MW01002669

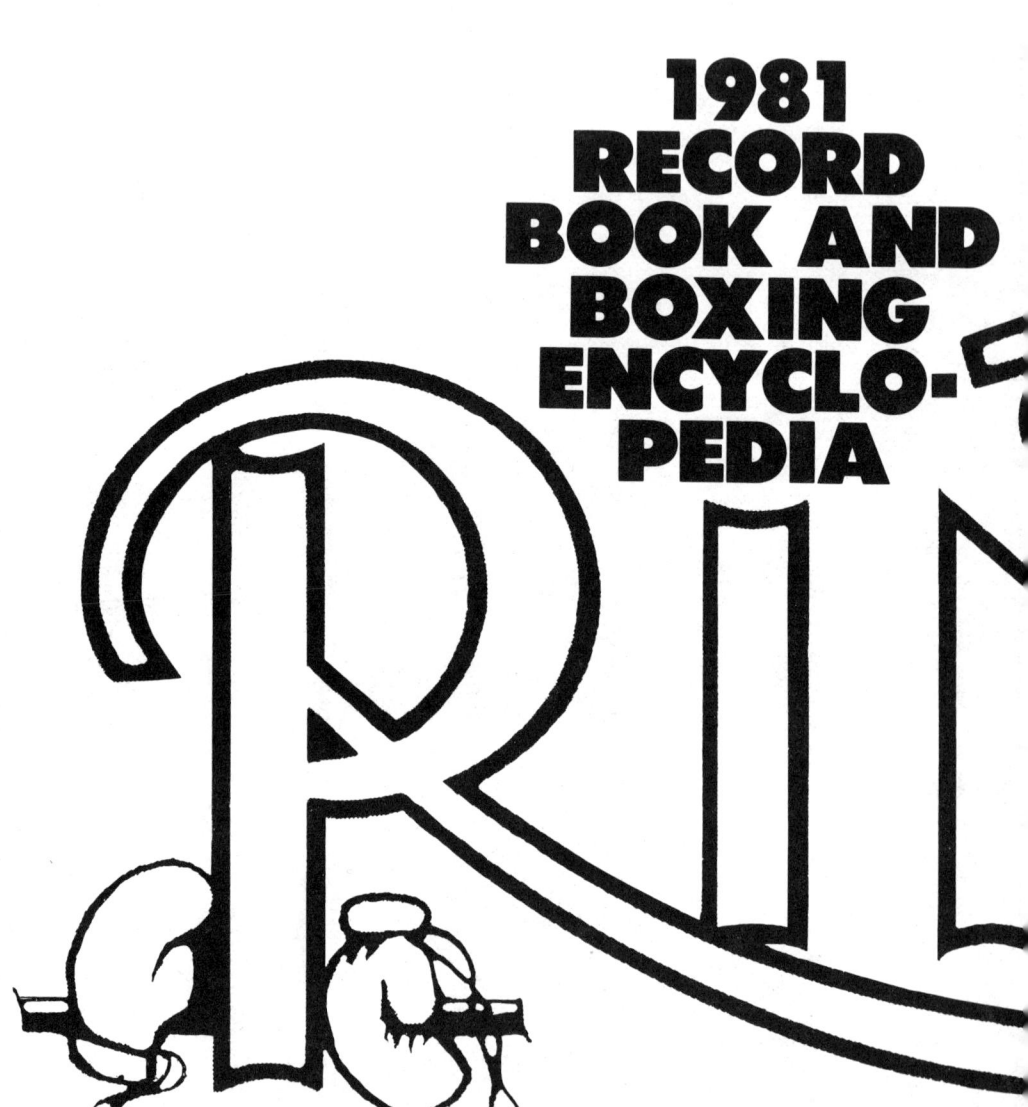

1981
RECORD
BOOK AND
BOXING
ENCYCLO-
PEDIA

ATHENEUM   NEW YORK

EDITOR-IN-CHIEF
Bert Randolph Sugar
EDITORS

Randy Gordon   **Herbert G. Goldman**
Current Fighters' Records   *Champions' Records*
ASSOCIATE EDITORS
Jack Goodman, Tom Hansen, John F. Johnson, Robert Yalen
ASSISTANT EDITORS
Richard H. Chudnoff, E.J. Gary, Louis Mesorana
DESIGN CONSULTANT
Richard Kubicz
ART
Donna Gates
CHAMPIONS' RECORDS
Jack Kinkaid, *Associate Editor,* **Gary Phillips**, *Associate Editor,* **Gilbert Odd**, *British Editor,*
Joe Y. Koizumi, *Japanese Editor;* David H. Bloch, Jerry Fitch, Robert Garry, Henry Hascup,
Hank Kaplan, Lawrence Roberts, Hy Rosenberg, Jan Skotnicki, N. Thorsen, Paul Zabala.
CONTRIBUTING EDITORS
Howard Albert, Frank Allnutt, Eduardo Amer G., Theo Angus Anitche, Eric Armit, Tony
Arnold, Eduardo Arroyo, Sybil Arum, Mike Avenenti, Mike Baker, Parker Beana, George C.
Beckles, Al Bernstein, Lloyd Blackmoore, George D. Blair, Dave Bloomberg, Johnny Bos, Debbie
Bozeat, Jim Brady, Jak Brami, Charles D. Brown, John Buchanan, Jim Buss, Gillie Campbell,
Bob Canobbio, George Canter, Robert Carson, Joseph Cassano, Gil Clancy, Ed Clark,
Christopher Coats, Dean Coleman, Nigel Collins, John F.X. Condon, Ron Copher, George Curcio,
Jacques Dechamps Jr., Patti Dreifuss, Angelo Dundee, Mike Dundee, Dan Duva, Kathy Duva,
Lou Duva, Laura Echeverri, Don Elbaum, Steve Farhood, Danny Feldman, Michael Feldman,
Dr. Sorrell Feldman, Shelly Finkel, Jack Fiske, Red Fortner, Don Fraser, Martin Gahan, Bob
Gerard, Michael Gitlitz, Velt Goldin, Steve Goldstein, Chris Gonzalez, Luis Gonzalez, Rene
Gonzalez, Bobby Goodman, Michael Goodwin, Malcolm Gordon, Helene Gordon, Jesoph Gramby,
Ben Green, J.T. Greenrose, Reg Gutteridge, Johnny Hanks, Dave Hartoon, Gary Hegyi, Ken
Hissner, Dr. Houslanger, Carlos Irusta, C.A. Jackson, Francis Jacobs, Jim Jacobs, Thomas
Jacobs, Jim Johnston, Mike Jones, Ron Katz, Brandon Kay, Wayne Kelly, Tom Kenville, George
Kimble, Michael Klahr, Alan Kornber, Stu Kroll, Chris LaPlacca, Wilson Larroseaux, Ruggles
Larson, Michael Leahy, Jim Leo, Frank Leonick, Mike Leonick, Glenn Leslie, Ketzel Levine, Stu
Levine, Joel Lipssitt, Steven Losch, Victor Machado, Jaran Manzanet, Sal Marchiano, Joe
Martino, Mario Rivera Maritino, Jerry McCarthy, Tresha McCormack, Gary L. Merritt, Ray
Mitchell, Sue Morgan, John Nolen, Shirley Norman, Ron Olver, Dan O'Malley, John E. O'Malley,
Erasmo Ortiz, Ira Packer, Charles Passero, Joe Pecoraro, Russell Peltz, Gabriel I. Penagaricano,
Gary Phillips, Grant Phillips, Eddie Pitcher, Bruce Posner, Dennis Rappaport, Bob Ritz, Allen
Rosenfeld, Jenny Rodriguez, Irving Rudd, Robert J. Ruiz, Norton Schultz, Frank Sciacca, Nancy
Sciacca, Frank Scrol, Ed Scullen, Frank Sgroi, Ben Sharav, J. Sheridan, Chuck Singer, David
Singer, Gerry Spears, Charlie Spina, Bob Surber, Pete Sussenns, Raquel Torres, Bruce
Trampler, Jack A. Tree, Ellis Dee Udechukwu, Rinze van der Meer, John Walcott, Harry
Warren, S. Weinberger, Ted Yamachika, Brian Zelley, Louis Zipkin.

PUBLISHED SIMULTANEOUSLY IN CANADA BY McCLELLAND AND STEWART LTD
MANUFACTURED BY HALLIDAY LITHOGRAPH CORPORATION,
WEST HANOVER AND PLYMPTON, MASSACHUSETTS
ISBN 0-689-11190-8   LCCN 81-66027
FIRST ATHENEUM EDITION

FOREWORD

1951 was a high water mark for boxing. That was the year when there were more great fights in the history of boxing than in any other year since James Figg first opened up his academy devoted exclusively to the pursuit of "The Gentlemanly Art of Self-Defence": Robinson-LaMotta, Saddler-Pep, Walcott-Charles, Gavilan-Bratton, Robinson-Turpin and Carter-Williams. It was also the end of an era which came to a close when Rocky Marciano "retired" Joe Louis. And it was the year another era began with the birth of future champion Roberto Duran.

But even more important to the future of boxing was the birth that year of the first modern computer. For it was that innovative breakthrough in data retrieval which was to insure the maintenance of boxing's valuable history for all time; the very mortar which holds the sport together — its records — could now be kept, corrected and updated on a systematized basis.

And along with the introduction of modern technology into boxing came the modernization of boxing's most valuable asset, THE RING RECORD BOOK. In an unending process which has been continuous since the first RING RECORD BOOK was issued in 1941, records have been computerized for the second straight year, allowing the editors to combine the same painstaking research which marked the earlier editions of THE RING RECORD BOOK with an un-

paralleled degree of completeness within individual entries.

Thus, we not only can take great pride in insuring that the original concept envisioned by Nat Fleischer lo those 40 years ago would remain essentially unaltered, but that the only changes in THE RECORD BOOK would occur in its general shape and comprehensiveness. In this manner the 1981 RING RECORD BOOK is but another chapter in the unending process which remains unbroken since that first RECORD BOOK. Albeit a more modern and thorough chapter.

In putting together the monthly editions of THE RING Magazine for the past two years we have felt a deep sense of responsibility as the custodians of boxing's great tradition — a tradition which takes its roots not only from the dedication and efforts of the boxers themselves who wrote these pages with their efforts, but also from the tradition started by Nat Fleischer. We believe that the fruits of our collective labors can be seen in the 1981 RING RECORD BOOK and that once again it is what it has always claimed to be: "The Bible of Boxing."

To many people a RECORD BOOK, such as this one, is a forbidding volume, a useful but bleak compendium to be referred to in haste for needed information — such as who fought whom when and where and with what result. And yet, what a RECORD BOOK ought to be is a treasury of information about every aspect of boxing, the most essential work in man's oldest and most elementary sport. And a necessity to the understanding of what goes on in that sport. It is a book to be picked up and read as if eating popcorn — just grab a handful and enjoy it. It is also meant to be dipped into and savored. For, in the final analysis, THE RING RECORD BOOK is a warehouse of information, and yet the very essence of the sport. To read it is to enjoy the sport, the sights, sounds and precious moments it has afforded each and every one of us.

Finally, a word about accuracy, which is always a concern. In an encyclopedic work this large it is an obsession and an obligation. We have endeavored to make this year's RECORD BOOK as error-free as humanly possible. We have taken out many of the legends "Previous Record Unavailable" which dotted last year's landscape and replaced them with full records where we could find them; we have added heretofore undiscovered fights found in moldering old yellow pages of yesteryear's champions; and we have even gone back to the computer to cross-rough current fighters' records and correct those inaccuracies which crept into the 1980 edition.

I wish it were possible to warrant that every one of the more than four million details represented here is exact and that every record is as complete as it should be. We who compiled and researched this material offer our humble disclaimer and remember the preface written by Peter Roget after he had completed the first edition of his famed THESAURUS back in 1852: "Notwithstanding all the pains I have bestowed on its execution, I am fully aware of its numerous deficiencies and imperfections, and of its falling far short of the degree of excellence that might be attained. But, in a work of this nature, where perfection is placed at so great a distance, I have thought it best to limit my ambition to that moderate share of merit which it may claim in its present form; trusting to the indulgence of those for whose benefit it is intended, and to the candor of critics who, while they find it easy to detect faults, can at the same time duly appreciate difficulties."

We, too, feel that although the 1981 RING RECORD BOOK is the greatest, most complete book on boxing ever compiled, it may still "fall far short of the degree of excellence that might be attained." But we're still trying. We and the computers. And feel in years to come this work will stand tall among reference works. And among RING RECORD BOOKS, both past and future.

BERT RANDOLPH SUGAR
EDITOR-IN-CHIEF

CONTENTS

A LIST
OF
DIVISIONAL
CHAMPIONS
AS OF
DEC. 31, 1980
FROM
EVERY
RANKING
ORGANIZATION

Ring's Champions
(as of 12/31/80)

HEAVYWEIGHT—LARRY HOLMES

LIGHT HEAVYWEIGHT—MATTHEW SAAD MUHAMMAD

MIDDLEWEIGHT—MARVIN HAGLER

JUNIOR MIDDLEWEIGHT—AYUB KALULE

WELTERWEIGHT—RAY LEONARD

JUNIOR WELTERWEIGHT—AARON PRYOR

LIGHTWEIGHT—TITLE VACANT

FEATHERWEIGHT—SALVADOR SANCHEZ

JUNIOR FEATHERWEIGHT—WILFREDO GOMEZ

BANTAMWEIGHT—JEFF CHANDLER

FLYWEIGHT—SHOJI OGUMA

	WBC	WBA	NABF
HEA	Larry Holmes	Mike Weaver	vacant
190	Carlos DeLeon	not recognized	S.T. Gordon
175	Matthew Saad Muhammad	Eddie Mustafa Muhammad	Jerry Martin
160	Marvin Hagler	Marvin Hagler	Sammy NeSmith
154	Maurice Hope	Ayub Kalule	Rocky Mosley
147	Sugar Ray Leonard	Thomas Hearns	Pepe Dominiguez
140	Saoul Mamby	Aaron Pryor	vacant
135	Jim Watt	Hilmer Kenty	Jorge Morales
130	Rafael Limon	Yasutsune Uehara	vacant
126	Salvador Sanchez	Eusebio Pedroza	Nico Perez
122	Wilfredo Gomez	Sergio Palma	Mike Ayala
118	Guadalupe Pintor	Jeff Chandler	vacant
115	Rafael Orono	not recognized	not recognized
112	Shoji Oguma	Peter Mathebula	Antonio Avelar
108	Hilario Zapata	Yoko Gushiken	Joey Olivo

	USBA	EBU	COMMONWEALTH
HEA	vacant	John L. Gardner	John L. Gardner
190	Bashiru Ali	not recognized	not recognized
175	Murray Sutherland	Rudi Koopman	Lotte Mwale
160	Curtis Parker	Tony Sibson	Tony Sibson
154	vacant	Marijan Benes	Kenny Bristol
147	vacant	Jorgen Hansen	Clyde Gray
140	Willie Rodriguez	Giuseppe Martinese	Obisia Nwakpa
135	Sean O'Grady	Charlie Nash	Langston Tinage
130	Robert Mullens	Carlos Hernandez	Johnny Aba
126	Rocky Lockridge	Roberto Castanon	Patrick Ford
122	not recognized	not recognized	not recognized
118	vacant	Valerio Nati	vacant
112	vacant	Charlie Magri	Stephen Muchoki
108	not recognized	not recognized	not recognized

	CANADA	GREATBRITAIN	ITALY
HEA	Trevor Berbick	vacant	Domenico Adinolfi
175	Gary Summernaya	Bunny Johnson	Christiano Cavina
160	Ralph Hollett	vacant	vacant
154	not recognized	Pat Thomas	Luigi Minchillo
147	Clyde Gray	Colin Jones	Pierangelo Pira
140	not recognized	Clinton McKenzie	Giuseppe Martinese
135	Gaetan Hart	Ray Cattouse	Lucio Cusma
130	not recognized	not recognized	Aristide Pizzo
126	vacant	Pat Cowdell	Marco Gallo
122	not recognized	not recognized	not recognized
118	vacant	vacant	Valerio Nati
112	vacant	Charlie Magri	Paolo Castrovilli
108	not recognized	not recognized	not recognized

	SPAIN	FRANCE	GERMANY
HEA	Felipe Rodriguez	Lucien Rodriguez	Georg Butzbach

175 Avenamar Peralta	Hocine Tafer	vacant
160 Andoni Amana	Jacques Chinon	Frank Wissenbach
154 Jose Hernandez	Louis Acaries	vacant
147 Antonio Casado	Roland Zenon	Jurgen Voss
140 Antonio Guinaldo	Christian Garcia	vacant
135 Jose Luis Heredia	Georges Cotin	Dieter Shantz
130 Ramon Maricnal	Charles Jurietti	vacant
126 Cecilo Lastra	Laurent Grimbert	vacant
122 not recognized	not recognized	not recognized
118 Esteban Eguia	Guy Caudron	vacant
112 Enrique Rodriguez	vacant	vacant
108 not recognized	not recognized	not recognized

WALES	SCOTLAND	IRELAND
HEA Neville Meade	vacant	vacant
175 Chris Lawson	vacant	vacant
160 vacant	vacant	vacant
154 Pat Thomas	Charlie Malarkey	vacant
147 Horace McKenzie	Dave Douglas	vacant
140 Billy Vivian	George Peacock	Davy Campbell
135 Martin Galleozzie	Willie Booth	Charlie Nash
130 not recognized	vacant	not recognized
126 Les Pickett	Gerry O'Neill	Damien McDermott
122 not recognized	not recognized	not recognized
118 vacant	Charlie Parvin	Davey Larmour
112 vacant	vacant	vacant
108 not recognized	not recognized	not recognized

OPBF	JAPAN	SOUTH KOREA
HEA vacant	vacant	vacant
175 vacant	vacant	vacant
160 Chong-Pal Park	James Callaghan	Byung-Rae Yuh
154 Tadashi Mihara	Michihiro Horihata	Sang-Ho Lee
147 Chung-Jae Hwang	Akio Kamoda	Jun-Sok Hwang
140 Thomas Americo	Eiichi Fukumoto	Kyung-Hwan Chae
135 Young-Ho Oh	Kiyoshi Kazama	Pil-Koo Lee
130 Ryu Fukida	Yasutsune Uehara	Tae-Jin Moon
126 Royal Kobayashi	Spider Nemoto	Son-Woo Chung
122 Willie Lucas	Hiroyuki Iwamoto	Chong-Woo Baek
118 Eijiro Murata	Hurricane Teru	Kyung-Joo Ha
115 William Develos	vacant	Chul-Ho Kim
112 Hong-Soo Yang	Kazumasa Tamaki	Kap-Chul Shin
108 Yong-Hyun Kim	Masaharu Inami	Soon-Yun Mah

PHILIPPINES	THAILAND	AUSTRALIA
HEA vacant	vacant	Tony Mundine
175 vacant	vacant	Tony Mundine
160 Joe Willisco	vacant	Wally Carr
154 Aquilino Nicolas, Jr.	vacant	Alex Temelkov
147 Mike de Guzman	Satanfa Pratip	Frank Ropis
140 Edward Heneral	Thom Singthanongsakdi	Jeff Malcolm
135 Nilo Acido	Jenrub Muangsurin	Barry Michael
130 Nene Jun	vacant	Paul Ferreri
126 Cesar Ligan	Nugprachun Kiatkumchai	Paul Ferreri
122 Rey Naduma, Jr.	Dejvarin Hollywood	Brian Roberts
118 Ronald Sumalis	Sakda Saksuree	Paul Ferreri
115 Diego de Villa	Phaktai Lipovitan-D	not recognized
112 Frank Cedeno	Dan Pisalchai	Steve Bell
108 Siony Carupo	Chukthep Chuvatana	Gerald Thompson

SOUTH PACIFIC / FIJI / SOUTH AFRICA

	SOUTH PACIFIC	FIJI	SOUTH AFRICA
HEA	Fossie Schmidt	vacant	Gerrie Coetzee
175	vacant	Joe Fabiano	Doug Lumley
160	vacant	Sakaria Ve	vacant
154	Sikeli Veitale	vacant	Bushy Bester
147	Ambika Prasad	Sakaria Ve	Harold Volbrecht
140	vacant	Sakaria Ve	Mziwandile Biyana
135	Robert Namana	Sakaria Ve	Peet Bothma
130	vacant	vacant	Evans Gwiji
126	vacant	Willie Tarika	Bashew Sibaca
122	not recognized	not recognized	Nkosomzi Moss
118	vacant	vacant	Welile Nkosinkolu
112	vacant	vacant	Peter Mathebula
108	not recognized	not recognized	Godfrey Nkate

ABU / NIGERIA / GHANA

	ABU	NIGERIA	GHANA
HEA	Ngozika Ekwelum	Eddie Cooper	Ray Arthur
175	Lotte Mwale	Abraham Tonica	vacant
160	Jean-Marie Emebe	Billy Savage	Richard Ofosu
154	Mimoun Mohatar	Grey Ibekwe	vacant
147	Joseph Bessala	Hunter Clay	Oblitey Commey
140	Obisia Nwakpa	Young Adiguin	vacant
135	Bossou Aziza	Davidson Andeh	Freddie Mensah
130	vacant	Kazeem Armah	vacant
126	Azuma Nelson	Victor Oseni	Henry Saddler
122	not recognized	not recognized	not recognized
118	vacant	Chris Emenogu	Raga Murphy
112	Stephen Muchoki	Ray Amoo	Everness Nortey
108	not recognized	not recognized	not recognized

RHODESIA / GUYANA / TRINIDAD [TOBAGO

	RHODESIA	GUYANA	TRINIDAD [TOBAGO
HEA	Ringo Starr	vacant	Wendell Joseph
175	Kid Power	Al Thomas	Carlos Mark
160	John Fisher	vacant	vacant
154	vacant	Kenny Bristol	vacant
147	Richard Rover	Vernon Lewis	Eddie Marcelle
140	vacant	vacant	vacant
135	Tadios Fisher	vacant	Claude Noel
130	vacant	vacant	vacant
126	Jey Nardo	Patrick Ford	vacant
122	not recognized	not recognized	not recognized
118	Stix Macloud	vacant	vacant
112	vacant	vacant	vacant
108	not recognized	not recognized	not recognized

MEXICO / PUERTO RICO / DOMINICAN REPUBLIC

	MEXICO	PUERTO RICO	DOMINICAN REPUBLIC
HEA	Mongol Ortiz	vacant	Bartolo Sony
175	David Cabrera	vacant	Luis Galvan
160	Petrolerio Macias	vacant	Jesus Castro
154	not recognized	vacant	Jesus Castro
147	Adolfo Sanjeado	vacant	Mario de la Rosa
140	not recognized	vacant	Miguel Montilla
135	Jose Luis Ramirez	vacant	Antonio Cruz
130	not recognized	vacant	Cocoa Sanchez
126	Gustavo Salgado	Felix Trinidad	Nelson Cruz Tamariz
122	not recognized	vacant	Leonardo Cruz
118	Norberto Cabrera	Andres Hernandez	Julio Solano
112	Pedro Flores	Orlando Maldonado	Julio Guerrero
108	German Torres	not recognized	Maximo Rodriguez

FECARBOX / LATIN AMERICA / AMERICAS

	FECARBOX	LATIN AMERICA	AMERICAS
HEA	Bernardo Mercado	Luis Acosta	Bernardo Mercado
190	vacant	not recognized	vacant
175	Leonardo Rogers	vacant	Oscar Rivadaneira
160	Fulgencio Obelmejias	vacant	Milton Owens
154	Nicanor Camacho	Nicanor Camacho	vacant
147	Mao de la Rosa	Wellington Wheatley	Segundo Murillo
140	Fitzroy Giuseppe	vacant	Jose Salazar
135	Edwin Viruet	Claude Noel	Orlando Romero
130	Reynaldo Hidalgo	Romualdo Garces	Luis Bendezu
126	Patrick Ford	Walter Gonzales	Denis Moran
122	Augustin Martinez	Augustin Martinez	Jose Cervantes
118	Enrique Sanchez	vacant	Cleo Garcia
115	Miguel Lora	Miguel Lora	Javier Brown
112	Prudencio Cardona	vacant	Luis Tapias
108	Rudy Crawford	Alfonso Lopez	Luis Beltran

FESUBOX / ARGENTINA / BRAZIL

	FESUBOX	ARGENTINA	BRAZIL
HEA	Domingo D'Elia	Domingo D'Elia	Luis Pires
190	Juan C. Sosa	Juan C. Sosa	Waldemar Paulino
175	Carlos F. Burlon	Abel Bailone	Clarismundo Silva
160	Ruben Pardo	Jacinto Fernandez	Luis Fabre
154	Walter Gomez	Walter Gomez	Joao Tavares
147	Tito Yanni	Ruben Lucero	Edson Lima
140	Roberto Alfaro	Roberto Alfaro	Diogenes Pacheco
135	Jesus Romero	Jesus Romero	Jose Carlos dos Santos
130	Victor Echegaray	Victory Echegaray	vacant
126	Juan Malvares	Juan Malvares	Jose DePaula
122	Sergio Palma	Cesar Villarruel	Danilo Batista
118	Jose Uziga	Jose Narvaez	vacant
112	Santos Laciar	Santos Laciar	Paulo Ribeiro
108	Rodolfo Rodriguez	Rodolfo Rodriguez	vacant

CHILE / COLOMBIA / COSTA RICA

	CHILE	COLOMBIA	COSTA RICA
HEA	vacant	vacant	vacant
190	not recognized	not recognized	Gilberto Acuna
175	Luis Alvarado	vacant	vacant
160	Antonio Garrido	Sigfredo Moreno	vacant
154	Nelson Torres	Manuel Saavedra	vacant
147	Victor Nilo	Carlos Mejia	Villaney Ruiz
140	Roberto Iluffi	Martin Rojas	Rudy Alpizar
135	Oscar Huerta	Eduardo Valdez	Luis Leon
130	Benedicto Villablanca	Victor Pacheco	Manuel Gonzales Maya
126	Juvenal Ordenes	Mario Miranda	Romualdo Vilchez
122	Hugo Fica	Julio Llerena	Daniel Cazan Solano
118	Benito Badilla	Jacinto Moreno	Luis Gonzalez
115	vacant	Raul Diaz	vacant
112	Jaime Miranda	vacant	vacant
108	Luis Beltran	Felipe Medrano	

ECUADOR / NICARAGUA / PANAMA

	ECUADOR	NICARAGUA	PANAMA
HEA	vacant	vacant	vacant
175	vacant	vacant	Tommy Ortiz
160	Luis Mora	vacant	vacant
154	vacant	Eddie Gazo	vacant
147	Segundo Murillo	Pedro Cisneros	Vianor Durango
140	vacant	vacant	Jose Salazar
135	vacant	Emilio Guerrero	vacant
130	Rafael Anchundia	vacant	Reynaldo Hidalgo
126	Hernando Mullo	Frank Joe	Carlos Nunez
122	vacant	Julio Hernandez	Ulises Morales

13

118	Klever Viteri	Carlos Bejarano	Ricardo Bennett
112	Jose Jimenez	Nestor Obregon	Pedro Romero
108	vacant	Rudy Crawford	Alfonso Lopez

	PERU	**URUGUAY**	**VENEZUELA**
HEA	vacant	vacant	vacant
175	Rumildo Bolivar	Carlos Flores	vacant
160	vacant	Jorge Flores	vacant
154	vacant	Jose Navarro	vacant
147	Fernando Castro	vacant	vacant
140	Alfredo Estrada	Carlos Alvarez	Jesus Navas
135	vacant	Gualberto Valdez	Luis Rodriguez
130	Luis Bendezu	Jose Arias	Ildefonso Bethelmy
126	Walter Gonzales	vacant	Ruben Veliz
122	vacant	Hugo Melgarejo	vacant
118	vacant	vacant	Edgar Roman
115	Luis Ibanez	vacant	Carlos Gutierrez
112	vacant	vacant	Jovito Rengifo
108	vacant	not recognized	Reinaldo Becerra

THE
1980
TITLE BOUTS
ON A
MONTH
-BY-
MONTH
BASIS

TITLE: WBC Light Flyweight
Champion: Sung-Jun Kim (Korea)
Challenger: Shigeo Nakajima (Japan)
Date: January 3rd
Place: Tokyo, Japan
Weights: Kim-107¾, Nakajima-107¾
Result: Nakajima won title by a unanimous decision
Referee: Dick Young (USA) 146-139 (SN)
Judge: Takeo Ugo (Japan) 148-143 (SN)
Judge: Renier Manoch (Indonesia) 145-141 (SN)

TITLE: WBC Super Featherweight
Champion: Alexis Arguello (Nicaragua)
Challenger: Ruben Castillo (USA)
Date: January 20th
Place: Tuscon, Arizona
Weights: Arguello-130, Castillo-129¾
Result: Arguello by a TKO at 2:03 of the 11th round
Referee: Octavio Meyran (Mexico)
Judge: Ricardo Rizo (Nicaragua) 97-96 (AA)
Judge: Juan Jose Guerra (Mexico) 97-96 (AA)
Judge: Bobby Cox (USA) 97-96 (RC)

TITLE: WBA Featherweight
Champion: Eusebio Pedroza (Panama)
Challenger: Spider Nemoto (Japan)
Date: January 22nd
Place: Tokyo, Japan
Weights: Pedroza-126, Nemoto-125½
Result: Pedroza by a unanimous decision
Referee: Nate Morgan (USA) 147-140 (EP)
Judge: Yusaku Yoshida (Japan) 147-146 (EP)
Judge: Emma Urrunaga (Panama) 148-138 (EP)

TITLE: WBA Junior Flyweight
Champion: Yoko Gushiken (Japan)
Challenger: Yong-Hyun Kim (Korea)
Date: January 27th
Place: Osaka, Japan
Weights: Gushiken-107½, Kim-107½
Result: Gushiken by a unanimous decision
Referee: Paul Field (USA) 149-141 (YG)
Judge: Kiyoaki Kurume (Japan) 150-140 (YG)
Judge: Sun Chou-Ik (Korea) 148-144 (YG)

TITLE: Vacant WBC Super Flyweight
Challenger: Rafael Orono (Venezuela)
Challenger: Seung-Hoon Lee (Korea)
Date: February 1st
Place: Caracas, Venezuela
Weights: Orono-113½, Lee-114¾
Result: Orono won vacant title by a split decision
Referee: Alfredo Fernandez (Argentina) 150-145 (RO)
Judge: Yong-Soo Chung (Korea) 148-147 (SHL)
Judge: Ladislao Sanchez (Venezuela) 148-143 (RO)

TITLE: WBC Featherweight
Champion: Danny Lopez (USA)
Challenger: Salvador Sanchez (Mexico)
Date: February 2nd
Place: Phoenix, Arizona
Weights: Lopez-125 ¾, Sanchez-125¼
Result: Sanchez won title by a TKO at 0:51 of the 13th round
Referee: Waldemar Schmidt (Puerto Rico)
Judge: Lou Fillipo (USA) 119-110 (SS)
Judge: Chuck Hassett (USA) 118-111 (SS)
Judge: Jorge Velasco (Mexico) 120-108 (SS)

TITLE: WBC Super Bantamweight
Champion: Wilfredo Gomez (Puerto Rico)
Challenger: Ruben Valdez (Colombia)
Date: February 3rd
Place: Las Vegas, Nevada
Weights: Gomez-122, Valdez-121¾
Result: Gomez by a TKO in 6 (could not answer bell for 7th)
Referee: Ferd Hernandez (USA)
Judge: Ismael Quinones Falu (Puerto Rico) 60-54 (WG)
Judge: Duane Ford (USA) 60-53 (WG)
Judge: Joe Swessel (USA) 60-52 (WG)

TITLE: WBC Heavyweight
Champion: Larry Holmes (USA)
Challenger: Lorenzo Zanon (Italy)
Date: February 3rd
Place: Las Vegas, Nevada
Weights: Holmes-213½, Zanon-215
Result: Holmes by a TKO at 2:39 of the 6th round
Referee: Raymundo Solis (Mexico)
Judge: Charles Minker (USA) 49-44 (LH)
Judge: Art Lurie (USA) 49-45 (LH)
Judge: Harold Buck (USA) 48-46 (LH)

TITLE: WBC Bantamweight
Champion: Guadalupe Pintor (Mexico)
Challenger: Alberto Sandoval (USA)
Date: February 9th
Place: Los Angeles, California
Weights: Pintor-116, Sandoval-117½
Result: Pintor by a TKO at 1:19 of the 12th round
Referee: Carlos Padilla (Philippines) 109-103 (GP)
Judge: Rudy Ortega (USA) 110-98 (GP)
Judge: Abraham Chavarria (Mexico) 110-102 (GP)

TITLE: WBC Flyweight
Champion: Chan-Hee Park (Korea)
Challenger: Arnel Arrozal (Philippines)
Date: February 10th
Place: Seoul, Korea
Weights: Park-111¾, Arrozal-111¼
Result: Park by a unanimous decision
Referee: Ken Morita (Japan) 147-144 (CHP)
Judge: Alfredo Quiazon (Philippines) 146-142 (CHP)
Judge: Kwang-Soo Kim (Korea) 149-145 (CHP)

TITLE: WBA Flyweight
Champion: Luis Ibarra (Panama)
Challenger: Tae-Shik Kim (Korea)
Date: February 16th
Place: Seoul, Korea
Weights: Ibarra-110¾, Kim-111¾
Result: Kim won title by a KO at 1:50 of the 2nd round
Referee: Servio Tulio Lay (Panama) 10-9 (TSK)
Judge: Martin Denkin (USA) 10-9 (TSK)
Judge: Chin-Kook Kim (Korea) 10-9 (TSK)

TITLE: WBC Super Lightweight
Champion: Sang-Hyun Kim (Korea)
Challenger: Saoul Mamby (USA)
Date: February 23rd
Place: Seoul, Korea
Weights: Kim-140, Mamby-139
Result: Mamby won title by a TKO at 1:44 of the 14th round
Referee: Harry Gibbs (England) 125-124 (SM)
Judge: Richard Steele (USA) 125-123 (SHK)

Judge: Takeo Ugo (Japan) 127-126 (SM)

TITLE: WBA Lightweight
Champion: Ernesto Espana (Venezuela)
Challenger: Hilmer Kenty (USA)
Date: March 2nd
Place: Detroit, Michigan
Weights: Espana-134¾, Kenty-134¼
Result: Kenty won title by a TKO at 2:53 of the 9th round
Referee: Larry Rozadilla (USA) 78-75 (HK)
Judge: Ismael Fernandez (Puerto Rico) 76-74 (EE)
Judge: Harold Lederman (USA) 78-74 (HK)

TITLE: WBC Lightweight
Champion: Jim Watt (Scotland)
Challenger: Charlie Nash (Ireland)
Date: March 14th
Place: Glasgow, Scotland
Weights: Watt-134¾, Nash-134¾
Result: Watt by a TKO at 2:10 of the 4th round
Referee: Sid Nathan (England) 29-28 (JW)
Judge: James Brimmell (Wales) 28-28 (--)
Judge: John Coyle (England) 29-28 (JW)

TITLE: World Middleweight
Champion: Vito Antuofermo (USA)
Challenger: Alan Minter (England)
Date: March 16th
Place: Las Vegas, Nevada
Weights: Antuofermo-158¼, Minter-159¾
Result: Minter won title by a split decision
Referee: Carlos Padilla (Philippines)
Judge: Charles Minker (USA) 144-141 (AM)
Judge: Roland Dakin (England) 149-137 (AM)
Judge: Ladislao Sanchez (Venezuela) 145-143 (VA)

TITLE: WBC Light Flyweight
Champion: Shigeo Nakajima (Japan)
Challenger: Hilario Zapata (Panama)
Date: March 24th
Place: Tokyo, Japan
Weights: Nakajima-108, Zapata-108
Result: Zapata won title by a unanimous decision
Referee: Hank Elespuru (USA) 144-143 (HZ)
Judge: Harold Lederman (USA) 144-141 (HZ)
Judge: Jose Escalante (Mexico) 146-144 (HZ)

TITLE: WBA Featherweight
Champion: Eusebio Pedroza (Panama)
Challenger: Juan Malvares (Argentina)
Date: March 29th
Place: Panama City, Panama
Weights: Pedroza-125½, Malvares-126
Result: Pedroza by a KO at 1:10 of the 9th round
Referee: Vincente Rainone (USA)
Judge: Roberto Ramirez (Puerto Rico)
Judge: Fernando Viso (Venezuela)

TITLE: WBA Junior Welterweight
Champion: Antonio Cervantes (Colombia)
Challenger: Miguel Montilla (Dominican Republic)
Date: March 29th
Place: Cartagena, Colombia
Weights: Cervantes-139¾, Montilla-139½
Result: Cervantes by a TKO at 1:28 of the 7th round
Referee: Waldemar Schmidt (Puerto Rico) 60-53 (AC)
Judge: Harold Lederman (USA) 60-53 (AC)
Judge: Marcos Antonio Torres (Panama) 60-55 (AC)

TITLE: WBC Light Heavyweight
Champion: Matthew Saad Muhammad (USA)
Challenger: John Conteh (England)
Date: March 29th
Place: Atlantic City, New Jersey
Weights: Muhammad-175, Conteh-175
Result: Muhammad by a TKO at 2:27 of the 4th round
Referee: Octavio Meyran (Mexico) 30-28 (MSM)
Judge: Charley Spina (USA) 29-28 (MSM)
Judge: Harry Gibbs (England) 30-28 (MSM)

TITLE: WBC Welterweight
Champion: Sugar Ray Leonard (USA)
Challenger: Dave Green (England)
Date: March 31st
Place: Landover, Maryland
Weights: Leonard-147, Green-147
Result: Leonard by a KO at 2:27 of the 4th round
Referee: Arthur Mercante (USA) 30-27 (SRL)
Judge: Harry Gibbs (England) 30-27 (SRL)
Judge: Larry Barrett (USA) 30-27 (SRL)

TITLE: WBA Light Heavyweight
Champion: Marvin Johnson (USA)
Challenger: Eddie Gregory (USA)
Date: March 31st
Place: Knoxville, Tennessee
Weights: Johnson-174½, Gregory-174
Result: Gregory won title by a TKO at 2:43 of the 11th round
Referee: Carlos Berrocal (Panama) 97-93 (EG)
Judge: Luis Sulbaran (Venezuela) 98-96 (EG)
Judge: Guillermo Bauza Romero (Mexico) 99-94 (EG)

TITLE: Vacant WBC Cruiserweight
Challenger: Marvin Camel (USA)
Challenger: Mate Parlov (Yugoslavia)
Date: March 31st
Place: Las Vegas, Nevada
Weights: Camel-185¾, Parlov-189
Result: Camel won vacant title by a unanimous decision
Referee: Fred Hernandez (USA)
Judge: Harold Buck (USA) 144-141 (MC)
Judge: Juan Jose Guerra (Mexico) 148-141 (MC)
Judge: Angelo Poletti (Italy) 149-141 (MC)

TITLE: WBA Heavyweight
Champion: John Tate (USA)
Challenger: Mike Weaver (USA)
Date: March 31st
Place: Knoxville, Tennessee
Weights: Tate-232, Weaver-207½
Result: Weaver won title by a KO at 2:15 of the 15th round
Referee: Ernesto Magana (Mexico) 138-133 (JT)
Judge: Nicasio Lorenzo Drake (Panama) 137-134 (JT)
Judge: Cesar Ramos (Puerto Rico) 136-133 (JT)

TITLE: WBC Heavyweight
Champion: Larry Holmes (USA)
Challenger: Leroy Jones (USA)
Date: March 31st
Place: Las Vegas, Nevada
Weights: Holmes-211, Jones-254½
Result: Holmes by a TKO at 2:56 of the 8th round
Referee: Richard Greene (USA)
Judge: Charles Minker (USA) 70-62 (LH)

Judge: Art Lurie (USA) 70-64 (LH)
Judge: Duane Ford (USA) 70-63 (LH)

TITLE: WBA Bantamweight
Champion: Jorge Lujan (Panama)
Challenger: Shuichi Isogami (Japan)
Date: April 2nd
Place: Tokyo, Japan
Weights: Lujan-118, Isogami-117¾
Result: Lujan by a TKO at 2:45 of the 9th round
Referee: Larry Rozadilla (USA) 80-72 (JL)
Judge: Medardo Villalobos (Mexico) 80-75 (JL)
Judge: Shuichi Uchida (Japan) 80-77 (JL)

TITLE: WBA Junior Lightweight
Champion: Samuel Serrano (Puerto Rico)
Challenger: Kiyoshi Kazama (Japan)
Date: April 3rd
Place: Nara, Japan
Weights: Serrano-129½, Kazama-129¾
Result: Serrano by a TKO at 0:45 of the 13th round
Referee: Stanley Christodoulou (South Africa) 119-113 (SS)
Judge: Allen Daniel (Puerto Rico) 119-112 (SS)
Judge: Ryoji Kashiwagi (Japan) 118-117 (SS)

TITLE: WBA Welterweight
Champion: Pipino Cuevas (Mexico)
Challenger: Harold Volbrecht (South Africa)
Date: April 6th
Place: Houston, Texas
Weights: Cuevas-146¼, Volbrecht-146¾
Result: Cuevas by a KO at 1:19 of the 5th round
Referee: Carlos Berrocal (Panama) 39-38 (PC)
Judge: Joe Bunsa (USA) 39-38 (HV)
Judge: Chris Jordan (USA) 39-38 (HV)

TITLE: WBC Featherweight
Champion: Salvador Sanchez (Mexico)
Challenger: Ruben Castillo (USA)
Date: April 12th
Place: Tucson, Arizona
Weights: Sanchez-126, Castillo-125½
Result: Sanchez by a unanimous decision
Referee: Marcelo Bertini (Italy)
Judge: James Jen Kim (USA) 145-141 (SS)
Judge: Jorge Velasco (Mexico) 147-144 (SS)
Judge: Ramon Berumeja (Mexico) 146-142 (SS)

TITLE: WBC Flyweight
Champion: Chan-Hee Park (Korea)
Challenger: Alberto Morales (Mexico)
Date: April 13th
Place: Taegu, Korea
Weights: Park-112, Morales-112
Result: Park by a unanimous decision
Referee: Takeshi Shimakawa (Japan) 150-139 (CHP)
Judge: Anselmo Escobedo (Mexico) 149-138 (CHP)
Judge: Kang Kyu-Soon (Korea) 150-143 (CHP)

TITLE: WBC Super Flyweight
Champion: Rafael Orono (Venezuela)
Challenger: Ramon Soria (Argentina)
Date: April 14th
Place: Caracas, Venezuela
Weights: Orono-114½, Soria-115
Result: Orono by a unanimous decision
Referee: Alberto Diaz Mendez (Nicaragua) 149-145 (RO)

Judge: Dimas Hernandez (Venezuela) 147-145 (RO)
Judge: Pedro Rodriguez Manzo (Venezuela) 145-143 (RO)

TITLE: WBA Junior Middleweight
Champion: Ayub Kalule (Uganda)
Challenger: Emiliano Villa (Colombia)
Date: April 17th
Place: Copenhagen, Denmark
Weights: Kalule-153½, Villa-150¾
Result: Kalule by a TKO in 11 (retired by corner after round)
Referee: Joe Santarpia (USA)
Judge: Carol Polis (USA)
Judge: James Rondeau (USA)

TITLE: WBC Super Featherweight
Champion: Alexis Arguello (Nicaragua)
Challenger: Rolando Navarette (Philippines)
Date: April 27th
Place: San Juan, Puerto Rico
Weights: Arguello-130, Navarette-130
Result: Arguello by a TKO in 5 (could not answer bell for 5th)
Referee: Roberto Ramirez (Puerto Rico) 39-37 (AA)
Judge: Samuel Conde (Puerto Rico) 40-37 (AA)
Judge: Cesar Ramos (Puerto Rico) 40-37 (AA)

TITLE: WBA Super Bantamweight
Champion: Ricardo Cardona (Colombia)
Challenger: Leo Randolph (USA)
Date: May 4th
Place: Seattle, Washington
Weights: Cardona-121½, Randolph-121¾
Result: Randolph won title by a TKO at 1:31 of the 15th round
Referee: Larry Rozadilla (USA) 138-132 (LR)
Judge: Rogelio Perez (Panama) 138-132 (LR)
Judge: John Nenizich (USA) 138-133 (LR)

TITLE: WBC Light Heavyweight
Champion: Matthew Saad Muhammad (USA)
Challenger: Louis Ngatchou Pergaud (Cameroon)
Date: May 11th
Place: Halifax, Nova Scotia
Weights: Muhammad-174½, Pergaud-174½
Result: Muhammad by a TKO at 1:19 of the 5th round
Referee: Rudy Ortega (USA) 40-36 (MSM)
Judge: Dick Young (USA) 40-36 (MSM)
Judge: Alec Nickerson (Canada) 39-37 (MSM)

TITLE: WBC Flyweight
Champion: Chan-Hee Park (Korea)
Challenger: Shoji Oguma (Japan)
Date: May 18th
Place: Seoul, Korea
Weights: Park-111¾, Oguma-111¾
Result: Oguma won title by a KO at 0:53 of the 9th round
Referee: Harold Nadaya (Philippines) 78-73 (SO)
Judge: Shoichi Uchida (Japan) 79-75 (SO)
Judge: Kwang-Soo Kim (Korea) 78-77 (SO)

TITLE: WBA Junior Flyweight
Champion: Yoko Gushiken (Japan)
Challenger: Martin Vargas (Chile)
Date: June 1st
Place: Kochi City, Japan
Weights: Gushiken-107¾, Vargas-107¾
Result: Gushiken by a TKO at 1:42 of the 8th round

Referee: Larry Hazzard (USA) 70-62 (YG)
Judge: Albert Tremari (USA) 70-58 (YG)
Judge: Rogelio Perez (Panama) 70-62 (YG)

TITLE: WBC Light Flyweight
Champion: Hilario Zapata (Panama)
Challenger: Chi-Bok Kim (Korea)
Date: June 7th
Place: Seoul, Korea
Weights: Zapata-107½, Kim-107
Results: Zapata by a unanimous decision
Referee: Richard Steele (USA) 149-138 (HZ)
Judge: Harmodio Cedeno (Panama) 149-140 (HZ)
Judge: Young-Soo Chung (Korea) 149-139 (HZ)

TITLE: WBC Lightweight
Champion: Jim Watt (Scotland)
Challenger: Howard Davis (USA)
Date: June 7th
Place: Glasgow, Scotland
Weights: Watt-134¾, Davis-133½
Result: Watt by a unanimous decision
Referee: Carlos Padilla (Philippines) 145-144 (JW)
Judge: Juan Jose Guerra (Mexico) 149-142 (JW)
Judge: Angel Custodio Tovar (Venezuela) 147-144 (JW)

TITLE: WBC Bantamweight
Champion: Guadalupe Pintor (Mexico)
Challenger: Eijiro Murata (Japan)
Date: June 11th
Place: Tokyo, Japan
Weights: Pintor-118, Murata-118
Result: Pintor retained title by a draw
Referee: Martin Denkin (USA) 144-144 (--)
Judge: Marcial Sosa Villamil (Mexico) 147-142 (GP)
Judge: Takeaki Kanaya (Japan) 146-144 (EM)

TITLE: WBA Junior Middleweight
Champion: Ayub Kalule (Uganda)
Challenger: Marijan Benes (Yugoslavia)
Date: June 12th
Place: Randers, Denmark
Weights: Kalule-153½, Benes-153
Result: Kalule by a unanimous decision
Referee: Max Strengfeld (Danish) 149-145 (AK)
Judge: Knud Jensen (Danish) 149-142 (AK)
Judge: Rinus Schulien (Dutch) 149-147 (AK)

TITLE: WBC Welterweight
Champion: Sugar Ray Leonard (USA)
Challenger: Roberto Duran (Panama)
Date: June 20th
Place: Montreal, Canada
Weights: Leonard-145, Duran-145¼
Result: Duran won title by a unanimous decision
Referee: Carlos Padilla (Philippines)
Judge: Harry Gibbs (England) 145-144 (RD)
Judge: Angelo Poletti (Italy) 148-147 (RD)
Judge: Raymond Baldeyrou (France) 146-144 (RD)

TITLE: WBC Featherweight
Champion: Salvador Sanchez (Mexico)
Challenger: Danny Lopez (USA)
Date: June 21st
Place: Las Vegas, Nevada
Weights: Sanchez-126, Lopez-126
Result: Sanchez by a TKO at 1:42 of the 14th round
Referee: Mills Lane (USA)
Judge: Harold Buck (USA) 125-122 (SS)
Judge: Anselmo Escobedo (Mexico) 127-120 (SS)

Judge: Benjamin Gonzalez (Mexico) 129-126 (SS)

TITLE: World Middleweight
Champion: Alan Minter (England)
Challenger: Vito Antuofermo (USA)
Date: June 28th
Place: Wembley, England
Weights: Minter-160, Antuofermo-159¼
Result: Minter by a TKO in 8 (retired by corner after round)
Referee: Octavio Meyran (Mexico) 80-73 (AM)
Judge: Kurt Halbach (West Germany) 80-72 (AM)
Judge: Jean Deswerts (Belgium) 80-71 (AM)

TITLE: WBA Flyweight
Champion: Tae-Shik Kim (Korea)
Challenger: Arnel Arrozal (Philippines)
Date: June 29th
Place: Seoul, Korea
Weights: Kim-112, Arrozal-112
Result: Kim by a unanimous decision
Referee: Ken Morita (Japan) 146-142 (TSK)
Judge: Takeo Ugo (Japan) 148-141 (TSK)
Judge: Renier Manoch (Indonesia) 145-142 (TSK)

TITLE: WBC Super Lightweight
Champion: Saoul Mamby (USA)
Challenger: Esteben DeJesus (Puerto Rico)
Date: July 7th
Place: Minneapolis, Minnesota
Weights: Mamby-139½, DeJesus-140
Result: Mamby by a TKO at 1:13 of the 13th round
Referee: Rudy Ortega (USA) 117-110 (SM)
Judge: Denny Nelson (USA) 117-112 (SM)
Judge: George Reiter (USA) 118-110 (SM)

TITLE: WBC Heavyweight
Champion: Larry Holmes (USA)
Challenger: Scott LeDoux (USA)
Date: July 7th
Place: Minneapolis, Minnesota
Weights: Holmes-214¼, LeDoux-226
Result: Holmes by a TKO at 2:05 of the 7th round
Referee: Davey Pearl (USA) 60-53 (LH)
Judge: Harold Lederman (USA) 60-53 (LH)
Judge: Richard Steele (USA) 60-53 (LH)

TITLE: WBC Super Welterweight
Champion: Maurice Hope (England)
Challenger: Rocky Mattioli (Italy)
Date: July 12th
Place: Wembley, England
Weights: Hope-153, Mattioli-151¾
Result: Hope by a TKO at 2:52 of the 11th round
Referee: Arthur Mercante (USA) 98-91 (MH)
Judge: Tony Perez (USA) 98-91 (MH)
Judge: Dick Young (USA) 98-92 (MH)

TITLE: WBC Light Heavyweight
Champion: Matthew Saad Muhammad (USA)
Challenger: Alvaro Lopez (USA)
Date: July 13th
Place: Great Gorge, New Jersey
Weights: Muhammad-174¼, Lopez 173¾
Result: Muhammad by a TKO at 2:03 of the 14th round
Referee: Waldemar Schmidt (Puerto Rico) 124-123 (MSM)
Judge: Frank Brunette (USA) 125-123 (MSM)
Judge: Paul Cavaliere (USA) 125-123 (MSM)

TITLE: WBA Featherweight
Champion: Eusebio Pedroza (Panama)
Challenger: Sa-Wang Kim (Korea)
Date: July 20th
Place: Seoul, Korea
Weights: Pedroza-126, Kim-125½
Result: Pedroza by a KO at 2:52 of the 8th round
Referee: Jesus Celis (Venezuela) 70-63 (EP)
Judge: Rodolfo Hill (Panama) 70-64 (EP)
Judge: Chin-Kook Kim (Korea) 69-66 (EP)

TITLE: WBA Light Heavyweight
Champion: Eddie Mustafa Muhammad (USA)
Challenger: Jerry Martin (USA)
Date: July 20th
Place: Great Gorge, New Jersey
Weights: Muhammad-175, Martin-175
Result: Muhammad by a TKO at 2:25 of the 10th round
Referee: Tony Perez (USA) 87-83 (EMM)
Judge: Eva Shain (USA) 88-82 (EMM)
Judge: Harold Lederman (USA) 85-85 (--)

TITLE: WBC Flyweight
Champion: Shoji Oguma (Japan)
Challenger: Sung-Jun Kim (Korea)
Date: July 28th
Place: Tokyo, Japan
Weights: Oguma-112, Kim-112
Result: Oguma by a split decision
Referee: Paul Field (USA) 148-145 (SO)
Judge: Shoji Nakamori (Japan) 147-145 (SO)
Judge: Man-Kim Kim (Korea) 149-146 (SJK)

TITLE: WBC Super Flyweight
Champion: Rafael Orono (Venezuela)
Challenger: Willie Jensen (USA)
Date: July 28th
Place: Caracas, Venezuela
Weights: Orono-114½, Jensen-115
Result: Orono retained title by a draw
Referee: Carlos Guzman (Argentina) 146-146 (--)
Judge: Horacio Castilla (Colombia) 146-146 (--)
Judge: Pedro Ramirez Manzo (Venezuela) 147-146 (RO)

TITLE: WBA Junior Lightweight
Champion: Samuel Serrano (Puerto Rico)
Challenger: Yasutsune Uehara (Japan)
Date: August 2nd
Place: Detroit, Michigan
Weights: Serrano-130, Uehara-129¾
Result: Uehara won title by a KO at 2:59 of the 6th round
Referee: Luis Sulbaran (Venezuela) 50-45 (SS)
Judge: Harold Lederman (USA) 50-45 (SS)
Judge: Stanley Berg (USA) 50-45 (SS)

TITLE: WBA Lightweight
Champion: Hilmer Kenty (USA)
Challenger: Young-Ho Oh (Korea)
Date: August 2nd
Place: Detroit, Michigan
Weights: Kenty-135, Oh-134½
Result: Kenty by a TKO at 2:15 of the 9th round
Referee: Ernesto Magana (Mexico) 79-74 (HK)
Judge: Michael Glenn (USA) 79-72 (HK)
Judge: Roberto Ramirez (Puerto Rico) 79-73 (HK)

TITLE: WBA Junior Welterweight
Champion: Antonio Cervantes (Colombia)

Challenger: Aaron Pryor (USA)
Date: August 2nd
Place: Cincinnati, Ohio
Weights: Cervantes-139¼, Pryor-138½
Result: Pryor won title by a KO at 1:47 of the 4th round
Referee: Larry Rozadilla (USA) 28-26 (AC)
Judge: Ismael Fernandez (Puerto Rico) 29-26 (AC)
Judge: Fernando Viso (Venezuela) 29-27 (AC)

TITLE: WBA Welterweight
Champion: Pipino Cuevas (Mexico)
Challenger: Thomas Hearns (USA)
Date: August 2nd
Place: Detroit, Michigan
Weights: Cuevas-146, Hearns-146½
Result: Hearns won title by a TKO at 2:39 of the 2nd round
Referee: Stanley Christodoulou (South Africa) 10-9 (TH)
Judge: Roberto Ramirez (Puerto Rico) 10-9 (TH)
Judge: Yusaku Yoshida (Japan) 10-9 (TH)

TITLE: WBC Light Flyweight
Champion: Hilario Zapata (Panama)
Challenger: Hector Melendez (Dominican Republic)
Date: August 4th
Place: Caracas, Venezuela
Weights: Zapata-108, Melendez-107¾
Result: Zapata by a unanimous decision
Referee: Rudy Jordon (USA) 147-141 (HZ)
Judge: Santos Arizmendi (Venezuela) 148-142 (HZ)
Judge: Umberto Figueroa (Panama) 148-139 (HZ)

TITLE: WBA Super Bantamweight
Champion: Leo Randolph (USA)
Challenger: Sergio Victor Palma (Argentina)
Date: August 9th
Place: Spokane, Washington
Weights: Randolph-122, Palma-121½
Result: Palma won title by a TKO at 1:12 of the 5th round
Referee: Stanley Christodoulou (South Africa)
Judge: Rudy Jordan (USA)
Judge: Luis Sulbaran (Venezuela)

TITLE: WBC Super Bantamweight
Champion: Wilfredo Gomez (Puerto Rico)
Challenger: Derrik Holmes (USA)
Date: August 22nd
Place: Las Vegas, Nevada
Weights: Gomez-121¾, Holmes-120¼
Result: Gomez by a TKO at 2:29 of the 5th round
Referee: Joey Curtis (USA)
Judge: Ismael Quinones Falu (Puerto Rico) 39-35 (WG)
Judge: Ray Solis (Mexico) 38-34 (WG)
Judge: Duane Ford (USA) 38-35 (WG)

TITLE: WBA Bantamweight
Champion: Jorge Lujan (Panama)
Challenger: Julian Solis (Puerto Rico)
Date: August 29th
Place: Miami Beach, Florida
Weights: Lujan-118, Solis-117¾
Result: Solis won title by a split decision
Referee: Jimmy Rondeau (USA) 144-143 (JS)
Judge: Medardo Villalobos (Panama) 148-144 (JL)
Judge: Waldemar Schmidt (Puerto Rico) 144-142 (JS)

TITLE: WBA Junior Middleweight
Champion: Ayub Kalule (Uganda)
Challenger: Bushy Bester (South Africa)
Date: September 6th
Place: Aarhus, Denmark
Weights: Kalule-153¼, Bester-152½
Result: Kalule by a unanimous decision
Referee: Davey Pearl (USA) 147-138 (AK)
Judge: Harold Buck (USA) 147-138 (AK)
Judge: Duane Ford (USA) 147-139 (AK)

TITLE: WBC Featherweight
Champion: Salvador Sanchez (Mexico)
Challenger: Patrick Ford (Guyana)
Date: September 13th
Place: San Antonio, Texas
Weights: Sanchez-126, Ford-126
Result: Sanchez by a split decision
Referee: Lou Filippo (USA)
Judge: Ramon Barumen (Mexico) 148-139 (SS)
Judge: Jose M. Escalante (Mexico) 145-145 (--)
Judge: A.D. 'Spider' Bynum (USA) 145-141 (SS)

TITLE: WBC Super Flyweight
Champion: Rafael Orono (Venezuela)
Challenger: Jovito Rengifo (Venezuela)
Date: September 15th
Place: Barquisamento, Venezuela
Weights: Orono-114¾, Rengifo-113½
Result: Orono by a TKO at 2:56 of the 3rd round
Referee: Zach Clayton (USA)
Judge: Jesus Celis (Venezuela)
Judge: Ladislao Sanchez (Venezuela)

TITLE: WBC Light Flyweight
Champion: Hilario Zapata (Panama)
Challenger: Shigeo Nakajima (Japan)
Date: September 17th
Place: Tokyo, Japan
Weights: Zapata-117¾, Nakajima-117¾
Result: Zapata by a TKO at 2:56 of the 11th round
Referee: Rudy Jordan (USA) 100-91 (HZ)
Judge: Humberto Figueroa (Panama) 100-91 (HZ)
Judge: Masao Kato (Japan) 100-95 (HZ)

TITLE: WBC Bantamweight
Champion: Guadalupe Pintor (Mexico)
Challenger: Johnny Owen (Wales)
Date: September 19th
Place: Los Angeles, California
Weights: Pintor-118, Owen-117½
Result: Pintor by a KO at 2:35 of the 12th round
Referee: Martin Denkin (USA) 107-102 (GP)
Judge: Chuck Hassett (USA) 105-103 (GP)
Judge: Dick Young (USA) 106-102 (GP)

TITLE: WBA Lightweight
Champion: Hilmer Kenty (USA)
Challenger: Ernesto Espana (Venezuela)
Date: September 20th
Place: San Juan, Puerto Rico
Weights: Kenty-135, Espana-135
Result: Kenty by a TKO at 2:57 of the 4th round
Referee: Martin Denkin (USA) 30-28 (HK)
Judge: Lou Tabat (USA) 29-28 (HK)
Judge: Larry Rozadilla (USA) 30-28 (HK)

TITLE: World Middleweight
Champion: Alan Minter (England)
Challenger: Marvin Hagler (USA)
Date: September 27th

Place: Wembley, England
Weights: Minter-159¾, Hagler-160
Result: Hagler won title by a TKO at 1:45 of the 3rd round
*Referee:*Carlos Berrocal (Panama) 20-19 (AM)
Judge: Marcelo Bertini (Italy) 20-19 (MH)
Judge: Juan Jose Guerra (Mexico) 20-19 (AM)

TITLE: WBC Super Lightweight
Champion: Saoul Mamby (USA)
Challenger: Maurice 'Termite' Watkins (USA)
Date: October 2nd
Place: Las Vegas, Nevada
Weights: Mamby 138½, Watkins-140
Result: Mamby by a unanimous decision
Referee: Mills Lane (USA)
Judge: Harold Buck (USA) 146-140 (SM)
Judge: Dimas Hernandez (Venezuela) 147-139 (SM)
Judge: Hank Elespuru (USA) 147-141 (SM)

TITLE: WBC Heavyweight
Champion: Larry Holmes (USA)
Challenger: Muhammad Ali (USA)
Date: October 2nd
Place: Las Vegas, Nevada
Weights: Holmes-211½, Ali-217½
Result: Holmes by a TKO in the 11th round (retired by corner after round)
Referee: Richard Greene (USA)
Judge: Chuck Minker (USA) 100-90 (LH)
Judge: Duane Ford (USA) 100-89 (LH)
Judge: Richard Steele (USA) 100-90 (LH)

TITLE: WBA Featherweight
Champion: Eusebio Pedroza (Panama)
Challenger: Rocky Lockridge (USA)
Date: October 4th
Place: at Gorge, New Jersey
Weights: Pedroza-126, Lockridge-126
Result: Pedroza by a split decision
Referee: Stanley Christodoulou (South Africa) 147-141 (EP)
Judge: Rodolfo Hill (Panama) 149-139 (EP)
Judge: Harold Lederman (USA) 144-142 (RL)

TITLE: WBA Junior Flyweight
Champion: Yoko Gushiken (Japan)
Challenger: Pedro Flores (Mexico)
Date: October 12th
Place: Kanazawa, Japan
Weights: Gushiken-107½, Flores-107¾
Result: Gushiken by a unanimous decision
Referee: Vincente Rainone (USA) 146-140 (YG)
Judge: Marcos Antonio Rodrigues (Mexico) 146-145 (YG)
Judge: Masao Kato (Japan) 146-142 (YG)

TITLE: WBC Flyweight
Champion: Shoji Oguma (Japan)
Challenger: Chan-Hee Park (Korea)
Date: October 18th
Place: Sendai, Japan
Weights: Oguma-111¾, Park-111½
Result: Oguma by a split decision
Referee: Harry Gibbs (England) 144-143 (SO)
Judge: Ken Morita (Japan) 146-145 (SO)
Judge: Kyu-Soon Kang (Korea) 148-144 (CHP)

TITLE: WBA Heavyweight
Champion: Mike Weaver (USA)
Challenger: Gerrie Coetzee (South Africa)

21

Date: October 25th
Place: Sun City, Bophuthatswana
Weights: Weaver-210, Coetzee-226½
Result: Weaver by a KO at 1:49 of the 13th rounds
(Venezuela) 117-113 (MW)
Judge: Ove Ovesson (Denmark) 116-115 (MW)
Judge: Harmodio Cedeno (Panama) 116-114 (MW)

TITLE: WBC Lightweight
Champion: Jim Watt (Scotland)
Challenger: Sean O'Grady (USA)
Date: November 1st
Place: Glasgow, Scotland
Weights: Watt-135, O'Grady-133
Result: Watt by a TKO at 2:37 of the 12th round
Referee: Raymond Baldeyrou (France) 109-105
(JW)
Judge: Harry Gibbs (England) 108-104 (JW)
Judge: Arthur Mercante (USA) 104-103 (JW)

TITLE: WBA Lightweight
Champion: Hilmer Kenty (USA)
Challenger: Vilomar Fernandez (Dominican
Republic)
Date: November 8th
Place: Detroit, Michigan
Weights: Kenty-135, Fernandez-134½
Result: Kenty by a unanimous decision
Referee: Waldemar Schmidt (Puerto Rico) 145-141
(HK)
Judge: Rogelio Perez (Panama) 147-141 (HK)
Judge: Guy Jutras (Canada) 146-141 (HK)

TITLE: WBA Super Bantamweight
Champion: Sergio Palma (Argentina)
Challenger: Ulises Morales (Panama)
Date: November 8th
Place: Buenos Aires, Argentina
Weights: Palma-121¾, Morales-119¾
Result: Palma by a TKO at 1:20 of the 9th round
Referee: Luis Sulbaran (Venezuela) 80-76 (SP)
Judge: Felix Dominguez (Argentina) 80-76 (SP)
Judge: Roberto Vecino (Uruguay) 80-76 (SP)

TITLE: WBA Bantamweight
Champion: Julian Solis (Puerto Rico)
Challenger: Jeff Chandler (USA)
Date: November 14th
Place: Miami, Florida
Weights: Solis-117½, Chandler-118
Result: Chandler won title by a TKO at 1:05 of the
14th round
Referee: Carlos Berrocal (Panama) 129-122 (JC)
Judge: Carol Polis (USA) 128-118 (JC)
Judge: Cesar Ramos (Puerto Rico) 125-124 (JC)

TITLE: WBA Junior Lightweight
Champion: Yasutsune Uehara (Japan)
Challenger: Leonel Hernandez (Venezuela)
Date: November 20th
Place: Tokyo, Japan
Weights: Uehara-129¾, Hernandez-129¼
Result: Uehara by a split decision
Referee: Chin-Kook Kim (Korea) 149-147 (YU)
Judge: Takeshi Shimakawa (Japan) 149-146 (YU)
Judge: Isidoro Rodriguez (Venezuela) 148-141 (LH)

TITLE: WBA Junior Welterweight
Champion: Aaron Pryor (USA)
Challenger: Gaetan Hart (Canada)
Date: November 22nd

Place: Cincinnati, Ohio
Weights: Pryor-138½, Hart-138¼
Result: Pryor by a TKO at 2:09 of the 6th round
Referee: Roberto Ramirez (Puerto Rico) 50-45 (AP)
Judge: Guy Jutras (Canada) 50-45 (AP)
Judge: Allen Daniel (Puerto Rico) 50-43 (AP)

TITLE: WBC Welterweight
Champion: Roberto Duran (Panama)
Challenger: Sugar Ray Leonard (USA)
Date: November 25th
Place New Orleans, Louisiana
Weights: Duran-146, Leonard-146
Result: Leonard won title by a TKO at 2:44 of the
8th round
Referee: Octavio Meyran (Mexico)
Judge: Mike Jacobs (England) 68-66 (SRL)
Judge: Jean Deswerts (Belgium) 68-66 (SRL)
Judge: James Brimmell (Wales) 67-66 (SRL)

TITLE: WBC Super Welterweight
Champion: Maurice Hope (England)
Challenger: Carlos Herrera (Argentina)
Date: November 25th
Place: Wembley, England
Weights: Hope-153½, Herrera-151¾
Result: Hope by a unanimous decision
Referee: Arthur Mercante (USA) 142-139 (MH)
Judge: Harry Gibbs (England) 145-142 (MH)
Judge: Horacio Lucena (Argentina) 147-146 (MH)

TITLE: WBC Cruiserweight
Champion: Marvin Camel (USA)
Challenger: Carlos DeLeon (Puerto Rico)
Date: November 25th
Place: New Orleans, Louisiana
Weights: Camel-182, DeLeon-182½
Result: DeLeon won title by a majority decision
Referee: Carlos Padilla (Philippines)
Judge: Roberto Ramirez (Puerto Rico) 145-142 (CD)
Judge: Ray Solis (Mexico) 145-145 (--)
Judge: Lucien Joubert (USA) 145-141 (CD)

TITLE: WBC Light Heavyweight
Champion: Matthew Saad Muhammad (USA)
Challenger: Lotte Mwale (Zambia)
Date: November 28th
Place: San Diego, California
Weights: Muhammad-175, Mwale-172½
Result: Muhammad by a KO at 2:25 of the 4th
round
Referee: Tony Perez (USA) 28-28 (--)
Judge: Roland Dakin (England) 29-29 (--)
Judge: Vince Delgado (USA) 29-28 (MSM)

TITLE: WBA Light Heavyweight
Champion: Eddie Mustafa Muhammad (USA)
Challenger: Rudi Koopmans (Holland)
Date: November 29th
Place: Los Angeles, California
Weights: Muhammad-175, Koopmans-175
Result: Muhammad by a TKO in 3 (retirement due
to cut eyelid)
Referee: Larry Rozadilla (USA) 30-27 (EMM)
Judge: James Jen Kin (USA) 30-28 (EMM)
Judge: Martin Denkin (USA) 30-27 (EMM)

TITLE: WBC Light Flyweight
Champion: Hilario Zapata (Panama)
Challenger: Reynaldo Becerra (Venezuela)
Date: December 1st

Place: Caracas, Venezuela
Weights: Zapata-108, Becerra-107
Result: Zapata by a split decision
Referee: Richard Steele (USA) 144-143 (HZ)
Judge: Humberto Figueroa (Panama) 146-143 (HZ)
Judge: Rafael Cayetano (Venezuela 146-146 (RB)

TITLE: WBA Welterweight
Champion: Thomas Hearns (USA)
Challenger: Luis Primera (Venezuela)
Date: December 6th
Place: Detroit, Michigan
Weights: Hearns-146½, Primera-146¾
Result: Hearns by a KO at 2:00 of the 6th round
Referee: Ismael Fernandez (Puerto Rico) 50-45 (TH)
Judge: Fernando Viso (Venezuela) 50-43 (TH)
Judge: Albert Tremari (USA) 49-44 (TH)

TITLE: Vacant WBC Super Featherweight
Challenger: Rafael Limon (Mexico)
Challenger: Ildefonso Bethelmy (Venezuela)
Date: December 11th
Place: Los Angeles, California
Weights: Limon-129¼, Bethelmy-129¼
Result: Limon by a TKO at 1:21 of the 15th round
Referee: Larry Rozadilla (USA)
Judge: Lou Fillipo (USA) 136-129 (RL)
Judge: Jorge Velasco (Mexico) 137-129 (RL)
Judge: Rafael Cartaya (Venezuela) 136-135 (RL)

TITLE: WBA Flyweight
Champion: Tae-Shik Kim (Korea)
Challenger: Peter Mathebula (South Africa)
Date: December 13th
Place: Los Angeles, California
Weights: Kim-111, Mathebula-112
Result: Mathebula won title by a split decision
Referee: Terry Smith (USA) 145-143 (PM)
Judge: Rudy Jordon (USA) 145-143 (PM)
Judge: James Jen Kim (USA) 145-141 (TSK)

TITLE: WBC Super Bantamweight
Champion: Wilfredo Gomez (Puerto Rico)
Challenger: Jose Cervantes (Colombia)
Date: December 13th
Place: Miami, Florida
Weights: Gomez-122, Cervantes-120½
Result: Gomez by a KO at 1:50 of the 3rd round
Referee: Ismael Quinones Falu (Puerto Rico) 20-18 (WG)
Judge: Eddie Eckert (USA) 20-18 (WG)
Judge: Horacio Castilla (Colombia) 19-19 (--)

TITLE: WBC Featherweight
Champion: Salvador Sanchez (Mexico)
Challenger: Juan LaPorte (USA)
Date: December 13th
Place: El Paso, Texas
Weights: Sanchez-126, LaPorte-124½
Result: Sanchez by a unanimous decision
Referee: Davey Pearl (USA)

Judge: Abraham Chavarria (Mexico) 148-142 (SS)
Judge: Vince Delgado (USA) 146-139 (SS)
Judge: A.D. 'Spider' Bynum (USA) 147-140 (SS)

TITLE: WBC Bantamweight
Champion: Guadalupe Pintor (Mexico)
Challenger: Alberto Davila (USA)
Date: December 19th
Place: Las Vegas, Nevada
Weights: Pintor-118, Davila-117½
Result: Pintor by a majority decision
Referee: Carlos Padilla (Philippines)
Judge: Anselmo Escobedo (Mexico) 143-142 (GP)
Judge: Angel Custodio Tovar (Venezuela) 146-142 (GP)
Judge: Duane Ford (USA) 143-143 (--)

Total number of title fights in 1980
WBC-51   WBA-37   Universal- 3

*number of title fights by division

	WBC	WBA	Universal
HEA	4	2	—
190	2	—	—
175	4	3	—
160	—	—	3
154	2	3	—
147	3	3	—
140	3	3	—
135	3	4	—
130	3	3	—
126	5	4	—
122	3	3	—
118	4	3	—
115	4	—	—
112	5	3	—
108	6	3	—
	51	37	3

*number of title fights by country

	WBC	WBA	Universal	Total
United States	26	19	1	46
Japan	6	7	—	13
Korea	5	3	—	8
England	2	0	2	4
Venezuela	6	0	—	6
Denmark	0	3	—	3
Scotland	3	0	—	3
Canada	2	0	—	2
Puerto Rico	1	1	—	2
Argentina	0	1	—	1
Colombia	0	1	—	1
Panama	0	1	—	1
South Africa	0	1	—	1
	51	37	3	91

THE RING'S UPDATED RECORDS OF ACTIVE FIGHTERS IN THE AMERICAS

BENNY ABARCA
Mexican Lightweight
(Previous Record Unavailable)
1980
May 10—Jose Luis Escalante, Mexico City .... W 10
July 12—Sergio Cabrera, Mexico City .... W 10

RICHARD ABBOTT
Los Angeles, Calif. Middleweight
1976
Sept. 23—Mike Hallacy, Wichita .... L 8
1977
Sept. 26—Ramon De Lao Canales, Stockton .... KO 3
Nov. 2—Greg McPherson, Concord .... L 6
1978
Jan. 4—Larry Muse, Las Vegas .... KO 3
Jan. 25—Steve Moyer, Las Vegas .... L 6
Jan. 28—Ernie Pope, Fresno .... W 6
Mar. 17—Ricky Weigel, Anaheim .... KO by 3
Apr. 19—Raul Dineros, Las Vegas .... L 6
May 18—James Waire, Los Angeles .... L 6
June 8—Ricky Weigel, Los Angeles .... L 6
1979
Mar. 22—Wally Yarborough, Los Angeles .... L 4
Mar. 29—Ted Sanders, Los Angeles .... L 6
May 4—John Vasquez, Pico Rivera .... L 4
Aug. 17—Dennis Mancino, San Diego .... L 6
1980
May 4—Jeff McCracken, Seattle .... L 6

MANUEL ABEDOY
Mexican Junior Lightweight
1974
Jan. 22—Leonardo Bermudez, Tijuana .... KO 1
Feb. 5—Alex Lopez, Tijuana .... W 10
Mar. 12—Eliu Hernandez, Tijuana .... KO 2
July 30—Pedro Jiminez, Tijuana .... W 10
Dec. 10—Valente Vera, Tijuana .... D 12
1975
Feb. 11—Carlos Barragan Vasquez, Tijuana ...... KO 2
Mar. 17—Saul Montana, Tijuana .... L 10
June 30—"Bobo" Gonzalez, Tijuana .... KO 8
Aug. 18—Victor Rios, Tijuana .... KO 5
Nov. 10—Lino Castillo, Tijuana .... KO 6
1976
Mar. 22—Tolquito Olivares, Tijuana .... W disq. 6
July 8—Alfredo Pitalua, Tijuana .... KO by 7
Oct. 22—Georges Cotin, Abidjan .... KO 5
1977
(Inactive)
1978
Jan. 9—Gerald Hayes, Tijuana .... W 10
Apr. 13—Jose Olivares, Los Angeles .... KO 6
Apr. 29—Fernando Cabanela, Los Angeles .... L 10
Oct. 25—Frank Ahumada, Las Vegas .... KO 5
1979
Dec. 13—Frankie Baltazar, Los Angeles .... L 10
1980
Apr. 14—Jaime Nava, Fresno .... W 10
June 30—Miguel Hernandez, Bakersfield .... KO 4
July 26—Ernesto Garfias, Los Angeles .... D 10

RAMON ABELDANO
Argentine Welterweight
1980
Feb. 1—Alberto Herrera, Brandsen .... W 6
Mar. 15—Manuel Alvarez, Buenos Aires .... L 6
Apr. 11—Felipe Baez, Brandsen .... W 6
June 27—Ramon E. Tevez, Villa Angela .... L 6
Aug. 16—Manuel Alvarez, Buenos Aires .... D 10
Oct. 10—Bernardo Narvaez, Concordia .... D 10
Dec. 12—Sergio Combis, Rosario .... L 10

VICTOR ABRAHAM
Los Angeles, Calif. Junior Welterweight
1973
July 5—Randy Shields, Los Angeles .... L 4
Sept. 19—Leroy Haley, Las Vegas .... L 6
Oct. 26—Tony Niebla, San Diego .... KO 5
Nov. 16—Julio Lopez, San Diego .... W 6
Dec. 20—Carlos Becerril, Los Angeles .... L 6

1974
Jan. 17—Randy Shields, Los Angeles .... L 6
Feb. 21—John Lujan, Los Angeles .... KO 6
Feb. 28—Claude Durden, Los Angeles .... KO 1
Mar. 15—Rudy Hernandez, San Diego .... L 6
Apr. 4—Trini Lopez, Los Angeles .... KO 4
May 2—Yosh Ogawa, Los Angeles .... W 10
Aug. 29—Robert Hernandez, Los Angeles .... L 10
Sept. 20—Miguel Mayan, San Diego .... L 10
Nov. 22—Miguel Mayan, San Diego .... W 8
1975
(Inactive)
1976
Mar. 18—Augustine Estrada, Stateline .... W 10
Mar. 25—Sigfrido Rodriguez, Los Angeles ...... KO by 6
June 16—Miguel Mayan, San Diego .... W 10
Aug. 10—Rado Broncano, Honolulu .... KO 2
Sept. 22—Mario Mendez, Honolulu .... W 10
Oct. 16—Francisco Rodriguez, San Juan .... KO 2
1977
May 5—Ramiro Bolanos', Los Angeles .... KO by 6
Aug. 25—Chris Gonzalez, Los Angeles .... W 10
1978
Jan. 19—Rudy Barro, Stockton .... W 10
Mar. 23—Pablo Baez, Los Angeles .... W 10
Apr. 11—Jimmy Rothwell, Philadelphia .... W 10
Aug. 31—Rudy Barro, Los Angeles .... L 10
1979
Jan. 14—Carlos Soto, San Juan .... KO 1
Apr. 5—Agapito Ramirez, Los Angeles .... W 10
1980
Aug. 23—J.J. Cottell, Inglewood .... KO 1
Mar. 22—Jose Duarte, Mexico City .... W 10
Apr. 25—Leonardo Bermudez, Culiacan .... W 10

JAMAL ABUBAKAR
Newark, N.J. Middleweight
1980
May 8—Bobby Czyz, Atlantic City .... L 4
July 16—Elwood Miller, Elizabeth .... KO 5
Aug. 27—Chris Rogers, Elizabeth .... W 6
Sept. 24—Abdul Sanda, Elizabeth .... W 4
Oct. 10—James Shuler, Newark .... L 4

PEDRO ACEVEDO
Bronx, N.Y. Middleweight
1980
Mar. 28—Carlton Swift, Tarrytown .... KO by 1
Sept. 18—Tommy Merola, Totowa .... KO by 1

MAURICIO ACEVES
Mexican Lightweight
1980
Feb. 16—Pedro Molina, Estado de Mexico .... KO 8
Mar. 22—Pedro Molina, Mexico City .... L disq. 3
June 7—Angel Mata, Mexico City .... KO by 2
Oct. 9—Cayetano Correa, Mexico City .... KO 8
Nov. 21—Armando Villalobos, Guadalajara ...... KO 4

ALEJO ACOSTA
Argentine Junior Welterweight
1980
June 14—Julio Sanchez, Baradero .... L 6
Aug. 22—Alfredo Palavecino, Mar del Plata ...... W 6
Nov. 28—Hugo Espinosa, Olavarria .... KO by 2

CANDIDO ACOSTA
Los Angeles, Calif. Welterweight
1977
Sept. 1—Jose Montanez, Los Angeles .... KO 2
Sept. 22—Howard Jackson, Los Angeles .... KO by 1
1978
(Inactive)
1979
Nov. 19—Chico Salinas, Bakersfield .... KO by 3
1980
Feb. 19—Sal Lopez, Sacramento .... KO by 4

EDUARDO ACOSTA
Argentine Lightweight
1980
Aug. 8—Alberto Castillo, San Juan .... W 10

LOUIS ACOSTA
Argentine Heavyweight, Based in Miami Beach, Fla.
1979
Nov. 27—Jimmy Jones, Miami Beach .... W 6

Dec. 18—Johnny Jackson, Miami Beach ....KO 1
1980
Jan. 29—Ron Harry, Miami ....KO 1
Feb. 12—John L. Johnson, Miami ....KO 2
Feb. 28—Jimmy Jones, Tampa ....W 6
Apr. 3—Terry Lee Wallace, Tampa ....KO 2
Apr. 15—Clinton Cochrane, Miami ....W 6
Apr. 27—Claman Parker, Greenville ....
June 14—Abdul Muhammad, Anaheim ....KO 6
Aug. 29—Al Byrd, Miami ....KO 4
Nov. 9—Gilberto Acuna, Santa Fe ....KO 4
(Latin American Heavyweight Title)

PEDRO ACOSTA
Colombian Welterweight
Born: May 24, 1956, Barranquilla
1975
Jan. 21—Victoriano Moya, Panama City ....KO 1
Feb. 23—Alfredo Junco, Cartagena ....KO 2
June 5—Rigoberto Pertuz, Cartagena ....W 6
Aug. 8—Eusebio Basquez, Cartagena ....W 6
1976
Feb. 8—Clemente Rojas, Cartagena ....W 10
May 16—Miguel Betruz, Cartagena ....D 12
(Colombian Lightweight Title Bout)
July 20—Enrique Maxwell, Cartagena ....W 10
Aug. 28—Miguel Betruz, Cartagena ....W 12
(Won Colombian Lightweight Title)
Oct. 16—Carlos Almanza, Cartagena ....KO 3
1977
Jan. 30—Alfonso Perez, Cartagena ....L 12
(Colombian Lightweight Title)
Feb. 26—Enrique Higgins, Cartagena ....KO 6
Mar. 18—Zenon Silgado, Cartagena ....D 10
Apr. 22—Luis Beltran, Cartagena ....KO by 8
May 14—Alfonso Frazer, Panama ....L 10
Oct. 29—Alfredo Junco, Panama City ....KO 4
Nov. 20—Pedro Rojas, Caracas ....KO by 8
1978
Mar. 4—Jose Ramirez, Caracas ....W 10
Oct. 21—Leonidas Asprilla, Cartagena ....W 12
(Latin American Lightweight Title)
Dec. 15—Claude Noel, Port of Spain ....L 10
1979
Feb. 17—Tommy Ortiz, Colon ....L 12
(Panamanian Junior Welterweight Title)
May 19—Leonidas Asprilla, Cartagena ....KO by 2
July 1—Lennox Blackmoore, Georgetown ....L 10
Oct. 9—Danny Stokes, Winnipeg ....W 10
Dec. 9—Johnny Summerhays, Winnipeg ....L 10
1980
Mar. 6—Ralph Racine, Winnipeg ....KO by 5
May 9—James Blevins, Chicago ....L 10
May 27—Charlie Nash, Belfast ....KO by 7
July 10—Johnny Lira, Chicago ....L 10
Aug. 8—Billy Moreno, Chicago ....W 10
Sept. 23—Gaetan Hart, Montreal ....L 10
Nov. 14—Juan Jose Giminez, Pesaro ....L 10
Nov. 19—Carlos Gonzales, Moline ....KO 3

ROMAN ACOSTA
Mexican Flyweight
1979
Jan. 13—Armando Perez, Mexico City ....L 10
Apr. 25—Rufino Hernandez, Merida ....KO 6
Aug. 12—Ricardo Finito, Tuxtla Gutierrez ....W 10
1980
May 14—Roberto Llanes, Merida ....W 10
July 30—Ricardo Lira, Merida ....KO 4
Oct. 14—Jorge DeJesus, Villahermosa ....L 10

VICTOR ACOSTA
Puerto Rican Featherweight
1980
Feb. 11—Jesus Rosado, San Juan ....W 4
Mar. 3—Pancho Chafrita, San Juan ....W 6
Apr. 21—Vicente Quinones, San Juan ....KO 8
July 3—Luis Rivera, Rio Piedras ....D 6
July 31—Luis Rivera, Rio Piedras ....L 8
Aug. 11—Luis Cueto, Trujillo ....KO 4
Sept. 11—Tito Roque, San Juan ....W 10

GILBERTO ACUNA
Costa Rican Heavyweight
1976
Sept. 28—Peter Muller, New York ....KO 1
Dec. 10—Dave Wilson, New York ....KO by 1

1977
Oct. 4—Billy Aird, London ....KO by 6
1978
Sept. 9—Tony Moore, Las Corogne ....KO 6
1979
July 11—Leroy Diggs, Rimini ....KO by 6
1980
Aug. 23—Joe Bugner, Inglewood ....KO by 6
Nov. 9—Luis Acosta, Sante Fe ....KO by 4
(Latin American Heavyweight Title)

JOAQUIN ACUNA
Mexican Featherweight
1976
May 1—Victor Diaz, Mexico City ....W 6
—Jacinto Gutierrez, Mexico City ....KO 1
Sept. 6—Fili Gonzalez, Mexico City ....KO 2
Dec. 12—Jorge Vera, Mexico City ....KO 2
1977
Jan. 14—Chamaco Leonard, Apatzingan ....KO 6
Mar. 16—Jose Sosa, Mexico City ....KO by 10
May 25—Jose Luis Valencia, Mexico City ....KO 4
July 6—Jose Luis Cruz, Mexico City ....KO by 6
1978
Jan. —Carlos Segura, Mexico City ....W 10
Mar. 22—Raul Valdez, Mexico City ....KO 2
May 10—Antonio Sanchez, Mexico City ....KO 1
May 24—Raul Reyes, Mexico City ....KO 3
July 5—Antonio Kiris, Mexico City ....KO 1
Sept. 16—Livio Nolasco, Mexico City ....KO 3
Nov. 11—Livio Nolasco, Mexico City ....KO 1
Dec. 2—Jorge Ramirez, Mexico City ....W 10
Dec. 19—Jorge Ramirez, Mexico City ....W 10
1979
Jan. 27—Jose Luis Cruz, Mexico City ....KO 7
Feb. 24—Condeario Bobadilla, Mexico City .....W 10
Mar. 28—Paulino Canche, Merida ....KO 8
May 5—Rafael Gandarilla, Mexico City ....W 10
Sept. 21—Jose Angel Cazares, Ciudad Juarez ... KO by 7
Nov. 23—Torito Melendez, Reynosa ....KO 6
1980
Feb. 2—Oscar Acuna, Phoenix ....L 10
Apr. 26—Hector Medina, Mexico City ....KO 5
May 16—Chuyin Lopez, Culiacan ....KO by 2
July 4—Mauricio Beltran, Culiacan ....KO by 2
Aug. 16—Gustavo Salgado, Mexico City ......KO by 5
Nov. 15—Federico Carreno, Mexico City ....KO 1
Dec. 21—Guillermo Morales, Tuxtla Gutierrez .....W 10

HUBERT (HERBERT) ADAMS
Cincinnati, Ohio Heavyweight
1979
May 21—Henry Porter, Belleville ....KO by 2
Dec. 19—George Mostardini, Rockford ....KO by 1
1980
Jan. 28—Mark Wickliff, Indianapolis ....KO by 1
May 17—Mike Schiebelhood, Dayton ....KO by 2
Sept. 12—Tom Fischer, Louisville ....KO by 1

DON ADDISON
Waterbury, Conn. Light Heavyweight
1978
June 29—Dan Veskovic, Springfield ....W 4
July 26—Tommy McNeece, New York ....L 4
Aug. 3—Frank Moore, Boston ....W 6
Sept. 20—John Powell, New York ....W 6
Nov. 21—Tony Tassone, Upper Darby ....W 8
Dec. 15—Marvin Lee, New York ....W 6
1979
Feb. 3—Dale Grant, Boston ....KO by 10
Feb. 28—Joe Maye, Hartford ....W 6
Apr. 3—Jerry Martin, Philadelphia ....KO by 3
May 18—Wilbur Henderson, Hartford ....D 8
July 27—Wilbur Henderson, Hartford ....D 8
Sept. 27—Joe Brown, Bristol ....KO 4
Nov. 5—Wilbur Henderson, Hartford ....KO 7
1980
Jan. 9—Matt Ross, Hartford ....W 10
Mar. 8—Murray Sutherland, Detroit ....KO by 4
May 23—Geoberto Almonte, Hartford ....KO 2
June 28—Reinaldo Oliveira, Manchester ....W 10
July 19—Mike Rossman, Atlantic City ....L 10
Sept. 12—Muhammad Shabazz, Hartford ....KO 11
(New England Light Heavyweight Title)
Oct. —Matt Ross, Providence ....W 10
Nov. 25—Cornell Chavis, Springfield ....KO by 4

JOEY ADELFIO
Chicago, Ill. Welterweight
1979
Oct. 10—Carlos Ramos, Las Vegas ....W 4

27

1980
Feb. 19—Eugene Jennings, Chicago ....KO 1

ASOR (AZOR) AGOSTO
Puerto Rican Lightweight
1976
Apr. 12—Jose Rivera, San Juan ....W 6
Aug. 12—Carlos DeLeon, San Juan ....L 8
1977
(Inactive)
1978
June 10—Jose Alejandro, Carolina, P.R. ....D 4
Aug. 14—Jose L. Latimer, Canovanas ....L 6
Aug. 26—Angel Nieto, Carolina ....L 6
Sept. 18—Angel Nieto, Rio Piedras ....D 6
Oct. 18—Antonio Cruz, Santo Domingo ....L 10
1979
Nov. 2—Leonel Hernandez, Caracas ....L 10
1980
May 22—Julio Guzman, Rio Piedras ....L 8

ALFREDO AGUAYO
Stockton, Calif. Junior Welterweight
1980
June 12—Jerry Reyes, Stockton ....KO 2
July 16—Eric Bonilla, Stockton ....KO 6
Oct. 16—Rosario Gonzales, Stockton ....W 10

ENRIQUE AGUERO
Argentine Lightweight
1980
Apr. 3—Geronimo Luque, Mendoza ....KO 4
May 23—Abraham Valenzuela, Mendoza ....D 10
Oct. 17—Abraham Valenzuela, San Luis ....D 10

RAUL AGUERO
Argentine Lightweight
1980
Feb. 1—Daniel Murua, Rio III ....L 10
Mar. 6—Oscar Frias, Cruz de Eje ....D 10
Apr. 24—Victor Echegary, San Juan ....L 10
May 9—Victor Zaya, S.Sal de Jujuy ....KO by 7
June 19—Hipolito Nunez, La Rioja ....KO by 9

DANNY AGUILAR
Stanton, Calif. Bantamweight
1979
Apr. 26—Aaron Morua, Pico Rivera ....W 6
May 25—Armando Ugalde, Pico Rivera ....W 6
June 14—Mario Cerda, Los Angeles ....W 6
Aug. 10—Eddie Estrada, San Diego ....W 4
Aug. 30—Lorenzo Ramirez, Los Angeles ....KO 5
1980
Mar. 6—Mario Cerda, Los Angeles ....D 6
Mar. 27—Ricardo Varela, Los Angeles ....L 10
July 15—Jose Luis Lopez, Anaheim ....KO 3
July 29—Frank Hesia, Honolulu ....KO 5
Aug. 13—Paz Mena, Las Vegas ....L 6
Sept. 5—Luis Avila, Inglewood ....L 10

LOBO AGUILAR
Mexican Flyweight
(Previous Record Unavailable)
1979
Mar. 1—Dario Ramirez, Puerto Vallarta ....W 10
1980
Jan. 15—Lorenzo Garcia, Puerto Vallarta .....KO by 3

LUIS (PAJARITO) AGUILAR
Mexican Flyweight
1976
Jan. 28—Raymundo Valdez, Halacho ....W 6
Jan. 31—Nacho Beltran, La Paz ....KO by 6
June 16—Raymundo Valdez, Merida ....L 6
1977
Feb. 14—Marco Ventura, Quintana ....KO 7
1978
Apr. 19—Manuel Acosta, Merida ....W 8
Aug. 12—Remigio Sulbaran, Maracay ....W 8
1979
Jan. 28—Jimmy Fernandez, Tuxtla Gutierrez .....W 12
June 3—Ulises Morales, Colon ....D 12
Aug. 12—Jimmy Fernandez, Tuxtla Gutierrez ......L 10
1980
Feb. 13—Jorge De Jesus, Merida ....KO 3
Apr. 5—Jose "Pepillo" Herrera, Mexico City ....L 10

ROBERTO AGUILAR
Argentine Heavyweight
1979
Mar. 10—Victor Galindez, San Miguel ....KO by 7

1980
Feb. 7—Antonio Musladino, San Juan ....D 10
May 17—Juan C. Sosa, Corrientes ....D 12
July 4—Antonio Musladino, Tucuman ....L 10
Sept. 12—Hugo Rufino, Cordoba ....L 8
Dec. 5—Antonio Musladino, Doblas ....W 10

JOAQUIN AGUILERA
Argentine Junior Welterweight
1980
June 2—Ruben Mansilla, Catrillo ....D 6
Aug. 1—Angel Heredia, Rio IV ....L 6
Oct. 17—Jorge Erramuspe, Trenel ....KO by 3

ALFONSO (LA CONESTA) AGUIRRE
San Antonio, Texas Welterweight
1979
Feb. 26—Ignacio Lopez, Houston ....L 6
June 2—Carlos Herrera, Albuquerque ....KO by 2
Nov. 6—Frank King, Corpus Christi ....KO by 3
1980
Apr. 14—Jose "Chichi" Santana ....KO 2

LUCIANO AGUIRRE
Argentine Lightweight
1980
July 4—Victor Altamirano, Cruz Alta ....W 6
July 25—Silverio Villalba, Rosario ....KO 3

RAUL (CONEJA) AGUIRRE
San Antonio, Texas Junior Welterweight
(Previous Record Unavailable)
1974
July 30—Gene Wells, Houston ....KO by 3
Sept. 16—Chris Baxter, Beaumont ....L 6
Nov. 14—Gene Wells, Beaumont ....KO by 4
1975
Apr. 22—Glenn Morgan, Orlando ....KO by 4
June 2—Jesse Lara, Piedras Negras ....W 8
July 5—Tony Moreno, Clovis, N.M. ....KO 5
July 24—Perry Abner, Philadelphia ....KO by 1
Oct. 4—Ike Fluellen, Mobile ....D 10
Oct. 14—David Wilson, Corpus Christi ....W 6
Nov. 4—Augie Gomez, Houston ....D 8
Nov. 18—Ray Sepulveda, Corpus Christi ....KO 4
Nov. 26—Lester Davis, Mobile ....W 8
1976
Jan. 20—Edgar Ross, Orlando ....KO by 5
Mar. 19—Sammy NeSmith, Indianapolis ....KO 4
Mar. 31—Augie Gomez, Galveston ....W 8
May 6—Sammy NeSmith, Indianapolis ....KO by 10
July 26—Tony Chiaverini, Topeka ....KO by 6
Oct. 27—Fate Davis, Cleveland ....KO by 2
Nov. 9—Bobby Thomas, Indianapolis ....KO 2
Nov. 24—Frankie Kolovrat, Cleveland ....KO by 7
1977
Jan. 21—Jose Duarte, Gomez Palacio ....W 10
Jan. 28—Jose Duarte, Gomez Palacio ....W 10
May 10—Steve Channel, Houston ....KO 1
May 17—Pete Tenorio, Corpus Christi ....KO 1
May 20—Adolfo Rivas, Marshall ....KO 1
July 17—Jesse Lara, Houston ....W 10
Sept. 6—Milton Owens, Orlando ....L 10
Oct. 11—Jesse Lara, Houston ....W 12
Nov. 5—Anthony Daniels, Kingsport ....L 10
Nov. 22—Jimmy Claar, Indianapolis ....W 6
1978
Feb. 11—Leroy Green, Kansas City ....L 10
May 16—Manuel Torres, Houston ....KO 2
July 20—Tommy Hearns, Detroit ....KO by 2
Aug. 25—Henry Walker, Dallas ....KO by 9
Nov. 22—Jerry Cheathan, Phoenix ....KO by 5
1979
Feb. 17—Gary Guiden, Indianapolis ....L 10
Mar. 31—Ron Pettigrew, San Antonio ....W 10
Apr. 24—Arturo Cirilos, Houston ....KO 3
Sept. 28—Basilio Guajardo, Monterrey ....KO 8
Oct. 3—Clarence Gilmore, Orlando ....KO 9
Nov. 13—Richard House, Orlando ....D 10
Dec. 29—Jose Duarte, Mexico City ....KO 2
1980
Feb. 29—Alberto Lopez, Monterrey ....KO by 10
Mar. 25—Larry Peterson, Jacksonville ....L 10
Apr. 14—Jose Santana, Chicago ....KO by 2
May 31—Jimmy Heair, El Paso ....KO by 9
(Texas Welterweight Title)
Sept. —Antonio Segurra ....KO 10
Oct. 10—Domingo Ayala, New York ....KO by 4
Nov. 8—Milton McCrory, Detroit ....KO by 1

RODRIGO AGUIRRE
Los Angeles, Calif. Featherweight
1977
May	25—Roberto Gutierrez, Las Vegas	L	6
June	23—Petronillo Velasquez, Los Angeles	W	4
Aug.	4—Fermin Navarro, Los Angeles	KO	2
Sept.	1—Paul Morales, Los Angeles	W	6

1978
Sept.	7—Petronillo Velasquez, Los Angeles	W	6
Nov.	8—Miguel Estrada, Las Vegas	W	10

1979
Aug.	9—Apollo Carbajal, Los Angeles	W	6
Aug.	16—Adolfo Hurtado, Los Angeles	W TD	6
Oct.	30—Alex Garcia, Bakersfield	W	8

1980
Jan.	18—Bob San Jose, San Bernardino	KO	2
Feb.	22—Sergio Nualarte, San Bernardino	KO	2
Apr.	4—Roman Contreras, San Bernardino	KO by	5
July	1—Fidel Fraijo, San Bernardino	TD	
Aug.	7—Gary Vinet, Los Angeles	W	4
Aug.	28—Juan Escobar, Los Angeles	W	10
Oct.	23—Roberto Garcia, Los Angeles	KO	6
Dec.	13—Jose Pacheco, El Paso	KO	4

TRINI AGUIRRE
Mexican Junior Lightweight
1980
Jan.	19—Sergio Aguirre, Mexio City	KO	3
Mar.	22—Cayetano Correa, Mexico City	KO by	1
Aug.	22—Beto Ramos, Acapulco	KO by	4

FRANK AHUMADA
Los Angeles, Calif. Junior Lightweight
1975
Jan.	24—Ruben Castillo, Tucson	KO by	4
Mar.	13—Ruben Castillo, Phoenix	L	6

1976
Feb.	12—Johnny Jenson, Los Angeles	L	6
Mar.	31—Lloyd Taylor, Las Vegas	L	6
Apr.	15—Scott Anderson, Las Vegas	D	6
Aug.	17—Ruben Castillo, Phoenix	L	12
	(Arizona State Featherweight Title)		

1977
Sept.	20—Simmie Black, New Orleans	KO	3

1978
Sept.	27—Miguel Estrada, Las Vegas	L	10
Oct.	25—Manuel Abedoy, Las Vegas	KO by	5

1979
Feb.	9—Roy Hernandez, Sacramento	W	10
Mar.	29—Frankie Baltazar, Los Angeles	L	10
June	2—Ruben Castillo, Albuquerque	L	10
Aug.	9—Frankie Baltazar, Los Angeles	L	10

u41980
Jan.	18—Rolando Navarette, Manila	L	10
Apr.	25—Rafael Limon, Anaheim	L	10

NATHANIEL AKBAR
Detroit, Michigan Junior Middleweight
1978
Oct.	26—Tommy Sacco, Detroit	KO	1
Dec.	9—Fred Reed, Detroit	W	4

1979
Feb.	2—Henry Sims, Chicago	W	6
Mar.	3—Ernie Davis, Detroit	W	6
May	8—Charley Peterson, Center Stage	W	4
May	24—Arthur Lee Body, Detroit	KO	3
July	12—Willie Brown, Detroit	KO	1
Sept.	20—Tommy Sacco, Detroit	W	8

1980
May	3—Willie Ray Taylor, Detroit	KO by	3

BOB AKERS
Waterville, Maine Heavyweight
1977
Jan.	6—Mike LaPointe, Portland	KO by	4
Nov.	24—Jimmy Ingalls, Portland	L	3

1978
Apr.	19—Mike LaPointe, Waterville	KO by	1

1979
May	17—Jesse Crown, Lubec, Me.	KO by	2

1980
Feb.	13—Paul Benjamin, Waterville	KO by	1

EDWIN ALARCON
Mexican Featherweight
1975
May	16—Ric Quijano, Manila	L	12

1979
Feb.	14—Erning Grafe, Cebu City	D	10
Feb.	21—Soo Hwang Hong, Seoul	KO by	4
June	11—Rey Cellano, Manila	D	10

1977
May	17—Santiago Hernandez, Honolulu	KO	1
June	28—Jose Del Rio, Honolulu	KO	5
Aug.	3—Mauricio Garcia, Honolulu	KO	2
Sept.	13—David Barrera, Honolulu	KO	8
Oct.	25—David Barrera, Honolulu	W	10
Nov.	29—Alex Oregel, Honolulu	W	10

1978
Feb.	25—Dong Kyun Yum, Seoul	L	10
Apr.	25—Jose Caba, Honolulu	KO by	2
July	18—Mike Ayala, San Antonio	L	10
Aug.	22—Danny Felizarde, San Antonio	KO	9
Nov.	21—Salvador Sanchez, San Antonio	KO by	8

1979
Mar.	24—Ernesto Gonzalez, Chicago	L	10
June	19—Virgilio Legaspi, Honolulu	KO	3
July	24—Juan Bautista, Honolulu	L	10

1980
Feb.	19—Ralph Aviles, Honolulu	L	10
Mar.	3—Ruben Castillo, Bakersfield	KO by	6

HUGO ALBAREZ
Argentine Welterweight
1980
Mar.	6—Simon Escobar, Bahia Blanca	KO by	7
Aug.	15—Ramon Oviedo, Mendoza	KO	9
Sept.	6—Juan C. Morales, Santa Fe	KO	9
Oct.	17—Simon Escobar, Cordoba	D	10

WILBERT (JUNIOR) ALBERS
Stockton, Calif. Heavyweight
1977
Mar.	9—Charles Terrell, San Carlos	KO	5
Mar.	31—Jim Castagnola, San Carlos	KO	2
June	3—Norman Sweeney, San Jose	KO by	6
July	20—Mustafa El Amin, Stockton	W	6
	—Ray Robinson, Las Vegas	KO	6
Sept.	17—Aldo Traversaro, Rome	L	8
Oct.	20—King David Smith, Eureka	L	10
Nov.	12—Leni Vanisi, Eureka	KO	7

1978
Mar.	2—King David Smith, Stockton	W	10
Mar.	10—Len Provo, San Diego	L	6
Apr.	14—Jim Ingram, San Diego	L	6
June	1—Bashiru Alli, Sacramento	W	6
Aug.	30—Ken Austin, Reno	W	7

1979
Jan.	17—Alvaro (Yaqui) Lopez, Stockton	KO by	3
Sept.	18—Harvey Steichen, Reno	KO by	8

1980
Jan.	9—James Williams, Las Vegas	KO by	6

MAURICIO ALDANA
Los Angeles, Calif. Welterweight
1978
Aug.	30—Donnie London, Las Vegas	KO	2
Oct.	25—Marvin Edwards, Las Vegas	W	8
Nov.	8—Pedro Pina, Las Vegas	L	8
Dec.	13—Ron Cummings, Oakland	L	8

1979
Jan.	10—Bruce Strauss, Las Vegas	KO	1
Jan.	17—Idika Nsofor, Las Vegas	KO	5
Feb.	1—Agapito Ramirez, Los Angeles	L	8
Mar.	14—Idika Nsofor, Las Vegas	W	6
Mar.	28—Leroy Jefferson, Las Vegas	L	8
Apr.	12—Danny Adams, Oakland	W	8
May	3—Agapito Ramirez, Los Angeles	L	10
May	30—Alfredo Logan, Honolulu	KO	3
June	12—Alfredo Logan, Honolulu	KO	4
Sept.	5—Marcy Atencio, Las Vegas	W	10
Sept.	19—Horace Shufford, Las Vegas	L	10
Oct.	31—Dick Fisher, Las Vegas	KO	7
Dec.	2—Randy Shields, Los Angeles	L	10

1980
May	1—Gary Giron, Las Vegas	W	10
May	29—Randy McGrady, Las Vegas	L	10
Aug.	5—Pete Ranzany, Sacramento	L	10
Dec.	4—Alejos Rodriguez, Los Angeles	D	10
Dec.	26—Clint Jackson, Las Vegas	KO by	7

JESSIE ALDRIDGE
San Matteo, California Light Heavyweight
1979
Dec.	11—Lee Burkey, Sparks	KO by	1

1980
Feb.	29—Joe Wade, Nanaimo	KO by	3
Mar.	27—Johnny Matthews, Stockton	KO by	3
Aug.	6—Larry Frazier, Las Vegas	KO by	1

FARRIED ALEDULLAH
Lakeland, Fla. Heavyweight
1980
Jan.	31—Tiger Brown, Orlando	KO 2
Feb.	28—Ernie Barr, Tampa	KO by 3

JOSE ALEJANDRO
Puerto Rican Featherweight
1978
Feb.	12—Chico Rosa, Carolina	L 8
June	10—Azor Agosta, Carolina	D 4
Aug.	28—Antonio Cruz, Santo Domingo	KO by 11

1979
Aug.	11—Angel Rosa, Trujillo	KO 5

1980
Feb.	11—Francisco Cruz, San Juan	W 10
May	19—Felix Trinidad, San Juan	W 10
July	17—Rafael Solis, Rio Piedras	KO by 9
Aug.	22—Elidez Ortiz, San Juan	W 10
Sept.	25—Daniel Rivera, San Juan	L 10

BOBBY (WILD MAN) ALEXANDER
New York City, N.Y. Junior Lightweight
1974
Aug.	5—Alfonso Taylor, New York	W 6
Oct.	7—Ruby Ortiz, New York	L 6
Nov.	19—Jose Resto, Paterson	W 6
Dec.	9—Hector Espinosa, N. Bergen	W 6

1975
Jan.	30—Hector Espinosa, N. Bergen	W 6

1976
(Inactive)
1977
Apr.	1—Leo Randolph, New York	KO 1
Apr.	15—Malcolm Driver, New York	W 4
May	20—Curtis Smith, New York	W 6
Sept.	23—Rufus Figueroa, New York	W 8

1978
Mar.	2—Alberto Collazo, Cleveland	W 10
Apr.	19—Angel Cruz, Allentown	KO by 5
May	20—Henry Rosa, Trenton	W 8
June	10—Clyde Beattie, Brooklyn	KO 2
Aug.	26—Ralph Racine, Pittsburgh	KO by 7
Oct.	19—Hank Rosa, Garfield	W 8
Oct.	27—Arcadio Suarez, New York	KO by 8
Dec.	5—Alfonso Evans, Philadelphia	D 6

1979
Feb.	8—Alberto Collazo, New Kensington	L 10
July	26—Antonio Cruz, Santo Domingo	L 10

1980
Jan.	25—Carmelo Negron, New York	KO by 10
Mar.	23—Greg Coverson, Grand Rapids	L 10
Aug.	25—Luis B. Rodriguez, Caracas	KO by 4

GARY ALEXANDER
Ohio Light Heavyweight
1974
Aug.	10—Jeff Wynne, Fairmont	W 6
Nov.	30—Dino Pellegrini, Toronto	D 4

1975
Feb.	15—Joe Blair, Alliance	W 6
Mar.	—Dino Pellegrini, Toronto	D 4
June	25—Pancho Ortiz, Indianapolis	KO 2
Sept.	7—Joe Henry, Toronto	L 8
Nov.	13—Eddie Queen	KO 6

1976
May	6—Harry Terrell, Cleveland	L 6
Aug.	26—Jimmy Owens, Canton	L 8
Oct.	2—Mayfield Pennington, Alliance	W 8
Nov.	6—Sylvester Wilder, Alliance	W 8

1977
May	7—Jamie Thomas, Cincinnati	L 6
Aug.	19—Johnny Heard, Pikeville	KO by 3
Sept.	24—Frankie Williams, Hamilton	D 6
Oct.	15—Anthony Jones, Salem	W 6
Oct.	29—Manuel Collazo, Hamilton	W 6
Dec.	—John Giroski, Pittsburg	W 10

1978
Feb.	16—Pat Cuillo, Cleveland	KO by 7
Mar.	31—Felton Woods, Saginaw	L 8
Apr.	29—Joe Klutz, Sebring	KO 5
May	27—Gary Summerhays, Brantford	L 8
Oct.	17—Murray Sutherland, Canton	L 8
Oct.	31—Gary Summerhays, Verdun	KO by 10

1979
(Inactive)
1980
May	3—Baker Tinsely, Canton	W 6
May	10—Al Bolden, Clarksburg	KO by 6
Aug.	23—Ed Temple, Alliance	KO 4

LARRY ALEXANDER
Memphis, Tenn. Heavyweight
1977
July	25—Don Martin, Memphis	KO 3
Sept.	20—Clifton Haynes, Memphis	KO 1
Nov.	8—Robert Echols, Memphis	KO by 5
Dec.	4—Raul Rodrigues, Memphis	KO 2
Dec.	7—Nick Wells, Topeka	KO by 7

1978
Jan.	10—James Dixon, Memphis	D 6
Jan.	29—Louis Tillman, Knoxville	KO 3
Feb.	8—Lynn Ball, Memphis	L 8
Mar.	21—Robert Reynosa, Greenville	KO 1
Apr.	4—Edward Baines, Greenville	KO 1
Apr.	25—Lee Holloman, Greenville	KO 3
May	9—Walter Santemore, Memphis	L 6
May	23—Carlton Morris, Greenville	KO 2
July	22—Willie (Le Roy) Brown, Knoxville	KO 1
Aug.	3—Joe (Gorilla) Griffen, Birmingham	KO 1
Sept.	21—Walter Santemore, Birmingham	L 10
Nov.	1—Rochelle Norris, White Plains	KO 7

1979
Feb.	9—Tom Nickson, Mobile	L 6
Feb.	16—A. J. Staples, Louisville	KO 2
May	24—John Hudson, Detroit	KO 6
Sept.	26—George Chaplin, Baltimore	L 12
Dec.	4—Marvin Stinson, Philadelphia	D 8

1980
Feb.	24—Jerry Thompkins, Atlantic City	KO 2
Apr.	15—Jeff Simms, Miami Beach	KO 6
Apr.	24—Bob Stallings, Totowa	KO 8
May	16—Greg Page, Lexington	KO by 6
Sept.	17—Renaldo Snipes, Westchester	KO by 2

ROBERTO ALFARO
Argentine Junior Welterweight
1980
Jan.	—Hugo Luero, Mar del Plata	W 12

(Won Argentine Junior Welterweight Title)
Mar.	22—Hugo Luero, Buenos Aires	W 12

(Won South American Junior Welterweight Title)
Apr.	17—Inocencio De La Rosa, Mendoza	W 10
May	23—Juan Merlo, Mendoza	W 12

(Retained Argentine Junior Welterweight Title)
July	11—Mario Martinez, Mendoza	KO 2
Aug.	8—Ramon Allende, Rio IV	D 10
Dec.	12—Nicolas Arkuszyn, San Juan	TD 7

JULIO ALFONSO
Dominican Rep. Welterweight
1975
Feb.	8—Jose Hernandez, Santo Domingo	KO 2

1976
Aug.	16—Teodoro Ozuna, La Roma	KO by 4

1977-1978
(Inactive)
1979
Mar.	10—Jorge Labrada, Los Angeles	L 4
Mar.	22—Tony Baltazar, Los Angeles	KO by 2
Mar.	30—Angel Maquilon, Barranquilla	W 8
May	9—Danny Adams, Oakland	KO by 2
Aug.	15—German Cuello, Las Vegas	KO by 4
Oct.	9—Vito Meredith, Honolulu	KO by 1
Nov.	21—Hedgemon Robertson, Los Angeles	KO by 1

1980
Feb.	6—Randy Clover, Las Vegas	KO by 2
July	17—Mario Tenio, Tucson	L disq. 2
Aug.	13—Pete Seward, Las Vegas	KO by 2
Oct.	7—Joe Maldonado, Bakersfield	KO by 5

BASHIRU ALI
San Carlos, Cal. Light Heavyweight
1978
June	1—Junior Albers, Sacramento	L 6
June	21—Charles Terrell, Concord	W 6
July	12—Jim Ingram, Oakland	L 6
July	22—William Tavake, Truckee	W 6
July	28—Reggie Phillips, San Diego	L 5
Dec.	6—Tony Stone, Stockton	W 6

1979
Feb.	27—Greg McPherson, San Carlos	L 10
Mar.	27—Basheer Wasud, San Carlos	W 6
Apr.	24—Greg McPherson, San Carlos	W 10
June	27—Pete McIntyre, Los Angeles	L 10
Oct.	4—Yaqui Lopez, San Carlos	L 10

1980
Jan.	31—Len Provo, San Carlos	KO 8
Feb.	29—David Smith, San Carlos	W 10
Apr.	11—Yaqui Meneses, San Carlos	W disq.
July	25—Jim Ingram, San Carlos	KO 7
Aug.	28—Byron Campbell, San Carlos	KO 5
Oct.	16—Alvaro Lopez, San Carlos	KO 10
Dec.	3—Jesse Burnett, Los Angeles	W 12

30

KATO ALI
(ANTHONY CURRY)
Philadelphia, Pa. Junior Lightweight
1979
Nov. 15—Antonio Nieves, Dover ....L 4
1980
Jan. 19—Martin Parham, Hempstead ....L 4
Feb. 13—Billy Costello, Westchester ....L 6
Apr. 16—Billy Costello, Westchester ....KO by 3
June 27—Tony Santana, New York ....L 6

MUSTAFA ALI
St. Thomas, V.I. Middleweight
1979
Jan. 27—Chico Santos, San Juan ....KO by 7
May 31—Eddie Marcelle, St. Thomas ....L 10
Oct. 19—Juan Cantres, St. Thomas ....W 10
1980
Jan. 27—Carlos Soto, San Juan ....KO by 8
May 31—Eddie Marcelle, St. Thomas ....W 12
(Won Caribbean Welterweight Title)
Oct. 19—Juan Cantres, St. Thomas ....W 10

ROBERTO ALE ALI
Argentine Welterweight
1980
Feb. 15—Martin Duran, Tucuman ....W 10
Mar. 7—Santiago Portillo, Tucuman ....L 6
Oct. 24—Jose Sanchez, Tucuman ....D 10
Dec. 12—Alberto Gonzalez, Tucuman ....KO 6
Dec. 26—Alberto Butiler, La Banda ....L 10

ALI ALLEN
Fairlawn, New Jersey Heavyweight
1979
June 12—Robert Evans, Totowa ....W 4
July 31—Rubio Rodriguez, Totowa ....W 6
Sept. 18—Rubio Rodriguez, E. Rutherford ....KO 1
Oct. 4—Terry Lee Kidd, N. Bergen ....KO 1
Oct. 26—Barry Funches, New York ....D 4
Nov. 28—Robert Evans, W. New York, N.J. ....D 4
1980
Jan. 25—Barry Funches, New York ....L 6
Feb. 27—Jerry Foley, Scranton ....W 8
Mar. 8—Melvin Epps, Great Gorge ....L 6
Mar. 26—Jerry Foley, Scranton ....W 8
May 28—Marty Capasso, Scranton ....L 8

LINWOOD ALLEN
Bronx, N.Y. Heavyweight
1980
Mar. 12—Paul Telesca, Westchester ....L 4
Apr. 26—Kerry Judge, Atlantic City ....KO by 3

LLOYD ALLEN
Cleveland, Ohio Junior Lightweight
1978
Jan. 12—Mike Johnson, Cleveland ....W 4
Feb. 16—Charles Buggs, Cleveland ....KO 2
Mar. 16—Ray Green, Cleveland ....KO 5
Apr. 6—Ron Furlow, Cleveland ....KO 6
Dec. 6—Alberto Collazo, Cleveland ....L 10
1979
May 16—Francisco Alvarado, Las Vegas ....W 8
Sept. 30—Willie Whipple, Canton ....L 10
1980
May 3—Chico Rodriguez, Canton ....KO 5

RAMON ALLENDE
Argentine Junior Welterweight
1980
Jan. 4—Sergio Loyola, Laboulaye ....W 10
Feb. 8—Sergio Loyola, Vdo Tuerto ....KO 5
Mar. 22—Ubaldo Sacco, Mar del Plata ....KO by 3
June 6—Pablo Vanegas, Laboulaye ....KO 10
July 4—Juan Namuncura, Cutralco ....L 10
Aug. 8—Roberto Alfaro, Rio IV ....D 10
Sept. 6—Jorge Paredes, Formosa ....W 10
Oct. 3—Juan Zuniga, Rio IV ....D 10
Dec. 11—Joaquin Moreyra, Formosa ....L 10

TERRANCE ALLI
Guyanan Junior Lightweight
1980
Aug. 1—Cleophus James, Port-of-Spain ....W 6
Oct. 17—Clyde Wilson, Port-of-Spain ....W 6

OMAR ALMADA
Argentine Junior Lightweight
1980
Mar. 11—Raul Bianco, Formosa ....L 10

June 6—Jorge M. Gomez, Neuquen ....L 10
July 8—Juan D. Malvarez, Catamarca ....L 10
Aug. 8—Armando Perez, Gral Pico ....L 10
Sept. 19—Hugo Villarruel, Rafaela ....L 10
Oct. 24—Hugo Villarruel, Ceres ....D 12

PEDRO ALONSO
1980
June 27—Evencio Rojas, Apatzingan ....KO 1
Sept. 2—Venado Tellez, Queretaro ....KO 5

RAFAEL (RATON) ALONSO
Mexico City Flyweight
1980
Jan. 12—Daniel Gonzalez, Mexico City ....KO 3
May 7—Jose Cordoba, Mexico City ....KO 5
June 21—Victor Palma, Mexico City ....KO 3
Aug. 30—Hipolito Hernandez, Mexico City ....W 8
Oct. 25—Juan Flores, Mexico City ....KO 2

ROBERTO (FURIA) ALONSO
Mexican Junior Featherweight
1980
Feb. 1—Alfonso Rodriguez, Guadalajara .....KO by 7
Mar. 28—Delfino Mendoza, Guadalajara ......KO by 5
May 28—Eduardo Torres, Mexico City ....KO by 2

ROSENDO (ROCKY) ALONSO
Mexican Flyweight
1978
Mar. —Mario Garcia, ...KO 2
May —Daniel Gruillon, Tuxtla Gutierrez ....L 10
May 22—Aragon Perez, Mexico City ....W 6
July 8—Baltazar Espana, Mexico City ....W 8
July 21—Rodolfo Quintero, Guadalajara ....W 10
Aug. 11—Kiko Bejines, Guadalajara ....W 10
Sept. 27—Francisco Gonzales, Mexico City ....KO 9
Oct. 27—Jorge Cruz, Mexico City ....KO 3
Dec. 9—Hector Cortez, Mexico City ....KO by 3
1979
Feb. 17—Jorge Vega, Mexico City ....KO 3
Mar. 7—Armando Perez, Mexico City ....W 10
Apr. 25—Manuel Luna, Mexico City ....KO by 5
July 6—Chuyin Lopez, Culiacan ....KO by 4
Aug. 3—Rodolfo Martinez, Guadalajara ....W 10
Sept. 14—Ambrosio Luna, Guadalajara ....W 10
Dec. 19—Kiko Bejinez, Guadalajara ....W 12
1980
Mar. 8—Guillermo Vallejo, Mexico City .....KO by 3
Apr. 25—Nicandro Martinez, Guadalajara ....KO 7
July 4—Ruben Mancilla, Guadalajara ....KO 1
Sept. 5—Juan Jose Guzman, Guadalajara ....KO 5

VICTOR ALTAMIRANO
Argentine Lightweight
1980
July 4—Luciano Aguirre, Cruz Alta ....L 6
Sept. 20—Ramon Bustos, Zarate ....KO by 2

CARLOS ALVARADO
Mexican Bantamweight
1980
Jan. 10—Vicente Villasano, Ocatlan ....KO 1
Jan. 17—Cecilio Estrada, Ocotlan ....KO 5
Mar. 21—Elpidio Infante, Acapulco ....KO by 1

FRANCISCO ALVARADO
El Paso, Texas Featherweight
1977
Nov. 2—Armando Hernandez, El Paso ....KO by 3
1978
Mar. 8—Arthur Jiminez, Las Vegas ,............KO 3
Apr. 4—Jesus Ruelas, El Paso ....W 6
May 25—Francisco Monzon, Denver ....KO 3
June 18—Leonel Valencia, Salt Lake City ....KO by 7
Sept. 28—Armando Hernando, El Paso ....KO 2
1979
Jan. 17—Jose Resendiz, Las Vegas ....W 10
Feb. 26—Valentin Holguin, Los Angeles ......KO by 3
Apr. 4—Chocolate Rueles, Las Angeles ....W 6
Apr. 25—Miguel Ruiz, Las Vegas ....KO 6
May 16—Lloyd Allen, Las Vegas ....L 8
June 18—Luis Loy, Los Angeles ....KO by 1
Oct. 4—Carlos Davila, Los Angeles ....W 4
Dec. 4—Jeff Chandler, Philadelphia ....KO by 7
1980
Jan. 24—Pablo Gomez, Los Angeles ....W 6
Feb. 26—Sal Ramirez, San Bernardino ....KO 5
Mar. 17—Juan Villasano, Bakersfield ....KO 6
June 5—Clark Duran, Los Angeles ....W TD 3

31

ROCKY ALVARADO
Mexican Flyweight
(Previous Record Unavailable)
1980
May   2—"Olivaritos" Olguin, Chihuahua .... L 12
     (Junior Flyweight Title of Chihuahua State)

OSCAR ALVARENGA
Argentine Lightweight
1980
Jan.   —Manuel Lopez, San Juan .... KO 7
Feb. 14—Miguel Figueroa, San Juan .... D 10
Mar. 21—Julio Melone, Rosario .... L 10
July 12—Juan Zuniga, Gral Pico .... KO 4
Aug.   8—Julio Melone, Cordoba .... L 10
Sept. 6—Justino Heredia, Gral Pico .... D 10

JUAN CÀRLOS ALVAREZ
Argentine Lightweight
1980
Jan.   —Victor Escobar, P.R.S. Oena .... KO by 3
July 18—Pedro Arm. Gutierrez, San Nicholas ...... L 10
Oct. 17—Julio Alegre, P.R.S. Pena .... L 10

JUAN ALVAREZ
Mexico City Bantamweight
1976
Jan. 10—Abundio Cortez, Mexico City .... W 10
Feb.   7—Pedro Flores, Mexico City .... W 10
Mar. 21—Mariano Garma, Mexico City .... KO 5
May   1—Luis Estaba, Caracas .... L 15
     (For WBC Junior Flyweight Title)
July   3—Ignacio Espinal, Mexico City .... W 10
Sept. 4—Valentin Martinez, Mexico City ...... KO by 6
     (Mexican Flyweight Title)
Nov. 13—Hermogene Prado, Managua .... KO 7
1977
Jan. 14—Julio Lopez, Coatzalcoalcos .... KO 5
Feb. 11—Jose Gallegos, Piedras Negras .... W 10
Apr.   9—Alberto Morales, Mexico City .... KO by 10
Aug. 21—Luis Estaba, Puerto La Cruz .... KO by 11
     (For WBC Junior Flyweight Title)
1978
Feb. 13—Ricardo Varela, Tuxtla Gutierrez .... W 10
Mar. 17—Jose Luis Cruz .... L 10
Mar. 25—Jose Luis Cruz, Mexico City .... L 10
Apr. 21—Pedro Galaviz, San Luis Potosi .... KO 2
     (North American Junior Flyweight Title)
July 29—Freddie Castillo, Merida .... KO by 10
Oct. 21—Lupe Madera, Merida .... L 10
Dec. 30—Pedro Galaviz, Mexico City .... KO 8
1979
Mar. 31—Gabriel Bernal, Mexicali .... L 10
Apr. 28—Jose Sosa, Mexico City .... L 10
July 20—Alfonso Zamora, San Luis Potosi .... W disq. 3
Sept. 20—Alberto Sandoval, Los Angeles .... L 10
Oct. 26—Tony Escobar, Culiacan .... KO 10
1980
Jan. 12—Jorge Ramirez, Mexico City .... W disq. 2
Mar.   8—Jorge Ramirez, Mexico City .... KO by 9
July 11—Jesus Chuyin Lopez, Culiacan .... KO by 3
Sept. 12—Horacio Pintado, Hermosillo .... KÒ 8

LUIS ALVAREZ
Argentine Junior Featherweight
1980
Jan.   —Urbano Villalba, Salta .... KO 2
Feb. 22—Carlos Betbeder, Salta .... W 10
Mar. 21—Ramon Dominguez, Salta .... W 10
Apr. 11—Diego Ramirez, Salta .... D 10
June 27—Americo Suarez, Salta .... L 10
Aug. 15—Juan Medina, S. Ped Jujuy .... W 10
Sept. 26—Carlos Totaro, Salta .... W 10
Dec.   5—Hugo Emer, Salta .... KO by 10

MANUEL ALVAREZ
Argentine Welterweight
1980
Mar. 15—Ramon Abeldano, Buenos Aires .... W 6
Apr.   5—Roberto Cornejo, Mar del Plata .... W 8
May   —Julio Sanchez, Buenos Aires .... D 6
June 14—Roberto Macial, Gral Belgrano .... W 6
Aug. 16—Ramon Abeldano, Buenos Aires .... D 10
Sept.   5—Jose Comolli, Tucuman .... W 8
Sept. 19—Martin Duran, Tucuman .... W 10
Oct.   3—Jose Guevara, Tucuman .... W 10
Oct. 24—Oscar San Juan, Tucuman .... KO 9
Nov. 14—Martin Duran, Tucuman .... W 10
Dec. 12—Ramon D. Moreyra, Tucuman .... W 10

MIKE ALVAREZ
Newark, N.J. Junior Welterweight
1980
Mar. 20—Ted White, North Bergen .... W 6
May 31—Ray Rosa, Elizabeth .... KO 3
Sept. 24—Bob Harvey, Halifax .... L 4

REYNALDO ALVAREZ
Texas Junior Lightweight
1980
Feb. 28—Johnny Contreras, McAllen .... KO by 2
Apr. 15—Jose Cabrera, Houston .... KO by 2

JAVIER AMARILLAS
Texas Bantamweight
1980
June 13—Jose Luis Soto, Los Mochis .... KO by 3
July 25—Antonio Lopez, Los Mochis .... KO by 2

TOM AMATO
Massapequa, New York Welterweight
1980
Aug. 15—James Donnelly, Glen Cove .... KO by 2
Oct.   2—Charles Thompson, Commack .... KÒ 2

ALVIN ANDERSON
Baltimore, Maryland, Junior Middleweight
1967
May 25—Sherman Mitchell, Baltimore .... W 4
July 10—George Scott, Baltimore .... KO 2
1968
(In U.S. Army)
1969
Oct. 13—Billy Garrett, Washington, D.C. .... KO 3
Nov. 25—Johnny Sanders, Philadelphia .... W 4
Dec. 11—Al Thomas, Baltimore .... KO 4
1970
Jan. 21—Roland Marshall, Leonardtown .... W 6
Mar. 19—Claude Wade, Baltimore .... W 4
Apr.   7—Roland Marshall, Philadelphia ...... KO by 4
May 28—Carlos Byrd, Baltimore .... KÒ 3
June 27—Claude Wade, Baltimore .... KO 1
Aug. 25—Richie Royal, Washington, D.C. .... KO 1
Sept. 22—Winston Noel, Washington, D.C. .... W 10
Nov. 10—Adrian Davis, Washington, D.C. .... W 10
1971
Aug. 10—Hector Perez, Baltimore .... W 10
Oct. 28—Herbie Lee, Baltimore .... KO 9
1972
Jan. 18—Art Kettles, Baltimore .... W 10
Apr. 20—Dick DiVeronica, Baltimore .... D 10
Nov. 20—Miguel Barreto, Philadelphia .... D 10
1973
Apr. 23—Elwood Townsend, Philadelphia .... KO 1
May 11—Mario Saurennan, Philadelphia .... L 10
July 23—James Taylor, Philadelphia .... KO 3
Oct. 16—Lamont Lovelady, Des Moines .... L 10
Nov. 26—Fausto Rodriguez, San Juan .... KO 4
1974
Apr. 15—Angel Espada, San Juan .... KO by 2
July 10—Maxwell Malinga, Durban .... D 10
Nov. 25—Fausto Rodriguez, Santo Domingo .... KO by 2
1975
(Inactive)
1976
Mar. 27—Bruce Cantrell, Owings Mill .... KO 9
July 29—Pablo Rodriguez, Baltimore .... KO 3
Sept. 16—John Harris, Baltimore .... KO 7
Oct. 28—Mike Baker, Baltimore .... KO 8
1977
Apr. 29—Bill Goodwin, Baltimore .... W 10
Oct.   6—Ayub Kalule, Copenhagen .... KO by 9
1978
Mar. 23—Wilson Bell, Portland, Me. .... KO 10
Aug.   8—Wilson Bell, Baltimore .... KO 7
Sept. 14—Dave Adkins, Baltimore .... W 10
Nov. 16—Rocky Mosley, Jr., Las Vegas ...... KO by 2
     (U.S. Vacant Junior Middleweight Title)
1979
Mar. 28—Dale Staley, Baltimore .... KO 3
May 10—Kenny Bristol, Georgetown, Guyana ...... L 10
May 25—Earl Liburd, Baltimore .... W 10
Aug. 30—Jerome L. Goodman, Richmond .... W 10
Oct. 11—Freddie Savage, Richmond .... KO 3
1980
May 10—Bushy Bester, Johannesburg .... KO by 2
Sept. 11—O'Dell Leonard, Washington, D.C. .... KO by 8

BRIAN ANDERSON
Montreal Welterweight
1979
Nov.   6—Don Marshall, Montreal .... L 4

Dec. 18—Ghyslain Deroy, Montreal .... W 4
1980
Jan. 21—Barry Marshall, Curling .... KO 2
Feb. 12—Nourredine Ben Salah, Montreal .... W 6
Mar. 11—Mario Cusson, Montreal .... KO by 3
Apr. 29—Allan Clarke, Halifax .... KO by 5

KELLY ANDERSON
(See Wayne Bobick)

ROBERT ANDERSON
Phoenix, Arizona Featherweight
1978
Sept. 28—Manuel Rueles, Phoenix .... W 4
Nov. 22—Manuel Rueles, Phoenix .... D 4
1979
Jan. 9—Al Rodriguez, Phoenix .... W 4
May 14—Omar Garcia, Phoenix .... W 4
June 27—Rafael Tejeda, Phoenix .... W 4
July 25—Francisco Pico, Phoenix .... W 4
Aug. 22—Juan Romero, Phoenix .... W 4
Sept. 22—Desi Newbill, Phoenix .... W 4
Oct. 18—Rafael Tejeda, Phoenix .... W 4
Nov. 13—Howard Sallis, Phoenix .... W 4
1980
Jan. 11—Darrell Stovall, Phoenix .... W 6
Feb. 3—Desi Newbill, Reno .... W 8
Mar. 20—Ruben Chavez, Phoenix .... KO 2
Apr. 9—Mike Rodriguez, Las Vegas .... W 6
Apr. 23—Mauro Fuentes, Las Vegas .... D 6
May 17—Eliu Hernandez, Las Vegas .... KO 4
June 3—Ramon Peralta, Phoenix .... W 6
June 26—Mario Casas, Las Vegas .... KO 2
Aug. 28—Francisco Rodriguez, Las Vegas .... W 4
Nov. 5—Frankie Grándos, Phoenix .... W 10
Nov. 20—Alberto Adiosa, Las Vegas .... W 4

ARCHIE ANDREWS
Philadelphia, Pa. Junior Middleweight
1974
Oct. 22—Victor Burton, Philadelphia .... L 4
Dec. 10—Willie Davis, Philadelphia .... KO 3
1975
Jan. 28—Robert Hughes, Philadelphia .... KO 1
Feb. 28—Bob Drewery, Philadelphia .... L 4
Apr. 9—Henry Hall, Binghamton .... KO 2
Apr. 22—Charles Stern, Philadelphia .... W 6
May 28—Don Morgan, Scranton .... L 6
July 9—William Mills, Binghamton .... W 6
Aug. 28—Larry Holland, Allentown .... KO by 1
1976
Apr. 13—Fred Jenkins, Philadelphia .... L 6
July 2—Guy Gargan, Atlantic City .... W 6
Nov. 30—Guy Gargan, Philadelphia .... W 6
1977
Feb. 1—Tyrone Demby, Philadelphia .... KO by 4
June 13—Rocky Estafire, Newark .... L 6
Aug. 25—Ray Kates, Vineland .... L 6
Sept. 17—Ruben Lopez, Philadelphia .... W 6
1978
Feb. 10—Guy Gargan, Philadelphia .... KO 6
Apr. 10—Rudy Donato, Philadelphia .... W 10
June 19—Tony Tassone, Philadelphia .... KO 6
Aug. 24—Tony Tassone, Philadelphia .... L 10
Nov. 21—Leo Saenz, Landover .... KO by 1
1979
May 14—Ted Mann, Philadelphia .... KO by 7
Sept. 26—Richie Bennett, Upper Darby .... KO by 2
1980
May 14—Ted Mann, Philadelphia .... KO by 7
Sept. 18—Tony Ayala, Jr., Totowa .... KO by 1

JOSE ANTONETTI
Bronx Lightweight
Managed by Steven Bos
1980
Mar. 21—Jose Rosado, New York .... W 4
May 4—Larry Savage, Kiamesha Lake .... KO 2
Oct. 2—David Vega, Commack .... KO 1
Oct. 23—Ron Jones, New York .... KO 1
Dec. 11—Keith York, New York .... KO 2

DOMINGO SANTOS ARAGON
Charta, Argentina Flyweight
1978
Aug. 4—Raul Paredi, Rosario .... W 6
Aug. 25—Mario Paniagua, Rosario .... W 6
Sept. 8—Luis Gimenez, Rosario .... KO 3
Oct. 20—Ramon Baez, Rosario .... W 8
Nov. 3—Ramon Baez, Rosario .... W 8
Nov. 17—Roberto Condori, Caldaos .... D 10
Dec. 22—Ramon Baez, La Rosas .... W 10

1979
Apr. 11—Jorge Gonzalez, Rosario .... W 10
June 1—Luis Gomez, Camilo Aldao .... W 10
June 22—Jose Izquierdo, Rosario .... W 10
July 27—Ruben Condori, Rosario .... D 10
Aug. 24—Hugo Emer, Camilo Aldao .... D 10
Sept. 28—Jose Izquierdo, Rosario .... W 10
Nov. 2—Hector Patri, Rosario .... W 10
Dec. 28—Ramon Rodriguez, Tucuman .... W 10
1980
Jan. 25—Luis Gomez, Tucuman .... KO 7
Mar. 8—Hector Patri, Buenos Aires .... L 10
Apr. 18—Santos Laciar, Cordoba .... L 10
May 16—Ruben Condori, Salta .... L 10
May 30—Carlos Reyes Sosa, Rosario .... W 10
June 19—Jorge Aguilar, P.R.S. Pena .... W 10
Aug. 1—Federico Condori, P.R.S. Pena ...... W disq. 7
Sept. 5—Jose Luis Lopez, P.R.S. Pena .... KO 9
Oct. 24—Miguel Lazarte, P.R.S. Pena .... W 10
Nov. 28—Miguel Lazarte, P.R.S. Pena .... D 10

JULIO ARANCIBIA
Argentine Middleweight
1980
Jan. 11—Miguel Castellini, V. Carlos Paz .... D 10
Mar. 7—Ruben Pardo, San Miguel .... D 10
Apr. 11—Irineo Cabrera, San Miguel .... W 10
May 2—Enrique Coronel, Salta .... W 10
May 23—Eduardo Contreres, Rosario .... D 10
June 13—Manuel F. Gonzalez, Rosario .... W 10
July 4—Eduardo Contreres, Rosario .... D 10
Aug. 9—Jose Duran, Gral Villegas .... W 10
Sept. 5—Luis Gutierrez, Rio Gallegos .... KO 3
Sept. 26—Roberto Ruiz, Buenos Aires .... D 10
Oct. 10—Oscar Ayala, Rio Gallego .... L 10
Dec. 12—Carlos Flores, Salta .... KO 6

RICARDO ARCE
Argentine, Middleweight
(Previous Record Unavailable
1980
Feb. 8—Jose A. Vega, Corrientes .... TD 2
(Retained Argentine Middleweight Title)
Apr. 11—Jose A. Vega, Corrientes .... KO 3
(Retained Argentine Middleweight Title)
May 9—Juan C. Bogado, Corrientes .... KO 1
June 21—Ruben Pardo, Buenos Aires .... L 12
(Lost Argentine Middleweight Title)
Aug. 8—Tommy Ortiz, Corrientes .... KO 4
Oct. 10—Jacinto Fernandez, Corrientes ...... KO by 9

OSCAR AREVALO
Argentine Junior Lightweight
1980
Jan 18—Victor Echegary, Tucuman .... L 10
Feb. 29—Victor Escobar, Tucuman .... KO by 9
June 5—Juan C. Herrera, Tucuman .... W 10
Aug. 8—Jose Funes, Tucuman .... L 10

ROQUE AREVALO
Argentine Junior Welterweight
1980
Feb. 22—Juan Barboza, Tucuman .... L 10
Mar. 21—Pedro Vanegas, Suardi .... L 10
Apr. 11—Hector Hernandez, Cordoba .... KO by 9
Oct. 3—Hugo Quartapelle, Villa Maria ...... KO by 5

BENNY ARGUELLES
Mexican Junior Featherweight
1977
Jan. 28—Jorge Mejia, Acapulco .... W 10
Mar. 4—Memo Ayala, Minatitlan .... KO by 7
May 6—Al Flores, Minatitlan .... KO 7
Nov. 29—Octavio Gomez, Minatitlan .... L 10
1978
Aug. 26—Pablo Ramirez, Coatzacoalcos .... L 10
1979
Sept. 22—Arturo Sanchez, Coatzacoalcos .... KO by 3
1980
Feb. 22—Romeo Anaya, Coatzacoalcos .... KO 4
June 5—Silvino Valencia, Salina Cruz .... L 10

MIGUEL ARGUELLO
Argentine Junior Middleweight
1980
Feb. 1—Ramon Tapia, Tucuman .... KO 4
July 25—Martin Duran, Tucuman .... D 8
Nov. 7—Osmar Ochoa, Tucuman .... KO by 7

RAMON ARGUELLO
Argentine Middleweight
1980
Aug. 9—Hugo Carriego, Gral Pico .... W 8

Sept. 12—Juan Panalillo, Oriente .... W 6
Oct. 17—Victor Robledo, Trenel .... D 6

NICOLAS ARKUZSYN
Argentine Junior Welterweight
Born: June 2, 1946 (Chaco)
1966
Oct. 15—Alberto Gallo, Buenos Aires .... W 6
Nov. 5—Alberto Gallo, Buenos Aires .... KO 5
Dec. 10—Antonio Romero, Buenos Aires .... W 6
1967
Apr. 8—Hector Morales, Buenos Aires .... D 6
May 27—Ramon Moreyra (Me. dec.) Bs. Aires ....KO 5
July 5—Hector Morales, Buenos Aires .... D 6
Oct. 14—Antonio Romero, Buenos Aires .... D 8
Nov. 4—Adolfo Robledo, Buenos Aires .... KO 8
1968
Apr. 6—Julio C. Lima, Buenos Aires .... KO 5
June 22—Antonio Romero, Buenos Aires .... KO 4
Dec. 6—Raul Leiva, Tucuman .... KO 2
1969
Apr. 26—Antonio Romero, Buenos Aires........... D 8
Aug. 16—Juan C. Almada, Olavarria............. D 10
1970
Feb. 5—Pedro Coria, Tres Arroyos................ D 10
Apr. 30—Jossue Moraes, Cipoletti .... D 10
Sept. 2—Alejandro Nievas, Buenos Aires .... W 10
Nov. 18—Luis H. Cabral, Buenos Aires .... L 10
1971
Jan. 28—Alejandro Nievas, Buenos Aires......... D 10
Aug. 16—Jose R. Sosa, Mendoza................. W 10
Oct. 29—Carlos Aro, Mendoza............... L. disq. 8
1972
Feb. 16—Nicolino Locche, Cruz del Eje .... L 10
Apr. 28—Juan Salinas, Rio Cuarto............... L 10
June 2—Luis H. Cabral, Neuquen............... L 10
Aug. 9—Juan Aranda, Buenos Aires............. L 10
Dec. 22—Mario Miranda, Rio Cuarto............. L 10
1973
Apr. 19—Hugo Gutierrez, Cordoba .... L 10
June 13—Ramon Duarte, Villa Angela............ W 12
1974
Mar. 30—Alfredo H. Coria, M. del Plata .... L 10
Sept. 19—Carlos Ibanez, Salta.................. L 10
Oct. 18—Ramon Duarte, Resistencia .... W 12
Nov. 8—Marciano Tura, Posadas .... W 10
1975
Feb. 7—Santiago Lopez, Resistencia............. W 12
Mar. 21—Hugo Gutierrez, Cordoba .... D 10
May 2—Gregorio Villavicencio, V. Maria........ D 10
Dec. 12—Hugo Gutierrez, San Luis .... D 12
(For the Argentine Lightweight Title)
1976
Feb. 26—Raul Ariza, Boulogne.................. KO 7
Apr. 4—Hugo Gutierrez, Bariloche.............. KO 12
(Won Argentine Lightweight Title)
Aug. 13—Abraham Valenzuela, San Luis .... L 10
Sept. 3—Armando Bustos, Rosario .... KO 8
1977
Jan. 20—Juan Zuniga, Tres Arroyos .... D 10
Feb. 4—Manuel Lopez, Tucuman .... W 10
Apr. 16—Mario Ortiz, Bs. Aires .... L 12
(Lost Argentine Lightweight Title)
Oct. 28—J. Dios Acosta, San Juan .... KO 8
Dec. 2—Oscar Alvarenga, Rosario .... KO 9
1978
Jan. 13—Juan M. Zuniga, Necochea .... W 10
Feb. 4—Jorge "P" Gomez, Sierras Bayas .... W 10
Mar. 10—Raul Venerdini, San Juan .... W 10
May 6—Marciano Tura, Sierras Bayas .... W 10
June 8—Juan M. Zuniga, Tres Arroyos .... L 10
July 14—Julio Melone, Rio Cuarto .... L 10
Aug. 4—Victor Escobar, R. S. Pena .... L 10
Nov. 2—Jorge Gomez, B. Blanca .... W 10
Dec. 7—Oscar Mendez, B. Blanca. .... L 12
(Argentine Lightweight Title)
1980
Mar. 14—Miguel Figueroa, San Juan .... W 10
Apr. 18—Rafael Zalazar, Rio III .... W 10
May —Hugo Luero, Buenos Aires .... W 10
July 4—Juan Barboza, Tucuman .... L 10
Aug. 7—Ruben Verdun, Posadas .... L 10
Aug. 29—Joaquin Moreyra, Formosa .... D 10
Oct. 10—Romulo Ibarra, Formosa .... W 10
Dec. 12—Roberto Alfaro, San Juan .... TD 7

KEN ARLT
Portland, Oregon Heavyweight
Born: May 22, 1957
Amateur record: 47 wins, 9 losses.
Quarterfinalist in 1977 National AAU tourney.
1977
June 11—Gary Keenan, Hillsboro, Ore. .... W 4
July 30—Fritz Krantz, Longview, Wash........... W 4

Sept. 3—Lew Lockwood, Ketchum, Idaho .... KO 3
Oct. 27—Bob Patterson, Portland .... KO 3
Nov. 19—Al Neumann, Hillsboro, Ore. .... W 8
1978
Apr. 7—D. J. Jones, Butte, Mont. .... L 6
June 3—Pat Stewart, Butte .... KO 3
July 19—Mustafa El Amin, Seattle .... KO 5
Aug. 29—Pinklon Thomas, Seattle .... L 6
Sept. 13—Mustafa El Amin, Butte .... KO 4
1979
Jan. 8—Mustafa El Amin, Seattle .... W 6
Apr. 12—Mike Westaway, Portland .... W 6
June 7—Bennett White, Portland .... W 8
July 26—John Kline, Portland .... W 8
July 31—Pat Duncan, Spokane .... L 8
Sept. 27—Len Lawson, Portland .... W 10
Nov. 7—Rich Kronich, Spokane .... W 2
Dec. 11—Harvey Steichen, Spokane .... L 10
1980
Jan. 23—Harvey Steichen, Portland .... W 8
Mar. 18—Al Neumann, Spokane .... L 8
Apr. 24—Harvey Steichen, Portland .... W 12

DAVEY ARMSTRONG
Tacoma, Washington Lightweight
Born: June 9, 1956. Height: 5 ft. 8½ in.
1980
Mar. 28—Gil Hernandez, Tacoma .... W 6
May 4—Edmundo Arrelano, Seattle .... KO 1
June 19—Ray Saldivar, Tacoma .... KO 3
Aug. 2—Miguel Flores, Detroit .... KO 1
Aug. 9—Eric Bonilla, Spokane .... KO 2
Aug. 29—Spencer Wilson, Miami .... KO 1
Sept. 20—Ray Gonzalez, San Juan .... KO 4
Oct. 24—Norberto Figueroa, Uniondale .... W 8
Nov. 8—Ed Murray, Detroit .... KO 2
Dec. 13—Ernesto Caballero, Miami .... KO by 4

VICTOR ARNAU
Hartford, Conn. Junior Lightweight
1975
Feb. 20—Benjamin Camacho, Bayamon .... KO 4
Mar. 14—Gilberto Mendez, San Juan .... W 6
1976
(Inactive)
1977
Oct. 22—Manny Quiles, Hartford .... KO 5
1978
(Inactive)
1979
Oct. 17—Angel Ortiz, Hartford .... KO 6
Nov. 15—Eddie Flores, Bristol .... KO 4
1980
Jan. 15—Benito Jiminez, W. Hartford .... KO 1
Feb. 5—Jose Matos, W. Hartford .... D 6
Apr. 22—Jorge Vasquez, W. Hartford .... W 8
May 29—Jorge Vasquez, W. Hartford .... L 8

CRAIG ARNOLD
St. Louis, Missouri Heavyweight
1978
Sept. 22—Mike Carun, St. Charles .... KO by 2
1979
Apr. 20—Hans Stoffregen, St. Louis .... KO by 1
Nov. 8—Jimmy Robertson, Indianapolis ..... KO by 1
1980
Jan. 21—Rick Innis, St. Charles .... KO by 1
May 12—Butch Wilkerson, Cape Girardea ... KO by 3

MARIO ARREGUEZ
Argentine Welterweight
1980
Mar. 13—Raul Torres, Bahia Blanca .... L 8
May 16—Ramon Franco, San Miguel .... L 8
June 13—Raul Fernandez, San Nicolas .... L 10
July 12—Ramon Fabias, Baradero .... L 8
Aug. 1—Jorge Palai, Mar del Plata .... L 8
Sept. 26—Alfredo Peralta, Tandil .... KO by 4
Oct. 31—Juan C. Beron, La Plata .... L 6

CHIVO ARRELLANO
Bantamweight
1979
July 16—Ramon Barrera, Bakersfield .... L 4
Aug. 20—Ramon Barrera, Bakersfield .... L 6
1980
Feb. 5—Billy Watkins, Houston .... KO by 3
Mar. 27—Mike Rodriguez, Los Angeles .... L 5

MEMO ARREOLA
Los Angeles, Calif. Lightweight
1979
June	21—Mike Rodriguez, Los Angeles	W	6
Aug.	23—Juan Sanchez, Los Angeles	L	6
Sept.	27—Ramon Coronado, Los Angeles	KO	6
Oct.	11—Rosendo Ramirez, Los Angeles	L	6

1980
Feb.	9—Aaron Morua, Los Angeles	L	6
Mar.	22—Davey "Fireball" Ramos,	W	6
Apr.	22—Bubba Blackwell, Sacramento	KO	2
May	2—Felipe Canela, San Bernardino	L	6
May	8—Mano Morua, Los Angeles	D	6
June	19—Ernesto Garfias, Los Angeles	L	10
Aug.	14—Arturo Frias, Los Angeles	L	10

NOEL ARRIESGADO
Philippine Featherweight
1978
Feb.	28—Jorge Torres, Honolulu	KO	3
Apr.	25—Jesus Hernandez, Honolulu	W	10
May	30—Jose Caba, Honolulu	KO	9
July	18—Jose Resendiz, Honolulu	KO	9
Nov.	2—Roger Buchelli, Los Angeles	W	10

1979
Jan.	30—Juan Manuel Meza, Honolulu	L	10

1980
Apr.	1—Felix Valencia, Honolulu	KO	3
June	17—Abdul Bey, Honolulu	W	10
July	19—Abdul Bey, Honolulu	W	10
Aug.	19—Gaby Cantera, Honolulu	W	10

DANIEL ARRIOLA
Argentine Junior Middleweight
1980
Feb.	15—Juan C. Valdez, Mar del Plata	KO	5
May	2—Omar Ochoa, Ciudadela	W	10
July	18—Miguel Garcia, Bahia Blanca	D	10

JUAN CARLOS ARRUA
Argentine Welterweight
1980
Apr.	5—Hector Rosales, Buenos Aires	W	4
May	15—Alberto Gojt, Chivilchoy	KO	3
June	5—Oscar Romero, Int. Alvear	KO by	3

OSCAR ARTAZA
Argentine Junior Welterweight
1980
Jan.	4—Alfredo Peralta, Mar del Plata	KO	6
Feb.	22—Orlando Frecini, Mar del Plata	KO by	5
Sept.	26—Ricardo Espinoza, Olavarria	L	6
Oct.	24—Ricardo Espinoza, Olavarria	KO by	2

EDDIE ARTHURS
Cliffside Park, N.J. Junior Welterweight
1979
Apr.	26—Benito Jiminez, North Bergen	KO by	2
Aug.	1—Kevin Renshaw, Secaucus	KO by	1
Sept.	29—Kevin Renshaw, Trenton	KO by	1
Nov.	14—Jeff Passero, Baltimore	KO by	1

1980
Mar.	20—Johnny Marrone, North Bergen	KO by	1

JEROME ARTIS
Philadelphia, Pa. Junior Lightweight
1972
Oct.	24—Hector Diaz, Philadelphia	D	4
Nov.	17—Hector Diaz, New York	W	4

1973
Jan.	15—Harvey Wilson, Philadelphia	KO	3
Feb.	3—Ricky Villaneuva, North Bergen	L	6
Apr.	23—George Snyder, Philadelphia	KO	5

1974
Apr.	8—Jesus Nieves, Philadelphia	KO	2
Apr.	29—Rafael Santana, Philadelphia	KO	2
Oct.	22—Willie Daniels, Philadelphia	W	8
Nov.	19—Eddie Rivera, Philadelphia	KO	1

1975
Jan.	14—Jose Nunez, Philadelphia	W	8
Mar.	11—Hector Espinoza, Philadelphia	W	8
Aug.	18—Alfonso Evans, Philadelphia	D	8
Oct.	28—Alfonso Evans, Philadelphia	KO	3
Dec.	2—Sammy Goss, Philadelphia	D	10

1976
Jan.	13—Sammy Goss, Philadelphia	W	10
Feb.	10—Johnny Copeland, Philadelphia	W	10
Apr.	6—Augustine Estrada, Philadelphia	W	10
June	8—Doc McClendon, Philadelphia	W	10
Aug.	16—Jose Fernandez, Philadelphia	D	10

1977
Jan.	17—Jose Fernandez, Philadelphia	W	10
June	28—William Berry, Philadelphia	W	10

Sept.	29—Alexis Arguello, New York	KO by	2

1978
Mar.	28—Ezequiel Sanchez, Santo Domingo	L	10

1979
Mar.	20—Charlie Nash, London	L	8
May	30—John Muwanga, Oslo	KO by	6
Oct.	18—Sammy Goss, Philadelphia	W	10
Dec.	12—Anthony Beverly, Washington D.C.	KO	1

1980
Feb.	29—Claude Noel, Trinidad	L	10
Mar.	14—Aristo Pizzo, Milan	W	10
Mar.	29—Rolando Navarette, Honolulu	KO by	7
June	7—Cornelius Boza-Edwards, Glasgow	KO by	3
July	28—Quenton Blackman, Philadelphia	KO	10
Sept.	18—Jose Gonzales, Philadelphia	W	12

JOSE ARUJO
Argentine Middleweight
1980
Mar.	22—Ricardo Ruiz, Buenos Aires	W	6
May	—Marcelino R. Diaz, Buenos Aires	L	6

STEVE ARVIN
Binghamton, N.Y. Middleweight
1977
Feb.	24—Tommy Mitses, Wilmington	KO	1
Apr.	21—Tommy Mitses, Wilmington	KO	3

1978
June	15—Russell Hart, Atlantic City	KO	3

1979
Jan.	9—Ray Crump, Philadelphia	KO	2
Mar.	17—Beau Jack, Elmira	W	6
Mar.	30—Daviel Tavares, Scranton	KO	5
Apr.	14—Ray Crump, Syracuse	KO	2
Oct.	24—Hank Whittmore, Scranton	KO	1
Nov.	21—Elijah Hamm, Scranton	KO	4
Dec.	12—Miguel Sanchez, Scranton	KO by	4

1980
Jan.	19—Charles Young, Syracuse	KO	2
Mar.	26—Pablo Rodriguez, Scranton	W	8
May	28—Ralph Mifka, Scranton	L	8
Aug.	21—Don Johnson, Halifax	L	8
Sept.	20—Leo Martinez, Bensalem, Pa.	W	8
Nov.	8—Alex Ramos, Lake Tahoe	KO by	

TITO ARZATE
Mexican Flyweight
1977
July	5—Ruben Solario, Tijuana	L	10
Sept.	28—Joey Olivo, Las Vegas	L	8
Oct.	27—Ernesto Rios, Los Angeles	KO by	4
Dec.	1—Demetrio Torres, Los Angeles	W	5

1978
Feb.	2—Santos Nunez, Los Angeles	L	6
Mar.	9—Paz Mena, Las Vegas	L	6
Mar.	22—Willie Jensen, Las Vegas	L	10
Apr.	26—Raul Ocha, Concord	L	6
June	14—Mario Chavez, Las Vegas	KO by	5

1979
(Inactive)
1980
May	5—Jose Torres, Phoenix	L	6
July	17—Jose Torres, Tucson	KO by	8

FRED ASKEW
Minneapolis, Minn. Heavyweight
Born: February, 1950
1966
Oct.	3—Ron Marsh, Milwaukee	KO by	2

1967
Jan.	18—Aaron Eastling, St. Paul	KO by	5

1968
Mar.	4—Eddie Dembry, Hammond	L	5
Mar.	29—Ed Hurley, St. Paul	D	6
July	25—Jim Howard, Bloomington	L	5
Dec.	4—Lee Estes, Rochester	W	5

1969
Jan.	20—Frank Steele, Chicago	L	4
June	25—Johnny Mac, La Crosse	L	6
July	1—George Foreman, Houston	KO by	1
July	31—Eddie Brooks, Milwaukee	L	6
Oct.	9—Ferrios King, La Crosse	KO	1
Nov.	19—Ted Gullick, Cleveland	KO by	2
Dec.	3—Lee Estes, Rochester, Minn.	W	4
Dec.	19—Orville Qualls, Omaha	W	4

1970
Mar.	3—Vic Brown, Buffalo	KO by	4
Mar.	17—Aaron Eastling, St. Paul	L	6
Oct.	1—John Esmey, Yuma	W	6
Nov.	26—Tony Anchaldo, Yuma	KO	2
Dec.	20—John Esmay, Yuma	W	6

35

```
                1971
Jan.   7—Charlie Hall, Yuma ....................KO  2
Apr.  23—Jose Lujan, Nogales ...................KO  3
                1972
              (Inactive)
                1973
Apr.  10—Joe Cable, Minneapolis ................KO  2
Aug.   6—Mike Shannon, Minneapolis ...........KO  2
                1974
Feb.   4—Cheeko Gardner, Minneapolis ...........W  4
June  26—T. J. Jones, St. Paul ....................W  6
Nov.  22—Larry Pennigar, Minneapolis ...........KO  1
                1975
May    7—Ron Stander, Minneapolis ..............W 10
                1976
Apr.   5—Larry Holmes, Landover ...........KO by  2
June   1—John Gardner, London .................LF  6
                1977
              (Inactive)
                1978
June  29—Chuck Gardner, St. Paul ..............KO  6
Sept. 27—Jim Beattie, St. Paul ...................NC 10
                1979
Feb.  14—John Kline, St. Paul ....................W  8
                1980
Mar.  19—Charles Atlas, St. Paul ................KO  7
Aug.  27—Marion Mitchell, S. Dakota ............KO  3
Sept.  6—Larry Joe Walsh, Sioux Falls, S.D. ......KO  3

               LEONIDAS ASPRILLA
          Cartagena, Colombia Lightweight
                1977
Jan.  30—Jairo Ortega, Cartagena ...............KO  3
May    7—Alfredo Junco, Cartagena .............KO  3
Sept. 16—Alvaro Marimon, Cartagena ............W  8
Sept. 30—Eusebio Vasquez, Cartagena ..........KO  6
Oct.  28—Rafael Pimental, Barranquilla ..........KO  3
Dec.   1—Julio Sanjuan, Barranquilla ...........KO  2
Dec.  15—Carlos Avila, Bogota ..................KO  1
                1978
Jan.  19—Miguel Betruz, Cartagena .............W 10
Feb.  18—William Blanco, Cartagena ............KO  3
May     —Luis Rivera, Cartagena ...............KO  2
June  30—Rafael Piamonte, Cartagena ...........KO  2
Sept.  2—Carlos Romero, Cartagena ............KO  4
Oct.  21—Pedro Acosta, Cartagena ..............L 12
          (Latin American Lightweight Title)
Dec.  29—Francisco Durango, Monteria ..........KO  2
                1979
Feb.  10—Miguel Betruz, Cartagena .............W 10
Mar.  31—Leonardo Bermudez, Cartagena .......W 10
May   19—Pedro Acosta, Cartagena .............KO  6
July  15—Alfonso Perez, Cartagena .............KO  6
        (Won Latin American Lightweight Title)
Sept.  1—Antonio Cruz, Cartagena ..............D 12
                1980
Feb.  23—Rafael Solis, Cartagena ................D 10
Apr.  13—Aaron Pryor, Kansas City .........KO by 10
June  28—Sergio Alvarez, Cartagena ..........KO by  4
Sept. 20—Orlando Romero, Ciudad Trujillo .....KO by  8
             (Lost Americas Title)

               OCTAVIANO ASPRILLA
             Panamanian Flyweight
                1980
Mar.  29—Tomas Hinestroza, Panama City .........L  4
Aug.   1—Antonio Mitre, Colon ...............KO by  5

                 JUAN ATILANO
            Mexico City, Mexico Flyweight
                1978
May     —Dionisio Balderas .....................KO  1
        —"Chiquelin" Garcia ....................KO  4
Nov.  18—Juventino Solis, Mexico City ...........W  4
                1979
Jan.   6—Gregorio Menchaca, Mexico ...........KO  2
Feb.  24—Federico Nunez, Mexico City ...........L  4
Apr.  25—Efrain Zepeda, Mexico City ...........KO  3
June  23—Mario Ochoa, Mexico City .........KO by  2
Nov.  14—Roberto Martinez, Mexico City .......KO by  2
                1980
Feb.  13—Martin Vidal, Mexico City ............KO  4
Mar.  12—Benny Flores, Mexico City .........KO by  1
July  16—Eligio Pena, Mexico City ..............KO  6
Oct.  11—Javier Esquivel, Mexico City ............D  8
Nov.  22—Carlos Morales, Mexico City ..........KO  2

                 CHARLES ATLAS
              Bastrop, La. Heavyweight
                1972
Nov.  25—Syl Murphy, Little Rock ................L  6
                1973
May   17—Clyde Brown, Memphis .................L 10

36
```

```
June  23—Bill Anderson, Bristol ...................L  4
Aug.  27—Bill Anderson, Monroe ................KO  7
Sept. 26—Ronnie Wright, Monroe ...............KO 10
Nov.  11—Ronnie Wright, Alexandria .............W  8
Dec.  10—Ray White, Monroe ....................L 10
                1974
Jan.  10—Frankie Evans, Baton Rouge ..........KO  4
Feb.   7—Johnny Boudreaux, Houston ............L  8
Feb.  19—Tom Berry, Oklahoma City .............W  6
Mar.  14—Brian Kelly, Oklahoma City ..........KO  3
Apr.  15—Jose Luis Garcia, Oklahoma City ....KO by  6
                1975
May   30—Memphis Al Jones, Memphis ...........W 10
Sept. 23—Johnny Boudreaux, Lake Charles ....KO by  8
                1976
Mar.  27—Jody Ballard, Tuscaloosa ...............L 10
Aug.  23—Al Hogan, New Orleans .................L  8
                1977
Mar.  30—Boom Boom Moorer, Cleveland ........KO  2
Apr.  26—Tom Prater, Orlando ...............KO by  4
May    7—Roy Williams, St. Louis ...........KO by  1
June  23—Chuck Gardner, Bloomington ...........L  6
July   7—Nick Wells, Shreveport .............KO by  3
                1978
Jan.  26—Boone Kirkman, Seattle ...........KO by  4
Apr.  28—Young Joe Louis, Chicago ..............L  8
Aug.  28—Calvin Cross, Chicago .............KO by  3
Nov.  29—Ron Stander, Omaha ..............KO by  1
                1979
Mar.   6—John Lee, Memphis .................KO by  8
June  18—Henry Lumpkin, Chicago ...........KO by  5
July  30—James Tillis, Chicago .............KO by  2
Aug.  16—Lupe Guerra, North Platte .........KO by  5
                1980
Mar.  19—Fred Askew, St. Paul ..............KO by  7
May   15—Floyd "Jumbo" Cummings, Chicago ..KO by  1
Oct.   9—Alfonso Ratliff, Chicago ..........KO by  1
Nov.  20—Monte Masters, Oklahoma City ....KO by  4

                 EMMETT ATLAS
              Bristol, Tenn. Welterweight
                1973
June  11—Mike West, Monroe ....................KO  3
June  14—Rey Santiago, Tampa ..............KO by  1
June  23—Charlie Ellis, Bristol .............KO by  2
July  24—Earl Young, Mobile ....................KO  2
Aug.  27—Alex Castro, Monroe ..................KO  2
Sept. 26—Skip Odom, Monroe ...................KO  3
Nov.   7—Carmelo Delgado, Alexandria ..........KO  6
Dec.  10—Romon Gonzalez, Monroe .............KO  1
Dec.  17—Kid Mexico, Mobile ...................KO  1
                1974
Feb.  19—Donnie Spencer, Oklahoma City .....KO by  5
Mar.  30—Donnie Spencer, St. Louis ..........KO by  5
Apr.  28—Frank Young, Houston .............KO by  3
July  30—Jackie Robertson, New Orleans ......KO by  5
Nov.  19—Tony Gardner, Oklahoma City ......KO by  4
                1975
Feb.   4—Bill Goodwin, Milwaukee ...........KO by  3
May    6—Larry Brasier, Oklahoma City .........W 10
Sept. 23—Ray Phillips, Lake Charles ..............L 10
                1976
Feb.  19—LeRoy Green, Kansas City ..........KO by  5
Mar.  26—Donnie Melancon, Tuscaloosa .........KO  5
May   25—Mike Box, Alexandria .................KO  2
June   3—Johnny Guerrero, Shreveport ..........KO  5
June   4—Bruce Cantrell, Tuscaloosa .............W  8
Aug.  23—Adam Moore, New Orleans .........KO by  3
Sept. 14—Gene Wells, Orlando ..................W  8
Nov.  16—Joey Vincent, Orlando .............KO by  3
                1977
Apr.  26—Gene Wells, Orlando ..............KO by  8
May     —Joe Barrientos, Shreveport .........KO by  3
May    5—Mike Box, Alexandria .................KO  2
July   7—Joe Barrientos, Shreveport .........KO by  3
                1978
Jan.  26—Ray Seales, Seattle .................KO by  2
June  19—Jimmy Heair, Orlando .............KO by  2
                1979
June  19—Jimmy Heair, Orlando .............KO by  2
                1980
Mar.  19—Gary Holmgren, St. Paul ..........KO by  2
Dec.   6—Marcus Dorsey, Bastrop ................W  6

                 RALPH AURIEMMO
           Margate, Fla. Junior Welterweight
                1980
May    1—Tony Ayala, Miami ....................KO  2
June   6—Ricky Lodge, Miami ....................W  4
July  25—Saul Guerra, Miami ....................W  6
```

RON AURIT
Philadelphia, Pa. Lightweight
1977
Feb.	21—Joey Wilder, Philadelphia	KO	4
Mar.	11—Billy Johnson, Philadelphia	KO	1
June	23—Larry Huffin, Philadelphia	W	4
Aug.	26—Larry Huffin, Allentown	W	4

1978
Oct.	24—Pedro Lebron, Philadelphia	W	4

1979
May	31—Larry Clark, Virginia Beach	KO	3
July	17—Ken Muse, Atlantic City	D	6
July	31—Rob Stevenson, Atlantic City	KO	5
Aug.	21—Ken Muse, Atlantic City	W	6
Oct.	18—Ken Loma, Philadelphia	KO	2
Nov.	14—Michael Ross, Philadelphia	KO by	6

1980
Apr.	26—Ira Robinson, Lynchburg	W	6
July	29—George Sydnor, Philadelphia	W	4
Sept.	18—Pedro Lebron, Philadelphia	KO	7

KEN AUSTIN
Lovelock, Nev. Heavyweight
1975
May	5—Mike Colbert, Carson City	KO by	3

1976
(Inactive)
1977
Oct.	30—Lew Lockwood, Carson City	W	4

1978
July	3—Fritz Krantz, Gardnerville	W	4
Aug.	5—Tony Stone, Elko	D	6
Aug.	30—Junior Albers, Reno	L	7
Oct.	30—Lew Lockwood, Carson City	W	7

1979
May	16—Steve Asher, Carson City	W	6
July	3—Harvey Steichen, Gardnerville	L	10
Sept.	11—Arnold Sam, Reno	KO	6
Oct.	30—Lew Lockwood, Carson City	W	7
Nov.	20—Harvey Steichen, Sparks	L	10

1980
Feb.	28—David Starkey, Tampa	W	4
Mar.	16—Andy Russell, Miami	KO	2
Apr.	15—Tony Servance, Miami	L	4

ANTONIO AVELAR
Mexican Flyweight
1975
Nov.	21—Raul Ochoa, Guadalajara	W	10

1976
Jan.	26—Angel Felix, La Paz	W	10
Mar.	20—Nacho Beltran, La Paz	KO by	2
Oct.	9—Fred Polanco, Guadalajara	KO	2
Nov.	12—Juan Jose Guzman, Guadalajara	KO by	7

1977
Feb.	4—Freddy Castillo, Guadalajara	L	10
May	21—Gabriel Bernal, Mexico City	L	10
June	24—Refugio Rojas, Guadalajara	KO	5
Aug.	24—Arturo Uruzquieta, Mexico City	KO	2
Sept.	10—Victor Aguirre, Mexico City	KO	10
Oct.	12—Jose Sosa, Mexico City	W	10

1978
Jan.	7—Samuel Machorro, Mexico City	L	10
Apr.	22—Fred Hernandez, San Luis Potosi	KO	8
July	29—Matias Marin, Merida	KO	8
Oct.	20—Freddy Castillo, Merida	KO by	10

1979
Feb.	10—Miguel Canto, Merida	L	15

(World Flyweight Title)
Aug.	25—Samuel Machorro, Mexico City	W	10
Dec.	1—Adelaido Galindo, Mexico City	KO	3

1980
Feb.	16—Alfonso Lopez, Mexico City	KO	5
Apr.	1—Aniceto Vargas, Houston	KO	4
Aug.	16—Alberto Morales, Merida	KO	10
Oct.	18—Rocky Mijares, Guadalajara	KO	2

ALLEN AVERY
Cleveland, Ohio
1980
Jan.	24—Don Thurman, Detroit	W	4
Dec.	2—Duane Thomas, Detroit	KO by	2
Dec.	9—Eddie Stokes, Kalamazoo	KO by	2

DANIEL AVERY
San Diego, Calif. Featherweight
1980
June	10—Len Castello, Tacoma	W	4
Aug.	2—Benny Silva, Cincinnati	W	4
Oct.	24—David Brown, Uniondale	W	4
Nov.	8—Clinton Harris, Detroit	KO by	4

CLAUDIO AVILA
Mexican Bantamweight
1980
May	10—Mario Nava, Mexico City	KO by	4

DIEGO AVILA
Mexico City, Mexico Flyweight
1980
Aug.	2—Victor Montero, Mexico City	W	4
Sept.	6—Eugenio Morgan, Mexico City	W	4
Nov.	5—Mario Nava, Mexico City	W	8

JOSE LUIS AVILA
Mexican Bantamweight
1980
Mar.	29—Julio Ruiz, Mexico City	KO	3
May	3—Victor Montero, Mexico City	L	4

LUIS AVILA
Los Angeles, Calif. Featherweight
1979
May	30—Lionel Harney, Las Vegas	L	4
Aug.	24—Dennis Quimayousie, Carson City	L	6
Sept.	13—Ray Salazar, Phoenix	W	4
Oct.	25—Mark Davis, Los Angeles	L	5
Dec.	12—Freddie Roach, Phoenix	L	6

1980
Mar.	6—Augustin Serros, San Jose	KO	5
Mar.	21—Jaime Garza, San Bernardino	KO by	8
May	13—Jaime Garza, Bakersfield	L	10
May	29—Rocky Garcia, Los Angeles	KO by	9
July	31—Eliu Hernandez, Los Angeles	KO	3
Aug.	14—Richard Savala, Los Angeles	L	6
Sept.	5—Danny Aguilar, Inglewood	W	10
Dec.	10—Ricardo Jimenez, Las Vegas	L	10
Dec.	19—Juan "Kid" Meza, Las Vegas	KO by	6

LUIS AVILA
Panamanian Junior Featherweight
1973
July	14—Luis A. Sanchez, Panama City	KO	2
Nov.	17—Adalidez Munoz, Panama City	W	6

1974
July	20—Rudy Gonzalez, Panama City		
Nov.	30—Mario Mendoza, Panama City	W	10

1975
Jan.	13—Rudy Gonzalez, Panama City	KO by	2
July	26—Jose Lugo, Panama City	KO	2
Aug.	23—Rigoberto Riasco, Panama City	L	12

1976
Aug.	8—Jose Pena, Colon	L	10

1977
(Inactive)
1978
July	1—Roberto Collins, Colon	KO	5

1979
June	30—Ulises Morales, Colon	D	12
Oct.	13—Dennis Morgan, Panama City	KO	12

(Latin American Junior Featherweight Title)
1980
Aug.	16—Ulises Morales, Panama City	L	10
Dec.	13—Agustin Martinez, Panama City	KO by	7

ADOLFO AVILES
Mexican Flyweight
1980
Jan.	23—Enrique Cordoba, Mexico City	W	4
Mar.	5—Julian Loria, Merida	D	6
May	14—Marco Ventura, Merida	L	8

RALPH AVILES
Hilo, Hawaii Lightweight
1979
Apr.	8—Mitsuo Shima, Tokyo	KO	3
June	5—Eliu Hernandez, Hilo	KO	2
July	3—Frank Cabanig, Hilo	KO	2
July	27—Domi Cruz, Hilo	KO	2
Sept.	1—Valentin Holquin, Hilo	KO	6
Oct.	16—Rolando Pastor, Honolulu	KO	5

1980
Feb.	19—Edwin Alarcon, Honolulu	W	10
Mar.	4—Nene Jun, Honolulu	W	10
May	6—Robert Vasquez, Honolulu	KO	7
May	27—Jose Cabrera, Honolulu	W	10
June	24—Celso Esmero, Honolulu	KO	7
July	29—Eddie Ballaran, Honolulu	KO	7
Sept.	16—Alfredo Pitalua, Honolulu	W	10
Nov.	11—Ernesto Garfias, Honolulu	W	10

DOMINGO AYALA
Puerto Rican Welterweight
1977
Sept.	10—Ismael Martinez, San Juan	KO	9

Oct.   8—Jorge Mojica Colon, Carolina, P.R. . . . . D 6
1978
Apr.   1—Carmelo Cruz, Carolina . . . . KO 5
May   20—Juan Berbere, Carolina . . . . KO 2
June   16—T.N.T. Gordon, St. Thomas . . . . KO 1
Aug.   14—Juan Cantres, Rio Predras . . . . KO 5
Sept.   9—Bruce Curry, San Juan . . . . KO 9
        (U.S. Junior Welterweight Title)
Oct.   28—Joe Turner, San Juan . . . . KO 2
1979
Jan.   14—Manuel Jiminez, San Juan . . . . L 10
1980
Feb.   24—Chong Ho Kim, S. Korea . . . . W 10
Apr.   19—Obisia Nwankpa, San Juan . . . . W 8
May   23—Ruby Ortiz, New York . . . . KO 10
June   27—Eddie Campbell, New York . . . . KO 3
Oct.   10—Raul Aguirre, New York . . . . KO 4
Dec.   12—Adriano Marrero, New York . . . . W 10

JAVIER AYALA
Los Angeles, Calif. Lightweight
Born: Aug. 30, 1943
1975
June   9—Frankie Benitez, San Juan . . . . L 10
Aug.   9—Nicolino Loche, Buenos Aires . . . . L 10
1976
Mar.   29—Art Leon, Tijuana . . . . L 10
Apr.   10—Angel Mayoral, Tijuana . . . . L 10
May   22—Antonio Cervantes, Maracay . . . . KO by 1
Oct.   11—Miguel Hernandez, Evanstown . . . . KO 3
1977
Mar.   1—Rudy Barro, Incline Village . . . .
1978
        (Inactive)
1979
Jan.   24—Miguel Estrada, Las Vegas . . . . W 10
Apr.   25—Jose Olivares, Lake Tahoe . . . . KO 9
June   27—Leroy Haley, Las Vegas . . . . L 10
Nov.   23—Chebo Hernandez, Juarez . . . . KO by 3
1980
Jan.   30—Dujuan Johnson, Las Vegas . . . . KO by 8
Mar.   19—Lou Bizzarro, Las Vegas . . . . L 10
May   21—Aundra Love, Las Vegas . . . . L 10
June   3—Jerry Cheatham, Phoenix . . . . L 10
July   23—Bruce Finch, Las Vegas . . . . KO by 3

MIKE AYALA
San Antonio, Tex. Featherweight
'73 Nat'l. GG Flyweight Champion,
'74 Nat'l. AAU Bantamweight Champion, and
'75 Nat'l. GG Bantamweight Champion.
Born: January 19, 1958
1975
Aug.   19—Raul Casarez, Corpus Christi . . . . KO 1
Sept. 16—Beto Avila, Corpus Christi . . . . KO 4
Oct.   3—Beto Avila, Piedras Negras . . . . KO 4
Nov.   12—Raul Jorres, Mobile, Ala. . . . . KO 1
Nov.   26—Bobby Dominguez, Mobile, Ala. . . . . KO 3
1976
Feb.   27—Miguel Castro, Negras . . . . KO 1
Apr.   13—Javier Moncivais, San Antonio . . . . W 10
May   21—Chamice Cuenca, Negras . . . . KO 2
June   22—Tony Rocha, San Antonio . . . . W 10
July   23—Goyo Vargas, San Antonio . . . . KO 4
Oct.   1—Chango Guillen, Negras . . . . W 10
Oct.   26—Ramon Elorde, San Antonio . . . . W 10
1977
Jan.   18—Cesar Deciga, San Antonio . . . . KO 7
Mar.   25—Romero Anaya, San Antonio . . . . KO 6
May   17—Rodolfo Martinez, San Antonio . . . . . . KO by 7
Aug.   9—Reynaldo Hidalgo, San Antonio . . . . W 10
Oct.   4—Raul Tirado, San Antonio . . . . W 10
Dec.   6—Tarcisio Gomez, San Antonio . . . . W 10
1978
Mar.   18—Ronnie McGarvey, San Antonio . . . . KO 1
July   18—Edwin Alarcon, San Antonio . . . . W 10
Aug.   22—Shig Fukuyama, San Antonio . . . . KO 6
Nov.   21—Edel Borunda, San Antonio . . . . W 12
1979
Feb.   24—Jose Nunez, Las Vegas . . . . W 10
June   17—Danny Lopez, San Antonio . . . . KO by 15
        (World Featherweight Title)
Nov.   23—Enrique Solis, New York . . . . W 10
1980
May   9—Marcial Santiago, Commack . . . . W 10
May   23—Nicky Perez, Pontiac . . . . W 12
Nov.   7—Javier Flores, San Antonio . . . . W 10

OSCAR AYALA
Argentine Junior Middleweight
1980
Apr.   5—Rogelio Zarza, Cdo Rivadavia . . . . W 10
May   17—Raul Guillermo, Rio Negro . . . . W 10

June   6—Hugo Salega, Rio Gallegos . . . . KO 6
Aug.   1—Rogelio Zarza, Rio Gallegos . . . . KO 3
Oct.   10—Julio C. Arancibia, Rio Gallegos . . . . W 10

SAMMY AYALA
San Antonio, Texas Junior Welterweight
Born: July 31, 1959
1977
July   21—Victor Villanueva, Laredo . . . . KO 5
Aug.   9—Edwardo Vega, San Antonio . . . . KO 1
1978
Jan.   30—Victor Villanueva, San Antonio . . . . KO 7
Feb.   17—Gabriel Urbina, Piedras Negras . . . . KO 3
May   2—Juan Ramirez, San Antonio . . . . KO 1
June   20—Mike Everett, San Antonio . . . . KO 10
Sept. 19—Lupe Galindo, San Antonio . . . . KO 3
Dec.   5—Jose Luis Baltazar, San Antonio . . . . W 10
1979
Jan.   30—Johnny Copeland, San Antonio . . . . W 10
June   17—Johnny Copeland, San Antonio . . . . KO 7
Aug.   28—Rafael Nunez, San Antonio . . . . KO 3
Sept. 14—Larry Stanton, Houston . . . . L 10
1980
June   17—Norberto Rodriguez, San Antonio . . . . . . KO 2
July   28—Ismael Moreno, Corpus Christi . . . . KO 2
Aug.   19—Mark Ibanez, San Antonio . . . . KO by 1

TONY AYALA, JR.
San Antonio, Texas Junior Middleweight
Born: February 13, 1963. Height: 5 ft. 7 in.
Managed by Shelly Finkel and Lou Duva
1980
June   17—Prisciliano "Zip" Castillo, San Antonio . . KO 1
July   15—German Marquez, San Antonio . . . . KO 1
July   28—Manuel Torres, Corpus Christi . . . . KO 1
Sept. 18—Archie Andrews, Totowa . . . . KO 1
Nov.   1—Mike Baker, Lake Tahoe . . . . W 8
Nov.   20—Lester Groves, Totowa . . . . KO 2
Dec.   20—Earl Liburd, Bronx . . . . KO 1

FELIPE AZAMAR
Mexico City, Mexico Featherweight
1977
Feb.   26—Ruben Soriano, Mexico City . . . . KO by 3
July   30—Moises Abad, Mexico City . . . . KO by 2
Oct.   15—Jose Luis Medel, Mexico City . . . . KO by 4
1978
        —Alfred Vasquez, Mexico City . . . . KO by 1
June   3—Roberto Castillo, Mexico City . . . . D 6
July   15—Roberto Castillo, Mexico City . . . . KO 1
        —Silvestre Dominguez, Mexico City . . . . . . W 6
Sept.   2—Maximo Calleje, Mexico City . . . . KO 1
1979
Jan.   6—Jose Chavez, Mexico City . . . . KO by 2
Feb.   8—Anillo Apestes, Churra . . . . KO 1
Mar.   3—Gonzalo Lovera, Mexico City . . . . W 6
Apr.   11—Jamie Rosas, Mexico City . . . . KO 1
Nov.   28—Jorge Zarate, Mexico City . . . . L 10
1980
Apr.   29—Chilango Pacheco, Mexico City . . . . . . KO by 7

CURTIS (ROCKY) AZEVEDO
Hilo, Hawaii Light Heavyweight
1979
Sept.   1—Eugene Gordon, Hilo . . . . W 4
Oct.   9—Mosese Halafuka, Honolulu . . . . KO 2
1980
Feb.   20—Danman Lacy, Hilo . . . . W 6
Apr.   8—Fomai Leota, Honolulu . . . . KO by 1
May   12—Alvaro Lopez, Honolulu . . . . KO 7
July   22—Charles Roye, Honolulu . . . . KO 1
Sept. 16—Karl Hess, Honolulu . . . . KO 5

JOHN BACA
Los Angeles, Calif. Heavyweight
1975
Dec.   4—Frank Pina, Los Angeles . . . . KO 1
1976
May   11—Tony Hernandez, Albuquerque . . . . KO 1
May   13—Angel Morgan, Albuquerque . . . . KO 1
May   19—Ismael Ruiz, Los Angeles . . . . KO 1
July   22—Filifili Alaiasa, Los Angeles . . . . KO 2
1977
Jan.   25—Gary Bates, Phoenix . . . . KO 2

38

Mar. 30—Chuck James, Phoenix ....KO 2
Apr. 27—Eric Sedillo, Phoenix ....L 6
1978
Nov. 3—Elliott Bryant, San Diego ....KO 2
Nov. 17—James Ingram, San Diego ....KO 2
1979
Aug. 2—Rahim Muhammad, Phoenix ....W 6
Sept. 13—Leon Shaw, Phoenix ....KO by 5
1980
July 11—Richard Jenson, Phoenix ....KO 2

FRED BACLAAN
Honolulu, Hawaii Lightweight
1979
June 5—Raymond Kelly, Hilo ....W 4
June 12—Raymond Kelly, Honolulu ....KO 3
July 3—Reuben Dudoit, Hilo ....KO by 3
July 27—Wyatt Coleman, Hilo ....D 3
Aug. 21—Wyatt Coleman, Honolulu ....W 3
Sept. 18—Ric Raquel, Honolulu ....D 3
1980
Apr. 8—Roger Reed, Honolulu ....D 3
May 27—Tino Savea, Honolulu ....KO by 2
July 8—Gordon Hanakani, Honolulu ....KO 3
Aug. 28—Gordon Hanakani, Honolulu ....W 4

FELIPE BAEZ
Argentine Featherweight
1980
Mar. 6—Jorge Gonzalez, Bâhia Blanca ....KO 8
Apr. 11—Ramon Abeldano, Brandsen ....L 6
May 2—Jorge M. Gomez, Gral Roca ....L 10
May 15—Faustino Barrios, San Nicolas ....L 10
June 7—Manuel Bustos, Zarate ....L 10
July 18—Omar Diaz, G. Belgarno ....L 8
Aug. 8—Mario Matthysse, Sunchales ....L 8
Sept. 26—Fernando Sosa, Mar del Plata ....L 8
Oct. 11—Adolfo Rossi, Dairiaux ....L 8
Dec. 19—Ricardo Espinosa, Olavarria ....D 8

PABLO BAEZ
Los Angeles, Calif. Welterweight
1977
June 24—Ovidio Zapata, San Diego ....KO 2
Sept. 26—Alejandro Garcia, San Diego ....KO 3
1978
Jan. 28—Joe Maldonado, Fresno ....L 6
Feb. 2—Rocky Fukumoto, Los Angeles ....KO 3
Mar. 2—Al Fletcher, Los Angeles ....KO 2
Mar. 14—Ron Cummings, Sacramento ....L 6
Mar. 23—Victor Abraham, Los Angeles ....L 10
Apr. 13—Agapito Ramirez, Los Angeles ....L 6
May 19—Fernando Lugo, San Diego ....KO 6
June 3—Esteban DeJesus, San Juan ......KO by 3
July 27—Jimmy Jackson, Los Angeles ....L 10
Aug. 25—Sultan Saladin, San Diego ....KO 8
Sept. 20—Horace Shufford, Las Vegas ....KO 9
Sept. 26—Rudy Barro, Pico Rivera ....L 10
1979
May 16—Leroy Jefferson, Las Vegas ....KO 7
Aug. 12—Ron Cummings, Las Vegas ....D 8
1980
Mar. 14—Leonardo Bermudez, Culiacan ....L 10
Apr. 25—Zeferino Gonzales, Los Angeles ....KO 6

JOE BAHASH
Huntington Beach, Calif. Welterweight
1980
Oct. 8—Nestor Pinango, Las Vegas ....D 4
Oct. 28—Abel Montelongo, Bakersfield ....L 4
Nov. 19—Andres Montoya, Las Vegas ....L 6
Dec. 10—Marty Tenio, Las Vegas ....L 6

ABEL CELESTINO BAILONE
Argentine Light Heavyweight
Born: December 19, 1952
1976
Mar. 12—Jorge Toledo, Villa Mercedes ....W 10
Apr. 9—Miguel Bergesi, Villa Mercedes ....KO 5
May 14—Juan Cuellar, Villa Mercedes ....W 8
July 8—Juan Cuellar, Villa Mercedes ....W 8
Sept. 10—Jorge Rivera, Villa Mercedes ....KO 3
Oct. 15—Anselmo Arrieto, Villa Mercedes ....KO 6
Dec. 18—Adolfo Salvatierra, Villa Mercedes ......W 10
1977
Feb. 11—Hector Altamirano, Villa Mercedes ......D 10
Apr. 9—Ramon Cerrezuela, San Luis ....L 10
Aug. 19—Gregorio Navarro, Villa Mercedes ......W 10
Sept. 16—Jorge Toledo, Villa Mercedes ....KO 6
Oct. 21—Carlos Flores, San Luis ....KO by 6
1978
May 12—Ramon Cerrezuela, San Luis ....W 12
(Won Argentine Title)

July 14—Ruben Zamarro, Villa Mercedes ....W 10
July 29—Ramon Cerrezuela, Buenos Aires .....KO by 9
Nov. 10—Ruben Zamarro, Villa Maria ....KO 12
(Retained Light Heavyweight Title)
Dec. 7—Hector Altamirano, G. Pinedo ....KO 7
1979
Jan. 11—Alberto Cardoza, San Luis ....KO 3
Apr. 6—Jorge Salgado, Mendoza ....L 10
June 22—Juan Espinola, Asuncion ....KO 8
(South American Light Heavyweight Title)
July 21—Natalio Ibarra, Villa Mercedes ....W 10
Aug. 10—Carlos Pouyannes, Rio Tercero ....W 10
Oct. 13—Juan Domingo Suarez, Buenos Aires ....KO 9
Nov. 23—Hugo Rossi, LaPlata ....KO 7
Dec. 22—Juan Domingo Suarez, Buenos Aires ....L 10
1980
May 23—Candido Barrera, Cordoba ....L 10
July 11—Juan C. Fernandez, Villa Mercedes ......L 10
Aug. 8—Carlos F. Burlon, Villa Mercedes ....L 12
Dec. 5—Cesar Duarte, Cdo. Rivadavia ....KO 10
(Retained Argentine Light Heavyweight Title)

JIMMY BAKER
Austin, Texas Middleweight
1980
Sept. 23—Hank Thomas, Indianapolis ....KO 3
Nov. 19—Felix Sifrientes, Moline ....KO 2
Dec. 10—Frank Anast, Moline ....KO 3

MIKE BAKER
Washington D.C. Middleweight
1973
Mar. 14—Skip Yeaton, Taunton ....KO 2
Mar. 21—Don Malosh, Taunton ....KO 2
Mar. 27—Harry Hippie, Boston ....KO 5
Mar. 29—Paul Christi, Portland, Me. ....KO 4
Mar. 31—Jose Pagon, North Adams ....W 6
Apr. 3—Marc Gervais, Quebec City ....W 10
Apr. 19—Oscar Freeman, Portland, Me. ....KO 7
Apr. 26—Bob Green, Portland, Me. ....KO 7
May 3—Jesus Alicia, Portland, Me. ....W 8
Aug. 2—Gary Broughton, Halifax ....KO by 7
Sept. 15—Oscar Freeman, Norfolk ....W 8
Oct. 10—Dave Wyatt, Richmond ....W 10
Nov. 15—Sonny Moore, Portland, Me. ....W 10
Nov. 23—Terry Hayward, Halifax ....D 8
1974
Jan. 17—Renaldo Olivera, Portland, Me. ....W 10
Mar. 21—Ott Wagner, Lincolnton ....KO 4
Apr. 5—Javier Carrabello, Richmond ....KO 3
May 7—Tony Licata, Houston ....L 10
(American Middleweight Title)
June 4—Fidel Gonzalez, Houston ....KO 4
July 29—Mike Rossman, New York ....L 8
Oct. 1—Robert Williams, Alexandria ....KO 1
Oct. 22—Sam Zohodi, Alexandria ....KO 3
Nov. —Matt Donovan, Boston ....L 10
Dec. 17—Dave Wyatt, Spartanburg ....KO 6
1975
Feb. 22—Leo Saenz, Largo ....W 10
Apr. 29—Leo Saenz, Largo ....L 10
July 10—Paul Osborne, Portland, Me. ....KO 8
(U.S. Junior Middleweight Title)
Sept. 11—Gary Bailey, Portland, Me ....W 10
(U.S. Junior Middleweight Title)
Sept. 16—Charlie Fullard, Richmond ....KO 3
(U.S. Junior Middleweight Title)
Oct. 28—Gene Wells, Orlando ....L 10
1976
Apr. 5—Larry Davis, Landover ....W 8
July 6—Nat King, Miami Beach ....L 10
Oct. 28—Alvin Anderson, Baltimore ....KO by 8
1977
Apr. 14—Ralph Palladin, Landover ....KO by 8
June 20—Billy Duquette, Peabody ....KO 6
Aug. 30—Jean-Claude LeClair, Montreal ....KO 1
Nov. 5—Mike Avans, Las Vegas ....W 10
1978
Mar. 15—Jimmy Savage, Washington D.C. ....W 10
Apr. 13—Frankie Kolovrat, Landover ....KO 2
Sept. 26—Freddy Johnson, Miami Beach ....L 10
Nov. 6—Charlie Weir, Durban ....L disq. 6
1979
Mar. 9—Casey Gacic, New York ....KO 6
Apr. 8—Ricky Weigel, Las Vegas ....W 10
June 22—Clarence Gilmore, New York ....KO 4
Aug. 10—Stanley Blythe, Spartanburg ....KO 6
Sept. 25—Maurice Hope, London ....KO by 7
(For WBC Junior Middleweight Title)
Oct. 10—Stanley Blythe, Spartanburg ....KO 4
Dec. 23—Claude Simpson, Spartanburg ....KO 2
1980
Nov. 1—Tony Ayala, Jr., Lake Tahoe ....L 8

MIKE BALDWIN
ALI MUHAMMAD
Newark, N.J. Light Heavyweight
1979

July	1—Harry Fryar, Rahway	W	4
Oct.	27—Mike Robinson, Rahway	L	6

1980

May	25—Junior Edmonds, Rahway	NC	2
Sept.	9—Sal San Filippo, Rahway	NC	1
Oct.	12—Bob Smith, Rahway	L	4

GUSTAVO BALEON
Mexican Lightweight
1979

Apr.	4—Jose Felix, Mexico City	KO	2
June	9—Ramiro Iniguez, Mexico City	KO	3
July	14—Mauricio Aceves, Mexico City	D	6
Oct.	13—Francisco Tapia, Mexico City	KO	2
	—Marcelo Vega, Mexico City	KO	2

1980

Mar.	8—Norberto Mendoza, Mexico City	KO	4
Apr.	5—Ray Beltran, Mexico City	KO by	4

LYNN BALL
Bossier, La. Heavyweight
1976

Aug.	4—James Dixon, Alexandria	W	6
Oct.	7—Ernie Smith, Fort Worth	KO	3
Nov.	27—Tommy Collins, Fort Worth	W	5

1977

Oct.	1—Henry Ray, Shreveport	KO	3
Oct.	22—Leroy Green, Lubbock	KO	2
Dec.	14—John Young, Wica	KO	2

1978

Feb.	8—Larry Alexander, Memphis	W	8
Apr.	19—Eddie Porett, Las Vegas	KO	3
Dec.	15—Morris Jackson, Omaha	KO	1

1979

Feb.	7—Jim Ingram, Las Vegas	L	6
Feb.	21—Lee Holloman, Las Vegas	KO	3
Mar.	14—Harry Terrell, Las Vegas	L	10
Nov.	8—Henry Porter, Tulsa	L	10
Dec.	12—Ron Lyle, Phoenix	KO	2

1980

Feb.	12—Vernon Johnston, Beaumont	W	10
Feb.	21—Lee Hollomon, Las Vegas	KO	3
May	31—Marty Monroe, El Paso	KO by	5
Nov.	7—Jody Ballard, San Antonio	W	10

MARCELLUS BALL
Cincinnati, Ohio Light Heavyweight
1980

Sept.	18—Phil Brown, Cleveland	L	4
Dec.	12—Ralph Thomas, Cleveland	L	4

EDDIE BALLARAND
Philippine Featherweight
1980

Feb.	8—Jesse Dariagan, Manila	W	10
June	24—Lionel Harney, Honolulu	W	10
July	16—Fili Ramirez, Las Vegas	W	10
July	29—Ralph Aviles, Honolulu	KO by	7
Sept.	25—Tony Baltazar, Los Angeles	KO by	4

JODY BALLARD
Houston, Texas Heavyweight
Born: Dec. 12, 1950
1974

Apr.	19—Ernie Smith, Dallas	W	4
June	4—Ernie Smith, Houston	KO	4
July	2—Charles Lee, Houston	KO	2
Aug.	13—Jimmy Cross, Houston	KO	2
Sept.	2—Rocky Robinson. Las Vegas	KO	2
Sept.	7—Carl Moore, Tucson	KO	2
Sept.	17—Charlie Lee, Houston	KO	2
Oct.	9—Al Hogan, Mobile	W	6
Oct.	19—Bobby Lee, Tucson	KO	1
Oct.	24—Young Sanford Houpe, Los Angeles	KO by	3
Nov.	13—Lee Mitchell, Albuquerque	KO	4
Nov.	26—Koli Vailea, Albuquerque	KO	6
Dec.	4—Ernie Smith, Dallas	KO	2

1975

Feb.	18—Henry Clark, San Jose	L	10
Mar.	11—Rodney Bobick, Miami Beach	W	10
Apr.	9—Pedro Lovell, Honolulu	L	10
May	6—Leon Shaw, Orlando	W	10
May	20—Bob Ellis, Orlando	W	10
June	3—Tommy Howard, Orlando	KO	8
July	8—O. T. Davies, Miami Beach	KO	5
July	16—Terry Kreuger, Houston	KO	3
Aug.	19—Gene Idlette, Orlando	KO	5
Oct.	1—Jimmy Gilmore, Las Vegas	W	8

Oct.	10—Jimmy Gilmore, Tucson	W	10

1976

Feb.	10—Al Jones, Miami Beach	L	10
Mar.	3—Leroy Jones, Las Vegas	KO by	4
Mar.	26—Charles Atlas, Tuscaloosa	W	10
Apr.	15—Tom Prater, Indianapolis	L	8
May	11—Leon Shaw, Orlando	KO by	1
June	4—Jimmy Phillips, Tuscaloosa	KO	2
July	14—Mike Weaver, Las Vegas	L	10

1977

Jan.	29—Stan Ward, Miami Beach	L	10
May	16—Dave Wilson, Landover	W	8
Sept.	14—Jimmy Young, Las Vegas	L	10

1978

Mar.	25—Dan Johnson, Las Vegas	W	4
June	9—Alfredo Evangelista, Las Vegas	L	10
Sept.	7—Leon Shaw, El Paso	L	10

1980

Oct.	1—Randy Mack, Las Vegas	KO by	10
Nov.	7—Lynn Ball, San Antonio	L	10

JOE BALLARD
Richmond, Va. Heavyweight
1980

Nov.	1—Brad Crane, Richmond	KO	2
Dec.	20—Anthony Washington, Richmond	KO	1

GUSTAVO BALLAS
Argentine Flyweight
1980

Feb.	8—Jose Ricord, Mar del Plata	KO	6
Mar.	7—Rigoberto Marcano, Buenos Aires	W	10
Apr.	3—Juan Arevena, Villa Maria	KO	5
Apr.	19—Rodolfo Rodriguez, Buenos Aires	W	10
May	16—Jorge Aguilar, Mendoza	W	10
June	6—Ramon Rodriguez, Villa Maria	KO	9
June	27—Hector Velazquez, San Juan	KO	2
Sept.	5—Ramon Rodriguez, Cordoba	KO	10
Sept.	19—Miguel Lazarte, Mendoza	W	10
Oct.	4—Rafael Pedroza, Buenos Aires	W	10
Nov.	22—Alfonso Lopez, Buenos Aires	W	10
Dec.	11—Ramon Rodriguez, Mendoza	KO	8

FRANKIE BALTAZAR
Los Angeles, Calif. Junior Lightweight
Born: April 14, 1958
1976

Apr.	22—Rafael Gonzalez, Los Angeles	W	4
May	7—Ignacio Bravo, San Bernardino	KO	4
June	3—Antonio Meza, Los Angeles	KO	1
Aug.	11—Reynaldo Zaragoza, Stockton	L	6
Sept.	9—Basilio Onate, Los Angeles	W	7
Oct.	28—Chango Cruz, Los Angeles	KO	9
Dec.	9—Memin Vega, Los Angeles	TD	4

1977

Feb.	3—Memin Vega, Los Angeles	W	10
Apr.	16—Francisco Villegas, Miami Beach	W	10
July	7—Miguel Ruiz, Los Angeles	KO	1
July	21—Delfino Rodriguez, Los Angeles	W	10
Oct.	6—Jorge Ramos, Los Angeles	KO	1
Nov.	3—Claude Durden, Los Angeles	KO	7
Dec.	15—Tony Sanchez, Los Angeles	KO	2

1978

Jan.	26—Jose Olivares, Los Angeles	KO	5
Feb.	23—Miguel Meza, Los Angeles	KO	4
Mar.	30—Shig Fukuyama, Los Angeles	KO	4
May	18—Jose Luis Solano, Los Angeles	KO	1
July	20—Leonico Meza, Los Angeles	KO	5
Aug.	3—Eliu Hernandez, Los Angeles	KO	3
Sept.	21—Ernesto Herrera, Los Angeles	KO	5
Nov.	9—Jaime Nava, Los Angeles	KO	6

1979

Mar.	29—Frank Ahumada, Los Angeles	W	10
June	21—Ignacio Campos, Los Angeles	KO	6
July	26—Tony Daniels, Los Angeles	W	6
Aug.	9—Frank Ahumada, Los Angeles	W	10
Nov.	1—Alejandro Lopez, Los Angeles	W	10

1980

Feb.	28—Miguel Etrada, Los Angeles	KO	6
May	9—Jaime Nava, Los Angeles	W	10
July	24—Rafael Limon, Los Angeles	KO by	4

JOSE LUIS BALTAZAR
Mexican Junior Middleweight
1965

Feb.	17—Jose Manzano, Mexico City	KO	3
July	21—Arturo Salas, Mexico City	L	8

1966

Mar.	16—Agustin Villada, Mexico City	KO	4
Apr.	23—Pancho Marin, Monterrey	W	10
June	3—Pancho Marin, Monterrey	W	10
Aug.	20—Joel Rangel, Mexico City	W	10

Oct.   1—Manuel (Tuxtepec) Garcia,
        Mexico City ....KO 6
1967
Jan.   13—Miguel Hernandez, Monterrey ....L 10
Mar.   4—Javier Espinosa, Mexico City ....KO 7
Apr.   22—Ray Reyes, Mexico City ....KO by 8
1968
June   12—Ruben Arocha, Tuxtla Gutierrez,
        Chiapas ....KO by 3
June   —(Chamaco) Cosgaya, Champoton,
        Campeche ....KO by 3
Sept. 18—Agustin Garcia, Mexico City ....KO 2
Oct.   30—Omar Chavez, Mexico City ....L disq. 5
1969
Sept. 10—Ruben Vazquez, Mexico City ....KO by 9
1970
Jan.   14—Gustavo Garcia, Mexico City ....L 10
Feb.   3—Mario Marquez, Tijuana ....KO 8
July   13—Manuel Fierro, Tijuana ....L 10
July   —Celso Olivas, Culiacan ....L 10
Aug.   1—Jose Angel Zamora, Monterrey ....W 10
Sept. 12—Lupe Torres, Monterrey ....KO 7
Oct.   28—Ruben Arocha, Mexico City ....W 10
1971
July   28—Mario Marquez, Mexico City ....L 10
Oct.   6—Faustino (Dinamita) Delgado,
        Merida, Yucatan ....L 10
1972
Mar.   28—Manuel (Sonrisas) Avitia, Reynosa ....W 10
Apr.   19—Chucho Garay, Mexico City ....KO 3
May   15—Isaac Quints, Reynosa ....L 10
July   19—Jose Palacios, Mexico City ....KO by 2
Aug.   18—Enrique Rodriguez, Aguascalientes ....W 10
Oct.   13—Hedgemon Lewis, San Diego ....L 10
Nov.   10—Ernie (Indian Red) Lopez, Los Angeles ...KO by 5
1973
Jan.   31—Samuel (Sammy) Garcia, Mexico City ....W 10
June   15—Margarito Martinez, Culiacan ....KO 3
Nov.   10—Nelson Ruiz, Maracay ....L 10
1974
Apr.   25—Rocky Mattioli, Melbourne ....L 10
May   17—Darryl Carrick, Melbourne ....L 10
1975
Apr.   23—Faustino (Dinamita) Delgado,
        Merida, Yucatan ....W 10
May   5—Pablo Cortina, Reynosa ....KO 1
May   24—Jose Baquedano, Monterrey ....L 10
July   18—Sergio Lozano, Ciudad Madero,
        Tamaulipas ....KO by 10
1976
Apr.   23—Jose Figueroa, Reynosa ....KO by 3
Oct.   29—Sergio Rodriguez, Reynosa ....KO 6
1977
Mar.   12—Ernesto Caballero, Manzanillo ....W 10
June   18—Jose Figueroa, Mexico City ....W 12
Sept.   3—Vianor Durango, Mexico City ....KO 9
Oct.   —Celso Olivas, Reynosa ....D 10
Nov.   22—Pete Ranzany, Sacramento ....L 10
1978
Feb.   10—Ernesto Caballero, Ciudad Diaz Ordaz ....W 12
        (Retained Mexican Welterweight Title)
May   12—Sivano Estopier, Poza Rica ....W 10
June   19—Salvador Garcia, Reynosa ....KO 1
July   14—Adan Chavarria, Monterrey ....L 10
Sept. 12—Jose Baquedano, Reynosa ....W 12
        (Retained Mexican Welterweight Title)
Oct.   21—Adolfo Sanjeado, Merida, Yucatan ....D 10
Dec.   5—Sammy Ayala, San Antonio ....L 10
1979
Apr.   10—Zeferino Gonzalez, Houston ....L 10
Aug.   31—Adan Chavarria, Monterrey ....KO by 8
        (Lost Mexican Welterweight Title)
Dec.   14—Leonardo Bermudez, Culiacan ....L 10
1980
Feb.   5—Jarvis Mayfield, Houston ....KO 4
Dec.   14—Leonardo Bermudez, Culiacan ....L 10

TONY BALTAZAR
La Puente, Calif. Junior Lightweight
1979
Feb.   8—Art Silvera, Los Angeles ....KO 1
Mar.   22—Julio Alfonso, Los Angeles ....KO 2
Apr.   19—Roberto Garcia, Los Angeles ....KO 2
May   10—Eric Bonilla, Los Angeles ....KO 2
June   21—Jaime Nava, Los Angeles ....W 6
July   26—Willie Daniels, Los Angeles ....W 6
Sept. 20—Clemente Enrique, Los Angeles ....KO 5
Nov.   8—Clemente Enrique, Los Angeles ....KO 1
1980
Feb.   19—Max Cervantes, Sacramento ....KO 1
May   15—Juan Campos, Los Angeles ....KO 2
July   10—Ruben Martinez, Los Angeles ....KO
Aug.   8—Rosario Gonzales, Los Angeles ....KO 1
Sept. 25—Eddie Ballarin, Los Angeles ....KO 4

Oct.   30—Chuy Rodriguez, Las Vegas ....D 4

CHARLIE BALTIMORE
Philadelphia, Pa. Heavyweight
1979
Aug.   30—Leroy Boone, Virginia Beach ....KO by 1
1980
May   16—Marty Capass, Chester ....KO by 2
Aug.   30—Leroy Boone, Virginia Beach ....KO by 1

DJATA BANKS
Philadelphia, Pa. Heavyweight
1979
June   12—Joe Louis Jones, Detroit ....KO 3
Sept. 12—Scott Lukachik, White Plains ....L 4
1980
May   9—Dennis Riley, Staten Island ....KO by 1

EMMETT AL BANKS
Dallas, Tex. Heavyweight
1979
July   21—Grover Robinson, Dallas ....KO by 5
Oct.   20—Eric Sedill, Pueblo ....KO by 3
1980
Aug.   16—Alvin Dominey, Odessa ....KO by 4

GERALD BANKS
Brooklyn, N.Y. Middleweight
1979
Nov.   23—Robert Rooney, Trenton ....W 4
1980
Feb.   8—Dalton Swift, Trenton ....D 4
Apr.   18—Danny Corbett, New York, N.Y. ....KO 4
Apr.   30—Ali Perez, Charleston ....W 6
Oct.   23—John Molander, New York, N.Y. .....KO by 1

JOE BANKS
Portland, Oregon Middleweight
1979
Oct.   20—Hudson Jackson, Portland ....KO 1
July   26—Tim Gockerell, Portland ....KO 3
1980
Jan.   23—Paddy Wilson, Portland ....KO 7
Oct.   23—Jeff McCracken, Spokane ....KO by 4
Dec.   27—Danny Pearson, North Bergen ....KO 1

WILLIAM BANKS
Las Vegas, Nev. Heavyweight
1978
Nov.   8—Eddie Atkinson, Las Vegas ....KO 2
Nov.   21—Eddie Wilson, Las Vegas ....KO by 1
1979
Jan.   17—Charles Roye, Las Vegas ....KO by 3
Dec.   12—Leslie Profit, Las Vegas ....KO by 1
1980
Jan.   16—Charles Roye, Las Vegas ....W 4
Feb.   3—James Williams, Reno ....KO by 2
May   21—Dennis Fikes, Las Vegas ....KO by 4
Aug.   13—Pascual Ramirez, Las Vegas ....KO by 2

JOSE BAQUEDANO
Mexican Welterweight
1970
Dec.   —E. Acosta, Merida ....D 4
1971
Jan.   —Kid Tekapan, Merida ....W 4
Feb.   —P. Martinez, Merida ....KO 5
Mar.   —P. Delgado, Merida ....W 8
Aug.   —Geronimo Ku, Merida ....KO 5
Oct.   —M. Gomez, Merida ....KO 2
1972
Mar.   5—Jose Figueroa, Merida ....KO 5
May   —Augustin Chavez, Merida ....KO by 2
June   28—Aguilar Fernandez, Merida ....KO 1
Aug.   16—Zurdo Canul, Merida ....KO 9
1973
Jan.   31—Pancho Tapia, Merida ....W 10
May   12—Fili Ascencio, Villahermosa ....KO 1
June   27—Jose Macias, Merida ....KO 6
Sept.   8—Mario Luna, Merida ....KO 1
1974
Mar.   23—Armando Alatore, Merida ....KO 2
Apr.   28—Ray Reyes, Merida ....KO 1
June   8—Dinamita Delgado, Merida ....W 10
1975
Mar.   9—Ramiro Ruvalcaba, Merida ....KO 4
May   24—Jose Luis Baltazar, Monterrey ....W 10
June   11—Gustavo Garcia, Merida ....NC 6
Aug.   23—Marcos Geraldo, Merida ....KO 1
Oct.   25—Alex Olguin, Merida ....KO 2
1976
May   10—Dinamita Caballero, Merida ....KO 6
        (Won Vacant Mexican Welterweight Title)

41

July 30—Andy Price, Los Angeles ....KO 6
Sept. 18—Johnny Gant, Los Angeles ....KO by 8
1977
(Inactive)
1978
Mar.   2—Babs McCarthy, Los Angeles ....KO by 1
Sept. 25—Jose Luis Baltazar, Reynosa ....L 12
(Lost Mexican Welterweight Title)
1979
Jan. 13—Jose Figueroa, Mexico City ....KO 1
Mar.   5—Robert Turner, Houston ....KO by 2
—Francisco Famoso, Merida ....KO 1
Aug. 18—Jose Duarte, Mexico City ....KO by 7
Oct. 19—Andres Nunez, Campeche ....KO 1
Dec. 21—Carlos Mark, Chetumal ....KO 2
1980
Mar.   7—Alberto Perez, Valladolid ....KO 3
Apr.   5—Ernesto Escalante, Mexico City ....KO 4
July 30—Ariel Favela, Merida ....KO 1
Aug. 30—Joaquin Macias, Mexico City ....KO by 8

MARCO BARAHONA
Nicaraguan Lightweight
Born: November 3, 1954; Height: 5'7"
1974
Sept. 16—Jose Resto, New York ....W 4
Nov. 25—Jimmy McCloud, New York ....KO 2
1975
Feb. 20—Arturo Rosa, North Bergen ....D 4
Sept. 8—Terrence Turner, New York ....W 4
Sept. 30—Jimmy McCloud, New York ....W 4
1976
Mar. 31—Jose Resto, Uniondale ....W 6
Apr. 14—Ron Meaweather, New York ....W 6
July 31—Arturo Guevara, Managua ....KO 2
Oct. 22—Danny Daniels, New York ....KO 4
1977
Feb.   2—Danny Daniels, New York ....W 4
Mar. 25—Larry Stanton, New York ....W 8
Aug.   9—Diablito Valdez, New York ....L 8
1978
June   6—Jose Resto, New York ....W 8
1979
Apr.   6—Ralph Racine, New York ....W 10
1980
Jan. 25—Pete Padilla, Felt Forum ....L 10
Nov. 12—Cocoa Sanchez, Felt Forum ....L 10

LOU BARBER
Baltimore, Md. Lightweight
1979
Apr. 26—Ricky Stinne, Virginia Beach ....L 4
May   17—Ricky Stinne, Virginia Beach ....L 4
Sept. 26—Ricky Patterson, Baltimore ....W 4
Oct. 24—Cliff Haywood, Baltimore ....L 4
Nov. 14—Ira Robinson, Baltimore ....W 4
1980
Mar. 26—Scotty Farmer, Baltimore ....W 4

JUAN BARBOZA
Argentine Welterweight
1980
Feb.   1—Martin Duran, Tucuman ....W 10
Feb. 22—Roque Arevalo, Tucuman ....W 10
Mar. 14—Viterman Sanchez, Tucuman ....W 10
Apr. 18—Sergio Loyola, Tucuman ....W 10
May   23—Americo Avalos, Tucuman ....KO 8
June   5—Hugo Luero, Tucuman ....W 10
July   4—Nicolas Arkuszyn, Tucuman ....W 10
Aug.   1—Hugo Luero, Tucuman ....D 10
Sept. 5—Raul Fernandez, Tucuman ....W 10
Oct. 10—Ricardo Monzon, Tucuman ....KO 3

HENRY BARCELLANO
Philippine Featherweight
1980
May   22—Warren Mathews, San Carlos ....KO by 5
July   8—Refugio Rojas, Honolulu ....KO by 4
Sept. 16—Tino Savea, Honolulu ....L 4

JUAN BARDI
Argentine Welterweight
1980
Apr. 12—Ruben Wilberger, Buenos Aires ....L 10
June 19—Jose L. Guevara, Villa Maria ....L 10
July 11—Santiago Portillo, Tucuman ....L 10
Dec. 12—Ramon Oviedo, Malargue ....L 12

RAY BARKSDALE
Chicago, Ill. Light Heavyweight
1979
Nov. 20—Wayne Green, Chicago ....KO 3
1980
Dec. 11—John Collins, Chicago ....KO by 5

GARY BARLOW
Lenoir, North Carolina Junior Lightweight
1977
Nov. 11—Woody Presswood, Fayetteville ....W 4
1978
Mar.   4—Billy McCreary, Lumberton ....KO 3
Apr. 24—Otis Locklear, Bellwood ....KO 2
May   27—Otis Locklear, Fallston ....KO 2
Sept. 21—Billy McCreary, Spartanburg ....KO 3
1979
Apr.   5—Robert Mullens, Spartanburg ....KO by 5
May   4—Sam Layton, Fayetteville ....KO by 3
1980
July 26—Rado Ray, Charlotte ....W 4
Sept. 20—Joe Smith, Charlotte ....W 4

BILL BARNES
Burnaby, British Columbia Welterweight
1980
Feb. 29—Charles LeCour, Nanaimo ....KO by 1
June   5—Pete Hendrege, Vancouver ....W 4
June 26—Billy Minnex, Bellingham ....KO by 1
Sept. 19—Mickey McMillan, Kamloops ....KO by 6

TONY BARNES
Newark, N.J. Junior Middleweight
1980
Oct.   4—Dennis Mulligan, Great Gorge ....KO by 2
Nov. 20—Dennis Mulligan, Totowa ....KO by 2

(ANDROS) ERNIE BARR
Light Heavyweight
Born: Mars-Bay, Andros, Bahama Islands
Age 21 yrs. Height: 6 ft. 3½ in.
1975 Florida Light Heavyweight Golden Glove Champion.
1976
Mar. 23—Ed (Savage) Turner, Orlando ....L 6
—Woody Starr, Nassau ....W 6
—Cephus Bowe, Nassau..................W 6
—K.O. Grant, Nassau ....KO 2
—Bobby Boyd, Hollywood ....KO 2
—Les Brown, Ft. Lauderdale ....KO 3
—Chris Braynham, Nassau ....KO 1
—Nat Gates, Orlando....................W 6
1977
Feb.   1—Ed Turner, Orlando ....KO 8
Feb. 11—Willie Goodman, Nassau ....KO 4
Apr. 16—Lee Royster, Miami Beach ....W 10
May   26—Glen Morgan, Tampa ....KO 7
July   8—Tony Mundine, Brisbane ....L 15
(Commonwealth Light Heavyweight Title)
1978
Jan. 14—Nat Gates, Nassau ....KO 4
Jan. 24—Tony Mundine, Melbourne ....L 10
Feb. 17—Jimmy Roper, Nassau ....KO 2
Mar.   2—Mustapha Wassaja ....L 8
Apr. 28—Boston Blackie, Nassau ....KO 8
June 20—Willie Allen, Miami Beach ....KO 2
July 20—Boston Blackie, Nassau ....KO 3
Dec. 30—John Girowski, Nassau ....KO 5
1979
Jan. 27—Bobby Lloyd, Nassau ....KO by 5
Mar. 16—Dynamite Fritz, Nassau ....W disq. 7
Sept. 1—Guillermo Escalera, Nassau ....KO 1
Sept. 12—Yaqui Lopez, Stockton ....KO by 3
1980
Feb. 12—Costello King, Miami Beach ....KO 2
Feb. 28—Fierod Abdullah, Tampa ....KO 3
Mar. 28—Baby Boy Rolle, Nassau ....W 10
Aug. 29—Bobby Lloyd, Nassau ....W 10
Dec. 13—Vonzell Johnson, Miami ....L 10

MIGUEL BARRAZA
Argentine Lightweight
1980
Jan.   —Federico Baez, Mar del Plata ....NC
July 11—Rodolfo Petrizani, Ciudadela ....L 10
Aug.   9—Ramon Fabaz, Baradero ....D 8

CANDIDO BARRERA
Argentine Light Heavyweight
1980
Mar.   7—Juan Suarez, Cordoba ....KO by 3
July 25—Alfredo Morales, Rio III ....W 12
Aug. 15—Juan Suarez, Cordoba ....KO by 9

RAMON BARRERA
Merida, Mexico Bantamweight
1979
July 16—Chivo Arrellano, Bakersfield ....W 4
Aug. 20—Chivo Arrellano, Bakersfield ....W 6
Sept. 25—Jaime Garza, Los Angeles ....KO by 3

42

May   21—Daniel Cruz, Las Vegas .... KO by 6

HECTOR BARRETO
Argentine Bantamweight
1980
Feb.   1—Felix Colman, Posadas .... L 10
May   9—Jose Izquirdo, Concordia .... D 10
Oct.   24—Ruben Condori, Salta .... L 10
Dec.   19—Hugo Fernandez, Concordia .... L 10

JOE BARRIENTES
Texas Junior Middleweight
1977
May   7—Emmett Atlas, Shreveport .... KO 3
Oct.   20—Donnie London, Marshall .... KO 3
Oct.   27—Ray Phillips, Dallas .... L 10
Nov.   30—Arnell Thomas, Topeka .... L 8
1978
Mar.   22—Ray Phillips, Dallas .... L 10
May   6—Norberto Cabrera, Viareggio .... L 8
1979
Mar.   31—Rodrigo Hernandez, Denver .... KO 6
Apr.   2—Mike Garcia, Dallas .... KO 5
June   23—Ron Brown, Denver .... KO by 8
July   9—Morris Jordan, Odessa .... W 8
July   21—Robert Powell, Dallas .... W 10
Aug.   14—Bennie Briscoe, Atlantic City .... KO by 6
Dec.   15—Ivy Brown, Kansas City .... KO by 5
1980
Mar.   17—Gary Guiden, Indianapolis .... KO by 3

ROBERTO BARRIENTOS
Argentine Featherweight
1980
Apr.   11—Pablo Lencina, San Cristobal .... W 10
July   11—Jorge M. Gomez, Gral Roca .... KO by 6
Sept.   6—Hugo Fernandez, Concordia .... KO by 8

FAUSTINO BARRIOS
Argentine Junior Lightweight
1980
Jan.   11—Ramon Franco, San Miguel .... D 8
Jan.   25—Pedro Burki, Camilo Aldao .... L 10
Mar.   22—Nestor Gundin, Zarate .... NC 1
Apr.   25—Ruben Stamuli, San Nicolas .... W 10
May   15—Felipe Baez, San Nicolas .... W 10
June   13—Mario Vizcaya, Rio IV .... L 10
June   27—Nestor Gundin, San Nicolas .... D 10
July   18—Jose Filipi, Camilo Aldao .... L 10
Aug.   9—Nestor Gundin, Baradero .... KO 3
Sept.   13—Ruben Stamuli, Mar del Plata .... L 10
Sept.   26—Santiago Lopez, Olavarria .... W 10
Oct.   11—Pedro Arm. Gutierrez, Buenos Aires ..... L 10
Dec.   12—Ruben Stamuli, Bolivar .... TD 9

RALPH BARRIOS
Florida Featherweight
1977
July   15—Willie Donahue, Tampa .... D 7
Dec.   15—Ben Chavez, Tampa .... KO 4
1978
Jan.   19—Arthur Clarke, Tampa .... L 8
Aug.   10—Frank Moultrie, Tampa .... KO by 7
Aug.   31—Terry Pizzarro, Tampa .... W 6
1979
Feb.   6—Tony Styles, Orlando .... W 6
June   21—Sipho Mange, Capetown .... L 8
1980
May   16—Oscar Muniz, San Bernardino .... KO by 1
Nov.   14—Ricardo Cardona, Miami Beach ...... KO by 1

RUDY BARRO
Welterweight
1979
Mar.   24—Jerry Cheatham, Tucson .... KO by 5
June   10—Daryl Penn, Stockton .... L 10
Oct.   25—Daryl Penn, Portland .... KO by 5
1980
Jan.   17—Victor Martinez, Los Angeles .... KO by 2
Apr.   21—Canela Salinas, Bakersfield .... W 10
July   29—Armando Ramirez, Honolulu .... KO by 7
Oct.   23—Lenny Hahn, Spokane .... L 10

PHILIP BATIE
Cleveland, Ohio Welterweight
1979
Sept.   26—Danny Jones, Windsor .... KO by 2
1980
Feb.   1—Louis Matco, Chicago .... KO by 1
Apr.   19—Billy Watkins, Muskegon .... KO 0
Apr.   30—Chuck Spicer, Youngstown .... KO 4
July   25—Nick Furlano, Smith Falls .... KO 4

Sept.   12—Pete Seward, Lorain .... KO by 1
Dec.   11—Terry Whitaker, Chicago .... KO by 1

JOSE BAUTISTA (FLORES)
Mexican Junior Featherweight
1979
Feb.   13—Manuel Ruelas, Houston .... KO 2
Mar.   20—Joe Nunez, Houston .... KO 2
Apr.   17—Hector Medina, Houston .... L 12
Sept.   22—Leo Randolph, Los Angeles .... L 10
1980
July   29—Sergio Reyes, Laredo .... L 10

JUAN BAUTISTA
Mexican Featherweight
1979
Mar.   30—Osvaldo Romero, Barranquilla .... W 10
Apr.   9—Juan Escobar, Los Angeles .... KO by 2
May   23—Gerald Hayes, Concord .... L 10
July   24—Edwin Alarcon, Honolulu .... W 10
Nov.   13—Jesus Nava, Maracaiba .... L 10
1980
Mar.   27—Warren Matthews, San Carlos .... L 10

CARLOS BAZAN
Argentine Middleweight
1980
Aug.   15—Juan C. Rodriguez, Cordoba .... D 6
Sept.   4—Luis Parodi, Mendoza .... W 6
Oct.   10—Teofilo Paez, Cordoba .... KO 3

RICKY BEARD
Jackson, Tennessee Welterweight
1980
Oct.   23—Charles White, Memphis .... KO 2

JESUS (CHUCHO) BECERRA
Mexico City, Mexico Flyweight
1980
Mar.   22—Miro Rosales, Mexico City .... D 4
Apr.   26—Neftali Ramirez, Mexico City .... W 4
June   21—Javier Saldana, Mexico City .... L 4
July   25—Roberto Llanes, Campeche .... L 10
Oct.   17—Venancio Rojas, Acapulco .... L 10

JOSE REINALDO BECERRA
Venezuelan Light Flyweight
1979
Apr.   29—Jesus Bastardo, Caracas .... W 4
June   16—Manual Teran, Caracas .... D 4
June   30—Prudencio Castillo, Caracas .... W 8
Oct.   6—Carlos Alvarez, Caracas .... L 8
Nov.   23—Santiago Moreno, Caracas .... W 10
1980
Mar.   10—Luis Sierra, Caracas .... W 10
May   19—Ricardo Lopez, Caracas .... W 10
June   16—Luis Sierra, Caracas .... KO 8
       (Won Venezuelan Light Flyweight Title)
Aug.   11—Prudencio Castillo, Caracas .... W 10
Sept.   15—Thomas Calderon, Barquisamento ...... KO 1
Dec.   1—Hilario Zapata, Caracas .... L 15
       (For WBC Junior Flyweight Title)

BUD BECKER
Wilmington, Del. Middleweight
1979
Jan.   11—Warren Fortune, Landover .... L 4
Oct.   24—Bill Harrington, Baltimore .... D 4
1980
Feb.   27—Eddie Gray, Washington D.C. .... W 4
Mar.   26—Bill Harrington, Baltimore .... L 4

EDDIE BEDNARICK
Pittsburgh, Pa. Heavyweight
1980
Feb.   9—Jesse Clark, Clarksburg .... KO 1
May   10—Phil Brown, Clarksburg .... KO 1
Aug.   2—Freddy Gore, Clarksburg .... KO 1

KIKO BEJINES
Mexican Bantamweight
1980
       —Hector Cortes, Guadalajara .... W 10
Oct.   11—Hector Cortes, Mexico City .... KO 1
Nov.   22—Freddy Hernandez, Guadalajara .... KO 3
Dec.   11—Oscar Mills, Los Angeles .... L 10

OSCAR (NEGRO) BEJINEZ
Mexican Flyweight
1980
Oct.   17—Victor Hernandez, Guadalajara .... KO 1

43

Nov. 21—Rosendo Alonso, Guadalajara .... KO 5

DINO BELANGER
Quebec, Canada Heavyweight
1979
Feb. 11—Charley Hord, Miami Beach .... KO 1
Feb. 19—Nat Pugh, Miami Beach .... KO 1
Mar. 5—Ted Simmons, Miami Beach .... KO 3
Mar. 19—Roy Campbell, Miami Beach .... KO 4
Apr. 10—Dennis Cardwell, Miami Beach .... KO 2
Sept. 25—Ron Majors, Miami Beach .... L 6
Nov. 20—Cowboy Walsh, Miami Beach .... KO 1
1980
Feb. 12—James Roper, Miami Beach .... W 6

OTIS BELL
Junior Middleweight
1979
June 21—Huberto De Los Rios, Los Angeles ... KO by 2
1980
May 2—Dave Portillo .... KO 2
Aug. 19—Fred Hutchings, Stockton .... L 4

WILSON BELL
Detroit, Mich. Junior Middleweight
1976
Jan. 17—Gregg Saunders, Detroit .... KO 2
Dec. 16—Glenn Nicholson, Inkster................ W 4
1977
Feb. 15—Kevin Dorian, Boston .... W 6
Oct. 27—Beau Jaynes, Portland, Me. .... L 8
Nov. 24—Joe Houston, Portland, Me. .... KO 5
Dec. 7—David Brooks, Mt. Clemens .... W 4
1978
Jan. 5—Beau Jaynes, Portland, Me. .... W 8
Mar. 23—Alvin Anderson, Portland, Me....... KO by 10
May 10—Marvin Jenkins, White Plains .... L 6
Aug. 8—Alvin Anderson, Baltimore .... KO by 7
Sept. 21—Odell Leonard, Washington D.C. .... KO 1
Oct. 10—Rocky Mosley, Las Vegas .... L 10
1979
Jan. 18—Rocky Mosley, Las Vegas .... L 12
(U.S. Junior Middleweight Title)
Mar. 3—Larry McCall, Detroit .... KO 8
Mar. 28—Kevin Moefield, Baltimore .... W 8
July 19—Jaime Rodriguez, Portland .... W 8
Aug. 7—Rocky Tassone, Baltimore .... KO 1
1980
Jan. 12—Dan Snyder, Atlantic City .... L 8
Feb. 5—Pate Ranzany, Sacramento .... KO by 7

JIMMY BELLA
Los Angeles, Calif. Welterweight
1980
Feb. 8—Ken Davis, San Bernardino .... KO 2
Feb. 19—Rafael Corona, Sacramento .... L 6
Apr. 17—Carlos Mura, Los Angeles .... W 6
May 27—Tim Harris, Sacramento .... L 6

MARIO BELLINI
Argentine Lightweight
1980
July 4—Rafael Gorosito, Mendoza .... D 6
July 18—Humberto Sanchez, Mendoza .... D 6
Sept. 5—Raul Gorosito, Tunuyan .... D 6

MAURICIO BELTRAN
Mexican Junior Featherweight
1980
July 4—Joaquin Acuna, Los Mochis .... KO by 5
Nov. 14—Horacio Pintado, Hermosillo .... KO 1

FARMER BENDER
Elroy, Wisconsin Heavyweight
1980
Aug. 8—Gary Sullins, Chicago .... KO by 1
Dec. 10—Alvin Manson, Moline .... KO by 1

PAUL BENJAMIN
Rockland, Me. Heavyweight
1980
Feb. 13—Bob Akers, Waterville .... KO 1
Feb. 23—John Odom, Rockland .... KO 1
Mar. 12—Frank Dunton, Waterville .... L 8
Apr. 20—James Smith, Portland .... KO by 5
June 26—Al Brooks, Revere .... KO by 5
Aug. 15—Ralph Cuomo, Glen Cove .... L 4
Sept. 9—Ulysses Doiron, Moncton .... L 10

RICARDO (LOCO LOCO) BENNETT
Panamanian Junior Featherweight
Born: 1958, Colon, Republic of Panama
1978
Mar. 4—Baby San Blas, III, Panama .... W 4
Apr. 16—Orlando Quijada, Panama .... W 4
Aug. 19—Orlando Rudas, Panama .... W 6
Sept. 16—Cesar Becerra, Panama .... KO 2
Sept. 30—Alfredo Thomas, Panama .... W 3
Oct. 13—Ringo Page, Panama .... KO 2
Dec. 2—Luis Gonzales, Panama .... KO 1
Dec. 30—John Cajina, Panama .... W 10
1979
Feb. 3—Gilbert Illueca, Panama City .... W 12
(Panamanian Junior Featherweight Title)
May 20—Aureliano Castillo, Colon .... W 10
Aug. 18—Roger Minor, Colon .... KO 6
Sept. 15—Carlos Bejarano, Colon .... L 10
1980
Sept. 20—Daniel Solano, Colon .... L 10

RICHIE BENNETT
Darby, Pa. Middleweight
1976
July 7—Roger Johnson, Philadelphia .... D 4
Nov. 3—Alex Coleman, Philadelphia .... KO 1
Nov. 10—Bob Patterson, South Orange, N.J. ... KO by 5
1977
Jan. 4—Roger Johnson, Bristol .... KO 2
Feb. 5—Roy Ingram, Bristol .... W 4
Mar. 7—Al Daniels, Upper Darby .... KO 1
Apr. 7—Roy Ingram, Upper Darby .... W 6
May 9—Jesse Freeman, Upper Darby .... KO 2
Sept. 15—Sidney Minott, Upper Darby .... KO 3
Oct. 20—Ed Warren, Upper Darby .... W 6
Nov. 15—Carlos Prigg, Upper Darby .... W 6
1978
Jan. 17—Ed Warren, Philadelphia .... KO 2
Feb. 10—Billy Early, Philadelphia .... KO 3
Mar. 7—David Dittmar, Upper Darby .... KO 3
Apr. 28—Ray Smith, Upper Darby .... KO 4
June 1—Dennis Brown, Upper Darby .... KO 1
July 15—Tyrone Freeman, Atlantic City .... W 6
Aug. 24—Tyrone Freeman, Philadelphia .... D 6
Nov. 21—Tyrone Freeman, Upper Darby .... KO 8
1979
Jan. 30—Jimmy Anderson, Upper Darby .... KO 8
Apr. 3—Tedd Mann, Philadelphia .... L 10
Aug. 21—George Lee, Atlantic City .... W 6
Sept. 26—Archie Andrews, Upper Darby .... KO 2
Oct. 30—Dan Snyder, Upper Darby .... KO 8
Dec. 4—Bob Patterson, Philadelphia .... KO 1
1980
Jan. 24—Bennie Briscoe, Upper Darby .... W 10
July 12—Skipper Jones, Atlantic City .... L 10
Aug. 25—Bennie Briscoe, Philadelphia .... L 10

MICHAEL BENNING
Trenton, N.J. Heavyweight
1978
Aug. 16—Billy Smith, Las Vegas .... W 4
Aug. 30—Baron Greenwood, Las Vegas .... KO 2
1979
July 1—Danny Williams, Rahway .... KO 1
1980
July 30—Mark Lee, Las Vegas .... W 4
Nov. 1—Chris McDonald, Lake Tahoe .... KO by 2
Sept. 17—Mike Creel, Las Vegas .... W 4

ALVIAR BENROS
Junior Middleweight
1979
Aug. 10—Ellis Miller, San Diego .... KO 1
Aug. 20—Javier Salomon, Bakersfield .... W 4
Nov. 2—Rafael Corona, San Diego .... W 6
Dec. 14—Gabriel Rico, San Bernardino .... KO 4
1980
Feb. 6—Mike True Hickman, Costa Rosa .... W 6
Mar. 20—Humberto de la Rosa, Los Angeles .... W 6

NORADEEN BEN SALLAH
Rennselaer, N.Y. Lightweight
1979
Oct. 25—Rafael Lopez, Latham .... KO by 3
Dec. 1—Eddie Lugo, Albany .... KO 3
1980
Jan. 15—Papo Figueroa, Hartford .... KO by 6
Feb. 12—Brian Anderson, Montreal .... L 6
Mar. 4—Dave Bolden, W. Hartford .... L 6
Apr. 16—Trevor Evelyn, White Plains .... KO by 1
Nov. 28—John Fanea, Providence .... KO by 2

44

STEVE BENTLEY
Long Beach, Calif. Middleweight
1978
Jan.	24—Mike Hallacy, Wichita	KO by	4
Mar.	2—Steve Moyer, Las Vegas	D	6
Mar.	31—Troy Vaughn, San Diego	W	5
Apr.	4—Robby Epps, Lake Tahoe	KO by	5
May	5—Ricky Weigel, San Diego	KO by	5
Dec.	1—Mustafa Shabazz, San Diego	L	6

1979
May	2—Len Harden, Las Vegas	L	8

1980
April	15—Gary Giron, Sparks	KO by	9

TREVOR BERBICK
Halifax, Canada Heavyweight
1976
Nov.	20—Angus Martin, Moncton	KO	5
Dec.	7—Bobby Halpern, Halifax	KO	2

1977
Jan.	9—Ace Lucas, New Glasgow	KO	2
Jan.	25—Joe Maye, Halifax	KO	7
Aug.	18—William Moore, Halifax	KO	3
Sept.	8—Eddie Owens, Halifax	KO	5
Dec.	8—Eugene Green, Halifax	W	10

1978
June	28—Horst Geisler, Halifax	KO	1
Aug.	1—Tony Moore, Halifax	KO	6
Sept.	12—Greg Johnson, Halifax	KO	4
Oct.	8—Greg Sorrentino, Halifax	KO	7

1979
Apr.	3—Bernardo Mercado, Halifax	KO by	1
May	26—Earl McLeay, Glace Bay	KO	7
June	14—Leroy Caldwell, Winnipeg	D	10
Dec.	11—Ngozika Ekwelum, Halifax	KO	5

1980
Mar.	11—Johnny Warr, Halifax	W	10
June	20—John Tate, Montreal	KO	9
Aug.	27—Ron Rousselle, Edmonton	KO	1

LEONARDO (CHINO) BERMUDEZ
Mexican Lightweight
(Previous Record Unavailable)
1977
Feb.	16—Ray Saldivar, Las Vegas	KO	6
Mar.	18—Rafael Limon, Culiacan	D	10
Apr.	6—Leroy Haley, Las Vegas	D	10
May	4—Leroy Haley, Las Vegas	L	12
May	13—Francisco Toro, Tucson	W	10
Aug.	9—German Cuello, Las Vegas	L	10
Sept.	—Cesar Savinon, Culiacan	W	10

1978
Feb.	10—Lupe Galindo, Mexico City	KO	7
Apr.	29—Juan Elizondo, Mexico City	KO by	2
June	3—Ernesto Davis, Mexico City	L	10
Sept.	1—Jose Luis Ramirez, Obregon	L	10
Dec.	23—Alfredo Pitalua, Mazatlan	D	10

1979
June	17—Rocky Ramon, San Antonio	L	10
Nov.	27—Monroe Brooks, Los Angeles	L	10

1980
Mar.	14—Pablo Baez, Culican	W	10
Apr.	25—Victor Abraham, Culiacan	L	10
May	30—Esteban Chupin, La Paz	KO	1
June	6—Jesse Lara, Mazatlan	KO	1
Sept.	5—Celso Olivas, Culiacan	KO	5

SALVADOR BERMUDEZ
1980
Mar.	3—Mauricio Bravo, Caracas	KO by	2
June	16—Mauricio Bravo, Caracas	KO by	6

JUAN BERNAL
1980
July	29—Arnulfo Hernandez, Laredo	KO	2
Sept.	1—Homero Gonzales, Laredo	W	6
Sept.	23—Magdalano Montoya, Houston	L	8

MARCIANO BERNARDI
White Plains, N.Y. Middleweight
1977
Feb.	18—Willie Bat, Adjuntas	KO	3
Mar.	19—Luis Torres, Adjuntas	KO	1
Apr.	16—Jose Collante, Caguas	KO by	4
Nov.	9—Joe Mascetta, White Plains	KO	1
Dec.	1—Ernie Johnson, Wharton	W	4

1978
Mar.	1—Rainer Thompson, White Plains	KO	1
Apr.	5—Ray Bryant, White Plains	KO	3
June	2—Joe Moreault, Boston	KO	3
June	14—Hilton Whitaker, White Plains	KO	4
Aug.	17—Rene Fontanez, Totowa	KO	4
Aug.	30—Raymond Mattos, Paramus	KO	1

Sept.	6—Tyrone Phelps, White Plains	W	6
Sept.	18—Carlos Betancourt, Rio Piedras	KO by	2
Sept.	26—Dan Staehle, Totowa	W	6
Oct.	5—James Phoenix, White Plains	KO	1
Oct.	19—Gil Davis, Garfield	KO	1
Nov.	14—Joe Tiberi, Totowa	KO by	4

1979
Feb.	14—Angel Perales, White Plains	KO	7
Mar.	13—Gordon Roland, Montreal	W	6
May	25—Joe Henry, Montreal	KO	3
June	3—Jean Ives Filion, Quebec	KO	3
Oct.	2—Vinnie Curto, Montreal	L	8
Aug.	28—Don Johnson, Halifax	KO	1
Nov.	15—Ben Serrano, Dover, N.J.	W	8
Dec.	23—Eddie Melo, Verdun	KO by	2

1980
Mar.	9—Chris Lange, Atlantic City	KO	2
Mar.	25—Willie Featherstone, Montreal	D	10
June	6—Tony Sibson, London	L	10
Nov.	20—Guy Kennedy, Totowa	L	10

JUAN C. BERON
Argentine Junior Welterweight
1980
Sept.	26—Jose Canceco, La Plata	KO	1
Oct.	31—Mario Arreguez, La Plata	W	6
Dec.	12—Norberto Ramirez, La Plata	W	6

CANDIDO BERRERA
Argentine Heavyweight
1980
May	23—Albel Celestino, Cordoba	W	10
June	6—Roque Molina, Mar del Plata	KO	7
Dec.	5—Juan Fernandez, Cordoba	D	10

RALPH BERRIOS
1980
Feb.	28—Tony Styles, Tampa	KO	3
Mar.	16—Terry Pizzarro, Miami	L	4
Apr.	3—Terry Pizzarro, Tampa	L	8

GASTON BERUBE
Montreal Heavyweight
1980
Mar.	16—Terry Wallace, Miami	KO	3
May	7—Red Milne, Montreal	KO	1
Sept.	23—Conroy Nelson, Montreal	KO by	1

DON BESTER
Chicago, Ill. Light Heavyweight
1978
Feb.	27—Lucky Patterson, Chicago	KO by	4
Nov.	11—Lee Thomas, Sterling	W	4

1979
Feb.	3—Jessie Wilson, Boston	KO	2
Dec.	15—Jamie Olatundie, Chicago	L	2

1980
Feb.	18—Jamie Olatundie, Chicago	L	6
June	27—Charlie Henderson, Chicago	L	4
Aug.	8—John Cox, Chicago	L	6
Dec.	9—Pierre Cormier, Montreal	W	4

CARLOS BETANCOURT
Puerto Rican Middleweight
1976
Oct.	16—Frank Calderon, San Juan	W	4

1977
June	25—Alex Porrata, Bayamon	L	4
Nov.	19—Vicent Figueroa, San Juan	KO	

1978
Mar.	4—Willie Llanes, Bayamon	KO	4
May	1—Edwin Soto, Carolina	KO	3
May	13—Gilbert Vega, Carolina	KO	2
Aug.	14—John Davis, Rio Piedras	KO	3
Sept.	18—Marciano Bernardi, Rio Piedras	KO	2
Nov.	27—Angel Ortiz, San Juan	W	10

1979
Jan.	27—Jose Collante, San Juan	W	8
Mar.	25—Sixto Gomez, San Juan	KO	2
Nov.	23—Manuel Melon, Felt Forum	L	8

1980
Jan.	25—John LoCicero, New York	KO by	1
Apr.	21—Jose Collante, San Juan	KO	7
June	27—Charlie Weir, New York	KO by	2

CARLOS BETBEDER
Argentine Junior Featherweight
1979
	—Sergio Palma, Comodoro Rivadavia	L	10
	—Francisco Acosta, Posadas	L	10
	—Ruben Granado, Rosario	L	10

1980
Feb.	22—Luis Alvarez, Salta	L	10

45

Apr.	5—Jose Narvaez, Buenos Aires	L 8
Oct.	3—Hugo Fernandez, Concordia	L 10

MELVIN BETHEA
Newark, N.J. Featherweight
1978

Nov.	30—Carmelo Negron, New York	KO by 2

1979

Feb.	14—Gino Perez, White Plains	D 4
Mar.	13—Rocky Lockridge, Totowa	KO by 1
June	27—Adonis Torres, New York	KO by 4
Oct.	4—Adonis Torres, New York	L 4

1980

Feb.	1—Jimmy Washington, Philadelphia	
July	25—Tom Elston, Rochester	KO 2
Sept.	9—Myron Taylor, Atlantic City	KO by 1

ILDELFONSO BETHELMY
Venezuelan Junior Lightweight
1974

July	13—Oscar Arnal, Caracas	L 4
Sept.	20—Jose Sulbaran, Valencia	W 4
Dec.	21—Ramon Salazar, Ciudad Bolivar	KO by 2

1975

Feb.	3—Raul Garcia, Caracas	KO 4
Apr.	12—Jose Pacheco, Cartagena	W 6
May	31—Leslie Moreno, Maracaibo	KO 3
July	14—Ricardo Cardona, Caracas	KO by 8
Nov.	6—Ramon Bido, Santo Domingo	KO 1
Nov.	17—Antonio Cruz, Santo Domingo	KO 3
Dec.	22—Leo Cruz, Santo Domingo	L 10

1976

Feb.	21—Jose Cervantes, Caracas	D 10
Nov.	7—Raul Garcia, Caracas	KO 9
Dec.	5—Adalberto Gomez, Caracas	KO 2
Dec.	19—Jorge Villarino, Caracas	KO 4

1977

Mar.	20—Enrique Maxwell, Caracas	W 10
May	29—Rafael Solis, Caracas	KO 1
June	19—Mario Martinez, Caracas	KO 9

(Won Central American & Caribbean
Junior Lightweight Title)

Dec.	4—Pedro Garcia, Caracas	KO 2
Dec.	18—Wilson Mosquera, Caracas	KO 5

1978

Mar.	12—Wilson Mosquera, Caracas	KO 6
May	28—Lorenzo Torres, Caracas	KO 6
June	25—Cocoa Sanchez, Caracas	D 12

(Retained Central American & Caribbean
Junior Lightweight Title)

1979

Mar.	25—Rioshi Takano, Caracas	KO 2
Dec.	21—Leonel Hernandez, Caracas	W 12

(Retained Central American & Caribbean
Junior Lightweight Title)

1980

Feb.	11—Francisco Aponte, Caracas	KO 1
July	14—Benito Jimenez, Caracas	KO 2
July	28—Costeno Mendoza, Caracas	W 10
Dec.	11—Rafael (Bazooka) Limon, Los Angeles	KO by 15

(For Vacant WBC Junior Lightweight Title)

MIGUEL (TURQUITO) BETRUZ
Colombian Welterweight
1972

Jan.	—Raul Maranda, Sincelejo	KO 4
Apr.	28—Milton Mendez, Cartagena	D 4
Nov.	24—Julio Sanjuan, Cartagena	KO 3
Dec.	15—Francisco Durango, Monteria	D 8

1973

Feb.	3—Manuel Cardales, Bogota	KO 4
July	15—Manuel Vargas, Sincelejo	KO 7
Aug.	3—Cipriano Zuluaga, Monteria	L 10
Dec.	16—Herman Torres Prens, Cartagena	KO 9

(Won Colombian Junior Lightweight Title)

1974

Feb.	9—Adalberto Gomez, Cartagena	W 10
Mar.	2—Carlos Foldes, Cartagena	W 10
Apr.	6—Barbulito Zuluaga, Monteria	
May	19—Jesus Sanctis, Sincelejo	KO 2
June	9—Herman Torres Prens, Cartagena	KO 12

(Lost Colombian Junior Lightweight Title)

July	27—Luis Davila, Cartagena	KO 1
Oct.	6—Francisco Durango, Cartagena	L 10
Dec.	17—Enrique Alonzo, Cartagena	W 10

1975

Jan.	22—Ramon Reyes, Cartagena	KO 9
Feb.	24—Gustavo Farinas, Cartagena	KO 6
Apr.	30—Julio Sanjuan, Barranquilla	KO 1

(Won Colombian Lightweight Title)

May	31—Antonio Gomez, Bogota	KO 10
Aug.	16—Josue Marquez, Cartagena	L 10
Nov.	1—Antonio Gomez, Caracas	D 10
Dec.	20—Hugo Barraza, Cartagena	L 10

1976

Jan.	24—Enrique Maxwell, Cartagena	KO 10
May	16—Pedro Acosta, Cartagena	D 12

(Colombian Lightweight Title)

Aug.	28—Pedro Acosta, Cartagena	L 12

(Colombian Lightweight Title)

Nov.	12—Alberto Merrera, Guayaquil	L 10

1977

Sept.	2—Rafael Anchundia, Cali	W 10

1978

Apr.	22—Alvaro Marimoun, Cartagena	KO by 5
Sept.	1—Saoul Mamby, Curacao	KO by 4
	—William Blanco, San Andres	L 10

1979

Feb.	9—Leonidas Asprilla, Caracas	L 10
May	19—Osvaldo Romero, Cartagena	L 10
Oct.	13—Miguel Montilla, San Juan	L 10

1980

May	18—Martin Rojas, Barranquilla	L 12
Sept.	20—Jose Salazar, Colon	L 10

ELLIS BETTS
St. Louis, Mo. Middleweight
1980

Nov.	18—Charlie Peterson, Belleville	W 8
Dec.	10—Larry Ward, Moline	D 6

JOHN BEVERIDGE
Fairmont, W. Va. Light Heavyweight
1978

Feb.	25—Percy Hairston, Kingsport	KO by 1
Mar.	2—Jimmy Caffrey, Cleveland	KO by 1
Aug.	17—Bradford Crane, Virginia Beach	KO by 1
Aug.	26—Rusty Rosenberger	KO by 1

1979

Jan.	12—Jesse Bennett, Weston, W. Va.	W 4

1980

Aug.	20—Jeff Lampkin, Warren	KO by 1
Sept.	18—Frank Draper, Cleveland	KO by 1
Dec.	5—Murray Sutherland, Columbus	KO by 1

ABDUL BEY
Los Angeles, Calif. Featherweight
Born: November 8, 1949
1974

Sept.	12—Ignacio Bravo, Los Angeles	W 5
Sept.	21—Mario Chavez, Santa Maria	KO 2
Sept.	26—Oscar Ortiz, San Diego	W 6
Oct.	11—Oscar Ortiz, San Diego	KO 3
Dec.	7—Peewee Emerson, Chicago	W 6
Dec.	10—Norman Goins, Indianapolis	KO by 4

1975

June	13—Jorge Torres, San Diego	L 6
July	18—Jorge Torres, San Diego	KO 6
Aug.	13—Seco Luna, Los Angeles	L 6
Sept.	20—Pascaual Calders, Fresno	W 8
Oct.	11—Roy Hernandez, Los Angeles	W 7
Nov.	4—Peter King, Las Vegas	L 10
Nov.	19—Manuel Lujan, San Diego	L 10

1976

Feb.	4—Saleamont Saksit, Las Vegas	KO 10
Feb.	25—Manuel Lujan, Las Vegas	L 10
Mar.	26—Adrian Villanueva, Los Angeles	KO 5
Apr.	21—Edgar Cabalhin, Los Angeles	W 10
June	19—Jose Torres, Los Angeles	D 10

1977

May	15—Jorge David Monzon, Tuxtla Gutierrez	NC 6
June	4—Antonio Nava, Mexico City	KO 6
June	27—Juan Escobar, Tijuana	KO 8
July	25—Jose Hernandez, Tijuana	KO 3
Sept.	16—Juan Escobar, Tijuana	KO 3
Oct.	25—Rodolfo Moreno, Los Angeles	KO 5

1978

Jan.	30—Roberto Torres, Tijuana	L 10
May	19—Isao Okahashi, Tokyo	KO 5
July	2—Susumu Okabe, Tokyo	KO 4
Oct.	22—Lee Yidano, Seoul	KO by 4
Mar.	6—Roger Bucheli, Honolulu	KO 1
Mar.	27—Alex Oregel, Honolulu	KO 7
May	15—Jesus Chuy Rocha, Honolulu	KO 2
June	12—Enrique Solis, Honolulu	W 10
July	3—Suktae Yun, Hilo	W 10
Aug.	21—Nene Jun, Honolulu	L 10
Dec.	8—Rolando Navarete, Honolulu	KO by 7

1980

June	17—Noel Arriesgado, Honolulu	L 10

RAUL BIANCO
Argentine Lightweight
1980
Mar. 11—Omar Almada, Formosa .... W 10
July 18—Ramon Moreyra, Formosa .... W 10
Oct. 3—Ruben Verdun, Posadas .... L 10

DON BICKFORD
Portland, Me. Middleweight
1976
Apr. 8—Peter Douvalle, Portland, Me. .... W 4
May 27—Joe DeFayette, Portland, Me. .... KO 6
June 3—Buddy Carr, Portland, Me. .... W 6
June 10—Joe DeFayette, Portland, Me. .... W 6
1977
June 4—Tony Pinette, Bath .... KO 3
1978
Apr. 19—Don Hackett, Waterville .... KO 1
July 19—Ben Sanchez, Waterville .... KO 6
Sept. 9—Roger Leonard, Providence .... KO by 2
1979
Mar. 28—Don Johnson, Waterville .... KO by 6
1980
Feb. 26—Dom DiMarzo, Woburn .... KO by 5
Apr. 16—Ralph Dumont, Waterville .... KO 2

ROBERTO BIDO
Dominican Republic Featherweight
1977
Feb. 2—Ricardo Manzanillo, La Vega .... KO 1
Mar. 3—Manuel Batista, Santiago .... KO 1
Apr. 18—Salvador Cosme, Santiago .... W 6
May 2—Hector Espinosa, Santiago .... KO 1
July 26—Hector Espinosa, Santo Domingo .... KO 1
Sept. 9—Salvador Cosme, Santo Domingo ...... W 6
1978
June 15—Jose Mora, Moca .... KO 1
Aug. 4—Patricio Nunez, Santo Domingo .... KO 1
Oct. 5—Nelson Cruz Tamariz, Santo Domingo KO by 10
Oct. 28—Manuel De La Rosa, Santo Domingo ...... L 6
Dec. 10—Salvador Cosme, Santo Domingo ...... KO 2
1979
May 10—Alberto Rodriguez, Moca .... KO 1
July 3—Pedro Martinez, Santo Domingo .... KO 3
July 26—Milciades Pena, Santo Domingo .... KO 5
1980
Apr. 12—Pedro Martinez, Santiago .... KO 3
May 26—Alejandro Arias, Santiago .... W 10
July 24—Angel Rodriguez, Santo Domingo .... KO 5
Aug. 25—Milciades Pena, Santo Domingo .... L 10
Nov. 15—Alejandro Garcia, Port-Au-Prince ...... KO 7
Dec. 20—Angel Rodriguez, Port-Au-Prince ...... KO 6

XAVIER BIGGS
Philadelphia, Pa. Welterweight
1979
Oct. 30—Bob Rooney, Upper Darby .... D 4
1980
Apr. 11—Jose Amaro, Chester .... KO 2
Sept. 4—Robert Sawyer, Atlantic City .... KO by 2

ERNEST BING
Pleasantville, N.J. Junior Lightweight
1973
Dec. 8—Ken Muse, Atlantic City .... W 4
1974
Apr. 8—Ron Meaweather, Philadelphia .... L 4
May 22—Lloyd Floyd, Philadelphia .... KO 2
Oct. 9—Alfonso Evans, Philadelphia .... L 6
1975
May 13—William Berry, Trenton .... D 4
1976
May 19—Lynwood Snowden, Philadelphia .... L 6
Sept. 23—Ron Branch, Wilmington, Dela. .... KO 6
Oct. 5—Ralph Racine, Scranton .... KO 1
Nov. 5—Jorge Rivera, New York .... W 4
Nov. 18—Luis Vega, Wilmington .... W 8
1977
Feb. 24—Carlos Duprey, Wilmington .... KO 5
Apr. 21—Ernesto Vann, Wilmington .... KO 1
June 23—Gerald Hayes, Philadelphia .... W 8
Aug. 24—Jose Resto, Vineland .... W 8
1978
Mar. 4—Rafael Limon, Los Angeles .... KO by 10
June 15—Morris Grant, Atlantic City .... KO 2
Oct. 20—Jose Pena, Atlantic City .... W 8
Nov. 24—Dan Daniels, Atlantic City .... W 12
1979
May 12—Jose Gonzalez, Atlantic City .... W 8

June 3—Gaeten Hart, Quebec .... D 10
July 24—Gaeten Hart, Atlantic City .... W 10
1980
Mar. 22—Anthony Banks, Atlantic City .... W 6
Apr. 26—Danny Daniels, Atlantic City .... W 12
(New Jersey State Lightweight Title)
Aug. 7—Willie Rodriguez, Atlantic City .... KO 9

LOU BIZZARRO
Erie, Pa. Junior Welterweight
1964
Nov. 5—Herman Dunbar, Erie .... W 4
1965
Feb. 25—Ken Rose, Erie .... W 4
Mar. 5—Ken Rose, Johnstown .... W 4
July 21—Billy Byrd, Uniontown .... W 4
Sept. 14—Billy Byrd, Erie .... W 6
1968
Sept. 2—Arnold Bush, Johannesburg .... KO 3
1969
(Inactive)
1970
Jan. 22—Andy Heimscgy, Mansfield .... W 4
July 21—Larry Kelly, Erie .... KO 4
1971
July 17—Ted Hamilton, Erie.................... KO 2
Aug. 21—Tommy Russell, Buffalo................. W 4
1972
Aug. 16—Tommy Russell, Erie .... KO 8
Sept. 27—Marcelino Alicia, Erie .... KO 3
1973
Apr. 5—Tony Berrios, Erie .... W 10
1974
(Inactive)
1975
Feb. 11—Don Boulter, Toronto .... W 8
Feb. 27—Bobby Crawford, Cincinnati .... KO 3
Mar. 20—Holandus Oliver, Cincinnati .... KO 3
Apr. 6—Beau Jaynes, Erie .... W 10
May 3—Lawrence Hafey, Erie .... W 10
June 3—Pablo Rodriguez, Fairview .... W 10
Aug. 13—Hector Matta, Erie .... W 10
Nov. 21—Benny Huertas, Erie .... W 10
1976
Apr. 15—Marion Thomas, Indianapolis .... W 10
May 22—Roberto Duran, Erie .... KO by 14
(World Lightweight Title)
1977
Jan. 21—Dom Monaco, Cincinnati .... W 10
Dec. 29—Ron Pettigrew, Pittsburgh .... W 10
1978
Aug. 22—Jose Resto, Erie .... W 10
1979
(Inactive)
1980
Mar. 19—Javier Ayala, Las Vegas .... W 10
Sept. 30—Larry Moore, Niles .... W 10

SIMMIE BLACK
Memphis, Tenn. Lightweight
1974
Nov. 5—Rito Torrez, Oklahoma City .... W 6
1975
Feb. 4—Elliott Santiago, Oklahoma City .... D 4
July 1—Sean O'Grady, Oklahoma City........ KO by 4
July 9—Earl Wilson, Memphis................... L 4
Aug. 5—Harvey Arnold, Oklahoma City .... L 4
Aug. 14—Al Franklin, St. Paul .... KO by 3
Aug. 19—Rocky Smith, Oklahoma City .... W 6
Sept. 16—Shannon Williams, Oklahoma City .... W 6
Nov. 25—Chuck Mitch, Globe, Ariz. .... L 6
1976
Mar. 2—Harvey Arnold, Oklahoma City....... KO by 4
May 15—Harvey Arnold, Joplin .... KO by 4
Aug. 4—Joey Vincent, Orlando............... L disq.
Aug. 17—Joey Vincent, Orlando.............. KO 3
Nov. 20—Ed Modicue, Marshall .... KO by 2
Nov. 30—Robert Vasquez, Memphis .... KO by 6
Dec. 18—Harvey Arnold, Marshall .... KO by 2
1977
Feb. 25—Scott Clark, Orlando .... KO by 2
Mar. 16—Chuck Mitch, Minneapolis .... L 6
Mar. 24—Frank Santore, Tampa .... KO by 3
May 23—Michael Theriot, Memphis .... W 4
July 9—Shannon Williams, Memphis .... W 4
July 25—Mike Mheriof, Memphis .... L 4
Aug. 20—Dennis Haggerty, Oklahoma City ..... KO by 5
Sept. 20—Frank Ahumada, New Orleans .... KO by 3
Oct. 25—Wardell Williams, Kansas City ...... KO by 1
Nov. 19—Larry Moore, Indianapolis .... KO by 4
Nov. 22—Danny Myers, Wheeling .... KO by 4
Nov. 27—Anthony Daniels, Knoxville .... KO by 3
1978
Jan. 27—Eddie Freeman, Greenville .... KO by 6

Mar. 21—Harold McMahan, Memphis .... L 4
Mar. 23—Dale Hernandez, Omaha .... KO by 1
Apr. 8—Max Horde, Fernandine Beach ...... KO by 4
Apr. 13—Shannon Williams, Memphis .... D 6
Apr. 25—Leon McCullum, Greenville .... L 4
May 3—Eddie Freeman, Blytheville .... KO by 5
May 8—Floyd Pearson, Chicago .... KO by 2
May 23—Shannon Williams, Little Rock .... W 6
June 3—Jerome Hill, Pikeville .... W 4
June 6—Earl Wilson, Memphis .... W 6
July 13—Richard Garcia, Hattisburg .... KO 2
Aug. 26—Norman Goins, Dayton .... KO by 2
Sept. 25—Ray Jackson, Little Rock .... L 4
Sept. 27—Jesse Baker, Memphis .... KO 3
1979
Feb. 28—Kenny Daniels, Chicago .... L 4
June 14—Jimmy Blevins, River Grove .... KO by 4
July 17—Al Fowler, Belleville .... L 8
Aug. 16—Joe Sosa, Kansas City .... KO by 1
Sept. 14—James Busceme, Houston .... KO by 3
Nov. 27—Al Fowler, Belleville .... L 10
Dec. 13—Al Thompson, Tulsa .... L disq. 8
Dec. 15—Billy Moreno, Chicago .... KO by 2
1980
Mar. 29—Bruce McIntyre, Johannesburg ...... KO by 5
May 9—Anthony Murray, Nashville .... KO by 3
May 15—Kenny Reed, Chicago .... KO by 4
June 13—Bubba Thompson, Tulsa .... L 8
June 24—Billy Watkins, Houston .... KO by 4
July 11—Otey Nations, Meridan .... L 6
Nov. 18—Benjamin Stiff, Belleville .... KO by 6
Dec. 9—Otey Williams, Birmingham .... KO by 1

LENNOX BLACKMOORE
Georgetown, Guyana Junior Welterweight
Born: July 10, 1950
1974
Jan. 27—Kid Carrington, Georgetown .... W 4
Mar. 31—Roy Smith, Georgetown .... W 4
May 5—Terry Greene, Georgetown .... L 6
June 30—Kid Carrington, Georgetown .... KO 6
Sept. 29—Terry Greene, Georgetown .... W 10
Nov. 17—Richardo Croquer, Georgetown .... KO 8
1975
Feb 2—Mike Drayton, Georgetown .... W 10
June 15—Terry Greene, Georgetown .... KO 14
(Won Guyanan Lightweight Title)
Sept. 7—Terry Greene, Georgetown .... W 15
(Retained Guyanan Lightweight Title)
1976
Feb. 8—Fitzroy Guissepi, Georgetown .... KO 10
Apr. 23—Percy Hayles, Georgetown .... KO 5
Oct. 29—Errol West, Georgetown .... KO 8
1977
Feb. 25—Claude Noel, Port of Spain .... KO 10
May 28—Claude Noel, Port of Spain .... KO 10
Oct. 1—Jonathon Dele, Lagos .... W 15
(Won British Commonwealth Lightweight Title)
1978
May 14—Desmond Thompson, Georgetown .... KO 5
Oct. 24—Hogan Jimoh, Lagos .... KO by 5
(Lost British Commonwealth Lightweight Title)
Nov. 28—Jose Fernandez, Georgetown .... KO 8
Dec. 26—Barry Michael, Georgetown .... KO 7
1979
Feb. 8—Adriano (Nani) Marrero, Georgetown .... W 10
July 1—Pedro Acosta, Georgetown .... W 10
Nov. 8—Dale Hernandez, Nebraska .... W 10
1980
May 2—Eddie Marcelle, Port-of-Spain .... W 10
Aug. 13—Fili Ramirez, Las Vegas .... KO 4
Aug. 22—Ron Cummings, Las Vegas .... W 10

JOHNNY BLAINE
Waterbury, Conn. Heavyweight
1976
Mar. 17—George Bradwell, Latham............. KO by 2
June 26—Biff Cline, Providence .... KO 2
July 29—George Chaplin, Baltimore .... KO by 2
Aug. 16—Greg Sorrentino, Utica .... KO by 4
Sept. 11—Doc Wilson, Waterbury .... L 4
Sept. 28—Greg Sorrentino, New York .... L 4
Dec. 2—Bill Sharkey, New York .... KO by 2
1977
Feb. 2—Bill Connell, New York .... KO by 3
Apr. 23—Bruce Grandham, Kalamazoo .... NC 2
May 13—Tyrone Harlee, New York .... D 6
May 26—Macka Foley, Portland, Me. ...... KO by 5
Sept. 9—Bobby Halpern, Nanuet .... KO by 3
Sept. 24—Ron Drinkwater, Boston .... KO by 5
1978
Apr. 7—Chuck Wepner, North Bergen .... KO by 3
May 13—Tom Fisher, Dayton .... KO by 2

June 13—Scott Frank, Totowa .... KO by 1
Aug. 16—Sergio Rodriguez, Nanuet .... W 6
Aug. 21—Charles Cox, Cape Cod .... KO by 3
Oct. 14—Steve Zouski, New Haven .... KO by 4
1979
Mar. 12—Steve Zouski, Providence .... KO by 2
May 26—Steve Zouski, Portland .... L 6
July 23—Alfredo Evangelista, Logrono .... KO by 2
—Dick Embelton, Hartford .... D 8
1980
May 3—Harry Terrell, Canton .... KO by 2
Sept. 13—Alfrede Evangelista, Malaga .... KO by 4
Nov. 28—Don Murphy, Providence .... W 6
Dec. 20—Bob Spellman, Richmond .... KO by 4

ALCIBIADES BLANDON
Panamanian Junior Featherweight
1980
Aug. 1—Humberto Mejia, Colon .... W 10
Oct. 4—Juvencio Monserrate, Colon .... W 10
Oct. 15—Pedro Moreno, Colon .... KO 5

JIMMY BLEVINS
Chicago, Ill. Junior Welterweight
1977
July 25—Newton Swain, Chicago .... W 4
Oct. 25—Santos Rodriguez, Chicago .... W 4
1978
Mar. 17—Bobby Plegge, Detroit .... W 6
Mar. 20—Jerry Strickland, Chicago .... W 4
May 13—Charlie Smith, Dayton .... KO 2
June 2—James Menefee, Kansas City .... W 4
July 9—Aundra Love, Indianapolis .... D 4
July 28—Tom Tarantino, Milwaukee .... W 8
1979
Jan. 16—Tom Tarantino, Waukesha .... L 8
Mar. 3—Johnny Summerhays, Detroit .... L 10
June 14—Simmie Black, River Grove .... KO 4
June 19—Larry Stanton, Orlando .... W 10
July 31—Rick Folstad, Orlando .... W 10
Oct. 4—Esteban DeJesus, New York .... L 10
1980
Mar. 3—Johnny Copeland, Chicago .... KO 7
Mar. 28—Manuel Torres, Chicago .... KO 5
Apr. 14—Raul Molina, Chicago .... L 10
May 9—Pedro Acosta, Chicago .... W 10
June 12—Billy Moreno, Chicago .... W 8
Nov. 22—Mike Blunt, Cincinnati .... W 10

MIKE BLUNT
Dayton, Ohio Junior Welterweight
Height: 5'10"
1979
Jan. 10—Larry Morgan, Richfield .... KO 1
Feb. 7—Greg Bender, Richfield .... KO 2
Apr. 13—Dale Gordon, Cincinnati .... KO 1
Apr. 27—Manning Galloway, Dayton .... W 6
May 11—Phil Bowman, Cincinnati .... KO 3
May 23—Mel Hauser, New Kensington .... KO by 1
July 6—Harvey Wilson, Dayton .... KO 3
Aug. 2—Dujuan Johnson, Detroit .... L 6
Sept. 18—Frankie Mills, Dayton .... W 4
Oct. 20—Jerry Strickland, Cincinnati .... KO 6
1980
Apr. 13—Tom Crowley, Kansas City .... W 6
May 17—Dave Bolden, Dayton .... W 10
June 20—Bobby Plegge, Cincinnati .... W 12
Aug. 2—Johnny Copeland, Cincinnati .... KO 3
Nov. 1—Pete Padilla, Dayton .... KO 4
Nov. 22—Jimmy Blevins, Cincinnati .... L 10

STANLEY BLYTHE
Gaffney, S.C. Middleweight
1980
July 26—Willie Ray Taylor, Charlotte .... L 6

WAYNE (KELLY ANDERSON) BOBICK
Vancouver, B.C. Light Heavyweight
1979
Feb. —Wayne McLay, Vancouver .... L 4
July 26—Scotty Welsh, Anchorage .... KO 2
Sept. 13—Jerry Reddick, Vancouver .... KO by 4
Oct. 27—Terry Jesmer, Regina .... KO 1
Nov. 27—Maurice Rice, Vancouver .... L 6
1980
Mar. 11—Wayne McLay, Vancouver .... L 4
July 26—Scotty Welsh, Anchorage .... KO 2
Sept. 13—Jerry Reddick, Vancouver .... KO by 4

KEN (BANG BANG) BOGNER
Trenton, N.J. Lightweight
1980
May 22—Robert Johnson, Totowa .... KO 2

June 5—Wayne Dabney, Atlantic City .... KO 1
June 19—Melvin Boynton, Totowa .... KO 1
July 13—Jose (Cheo) Ortiz, Great Gorge .... D 4
July 20—Jose (Cheo) Ortiz, Great Gorge .... W 4
Sept. 27—Robert Stevenson, Trenton .... KO 1
Nov. 7—Bill Geslocki, Trenton .... KO 1
Dec. 18—Jose Matos, Totowa .... W 6

DAVE BOLDEN
Brooklyn, N.Y. Lightweight
1977
Mar. 18—Ismael Maldonado, New York .... KO by 4
Apr. 21—Arnolfo Gallego, Dover .... W 4
May 5—Mike Keane, Albany .... KO 1
May 20—Merciades Jiminez, New York .... W 4
Nov. 25—Pee Wee Suarez, Providence .... L 6
1978
Jan. 14—Malcolm Driver, Hauppauge .... KO 3
Apr. 28—Paddy Dolan, Commack .... KO by 6
Apr. 29—Paddy Dolan, Commack .... KO by 6
June 13—Victor Mangual, Hartford .... L 6
Sept. 21—Pee Wee Suarez, Jersey City .... KO by 2
Oct. 12—George Cotin, Paris .... L 8
1979
Mar. 2—Victor Mangual, Albany .... KO by 1
Oct. 12—Bill Costello, Uniondale .... L 4
1980
Mar. 4—Noradine Ben Sallah, Hartford .... W 6
Mar. 28—Arcadio Suarez, Tarrytown .... L 10
Apr. 20—Fernando Fernandez, Portland .... L 10
May 9—Manny Simms, Staten Island .... KO 3
May 17—Mike Blunt, Dayton .... L 10
June 6—Bruce Strauss, Kansas City .... L 8
July 16—Gino Perez, Elizabeth .... KO by 7
Nov. 3—Marlon Starling, Hartford .... KO by 3

FRANKLIN BOMPART
Venezuelan Lightweight
1980
Apr. 28—Dangoberto Torres, Caracas .... KO 3
May 5—Jose Suarez, Caracas .... KO 2
June 13—Felix Pacheco, Pueato La Cruz .... KO 6

DWAYNE BONDS
Detroit, Mich. Heavyweight
1974
July 27—Fred Jones, Detroit..................... W 4
1975
May 30—Marty Monroe, San Diego.............. L 5
Sept. 5—Joe Garcia, Las Vegas .... W 5
Oct. 16—Frank Pina, Los Angeles............... KO 1
Dec. 18—Stan Ward, Stockton .... L 10
1976
Jan. 3—Angel Baggini, Las Vegas .... KO 6
May 4—Pedro Lovell, San Jose .... L 10
1977
Jan. 19—Mike Weaver, Las Vegas .... KO by 9
Nov. 25—David Johnson, Detroit .... W 4
1978
Jan. 25—Ron Gebere, Detroit .... KO 1
Feb. 10—Charley Johnson, Detroit .... L 8
July 24—Calvin Cross, Bridgeview .... KO by 2
Oct. 20—Bobby Williams, Pretoria .... W 6
1979
Mar. 27—Big J. McCauley, Michigan .... KO 1
June 2—Mike Schutte, Mmabatho .... D 8
1980
Mar. 31—Walter Santemore, Knoxville .... W 6
Apr. 20—Willie Shannon, Portland .... KO 9
Dec. 17—Renaldo Snipes, White Plains .... KO by 7

LARRY BONDS
Denver, Colo. Junior Middleweight
1973
May 12—Andy Sanchez, Denver.................. W 4
Aug. 15—Ward Jones, Denver .... W 4
Oct. 2—Ray Young, Denver .... KO 3
1974
Jan. 10—Steve St. Charles, Stateline .... W 6
Jan. 23—Demitra Salazar, Las Vegas............. KO 1
Feb. 13—Chuchu Mariscal, Las Vegas .... W 6
Mar. 19—Gildo Federico, Denver .... KO 5
June 5—Ezra Davis, Las Vegas .... KO by 2
Oct. 18—James Jackson, Stateline .... W 6
1975
Jan. 8—Ezra Davis, Las Vegas .... W 10
Jan. 29—Barreto Fernandez, Las Vegas........... W 6
Feb. 26—Angel Robinson Garcia, Las Vegas .... W 10
June 25—Quincy Daniels, Las Vegas............. KO 7
July 23—Mike Mayan, Las Vegas .... W 10
Sept. 13—Jessie Lara, Denver .... KO 7
Oct. 8—Jimmy Jackson, Las Vegas .... W 10

1976
Feb. 11—Antonio Levya, Las Vegas .... KO 7
Mar. 31—Julio Gomez, Las Vegas .... W 10
Apr. 21—Wayne Beale, Las Vegas................ W 10
1977
Apr. 4—Kevin Morgan, Las Vegas .... L 12
June 6—Bruce Finch, Milwaukee .... KO 5
Dec. 20—Rocky Mosley, Las Vegas .... W 12
1978
—Babs McCarthy, Las Vegas .... W 10
Mar. 16—Babs McCarthy, Stateline .... W 10
May 25—Rocky Mosley, Las Vegas .... L 12
1979
Mar. 16—Babs McCarthy, Lake Tahoe .... W 10
Apr. 16—Howard Jackson, Las Vegas .... W 12
July 14—Rodolfo Mendoza, Denver .... KO 3
Sept. 30—Jimmy Jackson, Reno .... W 10
1980
Apr. 19—Costello King, San Juan .... KO 7

ERIC BONILLA
San Diego, Calif. Lightweight
1977
July 8—Arturo Reyes, San Diego .... L 4
Sept. 16—Bill Matthis, San Diego .... L 4
Sept. 30—Bill Matthis, San Diego .... D 4
Nov. 4—Scipio Stubbs, San Diego .... L 5
Nov. 11—Fili Ramirez, San Diego .... W 4
Nov. 15—Carlos Garcia, Anaheim .... W 4
Dec. 16—Moses Armas, San Diego .... D 6
1978
Mar. 3—Jose Castro, San Diego .... W 5
May 19—Clinton Campbell, San Diego .... D 4
June 2—Gary Pittman, San Diego .... W 4
June 8—Irleis Perez, Los Angeles .... L 5
July 6—Daniel Patino, Los Angeles .... L 6
July 14—Robert Willcot, San Diego .... W 6
July 20—Irleis Perez, San Diego .... KO by 1
Nov. 3—Bernard Graham, San Diego .... L 4
Nov. 21—Alan Webb, Portland .... L 6
Dec. 1—Sergio Nualarte, San Diego .... W 4
1979
Apr. 6—Rubin Martinez, San Diego .... W 8
May 10—Tony Baltazar, Los Angeles .... KO by 2
Aug. 10—Armando Ramirez, San Diego .... L 6
Oct. 19—Spud Murphy, San Diego .... W 6
Nov. 23—Gil Rodriguez, San Diego .... L 6
Dec. 11—Lenny Hahn, Spokane .... L 10
1980
Feb. 22—Felipe Canela, San Bernardino .... L 6
Mar. 7—Felipe Canela, San Bernardino .... D 2
Apr. 4—John Montes, San Diego .... L 6
Apr. 24—Clark Duran, Los Angeles .... L 6
May 13—John Montes, Bakersfield .... L 6
May 30—Felipe Canela, San Bernardino ...... KO by 5
July 16—Alfredo Aguayo, Stockton .... L 6
Aug. 9—Davey Armstrong, Spokane .... L 6
Sept. 18—Robert Turner, San Diego .... KO by 3

LEROY BOONE
Norfolk, Va. Heavyweight
1977
Sept. 8—Bobby Jordon, Virginia Beach .... L 4
Oct. 18—David Rhodes, Virginia Beach .... KO 3
Nov. 3—Ray Mitchell, Virginia Beach .... W 4
Dec. 7—Ron Burton, Cleveland, Ohio .... W 4
1978
Jan. 19—Sam Collins, Virginia Beach .... KO 3
Feb. 23—David Johnson, Virginia Beach .... W 6
Mar. 16—Burt Reed, Virginia Beach .... KO 2
Apr. 6—Terry Mims, Cleveland .... KO 4
Apr. 20—John Jordan, Virginia Beach .... W 10
July 18—Harold Carter, Virginia Beach .... W 6
Oct. 9—Harold Carter, Hampton .... W 6
Nov. 9—Ira Martin, Virginia Beach .... W 6
1979
June 6—Marty Monroe, Los Angeles .... KO by 5
Aug. 30—Charue Baltimore, Virginia Beach ...... KO 1
Sept. 20—Bobby Jordan, Virginia Beach .... L 10
Dec. 14—Gerry Cooney, Atlantic City .... KO by 6
1980
Feb. 27—Steve Zouski, Scranton .... W 10
June 14—Earnie Shavers, Cincinnati .... L 10
Sept. 12—Greg Page, Louisville .... KO by 6

IRVING BOOTH
Newark, N.J. Welterweight
1979
Feb. 28—Sean Mannion, Belfast .... KO by 2
Mar. 13—Nino Gonzalez, Totowa .... KO by 1
June 28—Mike Duffy, Staten Island .... KO by 1
1980
Mar. 22—Ray (Poppy) Davis, Atlantic City ..... KO by 4

49

EDEL BORUNDA
Mexican Lightweight
1979
Feb. 21—Reuben Castillo, Lake Tahoe .... L 10
Mar. 25—Rafael Martinez, Monterrey .... KO 2
1980
Feb. 10—Amado Mendoza, Tuxtla Gutierrez .... L 10
May 2—Brigido Martinez, Chihuahua .... KO 5
July 11—Guillermo Morales, Chihuahua ..... KO by 3

MIKE BOSWELL
Rochester, N.Y. Heavyweight
1979
July 13—Tim Murphy, Rochester .... KO 3
1980
Oct. 29—Marty Capasso, Scranton .... L 6

GERALD BOUCHARD
Canadian Middleweight
1973
Feb. 20—Roger Phillips, Quebec .... KO 3
1976
Mar. 2—Jean LeClair, Montreal .... KO by 7
June 3—Cisco Kid, Verdun .... KO 3
Aug. 2—Tony Lopes, Peabody .... L 10
Aug. 31—Dave Downey, Montreal .... KO 6
1977
Jan. 25—Dave Downey, Halifax .... KO 8
Feb. 22—Jean-Yves Filion, Montreal .... KO 5
Mar. 9—Roland Cousins, Jonquiere .... KO 4
Apr. 26—Fernand Marcotte, Montreal .... W 10
June 28—Fernand Marcotte, Montreal .... L 10
Sept. 27—Marshall Butler, Montreal .... W 10
Dec. 13—Jean-Claude LeClair, Montreal ..... KO by 9
1978
Apr. 26—Ray Chavez, Montreal .... W 10
June 9—Benny Sanchez, Verdun .... KO 2
Dec. 19—Eddy Melo, Montreal .... KO by 3
1979
Mar. 13—Jimmy Gradson, Montreal .... KO by 7
1980
Jan. 21—Terry Roundeau, Quebec City .... KO 6
Mar. 11—Jimmy Grandson, Montreal .... W 8

GIOVANNI (JOHN) BOVENZI
Vineland, N.J. Middleweight
1979
May 14—Tony Suero, Philadelphia .... L 4
June 12—John Fanea, Totowa .... KO 3
July 10—Gregory Hackett, Atlantic City .... KO 1
July 17—Dorian Lisbona, Atlantic City .... W 4
July 24—Malik Muhammad, Atlantic City ..... KO 4
July 31—John Saxton, Totowa .... W 4
Aug. 7—Floyd Pittman, Baltimore .... W 4
Oct. 27—O'Dell Leonard, Baltimore .... KO by 1
Nov. 23—Bob Saxton, Trenton .... KO 1
1980
Jan. 18—Ray Coleman, Trenton .... KO 4
Mar. 14—Ernie Gladney, Trenton .... W 6
Apr. 1—John Molander, Totowa .... KO 3
Apr. 14—Steve Small, White Plains .... L 8
May 22—Nino Gonzales, Totowa .... L 8
Oct. 15—Feliciano Cintron, Totowa .... L 8

CHRISTOPHER BOWEN
Guyana Featherweight
1980
Mar. 30—Walter Smith, Georgetown .... W 6
Aug. 3—Colin Morgan, Georgetown .... W 8

CARLTON BOWERS
Belize Welterweight
1980
Mar. 1—Raul Molino, Bird's Island .... L 8
July 6—Henry Fever, Bird's Island .... W 8
Sept. 7—Cleophus Lord, Bird's Island .... KO 2

SCOTT BOWERS
Spokane, Wash. Middleweight
1979
Oct. 2—Glen Inlow, Spokane .... W 4
Dec. 11—Jim McAuley, Spokane .... W 6
1980
Mar. 18—Buddy McKay, Spokane .... L 6
June 2—Billy Minnix, Spokane .... KO by 1

FREDDIE BOYNTON
Middletown, N.J. Welterweight
Won N.J. Golden Glove 135 lbs. Title
1973 Won N.J. Golden Glove 147 lbs. Title
1973
Aug. 4—Bernaldo Almonte, New York .... KO 2

1974
Jan. 7—Jeff Holmes, New York .... W 4
Mar. 11—Leroy Jefferson, Philadelphia .... L 6
Mar. 18—Tyrone Phelps, New York .... D 6
July 26—Robert Adams, Asbury Park .... L 6
Oct. 29—Joe Huston, Walpole, Mass. .... KO 2
1975
Nov. 5—Al Fletcher, New York .... W 6
1976
Feb. 11—Jose Elias, New York .... L 8
1977
Apr. 1—Tyrone Phelps, New York .... W 6
Apr. 21—Randolf Scott, Philadelphia .... W 6
May 26—Joe Grier, Dover .... D 8
Oct. 25—Tyrone Demby, Philadelphia .... KO 4
Dec. 17—Johnny Gant, Washington, D.C. .... L 10
1978
Apr. 5—Sal Dragone, White Plains .... L 4
Sept. 29—Rocco Mattioli, Milan .... KO by 7
Dec. 15—Ray Hammond, New York .... L 8
1979
Jan. 12—Matteo Saloemini, Milan .... KO by 2
June 29—George Lee, Jersey City .... KO 2
Aug. 1—Derrick Wheeler, Asbury Park .... KO 3
Nov. 28—James McNally, West New York, N.J. ... KO 3
1980
Feb. 8—Ray Hammond, Harlem .... KO by 6
Mar. 29—Marijan Benes, Berlin .... KO by 1

MELVIN BOYNTON
Newark, N.J. Junior Lightweight
Born: June 18, 1954, Newark, N.J.
1977
July 8—Darrell Beattie, Geneva .... L 6
Aug. 25—Darrell Beattie, Syracuse .... KO 3
Oct. 8—Joe Phillips, Syracuse .... L 6
Nov. 7—Tony Stokes, Durham .... L 6
Nov. 19—Joe Phillips, Syracuse .... KO by 4
1978
Jan. 16—Pee Wee Stokes, Latham .... KO by 7
Mar. 1—Sal Dragone, White Plains .... KO by 2
Apr. 10—Sal Dragone, White Plains .... KO by 4
Apr. 27—Jimmy McNeece, New York .... L 4
May 13—Clyde Beattie, Utica .... D 6
June 2—Tommy Rose, Boston .... KO by 1
June 29—Louis Rivera, North Bergen .... L 4
Aug. 16—Sanford Ricks, Newark .... L 4
Aug. 25—Sal Dragone, New York .... L 4
Sept. 8—Jose Nieto, New York .... KO by 1
Oct. 21—Francisco Villegas, St. Thomas ...... KO by 4
Nov. 16—Jimmy Magnifico, North Bergen .... L 6
1979
Mar. 14—Robert Rucker, White Plains .... L 4
Apr. 17—Rocky Lockridge, Totowa .... KO by 2
—Tony Santana, N.Y.C. .... KO by 2
1980
June 19—Ken Bogner, Totowa .... KO by 1

RALPH BRACETTY
Lawrence, Mass. Junior Lightweight
1979
Oct. 27—Ed Lugo, Fitchburg ....W 4
1980
Feb. 26—Tom Brown, Woburn .... KO by 3
Mar. 26—Tom Gourley, Waterville .... KO by 3
May 1—Eduardo Lugo, Dorchester .... W 6
May 19—Manuel Dearce, Lawrence .... KO by 3
Aug. 18—Edwin Curet, Boston .... KO by 1

ALVIN BRACY
Philadelphia, Pa. Middleweight
1979
May 11—Phil Capobianco, Commack .... KO by 1
June 29—Wayne Kelly, Commack .... KO by 1
Sept. 27—Dana McCarthy, Bristol .... KO by 4
Nov. 29—Martin Briggs, Richmond .... NC 1
1980
Mar. 12—Steve Small, White Plains .... KO by 1

BILL BRADLEY
Muncie, Indiana Middleweight
1980
July 25—Dale Jackson, Chicago .... KO by 3
Sept. 12—Collins Keller, Columbus ....W 4
Dec. 13—Ponce Ortiz, El Paso ....KO 2

DAVE BRADLEY
Chicago, Ill. Light Heavyweight
1975
Aug. 22—Al Bell, Chicago ....L 4
Sept. 9—John Townsend, Chicago ....W 4
1976
Feb. 4—John Townsend, Waukesha .... L 6

Sept. 2—Al Fracker, Kalamazoo ....L 6
1977
Apr. 25—Tony Fritz, Chicago ....W 6
June 25—Hank Gregory, Chicago ....W 8
1978
Feb. 27—Gerald Abdul-Ahad, Chicago ....KO 1
1979
June 4—Stanley Scott, Bridgeview ....W 8
June 28—Anthony Jones, Ft. Mitchell ....L 6
Oct. 19—Greg McPherson, Chicago ....L 8
1980
Mar. 3—Stanley Scott, Chicago ....KO 2

GERALD BRADLEY
Louisiana Featherweight
1980
Aug. 9—Rufus Walter, Lake Charles ....W 4
Oct. 18—Victor Rodriguez, Lake Charles ....KO 2

MICHAEL BRADLEY
Columbus, Ohio Welterweight
1980
July 24—Luis Paine, Columbus ....KO 1
Sept. 25—Thomas Moody, Columbus ....W 6
Nov. 1—Tony Taylor, Dayton ....W 4

LIVINGSTON BRAMBLE
Passaic, N.J. Lightweight
1980
Oct. 16—Jesus Serrano, Totowa ....KO 1
Dec. 4—Bruce Williams, Atlantic City ....D 4

VINCE BRATCHER
California Heavyweight
1980
Apr. 18—James Manning, Santa Rosa ....W 4
Sept. 5—Mario Savala, Sacramento ....KO by 1

IGNACIO BRAVO
Mexican Featherweight
1980
Mar. 3—Salvador Bermudez, Caracas ....KO 2
Apr. 25—Ramon Perez, Caracas ....KO 2
May 5—Jose Ramirez, Caracas ....W 10
June 16—Salvador Bermudez, Caracas ....KO 6
July 21—Felix Pinto, Caracas ....W 10
Aug. 11—Ismael Martinez, Caracas ....D 10
Sept. 8—Ramon Perez, Caracas ....KO 3

DAVID BRAXTON
Detroit, Michigan Junior Middleweight
Born: June 24, 1953. Height: 5'10½"
Managed by Lon R. Jackson
1978
Apr. 19—Leonard Langley, Washington D.C. ....D 6
May 24—Bob Patterson, Philadelphia ....KO 5
June 3—Lou Benson, Baltimore ....W 6
Aug. 3—Gary Coates, Detroit ....W 4
Aug. 17—Smooth Jackson, Detroit ....KO 3
Aug. 24—Marvin Hagler, Philadelphia ....L 10
Nov. 3—Dale Gordon, Detroit ....KO 5
Nov. 9—Jaime Knox, Mt. Clemen ....KO 2
1979
Jan. 11—Larry McCall, Detroit ....W 8
Feb. 9—Larry Radford, Detroit ....W 8
Mar. 12—Bobby Bland, Saginaw ....KO 4
July 21—Daryl Penn, Pontiac ....W 8
Nov. 9—Bill Goodwin, Saginaw ....W 8
Nov. 15—Sammy Floyd, Detroit ....W 8
1980
(Inactive)

DWIGHT BRAXTON
Philadelphia Pa. Light Heavyweight
1978
Apr. 19—Leonard Langley, Washington D.C. ....D 6
June 3—Lou Benson, Baltimore ....W 6
Nov. 2—Johnny Davis, New York ....L 6
1979
May 25—Louis Butler, Baltimore ....W 6
July 3—Louis Butler, Atlantic City ....W 8
Sept. 26—Biff Cline, Baltimore ....KO 1
Nov. 14—Johnny Wilburn, Baltimore ....W 8
1980
Feb. 4—Theunis Kok, Johannesburg ....KO 10
Mar. 29—Cornell Chavis, Atlantic City ....KO 1
May 8—Leonard Langley, Atlantic City ....KO 2
June 5—Charlie Smith, Atlantic City ....KO 4
Aug. 14—Rick Jester, Chicago ....KO 3
Nov. 6—Tony Mesoraca, Atlantic City ....KO 6

ROGER BRAXTON
Seattle, Wash. Heavyweight
1978
Sept. 26—Roger Troupe, Pico Rivera ....L 4
1979
Jan. 8—Pinklon Thomas, Seattle ....KO by 6
May 18—Mark Westaway, Pico Rivera ....D 6
June 18—George Omara, Los Angeles ....L 4
June 24—Eddie Wilson, Las Vegas ....L 5
Dec. 7—Basheer Wadud, San Diego ....L 6
1980
May 2—George O'Mara, Inglewood ....L 6
May 17—Jesse Prieto, Las Vegas ....L 6
Sept. 19—John Ellis, Inglewood ....L 10

TONY BRAXTON
Camden, N.J. Junior Middleweight
1979
Oct. 27—Frank Fletcher, Rahway ....D 4
Dec. 1—Frank Fletcher, Rahway ....W 6
1980
May 25—Carlton Swift, Rahway ....W 8
Oct. 16—Ernie Johnson, Totowa ....KO 2
Dec. 18—Feliciano Cintron, Totowa ....KO 8

OTTO BREEDING
Indianapolis Featherweight
1980
Apr. 14—Carlos Serrano, Chicago ....KO by 5
June 27—Pajarito Marquez, Chicago ....KO by 4
Sept. 22—Ismael Santana, Chicago ....KO by 6

PAT BRENNAN
Plainedge, New York Lightweight
1979
June 29—Derrick Wheeler, Commack ....KO 2
Aug. 3—Larry Savage, Hempstead ....D 4
Aug. 31—Tommy Barr, Shirley ....KO 2
Sept. 30—Herman Ingram, Shirley ....W 4
Oct. 12—Sal Ramirez, Uniondale ....W 4
Nov. 28—Miguel Quiles, Hartford ....L 4
1980
Jan. 19—George Casher, Hempstead ....KO by 1
Mar. 21—Larry Savage, New York ....KO 2
Aug. 15—Robert Johnson, Glen Cove ....W 6
Dec. 6—Efran Oregel, Lake Tahoe ....KO by 2

HENRY BRENT
Brooklyn, New York Bantamweight
1980
Apr. 11—Angel Marrero, Staten Island ....W 6
Sept. 9—Robert Nixon, Memphis ....KO 3
Oct. 10—Julio Hernandez, New York ....KO 3

BENNIE BRISCOE
Philadelphia, Pa. Middleweight
Born: Feb. 8, 1943, Augusta, Ga.
1962
Sept. 10—Sam Samuel, Philadelphia ....W 4
Dec. 13—Dave Wyatt, Philadelphia..............KO 3
1963
Jan. 14—Charley Little, Philadelphia ....KO 1
Feb. 11—Bradford Silas, Philadelphia ....KO 4
Feb. 28—Joe Smith, Philadelphia ....KO 6
Mar. 25—Chuck McCreary, Philadelphia ....W 6
Apr. 25—Cash White, Philadelphia ....KO 2
July 22—Joe Clark, Las Vegas.................W 4
Oct. 11—Roosevelt Ware, Philadelphia ....KO 4
Dec. 2—Bobby Bell, Philadelphia ....KO 1
1964
Jan. 20—Johnny Clyde, Philadelphia ....W 6
Mar. 9—Charley Scott, Philadelphia ....KO 1
June 15—Percy Manning, Philadelphia ....KO 3
Nov. 30—Walter McDaniels, Philadelphia ....W 8
1965
Feb. 22—Dave Wyatt, Philadelphia..............KO 7
Mar. 29—Percy Manning, Philadelphia ....L 10
Apr. 19—Jimmy McMillan, Philadelphia ....KO 1
May 10—Doug McLeod, Philadelphia ....KO 1
Sept. 10—Tito Marshall, Philadelphia ....L 10
Dec. 6—Stanley Hayward, Philadelphia ....L 10
1966
July 25—C. L. Lewis, Philadelphia ....ND
Oct. 10—C. L. Lewis, Philadelphia ....KO 6
Dec. 5—George Benton, Philadelphia............KO 10
1967
Mar. 20—Luis Rodriguez, Philadelphia ....L 10
May 6—Carlos Monzon, Buenos Aires............D 10
May 29—Bobby Warthem, Philadelphia ....KO 7
Oct. 9—George Johnson, Philadelphia ....KO 4
Oct. 30—Ike White, Philadelphia ....KO 3
Nov. 20—Jimmy Lester, Philadelphia ....KO 6
Dec. 15—Luis Rodriguez, New York..............L 10

51

1968
Mar. 25—Yoland Leveque, Paris.............. L disq. 4
Aug. 7—Gene Bryant, Las Vegas................ KO 8
Aug. 20—Jose Gonzalez, New York............... W 10
Sept. 23—Vicente Rondon, San Juan............... L 10
Nov. 2—Pedro Miranda, San Juan............... KO 7
Nov. 18—Charlie Austin, Philadelphia........... W 10
1969
Jan. 26—Vicente Rondon, San Juan .... KO 8
Feb. 14—Juarez De Lima, New York............. L 10
Mar. 10—Jose Gonzalez, New York .... KO 5
May 19—Percy Manning, Philadelphia.......... KO 4
Sept. 30—Tito Marshall, Philadelphia .... KO 1
Nov. 18—Joe Shaw, Philadelphia................. L 10
1970
Mar. 16—Joe Shaw, Philadelphia............... KO 7
Sept. 23—Eddie Owens, Philadelphia............ KO 6
Nov. 2—Harold Richardson, Philadelphia .... KO 6
1971
Jan. 12—Ned Edwards, Philadelphia .... KO 2
Mar. 22—Tom Bethea, Philadelphia .... KO 7
May 3—Carlos Marks, Philadelphia .... KO 5
Aug. 10—Juarez de Lima, Philadelphia .... KO 2
Oct. 14—Charlie Austin, Philadelphia........... KO 1
Nov. 15—Rafael Gutierrez, Philadelphia .... KO 2
1972
Jan. 18—Al Quinney, Philadelphia............... KO 2
Mar. 21—Jorge Rosales, Philadelphia............ KO 1
Apr. 19—Luis Vinales, Scranton .... L 10
Oct. 11—Luis Vinales, Philadelphia............. KO 7
Nov. 11—Carlos Monzon, Buenos Aires........... L 15
(World Middleweight Title)
1973
Jan. 29—Carlos Salinas, Philadelphia .... KO 5
Mar. 26—Art Hernandez, Philadelphia........... KO 3
(North American Middleweight Title)
June 25—Bill Douglas, Philadelphia............. KO 8
Sept. 1—Rodrigo Valdez, Noumea .... L 12
Oct. 22—Ruben Arocha, Philadelphia........... KO 3
Dec. 8—Willie Warren, Atlantic City........... KO 7
1974
Feb. 25—Tony Mundine, Paris.................. KO 5
May 25—Rodrigo Valdez, Monte Carlo .... KO by 7
(WBC Vacant Middleweight Title)
Oct. 9—Emile Griffith, Philadelphia............ L 10
1975
Jan. 14—Lenny Harden, Philadelphia........... KO 10
Apr. 7—Vinnie Curto, Philadelphia............. D 10
June 16—Stanley Hayward, Philadelphia.......... W 10
Aug. 18—Eddie Gregory, Philadelphia........... W 10
Nov. 18—Eugene Hart, Philadelphia .... D 10
1976
Feb. 25—Jose Martin Flores, Philadelphia .... KO 7
Apr. 6—Eugene Hart, Philadelphia............. KO 1
June 26—Emile Griffith, Monte Carlo .... D 10
Aug. 18—Emeterio Villanueva, Philadelphia ...... KO 5
Dec. 20—Willie Warren, Nice .... D 10
1977
Jan. 17—Karl Vinson, Philadelphia .... W 10
Mar. 30—Jean Mateo, Paris .... KO 10
July 26—Sammy Barr, Philadelphia .... KO 8
Nov. 5—Rodrigo Valdez, Campione d'Italia .... L 15
(Vacant World Middleweight Title)
1978
Feb. 4—Vito Antuofermo, New York............ L 10
Mar. 31—Tony Chiaverini, Kansas City .... KO 8
May 24—Bob Patterson, Philadelphia........... KO 5
1979
Feb. 5—David Love, Philadelphia.............. L 10
May 23—Nick Ortiz, Washington, D.C........... W 10
Aug. 14—Joe Barrientes, Atlantic City .... KO 6
Sept. 11—Ted Mann, Philadelphia .... W 10
Oct. 20—Clemente Tshinza, Liege .... L 10
1980
Jan. 24—Richie Bennett, Upper Darby .... L 10
Aug. 25—Richie Bennett, Philadelphia........... W 10
Dec. 15—Vinnie Curto, Boston .... L 10

KENNY BRISTOL
Guyanan Junior Middleweight
(Guyana Record Unavailable)
1976
Oct. 22—John Locicero, New York .... W 4
Nov. 26—Nate Dixon, New York................. W 6
1977
Feb. 11—Bob Patterson, New York .... W 6
Apr. 29—Reuben Lopez, New York .... W 8
May 20—Angel Ortiz, New York .... W 10
June 9—Bob Patterson, North Bergen .... W 6
Sept. 20—Scorpion Ofusu, Accra .... L 10
1978
Apr. 5—Gil Rosario, White Plains .... W 6
May 28—Michael Paul, Georgetown .... W 10
Nov. 5—Sandy Torres, Georgetown .... W 10

1979
Apr. 29—Alvin Anderson, Georgetown .... W 10
July 29—Pat Thomas, Georgetown .... W 15
(Won British Commonwealth
Junior Middleweight Title)
Nov. 30—Ray Phillips, Trieste .... W 8
Dec. 8—Dick Fisher, ... W 8
1980
Feb. 24—Eddie Marcelle, Georgetown .... W 15
(Retained Commonwealth Light Middleweight Title)

JOE BRITT
Syracuse, N.Y. York Light Heavyweight
Managed by Billy Harris
1980
Jan. 19—Milt Hopkins, Syracuse .... KO 1
Apr. 19—Eric Winbush, Syracuse .... KO 2
July 25—Furgan Ali, Rochester .... KO 2

MARCOS BRITTON
Featherweight
1980
Jan. 18—Pat Ford, Port of Spain .... KO by 4
Aug. 1—Felix Rodriguez, Colon .... KO by 3

JUAN J. BRIZUELA
Argentine Junior Featherweight
1980
Apr. 11—Simon Ortigoza, Santa Rosa .... TD 6
May 9—Santo Laciar, Cordoba .... L 10
June 7—Sergio Palma, Pergamino .... L 10
Aug. 1—Jose Narvaez, Mendoza .... L 10
Sept. 26—Ramon Dominguez, P.R.S. Pena .... L 10
Dec. 12—Fernando Sosa, Mar del Plata .... KO by 10

AL BROOKS
Massachusetts Heavyweight
1980
June 26—Paul Benjamin, Revere .... KO 5
Oct. 16—Dino Dennis, Revere .... KO by 3

MONROE BROOKS
Los Angeles, Calif. Junior Welterweight
1972
Sept. 21—Javier Martinez, Los Angeles............ W 4
Oct. 24—Jose Miranda, Los Angeles .... D 6
Nov. 30—Tommy Velasquez, Los Angeles .... KO 3
Dec. 11—Jose Miranda, Woodland Hills........... W 6
1973
Feb. 8—Santiago Rosa, Los Angeles .... W 6
Feb. 20—Greg Potter, Bakersfield................. D 8
Mar. 22—Vicente Hernandez, Sacramento .... KO 5
Apr. 17—Jerry Jacobs, Sacramento .... KO 2
May 1—Raton Macias, Sacramento .... KO 1
May 22—Demitrio Salazar, Sacramento .... KO 6
June 12—Juan Collado, Sacramento .... W 10
July 24—Juan Collado, Sacramento .... KO 1
Aug. 7—Enrique Jana, Sacramento .... KO 10
Sept. 18—Raul Montoya, Sacramento .... W 10
Oct. 3—Miguel Mayon, Sacramento .... W 10
Oct. 23—Rudy Barro, Sacramento .... W 12
Dec. 6—Chucho Padilla, Sacramento .... KO 4
1974
Mar. 31—Jesus Alonso, Mexicali................. KO 2
May 11—Jose Angel Herrera, Monterrey.......... KO 6
June 2—Leoncio Ortiz, Mexicali .... L 10
June 25—Miguel Mayon, Sacramento .... KO 5
Aug. 15—Lino Cordero, Los Angeles .... KO 3
Sept. 5—Ruben Vasquez, Los Angeles .... KO 3
Nov. 7—Octavio Amparan, Los Angeles .... W 10
Dec. 20—Aurelio Muniz, Los Angeles .... KO 4
1975
Feb. 4—Jose Miranda, Sacramento .... KO 5
Mar. 18—David Oropeza, Sacramento .... TD 9
Apr. 22—Nacho Castaneda, Sacramento .... KO 4
June 10—David Oropeza, Sacramento .... KO 2
Aug. 29—Adolph Viruet, Las Vegas .... L 12
Sept. 23—Brooks Byrd, Sacramento .... KO 2
Nov. 15—Augustin Estrada, Los Angeles.......... KO 8
1976
Jan. 15—Alfonso Jiminez, Los Angeles .... KO 2
June 7—Augustine Estrada, Sacramento .... W 10
May 6—Miguel Estrada, Los Angeles............ KO 3
July 29—Rudy Barro, Honolulu .... W 10
Aug. 19—Pancho Del Toro, Los Angeles........... W 10
1977
Mar. 15—Saensak Muangsurin, Chiang-Mai ... KO by 15
(WBC Junior Welterweight Title)
Aug. 18—Jesse Lara, Los Angeles .... KO 4
Dec. 1—Abraham Perez, Los Angeles .... KO 3
1978
Jan. 19—Mario Mendez, Los Angeles .... KO 4
Feb. 22—Rafael Lopez, Anchorage .... KO 3

52

Mar.	18—Jose Gonzalez, Los Angeles	KO	2
Apr.	7—Bruce Curry, Los Angeles	KO by	9
	(U.S. Junior Welterweight Title)		
Sept.	7—Rafael Nunez, Los Angeles	KO	6
Dec.	8—Roberto Duran, New York	KO by	8

1979

May	15—Ron Cummings, Sacramento	D	10
Oct.	27—Howard Jackson, Los Angeles	KO	10
Nov.	27—Leonardo Bermudez, Los Angeles	W	10

1980

Jan.	26—Camilo Ibarra, Los Angeles	KO	5
Mar.	28—Miguel Sanchez, Tacoma	KO	2
May	4—Rafael Nunez, Seattle	W	10
June	14—Andres Ramirez, Cincinnati	KO	3
Aug.	23—Cristobal Torres, Inglewood	KO	3
Dec.	12—Rafael Nunez, Sacramento	KO	4

GARY BROUGHTON
Brantford, Canada Middleweight

1964

Oct.	19—Denny Stiletto, Sarnia	KO	4
Nov.	30—Vernon Lee, Indianapolis	KO	2

1965

Jan.	11—Colin Fraser, Toronto	L	8
Jan.	26—Colin Fraser, Sarnia	L	8
Feb.	22—Walter Kelly, Sarnia	D	6
Mar.	4—Walter Kelly, Sarnia	D	4
May	19—Tony Lopez, Toledo	KO by	5

1966

Jan.	25—Carl Jordan, Pittsburgh	W	6
Feb.	14—Henri Turner, Syracuse	W	6
Mar.	3—Walter Kelly, Toronto	L	8
May	9—Al Quinney, Toronto	KO	4
July	4—Walter Kelly, Toronto	L	8

1967

Feb.	15—Larry Tadum, McKeesport	L	6
Mar.	30—Larry Tadum, Pittsburgh	L	6
Apr.	10—Robert Tucker, Grand Rapids	L	6
May	22—Conrad Williams, Pittsburgh	L	6
June	15—Hedgemon Lewis, Detroit	L	8
Sept.	25—Don Cobbs, Detroit	L	10
Nov.	14—Walter Kelly, Buffalo	L	8

1968

Jan.	10—Carl Jordan, McKeesport	W	6
Apr.	16—Walter Kelly, Buffalo	L	8
May	8—Stu Gray, Toronto	W	8
June	1—Stu Gray, Toronto	KO	8
Oct.	16—Ed Derocher, Toronto	KO	2

1969

Feb.	4—Al Quinney, Buffalo	L	4
Mar.	4—Al Quinney, Oshawa	L	8
Apr.	11—Earl Johnson, Detroit	D	6
Apr.	21—Walter Kelly, Toronto	W	8
May	22—Al Jones, Detroit	L	6
Sept.	6—Earl Johnson, Cleveland	L	6
Nov.	25—Howard Youngblood, Detroit	KO	3
Dec.	10—Earl Johnson, Cleveland	L	6

1970

Feb.	27—Chuck McCreary, Detroit	L	6
Apr.	20—Columbus Lloyd, Windsor	W	8
May	28—Primus Williams, Windsor	W	8
Aug.	13—Dave Downey, Halifax	KO	9
	(Canadian Middleweight Title)		
Sept.	14—Joe Blair, Windsor	KO	3
Dec.	18—Dave Downey, Halifax	L	12
	(Canadian Middleweight Title)		

1971

May	7—Tom Hanna, Detroit	L	8
June	7—Nick Peoples, Windsor	D	8
Aug.	19—Stu Gray, Toronto	L	10
Oct.	4—Jimmy Meilleur, Windsor	W	12
	(Canadian Junior Middleweight Title)		
Nov.	3—Tom Hanna, Detroit	L	10

1972

Jan.	26—Dave Thach, Canton	W	10
Mar.	24—George McGee, Parma	KO	5
June	—Art Hernandez, Milwaukee	W	10
Oct.	12—Al Boldon, Pittsburgh	KO	3
Nov.	29—George McGhee, McKeesport	KO	9

1973

Apr.	10—Bobby Watts, Philadelphia	L	10
May	12—Sammy Ruckard, Windsor	KO	3
June	28—Roy McMillan, Toronto	KO	5
Aug.	2—Mike Baker, Halifax	KO	7
Aug.	30—Joey Durelle, Halifax	W	10
Sept.	27—Dave Downey, Halifax	L	12
	(Canadian Middleweight Title)		

1974

Feb.	18—Roy McMillan, Toronto	KO	4
Apr.	19—Kid Totas, Ottawa	L	8
June	10—Marshall Butler, Hull	KO	9
July	11—Tony Licata, New Orleans	L	10
Oct.	18—Kid Totas, Hull	L	10
Nov.	11—Jean-Claude Bouttier, New York	KO by	7

1975

Apr.	17—Sammy NeSmith, Indianapolis	KO by	3
June	12—Jean-Claude LeClair, Sorel	KO	7
Oct.	6—Jean-Claude LeClair, Sorel	KO	7
Nov.	4—Fernand Marcotte, Montreal	L	10
Dec.	1—Jean-Yves Fillion, Quebec City	W	10

1976

Apr.	5—Joe Henry, Toronto	D	10
Apr.	10—Gene Wells, Orlando	L	10
June	4—Clyde Gray, Halifax	L	10
Sept.	2—Christy Elliott, Halifax	L	10
Oct.	4—Fernand Marcotte, Quebec City	L	12
Oct.	26—Jean-Claude LeClair, Montreal	L	10

1977

Feb.	9—Bonifacio Avila, Quebec	KO by	7
Apr.	20—Doug Demmings, Minneapolis	L	10
May	18—Mayfield Pennington, Louisville	L	10
June	30—Claude Gauthier, Halifax	D	10
Aug.	18—Claude Gauthier, Halifax	W	10
Oct.	7—Roy Dale, Cincinnati	KO by	9

1978

Feb.	6—Joe Henry, Edmonton	L	8
Apr.	6—Gary Guiden, Cleveland	KO by	7
Sept.	12—Eddy Melo, Bradford	L	8
Oct.	17—Tap Harris, Canton	KO by	5

1979

Sept.	26—Rico Hoye, Windsor	W	10

1980

Jan.	21—Jimmy Gradson, Montreal	L	10

C. B. BROWN
Des Moines, Iowa Lightweight

1980

Apr.	13—Willie Turner, Kansas City	L	4
Aug.	3—Sylvester Price, North Platte	W	6
Aug.	8—Ralph Twinning, Chicago	KO by	3

C. J. BROWN
Seattle, Washington Middleweight

1976

May	13—Willie Baldwin, Portland	KO by	6
June	29—Willie Baldwin, Seattle	L	4
July	8—Willie Baldwin, Portland	L	6
Sept.	16—Larry Smith, Portland	L	6
Nov.	11—Steve Cole, Portland	KO	3

1977

May	26—John Sullivan, Portland	L	6
June	11—Daryl Penn, Hillsboro, Ore.	L	6
July	10—Rick Cece, Stateline	L	6
Dec.	8—Steve Moyer, Portland	L	6

1978

Jan.	26—Bobby Howard, Seattle	L	6
Apr.	8—Art Sinclair, Everett	KO	5
May	13—LeRoy Green, Kansas City	L	10
May	27—Doug Arlt, Missoula, Mont.	D	8
July	12—Gary Thomas, Kansas City	KO	3
Aug.	30—James Waire, Reno	KO by	7
Sept.	14—Paddy Wilson, Portland	D	6
Oct.	31—John L. Sullivan, Lacey	L	10
Nov.	11—Ken Camel, Missoula	L	10

1979

June	5—Kenny Camel, Missoula	L	8
June	14—Wayne Caplette, Winnipeg	L	8
June	21—Hudson Jackson, Seattle	KO	4

1980

Feb.	19—Scott Frank, Totowa	KO by	2
Apr.	13—Willie Turner, Kansas City	L	4

CHARLIE (CHOO CHOO) BROWN
Upper Darby, Pa. Lightweight

1979

Apr.	10—Wayne Dabney, Philadelphia	KO	1
May	22—Cortez Jackson, Upper Darby	KO	1
May	23—C. J. Faison, Washington, D.C.	KO	4
July	31—Henry Barber, Atlantic City	KO	3
Aug.	18—Danny Daniels, Atlantic City	KO	1
Sept.	11—Angel Cruz, Philadelphia	W	6
Nov.	8—Jerry Strickland, Indianapolis	KO	2
Nov.	21—Jose Gonzales, Allentown	KO	3
Nov.	29—Elliott Freeman, Virginia Beach	KO	3

1980

Feb.	18—Greg Netter, Upper Darby	D	6
June	5—Michael Ross, Atlantic City	KO	6
July	3—Gary Hinton, Atlantic City	W	10
Sept.	18—Curtis Harris, Totowa	KO by	4

CHARLEY BROWN
Welterweight

1980

Sept.	6—Randy Mitchell, Lincolnton	KO by	4
Sept.	20—David Dean, Charlotte	L	6

DAVID BROWN
Elizabeth, N.J. Featherweight
1980
Aug.	2—Diego Rosario, Totowa	D	4
Aug.	27—Edwin Santiago, Elizabeth	KO	2
Sept.	12—Hector Camacho, New York	L	4
Oct.	24—Daniel Avery, Uniondale	L	4
Dec.	17—Paul DeVorce, White Plains	W	6

FREDDIE BROWN
Norfolk, Va. Light Heavyweight
1977
June	2—Robert Gwynn, Virginia Beach	KO	1
July	2—Mel Grooms, Virginia Beach	KO	5
July	21—Jake Jenkins, Virginia Beach	W	6
Aug.	25—Willie Crews, Virginia Beach	W	6
Sept.	8—Micky Lewis, Virginia Beach	W	4
Sept.	21—Artie McCloud, Virginia Beach	L	6
Oct.	18—Mel Grooms, Virginia Beach	W	6
Feb.	23—Harry Savage, Virginia Beach	W	4
Mar.	2—Chuck Warfield, Cleveland	KO	8
Mar.	16—Leonard Langley, Virginia Beach	W	4
Apr.	6—Pat Cuillo, Cleveland	KO by	6
June	22—Odell Leonard, Virginia Beach	W	6
July	20—Charlie Brown, Virginia Beach	KO	3
Aug.	17—Jesse Carter, Virginia Beach	W	10
Sept.	9—James Scott, Rahway	KO by	4
Oct.	—Jerry Celestine, Memphis	L	10
Dec.	14—Don Wilson, Virginia Beach	W	6
	1979		
Jan.	10—Art Harris, Cleveland	L	10
Feb.	27—Jerome Jackson, Philadelphia	L	8
Apr.	26—Lou Benson, Virginia Beach	L	6
May	31—Lou Benson, Virginia Beach	D	8
July	16—Eddie Gregory, N.Y.	KO by	3
Aug.	30—Bob Saxton, Va. Beach	KO	2
Oct.	27—Pablo Ramos, Rahway	L	10
	1980		
May	29—Hocine Tafer, Grenoble	L	10
Nov.	1—Eddie Burke, Glasgow	KO by	1

GARY BROWN
Indianapolis, Ind. Junior Welterweight
1980
Aug.	13—Tony Travis, Indianapolis	W	4
Oct.	30—Shelby Wilkenson, Las Vegas	L	6

IVY BROWN
Kansas City, Mo. Light Heavyweight
1976
Mar.	—James Dixon, Memphis, Tenn.	W	4
Oct.	6—Julius Noble, Kansas City	W	4
Dec.	15—Cornell Verse, Kansas City	W	4
	1977		
Jan.	29—Tony McMinn, Kansas City, Mo.	KO by	4
Mar.	18—Ned Hallacy, Kansas City	W	6
Mar.	30—Pablo Ramos, Cleveland	L	6
Apr.	21—Dwight Morgan, Wichita	KO	1
Apr.	29—James Coleman, Wichita, Kansas	KO	1
June	17—Leon Washington, Kansas City, Mo.	KO	1
July	1—Ned Hallacy, Wichita, Kansas	KO by	7
Aug.	1—Robert Reynosa, Topeka	KO	3
Sept.	7—Larry Ward, Kansas City	KO	4
Oct.	11—Jerry Celestine, Memphis	L	10
Oct.	25—Leon Washington, Kansas City	KO	1
Dec.	15—Ron Burton, Kansas City	W	4
	1978		
Feb.	18—Bill Hollis, Saginaw	W	6
Mar.	15—Roberto Rockett, Memphis	W	8
Mar.	31—James Dixon, Kansas City	W	4
June	2—Savage Turner, Kansas City	W	8
June	26—Pat Cuillo, Detroit	KO	2
Sept.	27—Jerry Martin, Philadelphia	KO by	5
Dec.	2—Frankie Evans, Kansas City, Mo.	W	8
	1979		
Jan.	19—Ruben Bardot, Overland Park	KO	3
Feb.	27—Yaqui Lopez, Sacramento	KO by	3
May	12—Matt Ross, Wichita	KO	2
June	4—John Conteh, Liverpool	L	10
Aug.	3—Frank Evans, Tulsa	KO	6
Oct.	11—Gary Summerhays, Kansas City	W	10
Nov.	23—George Aidoo, Kansas City	KO	2
Dec.	15—Joe Barrientos, Kansas City	KO	6
	1980		
Feb.	9—Sydney Hoho, Johannesburg	KO	5
Mar.	9—Young Joe Louis, St. Paul	KO by	7
June	12—Sylvain Watbled, Paris	KO by	2
Aug.	6—S. T. Gordon, Santa Monica	KO by	2
Dec.	4—George Goforth, Kansas City	KO	6

JERRY BROWN
Chicago, Ill. Middleweight
1979
June	4—Imara Epesi, Bridgeview	W	4
June	13—Danny Murphy, Bridgeview	KO	1
	1980		
Aug.	8—Pat John, Chicago	KO	2
Nov.	7—Ricky Haynes, Chicago	L	6

JIMMY BROWN
Vineland, N.J. Middleweight
1980
Sept.	17—John Molander, White Plains	KO by	1

MIKE BROWN
Philadelphia, Pa. Lightweight
1979
June	8—Abdul Muhammad, Bermuda	KO	3
Aug.	30—Van Tate, Virginia Beach	W	4
Sept.	20—Lloyd Jones, Virginia Beach	KO	2
Oct.	18—Mustafa Muhammad, Philadelphia	KO	1
	1980		
Apr.	11—Larry Adkins, Chester	KO	2
June	11—Jose Figueroa, White Plains	W	6
Sept.	10—Bobby Johnson, Scranton	L	4

PHILLIP BROWN
New Orleans, La. Heavyweight
1980
Feb.	5—Walter Hayes, Memphis	KO	6
May	10—Ed Bednarik, Clarksburg	KO by	1
May	13—Michael Greer, Memphis	D	6
July	1—Ed Bangs, Memphis	KO	2
July	15—Bill Thomas, New Orleans	W	5
Aug.	9—Elton Armstrong, Lake Charles	KO	3
Sept.	18—Marcellus Ball, Cleveland	W	4
Oct.	18—Vernon Johnston, Lake Charles	W	8

RONNIE BROWN
Denver, Colorado Middleweight
1978
June	3—Adolfo Rivas, San Antonio	KO	1
Oct.	13—Mario Arzate, El Paso	KO	2
Nov.	17—Sonny Williams, Denver	KO	4
Dec.	8—Carlos Muro, El Paso	KO	1
Jan.	20—Pancho Carlos Hernandez, El Paso	KO	4
Feb.	17—Pancho Carlos Hernandez, El Paso	W	6
Mar.	24—John Robinson, Kansas City	KO	4
Apr.	27—Earl Reese, Kansas City	KO	2
June	8—George Carter, Denver	KO	2
June	23—Joe Barrientes, Dallas	W	8
July	20—Jim Ingram, Denver	W	8
	1980		
Jan.	16—Ted Sanders, Las Vegas	L	10
Mar.	17—Sammy Nesmith, Indianapolis	KO by	8
May	2—Rudy Robles, Las Vegas	KO by	3
Sept.	10—Rudy Robles, Las Vegas	KO by	1

TOMMY BROWN
Boston, Mass. Welterweight
1979
Nov.	7—Tom Jancsy, Boston	W	6
	1980		
Feb.	16—Jack Morrell, Portland	L	6
Feb.	26—Ralph Bracetty, Woburn	KO	3
June	20—Steve Hilliard, Boston	L	4
June	26—Jack Morrell, Revere	L	5

TONY BROWN
Cleveland, Ohio Junior Welterweight
1980
Mar.	21—Jesse Putman, Bellwood	W	6
Aug.	25—Terry Whittaker, Chicago	KO by	1

WILLIE BROWN
Akron, Ohio Junior Middleweight
1979
June	12—Lucky Clay, Detroit	D	
July	12—Nathaniel Akbar, Detroit	KO by	1
Aug.	24—Kenny Abbott, Cincinnati	W	4
	1980		
July	6—Eddie Temple, Columbus	KO by	1
Aug.	23—Kevin Straughter, Alliance	L	6

CARLOS BRYANT
California Lightweight
Sept.	17—Gerry Reyes, San Diego	W	4
Dec.	19—Mil Jiminez, San Diego	KO	3

JAMES BUCKLEY
St. Louis, Mo. Light Heavyweight
1980
May 12—Gene Spencer, Cape Girardeau .... KO 1
June 6—Willie Turner, Kansas City .... KO 4

VICTOR BULTRON
Puerto Rican Bantamweight
1977
Oct.   8—Ruben Vega, Carolino .... W 4
Oct. 15—Israel Melendez, Carolino .... L 4
Nov. 19—Israel Melendez, San Juan .... D 4
1978
Sept. 26—Julio Soto Solano, Santo Domingo .... L 10
1979
Feb. 26—Rafael Sosa, Santo Domingo .... L 10
Apr. 28—Luis Burgos, Trujillo .... L 10
1980
Sept. 9—Ramon Cruz, San Juan .... L 8

JOHNNY BUMPHUS
Nashville, Tenn. Junior Welterweight
Managed by Shelly Finkel & Lou Duva
1980
Nov.   8—Mike Michaud, Lake Tahoe .... KO 1
Dec.   4—Kenneth Long, Atlantic City .... KO 1
Dec. 20—Norberto Figueroa, New York .... W 6

HENRY BUNCH
Washington, D.C. Middleweight
1978
June 28—Charles Williams, Washington, D.C. ..... W 4
Nov. 21—Harry Savage, Landover .... W 5
1979
Feb. 12—Wilbur Crews, Washington, D.C. .... W 6
1980
Jan. 16—Malik Muhammad, Washington, D.C. ... KO 3

RICKY BURGESS
Waterville, Me. Welterweight
1980
Jan. 23—Charlie Jones, Waterville .... KO 5

EDUARDO BURGESS
Chilean Flyweight
1980
May   7—Antonio Villouta, Santiago .... KO 2
June 11—Pedro Jatib, Santiago .... KO 5
July 16—Eric Venegas, Santiago .... KO 5

LUIS BURGOS
Puerto Rican Bantamweight
1979
Apr. 28—Victor Bultron, Trujillo .... W 10
June 16—Orlando Maldonado, San Juan .... KO by 3
1980
Mar. 10—Wilfredo Padron, Caracas .... D 10
Mar. 24—Carlos Gutierrez, Caracas .... L 10
Apr. 14—Pedro Torres, Caracas .... L 10
Sept. 1—Jesus Esparragoza, Caracas .... L 10

SAMMY (ROCKY) BURKE
New Mexico Lightweight
1980
Jan. 18—Blas Chairez, El Paso .... KO 6
Mar.   7—Davey Lopez, El Paso .... KO 2
May   31—Roberto Garcia, El Paso .... D 6
Sept. 11—Jerry Reyes, El Paso .... W 6
Sept. 18—Francisco Monzon, El Paso .... KO 1

LEE BURKEY
Carson City, Nevada Light Heavyweight
1979
May   30—Bennett White, Las Vegas .... KO by 2
July 11—Bob Starbird, Las Vegas .... L 4
July 18—Eddie Gregg, Las Vegas .... KO by 2
Aug. 29—Charles Roye, Las Vegas .... W 4
Sept. 19—Carlos Muro, Las Vegas .... D 4
Oct.   3—Terry Bowman, Las Vegas .... L 6
Oct. 30—Frank Dabrowski, Carson City .... KO 3
Nov. 20—Leslie Robinson, Sparks .... KO 3
Dec. 11—Jessie Aldridge, Sparks .... KO 1
1980
Jan. 12—Henry Hearns, Lake Tahoe .... KO by 2
Feb. 19—Jimmy McCauley, Sparks .... KO 4
Mar. 16—Luke Capuano, Las Vegas .... W 8
Apr. 26—Jack Joy, Carson City .... KO 2
May   29—Mike Clark, Las Vegas .... L 6
July   3—Roger Phillips, Gardnersville .... KO 5
Aug   31—Mike Clark, Carson City .... KO by 5
Oct. 22—Paddy Wilson, Las Vega .... KO 2
Oct. 30—Lucky Patterson, Carson City .... W 10

Nov. 29—Greg McPherson, Lake Tahoe .... W 10

PEDRO BURKI
Argentine Junior Featherweight
1980
Jan.   —Faustino Barrios, Camilo Aldao .... W 10
Mar.   7—Alberto Castillo, Ordonez .... W 8
Apr. 11—Humberto Torres, Just. Posse .... KO 5
Aug.   8—Julio C. Saba, Villa Maria .... W 10
Sept. 6—Jorge Vargas, Villa Maria .... W 10
Oct. 24—Carlos Martinetti, Villa Maria .... W 10
Dec.   5—Raul Perez, Villa Maria .... D 10

CARLOS FLORES BURLON
Argentine Welterweight
1980
Jan. 18—Juan Carlos Fernandez, San Nicolas ...... D 10
Mar. 15—Jesus Ibanez, San Pedro .... D 10
Apr. 11—Angel Salinas, Ciudadela .... KO by 9
Aug.   8—Celestino Bailone, Villa Mercedes .... W 12
(Won South American Light Heavyweight Title)
Nov.   7—Abel Brera, Villa Constitucion .... KO 7

JOSE M. FLORES BURLON
Argentine Middleweight
1980
Apr. 24—Aldo Carmona, Pergamino .... W 8
May   24—Rogelio Zarza, Pergamino .... W 10
Sept. 6—Hugo Salega, San Miguel .... KO 3
Dec. 19—Rogelio Zarza, Tapiales .... W 10

JESSE BURNETT
Los Angeles, Calif. Light Heavyweight
Born: Feb. 8, 1946
1972
Apr. 13—Cisco Solario, Los Angeles............. TD 1
Apr. 24—Angel Baggini, Los Angeles .... W 6
June   5—Steve Stark, Los Angeles .... KO 4
July   1—Alvaro Lopez, Stockton .... W 8
July 24—Hildo Silva, Los Angeles................ W 6
Oct. 19—Ron Wilson, Los Angeles............... W 10
1973
Feb.   8—Jimmy Lester, Los Angeles .... W 10
Aug.   9—Felton Marshall, Los Angeles .... W 8
1974
Mar. 15—Ray White, San Diego .... KO 8
1975
Feb. 25—James Scott, Miami Beach................ L 10
July 31—Alvaro Lopez, Stockton .... W 12
Sept. 24—Alvaro Lopez, Stockton .... L 12
Nov. 28—Danny Brewer, Edmonton .... KO 3
1976
Apr.   8—Victor Galindez, Oslo .... L 10
May   3—Danny Brewer, Stockton .... KO 7
May   14—Tony Mundine, Brisbane .... KO 6
June   3—Willie Taylor, Copenhagen .... W 10
July 10—Eddie Jones, San Diego .... W 10
Dec.   9—Bobby Rascon, Tokyo .... KO 4
1977
Mar. 20—Al Bolden, Tokyo .... KO 10
May   21—Miguel Cuello, Monte Carlo .... KO by 9
(Vacant WBC Light Heavyweight Title)
Nov. 18—Lonnie Bennett, Las Vegas .... KO 6
1978
Feb. 15—Eddie Gregory, Las Vegas .... KO by 10
May   25—Mustapha Wassaja, Copenhagen .... L 10
July   2—Alvaro Lopez, Stockton .... L 15
(U.S. Light Heavyweight Title)
Nov.   8—Pete McIntyre, Stockton .... L 10
Nov. 28—Juan de la Garza, Billings .... KO 6
1979
Apr.   9—John Conteh, London .... D 10
Nov. 14—Jerry Martin, Philadelphia .... L 12
Nov. 24—Young Joe Louis, Bloomington .... L 10
Dec. 14—Clarence Geigger, Costa Mesa .... W 10
1980
Mar.   4—Lottie Mwale, Wembley .... L 12
Apr. 19—Dale Grant, Billings .... KO 7
June 14—Victor Galindez, Anaheim .... W 12
July 15—T.C. Bowman, Anaheim .... KO 6
Dec.   3—Bash Ali, Anaheim .... L 12

ELLIOTT BURTON
Jersey City, N.J. Light Heavyweight
1978
Apr.   6—Bill Connell, N. Bergen .... KO by 1
1979
Oct. 27—J.C. Moody, North Bergen .... KO by 4
1980
Sept. 24—Jimmy Anderson, Elizabeth .... KO by 1

GEORGE BURTON
Junior Welterweight
1980
Sept. 11—Reggie Davis, Washington ....KO 4
Oct. 18—Sanford Ricks, Atlantic City ....L 4

JAMES BUSCEME
Lightweight
1979
June 26—Roberto Tijerino, Beaumont ....KO 2
Aug. 15—Joe Webber, Beaumont ....KO 1
Sept. 14—Simmie Black, Houston ....KO 3
Oct. 10—Jose Cruz, Beaumont ....KO 3
1980
Jan. 9—John Morgan, Beaumont ....KO by 8

ESTEBAN BUSTOS
Argentine Bantamweight
1980
Feb. 3—Luis Gerez, Gral Acha ....W 10
June 27—Rolando Lahoz, San Juan ....L 10
Aug. 29—Americo Suarez, Santa Rosa ....D 10

MANUEL BUSTOS
Argentine Welterweight
1980
June 7—Felipe Baez, Zarate ....W 10
Aug. 23—Jose Funes, Zarate ....W 10
Oct. 4—Rodolfo Petrizani, Buenos Aires ....W 10
Dec. 12—Floro Zarza, Zarate ....KO 5

JOEY BUTCHER
Indianapolis, Ind. Heavyweight
1980
Sept. 13—Murray Sutherland, Milwaukee ......KO by 1
Sept. 23—Jimmy Claar, Indianapolis ....KO by 2.

ALBERTO BUTILER
Argentine Welterweight
1980
Apr. 19—Pedro Ant. Gutierrez, Buenos Aires .....KO 2
July 19—Manuel Lopez, La Banda ....W 10
Dec. 12—Jose Fures, La Banda ....W 10
Dec. 26—Roberto Ale Ali, La Banda ....W 10

RUBEN BUTILER
Argentine Featherweight
1980
May —Ramon Dominguez, Buenos Aires ....KO by 6
June 19—Hugo Fernandez, Concordia ....L 10
Aug. 8—Marcial Franco, Reconquista ....L 10
Sept. 6—Jose Uziga, Gualeguaychu ....KO by 2
Dec. 26—Hector Rosa, Salta ....D 10

BRATON BUTLER
Jersey City, N.J. Junior Welterweight
1980
May 25—Raymond Johnson, Rahway ....L 6

FRANK BUTLER
Heavyweight
1980
Dec. 20—John Navarro, Richmond ....W 4

LOUIS BUTLER
Baltimore, Md. Light Heavyweight
1977
Apr. 29—Joe Sprowl, Baltimore ....D 4
Aug. 5—Jimmy Williams, Richmond ....KO 1
Sept. 17—Eddie Johnson, Richmond ....KO
Nov. 30—Joe Sprowl, Baltimore ....KO 1
1978
Aug. 8—Johnny Wilburn, Baltimore ....L 6
Sept. 14—Vandell Woods, Baltimore ....D 6
Sept. 21—Darbell Miles, Washington, D.C. ....W 6
1979
Mar. 28—Leroy Johnson, Baltimore ....W 6
May 25—Dwight Braxton, Baltimore ....L 6
July 3—Dwight Braxton, Atlantic City ....L 8
Nov. 14—Ed Smith, Baltimore ....KO 5
1980
Mar. 26—Robert McFarland, Baltimore ....L 6

TOMMY BUTTS
Portland, Me. Light Heavyweight
1980
July 25—Ron Huston, New Bedford ....KO by 1
Dec. 3—Tommy James, Brunswick ....KO 3

AL BYRD
Greensboro, N.C. Heavyweight
1972
Apr. 5—Butch Chambers, Winston-Salem ....KO by 4
June 13—John Berry, Washington ....KO by 1
1973
Feb. —Louis Slaughter, Knoxville ....L 6
Feb. 28—Paul Minor, Baltimore ....KO by 1
Mar. 7—Bubba Winfield, Winston-Salem ....L 6
Sept. 17—Marvin Johnson, Fort Wayne ....KO by 1
Oct. 16—John Berry, Norfolk ....KO by 3
1974
Apr. 2—Bubba Winfield, Richmond ....KO by 3
1975
Sept. 16—Billy Howard, Richmond ....KO 1
Dec. 9—Joe Sprowell, Washington, D.C. ......KO by 2
1976
Apr. 5—Biff Cline, Landover ....KO by 1
Oct. 15—Gary Dokes, Hollywood, Fla. ....KO by 3
1977
June 2—Matt Robinson, Virginia Beach ....L 4
July 21—Don Spellman, Virginia Beach ....KO by 5
Aug. 7—John Jordan, Virginia Beach ....KO by 5
Sept. 8—John (Speedy) Jordan, Va. Beach ....KO by 5
1978
June 22—Bobby Jordan, Virginia Beach ....KO by 4
Aug. 26—Mike Wyant, Dayton ....KO by 2
1979
Jan. 22—Dave Johnson, Washington, D.C. .....KO by 2
May 16—Franco Thomas, Clarksburg ....L 10
1980
Aug. 29—Louis Acosta, Miami Beach ....KO by 4
Oct. 11—Claman Parker, Lincolnton ....L 6

JOSE CABA
Dominican Rep. Featherweight
(Previous Record Unavailable)
1978
Feb. 9—Jose Luis Lara, Los Angeles ....KO 3
Feb. 24—Francisco Grullon, Bakersfield ....KO 1
Mar. 24—Javier Flores, Ogden ....W 10
Apr. 25—Edwin Alarcon, Honolulu ....KO 2
May 30—Noel Arriesgado, Honolulu ....L 10
July 18—Robert Perez, Honolulu ....KO 2
Oct. 5—David Barrera, Los Angeles ....KO 4
Nov. 4—Isao Okahashi, Nagoya ....KO 8
1979
Jan. 30—Tereso Casas, Honolulu ....KO 3
Mar. 6—Miguel Meza, Honolulu ....W 10
May 15—Gustavo Castaneda Lara, Honolulu .....KO 1
Sept. 25—Danny Lopez, Los Angeles ....KO by 3
(For WBC Featherweight Title)
1979
Mar. 24—Javier Flores, Ogden ....W 10
Nov. 13—Jose Olivares, Phoenix ....KO 7
1980
Mar. 5—Gilbert Garza, Las Vegas ....KO 10
Apr. 23—Blaine Dickson, Las Vegas ....KO 7

FRANK CABANIG
1980
Feb. 20—Rey Carino, Hilo ....L 4
June 17—Ful Sumagaysay, Honolulu ....L 4

JUAN B. CABRAL
Argentine Welterweight
1980
Mar. 8—Pablo Ferreyra, Catrilo ....W 10
Mar. 21—Alberto Prieto, Rio IV ....W 10
Apr. 12—Simon Escobar, Gral Pico ....W 10
June 5—Raul Paz, Int. Alvear ....W 10
June 27—Alberto Prieto, Rio IV ....W 10
Aug. 1—Ramon Peralta, Rio IV ....L 10
Nov. 22—Simon Escobar, Villa Mercedes ....L 10
Dec. 12—Carlos Prieto, Hca Renanco ....TD 7

JUAN R. CABRAL
Argentine Welterweight
1980
Feb. 23—Juan C. Salomon, Caleufu ....KO 9
July 12—Juan C. Salomon, Guatrache ....KO 6

RAUL CABRAL
Argentine Middleweight
1980
June   4—Ruben Wilberger, Quemu-Quemu .... KO by 7
July 12—Ramon Quintana, Gral Villegras .... KO 9

DAVID (MACETON) CABRERA
Mexican Light Heavyweight
Born: Juchitan, Oaxaca, Mexico
1977
Mar. 18—Lalo Gonzalez, Acapulco .... KO 2
Apr. 22—Ismael Ruiz, Minatitlan .... KO by 1
Aug.   2—Bernardo Barron, Tezuitlan .... KO by 3
Nov.   4—Ruben Rivera, Monterrey .... TKO 4
Dec.   9—Manuel Fierro, Monterrey .... KO 6
    (Won Mexican Light Heavyweight Title)
1978
Mar. 11—Emeterio Villanueva, Mexico City .... KO by 3
May   5—Ruben Rivera, Monterrey .... KO by 2
June 11—Dave Dekers, Belize, B.H. .... KO 6
July 29—Emeterio Villanueva, Mexico City .... KO 3
    (Retained Mexican Light Heavyweight Title)
Sept. 23—Herminio (Loba) Ramirez, Mexico City .. KO 3
1979
Jan. 16—Johnny Baldwin, Houston .... KO 3
Mar. 20—Manuel Elizondo, Houston .... KO 5
July 12—Rogelio Cervantes, McAllen .... KO 3
Aug. 30—Marvin Camel, McAllen .... KO by 3
Nov. 13—Otis Gordon, Houston .... KO by 1
1980
Jan. 18—Julio Cruz, Acapulco .... KO
    (Retained Mexican Light Heavyweight Title)
Mar. 28—Raul Landeros, Acapulco .... KO 2
May 16—Eleno Fuentes, Ciudad Juarez .... KO 4
June 27—Ariel Favela, Ciudad Obregon .... KO 1
Oct. 12—Emeterio Villanueva, Mexico City ... W disq. 1
    (Retained Mexican Light Heavyweight Title)

HECTOR CABRERA
Argentine Junior Welterweight
1980
July   5—Ruben Mansilla, Catrilo .... L 6
July 18—Alberto Sosa, Villa Maria .... L 6
Sept. 5—Alberto Sosa, Tio Pujio .... L 6

IRINEO CABRERA
Argentine Middleweight
1980
Feb. 23—Ruben Wilberger, Doblas .... L 10
Mar. 28—Antonio Cara, Villa Angela .... L 10
Apr. 11—Julio Arancibia, San Miguel .... L 10
Dec. 12—Hugo A. Rossi, La Plata .... W 10

NORBERTO CABRERA
Mexican Bentamweight
(Previous Record Unavailable)
1979
Mar.   7—Auscencio Melendez, Hermosillo .... W 10
July 13—Hector Medina, Hermosillo .... KO 11
    (Won Mexican Bantamweight Title)
1980
Feb.   8—Manuel Lara, Hermosillo .... KO 5
    (Retained Mexican Bantamweight Title)
Mar. 28—Jose Angel Cazares, Hermosillo .... W 12
June 14—Francisco Manzo, Mexico City .... W 10
Oct. 11—Paulino Canche, Mexico City .... W 12
    (Retained Mexican Bantamweight Title)

NORBERTO CABRERA
Argentine Middleweight
Born: Sept. 11, 1952, Santa Fe
1972
Dec. 12—Ramon Vallejos, Santa Fe .... KO 1
Dec. 21—Rafael Lezcano, Santa Fe .... KO 3
1973
May 25—Salvatore Panunzio, Roma .... W 8
July 14—Mario Delgado, Buenos Aires .... W 8
Oct.   3—Hector Galven, Buenos Aires .... W 16
Dec. 28—Carlos Reato, Villaguay .... KO 2
1974
Feb.   9—Michel Chapier, Paris .... W 6
Mar. 23—Dante Rossi, Freyre, Cordoba .... KO 3
July 24—Orlando M. Nasul, Buenos Aires .... W 10
Sept. 6—Armando Vicente, Salta .... D 10
Nov. 13—Roberto Marziali, Buenos Aires .... W 10
Dec. 13—Octavio Escauriza, Rosario .... D 10
1975
Jan. 10—Rodolfo Rosales, Salta .... D 10
Mar. 15—Alberto Almiron, Posadas .... L 10
Apr. 11—Miguel A. Castellini, Salta .... KO by 5
June   6—Miguel A. Duro, Parana .... KO 7
Nov.   7—Hugo Corro, Tunuyan .... L 10
Dec. 26—Armando Vicente, Salta .... KO 3

1976
Jan. 23—Rodolfo Rosales, Salta .... D 10
Feb. 27—Rudecindo Chavez, Salta .... KO 5
Mar. 20—Rodolfo Rosales, Buenos Aires .... KO 5
Apr. 30—Roque Roldan, Salta .... L disq. 9
May 21—Hugo Corro, Buenos Aires .... W 10
Nov. 19—Roberto Benacquista, Milano .... KO 7
Dec. 17—Gerard Nosley, Milan .... KO by 2
1977
May 21—Wayne Bennett, Monte Carlo .... KO 4
June 17—Lucas Paz, San Pedro .... KO 6
July 30—Ali Perez, Monte Carlo .... KO 4
Dec.   8—Juan Carlos Bogado, Buenos Aires ...... KO 7
1978
Apr. 21—Gerard Nosley, Genova .... W 8
May   6—Joe Barrientes, Lido di Camaiore .... W 8
Dec.   2—Bobby Watts, Marsais .... L 8
1979
Mar. 31—Torito Melendez, Hermosillo .... W 10
Apr. 27—Abel Torres, Hermosillo .... KO 5
June 30—Marvin Hagler, Monte Carlo .... KO by 8
Oct.   5—Francisco Marquez, Hermosillo .... NC 9

SERGIO CABRERA
Mexican Lightweight
(Previous Record Unavailable)
1980
May 21—Memo Miranda, Mexico city .... KO by 7
July 12—Benny Abarca, Mexico City .... L 10

HECTOR CACERES
Argentine Junior Welterweight
1980
Jan. 11—Ricardo Magallanes, Pergamino .... L 10
Feb. 22—Horacio Saldano, S. Sal. de Jujuy .... L 10
Mar. 21—Enrique Coronel, S. Sal. de Jujuy .... L 10
Apr.   5—Jorge Medina, Buenos Aires .... L 10
May   2—Pablo Ferreyra, Mar del Plata .... LF 10
June   5—Carlos Nacimiento, Posadas .... L 10
June 19—Miguel A. Garcia, Bahia Blanca .... L 10
Oct. 24—Ramon Peralta, Rio Tercero .... L 10
Nov. 21—Miguel Fernandez, Rio Grande .... L 10
Dec.   5—Omar Ochoa, Tartagal .... L 10
Dec. 19—Mario Guilloti, Zarate .... L 10

JESUS CAICEDO
Colombian Bantamweight
1979
Aug.   4—Ernesto Gonzales, Chicago .... KO 3
1980
Mar.   2—Larry Turner, Detroit .... KO 1
Sept. 20—Jose L. Valiente, San Juan .... KO 2

LEROY CALDWELL
Milwaukee, Wisc. Heavyweight
1977
June   7—Bob Yarborough, Milwaukee .... W 10
1978
Apr. 18—Earl McLeay, Winnipeg .... W 6
June 20—Paul Nielsen, Winnipeg .... W 10
Oct.   3—Harold Carter, Winnipeg .... KO 8
Nov.   7—Johnny Mac, Waukesha .... W 8
Dec.   5—Eric Sedillo, Winnipeg .... L 8
1979
Jan. 16—Eddie Brooks, Milwaukee .... D 12
June 14—Trevor Berbick, Winnipeg .... D 10
July 11—Yaqui Meneses, Las Vegas .... KO 3
July 18—Pinklon Thomas, Las Vegas .... KO by 10
Aug. 22—Randy Mack, Las Vegas .... L 10
Sept. 27—Mircea Simon, Los Angeles .... W 10
Oct. 30—Willie Shannon, Las Vegas .... L 10
1980
Jan. 13—Kevin Isaac, Las Vegas .... D 10
Mar.   8—Stan Ward, Las Vegas .... L 10
July   9—Earl Tripp, Las Vegas .... L 10
Dec.   3—Randy Mack, Las Vegas .... W 10

BRUCE CALLOWAY
New Orleans, La. Middleweight
1980
July 15—Sam Wilson, New Orleans .... KO 2
Aug.   9—Tony Franklin, Lake Charles .... W 6
Sept. 23—Tyler Dupuy, New Orleans .... KO 2
Nov. 25—Mark Holmes, New Orleans .... KO by 5

OSVALDO CALVO
Argentine Featherweight
1980
Aug.   8—Hector Rodriguez, Villa Mercedes .... L 6
Oct. 31—Raul Inquin, La Plata .... L 6
Dec.   5—Carlos Olivera, Mar del Plata .... KO by 2

HECTOR CAMACHO
New York, N.Y. Featherweight
1980
Sept. 12—David Brown, New York ....W 4
Dec. 12—Benny Llanos, New York ....KO 1

MARCELO CAMACHO
Fresno, Calif. Junior Featherweight
1980
Feb. 5—Augie Serros, San Jose ....W 6
Apr. 14—Jose Torres, Fresno ....L 5
July 16—Cristobal Gutierrez, Stockton ....KO 2
Aug. 19—Bernie Mack, Stockton ....W 6
Oct. 16—Eleazar Ramos, Stockton ....KO 3

MARVIN CAMEL
Missoula, Mont. Light Heavyweight
Born: December 24, 1951
1973
Sept. 20—Joe Williams, Butte ....KO 2
1974
Feb. 20—James Jackson, Boise ....KO 4
1975
Jan. 22—George Clark, Las Vegas ....KO 4
Feb. 19—Chico Valdez, Las Vegas ....KO 2
Apr. 2—Jack Johnson, Las Vegas................W 8
Apr. 30—Amado Vasquez, Las Vegas ....KO 3
May 28—Fernando Jones, Las Vegas ....KO 6
Aug. 20—Ronnie Wilson, Las Vegas ....W 10
Sept. 24—Terry Lee, Las Vegas...................KO 8
Nov. 19—Danny Brewer, Las Vegas ....W 10
1976
Jan. 14—Pedro Vega, Stateline ....KO 1
Feb. 18—Don Melcon, Las Vegas................KO 3
Apr. 7—Rafael Gutierrez, Las Vegas ....W 10
May 8—Angel Oquendo, Missoula ....W 10
July 17—Matt Franklin, Stockton................L 10
Aug. 28—John Townsend, Missoula..............W 10
Sept. 25—John Townsend, Spokane ....W 10
Oct. 23—Matt Franklin, Missoula................W 10
Nov. 20—Larry Castaneda, Seattle ....W 10
1977
Jan. 24—Lionel Ford, Las Vegas ....W 10
Feb. 15—Dale Grant, Seattle ....D 10
May 6—Gary Summerhays, Missoula ....W 12
June 28—Danny Brewer, Seattle ....KO by 6
Aug. 29—Ron Wilson, Pablo, Mt.................W 10
Dec. 7—Karl Zurheide, Las Vegas ....KO 7
1978
Feb. 8—King David Smith, Las Vegas ....W 10
Mar. 9—Robert Lloyd, Wichita ....W 10
Apr. 7—Pete McIntyre, Butte, Mt. ....W 10
May 27—Chuck Warfield, St. Ignatius ....KO 5
Aug. 22—Ibar Arrington, Coeur d'Alene ....W 10
Sept. 12—Dale Grant, Butte ....W 12
Nov. 11—Tom Bethea, Missoula ....KO 2
1979
Jan. 3—Robert Heflin, Las Vegas ....KO 2
Feb. 22—Jim Ingram, Las Vegas ....KO 9
Apr. 24—David Smith, Missoula ....KO 3
June 6—Bill Sharkey, Missoula ....W 12
Aug. 1—Macka Foley, Las Vegas ....KO 2
Aug. 30—David Cabrera, McAllen ....KO 3
Dec. 8—Mate Parlov, Yugoslavia ....D 15
(For Vacant WBC Cruiserweight Title)
1980
Mar. 31—Mate Parlov, Las Vegas ....W 15
(Won Vacant WBC Cruiserweight Title)
Nov. 25—Carlos DeLeon, New Orleans ....L 15
(Lost WBC Cruiserweight Title)

BYRON CAMPBELL
Reno, Nev. Light Heavyweight
1978
May 30—Len Lawson, Incline Village ....KO by 1
1979
Mar. 10—Pascual Ramirez, Carson City ....W 4
Oct. 2—Pete Garcia, Reno ....D 4
Nov. 6—Leslie Robinson, Sparks ....W 6
1980
May 29—Carl Hess, Las Vegas ....D 6
July 15—Paddy Wilson, Reno ....W 10
Aug. 28—Bashiru Ali, San Carlos ....KO by 5

CHARLES CAMPBELL
Staten Island, N.Y. Heavyweight
1980
Mar. 7—Dennis Reilly, Staten Island ....W 4
Apr. 16—Paul Telesca, White Plains ....W 4

DANNY CAMPBELL
Kansas City, Mo. Welterweight
1979
Jan. 19—Bobby Orr, Overland Park ....W 4
Mar. 16—Steve Pruitt, Kansas City ....KO 1
July 26—Clyde Spencer, Overland Park ....KO 2
Aug. 16—Larry Puchta, Kansas City ....KO 1
Oct. 11—Charlie Peterson, Kansas City ....KO by 3
1980
June 6—Nick Miller, Kansas City ....KO 2
Aug. 1—Jesus Delgado, Las Vegas ....KO 4

EDDIE CAMPBELL
Brooklyn, N.Y. Junior Welterweight
1977
Jan. 7—Ben Camacho, New York ....KO 2
Jan. 21—Mike Thomas, New York ....W 4
Feb. 27—Marvin Jenkins, New York ....L 6
Mar. 11—Eddie Piton, New York ....KO 2
Apr. 19—Marco Harrez, White Plains ....L 6
May 5—Mike Thomas, Albany ....KO 3
June 24—Curtis Smith, Nanuet ....W 6
July 14—Willie Thompson, Dover ....KO 2
Sept. 8—Julio Cheualier, New York ....W 6
Oct. 27—Rufus Miller, New York ....L 4
1978
Feb. 27—Marvin Jenkins, New York ....L 6
Apr. 21—Benji Goldstone, Albany ....L 8
June 14—Don Johnson, White Plains ....W 6
Sept. 17—Chris Clarke, Sydney ....L 10
Nov. 1—Jesse Rogers, Westchester ....KO 2
1979
May 11—Julio Garcia, New York ....L 8
Nov. 24—Victor Mangual, Staten Island ....KO 6
1980
Feb. 9—Jo Kimpuani, Dunkirk ....KO by 2
May 23—Marlon Starling, Hartford ....L 8
June 27—Domingo Ayala, New York ....KO by 3

ALFREDO CAMPOS
Argentine Middleweight
1980
Feb. 2—Miguel Garcia, Monte Hermoso ....L 10
Mar. 7—Ramon Peralta, Rio III ....L 10
June 14—Pablo Ferreyra, Balcarce ....L 10
July 4—Tito Yanni, Mar del Plata ....L 10

JOSE CANCECO
Argentine Junior Welterweight
1980
Sept. 13—Jose Molina, Buenos Aires ....TW 3
Sept. 26—Juan Beron, La Plata ....KO by 1

PAULINO CANCHE
Mexican Bantamweight
(Previous Record Unavailable)
1980
Jan. 30—Austreberto "Beto" Perez, Merida ....D 10
Mar. 19—Jose (Shibata) Ruiz, Merida ....KO 8
Apr. 22—Jorge Avante, Villahermosa ....KO 5
June 14—Jorge Zarate, Merida ....KO 7
Oct. 11—Norberto Cabrera, Mexico city ....L 12
(Mexican Bantamweight Title)

FELIPE CANELA
Colton, Calif. Junior Welterweight
1980
Feb. 8—Willie Hall, San Bernardino ....KO 5
Feb. 22—Eric Bonilla, San Bernardino ....W 6
Mar. 7—Eric Bonilla, San Bernardino ....TD 6
May 2—Memo Arreola, San Bernardino ....KO 6
May 30—Eric Bonilla, San Bernardino ....KO 5
June 13—Alfredo Carranza, San Bernardino ......KO 7
July 1—Henry Gill, San Bernardino ....KO 5
Nov. 6—Petrolino Velasquez, Los Angeles ....KO 5

ARTURO (MANNY) CANO
Mexican Bantamweight
1980
Feb. 6—Guillermo Vallejo, Mexico City ......KO by 1
June 4—Paco (Gavilan) Ramos, Mexico City .....KO 2

RANULFO CANO
Mexican Flyweight
(Previous Record Unavailable)
1980
Jan. 30—Jose Esteban Quijano, Merida ....W 10
Apr. 26—Diego Franco, Merida ....L TD 7
(Junior Flyweight Title of Yucatan State)

MARTY CAPASSO
Aston Township, Pa. Heavyweight
1978
June	1—Roy Jones, Upper Darby	KO	1
June	19—Tyrone Harlee, Philadelphia	W	4
Sept.	27—Raquib Muhammad, Philadelphia	KO	1
Nov.	21—Vernon Coats, Upper Darby	W	4

1979
Feb.	21—Tyrone Harlee, Scranton	KO	6
Mar.	30—Johnny Warr, Scranton	W	8
Apr.	25—Jerry Foley, Scranton	KO	3
July	16—Jerry Thompkins, Philadelphia	W	8
Dec.	12—Serge Rodriguez, Scranton	KO	1

1980
May	16—Charlie Baltimore, Chester	KO	2
May	28—Ali Allen, Scranton	W	8
Oct.	29—Mike Boswell, Scranton	W	6

WAYNE CAPLETTE
Winnipeg, Canada Middleweight
1977
	—Terry Jesmer, Winnipeg	KO	3

1978
Apr.	18—Curt Yancy, Winnipeg	KO	2
June	20—Tommy Farrell, Winnipeg	KO	2
Oct.	3—Chuck Durham, Winnipeg	KO	3

1979
Feb.	9—Terry Jesmer, Winnipeg	KO	2
Mar.	16—Jimmy Hearn, St. Paul	KO	5
Apr.	20—Eddie Straight, Winnipeg	W	6
June	14—C. J. Brown, Winnipeg	W	8
Oct.	9—Harlan Holden, Winnipeg	KO	4
Oct.	27—Dave Simmonds, Regina	W	6
Dec.	8—Larry Ward, Winnipeg	KO	5

1980
Mar.	17—Steve Tohill, Edmonton	KO	4
July	25—Dave Reynolds, Winnipeg	KO	2
Nov.	11—Doug Demmings, Winnipeg	KO	8
Dec.	9—Eddie Melo, Montreal	L	8

DAVID CAPO
New York, N.Y. Featherweight
1978
Dec.	15—Juan LaPorte, New York	L	8

1979
Apr.	20—Leo Randolph, New York	W	8
Oct.	4—Jose Nieto, New York	L	8

1980
Feb.	29—Alberto Collazo, Commack	D	8
Apr.	18—Juan LaPorte, New York	L	10
June	2—Jesus Esparragoza, New York	W	8
Oct.	4—Nelson Azuma, Accra	L	10

JOHN CAPOBIANCO
Huntington, N.Y. Light Heavyweight
1973
July	9—Percy Halsey, New York	KO	1
Aug.	14—Paul Osborne, New Bedford	W	4
Oct.	15—Segundo Ochoa, New York	W	4
Oct.	26—Renaldo Oliviera, Brockton	W	4

1974
Jan.	14—Charles Stevens, New York	L	4
May	8—Julio Perez, New York	W	4

1975
Mar.	8—Barry Hill, Commack	W	6
May	23—John Molander, Commack	KO	6

1976
Jan.	24—Otis Gordon, New York	KO	5
Feb.	25—D.C. Walker, New York	W	6
Mar.	31—Carlos Novotny, Uniondale	W	6
Aug.	27—Dave Dittmar, Hempstead	W	10
Dec.	2—Otis Gordon, New York	KO by	8

1977
May	6—Segundo Ochoa, Commack	KO	1
June	18—Otis Gordon, Commack	KO	4
Aug.	27—Dave Dittmar, Hempstead	W	10

1978
Feb.	17—Mose Robinson, Commack	W	10
Oct.	14—Barry Hill, Commack	W	10

1979
Jan.	26—John Gallagher, New York	W	8
May	11—Bobby Cassidy, Commack	L	10
Oct.	12—Richie Kates, Uniondale	L	10

1980
Apr.	25—Reynaldo Oliveira, Commack	KO	7

PHIL CAPOBIANCO
Huntington, N.Y. Light Heavyweight
1979
May	11—Alvin Bracy, Commack	KO	1
Aug.	3—Jack Flowers, Hempstead, L.I.	KO	1
Aug.	31—James Anthony, Shirley	KO	1
Nov.	9—Jose Serrano, New York	W	4

1980
Apr.	18—Charles Hecker, New York	L	6
Aug.	15—Walter Driscoll, Glen Cove	KO	1

RAFAEL CAPRISIRO
Los Angeles, Calif. Lightweight
1980
Feb.	13—Francisco Rodriguez, Las Vegas	W	4
Mar.	3—Alonso Gonzales, Bakersfield	L	6
Mar.	26—Jose Torres, Las Vegas	L	6
May	16—Augustin Serros, San Jose	KO by	1
Dec.	16—Franco Gonzales, Los Angeles	W	6

LUKE CAPUANO
Chicago, Ill. Light Heavyweight
1978
Sept.	9—Bill Jackson, Chicago	KO	1
Sept.	27—Carl Halliburton, Chicago	KO	1
Oct.	25—Lamuel Moore, Chicago	KO	1
Nov.	18—Earl McLean, DePaul	KO	3
Dec.	15—Boom Boom Moorer, Chicago	W	6

1979
Feb.	2—Troy Bolden, Chicago	KO	1
Mar.	31—Baker Tinsley, Chicago	KO	3
Apr.	27—Bill Jackson, Chicago	KO	1
May	9—Juan de la Garza, Chicago	KO	2
June	18—George Aidoo, Highland Park	KO	5
July	20—Henry Sims, U. of Ill.	KO	6
July	30—Jose Gutierrez, Chicago	KO	3
Aug.	4—Obbie Garnett, Chicago	KO	1
Sept.	7—Don Kiser, Chicago	KO	1

1980
Feb.	24—Lee Royster, Atlantic City	L	8
Mar.	16—Lee Burkey, Las Vegas	L	8
Apr.	14—Adolph Rivas, Chicago	KO	2
May	9—Juan DeLa Garza, Chicago	KO	2
July	11—Jimmy Hearn, Chicago	KO	3
Aug.	14—Phil Wade, Chicago	KO	2
Sept.	10—George Goforth, Chicago	KO	1
Oct.	9—Don Masterson, Chicago	KO	2
Nov.	13—Mike Rossman, Chicago	L	10

BILLY CARABELLO
Paterson, N.J. Middleweight
1980
Jan.	8—Tom Merola, Totowa	L	4
Apr.	1—Tom Merola, Totowa	L	6

PAT CARDENAS
California Junior Featherweight
1980
Jan.	31—Sergio Castro, Los Angeles	L	6
Feb.	14—Len Jones, Los Angeles	W	4
June	26—Daniel Cruz, Los Angeles	KO by	2
Aug.	6—Francisco Reyes, Santa Monica	KO	1

RICARDO CARDENAS
Mexican Featherweight
1980
Jan.	18—Manuel Ruelas, El Paso	KO by	1
Mar.	7—Raul Ramirez, El Paso	KO by	5

PRUDENCIO CARDONA
Colombian Flyweight
Born: Dec. 22, 1951, San Basilio de Palenque
1973
Nov.	2—Luis Ramos, Barranquilla	W	4
Nov.	24—Humberto Ortega, Barranquilla	KO	4

1974
Jan.	18—Nestor Herrera, Barranquilla	W	6
May	10—Eliseo Padilla, Barranquilla	KO	1
June	13—Pedro Bendek, Barranquilla	KO	2
July	5—Roberto Lopez, Barranquilla	KO	7
Aug.	17—Abdon Peralta, Barranquilla	KO	1
Sept.	29—Henry Diaz, Cartagena	L	8
Nov.	23—Ben Villarreal, Bogota	KO	2

1975
Apr.	30—Nelson Vergaro, Barranquilla	KO	3
May	30—Calixto Perez, Cartagena	L	10
Aug.	9—Reyes Arnal, Caracas	KO	5
Sept.	5—Ricardo Estupinan, Barranquilla	KO	1
Oct.	4—Rogelio Minnott, Barranquilla	KO	5
Oct.	31—Enrique Torres, Barranquilla	W	10

1976
Mar.	26—Eduardo Oaraoan, Barranquilla	KO	5
Nov.	13—Henry Diaz, Cartagena	W	10

1977
Feb.	18—Nestor Jiminez, Cartagena	L	10
Mar.	12—Betulio Gonzalez, Maracaibo	KO by	3
Sept.	1—Justo Jorge, Barranquilla	KO	2
Oct.	20—Benjamin Villarreal, Barranquilla	KO	
Dec.	3—Pablito Jiminez, Barranquilla	W	10

1978

Mar. 10—Alfonso Lopez, Cartagena .... W 10
June 30—Luis Ibarra, Barranquilla .... W 10
Nov. 5—Jesus Caicedo, Maracay .... W 10

1979

Feb. 17—Luis Ibarra, Colon .... L 10
May 15—Sung-Hoon Lee, Seoul .... L 10
Dec. 15—Hector Patri, Barranquilla .... KO 8

1980

Nov. 14—Steve Whetstone, Miami .... KO 1
Dec. 13—Orlando Maldonado, Miami .... KO 7

ALBERTO CARDOZAO
Argentine Light Heavyweight
1980

Jan. 18—Cesar Duarte, S. Sal. de Jujuy .... KO by 8
Mar. 14—Cesar Duarte, S. Sal. de Jujuy .... KO by 7

ENRIQUE CARDOZO
Argentine Middleweight
1980

May 23—Ruben Wilberger, La Pampa .... KO by 8
Aug. 15—Hugo Rossi, La Plata .... KO by 7

ALDO CARMONA
Argentine Middleweight
1980

Feb. 12—Ruben Pardo, S. Sal. de Jujuy .... D 10
Apr. 11—Marcos Perez, Gral Alvear .... W 10
Apr. 24—Jose M. F. Burlon, Pergamino .... L 8
June 27—Juan D. Roldan, Salta .... KO by 3

CANDELARIO (CHANGUITO) CARMONA
Mexican Flyweight
1980

Feb. 8—Esteban Perez, Acapulco .... W 8
May 2—Rafael Morales, Acapulco .... W 8
July 11—Prospero (Popeye) Mendoza, Acapulco ... KO 6

ANGEL ANTONIO CARO
Argentine Middleweight
1980

Jan. 18—Hector Altamirano, P.R.S. Pena .... KO 4
Mar. 28—Irinio Cabrera, Villa Angela .... W 10
May 2—Roberto Marziali, P.R.S. Pena .... KO 4
May 16—Hugo Trujillo, P.R.S. Pena .... W 10
May 30—Marcelo Diaz, P.R.S. Pena .... W 10
July 25—Hugo Salega, P.R.S. Pena .... W 10
Sept. 6—Marcelo Diaz, P.R.S. Pena .... L 10
Oct. 31—Natalio Ibarra, P.R.S. Pena .... KO 9

OSCAR CARO
Argentine Light Heavyweight
1980

Mar. 14—Juan Jose Leiva, Tucuman .... W 4
Apr. 3—Juan Jose Leiva, Tucuman .... W 10

CLARENCE (TEE) CARPENTER
Trenton, N.J. Light Heavyweight
1977

Nov. 30—Eugene Green, Newark .... KO by 1

1978

Oct. 20—Robert Coley, Atlantic City .... KO by 3

1979
(Inactive)

1980

Jan. 8—Mike Fisher, Totowa .... KO by 3
Feb. 19—Mike Fisher, Totowa .... KO by 2

KEN CARPENTER
Upper Darby, Pa. Featherweight
1978

Apr. 28—Tony Still, Upper Darby .... W 4

1979

Jan. 30—Pete Torres, Upper Darby .... L 4
Mar. 30—Pedro Lebron, Scranton .... D 4
May 22—Heriberto Torres, Upper Darby .... KO 1
Aug. 21—Pedro Lebron, Atlantic City .... L 4
Sept. 11—Pedro Lebron, Philadelphia .... KO 6
Oct. 18—Jonathan Cook, Philadelphia .... KO 1
Oct. 27—Jerome Robinson, Rahway .... KO 3

1980

Jan. 24—Tim Daniels, Upper Darby .... KO 4
Feb. 11—Pedron Lebron, Upper Darby ...... KO by 2
Mar. 29—Confesor Rosales, Atlantic City ...... KO 1
May 4—Confesor Rosales, Atlantic City .... KO 5
July 3—Bobby Ingram, Atlantic City .... L 8
Nov. 6—Mike Frazier, Atlantic City .... KO by 3

DAVID CARR
Louisville, Ky. Heavyweight
1979

June 1—Jimmy Robertson, Louisville .... W 4

1980

Apr. 5—Conroy Nelson, Louisville .... W 4
May 16—Wilbert Johnson, Lexington .... KO by 4

JUAN CARRANZA
Argentine Featherweight
1980

Apr. 5—Pedro Arm. Gutierrez, Mar del Plata KO by 9
Sept. 13—Pedro Arm. Gutierrez, Gral Cabrera ...... L 10

MIKE CARRERE
Honolulu, Hawaii Junior Middleweight
1980

Apr. 8—Duane Molina, Honolulu .... KO 3
May 27—Rafael Zamora, Honolulu .... KO 1
June 24—Harold Neveau, Honolulu .... W 4
Sept. 16—Jose Rivera, Honolulu .... KO 3
Dec. 9—Edric Kerr, Honolulu .... KO 2

HUGO CARRIEGO
Argentine Middleweight
1980

May 23—Luis Lopez, Zarate .... L 8
Aug. 9—Ramon Arguello, Gral Pico .... L 6
Sept. 5—Miguel Maldonado, Mar del Plata .... L 6

AL (EARTHQUAKE) CARTER
Akron, Ohio Lightweight
1977

July 16—Gary Smith, Louisville .... KO 4
Aug. 12—Otto Palfy, Barberton .... KO 1
Oct. 15—George Adams, Salem .... KO 1
Nov. 26—Forest Winchester, Columbus .... KO by 5
Dec. 29—Willie Rankin, Pittsburgh .... KO 3

1978

Apr. 17—Jerry Strickland, Columbus .... KO 2
May 20—Earl Caldwell, Salem .... KO 1
Aug. 3—Eddie Murray, Detroit .... KO 6
Oct. 21—Chuck Spicer, Alliance .... KO 3
Nov. 29—Harvey Wilson, Richfield .... KO 4
Dec. 16—Ernest Payne, Alliance .... KO 3

1979

Jan. 10—Sid Blake, Richfield .... KO 3
Mar. 21—Hilbert Stevenson, Richfield .... KO 3
Apr. 27—Eddie Thomas, Dayton .... KO 1
July 6—Bobby Bath, Dayton .... KO 2
Oct. 20—Danny Daniels, Cincinnati .... KO 1
Nov. 16—Freddie Harris, Kansas City .... KO 7

1980

May 3—Calvin Slaughter, Canton .... KO 4
Nov. 1—Johnny Copeland, Dayton .... KO 4
Nov. 22—Ray Carrington, Cincinnati .... KO 2

JOHNNY CARTER
Philadelphia, Pa. Bantamweight
1977

June 15—Wayne King, Philadelphia .... W 4

1978

Jan. 24—Johnny Glover, Philadelphia .... W 6
Apr. 19—Angel Marrero, Allentown .... W 4
Nov. 4—Tony Hernandez, Atlantic City .... KO 5

1979

Jan. 31—Candy Iglecias, Las Vegas .... W 10
Mar. 28—Mario Chavez, Las Vegas .... W 10
May 16—Jose Villegas, Las Vegas .... W 10
July 17—Pedro LeBron, Atlantic City .... KO 10
Sept. 26—Pablo Lopez, Las Vegas .... KO 4
Oct. 17—Armando Ugalde, Las Vegas .... KO 2
Nov. 7—Juan Romero, Las Vegas .... W 10
Dec. 12—Pedro F. Lopez, Las Vegas .... KO 4

1980

Jan. 23—Mike Stuart, Las Vegas .... KO 9
(Won Nevada State Bantamweight Title)
Feb. 26—Ardon Peralta, Las Vegas .... KO 3
Mar. 26—Juan Garcia, Las Vegas .... W 10
June 19—Pedro Gonzalez, Tucson .... KO 4
June 25—Augo Partita, Las Vegas .... KO 3
Oct. 22—Sergio Castro, Las Vegas .... L 10
Dec. 5—Mark Pacheco, Las Vegas .... KO 6
(Won U.S. Bantamweight Title)

MARIO CASAS
Bantamweight
1979

Nov. 2—Lenny Jones, San Diego .... KO by 2

1980

June 26—Robert Anderson, Las Vegas .... KO by 2
Aug. 15—Ron Cisneros, Denver .... KO by 3

60

DOMINGO CASCO
Argentine Featherweight
1980
Feb. 9—Omar Mendoza, P.R.S. Pena .... KO 5
Mar. 14—Hipolito Nunez, P.R.S. Pena .... L 10

GEORGE CASHER
Hollis, N.Y. Welterweight
1979
Aug. 3—Tony Hedgemon, Hempstead .... KO 3
Aug. 31—Alphonso Belford, Shirley, L.I. .... L 4
Oct. 3—Papo Figueroa, Brooklyn .... D 4
Oct. 26—Billy Costello, New York .... L 4
1980
Jan. 19—Pat Brennan, Hempstead .... KO 1
Mar. 21—Fred Figueroa, New York .... L 6
May 2—Tony Santana, New York .... KO by 4

BOBBY CASSIDY
Levittown, N.Y. Light Heavyweight
Born: April 19, 1944, Levittown, N.Y.
1963
Mar. 19—Bobby Noble, New York .... KO 1
Apr. 20—Joe Falu, New York .... W 4
June 2—Al Sewell, New York .... W 4
June 18—James Jolly, New York .... KO 2
July 16—Al Sewell, New York .... KO 1
Aug. 13—Jesus Coma, New York .... W 4
Aug. 24—Danny Andrews, New York .... W 4
Sept. 24—Domingo Ortiz, New York............ W 4
Oct. 8—Domingo Ortiz, New York............... W 6
Oct. 25—Al Sewell, New York .... W 4
Nov. 26—Felix Santiago, New York .... W 6
Dec. 17—Felix Santiago, New York.............. W 6
1964
Feb. 4—Frankie Olivera, New York .... W 6
Feb. 28—Gil Diaz, New York .... D 8
Mar. 24—Johnny Torres, New York............. KO 4
May 15—Jesus Coma, New York .... KO 6
July 24—Tommy Saint, New York .... W 6
Oct. 6—Billy Collins, New York .... L 8
Nov. 24—Tommy Haynes, New York .... KO 8
Dec. 11—Frankie Olivera, New York .... KO 5
1965
Mar. 16—Ossie Marcano, New York .... L 8
June 7—Gil Diaz, New York .... W 10
Aug. 25—Isaac Logart, New York .... KO 4
Oct. 21—Bobby Bartels, New York .... KO 6
1966
Jan. 7—Pete Toro, New York .... KO by 2
Feb. 8—Danny Garcia, New York .... KO 3
Mar. 18—Pete Toro, New York .... L 10
June 22—Vince Martinez, Freeport .... W 8
Sept. 26—Clyde Taylor, Walpole .... W 8
Nov. 2—Celedonio Lima, New York.............. W 8
Nov. 29—Gordon Lott, Miami Beach .... W 10
1967
Jan. 6—Johnny Wood, Johannesburg........... L 10
Mar. 31—Carmelio Hernandez, New York .... W 10
Apr. 28—Bo Hogberg, Stockholm .... D 10
Oct. 11—Danny Perez, New York .... L 10
Oct. 30—Joe Harris, Philadelphia................ L 10
Dec. 26—Linnes Johnson, Miami Beach.......... W 10
1968
Apr. 5—Sandro Mazzinghi, Rome............ KO by 2
1969
May 23—Al Benoit, Worcester.................. L 10
July 30—Sonny Moore, Scranton .... KO 2
Sept. 24—Bob Bailey, Scranton .... KO 7
Oct. 13—Santiago Fernandez, New York .... KO 1
1970
Mar. 16—Bob Warthem, New York .... W 10
May 27—Bob Harrington, Scranton.............. KO 2
June 22—Sonny Floyd, Freeport, L.I.............. KO 1
July 16—Freddy Martinovick, Scranton .... W 8
Aug. 17—Luis Vinales, Freeport, L.I............... L 10
Oct. 13—Johnny Burnside, New York .... KO 5
Oct. 29—Carter Williams, Scranton .... KO 1
1971
Jan. 26—Luis Rodriguez, Miami Beach........... L 10
Mar. 30—Paul Kasper, Miami Beach............. ND 4
Apr. 26—Don Fullmer, New York .... W 10
Aug. 9—Rodrigo Valdez, New York .... KO by 6
1972
Mar. 1—Joe Jones, New York .... KO 6
Apr. 11—Gil Diaz, New York .... W 10
May 24—Jose Gonzalez, New York .... KO by 8
Oct. 20—Tom Bethea, New York .... W 10
1973
Mar. 21—Jimmy Dupree, Scranton .... D 10
May 2—Tommy Hicks, Scranton .... KO 9
June 20—Jimmy Dupree, Scranton .... L 10
Sept. 17—Jimmy Dupree, New York............ W 10

1974
Jan. 28—Jorge Ahumada, New York .... KO by 3
July 19—Juan Aguilar, New York................ KO 1
Nov. 13—Randy Stevens, Scranton .... KO 5
1975
Mar. 8—John Gerowski, Commack .... KO 4
Mar. 24—Karl Zurheide, Cleveland .... W 8
May 30—Reuben Figueroa, Commack .... KO 4
Sept. 30—Macka Foley, Uniondale .... W 10
Nov. 5—Luis Vinales, New York .... W 10
1976
Apr. 14—Dennis Cochrane, New York .... KO 3
May 22—Ramon Ronquillo, Erie .... KO by 10
Nov. 24—Ramon Ronquillo, New York.......... W 10
1977
Jan. 16—Willie Taylor, Pensacola .... W 8
(U.S. Championship Tournament)
June 18—Christy Elliott, Commack .... W 10
1978
Feb. 17—Dave Horne, Commack .... KO 1
Mar. 17—Ramon Ronquillo, Las Vegas .... W 10
1979
May 11—John Capobianco, Commack .... W 10
June 29—Dan Kaiser, Commack .... KO 2
1980
Jan. 19—Kid Samson, Hempstead .... KO 6

ROBERTO CASTANEDA
Hartford, Conn. Junior Welterweight
1980
Jan. 20—Jean LaPointe, Quebec City .... KO by 1
Feb. 5—Papo Figueroa, West Hartford .... KO by 1

ROGELIO CASTANEDA
Los Angeles, Calif. Lightweight
1975
Apr. 16—Nick Alfaro, Las Vegas .... W 10
May 17—Javier Muniz, Los Angeles............. D 8
June 12—Edwin Viruet, Los Angeles .... L 10
Aug. 29—Pete Vital, Las Vegas .... W 6
Oct. 16—Nacho Castaneda, Los Angeles .... W 10
1976
May 8—Julio Gomez, Los Angeles.............. W 10
June 18—Ray Lunny, Redwood City .... L 10
Aug. 31—Ben Villaflor, Honolulu .... L 10
Oct. 29—Juan Garcia, Los Angeles.............. W 10
1977
May 20—Victor De La Cruz, San Diego .... KO 4
June 10—Ricardo Arredondo, San Diego .... W 10
Oct. 25—Jorge Morales, Las Vegas .... W 10
1978
Jan. 23—Johnny Lira, Las Vegas .... L 10
Apr. 24—Jorge Morales, Las Vegas .... W 10
June 3—Alfredo Escalera, San Juan .... L 10
1979
Jan. 28—Jorge Morales, Reno .... L 10
Feb. 14—Horace Shufford, Las Vegas .... KO by 8
Apr. 11—Miguel Estrada, Las Vegas .... W 10
Apr. 26—Herron Rivera, Pico Rivera .... L 10
May 12—Ruby Ortiz, Las Vegas .... L 10
Nov. 14—Frankie Moultrie, Las Vegas .... L 10
1980
Mar. 7—Herman Montes, San Bernardino .... KO by 3
June 10—Frank Newton, Oklahoma City ...... KO by 6
July 22—Mark Ibanez, Honolulu .... KO by 2
Sept. 24—Armando Ramirez, Las Vegas ...... KO by 5

NORBERTO CASTELLANO
San Antonio, Texas Flyweight
1979
Oct. 30—Jose Luis Garcia, San Antonio .... KO 1
1980
Jan. 23—Mark Pacheco, Las Vegas .... L 10
June 17—Armando Loredo, San Antonio .... KO 1
Aug. 13—Jose Salas, San Antonio .... KO 4

JUAN CASTELLANOS
Texas Flyweight
1979
Feb. 20—Cecilio Cabrera, McAllen .... KO 2
Apr. 6—Jose Martinez, McAllen .... KO 6
July 12—Javier de la Rosa, Serda .... W 8
Aug. 24—Felipe Morales Martinez, McAllen ...... KO 7
1980
Dec. 2—Humberto Rodriguez, Houston .... L 10

ALBERTO CASTILLO
Argentine Lightweight
1980
Mar. 7—Pedro Burki, Ordonez .... L 8
June 13—Omar Gonzalez, Rio III .... W 10
Aug. 8—Eduardo Acosta, San Juan .... L 10
Sept. 6—Omar Gonzalez, Rio III .... D 10

61

FELIX CASTILLO
San Antonio, Texas Flyweight
1980
May	20—Jose Salas, San Antonio	KO	4
June	17—Joel Laredo, San Antonio	W	6
Aug.	12—Rosalio Guillen, San Antonio	KO	1
Nov.	7—Armando Hilario, San Antonio	KO	2
Nov.	20—Tim Daniels, Totowa	W	6

PRISCILIANO (ZIP) CASTILLO
Corpus Christi, Texas Junior Middleweight
1969
July	8—Israel Gomez, Corpus Christi	W	4
Aug.	12—Alvino Lopez, Corpus Christi	KO	4
Sept.	2—Alvino Lopez, Corpus Christi	W	4
Oct.	7—Armando Carillo, Corpus Christi	KO	4
Dec.	9—Lorenzo Trujillo, San Antonio	L	6

1970
May	10—Alfredo de la Rosa, Monterrey	W	10
July	17—Tony Reyes, Rio Bravo	KO	7
Sept.	9—Jose Martinez, Reynosa	KO	2

1971
July	20—Mike Ramirez, San Antonio	D	6
Nov.	30—Masataka Takayama, Honolulu	KO by	2

1972
Jan.	14—Mike Ramirez, San Antonio	L	6
Feb.	22—Lorenzo Ortiz, San Antonio	L	6
June	20—Luis Rodriguez, Corpus Christi	KO	6
July	18—Eddie Mitchell, Corpus Christi	KO	3
Sept.	12—Paul Garcia, Corpus Christi	KO by	5

1973
Sept.	18—Victor Rodriguez, Corpus Christi	W	6
Oct.	9—Abraham Ramirez, Corpus Christi	KO	6

1974
Apr.	4—Jaibo Lopez, Houston	KO by	6

1975
Jan.	13—Rogelio Flores, Corpus Christi	KO	6
Feb.	3—Eddie Mitchell, Corpus Christi	KO	2
Feb.	17—Danny Donatto, Corpus Christi	W	8
Mar.	21—Ike Fluellen, Jacinto City	W	8
July	21—Ray Sepulveda, Corpus Christi	W	10
Aug.	19—Oscar Balderas, Corpus Christi	KO	4
Sept.	16—Gilbert Galvan, Galveston	W	12
Nov.	21—Jean Piedvache, Paris	L	10

1976
Apr.	20—Rocky Ramon, Corpus Christi	KO by	8
Aug.	31—Oscar Balderas, Corpus Christi	KO by	2

1977
Mar.	22—Philip Sotello, Corpus Christi	KO	3
Mar.	25—Robert Vasquez, San Antonio	KO by	6
June	14—Jesse Lara, Houston	L	10
Aug.	2—Sultan Saladin, Corpus Christi	W	10

1978
Apr.	15—Zurdo Rojas, Monclova	W	10
June	10—Patalion Gonzales, Sabinas	W	10
Aug.	19—Leonides Palacios, Rio Bravo	W	10

1979
Feb.	13—Danny Donatto, Corpus Christi	KO by	4
Mar.	8—Fighting Jim, Rotterdam	KO by	3
Apr.	27—Marijan Benes, Belgrade	KO by	1
Nov.	6—Jessie Lara, Corpus Christi	KO	8

1980
May	9—Clint Jackson, Nashville	KO by	3
June	17—Tony Ayala, San Antonio	KO by	1

RUBEN CASTILLO
Tucson, Ariz. Featherweight
Born: December 19, 1957
1975
Jan.	24—Frank Ahumada, Tucson	KO	4
Feb.	22—Frank Castro, Tucson	KO	4
Mar.	13—Frank Ahumada, Phoenix	W	6
Mar.	31—Regis Rodriguez, Phoenix	KO	1
Apr.	16—Juan Aguilar, Las Vegas	KO	1
July	31—Manny Castro, Las Vegas	KO	1
Aug.	13—Reuben Aguilar, Las Vegas	KO	4
Aug.	22—Yuma Duran, Tecate	W	6
Sept.	24—Ray Thomas, Las Vegas	W	6
Oct.	10—Ray Thomas, Tucson	W	6
Nov.	12—Regis Rodriguez, Phoenix	KO	1
Nov.	25—Tony Alvarado, Eugene	W	6
Dec.	10—Danny Stennedo, Phoenix	KO	2
Dec.	17—Miguel Menza, Las Vegas	W	6

1976
Jan.	7—Simon Fontune, Phoenix	W	10
Apr.	8—Johnny Jensen, Los Angeles	W	10
May	11—Adrian Luna, Albuquerque	KO	2
May	26—Miguel Meza, Phoenix	W	10
Aug.	6—Roman Contreras, Los Angeles	W	10
Aug.	17—Frank Ahumada, Tucson	W	12
Sept.	1—Artemio Jeronimo, Las Vegas	W	10
Sept.	6—Ramon Contreras, Inglewood	KO	6
Nov.	10—Cookie Valencia, Las Vegas	KO	5

1977
Mar.	6—Kenny Weldon, Marion	W	8
	(U.S. Championship Tournament)		
Apr.	2—Walter Seeley, San Antonio	W	10
	(U.S. Championship Tournament)		
June	22—Alfredo Carranza, Las Vegas	KO	4
July	21—Jose Rodriguez, Las Vegas	KO	7
Aug.	17—Al Torres, Las Vegas	KO	1
Aug.	23—Elias Rodriguez, Las Vegas	W	6
Oct.	15—Miguel Meza, Palm Springs	W	10

1978
June	18—Jesus Reyes, Salt Lake City	W	10
June	26—Jesus Hernandez, Bakersfield	W	10
July	18—Roman Contreras, Pico Rivera	KO	5
Sept.	9—Julio Leal, Bakersfield	KO	8
Oct.	23—Juan Batista, Bakersfield	W	10
Dec.	11—Alex Oregel, Bakersfield	KO	2

1979
Jan.	27—Roberto Perez, Los Angeles	KO	3
Feb.	21—Edel Borunda, Lake Tahoe	W	10
Mar.	11—Warren Matthews, Reno	KO	7
Mar.	28—Tony Sanchez, Stateline	KO	3
Apr.	7—Roberto Quintanilla, Billings	KO	2
June	2—Frank Ahumada, Albuquerque	W	10
June	15—James Martinez, Las Vegas	W	12
July	21—Hector Carrasquillo, Houston	KO	3
Sept.	25—Roberto Torres, Los Angeles	KO	3
Oct.	18—Fel Clemente, Los Angeles	W	10
Nov.	19—Rolando Pastor, Bakersfield	KO	4
Dec.	10—Juan Escobar, Bakersfield	KO	9

1980
Jan.	20—Alexis Arguello, Tucson	KO by	11
	(For WBC Junior Lightweight Title)		
Mar.	3—Edwin Alarcon, Bakersfield	KO	6
Apr.	12—Salvador Sanchez, Tucson	L	15
	(For World Featherweight Title)		
Aug.	19—Roberto Garcia, Las Vegas	KO	6
Oct.	28—Lancelot Innis, Montreal	D	10
Nov.	11—James Martinez, Houston	D	10

JESUS (PECHO) CASTRO
Dominican Rep. Junior Middleweight
1977
Mar.	28—Wally Laso, Santo Domingo	KO	5
June	27—Fermin Guzman, Santo Domingo	L	12
Oct.	3—Fermin Guzman, Santo Domingo	W	12
Nov.	14—Nick Ortiz, Santo Domingo	W disq.	10
Dec.	19—Luis Arias, Santo Domingo	KO	9

1978
Feb.	24—Felix Velazquez, Santo Domingo	KO	1
Apr.	21—Ezequiel Ovando, Santo Domingo	W	10
June	10—Larry Davis, Brooklyn	KO	7
July	5—Rosario Matute, Santo Domingo	KO	1
Oct.	26—Santos Solis, Santo Domingo	KO	8

1979
Jan.	18—Sergio Lozano, New York	KO	4
Feb.	23—Sandy Torres, Santo Domingo	KO	6
Apr.	6—Sandy Torres, Santo Domingo	L	12
July	16—Al Styles Jr., New York	L	8
Dec.	10—Mario Buey Ramos, Romano, D.R.	KO by	3

1980
Apr.	26—Pedro Cisneros, Santo Domingo	KO	12
	(Latin American Junior Middleweight Title)		
June	12—Nicanor Camacho, Monteria	KO by	10
Aug.	29—John LoCicero, New York	KO by	1

MARCOS CASTRO
Tucson, Arizona Welterweight
1980
July	16—William Watson, Las Vegas	W	4
July	24—William Watson, Las Vegas	W	6
Sept.	3—Nestor Pinango, Las Vegas	W	4
Sept.	10—Paul Gonzales, Las Vegas	KO by	3

RAUL CASTRO
Argentine Welterweight
1980
Aug.	8—Miguel Dominguez, Mendoza	KO by	4
Oct.	3—Miguel Dominguez, Gral Alvear	L	10

SERGIO CASTRO
Los Angeles, Calif. Junior Featherweight
1977
Feb.	24—Antonio Adame, Salinas Cruz	KO by	4

1978
(Inactive)
1979
June	7—Ricardo Monzanto, Los Angeles	W	5
June	28—Delfino Cornejo, Los Angeles	W	6
Sept.	6—Desi Newbill, Los Angeles	W	6
Oct.	25—Mike Rodriguez, Los Angeles	W	5
Dec.	13—Bonnie Rodriguez, Los Angeles	KO	1

1980
Jan.	24—Doug Garcia, Los Angeles	KO	2
Jan.	31—Pat Cardenas, Los Angeles	W	6
Feb.	14—Desi Newbill, Los Angeles	KO	5
Feb.	21—Lorenzo Ramirez, Los Angeles	W	10
May	29—Jose Luis Lopez, Los Angeles	KO	2
July	24—Adrian Arreola, Los Angeles	L	6
Oct.	22—Johnny Carter, Las Vegas	W	10

JERRY CELESTINE
New Orleans, La. Light Heavyweight
1969
	—Sam Wilson, New Orleans	L	4
	—Ed Bangs, New Orleans	W	4

1970
	—Mike Wagner, New Orleans	KO	1

1971
	—Coleman, New Orleans	KO	1

1972-1975
(Inactive)
1976
Mar.	8—Nick Jones, New Orleans	KO	1
Apr.	19—Martin Lewis, New Orleans	W	4
Aug.	9—Willie Hicks, New Orleans	KO	1

1977
	—Jap Haynes, Pensacola, Fla.	KO	2
	—James Dixon, Memphis	KO	4
Apr.	19—Frank Bass, Pensacola	KO	4
Apr.	26—Tony McMinn, Memphis	KO	4
Aug.	23—Vonzell Johnson, New Orleans	W	10
Sept.	20—Melvin Mom, New Orleans	KO	5
Oct.	11—Ivy Brown, Memphis	W	10
Dec.	20—Juan De La Garza, New Orleans	KO	6

1978
Jan.	—Ivy Brown, Memphis	W	10
Apr.	18—John Townsend, New Orleans	KO	6
Sept.	15—Marvin Johnson, New Orleans	L	10
Oct.	24—Anthony Jones, New Orleans	KO	3
Dec.	6—Jerry Martin, Philadelphia	L	10

1979
Mar.	15—Mustapha Wassaja, Copenhagen	L	8
Apr.	14—Lonnie Bennett, New Orleans	KO	3
Oct.	27—James Scott, Rahway	L	10

1980
May	13—George Goforth, Memphis	KO	4
July	15—Richie Kates, New Orleans	KO by	3
Sept.	23—Richie Kates, New Orleans	KO	8
Nov.	25—Pablo Ramos, New Orleans	KO	9

HECTOR CENTURION
Argentine Middleweight
1980
Apr.	11—Geronimo Ramirez, Corrientes	L	10
Aug.	8—Emilio Rivera, Corrientes	KO	1
Oct.	10—Gregorio Ramirez, Corrientes	L	8

MARIO CERDA
California Flyweight
1979
June	14—Danny Aguilar, Los Angeles	L	6
Aug.	2—Armando Ugalde, Los Angeles	W	5

1980
Feb.	19—Mark Pacheco, Sparks	L	10
Mar.	6—Danny Aguilar, Los Angeles	D	6

TONY CERDA
Los Angeles, Calif. Junior Middleweight
1979
May	24—Rodney Harvey, Los Angeles	KO	2
June	14—Jorge Fernandez, Los Angeles	W	6
July	19—Mike Rundell, Los Angeles	KO	4
Sept.	20—Danny Adams, Los Angeles	W	6
Oct.	25—Gambino Rivera, Los Angeles	KO	3
Nov.	15—John Steve, Los Angeles	KO	4

1980
Jan.	17—Larry Myers, Los Angeles	W	6
Oct.	23—Mike Hutchinson, Las Vegas	KO	1
Nov.	29—Jose Guerrero, Las Vegas	KO	5

RAMON CERREZUELA
Argentine Heavyweight
1980
July	18—Juan D. Suarez, Mar del Plata	W	10
Aug.	16—Antonio Musladino, Mar del Plata	W	10

MAX CERVANTES
Oakland, Calif. Lightweight
1979
Apr.	12—Jorge Hernandez, Oakland	D	6
May	9—John Segura, Oakland	KO by	5
June	19—Gilbert Maldonado, San Carlos	KO by	2
Oct.	4—Julio Willis, San Carlos	KO by	0
Nov.	7—Juan Garcia, San Jose	L	6

Nov.	27—Earl Chaffin, Stockton	KO	3

1980
Feb.	19—Tony Baltazar, Sacramento	KO by	1
July	25—Golden Thomas, San Carlos	KO by	2

GEORGE CHAPLIN
Baltimore, Md. Heavyweight
1976
July	29—Johnny Blaine, Baltimore	KO	2
Sept.	16—Ken Hunter, Baltimore	KO	1
Oct.	28—Matt Robinson, Baltimore	KO	6
Dec.	10—Matt Robinson, Philadelphia	W	6

1977
Feb.	24—Robert Hill, Wilmington	W	4
Apr.	29—Bob Smith, Baltimore	KO	5
Aug.	5—John Jordan, Richmond	W	8
Sept.	17—Mike Koranicki, Richmond	L	10
Nov.	30—Don Wilson, Baltimore	KO	1

1978
Feb.	10—Leroy Diggs, Philadelphia	D	6
Aug.	8—Bobby Jordan, Baltimore	W	6
Sept.	14—Ira Martin, Baltimore	W	8

1979
Mar.	28—Jerry Thompkins, Baltimore	KO	9
May	25—Mike Koranicki, Baltimore	W	10
July	3—Duane Bobick, Atlantic City	KO	7
Sept.	26—Larry Alexander, Baltimore	W	12
Nov.	14—Wendell Bailey, Baltimore	W	12
Dec.	14—Henry Porter, Atlantic City	KO	5

1980
Apr.	5—Greg Page, Louisville	L	10
May	10—Jimmy Abbott, Johannesburg	D	10

DANNY CHAPMAN
New Paltz, N.Y. Welterweight
1980
Oct.	23—Jackie Sharpe, New York	W	4
Nov.	11—Herb Darity, West Hartford	W	6

ALFREDO CHAVES
Argentine Lightweight
1980
Apr.	19—Omar Garcia, Buenos Aires	TD	3
Dec.	13—Omar Garcia, Buenos Aires	D	6

JOSE CHAVEZ
Mexican Featherweight
1979
Apr.	17—Juan Venegas, Houston	L	6

1980
Jan.	16—Ricardo (Leoncito) Peralta, Merida	KO by	2
May	14—Juan Jimenez, Mexico City	KO by	8

MARIO CHAVEZ
Los Angeles, Calif. Flyweight
1975
Jan.	18—Danny O'Campo, Anaheim	KO by	2
Jan.	28—Martin Garcia, Tijuana	W	10
Feb.	12—Miguel Albornoz, Mexico City	W	10
Feb.	28—Francisco Nunez, Guadalajara	KO by	2
Mar.	19—Angel Salinas, Las Vegas	W	5

1976
(Inactive)
1977
Apr.	14—Silvano Lopez, Los Angeles	KO	4
Apr.	28—Oscar Muniz, Los Angeles	L	6
May	18—Arturo Silvano, Phoenix	KO	6
May	24—Tony Fernandez, Sacramento	KO	1
July	28—Johnny Mesa, Tucson	W	6
Sept.	13—Juan Herrera, Los Angeles	W	6
Sept.	23—Arturo Ulloa, San Jose	W	6
Oct.	19—Joe Garcia, Las Vegas	KO	6
Nov.	2—Kid Saldivar, Las Vegas	KO	3
Dec.	2—Jose Villegas, Bakersfield	W	8

1978
May	4—Paz Mena, Los Angeles	W	10
June	1—Raul Ochoa, Los Angeles	KO	7
June	14—Tito Arzate, Las Vegas	KO	5
Aug.	23—Raul Ochoa, Las Vegas	KO	4
Nov.	16—Oscar Muniz, Los Angeles	L	10
Dec.	14—Eddie Logan, Los Angeles	L	10

1979
Feb.	21—Blackie Sandoval, Las Vegas	KO	1
Mar.	27—Johnny Carter, Las Vegas	L	10
July	16—Aaron Morua, Bakersfield	KO	5
Aug.	20—Alfredo Gonzalez, Bakersfield	KO	2
Sept.	21—Carlos Canchola, San Diego	KO	4
Oct.	4—Ricardo Varela, Los Angeles	L	12
Oct.	23—Jose Merrera, Los Angeles	KO	2
Nov.	30—Willie Jenson, Las Vegas	L	10

1980
Feb.	14—Ricardo Varela, Los Angeles	L	12

(California Bantamweight Title)

Mar. 20—Lorenzo Ramirez, Los Angeles ....KO 3
Apr. 30—Ramon Grullon, Las Vegas ....W 10
May 24—Catalino Flores, Santa Monica ....KO 5
July 24—Luis Gonzales, Los Angeles ....KO 2
Oct. 29—Marcelo Camacho, Las Vegas ....KO 6
Nov. 11—Fred Jackson, Houston ....L 10

PEDRO CHAVEZ
Mexican Featherweight
1977
June 12—Daniel Felizardo, Matamoros ....KO by 5
1978
(Inactive)
1979
Apr. 6—Torito Melendes, McAllen ....KO by 1
1980
Oct. 9—Juan (Kid) Meza, Chicago ....KO by 1

RAY GUERRERO CHAVEZ
Venezuelan Welterweight
1970
Feb. 18—Cesar Chavez, Caracas ....KO 3
Mar. 30—Oscar Salazar, Caracas ....W 6
May 15—Guillermo Gonzales, Caracas...........KO 2
June 21—Julian Pacheco, Caracas ....KO 5
Aug. 7—Pedro Salina, Caracas ....W 8
Sept. 23—Oscar Salazar, Caracas ....W 8
Oct. 18—Pedro Nobriga, Maracaibo ....KO 4
Nov. 28—Juan Parra, Maracaibo ....KO 3
Dec. 23—Francisco Iturbe, Maracaibo.............KO 3
1971
Mar. 13—Antonio DeJesus, San Juan ....W 8
May 17—John Pearson, Boston..................KO 1
June 22—Eddie Parks, New York.................L 8
July 26—Eddie Parks, New York.................L 4
Sept. 2—Clyde Gray, Montreal ....D 10
Sept. 27—Fernando Marcotte, Quebec City.........D 10
Dec. 16—Felipe Cariaco, Maracaibo ....W 10
1972
Apr. 12—Dorman Crawford, Montreal ....W 10
May 27—Doug Charles, Sorel...................KO 2
June 15—Ray Rose, Montreal....................W 8
July 15—Eddie Parks, Montreal.................W 8
Aug. 24—Eddie Parks, Montreal.................W 8
Oct. 1—Joe Kimpuani, Istanbul.................KO 3
1973
Feb. 27—Donato Padunao, Montreal..............W 12
May 7—Fernand Marcotte, Quebec City ....W 10
June 25—Jose Rodriguez, New York..............L 10
Oct. 4—Doc McClendon, Montreal..............W 10
1974
July 20—Miguel Angel Campanino,
Buenos Aires ....L 10
Oct. 18—Rocky Mattioli, Melbourne ....L 10
1975
Mar. 15—Antonio Cervantes, Caracas..........KO by 2
June 15—Radamas Checo, Caracas ....KO 2
Aug. 25—Inocencio La Rosa, Caracas ....W 10
1976
Jan. 17—Beraldo Costa Acevedo, Caracas.........W 10
Feb. 21—Jose Bernardo Prada, Caracas............W 10
Nov. 17—Marcelino Alicia, Quebec ....KO 1
Dec. 14—Roy Johnson, Montreal ....KO 2
1977
Jan. 18—Al Franklin, Montreal ....KO 3
Mar. 23—Clyde Gray, Montreal ....KO 11
(Canadian Welterweight Title)
Aug. 3—Wilfred Benitez, New York ....KO by 15
(World Junior Welterweight Title)
1978
Jan. 24—Efisio Pinna, Montreal ....W 10
Apr. 26—Gerald Bouchard, Montreal ....L 10
June 13—Clyde Gray, Halifax ....KO by 7
1979
May 10—Ronald Zenon, Paris ....KO 3
1980
Feb. 7—Richard Rodriguez, Paris ....L 10

RICHIE CHAVEZ
Long Beach, California Middleweight
1980
Mar. 7—Randy McGrady, San Bernardino ....L 5
Mar. 21—Fahim Muhammad, San Bernardino ......L 5

CORNELL CHAVIS
New York, N.Y. Light Heavyweight
1978
Feb. 4—Tommy McNeece, New York ....L 4
Mar. 16—Ralph Cuomo, North Bergen ....KO 1
Apr. 7—Eddie Mallard, North Bergen ....KO 3
May 9—Junior Edmonds, Hartford ....L 4
Nov. 16—Pedro Rivera, New York ....W 4

64

1979
Jan. 26—Luis Guzman, New York ....L 6
June 27—Ramon Ronquillo, Secaucus ....W 8
Aug. 1—Sal San Filippo, Secaucus ....KO 5
Nov. 28—Johnny Wilburn, Hauppauge ....KO by 8
1980
Mar. 29—Dwight Braxton, Atlantic City ....KO by 1
Oct. 2—Ron Huston, New York ....L 6
Nov. 25—Don Addison, Springfield ....KO 5

JERRY CHEATHAM
Phoenix, Ariz. Junior Middleweight
Born: Aug. 16, 1958
1976
Aug. 16—Roberto Flores, Phoenix ....KO 1
Oct. 5—Leonardo Castillo, Phoenix ....KO 4
Nov. 16—Alfredo Sanchez, Phoenix ....L 6
1977
Jan. 25—Barantes Hernandez, Phoenix ....KO 2
Mar. 30—Joey Robles, Phoenix ....W 6
Apr. 27—Clarence Howard, Phoenix ....W 8
June 28—Abraham Perez, Phoenix ....KO 4
July 12—Bruce Henderson, Phoenix ....L 6
July 25—Bruce Henderson, Las Vegas ....L 6
Aug. 22—Ken Crooms, Phoenix ....D 6
Sept. 20—Ken Shepherd, Phoenix ....KO 3
Nov. 15—Alfredo Sanchez, Phoenix ....W 6
Dec. 14—Alfredo Sanchez, Tucson ....KO 1
1978
Jan. 24—Ramon Reyes, Phoenix ....KO 3
Feb. 28—Dave Oropeza, Phoenix ....KO 8
Mar. 7—Carmelo Garcia, Phoenix ....KO 3
Apr. 13—Steve Delgado, Phoenix ....W 10
May 23—Jaime Rios, Phoenix ....W 6
June 20—Joey Vincent, Phoenix ....W 10
Sept. 28—Gonzalo Rodriguez, Phoenix ....KO 3
Nov. 22—Raul Aguirre, Phoenix ....KO 5
1979
Feb. 13—Lamar Baskin, Phoenix ....KO 2
Mar. 17—Rudy Barro, Tucson ....KO 5
Apr. 10—Basil Buchanan, Phoenix ....KO 6
May 14—Agapito Ramirez, Phoenix ....W 10
June 27—Raymond Boyd, Phoenix ....KO 2
July 25—Noli Galicha, Phoenix ....KO 4
Aug. 22—Clarence Howard, Phoenix ....W 12
Sept. 18—Rafael Rodriguez, Phoenix ....L 10
Oct. 18—Aundra Love, Phoenix ....W 10
1980
Feb. 14—Ramiro Hernandez, Phoenix ....KO 1
June 3—Javier Ayala, Phoenix ....W 10
July 29—Rafael Rodriguez, Phoenix ....W 10
Nov. 5—Jose Figueroa, Phoenix ....W 10
Dec. 15—Mario Mendez, Phoenix ....KO 3

TONY CHIAVERINI
Kansas City, Mo. Junior Middleweight
1975
July 24—Charles Cook, Topeka ....KO 2
Aug. 13—Harry Smith, Topeka...................KO 3
Sept. 4—Monty Cady, Omaha...................W 4
Nov. 4—Dick Fowler, Topeka ....KO 2
Nov. 20—Holander Oliver, Omaha...............KO 1
1976
Jan. 8—Frank Freramo, Omaha, Neb............KO 2
Feb. 8—Doug Demmings, Minneapolis ....D 8
Feb. 20—Al Clay, Kansas City ....W 8
May 3—Doug Demmings, Minneapolis ....L 10
May 19—Roy Jones, Las Vegas, Nev. ....KO 6
June 22—Dennis Haggerty, Topeka, Ks...........KO 3
July 26—Raul Aguire, Topeka, Ks. ....KO 6
Aug. 26—Oscar Balderos, Kansas City ....KO 1
Sept. 22—James Parks, Cleveland, O. ....L 10
Oct. 6—Sammy NeSmith, Kansas City ....KO 9
Dec. 15—Vicente Medina, Kansas City ....W 10
1977
Jan. 29—Tony Gardner, Kansas City ....KO 2
Mar. 18—Willie Warren, Kansas City ....W 10
June 17—Vinnie Curto, Kansas City ....W 12
Aug. 1—Alfonso Aguirre, Topeka ....KO 3
Sept. 7—Al Bell, Kansas City ....W 4
Oct. 25—Billy Duquette, Kansas City ....W 10
Dec. 15—Jessie Garcia, Kansas City ....KO 5
1978
Jan. 29—Tony Gardner, Kansas City ....KO 2
Feb. 15—Marcelo Quinones, Las Vegas ....KO 3
Mar. 31—Bennie Briscoe, Kansas City ....KO by 3
May 8—Al Bell, Chicago ....KO 4
June 2—(King) George Aidoo, Kansas City ....KO 10
July 28—Renato Garcia, Kansas City ....W 10
Oct. 6—Mike Avans, Kansas City ....KO 5
Dec. 2—Elisha Obed, Kansas City ....W 10
1979
Feb. 13—Joe Gonsalves, Phoenix ....W 10
Mar. 16—Edgar Ross, Kansas City ....KO 10

Apr. 30—Bobby Patterson, Montreal .... KO 3
June 1—Rick Zarbatany, Kansas City .... KO 6
June 24—Ray Leonard, Las Vegas .... KO by 4
Aug. 16—Chris Lange, Kansas City .... KO 7
Sept. 22—Sandy Torres, Kansas City .... KO 9
Nov. 16—Joey Vincent, Kansas City .... KO 1
1980
Jan. 9—Charlie Peterson, Kansas City .... KO 2
Mar. 7—Alfonso Fraser, Kansas City .... W 10
June 6—Tony Licata, Kansas City .... W 10
Aug. 1—Wilfred Benitez, Las Vegas .... KO by 8
Nov. 12—Gary Coates, Kansas City .... W 10
Dec. 12—Odell Leonard, Kansas City .... KO by 6

JIM CHICOYNE
Winnipeg, Canada Heavyweight
1979
June 14—Lupe Guerra, Winnipeg .... L 4
1980
Mar. 6—Ken Nichols, Winnipeg .... KO 3
July 25—Brad Davis, Winnipeg .... KO 1

ALFREDO CICOPIEDI
Argentine Middleweight
1980
June 21—Miguel A. Castellini, Mar del Plata .... L 10
July 4—Miguel Castellini, San Nicolas .... KO by 7
Aug. 22—Miguel Castellini, Bahia Blanca ..... KO by 8

VICTOR CID
Corpus Christi, Texas Welterweight
1976
May 17—Aundra Love, Corpus Christi .... L 6
Aug. 3—Luis Valdez, Corpus Christi .... W 6
Aug. 24—Eddie Mitchell, Houston .... KO 4
Oct. 12—Frank Deltore, San Antonio .... L 6
1977
Jan. 25—Silverio Martinez, Corpus Christi .... L 8
May 17—Robert Rodriguez, Corpus Christi .... KO 3
May 31—Victor Villanueva, San Antonio .... D 6
June 28—Eduardo Vega, Corpus Christi .... W 6
Sept. 20—Eduardo Vega, Corpus Christi .... L 6
Dec. 13—Roberto Elizondo, Corpus Christi .... L 8
1978
(Inactive)
1979
Mar. 16—Steve Homan, Kansas City .... KO by 8
Nov. 20—Ezzard Charles Adams, Houston .... L 6
1980
Sept. 9—Frank Newton, Norman .... KO by 5

ANGEL CINTRON
New York, N.Y. Junior Welterweight
1979
Aug. 14—Victor Pappas, Atlantic City .... KO by 4
1980
Mar. 21—Norberto Figueroa, New York .... KO by 1

FELICIANO CINTRON
Boston, Mass. Junior Middleweight
1979
Nov. 7—Gary McGuire, Boston .... KO 6
Nov. 21—Ralph Mifka, Scranton .... D 6
1980
Feb. 16—Marvin Jenkins, Portland .... L 8
Apr. 8—Marlon Starling, Hartford .... KO by 6
June 26—Ben Serrano, Revere .... L 8
July 22—Allan Clarke, Halifax .... KO by 3
Oct. 16—Giovanni Bovenzi .... W 8
Dec. 18—Tony Braxton, Totowa .... KO by 8

ALFONSO CIRILLO
Mexican Junior Lightweight
1978
Feb. 14—Terry Strapnel, Houston .... W 6
Mar. 14—Armando Coronado, Houston .... L 8
May 1—Norman Goins, Indianapolis .... KO by 3
May 23—Jose Resendez, Denver .... KO by 4
July 5—Juan (Kid) Meza, Las Vegas .... KO by 4
1979
May 14—Leo Randolph, Philadelphia .... KO by 5
1980
Sept. 1—Refugio Rodriguez, Laredo .... L 4
Oct. 23—Rocky Garcia, Los Angeles .... KO by 5

RICARDO CISNEROS
Argentine Welterweight
1980
Mar. 14—Martin Duran, P.R.S. Pena .... W 8
Apr. 4—Enrique Coronel, P.R.S. Pena .... L 8
June 6—Enrique Coronel, P.R.S. Pena .... W 10
Aug. 22—Martin Duran, P.R.S. Pena .... W 10

Oct. 3—Hugo Trujillo, P.R.S. Pena .... KO 9
Oct. 24—Geronimo Ramirez, Villa Angela .... W 10

RON CISNEROS
Denver, Colorado Flyweight
Born: July 13, 1961. Height: 5 ft. 4 in.
1980
July 11—Armando Cruz, Denver .... W 6
Aug. 15—Mario Casias, Denver .... KO 3
Oct. 10—Alberto Cruz, Denver .... W 6
Nov. 7—Ricky Cortez, Denver .... W 6
Nov. 28—Luis Jimenez, Denver .... W 6
Dec. 19—Charles Anderson, Denver .... KO 2

GARY CLANCY
Huntington, N.Y. Heavyweight
1979
Oct. 12—Kid Samson, Uniondale .... W 4

GERALD CLARK
Philadelphia, Pa. Welterweight
1979
Sept. 26—Ronnie Green, Baltimore .... D 6
Oct. 26—Frankie Minigan, Rochester .... L 6
Nov. 29—Mel Hauser, Virginia Beach .... KO by 4
Dec. 18—Miguel Sanchez, Fairfield .... KO by 2
1980
Mar. 12—Ken Fusco, White Plains .... KO by 1
June 13—Jimmy McNeece, Harlem .... KO by 2

JAMES CLARK
Philadelphia, Pa. Welterweight
1979
Mar. 14—Junior Edmonds, White Plains .... KO by 3
1980
Jan. 19—Carl Wilson, Hempstead .... L 4

JESSE CLARK
Columbus, Ohio Heavyweight
1980
Feb. 9—Ed Bednarick, Clarksburg .... KO by 1
Aug. 25—Jumbo Cummings, Chicago .... KO by 1
Oct. 28—Randy Stephens, Warren .... KO by 1
Dec. 2—Tony Tucker, Toledo .... KO by 1
Dec. 5—Sam McGill, Clarksburg .... KO by 1

LANDER CLARK
Seattle, Wash. Middleweight
1979
Oct. 16—Perry Levoe, Sparks .... KO by 6
1980
Mar. 27—Perry Levoe, San Carlos .... L 8
May 4—J.B. Williamson, Seattle .... KO by 6

MIKE (KING) CLARK
Carson City, Nev. Middleweight
Managed by Ted Walker
1976
Sept. 22—Mustafa Shabazz, Las Vegas .... KO by 3
Nov. 4—Alvaro Lopez, Incline Village .... L 4
Nov. 18—Ronnie Whyte, Stateline .... W 4
1977
—Ernie Pope, Lake Tahoe .... L 4
1978
(Inactive)
1979
Aug. 24—Manny Gullatt, Carson City .... KO 4
Sept. 18—Gabino Rizzo, Reno .... KO 2
Sept. 26—Frank Reese, Las Vegas .... KO 3
Nov. 6—James Williams, Reno .... W 10
1980
Jan. 12—Rudy Cruz, Lake Tahoe .... W 10
Feb. 18—Henry Hearns, Carson City .... L 10
Apr. 26—Joe Gonzalez, Carson City .... W 10
May 29—Lee Burkey, Las Vegas .... W 10
June 26—Henry Hearns, Las Vegas .... L 10
Aug. 31—Lee Burkey, Carson City .... KO 5
Oct. 30—Al Patterson, Carson City .... W 10
Nov. 29—Greg McPherson, Lake Tahoe .... W 10

ALLAN CLARKE
Halifax, Nova Scotia, Canada Junior Welterweight
1975
Dec. 1—Ahmed Tosci, Halifax .... KO by 2
1976
July 12—Wayne Cormier, Shediac .... KO 2
Sept. 30—Reg McLean, New Glasgow .... W 4
1977
July 14—Ralph Hollett, Halifax .... L 6
Sept. 8—Ken Reddick, Halifax .... KO 2
Oct. 4—Paul Dorion, Halifax .... KO 1
Dec. 8—Geo Majors, Halifax .... KO 3

65

Apr. 11—Donald Johnson, Halifax .... W 6
June 13—Jim Henry, Halifax .... W 6
June 28—Roland Cousins, Halifax .... KO 2
Aug. 1—Don Morgan, Halifax .... W 8
Sept. 17—Charlie Benjamin, Sydney .... W 6
Oct. 8—Jesse Rogers, Glace Bay .... KO 1
1979
May 26—Rahim Muhammad, Glace Bay .... KO 1
June 5—Don Morgan, Halifax .... D 8
July 10—Earl Liburd, Halifax .... W 10
Aug. 28—Marvin Jenkins, Halifax .... W 8
Nov. 13—Quinton Blackman, Halifax .... W 8
Dec. 5—Marvin Jenkins, White Plains .... W 10
Jan. 22—Lawrence Hafey, Halifax .... L 10
Mar. 6—Al Ford, Winnipeg .... L 10
Apr. 29—Brian Anderson, Halifax .... KO 5
July 22—Feliciano Cintron, Halifax .... KO 3
Aug. 21—Clyde Gray, Halifax .... KO by 10

CHRIS CLARKE
Halifax, Canada Welterweight
1976
Sept. 30—Brian Linithorn, New Glasgow .... KO 3
Oct. 23—Allen Turenne, Charlottown .... KO 3
Nov. 4—Randy Milton, Stellerton .... KO 2
Mov. 23—Willie Davis, Halifax .... KO 5
1977
Jan. 9—Terry Summerhays, New Glasgow ..... KO 3
Jan. 25—Fred Legase, Halifax .... KO 2
June 1—Raymond Rouselleau, Montreal .... KO 3
July 3—Rey Mercado, New Glasgow .... KO 8
July 14—Bob Ryan, Halifax .... KO 6
Sept. 8—Al Romano, Halifax .... KO 5
Oct. 4—Sam Hailstock, Halifax .... KO 3
1978
Apr. 11—Ronald (Bo) Whyms, Halifax .... W 10
June 28—Billy Waith, Halifax .... W 10
Sept. 17—Eddie Campbell, Sydney .... W 10
Oct. 8—(Beau) Jaynes, Glace Bay .... KO 4
1979
June 5—Lawrence Hafey, Halifax .... W 10
July 10—Benji Goldstone, Halifax .... KO 1
Aug. 28—Clyde Gray, Halifax .... KO 10
(British Commonwealth Welterweight Title)
Nov. 13—Clyde Gray, Halifax ....KO by 10
(British Commonwealth Welterweight Title)
1980
Apr. 29—Ralph Hollett, Halifax .... W 12
(Canadian Middleweight Title)
Sept. 24—Ralph Hollett, Halifax .... KO by 2
(Lost Canadian Middleweight Title)

AL CLAY
Miami, Fla. Middleweight
1976
Feb. 19—Tony Chiaverini, Kansas City............. L 8
Apr. 6—Fred Reed, Chicago...................... W 6
Sept. 2—Jimmy Owens, Kalamazoo .... D 10
Dec. 16—Tommy Hanna, Inkster.................. L 10
1977
Aug. 8—Jimmy Carter, Chicago .... KO 3
May 23—Mike Hallacy, Chicago .... W 10
1978
Apr. 10—Johnny Heard, Chicago .... W 10
May 22—Lamont Lovelady, Chicago .... KO by 7
Aug. 28—Alex Porrata, Chicago .... KO 6
1979
Mar. 31—Alex Porrata, Chicago .... W 10
May 14—Tony Sibson, London .... KO by 7
1980
May 2—Matteo Salvemini, Rome .... KO by 4
Sept. 11—Fred Reed, Chicago .... W 10
Oct. 9—Kenny Heflin, Chicago .... KO 6

JAMES CLEVELAND
Dallas, Tex. Featherweight
1978
Dec. 16—Wilburn Lawson, Dallas .... L 4
1979
July 9—Alfonso Dominguez, Odessa .... KO by 3
Aug. 27—Donald James, Odessa .... KO 1
Oct. 20—James Ortega, Pueblo .... KO by 2
1980
May 19—Humberto Mendez, Odessa .... KO 3
July 18—Wilbur Lawson, Odessa .... W 4
Aug. 16—Roy Salazar, Odessa .... KO 4

RANDY CLOVER
Tucson, Ariz. Lightweight
1979
Sept. 5—Sterling McPherson, Las Vegas ...... KO by 3

Oct. 18—Rudy Matta, Phoenix .... KO 4
Oct. 25—Richard Fowler, Albuquerque .... W 4
Oct. 31—Henry Lopez, Phoenix .... KO 3
Nov. 13—Elieu Hernandez, Phoenix .... KO 3
Nov. 26—Mauro Fuentes, Las Vegas .... KO 2
Dec. 5—Ricky Samudio, Las Vegas .... KO 5
1980
Jan. 20—Angel Mendola, Tucson .... KO 1
Feb. 6—Julio Alfonso, Las Vegas .... KO 3
Mar. 5—Dave Ramos, Las Vegas .... KO 1
Mar. 13—Jaime Nava, Los Angeles .... W 6

GARY COATES
Cincinnati, Ohio Welterweight
1977
Mar. 26—Mike Wyant, Cincipnati .... L 4
May 7—Mike Wyant, Cincinnati .... L 6
Sept. 24—Jim Claar, Hamilton .... W 6
Oct. 15—Brislee Ross, Salem .... W 6
Oct. 29—Don Morgan, Hamilton .... L 6
Dec. 10—Dwight Davis, Grand Rapids .... L 4
1978
Mar. 31—Danny Paul, Saginaw .... L 6
Apr. 17—Tony Southerland, Columbus .... KO 1
Apr. 29—Jody Parker, Sebring .... W 6
June 28—Shane Bosley, Hamilton .... KO 4
Aug. 3—David Braxton, Detroit.................. L 4
1979
Feb. 24—Joe Lee, Alliance .... KO 2
Mar. 16—Luis Resto, Cincinnati .... KO by 4
Apr. 7—Anthony Daniels, Kingsport .... L 8
Apr. 13—Tony Gonzales, Cincinnati .... KO 4
May 17—Pete Seward, Columbus .... L 6
June 28—Jeff Gripper, Columbus .... W 6
Aug. 16—John LoCicero, Kansas City .... L 10
Sept. 30—Pete Seward, Canton .... KO 6
Nov. 16—Justice Ortiz, Kansas City .... W 8
Dec. 12—Sammy Rookard, Canton .... KO 7
1980
Apr. 5—Brian Muller, Akron .... L 6
Aug. 23—Greg Netter, Alliance .... W 8
Nov. 12—Tony Chiaverini, ... L 10

RANDALL (TEX) COBB
Philadelphia, Pa. Heavyweight
1977
Jan. 21—Pedro Vega, El Paso .... KO 1
Mar. 11—Tyrone Harlee, Philadelphia .... KO 2
Apr. 2—Trinidad Escamilla, San Antonio .... KO 1
May 10—Earnest Smith, El Paso .... KO 3
July 8—David Wynne, San Diego .... KO 2
1978
Mar. 17—Dave Martinez, Las Vegas .... KO 1
Apr. 7—Paul Solomon, Los Angeles .... KO 2
Nov. 11—Rodell Dupree, Boston .... KO 6
1979
Mar. —Vernon Johnston, Philadelphia .... KO
Apr. 3—Zack Ferguson, Philadelphia .... KO 1
Apr. 27—Jesse Crown, Newark .... KO 2
Aug. 28—Don Halpin, Atlantic City .... KO 3
Oct. 24—Terry Mims, Scranton .... KO 5
1980
Mar. 21—Chebo Hernandez, El Paso .... KO 1
May 9—Cookie Wallace, El Paso .... W 10
May 31—Robert Echols, El Paso .... KO 1
Aug. 2—Earnie Shavers, Detroit .... KO 8
Nov. 7—Ken Norton, San Antonio .... L 10

CLINTON COCHRANE
Charleston, W. Va. Heavyweight
1979
May 4—Tom Walker, Fayetteville .... KO 2
Dec. 29—John Molloy, Charleston .... KO 2
1980
Mar. 4—Rodell Dupree, Elizabeth .... L 8
Mar. 21—Jerry McIntyre, Belwood, N.C. .... KO 1
Apr. 15—Louis Acosta, Miami Beach .... L 6

ANDREW COE
Rahway Middleweight
1979
Mar. 10—Bill Day, Rahway .... KO 2
Apr. 27—Dan Staehle, Newark .... KO by 3
1980
Aug. 7—Reese Stradford, Atlantic City ...... KO by 2

JEROME (KID) COFFEE
Nashville, Tenn. Flyweight
Managed by Stan Allen
1980
Oct. 23—Tommy Wilson, Memphis .... W disq. 2

ALF COFFIN
Arlington, Va. Heavyweight
1979
Aug. 28—Melvin Epps, Atlantic City .... W 4
Nov. 24—John Green, Washington, D.C. .... KO 1
Dec. 12—Gary Williams, Washington, D.C. .... W 6
1980
Apr. 10—Rick Mills, Los Angeles .... KO by 4
June 13—Bashir Wadud,San Diego .... L 6

HILTON DAVID COHEN
Huntington, N.Y. Welterweight
Born: July 18, 1956 Height: 5'8"
1979
Oct. 19—Robert Taylor, Commack .... KO 1
Nov. 9—Dick Powell, New York .... KO 4
1980
May 4—Jesse Rogers, Kiamesha Lake .... KO 1

MIKE COLBERT
Portland Ore. Middleweight
1974
Aug. 16—Keith Newman, Portland .... W 6
Sept. 8—Bobby Adams, Gardnerville .... W 6
Nov. 8—Bobby Woods, Vancouver .... W 6
Dec. 11—Jake Nelson, Kennwick .... KO 4
1975
Feb. 6—Rocky Mosley, Portland................ KO 2
Apr. 10—Mardi Manuella, Portland............... W 6
May 7—Ken Austin, Carson City............... KO 3
June 11—Pete McIntyre, Stockton .... W 6
July 14—Steve Tohill, Seattle .... W 6
Aug. 9—Danny Brewer, Los Angeles............. W 5
Sept. 25—Karl Vinson, Portland .... W 10
Nov. 25—Vicente Medina, Seattle .... W 10
1976
Mar. 27—Casey Gacic, Owings Mill............. W 10
May 5—Rudy Cruz, Reno .... W 10
June 9—Vicente Medina, Reno .... W 10
Aug. 23—Tony Licata, New Orleans .... W 10
Nov. 20—Karl Vinson, Seattle .... W 10
1977
Jan. 16—Jackie Smith, Pensacola .... W 8
(U.S. Championship Tournament)
Apr. 10—Rocky Mosley Jr., Miami Beach .... W 10
(U.S. Championship Tournament)
May 26—Rudy Cruz, Portland .... W 10
Aug. 28—Mike Avans, Vancouver .... KO 7
Sept. 15—Joe Gonzalez, Portland .... KO 6
Nov. 26—Marvin Hagler, Boston .... KO by 12
(Massachusetts World Middleweight Title)
1978
Mar. 30—Clifford Wills, Portland .... W 10
Apr. 24—Edgar Wallace, Las Vegas .... KO 10
Sept. 17—Roy Dale, Reno .... W 10
Oct. 22—Rudy Robles, Reno .... KO by 5
1979
Jan. 28—Willie Baldwin, Reno .... KO 6
Mar. 24—Charlie Weir, Johannesburg .... L 10
Apr. 16—Rudy Robles, Las Vegas .... KO 11
June 21—Ray Seales, Seattle .... D 12
July 22—Rudy Robles, Pontiac .... W 10
Oct. 30—Renato Garcia, Las Vegas .... W 10
Nov. 30—Thomas Hearns, New Orleans .... L 10
1980
May 4—Curtis Parker, Atlantic City .... L 12
Sept. 9—Ted Sanders, Las Vegas .... W 12

MARTY COLE
Dartmouth, Nova Scotia, Canada Welterweight
1979
June 26—Reynald Savard, Montreal .... L 4
July 10—Derrick Cuttino, Halifax .... L 4
Dec. 11—Sanford Ricks, Halifax .... KO by 6
1980
Apr. 29—Brian Hawthorne, Halifax .... D 4
May 11—Bobby Harvey, Halifax .... L 4
Sept. 9—Paul Dorian, Moncton .... L 6

WYATT COLEMAN
Honolulu, Hawaii Lightweight
1979
July 27—Fred Baclaan, Hilo .... D 3
Aug. 21—Fred Baclaan, Honolulu .... L 3
1980
Nov. 18—Siaosi Poto, Honolulu .... KO

RAMON COLLADO
Argentine Lightweight
1980
July 11—Marcelo Romero, Mar del Plata .... L 6
Sept. 6—Luis Neyra, C. Rivadavia .... D 6

Oct. 11—Ricardo Espinoza, Buenos Aires ...... KO by 5

JOSE COLLANTE
Puerto Rican Welterweight
1978
Mar. 25—Carlos Santos, San Juan .... KO by 4
Apr. 8—Carlos Santos, San Juan .... KO by 3
1979
Jan. 27—Carlos Betancourt, San Juan .... L 6
1980
Apr. 21—Carlos Betancourt, San Juan .... KO by 7

ALBERTO COLLAZO
Pittsburgh, Pa. Featherweight
1976
Sept. 15—Willie Whipple, Cleveland .... L 4
Nov. 3—Jerry Strickland, Cleveland .... KO 2
Nov. 24—Scott Anderson, Cleveland .... KO 2
1977
Jan. 19—Otto Breeding, Cleveland .... KO 4
Mar. 8—Peanuts Emerson, Mentor .... W 6
Apr. 13—Elead Leal, Cleveland .... KO 2
May 17—Benny Marquez, Mentor .... W 6
Sept. 9—Mike Johnson, Mentor .... W 4
Sept. 29—Isaac Vega, Cleveland .... KO 4
Nov. 2—Frank Maldonado, Cleveland .... KO 4
Dec. 7—James Martinez, Cleveland .... W 10
1978
Mar. 1—Bobby Alexander, Cleveland .... L 10
July 15—Bennie Marquez, Chicago .... W 8
Sept. 19—Kent Seawell, Pittsburgh .... KO 1
Oct. 24—John Alexander, Pittsburgh .... KO 2
Nov. 16—Chuck Spicer, Pittsburgh .... KO 6
Dec. 6—Lloyd Allen, Cleveland .... W 10
1979
Feb. 8—Bobby Alexander, Pittsburgh .... W 10
July 19—Harvey Wilson, Pittsburgh .... KO 4
1980
Feb. 29—David Capo, Commack .... D 8
Mar. 28—Rodolfo Francis, New York .... KO 7
Apr. 25—Jose Nieto, Commack .... KO 9
Sept. 11—Francisco Manzo, Chicago .... L 10

ALBERT COLLINS
Inman, S. Carolina Heavyweight
1980
July 26—Claman Parker, Charlotte .... KO by 2
Sept. 6—Roby Jetton, Lincolnton .... KO by 4

ANTHONY COLLINS
Miami, Florida Lightweight
1980
May 2—Bean Chavez, Miami .... KO 1
June 6—Lonnie Lodge, Miami .... W 4
July 22—Emilio Diaz, Miami .... KO 2

EDDIE COLLINS
Meridian, Miss. Heavyweight
1980
Mar. 4—Dan Kiser, Memphis .... KO by 10
July 11—Franklin Otts, Meridian .... KO 3

JOHN COLLINS
Chicago, Ill. Middleweight
1980
Oct. 9—Lee Thomas, Chicago .... KO 3
Nov. 13—Robert Thomas, Chicago .... KO 2
Dec. 11—Ray Barksdale, Chicago .... KO 5

FELIX COLEMAN
Argentine Flyweight
1980
Feb. 1—Hector Barreto, Posadas .... W 10
Apr. 11—Jose T. Flores, Posadas .... W 10
June 19—Hector Patri, Posadas .... W 10

MARIO COLON
Puerto Rican Featherweight
1979
Aug. 4—Arturo Salas, Chicago .... KO 1
Aug. 11—Carlos Pinango, Caracas .... L 10
1980
Mar. 3—Herman Palacios, Caracas .... KO 6
Apr. 14—Raul Gonzales, Caracas .... L 10
July 3—Heriberto Olivares, Rio Piedras .... L 10
July 19—Jose Richardson, St. Thomas .... KO 8
Sept. 8—Juan Mijares, Caracas .... KO by 2

RAUL COLUMBO
Argentine Lightweight
1980
Mar. 28—Jose Colassi, Marcos Juarez .... D 10

Apr. 18—Lorenzo Garcia, San Pedro .... L 10
June 6—Jesus Romero, S. Sal. de Jujuy .... L 10
Aug. 15—Victor Escobar, P.R.S. Pena .... L 10

MIGUEL COMBI
Argentine Welterweight
1980
May 16—Alberto Prieto, Bell Ville .... L 10
June 27—Juan M. Suarez, Rosario .... KO 5
July 25—Juan D. Saucedo, Rosario .... L 10
Aug. 22—Juan D. Saucedo, Rosario .... L 10

SERGIO COMBIS
Argentine Lightweight
1980
July 25—Oscar Ruiz, Rosario .... W 6
Oct. 10—Hector Ruiz, Rosario .... W 8
Dec. 12—Ramon Abeldano, Rosario .... W 10

JOSE COMOLLI
Argentine Welterweight
1980
Aug. 22—Alfredo Gonzalez, Tucuman .... L 6
Sept. 5—Manuel Alvarez, Tucuman .... L 8

JOHNNY COMPO
Ft. Lauderdale, Fla. Welterweight
1979
June 22—Leon Williams, New York .... KO 3
Aug. 24—Angel Figueroa, Ft. Lauderdale .... KO 3
Sept. 25—Pedro Garcia, Miami Beach .... W 6
Oct. 5—Frankie Valdez, Ft. Lauderdale .... KO 3
Nov. 20—Alberto Sebilla, Miami Beach .... KO 3
Dec. 14—Bernard Johnson, Ft. Lauderdale ...... KO 3
1980
Jan. 13—Joe Johnson, Las Vegas .... W 6
Feb. 10—Johnny Torres, Miami .... W 8
Mar. 17—Jose Figueroa, Edmonton .... KO 7
Sept. 23—Bruce Strauss, Edmonton .... W 8
Oct. 17—Robert Thompson, W. Palm Beach ...... KO 2

MODESTO CONCEPCION
Los Angeles, Calif. Junior Welterweight
(Previous Record Unavailable)
1976
Feb. 17—Bobby Chacon, San Jose .... KO by 10
Apr. 10—Alexis Arguello, Managua .... KO by 2
1977
Feb. 16—Billy Turner, Las Vegas .... KO 6
Apr. 21—Roman Contreras, Los Angeles ...... KO by 7
Oct. 25—Johnny Copeland, Anaheim .... W 10
1978
Jan. 17—Miguel Estrada, Las Vegas .... W 10
May 15—Sigfriedo Rodriguez, Stockton .... L 10
Aug. 17—Jose Dominguez, Los Angeles .... TD 6
1979
June 15—Leroy Haley, Las Vegas .... TD 4
1980
Feb. 14—Gary Raymond, Phoenix .... W 10
May 5—Tyrone Rackley, Phoenix .... L 10
July 3—Rodolfo Gonzalez, Los Angeles ...... KO by 2

FEDERICO CONDORI
Argentine Bantamweight
1980
Jan. —Hector Patri, Salta .... L 10
June 19—Ruben Pasero, Salta .... KO 1
Aug. 1—Domingo Aragon, P.R.S. Pena ...... KO by 7

RUBEN CONDORI
Argentine Junior Featherweight
1980
Jan. 18—Raul Perez, Salta .... W 10
Feb. 29—Rodolfo Rodriguez, Salta .... W 10
Mar. 28—Santos Laciar, Cordoba .... D 10
Apr. 19—Adrian Roman, Buenos Aires .... D 10
May 16—Domingo Aragon, Salta .... W 10
June 6—Jorge O. Aguilar, Salta .... W 10
Aug. 1—Miguel Lazarte, Salta .... W 10
Sept. 5—Paulo Riveiro, Salta .... W 10
Oct. 24—Hector Barreto, Salta .... W 10
Dec. 12—Erik Vanegas, San Pedro .... KO 4

EVERETT CONKLIN
Long Island, N.Y. Light Heavyweight
Managed by Howard Davis, Sr.
.1980
Dec. 12—Dwight Triplett, New York .... KO 2

BILL CONNELL
Atlantic Highlands, N.J. Heavyweight
1977
Feb. 2—Johnny Blaine, New York .... KO 4

Mar. 2—Phil Brozier, New York .... W 4
Apr. 1—David Wilson, New York .... KO by 4
May 11—Guy Casale, New York .... L 4
Nov. 30—John Mitchell, Newark .... W 4
1978
Apr. 7—Elliott Burton, North Bergen .... KO 1
May 2—Mike Ruiz, Totowa .... KO 1
June 2—Terry Kidd, Jersey City .... KO 1
June 29—Jimmy Sykes, North Bergen .... KO 1
July 18—Ralph Mifka, Totowa .... KO 2
Oct. 28—Eddie Mallard, Jersey City .... D 6
1979
Jan. 27—Leon Whitehurst, Jersey City .... KO 2
Mar. 15—Eddie Mallard, North Bergen .... W 6
Apr. 17—Pedro Agosta, Totowa .... W 8
June 29—Robert Coley, Jersey City .... L 8
July 31—Lou Esa, Totowa .... W 8
Sept. 18—Scott Frank, East Rutherford .... KO by 7
1980
May 31—Brian O'Melia, Elizabeth .... KO 3
July 20—Pedro Soto, Great Gorge .... W 8

DAVID CONTEH
New York Light Heavyweight
Born: May 22, 1951 Wellingborough, England
1974
June —Roland Cousin, New York .... KO 3
Nov. —John Gallagher, New York .... W 6
1975
(Inactive)
1976
Oct. 29—Otis Gordon, Latham .... KO 5
Dec. 2—Eddie Phillips, New York .... L 8
1977
Apr. 19—Bobby Halpern, White Plains .... L 6
June 3—Leo Rogers, New York .... L 10
June 24—Eddie Phillips, Nanuet .... W 8
1978
Feb. 7—Bunny Johnson, London .... KO 3
1979
Jan. 26—Eddie Gregory, New York .... KO by 8
June 29—Pablo Ramos, Jersey City .... L 10
Aug. 24—Frankie Williams, Cincinnati .... W 10
1980
Apr. 18—Tony Mundine, Bologna .... L 10
Aug. 2—Michael Spinks, Baton Rouge .... KO by 8
Nov. 21—Hocine Tafer, Paris .... L 10

JORGE CONTI
Argentine Welterweight
1980
Jan. —Hector Rosales, Tandil .... KO 6
Mar. 7—Lorenzo Fernandez, Mar del Plata ... KO by 9
May 17—Roberto Cornejo, Tandil .... W 10
June 21—Hector H. Hernandez, Tandil .... W 6
Sept. 5—Lorenzo Fernandez, Tandil .... W 10

ALEX CONTRERAS
Texas Junior Welterweight
1979
May 17—Ramon Serrano, McAllen .... KO 3
Aug. 24—Alfredo Medrano, McAllen .... KO 6
1980
Feb. 28—Ramon Rodriguez, McAllen .... KO 1
Dec. 2—Steve Hearon, Houston .... KO by 3

EDUARDO CONTRERAS
Argentine Middleweight
1980
Apr. 18—Ruben Pardo, Rosario .... D 10
May 2—Raul Peralta, Cordoba .... W 10
May 23—Julio Arancibia, Rosario .... W 10
July 4—Julio Arancibia, Rosario .... D 10
July 25—Carlos Peralta, Cordoba .... W 10
Aug. 15—Carlos Peralta, Rosario .... L 10
Sept. 19—Raul Guillermo, Rosario .... W 10
Nov. 28—Nazereno Benitez, Rosario .... W 10
Dec. 18—Carlos Nacimiento, Posadas .... D 10

HENRY CONTRERAS
1980
June 19—Ramon Peralta, Tucson .... KO by 5
June 28—Corky Polandro, Rapid City .... KO 1
July 17—Francisco Rodriguez, Tucson .... KO 3

JOHNNY CONTRERAS
Texas Junior Lightweight
1979
Oct. 1—Victor Arguello, Corpus Christi .... KO 3
Nov. 6—Gilbert Garza, Corpus Christi .... KO 3
Dec. 11—Leonard Zapata, Corpus Christi ...... KO 5
1980
Feb. 28—Reynaldo Alvarez, McAllen .... KO 2

68

Apr. 15—Gustavo Rodriguez, Houston .... W 8

ENRIQUE CONTRERES
Argentine Junior Middleweight
1980
Mar. 7—Manuel F. Gonzalez, Rosario .... D 12
Oct. 17—Manuel F. Gonzalez, Rosario .... W 12

CALVIN COOK
Camden, N.J. Middleweight
1980
May 9—Euclides Valdez, Staten Island .... L 4
June 11—Doug DeWitt, White Plains .... L 4

JIMMY COOK
Memphis, Tenn. Middleweight
1977
Mar. 11—Joey Vincent, Orlando .... KO by 3
Mar. 15—Mickey Banks, Oklahoma City .... KO by 3
Apr. 2—Max Hord, Tallahassee .... L 6
May 14—David Tymes, Tallahassee .... KO 2
June 13—Phil Reed, Memphis .... L 6
1978
May 10—Max Hord, Fernandina Beach .... L 10
May 23—Phil Reed, Little Rock .... L 6
June 6—Terry Reed, Memphis .... KO 2
July 11—Glen Greenwell, Memphis .... L 4
Sept. 25—John Coleman, Little Rock .... L 4
Oct. 3—Bob Kidd, Memphis .... W 4
Nov. 14—Scott Allison, Memphis .... L 4
Dec. 19—Phil Reed, Memphis .... L 4
1979
Oct. 30—Lester Groves, Memphis .... L 4
Nov. 2—Bob Coolidge, Memphis .... KO by 3
1980
Oct. 7—David Miller, St. Charles .... L 4

ROLAND COOLEY
Philadelphia, Pa. Featherweight
Managed by Joe Frazier
1980
Nov. 28—Felix Thauriaux, New York .... W 4

BOB (ICEMAN) COOLIDGE
Foley, Minn. Middleweight
1979
May 4—Terry Jesmer, St. Paul .... W 4
June 25—Danny Murphy, Omaha .... KO 1
Aug. 2—Charlie Peterson, Omaha .... D 6
Aug. 10—Floyd Saunders, Evansville .... KO 1
Nov. 3—Jimmy Cook, Owensboro .... KO 3
Nov. 8—Jimmy Hearn, Omaha .... KO 4
1980
Mar. 19—Paul Johnson, St. Paul .... KO 1
June 28—Rodney Foster, Rapid City .... KO 2
July 11—Juan Ribota, Chicago .... KO 2
July 25—Joe Cumm, Winnipeg .... KO 3
Sept. 16—Carl Crowley, Winnipeg .... KO 5
Sept. 27—Tony Sibson, London .... KO by 7
Nov. 11—Charlie Peterson, St. Paul .... W 4

GERRY COONEY
Huntington, N.Y. Heavyweight
Born: August 24, 1956
Managed by Dennis Rappaport and Mike Jones
1977
Feb. 15—Bill Jackson, New York .... KO 1
Mar. 2—Jimmy Roberson, New York .... KO 2
Mar. 20—Jose Rosario, Louisville .... KO 2
Aug. 3—Matt Robinson, New York .... W 4
Nov. 18—Joe Maye, New York .... KO 4
Nov. 30—Quinnie Locklear, White Plains .... KO 1
Dec. 21—Jimmy Sykes, Brooklyn .... KO 1
1978
Jan. 14—Terry Kidd, Hauppauge .... KO 1
Jan. 27—Austin Johnson, Hempstead .... KO 1
Feb. 11—Gary Bates, Las Vegas .... KO 4
Mar. 17—S. T. Gordon, Las Vegas .... W disq. 4
June 22—G. G. Maldonado, New York .... KO 8
Oct. 5—Charles Polite, Westchester .... KO 4
Nov. 1—Sam McGill, Westchester .... W 8
Dec. 15—Grady Daniels, New York .... KO 5
1979
Jan. 13—Eddie Lopez, Miami Beach .... W 8
Feb. 26—Charlie Johnson, New York .... KO 1
June 29—Tom Prater, New York .... KO 2
Aug. 22—Broderick Mason, New York .... KO 4
Oct. 19—Malik Dozier, Commack .... KO 6
Nov. 9—John Denis, New York .... KO 3
Dec. 14—Leroy Boone, Atlantic City .... KO 6
1980
May 26—Jimmy Young, Atlantic City .... KO 4
Oct. 24—Ron Lyle, Uniondale .... KO 1

JOHNNY COOPER
Philadelphia, Pa. Welterweight
1976
July 28—Daryl Lampkin, Philadelphia .... D 4
Aug. 27—Tyrone Denby, Atlantic City .... L 4
Dec. 10—Jake Jenkins, Philadelphia............. W 4
1977
Jan. 19—Hibert Jackson, Bristol .... KO 4
Feb. 5—Kevin Meefield, Bristol .... W 4
Mar. 11—Al McBride, Philadelphia .... KO 1
May 14—O'Dell Leonard, Baltimore .... L 6
Sept. 16—Ray Davis, Wilmington .... W 6
1978
Dec. 14—Will Rankin, Virginia Beach .... KO 2
1979
Feb. 5—Mike Picciotti, Philadelphia .... D 8
Feb. 16—Josef Nsubuga, Oslo .... KO by 3
May 12—Frank Wells, Atlantic City .... KO 1
May 23—Tim (Blue) Walker, Washington, D.C. .. KO 3
July 31—Quasin Patrick, Atlantic City .... KO 3
Oct. 30—Kevin Howard, Upper Darby .... D 8
Dec. 14—Hubert Jackson, Atlantic City .... KO 1
1980
Mar. 9—Melvin Hauser, Atlantic City .... KO 8
Aug. 7—Melvin Hauser, Atlantic City .... KO 5
Sept. 4—Roger Stafford, Atlantic City .... L 10

JOHNNY COPELAND
Springfield, Mo. Junior Welterweight
1970
Apr. 11—Bernabe Lopez, Fort Worth .... KO 5
June 8—Bird Lopez, Dallas.................... W 6
Sept. 17—John White, Kalamazoo .... KO by 5
Oct. 31—Sammy Alvarez, Springfield, Mo........ W 6
Dec. 1—Rudy Barrientos, Dallas .... KO by 4
Dec. 5—Sammy Alvarez, Springfield, Mo........ W 6
1971
Feb. 10—Elijah Jones, Springfield, Mo. .... KO 2
Mar. 10—Ernesto Cokes, Joplin................. W 8
May 5—Marcos Geraldo, Las Vegas.......... KO by 3
May 19—Rocky Hoban, Las Vegas............... KO 2
June 9—Eduardo Mazon, Las Vegas.......... KO by 7
July 5—Richard Flores, Phoenix .... KO 7
Dec. 2—Dale Hernandez, Des Moines............ L 6
1972
Jan. 28—Rudy Bolds, St. Louis .... KO by 4
Apr. 21—Frankie Taylor, Springfield .... KO 3
May 16—Leoperdo Aguero, San Antonio .... KO by 4
July 17—Bennie McCall, New Orleans .... KO by 2
July 25—Gabriel Estrada, Houston .... KO by 6
Aug. 1—Carlos Ortiz, Oklahoma City .... KO by 3
Nov. 10—Marion Thomas, Indianapolis .... KO 6
Dec. 16—Mike Harris, Indianapolis............. KO 3
1973
Jan. 8—Simmie Black, Kansas City .... KO 5
Apr. 18—Dale Hernandez, Des Moines .... L 10
May 31—Marcus Anderson, Frankfurt........... L 10
June 18—Mike Harris, Des Moines .... KO 7
Sept. 22—Norman Goins, Indianapolis........ KO by 2
Oct. 16—Willie Williams, Des Moines .... KO 3
Oct. 24—Armando Rosales, Joplin.............. KO 8
Oct. 27—Marion Thomas, Indianapolis .... KO 3
Dec. 17—Alfredo Escalera, San Juan .... KO by 5
1974
Jan. 19—Charles Harvey, St. Louis............... KO 2
Feb. 26—Donnie Spencer, Joplin .... KO 5
Apr. 2—Ralph Coley, Joplin .... KO 5
May 21—Julio Lopez, Des Moines .... KO 5
Sept. 10—Juan Morales, Las Vegas .... KO by 4
Oct. 10—Hector Pena, Springfield.............. KO 3
Dec. 12—Angel Mayoral, Chicago............... L 10
Dec. 20—Tony Petronelli, Boston .... KO by 6
(American Junior Welterweight Title)
1975
Feb. 17—Mike Everett, Philadelphia .... KO 7
Mar. 1—Mike Wilson, Florissant .... KO 3
May 5—Mike Everett, Philadelphia........... KO by 8
June 27—James Busceme, Lake Charles .... KO 8
Aug. 18—Willie Daniels, Philadelphia .... KO 8
Aug. 28—Dennis Haggerty, Lake Charles .... KO 5
1976
Feb. 10—Jerome Artis, Philadelphia .... L 10
May 15—Robert Turner, Joplin .... KO 10
June 22—Cruz Ramos, Topeka .... KO 2
Nov. 11—Dennis Haggerty, Joplin .... KO 4
1977
Jan. 15—Robert Tijerina, Quapaw .... KO 5
Jan. 21—Larry Stanton, Cincinnati .... L 10
Feb. 24—Aundra Love, Cincinnati .... W 10
May 14—Dom Monaco, Baltimore .... KO 8
June 22—Miguel Montilla, Santo Domingo ... KO by 2
Oct. 20—Rocky Ramon, Marshall .... L 10

69

Oct. 25—Modesto Concepcion, Anaheim .... L 10
1978
Jan. 17—Wade Hinnant, Philadelphia .... L 10
Mar. 10—Antonio Cervantes, Caracas .... KO by 3
May 11—Rick Folstad, Bloomington .... W 10
July 9—Larry Stanton, Indianapolis .... KO by 5
Sept. 28—Tony Gonzalez, El Paso .... L 10
Nov. 11—Jorgen Hansen, Copenhagen .... KO by 7
1979
Jan. 30—Sammy Ayala, San Antonio .... L 10
Mar. 16—Aaron Pryor, Cincinnati .... KO by 7
June 17—Sammy Ayala, San Antonio .... KO by 7
Nov. 23—Steve Homan, Kansas City .... L 10
1980
Feb. 12—John Morgan, Beaumont .... L 10
Mar. 3—Jimmy Blevins, Chicago .... KO by 7
May 10—Pete Bothma, Johannesburg .... KO by 2
Aug. 2—Mike Blunt, Cincinnati .... KO by 3
Aug. 12—Pat Hallacy, Wichita .... KO by 6
Sept. 6—Wayne Burns, Sioux Falls .... KO 2
Oct. 23—Jimmy Heair, Memphis .... KO by 9
Nov. 1—Al Carter, Dayton .... KO by 4
Nov. 20—Frank Newton, Oklahoma City ..... KO by 7

KEITH CORBETT
Elizabeth, N.J. Junior Welterweight
1980
Oct. 18—Mike Passero, Atlantic City .... D 6

ABEL CORDOBA
Mexican Welterweight
1976
Feb. 26—Eugene Baldwin, Los Angeles .... KO 2
Mar. 12—Tommy Howard, San Bernardino......... D 8
Apr. 1—Mike Nixon, Los Angeles .... KO by 4
May 8—Armando Muniz, Los Angeles............. L 10
Sept. 2—Ruben Vasquez, Los Angeles............. KO 1
Oct. 21—Vicente Medina, Los Angeles .... W 10
1977
Jan. 22—Pete Ranzany, Los Angeles .... KO by 7
May 24—Pete Ranzany, Sacramento .... L 10
Sept. —Jose Figueroa, Mexico City .... KO by 3
Nov. 4—Elias Bautista, Salinas .... KO 4
Nov. 25—Adan Chavarria, Monterrey .... KO by 3
1978
Feb. 27—Fully Obel, Tuxtla .... W 10
June 12—Tito Cruz, Tuxtla .... W 10
July 17—Andres Fernandez, Tuxtla .... KO 3
Aug. 21—Cesar Savinon, Tuxtla .... KO 3
Oct. 8—Jose Figueroa, Tuxtla .... W 10
Nov. 27—Chucho Almazan, Tuxtla .... W 10
1979
Apr. 9—Fernando Lugo, Los Angeles .... KO 9
May 29—Kevin Finnegan, London .... L 8
1980
Apr. 1—Fulgencio Obelmejias, Caracas .... KO by 2

PIERRE CORMIER
Canadian Light Heavyweight
1980
Apr. 29—Paul Talbot, Halifax .... L 6
Dec. 9—Don Bester, Montreal .... L 4

ROBERTO CORNEJO
Argentine Welterweight
1980
Apr. 5—Manuel Alvarez, Mar del Plata .... L 8
May 17—Jorge Conti, Tandil .... L 10
Dec. 20—Jose Sosa, Gral Belgrano .... L 6

RAFAEL CORONA
California Junior Middleweight
1979
July 20—Hector Fernandez, San Diego .... KO 2
Aug. 3—Clint Jackson, Santa Monica .... L 4
Aug. 10—Robert Wilcot, San Diego .... KO 3
Aug. 17—Larry Meyers, San Diego .... W 4
Sept. 21—Danny Mancino, San Diego .... W 6
Nov. 2—Alvira Benrose, San Diego .... L 6
Nov. 15—Humberto DeLos Rios, Los Angeles .... L 6
1980
Jan. 22—Manny Gullatt, Sacramento .... KO 1
Feb. 5—Paul Jones, Sacramento .... KO by 3
Feb. 19—James Bella, Sacramento .... W 6

ENRIQUE CORONEL
Argentine Middleweight
1980
Feb. 1—Hugo Trujillo, S. Sal. de Jujuy .... W 10
Feb. 15—Ramon Quintana, S. Sal. de Jujuy .... W 10
Mar. 7—Jose A. Fernandez, S. Sal de Jujuy ...... W 10
Mar. 21—Hector Caceres, S. Sal de Jujuy .... W 10

Apr. 11—Ricardo Cisneros, P.R.S. Pena .... W 10
May 2—Julio Arancibia, Salta .... L 10
June 6—Ricardo Cisneros, P.R.S. Pena .... L 10
July 11—Antonio Juarez, San Ped. Jujuy .... D 10
Aug. 1—Jorge R. Valdez, Tartagal .... W 10
Oct. 11—Jorge Medina, Bolivar .... D 10
Nov. 21—Juan D. Roldan, Salta .... KO by 7
Dec. 19—Omar Ochoa, San Pedro .... L 10

UBALDO CORREA
Argentine Light Heavyweight
1980
July 18—Natalio Ibarra, Bahia Blanca .... KO 7
Aug. 16—Ruben Wilberger, Buenos Aires ...... KO by 5

HECTOR CORTEZ
Ecuadoran Featherweight
1974
—Francisco Corrosco, Guaquil .... KO 1
—Sergio Creyo, Guaquil .... KO 3
—William Rodriguez, Guaquil .... L 4
—Guencelao Ruiz, Guaquil .... KO 3
—Gustavo Altimirano, Guaquil .... D 8
—Platillo Soriano, Guaquil .... W 10
—Jaime Amaya, Guaquil .... D 10
—Ramiro Montaluo, Guaquil .... KO 4
—Washington Narbae, Guaquil .... KO 6
1975
—Hernando Mullo, Quito .... L 10
—Ramiro Montaluo, Cuenca .... KO 2
—Vincente Salecdo, Guaquil .... KO 3
—Tony Barbosa, Guaquil .... KO 3
—Renan Marota, Guaquil .... KO 10
—Roger Bucheilli, Guaquil .... W 10
—Raphael Anchundia, Guaquil .... W 12
1976
—Augustin Apablasa, Guaquil .... KO 4
—Ricardo Allendon, Guaquil .... KO 6
1977
Feb. 24—Sergio Ayala, Los Angeles .... W 10
May 6—Hector Molina, Guaquil .... W 10
—Gustavo Altimirano, Puerto Viejo ...... KO 3
Aug. 20—Alfredo Carranza, Los Angeles .... KO 1
Nov. 19—Jose Angel Casarez, Los Angeles .... KO 2
1978
Feb. 9—Ray Saldivar, Los Angeles .... KO 9
Aug. 13—Salvatore Sabchez, Mazatlan .... KO by 7
Dec. 4—Roberto Torres, Tijuana .... D 10
Dec. 19—Roberto Quintanilla, Houston .... W 10
1979
Apr. 24—Enrique Guerra, Houston .... W 10
June 5—Manny Castillo, Houston .... KO 5
Nov. 10—Francisco Marquez, Guadalajara .... KO 4
Nov. 27—Angel Gonzalez, Houston .... W 10
Dec. 8—Francisco Manzo, Los Angeles .... L 10
1980
Dec. 5—Santos Moreno, Las Vegas .... W 12
Dec. 12—Pedro Gonzalez, El Paso .... KO 1

JUAN C. CORTEZ
Argentine Flyweight
1980
Feb. 1—Hugo Saldubehere, Alta Gracia .... KO 4
Mar. 7—Juan Espindola, Alta Gracia .... W 10
Apr. 25—Ernesto Bustos, Alta Gracia .... W 10
May 15—Luis Gerez, Arrecifes .... L 10
Aug. 1—Raul Perez, Cordoba .... W 10
Sept. 19—Julio C. Saba, Cordoba .... W 10
Oct. 7—Ramon Soria, Mendoza .... L 10
Dec. 5—Ramon Soria, Cordoba .... D 10

BILL COSTELLO
New York, N.Y. Welterweight
Born: April 10, 1956, Managed by Mike Jones
1979
Aug. 22—Angel Ortiz, New York .... W 4
Sept. 12—Jose Gonzalez, White Plains .... KO 3
Oct. 12—Dave Bolden, Uniondale .... W 4
Oct. 19—John Jones, Commack .... KO 2
Oct. 26—George Casher, New York .... W 4
Dec. 5—Marvin Edwards, White Plains .... KO 1
1980
Feb. 13—Kato Ali, White Plains .... W 6
Apr. 16—Kato Ali, White Plains .... KO 3
May 4—Richie Garland, Kiamesha Lake ...... KO 5
May 14—Rich Sienni, White Plains .... W 6
Sept. 17—Paul Moore, White Plains .... KO 1
Oct. 2—Jose Green, Commack .... KO 5
Oct. 24—Orlando Montalvo, Uniondale .... W 8

J. J. COTTRELL
Denver, Colo. Welterweight
Born: February 29, 1956, Height: 5'8"
1978
May	23—Gabby Rivera, Denver	KO	2
June	3—Richard Flowers, Denver	KO	3
June	16—Carlos Muro, Ogden	KO	1
July	14—Dick Fisher, Ogden	W	6
Aug.	22—Jim Hearn, Omaha	KO	2
Sept.	8—Victor Martinez, Ogden	W	8
Oct.	14—Greg Stephens, Ogden	W	8
Dec.	8—Carlos Rodriguez, Denver	W	6

1979
Jan.	20—Pepe Dominguez, Ogden	L	10
Apr.	7—Daryl Penn, Billings	L	10
June	8—Sultan Saladin, Denver	W	8
June	16—Sultan Saladin, Colorado	KO	3
June	23—Clarence Hammock, Denver	KO	2
July	14—Billy Parks, Denver	D	6
Sept.	14—Carl Crowley, Ogden	KO	5
Oct.	20—Frank Lawson, Pueblo	D	10
Nov.	22—Julio Gomez, Las Vegas	KO by	4

1980
Feb.	6—Victor Martinez, Las Vegas	L	10
Feb.	23—Gabby Rivera, Greeley, Colo	KO	4
Mar.	15—Nick Miller, Denver	KO	1
Apr.	11—Rodrigo Hernandez, Denver	D	8
Apr.	19—Daryl Penn, Billings	W	10
May	23—Ron Brown, Denver	W	8
Aug.	23—Victor Abraham, Los Angeles	KO by	1
Nov.	7—Eddie Carrera, Denver	KO	3
Nov.	28—Jose Luis Pacheco, Denver	KO	2

GREG COVERSON
Kalamazoo, Mich. Junior Lightweight
Born: Dec. 6, 1956, Height: 5'8"
1976
Apr.	21—Young Casanova, Seattle	KO	3
May	25—Hideo Kitari, Seattle	KO	2
July	24—Harry Lee, Kalamazoo	KO	2
Sept.	22—Wilbur Young, Las Vegas	W	6
Oct.	6—Baby Soto, Las Vegas	KO	4
Oct.	20—Gustavo Saucedo, Las Vegas	KO	3
Nov.	3—Jorge Armin, Las Vegas	KO	8
Nov.	20—Jose Murciaga, Las Vegas	KO	4
Dec.	8—Manny Lopez, Las Vegas	KO	3

1977
Mar.	27—Jerry Kornele, San Antonio	W	8
	(U.S. Championship Tournament)		
Aug.	4—Johnny Summerhays, Wyoming	W	10
Nov.	26—Tony Johnson, Columbus	W	10
Dec.	10—Sammy Taylor, Grand Rapids	KO	1

1978
Feb.	16—Augustin Estrada, Houston	W	10
Mar.	16—Bennie Marquez, Kalamazoo	W	10
June	22—Dave White, Kalamazoo	KO	1
Nov.	9—Johnny Summerhays, Mt. Clemens	W	10

1979
Feb.	9—Scotty Foreman, Mt. Clemens	W	10
July	21—Ignacio (Negro) Campos, Pontiac	KO	7

1980
Jan.	9—Fausto Pena, Holland, Mich.	KO	1
Mar.	22—Bobby Alexander, Grand Rapids	W	10

JACK COWELL
Bridgeport, Conn. Junior Middleweight
1979
Oct.	17—Randy Davio, Hartford	L	4
Dec.	18—Ken Fusco, Fairfield	KO by	2

1980
Feb.	28—Randy Davio, Hartford	KO by	3
Apr.	8—Randy Davio, Hartford	L	4
May	23—Randy Davio, Hartford	L	5
Sept.	12—Randy Davio, Hartford	KO by	2
Oct.	16—Mark Mainero, Revere	KO by	3
Nov.	25—Derrick Dougherty, Springfield	L	4

CHARLES COX
Lowell, Mass. Heavyweight
1978
Jan.	16—Bobo Robinson, Waltham	KO	1
Mar.	20—Don Halpin, Boston	W	8
July	18—Sam Miller, Boston	W	6
Aug.	21—Johnny Blaine, Yarmouth	KO	3

1979
June	20—Reynaldo Snipes, White Plains	L	6

1980
July	20—Tim Witherspoon, Great Gorge	KO by	5

JOHN COX
Rockford, Ill. Light Heavyweight
1979
Dec.	19—Bill Hollis, Rockford	L	4

1980
Apr.	14—Stephen Shilaita, Chicago	L	6
June	27—Wilbur Johnson, Chicago	L	6
Aug.	8—Don Bester, Chicago	W	6
Sept.	12—Murray Sutherland, Milwaukee	KO by	2
Nov.	19—Charles Henderson, Moline	L	6

BRAD CRANE
Norfolk, Va. Heavyweight
1978
July	20—James Reid, Virginia Beach	L	4
Aug.	17—John Beverage, Virginia Beach	KO	1
Oct.	9—Quinnie Locklear, Hampton	L	6

1979
Apr.	26—Marc Moncure, Virginia Beach	KO	1
May	17—Lynn Jones, Virginia Beach	W	4
Sept.	20—Charlie Harris, Virginia Beach	KO	3

1980
Nov.	1—Joe Ballard, Richmond	KO by	2

MIKE CREEL
Las Vegas, Nev. Heavyweight
1977
July	12—Tony Razo, Phoenix	KO by	3
July	28—S. T. Gordon, Tucson	W	5

1978
Aug.	22—Ernie Smith, Odessa	L	4
Sept.	7—Kevin Isaac, El Paso	KO by	3
Sept.	17—Mike Weaver, Reno	KO by	2
Dec.	13—Lou Lockwood, Las Vegas	W	6

1979
Jan.	31—Dwight Hams, Las Vegas	KO	4
Feb.	14—Eddie Wilson, Las Vegas	KO by	1
Apr.	4—Dennis Haggerty, Las Vegas	KO	2
Apr.	18—Chuck Gardner, Las Vegas	L	5
June	20—Jeff Podgurski, Las Vegas	KO by	3

1980
Aug.	6—Ron Draper, Las Vegas	L	6
Sept.	17—Mike Benning, Las Vegas	L	4
Nov.	29—Tony Tubbs, Los Angeles	KO by	3

KEN CROOM
Los Angeles, Calif. Junior Middleweight
1979
Feb.	27—Larry Myers, San Carlos	KO	5
Mar.	16—Johnny Laine, San Diego	KO	4
Apr.	4—Robert Turner, Los Angeles	KO	2
June	6—Robert Wilcot, Los Angeles	KO	2
June	27—Larry Myers, Los Angeles	KO	2
Nov.	21—Marcy Atencio, Los Angeles	KO	4

1980
Aug.	28—Agapito Ramirez, Las Vegas	KO	4
Nov.	29—Jose Santana, Las Vegas	KO	1

JIMMY CROSS
Memphis, Tenn. Heavyweight
1971
Sept.	22—Clyce Brown, San Antonio	KO by	3
Nov.	12—Ray Vega, Memphis	W	10
Dec.	3—Jimmy Gillespi, Memphis	KO	1

1972
Jan.	13—Clyde Brown, Memphis	KO	5
Feb.	2—Mel Harris, Memphis	KO	1
Feb.	22—Buddy Chandler, Memphis	W	10
Mar.	30—Ray Vega, Memphis	W	10
Apr.	5—Ray Vega, Memphis	W	10
May	24—Henry Glass, Memphis	KO	3
July	17—Buddy Chandler, Memphis	KO by	8
Oct.	11—Jess Wolcott, Memphis	KO	1
Oct.	29—Tiffy Sugarplum, Memphis	KO	9
Nov.	14—Jimmy Phillips, Memphis	KO	10
Nov.	30—Ray Kelly, Memphis	L	10
Dec.	16—Jack Johnson, Memphis	KO	5

1973
May	17—Sylvester Murphy, Memphis	KO	4
May	22—Claude McBride, Oklahoma City	KO	4
May	30—Rudy Jones, Oklahoma City	KO	4
June	5—Brian Kelly, Oklahoma City	L	10
June	19—Bob Crutison, Oklahoma City	W	10
July	3—Pete Knight, Oklahoma City	W	10
July	17—Brian Kelly, Oklahoma City	L	10
Aug.	7—Billy Marsh, Oklahoma City	W	10
Sept.	4—Al Lewis, Oklahoma City	KO by	6
Oct.	16—Tom Berry, Oklahoma City	W	6
Nov.	13—Terry Hinke, Tokyo	KO by	2
Nov.	20—Tom Berry, Oklahoma City	D	6

1974
Feb.	19—Duane Bobick, Oklahoma City	KO by	3
Apr.	2—Duane Bobick, Minneapolis	KO by	10
May	11—Sam Vega, Little Rock	KO	3
Aug.	13—Jody Ballard, Houston	KO by	2

1975
June	27—John Dennis, Hamden	KO by	5

71

July 19—Alfio Righetti, Rimini .... KO by 1
1976
May 25—Bruce Grandham, Seattle .... KO by 2
1977
(Inactive)
1978
Jan. 24—Ron Stephens, Memphis .... W 4
May 23—Hubert McIntosh, Little Rock .... W 4
Sept. 1—Jeff Shellburg, Salt Lake City .... KO by 2
Dec. 20—Dan Kiser, Memphis .... NC 4
1979
June 14—George Mostardini, River Grove .... KO 4
Sept. 7—James Tillis, Chicago .... KO by 2
1980
Mar. 22—Lupe Guerra, N. Platte .... L 10
Aug. 2—Carl Halliburton, Millington .... KO 4

FRANKIE CROSSAN
Wilmington, Del. Light Heavyweight
Born: June 22, 1956
1976
Nov. 18—Elwood Townsend, Wilmington .... KO 3
1977
Jan. 27—Moses Robinson, Wilmington .... KO 1
Feb. 24—Clayton Ambrose, Wilmington .... L 4
Apr. 21—Al Daniels, Wilmington .... KO 1
1978
Apr. 28—Roy Jones, Upper Darby .... KO 1
May 18—Jesse Carter, Virginia Beach .... L 4
June 15—Derrick Ennis, Atlantic City .... KO by 2
Oct. 9—Jesse Carter, Hampton .... W 6
1979
Apr. 17—Dave Bird, Totowa .... L 6
1980
Mar. 14—Lindsay Page, Trenton .... KO 2
Apr. 11—Robert Grooms, Chester .... KO 1
Nov. 7—Chris Reeder, Trenton .... KO 2

TYRONE CROWLEY
Philadelphia, Pa. Lightweight
1980
Oct. 24—Isidro Ruiz, Philadelphia .... W 6
Dec. 11—Chris Harmon, Philadelphia .... KO 2

JESSE CROWN
Portland, Me. Heavyweight
1975
June 23—Kevin Isaac, New York .... KO by 1
1976
(Inactive)
1977
Nov. 24—Joe Velmure, Portland, Me. .... L 6
1978
Nov. 23—Ron Gabaree, Portland, Me. .... KO 6
Dec. 21—Al Brooks, Portland, Me. .... W 8
1979
Jan. 24—Vincent Smith, Waterville .... KO 2
Mar. 17—Bob Akers, Lubec, Me. .... KO 2
Apr. 27—Randy Cobb, Newark .... KO by 2
June 29—John Denis, Cranston .... KO by 2
1980
Nov. 27—James Van Kemren, Portland .... KO 2

ALBERT CRUZ
Dallas, Texas Bantamweight
1978
Aug. 25—Jose Luis Garcia, Dallas .... L 8
1979
Oct. 20—Felipe Garcia, Pueblo .... L 6
July 31—Jeff Chandler, Atlantic City .... KO by 3
      —James Ortega, Denver .... W 6
1980
Oct. 10—Ron Cisneros, Denver .... L 6

ANGEL CRUZ
Bethlehem, Pa. Lightweight
1977
July 14—Ken Twyne, Allentown .... W 4
Aug. 26—Ray Hall, Allentown .... W 4
1978
Apr. 9—Bobby Alexander, Allentown .... KO 5
June 4—Sandy Lemone, Allentown .... W 6
Oct. 22—Bernard Porter, Allentown .... KO 3
1979
Mar. 21—John McQueen, Allentown .... W 6
Apr. 10—Jorge Diaz, Philadelphia .... KO 4
May 7—Gaetan Hart, Buckingham .... L 10
Sept. 11—Charlie Brown, Philadelphia .... L 6
Nov. 22—Morris Grant, Allentown .... W 6
1980
Mar. 22—John McQueen, Bethlehem .... W 8
May 23—Anthony Fox, Bethlehem .... KO 1

ANTONIO (KID CAN) CRUZ
Dominican Rep. Lightweight
1977
Feb. 22—Rafael Andujar, Santo Domingo .... W 10
Apr. 1—Tony Arias, Santo Domingo .... W 10
Nov. 24—Rafael Andujar, Santo Domingo .... KO 7
1978
Feb. 24—Ezequiel Sanchez, Santo Domingo .... KO by 11
Aug. 28—Jose Alejandro, Santo Domingo .... KO 11
Oct. 16—Azor Agosto, Santo Domingo .... W 10
Nov. 6—Julio Serrano, Santo Domingo .... W 10
Nov. 30—Francisco Arias, Santo Domingo .... KO 5
1979
Feb. 26—Jorge Mojica, Santo Domingo .... W 10
July 26—Bobby Alexander, Santo Domingo .... W 10
1980
Mar. 10—Edwin Viruet, San Juan .... L 10
Aug. 25—Felix Reyes, Santo Domingo .... KO 3

DANIEL CRUZ
Los Angeles, Calif. Junior Lightweight
Managed by Jimmy Montaya
1980
Apr. 30—Rudy Mata, Las Vegas .... W 4
May 7—Jerry Reyes, Las Vegas .... L 4
May 21—Ramon Barrera, Las Vegas .... KO 6
June 11—Francisco Monzon, Las Vegas .... KO 1
June 18—Rigoberto Coria, Las Vegas .... W 6
July 2—Sergio Fierro, Las Vegas .... KO 1
July 16—Tony Villa, Las Vegas .... KO by 4
Aug. 20—Joey Rico, Las Vegas .... KO 1
Sept. 3—Grey Williams, Las Vegas .... KO 2
Sept. 25—Luis Pina, Los Angeles .... KO 5
Oct. 2—Lonnie Smith, Las Vegas .... L 4
Oct. 16—Carlos Garcia, Los Angeles .... KO 2
Nov. 8—Bernard Taylor, Lake Tahoe .... L 6
Nov. 29—Leonard Church, Los Angeles .... L 6

DENNIS CRUZ
New York City, N.Y. Junior Lightweight
1980
Aug. 29—Robert Sanchez, New York .... W 4
Dec. 20—Herman Ingram, Bronx .... KO 2

FRANCISCO CRUZ
Carolina, Puerto Rico Lightweight
1972
Apr. 8—Tony Tris, San Juan .... L 6
Nov. 16—Leo Cruz, Santo Domingo .... KO by 3
1973
May 12—Tony Tris, Carolina, P.R. .... L 8
July 14—Leo Cruz, Caguas .... L 10
Sept. 24—Wilson Yambo, San Juan .... W 8
Nov. 30—Orlando Amores, San Juan .... KO by 6
1974
Apr. 6—Leo Cruz, San Juan .... W 10
Apr. 27—Roberto Gomez, San Juan .... W 10
July 29—Santos Luis Rivera, San Juan .... KO by 7
Oct. 17—Carlos Zarate, Mexicali .... KO by 2
1975
Jan. 4—Felipe Pena, San Juan .... W 8
Feb. 8—Pedro Jose Diaz, San Juan .... W 8
June 16—Leo Cruz, Santo Domingo .... L 10
1976
Jan. 3—Enrique Solis, San Juan .... L 10
Apr. 5—Enrique Solis, San Juan .... L 10
Apr. 13—Baby Kid Chocolate, Philadelphia .... KO by 1
June 5—Quique Solis, San Juan .... L 10
June 17—Frankie Duarte, Los Angeles .... KO by 8
Oct. 15—Fidel Villalobos, Guadalajara .... KO 1
Oct. 26—Gaby Cantera, San Antonio .... KO by 9
1977
Feb. 11—Claude Noel .... KO by 3
Mar. 11—Elpidio Valdez, Guadalajara .... KO by 5
1978
May 13—Luis Rivera, Carolina .... L 8
1979
(Inactive)
1980
Feb. 11—Jose Alejandro, San Juan .... L 10
Oct. 10—Manuel de la Rosa, New York ...... KO by 3

HECTOR CRUZ
Puerto Rican Lightweight
1978
May 20—Raul Gonzalez, Carolina .... KO 1
June 2—Ray Viruet, San Juan .... W 4
Sept. 9—Rene Aviles, San Juan .... W 6
1979
Feb. 18—Ray Viruet, San Juan .... L 6
Apr. 28—Vicente Quinones, Trujillo .... L 6
Dec. 18—Vicente Quinones, Rio Piedras .... L 6

1980

Feb.	11—Fernando Ortiz, San Juan	L 8
May	29—Pelayito Hernandez, Rio Piedras	KO by 4
Sept.	19—Ivan Montalvo, San Juan	KO by 5

JIMMY CRUZ
New York City, N.Y. Lightweight
1977

Apr.	15—Jose (Cheo) Ortiz, Sunnyside	W 4
May	20—Jose Figueroa, Sunnyside	L 4

1978

June	6—Jose (Cheo) Ortiz, New York	KO by 6

1979
(Inactive)
1980

Apr.	11—Herman Boyd, Staten Island	KO 1
May	9—Robert Johnson, Staten Island	KO by 1

JOSE CRUZ
Jersey City, N.J. Middleweight
1980

Oct.	16—Hank Whitmore, Totowa	KO 1

JOSE LUIS CRUZ
Mexican Flyweight
1977

Mar.	8—Kimio Furesawa, Tokyo	KO by 6

1978

Dec.	9—Juan Reyna Lopez, Houston	KO 3

1979

Mar.	21—Juan Meza, Las Vegas	KO by 4
Apr.	6—Juan Guzman, McAllen	KO 2
May	17—Juan Reyna Lopez, McAllen	KO 2

JUAN RAMON CRUZ
Bronx, N.Y. Junior Lightweight
1980

May	23—Angel Vasquez, New York	KO 3

LEO CRUZ
Dominican Rep. Junior Featherweight
1972

Feb.	—Heriberto Oliveras, San Juan	W 4
Mar.	—Heriberto Oliveras, San Juan	W 4
July	—Diablito Valdez, Santo Domingo	W 4
Oct.	—Jorge Leo, Santo Domingo	W 6
Nov.	16—Francisco Cruz, Santo Domingo	KO 3

1973

Jan.	—Diablito Valdez, Santo Domingo	W 6
Feb.	—Diablito Valdez, Santo Domingo	KO 8
Mar.	—Felito Pena, Santo Domingo	W 8
Apr.	—Alfredo Campusano, Santo Domingo	KO 8
Apr.	7—Heriberto Oliveras, Carolina	KO 5
Apr.	28—Andres Torres, Carolina	D 10
May	—Francisco Cruz, San Juan	W 8
May	—Heriberto Oliveras, San Juan	KO 6
May	12—Luciano Santos, Carolina	W 10
July	14—Francisco Cruz, Caguas	W 10
Sept.	1—Hector Espinoza, San Juan	KO 7
Oct.	—Andres Torres, San Juan	KO 10
Nov.	30—Henry Maxwell, San Juan	W 10

1974

Apr.	6—Francisco Cruz, San Juan	L 10
July	—Inocencio Pena, Santo Domingo	KO 4
Aug.	14—Roberto Pena, Santo Domingo	KO 3
Sept.	9—Ben Ortiz, San Juan	KO 8
Dec.	19—Livio Nolasco, Santo Domingo	KO by 9

1975

June	16—Francisco Cruz, Santo Domingo	W 10
Sept.	1—Francisco Villegas, San Juan	W 10
Oct.	8—Patricio Nunez, Santo Domingo	KO 9
Dec.	22—Idelfonso Bethelmi, Santo Domingo	W 10

1976

Mar.	15—Tony Rocha, Santo Domingo	KO 6

1977

Jan.	15—Reynaldo Hidalgo, Panama City	KO by 6
Mar.	14—Nelson Cruz Tamariz, Santo Domingo	W 12
June	13—Nelson Cruz Tamariz, Santo Domingo	W 12
Sept.	—Rodrigo Ortiz, Acapulco	KO 3
Oct.	3—Manuel Batista, Santo Domingo	KO 3
Oct.	15—Aurelio Birriel, Carolina	L 10

Feb.	2—Guillermo Almengot, Santo Domingo	KO 9
Apr.	22—Jupe Pintor, San Juan	W 10
July	8—Cuban Kid, San Juan	KO 2
Sept.	9—Wilfredo Gomez, San Juan	KO by 13

(WBC Super Bantamweight Title)
1979

Feb.	18—Jose Cervantes, San Juan	W 10
Aug.	4—Ismael Santana, Chicago	KO 4

1980

	—Luis Barreto, Santo Domingo	KO 3
	—Niliberto Herrera, Santo Domingo	W 10

RAUL CRUZ
Las Vegas, Nevada Lightweight
1980

Apr.	23—Andres Montoya, Las Vegas	L 6
May	1—Joe Phillips, Las Vegas	L 6
May	28—Jaime Nava, Las Vegas	KO by 5

ROBERTO CRUZ
Mexican Light Heavyweight
1978

Jan.	24—Sammy NeSmith, Indianapolis	KO by 1
Apr.	12—Lobo Ramirez, Mexico City	KO by 1

1979

Feb.	3—Elias Equihua, Mexico City	W 8
Mar.	16—Jorge Vaca, Guadalajara	L 10
Apr.	14—Armando Alatorre, Mexico City	W 10
July	28—Efrain Marcano, Caracas	KO 3

1980

Mar.	28—Billy Ratliff, Chicago	KO by 6
July	6—Carlos Marks, Bird's Isle	W disq. 5

SANTOS CRUZ
Manhattan, N.Y. Featherweight
1978

Mar.	2—Juan LaPorte, New York	L 4

1979

Apr.	27—Benjamin Fuentes, New York	KO 1
June	29—Guillermo Guzman, New York	KO 2

1980

Jan.	18—Heriberto Torres, Trenton	W 4
Jan.	25—Jorge Vasquez, New York	L 4
Feb.	5—Rafael Lopez, W. Hartford	L 6
Oct.	1—Jimmy Washington, Atlantic City	L 8

GERMAN CUELLO
Los Angeles, Calif. Lightweight
1973

Apr.	27—Miguel Cruz, Tampico	W 10

1974

Apr.	6—Ruben Ruiz, Torreon	KO by 2
May	3—Jose Manuel Ursua, Monterrey	KO by 7
June	19—Chucho Flores, Mexico City	KO 7
Aug.	14—Jose Luis Hernandez, Mexico City	KO 7
Nov.	24—Clemente Mucino, Nogales	KO 6

1975
(Inactive)
1976

June	12—Juan Pablo Oropeza, Tampico	L 10

1977

Feb.	12—Abraham Perez, Tijuana	KO 7
Mar.	7—Ernesto Garfias, Tijuana	KO by 8
Aug.	9—Leonardo Bermudez, Las Vegas	W 10
Oct.	28—Julio Mendez, Las Vegas	KO 8

1978

Apr.	5—Miguel Estrada, Las Vegas	W 10
June	20—Andrew Ganigan, Honolulu	KO by 9
Sept.	27—Jose Isaac Marin, Las Vegas	W 10
Nov.	1—Leroy Haley, Las Vegas	KO by 10

1979

May	24—Herman Montes, Los Angeles	W 10
Aug.	15—Julio Alfonso, Las Vegas	KO 4
Dec.	5—Leroy Haley, Las Vegas	L 12

1980

Mar.	21—Luis Ramirez, Los Angeles	KO by 8

PAT CUILLO
Niagara Falls, Canada Light Heavyweight
1975

Aug.	23—Mustafa Hamsho, Binghamton	W 6
Oct.	23—Charlie Vivant, Binghamton	KO 2
Nov.	12—Charley Stern, Scranton	KO 6
Dec.	10—Billy Early, Scranton	KO 2

1976

Jan.	24—Philip Ali, Syracuse	KO 2
Mar.	31—Luis Rodriguez, Scranton	KO 5

1977

Sept.	7—Joe Sprowell, Virginia Beach, Va.	W 6

1978

Jan.	12—Sam Long, Cleveland	KO 3
Feb.	16—Gary Alexander, Cleveland	KO 7
Apr.	6—Fred Brown, Cleveland	KO 6
May	13—Diego Roberson, Utica	KO 4
June	26—Ivy Brown, Detroit	KO by 2
Aug.	26—Bernard McClean, Monaca	W 10
Sept.	29—Gary Summerhays, Hamilton	L 10
Dec.	5—Karl Zurheide, Winnepeg	KO 8

1979

Jan.	23—Bill Payne, Montreal	KO 1
Feb.	9—Grady Daniels, Winnipeg	KO 4
Feb.	26—Eddie Gregory, New York	L 10

1980

Apr.	4—Tony Mundine, Milan	KO by 5

FLOYD (JUMBO) CUMMINGS
Joliet, Ill. Heavyweight
1979
June 18—Dave Watkins, Highland Park .... KO 1
July 20—James Flynn, U. of Ill .... KO 1
July 30—George Goforth, Chicago .... KO 4
Nov. 20—Cornel Verse, Chicago .... KO 4
Dec. 15—Larry Sims, Chicago .... W 6
1980
Feb. 1—Sylvester Wilder, Chicago .... KO 2
Feb. 18—Amos Haynes, Chicago .... KO 2
Apr. 17—Vic Wallace, Chicago .... KO 2
May 15—Charles Atlas, Chicago .... KO 1
June 12—Razor Blade Jackson, Chicago .... KO 3
Aug. 25—Jesse Clark, Chicago .... KO 1
Sept. 10—Johnny Warr, Chicago .... W 10
Dec. 11—George Mostardini, Chicago .... KO 8

RON CUMMINGS
Sacramento, Calif. Junior Welterweight
1977
Oct. 21—Tiger Noji, Sacramento .... KO 5
Nov. 10—Curtis Lewis, Sacramento .... W 6
Nov. 22—Howard Jackson, Sacramento .... W 6
1978
Feb. 14—Al Fletcher, Sacramento .... W 6
Mar. 14—Pablo Baez, Sacramento .... W 6
May 2—Fred Lorona, Sacramento .... KO 7
June 1—Rafael Nunez, Sacramento .... W 6
July 13—Willie Hearne, Vallejo .... KO 2
Sept. 9—Albert Guevara, Sacramento .... W 6
Nov. 8—Jose Dominguez, Stockton .... D 8
Dec. 13—Mauricio Aldana, Oakland .... W 8
1979
Feb. 9—David Arrellano, Sacramento .... KO 5
May 15—Monroe Brooks, Sacramento .... D 10
Aug. 12—Pablo Baez, Las Vegas .... D 8
1980
May 6—Bruce Curry, Las Vegas .... L 10
Aug. 22—Lennox Blackmoore, Las Vegas .... L 10

RALPH CUOMO
Long Island, N.Y. Heavyweight
1977
Aug. 27—Paul Tellesco, Hempstead .... W 4
1978
Mar. 16—Cornell Chavis, N. Bergen .... KO by 1
Oct. 14—Floyd Anderson, Commack .... KO 2
1979
Apr. 20—Ron Cecchetti, New York .... L 4
May 11—Joe Manning, Commack .... KO 2
June 29—Pete Brodsky, Commack .... L 4
July 31—Ramon Ronquillo, Totowa .... KO by 1
1980
Apr. 1—Dave Bird, Totowa .... KO by 3
Aug. 15—Paul Benjamin, Glen Cove .... W 4
Oct. 24—Arnold Rodriguez, Uniondale .... L 4

EDWIN CURET
Chelsea, Mass. Featherweight
1980
Aug. 18—Ralph Bracetty, Boston .... KO 1
Sept. 5—Robert Johnson, Dorchester .... W 4
Nov. 25—Bobby Everett, Boston .... KO 2
Dec. 12—Robert Huff, Brocton .... W 4

BRUCE CURRY
Los Angeles, Calif. Junior Welterweight
1976
Sept. 9—Bruce Henderson, Los Angeles .... W 5
Oct. 5—Willie Hearne, San Carlos .... KO 1
Oct. 27—Kid Dynamita, Las Vegas............... W 6
Nov. 4—Chris Gonzalez, Los Angeles .... KO 1
Nov. 10—Clarence Howard, Las Vegas .... KO 3
Dec. 10—Kid Dinamita, Las Vegas .... W 6
1977
Feb. 21—Freddy Washington, Los Angeles .... W 10
Apr. 4—Jimmy Jackson, Las Vegas .... W 10
Apr. 15—Rafael Rodriguez, Jersey City .... W 10
May 13—Buffalo Suzuki, Tokyo.................. KO 7
May 25—Rudy Barro, Stockton .... KO 8
July 17—Lion Furuyama, Tokyo .... KO 5
Oct. 19—Julio Gomez, Stockton .... KO 3
Nov. 18—Wilfred Benitez, New York .... L 10
1978
Jan. 26—Minoru Sugiya, Tokyo................. KO 3
Feb. 4—Wilfred Benitez, New York .... L 10
Mar. 18—Luis Resto, Las Vegas .... KO 2
Apr. 7—Monroe Brooks, Los Angeles .... KO 9
(U.S. Junior Welterweight Title)
Sept. 9—Domingo Ayala, San Juan .... KO by 9
Oct. 27—Adolfo Viruet, New York .... L 10

Dec. 5—Wade Hinnant, Philadelphia .... W 10
1979
Feb. 24—Clinton McKenzie, Las Vegas .... W 10
Apr. 14—Willie Rodriguez, New Orleans .... KO 12
June 28—Thomas Hearns, Detroit .... KO by 3
Sept. 25—Greg Stephens, Las Vegas .... W 10
1980
Jan. 18—Jimmy Jackson, Las Vegas .... KO 7
May 6—Ron Cummings, Las Vegas .... W 10
June 3—Greg Stephens, Las Begas .... KO by 11
(NABF Welterweight Title)
Sept. 25—Andres Ramirez, Las Vegas .... KO 3

DAVID CURRY
Toledo, Ohio Welterweight
1980
Sept. 18—Tony Lane, Cleveland .... W 4

VINNIE CURTO
Boston, Mass. Middleweight
1972
Oct. 10—Victor Perez, Miami Beach............. KO 5
1973
Jan. 30—Lee Royster, Miami Beach .... KO 4
Feb. 20—Jimmy Williams, Miami Beach........... W 8
Mar. 13—John Jones, Miami Beach............... KO 2
Mar. 20—Calvin Holleman, Miami Beach .... KO 1
Apr. 3—Bernie Bennett, Miami Beach .... W 8
Apr. 10—Buillermo Escalera, Miami Beach......... W 8
May 1—Joe Hooks, Miami Beach .... W 8
May 29—Teddy Murray, Miami Beach .... KO 2
June 19—Casey Garic, Miami Beach .... W 10
July 31—Dennis Riggs, Miami Beach .... W 10
Aug. 28—Nat King, Miami Beach .... W 10
Sept. 18—Tommy Hicks, Miami Beach .... KO 8
Nov. 20—Terry Daniels, Miami Beach .... W 10
Dec. 18—Carlos Salinas, Miami Beach........... KO 7
1974
Jan. 22—Baby Boy Rolle, Miami Beach .... W 10
May 28—Luis Vinales, Miami Beach .... W 10
Oct. 25—Rodrigo Valdez, New York............. L 10
Nov. 2—Jessie Garcia, Miami Beach............. W 10
1975
Feb. 13—Tony Licata, New Orleans............... L 10
(American Middleweight Title)
Apr. 7—Bennie Briscoe, Philadelphia .... D 10
Aug. 8—Vito Antuofermo, Las Vegas........... L 10
Sept. 23—Johnny Pinney, Miami Beach........... D 10
1976
Feb. 18—Eddie Davis, Orlando .... W 10
July 20—Nat King, Miami Beach .... W 10
Aug. 17—Gene Wells, Orlando .... L 10
Dec. 22—Joe Grady, Boston.................... KO 6
1977
Jan. 29—Steve Smith, Boston .... W 10
Feb. 15—Dalton Swift, Boston .... KO 2
Mar. 12—D. C. Walker, Fitchburg .... W 10
Mar. 30—Henry Walker, Boston .... W 10
June 17—Tony Chiaverini, Kansas City .... L 12
July 20—Nat King, Miami Beach .... W 10
Aug. 17—Gene Wells, Orlando .... L 10
Aug. 27—Joe Houston, Bath .... W 10
1978
Mar. 7—Bob Payton, Upper Darby .... W 10
Apr. 27—Willie Classen, New York .... D 10
Dec. 5—Tommy Ellis, Miami Beach .... W 8
1979
Feb. 19—Starlin Woodside, Miami Beach .... KO 4
Apr. 30—Tony Daniels, Montreal .... KO 1
June 26—Ralph Hollett, Montreal .... W 8
July 17—Bill Ramsey, Dolbeau .... KO 6
Aug. 21—Dennis Waters, Montreal .... KO 2
Oct. 2—Marciano Bernardi, Montreal .... W 8
Nov. 6—Eddie Melo, Montreal .... W 10
1980
Jan. 20—Kelly Anderson, Montreal .... KO 3
May 29—Robert Davis, Revere .... W 10
Aug. 21—Danny Heath, Revere .... KO 9
Dec. 15—Bennie Briscoe, Boston .... W 10

MARIO CUSSON
Montreal, Canada Junior Welterweight
1978
June 6—Mel Domado, Montreal .... KO 1
June 9—Gerry Simpson, Verdun .... KO 1
Sept. 12—Robert Bath, Montreal .... KO 5
Oct. 31—Henry Rosa, Montreal .... D 6
Dec. 19—Robert Bath, Montreal .... KO 2
1979
May 25—Alex McNeil, Montreal .... W 6
June 26—Ron Henriksen, Montreal .... W 6
Aug. 21—Quentin Blackman, Montreal .... W 6
Nov. 6—L. C. Kolin, Montreal .... KO 1

1980

Mar.	11—Brian Anderson, Montreal	KO	3
Mar.	25—Ghyslain Deroy, Montreal	KO by	5
Dec.	9—Manuel Madera, Montreal	W	6

DERRICK CUTTINO
Paterson, N.J. Lightweight
1979

July	10—Marty Cole, Halifax	W	4
July	31—Vito Maselli, Totowa	L	4
Oct.	4—Benito Jimenez, N. Bergen	D	6
Oct.	30—Jesus Vasquez, Totowa	W	4
Nov.	15—Jose Green, Dover	W	6

1980

Jan.	24—Jack Rosas, Dover	L	6
Feb.	19—Jack Rosas, Totowa	L	4
Mar.	8—Jack O'Neill, Great Gorge	W	4
May	31—Arcadio Suarez, Elizabeth	L	8
July	22—Bob Harvey, Halifax	L	4
July	17—Herb Darity, New Bedford	L	4
Sept.	4—Anthony Fletcher, Atlantic City	L	6

BOBBY CZYZ
Wanaque, N.J. Middleweight
Born: February 10, 1962
Managed by Lou Duva
1980

Apr.	24—Hank Whitmore, Totowa	KO	1
May	8—Jamal Abubakar, Atlantic City	W	4
May	22—Dalton Swift, Totowa	KO	2
June	19—Roland Cousins, Totowa	KO	1
July	17—Bruce Strauss, Totowa	KO	4
Aug.	2—Leo Martinez, Totowa	W	8
Sept.	18—Johnny Davis, Totowa	KO	1
Oct.	16—Tommy Merola, Totowa	KO	2
Dec.	18—Skipper Jones, Totowa	KO	7

WAYNE DABNEY, JR.
Philadelphia, Pa. Lightweight
1978

Oct.	22—Arseneo Green, Allentown	KO by	2

1979

Apr.	10—Charley Brown, Philadelphia	KO by	1

1980

June	5—Ken Bogner, Atlantic City	KO by	1
Aug.	25—Dennis Howard, Philadelphia	KO by	2

FRANK J. DABROWSKI
Carson City, Nev. Light Heavyweight
1979

Aug.	1—Gary Yeats, Reno	KO	4
Sept.	18—Earl Shields, Reno	KO	1
Oct.	16—Lester Jackson, Reno	KO	1
Oct.	30—Lee Burkey, Carson City	KO by	3

1980

May	14—Charles Roye, Las Vegas	KO	

BOBBY DADE
Tallahassee, Fla. Heavyweight
1979

Oct.	23—Clyde Fussell, Orlando	KO by	3

1980

Mar.	18—Clyde Fussell, Orlando	KO by	3

ROY DALE
Cincinnati, Ohio, Middleweight
1969

May	1—Charlie Lewis, Fort Wayne	W	4
July	16—John Mason, Indianapolis	W	6
July	30—John Mason, Indianapolis	KO	4
Sept.	29—Al Jones, Detroit	KO by	5
Nov.	8—Walt Dolder, Lima	W	6

1970

Feb.	5—Charlie Lewis, Indianapolis	KO	2
Mar.	14—Howard Youngblood, Columbus	KO	8
Apr.	14—Stan Moore, Milwaukee	W	4
Apr.	27—Franklin Wilson, Chicago	W	6
May	23—Roy McMillan, Lima	W	6
June	16—Rich Kates, Philadelphia	KO by	1
Aug.	17—Jim Davis, Grain	L	5
Aug.	24—George McGee, Covington	KO	6
Sept.	28—George McGee, Lorain	KO	6
Oct.	4—Charlie Lewis, Newport	KO	2

Oct.	7—Charlie Lewis, Covington	KO	1

1971

Jan.	14—Tommy Shaffer, Huntington	W	8
May	15—James Park, Latonia	W	8
June	30—Jose Gabino, Huntsville	W	10
July	12—Don Cobbs, St. Louis	L	10
Aug.	13—Red Lacaze, New Orleans	KO	5
Oct.	3—Miguel de Oliveire, Sao Paulo	L	10
Nov.	8—Al Bolden, Cincinnati	W	8

1972

Mar	2—Tom Bogs, Copenhagen	L	10
Mar.	25—Juan Carlos Duran, Schio	L disq.	4
May	15—Phil Matthews, London	KO by	2
June	5—Octavio Romero, Caracas	L	10
Sept.	17—Carlos Duran, Turin	L	10
Nov.	28—Johnny Baldwin, Houston	L	10

1973

May	5—Carlos Monzon, Rome	KO by	1
July	5—Dave Downey, Halifax	L	10
Sept.	17—Bruce Cantrell, Ft. Wayne	W	10
Oct.	30—Tony Gay, Ft. Wayne	KO	3

1974
(Inactive)
1975

Mar.	20—Dave Wyatt, Cincinnati	KO	2
Nov.	26—Marcel Quinones, Lima	L	10

1976

Nov.	12—Joey Blair, Cincinnati	KO	5

1977

Jan.	21—Glen Morgan, Cincinnati	KO	10
Feb.	24—Burt Hayes, Cincinnati	KO	3
Mar.	26—Monty Bethan, Cincinnati	W	10
Oct.	7—Gary Broughton, Cincinnati	KO	9
Nov.	11—Larry Davis, Cincinnati	W	10

1978

Mar.	10—D.C. Walker, Cincinnati	KO	4
May	13—Gary Thomas, Dayton	W	8
Sept.	17—Mike Colbert, Reno	L	10

1979

May	25—Lamont Lovelady, Santa Monica	KO by	6
Apr.	14—Frank Formero, Cincinnati	KO	7

1980

Mar.	9—Lamont Lovelady, St. Paul	L	10
May	13—Gary Guiden, Indianapolis	KO by	6

KEN DALLAS
Detroit, Mich. Welterweight
1978

Apr.	21—John Lambe, Detroit	KO by	1
Aug.	17—Levant Wallace, Detroit	W	4

1979

Jan.	18—Ron Florek, Detroit	KO by	1
Nov.	1—Jeff White, Detroit	KO	2
Dec.	1—Scott Coleman, Detroit	W	4

1980

Sept.	27—Jerome Kinney, Detroit	KO by	3

DANIEL DANIELS
Newark, N.J. Lightweight
1973

May	7—Dave Smith, New York	W	4
June	18—Hugo Valazquez, New York	W	4
July	7—Hugo Valasquez, New York	W	4
July	16—Hector Diaz, New York	D	6
Aug.	7—Tommy Grant, Hartford	KO	6
Nov.	15—Charles Paterson, Scranton	KO	5
Nov.	26—Luis Rivera, San Juan	KO by	6

1974

Jan.	19—Danny Fryman, Waterbury	L	6

1975

Dec.	2—Carlos Duprey, Philadelphia	W	6

1976

Mar.	24—Ernest Vann, Philadelphia	L	6
May	29—Jeff Holmes, Waterbury	L	6
July	28—Ray Carrington, Utica	W	8
Aug.	16—Ruby Ortiz, Newark	KO by	2
Oct.	22—Marcos Barahona, New York	KO by	4

1977

Feb.	2—Marcos Barahona, New York	L	4
Mar.	18—Felix Perez, New York	L	8
Apr.	25—Salvatore Ramirez, Newark	W	8
May	13—Angel Rosa, New York	L	8
Dec.	8—Daniel Perez, North Bergen	KO by	1

1978

Feb.	22—Louie Hubela, Brooklyn	L	6
Feb.	23—Gino Perez, North Bergen	W	6
Mar.	2—Clyde Beattie, Cohoes	L	8
Mar.	19—Luis Davila, New Haven	L	8
Mar.	30—Joe Phillips, Cohoes	W	8
Apr.	18—Don Sennett, Cohoes	KO	3
Apr.	21—Raymond Roman, New York	W	7
May	26—Edward Bracetty, Boston	KO	3
June	13—Luis Davila, Hartford	KO by	6
Aug.	12—Joe Phillips, Alexandria Bay	D	8

75

Oct. 28—Louis Hubela, Jersey City .... L 6
Nov. 24—Ernest Bing, Atlantic City .... L 12
Dec. 12—Gaetan Hart, Verdun .... KO by 3
1979
Mar. 17—George Green, Elmira .... KO 1
Apr. 26—Bobby Mann, North Bergen .... W 6
May 24—Ron Bryant, Cohoes .... KO 2
June 22—Raymond Roman, New York .... L 6
July 16—Teo Ozuna, New York .... L 8
Aug. 18—Charlie Brown, Atlantic City .... KO by 1
Oct. 20—Al Carter, Cincinnati .... KO by 1
1980
Feb. 1—Jimmy Washington, Philadelphia .... L 6
Mar. 22—Jeffrey Langley, Atlantic City .... KO 1
Apr. 26—Ernest Bing, Atlantic City .... L 12
(New Jersey State Lightweight Title)
Oct. 16—Antonio Nieves, Totowa .... KO by 5
Dec. 17—Joseph Nieto, White Plains .... KO by 1

GRADY DANIELS
Sterling, Ill. Heavyweight
1976
July 27—Bill Jackson, Chicago .... KO 2
Aug. 22—Frank Brown, Flint .... L 4
1977
Jan. 26—Vic Brown, Cleveland .... KO 2
June 11—Robert Reynosa, Sterling .... KO 3
Aug. 8—Robert Yarborough, Chicago .... L 8
1978
Feb. 27—Chico Gardner, Chicago .... W 8
June 30—Pedro Agosta, Chicago .... W 10
Nov. 11—Jimmy Phillips, Sterling .... KO 5
Dec. 15—Gerry Cooney, New York .... KO by 5
1979
Feb. 9—Pat Cuillo, Winnipeg .... KO by 4
June 18—Jerry Thompkins, Highland Park .... W 10
Nov. 8—Morris Jackson, Omaha .... KO by 3
1980
Jan. 26—Marty Monroe, Los Angeles .... KO by 5
Apr. 14—Mongol Ortiz, Chicago .... L 10
Sept. 23—Jeff Sims, Edmonton .... KO by 2
Nov. 11—Johnny Townsend, Winnipeg .... W 8
Dec. 10—Robert McFarland, Moline .... L 8

LOU DANIELS
Trenton, N.J. Junior Welterweight
1977
Mar. 26—Eugene Brown, Bristol .... KO 2
May 9—Victor Pappas, Upper Darby .... KO by 2
1978
Apr. 17—Greg Winston, Philadelphia .... L 4
Sept. 13—Ted Westbrook, Las Vegas .... W 4
Sept. 27—Francisco Casas, Las Vegas .... W 4
Oct. 10—Gerardo Valencia, Las Vegas .... W 6
Oct. 18—Roger Baradat, Las Vegas .... W 4
Nov. 1—Fili Ramirez, Las Vegas .... KO 2
Dec. 5—Armando Ramirez, Las Vegas .... L 4
1979
Apr. 10—Gary Hinton, Philadelphia .... KO by 2
June 13—Idika Nsofor, Las Vegas .... L 6
June 20—Jose Osuna, Las Vegas .... KO by 3
Aug. 1—Joe Johnson, Las Vegas .... L 6
Aug. 15—Tyrone Rackley, Tucson .... KO by 1
Sept. 12—Joe Robles, Las Vegas .... L 4
Oct. 18—Sal Lopez, Los Angeles .... KO by 2
Nov. 13—Ray Mancini, Phoenix .... L 6
Nov. 21—Joe Willie Johnson, Las Vegas .... L 6
Nov. 27—Reynaldo Zaragoza, Stockton .... KO by 1
1980
Feb. 27—Jeff Passero, Washington, D.C. .... L 8
Apr. 9—Louie Hubela, Brooklyn .... KO by 1
June 11—Octavio Romero, Las Vegas .... W 6
June 25—Pablo Gomez, Las Vegas .... KO by 4

TIM DANIELS
Trenton, N.J. Featherweight
1979
Aug. 1—Ken Huston, Asbury Park .... KO 1
Sept. 29—Heriberto Torres, Trenton .... D 4
Nov. 23—Heriberto Torres, Trenton .... L 4
1980
Jan. 24—Ken Carpenter, Upper Darby .... KO by 4
Mar. 14—Paul Moore, Trenton .... KO 3
Apr. 26—Abdul Mason, Trenton .... L 5
June 20—John Verderosa, New York .... KO by 5
Nov. 7—Vegron Hill, Trenton .... L 6
Nov. 20—Felix Castillo, Totowa .... L 6
Nov. 28—Roberto Vinas, New York .... L 6

WILLIE DANIELS
Trenton, N.J. Lightweight
1970
Sept. 16—George Rielly, Scranton .... KO 2

Oct. 6—Billy Welbster, Philadelphia .... KO 2
Nov. 17—Lorrie Jackson, Philadelphia .... KO 2
1971
Feb. 9—George Green, Philadelphia .... KO 2
Mar. 29—Paul Boyd, Philadelphia .... W 4
Apr. 26—Jose Myers, Philadelphia .... KO 1
June 7—Saoul Mamby, Philadelphia .... L 8
June 22—Mickey Sherlock, Philadelphia .... W 6
Oct. 21—Johnny Howard, Philadelphia .... W 8
Nov. 30—Kent Holbrook, Philadelphia .... L 8
1972
Mar. 21—Miguel Hernandez, Philadelphia .... W 6
Apr. 18—Iveland Eastman, Philadelphia .... W 6
May 17—Johnny Summerhays, Scranton .... W 8
Sept. 13—Chu Chu Malave, Scranton .... L 10
1973
Mar. 24—Richie Villanueva, Atlantic City .... W 8
Apr. 9—Jimmy Lopez, Philadelphia .... D 6
Aug. 15—Angel Lopez, Philadelphia .... KO 1
Nov. 12—Tim Walker, Philadelphia .... L 6
1974
July 15—Jose Resto, New York .... L 6
July 29—Richie Harris, New York .... L 4
Oct. 22—Jerome Artis, Philadelphia .... L 8
1975
Jan. 28—Alfonso Evans, Philadelphia .... L 8
May 13—Jose Resto, Trenton .... D 4
Aug. 18—Johnny Copeland, Philadelphia ... KO by 8
1976
(Inactive)
1977
Aug. 23—Wade Hinnant, Philadelphia .... L 8
1978
July 26—Fili Ramirez, Las Vegas .... L 6
Aug. 2—Julio Mendez, Las Vegas .... L 6
Aug. 16—Moses Carbin, Las Vegas .... W 6
Sept. 13—Gonzalo Montellano, Las Vegas .... KO by 5
Oct. 11—Eddie Nuno, Las Vegas .... KO by 5
Dec. 13—Fili Ramirez, Las Vegas .... L 10
1979
Jan. 10—Al Hughes, Las Vegas .... L 10
Mar. 7—Julio Mendez, Las Vegas .... L 8
Apr. 4—Joe Valdez, Las Vegas .... D 6
Apr. 12—Irleis Perez, Los Angels .... KO by 2
May 9—Refugio Rojas, Las Vegas .... KO by 4
June 1—Danny Samudio, Los Angeles .... TL 4
June 6—Roberto Garcia, Las Vegas .... W 8
July 26—Tony Baltazar, Los Angeles .... L 6
Aug. 22—Santos Gutierrez, Las Vegas .... KO 4
Sept. 13—Irleis Perez, Los Angeles .... KO by 1
1980
May 9—John Verderosa, Staten Island .... KO by 2

HERB DARITY
1980
July 25—Derek Cuttino, New Bedford .... W 4
Sept. 9—Kevin Renshaw, Atlantic City .... KO 2
Oct. 14—Angel Ortiz, W. Hartford .... W 6
Oct. 30—William Hill, Atlantic City .... KO 1
Nov. 6—Danny Chapman, W. Hartford .... L 6

CHUCK DASKIEWICZ
1980
Mar. 9—Chuck Smith, St. Paul .... KO 2
July 7—Lynn Lustig, Bloomington .... KO 2

ALBERTO DAVILA
Los Angeles, Calif. Bantamweight
Born: August 10, 1954
1973
Mar. 1—Carlos Villareal, Los Angeles............. W 4
Mar. 15—Tomas Huerta, Los Angeles............. W 4
Apr. 6—Ruben Mozqueda, San Bernardino .... KO 5
Apr. 28—Tomas Huerta, Los Angeles............. W 5
May 31—Jose Marquecho, Los Angeles........... W 6
July 5—Alberto Cabanig, Los Angeles........... W 6
Aug. 23—Baby Corona, Los Angeles............. W 6
Oct. 4—Juan Lopez, Los Angeles............... W 6
Dec. 13—Juan Lopez, Los Angeles.............. KO 2
1974
Jan. 31—Dorteo Cubillias, Los Angeles .... W 10
Mar. 21—Mario Rogelio, Los Angeles .... KO 7
May 24—Rudy Gonzalez, Los Angeles .... KO 7
June 13—Tanny Amancio, Los Angeles .... W 10
July 25—Cecil Escobido, Los Angeles............ L 10
Dec. 12—Bonnie Necessario, Los Angeles .... W 10
1975
Apr. 10—Jose Del Rio, Los Angeles .... KO 5
May 21—Raul Pacheco, Las Vegas .... W 10
July 5—Eliseo Cosme, Los Angeles............. L 10
Dec. 4—Seco Luna, Los Angeles............... W 10
1976
Feb. 25—Lupe Pintor, Los Angeles .... W 10

Apr.   28—Raul Tirado, Los Angeles.................L 10
June   19—Jose Rosa, Los Angeles ....W 10
July   19—Wilfredo Gomez, San Juan ....KO by 9
Aug.   28—Cubano Hernandez, Los Angeles.........W 10
Nov.   19—Jose Medina, Los Angeles...............KO   3
1977
Apr.   28—Carlos Alcivar, Los Angeles ....W 10
June   9—Frank Duarte, Los Angeles ....KO   5
July   7—Manuel Vasquez, Los Angeles ....W 10
Aug.   25—Alberto Cabanig, Los Angeles ....KO 10
Nov.   17—Rodolfo Martinez, Los Angeles ....KO   7
1978
Feb.   25—Carlos Zarate, Los Angeles ....KO by   8
(WBC Bantamweight Title)
May   4—Ramon Aguinaga, Los Angeles..........KO   4
June   8—Manny Vasquez, Los Angeles ....KO   6
Sept. 15—Jorge Lujan, New Orleans ....L 15
(World Bantamweight Title)
Dec.   7—Mario Castro, Los Angeles ....KO   7
1979
Feb.   15—Ricardo Varela, Los Angeles ....W 10
Apr.   12—Patricio Nunez, Los Angeles ....KO   9
May   31—Frank Granados, Los Angeles ....W 10
July   12—Eddie Logan, Los Angeles ....W 10
Sept. 25—Jose Resendez, Los Angeles ....W 10
Dec.   14—Jose Resendez, San Bernardino ....W 10
1980
Feb.   2—Manuel Ruelas, Phoenix ....KO   8
Apr.   12—Melvin Johnson, Tucson ....KO   2
June   21—Richard Rozelle, Las Vegas ....KO   2
July   17—Miguel Flores, Los Angeles ....KO   4
Sept. 13—Terry Pizzaro, San Antonio ....KO   6
Dec.   19—Lupe Pintor, Las Vegas ....L 15
(For WBC Bantamweight Title)

RANDY DAVIO
Springfield, Mass. Junior Middleweight
1979
July   27—Angel Santiago, Hartford ....W   4
Aug.   18—Angel Santiago, Lowell ....KO   2
Sept.   7—Errol McNeil, Hartford ....KO by   1
Oct.   17—Jack Cowell, Hartford ....W   4
1980
Feb.   28—Jack Cowell, Hartford ....KO   3
Apr.   8—Jack Cowell, Hartford ....W   4
May   23—Jack Cowell, Hartford ....W   5
Sept. 12—Jack Cowell, Hartford ....KO   2
1980
Feb.   28—Jack Cowell, Hartford ....KO   3
Apr.   8—Jack Cowell, Hartford ....W   4
May   23—Jack Cowell, Hartford ....W   5
Sept. 12—Jack Cowell, Hartford ....KO   2
Nov.   25—Don Miller, Springfield ....KO by   5

ANTHONY DAVIS
Heavyweight
1979
Nov.   29—George O'Mara, Los Angeles ....KO by   3
1980
Apr.   23—Yaqui Meneses, Las Vegas ....KO   4
May   28—Ben Johnson, Las Vegas ....KO   1
Dec.   3—Ron Draper, Las Vegas ....W   6

EDDIE DAVIS
Freeport, N.Y. Light Heavyweight
Born: Oct. 4, 1951, Mgr.: Dennis Rappaport
1975
Sept. 12—Otis Gordon, Commack ....KO   2
Oct.   17—Al Ware, Commack ....KO   1
Nov.   28—Leo Rogers, Commack ....W disq.   2
1976
Jan.   24—Carlos Espada, New York ....KO   1
Mar.   31—D.C. Walker, Uniondale ....W   6
June   2—Sixto Martinez, Uniondale ....KO   3
Nov.   5—Mario Rosa, New York ....D 10
1977
Jan.   18—Jose Elias, New York ....W   8
Apr.   8—Bob Stewart, Syracuse ....KO   4
Aug.   27—Mario Rosa, Hempstead ....W 10
1978
Jan.   27—Luis Rodriguez, Hempstead ....W 10
Apr.   3—Marvin Johnson, Indianapolis ....KO by   7
1979
June   29—Luis Guzman, New York ....W   8
Aug.   3—George Aidoo, Hempstead ....KO   3
Oct.   19—Mike Tarasewich, Commack ....KO   1
1980
Feb.   23—Willie Taylor, Atlantic City ....W   8
May   9—Johnny Wilburn, Commack ....W   8
May   25—Curtis Goins, Atlantic City ,,,,,,,,,,KO   7
Sept. 07—Pete McIntyre, Los Angeles ....KO by   2

ERNESTO DAVIS
Panamanian Lightweight
1975
Jan.   26—Jesus Aparicio, Zacatecas ....KO by   6
1976
Apr.   10—Adolfo Sanjeado, Tuxtla Gutierrez ....W 10
May   14—Baltazar Garza, Tampico ....KO   5
July   20—Francisco Durando, Cartagena ....KO by   3
July   24—Aurelio Muniz, Mexico City ....W 10
Sept. 10—Jose Luis Madrid, Ciudad Mantes ....W 10
Oct.   16—Juan Elizondo, Mexico City ....D 10
1977
Mar.   4—Raton Montes, Laredo ....KO   5
Mar.   12—Julio Mendez, Mexico City ....W 10
May   13—Pedro Flores, Laredo ....W 10
June   25—Julio Mendez, Mexico City ....W 10
Aug.   12—Leoncio Ortiz, Coatzacoalcos ....W 10
1978
Mar.   18—Jose Medinan, Monctova ....NC   5
June   3—Leonardo Bermudez, Mexico City ....W 10
Aug.   11—Juan Cabrera, Tampico ....KO   5
1979
Apr.   4—Augustin Estrada, Juarez ....D 10
June   30—Gerardo Aceves, Mexico City ....KO by   2
1980
Nov.   29—Luis Rodriguez, Colon ....W 10

ERNIE (BULLA BULLA) DAVIS
Toledo, Ohio Middleweight
1979
Mar.   3—Nathaniel Akbar, Detroit L   6
Sept. 20—William Lee Jr., Detroit ....KO by   2
1980
Nov.   14—Leslie Gardner, Detroit ....L 10

HOWARD DAVIS, JR.
Glen Cove, N.Y. Lightweight
1976 Olympic Lightweight Gold Medalist
Born: Feb. 14, 1956
Managed by Dennis Rappaport and Michael R. Jones
1977
Jan.   15—Jose Resto, Las Vegas ....W   6
Mar.   20—Ricky Craney, Louisville ....KO   3
May   11—Carlos Gonzalez, New York ....W   6
July   17—Dom Monaco, Miami Beach ....KO   8
Sept. 13—Arturo Pineda, Los Angeles ....KO   4
1978
Feb.   4—Jose Fernandez, Las Vegas ....W   8
May   13—Larry Stanton, Orlando ....W 10
July   9—Norman Goins, Indianapolis ....W 10
Nov.   4—Luis Davila, Atlantic City ....W 10
1979
Apr.   21—Giancarlo Usai, New York ....KO   3
June   17—Jose Hernandez, San Antonio ....KO   7
Sept. 14—Maurice Watkins, Houston ....W 10
1980
Feb.   23—Vilomar Fernandez, Atlantic City ....W 12
June   7—Jim Watt, Glasgow ....L 15
(For WBC Lightweight Title)
Dec.   6—Johnny Lira, Lake Tahoe ....W 10

JOHN DAVIS
Hempstead, N.Y. Light Heavyweight
1978
Sept.   8—James Taylor, New York ....KO   1
Sept. 19—Kid Samson, New York ....W   6
Nov.   2—Dwight Braxton, New York ....W   6
Nov.   30—Beau Jack, New York ....W   6
1979
June   29—Kid Samson, Commack ....W   6
Sept.   8—William Turner, Shirley ....KO   3
Nov.   28—Roy Ingram, New York ....KO   3
1980
May   23—Bernard McClean, New York L   8
July   13—Tony Greene, Great Gorge ....W   6
Aug.   9—Vonzell Johnson, Atlantic City L   4
Sept. 12—Bernard McClean, New York ....W   8

JOHNNY DAVIS
Brooklyn, N.Y. Welterweight
1973
July   18—Billy Bell, Baltimore L   6
Aug.   15—Billy Bell, Baltimore L   6
Aug.   18—Justico Ortiz, New York L   4
Aug.   20—Justico Ortiz, New York ....KO by   4
Nov.   5—Hugo Velasquez, New York...............L   4
Nov.   6—Billy Bell, Baltimore L   6
Nov.   19—Thomas Williams, New York..............L   4
Dec.   5—Billy Bell, Baltimore L   4
Dec.   27—Bob Angus, New York...................L   4
1974
Jan.   7—Hugo Velasquez, New York ....KO   1
Jan.   16—Tim Walker, Baltimore ....KO by   2

Mar. 13—Jerry Snyder, Binghamton................D 4
Apr. 16—Johnny Rohland, Baltimore ....KO by 2
Aug. 27—Sparky Wheeler, Alexandria ....KO by 2
Oct. 9—Jerry Snyder, Scranton ....KO 2
Nov. 11—Pedro Acevedo, New York ....KO 1
Nov. 13—Jimmy Phoenix, Scranton............KO by 3
1975
Jan. 30—Larry Giello, North Bergen ....L 6
Mar. 24—Ronnie Gibbons, New York..........KO by 6
Nov. 11—Mario Saurennan, Philadelphia ......KO by 5
1976
Jan. 28—Mike Everett, Scranton ....KO by 4
May 24—Fernand Marcotte, Quebec ....KO by 4
Aug. 27—Alfonso Hayman, Atlantic City.......KO by 7
1977
(Inactive)
1978
Apr. 21—Mike Michaud, Albany ....KO by 6
Aug. 14—Carlos Betancourt, Rio Predras ......KO by 3
1979
Mar. 16—Andoni Amana, Barcelona ....KO by 5
1980
Jan. 25—Mark Medel, New York ....KO by 2
Feb. 28—Miguel Sanchez, Hartford ....KO by 5
Sept. 18—Bobby Czyz, Totowa ....KO by 1
Nov. 25—Alex Ramos, Hartford ....KO by 4

KEN DAVIS JR.
California Welterweight
1979
Sept. 27—Rodney Harvey, Los Angeles ....KO 1
Nov. 1—Sal Lopez, Los Angeles ....KO by 2
Dec. 14—Rodney Harvey, San Bernardino ....KO 1
1980
Jan. 18—Eddie Batiste, San Bernardino ....KO 1
Feb. 9—James Bella, San Bernardino ......KO by 2
Mar. 21—Ramon Sanchez, Los Angeles ....W 4
June 12—Jose Gomez, Los Angeles ....KO 1
July 10—Phil Leonin, Los Angeles ....KO 2

LARRY DAVIS
Elizabeth, N.J. Middleweight
1980
May 31—Abdul Sanda, Elizabeth ....L 4
June 6—Euclides Valdez, New York ....KO by 3
Aug. 27—Earl Liburd, Elizabeth ....L 4
Sept. 17—Doug DeWitt, White Plains ....L 6
Oct. 15—Merling Castellanos, White Plains ....L 4

MARK DAVIS
California Featherweight
1979
Sept. 27—Toshi Okuma, Los Angeles ....KO 4
Oct. 25—Luis Avila, Los Angeles ....W 5
Nov. 16—Musio Nava, Inglewood ....KO 2
1980
Jan. 18—Mil Jiminez, San Bernardino ....W 5
May 2—Gerardo Pena, Los Angeles ....KO 8
June 12—Jaime Nava, Los Angeles ....W 10
Nov. 13—Juan Manuel Hernandez, Los Angeles ...KO 5

NATHAN DAVIS
Bahamian Junior Lightweight
1979
Feb. 23—James Tynes, Nassau ....KO
Mar. 16—Freddie Majors, Nassau ....KO 5
Mar. 30—Mike Whyms, Nassau ....KO by 5
May 4—James Tynes, Nassau ....KO 3
Dec. 7—Danny Wilson, North Miami ....D 6
1980
Feb. 5—Robert Mullens, Charkeston ....KO by 5
Mar. 22—Maurice (Termite) Watkins,
Grand Rapids ....KO by 3

PERCELL DAVIS
Santa Monica, Calif. Heavyweight
1978
June 21—John Cline, Detroit ....W 4
Sept. 27—Jesse Harris, Flint ....W 4
Nov. 3—Bobby Watkins, Detroit ....KO 1
1979
May 25—Rahim Muhammad, Santa Monica ....W 8
Aug. 3—Abdul Kahn, Santa Monica ....W 10
Aug. 19—Pete Holm, Bloomington ....KO 2
Oct. 27—Reggie Phillips, Los Angeles ....KO 5
1980
Jan. 26—Bruce Scott, Los Angeles ....KO 1
Mar. 9—Charlie Johnson, St. Paul ....KO 7
Mar. 28—Raul Gorosito, Tacoma ....KO 1
May 4—Al Neumann, Seattle ....KO by 7
June 14—Harry Terrell, Cincinnati ....L 10

RAY (POPPY) DAVIS
Atlantic City, N.J. Welterweight
1971
Oct. 16—Glen Mason, Cherry Hill, N.J. ....KO 3
Nov. 9—Weldon Hudson, Philadelphia ....KO by 3
1972
(Inactive)
1973
Jan. 15—Mike Everett, Philadelphia ....KO by 1
1974-1975
(Inactive)
1976
Aug. 6—Tony Tassone, Atlantic City ....L 6
Sept. 23—Rudy Donato, Wilmington ....L 6
Oct. 14—Greg Mackett, Wilmington ....KO 6
Nov. 5—Mike Michaud, New York ....D 6
1977
Feb. 1—Jerome Goodman, Philadelphia ....L 6
Mar. 8—Ruben Lopez, Bristol ....L 8
Sept. 16—Johnny Cooper, Wilmington ....L 6
1978
Mar. 4—Jose Palacios, Los Angeles ....L 10
June 15—Elliott Freeman, Atlantic City ....W 8
Sept. 26—Nino Gonzalez, Totowa ....L 6
Oct. 20—Justice Ortiz, Atlantic City ....W 8
Nov. 24—Mike Jones, Atlantic City ....KO 3
1980
Mar. 22—Irving Booth, Atlantic City ....KO 4
Apr. 24—Nino Gonzalez, Totowa ....KO by 6

ROBERT DAVIS
Waterbury, Conn. Junior Middleweight
1979
Apr. 24—Muhammad Shabazz, Hartford ....L 4
May 18—Jose Diaz, Hartford ....KO 4
June 20—Steve Small, White Plains ....KO by 3
Sept. 27—Miguel Sanchez, Bristol ....L 4
Oct. 17—Miguel Sanchez, Hartford ....L 4
1980
May 14—Steve Small, White Plains ....W 8
May 23—Don Miller, Hartford ....KO 4
May 29—Vinnie Curto, Revere ....L 10
Oct. 15—Teddy Mann, White Plains ....W 8

DWIGHT DAVISON
Detroit, Mich. Middleweight
Born: March 18, 1955, Height: 6'0"
Managed by Luther Burgess
1977
June 11—Warren Coaston ....KO 1
July 1—Malcom Brown, Detroit ....KO 3
Aug. 9—Marvin Sanders, Las Vegas ....KO 5
Nov. 15—Rubin Riscon, Phoenix ....W 6
Nov. 26—Sam Long, Columbus ....KO 3
Dec. 10—Gary Coates, Grand Rapids ....W 6
1978
Mar. 16—Ali Muhammad, Kalamazoo ....W 6
Apr. 21—Dave Sutherland, Livonia ....KO 1
—Sammy Long, Columbus ....KO 1
May 17--Ron (Shane) Bosley, Flint ....KO 2
June 23—Ruby Cupe, Detroit ....KO 1
July 18—Andress Ramirez, Phoenix ....KO 2
July 20—Mike West, Detroit ....KO 1
Aug. 25—Tony Brooks, Houston ....W 8
Sept. 9—Lloyd Richardson, Detroit ....KO 8
Oct. 26—Ralph Moncrief, Detroit ....W 8
Nov. 9—Al Campbell, Detroit ....KO 1
Dec. 9—Jeff Morgan, Detroit ....KO 3
1979
Jan. 25—Ben Sanchez, Detroit ....KO 2
Feb. 9—Bob Patterson, Detroit ....KO 3
May 24—Tommy Hanna, Detroit ....KO 9
Sept. 15—Keith Broom, Detroit ....KO 2
Nov. 15—Willie Monroe, Detroit ....W 10
1980
Jan. 13—Simon Smith, Las Vegas ....KO 1
Jan. 24—Doug Demmings, Detroit ....KO 5
Feb. 22—Jamie Thomas, Detroit ....KO 6
May 23—Ray Seales, Clarkston ....W 10
Aug. 8—Curtis Parker, Las Vegas ....W 10

DAVID DEAN
Charlotte, N.C. Middleweight
1979
Apr. 5—Pee Wee Dunbar, Spartanburg ....KO 3
July 26—Leroy Miller, Charlotte ....W 4
1980
Aug. 18—Robbie Sims, Boston ....KO by 1
Sept. 20—Charlie Brown, Charlotte ....W 6

MANUEL DEARCE
Hartford, Conn. Junior Lightweight
1980
June	19—Ralph Bracetty, Lawrence	KO	3
July	25—Luis Robles, New Bedford	L	4
Sept.	12—Jose Ruiz, Hartford	W	4
Oct.	14—Jose Ruiz, W. Hartford	W	4

DARIO DE ASA
Florida Junior Middleweight
1980
May	2—Clauzell Longmire, Miami Beach	KO by	3
July	25—A. W. Muhammad, Miami	KO	2
Aug.	29—Carlos Mejia, Miami	W	10

JOHN DE GRAZIO
Toronto, Canada Welterweight
1980
May	31—Stephen Hughes, Lindsay	W	6
July	25—Reggie McKissac, Smith Falls	KO	1
Oct.	28—Frank Minnigan, Montreal	KO by	3

DARIO DE JESUS
Miami, Fla. Welterweight
1976
July	19—Carlos de Leon, San Juan	L	6
1977			
Oct.	29—Martin Ryals, Homestead	KO	3
1978			
Apr.	4—Dennis Green, North Miami Beach	KO	4
May	16—Dennis Green, Miami Beach	KO	5
July	18—Martin Ryals, Miami Beach	W	8
1979			
Jan.	13—Ron Hamilton, Miami Beach	D	8
Feb.	11—Kenny Abbott, Miami Beach	W	6
Oct.	4—Carlos Lozano, San Carlos	L	6
Nov.	27—Jorge Morales, Las Vegas	KO by	4
1980			
May	16—Marvin Huerta, San Jose	L	6
June	30—Chico Salinas, Bakersfield	KO by	5
Aug.	23—Jose Luis Ramirez, Inglewood	KO by	1

JUAN DE LA GARZA
Corpus Christi, Texas Light Heavyweight
1971
Aug.	31—William Brown, Beaumont	KO by	2
1972			
Oct.	24—Joe Barraza, Corpus Christi	KO	4
1973			
	—Ramon Juarez, Muskie	KO	3
	—Jose Davila, Rio Bravo	KO	2
	—Antonio Pulido, Saltillo	KO	1
	—Toro Gonzalez, Sabinas	KO	4
	—Rafael Solito, Cuidad Victoria	KO	5
	—Pancho Tuntaez, Nuevo Laredo	KO	3
1974			
	—Arturo Contreras, Monclova	W	10
	—Ezekiel Romano, Rio Bravo	KO	5
	—Mercano Aguilar, Sabinas	W	10
1975-1976			
	(Inactive)		
1977			
June	14—Joe Donatto, Houston	L	8
Aug.	2—Joe Donatto, Corpus Christi	L	10
Sept.	6—Jesus Sanchez, Houston	KO	3
Oct.	3—Vernon Johnson, Corpus Christi	D	6
Dec.	20—Jerry Celestine, New Orleans	KO by	6
1978			
Jan.	23—Young Joe Louis, Chicago	KO by	2
Feb.	27—Sylvan Watbled, Paris	KO by	3
Apr.	25—Ned Hallacy, Wichita	KO by	6
July	19—Alfio Righetti, Rimini	KO by	3
Sept.	19—Joe Donatto, Wichita	KO	4
Nov.	28—Jesse Burnett, Billings	KO by	5
1979			
Mar.	8—Ned Hallacy, Wichita	KO by	3
Aug.	7—Jesse Avila, Corpus Christi	L	8
Nov.	27—John Robinson, Kansas City	KO	3
1980			
May	9—Luke Capuano, Chicago	KO by	2
June	17—Eddie Gonzales, Houston	KO by	2

MANUEL DE LA ROSA
Dominican Rep. Lightweight
1978
Apr.	1—Ramon Cabral, Santo Domingo	W	6
May	11—Ramon Cabral, Santo Domingo	W	6
July	25—Felix Diaz, Santo Domingo	W	6
Aug.	20—Radames Rodriguez, Santo Domingo	W	4
Aug.	30—Felix Diaz, Santo Domingo	W	4
Oct.	26—Ramon Bido, Santo Domingo	W	6
Nov.	22—Ramon Bido, Santo Domingo	W	6

1979
May	11—Maximo Luciano, New York	W	4
June	27—Reggie James, New York	KO	1
1980			
Feb.	13—Felix Perez, White Plains	W	8
June	6—Ed Kinney, New York	KO	3
Oct.	10—Francisco Cruz, New York	KO	3
Dec.	12—Antonio Cruz, New York	L	10

JAVIER DE LA SERDA
Texas Flyweight
1979
July	12—Juan Castellano, McAllen	L	8
1980			
Apr.	1—Ernesto Guevara, Houston	L	6
June	17—Luis Jiminez, Houston	L	6
July	22—Luis Jiminez, Houston	L	6

CARLOS (SUGAR) DE LEON
Puerto Rican Light Heavyweight
1974
Aug.	3—Roy Harry, St. Thomas	KO	4
Oct.	19—Jessy Torres, St. Croix	KO	2
Nov.	2—Vernon Laws, St. Croix	KO	3
1975			
Feb.	3—Roberto Colon, Ponce	D	6
Mar.	17—Tripoti Guadalupe, St. Marteen	KO	5
Apr.	5—Kid Gavilan Jr., St. Marteen	KO	6
May	17—Top Cat Jackson, St. Marteen	KO	4
July	11—James Jackson, Trinidad	KO	3
Sept.	15—Larry Adkins, Trinidad	W	8
1976			
Apr.	5—Carlos Soto, St. Thomas	W	8
July	19—Dario DeJesus, San Juan	W	8
Aug.	12—Astor Agosto, San Juan	W	8
Oct.	14—Carlos Soto, San Juan	W	8
1977			
Feb.	12—Antonio Colon, San Juan	KO	6
June	25—Eddie Davis, San Juan	KO	3
Sept.	10—Ray Hammond, San Juan	L	8
Oct.	14—Battling Douglas, St. Thomas	KO	5
Nov.	8—Eddie Davis, Orlando	KO	5
1978			
Jan.	28—Ray Bryant, San Juan	KO	5
Mar.	25—Jesse Lara, Las Vegas	KO	2
Apr.	8—Tyrone Freeman, San Juan	KO	3
Sept.	26—Rennie Pinder, Miami Beach	KO	3
Nov.	18—Wendell Joseph, St. Thomas	W	10
1979			
Jan.	27—Bonifacio Avila, San Juan	KO	2
Apr.	8—Manny Freitas, Las Vegas	KO	1
Aug.	25—Willie McIntyre, San Juan	KO	1
Sept.	25—Christy Elliott, Ft. Lauderdale	KO	4
1980			
Apr.	25—Waldemar Paulino, Los Angeles	KO	1
June	28—Mario Rosa, San Juan	KO	8
Nov.	25—Marvin Camel, New Orleans	W	15
	(Won WBC Cruiserweight Title)		

ELIAS DE LEON
Mexican Bantamweight
1978
Apr.	15—Santos Nunez, Los Angeles	KO	2
Sept.	26—Enrique Muniz, Houston	KO	6
Oct.	17—Jiro Takada, Houston	KO	3
Dec.	19—Jose L. Garcia, Houston	KO	2
1979			
Feb.	26—Candelario Iglesia, Houston	KO	6
Apr.	10—Rodolfo Perez, Houston	KO	6
June	5—Calvin Shepard, Houston	W	10
1980			
Apr.	1—Gilberto Villacana, Houston	L	10
Sept.	23—Freddie Jackson, Houston	L	10

STEVE DELGADO
San Diego, Calif. Junior Middleweight
1977
Nov.	4—Greg Stephens, San Diego	KO	5
Nov.	11—Mustafa Shabazz, San Diego	W	6
Dec.	16—Greg Stephens, San Diego	L	6
1978			
Mar.	1—Joe Maldonado, Fresno	W	6
Apr.	13—Jerry Cheatham, Phoenix	L	10
June	1—Mario Neri, Los Angeles	KO	3
June	20—Clarence Howard, Phoenix	KO	2
July	18—Carlos Muro, Phoenix	W	8
Nov.	16—Henry Walker, Las Vegas	W	10
Dec.	15—Ted Sanders, San Diego	W	10
1979			
Mar.	7—James Waire, Las Vegas	W	10
Apr.	21—Roger Leonard, Phoenix	KO by	
May	1—Duddy Wilson, San Diego	KO	3
June	20—Jacinto Fernandez, Las Vegas	W	10

Aug. 10—Paddy Wilson, San Diego ....TD 10
Sept. 25—Mel Dennis, Las Vegas ....W 10
Dec. 12—Raul Nava, Phoenix ....KO 9
1980
Feb. 24—Nino Gonzales, Las Vegas ....W 10
May 6—Babs McCarthy, Las Vegas ....KO by 6
July 11—Henry Walker, Phoenix ....W 10
Oct. 7—Rocky Mosley, Las Vegas ....L 12
Nov. 28—Bushy Bester, Johannesburg ....L 10

DOMINGO D'ELIA
Argentine Heavyweight
Born: June 2, 1952 in Santa Fe
1973
Sept. 13—Ramon La Rosa, Resistencia ....KO 7
1974
Feb. 8—Ramon La Rosa, Coronda ....KO 4
Mar. 15—Armando Lascano, Resistencia ....KO 5
(Won Vacant Local Title)
June 28—Ruben Lopez, Resistencia ....KO 1
Nov. 8—Armando Lazcano, Resistencia ....W 10
1975
Feb. 28—Marcos Tosto, Resistencia ....W 10
Apr. 4—Ruben Gonzalez, Resistencia ....KO 5
July 11—Ruben Gonzalez, Resistencia ....D 10
Nov. 8—Ivan Rojas, Resistencia ....KO 4
1976
Feb. 28—Pablo Castellino, Resistencia ....L 10
Sept. 17—Juan Sosa II, Resistencia ....W 10
Nov. 12—Antonio Musladino, Resistencia ....W 10
Dec. 12—Pedro Sabadini, Resistencia ....KO 6
1977
Aug. 12—Pedro Sabadini, Resistencia ....W 10
Nov. 11—Raul Gorosito, Resistencia ....W 12
(Won Argentine Heavyweight Title)
1978
Feb. 10—Antonio Rossi, Resistencia ....KO 6
Mar. 17—Pablo N. Castellino, Resistencia ....KO 5
May 12—Luis F. Pires, Resistencia ....W 12
(Won South American Heavyweight Title)
Aug. 4—Juan C. Sosa, Santa Fe ....W 10
Nov. 10—Pablo Castellino, Resistencia ....W 12
(Retained Argentine Heavyweight Title)
1979
—Pablo Noe Castellino, Resistencia ....W 12
(Retained Argentine Heavyweight Title)
Feb. 9—Luis Pires, Resistencia ....KO 10
—Luis Pires, Resistencia ....W 12
(Retained Argentine Heavyweight Title)
—Antonio Musladino, Curuzu Cuatia ......W 10
—Marcos Tosto, Cordoba ....W 10
1980
Mar. 7—Norberto Fiori, Tandil ....D 12
(Retained Argentine Heavyweight Title)
Nov. 13—James (Quick) Tillis, Chicago ....KO by 4

HUMBERTO DE LOS RIOS
California Junior Middleweight
1979
June 21—Otis Bell, Los Angeles ....KO 2
July 19—Carlos Ramos, Los Angeles ....KO 3
Sept. 20—Joe Maldonado, Los Angeles ....KO 2
Nov. 15—Rafael Coron, Los Angeles ....W 6
Nov. 20—Rafael Corona, Los Angeles ....W 6
Dec. 6—Jose Luis Pena, Los Angeles ....KO 1
1980
Jan. 17—Joey Robles, Los Angeles ....L 6
Mar. 20—Benrus, Los Angeles ....L 6
June 26—T. Ficklin, Los Angeles ....KO 5
July 17—Sergio Lozano, Los Angeles ....KO 5

TYRONE DEMBY
Atlantic City, N.J. Junior Middleweight
1976
July 2—Daryl Lampkin, Atlantic City............D 4
Aug. 6—Daryl Lampkin, Atlantic City ....W 4
Aug. 11—Hubert Jackson, Philadelphia ....W 4
Aug. 27—John Cooper, Atlantic City ....W 4
Nov. 10—Mike Bullock, West Orange ....KO by 1
Nov. 18—Nikita Tarhocker, Wilmington ....KO 4
1977
Feb. 1—Archie Andrews, Philadelphia ....KO 4
Mar. 8—Jake Jenkins, Bristol ....KO 4
July 18—Norman Farrell, Philadelphia ....KO 1
Oct. 25—Fred Boynton, Philadelphia ....KO by 5
1978
(Inactive)
1979
May 12—James Sparks, Atlantic City ....KO 1
July 17—Greg Joiner, Atlantic City ....KO 1
Aug. 7—John Thompson, Atlantic City ....KO 1
1980
Mar. 22—Pat Pruitt, Atlantic City ....KO 1

Apr. 26—Curtis Taylor, Atlantic City ....KO 3
Aug. 9—Skipper Jones, Atlantic City ....KO by 6

DOUG DEMMINGS
St. Paul, Minn. Middleweight
1973
Aug. 6—Keith Deon, Minneapolis ....KO 2
Oct. 16—Larry Hauseman, Des Moines ....KO 4
Dec. 14—Danny Brewer, Chicago..............KO by 3
1974
Mar. 14—Roy Smith, Minneapolis ....L 5
May 15—Dick Ramsey, St. Paul.................W 4
May 23—Bobby Edwards, Minneapolis ....KO 6
June 22—Tony Johnson, Little Falls ....W 6
June 24—Tommy Sheehan, Providence...........KO 7
June 26—Ray Smith, St. Paul ....W 6
Oct. 8—George Jacob, Minneapolis ....W 6
Nov. 8—Donnie Stark, Crosby..................KO 3
1975
Feb. 3—Nick Peoples, Minneapolis ....W 8
Mar. 19—Barry Morris, Minneapolis ....W 6
May 7—Walter Tate, Minneapolis ....KO 1
May 14—John Diedel, St. Paul ....W 6
June 6—Jesse Smith, Minneapolis ....W 4
Oct. 28—Lee Barber, Minneapolis................W 6
1976
Feb. 7—Tony Chiaverini, Minneapolis............D 8
Mar. 9—Jimmy Owens, Minneapolis ....W 8
May 5—Tony Chiaverini, Minneapolis ....W 10
Nov. 30—Gary Thomas, Minneapolis.............KO 6
1977
Apr. 20—Gary Broughton, Minneapolis ....W 10
July 28—Clifford Wills, Bloomington ....W 6
Dec. 2—Ray Seales, Chicago ....L 15
1978
Apr. 7—Marvin Hagler, Los Angeles ....KO by 8
(U.S. Middleweight Title)
1979
Feb. 9—Jimmy Gradson, Winnipeg ....L 6
Apr. 4—George Aidoo, Winnipeg ....KO 5
June 14—James Williams, Winnipeg ....W 8
Oct. 23—Alan Minter, Wembley ....L 10
1980
Jan. 24—Dwight Davison, Detroit ....KO by 5
Nov. 11—Wayne Caplette, Winnipeg ....KO by 8

JOHN (DINO) DENIS
Attleboro, Mass. Heavyweight
1972
June 24—Henry Lawson, Providence ....W 4
Aug. 28—Henry Lawson, New Bedford ....KO 1
Sept. 15—Henry Lawson, Providence ....W 4
Oct. 11—Muhammad Ali, Boston ....Exh. 2
Dec. 7—Sonny Brown, Bayonne ....W 6
1973
Feb. 9—Brian O'Melia, New York ....W 6
Feb. 23—Tracy Morrison, Taunton ....KO 4
June 23—Paul Simonetti, Atlantic City ....KO 5
Aug. 8—Johnny Brown, Boston ....KO 2
Sept. 10—Claude McBride, Providence ....KO 1
Oct. 6—Sylvester Wilder, Brockton.............KO 5
Nov. 14—Cliff McDonald, Scranton ....KO 5
1974
Jan. 28—Billy Williams, New York................W 6
Feb. 9—Edmundo Stewart, Scranton ....W 10
Apr. 2—Enrique Rodriguez, West Hartford ....W 8
Apr. 24—Brian O'Melia, Scranton...............KO 10
June 24—Tommy Sheehan, New Bedford ....W 8
Aug. 28—Charlie Harris, Scranton................KO 5
Oct. 9—Tommy Kost, Scranton ....W 6
1975
Jan. 26—Terry Daniels, Scranton ....W 10
Feb. 3—Mike Boswell, Boston..................W 10
Mar. 24—Tony Burwell, Providence...............W 7
Apr. 11—Jerry Houston, New Bedford ....W 10
May 7—G. G. Maldonado, Scranton............KO 4
June 27—Jimmy Cross, Hamden..................KO 5
Aug. 26—Walker Smith, New Bedford ....KO 4
Sept. 30—Jose Roman, Providence ....W 10
Nov. 21—Joe Maye, Providence..................W 10
1976
Apr. 5—Obie English, Landover ....D 10
June 26—Scott LeDoux, Providence...............L 10
Oct. 15—George Foreman, Hollywood, Fla......KO by 4
1977
Mar. 27—Leroy Jones, San Antonio ....L 8
(U.S. Championship Tournament)
Nov. 25—Charley Polite, Providence ....W 10
1978
Jan. 28—C. J. Brown, Providence ....KO 8
Mar. 1—Jerry Thompkins, White Plains ....W 10
May 10—C. J. Bar Brown, White Plains ....W 10
June 28—Dave Wilson, Providence ....W 10

1979
June	20—Tyrone Harlee, White Plains	W	8
June	29—Jesse Crown, Cranston	KO	2
Nov.	9—Gerry Cooney, New York	KO by	3

1980
Oct.	16—Al Brooks, Revere	KO	3
Dec.	15—Chuck Findlay, Boston	W	10

MEL DENNIS
Houston, Texas Junior Middleweight
1970
Aug.	4—Ed Broussard, Houston	KO	1
Aug.	28—Jim Lopez, Phoenix	KO	2
Sept.	11—Ernesto Porter, Fort Worth	KO	4

1971
Feb.	15—Morris Crathin, Beaumont	KO	5
Mar.	15—Cuby Jackson, Dallas	D	6
Apr.	10—Ray Duran, New Orleans	W	6
Sept.	30—Don Smith, San Diego	D	6
Oct.	10—Bobby Stripling, Northridge	KO by	4

1972
Feb.	1—Augie Gomez, Houston	L	6
Apr.	4—Morris Crathin, San Antonio	W	6
July	17—Chuck Mince, New Orleans	L	10
Aug.	15—Sammy Ruckard, New Orleans	W	10
Oct.	9—Chuck Mince, New Orleans	W	10
Oct.	—Jack Tillman, Mobile	L	10

1973
Mar.	13—Jessie Avalos, San Antonio	L	12
Mar.	22—Tommy Van Hatten, New Orleans	KO	6
Oct.	31—Denny Moyer, New Orleans	W	10

1974
Mar.	7—Manuel Torres, Houston	KO	2
Apr.	23—Roy Barrientos, Houston	W	10
June	3—Vito Antuofermo, Rome	L	10
July	22—Lamont Lovelady, New Orleans	W	10
Aug.	5—Lamont Lovelady, New Orleans	KO	6
Sept.	18—Augie Gomez, Corpus Christi	KO	4
Nov.	18—Charlie Small, Galveston	W	10

1975
Jan.	17—Miguel Castellini, Belcarce	KO by	2
May	16—Alfredo Naveiras, Grivegnee	W	10
July	28—Charlie Small, New Orleans	W	10
Oct.	9—Eddie Davis, Mobile	KO	5

1976
Jan.	5—Eugene Hart, Philadelphia	KO by	3
July	9—Ante Barraza, Valle Hermosa	KO	4
Aug.	5—Jesse Pemado, Valle Hermosa	KO	4
Aug.	21—Jose Palacios, Mexico City	D	10
Sept.	17—Chu Chu Almazan, Matamoros	KO	5

1977
Mar.	6—Wilfred Benitez, Marion	L	8
	(U.S. Championship Tournament)		
Dec.	1—Johnny Heard, Houston	W	10

1978
Jan.	19—Roy Jones, Houston	KO	8
Apr.	4—Maurice Hope, London	L	10
May	16—Daryl Brumley, Houston	KO	11
Aug.	15—Frank Kolovrat, Houston	KO	1
Nov.	28—Jose Figueroa, Houston	W	10

1979
Feb.	13—George Aidoo, Houston	KO	5
Sept.	25—Steve Delgado, Las Vegas	L	10

1980
Feb.	9—Bruce McIntyre, Johannesburg	L	8
June	12—Loucif Hamani, Paris	L	10
Aug.	19—Gumersindo Gamez, Beaumont	W	12
	(Texas Middleweight Title)		
Nov.	25—Roger Leonard, New Orleans	L	10

CLEVELAND DENNY
Canadian Lightweight
1976
Dec.	14—Roland Beausoleil, Montreal	KO	2

1977
Feb.	9—Ron Pettigrew, Quebec	W	6
Feb.	22—Ronnie Hughes, Montreal	D	6
Apr.	27—Willie Davis, Montreal	W	6
June	1—Reggie McLean, Montreal	KO	4
June	28—Michel Rouleau, Montreal	W	6
July	26—Rick Craney, Montreal	KO	2
Sept.	27—Gaetan Hart, Montreal	W	10
Nov.	1—Jean LaPointe, Montreal	W	12
	(Canadian Lightweight Title)		

1978
Feb.	21—Clyde Beattie, Montreal	KO	6
Apr.	15—Gaetan Hart, Montreal	L	12
	(Canadian Lightweight Title)		

1979
Apr.	26—Ignacio Jimenez, Los Angeles	KO	3
May	10—Chuy Rodriguez, Los Angeles	TD	6

1980
June	20—Gaetan Hart, Montreal	KO by	10
	(Died of Injuries as Result of Bout)		

LYNDON DENNY
Brooklyn Lightweight
1980
Sept.	24—Dave Moore, Elizabeth	KO	2

GHYSLAIN DEROY
Quebec, Canada Welterweight
1979
June	3—Dennis Brisson, Quebec	KO	4
Dec.	18—Brian Anderson, Montreal	L	4

1980
Jan.	21—Donny Marshall, Montreal	W	6
Mar.	25—Mario Cusson, Montreal	KO	5
May	7—Lawrence Hafey, Montreal	KO	6
Sept.	25—Frank Minnigan, Montreal	KO	4
Dec.	9—Alphonso Contreras, Montreal	KO	3

BLAS DESCHAMP
Santo Domingo, Dominican Rep. Welterweight
1979
July	8—Frank Petti, New York	L	4
Sept.	19—Clyde Graves, New York	KO by	3

1980
June	6—Jimmy Donnolly, New York	W	4
June	20—Jimmy Longo, New York	D	4
Oct.	23—Kevin Rooney, Las Vegas	L	6

ELOY DE SOUZA
Brazilian Lightweight
(Previous Record Unavailable)
1979
Sept.	6—Ken Buchanan, Randers	L	8

1980
Jan.	4—Jean Marie Cotinaut, Carpi	L	8

PETE DEVANCE
Fort Worth, Texas Lightweight
1980
Mar.	3—Keith Wagoner, Oklahoma City	KO	1
July	11—Tim Lucero, Denver	KO by	2
Aug.	21—Robert Tijerina, Dallas	KO	1

PAUL DE VORCE
Yonkers, N.Y. Junior Lightweight
1980
Sept.	17—Anthony Fox, White Plains	KO	1
Oct.	15—Irwin Hazel, White Plains	KO	2
Dec.	17—David Brown, White Plains	W	4

DOUGLAS DEWITT
Yonkers, N.Y. Middleweight
1980
Mar.	28—Peter Pennello, Tarrytown	W	4
May	14—Charles Hecker, White Plains	KO	3
June	11—Calvin Clark, White Plains	W	4
Sept.	17—Larry Davis, White Plains	W	6
Oct.	15—Terry Duncan, White Plains	W	6
Dec.	17—Derrick Dougherty, White Plains	KO	1

ALBERTO DIAZ
Panamanian Bantamweight
1980
Nov.	1—Carlos Jiminez, Colon	W	4
Nov.	15—Domingo Castillo, Colon	KO	1

HUGO DIAZ
Argentine Lightweight
1980
Apr.	11—Horacio Mendez, Bahia Blanca	L	8
June	6—Mario Matthysse, Sunchales	L	10
June	19—Mario Matthysse, Esperanza	L	10

JOSE DIAZ
Hartford, Conn. Light Heavyweight
1977
May	5—Kevin Mahon, Albany	L	4

1978
(Inactive)
1979
May	18—Robert Davis, Hartford	L	4
July	27—Dana McCarthy, Hartford	KO by	1

1980
July	25—Mark Mainero, New Bedford	KO by	1

LUIS O. DIAZ
Argentine Lightweight
1980
Feb.	8—Nicolas Vera, L. de Zamora	D	6
Sept.	6—Alfredo Moyaho, Salto Argent	KO by	7
Dec.	5—Adolfo Rossi, Darraux	L	10
Dec.	19—Abel Musa, Gral Acha	L	10

81

MARCELO RUIZ DIAZ
Argentine Middleweight
1980
Mar. 7—Carlos Romero, Campna .... W 8
May —Jose Araujo, Buenos Aires .... W 6
May 30—Angel Caro, P.R.S. Pena .... L 10
June 19—Domingo Arriola, San Nicolas .... L 10
Sept. 6—Angel Caro, P.R.S. Pena .... W 10

PATRICIO DIAZ
Argentine Junior Middleweight
1980
Jan. —Rogelio Zarza, S. Sal. de Jujuy .... W 10
Feb. 14—Carlos Peralta, Mendoza .... L 10
Feb. 29—Walter Gomez, Mar del Plata .... W 10
May 2—Rogelio Zarza, Mendoza .... W 10
May 10—Jorge Ramirez, San Martin .... KO 6
May 31—Ricardo Magallanes, Pergamino .... W 10
June 25—Carlos Peralta, Buenos Aires .... D 10
Oct. 11—Walter Gomez, Buenos Aires .... TL 6
Dec. 5—Carlos Peralta, Rio Gallegos .... L 10
Dec. 19—Simon Escobar, Villa Mercedes .... L 10

RODOLFO R. DIAZ
Argentine Junior Lightweight
1980
Apr. 18—Jose Filippi, Correl Bustos .... KO by 11
Aug. 8—Ruben Riani, Rio III .... KO by 2
Sept. 12—Hector Lopez, Tucuman .... L 10

TOMAS DIAZ
Dominican Rep. Junior Lightweight
1979
Apr. 6—Carmelo Negron, New York .... KO by 3
Sept. 19—Martin Parham, New York .... L 4
1980
May 14—Robert Rucker, White Plains .... L 6

BLAINE DICKSON
Las Vegas, Nev. Junior Lightweight
1979
July 25—Ney Santiago, Las Vegas .... KO 2
Sept. 19—Mauro Fuentes, Las Vegas .... KO by 1
Nov. 1—Mory Cissy, Los Angeles .... W 6
Nov. 21—Vito Romero, Las Vegas .... KO 6
1980
Feb. 28—Rosendo Ramirez, Los Angeles .... W 6
Apr. 2—Ricardo Jiminez, Las Vegas .... W 10
Apr. 23—Jose Caba, Las Vegas .... KO by 7
June 26—Rosendo Ramirez, Las Vegas .... KO 10
July 24—Roberto Garcia, Las Vegas .... W 10
Sept. 25—Ken Saale, Las Vegas .... KO by 6
Nov. 29—Jaime Nava, Las Vegas .... W 10
Dec. 26—Ricardo Jiminez, Las Vegas .... KO 1

DOM DI MARZO
E. Boston, Mass. Middleweight
1977
May 21—Rodney Black, Boston .... KO 1
June 6—Bill Clark, Peabody .... W 4
June 27—Lorenzo Howard, Danvers .... W 4
Sept. 24—Jose Rodriguez, Boston .... W 6
1978
Mar. 4—Joe Houston, Boston .... KO 3
Mar. 16—Rocky Nino Cosmo, North Bergen .... KO 3
June 19—Joe Houston, Boston .... KO 8
July 12—Earl Harris, Boston .... KO 6
Sept. 9—Randy Milton, Providence .... L 8
Sept. 16—Joe Moreault, Cape Cod .... KO 4
Nov. 23—Joey Houston, Portland .... KO 2
Dec. 21—Benny Sanchez, Portland .... W 8
1979
Feb. 24—Harry White, Quincy .... KO 2
Mar. 12—Wilber Henderson, Providence .... L 6
Nov. 6—Juan Colon, Lowell .... KO 5
Nov. 28—George Lee, W. New York, N.J. .... KO 3
1980
Feb. 27—Don Bickford, Woburn .... KO 5
May 29—Joe Huston, Revere .... KO 3

JAMES DIXON
Philadelphia, Pa. Welterweight
1980
Oct. 1—Al Ferro, Atlantic City .... L 6
Oct. 30—Al Ferro, Atlantic City .... W 4
Nov. 22—Milton McCrory, Cincinnati .... KO by 5

JIMMY DIXON
Memphis, Tenn. Heavyweight
1976
June 25—Ivy Brown, Memphis .... L 6

Aug. 3—Memphis Al Jones, Memphis .... W 6
Aug. 4—Lynn Ball, Alexandria .... W 6
Sept. 1—John McClendon, Memphis .... W 6
Nov. 9—Robert Echols, Memphis .... L 8
Nov. 20—Alvin Cisco, Marshall .... KO 2
1977
Nov. 8—Roberto Rocket, Memphis .... L 4
Dec. 13—Steve Basse, Memphis .... W 4
1978
Jan. 10—Larry Alexander, Memphis .... D 6
Feb. 21—Dan Martin, Memphis .... W 4
Feb. 28—Alvin Dominey, Memphis .... L 4
Mar. 31—Ivy Brown, Kansas City .... L 4
Apr. 18—Ed Savage, Memphis .... L 4
Apr. 25—Russell Sloan, Greenville .... KO 2
May 3—Britt Grice, Blytheville .... KO 3
June 20—Nick Wells, Houston .... KO 2
Sept. 6—Eddie Gregory, White Plains .... KO by 1
1979
Feb. 1—Mircea Simon, Los Angeles .... KO by 2
Mar. 23—Tom Fischer, Rosemont .... KO by 6
Apr. 28—Ron Stander, Omaha .... W 10
June 25—Ron Stander, Omaha .... W 12
Sept. 21—Eric Sedillo, Denver .... KO by 6
1980
May 31—John Conteh, Liverpool .... KO by 5
Aug. 8—Steve Mormino, Chicago .... L 10
Oct. 25—Rudi Gauwe, Herenthais .... W 6
Dec. 10—Jimmy Hearns, Moline .... KO by 2
Dec. 19—Al Syben, Brussels .... L 10

MICHAEL DOKES
Akron, Ohio Heavyweight
Born: August 10, 1958
1976
Oct. 15—Al Byrd, Hollywood, Fla. .... KO 4
1977
Jan. 14—Sergio Rodriguez, Pensacola .... KO 2
Jan. 29—Dave Wilson, Miami Beach .... W 4
Mar. 5—Charlie Jordan, Marion .... KO 3
Apr. 10—Ed (Savage) Turner, Miami Beach ...... W 6
1978
Mar. 3—George Holden, Curacao .... KO 3
Mar. 25—Abdul Khan, Las Vegas .... W 8
Apr. 29—Dan Johnson, Inglewood .... W 6
Sept. 26—Terry Mims, Miami Beach .... W 8
Oct. 27—Eugene Green, New York .... W 8
Dec. 8—Ira Martin, New York .... W 8
1979
Mar. 23—Wendell Bailey, Las Vegas .... W 10
May 12—Greg Sorrentino, Las Vegas .... KO 3
July 20—Willie McIntyre, West Palm Beach ..... KO 2
Sept. 28—Jimmy Young, Las Vegas .... W 10
1980
Jan. 13—Earl Tripp, Las Vegas .... KO 1
Feb. 10—Lucien Rodriguez, Miami Beach .... W 10
Apr. 19—Ossie Ocasio, San Juan .... D 10
June 28—Ossie Ocasio, San Juan .... KO 1
Oct. 2—Tom Fischer, Las Vegas .... KO 7

ALVIN DOMINEY
Orlando, Fla. Light Heavyweight
1978
Feb. 28—James Dixon, Memphis .... W 4
May 23—Willie Shannon, Orlando .... KO by 2
June 20—Fritz Krantz, Phoenix .... KO 2
June 29—Danman Lacy, Odessa .... KO 1
July 18—Flash Geleim, Phoenix .... KO 1
July 31—Willie Stoglin, Odessa .... KO 1
Aug. 22—Frankie Evans, Odessa .... KO 6
Sept. 19—Clyde Mudget, Odessa .... L 12
1979
Mar. 16—Frank Williams, Cincinnati .... KO by 7
May 11—Frank Williams, Cincinnati .... L 10
July 9—Grover Robinson, Odessa .... W 10
Aug. 27—Zack Ferguson, Odessa .... KO 3
1980
Jan. 18—Jimmy Ingram, Las Vegas .... W 10
May 15—Rick Jester, Chicago .... KO by 1
July 18—Carl Ivy, Odessa .... KO 7
Aug. 16—Emmett Banks, Odessa .... KO 4
Aug. 30—Mike Quarry, Incline Village .... L 10

JOSE (PEPE) DOMINGUEZ
Los Angeles, Calif. Welterweight
1977
July 20—Dick Fisher, Las Vegas .... W 6
Dec. 20—Gary Raymond, Las Vegas .... W 7
1978
Jan. 23—Howard Jackson, Las Vegas .... D 8
Mar. 31—Jorge Morales, Las Vegas .... D 10
May 25—Fili Ramirez, Las Vegas .... W 8
July 27—Jose Luis Solano, Las Vegas .... KO 8

Aug. 17—Modesto Concepcion, Los Angeles .... TD 8
Aug. 25—Bert Lee, San Diego .... L 8
Oct. 27—Felix Pinto, New York .... W 8
Nov. 8—Ron Cummings, Stockton .... D 8
1979
Mar. 28—Curtis Ramsey, Lake Tahoe .... L 10
May 4—Horace Shufford, Pico Rivera .... W 10
May 25—Daryl Penn, Pico Rivera .... W 10
July 27—Howard Jackson, Las Vegas .... W 10
Oct. 30—Greg Stephens, Las Vegas .... L 10
Dec. 14—Bert Lee, Orange County .... L 10
1980
Jan. 23—Alan Webb, Portland .... W 10
May 5—Santiago Valdez, Phoenix .... L 10
May 28—Steve Chase, Portland, Ore. .... W 10
July 8—Greg Stephens, Las Vegas .... L 12
Nov. 11—Greg Stephens, Las Vegas .... W 12
(NABF Welterweight Title)

JOHN DOMINGUEZ
Los Angeles, Calif. Junior Welterweight
1979
June 13—Francisco Pico, Las Vegas .... KO 2
1980
June 18—Greg Williams, Las Vegas .... KO 5
Oct. 8—Jaime Nava, Las Vegas .... W 10

JUAN DOMINGUEZ
Los Angeles, Calif. Junior Lightweight
1979
June 13—Francisco Pico, Las Vegas .... KO 2
1980
Nov. 29—Dennis Quimayousie, Lake Tahoe .... L 10

MIGUEL DOMINGUEZ
Argentine Junior Welterweight
1980
Mar. 7—Juan Saucedo, Mendoza .... D 8
Apr. 17—Humberto Barloa, Mendoza .... D 8
Aug. 8—Raul Castro, Mendoza .... KO 4
Oct. 3—Raul Castro, Gral Alvear .... W 10

RAMON M. DOMINGUEZ
Argentine Featherweight
1980
Feb. 15—Julio C. Saba, Cordoba .... D 10
Mar. 7—Diego Ramirez, Trelew .... W 10
Mar. 21—Luis Alvarez, Salta .... L 10
May —Ruben Butiler, Buenos Aires .... KO 6
May 24—Marcelo Miranda, S. Sal. de Jujuy ...... KO 3
July 4—Heleno Ferreira, Salta .... D 10
Sept. 26—Juan Brizuela, P.R.S. Pena .... W 10
Dec. 13—Osvaldo Vallejos, Buenos Aires .... D 10

DANNY DONATTO
Houston, Texas Junior Middleweight
1974
Mar. 21—Bobby Smith, Houston .... W 6
July 22—Al Joseph, New Orleans .... KO 3
Aug. 6—Johnny Capitano, New Orleans .... W 6
1975
Feb. 17—Prisciliano Castillo, Corpus Christi .... L 8
June 16—Ike Fluellen, Jacinto City .... L 8
1975-1977
(Inactive)
1978
July 18—Jose Munoz, Houston .... KO 3
Sept. 19—Miguel Garcia, Houston .... D 6
Oct. 12—Martin Jiminez, Padadena .... KO 3
Nov. 12—Martin Jiminez, Pasadena .... KO 3
1979
Feb. 13—Priscilliano Castillo, Houston .... KO 4
Mar. 20—Jesse Lara, Houston .... KO 1
Apr. 17—Pete Seward, Houston .... L 10
May 22—Billy Miller, Beaumont .... L 10
1980
Jan. 8—Alejos Rodriguez, Houston .... KO by 4

DARRELL DORSEY
Sacramento, Calif. Junior Middleweight
1979
Apr. 12—Eddie Bearden, Lake Tahoe .... W 4
Apr. 21—Gary Giron, Elko .... KO by 2
1980
Jan. 17—Paul Jones, Stateline .... KO by 2

MARCUS DORSEY
Houston, Texas Middleweight
1978
Apr. 11—Mike Garcia, Houston .... W 6
Apr. 20—Robert Powell, Houston .... KO by 2
May 10—Mike Hallacy, Memphis .... KO by 0
June 27—Paul Stephens, Odessa .... KO by 3

July 18—Carl Ivy, Tyler .... L 6
Aug. 8—Leon McCullum, Houston .... D 6
1979
June 6—Herman Marquez, Laredo ....KO 1
July 21—Leon McCullum, Houston .... KO by 3
1980
Feb. 12—Manuel Torres, Beaumont .... KO by 4
Mar. 25—Manuel Torres, Houston .... L 10
June 17—Ignacio Lopez, Houston .... KO by 2
Oct. 18—Joe Pacheco, Lake Charles .... KO by 4
Dec. 6—Emmett Atlas, Bastrop .... L 6

RALPH DOUCETTE
(RALPH DUMONT)
Lowell, Mass. Junior Middleweight
1978
Jan. 5—Billy Burke, Portland .... KO by 2
Aug. 13—Dale Staley, Portland .... KO by 2
Sept. 29—Avelino Dos Reis, N. Providence ..... KO by 1
Nov. 23—Mark Mello, Portland .... W 6
Dec. 20—Charley Jones, Waterville .... L 6
1979
Jan. 11—Mike Rodriguez, Cohoes .... KO by 4
Apr. 4—Hector Ortiz, Springfield .... KO by 4
Apr. 18—Don Whipple, Waterville .... KO 4
May 18—Papo Figueroa, Hartford .... KO by 2
May 19—Mark Mello, Quincy .... W 4
May 25—Rusty Rosenberger, Montreal .... KO by 6
June 12—Rusty Rosenberger, Totowa .... KO by 2
Aug. 11—Augustin Killeen, N. Swanzey .... KO by 5
Aug. 21—Tom Jancy, Yarmouth .... L 4
Oct. 27—Juan Figarello, Fitchburg .... KO by 1
Oct. 30—Tom Merola, Totowa .... KO by 1
Dec. 1—John Griffin, Albany .... KO by 3
1980
Mar. 26—Rick Craney, Waterville .... L 8
Apr. 1—Larry Esaldo, Totowa .... KO by 2
Apr. 16—Don Bickford, Waterville .... KO by 2
June 28—Jack Morrell, Manchester .... KO by 3
Nov. 20—Rick Hamlisch, Totowa .... KO by 2

BILLY DOUGLAS
Columbus, Ohio Light Heavyweight
1967
Mar. 18—Arnold Bush, Newark .... KO 2
May 17—Arnold Bush, Columbus .... KO 2
June 6—Conrad Williams, Toledo .... L 6
Sept. 25—Art James, Detroit .... KO 3
Sept. 30—Davon Smith, Columbus .... KO 3
Oct. 3—Larry Tadum, McKeesport .... KO by 5
Dec. 2—Larry Tadum, Columbus .... W 8
1968
Jan. 27—Hilton Whittaker, Columbus .... W 10
June 1—Charlie Lewis, Columbus .... KO 2
Aug. 16—Leon Washington, New York .... L 6
1969
Feb. 15—Tommy Shaffer, Zanesville .... W 10
Apr. 21—Kenny Partlow, Columbus .... KO 2
June 11—Louis Vinales, Columbus .... KO 1
July 21—Pedro Miranda, San Juan .... KO by 7
Dec. 19—Sonny Floyd, Columbus .... KO 5
1970
Jan. 31—Skeeter McClure, Detroit .... KO 10
Mar. 4—Willie Warren, Columbus .... W 10
Apr. 29—James Parks, Cleveland .... W 8
July 12—Don Fullmer, Columbus .... D 10
Sept. 12—Tom Bethea, Columbus .... W 10
Nov. 18—Nojeem Adigun, Columbus .... KO 4
1971
Apr. 27—Bunny Sterling, London .... L 10
Sept. 29—Michael Paul, Pointe-A-Pitre .... KO 1
Dec. 4—Jose Gonzalez, San Juan .... L 10
1972
Feb. 7—Billy Lloyd, Philadelphia .... KO 1
Mar. 21—Carlos Marks, Philadelphia .... KO 10
Apr. 26—Sydney Hoho, Capetown .... W 10
May 15—Carlos Marks, Philadelphia .... W 10
Sept. 12—Al Quinney, Philadelphia .... KO 7
Nov. 29—Marion Connors, Cleveland .... KO 8
1973
Jan. 15—Nate Collins, Philadelphia .... KO 9
Mar. 18—Ricky Ortiz, Columbus .... KO 2
May 21—Steve Smith, Tokyo .... KO 3
June 25—Bennie Briscoe, Philadelphia ...... KO by 8
Nov. 15—Octavio Romero, Tampa .... KO 9
Dec. 22—Elijah Makathini, Durban .... L 10
1974
Aug. 19—Willie Monroe, Philadelphia .... L 10
Nov. 27—Danny Brewer, Columbus .... KO 2
1975
Feb. 15—Karl Zurheide, Columbus .... KO 3
Dec. 19—Lee Royston, Columbus .... KO 2

	1976	
Feb.	6—Pedro Soto, New York	W 10
Mar.	8—Tom Bethea, New York	L 10
July	—Angel Oquendo, Philadelphia	KO 7
Aug.	21—Victor Galindez, Buenos Aires	L 10
	1977	
July	16—Al Bell, Columbus	KO 1
Nov.	1—Marvin Johnson, Philadelphia	KO by 5
	1978	
Dec.	6—Charlie Smith, Cleveland	W 10
	1979	
Feb.	7—Pablo Ramos, Cleveland	L 10
May	9—Sylvester Wilder, Columbus	KO 3
July	2—Harold Riggins, Columbus	KO 5
Aug.	9—Jim Robinson, Columbus	KO 3
Sept.	18—Bobby Joe Anderson, Columbus	KO 2
Nov.	27—Fred Groves, Columbus	KO 2
	—Bob Robinson, Columbus	KO 2
	1980	
Feb.	18—Jerry Martin, Upper Darby	KO by 10
Aug.	21—Willie Kince, Columbus	KO 4

HANK DOUGLAS
East Orange, N.J. Middleweight
1980

June	19—Rick Hamlisch, Totowa	L 4
July	17—Rick Hamlisch, Totowa	D 4

TONY DOWLING
Vancouver, Canada Middleweight
1979

May	20—Ted Turner, Ft. St. John	W 6
Oct.	9—Terry Jesmer, Winnipeg	KO by 6
	1980	
Mar.	31—Rudi Koopmans, Rotterdam	KO by 1

MALIK DOZIER
Palmer Park, Md. Heavyweight
1977

Dec.	17—Dave Johnson, Washington, D.C.	L 4
	1978	
Nov.	17—Dave Johnson, Washington, D.C.	L 8
	1979	
Jan.	11—Quinnie Locklear, Landover	KO 1
July	3—Broderick Mason, Atlantic City	W 6
July	24—Wilbert Williams, Atlantic City	KO 2
Aug.	3—Mike Tarasewich, Atlantic City	W 6
Aug.	28—Robert Coley, Atlantic City	D 6
Oct.	19—Gerry Cooney, Commack	KO by 5
Nov.	25—Renaldo (Mr.) Snipes, Boston	KO by 5

SAL DRAGONE
White Plains, N.Y. Junior Welterweight
1978

Jan.	18—Ramon Torres, White Plains	KO 1
Mar.	1—Mel Boynton, White Plains	KO 2
Apr.	5—Mel Boynton, White Plains	W 4
May	10—Pete O'Keefe, White Plains	W 6
Aug.	25—Mel Boynton, New York	W 4
Oct.	5—Billy Rice, White Plains	KO 1
Nov.	1—Ronald Newby, White Plains	KO 1
Dec.	15—Peter O'Keefe, White Plains	W 4
	1979	
Mar.	14—Jay Micy, Westchester	KO 2
Apr.	11—Charles Smith, Westchester	KO 4
May	23—Ken Fusco, Westchester	W 8
Dec.	5—Ken Fusco, Westchester	L 8
	1980	
Feb.	13—Hassan Muhammad, White Plains	KO 3
May	31—Frank Jenco, Elizabeth	W 6
July	16—Joe Guzzo, Elizabeth	KO 2

LOUIS DRAKE
Kansas City, Mo. Heavyweight
1980

Aug.	12—Lon Dale Friesen, Wichita	W 4
Sept.	10—Lon Dale Friesen, Wichita	KO 1

FRANK DRAPER
Toledo, Ohio Light Heavyweight
1980

Sept.	18—John Beveridge, Cleveland	KO 1
Oct.	16—Darrell Hayes, Toledo	KO by 3
Dec.	2—Joe Bird, Jr., Toledo	W 4

RON DRAPER
Kansas City, Mo. Heavyweight
1973

Sept.	25—Duane Bobick, Kansas City	KO by 4
	1974	
Oct.	8—Scott LeDoux, Minneapolis	KO by 10

	1975	
Jan.	2—Marty Monroe, Los Angeles	L 6
Nov.	20—Randy Stevens, Omaha	L 8
	1976	
May	19—Oliver Phillips, Las Vegas	L 8
June	16—Gary Bates, Las Vegas	W 8
Oct.	20—Vic Brown, Cleveland	L 6
Nov.	17—Rodney Bobick, St. Paul	L 10
	1977	
July	29—Robert Echols, Memphis	L 6
	1978	
Jan.	14—Johnny Robinson, Kansas City	W 4
Feb.	11—Ron Burton, Kansas City	ND 2
Apr.	20—Johnny Boudreaux, Houston	L disq. 8
Dec.	9—John Tate, Detroit	KO by 5
	1979	
Feb.	20—Glenn Morgan, Bloomington	KO by 6
Mar.	16—Henry Porter, St. Louis	KO by 4
June	14—Young Joe Louis, River Grove	KO by 4
Dec.	14—George O'Mara, Orange County	KO by 2
	1980	
May	14—Samson N'Gata, Las Vegas	W 6
July	8—Steve Huntington, Las Vegas	L 6
July	16—Jeff Podgurski, Las Vegas	L 6
Aug.	6—Mike Creel, Las Vegas	W 6
Oct.	15—Tom Landry, Las Vegas	W 6
Nov.	7—Tony Tubbs, San Antonio	L 10
Nov.	26—Al Myles, Las Vegas	L 6
Dec.	3—Anthony Davis, Las Vegas	L 6
Dec.	17—Tony Perea, Las Vegas	KO by 4

BUSTER DRAYTON
Philadelphia, Pa. Middleweight
1978

Nov.	9—Charles Carey, Virginia Beach	D 4
Dec.	14—Jesse Carter, Virginia Beach	W 6
	1979	
May	31—Frank Moore, Virginia Beach	KO 1
July	3—Bob Saxton, Atlantic City	KO 1
Aug.	30—Jesse Carter, Virginia Beach	KO 6
Sept.	20—Julius Spell, Virginia Beach	W 4
Oct.	18—Clifford Smith, Philadelphia	KO 1
	1980	
Aug.	9—Bill Harrington, Atlantic City	KO 2
Oct.	1—Curtis Taylor, Atlantic City	ND 8
Nov.	6—Kevin Perry, Atlantic City	KO by 3

WALTER DRISCOLL
Brockton, Mass. Light Heavyweight
1980

Jan.	15—Marcus Jackson, W. Hartford	KO by 1
Jan.	23—Frank Button, Waterville	L 6
Mar.	4—Joe Vescio, W. Hartford	KO by 3
Apr.	1—Mike Fisher, Totowa	KO by 3
Aug.	15—Phil Capobianco, Glen Cove	KO by 1
Aug.	18—Louis Vallar, Boston	KO by 1

FRANKIE DUARTE
Los Angeles, Calif. Junior Featherweight
1973

Aug.	16—Tony Ramos, Los Angeles	KO 1
Sept.	27—Baby Corona, Los Angeles	KO 3
Oct.	18—Manny Gonzalez, Los Angeles	W 4
Oct.	23—Juan Lopez, Los Angeles	KO 4
Nov.	15—Joaquin Heredia, Los Angeles	KO 2
	1974	
Jan.	2—Johnny Meza, Las Vegas	KO 1
Jan.	10—Gasper Montejo, Los Angeles	KO 3
Jan.	26—Jorge Rodriguez, Tucson	KO 2
Feb.	7—Pedro Torres, Los Angeles	KO 3
Feb.	12—Jorge De La Rosa, Sacramento	KO 1
Mar.	21—Frankie Granados, Los Angeles	KO 5
May	24—Tetsuro Kawakimi, Los Angeles	W 10
July	11—Rufino Hernandez, Los Angeles	KO 3
Aug.	29—Antonio Garcia, Los Angeles	KO 5
Sept.	26—Tanny Amancio, Los Angeles	KO 5
Nov.	4—Cecil Escobido, Honolulu	KO 2
Dec.	3—Joe Guevara, Sacramento	L 12
	1975	
Mar.	13—Jorge Altamirano, Los Angeles	W 10
Apr.	24—Famosito Gomez, Los Angeles	W 10
May	28—Famosito Gomez, Los Angeles	L 10
Sept.	20—Jose Rosa, Los Angeles	KO 6
Jan.	8—Seco Luna, Los Angeles	W 10
Feb.	13—Santiago Hernandez, San Bernardino	KO 4
May	11—Erife Grafe, Honolulu	KO 6
June	17—Francisco Cruz, Los Angeles	KO 8
July	12—Jose Cazares, Tijuana	KO 4
Oct.	6—Al Diaz, Honolulu	W 10
Nov.	11—Alfonso Gutierrez, Los Angeles	KO 5
Dec.	9—Martin Buchanan, Los Angeles	KO 4

1977
Apr. 14—Jorge Carrasco, Los Angeles .... KO 9
June 9—Alberto Davila, Los Angeles .... KO by 5
1978
Feb. 12—Arturo Lopez, Los Angeles .... KO 9
Feb. 26—Daniel Ocampo, Los Angeles .... KO 9
Aug. 28—Peter King, Pico Rivera .... W 10
1979
Feb. 22—Francisco Flores, Los Angeles .... W 12
June 19—Rolando Navarrete, Honolulu .... L 10
1980
Feb. 11—Chamaco Lopez, Mexicali .... KO 9
Feb. 25—Daniel Ocampo, Los Angeles .... KO 9
Aug. 29—Peter King, Pico Rivera .... W 10

P. CESAR DUARTE
Argentine Light Heavyweight
1980
Jan. 18—Alberto Cardozao, S. Sal. de Jujuy ...... KO 8
Feb. 8—Natalio Ibarra, Trelew .... KO 5
Mar. 14—Alberto Cardozao, S. Sal. de Jujuy ..... KO 7
Mar. 28—Adolfo Salvatierra, S. Sal. de Jujuy ..... W 6
Apr. 26—Juan D. Suarez, Buenos Aires .... KO 4
July 12—Jesus Ibanez, Pergamino .... TD 5
Aug. 15—Jesus Ibanez, S. Sal. de Jujuy .... D 10
Dec. 5—Celestino Bailone, Cdo. Rivadavia ... KO by 10

ANDRE DUBIEN
Canadian Light Heavyweight
1979
June 3—Pierre Cormier, Quebec .... L 4
1980
Mar. 13—Ron Edwards, Hull .... KO 3
Apr. 21—Kelly Anderson, Hull .... L 6

FRED DUDLEY
Ft. Worth, Texas Light Heavyweight
1980
Aug. 8—Larry Jackson, Dallas .... KO 2

REUBEN DUDOIT
Honolulu, Hawaii Junior Lightweight
1979
July 3—Fred Baclaan, Hilo .... KO 3
Dec. 18—Roger Reed, Honolulu .... KO 2
1980
Feb. 20—Roger Reed, Honolulu .... KO 2
Apr. 1—Ful Sumagaysay, Honolulu .... W 5

MIKE DUFFY
Brooklyn, N.Y. Junior Middleweight
1978
Oct. 28—Peter Mancini, Jersey City .... KO 3
Dec. 1—Nino Cosme, Jersey City .... W 4
1979
Jan. 27—Pete O'Keefe, Jersey City .... KO 2
Mar. 15—Nino Cosme, North Bergen .... KO 2
1980
Feb. 29—Clyde Graves, Brooklyn .... D 4
May 23—Clyde Graves, New York .... KO by 5

ERNIE (PEE WEE) DUNBAR
Spartanburg, S.C. Middleweight
1979
Aug. 5—David Dean, Spartanburg .... KO by 3
Aug. 10—Henry Patterson, Spartanburg .... L 4
Dec. 2—Butch Chambers, Spartanburg .... L 4
1980
Feb. 5—Max Hord, Charleston .... KO 4
May 24—Jerry Miller, Union, S.C. .... KO by 3
July 26—Eddie Smith, Charlotte .... KO by 5
Aug. 8—Ray Phillips, Dallas .... KO by 1
Sept. 6—Maurice Moore, Lincolnton .... L 4
Sept. 25—Irwin Hines, Winston-Salem .... KO by 1
Dec. 21—Robey Jetton, Spartanburg .... L 4

PAT DUNCAN
Ruthdrum, Idaho Heavyweight
1979
July 3—Kim Edwards, Gardnerville .... KO 3
July 31—Ken Arlt, Spokane .... W 8
1980
July 3—Fred Muhammad, Gardnerville .... W 10
Aug. 31—Big Ed Smith, Carson City .... W 10
Oct. 22—Lee Mitchell, Crystal Bay .... W 10

TERRY DUNCAN
Winston-Salem, N.C. Middleweight
1979
Apr. 20—Mike Sacchetti, Fairmont .... L 6
Aug. 24—Clarence Gilmore, Memphis .... KO by 5
1980
Oct. 15—Doug DeWitt, White Plains .... L 6

FRANK DUNTON
1980
Mar. 12—Paul Benjamin, Waterville .... W 8

RODELL DUPREE
Jersey City, N.J. Heavyweight
1972
Apr. 6—Kevin Pantalow, North Bergen .... L 6
May 24—Henry Lawson, New York .... KO 3
Oct. 27—Henry Lawson, North Bergen .... L 6
Dec. 7—King David, Bayonne .... KO 4
1973
Mar. 21—Larry Holmes, Scranton .... L 4
June 23—Jerry Houston, Atlantic City .... L 4
Aug. 4—Kevin Pantalow, New York .... KO 1
Sept. 24—Kevin Isaacs, New York .... L 6
Oct. 10—Paul Simonetti, Scranton .... W 8
1974
May 29—Jerry Houston, Philadelphia .... W 8
1975
Aug. 15—Leroy Diggs, Atlantic City .... KO by 5
Sept. 13—Ken Robinson, New Bedford .... W 8
Oct. 14—Danny McAlinden, London .... KO by 3
1976
May 7—Ernie Lassiter, Kearny .... L 6
Sept. 11—Jerry Judge, Nutley .... W 8
Nov. 18—Rochelle Norris, Wilmington .... L 10
1977
Apr. 29—Obie English, Baltimore .... L 8
June 13—Mike Koranicki, Newark .... KO by 4
1978
Apr. 7—Joe Maye, North Bergen .... KO 3
June 2—Tyrone Harley, Jersey City .... W 4
Nov. 11—Randy Cobb, Boston .... KO by 6
1979
Feb. 26—Mike Tarasewich, New York .... W 10
1980
Mar. 4—Clinton Cochrane, Elizabeth .... W 8
Oct. 2—Steve Zouski, Boston .... L 10
Oct. 18—Renaldo Snipes, Atlantic City .... KO by 3

TYLER DUPUY
New Orleans, La. Junior Middleweight
1977
July 18—August Peters, New Orleans .... KO 3
Aug. 16—O.V. Emanuel, New Orleans .... W 4
Aug. 30—Kirk Kinard, New Orleans .... W 4
1978
Aug. 29—Lou Coleman, New Orleans .... KO 1
Oct. 24—Larry Rayford, New Orleans .... L 6
1979
Apr. 14—Larry Jackson, New Orleans .... KO 3
1980
July 15—Larry Rayford, New Orleans .... KO by 5
Sept. 23—Bruce Calloway, New Orleans .... KO by 2

CLARK DURAN
Los Angeles, Calif. Light Lightweight
1980
Jan. 31—Clemente Enrique, Los Angeles .... KO 3
Feb. 28—Jaime Nava, Los Angeles .... W 6
Apr. 24—Eric Bonilla, Los Angeles .... W 6
June 5—Frank Alvarado, Los Angeles .... KO by 3

FRANKIE DURAN
Seattle, Wash. Junior Middleweight
1978
July 13—Abraham Schwarze, Seattle .... KO 3
Aug. 9—Ken Martin, Seattle .... D 4
1979
Feb. 20—Manny Gullant, Seattle .... KO 1
Apr. 26—Hudson Jackson, Seattle .... W 6
1980
May 28—Robert Belton, Portland, Ore. .... KO 2

JOSE L. DURAN
Argentine Middleweight
1980
June 14—Manuel Flores, Gral Villegas .... W 4
Aug. 9—Julio Arancibia, Gral Villegas .... L 10
Nov. 14—Jose Vega, San Luis .... L 10
Dec. 5—Juan D. Roldan, San Francisco ...... KO by 6

MARTIN DURAN
Argentine Welterweight
1980
Feb. 1—Juan Barboza, Tucuman .... L 10
Feb. 15—Roberto Ale Ali, Tucuman .... L 10
Mar. 14—Ricardo Cisneros, P.R.S. Pena .... L 8
Mar. 28—Manuel Lopez, La Banda .... W 10
June 6—Santiago Portillo, San Nicolas ...... KO by 7
July 25—Miguel Arguello, Tucuman .... L 10

85

Aug.	22—Ricardo Cisneros, P.R.S. Pena	L 10
Sept.	19—Manuel Alvarez, Tucuman	L 10
Oct.	17—Tito Caceres, Tartagal	D 8
Nov.	14—Manuel Alvarez, Tucuman	L 10

PAT DURAN
Wichita Falls, Texas
Managed by Pat O'Grady
1980

June	17—Kenneth Connors, Oklahoma City	KO 1
July	1—Joe Presley, Oklahoma City	KO 2
July	15—Ray Nowdon, Oklahoma City	W 6
July	27—Ray Menafee, Oklahoma City	KO 3
Aug.	5—Rick Battles, Oklahoma City	KO 2
Aug.	19—Ray Nowdon, Oklahoma City	KO 2
Sept.	9—Ray Abrams, Norman	KO 3
Sept.	25—Clyde Spencer, Oklahoma City	W 6
Nov.	20—Clyde Atlas, Oklahoma City	W 6

RAFAEL DURAN
San Antonio, Texas Junior Featherweight
1977

Feb.	8—Valente Ramos, San Antonio	KO 5
Apr.	12—Tony Aranda, San Antonio	KO 1
May	31—Luis Rico, San Antonio	KO 2
June	11—Talan Monsivais, Laredo	KO 2
June	28—Rosendo Garcia, San Antonio	KO 2
Sept.	9—Guillermo Ayala, San Antonio	KO by 7
	1978	
Feb.	20—Calvin Sheppard, San Antonio	W 6
June	23—Famosito Gomez, Nuevo Laredo	L 10
	1979	
Jan.	30—Guillermo Ayala, San Antonio	KO 3
June	6—Ignacio Hernandez, Laredo	KO 2
Aug.	29—Jorge Monzon, Houston	KO by 3
	1980	
July	25—Steve Whetstone, Miami	KO by 1
July	29—Eduardo Flores, Laredo	KO 4
Oct.	14—Rigoberto Carillo, Laredo	W 10
Oct.	28—Victor Gordillo, Houston	KO 3

MIGUEL DURO
Argentine Middleweight
1980

Aug.	9—Osvaldo Figueredo, Segui	L 10
Oct.	10—Jose Orada, Parana	D 10

TODD DUSHANE
Los Angeles, Calif. Heavyweight
1980

Oct.	23—Ray Ruiz, Las Vegas	KO 2
Dec.	3—Chip Tyler, Anaheim	KO by 1

HAROLD DUTRA
California Heavyweight
1980

July	25—Len Lawson, San Carlos	KO by 4
Aug.	28—Steve Chase, San Carlos	KO 1
Oct.	16—Lew Lockwood, San Carlos	W 6

VICTOR ECHEGARAY
Argentine Junior Lightweight
Born: Sept. 16, 1945
1967

July	7—Humberto Villalobos, San Juan	KO 6
Oct.	20—Alfredo Recabarren, San Juan	KO 3
Nov.	5—Juan C. Diaz, San Juan	KO 3
Nov.	24—Wenceslao Lagos, San Juan	KO 2
Dec.	7—Miguel Pizarro, San Juan	KO 2
Dec.	22—Martin Juarez, San Juan	D 10
	1968	
Apr.	19—Juan D. Corradi, San Juan	D 10
Aug.	23—Alberto Mateo, San Juan	KO 4
Oct.	11—Moises Barbosa, San Juan	KO 4
Oct.	25—Fernando Porcel, San Juan	D 10
	1969	
Jan.	24—Ricardo Moreno, San Juan	D 10
Feb.	21—Ramon Luque, La Falda	KO 3
July	11—Leandro Pereyra, San Juan	D 10
Sept.	3—Venancio Gonzalez, Buenos Aires	KO by 6
Nov.	8—Luis A Reyes, Montevideo	W 10
Dec.	20—Juan D. Corradi, Buenos Aires	W 10
	1970	
Mar.	5—Carlos Aro, Mendoza	L 10

May	8—Gregorio Villavicencio, San Juan	W 10
May	30—Fermin Torres, Mexico City	KO 1
June	27—Pedro Dominguez, Mexico City	KO 7
July	18—Ricardo Arredondo, Mexico City	KO by 10
	1971	
Feb.	12—Juan Diaz, San Juan	KO 7
Mar.	5—Marelo Garrardo, San Juan	ND 1
Apr.	17—Juan D. Corradi, Buenos Aires	KO 3
June	26—Venancio Gonzalez, Buenos Aires	KO 5
July	16—Marcelo Gallardo, San Juan	KO 5
Sept.	3—Hugo Davila, San Juan	W 10
Nov.	6—Leoncio Ortiz, Buenos Aires	W 10
Dec.	10—Ramon Gomez, San Juan	KO 1
	1972	
Jan.	21—Marcelo Gallardo, Los Toldos	KO 4
Mar.	17—Leandro Pereyra, Laboulaye	KO 4
Apr.	14—Carlos Taborda, San Juan	KO 2
June	9—Leandro Pereyra, Gualeguaychu	W 10
Sept.	5—Ben Villaflor, Honolulu	D 15
	(World Junior Lightweight Title)	
Nov.	29—Juan D. Corradi, Buenos Aires	D 10
	1973	
Mar.	30—Kid Toledo, Buenos Aires	KO 9
May	10—Miguel Aguila, Neuguen	KO 2
June	19—Kuniaki Shibata, Tokyo	L 15
	(World Junior Lightweight Title)	
	1974	
Feb.	15—Carlos Martinez, Plaza Huincul	W 10
Mar.	7—Pedro Aguero, Mendoza	L 12
Apr.	11—Carlos Martinez, Pase de los Libres	KO 6
Apr.	26—Miguel Maldonado, San Salvador de Jujuy	KO 8
May	11—Jorge Gomez, San Juan	D 10
July	26—Jorge Gomez, San Juan	W 10
Aug.	29—Oscar Mendez, Bahia Blanca	D 10
Sept.	20—Pedro Aguero, San Juan	D 10
Nov.	1—Carlos Ibanez, Salta	W 10
	1975	
Jan.	7—Miguel Figueroa, Cordoba	L 10
Feb.	28—Miguel Figueroa, Cordoba	W 10
May	9—Ramon Duarte, San Juan	W 10
June	28—Sam Serrano, San Juan, Puerto Rico	L 15
Aug.	8—Alberto Herrera, Guayaquil	L 10
Oct.	25—Juan Garcia, Buenos Aires	L 10
	1976	
Feb.	13—Juan Olivera, Posadas	KO 7
Mar.	17—Pedro Aguero, Buenos Aires	W 12
	(Won Argentine Title)	
July	31—Cirilo Ruiz, Buenos Aires	KO 8
Aug.	19—Oscar Mendez, Bahia Blanca	L 10
Sept.	11—Antonio Ross, Bolivar	W 12
	(Retained Argentine Title)	
Nov.	3—Facundo Villalba, Catamarca	W disq. 9
Dec.	4—Oscar Mendez, Buenos Aires	W 10
	1977	
Feb.	11—Ramon Gonzalez, Mar del Plata	W disq. 3
July	5—Julio Melone, Cordoba	W 10
Sept.	3—Oscar Barrios, Bolivar	W 12
	(Retained Argentine Title)	
Oct.	7—Oscar Albarracin, Cordoba	W 10
Nov.	4—Oscar Mendez, San Juan	D 10
Dec.	16—Oscar Mendez, Necochea	ND 6
	1978	
Jan.	13—Martin Leiva, Tucuman	W 10
Feb.	9—Federico Godoy, Posadas	W 10
Mar.	9—Ramon Gonzalez, Posadas	W 12
	(Retained Argentine Title)	
Mar.	31—Miguel Figueroa, Cordoba	D 10
May	5—Facundo Villalba, Rafaela	D 10
June	8—Antonio Ross, Posadas	W 12
	(Retained Argentine Title)	
July	13—Miguel Figueroa, Rio Tercero	L 10
Oct.	13—Oscar Barrios, C. Cuatia	WF 8
Nov.	10—Jose M. Lopez, Chivilcoy	WF 6
Dec.	15—Jose Valdez, Venado Tuerto	KO 7
	(Retained Argentine Junior Lightweight Title)	
	1979	
Jan.	20—Benedicto Villablanca, Bariloche	KO 8
	(Retained South American Junior Lightweight Title)	
Apr.	12—Julio Melone, Cordoba	TD 4
May	18—Julio Melone, Cordoba	W 10
June	15—Emilcio Ortiz, Trelew	TW 5
July	20—Ruben Riani, Rosario	L 12
	(Lost Argentine Junior Lightweight Title)	
Oct.	26—Alfredo Moyand, Neuquen	KO 7
Nov.	17—Jose Arias, General Pico	KO 8
Dec.	14—Jorge Talquenca, San Salvador de Jujuy	TW 9
	1980	
Jan.	18—Oscar Arevalo, Tucuman	W 10
Apr.	24—Raul Aguero, San Juan	W 10
June	8—Bernabe Villablanca, San Juan	KO 7
	(Retained South American Junior Lightweight Title)	
Aug.	8—Emilcio Ortiz, San Juan	W 12
	(Retained South American Junior Lightweight Title)	

Nov.   7—Ruben Riani, San Juan .... W 12
(Regained Argentine Junior Lightweight Title)

ROBERT (IRONMAN) ECHOLS
Memphis, Tenn. Heavyweight
Height: 6'4"
1976
Mar.   1—Leroy Greer, Memphis .... KO 2
Apr. 14—Leroy Greer, Memphis .... KO 2
Aug.   3—Jesse Avila, Memphis.................. W 8
Sept. 9—Jesse Avila, Memphis.................. W 8
Oct. 12—Ernie Smith, Memphis .... KO 4
Nov.   9—James Dixon, Memphis .... W 8
1977
Feb. 10—Larry Alexander, Memphis .... KO 6
Apr. 28—Chico Gardner, Chicago .... W 8
May   14—Max Bear Smith, Chicago .... KO 2
June 16—Don Phillips, Chicago .... KO 1
July 28—Wolf Ray, Memphis .... KO 4
Sept. 20—Elton Armstrong, New Orleans .... D 4
Oct.   8—Ron Draper, Memphis .... W 6
Nov. 16—Walter Santamore, Memphis .... KO 6
1978
Apr. 10—Chico Gardner, Chicago .... W 8
May   17—Elton Armstrong, Memphis ....L 10
May   22 Max Smith, Chicago .... KO 2
July 26—Maurice Price, Greenville .... KO 7
Sept. 27—Elton Armstrong, Memphis ....L 10
1979
Sept. 13—Rahim Muhammad, Phoenix .... L 8
Sept. 25—Henry Porter, St. Louis ....L 10
1980
May   31—Randy Tex Cobb, El Paso .... KO by 1

DICK ECKLUND
Boston, Mass. Junior Welterweight
1975
Aug. 26—Joe DeFayette, New Bedford ....L 6
Sept. 30—Doug Romano, Boston .... W 4
Nov.   6—Eddie Hudson, Portland .... W 4
Nov. 21—Avelino Dos Reis, Providence ...... KO 3
Dec. 20—Jose Melendez, Boston .... W 4
1976
Jan. 31—Terry Rondeau, Waterbury .... W 6
Feb. 21—Frankie Benjamin, Waterbury .... W 6
Apr. 26—Carlos Garcia, Boston .... W 6
June 24—Randy Milton, Wallingford .... W 6
Sept. 30—Mike Michaud, Peabody .... W 8
Oct. 30—Rufus Miller, East Hartford .... W 8
1977
(Inactive)
1978
Jan. 16—Al Cruz, Latham .... KO 5
Mar.   4—Willie Rodriguez, Boston ....L 8
July 18—Ray Leonard, Boston ....L 10
1979
Aug. 18—Fernando Fernandez, Lowell .... W 10
Dec.   4—Dave Green, Wembley ....L 10
1980
June 20—Ferenado Fernandez, Boston ....L 10

JUNIOR EDMONDS
Newark, N.J. Light Heavyweight
1980
Mar. 22—Kid Samson, Atlantic City .... W 6
May   25—Muhammad Aziz, Rahway ....NC 2
Oct.   4—Bill Tuttle, Great Gorge .... W 6

BOBBY EDWARDS
Light Heavyweight
1980
Mar. 16—Pernall Farley, Los Angeles ....L 6
Mar. 26—Randy McGrady, Costa Mesa ....L 4
Apr. 12—Clayton Ross, Tucson ....L 6

DEMETRIUS EDWARDS
Miami Beach, Fla. Heavyweight
1979
Nov. 27—Greg Paine, Miami Beach ....D 6
1980
Jan. 29—Gabriel Science, Miami Beach .... KO 1
Feb. 28—Tony Sevirance, Tampa .... W 6
Apr. 27—Rocky Stevens, Greenville .... KO 1
Aug. 29—John Symonette, Miami Beach .... W 8

ROBERTO ELIZONDO
Corpus Christi, Texas Junior Lightweight
1977
Apr.   5—Roldolfo Perez, Corpus Christi .... KO 1
July 21—Enrique Contreras, Lardo .... KO 2
Aug.   2—Louis Gomez, Corpus Christi .... KO 1

Nov.   9—Gilbert Lara, Corpus Christi .... KO 1
Dec. 13—Victor Cid, Corpus Christi .... W 8
1978
Aug. 15—Juan Venegas, Houston .... KO 3
Dec. 15—Robert Perez, Corpus Christi .... KO 1
1979
Jan   16—Viterbo Romas, Houston .... KO by 7
Apr. 20—Jose Luis Medrano, Corpus Christi .... KO 1
Aug.   7—Arturo Leon, Corpus Christi .... W 10
Nov. 16—Ruben Moreno, Corpus Christi .... KO 2
Dec. 11—Juan Villisanna, Corpus Christi .... KO 4
1980
Mar. 13—Don Sennett, Los Angeles .... KO 1
Apr.   3—Alejandro Orejal, Los Angeles .... KO 4
Apr. 24—Antonio Nava, Los Angeles .... W 10
July   3—Antonio Nava, Los Angeles .... W 10
Aug.   7—Norman Goins, Los Angeles .... KO 2
Sept. 2—James Martinez, Los Angeles ....L 10
Oct. 19—Earl Young, Los Angeles .... KO 3
Dec. 19—Jesus Salledo, Las Vegas .... KO 3
Dec. 11—Marion Thomas, Los Angeles .... KO 2

JOHN ELLIS
Los Angeles, Calif. Heavyweight
1980
Mar. 21 Rick Mills, San Bernardino ....L 5
Apr.   4—Ron Tucker, San Bernardino .... KO 3
May   2—Zenith Thompson, Inglewood .... W 4
May   7—Zenith Thompson, San Bernardino .... KO 2
May   24—Zenith Thompson, Santa Monica .... KO 4
June 13—Vinnie Smith, San Diego .... W 4
June 30—Mike Bedford, Bakersfield .... KO 1
July 25—Abdullah Muhammad, San Bernardino ... W 5
Sept. 19—Roger Braxton, Inglewood .... W 10

RICHARD ELLIS
Baltimore, Md. Junior Lightweight
1979
Sept. 26—Clifford Haywood, Baltimore ....L 4
1980
Aug.   9—Ernest Jackson, Atlantic City .... KO by 2

DICK EMBLETON
Thomaston, Conn. Heavyweight
1979
May   25—Jose Verdejo, Portland ....L 6
June 29—Johnny Blaine, Hartford ....D 4
July 27—Tom Murphy, Hartford .... KO 4
Sept. 7—Baha Muhammad, Hartford .... KO 1
Sept. 27—Gary Williams, Bristol .... KO 2
Nov. 15—Calvin Langston, Bristol .... KO by 4
1980
Jan.   9—Bob Mladinich, Hartford .... KO 2
May   23—Melvin Epps, Hartford ....L 6

BARRY EMO
Toronto, Canada Heavyweight
1979
July 30—Albert Chard, Toronto .... KO 2
1980
Oct. 16—Tyrone Taylor, Toronto ....D 4

CLEMENTE ENRIQUEZ
Los Angeles, Calif. Lightweight
1979
Mar. 29—Vicente Barreto, Los Angeles .... KO 2
May   17—Fernando Reyes, Los Angeles .... TW 2
July 12—Masa Higa, Los Angeles .... W 4
Aug.   2—Francisco Pico, Los Angeles .... W 5
Sept. 6—Daniel Patino, Los Angeles ....L 6
Sept. 20—Tony Baltazar, Los Angeles .... KO by 5
Nov.   8—Tony Baltazar, Los Angeles .... KO by 1
1980
Jan. 31—Clark Duran, Los Angeles .... KO by 3

RAYMOND ENRIQUEZ
Mexican Junior Welterweight
1979
Apr. 20—Ray Serrano, Corpus Christi .... KO by 4
1980
Feb. 28—Alejandro Contreras, McAllen .... KO by 1
Dec.   5—Juan Ramirez, Cochristi .... KO 2

IMARA EPESI
Chicago, Ill. Middleweight
1979
Feb.   2—Pete Podgorski, Chicago ....L 4
Mar. 17—John Shavers, Chicago .... KO by 3
June 15—Jerry Brown, Belleville ....L 4
Dec. 15—Warren Thunder, Chicago .... KO by 6
1980
May   15—Jimmy Sansone, Chicago ....L 6

MELVIN EPPS
Brooklyn, N.Y. Heavyweight
1979

Aug.	28—Alf Coffin, Atlantic City	L	4
Dec.	11—Ron Rousell, Halifax	W	8
	1980		
Mar.	8—Ali Allen, Great Gorge	W	6
May	23—Dick Embleton, Hartford	W	6
June	6—Barry Funches, Felt Forum	L	8
June	13—John Clohessy, Harlem	W	6
June	20—Ken Schmidt, Hartford	L	6
Nov.	28—Peter Minot, Felt Forum	L	6

ROBBIE EPPS
Los Angeles, Calif. Middleweight
Born: July 7, 1958. Height: 6 ft. 2 in.
1977

June	22—Wally Rambeau, Las Vegas	KO	4
July	6—Carlos Muro, Tahoe	W	4
July	20—Frank Livingstone, Tahoe	KO	3
July	21—Dan Veskovic, Los Angeles	W	5
Aug.	12—Ted Sanders, San Diego	W	6
Sept.	6—John Pineada, Tahoe	KO	3
Sept.	28—Carmelo Garcia, Las Vegas	KO	3
Oct.	12—Zovek Barajas, Las Vegas	W	8
Nov.	1—Joe Ramos, Tahoe	W	8
Dec.	6—Henry Walker, Tahoe	W	10
	1978		
Jan.	24—Andre Beard, Sacramento	KO	5
Mar.	3—Lalo Barrientos, San Diego	KO	2
Mar.	15—Pat Wilson, Tahoe	KO	5
Apr.	4—Steve Bently, Tahoe	KO	4
May	3—Herman Marquez, Las Vegas	KO	4
June	27—Len Harden, Las Vegas	W	10
Aug.	9—Andre Beard, Las Vegas	W	10
Nov.	22—Gabe Peralta, Phoenix	KO	2
Dec.	12—Joe Gonzalves, Phoenix	W	10
	1979		
Jan.	9—Mike Hallacy, Phoenix	W	10
Mar.	15—Paddy Wilson, Lake Tahoe	KO	5
Apr.	10—Willie Warren, Phoenix	W	10
May	14—Henry Walker, Phoenix	L	10
July	20—Len Harden, El Paso	W	10
Sept.	18—Renato Garcia, Phoenix	W	10
Nov.	13—Henry Walker, Phoenix	W	10
	1980		
Aug.	27—Daryl Penn, Las Vegas	KO	6
Oct.	7—Ray Phillips, Las Vegas	KO	6

LARRY ESALDO
Woodbridge, N.J. Middleweight
1980

Jan.	8—Danny Corbett, Totowa	L	4
Apr.	1—Ralph Dumont, Totowa	KO	2

MARIANO ESCALERA
Featherweight
1980

May	22—Jose Cuadrado, Rio Piedras	D	4
June	12—Adolfo Jones, Rio Piedras	KO	2
June	19—Natalio Montalvo, Rio Piedras	KO	2
July	3—Dr. Julio Roman, Rio Piedras	KO	3
Oct.	2—Julio Guzman, San Juan	KO by	4
Oct.	23—Jose Rivas, Caguas	KO	1
Nov.	14—Juan Pizzaro, Miami Beach	W	6

REYES ESCALERA
Middleweight
1980

June	12—Pablo Rivera, Rio Piedras	KO by	4
Aug.	7—Alefandro Falo, Rio Piedras	W	6

MIGUEL ESTRADA
El Paso, Texas Lightweight
1976

Jan.	15—Ray Lampkin, Stateline	KO by	3
May	6—Monroe Brooks, Los Angeles	KO by	3
July	—Leoncio Ortiz, El Paso	W	10
Nov.	17—Paul Garcia, San Antonio	W	6
	1977		
May	10—Art Leon, El Paso	D	10
June	9—Bobby Chacon, Los Angeles	KO by	2
July	30—Art Leon, El Paso	KO by	6
	1978		
Jan.	17—Modesto Concepcion, Las Vegas	L	10
Mar.	26—Earl Young, Ogden	W	10
Apr.	5—German Cuello, Las Vegas	L	10
Apr.	12—Johnny Lira, Las Vegas	L	10
May	25—Roberto Perez, Denver	W	10
July	27—Jorge Morales, Las Vegas	KO by	5
Sept.	7—John Morgan, El Paso	KO	2

Sept.	27—Frank Ahumada, Las Vegas	W	10
Nov.	8—Rodrigo Aguirre, Las Vegas	L	10
	1979		
Jan.	24—Javier Ayala, Las Vegas	L	10
Feb.	7—Al Hughes, Las Vegas	W	10
Feb.	26—Rafael Limon, Houston	KO by	5
Apr.	11—Rogelio Castaneda, Las Vegas	L	10
Apr.	19—Herman Montes, Los Angeles	KO by	4
June	30—Roberto Perez, Albuquerque	KO	1
Dec.	19—Fili Ramirez, Las Vegas	L	10
	1980		
Jan.	18—Adolfo Rivas, El Paso	D	10
Feb.	28—Frank Baltazar, Los Angeles	KO by	6
May	27—Lito Pena, Honolulu	KO by	7

FREDDIE ESTRELLA
Honolulu, Hawaii Flyweight
1978

Aug.	1—Rey Carino, Honolulu	L	4
	1979		
Apr.	24—Julio Rodrigues III, Hilo	L	4
May	15—Caesar Zulueta, Honolulu	KO by	1
June	12—Julio Rodrigues, Honolulu	KO by	3
Dec.	18—Rey Carino, Honolulu	KO by	4
	1980		
May	13—Sam Guillermo, Honolulu	KO	3
June	24—Fanstino Zulueta, Honolulu	KO by	3
July	22—Ellchi Jumawan, Honolulu	KO by	2

JAMES ESTRELLA
Honolulu, Hawaii Flyweight
1979

Dec.	18—Caesar Zulueta, Honolulu	KO by	2
	1980		
May	6—Ely Manning, Honolulu	KO	1
July	22—Julio Rodriguez, Honolulu	KO by	2
Nov.	19—Steven Zulueta, Honolulu	KO by	1

ALFONSO EVANS
Philadelphia, Pa. Lightweight
1974

Feb.	18—Jose Resto, Philadelphia	W	4
Mar.	19—Ken Muse, Philadelphia	W	4
Apr.	29—Carlos Duprey, Philadelphia	W	4
June	4—Ron Meaweather, Philadelphia	W	4
Aug.	19—Carlos Duprey, Philadelphia	W	6
Oct.	9—Ernest Bing, Philadelphia	W	6
Nov.	19—Billy Wade, Philadelphia	KO	1
	1975		
Jan.	28—Willie Daniels, Philadelphia	W	8
Mar.	11—Ewell Hunter, Philadelphia	KO	2
Apr.	7—Ruby Ortiz, Philadelphia	L	8
May	22—Radames Ventura, Philadelphia	W	8
Aug.	18—Jerome Artis, Philadelphia	D	8
Oct.	28—Jerome Artis, Philadelphia	KO by	3
	1976		
Apr.	4—Warren Matthews, New Orleans	L	10
Sept.	23—Elviro Reyes Jajuja, Wilmington	W	8
	1977		
Apr.	18—William Berry, Philadelphia	L	10
Oct.	25—Sammy Goss, Philadelphia	W	10
	1978		
Sept.	27—Mike Frazier, Philadelphia	W	8
Dec.	5—Bobby Alexander, Philadelphia	D	6
	1979		
Aug.	18—Raymond Roman, Atlantic City	W	6
	1980		
July	13—Rocky Lockridge, Great Gorge	L	6

BILLY EVANS
Red Lake, Minn. Junior Middleweight
1979

Dec.	2—Bruce Strauss, Muncie	KO by	3
	1980		
May	13—Mark Lenerick, Indianapolis	KO by	1
June	20—Bruce Strauss, Fort Wayne	KO by	3
June	28—Marco Tineo, Rapid City	KO by	2
July	11—Jeffrey Madison, Chicago	KO by	2
Oct.	28—Mike Hollett, Indianapolis	L	4

CHARLIE EVANS
Omaha, Neb. Junior Welterweight
1978

July	26—C. B. Brown, Omaha	W	4
	1979		
June	25—C. B. Brown, Omaha	KO	3
Aug.	3—Tony Taylor, Omaha	W	5
Nov.	16—Joe Sosa, Kansas City	D	6

1980

Jan.	9—Joe Sosa, Omaha	W	6
Jan.	22—Ray Mancini, Indianapolis	KO by	2

ROBERT EVANS
Jersey City, N.J. Heavyweight
1979

Nov.	28—Ali Allen, West New York, N. J.	D	4

1980

Mar.	28—Scott Lukachek, Tarrytown	KO	1
May	9—Tim Witherspoon, Cammack	L	6
June	11—David Johnson, White Plains	W	6
Nov.	12—Harold Rice, Felt Forum	D	6

TREVOR EVELYN
Barbados Lightweight
1979

	—Orlando Santiago, Staten Island	W	4

1980

Feb.	29—Ken Lomax, Brooklyn	KO	3
Mar.	7—Gilberto Sanchez, Staten Island	W	4
Mar.	12—Richie Garland, White Plains	W	4
Apr.	16—Nordine Bensallah, White Plains	KO	1
June	18—Ray Mancini, Struthers	KO by	2
Oct.	23—Jimmy Longo, Felt Forum	W	6

RAMON FABAS
Argentine Lightweight
1980

Mar.	15—Omar Garcia, Buenos Aires	W	6
May	—Alberto Medina, Buenos Aires	D	6
July	12—Mario Arreguez, Baradero	W	8
Aug.	9—Miguel Barraza, Baradero	D	8

ROCKY FABRIZIO
Orlando, Florida Welterweight
Managed by stan Tommasello
1980

June	27—Frankie Millburn, Atlanta	KO	4
July	2—Jerry Bellman, Miami	KO	3
July	19—Lonnie Wilcox, Panama City, Fla.	W	4
July	25—Tony Foreman, N. Miami Beach	KO by	4
Sept.	2—Charles Thomas, N. Miami Beach	KO	3
Oct.	11—A.W. Muhammad, Ft. Myers	W	4
Nov.	8—A.W. Muhammad, Ft. Myers	W	6
Dec.	11—Rocky Stevens, Gainesville	W	4
Dec.	20—Mike Janus, Ft. Myers	W	6

PERNELL FAIRLEY
Light Heavyweight
1979

Sept.	20—Pete Garcia, Los Angeles	W	5
Oct.	18—Pete Garcia, Los Angeles	W	4
Dec.	6—Robert Guilbault, Los Angeles	W	4

1980

Feb.	21—George O'Mara, Los Angeles	W	6
Feb.	28—Bashir Wadud, Los Angeles	W	6
Mar.	13—Bobby Edwards, Los Angeles	W	8
Mar.	26—George O'Mara, Costa Mesa	W	8
Apr.	16—Len Lawson, Fresno	W	6
Aug.	20—Matt Ross, Las Vegas	KO	2

C. J. FAISON
Washington, D.C. Welterweight
1973

Aug.	31—Jackie Smith, Boston	W	4
Sept.	17—Tyrone Phelps, New York	KO by	4
Nov.	26—Ray Hammond, New York	L	6
Dec.	17—Kevin Dorian, New Bedford	W	8

1974

Mar.	14—Juan Rueda, North Bergen	W	8
June	3—Eddie Parks, New York	KO by	5
Aug.	27—Tyrone Phelps, Alexandria	W	6
Oct.	18—Jimmy Savage, Baltimore	W	6
Nov.	26—Ray Pitts, Largo	W	6

1975

Jan.	31—Jeff Holmes, Philadelphia	W	6
Feb.	22—Keith Averett, Largo	L	6
May	8—Floyd Mayweather, Baltimore	KO by	3

1976

Dec.	2—O'Dell Leonard, Baltimore	L	6
Dec.	17—Jimmy Rothwell, Philadelphia	L	8

1977

Jan.	19—Ruben Lopez, Bristol	L	8

1978

Feb.	8—Karim El-Amin, Washington D.C.	W	4
Mar.	15—Karim El-Amin, Washington D.C.	KO	1
May	24—Richard Jackson, Washington D.C.	W	6
June	28—Ron Pettigrew, Washington D.C.	W	6
Nov.	17—Steve Hughes, Washington D.C.	W	6

1979

Feb.	12—Butterfly Hughes, Washington, D.C.	KO	1
May	23—Charlie Brown, Washington, D.C.	KO by	3
Nov.	21—Johnny Turner, Scranton	KO by	3

1980

Jan.	30—Steve Michalerya, Allentown	KO by	3
Apr.	19—Rocky Fratto, Syracuse	KO by	1

MALO FALE
Samoan Lightweight
1977

Nov.	29—Artillery Menchaca, Honolulu	KO	3

1978

Feb.	7—Mario Manrique, Honolulu	W	5
Mar.	28—Jorge Zenquis, Honolulu	KO	5
Apr.	25—Virgilio Legaspi, Honolulu	W	6
June	20—Fili Ramirez, Honolulu	W	6
Aug.	1—Pascual Villareal, Honolulu	KO	3

1979

May	30—Virgilio Legaspi, Honolulu	W	6
July	31—Ful Sumagaysay, Honolulu	KO	1
Sept.	18—Mar Basa, Honolulu	W	10
Oct.	16—Ful Sumagaysay, Honolulu	KO	1

1980

Mar.	4—Joe Lim, Honolulu	KO by	7

DANNY FAVELLA
San Antonio, Texas Junior Welterweight
1979

Aug.	8—Oscar Rios, Corpus Christi	KO	1
Aug.	28—Leonardo Zapata, San Antonio	KO	2
Nov.	13—Billy Miller, Beaumont	KO by	6
Dec.	14—Billy Miller, Dallas	KO	2

1980

Aug.	13—Andres Ramirez, San Antonio	L	10

WILLIE FEATHERSTONE
Toronto, Canada Middleweight
(Previous Record Unavailable)
1978

Jan.	17—Murray Sutherland, Toronto	KO	3
Apr.	3—Al Bell, Toronto	KO	1
July	11—Harry White, Toronto	KO	1

1979

Feb.	5—Tyrone Freeman	W	8
Dec.	18—Bobby Lalonde, Montreal	KO	1

1980

Jan.	21—Jo Jo Dent, Montreal	KO	2
Feb.	12—Elisha Obed, Montreal	L	10
Mar.	25—Marciano Bernardi, Montreal	D	10

ADOLFO FELICE
Argentine Featherweight
1980

Jan.	4—Hugo Emer, V. Carlos Paz	KO	4
Jan.	18—Antonio Perez, Mar del Plata	D	8
Jan.	—Raul Perez, V. Carlos Paz	D	10
Feb.	27—Victor Velazquez, V. Carlos Paz	W	6
Mar.	14—Ruben Granado, Rosario	L	10
Apr.	3—Julio C. Saba, Cordoba	KO by	2
May	9—Marcelo Miranda, S. Sal de Jujuy	KO by	7
Oct.	24—Fernando Sosa, Mar del Plata	L	10
Dec.	5—Hector Rosa, San Pedro	W	10

ZACK FERGUSON
Houston, Texas Heavyweight
1978

Sept.	19—Vernon Johnston, Tyler	KO by	5

1979

Jan.	30—Victor Rodriguez, San Antonio	KO by	4
Apr.	3—Randy Cobb, Philadelphia	KO by	1
May	11—Charlie Johnson, Cincinnati	KO by	3
Aug.	27—Alvin Dominey, Odessa	KO by	3
	—Victor Rodriguez	L	6
Oct.	20—Fred Muhammad, Pueblo	L	6

1980

Aug.	16—Mike Hamby, Odessa	W	4
Sept.	23—Charles Hostetter, Odessa	L	4

FERNANDO FERNANDEZ
Pawtucket, R.I. Junior Middleweight
1977

Apr.	20—Lorenzo Howard, Taunton	W	4
Oct.	15—Joe O'Brien, Providence	KO	1

Oct. 22—Steve Toomey, Hartford ....W 6
Nov. 25—Al Cruz, Providence ....KO 3
Nov. 26—Jose Melendez, Boston ....W 8
1978
Mar. 20—Roberto Colon, Boston ....L 6
June 28—Randy Milton, Providence ....W 6
July 18—Beau Jaynes, Boston ....W 8
Aug. 3—Jessie Rogers, Boston ....W 6
Sept. 9—Bobby Brown, Providence ....KO 1
Sept. 29—Bill Ramsey, Providence ....W 8
Dec. 15—Charlie Benjamin, Providence ....W 8
1979
Feb. 3—Charlie Benjamin, Boston ....W 6
May 25—Steve Snow, Portland ....KO 4
Aug. 18—Dick Ecklund, Lowell ....KO 10
1980
Feb. 16—Jaime Rodriguez, Portland, Me. ....W 6
Apr. 20—Dave Bolden, Portland, Me. ....W 10
June 20—Dick Ecklund, Boston ....L 10
Aug. 18—Frank Minnigan, Boston ....L 10
Sept. 5—Jack Morrell, Dorchester ....W 10
Nov. 25—Joe Tiberi, Boston ....KO by 5

HECTOR FERNANDEZ
San Diego, Calif. Middleweight
1977
Dec. 16—James Waire, San Diego ....L 4
1978
Mar. 3—Ricky Weigel, San Diego ....KO by 2
May 5—Mike Hickman, San Diego ....L 5
1979
July 20—Rafael Corona, San Diego ....KO by 2
1980
Aug. 7—Perry Levoe, San Carlos ....KO 1
Aug. 9—Jeff McCracken, Spokane ....KO by 1

HUGO FERNANDEZ
Argentine Featherweight
1980
Jan. 18—Carlos de Leon, Buenos Aires ....KO 4
Feb. 8—Osvaldo M. Vallejo, Concordia ....L 10
June 19—Ruben Butiler, Concordia ....W 10
July 8—Marcial Franco, Reconquista ....L 10
Aug. 8—Jorge M. Gomez, Viedma ....L 10
Sept. 6—Roberto Barrientos, Concordia ....KO 8
Oct. 3—Carlos Betbeder, Concordia ....W 10
Nov. 21—Orlando Lucero, Concordia ....W 10
Dec. 19—Hector Barreto, Concordia ....W 10

JACINTO FERNANDEZ
Argentine Middleweight
1980
Mar. 14—Marcelino Quinonez, San Justo ....KO 8
Apr. 19—Crispin de Olivera, San Javier ....KO 9
Oct. 10—Ricardo Arce, Corrientes ....KO 9
(Won Argentine Middleweight Title)
Nov. 15—Jose Navarro, Santa Fe ....KO 4
Dec. 13—Carlos Marks, Parana ....KO 3
(Won Latin American Middleweight Title)

JACINTO FERNANDEZ
Tucson, Ariz. Middleweight
1979
Apr. 4—Len Harden, Las Vegas ....W 10
Apr. 25—Daryl Penn, Lake Tahoe ....KO 8
May 23—Len Harden, Las Vegas ....KO 6
June 20—Steve Delgado, Las Vegas ....L 10
Aug. 8—Rico Dineros, Las Vegas ....L 10
1980
July 22—Slick Mitchell, Miami Beach ....KO 2

JOSE FERNANDEZ
Dominican Rep. Lightweight
Born: October 13, 1947
(U.S. Record)
1970
Aug. 17—Jackie Stanton, Freeport, L.I. ....KO 2
Sept. 10—Chino Rodriguez, New York............KO 1
Nov. 2—Ray Hart, Philadelphia..................KO 1
Nov. 25—Alfonso Taylor, New York...............W 6
1971
Mar. 16—Benito Vega, New York..................KO 4
May 4—Carlos Santiago, New York..............KO 7
May 26—Felix Figueroa, New York.......... KO by 6
Aug. 21—Chuck Spencer, Buffalo ....W 6
Oct. 9—Walter Seeley, New York ....D 10
Nov. 25—Johnny Howard, New York ....KO 5
Dec. 10—Walter Seeley, New York ....W 10
1972
Jan. 13—Marion Thomas, New York ....KO 3
Feb. 24—Kenny Weldon, New York ....KO 5
Apr. 28—Vil Tumulak, New York.................W 10
May 26—Masa Takahashi, New York.............W 10

July 21—Jose Luis Lopez, New York ....W 12
(North American Junior Lightweight Title)
Aug. 28—Walter Seeley, New York................L 12
(North American Junior Lightweight Title)
Oct. 10—Pierre Deschenes, New York............KO 4
Nov. 22—Gustavo Birceno, New York.............W 10
1973
Mar. 12—Ould Makloufi, Paris....................D 8
May 7—Sammy Goss, New York..................L 10
July 7—Sammy Goss, New York..................L 12
(American Junior Lightweight Title)
Nov. 19—Eduardo Santiago, New York ....W 10
Dec. 14—Eliodoro Pitalua, Bogota................KO 4
1974
Mar. 4—Walter Seeley, New York................W 10
July 15—Sammy Goss, New York ....W 10
Dec. 19—Ezequiel Sanchez, Santo Domingo ....W 12
1975
Jan. 30—Ray Lunny, San Francisco ....L 10
Sept. 22—Domenico Monaco, New York ....W 10
Oct. 10—Ezequiel Sanchez, Santo Domingo ......L 12
Dec. 3—John Watson, New York ....W 10
1976
Feb. 20—Alfredo Escalera, San Juan ....KO by 13
(WBC Junior Lightweight Title)
Aug. 16—Jerome Artis, Philadelphia..............D 10
Sept. 18—Benito Ortiz, San Juan ....W 10
Nov. 5—Bobby Rodriguez, New York ....KO 1
Dec. 10—Gilbert Mares, New York ....KO 2
1977
Jan. 17—Jerome Artis, Philadelphia ....L 10
Apr. 15—Jose Gonzalez, New York ....W 10
May 20—Frank Toro, New York ....W 10
Aug. 3—Alexis Arguello, New York ....KO by 1
1978
Feb. 4—Howard Davis, Las Vegas ....L 8
July 9—Luis Beltran, Caracas ....L 10
1979
Jan. 9—James Martinez, Phoenix ....W 10
May 24—Jose Alvarez, Lugo ....L 8
June 14—Juan LaPorte, New York ....KO by 5
June 23—Aaron Pryor, Cincinnati ....KO by 1
1980
May 21—Nelson Torres, Santiago ....L 10
June 25—Victor Nilo, Santiago ....KO by 2

JUAN CARLOS FERNANDEZ
Argentine Light Heavyweight
1980
Jan. 18—Carlos F. Burlon, San Nicolas ....D 10
May 2—Jorge Salgado, Mendoza ....TW 3
May 30—Alfredo Morales, Cordoba ....W 10
July 11—Celestino Bailone, Villa Mercedes ....L 10
Sept. 12—Juan Suarez, Cordoba ....KO 5
Oct. 10—Carlos Flores, Cordoba ....TD 8
Dec. 5—Candido Berrera, Cordoba ....D 10

LORENZO FERNANDEZ
Argentine Welterweight
1980
Mar. 7—Jorge Conti, Mar del Plata ....KO 5
Mar. 28—Ricardo Magallanes, Colon ....L 10
Apr. 11—Carlos Ruiz, Camilo Aldao ....D 8
May 9—Jorge Medina, San Nicolas ....KO by 6
Sept. 5—Jorge Conti, Tandil ....L 10

RAUL FERNANDEZ
Argentine Lightweight
1980
Apr. 18—Raul Gonzalez, Gualeguaychu ....KO 6
June 13—Mario Arreguez, San Nicolas ....W 10
July 12—Ramon Franco, Gualeguaychu ....W 10
Aug. 9—Ubaldo Sacco, Bolivar ....L 10
Sept. 5—Juan Barboza, Tucuman ....L 10
Dec. 13—Jorge Erramuspe, Gral Pico ....L 10

SAUL FERNANDEZ
Los Angeles, Calif. Featherweight
1979
June 3—Leonardo Moreno, Las Vegas ....KO by 2
—James Ortega, Denver ....KO by 4
Sept. 16—Ben Carino, Honolulu ....KO by 1

VILOMAR FERNANDEZ
Bronx, N.Y. Lightweight
1971
May 24—Salvador Ramirez, New York............KO 2
July 20—Chino Rodriguez, New York............W 4
Oct. 2—Heribito Cintron, New York.............W 4
Nov. 25—Jose Serrano, New York ....W 4
1972
Jan. 13—David Smith, New York ....KO by 4

Mar.   1—Jose Resto, New York.................... W   6
Apr. 17—Jose Resto, New York.................... W   6
Apr. 28—Jose Resto, New York.................... W   6
June   5—Gilberto Mendez, New York............. W   6
July 28—Luke Erwin, New York................... KO 2
Sept. 20—Herb Cintron, New York................ KO 4
Nov. 10—Azael Curot, New York.................. W   8
Nov. 17—Gregory Benitez, New York............. W   6
1973
Jan. 19—Jose Rivera, New York.................. KO 2
Feb. 24—Eduardo Santiago, New York............. D 10
July 23—Eduardo Santiago, New York............. W 10
Oct. 22—Walter Seeley, New York................ L 10
1974
Mar.   8—Edwin Viruet, New York.................. L 10
June 15—Cocoa Sanchez, Santo Domingo........... L 12
1975
Jan.   7—Frankie Otero, Miami Beach............. W 10
Feb. 11—Frankie Otero, Miami Beach............. W 10
Apr. 28—Antonio Amaya, Santo Domingo.......... W 10
Aug. 22—Ray Lunny, San Francisco............... W 10
1976
Feb.   6—Ray Lampkin, New York.................. W 10
June 15—Vicente Saldivar, New York............. L 10
1977
Jan. 29—Roberto Duran, Miami Beach........ KO by 13
  (World Lightweight Title)
Apr.   1—Jose Melendez, New York.............. KO 2
Apr. 29—Jose Toro, New York................... KO 3
Aug. 12—Rocky Orengo, New York............... KO 7
1978
Mar.   2—Larry Stanton, New York................ D 10
July 26—Alexis Arguello, New York............. W 10
1979
Nov. 28—Gino Perez, W. New York, N.J........... W 10
1980
Feb. 23—Howard Davis, Jr., Atlantic City........ L 12
Nov.   8—Hilmer Kenty, Detroit................... L 15
  (WBA Lightweight Title)

HELENO FERREIRA
Argentine Featherweight
1980
Apr. 11—Ruben Granado, Rosario................. D 10
May   2—Julio Saba, Cordoba.................... L 10
June   7—Roberto Haidar, Gral Pico............. L 10
July   4—Ramon Dominguez, Salta............... D 10
Aug.   8—Ramon Soria, Mendoza.................. L 10
Aug. 22—Hugo Emer, Rio IV..................... W 10
Sept. 19—Hugo Emer, Rio IV..................... W 10

PABLO FERREYRA
Argentine Welterweight
1980
Jan. 11—Carlos Peralta, S. Sal de Jujuy........... L 10
Mar.   8—Juan B. Cabral, Catrilo................. L 10
May   2—Hector Caceres, Mar del Plata.......... WF 3
June 14—Alfredo Campos, Balcarce.............. W 10
July 11—Mario Guilloti, Chacabuco............. L 10
Sept. 5—Oscar Vallejo, Concordia............... L 10
Oct. 17—Alfredo Lucero, Salta............. KO by 4

TONY FICKLIN
California Welterweight
1980
May   30—Scott Wilson, San Bernardino............ W   4
June 26—Humberto De La Rosa, Los Angeles .. KO by 5

OSVALDO FIGUEREDO
Argentine Middleweight
1980
Aug.   9—Miguel Duro, Segui................... W 10
Sept. 5—Roberto Benitez, Parana................ D 10
Oct. 10—Hector Rios, Parana................... L 10
Dec.   5—Aldo Zurawski, Laguna Paiva............ L 10

FREDDIE FIGUEROA
New York, N.Y. Featherweight
1978
Aug.   3—Levant Williams, Detroit................. L   4
Aug. 25—Jose Nieto, New York................ KO by 2
1980
Mar. 21—George Casher, New York............... W   6

JOSE FIGUEROA
Mexican Welterweight
1973
Aug.   4—Pipino Cuevas, Mexico City......... KO by 3
1974
Feb.   3—Ignacio Sanchez, Delicias............... KO 8
Feb. 26—Filia DeLos Santos, Delicias........... KO 3
Apr. 17—Sugar Sanders, Salinas............. KO 2
May   11—Jose Aragon, Mexico City............. W   4

1975
Feb. 24—Sandy Torres, San Juan ....L 10
Dec. 20—Felipe Brites, Villaguay ....KO   4
1976
Jan. 16—Gustavo Garcia, Apatzingan .... KO 10
Apr. 23—Jose Luis Baltazar, Reynosa .... KO   7
May   13—Daniel Gonzalez, Paris ....D 10
Sept. 17—Jimmy Jackson, Los Angeles .... KO by   2
1977
Mar. 12—Jose Palacios, Mexico City .... KO   7
June 18—Jose Luis Baltazar, Mexico City .... L 12
Sept.   —Pedro Martinez, Salina Cruz .... KO   2
Sept.   —Abel Cordoba, Mexico City .... KO   3
1978
Jan. 14—Julio Gomez, Mexico City .... KO   1
Mar. 25—Celso Olivas, Mexico City .... KO   4
May   6—Cesar Savinon, Mexico City .... KO   6
May   18—Rodney Harvey, Los Angeles .... KO   3
June   8—Larry Duran, Los Angeles .... W   5
June 24—Antonio Adame, Mexico City .... KO   2
Oct.   8—Abel Cordoba, Tuxtla .... L 10
Nov. 28—Mel Dennis, Houston .... L 10
1979
Jan. 13—Jose Baquedano, Mexico City .... KO by   3
Mar. 13—Alejo Rodriguez, San Antonio .... L 10
Aug.   3—Andy Price, Santa Monica .... L 10
Sept. 22—Thomas Hearns, Los Angeles .... KO by   3
Nov. 27—Zeferino Gonzalez, Los Angeles .... L 10
1980
Feb.   1—Adan Chavarria, Monterrey .... KO 11
  (Won Mexican Welterweight Title)
Mar. 17—Johnny Compo, Edmonton .... KO by   7
Mar. 28—Celso Olivas, Obregon .... L 12
May   2—Randy Shields, Los Angeles .... KO by   3
Nov.   5—Jerry Cheatham, Phoenix .... L 10

JOSE FIGUEROA
Nanagualo, Puerto Rico Featherweight
1977
May   20—Jimmy Cruz, New York .... W   4
1978
May   5—Jose Maldonado, Brooklyn .... KO   3
June 10—Jose Ortiz, Brooklyn .... D   6
Sept. 20—Jose Ortiz, New York L   6
1979
May   5—Ernesto Gonzalez, Chicago .... D 10
June 14—Juan LaPorte, New York .... KO by   5
1980
June 11—Mike Brown, White Plains L   4
Aug. 29—Dennis Cruz, New York .... KO by   1
Sept. 12—Jorge Vasquez, New York .... KO   1
Nov.   6—Myron Taylor, Atlantic City .... KO by   1

MIGUEL FIGUEROA
Argentine Lightweight
1980
Feb. 14—Oscar Alvarenga, San Juan .... D 10
Feb. 29—Jesus Romero, Salta .... L 10
Mar. 14—Nicolas Arkuszyn, San Juan .... L 10

NORBERTO FIGUEROA
Bronx, N.Y. Junior Welterweight
1980
Feb.   8—Keith York, New York .... KO   2
Mar. 21—Angel Cintron, New York .... KO   1
May   2—Eduardo Mejia, New York .... KO   1
June 27—Jimmy Longo, New York .... W   4
Sept. 12—Jimmy Longo, New York L   4
Oct. 24—Davey Armstrong, Uniondale L   8
Nov.   3—Marcus Starks, Hartford .... W   6
Dec. 20—Johnny Bumphus, Bronx L   6

PAPO FIGUEROA
Hartford, Conn. Welterweight
1979
Apr. 24—Richie Casale, Hartford .... KO   3
May   18—Ralph Doucette, Hartford .... KO   2
June 29—Angel Ortiz, Hartford .... W   8
July 27—Richie Casale, Hartford .... KO   1
Sept. 7—Wilfredo Franco, Hartford .... D   4
Oct.   3—George Casher, Brooklyn .... D   4
Oct. 17—Steve Snow, Hartford .... W   6
Nov.   5—Charlie Newell, Hartford L   6
1980
Jan. 15—Noradene Bensalah, W. Hartford .... KO   6
Feb.   5—Bobby Castaneda, W. Hartford .... KO   1
Mar.   4—Hector Ortiz, W. Hartford .... D   8
Apr. 22—Hector Ortiz, W. Hartford .... KO   4
May   29—Walter Smith, W. Hartford .... KO   2
       —Jaime Rodriguez, Hartford .... KO   7

JOSE FILIPPI
Argentine Junior Lightweight
1980
Apr.	18—Rodolfo Diaz, Corral Bustos	KO 11
June	19—Santiago Lopez, Corral Bustos	W 10
July	18—Faustino Barrios, Camilo Aldao	W 10
Sept.	5—Juan Malvarez, Rosario	D 10
Oct.	3—Gabriel Sanchez, Rosario	L 10
Dec.	12—Juan D. Malvarez, Trelew	L 10

BRUCE FINCH
Milwaukee, Wisc. Welterweight
1973
Sept.	25—Jeff Morgan, Milwaukee	D 4

1974
May	23—Gary Holmgren, Minneapolis	W 5
Nov.	20—Ricardo Thomatis, Milwaukee	KO 3

1975
Oct.	20—Candy Smith, Milwaukee	KO 1
Dec.	10—Robert Williams, Milwaukee	KO 1

1976
Feb.	2—Don Boulter, Milwaukee	KO 3

1977
Feb.	14—Charles Walters, Milwaukee	KO 1
Mar.	25—Tyrone Phelps, Milwaukee	W 8
May	4—Pete Ranzany, San Francisco	KO by 5
June	6—Larry Bonds, Milwaukee	KO by 5

1978
Apr.	18—Freddie Johnson, New Orleans	W 10
June	28—Daryl Penn, Las Vegas	KO 6
Aug.	23—Quincy Daniels, Las Vegas	KO 3
Sept.	7—Thomas Hearns, Detroit	KO by 2

1979
June	25—Ed Modique, Milwaukee	KO 9
Nov.	20—Curtis Taylor, Chicago	KO 8

1980
Feb.	1—Jose Santana, Chicago	W 10
July	23—Javier Ayala, Las Vegas	KO 3
Sept.	16—Rafael Rodriguez, Winnipeg	W 10
Dec.	17—Victor Martinez, Las Vegas	KO 1

CHARLES (CHUCK) FINDLAY
Toronto, Canada Heavyweight
1977
Mar.	7—Dave Darrell, Toronto	KO 1

1978
Dec.	11—Conroy Nelson, Toronto	W 6

1979
(Inactive)
1980
May	26—Bob Felstein, Ontario	W 10
Nov.	11—Trevor Berbick, Boston	KO by 1
Dec.	15—John "Dino" Denis, Boston	L 10

NORBERTO FIORI
Argentine Heavyweight
1980
Mar.	7—Domingo D'Elia, Tandil	D 12
May	24—Antonio Musladino, Tandil	W 10

TOM (ROUGHHOUSE) FISCHER
Dayton, Ohio Heavyweight
1976
Aug.	13—Mayfield Pennington, Pikesville	L 4
Oct.	6—Kenny Moore, Cleveland	L 4
Oct.	20—Boom Boom Moorer, Cleveland	KO by 3
Nov.	27—Bill Jackson, Lincoln	KO 3

1977
Feb.	15—Charlie Jordan, Toledo	W 4
Mar.	12—Charley Jordan, Toledo	W 4
Mar.	25—Richard Christmas, Dayton	KO 3
May	18—Danny Lee, Louisville	KO 8
Sept.	30—Charlie Jordan, Dayton	W 10
Oct.	7—Charlie Jordan, Cincinnati	W 4
Oct.	25—Boom Boom Moorer, Chicago	KO 3
Nov.	22—Danny Davis, Chicago	KO 1

1978
Feb.	27—Baker Tinsley, Chicago	W 8
Mar.	10—Jeff Isabel, Cincinnati	KO 1
Apr.	28—George Mostardini, Chicago	L 6
May	13—Johnny Blaine, Dayton	KO 2
June	30—Jim Beattie, Chicago	W 8
Aug.	26—Terry Daniels, Dayton	KO 4
Sept.	27—Johnny Mac, St. Paul	KO 4
Nov.	11—Pete Holms, Beaver Dam	KO 2
Nov.	18—Harold Carter, DePaul	W 10

1979
Mar.	23—James Dixon, Rosemont	W 10
June	14—Joe Maye, River Grove	KO 6
Aug.	24—Ron Stander, Cincinnati	W 10
Sept.	18—Mike Tarasewich, Dayton	KO 1
Nov.	8—Tim Tankersley, Indiana	KO 1
Dec.	19—Frank Brown, Rockford	KO 9

1980
Apr.	5—Baker Tinsley, Louisville	W 8
May	17—Lupe Guerra, Dayton	L 10
Sept.	6—Baker Tinsley, Jenkins	KO 1
Sept.	12—Herb Adams, Louisville	KO 1
Oct.	2—Michael Dokes, Las Vegas	KO by 7

MIKE FISHER
Paterson, N.J. Light Heavyweight
1979
Apr.	24—Wilber Henderson, Hartford	L 6
June	28—Ron Cicchetti, Staten Island	KO 4
July	31—Darryl Freedman, Totowa	KO 1
Aug.	27—Jeremia Cabollaro, Atlantic City	KO 1
Sept.	18—Harry Fryar, Meadowlands	L 6

1980
Jan.	8—Clarence Carpenter, Totowa	KO 3
Feb.	19—Clarence Carpenter, Totowa	KO 2
Mar.	8—Joe Peoples, Great Gorge	KO 1
Apr.	1—Walter Driscoll, Totowa	KO 3
Apr.	5—Jodie Parker, Louisville	KO 2
May	22—David Bird, Totowa	L 8
Dec.	27—Sal San Filippo, N. Bergen	KO 1

MIKE FISHER
Dayton, Ohio Middleweight
1980
Apr.	5—Jodie Parker, Louisville	KO 2
Sept.	6—Jodie Parker, Jenkins	KO 1
Dec.	9—Charlie Peterson, Warren	KO by 4

JACKIE FIX
Albuquerque, N.M. Welterweight
1980
Sept.	7—Steve Lopez, Albuquerque	KO 1
Dec.	17—Irwin Hazel, Steubenville	KO 2

ANTHONY FLETCHER
Philadelphia, Pa. Lightweight
1980
June	5—Ronald Jones, Atlantic City	KO 1
July	3—Dennis Howard, Atlantic City	W 6
Aug.	7—Chris Harmon, Atlantic City	KO 1
Sept.	4—Derek Cuttino, Atlantic City	W 6
Oct.	30—Jack Rosas, Atlantic City	W 6

FRANK (THE ANIMAL) FLETCHER
Philadelphia, Pa. Middleweight
1976
Oct.	7—Charles Stern, Allentown	W 4

1977
June	15—Jodie White, Philadelphia	KO 4
Oct.	20—Dan Snyder, Upper Darby	KO 2
Oct.	25—Art McCloud, Philadelphia	L 6

1978
Mar.	21—John Scott, Philadelphia	KO 2

1979
Oct.	27—Tony Braxton, Rahway	D 6
Dec.	1—Tony Braxton, Rahway	L 6

1980
Apr.	10—Ben Serrano, Atlantic City	W 8
May	8—Jerome Jackson, Atlantic City	KO 4
July	3—William Lee, Atlantic City	KO 4
Sept.	4—Randy McGrady, Atlantic City	KO 7
Dec.	4—Sammy NeSmith, Atlantic City	KO 6

ALEJANDRO FLORES
1980
Jan.	10—Candido Tellez, Mexico City	KO by 6
May	24—Candido Tellez, Mexico City	KO by 3

CARLOS FLORES
Argentine Middleweight
1980
Mar.	22—Roberto Ruiz, Buenos Aires	KO by 7
Apr.	18—Roberto Ruiz, Tucuman	L 4
July	4—Luis Peralta, Concepcion	KO by 4
Aug.	29—Hugo Trujillo, Salta	W 10
Oct.	3—Hugo Rossi, La Plata	L 10
Oct.	10—Juan Fernandez, Cordoba	TD 8
Dec.	12—Julio Arrancibia, Salta	KO by 6

CATALINO FLORES
Los Angeles, Calif. Bantamweight
1978
Apr.	7—Oscar Muniz, Los Angeles	KO by 3
Aug.	6—Ernesto Rios, Stockton	KO by 5

1979
Apr.	19—Carlos Zuniga, Stockton	KO by 7
July	12—Oscar Muniz, Los Angeles	L 10
Aug.	23—Ricardo Varela, Los Angeles	L 10
Nov.	29—Alberto Sandoval, Los Angeles	TD

1980
Mar. 24—Mario Chavez, Santa Monica ....KO by 5

EDDIE FLORES
Connecticut Junior Lightweight
1979
Sept. 27—Marcus Starks, Bristol ....L 4
Oct. 17—Manuel Sanchez, Hartford ....L 4
Nov. 15—Victor Arnau, Bristol ....KO by 4
1980
Jan. 9—Manuel Wuiles, Hartford ....L 4

JAVIER FLORES
Salt Lake City, Utah Bantamweight
Born: April 5, 1956
1974
Oct. 9—Candy Iglesias, Las Vegas ....KO 3
1975
—Pedro Rodriguez, Chihuahua ....KO 3
—Danny Young, Las Vegas ....KO 3
1976
June 17—Johnny Mesa, Salt Lake City ....KO 2
—Raymond Diaz, Salt Lake City ....KO 2
1977
Jan. 15—Johnny Mesa, Salt Lake City ....KO 4
Feb. 8—Shiki Kambora, Salt Lake City ....W 8
Mar. 9—Delfino Martinez, Salt Lake City ......W 6
Apr. 2—Danny Young, Ogden ..:..............KO 2
Apr. 27—Earl Large, Las Vegas ....D 8
May 11—Rafael Rodriguez, Las Vegas ....KO 4
May 21—Julio Mendez, Salt Lake City ....KO 6
June 1—Oscar Muniz, Las Vegas ....D 8
June 17—Jose Davey Rodriguez, Ogden ....KO 1
July 20—Elias Rodriquez, Las Vegas ....W 8
Aug. 10—Bobo Gonzalez, Las Vegas ....KO 3
Nov. 2—Jose (The Indian) Resendez, Las Vegas ....D 8
1978
Jan. 14—Frank Manzone, Salt Lake City ....KO 2
Feb. 4—Jose Resendez, Salt Lake City ....W 10
Mar. 24—Jose Caba, Ogden ....L 10
July 1—Dave Pierson, Salt Lake City ....KO 2
July 27—Earl Large, Las Vegas ....W 12
Sept. 22—Miguel Degarana, Salt Lake City ......KO 1
Oct. 10—Nicky Perez, Las Vegas ....L 12
Nov. 11—Ramon Aguinaga, Salt Lake City ....KO 6
Dec. 9—Eliu Hernandez, Salt Lake City ....KO 2
1979
Feb. 14—Ad Zapanta, Salt Lake City ....KO 4
Feb. 21—Melvin Johnson, Stateline ....KO 9
Mar. 11—Nico Perez, Reno ....L 12
June 28—Roberto Morela, Los Angeles ....KO 5
July 19—Alberto Sandoval, Los Angeles ....L 10
Oct. 13—Cookie Valencia, Salt Lake City ....W 12
Dec. 8—Cookie Valencia, Salt Lake City ....W 12
1980
Feb. 1—Jeff Chandler, Philadelphia ....L 10
Mar. 22—Jose Resendez, Salt Lake City ....L 10
June 3—Jose Osuna, Las Vegas ....W 12
July 8—Ricardo Varela, Las Vegas ....W 12
Aug. 22—Edwin Rosario, Las Vegas ....KO by 9
Nov. 7—Mike Ayala, San Antonio ....L 10

PEDRO FLORES
Born: Jan. 14, 1951, Guadalajara, Jalisco, Mexico.
Weight: 108 lbs. Height: 5 ft. 2 in.
Managed by Lupe Sanchez.
1973
Nov. 7—Ramon Novelo, Colima ....KO 7
Nov. 30—Teo Jimenez, Colima ....KO 2
1974
June 7—Francisco Javier Nunez, Guadalajara ...KO 9
July 12—Juan Alvarez, Guadalajara ....W 10
Sept. 15—Jose Luis Cetina, Merida ....W 10
1975
Mar. 5—Evaristo Perez, Mexico City ....W 10
May 28—Manuel Montiel, Mexico City ....W 10
July 19—Alberto Morales, Acapulco ....L 12
(For Mexican Flyweight Title)
Nov. 1—Valentin Martinez, Mexico City ......KO by 7
1976
Feb. 7—Juan Alvarez, Mexico City ....W 10
Apr. 21—Roberto Marin, Tecoman ....W 10
July 3—Adelaido Galindo, Mexico City ....KO by 3
1977
June 15—Matias Marin, Merida ....W 10
July 6—Freddie Castillo, Merida ....L disq. 8
1978
(Inactive)
1979
Mar. 24—Samuel Machorro, Mexico City ....W 10
June 9—Jose Luis Valencia, Mexico City ....W 10
Sept. 8—Pedro Coloria, Mexico City ....W 10
1980
Feb. 2—Jose Luis Cruz, Mexico City ....W 10

June 13—Jose Gallegos, Monterrey ....W 12
(Won Mexican Flyweight Title)
Oct. 12—Yoko Gushiken, Kanazawa ....L 15
(For WBA Junior Flyweight Title)

ROBERTO FLORES
Houston, Texas Junior Lightweight
1978
Apr. 11—Daniel Felizardo, Houston ....KO 5
Oct. 17—Romeo Anaya, Houston ....KO by 4
1979
Aug. 23—Hilmer Kenty, Detroit ....KO by 1
Oct. 1—Florentino Falcon, Corpus Christi ....KO 7
1980
Jan. 23—Freddie Roach, Las Vegas ....KO by 1
Mar. 7—Isaac Vega, Chicago ....KO by 2
Sept. 30—Jose Portillo, Houston ....KO by 9

JAMES FLYNN
Chicago, Ill. Heavyweight
1979
July 20—Jumbo Cummings, Univ. of Ill. ......KO by 1
Sept. 25—Rick Meyer, Belleville ....L 6
1980
May 9—Tommy Stevenson, Chicago ....L 6
July 27—Lupe Guerra, Omaha ....L 8
Aug. 25—Alfonso Ratliff, Chicago ....KO by 1

TERRY FLYNN
Grand Rapids, Mich. Middleweight
1980
Mar. 22—Lynn Lustig, Grand Rapids ....KO 2
Apr. 19—Charlie Peterson, Muskegon ....W 6
May 22—Danny Fields, Holland ....KO 1

JERRY FOLEY
Scranton, Pa. Heavyweight
1976
Jan. 28—Bob Silverman, Scranton ....KO 1
Aug. 15—Kenny Jones, Scranton ....KO 1
Oct. 5—Alex Carr, Scranton ....KO 3
1977
May 20—Johnny Warr, Binghamton ....L 6
1978
May 2—Guy Casale, Totowa ....ND
June 13—Conrad Tooker, Totowa ....L 6
Sept. 20—Bob Bird, Scranton ....KO 4
Oct. 25—Tom Healy, Scranton ....KO 4
Nov. 20—Joe Maye, Scranton ....W 6
1979
Apr. 25—Marty Capasso, Scranton ....KO by 3
June 24—Sylvain Watbled, Monte Carlo ......KO by 6
Sept. 19—Quinnie Locklear, Scranton ....KO 6
Oct. 24—Calvin Langston, Scranton ....KO 5
Nov. 21—Bob Coley, Scranton ....KO 5
1980
Feb. 27—Ali Allen, Scranton ....L 8
Mar. 26—Ali Allen, Scranton ....L 8
May 28—Jimmy Smith, Scranton ....L 8
Sept. 20—Kerry Judge, Ben Salem, Pa. ....L 8
Nov. 8—Mitchell Green, Lake Tahoe ....KO by 1

AL FORD
Edmonton, Canada, Junior Welterweight
1967
Oct. 20—Joe Hogue, Edmonton ....KO 3
Nov. 17—Milton Gabriel, Edmonton ....KO 3
Dec. 15—Ron Lykes, Edmonton ....KO 1
1968
Feb. 9—Gene Green, Edmonton ....KO 2
Mar. 8—Mickey McMillian, Edmonton ....W 8
Mar. 25—Tony Mesi, Portland ....KO 2
Apr. 8—Denny Barthuly, Edmonton ....KO 2
Apr. 30—Andy Anderson, Portland ....W 6
June 1—Joe Gray, Edmonton ....KO 5
June 10—Ismeal Rivera, Portland ....KO 4
June 26—Michel Godin, Edmonton ....KO 3
Sept. 27—Julio Mandell, Edmonton ....W 12
(Canadian Lightweight Title)
Nov. 13—Jimmy Fields, Edmonton ....W 10
Nov. 21—Dave White, Portland ....KO 5
1969
Jan. 31—Ben Joseph, Edmonton ....W 8
Feb. 19—Bobby Brooks, Edmonton ....W 8
Apr. 12—Jean Marie Huard, Edmonton ....KO 2
May 30—Felix Jasso, Edmonton ....W 8
Aug. 17—Fernand Durelle, Lethbridge ....W 12
Aug. 29—Beto Maldonado, Edmonton ....W 10
Oct. 23—Rene Macias, Portland ....W 10
Nov. 19—Ray Adigun, Honolulu ....W 10

Dec.	4—Jose Castillo, Honolulu	KO	2
1970			
Jan.	13—Fermin Soto, Honolulu	W	10
Feb.	11—Flash Gallego, Honolulu	W	10
Feb.	20—Frisco Montemayor, Hilo	KO	9
Apr.	8—Luis Baez, Edmonton	W	10
May	13—Len Kesey, Edmonton	W	10
May	30—Lawrence Hafey, New Glasgow	W	12
	(Canadian Lightweight Title)		
June	10—Angel Rivera, Edmonton	W	10
Sept.	29—Percy Hayles, Edmonton	W	10
Oct.	27—Raul Montoya, Edmonton	W	10
1971			
Jan.	20—Chichi Ontiveros, Edmonton	KO	5
Feb.	14—Gabriel Branvilla, Seattle	KO	6
Feb.	25—Juan Montoya, Portland	W	10
Mar.	22—Willy Reilly, Edmonton	W	10
May	3—Leo Noel, Moncton	KO	8
July	12—Percy Hayles, Kingston	L	15
	(British Empire Lightweight Title)		
Sept.	23—Nick Agahi, Portland	W	10
Oct.	23—Fermin Soto, Mexico City	W	10
Dec.	9—Moses Diamond, Seattle	KO	1
1972			
Mar.	1—Joe Espinosa, Seattle	KO	4
Mar.	28—Ken Buchanan, London	L	10
June	17—Alfonso Frazier, Panama City	KO by	5
	(World Junior Welterweight Title)		
Nov.	29—Raul Montoya, Edmonton	W	10
1973			
Jan.	22—Percy Hayles, Kingston	KO by	12
	(British Empire Lightweight Title)		
1974			
	(Inactive)		
1975			
July	12—Jo Jo Jackson, Slave Lake	W	10
Aug.	3—Roscoe Frazier, Slave Lake	W	10
Oct.	20—Victor de la Cruz, Edmonton	W	10
Nov.	28—Johnnie Summerhays, Edmonton	L	12
	(Canadian Lightweight Championship)		
1976			
	(Inactive)		
1977			
Feb.	27—Nick Alfaro, Calgary	W	8
Apr.	4—Ralph Racine, Winnipeg	L	10
May	24—Nick Furlano, Winnipeg	W	12
June	29—Octavio Anparon, Thompson, Man.	W	10
1978			
Feb.	6—Bobby Hughes, Edmonton	W	10
June	20—Ralph Racine, Winnipeg	L	10
Dec.	5—Tom Tarantino, Winnipeg	W	10
1979			
Feb.	9—Nick Furlano, Winnipeg	KO by	14
	(For Canadian Junior Welterweight Title)		
May	11—Aaron Pryor, Cincinnati	KO by	3
Dec.	8—Danny Stokes, Winnipeg	KO	2
Dec.	18—Ralph Racine, Montreal	L	8
1980			
Mar.	6—Allan Clarke, Winnipeg	W	10
Mar.	17—Johnny Summerhays, Edmonton	L	10

PATRICK FORD
Georgetown, Guyana Featherweight
Born: December 15, 1955. Height: 5 ft. 10 in.

1976			
Nov.	26—Compton Canzius, Georgetown	KO	2
1977			
Mar.	17—Roy Smith, Georgetown	W	6
Sept.	9—Charles Quintin, Georgetown	KO	3
1978			
Jan.	23—Clyde Wilson, Georgetown	KO	4
Feb.	4—Tiger Green, Georgetown	W	15
	(Guyana Featherweight Title)		
June	17—Michael Drayton, Georgetown	KO	5
Sept.	9—Diego Alcala, Georgetown	KO	9
Nov.	27—Harold Bernard, Georgetown	W	10
1979			
Mar.	30—Jean LaPointe, Port-of-Spain	KO	4
Oct.	19—Enrique Solis, Georgetown	W	12
	(FECARBOX Featherweight Title)		
Dec.	12—Cecil Fernandez, Georgetown	KO	10
1980			
Jan.	17—Marcos Britton, Port-of-Spain	KO	4
Feb.	19—Fernando Jiminez, Port-of-Spain	W	10
May	20—Nelson Cruz Tamarez, Georgetown	KO	4
	(Retained FECARBOX Title)		
Aug.	1—Eddie Ndukwu, Lagos	KO	8
	(Won British Commonwealth Title)		
Sept.	13—Salvador Sanchez, San Antonio	L	15
	(For World Featherweight Title)		

RONNIE FORD
Texas Junior Middleweight

1977			
Apr.	29—Dave McMinn, Fort Worth	L	4
1978			
Feb.	21—Rocky McCullum, Greensville	L	4
Aug.	27—Carlos Black, Odessa	KO	1
1979			
Nov.	13—Steve Hearon, Houston	L	4
Dec.	15—Larry Mayes, Kansas City	D	6
1980			
May	19—Raul Flores, Odessa	KO	3
July	19—Homer Jackson, Panama City, Fla.	KO by	1

SCOTTY FOREMAN
New Orleans, La. Junior Welterweight

1976			
Mar.	8—Joe Bradley, New Orleans	KO	2
Apr.	4—Adrian Luna, New Orleans	KO	2
Apr.	19—Fred Harris, New Orleans	KO by	3
May	19—Frank Santore, New Orleans	KO	1
Aug.	9—Joe Madranos, New Orleans	KO	1
1977			
June	16—Mike Ramirez, Mobile	KO	3
July	18—Aundra Love, New Orleans	W	7
Aug.	23—Jimmy Heair, Memphis	KO by	7
Dec.	20—Silverio Martinez, New Orleans	KO	2
1978			
Mar.	14—Jose Luis Valdez, New Orleans	KO	2
May	3—Aaron Pryor, Miami Beach	KO by	6
Aug.	22—Frank Santore, Orlando	W	10
Sept.	5—Wayne Battle, Orlando	KO	2
Sept.	19—Norman Goins, Orlando	W	10
Oct.	24—Claude Noel, Orlando	KO by	2
1979			
Aug.	2—Dale Hernandez, Omaha	KO by	10
Nov.	30—Hilmer Kenty, New Orleans	KO by	3
1980			
June	10—Sean O'Grady, Oklahoma City	KO by	2
July	15—John Morgan, Beaumont	KO	2

TONY FOREMAN
Florida Middleweight

1979			
Dec.	14—Costello King, Sunrise	L	4
1980			
July	25—Rocky Fabrizio, Miami	KO	4
Aug.	19—Cyril Withers, Miami	L	4

WARREN FORTUNE
Washington, D.C. Junior Welterweight

1978			
May	24—Nathan Slye, Washington, D.C.	KO	2
1979			
Jan.	11—Bud Becker, Landover	W	4
Apr.	6—Dale Fortune, Washington, D.C.	W	6
1980			
Jan.	16—Ken Lomax, Washington, D.C.	KO	3
Sept.	11—Larry Spriggs, Washington, D.C.	W	4

JIMMY (JUNIOR) FOSTER
Las Vegas, Nev. Junior Welterweight

1979			
Sept.	28—Idika Nsofor, Las Vegas	KO by	4
1980			
Apr.	9—Bobby Krueger, Las Vegas	KO	11
Sept.	10—Ronnie Romero, Las Vegas	KO by	3
Nov.	26—Pete Garcia, Las Vegas	L	4
Dec.	19—Jimmy Vozar, Las Vegas	KO by	1

RODNEY FOSTER
Minneapolis, Minn. Junior Middleweight

1980			
May	13—Bruce Strauss, Indianapolis	KO by	3
June	20—Danny Myers, Ft. Wayne	KO by	2
June	28—Bob Coolidge, Indianapolis	KO by	2
Oct.	28—Billy Carr, Indianapolis	KO	3

AL FOWLER
St. Louis, Mo. Welterweight

1979			
Mar.	16—Rick Freeman, St. Louis	W	6
Apr.	20—Jerry Strickland, St. Louis	W	6
May	21—Rod Kennebrew, Belleville	KO	5
June	5—Joe Styles, Memphis	W	6
July	17—Simmie Black, Belleville	W	8
Sept.	25—Terry Stratnel, Belleville	KO	7
Nov.	8—Bubba Thompson, Tulsa	L	8
Nov.	27—Simmie Black, Belleville	W	10
1980			
Jan.	21—Kelvin Lampkin, St. Charles	L	6
Mar.	16—Elmer Suttington, Kansas City	L	6
Dec.	10—Efraim Nieves, Moline	KO by	4

ANTHONY FOX
Philadelphia, Pa. Featherweight
1980

May	23—Angel Cruz, Bethlehem	KO by 1
Sept.	17—Paul DeVorce, White Plains	KO by 1
Nov.	28—Todd Longmire, Providence	KO by 3

AL FRACKER
Detroit, Mich. Light Heavyweight
1976

Apr.	23—Dick Morgan, Flint	KO 3
June	23—Ted Paxton, Mentor	W 6
July	24—Billy Williams, Kalamazoo	KO 1
Aug.	22—Charles Jordan, Flint	W 6
Sept.	2—Dave Bradley, Kalamazoo	W 6
	1977	
Apr.	23—Bill Ratcliff, Kalamazoo	W 10
June	11—Oscar Freeman, Michigan Center	W 10
Aug.	4—Hank Gregory, Grand Rapids	KO by 5
	1978	
Mar.	16—Julian Estrada, Kalamazoo	KO 5
Sept.	2—Percy Hairston, Detroit	W 6
	1979	
Jan.	24—Willy Crawford, Cleveland	KO by 7
	1980	
July	26—Eddie Temple, Kalamazoo	KO 4

CARMELO FRANCO
Puerto Rican Junior Welterweight
1980

Feb.	18—Jose Luis Torres, San Juan	L 4
Apr.	—Jose Vidal, San Juan	KO by 2

MARCIAL FRANCO
Argentine Featherweight
1980

July	8—Hugo Fernandez, Reconquista	W 10
Aug.	8—Ruben Butiler, Reconquista	W 10

ORLANDO FRANCO
Argentine Lightweight
1980

Jan.	—Norberto Ramirez, San Miguel	W 6
Feb.	15—Eduardo Lopez, Junin	KO 6
Mar.	6—Carlos Villanueva, Zarate	D 8
Apr.	12—Ramon Franco, Buenos Aires	D 8
May	23—Carlos Villanueva, San Nicolas	W 10
July	4—Carlos Villanueva, Campana	KO 3
Aug.	8—Alberto Pilli, Mar del Plata	D 10
Sept.	13—Orlando Frecini, Buenos Aires	L 8
Dec.	20—Oscar A. Rossi, Dariaux	KO by 7

RAMON FRANCO
Argentine Welterweight
1980

Jan.	—Faustino Barrios, San Miguel	D 8
Apr.	12—Orlando Franco, Buenos Aires	D 8
May	16—Mario Arrueguez, San Miguel	W 8
July	12—Raul Fernandez, Gualeguaychu	L 10
Dec.	12—Carlos Olivera, Mar del Plata	L 6

WILFREDO FRANCO
New Haven, Conn. Welterweight
1979

Sept.	7—Papo Figueroa, Hartford	D 4
Nov.	5—Fred Petschke, Hartford	KO 1
Nov.	28—Charlie Newell, Hartford	KO by 5
	1980	
Feb.	28—Roberto Vasquez, Hartford	KO 4
June	20—Steve Snow, Hartford	W 6

SCOTT FRANK
Oakland, N.J. Heavyweight
1978

May	2—Joe Maye, Totowa	W 6
May	20—Bob Coley, Trenton	KO 2
June	13—Johnny Blaine, Totowa	KO 1
Aug.	30—John McGrath, Paramus	KO 2
Sept.	26—Chuck Wepner, Totowa	W 12
Nov.	14—Charles Harris, Totowa	KO 3
	1979	
Mar.	13—Guy Casale, Totowa	KO 9
Apr.	11—James Reid, White Plains	W 8
July	31—Don Martin, Totowa	KO 4
Sept.	18—Bill Connell, E. Rutherford	KO 8
	1980	
Jan.	8—Ron Stander, Totowa	KO 1
Feb.	19—C.J. Bar Brown, Totowa	KO 0
Nov.	20—Randy Willis, Totowa	KO 1

ROCKY FRATTO
Geneva, N.Y. Middleweight
1976

Nov.	20—Joe Grady, Utica	W 6
	1977	
Jan.	21—Lorenzo Howard, Rochester	KO 2
Apr.	8—Johnny Taylor, Syracuse	KO 2
June	3—D. C. Walker, Syracuse	W 8
July	8—Al Romano, Geneva	W 8
Aug.	25—Ray Bryant, Syracuse	W 8
Oct.	8—Renaldo Oliveria, Geneva	W 10
Nov.	19—Ricky Burgess, Syracuse	KO 3
	1978	
Mar.	25—Tyrone Phelps, Syracuse	W 10
July	15—Pablo Rodriguez, Alexandria Bay	W 10
Aug.	12—Justice Ortiz, Alexandria Bay	W 10
Oct.	4—Pablo Rodriguez, Elmira	KO 4
Dec.	8—Everaldo Costa Azevedo, Syracuse	W 10
	1979	
Mar.	17—Steve Michalerya, Elmira	W 10
Apr.	14—Beau Jaynes, Syracuse	KO 7
June	2—Sammy Masias, Syracuse	W 10
July	13—Pat Murphy, Rochester	KO 7
Oct.	26—Steve Michalerya, Rochester	W 10
	1980	
Jan.	19—Jaime Rodriguez, Syracuse	W 10
Feb.	29—Sammy Masias, Rome, N.Y.	W 8
Apr.	19—C.J. Faison, Syracuse	KO 1
July	25—Rick Zarbatany, Rochester	KO 7

LARRY FRAZIER
San Francisco, Calif. Heavyweight
1972

Aug.	10—Budda Brooks, San Francisco	KO 2
Sept.	29—Sam Wilson, San Carlos	KO 1
	1973	
Feb.	27—Dave Sherman, San Francisco	KO 1
July	12—John Marbury, Seattle	KO 2
Sept.	21—Orville Qualls, Las Vegas	KO 1
Dec.	12—Mike Weaver, San Francisco	KO 2
	1974	
Jan.	10—Leroy Jones, Stateline	L 6
	1975	
July	9—Leroy Jones, Las Vegas	L 10
	1976	
June	16—Oliver Phillips, Las Vegas	KO 2
Sept.	30—Young Sekona, Honolulu	KO by 1
	1978	
Oct.	5—Bisher Wadud, Seattle	KO 8
	1979	
Feb.	20—Earl McLeay, Seattle	KO 1
June	21—Lee Black, Seattle	KO 1
	1980	
Aug.	6—Jesse Aldridge, Las Vegas	KO 1
Aug.	29—Jeff Sims, W. Palm Beach	NC 1
Dec.	6—Terry Krueger, Lake Tahoe	KO 3

MARVIS FRAZIER
Philadelphia, Pa. Heavyweight
Managed by Joe Frazier
Born: September 12, 1960
1980

Sept.	12—Roger Troupe, New York	KO 3
Oct.	10—Dennis Rivers, New York	KO 2

MIKE FRAZIER
Philadelphia, Pa. Featherweight
1975

Sept.	16—Billy Abel, Philadelphia	KO by 4
	1976	
May	10—Mike Dowling, Philadelphia	KO 1
June	8—Jeff Chandler, Philadelphia	L 4
Aug.	16—Tony Stokes, Philadelphia	L 4
	1977	
Feb.	1—John Glover, Philadelphia	W 6
July	18—Billy Abel, Philadelphia	W 8
Oct.	6—Jim Washington, Philadelphia	L 8
	1978	
Apr.	22—Sammy Goss, Trenton	L 8
Sept.	21—Otis Hooper, Washington D.C.	KO 4
Sept.	27—Alfonso Evans, Philadelphia	L 8
	1979	
Apr.	6—Jose Nieto, New York	KO by 1
	1980	
Jan.	30—Jose Gonzales, Allentown	L 8
Nov.	9—Ken Carpenter, Atlantic City	KO 3

ORLANDO FRECINI
Argentine Junior Middleweight
1980

Feb.	22—Omar Antena, Mar del Plata	KO 5
Apr.	26—Carlos Villanueva, Buenos Aires	KO 5

95

May	15—Norberto Oliveto, Chivilchoy	W 10
June	21—Victor Zaya, Buenos Aires	KO 4
July	12—Santiago Lopez, Baradero	W 10
Sept.	13—Orlando Franco, Buenos Aires	W 8

LEOPOLDO FRIAS
Dominican Rep. Junior Featherweight
(Previous Record Unavailable)
1977

Mar.	28—Salvadore Cosme, Santo Domingo	KO 3
Apr.	15—Juan Sierra, Santo Domingo	KO 1
Sept.	16—Ramon Santana, Santo Domingo	W 8
Oct.	14—Miguel Rivera, Santo Domingo	KO 1
Oct.	27—Enrique Mateo, Santo Domingo	W 10
Dec.	19—Enrique Mateo, Santo Domingo	W 10
1978		
Feb.	2—Enrique Sanchez, Santo Domingo	L 10
Mar.	15—Julian Solis, Santo Domingo	L 10
June	23—Guillermo Almengot, Santo Domingo	W 10
Oct.	26—Jose Jiminez, Santo Domingo	KO by 9
1979		
May	4—Juan Castro, Santo Domingo	W 10
1980		
Feb.	18—Edwin Rosario, Puerto Rico	KO by 2
Aug.	18—Ramon Santana, Santo Domingo	KO 8
Sept.	26—Manuel Paul, Santo Domingo	KO 1

LON DALE FRIESEN
Wichita, Kans. Heavyweight
1979

Sept.	18—Louis Brown, Wichita	KO 2
1980		
June	13—Jimmy Pearish, Tulsa	KO 3
Aug.	12—Louis Drake, Wichita	L 4
Sept.	10—Louis Drake, Wichita	KO by 1

TONY FRITZ
Chicago, Ill. Heavyweight
1976

Nov.	30—Dick Morgan, Indianapolis	L 6
1977		
Apr.	25—David Bradley, Chicago	L 6
June	25—Julius Nobles, Chicago	KO by 1
1978		
(Inactive)		
1979		
Apr.	27—Lucky Patterson, Chicago	D 4
June	4—Dan Murphy, Bridgeview	KO by 2
Dec.	18—Jeff Simms, Miami Beach	KO by 1
1980		
Aug.	22—Frank Monaco, Chicago	KO by 3

HARRY FRYAR
Trenton, N.J. Light Heavyweight
1978

Jan.	24—Curtis Parker, Philadelphia	KO by 1
1979		
Jan.	23—Daryl White, Philadelphia	L 4
July	1—Mike Baldwin, Rahway	L 4
July	24—Tony Mesoraca, Atlantic City	W 4
July	31—Ron Huston, Totowa	KO by 4
Sept.	18—Mike Fisher, E. Rutherford	W 6
1980		
Feb.	24—Tony Mesoraca, Atlantic City	L 6
Mar.	7—Al Styles, Staten Island	KO by 2

MAURO FUENTES
Los Angeles, Calif. Featherweight
1978

Sept.	28—Robert Anderson, Phoenix	L 4
Nov.	22—Kid Meza, Phoenix	KO by
1979		
Mar.	24—Hector Martinez, Tucson	L 4
Aug.	22—Ricardo Jiminez, Phoenix	KO by 2
Sept.	19—Blaine Dickson, Las Vegas	KO 1
Nov.	24—Randy (Clover) McNurlin, Las Vegas	KO by 2
1980		
Mar.	20—Julian Fuentes, Phoenix	W 8
Apr.	23—Robert Anderson, Las Vegas	D 6
July	9—Vito Romero, Las Vegas	KO by 4
Aug.	16—Ruben Munoz, Odessa	KO by 2
Dec.	16—Darrell Stovall, Phoenix	KO by 5

ROBERTO FUERTE
Argentine Lightweight
1980

Sept.	5—Juan Herrera, Tartagal	W 10
Oct.	3—Juan Herrera, S. Ped. Jujuy	D 10

BARRY FUNCHES
Manhattan, N.Y. Heavyweight
1979

Apr.	27—Mike Adams, New York	KO 2
May	23—Renaldo Snipes, White Plains	KO by 3
Oct.	26—Ali Allen, New York	D 4
1980		
Jan.	25—Ali Allen, New York	W 6
Apr.	18—Lou Esa, New York	KO 5
June	6—Melvin Epps, New York	W 8
Aug.	29—Tony Murillo, New York	KO 1
Oct.	23—Ossie Ocasio, New York	L 10

JOSE I. FUNES
Argentine Lightweight
1980

June	13—Victor Escobar, P.R.S. Pena	L 10
Aug.	8—Oscar Arevalo, Tucuman	W 10
Aug.	23—Manuel Bustos, Zarate	L 10
Sept.	26—Julio Melone, Pilar	L 12
Dec.	12—Alberto Butiler, La Banda	L 10

JUAN V.O. FUNES
Argentine Welterweight
1980

May	16—Jose Oroda, San Francisco	W 8
June	19—Diego Medina, Salta	KO 4
July	8—Osvaldo Barredo, San Francisco	D 10
Oct.	3—Ricardo Ruiz, San Francisco	L 10

NICK FURLANO
Toronto, Canada Junior Welterweight
1976

Oct.	23—Danny Stokes, Toronto	W 8
1977		
Jan.	18—Chuck Spicer, Toronto	KO 2
Mar.	7—Ralph Racine, Toronto	W 8
Mar.	25—Danny Stokes, Winnipeg	KO 8
Apr.	28—Tony Johnson, Toronto	W 8
May	24—Al Ford, Winnipeg	L 12
Nov.	1—Al Franklin, Toronto	KO 6
Dec.	8—Larry Moore, Toronto	KO 3
Dec.	13—Jim Henry, Toronto	W 8
1978		
Jan.	24—Jean LaPointe, Montreal	D 8
Apr.	28—Leo Marsh, Toronto	W 10
June	6—Jean LaPointe, Montreal	L 10
1979		
Feb.	9—Al Ford, Winnipeg	KO 14
	(For Canadian Junior Welterweight Title)	
Apr.	20—Freddie Harris, Winnipeg	W 10
May	25—Jose Gonzales, Montreal	W 8
	—Jean LaPointe, Montreal	KO 6
June	26—Gaetan Hart, Montreal	L 8
Aug.	21—Gaetan Hart, Montreal	W 12
	(Won Canadian Lightweight Title)	
Oct.	2—Jean LaPointe, Montreal	KO 6
1980		
Feb.	12—Chuck Spicer, Montreal	KO 3
Mar.	25—Gaetan Hart, Montreal	L 12
	(Canadian Lightweight Title)	
May	26—Danny Jones, Toronto	W 12
June	5—Benny Marquez, Winnipeg	W 10
July	25—Phil Batie, Smith Falls	KO 4
Aug.	27—Al Ford, Edmonton	W 10
Dec.	9—Ricky Camaro, Montreal	L 8

RONNIE FURLOW
Canadian Junior Lightweight
1977

Apr.	2—Willie Johnson, Tallahassee	KO 1
July	25—Isaac Vega, Chicago	KO by 4
Aug.	28—George Maldonado, Stateline	KO by 3
1978		
Jan.	23—Carlos Serrano, Chicago	L 4
Jan.	24—Jean LaPointe, Montreal	D 6
Feb.	13—Joey Mayes, Cleveland	L 6
Apr.	6—Lloyd Allen, Cleveland	KO by 6
June	6—Jean LaPointe, Montreal	L 10
Oct.	4—Steve Crow, Waukegan	KO 2
Nov.	18—Billy Moreno, DePaul	KO by 1
1979		
July	3—Dennis Quimayousie, Gardnerville	KO by 3
Sept.	18—Lionel Harney, Reno	L 6
Oct.	2—Lionel Harney, Reno	KO by 7
Nov.	13—Francisco Velez, Sparks	W 8
Dec.	18—Leonardo Mareno, Sparks	KO by 2
1980		
Feb.	29—Richard Savala, San Carlos	KO by 8

KEN FUSCO
White Plains, N.Y. Welterweight
1978
June	14—Stan Jackson, White Plains	KO 2
Sept.	6—Mel Young, White Plains	KO 1
Oct.	5—Jose Maldonado, White Plains	KO 3
Dec.	15—Derrick Wheeler, White Plains	KO 3

1979
Feb.	14—Keith York, White Plains	KO 1
Mar.	14—Carlos Plumas, White Plains	KO 2
Apr.	20—Duane Thomas, New York	L 4
May	23—Sal Dragone, White Plains	L 8
Oct.	10—James Macey, White Plains	KO 1
Nov.	5—Sal Dragone, White Plains	W 8

1980
Feb.	13—Tim LaValley, White Plains	W 6
Mar.	12—Gerald Clark, White Plains	KO 1

CLYDE FUSSELL
Lakeland, Fla. Heavyweight
1978
May	13—Al Migliorato, Orlando	KO 1
June	10—Ron Hill, Miami Beach	KO 3
July	25—Mark Orman, Orlando	KO 1
Oct.	3—Richard Majors, Orlando	KO 6

1979
Feb.	19—Joey Little, Tampa	KO 1
Mar.	13—Joey Little, Orlando	KO 2
Oct.	23—Bobby Dade, Orlando	KO 3

1980
Jan.	18—Johnny Jackson, Orlando	KO 5
Mar.	18—Bobby Dade, Orlando	KO 3

RON GABAREE
(GEBERE, GERBERE, GARBAREE)
Clinton, Mass. Heavyweight
1975
Sept.	11—Rick Wynn, Portland, Me.	KO by 3
Sept.	17—Bill Carson, Ottowa	KO by 1
Sept.	30—Danny O'Malley, Boston	L 4
Oct.	9—Ron McGraw, Portland, Me.	L 6
Oct.	23—Don Wigfall, Portland, Me.	KO by 3
Nov.	21—Danny O'Malley, Providence	KO by 1

1976
(Inactive)
1977
Mar.	12—Ed Chase, Fitchburg	KO 3
Mar.	30—Paul St. Louis, Boston	KO 3
June	6—Ron Drinkwater, Peabody	KO by 1

1978
Apr.	29—Joe Velmure, Lowell	L 8
Nov.	23—Jesse Crown, Portland	KO by 6
Dec.	8—Tyrone Harlee, Syracuse	KO by 1

1979
Jan.	11—Greg Sorrentino, Choes	KO by 3
Jan.	25—Dwain Bonds, Detroit	KO by 1
Feb.	22—Jose Ortiz, Cohoes	KO 2
Feb.	24—Don Halpin, Quincy	KO by 2
Nov.	28—Mike Garrahan, Hauppauge	KO by 1

1980
Nov.	28—Jimmy Smith, Providence	KO by 2

ROCKY GADSON
Philadelphia, Pa. Featherweight
1980
Apr.	11—Pedro Lebron, Chester	W 6
May	16—Pedro Lebron, Chester	W 6

NOLI GALICHA
Honolulu, Hawaii Welterweight
1975
Aug.	15—Ross Eadie, Port Moresby	KO by 7
Sept.	25—Dally Law, Port Moresby	W 10

1976
(Inactive)
1977
Jan.	10—Gideon Toyogon, Manila	L 12

(Philippine Welterweight Title)
1978
Apr.	15—Gideon Toyogon, Balagtas	L 12

(Philippine Welterweight Title)
1979
May	15—Alfredo Logan, Honolulu	KO by 8
July	25—Jerry Cheatham, Phoenix	KO by 4

Aug.	21—Terry Welch, Honolulu	KO 1
Sept.	18—Dave Meadows, Honolulu	W 10
Oct.	16—Randy Shields, Honolulu	KO by 1

1980
May	27—Young Kennedy, Honolulu	W 6
July	19—Abdul Bey, Hilo	W 10
Dec.	9—Dave Meadows, Honolulu	W 8

ADELAIDO GALINDO
Mexican Flyweight
1974
Aug.	26—Jose Lugo, Tijuana	KO 4
Sept.	16—Jose Luis Lizarga, Tijuana	W 10
Nov.	14—Tony Escobar, Tijuana	KO 5
Dec.	2—Santos "Cora" Rodriguez, Tijuana	KO 1

1975
Jan.	20—Francisco J. Nunez, Tijuana	KO 9
Feb.	11—Jorge Padron, Tijuana	W disq. 3
Mar.	9—Roberto Alvarez, Tijuana	W 10
June	23—Juan Zarate, Tijuana	KO 1
Aug.	2—Willie Jensen, Los Angeles	L 10
Oct.	6—Aniceto Vargas, Honolulu	KO 3
Dec.	14—Francisco Cruz, Honolulu	TD 3

1976
Feb.	21—Juan Jose Guzman, Mexico City	W 10
Apr.	25—Raul Pacheco, Mexico City	KO 2
May	15—Gonzalo Gonzalez, Merida	KO 8
July	3—Pedro Flores, Mexico City	KO 3
July	21—Francisco Granados, Tijuana	KO 1
Sept.	3—Alfonso Gutierrez, Mexicali	KO 4
Dec.	13—Esteban Salas, Tuxtla Gutierrez	KO 3

1977
Feb.	12—Francisco "Trompo" Marquez, Mexico City KO 9
Apr.	17—Aurelio "Pulga" Sanchez, Oaxaca	KO 3
Apr.	30—Freddy Castillo, Mexico City	KO by 8
Aug.	16—"Corderito" Gonzalez, Juarez	KO 2
Sept.	17—Freddy Hernandez, Merida	W 10
Dec.	2—"Moro" Rodriguez, Madrid	W 10

1978
Mar.	31—Ubaldo Gonzalez, Mazatlan	L 10
May	2—Sergio Reyes, San Antonio	W 10
July	15—Sergio Reyes, Tampico	KO 1
Aug.	16—Leonel Rojas, Matamoros	KO 3
Dec.	23—Leonel Rojas, Celaya	KO 2

1979
Mar.	10—Eleoncio Mercedes, Los Angeles	W 10
May	1—Gilbert Villisana, Houston	KO 4
June	3—Mike Stuart, Las Vegas	TW 6
Aug.	29—Candy Iglesias, Houston	W 10
Dec.	1—Antonio Avelar, Mexico City	KO by 3

1980
Sept.	19—Carlos Zuniga, Los Angeles	KO 6

RAMON GALLARCE
Argentine Junior Featherweight
1980
July	11—Jose A. Gomez, Ros. Frontera	L 6
Aug.	1—Jose A. gomez, Tucuman	D 6

TONY GALLO
Everett, Washington Heavyweight
1980
June	2—Rod George, Spokane	KO 2
Dec.	23—Zeke Thompson, Tacoma	KO 1

MANNING GALLOWAY
Columbus, Ohio Junior Welterweight
1978
Dec.	6—Gene Ellington, Cleveland	W 6

1979
Jan.	24—Mel Hauser, Cleveland	W 6
Apr.	27—Mike Blunt, Dayton	L 6
May	9—Calvin Straughter, Columbus	W 6
May	17—Forrest Winchester, Columbus	L 6
June	28—Phil Beattie, Columbus	KO 2
Sept.	30—Larry McCall, Canton	W 8
Dec.	1—Woody Harris, Detroit	W 6
Dec.	28—Greg Netter, Columbus	W 10

1980
Feb.	9—Dale Gordon, Clarksburg	W 6
May	16—Curtis Taylor, Lexington	KO by 2

MARTIN GALLOZA
Philadelphia, Pa. Bantamweight
1980
Mar.	22—Angel Marrero, Bethlehem	KO by 1

JUAN J. GALVEZ
Argentine Welterweight
1980
May	30—Nestor Gundin, San Nicolas	L 10

June 27—Ruben Mendoza, Rosario ....W 10
Aug. 1—Gabriel Sanchez, Tucuman ....KO by 3

ANDREW GANIGAN
Honolulu, Hawaii Lightweight
1976
Feb. 24—Felipe Avila, Honolulu ....KO 3
Apr. 13—Dave Bernal, Honolulu ....KO 1
June 10—Rado Broncano, Honolulu ....KO 1
Sept. 15—Rafael Nunez, Honolulu ....KO 2
Oct. 6—Jose Luis Lopez, Honolulu ....KO 3
Nov. 16—Chichie Pineda, Honolulu ....KO 1
1977
Feb. 8—Jose Posos, Honolulu ....KO 3
Mar. 1—Jose Luis Gonzalez, Honolulu ....KO 10
May 17—Turi Pineda, Honolulu ....KO 2
May 31—Tom Tarantino, Honolulu ....KO 7
June 14—Jose Talamantez, Honolulu ....KO 5
Aug. 4—Juan Garcia, Los Angeles ....KO 8
Sept. 14—Roman Contreras, Honolulu ....KO 3
Oct. 26—Gerardo Ferrat, Honolulu ....KO 5
Nov. 29—Ernesto Garfias, Honolulu ....W 10
1978
Feb. 7—Ignacio Campos, Honolulu ....KO 6
Mar. 28—Vicente Saldivar, Honolulu ....KO 8
May 30—Carlos Becerril, Honolulu ....KO 2
(U.S. Lightweight Title)
June 20—German Cuello, Honolulu ....KO 9
Aug. 1—Johnny Lira, Honolulu .... KO by 6
(U.S. Lightweight Title)
1979
Jan. 30—Elpidio Valdez, Honolulu ....KO 2
Mar. 6—David Madrid, Honolulu ....KO 2
Mar. 27—Vicente Mijares, Honolulu ....W 12
May 30—Hyung Kil Chun, Honolulu ....W 12
July 31—Robert Vasquez, Honolulu ....KO by 7
1980
Feb. 19—Roberto Vasquez, Honolulu ....KO 7
Nov. 12—Gerardo Venzor, Honolulu ....KO 6
Dec. 9—Curtis Ramsey, Honolulu ....KO 2

JOHNNY GANT
Washington, D.C. Welterweight
1968
Aug. 27—Hurricane Herbert, Washington, D.C. .....KO 4
Sept. 9—Dave Mosby, Washington, D.C..........KO 4
Oct. 21—Milton Carr, Alexandria ....KO 2
Oct. 31—Roland Trottman, Baltimore ....D 4
Nov. 18—Winston Noel, Alexandria ....KO 5
Dec. 16—Benny Huertas, Alexandria ....L 6
1969
Feb. 10—Billy Elliott, Alexandria ....KO 6
Mar. 10—Chuck Johns, Alexandria ....KO 1
Mar. 31—Tom Richardson, Alexandria ....KO 3
Apr. 28—Bobby Hayman, Washington, D.C........W 6
May 12—Nikita Harhocker, Washington, D.C. ....KO 4
June 9—Frankie Steele, Washington, D.C. ....KO 5
June 30—Dave Wyatt, Washington, D.C. ....KO 7
Aug. 18—Teddy Cooper, Washington, D.C. ....W 10
Sept. 15—Jose Myers, Washington, D.C...........KO 6
1970
Feb. 14—Dario Hidalgo, San Juan ....L 10
Apr. 16—Larry Adkins, Baltimore...............W 10
May 28—Adrian Davis, Baltimore............ KO by 2
July 30—Winston Noel, Baltimore................W 10
Sept. 16—Herbie Lee, Washington, D.C............W 10
1971
Jan. 19—Pat McCormack, London.................KO 3
Mar. 22—Joe Bessala, Paris.....................D 10
Apr. 26—Ivelaw Eastman, Washington, D.C.......KO 4
June 23—Clyde Tyler, Washington, D.C..........KO 6
July 13—Bob Payzant, Washington, D.C. ....KO 2
Sept. 28—Marcelino Alicia, Washington, D.C.......KO 4
Nov. 16—Otho Tyson, Baltimore..................KO 6
1972
Jan. 18—Vernon Mason, Baltimore ....L 10
Apr. 20—Vernon Mason, Baltimore...............W 12
May 16—Don McClendon, Washington, D.C. ......W 10
Aug. 24—Bobby Hayman, Baltimore..............W 10
1973
Feb. 1—Ely Yares, Los Angeles ....W 10
Feb. 14—Hipolito Barajas, Honolulu...............W 10
Apr. 16—Esteban DeJesus, San Juan.............L 10
May 8—Andre Reed, Washington, D.C..........KO 3
Dec. 10—Hedgemon Lewis, New York............L 10
1974
Jan. 16—Chris Fernandez, Baltimore..............W 10
May 10—Hector Thompson, Brisbane.............L 10
May 21—Mario Saurenann, Largo................W 10
July 18—Angel Robinson Garcia, Baltimore.......W 10
Aug. 27—Jim Henry, Alexandria ....KO 8
Nov. 28—Alfonso Hayman, Largo .... KO by 10

1975
Feb. 22—Clyde Washington, Largo ....KO 5
Apr. 29—Keith Averett, Largo ....W 10
June 17—Alfonso Hayman, Largo.................W 10
Aug. 26—Harold Weston, Largo....................D 10
Oct. 11—Angel Espada, Ponce....................L 15
(WBA Welterweight Title)
1976
Apr. 2—Joe Grier, Washington D.C...............KO 8
May 24—Fausto Rodriguez, Santo Domingo........L 10
June 26—Daniel Gonzalez, Monte Carlo ....W 10
Sept. 17—Jose Baquedano, Los Angeles ....KO 8
1977
Feb. 13—Anthony House, Annapolis ....KO 2
(U.S. Championship Tournament)
Nov. 18—Eddie Marcelle, Port of Spain ....L 10
Dec. 17—Freddie Boynton, Washington D.C. ....W 10
1978
Feb. 4—Victor Perez, Baltimore ....W 10
Apr. 13—Justice Ortiz, Landover ....W 8
May 10—Roland Pryor, Washington D.C. ....KO 8
Nov. 21—Sammy Ruckard, Landover ....KO 10
1979
Jan. 11—Ray Leonard, Landover .... KO by 8
June 2—Harold Volbrecht, Mmabathosa ....L 10
1980
Feb. 27—Larry Moore, Washington, D.C. ....KO 3
Mar. 31—Roger Leonard, Landover ....L 8

MIKE GANS
San Francisco, Calif. Heavyweight
1980
Aug. 28—Andrew Shears, San Carlos ....KO 1
Nov. 19—Ken Lakusta, Crystal Bay ....W 6

ALBERTO GARCIA
Mexican Flyweight
1980
Feb. 23—Francisco Sanchez, Mexico City ....L 4
Apr. 19—Ramon Lopez, Mexico City ....KO 2
June 25—Antonio Zamora, Mexico City ....KO 1

ALEX GARCIA
Las Vegas, Nev. Junior Lightweight
1978
Apr. 13—Nicky Perez, Phoenix ....L 8
May 25—Nicky Perez, Phoenix ....L 10
1979
May 30—Francisco Ponce, Las Vegas ....W 10
Sept. 12—Roy Hernandez, Stockton ....KO by 6
Oct. 30—Rodrigo Aguirre, Bakersfield ....L 8
1980
Mar. 8—Ricardo Jiminez, Las Vegas ....KO by 4
May 22—Juan (Kid) Mesa, Los Angeles ....KO by 3

CARLOS GARCIA
Norfolk, Va. Welterweight
1979
Aug. 21—Jimmy Corkum, S. Yarmouth ....L 10
1980
Oct. 16—Danile Cruz, Los Angeles ....KO by 2
Dec. 15—Jack Morrell, Boston ....KO 6

CLEO GARCIA
Nicaraguan Bantamweight
(Previous Record Unavailable)
1979
Apr. 8—Jorge Lujan, Las Vegas ....KO by 15
(World Bantamweight Title)
1980
Dec. 11—Jose Quijana, Los Angeles ....KO 4

DOUG GARCIA
Los Angeles, Calif. Junior Featherweight
1979
Oct. 11—Desi Newbill, Los Angeles ....KO by 2
1980
Jan. 24—Sergio Castro, Los Angeles ....KO by 2
May 30—Felipe Cisneros, Bakersfield ....KO by 3
Aug. 14—Miguel Saucedo, Los Angeles ....L 4

GEORGE (ROCKY) GARCIA
Los Angeles, Calif. Featherweight
1978
Sept. 7—Adan Aguilar, Los Angeles ....KO 2
Sept. 21—Jose Claudio, Los Angeles ....KO 2
Sept. 28—Pascual Villarreal, Los Angeles ....W 6
Nov. 9—Noe Rivera, Los Angeles ....KO 3
Nov. 16—Adolfo Hurtado, Los Angeles ....W 6
Nov. 30—John Papin, Los Angeles ....W 6
Dec. 14—David Barrera, Los Angeles ....W 6

1979
Feb. 15—Arturo Rojas, Los Angeles ....W 6
Mar. 15—Eliu Hernandez, Los Angeles ....KO 3
May 20—Manuel Rodriguez, Las Vegas ....W 6
Aug. 9—Eddie Freeman, Los Angeles ....KO 3
Sept. 13—Roberto Garcia, Los Angeles ....W 10
Dec. 6—Roberto Merida, Los Angeles ....KO 7
1980
Feb. 21—Humberto Lara, Los Angeles ....KO 3
Mar. 20—Pipinto Jiminez, Phoenix ....KO by 3
Apr. 17—Fel Clemente, Los Angeles ....W 10
May 29—Luis Avila, Los Angeles ....KO 9
June 19—Tony Styles Diaz, Los Angeles ....KO 4
July 31—Armando Ugalde, Los Angeles ....WTD 9
Aug. 7—Roberto Torres, Los Angeles ....W 10
Nov. 6—Ricardo Varela, Los Angeles ....W 10
Dec. 6—Roberto Merida, Los Angeles ....KO 7

JORGE GARCIA
Argentine Junior Middleweight
1980
Jan. —Juan Valdez, Tandil ....W 10
Oct. 17—Floro Zarza, Centenario ....KO 2
Dec. 19—Juan Monzon, Neuquen ....KO 2

JORGE GARCIA
Los Angeles, Calif. Bantamweight
1978
June 15—Juan Ramos, Los Angeles ....KO 2
June 29—Lorenzo Ramirez, Los Angeles ....W 4
Aug. 17—Jose Claudio, Los Angeles ....KO 2
Aug. 24—Lorenzo Ramirez, Los Angeles ....W 5
Dec. 7—Manuel Ruelas, Los Angeles ....D 6
1979
July 12—Antonio Medina, Los Angeles ....W 6
Sept. 13—Jose Villegas, Los Angeles ....W 6
Oct. 25—Johnny Papin, Los Angeles ....W 10
1980
June 19—Tony Styles Diaz, Los Angeles ....KO 4

JOSE LUIS GARCIA
San Antonio, Texas Flyweight
1975
Oct. 14—Luis Rico, Corpus Christi ....W 6
1976
Dec. 7—Virgil Sweeney, Galveston ....KO 1
1977
Jan. 4—Jesse Hernandez, Corpus Christi ....W 4
Jan. 21—Ernesto Rodriguez, Laredo ....KO 4
Feb. 25—Carlos Cantu, Laredo ....L 10
June 11—Carlos Cantu, Laredo ....KO by 6
1978
Apr. 11—Joe Nunez, Houston.....................KO 5
May 2—Calvin Sheppard, San Antonio ....W 8
June 20—Calvin Sheppard, San Antonio ....W 10
Aug. 25—Alberto Cruz, Dallas ....W 8
Dec. 19—Elias DeLeon, Houston ....KO by 2
1979
May 26—Jose Gallegos, Merida ....KO by 6
July 3—Ignacio Espinal, Santo Domingo .....KO by 2
Aug. 8—Willie Jensen, Las Vegas ....KO by 3
—Johnny Owens, Cardiff ....KO by 5
1980
Aug. 19—Freddie Jackson, Beaumont ....KO by 3
Oct. 9—Jose Luis Cruz, Mc Allen ....KO by 3

JUAN GARCIA
Mexicali, Mexico Flyweight
1979
July 2—Jose Herrera, Los Angeles ....KO by 8
Aug. 28—Flash Jagdon, Honolulu ....L 10
1980
Nov. 28—Candido Tellez, San Diego ....KO by 2

JULIO GARCIA
Newark, N.J. Welterweight
1979
Dec. 12—Johnny Turner, Scranton ....L 10
1980
Sept. 4—Ismael Martinez, Rio Piedras ....L 10

JUSTO GARCIA
California Junior Featherweight
1979
Nov. 29—Ruben Solorio, Los Angeles ....KO 4
1980
Mar. 21—Juan Escobar, Los Angeles ....W 10
Nov. 28—Warren Matthews, San Diego ....W 10

LORENZO GARCIA
Argentine Lightweight
1980
Feb. 1—Rodolfo Petrizani, San Pedro ....W 4

Mar. 21—Jean Zuniga, San Pedro ....D 10
Apr. 18—Paul Columbo, San Pedro ....W 10
June 14—Pedro A. Gutierrez, Baradero ....W 10
July 25—Santiago Lopez, San Pedro ....W 10
Dec. 5—Jesus Romero, San Pedro ....W 12
(Won Argentine Lightweight Title)

LUIS ENRIQUE GARCIA
Mexican Flyweight
1980
Mar. 29—Pedro Moreno, Mexico City ....W 10
May 16—Luis Castillo, Villahermosa ....KO 3

MARCOS GARCIA
San Diego, Calif. Middleweight
1980
June 23—J.W. Stewart, San Diego ....D 4
July 16—J.W. Stewart, San Diego ....KO 2
Aug. 19—Sylvester Green, San Diego ....L 5
Nov. 28—Sylvester Green, San Diego ....KO 1

MIGUEL A. GARCIA
Argentine Welterweight
1980
Jan. 11—Carlos Prieto, Gral Villegas ....W 10
Feb. 2—Alfredo Campos, Monte Hermoso ....W 10
Apr. 12—Antonio Juarez, Gral Villegas ....W 10
June 19—Hector Caceres, Bahia Blanca ....W 10
July 18—Daniel Arriola, Bahia Blanca ....D 10
Aug. 8—Antonio Juarez, Neuquen ....W 10

MIGUEL (MIKE) GARCIA
Houston, Texas Middleweight
1978
Apr. 11—Marcus Dorsey, Houston ....L 6
May 2—Adolfo Rivas, San Antonio ....D 4
July 18—Leon McCullum, Houston ....W 6
Sept. 19—Danny Donatto, Houston ....D 6
Oct. 10—Leon McCullum, Houston ....TL 10
Nov. 28—Wilford Scypion, Houston ....KO by 4
1979
Apr. 2—Joe Barrientes, Dallas ....KO by 5
1980
Jan. 17—Babs McCarthy, Stateline ....KO by 4
Aug. 12—Tyrone Wren, Wichita ....D 8
Sept. 10—Larry Martin, Wichita ....KO by 3
Nov. 11—Eddie Green, Houston ....KO by 5

OMAR GARCIA
Argentine Lightweight
1980
Mar. 15—Ramon Fabas, Buenos Aires ....L 6
Apr. 19—Alfredo Chaves, Buenos Aires ....TD 3
June 21—Alberto Musa, Buenos Aires ....L 6
Dec. 13—Alfredo Chaves, Buenos Aires ....D 6

PEDRO (PETE) GARCIA
Los Angeles, Calif. Light Heavyweight
1978
Mar. 15—Nick Probencia, Las Vegas ....KO 1
June 21—Len Lawson, Concord ....L 6
Aug. 18—James Ingram, San Diego ....KO by 3
1979
July 11—Charles Roye, Las Vegas ....KO 5
Sept. 20—Parnell Fairley, Los Angeles ....L 5
Oct. 2—Byron Campbell, Reno ....D 4
Oct. 18—Parnell Fairley, Los Angeles ....L 4
1980
Nov. 8—Victor Callejas, Detroit ....KO 2
Nov. 26—Junior Foster, Las Vegas ....W 4

CHUCK GARDNER
Minneapolis, Minn. Heavyweight
1976
Nov. 9—Bill Jackson, St. Paul ....KO 1
Nov. 30—Wilson Williams, Minneapolis ....W 4
1977
Apr. 20—Charley Jordon, Minneapolis ....W 4
May 7—J. D. McCauley, St. Louis ....KO 4
June 23—Charles Atlas, Bloomington ....W 6
Dec. 2—Baker Tinsley, Chicago ....KO 1
1978
Feb. 27—Grady Daniels, Chicago ....L 8
Apr. 7—Robert Echols, Chicago ....L 8
May 11—Jim Beattie, Bloomington ....L 10
June 24—Fred Askew, St. Paul ....KO by 6
1979
Feb. 28—Ernie Smith, Las Vegas ....W 5
Mar. 21—Lee Holloman, Las Vegas ....W 6
Apr. 18—Mike Creel, Las Vegas ....W 5
Sept. 19—Jesus Meneses, Las Vegas ....KO by 9
Oct. 31—Jerry Thompkins, Phoenix ....W 4

99

July	10—Sugar Bear Williams, Chicago	KO	2
Sept.	6—Ken James, Sioux Falls	KO	1
Nov.	1—Tony Tucker, Lake Tahoe	KO by	3

LESLIE GARDNER
Detroit, Mich. Middleweight
1978
Nov.	3—John Beverage, Detroit	KO	1
Nov.	10—Rodney Green, Detroit	L	6
Sept.	27—Jess Griggin, Flint	KO	1
Dec.	1—Dwight Curtis, Detroit	KO	2
1979
Jan.	18—Tiger Coupe, Detroit	KO	3
Nov.	1—Don Cobbs, Detroit	W	8
1980
Jan.	24—Clifton Askew, Detroit	KO	2
May	23—Sammy Floyd, Pontiac	L	8
Oct.	18—Willie Crawford, Pontiac	KO	1
Nov.	14—Ernie Davis, Detroit	W	10
Nov.	—Terry Gaines, Detroit	KO	1

MARTY JOE GARELIK
Denver, Colo. Welterweight
1979
July	14—Sultan Saladin, Denver	W	6
1980
Mar.	15—Chris Johnson, Ogden	KO by	3

VERBIE GARLAND
Toledo, Ohio Heavyweight
1973
July	27—Bob Conway, Toledo	W	4
Nov.	17—Lloyd Richardson, Detroit	KO	3
1974
Mar.	13—Frank Schram, Toledo	W	6
May	25—Tom Prater, Detroit	L	6
1975
May	10—Fred Jones, Toledo	W	6
1976
May	13—William Anderson, Toledo	KO by	5
Dec.	11—Charlie Johnson, Alliance	L	10
1977
Mar.	22—Harry Terrell, Cleveland	L	6
May	23—Walter Moore, Chicago	L	10
1978
May	17—Frank Brown, Flint	L	6
1980
Sept.	18—Larry Sims, Cleveland	KO by	3

OBBIE GARNETT
Cincinnati, Ohio Light Heavyweight
1978
Oct.	31—Clyde Mudgett, Indianapolis	KO by	1
Nov.	11—Billy Ratliff, Beaver Dam	KO by	1
Dec.	15—Henry Sims, Chicago	KO by	1
1979
May	19—Stan Scott, Findlay	KO by	1
Aug.	4—Luke Capuano, Chicago	KO by	1
Sept.	8—Johnny Wilburn, Kingsport	KO by	1
1980
Sept.	12—Garland Tipton, Louisville	KO by	1
Oct.	30—James Spear, Louisville	KO by	1

DONNIE GARRETT
Muncie, Ind. Junior Middleweight
Born: January 2, 1953
1977
Apr.	22—Bob Barnes, Indianapolis	KO	2
May	4—Eugene Bridges, Cleveland	KO	3
1978
June	3—Charlie Smith, Muncie	KO by	1
June	21—Frankie Mills, Detroit	KO	2
1979
Apr.	17—Cicero Blake, Waukesha	KO by	2
June	1—Chuck Walker, Louisville	KO	1
Dec.	2—Louis Brown, Muncie	KO	3
1980
Jan.	22—Larry Puchta, Indianapolis	W	5
Mar.	17—Mark McCullough, Indianapolis	L	4
Aug.	13—Don Williams, Indianapolis	KO	4

DAVID GARZA
San Carlos, Calif. Junior Middleweight
1978
Mar.	14—Jorge Fernandez, Sacramento	L	6
1979
Feb.	6—Danny Adams, San Carlos	L	6
1980
Mar.	6—Rocky Grunon, San Jose	KO	3
Apr.	11—Juan Huerta, San Jose	W	6
Oct.	24—Ricky Wynn, Oakland	D	5

GILBERT GARZA
San Antonio, Texas Junior Lightweight
1979
Mar.	13—Jose Luis Escamilla, San Antonio	KO	3
Mar.	16—Wardell Williams, Kansas City	KO by	3
Mar.	31—Antonio Soria, San Antonio	KO	2
June	27—Jose Pena, New York	KO by	3
July	31—Ruben Moreno, San Antonio	L	6
Sept.	20—Ruben Moreno, San Antonio	L	6
Nov.	6—Johnny Contreras, Corpus Christi	KO by	3
Nov.	20—Juan Venegas, Houston	W	6
1980
Feb.	18—Dennis Quimayousie, Carson City	L	10
Feb.	25—Dave Larmour, Belfast	L	8
Mar.	5—Jose Caba, Las Vegas	KO by	10
Mar.	25—Tony Sanchez, Houston	KO by	2
Dec.	5—Joel Loredo, Corpus Christi	KO by	6

JAIME GARZA
Los Angeles, Calif. Bantamweight
Born: September 10, 1959
Height: 5'7"
Managed by Bennie Georgino
1978
Feb.	7—Eduardo Villareal, Reynosa	KO	1
Mar.	2—Francisco Silva, Reynosa	KO	1
Nov.	30—Miguel Bejarano, Los Angeles	KO	1
Dec.	14—Augustin Sanchez, Los Angeles	KO	2
1979
Jan.	11—Delfino Cornejo, Los Angeles	KO	2
Jan.	18—Jose Villegas, Los Angeles	KO	4
Aug.	23—Jose Villegas, Los Angeles	W	6
Sept.	25—Ramon Barrera, Los Angeles	KO	3
Nov.	2—Fernando Reyes, San Diego	KO	2
Dec.	8—Ernesto Rios, Los Angeles	KO	3
Dec.	14—Jose Luis Lopez, San Bernardino	KO	1
1980
Feb.	2—Joe Lopez, Phoenix	KO	1
Feb.	22—Jose Hernandez, San Bernardino	KO	2
Mar.	21—Luis Avila, San Bernardino	KO	8
Apr.	12—Pedro Gonzales, Tucson	KO	3
May	2—Jose Reyna, San Bernardino	KO	1
May	13—Luis Avila, Bakersfield	W	10
June	21—Augustine Granados, Las Vegas	KO	1
July	17—Luis Sandoval, Los Angeles	KO	3
Aug.	7—Lorenzo Ramirez, Los Angeles	KO	4
Sept.	13—Calvin Sheppard, San Antonio	KO	4
Oct.	30—Jose Luis Valente, Los Angeles	KO	3
Dec.	13—Manuel Ruelas, El Paso	KO	1

CURTIS GASKIN
Orlando, Fla. Heavyweight
1978
May	23—Nick Wells, Orlando	L	8
June	23—Eugene Idoletti, Orlando	W	8
Oct.	3—Eugene Idoletti, Orlando	W	6
1979
(Inactive)
1980
Dec.	12—Tony Severance, Gainesville	L	6

ROQUE R. GASTALDO
Argentine Junior Middleweight
1980
Sept.	5—Hector Quintero, Parana	W	10
Oct.	10—Juan M. Suarez, Parana	KO	8

JOEL GATICA
Mexican Featherweight
1975
Feb.	14—Carmelo Montes, Acapulco	D	4
1976
Apr.	23—Anastacio Gil, Acapulco	KO	3
May	21—Leo Cisneros, Acapulco	KO	2
June	4—David Escobedo, Monterrey	KO by	2
1977
Jan.	—Mario Nava, Acapulco	KO by	2
Mar.	25—Rodolfo Lara, Acapulco	KO	2
Apr.	22—Miguel Alvarez, Acapulco	KO	4
Aug.	19—Miguel Gonzalez, Acapulco	KO by	1
1978
June	9—Mario Nava, Acapulco	KO by	2
1979
(Inactive)
1980
Jan.	26—Bernardino Pena, Mexico City	L	8
Mar.	7—Victor Hernandez, Acapulco	KO by	3
May	23—Victor Hernandez, Acapulco	KO by	1
Aug.	29—Javier Hernandez, Acapulco	KO by	7

LLOYD (SHADOW) GEORGE
Trinidad Lightweight
1979
—Preston Carrington, Port-of-Spain	.... W	8
—Compton Carzuis, Diego Martin	.... KO	2
—Ricardo Croque, Diego Martin	.... KO	6

1980
Feb.	29—Roy Smith, Port-of-Spain	.... W	8
Mar.	28—Jose Lopez, Port-of-Spain	.... W	8

MARCOS (LOPEZ) GERALDO
Mexican Middleweight
Born: September 28, 1954, Guaymas, Sonora, Mexico
1970
Sept.	29—Albaro Parra, Fresno	.... W	4
Oct.	16—Eddie Parks, San Diego	.... KO by	1

1971
Jan.	23—Tony Sanchez, Woodland Hills	.... W	4
Feb.	10—Dave White, Las Vegas	.... W	6
Apr.	8—Agapito Villegas, Los Angeles	.... W	4
Apr.	14—Billy Ray, Las Vegas	.... KO by	1
Apr.	30—Dave White, San Diego	.... KO	3
May	5—Johnny Copeland, Las Vegas	.... KO	3
May	15—Efren Cisneros, Woodland Hills	.... KO	2
May	20—Lou Blades, Los Angeles	.... KO by	3
May	28—Billy Ray, Stateline	.... W	6
June	19—Leroy Broussard, Santa Monica	.... KO	6
July	17—Jimmy Nelson, Santa Monica	.... W	6
Aug.	25—Chuy Ramirez, Las Vegas	.... KO	9
Oct.	6—Tony Perez, Las Vegas	.... KO	6
Oct.	14—Freddie Mills, Las Vegas	 L	10
Dec.	8—Robert Carrillo, Las Vegas	.... KO	3
Dec.	22—Rosario Morrilo, Las Vegas	.... KO	2

1972
Jan.	12—Leon Linscomb, Las Vegas	.... KO	5
Jan.	19—Chu Chu Cebrores, Las Vegas	.... KO	3
Feb.	17—Miguel Hernandez, Stateline	.... W	10
May	3—Miguel Aguilar, Las Vegas	.... KO	10
Oct.	4—Willie Thomas, Las Vegas	.... W disq.	9
Oct.	26—John L. Sullivan, Stateline	 L	10
Nov.	30—Johnny Rico, Las Vegas	.... W	10

1973
Feb.	28—Peter Cobblah, Las Vegas	.... KO by	1
June	22—David Love, San Diego	 L	10
July	6—David Love, San Diego	 L	10
July	27—Steve Ewell, San Francisco	.... KO	7
Sept.	14—Renato Garcia, San Diego	.... KO by	9
Nov.	23—John Huntley, San Diego	.... KO	4
Dec.	6—Vicente Medina, Sacramento	.... W	6

1974
Jan.	10—Andre Beard, Los Angeles	.... W	6
Mar.	14—Andre Beard, Los Angeles	.... W	6
Apr.	18—Armando Muniz, Los Angeles	.... W	10
Aug.	16—James Caffey, San Diego	.... W	10
Sept.	27—Mike Evans, San Diego	.... W	10
Oct.	16—James Marshall, Las Vegas	.... W	10
Dec.	6—Jean Mateo, San Francisco	.... KO by	1

1975
Feb.	13—Willie Warren, Las Vegas	.... W	10
May	20—Manuel Fierro, Guaymas	.... KO	8
Aug.	23—Jose Baquedano, Merida, Yucatan	.... KO by	1

1976
Apr.	5—Chucho Almazan, Guaymas	.... W	10
Apr.	29—Jose Palacios, Guaymas	.... TKO	6
Sept.	3—Ernesto Caballero, Guaymas	.... W disq.	4
Oct.	30—Ernesto Caballero, Mexico City	.... KO	1
Dec.	4—Jose Figueroa, Mexico City	.... KO by	6

1977
Mar.	11—Herminio (Loba) Ramirez, Guaymas	..... KO	2
Oct.	22—Emeterio Villanueva, Mexico City	...... KO	2

1978
Jan.	22—Alex Olguin, Guaymas	.... KO	1
Mar.	4—Renato Garcia, Los Angeles	.... TKO	9
May	20—Joaquin (Petrolero) Macias, Los Angeles	TKO	5

(Retained Mexican Middleweight Title)
Sept.	9—George Cooper, Sacramento	.... TKO	6

(Won California Middleweight Title)
1979
Mar.	31—Renato Garcia, Mexicali	.... KO	6
May	20—Ray Leonard, New Orleans	 L	10
Aug.	25—Lorenzo Benitez, Tijuana	.... KO	2

1980
Feb.	16—John LoCicero, Portland, Me.	.... KO	10
May	17—Marvin Hagler, Las Vegas	.... KO	11
Sept.	11—Caveman Lee, Chicago	.... KO by	1

LUIS GEREZ
Argentine Flyweight
1980
Feb.	3—Esteban Bustos, Gral Acha	 L	10
Feb.	20—Raul Davis, Arrecifes	.... W	10
Apr.	3—Jorge Martinez, Arrecifes	.... W	10
May	15—Juan Cortez, Arrecifes	.... W	10

July	3—Ramon Baez, Arrecifes	.... KO	1
Sept.	12—Jose Narvaez, Mendoza	 L	12
Oct.	10—Raul Perez, Arrecifes	.... W	10

SAM GERVIN
Akron, Ohio Welterweight
1980
July	6—Greg Netter, Columbus	.... KO by	6
Aug.	21—Greg Netter, Columbus	 L	6
Sept.	18—Earl Jewell, Cleveland	 L	4
Sept.	24—Razor Rosenberger, Struthers	.... KO by	5
Sept.	30—Rick Noggle, Niles	 L	10
Oct.	18—Jerome Kinney, Pontiac	.... KO by	4

RONNIE GIBBONS
New Hyde Park, N.Y., Junior Welterweight
1974
Jan.	10—Fernando Saenz, Las Vegas	.... KO	3
Jan.	17—Tony Saenz, Las Vegas	.... KO	1
Jan.	24—Robert Ramierez, Las Vegas	.... KO	3
Feb.	11—Juan Morales, Las Vegas	.... W	8
Feb.	25—Mike Swiger, Las Vegas	.... KO	3
Mar.	5—Robert Turner, Las Vegas	.... KO	3
Mar.	19—Kevin Morgan, Las Vegas	.... W	6
Apr.	1—Jim Montague, Las Vegas	.... KO	7
May	8—George Fakaras, New York	.... KO	3
June	10—Henry Gracio, New York	.... D	4
Nov.	22—Oresto Lebron, New York	.... W	6

1975
Mar.	24—Johnny Davis, New York	.... KO	6
July	23—Angel Citron, Largo	.... KO	3
Aug.	26—Joe Hrbcha, Largo	.... KO	1
Sept.	12—Pablo Rodriguez, Commack	.... W	8
Sept.	30—Oresto Lebrun, New York	.... W	6
Oct.	17—Marcelino Alicia, Commack	.... KO	1
Nov.	7—Pablo Rodriguez, Latham	.... W	8
Dec.	12—Fernand Marcotte, New York	.... KO by	1

1976
Feb.	29—Papo Melendez, Commack	.... KO by	4
Mar.	17—Charlie Benjamin, Albany	.... KO	4
Aug.	27—Danny McAloon, New York	.... KO by	9

1980
Nov.	3—Steve Snow, Hartford	.... KO	3

GARY GIRON
1980
Feb.	20—Rodrigo Hernandez, Las Vegas	 L	10
Apr.	15—Steve Bentley, Sparks	.... KO	9
May	2—Mauricio Aldana, Las Vegas	 L	10
June	14—Chris Lange, Yerington	.... KO	8

ERNIE GLADNEY
Philadelphia, Pa. Welterweight
1977
Mar.	7—Mike Picciotti, Upper Darby	.... KO by	2
May	9—Greg Singleton, Newark	 L	4
May	26—Alonzo Green, Allentown	.... W	4
July	20—Will Rankin, Virginia Beach	.... W	4
Aug.	3—Victor Pappas, Philadelphia	.... W	4

1978
Mar.	14—Victor Pappas, Philadelphia	 L	6
Apr.	19—Craig Stevenson, Washington D.C.	 L	6
Oct.	26—Danny Paul, Detroit	.... KO by	1

1979
Mar.	14—Giovanni Bovenzi, Trenton	 L	6

1980
Mar.	12—Trevor Evelyn, White Plains	.... *L	4
Mar.	14—Giovanni Bovenzi, Trenton	 L	6
May	4—Billy Costello, Kiamesha Lake	.... KO by	5
July	29—Kevin Howard, Philadelphia	.... KO by	3
Sept.	10—Ralph Mifka, Scranton	 L	8

(*Fought under the name "Richie Garland")

GEORGE GOFARTH
St. Louis, Mo. Light Heavyweight
1979
Apr.	20—Dan Kiser, St. Louis	.... W	6
June	11—James Tillis, Chicago	.... KO by	5
July	26—Floyd Cross, Overland Park	.... W	4
July	30—Jumbo Cummings, Chicago	.... W	4
Sept.	25—Robert McFarland, Belleville	.... KO by	3
Nov.	27—Rick Meyer, Belleville	.... W	6

1980
Jan.	21—Rick Meyer, St. Charles	.... D	4
Mar.	17—Tracy Morrison, Kansas City	 L	8
Mar.	17—Clyde Mudgett, Indianapolis	 L	6
Apr.	22—Dan Kiser, Memphis	.... W	10
May	12—Franklin Otts, Cape Girardeau	.... KO	3
May	13—Jerry Celestine, Memphis	.... KO by	4
Sept.	16—Lalu Capuano, Cicero	.... KO by	1
Oct.	7—Phil Wade, St. Charles	.... W	6

101

CURTIS GOINS
Brooklyn, N.Y. Light Heavyweight
1976
Sept. 13—Ray James, Peabody .... W 4
Oct. 8—Willie Stallings, Sunnyside .... L 4
Nov. 19—Johnny Davis, Sunnyside .... L 4
1977
Oct. 27—Hilliard Edmonds, Elizabeth .... W 6
Nov. 3—Melvin Richardson, Durban .... L 8
1978
(Inactive)
1979
Oct. 4—Ron Huston, New York .... KO by 4
1980
Feb. 29—Johnny Wilburn, Commack .... KO by 8
Apr. 25—Bernard McClean, Commack .... L 8
May 25—Eddie Davis, Atlantic City .... KO by 7
Oct. 10—Euclides Valdez, New York .... L 6

NORMAN GOINS
Indianapolis, Ind. Lightweight
1972
Nov. 10—Willie Williams, Indianapolis .... KO 4
Dec. 16—Curtis Burks, Indianapolis .... KO 2
1973
Apr. 17—Julie Mandell, Indianapolis .... W 6
May 22—Johnny Howard, Indianapolis .... KO 2
Aug. 24—Hubert Stevenson, Indianapolis .... KO 3
Sept. 22—Johnny Copeland, Indianapolis .... KO 2
Oct. 27—Marcus Anderson, Indianapolis .... KO 3
Nov. 8—Charley Harvey, Indianapolis .... KO 1
Nov. 15—Cocoa Kid, Tampa..................... NC 8
1974
Feb. 16—Willie Williams, New Castle .... KO 2
July 27—Danny Starks, Union City .... KO 2
Aug. 26—Angel Mayoral, Chicago .... KO by 7
Nov. 12—Richie Pettigrew, Indianapolis......... KO 3
Dec. 10—Abdul Bey, Indianapolis .... KO 4
1975
Apr. 17—Brooks Byrd, Indianapolis .... KO 2
June 6—Lorenzo Trujillo, Indianapolis .... W 10
Sept. 24—Rocky Ramon, Indianapolis .... W 10
Oct. 28—Art Leon, Honolulu .... W 10
1976
Mar. 9—Mike Everett, Philadelphia .... L 10
Apr. 17—Nkosana Mgaxsi, E. London......... KO by 9
May 28—Abdul Fakly, Abidjan .... D 10
July 30—Sigfrido Rodriguiz, Los Angeles...... KO by 4
Nov. 30—Marion Thomas, Indianapolis .... W 10
1977
Mar. 22—Maurice (Termite) Watkins,
Corpus Christi .... ND 3
May 24—Bobby Hughes, Winnipeg .... L 8
Sept. 16—John Powell, New York .... KO 2
1978
Jan. 24—Gilberto Mares, Indianapolis .... KO 1
Feb. 20—Wade Hinnant, Philadelphia .... KO by 9
May 1—Alphonso Cirullo, Indianapolis .... KO 3
June 5—Willie Rodriguez, Allentown .... L 10
July 9—Howard Davis, Indianapolis .... L 10
Aug. 26—Simmie Black, Dayton .... KO 2
Sept. 19—Scotty Foreman, Orlando .... L 10
Oct. 11—Roberto Perez; Indianapolis .... W 7
Nov. 11—Sonny Floyd, Beaver Dam .... KO 6
1979
Mar. 9—Saoul Mamby, New York .... L 10
Apr. 13—Aaron Pryor, Cincinnati .... KO by 9
1980
May 13—Don Snow, Indianapolis .... KO 1
July 10—Juan Graciano, Los Angeles .... KO 4
Aug. 7—Roberto Elizondo, Los Angeles ...... KO by 2
Dec. 16—Rodolfo Gonzalez, Los Angeles ..... KO by 1

ALBERTO GOJT
Argentine Junior Middleweight
1980
Apr. 17—Juan Namuncura, Neuquen .... L 10
May 15—Juan C. Arrus, Chivilchoy .... KO by 3

BENJI GOLDSTONE
Albany, N.Y. Welterweight
1976
Oct. 1—Mike Estafire (Mustafa Hamsho), Utica ... L 4
Nov. 20—L.C. Stromin, Utica .... KO 4
1977
Jan. 21—Raham Muhammad, Rochester .... KO 2
May 20—Don Melosh, Binghamton .... KO 5
July 8—Sam Hailstock, Geneva .... L 6
Nov. 13—Ben Sanchez, Albany .... W 6
Dec. 13—Willie Davis, Cohoes .... KO 1
1978
Apr. 21—Eddie Campbell, Albany .... W 8
May 13—Tyrone Phelps, Utica .... KO 5

1979
Jan. 23—Alain Turenne, Montreal .... W 8
May 1—Bernardo Prada, Montreal .... KO by 7
July 10—Chris Clarke, Halifax .... KO by 1
1980
June 20—Marlon Starling, Hartford .... KO by 5
July 25—Frank Minnigan, Rochester .... L 6

ALBERTO GOMEZ
Brooklyn, N.Y. Lightweight
1979
Oct. 27—Benito Jiminez, North Bergen .... L 6
1980
Mar. 20—Russ Riccardi, N. Bergen .... L 4
May 31—Russ Riccardi, Elizabeth .... L 4

GUMERSINDO TACHO GOMEZ
Houston, Texas Middleweight
1979
Apr. 24—Robert Powell, Houston .... L 6
1980
Aug. 19—Melvin Dennis, Beaumont .... L 12

JESUS GOMEZ
Puerto Rican Junior Featherweight
1979
Feb. 23—Julio Solano, Santo Domingo .... KO by 2
1980
July 17—Matuzalem Rivera, Rio Piedras .... L 8

JORGE GOMEZ
Argentine Featherweight
1980
Feb. 28—Carlos Romero, Gral Roca .... W 10
Mar. 14—Carlos Totaro, Gral Roca .... KO 8
Mar. 28—Victor Velazquez, Cipoletti .... KO 3
Apr. 17—Juan J. Espindola, Bahia Blanca .... W 10
May 2—Felipe Baez, Gral Roca .... W 10
June 6—Omar Almada, Neuquen .... W 10
July 11—Roberto Barrientos, Gral Roca .... KO 6
Aug. 8—Hugo Fernandez, Viedma .... W 10
Sept. 6—Orlando Lucero, San Antonio .... KO 9
Sept. 19—Armando Perez, Buenos Aires .... W 10
Oct. 17—Ricardo Poncini, Gral Roca .... KO 3
Nov. 21—Benicio Sosa, Gral Roca .... KO 4

JORGE GOMEZ
Argentine Lightweight
1980
Apr. 17—Julio Melone, Rio IV .... L 10
Sept. 6—Mario Vizcaya, Rio IV .... L 10

JOSE A. GOMEZ
Argentine Flyweight
1980
June 19—Armando Romero, Salta .... D 6
July 11—Ramon Galarce, Ros Frontera .... L 6
Aug. 1—Ramon Galarce, Tucuman .... D 6
Sept. 26—Juan Godoy, Salta .... L 6
Oct. 10—Humberto Torres, Salta .... L 6
Dec. 19—Froilan Nieva, San Pedro .... D 8

JULIO GOMEZ
Los Angeles, Calif. Welterweight
1974
Mar. 7—Jose Martin Flores, Los Angeles .... D 6
Apr. 15—Kevin Morgan, Sacramento .... KO 2
Oct. 18—Johnny Montagne, San Diego .... W 6
Oct. 31—Jose Duarte, Los Angeles .... W 6
Nov. 15—James Jackson, San Diego .... KO 3
Nov. 21—Jose Duarte, Los Angeles .... W 6
Dec. 11—David Arrellano, Las Vegas............. W 10
1975
Jan. 15—Chu Chu Garcia, Las Vegas .... D 10
Apr. 5—Julio Medina, Santiago .... KO 3
May 23—Ricardo Molina, Santiago .... W 10
June 27—Manuel Lira, Santiago............... KO 5
Aug. 8—Ricardo Molina, Santiago............. W 11
Sept. 5—Eduardo de la Cruz, Santiago .... KO 1
Oct. 31—Francisco Lopez, Santiago............. W 10
Dec. 12—Julio Medina, Valparaiso .... W 10
1976
Mar. 31—Larry Bonds, Las Vegas .... L 10
May 8—Rogelio Castaneda, Los Angeles......... L 10
Oct. 29—Andy Price, Los Angeles .... W 10
Dec. 7—Pete Ranzany, Sacramento .... TL 7
1977
Mar. 11—Pete Ranzany, Sacramento .... L 12
Apr. 29—Mike Avans, San Diego .... W 10
June 2—Kevin Morgan, Las Vegas .... KO 4
July 25—Mario Mendez, Las Vegas .... KO 5
Oct. 19—Bruce Curry, Stockton .... KO by 3

102

Dec. 2—Antonio Leyva, San Diego .... KO 3
1978
Jan. 14—Jose Figueroa, Mexico City .... KO by 1
Mar. 18—Andy Price, Los Angeles .... KO by 2
1979
Nov. 21—J. J.Cottrell, Las Vegas .... KO 4
1980
Jan. 9—Daryl Penn, Las Vegas .... KO by 7

PABLO GOMEZ
Los Angeles, Calif. Junior Welterweight
1980
Jan. 24—Frank Alvarado, Los Angeles .... L 6
Feb. 5—Ricky Wynn, Sacramento .... KO by 5
Mar. 13—Bobby Krueger, Las Vegas .... KO by 2
Apr. 10—Ramon Sanchez, Los Angeles .... W 4
Apr. 21—Phillip Montellano, Bakersfield ...... KO by 2
June 4—Pedro Tarango, Las Vegas .... KO 3
June 25—Lou Daniels, Las Vegas .... KO 4
July 8—Lito Pena, Honolulu .... L 10
Aug. 1—Pat Jefferson, Las Vegas .... L 8
Aug. 9—Lenny Hahn, Spokane .... KO by 6
Sept. 24—Lenny Hahn, Boise .... D 10
Nov. 12—Lou Celedon, Las Vegas .... KO by 6
Dec. 12—Jeff McCracken, Sacramento .... KO by 2

RAUL GOMEZ
Argentine Junior Welterweight
1980
Feb. 7—Angel Olea, Belle Ville .... D 10
Mar. 7—Roberto Petrizani, Villa Maria .... L 8

WALTER GOMEZ
Argentine Junior Middleweight
1980
Feb. 1—Victor Milo, Santa Rosa .... KO 3
Feb. 29—Patricio Diaz, Mar del Plata .... L 10
May 16—Carlos Peralta, Santa Rosa .... KO 8
(Won Vacant Argentine Junior Middleweight Title)
Aug. 15—Joao Tabares, San Nicolas .... KO 4
(Won Vacant South American Junior Middleweight Title)
Oct. 11—Patricio Diaz, Buenos Aires .... TW 6
(Retained Argentine Junior Middleweight Title)
Dec. 19—Nelson Torres, Venado Tuerto .... D 12
(Retained South American Junior Middleweight Title)

JOE GONSALVES
Middleweight
1979
July 7—David Love, San Diego .... L 10
1980
Apr. 26—Mike Clark, Carson City .... L 10

ALONZO GONZALES
Los Angeles, Calif. Flyweight
1978
Feb. 9—Francisco Rodriguez, Los Angeles .... KO 2
Feb. 24—Jorge Ayala, Bakersfield .... W 6
Apr. 24—Augustin Sanchez, Bakersfield .... W 6
May 19—Armando Ugalde, Bakersfield .... L 6
June 15—Eleazar Soto Ramos, Los Angeles ...... KO 3
July 5—Augustin Sanchez, Las Vegas .... W 10
July 26—Jorge Ayala, Las Vegas .... W 10
Oct. 4—Fernando Hernandez, Las Vegas .... TD 3
Nov. 15—Candy Iglecias, Las Vegas .... L 10
1979
May 31—Jose Gonzales, Los Angeles .... KO by 1
June 18—Augustin Sanchez, Los Angeles .... KO 9
Aug. 10—Mario Chavez, Bakersfield .... KO by 2
1980
Mar. 3—Rafael Capristro, Bakersfield .... L 6
Oct. 7—Cristobal Gutierrez, Bakersfield .... KO 6
Oct. 28—Evaristo Morales, Bakersfield .... KO 6

VICTOR GONZALES
Texas Flyweight
1979
Nov. 6—Armando Loredo, Corpus Christi .... L 6
1980
Feb. 5—Simon Torres, Houston .... KO by 3
May 20—Jose Perez, San Antonio .... KO by 4
Sept. 30—Eulilio Anguino, Houston .... KO 3
Oct. 24—Arturo Pedroza, Dallas .... KO by 2
Dec. 5—Adam Franco,Corpus Christi .... KO by 3

ALFREDO GONZALEZ
Argentine Welterweight
1980
July 11—Hugo Vicente, Tucuman .... KO by 1
Aug. 22—Jose Comolli, Tucuman .... W 6

EDWARD (EDDIE) GONZALEZ
Houston, Texas Light Heavyweight
1978
Apr. 20—Frank Allarate, Houston .... W 4
May 16—Bruce Kaposta, Houston .... KO 1
July 18—Barry Smith, Houston .... W 4
Aug. 8—Oscar Balderas, Houston .... KO 6
Aug. 15—James Kelly, Houston .... KO 2
1979
Jan. 16—Antonio Adame, Houston .... KO 3
Feb. 6—Sterling Benjamin, Orlando .... KO 1
Mar. 20—Milton Jarrels, Houston .... W 6
June 12—Grover Robinson, Beaumont .... KO by 5
Dec. 11—Donnie Melancon, Houston .... KO 3
1980
Jan. 9—Stan Scott, Holland, Mich. .... W 8
Mar. 18—Adolfo Rivas, Houston .... KO 3
Apr. 29—Charlie Smith, Houston .... KO 7
June 17—Juan de la Garza, Houston .... KO 2
July 15—Ramon Yera, Beaumont .... KO 1
July 22—Gary Bradshaw, Houston .... KO 7
July 29—Larry Strogen, Houston .... W 8

ERNESTO GONZALEZ
Durando, Mexico Featherweight
1976
Nov. 30—Otto Breeding, Indianapolis .... L 4
1977
May 23—Octavio Amparan, Chicago .... KO by 8
Aug. 19—Rodriguez, Chicago .... W 6
1978
Mar. 16—Forrest Winchester, Kalamazoo ...... KO by 3
June 2—Wardell Williams, Kansas City .... L 4
July 21—Chuck Spicer, Chicago .... KO 3
Dec. 2—Tom Crowley, Aurora .... L 6
1979
Mar. 24—Edwin Alarcon, Chicago .... W 10
May 5—Jose Figueroa, Chicago .... D 10
Aug. 4—Jesus Caicedo, Chicago .... KO by 3
1980
Aug. 22—Curtis Hampton, Chicago .... L 8

HOMERO GONZALEZ
Mexican Junior Featherweight
1979
Dec. 11—Felipe Avila, Corpus Christi .... KO 2
1980
May. 20—Alberto Favella, San Antonio .... KO by 2
July 15—Roberto Sandoval, Laredo .... KO 1
July 28—Adam Franco, Corpus Christi .... L 6
Sept. 1—Juan Bernal, Laredo .... L 6
Oct. 14—Refugio Rodriguez, Laredo .... KO by 1

JOSE GONZALEZ
San Diego, Calif. Junior Welterweight
1979
Feb. 13—Tony Chiaverini, Kansas City .... L 10
Apr. 21—Hedgemon Robertson, Las Vegas ..... KO by 4
May 25—Gary Stewart, San Diego .... KO 4
May 31—Alfredo Gonzalez, Los Angeles .... KO by 1
Aug. 10—Robert Turner, San Diego .... KO by 6
Oct. 19—Roberto Rodriguez, San Diego .... L 6
Nov. 2—Spud Murphy, San Diego .... TD
1980
Nov. 2—Spud Murphy, San Diego .... TD 2

JOSE (SPEEDY) GONZALEZ
Allentown, Pa. Lightweight
1975
June 3—Eladio Leal, Miami Beach .... W 6
July 8—Henry Thomas, Miami Beach .... W 6
July 22—Rafael Nicasio, Miami Beach .... W 6
Sept. 16—Leo Lopez, Philadelphia .... KO 6
Nov. 25—Juan Hidalgo, Miami Beach .... L 10
1976
Jan. 20—Pedro Diaz, Miami Beach .... W 10
June 5—Benjamin Ortiz, Caugas .... L 10
Oct. 7—Kerry Graham, Allentown .... W 4
Dec. 28—Frankie Santore, Orlando .... W 8
1977
Feb. 16—Maurice (Termite) Watkins, Orlando ...... L 10
Mar. 11—Manuel Lujan, San Diego .... W 10
Apr. 15—Jose Fernandez, New York .... L 10
1978
(Inactive)
1979
Jan. 25—Hilmer Kenty, Detroit .... KO by 7
May 12—Ernest Bing, Atlantic City .... L 8
May 25—Nick Furlano, Montreal .... L 8
Sept. 12—Billy Costello, White Plains .... KO by 3
Nov. 3—Cornelius Boza Edwards, Glasgow ... KO by 0
Nov. 21—Charlie (Choo Choo) Brown, Allentown ... W 6

103

1980

Jan.	30—Mike Frazier, Allentown	W 8
Mar.	22—Michael Ross, Allentown	D 6
Apr.	11—John Verderosa, Staten Island	L 8
June	27—Arcadio Suarez, New York	L 10
Sept.	18—Jerome Artis, Philadelphia	L 12
Oct.	18—Quenton Blackman, Philadelphia	W 6

MANUEL GONZALEZ
Argentine Junior Middleweight
Born: March 15, 1953 Rodeo del Medio (Mendoza)

1973

	—Juan Galletari, Tunuyan	KO 3
Nov.	16—Alberto H. Maldonado, Tunuyan	W 6

1974

Feb.	1—Hugo Ibarra, Mendoza	W 8
Mar.	7—Juan Galletari, Mendoza	TKO 2
Apr.	19—Francisco Fernandez, Mendoza	W disq. 7
May	31—Ramon Pereyra, Mendoza	KO 4
July	12—Juan D. Alvarez, Rio Gallegos	W 3
Aug.	23—Alfredo Cicopiedi, Mendoza	W 10
Oct.	5—Armando Vicente, Buenos Aires	W 10
Oct.	25—Hugo Obregon, Mendoza	W 10
Dec.	13—Pedro Bazan, Mendoza	D 10

1975

Jan.	23—Rogelio Zarza, Mendoza	W 10
May	30—Pedro Acuna, Mendoza	KO 2
Aug.	9—Alfredo Cicopiedi, Mendoza	W 10
Sept.	5—Pedro Bazan, Mendoza	W 10
Sept.	19—Mario Delgado, San Luis	W 10
Nov.	21—Alberto Almiron, Mendoza	TKO 7
Dec.	23—Juan Garcia, Mendoza	W 10

1976

Feb.	17—Jacinto Fernandez, Salta	W 10
Mar.	5—Alejandro Garrido, Mendoza	TKO 5
Apr.	14—Hugo Obregon, Buenos Aires	W 10
May	7—Esteban Osuna, Mendoza	W 10
June	15—Roque Roldan, Salta	W 10
July	2—Rudecindo Chavez, Mendoza	TKO 5
Aug.	13—Juan Garcia, Salta	TKO 2
Sept.	10—Roque Roldan, Mendoza	TKO 7
Oct.	23—Esteban Osuna, Buenos Aires	W 12
	(Won Argentine Junior Middleweight Title)	
Nov.	12—Alberto Almiron, Reconquista	W 10

1977

Feb.	16—Hugo Saavedra, Mendoza	W 10
Mar.	2—Porcel de Peralta, Buenos Aires	D 10
May	20—Roque Roldan, Tucuma	W 10
June	15—Raul A. Paez, Carlos Paz	KO 5
July	7—Rogelio Zarza, La Rioja	W 10
Aug.	12—Jose A. Vega, Mendoza	KO 3
Sept.	24—Esteban Osuna, Buenos Aires	W 12
	(Retained Argentine Title)	
Oct.	22—Rogelio Zarza, Carlos Paz	W 10
Dec.	9—Esteban Osuna, La Rioja	W 10

1978

Mar.	3—Ramon Perez, Cordoba	W 10
Apr.	1—Roque Roldan, Buenos Aires	W 10
May	6—Rogelio Zarza, Villa Maria	W 10
May	24—Joao Mendonca, San Pablo	W 12
	(Won South American Title)	
July	7—Alfredo Cruz, Mendoza	D 10
Sept.	16—Manuel Gonzalez II, Buenos Aires	W 10
Nov.	25—R. Porcel Peralta, Buenos Aires	W 12
	(Retained Junior Middleweight Title)	
Dec.	15—Crispin de Oliveira, Mendoza	KO 9

1979

Jan.	26—Jose Vega, Buenos Aires	D 10
Mar.	14—Masashi Kudo, Tokyo	L 15
	(For WBA Junior Middleweight Title)	
June	20—Masashi Kudo Yokkaichi	KO by 12
	(For WBA Junior Middleweight Title)	

1980

Mar.	7—Enrique Contreres, Rosario	D 12
June	13—Julio Arancibia, Rosario	L 10
Aug.	15—Luis Peralta, Santa Fe	L 10
Sept.	12—Jorge Morello, Rosario	W 10
Oct.	17—Enrique Contreras, Rosario	L 12
Dec.	26—Alfredo Lucero, Salta	KO by 2

MIGUEL A. GONZALEZ
Argentine Lightweight

1980

Mar.	8—Ramon M. Gonzalez, Bahia Blanca	W 10
Apr.	5—Juan Zuniga, Bahia Blanca	L 10
Nov.	7—Angel Olea, Cutral	W 10
Dec.	5—Juan Namuncura, Cutralco	W 10

MIKE (NINO) GONZALEZ
Bayonne, N.J. Junior Middleweight

1978

May	2—Enrique Rosa, Totowa	W 4
June	13—Jesse Rogers, Totowa	W 6

June	29—Jose Matos, North Bergen	W 4
Aug.	2—Keith York, Bayonne	KO 1
Sept.	26—Red Davis, Totowa	W 6
Nov.	16—Donnell McCrea, North Bergen	W 6

1979

Jan.	27—Donnell McCrea, Jersey City	KO 5
Mar.	13—Irving Booth, Totowa	KO 1
Apr.	17—Joe Grier, Totowa	KO 5
Aug.	1—Justice Ortiz, Secaucus	KO 6
Sept.	18—Rusty Rosenberger, E. Rutherford	W 10
Oct.	30—Tommy Sacco, Totowa	KO 2

1980

Jan.	8—Mike Michaud, Totowa	KO 7
Feb.	24—Steve Delgado, Las Vegas	L 10
Apr.	1—Bruce Strauss, Totowa	KO 8
Apr.	24—Ray (Poppy) Davis, Totowa	KO 6
May	22—Giovanni Bovenzi, Totowa	W 10
June	28—Costello King, San Juan	W 10
July	16—Winston Noel, Elizabeth	KO 2
Aug.	21—Skipper Jones, Totowa	W 10
Oct.	4—Earl Liburd, McAfee	W 10
Nov.	25—Luis Resto, New York	KO 9

OMAR GONZALEZ
Argentine Lightweight

1980

June	13—Alberto Castillo, Rio III	L 10
July	18—Marcelo Miranda, San Ped. Jujuy	D 10
Sept.	6—Alberto Castillo, Rio III	D 10

RAMON GONZALEZ
Texas Junior Welterweight

1979

Aug.	24—Kenneth Sheppard, McAllen	W 6

1980

Feb.	28—Silvario Martinez, McAllen	W 8
Apr.	6—Julio Mendez, Houston	W 10
Dec.	2—Rene Pagan, Houston	L 8

RAUL GONZALEZ
Argentine Lightweight

1980

Feb.	8—Jesus Romero, San Pedro	L 6
Apr.	18—Raul Fernandez, Gualeguaychu	KO by 6
June	13—Hugo Hernandez, Bariloche	KO by 1

RAUL GONZALEZ
Venezuelan Bantamweight

1980

Apr.	14—Mario Colon, Caracas	KO 2
May	19—Santiago Perez, Caracas	KO 2
June	16—Fernando Bustos, Caracas	KO 3
Aug.	18—Johnny Jackson, Caracas	KO 3

RAY GONZALEZ
Puerto Rican Junior Welterweight

1980

Mar.	31—Albert Sevilla, San Juan	KO 1
Apr.	21—Angel Hernandez, San Juan	D 4
Sept.	20—Davey Armstrong, San Juan	KO by 4

RICHARD GONZALEZ
Florida Junior Welterweight

1977

Feb.	16—John Morgan, Orlando	KO 2
May	17—John Morgan, Orlando	KO 2
Oct.	29—Lloyd Harvey, Homestead	W 6

1978

Feb.	21—Dennis Green, Hollywood	KO 2
Mar.	28—Calvin Washington, Orlando	KO 5
Apr.	11—Richie Lee Roberts, Miami Beach	D 4
Dec.	5—Leon Williams, Miami Beach	W 4

1979

Apr.	10—Doreen Lisborne, Miami Beach	KO 2
May	20—Maurice Quillens, Baton Rouge	KO by 3
Nov.	27—Leon Williams, Miami Beach	KO 4
Dec.	18—Richie Lee Roberts, Miami Beach	D 6

1980

Jan.	29—Clauzell Longmire, Miami	L 4

RODOLFO (GATO) GONZALEZ
Mexican Lightweight

1978

Oct.	21—Manuel Ferrer, Mexico City	KO 5
Dec.	23—Jose Tolosa, Mazatlan	KO 4

1979

Feb.	10—Juan Hernandez, Merida	KO 4
Mar.	16—Chucho Saucedo, Mazatlan	KO 4
May	26—Guadalupe Perez, Merida	KO 6
July	7—Rafael Rojas, Mazatlan	KO 3
July	22—Jose Luis Escalante, San Luis Potosi	KO 4
Aug.	25—Juan Elizondo, Tijuana	KO 6

Oct.	6—Humberto Caicedo, McAllen	KO 1
Nov.	10—Salvador Torres, Guadalajara	KO 1
Dec.	8—Curtis Ramsey, Los Angeles	KO 3
1980		
Feb.	16—Alfredo Pitalua, Estado de Mexico	KO 10
Apr.	2—Nacho Jiminez, Los Angeles	KO 3
July	3—Modesto Concepcion, Los Angeles	KO 2
July	26—Herman Montes, Los Angeles	TD 3

ZEFERINO (SPEEDY) GONZALEZ
Los Angeles, Calif. Junior Middleweight
1975

June	21—Carmelo Cruz, Los Angeles	W 4
Aug.	2—Derold Garbutt, Los Angeles	KO 4
Aug.	23—Juan Morales, Los Angeles	KO 2
1976		
Feb.	25—Francisco Ortega, Los Angeles	KO 2
Mar.	11—Gil Pedroza, Los Angeles	W 6
Apr.	1—Eugene Baldwin, Los Angeles	KO 3
Apr.	15—Lupe Hernandez, Los Angeles	KO 1
June	10—Freddie Washington, Los Angeles	D 7
July	29—Bob Medina, Los Angeles	W 7
1977		
Mar.	17—Marvin Sanders, Los Angeles	W 6
Apr.	5—Marvin Sanders, San Diego	L 6
May	25—Jimmy Owens, Las Vegas	W 10
June	29—David Oropeza, Las Vegas	W 10
Nov.	9—Rocky Mosley, Las Vegas	L 10
1978		
Mar.	18—Greg Stephens, Los Angeles	W 6
May	25—Kevin Morgan, Las Vegas	W disq. 6
July	18—Rudy Barro, Pico Rivera	W 10
Aug.	31—Jimmy Jackson, Los Angeles	W 10
Sept.	26—Agapito Ramirez, Pico Rivera	W 10
Dec.	1—Antonio Adame, San Diego	W 10
1979		
Apr.	10—Jose Luis Baltazar, Houston	W 10
Sept.	28—Roberto Duran, Las Vegas	L 10
Nov.	27—Jose Figueroa, Los Angeles	W 10
1980		
Apr.	25—Pablo Baez, Los Angeles	KO by 6

LARRY GOODMAN
El Paso, Texas Middleweight
1980

May	9—Phillip Reed, El Paso	KO 2
Sept.	11—Larry Meyers, El Paso	KO 6

DANA GOODSON
Hawaiian Heavyweight
1978

Feb.	28—Sam N'Gata, Honolulu	W 5
Mar.	28—Sam N'Gata, Honolulu	W 5
1979		
Mar.	6—Fetulima Nuuvali, Honolulu	KO 2
July	31—Abdullah Muhammad, Honolulu	W 6
1980		
Feb.	19—Sefalu Togafau, Honolulu	NC 2

MICKEY GOODWIN
Detroit, Mich. Middleweight
1977

Nov.	25—Willie Williams, Detroit	KO 1
Dec.	7—Jessie Willis, Mt. Clemens	KO 1
Dec.	16—Warren Costen, Detroit	KO 1
1978		
Jan.	29—Danny Norwood, Knoxville	KO 1
Feb.	10—Eddie Phillips, Detroit	W 6
Feb.	17—Robert Armstrong, Saginaw	KO 1
May	8—Sonny Floyd, Detroit	W 10
June	8—Sonny Floyd, Detroit	W 6
July	20—Robert Thomas, Detroit	KO 1
Aug.	3—Gary Bailey, Detroit	KO 2
Sept.	7—Moses Robinson, Detroit	KO 1
Oct.	26—Don Cobbs, Detroit	W 10
Dec.	9—Johnny Wise, Detroit	KO 2
1979		
Jan.	25—Al Campbell, Detroit	KO 1
Jan.	31—Sam Blyth, Saginaw	KO 5
Feb.	13—Gus Vasquez, Phoenix	KO 1
Mar.	27—Percy Hairston, Detroit	KO 1
May	8—Jimmy Claar, Detroit	KO 2
May	20—Ted Sanders, Las Vegas	L 10
Aug.	23—Willie Warren, Detroit	W 10
Nov.	1—Willie Warren, Detroit	W 10
1980		
Feb.	7—Fermin Guzman, Wyandotte	W 10
Mar.	2—Leo Saenz, Detroit	KO 1
Sept.	30—Lester Davis, Niles	KO 1
Nov.	8—Herman Barrientes, Detroit	KO 3

DALE GORDON
West Virginia Welterweight
1978

Sept.	19—Geraldo Weaver, Pittsburgh	L 4
Nov.	3—David Braxton, Detroit	KO by 5
Nov.	29—Larry Morgan, Richfield	L 4
1979		
Feb.	7—Chris Carney, Richfield	L 4
Feb.	9—Ron Florey, Mt. Clemens	L 6
Apr.	6—Warren Fortune, Washington	L 6
Apr.	10—Clyde Mudgett, Beaumont	KO 9
Apr.	13—Mike Blunt, Cincinnati	KO by 1
May	16—Larry Stover, Clarksburg	KO 1
May	23—Leon Garner, New Kensington	L 4
Sept.	8—Rick Patterson, Kingsport	L 6
Sept.	22—Hilbert Stevenson, Kingsport	L 6
Dec.	12—Bobby Plegge, Canton	L 6
1980		
Jan.	15—Ray Mancini, Youngstown	KO by 1
Feb.	9—Manning Galloway, Clarksburg	L 6
Aug.	20—John Myers, Las Vegas	L 6
Sept.	9—John Myers, Warren	L 6
Sept.	30—Harry Arroyo, Niles	KO by 4
Dec.	9—Brian Brunette, Warren	L 4
Dec.	17—Spencer Wilson, Youngstown	KO 1

EUGENE GORDON
Honolulu, Hawaii Heavyweight
1979

Sept.	1—Curtis Azevedo, Hilo	L 4
1980		
Feb.	19—Moses Halafuka, Honolulu	L 3
Mar.	4—Carl Poff, Honolulu	L 3

OTIS GORDON
Houston, Texas Light Heavyweight
1975

Aug.	26—Jimmy Smith, Albany	KO by 4
Sept.	12—Eddie Davis, Commack	KO by 2
Dec.	17—John O'Donoghue, New York	KO 1
1976		
Jan.	24—John Capobianco, New York	KO by 5
Mar.	17—Bob Stewart, Albany	KO by 4
June	24—Peachy Davis, Wallingford	KO 2
June	28—Eddie Gregory, New York	KO by 4
July	29—Johnny Wilburn, Baltimore	KO by 4
Sept.	28—Kevin Smith, New York	KO 1
Oct.	29—David Conteh, Latham	KO by 5
Dec.	2—John Capobianco, New York	KO 8
1977		
Jan.	21—Leo Rogers, New York	L 10
Mar.	12—Matt Ross, Fitchburg	KO by 5
June	9—Kevin Smith, North Bergen	KO by 3
June	18—John Capobianco, Commack	KO by 4
1978		
Mar.	20—Matt Ross, Boston	KO 5
Apr.	29—Matt Ross, Lowell	KO by 4
June	20—Eddie Mitchell, Houston	KO 2
Oct.	14—Donnie Melancon, Houston	KO 1
Dec.	9—Jesse Joyner, Houston	KO 1
1979		
Feb.	13—Don Melancon, Houston	KO 1
Apr.	10—Clyde Mudgett, Beaumont	KO 9
June	12—Manuel Elizondo, Beaumont	KO 4
Nov.	13—David Cabrera, Houston	KO 1
1980		
Jan.	22—Carl Ivy, Houston	KO 4

S. T. GORDON
Los Angeles, Calif. Light Heavyweight
1977

Feb.	23—Alvaro Lopez, Las Vegas	L 5
Mar.	23—Abelardo Meraz, Las Vegas	KO 1
Apr.	20—Richard Dean, Las Vegas	KO 1
June	15—Howard Snyder, Las Vegas	KO
July	28—Mike Creel, Tucson	L 5
1978		
Jan.	17—Vaiao Suafoa, Las Vegas	KO 5
Mar.	17—Gerry Cooney, Las Vegas	L disq. 4
Aug.	29—Eddie Lopez, Pico Rivera	L 10
Oct.	18—Earl Tripp, Las Vegas	L 10
Nov.	11—Young Sanford, Salt Lake City	KO 5
1979		
Feb.	23—Alvaro Lopez, Las Vegas	L 5
Mar.	23—Abelardo Meraz, Las Vegas	KO 1
Apr.	20—Richard Dean, Las Vegas	KO 1
June	6—Earl Tripp, Las Vegas	KO 7
June	15—Howard Snyder, Las Vegas	KO 1
July	28—Mike Creel, Tucson	L 4
Nov.	9—David Ocha, Las Vegas	KO 1
1980		
Mar.	15—Eric Sedillo, Ogden	KO 5
May	24—Niva Tofaeono, Santa Monica	KO 2

Aug.	6—Ivy Brown, Santa Monica	KO 2
Oct.	22—Earl Tripp, Santa Monica	KO 4

RAUL GOROSITO
Argentine Heavyweight
1971 N.Y. Golden Gloves Champion
1971

Apr.	19—Edmundo Stewart, New York	KO 4
May	13—Randy Neumann, North Bergen	L 8
May	26—Ned Edwards, New York	KO 4
July	16—Nasper Evans, New York	KO 4
Sept.	23—Richard Pittman, Paterson	KO 3
Oct.	21—Paul Simonetti, Paterson	W 8
Nov.	17—Randy Neumann, New York	L 10

1972

Feb.	11—Marc Hans, New York	KO 2
Nov.	14—Carl Baker, San Juan	W 8
Dec.	26—Johnny Hudgins, Miami Beach	W 10

1973

Feb.	16—Russ Baker, San Juan	W 10
Mar.	6—Jimmy Summerville, Miami Beach	D 8
Mar.	13—Les Stevens, London	L 8
June	18—Rodney Bobick, New York	W 10
Aug.	21—Oliver Wright, Miami Beach	KO 1
Sept.	25—Oliver Wright, Miami Beach	L 10
Nov.	5—Randy Neumann, New York	L 10

1974

June	17—Rodney Bobick, Minneapolis	L 10
Aug.	12—John Berry, New York	W 8
Nov.	4—Kevin Isaacs, New York	L disq. 5
Nov.	14—Howard Smith, Los Angeles	L 10

1975

Apr.	23—Duane Bobick, Bloomington	L 10
Sept.	1—Pablo Castellino, Buenos Aires	KO 1
Nov.	1—Oscar Bonavena, Buenos Aires	L 10
Dec.	12—Pablo Castellino, Mendoza	D 10

1976

Feb.	27—Antonio Musladino, Resistencia	D 10
June	10—Antonio Musladino, Bahia Blanca	W 12
	(Won Argentine Heavyweight Title)	
Sept.	16—Pablo Sarmiento, Bahia Blanca	KO 1
Oct.	1—Kallie Knoetze, Johannesburg	W disq. 8
Nov.	19—Ngozika Ekwelum, Madrid	D 8

1977

Jan.	14—Antonio Musladino, Cordoba	D 12
	(Retained Argentine Heavyweight Title)	
Mar.	4—Kallie Knoetze, Pretoria	L 10
July	13—Pablo Castellino, Villa Regina	D 12
	(Retained Argentine Heavyweight Title)	
Nov.	11—Domingo D'Elia, Resistencia	L 12

1978

May	13—John Tate, Orlando	KO by 2
July	22—Ismael Ruiz, Mexico City	W 10

1979

June	24—Luis Lopez, Panama City	L 10
Nov.	28—Gilberto Acuna, San Jose	KO by 5

1980

Mar.	28—Percell Davis, Tacoma	KO by 1

SAMMY GOSS
Trenton, N.J. Junior Lightweight
1969

Feb.	20—Henry Wickham, Portland, Me.	KO 2
Feb.	22—Jose Garcia, North Adams	KO 2
Mar.	3—Jeff Guy, Philadelphia	KO 1
Mar.	15—Kid Pitito, North Adams	KO 4
May	1—Leo Di Fiore, Portland	W 10
May	29—Leo Di Fiore, Portland, Me.	W 10
June	26—Beau Jaynes, Portland, Me.	W 10
July	11—Ivelaw Eastman, Syracuse	W 6
Sept.	24—Ken Campbell, Portland, Me.	L 10
Oct.	14—Ivelaw Eastman, Philadelphia	KO 7
Nov.	11—Billy Wade, Philadelphia	W 10
Nov.	25—Castro Ramirez, Philadelphia	KO 8
Dec.	9—Clyde Tyler, Philadelphia	KO 3

1970

Feb.	25—Ron Miller, Philadelphia	KO 5
Apr.	14—Adolfo Martis, Philadelphia	KO 5
May	4—Billy Wade, Philadelphia	KO 2
June	15—Marion Thomas, Philadelphia	W 10
July	20—Ruben DeJesus, Philadelphia	KO 5
Sept.	12—Jose Marin, Trenton	W 10
Oct.	6—Augie Pantellas, Philadelphia	W 10
Nov.	17—Ricardo Arrendondo, Philadelphia	KO by 6

1971

Feb.	9—Carlos Zayas, Philadelphia	KO 5
Mar.	29—Bill Whittenburg, Philadelphia	W 10
Apr.	21—Beau Jaynes, Philadelphia	KO 1
May	17—Lorenzo Trujillo, Philadelphia	W 10
June	22—Miguel Herrera, Philadelphia	W 10
Aug.	10—Lloyd Marshall, Philadelphia	KO 7
	(North American Featherweight Title)	
Oct.	14—Jose Lopez, Philadelphia	KO by 6

Nov.	17—Jo Jo Jackson, Scranton	KO 5

1972

Feb.	28—Felix Figueroa, Philadelphia	W 10
Apr.	18—Luis Lopez, Philadelphia	W 10
June	5—Chino Jiminez, Philadelphia	KO 9
Sept.	12—Carlos Vasquez, Philadelphia	KO 7
Oct.	25—Eluid Garves, Philadelphia	KO 8
Nov.	20—Jose Luis Lopez, Philadelphia	W 10

1973

Jan.	15—Raul Cruz, Philadelphia	KO 2
Mar.	9—Walter Seeley, New York	W 12
Apr.	17—Jorge Ramos, Philadelphia	W 10
May	7—Jose Fernandez, New York	W 10
July	7—Jose Fernandez, New York	W 12
	(American Junior Lightweight Title)	
Aug.	18—Edwin Viruet, New York	W 10

1974

Mar.	11—Clemente Mucine, Philadelphia	W 10
May	13—Tyrone Everett, Philadelphia	L 12
	(U.S. Junior Lightweight Title)	
July	15—Jose Fernandez, New York	L 10
Sept.	10—Flipper Uehara, Okinawa	D 10
Nov.	9—Happy Boy Mgxaji, East London	L 10

1975

Feb.	17—Fernando Jiminez, Philadelphia	W 10
Mar.	18—Ray Lunny, San Carlos	KO by 8
May	13—Felix Figueroa, Trenton	W 10
June	17—Ronnie McGarvey, Largo	KO by 6
Dec.	2—Jerome Artis, Philadelphia	D 10

1976

Jan.	13—Jerome Artis, Philadelphia	L 10

1977

Oct.	25—Alfonso Evans, Philadelphia	L 10

1978

Apr.	22—Michael Frazier, Trenton	W 8

1979

Jan.	30—Augie Pantellas, Upper Darby	L 10
Sept.	29—Robert Grant, Trenton	W 8
Oct.	18—Jerome Artis, Philadelphia	L 10

1980

Jan.	8—Rocky Lockridge, Totowa	KO by 5

TOM GOURLEY
Halifax, Nova Scotia Featherweight
1979

Nov.	13—Ron Nesmith, Halifax	KO 4
Feb.	13—Ray McClure, Waterville	KO 1
Mar.	26—Ed Bracetty, Waterville	KO 3
May	11—Lennie Pennock, Halifax	L 10
July	22—Eddie Kenney, Halifax	W 4
Nov.	21—Jeff Day, Moncton	W 10

JUAN GRACIANO
Mexican Lightweight
1978

July	21—Guyo Iracheta, Guadalajara	KO 5
Sept.	1—Jose L. Escalante, Guadalajara	KO 8

1979

May	4—Aurelio Muniz, Guadalajara	KO 4
Nov.	30—Juan Elizondo, Guadalajara	KO 3

1980

July	10—Norman Goins, Los Angeles	KO by 4

JIMMY GRADSON
Toronto, Canada Welterweight
1978

June	27—Lancelot Innis, Montreal	L 6
Aug.	16—Dave Vent, Toronto	KO 3
Sept.	12—Johnny Lambe, Montreal	W 6
Sept.	29—John Lambie, Hamilton	W 6
Oct.	8—Ralph Hollett, Halifax	W 6

1979

Feb.	9—Doug Demmings, Winnipeg	W 6
Mar.	13—Gerald Bouchard, Montreal	KO 7
Aug.	21—Lancelot Innis, Montreal	D 8
Oct.	2—Papo Villa, Montreal	W 8
Nov.	6—Bobby Marsh, Montreal	KO 1
Dec.	18—Joe Henry, Montreal	KO 7

1980

Jan.	21—Gary Broughton, Montreal	W 10
Feb.	12—Jim Henry, Montreal	KO 4
Mar.	11—Gerald Bouchard, Montreal	L 8
Mar.	16—Tony Falu, Miami	KO 2
May	7—Donato Paduano, Montreal	W 10

GEORGE GRAHAM
Texas Heavyweight
1980

June	17—Harold Campbell, Houston	KO 1
June	24—Willie Stoglin, Houston	KO 1
July	15—Larry Jones, Beaumont	KO 1

JERRY GRAHAM
Philadelphia, Pa. Lightweight
1976

Oct.	7—Jose Gonzalez, Allentown	L 4
Dec.	17—Micky Diflo, Philadelphia	KO 1

1977

Jan.	4—Mike Williams, Bristol	KO 3
Feb.	1—Ricky Norton, Philadelphia	W 4
Feb.	19—George McCarthy, Bristol	KO 2
Apr.	21—Barry Price, Wilmington	KO 1
June	15—Quenton Blackman, Philadelphia	W 6
Aug.	24—Eddie James, Vineland	W 4
Sept.	16—Al Hughes, Wilmington	KO 4

1978

Feb.	10—Don Wise, Philadelphia	KO 2
June	6—Jimmy Shedwick, Philadelphia	D 8
June	15—George Sydnor, Atlantic City	W 6

1979

Nov.	14—Gary Hinton, Philadelphia	L 6

1980

Jan.	30—Sam Hailstock, Allentown	KO 6
Oct.	1—John Muwanga, Oslo	KO by 8
Nov.	12—Gary Hinton, Philadelphia	L 8

RUBEN GRANDAO
Argentine Featherweight
1980

Mar.	14—Adolfo Felice, Rosario	W 10
Apr.	11—Heleno Ferreira, Rosario	D 10
Sept.	19—Cesar Villarreul, Tandil	L 12

FRANKIE GRANADOS
1980

Jan.	1—Mario Castro, Gomez Palacios	KO by 7
June	3—Jose Torres, Phoenix	L 8
June	12—Carlos Zuniga, Stockton	KO by 8
June	21—Jaime Garza, Las Vegas	KO by 1
Sept.	18—Abdul Bey, Las Vegas	KO by 7
Nov.	5—Robert Anderson, Phoenix	L 10

ROBERT (BRUCE) GRANDHAM
Houston, Texas Heavyweight
1975

July	15—Vernon Johnston, Oklahoma City	KO 3
Aug.	13—Pete Young, Kansas City	KO 5

1976

Mar.	9—Ibar Arrington, Seattle	L 10
Apr.	21—Ernie Smith, Seattle	KO 3
May	25—Jimmy Cross, Seattle	KO 2
July	24—Willie Anderson, Kalamazoo	W 8
Sept.	22—Eddie Lopez, Las Vegas	KO by 3
Nov.	20—Ernie Smith, Marshall	W 6

1977

Apr.	23—John Blaine, Kalamazoo	NC 2
Aug.	9—Derrick Simpkin, Liverpool	KO 6
Oct.	6—Franco Carmona, Liverpool	KO 4
Nov.	10—John DePledge, Liverpool	KO 2
Dec.	8—Neville Meade, Liverpool	KO by 3

1978

Mar.	31—Neville Meade, Liverpool	KO 3

1979
(Inactive)

1980

Jan.	9—Jerry McIntyre, Holland, Mich.	KO 1
May	22—Larry Beilfuss, Holland, Mich	KO 4

DALE GRANT
Santa Rosa, Calif. Light Heavyweight
1973

Oct.	13—David Arrellano, Santa Rosa	W 6
Nov.	28—Manuel Elizondo, Oakland	KO 3
Dec.	12—Charlie Austin, Seattle	W 6

1974

Mar.	7—Chuck Zellers, Reno	KO 3
Apr.	16—James Jackson, Tacoma	W 10
May	23—Pedro Barazza, Las Vegas	KO 3
July	7—Bruce Scott, Gardnerville	W 8
July	29—King George Aidoo, Las Vegas	KO by 1
Sept.	16—Karl Vinson, Stockton	W 6
Sept.	30—Hildo Silva, Las Vegas	KO by 8

1975

June	10—Karl Vinson, Sacramento	KO by 4

1976
(Inactive)

1977

Feb.	15—Marvin Camel, Seattle	D 10
Mar.	23—Al Banks, Anchorage	KO 4
Apr.	26—Mustafa El-Amin, Seattle	KO 2
May	25—Fred Wallace, Anchorage	KO 2
June	3—Richie Ortiz, Butte	W 10
June	29—Bobby Rascon, Anchorage	KO 8
Oct.	25—Al Newmann, Seattle	KO 4

1978

Jan.	26—Johnny Wilburn, Seattle	W 10
Feb.	28—Stanley Johnson, Seattle	KO 10
June	3—Johnny Townsend, Butte	KO 5
June	19—Matt Franklin, Philadelphia	KO by 5
Sept.	12—Marvin Camel, Butte	L 12

1979

Feb.	3—Donny Addison, Boston	W 10
July	27—Tommy Evans, Oakland	KO by 7
Aug.	7—Jerry Martin, Atlantic City	KO by 2

1980

Apr.	19—Jesse Burnett, Billings	KO 7

MICHAEL GRANT
Philadelphia, Pa. Middleweight
1978

Nov.	24—Robert Morris, Atlantic City	W 4

1979

Nov.	23—Mario Maldonado, Trenton	L 4
Nov.	28—J. C. Moody, W. New York, N.J.	KO by 3
Dec.	4—Tony Mesoraca, Philadelphia	KO by 2

1980

Jan.	16—Bill Tuttle, Washington, D.C.	KO by 1
Mar.	16—Ken Moody, Omaha	L 4
Apr.	24—Tommy Merola, Totowa	KO by 2
Sept.	10—Ralph Mifka, Scranton	L 8
Oct.	15—Steve Small, White Plains	KO by 4
Dec.	12—Rodney Trusel, Detroit	KO by 1

ROBERT GRANT
Paterson, N.J. Lightweight
1978

May	20—Keith Bennett, Trenton	KO 1
May	26—Terry McCoy, Lawrenceville	W 4
June	29—Steve Snow, Springfield	W 4
Nov.	2—Jose Pena, New York	L 6
Nov.	16—Jose Matos, North Bergen	W 6

1979

Feb.	23—Rocky Ortiz, Springfield	L 4
Apr.	24—Luis Davila, Hartford	KO by 7
Sept.	29—Sammy Goss, Trenton	L 8
Oct.	10—Tony Arias, White Plains	W 10

1980

Mar.	20—Gino Perez, N. Bergen	L 12
(Vacant N.J. State Lightweight Title)		

CLYDE GRAVES
Irvington, N.J. Welterweight
1979

Sept.	19—Blas Deschamp, N.Y.	KO 3

1980

May	23—Mike Duffy, New York	KO 5
Feb.	29—Mike Duffy, Brooklyn	D 4
June	27—Kevin Rooney, New York	L 6
Oct.	23—Pedro Vilella, New York	L 6

RANDY GRAVES
Pittsburgh, Pa. Middleweight
1977

Nov.	25—David Brooks, Detroit	W 4

1978

May	10—Tyrone Rackley, Salem	L 4

1979

Feb.	24—Charlie Cross, Alliance	KO 3
Apr.	19—Willie Brown, Richfield	W 4
Apr.	28—Larry Duncan, Sebring	W 6
Oct.	3—Larry Myers, Las Vegas	W 4
Oct.	17—Gary Hall, Las Vegas	KO 2
Nov.	28—Randy McGrady, Las Vegas	L 6

1980

Jan.	30—Dennis Mancino, Las Vegas	W 6
Feb.	20—Rick Noggle, Las Vegas	W 6
Aug.	27—O'Dell Hadley, Las Vegas	KO by 2

BILLY GRAY
Staten Island, N.Y. Light Heavyweight
1979

Nov.	24—Curtis Richardson, Staten Island	KO 4

1980

Dec.	12—Harold Williams, New York	KO by 4

CLYDE GRAY
Toronto, Canada Welterweight
Born: March 10, 1947
1968

Mar.	13—Mike Belski, McKeesport	KO 2
May	8—Bobby Scott, Toronto	KO 1
June	1—Primus Williams, Toronto	W 6
July	10—J. J. Phillips, Baltimore	KO 3
Aug.	21—Luc Pivin, Montreal	W 6
Sept.	17—Jason Smith, Toronto	KO 1
Oct.	16—Julie Mandell, Toronto	W 8

Nov. 12—Arnold Sparks, Toronto ....KO 7
Dec. 10—J. Phillips, Baltimore...................KO 3
1969
Jan. 14—Jerry Wells, Miami Beach...............W 6
Feb. 3—Lorenzo Harris, New York ....W 6
Apr. 21—Serge Proulx, Toronto....................W 8
May 15—Clermont Bureau, Montreal............KO 3
May 26—Al Bashir, Toronto ....KO 5
June 9—Freddie Cobb, Toronto ....KO 3
Aug. 14—Juan Ramos, Toronto ....W 8
Oct. 2—Jack Clements, Montreal ....KO 1
Nov. 4—Dave Dittmar, Toronto ....KO 7
1970
Jan. 27—Humberto Trottman, Toronto........W disq. 5
Feb. 16—Luigi Colovita, Toronto ....KO 1
Apr. 7—Nick Peoples, Toronto ....KO 5
Apr. 15—Dave Hilton, Montreal...................W 10
Apr. 27—Eddie Perkins, Chicago................L 10
Aug. 20—Eddie Wilson, Toronto ....KO 2
Oct. 15—Frank Steele, Toronto ....KO 7
Oct. 26—Benito Juarez, Toronto ....KO 5
1971
Feb. 18—Donato Paduano, Montreal..............W 12
(Canadian Welterweight Title)
Apr. 14—Don Ross, Toronto.....................KO 4
June 11—Walter Arsenault, Kitchener............KO 2
June 25—Gene Herrick, Moncton ....KO 2
Aug. 19—Vic Doucette, Toronto ....KO 2
(Canadian Welterweight Title)
Sept. 2—Ray Chavez, Montreal ....D 10
Nov. 19—Armando Muniz, Long Beach........KO by 9
1972
Jan. 28—Lonnie States, Vancouver...............KO 4
Feb. 11—Marcel Cerdan, Marseilles ....W 10
May 1—Manuel Gonzalez, Vancouver...........KO 6
Aug. 16—Ray Rose, Toronto.....................KO 8
Nov. 21—Otho Tyson, Toronto....................KO 2
Dec. 4—Pat Murphy, Halifax....................W 10
1973
Feb. 12—Eddie Blay, Toronto ....W 15
(British Empire Welterweight Title)
Mar. 10—Papo Villa, Halifax......................W 10
Apr. 11—Jimmy Hamm, Toronto ....KO 10
June 1—Tony Berrios, Halifax...................KO 6
Aug. 15—Roscoe Bell, Toronto...................KO 4
Sept. 22—Jose Napoles, Toronto..................L 15
(World Welterweight Title)
Dec. 3—Fernando Marcotte, Montreal ....KO 9
(Canadian Welterweight Title)
1974
Feb. 18—Bunny Grant, Toronto..................KO 9
(British Empire Welterweight Title)
Apr. 29—Art Kettles, Toronto....................W 10
June 17—Gil King, Toronto.......................KO 4
Aug. 14—Fate Davis, Toronto ....KO 7
1975
Feb. 8—Beau Jaynes, Toronto...................KO 7
Mar. 1—Marc Gervais, Calgary.................KO 5
(Canadian Welterweight Title)
Apr. 9—Robert Williams, Hull ....KO 3
Apr. 26—Sammy Ruckard, Toronto ....KO 3
June 28—Angel Espada, San Juan ....L 15
(WBA Vacant Welterweight Title)
Dec. 3—Lawrence Hafey, Toronto ....KO 8
(Canadian Welterweight Title)
1976
Apr. 5—Jim Henry, Toronto....................KO 3
May 10—David Oropeza, Toronto................KO 1
June 4—Gary Broughton, Halifax ....W 10
Sept. 2—Angel Robinson Garcia, Halifax.........W 10
Nov. 14—Roy Johnson, Toronto..................KO 8
Nov. 23—Kevin Odus, Halifax ....KO 5
(Commonwealth Welterweight Title)
1977
Jan. 18—Rafael Rodriguez, Montreal ....W 10
Feb. 27—Al Romano, Toronto ....W 6
Mar. 23—Guerrero Chavez, Montreal ....KO by 11
(Canadian Commonwealth Welterweight Title)
Aug. 6—Jose Cuevas, Los Angeles ....KO by 2
(WBA Welterweight Title)
—Larry Smith, Winnipeg...............KO 4
Dec. 9—Vernon Lewis, Port of Spain ....W 15
(British Commonwealth Welterweight Title)
1978
Feb. 6—Johnny Stef, Edmonton ....KO 6
Apr. 11—Alfonso Hayman, Halifax ....KO 5
June 13—Ray Chavez, Halifax....................KO 7
Aug. 19—Salaraia Ve, Halifax....................KO 8
(British Commonwealth Welterweight Title)
Dec. 2—Salaraia Ve, Lautoka....................KO 8
(British Commonwealth Welterweight Title)
1979
Jan. 11—Thomas Hearns, Detroit ....KO by 10
June 13—Pete Ranzany, sacramento ....KO by 5

Aug. 28—Chris Clarke, Halifax ....KO by 11
(Lost British Commonwealth Welterweight Title)
Nov. 13—Chris Clarke, Halifax ....KO 10
(Regained British Commonwealth Welterweight Title)
1980
May 11—Mike Herron, Halifax ....W 10
May 31—Cecil King, Lindsay ....W 10
June 20—Roger Leonard, Montreal ....L 10
Aug. 21—Allan Clarke, Halifax ....KO 10

ARSENEO GREEN
Allentown, Pa. Junior Welterweight
1977
May 26—Ernest Gladney, Allentown ....L 4
July 14—Mike Ross, Allentown ....W 4
Aug. 26—Ken Muse, Allentown ....W 4
1978
June 4—Pete O'Keefe. Allentown ....W 4
June 22—Ismael Maldonado, New York ....KO 2
Oct. 22—Wayne Dabney, Allentown ....KO 2
1979
Feb. 2—Morris Grant, Allentown ....KO 2
Mar. 17—Frank Minigan, Elmira ....W 6
May 7—Ricky Camaro, Buckingham ....L 8
Nov. 14—Victor Pappa, Philadelphia ....KO by 7
1980
Jan. 30—Maurice Young, Allentown ....KO 1
May 4—Victor Pappa, Atlantic City ....KO by 3
Sept. 10—Juan Jose Giminez, San Remo ....KO 3

DARRELL GREEN
Columbus, Ohio Welterweight
1980
Apr. 5—Larry Rushin, Louisville ....W 4
May 3—John Meyers, Canton ....L 6
May 16—Tyrone Moore, Lexington ....KO by 2

DENNIS GREEN
Miami, Fla. Junior Welterweight
1978
Feb. 21—Richard Gonzalez, Hollywood ....KO by 2
Mar. 25—Bean Chavez, Homestead ....W 4
Apr. 4—Dario DeJesus, North Miami Beach .. KO by 2
May 3—Eladio Leal, Miami Beach ....KO 3
May 16—Dario DeJesus, Miami Beach ....KO by 5
July 18—Chris Rizzo, Miami Beach ....KO by 5
Aug. 22—Chris Rizzo, Orlando ....KO by 4
Sept. 19—Kid Chocolate, Orlando ....L 4
Sept. 26—Terry Pizzaro, Miami Beach ....L 4
Oct. 9—Larry Peterson, Jacksonville ....KO by 3
1979
Mar. 16—Bobby Grady, Savannah ....KO by 1
Apr. 10—Juan Torres, Miami Beach ....L 6
Aug. 24—Johnny Torres, Sunrise ....L 4
Feb. 10—Clauzell Longmire, Miami ....KO by 2

JOHN GREEN
Richmond, Va. Heavyweight
1979
Nov. 24—Alf Coffin, Washington, D.C. ....KO by 1
1980
Nov. 1—Al Monday, Richmond ....KO 2
Dec. 20—Kid Samson, Richmond ....KO by 4

JOSE GREEN
Warminster, Pa. Junior Welterweight
1978
Feb. 17—Arcadio (Pee Wee) Suarez, Commack KO by 1
1979
Sept. 19—Garland Wright, Scranton ....KO by 3
Nov. 15—Derrick Cuttino, Dover ....L 6
1980
Jan. 24—Ernest Jackson, Upper Darby ....L 4
Apr. 10—Kevin Renshaw, Atlantic City ....KO 3
Sept. 20—Scott Wolfertz, Bensalem ....KO 5
Oct. 2—Billy Costello, Commack ....KO by 5

LEROY GREEN JR.
Kansas City, Mo. Junior Middleweight
1973
—Billy Goodwin ....KO 3
—Bobby Crawford.......................KO 4
Nov. 3—Skip Odem, Topeka ....KO 3
1974
—Joe Armour ....W 6
—P. D. Wade ....KO 4
1975
—Hector Pena ....KO 4
—Emmett Atlas.........................KO 5
1976
Feb. 19—Emmett Atlas, Kansas City ....KO 5

1977
(Inactive)
1978

Jan.	14—Johnny Heard, Kansas City	KO	7
Feb.	11—Raul Aguirre, Kansas City	W	10
Mar.	17—Toro Rivas, Kansas City	KO	1
Apr.	21—Tony Gardner, Kansas City	KO	1
May	13—C. J. Brown, Kansas City	W	10
Dec.	11—Pancho Rios, Topeka	KO	2

1979

Nov.	27—Willie Warren, Kansas City	W	10

1980

May	3—Ralph Moncrief, San Carlos	L	10
Aug.	8—James Waire, Las Vegas	L	10
Oct.	31—Fulgencio Obelmejias, Rome	KO by	3

MITCHELL GREEN
Bronx, N.Y. Heavyweight
Height: 6 ft. 5 in.
Managed by Shelly Finkel and Lou Duva
1980

Nov.	8—Jerry Foley, Lake Tahoe	KO	1
Nov.	25—Johnny Pitts, Hartford	KO	3
Dec.	20—Harold Rice, Bronx	KO	5

RICHARD GREEN
Tulsa, Oklahoma Middleweight
Managed by Ed Duncan
1980

June	13—Antonio Campbell, Tulsa	KO	1
Sept.	10—Earl McFadden, Wichita	L	4

RONNIE GREEN
Philadelphia, Pa. Middleweight
1979

May	31—Rocky Lockridge, Philadelphia	KO by	1
Aug.	30—Charles Carey, Virginia Beach	L	4

1980

June	5—Gary Hinton, Atlantic City	L	8
June	28—Cornelius Boza-Edwards, Wembley	KO by	6
Sept.	11—Craig Stevens, Washington, D.C.	W	6
Oct.	30—Victor Pappa, Atlantic City	L	8

ROOSEVELT GREEN
Chicago, Ill. Middleweight
1978

Sept.	27—Imara Epesi, Chicago	W	4
Dec.	15—Chief Ketchinakow, Chicago	KO	1

1979

Feb.	2—Warren Thunder, Chicago	KO	1
Mar.	17—Lynn Lustig, Chicago	KO	1
June	11—Lee Thomas, Chicago	KO	1
July	20—John Shavers, U. of Ill.	W	6
Sept.	7—Billy Goodwin, Chicago	W	6
Dec.	15—Charles Cross, Chicago	KO	3

1980

Apr.	17—Larry Martin, Chicago	KO by	2
Aug.	23—Tony Powell, Inglewood	W	4
Aug.	25—Jimmy Flynn, Chicago	KO	3
Sept.	27—Mickey Jones, Los Angeles	W	4
Oct.	9—Santiago Valdes, Chicago	W	10
Dec.	11—Louis Mateo, Chicago	KO	7

SYLVESTER (SILVER) GREEN
San Diego, Calif. Light Heavyweight
1979

Mar.	9—Niua Tofaeono, San Diego	KO by	4

1980

Mar.	26—Ken Hodges, Costa Mesa	D	4
Apr.	21—Rafael Zamora, Bakersfield	KO	2
May	16—Scott Wilson, San Bernardino	D	4
May	30—Carlos Mura, San Bernardino	W	4
Aug.	19—Marcos Garcia, San Diego	W	5
Sept.	5—Kenny Hodges, Inglewood	KO by	3
Nov.	28—Marcos Garcia, San Diego	KO by	1

RAY GREENE
Akron, Ohio Junior Lightweight
1977

Apr.	5—Chuck Spicer, Westlake	W	4
Apr.	24—John Sparks, Portsmouth	L	6
May	7—Robert (Pee Wee) Emerson, Cincinnati	L	6
Aug.	12—Gary Smith, Barberton	KO	2
Sept.	21—Charles Buggs, Cleveland	W	4
Oct.	12—Forest Winchester, Columbus	KO by	3
Nov.	26—Rich Lane, Columbus	L	4

1978

Mar.	16—Lloyd Allen, Cleveland	KO by	5
Sept.	20—Scott Coles, Strongville	L	6
Nov.	6—Joey Mayes, Cleveland	L	6

1979
(Inactive)

1980

Apr.	5—Bobby Plegge, Akron	L	6
Sept.	18—Louis Self, Cleveland	KO by	1

MICHAEL GREER
Memphis, Tenn. Heavyweight
1980

Apr.	22—Steve Mormino, Memphis	W	4
May	13—Phillip Brown, Cape Girardeau	D	6
July	1—John Pinney, Memphis	KO	6
Sept.	9—Arthur Pruitt, Memphis	KO	6

EDDIE GREGG
Las Vegas, Nev. Heavyweight
1979

July	18—Lee Burkey, Las Vegas	KO	2
Aug.	29—Lee Holloman, Las Vegas	KO	2
Sept.	12—Lew Lockwood, Las Vegas	KO	3
Nov.	28—Danny Lee Underwood, Las Vegas	KO	1
Dec.	19—Viaio Suafoa, Las Vegas	KO	4

1980

May	25—Oliver Wright, Atlantic City	D	6

STEVE GREGORY
Columbus, Ohio Junior Middleweight
Born: January 30, 1955, Columbus, Ohio
1977

May	11—James Brown, Cleveland	KO	1
May	20—Ray Caruthers, Marion	KO	2
May	25—Birsee Ross, Cleveland	W	4
June	11—Ernie Whitt, Columbus	KO	1
July	16—Bobby Orr, Columbus	KO	3
Aug.	12—Dave Donaldson, Barberton	KO	2
Sept.	24—Shane Bosley, Columbus	KO	7
Dec.	3—Joe Blair, Beckley	KO	1
Dec.	15—Larry McCall, Hamilton	W	6

1978

Feb.	16—John Taylor, Cleveland	KO	5
Mar.	1—Jaime Thomas, Dayton	W	6
Apr.	17—Lloyd (Blue) Richardson	W	8
June	3—Sammy Floyd, Pikeville	W	8
July	18—Randy Milton, Boston	D	8
July	27—Ken Baity, Canton	KO	6
Dec.	6—Henry Hall, Miami Beach	KO	1

1979

Jan.	10—Mike Wyant, Cleveland	W	10
Feb.	19—Ron Hamilton, Ft. Lauderdale	KO	2
Mar.	5—Rene Pinder, Ft. Lauderdale	D	8
May	17—Charlie Benjamin, Columbus	KO	5
June	28—Frankie Kolovrat, Columbus	KO	2
Sept.	20—Sammy Masias, Cleveland	KO	3
Dec.	6—Ayub Kalule, Copenhagen	L	15

(For WBA Junior Middleweight Title)
1980

June	5—Eddie Bergin, Columbus	KO	1
July	24—Elisha Obed, Columbus	W	10
Sept.	12—Steve Moyer, Columbus	W	10
Nov.	25—Pat Hallacy, New York	W	10

JOHN GRIFFIN
New York, N.Y. Middleweight
1978

Dec.	1—Larry Allen, Cohoes	W	6

1979

Dec.	1—Ralph Doucette, Albany	KO	3

1980

Jan.	9—Miguel Sanchez, Hartford	KO by	1
Feb.	13—Freddie Spry, White Plains	KO by	2

LESTER GROVES
1979

Oct.	30—Jimmy Cook, Memphis	W	6

1980

Mar.	4—Russell Nations, Memphis	KO by	6
Apr.	22—Wood Pruitt, Memphis	KO	3
May	13—Bob Stevenson, Memphis	KO	3
June	28—Larry McCall, Bowling Green	KO by	5
July	11—Charlie Smith, Meridian	D	6
Sept.	6—Ken Heflin, Jenkins	L	6
Sept.	9—Bossie Jamison, Memphis	D	6
Oct.	7—Sid Taylor, St. Charles	L	6
Nov.	20—Tony Ayala, Jr., Totowa	KO by	2
Dec.	9—Gene McCombs, Birmingham	L	6

LUPE GUERRA
North Platte, Nebr. Heavyweight
1978

Mar.	23—Charles Smith, Omaha	W	4
May	1—Kent Meyer, Omaha	KO	3
July	26—Paus Tumi, Omaha	KO	2
Oct.	25—Pete Holm, Omaha	W	6
Nov.	29—Jimmy Pearish, Omaha	W	6

1979

Apr. 28—Luis Brown, Omaha	KO 5
May 11—Les Myers, Wichita	W 5
May 31—Jerry Day, Brandon	W 4
June 14—Jimmy Chycone, Winnipeg	W 4
June 25—Dan Keiser, Omaha	W 6
Aug. 2—Jim Robertson, Omaha	W 8
Aug. 18—Charles Atlas, North Platte	KO 5
Nov. 8—L. J. Harvey, Omaha	W 6

1980

Mar. 22—Jimmy Cross, N. Platte	W 10
May 17—Tom Fischer, Dayton	L 10
July 27—Jim flynn, Omaha	W 8

JULIO GUERRERO
Dominican Rep. Bantamweight
(Previous Record Unavailable)
1978

Mar. 15—Tito Roque, Santo Domingo	L 8
July 5—Juan Sierra, Santo Domingo	W 10
Aug. 28—Juan Sierra, Santo Domingo	KO 11
Oct. 16—Orlando Maldonado, Santo Domingo	L 8

1979

Jan. 14—Orlando Maldonado, San Juan	L 8

1980

June 2—Carlos Acrazal, Colon	W 10
July 12—Prudencio Cardona, Barranquilla	L 10
Sept. 16—Ismael Torres, Santo Domingo	KO 7

ALBERT GUEVARA
Mexican Junior Welterweight
1974

Mar. 19—Fidel Guzman, Sacramento	W 6

1975

Feb. 4—Nacho Jiminez, Sacramento	L 6
Oct. 14—Isidrio Salinas, Sacramento	KO 3
Nov. 11—Juan Arcos, Sacramento	W 6

1976

Feb. 24—Pete Constancio, Sacramento	D 6
Sept. 14—Dave Kibby, Sacramento	KO 4
Nov. 9—Kid Dynamita, Sacramento	KO by 2

1977

Nov. 10—Howard Jackson, Sacramento	L 6
Dec. 13—Vicente Hernandez, Sacramento	L 6

1978

Mar. 8—Abraham Perez, Las Vegas	L 8
July 13—Willie Ray, Seattle	KO 3
Aug. 9—Steve Chase, Seattle	L 6
Sept. 9—Ron Cummings, Sacramento	L 6
Dec. 14—Noe Rivera, Los Angeles	KO 2

1980

Aug. 5—Golden Thomas, Sacramento	L 6
Sept. 5—Golden Thomas, Sacramento	KO 1
Sept. 23—Mark Ibanez, Honolulu	KO by 6

JOSE L. GUEVARA
Argentine Welterweight
1980

Mar. 7—Roberto T. Ortiz, Villa Maria	KO 6
Apr. 3—Jorge Zalazar, Villa Maria	W 8
June 19—Juan Bardi, Villa Maria	W 10
July 5—Oscar L. Romero, Catrilo	L 10
Aug. 1—Romulo Ibarra, Corrientes	L 10
Oct. 3—Manuel Alvarez, Tucuman	L 10
Nov. 1—Oscar Romero, Santa Rosa	L 10

RODOLFO GUEVERRA
San Antonio, Texas Junior Welterweight
1980

Jan. 9—Juan Venegas, Beaumont	KO by 5
July 15—Abel Herrera, San Antonio	L 6
Aug. 12—Erasmo Gonzalez, San Antonio	KO by 3

GARY GUIDEN
Muncie, Ind. Middleweight
Born: August 24, 1955, Muncie, Indiana
1975

Apr. 17—Candy Smith, Indianapolis	KO 2
May 10—Ernie (Bubba) Davies, Toledo	L 4
May 22—Cisco (Kid) Oliver, Cincinnati	KO 1
June 6—Donald Webster, Indianapolis	KO 1
June 20—Bobby Crawford, Dayton	KO 1
July 16—Rory O'Shea, St. Paul	W 6
Aug. 5—Al (Fire Brand) Clay, Chicago	KO 6
Sept. 6—Mike Wyant, Hamilton	KO 5
Sept. 24—Robert Strong, Indianapolis	W 6
Oct. 4—Baby Ray Smith, Chicago	KO 2
Nov. 13—Sammy Floyd, Indianapolis	KO 4

1976

Feb. 28—Tommy Ellis, Muncie	KO 2
Mar. 20—Alfonso Aguirre, Indianapolis	KO 2
Apr. 23—Auadis Kassibian, Flint	KO 2
May 6—Don Meloncon, Indianapolis	KO by 2

1976

May 25—Leon Futch, Orlando	KO 2
Oct. 6—Henry Gregory, Kansas City	KO 5
Nov. 24—Ron West, Cleveland	W 6

1977

Feb. 1—Sammy NeSmith, Indianapolis	KO 3
Mar. 18—Nick Ortiz, Kansas City	KO 7
July 27—Joey Blair, Cleveland	KO 2
Sept. 6—Dick McIntosh, Orlando	KO 2

1978

Jan. 14—Angel Espada, Kansas City	KO 2
Apr. 6—Gary Broughton, Cleveland	KO 7
June 3—Rodney Cupe, Muncie	KO 2
July 19—Lloyd Richardson, Dayton	KO 3
Oct. 10—Lonnie Washington, Indianapolis	KO 3
Nov. 11—Sammy (King) Floyd, Beaver Dam, Ky.	KO 7
Dec. 13—Erwin Williams, Oakland	KO 9

1979

Feb. 17—Raul Aguirre, Indianapolis	W 10
June 2—Tap Tap Makathini, Mmabatho	KO by 4
Sept. 20—Jerome Jackson, Indianapolis	L 10
Nov. 14—Curtis Parker, Philadelphia	KO by 5

1980

Mar. 17—Joe Barrientes, Indianapolis	KO 3
May 13—Roy Dale, Indianapolis	KO 6

RAUL GUILLERMO
Argentine Junior Middleweight
1980

Apr. 12—Bernardo Narvaez, Condordia	D 10
May 17—Oscar Ayala, Rio Negro	L 10
Sept. 19—Eduardo Contreras, Rosario	L 10
Oct. 17—Carlos Nacimento, Posadas	L 10

MARIO GUILLOTTI
Argentine Welterweight
Born: August 28, 1939
1969

Mar. 21—Avelino Alegre, Junin	KO 5
July 11—Miguel Bravo, Junin	KO 7
Aug. 13—Ricardo Veron, Buenos Aires	W 10
Aug. 29—Antonio Vargas, Junin	KO 3
Sept. 13—Juan Garcia, Buenos Aires	KO 3
Oct. 24—Andres Martinez, Junin	KO 4
Nov. 12—Antonio Deleo, Buenos Aires	KO 6

1970

Jan. 30—Jose Cisneros, Junin	KO 6
Feb. 21—Adolfo Montenegro, Buenos Aires	W 10
Apr. 3—Ramon Oliva, Junin	W 10

1971

Feb. 11—Adolfo Montenegro, Junin	KO 1
Feb. 24—Chucho Almazan, Mar del Plata	W 10
Apr. 16—Anibal DiLella, Junin	W 10
Oct. 15—Eduardo Caballero, Junin	KO 4

1972

Jan. 8—Raul Sosa, Mar del Plata	KO 7
Feb. 11—Octavio Escauriza, Laboulaye	D 10
Apr. 22—Ramon LaCruz, Buenos Aires	W 10
June 2—Oscar Gonzalez, Laboulaye	KO 3
July 8—Horacio Saldano, Buenos Aires	W disq. 3
Dec. 8—Octavio Escauriza, Junin	KO 9

1973

May 11—Rafael Lascano, Chacabuco	KO 5
June 8—Francisco Fernandez, Junin	KO 2
Aug. 10—Martin Juarez, Junin	KO 3
Sept. 1—Miguel A. Campanino, Buenos Aires	KO by 5
Oct. 10—Hugo Espindola, Chacavbuco	KO 4

1974

Mar. 15—Miguel Priento, Junin	KO 6
Apr. 17—Juan Aranda, Buenos Aires	D 10
June 15—Miguel A. Campanino, Buenos Aires	L 10
July 12—Miguel Fernandez, Resistencia	W 10
Aug. 16—Carlos Villalba, Junin	W 10
Sept. 6—Aladino Sanbran, Junin	KO 8
Sept. 28—Horacio Saldano, Buenos Aires	D 10
Dec. 14—Arturo Zuniga, Mexico City	KO 7

1975

Jan. 18—Julio Paletta, Posadas	KO 4
Feb. 7—Miguel Fernandez, Junin	W 10
Mar. 15—Miguel A. Campanino, Buenos Aires	L disq. 1
May 9—Orlando Miranda, S. S. de Jujuy	KO 1
June 21—Miguel A. Campanino, Buenos Aires	L 12
	(For the Argentine Welterweight Title)
Oct. 11—Daniel Gonzalez, Buenos Aires	D 9
	(Medical Decision)
Nov. 22—Daniel Gonzalez, Buenos Aires	D 10
Dec. 12—Orlando Miranda, Tucuman	KO 2

(For the Argentine Welterweight Title)

May 14—Oscar Aparicio, Rome	W 8
Aug. 21—Giuseppe Minotti, Chiavari	W 8
Oct. 15—Oscar Aparicio, Milan	W 8
Nov. 12—Everaldo Azevedo, Milano	D 8

1977

Jan.	9—Everaldo Azevedo, Como	L 10
Feb.	22—David Green, London	L 10
Apr.	15—Antonio Casado, Genova	KO 7
May	7—Oscar Aparicio, Rimini	KO 2
June	18—Nelson Gomez, Rome	W 8
Oct.	22—Antonio Tosello, Turin	KO 7

1978

Apr.	22—Luis Resto, San Remo	W 8
May	25—E. Costa Azevedo	W 8
July	26—Pablo Zito, Italia	W 8
Oct.	7—Horacio Saldano, Buenos Aires	D 10
Nov.	18—Horacio Saldano, Buenos Aires	D 10
Dec.	8—Hector Caooros, Junin	W 10

1979

	—Hector Caceres, Junin	W 10
	—Horacio Saldano, Buenos Aires	D 10

1980

Apr.	11—Jorge Tito Yanni, Buenos Aires	KO 12
	(Won Argentine Welterweight Title)	
June	13—Nelson Torres, Junin	KO 5
July	11—Pablo Ferreyra, Chacabuco	W 10
Sept.	26—Alfredo Lucero, Buenos Aires	KO by 8
Dec.	19—Hector Caceres, Zarate	W 10

FITZROY GUISSEPPI
Trinidad, B.W.I. Lightweight

1967

Dec.	12—Mervyn George, Port of Spain	D 6

1968

Mar.	29—Johnny Isaacs, Port of Spain	KO 4
July	12—Mervyn George, Port of Spain	W 6
Nov.	1—Charley James, Port of Spain	L 8

1969

Mar.	14—Charlie James, Port of Spain	L 8
May	16—Trevor Glasgow, Port of Spain	D 10
June	21—Barry Mason, Kingston	L 10
Nov.	28—Trevor Glasgow, Port of Spain	L 10

1970
(Inactive)

1971

Apr.	30—Charles James, Port of Spain	W 10
Aug.	23—Charlie James, Port of Spain	D 10

1972

Sept.	3—Fitzgerald King, Kingston	KO 7

1973

Jan.	14—Kid Tepakan, Belize	W 10
Apr.	29—Lupe Galendo, Belize	KO by 10
July	22—Chamaco Ortiz, Belize	KO 9
Sept.	2—Joe Cartwright, Belize	W 10

1974

Feb.	27—Percy Hayles, Belize	W 10
July	18—Zordo Canul, Belize City	KO 7
Aug.	18—Dinemita Delgado, Belize City	W 10

1975

Feb.	15—Julio Mendez, Mexico City	KO by 3
May	16—Monkey Gomez, Chetumal	KO 9

1976

Nov.	26—Claude Noel, Port of Spain	KO by 10

1977

May	12—Rudolph Fuentes, Belize	W 10

1978

Feb.	10—Claude Noel, Port of Spain	KO by 8
Oct.	6—Eddie Marcelle, Port of Spain	L 10

1980

Mar.	15—Ernesto Davis, Belize	L 10
Mar.	28—Michael Parsons, Port-of-Spain	L 10
	—Adolfo Sanjeado, Belize	W 10
Sept.	7—Julio Mendez, Bird's Isle	W 10

MANNY GULLATT
Carson City, Nev. Middleweight

1978

June	3—Dick Fisher, Butte	KO by 3
July	3—Abraham Schwartz, Gardnerville	KO by 3
Oct.	31—Eddie Bearden, Carson City	W 4

1979

Feb.	14—Mel McKay, Spokane	L 4
Feb.	20—Frank Duran, Seattle	KO by 1
Apr.	21—Danny Edgar, Elko	L 7
May	16—Kid Hinestroza, Carson City	KO by 2
July	3—Gary Giron, Gardnerville	KO by 3
Aug.	24—Mike Clark, Carson City	KO by 4
Oct.	4—Perry Levoe, San Carlos	KO by 4
Oct.	20—Perry Levoe, Sparks	L 4

1980

Jan.	22—Rafael Corono, Sacramento	KO by 1
Feb.	29—Perry Levoe, San Carlos	W 4
Apr.	15—Leonard Thomas, Sparks	KO by 2

NESTOR GUNDIN
Argentine Lightweight

1980

Feb.	1—Carlos Villanueva, San Pedro	D 10
Mar.	21—Faustino Barrios, Zarate	NC 1
May	30—Juan Galvez, San Nicolas	W 10
June	27—Faustino Barrios, San Nicolas	D 10
Aug.	9—Faustino Barrios, Baradero	KO by 3

CRISTOBAL GUTIERREZ
Los Angeles, Calif. Junior Featherweight

1979

Mar.	15—Desi Newbill, Los Angeles	KO by 1

1980

Mar.	7—Jose Luis Lopez, San Bernardino	KO 4
Mar.	21—Salvador Ugalde, San Bernardino	KO 3
July	16—Marcelo Camacho, Stockton	KO by 2
Oct.	7—Alonso Gonzales, Bakersfield	KO by 6

JOSE GUTIERREZ
Lorain, Ohio Light Heavyweight

1977

Apr.	27—Johnny Fields, Lorain	KO by 3
Nov.	2—Moses Robinson, Cleveland	W 6
Dec.	7—Tony Curovic, Cleveland	L 6

1978

Jan.	6—Frankie Williams, Cincinnati	KO by 3
Feb.	1—Pat Cuillo, Cleveland	KO by 4
Apr.	26—Pablos Ramos, Youngstown	KO by 5
May	23—Al Bolden, New Kensington	L 6

1979

July	30—Luke Capuano, Chicago	KO by 3
Sept.	20—Zeke Zelichowski, Detroit	L 4

1980

Apr.	5—Mike Schiebelhood, Akron	KO by 2

PEDRO ANTONIO GUTIERREZ
Argentine Junior Welterweight

1980

Apr.	19—Alberto Butiler, Buenos Aires	KO by 2
June	6—Manuel Roca, Mar del Plata	D 6
June	14—Lorenzo Garcia, Baradero	L 10
July	4—Manuel Roca, Mar del Plata	KO by 4
Sept.	6—Aniceto Caceres, Virreyes	KO by 2

PEDRO ARMANDO GUTIERREZ
Argentine Lightweight

1980

Apr.	5—Juan Carranza, Mar del Plata	KO 9
Apr.	18—Hipolito Nunez, Salta	D 10
May	16—Daniel Murua, Bolivar	KO by 9
July	18—Juan Alvarez, San Nicolas	W 10
Sept.	13—Juan Carranza, Gral Cabrera	W 10
Oct.	11—Faustino Barrios, Buenos Aires	W 10

FERMIN GUZMAN
Santo Domingo Middleweight
(Previous Record Unavailable)

1977

June	27—Jesus Castro, Santo Domingo	W 12
Aug.	29—Felix Velasquez, Santo Domingo	W 10
Oct.	3—Jesus Castro, Santo Domingo	L 12

1978

Apr.	24—Miro Campusano, Santo Domingo	KO 4
June	23—Inocencio De La Rosa, Santo Domingo	L 10
June	30—Fighting Jim, Curacao	L 10

1979

Sept.	19—Mustafa Hamsho, New York	KO by 7

1980

Oct.	2—Wilford Scypion, Commack	KO by 8
Dec.	11—Youngblood Williams, Philadelphia	L 10

JULIO GUZMAN
Puerto Rican Featherweight

1980

Feb.	4—Pablo Hernandez, San Juan	W 4
Feb.	18—Victor Santos, San Juan	W 4
Apr.	28—Angel Rivera, San Juan	KO 6
May	22—Azor Agosto, Rio Piedras	W 8
Oct.	2—Mariano Escalera, San Juan	KO 4

111

LAWRENCE HAFEY
Stellarton, Nova Scotia Welterweight
Born: New Glasgow
1967
Jan.   12—Gary McNeil, New Glasgow .... W 6
Feb.   19—Ken MacIntyre, St. Annes .... L 6
Mar.   8—Ken MacIntyre, St. Annes .... D 6
June   12—Gary McNeil, New Glasgow .... W 6
1968
May   11—Mike Supple, New Glasgow .... KO 2
May   25—Leo Noel, New Glasgow .... L 8
June   8—Lonnie States, New Glasgow .... L 6
July   12—Lonnie States, Windsor .... W 6
Aug.   3—Fernand Durelle, New Glasgow........... W 8
Oct.   5—Les Gillis, New Glasgow................. L 12
Oct.   15—Carlos Garcia, New Glasgow .... KO 5
Oct.   19—Henry Wickham, New Glasgow........... KO 5
Dec.   16—Benny Randell, New Glasgow .... W 10
1969
Jan.   30—Marcellino Alicea, Taunton .... W 8
Feb.   6—Fernandes Santiago, Taunton .... KO 6
June   21—Art Jones, New Glasgow .... W 10
Aug.   2—Fernand Durelle, New Glasgow.......... W 8
Oct.   27—Walter Arsenault, New Glasgow......... W 10
Nov.   11—Les Gillis, Glace Bay................... L 10
1970
Feb.   8—Walter Arsenault, Dartmouth........... W 10
Mar.   8—Lonnie States, Dartmouth .... W 10
May   11—Fernand Durelle, Saint John .... W 10
May   16—Dick French, New Glasgow .... KO 6
May   30—Al Ford, New Glasgow .... L 12
        (Canadian Lightweight Title)
July   18—Rocky McDougall, New Glasgow........ KO 4
Aug.   8—Art Jones, New Glasgow .... L 10
Aug.   10—Art Jones, New Glasgow .... L 10
1971
June   24—Tiger Lo, Moncton...................... KO 5
Aug.   7—Don Boutler, New Glasgow .... KO 7
Aug.   16—Fernand Marcotte, Quebec City .... L 10
1972
June   1—Ray Rose, Halifax...................... L 6
June   22—Gerald Bouchard, Halifax .... W 8
July   13—Marco Gervais, Halifax .... W 10
1973
Mar.   31—Gonzalo Rodriguez, San Diego.......... L 4
July   5—Morris Jordan, Halifax.................. W 6
July   8—Don Boulter, Badeque .... KO 2
Aug.   2—Freytes Caban, Halifax .... W 10
Sept. 30—Hank Robinson, New Glasgow.......... KO 4
Oct.   23—Marco Gervais, Halifax .... W 10
Nov.   23—Raul Sosa, Halifax .... W 10
Dec.   3—Kid Totas, Montreal .... W 10
1974
May   28—Henry Thomas, Miami Beach .... KO 5
June   10—Marco Gervais, Quebec City .... D 10
July   24—Kid Totas, Halifax .... W 10
July   30—Clyde Washington, New Orleans .... W 10
Aug.   15—Ernie Witcher, Dartmouth .... KO 4
Nov.   16—Reinaldo Olivera, Brockton .... W 10
Nov.   18—Curtis Phillips, Boston .... W 6
Dec.   2—Wilfredo Benitez, New York .... L 8
Dec.   15—Bruno Arcari, Milan .... L 10
Dec.   21—Clyde Stevens, New Glasgow .... KO 3
1975
May   3—Lou Bizzarro, Erie .... L 10
May   29—Dave Downey, Halifax.................. W 12
        (Canadian Middleweight Title)
Aug.   27—Clyde Washington, New Orleans .... KO 4
Sept.   9—Paul Osborne, Montreal .... KO 1
Dec.   1—Clyde Gray, Toronto .... KO by 8
        (Canadian Welterweight Title)
1976
Mar.   2—Fernand Marcotte, Montreal .... KO by 10
1977
Dec.   8—Johnny Stef, Halifax .... L 10
1978
June   13—Don Johnson, Halifax .... KO 6
Sept. 12—Eddie Parks, Halifax .... W 10
Oct.   8—Nelson Alphonso, Halifax .... W 10
1979
Apr.   3—Al Little, Halifax .... KO 6
May   5—Dave Green, Wembley .... KO by 1
June   5—Chris Clarke, Halifax .... L 10

1980
Mar.   11—Sean Mannion, Halifax .... L 10
May   7—Ghyslain Deroy, Montreal .... KO by 6

LENNY HAHN
Spokane, Wash. Welterweight
1978
Aug.   22—Mike Lamphere, Seattle .... KO 3
Sept. 14—Paul Jones, Portland .... KO 1
1979
Feb.   14—Ron Mendola, Spokane .... KO 2
Mar.   31—Mike Tolang, Spokane .... KO 2
July   31—Andres Obregon, Spokane .... KO 2
Oct.   3—Victor Hernandez, Spokane .... KO 3
Dec.   11—Eric Bonilla, Spokane .... W 10
1980
Mar.   18—Vicente Hernandez, Spokane .... KO 7
June   2—Len Thomas, Spokane .... KO 7
Aug.   9—Pablo Gomez, Spokane .... KO 6
Oct.   23—Rudy Barro, Spokane .... W 10

ROBERTO HAIDAR
Argentine Featherweight
1980
Jan.   11—Geronimo Luguez, Mendoza .... KO 2
Feb.   28—Hipolito Nunez, Mendoza .... L 10
Apr.   24—Marcelo Miranda, S. Sal de Jujuy .... KO by 7
June   7—Heleno Ferreira, Gral Pico .... L 10

SAM HAILSTOCK
Allentown, Pa. Welterweight
1975
Dec.   11—Earl Nelson, Allentown .... KO 1
1976
Jan.   29—Darryl Lampkin, Easton................. D 4
Mar.   8—Darryl Lampkin, Allentown .... W 4
May   12—Larry O'Donnell, Scranton .... W 4
June   30—Pee Wee Murphy, Scranton .... W 4
Aug.   26—Paul Moore, Allentown .... KO 2
Oct.   7—Kevin Moefield, Allentown............. KO 4
1977
May   9—Miguel Hernandez, Newark .... KO by 3
June   18—Luis Resto, Commack .... D 6
July   8—Benji Goldstone, Geneva .... W 6
Aug.   1—Kelly Oickle, Sydney .... L 10
Oct.   4—Chris Clarke, Halifax .... KO by 4
Dec.   1—Mike Bullock, Wharton .... W 8
1978
June   4—Bruce Thompson, Allentown .... W disq. 4
1979
Feb.   18—Angel Espada, San Juan .... KO by 9
Apr.   3—Colin Jones, Wales .... KO by 2
May   10—Roberto Gambini, Paris .... KO by 3
1980
Jan.   30—Jerry Graham, Allentown .... KO 6
Oct.   30—Mike Picciotti, Atlantic City ...... KO by 7

MOSES HALAFUKA
Honolulu, Hawaii Light Heavyweight
1979
July   27—Leo Arrington, Hilo .... KO 1
July   31—Carl Poff, Honolulu .... KO 2
Sept.   1—Fetulima Nuuvali, Hilo .... KO 2
Oct.   9—Curtis Azevedo, Honolulu .... KO by 2
1980
Feb.   19—Eugene Gordon, Honolulu .... W 3
July   8—Kenneth Oki, Honolulu .... KO 1
July   22—Calvin Mobley, Honolulu .... KO 5
Aug.   26—Glen Li, Honolulu .... KO 2
Nov.   12—Sefulu Togafau, Honolulu .... KO 3

LEROY HALEY
Las Vegas, Nev. Junior Welterweight
1973
Jan.   10—Carlos Gonzalez, Las Vegas .... W 6
May   1—Manny Casrillo, Las Vegas............. W 4
May   23—Joe Falcone, Las Vegas .... W 5
June   7—Ezra Davis, Las Vegas................. W 4
June   21—Demetrio Salazar, Las Vegas .... W 8
July   9—Bart Spencer, Las Vegas .... KO 3
Aug.   5—Moses Carbin, Las Vegas .... W 5
Aug.   27—Philipe Mendez, Las Vegas .... W 6
Sept. 14—Jose Fernandez, Las Vegas............. KO 5
Sept. 19—Victor Abraham, Las Vegas .... W 6
Oct.   3—Demetrio Salazar, Las Vegas .... KO 5
Oct.   25—Abby Espinoza, Las Vegas .... KO 5
Nov.   21—Danny Castro, Las Vegas .... W 8
Dec.   20—Carlos Barrington, Las Vegas .... KO 4
1974
Mar.   21—Earl Young, Las Vegas .... W 6
Oct.   16—Danny Stennado, Las Vegas .... KO 3
Nov.   7—Don Contro, Las Vegas .... KO 3
1975
Jan.   10—Brad Silas, Las Vegas .... KO 6

112

Feb.	8—Camel Enqui, Las Vegas	KO	2
Mar.	26—Roy Holloway, Las Vegas	W	8
May	14—Roy Holloway, Las Vegas	L	8
Aug.	27—Eddie Murry, Las Vegas	W	8
Sept.	17—Gene Prado, Las Vegas	W	10

1976

May	5—Alejo Sanchez, Las Vegas	W	8
May	12—Rafael Nunez, Las Vegas	W	8
June	2—Gene Prado, Las Vegas	W	10
June	30—Audo Love, Las Vegas	W	10
Aug.	18—Rudy Barro, Las Vegas	W	10
Sept.	8—Pete Constancia, Las Vegas	W	10
Dec.	1—Earl Young, Las Vegas	W	10

1977

Feb.	2—Augustin Estrada, Las Vegas	W	10
Apr.	6—Leonardo Bermudez, Las Vegas	D	10
May	4—Leonardo (Chino) Bermudez, Las Vegas	W	12
Oct.	19—Victor Barrata Hernandez, Las Vegas	W	10
Nov.	2—David (Little Horse) Barnel, Las Vegas	W	10

1978

Jan.	4—Hector Rivera, Las Vegas	KO	8
Mar.	8—Augustin Estrada, Las Vegas	W	10
May	17—Jorge Morales, Las Vegas	NC	9
Aug.	9—Tony Martinez, Las Vegas	KO	3
Nov.	1—German Cuello, Las Vegas	KO	10

1979

Feb.	2—Willie Rodriguez, Allentown	KO by	9
June	15—Modesto Concepcion, Las Vegas	TD	4
June	27—Javier Ayala, Las Vegas	W	10
Aug.	2—Hector Rivera, Phoenix	W	10
Dec.	5—German Cuello, Las Vegas	W	12

1980

Oct.	15—Rosendo Ramon, Las Vegas	W	12

HENRY HALL
Eustis, Fla. Junior Middleweight

1975

Jan.	30—Willie Chaney, Tampa	W	4
Feb.	11—Edgar Ross, Orlando	KO by	5
Feb.	20—Willie Chaney, Orlando	KO by	1
Apr.	9—Archie Andrews, Binghamton	KO by	2
May	28—Bernard Bryant, Scranton	L	6
July	9—Frank Mattera, Binghamton	KO by	5
Sept.	9—Clarence Henderson, Orlando	KO by	2
Dec.	18—Willie Chaney, Tampa	KO by	1

1976

May	25—Scott Clark, Orlando	L	4

1977

Jan.	14—Sammy Masias, Orlando	KO by	5
May	10—David Graham, Orlando	KO	3
May	17—James Salerno, Orlando	L	4
July	8—Spook Jackson, St. Augustine	KO by	3
Aug.	4—Ron Royer, Tampa	KO	4
Aug.	25—Rick Urso, Tampa	KO	4
Sept.	22—Kenny Ryals, Tampa	L	6
Oct.	15—Jerome Brooks, Ft. Lauderdale	L	6
Oct.	29—Sammy Masias, Homestead	KO by	8
Nov.	8—Danny Corbett, Orlando	L disq.	1
Nov.	15—Jerome Brooks, West Palm Beach	L	6
Dec.	1—Frankie Suarez, Tampa	L	8

1978

Jan.	17—Robert Spencer, Orlando	L	4
Apr.	6—Ted Mann, Miami Beach	KO by	5
June	10—Sammy Masias, Miami Beach	KO by	8
Nov.	2—Arnell Thomas, Orlando	W	4
Dec.	6—Steve Gregory, Miami Beach	KO by	1

1979

Jan.	30—Dennis Riggs, Jacksonville	L	10
Feb.	19—Slick Mitchell, Tampa	L	6
Mar.	15—Larry Peterson, Palatka	L	8

1980

Oct.	11—Homer Jackson, Ft. Meyers	KO by	2
Dec.	20—Mike Wilcox, Ft. Meyers	KO by	3

WILLIE HALL
San Diego, Calif. Lightweight

1979

Sept.	18—Francisco Pico, Phoenix	L	4
Oct.	11—Ruben Munoz, Phoenix	L	4
Dec.	7—Timmy Martinez, San Diego	L	5
Dec.	14—John Montes, San Bernardino	L	5
Dec.	19—Mano Morua, San Diego	L	6

1980

Jan.	18—Sal Ramirez, San Bernardino	L	6
Feb.	8—Felipe Canella, San Bernardino	KO by	5

PAT HALLACY
Wichita, Kans. Welterweight

1977

Mar.	18—Steve Channell, Itanous City	KO	1
Sept.	21—Simmie Black, Wichita	KO	2
Dec.	14—Dennis Haggerty, Wichita	W	5

1978

Jan.	24—Dennis Horn, Wichita	W	4
Feb.	28—Ralph Peterson, Wichita	KO	1
Mar.	14—Dennis Haggerty, Wichita	W	4
Apr.	26—Tyrone Wren, Wichita	W	6
May	10—Michael Hearon, Memphis	W	6
May	24—Jimmy Hearn, Omaha	W	6
June	3—Martin Jiminez, Wichita	KO	3
June	10—Frank Crosby, Memphis	KO	4
July	11—Eddie Gilmore, Memphis	W	6
Aug.	3—Larry Mayes, Wichita	KO	2
Sept.	5—Larry Rayford, New Orleans	W	6
Sept.	18—Frank Crosby, Wichita	KO	4
Dec.	1—John Morgan, New Orleans	KO	4

1979

Jan.	10—Clarence Howard, Phoenix	L	8
Mar.	8—Clarence Howard, Wichita	W	10
May	12—Johnny Davis, Wichita	W	8
Aug.	4—Johnny Moore, Tulsa	KO	3
Sept.	18—Bruce Strauss, Wichita	W	10
Oct.	26—Luis Resto, New York	L	10
Nov.	1—Justice Ortiz, Wichita	W	10
Dec.	20—Dave Bolden, Wichita	W	10

1980

Feb.	9—Bushy Bester, Johannesburg	L	8
May	10—Harold Volbrecht, Johannesburg	L	8
Aug.	12—Johnny Copeland, Wichita	KO	6
Sept.	10—Tyrone Wren, Wichita	KO	7
Oct.	2—Johnny Turner, New York	D	10
Nov.	25—Steve Gregory, New York	L	10

CARL HALLIBURTON
Millington, Wisc. Heavyweight

1978

June	30—Frank Monaco, Chicago	KO by	2
Sept.	27—Luke Capuano, Chicago	KO by	1
Nov.	18—Renaldo Snipes, Sheffield	KO by	1

1979

May	1—John Lee, Memphis	KO by	1

1980

May	12—Gary Sullins, Cape Girardeau	KO by	3
June	17—Monte Masters, Oklahoma City	KO by	1
Aug.	2—Jimmy Cross, Millington	KO by	4
Oct.	7—Butch Wilkinson, St. Charles	KO by	1

DON HALPIN
Lowell, Mass. Heavyweight

1977

June	20—Barry Proctor, Peabody	W	8
Nov.	11—Bill Payne, Cohoes	KO	2

1978

Mar.	11—Al Brooks, Lowell	W	6
Mar.	20—Charles Cox, Boston	L	8
May	13—Ron Drinkwater, Boston	L	8
June	19—Tom Landry, Boston	KO	1

1979

Feb.	24—Ron Gebere, Quincy	KO	2
May	18—Dennis Jordan, Hartford	KO by	3
Aug.	14—Felipe Rodriguez, Pontevedra	KO by	4
Aug.	28—Randy Cobb, Atlantic City	KO by	3
Nov.	10—Rudi Gauwe	KO by	3

1980

Jan.	19—Greg Sorrentino, Syracuse	L	10
Mar.	8—Jimmy Young, Great Gorge	KO by	2
Apr.	20—Steve Zouski, Portland, Me.	KO by	7

JERRY HALSTEAD
Midwest City, Oklahoma

1980

June	10—Leonard Patterson, Oklahoma City	KO	3
June	17—Fred Williams, Oklahoma City	KO	3
July	1—Tim Moore, Oklahoma City	KO	1
July	15—Russell Fitzgerald, Oklahoma City	W	4
Aug.	5—Pete Lewis, Oklahoma City	W	4
Aug.	19—Dick Chesio, Oklahoma City	KO	2
Sept.	9—Jodie Long, Norman	KO	1
Sept.	25—James Brown, Oklahoma City	KO	2
Nov.	20—Andrew McNeil, Oklahoma City	KO	3

RICK HAMLISCH
Belleville, N.J. Middleweight

1980

June	19—Hank Douglas, Totowa	W	4
July	17—Hank Douglas, Totowa	D	4
Sept.	18—Dennis Mulligan, Totowa	L	4
Oct.	16—Larry Tann, Totowa	KO	1
Nov.	20—Ralph Dumont, Totowa	KO	2
Dec.	18—Andy Riccardi, Totowa	L	4

ELIJAH HAMM
Paterson, N.J. Middleweight

1979

Oct.	12—Frank Sumpter, Rahway	KO by	3

Nov. 21—Steve Arvin, Scranton .... KO by 4
1980
Jan. 24—Hank Whitmore, Dover .... KO   3
Mar. 8—John Molander, Great Gorge .... KO by 1
Aug. 15—Tommy McNeece, Glen Cove .... KO by 1

RAY HAMMOND
Bronx, N.Y. Junior Middleweight
1973
Oct. 15—Tyrone Phelps, New York .... KO   3
Nov. 26—C. J. Faison, New York .... W   6
1974
Feb. 11—Jeff Holmes, New York .... W   6
Apr. 8—Tyrone Phelps, New York .... W   6
Apr. 22—Eddie Parks, New York................. L   6
Dec. 2—Jeff Holmes, New York .... W   6
1975
Mar. 14—Don Morgan, Elizabeth .... W   6
June 23—Don Morgan, New York................ W   8
1976
Mar. 30—Al Fletcher, New York .... KO   2
July 2—Larry Holland, Atlantic City........... KO   4
Aug. 6—Dave Huckaby, New York.............. W   8
1977
June 30—D. C. Walker, Halifax .... KO   3
Aug. 27—Angel Espada, San Juan .... L 10
Sept. 10—Carlos DeLeon, San Juan .... W   8
Dec. 2—Osbaldo Romero, Willemstad .... W 10
1978
July 29—Pedro Rojas, Caracas .... L 10
Dec. 15—Fred Boynton, New York .... W   8
1979
June 28—Ayub Kalule, Randers L   8
—Eddie Marcelle, St. Croix .... L 10
1980
Feb. 8—Fred Boynton, New York .... KO   6
Mar. 31—Earl Thomas, New York .... KO   2
Apr. 30—Ken Dunn, Charleston .... KO   1
May 27—Pete Ranzany, Sacramento .... TD   3
Aug. 1—Clint Jackson, Las Vegas .... KO by 10
Oct. 25—Charlie Weir, Bophuthatswana ...... KO by 6

MUSTAFA HAMSHO
(ROCKY ESTAFIRE, MIKE ESTAIRE,
AND MIKE ESTAFIRE)
New York, N.Y. Middleweight
1975
Aug. 23—Pat Cuillo, Binghamton L   6
Oct. 23—Danny McNevin, Binghamton .... D   4
1976
Apr. 14—Ray Villanueva, Sunnyside, N.Y......... KO   3
Apr. 28—Carlos Novotney, Sunnyside, N.Y........ KO   4
May —Chuck Small, Utica.................... W   6
*June 26—Roger Philips, No. Providence .... KO by 2
Aug. 16—Reggie Jones, Newark.................. D   8
Sept. 11—Cove Green, Utica .... KO   2
Oct. 1—Benji Goldstone, Utica .... W   4
Oct. 29—Bernard McLean, Sunnyside N.Y....... W   6
1977
Apr. 29—Lester Camper, Baltimore .... W   8
May 20—Lorenzo Howard, Binghamton .... KO   1
June 13—Archie Andrews, Newark .... W   6
Sept. 27—Gil Rosario, West New York .... W   6
Nov. 9—Antonio Adame, Las Vegas .... W 10
1978
Jan. 21—Rocky Mosley, Las Vegas .... W 10
June 28—Frankie Moore, Providence .... KO   2
Sept. 21—Bobby Watts, Jersey City .... W   6
Oct. 28—Eddie Parks, Jersey City .... KO   5
Dec. 1—Don Johnson, Jersey City .... KO   5
1979
Jan. 27—Pat Murphy, Jersey City .... KO   3
Mar. 15—Winston Noel, North Bergen .... KO   2
Apr. 11—Tyrone Freeman, White Plains .... KO   1
Apr. 26—Domingo Ortiz, North Bergen .... KO   8
June 27—Domingo Ortiz, Secaucus .... KO   7
Sept. 19—Fermin Guzman, New York .... KO   7
Oct. 4—Barry Hill, North Bergen .... KO   1
1980
Mar. 29—Reggie Jones, Atlantic City .... KO   6
June 15—Wilford Scypion, Clarkson .... W disq. 10
Sept. 24—Bob Patterson, Elizabeth .... KO   4
Nov. 25—Rudy Robles, New York .... W 10
* Result in dispute

GORDON HANAKAHI
1980
July 8—Fred Baclaan, Honolulu .... KO by 3
July 29—Lawrence Gallard, Honolulu .... W   3
Aug. 25—Fred Baclaan, Honolulu L   4
Nov. 12—Roger Reed, Honolulu .... W   3

MIKE HARDEN
Dayton, Ohio Light Heavyweight
1979
Feb. 7—Charley Williams, Richfield .... D   4
Apr. 19—Randy Graves, Richfield L   4
July 6—Chester Williams, Dayton .... KO   1
1980
Sept. 10—Jesse Hicks, Cicero .... KO   2
Sept. 17—Charlie Williams, Dayton .... D   6
Nov. 1—Clem McLittle, Detroit L   8

EARL HARGROVE
Philadelphia, Pa. Junior Middleweight
Managed by Gary Hegyi
1979
Nov. 29—John Saxton, Virginia Beach .... KO   2
1980
Jan. 18—Carl Izzard, Trenton .... KO   1
Mar. 14—Perry Freeman, Trenton .... KO   1
Apr. 11—Wayne Kirkland, Chester .... KO   1
Apr. 26—Wayne Flemming, Trenton .... KO   1
Aug. 21—Fernando Collazo, Revere .... KO   1
Sept. 27—Matador Loving, Trenton .... KO   5
Oct. 16—Donnie Miller, Revere .... KO   2
Dec. 15—Paul Grant, Boston .... KO   2

LIONEL (FLAPPING EAGLE) HARNEY
Carson City, Nev. Featherweight
Managed by Ted Walker
1979
Mar. 10—Scott Anderson, Carson City .... W   4
May 2—Sal Huerta, Las Vegas .... W   4
May 9—Egilio Montalvo, Carson City .... W   4
May 30—Luis Avila, Las Vegas .... W   4
June 16—Eliu Hernandez, Yerington .... KO   3
July 3—Bobby Mercado, Gardnerville .... W   6
July 18—Francisco Pico, Las Vegas .... W   6
Aug. 1—Sergio Serabia, Reno L   6
Aug. 24—Freddie Short, Carson City .... KO   3
Sept. 18—Ronnie Furlow, Reno .... W   6
Oct. 2—Ronnie Furlow, Reno .... KO   7
Oct. 30—Francisco Pico, Carson City .... W 10
Dec. 11—Carlos Zuniga, Reno .... KO by 1
1980
Jan. 22—Joe Phillips, Reno .... L 10
Feb. 20—Jaime Nava, Las Vegas .... W 10
Apr. 16—Freddie Roach, Las Vegas .... KO by 6
June 14—Bonnie Necessario, Yerington .... KO   4
June 24—Eddie Ballaran, Honolulu .... L 10
July 3—Jose Luis Lara, Gardnerville .... W 10
Sept. 5—Richard Savala, Sacramento .... KO by 1
Nov. 8—Fili Ramirez, Lake Tahoe .... W   8

BILL HARRINGTON
Baltimore, Md. Middleweight
1979
Sept. 26—Charlie Tuttle, Baltimore .... KO   1
Oct. 24—Bud Becker, Baltimore .... D   4
Nov. 14—Martin Spriggs, Baltimore .... KO by 2
1980
Mar. 26—Bud Becker, Baltimore .... W   4
Aug. 9—Buster Drayton, Atlantic City .... KO by 2

ART (TAP) HARRIS
Akron, Ohio Middleweight
1970
May 27—Willie Williams, Cleveland .... W   4
June 24—Willie Williams, Cleveland .... W   4
July 22—Willie Williams, Akron .... KO   1
Aug. 3—Rick Wheeler, Norton .... W   4
Aug. 19—Vic Therpe, Cleveland .... W   4
Sept. 29—Terry Summerhays, Buffalo .... W   6
Oct. 21—Bob O'Neil, Akron .... W   4
Nov. 11—Jeff Morgan, Cleveland .... W   4
Nov. 25—Vince Neretka, Cleveland .... W   4
1971
Feb. 10—Vince Neretka, Minge Junction .... KO   5
Mar. 17—Nick Peoples, Akron .... W   6
Apr. 28—Otis Goode, Cleveland .... KO   5
May 26—Dick Topinke, Cleveland .... W   8
Sept. 10—Earl Robinson, Toledo .... KO   4
Sept. —Kenny Baker, Akron .... W   6
Oct. 19—Fred Jimenez, Cleveland .... W   8
Nov. 10—Cecea Kid, Akron .... KO   4
1972
Feb. 8—Sammy Maul, Cleveland .... W   8
Apr. 17—Billy Goodwin, Chicago .... W   8
Apr. 26—Frank Kolovrat, Cleveland .... W 10
Aug. 28—Marcelina Alicia, Cleveland .... KO   5
Oct. 12—Tony Berries, Pittsburgh .... W 10
1976
July 5—Eddie Witt, Marion .... KO   3
Sept. 7—Shane Besley, Marion .... KO   4

1977
Mar. 3—Johnny Heard, Marion .... KO 4
Aug. 28—Gary Alexander, Marion .... W 6
1978
Oct. 17—Gary Broughton, Canton .... KO 5
1979
Jan. 24—Fred Brown, Cleveland .... W 10
Mar. 21—Willie Warren, Richfield .... W 10
May 25—Renato Garcia, Richfield .... W 10
Sept. 20—Leo Saenz, Richfield .... W 10
1980
Apr. 5—Ray Seales, Akron .... KO by 6

CLINT HARRIS
Windsor, Ontario, Canada Junior Welterweight
Managed by Jerry McCarthy
1980
May 7—Bobby Buscombe, Windsor .... W 4
July 26—Robbie Houle, S. Falls, Ont. .... L 4
Sept. 22—Terry Whitaker, Chicago .... L 4
Sept. 27—Joe Lyle, Detroit .... L 4
Nov. 8—Daniel Avery, Detroit .... KO 4
Dec. 16—Ricky Pappa, Toronto .... D 6

CURTIS HARRIS
Paterson, N.J. Lightweight
1975
Sept. 8—Hector Sanchez, New York .... W 4
Sept. 22—Roberto Medina, New York .... W 4
1976
Sept. 24—Carlos Soto, New York .... KO 4
1977
(Inactive)
1978
Sept. 8—Milciades Jiminez, New York .... KO 2
1979
June 27—Herman Boyd, New York .... KO 1
Oct. 30—Ed Rivera, Totowa .... KO 1
Nov. 15—Confesor Rosales .... W 4
1980
Apr. 10—Michael Ross, Atlantic City .... L 6
June 19—Tim LaValley, Totowa .... KO 6
July 17—Martin Parham, Totowa .... NC
Sept. 18—Charlie Brown, Totowa .... KO 4

FRED (THE STEPPER) HARRIS
Bossier City, La. Junior Welterweight
1975
Feb. 4—Tom Tarantino, Milwaukee .... W 6
Apr. 22—Tim Miller, Sacramento .... L 6
Nov. 15—Marion Thomas, Chicago .... KO 4
1976
Feb. 21—George Anderson, Chicago .... KO 6
Apr. 6—Bobby Orr, Chicago................... W 6
Apr. 19—Scotty Foreman, New Orleans........... KO 3
June 3—Demetrio Tovar, Shreveport............. W 10
Aug. 4—Maurice Quillens, Alexandria .... W 10
Aug. 22—Ron Pettigrew, Flint .... L 6
Nov. 4—Tom Pinner, Fort Worth .... W 5
Nov. 20—Shannon Williams, Marshall .... KO 2
Nov. 27—Tommy Young, Fort Worth .... ND
Dec. 18—Robert Tijerina, Marshall .... KO 5
1977
Feb. 8—Pedro Flores, San Antonio .... L 10
Feb. 28—Joe Medrano, Houston .... W 10
Mar. 5—James Pixley, Marshall .... W 5
Mar. 18—Steve Homan, Kansas City .... L 6
Apr. 2--Robert Tijerina, Marshall .... KO 4
Apr. 26—Jimmy Heair, Memphis .... L 10
May 3—Rocky Ramon, Marshall .... KO by 10
July 7—Jimmy Heair, Memphis .... L 10
Aug. 16—Aundre Love, New Orleans .... L 10
Aug. 25—Rosendo Ramon, Marshall .... L 10
Sept. 6—Silvero Martinez, Houston .... L 10
Sept. 28—Rick Folstad, Minneapolis .... L 10
Oct. 25—Termite Watkins, Orlando .... L 10
1978
Jan. 10—Jimmy Heair, Memphis .... KO by 6
May 1—Dale Hernandez, Omaha .... KO by 3
Oct. 3—Mike Herron, Memphis .... L 10
Nov. 16—Sean O'Grady, Oklahoma City .... KO by 7
1979
Apr. 27—Aaron Pryor, Dayton .... KO by 6
Apr. 20—Nick Furlano, Winnipeg .... L 10
Nov. 16—Al Carter, Kansas City .... KO by 7
1980
Feb. 16—Frank Lawson, Fayetteville .... KO by 1
Mar. 7—Tom Crowley, Kansas City .... L 6
July 29—Bill Watkins, Houston .... L 0
Sept. 23—Ruben Munoz, Odessa .... KO by 4
Nov. 11—James Busceme, Beaumont .... KO by 5

RONNIE HARRIS
Canton, Ohio Middleweight
1971
Nov. 11—Joe Blair, Canton .... KO 1
Dec. 29—Otis (Lightning) Goode, Canton .... KO 2
1972
Jan. 15—Ted Hamilton, Canton.................. KO 2
Feb. 12—Ellis Poole, Canton .... W 6
Feb. 19—Morris Jordan, Canton.................. W 6
May 2—Bobby Haymon, Detroit................... W 8
1973
Mar. 1—Rubin Arotha, Detroit.................. W 10
May 2—Rowland Pryor, New York .... W 10
Aug. 5—Leon Washington, New York............ W 10
1974
Apr. 20—Chu Chu Garcia, Toronto .... W 10
June 20—Frank Davila, Montreal .... W 10
Aug. 20—Peter Cobblah, Las Vegas .... W 10
1975
July 22—John Taylor, Quebec City .... KO 1
Aug. 22—Tony Garcia, Quebec City.............. KO 2
Sept. 9—Alan Kemp, Hull..................... KO 1
Oct. 10—Gary Bailey, Hull .... W 10
1976
Jan. 24—Tommy Hanna, Las Vegas .... W 10
Aug. 26—Marion Conner, Canton .... KO 11
Oct. 22—Sandy Torres, New York............... W 10
1977
Feb. 15—James Parks, New York .... W 10
Mar. 2—Ray Seales, New York .... W 10
Apr. 12—Alan Minter, London .... KO 8
July 17—Frank Reiche, Miami Beach .... KO 2
Sept. 28—Cliff Wills, Canton .... KO 10
1978
Jan. 27—Angel Ortiz, Hempstead .... W 10
Feb. 24—Gratien Tonna, Las Vegas .... W 12
Aug. 5—Hugo Corro, Buenos Aires .... L 15
(World Middleweight Title)
1979
Apr. 10—Edgar Wallace, Phoenix .... W 12
July 22—Bob Patterson, Canton .... W 10
Dec. 12—Leo Saenz, Canton .... KO 7
1980
May 13—Sammy NeSmith, Indianapolis ...... KO by 10

TIM HARRIS
Sacramento, Calif. Middleweight
1980
May 27—James Bella, Sacramento .... W 6
July 1—Antonio Correa, Sacramento .... KO 1
Aug. 25—Rafael Zamora, Sacramento .... KO 2
Sept. 5—Bobby Howard, Sacramento .... W 6
Oct. 16—Perry LeVoe, San Carlos .... W 6

GAETAN HART
Canadian Lightweight
Born: November 9, 1953
1973
Apr. 16—Paul Collette, Montreal................L 6
June 4—Tony Tamborello, Toronto.............. KO 3
Aug. 26—Tommy Jackson, Montreal .... W 6
Oct. 23—JoJo Jackson, Montreal .... D 4
Nov. 12—Jimmy Henry, Montreal .... L 8
1974
Mar. 5—Jose Maryiner, Montreal.............. KO by 4
Apr. 10—Tony Johnson, Hull.................... W 8
May 11—Ron Pettigrew, Hull .... KO 6
June 15—Royal Boutin, Quebec................. KO 5
July 5—Barry Sponagle, Halifax .... KO by 7
Aug. 12—Al Mendina, Boston .... W 8
Sept. 2—Ron Pettigrew, Dartmouth............ KO 8
Sept. 18—Rudy Bolds, Pittsburgh .... KO by 3
Oct. 10—Cornell Hall, Hull................... W 10
Oct. 29—Robert Medina, Walpole .... W 6
Nov. 14—Eddie Heckbert, Hull................. KO 5
1975
Jan. 11—Danny Stokes, Toronto .... L 8
Apr. 1—Bruno Arcari, Genoa .... KO by 7
Apr. 30—Daniel Levesque, Montreal........... KO by 3
June 8—Cornell Hall, Ottawa .... L 8
June 18—Larry Moore, Hull................. KO 3
July 12—Danny Stokes, Toronto................. W 8
July 15—Ron Jones, Chicago................. W 4
July 28—George Anderson, Minneapolis .... W 8
Aug. 12—Paul Sigman, Hull .... KO 2
Aug. 24—Ricky Tomatis, Chicago............. L 8
Sept. 16—Al Franklin, St. Paul .... D 10
Oct. 28—Al Franklin, Minneapolis .... D 10
Nov. 17—Alfredo Escalera, San Juan .... KO by 6
Dec. 20—Larmar Baskin, Gatineau............. KO 3
1976
Jan. 26—Louis Davila, Quebec................. KO 5
Feb. 16—Leo DiFiore, Quebec................. KO 5

Mar. 17—Tony Petronelli, Boston.............KO by 12
Apr. 22—Al Franklin, Minneapolis................L 8
May 3—Jimmy King, Hull...................KO 3
May 21—Dom Monaco, Brooklyn ....L 10
1977
July 26—Ricky Camara, Montreal ....W 8
Sept. 27—Cleveland Denny, Montreal ....L 10
Oct. 24—Willie Davis, Buckingham ....W 8
Nov. 1—Barry Sponacle, Montreal ....W 10
Nov. 22—Jim Henry, Buckingham ....W 10
Dec. 13—Michel Rouleau, Montreal ....W 8
1978
Jan. 24—Ralph Racine, Montreal ....W 10
Feb. 21—Rocky Orango, Montreal ....W 10
Apr. 5—Cleveland Denny, Montreal ....W 10
(Canadian Lightweight Title)
June 1—Leo Marsh, Hull.....................KO 2
(Canadian Lightweight Title)
June 27—Jean Lapointe, Montreal ....KO 10
(Canadian Lightweight Title)
Aug. 31—Quenton Blackman, Buckingham ....W 10
Sept. 26—Ron Meaweather, Montreal ....KO 8
Nov. 20—Al Franklin, Buckingham ....KO 8
Dec. 5—Johnny Summerhays, Montreal ....W 12
(Canadian Lightweight Title)
Dec. 12—Danny Daniels, Verdun ....KO 3
1979
Feb. 5—Tommy Rose, Hull ....W 10
Mar. 30—Claude Noel, Trinidad ....L 10
May 7—Angel Cruz, Gatineau ....W 10
June 3—Ernest Bing, Port Cartier ....D 10
June 26—Nick Furlano, Montreal ....W 8
July 24—Ernest Bing, Atlantic City ....L 10
Aug. 26—Nick Furlano, Montreal ....L 12
Nov. 6—Benito Jimenez, Montreal ....KO 4
Nov. 23—Roberto Colon, Verdun ....KO 4
1980
Jan. 20—Kenny Muse, Quebec City ....W 10
Mar. 13—Tim LaValley, Hull ....KO 8
Mar. 25—Nick Furlano, Montreal ....W 12
(Regained Canadian Lightweight Title)
May 7—Ralph Racine, Montreal ....KO 12
June 20—Cleveland Denny, Montreal ....KO 10
Sept. 23—Pedro Acosta, Montreal ....W 10
Nov. 22—Aaron Pryor, Cincinnati ....KO by 6
(For World Junior Welterweight Title)

BOB HARVEY
Truro, Nova Scotia, Canada Junior Welterweight
1980
May 11—Marty Cole, Halifax ....W 4
July 22—Derrick Cuttino, Halifax ....W 4
Aug. 21—Randy Mitchum, Halifax ....KO 6
Sept. 9—Wayne Cormier, Moncton ....KO 1
Sept. 24—Mike Alvarez, Halifax ....W 6
Nov. 21—Brian Linthorn, Moncton ....KO 3

MELVIN (AL) HAUSER
Pittsburgh, Pa. Welterweight
Born: June 21, 1954
1978
Sept. 8—Earl Caldwell, Pittsburgh ....KO 1
Dec. 19—Phil Batie, Pittsburgh ....KO 1
1979
Jan. 24—Manning Galloway, Cleveland ....L 6
Feb. 8—Abel Santiago, New Kensington ....KO 3
May 23—Mike Blunt, Cleveland ....KO 1
July 17—Charles Cross, Pittsburgh ....KO 3
Nov. 29—Gerald Clark, Va. Beach ....KO 4
1980
Mar. 9—Johnny Cooper, Atlantic City ....KO by 7
May 14—Al Fletcher, White Plains ....D 6
Aug. 7—Johnny Cooper, Atlantic City ....KO by 5

DARNELL HAYES
Columbus, Ohio Light Heavyweight
1980
June 1—Willie White, Columbus ....W 4
Aug. 21—Steve Jones, Columbus ....KO 3
Sept. 10—Zeke Zelichowsky, Detroit ....KO 2
Sept. 12—Donnie Townsend, Columbus ....KO 2
Sept. 25—Jeff Jordan, Columbus ....KO by 3
Oct. 16—Frank Draper, Toledo ....KO by 2

GERALD HAYES
Newark, N.J. Featherweight
1975
Sept. 24—Joe Roman, Bayonne ....D 4
Nov. 18—Billy Abel, Philadelphia ....W 4
Dec. 17—Joey Saldano, New York ....D 4
1976
Jan. 13—Johnny Barr, Philadelphia ....W disq. 4
Jan. 31—Ural Hunter, Waterbury ....KO 1

116

Mar. 20—Leo DiFiore, Waterbury ....KO 1
Apr. 3—Ralph Racine, Utica ....KO by 5
May 29—Francisco Maldonado, Waterbury ....KO 2
Aug. 16—Malanga Torres, San Juan ....L 8
1977
Feb. 1—William Berry, Philadelphia ....L 10
Mar. 2—Elviro Jajuja, Philadelphia ....W 6
Apr. 15—Manuel Lujan, San Diego ....KO 1
Apr. 23—Nacho Jiminez, Los Angeles ....L 5
May 30—Ad Zapanta, San Diego ....KO 2
June 23—Ernest Bing, Philadelphia ....L 8
Sept. 10—Heriberto Olivares, San Juan ....L 8
Sept. 28—Ralph Racine, Scranton ....L 10
Oct. 28—Rufus Miller, Elizabeth ....W 8
1978
Jan. 9—Manuel Abedoy, Tijuana ....L 10
Feb. 10—Santiago Mesa, San Diego ....KO 8
Feb. 25—Lupe Pintor, Inglewood ....L 10
May 4—William Berry, North Bergen ....W 12
June 30—Jose Resto, Newark ....W 10
July 22—Tony Trys, Caracas ....L 10
Sept. 26—Jean LaPointe, Montreal ....L 10
Oct. 19—Joe Rivera, Garfield ....KO 4
Dec. 6—Bobby Chacon, Stockton ....L 10
1979
Feb. 27—Antonio Medina, Los Angeles ....KO 2
Mar. 27—Arturo Rojas, San Carlos ....KO 3
May 23—Juan Bautista, Concord ....W 10
July 16—Tommy Barr, Jersey City ....KO 1
Aug. 7—Derrik Holmes, Atlantic City ....D 8
Sept. 18—Rocky Lockridge, Giants' Stadium ....L 12
Nov. 23—Jose Nieto, New York ....KO 1
1980
Jan. 16—James Martinez, Odessa ....L 10
Mar. 31—Alexis Arguello, Las Vegas ....L 10
June 4—Bashew Sibaca, Capetown ....W 10
Oct. 4—Jorge Alvarado, McAfee ....L 10

ALFONSO HAYMAN
Philadelphia, Pa. Welterweight
1970
July 29—Roy Ingram, Philadelphia ....D 4
Sept. 16—Roy Ingram, Philadelphia ....L 4
Oct. 14—Johnny Rohland, Scranton ....KO 6
Dec. 9—Mel Mayfield, Philadelphia ....KO 1
1971
Jan. 12—Roy Ingram, Philadelphia ....W 6
Jan. 25—Art Kettles, Philadelphia ....W 6
Apr. 5—Robert Ziegler, Philadelphia.............W 6
May 26—Roy Ingram, Philadelphia ....D 4
Sept. 21—Hector Perez, Philadelphia ....W 6
1972
Jan. 18—William Watson, Philadelphia ....L 8
May 5—Hector Perez, New York ....L 8
Dec. 5—William Watson, Philadelphia ....KO 8
1973
Mar. 26—Gabe Bowens, Philadelphia ....KO 7
May 14—Miguel Barreto, Philadelphia ....D 10
Aug. 6—Roberto Sosa, Philadelphia ....KO 7
Aug. 31—Papo Villa, Philadelphia................KO 6
Nov. 12—Eddie Davis, Philadelphia ....W 10
1974
Jan. 14—William Watson, Philadelphia...........KO 7
Feb. 18—J. T. Dowe, Philadelphia...............W 10
May 22—Roy Barrientes, Philadelphia ....W 10
Sept. 10—Mario Saurennann, Philadelphia ....W 12
Nov. 26—Johnny Gant, Largo..................KO 10
1975
June 17—Johnny Gant, Landover, Md.............L 10
Oct. 21—Miguel Barreto, Philadelphia ....L 10
1976
Mar. 11—Hector Thompson, Brisbane.............L 10
Apr. 27—Angel Espada, San Juan ....KO by 8
June 11—Pete Ranzany, Sacramento ....KO by 9
Aug. 27—Johnny Davis, Atlantic City ....KO 6
Dec. 3—Rocky Mattioli, Milan ....KO by 10
1977
June 27—Youngblood Williams, Philadelphia ....D 10
Aug. 8—Fausto Rodriguez, Santo Domingo ......L 10
Dec. 7—Santos Solis, San Juan ....L 10
1978
Feb. 10—Efren Conzalez, Philadelphia ....KO 1
Mar. 14—Jimmy Rothwell, Philadelphia ....L 10
Apr. 12—Clyde Gray, Halifax ....KO by 5
Sept. 26—Maurice Hope, London ....KO by 5
Nov. 9—Bobby Acey, Virginia Beach ....KO 7
Dec. 14—Ron Pettigrew, Virginia Beach ....W 8
1979
Apr. 3—Thomas Hearns, Philadelphia ....L 10
May 30—Josef Nsubuga, Oslo ....L 8
Sept. 20—Bobby Acey, Virginia Beach ....KO 8
1980
Sept. 10—Johnny Turner, Scranton ....KO by 7
Dec. 12—Milton McCrory, Detroit ....KO by 2

AMOS HAYNES
Youngstown, Ohio Heavyweight
1980
Jan. 15—Vic Wallace, Youngstown .... KO 3
Feb. 18—Jumbo Cummings, Chicago .... KO by 2
Apr. 30—Stan Scott, Youngstown .... KO 6
Sept. 11—George Mostardini, Chicago .... KO by 3
Sept. 24—Baker Tinsley, Struthers .... W 8

BOB HAZELTON
Los Angeles, Calif. Heavyweight
1969
June 3—Jose Perra, Los Angeles .... KO 5
July 16—Tunka Kid, Oklahoma .... KO by 4
Aug. 17—Jack Riley, Los Angeles .... W 4
Sept. 10—Dick Hammett, Los Angeles .... W 4
Oct. 12—Steve Carter, San Jose .... KO by 2
Dec. 6—George Foreman, Las Vegas .... KO by 1
1970-1971
(Inactive)
1972
Dec. 12—Ray White, San Diego .... KO by 7
1973-1974
(Inactive)
1975
Feb. 11—Larry Stevenson, Taos .... KO 5
Aug. 22—Jose Luis Garcia, Caracas .... KO by 3
Oct. —Bob Smith, Taos .... KO 2
Dec. 12—Mike Rogers, Farmington .... KO 2
1976
Dec. 12—Jack Thomas, Grants .... KO 2
1977
Jan. 28—Jose Perez, Roxwell .... KO 3
Feb. 15—Shotgun Fowler, Oklahoma City .... KO 1
Mar. 5—Verlee Price, Marshall .... KO 2
Apr. 2—Jose Rodriguez, Marshall .... KO 2
May 20—Al Bolden, Marshall .... KO 2
June 21—Jerry McIntyre, Oklahoma City .... KO 1
June 30—Manuel Ramos, Marshall .... KO 2
Sept. 2—Bob Foster, Curacao .... KO by 10
1978
Mar. 9—Carl Baker, Wichita .... KO 1
Apr. 25—Willie Harvey, Wichita .... KO 2
June 3—Bob Foster, Wichita .... KO 2
Sept. 18—Chuck Warfield, Wichita .... KO 2
1979
May 12—Lucien Rodriguez, Wichita .... KO by 3
1980
Feb. 21—Bob Sutton, Gainesville .... KO 2

JIMMY HEAIR
Memphis Tenn. Welterweight
1971
July 22—George Rivera, Los Angeles .... W 4
Aug. 7—Val Chapron, Santa Monica .... W 4
Aug. 12—Jorge Rivera, Los Angeles............... W 4
Aug. 14—Julio Lopez, Anaheim.................. W 4
Aug. 19—Julio Lopez, Los Angeles............... W 4
Aug. 29—Julio Lopez, Santa Monica .... W 4
1972
Mar. 12—Richard Puentes, Farmington .... W 6
Mar. 25—Agapito Villegas, Long Beach .... W 6
Apr. 3—Antonio Alcala, Los Angeles .... W 5
Apr. 10—Gabriel Vega, Los Angeles............. KO 1
Apr. 17—David Herrera, Los Angeles............. KO 6
May 1—Ray Llamas, Los Angeles .... KO 2
May 8—Chi Chi Ontiveros, Los Angeles .... KO 1
May 15—Lupe Orantes, Los Angeles.............. KO 5
June 5—Alberto Maldonado, Los Angeles........ KO 1
June 19—Ben Hernandez, Los Angeles .... KO 3
June 30—Jaime Campos, Los Angeles .... W 10
July 24—Ignacio Casteneda, Los Angeles .... W 10
Aug. 28—Sugar Montgomery, Los Angeles .... W 10
Sept. 11—Cesar Sinda, Anaheim................... KO 10
Oct. 9—Juan Collado, Northridge .... KO 3
Oct. 31—Mike Mayon, Bakersfield .... W 10
Nov. 28—Angel Mayoral, Los Angeles .... KO 9
1973
Jan. 29—Hiroyuki Murakami, Anaheim .... KO 5
Mar. 17—Chango Carmona, Los Angeles .... W 10
June 1—Clemente Mucino, Los Angeles........... KO 5
June 23—Rene Morgan, Los Angeles .... KO 2
July 20—Mike Mayan, San Diego .... W 10
Aug. 17—Raul Montoya, Los Angeles .... W 10
Oct. 5—Constinto Rodriguez, Los Angeles........ KO 5
Oct. 27—Arturo Pineda, Los Angeles............. KO 4
Dec. 13—Nacho Castenada, Los Angeles .... KO 9
1974
Jan. 1—Clemente Mucino, Mexicali .... KO 5
May 9—Rudy Barra, Los Angeles .... L 10
June 6—Rito Torres, Oklahoma City .... KO 3
July 19—Raul Montoya, San Diego .... W 10
Aug. 9—Nacho Castenada, San Diego........... KO 8
Aug. 30—Hector Thompson, Brisbane.............. L 10

Oct. 11—Miguel Mayan, San Diego .... L 10
Nov. 22—Juan Collado, San Diego............... KO 8
1975
Jan. 18—Art Leon, Anaheim .... L 10
Feb. 28—Gerardo Ferratt, San Diego .... KO 5
Mar. 14—Antonio Hernandez, San Diego .... W 10
Apr. 16—Lorenzo Trujillo, El Paso................ W 10
May 2—Jose Peterson, San Diego .... L 10
July 11—Sigfredo Rodriguez, Durango............. L 10
July 28—Laudial Negron, San Juan .... KO 5
Sept. 10—Nicolino Loche, Buenos Aires .... L 10
Oct. 7—Jorge Rodriquez, Juarez .... KO 2
Dec. 18—Rudy Hernandez, Los Angeles............ W 10
1976
Jan. 10—Andreas Gonzalez, Las Vegas .... W 10
Feb. 5—Javier Muniz, Los Angeles............... W 10
Mar. 4—Art Leon, Los Angeles................. D 10
Mar. 16—Jesus Alonzo, Tijuana .... KO 5
Apr. 2—Jose Soberaives, Tijuana .... KO by 7
May 26—Tonga Kiatvayupak, Bangkok .... L 10
June 17—Armando Muniz, El Paso .... L 12
July —Rodnay Cooper, El Paso................. KO 2
Aug. 3—Lorenzo Trujilio, Corpus Christi .... W 10
Sept. 18—Santos Solis, San Juan .... L 10
Oct. 12—Rosendo Ramon, San Antonio .... W 10
Nov. 6—Augustin Estrada, Ignacio .... KO 5
Nov. 9—David Green, London .... L 10
Dec. 11—Richard Puentes, Ignacio .... KO 5
1977
Jan. 10—Art Leon, El Paso .... L 10
Mar. 2—Harold Weston, New York .... L 10
Apr. 26—Freddie Harris, Memphis .... L 10
May 13—Rudy Hernandez, Tucson .... KO 3
May 23—Dennis Haggerty, Memphis .... KO 2
June 13—Joe Medrano, Memphis .... KO 4
July 7—Freddie Harris, Memphis .... W 10
Aug. 23—Scottie Foreman, Memphis .... KO 7
Sept. 20—Jerry Strickland, Memphis .... KO 1
Oct. 15—Juan Garcia, Palm Springs .... KO 10
Nov. 8—Robert Turner, Memphis .... KO 5
Dec. 13—Mike Romeriz, Memphis .... KO 4
1978
Jan. 10—Freddie Harris, Memphis .... KO 6
Jan. 25—Donnie London, Greenville .... KO 1
Feb. 7—Robert Tijerina, Memphis .... KO 3
Feb. 21—John Morgan, Greenville .... KO 3
Mar. 21—Paul Garcia, Memphis .... KO 4
Apr. 25—George Madison, Greenville .... KO 1
May 23—Clyde Spencer, Little Rock .... KO 3
June 20—Jessie Martinez, Little Rock .... KO 2
July 13—Jimmy Corkum, Hattisburg .... KO 3
Oct. 12—Adriano Marrero, Memphis .... L 10
Nov. 2—Kelvin Jackson, Orlando .... W 10
Dec. 12—Pete Ranzany, Sacramento .... L 12
(U.S. Welterweight Title)
1979
Feb. 6—Roberto Spencer, Orlando .... KO 3
Feb. 20—Juan Roman Panchi, Orlando .... KO 5
Apr. 8—Roberto Duran, Las Vegas .... L 10
May 29—Tony Johnson, Memphis .... KO 1
June 19—Emmett Atlas, Orlando .... KO 2
July 10—Don Morgan, Memphis .... W 10
Aug. 24—Marvin Ladson, Memphis .... KO 1
Oct. 3—Richard House, Orlando .... L 10
Dec. 7—Freddie Harris, Memphis .... KO 5
1980
Mar. 31—Clint Jackson, Knoxville .... KO by 9
May —Javier Rivas, El Paso .... W 10
May 31—Raul Aguirre, El Paso .... KO 7
July 1—Sal Lopez, Sacramento .... KO by 5
Sept. 9—Maurice Quillen, Memphis .... W 10
Oct. 23—Charley Copeland, Memphis .... KO 9
Nov. 18—Robert Culp, Belleville .... KO 2
Dec. 9—Billy White, Birmingham .... KO 3

JOHNNY HEARD
Chicago, Ill. Middleweight
1976
July 26—George Madison, Indianapolis .... W 4
Sept. 20—Eddie Davis, Orlando .... W 8
Oct. 10—Larry Ward, Milwaukee .... W 6
Oct. 20—James Parks, Cleveland .... L 10
Nov. 9—Mike West, Indianapolis .... KO 3
Nov. 30—Herman Graham, Indianapolis .... L 4
1977
Mar. 6—Art Harris, Marion .... KO by 4
May 26—Billy Goodwin, Waukesha .... KO 2
June 9—Ray Seales, Butte .... KO by 2
June 20—Mike Hallacy, Wichita .... KO 7
Aug. 0—Richard Leeds, Chicago .... KO 2
Sept. 7—George Jacobs, Kansas City .... KO 2
Sept. 28—James Parks, Canton .... L 10
Dec. 1—Mel Dennis, Houston .... L 10

1978

Jan.	14—Leroy Green, Kansas City	KO by	7
Mar.	2—Robbie Davies, Liverpool	W	8
Mar.	30—Leo Saenz, Baltimore	W	10
Apr.	10—Al Clay, Chicago	L	10
June	3—Bobby Watts, Baltimore	L	10
June	28—Ray Seales, Washington D.C.	L	10
July	12—Tony McMinn, Kansas City	KO	2
Sept.	17—Fulgencio Obel, Caracas	KO by	7
Oct.	25—King George Aidoo, Chicago	KO	5
Nov.	29—Ralph Moncrief, Richfield	L	8

1979

Mar.	3—Bobby Hoye, Detroit	KO by	7
Apr.	10—Wilford Scypion, Beaumont	KO by	2
May	14—Tony Danza, Phoenix	KO by	3
June	14—Marcelo Quinones, Lima	KO	9
Sept.	7—Fred Reed, Illinois	D	8

1980

Feb.	21—Robbie Davies, Liverpool	KO	7
Mar.	27—Eddie Smith, Liverpool	KO by	5
July	25—Mark Hughes, Chicago	KO	2
Aug.	16—Charlie Weir, Johannesburg	KO by	1
Oct.	31—Nicola Cirelli, Rome	KO by	2

HENRY HEARNS
Los Angeles, Calif. Middleweight
1978

June	8—Chon Arias, Los Angeles	KO by	3
July	12—Bret Ellison, Las Vegas	KO	2
Aug.	17—Lee Kahey, Los Angeles	W	4
Aug.	31—Lee Kahey, Los Angeles	KO	4
Sept.	12—Mike Hickman, Pico Rivera	KO	3

1980

Jan.	12—Lee Burkey, Lake Tahoe	KO	2
Feb.	18—Mike Clark, Carson City	W	10
May	29—Clyde Mudgett, Las Vegas	KO	2
June	26—Mike Clark, Las Vegas	W	10
Aug.	28—Tony Mesoraca, Las Vegas	KO by	2

JIMMY HEARNS
1980

Apr.	21—Eddie Melo, Hull	KO by	2
May	13—Bill Carr, Indianapolis	KO by	3
June	18—Jeff Lampkin, Struthers	KO by	1
June	28—Rick Nelson, Rapid City	D	4
July	11—Luke Capuano, Chicago	KO by	3
Nov.	11—Rick Nelson, St. Paul	KO by	2
Dec.	10—James Dixon, Moline	KO by	2

STEVE HEARON
Texas Junior Middleweight
1979

Nov.	13—Ronald Ford, Houston	W	4
Nov.	20—Pedro Garza, Houston	KO	4

1980

Jan.	8—Tom Pinner, Houston	W	3
Mar.	18—Jarvis Mayfield, Houston	KO by	4
Apr.	29—Rufus Walker, Houston	W	6
June	24—Abraham Ramirez, Houston	KO	3
July	22—Rene Pagan, Houston	W	6
July	29—Don Duncan, Houston	KO	1
Aug.	19—Leon McCullum, Beaumont	KO	5
Nov.	11—Melvin Wynn, Beaumont	KO	5

DANNY HEATH
Lowell, Mass. Junior Middleweight
1979

June	29—Larry Carpenter, Cranston	KO	4
Aug.	11—Claudis Taylor, N. Swanzey	KO	2
Aug.	21—Saxton Boynton, Yarmouth	W	8
Sept.	8—Jaime Rodriguez, N. Swanzey	L	8
Oct.	27—Jaime Rodriguez, Fitchburg	L	10
Nov.	10—Alois Carmeliet, Zele	KO by	1

1980

June	28—Jaime Rodriguez, Manchester	L	10
Aug.	21—Vinnie Curto, Revere	KO by	9
Oct.	2—Robbie Sims, Boston	KO by	1

CHARLES HECKER
Brooklyn, N.Y. Middleweight
1980

Apr.	18—Phil Capobianco, New York	W	4
May	2—Herb Wilens, New York	W	6
May	14—Doug DeWitt, White Plains	KO by	3
Aug.	15—John Molander, Glen Cove	KO by	2
Nov.	28—James Shuler, New York	KO by	3

KENNY HEFLIN
Louisville, Ky. Middleweight
1979

June	5—Glen Greenwall, Memphis	KO	3
	—Ronnie Walker, Louisville	KO	1
June	28—Floyd Saunders, Kentucky	W	6

118

Aug.	10—Ray Morgan, Evansville	KO	1
Sept.	8—Rodney Coupe, Wheeling	L	6
Nov.	3—Gary Thomas, Owensboro	W	6

1980

Feb.	1—Duane Strotar, Louisville	KO	1
Apr.	5—Eddie O'Ryan, Louisville	W	4
May	3—Rick Noggle, Canton	L	8
May	16—Franklin Mills, Lexington	KO by	3
Sept.	6—Lester Groves, Jenkins	W	6
Sept.	11—Clem Tucker, Chicago	KO	6
Oct.	9—Al Clay, Chicago	KO by	6
Dec.	13—Larry McCall, El Paso	W	8

CHARLES HENDERSON
Kansas City, Mo. Light Heavyweight
Born: April 28, 1958
1980

June	26—Don Bester, Chicago	W	4
Nov.	19—John Cox, Moline, Ill.	W	6
Dec.	4—Phil Wade, Kansas City	KO	2
Dec.	19—Tommy Green, Peoria	KO	1

CRAIG HENDERSON
Miami Beach, Fla. Heavyweight
1979

Feb.	11—Jeff Podgurski, Miami Beach	L	4

1980

June	6—Ken Lakusta, Miami	L	4
Sept.	23—Ken Lakusta, Edmonton	KO by	4

WILBUR HENDERSON
Hartford, Conn. Middleweight
1979

Feb.	28—Jesse Walker, Hartford	KO	4
Mar.	12—Dom DiMarzo, Providence	W	6
Mar.	29—Greg Burdette, Hartford	KO	1
Apr.	24—Mike Fisher, Hartford	W	6
May	18—Don Addison, Hartford	D	8
July	27—Don Addison, Hartford	D	4
Sept.	7—Ali Muhammad, Hartford	KO by	7
Nov.	5—Don Addison, Hartford	KO by	7

1980

May	29—Jesse Wilson, W. Hartford	KO	1

JOE HENRY
Toronto, Canada Middleweight
1975

June	10—Roy Johnson, Sorel	L	4
Sept.	16—Roy Johnson, Granby	KO	8

1976

Apr.	5—Clyde Gray, Toronto	KO by	3
May	10—Roy Johnson, Toronto	D	10
July	27—Tony Lopez, Lawrence	L	10
Aug.	23—Beau Jaynes, Peabody	L	10

1977

May	3—Gerald Bouchard, Montreal	L	6
May	21—Jimmy Corkum, Boston	KO by	5
June	28—Jean Claude LeClair, Montreal	KO by	7
June	30—Don Boulter, Halifax	D	10
Oct.	15—Marvin Hagler, Providence	L	10
Nov.	22—Gatean Hart, Buckingham	L	10
Dec.	13—Nick Furlano, Toronto	L	8

1978

Feb.	6—Gary Broughton, Edmonton	W	8
June	1—Alain Turenne, Hull	W	8
June	13—Allan Clarke, Halifax	L	6

1979

May	25—Marciano Bernardi, Montreal	KO by	3
Dec.	18—Jimmy Gradson, Montreal	KO by	7

1980

Feb.	12—Jimmy Gradson, Montreal	KO by	4
Mar.	13—Steve Spatafuria, Hull	KO	3
May	31—Jean Paul Seguin, Smith Falls	L disq.	3
July	25—Jean Paul Seguin, Smith Falls	KO	4
Oct.	28—Mike Knox, Montreal	KO	3
Nov.	11—Don Johnson, Halifax	L	8

ANGEL HEREDIA
Argentine Lightweight
1980

June	2—Luis Rodriguez, Catrilo	W	6
Aug.	1—Joaquin Aguilera, Rio IV	W	6
Sept.	6—Jorge Erramuspe, Gral Pico	L	8

JUSTINO HEREDIA
Argentine Lightweight
1980

Mar.	1—Juan Zuniga, Gral Pico	L	10
May	9—Emilcio Ortiz, La Pampa	W	10
June	2—Juan Zuniga, La Pampa	L	10
Sept.	6—Oscar Alvarenga, Gral Pico	D	10
Oct.	10—Mario Vizcaya, Rio IV	L	10

ANDRES HERNANDEZ
Puerto Rican Bantamweight
1969
June	22—Willie Pastrana, San Juan	W	4
Aug.	16—Santos Rivera, San Juan	L	6
Nov.	1—Santos Rivera, San Juan	W	6

1970
Feb.	14—Jose Rosado, San Juan	W	4
Apr.	18—Santos Rivera, San Juan	L	6

1971
Feb.	11—Tomas Rivera, Ponce	D	4
May	1—Hiram Morales, San Juan	W	8
May	22—Johnny Sandoval, San Juan	W	8
July	24—Eddie Rivera, San Juan	KO	1

1972
May	13—Jose Luis Cetina, Chicago	KO	6
June	3—Jose Sanchez, Chicago	W	10
July	3—Jose Medina, Chicago	W	10
Oct.	7—Benny Ramirez, San Juan	W	10

1973
Apr.	23—Jesus Nieves, San Juan	W	10
June	29—Chuy Rocha, San Juan	W	10
Aug.	4—Vicente Warren, San Juan	KO	6
Sept.	8—Gilbert Illueca, Panama City	L	10

1974
Mar.	3—Erasmo Flores, San Juan	KO	4
July	15—Andres Torres, San Juan	W	12
Aug.	12—Johnny Watson, San Juan	W	10

1975
Feb.	17—Jose Valdez, San Juan	KO	1
Mar.	24—Benito Estrella, San Juan	W	10
June	6—Jaime Perez, Altamirano	KO	1
Aug.	13—Ben Ali, Erie	KO	2
Nov.	6—Bobby Holderfield, San Juan	KO	3
Dec.	20—Wilfredo Gomez, San Juan	KO by	8

1976
Oct.	11—Andres Torres, San Juan	W	10

1977
May	21—Eirberto Sanchez, San Juan	KO	2
July	11—Famosito Gomez, San Juan	W	10

1978
Feb.	18—Coty Garcia, San Juan	W	10
Mar.	5—Young Brance, San Juan	KO	1
Apr.	22—Carlos Zarate, San Juan	KO by	13
	(WBC Bantamweight Title)		

1979
Feb.	26—Enrique Sanchez, Santo Domingo	W	10
July	3—Jose Jiminez, Santo Domingo	L disq.	6
Sept.	22—Edwin Rivera, San Juan	KO	6

1980
Mar.	29—Jeff Chandler, Atlantic City	L	12

ANGEL HERNANDEZ
Puerto Rican Lightweight
1980
Feb.	18—Luis Mejias, San Juan	W	4
Mar.	3—Luis Adorno, San Juan	W	4
Apr.	21—Ray Gonzales, San Juan	D	4
July	24—Efrain Acosta, Rio Piedras	W	6
Dec.	13—Raul Morales, El Paso	W	6

CARLOS HERNANDEZ
Mexican Flyweight
1980
Jan.	10—Librado Roman, Ocotlan	W	4
July	25—Emilio Zamora, Acapulco	KO by	6

CHI CHI HERNANDEZ
Hartford, Conn. Welterweight
1980
June	19—Jack Morrell, Lawrence	D	4
July	25—Felix Nance, New Bedford	L	4
Nov.	11—Angel Ortiz, W. Hartford	W	6

DALE HERNANDEZ
Omaha, Nebr. Junior Welterweight
Born: Jan. 22, 1951
1970
June	8—Terry Chrapko, Omaha	KO	3
July	17—Sonny Oliver, Omaha	W	4
Aug.	28—Calvin Fowler, Omaha	KO	1
Sept.	17—Robert Taylor, Omaha	KO	1
Dec.	16—Jo Jo White, Omaha	KO	2

1971
Jan.	18—Willie Williams, Norfolk, Nebr.	KO	2
Mar.	30—Fred Jimenez, Omaha	W	6
Apr.	23—Jimmy Morton, Omaha	KO	2
May	24—Willie Williams, Omaha	KO	4
Dec.	2—Johnny Copeland, Des Moines	W	6

1972
May	25—Ringo Carrington, Omaha	KO	5
July	10—Rudy Valdez, Denver	KO	3
Sept.	6—Tom Tarantino, Des Moines	KO	5

Sept.	29—Carlos Gonzalez, Denver	KO	1

1973
Jan.	31—Raul Manjarrez, Denver	W	8
Apr.	18—John Copeland, Des Moines	W	10
May	13—Johnny Howard, Pierre	W	10
June	18—Joe Cartwright, Des Moines	W	10

1974
Mar.	22—Ron Pettigrew, Omaha	KO	5
July	14—Roy Holloway, Las Vegas	KO	5
Oct.	16—John North, Chicago	KO	8
Nov.	27—Art Leon, Las Vegas	W	12

1975
Apr.	16—Rodrigo Contreras, Las Vegas	KO	5
Oct.	1—Miguel Mayan, Las Vegas	W	10
Nov.	18—Rafael Nunez, Las Vegas	KO	1
Dec.	3—Tony Martinez, Las Vegas	W	10
Dec.	17—Concepcion Martinez, Las Vegas	W	10

1976
Jan.	28—Jose Gonzalez, Las Vegas	KO	9
Apr.	26—Tony Petronelli, Boston	L	12
Sept.	14—Mike Everett, Philadelphia	L	10

1977
(Inactive)
1978
Mar.	23—Simmie Black, Omaha	KO	1
May	1—Freddie Harris, Omaha	KO	3
July	26—Johnny Summerhays, Omaha	W	10
Oct.	25—Don Sennett, Omaha	KO	6

1979
June	25—Bobby Hughes, Omaha	W	10
Aug.	2—Scotty Foreman, Omaha	KO	10
Nov.	8—Lennox Blackmoore, Omaha	L	10

1980
Jan.	9—Red Garcia, Kansas City	KO	2
Mar.	22—Simmie Black, N. Platte	KO	2
Apr.	13—Ralph Racine, Kansas City	KO by	8

ELIOU HERNANDEZ
Mexican Featherweight
1978
Aug.	24—Frankie Baltazar, Los Angeles	KO by	3
Dec.	9—Javier Flores, Salt Lake City	KO by	2

1979
Mar.	15—Rocky Garcia, Los Angeles	KO by	3
June	5—Ralph Aviles, Hilo	KO by	2
June	16—Lionel Harney, Yerington	KO by	2
Aug.	10—Carlos Ortiz, San Diego	KO by	1
Oct.	4—Louis Loy, Los Angeles	KO by	3
Nov.	13—Randy Clover, Phoenix	KO by	3

1980
Jan.	20—Ricardo Jiminez, Las Vegas	KO by	1
Mar.	6—Felipe Urquiza, San Jose	KO by	4
Apr.	14—Roy Hernandez, Fresno	KO by	4
May	17—Robert Anderson, Las Vegas	KO by	4
July	24—Darrell Stovall, Las Vegas	L	4
July	31—Luis Avila, Los Angeles	KO by	3

FREDDY (RIEL) HERNANDEZ
Colombian Bantamweight
(Previous Record Unavailable)
1980
June	7—Gustavo Martinez, Mexico City	W	10
Oct.	12—Javier Nunez, Mexico City	KO	9

HECTOR (YEYE) HERNANDEZ
Argentine Welterweight
Born: July 9, 1957, S.C. de Bariloche, Arg.
1975
July	25—Galindo Gonzalez, Bariloche	KO	2
Aug.	29—Manuel Cisternas, Santiago, Chile	KO	3
Sept.	26—Manuel Pena, Santiago, Chile	KO	7
Oct.	25—Pablo Mella, Monte Montt, Chile	KO	1
Nov.	14—Raul Sosa, Santiago, Chile	W	8
Dec.	5—Pascual Zabala, Bariloche	W	10
Dec.	19—Omar Zarza, Bariloche	W	10

1976
Jan.	16—Abel Funes, Bariloche	KO	1
Feb.	20—Miguel Figueroa, Bariloche	D	10
Mar.	12—Hugo Gutierrez, Bariloche	KO	3
Apr.	2—Miguel Figueroa, Bariloche	KO	4
Apr.	28—Ceferino Morales, Buenos Aires	L	10
May	21—Floro Zarza, Bariloche	W	10
July	2—Juan J. Gimenez, Bariloche	W	10
July	16—Hector Caceres, Bariloche	W	10
Sept.	9—Juan J. Gimenez, Bahia Blanca	L	10
Sept.	24—Floro Zarza, Bariloche	W disq.	9
Oct.	8—Jose I. Funes, Bariloche	W	10

1977
Apr.	6—Juan Olivera, Bariloche	W	10
May	20—Mario Miranda, Bariloche	KO	3
July	7—Ramon Allende, Bariloche	KO	0
Aug.	5—Jorge Gomez, Bariloche	KO	6

Aug. 26—Joao Merencio, Bariloche ....KO 1
Sept. 9—Jorge Gomez, Bariloche ....D 10
Oct.   7—Nicolas Arkuzsyn, Bariloche ....W 10
Oct. 21—Hugo Albarez, Neuquen ....KO 4
Nov. 21—Ramon Allende, Buenos Aires ....KO 2
Dec. 17—Carlos Gimenez, Buenos Aires ....KO 1
        (Won Argentine Junior Welterweight Title)
1978
Jan. 13—Miguel Maldonado, Bariloche ....W 10
Jan. 27—Cirilo Ruiz, Mar del Plata ....KO 9
Feb. 24—Ernesto Ibarra, C. Rivadavia ....W 10
Apr.   8—Juan R. Olivera, C. Rivadavia ....W 10
May   5—Romulo Ibarra, Cordoba ....W 10
July   7—Juan A. Merlo, La Plata ....W 12
        (Retained Argentine Title)
July 28—Hector Caceres, Neuquen ....W 10
Sept. 23—Hugo Luero, Buenos Aires ....L 12
        (Lost Argentine Junior Welterweight Title)
Nov.   3—Cirilo Ruiz, Bariloche ....KO 5
Dec. 29—Tito del Barco, Bariloche ....D 10
1979
June   8—Juan Olivera, Bariloche ....W 10
July   6—Antonio Juarez, Bariloche ....W 10
Aug.   4—Antonio Juarez, Villa Regina ....D 10
Nov. 17—Hugo Luero, Buenos Aires ....L 12
        (For Argentine Junior Welterweight Title)
1980
Feb.   1—Romulo Ibarra, Bariloche ....W 10
Feb. 22—Hugo Quartapelle, Mar del Plata ....L 10
Apr. 11—Roque Arevalo, Cordoba ....KO 9
July   8—Rafael Zalazar, Cordoba ....KO 5
Oct.   3—Ramon Perez, Cordoba ....L 10
Nov. 14—Nelson Torres, Cordoba ....W 10
Nov. 28—Ramon Peralta, Tucuman ....W 10
Dec. 19—Ramon Peralta, Rio III ....L 10

HIPOLITO HERNANDEZ
Mexican Flyweight
1979
July 11—Hugo Partida, Mexico City ....KO by 2
1980
Jan. 23—Jose Cordoba, Mexico City ....KO 3
Feb. 20—Juan Flores, Mexico City ....L 8
June 27—Felix Palacios, Apatzingan ....KO 2
July 19—Jesus Rodriguez, Mexico City ....L 8

HUGO (PAJ) HERNANDEZ
Argentine Lightweight
1980
June 13—Raul Gonzalez, Bariloche ....KO 1
July 11—Roberto Maciel, Bariloche ....KO 4
Aug. 15—Angel Olea, Mendoza ....W 8
Sept. 12—Carlos Canete, Mendoza ....KO 8
Oct. 10—Juan Huale, Bariloche ....KO 1
Dec.   5—Cirilo Ruiz, Bariloche ....KO 7

JULIO HERNANDEZ
Nicaraguan Junior Featherweight
1976
June 27—Juan Antonio Lopez, Culiacan ....L 10
Oct.   3—Nestor Jiminez, Cartagena ....L 12
1977
(Inactive)
1978
Nov. 17—Blas Chairez, Las Vegas ....KO by 1
1979
Jan. 28—Francisco Figueroa, Managua ....KO 7
June 16—Wilfredo Gomez, San Juan ....KO by 5
        (World Junior Featherweight Title)
1980
Oct. 10—Henry Brent, New York ....KO by 3

LEONEL HERNANDEZ
Born: July 5, 1948, Anzoategui, Venezuela.
Weight: 130 lbs. Height: 5 ft. 3½ in.
Managed by Rafito Cedeno.
1969
Feb. 10—Luis Chourio, Caracas ....KO 1
Mar. 14—Rafael Rodriguez, Caracas ....W 4
Mar. 31—Alberto Hurtado, Caracas ....KO 1
Apr. 18—Silvino Galarraga, Caracas ....KO 1
May   16—Euro Partidas, Caracas ....KO 1
June   3—Modesto Santos, Caracas ....W 6
July   1—Orlando Natera, Caracas ....KO 8
Aug.   4—Frankie Holder, Caracas ....KO 4
Sept. 15—Eligio Pirela, Caracas ....W 8
1970
Apr. 10—Claudio Lopez, Caracas ....W 10
Apr. 24—Silvino Galarraga, Caracas ....KO 10
1971
Apr. 16—Orlando Natera, Caracas ....W 10
May   3—Esteban DeJesus, Caracas ....L 10

Aug.   9—Andres Torres, Caracas ....KO 6
Sept. 6—Enrique Warren, Caracas ....KO 2
Oct. 29—Felipe Lopez, Caracas ....KO 1
Nov. 29—Silvino Galarraga, Caracas ....KO 11
        (Won Venezuelan Featherweight Title)
1972
Feb.   5—Jose Jimenez, Maracay ....KO 2
Mar. 20—Manuel Roque, Caracas ....KO 7
May   27—Raul Martinez Mora, Maracay ....KO 5
Aug. 12—Jose Salas, Monterrey ....KO by 7
Dec. 15—Benjamin Ramirez, Barquisamento .....KO 9
1973
Mar. 17—Ernesto Marcel, Maracay ....W 10
July 14—Rigoberto Riasco, Panama City ....L 10
Aug. 18—Bert Nabalatan, Caracas ....W 10
Sept. 1—Ray Echevarria, Caracas ....KO 3
1974
Feb. 19—Santos Luis Rivera, Maracay ....W 10
Mar. 26—Tomas Frias, Caracas ....W 10
May   10—Benjamin Ortiz, Maracay ....W 10
July 13—Tanny Amancio, Caracas ....KO 1
Sept. 17—Enzo Farinelli, Maracay ....KO 2
Nov. 16—Rodolfo Fuentes, Ciudad Bolivar ....W 10
1975
Mar. 15—Alexis Arguello, Caracas ....KO by 8
        (For WBA Featherweight Title)
June 15—Mario Mendez, Caracas ....KO 10
Aug. 11—Angel Cure, Caracas ....KO 2
Sept. 20—Alfredo Escalera, Caracas ....D 15
        (For WBC Junior Lightweight Title)
1976
Feb. 21—Felix Figueroa, Maracay ....W 10
Apr.   —Rafael Andujar, Carupano ....KO 4
July   —Tony Tris, Cumana ....W 10
Sept. 13—Adalberto Gomez, Maracay ....W 10
1977
Jan. 23—Octavio (Famoso) Gomez, Caracas ......W 10
June 26—Samuel Serrano, Puerto la Cruz ....L 15
        (For World Junior Lightweight Title)
1978
Apr. 22—Lorenzo Torres, Caracas ....KO 8
June   5—Niliberto Herrera, Caracas ....KO 5
Oct. 22—Guillermo Gomez, Caracas ....W 10
1979
July 14—Raul Molina, Caracas ....KO 7
Aug. 18—Roberto Diaz, Caracas ....KO 2
Aug. 25—Raul Astorga, Caracas ....W 10
Oct.   6—Francisco Cruz, Caracas ....KO 7
Nov.   2—Azor Agosto, Caracas ....W 10
Dec. 21—Ildefonso Bethelmy, Caracas ....L 12
        (For Central American & Caribbean
        Junior Lightweight Title)
1980
July   7—Carlos Pinango, Caracas ....KO 8
Nov. 20—Yasutsune Uehara, Tokyo ....L 15
        (For World Junior Lightweight Title)

MIGUEL HERNANDEZ
New York, N.Y. Welterweight
1976
Aug. 27—Raham Muhammad, New York..........KO 1
Oct. 22—Tyrone Phelps, New York ....W 6
Dec. 10—Don Morgan, New York ....KO 1
1977
Jan. 21—D.C. Walker, New York ....W 6
Apr. 25—Jeff Holmes, Newark ....KO 5
May   9—Sam Hailstock, Newark ....KO 3
May   26—Tyrone Phelps, McAfee ....W 6
Sept. 16—Jake Jenkins, New York ....W 8
Dec. 16—John Redford, Detroit ....KO 1
1978
Mar. 17—Ernie Davis, Detroit ....KO 2
May   5—Frank Minigan, Brooklyn ....KO 1
May   8—Larry McCall, Detroit ....KO by 8
July 20—Larry McCall, Detroit ....W 8
1979
June 27—Charlie Benjamin, New York ....KO 1
1980
July 13—Earl Liburd, Great Gorge ....W 6

MIGUEL HERNANDEZ
Mexican Lightweight
1978
Nov. 17—Ricardo Gonzalez, El Paso ....W 10
1979
Nov.   6—Juan Antonio Lopez, Tijuana ....KO by 5
1980
June 30—Manuel Abedoy, Bakersfield ....KO by 4
Oct.   9—Roland Harmon, Los Angeles ....TD 3

RAFAEL HERNANDEZ
Mexican Flyweight
1980
May   14—Fili Gonzalez, Mexico City ....KO 1

June 18—Roberto Arredondo, Mexico City .... W 4

RAMIRO HERNANDEZ
Junior Welterweight·
1979
Oct. 1—Roberto Perez, Corpus Christi .... L 10
Dec. 15—Sean O'Grady, Oklahoma City ...... KO by 4
1980
Feb. 14—Jerry Cheatham, Phoenix .... KO by 1
Mar. 18—Roberto Madrid, Houston .... KO by 6
Apr. 29—Billy Watkins, Houston .... KO by 4
June 24—Jerry Smith, Houston .... L 6
Aug. 19—Ronnie Shields, Beaumont .... KO by 1

RODRIGO HERNANDEZ
Denver, Colo. Junior Middleweight
1978
June 3—Mike Benelli, Denver .... L 4
Oct. 13—Sonny Williams, Denver .... KO 2
1979
Feb. 17—Marcy Atencio, Denver .... KO 1
Mar. 31—Joe Barrientes, Denver .... KO by 6
July 14—Bobby Ray Flores, Denver .... W 4
Aug. 13—Sonny Williams, Denver .... KO 2
Oct. 3—Dick Fisher, Las Vegas .... L 10
1980
Feb. 20—Gary Giron, Las Vegas .... W 10
Apr. 11—J.J. Cottrell, Denver .... D 8
May 2—Randy McGrady, Las Vegas .... L 10

ROY HERNANDEZ
San Antonio, Texas Junior Lightweight
1975
Mar. 27—Tino Gonzalez, Los Angeles .... KO by 3
July 11—Paul Teibl, San Diego .... KO 5
July 26—Paco Zavala, Los Angeles .... KO 2
Aug. 30—Ignacio Bravo, Los Angeles .... KO 5
Oct. 11—Abdul Bey, Los Angeles .... L 7
1976
Mar. 11—Jose Luis Navarette, Los Angeles........ W 10
Mar. 26—Santiago Hernandez, San Bernardino .... KO 9
June 12—Ray Thomas, Fresno.................... KO 4
Aug. 28—Jorge Mejia, Fresno .... KO 5
Nov. 2—Phil Howard, Fort Worth .... KO 2
Nov. 9—Eddie Freeman, Memphis .... KO 5
Dec. 8—Artemio Jeronimo, Stockton............. W 10
1977
Jan. 4—Roberto Quintanilla, Corpus Christi ..... KO 4
Feb. 1—Ricky Ramos, Corpus Christi .... KO 4
Oct. 4—Roberto Quintanilla, San Antonio .... W 10
Dec. 6—Victor Rocha, San Antonio .... KO 5
1978
Feb. 20—Carlos Mendoza, San Antonio .... KO by 6
1979
Feb. 9—Frank Ahumada, Sacramento .... L 10
Feb. 27—Juan Villa, Sacramento .... W 8
Apr. 19—Daryl Jones, Stockton .... W 10
June 10—Francisco Ponce, Stockton .... KO by 1
Sept. 12—Alex Garcia, Stockton .... KO 6
Nov. 2—Juan Meza, Los Angeles .... KO by 1
1980
Mar. 6—Benny Silva, San Jose .... KO 10
Apr. 14—Eliou Hernandez, San Jose .... KO 4
Aug. 26—Johnny Sato, Honolulu .... L 10

VICTOR (COSTENO) HERNANDEZ
Mexican Flyweight
1980
Mar. 7—Joel Gatica, Acapulco .... KO 3
Apr. 2—Jose Garibo, Mexico City .... KO by 3
May 23—Joel Gatica, Acapulco .... KO 3
May 30—Roberto Ramirez, Guadalajara ...... W disq. 3
June 13—Salvador (Raton) Estrada .... KO by 4

ABEL HERRERA
Texas Featherweight
1980
June 17—Joaquin Rosas, San Antonio .... KO 1
July 15—Rudy Guevara, San Antonio .... W 6

ALBERTO HERRERA
Argentine Welterweight
1980
Feb. 1—Ramon Abeldano, Brandsen .... L 6
May 17—Alberto Pilli, Mar del Plata .... L 8
Oct. 10—Hector Quintero, La Plata .... KO 7

CARLOS HERRERA
Argentine Junior Middleweight
1974
Sept. 6—Rene Campos, San Justo .... L 6
Nov. 15—Eduardo Galvan, San Justo .... W 6

Dec. 27—Americo Munoz, Helvecia .... KO 4
1975
Feb. 7—Bruno Gualtieri, Balcarce .... KO 5
Mar. 7—Americo Munoz, Rafaela .... W 8
July 9—Ramon Acosta, San Justo .... KO 3
Sept. 5—Ramon Peralta, Reconquista .... KO 9
Nov. 8—Omar Zarza, San Justo .... W 10
Dec. 5—Raul Sosa, Rafaela .... W 10
Dec. 19—Carlos Villalba, San Justo .... W 12
1976
Feb. 19—Walter Gomez, Salta .... KO by 2
Apr. 23—Ramon Tevez, Charta .... KO 7
June 13—Rodolfo Rojas, Concordia .... L disq. 7
Sept. 24—Mario Miranda, San Justo .... W disq. 3
Dec. 10—Raul Sosa, San Justo .... KO 2
1977
Jan. 28—Leo Chazarreta, Santa Fe .... KO 4
Mar. 11—Carlos Casal, Santa Fe .... KO 10
Apr. 1—Luis Sosa, San Justo .... KO 8
July 15—Nelson Torres, Santa Fe .... W 10
Sept. 2—Juan Jose Perez, Benito Juarez .... W 10
Sept. 30—Juan C. Morales, General Pinedo .... W 10
1978
Jan. 27—Hector Caceres, San Justo .... KO 4
Feb. 17—Rogelio Zarza, San Justo .... W 10
Mar. 17—Walter Gomez, Santa Rosa .... TL 1
Apr. 13—Juan Arana, Esperanza .... KO 3
June 16—Tito Del Barco, San Justo .... W 10
Oct. 13—Miguel Curbelo, San Justo .... KO 9
Nov. 10—Marcos Perez, San Justo .... KO 6
Dec. 10—Pedro Bazan, San Justo .... KO 4
1979
Feb. 9—Juan Carlos Bogado, San Justo .... W 10
Mar. 24—Ariel Fabela, Tucson .... KO 4
Apr. 18—Hipolito Barajas, Las Vegas .... KO 3
May 2—Norris McKinney, Las Vegas .... KO 6
June 2—Alfonso Aguirre, Albuquerque .... KO 2
June 24—Henry Walker, Las Vegas .... KO 6
Aug. 10—Mauro Fernando, San Justo .... KO 4
Dec. 14—Sandy Torres, Buenos Aires .... KO 2
1980
Feb. 15—Miguel A. Hernandez, San Justo .... KO 6
Mar. 14—Joao Tavares, San Justo .... KO 4
Aug. 19—Costello King, Miami Beach .... KO 5
Oct. 24—Tommy Ellis, San Justo .... KO 4
Nov. 25—Maurice Hope, London .... L 15
(WBC Junior Middleweight Title)

DANIEL HERRERA
Mexican Featherweight
1980
June 6—Luis Coral, Chetumal .... KO 3
Sept. 12—Fidel Trejo, Campeche .... KO 4

JOSE HERRERA
Mexican Flyweight
1978
July 28—Jorge Rodriguez, Tampico .... KO 1
Sept. 14—Augustin Sanchez, Los Angeles .... KO 5
Oct. 21—Carlos Gomez, Obregon .... KO 4
1979
July 2—Juan Garcia, Los Angeles .... KO 8
Oct. 23—Mario Chavez, Los Angeles .... KO by 2
1980
May 2—Augustin Sanchez, Los Angeles .... KO 3

JOSE HERRERA
Denver, Colo. Heavyweight
1978
Oct. 13—Fred Grogan, Denver .... W 4
Nov. 17—David Ochoa, Denver .... KO 2
Dec. 8—Tony Frunchy, Denver .... KO 3
1979
June 8—Fred Grogan, Denver .... L 4
1980
Jan. 16—Jesse Prieto, Las Vegas .... L 6

JUAN HERRERA
Mexican Flyweight
1980
Jan. 23—Fidel Martinez, Merida .... KO 4
Feb. 27—Roberto Ruiz, Merida .... W 10
Apr. 26—Tony Escobar, Merida .... W 10
June 14—Jimmy Hernandez, Merida .... KO 3

JUAN C. HERRERA
Argentine Lightweight
1980
June 5—Oscar Arevalo, Tucuman .... L 10
Sept. 5—Roberto Fuerte, Tartagal .... L 10
Oct. 3—Roberto Fuerte, S. Ped. Jujuy .... D 10
Oct. 24—Sebastian Mosqueira, S. Ped. Jujuy ...... L 10

121

MICHAEL HERRON
Memphis, Tenn. Welterweight
Managed by Roy Dean
1978
Apr.	4—Frank Crosby, Greenville	W	6
Apr.	18—Tom Bradley, Memphis	KO	1
Apr.	25—Richard Tomlin, Greenville	KO	1
May	9—Pat Hallacy, Memphis	L	6
May	23—James Wallace, Memphis	KO	2
June	2—Tyrone Wren, Kansas City	L	6
July	21—Don Morgan, Knoxville	L	10
Oct.	3—Freddie Harris, Memphis	W	10

1979
Jan.	16—Billy Milly, Little Rock	W	10
Apr.	7—Donnie Norwood, Kingsport	KO	4
May	1—Carl Crowley, Memphis	W	8
July	17—Ed Modicue, Memphis	W	12
Aug.	28—Don Morgan, Memphis	W	10
Oct.	30—Tyrone Wren, Memphis	W	10
Dec.	15—Larry Martin, Kansas City	KO by	2

1980
Feb.	18—Roger Stafford, Upper Darby	L	8
Mar.	9—Kevin Howard, Atlantic City	KO by	5
May	11—Clyde Gray, Halifax	L	10
June	5—Kevin Howard, Atlantic City	L	8
July	12—Mike Picciotti, Atlantic City	D	10
Oct.	24—Wilford Scypion, Uniondale	KO by	4

FRANK HESIA
Kaneohe, Hawaii Bantamweight
1979
Sept.	1—Jose Zaldivar Panulaya, Hilo	KO	3
Oct.	9—Ceaser Zulueta, Honolulu	KO	2

1980
Feb.	20—Caesar Zulueta, Hilo	KO	3
Apr.	8—Corky Polando, Honolulu	KO	2
July	29—Danny Aguilar, Honolulu	KO by	5
Nov.	19—Caesar Zulueta, Honolulu	KO	2

CARL HESS
Tucson, Arizona Light Heavyweight
1980
Mar.	5—Rafael Zamora, Las Vegas	D	4
Apr.	16—Troy Vaughn, Las Vegas	D	4
May	2—Troy Vaughn, Las Vegas	W	4
May	29—Byron Campbell, Las Vegas	D	6
July	2—Ruben Rascon, Las Vegas	W	6
July	17—James Williams, Tucson	KO	3
July	24—Lee Burkey, Las Vegas	KO by	4
Aug.	26—Fomai Leota, Honolulu	W	8
Sept.	16—Curtis Azevedo, Honolulu	KO by	5
Nov.	12—Vincente Medina, Las Vegas	L	8

LEROY HESTER
Miami Beach Light Heavyweight
1980
July	22—Oscar Florentin, Miami	KO	2
Dec.	16—Costello King, Miami	KO	5

MIKE TRUE HICKMAN
San Diego, Calif. Middleweight
1978
May	5—Hector Fernandez, San Diego	W	5
June	30—Dennis Mancino, San Diego	W	4
July	28—Dean McCartin, San Diego	KO by	3
Sept.	12—Henry Hearns, Pico Rivera	KO by	3

1979
Nov.	27—J. B. Williamson, Los Angeles	KO by	1

1980
Jan.	31—Perry LeVoe, San Carlos	L	6
Feb.	6—Alviar Benros, Costa Mesa	L	6
May	22—Perry LeVoe, San Carlos	KO by	4
Sept.	19—O'Dell Hadley, Inglewood	KO by	2

JUAN HIDALGO
1980
May	2—Richard House, Miami	W	10
June	6—Luis Resto, New York	L	10
Dec.	16—Clauzell Longmire, Miami	KO by	6

REYNALDO HIDALGO
Panamanian Featherweight
1975
Feb.	15—Francisco Castro, Panama City	KO	4
Mar.	2—Roberto Suarez, Panama City	W	10
May	3—Alfonso Perez, Panama City	W	10
Aug.	16—Jesus Rodriguez, Panama City	KO	3
Oct.	4—Mauricio Estrada, Guatamala	KO	3

1976
Jan.	17—Rafael Ortega, Panama City	KO by	8

1977
Jan.	15—Leo Cruz, Panama City	KO	6
May	14—Eusebio Pedroza, Panama City	KO by	9

Aug.	9—Mike Ayala, San Antonio	L	10
Nov.	20—Rodolfo Francis, Panama City	KO by	1

1978
Apr.	15—Rigoberto Garibaldo, Panama City	KO	5
	(Won Panamanian Junior Lightweight Title)		
July	2—Hector Carrasquillo, Panama City	W	10
Sept.	1—Felix Sune, Panama City	W	10

1979
May	19—Antonio Nava, Panama City	W	10

1980
Aug.	16—Enrique Maxwell, Panama City	W	10
Dec.	13—Federico Latino, Panama City	KO	9

VEGRON HILL
Trenton, N.J. Bantamweight
1980
Sept.	27—Tony Hernandez, Trenton	KO	3
Nov.	7—Tim Daniels, Trenton	W	6
Dec.	18—Diego Rosario, Totowa	KO by	4

STEVE HILLIARD
Boston, Mass. Lightweight
1980
June	20—Tommy Brown, Boston	W	4
Dec.	12—Charley McFarline, Brockton	KO	1

GARY HINTON
West Philadelphia, Pa. Lightweight
1978
Jan.	24—Billy Jones, Philadelphia	W	4
June	6—Daryl Guyton, Philadelphia	KO	3
Sept.	21—Chuck Simms, Philadelphia	W	4
Oct.	24—Chuck Simms, Philadelphia	KO	2

1979
Jan.	23—Michael Ross, Philadelphia	W	6
Apr.	10—Lou Daniels, Philadelphia	KO	2
July	16—Jorge Nina, Philadelphia	W	6
Nov.	14—Jerry Graham, Philadelphia	W	6

1980
June	5—Ronnie Green, Atlantic City	W	8
July	3—Charles Brown, Atlantic City	L	10
Oct.	1—Ernest Jackson, Atlantic City	D	8
Nov.	12—Jerry Graham, Philadelphia	W	8

KEN HODGE
Los Angeles, Calif. Middleweight
1980
Jan.	9—Joe Valle, Las Vegas	W	4
Mar.	26—Sylvester Green, Baltimore	W	4
Apr.	21—Clint Modisett, Bakersfield	W	4
June	13—John Steve, San Bernardino	TD	1
Aug.	6—Al Chavez, Santa Monica	W	4
Sept.	5—Sylvester Green, Inglewood	KO	3
Oct.	22—Larry Meyers, Santa Monica	KO by	2

HARLEN HOLDEN
Chicago, Ill. Middleweight
1979
Dec.	8—Terry Jesmer, Winnipeg	W	6
Dec.	15—Elvis Parks, Chicago	L	4

1980
Feb.	18—Warren Thunder, Chicago	L	6
June	27—Larry Puchta, Chicago	KO	2
July	25—Charles Peterson, Chicago	KO	2
Aug.	22—Terry Jesmer, Chicago	KO	6

RALPH HOLLETT
Halifax, Nova Scotia Middleweight
1977
July	14—Allan Clarke, Halifax	W	6
Dec.	8—Ron Johnson, Halifax	L	6

1978
May	6—Eddei Warner, New Glasgow	KO	5
June	13—Kerry Patterson, Halifax	KO	4
June	30—Lenny Carter, Halifax	KO	7
Sept.	12—Al Little, Halifax	W	7
Oct.	8—Jim Gradson, Halifax	L	6

1979
Apr.	3—Donnie Johnson, Halifax	L	10
June	5—Dan Long, Halifax	L	8
June	26—Vinnie Curto, Montreal	L	8

1980
Jan.	22—Fernand Marcotte, Halifax	W	12
Mar.	11—Lancelot Innis, Halifax	W	10
Apr.	29—Chris Clarke, Halifax	L	12
	(Canadian Middleweight Title)		
May	11—Terry Jesmer, Halifax	KO	5
Sept.	24—Chris Clarke, Halifax	KO	2
Nov.	11—Danny Jones, Halifax	KO	8

BILL HOLLIS
Flint, Michigan Light Heavyweight
1976
Apr. 23—Lionel Ford, Flint ....L 4
1977
(Inactive)
1978
Feb. 4—Sonny Woods, Flint ....KO 1
Feb. 17—Ivy Brown, Saginaw ....L 6
May 17—Jeff Harris, Flint ....L 4
Sept. 27—Billy Ratliff, Flint ....KO by 2
Dec. 4—Murray Sutherland, Saginaw ....KO by 3
1979
Dec. 19—Johnny Cox, Rockford ....W 4
1980
May 23—Vonzell Johnson, Pontiac ....KO by 3
Nov. 14—Lemuel McLittle, Detroit ....L 8

LEE HOLLOMAN
(ABDULLAH MUHAMMAD)
Dallas, Texas Heavyweight
1977
Apr. 2—Wolf Ray, Marshall ....KO by 3
Apr. 29—Carl Ivy, Fort Worth ....L 4
May 3—Henry Ray, Marshall ....KO by 3
July 29—Ron Draper, Wichita ....KO by 3
Sept. 22—Claman Parker, Fayetteville ....L 10
Oct. 26—Carl Ivey, Dallas ....L 4
1978
Apr. 25—Larry Alexander, Greenville ....KO by 3
1979
Feb. 21—Lynn Ball, Las Vegas ....KO by 3
Mar. 21—Chuck Gardner, Las Vegas ....L 6
Apr. 18—Walter Cloud, Las Vegas ....D 4
Apr. 26—Jesse Prieto, Pico Rivera ....L 6
May 23—Pinklon Thomas, Las Vegas ....KO by 2
July 31—Dana Goodson, Honolulu ....L 6
Aug. 8—Mike Kachar, Las Vegas ....D 4
Aug. 15—Jesus (Yaqui) Meneses, Las Vegas ....W 6
Aug. 29—Ed Gregg, Las Vegas ....KO by 2
Oct. 2—H. Steichen, Spokane ....KO by 5
Nov. 13—Ed (Too Tall) Jones, Phoenix ....KO by 6
1980
Mar. 7—Tony Perez, El Paso ....KO by 3
June 14—Luis Acosta, Anaheim ....KO by 6
July 15—John Ellis, Anaheim ....L 6

DERRIK HOLMES
Washington, D.C. Featherweight
Born: August 23, 1955. Height: 5 ft. 7 in.
Amateur Record: 129-10 (75 KO's)
1978
June 28—Jimmy Jones, Washington, D.C. ....KO 3
Nov. 17—Robert Matos, Washington, D.C. ....W 6
1979
Jan. 11—Tony Hernandez, Landover ....KO 6
Jan. 22—Rodell Stevenson, Washington, D.C. .....KO 3
Apr. 6—Ronnie Newby, Washington, D.C. ......KO 1
Apr. 20—Juan Marquez, New York ....W 6
May 23—Felix Rodriguez, Washington, D.C. ......KO 2
May 31—Bruce Haines, Philadelphia ....KO 1
July 24—Fernando Martinez, Atlantic City ....KO 1
Aug. 7—Gerald Hayes, Atlantic City ....D 10
Oct. 24—Leo Lopez, Baltimore ....W 10
Dec. 12—Earl Large, Washington, D.C. ....KO 3
1980
Jan. 12—Livio Nolasco, Atlantic City ....KO 2
Mar. 12—Marcial Santiago, Washington, D.C. .....W 10
Mar. 31—Isaac Vega, Landover ....KO 1
Aug. 22—Wilfredo Gomez, Las Vegas ....KO by 5
(For World Junior Featherweight Title)

LINDELL HOLMES
Detroit, Mich. Middleweight
Managed by Emanuel Steward
1979
Nov. 15—Rodney Coupe, Detroit ....KO 1
1980
Feb. 7—Dave Roberts, Wyandotte ....KO 3
Mar. 2—Clifford Askew, Detroit ....KO 1
May 3—Willie Torres, Detroit ....KO 1
July 17—Vernon Cunningham, Maumee ....KO 4
Sept. 10—Benny Mitchell, Detroit ....KO 3
Oct. 18—George Madison, Toledo ....KO 4
Dec. 12—Gary Thomas, Detroit ....KO 4

MARK HOLMES
Easton, Pa. Middleweight
1980
July 7—Robbie Robinson, Bloomington ....KO 2
Aug. 8—L.G. Hudson, Las Vegas ....W 4
Aug. 22—Mario Neri, Las Vegas ....KO 3
Oct. 2—Randy Rivers, Las Vegas ....W 6

Nov. 25—Bruce Calloway, New Orleans ....KO 5

STEVE (THE HAMMER) HOMAN
Raytown, Kansas Lightweight
Managed by Peyton Sher
1976
Aug. 7—Bob Shaw, Hutchinson ....KO 1
Aug. 25—Lamar Baskins, Kansas City ....KO 2
Oct. 6—Marion Thomas, Kansas City ....W 4
Dec. 15—Santos Rodriguez, Kansas City ....KO 4
1977
Jan. 29—Charles Worman, Kansas City ....KO 1
Mar. 18—Freddie Harris, Kansas City ....W 6
June 17—Jerry Strickland, Kansas City ....KO 2
June 30—Robert Turner, Wichita ....W 6
Franklin, Kansas City ....W 6
Sept. 7—Al Franklin, Kansas City ....W 6
Oct. 3—James Kenty, Columbus ....L 6
Dec. 1—Maurice (Termite) Watkins, Houston .....L 10
1978
Mar. 31—Benny Marquez, Kansas City ....W 8
Oct. 6—Harvey Wilson, Kansas City ....KO 3
1979
Jan. 19—Eddie Murray, Overland Park, Kans. ...KO 5
Mar. 16—Victor Cid, San Antonio ....KO 8
June 1—Silverio Martinez, Kansas City ....KO 2
July 26—Tom Crowley, Overland Park ....KO 6
Oct. 11—John Summerhays, Ontario ....W 10
Nov. 23—Johnny Copeland, Overland Park ....W 10
1980
Mar. 16—Ken Saale, Kansas City ....W 10

W. C. HONEYCUTT
Detroit, Mich. Light Heavyweight
1978
June 22—Dwight Curtis, Detroit ....KO 2
1979
Nov. 1—Zeke Zelichowski, Detroit ....KO 1
Dec. 1—Earl Caldwell, Detroit ....KO by 3
1980
Jan. 12—Gary Hunter, Detroit ....KO 2
Feb. 22—John Maschek, Detroit ....KO 1

MANUEL HONG
Mexican Flyweight
1980
Jan. 23—Eloy Cardenas, Merida ....KO 6
Mar. 19—Chucho Gutierrez, Merida ....KO 3
June 6—Juan Bernal, Campeche ....KO 4
June 28—Pablo Ibarra, Campeche ....KO 6

LAMONT HOPKINS
Flint, Mich. Welterweight
1979
Mar. 27—Charley Peterson, Michigan ....KO by 4
1980
Jan. 24—Bernard Mays, Detroit ....L 6
Feb. 22—Duane Thomas, Detroit ....KO by 3
Oct. 28—Razor Rosenberger, Warren ....L 6

MILTON HOPKINS
Newark, New Jersey Light Heavyweight
1977
May 23—Steve Small, White Plains ....KO by 1
1978
(Inactive)
1979
June 28—Charlie Young, Staten Island ....KO by 4
1980
Jan. 19—Joe Britt, Syracuse ....KO by 1
Mar. 22—Richard Giquinto, Atlantic City .....KO by 1

RICK HORAN
Brockton, Mass. Junior Middleweight
1979
Feb. 22—John Griffin, Cohoes ....L 4
Mar. 1—George Crosswell, White Plains ....KO 1
Mar. 29—Larry Allen, Cohoes ....W 6
1980
Mar. 25—Donato Paduano, Montreal ....KO by 3

MAX HORD
Fernandina Beach, Fla. Middleweight
1974
Oct. 16—Prentice Clark, Lake City...............KO 2
Nov. 12—Harold Solomon, Lake City..............W 4
1975
Aug. 19—Edgar Ross, Orlando ....KO by 2
Oct. 28—Joey Vincent, Orlando ....KO by 2
Dec. 11—Joey Vincent, Fernandina Beach .....KO by 4
1976
Feb. 28—Al Hughes, Muncie..................KO by 5

123

July   20—Scott Clark, Orlando................KO by 2
Sept.   9—Jimmy Thomas, Fernandina Beach......KO 2
Oct.   13—Eddie Brown, Fernandina Beach........KO 3
Dec.   1—Al Young, Fernandina Beach...........KO 2
1977
Jan.   5—Andy Walsh, Fernandina Beach........KO 1
Feb.   23—Gene Wells, Fernandina Beach......KO by 8
Apr.   2—Jimmy Cook, Tallahassee................W 6
May   14—Tony Gardner, Tallahassee..............L 10
Nov.   25—Don Singleton, Fernandina Beach.......KO 3
1978
Feb.   23—Tony Gardner, Fernandina Beach.......W 10
Apr.   8—Simmie Black, Fernandina Beach.......KO 4
May   10—Jimmy Cook, Fernandina Beach.........W 10
July   12—Tony Gardner, Fernandina Beach.......W 12
Sept.   27—Joe Hooks, Fernandina Beach..........KO 1
1979
Jan.   17—Jimmy Cook, Fernandina Beach........KO 6
Apr.   27—Tony Danza, New York..............KO by 1
May   12—Simmie Black, Fernandina Beach.......KO 5
July   25—Lee Thomas, Fernandina Beach........KO 7
Dec.   7—Tony Daniels, North Miami.........L disq. 4
Dec.   28—Lee Thomas, Fernandina Beach.......KO 3
1980
Feb.   5—Ernie Dunbar, Charleston.........KO by 4
Feb.   21—Mike Wilcox, Gainesville..............KO 2
Mar.   26—Joey Vincent, Fernandina Beach.....KO by 5
June   26—Mike Wilcox, Gainesville................W 8
July   19—Al Hughes, Panama City...............KO 3

DENNIS HORNE
Oklahoma City, Okla. Middleweight
1977
July   19—Steve Channell, Oklahoma City.........W 4
Aug.   2—Paul Knight, Oklahoma City..........KO 1
Aug.   16—Rocky Matthews, Oklahoma City........KO 2
Sept.   6—Clyde Spencer, Oklahoma City..........L 4
Oct.   4—Dennis Smedley, Oklahoma City........W 4
Oct.   18—Rocky Matthews, Oklahoma City........W 4
Nov.   15—Wendell Helm, Oklahoma City.........KO 1
Dec.   5—Gary Chiaverini, Kansas City..........W 4
1978
Jan.   24—Pat Hallacy, Wichita...................L 4
June   10—Clyde Spencer, Oklahoma City.........KO 2
July   25—Donnie London, Little Rock...........KO 6
Sept.   6—Clyde Spencer, Oklahoma City..........L 4
1979
Jan.   16—Johnny Morgan, Little Rock............W 4
Feb.   20—Richie Roberts, Orlando................L 6
Aug.   3—Don Masterson, Tulsa.................KO 2
Dec.   20—Odell Willis, Wichita.................KO 6
1980
Mar.   3—Lorenzo Jones, Oklahoma City.........KO 2
Apr.   3—Rocky Matthews, Oklahoma City........KO 6
June   10—Pete Knight, Oklahoma City...........KO 4

SAMMY HORNE
Anderson, S.C. Welterweight
Height: 5 ft. 9 in.
1979
Dec.   23—Tony Thomas, Spartanburg.............KO 4
1980
Jan.   16—Jim Van Zandt, Las Vegas.............KO 1
Feb.   20—Mario Tenio, Las Vegas................W 6
July   18—Sam Lantion, Spartanburg.............KO 3
Oct.   4—Paul Gentry, Union, S.C..............KO 1
Nov.   6—Roosevelt Moss, Spartanburg..........KO 2
Dec.   9—James Reed, Kalamazoo................KO 4
Dec.   21—Randy Mitchum, Spartanburg...........W 6

MELVIN HOSEY
Dayton, Ohio Heavyweight
1980
Feb.   1—George Mostardini, Louisville...........L 4
May   17—Jamie Knox, Dayton...................KO 3
July   17—Ali Haakim, Maumee.................KO by 4
Aug.   27—Stan Johnson, Edmonton................L 6
Sept.   10—Terry Nicopolis, Cicero................L 4
Nov.   13—Alfonso Ratliff, Chicago............KO by 5

CHARLES HOSTETTER
Odessa, Texas Heavyweight
1980
Sept.   23—Zack Freeman, Odessa..................W 4
Dec.   16—Paul Lawson, Odessa..................KO 2

RICHARD HOUSE
St. Louis, Mo. Welterweight
1979
Oct.   3—Jimmy Heair, Orlando.................W 10
1980
Aug.   14—Floyd Pearson, Chicago...............KO 8
Sept.   11—Jose Santana, Chicago.............KO by 8

JOE HOUSTON
Boston, Mass. Welterweight
1974
Mar.   1—Donnie Sennett, Worcester...............L 6
Mar.   7—L. C. Mack, Portland, Me...........KO by 3
Apr.   24—Jackie Smith, Waltham.............KO by 3
Oct.   29—Fred Boynton, Walpole..............KO by 2
Nov.   15—L. C. Mack, Worcester..................W 4
Nov.   23—Vinnie DeBorros, Waterbury........KO by 1
1975
Apr.   11—Jesse Bender, New Bedford..............L 6
Apr.   14—Billy Duquette, Boston.............KO by 1
May   8—Bob Pompeo, Portland.............KO by 4
May   10—Billy Duquette, Brockton...............W 4
May   24—Dana McCarthy, Middleton.........KO by 4
July   3—Frank Moore, Chelsea....................D 6
July   17—Billy Duquette, Portland, Me..........W 6
Oct.   23—Juan Colon, Portland...................L 6
Nov.   21—Rocky Estafire, Providence........KO by 2
Nov.   27—Roger Phillips, Portland..............W 8
Dec.   20—Bobby Asack, Boston...................W 4
1976
Jan.   15—Larry Butler, Portland.............KO by 3
Jan.   24—Don Wigfall, Brockton..............KO by 1
Mar.   17—Billy Duquette, Boston.................L 4
Mar.   23—Kenny Nelson, Boston...................L 4
May   19—Jackie Smith, Taunton..................L 8
June   6—Roland Cousins, Taunton...............W 6
Aug.   31—Marshall Butler, Montreal.........KO by 4
Nov.   25—Rick Burgess, Portland, Me........KO by 2
1977
Apr.   20—Frank Moore, Taunton...................L 6
Aug.   27—Vinnie Curto, Bath...................L 10
Oct.   7—Bob Santos, Lowell...................KO 5
Nov.   13—Lorenzo Howard, Albany................W 6
Nov.   18—Ray Bryant, Lowell................KO by 4
Nov.   24—Wilson Bell, Portland.............KO by 5
1978
Feb.   24—Ricky Zarbatany, Chicoutimi...........L 8
Mar.   4—Dom DiMarzo, Boston..............KO by 3
June   19—Dom DiMarzo, Boston...................L 8
Sept.   13—Ricky Burgess, Waterville.........KO by 4
1979
Oct.   2—Daniel Levesque, Montreal.........KO by 3
1980
May   29—Dom DiMarzo, Revere..............KO by 3
(Retired by Massachusetts Commission due to number of knockout losses)

BOBBY HOWARD
Seattle, Wash. Middleweight
1977
Feb.   12—Tommy Howard, Lacey..................L 4
Mar.   25—Les Vegas, Seattle................KO by 1
June   23—Steve Tohill, Vancouver................L 6
July   2—Pat Wilson, Salem......................W 6
1978
Jan.   26—C. J. Brown, Seattle...................W 6
Feb.   12—Joe Williams, Seattle...............Exh. 3
Mar.   2—Doug Arlt, Everett.....................D 6
May   4—Doug Arlt, Portland....................W 6
May   9—Eugene White, Seattle................KO 6
Aug.   29—Daryl Penn, Seattle..................W 12
Oct.   31—Doug Arlt, Seattle...................KO 4
1979
Jan.   18—Daryl Penn, Portland...................L 8
Apr.   7—Ken Foren, Billings..................KO 1
July   2—Les Riggins, Washington...............W 6
1980
June   13—Gordie Lawson, Nanaimo.................D 6
June   26—Gordie Lawson, Bellingham..............D 6
Aug.   6—Felton Marshall, Santa Monica.........L 10
Sept.   5—Tim Harris, Sacramento.................L 6
Oct.   11—Charles LeCour, Nanaimo...............ND 6
Nov.   19—Jimmy Owens, Las Vegas..............W-4

DENNIS HOWARD
Philadelphia, Pa. Lightweight
1980
July   3—Anthony Fletcher, Atlantic City.........L 6
Aug.   25—Wayne Dabney, Philadelphia...........KO 2
Oct.   24—David Bookman, Philadelphia...........W 4

KEVIN HOWARD
Philadelphia, Pa. Welterweight
1978
Oct.   22—Abel Santiago, Allentown.............KO 4
1979
Feb.   5—William Burton, Philadelphia...........W 4
Apr.   3—Marvin Edwards, Philadelphia.........KO 1
May   22—Mario Williams, Upper Darby...........W 6
Sept.   26—Malik Muhammad, Upper Darby.......KO 2

124

Oct. 30—John Cooper, Upper Darby ....D 8
1980
Jan. 12—Joe Tiberi, Atlantic City ....W 6
Mar. 9—Michael Herron, Atlantic City ....KO 5
June 5—Michael Herron, Atlantic City ....W 8
July 28—Ernie Gladney, Philadelphia ....KO 4
Oct. 24—Tim LaValley, Philadelphia ....KO 2

BOBBY RICO HOYE
Detroit, Mich. Middleweight
1978
Dec. 9—Pablo Rodriguez, Detroit ....KO 4
1979
Mar. 3—Johnny Heard, Detroit ....KO 7
May 8—Eddie Philips, Center Stage ....W 10
July 12—Sammy Floyd, Detroit ....W 6
Sept. 26—Gary Broughton, Windsor ....L 10
1980
Oct. 30—Ernie Singletary, Atlantic City ......KO by 2

LOUIE HUBELA
Brooklyn, N.Y. Lightweight
Born: Aug. 20, 1954
1977
Nov. 18—Jose Ortiz, New York ....W 4
Dec. 21—Mike Leonard, Brooklyn ....KO 1
1978
Jan. 25—Rich Garland, Brooklyn ....W 4
Feb. 22—Dan Daniels, Brooklyn ....W 6
Apr. 19—David Vega, Brooklyn ....W 4
Apr. 27—Iggy Villanueva, New York ....W 4
May 26—Ed Leahy, Brooklyn ....KO 5
July 26—Clyde Beattie, New York ....W 4
Aug. 25—Jimmy McNeece, New York ....W 6
Oct. 28—Dan Daniels, Jersey City ....W 6
1979
Jan. 26—David Vega, New York ....W 4
Feb. 22—Ralph Dumont, Cohoes ....KO 3
May 11—Benito Jimenez, New York ....W 6
May 24—Benny Fuentes, Cohoes ....W 6
June 28—Ronnie Newby, Staten Island ....KO 1
Oct. 26—Reggie James, Staten Island ....KO 2
1980
Feb. 29—Jorge Nina, Brooklyn ....W 8
Apr. 9—Lou Daniels, Brooklyn ....KO 1
Apr. 19—Jean LaPointe, Syracuse ....W 8
June 18—Kelvin Lampkin, Struthers ....W 6
Sept. 12—John Verderosa, New York ....KO by 7

JUAN HUERTA
1980
Apr. 12—Dave Garza, San Jose ....L 6
Apr. 22—Paul Jones, Sacramento ....KO by 2
July 16—Fred Hutchins, Stockton ....KO by 6

BOBBY HUFF
Brockton, Mass. Lightweight
1979
June 18—Salvatore Ramos, Cohoes ....KO by 5
Sept. 30—Walter Seeley, Suffolk ....KO by 4
1980
Dec. 12—Edwin Curet, Brockton ....L 4

AL HUGHES
Selma, Ind. Welterweight
Born: April 24, 1953
1975
Apr. 17—Jim Claar, Indianapolis..................W 4
May 10—Willie Wren, Toledo....................L 4
May 22—Bobbie Orr, Cincinnati ....D 4
June 6—Bobbie Crawford, Indianapolis..........W 4
June 20—Arthur Shelly, Dayton.................KO 1
Oct. 4—Reuben Green, Chicago ....KO 2
Nov. 22—Bobby Plegge, Chicago ....D 4
Dec. 16—Robert Strickland, Indianapolis..........W 4
1976
Feb. 28—Max Horde, Muncie ....KO 5
Mar. 20—Dave Adkins, Indianapolis ....L 5
Nov. 9—Frank Santore, Indianapolis ....KO by 1
Nov. 13—Steve Horten, Indianapolis ....KO 2
Nov. 30—Clancy Morgan, Indianapolis ....D 4
1977
July 25—Benny Marquez, Chicago ....KO by 1
Sept. 16—Jerry Graham, Wilmington ....KO by 5
1978
Feb. 23—Bobby Acey, Virginia Beach ....KO by 2
Oct. 6—Ronnie Branch, Baltimore ....D 6
Nov. 21—Craig Stevens, Landover ....L 5
Dec. 9—Jimmy Corkum, Springfield ....L 10
1979
Jan. 10—Willie Daniels, Las Vegas ....W 10
Feb. 7—Miguel Estrada, Las Vegas ....L 10
Dec. 2—Ernie Wicher, Muncie ....W 6

1980
July 19—Max Hord, Panama City, Fla.........KO by 3

MARK HUGHES
Texas Middleweight
1978
Dec. 5—Robert Thomas, San Antonio ....KO by 1
1979
July 21—Joseph Davila, Dallas ....W 4
1980
July 25—Johnny Heard, Chicago ....KO by 2

ROBERT HUGHES
Aurora, Ill. Welterweight
1979
Mar. 17—Pete Podgorski, Chicago ....W 4
Apr. 27—Harold Skully, Chicago ....W 4
June 13—Chief Ketchinakow, Bridgeview ....KO 1
Oct. 19—Louis Mateo, Chicago ....W 4
Dec. 15—Bobby Orr, Chicago ....W 4
1980
Mar. 3—Louis Mateo, Chicago ....L 6
Apr. 17—Lloyd Pearson, Chicago ....KO by 2
July 10—Steve Williams, Chicago ....L 6

STEVE (BUTTERFLY) HUGHES
Palmer Park, Md. Welterweight
1978
Nov. 3—Sean Mannion, Portland, Me............L 6
Nov. 17—C. J. Faison, Washington, D.C. ....L 6
Nov. 21—Tim Walker, Landover ....W 5
1979
Jan. 11—Tim Walker, Landover ....L 6
Feb. 12—C. J. Faison, Washington, D.C. .....KO by 1
1980
May 31—John DeGrazio, Lindsay ....L 6

FIGHTING HUNKS
St. Kitts, B.W.I. Welterweight
1972
Aug. 24—Sporting Richards, St. Kitts ....KO 3
Dec. 21—Sporting Richards, St. Kitts ....W 4
1973
Aug. 25—Chit Barrow, St. Kitts ....W 6
Sept. 15—Road Runner, St. Croix ....KO 1
Oct. 20—T.N.T. Gordon, St. Croix ....L 6
Oct. 29—Young Dorsett, St. Kitts ....W 8
Dec. 15—Chu-Chu, St. Martin ....W 6
1974
Aug. 28—Reliance Roy, St. Kitts ....W 6
Sept. 28—Easy Boy Ken, St. Kitts ....KO 9
Dec. 28—Easy Boy Ken, St. Kitts ....W 10
1975
Feb. 14—Skipping Tennis, St. Martin ....KO 6
Feb. 19—St. Jean Yves, Guadaloupe ....KO 1
Feb. 25—Frankie Romero, St. Croix ....L 6
Apr. 4—Dermel, Guadaloupe ....W 4
Apr. 11—Skipping Tennis, St. Martin ....KO 7
—Frankie Gonzales, St. Martin ....KO by 2
May 9—Coniver Francis, Guadaloupe ....W 4
Sept. 6—Young Dorsett, St. Kitts ....KO 4
Oct. 31—Easy Boy Lake, St. Martin ....W 10
Dec. 31—Chu-Chu, St. Kitts ....KO 4
1976
Jan. 9—Easy Boy Lake, St. Martin ....L 10
Feb. 13—Yves Jeudi, St. Martin ....KO 5
Mar. 26—Jesse Torres, St. Martin ....L 10
May 14—Robinson Junior, St. Martin ....D 10
July 16—Rubella Duran, St. Martin ....KO by 8
Sept. 15—Skipping Tennis, St. Martin ....KO 3
Oct. 29—Easy Boy Lake, St. Thomas ....KO 10
1977
Jan. 21—Ramon Kid Serrano, St. Thomas ....W 10
Feb. 26—Joe Walcott, St. Kitts ....W 12
June 10—Mao De La Rosa, Curacao ....D 10
Oct. 14—Domingo Ayala, St. Thomas ....KO by 3
Dec. 17—Luis Resto, St. Thomas ....L 10
1978
Mar. 3—Skipping Tennis, Guadaloupe ....W 6
Apr. 27—Freitas Caban, Curacao ....D 10
June 30—Kaky Ramos, Curacao ....KO 3
July 28—Earl Liburd, St. Thomas ....L 12
Aug. 5—Joe Walcott, St. Kitts ....W 12
Oct. 20—Earl Liburd, St. Thomas ....W 12
Nov. 3—Turco Betruz, Curacao ....W 10
Dec. 12—Toughfeller, St. Kitts ....KO 4

125

1979
Feb.   8—Segundo Murillo, Ecuador .... L 12
Nov.   —Rocky Orango, St. Thomas .... W 10
1980
May   23—Juan Serrano, St. Thomas .... L 10

GARY HUNTER
Windsor, Canada Light Heavyweight
1979
Sept. 26—John Kubinec, Windsor .... L 4
Oct.   18—Zeke Zelichowski, Detroit .... KO by 1
1980
Jan.   12—W.C. Honeycutt, Detroit .... KO by 2
Apr.   17—Jamie Olatunde, Chicago .... KO by 1
Sept. 27—Al Rodriguez, Detroit .... KO by 1
Dec.   11—Leroy Murphy, Chicago .... KO by 1

JERRY HUNTER
Louisville, Ky. Heavyweight
1979
       —Jimmy Robertson, Evansville .... D 6
1980
Jan.   12—W.C. Honeycutt, Detroit .... KO by 2
Apr.   17—Jamie Olatunde, Chicago .... KO by 1
May   13—Clyde Mudgett, Indianapolis .... KO by 3
Aug.   2—Tony Tubbs, Cincinnati .... KO by 4
Sept.   6—Tom Stevenson, Jenkins .... L 6
Oct.   28—Ric Innis, Indianapolis .... KO by 1

STEVE HUNTINGTON
West Jordan, Utah Heavyweight
Born: Sept. 24, 1957
1978
Dec.   9—Sam Aione, Salt Lake City .... W 4
1979
Jan.   20—Gary Coonradt, Ogden .... KO 1
Feb.   14—John Hoke, Salt Lake City .... KO 2
Mar.   10—Darrell Patterson, Salt Lake City ...... KO 5
Apr.   21—Roger Troupe, Las Vegas .... KO 5
Oct.   13—Samson Nagata, Salt Lake City .... W 6
1980
Mar.   22—Freddie News, Salt Lake City .... KO 2
Apr.   17—T.C. Bowman, Las Vegas .... W 8
May   16—Franco Morales, Ogden .... KO 1
July   8—Ron Draper, Las Vegas .... W 6

ADOLFO HURTADO
Los Angeles, Calif. Junior Lightweight
1978
Nov.   16—George Garcia, Los Angeles .... KO by 5
1979
July   25—Fred Roach, Las Vegas .... L 6
Aug.   16—Rodrigo Aguirre, Los Angeles .... L TD 6
Nov.   1—Apollo Carbajal, Los Angeles .... W 4
Nov.   8—Ricardo Martinez, Los Angeles .... W 4
Dec.   12—Juan Rodriguez, Las Vegas .... KO 2
1980
Feb.   5—Richard Savala, Sacramento .... KO by 4
Apr.   18—Mario Portillo, Sacramento .... L 6

RON HUSTON
Weehawken, N. J. Light Heavyweight
1979
May   21—John Powell, New York .... KO 4
July   31—Harry Fryar, Totowa .... KO 4
Oct.   4—Curtis Goins, New York .... KO 4
Nov.   9—Gene Muldrow, New York .... KO 1
1980
Mar.   21—Henry Patterson, Fall River .... W 10
July   25—Tommy Butts, New Bedford .... KO 1
Oct.   2—Cornell Chavis, New York .... W 6
Nov.   28—Eric Winbush, New York .... W 8

MIKE HUTCHINSON
Texas Light Heavyweight
1979
June   17—Bobby Thomas, San Antonio .... KO 1
July   9—Jimmy Stringer, Odessa .... KO 1
July   21—Carlos Black, Dallas .... KO 1
Dec.   14—Manuel Garcia, Dallas .... KO by 4
1980
Aug.   8—Roy Barrientos, Dallas .... W 4
Oct.   16—Randall Jackson, Toledo .... W 4
Oct.   23—Tony Cerda, Las Vegas .... KO by 1
Dec.   3—Dennis Fikes, Las Vegas .... KO by 1
Dec.   6—Danny Paul, Detroit .... KO by 4
Dec.   9—T.C. Williams, Birmingham .... W 4

JESUS IBANEZ
Argentine Light Heavyweight
1980
Mar.   14—Carlos F. Burlon, San Pedro .... D 10
May   17—Alfredo Morales, La Pampa .... L 10
July   12—Cesar Duarte, Pergamino .... TD 5
Aug.   15—Cesar Duarte, S.Sal. de Jujuy .... D 10

MARK IBANEZ
Honolulu, Hawaii Junior Welterweight
1978
June   20—Clinton Campbell, Honolulu .... KO 3
July   18—Alfredo Logan, Honolulu .... W 5
       30—Ful Sumagaysay, Honolulu .... W 6
June   12—Frankie Balasi, Honolulu .... KO 4
July   27—Jose Osuna, Hilo .... L 8
1980
Feb.   19—Vito Meredith, Honolulu .... KO 2
Mar.   4—Rudy Mata, Honolulu .... KO 1
Apr.   8—Joe Lim, Honolulu .... W 10
May   12—Danny Patino, Honolulu .... KO 4
June   17—Jale Fotu, Honolulu .... KO 1
July   22—Rogelio Castaneda, Honolulu .... KO 2
Aug.   19—Sammy Ayala, Honolulu .... KO 1
Sept. 23—Albert Guevara, Honolulu .... KO 6
Nov.   19—Armando Ramirez, Honolulu .... KO 3

CAMILIO IBARRA (FLORES)
Mexican Lightweight
1979
Jan.   12—Salvador Torres, Coatzacoalcos .... KO 6
Jan.   27—Nacho Saucedo, Coatzacoalcos .... KO 5
Mar.   13—Rosendo Ramon, San Antonio .... TD 3
Apr.   17—John Morgan, Houston .... KO 6
Oct.   27—Herman Montes, Los Angeles .... L 10
1980
Jan.   26—Monroe Brooks, Los Angeles .... KO by 5
May   10—Ernesto Davies, Mexico City .... W disq. 3

CARLOS IBARRA
Mexican Featherweight
1979
Oct.   10—Pablo Ramirez, Mexico City .... W 10
Nov.   24—Pablo Ramirez, Mexico City .... KO by 6
1980
Feb.   6—Delfino Mendoza, Mexico City ...... KO by 7
Mar.   26—Antonio Arcos, Mexico City .... W 10
Aug.   2—Raul Decaro, Mexico City .... L disq. 5

DEMETRIO IBARRA
Argentine Lightweight
1980
May   2—Sebastien Mosqueira, Corrientes .... L 10
Aug.   1—Carlos Escurra, Corrientes .... KO 9
Aug.   15—Ramon Gonzalez, Corrientes .... W 10

NATALIO IBARRA
Argentine Light Heavyweight
1980
Feb.   8—Cesar Duarte, Trelew .... KO by 5
July   18—Ubaldo Correa, Bahia Blanca .... KO by 7
Sept.   6—Hugo Rossi, La Plata .... L 10
Oct.   18—Ruben Wilberger, Trenel .... KO by 9
Oct.   31—Angel Caro, P.R.S. Pena .... KO by 9

ROMULO IBARRA
Argentine Welterweight
1980
Feb.   1—Hector Hernandez, Bariloche .... L 10
Aug.   1—Jose Guevara, Corrientes .... W 10
Sept.   5—Rodolfo Petrizani, Corrientes .... W 10
Oct.   10—Nicolas Arkuszyn, Formosa .... L 10
Nov.   14—Joaquin Moreyra, Formosa .... L 10
Dec.   10—Ruben Verdun, Posadas .... KO 5

JOSE IBIRIS
Argentine Flyweight
1980
Feb.   8—Hector Patri, Mar del Plata .... L 8
Sept. 26—Hector Patri, Le Plata .... L 10

126

CANDELARIO (CANDY) IGLECIAS
Phoenix, Ariz. Flyweight
1977
Jan.	25—Johnny Mesa, Phoenix	D	6
Feb.	8—Tony Moreno, San Antonio	L	10
Apr.	27—Fred Hutchinson, Phoenix	KO	2
May	18—Johnny Love, Phoenix	KO	2
June	2—Danny Young, Phoenix	KO	5
June	14—Raul Ochoa, Phoenix	L	6
July	12—Alberto Martinez, Phoenix	KO	2

1978
Feb.	25—Joey Olivo, Los Angeles	L	6
Apr.	12—Alfonso Del Gadillo, Las Vegas	KO	7
May	19—Joey Olivo, Concord	L	10
Sept.	14—Javier Mendoza, Los Angeles	KO by	3
Nov.	15—Alonso Gonzalez, Las Vegas	W	10

1979
Jan.	31—Johnny Carter, Las Vegas	L	10
Feb.	26—Elias DeLeon, Houston	KO by	6
Apr.	24—Johnny Mesa, Houston	W	10
May	18—Joey Olivo, Pico Rivera	L	10
June	6—Raul Pacheco, Los Angeles	W	10
Aug.	29—Adelaido Galindo, Houston	L	10

1980
Jan.	22—Humberto Rodriguez, Houston	W	10
Apr.	1—Pedro Galaviz, Houston	KO by	6
June	18—Augustin Sanchez, Las Vegas	KO	7
July	31—Joey Olivo, Los Angeles	L	10
Oct.	9—Juan Garcia, Los Angeles	L	10
Nov.	7—Candido Tellez, San Antonio	KO by	5

JIM INGRAM
Los Angeles, Calif. Light Heavyweight
1978
Jan.	27—Lenis Provo, San Diego	L	5
Feb.	10—Hillard Edmonds, San Diego	D	4
Feb.	24—Lenis Provo, San Diego	L	5
Apr.	14—Junior Albers, San Diego	W	6
Apr.	28—David Smith, San Diego	W	6
May	5—Hector Torres, San Diego	KO	3
July	12—Bashiru Ali, Oakland	W	6
Aug.	18—Pedro Garcia, San Diego	KO	3
Sept.	12—Alvaro (Yaqui) Lopez, Pico Rivera	W	10
Oct.	22—Franco Thomas, Reno	W	10
Nov.	17—John Baca, San Diego	KO by	2

1979
Jan.	19—Eric Sedillo, Ogden	L	10
Feb.	7—Lynn Ball, Las Vegas	W	6
Feb.	28—Marvin Camel, Las Vegas	L	10
Mar.	11—Tony Licata, Reno	D	10
Mar.	28—Emeterio Villanueva, Stockton	KO	8
Apr.	12—Willie Shannon, Portland	L	10
May	9—Tommy Evans, Oakland	L	10
May	18—Earl Tripp, Pico Rivera	KO by	9
July	14—Ron Brown, Denver	L	8
Aug.	1—Marty Monroe, Los Angeles	L	10
Sept.	28—Clarence Geigger, Las Vegas	W	6
Nov.	27—Alvaro Lopez, Las Vegas	KO	5

1980
Jan.	18—Alvin Dominey, Las Vegas	W	10
Feb.	24—Willie Shannon, Las Vegas	KO by	3
May	3—Stan Ward, San Carlos	KO by	10
June	3—Raheem Muhammad, Las Vegas	L	8
July	25—Bashiru Ali, San Carlos	KO by	7
Sept.	11—Tony Perea, El Paso	L	8
Dec.	5—Franco Thomas, Clarksburg	KO by	5

BOB INGRAS
1980
Jan.	24—Joe Rivera, Dover	KO by	2
July	3—Ken Carpenter, Atlantic City	W	8
July	25—Tony Salvatore, Rochester	L	8
Dec.	20—Dennis Cruz, Bronx	KO by	2

GLEN INLOW
Kellogg, Idaho Junior Middleweight
1979
Oct.	2—Scott Bowers, Spokane	L	4
Dec.	11—Rich Kronich, Spokane	KO	2

1980
Mar.	18—Rich Kronich, Spokane	KO by	4

LANCELOT INNIS
Canadian Junior Middleweight
Born: July 20, 1954 Guyana
1977
Dec.	13—Jean Guy Binnette, Quebec	KO	4

1978
June	1—Ron Pettigrew, Hull	D	6
June	27—Jimmy Grandson, Montreal	D	6
Dec.	5—Ricky Camora, Montreal	W	8

1979
Apr.	30—Raymond Rousselot, Montreal	W	6
Aug.	21—Jimmy Gradson, Montreal	D	8

1980
Jan.	22—Dan Long, Halifax	L	8
Mar.	11—Ralph Hollett, Montreal	L	10
May	30—Nicola Cirelli, Rome	L	8
Oct.	28—Eddie Melo, Montreal	D	10

RIC INNIS
Indianapolis, Ind. Heavyweight
1979
Dec.	14—Jimmy Higginson, Evansville	KO	1

1980
Jan.	21—Craig Arnold, St. Charles	KO	1
Aug.	13—Tommy Stevenson, Indianapolis	KO by	1
Oct.	28—Jerry Hunter, Indianapolis	KO	1

JOSE ISAAC
Puerto Rican Middleweight
1980
Mar.	31—Alejandro Falu, San Juan	KO	4
Apr.	7—Alejandro Falu, San Juan	KO	5
June	19—Adolfo Hunter, Rio Piedras	W	8
Aug.	7—Manuel Navarro, Rio Piedras	KO	6

KEVIN ISAAC
New York, N.Y. Heavyweight
1973
Sept.	24—Rodell Dupree, New York	W	6
Oct.	30—John Jackson, Buffalo	KO	1
Nov.	28—Larry Holmes, Cleveland	KO by	3
Dec.	26—Gianni Franzolin, Milano	KO	3

1974
Jan.	25—Ennio Cometti, Milano	D	8
Apr.	20—Obie English, Norfolk	L	6
Aug.	12—Willie Moore, New York	W	6
Nov.	4—Raul Gorosito, New York	W disq.	5

1975
Mar.	11—Billy Aird, London	L	8
June	23—Jesse Crown, New York	KO	1
Oct.	23—Bob Cruiston, Binghamton	W	6
Nov.	5—Bobby Mashburn, Sunnyside	KO	4
Dec.	3—Alex Carr, New York	KO	1

1976
Apr.	5—Greg Johnson, Landover	W	8
Sept.	11—Ron Lyle, Utica	KO by	7

1977
Mar.	6—Stan Ward, Marion	L	8
	(U.S. Championship Tournament)		

1978
Jan.	21—Joe Alexander, Las Vegas	W	10
Apr.	8—Ozzie Ocasio, San Juan	L	10
June	9—Ellis Sanders, Las Vegas	KO	3
Sept.	7—Mike Creel, El Paso	KO	3

1979
Mar.	23—Earl Tripp, Las Vegas	W	10

1980
Jan.	13—Leroy Caldwell, Las Vegas	D	10
May	3—Leon Spinks, San Carlos	KO by	8

JESSE ISLAND
San Diego, Calif. Light Heavyweight
1979
Apr.	6—John Steve, San Diego	KO by	1
May	20—Niva Tofaeono, Las Vegas	KO by	4
Aug.	27—Niva Tofaeono, San Diego	KO by	2

1980
Mar.	27—Billy Tavake, San Carlos	L disq.	2
June	14—Leo Oliver, Anaheim	W	4
Aug.	18—John Steve, San Diego	KO	1

CARL IVY
Marshall, Texas Light Heavyweight
1975
Apr.	21—Zack Page, Dallas	KO by	5

1976
(Inactive)
1977
Apr.	29—Lee Holloman, Fort Worth	W	4
Aug.	25—Randy Kirkland, Marshall	W	4
Oct.	20—Trinidad Escamilla, Marshall	KO	3
Oct.	26—Lee Holloman, Dallas	W	4

1978
Mar.	22—Fred Wallace, Dallas	W	6
Apr.	4—Roberto Rockett, Greenville	L	8
May	30—Frankie Evans, Tyler	W	10
July	18—Marcus Dorsey, Tyler	W	6
Aug.	—Leon Puente, El Paso	W	10
Dec.	5—Victor Rodriguez, San Antonio	KO	6

1979
(Inactive)

1980

Jan.	22—Otis Gordon, Houston	KO by 4
July	18—Al Dominey, Odessa	KO by 7
Sept.	23—Winston Chalmers, Odessa	KO 1
Nov.	29—Yaqui Lopez, Lake Tahoe	KO by 3

JOSE IZQUIERDO
Argentine Flyweight
1980

Mar.	14—Adrian Roman, Cordoba	L 10
May	9—Hector Barretto, Concordia	D 10
June	4—Americo Suarez, Quemu-Quemu	KO by 8

BILL JACKSON
Texas Junior Middleweight
1980

Feb.	9—Gene McCombs, Dallas	W 5
Apr.	5—Juan Martinez, Dallas	KO 2
May	31—Leander Floyd, El Paso	W 5

CLINT JACKSON
Nashville, Tenn. Junior Middleweight
Born: May 20, 1954
Managed by Stan Allen
1979

Aug.	3—Rafael Corona, Santa Monica	W 4
Aug.	28—Jim Wallace, Memphis	KO 2
Oct.	30—Larry Martin, Memphis	KO 2
Nov.	30—Larry Rayford, New Orleans	KO 7

1980

Mar.	8—Jamie Knox, Nashville	KO 1
Mar.	31—Jimmy Heair, Knoxville	KO 9
May	9—Priscialiano Castillo, Nashville	KO 3
Aug.	1—Ray Hammond, Las Vegas	KO 10
Dec.	26—Mauricio Aldana, Las Vegas	KO 7

DALE JACKSON
1980

July	25—Bill Bradley, Chicago	KO 3
Aug.	22—Frank Anest, Chicago	KO 2
Oct.	9—Pat John, Chicago	KO 4

EARNEST JACKSON
Philadelphia, Pa. Junior Welterweight
1980

Jan.	24—Jose Green, Upper Darby	W 4
May	9—Jack O'Neill, Atlantic City	KO 2
July	3—Paul Moore, Atlantic City	L 4
Aug.	9—Richard Ellis, Atlantic City	KO 2
Oct.	1—Gary Hinton, Atlantic City	D 8

FREDDY (THE PEBBLE) JACKSON
Houston, Texas Bantamweight
1980

Mar.	25—Silvero Martinez, Houston	KO 4
July	22—Piedrita Vasquez, Houston	KO 1
Aug.	19—Jose Luis Garcia, Beaumont	KO 3
Sept.	16—Humberto Rodriguez, Beaumont	KO 2
Sept.	23—Elias DeLeon, Houston	W 10

HOMER JACKSON
Florida Welterweight
1979

June	19—Mickey Jones, Orlando	W 4
Aug.	9—Ken Taylor, Gainesville	KO 2
Oct.	23—Melvin Wynn, Orlando	L 6
Nov.	13—Kelvin Jackson, Orlando	W 8
Dec.	13—Melvin Wynn, Gainesville	L 6
Dec.	19—Jim Winter, Fernandina Beach	KO 2

1980

Jan.	18—Armando Ramirez, Orlando	W 6
Feb.	21—Bob Johnson, Gainesville	KO 3
Mar.	25—Melvin Wynn, Jacksonville	L 6
Apr.	3—Archie Cruz, Tampa	KO 6
July	19—Ron Ford, Panama City, Fla.	KO 1
Oct.	11—Henry Hall, Ft. Meyers	KO 2

HUBERT JACKSON
Newark, N.J. Welterweight
1976

July	7—Jeremiah King, Philadelphia	KO by 1
Aug.	11—Tyrone Demby, Philadelphia	L 4

1977

Jan.	21—Jimmy Williams, Rochester	W 4
Jan.	27—Frank Duck, Syracuse	KO 3
Feb.	4—Raul Adams, Sunnyside	KO by 3
Feb.	16—Gene Ellington, Cleveland	KO 3

1978
(Inactive)
1979

Sept.	7—Marlon Starlin, Hartford	L 4
Sept.	30—Alfonso Belford, Shirley	KO 1
Oct.	25—Larry Farmer, Staten Island	KO 2
Dec.	11—Don Downey, Halifax	KO 2
Dec.	14—Johnny Cooper, Atlantic City	KO by 1

1980

Feb.	1—Mike Picciotti, Philadelphia	L 8
Mar.	9—Mike Picciotti, Atlantic City	KO by 4
July	17—Robert Sawyer, Totowa	KO by 1

JEROME JACKSON
Philadelphia, Pa. Middleweight
1977

Aug.	23—Jake Jenkins, Philadelphia	D 4
Nov.	15—Guy Gargan, Upper Darby	L 6

1978

Jan.	17—Ted Mann, Philadelphia	W 4
Feb.	20—Dan Snyder, Philadelphia	KO 6
Apr.	17—Tyrone Taylor, Philadelphia	W 6
Sept.	21—Bob Wert, Philadelphia	KO 2
Nov.	1—Ali Perez, White Plains	W 8
Dec.	12—Billy Freeman, Philadelphia	W 8

1979

Feb.	27—Fred Brown, Philadelphia	W 8
Apr.	10—Clifford Wills, Philadelphia	W 8
Sept.	20—Gary Guiden, Indianapolis	L 10
Nov.	8—Sammy NeSmith, Indianapolis	L 10

1980

Jan.	24—Sammy Floyd, Upper Darby	KO 8
Feb.	23—Wilford Scypion, Atlantic City	L 8
Apr.	10—Bob Patterson, Atlantic City	W 4
May	8—Frank Fletcher, Atlantic City	KO by 5

JIMMY JACKSON
Los Angeles, Calif. Welterweight
1974

Feb.	20—John Shufford, Las Vegas	KO by 2
Apr.	11—Mario Garcia, Los Angeles	KO by 2
July	9—Roy Hollis, Los Angeles	KO by 2
Aug.	27—Johnny Pineda, Santa Maria	D 5
Aug.	29—Pete Ranzany, Los Angeles	L 5
Sept.	7—Johnny Pinedo, Richmond	KO by 2
Oct.	27—Pete Ranzany, Sacramento	W 8
Nov.	5—Jim Burchett, Sacramento	L 8
Nov.	15—Julio Gomez, San Diego	KO by 3

1975

Jan.	23—Salvador Castaneda, Los Angeles	W 5
Jan.	30—Arthur Roddy, Los Angeles	W 5
Feb.	4—Pete Ranzany, Sacramento	L 6
Feb.	28—Art Roddy, San Diego	L 5
Mar.	4—Eddie Alexander, Sacramento	W 6
Mar.	14—Dave Lopez, San Diego	W 6
Mar.	26—Tony Harrington, San Diego	W 6
Apr.	10—Jesus Burciago, Los Angeles	KO 2
Apr.	18—Allan Gantt, San Diego	W 8
Apr.	22—Pete Ranzany, Sacramento	KO by 8
June	10—Larry Smith, Sacramento	W 6
Aug.	13—Juvencio Bernal, Los Angeles	W 5
Aug.	26—Young Kennedy, Honolulu	W 8
Oct.	8—Larry Bonds, Las Vegas	L 10

1976

Jan.	20—John Pinedo, Sacramento	KO 2
Feb.	24—Roger Buckskin, Sacramento	W 8
Apr.	2—Andy Price, Los Angeles	L 10
July	10—Arture Zuniga, Juarez	KO 4
Sept.	17—Jose Figueroa, Los Angeles	KO 2
Oct.	29—Roberto Sosa, Los Angeles	KO 3

1977

Feb.	21—Rocky Mosley Jr., Las Vegas	L 12
Apr.	4—Bruce Curry, Las Vegas	L 10
Dec.	15—Gustavo Garcia, Los Angeles	W 10

1978

Feb.	11—Rudy Barro, Las Vegas	KO 5
Mar.	18—Tony Gonzales, Las Vegas	KO 6
July	6—Sultan Saladin, Las Vegas	KO 4
July	27—Pablo Baez, Los Angeles	W 10
Aug.	31—Zeferino Gonzalez, Los Angeles	L 10
Nov.	16—Kevin Morgan, Las Vegas	W 12

1979

Mar.	2—Howard Jackson, Las Vegas	W 12
Sept.	30—Larry Bonds, Reno	L 10
Oct.	27—Jose Duarte, Mexico City	KO by 5

1980

Jan.	18—Bruce Curry, Las Vegas	KO by 7

JOHNNY JACKSON
Las Vegas, Nev. Bantamweight
1978
Mar. 15—Salvatore Ogolde, Las Vegas .... KO by 2
Apr. 19—Desi Newbill, Las Vegas .... KO by 2
1979
May 11—Aaron Morua, Pico Rivero .... KO by 2
Nov. 7—Augustin Serros, San Jose .... KO by 1
1980
Jan. 10—Augie Serros, Santa Rosa .... KO by 1
Mar. 6—Doug Trichel, Santa Rosa .... KO 1
Apr. 24—Franco Torregoza, Stockton .... KO by 1
June 30—Armando Ugalde, Bakersfield .... KO by 3
Aug. 18—Raul Gonzales, Caracas .... KO by 3
Nov. 1—James Manning, Rosebud .... KO by 2

LARRY JACKSON
New Orleans, La. Light Heavyweight
1978
Feb. 28—Larry Mayes, Wichita .... KO by 2
Mar. 22—David Kuykendall, Dallas .... KO by 4
July 18—Robert Perry, Houston .... KO by 1
1979
Feb. 9—Mike Ramirez, Mobile .... KO by 2
Apr. 2—Grover Robinson, Dallas .... KO by 1
Apr. 14—Tyler Dupuy, New Orleans .... KO by 3
Aug. 28—Manuel Garcia, San Antonio .... KO by 2
1980
Mar. 11—Bill Mercier, Seattle .... KO by 1
Aug. 8—Fred Dudley, Dallas .... KO by 2

MARCUS JACKSON
Hartford, Conn.
1979
Sept. 7—Sonny Assani, Hartford .... W 4
1980
Jan. 15—Walter Driscoll, W. Hartford .... KO 1
Nov. 11—Ray James, W. Hartford .... KO 2

SAMMY JACKSON
Memphis, Tenn. Middleweight
1979
Aug. 10—George Madison, Evansville .... KO by 1
1980
July 15—Monte Masters, Oklahoma City ...... KO by 1

TYRONE JACKSON
Metairie, La. Junior Welterweight
1977
Aug. 16—Juan Canto, New Orleans .... KO 3
1978
Mar. 14—Frank Crosby, New Orleans .... W 4
1979
Feb. 14—Andre Mordecai, Washington .... KO by 1
Nov. 30—Joe Webber, New Orleans .... KO 2
1980
July 15—Maurice Quillens, New Orleans .... D 5

MIKE JAMESON
Cupertino, Calif. Heavyweight
1980
Jan. 31—Marlyn Johnson, San Carlos .... W 5
Mar. 27—Marlyn Johnson, San Carlos .... KO 2
July 25—Lew Lockwood, San Carlos .... W 6
Oct. 16—Ronald Gibbs, San Carlos .... KO 1

TOM JANCSY
Everett, Mass. Welterweight
1979
Aug. 21—Ralph Dumont, Yarmouth .... W 4
Nov. 7—Tom Brown, Boston .... L 6
1980
Feb. 22—Ray Rosa, Fall River .... L 4
May 1—Verne Campbell, Dorchester .... KO 1
Nov. 22—Billy Hill, Scranton .... L 4

PAT JEFFERSON
Rapid City, S.D. Junior Welterweight
1980
June 28—Rudy Matta, Rapid City .... KO 3
July 24—Pancho Monzon, Las Vegas .... KO 1
Aug. 1—Pablo Gomez, Las Vegas .... W 8

MARVIN (KID HARLEM) JENKINS
New York, N.Y. Junior Welterweight
1977
Sept. 27—Lloyd Blake, Passaic .... W 6
1978
Jan. 23—Alfred Franklin, St. Paul .... W 6
Feb. 27—Eddie Campbell, New York .... W 6
Mar. 27—Larry Puchta, St. Paul .... KO 3

May 10—Wilson Bell, White Plains .... W 6
July 18—Ike Hooks, Miami Beach .... D 8
1979
Jan. 14—Jesse Rogers, White Plains .... KO 1
Mar. 14—Marvin Edwards, White Plains .... W 8
May 21—Santos Gimenez, New York .... L 10
July 16—Jesse Lara, New York City .... KO 1
Aug. 28—Allan Clarke, Halifax .... L 8
Sept. 12—Mike Ross, White Plains .... W 8
Dec. 5—Allan Clarke, White Plains .... L 10
1980
Feb. 16—Feliciano Cintron, Portland, Me. .... W 8
Apr. 25—Willie Rodriguez, Commack .... L 12
Nov. 28—Ruby Ortiz, New York .... W 10

WILLIE (BIRDLEGS) JENSEN
Las Vegas, Nev. Flyweight
1973
May 2—Mato Espinoza, Las Vegas .... KO 3
May 16—Jewell Chappell, Las Vegas .... W 5
May 30—Flash Zaldivar, Las Vegas .... W 6
Sept. 12—Joe Saldivar, Las Vegas .... W 8
Oct. 3—Reynaldo Gutierrez, Las Vegas .... KO 2
Oct. 28—Jesse Trujillo, Stateline .... W 8
Nov. 21—Danny Young, Las Vegas .... KO 5
Nov. 28—Willie Vasquez, Las Vegas .... W 8
1974
Jan. 23—Pedro Torres, Las Vegas .... W 8
Mar. 13—Johnny Mesa, Las Vegas .... W 8
1975
Feb. 5—Harvey Wilson, Las Vegas .... W 6
May 14—Seco Luna, Las Vegas .... W 4
June 25—Candy Iglesias, Las Vegas .... W 6
Aug. 2—Lalo Galindo, Los Angeles .... W 10
Sept. 20—Lupe Pintor, Las Vegas .... KO by 7
Dec. 11—Tony Rocha, Las Vegas .... W 10
(U.S. Flyweight Title)
1976
May 8—Guty Espada, Los Angeles............... D 10
1977
(Inactive)
1978
Mar. 22—Tito Arzate, Las Vegas .... W 10
May 10—Jose Carranza, Las Vegas .... KO 7
1979
Aug. 8—Jose L. Garcia, Las Vegas .... KO 3
Nov. 30—Mario Chaves, Las Vegas .... W 10
1980
Feb. 19—Sergio Reyes, Sparks .... KO 6
Mar. 27—Mark Pacheco, Las Vegas .... KO 5
July 28—Rafael Orono, Caracas .... D 15
(For WBC Super Flyweight Title)

GEORGE (JOYAL) JEROME
Vancouver, Canada Heavyweight
1968
—Russell Baer, Headingly.................. W 4
1969
—Marcel Malloy, Windsor.................. W 6
—George Poitras, Stony Plain .... W 6
1970
Dec. 3—Chuck Miller, Winnipeg .... L 6
1971
—Chuck Miller, Winnipeg .... D 6
Apr. —Chuck Miller, Grand Rapids.......... W 6
1972
—Sonny Harris, Windsor................. KO 2
—Elmer Parenteau, Creston................ W 6
—Bob Avery, Bisbee .... D 4
1973
(Inactive)
1974
Apr. 4—Chuck Borden, Chilliwack .... KO 2
June 8—Gary (Hobo) Wiler, Olympia......... KO by 3
Oct. 25—Hugh Mercier, Saskatoon .... KO 6
(Western Canada Heavyweight Title)
1975
Mar. 5—Bob Patterson, Richmond .... KO 2
Apr. 14—Young Sekona, Auckland .... KO by 4
Nov. 8—Eddie Ostapovich, Richmond............. D 8
1976
May 10—Horst (Him) Geisler, Toronto........... KO 6
Oct. 12—Pat Duncan, Seattle .... KO by 8
Nov. 1—Jean Pierre Coopman, Izegem .... KO by 4
Dec. 10—Paul Neilson, Toronto .... KO by 8
(Canadian Heavyweight Title)
1977
Feb. 27—Earl McLeay, Calgary .... D 12
Mar. 25—Bob Patterson, Winnipeg .... W 10
Sept. 28—Jack Martin, Vancouver .... Exh. 4
Oct. 1—Joe (King) Roman, Butte .... KO by 9
Nov. 4—Al Sparks, Winnipeg .... L 8
1978
Apr. 18—Ibar Arrington, Everett .... KO by 8

May	23—Jose Roman, Bellingham	L 8
July	4—Mustafa El Amin, Vancouver	D 4
Sept.	5—Hennie Thoonen, Rotterdam	KO by 4
Dec.	11—George Chuvalo Toronto	KO by 2
	(Canadian Heavyweight Title)	

1979

June	7—Pinklon Thomas, Portland	KO by 2
July	26—Pat Stewart, Anchorage	W 8
Oct.	27—Ron Douglas, Regina	KO 4

1980

May	21—Ron Rousselle, Kelowna	KO by 5

TERRY JESMER
Winnipeg, Canada Middleweight

1977

Nov.	4—Wayne Caplette, Winnipeg	KO by 3

1978

Apr.	18—Larry Puchta, Winnipeg	KO 4
June	20—Henry Mason, Winnipeg	KO 2
June	29—Gordy Kampa, St. Paul	L 4
Aug.	30—Steve Krueger, Bloomington	KO by 1
Oct.	3—Clem Tucker, Winnipeg	KO by 5
Oct.	25—Mike Morgan, Grand Forks	L 8
Dec.	5—Mike Morgan, Winnipeg	L 8

1979

Feb.	9—Wayne Caplette, Winnipeg	KO by 2
June	14—Bruce Strauss, Winnipeg	D
Aug.	10—Gary Thomas, Evansville	KO by 4
Oct.	9—Tony Dowling, Winnipeg	KO 6
Oct.	27—Kelly Anderson, Regina	KO 1
Nov.	27—Harland Holden, Winnipeg	L 6
Dec.	9—Harlen Holden, Winnipeg	L 6

1980

Mar.	6—Joe Gardai, Winnipeg	KO 8
Mar.	17—Costello King, Edmonton	L 8
May	12—Ralph Hollett, Halifax	KO by 5
July	25—Larry Puchta, Winnipeg	KO 3
Aug.	22—Harlen Holden, Chicago	KO by 6

RICK JESTER
Detroit, Mich. Light Heavyweight

1978

Dec.	4—Willie Williams, Saginaw	KO 2
Dec.	9—Lucky Patterson, Detroit	KO 1

1979

Jan.	25—Bobby Edwards, Detroit	KO 1
Jan.	31—Murray Sutherland, Saginaw	KO by 1
Mar.	27—Ben Mitchell, Michigan	KO 2
May	24—Joe Griffin, Detroit	KO 1

1980

May	15—Alvin Dominey, Chicago	KO 1
June	12—Jamie Olatunde, Chicago	KO 7
Aug.	14—Dwight Braxton, Chicago	KO by 3

ROBEY JETTON
Lincolnton, N.C. Light Heavyweight

1980

Sept.	6—Al Collins, Lincolnton	KO 4
Dec.	21—Pee Wee Dunbar, Spartanburg	W 4

MILCIADES JIMENEZ
Brooklyn, N.Y. Junior Lightweight

1977

Mar.	24—Igg Villanueva, Dover	KO 2
May	20—Dave Bolden, New York	L 4

1978

June	6—Carlos Paneto, New York	KO 2
Sept.	8—Curtis Harris, New York	KO by 2

1979

Apr.	27—Kelvin Lewis, Newark	L 4
July	10—Jorge Diaz, Atlantic City	W 4
Oct.	3—Tomas Diaz, Brooklyn	L 6

1980

Jan.	18—Mark David, Los Angeles	L 5
Jan.	31—Paul Morales, Los Angeles	KO by 2
Apr.	24—Mike Rodriguez, Los Angeles	L 4
May	9—Francisco Nunez, Los Angeles	KO 5
May	22—Tony Armas, Los Angeles	KO 5
May	30—Rosario Gonzales, San Bernardino	KO 7
July	1—Richard Savala, Sacramento	KO by 2
Dec.	19—Carlos Bryant, San Diego	KO by 3

NESTOR (BABA) JIMENEZ
Colombian Junior Featherweight
Born: October 24, 1947, Cartagena

1967

Oct.	24—Luis Gonzalez, Sincelejo	W 4
Nov.	20—Roberto Lopez, Sincelejo	W 4
Dec.	3—Hugo Barraza, Barranquilla	W 4
Dec.	17—Ney Padilla, Sincelejo	W 4

1968

Jan.	13—Luis Zuniga, Sincelejo	KO 5
Jan.	21—Hugo Barraza, Cartagena	W 6
Feb.	2—Nelson Torres, Sincelejo	W 6
Feb.	17—Fernando Ramirez, Barranquilla	W 6
Feb.	28—Miguel Zabaleta, Maicao	W 6
Mar.	10—Nelson Torres, Cartagena	KO 5
Mar.	23—Ney Padilla, Sincelejo	KO 4
May	12—Miguel Zabaleta, Cartagena	KO 3
June	28—Luis Zuniga, Sincelejo	W 6
July	13—Luis Zuniga, Barranquilla	W 6
Aug.	3—German Espinosa, Bogota	L 6
Oct.	25—Hugo Barraza, Cartagena	W 8
Dec.	22—Marion de Leon, Barranquilla	KO by 7
Dec.	29—Henry William Gonzalez, Sincelejo	W 10

1969

Jan.	19—Juan Martinez, Sincelejo	D 10
Jan.	26—Luis Zuniga, Cartagena	W 8
Mar.	1—Henry William Gonzalez, Barranquilla	KO 5
Apr.	11—Adalberto Iriarte, Barranquilla	W 10
May	3—Alvaro Lopez, Barranquilla	W 10
June	20—Roberto Lopez, Sincelejo	KO 2
June	27—Herbert Locket, Sincelejo	W 10
July	4—German Espinosa, Bogota	KO by 4

1970

Mar.	21—Mario de Leon, Monteria	W 10
Apr.	7—Herbert Locket, Monteria	W 10
Apr.	17—Betulio Gonzalez, Caracas	L 10
June	20—Orlando Amores, Panama	L 10
Aug.	17—Enrique Pinder, Colon	L 10
Oct.	9—Salvador Lozano, San Jose, Costa Rica	W 10
	—Roberto Pato Fuentes	L 10

1971

Feb.	18—Eduardo Raton, Mojica, Managua	W 10
May	14—Justo Valdez, Barranquilla	W 10
May	3—Mario de Leon, Cartagena	KO 7
July	16—Rafael Achundia, Guayaquil	L 10
Aug.	—Jorge Reyes, Monterrey	W 10
Sept.	11—Vale Valles, Barranquilla	W 10
Oct.	1—Fernando Bustos, Cartagena	KO 3
Oct.	22—Edmundo Martinez, Barranquilla	KO 3
Nov.	26—Pedro Bendek, Cartagena	KO 3

1972

Jan.	2—Romeo Anaya, Tuxtla, Mexico	L 10
Mar.	10—Pedro Bendek, Barranquilla	KO 4
Apr.	26—Jose Villaneuva, Barranquilla	KO 1
June	11—Jorge Benitez, Barranquilla	KO 1
July	17—Antonio Medina, Caracas	KO by 6
Sept.	29—Renan Marotto, Cartagena	W 10
Dec.	15—Miguel Espinosa, Cartagena	W 10

1973

Mar.	11—Nilberto Herrara, Cartagena	W 10
May	4—Jaime Amaya, Barranquilla	W 12
	(Won Colombian Bantamweight Title)	
July	9—Ismael Escobar, Bogota	KO 9
Sept.	8—Senen Rios, Bogota	KO 1
Dec.	2—Jaime Ricardo, Sincelejo	KO 5

1974

Feb.	10—Miguel Espinosa, Cartagena	W 10
Mar.	1—Henry Castillo, Cartagena	W 10
June	9—Orlando Amores, Cartagena	W 10
Aug.	21—Ruben Valdez, Cartagena	KO 4
	(Retained Colombian Bantamweight Title)	
Oct.	31—Jaime Amaya, Barranquilla	W 10
Dec.	5—Fernando Bustos, Bogota	KO 2
Dec.	27—Sigifredo Moreno, Bogota	KO 9

1975

Jan.	10—Sigifredo Moreno, Bogota	KO 9
Mar.	10—Jorge Madrigal, Bogota	KO 1
May	31—Rodolfo Martinez, Bogota	KO by 8
	(WBC Bantamweight Title)	
July	26—Enrique Pinto, Cartagena	L 10
Dec.	7—Carlos Zarate, Mexicali	KO by 2

1976

Feb.	29—Carlos Arturo Osorio, Cartagena	W 12
	(Bantamweight Title of Colombia)	
June	17—Enrique Pinto, Cartagena	W 12
	(Colombian Bantamweight Title)	
Aug.	17—Cleo Garcia, Cartagena	W 12
	(Won Central American Super Bantamweight Title)	
Oct.	1—Julio Hernandez, Cartagena	W 12

1977

Feb.	18—Ricardo Cardona, Cartagena	W 12
May	—Rene Silva, Cartagena	KO 5
July	1—Jose Cervantes, Cartagena	W 12
	(Won Colombian Super Bantamweight Title)	
Sept.	16—Nelson Cruz Tamariz, Cartagena	W 12
	(Central American Title)	
Oct.	7—Nelson Cruz Tamariz, Cartagena	W 10
Oct.	28—Juan Mayoral, Barranquilla	KO 4
Dec.	15—Johnny Castro, Bogota	W 12
	(Central American Title)	

1978

	—Raul Tirado, Cartagena	W 10
	—Pedro Rodriguez, Cartagena	W 10

1979

Mar.   9—Wilfredo Gomez, New York .... KO by 5
(For World Junior Featherweight Title)
1980
Mar. 29—Jose Lora Patricio, Cartagena .... KO 7

RAMON JIMENEZ
Mexican Junior Featherweight .
1980
Mar.   1—Raul Morales, Mexico City .... KO 3
Apr.   5—Gustavo Chavez, Mexico City .... KO 1

RICARDO JIMENEZ
Los Angeles, Calif. Junior Lightweight
1979
July 18—Harvard Betts, Las Vegas .... KO 4
July 25—Darrell Stovall, Phoenix .... W 4
Aug.   1—Roy Mata Barajas, Las Vegas .... W 4
Aug. 15—Jose Pacheco, Las Vegas .... KO 2
Aug. 22—Mauro Fuentes, Phoenix .... KO 2
1980
Jan.   9—Andres Armendariz, Las Vegas .... KO 2
Jan. 30—Eliou Hernandez, Las Vegas .... KO 1
Feb. 13—Joe Phillips, Las Vegas .... KO 3
Mar.   8—Alex Garcia, Las Vegas .... KO 4
Mar. 20—Gilbert Garza, Phoenix .... KO 3
Apr.   2—Blaine Dickson, Las Vegas .... L 10
May   7—Emil Polanco, Las Vegas .... KO 5
May 14—Rosendo Ramirez, Las Vegas .... L 10
June 11—Julio Mendez, Las Vegas .... KO 2
July   2—Danny Patino, Las Vegas .... KO 3
July 27—Leonardo Moreno, Las Vegas .... KO by 1
Sept.   3—Pascual Villareal, Las Vegas .... KO 4
Sept. 11—Roberto Torres, Los Angeles .... D 10
Oct.   8—Jose Luis Piceno, Las Vegas .... KO 4
Nov.   5—Darryl Stovall, Phoenix .... W 8
Dec. 10—Luis Avila, Las Vegas .... W 10
Dec. 26—Blaine Dickson, Las Vegas .... KO by 1

IGNACIO (NACHO) JIMENEZ
Stockton, Calif. Lightweight
1979
Jan. 17—Chuy Rodriguez, Stockton .... L 10
Oct. 11—Juan Escobar, Los Angeles .... KO by 9
1980
Jan. 31—Warren Matthews, San Carlos ...... KO by 8
Apr. 24—Rodolfo Gonzalez, Los Angeles ..... KO by 1
Dec. 13—Nak-Yung Choi, San Pedro .... L 10

JOSE (MONITA) JIMINEZ
Dominican Rep. Bantamweight
(Previous Record Unavailable)
1977
Feb. 20—Ruben Marin, Mexico City .... KO 3
Mar. 19—Ramon Cabral, Santo Domingo .... KO 5
Aug.   5—Juanito Herrera, Baranquilla .... L 10
Oct.   3—Julio Soto Solano, Santo Domingo .... W 12
1978
Feb. 24—Julio Soto Solano, Santo Domingo .... L 12
Apr. 25—Julio Soto Solano, Santo Domingo .... L 12
June 10—Julian Solis, Carolino .... KO by 2
Sept. 21—Jorge Mejia, Guayaquil .... L 10
(Ecuadorian Flyweight Title)
Oct. 26—Leopoldo Frias, Santo Domingo .... KO 9
1979
Apr.   2—Luis Rosario, Santo Domingo .... W 10
June 28—Mario Miranda, Barranquilla .... L 8
July   3—Andres Hernandez, Santo Domingo .. W disq. 6
Aug. 22—Jose Nieto, New York .... KO by 7
1980
Sept. 16—Emilio Hernandez, Santo Domingo .... L 10
Oct. 14—Wilfredo Gomez, Panama City .... KO by 1

LUIS JIMENEZ
Houston, Texas Bantamweight
1980
June 17—Javier de la Cerda, Houston .... W 6
July 22—Javier de la Cerda, Houston .... W 6
Aug. 24—Ernesto Guevarra, McAllen .... L 8
Sept. 30—Jose Reyna, Houston .... TD 1

MANUEL (YUCA) JIMINEZ
Puerto Rican Welterweight
1977
Mar. 11—Mike Thomas, New York .... KO 5
Mar. 19—Jose Toro, Adjuntas .... W 10
July 16—Arnaldo Santiago, Adjuntas .... KO 3
Oct. 15—Jose A. Rosa, Carolino .... W 8
1978
Jan. 14—Chester McFarland, Carolina, P.R. ..... KO 1
Feb. 12—Juan Barbosa, Carolino .... KO 7
Mar.   5—Hurricane Jackson, Carolino .... KO 1
June 26—Julio Serrano, Rio Piedras .... KO 2

July 12—Jose Rosa, San Juan .... W 10
Aug.   1—J. C. Smith, Rio Piedras .... KO 1
Aug. 26—Miguel Morales, Carolino .... KO 3
Nov. 27—Luis Rodriguez, San Juan .... W 10
1979
Jan. 14—Domingo Ayala, San Juan .... W 10
Apr. 28—George Mejia, Trujillo Alto .... KO 5
May 21—Marvin Jenkins, New York .... W 10
1980
Mar. 24—Felix Reyes, San Juan .... KO 2
Apr. 27—Jesus De La Rosa, San Juan .... KO 6
July 31—Jose Vallejo, Rio Piedras .... W 10
Oct. 27—Felix Pinto, Alto Trujillo .... W 10

MARTIN JIMINEZ
Welterweight
1977
May 23—Leon McCullum, Houston .... W 4
July 19—Leon McCullum, Houston .... W 6
1978
June   3—Pat Hallacy, Wichita .... KO by 3
Oct. 12—Danny Donatto, Pasadena .... KO by 3
1979
Apr. 10—Mario Medina, Beaumont .... KO by 4
1980
Feb. 12—Billy Watkins, Beaumont .... KO by 1

CHARLIE JOHNSON
Alliance, Ohio Heavyweight
1973
June 16—Lou Rogan, Alliance .... W 6
Sept. 29—Sylvester Wilder, Alliance .... W 10
Nov. 10—Ted Paxton, Alliance .... W 8
1974
Apr.   6—Reggie Flemming, Alliance .... KO 3
May 25—Sylvester Wilder, Alliance .... W 8
1975
Feb. 15—Frankie Rodgers, Alliance .... KO 2
May 18—Charlie Jordan, Canton .... W 10
1976
Mar. 12—Phil Fritz, Toronto .... KO 3
Apr.   3—Tom Prater, Indianapolis .... KO by 1
Oct.   2—Jesse Clark, Alliance .... KO 2
Nov.   6—Charlie Jordan, Alliance .... W 8
Dec. 11—Verbie Garland, Alliance .... W 10
1977
June 25—Walter Moore, Chicago .... KO by 4
1978
Feb. 10—Dwain Bonds, Detroit .... W 8
Apr. 29—Percy Hairston, Sebring .... KO 8
Oct.   5—Ibar Arrington, Seattle .... W 10
Nov. 29—Harry Terrell, Richfield .... KO by 8
1979
Feb. 26—Gerry Cooney, New York .... KO by 1
Apr. 28—Charley Boston, Sebring .... KO 3
May 11—Zack Ferguson, Cincinnati .... KO 3
Aug. 30—Mircea Simon, Los Angeles .... KO by 4
1980
Mar.   9—Percell Davis, St. Paul .... KO by 7
Oct. 28—Lamar Robinson, Warren .... W 6

CHRIS JOHNSON
Denver, Colo. Lightweight
1979
    —Wilborn Lawson, Denver .... W 4
Aug. 16—Ray Menefee, North Platte .... W 6
Sept. 21—Clemente Rodriguez, Denver .... W 4
1980
Mar. 15—Marty Garelick, Ogden .... KO 3
Apr. 19—Billy Clark, Billings .... KO 2

DAVE (BIG FOOT) JOHNSON
Bowie, Md. Heavyweight
1977
Sept. 21—Bobby Jordan, Virginia Beach .... W 6
Oct. 27—Mike LaPointe, Portland, Me. .... KO
Nov.   3—Matt Robinson, Virginia Beach .... W 6
Nov. 25—Dwain Bonds, Detroit .... L 4
Dec. 17—Malik Dozier, Washington D.C. .... W 4
1978
Jan. 25—Tito Fontano, Washington D.C. .... KO 4
Feb. 23—Leroy Boone, Virginia Beach .... L 6
Apr. 19—Art Savage, Washington D.C. .... W 6
Apr. 20—Don Spellman, Virginia Beach .... W 6
May 10—Eugene Green, Washington D.C. .... W 6
May 22—George Williams, Washington D.C. ...... W 6
Oct.   6—Wendell Bailey, Baltimore .... L 6
Nov. 17—Malik Dozier, Washington D.C. .... W 6
1979
Jan. 22—Al Byrd, Washington D.C. .... KO 2
May 17—Eddie Benson, Virginia Beach .... KO 1
June   2—Jimmy Abbott, Mmabatho .... KO by 3

1980

Apr.	16—Renaldo Snipes, White Plains	L 8
June	11—Robert Evans, White Plains	L 6
Oct.	2—Greg Page, Mad. Sq. Garden, N.Y.	KO by 6

DON JOHNSON
Halifax, Canada Welterweight
1977

June	30—Baldav Singh, Halifax	W 4
July	3—Bob Brake, New Glasgow	KO 1
July	31—Wayne Cormier, Sydney	KO 1
Sept.	8—Reg McLean, Halifax	KO 2
Oct.	4—Angel Cintron, Halifax	W 8
Dec.	8—Ralph Hollett, Halifax	W 6

1978

May	6—George Majers, New Glasgow	KO 2
June	13—Lawrence Hafey, Halifax	KO by 6
Aug.	1—Don Johnson (New York), Halifax	W 8
Sept.	17—Ray Rosa, Sydney	KO 5

1979

Mar.	28—Don Bickford, Waterville	KO 5
Apr.	3—Ralph Hollett, Halifax	W 10

(Eastern Canadian Middleweight Title)

Aug.	28—Marciano Bernardi, Halifax	KO by 1
Dec.	18—Bernardo Prada, Montreal	KO by 2

1980

Aug.	21—Steve Arvin, Halifax	W 8
Sept.	24—Kerry Patterson, Halifax	KO 2
Nov.	11—Jim Henry, Halifax	W 8
Nov.	21—Ulysses Dorian, Moncton	KO by 3

DUJUAN JOHNSON
Detroit, Mich. Junior Welterweight
1979

June	12—Larry Savage, Detroit	KO 2
June	28—Larry Morgan, Detroit	KO 1
July	12—Donzell Smith, Detroit	KO 1
Aug.	2—Mike Blunt, Detroit	W 6
Sept.	20—Ron Pettigrew, Detroit	KO 5
Oct.	18—Pethayani Petcharoen, Detroit	W 8

1980

Jan.	30—Javier Ayala, Las Vegas	KO 8
Feb.	5—Paul Jones, Wyandotte	KO 1
May	3—Mario Martinez, Detroit	W 10
Sept.	10—Greg Netter, Detroit	KO 9
Dec.	—Miguel Montilla, Detroit	W 10

EMMETT JOHNSON
Philadelphia, Pa. Middleweight
1979

Aug.	14—Jimmy Sykes, Atlantic City	KO by 6
Sept.	26—Willie Torres, Upper Darby	KO by 2
Dec.	4—Willie Torres, Philadelphia	KO by 4

1980

Sept.	4—Emilio Narvaez, Atlantic City	L 4
Nov.	22—Mike Adessa, Scranton	KO by 2

FRED JOHNSON
(See SIMMIE BLACK)

FREDDIE JOHNSON
New Orleans, La. Middleweight
1976

July	27—Larry Rayford, New Orleans	W 4
Dec.	15—Robert Perry, Pensacola	W 6

1977

May	5—Leon McCullum, Mobile	W 6
May	23—Philip Reed, Memphis	W 6
July	18—Ed Modicue, New Orleans	W 6
Aug.	30—Anthony House, New Orleans	KO 6

1978

Feb.	27—Manuel Torres, New Orleans	KO 6
Mar.	21—Clarence Gilmore, Memphis	W 8
Apr.	8—Bruce Finch, New Orleans	L 10
Aug.	8—Sammy Masias, Orlando	NC 4
Sept.	26—Mike Baker, Miami Beach	W 10
Nov.	14—Paul Stephens, New Orleans	W 10
Dec.	—Larry Hafey, Halifax	L 10

1979

Jan.	16—Wilford Scypion, Houston	KO by 8
Apr.	14—Tony Licata, New Orleans	KO 4

1980

Mar.	29—Bruce McIntyre, Johannesburg	KO by 5
Sept.	10—Fulgencio Obelmejias, San Remo	KO by 3

JOE JOHNSON
Las Vegas, Nev. Junior Welterweight
1979

July	11—Jesus Huerta, Las Vegas	L 4
Aug.	1—Louis Daniels, Las Vegas	W 4
Aug.	22—Vicente Barreto, Las Vegas	KO 2
Sept.	26—Roberto Garcia, Las Vegas	L 4
Oct.	24—Santos Gartierrez, Las Vegas	KO 1

Nov.	7—Hector Martinez, Las Vegas	W 4
Nov.	21—Louis Daniels, Las Vegas	W 6
Dec.	5—Mario C. Tineo, Las Vegas	W 4

1980

Jan.	13—Johnny Compo, Las Vegas	L 6
Jan.	23—Sterling McPherson, Las Vegas	KO by 3

JOHN L. JOHNSON
Miami, Florida Heavyweight
1973

May	1—Eddie Mitchell, Miami Beach	KO 2
May	29—Leon Shaw, Miami Beach	W 4
June	19—Leon Shaw, Miami Beach	KO 3
July	3—Virgil Farthing, Miami Beach	KO 2
July	31—Larry McGee, Miami Beach	KO 2
Aug.	21—Rene Kinsey, Miami Beach	W 8
Sept.	18—Bob Crutison, Miami Beach	KO 5

1974

Jan.	22—James Scott, Miami Beach	L 6
Mar.	4—John Berry, Largo	L 6
June	4—Mike Koranicki, Miami Beach	KO by 5
Oct.	8—Robert Lloyd, Miami Beach	L 10
Nov.	22—Scott LeDoux, Minneapolis	KO by 5
Dec.	10—Mike Koranicki, Miami Beach	L 10

1975

Jan.	7—O.T. Davies, Miami Beach	W 8
Jan.	21—O.T. Davies, Miami Beach	KO by 4
Mar.	11—O.T. Davies, Miami Beach	KO 2
Mar.	18—Robert Lloyd, Miami Beach	L 10
Aug.	5—Eddie Neilson, Miami Beach	L 8
Sept.	23—Oliver Wright, Miami Beach	L 8
Nov.	1—Alfio Righetti, Milan	KO by 6

1976
(Inactive)
1977

June	14—Lou Esa, Orlando	KO by 2

1978

Mar.	16—Rocky McCaleb, Hollywood	L 4
Apr.	4—Richard Majors, North Miami Beach	D 4

1979
(Inactive)
1980

Jan.	29—Richard Majors, Miami Beach	KO 1
Feb.	12—Luis Acosta, Miami Beach	KO by 2
Aug.	29—Earl Tripp, Miami Beach	KO by 2
Nov.	14—Tony Tubbs, Miami Beach	KO by 1

MARLYN JOHNSON
Los Angeles, Calif. Heavyweight
1979

Feb.	6—Basheer Wadud, San Carlos	KO by 2
June	27—Rick Mills, Los Angeles	KO by 1

1980

Jan.	31—Mike Jamison, San Carlos	L 5
Mar.	27—Mike Jamison, San Carlos	KO by 2

MELVIN JOHNSON
Clovis, N.M. Bantamweight
1973

July	30—Frolin Martinez, Albuquerque	KO by 4
Sept.	26—John Rodriguez, Houston	W 4
Nov.	13—Cantalino Flores, El Paso	L 10
Dec.	18—Jose Navarette, El Paso	W 10

1974

Jan.	10—Ray Mendoza, Houston	W 6
Jan.	17—Roberto Rodriguez, Houston	KO 1
Feb.	10—Erasmo Flores, Houston	W 12
Apr.	17—Jose Ybarry, Houston	W 10

1975
(Inactive)
1976

May	3—James Martinez, Topeka	L 10

1977

Apr.	30—Sergio Reyes, Laredo	KO by 3

1978

Oct.	12—Oscar Muniz, Los Angeles	L 10

1979

Jan.	28—Nicky Perez, Reno	L 10
Feb.	21—Javier Flores, Lake Tahoe	KO by 9
Apr.	16—Nicky Perez, Las Vegas	L 12

(For U.S. Junior Featherweight Title)

Aug.	21—Rudy Patalinghug, Honolulu	W 10

Feb.	8—Oscar Muniz, San Bernardino	KO by 7
Apr.	12—Alberto Davila, Tucson	KO by 2
July	12—Alfonso Zamora, Los Angeles	KO by 3

RAYMOND JOHNSON
New York City, N.Y. Junior Lightweight
1980

Apr.	25—Jose Rosado, Commack	W 4
May	25—Braton Butler, Rahway	W 6

RICKY JOHNSON
Queens, N.Y. Welterweight
1979
Mar.	2—Hugo Fuat, Albany	W	4
Apr.	6—Jamel Love, Albany	KO	2
July	8—Charles Young, New York	W	4
Oct.	24—Garland Wright, Scranton	D	4
Nov.	21—Frank Minigan, Scranton	W	6

1980
Nov.	12—Mark Medel, New York	KO by	1

ROBERT JOHNSON
Lakewood, N.J. Junior Lightweight
1980
May	9—Jimmy Cruz, Staten Island	KO	1
May	22—Ken Bogner, Totowa	KO by	2
July	20—Jimmy McNeece, Great Gorge	L	4
July	31—Pedro Lebron, Atlantic City	D	4
Aug.	15—Pat Brennan, Glen Cove	L	6
Sept.	5—Edwin Curet, Dorcester	L	4
Sept.	12—Tony Santana, New York	L	6
Oct.	18—Terry Silvers, Atlantic City	L	4
Dec.	17—Mark Cerenzie, White Plains	L	4

ROY JOHNSON
Bermudian Welterweight
1975
June	10—Jim Henry, Sorel	W	6
July	3—Ray Rosario, Trois River	W	6
July	22—Julius Mendell, Montreal	W	6
Aug.	4—Alfred Lagace, Montreal	W	6
Sept.	16—Jim Henry, Granby	KO by	8
Oct.	10—Ricky Zarbatany, Quebec	W	10
Nov.	4—Carl Winston, Montreal	W	6
Dec.	22—Keith (Voodoo Man) Everette, Hull	D	10

1976
May	3—Marc Gervais, Hull	W	10
May	10—Joe Henry, Toronto	D	10
May	26—Ruby Orr, Verdun	W	10
July	3—David William, Moncton	KO	3
Aug.	3—Donnie Sennett, Moncton	W	10
Oct.	23—Don Boulter, Charlottown	L	8
Nov.	14—Clyde Gray, Toronto	KO by	8
Dec.	14—Guerrero Chavez, Montreal	KO by	2

1977
Apr.	26—Marc Gervais, Montreal	KO	5
June	29—Cecil King, Montreal	D	6

1978
Feb.	21—David Green, London	KO by	4

1979
Oct.	30—Ronald Zenon, Paris	L	10

TYRONE JOHNSON
Philadelphia, Pa. Featherweight
1979
Feb.	12—Andre Mordecai, Washington, D.C.	KO by	1

VONZELL JOHNSON
Indianapolis, Ind. Light Heavyweight
1974
Nov.	12—Sylvester Wilder, Indianapolis	W	4
Dec.	9—Charlie Jordan, Highland Park	KO	3

1975
May	8—Smokey Middleton, Baltimore	W	6
May	22—Wayne McGee, Baltimore	W	6
June	17—Smokey Middleton, Largo	W	6
June	25—George McGee, Toledo	W	8

1976
Apr.	22—Bruce Scott, Seattle	KO	3
May	5—Terry Lee, Lake Tahoe	KO	6
May	25—Eddie Owens, Seattle	KO	7
Oct.	6—Buddha Brooks, Las Vegas	KO	7
Oct.	27—Vern McIntosh, Las Vegas	KO	7
Nov.	24—Hildo Silva, Las Vegas	W	10

1977
Mar.	27—Tony Greene, San Antonio	KO	4
June	22—Gary Summerhays, Columbus	W	10
Aug.	23—Jerry Celestine, New Orleans	L	10
Oct.	13—Ron Wilson, Columbus	KO	10
Nov.	26—Hank Gregory, Columbus	KO	2

1978
June	22—Chuck Warfield, Kalamazoo	KO	7

1979
Sept.	26—Larry Sims, Windsor	W	10

1980
May	23—Bill Hollis, Pontiac	KO	3
Aug.	9—John Davis, Atlantic City	W	8

VERNON JOHNSTON
Tyler, Texas Heavyweight
1979
Jan.	13—Greg Monroe, Beaumont	KO	2
Feb.	17—Claman Parker, Beaumont	KO by	5

1976
Aug.	14—Tommy Collins, Houston	KO by	2
Nov.	4—Juan DeLaGarza, Corpus Christi	D	6

1977
Apr.	25—Doug Ahonen, Conroe	L	6
Oct.	4—Juan De La Garza, Corpus Christi	D	6

1978
Feb.	20—Victor Rodriguez, San Antonio	KO by	3
July	18—Henry Ray, Tyler	L	6
Sept.	19—Zack Ferguson, Tyler	KO	5

1979
June	19—Henry Ray, Houston	KO	5
June	26—Bruce Scott, Beaumont	W	6
Aug.	15—Henry Ray, Beaumont	KO	1
Oct.	10—Clarence Allen, Beaumont	KO	2

1980
Jan.	9—Bruce Scott, Beaumont	L	8
Feb.	12—Lynn Ball, Beaumont	L	10
Apr.	28—Harold Campbell, Houston	KO	2
June	3—Verlee Price, Houston	W	8
July	15—Ernie Smith, Beaumont	L	10
Sept.	16—Verlee Price, Beaumont	W	8
Oct.	18—Phillip Brown, Lake Charles	L	8

GREG JOINER
New York, N.Y. Middleweight
1979
July	17—Tony Demby, Atlantic City	KO by	1

1980
July	17—Tyrone Denby, Atlantic City	KO by	1

(MEMPHIS) AL JONES
Heavyweight
1979
Nov.	27—Henry Porter, Belleville	KO by	5
Dec.	13—James Tillis, Tulsa	KO by	4

BOBBY JONES
Long Island, N.Y. Light Heavyweight
1979
Sept.	28—Steve Zouski, Taunton	KO by	2

CHARLES JONES
Maine Welterweight
1976
Dec.	16—Pat Burke, Portland	L	4

1977
Jan.	6—Jimmy Corkum, Portland	KO by	4

1978
Dec.	20—Ralph Dumont, Waterville	W	6

1979
Feb.	17—Rick Craney, Belfast, Me.	L	6
Mar.	28—Dana Knight, Waterville	KO by	7

1980
Jan.	23—Ricky Burgess, Waterville	KO by	5
Apr.	16—Rick Grivies, Waterville	KO	2
June	22—Rick Craney, Wiscasset	KO	5
Sept.	24—Bob Quirion, Waterville	D	6

DANNY JONES
Windsor, Ontario, Canada Welterweight
1979
June	28—Kevin Abney, Detroit	W	4
Aug.	23—Tony Taylor, Detroit	W	6
Sept.	26—Philip Batie, Windsor	KO	2
Nov.	23—Ricky Camaro, Verdun	KO by	4

1980
Feb.	22—Larry McCall, Detroit	W	6
May	5—Mark McCullough, Windsor	W	8
Aug.	25—Roosevelt Green, Chicago	KO by	3
May	26—Nick Furlano, Toronto	L	12
	(For Canadian Junior Welterweight Title)		
Nov.	11—Ralph Hollett, Halifax	KO by	8

DARYL (PEE MAN) JONES
Los Angeles, Calif. Junior Featherweight
1979
Sept.	23—Joel Valdez, San Jose	W	6
Oct.	4—Jose Resendez, Oroville	L	5
Oct.	27—Tony Fernandez, Stockton	W	6

1978
Apr.	28—Ramon Aguinaga, San Diego	W	10
May	15—Carlos Zuniga, Stockton	W	6
June	7—Alfonso Delgadillo, Stockton	W	6
July	2—Eleoncio Mercedes, Stockton	L	6
July	31—Raymundo Osorio, Bakersfield	W	8
Aug.	26—Ernesto Rios, Fresno	KO by	9
Nov.	27—Freddie Gonzalez, Bakersfield	L	12

1979
Apr.	4—Jose Resendez, Los Angeles	W	10
Apr.	19—Ray Hernandez, Stockton	L	10
May	25—Leo Randolph, Santa Monica	L	10
Oct.	26—Orlando Maldonado, New York	L	10

133

1980
Mar. 28—Raul Pacheco, Tacoma .... W 10

ED (TOO TALL) JONES
Jackson, Tenn. Heavyweight
1979
Nov. 3—Yaqui Meneses, Las Cruces .... W 6
Nov. 13—Abdullah Muhammad, Phoenix .... KO 6
Nov. 24—Fernando Montes, Washington, D.C. .... KO 1
Dec. 14—Jim Wallace, Dallas .... KO 2
1980
Jan. 22—Billy Joe Thomas, Indianapolis .... KO 4
Jan. 26—Rocky Gonzales, Jackson, Miss. .... KO 1

LENNY JONES
Calif. Featherweight
1979
Nov. 2—Mario Casas, San Diego .... KO 2
Nov. 23—Sergio Naularte, San Diego .... W 4
1980
Feb. 6—Fernando Reyes, Costa Mesa .... W 6
Feb. 14—Pat Cardenas, Los Angeles .... L 4
June 13—Adan Uribe Perez, San Diego .... L 4
Sept. 18—Fernando Reyes, San Diego .... W 6
Nov. 5—Lewis Cese, San Diego .... W 5

LEROY JONES
Denver, Colo. Heavyweight
1973
July 30—John Scroggins, Cheyenne .... KO 3
1974
Jan. 10—Larry Frazier, Stateline................. W 6
Jan. 23—Joe Anderson, Las Vegas .... KO 1
Feb. 13—Paul Solomon, Las Vegas .... KO 1
Mar. 19—Lou Rogan, Denver.................... KO 3
June 5—Bob Crutison, Las Vegas............... KO 2
July 2—Johnny Gilmore, Las Vegas .... W 8
Aug. 26—Henry Culpeper, Las Vegas .... W 8
Sept. 24—Koli Vaile, Las Vegas .... KO 4
Oct. 18—Chu Hernandez, Stateline.............. KO 6
1975
Jan. 29—Rico Brooks, Las Vegas................. W 10
Feb. 11—Jimmy Gilmore, Honolulu............... W 8
Mar. 18—George Johnson, Honolulu.............. W 10
July 9—Larry Frazier, Las Vegas .... W 10
Sept. 13—Arthur Robinson, Denver .... KO 2
1976
Mar. 3—Jody Ballard, Las Vegas .... KO 4
May 13—Mogel Ortiz, Albuquerque .... KO 6
July 10—Pedro Lovell, San Diego................ D 10
1977
Jan. 22—Cookie Wallace, Pensacola .... KO 9
Mar. 27—John Dennis, San Antonio .... W 8
(U.S. Championship Tournament)
Sept. 14—Greg Johnson, Las Vegas .... W 10
1978
Aug. 19—Mike Weaver, Las Vegas .... W 10
1979
Jan. 26—Fili Moala, San Diego .... W 10
May 12—Harry Terrell, Las Vegas .... W 10
July 14—Jim Beattie, Denver .... KO 4
1980
Mar. 31—Larry Holmes, Las Vegas .... KO by 8
(For World Heavyweight Title)

LLOYD JONES
Atlantic City, N.J. Junior Lightweight
1979
Sept. 20—Mike Brown, Virginia Beach .... KO 2
Oct. 18—Robert (Pee Wee) Rucker, Philadelphia KO by 2
1980
Apr. 8—Marcus Starks, Hartford .... KO by 3

LORENZO JONES
Oklahoma City, Okla. Middleweight
1979
Sept. 20—Larry Smith, Tulsa .... KO 4
Oct. 23—Steve Channell, Oklahoma City .... KO 1
Dec. 15—Frank Lawson, Oklahoma City .... KO 4
1980
Feb. 9—Clyde Spencer, Oklahoma City .... KO 4
Mar. 3—Dennis Horne, Oklahoma City .... KO by 2
July 1—Mike Williams, Oklahoma City .... W 4

NORMAN JONES
New York Middleweight
1979
Nov. 28—Nick Coffman, Smithtown .... L 4
1980
Mar. 7—Kevin Rooney, Staten Island .... L 6
Apr. 19—Frank Minnigan, Syracuse .... KO by 6

PAUL JONES
Sacramento, Calif. Junior Middleweight
1978
Sept. 14—Lenny Hahn, Portland .... KO by 2
1979
Sept. 18—Gary Giron, Reno .... KO by 4
1980
Jan. 17—Daryl Dorsey, Stateline .... KO 2
Feb. 5—Adolfo Hurtado, Stateline .... KO by 4
Feb. 7—Dujuan Johnson, Wyandotte .... KO by 1
Apr. 22—Juan Huertas, Sacramento .... KO 2

REGGIE JONES
(REGGIE AMIN MUHAMMAD)
Newark, N.J. Middleweight
1974
Jan. 17—Carlos Stevens, North Bergen.......... KO 4
June 20—Walter Riley, North Bergen............ KO 1
Oct. 28—Chris Black, New York .... KO by 1
1975
Feb. 20—Bob Payton, Upper Darby................ L 6
Aug. 5—Ali Perez, Elizabeth .... W 6
Sept. 26—Ali Perez, Latham .... L 6
1976
Jan. 31—John Harris, Waterbury .... L 6
Apr. 4—Charles Buckner, New Orleans.......... W 6
May 25—Butch Bostich, Alexander.............. KO 1
July 26—Alfonso Aguirre, New Orleans .... W 10
Aug. 16—Rocky Estafire, Newark .... D 6
1977
Apr. 25—Ali Perez, Newark .... W 10
May 26—Matt Donovan, McAfee .... KO 5
Nov. 7—Roland Cousins, Durham .... KO 3
Nov. 30—John Martino, Newark .... W 10
1978
Aug. 16—Ray Smith, Newark .... L 8
Sept. 9—Charles Carey, Rahway .... W 8
1979
Mar. 10—Ray Kates, Rahway .... W 12
Apr. 27—Rusty Rosenberger, Newark .... L 12
June 29—Tyrone Freeman, Jersey City .... KO 3
1980
Mar. 29—Mustafa Hamsho, Atlantic City ...... KO by 6
Dec. 18—Greg Thomas, Totowa .... KO 2

SKIPPER JONES
1980
Mar. 4—Muhammad Shabazz, W. Hartford .... L 8
May 16—Robert Thomas, Chester .... W 6
May 29—Muhammad Shabazz, W. Hartford .... KO 8
July 12—Richie Bennett, Atlantic City .... W 10
Aug. 9—Tyrone Demby, Atlantic City .... L 10
Aug. 21—Nino Gonzales, Totowa .... L 10
Dec. 18—Bobby Czyz, Totowa .... KO by 7

ANTONIO JUAREZ
Argentine Welterweight
1980
Jan. —Raul Paz, Monte Hermoso .... W 10
Mar. 8—Ramon Quintana, Buenos Aires .... W 10
Apr. 12—Miguel Garcia, Gral Villegas .... L 10
May 17—Ramon Peralta, Rio III .... D 12
July 11—Enrique Coronel, San Pedro .... D 10
Aug. 8—Miguel Garcia, Neuquen .... L 10

KERRY JUDGE
Warminster, Pa. Heavyweight
1980
Apr. 26—Linwood Allen, Atlantic City .... KO 3
May 25—Roger Troupe, Atlantic City .... W 4
Sept. 20—Jerry Foley, Bansalen, Pa. .... W 4
Oct. 4—Kid Samson, Great Gorge .... W 4
Nov. 12—King Edward Range, New York .... W 4

EIICHI JUMAWAM
Wahiawa, Hawaii Junior Featherweight
1980
July 22—Fred Estrella, Honolulu .... KO 2
Dec. 9—Cuco Talamantes, Honolulu .... KO 1

MIKE KACHER
Milwaukee, Wisc. Heavyweight
1979
Aug. 8—Lee Holloman, Las Vegas .... D 4

July   11—Bill Preisol, Chicago ....KO by 2

RICHIE KATES
Brighton, N.J. Light Heavyweight
1969
Dec.   11—Bobby Haynes, Baltimore ....W   4
1970
Mar.   16—Willie Hoover, Philadelphia.............KO   1
Apr.   16—Bobby Haynes, Baltimore ....W   4
June   16—Roy Dale, Philadelphia ....KO   1
Sept.   1—Tony Beckham, Washington, D.C. ......KO   1
Sept. 11—Rocky Salerno, Boston..................KO   1
Sept. 22—Joe Jones, Washington, D.C. ....KO   1
Nov.   24—Paul Dickinson, Philadelphia...........KO   2
1971
Jan.   12—Mel Ward, Philadelphia ....KO   2
Jan.   18—Bob Simmons, Philadelphia ....W   6
Apr.   5—Bob Simmons, Philadelphia ....W   8
May   17—Johnny Rouse, Philadelphia............KO   4
Sept. 21—Bob Avena, Philadelphia.................KO   2
Oct.   5—Jimmy Cherico, Philadelphia............KO   2
Nov.   15—Len Hutchins, Philadelphia ....W   8
1972
Jan.   18—Elliot Miller, Philadelphia ....KO   3
Feb.   28—Roger Rouse, Philadelphia ....KO   8
Oct.   11—Eddie Owens, Philadelphia...........KO by 7
1973
Feb.   14—Bill Freeman, Philadelphia ....W 10
Mar.   24—Ron Oliver, Atlantic City ....KO   2
Apr.   10—Paul Cardoza, Philadelphia ....W 10
June   2—Roger Russell, Atlantic City ....W 10
July   23—Eddie Owens, Philadelphia...............W 10
Sept. 24—Don Fullmer, Philadelphia ....W 10
1974
Jan.   7—Jose Gonzalez, New York ....W 10
May   29—Jimmy Dupree, Philadelphia............KO   1
July   19—James Mathatota, Durban ....KO   4
1975
Jan.   9—Robert Lloyd, Wilmington ....W 10
Feb.   21—Paul Cardoza, Philadelphia ....W 10
May   4—Muhammad Alonzo, Durban ....W 10
Sept. 23—Ron Wilson, Philadelphia...............KO   7
Nov.   29—Pierre Fourie, Johannesburg ....W 10
1976
May   22—Victor Galindez, Johannesburg.......KO by 15
(WBA Light Heavyweight Title)
Aug.   27—Don Rucker, Atlantic City ....KO   2
1977
June   18—Victor Galindez, Rome ....L 15
(WBA Light Heavyweight Title)
Aug.   25—Harold Carter, Vineland ....KO   3
1978
Feb.   10—Matt Franklin, Philadelphia ....KO by 6
Nov.   4—Carlos Marks, Atlantic City ....KO   9
1979
Mar.   10—James Scott, Rahway ....KO by 10
July   21—Murray Sutherland, Pontiac ....W 10
Aug.   21—Mario Rosa, Atlantic City ....W 10
Oct.   12—John Capobianco, Uniondale ....W 10
1980
July   15—Jerry Celestine, New Orleans ....KO   5
Sept. 23—Jerry Celestine, New Orleans ....KO by 8

KEITH KELLY
Miami, Florida Heavyweight
1976
June   1—Mal Thomas, Miami Beach ....KO   1
June   8—Johnny Evans, Miami Beach ....W   6
Sept. 14—Tracy Steele, Miami Beach ....W   4
Oct.   15—Willie Johnson, Hollywood, Fla. ....W   6
1977
Jan.   29—Steve Basse, Miami Beach ....W   4
1978-1979
(Inactive)
1980
Jan.   24—Larry Sims, Detroit ....KO   6
Feb.   22—Ali Haakim, Detroit ....KO by 5

RODNEY KENNEBREW
Cincinnati, Ohio Lightweight
1979
Jan.   10—Joe Mayes, Richfield L   6
May   19—Ron Pensrow, Findlay L   6
May   21—Al Fowler, Belleville ....KO by 5
1980
Feb   1—Gene Stevens, Louisville L   6
July   17—Kevin Straughter, Maumee ....KO by 4
Sept. 20—Milton McCrory, San Juan ....KO by 1
Nov.   7—Tyrone Moore, Clarksville ....KO by 6

GUY KENNEDY
Bronx, N.Y. Middleweight
1979
Apr.   11—Jack Flowers, White Plains ....W   4
May   23—Mario Maldonado, White Plains ....W   4
Aug.   26—John Depts, Rahway ....KO   4
Nov.   15—Juan Figueroa, Bristol ....W   4
1980
Apr.   9—Eddie Romero, Prospect Hall ....KO   4
Apr.   24—Miguel Sanchez, Totowa ....KO   8
May   22—Mario Maldonado, Totowa ....KO   8
July   24—Randy McGrady, Las Vegas ....KO by 4
Nov.   20—Marciano Bernardi, Totowa ....W 10

COSTELLO KING
Florida Middleweight
1979
Oct.   5—Jerome Brooks, Ft. Lauderdale ....W   6
Dec.   14—Tony Foreman, Ft. Lauderdale ....W   4
Dec.   18—Demetrius Edwards, Miami Beach L   4
1980
Feb.   10—John Symonette, Miami Beach L   4
Feb.   12—Ernie Barr, Miami Beach ....KO by 2
Mar.   17—Terry Jesmer, Edmonton ....W   8
June   28—Nino Gonzalez, San Juan L   8
July   25—Mike Janus, Miami ....W   4
Aug.   19—Carlos Herrera, Miami ....KO by 5

DONALD KING
Indianapolis, Ind. Middleweight
1980
Sept. 23—Charlie Peterson, Indianapolis ....KO   1
Oct.   28—Garland Tipton, Indianapolis ....KO   3
Nov.   22—Steve Woods, Cincinnati ....KO   2

JOSHUA KING
Brooklyn, N.Y. Lightweight
1979
June   28—Ronnie Bryant, Staten Island ....KO   1
Aug.   28—Luis Isaac, Atlantic City ....W   4
Oct.   12—Miguel Rivera, Uniondale ....KO   1
Dec.   11—Julius Dozier, Halifax ....KO   1
1980
Apr.   19—Tony Salvatore, Syracuse L   6
May   9—Jose Matos, Commack ....D   6
June   20—Marcus Starks, Hartford L   6

NAT KING
1980
Jan.   29—George Lee, Miami Beach ....KO   1
Feb.   12—Eddie Melo, Montreal ....KO by 3

JEROME KINNEY
Detroit, Mich. Junior Welterweight
1980
Sept. 27—Ken Dallas, Detroit ....KO   3
Oct.   18—Sam Gervin, Pontiac ....KO   4
Nov.   1—Larry Johnson, Detroit ....KO   3
Nov.   14—Gary Stallworth, Detroit ....KO   1

DAN KISER
Memphis, Tenn. Light Heavyweight
1979
Sept.   7—Luke Capuano, Chicago ....KO   1
1980
Mar.   4—Eddie Collins, Memphis ....KO 10
Mar.   26—Phil Wade, Fayetteville ....KO   6
Apr.   22—George Goforth, Memphis ....L 10
Aug.   2—Robert Thomas, Millington ....KO   8
Aug.   25—Henry Sims, Chicago ....KO by 3

KENNY KLINGMAN
Miami Beach, Fla. Middleweight
Born: February 23, 1960
1977
Oct.   15—Al Walker, Ft. Lauderdale ....KO   1
Oct.   23—Joe Kidd, Miami Beach ....KO   2
Oct.   25—Johnny Walker, Homestead ....KO   1
1978
Feb.   21—Willie Allen, Hollywood ....KO   3
Mar.   16—Mike Ethridge, Hollywood ....KO   2
Apr.   14—Jess Hayman, Ft. Lauderdale ....KO   2
May   12—Frank Wallace, Ft. Lauderdale ....KO   2
June   20—James Taylor, Miami ....KO   1
July   18—Paul Novek, Miami Beach ....KO   1
Sept. 26—Don Cobbs, Miami Beach ....KO   1
1979
Jan.   13—Jim White, Miami Beach ....KO   1
Mar.   5—James Roper, Sunrise ....KO   4
July   29—Leon Sheffield, W. Palm Beach ....W   4
Aug.   24—Tony Daniels, Sunrise ....HO   1
Oct.   5—Rocky Stevens, Ft. Lauderdale ....KO   1

135

1980
Feb.   5—Tony Daniels, Charleston ....W   8
Oct. 17—Buddy Walker, W. Palm Beach ....KO   1

MIKE KNOX
Hartford, Conn. Lightweight
1979
July 27—Marcus Starks, Hartford L   4
Sept. 7—Marcus Starks, Hartford ....KO by   4
1980
Sept. 23—Michael Lalonde, Montreal L   8
Oct. 28—Jim Henry, Montreal ....KO by   3

MIKE KORANICKI
Philadelphia, Pa. Heavyweight
1973
June 19—Larry McGee, Miami Beach............KO   1
June 26—Carlos Dunston, Miami Beach..........KO   3
July 17—Calvin Hollaman, Miami Beach ....KO   2
1974
Apr.   2—Lou Howard, Miami Beach..............KO   5
Apr.   9—O. T. Davis, Miami Beach...............W   8
Apr. 23—O. T. Davis, Miami Beach..............KO   4
June   4—John L. Johnson, Miami Beach.........KO   5
July   9—Charlie Boston, Miami Beach ....KO   3
July 30—Jimmy Summerville, Miami Beach ......W 10
Aug. 20—Jimmy Summerville, Miami Beach ......W 10
Sept. 18—Reggie Fleming, Pittsburgh ....KO   2
Nov.   4—Rochell Norris, New York L   6
Dec. 10—John L. Johnson, Miami Beach.........W 10
1975
Dec.   9—John Berry, Washington, D.C........KO by   7
1976
Mar.   9—Harold Carter, Allentown...............W 10
Sept. 3—Joe Gholston, Philadelphia ....W   8
Sept. 16—Wendell Bailey, Baltimore..............L   8
Dec. 10—Joe Gholston, Philadelphia ....D   8
1977
Jan. 21—John Warr, Rochester, N.Y. ....W   8
Mar. 15—Tom Prater, Miami Beach ....W 10
Apr. 29—Nick Wells, Fort Worth ....KO   9
June 13—Rodell Dupree, Newark ....KO   4
July 26—Dave Wilson, Philadelphia ....KO   4
Sept. 16—George Chaplin, Richmond ....W 10
Oct. 15—Fili Moala, Palm Springs ....D 10
1978
June 19—Jerry Thompkins, Philadelphia ....W 10
1979
Feb. 20—John L. Gardner, London ....KO by 10
May   25—George Chaplin, Baltimore.............L 10
Dec. 19—Kallie Knoetze, Cape Town ....KO 10
1980
Apr. 19—Gerrie Coetzee, Johannesburg ....KO by   1
Aug. 14—James (Quick) Tillis, Chicago ....L 10

RAUL KRENS
Argentine Junior Middleweight
1980
Apr. 26—Carlos Velazquez, Buenos Aires ......KO by   1
Oct. 18—Norberto Garcia, Junin ....KO by   3
Dec. 19—Ruben Wilberger, Gral Acha ....TD   2

RICH KRONICH
Spokane, Wash. Junior Welterweight
1977
Oct. 22—Roger Stafford, Las Vegas ....KO by   1
Dec.   8—Hedgemon Robertson, Las Vegas .....KO by   2
1978
(Inactive)
1979
Feb. 14—Gary Pittman, Spokane ....KO by   2
Dec. 11—Glen Inlow, Spokane ....KO by   2
1980
Mar. 18—Glen Inlow, Spokane ....KO   4
June   2—Francisco Rivera, Spokane ....W   6
Oct. 23—Gary Pittman, Spokane L   6

ROBERT KRUEGER
Phoenix, Ariz. Lightweight
1980
Jan. 11—Johnny Rico, Phoenix ....KO   1
Feb.   1—Rudy Matta, Phoenix ....W   6
Jan. 20—Rafael Tejeda, Tucson ....KO   2
Mar. 13—Pablo Gomez, Las Vegas ....KO   2
Apr.   9—Junior Foster, Las Vegas ....KO by   1
May   29—Rocky Matta, Las Vegas ....KO by   4
Sept. 24—Carlton Sparrow, Las Vegas ....KO by   3

TERRY KRUEGER
Dallas, Texas Heavyweight
1978
July 14—Fili Moala, San Diego ....KO by   3
Sept. 19—Ismael Ruiz, Houston ....W 10

136

1979
June 12—Ernie Smith, Beaumont ....KO by   8
1980
Dec.   6—Larry Frazier, Lake Tahoe ....KO by   3

ROCKY KUTULAS
Spokane, Washington Welterweight
1980
June   2—Eddie Mendoza, Spokane ....KO   3
Aug.   9—Francisco Rivera, Spokane ....W   4

SANTOS (FALUCHO) LACIAR
Argentina Flyweight
Born: January 31, 1959, Huinca Renanco, Cordoba
1976
Dec.   3—Carlos Maliene, Huinca Renanco ....KO   2
Dec.   —Angel Tito Pereyra, Huinca Renanco ...KO   4
1977
Feb.   5—Amada Chavez, Realico ....KO   5
Feb. 25—Jose Flores, Huinca Renanco ....KO   4
Mar. 26—Alejandro Olguin, Ing. Luiggi ....D 10
Apr. 22—Alberto Martin, Huinca Renanco ....W 10
May   7—Jose Izquierdo, Realico ....W 10
June 18—Jose L. Zarate, Huinca Renanco ....KO   1
July   8—Jose Ibiris, Huinca Renanco ....D 10
Sept. 9—Carlos Reyes Sosa, Villa Maria ....W 12
(Won Cordoba State Flyweight Title)
Sept. 30—Manuel Quinteros, Huinca Renanco .....KO   8
Oct. 22—Carlos Reyes Sosa, Villa Carlos Paz .....KO   8
Nov.   4—Jose Izquierdo, Huinca Renanco ....W 10
Dec. 17—Enrique Navarro, Realico ....KO   6
1978
Jan. 13—Luis Gerez, Huinca Renanco ....W 10
Feb. 10—Jose Ibiris, Huinca Renanco ....W 10
Apr. 14—Ramon Soria, Huinca Renanco ....D 10
May   19—Carlos Aguero, Huinca Renanco ....W 10
June   2—Reynaldo Romero, Huinca Renanco ......W 10
July   8—Hector Barreto, Huinca Renanco ....W 10
Sept. 6—Jose Izquierdo, Villa Carlos Paz ....W 10
Sept. 20—Jose Luis Lopez, Villa Carlos Paz .....KO   4
Oct.   6—Luis Gerez, Villa Maria ....D 10
Oct. 21—Angel Luis Fernandez, Buenos Aires .....W 10
Nov.   9—Felipe Rojas, Villa Carlos Paz ....KO   5
Dec.   1—Ramon Soria, Mendoza ....L 10
Dec. 14—Raul Perez, Villa Carlos Paz ....W 10
1979
Jan. 26—Jose Ibiris, Villa Carlos Paz ....W 10
Feb. 14—Juan Carlos Rios, Villa Carlos Paz .....W 10
Mar. 16—Raul (Nico) Perez, Huinca Renanco ......L 10
Apr. 11—Gilberto Lopez, Villa Carlos Paz ....W 10
Apr. 26—Jose Flores, Villa Carlos Paz ....KO   7
May   25—Raul Perez, Villa Carlos Paz ....L 10
June 22—Juan Jose Espindola, Cordoba ....W 10
Aug.   2—Miguel A. Lazarte, Villa Carlos Paz .....D 10
Sept. 6—Luis Gomez, Villa Carlos Paz ....W 10
Oct. 12—Hector Velasquez, Villa Carlos Paz ......W 10
Nov.   3—Gustavo Ballas, Buenos Aires ....L 10
Dec.   7—Gederico Condori, Buenos Aires ....W 10
1980
Feb. 27—Miguel Lazarte, Villa Carlos Paz ....W 12
(Won Vacant Argentine Flyweight Title)
Mar. 28—Ruben Condori, Cordoba ....D 10
Apr. 18—Domingo Aragon, Cordoba ....W 10
May   6—Adrian Roman, Cordoba ....KO   3
May   9—Juan J. Brizuela, Cordoba ....W 10
July 23—Miguel A. Velez, Villa Carlos Paz ......KO   6
Aug. 30—Jaime Miranda, Santiago ....TD   8
(For South American Flyweight Title)
Nov.   6—Federico Condori, Huinca Renanco ......W 10
Nov. 22—Jaime Miranda, Villa Carlos Paz ....W 12
(Won South American Flyweight Title)
Dec.   8—Charlie Magri, London ....L 10

CHARLES LACOUR
Seattle, Washington Junior Middleweight
1980
Feb. 29—Bill Barnes, Nanaimo ....KO   1
Apr. 24—Manny Gonzales, Portland ....D   6
May   21—Jimmy Millan, Kelowna ....KO   4
June 13—Bruce Strauss, Nanaimo ....W   8
Sept. 23—Craig Henderson, Edmonton ....KO   4
Oct. 11—Bobby Howard, Nanaimo ....ND   4
Oct. 22—Leonard Thomas, Crystal Bay ....W   8
Nov. 19—Reinaldo Roque, Las Vegas L   6

DANMAN LACY
Los Angeles, Calif. Light Heavyweight
1978
June	27—Alvin Dominey, Odessa	KO by	1
July	31—Daniel Lopez, Odessa	KO	5
Sept.	19—Art Henderson, Odessa	KO	3

1979
Aug.	28—Tom Westbrook, Honolulu	KO	6
Sept.	30—Niva Tofaeono, Odessa	KO	5
Nov.	15—George O'Mara, Los Angeles	KO by	3

1980
Feb.	20—Curtis Azevedo, Hilo	KO by	6
May	19—Grover Robinson, Odessa	KO by	1

MARVIN LADSON
Winston-Salem, N.C. Junior Welterweight
1977
June	2—Willie Rankin, Virginia Beach	W	4
July	21—Hilbert Stevenson, Virginia Beach	KO by	2

1978
Nov.	25—Hilbert Stevenson, Kingsport	KO by	4

1979
Jan.	22—Dale Staley, Washington, D.C.	KO by	2
Aug.	24—Jimmy Heair, Memphis	KO by	1
Sept.	22—John Myers, Winston-Salem	KO	2

1980
Sept.	25—Paul Gentry, Winston-Salem	KO	2
Dec.	17—Ray Mancini, Youngstown	KO by	1

ROLANDO LAHOZ
Argentine Bantamweight
1980
Feb.	21—Jose Uziga, Carlos Paz	L	12
June	27—Esteban Bustos, San Juan	W	10
Aug.	8—Raul Pared, San Juan	KO	10
Sept.	4—Raul Perez, Mendoza	L	10
Dec.	19—Julio C. Saba, San Juan	W	10

KEN LAKUSTA
Edmonton, Canada Heavyweight
1980
Apr.	15—Ron Harry, Miami Beach	KO by	1
Mar.	17—Ron Rousselle, Edmonton	KO by	2
May	2—Johnny Jackson, Miami Beach	W	4
June	6—Craig Henderson, Miami Beach	W	4
Aug.	19—Mike Bennett, Miami Beach	KO	1
Nov.	19—Mike Gans, Crystal Bay	L	6

MICHEL LALONDE
Hull, Canada Junior Welterweight
1980
Mar.	13—Kenny Dunn, Hull	KO	2
Apr.	21—Tommy Holder, Hull	W	6
May	7—Kenny Muse, Montreal	W	8
Sept.	23—Mike Knox, Montreal	W	8
Oct.	28—Joe Bolarino, Montreal	W	6
Dec.	9—Jean LaPointe, Montreal	W	8

JEFF LAMPKIN
Youngstown, Ohio Light Heavyweight
1980
June	11—Jimmy Hearn, Struthers	KO	1
Aug.	20—John Beveridge, Warren	KO	1
Sept.	9—Wes Rowe, Warren	KO	3
Sept.	24—Earl Caldwell, Struthers	KO	1
Oct.	28—Eddie Temple, Warren	KO	1
Dec.	9—Willie Crawford, Warren	KO	4
Dec.	16—Stan Scott, Cleveland	KO	3

KELVIN LAMPKINS
Muncie, Ind. Lightweight
1979
Sept.	20—Eric Tribeau, Indianapolis	W	4

1980
Jan.	21—Alvin Fowler, St. Charles	W	6
Mar.	8—Anthony Murray, Nashville	L	6
Mar.	22—Willie McIntosh, Grand Rapids	L	6
May	9—Pajarito Marquez, Chicago	L	6
May	22—Willie McIntosh, Holland, Mich.	W	4
June	18—Louis Hubela, Struthers	L	6
July	11—Efrain Nieves, Chicago	L	4
Aug.	3—Ernie Trimmonds, N. Platte	KO	2
Nov.	7—Eladio Leal, Chicago	KO	2
Oct.	25—Dave Williams, Herenthais	KO by	5
Dec.	9—Ray Mancini, Warren	KO by	2

TOM LANDRY
Massachusetts Heavyweight
1977
June	20—Eddie Chase, Peabody	KO	1
Nov.	18—Joe Velmure, Lowell	L	4

1978
Mar.	11—Alex Carr, Lowell	KO	1
May	9—Al Brooks, Hartford	L	6
May	13—Joe Velmure, Boston	L	8
June	19—Don Halpern, Boston	KO by	1
Nov.	11—Steve Zouski, Boston	KO by	2

1979
(Inactive)
1980
Aug.	20—Bobby Wonder, Las Vegas	KO	1
Oct.	15—Ron Draper, Las Vegas	L	6

CHRIS LANGE
Columbus, Ga. Middleweight
1977
Sept.	6—Bob Franchino, Orlando	W	4
Sept.	27—Bob Franchino, Orlando	W	4
Oct.	25—Babe Clark, Orlando	W	4
Nov.	22—Slick Mitchell, Orlando	KO by	5

1978
Jan.	17—Larry Saffeels, Columbus	KO	3
Jan.	31—Earthy Ellis, Orlando	W	4
Feb.	13—Larry Saffeels, Columbus	KO	5
Feb.	28—Dennis Whittfield, Jacksonville	KO	2
Mar.	16—Willie Allen, Ft. Lauderdale	KO	3
Apr.	6—Solomon Brown, Palatka	KO	2
May	6—Rock Stevens, Palatka	W	6
June	3—Howard Soloman, Jacksonville	KO	1
June	17—Major Lambert, Jacksonville	KO	4
July	1—Willie Goodman, Jacksonville	W	6
July	18—Slick Mitchell, Jacksonville	D	8
Aug.	25—Solomon Brown, Columbus	KO	5
Sept.	27—Pat Dorsey, Columbus	KO	6
Nov.	14—Gary Smith, Columbus	W	10
Dec.	5—Rock Stevens, Jacksonville	W	6

1979
Feb.	10—Gary Smith, Palatka	W	6
May	15—Tiger Hall, Jacksonville	KO	8
May	26—Rock Stevens, Columbus	KO	2
June	6—A. W. Muhammad, Jacksonville	W	6
Aug.	16—Tony Chiaverini, Kansas City	KO by	7
Sept.	20—Sammy NeSmith, Indianapolis	L	10

1980
Mar.	9—Marciano Bernardi, Atlantic City	KO by	2
May	28—Paddy Wilson, Portland, Ore.	D	8
June	14—Gary Giron, Yerington	KO by	8

LEONARD LANGLEY
Washington, D.C. Light Heavyweight
1977
June	21—Frankie Elam, Largo	KO by	1
Sept.	18—Franco Thomas, Fairmont	L	6

1978
Mar.	15—Dave Little, Washington, D.C.	KO	1
Mar.	16—Fred Brown, Virginia Beach	L	4
Apr.	19—Dwight Braxton, Washington, D.C.	D	6

1979
Apr.	26—Al Yasbick, Virginia Beach	L	6
May	31—Chris Reederm, Virginia Beach	L	6

1980
May	8—Dwight Braxton, Atlantic City	KO by	2

CALVIN LANGSTON
Bridgeport, Conn. Heavyweight
1979
June	29—Robert Evans, New York	L	4
Oct.	10—C. J. Vesco, White Plains	D	4
Oct.	24—Jerry Foley, Scranton	KO by	5
Nov.	7—Jimmy Smith, Boston	L	4
Nov.	15—Dick Embleton, Bristol	KO	4
Dec.	1—Alfredo Evangelista, Pamplona	KO by	3

1980
Feb.	27—Jimmy Smith, Scranton	L	6
Feb.	28—Ralph Kelly, Hartford	L	4
Mar.	26—Mike Boswell, Scranton	KO by	2
Apr.	24—Dave Bird, Totowa	L	6
May	4—Conroy Nelson, Kiamesha Lake	KO by	1
Nov.	3—Ken Schmidt, Hartford	KO by	1

SAM LANTION
Spartanburg, S.C. Welterweight
1977
June	—Robert Mullins, Spartanburg	KO by	2

1978
June	7—Sammy Ruckard, Spartanburg	KO by	4
Aug.	—Robert Mullins, Spartanburg	KO by	5
Dec.	23—Hawthorne Davis, Spartanburg	KO	4

1979
Apr.	5—Super Bug Williams, Spartanburg	KO	2
May	4—Gary Barlow, Fayetteville	KO	3

1980
Feb.	5—Calvin Watt, Charleston	KO	2
Feb.	9—Thierry Samo, Calais	KO by	1

Mar. 22—Floyd Mayweather, Grand Rapids .... KO by 4
May 24—Robert Mullins, Union, S.C. .... KO by 4
July 18—Sammy Horne, Spartanburg .... KO by 3
Sept. 25—Ted Hadfield, Winston-Salem .... KO by 4

WILFREDO LANZO
New York, N.Y. Featherweight
1978
Feb. 27—Luis Rivero, New York .... L 6
June 6—Saul Grullion, New York .... KO 2
June 22—Jose Ortiz, New York .... W 4
Nov. 30—Nelson Diaz, New York .... W 6
1979
Apr. 6—Jose Ortiz, New York .... W 6
July 8—Joe Rivera, New York .... W 8
Oct. 26—Cocoa Sanchez, New York .... L 8
1980
Mar. 3—Carlos Pinango, Caracas .... KO by 2
May 23—Tirso de la Rosa, New York .... KO 3

JEAN LAPOINTE
Montreal, Quebec, Canada Featherweight
Born: April 10, 1951
1975
Nov. 7—Jocelyn Marcotte, Sorec .... KO 4
1976
May 4—Jose Martinez, Montreal .... W 6
June 3—Otto Brading, Verdua .... KO 4
July 9—Papo Melandez, Montreal .... KO 4
July 21—Kevin Cabin, Montreal .... KO 3
Aug. 14—Papo Melandez, Montreal .... KO 3
Sept. 21—Barry Sponacle, Montreal .... W 10
Nov. 26—Jose Martinez, Montreal .... W 10
1977
Mar. 22—Barry Sponacle, Montreal .... W 12
June 1—Danny Stokes, Montreal .... KO 4
July 5—Ralph Racine, Montreal .... KO by 3
Aug. 30—Cleveland Denny, Montreal .... L 12
1978
Jan. 24—Nicky Furlano, Montreal .... D 8
Feb. 26—Barry Mason, Montreal .... KO 8
Mar. 28—Jose Ortez, Montreal .... KO 10
June 6—Nicky Furlano, Montreal .... W 10
June 27—Gaetan Hart, Montreal .... KO by 10
Sept. 26—Gerald Hayes, Montreal .... W 10
Dec. 5—Joe Phillips, Montreal .... W 10
Dec. 12—Jose Rantas, Verdun .... KO by 3
1979
Mar. 13—Pinnock Leonard, Montreal .... KO 5
Mar. 30—Pat Ford, Port of Spain .... KO by 4
May 25—Joe Bolarino, Montreal .... W 8
Oct. 2—Nick Furlano, Montreal .... KO by 6
1980
Jan. 20—Roberto Castaneda, Quebec City .... KO 1
Jan. 25—Juan LaPorte, New York .... KO by 7
Dec. 9—Michel Lalonde, Montreal .... L 8

JUAN LAPORTE
New York, N.Y. Featherweight
Born: Nov. 24, 1959
1977
Oct. 29—John Green, Hamilton .... KO 1
Nov. 11—Jerry Strickland, Cincinnati .... W 4
Dec. 15—Charlie Buggs, Hamilton .... KO 3
1978
Mar. 2—Santos Cruz, New York .... W 4
May 29—Jose Rodriguez, Los Angeles .... L 6
July 26—Ray Viruet, New York .... W 6
Dec. 15—David Capo, New York .... W 8
1979
Apr. 27—Lazaro Fabian, New York .... KO 1
June 14—Jose Figueroa, New York .... KO 5
Aug. 16—Wardell Williams, Kansas City .... KO 2
Aug. 22—Andres Malanga Torres, New York ..... KO 6
Sept. 19—Joe Rivera, New York .... W 8
1980
Jan. 25—Jean LaPointe, New York .... KO 7
Apr. 18—David Capo, New York .... W 10
June 20—Fel Clemente, New York .... KO 10
Sept. 13—Mano Morua, San Antonio .... W 10
Dec. 13—Salvador Sanchez, El Paso .... L 15
(For World Featherweight Title)

HUMBERTO LARA
Mexican Featherweight
1975
Jan. 15—Paulino Canche, Merida .... D 8
Feb. 25—Miguel Fernandez, Merida .... W disq. 10
1976
(Inactive)
1977
Feb. 7—Lonny Pacheco, Halaxho .... D 10
Sept. 17—Vincent Pool, Merida .... L 10

1978
Feb. 28—Conrado Vasquez, Honolulu .... L 10
Mar. 4—Roberto Barrientos .... L 10
May 30—Nick Perez, Incline Village .... L 10
Nov. 11—Earl Young, Salt Lake City .... L 10
1979
June —Nicky Perez, Albuquerque .... L 10
Aug. 16—Juan Meza, Los Angeles .... KO by 4
1980
Feb. 21—Rocky Garcia, Los Angeles .... KO by 3
Apr. 1—Richard Savala, Sacramento .... L 6
Apr. 10—Louis Loy, Los Angeles .... L 10

JESSIE LARA
Houston, Texas Junior Middleweight
1968
Mar. 26—Baldomar Garcia, Corpus Christi .... L 4
Apr. 26—Lawrence Brown, Corpus Christi .... D 4
Oct. 7—Al Jackson, New Orleans .... KO by 3
—Mauro Martinez, Nueva Rosita .... W 8
—Pedro Kanguro Pina, Nueva Rosita ..... KO 8
—Robelde Reyna, Nueva Rosita .... KO 4
—Piri Alvarado, Nueva Rosita .... W 8
—Chicharito Martinez, Nueva Rosita ..... KO 9
—Daniel Lopez, Acuna .... KO 8
—Mocho Hernandez, Acuna .... KO 5
1969
Feb. 6—Pajarito Corona, Los Angeles .... L 6
Mar. 30—Jimmy Robertson, Los Angeles ...... KO by 4
—Beto Estrada, Nueva Rosita .... W 10
—Mauro Martinez, Nueva Rosita .... W 10
—Miguel Hernandez, Acuna .... L 10
—Cordobles Rodriguez, Saltillo .... W 10
—Beto Licraga, Monclova .... KO 7
—Bolerito Padilla, Monclova .... KO 8
—Lupe Torres, Acuna .... KO 6
—Miguel Hernandez, Acuna .... KO 9
Oct. 7—Ruben Leyva, San Antonio .... KO 5
Oct. 28—Casar Narvaez, San Antonio .... KO 2
Dec. 9—Magdeleno Puentes, San Antonio .... W 8
1970
—Lobito Enriquez, Acuna .... KO 5
—Gabby Estrada, Nueva Rosita .... W 10
—Victor Valero, Piedras Negras .... KO 5
Mar. 30—Billy Vining, New Orleans .... D 8
Apr. 14—Albert Armendarez, Corpus Christi .... KO 8
May 5—Koichi Otomaru, Honolulu .... D 6
May 26—Bob Mielke, Honolulu .... W 5
June 16—Walter Charles, Honolulu .... KO by 6
Sept. 29—Bob Mielke, Honolulu .... W 5
1971
—Isaac Quintas, Piedras Negras .... KO by 7
—Barnabe Vasquez, Piedras Negras ...... L 10
—Jose Hererra, Monclova .... W 10
Apr. 17—Roy Barrientos, San Antonio .... KO by 6
June 18—Gilbert Mares, San Antonio .... W 10
Aug. 16—Jimmy Hamm, New Orleans .... L 8
Sept. 30—Raymond Boyd, San Antonio .... W 10
1972
—Tony Morales, Piedras Negras .... KO 5
June 26—Frank Young, Houston .... KO by 3
Dec. 5—Roy McMillian, Clovis .... L 6
1973
Apr. 23—Jerry Kornele, Jacinto City .... KO by 2
July 30—Brooks Byrd, Albuquerque .... L 8
Oct. 2—Alfonso Aguirre, San Antonio .... L 8
Nov. 13—Efrain Gonzalez, San Antonio .... KO 7
1974
Feb. 19—Augie Gomez, San Antonio .... D 10
Nov. 19—Irish Gene Wells, Houston .... KO by 10
Dec. 16—Frank Young, Jacinto City .... L 10
1975
—Mickey Jones, Mobile .... W 10
Mar. 15—Esteban De Jesus, Caracas .... KO by 3
July 24—Frank Young, Jacinto City .... KO by 5
Sept. 13—Larry Bonds, Denver .... KO by 7
1976
—Cubanito Medrano, Nueva Rosita .... KO 5
—Panchito Reyes, Nueva Rosita .... KO 4
—Antonio Leyva, Sabinas .... KO 5
—Paino Gonzalez, Piedras Negras .... KO 2
—Alex Aguirre, Piedras Negras .... W 10
—Manuel Avitia, Piedras Negras .... W 10
1977
Apr. 2—Jo Kimpuani, Dunkerque .... KO by 3
June 14—Prisciliano Castillo, Houston .... W 10
June 16—Lester Davis, Mobile .... KO by 3
July 19—Raul Aguirre, Houston .... L 10
Aug. 18—Monroe Brooks, Los Angeles .... KO by 4
Oct. 11—Raul Aguirre, Houston .... L 12
Dec. 13—Eddie Mitchell, Houston .... W 8
1978
Feb. 17—Alois Carmeliet, Zele .... L 10

Mar. 3—Fighting Jim, Curacao .... KO by 3
Mar. 25—Carlos DeLeon, Las Vegas .... KO by 3
July 7—Bruno Arcari, Genoa .... KO by 5
Oct. 10—Adolfo Rivas, Houston .... W 10
1979
Mar. 20—Danny Donatto, Houston .... KO by 1
May 9—Victor Martinez, Las Vegas .... KO by 2
July 16—Marvin Jenkins, New York .... KO by 1
Nov. 6—Prisciliano Castillo, Corpus Christi ... KO by 8
Dec. 7—Jose Duarte, Acapulco .... KO by 5
1980
Feb. 21—Andy Price, Tulsa .... KO by 4
Apr. 29—Leon McCullum, Houston .... W 8
July 15—Antonio Munoz, Laredo .... KO 2
Sept. 1—Oscar Albarado, Laredo .... KO by 6

JOSE LUIS LARA
Mexican Featherweight
1977
Feb. 28—Jose Luis Luna, Tuxtla Gutierrez .... KO 1
Apr. 18—Amadeo Mendoza, Tuxtla Gutierrez .... L 10
May 12—Jose Luis Diaz, Los Angeles .... W 4
May 19—Jose Valencia, Los Angeles .... W 5
May 26—Jose Rodriguez, Los Angeles .... L 6
June 15—Federico Carrena, Mexico City .... KO by 1
June 16—Eulogio Bojorguez, Los Angeles .... L 5
July 14—David Barrera, Los Angeles .... L 5
Oct. 6—Spud Murphy, Los Angeles .... KO by 3
1978
Feb. 2—Salvador Gonzalez, Los Angeles .... W 5
Feb. 9—Jose Caba, Los Angeles .... KO by 3
Mar. 17—Salvador Gonzalez, Bakersfield .... W 6
Apr. 4—Manuel Ferrer, Mexico City ....KO 8
July 6—Juan Manuel Sanchez, Los Angeles ...... L 6
July 29—Alfredo Vasquez, Mexico City ....KO 2
Aug. 23—Rafael Alonso, Las Vegas .... L 4
Aug. 26—Francisco Velez, Fresno .... W 6
Sept. 8—John Papin, Los Angeles .... L 6
Sept. 26—Rudy Ramirez, Pico Rivera .... W 6
Sept. 30—Rodolfo Castillo, Mexico City ....KO 2
Oct. 5—Rocky Lockridge, Seattle .... L 6
Nov. 2—Johnny Papin, Los Angeles .... W 6
Nov. 15—Juan Meza, Las Vegas .... KO by 5
Nov. 22—Pablo Ramirez, Mexico City .... L 10
1979
Jan. 28—Antonio Lara, Tuxtla Gutierrez ....KO 7
Jan. 29—Juan Escobar, Los Angeles .... KO by 4
Mar. 14—Juan Garcia, Mexico City .... KO by 1
May 17—Juan Villa, Los Angeles .... L 10
Oct. 4—John Papin, Los Angeles .... D 10
1980
July 3—Lionel Harney, Gardnerville .... L 10
July 7—Edwin Rosario, Bloomington .... KO by 2

JOSE LATIMER
Puerto Rican Junior Welterweight
1977
Oct. 15—Saul Melendez, San Juan .... KO 1
1978
Jan. 14—Ismael Santana, Carolina, P.R. ...... KO by 3
May 13—Alejandro Diaz, Carolina, P.R. ....KO 3
June 10—Angel Nieto, Carolina, P.R. ....KO 3
June 26—Jose Rentas, Rio Piedras ....KO 2
Aug. 14—Azor Agosto, Canovanas .... W 6
1979
(Inactive)
1980
Feb. 18—Vincent Quinones, San Juan .... KO 6

TIM LA VALLEY
Troy, N.Y. Junior Welterweight
1979
Mar. 29—Jose Rivera, Cohoes ....KO 1
Apr. 4—Benny Benitez, Springfield .... L 6
May 23—Felix Perez, White Plains .... KO by 1
June 18—Billy Burke, Cohoes ....KO 3
July 13—Frank Minigan, Rochester .... L 6
July 27—Marlon Starling, Hartford .... KO by 3
Oct. 25—Salvadore Ramos, Latham .... W disq. 6
Dec. 1—Ray Rivera, Albany ....KO 4
1980
Jan. 9—Hector Ortiz, Hartford .... KO by 5
Jan. 19—Frank Minigan, Syracuse .... W 6
Feb. 13—Ken Fusco, White Plains .... L 6
Mar. 13—Gaetan Hart, Hull .... KO by 8
May 4—Orlando Montalvo, Kiamasha Lake .... W 6
June 19—Curtis Harris, Totowa .... KO by 6
Oct. 24—Kevin Howard, Philadelphia .... KO by 2
Nov. 28—Don Carney, Providence ....KO 3

FRANK LAWSON
Dallas, Texas Welterweight
1978
Feb. 23—Charles Carey, Virginia Beach ....L 4
Sept. 19—Luis Alonzo, Tyler ....KO 3
Sept. 21—Daryl White, Philadelphia .... KO by 2
Nov. 4—Tony Demby, Atlantic City ....L 4
Dec. 16—Robert Madrid, Dallas ....L 6
1979
Apr. 2—Ward Jones, Dallas ....KO 6
Aug. 27—Joe Davila, Odessa ....KO 3
Oct. 20—J. J. Cottrell, Pueblo ....D 8
Dec. 15—Lorenzo Jones, Oklahoma City .... KO by 4
1980
Feb. 16—Fred Harris, Fayetteville ....KO 1
Sept. 16—Ronnie Shields, Beaumont .... KO by 3
Dec. 16—Charles Hostetter, Odessa .... KO by 3

GORDIE LAWSON
Vancouver, Canada Middleweight
1980
May 17—Maurice Rice, Kelowna .... W 6
June 5—Brian West, Vancouver .... W 4
June 13—Tommy Howard, Nanaimo .... D 6
June 26—Tommy Howard, Bellingham .... D 6
Nov. 17—Monty Betham, Aukland .... KO by 5

LEN LAWSON
Stockton, Calif. Heavyweight
1978
May 30—Byron Campbell, Incline Village ....KO 1
June 21—Pedro Garcia, Concord .... W 6
July 13—Tony Stone, Vallejo .... W 6
Dec. 13—Leni Vanisi, Oakland ....KO 7
1979
Jan. 17—Tony Stone, Stockton .... W 6
Feb. 6—Tony Stone, San Carlos .... D 6
Feb. 27—Tony Stone, San Carlos .... W 8
Apr. 26—Franco Thomas, Seattle .... L 10
June 19—Basheer Wadud, San Carlos .... D 8
Sept. 27—Ken Arlt, Portland .... L 10
1980
Apr. 1—Tony Marciano, Sacramento ....KO 5
Apr. 16—Parnell Fairley, Fresno .... L 6
July 25—Harold Dutra, San Francisco .... WTD 4
Sept. 5—Jim Restauri, Sacramento .... D 6

PAUL LAWSON
Ft. Worth, Texas Heavyweight
1979
Dec. 15—Monty Masters, Oklahoma City ...... KO by 4
1980
Jan. 8—Tom Trimm, Houston .... KO by 3
Feb. 16—Phil Wade, Fayetteville .... W 6
July 18—Mike Hamby, Odessa .... KO by 1
Aug. 21—Joe Graham, Dallas .... KO by 3

WILBURN LAWSON
Dallas, Texas Lightweight
1978
Dec. 16—James Cleveland, Dallas .... W 4
1979
Mar. 5—Juan Venegas, Houston .... KO by 5
July 21—John Morgan, Dallas .... L 6
Aug. 21—Frank Newton, Oklahoma City .... D 6
Aug. 27—Ruben Munoz, Odessa .... KO by 3
—Chris Johnson, Denver .... L 4
1980
July 18—James Cleveland, Odessa .... L 4
Aug. 21—Jerry Smith, Dallas .... L 6
Sept. 16—Ezzard Charles Adams, Beaumont ... KO by 4

MIGUEL A. LAZARTE
Argentine Flyweight
1980
Jan. 4—Rodolfo Rodriguez, Mar del Plata .... W 10
Feb. 27—Carlos Lacair, V. Carlos Paz .... L 12
May —Joaquin Miranda, Santiago .... L 10
June 6—Hector Patri, Gral Acha .... D 10
Aug. 1—Ruben Condori, Salta .... L 10
Aug. 15—Enrique Navarro, Mar del Plata ....KO 5
Sept. 19—Gustavo Ballas, Mendoza .... L 10
Oct. 24—Domingo Aragon, P.R.S. Pena .... L 10
Nov. 7—Luis Lopez, Allen ....KO 2
Nov. 28—Domingo Aragon, P.R.S. Pena .... D 10
Dec. 13—Juan J. Lopez, Olavarria .... W 10

PEDRO LEBRON
Kennett Square, Pa. Junior Lightweight
1977
Dec. 6—Tony Still, Philadelphia ....D 4

139

1978
Jan. 31—Mark Christian, Upper Darby .... KO 4
Mar. 14—Tony Still, Philadelphia .... W 4
Apr. 22—Keith Bennett, Trenton .... KO 3
May 26—Mark Christian, Trenton .... W 4
Oct. 24—Ron Aurit, Philadelphia .... L 4
Nov. 24—Tommy Nellom, Philadelphia .... W 4
1979
Jan. 30—Heriberto Torres, Upper Darby .... L 4
Mar. 30—Ken Carpenter, Scranton .... D 4
May 22—Tony Edwards, Upper Darby .... KO 1
July 17—John Carter, Atlantic City .... KO by 4
Aug. 21—Ken Carpenter, Atlantic City .... W 4
Sept. 11—Ken Carpenter, Philadelphia .... KO by 6
1980
Jan. 12—Heriberto Torres, Atlantic City .... D 6
Feb. 18—Ken Carpenter, Upper Darby ...... KO by 2
Apr. 11—Rocky Gadson, Chester .... L 6
May 16—Rocky Gadson, Chester .... L 6
July 31—Robert Johnson, Atlantic City .... D 4
Sept. 18—Ron Aurit, Philadelphia .... KO by 7

SCOTT LE DOUX
Minneapolis, Minn. Heavyweight
1974
Feb. 4—Arthur Pullens, Minneapolis .... KO 3
Mar. 14—Floyd Cox, Minneapolis .... KO 3
Apr. 23—Steve Patterson, Minneapolis .... W 6
May 15—Reggie Flemmings, St. Paul .... KO 3
May 23—Larry Penniger, Minneapolis .... KO 6
July 31—Joe Batton, Minneapolis .... KO 6
Aug. 13—Tom Berry, St. Paul .... KO 10
Oct. 8—Ron Draper, Minneapolis .... KO 10
Nov. 8—Lou Rogan, Crosby .... W 10
Nov. 22—John L. Johnson, Minneapolis .... KO 5
1975
Jan. 18—C. J. Brown, Boston .... W 6
Jan. 29—Larry Renault, Rochester, Minn. .... KO 2
Mar. 14—Cookie Wallace, St. Paul .... KO by 2
Apr. 23—Rodney Bobick, Bloomington .... W 10
July 8—Terry Daniels, Orlando .... KO 6
Aug. 14—George Johnson, St. Paul .... D 10
Sept. 23—Brian O'Melia, St. Paul .... W 10
Dec. 10—Ron Stander, Minneapolis .... W 10
1976
Feb. 7—Bill Carson, Minneapolis .... KO 9
Mar. 9—Larry Middleton, Minneapolis .... W 10
Apr. 22—Duane Bobick, Minneapolis .... L 10
June 26—John Dennis, Providence .... L 10
Aug. 16—George Foreman, Utica .... KO by 3
Nov. 30—Junior Bentley, Minneapolis .... KO 2
1977
Feb. 13—Johnny Boudreaux, Annapolis .... L 8
(U.S. Championship Tournament)
Mar. 2—Pedro Soto, New York .... W 10
June 23—Tom Prater, Bloomington .... KO 7
July 28—Duane Bobick, Bloomington .... KO by 8
Oct. 22—Leon Spinks, Las Vegas .... D 10
Dec. 2—Muhammad Ali, Chicago .... Exh. 5
1978
Sept. 26—Bill Sharkey, Miami Beach .... D 10
Oct. 3—Sylvester Wilder, Winnipeg .... KO 2
Nov. 10—James Brown, Las Vegas .... KO 2
Dec. 15—Joe Donatto, Omaha .... KO 3
1979
Feb. 20—Jim Beattie, Bloomington .... KO 3
May 12—Ron Lyle, Las Vegas .... L 10
Aug. 19—Ken Norton, Bloomington .... D 10
Nov. 24—Mike Weaver, Bloomington .... L 12
1980
Mar. 9—Marty Monroe, St. Paul .... W 10
July 7—Larry Holmes, Bloomington .... KO by 7

BERT LEE
San Diego, Calif. Junior Middleweight
1977
Feb. 25—Jorge Falaro, San Diego .... W 4
Mar. 25—David Ocequeda, San Diego .... KO 1
Apr. 1—Tony Adame, San Diego .... W 4
Apr. 29—Greg Stephens, San Diego .... KO by 2
June 24—Ronald Turner, San Diego .... W 5
July 15—Curtis Lewis, San Diego .... D 4
July 22—Francisco Ortega, San Diego .... KO by 4
Sept. 16—Gil Valdez, San Diego .... W 4
Sept. 30—Ronald Turner, San Diego .... KO 4
Oct. 29—Victor Martinez, Fresno .... L 6
Nov. 11—Roger Wells, San Diego .... KO 1
Dec. 2—James Bella, San Diego .... D 6
1978
May 19—Eugene Baldwin, San Diego .... KO 2
June 2—Gil Valdez, San Diego .... W 8
June 30—Cisco Ortega, San Diego .... D 6
July 14—Joel Carranza, San Diego .... W 6
Aug. 25—Jose Dominguez, San Diego .... W 8

Sept. 26—Carmen Garcia, Pico Rivera .... KO 5
Nov. 17—Jose Isaac Marin, San Diego .... W 10
1979
Jan. 26—Jorge Fernandez, San Diego .... KO 9
Feb. 8—Victor Martinez, Los Angeles .... L 10
Dec. 14—Pepe Dominguez, Orange County .... W 10
1980
Feb. 6—Agapito Ramirez, Costa Mesa .... W 10
Apr. 25—Leo Arguello, Los Angeles .... KO 3
June 14—Steve Moyer, Anaheim .... TD 6
Dec. 3—Fernando Lugo, Anaheim .... KO 2

GEORGE LEE
Perth Amboy, N.J. Middleweight
1979
Feb. 26—Al Lockard, New York .... W 4
Mar. 15—Gil Rosario, North Bergen .... L 4
June 29—Fred Boynton, Jersey City .... KO by 2
Aug. 3—Frank Petti, Hempstead .... L 4
Aug. 21—Richie Bennett, Atlantic City .... L 6
Oct. 26—Fulgencio Obelmejias, Caracas ...... KO by 1
Nov. 17—Fulgencio Obelmejias, Caracas ...... KO by 1
Nov. 23—Harry Sterling, Trenton .... D 4
Nov. 28—Dom DiMarzo, W. New York, N.J. ... KO by 3
Dec. 14—Jacinto Fernandez, Buenos Aires ...... KO 2
1980
Jan. 6—Andoni Amana, Bilboa .... KO by 6

MARK LEE
Carson City, Nevada Heavyweight
1979
July 3—Don Ohotto, Gardnerville .... KO 3
July 15—Samson N'Gata, Reno .... KO 2
July 30—Mike Benning, Las Vegas .... L 4
Aug. 31—Willie Stoglin, Carson City .... KO 3
Oct. 30—Bruce Morriseau, Carson City .... KO 3
Nov. 19—Garland Barnes, Lake Tahoe .... KO 1

CAVEMAN LEE
(AKA WILLIAM LEE, WILLIAM LEE JR.)
Philadelphia, Pa. Middleweight
1976
Feb. 25—Wallace Smith, Philadelphia .... KO 1
June 16—Fred Robinson, Philadelphia .... KO 1
July 14—Jimmy Dean, Philadelphia .... KO 1
Nov. 3—Jimmy Howard, Philadelphia .... KO 1
1977
June 23—Ray Bryant, Philadelphia .... KO 2
Sept. 14—Henry Walker, Las Vegas .... KO 1
Nov. 5—Henry Walker, Las Vegas .... KO 1
1978
Dec. 15—Don Addison, New York .... L 6
1979
Aug. 30—Reggie Lee Inman, Richmond .... KO 1
Sept. 20—Ernie Davis, Detroit .... KO 2
Oct. 18—Lloyd Richardson, Detroit .... KO 5
Nov. 29—Charles Cary, Virginia Beach .... KO 1
1980
Jan. 16—O'Dell Leonard, Washington, D.C. ...... W 8
Apr. 17—Alex Poratta, Chicago .... KO 8
May 15—Larry Martin, Chicago .... KO 2
July 3—Frank Fletcher, Atlantic City .... KO by 4
Sept. 11—Marcos Geraldo, Chicago .... KO 1

JUAN JOSE LEIVA
Argentine Light Heavyweight
1980
Mar. 14—Oscar Caro, Tucuman .... L 4
Apr. 3—Oscar Caro, Tucuman .... L 10

MARK LEMERICK
Anderson, Ind. Welterweight
1979
Nov. 8—Jamie Knox, Indianapolis .... W 4
1980
Jan. 22—Tony Taylor, Indianapolis .... L 6
Jan. 21—Rick Freeman, St. Charles .... W 4
Mar. 17—Ricky Davis, Indianapolis .... KO 3
May 13—Billy Evans, Indianapolis .... KO 1
May 16—Tony Teague, Lexington .... KO by 4

PABLO LENCINA
Argentine Featherweight
1980
Apr. 11—Pablo Barrientos, San Cristobal .... L 10
Aug. 15—Hugo Villarruel, Rafaela .... KO by 6

ARTURO LEON
Phoenix, Ariz. Junior Lightweight
1972
Apr. 8—Jorge Reyes, Mexico City .... KO 8
June 1—Benny Rodriguez, Los Angeles .... L 10

1973
Oct. 17—Davey White, Las Vegas .... KO 8
Nov. 20—Moses Carbin, Las Vegas .... L 8
1974
Feb. 18—Nick Alfaro, Albuquerque .... W 6
Mar. 15—Ed Alwin, Tucson .... KO 2
Apr. 18—Angel Robinson Garcia, Reno .... L 6
May 1—Pete Vital, Las Vegas .... W 10
July 8—Fernando Gil, Las Vegas .... L 6
Sept. 2—Dave Kibby, Las Vegas .... W 10
Sept. 17—Tony Sanchez, Houston .... W 10
Oct. 13—Lorenzo Trujillo, Corpus Christi .... L 10
Nov. 27—Dale Hernandez, Las Vegas .... L 12
1975
Jan. 18—Jimmy Heair, Anaheim .... W 10
Mar. 1—Randy Shields, Los Angeles .... L 10
June 19—Rudy Hernandez, San Diego .... L 10
Nov. 19—Eddie Murray, Las Vegas .... W 8
1976
Jan. 14—Augustin Estrada, Las Vegas .... W 10
Feb. 9—Ray Lunny III, San Francisco .... L 10
Mar. 4—Jimmy Heair, Los Angeles .... D 10
Mar. 27—Javier Ayala, Tijuana .... KO 4
Aug. 25—Alberto Reyes, Las Vegas .... W 10
Sept. 21—Maurice Watkins, Corpus Christi .... L 10
1977
Jan. 10—Jimmy Heair, El Paso .... W 10
Mar. 31—Jose Talamantez, San Antonio .... L 12
May 10—Miguel Estrada, El Paso .... D 10
June 1—Jorge Ramos, Incline Village .... W 10
July 30—Miguel Estrada, El Paso .... KO 6
Nov. 15—Bobby Chacon, Anaheim .... W 10
1978
June 1—Tiger Noji, Los Angeles .... KO 4
June 21—Julio Mendez, Las Vegas .... KO 7
Nov. 10—Alexis Arguello, Las Vegas .... L 15
(WBC Junior Lightweight Title)
1979
Jan. 23—Jose Luis Medrano, Tucson .... W 10
Feb. 14—Danny Samudio, Las Vegas .... W 10
Apr. 24—Ernesto Herrera, Houston .... W disq. 10
June 28—Hilmer Kenty, Detroit .... L 10
Aug. 7—Roberto Elizondo, Corpus Christi .... L 10
Oct. 23—Sean O'Grady, Oklahoma City .... L 15
1980
Jan. 22—Roberto Madrid, Houston .... W 10
Mar. 27—Jorge Morales, Las Vegas .... W 12

ODELL LEONARD
Palmer Park, Md. Middleweight
1976
Dec. 2—C. J. Faison, Baltimore .... W 6
1977
Feb. 5—Stanley Jackson, Baltimore .... W 4
May 14—Johnny Cooper, Baltimore .... W 6
June 10—John Harris, Hartford .... W 6
Sept. 24—Ronnie Pettigrew, Baltimore .... KO 3
Dec. 17—Julio Garcia, Washington, D.C. .... W 6
1978
Jan. 25—Sylvester Harris, Washington D.C. ...... KO 1
Feb. 4—Ruben Lopez, Baltimore L
Mar. 15—Stanley Jackson, Washington D.C. ...... W 4
Apr. 13—Ronnie West, Landover .... W 4
Apr. 19—Kevin Armstrong, Washington D.C. ...... KO 2
May 10—Wilbert Crews, Washington D.C. .... W 6
May 24—Keith Broom, Washington D.C. .... KO by 2
June 22—Fred Brown, Virginia Beach .... L 6
Sept. 21—Wilson Bell, Washington D.C. ...... KO by 1
Dec. 9—Johnny Harris, Springfield .... D 6
1979
Jan. 11—Ted Mann, Landover .... L 6
Jan. 22—Don Norwood, Washington D.C. .... KO 2
May 31—Al Styles Jr., Philadelphia .... L 8
Oct. 24—Giovanni Bovenzi, Baltimore .... KO 1
1980
Jan. 16—Caveman Lee, Washington D.C. .... L 8
Sept. 11—Alvin Anderson, Washington D.C. ...... KO 8
Dec. 12—Tony Chiaverini, Kansas City .... KO 6

ROGER LEONARD
Palmer Park, Md. Middleweight
1978
Sept. 9—Don Bickford, Providence .... KO 2
Oct. 6—Elliott Freeman, Baltimore .... KO 3
Nov. 21—Stanley Blythe, Landover .... W 5
Dec. 9—Sean Mannion, Springfield .... W 6
1979
Jan. 11—Mario Maldonado, Landover .... KO 2
Feb. 11—Jody Parker, Miami Beach .... KO 3
Apr. 21—Oscar Delgado, Phoenix .... KO
May 20—Ray Daordin, Baton Rouge .... KO 6
June 24—Wayne Beale, Las Vegas .... W 8
Aug. 12—Wayne Beale, Las Vegas .... W 8
Nov. 30—Rudy Robles, Las Vegas .... W 8

1980
Jan. 16—Tyrone Phelps, Washington D.C. .... KO 3
Mar. 31—Johnny Gant, Landover .... W 8
June 20—Clyde Gray, Montreal .... W 10
Nov. 25—Mel Dennis, New Orleans .... W 10

PHILLIP LEONIN
Los Angeles, Calif. Junior Welterweight
1980
May 2—Raul Salazar, Los Angeles .... D 6
May 15—Raul Salazar, Los Angeles .... L 6
July 10—Ken Davis, Los Angeles .... KO by 2

FONAI LEOTA
Los Angeles, Calif. Light Heavyweight
1976
Apr. 15—Baby Leroy, Los Angeles .... L 4
June 3—Baby Leroy, Los Angeles .... KO 1
June 17—Lee Kahey, Los Angeles .... KO 3
Aug. 26—Fabian Falconett, Los Angeles .... KO 2
1977
(Inactive)
1978
Mar. 31—Leni Vanisi, San Diego .... D 8
Apr. 14—Len Provo, San Diego .... KO by 2
1980
Apr. 9—Curtis Azevedo, Honolulu .... KO 1
Aug. 26—Karl Hess, Honolulu .... L 8

PERRY LEVOE
Cupertino, Calif. Middleweight
1979
Aug. 24—Gary Giron, Carson City .... L 6
Oct. 4—Manny Gullatt, San Carlos .... KO 4
Oct. 16—Lander Clark, Sparks .... KO 6
Nov. 20—Manny Gullatt, Sparks .... W 4
Dec. 18—Azell James, Sparks .... KO 2
1980
Jan. 31—Mike Hickman, Sparks .... W 6
Feb. 29—Manny Gullatt, San Carlos .... KO 4
Mar. 27—Lamar Clark, Sparks .... W 8
May 22—Mike Hickman, Sparks .... KO 4
Aug. 7—Hector Fernandez, San Carlos .... KO by 1
Oct. 16—Tim Harris, San Carlos .... L 6

EARL LIBURD
St. Thomas, V.I. Welterweight
(Previous Record Unavailable)
1978
July 1—Easy Boy Lake, St. Thomas .... KO 10
July 28—Fighting Hunks, St. Thomas .... W 10
Aug. 26—Mustafa Ali, St. Thomas .... W 12
Oct. 21—Fighting Hunks, St. Thomas .... L 12
Nov. 16—Justice Ortiz, North Bergen .... KO 7
1979
Apr. 6—Luis Resto, New York .... L 8
May 25—Alvin Anderson, Baltimore .... L 10
July 10—Allan Clarke, Halifax .... L 10
Sept. 22—Eddie Marcelle, St. Thomas ...... KO by 6
1980
May 23—Jose A. Rivera, New York .... KO 2
July 13—Miguel Hernandez, Great Gorge .... L 6
Aug. 27—Larry Davis, Elizabeth .... W 4
Oct. 4—Nino Gonzales, Great Gorge .... L 10
Dec. 20—Tony Ayala, Jr., Bronx .... KO by 1

TONY LICATA
New Orleans, La. Middleweight
1969
May 22—Bernard Bennett, Tampa .... KO 2
June 9—Sammy Wilson, New Orleans .... KO 2
June 30—Jim Mells, Tampa .... W 6
Aug. 29—Charlie Fullard, Tampa .... KO 1
Nov. 13—Jose Gabino, Tampa .... W 8
Dec. 4—Robert Williams, Tampa .... W 8
1970
Feb. 2—Gilbert de los Santos, Tampa .... W 8
Mar. 9—Johnny Brooks, New Orleans .... W 4
Apr. 6—Teddy Cooper, New Orleans .... W 8
Apr. 20—Al Bashir, Tampa .... KO 2
May 11—Mike Pusateri, New Orleans .... W 10
June 8—Candy Rosa, Tampa .... W 8
June 22—Luis Vinales, Arabi .... D 8
July 22—Luis Vinales, New Orleans .... W 8
Aug. 19—Tom Hanna, New Orleans .... W 8
Sept. 30—Rocky Halliday, New Orleans .... KO 7
Nov. 5—Jimmy Williams, Tampa .... W 8
1971
Feb. 1—Walter Opshinsky, New Orleans ...... KO 7
Feb. 23—Gene Wells, Tampa .... W 8
Mar. 15—Danny McAloon, Arabi .... W 10
Apr. 24—Gene Wells, Tampa .... W 8
May 17—Larry Carney, Tampa .... KO 4
June 20—Dave Adkins, New Orleans .... W 10

Aug. 10—Bob O'Brian, New Orleans .... W 10
1972
Feb. —Luis Galvan, Tampa .... KO 8
Mar. 20—Dennis Riggs, New Orleans .... KO 4
Apr. 26—Jose Chirino, New Orleans .... KO 9
Oct. 11—Juan Ramos, Boston .... KO 2
Oct. 28—John Coiley, New Orleans .... W 10
Nov. 28—Alvin Phillips, New Orleans .... D 10
Dec. 12—John Coiley, Boston .... KO 1
1973
Mar. 6—Dennis Riggs, Jacksonville .... D 10
Apr. 9—Alvin Phillips, New Orleans .... W 10
Apr. 26—Ernie Burns, Tampa .... W 10
June 1—Dennis Riggs, Tampa .... W 12
July 11—Art Hernandez, New Orleans .... KO 8
July 21—Tony Gardner, Tampa .... KO 2
Sept. 10—Luis Vinales, Boston .... KO 9
Oct. 2—Denny Moyer, New Orleans .... W 10
Nov. 14—Bruce Scott, Orlando .... KO 4
Dec. 5—Nat King, Orlando .... KO 8
1974
Feb. 5—Emile Griffith, Boston .... W 12
(American Middleweight Title)
Mar. 29—Roy McMillian, Rome................. W 10
Apr. 23—Cuby Top Cat Jackson, Houston .... KO 8
(American Middleweight Title)
May 7—Mike Baker, Houston................. W 10
(American Middleweight Title)
June 3—Willie Warren, Toronto .... W 10
July 11—Gary Broughton, New Orleans .... W 10
Aug. 15—Vicente Medina, Albuquerque .... KO 2
Oct. 9—Gene Wells, Mobile.................. W 10
(American Middleweight Title)
1975
Jan. 30—Marcel Clay, Tampa .... W 10
(U.S. Middleweight Title)
Feb. 13—Vinnie Curto, New Orleans .... W 10
(U.S. Middleweight Title)
Mar. 21—Ramon Mendez, Milan .... L 10
Apr. 21—Ramon Mendez, New Orleans .... W 10
June 30—Carlos Monzon, New York .... KO by 10
(World Middleweight Title)
1976
Mar. 6—Jean Mateo, Paris.................... KO by 8
Apr. 19—Jose Luis Duran, New Orleans .... KO 10
May 19—Gene Wells, New Orleans............... KO 7
(U.S. Middleweight Title)
June 12—Mike Rossman, New Orleans .... W 10
Aug. 23—Mike Colbert, New Orleans .... L 10
Sept. 22—Mike Nixon, New Orleans .... W 10
Nov. 9—Alan Minter, London .... KO by 6
1977
Dec. 1—J. T. Dowe, Tampa .... W 10
1978
Sept. 5—Ned Hallacy, New Orleans .... KO 10
Nov. 14—Bob Patterson, New Orleans .... KO 4
Dec. 1—Jaime Thomas, New Orleans .... W 10
1979
Jan. 22—Mel Dennis, New Orleans .... W 10
Mar. 11—Jim Ingram, Reno .... D 10
Apr. 14—Freddie Johnson, New Orleans .... KO by 4
1980
Feb. 28—Sammy Barr, Tampa .... KO 4
Apr. 3—Gene Wells, Tampa .... KO 8
June 6—Tony Chiaverini, Kansas City .... L 10

CHRIS LINSON
Sante Fe, N.M. Welterweight
1980
Mar. 7—Jose Hernandez, El Paso .... L 8
May 9—Norman Thompson, Chicago .... KO 7
June 27—Frank Mills, Chicago .... KO 2
Oct. 23—Carlos Ramos, Las Vegas .... KO 6
Nov. 29—Joey Robles, Las Vegas .... KO 10

BRIAN LINTHORNE
New Glasgow, Canada Welterweight
1980
Apr. 30—Marty Cole, Halifax .... D 6
Nov. 21—Bob Harvey, Moncton .... KO by 2

JOHNNY LIRA
Chicago, Ill. Lightweight
1976
Nov. 17—Genaro Gloria, Las Vegas .... KO 4
Nov. 24—Allen Gantt, Las Vegas .... KO 3
Dec. 1—Tony Terraciano, Las Vegas .... W 6
1977
Jan. 20—Jimmy Ligons, Las Vegas .... W 10
Feb. 9—Canela Salinas, Las Vegas .... KO 7
Feb. 16—Frank Peralta, Las Vegas .... KO 6
Mar. 2—Nacho Castaneda, Las Vegas .... KO 5
Mar. 10—Jose Infante, Las Vegas .... KO 1
Mar. 16—Juan Arcos, Las Vegas .... KO 9

Apr. 27—Miguel Estrada, Las Vegas .... W 10
May 27—Victor Hernandez, Las Vegas .... W 10
June 8—Victor Hernandez, Las Vegas .... KO 7
Aug. 3—Manny Lopez, Las Vegas .... D 10
Aug. 24—Manny Lopez, Las Vegas .... W 10
1978
Jan. 23—Rogelio Castaneda, Las Vegas .... W 10
Aug. 1—Andrew Ganigan, Honolulu .... KO 6
(U.S. Lightweight Title)
Dec. 8—Larry Stanton, New York .... W 10
1979
Apr. 27—Tom Tarrantino, Chicago .... KO 7
Aug. 4—Ernesto Espana, Chicago .... KO by 10
(For WBA Lightweight Title)
1980
July 10—Pedro Acosta, Chicago .... W 10
Aug. 14—Leon Mesa, Chicago .... KO 4
Sept. 10—Chico Rodriguez, Cicero .... KO 1
Dec. 6—Howard Davis, Jr., Lake Tahoe .... L 10

AL LITTLE
East Orange, N.J. Junior Middleweight
1977
Mar. 26—Jose Tiberi, Bristol .... L 4
Apr. 25—Gil Rosario, Newark .... W 4
May 9—Jake Jenkins, Newark .... D 4
1978
Sept. 12—Ralph Hollett, Halifax .... L 8
Sept. 26—Alain Turenne, Montreal .... D 8
1979
Apr. 3—Lawrence Hafey, Halifax .... L disq. 6
Oct. 26—Norberto Sabater, New York .... L 4
1980
Aug. 2—Tony Suero, Totowa .... L 8

BENNY LLANOS
Union City, N.J. Junior Featherweight
1979
June 29—Herberto Torres, Jersey City .... L 4
1980
Dec. 12—Hector Camacho, New York .... KO by 1

JOHN LOCICERO
New York, N.Y. Middleweight
1976
Aug. 8—Joe Grady, New York.................... W 4
Sept. 10—Johnny Grant, New York .... KO 2
Oct. 1—Tony Danza, New York .... KO 1
Oct. 22—Kenny Bristol, New York .... L 4
1977
Apr. 1—Morris Watkins, New York .... KO 2
May 11—Barry Hill, New York .... KO 2
June 22—Manuel Melon, New York .... KO 4
Aug. 12—Reggie Ford, New York .... L 6
Nov. 18—King George Aidoo, New York .... KO 2
1978
May 27—James Waire, Los Angeles .... W 6
Sept. 6—Ali Muhammad, White Plains .... KO 2
1979
Feb. 26—Ali Perez, New York .... KO 2
Mar. 14—Roberto Rivera, White Plains .... KO 1
Apr. 16—Willie Classen, New York .... KO 8
June 29—Ray Villanueva, New York .... KO 2
Aug. 16—Gary Coates, Kansas City .... W 10
Nov. 9—Gilbert Cohen, New York .... KO 2
1980
Jan. 25—Carlos Betancourt, New York .... KO 1
Feb. 16—Marcos Geraldo, Portland, Me. ..... KO by 10
May 2—Ted Mann, New York .... W 10
Aug. 29—Jesus Castro, New York .... KO 1
Oct. 23—Norberto Sabater, New York .... L 10

QUINNIE LOCKLEAR
Baltimore, Md. Heavyweight
1977
Sept. 21—Don Spellman, Virginia Beach .... L 4
Nov. 30—Gerry Cooney, White Plains .... KO by 1
1978
Apr. 13—Lou Benson, Landover .... L 4
May 24—Darnell Miles, Washington D.C. .... KO 1
Aug. 8—Dennis McAllister, Baltimore .... L 6
Sept. 14—James Reid, Baltimore .... KO by 6
Sept. 19—Jerry Foley, Scranton .... KO by 6
Oct. 9—Brad Crane, Hampton .... W 6
Nov. 9—James Reid, Virginia .... W 6
1979
Jan. 11—Malik Dozier, Landover .... KO by 2
Aug. 7—Charles Smith, Baltimore .... KO by 6
Sept. 19—Jerry Foley, Scranton .... KO by 6
1980
Mar. 31—George Williams, Landover .... KO by 2

ROCKY LOCKRIDGE
Paterson, N.J. Featherweight
Born: January 30, 1959
1978
Aug.	9—Tony Reed, Seattle	KO	2
Oct.	5—Jose Luis Lara, Seattle	W	6
Nov.	14—Tony Hernandez, Totowa	KO	1

1979
Mar.	13—Melvin Bethea, Totowa	KO	1
Apr.	17—Melvin Boynton, Totowa	KO	2
Apr.	27—Mike Maldonado, Newark	KO	2
May	31—Ronnie Green, Philadelphia	KO	1
Sept.	18—Gerald Hayes, Giants Stadium	W	12
Oct.	30—Jose Cheo Ortiz, Totowa	KO	2

1980
Jan.	8—Sammy Goss, Totowa	KO	5
Feb.	19—Fel Clemente, Totowa	KO	7
Mar.	8—Richard Rozelle, Great Gorge	KO	2
Apr.	1—Joey Mayes, Totowa	KO	2
June	19—Marcial Santiago, Totowa	KO	3
July	13—Alfonso Evans, Great Gorge	KO	5
Aug.	2—Livio Nolasco, Totowa	KO	4
Oct.	4—Eusebio Pedroza, Great Gorge	L	15
	(For WBA Featherweight Title)		
Dec.	18—Benny Marquez, Totowa	KO	3

LEW LOCKWOOD
Seattle, Wash. Heavyweight
1977
May	31—Paul Guyness, Incline Village	L	4
Sept.	3—Ken Arlt, Ketchum	KO by	3
Oct.	30—Ken Austin, Carson City	L	4

1978
July	3—Arnold Sam, Las Vegas	KO	2
Aug.	5—Alex Rios, Elko	W	4
Aug.	30—Bennett White, Reno	W	4
Oct.	30—Ken Austin, Carson City	L	7
Dec.	13—Mike Creel, Las Vegas	L	6

1979
Feb.	20—Pinklon Thomas, Seattle	KO by	4
May	16—Bennett White, Carson City	L	6
May	23—Walter Cloud, Las Vegas	L	6
June	16—Arnold Sam, Yerington	W	6
July	4—Jeff Podgurski, Las Vegas	KO by	3
Sept.	12—Eddie Gregg, Las Vegas	KO by	3
Oct.	30—Ken Austin, Carson City	L	7

1980
Feb.	29—Gord Racette, Nanaimo	KO by	2
Apr.	16—Jim Restauri, Fresno	L	4
May	13—Jim Restauri, Sacramento	L	5
July	1—Jim Restauri, Sacramento	W	6
July	25—Mike Jameson, San Carlos	L	6
Aug.	5—Jim Restauri, Sacramento	L	6
Oct.	16—Harold Dutra, San Carlos	L	6

KEN LOMAX
Philadelphia, Pa. Welterweight
1979
Oct.	18—Ron Aurit, Philadelphia	KO by	2
Oct.	26—Tony Salvatore, Rochester	KO by	1
Nov.	28—Peter Pennello, W. New York, N.J.	KO by	2

1980
Jan.	16—Warren Fortune, Washington	KO by	3
Feb.	29—Trevor Evelyn, Brooklyn	KO by	3
Aug.	21—Greg Joseph, Revere	KO by	1
Sept.	20—David Bookman, Ben Salem	KO by	3
Nov.	1—Ira Robinson, Richmond	KO by	4

DANNY LONG
Boston, Mass. Middleweight
1979
Jan.	15—Reynaldo Olivera, Boston	KO	1
Feb.	3—Jose Ortiz, Boston	KO	3
Apr.	20—Hugo Fuat, New York	KO	2
June	5—Ralph Hollett, Halifax	W	8
Sept.	19—Danny Pate, Scranton	W	6
Nov.	7—Tommy Molloy, Boston	KO	1

1980
Jan.	22—Lancelot Innis, Halifax	W	8
Feb.	22—Dan Staehle, Fall River	KO	4
Mar.	26—Ralph Mifka, Scranton	W	8
May	1—Kevin Mofield, Dorchester	W	10

SONNY LONG
Santa Monica, California Bantamweight
1980
Sept.	27—Adan Uribe, Inglewood	W	4
Nov.	22—James Tolliver, Cincinnati	D	4

CLAUZELLE (BEAVER) LONGMIRE
Ft. Lauderdale, Florida Welterweight
1980
Jan.	29—Richie Gonzales, Miami	W	4

Feb.	10—Dennis Green, Miami	KO	2
Apr.	15—Jose Torres, Miami	W	6
May	2—Dario DeJesus, Miami	KO	3
June	6—Robert Spencer, Miami	KO	2
July	25—Larry Spasser, Miami	KO	1
	—Angel Figueroa, Ft. Lauderdale	KO	1
Aug.	19—Ceferino Morales, Miami	KO	5
Oct.	17—Juan Panchi, W. Palm Beach	KO	4
Dec.	16—Juan Hidalgo, Miami	KO	6

JIMMY LONGO
New Paltz, N.Y. Junior Welterweight
1978
Apr.	21—Jose (Cheo) Ortiz, Albany	L	4

1979
(Inactive)
1980
Mar.	28—Trevor Evelyn, New York	L	4
June	20—Blas Deschamps, New York	D	4
June	27—Norberto Figueroa, New York	L	4
Sept.	12—Norberto Figueroa, New York	W	4
Oct.	14—Luis Vargas, W. Hartford	W	4
Oct.	23—Trevor Evelyn, New York	L	6
Dec.	20—Tim LaValley, N. Adams	W	6

ALVARO LOPEZ
San Diego, Calif. Light Heavyweight
1976
Apr.	1—Lee Kahey, Los Angeles	KO	1
Apr.	29—Leroy Danford, Los Angeles	L	4
May	21—Lee Kahey, San Bernardino	W	5
Sept.	15—Ray Robinson, Las Vegas	KO by	3
Nov.	4—Mike Clark, Incline Village	W	6

1977
Feb.	3—Leni Vanisi, Los Angeles	W	6
Feb.	28—S. T. Gordon, Las Vegas	W	5
July	6—Ronnie Wilson, Las Vegas	L	10
Sept.	23—Benny Barra, Las Vegas	KO	5

1978
Jan.	12—Gene Miera, Los Angeles	KO	2
Feb.	9—Pete McIntyre, Los Angeles	L	10
Sept.	12—Jim Ingram, Pico Rivera	L	10

1979
June	3—Bernardo Barron, Las Vegas	KO	10
Aug.	12—James Salerno, Las Vegas	L	10
Nov.	27—Jimmy Ingram, Las Vegas	KO by	5

1980
May	12—Curtis Azevedo, Honolulu	KO by	7
Oct.	16—Bashiru Ali, San Carlos	KO by	10
Nov.	29—Carl Ivy, Lake Tahoe	KO	3

ALVARO (YAQUI) LOPEZ
Stockton, Calif. Light Heavyweight
Born: May 21, 1951
1972
Apr.	24—Herman Hampton, Stockton	W	6
June	2—Herman Hampton, Carson City	KO	3
June	16—Cisco Solorio, Stockton	KO	6
July	1—Jesse Burnett, Stockton	L	8
Oct.	24—King Henry Tavako, San Carlos	W	6
Nov.	6—Mack Hearn, Eugene	KO	6
Nov.	29—Herman Hampton, Stockton	KO	7
Dec.	11—Van Sahib, Eugene	KO	2

1973
Feb.	8—Polo Ramirez, Stockton	KO	7
Mar.	15—Al Bolden, Seattle	L	10
Apr.	21—Hildo Silva, Santa Rosa	W	10
June	9—Ron Wilson, Santa Rosa	W	10
July	6—Dave Rogers, Gardnerville	KO	5
Aug.	3—Ron Wilson, Reno	KO	6
Aug.	22—Herman Hampton, Tacoma	KO	6
Sept.	20—Budda Brooks, Stockton	KO	5
Nov.	1—Alfonso Gonzalez, Portland	KO	2
Dec.	6—Al Bolden, Portland	W	10

1974
Feb.	14—Andy Kendall, Portland	KO	5
Mar.	7—Willie Warren, Reno	W	10
May	10—Hildo Silva, Stockton	W	12
July	7—Joe Cokes, Gardnerville	W	12
Oct.	11—Bobby Rascon, Portland	KO	6
Nov.	13—Hildo Silva, Stockton	W	10

1975
Mar.	4—Terry Lee, Sacramento	KO	9
Apr.	8—Lee Mitchell, Sacramento	KO	6
May	14—Mike Quarry, Stockton	W	10
July	3—Gary Summerhays, Gardnerville	W	10
July	31—Jesse Burnett, Stockton	L	12
Sept.	24—Jesse Burnett, Stockton	W	12

1976
Feb.	12—Terry Lee, Portland	W	10
May	3—David Smith, Stockton	W	10
June	30—Karl Zurheide, Stockton	KO	6
July	17—Larry Castaneda, Stockton	KO	9

143

Oct.	9—John Conteh, Copenhagen .... L 15	
	(WBC Light Heavyweight Title)	
Dec.	8—Pete McIntyre, Stockton .... KO 6	

1977

Feb.	17—Danny Brewer, Stateline .... KO 6	
Mar.	7—Larry Castaneda, Stockton .... KO 8	
Apr.	5—Ron White, Incline Village .... W 8	
Apr.	22—Lonnie Bennett, Indianapolis .... KO by 3	
June	17—Bobby Lloyd, Miami Beach .... KO 5	
July	20—Manuel Fierro, Stockton .... KO 3	
Sept.	17—Victor Galindez, Rome .... L 15	
	(WBA Light Heavyweight Title)	
Oct.	27—Chuck Warfield, Stockton .... KO 4	
Nov.	—Clarence Geigger, Stateline .... KO 6	
Dec.	15—Clarence Geigger, Stockton .... KO 4	

1978

Jan.	12—Fabian Falconette, Los Angeles .... KO 2	
Mar.	2—Mike Rossman, New York .... KO 6	
Mar.	17—Ned Hallacy, Las Vegas .... W 10	
May	6—Victor Galindez, Lido DiCamaiore .... L 15	
	(WBA Light Heavyweight Title)	
July	2—Jesse Burnett, Stockton .... W 15	
	(U.S. Light Heavyweight Title)	
Oct.	24—Matt Franklin, Philadelphia .... KO by 11	
	(U.S. Light Heavyweight Title)	

1979

Jan.	17—Junior Albers, Stockton .... KO 3	
Feb.	27—Ivy Brown, Sacramento .... KO 3	
Sept.	12—Ernie Barr, Stockton .... KO 3	
Oct.	4—Bashiru Ali, Redwood City .... W 10	
Dec.	1—James Scott, Rahway .... L 10	

1980

Apr.	16—Pete McIntyre, Fresno .... KO 8	
May	20—Bobby Lloyd, Fresno .... KO 8	
July	13—Matthew Saad Muhammad,	
	Great Gorge .... KO by 14	
	(For World Light Heavyweight Title)	
Oct.	18—Michael Spinks, Atlantic City .... KO by 7	
Nov.	29—Carl Ivy, Lake Tahoe .... KO 3	

EDDIE (ANIMAL) LOPEZ
Los Angeles, Calif. Heavyweight

1976

Apr.	8—John Phillips, Los Angeles .... KO 4	
Apr.	29—Jed Walls, Los Angeles .... KO 1	
June	24—Marlyn Johnson, Los Angeles .... KO 1	
Aug.	22—Bob Swoopes, Los Angeles.............. W 4	
Sept.	22—Bruce Grandham, Las Vegas .... KO 3	
Oct.	13—Oliver Phillips, Las Vegas .... KO 8	
Oct.	28—Phelps Se'e, Los Angeles .... W 7	

1977

Jan.	5—Earl McLeay, Las Vegas .... KO 1	
Feb.	9—Bob Swoopes, Las Vegas .... W 8	
July	22—Dan Johnson, San Diego .... KO 5	
Sept.	13—John Tate, Los Angeles .... L 6	
Oct.	29—Fernando Montez, Los Angeles .... KO 4	

1978

Aug.	29—S. T. Gordon, Pico Rivera .... W 10	

1979

Jan.	13—Gerry Cooney, Miami Beach .... L 8	
Mar.	1—Mircea Simon, Los Angeles .... D 10	
Aug.	17—Abdul Khan, San Diego .... KO 4	
Sept.	14—Jimmy Abbott, Durban .... W 10	
Nov.	27—Fili Moala, Los Angeles .... W 10	

1980

Mar.	8—Leon Spinks, Las Vegas .... D 10	
Sept.	27—Marty Monroe, Los Angeles .... KO by 5	

HECTOR LOPEZ
Argentine Lightweight

1980

Mar.	7—Luis Zarate, La Banda .... D 10	
June	14—Juan Malvares, Mar del Plata .... KO by 9	
Aug.	1—Marcelo Miranda, S. Sal. de Jujay ..... L 10	
Sept.	12—Rodolfo Diaz, Tucuman .... W 10	

IGNACIO LOPEZ
Houston, Texas Light Heavyweight

1977

May	17—Adolfo Rivas, Corpus Christi .... KO 3	
June	28—Adolfo Rivas, Corpus Christi .... KO 2	
July	26—Robert Chavez, Corpus Christi .... KO 1	
Oct.	4—Robert Perry, Corpus Christi .... KO 6	

1978

Mar.	14—Regino Maybit, Houston .... KO 1	
Apr.	20—Eddie Mitchell, Houston .... W 6	
June	20—Paul Stephens, Houston .... L 6	
Oct.	14—Arthur Henderson, Houston .... KO 1	

1979

Jan.	16—Sharif DeLaRam, Houston .... W 6	
Feb.	26—Alfonso Aguirre, Houston .... W 6	

1980

June	17—Marcus Dorsey, Houston .... KO 2	
Sept.	23—Paul Stephens, Houston .... W 8	

JOSE LUIS LOPEZ
Argentine Flyweight

1980

Aug.	8—Ramon Rodriguez, Tucuman .... KO by 5	
Aug.	22—Hector Patri, La Plata .... L 10	
Sept.	5—Domingo Aragon, P.R.S. Pena .... KO by 9	

JOSE L. LOPEZ
Los Angeles, Calif. Featherweight

1979

Oct.	24—Joe Phillips, Las Vegas .... KO by 3	
Dec.	14—Jaime Garza, San Bernardino .... KO by 1	

1980

Feb.	2—Jaime Garza, Phoenix .... KO by 1	
Mar.	7—Chris Gutierrez, San Bernardino ..... KO by 4	
May	16—Desi Newbill, San Bernardino .... L 4	

JOSE MARIA P. LOPEZ
Argentine Lightweight

1980

June	6—Santiago Lopez, Chivilcoy .... D 10	
Oct.	3—Alfredo Moyano, Rio Gallegos .... L 10	

JOSE MARIO LOPEZ
Argentine Featherweight

1980

Mar.	7—Jose Casas, Rio IV .... W 12	
Mar.	22—Pedro Vargas, Centenario .... W 10	
Apr.	3—Hugo Emer, Rio IV .... L 10	
Aug.	8—Victoriano Garcia, San Luis .... KO 5	
Oct.	3—Victoriano Garcia, San Luis .... D 6	
Dec.	19—Rodolfo Gonzalez, San Juan .... KO 4	

LUIS G. LOPEZ
Argentine Middleweight

1980

Feb.	21—Santos Medina, Zarate .... W 8	
May	23—Hugo Carrizo, San Nicolas .... W 8	
Aug.	8—Carlos Schultz, Rosario .... L 6	
Sept.	19—Luis Guillermo, Rosario .... KO by 2	

MANNY LOPEZ
Salt Lake City, Utah Junior Welterweight

1980

Feb.	23—Sultan Saladin, Greeley .... W 8	
Mar.	15—Sultan Saladin, Denver .... W 10	
Apr.	2—Sterling McPherson, Las Vegas ...... KO by 1	
June	11—Victor Martinez, Las Vegas .... KO by 4	
	—Nick Miller, Denver .... KO 1	

MANUEL LOPEZ
Argentine Junior Middleweight

1980

Jan.	—Oscar Alvarenga, San Juan .... KO by 7	
Mar.	28—Martin Duran, La Banda .... L 10	
July	18—Alberto Butiler, La Banda .... L 10	

RAPHAEL LOPEZ
Pawtucket, R.I. Junior Lightweight

1979

June	29—Francisco Maldonado, Cranston .... KO 2	
Aug.	21—Ed Lugo, Dennisport .... KO 2	
Sept.	28—Andy Barboza, Taunton .... KO 6	
Oct.	25—Noradene Bensalah, Latham .... KO 3	
Nov.	28—Spider Blackwell, Hartford .... KO 2	

1980

Feb.	5—Santos Cruz, W. Hartford .... W 6	
Feb.	22—Antonio Nieves, Fall River .... W 4	
May	22—Jose Morales, Revere .... W 8	
June	26—Jose Morales, Revere .... W 5	
Sept.	18—Edwin DeJesus, San Juan .... KO 1	
Oct.	2—Tom Brown, Providence .... KO 4	
Oct.	16—Jose Rosa, Caguas .... W 4	
Nov.	28—Ahmet Tosci, Providence .... KO 2	

RIGOBERTO LOPEZ
Los Angeles, Calif. Welterweight

1980

Oct.	15—Steve Johnson, Las Vegas .... D 4	
Nov.	8—Wayne Walker, Lake Tahoe .... D 4	
Dec.	12—Roosevelt Green, Sacramento .... L 4	

SAL LOPEZ
Los Angeles, Calif. Junior Welterweight

1978

Sept.	9—Roland Brookter, Sacramento .... KO 3	

1979

Jan.	29—Luis Piceno, Los Angeles .... KO 3	
Apr.	19—Alfredo Carranza, Stockton .... KO 1	
May	15—Jaime Nava, Sacramento .... W 6	
June	13—Julio Alonso, Sacramento .... KO 1	
June	27—Joe Maldonado, Oakland .... W 6	

Oct. 18—Lou Daniels, Los Angeles ....KO 2
Nov. 1—Adrian Boizo, Los Angeles ....KO 2
Nov. 15—Ken Davis Jr., Los Angeles.............KO 2
Nov. 29—Ron Turner, Los Angeles ....KO 1
Dec. 13—Rafael Nunez, Los Angeles ....KO 6
1980
Jan. 10—Juan Garcia, Los Angeles ....KO 6
Jan. 22—David Madrid, Sacramento ....KO 6
Feb. 19—Candido Acosta, Sacramento ....KO 4
Apr. 1—Curtis Ramsey, Sacramento ....KO 6
May 13—Ed Modicue, Sacramento ....KO 6
July 1—Jimmy Heair, Sacramento ....KO 5
Aug. 14—Hector Rivera, Los Angeles ....KO 8
Sept. 5—Pete Ranzany, Sacramento ....KO by 8

SANTIAGO LOPEZ
Argentine Lightweight
1980
Feb. 29—Carlos Martinetti, Saenz Pena ....W
Mar. 21—Victor Escobar, P.R.S. Pena ....L 10
May 16—Hipolito Nunez, San Miguel ....L 10
June 6—Jose M.P. Lopez, Chivilcoy ....D 10
June 19—Jose Filippi, Corral Bustos ....L 10
July 12—Orlando Frecini, Baradero ....L 10
July 25—Lorenzo Garcia, San Pedro ....L 10
Sept. 6—Juan Namuncura, Neuquen ....L 10
Sept. 26—Faustino Barrios, Olavarria ....L 10
Nov. 7—Juan D. Malvarez, Panama ....L 10

RICHARD LORD
Austin, Texas
1980
July 18—James Phillips, Odessa ....KO 2
Aug. 8—Humberto Mandez, Dallas ....KO 3
Aug. 16—Reyes Pelendo, Odessa ....KO 6
Sept. 23—Joe Brown, Odessa ....KO 3
Oct. 24—Victor McCray, Dallas ....KO 1
Dec. 16—Gaby Macias, Odessa ....KO 4

ARMANDO LOREDO
Texas Flyweight
1979
Nov. 6—Victor Gonzales, Corpus Christi ....W 6
1980
Sept. 2—Juan Ortega, Corpus Christi ....KO 3
Dec. 5—Arturo Pedroza, Corpus Christi ....W 8

JOEL LOREDO
Texas Flyweight
1979
Dec. 11—Jose Salas, Corpus Christi ....L 4
1980
June 18—Felix Castillo, San Antonio ....L 6
Sept. 2—Augustin Garcia, Corpus Christi ....KO 3
Dec. 5—Gilbert Garza, Corpus Christi ....KO 6

YOUNG JOE LOUIS
(EDDIE TAYLOR)
Chicago, Ill. Heavyweight
1975
July 25—Bob Yarbrough, Chicago ....Exh. 4
Aug. 1—Roland Mitchell, Chicago ....KO 1
Oct. 4—Sylvester Wilder, Chicago ....KO 2
Oct. 20—Joe Batton, Chicago ....W 6
Nov. 22—Art Pulliam, Chicago ....W 7
1976
(Inactive)
1977
Apr. 25—Danny Davis, Chicago ....KO 1
July 25--Larry Beilfess, Chicago ....KO 6
1978
Jan. 23—Juan De La Garza, Chicago ....KO 2
Apr. 28—Charles Atlas, Chicago ....W 8
Oct. 25—Terry Daniels, Chicago ....KO 3
1979
Mar. 17—Henry Lumpkin, Chicago ....W 10
Mar. 23—Tiger Joe Harris, Rosemont ....KO 4
June 14—Ron Draper, River Grove ....KO 4
Aug. 19—Oliver Phillips, Bloomington ....W 10
Nov. 24—Jesse Burnett, Bloomington ....W 10
1980
Mar. 9—Ivy Brown, St. Paul ....KO 7

AUNDRA LOVE
Houston, Texas Middleweight
1975
Nov. 4—Lamar Baskin, Houston ....KO 3
Nov. 18—Rogelio Flores, Houston ....W 4
1976
Jan. 5—Al Banks, Jacinto City ....KO 1
Mar. 8—Maurice Quillens, New Orleans ....L 6
Mar. 26—Rogelio Flores, Tuscaloosa ....W 6

Apr. 20—Martin Jiminez, Corpus Christi ....KO 1
May 6—Santiago Valdez, Indianapolis...........KO 3
May 17—Victor Sid, Corpus Christi.................W 6
July 28—Bobby Crawford, Indianapolis ....W 6
Aug. 21—Floyd Meaweather, Flint ....L 10
1977
Feb. 1—Jerry Strickland, Indianapolis ....KO 2
Feb. 24—Johnny Copeland, Cincinnati ....L 10
Apr. 22—Sammy Taylor, Indianapolis ....KO by 1
May 7—Sammy Taylor, Cincinnati ....KO 5
May —Ed Modicue, Shreveport ....L 8
July 18—Scott Foreman, New Orleans ....L 7
1978
Jan. 19—Pete Seward, Houston ....L 8
Feb. 16—Louis Acaries, Paris ....L 10
July 9—Jimmy Blevins, Indianapolis ....D 6
Nov. 7—David Green, London ....KO by 8
1979
Jan. 23—Jimmy Bratten, London ....L 8
—Gilbert Galvan, Houston ....W 6
June 26—Gilbert Galvan, Houston ....W 8
Nov. 1—Rafael Rodriguez, Phoenix ....W 10
1980
Jan. 11—Tyrone Rackley, Phoenix ....L 10
Mar. 13—Rocky Mosley, Las Vegas ....L 10
May 7—Fernando Lugo, Las Vegas ....W 10
July 2—Victor Martinez, Las Vegas ....KO by 9

DAVID LOVE
San Diego, Calif. Middleweight
1970
Oct. 24—Jessie Reed, Los Angeles.............KO by 3
1971
Aug. 13—John Huntley, San Diego ....L 4
Aug. 21—Hildo Silva, Santa Monica ....L 4
Oct. 27—John Dunn, San Diego.....................W 4
Dec. 4—Manuel Caballero, Long Beach ....KO 3
1972
Feb. 17—Eleazar Juarez, San Diego ....W 6
Mar. 4—Raul Pacheco, Long Beach ....KO 4
Apr. 12—John Dunn, San Diego.....................L 6
Apr. 19—David Arrellino, Las Vegas ....W 10
May 18—Frank Gastelum, Los Angeles ....W 6
June 8—Roberto Villanueva, Los Angeles .....W 6
June 16—Nick Garcia, San Diego.................KO 2
July 21—Miguel Aguilar, San Diego.............KO 7
Aug. 9—Robert Stripling, San Diego.............KO 6
Sept. 13—Polo Corona, San Diego.................W 10
Oct. 20—John Dunn, San Diego.....................W 10
Dec. 13—Alfonso Gonzalez, San Diego ....W 10
1973
Jan. 29—Perry Abner, Philadelphia ....W 10
Mar. 15—Mike Seyler, Seattle.....................KO 7
Mar. 27—Billy Walker, Stockton ....KO 9
June 22—Marco Gerardo, San Diego ....W 10
July 6—Marco Gerardo, San Diego ....W 10
Aug. 25—Vicente Medina, Santa Rosa ....W 10
Oct. 13—George Cooper, Santa Rosa..........KO by 8
Nov. 23—Renato Garcia, San Diego ....L 10
Dec. 14—Renato Garcia, San Diego ....KO by 2
1974
Feb. 8—Jose Martin Flores, San Diego ....W 10
Feb. 22—Chuchu Garcia, San Diego ....W 10
Mar. 30—Don Cobbs, St. Louis ....W 10
May 10—Mario Marquez, San Diego.............W 10
June 14—Vicente Medina, San Diego.............KO by 1
Aug. 6—Ray Seales, Tacoma ....KO by 12
Nov. 8—Rudy Robles, San Francisco.............L 10
Dec. 6—Mike Nixon, San Diego ....ND
1975
Feb. 7—Mike Avans, San Diego.................KO 5
Mar. 6—Rudy Cruz, San Jose ....ND
Apr. 11—George Cooper, San Jose ....KO by 9
Aug. 23—Jan Kies, Johannesburg ....W 10
Dec. 12—Bruno Arcari, Turin ....KO by 5
1976
June 14—Tap Tap Makhathini, Jabulani ....W 1
Aug. 16—Willie Monroe, Philadelphia ....KO 4
1977
Mar. 27—Bobby Watts, San Antonio ....KO 4
(U.S. Championship Tournament)
1978
Jan. 24—Edgar Wallace, Phoenix ....KO 5
June 5—Loucif Hamani, Paris ....L 10
Aug. 5—Alfredo Cabral, Buenos Aires ....L 10
Nov. 22—Edgar Wallace, Phoenix ....KO by 2
1979
Feb. 5—Bennie Briscoe, Philadelphia ....W 10
July 7—Joe Gonsalves, San Diego.................W 10
Sept. 6—Ayub Kalule, Copenhagen ....L 10
1980
Mar. 9—Curtis Parker, Atlantic City ....KO by 4
May 21—Javier Ayala, Las Vegas ....W 10
Aug. 16—Bruce McIntyre, Johannesburg ......KO by 1

145

LAMONT LOVELADY
Baltimore, Md. Middleweight
1978
May   22—Al Clay, Chicago ....KO 7
Oct.   6—Leo Saenz, Baltimore ....KO 7
1979
May   25—Roy Dale, Santa Monica ....KO 6
Aug. 19—Ralph Moncrief, Bloomington ....L 10
1980
Mar.   9—Roy Dale, St. Paul ....W 10
May   24—Fulgencio Obelmejias, Caracas ......KO by 3

LOUIS LOY
Los Angeles, Calif. Junior Lightweight
1979
May   17—Francisco Pico, Los Angeles ....W 4
June 18—Francisco Alvarado, Los Angeles ....KO 1
Aug. 20—Roberto Garcia, Bakersfield ....W 10
Sept. 13—Apollo Carbajal, Los Angeles ....KO 1
Sept. 21—James Sowell, San Diego ....KO 5
1980
Jan.   24—Francisco Ponce, Los Angeles ....KO 4
Apr.   10—Humberto Lara, Los Angeles ....W 10
Dec.   4—Roland Harmon, Los Angeles ....KO 1

SERGIO LOYOLA
Argentine Junior Welterweight
1980
Jan.   4—Ramon Allende, Laboulaye ....L 10
Feb.   8—Ramon Allende, Vdo Tuerto ....KO by 5
Apr. 18—Juan Barboza, Tucuman ....L 10
June 19—Ramon Peralta, Vdo Tuerto ....D 10
Dec. 19—Marcelo Romero, Vdo Tuerto ....KO by 4

CARLOS LOZANO
Sacramento, Calif. Junior Welterweight
1979
Mar. 27—Luis Piceno, Sacramento ....W 6
June 27—Dave Portilla, Oakland ....W 6
Nov.   7—Victor Garvin, San Jose ....KO 4
1980
Jan.   10—Adrian Boizo, Los Angeles ....W 6
Jan.   31—Gilberto Rodriguez, Los Angeles ....W 8
Mar.   6—Juan Morales, Los Angeles ....KO 3
Mar. 27—Ruben Martinez, Los Angeles ....KO 3
Apr.   3—Alberto Cota, Los Angeles ....KO 6
Apr. 22—Silverio Martinez, Sacramento ....KO 1
May   13—Manuel Leal, Sacramento ....W 10
June 12—Manuel Leal, Los Angeles ....W 10
Aug. 28—Horace Shufford, Las Vegas ....L 10

HUGO LOZANO
Houston, Texas Junior Lightweight
1980
Mar. 25—Ruben Chavarria, Houston ....KO 1
Apr. 15—Willie Sheppard, Houston ....KO 3

SERGIO LOZANO
Mexican Junior Middleweight
1979
Jan.   18—Jesus Castro, New York ....KO by 4
1980
July   17—Humberto de los Rios, Los Angeles ...KO by 5

ANTONIO LUCENA
Argentine Lightweight
1980
Apr. 12—Hector Romero, Buenos Aires ....KO by 5
June   6—Jorge Palai, Mar del Plata ....L 6
July   8—Mario Matthysse, Villa Trinidad .....KO by 8

ALFREDO LUCERO
Argentine Welterweight
Previous record: 38 fights Won 31 Lost 3
Drew 4 18 KOs
1980
Mar.   7—Rogelio Zarza, Salta ....KO 7
Mar. 28—Hugo Trujillo, Salta ....KO 3
May   2—Marcos Perez, Jujuy ....ND 7
May   23—Carlos Nacimiento, Salta ....W 10
Aug. 15—Ricardo Magallanes, Salta ....KO 1
Sept. 27—Mario Guillotti, Buenos Aires ....KO 8
(Won Argentine Welterweight Title)
Oct.   17—Pablo Ferreyra, Salta ....KO 4
Dec. 26—Manuel F. Gonzalez, Salta ....KO 2

ORLANDO LUCERO
Argentine Featherweight
1980
Sept. 6—Jorge M. Gomez, San Antonio ....KO by 9
Nov. 21—Hugo Fernandez, Concordia ....L 10

TIM LUCERO
Denver, Colorado Junior Lightweight
Born: April 5, 1961. Height: 5 ft. 7 in.
1980
May   23—Richard Cary, Denver ....KO 3
July   11—Pete DeVance, Denver ....KO 2
Aug. 15—Ray Menefee, Denver ....W 6
Oct.   10—Joe Brown, Denver ....W 6
Nov.   7—Joaquin Alvarado, Denver ....W 6
Nov. 28—Gabby Mascias, Denver ....KO 2
Dec. 19—Joe Brown, Denver ....KO 5

MAXIMO LUCIANO
Dominican Republic Junior Lightweight
1979
May   11—Manuel de la Rosa, New York ....L 4
1980
Jan.   19—John Verderosa, Hempstead ....KO by 5

HUGO LUERO
Argentine Junior Welterweight
1978
Mar.   3—Epifanio Pavon, La Plata ....W 10
Apr.   7—Ramon Allende, La Plata ....KO 7
May   5—Jose Villanueva, La Plata ....KO 5
May   27—Luis Correa, G. Madariaga ....KO 8
June 23—Romulo Ibarra, Dolores ....W 10
July 29—Rafael Galeano, Santa Teresita ....KO 2
Aug. 26—Juan Olivera, Buenos Aires ....W 10
Sept. 23—Hector (Y) Hernandez, Buenos Aires ....W 12
(Won Argentine Junior Welterweight Title)
1979
     —Carlos C. Canete, La Plata ....KO 10
     —Cirilo Ruiz, General Belgrano ....W 10
1980
Jan.   25—Roberto Alfaro, Mar del Plata ....L 12
(Lost Argentine Junior Welterweight Title)
Mar. 21—Roberto Alfaro, Buenos Aires ....L 12
(Lost South American Junior Welterweight Title)
May   —Nicolas Arkuszyn, Buenos Aires ....W 10
June   5—Juan Barboza, Tucuman ....L 10
July   11—Juan I. Funes, San Miguel ....W 10
Aug.   1—Juan Barboza, Tucuman ....D 10
Sept. 13—Ubaldo Sacco, Buenos Aires ....KO by 6
Nov. 21—Manuel Pena, La Plata ....KO 5
Dec. 11—Hugo Quartapelle, Mendoza ....KO 5

EDDIE LUGO
Lowell, Mass. Featherweight
1979
Oct.   27—Ralph Bracetty, Fitchburg ....L 4
Dec.   1—Noradeen Bennsallah, Albany ....KO by 3
1980
May   1—Ralph Bracetty, Dorchester ....L 6
June 19—Joe Pelletier, Lawrence ....KO by 1

FERNANDO LUGO
San Diego, Calif. Welterweight
1978
May   10—Anthony Daniels, Anchorage ....KO 6
May   19—Pablo Baez, San Diego ....KO by 6
1979
Apr.   9—Abel Cordova, Los Angeles ....KO by 9
May   25—Eddie Nuno, Pico Rivera ....KO by 4
1980
May   7—Aundra Love, Las Vegas ....L 10
Dec.   3—Bert Lee, Anaheim ....KO by 2

SCOTT LUKACHIK
Bridgeport, Conn. Heavyweight
1978
Dec. 15—Sam Miller, White Plains ....KO 1
1979
     —Djata Banks, White Plains ....W 4
1980
Feb. 28—Vinnie Smith, Hartford ....KO 2
Mar. 28—Robert Evans, Tarrytown ....KO by 1

(LIGHTNING) WAYNE LUNUM
Chicago Bantamweight
1977 National Golden Gloves Champion
1980
Sept. 30—Juan Rosario, Niles ....KO 2

LYNN LUSTIG
Cleveland, Ohio Middleweight
1979
Mar. 17—Roosevelt Green, Chicago ....KO by 1
1980
Mar. 22—Terry Flynn, Grand Rapids ....KO by 2
Apr. 19—Floyd Mayweather, Muskegon ....KO by 2
July   7—Kid Pollack, Bloomington ....KO by 2

RON LYLE
Denver, Colo. Heavyweight
Born: Feb. 11, 1942
1971
Apr.	23—A. J. Staples, Denver	KO 2
May	22—Art Miller, Boston	KO 5
June	22—Gary Bates, Stateline	KO 4
July	16—Edmundo Stewart, New York	KO 2
July	24—Leroy Caldwell, Lake Geneva	W 5
Aug.	11—Frank Niglett, Las Vegas	KO 9
Sept.	1—Eddie Land, Las Vegas	KO 7
Oct.	10—Manuel Ramos, Denver	W 10
Nov.	10—Joe E. Lewis, Las Vegas	KO 3
Nov.	26—Jack O'Halloran, Denver	KO 4
Dec.	18—Bill Drover, Denver	KO 2
1972
Jan.	22—Chuck Leslie, Denver	KO 3
Mar.	25—George Johnson, Denver	KO 3
May	10—Mel Turnbow, Las Vegas	KO 7
May	25—Mike Boswell, Omaha	KO 4
July	11—Vicente Rondon, Denver	KO 2
Sept.	30—Buster Mathis, Denver	KO 2
Oct.	29—Luis Pirez, Denver	KO 3
Dec.	9—Larry Middleton, Denver	KO 3
1973
Feb.	9—Jerry Quarry, New York	L 12
Apr.	14—Bob Stallings, Missoula	W 10
May	12—Gregorio Peralta, Denver	W 10
June	11—Wendell Newton, Philadelphia	W 10
July	3—Lou Bailey, Oklahoma City	W 10
Aug.	15—Jose Luis Garcia, Denver	KO 3
Oct.	4—Jurgin Blin, Denver	KO 2
Oct.	31—Larry Middleton, Baltimore	W 10
Nov.	17—Gregorio Peralta, Frankfurt	D 10
1974
Mar.	19—Oscar Bonavena, Denver	W 12
May	21—Larry Middleton, Baltimore	W 12
July	16—Jimmy Ellis, Denver	W 12
Sept.	17—Boone Kirkman, Seattle	KO 8
Dec.	1—Al (Memphis) Jones, New Orleans	KO 5
1975
Feb.	11—Jimmy Young, Honolulu	L 10
May	16—Muhammad Ali, Las Vegas	KO by 11
	(World Heavyweight Title)	
Sept.	13—Earnie Shavers, Denver	KO 6
1976
Jan.	24—George Foreman, Las Vegas	KO by 4
	(U.S. Heavyweight Title)	
Sept.	11—Kevin Isaac, Utica	KO 7
Nov.	6—Jimmy Young, San Francisco	L 12
1977
Mar.	20—Joe Bugner, Las Vegas	W 12
Sept.	14—Stan Ward, Las Vegas	W 10
1978
June	3—Horacio Robinson, Denver	KO 8
1979
Apr.	7—Fili Moala, San Diego	KO 8
May	12—Scott LeDoux, Las Vegas	W 10
Dec.	12—Lynn Ball, Phoenix	KO by 2
1980
June	19—Al Neumann, Tacoma	KO 10
Aug.	23—George O'Mara, Inglewood	KO 10
Oct.	24—Gerry Cooney, Uniondale	KO by 1

ROCKY McCALEB
Miami, Florida Heavyweight
1976
July	6—Larry Karajalia, Miami Beach	KO 2
July	20—Don Samuels, Miami Beach	KO 2
1977
May	6—Tracy Steele, Miami Beach	W 4
June	23—Walter Burkhart, Bloomington	W 4
Sept.	28—Jimmy Roberts, Minneapolis	D 4
1978
Mar.	16—John L. Johnson, Hollywood, Fla.	W 4
June	29—Marc Hans, St. Paul	W 4
1979
(Inactive)
1980
Oct.	29—Eddie Williams, St. Paul	L 6

LANNY McCALL
Cincinnati, Ohio Junior Welterweight
1976
Nov.	12—Cookie Clayton, Cincinnati	KO 1

1977
June	22—Pete Seward, Columbus	L 6
Dec.	15—Steve Gregory, Hamilton	L 6
1978
Jan.	12—Bobby Haymon, Cleveland	KO by 7
Apr.	15—Art McKnight, Mansfield	L 10
May	8—Miguel Hernandez, Detroit	KO 8
July	20—Miguel Hernandez, Detroit	L 8
Sept.	9—Art McKnight, Strongsville	KO by 4
1979
Mar.	3—Wilson Bell, Detroit	KO by 8
Nov.	3—Frankie Mills, Owensboro	W 8
1980
Feb.	22—Danny Jones, Detroit	L 6
May	30—Nino LaRocco, Rome	KO by 5
June	28—Lester Groves, Bowling Green	KO 5
Dec.	13—Kenny Heflin, El Paso	L 8

BABILAH (BABS) McCARTHY
Sacramento, Calif. Welterweight
1976
Apr.	21—Jesse Lopez, Stockton	KO 1
Apr.	27—Chris Gonzalez, Sacramento	KO by 2
July	1—Chris Gonzalez, Los Angeles	KO 3
July	24—Roger Buckskin, Crescent City	W 8
Aug.	5—Chris Gonzalez, Los Angeles	D 7
Aug.	17—Larry Smith, Seattle	L 8
Oct.	12—Larry Smith, Seattle	KO 9
Dec.	15—Rocky Mosley, Las Vegas	KO by 6
1977
June	—Pete Ranzany, Incline Village	L 10
July	—Rudy Barro, Stateline	L 10
Aug.	2—Pete Ranzany, Sacramento	L 12
Nov.	10—Rudy Barro, Sacramento	L 10
1978
Jan.	23—Larry Bonds, Las Vegas	L 10
Mar.	2—Jose Baquedano, Los Angeles	KO 1
Mar.	16—Larry Bonds, Stateline	L 10
June	1—Randy Shields, Sacramento	L 10
June	25—Paddy Wilson, Stateline	KO 2
Sept.	9—Jose Palacios, Sacramento	W 10
Nov.	14—Wayne Beale, Sacramento	W 10
1979
Feb.	27—Henry Walker, Sacramento	W 10
Mar.	16—Larry Bonds, Lake Tahoe	L 10
Aug.	12—Billy Miller, Las Vegas	KO 2
1980
Jan.	17—Miguel Garcia, Stateline	KO 4
Feb.	3—Rocky Mosley, Reno	L 10
May	6—Steve Delgado, Las Vegas	KO 6

JIMMY McCAULEY
Columbus, Ohio Heavyweight
1979
Mar.	27—Dwain Bonds, Michigan	KO by 1
1980
Feb.	19—Lee Burkey, Sparks	KO by 4

GENE McCOMB
Lake Charles, Louisiana Junior Middleweight
1980
Oct.	18—Junior Harris, Lake Charles	KO 1
Dec.	6—Carl Watson, Bastrop, La.	KO 2
Dec.	9—Lester Groves, Birmingham	W 6

JEFF McCRACKEN
Sand Point, Idaho Middleweight
1980
May	4—Richard Abbott, Seattle	W 6
June	19—J.W. Stewart, Tacoma	TD 4
Aug.	2—J.W. Stewart, Cincinnati	KO 2
Aug.	9—Francisco Rivera, Spokane	KO 1
Sept.	27—Fahim Muhammad, Inglewood	KO 6
Oct.	23—Joe Banks, Spokane	KO 4
Nov.	29—Larry Myers, Los Angeles	KO 4
Dec.	12—Pablo Gomez, Sacramento	KO 2

MILTON McCRORY
Detroit, Michigan Welterweight
Born: Feb. 7, 1962. Height: 6 ft. 1 in.
Managed by Emanuel Steward
1980
Sept.	10—Kevin Straughter, Detroit	KO 1
Sept.	20—Rodney Kennebrew, San Juan	KO 1
Oct.	16—Chuck Smith, Toledo	KO 1
Oct.	23—William Hodges, Detroit	KO 1
Nov.	8—Raul Aguirre, Detroit	KO 1
Nov.	22—James Dixon, Cincinnati	KO 5
Dec.	2—Bill Roberts, Toledo	KO 1
Dec.	12—Alfonso Hayman, Detroit	KO 3

147

CHRIS McCRUGDDEN
Rochester, N.Y. Light Heavyweight
1980
Feb. 13—Paul Telesco, White Plains .... KO by 1
Sept. 9—Mike Adessa, Scranton .... KO by 1

MARK McCULLOUGH
Columbus, Ohio Middleweight
1980
Feb. 28—Ricky Davis, Washington, D.C. .... W 4
Mar. 17—Donnie Garrett, Indianapolis .... W 4
Apr. 5—Tony Moore, Louisville .... L 6
May 10—Mike Sacchetti, Clarksburg .... KO by 1
—Danny Jones, Windsor .... L 8
Sept. 18—Ron Ayres, Cleveland .... L 4
Sept. 24—Jimmy Villers, Struthers .... KO by 4

LEON McCULLUM
Beaumont, Texas Middleweight
1976
Sept. 21—Bill Watkins, Jr., Corpus Christi .... L 6
Oct. 21—Phil Sotelo, Fort Worth .... L 5
Oct. 26—Robert Perez, Corpus Christi .... KO by 2
1977
Feb. 28—Alfonso Verela, Houston .... W 4
May 5—Freddie Johnson, Mobile .... L 6
May 23—Martin Jiminez, Houston .... L 4
July 19—Martin Jiminez, Houston .... L 6
Sept. 6—Charles Adams, Houston .... Exh. 6
Oct. 11—Efren Gonzalez, Houston .... L 6
Dec. 13—Paul Arriage, Houston .... KO 2
1978
Feb. 14—Adolfo Rivas, Houston .... KO 2
Feb. 28—Tommy Howard, Seattle .... KO by 7
July 18—Miguel Garcia, Houston .... L 6
Aug. 8—Marcos Dorsey, Houston .... D 6
Oct. 10—Mike Garcia, Houston .... TW 10
1979
May 22—Norris McKinney, Beaumont .... L 8
July 21—Marcus Dorsey, Houston .... KO 3
Aug. 29—Othun Guzman Iturbe, Houston ... KO by 10
Oct. 12—Rocky Mattioli, Rome .... KO by 5
Dec. 11—Jose Gamez, Houston .... L 10
1980
Apr. 22—Gilbert Miranda, Memphis .... W 4
Apr. 29—Jesse Lara, Houston .... L 8
June 3—Andre Ramirez, Houston .... L 8
July 1—Bossy Jamison, Memphis .... L 4
July 11—Russell Nations, Meridian .... KO by 3
July 15—Gonzallo Montes, Laredo .... KO by 6
Aug. 19—Steve Hearon, Beaumont .... KO by 5

LEON McDONALD
Florida Light Heavyweight
1979
Aug. 24—Ron Harry, Ft. Lauderdale .... KO 1
Sept. 25—Leon Sheffield, Miami Beach .... KO 1
Oct. 5—James Roper, Ft. Lauderdale .... KO 1
Nov. 20—Tanny Santiago, Miami Beach .... KO by 2
1980
Jan. 29—James Salerno, Miami .... W 10
June 6—Anthony Phillips, Miami .... KO 3
Oct. 17—Eddie Mack, W. Palm Beach .... KO 3
Dec. 16—Junior Royster, Miami .... W 10

EARL McFADDEN
Hugo, Oklahoma Middleweight
1980
June 13—Ronnie Martin, Tulsa .... KO 1
Aug. 12—Robert Powell, Wichita .... W 8
Sept. 10—Richard Green, Wichita .... W 4

ROBERT McFARLAND
Memphis, Tenn. Light Heavyweight
1979
July —Bobby Powell, Memphis .... KO 4
July —Louis Tillman, Memphis .... KO 2
Aug. —Bobby Mitchum, Memphis .... KO 3
Sept. 18—Charles Smith, Memphis .... KO 2
Sept. 25—George Goforth, Belleville .... TW 3
Oct. 24—Bill Tuttle, Baltimore .... KO by 1
1980
Dec. 10—Grady Daniels, Moline .... W 8
Dec. 19—Jamie Olatunde, Peoria .... W 10

ROBERT McFARLAND
Trenton, N.J. Light Heavyweight
1980
Jan. 24—Broderick Mason, Upper Darby ...... KO by 1
Feb. 27—Javon Pratt, Washington, D.C. .... KO 2
Mar. 4—Reggie Patrick, Elizabeth .... KO 6
Mar. 26—Lou Butler, Baltimore .... W 6
Apr. 9—Negro Rivera, Brooklyn .... KO by 2

148

SEAN McGARRY
Philadelphia, Pa. Junior Welterweight
1978
June 1—Leo Randolph, Upper Darby .... KO 2
1979
(Inactive)
1980
Apr. 10—Victor Pappa, Atlantic City .... KO by 8
July 31—Mike Passero, Atlantic City .... D 4

ROBERT McGILL
Lancaster, Ohio Junior Welterweight
1980
June 5—Randy Smith, Columbus .... KO 2
Aug. 21—Chico Rodriguez, Columbus .... KO 3
Sept. 18—Isaac Hubbard, Cleveland .... KO 3
Sept. 24—Fred Bowman, Struthers .... L 4
Sept. 25—Junie Johnson, Columbus .... D 4

SAM McGILL
Pittsburgh, Pa. Heavyweight
1978
Aug. 22—Harold Porter, Erie .... W 8
Nov. 1—Gerry Cooney, White Plains .... L 8
1979
Mar. 17—Alfio Righetti, Rimini .... L 10
1980
Dec. 5—Jesse Clark, Clarksburg .... KO 1

RANDY McGRADY
California Middleweight
1978
Mar. 7—Mike Westrich, Las Vegas .... KO 3
May 23—Tom Brooks, Concord, Calif. .... W 6
1979
May 4—Fahim Muhammad, Pico Rivera .... W 6
Nov. 16—William Rodriguez, Inglewood .... L 5
Nov. 28—Randy Graves, Las Vegas .... W 6
1980
Mar. 7—Richie Chavez, San Bernardino .... W 5
Mar. 26—Bobby Edwards, Costa Mesa .... W 4
Mar. 29—Mauricio Aldana, Las Vegas .... W 10
Apr. 17—Mario Luna, Los Angeles .... W 6
May 2—Rodrigo Hernandez, Las Vegas .... W 10
July 24—Guy Kennedy, Las Vegas .... KO 4
Sept. 4—Frank Fletcher, Atlantic City .... KO by 7

WILLIE McINTOSH
Grand Rapids, Mich. Middleweight
1980
Mar. 22—Kelvin Lampkins, Grand Rapids .... W 6
May 22—Kelvin Lampkins, Holland, Mich. .... L 4

PETE McINTYRE
Los Angeles, Calif. Light Heavyweight
1973
Oct. 24—King David Smith, Los Angeles .... L 5
1974
(Inactive)
1975
Apr. 25—Larry Castaneda, San Diego .... KO 2
June 11—Mike Colbert, Stockton .... L 6
June 27—Jose Macias, San Diego .... L 6
Nov. 24—Danny Brewer, Las Vegas .... L 6
1976
Feb. 19—Paul Guyness, Eugene .... KO 1
Apr. 15—Daniel Brewer, San Jose .... D 6
July 15—Fabian Falconett, Los Angeles .... KO 2
Sept. 29—Butch Geigger, Las Vegas .... L 10
Dec. 8—Alvaro (Yaqui) Lopez, Stockton ...... KO by 6
1977
Mar. 25—Norman Sweeney, San Diego .... W 10
May 27—Danny Brewer, San Diego .... KO by 8
1978
Feb. 9—Alvaro (Yaqui) Lopez, Los Angeles ...... W 10
Mar. 10—Mike Quarry, San Diego .... KO 5
Apr. 7—Marvin Camel, Butte .... L 10
Nov. 8—Jesse Burnett, Stockton .... W 10
1979
Feb. 27—Lenis Provo, San Carlos .... W 10
June 27—Bashiru Ali, Los Angeles .... W 10
Aug. 3—Tony Mundine, Sydney .... KO by 5
1980
Apr. 16—Alvaro (Yaqui) Lopez, Fresno ...... KO by 8
Sept. 11—Pete Riddles, El Paso .... W 6
Sept. 27—Eddie Davis, Inglewood .... KO 2

BUDDY McKAY
Coeur d'Alene, Idaho Junior Middleweight
1979
Feb. 14—Manny Gullatto, Spokane .... W 4
Mar. 31—Eddie Bearden, Spokane .... W 4

May 16—Gary Giron, Carson City .... KO by 2
July 31—Hudson Jackson, Spokane .... KO by 5
1980
Mar. 18—Scott Bowers, Spokane .... W 6
Oct. 23—Dave Zimmerle, Spokane .... KO 3

NORRIS McKINNEY
Dallas, Texas Middleweight
1978
June 21—Lloyd Richardson, Detroit .... KO by 2
1979
May 2—Carlos Herrera, Las Vegas .... KO by 6
May 22—Leon McCullum, Beaumont .... W 8
July 21—Arthur Henderson, Dallas .... KO 2
Nov. 8—Don Masterson, Tulsa .... KO 1
1980
Jan. 9—Wilford Scypion, Beaumont .... KO by 3

ART McKNIGHT
Mansfield, Ohio Welterweight
1977
Mar. 8—Nate Lenore, Mentor .... KO 3
Mar. 29—Jerry Strickland, Westlake, Oh. .... W 4
Mar. 30—Larry Moore, Cleveland .... KO 3
Apr. 27—Richard Woods, Lorain .... KO 1
May 11—Willie Wren, Cleveland .... W 4
May 18—Ron Pettigrew, Lorain .... KO 6
May 25—Mike Gray, Cleveland .... KO 3
Sept. 9—Larry McCall, Strongsville, Oh. ...... KO 4
Nov. 2—Ron Pettigrew, Cleveland .... W 6
Dec. 7—Will Rankin, Cleveland .... KO 3
1978
Feb. 8—Roland Pryor, Washington D.C. .... L 10
Mar. 1—Ray Leonard, Dayton .... KO by 7
Apr. 15—Larry McCall, Mansfield .... W 10
Apr. 29—Larry McCall, Sebring .... W 8
May 13—Larry Moore, Dayton .... KO 4
Aug. 25—Floyd Maeweather, Houston .... L 10
1979
Jan. 10—Danny Paul, Richfield .... L 6
Apr. 19—Bobby Plegge, Richfield .... W 10
May 19—Ron Pettigrew, Findlay .... W 10
Sept. 19—Willie Rodriguez, Scranton .... L 12
1980
Apr. 30—Greg Netter, Youngstown .... D 10

EARL McLEAY
Canadian Heavyweight
1977
Feb. 27—George Jerome, Calgary .... D 12
Dec. 8—George Chuvalo, Toronto .... KO by 1
1978
Sept. 27—George Mostardini, Chicago .... KO 3
Nov. 18—Luke Capuano, DePaul .... KO by 3
1979
Feb. 20—Larry Frazier, Seattle .... KO by 1
May 9—Yaqui Meneses, Las Vegas .... KO by 5
May 26—Trevor Berbick, Glace Bay .... KO by 7
1980
June 13—Gord Racette, Nanaimo .... KO by 1

LEMUEL McLITTLE
Detroit, Mich. Light Heavyweight
1980
Sept. 27—Ed Temple, Detroit .... KO 2
Nov. 1—Mike Harding, Detroit .... W 8
Nov. 14—Bill Hollis, Detroit .... W 8

TONY McMINN
Topeka, Kans. Light Heavyweight
1976
May 3—Titus Shelby, Topeka .... KO 1
June 2—Richard Bardot, Topeka .... KO by 3
Sept. 15—Don Masterson, Nowata .... KO 1
Oct. 14—Robert Thomas, Quapaw .... KO 1
Oct. 25—Ron Cichon, Miami, Okla. .... KO 2
Nov. 12—Bruce Scott, Joplin .... KO 4
Dec. 9—Moses Brown, Quapaw .... KO 1
1977
Jan. 15—Barry Smith, Quapaw .... KO 3
Jan. 29—Ivy Brown, Kansas City .... KO 4
Mar. 5—Al Banks, Quapaw .... KO 2
Mar. 18—Mike Hallacy, Kansas City .... KO by 1
Mar. 29—Mayfield Pennington, Memphis .... W 8
Apr. 5—Mickey Banks, Oklahoma City .... KO 10
Apr. 19—Jose Luis Gonzalez, Oklahoma City ... KO 5
Apr. 26—Jerry Celestine, Memphis .... KO by 4
June 21—Rocky Matthews, Oklahoma City ...... KO 1
July 19—Mickey Banks, Oklahoma City .... KO 3
Aug. 2—Alfonso Aguirre, Oklahoma City ...... KO 2
Aug. 16—Phillip Sotello, Oklahoma City .... KO 2
Sept. 6—Troy Vaughn, Oklahoma City .... W 6
Oct. 4—Dennis Haggerty, Oklahoma City ...... KO 2

Oct. 18—Roy Christian, Oklahoma City .... KO 4
Nov. 15—Chuck Walker, Phoenix .... L 10
Dec. 6—Pete Knight, Oklahoma City .... KO 4
1978
Mar. 9—Leroy Washington, Wichita .... KO 2
Mar. 18—Kid Tinero, Kansas City .... KO 1
Apr. 11—Dennis Haggerty, Wichita .... KO 2
May 13—Jim Coleman, Kansas City .... KO 3
June 10—Frank Formaro, Oklahoma City .... KO 7
July 12—Johnny Heard, Kansas City .... KO by 2
Nov. 18—Hurricane Lacy, Joplin .... KO 3
1979
Jan. 12—Ron Wilson, St. Louis .... KO 3
Jan. 30—Robert Vance, Memphis .... KO 3
Mar. 6—Ray Masterson, Memphis .... KO 2
Mar. 16—George Aidoo, St. Louis .... KO 9
Apr. 20—Eddie Smith, St. Louis .... KO by 2
May 1—Frankie Evans, Memphis .... W 10
Aug. 24—Pascual Ramirez, Carson City .... L 8
1980
Sept. 20—Dave Watkins, Lake Ozark, Mo. .... KO 4
Oct. 23—Bill Payton, Memphis .... KO 3
Nov. 15—Ed Johnson, Miami, Ok. .... KO 2
Dec. 13—Mark Hughes, Bartlesville .... KO 4

FRED McMUNN
Kensington, Pa. Middleweight
1980
Feb. 1—Luis Carrasquillo, Philadelphia .... KO 2
Mar. 9—Leo Martinez, Atlantic City .... W 4
May 4—Bob Rooney, Atlantic City .... KO 1
July 3—Leo Martinez, Atlantic City .... W 6

JIMMY McNALLY
Wilmington, Mass. Light Heavyweight
1979
Mar. 1—Mike Corsetti, White Plains .... KO 2
Mar. 12—Danny Tavares, Providence .... W 4
Mar. 15—Joe Moreault, Hartford .... W 4
June 29—Eddie Phillips, Hartford .... W 8
Aug. 21—Ben Ferguson, Yarmouth .... KO 2
Nov. 6—Jose Rivera, Lowell .... W 8
Nov. 28—Fred Boynton, W. New York, N.J. ..... KO by 3
1980
Feb. 26—Jose Pagan, Woburn .... W 8
Aug. 21—Reinaldo Oliviera, Revere .... W 4
Dec. 15—Reinaldo Oliviera, Boston .... KO 10

JIMMY McNEECE
Oakdale, L.I., N.Y. Lightweight
1978
Apr. 27—Mel Boynton, New York .... W 4
Aug. 25—Louie Hubela, New York .... L 6
1979
Jan. 26—Sergio Nualarte, San Diego .... W 6
Feb. 8—Daniel Patino, Los Angeles .... L 6
1980
June 13—Gerald Clark, New York .... KO 2
July 20—Robert Johnson, Great Gorge .... W 4

TOMMY McNEECE
Oakdale, L.I., N.Y. Light Heavyweight
1977
June 9—Mike Pittman, North Bergen .... KO 1
June 22—Al Ware, New York .... W 4
Oct. 25—Dave Horn, West New York .... W 4
Nov. 18—Jose Zabala, Commack .... KO 2
1978
Jan. 14—Angel Ortiz, Hauppauge .... W 4
Feb. 4—Cornell Chavis, New York .... W 4
Mar. 2—Mike Robinson, New York .... D 4
Apr. 21—Sixto Martinez, Albany .... KO 2
July 26—Don Addison, New York .... W 4
1979
Aug. 14—Kid Samson, Atlantic City .... D 6
Aug. 31—Sam Bell, Shirley .... KO 2
1980
May 22—Tony Mesoraca, Totowa .... KO by 8
Aug. 15—Elijah Hamm, Glen Cove .... KO 1
Dec. 12—Euclides Valdez, New York .... KO by 5

STERLING McPHEARSON
Las Vegas, Nev. Lightweight
1979
Feb. 14—Rock Samudio, Las Vegas .... D 4
Mar. 14—Rick Fager, Las Vegas .... KO 1
June 27—Arturo Chihuahua, Las Vegas .... KO 3
Sept. 5—Randy McNurlin, Las Vegas .... KO 3
1980
Jan. 23—Joe Willie Johnson, Las Vegas .... KO 3
Feb. 3—Jaime Nava, Las Vegas .... W 6
Apr. 2—Manny Lopez, Las Vegas .... KO 1
Oct. 1—Rene Mejia, Las Vegas .... KO 2

149

GREG McPHERSON
Waukeegan, Ill. Middleweight
1977
Mar. 31—Frank Livingstone, San Carlos .... KO 2
Apr. 20—Charles Terrell, San Carlos .... KO 3
June 3—Leroy Dansford, San Jose .... KO 2
1978
Mar. 16—Johnny Sullivan, Stateline .... L 8
1979
Feb. 6—Charles Terrell, San Carlos .... KO 1
Feb. 27—Bashiru Ali, San Carlos .... W 10
Mar. 16—Johnny Sullivan, Lake Tahoe .... L 8
Mar. 27—Leni Vanisi, San Carlos .... KO 4
Apr. 24—Bashiru Ali, San Carlos .... L 10
June 18—Maurice Rice, San Carlos .... KO 3
Oct. 19—David Bradley, Chicago .... W 8
Nov. 20—Alex Porratta, Chicago .... L 10
1980
Feb. 1—Henry Sims, Chicago .... L 10
Aug. 7—King David Smith, San Carlos .... L 10
Nov. 29—Mike Clark, Lake Tahoe .... L 10

RODDY MacDONALD
New Waterford, Nova Scotia Light Heavyweight
1978
Sept. 17—Larry Allen, Sydney .... W 6
Oct. 8—Greg Burdett, Glace Bay .... KO 1
1979
Mar. 12—Akbar Muhammad, Chicago .... W 6
May 26—Hilliard Edmond Jr., Glace Bay .... KO 7
July 10—Mustafa Bayeh, Halifax .... KO 2
Aug. 28—Eddie Smith, Halifax .... KO 5
Nov. 13—Johnny Gallagher, Halifax .... W 8
1980
Feb. 23—Fred Picotte, Fall River .... KO 1
Mar. 11—Kelly Anderson, Halifax .... KO 1
Apr. 16—Kid Samson, White Plains .... W 10
July 22—Gary Summerhays, Halifax .... KO by 7
(Canadian Light Heavyweight Title)
Sept. 24—Maurice Moore, Halifax .... KO 2
Dec. 16—Lew Alexander, Toronto .... KO 1

RANDY MACK
Philadelphia, Pa. Heavyweight
1975
Nov. 13—Luis Rodriguez, Allentown .... W 6
1976
Apr. 15—C. J. Bar Brown, Allentown .... L 8
May 10—Gene Owens, Philadelphia .... L 6
Sept. 14—Marty Monroe, Philadelphia .... L 8
1977
(Inactive)
1978
Mar. 21—Tyrone Harlee, Philadelphia .... KO 1
Apr. 10—David Smith, Philadelphia .... KO 2
June 6—Joe Maye, Philadelphia .... KO 3
July 15—Jerry Thompkins, Atlantic City .... KO 7
Sept. 27—Sam McGill, Philadelphia .... W 8
Dec. 5—Marvin Stinson, Philadelphia .... D 8
1979
Feb. 21—Leon Shaw, Las Vegas .... KO 3
May 16—Terry Mims, Las Vegas .... W 10
Aug. 22—Leroy Caldwell, Las Vegas .... W 10
Nov. 7—Fili Moala, Las Vegas .... W 10
1980
Feb. 21—Leon Shaw, Las Vegas .... KO 3
Feb. 27—Mike Rogers, Las Vegas .... KO 1
May 25—Marvin Stinson, Atlantic City .... D 10
Oct. 1—Jody Ballard, Las Vegas .... KO 10
Dec. 3—Leroy Caldwell, Las Vegas .... L 10

MANUEL MADERA
Lowell, Mass. Junior Welterweight
1979
Oct. 27—Louis Castro, Fitchburg .... W 4
1980
Nov. 11—Papo Figueroa, W. Hartford .... L 10
Dec. 9—Mario Cusson, Montreal .... L 6

RAY MADERA
Brooklyn, N.Y. Junior Welterweight
Managed by Al Gavin
1979
Apr. 26—Jimmy Martinez, N. Bergen .... KO 2
Oct. 27—Donnell McCrea, N. Bergen .... W 6
1980
Feb. 27—Garland Wright, Scranton .... L 6
Nov. 28—Danny Pearson, New York .... L 4

GEORGE MADISON
Evansville, Ill. Middleweight
1976
May 3—Richard Barnes, Topeka .... KO 2

May 25—Joey Vincent, Orlando .... KO 1
July 8—Victor (Taco) Perez, Orlando .... KO 1
July 28—Johnny Herd, Indianapolis .... L 4
Aug. 31—Victor (Taco) Perez, Orlando .... KO by 5
Nov. 9—Clem Tucker, St. Paul .... KO by 1
1977
Feb. 1—Herman Graham, Indianapolis .... L 4
1978
Feb. 25—Anthony Daniels, Kingsport .... KO by 3
Apr. 25—Jimmy Heair, Greenville .... KO by 1
1979
Nov. 3—Floyd Saunders, Owensboro .... KO by 4
1980
Oct. 18—Lindell Holmes, Toledo .... KO by 3

JEFFREY MADISON
St. Louis, Mo. Junior Middleweight
1980
July 11—Billy Evans, Chicago .... KO 2
Aug. 8—Steve Wetzel, Chicago .... W 4
Aug. 13—Charles Peterson, Indianapolis .... L 6
Sept. 22—Steve Williams, Chicago .... L 6
Nov. 19—Carl Crowley, Moline .... L 8
Dec. 19—Billy Page, Peoria .... W 8

ROBERTO MADRID
Houston, Texas Lightweight
1980
Jan. 22—Arturo Leon, Houston .... L 10
Mar. 18—Ramiro Hernandez, Houston .... KO 6
Apr. 15—Kenneth Sheppard, Houston .... KO 5
June 17—Juan Venegas, Houston .... W 10
Oct. 28—Faustino Pena, Houston .... W 10

RICARDO (PALITO) MAGALLANES
Argentine Middleweight
1980
Jan. 11—Hector Caceres, Pergamino .... W 10
Mar. 28—Lorenzo Fernandez, Colon .... W 10
May 31—Patricio Diaz, Pergamino .... L 10
July 25—Jorge Medina, San Nicolas .... W 10
Aug. 15—Alfredo Lucero, Concordia .... KO by 1

JIMMY MAGNIFICO
Hasbrouck Hgts., N.J. Bantamweight
1977
May 26—John Glover, Denver .... L 4
June 9—Isaias Villanueva, North Bergen .... W 4
June 24—Heriberto Sanchez, New York .... W 4
Sept. 27—Roberto Sanchez, W. New York .... W 4
Dec. 8—Luis Riveria, N. Bergen .... W 4
1978
Jan. 19—Edwin Rivera, North Bergen .... L 4
Mar. 16—Isaias Villanueva, North Bergen .... W 6
May 4—Johnny Britt, North Bergen .... W 6
Nov. 16—Mel Boynton, North Bergen .... W 6
Dec. 1—Louis Edwin Rivera, Jersey City .... L 12
1979
June 27—Fernando Martinez, Secaucus .... D 8
1980
Jan. 15—Pepe Vasquez, W. Hartford .... D 6
Mar. 4—Pepe Vasquez, W. Hartford .... D 6
Mar. 20—Bille Wade, N. Bergen .... KO 3
May 31—Joe Rivers, Elizabeth .... L 8

MARK MAINERO
Boston, Mass. Middleweight
1980
Feb. 26—David Ortiz, Woburn .... W 4
May 1—Sean Mannion, Dorchester .... Exh 4
May 29—Jorge Santana, Revere .... W 6
June 26—Matador Loving, Revere .... W 5
July 25—Jose Diaz, New Bedford .... KO 2
Sept. 12—Ronnie Pilgrim, W. Hartford .... W 4
Oct. 2—Greg Joseph, Boston .... W 6
Oct. 16—Jack Cowell, Revere .... KO 3
Dec. 15—Donny Miller, Boston .... W 6

RICHARD MAJORS
Miami, Florida Heavyweight
1978
Feb. 21—Eli Smith, Hollywood, Fla. .... W 4
Apr. 4—John L. Johnson, Miami .... D 4
Oct. 3—Clyde Fussell, Orlando .... KO by 6
1979
Mar. 19—Jeff Podgurski, Sunrise .... D 10
Dec. 7—Pat Streichen, N. Miami .... KO by 2
1980
Jan. 29—John L. Johnson, Miami .... KO by 1

FRANCISCO MALDONADO
Boston, Mass. Junior Lightweight
1975
Jan.	16—Jimmy Lopez, Portland, Me.	L	6
Sept.	5—Jimmy Lopez, Lewiston	KO by	4

1976
July	20—Jimmy Lopez, Lawrence	KO by	2
July	26—Jimmy Farrell, Peabody	L	6
Oct.	24—Jimmy Farrell, Brockton	L	8

1977
Mar.	12—Papo Melendez, Fitchburg	KO by	5
Apr.	20—Michael Rae, Taunton	KO by	3
Aug.	8—Michel Rouleau, Montreal	KO by	2
Oct.	7—Jimmy Lopez, Lowell	L	4
Nov.	2—Alberto Collazo, Cleveland	KO by	4
Nov.	26—Daryl Beattie, Albany	KO by	6

1978
Apr.	29—Charles McFarline, Lowell	KO	1
June	18—Bobby Everett, Boston	KO by	2
Aug.	13—Dave Ramalho, Portland, Me.	KO by	4

1979
Mar.	29—Ed Welcome, Cohoes	KO by	4

1980
June	28—Dave Ramahlo, Manchester	KO by	1

JOE MALDONADO
Fresno, Calif. Welterweight
1977
Oct.	29—Kenny Sheppard, Fresno	W	4
Dec.	17—Curtis Lewis, Fresno	W	6

1978
Jan.	28—Pablo Baez, Fresno	W	6
Mar.	1—Steven Delgado, Fresno	L	6
May	2—Gilbert Valdez, Sacramento	L	6
Dec.	6—Leonard Thomas, Stockton	W	6

1979
June	27—Salomon Lopez, Oakland	L	4
Sept.	20—Humberto DeLos Rios, Los Angeles	KO by	2
Dec.	11—Willie Hearne, San Jose	W	6

1980
Feb.	19—Ricky Wayne, Sacramento	W	6
Mar.	27—Lem Thomas, Stockton	W	4
Apr.	16—Chico Ortega, Fresno	KO by	2
May	20—Lem Thomas, Fresno	W	6
Oct.	7—Julio Alfonso, Bakersfield	KO	5

MARIO MALDONADO
Vineland, N.J. Junior Middleweight
1979
Jan.	11—Roger Leonard, Landover	KO by	2
May	22—Leo Martinez, Upper Darby	W	4
May	23—Guy Kennedy, White Plains	L	4
July	10—Jimmy Sykes, Atlantic City	L	4
Sept.	30—James Murphy, Trenton	W	4
Nov.	23—Michael Grant, Trenton	W	4
Dec.	4—Jimmy Sykes, Philadelphia	W	6

1980
Jan.	18—Joe Brown, Trenton	KO	1
Feb.	1—Willie Torres, Philadelphia	D	4
Feb.	27—Keith Jackson, Washington, D.C.	KO	3
Mar.	12—Curtis Pittman, Washington, D.C.	KO	1
Mar.	26—Larry Spriggs, Baltimore	KO	2
Apr.	24—Norberto Sabater, Totowa	L	9
May	22—Guy Kennedy, Totowa	L	10
Sept.	4—Ben Serrano, Atlantic City	W	6
Sept.	18—Al Styles, Philadelphia	L	8
Oct.	18—Miguel Sanchez, Atlantic City	KO	3

MIGUEL MALDONADO
Argentine Middleweight
1980
June	6—Ricardo Ruiz, Mar del Plata	L	6
June	21—Ricardo Ruiz, Mar del Plata	D	6
Aug.	1—Carlos Romero, Mar del Plata	W	6
Sept.	5—Hugo Carriego, Mar del Plata	W	6
Oct.	10—Jose Gigena, Mar del Plata	KO by	7

ORLANDO MALDONADO
Puerto Rican Flyweight
Born, November 22, 1959, Bayamon, P.R.
1977
May	6—Roberto Pina, Curacao	KO	2
June	9—Tim Alexander, St. Martin	KO	3
July	10—Ramon L. Perez, San Juan	W	4
Aug.	21—Peterson Marin, Carolina, P.R.	KO	4

1978
Mar.	30—Jose Latimer, San Juan	W	4
Apr.	18—Jose Latimer, San Juan	KO	4
July	16—Ramon Perez, San Juan	W	6
Aug.	14—Jose Lattimer, Rio Predras	W	4
Oct.	8—Peterson Marin, Carolina	D	4
Oct.	20—Julio Guerrero, Santo Domingo	D	8
Dec.	28—Julio Guerrero, San Juan	W	8

1979
Apr.	28—Elpidio de Paula, Trujillo Alto, P.R.	W	8
June	22—Luis A. Burgos, San Juan	KO	3

(Flyweight Championship of Puerto Rico)
Aug.	16—Renzo Pena, Trujillo Alto	KO	3
Sept.	22—Jose Ortiz, San Juan	KO	3
Oct.	26—Daryl Jones, New York	W	10

1980
Feb.	3—Arturo Tebaqui, Las Vegas	KO	10
Apr.	27—Tito Roque, San Juan	W	10
June	12—Maximo Rodriguez, San Juan	KO	2
July	10—Pascual Polanco, San Juan	W	10
Aug.	23—Enrique Guadamuz, San Juan	KO	1

(Won FECARBOX Flyweight Title)
Oct.	18—Miguel Canto, Guadalajara	L disq.	6
Dec.	13—Prudencio Cardona, Miami	KO by	7

RICARDO MALDONADO
Mexican Lightweight
1980
Jan.	19—Feliciano Soto, Mexico City	KO	1
Mar.	15—Adolfo Gasca, Mexico City	KO by	3
Nov.	15—Armando Lopez, Mexico City	KO	1

EDDIE MALLARD
Jersey City, N.J. Heavyweight
1975
June	19—Roman Ranquallo, North Bergen	KO	1
Nov.	28—Marcos Larrios, Commack	KO	3

1976
Mar.	30—Leo Rogers, New York	KO by	2

1977
May	9—Melvin Richarson, Newark	L	4

1978
Apr.	7—Cornell Chavis, North Bergen	KO by	3
June	2—Richard Roy, Jersey City	L	6
Oct.	28—Bill Connell, Jersey City	D	6

1979
Mar.	15—Bill Connell, North Bergen	L	6

1980
Feb.	24—Conroy Nelson, Atlantic City	D	4

JUAN DOMINGO MALVAREZ
Argentine Featherweight
Born: Oct. 7, 1952, Trelew (Chubut), Argentina
1971
Jan.	8—Jose Almonacid, Esquel	L	6

1972
Sept.	8—Jose Almonacid, Trelew	D	6
Sept.	22—Carlos Arguello, Trelew	KO	1
Nov.	10—Jose Almonacid, Gaiman	KO by	2

1973
Nov.	23—Rodolfo Uncos, Trelew	KO	3

1974
Feb.	8—Juan Bega, Trelew	KO	3
Apr.	11—Andres Abalos, Trelew	KO	3
May	31—Ruben Granado, Gayman	D	8
July	19—Alfredo Flores, Trelew	KO	3
Aug.	2—Ruben Grando, Trelew	D	10
Sept.	20—Tomas Lima, Trelew	KO	6
Nov.	22—Marcos Urquiza, Trelew	KO	3
Dec.	20—Ruben Granado, Trelew	KO	10

1975
Jan.	17—Jose Martino, Gayman	KO	5
Mar.	14—Rodolfo Calderolli, Posadas	KO	1
Apr.	4—Hipolito Nunez, Salta	D	10
July	5—Hipolito Nunez, Salta	L	10
July	18—Enrique Tomas, Aquero	L	10
Aug.	8—Ramon Benitez, Salta	KO	3
Aug.	14—Carlos Portillo, Salta	KO	1
Aug.	29—Ruben Granado, Salta	KO	7
Sept.	19—Julio Alegre, Salta	KO	1
Oct.	31—Enrique Aguero, Salta	L	10
Dec.	12—Benicio Sosa, Salta	L	10

1976
Jan.	30—Carlos Portillo, Trelew	KO	5
Feb.	27—Ramon Gonzalez, Trelew	W	10
Apr.	2—Facundo Villalba, Salta	TD	4
Apr.	23—Hugo Melgarejo, Salta	W	10
July	16—Miguel Escobares, Trelew	KO	5
Aug.	6—Julio Alegre, Trelew	W	10
Aug.	28—Benicio Sosa, Buenos Aires	W	10
Sept.	24—Hugo Melgarejo, Trelew	W	10
Oct.	22—Facundo Villalba, Trelew	W	10
Dec.	3—Ramon Gonzalez, Trelew	W	10

1977
Jan.	14—Benicio Sosa, Mar del Plata	W	12

(Won Argentine Featherweight Title)
Feb.	11—Raul Colombo, Trelew	W	10
Feb.	23—Miguel Escobares, Carlos Paz	W	10
Mar.	18—Osvaldo Fleurabuena, Salta	KO	9
Apr.	9—Eduardo Echeverria, C. Rivadevia	KO	7
May	21—Ramon Gonzalez, Buenos Aires	W	10

June 10—Luis Valdez, Gral Roca .... KO 5
Sept. 8—Oscar Silva, Trelew .... KO 5
Oct. 29—Eduardo Prieto, Valparaiso .... L 12
(South American Featherweight Title)
Dec. 23—Antonio Ross, Trelew .... W 8
1978
Jan. 22—Emilcio R. Ortiz, Caleta Olivia .... W 10
Feb. 10—Juan C. Alvarez, Mar del Plata .... KO 8
Mar. 11—Manuel Almada, Buenos Aires .... KO 7
Mar. 23—Facundo Villalba, Bahia Blanca .... W 10
Apr. 15—Hipolito Nunez, Buenos Aires .... W 12
May 19—Modesto Gomez, Neuquen .... KO 1
June 9—Manuel Almada, C. Rivadavia .... W 10
July 14—Manuel Almada, Trelew .... KO 4
Aug. 4—Juan Reyes, San Juan .... D 10
Sept. 15—Danny Lopez, New Orleans .... KO by 2
(WBC Featherweight Title)
Nov. 4—Julio Alegre, Buenos Aires ...... KO 11
(Retained Argentine Featherweight Title)
Nov. 24—Ramon Lorenzo, Salta .... KO 6
Dec. 8—Ramon Duarte, Formosa .... KO 8
Dec. 22—Santiago Lopez, Tucuman .... W 10
1979
Feb. 9—Juan Reyes, Mar del Plata .... KO 4
Feb. 23—Hector Lopez, Tucuman .... KO 2
Mar. 16—Roberto Haidar, Mendoza .... D 10
Apr. 4—Jose F. DePaula, Trelew .... KO 7
(Won South American Featherweight Title)
May 19—Hipolito Nunez, Trelew .... W 12
(Retained South American Featherweight Title)
July 6—Armando Perez, Trelew .... TD 2
Nov. 2—Hector Lopez, S. Sal. de Jujay .... W 10
Nov. 16—Domingo Casco, Trelew .... KO 5
Dec. 7—Juan Medina, San Miguel .... KO 5
Dec. 21—Julio Alegre, P.R.S. Pena .... KO 4
1980
Jan. 11—Frank Joe, Mar del Plata .... KO 5
Mar. 29—Eusebio Pedroza, Panama .... KO by 9
(For WBC Featherweight Title)
June 14—Hector Lopez, Mar del Plata .... KO 3
July 7—Omar Almada, Catamarca .... KO 10
Aug. 16—Hipolito Nunez, Buenos Aires .... W 12
(Retained Argentine Featherweight Title)
Sept. 5—Jose Filippi, Rosario .... D 10
Sept. 19—Luis A. Zarate, Salta .... D 10
Nov. 7—Santiago Lopez, Parana .... W 10
Dec. 12—Jose Filippi, Trelew .... W 10

RUBEN (GATO) MANCILLA
Mexican Flyweight
(Previous Record Unavailable)
1979
Feb. 10—Guty Espadas, Merida .... KO by 3
Apr. 18—Augustin Macias, Mexico City .... L 10
May 30—Miguel Gonzales, Mexico City .... W disq. 7
July 13—Roberto Ramirez, Guadalajara .... KO by 6
Aug. 17—Elegio Lopez, Acapulco .... KO by 7
Sept. 7—Arturo Gonzalez, Coatzacoalcos ..... KO by 7
Nov. 16—Jose Luis Cruz, Reynosa .... KO by 1
1980
Apr. 5—Ismael (Zorro) Morales, Tapachula ... KO by 5
July 4—Rocky Alonso, Guadalajara .... KO by 1

RAY (BOOM BOOM) MANCINI
Youngstown, Ohio Lightweight
Born: March 4, 1961 Managed by Dave Wolf
1979
Oct. 18—Phil Bowen, Struthers .... KO 1
Nov. 13—Lou Daniels, Phoenix .... W 6
Nov. 24—Rick Patterson, Washington .... KO 2
Dec. 14—Roberto Perez, Dallas .... KO 1
1980
Jan. 15—Dale Gordon, Youngstown .... KO 1
Jan. 22—Charlie Evans, Indianapolis .... KO 2
Jan. 26—Ramiro Hernandez, Jackson .... KO 3
Mar. 17—Tony Rutledge, Indianapolis .... KO 1
Apr. 30—Bobby Sparks, Youngstown .... KO 1
June 18—Trevor Evelyn, Struthers .... KO 2
July 23—Leon Smith, Las Vegas .... W 10
July 30—Jaime Nava, Las Vegas .... W 10
Sept. 9—Johnny Summerhays, Warren .... W 10
Oct. 28—Bobby Plegge, Warren .... KO 6
Dec. 9—Kelvin Lampkin, Warren .... KO 2
Dec. 17—Marvin Ladson, Youngstown .... KO 1

DENNIS MANCINO
Los Angeles, California Middleweight
1978
June 30—Mike Hickman, San Diego .... W 4
1979
Mar. 10—Paddy Wilson, Los Angeles .... L 4
Aug. 17—Richard Abbott, San Diego .... W 4
Sept. 21—Rafael Corona, San Diego .... L 6

Oct. 27—J.B. Williamson, Los Angeles .... L 4
1980
Jan. 30—Randy Graves, Las Vegas .... L 6

TED MANN
Philadelphia, Pa. Middleweight
1977
Aug. 24—Joe Washington, Vineland .... KO 3
Sept. 16—Jesse Goodmond, Wilmington .... KO 4
Sept. 28—Daran Ali Muhammad, Passaic .... KO 1
Nov. 1—Titus Burgess, Philadelphia .... W 4
1978
Jan. 16—Jerome Jackson, Philadelphia .... L 4
Mar. 16—Bill Ryan, Ft. Lauderdale .... KO 3
Mar. 27—Jerome Brooks, Homestead .... KO 5
Apr. 6—Tiger Hall, Miami Beach .... KO 5
Apr. 27—Larry Peterson, Jacksonville .... KO 6
June 1—Marvin Lee, Upper Darby .... KO 1
June 14—Dave Dittmar, White Plains .... KO 3
Oct. 14—Dan Lowery, Ft. Lauderdale .... KO 2
Oct. 24—Frankie Suarez, Orlando .... KO 7
Dec. 29—Tyrone Phelps, Vineland .... W 6
1979
Jan. 11—Odell Leonard, Landover .... W 6
Feb. 14—Ray Bryant, White Plains .... W 6
Apr. 3—Richie Bennett, Philadelphia .... W 10
May 14—Archie Andrews, Philadelphia .... KO 7
July 16—Li'l Abner, Philadelphia .... KO 6
Sept. 11—Bennie Briscoe, Philadelphia .... L 10
Nov. 14—Rocky Tassone, Philadelphia .... W 10
1980
May 2—John LoCicero, New York .... L 10
May 14—Archie Andrews, Philadelphia .... KO 7
July 31—Ernie Singletary, Atlantic City .... L 10
Oct. 15—Robert Davis, White Plains .... L 8
Dec. 17—Steve Small, White Plains .... W 8

SEAN MANNION
South Boston, Mass. Welterweight
1978
June 6—Danny Torres, Providence, R.I. .... W 6
July 10—Tommy Pyke, Boston .... KO 1
Aug. 24—Steve Coupe, Boston .... W 6
Sept. 10—Jose Ortiz, New Haven .... KO 5
Nov. 3—Steve Hughes, Portland, Me. .... W 6
Nov. 11—Jose Ortiz, Boston .... W 6
Dec. 9—Roger Leonard, Springfield .... L 6
Dec. 15—Jessie Rogers, North Providence, R.I. ..... KO 6
1979
Jan. 15—Fernando Fernandez, Boston .... W 6
Feb. 24—Jamie Rodriguez, Quincy .... W 6
Feb. 28—Irving Booth, Belfast .... KO 2
May 19—Jamie Rodriguez, Quincy .... W 8
Nov. 7—Jimmy Corkum, Boston .... KO 6
1980
Feb. 22—Pat Maloney, Fall River .... KO 7
1980
Feb. 22—Pat Maloney, Fall River .... KO 7
Mar. 11—Larry Hafey, Halifax .... W 10
Apr. 18—Ruby Ortiz, New York .... L 10
Aug. 2—Steve Snow, Totowa .... KO 5
Sept. 18—Tony Suero, Totowa .... KO by 8

RUBEN MANSILLA
Argentine Lightweight
1980
June 2—Joaquin Aguilera, Catrilo .... D 6
July 5—Hector Cabrera, Catrilo .... W 6
Sept. 20—Albert Sosa, Catrilo .... KO by 6

ALVINO MANSON
Anderson, Indiana Middleweight
1980
Oct. 28—Jody Parker, Indianapolis .... KO 1
Dec. 10—Virgil Bender, Moline .... KO 1

FRANCISCO MANZO
Mexico City, Mexico Featherweight
1977
Jan. 28—Nacho Rivera, Mexico City .... W 8
Apr. 16—Pablo Rodriguez, Mexico City .... KO by 5
June 18—Jose Cabrera, Mexico City .... D 8
Sept. 3—Cosmo Corcuion, Mexico City .... KO 1
1978
Mar. 1—Gustavo Salgado, Mexico City .... KO 5
Mar. 29—Benny Abarca, Mexico City .... KO 3
May 3—Fernando Martinez, Mexico City .... KO 3
July 8—Miguel Lopez, Mexico City .... KO by 5
Oct. 4—Rocky Martinez, Mexico City .... KO 1
Dec. —Victor Ramirez, Mexico City .... KO 9
1979
Mar. 31—Bonny Mujan, Mexico City .... KO 3
July 30—Benny Marquez, Chicago .... KO 3

Dec.   8—Hector Cortez, Los Angeles .... W 10
1980
Feb.   10—Guillermo Morales, Tuxtla Gutierrez   KO by 9
        (For Mexican Featherweight Title)
June   14—Norberto Cabrera, Mexico City .... L 10
Sept. 11—Alberto Collazo, Chicago .... W 10

RIGOBERTO MARCANO
Venezuelan Flyweight
1977
Feb.   20—Samuel Machorro, Caracas .... W 10
May   21—Yoko Gushiken, Sapporo .... L 15
        (WBA Junior Flyweight Title)
1978
        (No Record)
1979
Jan.   7—Yoko Gushiken, Kawasaki ....KO by 7
        (WBA Junior Flyweight Title)
1980
July   4—Ismael Torres, Cumano .... W disq. 7

PIERRE MARCHARD
San Diego, California Heavyweight
1980
Aug.   19—Zeanous Thompson, San Diego .... KO 3
Sept. 18—Len Tucker, San Diego .... KO 2
Nov.   5—Leonard Santana, San Diego .... KO 2

FERNAND MARCOTTE
Montreal, Canada Middleweight
1970
Nov.   8—Al Barau, Quebec...................... KO 2
Dec.   1—Sandy Jeffries, Miami Beach........... KO 4
Dec.   15—Jack Clements, Quebec City .... W 10
1971
Feb.   9—Don Ross, Quebec City................... W 10
Mar.   10—Jack Clements, Quebec................... W 10
May   16—Jose Pagan, Quebec City................ KO 3
May   31—Al Durate, Quebec City................. KO 5
Aug.   16—Lawrence Hafey, Quebec City .... W 10
Sept.   2—Ricky Skylark, Montreal................ KO 2
Sept. 27—Ray Chavez, Quebec .... D 10
Nov.   4—Donato Paduano, Montreal .... D 10
Dec.   6—Reynald Cantin, Quebec................. W 10
1972
Feb.   15—Donato Paduano, Montreal .... L 10
Apr.   10—Juan Ramos, Quebec .... W 10
May   10—Mike Brown, Quebec.................... KO 5
Aug.   21—Al Romano, Quebec..................... KO 1
Oct.   9—Joey Durelle, Quebec.................. KO 1
Nov.   16—Joey Durelle, Montreal .... W 10
1973
Jan.   17—Eddie Davis, Miami Beach........... KO 6
May   7—Ray Chavez, Quebec City............... L 10
Aug.   21—Dave Wyatt, Montreal................. KO 4
Oct.   9—Fermin Guzman, Miami Beach .... KO 9
Dec.   3—Clyde Gray, Montreal................ KO by 9
        (Canadian Welterweight Title)
1974
May   13—Don Melosh, Quebec................... KO 5
June   10—Art Kettles, Quebec City................ W 10
Sept.   9—Bob Shellings, Montreal .... KO 5
Nov.   4—Gary Broughton, Montreal .... W 10
Dec.   10—Joey Durelle, Montreal.................. D 10
1975
Jan.   21—Elisha Obed, Miami Beach........... KO by 11
Aug.   22—Rocky Mattioli, Melbourne.......... KO by 9
Sept.   5—Rudy McCurdy, Quebec City .... KO 3
Dec.   12—Ronnie Gibbons, New York .... KO 1
1976
Mar.   2—Larry Hafey, Montreal .... KO 10
Dec.   14—Jean-Claude LeClair, Montreal.......... KO 6
1977
Jan.   18—Elisha Obed, Montreal .... L 10
Apr.   26—Gerald Bouchard, Montreal .... L 10
June   28—Gerald Bouchard, Montreal .... W 10
Aug.   30—Frank Kolovrat, Montreal .... KO 3
1978
Jan.   24—Ken Blackwell, Montreal .... KO 9
Feb.   21—Ernie Burns, Hollywood, Fla............. KO 5
Apr.   5—Wilbert Crews, Montreal .... W 10
June   27—Jean Claude LeClair, Montreal .... KO 9
        (Canadian Middleweight Title)
Oct.   31—Eddy Melo, Quebec .... L 10
1979
Feb.   11—Ray Leonard, Miami Beach .... KO by 8
June   26—Eddy Melo, Montreal .... W 12
1980
Jan.   22—Ralph Hollett, Halifax .... L 12
        (Lost Canadian Middleweight Title)
June   20—Eddy Melo, Montreal .... D 10

PASCUAL MARGARA
Argentine Flyweight
1980
June   19—Miguel Velez, Villa Maria .... W 6
Aug.   8—Armando Romero, Villa Maria .... W 6
Sept.   5—Armando Romero, Cordoba .... D 6

CARLOS MARKS
Trinidad, B.W.I. Middleweight
1965
July   29—Neil Welsh, Trinidad .... W 6
Nov.   5—Johnny Thomas, Trinidad.............. W 6
Nov.   27—Rufus Figaro, Port of Spain .... W 8
1966
Apr.   29—Anthony Gay, Trinidad.................. W 10
July   7—Barry Foster, Port of Spain .... W 10
Sept.   8—Yalhone Arez, Port of Spain............. W 10
1967
Mar.   3—Johnny DePeiza, Port of Spain .... W 10
May   1—Grady Ponder, Port of Spain .... L 10
June   4—Johnny DePeiza, Port of Spain .... KO 9
July   27—Lennox Beckles, Port of Spain .... L 10
Dec.   2—Anthony Gay, Port of Spain .... W 10
1968
Jan.   19—Juan Ramos, New York.................. W 8
Feb.   16—David Melendez, New York............. L 8
Apr.   15—Freddie DeVore, New York............. W 8
May   21—Dave Adkins, Walpole................. W 10
June   10—Vince Shomo, New York .... D 10
July   12—Matt Donovan, Port of Spain .... L 10
Nov.   1—Matt Donovan, Port of Spain............ L 15
Dec.   10—Percy Hayles, Kingston............... W 10
1969
Apr.   9—Joe Shaw, New York .... W 10
June   14—Bunny Grant, Kingston .... L 10
Sept. 23—Bunny Grant, Kingston .... L 10
Oct.   2—Bobby Warthem, Halifax .... W 10
Nov.   6—Billy Lloyd, Philadelphia .... KO 9
1970
Jan.   16—Tom Bethea, New York................ KO 6
Feb.   23—Luis Vinales, New York .... W 10
Mar.   11—Emile Griffith, New York .... L 12
June   8—Jacques Kechichian, Paris............. L 10
Oct.   2—Young Badow, Port of Spain .... W 10
Dec.   2—Noel Burgess, Port of Spain .... W 10
1971
May   3—Bennie Briscoe, Philadelphia .... KO by 5
Oct.   10—Luis Galvan, St. Thomas................ W 10
1972
Feb.   10—Tom Berrios, Portland, Me............. KO 3
Mar.   21—Bill Douglas, Philadelphia .... KO by 10
Apr.   20—Matt Donovan, Port of Spain........... L 15
May   15—Bill Douglas, Philadelphia .... L 10
Sept. 26—Mark Rowe, London................... L 10
Oct.   17—Tom Imrie, London.................... W 10
Nov.   7—Kevin Finnegan, London .... L 8
Nov.   19—Tom Bogs, Aarhms................... KO 8
Dec.   18—Rodrigo Valdez, Paris .... L 10
1973
Apr.   2—Wayne Bannister, Melbourne .... W 10
June   10—Miguel Angel Castellini, Buenos Aires ..... L 10
June   22—Miguel de Oliveire, Sao Paulo .... L 10
Aug.   3—Tony Mundine, Brisbane............ KO by 10
Sept. 28—Tony Mundine, Brisbane .... L 15
        (British Empire Middleweight Title)
Dec.   14—Tony Santiago, Port of Spain .... W 10
1974
Apr.   29—David Dakers, Belize City .... KO 3
July   10—Ike Martinez, Port of Spain .... W 10
July   11—Elisha Obed, Nassau .... L 10
Nov.   18—Battling Laavasa, Auckland .... W 10
Dec.   5—Sammy Barr, Nassau .... W 10
1975
Feb.   3—Monty Betham, Auckland................ W 10
Mar.   18—Eckhard Dagge, Berlin................. W 10
Apr.   4—Ronnie Pinder, Port of Spain .... W 10
June   2—Willie Monroe, Philadelphia .... L 10
July   24—Monty Betham, Wellington .... L 15
        (British Empire Middleweight Title)
Oct.   10—Frank Reiche, Berlin................... L 10
Nov.   29—Doc Holliday, Port of Spain .... W 10
1976
Jan.   28—Willie Monroe, Philadelphia .... L 10
Mar.   2—Ashton Antoine, Port of Spain .... W 15
June   18—Ashton Antoine, Port of Spain........... W 15
July   31—Monty Betham, Auckland............... L 15
        (British Commonwealth Middleweight Title)
1977
June   17—Michael Paul, Port of Spain .... L 15
1978
May   26—Wendell Joseph, Port of Spain .... W 15
July   14—Ashton Antoine, Port of Spain .... W 10
Nov.   4—Richie Kates, Atlantic City .... KO by 9

153

1979
Feb. 16—Wilson Perez, Oslo ....D 8
Sept. —David Cabrera, Mexico City ....L 10
Sept. 21—Marvin Johnson, Indianapolis ....L 10
Oct. 9—Lotte Mwale, London ....KO by 2
Oct. 19—Julius Noble, Chicago ....L 10
Dec. 21—Jose Baquedano, Chetumal ....KO by 2
1980
Mar. 1—Emeterio Villanueva, Bird's Isle ....W 10
Apr. 24—Elias Equillvia, Belize City ....KO 5
July 6—Roberto Cruz, Bird's Isle ....L disq. 5
Aug. 1—Ed Wilson, Port-of-Spain ....W 10
Oct. 17—Michael Paul, Port-of-Spain ....L 15
Dec. 13—Jacinto Fernandez, Parana ....KO by 3

BENNY MARQUEZ
Chicago, Ill. Featherweight
1977
Apr. 25—Santos Rodriguez, Chicago ....W 4
May 17—Alberto Collazo, Mentor ....L 6
June 11—Joe Medrano, Sterling ....W 6
July 25—Al Hughes, Chicago ....KO 1
Aug. 19—Joe Medrano, Chicago ....W 8
1978
Jan. 19—Maurice Watkins, Houston ....L 10
Jan. 23—Raton Montes, Chicago ....W 8
Mar. 16—Greg Coverson, Kalamazoo ....L 10
Mar. 31—Steve Homan, Kansas City ....L 8
Apr. 28—Alberto Collazo, Chicago ....L 10
July 21—Gustavo Martinez, Chicago ....KO 1
Sept. 9—Robert Perez, Chicago ....KO 8
1979
Mar. 24—Virgilio Legaspi, Chicago ....KO 4
May 5—Roberto Torres, Chicago ....L 10
July 30—Francisco Manzo, Chicago ....KO by 3
1980
Mar. 7—Emilio Palacios, Chicago ....W 10
Mar. 27—Roberto Perez, Chicago ....KO 3
Apr. 22—Cornelius Boza-Edwards, London ....KO by 4
June 5—Nick Furlano, Winnipeg ....L 10
July 11—Eddie Murray, Chicago ....KO by 4
July 27—Frank Newton, Omaha ....KO by 5
Aug. 21—Juan (Kid) Mesa, Los Angeles ......KO by 1
Dec. 18—Rocky Lockridge, Totowa ....KO by 3

GERMAN MARQUEZ
Laredo, Texas Middleweight
1979
Apr. 20—Norberto Rodriguez, Laredo ....KO 5
June 6—Marcus Dorsey, Laredo ....KO by 1
Aug. 15—Wilford Scypion, Beaumont ....KO by 2
1980
Oct. 14—Oscar Albarado, Laredo ....KO by 2

ADRIANO (NANI) MARRERO
Dominican Rep. Junior Welterweight
1973
Feb. 17—Julio Valdes, Santo Domingo ....W 4
Mar. 3—Inocencio Pena, Santo Domingo..........W 6
Apr. 6—Rafael Salcedo, Santo Domingo ....W 8
May 14—Guillermo Amengol, Santo Domingo .....W 8
July 16—Guillermo Amengol, Santo Domingo .....W 8
Aug. 1—Julio Valdes, Santo Domingo ....W 8
Aug. 16—Patricio Nunez, Santo Domingo..........W 8
Sept. 10—Tony Triz, Santo Domingo ....W 8
Sept. 29—Livio Nolasco, Santo Domingo ....L 12
Oct. 24—Enrique Solis, San Juan..................D 8
Nov. 12—Willie Carrasco, San Juan ....W 8
Nov. 20—Eladio Leal, Miami......................W 8
Nov. 29—Tony Sanchez, Tampa, Fla................W 8
1974
May 14—Jose Peterson, Miami Beach ....L 10
June 11—Freddy Majors, Miami Beach............KO 1
Oct. 8—Jose Peterson, Miami Beach ....W 10
1975
Feb. 25—Jose Peterson, Miami Beach ....KO 4
Mar. 18—Ike Hooks, Miami Beach ....W 10
June 28—Josue Marquez, San Juan................W 10
Aug. 5—Angel Robinson Garcia, Miami Beach....W 10
Aug. 30—Norman Sekgapane, Johannesburg........L 10
Oct. 10—Hector Thompson, Melbourne............L 10
1976
Mar. 16—Termite Watkins, Miami Beach ....W 10
Apr. 17—Jose Rosa, San Juan ....KO 5
Apr. 26—Ceferino Burbuja, Santo Domingo ....W 10
June 8—Saoul Mamby, Miami Beach ....L 10
June 13—Carlos Giminez, Santo Domingo ....W 10
Sept. 18—Josue Marquez, San Juan ....L 10
1977
Mar. 19—Antonio Cervantes, Maracay ....L 10
May 31—Saoul Mamby, Santo Domingo ....W 10
Sept. 26—Jose Batista, Santo Domingo ....W 10
Nov. 5—Antonio Cervantes, Maracay ....L 15
(WBA Junior Welterweight Title)

1978
—Zenon Silgado, Cartagena ....W 10
Oct. 12—Jimmy Heair, Memphis ....W 10
1979
Feb. 4—Lennox Blackmoore, Georgetown ....L 10
May 4—Calvin King, Santo Domingo ....KO 3
1980
Nov. 28—Enrique Sanchez, New York ....L 10
Dec. 12—Domingo Ayala, New York ....L 10

ANGEL MARRERO
Bethlehem, Pa. Bantamweight
1978
Apr. 9—Johnny Carter, Allentown ....L 4
June 4—Edwin Rivera, Allentown ....W 4
Oct. 22—Wayne Howard, Allentown ....W 4
1979
Mar. 21—Gilbert Gans, Allentown ....W 4
Sept. 11—Jose Muniz, Philadelphia ....D 4
Nov. 22—Jose Muniz, Allentown ....KO 6
1980
Mar. 22—Martin Galloza, Allentown ....KO 1
Apr. 22—Henry Brent, Staten Island ....L 6
Nov. 28—Enrique Sanchez, New York ....L 10

JOHNNY MARRONE
Bayonne, N.J. Junior Welterweight
1980
Mar. 20—Eddie Arthurs, N. Bergen ....KO 1
Sept. 24—Don Marchesani, Elizabeth ....KO 1
Dec. 27—John Passante, N. Bergen ....KO 1

DON MARSHALL
Toronto, Canada Light Heavyweight
1979
Oct. 22—Jerry Reddick, Edmonton ....KO by 1
Nov. 6—Brian Anderson, Montreal ....W 4
1980
Jan. 21—Ghyslain Deroy, Montreal ....L 6
May 31—Michel Douces, Lindsay ....W 5
Aug. 27—Randy Jackson, Edmonton ....L 6

JAMES MARSHALL
Harlem, N.Y. Junior Featherweight
1980
Feb. 8—Adonis Torres, New York ....KO by 3
Sept. 17—Edwin Oquendo, White Plains ....L 4
Dec. 20—Edwin Oquendo, New York ....KO by 1

JERRY (THE BULL) MARTIN
Philadelphia, Pa. Light Heavyweight
1976
Feb. 25—Sixto Martinez, Philadelphia ....KO 1
Apr. 13—Paul White, Philadelphia ....KO 1
June 8—Moses Robinson, Philadelphia ....W 4
Sept. 2—Moses Robinson, Philadelphia ....KO 1
Sept. 16—John Wilburn, Baltimore................W 6
1977
Apr. 14—Smokey Middleton, Landover ....KO 8
May 25—Pablo Ramos, Cleveland ....L 10
Nov. 3—Charlie Smith, Virginia Beach ....W 6
Dec. 6—Diego Roberson, Philadelphia ....KO 1
1978
June 19—Bernard McClean, Philadelphia ....W 6
Sept. 27—Ivy Brown, Philadelphia ....KO 5
Dec. 6—Jerry Celestine, Philadelphia ....W 10
Apr. 3—Don Addison, Philadelphia ....KO 4
Apr. 29—Al Bell, Indianapolis ....KO 3
July 15—Willie Taylor, Philadelphia ....KO 8
Aug. 7—Dale Grant, Atlantic City ....KO 12
Sept. 11—Leo Rogers, Philadelphia ....KO 4
Nov. 14—Jesse Burnett, Philadelphia ....W 12
Feb. 18—Billy Douglas, Upper Darby ....KO 10
May 25—James Scott, Rahway ....L 10
July 20—Eddie Mustafa Muhammad, McAfee ..KO by 10
(For WBA Light Heavyweight Title)
—Otis Gordon, London ....KO

LARRY MARTIN
Kansas City, Mo. Middleweight
1979
June 1—Jimmy Hearns, Kansas City ....KO 1
July 26—Larry Ward, Overland Park ....W 6
Oct. 30—Clint Jackson, Memphis ....KO by 2
Dec. 15—Michael Herron, Kansas City ....KO 2
1980
Feb. 23—Clarence Gilmore, Memphis ....KO 6
Apr. 17—Roosevelt Green, Chicago ....KO 2
May 15—Caveman Lee, Chicago ....KO by 2
Sept. 10—Mike Garcia, Wichita ....KO 3

154

CARLOS MARTINETTI
Argentine Featherweight
1980
Jan. 18—Hipolito Nunez, Mar del Plata .... L 10
Feb. 29—Santiago Lopez, Saenz Pena .... L 10
Oct. 24—Pedro Burki, Villa Maria .... L 10

FERNANDO MARTINEZ
Paterson, N.J. Bantamweight
1978
Aug. 2—Tony Saladen, Bayonne .... KO 2
Nov. 14—Leo Randolph, Totowa .... L 8
1979
Apr. 17—Charlie Brown, Totowa .... KO 4
June 12—Larry Adkins, Totowa .... KO 1
June 27—Jimmy Magnifico, Secaucus .... D 8
July 24—Derrik Holmes, Atlantic City .... KO by 1
1980
Aug. 2—Antonio Nieves, Totowa .... D 4

GUSTAVO MARTINEZ
Argentine Featherweight
1980
Feb. 15—Hipolito Nunez, Tucuman .... KO by 7
May 2—Antonio Zarate, Tucuman .... L 10
Oct. 3—Luis Zarate, Salta .... KO by 5

GUSTAVO MARTINEZ
Mexican Featherweight
1978
July 21—Bennie Marquez, Chicago .... KO by 1
Oct. 17—Tarcisio Gomez, Houston .... L 10
1979
July 21—Calvin Sheppard, Houston .... W 10
1980
Feb. 5—Calvin Sheppard, Houston .... W 10
Apr. 1—Francisco Marquez, Houston .... D 10
July 31—Jeff Chandler, Atlantic City .... KO by 8

JAMES MARTINEZ
Houston, Texas Junior Featherweight
1973
Mar. 5—Eddie Mitchell, Jacinto City .... KO 4
July 17—Billy Holliday, Oklahoma City .... KO 2
Aug. 30—Carlos Santos, Tampa .... D 6
Nov. 20—Earl Wilson, Little Rock .... W 4
Dec. 17—Wayne Cook, Jacinto City .... W 6
1974
Jan. 10—Rodolfo Ibarra, Houston .... KO 5
Jan. 24—Francisco Garcia, Houston .... W 8
Mar. 4—Jose de la Rocha, Dallas .... W 10
Apr. 8—Harvey Wilson, Dallas................... W 10
May 7—Domingo Luna, Oklahoma City.......... KO 6
May 9—Willie Johnson, Enid .... KO 1
May 22—Rito Torres, Oklahoma City.............. W 10
June 6—Tommy Tucker, Oklahoma City .... KO 3
June 13—Genaro Morones, Memphis.............. KO 4
Oct. 11—Johnny Moreno, San Antonio .... W 10
Nov. 23—Carlos Zarate, Los Angeles.......... KO by 7
1975
July 1—Billy Miller, Kansas City .... W 10
July 24—Kid Turazon, Topeka .... KO 9
Sept. 30—Vernon Solis, London................ KO by 7
1976
Mar. 17—Baby Kid Chocolate, Philadelphia........ L 10
May 3—Mel Johnson, Topeka .... W 10
May 13—Art Silvera, Albuquerque .... W 8
June 2—Earl Large, Topeka..................... W 10
July 27—Jose Luis Medrano, Topeka .... W 10
Oct. 6—Ray Carrington, Cleveland............... W 10
Nov. 10—William Berry, Cleveland............... W 10
1977
Mar. 27—Warren Matthews, San Antonio .... W 8
(U.S. Championship Tournament)
Apr. 10—Richard Rozelle, Miami Beach .... L 10
(U.S. Championship Tournament)
May 23—Shannon Williams, Houston .... KO 3
Oct. 1—John Morgan, Shreveport .... KO 5
Dec. 7—Albert Collazo, Cleveland .... L 10
1978
June 27—Jose Medrano, Odessa .... KO 8
July 31—Enrique Munoz, Odessa .... W 10
Sept. 19—Juan Villasana, Odessa .... KO 5
Sept. 28—Juan Rodriguez, Phoenix .... KO 7
Dec. 10 Juan Rocha, Dallas.................... W 10
1979
Mar. 13—Salvador Sanchez, San Antonio .... L 10
June 15—Reuben Castillo, Las Vegas .... L 12
(U.S. Featherweight Title)
Nov. 13—Juan Garcia, Houston .... L 10

1980
May 19—Manuel Flores, Odessa .... KO 3
July 18—Robert Mullens, Spartanburg .... L 12
Sept. 2—Roberto Elizondo, Corpus Christi .... L 10
Oct. 24—Roque Montoya, Dallas .... W 10
Nov. 11—Ruben Castillo, Houston .... D 10
Dec. 16—Gerald Hayes, Toronto .... W 10

JERRY MARTINEZ
Junior Middleweight
1979
Oct. 27—Roberto Torrez, Albuquerque .... KO 2
1980
Oct. 1—Pete Seward, Las Vegas .... KO by 4

JORGE MARTINEZ
Argentine Flyweight
1980
Feb. 14—Humberto Torres, Mendoza .... D 8
Apr. 3—Luis Gerez, Arrecifes .... L 10
Apr. 24—Hector Rosa, S. Sal de Jujuy .... KO by 7
June 6—Aldo Caldorelli, Reconquista .... D 10
July 4—Humberto Torres, Mendoza .... D 10
Aug. 15—Jose Narvaez, La Rioja .... L 10
Oct. 3—Bernabe Mendez, Trelew .... L 10

LEO MARTINEZ
Philadelphia, Pa. Middleweight
1979
Apr. 10—Atum Ali, Philadelphia .... KO 1
May 22—Mario Maldonado, Upper Darby .... L 6
1980
Jan. 24—Luis Carrasquillo, Upper Darby .... W 4
Mar. 9—Fred McMunn, Atlantic City .... L 4
July 3—Fred McMunn, Atlantic City .... L 6
Aug. 21—Bobby Czyz, Totowa .... L 8
Sept. 20—Steve Arvin, Ben Salem .... L 8
Dec. 20—Alex Ramos, Bronx .... KO by 1

LEONARDO MARTINEZ
El Paso, Featherweight
1980
Jan. 18—Justo Ruiz, El Paso .... KO 2
Mar. 7—Victor Lopez, El Paso .... KO 1
Mar. 21—Simon Fortunel, El Paso .... KO 4
May 9—Arturo Vasquez, El Paso .... TD 2
May 31—Joaquin Alvarado, El Paso .... KO 3
Sept. 11—Hernando Salinas, El Paso .... W 6
Dec. 13—Salvador Ugalde, El Paso .... L 6

ROBERTO MARTINEZ
Mexican Featherweight
1979
Mar. 17—Alejandro Romero, Mexico City .... W 4
Mar. 23—Roberto Ramos, Guadalajara .... W 10
July 25—Javier Esquival, Mexico City .... W 6
Oct. 22—Jorge Torres, Mexico City .... KO 5
1980
June 11—Juan Arias, Mexico City .... KO 5
Aug. 6—Juan Hernandez, Mexico City .... KO 2
Oct. 22—Jorge Torres, Mexico City .... KO 5

RUBEN MARTINEZ
San Diego, Calif. Junior Welterweight
1977
Mar. 20—Gonzalo Montellano, Las Vegas ...... KO by 1
July 22—Herman Montes, San Diego .... KO by 2
Oct. 13—Rocky Fukumoto, Los Angeles .... KO by 2
1978
Jan. 27—Oscar Armas, San Diego .... W 6
Feb. 7—Amie Peregrino, Honolulu .... W 8
Mar. 10—Bill Matthis, San Diego .... L 6
1979
Feb. 23—Carlos Barragon, San Diego .... D 8
Apr. 6—Eric Bonilla, San Diego .... L 8
May 4—Hedgemon Robinson, San Diego ...... KO by 1
1980
Mar. 27—Carlos Lozano, Los Angeles .... KO by 3
July 10—Tony Baltazar, Los Angeles .... KO by 1

SILVERIO MARTINEZ
Corpus Christi, Texas, Junior Featherweight
(Mexican Record 7-0)
1976
Jan. 5—Eddie Mitchell, Corpus Christi .... W 6
Apr. 20—Raul Cervantes, Corpus Christi .... KO 1
May 17—Rogelio Flores, Corpus Christi.......... KO 2
Sept. 21—Carmelio DeLeon, Corpus Christi........ W 6
Oct. 26—Robert Perry, Corpus Christi .... KO by 2
1977
Jan. 25—Victor Cid, Corpus Christi .... W 8
Mar. 22—John Morgan, Corpus Christi .... KO 3

155

Sept.	6—Freddie Harris, Houston	W	10
Oct.	3—Tom Pinner, Corpus Christi	KO by	6
Dec.	20—Scotty Foreman, New Orleans	KO by	2

1978

July	8—Chaparo Mendiola, Valle, Mexico	W	10
Sept.	16—Venturo Guerrera, San Fernando, Mex.	W	10

1979

June	1—Steve Homan, Kansas City	KO by	2
Aug.	14—Tony Rocha, Houston	KO by	3
Oct.	10—Freddy Jackson, Beaumont	L	6

1980

Feb.	28—Raymond Gonzalez, McAllen	L	8
Mar.	25—Freddie Jackson, Houston	KO by	4
Apr.	22—Carlos Lozano, Sacramento	KO by	1

TIMMY MARTINEZ
Pasadena, Calif. Lightweight
1977

Oct.	27—Lupe Amaniego, Los Angeles	KO by	1

1978

May	24—Fernando Reyes, Los Angeles	W	10

1979

May	24—Fernando Reyes, Los Angeles	W	5
May	31—Roberto Garcia, Los Angeles	L	5
June	13—Danny Patino, Las Vegas	L	8
July	26—Takashi Sugimoto, Los Angeles	TD	2
Sept.	6—Salvador Ramirez, Los Angeles	KO by	4
Oct.	18—John Montes, Jr., Los Angeles	KO by	2
Nov.	23—Robert San Jose, San Diego	W	5
Dec.	7—Willie Hall, San Diego	W	5
Dec.	19—Juan Garcia, San Diego	L	6

1980

Jan.	17—Chris Duran, Los Angeles	KO by	2

VICTOR (KID ZORRITO) MARTINEZ
Los Angeles, Calif. Welterweight
1977

Oct.	4—Leo Oliver, Oroville	KO	1
Oct.	19—Joe Russell, Las Vegas	KO	
Oct.	26—Hernando Cervantes, Las Vegas	KO	1
Oct.	29—Bert Lee, Fresno	W	6
Dec.	15—Francisco Ortega, Los Angeles	W	4
Dec.	17—Miguel De La Mora, Fresno	KO	2

1978

Mar.	3—Mike Rundell, San Diego	KO by	3
Apr.	13—Clarence Howard, Phoenix	L	8
June	2—Robert Willcot, San Diego	KO	1
June	21—Gregory Stephens, Concord	KO	7
July	12—Fernando Arechiga, Las Vegas	KO	1
Aug.	3—Howard Jackson, Los Angeles	KO by	7
Oct.	18—Gilberto Mares, Las Vegas	KO	1
Nov.	21—Mando Cordova, Las Vegas	KO	2

1979

Feb.	8—Bert Lee, Los Angeles	W	10
Mar.	21—Mario Valencia, Las Vegas	KO	1
Apr.	18—Francisco Del Toro, Las Vegas	W	10
May	9—Jessie Lara, Las Vegas	KO	2
Sept.	5—Jose Rodriguez, Las Vegas	KO	2
Dec.	10—Marcy Atencio, Las Vegas	KO	7

1980

Jan.	17—Rudy Barro, Los Angeles	KO	2
Feb.	6—J.J. Cottrell, Las Vegas	W	10
May	15—Agapito Ramirez, Los Angeles	W	10
June	11—Manny Lopez, Las Vegas	KO	4
July	2—Aundra Love, Las Vegas	KO	9
Nov.	26—Chuy Rodriguez, Mexico City	KO	3
Dec.	17—Bruce Finch, Las Vegas	KO by	1

ROBERTO MARZIALI
Argentine Middleweight
1980

May	2—Angel Caro, P.R.S. Pena	KO by	4
Aug.	22—Juan Roldan, La Villaras	KO by	1

SAMMY MASIAS
Orlando, Fla. Welterweight
Born: Nov. 23, 1952, San Antonio, Texas
1976

Sept.	14—Jose Gonzalez, Miami Beach	KO	1
Oct.	15—James Hughes, Hollywood	KO	2
Nov.	9—Don Collins, Miami Beach	KO	2
Dec.	7—Billy Vasser, Orlando	KO	1
Dec.	28—Willie O'Brien, Orlando	KO	2

1977

Jan.	1—Tiger Hall, Miami Beach	KO	5
Jan.	14—Tiger Hall, Orlando	KO	5
Jan.	25—Scott Clark, Orlando	L	8
Mar.	15—Larry Llwellyn, Miami Beach	D	4
May	6—Richie Gonzales, Miami Beach	W	4
June	17—James Hughes, Miami Beach	KO	1
July	17—Richard Gonzalez, Miami Beach	KO	1
Aug.	26—Charlie Fullard, Orlando	KO	2
Sept.	27—Cliff Johnson, Orlando	KO	3

Oct.	5—Eddie Marcelle, Port of Spain	L	8
Oct.	29—Tiger Hall, Homestead	KO	8
Nov.	22—Scott Clark, Orlando	L	10
Dec.	9—Randy Armstrong, Homestead	KO	2

1978

Jan.	17—Eddie Davis, Orlando	KO	7
Apr.	4—Daniel Levesque, North Miami Beach	W	8
May	16—Ike Hooks, Miami Beach	L	10
June	10—Henry Hall, Ocala	L	8
June	20—Ike Hooks, Miami Beach	L	10
Aug.	8—Freddie Johnson, Orlando	NC	4
Oct.	14—Harold Weston, Houston	KO by	5
Dec.	5—Dave Green, Kensington	KO by	1

1979

Feb.	9—Pete Ranzany, Sacramento	KO by	3
June	2—Rocky Fratto, Syracuse	L	10
Sept.	20—Steve Gregory, Cleveland	KO by	3
Dec.	14—Mando Ramirez, Sunrise	KO	2

1980

Feb.	29—Rocky Fratto, Rome	L	8

BRODERICK MASON
Philadelphia, Pa. Heavyweight
1977

Feb.	9—Wayne Bailey, Philadelphia	KO	1
Mar.	23—Matt Robinson, Philadelphia	W	4
Dec.	6—Leroy Diggs, Philadelphia	W	6

1978

Jan.	24—Burt Reid, Philadelphia	KO	1
May	26—Frank Williams, Trenton	KO	1
June	6—Art Savage, Philadelphia	W	6
Oct.	12—Bob Stallings, Rahway, N.J.	L	4
Oct.	20—Tyrone Harlee, Atlantic City	L	6
Dec.	12—Art Savage, Philadelphia	KO	5

1979

May	23—G. Williams, Washington, D.C.	W	4
July	3—Malik Dozier, Atlantic City	L	6
July	17—Mike Tarasewich, Atlantic City	W	6
Aug.	7—Munit Gasim, Atlantic City	KO	2
Aug.	22—Gerry Cooney, New York	KO by	4

1980

Jan.	24—Robert McFarland, Upper Darby	KO	1
Oct.	24—Roger Troupe, Philadelphia	KO	1

MONTE MASTERS
Oklahoma City, Okla. Heavyweight
1979

July	19—Mark Smith, Oklahoma City	KO	1
Dec.	15—Paul Lawson, Oklahoma City	KO	4

1980

Feb.	9—Steve Megliaccio, Oklahoma City	KO	3
Mar.	3—Larry Montgomery, Oklahoma City	KO	2
Apr.	3—Michael Ford, Oklahoma City	KO	1
June	10—Henry Johnson, Oklahoma City	NC	2
June	17—Carl Halliburton, Oklahoma City	KO	1
July	1—Otis Hardy, Oklahoma City	KO	4
July	15—Sam Jackson, Oklahoma City	KO	1
Aug.	5—Lewis Anderson, Oklahoma City	KO	2
Aug.	19—Charles Roper, Oklahoma City	KO	1
Sept.	9—Carl Bradshaw, Norman	KO	4
Sept.	25—Bruce Scott, Oklahoma City	KO	5

DON MASTERSON
Muskogee, Okla. Middleweight
1975

Dec.	2—Humphrey McBride, Oklahoma City	KO by	2
Dec.	16—Jerry McIntyre, Oklahoma City	KO by	1

1976

Jan.	6—Harold Brown, Houston	KO	3
Feb.	17—Wayne Lewis, Oklahoma City	L	4
May	18—Wayne Lewis, Oklahoma City	D	4
Oct.	25—Hank Gregory, Oklahoma City	KO by	4

1977
(Inactive)
1978

Jan.	24—Roy Taylor, Wichita	KO	2

1979

Aug.	3—Dennis Horne, Tulsa	KO by	2
Sept.	18—John McDuff, Wichita	KO	3
Nov.	1—Glen Ridgepath, Wichita	L	4
Nov.	8—Norris McKinney, Tulsa	KO by	1
Dec.	15—Tyrone Wren, Kansas City	L	6

1980

Aug.	12—Roy Taylor, Wichita	KO	1
Oct.	9—Luke Capuano, Chicago	L	10

FRANCISCO MASTRI
Puerto Rican Welterweight
1979

Oct.	19—Larry Rowland, Commack	W	4

1980

Oct.	10—Manny Sims, New York	KO by	2

ANGEL MATA
Mexican Lightweight
1977
Apr.	9—Melchor Mendoza, Mexico City	KO	5
May	20—Miguel Cruz, Ciudad Madera	KO by	8
Aug.	—Jose Luis Tapia, Mexico City	KO by	4
Nov.	30—Nacho Cabrera, Mexico City	KO	4

1978
Jan.	11—Bernal Bravo, Mexico City	KO	2
Jan.	28—Raul Molina, Mexico City	KO by	4
Feb.	21—Rancho Ramirez, Mexico City	KO	1
July	20—Roberto Villasana, Apatzingan	KO	1
Aug.	5—Melesio Perez, Mexico City	KO	3
Aug.	25—Andres Lobera, Mexico City	L	10

1979
Mar.	3—Chuy Montes, Mexico City	KO	2
Mar.	16—Negro Torres, Apatzingan	KO	1
May	12—Arturo Guzman, Mexico City	KO by	2
July	11—Juan Hernandez, Mexico City	TD	1
Sept.	19—Francisco Santilla, Mexico City	KO	5
Oct.	5—Yuyu Copala, Acapulco	L	10
Oct.	30—Rocky Ramon, San Antonio	L	10

1980
Jan.	23—Reyes Gonzalez, Mexico City	KO	2
Mar.	12—Jose Luis Escalante, Mexico City	L	10
June	7—Mauricio Aceves, Mexico City	KO	2
June	21—Jose Luis Tapia, Mexico City	KO by	8

RUDOLFO MATA
(Roy Mata Barajas)
1979
Feb.	13—Ricardo Hurtado, Phoenix	KO	2
Aug.	1—Ricardo Jiminez, Las Vegas	L	4
Aug.	15—Darrell Stovall, Phoenix	L	4
Aug.	22—Darrell Stovall, Phoenix	L	4
Oct.	19—Andy Glover, Phoenix	KO by	4

1980
Mar.	4—Mark Ibanez, Honolulu	KO by	1
Apr.	30—Daniel Cruz, Las Vegas	L	4
May	29—Bobby Krueger, Las Vegas	KO	4
June	28—Pat Jefferson, Rapid City	KO by	3
Oct.	23—Alex Celedon, Las Vegas	W	6
Oct.	29—Ronnie Romero, Las Vegas	KO by	4

LOUIS MATEO
Chicago, Ill. Welterweight
1978
Jan.	14—Jorge Mojica, Carolina	W	4

1979
Oct.	19—Robert Hughes, Chicago	L	4
Dec.	15—Eugene Jennings, Chicago	KO	1

1980
Feb.	1—Phil Batie, Chicago	KO	2
Feb.	18—Larry Porterfield, Chicago	KO	1
Mar.	3—Robert Hughes, Chicago	W	6
Mar.	28—Jerry Strickland, Chicago	KO	2
Apr.	14—Evaristo Serrano, Chicago	KO	2
May	9—Arnell Thomas, Chicago	KO	1
June	27—Larry Mayes, Chicago	W	10
Aug.	14—Randy Shields, Chicago	L	10
Sept.	22—Gary Smith, Chicago	KO	1
Dec.	11—Roosevelt Green, Chicago	KO by	7

JOSE MATOS
Newark, N.J. Lightweight
1977
Dec.	8—Gino Perez, N. Bergen	L	4

1978
June	2—Bobby Mann, Jersey City	W	4
June	29—Nino Gonzalez, N. Bergen	L	4
Sept.	9—Tony Braxton, Rahway	L	4
Nov.	16—Robert Grant, N. Bergen	L	6

1979
Oct.	27—Martin Parham, North Bergen	L	6

1980
Feb.	5—Victor Arnau, West Hartford	D	6
Mar.	4—Martin Parham, Elizabeth	L	6
May	9—Joshua King, Commack	D	6
Dec.	18—Ken Bogner, Totowa	L	6

JOHNNY MATTHEWS
Stockton, California Heavyweight
1980
Mar.	27—Jessie Aldrich, Stockton	KO	3
May	20—George O'Mara, Fresno	KO by	3

WARREN MATTHEWS
New Orleans, La. Featherweight
1972
Mar.	20—Cisco Reyes, New Orleans	W	4
Apr.	26—Cisco Reyes, New Orleans	W	4
June	6—Tony Rocha, Houston	D	6
Sept.	6—Ricky Capitano, New Orleans	KO by	2

Oct.	9—Ron Billiot, New Orleans	W	4

1973
July	11—Juan Cantu, New Orleans	L	6
Oct.	2—Gerald Bradley, New Orleans	W	6
Oct.	30—Tony Sanchez, New Orleans	L	6
Nov.	28—Cisco Reyes, New Orleans	KO	2

1974
Mar.	15—Atliano Sanchez, Alexandria	W	10
July	10—Tony Sanchez, New Orleans	W	8
July	22—Bennie McCall, New Orleans	KO	3
Dec.	13—Juan Barra, New Orleans	KO	2

1975
July	28—Frank Palafox, New Orleans	KO	3
Aug.	27—John North, New Orleans	KO	2
Sept.	2—James Busceme, Lake Charles	KO	6

1976
Mar.	8—Tony Sanchez, New Orleans	KO	1
Apr.	4—Alonso Evans, New Orleans	W	10
May	25—Roberto Quintanilla, New Orleans	W	10
July	26—Gaby Cantrera, New Orleans	W	10

1977
Mar.	27—James Martinez, San Antonio	L	8

(U.S. Championship Tournament)
Apr.	19—Bob Tjekina, Pensacola	KO	2
May	5—Willie Donahue, Mobile	KO	4
July	18—Bill Pearish, New Orleans	KO	3
Aug.	30—Hilbert Stevenson, New Orleans	KO	3
Sept.	20—Fleber Viteri, New Orleans	KO	9

1978
Feb.	27—Kenny Weldon, New Orleans	KO	6
Aug.	8—Claude Noel, Orlando	KO by	2

1979
Mar.	11—Reuben Castillo, Reno	KO by	7

(U.S. Featherweight Title)

1980
Jan.	31—Nacho Jiminez, San Carlos	W	10
Mar.	27—Juan Bautista, San Carlos	W	10
May	22—Henry Barcellano, San Carlos	KO	5
Nov.	28—Justo Garcia, San Diego	L	10

MARIO MATTHYSSE
Argentine Lightweight
1980
June	6—Hugo Diaz, Sunchales	W	10
June	19—Hugo Diaz, Esperanza	W	10
July	8—Antonio Lucena, Villa Trinidad	KO	8
Aug.	8—Felipe Baez, Sunchales	W	10
Sept.	26—Juan Saucedo, Rosario	W	10

JOE MAYE
Hartford, Conn. Heavyweight
1973
Nov.	3—Greg Osoweicki, Waterbury	KO	1
Dec.	1—Greg Osoweicki, Waterbury	KO	1

1974
June	25—Howie Hall, West Hartford	W	4
Aug.	27—Rick Wyan, New Bedford	L	6
Sept.	21—Leroy Diggs, Waterbury	KO by	2

1975
Aug.	26—Dennis Jordan, Albany	W	4
Sept.	8—Gregory Johnson, New York	L	6
Sept.	30—Dennis Jordan, Hartford	KO by	6
Nov.	21—John Dennis, Providence	L	10
Dec.	12—Greg Johnson, New York	L	4
Dec.	20—Ricky Wynn, Boston	L	10

1976
Feb.	25—Roy Williams, Philadelphia	KO by	8
May	7—Brian O'Melia, Kearny	L	8
May	21—Bill Sharkey, Brooklyn	L	8
June	24—Macka Foley, Wallingford	L	6
Sept.	28—Bill Sharkey, New York	L	4
Oct.	30—Dennis Jordan, E. Hartford	L	8
Dec.	2—Wendell Bailey, Baltimore	L	6

1977
Jan.	25—Trevor Berbick, Halifax	KO by	7
Mar.	1—Dennis Jordan, Albany	L	6
Apr.	8—Hal Carroll, Syracuse	L	8
Apr.	14—Ira Martin, Landover	L	6
Apr.	21—Matthew Saad Muhammad, Wilmington	L	10
Nov.	18—Jerry Cooney, New York	KO by	4
Nov.	25—Joe Velmure, Boston	L	6
Dec.	19—Joe Velmure, Boston	L	6
Dec.	21—Guy Casale, Brooklyn	L	6

1978
Feb.	28—Al Brooks, Hartford	D	6
Mar.	4—Al Brooks, Boston	L	6
Mar.	11—Joe Velmure, Lowell	D	8
Mar.	21—Al Brooks, New Orleans	W	4
Apr.	7—Rodell Dupree, North Bergen	KO by	3
May	2—Scott Frank, Totowa	L	6
May	13—Eddie Casey, Boston	L	6
May	26—Eddie Owens, Boston	L	8

157

June	6—Randy Mack, Philadelphia	KO by	3
Aug.	3—Steve Zouski, Boston	L	4
Sept.	9—Alfredo Evangelista, Las Cornoa	KO by	3

1979

Jan.	15—Steve Zouski, Boston	KO by	8
Feb.	3—Steve Zouski, Boston	KO by	6
Feb.	28—Don Addison, Hartford	L	6
May	10—Sylvain Watbled, Paris	KO by	3
May	25—Vinnie Smith, Portland	L	6
June	14—Tom Fisher, River Grove	KO by	6
July	28—Mate Parlov, Munich	KO by	5

1980

Apr.	21—Conroy Nelson, Hull	KO by	2
Apr.	30—Jimmy Smith, Scranton	L	6

JOEY MAYES
Cleveland, Ohio Featherweight

1976

May	5—John Alexander, Cleveland	W	4
June	28—Tony Reed, Mentor	KO	3
Sept.	8—Harry Lee, Cleveland	KO	1
Sept.	22—Tony Reed, Cleveland	KO	6
Oct.	13—John Alexander, Cleveland	KO	1
Oct.	27—Peanuts Emerson, Cleveland	L	6
Nov.	10—John Glover, Indianapolis	L	6

1977

Jan.	26—Scott Anderson, Cleveland	W	6
Mar.	8—John Green, Mentor	KO	2
Mar.	30—Bill Pearish, Cleveland	KO by	6
May	17—Isaac Vega, Mentor	L	6

1978

Jan.	12—Tony Reed, Cleveland	KO	3
Feb.	12—Ron Furlow, Cleveland	W	6
Mar.	29—James Saunders, Westlake	KO	1
Apr.	15—Mike Johnson, Mansfield	L	6

1979

Jan.	10—Rodney Kennebrew, Richfield	W	6

1980

Apr.	1—Rocky Lockridge, Totowa	KO by	2

LARRY MAYES
Miami, Oklahoma Welterweight

1977

Mar.	5—Bubba Johnson, Quapaw	KO	2
June	21—Steve Channell, Oklahoma City	KO	3
July	29—Arturo Cirillo, Wichita	W	4

1978

Jan.	24—Tony Chiaverini, Wichita	W	4
Feb.	28—Larry Jackson, Wichita	KO	2
Mar.	31—Tyrone Wren, Kansas	L	6
Aug.	3—Pat Hallacy, Wichita	KO by	2
Sept.	22—Sammy Taylor, St. Louis	KO by	6
Nov.	19—Billy Miller, Joplin	L	8

1979

May	12—Bruce Strauss, Wichita	KO by	5
Nov.	23—Cicero Blake, Kansas City	KO	4

1980

May	9—Shelvy Wilkerson, Nashville	KO	1
June	12—Claude Lancaster, Paris	KO by	5
June	27—Louie Mateo, Chicago	L	10
Aug.	22—Larry Tyson, Chicago	KO	3
Oct.	30—Herol Graham, Liverpool	KO by	4

RUBEN MAYET
San Antonio, Texas Featherweight
Managed by Tony Ayala, Sr.

1980

July	15—Juan Ortega, San Antonio	KO	3
Aug.	12—Benjamin Salis, San Antonio	KO	1
Dec.	20—Andres Tena, Bronx	KO by	1

JARVIS MAYFIELD

1980

Feb.	5—Jose Luis Baltazar, Houston	KO by	4
Mar.	18—Steve Hearon, Houston	KO by	4

BERNARD MAYS
Detroit, Michigan Middleweight

1979

Dec.	1—Sammy Myatt, Detroit	KO	2

1980

Jan.	12—Ron Vaughn, Detroit	KO	1
Jan.	24—Lamont Hopkins, Detroit	W	6
Feb.	22—Sanford Smith, Detroit	KO	1
Sept.	27—Randall Jackson, Detroit	KO	1
Nov.	1—Clifford Wills, Detroit	W	10
Nov.	14—Ponce Ortiz, Detroit	KO	3

FLOYD MAYWEATHER
Cleveland, Ohio Welterweight

1974

Nov.	21—Ron Pettigrew, Highland Park	W	4

1975

Apr.	11—Sparky Wheeler, Baltimore	KO	2
Apr.	29—Ernie Witt, Largo	KO	1
May	8—C. J. Faison, Baltimore	KO	3
May	22—Tyrone Phelps, Baltimore	KO by	2
July	23—Tyrone Phelps, Largo	W	8

1976

Apr.	21—Darrell Penn, Seattle	KO	4
Apr.	23—Bobby Orr, Flint	KO	8
July	24—Joe Armour, Kalamazoo	W	8
Aug.	22—Aundra Love, Flint	W	10
Sept.	17—Toni Ortiz, Pittsburgh	KO	3

1977

Mar.	27—Miguel Barreto, San Antonio	W	8

(U.S. Championship Tournament)

June	11—Ron Pettigrew, Jackson	KO	7
Aug.	4—Sammy Ruckard, Wyoming	KO	10
Dec.	10—Pablo Rodriguez, Grand Rapids	W	10

1978

Aug.	25—Art McKnight, Houston	W	10
Sept.	9—Ray Leonard, Providence	KO by	9

1980

Jan.	9—Calvin Straughter, Holland, Mich.	KO	3
Mar.	22—Sam Lantion, Grand Rapids	KO	4
Apr.	19—Lynn Lustig, Muskegon	KO	2
May	22—Bobby Crawford, Holland, Mich.	KO	3

BRIAN MEADE
Columbus, Ohio Middleweight

1980

June	5—Sammy Vance, Columbus	KO	3
June	24—Sammy Vance, Columbus	KO	2
Sept.	25—Bill Chaplin, Columbus	W	4

DAVE MEADOWS
Las Vegas, Nev. Middleweight

Aug.	24—Aispeli Poto, Jr., Honolulu	W	4
Aug.	31—Toshio Azuki, Honolulu	W	4
Sept.	14—Sekona Kid, Honolulu	W	4

1977

Feb.	8—Stanley Gonzalez, Honolulu	D	4
Sept.	13—Tama Elasi, Honolulu	W	4
Oct.	25—Tala Taito, Honolulu	W	5

1978

Mar.	28—Vai Afa, Honolulu	W	6
May	30—Vai Afa, Honolulu	W	6
June	20—Tony Franco, Honolulu	W	6
July	18—Terry Texidor, Honolulu	KO	3
Aug.	1—James Waire, Honolulu	KO by	3

1979

Apr.	24—Tala Taito, Honolulu	W	10
Sept.	12—Noli Galicha, Honolulu	L	10

1980

Mar.	16—Agapito Ramirez, Las Vegas	W	10
May	17—Rocky Mosley, Las Vegas	L	10
Dec.	9—Noli Galicha, Honolulu	L	8

MARK MEDEL
Jersey City, N.J. Welterweight

1979

Oct.	4—Hugo Fuat, New York	W	4
Nov.	23—Pat Esposito, New York	KO	1

1980

Jan.	25—Johnny Davis, New York	KO	2
Mar.	4—Kevin Perry, Elizabeth	KO by	1
Sept.	24—Herb Wilens, Elizabeth	KO	4
Nov.	12—Ricky Johnson, New York	KO	2

HECTOR (YOUNG CASANOVA) MEDINA
Mexican Bantamweight

1974

Aug.	15—Johnny Jensen, Los Angeles	L	5
Sept.	16—Gasper Montejo, Los Angeles	W	5
Oct.	17—Antonio Sanchez, Los Angeles	TD	4
Oct.	24—Baby Corona, Los Angeles	W	6
Nov.	7—Danny O'Campo, Los Angeles	L	6
Nov.	21—Raul Rosette, Los Angeles	L	6

1975

Feb.	7—Jose Gutierrez, Los Angeles	L	6
Feb.	13—Jose Gutierrez, Los Angeles	L	6
Feb.	27—Jose Gutierrez, Los Angeles	W	6
June	12—Gary Ferrari, Portland, Ore.	KO by	3
July	18—Mario Mendez, San Francisco	W	10

1976

Apr.	23—Juan Jose Guzman, San Bernardino	KO	5
June	24—Jose Del Rio, Los Angeles	KO by	6
Oct.	14—Alberto Sandoval, Los Angeles	L	10
Nov.	28—Richard Rozelle, Las Vegas	L	8

1977

Mar.	15—Orlando Javierto, Honolulu	W	10
Mar.	31—Alberto Sandoval, Los Angeles	KO by	3
Sept.	2—Delfino Mendoza, Obregon	W	10

Sept.	—Manuel Montiel, Obregon	KO 4

1978

Feb.	3—Lupe Hernandez, Obregon	W 10
Mar.	12—Manuel Vasquez, Obregon	KO 7
June	23—Alfonso Zamora, Obregon	KO by 6
Oct.	6—Rafael Gandarilla, Obregon	W 12

1979

Mar.	9—Fabian Palma, Obregon	W 10
Apr.	17—Jose Bautista, Houston	W 12

1980

Mar.	1—Hector Cortes, Mexico City	W 10
Apr.	26—Joaquin Acuna, Mexico City	KO by 5

JORGE MEDINA
Argentine Junior Middleweight
1980

Jan.	19—Ramon Quintana, Ciudadela	W 10
Feb.	14—Carlos Nacimiento, Posadas	D 10
Apr.	5—Hector Caceres, Buenos Aires	W 10
May	9—Lorenzo Fernandez, San Nicolas	KO 6
July	5—Bernardo Narvaez, Zarate	W 10
July	25—Ricardo Magallanes, San Nicholas	L 10
Oct.	11—Enrique Coronel, Bolivar	D 10

JUAN MEDINA
Argentine Featherweight
1980

June	6—Luis Zarate, Metan	KO by 2
July	25—Hector Rosa, San Pedro	L 10
Aug.	15—Luis Alvarez, San Pedro	L 10
Oct.	3—Marcelo Miranda, San Pedro	KO by 8

SANTOS MEDINA
Argentine Welterweight
1980

Feb.	21—Luis Lopez, Zarate	L 8
Aug.	1—Manuel Roca, Mar del Plata	L 6
Dec.	20—Luis Suarez, Federal	KO by 2

TERRY MEDLEY
Gaffney, S.C. Junior Welterweight
Born: August 19, 1956. Height: 5 ft. 8½ in.
1979

Dec.	22—James Nash, Spartanburg	KO 1

1980

July	18—Tim Norman, Spartanburg	KO 2
Sept.	6—Johnny Wilson, Lincolnton, N.C.	KO 2
Sept.	25—Larry Stevenson, Winston-Salem	KO 2
Oct.	4—Robert Hamler, Union, S.C.	KO 1
Nov.	6—Paul Gentry, Spartanburg	KO 1
Dec.	21—James McCombs, Spartanburg	KO 1

REY MELENDEZ
Dominican Rep. Junior Featherweight
(Previous Record Unavailable)
1979

Mar.	31—Sung-Jun Kim, Seoul	D 15
	(WBC Junior Featherweight Title)	
Oct.	21—Sung-Jun Kim, Seoul	L 15
	(WBC Junior Featherweight Title)	

1980

Aug.	9—Hilario Zapata, Caracas	L 15
	(For WBC Junior Flyweight Title)	

MARK MELLO
Dracut, Mass. Junior Welterweight
1977

Oct.	27—Dave Ramalho, Portland	KO by 2

1978

Nov.	23—Ralph Dumont, Portland	L 6

1979

Mar.	29—Danny Ferris, Cohoes	KO by 1
May	19—Ralph Doucette, Quincy	L 4
June	29—Danny Ferris, Cranston	KO by 2
Oct.	27—Jack O'Neill, Fitchburg	KO by 1
Dec.	15—Freddie Picotte, Kittery	KO by 1

1980

Feb.	26—Jack Morrell, Woburn	KO by 3

EDDY MELO
Canadian Light Heavyweight
1978

Mar.	7—Joe Mainfils, Montreal	KO 1
Mar.	14—Billy Avens, Montreal	KO 1
Apr.	26—Frank Bullard, Montreal	KO 2
May	15—Otto Inglesberger, Verdun	KO 2
June	5—John Powell, Montreal	KO 1
June	27—Kervin Moss, Montreal	KO 4
Aug.	15—Roland Cousin, Montreal	KO 2
Aug.	31—Ken Blackwell, Hull	KO 1
Sept.	12—Gary Broughton, Bradford	W 8
Oct.	31—Fernand Marcotte, Quebec	W 10
Dec.	19—Gerald Bouchard, Montreal	KO 3

1979

Jan.	23—Pablo Rodriguez, Montreal	KO 1
Mar.	13—Jean-Claude LeClair, Montreal	KO 1
May	25—Bonifacio Avila, Montreal	KO 6
June	26—Fernand Marcotte, Montreal	L 12
Oct.	2—Ali Perez, Montreal	KO 9
Nov.	6—Vinnie Curto, Montreal	L 10
Nov.	27—Les Riggins, Vancouver	KO 6
Dec.	23—Marciano Bernardi, Verdun	KO 2

1980

Feb.	12—Nat King, Montreal	KO 3
Mar.	11—Gary Summerhays, Montreal	KO by 11
	(For Canadian Light Heavyweight Title)	
Apr.	21—Jimmy Hearns, Hull	KO 2
June	20—Fernand Marcotte, Montreal	D 10
Oct.	28—Lancelot Innis, Montreal	D 10
Dec.	9—Wayne Caplette, Montreal	W 8

MANUEL MELON
New York Middleweight
1976

June	28—A.J. Fermin, New York	KO 2
July	26—Joe Grady, New York	D 6
Aug.	27—Joe Grady, New York	W 4

1977

Apr.	15—Tyrone Phelps, New York	W 6
June	6—Austin Killeen, Peabody	W 4
June	22—John LoCicero, New York	W 4
Nov.	30—Reggie Ford, White Plains	L 8

1978
(Inactive)
1979

Nov.	23—Carlos Betancourt, New York	W 8

1980

Aug.	27—Carlton Swift, Elizabeth	W 8

JULIO MELONE
Argentine Featherweight
1980

Mar.	21—Oscar Alvarenga, Rosario	W 10
Apr.	17—Jorge P. Gomez, Rio IV	W 10
May	—Juan Zuniga, Buenos Aires	L 10
May	30—Emilcio Ortiz, Rio IV	W 10
Aug.	8—Oscar Alvarenga, Cordoba	W 10
Sept.	26—Jose I. Funes, Pilar	W 12
Oct.	31—Oscar Albarracan, Cordoba	W 12
Dec.	5—Luis Zarate, Salta	W 10

BERNABE MENDEZ
Argentine Junior Featherweight
1980

Sept.	5—Luis Piccioti, Trelew	KO 5
Oct.	3—Jorge Martinez, Trelew	W 10

HORACIO MENDEZ
Argentine Welterweight
1980

Mar.	7—Juan Namuncura, Cutralco	KO by 7
Apr.	11—Hugo Diaz, Bahia Blanca	W 8
Apr.	24—Raul Torres, Bahia Blanca	D 8
Aug.	1—Adolfo Rossi, Dariaux	L 8
Aug.	22—Jorge Palai, Bahia Blanca	L 6
Dec.	18—Ramon Traba, Bahia Blanca	L 6

JULIO MENDEZ
Mexico City, Mexico Lightweight
1978

Jan.	12—Al Fletcher, Incline Village	KO by 4
June	21—Arturo Leon, Las Vegas	KO by 7
Aug.	2—Willie Daniels, Las Vegas	W 6
Sept.	13—Jose Osuna, Las Vegas	KO by 2

1979

Jan.	29—Alfredo Carranza, Los Angeles	W 8
Mar.	7—Willie Daniels, Las Vegas	W 8
Mar.	22—Chuy Rodriguez, Los Angeles	KO by 1
July	30—Al Guevara, Chicago	W disq. 5

1980

Apr.	6—Ramon Gonzalez, Houston	L 10
June	11—Ricardo Jiminez, Las Vegas	KO by 2
Sept.	7—Fitzroy Guissippi, Bird's Isle	L 10

OSCAR (CACHIN) MENDEZ
Argentine Lightweight
1980

Feb.	1—Hector Carrasquilla, Mar del Plata	W 10
May	9—Jesus Romero, S. Sal. de Jujuy	L 12
	(Lost Argentine Lightweight Title)	
June	27—Victor Escobar, P.R.S. Pena	KO by 0

159

OMAR MENDOZA
Argentine Featherweight
1980
Feb. 9—Domingo Casco, P.R.S. Pena .... KO by 5
Mar. 9—Hector Ferreira, Gral Pinedo .... W 6
May 23—Hipolito Nunez, Villa Angela .... L 10
Sept. 6—Benicio Sosa, Villa Angela .... L 10

RUBEN MENDOZA
Argentine Welterweight
1980
Feb. 15—Victor Escobar, P.R.S. Pena .... L 8
May 9—Jorge Paredes, Formosa .... L 10
June 27—Juan Galvez, Rosario .... L 10

RAY MENEFEE
Lincoln, Nebr. Lightweight
1978
June 2—Jimmy Blevins, Kansas City .... L 4
Sept. 18—Paul Goseland, Wichita .... L 4
Oct. 6—Kareem Ali, Kansas City .... KO 4
Oct. 25—C.B. Brown, Omaha .... KO by 3
Dec. 15—Kareem Ali, Omaha .... KO 2
1979
Jan. 19—Wardell Williams, Kansas City .... L 6
June 1—Wardell Williams, Kansas City .... L 6
Aug. 3—Sylvester Price, Omaha .... L 5
Aug. 16—Chris Johnson, North Platte .... L 6
Dec. 20—Jerry Magdalena, Wichita .... L 4
1980
Mar. 16—Mark Villa, Omaha .... W 8
Mar. 26—Kenny Moody, N. Platte .... KO 4
Aug. 15—Tim Lucero, Denver .... L 6

JESUS (YAQUI) MENESES
Mexican Heavyweight
1978
Jan. 28—Elias Equihua, Mexico City .... KO 2
Apr. 8—Jorge (Martillo) Flores, Mexico City ..... KO 5
May 19—Polo Najera, Guadalajara .... L 10
June 14—Roberto Ramirez, Mexico City .... KO by 3
July 8—Herminio (Loba) Ramirez, Mexico City KO by 3
1979
May 9—Earl McLeay, Las Vegas .... KO 5
May 30—Korosetta Kid, Honolulu .... KO by 5
July 4—Walter Cloud, Las Vegas .... KO 3
July 11—Leroy Caldwell, Las Vegas .... KO by 5
Aug. 16—Lee Holliman, Las Vegas .... L 6
Sept. 19—Chuck Gardner, Las Vegas .... KO 5
Nov. 3—Ed (Too Tall) Jones, Las Cruces .... L 6
1980
Jan. 18—Tony Perea, El Paso .... L 6
Apr. 11—Bash Ali, San Jose .... L disq. 8
Apr. 23—Anthony Davis, Las Vegas .... KO by 4

BERNARDO MERCADO
Colombian Heavyweight
Born: July 16, 1953, Monteria, Colombia
1975
Nov. 15—Harry Washington, Los Angeles .... KO 1
Dec. 11—Kenny Charles, Los Angeles .... KO 1
1976
Jan. 8—Marvin Johnson, Los Angeles .... KO 1
Feb. 12—Dave Martinez, Los Angeles .... KO 3
Feb. 26—Mark White, Reno .... KO 1
May 10—Manuel Ramos, Albuquerque............ KO 5
Aug. 19—Johnny Mack, Nevada .... W 8
Sept. 22—Bob Smith, Las Vegas .... KO 1
Sept. 28—James J. Woody, New York .... KO 3
Oct. 7—Earl McClean .... KO 1
Oct 22—Dan Johnson .... KO 6
Nov. 3—Johnny Pouha, Las Vegas............... KO 1
1977
Feb. 15—Paul Solomon, Sacramento .... KO 1
Mar. 10—Dan Johnson, Los Angeles .... KO 7
Apr. 29—Randy Stephens, Fort Worth .... KO 2
May 13—Horace Robinson, New York .... KO 1
July 22—Bob Smith, Cartagena .... KO 2
Sept. 29—Roger Russell, New York .... KO 1
Nov. 14—Muhammad Ali, Bogota .... Exh. 4
Nov. 18—Fili Moala, Las Vegas .... KO 8
1978
Feb. 24—Horace Robinson, Las Vegas .... W 10
June 22—John Tate, New York .... KO by 2
Oct. 22—Mike Weaver, Reno .... KO by 5
1979
Apr. 3—Trevor Berbick, Halifax .... KO 1
May 25—Fili Moala, San Diego .... KO 6
Aug. 3—Henry Clark, Santa Monica .... W 10
—Tony Pulu, Salt Lake City .... KO 5
1980
Feb. 2—Tony Pulu, Salt Lake City .... KO 8
Mar. 8—Earnie Shavers, Great Gorge .... KO 7

ELEONCIO MERCEDES
Mexican Flyweight
1978
July 2—Pee Man Daryl Jones, Stockton .... W 6
July 13—Juan Garcia, Los Angeles .... W 6
Aug. 10—Joey Olivo, Los Angeles .... L 10
Aug. 30—Aaron Morua, Las Vegas .... L 10
1979
Mar. 10—Adelaido Galinda, Los Angeles .... L 10
Dec. 21—Jose Gallegos, Reynosa .... L 10
1980
Sept. 6—Rafael Morales, Mexico City .... W 10

VITO MEREDITH
Honolulu, Hawaii Welterweight
1977
Oct. 25—Edward Gouveis, Honolulu .... KO 1
Nov. 29—Stanley Gonsalves, Honolulu .... KO 1
1978
Apr. 25—Amie Pellegrino, Honolulu .... W 6
1979
Jan. 30—Alfredo Logan, Honolulu .... L 5
June 19—Kazunori Shiratori, Honolulu .... KO 5
July 24—Armando Ramirez, Honolulu .... KO by 2
Oct. 9—Julio Alfonso, Honolulu .... KO 1
1980
Feb. 19—Mark Ibanez, Honolulu .... KO by 2
May 12—Katsuhiro Okubo, Honolulu .... KO by 2

JUAN MERLO
Argentine Junior Welterweight
1980
Apr. 11—Julio Duarte, Gral Madariaga .... KO 7
May 23—Roberto Alfaro, Mendoza .... L 12
(For Argentine Junior Welterweight Title)

TOMMY MEROLA
Newark, N.J. Junior Middleweight
1979
Sept. 18—Ray Rosa, E. Rutherford .... KO 2
Oct. 30—Ralph Dumont, Totowa .... KO 1
1980
Jan. 8—Billy Carrabello, Totowa .... W 4
Mar. 8—Charles Young, Great Gorge .... KO 2
Apr. 1—Billy Carrabello, Totowa .... W 6
Apr. 24—Mike Grant, Totowa .... KO 2
May 22—Dan Staehle, Totowa .... W 6
June 19—Harold White, Totowa .... KO 1
Sept. 18—Pedro Acevedo, Totowa .... KO 1
Oct. 16—Bobby Czyz, Totowa .... KO by 2

JUAN (KID) MESA
Las Vegas, Nev. Junior Featherweight
1977
Sept. 23—Elias Rodriguez, Tucson .... KO 3
Oct. 4—Terry Allen, Oroville .... L 4
Oct. 13—Valentin Holguin, Los Angeles .... L 4
Oct. 19—Davey White, Las Vegas .... W 6
Oct. 27—Valentin Holguin, Los Angeles .... W 4
Nov. 3—Horacio Pintado, Los Angeles .... KO 1
Nov. 18—Carlos Ortiz, San Diego .... L 4
Dec. 16—Carlos Ortiz, San Diego .... KO 1
1978
Apr. 28—Rodolfo Ambriza, San Diego .... W 4
May 10—Adan Aguilar, Las Vegas .... KO 1
June 14—Jose Martin Garcia, Las Vegas .... KO 1
June 28—Pascual Villareal, Bakersfield .... KO 2
July 5—Alfonso Cirillo, Las Vegas .... KO 1
Aug. 2—William Berry, Las Vegas .... L 10
Nov. 15—Jose Luis Lara, Las Vegas .... KO 5
Nov. 22—Mauro Fuentes, Phoenix .... KO 2
Dec. 12—Leonel Valencia, Sacramento .... KO 2
1979
Jan. 2—James Martinez, Phoenix .... W 10
Jan. 30—Noel Arriesgado, Honolulu .... W 10
Mar. 21—Jose Cruz, Las Vegas .... KO 4
June 14—Rosendo Ramirez, Las Vegas .... KO 5
Aug. 17—Humberto Lara, Los Angeles .... KO 4
Oct. 3—Mucio Nava, Las Vegas .... KO 2
Oct. 24—Carlos Cantu, Las Vegas .... KO 3
Nov. 9—Roy Hernandez, Los Angeles .... KO 1
1980
Jan. 20—Simon Fortunel, Tucson .... KO 2
Mar. 6—Ruben Moreno, Los Angeles .... KO 6
Mar. 26—Jorge Altamirano, Las Vegas .... KO 3
May 22—Alex Garcia, Los Angeles .... KO 3
June 26—Carlos Mendoza, Los Angeles .... L 10
Aug. 21—Francisco Marquez, Los Angeles .... KO 1
Oct. 9—Pedro Chavez, Los Angeles .... KO 1
Nov. 21—Brujo Rodriguez, Los Angeles .... W 10

Dec. 19—Luis Avila, Las Vegas .... KO 6

TONY MESORACA
Philadelphia, Pa. Light Heavyweight
1979
Apr. 14—Dennis Haggerty, New Orleans .... KO 3
May   12—Daryl Freeman, Atlantic City .... KO 2
July   3—Billy Early, Atlantic City .... KO 3
July 24—Harry Fryar, Atlantic City .... L 4
Oct. 30—Sonny Grooms, Upper Darby .... KO 3
Dec.   4—Mike Grant, Philadelphia .... KO 2
1980
Feb. 24—Harry Fryar, Atlantic City .... W 6
May   22—Tommy McNeece, Totowa .... KO 2
July 17—Dave Bird, Totowa .... KO 8
Aug. 28—Henry Hearns, Las Vegas .... W TD 5
Nov.   1—Dwight Braxton, Atlantic City .... KO by 6

RICK MEYER
Colombian Light Heavyweight
1979
May   21—Hans Stoffregen, Belleville .... L 4
July 17—Wood Pruitt, Belleville .... KO 2
Sept. 25—Jim Flynn, Belleville .... W 6
Nov. 27—George Goforth, Belleville .... L 6
1980
Jan. 21—George Goforth, St. Charles .... D 4
May   12—Arthur Pruitt, Cape Girardeau .... L 6
Oct.   7—Earl Thomas, St. Charles .... W 4

JOHNNY MEYERS
Warren, Ohio Welterweight
1979
July   6—Dave Myrick, Dayton .... W 4
Sept. 22—Marvin Ladson, Winston-Salem ...... KO by 2
1980
Jan. 24—Jeff White, Detroit .... W 4
May   3—Darrell Green, Canton .... W 6
Aug. 20—Dale Gordon, Las Vegas .... W 6
Sept. 9—Dale Gordon, Warren .... W 6
Oct. 28—Curtis Burkes, Warren .... W 6

LARRY MEYERS
Los Angeles, Calif. Middleweight
1977
Apr. 28—Don Vaskovic, Los Angeles .... L 5
May   20—Greg Stephens, San Diego .... KO by 3
1978
(Inactive)
1979
Jan. 11—Rodney Harvey, Los Angeles .... KO 5
Jan. 25—Enrique Silva, Los Angeles .... L 6
Feb. 27—Kenny Crooms, San Carlos .... KO by 4
June 27—Kenny Crooms, Los Angeles .... KO by 2
Aug. 17—Rafael Corona, San Diego .... L 4
Oct.   3—Rudy Graves, Las Vegas .... L 4
Oct. 18—Sammy NeSmith, Phoenix .... KO by 1
1980
Jan. 17—Tony Cerda, Los Angeles .... L 6
Mar. 26—Mario Luna, Costa Mesa .... L 6
May   15—Steve Moyer, Los Angeles .... L 6
Sept. 11—Larry Goodman, El Paso .... KO by 6
Oct. 22—Kenny Hodge, Santa Monica .... KO 2
Nov. 29—Jeff McCracken, Los Angeles .... KO by 4

LEONCIO MEZA
Mexican Junior Welterweight
1978
Mar. 29—Jimmy Ligons, Las Vegas .... L 8
Apr. 12—Don Juan Cornelius, Las Vegas .... KO 4
May   10—Jose Osuna, Las Vegas .... W 8
May   25—Herman Montes, Los Angeles .... L 10
July 20—Frankie Baltazar, Los Angeles .... KO by 5
Nov. 21—Tony Martinez, Las Vegas .... KO 6
1979
July 16—Robert Vasquez, Bakersfield .... L 10
July 25—Nick Alfaro, Las Vegas .... W 10
Sept. 12—Idika Nsofor, Las Vegas .... L 8
1980
Apr. 16—Jose Osuna, Las Vegas .... KO by 5
Aug. 14—Johnny Lira, Chicago .... KO by 4

MIGUEL MEZA
Los Angeles, Calif. Featherweight
1974
Sept. 7—Ruben Coria, Richmond .... D 6
Oct.   3—Yosh Shikauchi, Los Angeles .... W 6
Nov.   2—German Lopez, Los Angeles .... D 5
1975
Aug. 28—Carlos Garcia, Los Angeles .... D 5
Sept. 00—Delfino Rodriguez, Los Angeles .... L 4
Oct. 16—Alex Cota, Los Angeles .... W 6
Dec. 17—Reuben Castillo, Las Vegas .... L 6

1976
Apr. 15—Roman Contreras, San Jose............. L 10
July 10—Manuel Lujan, San Diego............... L 8
Aug. 12—Manuel Lujan, San Diego .... D 10
Oct. 29—Manuel Lujan, Los Angeles.............. D 12
Dec. 16—Bobby Chacon, Los Angeles .... KO by 3
1977
June 21—Ronnie McGarvey, Landover .... KO by 6
Oct. 15—Ruben Castillo, Palm Springs .... L 10
Dec. 15—Fel Clemente, Stockton .... W 10
1978
Jan. 19—Fel Clemente, Stockton .... L 12
Feb. 23—Frank Baltazar, Los Angeles .... KO by 4
Apr. 29—Diego Alcala, Los Angeles .... L 10
June 21—Jose Resendiz, Concord .... W 10
Sept. 6—William Berry, Las Vegas .... L 10
Sept. 19—Reynaldo Zaragoza, Stockton .... KO 7
Nov. 27—Juan Escobar, Bakersfield .... L 12
1979
Mar.   6—Jose Caba, Honolulu .... L 10
Aug. 28—Rolando Navarette, Honolulu .... KO by 7
1980
Apr. 24—Johnny Sato, Stockton .... L 10
July   3—Juan Escobar, Los Angeles .... KO by 2
Sept. 1—Jose Canizales, Laredo .... KO by 2

STEVE MICHALERYA
Allentown, Pa. Junior Middleweight
Managed by John Florio
1975
Aug. 25—Greg Joiner, Allentown .... W 4
Dec. 11—Tom Brown, Allentown .... KO 1
1976
Jan. 29—Smiley Williams, Easton .... W 4
Apr. 15—Pee Wee Murphy, Allentown .... W 4
May   20—Daryl Lampkin, Allentown .... L 4
Aug. 26—Fred Robinson, Allentown .... W 4
Oct.   7—Smiley Williams, Allentown .... KO 3
1977
Feb.   3—Daryl Lampkin, Allentown .... L 4
May   14—Robert Hart, Allentown .... KO 1
July 14—Kevin Moefield, Allentown .... KO by 6
1978
Feb. 27—(Irish) Johnny Sears, New York City .....W 8
Apr.   9—Elliot Freeman, Allentown .... W 8
June   4—James Anderson, Allentown .... W 8
Sept. 20—Johnny Turner, Scranton .... KO by 1
Oct. 22—Kevin Moefield, Allentown .... W 8
Nov. 16—Josef Nsubuga, Copenhagen .... KO by 4
1979
Feb.   3—Tony Edward, Allentown .... KO 3
Mar. 17—Rocky Fratto, Elmira .... L 10
Sept. 25—Dave Green, London .... KO by 3
Oct. 26—Rocky Fratto, Rochester .... L 10
1980
Jan. 30—C.J. Faison, Allentown .... KO 3
Mar. 22—Elwood Townsend, Bethlehem .... KO 2
May   23—Mike Baker, Bethlehem .... W 10
Sept. 10—Carlos Santos, San Remo .... KO by 8

MIKE MICHAUD
East Meadow, L.I., N.Y. Welterweight
1975
Sept. 22—Julio Garcia, New York.................. W 4
Oct. 20—Don Shamberger, New York .... KO 2
Nov. 26—Marcos Larios, Commack .... KO 6
1976
Jan. 24—Charlie Benjamin, New York............ W 4
Mar. 31—Heriberto Vasquez, Uniondale .... KO 1
Apr. 28—Juan Cantres, New York .... L 6
June   2—George Fakaris, New York............... KO 5
Sept. 20—Dick Ecklund, Peabody .... L 8
Nov.   5—Poppy Davis, New York .... D 6
Dec. 20—Julio Garcia, Harlem .... L 8
1977
Feb. 18—Lloyd Blake, New York .... KO 7
Mar.   1—Curtis Phillips, Albany .... KO 3
Apr. 21—Lloyd Blake, Dover .... W 8
1978
Feb.   4—Justice Ortiz, New York .... L 6
Apr. 21—Johnny Davis, Albany .... KO 6
Dec. 15—Danny McAloon, White Plains .... L 8
1979
Apr.   6—Jesse Rogers, Albany .... KO 3
June 24—Mike Wyant, Cincinnati .... KO by 8
Oct.   3—George Fakaris, Brooklyn .... W 10
1980
Jan.   8—Nino Gonzalez, Totowa .... KO by 7
Mar. 01—Jaime Rodriguez, Fall River .... W 8
June 20—Johnny Turner, New York .... KO by 8
Nov.   8—Johnny Bumphus, Lake Tahoe .... KO by 1

161

RALPH MIFKA
Scranton, Pa. Middleweight
1976
Mar. 31—Mose Robinson, Scranton .... KO 3
1977
Sept. 28—Diego Roberson, Scranton .... L 6
1978
July 18—Bill Connell, Totowa .... KO by 2
Sept. 20—Wallace McFarland, Scranton .... W 6
Oct. 25—Joe Stock, Scranton .... W 6
Nov. 22—Pancho Stratton, Scranton .... W 6
1979
Apr. 25—Kid Samson, Scranton .... W 6
Sept. 19—Guy Gargan, Scranton .... L 6
Oct. 24—Danny Long, Scranton .... L 6
Nov. 21—Feliciano Cintron, Scranton .... D 6
Dec. 12—Dan Staehle, Scranton .... W 6
1980
Feb. 27—Dalton Swift, Scranton .... KO 2
Mar. 26—Danny Long, Scranton .... L 8
Apr. 30—Ernie Johnson, Scranton .... KO 3
May 28—Steve Arvin, Scranton .... W 8
Sept. 10—Ernie Gladney, Scranton .... W 8
Oct. 29—Tony Tassone, Scranton .... KO 5
Nov. 22—Steve Small, Scranton .... L 8

DON MILLER
Bridgeport, Conn. Junior Middleweight
1980
May 23—Robert Davis, Hartford .... KO by 4
Sept. 12—Abdul Sanda, Hartford .... KO by 3
Oct. 14—Jack Johns, W. Hartford .... D 4
Oct. 16—Earl Hargrove, Revere .... KO by 2
Nov. 25—Randy Davio, Springfield .... KO 5

ELLIS MILLER
Welterweight
1979
Aug. 10—Alviar Benros, San Diego .... KO by 1
1980
Nov. 5—Reynaldo Roque, San Diego .... L 4
Dec. 19—Jerry Ballon, San Diego .... KO 3

FRANKIE MILLS
Liberty, Ind. Welterweight
1978
June 21—Donnie Garrett, Detroit .... KO by 2
July 22—Danny Myers, Knoxville .... KO by 3
Oct. 17—Rick Nogle, Canton .... L 6
Nov. 7—Tom Tarantino, Waukesha .... KO by 3
1979
Sept. 18—Mike Blunt, Dayton .... L 4
Oct. 11—Tyrone Wren, Kansas City .... L 6
Oct. 18—Jim Oillers, Struthers .... L 4
Nov. 3—Larry McCall, Owensboro .... L 8
1980
Jan. 21—Richard House, St. Charles .... KO by 2
May 16—Ken Heflin, Lexington .... KO 3
May 22—Billy Watkins, Jr., Holland, Mich .... KO by 3
June 27—Chris Linson, Chicago .... KO by 2

RICK MILLS
San Diego, Calif. Heavyweight
1977
Apr. 29—Kelly Perkins, San Diego .... KO 3
1978
Apr. 14—Rocky Jones, San Diego .... W 5
May 19—Elliott Bryant, San Diego .... KO 3
Aug. 25—Rahim Muhammad, San Diego .... W 6
Aug. 29—Bashir Wadud, Pico Rivera .... L 6
1979
June 27—Marlyn Johnson, Los Angeles .... KO 1
1980
Mar. 21—John Ellis, San Bernardino .... W 5
Apr. 11—Alf Coffin, Los Angeles .... KO 3
July 16—Bashir Wadud, San Diego .... L 8

TERRY MIMS
Cleveland, Ohio Heavyweight
1977
Aug. 12—Phil Brozier, Barberton .... KO 1
Nov. 2—Gus Turner, Cleveland .... KO 1
Dec. 7—Lamar Robinson, Cleveland .... W 4
1978
Jan. 12—Vic Brown, Cleveland .... KO 1
Feb. 12—Donnie Sherman, Cleveland .... W 6
Mar. 2—Tim Johnson, Cleveland .... KO 1
Mar. 16—Rufus Brassell, Cleveland .... W 10
Apr. 6—Leroy Boone, Cleveland .... KO by 4
Sept. 26—Mike Dokes, Miami Beach .... L 8
Nov. 30—Duane Bobick, Indianapolis .... KO by 7
1979
May 16—Randy Mack, Las Vegas .... L 10

1980
Jan. 25—Alfio Righetti, Bologna .... KO 1
May 22—Domenico Adinolfi, Bologna .... KO by 4

FRANKIE MINIGAN
Rochester, N.Y. Welterweight
1977
Nov. 19—Bubba Chavis, Syracuse .... KO 3
Dec. 13—Jimmy Corkum, Cohoes .... L 8
1978
Mar. 25—Donald Johnson, Syracuse .... L 6
May 5—Miguel Hernandez, Brooklyn .... KO by 1
July 15—Tyrone Phelps, Alexandria Bay .... L 6
Aug. 12—Tyrone Phelps, Alexandria Bay .... W 6
Sept. 16—Tyrone Phelps, Elmira .... L 6
1979
Mar. 2—Patrick Maloney, Albany .... L 8
Mar. 17—Arseneo Green, Elmira .... L 6
Apr. 14—Sanford Ricks, Syracuse .... L 6
June 2—Bobby Hughes, Syracuse .... W 8
July 13—Tim LaValley, Rochester .... W 6
Oct. 26—Gerald Clark, Rochester .... L 6
Nov. 21—Ricky Johnson, Scranton .... L 6
1980
Jan. 19—Tim LaValley, Syracuse .... L 6
Feb. 28—Marlon Starling, Hartford .... KO by 4
Apr. 19—Norman Jones, Syracuse .... KO 6
Apr. 30—Kevin Rooney, Scranton .... KO by 5
July 25—Benji Goldstone, Rochester .... W 6
Aug. 18—Fernando Fernandez, Boston ....W 10
Sept. 23—Ghyslain Deroy, Montreal .... KO by 4
Oct. 28—Johnny DeGrazio, Montreal .... KO 3

RAMON MIRABAL
Argentine Lightweight
1980
May 9—Rafael Zalazar, Rio III .... W 10
May 23—Jorque Talquenca, Mendoza .... W 10

MARCELO MIRANDA
Argentine Featherweight
1980
Mar. 14—Raul Perez, La Rioja .... L 10
Apr. 24—Roberto Haidar, S. Sal. de Jujuy .... KO 7
May 9—Adolfo Felice, S. Sal. de Jujuy .... KO 7
May 23—Ramon Dominguez, S. Sal. de Jujuy .. KO by 3
July 18—Omar Gonzalez, San Pedro .... D 10
Aug. 1—Hector Lopez, S. Sal. de Jujuy .... W 10
Aug. 29—Armando Perez, S. Sal. de Jujuy ...... W 10
Sept. 12—Dacio Perez, S. Sal. de Jujuy .... KO 7
Oct. 3—Juan Medina, S. Sal. de Jujuy .... KO 8

MARIO MIRANDA
Barranquilla, Colombia Featherweight
Born: April 15, 1959
1979
June 9—Edelmiro Cassiani, Barranquilla .... W 6
Nov. 4—Pablo Vizcaino, Barranquilla .... KO 7
Feb. 23—Jaime Ricardo, Barranquilla .... KO 4
Mar. 29—Humberto Castilla, Cartagena .... W 10
May 18—Francisco Castro, Barranquilla .... KO 5
June 27—Manuel Gonzalez, Barranquilla .... KO 2
Aug. 14—Raul Silva, Barranquilla .... KO 8
Oct. 31—Armando Perez, Barranquilla .... KO 11
(Won Colombian Featherweight Title)

BEN MITCHELL
Columbus, Ohio Light Heavyweight
1979
Mar. 27—Rick Jester, Michigan .... KO by 2
July 2—Sam Bryant, Columbus .... KO 2
Nov. 27—Pete Henry, Columbus .... KO 6
Dec. 28—Pete Henry, Columbus .... KO 4
1980
Feb. 18—Ernie Singletary, Upper Darby .... L 8
Apr. 30—Rusty Rosenberger, Youngstown .... KO 2
Sept. 10—Lindell Holmes, Detroit .... KO by 3

RANDY MITCHEM
Junior Welterweight
1979
Dec. 12—Jeff Passero, Washington, D.C. ...... KO by 5
1980
Aug. 21—Bob Harvey, Halifax .... KO by 6
Sept. 6—Charley Brown, Lincolnton .... KO 4
Dec. 21—Sammy Horne, Spartanburg .... L 6

CALVIN MOBLEY
Honolulu, Hawaii Middleweight
1979
Apr. 24—Bernie D'Zurella, Hilo .... W 4

May 15—Bernie D'Zurella, Honolulu .... W 4
May 30—Bernie D'Zurella, Honolulu .... W 5
Sept. 1—Carl Poff, Hilo .... KO 3
1980
July 22—Moses Halafuka, Honolulu .... KO by 5

KEVIN MOFIELD
Philadelphia, Pa. Middleweight
1974
Aug. 19—Ron Branch, Philadelphia .... KO by 2
Nov. 12—John Florio, Philadelphia .... L 4
1975
(Inactive)
1976
Oct. 7—Sam Hailstock, Allentown .... KO by 3
Oct. 14—Dan Snyder, Wilmington .... L 4
1977
Feb. 5—Johnny Cooper, Bristol .... L 4
July 14—Steve Michalerya, Allentown .... KO 6
Sept. 15—Mike Picciotti, Upper Darby .... L 6
1978
Jan. 31—Mike Picciotti, Upper Darby .... D 6
Apr. 10—Mike Picciotti, Philadelphia .... L 8
Oct. 22—Steve Michalerya, Allentown .... L 8
Oct. 28—Angel Espada, San Juan .... KO by 4
1979
Mar. 28—Wilson Bell, Baltimore .... L 8
1980
May 1—Danny Long, Dorchester .... L 10

JORGE MOJICA
Puerto Rican Lightweight
1978
Jan. 14—Rocky Mateo, Carolina, P.R. .... L 4
May 13—Jose L. Santana, Carolina, P.R. .... W 4
July 1—Mao de la Rosa, Curacao .... L 10
1979
Feb. 26—Antonio Cruz, Santo Domingo .... L 10
Apr. 28—Manuel Jiminez, Trujillo .... KO by 5
1980
Oct. 9—Luis Resto, Rio Piedras .... KO by 8

JOHN MOLANDER
Huntington, N.Y. Middleweight
Born: November 16, 1951
1975
May 23—John Capobianco, Commack .... KO by 6
1976-1978
(Inactive)
1979
Oct. 3—Ali Gregory, Brooklyn .... KO 3
1980
Jan. 19—Malik Muhammad, Hempstead .... KO 1
Mar. 8—Elijah Hamm, Great Gorge .... KO 1
Apr. 1—Giovanni Bovenzi, Totowa .... KO by 3
June 13—Ali Perez, Harlem .... L 6
Aug. 15—Charles Hecker, Glen Cove .... KO 2
Sept. 17—Jimmy Brown, White Plains .... KO 1
Oct. 23—Gerald Banks, New York .... KO 1

TOM MOLLOY
New York, N.Y. Middleweight
1977
May 6—Tony Danza, Commack .... KO by 3
1978
Jan. 14—Earl Harris, Hauppauge .... W 4
Jan. 25—Dennis Taglianetti, Brooklyn .... L 4
Oct. 14—George Fakaris, Commack .... D 4
1979
May 11—James Anthony, Commack .... W 4
June 29—Sam Bell, Commack .... W 4
Oct. 12—Nick Coffman, Uniondale .... W 4
Nov. 7—Danny Long, Boston .... KO by 1
1980
Dec. 11—Johnny Sears, New York .... L 4

RALPH MONCRIEF
Cleveland, Ohio Middleweight
1972
Sept. 14—Ottis Goode, Cleveland .... KO 4
Sept. 18—Joe Blair, Cleveland..................... W 4
Dec. 14—Lionell Ford, Kalamazoo................. KO 5
1973
Mar. 3—Lee Barber, Detroit.................. KO by 5
Oct. 16—Frank Foramero, Des Moines........... W 6
Nov. 24—Dave Vent, Toronto .... KO 5
1974
Mar. 20—Al Styles, Scranton..................... L 6
1975
(Inactive)
1976
Feb. 16—Damiano Pelligrino, Toronto .... KO 2
Sept. 8—Bill Williams, Cleveland................. KO 1

Sept. 22—Al Tigerbell, Cleveland .... KO 5
Oct. 6—Eddie Burgin, Cleveland................ KO 1
1977
Apr. 13—Lee Barber, Cleveland .... KO 7
Sept. 28—Ernie Singletary, Canton .... W 10
1978
Oct. 26—Dwight Davison, Detroit .... L 8
Nov. 29—Johnny Heard, Richfield .... W 8
1979
Jan. 15—Ernie Singletary, Philadelphia .... L 10
Aug. 19—Lamont Lovelady, Bloomington .... W 10
1980
May 3—Leroy Green, San Carlos .... W 10
Sept. 15—Bruce McIntyre, Durban .... KO 10
Nov. 3—Gert Steyn, Durban .... KO 7

MARTY MONROE
Los Angeles, Calif. Heavyweight
1974
May 2—King David Smith, Los Angeles .... W 5
Dec. 18—Lee Thomas, Las Vegas .... KO 1
1975
Jan. 9—Ron Draper, Los Angeles................ W 6
Jan. 16—Tony Pulu, Los Angeles................ W 4
Feb. 7—Tony Pulu, San Diego................... D 5
Apr. 18—Fernando Jones, San Diego .... KO 2
May 30—Dwain Bonds, San Diego................ W 5
Aug. 1—Tony Pulu, Las Vegas .... KO 2
Aug. 8—Mel Rush, Las Vegas .... KO 5
1976
Jan. 24—Greg Johnson, Las Vegas .... W 6
Aug. 16—Willie Moore, Philadelphia .... KO 4
Sept. 14—Randy Mack, Philadelphia .... W 8
1977
Jan. 17—C. J. Bar Brown, Philadelphia .... KO 1
July 26—Joe Gholston, Philadelphia .... W 10
1978
Feb. 4—Fraser Memela, Johannesburg .... KO 4
Apr. 22—Larry Cruz, Salt Lake City .... KO 2
1979
Apr. 4—Gary Gahan, Los Angeles .... KO 2
June 6—Leroy Boone, Los Angeles .... KO 5
Aug. 1—Jimmy Ingram, Los Angeles .... W 10
Nov. 27—Henry Lumpkins, Los Angeles .... KO 7
1980
Jan. 26—Grady Daniels, Los Angeles .... KO 5
Mar. 9—Scott LeDoux, St. Paul .... L 10
May 31—Lynn Ball, El Paso .... KO 5
Sept. 27—Eddie Lopez, Los Angeles .... KO 5

WILLIE (THE WORM) MONROE
Philadelphia, Pa. Middleweight
Born: June 5, 1948
1969
Nov. 11—Vince Neratka, Philadelphia........... KO 1
Dec. 9—Joe Williams, Philadelphia............. KO 4
1970
Feb. 25—Fred Thomas, Philadelphia .... KO 1
Mar. 23—Louis Rivera, Philadelphia .... KO 1
Apr. 23—Ted Hamilton, Philadelphia............ KO 1
May 18—Alberto Millan, Philadelphia .... KO 3
June 16—Ruben Figueroa, Philadelphia .... KO 2
July 7—Willie Caldwell, New Orleans .... KO 2
July 13—Sanchez Rosa, Tampa................. KO 2
July 20—Oscar Coor, Philadelphia .... KO 2
Sept. 14—Adam Moore, New Orleans .... KO 3
Oct. 6—Moteen Adignu, Philadelphia .... KO 4
Nov. 18—Luis Vinales, Philadelphia............ KO 6
1971
Jan. 18—Alvin Phillips, Philadelphia............ W 10
Apr. 12—Adam Moore, Tampa................ KO 10
May 27—Abe Cabrera, Philadelphia .... KO 3
July 14—Elgie Walters, Houston .... KO 4
Oct. 19—Willie Warren, Houston .... W 10
1972
Jan. 15—Alvin Phillips, New Orleans .... W 10
Mar. 21—Luis Galvan, Houston .... W 10
Mar. 27—Max Cohen, Paris..................... L 10
Sept. 6—Alvin Phillips, New Orleans .... L 10
Oct. 24—Leroy Roberts, Philadelphia .... KO 1
Dec. 5—George Davis, Philadelphia .... KO 6
1973
Jan. 22—Roy Lee, Kingston .... KO 1
Mar. 6—Don Cobbs, Philadelphia .... W 10
May 11—Roy McMillan, Philadelphia .... KO 3
Aug. 15—Jose Gonzalez, Philadelphia.......... W 10
Nov. 5—Fabio Bettini, Paris................... D 10
1974
Feb. 18—Eugene Hart, Philadelphia............ W 10
Apr. 9—Stanley Hayward, Philadelphia........ KO 7
Aug. 19—Billy Douglas, Philadelphia .... W 10
Nov. 12—Bobby Watts, Philadelphia .... L 10

163

May —Rennie Pinder, Philadelphia.............KO 4
June 2—Carlos Marks, Philadelphia..............W 10
1976
Jan. 28—Carlos Marks, Philadelphia..............W 10
Mar. 9—Marvin Hagler, Philadelphia............W 10
May 19—Felton Marshall, Philadelphia..........KO 7
Aug. 16—Dave Love, Philadelphia............KO by 4
Dec. 3—Angel Robinson Garcia, Rochester, N.Y....KO 8
1977
Jan. 21—Lenny Harden, Rochester, N.Y. ....KO 3
Feb. 15—Marvin Hagler, Boston..............KO by 12
June 15—Larry Davis, Philadelphia..............W 10
Aug. 23—Marvin Hagler, Philadelphia........KO by 2
1978
Apr. 22—Frank Lucas, Milan....................KO 9
1979
Mar. 3—Scorpion Ofuso, Accra ....L 10
May 31—Keith Broom, Philadelphia ....W 10
July 15—Curtis Parker, Philadelphia ....L 10
Nov. 15—Dwight Davison, Detroit ....L 10
1980
July 28—Jimmy McClain, Philadelphia ....W 10

RICO MONTALBAN
Richmond, Virginia Heavyweight
1980
Sept. 17—Tony Childs, Strongville ....KO 1
Nov. 1—Kid Samson, Richmond ....W 4

ORLANDO MONTALVO
Puerto Rican Welterweight
1979
Aug. 7—Adan Chavarria, Houston ....KO by 5
1980
Feb. 11—Jose A. Rivera, San Juan ....L 6
May 4—Tim La Valley, Kiamesha Lake..........L 6
Sept. 19—Jose A. Rivera, San Juan ....W 8
Oct. 24—Billy Costello, Uniondale ....L 8

GONZALLO MONTELLANO
Bakersfield, Calif. Lightweight
1976
Jan. 22—Juan Arcos, Los Angeles.................W 5
Feb. 13—Ray Saldivar, San Bernardino..........KO 5
Mar. 25—Jose Zatarain, Los Angeles..............KO 1
Apr. 9—Jose Luis Lopez, San Bernardino........W 8
May 6—Waymon Young, Los Angeles.............W 6
Nov. 11—Guillermo Gonzalez, Los Angeles......KO 3
Dec. 16—Ruben Martinez, Los Angeles ....KO 4
1977
Feb. 17—Canelo Salinas, Los Angeles ....KO 3
Mar. 20—Ruben Martinez, Las Vegas ....KO 1
Apr. 14—Rafael Nunez, Los Angeles ....W 10
Sept. 1—Tiger Noji, Los Angeles ....KO 5
Oct. 27—Vicente Hernandez, Los Angeles ......KO 7
Dec. 2—Roman Contreras, Bakersfield ....W 10
1978
Mar. 17—Claude Durden, Bakersfield ....W 10
July 31—Jose Marin, Bakersfield ....W 10
Aug. 28—Teodoro Pineda, Bakersfield ....KO 2
Sept. 13—Willie Daniels, Las Vegas ....KO 5
Oct. 23—Moses Carbin, Bakersfield ....KO 5
Nov. 14—Julio Mendez, Bakersfield ....KO 2
1979
Feb. 5—Moses Carbin, Bakersfield ....W 10
Apr. 16—Abraham Perez, Bakersfield ....KO 4
May 21—Jose Osuna, Bakersfield ....KO 4
June 15—Tom Pinner, Laredo ....KO 4
July 16—Frankie Balaski, Bakersfield ....W 10
Oct. 30—Fili Ramirez, Bakersfield ....W 10
1980
Mar. 17—Tony Tejeda, Bakersfield ....KO 1
May 13—Herman Montes, Bakersfield ....D 12
July 27—Sean O'Grady, Omaha ....L 12
Oct. 7—Salvador Torres, Bakersfield ....W 10

PHILLIP MONTELLANO
Bakersfield, Calif. Junior Middleweight
1980
Mar. 3—Jose Rivera, Bakersfield ....KO 1
Mar. 17—Marcos Jiminez, Bakersfield ....KO 1
Apr. 21—Pablo Gomez, Bakersfield ....KO 2
May 13—Ramon Sanchez, Bakersfield ....W 6
May 30—Chico Salinas, Bakersfield ....KO by 4

HERMAN MONTES
Los Angeles, Calif. Lightweight
1977
June 2—Arturo Reyes, Los Angeles ....KO 2
July 22—Ruben Martinez, San Diego ....KO 2
Aug. 11—Jose Rodriguez, Los Angeles ....KO 5
Sept. 29—Simon Gurrola, Los Angeles ....KO 3

Oct. 8—Tony Sanchez, Los Angeles ....W 6
Nov. 17—Johnny Jenson, Los Angeles ....KO 5
Dec. 10—Fidel Fraijo, Los Angeles ....W 5
1978
Mar. 9—Jose Olivares, Los Angeles ....W 10
Apr. 7—Sergio Nualarte, Los Angeles ....KO 2
Apr. 23—Tony Sanchez, Los Angeles ....KO 5
May 11—Mariano Alanzo, Los Angeles ....W 10
May 25—Leoncio Meza, Los Angeles ....W 10
July 6—Jose Marin, Los Angeles ....W 10
Nov. 30—Jose Osuna, Los Angeles ....KO 2
1979
Jan. 11—Fili Ramirez, Los Angeles ....W 10
Mar. 22—Augustin Rivera, Los Angeles ....W 10
Apr. 22—Ney Gordillo, Los Angeles ....KO 4
May 24—German Cuello, Los Angeles ....L 10
Aug. 2—Curtis Ramsey, Pico Rivera ....D 10
Sept. 22—Ney Gordillo, Los Angeles ....KO 4
Oct. 27—Camilo Ibarra, Los Angeles ....W 10
Dec. 10—Petronillo Velasquez, Bakersfield ....KO 2
1980
Jan. 18—Chuy Rodriguez, San Bernardino ......KO 1
Jan. 26—Fili Ramirez, Los Angeles ....W 10
Mar. 7—Rogelio Castaneda, San Bernardino .....KO 3
Apr. 18—Jerry Venzor, Bakersfield ....KO 4
May 13—Gonzallo Montellano, Bakersfield ....D 12
July 26—Rodolfo (Gato) Gonzalez, Los Angeles ...TD 3
Dec. 13—Rosario Gonzalez, El Paso ....KO 2

JOHN MONTES JR.
Lightweight
1979
Oct. 18—Timmy Martinez, Los Angeles ....KO 2
Dec. 14—Willie Hall, San Bernardino ....W 5
1980
Apr. 4—Eric Bonilla, San Bernardino ....W 6
May 13—Eric Bonilla, Bakersfield ....W 6
July 1—Gary Vinet, San Bernardino ....KO 3
July 3—Juan Jiminez, Los Angeles ....KO 1
Aug. 28—Fidel Fraijo, Los Angeles ....KO 6
Oct. 16—Fili Ramirez, Los Angeles ....W 10
Nov. 6—Jose Osuna, Los Angeles ....KO 1
Dec. 13—Jerry Venzor, El Paso ....KO 1

LARRY MONTGOMERY
Beaumont, Texas Heavyweight
1979
May 22—Willie Stoglin, Beaumont ....W 4
Aug. 3—Louis Brown, Clarksburg ....L 6
Sept. 14—Tom Trim, Houston ....KO by 1
Nov. 8—Louis Brown, Tulsa ....KO by 4
1980
Mar. 3—Monte Masters, Oklahoma City ......KO by 2
May 9—Tony Perea, El Paso ....KO by 2

MIGUEL MONTILLA
Dominican Rep. Junior Welterweight
1972
Jan. —Roberto Ayala, Tampa ....W 8
Feb. 19—Eduardo Trinidad, San Juan............D 6
Feb. —Ricky Capitano, Tampa ....KO 1
Apr. 7—Nestor Rojas, Miami Beach..............D 10
June 6—Joey Cartwright, Miami..................L 10
1973
Feb. 19—Radames Checo, Santo Domingo.........W 12
(Dominican Rep. Lightweight Title)
Mar. 17—Alfredo Escalera, Carolina ....W 10
Apr. 7—Angel Rivera, Carolina ....KO 7
Apr. —Easy Boy Lee, St. Thomas..............KO 2
May —Joe Cartwright, Miami..................W 10
May 28—Jose Resto, San Juan ....W 10
July —Jose Resto, San Juan ....KO 8
July 14—Alfredo Escalera, Caguas ....KO by 8
Sept. 1—Santiago Rosa, San Juan ....W 10
Nov. 12—Carlos Gil, San Juan ....W 12
1974
Feb. 23—Hector Median, Santo Domingo ....L 12
(Dominican Junior Welterweight Title)
June 8—Oscar Salazar, Santo Domingo ....KO 2
Sept. 30—Chris Fernandez, Santo Domingo ....KO 6
1975
Feb. 17—Antonio Amaya, Santo Domingo ....W 10
Oct. 8—Carlos Gil, Santo Domingo..............KO 11
Dec. 22—Gustavo Briceno, Santo Domingo ....KO 3
1976
June 25—Manuel Irrizarry, Santo Domingo........KO 1
1977
Apr. 15—Mike Everett, Santo Domingo ....KO 1
May 30—Bernardo Diaz, Santo Domingo ....KO 2
June 10—Jose Batista, Santo Domingo ....KO 3
June 23—Johnny Copeland, Santo Domingo ....KO 2
July 16—Adolfo Marte, Santo Domingo ....KO 2
Sept. 16—Ricardo Arredondo, Santo Domingo .....W 10
Oct. 27—Mario Mendez, Santo Domingo ....KO 2

1978
Feb. 18—Bobby Hughes, San Juan .... KO 7
Apr. 14—Emilio Guerrero, Santo Domingo .... KO 6
Aug. 14—Memo Cruz, Santo Domingo .... KO 4
Aug. 28—Aurelio Muniz, Santo Domingo .... KO 2
1979
Jan. 18—Antonio Cervantes, New York .... L 15
(For World Junior Welterweight Title)
May 5—Juan Cantres, Santo Domingo .... KO 2
June 29—Daniel Lake, Santo Domingo .... KO 3
1980
Mar. 29—Antonio Cervantes, Cartagena .... KO by 7
(For World Junior Welterweight Title)
Oct. 20—Alfonso Frazer, Santo Domingo .... KO 9
Dec. 6—Dujuan Johnson, Detroit .... L 10

ANDRES MONTOYA
Las Vegas, Nev. Junior Welterweight
1979
Jan. 24—Arturo Silveria, Las Vegas .... W 4
Feb. 7—Angel Garcia, Las Vegas .... W 4
Apr. 11—Angel Garcia, Las Vegas .... W 4
Apr. 18—Johnny Segura, Las Vegas .... W 4
Nov. 14—Juan Garcia, Las Vegas .... D 4
1980
Apr. 23—Raul Cruz, Las Vegas .... W 6
Nov. 19—Joe Bahash, Las Vegas .... D 6

MAGDALENO MONTOYA
Mexican Bantamweight
1980
Sept. 23—Juan Bernal, Houston .... W 8
Oct. 24—Miguel Torres, Dallas .... W 8

ROQUE MONTOYA
Mexican Featherweight
1979
June 5—Juan Escobar, Houston .... KO by 5
1980
Feb. 5—Ken Sheppard, Houston .... W 8
Sept. 23—Jorge Zuniga, Houston .... KO 8
(Texas Featherweight Title)
Oct. 24—James Martinez, Dallas .... L 10

J. C. MOODY
New York, N.Y. Light Heavyweight
1979
June 29—Gene Muldrow, New York .... W 4
Oct. 4—Charles Brown, N. Bergen .... KO 1
Oct. 27—Elliott Burton, N. Bergen .... KO 4
Nov. 28—Michael Grant, W. New York, N.J..... KO 3
1980
Jan. 15—Muhammad Shabazz, W. Hartford ... KO by 1
Feb. 29—Sam Bell, Brooklyn .... KO by 1
Mar. 9—Euclides Valdez, Brooklyn .... KO by 1
July 16—Gene Muldrow, Elizabeth .... KO 3
Aug. 29—Euclides Valdez, New York .... KO by 1

THOMAS MOODY
Columbus, Ohio Welterweight
1980
Aug. 21—James Leftwich, Columbus .... KO 4
Sept. 10—Lanny Edmond, Detroit .... KO 6
Sept. 25—Michael Bradley, Columbus .... L 6
Nov. 1—Gary Barbour, Dayton .... KO 3

DAVEY MOORE
New York City, N.Y. Welterweight
1980
Nov. 1—Chucho Saucedo, Lake Tahoe .... W 6
Dec. 20—Ted White, Bronx .... W 6

MAURICE MOORE
Charlotte, N. Carolina Middleweight
1980
Sept. 6—Pee Wee Dunbar, Lincolnton .... W 4
Sept. 24—Roddy Mac Donald, Halifax .... KO by 2
Oct. 11—Gaither Brannon, Lincolnton .... L 8

PAUL MOORE
Philadelphia, Pa. Junior Welterweight
1976
Aug. 26—Sam Hailstock, Allentown .... KO by 2
1977
Nov. 15—Mickey DiFlo, Upper Darby .... D 6
1978
Mar. 21—Billy Jones, Philadelphia .... L 4
1979
Nov. 23—Benny DeJesus, Trenton .... W 4
1980
Jan. 30—Scott Farmer, Allentown .... W 4
Mar. 14—Tim Daniels, Trenton .... KO by 3

Mar. 22—Anibal Santiago, Bethlehem .... L 4
Mar. 28—Kevin Rooney, Scranton .... L 6
July 3—Ernest Johnson, Atlantic City .... L 4
Sept. 17—Billy Costello, White Plains .... KO by 1

TYRONE MOORE
Louisville, Ky. Junior Welterweight
1979
Oct. 18—Darnell Smith, Philadelphia .... KO 1
Nov. 24—Lalo Hernandez, Bloomington .... KO 1
1980
Feb. 1—Jerry Strickland, Louisville .... W 6
Mar. 12—Jeff Passero, Washington, D.C. ...... KO by 1
Apr. 5—Mark McCullough, Louisville .... W 6
May 16—Darryl Green, Lexington .... KO 2
Sept. 12—Kenneth Hill, Louisville .... KO 1
Nov. 7—Rodney Kennebrew, Clarksville .... KO 6
Dec. 12—Don Morgan, Louisville .... W 8

ALFREDO MORALES
Argentine Light Heavyweight
1980
May 17—Jesus Ibanez, La Pampa .... W 10
May 30—Juan Fernandez, Cordoba .... L 10
July 25—Candido Barrera, Rio III .... L 12
Sept. 5—Angel Salinas, Bolivar .... KO by 5
Dec. 12—Jorge Salgado, La Plata .... KO by 2
Dec. 26—Jesus Romero, San Pedro .... L 10

JORGE MORALES
(KID DYNAMITA)
Los Angeles, Calif. Lightweight
1976
Aug. 5—Fernando Urlich, Los Angeles .... W 4
Aug. 26—Romualdo Juarez, Los Angeles .... KO 1
Sept. 30—Gil Valdez, Los Angeles .... W 5
Oct. 27—Bruce Curry, Las Vegas .... L 6
Nov. 9—Albert Guevara, Sacramento .... KO 2
Dec. 7—Vicente Hernandez, Sacramento .... KO 6
1977
Feb. 21—Clarence Howard, Las Vegas .... KO 6
Apr. 4—Mario Mendez, Las Vegas .... L 10
July —Abraham Perez, Las Vegas .... KO by 2
Oct. 25—Rogelio Castaneda, Las Vegas .... L 10
1978
Mar. 31—Joey Dominquez, Las Vegas .... D 10
Apr. 24—Rogelio Castaneda, Las Vegas .... L 10
May 17—Leroy Haley, Las Vegas .... NC
June 27—Rudy Hernandez, Las Vegas .... KO 6
July 27—Miguel Estrada, Las Vegas .... KO 5
Aug. 19—Curtis Ramsey, Las Vegas .... KO 5
Oct. 10—Howard Jackson, Las Vegas .... W 10
Dec. 5—Joe Talamantez, Reno .... KO 5
1979
Jan. 28—Rogelio Castaneda, Reno .... W 10
Feb. 21—Hector Rivera, Lake Tahoe .... W 12
Apr. 25—Ignacio Campos, Lake Tahoe .... W 10
July 27—Chuy Rodriguez, Las Vegas .... KO 5
Sept. 25—Curtis Ramsey, Las Vegas .... W 10
Nov. 27—Dario DeJesus, Las Vegas .... KO 4
1980
Mar. 27—Arturo Leon, Las Vegas .... L 12
June 3—Jose Osuna, Las Vegas .... KO 7
July 8—Jerry Venzor, Las Vegas .... KO 3
Aug. 19—Frankie Moultrie, Las Vegas .... KO 7
Sept. 9—Jose Cirilos, Las Vegas .... KO 2
Nov. 11—Jesus Salcedo, Las Vegas .... KO 3

PAUL MORALES
Los Angeles, Calif. Junior Lightweight
1977
Jan. 13—Jose Valencia, Los Angeles .... W 4
Jan. 27—Martin Avila, Los Angeles .... L 5
Apr. 7—Martin Avila, Los Angeles .... KO 5
June 1—Chelene Hernandez, Las Vegas .... L 8
1978
Mar. 23—Jose Rodriguez, Los Angeles .... KO 4
1979
(Inactive)
1980
Jan. 31—Mil Jiminez, Los Angeles .... KO 2
Feb. 20—Ronald Strode, Hilo .... W 6
June 13—Gary Vinet, San Bernardino .... L 4

DENIS MORAN
Nicaraguan Bantamweight
1978
Jan. 28—Tony Stokes, San Juan .... KO 5
June 3—Andres Torres, San Juan .... L 10
1979
Apr. 8—Mauricio Aldana, Las Vegas .... KO 2
1980
Dec. 16—Gustavo Salgado, Los Angeles .... KO by 1

165

JORGE MORELLO
Argentine Junior Middleweight
1980
Jan.	4—Hugo Quieroga, Cafferatta	KO	5
Mar.	21—Ramon Peralta, Vdo Tuerto	L	10
Sept.	12—Manuel Gonzalez, Rosario	L	10

BILLY MORENO
Chicago, Ill. Lightweight
1978
May	8—Warren Thunder, Chicago	KO by	2
Aug.	28—Chief Ketchinakow, Chicago	L	4
Nov.	18—Ron Furlow, DePaul	KO	1
Dec.	2—Carl Crowley, Aurora	L	6
Dec.	15—Carl Crowley, Chicago	L	4
1979
Feb.	28—Tom Crowley, Chicago	KO	1
June	4—Kenny Daniels, Bridgeview	W	4
Dec.	15—Simmie Black, Chicago	KO	2
1980
Feb.	18—Eddie Murray, Chicago	L	6
June	12—Jimmy Blevins, Chicago	L	8
Aug.	8—Pedro Acosta, Chicago	L	10
Sept.	25—Frank Newton, Oklahoma City	KO by	9

CHANGO MORENO
Featherweight
1979
June	3—Saul Hernandez, Las Vegas	KO	2
July	26—Toshi Okuma, Los Angeles	W	5
Dec.	18—Ronnie Furlow, Sparks	KO	2
1980
Mar.	21—Jaime Nava, Los Angeles	W	4
July	26—Ricardo Jiminez, Los Angeles	W	10
Sept.	11—Jaime Nava, Los Angeles	W	10

RUBEN MORENO
Texas Featherweight
1979
July	31—Gilbert Garza, San Antonio	W	6
Aug.	15—Jerry Kornele, Beaumont	W	10
Oct.	24—Fred Roach, Las Vegas	L	6
Nov.	16—Roberto Elizondo, Corpus Christi	KO by	2
1980
Mar.	6—Juan (Kid) Mesa, Los Angeles	KO by	6

JOAQUIN MOREYRA
Argentine Junior Welterweight
1980
May	9—Oscar Godoy, Formosa	KO	4
Aug.	1—Angel Olea, Formosa	W	10
Aug.	29—Nicolas Arkuszyn, Formosa	D	10
Nov.	14—Romulo Ibarra, Formosa	W	10
Dec.	11—Ramon Allende, Formosa	W	10

RAMON MOREYRA
Argentine Lightweight
1980
Sept.	5—Gabriel Sanchez, Rosario	L	10
Sept.	26—Eduardo Echeverria, Rosario	KO	7
Dec.	12—Manuel Alvarez, Tucuman	L	10

DON MORGAN
Nashville, Tenn. Welterweight
1974
Nov.	11—Robert Adams, New York	L	4
1975
Mar.	14—Ray Hammond, Elizabeth	L	6
May	28—Archie Andrews, Scranton	W	6
June	23—Ray Hammond, New York	L	8
1976
Feb.	11—Jeff Holmes, New York	KO	5
Mar.	30—Maximo Pierret, New York	L	6
Aug.	6—Tyrone Phelps, New York	KO by	5
Dec.	10—Miguel Hernandez, New York	L	6
1977
Sept.	18—Mark Harrez, New York	W	6
Oct.	29—Gary Coates, Hamilton	W	6
1978
July	9—Sammy NeSmith, Indianapolis	KO by	5
Aug.	1—Allan Clarke, Halifax	L	8
Sept.	—Roy Goss, Birmingham	L	10
1979
June	15—Allan Clarke, Halifax	D	8
Oct.	3—Billy Miller, Orlando	KO	10
Oct.	23—Ray Jackson, Orlando	W	10
1980
Mar.	8—Bruce Thompson, Nashville	L	10
May	9—Tyrone Wren, Nashville	KO	9
Dec.	12—Tyrone Moore, Louisville	L	8

JOHN MORGAN
Houston, Texas Junior Welterweight
1977
Feb.	16—Richard Gonzalez, Orlando	KO by	2
Feb.	28—Gilbert Galvan, Galveston	KO by	2
Mar.	22—Silverio Martinez, Corpus Christi	KO by	3
Apr.	29—Billy Miller, Fort Worth	KO by	3
May	16—Richard Gonzalez, Orlando	KO by	2
Sept.	22—Hilbert Stevenson, Cumberland	L	8
Oct.	1—James Martinez, Shreveport	KO by	5
1978
Feb.	21—Jimmy Heair, Memphis	KO by	3
Apr.	20—Termite Watkins, Houston	KO by	4
July	18—Bobby Vascocu, Tyler	L	10
Dec.	1—Pat Hallacy, New Orleans	KO by	4
1979
July	9—Ruben Munoz Jr., Odessa	L	4
July	21—Wilbur Lawson, Dallas	W	10
1980
Jan.	9—James Busceme, Beaumont	KO	8
Feb.	12—Johnny Copeland, Beaumont	W	10
June	12—Ken Saale, Chicago	L	10
July	15—Scotty Foreman, Beaumont	KO	2
Sept.	16—Jose Cabrera, Beaumont	KO	9

JOHN MORGAN
(See MUSTAFA SHABAZZ)
Los Angeles, Calif. Middleweight

STEVE MORMINO
St. Louis, Mo. Heavyweight
1979
Sept.	25—Billy Joe Thomas, Belleville	KO	2
Dec.	15—Steve Osborn, Kansas City	KO	1
1980
Jan.	21—Jimmy Robertson, St. Charles	W	6
Mar.	17—Mark Wyckliff, Indianapolis	KO	2
Apr.	22—Michael Greer, Memphis	L	4
Aug.	8—James Dixon, Chicago	W	10
Oct.	7—Al Jones, St. Charles	KO	8

JACK MORRELL
Lowell, Mass. Junior Welterweight
1979
Oct.	27—Angel Rivera, Fitchburg	KO	2
Nov.	6—Julio Andrade, Lowell	L	8
Nov.	8—Charles McFarlane, Lowell	KO	2
Dec.	1—Heriberto Vasquez, Albany	KO	2
Dec.	15—Ralph Dumont, Kittery	KO	3
1980
Feb.	16—Tommy Brown, Portland, Me.	W	6
Feb.	26—Mark Mello, Woburn	KO	3
Apr.	20—Rick Craney, Portland, Me.	L	6
June	19—Chi Chi Hernandez, Lawrence	D	4
June	26—Tom Brown, Revere	W	5
June	28—Ralph Doucette, Manchester	KO	3
Sept.	5—Fernando Fernandez, Dorchester	L	10
Dec.	15—Carlos Garcia, Boston	KO by	6

MAURICIO (MANO) MORUA
Pomona, Calif. Lightweight
1979
Nov.	14—Juan Rivera, Las Vegas	KO	2
1980
Apr.	3—Leon Smith, Los Angeles	KO	4
Apr.	18—Pancho Velez, San Bernardino	KO	6
May	2—Frank Lopez, San Bernardino	KO	5
May	8—Memo Arreola, Los Angeles	D	6
June	21—Carlos Ibarra, Las Vegas	W	6
Aug.	21—Rodrigo Flores, Los Angeles	KO	4
Sept.	13—Juan LaPorte, San Antonio	L	10

ROCKY MOSLEY JR.
Las Vegas, Nev. Junior Middleweight
1975
Aug.	12—Tony McDaniels, Seattle	KO	1
Sept.	23—Al Foster, Everett	KO	2
1976
Feb.	11—Antonio Adame, Las Vegas	KO	3
Feb.	18—Rico Dineros, Las Vegas	W	4
Mar.	3—Ike Shipman, Las Vegas	W	6
Apr.	28—Pedro Garcia, Las Vegas	KO	1
May	11—Juan Ramirez, Las Vegas	KO	3
June	9—Robert Sollis, Las Vegas	W	6
June	23—Chucho Garcia, Las Vegas	W	10
July	12—Babala McCarthy, Las Vegas	W	8
Sept.	1—Armando Allatore, Las Vegas	KO	2
Sept.	15—Vicente Medina, Las Vegas	KO	6
Oct.	20—David Oropeza, Las Vegas	KO	1
Dec.	15—Babala McCarthy, Las Vegas	KO	6
1977
Feb.	21—Jimmy Jackson, Las Vegas	W	12

Mar.	6—Johnny Baldwin, Marion .... KO	4
	(U.S. Championship Tournament)	
Apr.	10—Mike Colbert, Miami Beach L	10
	(U.S. Championship Tournament)	
Aug.	9—Edgar Wallace, Las Vegas .... KO by	4
Oct.	25—Freddie Washington, Las Vegas .... W	10
Nov.	9—Zeferino Gonzalez, Las Vegas .... W	10
Dec.	20—Larry Bonds, Las Vegas L	12
	1978	
Jan.	21—Mustafa Hamsho, Las Vegas L	8
Mar.	15—Pedro Pina, Las Vegas .... KO	2
Mar.	31—Lenny Harden, Las Vegas .... W	10
May	25—Larry Bonds, Las Vegas .... W	12
June	27—Henry Walker, Las Vegas .... W	12
Oct.	10—Wilson Bell, Las Vegas .... W	10
Nov.	16—Alvin Anderson, Las Vegas .... KO	2
	(U.S. Vacant Junior Middleweight Title)	
	1979	
Jan.	18—Wilson Bell, Las Vegas .... W	12
	(U.S. Junior Middleweight Title)	
Mar.	2—Ray Phillips, Las Vegas .... KO	1
	(U.S. Junior Middleweight Title)	
June	15—Daryl Penn, Las Vegas .... W	12
	(U.S. Junior Middleweight Title)	
Nov.	27—Nick Ortiz, Las Vegas .... KO by	4
	(Lost U.S. Junior Middleweight Title)	
	1980	
Jan.	11—Ruben Rascon, Phoenix .... W	10
Feb.	3—Babs McCarthy, Reno .... W	10
Mar.	13—Aundra Love, Las Vegas .... W	10
Mar.	27—Tyrone Rackley, Las Vegas L	10
May	17—Dave Meadows, Las Vegas .... W	10
Aug.	1—Ted Sanders, Las Vegas .... W	10
Oct.	7—Steve Delgado, Las Vegas .... W	12

SEBASTIEN MOSQUEIRA
Argentine Lightweight
1980

May	2—Demetrio Ibarra, Corrientes .... W	10
Aug.	7—Gualberto Valdez, Asuncion .... W TD	5
	(Won South American Lightweight Title)	
Oct.	24—Juan Herrera, San Pedro .... W	10

GEORGE MOSTARDINI
Chicago, Ill. Heavyweight
1977

July	12—Harold Brown, Orlando .... KO	1
Oct.	25—Troy Bolden, Chicago .... KO	1
Nov.	22—Danny George, Chicago .... KO	1
Dec.	2—Henry Williams, Chicago .... KO	1
Dec.	13—Troy Bolden, Chicago .... KO	2
	1978	
Jan.	23—Dwight Sims, Chicago .... KO	1
Mar.	20—Baker Tinsley, Chicago .... KO	1
Apr.	28—Tom Fischer, Chicago .... W	6
June	30—Leon Spinks, Chicago .... Exh.	4
July	20—Danny Davis, Detroit .... KO	1
July	28—Dennis Halliburton, Kansas City .... KO	2
Sept.	27—Earl McLean, Chicago .... KO by	3
Dec.	15—Sylvester Wilder, Chicago .... KO	1
	1979	
Feb.	2—Paosi Tuiono, Chicago .... KO	1
Mar.	23—Trinidad Escamilla, Rosemont .... KO	2
June	14—Jimmy Cross, River Grove .... KO by	4
Dec.	19—Herbert Adams, Rockford .... KO	1
	1980	
Feb.	1—Melvin Hosea, Louisville .... W	8
Mar.	7—Gene Abbott, Chicago .... KO	1
Mar.	28—Mongol Ortiz, Chicago .... W	10
July	10—Max Baer Smith, Chicago .... KO	3
Aug.	25—Bob Whaley, Chicago .... KO	1
Sept.	11—Amos Hayes, Chicago .... KO	3
Dec.	11—Jumbo Cummings, Chicago .... KO by	8

ALFREDO MOYANO
Argentine Lightweight
1980

Sept.	6—Luis Diaz, Salto Argent .... KO	7
Oct.	3—Jose M.P. Lopez, Rio Gallegos .... W	10
Nov.	13—Juan Zuniga, Tres Arroyos L	10

CLYDE MUDGETT
(See LEE ROY JONES)
Houston, Texas Light Heavyweight
1977

Apr.	22—Dick Morgan, Indianapolis L	4
May	23—Lucky Patterson, Chicago .... W	4
June	23—Joey Butcher, Thompson .... KO	3
Sept.	6—Willie Goodman, Orlando .... W	4
Sept.	29—Risto Beckovich, Cleveland L	6
Nov.	22—Julio Estrada, Indianapolis .... KO	1
	1978	
Jan.	31—Mike West, Indianapolis .... KO	3

Feb.	14—Roy (Cookie) Wallace, Houston .... KO by	2
Mar.	18—Ron Burton, Kansas City .... KO	2
Mar.	23—Ron Stander, Omaha .... KO by	4
May	1—Alvin Yates, Indianapolis .... KO	1
May	3—George Clark, Las Vegas .... KO	1
May	15—Kevin Smith, New York L	8
July	9—Tom Prator, Indianapolis .... KO by	5
Aug.	25—Zack Page, Dallas .... W	8
Sept.	19—Alvin Dominey, Odessa .... W	12
Oct.	11—Al Bell, Indianapolis .... KO	5
Oct.	31—Obie Garnett, Indianapolis .... KO	1
Nov.	1—King David Smith, Las Vegas L	10
Dec.	15—Jose Luis Gonzalez, Corpus Christi ...... W	6
	1979	
Apr.	10—Otis Gordon, Beaumont .... KO by	9
Mar.	17—George Goforth, Indianapolis .... W	6
Mar.	21—Domenico Adinolfi, Bologna .... KO by	2
May	13—Jerry Hunter, Indianapolis .... KO	3
May	29—Henry Hearns, Las Vegas .... KO by	2
Oct.	28—Baker Tinsley, Indianapolis L	8
Dec.	13—Baker Tinsley, Louisville .... KO by	6

FAHIM MUHAMMAD
Los Angeles, California Middleweight
1980

Feb.	2—Leon Shaw, Phoenix .... W	10
Mar.	21—Richie Chavez, San Bernardino .... W	5
Mar.	26—John Steve, Costa Mesa .... KO	4
May	2—John Vasquez, Inglewood .... W	4
May	20—Miguel Mora, Fresno .... KO	3
June	5—Jimmy Ingram, Las Vegas .... W	8
Aug.	6—Randy Rivers, Las Vegas .... W	6
	1980	
Aug.	28—Dan Sanders, Los Angeles .... KO	6
Sept.	3—Randy Rivers, Las Vegas L	6
Sept.	27—Jeff McCracken, Los Angeles .... KO by	6

FRED MUHAMMAD
(FRED GROGAN)
Denver, Colo. Heavyweight
1978

Sept.	1—Freddie News, Salt Lake City .... KO by	1
Oct.	13—Jose Herrera, Denver L	4
	1979	
June	8—Jose Herrera, Denver .... W	4
Oct.	20—Zack Ferguson, Pueblo .... W	6
	1980	
Feb.	23—Jeff Shelburg, Greeley .... KO by	6
July	3—Pat Duncan, Gardnerville L	10

MALIK MUHAMMAD
Philadelphia, Pa. Middleweight
1979

Mar.	14—Roger Stafford, White Plains .... KO by	2
June	29—Clifford Smith, Commack .... KO	4
July	24—John Bonzei, Atlantic City .... KO by	4
Aug.	3—Stan Williams, Hempstead .... KO	2
Aug.	30—Charlie Tuttle, Richmond .... KO by	2
Sept.	26—Kevin Howard, Upper Darby .... KO by	2
	1980	
Jan.	16—Henry Bunch, Washington, D.C. ..... KO by	
Jan.	19—John Molander, Hempstead .... KO by	1

GENE MULDROW
Jersey City, N.J. Light Heavyweight
1977

Dec.	8—Chris Costanza, North Bergen .... KO	3
	1978	
Feb.	23—Rusty Rosenberger, North Bergen L	4
June	29—Harry DeCosey, N. Bergen L	4
Sept.	9—John Depts, Rahway .... KO by	3
	1979	
June	27—Harry DeCosey, Secaucus L	6
June	29—J.C. Moody, New York L	4
Nov.	9—Ron Huston, New York .... KO by	1
	1980	
July	16—J.C. Moody, Elizabeth .... KO by	3

BRIAN MULLER
Guyanan
Born: June 23, 1954, Amateur Record: 54-7, 38 KO's
1979

Feb.	4—Terrence Clarke, Georgetown .... KO	6
Mar.	25—Selwyn Figaro, Georgetown .... KO	5
May	27—Lennox Beckles, Georgetown .... W	10
July	30—Michael Baptise, Port-of-Spain .... KO	5
Aug.	29—Roy Harry, Port-of-Spain .... KO	5
Sept.	30—Mark Harris, Georgetown .... W	10
Dec.	26—Regginald Forde, Georgetown .... D	10
	1980	
Mar.	16—Clarence Howard, Las Vegas .... KO	9
Apr.	5—Gary Coates, Akron .... W	8

DENNIS MULLIGAN
Emerson, N.J. Junior Middleweight
1980

Nov.	20—Tony Barnes, Totowa	KO	2
Sept.	18—Rick Hamlisch, Totowa	W	4
Oct.	4—Tony Barnes, Great Gorge	KO	2

ROBERT MULLINS
Spartanburg, S.C. Lightweight
Born: August 21, 1951
1975

Sept.	—Super Bug Williams, Spartanburg	KO	2
Nov.	—Rondell Stephenson, Spartanburg	KO	2
Nov.	—Willie Smithe, Lenoir	KO	1
1976			
(Inactive)			
1977			
June	—Sam Lantion, Spartanburg	KO	2
Aug.	—Carey Palmer, Spartanburg	KO	5
1978			
Mar.	—Lu El Sheba, Palatka	KO	2
Mar.	—Frankie Moultrie, Orlando	W	8
Apr.	—Andrea Overdon, Palatka	KO	2
Apr.	—Leon Gilliard, St. Augustine	KO	4
Aug.	—Sam Lantion, Spartanburg	KO	5
Sept.	—Ed Conners, Spartanburg	KO	3
Oct.	—Johnny Wilson, Caesar	KO	2
Dec.	—Gary Barlow, Spartanburg	KO	5
1979			
Feb.	22—Johnny Summerhays, Saginaw	W	10
Apr.	5—Gary Barlow, Spartanburg	KO	5
June	—Hilbert Stevenson, Spartanburg	W	10
Nov.	8—Norman Banner, Spartanburg	KO	2
Dec.	12—Willie Whipple, Canton	W	10
1980			
Feb.	5—Nat Davis, Charleston	KO	5
May	24—Sam Lantion, Union, S.C.	KO	4
July	18—James Martinez, Spartanburg	W	12
Nov.	6—Boycie Tolliver, Spartanburg	KO	1
Dec.	21—Speedy Brown, Spartanburg	KO	4

JOSE MUNIZ
Warminster, Pa. Bantamweight
1979

Sept.	11—Angel Marreno, Philadelphia	D	4
Nov.	15—Hassan Ali, Dover	D	4
Nov.	21—Angel Marrero, Philadelphia	D	4
1980			
Oct.	2—Tony Santana, Commack	KO by	1

OSCAR MUNIZ
Los Angeles, Calif. Bantamweight
1976

Aug.	19—Carlos Alcivar, Los Angeles	W	4
Oct.	7—Arnulfo Martinez, Los Angeles	KO	5
Oct.	13—Richard Rozelle, Las Vegas	L	8
Nov.	18—Mauricio Garcia, Los Angeles	KO	2
1977			
Mar.	3—Rene Silva, Los Angeles	W	6
Apr.	28—Mario Chavez, Los Angeles	W	6
June	1—Javier Flores, Las Vegas	D	8
June	23—Jose Rosa, Los Angeles	KO	1
July	29—Raul Pacheco, San Diego	KO	10
Sept.	29—Santiago Hernandez, Los Angeles	TD	8
Oct.	8—Jorge Altamirano, Los Angeles	KO	6
1978			
Mar.	9—Santiago Hernandez, Los Angeles	TD	7
Apr.	7—Catalino Flores, Los Angeles	KO	3
Apr.	20—Danny Ocampo, Los Angeles	KO	5
May	25—Antonio Sanchez, Los Angeles	KO	9
July	13—Ruben Solorio, Los Angeles	W	10
Aug.	10—Francisco Ponce, Los Angeles	KO	7
Oct.	12—Mel Johnson, Los Angeles	W	10
Nov.	16—Mario Chavez, Los Angeles	W	10
1979			
Jan.	18—Eddie Logan, Los Angeles	W	10
Feb.	2—Joaquin Acuna, Phoenix	W	10
Feb.	8—Melvin Johnson, San Bernardino	KO	7
Mar.	10—Catalino Flores, Salt Lake City	KO	8
Apr.	19—Jose Resendez, Los Angeles	KO	6
July	12—Catalino Flores, Los Angeles	W	10
Sept.	6—Eddie Logan, Los Angeles	KO	6
Oct.	27—Leo Randolph, Los Angeles	L	10
1980			
Feb.	2—Joaquin Acuna, Phoenix	W	10
Feb.	8—Melvin Johnson, San Bernardino	KO	7
Mar.	12—Juan Romero, Tucson	KO	9
May	16—Ralph Berrios, San Bernardino	KO	1
June	21—Ruben Solario, Las Vegas	L	10
Sept.	13—Miguel Flores, San Antonio	KO	3
Dec.	11—Kiko Bejines, Los Angeles	W	10

ARTURO MUNOZ
Texas Junior Lightweight
1979

Nov.	27—Efraim Flores, Houston	L	4
1980			
Jan.	8—Efraim Flores, Houston	D	6
Apr.	6—Jorge Zuniga, Houston	L	4
Aug.	26—Juan Campos, Houston	KO	3
Nov.	11—Tony Tamez, Beaumont	L	6

RUBEN MUNOZ JR.
Texas Junior Lightweight
1979

July	9—John Morgan, Odessa	W	4
Aug.	27—Wilburn Lawson, Odessa	KO	3
Oct.	11—Willie Hall, Phoenix	W	4
Nov.	13—Ramon Comey, Houston	KO	2
1980			
Feb.	12—Ezzard Charles Adams, Beaumont	W	6
May	19—Ramon Guillen, Dallas	KO	4
July	28—Tony Sanchez, Odessa	KO	2
Aug.	16—Mauro Fuentes, Odessa	KO	2
Aug.	30—Dennis Quimayousie, Incline Village	L	8
Sept.	23—Fred Harris, Odessa	KO	4

QUADIR MUNTAQUIM
Camden, N.J. Light Heavyweight
1980

Feb.	23—Novel Renta, Atlantic City	W	4
Mar.	14—Dwight Triplett, Trenton	L	4
May	16—Dwight Triplett, Chester	KO by	4

LUIS CARLOS MURA
Tucson, Ariz. Junior Middleweight
1977

July	6—Bobby Epps, Las Vegas	L	6
July	20—Bobby Epps, Lake Tahoe	L	4
1978			
Jan.	24—Len Harden, Phoenix	KO by	3
Mar.	24—Troy Vaughn, Ogden	D	4
Apr.	4—Raul Gomez, El Paso	KO	1
July	26—Bobby Swanson, Las Vegas	W	4
Aug.	31—Edgar Ross, Tampa	KO by	5
Oct.	28—Xavier Garcia, Tucson	W	8
Nov.	15—Fahim Muhammad, Las Vegas	L	6
Nov.	25—Xavier Garcia, Tucson	L	8
Dec.	8—Ron Brown, Denver	KO by	1
1979			
Sept.	5—Dick Fisher, Las Vegas	L	8
Sept.	19—Lee Burkey, Las Vegas	D	4
1980			
Apr.	14—Pascual Ramirez, Fresno	D	6
Apr.	17—James Bella, Los Angeles	L	6
May	5—Clayton Ross, Phoenix	L	6
May	30—Sylvester Green, San Bernardino	L	6

LEROY MURPHY
Chicago, Ill. Light Heavyweight
1980

Nov.	13—Roger Moore, Chicago	KO	2
Dec.	11—Gary Hunter, Chicago	KO	1

SEGUNDO MURILLO
Born: January 16, 1955, Loja, Ecuador.
Weight: 147 lbs.
1974

Aug.	2—Jose Tupiza, Guayaquil	W	4
Aug.	17—Jorge Criollo, Guayaquil	D	4
Oct.	28—Jorge Moreno, Cuenca	KO	5
Dec.	18—Osvaldo Davalos, Guayaquil	W	8
1975			
Feb.	1—Jose Tupiza, Guayaquil	KO	3
Mar.	13—Osvaldo Davalos, Guayaquil	W	8
Aug.	8—Wellington Wheatley, Guayaquil	W	6
Dec.	19—Wellington Wheatley, Guayaquil	L	8
1976			
May	22—Marco Jurado, Quito	L	8
Oct.	16—Jose Tupiza, Quito	W	8
Dec.	3—Eduardo Aracena, Guayaquil	W	10
Dec.	16—Vicente Salcedo, Portoviejo	W	8
1977			
Jan.	15—Luis Castro, Guayaquil	KO	3
Mar.	10—Rafael Anchunadia, Portoviejo	L	8
Apr.	22—Jose Grijalba, Loja	W	12
May	7—Manuel Gongora, Portoviejo	KO	7
May	27—Carlos Renterias, Loja	KO	3
July	9—Rafael Piamonte, Quito	L	10
July	29—Wellington Wheatley, Portoviejo	L	12
(For Ecuadorian Junior Welterweight Title)			
Sept.	17—Victor Nilo, Quito	W	10
Dec.	20—Francisco Quinonez, Guayaquil	W	10

1978
Apr. 15—Alberto Herrera, Quevedo .... W 8
Apr. 27—Eduardo Aracena, Guayaquil .... W 10
July 6—Luis Rodriguez, Guayaquil .... KO 4
     (Won American Welterweight Title)
Aug. 31—Julio Medina, Guayaquil .... KO 6
Dec. 1—Ramiro Bolanos, Guayaquil .... W 10
Dec. 21—Tony Montano, Portoviejo .... W 10
1979
Feb. 8—Fighting Hunks, Guayaquil .... W 12
     (Retained American Welterweight Title)
Mar. 3—Thomas Hearns, Detroit ....KO by 8
June 2—Rafael Anchunadia, S.D. de los Colorados D 8
July 19—Osvaldo Romero, Guayaquil .... W 12
     (Retained American Welterweight Title)
Sept. 17—Victor Nilo, Quito .... W 10
Nov. 2—Osvaldo Romero, Guayaquil .... W 12
     (Retained American Welterweight Title)
Dec. 21—Rosendo Vidal, Guayaquil .... W 10
1980
Aug. 31—Mercedes Espinoza, Quito .... W 10

EDDIE MURRAY
Chicago, Ill. Junior Lightweight
1978
Aug. 3—Al Carter, Detroit .... KO by 6
Dec. 9—Hilmer Kenty, Detroit .... KO by 3
1979
Jan. 19—Steve Homan, Kansas .... KO by 5
1980
Feb. 18—Billy Moreno, Chicago .... W 6
July 11—Benny Marquez, Chicago .... KO 4
Nov. 8—Davey Armstrong, Detroit .... KO by 2

KENNY MUSE
Camden, N.J. Junior Lightweight
Born: October 25, 1951, Camden N.J.
1973
Dec. 8—Ernest Bing, Atlantic City .... L 4
1974
Jan. 14—Carlos Duprey, Philadelphia .... L 4
Mar. 19—Alfonso Evans, Philadelphia .... L 4
June 26—Carlos Duprey, Camden .... L 6
1975
Dec. 10—George Reilly, Scranton .... KO 3
1976
(Inactive)
1977
Apr. 21—Mike Dowling, Wilmington .... L 4
May 9—Mike Picciotti, Philadelphia .... L 4
Aug. 26—Arseneo Green, Allentown .... L 4
Sept. 15—Victor Pappas, Philadelphia .... L 6
Oct. 25—Alseneo Green, Allentown .... L 4
1978
Apr. 28—Michael Ross, Upper Darby .... L 4
Oct. 24—Mickey Diflo, Philadelphia .... W 4
1979
June 3—Ricky Camora, Quebec .... L 8
July 17—Ron Aurit, Atlantic City .... D 6
Aug. 5—Ron Aurit, Atlantic City .... L 6
1980
Jan. 18—Gaetan Hart, Quebec City .... L 10
Feb. 23—Confesor Rosales, Atlantic City .... W 4
Mar. 11—Jean LaPointe, Montreal .... L 8
May 7—Michael Lalonde, Montreal .... L 8

JOHN MYER
Warren, Ohio Welterweight
1979
May 23—Lynn Lustig, New Kensington .... W 4
1980
Aug. 20—Dale Gordon, Warren .... W 6
Sept. 17—Chuck Spicer, Strongville .... W 4

DANNY MYERS
Muncie, Ind. Welterweight
Born: August, 15, 1951
1977
Nov. 22—Simmie Black, Indianapolis .... KO 3
1978
Jan. 25—Nicky Wills, Indianapolis .... KO 2
Apr. 3—Melvin Young, Indianapolis .... KO 1
Apr. 5—Joey Hrbcha, Cleveland .... W 4
May 1—Phil Bowen, Indianapolis .... KO by 1
June 3—Joey Hrbcha, Muncie .... KO 1
July 9—Charley Smith, Indianapolis .... KO 3
July 22—Frankie Mills, Knoxville .... KO 3
Oct. 10—Dave Harris, Indianapolis .... HO 1
Oct. 17—Joey Hrbcha, Canton .... KO 1

Oct. 31—Roberto Garcia, Indianapolis .... KO 1
Nov. 30—Cicero Blake, Indianapolis .... KO 4
1979
Feb. 17—Simmie Black, Indianapolis .... KO 3
Apr. 22—Curtis Stevens, Indianapolis .... KO 2
July 18—Norman Withers, Indianapolis .... KO 2
Sept. 20—Joe Suguro, Indianapolis .... KO 2
Dec. 2—Phil Bowen, Muncie .... KO 2
1980
Jan. 22—Marion Thomas, Indianapolis .... L 12
June 20—Rodney Foster, Ft. Wayne .... KO 2
Sept. 23—Al Conti, Indianapolis .... KO 3
Nov. 1—Aaron Pryor, Dayton .... KO by 3

CARLOS NACIMIENTO
Argentine Welterweight
1980
Feb. 14—Jorge Medina, Posadas .... D 10
Apr. 18—Rogelio Zarza, Mar del Plata .... L 10
May 23—Alfredo Lucero, Salta .... L 10
June 5—Hector Caceres, Posadas .... W 10
July 4—Hugo Gomez, Posadas .... W 6
Sept. 4—Carlos Peralta, Posadas .... L 10
Oct. 17—Raul Guillermo, Posadas .... W 10
Dec. 18—Eduardo Contres, Posadas .... D 10

JUAN NAMUNCURA
Argentine Junior Welterweight
1980
Mar. 7—Horacio Mendez, Cutralco .... KO 7
Apr. 17—Alberto Gojt, Neuquen .... W 10
July 4—Ramon Allende, Cutralco .... W 10
Sept. 6—Santiago Lopez, Neuquen .... W 10
Dec. 5—Miguel Gonzalez, Cutralco .... L 10

FELIX NANCE
Norwich, Conn. Junior Welterweight
1979
Nov. 28—Tony Rodriguez, Hartford .... KO 2
1980
Jan. 9—Rocky Ortiz, Hartford .... D 4
July 25—Chi Chi Hernandez, New Bedford .... W 4

BERNARDO NARVAEZ
Argentine Welterweight
1980
Apr. 12—Raul Guillermo, Buenos Aires .... D 10
July 5—Jorge Medina, Zarate .... L 10
Aug. 8—Rodolfo Rojas, Concordia .... W 10
Oct. 10—Ramon Abeldano, Concordia .... D 10
Dec. 12—Oscar Vallejos, Concordia .... D 10

JOSE NARVAEZ
Argentine Bantamweight
1980
Feb. 21—Carlos Huilli, Mendoza .... W 6
Mar. 7—Julio C. Saba, Pilar .... W 10
Apr. 5—Carlos Betbeder, Buenos Aires .... W 8
May 17—Jose Uziga, Pergamino .... W 12
     (Won Argentine Bantamweight Title)
July 4—Hermogenes Prado, Mendoza .... W 10
Aug. 1—Juan Brizuela, Mendoza .... W 10
Aug. 15—Jorge Martinez, La Rioja .... W 10
Sept. 12—Luis Gerez, Mendoza .... W 12
     (Retained Argentine Bantamweight Title)
Oct. 17—Jorge Araya, Mendoza .... TW 5
Nov. 14—Juan C. Cortez, San Juan .... L 10

OTEY NATIONS
Birmingham, Alabama Middleweight
1980
Mar. 4—Chester Jackson, Memphis .... KO 3
July 11—Simmie Black, Meridian .... W 6
Dec. 9—Simmie Black, Birmingham .... KO 1

RUSSELL NATIONS
Birmingham, Alabama Welterweight
1979
Mar. 6—Simmie Black, Memphis .... D 4
Mar. 29—Mike Ramirez, Mobile .... L 6
1980
Mar. 4—Lester Groves, Memphis .... KO 6
July 11—Rocky McCollum, Meridian .... KO 3
Dec. 9—Rufus Walters, Birmingham .... W 6

JAIME NAVA
Los Angeles, Calif. Lightweight
1977
Feb. 19—Rodolfo Castillo, Guadalajara .... W 10
June 11—Jesus Ramirez, Guadalajara .... KO by 9
1978
Apr. 10—Fili Ramirez, Fresno .... W 8
May 20—Jose Osuna, Fresno .... W 8
Aug. 26—Rafael Limon, Fresno .... KO by 10
Nov. 9—Frankie Baltazar, Los Angeles .... KO by 6
1979
May 15—Sal Lopez, Sacramento .... L 6
May 21—Petronillo Velasquez, Bakersfield .... KO by 8
June 21—Tony Baltazar, Los Angeles .... L 6
July 4—Frank Moultrie, Las Vegas .... KO by 6
1980
Feb. 3—Sterling McPhearson, Las Vegas .... L 6
Feb. 13—Jesse Castelberry, Las Vegas .... W 6
Feb. 20—Lionel Harney, Las Vegas .... L 10
Feb. 28—Clark Duran, Los Angeles .... L 6
Mar. 13—Randy Clover, Los Angeles .... L 6
Mar. 18—Dennis Quimayousie, Sparks .... W 10
Mar. 21—Leonardo Moreno, Los Angeles .... L 4
Apr. 14—Manuel Abedoy, Fresno .... L 10
May 9—Frankie Baltazar, Los Angeles .... L 10
May 28—Raul Cruz, Las Vegas .... KO 5
June 12—Mark Daniels, Los Angeles .... L 10
July 30—Ray Mancini, Las Vegas .... L 10
Sept. 11—Chango Moreno, Los Angeles .... L 10
Oct. 8—Juan Dominguez, Los Angeles .... L 10
Nov. 19—Frankie Moultrie, Las Vegas .... W 10
Nov. 29—Blaine Dickson, Las Vegas .... L 10
Dec. 6—Hedgemon Robertson, Lake Tahoe .... L 8

ROLANDO NAVARETTE
Honolulu, Hawaii Junior Lightweight
1978
May 27—Tony Jumao-as, Cebu .... KO by 4
July 15—Wine Jon, Chrlsantos .... W 12
1979
Feb. 16—Rey Tam, Manila .... KO 4
June 19—Frankie Duarte, Honolulu .... W 10
1979
July 24—Jose Torres, Honolulu .... W 10
Aug. 28—Miguel Meza, Honolulu .... KO 2
Oct. 9—Junichi Okubo, Honolulu .... KO 3
Dec. 18—Abdul Bey, Honolulu .... KO 7
1980
Jan. 18—Frank Ahumada, Manila .... W 10
Apr. 1—Jerome Artis, Honolulu .... KO 7
Apr. 27—Alexis Arguello, San Juan .... KO by 4
(For WBC Junior Lightweight Title)

AGUSTIN NAVARRO
Argentine Junior Featherweight
1980
Feb. 9—Luciano Azcona, Tandil .... W 8
Mar. 7—Jorge Dominguez, Tandil .... KO 7
Apr. 26—Roberto Poncini, Tandil .... W 10
May 24—Luciano Azcona, Tandil .... W 8

CARMELO NEGRON
New York, N.Y. Featherweight
1978
Sept. 19—Henry Jones, New York .... KO 2
Oct. 5—Tony Still, White Plains .... KO 2
Nov. 30—Melvin Bethea, New York .... KO 2
1979
Jan. 9—Glenn Guy, Philadelphia .... KO 1
Mar. 2—Felix Rodriguez, Albany .... KO 1
Apr. 6—Tomas Diaz, New York .... KO 3
May 21—Bobby Everett, New York .... KO 1
June 14—Marcial Santiago, New York .... KO 6
June 27—Jose Luis Medrano, New York .... KO 1
Sept. 19—Livio Nolasco, New York .... KO 6
1980
Jan. 25—Bobby Alexander, New York .... KO 10
Apr. 18—Terry Pizzarro, New York .... KO 7
June 20—Davey Vasquez, New York .... KO 6
Oct. 2—Baby Kid Chocolate, New York .... KO 7

CONROY NELSON
Ottowa, Canada Heavyweight
1978
Nov. 20—Sylvester Wilder, Buckingham .... KO 2
Dec. 11—Chuck Findlay, Toronto .... L 6
1979
Feb. 5—Djata Banks, Hull .... KO 2
1980
Feb. 24—Eddie Mallard, Atlantic City .... D 4
Mar. 13—Joe Dinardo, Hull .... KO 1

Apr. 6—David Carr, Louisville .... W 4
Apr. 21—Joe Maye, Hull .... KO 2
May 4—Calvin Langston, Monticello .... KO 1
May 23—Harold Rice, Hartford .... KO by 2
July 25—Larry Simms, Ontario .... W 6
Sept. 23—Gaston Berube, Montreal .... KO 1
Nov. 11—Leroy Caldwell, Halifax .... W 10

SAMMY NeSMITH
Indianapolis, Ind. Middleweight
1973
Sept. 22—Shane Bosley, Indianapolis .... KO 1
Oct. 27—Bobby Crawford, Indianapolis .... KO 1
Nov. 8—Lionel Ford, Indianapolis .... W 4
Nov. 15—Sammy Barr, Tampa .... KO 2
1974
Feb. 16—Gehe Simelton, New Castle .... KO 1
Apr. 13—Joe Armour, New Castle .... W 4
Nov. 12—Jimmy Jones, Indianapolis .... KO 1
Dec. 11—Bobby Orr, Indianapolis .... KO 1
1975
Jan. 29—Ray Smith, Indianapolis .... KO 1
Apr. 17—Gary Broughton, Indianapolis .... KO 3
June 6—Willie Warren, Indianapolis .... KO 2
Dec. 16—Juan Garcia, Indianapolis .... KO 2
1976
Mar. 19—Raoul Aguirre, Indianapolis .... KO by 3
May 6—Raoul Aguirre, Indianapolis .... KO 10
May 25—Al Cook, Orlando .... KO 3
July 28—Donnie Meloncon, Indianapolis .... KO 3
Oct. 6—Tony Chiaverini, Kansas City .... KO by 9
Nov. 13—Jimmy Carter, Indianapolis .... KO 1
Nov. 30—Oscar Balderis, Indianapolis .... KO 1
1977
Feb. 1—Gary Guiden, Indianapolis .... KO by 3
Mar. 11—Al Moss, Orlando .... KO 1
Sept 6—Major Lambert, Orlando .... KO 2
Nov. 22—Prino Gonzalez, Indianapolis .... KO 1
1978
Jan. 24—Roberto Cruz, Indianapolis .... KO 1
Apr. 3—Ruben Lopez, Indianapolis .... KO 2
May 1—Larry Davis, Indianapolis .... KO 3
July 9—Don Morgan, Indianapolis .... KO 5
Aug. 29—Ray Seales, Seattle .... KO by 5
Nov. 30—Tyrone Phelps, Indianapolis .... KO 7
1979
Feb. 17—Keith Broom, Indianapolis .... KO 5
Apr. 22—Bennie Sanchez, Indianapolis .... KO 2
July 18—Jim Hearn, Indianapolis .... KO 2
Sept. 20—Chris Lange, Indianapolis .... W 10
Oct. 19—Larry Myers, Phoenix .... KO 1
Nov. 8—Jerome Jackson, Indianapolis .... W 10
1980
Jan. 22—Robert Powell, Indianapolis .... KO 2
Mar. 17—Ronnie Brown, Indianapolis .... KO 8
May 13—Ronnie Harris, Indianapolis .... KO 10
Oct. 28—Joe Martin, Indianapolis .... KO 1
Dec. 4—Frank Fletcher, Atlantic City .... KO by 6

GREG NETTER
Columbus, Ohio Welterweight
1977
Sept. 24—Earl Caldwell, Columbus .... W 4
1978
(Inactive)
1979
Sept. 18—Kevin Straughter, Columbus .... W 4
Nov. 27—Kevin Straughter, Columbus .... KO 3
Dec. 28—Manning Galloway, Columbus .... L 10
1980
Feb. 18—Charlie Brown, Upper Darby .... D 6
Apr. 30—Art McKnight, Youngstown .... D 10
June 1—Kevin Straughter, Columbus .... KO 5
July 6—Sam Gervin, Columbus .... KO 6
Aug. 21—Sam Gervin, Columbus .... W 6
Aug. 23—Gary Coates, Alliance .... L 8
Sept. 10—Dujuan Johnson, Detroit .... KO by 9

AL NEUMANN
Seattle, Wash. Heavyweight
1977
Feb. 12—Tom Sullivan, Lacey .... KO by 1
Mar. 25—Tom Sullivan, Seattle .... D 4
June 11—Paul Guyness, Hillsboro .... W 4
June 28—Stan Johnson, Seattle .... KO by 3
Aug. 16—Richard Gosha, Seattle .... KO by 1
Oct. 6—Dale Grant, Seattle .... KO by 4
Nov. 19—Ken Arlt, Hillsboro .... L 6
1978
Feb. 22—Vic Van Fleet, Anchorage .... W 4
Mar. 2—Jack Martin, Everett .... KO 2
Mar. 16—Franco Thomas, Anchorage .... L 8
Apr. 10—Scotty Welsh, Everett .... W disq. 1

May 10—Tony Franco Thomas, Anchorage ..... KO by 9
Aug. 22—Mustapha Allimean, Seattle .... KO by 6
1979
Feb. 14—Harvey Steichen, Spokane .... W 8
Oct. 31—Earl Tripp, Las Vegas .... L 10
1980
Mar. 11—Nate Stewart, Seattle .... KO 4
Mar. 18—Ken Arlt, Spokane .... W 8
May 4—Perscell Davis, Seattle .... KO 7
June 19—Ron Lyle, Tacoma .... KO by 10

HAROLD NEVEAU
Carson City, Nevada Junior Middleweight
1980
Apr. 24—Joey Roybal, Portland .... W 6
June 24—Mike Carrerre, Honolulu .... L 4
July 15—Richard Schneider, Reno .... W 4
Aug. 31—Richard Schneider, Carson City .... W 6
Oct. 11—Robert Johnson, Nanaimo .... KO 5
Oct. 30—Tommy Carrasco, Carson City .... KO 3
Nov. 19—Leroy Miller, Lake Tahoe .... KO 3

DESI NEWBILL
Los Angeles, Calif. Junior Featherweight
1978
Apr. 19—Johnny Jackson, Las Vegas .... KO 2
May 10—Salvador Ugalde, Las Vegas .... W 4
June 28—Salvador Ugalde, Las Vegas .... KO by 1
1979
Feb. 15—Delfino Cornejo, Los Angeles .... W 4
Feb. 22—Jose Villegas, Los Angeles .... D 4
Mar. 1—Jose Villegas, Los Angeles .... L 6
Mar. 15—Cristobal Gutierrez, Los Angeles .... KO 1
Mar. 22—Lino Castillo, Los Angeles .... W 6
Apr. 5—Francisco Sanchez, Los Angeles .... TD 2
May 3—Lorenzo Ramirez, Los Angeles .... D 6
May 10—Salvador Ugalde, Los Angeles .... L 6
June 13—Jose Villegas, Sacramento .... L 10
Aug. 10—Fred Roach, San Diego .... L 6
Sept. 9—Sergio Castro, Los Angeles .... L 6
Sept. 18—Robert Anderson, Phoenix .... L 6
Oct. 11—Doug Garcia, Los Angeles .... KO 2
Oct. 18—Yoshi Sunagawa, Los Angeles .... D 6
1980
Feb. 3—Robert Anderson, Reno .... L 8
Feb. 14—Sergio Castro, Los Angeles .... KO by 5
May 16—Jose Luis Lopez, San Bernardino .... W 4
June 19—Richard Savala, Los Angeles .... KO by 5

CHARLIE NEWELL
Somers, Conn. Junior Welterweight
1979
June 29—Miguel Sanchez, Hartford .... KO by 1
Nov. 5—Papo Figueroa, Hartford .... W 6
Nov. 15—Marcus Starks, Bristol .... L 4
Nov. 28—Wilfredo Franco, Hartford .... KO 5
1980
Jan. 9—Marlon Starling, Hartford .... KO by 7
(Died on Jan. 18 of injuries sustained in Starling fight.)

FREDDIE NEWS
Salt Lake City, Utah Heavyweight
1978
Sept. 1—Fred Grogan, Salt Lake City .... KO 1
Dec. 9—Tony Pulu, Salt Lake City .... KO by 1
1979
Mar. 10—Tony Pulu, Salt Lake City .... KO by 5
1980
Mar. 22—Steve Huntington, Salt Lake City .... KO by 2

FRANK NEWTON
Oklahoma City, Okla. Lightweight
1978
Aug. 1—Sean O'Grady, Oklahoma City .... Exh. 4
Sept. 6—Tom Crowley, Oklahoma City .... W 6
Nov. 16—Alvin Fowler, Oklahoma City .... W 6
Dec. 7—Johnny Sanchez, Oklahoma City .... W 6
1979
Mar. 17—Shannon Williams, Oklahoma City ..... KO 3
Aug. 3—Herman Page, Tulsa .... KO 1
Sept. 20—Al Thompson, Tulsa .... KO 3
Oct. 23—Simmie Black, Oklahoma City .... KO 2
Dec. 15—Wilburn Lawson, Oklahoma City .... D 6
1980
Feb. 9—Gustavo Rodriguez, Oklahoma City .... KO 3
Mar. 3—Adolfo Rivas, Oklahoma City .... KO 6
Apr. 3—Ken Saale, Oklahoma City .... W 12
(Won State Lightweight Title)
June 10—Rogelio Castaneda, Oklahoma City .... KO 6
July 27—Benny Marquez, Omaha .... KO 5
Sept. 9—Victor Cid, Oklahoma City .... KO 5
Sept. 25—Billy Moreno, Norman .... KO 9
Nov. 20—Johnny Copeland, Oklahoma City .... KO by 7

LUIS NEYRA
Argentine Lightweight
1980
Aug. 9—Victor Ojeda, Caleta Olivia .... W 6
Sept. 6—Ramon Collado, Cdo. Rivadavia .... D 6
Dec. 5—Roberto Guerrero, Cdo. Rivadavia .... W 6

JOSE NIETO
Bronx, N.Y. Super Bantamweight
Born: December 2, 1954, Height: 5 ft. 3 in.
Managed by Adonis Torres
1978
Jan. 25—Jose (Cheo) Ortiz, Brooklyn .... W 4
May 5—George Nieves, Brooklyn .... KO 2
Aug. 25—Freddy Figueroa, New York .... KO 2
Sept. 8—Melvin Boynton, New York .... KO 1
Nov. 2—Jose (Cheo) Ortiz, New York .... KO 7
Nov. 30—Bob Ingras, New York .... KO 2
1979
Apr. 6—Mike Frazier, New York .... KO 1
Apr. 27—Roy Taylor, New York .... KO 2
May 21—Jimmy Washington, New York .... W 6
June 14—Leo Lopez, New York .... KO 4
Aug. 22—Monito Jimenez, New York .... KO 7
Oct. 4—David Capo, Felt Forum .... W 8
Nov. 23—Gerald Hayes, New York .... KO by 1
1980
Mar. 4—Salvatore Ramirez, Elizabeth .... KO 2
Apr. 25—Alberto Collazo, Commack .... KO by 7
Dec. 17—Danny Daniels, White Plains .... KO 1

ANTONIO NIEVES
Paterson, N.J. Featherweight
1979
Nov. 15—Kato Ali, Dover .... W 4
1980
Feb. 22—Rafael Lopez, Fall River .... L 4
Mar. 8—Ron Meaweather, Great Gorge .... W 4
May 25—Tony Santana, Atlantic City .... L 6
Aug. 2—Fernando Martinez, Totowa .... W 6
Oct. 16—Danny Daniels, Totowa .... KO 5

EFRAIN NIEVES
Milwaukee, Wisc. Junior Lightweight
1980
July 11—Kelvin Lampkin, Chicago .... W 4
Aug. 22—Ben Stiff, Chicago .... KO 3
Dec. 10—Alvin Fowler, Moline .... KO 4

VICTOR NILO
Chilean Welterweight
1980
Feb. 1—Walter Gomez, Santa Rosa .... KO by 3
June 25—Jose Fernandez, Santiago .... KO 3
Sept. 5—Tito Yanni, Mar del Plata .... TL 2
Oct. 10—Tito Yanni, Mar del Plata .... KO by 4

JORGE NINA
Passaic, N.J. Junior Lightweight
1979
—Rocky Ortiz, Staten Island .... L 4
1980
Feb. 29—Louis Hubela, Brooklyn .... L 8
June 11—John Verderosa, White Plains ... L disq. 6
Dec. 11—Robert Rucker, New York .... L 8

JULIUS NOBLE
Chicago, Ill. Light Heavyweight
1976
Oct. 6—Ivy Brown, Kansas City .... L 4
Nov. 10—Dick Morgan, Indianapolis .... D 4
1977
Jan. 19—Paul Ramos, Cleveland .... L 6
Apr. 25—Mike West, Chicago .... W 4
June 25—Tony Fritz, Chicago .... KO 2
July 25—Mike West, Chicago .... KO 3
Oct. 25—Henry Sims, Chicago .... KO 5
Dec. 13—Lee Thomas, Chicago .... KO 1
1978
May 8—Tony Curovis, Chicago .... KO 4
July 24—Percy Hairston, Bridgeview .... KO 3
Oct. 6—Karl Zurheide, Waukegan .... D 10
1979
Feb. 28—Ronnie Wright, Chicago .... KO 2
Mar. 20—Bill Radcliff, Chicago .... W 6
June 11—Chuck Warfield, Chicago .... KO 1
Oct. 19—Carlos Marks, Chicago .... W 10
1980
Feb. 1—Murray Sutherland, Chicago .... KO by 4

CLAUDE NOEL
Trinidad, W.I. Lightweight
1973
Nov.　13—Art de Freitas, Port of Spain　..........KO　2
1974
(Inactive)
1975
June　16—Michael Baptiste, Port of Spain　........KO　4
Oct.　23—Cleve Nichols, Port of Spain　...........KO　6
1976
Sept.　20—Selwyn Figarro, Port of Spain　........KO　8
Nov.　26—Fitzroy Guiseppi, Port of Spain　........KO　10
(T & T Lightweight Title)
1977
Feb.　11—Francisco Cruz, Guadeloupe　...........KO　3
Feb.　25—Lennox Blackmoore, Port of Spain　...KO by　10
May　17—Easy Boy Lake, St. Croix　..............KO　4
May　29—Lennox Blackmoore, Port of Spain　...KO by　10
June　3—Raphael Solis, Guadeloupe　.............W　10
July　3—Vinnie DeBarros, Port of Spain　.........KO　4
Oct.　7—Larry Stanton, Port of Spain　...........W　10
Dec.　16—Hector Medina, Port of Spain　..........KO　10
1978
Feb.　10—Fitzroy Guisseppi, Port of Spain　........KO　8
(T & T Lightweight Title)
June　6—Frankie Moultrie, Orlando　.............KO　2
July　25—Hilbert Stevenson, Orlando　............KO　3
Aug.　8—Warren Matthews, Orlando　.............KO　2
Oct.　24—Scotty Foreman, Orlando　..............KO　2
Nov.　7—Augustine Estrada, Orlando　...........W　10
Dec.　15—Pedro Acosta, Port of Spain　...........W　10
1979
Mar.　30—Gratien Hart, Port of Spain　...........W　10
June　16—Ernesto Espana, San Juan　.........KO by　13
(Vacant WBA Lightweight Title)
1980
Jan.　18—Francisco Becerra, Port-of-Spain　.......KO　5
Feb.　29—Jerome Artis, Port-of-Spain　............W　10
Mar.　28—Michael Reid, Port-of-Spain　...........W　10

DAVID NOEL
Trinidad Junior Middleweight
1980
May　2—Ivor Simmons, Port-of-Spain　...........KO　6
Aug.　1—Teachor McKenzie, Port-of-Spain　.......W　8
Oct.　17—Roy Harry, Port-of-Spain　...............W　8

WINSTON NOEL
Brooklyn, N.Y. Welterweight
1968
Sept.　26—Lou Falu, Taunton　....................KO　2
Oct.　18—Bobby Hughes, New York　...............L　4
Nov.　18—Johnny Gant, Alexandra　.............KO by　5
1969
Jan.　13—Otho Tyson, Secaucus　..................L　6
Jan.　28—Danny Cocoran, New York　.............KO　4
Mar.　14—Juan Rueda, New York　.................L　4
Mar.　25—Colin Fraser, Montreal　.................L　6
Apr.　5—Marcelino Alicia, Plymouth　............KO　6
Apr.　25—Reuben Cortez, Syracuse　...............W　6
Nov.　12—Marcelino Alicia, Worcester　............L　8
Dec.　4—Bobby Hughes, Taunton　................L　8
Dec.　19—Jose Nieves, New York　.................L　8
1970
July　13—Ron Miller, Washington, D.C.　..........L　10
July　30—Johnny Gant, Baltimore　................L　10
Sept.　22—Alvin Anderson, Washington, D.C.　......L　10
Nov.　2—Ricky Thomas, Philadelphia　...........D　6
Nov.　24—Ricky Thomas, Philadelphia　...........W　8
1971
Feb.　22—Otho Tyson, Providence　................L　4
1972
Feb.　16—Hector Perez, New York　................L　8
Feb.　24—Chuck Wilburn, Portland, Me.　..........L　10
Apr.　15—Pat Murphy, Jersey City　...............L　8
Apr.　25—Adrian Davis, Baltimore　...............L　10
1973
Apr.　16—William Watson, Philadelphia　..........L　8
May　28—Fausto Rodriguez, San Juan　..........KO by　1
1974
Nov.　6—Pedro Fernandez, Madrid　...........KO by　4
Nov.　21—Ken Buchanan, Copenhagen　.........KO by　2
1975
Feb.　8—Frankie Benitez, San Juan　...........KO by　2
1976
Aug.　16—Tyrone Phelps, Newark　................L　6
Aug.　19—Tyrone Phelps, New York　..............L　6
1977
Dec.　10—Pete Seward, Grand Rapids　............L　8
1978
Apr.　15—Nelson Ruiz, Caracas　.............KO by　1
Sept.　21—Pat Murphy, Jersey City　...............L　8

1979
Mar.　15—Mustafa Hamsho, North Bergen　.....KO by　2
Apr.　6—Ernie Johnson, Albany　..............KO by　3
1980
July　16—Nino Gonzales, Elizabeth　............KO by　2

RICK NOGGLE
Dayton, Ohio Middleweight
1978
Aug.　22—Earl Harris, Erie　......................KO　4
Oct.　17—Frankie Mills, Canton　.................W　6
Nov.　29—Theron Smallridge, Richfield　..........KO　2
1979
Apr.　19—Ivan McCoy, Richfield　.................KO　2
May　25—Calvin Howard, Richfield　..............KO　1
Oct.　18—Charles Patterson, Struthers　...........KO　3
1980
Jan.　15—Eddie Harris, Youngstown　.............KO　4
Feb.　20—Randy Graves, Las Vegas　..............L　6
Apr.　5—Tommy Sacco, Akron　..................KO　4
May　4—Kenney Heflin, Canton　...............W　8
June　14—Earl Caldwell, Cincinnati　..............KO　1
Sept.　30—Sam Gervin, Niles　.....................W　10

LIVIO NOLASCO
Dominican Rep. Featherweight
Born: April 23, 1952
1972
Oct.　17—Tomas Rivera, Ponce　..................KO　7
1973
Feb.　19—Nelson Cruz Tamariz, Santo Domingo　.....L　10
1974
Apr.　1—Eduardo Santiago, New York　...........L　10
May　6—Eduardo Santiago, New York　..........W　10
May　25—Eduardo Santiago, New York　..........L　10
Sept.　9—Dom Monaco, New York　..............W　10
Dec.　19—Leo Cruz, Santo Domingo　.............KO　9
1975
June　9—Nelson Tamariz, Santo Domingo　........L　10
Aug.　30—Ben Lelake, Johannesburg　...........KO by　7
1976
Apr.　3—Marcos Britton, Panama City　..........KO　6
June　12—Rigoberto Riasco, Panama City.　......KO by　10
(WBA Super Bantamweight Title)
1977
Aug.　7—Ruben Valdes, Barranquilla　.............L　12
Nov.　20—Oscar Arnal, Caracas　..............KO by　4
1978
Feb.　12—Julian Solis, Carolino　.................L　10
Aug.　5—Raul DeCaro, Mexico City　.............KO　8
Sept.　11—Joaquin Acuna, Mexico City　..........KO by　3
Nov.　11—Joaquin Acuna, Mexico City　..........KO by　1
Dec.　2—Joaquin Acuna, Culiacan　............KO by　1
1979
Mar.　10—Lupe Pintor, Los Angeles　...........KO by　6
Sept.　19—Carmelo Negron, New York　.........KO by　6
Oct.　18—Jose Luis Suto, Los Mochis　............L　10
1980
Jan.　12—Derrick Holmes, Atlantic City　.......KO by　2
Aug.　2—Rocky Lockridge, Totowa　...........KO by　4

ROCHELL NORRIS
Atlantic City, N.J. Heavyweight
1973
Mar.　24—Henry Lawson, Atlantic City　...........KO　3
May　2—Paul Simonetti, Scranton　..............KO　1
June　2—Sonny Brown, Atlantic City　............W　6
June　25—Don Branch, Philadelphia　..............W　4
Aug.　10—Ben Benjamin, Atlantic City　...........KO　3
Oct.　10—Mike Burks, Scranton　.................KO　2
Oct.　22—Obie English, Philadelphia　..........KO by　4
1974
Oct.　18—John Clohessey, Baltimore　.............KO　5
Nov.　4—Mike Koranicki, New York　.............W　6
Nov.　13—Charlie Green, Scranton　...............W　8
1975
Jan.　26—Ernie Lassiter, Scranton　...............W　8
Feb.　10—Mose Harrell, Camden　................W　8
Apr.　9—Earnie Shavers, Binghamton　........KO by　10
July　9—Larry Middleton, Binghamton　........KO by　9
Oct.　21—Duane Bobick, Philadelphia　.........KO by　2
1976
Aug.　19—Bob Smith, New York　..................L　8
Nov.　18—Rodell Dupree, Wilmington, Del.　........W　8
1977
Sept.　16—Matt Robinson, Wilmington　.............W　6
1978
Nov.　1—Larry Alexander, White Plains　......KO by　7

1979
(Inactive)
1980
Feb. 23—John Warr, Atlantic City .... W 6

SERGIO NUALARTE
San Diego, Calif. Featherweight
1978
Feb. 23—Jose Rodriguez, Los Angeles .... KO by 10
Mar. 31—Jose Resendiz, San Diego ....L 8
Apr. 7—Herman Montes, Los Angeles .... KO by 2
Dec. 1—Eric Bonilla, San Diego ....L 4
1979
Jan. 8—Gary Pittman, Seattle .... KO 7
Jan. 26—Jimmy McNeece, San Diego ....L 6
Feb. 9—Arturo Vidrio, San Diego .... W 6
Feb. 15—Irleis Perez, Los Angeles .... KO by 2
June 10—Reynaldo Zaragoza, Stockton .... KO by 3
June 16—Eddie Freeman, Memphis .... KO by 7
Nov. 2—Ricardo Martinez, San Diego ....L 6
Nov. 23—Lenny Jones, San Diego .... W 4
Dec. 18—Dennis Quimayousie, Sparks ....L 10
1980
Feb. 22—Rodrigo Aguirre, San Bernadino ..... KO by 2

RUBEN NUNCIO
Houston, Texas Middleweight
1977
Apr. 5—Lamar Zaskin, Houston ....KO 3
May 10—Arturo Cirillo, Houston ....KO 3
1979
June 27—Clarence Howard, Phoenix .... W 8
1980
Oct. 28—Rene Pagan, Houston .... W 6

FRANCISCO JAVIER NUNEZ
Mexican Junior Featherweight
1979
May 17—Ernesto Ruiz, McAllen .... W 10
1980
May 9—Mil Jiminez, Los Angeles .... KO by 4

HIPOLITO NUNEZ
Argentine Featherweight
1980
Jan. 18—Carlos Martinetti, Mar del Plata .... W 10
Feb. 15—Gustavo Martinez, Tucuman ....KO 7
Feb. 28—Roberto Haidar, Mendoza .... W 10
Mar. 14—Domingo Casco, P.R.S. Pena .... W 10
Apr. 18—Pedro Gutierrez, Salta ....D 10
May 2—Hector Lopez, Tucuman .... W 10
May 16—Santiago Lopez, San Miguel .... W 10
May 23—Omar Mendoza, Villa Angela .... W 10
June 19—Raul Aguero, La Rioja ....KO 9
Aug. 16—Juan Malvarez, Buenos Aires ....L 12
(For Argentine Featherweight Title)
Oct. 17—Ricardo Rivarola, S.Sal. De Jujuy ...... KO 10
Oct. 31—Gabriel Sanchez, Cordoba ....L 10
Dec. 5—Carlos Sanchez, Trelew .... W 10

RAFAEL NUNEZ
Sacramento, Calif. Junior Welterweight
1975
Nov. 12—Dale Hernandez, Las Vegas .... KO by 2
1976
Jan. 7—Tony Baretta, Las Vegas................KO 2
Feb. 13—Octavio Amparan, Los Angeles .... KO by 4
May 11—Leroy Haley, Las Vegas ....L 8
Sept. 15—Andrew Ganigan, Honolulu .... KO by 2
Dec. 16—Carlos Becerrill, Los Angeles........ KO by 1
1977
Apr. 1—Mike Mayan, San Diego ....D 10
Apr. 14—Gonzale Montellano, Los Angeles ....L 10
June 2—Fidel Fraijo, Los Angeles .... W 10
July 21—Teruyoshi Noji, Los Angeles ....KO 5
Aug. 11—Arturo Pineda, Los Angeles .... W 10
1978
June 1—Ron Cummings, Sacramento ....L 6
Sept. 7—Monroe Brooks, Los Angeles .... KO by 6
1979
July 19—Irleis Perez, Los Angeles ....L 10
Aug. 28—Sammy Ayala, San Antonio .... KO by 3
Dec. 7—Gil Rodriguez, San Diego ....D 10
Dec. 13—Sal Lopez, Los Angeles .... KO by 6
1980
June 19—Jose Luis Ramirez, Tijuana ....KO by 1
Dec. 12—Monroe Brooks, Sacramento .... KO by 4

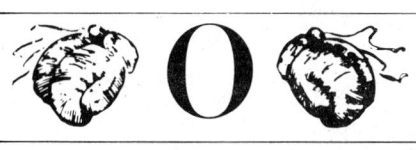

FULGENCIO OBELMEJIAS
("FULLY OBEL")
Venezuelan Middleweight
1977
Jan. 3—Franklin Zuzarra, Caracas ....KO 1
Apr. 3—Franklin Zuzarra, Caracas ....KO 1
Oct. 22—Jesus Ortiz, Mexico ....KO 9
Nov. 18—Andry Beerd, San Diego ....KO 2
Dec. 17—Rogelio Vera, Mexico ....KO 2
1978
Feb. 5—Vicente Pinon, Mexico ....KO 2
Mar. 1—Abel Cordova, Mexico .... W 10
Apr. 6—Rudy Robles, Mexico ....KO 4
Apr. 30—Rolando Martinez, Caracas ....KO 1
June 4—Jose Anglada, Caracas ....KO 1
July 15—Sandy Torres, Caracas ....KO 4
July 29—Willie Warren, Caracas ....KO 8
Sept. 17—Johnny Heard, Caracas ....KO 8
Nov. 12—Kenny Bladwell, Caracas ....KO 3
Dec. 17—Carlos Marks, Caracas ....KO 9
(For Central American and Caribbean Middleweight Title)
1979
Mar. 10—Angel Ortiz, Caracas ....KO 3
Apr. 1—Jamie Thomas, Caracas ....KO 4
Aug. 7—Luis Antonio Arias, Caracas ....KO 2
Sept. 16—Sammy Floyd, Caracas ....KO 10
Nov. 17—George Lee, Caracas ....KO 1
Dec. 17—Ray Phillips, Caracas ....KO 4
1980
Mar. 3—Elisha Obed, Caracas ....KO 3
Apr. 1—Abel Cordova, Caracas ....KO 2
Apr. 14—Walter Miranda, Caracas ....KO 1
May 24—Lamont Lovelady, Caracas ....KO 3
June 30—Clifford Wills, Caracas ....KO 3
Aug. 18—Felton Marshall, Caracas .... W 10
Sept. 10—Freddie Johnson, San Remo ....KO 3
Oct. 31—Leroy Green, Jr., Rome ....KO 3

OSVALDO (OSSIE) OCASIO
(JAWS)
Puerto Rican Heavyweight
1976
Feb. 20—Heriberto Lorenzo, San Juan ....KO 3
Apr. 5—Rafael Guerrero, San Juan ....KO 2
Apr. 27—Joe Rene, San Juan ....KO 1
July 17—Ed Turner, San Juan .... W 8
Aug. 16—Aaron Solomon, San Juan ....KO 1
1977
Feb. 12—Ed Turner, San Juan ....KO 2
Mar. 17—Gene Idolette, San Jian ....KO 1
June 14—Roy Morris, Orlando ....KO 2
June 25—Frank Schram, San Juan ....KO 4
July 12—Tommy Nickson, Orlando ....KO 4
1978
Mar. 25—Kevin Isaac, San Juan .... W 10
Apr. 8—Kevin Isaac, San Juan .... W 10
June 9—Jimmy Young, Las Vegas .... W 10
1979
Jan. 27—Jimmy Young, San Juan .... W 10
Mar. 23—Larry Holmes, Las Vegas .... KO by 7
(For WBC Heavyweight Title)
Nov. 20—Jack Sterling, Miami ....KO 1
1980
Apr. 19—Michael Dokes, San Juan ....D 10
June 28—Michael Dokes, San Juan .... KO by 1
Oct. 23—Barry Funches, New York .... W 10

MARIO OCHOA
Mexican Bantamweight
1980
Jan. 23—Javier Esquivel, Mexico City .... KO by 3
Feb. 23—Federico Nunez, Mexico City ....D 8
Mar. 15—Severiano Mendoza, Mexico City ......KO 5
Apr. 5—Alfredo Segura, Mexico City ....KO 1
June 28—Javier Esquivel, Mexico City ....D 8

OSMAR OCHOA
Argentine Junior Middleweight
1980
Apr. 11—Hector Rios, Camilo Aldao .... W 10
May ?—Daniel Ariola, Ciudadela ....L 10
Aug. 1—Santiago Portillo, Tucuman ....L 10

Nov. 7—Miguel Arguello, Tucuman .... KO 7
Dec. 5—Tito Caceres, Tartagal .... W 10
Dec. 19—Enrique Coronel, San Pedro .... W 10

DR. HERBERT ODOM
Chicago, Ill. Welterweight
1979
July 30—Eddie Partee, Chicago .... KO 2
Sept. 7—Keith Lognoon, Chicago .... KO 4
1980
Mar. 3—Larry Puchta, Chicago .... W 4

SEAN O'GRADY
Oklahoma City, Okla. Lightweight
Born: February 10, 1959
1975
Jan. 21—David Tymes, Oklahoma City .... KO 1
Feb. 4—Willie Johnson, Oklahoma City .... KO 1
Feb. 18—Joe Matthews, Oklahoma City .... KO 1
Mar. 4—James Word, Oklahoma City .... KO 1
Mar. 18—Muhammad Muffleh, Oklahoma City .... KO 1
Apr. 1—Rocky Matthews, Oklahoma City ...... KO 2
Apr. 15—Tyrone Taylor, Oklahoma City .... KO 1
May 6—Earl Booth, Oklahoma City .... KO 1
May 17—David Williams, Little Rock........... KO 1
May 20—Ramon Campos, Oklahoma City .... W 6
June 3—Baby Perez, Oklahoma City .... KO 3
June 9—Earl Booth, Dallas .... KO 1
June 17—Ezekiel Campos, Oklahoma City....... KO 1
July 1—Simmie Black, Oklahoma City .... KO 4
July 9—Ramon Reyes, Memphis .... KO 3
July 15—Ramon Campos, Oklahoma City....... W 10
Aug. 5—Victor Luna, Oklahoma City .... KO 1
Aug. 19—Harvey Wilson, Oklahoma City .... W 10
Sept. 2—Billy Miller, Oklahoma City .... KO 3
Sept. 4—Harvey Wilson, Omaha .... W 8
Oct. 21—Raul Carrez, Oklahoma City .... KO 1
Nov. 4—Ramon Reyna, Oklahoma City .... KO 3
Nov. 18—Tony Ramirez, Oklahoma City .... KO 3
Nov. 20—Robert Rodriguez, Omaha............. KO 3
Dec. 2—Lucano Medina, Oklahoma City .... KO 4
Dec. 16—Bubba Thompson, Oklahoma City ..... KO 3
1976
Jan. 6—Shannon Williams, Oklahoma City ..... KO 2
Jan. 20—Ken Connors, Oklahoma City .... KO 1
Feb. 3—Luis Martinez, Oklahoma City .... KO 1
Feb. 25—Danny Lopez, Los Angeles .... KO by 5
(U.S. Featherweight Title)
Apr. 6—Domingo Luna, Oklahoma City......... KO 3
Apr. 20—Manuel Tarazon, Oklahoma City ...... KO 3
May 4—Frank Amano, Oklahoma City .... KO 1
May 18—Eliseo Estrada, Oklahoma City ...... KO 3
June 1—Blackie Sandoval, Oklahoma City ..... KO 3
Sept. 7—Joe Medrano, Oklahoma City .... KO 3
Sept. 21—Rickie Puentes, Oklahoma City .... KO 2
Oct. 5—Danny Young, Oklahoma City .... KO 1
Oct. 19—William Curtis, Oklahoma City .... KO 2
Nov. 2—Esteban Olvera, Oklahoma City....... KO 6
Nov. 16—Jose Cazares, Oklahoma City .... KO 3
Dec. 7—Raul Carreon, Oklahoma City......... KO 5
Dec. 21—Francisco Robles, Oklahoma City....... KO 2
1977
Mar. 1—Earl Large, Oklahoma City .... KO 9
Mar. 15—Melvin Jameson, Oklahoma City ...... KO 1
Apr. 5—Chango Guillen, Oklahoma City ...... KO 1
May 17—Tony Sanchez, Oklahoma City .... KO 2
June 6—Jerome Smith, Oklahoma City .... KO 1
June 22—David Vasquez, New York .... W 10
July 19—Ricardo Flores, Oklahoma City .... KO 2
Sept. 6—Gilberto Lara, Oklahoma City .... KO 1
Oct. 25—Jose Olivares, Anaheim .... KO 5
Dec. 6—Bill Pearish, Oklahoma City .... KO 2
1978
Mar. 17—Eddie Freeman, Las Vegas .... KO 1
Mar. 23—Ramon Campos, Omaha .... KO 1
Apr. 15—Romeo Anaya, Los Angeles .... KO 3
May 1—Harvey Wilson, Omaha .... KO 2
June 10—Shig Fukuyama, Oklahoma City ...... KO 5
Oct. 11—Al Franklin, Denver .... KO 6
Nov. 16—Freddie Harris, Oklahoma City ...... KO 7
Nov. 29—Paul Garcia, Council Bluffs .... KO 5
Dec. 7—Beau Jaynes, Oklahoma City .... KO 2
1979
Jan. 25—Marion Thomas, Oklahoma City .... KO 2
Feb. 16—Juan Garcia, Oklahoma City .... KO 2
Mar. 17—Jose Hernandez, Oklahoma City .... W 10
Apr. 28—Rodriguez Perez, Omaha .... KO 5
July 19—Dieter Schantz, Oklahoma City .... KO 2
Sept. 21—Jose Martinez, Tulsa .... KO 4
Oct. 23—Arturo Leon, Oklahoma City .... W 15
Dec. 15—Ramiro Hernandez, Oklahoma City ..... KO 5
1980
July 27—Gonzallo Montellano, Omaha .... W 12

Sept. 9—Carlos Villacana .... KO 6
Sept. 25—Jose Gonzalez, Oklahoma City .... KO 3
Nov. 1—Jim Watt, Glasgow .... KO by 12
(For WBC Lightweight Title)

KENNETH OKI
Honolulu, Hawaii Heavyweight
1980
Apr. 8—Carl Poff, Honolulu .... W 4
May 6—Carl Poff, Honolulu .... KO 1
July 8—Moses Halafuka, Honolulu .... KO by 1

JAMIE OLATUNDE
Chicago, Ill. Light Heavyweight
1979
July 19—Slick Mitchell, Orlando .... KO 3
Oct. 19—Art Henderson, Chicago .... KO 1
Dec. 15—Don Bester, Chicago .... W 4
1980
Feb. 18—Don Bester, Chicago .... W 6
Apr. 17—Jerry Hunter, Chicago .... KO 1
May 15—Dave Bradley, Chicago .... KO 8
June 12—Rick Jester, Chicago .... KO by 7
Dec. 19—Robert McFarland, Peoria .... L 10

ANGEL OLEA
Argentine Junior Welterweight
1980
Feb. 7—Raul Gomez, Bell Ville .... D 10
Feb. 29—Miguel Barraza, San Del Estero L
May 16—Pedro Vanegas, San Francisco .... L 10
Aug. 1—Joaquin Moreyra, Formosa .... L 10
Aug. 15—Hugo Hernandez, Mendoza .... L 8
Sept. 19—Martin Leiva, Tucuman .... L 10
Nov. 7—Miguel A. Gonzalez, Cutral .... L 10

CARLOS OLIVERA
Argentine Junior Welterweight
1980
Oct. 17—Jose Molina, Buenos Aires .... KO 3
Dec. 5—Osvaldo Calvo, Mar del Plata .... KO 2
Dec. 12—Ramon Franco, Mar del Plata .... W 6

VICTOR OLIVERA
Argentine Featherweight
1980
Sept. 26—Horacio Valdez, Buenos Aires .... KO 6
Oct. 18—Carlos Rodriguez, Junin ....L 6
Nov. 15—Ramon Crespin, Buenos Aires .... KO 1
Dec. 20—Horacio Valdez, Gral Belgrano .... D 6

HERIBERTO OLIVARES
Puerto Rican Featherweight
1972
Feb. 4—Juan Ocasio, Ponce .... W 4
Feb. 6—Antonio Birriez, San Juan .... KO 1
Apr. 3—Leo Cruz, San Juan .... D 4
Apr. 10—Ruben Santiago, San Juan .... D 4
Sept. 4—Jose Rosa, San Juan .... KO by 6
1973
Apr. 7—Leo Cruz, Carolina .... KO by 5
1974
Apr. 6—Ivan Jose Ocasio, San Juan .... KO by 6
1975-1976
(Inactive)
1977
Sept. 10—Gerald Hayes, San Juan .... W 8
Dec. 3—Fernando Rivera, San Juan .... W 8
1978
June 26—Fernando Rivera, Rio Piedras ....L 8
Sept. 18—Ken Agosto, Rio Piedras .... KO by 8
1979
Apr. 2—Pedro Vizcaino, Santo Domingo .... W 10
Apr. 22—Francisco Aponte, Trujillo .... KO 5
Sept. 22—Ramon Santana, San Juan .... W 10
1980
May 22—Enrique Solis, Rio Piedras ....L 10
July 3—Mario Colon, Rio Piedras .... W 10

REYNALDO OLIVIERA
Carver, Mass. Middleweight
1973
May 18—Chris Pina, Brockton .... D 4
June 15—Chris Pina, Brockton .... W 4
Oct. 6—Cove Green, Brockton ....L disq. 5
Oct. 26—John Capaliano, Brockton ....L 4
Nov. 17—Paul Osborne, Brockton .... W 6
Dec. 18—Paul Christie, Boston .... KO 4
1974
Jan. 17—Mike Baker, Portland, Me. ....L 10
Jan. 28—Hector Ortiz, Boston .... W 6
Feb. 5—Eddie Parka, Boston .... D 6

Oct.	29—Ernie Witcher, Walpole	W	6
Nov.	16—Lawrence Hafey, Brockton	L	6

1975

Feb.	15—Jesse Bender, Brockton	KO	2
Mar.	7—Jesse Bender, Brockton	KO by	4
Apr.	14—Jesse Bender, Boston	L	4
May	10—Frank Moore, Brockton	W	4
May	24—Jerry Tramantano, Brockton	W	6
June	6—Vito Antuofermo, Naples	KO by	6
Sept.	11—Zhodi Zhodi, Portland, Me.	KO	3

1976
(Inactive)
1977

Oct.	8—Rocky Fratto, Geneva	L	10

1978

June	19—Roberto Rivera, Boston	KO	3
July	12—Ben Sanchez, Boston	L	8
Sept.	16—Bill Ramsey, Cape Cod	KO	2
Nov.	11—John Harris, Boston	KO by	1
Dec.	21—Danny Long, Portland	KO by	5

1979

Jan.	15—Danny Long, Boston	KO by	1
Aug.	21—Manny Freitas, Yarmouth	KO by	2
Nov.	6—Manny Freitas, Boston	KO	5

1980

Apr.	25—John Capobianco, Commack	KO by	7
June	28—Don Addison, Manchester	L	10

JOEY OLIVO
Los Angeles, Calif. Flyweight
1976

June	19—Paz Mena, Los Angeles	W	4
Aug.	6—Jorge Ayala, Los Angeles	W	4
Oct.	2—Ramon Munoz, Los Angeles	W	4

1977

Apr.	23—Demetrios Torres, Los Angeles	W	4
May	11—Santes Nunez, Las Vegas	W	6
June	8—Joe Kid Saldivar, Las Vegas	W	6
June	29—Demetrios Torres, Stockton	KO	2
July	29—Santos Nunez, San Diego	KO	6
Aug.	20—Ramon Munoz, Los Angeles	KO	1
Sept.	28—Tito Arzate, Las Vegas	W	8
Nov.	17—Ken Yamato, Los Angeles	W	8
Dec.	14—Johnny Mesa, Tucson	W	8

1978

Feb.	25—Candy Iglesias, Los Angeles	W	6
Mar.	17—Victor Diaz, Anaheim	W	10
May	19—Candy Iglesias, Concord	W	10
Aug.	10—Eleoncio Mercedes, Los Angeles	W	10
Sept.	12—Rafael Rubio, Pico Rivera	KO	10

1979

Mar.	5—Lupe Mierra, Houston	W	12
May	18—Candy Iglesias, Pico Rivera	W	10
Aug.	30—Florencio Barboza, Los Angeles	KO	1
Oct.	23—Javier Mendoza, Los Angeles	W	10
Nov.	16—Martin Vargas, Santiago	L	10

1980

Feb.	9—Amado Ursua, Los Angeles	W	12
	(Retired NABF Light Flyweight Title)		
June	5—Pedro Galaviz, Los Angeles	KO	9
July	31—Candy Iglesias, Los Angeles	W	10

GEORGE OMARA
Heavyweight
1979

June	18—Roger Braxton, Los Angeles	W	4
Oct.	10—Jessie Prieto, Las Vegas	KO	5
Oct.	19—Glen Williams, San Diego	KO	2
Nov.	15—Hurricane Lacy, Los Angeles	KO	3
Nov.	23—Sam Wilson, San Diego	KO	2
Nov.	29—Anthony Davis, Los Angeles	KO	3
Dec.	14—Ron Draper, Orange County	KO	2

1980

Feb.	21—Parnell Fairely, Los Angeles	L	6
Mar.	26—Parnell Fairely, Costa Mesa	L	8
May	2—Roger Braxton, Inglewood	W	6
May	20—John Matthews, Fresno	KO	3
May	28—Harvey Steichen, Las Vegas	W	10
Aug.	23—Ron Lyle, Inglewood	KO by	10

JACK O'NEILL
Lowell, Mass. Junior Welterweight
1979

Oct.	27—Mark Mello, Fitchburg	KO	1

1980

Mar.	8—Derrick Cuttino, Great Gorge	L	4
May	8—Ernest Jackson, Atlantic City	KO	2
June	5—Earnest Jackson, Atlantic City	KO by	2

EDWIN (PIPINO) OQUENDO
Bronx, N.Y. Featherweight
1980

July	16—Edwin Santiago, Elizabeth	L	4

Sept.	17—James Marshall, White Plains	W	4
Nov.	12—Adonis Torres, New York	KO	2

ALEX OREGEL
Los Angeles, Calif. Junior Lightweight
1978

July	12—Jesus Hernandez, Las Vegas	KO	4
Aug.	3—Jose Posos, Los Angeles	KO	2
Sept.	28—Jose Valdez, Los Angeles	KO	5
Nov.	9—Jose Rodriguez, Los Angeles	ND	4
Dec.	11—Reuben Castillo, Bakersfield	KO by	2

1979

Feb.	5—Roger Bucheli, Bakersfield	W	10
Mar.	27—Abdul Bey, Honolulu	KO by	7
June	28—Robert Vasquez, Los Angeles	D	10
Nov.	15—Rosendo Ramirez, Los Angeles	ND	8

1980

Apr.	3—Roberto Elizondo, Los Angeles	KO by	2

JOSE ORODA
Argentine Welterweight
1980

Apr.	11—Ramon Peralta, Berrotan	L	10
May	16—Juan Funes, San Francisco	L	8
Oct.	10—Miguel Duro, Parana	D	10

RAFAEL ORONO
Venezuelan Bantamweight
1979

Feb.	18—Victor Idrogo, Caracas	W	4
Mar.	18—Hernan Palacios, Caracas	W	4
May	6—Alfredo Mendoza, Caracas	KO	3
June	2—Henry Diaz, Caracas	W	10
July	21—Enrique Pinto, Caracas	KO	3
Aug.	11—Aureliano Castillo, Caracas	W	10
Sept.	15—Edgar Roman, Caracas	W	12
	(Won Venezuelan Bantamweight Title)		
Sept.	29—Jorge Cruz, Santa Barbara, Ven.	KO	2
Oct.	25—Luis Burgos, Caracas	W	10
Dec.	19—Jorge Vargas, Caracas	KO	9

1980

Feb.	1—Seung-Hoon Lee, Caracas	W	15
	(Won Vacant WBC Super Flyweight Title)		
Apr.	14—Ramon Soria, Caracas	W	15
	(Retained WBC Super Flyweight Title)		
July	28—Willie Jensen, Caracas	D	15
	(Retained WBC Super Flyweight Title)		
Sept.	15—Jovito Rengifo, Barquisamento	KO	3
	(Retained WBC Super Flyweight Title)		

ANGEL ORTEGA
Mexican Flyweight
1980

Feb.	2—Juan Flores, Mexico City	W	6
Apr.	12—Jose Cordoba, Mexico City	L	6
June	7—Paco Sanchez, Mexico City	KO	3
July	9—Jose Cordoba, Mexico City	W disq.	6

FELIPE OROZCO
Colombian Featherweight
1980

June	12—Jose Zuniga, Monteria	W	6
Dec.	6—Pedro Perez, Barranquilla	KO	3

FRANCISCO ORTEGA
San Diego, Calif. Welterweight
1978

June	30—Bert Lee, San Diego	D	6
Aug.	31—Rodney Harvey, Los Angeles	KO	2

1979

May	4—Bernardo Graham, San Diego	KO	2

1980

Apr.	16—Joe Maldonado, Fresno	KO	2
June	13—Hector Rivera, San Bernardino	KO	8

SIMON ORTIGOZA
Argentine Lightweight
1980

Mar.	7—Hector Rosa, S. Sal. de Jujuy	KO by	7
Apr.	11—Juan Brizuela, Santa Rosa	TD	9
June	19—Diego Ramirez, Bolivar	W	10
Aug.	22—Cesar Villarruel, Tandil	L	10

ANGEL ORTIZ
Springfield, Mass. Junior Welterweight
1976

July	26—Pee Wee Stokes, New York	D	6

1977

Feb.	11—Marcial Santiago, New York	W	6
Sept.	16—Ray Roman, New York	KO by	4
Dec.	15—Rodney Coop, Hamilton	L	4

1978

Jan. 19—Pablo Nieves, North Bergen .... KO 5
Jan. 25—Joe Nieto, Brooklyn .... L 4
June 2—Arcadio Suarez, Jersey City .... KO by 6

1979

Sept. 19—Manny Sims, New York .... L 4
—Papo Figueroa, Hartford .... W 8

1980

Nov. 11—Chi Chi Hernandez, W. Hartford .... L 6

EMILCIO ORTIZ
Argentine Welterweight
1980

Apr. 3—Jesus Romero, S. Sal. de Jujuy .... L 10
May 30—Julio Melone, Rio IV .... L 10
Aug. 8—Victor Echegaray, San Juan .... L 12
Dec. 5—Victor Escobar, P.R.S. Pena .... L 10

FERNANDO ORTIZ
Puerto Rican Featherweight
1980

Feb. 11—Hector Cruz, San Juan .... W 8
Mar. 24—Victor Acosta, San Juan .... L 8
July 3—Edwin Rivera, Rio Piedras .... W 8
July 24—Sonny Agosto, Rio Piedras .... W 8
Oct. 27—Francisco Rodriguez, Alto Trujillo .... W 8

HECTOR ORTIZ
Hartford, Conn. Welterweight
1979

Sept. 7—Steve Snow, Hartford .... L 7
Nov. 28—Steve Snow, Hartford .... W 8
—Steve Snow, Hartford .... D 8

1980

Jan. 9—Tim LaValley, Hartford .... KO by 5
Mar. 4—Papo Figueroa, W. Hartford .... D 8
Apr. 22—Papo Figueroa, W. Hartford .... KO by 4
June 19—Roberto Colon, Lawrence .... KO by 4

JOSE (CHEO) ORTIZ
Brooklyn, N.Y. Featherweight
1976

July 20—Jimmy Corkum, Lawrence .... L 4

1977

Apr. 1—Carlos Paneto, New York .... KO by 4
Apr. 15—Jimmy Cruz, New York .... L 4
Apr. 20—Jimmy Corkum, Taunton .... KO by 2
Apr. 29—Torrence Turner, New York .... D 4
May 13—Curtis Smith, New York .... W 4
May 26—Greg Williams, Dover .... L 4
June 27—Victor Papas, Philadelphia .... KO by 2
Oct. 7—Jimmy Corkum, Lowell .... L 8
Nov. 18—Louie Hubela, New York .... L 4

1978

Jan. 25—Jose Nieto, Brooklyn .... L 4
Feb. 18—Juanito Guzman, San Juan .... W 10
Feb. 21—Jean LaPointe, Montreal .... KO by 8
Mar. 28—Jean LaPointe, Montreal .... KO by 10
Apr. 21—Jimmy Longo, Albany .... W 4
June 6—Jimmy Cruz, New York .... KO 6
June 10—Jose Figueroa, Brooklyn .... D 6
June 22—Wilfredo Lenzo, New York .... W 6
Sept. 20—Jose Figueroa, New York .... W 6
Oct. 14—Sean Mannion, New Haven .... KO by 5
Nov. 2—Jose Nieto, New York .... KO by 7
Nov. 11—Sean Mannion, Boston .... L 6
Dec. 9—Steve Snow, Springfield .... L 4

1979

Apr. 6—Wilfredo Lanzo, New York .... L 6
Oct. 30—Rocky Lockridge, Totowa .... KO by 2

1980

July 13—Ken Bogner, Great Gorge .... D 4
July 20—Ken Bogner, Great Gorge .... L 4

NICK ORTIZ
Puerto Rican Junior Middleweight
1973

Jan. 8—Steve Sims, New York .... W 6
Apr. 23—Santos Solis, San Juan .... L 6
May 30—Max Rodriguez, San Juan............... KO 2

1974

June 22—Reynaldo Ortiz, San Juan .... KO 1
Aug. 3—Eddie Correa, San Juan .... KO 2
Sept. 9—Fermin Guzman, San Juan .... KO 8
Dec. 9—Curtis Phillips, New York .... KO 5

1975

Jan. 4—Juan Serrano, San Juan .... KO 5
Jan. 18—Frankie Gonzalez, San Juan .... KO 2
Feb. 24—Wilbert Seales, San Juan .... KO 8
Mar. 31—Diablillo Trinidad, San Juan .... KO 6
Apr. 28—Fausto Rodriguez, San Juan .... W 10
June 2—Manny Torres, San Juan................ KO 5

Aug. 2—Jorge Sander, Managua................ KO 1
Sept. 19—Kevin Morgan, San Juan .... KO by 4
Nov. 3—Kevin Morgan, San Juan .... KO by 4

1976

Sept. 18—Wilbert Seales, San Juan .... KO 3

1977

Mar. 18—Gary Guiden, Kansas City .... KO by 7
June 18—Sam Danier, Caguas .... KO 3
Nov. 14—Jesus Castro, Santo Domingo .... L disq. 10

1978

Sept. 9—Tony Lopes, Providence .... KO 4
Oct. 14—Jimmy Brown, New Haven .... KO 1
Oct. 21—Mayfield Pennington, Louisville .... KO 5
Oct. 28—Mayfield Pennington, Louisville .... KO 3

1979

Feb. 23—Ray Bryant, Springfield .... KO 2
Mar. 29—Jose Pagan, Hartford .... KO 3
May 23—Bennie Briscoe, Washington, D.C. ..... L 10
Nov. 27—Rocky Mosley Jr., Las Vegas .... KO 4

1980

Jan. 18—Steve Delgado, Las Vegas .... L disq. 5
(No. Amer. Federation Junior Middleweight Title)
July 25—Milton Owens, Kissimmee .... L 10

ROBERTO ORTIZ
Argentine Middleweight
1980

Jan. —Juan Roldan, San Francisco .... KO by 2
Mar. 7—Jose Luis Cuevara, Villa Maria ...... KO by 6
Apr. 18—Ramon Tapia, Catamarca .... W 6

RUBY (THE SNAKE) ORTIZ
Bronx, N.Y. Junior Welterweight
1973

Aug. 25—Richie Harris, New York .... L 4
Nov. 26—Richie Harris, New York .... L 4

1974

Feb. 18—Jose Rosado, New York................ KO 4
Mar. 18—Rafael Santana, New York............. KO 2
Apr. 22—Rafael Santana, New York............... D 4
May 13—John Tutino, New York................ KO 3
May 23—Jose Rivera, North Bergen............... D 4
June 10—Terance Turner, New York.............. W 4
June 24—Benito Vega, New York................. W 4
Aug. 4—Jose Resto, New York.................. W 6
Oct. 7—Bobby Alexander, New York .... W 6
Oct. 28—Hector Espinoza, New York............. D 6
Nov. 11—Hector Espinoza, New York............. W 6
Dec. 2—Salvador Ramirez, New York............ KO 3

1975

Apr. 7—Alfonso Evans, Philadelphia............. W 8
Sept. 12—Jose Resto, Commack................... W 8
Dec. 5—Wilson Yambo, New York .... KO 6

1976

May 23—Larry Stanton, Erie.................... W 8
Aug. 16—Dan Daniels, Newark.................. KO 2

1977

Jan. 18—Leo DiFiore, New York .... KO 2
Mar. 6—Vinnie DeBarros, Marion .... W 8
(U.S. Championship Tournament)
Apr. 2—Johnny Sullivan, San Antonio .... W 10
(U.S. Championship Tournament)

1978
(Inactive)

1979

Mar. 9—Hugo Rengifo, New York .... W 10
May 12—Rogelio Castaneda, Las Vegas .... W 10
June 22—Willie Rodriguez, New York .... L 8
Aug. 25—Manuel (Yuca) Jiminez, San Juan .... W 10
Nov. 9—Esteban DeJesus, New York .... L 10

1980

Apr. 18—Sean Mannion, New York .... W 10
May 23—Domingo Ayala, New York .... KO by 10
Aug. 27—Adolfo Viruet, Elizabeth .... L 10
Nov. 28—Marvin Jenkins, New York .... L 10

CARLOS OSORIO
Venezuelan Flyweight
1978

July 29—Jovito Rengifo, Caracas................ L 10
Sept. 11—Jovito Rengifo, Caracas................ L 10

1980

Feb. 10—Raul Diaz, Bucarananga .... KO by 4
June 27—Homer Mesa, Barranquilla .... KO by 3

JOSE OSUNA
Los Angeles, Calif. Junior Welterweight
1978

May 10—Leoncio Meza, Las Vegas .... L 8
May 20—Jaime Nava, Fresno .... L 8
Aug. 10—Irleis Perez, Los Angeles .... KO by 1
Sept. 13—Julio Mendez, Las Vegas .... KO 2

Sept. 20—Ricky Samudio, Las Vegas ....W 8
Oct. 5—Petronillo Velasquez, Los Angeles ....KO by 6
Nov. 14—Jose Castaneda, Bakersfield ....L 8
Nov. 30—Herman Montes, Los Angeles ....KO by 2
1979
Mar. 28—Tommy Cisneros, Las Vegas ....KO by 6
May 2—Pancho Del Toro, Las Vegas ....L 8
May 21—Gonzalo Montellano, Bakersfield .....KO by 4
June 20—Lou Daniels, Las Vegas ....KO 3
June 27—Sammy Davila, Las Vegas ....W 8
July 24—Mark Ibanez, Honolulu ....W 8
Aug. 15—Frankie Moultrie, Las Vegas ....L 10
Sept. 18—Winnie Guinieta, Honolulu ....W 10
Nov. 8—Armando Ramirez, Los Angeles ......KO by 5
1980
Apr. 16—Leon Mesa, Las Vegas ....KO 5
June 3—Jorge Morales, Las Vegas ....KO by 7
Sept. 25—Rosendo Ramirez, Las Vegas ....W 10
Nov. 6—John Montes, Los Angeles ....KO by 1

RAMON OVIEDO
Argentine Welterweight
1980
Jan. 11—Horacio Saldano, Mendoza ....W 10
Feb. 21—Redomirez Madariaga, Mendoza ....W 10
Aug. 15—Hugo Albarez, Mendoza ....KO by 9
Dec. 12—Juan Bardi, Malargue ....W 12

JIMMY OWENS
Las Vegas, Nev. Middleweight
1972
Jan. 12—Howard Black, Windsor..................W 6
Mar. 12—Teddy Martin, Halifax...................W 6
Apr. 6—Felix Sanchez, Memphis ....KO 2
June 10—Bill Campbell, Mobile ....KO 1
June 17—Rex Townsend, Mobile ....W 6
July 4—Ray Bell, Memphis ....KO 4
July 31—Wade Smith, Jacksonville...............KO 6
Sept. 20—Lonnie Crosby, Lincoln ....KO by 2
Nov. 14—Tony Gardner, Memphis ....L 10
Dec. 12—Gary James, Lincoln....................W 6
1973
Feb. 18—Terry Ball, Jacksonville..................W 8
Apr. 5—Les Pitten, Mobile......................KO 1
June 14—Nelson Alphonso, Tampa..............KO by 1
Sept. 4—Pat Durden, Kansas City ....KO 7
Sept. 28—Mack Jones, Kansas City ....W 8
Oct. 3—Roy McMillian, Toronto ....L 8
Oct. 11—Keith Averett, Toronto ....KO 4
1974
Mar. 22—John Mangum, Detroit ....KO 8
Apr. 12—Marcu Bouchard, Halifax...............KO 6
May 25—John Mangum, Detroit ....KO 7
Dec. 10—Jean Pierre, Sorel ....KO 4
1975
Apr. 14—Marvin Hagler, Boston ....L 10
May 24—Marvin Hagler, Brockton ....L disq. 6
1976
Mar. 9—Doug Demmings, Minneapolis..........L 8
June 12—Tom Hanna, Highland Park ....L 10
Aug. 3—Scott Clark, Orlando...................W 6
Aug. 10—Pedro Santiago, Miami Beach ....KO 4
Aug. 26—Gary Alexander, Canton ....W 8
Sept. 2—Al Clay, Kalamazoo ....D 10
Oct. 1—Eddie Gregory, New York..........KO by 10
1977
Mar. 9—Vicente Medina, Las Vegas ....W 8
Mar. 29—Armando Alatoore, Las Vegas ....KO 2
May 6—Karl Zurheide, Missoula ....L 10
May 25—Zeferino Gonzalez, Las Vegas ....L 10
July 12—Rudy Robles, Phoenix ....KO by 6
1978
Feb. 24—James Parks, Las Vegas ....KO by 3
Oct. 3—Scott Clark, Orlando ....KO by 4
1979
Jan. 10—Mike Westrich, Las Vegas ....KO by 2
1980
Nov. 19—Bobby Howard, Las Vegas ....L 4

MILTON OWENS
Orlando, Florida Middleweight
1975
Dec. 9—Slick Mitchell, Orlando ....W 6
1976
Feb. 3—George Clark, Orlando ....W 6
Aug. 31—Gary Thomas, Orlando ....KO 1
Sept. 14—Chris Brantley, Orlando ....KO 1
Sept. 21—Eddie Davis, Orlando ....W 6
Oct. 12—Johnny Evans, Orlando ....W 6
Nov. 16—Buddy Niles, Orlando ....KO 1
Nov. 7—Al Moss, Orlando ....KO 2

1977
Jan. 14—Eddie Davis, Orlando ....W 6
Feb. 1—Randy Armstrong, Orlando ....KO 3
Feb. 25—Johnny Evans, Orlando ....W 8
Mar. 11—Sammy Barr, Orlando ....W 8
Mar. 24—Eddie Davis, Tampa ....W 8
Apr. 12—Rennie Pinder, Orlando ....KO 6
Apr. 28—Jose Luis Gonzalez, Tampa ....KO 4
Aug. 25—Major Lambert, Tampa ....KO 4
Sept. 6—Raul Aguirre, Orlando ....W 10
Nov. 22—Ernie Burns, Orlando ....KO 4
Dec. 13—Nat King, Orlando ....KO 5
1978
Jan. 17—J.T. Dowe, Orland ....KO 3
June 6—Slick Mitchell, Orlando ....KO 3
July 25—Irwin Hines, Orlando ....W 10
Aug. 10—Ayub Kalule, Copenhagen ....KO by 7
Dec. 12—Billy McIntyre, Orlando ....KO 4
1979
Jan. 10—Mike West, Las Vegas ....KO by 2
Feb. 6—Tony Greene, Orlando ....W 10
Feb. 19—Willie Goodwin, Tampa ....W 6
May 15—Dennis Riggs, Jacksonville ....KO by 6
1980
July 25—Nick Ortiz, Kissimmee ....W 10

TEODORO OZUNA
Dominican Junior Welterweight
Born: Dec. 23, 1941
Managed by Frank Sciacca
1975
Dec. 15—Jose Fernandez, Santo Domingo ....KO 2
1976
Mar. 15—Leo Lorenzo, Santo Domingo ....KO 2
July 1—Felipo Pena, Santo Domingo ....KO 1
Aug. 16—Julio Alfonso, Santo Domingo ....KO 4
Oct. 19—Tony Arias, Santo Domingo ....W 10
Nov. —Salvador Gomez, Santo Domingo ....W 6
1977
Feb. 26—Pica Piedra, Santo Domingo ....W 8
June 13—Rafael Andujar, Santo Domingo ....KO 7
Oct. 10—Rafael Solis, Santo Domingo ....L 10
1978
Mar. 11—Harold Bernard, Port of Spain ....W 6
Apr. 1—Chico Rosa, Carolina, P.R. ....L 10
May 13—Chico Rosa, Carolina, P.R. ....KO 7
July 8—Ernesto Espana, San Juan ....KO by 1
Oct. 2—Raymond Roman, New York ....W 8
Oct. 30—Mike Thomas, New York ....KO 2
1979
Jan. 9—Wade Hinnant, Philadelphia ....L 10
Mar. 7—Maurice Watkins, New York ....W 10
May 11—Arcadio Suarez, New York ....W 10
July 16—Dan Daniel, New York ....W 8
1980
Feb. 29—Larry Stanton, Commack ....W 10

JOSE PACHECO
Los Angeles, Calif. Featherweight
1979
Aug. 15—Ricardo Jimenez, Las Vegas ....KO by 2
Sept. 21—James Ortega, Denver ....KO by 2
Oct. 2—Dennis Quimayousie, Reno ....L 8
Oct. 30—Dennis Quimayousie, Carson City ....KO by 3
Dec. 11—Danny Cortez, Bakersfield ....L 6
1980
Sept. 30—Eddie Carter, Houston ....L 8
Dec. 13—Rodrigo Aguirre, El Paso ....KO by 4
Dec. 16—Chato Ramos, Odessa ....L 6

MARK PACHECO
Reno, Nev. Flyweight
1979
July 3—Antonio Reyes, Gardnerville ....D 4
Aug. 1—Oscar Cristerna, Reno ....KO 3
Sept. 11—Francisco Rodriguez, Reno ....KO 3
Oct. 2—Dennis Quimayousie, Reno ....L 8
Nov. 6—Augustine Sanchez, Sparks ....W 6
Nov. 20—Armando Ugalde, Sparks ....W 8
Dec. 18—Augustine Sanchez, Sparks ....W 9
1980
Jan. 22—Norberto Castellano, Sparks ....W 10
Feb. 10—Mario Ocida, Sparks ....W 10
Mar. 27—Willie Jensen, Las Vegas ....KO by 5

May 22—German Torres, Los Angeles .... KO by 6
July 15—Panterito Chavez, Reno .... W 10
Sept. 9—Richard Varela, Las Vegas .... L 10

PETE PADILLA
Bronx, N.Y. Junior Welterweight
Born: Oct. 26, 1956
Managed by Guillermo Robert
1975
Apr. 22—Charles Sampson, Philadelphia .... D 4
Aug. 18—Tom Brown, Philadelphia .... KO 2
Nov. 18—Rogelio Perez, Philadelphia .... W 4
1976-1978
(Inactive, Military Service)
1979
Apr. 22—David Vega, New York .... W 4
May 11—Manny Simms, New York .... W 4
July 8—Jorge Nina, New York .... W 4
Sept. 22—Pettis Withers, Kansas City .... W 6
Oct. 4—David Vega, New York .... W 6
1980
Jan. 25—Marco Barahona, New York .... W 10
May 2—Cocoa Sanchez, New York .... L 10
Nov. 1—Mike Blunt, Dayton .... KO by 3

JOSE PAGAN (RIVERA)
Lowell, Mass. Middleweight
1970
Mar. 12—Ricky Burgess, Portland, Me. .... L 4
Mar. 19—Ricky Burgess, Portland .... D 4
Mar. 26—Ricky Burgess, Portland .... L 6
Oct. 8—Ricky Burgess, Portland .... W 4
Oct. 22—Bob Richards, Portland .... KO by 3
Oct. 29—Willie Williams, Portland .... KO by 2
Nov. 5—Santiago Crespo, Portland .... L 2
Nov. 12—Tommy Connors, Boston .... KO by 2
Nov. 23—Bob Richards, Portland .... L 8
Dec. 3—Dick DiVola, Portland .... KO by 1
Dec. 10—Phil St. Cyr, Portland .... L 4
1971
Jan. 7—Richie Seeley, Portland .... L 4
Jan. 11—Johnny Reno, Providence............... W 4
Jan. 21—Tom Connors, Portland .... KO by 2
Jan. 28—Eddie Ahlmeyer, Portland.............. D 4
Feb. 1—Marcelino Alicia, Providence .... KO by 3
Feb. 4—Phil St. Cyr, Portland .... KO by 4
Apr. 22—Bob Payzant, Portland............. L 4
Apr. 29—Bob Payzant, Portland .... W 4
May 3—Tommy Connor, Boston................. KO 4
May 10—Felix Losado, Boston .... KO 4
May 16—Fernand Marcotte, Quebec .... KO by 3
May 20—Phil Hudson, Portland.................. L 6
May 22—Tommy Grant, Boston .... KO by 4
May 29—Don Sennett, Hyannis .... L 6
June 10—Bob Payzant, Portland .... D 4
June 14—Ken Tavares, Providence .... KO by 4
June 21—Don Sennett, New Bedford .... KO by 1
July 8—Jimmy Jaynes, Portland .... L 6
July 22—Bob Richards, Portland .... KO by 4
Aug. 2—Paul Christie, New Bedford .... W 4
Aug. 12—Leo DiFiore, Portland .... L 6
Aug. 26—Leo DiFiore, Portland .... L 6
Aug. 27—Jerry Tramp, Providence .... L 6
Aug. 30—Tommy Grant, New Bedford .... L 4
Sept. 9—Roger Phillips, Portland .... L 4
Oct. 13—Billy Wade, Waltham ....W 6
Oct. 20—Larry Michaud, Worcester .... KO 2
Oct. 27—Azael Curet, Walpole .... L 4
Oct. 28—Azael Curet, Portland .... D 8
Nov. 3—Ivelaw Eastman, Waltham .... W 8
Nov. 18—Jesus Alicia, Portland .... KO by 3
Nov. 24—Roger Phillips, Waltham................. W 4
Dec. 11—Tommy Grant, Boston .... KO by 4
1972
Jan. 6—Jose Curet, Portland..................... W 4
Jan. 10—Paul Osborne, Waltham............... W 4
Jan. 17—Tommy Grant, Waltham .... KO by 7
Jan. 20—Larry Michaud, Portland................. W 4
Jan. 27—Larry Michaud, Portland................. W 6
Feb. 7—Angel Torres, Waltham .... L 6
Feb. 10—George Gosselin, Waltham .... W 6
Feb. 14—Al Romano, Waltham .... L 6
Feb. 21—Angel Torres, Waltham .... KO by 4
Mar. 2—Larry Michaud, Portland .... L 6
Apr. 3—Mike Brown, Waltham .... W 4
Apr. 5—Don Maloch, Boston .... W 4
Apr. 20—Willie Williams, Portland .... D 6
Apr. 29—Bobby Haymon, Cleveland .... KO by 3
May 18—Otho Tyson, Portland .... D 6
June 22—Don Melsoh, Portland .... W 6
June 27—Kevin Dorian, Portland .... L 4
July 6—Mike Brown, Portland .... L 6
July 20—Mike Brown, Portland .... KO by 3
July 24—Angel Torres, Waltham .... L 8

July 27—Tony Petronelli, Portland .... KO by 1
Aug. 22—Tony Petronelli, Waltham............... KO by 4
Aug. 24—Steve Bretton, Portland.................W 4
Aug. 31—Kevin Dorian, Portland .... W 6
Sept. 16—Eddie Gregory, Boston .... KO by 1
Nov. 17—Beau Jaynes, Lowell .... L 8
Nov. 30—Gene Roberts, Portland .... L 6
Dec. 7—Gene Roberts, Portland .... W 6
Dec. 14—Gene Roberts, Portland .... L 6
Dec. 18—Paul Osborne, Waltham .... L 6
1973
Jan. 11—Cal Ware, Portland .... L 6
Jan. 15—Terry Rondeau, Waltham .... W 6
Feb. 7—Angel Torres, Taunton .... L 6
Feb. 22—Marc Gervais, Quebec .... L 10
Feb. 23—Jesus Alicia, Taunton .... L 8
Mar. 27—George Green, Boston .... W 6
Mar. 31—Mike Baker, North Adams .... L 6
Apr. 6—Babe Winston, Portland .... KO 4
May 10—Bob Richard, Portland .... W 8
May 17—Donato Paduano, Verdun .... KO by 6
June 14—Paul Poirier, Portland................... L 6
June 15—Jose Garcia, Brockton .... W 8
June 28—Jackie Smith, Portland .... KO by 3
Aug. 7—Steve Sims, Hartford .... L 6
Sept. 25—Jose Carabello, Hartford .... L -6
Oct. 6—Paul Poirier, Brockton .... L 6
Oct. 12—Juan Colon, Worcester .... W 6
Oct. 16—Steve Sims, Hartford .... L 6
Oct. 26—Juan Carlos Garcia, Brockton .... KO by 4
1974
Mar. 16—Jeff Holmes, Waterbury .... L 6
Apr. 4—Paul Poirier, Worcester .... KO by 4
Oct. 12—Dave Huckaby, Waterbury .... KO by 5
Oct. 18—Leo Saenz, Baltimore .... KO by 2
Oct. 22—Jeff Holmes, West Hartford .... KO by 4
1975
Mar. 1—Jose Carabello, Bristol .... D 6
Mar. 20—Dana McCarthy, Waterbury .... KO by 3
Mar. 24—Hector Matta, San Juan .... L 10
Apr. 11—Dana McCarthy, Waterbury .... KO by 2
Apr. 12—Pablo Rodriguez, Waterbury .... L 6
May 1—Vinnie De Borros, Bristol .... L 6
May 10—Donnie Nelson, Manchester .... L 6
July 17—John Harris, Portland .... L 6
July 24—Tony Lopes, Portland .... L 6
July 28—Hector Medina, San Juan .... KO by 1
1976
June 29—Mike Bullock, Lawrence .... L 4
July 26—Al Romano, Peabody .... L 8
1977
Mar. 23—Tony Lopes, Boston .... L 8
Apr. 23—Tony Lopes, Fitchburg .... L 10
1978
July 18—Roosevelt Brown, Boston .... KO by 5
1979
Mar. 1—Manny Freitas, White Plains .... KO 6
Mar. 13—Rusty Rosenberger, Totowa .... L 6
Mar. 29—Nick Ortiz, Hartford .... KO by 3
Nov. 6—Jimmy McNally, Lowell .... L 8
1980
Feb. 26—Jimmy McNally, Woburn .... L 8

RENE PAGAN
Beaumont, Texas Middleweight
1979
May 22—William J. Jones, Beaumont .... KO 3
June 26—Eddie Carter, Houston .... L 6
Dec. 11—Daryl Brumley, Houston .... L 6
1980
July 22—Steve Hearon, Houston .... L 6
Oct. 28—Ruben Nuncio, Houston .... L 6
Dec. 2—Ramon Gonzales, Houston .... W 8

GREG PAGE
Louisville, Ky. Heavyweight
Amateur Record: 90-11, 55 knockouts
1979
Feb. 16—Don Martin, Louisville .... KO 2
June 1—Jerry McIntyre, Louisville .... KO 2
Aug. 19—James Knox, Minneapolis .... KO 2
Sept. 22—Oliver Phillips, Los Angeles .... KO 4
Oct. 18—Frankie Brown, Philadelphia .... KO 3
Nov. 2—James Reid, Bloomington .... KO 1
Dec. 14—Ira Martin, Atlantic City .... KO 1
1980
Feb. 1—Victor Rodriguez, Louisville .... KO 3
Mar. 8—Claman Parker, Las Vegas .... KO 1
Apr. 5—George Chaplin, Louisville .... W 10
May 16—Larry Alexander, Lexington .... KO 6
Sept. 12—Leroy Boone, Louisville .... KO 6
Oct. 2—Dave Johnson, New York .... KO 6

LINDSAY PAGE
Trenton, N.J. Light Heavyweight
1979
Sept. 29—James Wilson, Trenton ....KO 1
Nov. 23—Curtis Pittman, Trenton ....W 4
1980
Aug. 7—Roger Troupe, Atlantic City ....KO by 1

JORGE PALAI
Argentine Welterweight
1980
June 6—Antonio Lucena, Mar del Plata ....W 6
Aug. 1—Mario Arreguez, Mar del Plata ....W 6
Aug. 22—Horacio Mendez, Mar del Plata ....W 8
Sept. 5—Alejo Acosta, Mar del Plata ....W 6
Sept. 26—Manuel Olivera, Olavarria ....KO 2
Oct. 10—Marcelo Romero, Mar del Plata ....W 8

OTTO PALFY
Akron, Ohio Lightweight
1974
Apr. 5—Tony Johnson, Akron ....L 6
1975
Oct. 23—Peanuts Emerson, Erie ....L 6
1976
(Inactive)
1977
May 20—Charley Spiecer, Marion ....KO 4
Aug. 12—Al Carter, Barberton ....KO by 1
1978
*Feb. 21—Arnold Palmer, Strongville ....KO 1
*Feb. 21—Harvey Wallbanger, Strongville ....W 4
*Both fights on same card.
1979
Jan. 10—Bobby Sparks, Richfield ....KO by 5
1980
Apr. 5—Louis Payne, Akron ....W 4

JOHNNY PAPIN
Los Angeles, Calif. Featherweight
1978
July 26—Angel Garcia, Las Vegas ....D 4
Aug. 16—Juan Castro, Las Vegas ....KO 4
Sept. 8—Jose Luis Lara, Los Angeles ....L 4
Nov. 1—Jose Luis Lara, Los Angeles ....L 6
Nov. 30—George Garcia, Los Angeles ....L 6
1979
Mar. 16—Jorge Portela, San Diego ....D 5
Mar. 28—Francisco Pico, Las Vegas ....W 6
June 27—Fred Roach, Las Vegas ....L 6
Oct. 4—Jose Luis Lara, Los Angeles ....D 10
Oct. 25—George Garcia, Los Angeles ....L 10
1980
Sept. 10—Elmer Suddington, Wichita ....L 4

VICTOR PAPPA
Upper Darby, Pa. Lightweight
1977
Mar. 7—Billy Johnson, Upper Darby ....KO 1
Apr. 7—Hector Pereira, Upper Darby ....KO 3
May 9—Lou Daniels, Upper Darby ....KO 1
June 27—Jose Ortiz, Philadelphia ....KO 2
Aug. 3—Ernie Gladney, Philadelphia ....L 4
Sept. 15—Ken Muse, Upper Darby ....W 6
1978
Jan. 31—Keith Bennett, Upper Darby ....KO 1
Mar. 14—Ernie Gladney, Philadelphia ....W 6
1979
Jan. 30—Billy Abel, Upper Darby ....KO 3
Feb. 27—John McQueen, Blue Horizon ....W 6
May 14—John McQueen, Philadelphia ....W 8
Aug. 14—Angel Cintron, Atlantic City ....KO 4
Sept. 26—Marvin Edwards, Upper Darby ....KO 2
Nov. 14—Arseneo Green, Philadelphia ....KO 7
1980
Feb. 9—Armando Ramirez, Miami Beach ....KO 2
Apr. 10—Sean McGarry, Atlantic City ....KO 8
May 4—Arseneo Green, Atlantic City ....KO 3
Oct. 30—Ron Green, Atlantic City ....W 8

BOBBY PAPPION
New Orleans, La. Lightweight
1978
Mar. 29—Eddie Richardson, Mobile ....L 6
Dec. 1—Joe Webber, New Orleans ....W 4
1979
(Inactive)
1980
June 3—Ron Perkins, Houston ....W 4
June 24—Miguel Flores, Houston ....W 6
Aug. 26—Roberto Perez, Houston ....KO 2
Sept. 23—Melvin Paul, New Orleans ....L 6

RUBEN HECTOR PARDO
Argentine Middleweight
Born: June 22, 1950, Buenos Aires
(Previous Record Unavailable)
1976
June 5—Alejandro Garcia, Buenos Aires ....W 8
Aug. 21—Oscar Perez, Buenos Aires ....KO 1
Oct. 5—Smiley Geising, Johannesburg ....KO 3
Oct. 20—Hugo Obregon, Buenos Aires ....W 10
Nov. 26—Alfredo Cruz, Carlos Paz ....D 10
1977
Apr. 15—Juan C. Bogardo, Concordia ....KO 9
July 6—Natalio Ibarra, Carlos Paz ....KO 4
July 27—Adolfo Cruz, Carlos Paz ....D 10
Sept. 17—Salvatore Russo, Roma ....KO 4
Oct. 17—Camilo Gaitan, Buenos Aires ....W 10
1978
Jan. 20—Luis Carcacha, Pergamino ....KO 2
Mar. 3—Miguel Obregon, Azul ....W 10
Mar. 17—Juan Mora, Villa Maria ....KO 4
May 27—Juan M. Flores Burlon, Buenos Aires ....L 10
July 1—Pedro C. Duarte, Buenos Aires ....W 10
Oct. 6—Alberto Almiron, Trelaw ....W 10
Nov. 3—Antonio Lopez, Rosario ....W 10
Nov. 25—Raul A. Paez, Mar del Plata ....KO 6
1979
Jan. 1—Jose Maria Flores, San Carlos de Bariloche KO 4
(Won South American Middleweight Title)
Mar. 9—Alberto Almiron, Curuzu Cuaita ....W 10
Mar. 22—Alberto Almiron, Bahia ....D 10
May 25—Juan Carlos Bogado, Mar del Plata .....W 10
June 30—Gerard Nosley, Monte Carlo ....KO 4
—Raul A. Paez, Mar del Plata ....KO 6
Aug. 3—Juan Carlos Bogado, Mar del Plata .....W 10
—Ricardo Arce, Buenos Aires ....L 12
(Lost Argentine Middleweight Title)
Oct. 20—Gert Steyn, Pretoria ....KO 5
1980
Feb. 12—Aldo Carmona, S.Sal. de Jujuy ....D 10
Mar. 7—Julio Arancibia, San Miguel ....D 10
Apr. 18—Eduardo Contreras, Rosario ....D 10
May 3—M. Quentin, Johannesburg ....W 10
June 21—Ricardo Arce, Buenos Aires ....W 12
(Retained South American Middleweight Title)
Oct. 3—Jose Vega, San Luis ....L 10
Oct. 25—Al Styles, Sun City ....W 10

RAUL PARED
Argentine Junior Featherweight
1980
Feb. 16—Americo Suarez, Toay ....L 10
Mar. 8—Humberto Torres, Buenos Aires ....L 6
Apr. 3—Raul Perez, La Rioja ....L 10
Apr. 18—Jose Uziga, Gualeguaychu ....L 10
May 31—Ricardo Poncini, Pergamino ....KO by 4
Aug. 8—Rolando Lahoz, San Juan ....KO by 10

JORGE PAREDES
Argentine Welterweight
1980
May 9—Ruben Mendoza, Formosa ....W 10
Sept. 6—Ramon Allende, Formosa ....L 10

MARTIN PARHAM
New York, N.Y. Lightweight
Born: Aug. 25, 1957
Managed by Bob Jackson
1979
Sept. 19—Tommy Diaz, New York ....W 4
Oct. 4—Keith York, N. Bergen ....KO 3
Oct. 27—Jose Matos, N. Bergen ....W 6
Nov. 9—Jose Rosado, New York ....W 4
1980
Jan. 19—Kato Ali, Hempstead ....W 4
Mar. 4—Jose Matos, Elizabeth ....W 6
June 19—Jeff Passero, Totowa ....W 8
July 17—Curtis Harris, Totowa ....NC
Dec. 11—Jack Rosas, New York ....W 8

CLAYMAN (SANDMAN) PARKER
Spartanburg, S.C. Heavyweight
1974
Nov. 11—Sylvester Kelly, Lenoir ....KO by 5
Dec. 17—Scokomite Lyles, Spartanburg ....KO 1
1975
Feb. 17—Vernon Johnson, Beaumont ....KO 5
July 10—Ricky Ballanger, Blacksburg ....L 12
Aug. 20—Jessie Byrd, Lenoir ....KO 1
Sept. 21—James Brown, Spartanburg ....KO 2
Oct. 4—Terry Denny, Lenoir ....KO 1
1976
Nov. 27—Bump Kelly, Charlotte ....L 12

179

1977

Feb.	15—Bulldog Patterson, Lenoir	KO	8
Mar.	29—Rocky Bentley, Lenoir	W	8
July	9—Ray Timmons, Bellwood	W	6
Aug.	13—Billy Howard, Bellwood	KO	1
Aug.	27—Butch Chambers, Bellwood	W	6
Sept.	22—Lee Holloman, Fayetteville	W	10
Nov.	3—Terry Denny, Cumberland	W	10
Dec.	15—Rocky Bentley, Charlotte	L	8

1978

Jan.	14—Paul Admas, Spartanburg	KO	2
Feb.	10—Choo Choo Sims, Bellwood	W	6
Mar.	3—Tom Walker, Lumberton	KO	3
Mar.	24—Terry Denny, Lenior	W	6
Apr.	1—Butch Chambers, Lenoir	W	8
Apr.	21—Don Collins, Bellwood	KO	2
May	27—Monte Baker, Fallston	KO	3
July	1—Steve Hoskins, Crossroads	D	8
Aug.	17—Jimmy Brannon, Spartanburg	W	6
Dec.	23—James Brannon, Spartanburg	KO	4

1979

Feb.	3—Jo Jo Waddell, Bellwood	KO	2
May	4—Rocky Bentley, Fayetteville	W	12
Dec.	1—Joe Dean Wright, Fayetteville	KO	1
Dec.	14—Lorenzo Zanon, Milan	KO by	7
Dec.	23—Joe Waddell, Spartanburg	KO	2
Dec.	29—Tom Walker, Charlestown	KO	2

1980

Mar.	8—Greg Page, Las Vegas	KO by	1
Apr.	27—Luis Acosta, Greenville	L	5
July	26—Albert Collins, Charlotte	KO	2
Sept.	6—Butch Chambers, Lincolnton	W	8
Sept.	20—Terry Denny, Charlotte	W	10
Oct.	11—Al Byrd, Lincolnton	W	6
Oct.	17—Jeff Sims, West Point	KO by	7

CURTIS PARKER
Frankford, Pa. Middleweight

1977

Dec.	6—Frank Williams, Philadelphia	KO	1

1978

Jan.	24—Harry Fryer, Philadelphia	KO	3
Feb.	10—Kid Samson, Philadelphia	W	6
Mar.	21—Jody White, Philadelphia	KO	4
June	8—Sam Long, Detroit	KO	2
Aug.	24—Dan Snyder, Philadelphia	KO	3
Sept.	21—Jerome Goodman, Philadelphia	KO	8
Oct.	31—Larry Davis, Philadelphia	KO	1
Dec.	5—Ray Smith, Philadelphia	KO	5

1979

Feb.	27—Charles Carey, Philadelphia	KO	1
Apr.	3—Arnell Thomas, Philadelphia	KO	3
May	14—Willie Warren, Philadelphia	KO	5
July	16—Willie Monroe, Philadelphia	W	10
Sept.	11—Elisha Obed, Philadelphia	KO	7
Nov.	14—Gary Guiden, Philadelphia	KO	5

1980

Mar.	9—David Love, Atlantic City	KO	9
May	4—Mike Colbert, Atlantic City	W	12
Aug.	8—Dwight Davison, Las Vegas	L	10

JODY PARKER
Louisville, Ky. Middleweight

1977

May	6—Willie Harp, Miami Beach	L	4
Dec.	9—Bobby Niles, Homestead	W	6
Dec.	15—Tommy Ellis, Tampa	L	6

1978

Jan.	19—Henry Tiger Hall, Tampa	W	4
Feb.	21—Danny Corbett, Hollywood, Fla	KO by	3
Apr.	14—Irvin Hines, Cincinnati	KO by	2
Apr.	29—Gary Coates, Sebring	L	6
Nov.	1—Ray House, Beaver Dam	KO by	3

1979

Feb.	11—Roger Leonard, Miami Beach	KO by	3

1980

Apr.	5—Mike Fisher, Louisville	KO by	2
Sept.	6—Mike Fisher, Jenkins	KO by	1
Oct.	28—Alvino Manson, Indianapolis	KO by	1

BILLY PARKS
Denver, Colo. Lightweight

1975

June	2—Guillermo Gonzalez, Las Vegas	W	5
July	9—Tony Martinez, Las Vegas	W	5
July	23—Gene Prado, Las Vegas	D	6
Sept.	13—Cisco Garcia, Denver	KO	2
Oct.	8—Eddie Murray, Las Vegas	L	6

1976

Mar.	3—Manny Lopez, Las Vegas	W	6
Mar.	31—Senora Fortinel, Las Vegas	W	6
Apr.	3—Teo Pineda, Las Vegas	KO	3
Apr.	21—Waymon Young, Las Vegas	W	6

May	5—Miguel Mayan, Las Vegas	D	8
June	2—Clarence Howard, Las Vegas	W	8

1977

June	6—Ed Modicue, Milwaukee	W	8

1978

Mar.	18—Billy Pearish, Denver	KO	5
May	3—Fili Ramirez, Denver	W	8
Sept.	1—Wayne Lewis, Salt Lake City	KO	3

1979

July	14—J.J. Cottrell, Denver	D	6

1980

Aug.	6—Forrest Winchester, Las Vegas	D	10

ELVIS PARKS
Chicago, Ill. Middleweight

1979

July	17—Danny Murphy, Belleville, Ill.	KO	3
July	20—Warren Thunder, Chicago	L	6
Dec.	15—Harlan Holden, Chicago	W	4

1980

Apr.	17—Warren Thunder, Chicago	KO	2
June	12—Pat Jones, Chicago	W	4
Aug.	25—Jimmy Sansone, Chicago	W	6
Dec.	11—Jeff Stoudemire, Chicago	KO by	3

LUIS PARODI
Argentine Middleweight

1980

Sept.	4—Carlos Bazan, Mendoza	L	6
Dec.	20—Juan Ramirez, Mendoza	W	6

JOSE PARRILLA
Puerto Rican Flyweight

1978

Oct.	2—Luis Colon, Rio Piedras	W	4

1979

Jan.	14—Jimmy Maldonado, San Juan	KO	2
Feb.	18—Victor Callejas, San Juan	W	6
Apr.	28—Rene Aviles, Trujillo	W	6
Oct.	13—Alfredo Herrera, Trujillo	KO	3
Feb.	4—Tottie Villegas, San Juan	KO	1
Mar.	10—Tito Roque, San Juan	W	10
May	5—Victor Bultron, San Juan	W	10
June	19—Ramon Perez, Rio Piedras	KO by	7

JEFF PASSERO
Hillcrest Heights, Md. Junior Welterweight
Born: July 5, 1959

1979

Aug.	7—Van Tate, Baltimore	W	4
Sept.	26—Floyd Pittman, Baltimore	W	4
Oct.	24—Van Tate, Baltimore	KO	1
Nov.	14—Eddie Arthurs, Baltimore	KO	1
Nov.	24—Keith York, Washington, D.C.	KO	1
Dec.	12—Randy Mitchem, Washington, D.C.	KO	5
Jan.	16—Clifford Smith, D.C. Armory	KO	3
Feb.	27—Lou Daniels, D.C. Armory	W	8
Mar.	12—Tyrone Moore, Washington	KO	1
Mar.	26—Richie Garland, Baltimore	KO	1
Apr.	16—Victor Mangual, White Plains	W	6
June	19—Martin Parham, Totowa	L	8
Oct.	15—Marcus Starks, White Plains	W	8

MIKE PASSERO
Mitchellville, Maryland Junior Welterweight

1980

July	31—Sean McGarry, Atlantic City	D	4
Sept.	17—Glen Monick, White Plains	KO	1
Oct.	18—Keith Corbett, Atlantic City	D	4

DANNY PATINO
Los Angeles, Calif. Lightweight

1978

June	26—Jose Claudio, Bakersfield	KO	2
July	6—Eric Bonilla, Los Angeles	W	6
July	20—Fernando Flores, Los Angeles	W	4
Aug.	10—Noe Rivera, Los Angeles	W	4
Aug.	28—Fili Ramirez, Bakersfield	W	6
Oct.	23—Jose Castaneda, Bakersfield	L	6
Nov.	9—Valentin Holguin, Los Angeles	L	6
Nov.	21—Alfredo Sosa, Las Vegas	W	6

1979

Feb.	8—Jimmy McNeece, Los Angeles	W	6
Feb.	20—Red Wiles, Seattle	W	6
Mar.	14—Tommy Cisneros, Las Vegas	KO by	5
Apr.	16—Carlos Contreras, Bakersfield	KO by	5
Apr.	25—Fili Ramirez, Las Vegas	KO by	5
June	13—Tim Martinez, Las Vegas	W	6
June	21—Manny Gonzales, Seattle	KO by	3
Sept.	6—Clemente Enrique, Los Angeles	W	6
Oct.	10—Refugio Rojas, Las Vegas	KO by	4

1980
May   12—Mark Ibanez, Honolulu .... KO by 4
July   2—Ricardo Jiminez, Las Vegas .... KO by 3

REGGIE PATRICK
Elizabeth, N.J. Light Heavyweight
1980
Feb.   5—Danny Perez, W. Hartford ....D 6
Mar.   4—Robert McFarland, Elizabeth ....KO 6
Aug.   29—Eddie Smith, New York .... KO by 4
Oct.   18—Dwight Triplett, Atlantic City ....KO 1
Dec.   27—Walter Saxton, N. Bergen ....W 4

HECTOR PATRI
Argentine Flyweight
Previous Record—11 fights: Won 7, Lost 3, Drew 1, 3 KOs
1980
Jan.   25—Federico Condori, Salta ....W 10
Feb.   8—Jose Ibiris, Mar del Plata ....W 10
Mar.   8—Domingo Aragon, Buenos Aires ....W 10
Apr.   6—Fernando Sagredo, Santiago ....D 10
June   3—Miguel Lazarte, Gral. Acha ....D 10
June   19—Felix Colman, Posadas ....L 10
July   18—Carlos Sosa, Villa Maria ....L 10
Aug.   22—Jose Lopez, La Plata ....W 10
Sept. 26—Jose Ibiris, La Plata ....W 10
Nov.   8—Hermogenes Murillo, Buenos Aires ......W 10

BOB PATTERSON
Paterson, N.J. Middleweight
1976
Feb.   11—Gilberto Vega, New York ....W 4
May   21—Ali Perez, Paterson ....D 6
June   8—Jerome Goodman, Philadelphia ....D 4
Aug.   16—Dom Ortiz, Newark ....W 6
Aug.   26—Fred Daniels, Allentown ....W 6
Nov.   10—Dennis Bennett, West Orange ....KO 4
1977
Feb.   11—Ken Bristol, New York ....L 6
Mar.   31—Curtis Phillips, North Bergen ....KO 5
May   9—Larry Davis, Newark ....W 10
June   9—Richard Hicks, N. Bergen ....KO 1
June   23—Reggie Jones, Newark ....L 12
Oct.   28—Matt Donovan, Elizabeth ....KO 4
Nov.   5—Hugo Corro, Buenos Aires ....KO by 5
1978
Feb.   21—Bonifacio Avila, Montreal ....KO 10
May   24—Bennie Briscoe, Philadelphia ...... KO by 5
Sept. 26—Kevin Finnegan, Wembley ....L 8
Nov.   14—Tony Licata, New Orleans .... KO by 4
1979
Feb.   9—Dwight Davison, Mt. Clemens ...... KO by 3
Mar.   12—Marvin Hagler, Providence .... KO by 3
May   1—Tony Chiaverini, Montreal .... KO by 3
July   22—Ronnie Patterson, Canton ....L 10
Oct.   30—Kevin Smith, Totowa ....KO 1
Dec.   4—Richie Bennett, Philadelphia .... KO by 10
1980
Mar.   26—Joe Tiberi, Baltimore ....KO 7
Apr.   10—Jerome Jackson, Atlantic City ....L 8
May   4—Ernie Singletary, Atlantic City ....L 8
May   25—Wilford Scypion, Atlantic City ...... KO by 6
July   17—Ben Serrano, Totowa ....W 8
Sept. 24—Mustafa Hamsho, Elizabeth .... KO by 4

HENRY (BULLDOG) PATTERSON
Fayetteville, N.C. Heavyweight
1977
Feb.   15—Clayman Parker, Lenior .... KO by 8
Nov.   11—Richard Benjamin, Fayetteville ....W 8
1978
Sept.   9—Henry McIntyre, Harris, N.C. ....KO 2
Dec.   23—Duane Bobick, Spartanburg .... KO by 2
1979
Aug.   10—Pee Wee Dunbar, Spartanburg ....W 4
Nov.   7—Jerry Williams, Spartanburg ....L 6
Nov.   15—Sylvain Watbled, Paris .... KO by 2
1980
Mar.   21—Ron Huston, Fall River ....L 10
Aug.   2—Tommy (Franco) Thomas, Clarksburg KO by 7
Dec.   12—Steve Zouski, Brockton .... KO by 3
Dec.   17—Randy Stephens, Youngstown ....L 10

KERRY PATTERSON
Halifax, N.S. Welterweight
1977
Aug.   18—Zaldi Sinchma, Halifax ....KO 1
1978
June   13—Ralph Hollett, Halifax .... KO by 4
1979
(Inactive)
1900
Sept. 24—Don Johnson, Halifax .... KO by 2
Nov.   21—Paul Dorian, Moncton .... KO by 3

LUCKY PATTERSON
Chicago, Ill. Light Heavyweight
1978
Feb.   27—Don Bester, Chicago ....KO 4
Apr.   28—Henry Sims, Chicago ....L 4
June   30—Henry Sims, Chicago ....L 4
Dec.   9—Rick Jester, Detroit .... KO by 1
1979
Apr.   27—Tony Fritz, Chicago ....D 4
1980
Oct.   30—Mike Clark, Carson City ....L 10

RICKY PATTERSON
Washington, D.C. Junior Lightweight
1978
Apr.   5—Robert Gibson, Washington, D.C. ....W 4
1979
Apr.   6—Tony Edwards, Washington, D.C. ....W 6
Sept. 26—Lou Barber, Baltimore ....L 4
Nov.   24—Ray Mancini, Washington, D.C. ..... KO by 2
1980
Sept. 11—Lloyd Taylor, Washington, D.C. ..... KO by 3

DANNY (MAD DOG) PAUL
Detroit, Mich. Welterweight
1978
Feb.   10—Johnny Ace, Detroit ....W 6
Mar.   17—Willie Wren, Detroit ....KO 4
Mar.   31—Gary Coates, Saginaw ....W 6
June   8—Santiago Valdez, Detroit .... KO by 3
Aug.   3—Ron Flack, Detroit ....KO 6
Sept.   7—Santiago Valdez, Detroit ....W 6
Oct.   26—Ernie Gladney, Detroit ....KO 1
1979
Jan.   10—Art McKnight, Richfield ....W 6
Jan.   31—John Lamb, Saginaw ....W 4
Feb.   13—Clarence Howard, Phoenix ....W 7
1980
Feb.   7—Jeff Grant, Wyandotte ....KO 4
May   3—Greg Thomas, Detroit ....KO 1
Aug.   2—Jose Palacios, Detroit ....W 10
Sept. 30—Bruce Strauss, Niles ....KO 4
Dec.   6—Mike Hutchinson, Detroit ....W 10

GREG PAYNE
Orlando, Fla. Heavyweight
1979
Nov.   27—Demetrius Edwards, Miami Beach ....W 10
1980
Jan.   18—Tony Severance, Orlando ....D 6
Feb.   21—Tony Severance, Gainesville ....L 6
Mar.   18—Danny Mac, Orlando ....L 6

LOUIS PAYNE
Columbus, Ohio Junior Welterweight
1980
Apr.   5—Otto Palfy, Akron ....W 4
July   24—Michael Bradley, Columbus .... KO by 1
Sept. 13—Chuck Spicer, Lorain ....KO 4

RAUL PAZ
Argentine Welterweight
1980
Jan.   —Antonio Juarez, Monte Hermoso ....L 10
June   5—Juan Cabral, Int. Alvear ....L 10
July   11—Simon Escobar, Villa Mercedes ....L 10
Dec.   5—Osvaldo Barreda, Olavarria ....L 10

JIM PEARISH
Joplin, Mo. Heavyweight
1977
Mar.   5—Squirrel Barnes, Quaqua ....W 4
Apr.   5—Wayne Lewis, Oklahoma City ....W 4
Oct.   11—Steve Basse, Memphis ....L 4
Dec.   6—Ike McIntosh, Oklahoma City ....KO 1
1978
Mar.   18—Jeff Shelburg, Denver .... KO by 4
Nov.   18—Willie Stoglin, Joplin ....W 4
Nov.   29—Lupe Guerra, Omaha ....L 6
1979
        —Ron Stander, North Platte .... KO by 5
Dec.   13—Louis Brown, Tulsa .... KO by 3
1980
June   13—Lon Dale Freissen, Tulsa .... KO by 3

DANNY PEARSON
Jersey City, N.J. Welterweight
1980
Sept. 24—Eddie Sanchez, Elizabeth ....KO 1
Nov.   28—Ray Madera, New York ....W 4
Dec.   27—Joe Banks, N. Bergen .... KO by 1

181

FLOYD PEARSON
Blue Island, Ill. Welterweight
1977
Nov. 22—Warren Thunder, Chicago .... KO 2
1978
Mar. 20—Gene Stevens, Chicago .... L 4
May 8—Simmie Black, Chicago .... KO 2
Aug. 28—Jerry Strickland, Chicago .... KO 3
Nov. 11—Eddie Thomas, Sterling .... KO 5
1979
Feb. 28—Carl Crowley, Chicago .... L 6
June 11—Bruce Strauss, Chicago .... L 6
1980
Apr. 17—Robert Hughes, Chicago .... KO 2
May 2—Niwa LaRocca, Rome .... KO 2
Aug. 14—Richard House, Chicago .... KO by 8

JORGE PECH
Mexican Flyweight
1980
Feb. 13—Jorge Alberto May, Merida .... L 10
Feb. 24—Raul Armando Koh, Tenosique .... W 6

RAFAEL PEDROZA
Panamanian Flyweight
1975
Jan. 21—Luis Sotomayor, Panama City .... KO 2
Apr. 26—Adriano Mendoza, Panama City ...... KO 1
Aug. 23—Candelario Guzman, Panama City ..... KO 7
1976
Nov. 13—Domingo Torres, Panama City .... KO 4
1977
Feb. 5—Felipe Perez, Panama City .... KO 7
Apr. 25—Luis Estaba, Caracas .... L 15
(WBC Light Flyweight Title)
May 15—Luis Estaba, Caracas .... L 15
Oct. 1—Luis Ibarra, Colon .... L 10
1978
July 1—Eusebio Urcuyo, Panama City .... KO 1
1979
Apr. 7—Alex Santana Guido, Panama City ..... KO 1
July 29—Yoko Gushiken, Kitakyushi .... L 15
(WBA Junior Flyweight Title)
Sept. —Martin Vargas, Santiago .... KO by 4
1980
Mar. 1—Javier Gonzales, Panama City .... W 12
Aug. 16—Fausto Gomez, Panama City .... KO 5
Aug. 30—Miguel Iriarte, Colon .... L 10
Oct. 4—Gustavo Ballas, Buenos Aires .... L 10

BERNARDINO PENA
Mexican Flyweight
1980
Jan. 26—Joel Gatica, Mexico City .... W 8
Feb. 27—Fidel Martinez, Mexico City .... L 8
May 3—Augustin Lopez, Mexico City .... W 8
May 28—Rodolfo Ortega, Mexico City .... D 10
July 9—Camilo (Gentil) Ortiz, Mexico City .... L 10
Aug. 6—Pablo Flores, Mexico City .... KO 6

FAUSTINO PENA
Texas Junior Lightweight
1979
Nov. 27—Rafael Limon, Houston .... L 10
1980
Jan. 9—Greg Coverson, Holland, Mich. .... KO by 1
Oct. 28—Roberto Madrid, Houston .... L 10

GERARDO PENA
Mexican Featherweight
1977
Mar. 20—Jose Luna, Nuevo, Laredo .... KO 3
1978
Apr. 1—Mario Najera, Tampico .... KO 2
July 28—Juan Villanueva, Tampico .... KO 2
Sept. 14—Alex Garcia, Los Angeles .... KO 5
1979
Feb. 23—Mario Castro, Aguascalientes .... KO 4
July 2—Benny Silva, Los Angeles .... KO 4
Oct. 23—Refugio Rojas, Los Angeles .... W 10
Nov. 16—Francisco Pena, Inglewood .... KO 6
1980
Feb. 9—Robert Garcia, Los Angeles .... KO 8
May 2—Mark Davis, Los Angeles .... KO by 8

MILCIADES PENA
Dominican Rep. Featherweight
1978
Feb. 2—Bienvenido Rijo, Santo Domingo .... W 4
July 26—Roberto Bido, Santo Domingo .... KO by 6
Aug. 28—Juan Rijo, Santo Domingo .... KO 1
Oct. 16—Juan Pimentel, Santo Domingo .... KO 1

182

1979
Mar. 25—Ray Viruet, San Juan .... W 6
1980
Aug. 25—Roberto Bido, Santo Domingo .... W 10

DARYL PENN
Portland, Ore. Middleweight
1975
Aug. 12—Eugene White, Seattle .... W 6
Oct. 6—Lester Bordon, River Bend .... KO 1
Nov. 20—Steve St. Charles, Portland .... KO 1
1976
Feb. 10—Steve Tohill, Seattle..................... KO 6
Feb. 19—Ricardo Rodriguez, Eugene.............. KO 1
Mar. 9—Larry Smith, Seattle..................... L 6
Apr. 9—Raul Reyes, Salt Lake City............. W 4
Apr. 21—Floyd Mayweather, Seattle .... L 6
June 9—Babala McCarthy, Stateline .... KO by 3
Sept. 15—Larry Smith, Everett .... KO by 3
Oct. 12—Steve Tohill, Seattle.................... W 6
1977
Feb. 12—John L. Sullivan, Lacey .... KO 2
June 11—C. J. Brown, Hillsboro .... W 6
June 23—Tommy Howard, Vancouver .... L 10
Aug. —David Rodriguez, Vancouver .... KO 2
Oct. 28—Augie Gomez, Portland .... W 10
1978
May 5—Steve Chase, Portland .... D 8
June 28—Bruce Finch, Las Vegas .... KO by 6
Aug. 5—Rudy Barro, Elko .... L 10
Aug. 29—Bobby Howard, Seattle .... L 12
1979
Jan. 18—Bobby Howard, Portland .... W 8
Apr. —J. J. Cottrell, Billings .... W 10
Apr. 25—Jacinto Fernandez, Lake Tahoe ...... KO by 8
May 25—Jose Dominguez, Pico Rivera .... L 10
June 10—Rudy Barro, Stockton .... W 10
June 15—Rocky Mosley, Las Vegas .... L 12
(U.S. Junior Middleweight Title)
July 21—David Braxton, Pontiac .... L 10
Oct. 25—Rudy Barro, Portland .... KO 5
1980
Jan. 9—Julio Gomez, Las Vegas .... KO 7
Mar. 20—Chuck Walker, Phoenix .... KO 4
Apr. 19—J. J. Cottrell, Billings .... KO 4
Aug. 27—Bobby Epps, Las Vegas .... L disq. 6
Nov. 11—Scott Papasoderea, Winnipeg .... W 4

PETER PENNELLO
Jersey City, N.J. Middleweight
1979
Oct. 4—Hank Whittmore, N. Bergen .... D 4
Nov. 28—Ken Lomzx, W. New York, N.J. .... KO 2
1980
Mar. 20—Hank Whitmore, N. Bergen .... D 4
Mar. 28—Doug DeWitt, Tarrytown .... L 4

ALFREDO PERALTA
Argentine Junior Welterweight
1980
Jan. 4—Oscar Artaza, Mar del Plata .... KO by 6
Sept. 26—Mario Arreguez, Tandil .... KO 4

CARLOS PERALTA
Argentine Middleweight
1980
Jan. 11—Pablo Ferreyra, S. Sal. de Jujuy .... W 10
Feb. 14—Patricio Diaz, Mendoza .... W 10
Apr. 3—Oscar Barrios, Rio III .... KO 9
May 16—Walter Gomez, Santa Rosa .... L 8
June 25—Patricio Diaz, Buenos Aires .... D 10
July 25—Eduardo Contreras, Cordoba .... D 10
Aug. 15—Eduardo Contreras, Rosario .... W 10
Sept. 4—Carlos Nacimiento, Posadas .... W 10
Sept. 26—Ramon Ozuna, Rio III .... W 10
Dec. 5—Patricio Diaz, Rio Gallegos .... W 10
Dec. 18—Juan D. Roldan, Cordoba .... D 12

LUIS PERALTA
Argentine Middleweight
1980
June 6—Hugo Trujillo, La Banda .... W 10
July 4—Carlos Flores, Concepcion .... KO 4
Aug. 15—Manuel Gonzalez, Santa Fe .... W 10
Oct. 3—Rogelio Zarza, Santa Fe .... W 10

RAMON S. PERALTA
Argentine Welterweight
1980
Mar. 7—Alfredo Campos, Rio III .... W 10
Mar. 21—Jorge Morello, Vdo Tuerto .... W 10
Apr. 11—Jose Oroda, Berrotan .... W 10
May 17—Antonio Juarez, Rio III .... D 12

June 19—Sergi Loyola, Vdo Tuerto ....D 10
Aug. 1—Juan Cabral, Rio IV ....W 10
Sept. 12—Santiago Portillo, Tucuman ....D 10
Oct. 24—Hector Caceres, Tio Tercero ....W 10
Nov. 28—Hector Hernandez, Tucuman ....L 10
Dec. 19—Hector Hernandez, Rio III ....W 10

RAUL PORCEL PERALTA
Argentine Middleweight
1980
Feb. 8—Ezequiel Obando, Cordoba ....KO 4
May 2—Eduardo Contreras, Cordoba ....L 10

ERIC PEREA
Panama City, Panama Welterweight
1980
Mar. 29—Reynaldo Ortega, Panama City ....KO 1
June 28—Marino Alabarca, Panama City ....KO 2
Aug. 1—Ricardo Davies, Colon ....KO 3
Oct. 4—Robert Sawyer, Great Gorge ....KO by 2

TONY PEREA
Texas Heavyweight
1979
July 20—John Wages, El Paso ....KO 2
Sept. 12—Verlee Price, El Paso ....KO 4
1980
Jan. 18—Yaqui Meneses, El Paso ....W 6
Mar. 7—Abdullah Muhammad, El Paso ....KO 3
May 9—Larry Montgomery, El Paso ....KO 2
Sept. 11—Jimmy Ingram, El Paso ....W 8
Dec. 17—Ron Draper, Las Vegas ....KO 4

ALBERTO PEREYRA
Argentine Featherweight
1980
Apr. 24—Renicio Sosa, Corrientes ....KO 5
June 21—Ovidio Szkarlatiuk, Buenos Aires ....L 6
July 18—Benicio Sosa, Villa Angela ....KO by 8
Oct. 3—Jorge Perez, Posadas ....L 8

ALFREDO PEREZ
Corpus Christi, Texas, Welterweight
1977
Dec. 13—Ralph Torres, Corpus Christi ....KO 2
1978
Feb. 20—Glen Mitchell, San Antonio ....KO 1
Mar. 31—Jose Angel Villasana, San Antonio ....W 6
1979
July 31—Al Davila, San Antonio ....KO 3
1980
Oct. 14—Jose Medina, Laredo ....KO by 7

ALI PEREZ
New York, N.Y. Middleweight
1974
Oct. 15—Greg Singleton, Paterson ....KO 4
Dec. 9—Melvin Cherry, New York ....KO 1
1975
Jan. 7—Christy Elliott, Paterson ....KO by 6
Aug. 5—Reggie Jones, Elizabeth ....L 6
Sept. 26—Reggie Jones, Latham ....W 6
Nov. 7—John Harris, Latham ....L 6
1976
Feb. 25—Larry Davis, New York ....W 8
May 21—Robert Patterson, Paterson ....D 6
June 26—John Pinney, Monte Carlo ....D 8
Aug. 12—Emerito Morales, Paterson ....KO 5
Aug. 19—Pepe Ortiz, New York ....KO 5
Sept. 3—Dom Ortiz, Philadelphia ....W 6
Nov. 10—Nikita Tarhocker, West Orange ....KO 3
1977
Feb. 3—Ruben Lopez, Allentown ....L 10
Apr. 25—Reggie Jones, Newark ....L 10
June 9—Sixto Morales, North Bergen ....KO 5
July 30—Norberto Cabrera, Monte Carlo ......KO by 4
Nov. 30—Hilton Whitaker, Newark ....W 8
1978
Feb. 2—Jean Claude LeClair, Montreal ....L 10
Sept. 8—Jimmy Anderson, New York ....KO 5
Nov. 1—Jerome Jackson, Westchester ....L 8
1979
Feb. 26—John LoCiccero, New York ....KO by 2
Oct. 2—Eddie Melo, Montreal ....KO by 6
1980
Mar. 21—Carlton Perez, New York ....L 6
Apr. 30—Gerald Banks, Charleston ....L 6
June 13—John Molander, New York ....W 6

ARMANDO PEREZ
Argentine Featherweight
1980
Aug. 9—Omar Almada, Gral Pico ....W 10

Aug. 29—Marcelo Miranda, S. Sal. de Jujuy ....L 10
Sept. 20—Jorge M. Gomez, Buenos Aires ....L 10
Dec. 20—Ruben Araya, Resistencia ....KO 8

DANNY PEREZ
Hoboken, N.J., Middleweight
1977
Oct. 25—Paddy Young, New York ....L 4
Dec. 8—Danny Daniels, North Bergen ....KO 1
1978
Mar. 16—Francisco Lopez, North Bergen ....KO 1
June 28—Sean Mannion, Providence ....L 6
Sept. 28—Manuel Ruelas, Phoenix ....L 6
Nov. 16—Kevin Mahon, North Bergen ....W 4
1979
(Inactive)
1980
Feb. 5—Reggie Patrick, W. Hartford ....D 6
Mar. 28—Herbie Wilens, Tarrytown ....KO by 3

FELIX PEREZ
New York, N.Y. Lightweight
1974
Apr. 8—John Tutino, New York ....W 4
Apr. 18—John Tutino, North Bergen...............W 4
May 13—Felix Flores, New York.................L 4
May 26—Charlie Glenn, Portland, Me. ....KO 6
Sept. 6—Jose Roberto, Portland, Me. ....W 6
Nov. 11—Patrick Maloney, New York ....L 4
1975
Jan. 7—Art Rosa, Paterson.....................D 4
Mar. 24—Marco Larios, New York ....W 4
Apr. 25—Ahmet Tosci, Kingston.................W 6
May 3—Jim Roan, New Bedford ....W 6
1976
Mar. 30—Mike Vasquez, New York ....KO 1
Apr. 28—Celia Romero, New York ....W 4
June 23—Kid Camanche, East Hartford ....KO 7
Dec. 2—Luis Rivera, New York ....KO 1
1977
Mar. 18—Dan Daniels, New York ....W 8
May 24—Jose Resto, White Plains, N.Y. ....W 8
Sept. 8—Billy Wade, New York ....W 8
Oct. 27—Cocoa Sanchez, New York ....KO by 7
1978
Jan. 18—Lloyd Wilson, White Plains ....W 6
Apr. 5—Benito Jiminez, White Plains ....KO 7
July 26—Paddy Dolan, New York ....W 8
Nov. 6—Jesus de la Rosa, Santo Domingo ....KO by 4
1979
May 23—Tim LaValley, White Plains ....KO 1
1980
Feb. 13—Manuel de la Rosa, White Plains ....L 8
Nov. 12—John Verderosa, New York ....KO by 7

IRLEIS PEREZ
Los Angeles, Calif. Lightweight
1978
May 25—Pedro Osuna, Los Angeles ....KO 1
June 8—Eric Bonilla, Los Angeles ....W 5
July 20—Eric Bonilla, Los Angeles ....KO 1
Aug. 10—Jose Osuna, Los Angeles ....KO 1
Sept. 28—Genaro Gloria, Los Angeles ....W 6
Nov. 16—Alfredo Carranza, Los Angeles ....KO 3
Dec. 7—Genaro Gloria, Los Angeles ....KO 1
1979
Feb. 15—Sergio Nualarte, Los Angeles ....KO 2
Mar. 15—Elpidio Valdez, Los Angeles ....KO 1
Apr. 12—Willie Daniels, Los Angeles ....KO 2
June 14—Jesus Hernandez, Los Angeles ....KO 4
July 19—Rafael Nunez, Los Angeles ....W 10
Sept. 13—Willie Daniels, Los Angeles ....KO 1
1980
May 29—Fili Ramirez, Los Angeles ....KO 9

ISIDRO GINO PEREZ
West New York, N.J. Lightweight
1977
Oct. 25—Lou Parks, West New York ....KO 2
Dec. 8—Jose Matos, North Bergen ....W 4
1978
Jan. 19—James Kolb, North Bergen ....KO 1
Feb. 23—Dan Daniels, North Bergen ....KO 1
Oct. 4—Tommy Barr, White Plains ....KO 1
Dec. 15—Tony Still, White Plains ....L 4
1979
Feb. 14—Melvin Bethea, White Plains ....D 4
Mar. 14—Lamont Waddy, White Plains ....W 4
Nov. 28—Vilomar Fernandez, W. New York, N.J. ....L 10
Dec. 5—Larry Savage, White Plains ....KO 4
1980
Mar. 20—Robert Grant, North Bergen ....W 12
July 16—Dave Bolden, Elizabeth ....KO 7

183

JOSE PEREZ
Texas Junior Featherweight
1980
May 20—Victor Gonzales, San Antonio .... KO 4
June 17—Ruben Chiaverria, San Antonio .... KO 4
Sept. 5—Jesse Renteria, Inglewood .... L 4
Nov. 6—Joe Eaton, Los Angeles .... L 5
Dec. 4—Frank Lopez, Los Angeles .... L 4

LUIS PEREZ
Argentine Lightweight
1980
Feb. 22—Luis A. Zarate, Tucuman .... W 10
Apr. 3—Luis A. Zarate, Tucuman .... D 10
June 19—Luis A. Zarate, La Banda .... W 10
Sept. 5—Luis A. Zarate, S. Ped. Jujuy .... W 10
Nov. 7—Luis A. Zarate, Salta .... D 10

NICKY PEREZ
Tucson, Ariz. Junior Featherweight
1977
June 25—Luis Rosario, Bayamon .... KO by 4
July 13—Artemio Rodriguez, Las Vegas .... KO 3
July 20—Carlos Perez, Las Vegas .... KO 5
Aug. 3—Elias Rodriguez, Las Vegas .... W 6
Aug. 10—Joey Rico, Las Vegas .... KO 3
Aug. 25—Danny Young, Tucson .... KO 2
Sept. 6—John Pineda, Lake Tahoe .... KO 3
Sept. 7—Jose Luis Vieyra, Las Vegas .... W 6
Sept. 23—Jose Rodriguez, Tucson .... KO 5
Oct. 5—Genaro Lugo, Las Vegas .... KO 5
Oct. 22—Alfonso Dominguez, Lubbock .... KO 5
Nov. 9—Francisco Grullon, Tucson .... KO 5
Dec. 14—Genaro Lugo, Tucson .... KO 7
1978
Jan. 17—John Luna, Las Vegas .... W 6
Jan. 24—Genaro Lugo, Phoenix .... KO 4
Feb. 8—Andreo Provencio, Phoenix .... KO 1
Mar. 7—Reuben Cofia, Phoenix .... KO 3
Mar. 22—Jose Claudio, Las Vegas .... KO 4
Apr. 4—Daniel Perez, El Paso .... KO 2
Apr. 13—Alex Garcia, Phoenix .... KO 3
Apr. 25—Jesus Barrientos, El Paso .... W 8
May 15—Alex Garcia, Denver .... W 10
May 30—Humberto Lara, Incline Village .... W 10
June 20—Alfonso Dominguez, Phoenix .... W 8
July 19—Cesario Quinnones, Las Vegas .... KO 2
Aug. 16—Tony Hernandez, Las Vegas .... W 10
Aug. 27—Regis Rodriguez, Tucson .... KO 3
Sept. 9—Antonio Hernandez, Bakersfield .... W 10
Oct. 10—Javier Flores, Las Vegas .... W 12
Oct. 28—Ray Salcedo, Tucson .... KO 6
Nov. 25—Mario Servin, Tucson .... W 10
1979
Jan. 28—Melvin Johnson, Reno .... W 10
Mar. 11—Javier Flores, Reno .... W 12
Mar. 28—Ramon Aguinaga, Stateline .... KO 3
Apr. 16—Melvin Johnson, Las Vegas .... W 12
June 2—Humberto Lara, Albuquerque .... W 10
June 30—Carlos Cantu, Albuquerque .... KO 4
July 27—Carlos Cantu, Las Vegas .... KO 3
Aug. 15—Benny Silva, Tucson .... W 10
Aug. 27—Regis Rodriguez, Tucson .... KO 3
Sept. 12—Manuel Rueles, El Paso .... W 10
Sept. 27—Regis Rodriguez, Tucson .... KO 3
Oct. 26—Wilfredo Gomez, New York .... KO by 5
(For World Junior Featherweight Title)
1980
Jan. 20—Angel Salinas, Tucson .... KO 2
Apr. 12—Ruben Solario, Tucson .... W 10
May 23—Mike Ayala, Clarkson .... L 12
(For North American Junior Featherweight Title)
Oct. 7—Ricardo Varela, Las Vegas .... W 10
Nov. 11—Cookie Valencia, Las Vegas .... KO 3

RAMON PEREZ
Puerto Rican, Flyweight
1977
July 11—Orlando Maldonado, San Juan .... L 4
Oct. 3—Juan Sierra, Santo Domingo .... L 10
1978
Mar. 4—Victor Bultron, Carolina .... D 4
Apr. 1—Luis Burgos, Carolina .... D 6
Apr. 14—Enrique Sanchez, Santo Domingo .... KO by 9
Oct. 28—Jose Anada, San Juan .... W 6
1979
Jan. 14—Hilario Zapata, San Juan .... L 10
June 29—Jose Vallejo, Santo Domingo .... L 10
1980
Apr. 7—Felix Llanos, San Juan .... KO 4
Apr. 28—Mauricio Bravo, Caracas .... KO by 2
June 19—Jose Parilla, Rio Piedras .... KO 7
Sept. 8—Mauricio Bravo, Caracas .... KO by 3

Oct. 16—Bazooka Sosa, Caguas .... W 10

RAMON E. PEREZ
Argentine Middleweight
1980
Apr. 11—Juan D. Roldan, San Francisco ...... KO by 8
Sept. 5—Alfredo Sosa, Tunuyan .... L 10
Oct. 3—Hector Hernandez, Cordoba .... W 10

RAUL (NICO) PEREZ
Argentine Junior Featherweight
1980
Jan. —Adolfo Felice, V. Carlos Paz .... D 10
Feb. 28—Luis Gerez, Arrecifes .... L 10
Mar. 14—Marcelo Miranda, La Rioja .... W 10
Apr. 3—Raul Pared, La Rioja .... W 10
May —Cesar Villarruel, Buenos Aires .... W 10
June 13—Jose Flores, Mendoza .... W 10
July 8—Julio C. Saba, S. Sal de Jujuy .... W 10
July 18—Hermogenes Prado, Mendoza .... W 10
Aug. 1—Juan C. Cortez, Cordoba .... L 10
Sept. 4—Rolando Lahoz, Mendoza .... W 10
Oct. 10—Luis Gerez, Arrecifes .... L 10
Dec. 5—Pedro Burki, Villa Maria .... D 10

ROBERTO PEREZ
Houston, Texas Lightweight
1975
June 3—Sean O'Grady, Oklahoma City ...... KO by 3
Aug. 19—Ricky Gutierrez, Corpus Christi .... L 4
Sept. 16—Ricky Gutierrez, Corpus Christi .... D 6
Nov. 18—Ricky Gutierrez, Corpus Christi ..... KO by 2
1976
Mar. 31—Harrison Kiger, Galveston .... L 4
Oct. 26—Leon McCullum, Corpus Christi .... KO 2
1977
Jan. 25—Sultan Saladin, Corpus Christi ...... KO by 5
May 26—Billy Miller, Austin .... KO by 2
June 11—Rodolfo Perez, Sterling .... KO 2
July 19—Rommel Mendoza, Houston .... W 8
Aug. 1—Wardell Williams, Topeka .... KO by 1
1978
Feb. 14—Rommel Mendoza, Houston .... KO 5
Mar. 14—Jimmy Martinez, Houston .... W 10
July 18—Jose Caba, Honolulu .... KO by 2
Aug. 8—James Martinez, Houston .... KO 6
Sept. 5—Bennie Marquez, Chicago .... KO by 8
Oct. 11—Norman Goins, Indianapolis .... L 7
Dec. 15—Roberto Elizondo, Corpus Christi ... KO by 1
1979
Jan. 25—Ruben Castillo, Los Angeles .... KO by 3
Feb. 26—Ricardo Arredondo, Houston .... KO by 4
Apr. 10—Elias De Leon, Houston .... KO by 4
Apr. 20—Florentino Falcon, Corpus Christi ...... L 10
Apr. 28—Sean O'Grady, Omaha .... KO by 5
Aug. 15—Maurice Watkins, Beaumont .... KO by 1
Oct. 1—Ramiro Hernandez, Corpus Christi ... W 10
—Maurice Watkins, Beaumont .... KO by 7
Dec. 14—Ray Mancini, Dallas .... KO by 1
1980
Mar. 28—Benny Marquez, Chicago .... KO by 3
Aug. 25—Bobby Pappion, Houston .... KO by 2
Oct. 9—Javier Gonzalez, McAllen .... L 6
1980
Aug. 26—Bobby Pappion, Houston .... KO by 2

RODOLFO PEREZ
Houston, Texas Junior Featherweight
1977
Jan. 25—Antonio Vargas, Houston .... KO 6
Feb. 1—Roberto Vazquez, Corpus Christi .... KO by 2
Feb. 24—Chamaco Limon, Piedras Negras .... W 10
Apr. 5—Robert Elizondo, Corpus Christi .... KO by 1
May 11—Sefafin Pacheco, Mexico City .... KO 3
June 11—Roberto Perez, Sterling .... KO by 2
Oct. 4—Ricky Gutierrez, San Antonio .... KO by 2
1978
(Inactive)
1979
Apr. 10—Elias DeLeon, Houston .... KO by 6
May 11—Jose Villegas, Pico Rivero .... L 10
1980
Apr. 24—Carlos Zuniga, Stockton .... L 10

BRUCE PERRY
Massachustts Heavyweight
1980
June 26—Frank Rocco, Revere .... KO by 5
Aug. 21—Curtis Whitner, Revere .... W 4
Oct. 16—Curtis Whitner, Revere .... L 4
Dec. 15—Paul Bissonnette, Boston .... L 4

KEVIN PERRY
Philadelphia, Pa. Middleweight
1979
June	29—Dan Staehle, Jersey City	KO 1
July	31—Ben Serrano, Atlantic City	W 4
Sept.	26—Jimmy Anderson, Upper Darby	KO 1

1980
Mar.	4—Mark Medel, Elizabeth	KO 1
Oct.	1—Willie Ray Taylor, Atlantic City	KO 4
Nov.	6—Buster Drayton, Atlantic City	KO 3

BERNARD PETERSON
Philadelphia, Pa. Junior Welterweight
1979
Sept.	29—Kevin Bell, Trenton	KO 2
Nov.	23—Willie Thomas, Trenton	KO 3

1980
Jan.	24—Manny Simms, Upper Darby	KO 3
May	16—Roger Stafford, Chester	D 8
Aug.	7—Roger Stafford, Atlandit City	W 8

CHARLEY PETERSON
Muncie, Ind. Junior Middleweight
1979
Mar.	27—Lamont Hopkins, Michigan	KO 4
Apr.	17—Tom Crowley, Waukesha	L 4
May	8—Nathaniel Akbar, Center Stage	L 4
June	24—Steve Woods, Cincinnati	W 8
July	18—Bruce Strauss, Indianapolis	W 8
Aug.	3—Bob Coolidge, Omaha	D 8
Aug.	24—Steve Woods, Cincinnati	W 6
Oct.	11—Danny Campbell, Kansas City	KO 3
Dec.	14—Gary Thomas, Evansville	W 6

1980
Jan.	9—Tony Chiaverini, Kansas City	KO by 2
Mar.	8—Shelvy Wilkerson, Nashville	KO by 3
Apr.	19—Terry Flynn, Muskegon	L 6
June	27—Juan Ribota, Chicago	D 4
July	28—Harlen Holden, Chicago	KO by 2
Aug.	13—Jeff Madison, Indianapolis	W 6
Sept.	6—Garland Tipton, Kensington, Ky.	L 6
Sept.	23—Don King, Indianapolis	KO by 1
Oct.	30—Nick Wills, Louisville	KO 4
Nov.	1—Winfield Braithwaite, Dayton	KO by 3
Nov.	11—Bob Coolidge, St. Paul	L 8

LARRY PETERSON
Jacksonville, Fla. Welterweight
(Previous Record Unavailable)
1977
Nov.	29—Jerry Powers, Jacksonville	W 10

1978
Feb.	14—Wayne Battle, Jacksonville	KO 6
Apr.	27—Ted Mann, Jacksonville	KO by 6
May	16—Eddie Walker, Jacksonville	KO 4
June	27—Gary Smith, Jacksonville	W 10
Oct.	9—Dennis Green, Jacksonville	KO 3
Dec.	5—Martin Ryals, Jacksonville	KO 3

1979
Mar.	15—Henry Hall, Palatka	W 8
Oct.	4—Johnny Turner, New York	KO by 4

1980
Mar.	25—Raul Aguirre, Jacksonville	W 10
Sept.	25—Mauricio Bravo, Caracas	KO by 7

RODOLFO PETRIZANI
Argentine Lightweight
1980
Feb.	1—Lorenzo Garcia, San Pedro	L 4
Apr.	18—Victor Escobar, P.R.S. Pena	L 10
May	2—Hugo Quartapelle, Villa Maria	L 10
July	11—Miguel Barraza, Ciudadela	W 10
Sept.	5—Romulo Ibarra, Corrientes	L 10
Oct.	4—Manuel Bustos, Buenos Aires	L 10

TYRONE PHELPS
New York, N.Y. Junior Middleweight
1973
Sept.	17—C. J. Faison, New York	KO 3
Oct.	15—Ray Hammond, New York	KO by 3
Dec.	10—Max Pierret, New York	W 6

1974
Jan.	7—Max Pierret, New York	KO 4
Mar.	18—Fred Boynton, New York	D 6
Apr.	8—Ray Hammond, New York	L 6
May	7—Kid Sampson, Philadelphia	W 6
May	13—Omar Piton, New York	L 8
Aug.	27—C. J. Faison, Alexandria	L 6

1975
Mar.	24—Omar Piton, New York	L 8
Apr.	4—Jeff Holmes, Uniondale	W 6

May	22—Floyd Mayweather, Baltimore	KO 2
July	23—Floyd Mayweather, Largo	L 8
Nov.	21—Lloyd Richardson, Kingston	L 8

1976
Apr.	3—Johnny Stiff, Utica	D 8
June	28—Dave Huckaby, New York	L 8
July	28—Ernie Singletary, Philadelphia	L 6
Aug.	6—Don Morgan, New York	KO 5
Aug.	13—D. C. Walker, Sunnyside	D 8
Aug.	16—Winston Noel, Newark	W 6
Aug.	19—Winston Noel, New York	W 6
Oct.	22—Miguel Hernandez, New York	L 6
Dec.	2—Leo Saenz, Baltimore	KO by 9

1977
Feb.	15—Mike Bullock, New York	W 6
Mar.	25—Bruce Finch, Milwaukee	L 8
Apr.	1—Fred Boynton, New York	L 6
Apr.	15—Manuel Melon, New York	L 6
Apr.	21—Mike Bullock, Dover	L 6
May	26—Miguel Hernandez, McAfee	L 6
June	3—Luis Resto, New York	KO by 4

1978
Jan.	14—Roy Edmonds, Hauppauge	KO by 2
Mar.	25—Rocky Fratto, Syracuse	L 8
Mar.	31—Tommy Hearns, Saginaw	KO by 3
May	6—Frank Wissenbach, Berlin	L 10
May	13—Benji Goldstone, Utica	KO by 5
July	15—Frank Minigan, Alexandria Bay	W 6
July	29—Fighting Jim, St. Martin	KO by 8
Aug.	12—Frankie Minigan, Alexandria Bay	L 6
Sept.	6—Marciano Bernardi, White Plains	L 6
Sept.	10—James Williams, Elmira	W 6
Oct.	28—Carlos Santos, San Juan	KO by 4
Nov.	2—Edgar Ross, Birmingham	L 10
Nov.	3—Sammy NeSmith, Indianapolis	KO by 7

1979
Feb.	3—Andoni Amana, Madrid	L 8
Feb	12—Roland Pryor, Washington, D.C.	KO by 9
Apr.	14—Danny Patino, Syracuse	L 6

1980
Jan.	16—Roger Leonard, Washington, D.C.	KO by 3

JIMMY PHILLIPS
Ft. Worth, Texas Featherweight
1978
Aug.	22—Jesse Montemayor, Odessa	KO by 3

1979
June	12—James Smith, Beaumont	KO by 2

1980
July	18—Richard Lord, Odessa	KO by 2

JOE PHILLIPS
Pittsfield, Mass. Junior Lightweight
1977
Oct.	8—Mel Boynton, Geneva	W 4
Oct.	29—Steve Snow, Hartford	D 4
Nov.	10—Eduardo Rivera, Cohoes	KO 2
Nov.	19—Mel Boynton, Syracuse	KO 4
Dec.	8—Dan Tratzinski, Cohoes	W 6

1978
Jan.	14—Mike Rae, Albany	KO 2
Mar.	2—Ron Meaweather, Cohoes	W 8
Mar.	30—Dan Daniels, Cohoes	L 8
Apr.	18—Clyde Beattie, Cohoes	W 1
July	15—Tony Stokes, Alexandria Bay	W 6
Aug.	12—Dan Daniels, Alexandria Bay	D 8
Sept.	16—Jimmy Lopez, Cape Cod	L 10
Dec.	5—Jean LaPointe, Montreal	L 10

1979
Jan.	26—Paddy Dolan, New York	L 8
Feb.	28—Luis Davila, Hartford	L 10
Oct.	24—Jose L. Lopez, Las Vegas	KO 3
Nov.	14—Robert Garcia, Las Vegas	L 10
Dec.	11—Sergio Serabia, Sparks	L 6

1980
Jan.	22—Lionel Harney, Sparks	W 10
Feb.	13—Ricardo Jiminez, Las Vegas	KO by 3
May	2—Raul Cruz, Las Vegas	W 6
May	24—Santos Moreno, Salt Lake City	KO by 4
Dec.	20—Manuel D'Arcie, N. Adams	W 8

OLIVER PHILLIPS
Jamaica, W.I. Heavyweight
1975
Nov.	26—Jimmy Gilmore, Las Vegas	W 6

1976-1977
(Inactive)
1978
Aug.	19—Franco Thomas, Las Vegas	W 10
Oct.	26—Mircea Simon, Los Angeles	KO by 2

1979
Mar.	2—Mike Weaver, Las Vegas	KO by 4
Aug.	19—Young Joe Louis, Bloomington	L 10

Sept. 22—Greg Page, Los Angeles .... KO by 4
1980
May 25—Eddie Gregg, Atlantic City .... D 6

(SUGAR) RAY PHILLIPS
Dallas, Texas Junior Middleweight
1975
June 27—Charles Cook, Lake Charles.............. W 8
July 15—Joe Parson, Oklahoma City .... W 4
Aug. 28—Willie Hicks, Lake Charles.............. W 8
Sept. 23—Emmett Atlas, Lake Charles............. W 10
1976
May 3—Hank Gregory, Topeka.................... W 6
June 2—Alfonso Aguirre, Topeka................ KO 1
June 22—Hank Gregory, Topeka................... W 6
Oct. 7—David Tynes, Fort Worth .... KO 1
Oct. 21—Dennis Haggerty, Fort Worth .... KO 3
Nov. 2—Barry Smith, Fort Worth............... W 5
Nov. 4—Charles Smith, Fort Worth............. W 5
1977
Sept. 24—Marvin Hagler, Boston .... KO by 7
Oct. 26—Joe Barrientos, Dallas .... W 10
1978
Mar. 22—Joe Barrientos, Dallas .... W 10
1979
Mar. 2—Rocky Mosley Jr., Las Vegas .... KO by 1
(U.S. Junior Middleweight Title)
Dec. 17—Fulgencio Obelmejias, Caracas ...... KO by 4
1980
Aug. 8—Ernie Dunbar, Dallas .... KO 1
Oct. 7—Robbie Epps, Las Vegas .... KO by 6

MIKE PICCIOTTI
Upper Darby, Pa. Welterweight
1976
Nov. 19—Hector Pereira, Philadelphia .... W 4
1977
Mar. 7—Ernie Gladney, Upper Darby .... KO 2
Apr. 7—Morris Grant, Upper Darby .... KO 3
May 9—Ken Muse, Upper Darby .... W 4
July 26—Donald Leery, Philadelphia .... W 4
Sept. 15—Kevin Moefield, Upper Darby .... W 6
Oct. 20—Morris Grant, Upper Darby .... KO 2
Nov. 15—Elliott Freeman, Upper Darby .... W 6
1978
Jan. 31—Kevin Moefield, Upper Darby .... D 6
Mar. 7—Elliott Freeman, Upper Darby .... W 6
Apr. 10—Kevin Moefield, Philadelphia .... KO 8
Apr. 28—Don Johnson, Upper Darby .... KO 4
June 4—Joe Tiberi, Upper Darby .... KO 3
Aug. 24—Luis Vega, Philadelphia .... W 6
Sept. 27—Don Johnson, Philadelphia .... L 6
Nov. 21—Tyrone Phelps, Upper Darby .... W 8
1979
Feb. 5—Johnny Cooper, Philadelphia .... D 8
Dec. 4—Darnell Smith, Upper Darby .... KO 1
1980
Feb. 1—Hubert Jackson, Philadelphia .... W 8
Mar. 9—Hubert Jackson, Atlantic City .... KO 4
Apr. 10—Dale Staley, Atlantic City .... KO 6
July 12—Michael Herron, Atlantic City .... D 10
Sept. 9—Curtis Taylor, Atlantic City .... W 10
Oct. 30—Sam Hailstock, Atlantic City .... KO 7

LUIS PICENO
Los Angeles, Calif. Junior Welterweight
1979
Jan. 29—Salomon Lopez, Los Angeles .... KO by 3
Mar. 27—Carlos Lozano, Sacramento .... L 1
1980
Aug. 20—Refugio Rojas, Las Vegas .... KO by 5
Oct. 8—Ricardo Jiminez, Las Vegas .... KO by 4

LUIS PINA
Calif. Junior Featherweight
1980
Sept. 4—Jose F. Rodriguez, Los Angeles .... W 4
Sept. 25—Daniel Cruz, Los Angeles .... KO by 5

CARLOS PINANGO
Venezuelan Junior Lightweight
1979
Jan. 28—Hector Pinto, Caracas .... W 4
Mar. 25—Pedro Pablo Torres, Caracas .... KO 2
Apr. 21—Pedro Pablo Torres, Caracas .... KO 2
July 7—Federico Carreno, Caracas .... KO 6
Aug. 4—Federico Carreno, Caracas .... KO 6
Aug. 18—Pablo Marquez, Caracas .... KO 5
Aug. 25—Gustavo Salgado, Caracas .... W 10
Sept. 29—Azor Agosto, Caracas .... W 10
Nov. 2—Mario Colon, Caracas .... W 10
Dec. 17—Jacinto Fuentes, Caracas .... KO 2

1980
Mar. 3—Wilfredo Lanzo, Caracas .... KO 2
Apr. 1—Guillermo Morales, Caracas .... KO 6
Apr. 21—Manuel Rodriguez, Caracas .... KO 2
June 9—Pedro Pablo Torres, Caracas .... KO 2
July 7—Leonel Hernandez, Caracas .... KO by 8
Aug. 18—Felix Trinidad, Caracas .... KO 8
Sept. 22—Norberto Ramirez, Barquisamento ..... KO 1

NESTOR PINANGO
Las Vegas, Nevada Junior Welterweight
1980
Oct. 8—Joe Bahash, Las Vegas .... D 4
Nov. 5—Pat Barry, Las Vegas .... KO 4

ROBERTO PINEIRO
Puerto Rican Junior Lightweight
1979
Aug. 11—Fernando Ortiz, Trujillo .... L 4
1980
Mar. 24—Americo Rivera, San Juan .... D 4
May 22—Ray Viruet, Rio Piedras .... W 6
June 19—Americo Rivera, Rio Piedras .... W 6
Sept. 4—Angel Rivera, Rio Piedras .... KO 7

TOM PINNER
Houston, Texas Welterweight
1975
Nov. 18—Dennis Haggerty, Galveston .... KO 3
1976
Jan. 21—Gilbert Galvan, Beaumont............... L 10
June 12—Maurice Quiellens, New Orleans .... L 6
June 22—Beto Avila, Galveston................... L 10
Nov. 4—Fred Harris, Fort Worth............... L 5
Nov. 30—Jimmy Martinez, Houston........... KO by 5
1977
Oct. 4—Sylverio Martinez, Corpus Christi .... KO 6
1978
May 30—Ray Barrett, Tyler .... KO 1
Sept. 19—Alejos Rodriguez, San Antonio ...... KO by 5
1979
Jan. 31—Juan Villasana, Laredo .... KO 4
Apr. 20—Juan Ramirez, Laredo .... KO 1
June 6—Gonzalo Montes, Laredo .... KO by 4
Oct. 10—Jose Mireles, Beaumont .... W 6
1980
Jan. 8—Steve Hearon, Houston .... KO by 3
Aug. 21—Tyrone Cotton, Dallas .... KO by 4

LEONARD PINNOCK
Montreal, Canada Junior Featherweight
1979
Mar. 13—Jean LaPointe, Montreal .... KO by 5
1980
Jan. 20—Tony Salvatore, Quebec .... L 6
Mar. 13—Jean LaPointe, Montreal .... KO by 5
May 11—Tom Gourley, Halifax .... L 10

ALFREDO PITALUA
Colombian Lightweight
Born: December 17, 1955
1972
Oct. 23—Lorenzo Torres, Cartagena .... W 4
1973
Mar. 16—Nelson Torres, Cartagena .... KO 1
May 4—Armando Perez, Barranquilla .... L 10
July 12—Francisco (Yata) Durango, Monteria ...... L 8
1974
Nov. 2—Lorenzo Torres, Bogota .... KO 3
Nov. 16—Eduardo Herrera, Bogota .... KO 1
Dec. 14—Jacob Torres, Bogota .... W 8
Dec. 27—Manuel Vargas, Bogota .... KO 1
1975
Feb. 14—Olimpo Santos, Bogota .... KO 5
Mar. 2—Wilfredo Castro, Cartagena .... W 10
Apr. 18—Salvador Silva, Bogota .... KO 1
May 31—Glisorio Velasco, Cali .... KO 6
Oct. 11—Macario Jimenez, Guadalajara .... KO 7
Nov. 22—Victor Ramirez, Mexico .... KO 6
1976
Jan. 17—Macario Jimenez, Mexico City .... KO 2
Jan. 31—Ney Gordillo, Mexico City .... KO by 2
Mar. 19—Eloy Yepez, Chetumal .... KO 1
Apr. 4—Rosalio Muro, Mexicali .... KO 4
Apr. 21—Johnny Wason, Los Angeles .... KO 8
June 2—David Sotelo, Los Angeles .... KO 6
July 7—Manuel Abedoy, Tijuana .... KO 7
Sept. 18—Jose Herrera, Reynosa .... KO 6
Dec. 4—Enrique Maxwell, Bogota .... KO 1
1977
Feb. 5—Ernesto Herrera, Mexico City .... KO by 7
Apr. 17—Carlos Romero, Tuxtla Gutierrez .... KO 3
June 10—Lupe Galindo, Piedras Negras .... KO 6

July 18—Ignacio Campos, Tijuana .... KO 6
Aug. 26—Juan Elizondo, Mante City .... KO 8
Nov. 4—Leonardo Bermudez, Culiacan .... W 10
Nov. 21—Jose L. Soberanes, Culiacan .... KO 8
1978
Feb. 12—Vicente Mijares, Mexicali .... W 10
July 15—Jese L. Soberanes, Mexico City .... KO 5
Sept. 30—Betillo Gutierrez, Mexico City .... KO 4
Dec. 23—Leonardo Bermudez, Mazatlan .... D 10
1979
—Aurelio Muniz, Matomaros .... W 10
Dec. 9—Betillo Gutierrez, Los Moshis .... L 10
1980
Feb. 16—Rodolfo Gonzalez, Estado de Mexico .. KO by 10
May 24—Juan Graciano, Guadalajara .... KO by 2
Sept. 16—Ralph Aviles, Honolulu .... L 10

GARY PITTMAN
Seattle, Wash. Lightweight
1978
Mar. 10—Arturo Vidrio, San Diego .... W 4
Apr. 26—Noe Rivera, Concord .... KO 2
May 5—Clinton Campbell, San Diego .... L 5
June 2—Eric Bonilla, San Diego .... L 4
1979
Jan. 8—Sergio Nualarte, Seattle .... KO by 7
Feb. 14—Rich Kronich, Spokane .... KO 2
Apr. 24—Johnny Sanchez, Missoula .... W 4
1980
Oct. 23—Rich Kronich, Spokane .... W 6

TERRY PIZZARO
Florida Lightweight
1978
Aug. 22—Kid Baby Chocolate, Orlando .... L 4
Aug. 24—Danny Wilcox, Ft. Lauderdale .... KO 4
Aug. 31—Ralph Berrios, Tampa .... L 6
Sept. 26—Dennis Green, Miami .... W 4
Oct. 5—Danny Wilcox, Ft. Lauderdale .... L 6
1979
(Inactive)
1980
Jan. 29—Tony Styles Diaz, Miami .... W 4
Mar. 16—Ralph Berrios, Miami .... W 4
Apr. 3—Ralph Berrios, Tampa .... W 8
Apr. 18—Carmelo Negron, New York .... KO by 7
Sept. 13—Albert Davila, San Antonio .... KO by 6
Oct. 17—Terry Kemp, W. Palm Beach .... D 6

BOBBY PLEGGE
Portsmouth, Ohio Junior Welterweight
1975
Aug. 29—Rocky Clayton, Charleston .... W 6
Nov. 22—Al Hughes, Chicago .... D 4
1976
July 24—Jerry Strickland, Kalamazoo .... W 6
Aug. 26—Steve Adams, Canton .... W 4
Sept. 2—Eric Trabue, Kalamazoo .... L 4
Oct. 13—Steve Adams, Cleveland .... L 6
Nov. —Jeff Gaines, Alliance..................... KO 1
Dec. 11—Steve Adams, Alliance................... KO 3
1977
June 11—Jerry Strickland, Jackson .... W 4
Aug. 4—Forest Winchester, Wyoming .... KO 1
Oct. 15—Jerry Strickland, Salem .... W 10
1978
Mar. 17—Jimmy Blevins, Detroit .... L 6
May 20—Chuck Gregory, Salem .... W 12
(Ohio State Junior Welterweight Title)
1979
Jan. 10—Phil Bowen, Richfield .... KO 6
Feb. 7—Joe Kirkwood, Richfield .... KO 3
Feb. 24—Phil Batie, Alliance .... KO 2
Mar. 21—Willie Wren, Richfield .... KO 1
Apr. 19—Art McKnight, Richfield .... KO 1
Apr. 28—Larry Stover, Sebring .... KO 1
June 24—Jerry Strickland, Cincinnati .... L 6
Sept. 20—Harvey Wilson, Richfield .... KO 2
Sept. 30—Forrest Winchester, Canton .... L 8
Dec. 12—Dale Gordon, Canton .... W 6
1980
Apr. 5—Ray Green, Akron .... W 6
June 20—Mike Blunt, Cincinnati .... L 12
Oct. 28—Ray (Boom Boom) Mancini, Warren .. KO by 7

JEFF PODGURSKI
Las Vegas, Nev. Heavyweight
Born: November 5, 1954
Height: 6 ft. 2 in., Weight: 200 lbs.
Manager: Stan Tischler
1979
Feb. 12—Craig Henderson, Miami Beach .... W 4

Feb. 19—Craig Henderson, Miami Beach .... KO 4
Mar. 20—Richard Majors, Miami Beach .... D 4
June 19—Mike Creel, Las Vegas .... KO 3
July 4—Lou Lockwood, Las Vegas .... KO 3
Aug. 8—Arnold Sam, Las Vegas .... KO 4
Oct. 31—Arnold Sam, Las Vegas .... KO 5
Dec. 12—Keith Moore, Las Vegas .... KO 2
1980
Feb. —Jimmy Wallace, Las Vegas .... KO 1
Mar. 19—Harvey Steichen, Las Vegas .... L 8
July 16—Ron Draper, Las Vegas .... W 6
Aug. 29—Ray Thomas, W. Palm Beach .... KO by 1

CARL POFF
St. Louis, Mo. Light Heavyweight
1979
Mar. 27—Tofi Mika, Honolulu .... D 5
June 5—Bernie D'Zurella, Hilo .... L 4
July 31—Mosese Halafuka, Honolulu .... KO by 2
Aug. 16—Mike Graves, Honolulu .... L 3
Sept. 1—Calvin Mobley, Hilo .... KO by 3
1980
Mar. 4—Eugene Gordon, Honolulu .... W 3
Apr. 8—Kenneth Oki, Honolulu .... L 4
May 6—Kenneth Oki, Honolulu .... KO by 1

FRANCISCO PONCE
Los Angeles, Calif. Junior Lightweight
1977
Feb. 14—Antonio Hernandez, Tijuana .... W 10
Mar. 15—Manuel Ruelas, Tijuana .... L 10
Aug. 23—Candelario Bobadilla, Tijuana .... W 10
Nov. 19—Andres Hernandes, San Juan .... KO by 9
1978
Mar. 4—Jose Resendiz, Los Angeles .... W 4
Apr. 19—Earl Large, Las Vegas .... L 10
Aug. 10—Oscar Muniz, Los Angeles .... KO by 7
Sept. 26—Salvatore Sanchez, Houston .... KO by 2
Dec. 12—Juan Villa, Sacramento .... KO by 5
1979
May 30—Alex Garcia, Las Vegas .... L 10
June 10—Roy Hernandez, Stockton .... KO 1
1980
Jan. 24—Luis Loy, Los Angeles .... KO by 4

ROBERTO PONCINI
Argentine Junior Featherweight
1980
Apr. 26—Agustin Navarro, Tandil .... L 10
May 31—Raul Pared, Pergamino .... KO 4
Oct. 17—Jorge Gomez, Gral Roca .... KO by 3

ALEX PORRATA
Puerto Rican Junior Middleweight
1977
Feb. 12—Carlos Santos, San Juan .... L 4
July 11—Carlos Santos, San Juan .... L 6
1978
Apr. 10—Mauro Galvan, Chicago .... W 8
July 24—Eddie Roberts, Bridgeview .... KO 2
Aug. 28—Al Clay, Chicago .... KO by 6
1979
Mar. 31—Al Clay, Chicago .... L 10
June 4—Akbar Ali Muhammad, Bridgeview ..... KO 8
Nov. 20—Greg McPherson, Chicago .... W 10
1980
Apr. 17—Caveman Lee, Chicago .... KO by 6

HENRY PORTER
St. Louis, Mo. Heavyweight
1978
Sept. 22—David Watkins, St. Charles .... KO 2
1979
Jan. 12—Don Martin, St. Louis .... KO 2
Mar. 16—Ron Draper, St. Louis .... KO 5
Apr. —Ron Williams, Cedar Rapids .... KO 2
May 21—Herbert Adams, Belleville .... KO 2
July 25—James Tillis, Chicago .... KO by 6
Sept. 25—Robert Echols, Belleville .... W 10
Nov. 8—Lynn Ball, Tulsa .... W 10
Nov. 27—Al Jones, Belleville .... KO 4
Dec. 14—George Chaplin, Atlantic City .... KO by 5
1980
Apr. 14—Jimmy Abbott, Cape Town .... KO by 4
Aug. 19—Fossie Schmidt, Honolulu .... KO by 2

DAVE PORTILLO
Los Angeles, Calif. Welterweight
1977
Aug. 12—Guillermo Gonzales, San Diego .... W 5
Aug. 19—Guillermo Gonzales, San Diego .... W 5

Oct.   25—Moses Armas, Los Angeles L   4
1978
(Inactive)
1979
May   31—Jorge Labrado, Los Angeles ....KO   3
June   27—Carlos Lozano, Oakland L   6
1980
May   2—Otis Bell, Los Angeles ....KO by   2

MARIO PORTILLO
1980
Feb.   8—Chris Gutierrez, San Bernardino ....W   4
Mar.   3—Juan Villasana, Bakersfield ....W   5
Apr.   4—Fernando Reyes, San Bernardino ....W   6
Apr.   18—Adolfo Hurtado, San Bernardino ....W   6
May   16—Fernando Reyes, San Bernardino ....KO by   1
July   3—Adrian Arreola, Los Angeles L   6

SANTIAGO PORTILLO
Argentine Welterweight
1980
Mar.   7—Roberto Ale Ali, Tucuman ....W   6
Mar.   21—Rodolfo Rojas, Tucuman ....KO   2
June   6—Martin Duran, San Nicolas ....KO   7
July   11—Juan Bardi, Tucuman ....W 10
Aug.   1—Omar Ochoa, San Nicolas ....W 10
Aug.   22—Omar Salguero, Tucuman ....KO   6
Sept. 12—Ramon Peralta, Tucuman ....D 10

CARLOS POUYANNES
Argentine Light Heavyweight
1980
Mar.   14—Jorge Salgado, Mendoza ....L 10
Apr.   5—Juan D. Suarez, Mar del Plata ....KO by   1

ROBERT POWELL
Houston, Texas Middleweight
1977
—Kurt Kennard, Shreveport L   4
1978
Apr.   20—Marcus Dorsey, Houston ....KO   2
Oct.   10—Al Davila, Houston ....W   6
Nov.   24—Jean Simos (Simon) Liege, Belgium .....KO   9
1979
Mar.   20—Paul Stephens, Houston ....W   8
Apr.   24—Tacho Gomez, Houston ....W   6
July   21—Joe Barrientes Jr., Dallas ....L 10
Aug.   29—Ted Sanders, Las Vegas ....L 10
Nov.   29—Tony Sibson, Liverpool ....KO by   1
1980
Jan.   22—Sammy NeSmith, Indianapolis ....KO by   2
Aug.   12—Earl McFadden, Wichita L   8

TOM PRATER
Indianapolis, Ind. Heavyweight
1973
Oct.   30—Lou Rogan, Ft. Wayne ....W   4
Nov.   8—Art Robinson, Indianapolis ....W   4
1974
Feb.   16—Reggie Fleming, New Castle ....KO by   3
Apr.   13—Danny George, New Castle ....KO   3
May   25—Verbie Garland, Detroit.................W   6
July   17—Reggie Flemming, Chicago ....KO   6
Nov.   12—Bill Hurt, Indianapolis L   4
Dec.   11—Robert Yarbrough, Indianapolis ....W   6
1975
Jan.   29—Bobby Smith, Indianapolis ....KO   2
Feb.   15—J. D. McCauley, Columbus ....KO   4
Apr.   17—Wayne Lewis, Indianapolis ....KO   2
June   6—Robert Yarbrough, Indianapolis ....W   4
June   25—Verbie Garland, Toledo..................L   6
Sept.   6—Lou Rogan, Hamilton ....W   8
Sept. 24—Terry Daniels, Indianapolis ....W 10
1976
Apr.   3—Charley Johnson, Indianapolis ....KO   1
Apr.   15—Jody Ballard, Indianapolis ....W   8
July   20—Lou Esa, Miami Beach ....D   8
Aug.   10—Randy Stevens, Miami Beach ....W 10
Sept. 14—Big Al Jones, Miami Beach ....KO   4
Nov.   9—Mongol Ortiz, Miami Beach ....KO   3
1977
Jan.   16—Larry Holmes, Pensacola L   8
(U.S. Championship Tournament)
Mar.   15—Mike Koranicki, Miami Beach ....L 10
Apr.   26—Charles Atlas, Orlando ....KO   4
June   23—Scott LeDoux, Bloomington ....KO by   7
Oct.   29—Gerrie Coetzee, Johannesburg ....KO by   4
1978
Mar.   22—Randy Stephens, Dallas ....KO by   2
July   9—Clyde Mudgett, Indianapolis ....KO   5
Oct.   31—Duane Bobick, Indianapolis ....KO by   5

1979
Feb.   4—Alfio Righetti, Rimini ....L 10
June   29—Gerry Cooney, New York ....KO by   2
Dec.   20—Walter White, Belle Glade ....KO   5
1980
Jan.   29—Jeff Sims, Miami Beach ....KO by   6
Apr.   27—Jerry McIntyre, Greenville ....KO   1
Aug.   12—Bernardo Mercado, Bogota ....KO by 12

JAVON PRATT
Washington, D.C. Light Heavyweight
1978
Nov.   17—Biff Cline, Washington, D.C. ....D   6
1979
Jan.   22—Bobby Watkins, Washington, D.C. ......KO   1
Feb.   12—Donald Wilson, Washington, D.C. ....W   6
Sept.   8—Vince Edwards, Kingsport ....KO   1
1980
Jan.   16—Al Winston, Washington, D.C. ....KO   2
Feb.   27—Robert McFarland, Washington, D.C. KO by   2

ANDY PRICE
Los Angeles, Calif. Welterweight
1972
Oct.   13—Gonzalo Rodriguez, San Diego ....D   4
Oct.   30—Felix Alvarado, Woodland Hills..........W   5
Nov.   14—Javier Martinez, Bakersfield ....W   6
Dec.   4—Efren Cisneros, Woodland Hills..........W   4
Dec.   13—Manny Parejo, San Diego ....W   6
1973
Jan.   11—Tim Walker, Los Angeles ....W   6
Feb.   2—Frank Davila, San Bernardino ....W   6
Feb.   20—Carlos Gonzalez, Bakersfield ....KO   5
Apr.   19—Akira Fujikura, Los Angeles ....KO   3
May   17—Benny Reyes, Los Angeles...............D   6
June   28—Lou Blades, Los Angeles ....W   6
Aug.   30—Demitrico Salazar, Los Angeles..........W   6
Oct.   25—Renaldo Victoria, Los Angeles...........D   6
Nov.   8—Javier Muniz, Los Angeles...............D   6
1974
Jan.   24—Julio Lopez, Los Angeles ....KO 10
Feb.   7—Rudy Barro, Los Angeles..............KO by   2
Aug.   2—Carlos Palomino, San Diego............W 10
Aug.   19—Fred Jiminez, Las Vegas..............KO   5
Nov.   6—David Oropeza, Las Vegas ....W 10
1975
Jan.   23—Centavito Hernandez, Los Angeles.......KO   7
Feb.   20—Eagle Sato, Los Angeles ....KO   6
Mar.   27—Ernesto Caballero, Los Angeles..........W 10
1976
Jan.   29—Rudy Barro, Los Angeles ....W 10
Apr.   2—Jimmy Jackson, Los Angeles ....W 10
June   2—Pipino Cuevas, Los Angeles.............W 10
July   30—Jose Baquedano, Los Angeles ....KO by   6
Oct.   29—Julio Gomez, Los Angeles ....L 10
1977
Mar.   29—Tony Gonzalez, Las Vegas ....W 10
June   22—Harold Weston, New York ....L 10
July   30—Rudy Barro, El Paso ....KO   5
Sept. 29—David Green, London ....L 10
1978
Mar.   18—Julio Gomez, Los Angeles ....KO   2
1979
Mar.   16—Billy Miller, San Diego ....W 10
May   25—Vicente Hernandez, Santa Monica ....KO   4
Aug.   3—Jose Figueroa, Santa Monica ....W 10
Sept. 28—Ray Leonard, Las Vegas ....KO by   1
1980
Feb.   21—Jesse Lara, Tulsa ....KO   4

SYLVESTER PRICE
Muncie, Ind. Junior Lightweight
1979
Aug.   3—Ray Menefee, Omaha ....W   5
1980
June   27—Armando Garcia, Chicago ....W   4
July   26—Carlos Serrano, Chicago ....W 10
Aug.   3—C. B. Brown, N. Platte L   6

VERLEE PRICE
Las Vegas, Nev. Heavyweight
1976
May   27—Carlos Barona, Los Angeles ....KO   4
July   8—Ismael Ruiz, Los Angeles ....KO by   3
Nov.   4—Fili Moala, San Carlos ....KO by   1
1977
Mar.   5—Bob Hazelton, Marshall ....KO by   2
May   26—Sonny Kissman, Austin ....W   8
Oct.   1—Nick Wells, Shreveport ....KO by   1
1978
May   3—Eric Sedillo, Denver ....KO by   4
July   7—Jeff Shelburg, Salt Lake City ....KO by   7
Aug.   2—Earl Tripp, Las Vegas ....KO by   2

1979
June 30—Jeff Shelburg, Colorado Springs ...... KO by 2
Sept. 12—Tony Perea, El Paso .... KO by 4
1980
June 3—Vernon Johnston, Houston .... L 8
July 1—John Lee, Memphis .... KO by 7
Sept. 16—Vernon Johnston, Beaumont .... L 8

ALBERTO PRIETO
Argentine Welterweight
1980
Feb. 8—Juan Salomon, Laboulaye .... W 10
Mar. 21—Juan B. Cabral, Rio IV .... L 10
May 16—Miguel Combi, Bell Ville .... W 10

CARLOS PRIETO
Argentine Welterweight
1980
Jan. 11—Miguel Garcia, Gral Villegas .... L 10
Dec. 12—Juan B. Cabral, HcaRenanco .... TD 7

JESSE PRIETO
Los Angeles, Calif. Heavyweight
1978
Sept. 20—Walter Cloud, Reno .... W 4
1979
Apr. 26—Lee Holloman, Pico Rivera .... W 6
June 1—Seifu Mak, Los Angeles .... W 5
Oct. 10—George O'Mara, Las Vegas .... KO by 5
1980
Jan. 16—Jose Herrera, Las Vegas .... W 6
May 2—Jimmy Wallace, Las Vegas .... KO 1
May 17—Rogert Braxton, Las Vegas .... W 6

LUIS PRIMERA
Venezuelan Welterweight
1977
Mar. 13—Pedro Lugo, Caracas .... KO 2
Aug. 14—Nelson Perez, Caracas .... W 4
1978
May 7—Rafael Donado, Caracas .... KO 1
May 28—Pedro Acosta, Caracas .... KO 7
June 11—Bo Whyms, Caracas .... KO 1
July 15—Juan Disla, Caracas .... KO 3
July 29—Luis Resto, Caracas .... W 10
Dec. 17—Juan Batista, Caracas .... KO 3
1979
Mar. 18—Taisnin Takeda, Caracas .... KO 2
May 6—Jose Ramirez, Caracas .... W 10
Oct. 26—Bobby Mudgett, Caracas .... KO 2
Dec. 17—Jose Luis Ortiz, Caracas .... KO 1
1980
Feb. 1—Felix Pintor, Caracas .... KO 6
June 9—Papo Villa, Caracas .... KO 2
Sept. 29—Dario De Asa, Caracas .... KO 3
Dec. 6—Thomas Hearns, Detroit .... KO by 6
(For WBA Welterweight Title)

LENIS (LEN) PROVO
San Carlos, Calif. Light Heavyweight
1977
Nov. 18—DeWayne Wiley, San Diego .... W 4
Dec. 2—DeWayne Wiley, San Diego .... W 4
Dec. 16—Amado Vasquez, San Diego .... KO 2
1978
Jan. 27—Jim Ingram, San Diego .... W 5
Feb. 24—Jim Ingram, San Diego .... W 5
Mar. 10—Junior Albers, San Diego .... W 6
Apr. 14—Foma Leota, San Diego .... KO 2
June 30—Ron Wilson, San Diego .... W 10
July 28—Ron Wilson, San Diego .... KO by 10
Dec. 15—Gene Miera, San Diego .... KO 1
1979
Feb. 27—Pete McIntyre, San Carlos .... L 10
Apr. 12—Tommy Evans, Oakland .... KO by 3
Oct. 19—Nuia Tofaeona, San Diego .... KO by 2
1980
Jan. 31—Bashiru Ali, San Carlos .... KO by 8
July 16—King David Smith, San Diego .... L 10

ARTHUR PRUITT
New Orleans, La. Heavyweight
1980
Apr. 22—Derrick Harrison, Memphis .... L 6
May 12—Rick Meyer, Cape Girardeau .... W 6
Sept. 9—Michael Greer, Memphis .... KO by 6

WOOD PRUITT
St. Louis, Mo. Light Heavyweight
1979
July 17—Rick Meyer, Belleville, Ill. .... KO by 2
1980
Apr. 22—Lester Groves, Memphis .... KO by 3

LARRY PUCHTA
Minneapolis, Minn. Welterweight
1977
Apr. 20—Bobby Rodriguez, Minneapolis .... KO by 3
1978
Jan. 23—Mike Morgan, Minneapolis .... KO by 3
Mar. 27—Marvin Jenkins, St. Paul .... KO by 3
Apr. 18—Terry Jesmer, Winnipeg .... KO by 4
Oct. 25—Carl Crowley, Grand Forks .... KO by 3
1979
May 4—Bruce Strauss, St. Paul .... L 5
Aug. 16—Danny Campbell, Kansas City .... KO by 1
Oct. 20—Kevin Connors, Cincinnati .... KO by 2
1980
Mar. 3—Dr. Herbert Odom, Chicago .... L 4
Mar. 19—Ossie Quast, St. Paul .... W 4
June 27—Harlen Holden, Chicago .... KO by 2
July 25—Terry Jesmer, Winnipeg .... KO by 3
Nov. 11—Wayne Grant, St. Paul .... KO 5

TONY PULU
Tonga Heavyweight
Born: April, 13, 1954, Kolonga, Tonga
(Complete Record Unavailable)
1970
—Maile Haumona, Nukualofa .... W 10
—Viliami Sefokali, Nukualofa .... KO 5
—Moefili Salesi, Nukualofa .... KO 9
—Viliami Sefokali, Nukualofa .... W 10
1971
—Fonomanu Sekona, Samoa .... L 10
—Koli Vailea, Nukualofa .... KO 8
1972
—Luke Veikoso, Nukualofa .... W 10
—Natumu Bonbon, Nukualofa .... KO 5
—Ang Augese, Nukualofa .... KO 5
—Fala Angavale, Nukualofa .... W 6
1973
July 12—Charles Brooks, Los Angeles .... L 6
Oct. 11—Mike Weaver, Los Angeles .... KO by 4
Nov. 15—Charles Brooks, Los Angeles .... W 6
1974
Jan. 24—Bob Crutison, Los Angeles .... KO 6
Jan. 31—Charles Brooks, Los Angeles .... W 6
Feb. 7—David Smith, Los Angeles .... W 6
1975
Jan. 31—Henry Washington, San Diego .... KO 2
Feb. 7—Marty Monroe, San Diego .... D 5
Feb. 20—Alan Bourse, Los Angeles .... KO 4
Aug. 1—Marty Monroe, Las Vegas .... KO by 2
1976-1977
(Inactive)
1978
Jan. 16—Marty Monroe, Los Angeles .... L 4
Aug. 23—Earl Tripp, Las Vegas .... KO by 1
Sept. 22—Jeff Shelburg, Salt Lake City .... W 10
Nov. 11—Jeff Shelburg, Salt Lake City .... W 10
Dec. 9—Freddie News, Salt Lake City .... KO 1
(Utah State Heavyweight Championship)
1979
Mar. 10—Freddie News, Salt Lake City .... KO 5
Apr. 21—Reggie Phillips, Las Vegas .... KO 5
June 14—Mircea Simon, Los Angeles .... KO by 3
1980
Feb. 2—Bernardo Mercado, Salt Lake City ... KO by 8
Aug. 22—Stan Ward, Las Vegas .... KO by 6

MIKE QUARRY
Orlando, Fla. Light Heavyweight
Born: March 5, 1951
1969
Apr. 11—Butch McCarthy, Woodland Hills .... KO 2
Apr. 18—James Dick, Inglewood, Calif. .... W 5
Apr. 29—William Marden, Woodland Hills .... KO 1
May 14—Bob Matthews, Los Angeles .... W 6
May 19—La Verne Williams, San Diego .... KO 3
May 27—Ernie Gipson, Oakland .... KO 5
June 23—Ruben Figueroa, New York .... W 6
Aug. 1—Larry Greg, St. Paul .... KO 2
Aug. 15—Ken Watkins, San Bernardino .... W 6
Sept. 3—George Thomas, Oakland .... W 8
Sept. 5—Ben Watkins, Woodland Hills .... W 6
Sept. 18—Jeff Wall, Seattle .... KO 3

Oct.	6—Dean Whitlock, Minneapolis	KO 6
Oct.	9—Vidal Flores, La Crosse	W 8
Oct.	14—George Holden, Orlando	KO 7
Oct.	21—Teddy Murray, Orlando	W 6
Oct.	31—Ruben Figueroa, New York	W 8

1970

Jan.	26—George Thomas, Los Angeles	W 8
Feb.	19—Bob Matthews, Los Angeles	W 6
Mar.	3—George Holden, Miami Beach	W 10
Mar.	24—Filifili Alaiasi, Honolulu	W 8
Apr.	25—Jesse Hill, Santa Barbara	W 10
June	7—Eddie Avoth, Woodland Hills	W 10
June	17—Ray Ayala, New York	W 10
Nov.	14—Enrique Villareal, Woodland Hills	KO 9
Dec.	19—Amado Vazquez, Woodland Hills	W 10

1971

Jan.	24—Andy Kendall, Woodland Hills	W 10
Feb.	27—Ron Wilson, Woodland Hills	W 10
Apr.	14—Larry Cruz, Stateline	KO 1
Apr.	28—Hill Chambers, Las Vegas	W 10
May	15—Ron Wilson, Los Angeles	W 10
May	31—Armado Vasquez, National City	KO 9
Aug.	14—Chuck Hamilton, Anaheim	W 10
Oct.	30—Jimmy Dupree, Anaheim	W disq. 5

(North American Light Heavyweight Title)

1972

Mar.	10—Tommy Hicks, New York	W 10
Apr.	3—Chuck Hamilton, Los Angeles	KO 8
June	27—Bob Foster, Las Vegas	KO by 4

(World Light Heavyweight Title)

Dec.	12—Frankie Evans, Miami Beach	D 10

1973

Jan.	11—Paul Kasper, Orlando	KO 5
Jan.	29—Ray White, Anaheim	W 12
Apr.	4—Walter White, Orlando	W 10
Apr.	23—Hal Carroll, New York	D 10
May	10—Tom Bogs, Denmark	L 10
July	12—Billy Wagner, New York	D 12

(American Light Heavyweight Title)

Oct.	3—Andy Kendall, Orlando	L 10
Nov.	13—Chris Finnegan, London	L 10
Dec.	18—Karl Zurheide, Milwaukee	W 10

1974

Feb.	5—Brian Kelly, Oklahoma City	W 10
Feb.	15—Bobby Rascon, Albuquerque	W 10
Mar.	2—Pierre Fourie, Johannesburg	L 10
Apr.	11—Gary Summerhays, Orlando	W 12
May	21—Karl Zurheide, Houston	W 10
Nov.	27—Bobby Rascon, Albuquerque	W 10
Dec.	9—Pedro Soto, New York	W 8

1975

Jan.	3—Jose Roman, Tampa	W 10
Feb.	17—Bobby Rascon, Corpus Christi	W 10
Apr.	21—Melvin Mott, Dallas	W 10
May	14—Alvaro Lopez, Stockton	L 10
June	3—Vernon McIntosh, Orlando	W 10
July	8—Vernon McIntosh, Miami Beach	KO 6
July	25—Pedro Soto, Las Vegas	L 10
Sept.	9—Tami Santiago, Orlando	W 10
Sept.	30—Mike Rossman, New York	W 10

1976

May	11—Nat Gates, Albuquerque	W 10
June	8—Chuck Warfield, Orlando	W 10
June	22—Syl Wilder, Orlando	KO 5
Aug.	3—Billy Freeman, Orlando	KO 8
Aug.	24—Tony Greene, Miami Beach	D 10
Oct.	5—Eddie Owens, Scranton	W 10
Oct.	30—Tom Bethea, Las Vegas	W 10
Dec.	11—Mike Rossman, Las Vegas	L 10

1977

Mar.	23—Fred Wallace, Anchorage	W 10
May	11—Mike Rossman, New York	KO by 6

1978

Jan.	24—Ned Hallacy, Wichita	D 10
Feb.	24—Ronnie Wilson, San Diego	W 10
Mar.	10—Pete McIntyre, San Diego	KO by 5
June	13—Kevin Smith, Totowa	D 10
July	12—Tommy Evans, Oakland	KO by 8

1979

Nov.	23—Pascual Ramirez, Incline Village	KO 8

1980

Aug.	30—Alvin Dominey, Incline Village	W 10

HUGO QUARTAPELLE
Argentine Junior Welterweight
Previous Record—29 fights: Won 25, Lost 3, Drew 1, 10 KOs

1980

Feb.	22—Hector Hernandez, Mar del Plata	W 10
Mar.	21—Rafael Zalazar, Villa Maria	W 12
Apr.	5—Ubaldo Sacco, Buenos Aires	W 10
May	2—Rodolfo Petrizani, Buenos Aires	W 10
June	13—Romulo Ibarra, Mendoza	W 10
Oct.	3—Roque Arevalo, Villa Maria	KO 6

Nov.	21—Ramon Bustos, Mendoza	D 10
Dec.	11—Hugo Luero, Mendoza	KO by 5

OSSIE QUAST
Minneapolis, Minn. Junior Middleweight

1976

May	5—John Ryan, Minneapolis	KO 1
June	30—Paul Johnson, Minneapolis	KO by 4
Nov.	9—Paul Johnson, St. Paul	KO by 3

1977
(Inactive)

1978

Oct.	25—John Ryan, Grand Forks	KO 1

1979

Feb.	14—Bruce Strauss, St. Paul	L 6
Apr.	20—Bruce Strauss, Winnipeg	W 6

1980

Mar.	19—Larry Puchta, St. Paul	L 4
Oct.	29—Bernie Melchor, St. Paul	KO by 4

MANNY QUILES
Hartford, Conn. Lightweight

1977

Sept.	23—Marcial Santiago, New York	W 6
Aug.	12—Marcial Santiago, New York	W 4
Oct.	22—Victor Arnau, Hartford	KO by 4
Nov.	26—Eddie Cruz, Waterbury	W 6

1978

Apr.	22—Felix Trinidad, San Juan	KO by 4

1979

Oct.	17—Eddie Flores, Hartford	W 4
Nov.	28—Pat Brennan, Hartford	W 4

1980

Jan.	9—Eddie Flores, Hartford	W 4

MAURICE (TIGER) QUILLENS
New Orleans, La. Junior Welterweight

1975

Apr.	21—Sam Wilson, New Orleans	W 4
Aug.	27—Al Banks, New Orleans	KO 2

1976

Mar.	8—Aundra Love, New Orleans	W 6
June	12—Tom Pinner, New Orleans	W 6
Aug.	4—Freddie Harris, Alexandria	L 10

1977

Aug.	23—Larry Raymond, New Orleans	D 4

1978

Oct.	24—Frank Crosby, New Orleans	W 4
Nov.	4—Larry Rayford, New Orleans	KO by 3

1979

May	20—Richard Gonzales, Baton Rouge	KO 3

1980

July	15—Tyrone Jackson, New Orleans	D 5

DENNIS QUIMAYOUSIE
Carson City, Nev. Junior Featherweight

1979

Apr.	12—Bobby Chudian, Lake Tahoe	KO 2
May	30—Mike Rodriguez, Las Vegas	W 4
June	16—Randall Lanza, Yerington	KO 2
July	3—Ron Furlow, Gardnerville	KO 2
Aug.	1—Jose L. Corona, Reno	KO 2
Aug.	24—Luis Avila, Carson City	W 6
Sept.	11—Francisco Vellez, Incline Village	W 8
Oct.	2—Jose Pacheco, Reno	W 8
Oct.	30—Jose Pacheco, Carson City	KO 3
Nov.	23—Francisco Velez, Lake Tahoe	W 8
Dec.	18—Sergio Nualarte, Reno	W 10

1980

Jan.	22—Roberto Garcia, Sparks	L 10
Feb.	18—Gilbert Garza, San Antonio	W 10
Mar.	18—Jaime Nava, Sparks	W 10
Apr.	26—Ronnie Johnson, Carson City	KO 1
July	30—Refugio Rojas, Las Vegas	KO by 8
Aug.	30—Ruben Munoz, Incline Village	W 8

MIKE QUINSEY
Vancouver, Canada Heavyweight

1979

Oct.	22—Ron Rousselle, Edmonton	KO by 1

1980

June	13—Joe Wade, Nanaimo	KO by 2
Jan.	31—Brent Racette, Vancouver	KO by 1

RAMON QUINTANA
Argentine Junior Middleweight

1980

Jan.	—Jorge Medina, Ciudadela	L 10
Feb.	15—Enrique Coronel, S. Sal. de Jujuy	L 10
Mar.	8—Antonio Juarez, Buenos Aires	L 10
July	12—Raul Cabral, Gral Villegas	KO by 9

HECTOR QUINTERO
Argentine Junior Middleweight
1980
Sept.	5—Roque Gastaldo, Parana	L	10
Dec.	12—Horacio Saldano, San Miguel	KO by	8

POPEYE QUIRRION
Waterville, Maine Junior Middleweight
1980
Feb.	13—Steve Mosher, Waterville	KO	2
Mar.	12—Gordon Johnstone, Waterville	KO	3
Apr.	16—Joey Richardson, Waterville	KO	3
Sept.	24—Charley Jones, Waterville	D	6
Oct.	2—Jack Morrell, Boston	L	10

R

ERNIE RABOTTE
Middleweight
1979
Nov.	21—Ed Batista, Los Angeles	KO	5

1980
Feb.	6—John Steve, Costa Mesa	W	4
Jan.	26—J. B. Williamson, Los Angeles	L	6

BRENT RACETTE
Victoria, B.C., Canada Heavyweight
Height: 6ft. 4 in. Weight: 225 lbs.
1980
Jan.	31—Mike Quinsey, Vancouver	KO	1
Mar.	15—Fili Savini, Vancouver	W	4

GORD RACETTE
Nanaimo, B.C., Canada Heavyweight
Height: 6 ft. 2 in.
1979
June	15—Bill Pepper, Delta	KO	2
June	15—Wayne Pickerton, Delta	W	3
	(Won Heavyweight Tournament)		
June	28—Pat Garat, Vancouver	KO	1
June	28—Billy Graham, Vancouver	KO	2
June	28—Roger Dagge, Vancouver	W	4
	(Won Heavyweight Tournament)		
July	8—Hans De Goode, Campbell	W	3
July	19—Marlan Sears, Nanaimo	KO	1
July	19—Dave Barnley, Nanaimo	KO	1
July	19—Rick Humphrey, Nanaimo	KO	1
	(Won Heavyweight Tournament)		
Aug.	30—Mike Maroon, Bellingham	KO	1
Aug.	30—Corky Cornellius, Bellingham	KO	3
	(Won Heavyweight Tournament)		
Sept.	13—Corky Cornellius, Vancouver	W	4
Nov.	27—Steve Asher, Vancouver	W	6

1980
Feb.	29—Lew Lockwood, Nanaimo	KO	2
Mar.	15—Mike Silva, Vancouver	KO	1
May	21—John Hagen, Kelowna	KO	1
May	29—Nat Stewart, Vancouver	KO	1
June	26—Val Gassaway, Bellington	KO	1
June	13—Earl McLeay, Nanaimo	KO	1
Aug.	27—Lou Alexander, Edmonton	KO	1
Oct.	11—Harvey Steichen, Nanaimo	KO	5
Nov.	27—Steve Asher, Vancouver	W	6
Dec.	17—Ernie Smith, Crystal Bay	KO	1

RALPH RACINE
Canadian Lightweight
1975
May	3—Robert Emerson, Erie	W	6
May	28—John McQueen, Scranton	W	6
Sept.	10—Ray Hall, Scranton	KO	4
Nov.	12—Luis Vega, Scranton	W	6
Nov.	—Julie Mandell, Toronto	W	6

1976
Jan.	24—Ron Meaweather, Syracuse	W	6
Feb.	25—Luis Vega, Scranton	W	6
Mar.	31—Mike Davis, Scranton	W	6
Apr.	3—Gerald Hayes, Utica	KO	5
May	12—Quentin Blackman, Scranton	KO by	7
Oct.	5—Ernest Bing, Scranton	KO by	2
Nov.	10—Ray Carrington, Cleveland	L	6

1977
Jan.	26—Paul Marcum, Cleveland	KO	4
Mar.	7—Nick Furlano, Toronto	L	8
Mar.	22—Marion Thomas, Cleveland	KO	7

May	6—Paddy Dolan, Commack	KO	9
May	17—Ray Carrington, Mentor	KO	5
Aug.	30—Jean LaPointe, Montreal	KO	3
Sept.	28—Gerald Hayes, Scranton	W	10
Nov.	4—Al Ford, Winnipeg	W	10
Dec.	8—Bobby Hughes, Toronto	D	10

1978
Jan.	24—Gaetan Hart, Montreal	L	10
Apr.	18—Tom Tarantino, Winnipeg	KO	2
June	20—Al Ford, Winnipeg	W	10
Aug.	26—Bobby Alexander, Monaca	KO	7
Oct.	14—Larry Stanton, Commack	W	10
Dec.	5—Henry Rosa, Montreal	KO	9

1979
Jan.	23—Georges Cotin, Montreal	KO	8
Feb.	26—Cocoa Sanchez, New York	KO	10
Apr.	6—Marco Barahona, New York	L	10
Apr.	20—Billy Pearish, Winnipeg	KO	1
May	21—Julio Valdez, New York	L	10
Aug.	2—Hilmer Kenty, Detroit	L	10
Dec.	18—Al Ford, Montreal	W	8

1980
Mar.	6—Pedro Acosta, Winnipeg	KO	5
Apr.	13—Dale Hernandez, Kansas City	KO	8
Apr.	24—Bruce Strauss, Winnipeg	KO	5
May	7—Gaetan Hart, Montreal	KO by	12

TYRONE RACKLEY
Phoenix, Ariz. Welterweight
1978
May	20—Randy Graves, Salem	W	4
June	28—Ivan McCoy, Hamilton	KO	3

1979
May	23—Steve Richardson, Las Vegas	W	4
June	6—Steve Richardson, Las Vegas	W	6
June	20—Mike Murray, Las Vegas	KO	2
June	30—Adolfo Rivas, Albuquerque	KO	2
July	25—Gary Giron, Las Vegas	KO	4
Aug.	15—Lou Daniels, Tucson	KO	1
Aug.	22—Julio Mendez, Phoenix	KO	1
Aug.	27—Martin Garibay, Tucson	W	6
Oct.	18—Raul Nava, Phoenix	KO	2
Oct.	31—Ernesto Barreto, Phoenix	KO	4
Nov.	7—Tony Suero, Las Vegas	D	4
Nov.	27—Adam Chavarria, Houston	L	10

1980
Jan.	11—Aundra Love, Phoenix	W	10
Mar.	27—Rocky Mosley, Las Vegas	W	10
May	5—Modesto Concepcion, Phoenix	W	10
Dec.	16—Mario Tineo, Phoenix	W	10

DAVID RAMAHLO
Lowell, Mass. Featherweight
1976
June	29—Jose Roman, Lawrence	KO	2
July	20—Ramon Garcia, Lawrence	KO	2
July	26—Ben Ali, Lawrence	W	6
Aug.	16—Jose Montenez, Peabody	KO	2
Aug.	30—George Michel, Peabody	W	6
Nov.	25—Juan Sanchez, Portland, Me.	W	6
Dec.	9—George Butts, Portland	W	6

1977
Jan.	29—Humberto Sanchez, Boston	W	6
Feb.	29—H. Vance, Boston	KO	6
Mar.	12—Pedro Martinez, Fitchburg	W	6
Mar.	22—Humberto Sanchez, Boston	W	6
Apr.	22—Mimun Ben Ali, Manchester	KO	8
June	27—D. C. Cunningham, Peabody	KO by	1
Aug.	27—Mickey Owens, Bath	KO	3
Oct.	7—Shorty Sanchez, Lowell	W	8
Oct.	7—Mike Melon, Portland, Me.	KO	2
Nov.	18—Ben Ali, Lowell	KO	7
Dec.	19—Heriberto Sanchez, Boston	W	10

1978
Jan.	28—Mike Thomas, Providence	KO	2
Mar.	11—Jimmy Farrell, Lowell	D	12
July	10—Jimmy Farrell, Boston	W	12
July	19—Frank Camaro, Waterville	KO	6
Aug.	13—Francisco Maldonado, Portland, Me.	KO	4
Dec.	1—Joe Rivera, Cohoes	KO	2
Dec.	20—Ernesto Muniz, Waterville	KO	1

1979
Jan.	11—Ramon Cruz, Cohoes	KO	1
Feb.	22—Papo Melendez, Cohoes	KO	1
Aug.	11—Leon Hall, N. Swansey	KO	3

1980
June	19—Ed Welcome, Lawrence	KO	1
June	28—Francisco Maldonado, Manchester	KO	1

AGAPITO RAMIREZ
Los Angeles, Calif. Junior Middleweight
1977
Feb.	11—Juan Ramirez, Guadalajara	KO by	7

1978

Mar.	2—Jorge Alfaro, Los Angeles	W 5
Mar.	17—Mario Neri, Bakersfield	W 5
Apr.	13—Pablo Baez, Los Angeles	W 6
Apr.	24—Gil Valdez, Bakersfield	W 8
May	9—Tiger Noji, Bakersfield	KO by 6
June	26—Larry Duran, Bakersfield	W 6
July	27—Curtis Lewis, Los Angeles	TD 2
Aug.	28—Ricky Weigel, Bakersfield	L 10
Sept.	26—Zeferino Gonzalez, Pico Rivera	L 10

1979

Feb.	1—Mauricio Aldana, Los Angeles	W 10
Feb.	26—Kazunori Shiratori, Los Angeles	KO 9
Apr.	5—Victor Abraham, Los Angeles	L 10
May	3—Mauricio Aldana, Los Angeles	W 10
May	14—Jerry Cheatham, Phoenix	L 10

1980

Feb.	6—Bert Lee, Costa Mesa	L 10
Mar.	16—Dave Meadows, Las Vegas	L 10
Apr.	22—Pete Ranzany, Sacramento	L 10
June	3—Horace Shufford, Las Vegas	L 10
Aug.	23—Kenny Crooms, Las Vegas	KO by 4
May	15—Victor Martinez, Los Angeles	L 10

ANDRE RAMIREZ
Junior Welterweight
1980

May	20—Alejos Rodriguez, San Antonio	W 10
June	3—Leon McCullum, Houston	W 8
June	14—Monroe Brooks, Cincinnati	KO by 3
Aug.	13—Danny Favela, San Antonio	W 10
Sept.	4—Jorge Morales, Los Angeles	L 10
Sept.	25—Bruce Curry, Las Vegas	KO by 3

ARMANDO RAMIREZ
Los Angeles, Calif. Lightweight
Managed by Maurico Morales
1978

Oct.	4—Joe Turner, Las Vegas	KO 3
Dec.	5—Lou Daniels, Las Vegas	W 4

1979

July	24—Vito Meredith, Honolulu	KO 2
Aug.	1—Leslie Powell, Los Angeles	KO 3
Aug.	10—Eric Bonilla, San Diego	W 6
Nov.	8—Jose Osuna, Los Angeles	KO 5
Dec.	14—Robert Turner, Orange County	W 6

1980

Jan.	24—Adrian Boizo, Los Angeles	KO 5
July	8—Joe Lim, Honolulu	W 10
July	29—Rudy Barro, Honolulu	KO 7

ARTEMIO RAMIREZ
Mexican Bantamweight
1980

Feb.	13—Javier Solis, Mexico City	KO 7
May	3—Antonio de la Paz, Mexico City	L 10

DIEGO VEGA RAMIREZ
Argentine Featherweight
1980

Jan.	18—Hector Rosa, S. Sal. de Jujuy	L 10
Feb.	1—Hector Rosa, S. Sal. de Jujuy	L 10
Mar.	7—Ramon Dominguez, Trelew	L 10
Apr.	11—Luis Alvarez, Salta	D 10
June	19—Simon Ortigoza, Bolivar	W 10

FILI RAMIREZ
Los Angeles, Calif. Lightweight
1977

Nov.	4—Carlos Ortiz, San Diego	L 4
Nov.	11—Eric Bonilla, San Diego	L 4

1978

Feb.	8—Oscar Burboa, Phoenix	L 4
Feb.	24—Salvador Gonzalez, Bakersfield	W 6
Mar.	1—Alex Rodriguez, Fresno	W 6
Mar.	17—Mike Maturino, Bakersfield	KO 2
Apr.	10—Jaime Nava, Fresno	L 8
Apr.	22—Francisco Pico, Denver	KO 3
Apr.	26—Rudulfo Ortiz, Las Vegas	KO 5
May	8—Billy Parks, Denver	L 8
May	25—Joey Dominguez, Las Vegas	L 8
June	20—Malo Fane, Honolulu	L 6
July	26—Willie Daniels, Las Vegas	W 6
July	31—Juan Sanchez, Bakersfield	D 8
Aug.	28—Daniel Patino, Bakersfield	L 6
Sept.	6—Eddie Nuno, Las Vegas	L 8
Oct.	18—Marvin Edwards, Las Vegas	W 6
Nov.	1—Louis Daniels, Las Vegas	KO by 2
Nov.	30—Jose Rodriguez, Las Vegas	KO 1
Dec.	13—Willie Daniels, Las Vegas	W 10

1979

Jan.	11—Herman Montes, Los Angeles	L 10

Mar.	7—Ray Saldivar, Las Vegas	D 10
Apr.	25—Danny Patino, Las Vegas	KO 5
Aug.	22—Idika Nsofor, Las Vegas	L 8
Sept.	12—Frankie Moultrie, Las Vegas	L 10
Oct.	30—Gonzalo Montellano, Bakersfield	L 10
Dec.	7—Spud Murphy, San Diego	W 6
Dec.	19—Miquel Estrada, Las Vegas	W 10

1980

Jan.	26—Herman Montes, Los Angeles	L 10
Mar.	16—Cornelius Boza-Edwards, Las Vegas	KO by 7
Apr.	30—Rosendo Ramirez, Las Vegas	L 10
May	29—Irleis Perez, Los Angeles	KO by 9
July	16—Eddie Ballarin, Las Vegas	L 10
Aug.	13—Lennox Blackmoore, Las Vegas	KO by 4
Oct.	16—John Montes, Los Angeles	L 10
Nov.	8—Lionel Harney, Lake Tahoe	L 8

GERONIMO RAMIREZ
Argentine Middleweight
1980

Apr.	11—Hector Centurion, Corrientes	W 10
June	19—Roberto Ruiz, Tucuman	KO by 7
Oct.	24—Ricardo Cisneros, Villa Angela	L 10

JORGE RAMIREZ
Mexican Flyweight
1977

Jan.	28—Esteban Guadras, Mexico City	KO 1
Mar.	23—Felipe Fernandez, Mexico City	W 6
Apr.	1—Rigoberto Estrada, Juarez	L 10
Apr.	15—Ricardo Lira, Salinas	KO by 5
June	2—David Escobedo, Monterrey	D 10

1978

June	24—Fernando Gomez, Mexico City	W 10
Aug.	12—Jose Ruiz, Mexico City	W 10
Sept.	23—Francisco Nunez, Mexico City	KO 8
Nov.	1—Jose Bautista, Mexico City	W 10
Dec.	9—Joaquin Acuna, Mexico City	L 10

1979

Apr.	21—Jose Luis Soto, Mexico City	W 10
June	16—Fabian Palma, Mexico City	W 10
Aug.	11—Jose Bautista, Mexico City	W 10
Sept.	28—Chuyin Lopez, Culiacan	L 10
Dec.	7—Ray Rodriguez, Guadalajara	W 10

1980

Jan.	12—Juan Alvares, Mexico City	L disq. 2
Mar.	8—Juan Alvares, Mexico City	KO 9
May	7—Manual Vasquez, Mexico City	W 10
June	7—Antonio De LaPaz, Mexico City	W 10
Aug.	9—Hector Medina, Mexico City	W 10
Oct.	18—Antonio De LaPaz	L 10

JOSE LUIS RAMIREZ
Mexican Lightweight
(Previous Record Unavailable)
1979

Nov.	26—Ignacio Campos, Tijuana	KO 12

(Retained Mexican Lightweight Title)

1980

June	19—Rafael Nunez, Tacoma	KO 1
Aug.	23—Dario DeJesus, Inglewood	KO 1

JUAN RAMIREZ
Laredo, Texas Junior Welterweight
1976

Feb.	27—Juan Carlos Canete, Pinedo	D 6

1977

Feb.	11—Agapito Ramirez, Guadalajara	KO 7
Apr.	30—Johnny Flores, Laredo	KO 4
May	6—Juan Panchi, Acapulco	KO by 5
May	17—Tony Aranda, San Antonio	L 10

1978

Jan.	1—Andres Ramirez, Gomez Palacios	KO by 1
May	2—Sammy Ayala, San Antonio	KO by 1

1979

Jan.	31—Tony Aranda, Laredo	W 8
Apr.	20—Tom Pinner, Laredo	KO by 1

1980

Dec.	5—Ramon Enriques, Corpus Christi	KO by 2

LORENZO RAMIREZ
Los Angeles, Calif. Junior Featherweight
1977

Aug.	20—Eduardo Plata, Los Angeles	L 4
Sept.	29—Eduardo Plata, Los Angeles	L 5

1978

June	15—Alfonso Delgadillo, Los Angeles	W 4
June	29—Jorge Garcia, Los Angeles	L 4
Aug.	24—Jorge Garcia, Los Angeles	L 5
Nov.	30—Mike Gmarza, Los Angeles	TD 4

1979

May	3—Desi Newbill, Los Angeles	D 6

May 10—Delfino Cornejo, Los Angeles ....D 6
May 24—Delfino Cornejo, Los Angeles ....KO 6
July 2—Rafael Pena, Los Angeles ....KO by 7
Aug. 30—Danny Aquilar, Los Angeles ....KO by 5
Sept. 7—Porfirio Hernandez, Monterrey ....KO 2
1980
Jan. 10—Rafael Alonzo, Los Angeles ....KO 3
Feb. 21—Sergio Castro, Los Angeles ....L 10
Mar. 20—Mario Chavez, Los Angeles ....KO by 3
Aug. 7—Jaime Garza, Los Angeles ....KO by 4

PABLO RAMIREZ
Mexican Flyweight
1979
Oct. 10—Carlos Ibarra, Mexico City ....L 10
Nov. 24—Carlos Ibarra, Mexico City ....KO 6
1980
Feb. 20—Fidencio Gonzalez, Mexico City ....L 10
Apr. 23—Delfino Mendoza, Mexico City ....KO 6
July 5—Marcos Villasana, Mexico City ....KO by 1

PASQUAL RAMIREZ
Fresno, Calif. Light Heavyweight
1977
Dec. 17—Ernie Pope, Fresno ....L 5
1978
Jan. 19—Ricky Weigel, Los Angeles ....KO by 3
Mar. 1—Coleman Blackmun, Fresno ....KO 5
Apr. 10—Troy Vaughn, Fresno ....W 6
May 20—Charles Terrell, Fresno ....D 6
Aug. 26—Charles Terrell, Fresno ....KO by 4
Dec. 6—Azell James, Stockton ....KO 3
1979
Mar. 10—Byron Campbell, Carson City ....L 4
Mar. 14—Gary Yeats, Oakland ....KO 4
Aug. 24—Tony McMinn, Carson City ....W 8
Nov. 23—Mike Quarry, Incline Village ....KO by 8
1980
Apr. 14—Carlos Muro, Fresno ....D 6
Aug. 13—William Banks, Las Vegas ....KO 2

ROBERTO (LOBITA) RAMIREZ
Mexican Flyweight
1979
July 13—Ruben Mancilla, Guadalajara ....KO 6
Oct. 19—Juan Zarate, Guadalajara ....KO 5
1980
Mar. 14—Ubaldo Gonzalez, Guadalajara ....KO by 2
May 30—Victor Hernandez, Guadalajara ......L disq. 3

ROSENDO (ROCKY) RAMIREZ
Bakersfield, Calif. Lightweight
1979
Feb. 5—Valentin Holquin, Bakersfield ....L 6
Feb. 26—Takashi Sugimoto, Los Angeles ....KO 4
Mar. 27—Rolando Pastor, Honolulu ....L 6
May 30—Jose Valdez, Las Vegas ....W 10
June 13—Juan Mesa, Las Vegas ....KO by 5
—Memo Arreola,.........................W 6
Nov. 15—Alex Oregel, Los Angeles ....ND 8
1980
Mar. 22—Willie Rodriguez, Bethlehem ....L 12
(For USBA Junior Welterweight Title)

SAL RAMIREZ
Los Angeles, California Lightweight
1978
Jan. 19—Simon Gurrola, Los Angeles ....W 5
1979
Aug. 16—Miguel Gonzales, Los Angeles ....L 5
Oct. 11—Roberto San Jose, Los Angeles ....KO 3
Sept. 6—Timmy Martinez, Los Angeles ....KO 4
Dec. 10—James Castillo, Bakersfield ....W 5
1980
Jan. 18—Willie Hall, Los Angeles ....W 6
Feb. 22—Frank Alvarado, San Bernardino ....KO by 5
May 16—Leon Smith, San Bernardino ....KO by 2

SAL RAMIREZ
Newark, N.J. Featherweight
1979
Oct. 12—Pat Brennan, Uniondale ....L 4
Oct. 25—Tim LaValley, Latham ....L disq. 6
1980
Mar. 4—Jose Nieto, Elizabeth ....KO by 2

ALEX (THE BRONX BOMBER) RAMOS
Bronx, N.Y. Middleweight
Born: January 17, 1961 Height: 5 ft. 10 in.
1980
Nov. 8—Steve Arwin, Lake Tahoe ....KO 5
Nov. 25—Johnny Davis, Hartford ....KO 4
Dec. 20—Leo Martinez, Bronx ....KO 1

CARLOS RAMOS
Los Angeles, Calif. Junior Middleweight
1979
Apr. 12—Gumara Martinez, Los Angeles ....W 6
May 3—Gumara Martinez, Los Angeles ....W 6
June 16—Gary Giron, Yerington ....KO by 2
July 19—Humberto DeLos Rios, Los Angeles ..KO by 3
Oct. 10—Joey Adelfio, Las Vegas ....L 4
Oct. 30—Chico Salinas, Bakersfield ....KO by 8
Dec. 10—Chico Salinas, Bakersfield ....L 10
1980
Jan. 10—Vic Kelly, Los Angeles ....L 6
Sept. 24—Lenny Hahn, Boise ....D 10
Oct. 23—Chris Linson, Las Vegas ....KO by 6

CHATO RAMOS
Odessa, Texas Middleweight
1980
May 19—Macario Estorga, Odessa ....KO by 3
July 18—Paul Stephens, Odessa ....KO 2
Sept. 23—Lovell Chalmer, Odessa ....KO 1
Dec. 16—Jose Pacheco, Odessa ....W 6

DAVE RAMOS
Salt Lake City, Utah Lightweight
1979
July 1—L. J. Simpson, Salt Lake City ....KO 1
Oct. 13—John Bradley, Salt Lake City ....KO 2
Dec. 8—Rocky Haines, Salt Lake City ....KO 2
1980
Mar. 5—Randy Clover, Las Vegas ....KO by 1
Mar. 15—Antonio Garcia, Ogden ....KO 1
Mar. 22—Memo Arreola, Salt Lake City ....L 8
Aug. 23—Sultan Saladin, Salt Lake City ....L 8

MARIO (EL BUEY) RAMOS
Dominican Rep. Junior Middleweight
(Previous Record Unavailable)
1977
Mar. 19—Miro Campusano, Santo Domingo ....W 10
May 2—Omar Lora, Santo Domingo ....KO 2
1978
Oct. 16—Julio Vizcaino, Santo Domingo ....KO 3
Nov. 6—Juan Serrano, Santo Domingo ....KO
Nov. 30—Inocencio De La Rosa, Santo Domingo ....L 12
1979
Feb. 26—Jose Vallejo, Santo Domingo ....L 10
Apr. 2—Carlos Santos, Santo Domingo ....KO by 8
1980
Nov. 15—Michael Dewar, Port-Au-Prince ....L 10

PABLO RAMOS
Cleveland, Ohio Light Heavyweight
1976
Oct. 20—Lucky Patterson, Cleveland ....KO 2
Nov. 3—Danny Davis, Cleveland ....KO 1
Nov. 17—Bill Radcliff, Cleveland ....KO 5
1977
Jan. 5—Al Bell, Cleveland ....W 6
Jan. 19—Julius Noble, Cleveland ....W 6
Mar. 8—Mayfield Pennington, Mentor ....KO 6
Mar. 30—Ivy Brown, Cleveland ....W 6
Apr. 27—Larry Perdue, Lorain ....KO 1
May 25—Jerry Martin, Cleveland ....W 10
July 27—Dick Morgan, Cleveland ....KO 5
1978
Apr. 26—Jose Gutierrez, Youngstown ....KO 5
Dec. 4—Gary Summerhays, Saginaw ....W 10
1979
Feb. 7—Billy Douglas, Richfield ....W 10
June 29—David Conteh, Jersey City ....W 10
Oct. 27—Freddie Brown, Rahway ....W 10
1980
July 7—Johnny Townsend, Bloomington ....W 10
Sept. 13—Willie Crawford, Lorain ....KO 3
Oct. 1—Rudy Robles, Las Vegas ....W 10
Oct. 25—Murray Sutherland, Pontiac ....L 12
(For NABF Light Heavyweight Title)
Nov. 25—Jerry Celestine, New Orleans ....KO by 9

CURTIS RAMSEY
Portland, Ore. Junior Welterweight
1976
Aug. 17—Hideo Kitani, Seattle ....KO 2
Sept. 15—Denny Almieda, Portland, Ore..........W 6
Dec. 8—Mario Valdez, Everett ....W 6
1977
Jan. 26—Horace Shufford, Las Vegas ....D 5
Feb. 17—Vicente Hernandez, Portland ....W 6
Apr. 14—Jimmy Ligons, Portland ....KO 2
May 26—Steve Chase, Portland ....KO by 4
Oct. 30—Harvey Arnold, Carson City ....W 10

1978
Jan. 12—Jose Hernandez, Incline Village.......... L 10
Mar. 29—Scipio Stubbs, Las Vegas .... KO 3
Apr. 4—Jose Hernandez, Incline Village.......... L 10
May 25—Horace Shufford, Las Vegas .... L 10
Aug. 19—Jorge Morales, Las Vegas .... KO by 5
1979
Feb. 22—Allan Webb, Portland .... KO 10
Mar. 28—Joey Dominguez, Lake Tahoe .... W 10
May 11—Eddie Nuno, Pico Rivera .... D 10
June 7—Steve Chase, Portland .... D 12
Aug. 2—Herman Montes, Pico Rivera .... D 10
Sept. 25—Jorge Morales, Las Vegas .... L 10
Oct. 25—Eddie Nuno, Portland .... W 10
Dec. 8—Rodolfo Gonzalez, Los Angeles .... KO by 2
1980
Apr. 1—Sal Lopez, Sacramento .... KO by 6
Sept. 24—Pablo Gomez, Boise .... KO 4
Dec. 9—Andy Ganigan, Honolulu .... KO by 2

(KING) EDWARD RANE
Yonkers, N.Y. Heavyweight
1980
Sept. 12—Dennis Reilly, New York .... KO 1
Nov. 12—Kerry Judge, New York .... L 4
Nov. 25—Harold Rice, Hartford .... KO by 1

PETE RANZANY
Sacramento, Calif. Welterweight
Born: April 6, 1952
1973
Oct. 2—Marc Thomas, Sacramento.............. KO 3
1974
Feb. 26—Kevin Morgan, Sacramento .... KO 2
Mar. 19—Benny Reyes, Sacramento............... KO 3
Apr. 2—Tommy Howard, Sacramento............. KO 3
Apr. 30—Roger Buckskin, Sacramento............. KO 2
Aug. 29—Jimmy Jackson, Los Angeles .... W 5
Oct. 22—Jimmy Jackson, Sacramento .... L 8
Dec. 3—Dan Kibby, Sacramento .... KO 3
1975
Jan. 16—Jesus Burciaga, Los Angeles .... KO 1
Feb. 4—Jimmy Jackson, Sacramento .... W 6
Mar. 4—Harry Brown, Sacramento .... KO 1
Mar. 18—Gonzalo Rodriguez, Sacramento........... W 8
Apr. 8—Gonzalo Rodriguez, Sacramento .... W 10
Apr. 22—Jimmy Jackson, Sacramento .... KO 8
July 14—Toshi Hara, Sacramento .... KO 6
Oct. 14—David Oropeza, Sacramento .... KO 5
Nov. 1—Renato Garcia, Los Angeles............. KO 5
Nov. 11—Fred Jones, Sacramento .... KO 5
Dec. 2—Ruben Vasquez, Sacramento.............. KO 7
1976
Jan. 20—Mike Avans, Sacramento .... W 10
Feb. 10—Manuel Leal, Sacramento............... KO 1
Feb. 24—Adolph Viruet, Sacramento .... W 10
Apr. 27—Benny Huertas, Sacramento .... KO 2
June 7—Alfonso Hayman, Sacramento .... KO 9
July 26—Keith Averett, Sacramento .... KO 3
Sept. 14—Rudy Barro, Sacramento................ KO 2
Nov. 9—Gene Wells, Sacramento .... W 10
Dec. 7—Julio Gomez, Sacramento .... TW 7
1977
Jan. 22—Abel Cordova, Los Angeles .... KO 7
Mar. 11—Julio Gomez, Sacramento .... W 12
May 4—Bruce Fitch, San Francisco .... KO 5
May 24—Abel Cordova, Sacramento .... W 10
June —Babs McCarthy, Incline Village .... W 10
Aug. 2—Babs McCarthy, Sacramento .... W 12
Oct. 21—Randy Shields, Sacramento .... TD 2
Nov. 22—Jose Luis Baltazar, Sacramento .... W 10
Dec. 13—Armando Muniz, Sacramento .... KO by 6
1978
Feb. 14—Randy Shields, Sacramento .... KO 11
Mar. 14—Joe Grier, Sacramento .... KO 4
May 2—Rafael Rodriguez, Sacramento .... W 10
June 25—Santiago Valdez, Stateline .... KO 2
Sept. 9—Jose Cuevas, Sacramento .... KO by 2
(WBA Welterweight Title)
Nov. 14—Rafael Rodriguez, Sacramento .... W 10
Dec. 12—Jimmy Heair, Sacramento .... W 12
(U.S. Welterweight Title)
1979
Feb. 9—Sammy Masias, Sacramento .... KO 3
Mar. 27—Bernardo Prada, Sacramento .... W 10
June 13—Clyde Gray, Sacramento .... KO 5
Aug. 10—Ray Leonard, Las Vegas .... KO by 4
1980
Feb. 5—Wilson Bell, Sacramento .... KO 7
Apr. 22—Agapito Ramirez, Sacramento .... W 10
May 27—Ray Hammond, Sacramento .... TD 3
Aug. 5—Mauricio Aldana, Sacramento .... W 10
Sept. 5—Sal Lopez, Sacramento .... KO 6
Dec. 12—Wilfred Benitez, Sacramento .... L 10

ALFONSO RATLIFF
Chicago, Ill. Heavyweight
1980
Aug. 25—Jim Flynn, Chicago .... KO 1
Sept. 22—Mike Chrun, Chicago .... KO 2
Oct. 9—Charles Atlas, Chicago .... KO 1
Nov. 13—Melvin Hosey, Chicago .... KO 5

BILLY RATLIFF
Louisville, Ky. Light Heavyweight
1976
Oct. 27—Sylvester Wilder, Cleveland .... W 6
Nov. 17—Paul Raymond, Cleveland .... KO by 5
1977
Apr. 23—Al Fracker, Jackson .... L 10
July 16—Terry Hairston, Louisville .... W 5
Nov. 10—Sam Gonzalez, Cincinnati .... KO 3
1978
Mar. 20—Julius Noble, Chicago .... L 4
Apr. 8—Ted Hamilton, Pikesville .... KO 2
Sept. 27—Billy Hollis, Flint .... KO 2
Oct. 28—Al Bell, Louisville .... W 6
Nov. 11—Obie Garnett, Beaver Dam .... KO 1
1979
Jan. 31—Gary Summerhays, Saginaw .... L 10
July 22—Mario Rosa, Canton .... L 10
1980
Feb. 27—Rico Castillo, Las Vegas .... KO 6
Mar. 28—Roberto Cruz, Chicago .... KO 6
Nov. 9—Risto Bekovich, Saginaw .... L 10

LARRY RAYFORD
New Orleans, La. Junior Middleweight
1976
July 26—Freddy Johnson, New Orleans .... KO by 4
1977
June 16—Mike Box, Mobile .... KO 2
Aug. 23—Maurice Quillens, New Orleans .... D 4
Sept. 23—Roy Robinson, New Orleans .... W 4
1978
Sept. 11—Pat Hallacy, New Orleans .... L 6
Sept. 18—Mike Bonelli, Wichita .... KO 5
Oct. 24—Tyler Dupuy, New Orleans .... W 6
Nov. 14—Manuel Quillen, New Orleans .... KO 3
Dec. 1—John English, New Orleans .... KO 4
1979
Jan. 22—Melvin Dennis, New Orleans .... W 6
Feb. 9—David Braxton, Mt. Clemens .... L 8
Apr. 14—Chuck Mince, New Orleans .... L 10
May 20—Joaquin Macias, Baton Rouge .... KO by 10
Nov. 30—Clint Jackson, New Orleans .... KO by 7
1980
July 15—Tyler Dupey, New Orleans .... KO 5
Sept. 9—Norberto Sabater, Memphis .... L 10
Sept. 23—Robert Kinchen, New Orleans ...... KO by 3

GARY RAYMOND
Phoenix, Arizona Welterweight
1977
May 23—Joe Hernandez, Tucson .... W 4
June 14—Larry Monteith, Phoenix .... KO 2
Aug. 22—Larry Roldan, Phoenix .... KO 1
Nov. 15—Hedgemon Robertson, Phoenix .... W 4
Dec. 20—Jose (Pepe) Dominguez, Las Vegas .... L 7
1978
May 23—Carmelo Garcia, Phoenix .... W 6
1979
May 14—Ronald Taylor, Phoenix .... W 6
Aug. 2—Alfredo Carranza, Phoenix .... W 8
Oct. 11—Hector Rivera, Phoenix .... KO 8
1980
Feb. 14—Modesto Concepcion, Phoenix .... L 10
Oct. 9—Joe Mociera, Phoenix .... KO by 7

JERRY REDDICK
Halifax, Canada Light Heavyweight
1979
Oct. 22—Don Marshall, Edmonton .... KO 1
—Tommy Boyce, Vancouver .... KO 2
1980
Mar. 15—Dave Simmons, Vancouver .... KO 2
May 29—Ron Cichon, Vancouver .... KO 1
—Mustafa El-Amin, Juneau .... KO 2
Sept. 18—Paddy Wilson, Nanaimo .... KO 5
Dec. 23—Bobby Young, Tacoma .... KO 2

FRED REED
Chicago, Ill. Middleweight
Height: 5 ft. 10 in.
1978
July 24—Danny Cohen, Bridgeview .... KO 1
Nov. 11—Mike West, Sterling .... KO 2

Dec. 2—John Shavers, Aurora ....W 6
Dec. 9—Nathaniel Akbar, Detroit ....L 4
1979
June 13—Billy Goodwin, Bridgeview ....W 10
Aug. 2—Tommy Hannah, Detroit ....KO by 9
Sept. 7—Johnny Heard, Chicago ....D 8
1980
Sept. 11—Al Clay, Chicago ....L 10
Dec. 4—Nicola Cirelli, Rome ....L 8

JIM REED
Tulsa, Okla. Middleweight
1979
Nov. 1—O'Dell Willis, Wichita ....KO by 1
1980
Dec. 9—Sammy Horne, Kalamazoo ....KO by 4

KEN REED
Chicago, Ill. Lightweight
1980
May 15—Simmie Black, Chicago ....KO 4
Aug. 25—Pete Sanchez, Chicago ....W 4
Oct. 3—Jimmy Paul, Detroit ....KO by 5

ROGER REED
Honolulu, Hawaii Lightweight
1979
Dec. 18—Rueben Dudoit, Honolulu ....KO by 2
1980
Feb. 19—Rick Marquez, Honolulu ....KO by 2

CHRIS REEDER
Philadelphia, Pa. Heavyweight
1979
Mar. 28—Stan Williams, Philadelphia ....KO 3
May 25—Ronnie Stevens, Baltimore ....KO 2
May 31—Leonard Langley, Virginia Beach ....W 6
July 3—Walter Foster, Atlantic City ....W 4
Sept. 20—Charlie Smith, Virginia Beach ....L 6
1980
Apr. 11—Charlie Smith, Chester ....KO by 5
Nov. 7—Frankie Crossan, Trenton ....KO by 2

JAMES REID
Richmond, Va. Heavyweight
1978
June 22—Ben Carr, Virginia Beach ....KO 2
July 20—Brad Craig, Virginia Beach ....W 4
Aug. 17—Ted Hamilton, Virginia Beach ....KO 3
Sept. 14—Quinnie Locklear, Baltimore ....KO 5
Nov. 9—Quinnie Locklear, Virginia Beach ....L 6
1979
Nov. 24—Greg Page, Bloomington ....KO by 1
1980
May 14—Renaldo Snipes, White Plains ....KO by 3
Dec. 11—Tim Witherspoon, Philadelphia .....KO by 6

DENNIS REILLY
Staten Island, N.Y. Heavyweight
1980
Mar. 7—Charles Campbell, Staten Island ....L 4
May 9—Djata Banks, Staten Island ....KO 1
July 16—Elis Sipiro, Elizabeth ....KO 1
Sept. 12—King Edward Range, New York ......KO by 1

JOVITO RENGIFO
Venezuelan Flyweight
1977
May 28—Robinson Sanchez, Catia La Mar ....W disq. 2
June 30—Robinson Sanchez, Edo. Yaracu ....KO 3
Oct. 9—Israel Torres, Caracas ....W 6
Nov. 28—Robinson Sanchez, San Felipe ....W 6
1978
Apr. 23—Robinson Sanchez, Caracas ....KO 6
June 4—Eduardo D'Luis, Caracas ....KO 2
July 29—Carlos Osorio, Caracas ....W 10
Sept. 10—Carlos Osorio, Caracas ....W 10
Sept. 24—Henry Diaz, Caracas ....W 10
Oct. 22—Freddy Moran, Caracas ....W 10
Nov. 26—Oscar Gomez, Caracas ....KO 4
1979
Feb. 18—Jose Ortiz, Caracas ....KO 1
Apr. 8—Farsithrong Fairtex, Caracas ....W 10
June 30—Luis Sierra, Caracas ....KO 1
July 21—Mario Gatica, Caracas ....KO 5
Sept. 1—Remigio Suloaran, Caracas ....KO 4
Sept. 22—Carlos Gutierrez, Caracas ....KO 11
(Won Venezuelan Flyweight Title)
Sept. 29—Humberto Mayorga, Edo. Zulla ....W 10
Nov. 9—Jorge Cruz, Caracas ....KO 6
Dec. 17—Carlos Huilli, Caracas ....KO 4
1980
Feb. 1—Juan Jose Guzman, Caracas ....KO 3

Mar. 24—Rodolfo Rodriguez, Caracas ....W 10
Apr. 14—Jimmy Fernandez, Caracas ....TW 7
June 2—Alberto Mendez, Caracas ....KO 8
July 20—Daniel Guillen, Caracas ....W 10
Sept. 15—Rafael Orono, Barquisamento ....KO by 3
(For WBC Super Flyweight Title)
Dec. 1—Alfonso Lopez, Caracas ....L 10

KEVIN RENSHAW
Gloucester, N.J. Lightweight
1979
Sept. 29—Eddie Arthurs, Trenton ....KO 1
Nov. 21—Scott Wolfertz, Allentown ....KO by 3
1980
Jan. 30—Bob Johnson, Allentown ....L 4
Feb. 18—Eddie Ortiz, Upper Darby ....W 4
Mar. 14—Quinto Benvenida, Trenton ....KO 2
Apr. 10—Jose Green, Atlantic City ....KO by 3
July 12—Greg Cook, Atlantic City ....W 4
Aug. 9—Robert Stevenson, Atlantic City ....D 4
Sept. 9—Herb Darity, Atlantic City ....KO by 2

JOSE RENTA
Puerto Rican Welterweight
1979
June 29—Jose Vallejo, Santo Domingo ....KO by 3
1980
Oct. 24—Tony Santana, Uniondale ....KO by 3

JOSE RESENDEZ
Los Angeles, Calif. Junior Featherweight
1977
Mar. 6—Ernesto Rios, San Luis ....KO by 7
Oct. 4—Pee Man Jones, Oroville ....W 5
Oct. 29—Eduardo Plata, Los Angeles ....W 4
Nov. 2—Javier Flores, Las Vegas ....D 8
Dec. 15—Horacio Pintado, Los Angeles ....W 4
1978
Jan. 12—Eduardo Plata, Los Angeles ....W 6
Feb. 4—Javier Flores, Salt Lake City ....L 10
Feb. 14—Tony Fernandez, Sacramento ....KO 3
Mar. 4—Francisco Ponce, Los Angeles ....L 4
Mar. 17—Antonio Sanchez, Anaheim ....KO 3
Mar. 31—Sergio Nualarte, San Diego ....W 8
Apr. 23—Jesse Trujillo, Denver ....W 10
May 23—Alfonso Cirilos, Denver ....W 10
June 21—Miguel Meza, Concord ....L 4
July 18—Noel Arriesgado, Honolulu ....KO by 9
Dec. 5—Earl Large, Las Vegas ....L 10
1979
Jan. 16—Francisco Alvarado, Las Vegas ....L 10
Apr. 4—Daryl Jones, Los Angeles ....L 10
Apr. 19—Oscar Muniz, Los Angeles ....KO by 6
Sept. 25—Alberto Davila, Los Angeles ....L 10
Dec. 8—Melvin Johnson, Salt Lake City ....L 10
Dec. 14—Alberto Davila, San Bernardino ....L 10
1980
Mar. 22—Javier Flores, Salt Lake City ....W 10
June 3—Javier Flores, Las Vegas ....L 12
Aug. 19—Nicky Perez, Las Vegas ....L 10
Aug. 27—Freddie Roach, Las Vegas ....L 10
Sept. 11—Luis Gonzalez, Los Angeles ....W 10
Nov. 1—Freddie Roach, Lake Tahoe ....L 8

JIM RESTAURI
1980
Apr. 1—Val Gassaway, Sacramento ....KO 1
Apr. 16—Lew Lockwood, Fresno ....W 4
May 13—Lew Lockwood, Sacramento ....W 5
July 1—Lew Lockwood, Sacramento ....L 6
Aug. 5—Lew Lockwood, Sacramento ....W 6
Sept. 5—Len Lawson, Sacramento ....D 6

LUIS RESTO
New York, N.Y. Welterweight
1977
Feb. 4—Julio Chevalier, New York ....W 4
Apr. 19—Bo Whyms, White Plains ....W 6
June 3—Tyrone Phelps, New York ....KO 4
June 18—Sam Hailstock, Commack ....D 6
Nov. 18—Anthony Daniels, New York ....W 6
Dec. 12—Fighting Hunks, St. Thomas ....W 10
1978
Mar. 18—Bruce Curry, Las Vegas ....KO by 2
Apr. 22—Mario Guilloti, San Remo ....L 8
Oct. 1—Mark Harris, Georgetown ....KO 7
—Luis Primera, Caracas ....KO by 1
1979
Feb. 4—Reggie Ford, Georgetown ....W 10
Mar. 16—Gary Coates, Cincinnati ....KO 4
Apr. 6—Earl Liburd, New York ....W 8
Sept. —Vernon Lewis, Guyana ....L 10
Oct. 26—Pat Hallacy, New York ....W 10

195

1980
Mar. 28 Adolfo Viruet, New York ....D 10
June   6—Juan Hidalgo, New York ....W 10
Oct.   9—George Mojica, San Juan ....KO 8
Nov.   6—Ismael Martinez, San Juan ....W 10
Nov. 25—Nino Gonzales, New York ....KO by 9

FERNANDO REYES
San Diego, Calif. Junior Lightweight
1979
Mar.   9—Francisco Pico, San Diego ....L 4
May   4—Vicente Barreto, San Diego ....D 4
May   17—Clemente Enriques, Los Angeles ....TL 2
May   24—Tim Martinez, Los Angeles ....L 5
Nov.   2—Jaime Garza, San Diego ....KO by 2
1980
Feb.   6—Lenny Jones, Costa Mesa ....L 6
Apr.   4—Mario Portillo, San Bernardino ....L 6
May   2—Tommy Rodriguez, San Bernardino ....KO 4
May   16—Mario Portillo, San Bernardino ....KO 1
Sept. 17—Lenny Jones, San Diego ....L 6
Dec. 16—Alvin Reyes, Los Angeles ....KO by 1

JERRY REYES
Inglewood, Calif. Junior Welterweight
1980
May   7—Daniel Cruz, Las Vegas ....W 4
May   13—Golden Thomas, Sacramento ....KO by 2
June 12—Alfredo Aquayo, Stockton ....KO by 2
Sept. 11—Rocky Burke, El Paso ....L 6
Sept. 17—Carlos Bryant, San Diego ....L 4
Sept. 24—Dan Ditoff, Boise ....W 6
Oct.   7—Joe Sanchez, Bakersfield ....L 4
Oct. 23—Joe Sanchez, Los Angeles ....L 6
Nov. 11—Ronnie Shields, Houston ....KO by 4

SERGIO REYES
Laredo, Texas Bantamweight
Born: May 23, 1953
1974
Aug.   8—Miguel Reyna, Sabinas ....W 4
Oct. 11—Luis Rico, San Antonio ....KO 2
1975
July 21—Frank Garza, Corpus Christi ....KO 5
Sept. 16—Raul Casarez, Corpus Christi ....KO 5
1976
Feb.   3—Bernardo Darra, Laredo ....KO by 7
Mar.   9—Juan Lara, Laredo ....W 10
Apr. 30—Gerardo Heredia, Monterrey ....L 10
May   30—Joe Garcia, Laredo ....KO 5
July 16—Noe Hernandez, Laredo ....KO 2
Sept. 23—Baby Kid Chocolate, Wilmington ....L 10
1977
Jan. 21—Manuel Rodriguez, Laredo ....KO by 3
Feb. 25—Manuel Rodriguez, Laredo ....W 10
Apr. 30—Mel Johnson, Laredo ....KO 3
June 16—Arturo Romero, Laredo ....KO 3
July 21—Rodolfo Ibarra, Laredo ....KO 2
Oct. 13—Fili Gonzales, Laredo ....KO 7
1978
May   2—Adelaido Galindo, San Antonio ....L 10
July 15—Adelaido Galindo, Tampico ....KO by 1
Aug. 24—Jeff Chandler, Philadelphia ....L 8
Oct. 26—Calvin Sheppard, Laredo ....W 10
Nov. 28—Josie Bautista, Houston ....KO by 6
1979
Jan. 31—Mario Rogelio, Laredo ....KO 5
Apr. 20—Calvin Reyes, Laredo ....KO 3
May   1—Ad Zapanta, Houston ....KO 9
Dec. 14—Tommy Young, Dallas ....L 12
1980
Feb. 19—Willie Jensen, Sparks ....L NC
Apr. 25—Ruben Olivares, Nuevo Laredo ....KO by 7
July 29—Jose Batista, Laredo ....W 10
Sept. 1—Rafael Gonzalez, Laredo ....L 10
Dec.   5—Elias DeLeon, Corpus Christi ....W 10

ROBERTO REYNOSA
Houston, Texas Heavyweight
1977
Apr.   5—Jose Luis Gonzalez, Houston ....KO by 3
June 11—Grady Daniels, Sterling ....KO by 3
Aug.   1—Ivy Brown, Topeka ....KO by 3
Aug. 31—William Kissman, Austin ....KO by 3
1978
Jan. 25—Marvin Johnson, Indianapolis ....KO by 1
Feb. 14—Christino Zaragoza, Houston ....KO by 1
Mar. 21—Larry Alexander, Greenville ....KO by 1
1979
Apr. 20—Elmo Henderson, Corpus Christi ....TD 4
July 31—Charlie Parker, San Antonio ....KO 1
Nov. 28—Earl Tripp, Las Vegas ....KO 2
1980
Jan. 26—Ed (Too Tall) Jones, Jackson ....KO by 1

RUBEN RIANI
Argentine Junior Lightweight
1980
Mar.   7—Ruben Stamuli, Mar del Plata ....KO 5
June   7—Daniel Murua, Gral Pico ....D 10
July 11—Daniel Murua, Rosario ....W 10
Aug.   8—Rodolfo Diaz, Rio III ....KO 2
Nov.   7—Victor Echegary, San Juan ....L 12
(For Argentine Junior Lightweight Title)

JUAN RIBOTA
Durando, Mexico Welterweight
1979
Mar. 24—Robert Green, Chicago ....KO 3

June 27—Charles Peterson, Chicago ....D 4
July 11—Bob Coolidge, Chicago ....KO by 2

RUSS RICCARDI
Hoboken, N.J. Lightweight
1980
Mar. 20—Al Gomez, N. Bergen ....W 4
May   31—Al Gomez, Elizabeth ....W 4
Sept. 24—Dave Donald, Elizabeth ....KO 2
Dec. 27—Dave Donald, N. Bergen ....KO 2

MAURICE RICE
Light Heavyweight
1978
Oct. 30—Mustafa El-Amin, Seaside, Ore. ....L 10
1979
June 19—Greg McPherson, San Carlos ....KO by 3
Nov. 27—Kelly Anderson, Vancouver ....W 6
1980
May   17—Gordie Lawson, Kelowna ....L 6

STEVE RICHARDSON
Trenton, N.J. Middleweight
1979
May   23—Tyrone Rackley, Las Vegas ....L 4
June   6—Tyrone Rackley, Las Vegas ....L 6
June 27—Packy Paulson, Phoenix ....KO by 3
1980
Dec. 16—Don Poole, Toronto ....KO by 1

SANFORD RICKS
East Orange, N.J. Junior Welterweight
1978
June 30—David Vega, Newark ....KO 1
Aug. 16—Mel Boynton, Newark ....W 4
Sept. 16—Pedro Torres, Elmira ....W 4
1979
Jan. 11—Levant Williams, Detroit ....KO 5
Apr. 14—Frankie Minigan, Syracuse ....W 6
May   24—Keith Stokes, Cohoes ....KO 2
Sept. 30—Fermin Wilson, Suffolk ....KO 1
Dec. 11—Marty Cole, Halifax ....KO 6
1980
Oct. 18—George Burton, Atlantic City ....W 4

JOEY RICO
Tucson, Ariz. Lightweight
1975
Jan. 11—Mike Avans, Tucson ....W 10
June 18—Ruben Aguilar, Las Vegas ....KO by 5
1976
(Inactive)
1977
Aug. 10—Nicky Perez, Las Vegas ....KO by 3
1978
(Inactive)
1979
Jan. 23—Jaime Castillo, Tucson ....L 4
Apr. 12—Jerry Wiles, Lake Tahoe ....KO by 3
1980
Aug. 20—Daniel Cruz, Las Vegas ....KO by 3

HECTOR RIOS
Argentine Junior Middleweight
1980
Apr. 11—Osmar Ochoa, Camilo Aldao ....L 10
Oct. 10—Osvaldo Figueredo, Parana ....W 10

RICARDO RIVAROLA
Argentine Junior Featherweight
1980
Apr. 17—Pedro Munoz, Posadas ....W 10
Oct. 17—Hipolito Nunez, S. Sal. de Jujuy .....KO by 10

196

ADOLFO RIVAS
Houston, Texas Middleweight
1977
May	17—Ignacio Lopez, Corpus Christi	KO by 3
May	20—Raul Aguirre, Marshall	KO by 1
June	28—Ignacio Lopez, Corpus Christi	KO by 2

1978
Feb.	14—Leon McCullum, Houston	KO by 2
Apr.	11—John English, Houston	NC 3
May	2—Miguel Garcia, San Antonio	D 4
May	30—Pedro Torres, El Paso	KO by 1
June	3—Ronnie Brown, Denver	KO by 1
June	20—Clarence Gilmore, Corpus Christi	KO by 3
Aug.	8—John English, Houston	W 10
Oct.	12—Jesse Lara, Houston	L 10
Oct.	31—Jim Claar, Indianapolis	KO by 4
Dec.	11—Leroy Green, Topeka	KO by 2
Dec.	15—Gus Oropeza, Corpus Christi	KO by 2

1979
June	5—Raymond Boyd, Houston	KO by 3

1980
Jan.	18—Miguel Estrada, El Paso	D 10
Mar.	3—Frank Newton, Oklahoma City	KO by 6
Mar.	18—Eddie Gonzales, Houston	KO by 3
Apr.	14—Luke Capuano, Chicago	KO by 2
June	3—Larry Strogen, Houston	KO by 3

JAVIER RIVAS
Texas Junior Welterweight
1979
Sept.	12—Francisco Del Toro, El Paso	KO 10

1980
Sept.	18—Eduardo Carrera, El Paso	KO 5
May	9—Jimmy Heair, El Paso	L 10

AMERICO RIVERA
Puerto Rican Junior Featherweight
1980
Mar.	24—Roberto Pinerio, San Juan	D 4
Apr.	28—Efrain Cotto, San Juan	W 4
May	29—Francisco Aponte, Rio Piedras	KO 5
July	10—Ramon Cruz, Rio Piedras	L 6
Aug.	7—Manuel Santos, Rio Piedras	W 6
Sept.	11—Edwin Salgado, San Juan	L 6

ANGEL RIVERA
Lawrence, Mass. Welterweight
1978
May	20—Jose Alejandro, Carolina	

1979
Oct.	27—Jack Morrell, Fitchburg	KO by 2

1980
Apr.	28—Julio Guzman, San Juan	KO by 6
Sept.	4—Roberto Pineiro, Rio Piedras	KO by 7 r

AUGUSTIN RIVERA
Mexican Lightweight
1979
Feb.	9—David Madrid, San Diego	W 10
Mar.	22—Herman Montes, Los Angeles	L 10

1980
Nov.	28—Roberto Garcia, San Diego	D 10

FERNANDO RIVERA
Puerto Rican Featherweight
1977
Mar.	25—Marcial Santiago, New York	W 6
Feb.	27—Zenon Silgado, Sincelejo	KO by 2

1978
Jan.	14—Felix Trinidad, Carolina	W 6
Mar.	4—Francisco Aponte, Carolina	W 8
May	13—Francisco Cruz, Carolina	W 8
June	26—Heriberto Olivares, Rio Piedras	W 8
Aug.	26—Wilson Yambo, Carolina	KO 3
Oct.	2—Ken Agosto, Rio Piedras	L 10
Nov.	27—Felix Trinidad, San Juan	L 12
	(Puerto Rican Featherweight Title)	

1980
Feb.	4—Edwin Rivera, San Juan	W 10
Mar.	3—Juan Castro, San Juan	KO 3
Mar.	31—Santos Luis Rivera, San Juan	W 10
July	24—Quique Solis, Rio Piedras	W 10

HECTOR RIVERA
Los Angeles, Calif. Junior Lightweight
1977
June	9—Francisco Flores, Los Angeles	KO 2
June	30—Eulogio Bojorquez, Los Angeles	KO 1
July	12—Larry Fuentes, Honolulu	W 10
Sept.	29—Dave Bernal, Los Angeles	KO 7
Oct.	13—Abraham Perez, Los Angeles	L 10

1978
Jan.	4—Leroy Haley, Las Vegas	KO by 8

Apr.	13—Ray Saldivar, Los Angeles	KO 2
Apr.	22—Manny Lopez, Salt Lake City	L 10
June	7—Augustin Estrada, Las Vegas	W 10
Sept.	12—Jose Isaac Marin, Pico Rivera	L 10
Nov.	27—Vicente Saldivar, Bakersfield	TL 6

1979
Feb.	21—Jorge Morales, Lake Tahoe	L 12
Aug.	2—LeRoy Haley, Phoenix	L 10
Oct.	11—Gary Raymond, Phoenix	KO by 8

1980
June	13—Cisco Ortega, San Bernardino	KO by 8
Aug.	14—Sal Lopez, Los Angeles	KO by 8

JOSE RIVERA
Brooklyn, N.Y. Junior Lightweight
1978
Aug.	21—Jimmy Lopez, Cape Cod	W 8
Oct.	19—Gerald Hayes, Garfield	KO by 4
Dec.	1—Dave Ramalho, Cohoes	KO by 2

1979
Mar.	29—Tim LaValley, Cohoes	KO by 1
Sept.	19—Juan LaPorte, New York	L 8

1980
Jan.	24—Bob Ingram, Dover	KO 2
May	31—Jimmy Magnifico, Elizabeth	W 8

NOE RIVERA
Concord, Calif. Lightweight
1978
Apr.	10—Daniel Patino, Los Angeles	L 6
Apr.	24—Petronillo Vezasquez, Los Angeles	KO by 2
Apr.	26—Gary Pittman, Concord	KO by 1
June	8—Eddie Rodgers, Los Angeles	KO by 3
Sept.	28—Tony Tijeda, Phoenix	KO 1
Nov.	9—George (Rocky) Garcia, Los Angeles	KO by 3
Dec.	14—Albert Guevara, Los Angeles	KO by 2

1979
Mar.	21—Vicente Barreto, Los Angeles	L 4

1980
Mar.	10—Jesus Montanes, San Juan	W 4
Mar.	24—Wilfredo Colon, San Juan	KO by 2
June	12—Manuel Santòs, Rio Piedras	D 6
Aug.	7—Milton Torres, Rio Piedras	L 4

RANDY RIVERS
Trenton, N.J. Middleweight
1978
Aug.	16—Bobby Gill, Las Vegas	KO 1
Aug.	23—Rahim Muhammad, Las Vegas	D 4
Aug.	30—Jimmy Coleman, Las Vegas	KO 2

1979
July	1—Larry Lynch, Rahway	D 4

1980
Apr.	26—Wilbur Thomas, Trenton	KO 3
July	30—H. L. Hudson, Las Vegas	W 4
Aug.	6—Fahim Muhammad, Las Vegas	L 6
Sept.	3—Fahim Muhammad, Las Vegas	W 6
Oct.	2—Mark Holmes, Las Vegas	L 6

CHRIS RIZZO
Orlando, Fla. Lightweight
Born: May 5, 1959, Rochester N.Y.
1978
May	13—Andre Obregon, Orlando	KO 1
July	8—Billy Lopez, Orlando	KO 1
July	18—Dennis Green, Miami Beach	KO 2
Aug.	22—Dennis Green, Orlando	KO 4
Aug.	31—Billy Wallace, Tampa	W 4
Oct.	24—Arthur Clarke, Orlando	W 8
Nov.	21—Harry Ryals, Orlando	KO 2
Dec.	12—Frankie Moultrie, Orlando	L 10

1979
June	19—Clyde Spencer, Orlando	KO 8
July	31—Simmie Black, Orlando	W 10

1980
June	13—Victor Mangual, Harlem	KO by 9

FREDDIE ROACH
Dedham, Mass. Featherweight
Born: March 5, 1960
Managed by Eddie Futch
1978
Aug.	24—Roberto Vasquez, Boston	W 6
Sept.	16—Jose Maldonado, Yarmouth	KO 6
Dec.	21—Eddie Bracetty, Portland	W 6

1979
Feb.	3—Ed Bracetty, Boston	W 6
June	6—Ney Santiago, Las Vegas	KO 6
June	27—John Pappe, Las Vegas	W 6
July	25—Adolfo Hurtado, Las Vegas	W 6
Aug.	2—Ricardo Hurtado, Phoenix	KO 1
Aug.	10—Deal Newhill, San Diego	W 6
Aug.	29—Francisco Pico, Las Vegas	W 6

Sept.	13—Beto Nunez, Phoenix	L 6
Oct.	24—Ruben Moreno, Las Vegas	W 6
Dec.	12—Louis Villa, Las Vegas	W 6
1980		
Jan.	23—Roberto Flores, Las Vegas	KO 1
Apr.	2—Billy Martinez, Las Vegas	KO 2
Apr.	16—Lionel Harney, Las Vegas	KO 6
July	11—Manuel Martinez, Phoenix	KO 3
Aug.	27—Jose Resendez, Las Vegas	W 10
Oct.	9—Pedro Gonzales, Phoenix	KO 4
Nov.	1—Jose Resendez, Lake Tahoe	W 8

EDDIE ROBERTS
Kingsport, Tenn. Junior Middleweight
1977

Nov.	5—Wayne Brooks, Kingsport	KO 2
Nov.	19—Ron Vaughn, Wheeling	W 6
Nov.	27—Johnny Ace, Knoxville	D 4
1978		
Feb.	25—Sylvester Harris, Kingsport	W 6
Apr.	25—Trevor Harvey, Orlando	W 6
July	24—Alex Porrata, Bridgeview	KO by 2
1979		
Sept.	8—Willie Taylor, Kingsport	L 6
1980		
Jan.	15—Rick Noggle, Youngstown	KO by 4

HEDGEMON ROBERTSON
Los Angeles, Calif. Lightweight
1977

July	15—Arturo Reyes, San Diego	KO 1
Nov.	15—Gary Ramon, Phoenix	L 4
Dec.	8—Rich Kronich, Las Vegas	KO 2
1978		
Sept.	8—Scipio Stubbs, Los Angeles	KO 4
1979		
Apr.	21—Jose Gonzalez, Las Vegas	KO 4
May	4—Ruben Martinez, San Diego	KO 1
June	19—John Willis, San Carlos	KO 1
Aug.	1—Jose Castenada, Los Angeles	KO 2
Nov.	21—Julio Alfonso, Los Angeles	KO 1
1980		
Aug.	27—Chucho Salcedo, Las Vegas	D 8
Oct.	22—Jesus Delgado, Las Vegas	KO 2

(SMOKIN') JIMMY ROBERTSON
Muncie, Ind. Light Heavyweight
1977

Sept.	28—Rocky McCaleb, Minneapolis	D 4
1978		
Jan.	25—Baker (Bear) Tinsley, Indianapolis	W 4
Apr.	3—Joe Brown, Indianapolis	D 4
June	3—Tim Johnson, Muncie	KO 3
July	19—Jerry Daniels, Dayton	L 4
1979		
Feb.	16—Baker Tinsley, Louisville	L 6
Mar.	27—Jimmy Olszewski, Detroit	W 4
June	1—David Carr, Louisville	L 4
Aug.	3—Lupe Guerra, Omaha	L 8
Aug.	10—Jerry Hunter, Evansville	D 6
Aug.	23—Dave McCann, Detroit	W 4
Nov.	8—Craig Arnold, Indianapolis	KO 1
Nov.	15—Young Louis, Detroit	L 6
1980		
Jan.	21—Steve Mormino, St. Charles	L 6

GROVER ROBINSON
Dallas, Texas Light Heavyweight
1973

June	23—Sonny Floyd, Bristol	L 4
July	24—Ernie Davis, Mobile	W 6
Oct.	15—Robert Hoye, Kalamazoo	KO by 6
Dec.	10—Johnny Donatto, Monroe	KO 3
1974		
July	30—Edgar Ross, New Orleans	KO 3
1975-1978		
(Inactive)		
1979		
Apr.	2—Larry Jackson, Dallas	KO 1
Apr.	10—Matt Ross, Beaumont	KO by 6
June	12—Eddie Gonzalez, Beaumont	KO 5
July	9—Alvin Dominey, Odessa	L 10
July	21—Emmett Al Banks, Dallas	KO 5
1980		
May	19—Danman Lacy, New Orleans	KO 1

IRA ROBINSON
Richmond, Va. Lightweight
1979

Nov.	14—Lou Barber, Baltimore	L 4
Nov.	29—Van Tate, Virginia Beach	L 4
1980		
Apr.	26—Ron Aurit, Lynchburg	L 6

Sept.	17—Charles Triplett	W 4
Dec.	20—Scott Farmer, Richmond	W 4

LAMAR ROBINSON
Ohio, Heavyweight
1977

Dec.	7—Terry Mims, Cleveland	L 4
1978		
Apr.	26—Amos Haynes, Youngstown	L 6
1979		
Oct.	18—Amos Haynes, Struthers	L 6
1980		
Aug.	20—Robert White, Warren	KO 1
Oct.	28—Charlie Johnson, Warren	L 6

RUDY ROBLES
Los Angeles, Calif. Middleweight
1970

Apr.	16—Chon Arias, Los Angeles	W 5
May	21—Lee Flowers, Los Angeles	W 4
June	11—Roberto Villanueva, Los Angeles	KO 1
Sept.	17—Tommy James, Los Angeles	W 4
Oct.	15—Steve Papp, Los Angeles	W 6
Nov.	19—Steve Papp, Los Angeles	W 5
Dec.	14—Frankie Bueno, National City	KO 5
1971		
Jan.	14—Tommy Kearse, Los Angeles	W 6
Jan.	28—Tommy Kearse, Los Angeles	W 6
Feb.	12—Chuck Jefferson, Los Angeles	KO 3
Mar.	11—Al Stankie, Los Angeles	W 10
May	27—Mario Marquez, Los Angeles	W 10
June	24—Cipriano Hernandez, Los Angeles	W 10
Aug.	5—Jessie Reid, Los Angeles	W 10
Sept.	2—Coneji Aguirre, Los Angeles	KO 6
Oct.	28—Willie Warren, Los Angeles	W 10
1972		
Jan.	6—Jorge Rosales, Los Angeles	KO 7
Feb.	11—Ron Wilson, Los Angeles	W 10
Mar.	23—Ron Wilson, Los Angeles	W 10
1973		
July	11—Clarence Geigger, Las Vegas	KO 1
Aug.	31—George Davis, Los Angeles	KO 9
Oct.	4—Dave Adkins, Las Vegas	W 10
1974		
Mar.	4—Al Stankie, Oakland	KO 8
Apr.	8—George Cooper, Oakland	L 12
Apr.	22—Joe Gonzalez, San Jose	W 10
July	23—George Davis, Oakland	W 10
Sept.	20—Felton Marshall, Richmond	KO 5
Nov.	8—Dave Love, San Francisco	W 10
Nov.	14—Kim Booker, San Francisco	W 10
Dec.	7—Rudy Cruz, San Jose	L 10
1975		
Jan.	17—Rudy Cruz, San Jose	W 10
Feb.	28—Tony Mundine, Brisbane	W 10
Apr.	29—George Davis, Stockton	W 10
Aug.	16—Rodrigo Valdez, Cartagena	L 15
	(WBC Middleweight Title)	
1976		
Apr.	13—Loucif Hamani, Paris	L 10
July	17—Karl Vinson, Stockton	L 10
Mar.	30—Edgar Wallace, Phoenix	KO by 6
July	12—Jimmy Owens, Phoenix	KO 6
July	28—Mario Luna, Tucson	KO 3
Sept.	8—Ayub Kalule, Copenhagen	L 10
Oct.	4—George Cooper, Oroville	D 12
1978		
Apr.	3—Fully Obel, Tijuana	KO by 4
Oct.	22—Mike Colbert, Reno	KO 5
Dec.	5—Dave Adkins, Reno	KO 4
1979		
Feb.	6—Alan Minter, London	L 10
Apr.	16—Mike Colbert, Las Vegas	KO by 11
July	11—Josef Kossman	KO 4
Oct.	17—James Waire, Las Vegas	W 10
Nov.	30—Roger Leonard, Las Vegas	L 8
1980		
May	2—Ron Brown, Las Vegas	KO 3
May	24—James Waire, Santa Monica	L 10
Sept.	11—Ron Brown, Las Vegas	KO 1
Oct.	1—Paul Ramos, Las Vegas	L 10
Nov.	25—Mustafa Hamsho, New York	L 10

MANUEL ROCA
Argentine Junior Welterweight
1980

June	6—Pedro A. Gutierrez, Mar del Plata	D 6
July	4—Pedro A. Gutierrez, Mar del Plata	KO 4
Aug.	1—Santos Medina, Mar del Plata	W 6

TONY ROCHA
Texas Junior Featherweight
1979
Aug. 14—Silverio Martinez, Houston ....KO 3
1980
Jan. 22—Francisco Vasquez, Houston ....KO 3
Mar. 28—Leo Randolph, Tacoma ....KO by 2

JULIO RODRIGUES
Wainae, Hawaii Flyweight
1979
Apr. 24—Freddy Estrella, Hilo ....W 4
June 5—Carlos Canchola, Hilo ....W 8
June 12—Freddy Estrella, Honolulu ....KO 3
July 31—Aniceto Vargas, Honolulu ....W 8
Oct. 9—Jose Zaldivar Panulaya, Honolulu ....W 8
1980
July 22—James Estrella, Honolulu ....KO 2
Aug. 19—Caesar Zulueta, Honolulu ....KO 2
Sept. 23—Armando Ugalde, Honolulu ....W 10
Oct. 16—Candido Tellez, Los Angeles ....KO by 2

ALEJOS RODRIGUEZ
San Antonio, Texas Welterweight
1977
Apr. 12—Victor Villanueva, San Antonio ....KO 4
May 26—James Wallace, Austin ....KO 2
June 28—Norberto Rodriguez, San Antonio ....KO 1
Sept. 9—Mike Torres, San Antonio ....KO 3
1978
June 20—Paulino Garcia, San Antonio ....KO 3
July 18—Paul Garcia, San Antonio ....KO 2
Aug. 22—Ray Sepulveda, San Antonio ....KO 3
Sept. 19—Tom Pinner, San Antonio ....KO 5
1979
—Jose Figueroa, San Antonio ....W 10
Aug. 8—Gus Orpheza, Corpus Christi ....KO 1
Aug. 28—David Madrid, San Antonio ....KO 4
Oct. 30—Jose Mireles, San Antonio ....KO 3
1980
May 20—Andres Ramos, San Antonio ....L 10

CHICO RODRIGUEZ
Columbus, Ohio Lightweight
1978
Apr. 17—Bobby Sparks, Columbus ....KO by 3
June 28—Leon Gardner, Hamilton ....L 4
Oct. 24—Leon Gardner, Pittsburgh ....KO by 2
1979
Jan. 18—Johnny Ace Smith, Detroit ....KO by 2
Feb. 22—Ron Florek, Saginaw ....KO by 2
May 9—Richard Rozelle, Columbus ....KO by 5
Sept. 18—Alvin Straughter, Columbus ....KO by 4
Nov. 27—David Alexander, Columbus ....KO 2
Dec. 28—Tony Rutledge, Columbus ....L 6
1980
Apr. 30—Mike Johnson, Youngstown ....L 6
May 3—Lloyd Allen, Canton ....KO by 5
Aug. 21—Kean McGill, Columbus ....KO by 3
Sept. 10—Johnny Lira, Cicero ....KO by 1

CHUY RODRIGUEZ
Mexican Lightweight
1979
Jan. 17—Nacho Jiminez, Stockton ....W 10
Mar. 22—Julio Mendez, Los Angeles ....KO 1
May 10—Cleveland Denny, Los Angeles ....TD 6
July 27—Jorge Morales, Las Vegas ....KO by 5
Oct. 11—David Oropeza, Phoenix ....L 8
1980
Jan. 18—Herman Montes, San Bernardino ....KO by 1
May 6—Mike Lopez, Las Vegas ....KO 7
Oct. 30—Tony Baltazar, Los Angeles ....TD 4

FELIX RODRIGUEZ
Springfield, Mass. Bantamweight
1979
Mar. 2—Carmelo Negron, Albany ....KO by 2
Apr. 6—Nelson Cruz Tamariz, Albany ....KO by 4
May 23—Derrik Holmes, Washington, D.C. ....KO by 2
June 18—Eddie Welcome, Cohoes ....L 6
July 13—Tony Salvatore, Rochester ....KO by 2
1980
Apr. 22—Pepe Vasquez, Hartford ....W 4
Aug. 30—Jose Cueto, Colon ....W 10

FRANCISCO RODRIGUEZ
Los Angeles, Calif. Junior Lightweight
1977
Mar. 1—Jaime Avarte, Houston ....KO by 2
May 6—Jose Soto, Houston ....L 0
June 9—Dave Bernal, Los Angeles ....KO by 3

1978
Feb. 9—Alonso Gonzalez, Los Angeles ....KO by 2
Oct. 17—Freddie Roach, Houston ....KO by 3
1979
Sept. 11—Mark Pacheco, Reno ....KO by 3
1980
Feb. 13—Rafael Capristo, Las Vegas ....L 4
Mar. 13—Rafael Tejeda, Las Vegas ....KO by 5
May 28—James Manning, Portland ....L 6
July 17—Henry Contreras, Tucson ....KO by 3
Aug. 28—Robert Anderson, Las Vegas ....L 4
Sept. 4—Jose Pena, Los Angeles ....L 6

GIL RODRIGUEZ
California Junior Welterweight
1979
Jan. 9—Oscar Borboa, Phoenix ....L 4
Oct. 19—Jose Luis Gonzales, San Diego ....W 6
Nov. 23—Eric Bonilla, San Diego ....W 6
Dec. 7—Rafael Nunez, San Diego ....D 10
1980
Jan. 31—Carlos Lozano, Los Angeles ....L 8

HUMBERTO RODRIGUEZ
Mexican Flyweight
1979
Apr. 6—Felipe Morales, McAllen ....KO 6
Aug. 14—Calvin Sheppard, Houston ....L 10
Nov. 13—Gilberto Villicana, Houston ....W 8
1980
Jan. 22—Candy Iglesias, Houston ....L 10
Sept. 16—Freddie Jackson, Beaumont ....KO by 2

JAIME RODRIGUEZ
Lawrence, Mass. Junior Middleweight
1979
Feb. 24—Sean Mannion, Quincy ....L 6
June 12—Joe Tiberi, Totowa ....L 8
Oct. 27—Danny Heath, Fitchburg ....W 10
1980
Jan. 19—Rocky Fratto, Syracuse ....L 10
Feb. 16—Fernando Fernandez, Portland ....L 6
Feb. 26—Jorge Santana, Woburn ....L 4
Mar. 21—Mike Michaud, Fall River ....L 8
Apr. 30—Johnny Turner, Scranton ....L 10
June 28—Danny Heath, Manchester ....W 10
Sept. 12—Papo Figueroa, Hartford ....KO by 7

JULIO RODRIGUEZ
Mexican Flyweight
1979
Oct. 28—Netrnoi Vorasingh, Bangkok ....L 10
1980
May 13—Siony Carupo, Honolulu ....W 10
July 22—James Estrella, Honolulu ....KO 2
Aug. 19—Caesar Zulueta, Honolulu ....KO 2
Sept. 23—Armando Ugalde, Honolulu ....W 10
Oct. 16—Candido Tellez, Los Angeles ....KO by 2

LUIS BELTRAN RODRIGUEZ
Venezuelan Lightweight
1977
Feb. 27—Hugo Barrara, Caracas ....L 10
Apr. 22—Pedro Acosta, Cartagena ....KO 8
July 1—Alfonso Perez, Cartagena ....L 10
Oct. —Otoniel Martinez, Caracas ....KO by 4
1978
Mar. 18—Wilfredo Castro, Cartagena ....L 10
July 8—Jose Fernandez, Caracas ....W 10
Oct. 15—Alfonso Torres, Caracas ....L 10
1979
Aug. 25—Juan Campos, Caracas ....KO 3
Oct. 13—Pablo Manon, Caracas ....L 10
Nov. 17—Hugo Rengifo, Maracay ....KO 1
1980
Jan. —Jorge Diaz ....KO 2
Mar. 10—Jose Isturiz, Caracas ....W 12
(Venezuelan Lightweight Title)
Apr. 21—Ronald Alvarez, Caracas ....KO 5
June 30—Marion Thomas, Caracas ....KO 3
Aug. 25—Robert Alexander, Caracas ....KO 4

MIKE RODRIGUEZ
Los Angeles, Calif. Junior Featherweight
1979
May 30—Dennis Quimayousie, Las Vegas ....L 4
June 21—Memo Arreola, Los Angeles ....L 6
Oct. 25—Sergio Castro, Los Angeles ....L 5
1980
Mar. 27—Chivo Arrellano, Los Angeles ....W 5
Apr. 3—Adam Uribe, Los Angeles ....L 4
Apr. 9—Robert Anderson, Las Vegas ....L 6
Apr. 24—Mil Jiminez, Los Angeles ....W 4

199

June 12—Richard Savala, Los Angeles .... KO by 1
Dec. 26—Bernard Taylor, Las Vegas .... KO by 3

NORBERTO RODRIGUEZ
Mexican Junior Middleweight
1977
June 28—Alejos Rodriguez, San Antonio .... KO by 1
1978
(Inactive)
1979
Apr. 20—Herman Marquez, Laredo .... KO by 5
1980
June 17—Sammy Ayala, San Antonio .... KO by 2

PABLO RODRIGUEZ
Holyoke, Mass. Middleweight
1968
Sept. 26—Bob Akerson, Taunton.................L 4
Oct. 7—Felix Guzino, Taunton ....W 4
1969
Apr. 19—Ace Roberts, North Adams ....W 4
June 28—Juan Pizzaro, North Adams ....W 6
Aug. 25—Walter Moore, North Adams ....L 4
1970
Apr. 18—Kevin McGrath, North Adams........... W 6
1971
Feb. 22—Arthur Kettles, Providence.......... KO by 5
Apr. 3—Vince Malave, North Adams ....W 4
Apr. 20—Vince Malave, North Adams ....W 6
Aug. 30—Juan Ruiz, New Bedford .... KO by 1
1972
Nov. 3—Cocoa Kid, Springfield ....W 6
Nov. 21—Cocoa Kid, Springfield ....NC 5
1973
Mar. 10—Hector Maita, San Juan ....L 10
June 2—William Watson, Philadelphia........ KO by 1
Nov. 13—Jose Carabello, New Haven..............D 6
Dec. 5—Leo Saenz, Baltimore .... KO by 3
1974
Feb. 23—Cocoa Kid, Waterbury ....W 6
Apr. 2—Oscar Piton, West Hartford ....L 6
Apr. 4—Paul Osborne, Worcester ....D 6
Nov. 2—Steve Toomey, Waterbury...............W 6
Nov. 23—Danny Fyman, Waterbury ....W 6
1975
Apr. 9—Pete Pagan, Paterson....................L 6
Apr. 12—Jose Pagan, Waterbury ....W 6
June 3—Lou Bizzarro, Fairview ....L 10
Sept. 12—Ronnie Gibbons, Commack...............L 8
Nov. 19—Sandy Torres, New York.................L 8
1976
Jan. 24—Billy Backus, Syracuse ....L 10
July 29—Alvin Anderson, Baltimore........... KO by 3
Oct. 1—Rocky Mattioli, Milan .... KO by 2
Dec. 2—Vito Antuofermo, New York .... KO by 4
1977
Feb. 9—Jean-Claude LeClair, Quebec .... KO by 4
Mar. 5—Gratien Tonna, St. Quentin .... KO by 1
Oct. 8—Alfredo Naueiras, Liege ....L 10
Dec. 10—Floyd Mayweather, Grand Rapids ....L 10
1978
July 15—Rocky Fratto, Alexandria Bay ....L 10
Oct. 4—Rocky Fratto, Elmira .... KO by 4
Dec. 9—Rico Hoye, Detroit ....KO by 4
1979
Jan. 23—Eddy Melo, Montreal .... KO by 1
Apr. 21—Elisha Obed, Bahamas .... KO by 5
July 28—Georg Steinherr, Munich .... KO by 5
1980
Mar. 26—Steve Arvin, Scranton ....L 8

RAFAEL RODRIGUEZ
Minneapolis, Minn. Welterweight
1970
Dec. 3—Kasmun Pushkar, Minneapolis ....W 5
1971
Aug. 19—Billy Goodwin, Minneapolis .... KO 8
Aug. 26—Primus Williams, Minneapolis ....KO 2
1972
Feb. 23—Clem Tucker, Minneapolis ....KO 1
Mar. 8—Billy Goodwin, St. Paul .... KO by 4
1973
Aug. 24—Bobby Crawford, Rochester, Minn........ W 5
Sept. 26—Steve St. Charles, Las Vegas ....W 5
Dec. 14—Tim Adams, Chicago ....W 6
1974
Feb. 1—John Fuller, Minneapolis ....KO 2
Feb. 15—Keith Averett, Chicago..................D 4
Apr. 23—Johnny Montagne, Minneapolis ....W 10
May 23—Mike Morfan, Minneapolis...............KO 1
June 26—Chuck Wilburn, St. Paul ....W 10
Aug. 13—Keith Averett, St. Paul ....KO 1
Aug. 28—Joe Espinoza, St. Paul ....KO 4

1975
Feb. 3—Denny Moyer, Minneapolis...............W 10
Mar. 19—Hedgemon Lewis, Minneapolis............L 10
May 7—Hedgemon Lewis, Minneapolis............L 10
1976
Feb. 7—Tom Howard, Minneapolis ....W 10
Mar. 9—Chuchu Garcia, Minneapolis.............W 10
May 5—Angel Robinson Garcia, Minneapolis......W 10
June 2—Harold Weston, Uniondale................L 10
Sept. 8—Frank Kolovrat, Cleveland...............W 10
Nov. 30—Sammy Ruckard, Minneapolis............W 10
1977
Jan. 18—Clyde Gray, Montreal ....L 10
Apr. 15—Bruce Curry, Jersey City ....L 11
June 3—Billy Backus, Syracuse ....L 12
1978
Jan. 23—Pat O'Connor, St. Paul ....W 10
Mar. 27—Pat O'Connor, St. Paul ....W 10
May 2—Pete Ranzany, Sacramento ....L 10
June 3—Ray Leonard, Baltimore ....L 10
Sept. 27—Arnell Thomas, St. Paul ....KO 1
Nov. 14—Pete Ranzany, Sacramento ....L 10
1979
Mar. 21—Len Harden, Las Vegas ....L 8
May 15—Dave Green, London ....KO by 8
Sept. 18—Jerry Cheatham, Phoenix ....W 10
Nov. 1—Aundra Love, Phoenix ....L 10
1980
Apr. 13—Tony Chiaverini, Kansas City ....L 10
May 30—Rocky Mattioli, Rome ....KO by 8
Sept. 16—Bruce Finch, Winnipeg ....L 10

RAMON RODRIGUEZ
Argentine Flyweight
1980
Jan. 4—Miguel Lazarte, Mar del Plata ....L 10
Feb. 1—Reynaldo Romero, La Banda ....W 10
Mar. 21—Jorge Alegre, Tucuman ....KO 1
June 6—Gustavo Ballas, Villa Maria .... KO by 9
Aug. 8—Jose Lopez, Tucuman ....KO 5
Sept. 5—Gustavo Ballas, Cordoba .... KO by 10
Dec. 11—Gustavo Ballas, Mendoza ....KO by 8

REFUGIO RODRIGUEZ
Texas Bantamweight
1979
Apr. 20—Juan Carlos Aguilar, Laredo ....KO 2
June 6—Esteban Barrentes, Laredo ....KO 2
Aug. 29—Antonio Soria, Houston ....KO 3
1980
July 29—Sergio Reyna, Laredo ....KO 1
Oct. 28—Tony Tamez, Houston ....KO by 2

RODOLFO RODRIGUEZ
Argentine Flyweight
Born: Aug. 24, 1953
1974
Apr. 6—Jose Izquiedo, Pehuajo...................KO 3
May 11—Jose Silva, Buenos Aires ....W 6
June 15—Angel Fernandez, Buenos Aires............W 6
July 26—Jose Arias, Cordoba ....KO 7
Sept. 9—Jose Flores, Salta ....KO 4
Oct. 6—Alberto Correa, San Pedro ....KO 2
Oct. 23—Juan C. Rios, Buenos Aires...............W 10
Nov. 20—Gilberto Lopez, Buenos Aires............W 10
1975
Mar. 7—Felix Gonzalez, Bariloche ....W 10
Apr. 4—Felix Lopez, Rio Cuarto ....D 10
May 3—Angel Fernandez, Bariloche..............W 10
June 13—Hector Velasquez, Bariloche ....W 10
Sept. 13—Juan C. Rios, Buenos Aires ....W 10
Oct. 10—Gilberto Lopez, Huinca Renanco..........W 10
Nov. 29—Juan J. Brizuela, Buenos Aires............W 10
(Won Argentine Flyweight Title)
Dec. 19—Carlos Leyes, Parana ....W 10
1976
Feb. 1—Benigno Rodriguez, Panama ....KO 1
Mar. 11—Raul Perez, Mendoza ....W 10
Apr. 10—Carlos Escalante, Buenos Aires...........W 12
(Retained Argentine Flyweight Title)
May 7—Carlos Leyes, Tres Arroyos........ W disq. 5
June 11—Alberto Martin, Posadas ....W 10
Aug. 8—Alberto Martin, Huinca Renanco ....W 10
Aug. 18—Reyes Arnal, Caracas ....TKO 8
Sept. 13—Felix Gonzalez, Catamarca ....W 10
Sept. 26—Luis Estaba, Caracas ....TKO 11
(WBA Junior Flyweight Title)
Dec. 17—Gilberto Lopez, Cordoba ....W 10
1977
Jan. 5—Vega Ramirez, Carlos Paz ....KO 9
Mar. 19—Miguel Lazarte, Buenos Aires ....W 10
June 6—Felix Gonzalez, Villa Maria ....KO 4
Aug. 27—Carlos Escalante, Buenos Aires ....W 12
(Retained Argentine Flyweight Title)

Sept. 17—Luis Gerez, General Pico .... W 10
Oct. 8—A. Lois Fernandez, Buenos Aires .... W 10
Oct. 21—Raul (Nico) Perez, Carlos Paz ....D 10
Dec. 10—Ramon Soria, Buenos Aires .... L 12
(Lost Argentine Flyweight Title)
1978
Jan. 21—Alberto Martin, Mar de Ajo .... W 10
Apr. 13—Juan C. Rios, Posadas .... W 10
June 11—Felipe Rojas, General Madariaga .... D 10
July 22—Ramon B. Soria, Buenos Aires .... L 10
Aug. 18—Jose Ibiris, Tucuman .... KO 10
Sept. 2—Miguel A. Lazarte, Buenos Aires .... D 10
Oct. 10—A. Lois Fernandez, Buenos Aires .... D 10
Nov. 24—Carlos Escalante, C. Cuatia .... D 10
Dec. 28—Carlos Escalante, Villa Maria .... W 10
1979
—Ramon Rodriguez, Tucuman .... KO 8
—Carlos Escalante, Villa Maria .... W 10
—Luis Gerez, Arrecifes .... D 10
—Ramon Balbino Soria, Buenos Aires .... L 12
(For Argentine and South American Flyweight Title)
—Miguel Lazarte, Rosario .... W 10
1980
Jan. 4—Miguel Lazarte, Mar del Plata .... L 10
Feb. 29—Ruben Condori, Salta .... L 10
Mar. 24—Jovito Rengifo, Caracas .... L 10
Apr. 19—Gustavo Ballas, Buenos Aires .... L 10
July 12—Wilfredo Patron, Caracas .... KO 3
July 28—Ricardo Lopez, Caracas .... KO 9
Aug. 11—Armando Ugalde, Caracas .... KO 3
Sept. 29—Humberto Mallarga, Caracas .... W 10

RUBIO RODRIGUEZ
Brooklyn, N.Y. Heavyweight
1979
July 31—Ali Allen, Totowa .... L 6
Sept. 18—Ali Allen, E. Rutherford .... KO by 1
1980
Oct. 24—Ralph Cuomo, Uniondale .... W 4

SERGIO RODRIGUEZ
Haitian Heavyweight
1976
Mar. 30—Greg Johnson, Sunnyside .... L 8
1977
Jan. 16—Michael Dokes, Pensacola .... KO by 2
Nov. 27—Dane Wilson, Waterbury .... KO by 4
1978
Apr. 6—Conrad Tooker, North Bergen .... KO 2
Aug. 16—Johnny Blaine, Nanuet .... L 6
1979
(Inactive)
1980
Dec. 12—Marty Capasso, Scranton .... KO by 1

VICTOR RODRIGUEZ
San Antonio, Texas Heavyweight
1977
Aug. 31—Abel Escamilla, Austin .... KO 1
Nov. 8—Robert Reynosa, San Antonio .... KO 3
1978
Jan. 17—Francisco Garcia, Jorrean, Mex. .... KO 1
Feb. 20—Vernon Johnston, San Antonio .... KO 3
Apr. 7—Rodolfo Paloma, Piedras Negras .... KO 2
May 2—Jimo Zaragoza, San Antonio .... W 4
July 13—Walter Santemore, Hattiesburg, Mex. .....L 8
Oct. 26—Carlos De Angel, Laredo .... KO 3
Dec. 3—Carl Ivy, San Antonio .... KO 7
1979
Jan. 30—Zack Ferguson, San Antonio .... KO 4
Aug. 28—Fernando Montes, San Antonio .... L 10
Nov. 13—Bruce Scott, Beaumont .... L 8
1980
Feb. 1—Greg Page, Louisville .... KO by 3
Oct. 18—Gerald Bradley, Lake Charles .... KO by 2

WILLIE RODRIQUEZ
Allentown, Pa. Junior Welterweight
1975
Nov. 13—Bob Edison, Allentown .... KO 2
Dec. 11—John Barr, Allentown.................... W 4
1976
Jan. 29—Jose Perez, Easton .... KO 2
Mar. 8—Ron Mayberry, Allentown................ KO 1
Apr. 15—Rufus Miller, Allentown................. L 6
May 20—Ron Branch, Allentown .... W 6
June 30—George Snyder, Allentown............... W 6
Aug. 26—Luis Vega, Allentown................... W 6
Oct. 7—Luis Vega, Allentown................... W 8
Nov. 18—Jose Resto, Allentown.................. W 8
1977
Feb. 3—Rufus Miller, Allentown .... W 10

May 14—Sugar Ray Leonard, Baltimore ....L 6
Aug. 26—Quenton Blackman, Allentown .... W 10
Oct. 25—Tommy Rose, Richmond .... KO 4
1978
Mar. 4—Dick Ecklund, Boston .... W 8
April 9—Rocky Orengo, Allentown .... W 10
June 5—Norman Goins, Allentown .... W 10
Sept. 18—Charlie Nash, London .... L 10
Nov. 16—Nkosana Mgxaji, Capetown .... L 10
1979
Feb. 2—Leroy Haley, Allentown .... KO 12
Mar. 21—Mike Everett, Allentown .... KO 4
Apr. 14—Bruce Curry, New Orleans .... KO by 10
June 22—Ruby Ortiz, New York .... W 8
Sept. 19—Art McKnight, Scranton .... W 12
Nov. 22—Willie Daniels, Allentown .... KO 2
1980
Mar. 22—Rocky Bannon, Bethlehem .... W 12
(For USBA Junior Welterweight Title)
Apr. 25—Marvin Jenkins, Commack .... W 12
(Retained USBA Junior Welterweight Title)
Aug. 7—Ernest Bing, Atlantic City .... KO by 9

CHRIS ROGERS
Elizabeth, N.J. Welterweight
1979
Sept. 29—Rahman Farad, Trenton .... L 4
1980
Aug. 27—Jamal Arbubakar, Elizabeth .... L 6
Sept. 12—James Shuler, New York .... KO by 2

JESSE ROGERS
Hartford, Conn. Junior Welterweight
1978
May 26—Pedro Torres, Boston .... L 4
June 13—Nino Gonzalez, Totowa .... L 6
Aug. 3—Fernando Fernandez, Boston .... L 6
Aug. 21—Bill Ramsey, Cape Cod .... W 6
Aug. 16—Rufus Miller, Nanuet .... L 6
Oct. 8—Allan Clarke, Glace Bay .... KO by 1
Oct. 14—Al Smith, New Haven .... KO 2
Oct. 26—Hilmer Kenty, Detroit .... KO by 1
1979
—Manny Simms, Shirley .... KO by 3
Feb. 10—Marvin Jenkins, White Plains ...... KO by 1
Dec. 12—Kevin Rooney, Scranton .... KO by 1
1980
May 4—Hilton Cohen, Kiamesha Lake ...... KO by 1

LEO ROGERS
Dominican Rep. Light Heavyweight
1975
Sept. 22—Don Powell, New York .... KO 1
Oct. 20—Bob Lewis, New York .... KO 3
Nov. 28—Eddie Davis, Commack ....L disq. 2
1976
Mar. 30—Eddie Mallard, New York .... KO 2
Sept. 10—Bob Smith, New York .... KO 1
Oct. 8—Mario Rosa, New York .... L 10
Nov. 3—Boom Boom Moorer, Cleveland .... KO by 4
1977
Jan. 21—Otis Gordon, New York .... W 10
Mar. 11—Eddie Phillips, New York .... W 10
June 3—David Conteh, New York .... W 10
1978
Feb. 2—Mario Rosa, Santo Domingo .... KO 7
June 25—Faustino Quinales, Caracas .... KO 2
Sept. 26—John Conteh, London .... KO by 7
1979
Sept. 11—Jerry Martin, Philadelphia .... KO by 4
Apr. 26—Avenemar Peralta, Dakar .... W 10
May 10—Ba Sounkalo, Bamaka .... W 10
Oct. 31—Domenico Adinolfi, Rome .... KO by 9

REFUGIO ROJAS
Los Angeles, Calif. Lightweight
1979
Jan. 31—Ricky Samudio, Las Vegas .... W 6
Feb. 22—Arturo Vidrio, Los Angeles .... KO 6
Mar. 28—Fel Clemente, Stockton .... L 10
May 9—Willie Daniels, Las Vegas .... KO 4
June 7—Cookie Valencia, Los Angeles .... KO 8
Aug. 23—Roberto Torres, Los Angeles .... W 10
Aug. 25—Negro Torres, Los Angeles .... W 10
Sept. 26—Roberto Merida, Las Vegas .... KO 3
Oct. 10—Danny Patino, Las Vegas .... KO 4
Oct. 23—Gerardo Pena, Los Angeles .... L 10
1980
June 18—Leon Smith, Las Vegas .... KO 2
July 8—Henry Barcellano, Honolulu .... KO 4
July 30—Dennis Quimayousie, Las Vegas ..... KO by 8

Aug.	20—Jose Luis Piceno, Las Vegas	KO 5
Nov.	5—Rosendo Ramirez, Las Vegas	W 10

JUAN D. ROLDAN
Argentine Middleweight
Previous Record—15 fights: Won 14, Lost 1, 11 KO's
1980

Jan.	18—Roberto Troilo Ortiz, San Francisco	KO 2
Feb.	8—Juan Bogado, San Francisco	W 10
Feb.	22—Marcos Perez, Cordoba	KO 6
Mar.	15—Adolfo Cruz, Buenos Aires	KO 7
Apr.	11—Ramon Perez, San Francisco	KO 8
May	16—Ricardo Ortiz, San Francisco	W 10
June	6—Jorge Salgado, San Francisco	KO 7
June	27—Aldo Carmona, Salta	KO 3
July	8—Rogelio Zarza, San Francisco	W 10
Aug.	22—Roberto Marziali, Las Varillas	KO 1
Oct.	3—Ricardo Ortiz, San Francisco	W 10
Nov.	7—Ramon Perez, Cordoba	W 12
Nov.	21—Enrique Coronel, Salta	KO 7
Dec.	5—Jose Duran, San Francisco	KO 6
Dec.	19—Carlos Peralta, Cordoba	D 12

ADIRAN ROMAN
Argentine Flyweight
1980

Mar.	14—Jose Izquirdo, Cordoba	W 10
Apr.	19—Ruben Condori, Buenos Aires	D 10
June	6—Santos Laciar, Cordoba	KO by 3
Aug.	22—Carlos Sosa, Cordoba	KO 12

AL ROMANO
N. Adams, Me. Welterweight
1966

Dec.	8—Ronnie Butts, Portland, Me.	W 4
Dec.	15—Curt Simmons, Portland, Me.	W 4
Dec.	19—Ronnie Butts, Worcester	W 4

1967

Jan.	16—Hank Mandeville, Worcester	W 4
Feb.	20—Winston Cooke, Worcester	KO 1
Mar.	13—Frank Sanson, Worcester	KO 1
Apr.	24—Danny Heath, Worcester	L 4
May	1—Todd Pertell, Worcester	W 4
June	1—Gary O'Neil, Portland, Me.	W 4
June	23—Dan Corcoran, Pittsfield	KO 1
July	20—Ted Farmer, Portland, Me.	W 4
Aug.	31—Armand Albert, Portland, Me.	L 4
Oct.	2—Hugh Connor, Worcester	KO by 1
Oct.	12—Todd Pertell, Portland, Me.	W 4

1968

Feb.	1—Jerry Graci, Portland, Me.	L 8
Feb.	8—Eddie Beaudin, Portland, Me.	KO 6
Mar.	26—Danny Heath, Boston	KO by 1
May	23—Beau Jaynes, Portland, Me.	L 10
July	4—George Ayala, Portland, Me	KO 6
Oct.	2—Aime Moran, Lewiston	KO 1
Oct.	5—Paul Hamilton, Portland, Me.	KO 5
Nov.	7—Dave Mosby, Portland, Me.	W 8
Nov.	23—Herb Walker, North Adams	KO 1
Dec.	7—Johnny Keulian, North Adams	KO 4

1969

Jan.	2—Gene Herrick, Portland, Me.	KO 10
Jan.	11—Dave Mosby, North Adams	W 10
Feb.	12—Roy Williams, Portland, Me.	W 10
Feb.	22—Gabe LaMarca, North Adams	KO 10
Mar.	15—Johnny Pilla, North Adams	W 10
Apr.	6—Isadro Perez, North Adams	W 10
Apr.	19—Al Baschir, North Adams	W 10
May	8—Danny Heath, Portland, Me.	L 10
June	28—Isadro Perez, North Adams	W 10
July	14—Al DeJanette, North Adams	KO 1
Aug.	5—Ernie Dew, North Adams	KO 2
Aug.	18—Luc Pivin, North Adams	W 10
Aug.	25—Roy Williams, North Adams	W 10
Sept.	15—Roy Williams, North Adams	W 10
Nov.	13—Jean Maria Avena, Portland, Me.	KO 2

1970

Jan.	24—Gene Roberts, North Adams	W 10
Feb.	28—Kid Bassey II, North Adams	L 10
Mar.	21—Kid Bassey II, North Adams	W 10
Apr.	5—Walter Arsenault, North Adams	W 12
Apr.	19—Kid Bassey II, North Adams	W 12
June	8—Roy Williams, North Adams	W 12
June	22—Buddy Carr, North Adams	KO 6
July	17—Paco Flores, Tucson	KO by 2
Oct.	17—Frank Smede, Pittsfield	KO 2
Nov.	7—Arnold Sparks, Pittsfield	D 8
Nov.	21—Arnold Sparks, Pittsfield	W 12

1971

Jan.	14—Ivelaw Eastman, Pittsfield	W 12
Mar.	14—Danny Heath, North Adams	KO 9
Apr.	3—Jesus Alicia, North Adams	W 10
Apr.	20—Tom Doby, North Adams	KO 7
May	7—Jesus Alicia, North Adams	KO 8

June	28—Bob Payzant, New Bedford	KO 8
July	22—Skip Yeaton, Portland, Me.	L 10
Sept.	9—Jimmy Jaynes, Portland, Me.	W 8
Nov.	9—Jackie Turpin, Wolverhampton	KO by 2

1972

Feb.	14—Jose Pagan, Waltham	W 6
Mar.	6—Randolph Harvin, Waltham	KO 1
Mar.	24—Bruno Arcari, Turin	KO by 4
May	15—Dom Maloch, Waltham	W 8
May	22—Tony Porter, Waltham	W 8
June	24—Juan Botta, Walpole	KO by 2
July	24—Roger Phillips, Waltham	W disq. 2
Aug.	21—Fernand Marcotte, Quebec	KO by 1
Sept.	14—Larry Butler, Portland, Me.	L 10
Sept.	29—Don Cherry, Portland, Me.	KO 2
Nov.	3—Roger Phillips, Springfield	L 8
Dec.	18—Donny Sennett, Waltham	KO 10

1973

Jan.	4—Bob Richards, Portland, Me.	W 10
Mar.	31—Roger Phillips, North Adams	W disq. 2
May	31—Larry Butler, Portland	L 10
Aug.	8—Tony Petronelli, Boston	KO by 3
Sept.	10—Paul Osborne, Burlington	W 10
Oct.	12—Billy Backus, Syracuse	KO by 3

1974

Jan.	28—Chris Pina, Boston	L 10
May	7—Paul Poirier, Worcester	L 8
June	17—Jackie Smith, Worcester	KO by 7
Oct.	29—Paul Osborne, Pittsfield	KO by 4

1975

Mar.	25—Gerry Anson, Boston	W 8
July	10—Bob Pompeo, Portland, Me.	W 8
Aug.	7—Bob Pompeo, Portland, Me.	L 10

1976

Mar.	23—Jackie Smith, Boston	L 8
July	26—Jose Pagan, Peabody	W 8
Oct.	24—Billy Duquette, Brockton	W 8

1977

Feb.	27—Clyde Gray, Toronto	KO by 6
July	8—Rocky Fratto, Geneva	L 8
Sept.	8—Chris Clark, Halifax	KO by 5

1978

Jan.	28—Ricky Burgess, Albany	KO 2
Mar.	2—Ray Bryant, Cohoes	W 8
Mar.	30—Kid White, Cohoes	KO 2

1979

Dec.	1—Terry Rondeau, Albany	W 8

1980

Dec.	20—Terry Rondeau, N. Adams	W 10

ARMANDO ROMERO
Argentine Flyweight
1980

June	19—Jose Gomez, Salta	D 6
Aug.	8—Pascual Margaro, Villa Maria	L 6
Sept.	5—Pascual Margaro, Cordoba	D 6

CARLOS ROMERO
Argentine Middleweight
1980

Mar.	7—Marcelino Diaz, Campana	L 8
July	4—Jose Huala, Mar del Plata	KO 2
Aug.	1—Miguel Maldonado, Mar del Plata	L 6
Dec.	19—Jose Gigena, Tapiales	D 4

JESUS ROMERO
Argentine Lightweight
1980

Feb.	8—Raul Gonzalez, San Pedro	W 6
Feb.	29—Miguel Figueroa, Salta	W 10
Apr.	3—Emilcio Ortiz, S. Sal de Jujuy	W 10
May	9—Oscar Mendez, S. Sal de Jujuy	W 12
	(Won Argentine Lightweight Title)	
June	6—Raul Columbo, S. Sal de Jujuy	W 10
July	4—Julio Melone, Cordoba	D 10
Aug.	8—Luis Zarate, Salta	W 10
Sept.	5—Augusto Denis, S. Sal de Jujuy	KO 3
Nov.	14—Sebastien Mosqueira, Jujuy	KO 8
	(Won South American Lightweight Title)	
Dec.	5—Lorenzo Garcia, San Pedro	L 12
	(Lost Argentine Lightweight Title)	
Dec.	26—Alfredo Morales, San Pedro	W 10

MARCELO ROMERO
Argentine Junior Welterweight
1980

Mar.	8—Ruben Lizarra, Buenos Aires	KO 4
June	13—Alberto Gotz, Junin	W 4
July	11—Ramon Collado, Mar del Plata	KO 4
Aug.	16—Alberto Medisa, Buenos Aires	W 6
Sept.	19—Hugo Vicente, Salta	D 8
Oct.	10—Jorge Palais, Mar del Plata	L 8
Dec.	19—Sergio Loyola, Venada Tuerto	KO 4

ORLANDO ROMERO
Trujillo, Peru Lightweight
Born: March 23, 1960, Trujillo, Peru.
Weight: 135 lbs. Height: 5 ft. 6½ in. Southpaw.
1979

Feb.	24—Rafael Pando, Lima	W 6
June	9—Benjamin Burga, Lima	W 6
June	23—Toribio Quinto, Lima	KO 3
July	7—Florencio Huaman, Lima	KO 3
July	21—Miguel Macias, Lima	D 6
Aug.	3—Luis Carhuamaca, Lima	W 6
Aug.	17—German Calderon, Lima	KO 6
Aug.	31—Luis Granda, Lima	W 6
Oct.	22—Carlos Soriano, Trujillo	KO 2
Nov.	3—Luis (Cholo) Castro, Trujillo	KO 3
Nov.	17—Vicente Salcedo, Trujillo	KO 1
Nov.	29—Julio Sandoval, Trujillo	W 10

1980

Mar.	8—Mentor Sotilo, Lima	KO 2
Apr.	19—Domingo Gonzalez, Lima	KO 6

(Won Peruvian Lightweight Title)

June	7—Rafael Prieto, Trujillo	W 10
July	5—Carlos Avila, Trujillo	KO 2
Sept.	20—Leonidas Asprilla, Trujillo	W 12

(Won American Lightweight Title)

OSCAR L. ROMERO
Argentine Welterweight
1980

May	17—Juan C. Salomon, La Pampa	W 10
June	5—Juan C. Arrua, La Pampa	KO 3
July	5—Jose Luis Guevara, Catrilo	W 10
Nov.	15—Jose Luis Guevara, Santa Rosa	W 10

RICARDO ROMERO
Argentine Junior Welterweight
1980

Aug.	1—Hugo Vicente, Tucuman	L 6
Oct.	3—Jorge Zalazar, Tucuman	KO 2
Oct.	24—Hugo Vicente, Ros Frontera	KO by 4

RONNIE ROMERO
Salt Lake City, Utah Junior Lightweight
1980

Aug.	2—Jose Pacheco, Salt Lake City	W 4
Sept.	10—Junior Foster, Las Vegas	KO 3
Oct.	29—Rudy Mata, Las Vegas	KO 3
Nov.	26—Nestor Pinango, Las Vegas	W 6

TERRY RONDEAU
Stonehill, Mass. Lightweight
1967

Nov.	2—Bobby Diamond, Portland	W 4
Nov.	16—Henry Wickham, Portland	L 6

1968
(Inactive)
1969

Feb.	15—Paul Barrabee, Groten	W 4
Mar.	15—Jose Cruz, North Adams	W 4
Mar.	25—Rafael Santiago, Boston	W 6
Apr.	11—Eulillio Garcia, Worcester	W 4
Apr.	19—Joe Vano, North Adams	W 4
Apr.	24—Joe Croteau, Portland	KO 2
May	23—Eulilio Garcia, Worester	KO 2
June	26—Joe Croteau, Portland	KO 4
June	28—Tony Rivers, North Adams	W 10
July	14—Carlos Garcia, North Adams	W 10
Aug.	5—Carlos Garcia, North Adams	KO 6
Aug.	18—Johnny Keulian, North Adams	KO 2
Aug.	25—Tony Cruz, North Adams	W 10
Sept.	15—Norman Sanchez, North Adams	KO 2
Sept.	29—Jean LaRoux, North Adams	W 10
Nov.	13—Gaston Pelletier, Portland	KO 6
Dec.	18—Ronald Sanchagrin, Portland	KO 3

1970

Jan.	8—Bobby Singleton, Portland	W 8
Jan.	24—Henry Wickham, North Adams	KO 4
Feb.	21—Jimmy Jaynes, North Adams	L 10
Mar.	21—Gaston Pelletier, North Adams	KO 6
Apr.	4—Ivelaw Eastman, North Adams	W 10
June	8—Angel Vasquez, North Adams	KO 4
Oct.	17—Phil St. Cyr, Pittsfield	W 8
Oct.	29—Pat Maloney, Portland	W 8
Nov.	7—Phil St. Cyr, Pittsfield	W 8
Nov.	12—Bobby Richards, Portland	L 10
Dec.	5—Pat Maloney, Pittsfield	KO 2
Dec.	10—Bobby Richards, Portland	W 10

1971

Jan.	14—Bobby Richards, Pittsfield	L 2
Apr.	3—Jesus Gomez, North Adams	L 10
Apr.	00—Leo DiFiore, Portland	L 10
May	7—Ivelaw Eastman, North Adams	L 8
Dec.	11—Don Sennett, Boston	L 10

1972

Jan.	6—Phil Hudson, Portland	L 10
Jan.	10—Roger Zami, Paris	KO by 4
Jan.	20—Carlos Ortiz, Portland	KO by 4
Feb.	7—Jose Curet, Waltham	KO 4
Feb.	14—Tommy Grant, Waltham	KO by 3
Mar.	6—Ivelaw Eastman, Waltham	KO by 5
July	27—Kevin Dorian, Portland	L 6
Nov.	30—Leo DiFiore, Portland	L 8
Dec.	12—Eddie Avila, Lowell	L 6

1973

Jan.	15—Jose Pagan, Waltham	L 6
Jan.	22—Eddie Avila, Boston	L 6
Mar.	31—Leo DiFiore, North Adams	W 8
Apr.	14—Samuel Serrano, Carolina, P.R.	KO by 2

1974
(Inactive)
1975

Mar.	20—Vinnie DeBorros, Waterbury	L 6
Apr.	12—Vinnie DeBorros, Waterbury	L 6
May	1—Steve Toomey, Bristol	L 6
May	19—Dom Monaco, Binghamton	L 8

1976

Jan.	24—Johnny Harp, Syracuse	L 6
Jan.	31—Dick Ecklund, Waterbury	L 6
Feb.	16—Marc Gervais, Aylmer	KO by 7

1977
(Inactive)
1978

Mar.	2—Jimmy Corkum, Cohoes	L disq. 3

1979

Feb.	21—Ricky Burgess, Waterville	L 10
May	4—Elisha Obed, Nassau	KO by 6
Dec.	1—Al Romano, Albany	L 8
Dec.	11—Gary Giron, Sparks	KO by 3

1980

Jan.	21—Gerald Bouchard, Montreal	KO by 6

RAMON RONQUILLO
West New York, N.J. Light Heavyweight
1975

May	29—Robert Lewis, North Bergen	W 4
June	19—Eddie Mallard, North Bergen	KO by 1
June	27—Kenny Jones, Hamden	KO 1
Aug.	23—Dan McNevin, Binghamton	L 4
Sept.	24—John Gallagher, Bayonne	D 4
Nov.	5—Emerito Morales, Sunnyside	D 4
Dec.	3—Bob Green, New York	KO 6

1976

Feb.	11—Bill Sharkey, New York	L 6
May	22—Bobby Cassidy, Erie	KO 10
Nov.	24—Bobby Cassidy, New York	L 10

1977

June	24—Bob Smith, New York	W 8
Sept.	27—Bob O'Brien, West New York	KO 1
Dec.	8—Mel Richardson, North Bergen	KO 4

1978

Feb.	23—Jose Morales, North Bergen	KO 2
Mar.	17—Bobby Cassidy, Las Vegas	L 10
June	2—John Kane, Jersey City	KO 5
Dec.	1—Jimmy McClain, Jersey City	KO 5

1979

Jan.	27—Ray J. Elson, Jersey City	KO 3
June	27—Cornell Chavis, Secaucus	L 8
July	31—Ralph Cuomo, Totowa	KO 1
Sept.	18—Mike Rossman, East Rutherford	KO 6
Nov.	28—Jimmy Claar, W. New York, N.J.	KO 3

1980

Feb.	24—Michael Spinks, Atlantic City	KO by 6
July	16—Willie Taylor, Elizabeth	KO by 3

KEVIN ROONEY
Catskill, N.Y. Welterweight
1979

	—Heriberto Vasquez, Staten Island	KO 1
Dec.	12—Jessie Rogers, Scranton	KO 1

1980

Mar.	7—Norman Jones, Staten Island	W 6
Apr.	30—Frank Minigan, Scranton	KO 5
May	9—Charles Thomas, Staten Island	KO 3
May	25—Paul Moore, Scranton	W 6
July	27—Clyde Graves, New York	W 6
Oct.	23—Blas Deschamps, New York	W 6
Oct.	29—Curtis Pittman, Scranton	KO 1
Nov.	22—Jeff Passero, Scranton	W 8

ROBERT ROONEY
Philadelphia, Pa. Junior Middleweight
1976

May	7—Bo Williford, Kearny	W 4

1977 1978
(Inactive)

203

Oct. 30—Xavier Biggs, Upper Darby .... D 4
Nov. 23—Jerry Banks, Trenton .... L 4
1980
May 4—Fred McMunn, Atlantic City .... KO by 4

JOHNNY ROPER
Florida Light Heavyweight
1977
Jan. 25—John Tallarico, Orlando .... KO by 1
1978
Feb. 17—Ernie Barr, Saginaw .... KO by 2
May 12—Ted Pryor, Miami Beach .... L 4
May 16—Willie Lee Allen, Miami Beach .... L 4
July 17—Rocky Casolo, Miami Beach .... W 3
1979
Apr. 10—Bob Francino, Miami Beach .... KO by 2
Oct. 1—Leon McDonald, Ft. Lauderdale ..... KO by 1
1980
Feb. 12—Dino Belanger, Miami Beach .... L 6

TITO ROQUE
Dominican Republic Flyweight
1978
Mar. 15—Julio Guerrera, Santo Domingo .... L 6
June 23—Quiro Hernandez, Santo Domingo .... W 8
July 14—Quiro Hernandez, Santo Domingo .... W 10
Sept. 15—Elipidio DePaula, Santo Domingo .... KO by 6
Nov. 30—Ignacio Espinal, Santo Domingo ... KO by 5
1980
Mar. 10—Jose Parilla, San Jose .... L 10
Apr. 27—Orlando Maldonado, San Juan .... L 10
July 24—Ramon Cruz, Rio Piedras .... L 8
Sept. 11—Victor Acosta, San Juan .... L 10

HECTOR ROSA
Argentine Junior Featherweight
1980
Jan. 18—Diego Ramirez, S. Sal de Jujuy .... W 10
Feb. 1—Diego Ramirez, S. Sal de Jujuy .... W 10
Mar. 7—Simon Ortigoza, S. Sal de Jujuy .... KO 7
Mar. 28—Ubaldo Villalba, S. Sal de Jujuy .... KO 1
Apr. 24—Jorge Martinez, S. Sal de Jujuy .... KO 7
May 9—Juan Espindola, S. Sal de Jujuy .... KO 7
May 30—Julio C. Saba, S. Sal de Jujuy .... L 10
July 25—Juan Medina, S. Pedro .... W 10
Sept. 12—Miguel Lovera, S. Sal de Jujuy .... KO 7
Oct. 10—Americo Suarez, S. Sal de Jujuy .... D 10
Dec. 5—Adolfo Felice, San Pedro .... L 10
Dec. 26—Ruben Butiler, Salta .... D 10

MARIO ROSA
Paterson, N.J. Light Heavyweight
1970
Apr. 13—Arthur Young, Boston .... KO 6
May 7—Jimmy Hogan, North Bergen .... L 4
June 29—Dom Ortiz, Jersey City .... W 6
Sept. 16—Roland Marshall, Philadelphia .... W 6
Nov. 10—Orlando Fuller, Philadelphia............ KO 3
1971
Jan. 25—Clarence Finney, Philadelphia .... KO 4
Mar. 18—Ernesto Ortiz, North Bergen .... W 6
Oct. 28—Dave Ivory, North Bergen................ W 8
1972
Feb. 17—Len Harden, North Bergen .... L 10
Apr. 6—Ricky Ortiz, North Bergen .... W 10
May 25—Len Harden, North Bergen.......... KO by 3
Oct. 10—Willie Mack, New York.................. KO 2
1973
Mar. 23—Len Harden, Elizabeth.................... W 12
May 17—Jose Chirino, North Bergen .... W 12
Nov. 8—King George Aidoo, North Bergen .... KO 9
Dec. 17—Bobby Watts, New York.................. L 10
1974
Mar. 11—Dave Adkins, Philadelphia............... W 10
July 19—Leon Washington, New York.......... KO 9
Oct. 15—Angel Ortiz, Paterson .... KO 6
Nov. 25—Eddie Gregory, New York.......... KO by 8
1975
Mar. 20—Chris Black, North Bergen............ W 10
May 10—Eugene Hart, Philadelphia.......... KO by 4
Sept. 8—Chris Black, New York .... W 10
1976
May 21—Raymond Beras, Paterson............... KO 2
Nov. 5—Eddie Davis, New York .... D 10
1977
Feb. 4—Bob Smith, New York .... KO 4
Mar. 24—Jose Elias, Dover .... W 10
Aug. 27—Eddie Davis, Hempstead .... L 10
Sept. 27—Vandell Woods, Paterson .... W 10
1978
Feb. 2—Leonardo Rogers, Santo Domingo .... KO by 7
Feb. 16—Johnny Baldwin, Houston .... KO by 6

July 22—Billy Raiziff, Canton .... W 10
Aug. 1—Harry DeCosey, Secausus .... KO 5
Aug. 21—Richie Kates, Atlantic City .... L 10
1980
June 28—Sugar DeLeon, San Juan .... KO by 8

JESUS ROSADO
Puerto Rican Featherweight
1980
Feb. 11—Victor Acosta, Puerto Rico .... L 4
Apr. 21—Ricardo Santiago, San Juan .... D 4
July 3—Edwin De Jesus, Rio Piedras .... D 4
July 17—Edwin De Jesus, Rio Piedras .... W 6
July 31—Jose Rivas, Rio Piedras .... W 4

JOSE ROSADO
New York Lightweight
1979
Nov. 9—Martin Parham, New York, N.Y. .... L 4
1980
Feb. 5—Jack Johns, West Hartford .... L 4
Mar. 21—Jose Antonetti, New York .... L 4
Apr. 25—Raymond Johnson, Commack .... L 4

CONFESOR ROSALES
Warminster, Pa. Lightweight
1979
Nov. 15—Curtis Harris, Dover .... L 4
1980
Feb. 23—Ken Muse, Atlantic City .... L 4
Mar. 29—Ken Carpenter, Atlantic City .... KO by 1
May 4—Ken Carpenter, Atlantic City .... KO by 5

DIEGO ROSARIO
Paterson, N.J. Junior Featherweight
1980
July 17—Don Nisivoccia, Totowa .... KO 4
Aug. 1—David Brown, Totowa .... D 4
Oct. 16—Quylidil Hart, Totowa .... KO 2
Nov. 20—Edwin Santiago, Totowa .... KO 4
Dec. 18—Vegron Hill, Totowa .... KO 3

EDWIN ROSARIO
Puerto Rican Junior Featherweight
Managed by Jim Jacobs
1979
July 20—Jose Villegas, San Diego .... KO 5
Aug. 1—James Sowell, Los Angeles .... KO 2
Sept. 22—Pancho Muletta, San Juan .... KO 2
1980
Feb. 18—Leopoldo Frias, Puerto Rico .... KO 2
Mar. 10—Pascual Polanco, San Juan .... KO 4
July 7—Jose Luis Lara, Bloomington .... KO 2
Aug. 22—Javier Flores, Las Vegas .... KO 9

GIL ROSARIO
Hoboken, N.J. Middleweight
1977
Mar. 24—Tony Reid, Dover .... KO 2
Apr. 25—Al Little, Newark .... L 4
May 26—Pat Esposito, Dover .... W 4
June 9—Mike Bullock, North Bergen .... W 6
Sept. 27—Mustafa Hamsho, West New York, N.J. ...L 6
Dec. 1—Ray Villanueva, Wharton .... W 6
1978
Apr. 5—Ken Bristol, White Plains .... L 6
1979
Mar. 15—George Lee, North Bergen .... W 4
1980
Feb. 5—Muhammad Shabazz, W. Hartford ... KO by 2

JACK ROSAS
New Jersey Lightweight
1980
Jan. 24—Derrik Cuttino, Dover .... W 6
Feb. 8—Willie Hernandez, New York .... KO 3
Feb. 19—Derrik Cuttino, Totowa .... W 4
Oct. 30—Anthony Fletcher, Atlantic City .... L 6

RAZOR ROSENBERGER
Wayne, N.J. Welterweight
1978
Jan. 19—Donnel McGrea, North Bergen .... KO 3
Jan. 25—Russell Hart, Brooklyn .... KO 1
Feb. 22—Gene Muldrow, North Bergen .... W 4
Apr. 26—Bill Calabro, Youngstown .... W 6
1979
June 12—Ralph Dumont, Totowa .... KO 2
1980
Sept. 24—Sam Gervin, Struthers .... KO 5
Oct. 28—Lamont Hopkins, Warren .... W 6

RUSTY ROSENBERGER
Paterson, N.J. Middleweight
1978
Jan.	19—Ray Garcia, North Bergen	KO	1
Feb.	23—Gene Muldrow, North Bergen	W	4
May	20—Billy Perez, Trenton	KO	2
June	13—Dan Stahle, Totowa	W	6
July	18—Harry White, Totowa	KO	1
Aug.	17—Greg Duran, Totowa	KO	2
Aug.	22—John Beverage, Monaca	KO	1
Aug.	30—William Ramsay, Paramus	KO	3
Oct.	19—Bill Day, Garfield	KO	3
Dec.	15—Angel Perales, New York	W	6

1979
Mar.	13—Jose Pagan, Totowa	W	6
Apr.	27—Reggie Jones, Newark	W	12
May	25—Ralph Doucette, Montreal	KO	2
June	12—Tommy Sacco, Totowa	W	8
Sept.	18—Nino Gonzales, Giants' Stadium	L	10

1980
Apr.	30—Benny Mitchell, Youngstown	KO by	3

CLAYTON ROSS
Phoenix, Arizona Light Heavyweight
1980
Jan.	11—Rico Castillo, Phoenix	KO	3
Feb.	14—Charles Roye, Phoenix	KO	6
Apr.	12—Bobby Edwards, Tucson	W	6
May	5—Carlos Mura, Phoenix	W	6

MATT ROSS
Lawrance, Mass. Light Heavyweight
1976
June	2—Mike Benoit, Portland, Me.	W	4
June	9—Mike LaPointe, Portland, Me.	W	4
June	29—Allen Jones, Lawrence	W	4
July	20—Bill Thompson, Lawrence	KO	2
July	27—Bob Smith, Lawrence	W	6
Nov.	25—Mike LaPointe, Portland, Me.	KO	1

1977
Mar.	12—Otis Gordon, Fitchburg	KO	5
Apr.	23—Barry Proctor, Fitchburg	KO	1
June	6—Eddie Owens, Peabody	W	9
June	27—Dave Adkins, Danvers	W	10
Oct.	7—Jimmy Robertson, Lowell	KO	3
Dec.	19—Eddie Phillips, Boston	W	10

1978
Mar.	20—Otis Gordon, Boston	KO by	5
Apr.	29—Otis Gordon, Lowell	KO	4
July	15—Mike Rossman, Atlantic City	KO by	2

1979
Apr.	10—Grover Robinson, Beaumont	KO	6
May	12—Ivy Brown,	KO by	2
Oct.	30—Sylvain Watbled, Paris	KO by	1

1980
Jan.	9—Don Addison, Hartford	L	10
Apr.	29—Kid Samson, Halifax	W	10
Aug.	20—Parnell Fairley, Las Vegas	KO by	2
Oct.	2—Don Addison, Providence	L	10

MICHAEL ROSS
Philadelphia, Pa. Junior Welterweight
1977
July	14—Alseneo Green, Allentown	L	4
Oct.	6—Ken Twyne, Philadelphia	KO	1

1978
Apr.	28—Ken Muse, Upper Darby	W	4

1979
Jan.	23—Gary Hinton, Philadelphia	L	6
July	16—Greg Winston, Philadelphia	D	6
Sept.	12—Marvin Jenkins, White Plains	L	8
Nov.	14—Ron Aurit, Philadelphia	KO	6
Dec.	1—Archie Lee Matthews, Rahway	KO	2

1980
Mar.	22—Jose Gonzales, Bethlehem	D	6
Apr.	10—Curtis Harris, Atlantic City	W	6
June	5—Charlie Brown, Atlantic City	KO by	6

ADOLFO O. ARCE ROSSI
Argentine Welterweight
1980
Aug.	2—Horacio Mendez, Dariaux	W	8
Sept.	5—Antonio Brandan, Pigue	KO	8
Oct.	11—Felipe Baez, Dairiaux	W	8
Dec.	5—Luis Diaz, Dariaux	W	10
Dec.	20—Orlando Franco, Dariaux	KO	7

HUGO ARCE ROSSI
Argentine Middleweight
1980
Aug.	15—Enrique Cardozo, La Plata	KO	7
Oct.	3—Carlos Flores, La Plata	W	10
Dec.	12—Irineo Cabrera, La Plata	L	10

RON ROUSSELLE
Canadian Heavyweight
1977
Mar.	7—Toronto	KO by	1
June	1—Chris Clarke, Montreal	KO by	2
July	1—Eugene Green, Toronto	KO by	1

1978
Jan.	31—Mike Chrun, Toronto	W	6
Mar.	20—Mike Rodgers, Toronto	KO	1
July	11—Eugene Green, Toronto	KO by	1

1979
July	30—Sylvester Wilder, Toronto	KO	1
	—Mike Quinsey, Edmonton	KO	1
Dec.	11—Melvin Epps, Halifax	L	8

1980
Mar.	17—Ken Lakusta, Edmonton	KO	2
May	22—George Jerome, Kelowna	KO	5
Aug.	27—Trevor Berbick, Edmonton	KO by	1

CHARLES ROYE
Las Vegas, Nev. Light Heavyweight
1979
Jan.	17—William Banks, Las Vegas	KO	3
Feb.	28—Gary Keates, Las Vegas	L	4
Apr.	4—Niua Tofaeono, Las Vegas	KO by	1
July	11—Pete Garcia, Las Vegas	KO by	5
Aug.	29—Lee Burkey, Las Vegas	L	4

1980
Jan.	16—William Banks, Las Vegas	L	4
Feb.	6—Ron Tucker, Las Vegas	KO	2
Feb.	14—Clayton Ross, Phoenix	KO by	6
May	14—Frank Dabrowski, Las Vegas	KO by	4
July	22—Curtis Azevedo, Honolulu	KO by	1

LEE (JUNIOR) ROYSTER
(ROYSTON)
Miami, Fla. Light Heavyweight
1972
Dec.	12—Angel Estevez, Miami	L	4

1973
Jan.	30—Vinnie Curto, Miami Beach	KO by	4
	—Baby Rolle, Nassau	KO by	3

1974
June	6—Tony Greene, Tampa	W	8
July	18—Walter White, Tampa	L	10
Sept.	10—James Scott, Miami Beach	D	10

1975
Nov.	15—Walter White, Fort Lauderdale	KO	4
Dec.	19—Bill Douglas, Columbus	KO by	6

1976
July	6—Wayne McGee, Miami Beach	KO	5
Aug.	18—Robert Lloyd, Fort Lauderdale	KO by	10

1977
Apr.	10—Nat Gates, Miami Beach	W	6
Apr.	16—Ernie Barr, Miami Beach	L	10
July	21—Al Korovou, Port Moresby	W	10
July	28—Tony Mundine, Port Moresby	KO	1
Sept.	9—Tony Mundine, Brisbane	L	10
Nov.	1—Matt Franklin, Philadelphia	L	10

1978
May	19—Louis Pergaud, Essen	L	8

1979
June	4—Lottie Mwale, Liverpool	KO by	4
July	10—Eddie Gregory, Atlantic City	KO by	5

1980
Feb.	24—Luke Capuano, Atlantic City	W	8
Sept.	9—Marvin Johnson, Atlantic City	KO by	4

RICHARD (THE FLY) ROZELLE
Detroit, Mich. Bantamweight
1974
Aug.	4—Jose Davila, Seattle	KO	4
Sept.	8—Tony Miera, San Francisco	W	6
Nov.	28—Young Casanova, Las Vegas	W	8
Dec.	8—Baby Soto, Las Vegas	W	8

1976
July	24—Johnny Alexander, Kalamazoo	KO	2
Sept.	26—Mauricio Garcia, Las Vegas	KO	2
Oct.	13—Oscar Muniz, Las Vegas	W	8
Oct.	23—Jorge Flores, Las Vegas	W	8
Nov.	10—Alex Oregel, Las Vegas	W	8
Nov.	17—Alex Cota, Las Vegas	W	8

1977
Feb.	13—David Vasquez, Annapolis	W	8
	(U.S. Championship Tournament)		
Apr.	10—James Martinez, Miami Beach	W	10
	(U.S. Championship Tournament)		
June	22—Peanuts Emerson, Columbus	W	10
Oct.	13—Wardell Williams, Columbus	W	10
Dec.	1—Carlos Zayas, Houston	KO	2

1978
Jan.	19—Wardell Williams, Houston	KO	5
July	18—Lupe Pintor, Houston	KO by	5

205

Dec.	9—Jose Batista, Houston	KO by 8

1979

Mar.	14—Andrew Hill, Detroit	KO 2
May	9—Chico Rodriguez, Columbus	KO 5
July	2—Harvey Wilson, Columbus	KO 4
July	22—Willie Whipple, Canton	KO
Sept.	25—Salvador Sanchez, Los Angeles	KO by 3

1980

Mar.	8—Rocky Lockridge, Great Gorge	KO by 2
June	21—Alberto Davila, Las Vegas	KO by 2

ROBERTO (RUVALDINO) RUBALDINO
Mexican Bantamweight
(Previous Record Unavailable)

1976

Sept.	18—Rodolfo Martinez, Reynosa	KO 4

1977

Apr.	3—Cuervo Martinez, Matamoros	KO 3
Apr.	23—Socrates Batoto, Los Angeles	KO 2
May	28—Shiji Kambara, Monterrey	KO 2
July	1—Fabian Palma, Mazatlan	L 10
Aug.	5—Orlando Javierto, Matamoros	KO 6
Sept.	9—Pedro Rodriguez, Reynosa	KO 4
Nov.	19—Antonio Paisano, Los Angeles	W 10

1978

Mar.	18—Jorge Lujan, San Antonio	KO by 11
	(World Bantamweight Title)	
July	21—Cesar Desiga, Chicago	KO 4
Nov.	11—Conrado Vasquez, Houston	KO 8
Dec.	16—Enrique Muniz, Dallas	KO 8

1979

Feb.	26—Kid Shapper, Reynosa	KO 5
Apr.	10—Frank Granados, Houston	W 10
July	7—Antonio (Tono) Becerra, Mazatlan	KO 10
Oct.	6—Jorge Lujan, McAllen	KO by 15
	(For World Bantamweight Title)	

1980

Oct.	31—Enrique Muniz, Monterrey	KO 8
Dec.	29—Sergio Reyes, Reynosa	KO 6

SAMMY RUCKARD
Spartanburg, S.C. Middleweight

1971

Apr.	15—James Brown, Spartanburg	KO 5
Aug.	6—Moby Dick, Shelby	KO 3
Aug.	7—Buck Jessup, Mt. Holly	L 6
Aug.	9—Willie Gillis, Shelby	KO 3
Sept.	23—Holandus Anderson, Spartanburg	KO 4
Sept.	30—Rudy Bolds, North Braddock	L 8
Nov.	13—Marion Thomas, Brydstown	L 10

1972

Jan.	27—Johnny Howard, Norfolk	KO 7
Feb.	28—Art Kettles, Washington, D.C.	L 8
Apr.	5—Adrian Davis, Baltimore	KO by 4
Apr.	9—Anthony House, Durham	W 6
Apr.	11—Jose Gabino, Beaumont	W 10
May	16—Frank Eiselee, Beaumont	KO 2
Aug.	15—Mel Dennis, New Orleans	L 10
Aug.	22—Jimmy Owens, Beaumont	KO 8
Sept.	28—Bobby Hayman, Cleveland	L 10

1973

Feb.	12—Frank Young, Beaumont	W 10
Apr.	15—Johnny Mangum, Detroit	L 10
May	12—Gary Broughton, Windsor	KO by 3
Oct.	27—Don Cobbs, St. Louis	KO by 9

1974

Dec.	17—Larry Duncan, Spartanburg	KO 2
Dec.	25—Elisha Obed, Nassau	L 10

1975

Feb.	17—Efren Gonzalez, Beaumont	KO 4
Mar.	31—Charlie Cook, Beaumont	KO 7
Apr.	26—Clyde Gray, Toronto	KO by 3
June	16—Mike Everett, Philadelphia	L 10
July	10—Hoisa Phillips, Blacksburg	KO 1
Aug.	22—Danny Norwood, Lenoir	KO 3
Sept.	21—Cho Cho Sims, Spartanburg	KO 4
Oct.	4—Willie Smith, Lenoir	KO 3
Nov.	2—Danny Norwood, Spartanburg	KO 5

1976

Mar.	23—Gene Wells, Orlando	KO by 10
July	6—Edgar Ross, Orlando	L 10
Nov.	30—Ralph Rodriguez, Minneapolis	L 10

1977

July	15—Edgar Ross, Tampa	L 10
Aug.	5—Floyd Mayweather, Wyoming	KO by 10

1978

June	7—Sam Layton, Atlanta	KO 4
Nov.	4—Curtis Taylor, Atlanta	L 10
Nov.	21—Johnny Gant, Landover	KO by 10

1979

Jan.	31—Thomas Hearns, Saginaw	KO by 8
Aug.	10—Sam Larion, Spartanburg	KO 5
Nov.	15—Ronald Zenon, Paris	KO by 3

Dec.	12—Gary Coates, Canton	KO by 7
Dec.	23—Roosevelt Moss, Spartanburg	L 4

1980

Jan.	24—Tidjani Sidibe, Genova	KO by 3
Apr.	6—Maurice (Termite) Watkins, Houston	KO by 4

ROBERT (PEE WEE) RUCKER
Harlem, N.Y. Lightweight

1978

Sept.	8—Pete O'Keefe, New York	KO 3
Oct.	20—Bernard Porter, Atlantic City	W 4
Nov.	2—Richie Garland, New York	W 4
Nov.	20—Tony Hedgemon, New York	W 4

1979

Mar.	2—Carlos Espada, Albany	KO 1
Mar.	14—Melvin Boynton, White Plains	W 4
May	23—Benito Jiminez, White Plains	W 6
June	20—Benny Benitez, White Plains	W 6
July	16—Glen Guy, New York	KO 5
Aug.	22—Johnny Barretto, New York	W 4
Sept.	12—Mike Thomas, White Plains	KO 3
Oct.	18—Lloyd Jones, Philadelphia	KO 2

1980

Jan.	11—Tony Hernandez, White Plains	KO 1
May	14—Tomas Diaz, White Plains	W 6
July	17—Jerry Strickland, Maumee	KO 3
Sept.	17—John McQueen, White Plains	W 3

MANUEL RUELAS
Mexican Featherweight

1979

Jan.	18—Juan Sanchez, Los Angeles	KO by 1
Feb.	13—Jose Bautista, Houston	KO by 2
Apr.	4—Francisco Alvarado, Las Vegas	L 6
Apr.	11—Omar Garcia, Las Vegas	KO 2
Apr.	16—Joe Villegas, Bakersfield	D 8
Apr.	25—Ricardo Varela, Las Vegas	D 10
Sept.	12—Nicky Perez, El Paso	L 10

1980

Jan.	18—Ricardo Cardenas, El Paso	KO 1
Feb.	2—Alberto Davila, Phoenix	KO by 8
Dec.	13—Jaime Garza, El Paso	KO by 1

HUGO RUFINO
Argentine Heavyweight

1980

May	9—Ernesto Zalazar, P.R.S. Pena	L 8
Aug.	15—Roque Molina, Cordoba	KO 5
Sept.	12—Roberto Aguilar, Cordoba	W 8

BOBBY RUIZ
Mexican Flyweight

1979

Mar.	5—Guty Espadas, Houston	KO by 7

1980

Jan.	19—Armando Perez, Mexico City	L 10
Feb.	16—Pedro Flores, Monclova	W 10
Feb.	27—Juan Herrera, Merida	L 10

CIRILO RUIZ
Argentine Junior Middleweight

1980

Mar.	7—Jose Sanchez, Mendoza	KO 6
Mar.	28—Omar Salguero, Rosario	L 6
June	6—Omar Salguero, Rosario	L 12
Dec.	5—Hugo Hernandez, Bariloche	KO by 7

HECTOR RUIZ
Argentine Welterweight

1980

June	19—Hugo Vicente, Salta	W 6
Sept.	5—Geronimo Maldonado, Cordoba	W 8
Oct.	10—Sergio Combis, Rosario	L 8

ISMAEL RUIZ
Los Angeles, Calif. Heavyweight

1976

Feb.	22—Roberto Najona	KO 2
July	8—Verlee Price, Los Angeles	KO 3
July	15—John Baca, Los Angeles	KO by 1

1977

Mar.	5—Moi Martinez, Mexico City	KO 1
Mar.	25—Fernando Montes, Laredo	KO by 4
Apr.	22—David Cabrerra	KO 1
May	27—Roberto Najera, Mazatlan	KO 1
June	11—Joe Donato, Mexico City	KO 2
July	2—Jorge Flores, Los Mochis	KO 1
Aug.	27—Polo Najera, Mexico City	KO 9
Nov.	18—David Wynne, San Diego	KO 1

1978

Jan.	9—Johnny Robinson, Tijuana	KO 3
Feb.	4—Bump Kelly, Mexico City	L 10

Mar. 17—Dan Johnson, Anaheim ....W 10
Apr. 24—Macka Foley, Tijuana ....KO 4
May 12—Johnny Robinson, Mazatlan ....KO 2
Sept. 19—Terry Krueger, Houston ....L 10
Dec. 8—Nacho Villa, Juarez ....KO 3
1979
Mar. 25—Ruben Rivera, Monterrey ....KO 5
June 28—Chobo Hernandez, Juarez ....KO by 8
1980
Feb. 23—Alfredo (Mongol) Ortiz, Mexico City ......W 10
June 21—Jorge (Martillo) Flores, Mexico City .. KO by 9
(For Vacant Mexican Heavyweight Title)

MIGUEL RUIZ
Los Angeles, Calif. Junior Lightweight
1979
Apr. 25—Francisco Alvarado, Las Vegas ......KO by 6
1980
Feb. 5—Hector Cortez, San Jose ....KO by 1

RICARDO RUIZ
Argentine Middleweight
1980
Mar. 22—Jose Arajo, Buenos Aires ....L 6
June 6—Miguel Maldonado, Mar del Plata ....W 6
June 21—Miguel Maldonado, Mar del Plata ....D 6
Aug. 16—Juan Rivera, Buenos Aires ....KO 6
Oct. 3—Juan V.O. Funes, San Francisco ....W 10

ROBERTO RUIZ
Argentine Middleweight
1980
Mar. 7—Oscar Aguero, Tucuman ....KO 2
Mar. 22—Carlos Flores, Buenos Aires ....KO 7
Apr. 18—Carlos Flores, Tucuman ....TW 4
June 19—Geronimo Ramirez, Tucuman ....KO 7
July 25—Luis Gutierrez, Tucuman ....KO 7
Sept. 26—Julio Arancibia, Buenos Aires ....D 10

MIKE RUNDELL
San Diego, Calif. Junior Middleweight
1977
Nov. 18—Ronald Florek, San Diego ....KO 1
1978
Jan. 27—Bob Willcot, San Diego ....KO 2
Feb. 10—Lawrence Roldan, San Diego ....KO 1
Mar. 3—Victor Martinez, San Diego ....KO 3
May 11—Mario Neri, Los Angeles.................W 6
May 27—Gil Valdez, Los Angeles.................D 4
June 29—Eugene Baldwin, Los Angeles ....KO by 1
Dec. 15—Lalo Hernandez, San Diego ....W 6
1979
Mar. 16—Bob Willcot, San Diego ....W 5
July 7—Al Garbett, San Diego ....KO 1
July 19—Tony Certa, Jr., Los Angeles ....KO by 4
1980
Dec. 19—Charles LaCour, San Diego ....W 4

LARRY RUSHIN
Louisville, Ky. Welterweight
1979
June 1—Bobby Powell, Louisville ....KO 2
June 14—Willie Settles, River Grove ....KO 2
1980
Feb. 1—Steve Chaney, Louisville ....KO 1
Apr. 5—Darrell Green, Louisville ....L 4
July 10—Jose Santana, Chicago ....KO by 1
Dec. 12—Larry Tyson, Louisville ....KO 2

TONY RUTLEDGE
Columbus, Ohio Lightweight
1979
Dec. 28—Chico Rodriguez, Columbus ....W 6
1980
Mar. 17—Ray Mancini, Indianapolis ....KO by 1
June 1—David Alexander, Columbus ....KO 1
Sept. 18—Chuck Spicer, Cleveland ....W 4
Sept. 24—Walter Perez, Struthers ....L 4
Oct. 18—Billy Madison, Pontiac ....W 6

KEN SAALE
St. Louis, Mo. Lightweight
1980
Mar. 16—Steve Homan, Kansas City ....L 10

Apr. 3—Frank Newton, Oklahoma City ....L 12
(Oklahoma State Lightweight Title)
June 12—John Morgan, Chicago ....W 10
Sept. 25—Blaine Dickson, Las Vegas ....KO 6

JULIO CESAR SABA
Cordoba, Argentina Junior Featherweight
Born: Nov. 9, 1955
1973
Sept. 7—Juan Bega, Cordoba....................KO 2
Sept. 21—Alberto Correa, Cordoba................KO 1
Nov. 2—Manuel Munoz, Cordoba................KO 3
Nov. 23—Roberto Urretaviscaya, Cordoba ....D 10
1974
Jan. 18—Juan C. Rios, Cordoba ....D 10
Feb. 22—Roberto Urretaviscaya, Cordoba ....W 10
Apr. 19—Marcos Urquiza, Cordoba ....W 11
May 3—Felix Gonzalez, Cordoba.................D 10
June 7—Jose Arias, Cordoba....................D 10
June 28—Jose Arias, Cordoba ....W 10
Aug. 16—Juan C. Rios, Cordoba ....W 10
Sept. 27—Tito Pereyra, Cordoba..................D 10
Oct. 25—Ruben Ramirez, Cordoba................W 10
Nov. 15—Diego Vega Ramirez, Cordoba ....W 10
Dec. 20—Felix Gonzalez, Cordoba ....W 12
1975
Feb. 21—Carlos Cordoba, Cordoba................W 10
Mar. 14—Gilberto Lopez, Cordoba................D 10
Apr. 18—Carlos Lopez, La Rioja ....D 10
May 23—Roberto Barrientos, Cordoba ....W 10
June 13—Carlos Cordoba, Cordoba................W 10
Aug. 29—Gilberto Lopez, Cordoba ....W 10
Nov. 7—Jose Flores, Salta......................L 10
Dec. 5—Jose Flores, Cordoba ....W 10
1976
Jan. 16—Juan J. Brizuela, Cordoba ....W 10
Apr. 9—Juan C. Rios, Cordoba ....W 12
(Won Vacant Argentine Bantamweight Title)
May 21—Gilberto Lopez, Cordoba ....W 10
July 23—Gilberto Lopez, Cordoba ....W 10
Aug. 5—Alberto Martin, Cordoba ....W 10
Sept. 4—Juan C. Rios, Buenos Aires ....D 10
Oct. 9—Arnoldo Aguero, Cordoba ....W 12
(Retained Title)
Nov. 5—Rolando Lahoz, Cordoba ....W 10
Dec. 10—Jose Vicario, Catamarca ....W 10
1977
Feb. 4—Angel Zalazar, Cordoba ....W 12
(Retained Title)
Mar. 2—Hugo Emer, Carlos Paz ....W 10
Oct. 14—Jose T. Flores, Cordoba ....W 10
Nov. 19—Juan C. Rios, Cordoba ....W 10
Dec. 16—Raul Perez, Cordoba ....W 10
1978
Jan. 6—Juan C. Rios, Mar del Plata ....W 12
(Retained Title)
Feb. 10—Raul Perez, Cordoba ....D 10
Feb. 24—Danilo Batista, Cordoba ....W 12
(Won South American Bantamweight Title)
May 12—Diego Vega Ramirez, Cordoba ....L 10
July 13—Raul Perez, Cordoba ....W 12
(Retained Argentine Title)
Aug. 11—Esteban Bustos, Rio Tercero ....W 10
Sept. 8—Arnoldo Aguero, Cordoba ....W 10
Oct. 13—Danilo Batista, Cordoba ....W 12
(Retained South American Title)
Nov. 10—D. Vega Ramirez ....W 12
Dec. 9—Rolando Lahoz, Cordoba ....D 12
(Retained Argentine Title)
1979
Jan. 26—Carlos Sosa ....KO 4
Mar. 16—Jose Casas ....KO 10
June 2—Julian Solis, Buenos Aires ....KO by 8
1980
Feb. 15—Ramon M. Dominguez, Cordoba ....D 10
Mar. 7—Jose Narvaez, Mendoza ....L 10
Apr. 3—Adolfo Felice, Cordoba ....KO 2
May 2—Heleno Ferriero, Cordoba ....W 10
May 30—Hector Rosa, S. Sal de Jujuy ....W 10
June 13—Jose Casas, Cordoba ....W 10
July 4—Raul Perez, S. Sal de Jujuy ....L 10
Aug. 8—Pedro Burki, Villa Maria ....L 10
Sept. 12—Juan C. Cortez, Cordoba ....L 10
Nov. 7—Ceasar Villarruel, Tandil ....TL 3
(For Vacant Argentine Junior Featherweight Title)
Dec. 19—Rolando Lahoz, San Juan ....L 10

NORBERTO SABATER
Brooklyn, N.Y. Middleweight
1979
Feb. 26—Danny Pate, New York..................W 4
Apr. 6—Jesse Goodmond, New York ....W 4
Apr. 27—Gregory Ruman, New York ....W 6
June 27—Raymond Crump, New York ....KO 2

207

July	10—Danny Snyder, Atlantic City	W	6
Aug.	22—Miguel Sanchez, New York	W	6
Aug.	31—Robert Hart, New York	KO	3
Oct.	3—Tommy Sparr, New York	KO	1
Oct.	26—Al Little, New York	W	4

1980

Feb.	29—Carlton Swift, Brooklyn	W	6
Mar.	12—Jesse Carter, White Plains	KO	5
Apr.	9—Willie Ray Taylor, Brooklyn	W	8
Apr.	24—Mario Maldonado, Totowa	W	6
July	1—Garland Tipton, Memphis	KO	1
July	20—Dan Snyder, Great Gorge	KO	5
Sept.	9—Larry Rayford, Memphis	W	10
Oct.	23—John LoCicero, New York	W	10

MIKE SACCHETTI
Fairmont, W. Virginia Middleweight
1979

| Apr. | 20—Terry Duncan, Fairmont | W | 6 |

1980

May	10—Mark McCullough, Clarksburg	KO	1
Aug.	2—Speedy Brown, Clarksburg	KO	4
Aug.	17—Bernard Mays, Wyandotte	L	8
Sept.	18—Jeff Stoudemire, Cleveland	W	4
Nov.	29—Greg Harbert, Columbus	W	4
Dec.	5—Lewis Jones, Clarksburg	W	6
Dec.	16—Gerald Boiner, Cleveland	W	6

TOMMY SACCO
Alliance, Ohio Middleweight
1976

| Oct. | 2—Ernie Wicher, Alliance | W | 4 |

1977

Apr.	13—J. H. Foster, Cleveland	KO	3
May	20—Eddie West, Marion	W	4
Sept.	24—Mike Wyant, Hamilton	KO by	3

1978

| Oct. | 26—Nat Akbar, Detroit | KO by | 1 |
| Dec. | 16—Ronnie Vaughn, Alliance | KO | 3 |

1979

Jan.	11—Al Clay, Detroit	L	4
Feb.	24—Willie Brown, Alliance	W	6
Mar.	16—Steve Woods, Cincinnati	L	4
Apr.	13—Steve Woods, Cincinnati	L	4
Apr.	27—James Wallace, Dayton	KO	4
June	12—Rusty Rosenberger, Totowa	L	8
Sept.	20—Nat Akbar, Detroit	L	8
Sept.	30—Willie Brown, Canton	L	6
Oct.	30—Nino Gonzalez, Totowa	KO by	2

1980

| Apr. | 5—Rick Noggle, Akron | KO by | 4 |

UBALDO SACCO
Argentine Junior Welterweight
Previous Record—15 fights: Won 15, Lost 0, 8 KOs
1980

Feb.	16—Carlos Sulquehilde, Pinamar	KO	2
Mar.	22—Ramon Allende, Mar del Plata	KO	3
Apr.	5—Hugo Quartapelle, Buenos Aires	L	10
May	17—Juan Saucedo, Com. Rivadavia	W	10
July	11—Roberto Iluffi, Mar del Plata	KO	7
Aug.	9—Raul Fernandez, Bolivar	W	10
Sept.	13—Hugo Luero, Buenos Aires	KO	6
Oct.	17—Joel Gomez, Mar del Plata	KO	4
Nov.	14—Juan Saucedo, Tucuman	KO	6
Dec.	5—Felix Sune, Mar del Plata	W	10

LEO SAENZ
Baltimore, Md. Middleweight
1973

Apr.	25—Ivelaw Eastman, Baltimore	KO	2
May	16—Roger Phillips, Baltimore	KO	2
May	29—Clarence Finney, Baltimore	W	6
June	26—Johnny Shufford, Baltimore	KO	2
July	18—Jim Redford, Baltimore	W	6
Aug.	1—Clay Butts, Baltimore	KO	2
Aug.	15—Roger Phillips, Baltimore	KO	2
Sept.	19—Jerry Carabello, Baltimore	KO	2
Oct.	31—Johnny Simpson, Baltimore	W	6
Nov.	14—Nikita Tarhocker, Baltimore	KO	2
Dec.	5—Pablo Rodriguez, Baltimore	KO	3

1974

Jan.	16—Dave Dittmar, Baltimore	W	8
Feb.	20—Dave Dittmar, Baltimore	W	8
Mar.	4—Willie Williams, Largo	KO	2
Apr.	16—Julie Dickens, Baltimore	KO	4
May	21—Juan Ramos, Largo	KO	2
Aug.	27—Les Davis, New Orleans	KO	2
Oct.	2—Jose Anglada, Baltimore	KO	1
Oct.	18—Jose Pagan, Baltimore	KO	2
Nov.	26—Bruce Cantrell, Largo	W	10
Dec.	18—Willie Mack, Baltimore	D	10

1975

Jan.	21—Bruce Cantrell, Largo	W	10
Feb.	22—Mike Baker, Largo	L	10
Apr.	29—Mike Baker, Largo	W	10
July	23—Emile Griffith, Largo	L	10

1976

| Dec. | 2—Tyrone Phelps, Baltimore | KO | 9 |

1977

| Feb. | 13—Casey Gacic, Annapolis | L | 8 |

(U.S. Championship Tournament)

Apr.	14—Jimmy Savage, Landover	D	10
June	21—Bobby Payton, Landover	KO	5
Sept.	24—Jimmy Savage, Baltimore	W	10
Nov.	30—Rennie Pinder, Baltimore	KO	2

1978

Mar.	30—Johnny Heard, Baltimore	L	10
Oct.	6—Lamont Lovelady, Baltimore	KO by	7
Nov.	21—Archie Andrews, Landover	KO	1

1979

| July | 17—Mustafa Hamsho, Atlantic City | KO by | 6 |
| Dec. | 12—Ronnie Harris, Canton | KO by | 7 |

1980

| Mar. | 2—Mickey Goodwin, Detroit | KO by | 10 |

SULTAN SALADIN
(See EUGENE BALDWIN)
1980

Feb.	23—Manny Lopez, Greeley	L	8
Mar.	15—Manny Lopez, Denver	L	10
Aug.	23—Dave Ramos, Salt Lake City	W	8
Sept.	10—Joe Robles, Las Vegas	KO by	3

JOSE SALAS
Mexican Flyweight
1979

| Dec. | 11—Joel Loredo, Corpus Christi | W | 4 |

1980

May	20—Felix Castillo, San Antonio	KO by	4
July	15—Jose Canizales, Laredo	KO by	2
Aug.	13—Norberto Castellanos, San Antonio	KO by	4

JOSE SALAZAR
Panamanian Junior Welterweight
Amateur Record: Total Number of Fights 21,
Won, 21 Lost, 0
1977

Jan.	3—Enrique Alvia, Panama	KO	2
Jan.	30—Mauricio Quiros, Panama	KO	2
Feb.	25—Wilbert Delgado, Panama	KO	3
Mar.	20—Haydee Stewart, Panama	D	10
Apr.	10—Alfredo Junco, Panama	KO	5
May	15—Haydee Stewart, Panama	KO	9
June	20—Unknown, Panama	L	10
July	15—Antonio Amaya, Panama	W	10
Aug.	25—Rogelio Galaway, Panama	KO	6
Sept.	30—Roberto Collin, Panama	KO	3
Dec.	15—Antonio Paulet, Panama	KO	2

1978

Jan.	3—Jorge Richard, Panama	KO	5
Mar.	15—Benito Estrada, Panama	KO	3
Apr.	30—Antonio Amaya, Colon	L	12
May	15—Antonio Chifundo, Panama	KO	1
July	30—Pedro Romero, Panama	KO	2
Dec.	30—Rogelio Caloway, Panama	KO	5

1979

| Feb. | 10—Osvaldo Romero, Cartagena | KO by | 7 |
| June | 30—Luis Herazo, Colon | KO | 3 |

1980

| Sept. | 20—Miguel Betruz, Colon | W | 10 |

RAUL SALAZAR
Culver City, Calif. Junior Welterweight
1980

Mar.	27—Robert San Jose, Los Angeles	KO	3
Apr.	17—Juan Garcia, Los Angeles	W	4
May	2—Phillip Leonin, Los Angeles	D	6
May	15—Phillip Leonin, Los Angeles	W	6
July	24—Danny Plegge, Los Angeles	KO	3
Aug.	21—Ken Davis, Jr., Los Angeles	KO	3

HORACIO SALDANO
Argentine Welterweight
Born: Oct. 17, 1947
Previous Record—67 fights: Won 51, Lost 1, Drew 15, 31 KOs
1976

	—C. Molina Ortiz, Buenos Aires	W	10
Dec.	11—Ramon Mendez, Buenos Aires	W	10
Dec.	23—Vicente Martinez, Tucuman	KO	10

1977

Apr.	7—Carlos Villalba, Tucuman	W	10
Apr.	22—Hector Caceres, Tucuman	W	10
Sept.	17—Hector Caceres, Tucuman	D	10
Oct.	17—Adolfo Montenegro, Salta	KO	5

Nov. 12—Miguel A. Campanino, Buenos Aires ......L 10
1978
Mar. 31—Carlos Sosa, Santiago del Estero ....W 10
May 20—Carlos M. Gomenez, Buenos Aires ....L 10
Oct. 7—Mario Guilloti, Buenos Aires ....D 10
Nov. 18—Mario Guilloti, Buenos Aires ....D 10
1979
June 16—Simon Escobar, Buenos Aires ....D 10
Dec. 28—Hector Caceres, Tartagal ....W 10
1980
Jan. 17—Ramon Iviedo, Mendoza ....L 10
Feb. 22—Hector Caceres, S. Sal de Jujuy ....W 10
Mar. 15—Tito Yanni, Buenos Aires ....KO by 6
Nov. 15—Tito Yanni, Buenos Aires ....KO 4
Dec. 12—Hector Quintero, San Miguel ....KO 8

RAY SALDIVAR
Los Angeles, Calif. Lightweight
1976
Jan. 15—Martin Avila, Los Angeles ....W 5
Jan. 22—Guillermo Gonzales, Los Angeles ....W 5
Feb. 13—Gonzalo Montellano, San Bernardino..KO by 5
Apr. 9—Martin Avila, San Bernardino...........W 8
Apr. 21—Manny Mora, Los Angeles ....W 6
June 12—Ignacio Bravo, Fresno..................W 5
June 17—Martin Avila, Los Angeles ....W 7
June 30—Billy Turner, Stockton..................L 6
July 8—Moses Armas, Los Angeles...............L 5
Aug. 18—Dave Kibby, Las Vegas ....W 8
Sept. 16—Johnny Jenson, Los Angeles.........KO by 5
Nov. 19—Tony Sanchez, Stewart, Nev. ....W 8
Dec. 15—Richie Alvarado, Las Vegas ....W 8
1977
Jan. 19—Harvey Arnold, Las Vegas ....W 8
Feb. 16—Leonardo Bermudez, Las Vegas ......KO by 6
Mar. 23—Canelo Salinas, Las Vegas ....W 8
Apr. 5—Nick Alfaro, Incline Village ....W 10
Apr. 21—Pete Constancio, Las Vegas ....D 8
Aug. 18—Jimmy Martinez, Los Angeles ....KO 10
Oct. 8—Rafael (Bazooka) Limon, Los Angeles KO by 4
Dec. 1—Art Frias, Los Angeles ....L 10
1978
Feb. 9—Hector Cortez, Los Angeles ....KO by 9
Apr. 13—Hector Rivera, Los Angeles ....KO by 2
1979
Mar. 7—Fili Ramirez, Las Vegas ....D 10
Sept. 13—Luis Avila, Phoenix ....L 4
1980
June 19—Davey Armstrong, Tacoma ....KO by 3

HUGO SALEGA
Argentine Middleweight
1980
June 6—Oscar Ayala, Rio Gallegos ....L 6
July 25—Angel Caro, P.R.S. Pena ....L 10
Sept. 6—Jose Burlon, San Miguel ....KO by 3

JAMES SALERNO
Orlando, Fla. Light Heavyweight
Born: July 12, 1961
1977
May 24—Tiger Hall, Orlando ....W 4
June 14—Mike Rivers, Orlando ....KO 1
June 28—Frank Bass, Orlando ....W disq. 2
June 29—Billy O'Dell, Gainesville ....KO 1
July 12—Leon Futch, Orlando ....W 6
July 27—Billy Rich, Cleveland ....W 4
Sept. 15—Babe Clark, Daytona Beach ....W 6
Sept. 27—Willie Chaney, Orlando ....KO 3
Oct. 25—Jody Booth, Orlando ....KO 4
Nov. 22—Timmy Torken, Orlando ....KO 4
1978
Mar. 16—Willie Brown, Hollywood ....KO 2
June 23—Willie Goodwin, Orlando ....W 6
Aug. 22—Gary Smith, Orlando ....KO 5
Sept. 19—Rock Stevens, Orlando ....KO 2
Dec. 12—Sam Bowen, Orlando..................KO 4
1979
Jan. 17—Willie Goodman, Orlando ....W 6
Mar. 16—Henry Mitchell, Savannah ....KO 8
Mar. 19—Rodney Moore, Ft. Lauderdale ....KO 3
Apr. 10—Frank Bass, Miami Beach ....KO 5
Apr. 19—Willie McIntyre, Savannah ....W 8
Aug. 12—Alvaro Lopez, Las Vegas ....W 10
Nov. 27—Starlin Woodside, Miami Beach ....KO 7
Dec. 18—Carl Baker, Miami Beach ....KO 6
1980
Jan. 29—Leon McDonald, Miami ....L 10

JORGE SALGADO
Argentine Light Heavyweight
1980
Mar. 14—Carlos Pouyannes, Mendoza ....W 10

June 6—Juan D. Roldan, San Francisco ......KO by 7
Oct. 24—Angel Salinas, Ciudadela ....W 10
Nov. 28—Juan Cuellar, Tapiales ....KO 2
Dec. 12—Alfredo Morales, La Plata ....KO 2

OMAR SALGUERO
Argentine Welterweight
Mar. 28—Cirilo Ruiz, Rosario ....W 6
Apr. 25—Juan Saucedo, Rosario ....W 10
June 6—Cirilo Ruiz, Rosario ....W 12
Aug. 22—Santiago Portillo, Tucuman ....KO by 6

ANGEL SALINAS
Argentine Light Heavyweight
1980
Apr. 11—Carlos Burlon, Ciudadela ....KO 9
Sept. 5—Alfredo Morales, Mar del Plata ....KO 5
Oct. 24—Jorge Salgado, Ciudadela ....L 10

ANGEL SALINAS
Phoenix, Ariz. Junior Welterweight
1979
Dec. 18—Ronald Strode, Honolulu ....KO by 3
1980
Jan. 20—Nicky Perez, Tucson ....KO by 2

CHICO SALINAS
California Welterweight
1979
Oct. 30—Carlos Ramos, Bakersfield ....KO 8
Nov. 19—Candido Acosta, Bakersfield ....KO 3
Dec. 10—Carlos Ramos, Bakersfield ....W 10
1980
May 30—Phillip Montellano, Bakersfield ....KO 4
Mar. 26—Idika Nsofor, Las Vegas ....KO 7
Apr. 21—Rudy Barro, Bakersfield ....L 10
June 30—Dario De Jesus, Bakersfield ....KO 5
July 26—Joey Robles, Los Angeles ....L 10

ENRIQUE SALLAGO
Argentine Welterweight
1980
June 6—Jose Alvarado, Trelew ....KO 6
Aug. 8—Nestor Vittadini, Trelew ....KO 7
Oct. 10—Juan Olivera, Trelew ....KO 8

JUAN C. SALOMON
Argentine Welterweight
1980
Feb. 8—Alberto Prieto, Laboulaye ....L 10
Feb. 23—Juan R. Cabral, Calefu ....KO by 9
May 9—Jorge Zalazar, Rio III ....KO by 4
May 17—Oscar Romero, La Pampa ....L 10
July 12—Juan R. Cabral, Guatrache ....KO by 6

TONY SALVATORE
Montreal, Canada Featherweight
1979
Apr. 30—Guy Boutin, Montreal ....D 4
June 2—Herman Ingram, Syracuse ....W 6
July 13—Felix Rodriguez, Rochester ....KO 2
Oct. 26—Ken Lomax, Rochester ....KO 1
1980
Jan. 20—Leonard Pinnock, Quebec City ....W 6
Mar. 25—Maurice Deroy, Montreal ....W 6
Apr. 19—Joshua King, Syracuse ....W 6
July 25—Bob Ingram, Rochester ....W 8

ARNOLD SAM
Yerington, Nev. Heavyweight
1978
July 3—Lew Lockwood, Gardnerville ....KO by 2
Aug. 22—Harvey Steichen, Couer d'Alene .....KO by 4
Sept. 14—Harvey Steichen, Portland ....KO by 6
Oct. 30—Alex Rios, Carson City ....D 4
1979
Jan. 18—Gary Phillips, Portland ....L 4
Apr. 21—Bennett White, Elko ....L 5
Apr. 21—Steve Asher, Couer d'Alene ....W 4
June 16—Lew Lockwood, Yerington ....L 6
July 4—James Hoover, Las Vegas ....W 4
Aug. 8—Jeff Podgurski, Las Vegas ....KO by 4
Sept. 11—Ken Austin, Reno ....KO by 6
Oct. 31—Jeff Podgurski, Las Vegas ....KO by 5
1980
Jan. 17—Val Gassaway, Stateline ....KO 3
Mar. 10—John Zuroggen, Sparks ,,,,,,,,,,,,,L 6
June 14—Steve Chase, Yerington ....W 0
Dec. 17—Larry Ware, Crystal Bay ....L 6

KID SAMSON
(RONALD SESSIONS)
Philadelphia, Pa. Light Heavyweight
1974
Apr.	8—Bob Payton, Philadelphia	L	4
May	22—John Martino, Philadelphia	KO	1
June	4—Tyrone Phelps, Philadelphia	L	6
Oct.	22—Bob Payton, Philadelphia	L	6
Nov.	12—Rudy Donato, Philadelphia	KO by	2

1975
Jan.	28—Eddie Benson, Philadelphia	W	4
Mar.	28—Tim Kirk, Philadelphia	KO	1
Nov.	18—Youngblood Williams, Philadelphia	L	6

1976
Nov.	3—Scotty Tate, Philadelphia	KO	1

1977
Feb.	3—Louis Rodriguez, Allentown	L	6
May	16—Charlie Singleton, Chester	L	6

1978
Feb.	10—Curtis Parker, Philadelphia	L	6
Sept.	19—John Davis, New York	L	6

1979
Apr.	25—Ralph Mifka, Scranton	L	6
May	11—Butch Turner, Commack	L	6
June	29—John Davis, Commack	L	6
Aug.	3—Willie Stallings, Hempstead	L	8
Aug.	14—Tom McNeece, Atlantic City	D	6
Oct.	12—Gary Clancy, Uniondale	L	4
	—James Anthony, Shirley	KO	1
Nov.	28—Eddie Gregory, Hauppauge	KO by	4

1980
Jan.	19—Bobby Cassidy, Hempstead	KO by	6
Mar.	22—Junior Edmonds, Atlantic City	L	6
Apr.	16—Roddy Mac Donald	L	6
Apr.	29—Matty Ross, Hull	L	10
May	16—Charlie Singleton, Chester	L	6
Sept.	5—Steve Zouski, Dorchester	L	10
Oct.	4—Kerry Judge, McAfee	L	4
Nov.	1—Rico Montalban, Richmond	L	4
Dec.	20—John Green, Richmond	KO	4

AUGUSTIN SANCHEZ
Los Angeles, Calif. Flyweight
1978
Apr.	24—Alonzo Gonzalez, Bakersfield	L	6
July	5—Alonso Gonzalez, Las Vegas	L	10
Sept.	14—Jose Herrera, Los Angeles	KO by	5
Nov.	25—Arturo Tebaqui, Las Vegas	L	6
Dec.	14—Jaime Garza, Los Angeles	KO by	2

1979
June	18—Alonzo Gonzales, Los Angeles	KO by	9
Nov.	6—Mark Pacheco, Sparks	L	6
Dec.	18—Mark Pacheco, Sparks	KO by	9

1980
May	2—Jose Herrera, Los Angeles	KO by	3
June	18—Candy Iglesias, Las Vegas	KO by	7
Aug.	19—Eduardo Acosta, Stockton	KO by	5

ENRIQUE SANCHEZ
Dominican Rep. Bantamweight
(Previous Record Unavailable)
1977
Mar.	5—Francisco Leta, Santo Domingo	KO	4
Mar.	26—Alberto Rodriguez, Santo Domingo	KO	4
Nov.	14—Rafael Sosa, Santo Domingo	KO	2

1978
Feb.	2—Leopoldo Frias, Santo Domingo	W	10
Mar.	15—Felix Llanos, Santo Domingo	KO	1
Apr.	14—Ramon Perez, Santo Domingo	KO	9
June	23—Lazaro Fabian, Santo Domingo	KO	3
July	14—Manuel Vasquez, Santo Domingo	W	10
Aug.	28—Justo Garcia Fernandez, Santo Domingo	KO	3
Sept.	26—Ben Ramirez, Santo Domingo	KO	8

1979
Feb.	26—Andres Hernandez, Santo Domingo	L	10

1980
Aug.	25—Andres (Malanga) Torres, Santo Domingo	KO	2
Oct.	20—Enrique Brown, Santo Domingo	KO	1
Nov.	28—Angel Marrero, New York	W	10

GABRIEL SANCHEZ
Argentine Lightweight
1980
Mar.	7—Luis Quevedo, San Lorenzo	W	10
May	23—Victor Escobar, P.R.S. Pena	L	10
Aug.	1—Juan J. Galvez, Rosario	KO	3
Sept.	5—Ramon Moreyra, Rosario	W	10
Oct.	3—Jose Filippi, Rosario	W	10
Oct.	31—Hipolito Nunez, Cordoba	W	10

HUMBERTO SANCHEZ
Argentine Junior Lightweight
1980
June	'13—Juan Ocana, San Luis	KO	5
July	18—Mario Bellini, Mendoza	D	6
Oct.	7—Norberto Reyna, Mendoza	W	6

JUAN SANCHEZ (MANUEL)
Bakersfield, Calif. Featherweight
1977
Jan.	15—Richard Fowler, Las Vegas	KO	5
Sept.	22—Roman Almaguer, Los Angeles	W	4
Oct.	6—Horacio Pintado, Los Angeles	W	5
Nov.	22—Eulogio Bojorquez, Sacramento	L	6
Dec.	13—Eulogio Bojorquez, Sacramento	D	6

1978
May	19—Valentin Holguin, Bakersfield	L	8
May	25—Juaquin Alvarado, Denver	KO	5
July	6—Jose Luis Lara, Los Angeles	KO	6
July	31—Fili Ramirez, Bakersfield	D	8
Dec.	7—Jose Posos, Los Angeles	KO	4
Dec.	—Frank Newton, Oklahoma City	L	6

1979
Jan.	18—Manuel Ruelas, Los Angeles	KO	1
Feb.	1—Arturo Rojas, Los Angeles	L	8
Apr.	24—Gary Pittman, Missoula	L	6
Aug.	2—Pancho Vellez, Los Angeles	KO	3
Aug.	23—Memo Arsola, Los Angeles	W	6
Nov.	1—Tony Tejera, Albuquerque	KO	2

1980
June	26—Arturo Frias, Los Angeles	KO by	1

JULIO SANCHEZ
Argentine Welterweight
1980
Apr.	26—Carlos Chacon, Buenos Aires	KO	1
May	—Manuel Alvarez, Buenos Aires	D	6
June	14—Alejo Acosta, Baradero	W	6

MIGUEL SANCHEZ
Bridgeport, Conn. Junior Middleweight
1979
Aug.	18—Ray Rivera, Lowell	KO	2
Sept.	22—Norberto Sabater, Bristol	L	4
Sept.	27—Robert Davis, Bristol	W	4
Oct.	10—Darnell Smith, White Plains	KO	1
Oct.	17—Robert Davis, Hartford	W	4
Nov.	5—Brian Smith, Hartford	KO	1
Nov.	15—Felix Campos, Bristol	KO	2
	—Charles Newell, Hartford	KO	1
Dec.	12—Steve Arvin, Scranton	KO	4
Dec.	18—Gerald Clark, Fairfield	KO	2

1980
Jan.	9—John Griffin, Hartford	KO	1
Feb.	28—Johnny Davis, Hartford	KO	5
Apr.	24—Guy Kennedy, Totowa	KO by	8

SERGIO SANCHEZ
Mexican Welterweight
1980
Feb.	23—Andres Fernandez, Mexico City	KO	3
Mar.	15—Francisco Torres, Mexico City	KO	5
Apr.	19—Raul Arroyo, Mexico City	KO	3
June	7—Nicolas Herrera, Mexico City	KO	8
July	30—Jaime Chavez, Mexico City	KO	2

TONY SANCHEZ
Houston, Texas Junior Lightweight
1972
	—Enrique Muniz, Monterrey	KO	4
	—Carlos Hernandez, Monterrey	KO	1
	—Ernesto Ruiz, Piedras Negras	KO	3
	—Hector Pena Duque, Musquiz	KO	2
	—Marcelo Dimas, Linares	KO	3
	—Joe Contreras, Monterrey	KO	5
	—Javier Moncalves, Piedras Negras	KO	6
	—Jose Luis Gonzalez, Monterrey	KO	5
	—Jose Luis Castillo, Monterrey	KO	2
July	10—Baby Ruiz, Piedras Negras	KO	2
July	28—Ichi Hernandez, Monterrey	KO	2
	—Valente Morales, Monterrey	KO	2
Oct.	30—Warren Matthews, New Orleans	W	6
	—George Tobias, Houston	KO	2

1973
	—Lorenzo Zarzosa, Houston	KO	3
	—George Tobias, Houston	KO	1
Feb.	7—Chamaco Medrano, Houston	W	10
May	29—Rodolfo Ibarra, Houston	KO	3
Nov.	7—Bobby Holderfield, Alexandria	KO	3
Nov.	29—Nani Marrero, Tampa	D	8
Dec.	20—Tony Rocha, Houston	KO	3

1974

Mar.	7—Apolonio Salinas, Houston	KO	2
Mar.	15—Warren Matthews, Alexandria	L	10
May	6—Santos Luis Rivera, San Juan	KO by	7
May	14—Lupe Cantu, Corpus Christi	KO	2
June	1—Tony Rocha, Corpus Christi	D	10
July	16—Gus Rodriguez, Houston	KO	9
Aug.	27—Ismael Gallegos, Houston	KO	6
Sept.	17—Art Leon, Houston	L	10

1975

July	16—Valente Ramos, Houston	W	12

1976

Mar.	8—Warren Matthews, New Orleans	KO by	1
Sept.	9—Gaby Cantera, San Antonio	KO by	3

1977

Apr.	1—Felix Greaves, New York	L	4
May	17—Sean O'Grady, Oklahoma City	KO by	2
Aug.	27—Aureliano Castillo, Mexico City	NC	7

1978

Mar.	2—Abraham Perez, Stockton	KO by	5
Apr.	23—Herman Montes, Los Angeles	KO by	5
June	7—Reynaldo Zaragoza, Stockton	KO by	2

(Retired after above bout.)

1979

Mar.	28—Ruben Castillo, Lake Tahoe	KO by	2

1980

Mar.	25—Gilberto Garza, Houston	KO	2
July	18—Reuben Muniz, Odessa	KO by	2

ABDUL SANDA
New Paltz, N.Y. Light Heavyweight

1980

May	31—Larry Davis, Elizabeth	W	4
June	26—Steve Valencia, New York	KO	1
Aug.	29—Steve Valencia, New York	KO	1
Sept.	12—Don Miller, Hartford	KO	3
Sept.	24—Jamal Arbubakar, Elizabeth	L	4
Oct.	14—Fernando Collazo, W. Hartford	KO	1

TED SANDERS
Los Angeles, Calif. Middleweight

1977

June	24—Greg Stephens, San Diego	KO by	3
Aug.	6—Russell Pope, Fresno	D	6
Aug.	12—Robby Epps, San Diego	L	6

1978

Apr.	24—Len Harden, Las Vegas	L	8
June	29—Ricky Weigel, Los Angeles	L	6
July	20—James Waire, Los Angeles	L	6
Nov.	16—James Waire, Los Angeles	L	6
Dec.	15—Steve Delgado, San Diego	L	10

1979

Jan.	17—Chris Black, Las Vegas	KO by	2
Mar.	14—Len Harden, Las Vegas	D	8
Mar.	29—Richard Abbott, Los Angeles	W	6
Apr.	24—James Waire, San Carlos	L	4
May	20—Mickey Goodwin, Las Vegas	W	10
July	25—Chris Black, Las Vegas	KO	3
Aug.	10—Renato Garcia, San Diego	W	10
Aug.	29—Robert Powell, Las Vegas	W	10

1980

Jan.	16—Ron Brown, Las Vegas	W	10
Apr.	19—Ray Seales, Billings	KO by	7
Aug.	1—Rocky Mosley, Las Vegas	D	10
Sept.	9—Mike Colbert, Las Vegas	L	12

(Nevada State Middleweight Title)

Nov.	29—J. B. Williamson, Los Angeles	L	10

ALBERTO SANDOVAL
Los Angeles, Calif. Bantamweight

1975

Aug.	23—Rufino Hernandez, Los Angeles	W	6
Sept.	13—Ignacio Osornio, Los Angeles	KO	1
Sept.	27—Rufino Hernandez, Los Angeles	W	6
Dec.	18—Sergio Martinez, Los Angeles	W	6

1976

Feb.	5—Bobby Holderfield, Los Angeles	KO	3
Mar.	4—Juan Lopez, Los Angeles	KO	5
Mar.	18—Juan Rodriguez, Los Angeles	KO	4
Apr.	1—Catalino Flores, Los Angeles	KO	5
Apr.	29—Juan Rodriguez, Los Angeles	KO	3
July	1—Alberto Cabanig, Los Angeles	W	10
July	22—Raul Ochoa, Los Angeles	KO	2
Aug.	12—Johnny Meza, Los Angeles	KO	2
Sept.	9—Raul Pacheco, Los Angeles	KO	5
Oct.	14—Young Casanova, Los Angeles	W	10
Dec.	2—Jose Del Rio, Los Angeles	KO	5

1977

Jan.	27—Frankie Granados, Los Angeles	W	10
Mar.	2—Halimi Gutierrez, Los Angeles	KO	9
Mar.	31—Young Casanova, Los Angeles	KO	3
May	21—Paddy Maguire, Los Angeles	KO	3
June	30—Tony Moreno, Los Angeles	KO	3
July	28—Alberto Morales, Los Angeles	W	10

Sept.	13—Rafael Rubio, Los Angeles	KO	3
Nov.	3—Catalino Flores, Los Angeles	KO	4
Dec.	10—Orlando Javierto, Los Angeles	KO	6

1978

Feb.	2—Eliseo Cosme, Los Angeles	TL	4
Mar.	23—Eliseo Cosme, Los Angeles	KO	5
Apr.	23—Socrates Batoto, Los Angeles	KO	6
June	15—Freddie Gonzalez, Los Angeles	KO	1
Oct.	5—Raul Pacheco, Los Angeles	KO	2
Oct.	26—Alfonso Zamora, Los Angeles	KO by	9

1979

Mar.	15—Eddie Logan, Los Angeles	L	10
May	3—Eddie Logan, Los Angeles	W	10
July	19—Javier Flores, Los Angeles	W	10
Sept.	20—Juan Alvarez, Los Angeles	W	10
Nov.	29—Catalino Flores, Los Angeles	W	TD

1980

Feb.	9—Lupe Pintor, Los Angeles	KO by	12

(For WBC Bantamweight Title)

BLACKIE SANDOVAL
Albuquerque, N.M. Bantamweight

1979

Feb.	21—Mario Chavez, Las Vegas	KO by	1

1980

May	5—Isaac Vega, Chicago	KO by	2

LUIS SANDOVAL
Tijuana, Mexico Bantamweight
(Previous Record Unavailable)

1979

May	5—Ismael Santana, Chicago	KO by	3

1980

June	3—Mike Barry, Las Vegas	KO	2
July	17—Jaime Garza, Los Angeles	KO by	3

RICARDO (RICHARD) SANDOVAL
Pomona, Calif. Flyweight

1980

Nov.	5—Gerardo Pedroza, Las Vegas	KO	2
Dec.	26—Miguel Juarez, Las Vegas	KO	1

ISMAEL SANTANA
Puerto Rican Junior Featherweight

1979

May	5—Luis Sandoval, Chicago	KO	3
Aug.	4—Leo Cruz, Chicago	KO by	4

1980

Sept.	22—Otto Breeding, Chicago	KO	6

JOSE SANTANA
Panamanian Featherweight

1977

Jan.	29—Carlos Mimila, Panama City	W	10
Apr.	2—Eusebio Pedroza, Panama City	L	10
Dec.	3—Domingo Ayala, San Juan	KO	7

1978

Feb.	12—Hector Colon, Carolina	W	4
May	13—Jorge Mojica, Carolina	L	4
July	30—Jacob Torres, San Juan	KO	9
Sept.	9—Manny Torres, Chicago	KO	1
Dec.	16—Salvatore Sanchez, Mexico City	KO by	2

1979

Mar.	24—Amie Peregrino, Chicago	KO	6
May	6—Ruben Vasquez, Chicago	W	10
June	6—Carlos Nunez, City of David	L	12
July	30—Jose Palacios, Chicago	KO by	7

1980

Jan.	30—Rosendo Ramirez, Las Vegas	L	8
Nov.	15—Francisco Perez, Chiriqui	L	10

RAMON (CHICO) SANTANA
Dominican Rep. Featherweight

1977

Apr.	15—Inocencio Pena, Santo Domingo	L	10
June	24—Ramoncito Cruz, Santo Domingo	W	6
Sept.	16—Leopoldo Frias, Santo Domingo	L	8

1978

Feb.	2—Jose Pena, Santo Domingo	L	10

1979

Sept.	22—Heriberto Olivares, San Juan	L	10

1980

Aug.	18—Leopoldo Frias, San Juan	KO by	8

TONY SANTANA
Brooklyn, N.Y. Lightweight
Managed by Michael R. Jones

1979

	—Melvin Boynton, New York	KO	2
Oct.	10—Ron Newby, White Plains	KO	1
Oct.	25—Felix Matos, Staten Island	KO	3

1980

Feb.	29—John Jones, Brooklyn	KO	1

Apr.	9—Tony Hernandez, Brooklyn	KO	2
May	2—George Casher, New York	KO	4
May	25—Antonio Nieves, Atlantic City	W	6
June	27—Kato Ali, New York	W	6
Sept.	12—Robert Johnson, New York	W	6
Oct.	2—Jose Muniz, Commack	KO	1
Oct.	24—Jose Rentas, Uniondale	KO	3
Dec.	12—Jose Rivera, New York	W	8

WALTER SANTEMORE
New Orleans, La. Heavyweight
1976

Apr.	19—Tom Nicks, Pensacola	W	6
Aug.	23—John Tate, Memphis	L	6
Dec.	15—Tommy Collins, New Orleans	W	6

1978

Apr.	18—Charles Smith, New Orleans	W	6
May	9—Larry Alexander, Memphis	W	6
July	7—John Tate, Orlando	KO by	6
July	13—Victor Rodriguez, Hattiesburg	W	8
Aug.	8—Willie Shannon, Orlando	KO by	2
Sept.	21—Larry Alexander, Birmingham	W	10

1979

| Mar. | 23—Roy Williams, Rosemont | KO by | 5 |

1980

Feb.	12—Jeff Sims, Miami	KO by	1
Mar.	31—Dwain Bonds, Knoxville	L	6
May	15—James Tillis, Chicago	L	10

ABEL SANTIAGO
Allentown, Pa. Welterweight
1978

| Sept. | 20—Galand Wright, Scranton, Pa. | L | 4 |
| Oct. | 22—Kevin Howard, Allentown, Pa. | KO by | 4 |

1979

Feb.	8—Melvin Al Hauser, New Kensington	KO by	3
Mar.	21—Jose Amaro, Allentown	W	4
Aug.	18—Tony Suero, Atlantic City	L	4

1980

Jan.	30—Darnell Smith, Allentown	W	4
Mar.	22—Paul Moore, Bethlehem	W	4
May	23—Kevin Griffith, Bethlehem	KO by	2
Nov.	20—James Green, Totowa	KO by	1

EDWIN SANTIAGO
Hoboken, N.J. Bantamweight
1980

July	16—Pipino Oquendo, Elizabeth	W	4
Aug.	27—David Brown, Elizabeth	KO	2
Nov.	20—Diego Rosario, Totowa	KO by	4

MARCIAL SANTIAGO
Brooklyn, N.Y. Featherweight
1975

| Dec. | 5—Luis Cabrera, New York | KO | 1 |

1976

| Feb. | 25—Dan Tratzinski, New York | W | 6 |

1977

Jan.	18—Thomas Ackree, New York	KO	1
Feb.	11—Angel Ortiz, New York	L	6
Mar.	25—Fernand Rivera, New York	L	6
Aug.	12—Manuel Quiles, New York	D	4
Sept.	23—Manuel Quiles, New York	L	6

1978

| Aug. | 17—Leo Randolph, Totowa | L | 6 |

1979

| June | 14—Carmelo Negron, New York | KO by | 6 |

1980

Mar.	12—Derrik Holmes, Washington, D.C.	L	10
May	9—Mike Ayala, Commack	L	10
June	19—Rocky Lockridge, Totowa	KO by	3
Oct.	28—Ron White, New York	W	4

CARLOS SANTOS
Puerto Rican Junior Middleweight
1977

| May | 22—Juan Polanco, San Juan | KO | 2 |
| July | 11—Alex Porrata, San Juan | W | 6 |

1978

Mar.	25—Jose Collamtes, San Juan	KO	4
June	3—Feliciano Cintron, San Juan	KO	3
Sept.	9—Ricky Weigel, San Juan	W	8
Oct.	28—Tyrone Philps, San Juan	KO	4

1979

Jan.	27—Mustafa Ali, San Juan	KO	7
Apr.	2—Mario Ramos, Santo Domingo	KO	8
June	16—Felix Pagan Pintor, San Juan	W	8
Aug.	11—Gilberto Almonte, Trujillo	KO	3

1980

| Apr. | 4—Charley Peterson, Milan | KO | 2 |

JOHNNY SATO
Stockton, Calif. Junior Lightweight
1977

| Nov. | 28—Ray Banash, Cagayon | KO | 5 |

1978

Feb.	4—Tony Jumao-ao, Cebu City	W	10
May	13—Neme Jun, Cag do Oro	L	10
June	30—Leo Viajedor, Manila	W	10
Nov.	4—Arman Bangoyan, Cag do Oro	W	10

1979

Jan.	20—Nardito Adrayan, Santos City	KO	6
Feb.	23—Max Boy Toyogon, Manila	KO	5
Mar.	11—Hurricane Teru, Tokyo	L	10
Apr.	21—Nitoy Bantilan, Santos City	KO	7
June	22—Ryu Fukida, Manila	W	10
Sept.	26—Roger Henry, Manila	KO	5

1980

Mar.	27—Roberto Garcia, Stockton	W	10
Apr.	24—Miguel Mesa, Stockton	W	10
July	16—Antonio Becerra, Stockton	W	10
Aug.	26—Roy Hernandez, Honolulu	W	10
Nov.	5—Reynaldo Zaragoza, Stockton	KO	8

JOHNNY SAUCEDO
Sacramento, Calif. Junior Featherweight
1979

May	15—Richard Savala, Sacramento	KO by	4
Sept.	11—Jose Corona, Reno	KO	4
Dec.	11—Augustin Serros, San Jose	L	6

1980

| Apr. | 18—Eduardo Pagan, Santa Rosa | W | 6 |

JUAN SAUCEDO
Argentine Welterweight
1980

Mar.	7—Miguel Dominguez, Mendoza	D	8
Apr.	25—Omar Salguero, Rosario	L	10
May	17—Ubaldo Sacco, Rio Negro	L	10
July	25—Miguel Combi, Rosario	W	10
Aug.	22—Miguel Combi, La Villaras	W	10
Sept.	26—Mario Matthysse, Rosario	L	10

LARRY SAVAGE
Philadelphia, Pa. Lightweight
1979

June	12—Dujuan Johnson, Detroit	KO by	2
Aug.	—Pat Brennan, Hempstead	D	4
Dec.	5—Gino Perez, White Plains	KO by	4

1980

| Mar. | 21—Pat Brennan, New York | KO by | 2 |
| May | 4—Jose Antonetti, Kiamesha Lake | KO by | 2 |

MARIO SAVALA
Sacramento, Calif. Bantamweight
1980

Apr.	1—Gil Brown, Sacramento	KO	1
May	27—George Maldonado, Sacramento	KO	2
July	1—Mario Cortez, Sacramento	KO	2
Sept.	5—Vince Bratcher, Sacramento	KO	1

RICHARD SAVALA
Sacramento, Calif. Featherweight
1979

May	15—Johnny Saucedo, Sacramento	KO	4
Sept.	12—Bobby Mercado, Stockton	W	6
Nov.	7—Arsenio M. Gonzales, San Jose	W	6

1980

Feb.	5—Adolfo Hurtado, Sacramento	KO by	4
Feb.	29—Ronnie Furlow, San Carlos	KO	8
Apr.	1—Humberto Lara, Sacramento	W	6
June	12—Mike Rodriguez, Los Angeles	KO	1
June	19—Desi Newbill, Los Angeles	KO	5
July	1—Milciades Jiminez, Sacramento	KO	3
Sept.	5—Lionel Harney, Sacramento	KO	1
Sept.	30—Gary Spencer, Sacramento	W	10

ROBERT SAWYER
Washington, D.C. Welterweight
1980

July	17—Hubert Jackson, Totowa	KO	1
Sept.	4—Xavier Biggs, Atlantic City	KO	2
Oct.	4—Eric Perea, McAfee	KO	2

MIKE SCHEIBLEHOOD
Akron, Ohio Heavyweight
1975

| Feb. | 11—Dave Vent, Toronto | KO | 6 |

1976

| May | 18—Skippy Gray, Ashtabula | KO | 2 |

1979

| Feb. | 7—Tony Corovic, Richfield | W | 4 |
| Sept. | 20—Maurice Marcellus, Richfield | W | 4 |

1980

Apr.	5—Jose Gutierrez, Akron	KO 2
May	17—Herb Adams, Dayton	KO 2
June	20—Ray Joseph, Cincinnati	KO 6
Aug.	2—Baker Tinsley, Cincinnati	W 6
Dec.	16—Vic Wallace, Cleveland	KO 3

FOSSIE SCHMIDT
Honolulu, Hawaii Heavyweight
1980

June	17—Scotty Welsh, Honolulu	KO by 1
Aug.	19—Henry Porter, Honolulu	KO 2
Sept.	23—Robert Echols, Honolulu	KO 6
Nov.	18—Henry Porter, Honolulu	KO 2

KEN SCHMIDT
Hamden, Conn. Heavyweight
1979

Feb.	28—Al White, Hartford	W 4
Mar.	29—Billy Grant, Hartford	KO 1
Apr.	24—Mike Baker, Hartford	KO 3
May	18—Alex Carr, Hartford	KO 1
May	25—Ray Rodriguez, Portland	KO 4
June	29—Jose Verdejo, Hartford	W 4
Nov.	5—Jimmy Harris, Hartford	KO by 1

1980

Apr.	8—Jimmy Harris, Hartford	KO 2
June	20—Melvin Epps, Hartford	W 6
Nov.	3—Calvin Langston, Hartford	KO 1

STEVE SCHWAN
Austin, Texas Middleweight
1980

Aug.	16—Joe Vargas, Odessa	KO 3
Sept.	23—Anderson Harris, Odessa	KO 1
Oct.	24—Nacho Torres, Dallas	KO 2

CHRIS SCHWENKE
Midvale, Utah Light Heavyweight
1980

July	23—Bill Fallow, Las Vegas	W 4
Aug.	2—Earl Lanier, Salt Lake City	KO 1
Aug.	23—Bill Fallow, Salt Lake City	KO 2
Sept.	24—Harry Rayton, Las Vegas	KO 1
Oct.	29—Joseph Rivera, Las Vegas	KO 1
Nov.	26—James Williams, Las Vegas	KO 3

BRUCE SCOTT
Beaumont, Texas Light Heavyweight
1969

June	9—Speedy King, New Orleans	L 4
June	17—Gilbert Martinez, Houston	KO 2
July	10—Sam Wilson, New Orleans	KO by 3
July	21—Speedy King, New Orleans	L 4
Aug.	11—Freddie Callaway, New Orleans	W 4
Sept.	2—Severo Balboa, Corpus Chr.	KO by 8
Sept.	29—Freddie Calloway, New Orleans	W 4
Dec.	1—Ronnie Wright, Austin	KO by 3

1970

Jan.	20—Dean Whitlock, Houston	KO by 2
Jan.	23—Floyd Dalfrey, Beaumont	L
Feb.	2—Gilbert Gutierrez, Austin	KO by 3
Apr.	21—Sammy Lockley, Beaumont	W 4
June	8—Ricardo Williams, Dallas	L 6
June	16—Johnny Baldwin, Houston	KO by 1
July	27—Terry Sorrell, Beaumont	W 4
Aug.	31—Johnny Baldwin, Beaumont	KO by 3
Oct.	7—Chuck Mince, New Orleans	L 6

1971

Jan.	25—Adam Moore, New Orleans	KO by 3
Apr.	27—James Breaux, Beaumont	KO by 2
June	1—Frankie Evans, Beaumont	W 6
Aug.	3—Paul Patin, Beaumont	L 10
Oct.	2—Brian Kelly, Cushing	L 10
Nov.	16—Johnny Baldwin, Beaumont	KO by 5

1972

Jan.	18—Frankie Evans, Beaumont	L 12
Mar.	28—Elgie Walters, Beaumont	W 6

1973

Feb.	2—Ruediger Schmidtke, Kelkheim	KO by 8
Feb.	23—John Penny, Dallas	L 6
May	21—Dave Rodgers, Eugene	D 8
Sept.	5—Terry Daniels, Orlando	L 10
Sept.	25—John Words, Kansas City	L 8
Oct.	12—Terry Daniels, Dallas	L 10
Nov.	14—Tony Licata, Orlando	KO by 4

1974

Mar.	8—Terry Daniels, Hot Springs	L 10
May	21—Lonnie Bennett, Houston	KO by 7
July	6—Dale Grant, Gardnersville	L 0

1975

Apr.	11—Ibar Arrington, Everett	L 10
May	20—Ned Hallacy, Oklahoma City	W 10

Aug.	5—Ron Stander, Oklahoma City	KO by 2
Nov.	18—Jimmy Fletcher, Oklahoma City	L 10

1976

Feb.	26—Eddie Jones, Reno	KO by 8
Apr.	21—Vonzell Johnson, Seattle	KO by 3
June	22—Pete Young, Topeka	L 6
Sept.	14—Ibar Arrington, Everett	KO by 2
Nov.	11—Tony McMinn, Joplin	KO by 4
Nov.	20—Dennis Haggerty, Marshall	W 4
Dec.	7—Ray Storie, Oklahoma City	KO by 3

1977

June	1—Leon Spinks, Montreal	KO by 3

1978

Nov.	1—Jerome Tunsall, St. Louis	L 6

1979

June	26—Vernon Johnson, Beaumont	L 6
Nov.	13—Victor Rodriguez, Beaumont	W 8

1980

Sept.	25—Monte Masters, Oklahoma City	KO by 5
Dec.	17—Harvey Steichen, Crystal Bay	KO by 3

JAMES SCOTT
Rahway, N.J. Light Heavyweight
1974

Jan.	22—John L. Johnson, Miami Beach	KO 4
Feb.	5—Hydra Lacey, Miami Beach	KO 3
Feb.	19—Willie Johnson, Miami Beach	KO 4
Mar.	5—Baby Boy Rolle, Miami Beach	KO 8
Apr.	2—Frankie Evans, Miami Beach	W 10
Apr.	23—Ray Anderson, Miami Beach	W 10
May	14—Koli Vailea, Miami Beach	KO 5
July	9—Robert Lloyd, Miami Beach	W 10
Sept.	10—Lee Royston, Miami Beach	D 10
Nov.	19—Raul Loyola, Miami Beach	W 10

1975

Feb.	25—Jesse Burnett, Miami Beach	W 10

1976-1977
(Inactive)
1978

May	24—Jimmy Diego Robinson, Rahway	KO 2
Sept.	9—Freddie Brown, Rahway	KO 4
Oct.	12—Eddie Gregory, Rahway	W 12

1979

Mar.	10—Richie Kates, Rahway	KO 10
July	1—Bunny Johnson, Rahway	KO 7
Aug.	26—Ennio Cometti, Rahway	KO 6
Oct.	27—Jerry Celestine, Rahway	W 10
Dec.	1—Yaqui Lopez, Rahway	W 10

1980

May	25—Jerry Martin, Rahway	L 10

STANLEY SCOTT
Cleveland, Ohio Light Heavyweight
1978

June	28—Slim Ali, Washington, D.C.	L 4
Aug.	26—Bill Hollis, Dayton	KO 2
Sept.	14—Greg Lamarr, Virginia Beach	KO 4
Oct.	9—Al Yasbick, Hampton	L 8
Oct.	17—Wes Rowe, Canton	KO 3
Nov.	24—Tim Johnson, West Lake	KO 2

1979

Jan.	24—Tim Johnson, Strongsville	KO 2
Feb.	21—John Williams, Strongsville	KO 1
Mar.	7—Willie Crawford, Strongsville	KO 1
May	19—Obie Garnett, Findlay	KO 1
June	4—Dave Bradley, Chicago	L 6

1980

Jan.	9—Eddie Gonzales, Holland, Mich.	L 6
Mar.	3—Dave Bradley, Chicago	KO by 2
Apr.	30—Amos Hayes, Youngstown	KO by 3
July	26—Len Hutchins, Kalamazoo	KO by 5
Aug.	15—Murray Sutherland, Muskegon	KO by 2
Dec.	16—Jeff Lampkin, Cleveland	KO by 3

WILFORD SCYPION
New York Middleweight
1978

July	18—Dennis Haggerty, Houston	KO 1
Aug.	15—Calvin Todd, Houston	KO 4
Sept.	19—Carlos Terrazas, Houston	KO 2
Oct.	12—Oscar Rios, Pasadena	KO 1
Nov.	28—Miguel Garcia, Houston	KO 4

1979

Jan.	16—Fred Johnson, Houston	KO 8
Apr.	10—Johnny Heard, Beaumont	KO 2
May	22—Jesse Edwards, Beaumont	KO 2
June	26—Arnel Thomas, Beaumont	KO 2
Aug.	15—Herman Marquez, Beaumont	KO 2
Sept.	14—Jose Gomez, Houston	KO 6
Oct.	10—Manuel Torres, Houston	KO 2
Nov.	23—Willie Classen, New York	KO 10

1980

Jan.	9—Norris McKinney, Beaumont	KO 3

Feb.	23—Jerome Jackson, Atlantic City	W	8
May	25—Bob Patterson, Atlantic City	KO	6
June	15—Mustapha Hamsho, Clarksburg	L disq.	10
Oct.	2—Fermin Guzman, Commack	KO	8
Oct.	24—Michael Herron, Uniondale	KO	4
Dec.	13—Willie Ray Taylor, Miami	KO	4

(SUGAR) RAY SEALES
Tacoma, Wash. Middleweight
1973
Jan.	11—Gonzalez Rodriguez, Tacoma	W	8
Feb.	12—Conrad Green, Eugene	KO	2
Mar.	1—Sugar Montgomery, Stockton	KO	6
Mar.	15—Felix Alvarado, Seattle	W	8
Mar.	26—Jose Miranda, Eugene	W	8
Apr.	12—Chico Andrade, Reno	KO	4
May	20—Roger Buckskin, Hoquiam	KO	5
June	25—Leroy Romero, Butte	W	10
July	7—Frank Davila, Gardnerville	W	10
Aug.	22—Chu Chu Garcia, Tacoma	W	10
Oct.	12—Roy Barrientos, Dallas	W	10
Nov.	2—Dave Coventry, Portland	KO	4
Dec.	12—Jose Miranda, San Francisco	W	10
	1974		
Feb.	13—Angel Robinson Garcia, Las Vegas	W	10
Feb.	28—Omar Chavez, Las Vegas	KO	8
Mar.	7—Beto Gonzalez, Reno	KO	3
Mar.	19—Jose Espinoza, Denver	KO	4
Apr.	16—Jose Martin Flores, Tacoma	KO	10
June	8—John Sullivan, Lacey	KO	2
Aug.	6—Dave Love, Tacoma	KO	12
Aug.	30—Marvin Hagler, Boston	L	10
Sept.	18—Les Riggins, Seattle	KO	1
Nov.	26—Marvin Hagler, Seattle	D	10
	1975		
Feb.	11—Mike Nixon, Seattle	W	10
Mar.	28—Johnny Rico, Tucson	W	10
Apr.	22—Manuel Elizondo, Sacramento	KO	2
May	14—Rudy Cruz, Sacramento	W	10
Aug.	15—Eugene Hart, Atlantic City	L	10
Oct.	21—Mike Lancaster, Seattle	KO	2
Dec.	2—Renato Garcia, Seattle	W	10
	1976		
Mar.	9—George Cooper, Seattle	W	12
May	25—Rico Hoye, Seattle	KO	4
Oct.	15—Gianni Mingardi, Milan	KO	6
Dec.	7—Alan Minter, London	KO by	5
	1977		
Mar.	2—Ronnie Harris, New York	L	10
Apr.	26—George Davis, Seattle	KO	2
May	25—Tony Gardner, Anchorage	KO	4
June	23—Cliff Wills, Vancouver	W	10
June	29—Vicente Medina, Anchorage	W	10
July	19—Nate Lenoir, Seattle	KO	2
Sept.	6—Eddie Davis, Memphis	KO	7
Sept.	21—Mike Hallacy, Wichita	W	10
Oct.	25—Joe Gonzalez, Seattle	KO	4
Dec.	2—Doug Demmings, Chicago	W	15
	1978		
Jan.	26—Emmett Atlas, Seattle	KO	2
Feb.	28—Willie Warren, Seattle	D	10
Apr.	8—Mayfield Pennington, Pikeville	KO	8
May	9—Dale Grant, Seattle	D	4
May	23—Dale Grant, Bellingham	L	4
June	9—David Heard, Butterfield	KO	2
June	20—Tommy Howard, Seattle	W	12
June	28—Johnny Heard, Washington D.C.	W	10
Aug.	29—Sammy NeSmith, Seattle	KO	5
Nov.	9—Ayub Kalule, Copenhagen	L	10
	1979		
Feb.	3—Marvin Hagler, Boston	KO by	1
June	21—Mike Colbert, Seattle	D	12
	1980		
Apr.	5—Art (Tap) Harris, Akron	KO	6
Apr.	19—Ted Sanders, Billings	KO	7
May	23—Dwight Davison, Clarkston	L	10
Aug.	2—Jamie Thomas, Baton Rouge	W	10
Dec.	23—James Williams, Tacoma	W	10

ERIC SEDILLO
Denver, Colo. Heavyweight
1976
Feb.	3—Don Meloncon, Albuquerque	KO	3
	1977		
Mar.	9—Tom Sullivan, Las Vegas	KO by	1
Apr.	27—John Baca, Phoenix	W	6
June	14—Frank Battaglia, Phoenix	KO	2
	1978		
Apr.	22—Hank Gregory, Denver	KO	3
May	3—Verlee Price, Denver	KO	4
May	23—Fred Wallace, Denver	KO	3
June	22—Ernie Smith, Denver	KO	1
Sept.	8—Mustafa El Amin, Ogden	KO	1
Dec.	5—Leroy Caldwell, Winnipeg	W	8

1979
Jan.	20—Jim Ingram	W	10
June	23—Cookie Wallace, Denver	KO	1
Sept.	21—James Dixon	KO	6
Oct.	20—Al Banks, Pueblo	KO	3
	1980		
Mar.	15—S. T. Gordon, Ogden	L	10
June	12—James Tillis, Chicago	KO by	3

JOHNNY SEGURA
Los Angeles, Calif. Junior Welterweight
1979
Apr.	18—Andres Montoya, Las Vegas	L	4
May	9—Max Cervantes, Oakland	KO	5
	1980		
Apr.	18—Kelly Pickering, Santa Rosa	KO by	3

LOUIS SELF
Toledo, Ohio Lightweight
1977
Feb.	15—Jerry Strickland, Toledo	W	4
	1978-1979		
	(Inactive)		
	1980		
Sept.	18—Ray Green, Cleveland	KO	1
Oct.	16—Chico Rodriguez, Toledo	KO	2
Dec.	6—Forrest Winchester, Detroit	KO by	2

MICHAEL SENEGAL
Lake Charles, La. Welterweight
1980
Aug.	9—T. C. Williams, Lake Charles	KO	3
Oct.	18—Enrique Garcia, Lake Charles	KO	4
Oct.	23—Benny Ray Trusel, Detroit	L	4
Dec.	6—Tom Pinner, Bastrop, La.	KO	3
Dec.	9—Terry Stevenson, Birmingham	KO	2

BEN SERRANO
Warminster, Pa. Middleweight
1979
July	31—Kevin Perry, Atlantic City	L	4
Aug.	28—Herb Wilens, Atlantic City	L	4
Sept.	26—Leo Martinez, Upper Darby	KO	1
Nov.	15—Marciano Bernardi, Dover	L	8
	1980		
Apr.	10—Frank Fletcher, Atlantic City	L	8
June	26—Feliciano Cintron, Revere	W	8
July	17—Bob Patterson, Totowa	L	8
Sept.	4—Mario Maldonado, Atlantic City	L	6

JESUS SERRANO
Bronx, N.Y. Lightweight
1980
Sept.	18—Eddie Kinney, Totowa	KO	2
Oct.	16—Livingston Bramble, Totowa	KO by	1

AUGUSTIN SERROS
California Junior Featherweight
1979
Nov.	7—Johnny Jackson, San Jose	KO	1
Dec.	11—Johnny Saucedo, San Jose	W	6
	1980		
Jan.	10—Johnny Jackson, Santa Rosa	KO	2
Feb.	5—Marcelo Camacho, San Jose	L	6
Mar.	6—Luis Avila, San Jose	KO by	5
May	16—Rafael Capristro, San Jose	KO	1

RONALD SESSIONS
(See KID SAMPSON)

WILLIE JOE SETTLES
Parkin, Ark. Junior Middleweight
1978
Dec.	16—Simmie Black, Memphis	D	4
	1979		
May	1—Joe Cook, Memphis	W	4
June	5—Alvin Fowler, Memphis	L	6
June	14—Larry Rushin, River Grove	KO by	2
July	17—Tom Crowley, Belleville, Ill.	L	6
Sept.	18—Lester Gloves, Memphis	L	4
	1980		
Mar.	4—Charles Smith, Memphis	KO by	6

TONY SEVERANCE
Gainesville, Fla. Heavyweight
1980
Jan.	18—Greg Payne, Orlando	D	6
Feb.	21—Greg Payne, Gainesville	W	6
Feb.	28—Demetrius Edwards, Tampa	L	6
Apr.	15—Ken Austin, Miami	W	4
June	26—Paul Kasper, Gainesville	KO	1
Dec.	11—Curtis Gaskins, Gainesville	W	6

MILTON (PETE) SEWARD
Kalamazoo, Mich. Welterweight
Born: May 3, 1954, Height: 5 ft. 9 in.
1977
June	11—Larry Moore, Jackson	KO	3
June	22—Larry McCall, Columbus	W	6
Aug.	4—Juan Regato, Wyoming	W	6
Oct.	13—Tyrone Wren, Columbus	W	6
Dec.	10—Winston Noel, Grand Rapids	W	8
1978
Jan.	19—Aundra Love, Houston	W	8
June	21—Ron Pettigrew, Detroit	W	8
Aug.	25—Charlie Benjamin, Houston	KO	4
Sept.	13—Ken Arlt, Butte	KO by	2
Oct.	6—Tyrone Wren, Kansas City	W	8
1979
Feb.	9—Ernest Payne, Mt. Clements	KO	6
Apr.	17—Danny Donatto, Houston	W	10
May	17—Gary Coates, Columbus	W	6
Sept.	30—Gary Coates, Canton	KO by	6
1980
Aug.	13—Julio Alfonso, Las Vegas	KO	2
Sept.	13—Phil Batie, Lorain	KO	1
Oct.	1—Jerry Martinez, Las Vegas	KO	4

MUHAMMAD SHABAZZ
Hartford, Conn. Light Heavyweight
1979
Feb.	28—Joe Morey, Hartford	W	4
Mar.	29—Beau Jack, Hartford	W	4
Apr.	24—Robert Davis, Hartford	W	4
May	18—Ali Muhammad, Hartford	KO by	3
May	26—Mickey McDonald, Glace Bay	KO	4
June	14—Charlie Singleton, Felt Forum, N.Y.	KO by	4
Nov.	15—Dana McCarthy, Bristol	KO	5
1980
Jan.	15—J. C. Moody, W. Hartford	KO	1
Feb.	5—Gil Rosario, W. Hartford	KO	2
Mar.	4—Skipper Jones, W. Hartford	W	8
May	29—Skipper Jones, W. Hartford	W	8
Sept.	12—Don Addison, Hartford	KO by	11

WILLIE SHANNON
Portland, Ore. Heavyweight
1977
Sept.	15—George Holden, Daytona Beach	W	4
Oct.	7—Doug Farrell, St. Augustine	KO	1
Oct.	25—Willie Goodman, Orlando	KO	3
Nov.	18—Charles Banks, Gainesville	KO	1
1978
Jan.	17—George Holder, Orlando	W	4
Apr.	10—Rocky Stevens, Jacksonville	KO	1
May	23—Alvin Dominey, Orlando	KO	2
July	27—Willie Goodman, Palatka	KO	2
Aug.	8—Walter Santemore, Orlando	KO	2
Oct.	3—Tom Nickson, Orlando	KO	2
Dec.	12—Elton Armstrong, Orlando	KO	1
1979
Feb.	22—John Kline, Portland	KO	4
Mar.	22—Steve Moyer, Portland	D	4
Apr.	12—Jimmy Ingram, Portland	W	10
July	26—Charley Polite, Portland	KO	4
Oct.	30—Leroy Caldwell, Las Vegas	W	10
1980
Feb.	24—Jimmy Ingram, Las Vegas	KO	3
Apr.	20—Dwain Bonds, Portland, Me.	KO	9

EARNIE SHAVERS
Warren, Ohio Heavyweight
Born: August 31, 1945, Garland, Ala.
AAU Heavyweight Champion in 1969
1969
Nov.	6—Red Howell, Akron	KO	2
Nov.	11—George Holden, Orlando	KO	1
Nov.	14—Stan Johnson, Seattle	L	6
Nov.	21—Lee Roy, Rapid City	KO	3
Dec.	4—J. D. McCauley, Akron	KO	2
Dec.	18—Chico Froncano, Canton	KO	1
Dec.	26—Gene Idolette, Orlando	KO	2
1970
Jan.	7—Tiger Brown, Akron	KO	1
Jan.	24—Joe Byrd, Canton	KO	3
Jan.	27—Tiger Brown, Orlando	KO	5
Mar.	6—Art Miller, Canton	KO	1
Mar.	23—Ray Asher, Youngstown	KO	1
Apr.	14—Frank Smith, Canton	KO	4
May	11—Ron Stander, Omaha	KO by	5
Aug.	29—Jim Daniels, Youngstown	KO	1
Sept.	12—Don Branch, Columbus	KO	1
Oct.	14—Johnny Hudgins, Canton	KO	1
Nov.	18—Johnny Mac, Youngstown	KO	4
Dec.	7—Bunky Akins, New York	KO	2

1971
Jan.	6—Lee Estes, Akron	KO	2
Jan.	15—Nat Shaver, Miami Beach	KO	1
Feb.	3—Johnny Mac, Las Vegas	KO	3
Feb.	17—Richard Gosha, Akron	KO	5
Mar.	3—Steve Carter, Las Vegas	KO	1
Mar.	24—Young Agabab, Las Vegas	KO	1
Apr.	21—Mac Harrison, Akron	KO	2
Apr.	24—Willie Johnson, Tampa	KO	4
May	14—Jimmy Brown, Las Vegas	KO	1
June	1—Chuck Leslie, Stateline	KO	10
June	30—Bill Hardney, Warren	KO	1
July	13—Bill McMurray, Stateline	KO	1
Sept.	28—Pat Duncan, Reno	KO	5
Oct.	17—Charlie Boston, Akron	KO	2
Oct.	29—Elmo Henderson, Stateline	KO	4
Nov.	23—Cleo Daniels, Warren	KO	2
Nov.	30—Del Morris, Bryant	KO	3
1972
Feb.	1—Ted Gullick, Warren	KO	6
Feb.	15—Elgie Walters, Beaumont	KO	2
Apr.	6—Charlie Polite, Warren	KO	3
Apr.	22—Bob Felstein, Akron	KO	5
May	5—Lou Bailey, Akron	KO	2
Aug.	26—Vicente Rondon, Canton	W	10
Sept.	22—A. J. Staples, Canton	KO	1
Oct.	25—Leroy Caldwell, Newton Falls	KO	1
1973
Feb.	19—Jimmy Young, Philadelphia	KO	3
May	12—Harold Carter, Windsor	KO	1
June	18—Jimmy Ellis, New York	KO	1
Dec.	14—Jerry Quarry, New York	KO by	1
1974
May	16—Cookie Wallace, San Jose	KO	1
Nov.	4—Bob Stallings, New York	L	10
Nov.	26—Jimmy Young, Largo	D	10
1975
Feb.	11—Leon Shaw, Orlando	KO	1
Apr.	9—Rochell Norris, Binghamton	KO	10
May	8—Oliver Wright, Baltimore	KO	3
Sept.	13—Ron Lyle, Denver	KO by	6
Nov.	13—Tommy Howard, Monroeville	KO	3
1976
Mar.	28—Henry Clark, Paris	W	10
Sept.	28—Henry Clark, New York	KO	2
Dec.	11—Roy Williams, Las Vegas	KO	10
1977
Apr.	17—Howard Smith, Las Vegas	KO	2
Sept.	29—Muhammad Ali, New York	L	15
	(World Heavyweight Title)		
1978
Mar.	25—Larry Holmes, Las Vegas	L	12
July	20—Harry Terrell, Virginia Beach	KO	2
Oct.	9—John Gerowski, Hampton	KO	1
Dec.	4—Harold Carter, Saginaw	KO	3
1979
Mar.	23—Ken Norton, Las Vegas	KO	1
May	25—Eddie Porette, Richfield	KO	3
Sept.	28—Larry Holmes, Las Vegas	KO by	11
	(For WBC Heavyweight Title)		
1980
Mar.	8—Bernardo Mercado, Great Gorge	KO by	7
June	14—Leroy Boone, Cincinnati	W	10
Aug.	2—Randall (Tex) Cobb, Detroit	KO by	8
Oct.	17—Art Miller, West Palm Beach	KO	2

LEON SHAW
Jacksonville, Fla. Heavyweight
1971
May	18—Nap Smith, Tampa	KO	3
July	18—Alton Diggs, Jacksonville	KO	2
Aug.	24—Henry Hall, Jacksonville	D	6
1972
Aug.	29—Paul Kasper, Jacksonville	KO by	3
1973
May	29—James J. Johnson, Miami Beach	L	4
June	19—James J. Johnson, Miami Beach	KO by	3
July	3—Henry Hall, Miami Beach	W	6
Sept.	5—Joe Gholston, Atlanta	L	8
1974
Oct.	13—Paul Kasper, Macon	KO	3
Dec.	3—Johnny Boudreaux, Orlando	L	10
1975
Feb.	11—Earnie Shavers, Orlando	KO by	1
Mar.	7—Larry Renaud, Tampa	W	8
May	6—Jody Ballard, Orlando	L	10
May	20—Tommy Howard, Orlando	W	10
Sept.	9—O. T. Davies, Orlando	KO	2
Dec.	9—Larry Holmes, Washington, D.C.	KO by	1
1976
May	11—Jody Ballard, Orlando	KO	1
Sept.	14—Hurricane Grant, Miami Beach	KO	4
1977
June	15—George Montgomery, St. Augustine	KO	3

Aug. 17—Tommy Howard, St. Augustine .... KO 5
Oct. 1—Clarence Morris, Gainesville .... KO 3
Oct. 7—Tom Nickson, St. Augustine .... W 8
Oct. 19—Paul Kasper, Jacksonville .... W 6
Nov. 16—Carl Baker, St. Augustine .... W 8
1978
Feb. 6—Carl Baker, Jacksonville .... W 10
Feb. 27—Bobby Lloyd, Jacksonville .... L 12
Sept. 7—Jody Ballard, El Paso .... W 10
1979
Jan. 26—Rene Kinsey, Jacksonville .... W 10
Feb. 21—Randy Mack, Las Vegas .... KO by 3
Nov. 13—Jimmy Abbott, Capetown .... KO by 4
1980
Feb. 2—Rahim Muhammad, Phoenix .... L 10
Feb. 21—Randy Mack, Las Vegas .... KO by 3

JEFF SHELBURG
Salt Lake City, Utah Heavyweight
Born: November 8, 1955
1977
June 17—Pete Anada, Ogden .... KO 1
Aug. 19—J. D. Smith, Ogden .... KO 2
Nov. 12—Charlie (Budda) Brooks .... W 6
1978
Jan. 14—Dave Gilmore, Salt Lake City .... KO 3
Feb. 4—Donnie Greenfield, Salt Lake City ...... KO 1
Mar. 18—Jimmy Pearish, Denver .... KO 4
Mar. 24—Terry La Salle, Ogden .... KO 1
Apr. 22—Dave Martinez, Salt Lake City .... KO 2
May 3—Ellis Sanders, Denver .... KO 6
July 7—Verlee Price, Salt Lake City .... KO 7
July 14—Johnny Robinson, Salt Lake City ...... KO 3
Sept. 1—Jimmy Cross, Salt Lake City .... KO 3
Sept. 8—Charlie (Budda) Brooks, Ogden ...... KO 1
Sept. 22—Toni Pulu, Salt Lake City .... L 10
Nov. 11—Toni Pulu, Salt Lake City .... L 10
1979
Mar. 31—Frankie Evans, Denver .... KO 5
June 16—Verlee Price, Colorado Springs .... KO 2
Sept. 14—Joe Donatto, Ogden .... KO 2
1980
Feb. 23—Fred Muhammad, Greeley .... KO 6
Mar. 15—Harvey Steichen, Denver .... W 10
May 24—Ron Stander, Salt Lake City .... W 10
Aug. 23—Harvey Steichen, Salt Lake City .... KO 1
Oct. 23—Marvin Stinson, Las Vegas .... L 10

CALVIN SHEPPARD
Laredo, Texas Bantamweight
1978
Feb. 20—Rafael Duran, San Antonio .... L 6
May 2—Jose Luis Garcia, San Antonio .... L 8
June 20—Lucio Garcia, San Antonio .... L 10
Oct. 26—Sergio Reyes, Laredo .... L 10
1979
Apr. 20—Sergio Reyes, Laredo .... KO by 3
June 5—Elias DeLeon, Houston .... L 10
July 21—Gustavo Martinez, Houston .... L 10
Aug. 14—Humberto Rodriquez, Houston .... W 10
1980
Feb. 5—Gustavo Martinez, Houston .... L 10
Sept. 13—Jaime Garza, San Antonio .... KO by 4
Oct. 30—Gigio Estrada, Los Angeles .... W 10

KENNETH SHEPPARD
Fresno, Calif. Welterweight
1976
Oct. 27—Kenny Crooms, Las Vegas .... KO by 1
1977
Jan. 22—Russell Pope, Fresno .... KO by 3
May 13—Greg Stephens, San Diego .... KO by 2
Sept. 20—Jerry Cheatham, Phoenix .... KO by 4
Oct. 29—Joe Maldonado, Fresno .... L 4
1978
(Inactive)
1979
Aug. 24—Ramon Gonzalez, McAllen .... L 6
1980
Feb. 5—Roque Montoya, Houston .... L 8
Apr. 15—Roberto Madrid, Houston .... KO by 5

RANDY SHIELDS
No. Hollywood, Calif. Welterweight
1973 National Golden Gloves Lightweight Champion
1974
Jan. 17—Victor Abraham, Los Angeles .... W 6
Feb. 14—Tony Sanchez, Portland............... KO 4
Mar. 4—Armando Cordova, Los Angeles.......... W 6
Apr. 19—Dave Kirby, Portland.................... W 6
May 17—Felix Jasso, San Diego .... KO 4
May 24—Moses Carbin, San Diego .... KO 4
June 7—Jose Katon Macias, San Diego.......... KO 8

June 13—Al Doster, Portland.................... KO 3
July 5—Felix Alvarado, San Diego .... KO 2
July 12—Jose Macias, San Diego .... KO 4
Aug. 2—Rocky Cruz, San Diego .... KO 8
Aug. 30—Raul Montoya, San Diego .... W 10
Sept. 9—Juan Morales, Los Angeles .... KO 3
Oct. 17—Dave Kibby, Los Angeles .... W 10
Nov. 14—Roy Holloway, Los Angeles .... KO 4
Dec. 5—Leoncio Meza, Los Angeles .... KO 4
Dec. 12—Alberto Reyes, Portland .... W 10
1975
Jan. 16—Carlos Barajas, Los Angeles............. KO 5
Mar. 1—Art Leon, Los Angeles.................. W 10
Mar. 20—Armando Montemayor, Los Angeles ...... KO 2
Apr. 9—Miguel Mayan, Portland................. W 10
May 16—Octavio Amaparan, Los Angeles........ KO 9
June 12—Miguel Mayan, Portland................. W 10
June 28—Centavito Hernandez, Los Angeles...... W 10
Aug. 23—Tury Pineda, Los Angeles............... W 10
Oct. 11—Alfonso Jiminez, Los Angeles .... W 10
Nov. 29—Vicente Saldivar, Los Angeles........ KO by 8
1976
Feb. 19—Vicente Saldivar, Los Angeles .... L 10
Sept. 30—Ramiro Bolanos, Los Angeles .... W 10
Nov. 11—Ray Lampkin, Portland................. KO 3
1977
Jan. 16—Juan Cantres, Pensacola .... W 8
(U.S. Championship Tournament)
June 16—Pancho Del Toro, Los Angeles.......... KO 5
Oct. 21—Pete Ranzany, Sacramento .... TD 2
1978
Feb. 14—Pete Ranzany, Sacramento .... KO by 11
June 1—Babs McCarthy, Sacramento .... W 10
Aug. 25—Wilfred Benitez, New York .... KO by 6
Oct. 6—Ray Leonard, Baltimore .... L 10
Dec. 14—David Madrid, Los Angeles .... KO 4
1979
Jan. 29—Jose Palacios, Los Angeles .... W 10
July 30—Pipino Cuevas, Chicago .... L 15
(WBA Welterweight Title)
Oct. 16—Noli Galicha, Honolulu .... KO 1
Dec. 8—Mauricio Aldana, Los Angeles .... W 10
1980
May 2—Jose Figueroa, Los Angeles .... KO 3
Aug. 14—Louie Mateo, Chicago .... W 10

RONNIE SHIELDS
Port Arthur, Texas Junior Welterweight
1980
Aug. 19—Ramiro Hernandez, Beaumont .... KO 1
Sept. 16—Frank Lawson, Beaumont .... KO 1
Nov. 11—Jerry Reyes, Houston .... KO 4

STEVE SHILAITA
Chicago, Ill. Light Heavyweight
1980
Feb. 18—Dan Murphy, Chicago .... KO 1
Mar. 28—Warren Coaston, Chicago .... KO 1
Apr. 14—John Cox, Chicago .... W 6
July 25—Wilbert Johnson, Chicago .... W 6
Nov. 7—Don Green, Chicago .... KO 3
Dec. 11—Lenny Lapaglia, Chicago .... KO by 1

HORACE SHUFFORD
Las Vegas, Nev. Junior Welterweight
1977
Apr. 6—Gil Valdez, Las Vegas .... W 6
June 22—Richard Contreras, Las Vegas .... W 6
Aug. —Curtis Lewis, Las Vegas .... W 6
1978
Jan. 17—Al Fletcher, Las Vegas .... W 8
Apr. 26—Jimmy Ligons, Las Vegas .... KO 2
May 25—Curtis Ramsey, Las Vegas .... W 10
Sept. 20—Pablo Baez, Las Vegas .... KO by 9
Dec. 13—Eddie Nuno, Las Vegas .... KO 5
1979
Feb. 14—Rogelio Castaneda, Las Vegas .... KO 8
May —Joey Dominguez, Pico Rivera .... L 10
Sept. 19—Mauricio Aldana, Las Vegas .... W 10
1980
Mar. 19—Steve Chase, Las Vegas .... W 10
June 4—Agapito Ramirez, Las Vegas .... W 10
Aug. 28—Carlos Lozano, Las Vegas .... W 10

JAMES SHULER
Philadelphia, Pa. Middleweight
Born: May, 1959. Height: 6 ft. 1 in.
1980
Sept. 12—Chris Rogers, New York .... KO 2
Oct. 10—Jamal Arbubakar, New York .... W 4
Nov. 28—Charles Hecker, New York .... KO 3

216

BENNY SILVA
Tijuana, Mexico Junior Lightweight
1979
July 2—Gerardo Pena, Los Angeles ....KO by 4
Aug. 15—Nicky Perez, Tucson ....L 10
1980
Mar. 6—Roy Hernandez, San Jose ....KO by 10
May 16—Roberto Garcia, San Jose ....KO by 10
Aug. 2—Daniel Avery, Cincinnati ....L 4

TERRY SILVER
Louisville, Ky. Junior Welterweight
1980
Sept. 12—Jeff Foster, Louisville ....KO 2
Oct. 18—Robert Johnson, Atlantic City ....W 4
Nov. 7—Clarence Brown, Clarksville ....KO 2
Dec. 12—Darrell Owens, Louisville ....KO 2

DAVE SIMMONDS
Vancouver, Canada Middleweight
1972
Aug. 10—Tom DelVechio, Nelson ....KO 1
1973
Apr. —Benito Juarez, Las Vegas ....KO 8
—Fustin Perez, Las Vegas ....KO 4
—Jesus Gonzales, Las Vegas ....KO 6
1974
(Inactive)
1975
Jan. 20—Jan Magziarz, Mayfair ....W 8
—Gus Farrell, Manchester ....W 8
1976-1978
(Inactive)
1979
Oct. 27—Wayne Caplette, Regina ....L 6
Nov. 27—Paul Guyness, Vancouver ....KO 3
1980
Feb. 29—Bruce Strauss, Nanaimo ....W 10
Mar. 15—Jerry Reddick, Vancouver ....KO by 2

IVOR (BABA) SIMMONS
Georgetown, Guyana Junior Middleweight
Born: June 11, 1959
1978
Nov. 28—Terrence Clarke, Guyana ....W 6
Dec. 26—D. J. Hammer, Guyana ....KO 4
1979
Feb. 8—Keith Smarte, Guyana ....KO 6
July 10—Terrence Clarke, Guyana ....KO 2
1980
Feb. 24—Clifford Jones, Georgetown ....W 6
Mar. 16—Bomber Williams, Georgetown ....W 10
Apr. 27—Mortimer Cornell, Georgetown ....W 8
May 2—David Noel, Trinidad ....KO by 4
Sept. 7—Albert Brown, Georgetown ....L 12
(For Middleweight Championship of Guyana)

MANNY SIMMS
New York Welterweight
1979
May 11—Pete Padilla, Felt Forum, N.Y. ....L 4
Sept. 19—Angel Ortiz, New York ....W 4
Oct. 19—John Saxton, Commack ....W 6
—Jesse Rogers, Shirley ....KO 3
1980
Jan. 24—Bernard Petersen, Upper Darby ......KO by 3
May 9—Dave Bolden, Staten Island ....KO by 3
Oct. 10—Francisco Maestre, New York ....KO 2

HENRY SIMS
Chicago, Ill. Light Heavyweight
1978
Apr. 28—Lucky Patterson, Chicago ....W 4
June 30—Lucky Patterson, Chicago ....W 4
Sept. 27—Lee Thomas, Chicago ....KO 3
Oct. 25—Cecil Peck, Chicago ....KO 2
Dec. 15—Obie Garnett, Chicago ....KO 1
1979
Feb. 2—Akbar Muhammad, Chicago ....L 6
Apr. 27—Gus Turner, Chicago ....W 6
July 20—Luke Capuano, Univ. of Ill. ....KO by 6
1980
Feb. 1—Greg McPherson, Chicago ....W 10
Aug. 25—Dan Kiser, Chicago ....KO 3
Sept. 10—Johnny Townsend, Cicero ....KO 4

JEFF SIMS
Belle Glade, Fla. Heavyweight
1979
Mar. 19—Greg Henderson, Fort Lauderdale ....KO 0
Apr. 19—Jimmy Lee Nixon, Savannah ....KO 1
Apr. 30—Carl Baker, Miami ....KO 2
Nov. 27—Glen Morgan, Miami Beach ....KO 2

Dec. 18—Phil Fritz, Miami Beach ....KO 1
Dec. 28—Al Leticky, Belle Glade ....KO 1
1980
Jan. 29—Tom Prater, Miami ....KO 2
Feb. 12—Walter Santemore, Miami ....KO 1
Mar. 18—Nick Wells, Orlando ....KO 5
Apr. 15—Larry Alexander, Miami ....KO by 6
Aug. 29—Larry Frazier, W. Palm Beach ....NC 1
Sept. 23—Grady Daniels, Edmonton ....KO 2
Oct. 17—Claman Parker, W. Palm Beach ....KO 7

LARRY SIMS
Cleveland, Ohio Heavyweight
1979
May 25—Carl Norfleet, Richfield ....KO 3
July 12—Joe Louis Jones, Detroit ....D 4
Sept. 26—Vonzell Johnson, Windsor ....L 10
Dec. 15—Jumbo Cummings, Chicago ....L 6
1980
Jan. 24—Keith Kelly, Detroit ....KO by 6
July 25—Conroy Nelson, Smith Falls ....L 6
Sept. 18—Verbie Garland, Cleveland ....KO 3
Nov. 22—Tony Tubbs, Cincinnati ....KO by 3
Dec. 12—Ali Haakim, Detroit ....KO by 2

ROBBIE SIMS
Brockton, Mass. Middleweight
1980
May 17—Troy Vaughn, Las Vegas ....KO 3
Aug. 18—Dave Dean, Boston ....KO 1
Oct. 2—Danny Heath, Boston ....KO 1
Nov. 25—Robert Thomas, Boston ....KO 4

ERNIE SINGLETARY
Philadelphia, Pa. Middleweight
1974
Oct. 24—Tim Kirk, Wilmington, Del. ....KO 1
1975
Jan. 9—Ed Motten, Wilmington, Del............KO 1
Apr. 17—Roy Ingram, Upper Darby.............W 6
May 5—Ed Benson, Philadelphia...............W 4
Sept. 16—Tyrone Freeman, Philadelphia ....W 6
Dec. 2—Dave Dittmar, Philadelphia ....KO 5
1976
July 28—Tyrone Phelps, Philadelphia............W 6
1977
Jan. 5—James Parks, Cleveland ....W 10
Feb. 19—Fred Daniels, Bristol ....KO 5
Apr. 18—Bob Payton, Philadelphia ....W 8
July 18—Dave Dittmar, Philadelphia ....KO 2
Sept. 28—Ralph Moncrief, Canton ....L 10
1978
Mar. 21—Jerome Goodman, Philadelphia ....W 10
Apr. 17—Eddie Phillips, Philadelphia ....W 8
June 13—Dino Del Cid, Philadelphia ....KO 4
Oct. 24—Ray Villanueva, Philadelphia ....W 10
1979
Feb. 5—Ralph Moncrief, Philadelphia ....W 10
June 8—Tyrone Freeman, Bermuda ....W 10
Oct. 18—Al Styles Jr., Philadelphia ....W 10
1980
Feb. 18—Benny Mitchell, Upper Darby ....W 8
Mar. 3—Cameron Adams, Capetown ....W 10
May 4—Bob Patterson, Atlantic City ....W 8
July 31—Teddy Mann, Atlantic City ....W 10
Oct. 30—Bobby Hoye, Atlantic City ....KO 2

CHARLES SINGLETON
Philadelphia, Pa. Light Heavyweight
1979
Apr. 6—Moe Wilson, New York ....KO 4
June 14—Hamad Amin Shabazz, New York ....KO 4
Sept. 8—Floyd Saunders, Wheeling ....KO 4
1980
May 16—Kid Samson, Chester ....W 6
Sept. 9—Furgan Ali, Atlantic City ....KO 3
Nov. 12—Eddie Harris, Philadelphia ....KO 4

CHARLES SMITH
Virginia Beach, Va. Light Heavyweight
1977
June 2—Oscar Freeman, Virginia Beach ....W 6
Aug. 2—Joe Sprowl, Virginia Beach ....W 6
Oct. 18—Al Yasbick, Virginia Beach ....W 6
Nov. 3—Jerry Martin, Virginia Beach ....L 6
Dec. 1—Al Yasbick, Virginia Beach ....W 6
1978
Jan. 19—Jasper Brisbane, Virginia Beach ....W 6
Jan. 24—Franklin Otis, Greenville ....KO 1
Mar. 23—Lupe Guerra, Omaha ....L 4
Apr. 18—Walter Santemore, New Orleans ....L 6
1979
Feb. —Bill Douglas, Cleveland ....L 10

217

Apr. 26—Homer Jones, Virginia Beach ....KO 1
May 31—Darrell Freeman, Virginia Beach ....KO 2
July 17—Lou Benson, Virginia Beach ....L 6
Aug. 7—Quinnie Locklear, Baltimore ....KO 6
Sept. 20—Chris Reeder, Virginia Beach ....W 6
1980
May 8—Bill Tuttle, Atlantic City ....W 8
June 5—Dwight Braxton, Atlantic City ....KO by 4
Dec. 6—Grover Robinson, Bastrop ....KO by 6

CLIFFORD SMITH
Philadelphia, Pa. Junior Middleweight
1979
Apr. 11—Sal Dragone, White Plains ....KO by 4
May 14—Kevin Abney, Philadelphia ....KO by 2
June 29—Malik Muhammad, Commack ....KO by 1
Aug. 14—Gregory Winston, Atlantic City .....KO by 2
Oct. 18—Buster Drayton, Philadelphia ....KO by 1
Dec. 2—Johnny Barr, Washington, D.C. ......KO by 2
1980
Jan. 16—Jeff Passero, Washington, D.C. ......KO by 3
Feb. 29—Pat Esposito, Brooklyn ....KO by 3

DARNELL SMITH
Philadelphia, Pa. Junior Middleweight
1979
June 8—Bob Saxton, Hamilton ....L 6
Oct. 10—Miguez Sanchez, White Plains ....KO by 1
Oct. 18—Tyrone Moore, Philadelphia ....KO by 1
Nov. 29—Larry Sprigos, Richmond ....KO by 4
Dec. 4—Mike Picciotti, Philadelphia ....KO by 1
1980
Jan. 30—Abel Santiago, Allentown ....L 4
Oct. 1—Marvin Richardson, Atlantic City ....KO by 3

ED SMITH
Charlotte, N.C. Light Heavyweight
1977
Aug. 23—Al Hogan, New Orleans ....KO by 4
1978
Jan. 3—Jimmy Richards, Shelby ....W 8
Apr. 13—Murray Sutherland, Huntington .....KO by 4
Apr. 20—Tony McMinn, St. Louis ....KO 4
May 4—Joel Patterson, Fayetteville ....W 6
May 17—Al Yasbeck, Virginia ....L 6
Aug. 28—Roddie McDonald, Halifax ....KO by 5
Nov. 14—Lou Butler, Baltimore ....KO by 5
1979
Aug. 28—Roddy MacDonald, Halifax ....KO by 5
Nov. 14—Lou Butler, Norfolk ....KO by 5
1980
Feb. 29—Bernard McClean, Commack ....KO by 6
Mar. 31—Irwin Hines, Knoxville ....KO by 2
July 26—Ernest Dunbar, Charlotte ....KO by 5
Aug. 29—Reggie Patrick, New York ....KO 4
Sept. 20—Freddie Gore, Charlotte ....KO 1

ERNIE (BIG E) SMITH
Dallas, Texas Heavyweight
1975
Feb. 10—Clint Walker, Dallas ....KO 3
Feb. 21—John Balla, Dallas ....KO 1
1976
Apr. 6—George Palmer, Oklahoma City ....KO 1
Apr. 21—Bruce Grandham, Seattle ....KO by 3
Oct. 7—Lynn Ball, Fort Worth ....KO by 3
Nov. 4—Nick Wells, Fort Worth ....KO by 3
Nov. 20—Bruce Grandham, Marshall ....L 6
Dec. 9—Jim Beattie, St. Paul ....KO by 2
1977
Feb 1—James Beattie, Oklahoma City ......KO by 3
Mar. 5—Randy Kirkland, Marshall ....KO by 2
Mar. 23—Jose Roman, Anchorage ....KO by 3
May 10—Randy Cobb, El Paso ....KO by 3
1978
June 22—Eric Sedillo, Denver ....KO by 1
Aug. 22—Mike Creel, Odessa ....W 4
Sept. 19—Willie Stoglin, Odessa ....W 4
Nov. 14—Walter St. Amant, New Orleans ....L 6
1979
Feb. 28—Chuck Gardner, Las Vegas ....L 5
June 12—Terry Krueger, Beaumont ....KO 8
Oct. 16—Harvey Steichen, Sparks ....KO 1
Nov. 13—Bob Stallings, Beaumont ....KO by 3
Dec. 12—Leon Shaw, Phoenix ....L 8
1980
Apr. 15—Harvey Steichen, Sparks ....KO by 1
July 15—Vernon Johnston, Beaumont ....W 10
Aug. 31—Pat Duncan, Carson City ....L 10
Dec. 17—Gord Racette, Crystal Bay ....KO by 1

GARY SMITH
Miami, Fla. Welterweight
1977
July 16—Al Carter, Orlando ....KO by 4
Aug. 12—Ray Green, Barberton ....KO by 2
1978
Feb. 6—Kelvin Jackson, Jacksonville ....L 6
Apr. 10—Kelvin Jackson, Jacksonville ....L 6
June 27—Larry Peterson, Jacksonville ....L 10
Aug. 22—James Salerno, Orlando ....KO by 5
Nov. 7—Robert Spencer, Orlando ....L 6
1979
Jan. 13—Elisha Obed, Miami Beach ....NC
Mar. 13—Robert Saewcer, Orlando ....L 6
Nov. 21—Maurice (Termite) Watkins, Orlando KO by 5
1980
Sept. 22—Louie Mateo, Chicago ....KO by 1

JAMES SMITH
Shreveport, La. Lightweight
1979
June 12—James Phillips, Beaumont ....KO 2
1980
May 31—Joe Zamora, El Paso ....W 4
June 24—Ramiro Hernandez, Beaumont ....W 6
July 15—Joe Pressley, Beaumont ....KO 1
Aug. 21—Wilburn Lawson, Dallas ....W 6
Nov. 19—Earl Young, Crystal Bay ....KO 2

JIMMY SMITH
Wilkes-Barre, Pa. Heavyweight
1975
Aug. 5—Robert Connors, Elizabeth ....KO 3
Aug. 26—Otis Gordon, Albany ....KO 4
Nov. 12—Dom Grandinetti, Scranton ....KO 6
1976-1978
(Inactive)
1979
Oct. 27—Dave Song, North Bergen ....KO 1
Nov. 7—Calvin Langston, Boston ....W 4
Nov. 28—Chuck Barone, West New York ....KO 1
1980
Feb. 27—Calvin Langston, Scranton ....W 6
Apr. 20—Paul Benjamin, Portland, Me. ....KO 5
Apr. 30—Joe Maye, Scranton ....W 6
May 28—Jerry Floey, Scranton ....W 8
Nov. 28—Ron Gabaree, Providence ....KO 2

LEON SMITH
Pasadena, California Lightweight
1980
Feb. 14—Alex Fernandez, Los Angeles ....D 4
Mar. 6—Alejandro Hernandez, Los Angeles ....W 4
Mar. 20—Francisco Nunez, Los Angeles ....KO 5
Apr. 3—Mano Morua, Los Angeles ....KO by 4
May 16—Sal Ramirez, San Bernardino ....KO 2
June 5—Manuel Moreno, Los Angeles ....W 4
June 13—Mario Del Valle, San Bernardino ....KO 1
June 18—Refugio Rojas, Las Vegas ....KO by 2
July 23—Ray Mancini, Las Vegas ....KO by 1

VINNIE SMITH
Portland, Me. Middleweight
1979
May 26—Joe Maye, Portland, Me. ....W 6
1980
Feb. 28—Scott Lukachek, Hartford ....KO by 2
June 13—John Ellis, San Diego ....L 4

REYNALDO (MISTER) SNIPES
White Plains, N.Y. Heavyweight
Height: 6 ft. 2½ in.
1978
Nov. —Carl Hulberton, Chicago ....KO 1
Dec. 10—Hal Emerson, White Plains ....W 4
1979
Feb. 10—Sam Miller, White Plains ....KO 3
Mar. 14—Ron Hope, White Plains ....W 4
Apr. 11—Dave Smith, White Plains ....KO 3
May 23—Barry Funches, White Plains ....KO 3
June 28—Charles Cox, White Plains ....W 6
July 8—Eugene Green, New York ....W 6
Oct. 10—Mike Tarasewich, White Plains ....KO 4
Dec. 5—Tyrone Harlee, White Plains ....KO 4
1980
Apr. 16—Dave Johnson, White Plains ....W 8
May 14—James Reid, White Plains ....KO 8
June 11—Johnny Warr, White Plains ....W 8
Aug. 9—Robert Coley, Atlantic City ....KO 2
Sept. 17—Larry Alexander, White Plains ....KO 2
Oct. 18—Rodell Dupree, Atlantic City ....KO 3
Nov. 25—Malik Dozier, Boston ....KO 5
Dec. 17—Dwaine Bonds, White Plains ....KO 8

218

STEVE SNOW
Hartford, Conn. Lightweight
1977
May 21—Alfonso Griggs, Hartford..............KO 2
June 10—Curtis Smith, Hartford.............KO by 2
Oct. 22—Joe Phillips, Hartford....................D 4
Nov. 26—Jose Vasquez, Waterbury.............KO 3
1978
Feb. 28—Benny Benitez, Hartford.................L 4
May 26—Mike Rae, Boston.......................W 4
June 29—Bobby Grant, Springfield................L 4
Dec. 9—Jose Ortiz, Springfield...................W 4
1979
Feb. 28—Hector Ortiz, Hartford...................L 4
Apr. 4—Luis Rodriguez, Springfield............KO 2
Apr. 24—Hector Ortiz, Hartford...................W 6
May 29—Angel Ortiz, Hartford.................KO by 4
June 29—Angel Ortiz, Hartford....................L 4
Sept. 7—Hector Ortiz, Hartford..................W 7
Oct. 17—Hector Ortiz, Hartford...................L 8
Nov. 28—Hector Ortiz, Hartford...................L 8
1980
Apr. 8—Bob Tomasetti, Hartford ....KO 2
June 20—Willie Franco, Hartford ....L 6
Aug. 2—Sean Mannion, Totowa ....KO by 5
Nov. 3—Ronnie Gibbons, Hartford ....KO by 3

DAN SNYDER
Philadelphia, Pa. Middleweight
1976
June 8—Carlos Prigg, Philadelphia..............W 4
Aug. 27—Robert Hart, Atlantic City..............W 4
Sept. 14—Jackie Thornton, Philadelphia..........W 4
Oct. 14—Kevin Moefield, Wilmington.............W 4
1977
Jan. 17—Daryl Lampkin, Philadelphia...........W 6
Feb. 5—Robert Hart, Bristol ....KO 2
Feb. 19—Speedy Robinson, Bristol..............KO 1
Mar. 11—Billy Goodman, Philadelphia.......KO by 4
Apr. 29—George Jacobs, Baltimore..............W 6
June 23—Clayton Ambrose, Philadelphia.........W 6
Sept. 15—Jerome Goodman, Upper Darby..........L 8
Oct. 20—Frank Fletcher, Upper Darby.......KO by 2
1978
Feb. 20—Jerome Jackson, Philadelphia......KO by 6
Apr. 7—Frank Wissenbach, Berlin.........KO by 6
July 15—Fred Daniels, Atlantic City............KO 1
July 31—Daniel Mapanya, Capetown..........L 10
Aug. 24—Curtis Parker, Philadelphia.......KO by 3
1979
Jan. 23—John Howard, Philadelphia.........KO by 4
May 12—Stanley Williams, Atlantic City.......KO 1
July 10—Norberto Sabater, Atlantic City ....L 6
Sept. 25—Prince Rodney, Wembley..........KO by 3
Oct. 30—Richie Bennett, Upper Darby........KO by 8
1980
Jan. 12—Wilson Bell, Atlantic City..............W 8
Feb. 29—Matteo Salvemini, Rome............KO by 4
July 20—Norberto Sabater, Great Gorge......KO by 5

JULIO SOTO SOLANO
Dominican Republic Bantamweight
1975
Oct. 8—Domonco Polanco, Santo Domingo ....W 4
1976
(Inactive)
1977
Mar. 28—Enrique Mateo, Santo Domingo ....W 10
June 27—Pedro Jose Diaz, Santo Domingo ....W 12
Aug. 8—Jose Ortiz, Santo Domingo ....KO 1
Oct. 3—Jose Jiminez, Santo Domingo ....L 12
Dec. 19—Ramon Cruz, Santo Domingo ....KO 7
1978
Feb. 24—Jose Jiminez, Santo Domingo ....W 12
Apr. 25—Jose Jiminez, Santo Domingo ....W 12
July 5—Edgardo Cuadrado, Santo Domingo .....KO 10
Sept. 26—Victor Bultron, Santo Domingo ....W 10
Oct. 16—Julian Solis, Santo Domingo ....L 12
1979
Feb. 24—Jesus Gomez, Santo Domingo ....KO 2
Apr. 6—Rafael Sosa, Santo Domingo ....W 9
June 29—Ramon L. Perez, Santo Domingo ....W 10
June 30—Ramon Perez, Santo Domingo ....W 10
Dec. 10—Emillio Hernandez, Romana ....W 12
1980
June 12—Miguel Lora, Monteria ....L 12
(Central American & Caribbean Bantamweight Title)
Oct. 20—Patricio Nunez, Santo Domingo ....KO 6

RAFAEL SOLIS
Puerto Rican Featherweight
1974
Aug. 12—Luis Rosario, San Juan ....D 4

1975
(Inactive)
1976
Apr. 27—Carlos Rodriguez, San Juan ....KO 7
June 5—Asar Agosta, San Juan ....W 6
1977
Feb. 22—Roberto Calixto, Santo Domingo ....KO 2
May 29—Ildrfonso Zethelmy, Caracas ....KO by 1
June 14—Claude Noel, Guadeloupe ....L 10
Aug. 8—Hector Montas, Santo Domingo ....KO 6
Oct. 14—Teo Ozuna, Santo Domingo ....W 10
Oct. 29—Ernesto Herrera, Los Angeles ....ND
1978
Apr. 14—Gregorio Severino, Santo Domingo ......KO 5
May 20—Jose Roman, Carolina ....KO 4
Aug. 14—Delio Mercedes, Santo Domingo ....KO 7
1979
Feb. 23—Adolfo Marte, Santo Domingo ....KO 3
1980
Feb. 23—Leonidas Asprilla, Cartagena ....D 10
July 17—Jose Alejandro, Rio Piedras ....KO 9
Aug. 29—Anthony House, Miami ....KO 3

RAMON SORIA
Argentine Bantamweight
Born: May 14, 1955, Villa Dolores
Previous record — 14 fights:
Won 10, Lost 1, Drew 3, 2 KOs.
1975
Oct. 24—Luis Cortez, Mendoza ....W 6
Nov. 21—Juan Ruarte, Mendoza ....W 6
1976
Feb. 13—Felix Ruarte, Villa Dolores ....KO 5
Feb. 28—Martin Devia, Guaymallen ....ND
July 23—Ruben Pasero, Rio III ....W 10
Aug. 20—Miguel A. Veliz, Mendoza ....KO 5
Sept. 15—Carlos Leyes, Buenos Aires ....W 10
Oct. 27—Luis Gerez, Buenos Aires ....W 10
Nov. 12—Tito Pereyra, C. Sarmiento ....KO 5
Dec. 3—Raul (Nico) Perez, Mendoza ....W 10
1977
Jan. 28—Carlos Escalante, Mar del Plata ....W 10
Feb. 25—A. Lois Fernandez, Mar del Plata ....W 10
Apr. 9—Ruben Pasero, Buenos Aires ....W 10
Apr. 22—Martin Devia, Villa Dolores ....KO 4
May 6—Juan C. Rios, Mendoza ....W 10
June 10—Ricardo Gomez, Villa Dolores ....KO 4
June 24—Juan C. Rios, Villa Dolores ....W 10
Aug. 19—Jose Flores, Villa Dolores ....W 10
Oct. 7—Alberto Martin, Maipu ....W 10
Nov. 18—Raul Perez, Mendoza ....W 10
Dec. 10—Rodolfo Rodriguez, Buenos Aires ....W 12
(Won Argentine Flyweight Title)
1978
Feb. 17—Miguel A. Lazarte, Mar del Plata ....W 12
(Retained Argentine Flyweight Title)
Mar. 9—Gilberto Lopez, Mendoza ....W 10
Mar. 30—Felipe Rojas, Mendoza ....W 10
Apr. 14—Santos Laciar, Huinca Renanco ....D 10
May 27—Felipe Rojas, San Julian ....W 10
June 9—Americo Suarez, Bolivar ....W 10
July 22—Rodolfo Rodriguez, Buenos Aires ....W 12
(Retained Argentine Flyweight Title)
Aug. 11—C. Reyes Sosa, San Juan ....KO 4
Sept. 22—Ramon Rodriguez, Tucuman ....D 10
Dec. 1—Santos Laciar, Mendoza ....W 10
1979
Nov. 10—Freddy Castillo, Buenos Aires ....KO by 5
1980
May 14—Rafael Orono, Caracas ....L 15
(For WBA Junior Featherweight Title)
Aug. 8—Heleno Ferreira, Mendoza ....W 10
Sept. 12—Carlos Huilli, V. Carlos Pax ....W 10
Oct. 7—Juan C. Cortez, Mendoza ....W 10
Oct. 25—Welille Nkusunkulu, Sun City ....L 8
Dec. 10—Juan C. Cortez, Cordoba ....D 10

GREG SORRENTINO
Syracuse, N.Y. Heavyweight
1976
July 28—Bob Smith, Utica ....D 4
Aug. 16—Johnny Blaine, Utica ....KO 4
Sept. 11—Johnny Warr, Utica ....W 4
Sept. 28—Johnny Blaine, New York ....W 6
Oct. 2—Johnny Warr, Utica ....W 6
Oct. 29—Eddie Phillips, Latham ....W 4
Nov. 6—Dave Wilson, Waterbury ....L 6
Dec. 3—Johnny Warr, Rochester ....W 6
1977
Jan. 27—Humberto Molyouex, Syracuse ....W 8
May 7—Lee Conalito, St. Louis ....L 4
June 3—Bob Smith, Syracuse ....W dlsq 0
Aug. 16—Ibar Arrington, Seattle ....W 10

1978

Mar.	25—Vic Brown, Syracuse		W	10
May	15—Billy Sharkey, New York		W	10
Aug.	16—Johnny Warr, Newark		W	10
Oct.	8—Trevor Berbick, Halifax		KO by	7
Dec.	5—John L. Gardner, London		KO by	7

1979

Jan.	11—Ron Gebere, Cohoes		KO	3
Mar.	29—Bob Stallings, Cohoes		W	8
Mar.	31—Jim Beattie, Chicago		W	10
May	12—Mike Dokes, Las Vegas		KO by	3
Oct.	17—Dennis Jordan, Hartford		W	10

1980

Jan.	19—Don Halpin, Syracuse		W	10
Aug.	18—Steve Zouski, Boston		KO by	10

ALBERTO P. SOSA
Argentine Junior Welterweight
1980

July	18—Hector Cabrera, Villa Maria		W	6
Sept.	5—Hector Cabrera, Tio Pujio		W	6
Sept.	20—Ruben Mansilla, Catrilo		KO	6

BENICIO SOSA
Argentine Featherweight
1980

Apr.	24—Alberto Pereyra, Corrientes		KO by	5
July	18—Alberto Pereyra, Villa Angela		KO	8
Sept.	6—Omar Mendoza, Villa Angela		W	10
Oct.	3—Angel Zalazar, Formosa		D	10
Nov.	7—Angel Zalazar, Villa Angela		KO	6
Nov.	21—Jorge Gomez, Gral Roca		KO by	4

FERNANDO R. SOSA
Argentine Featherweight
1980

July	25—Ramon Galarce, Rio Hondo		KO	6
Aug.	22—Hector Ayala, La Banda		W	6
Sept.	5—Ovidio Szkartziuk, Mar del Plata		KO	2
Sept.	26—Felipe Baez, Mar del Plata		W	8
Oct.	24—Adolfo Felice, Mar del Plata		W	10
Dec.	12—Juan J. Brizuela, Mar del Plata		KO	10

JOE SOSA
Kansas City Lightweight
1979

Aug.	16—Simmie Black, Kansas City		KO	4
Nov.	16—Charlie Evans, Kansas City		D	6

1980

Jan.	9—Charlie Evans, Kansas City		L	6

JUAN C. SOSA
Argentine Light Heavyweight
1980

Mar.	14—Miguel Paez, Tandil		W	12
	(Won Argentine Light Heavyweight Title)			
Apr.	24—Ruben Zamaro, Tucuman		L	10
May	17—Roberto Aguilar, Corrientes		D	12
July	11—Raul Zalazar, P.R.S. Pena		KO	7
Aug.	15—Francisco Bono, Los Toldos		KO	3
Oct.	10—Waldemar Paulino, Tandil		W	12
	(Won South American Light Heavyweight Title)			
Dec.	19—Ruben Zamaro, Junin		L	12
	(Lost Argentine Light Heavyweight Title)			

JOSE SOTO
Texas Junior Lightweight
1979

July	21—Juan Venegas, Houston		KO by	5
Sept.	12—Charlie Carroll, El Paso		W	4

1980

Oct.	28—Miguel Flores, Houston		W	8
Nov.	11—Obie Garnett, Louisville		KO	1

BOBBY SPARKS
Alliance, Ohio Lightweight
1976

Sept.	7—Charley Buggs, Portsmouth		L	6
Dec.	11—John Alexander, Alliance		W	4

1977

Jan.	22—Paul Stewart, Portsmouth		KO	3
Mar.	5—Chuck Spicer, Portsmouth		W	6
Apr.	30—Ray Greene, Portsmouth		W	6
May	28—Cookie Claytor, Portsmouth		KO	2
July	16—Calvin Straughter, Columbus		W	4
Sept.	24—Calvin Straughter, Columbus		W	4
Oct.	8—Johnny Green, Portsmouth		KO	3

1978

Apr.	17—Chico Rodriguez, Columbus		KO	3
Nov.	29—Charlie Buggs, Richfield		KO	3

1979

Jan.	10—Otto Palfy, Richfield		KO	6
Mar.	21—Jerry Strickland, Richfield		KO	1

Apr.	19—Bobby Thomas, Richfield		KO	1
May	25—Phil Bowen, Richfield		KO	2
July	26—Mike Johnson, Dayton		KO	5

1980

Apr.	30—Ray Mancini, Youngstown		KO by	1

CARLTON SPARROW
Las Vegas, Nev. Junior Lightweight
1980

Sept.	10—George Crawford, Las Vegas		KO	2
Sept.	24—Bobby Krueger, Las Vegas		KO	3
Nov.	12—Larry Hernandez, Las Vegas		KO	2
Dec.	3—Albert Jones, Las Vegas		KO	1

DON SPELLMAN
Virginia Beach, Va. Heavyweight
1977

June	2—Billy Howard, Virginia Beach		KO	1
Aug.	5—Ira Martin, Richmond		L	6
	—Charlie Harris, Virginia Beach		W	6
Aug.	21—Matt Robinson, Virginia Beach		W	6
Sept.	23—Quinnie Locklear, Virginia Beach		W	4

1978

Jan.	19—Art Savage, Virginia Beach		W	6
Apr.	20—Dave Johnson, Virginia Beach		L	6
Dec.	14—Bob Stallings, Virginia Beach		L	6

1979

Oct.	11—Ali Ben Franklin, Richmond		W	6

1980

Nov.	1—Charlie Smith, Richmond		W	8
Dec.	20—Johnny Blaine, Richmond		KO	6

CLYDE SPENCER
McAlester, Okla. Middleweight
1976

Sept.	7—Mickey Bants, Oklahoma City		L	4
Sept.	21—Rocky Matthews, Oklahoma City		W	4
Oct.	5—Bill Pearish, Oklahoma City		KO by	3
Nov.	2—Steve Channell, Oklahoma City		W	4

1977

Aug.	20—Wendell Helm, Oklahoma City		KO	2
Sept.	6—Dennis Horne, Oklahoma City		W	4
Oct.	4—Phil Reed, Oklahoma City		D	4
Oct.	18—Phil Reed, Oklahoma City		W	4
Nov.	15—Ruben Bardot, Oklahoma City		KO by	3
Dec.	6—Curtis Williams, Oklahoma City		KO	4

1978

May	23—Jimmy Heair, Little Rock		KO by	3
June	10—Dennis Horne, Oklahoma City		KO by	2
Oct.	11—Dwaine Pice, Oklahoma City		KO	2
Nov.	16—Tom Crowley, Oklahoma City		L	4

1979

Mar.	17—Mike Glur, Oklahoma City		D	4
Apr.	28—Bruce Strauss, Omaha		KO by	6
June	19—Chris Rizzo, Orlando		KO by	8
July	26—Danny Campbell, Overland Park		KO by	2

1980

Feb.	9—Lorenzo Jones, Oklahoma City		KO by	4
Aug.	26—Billy Watkins, Houston		KO by	2
Sept.	25—Pat Duran, Oklahoma City		L	6
Nov.	20—Pat Duran, Oklahoma City		L	6

GARY SPENCER
Sacramento, Calif. Junior Lightweight
1980

Mar.	18—Vicente Manzanares, Sparks		W	6
June	12—Jose Ortega, Stockton		W	6
July	16—Francisco Velez, Stockton		KO	1
Aug.	30—Gary Garcia, Incline Village		D	6
Aug.	7—Puma Medina, San Carlos		W	6
Sept.	30—Richard Savala, Sacramento		L	10

GENE SPENCER
Memphis, Tenn. Lightweight
1979

Dec.	19—Tom Crowley, Rockford		KO by	3

1980

Mar.	7—Pajarito Marquez, Chicago		KO by	1
May	12—James Buckley, Cape Girardeau		KO by	1

ROBERT SPENCER
Zellwood, Fla. Junior Middleweight
1976

Feb.	3—Frankie Santore, Orlando		KO by	3

1977
(Inactive)

1978

Jan.	17—Tiger Hall, Orlando		W	4
Jan.	31—Joey Vincent, Orlando		W	10
Nov.	7—Gary Smith, Orlando		W	6

1979

Feb.	6—Jimmy Heir, Orlando		KO by	3
Mar.	13—Gary Smith, Orlando		W	6

June 6—Clauzell Longmire, Miami ....KO by 2
July 19—Willie Vasser, Panama City, Fla. ....KO 2

MICHAEL SPINKS
St. Louis, Mo. Light Heavyweight
1976 Middleweight Gold Medalist in Montreal Olympics
Born: July 13, 1956
1977
Apr. 17—Eddie Benson, Las Vegas ....KO 1
May   7—Luis Rodriguez, St. Louis ....W 6
June 1—Joe Bordon, Montreal ....KO 2
Aug. 23—Jasper Brisbane, Philadelphia ....KO 1
Sept. 13—Ray Elson, Los Angeles ....KO 1
Oct. 22—Gary Summerhays, Las Vegas ....W 10
1978
Feb. 15—Tom Bethea, Las Vegas ....W 10
Dec. 15—Eddie Phillips, White Plains ....KO 4
1979
Nov. 24—Marc Hans, Bloomington ....KO 1
1980
Feb. 1—Johnny Wilburn, Louisville ....W 10
Feb. 24—Ramon Ronquillo, Atlantic City ....KO 6
May   4—Murray Sutherland, Kiamesha Lake .....W 10
Aug. 2—Dave Conteh, Baton Rouge ....KO 7
Oct. 18—Yaqui Lopez, Atlantic City ....KO 7

MARTIN SPRIGGS
Baltimore, Md. Middleweight
1979
Nov. 14—Bill Harrington, Baltimore ....KO 2
Nov. 29—Al Bracy, Richmond ....NC 1
1980
Sept. 11—Anthony Petrie, Washington, D.C. ......W 4
Nov. 1—Paul Grant, Richmond ....KO 2
Dec. 20—Richard Williams, Richmond ....KO 1

FRED SPRY
Peekskill, N.Y. Middleweight
1980
Feb. 13—John Griffin, White Plains ....KO 2
Mar. 12—Jack Flowers, White Plains ....KO 2
Apr. 16—Lee Grant, White Plains ....KO 1
May   14—Lenny Villers, White Plains ....L 4
Dec. 17—Charley Young, White Plains ....KO 3

DAN STAEHLE
Paterson, N.J. Middleweight
1978
May   20—Carl Viel, Trenton ....W 4
June 13—Rusty Rosenberger, Totowa ....L 6
June 20—Carl Viel, Trenton ....W 4
July 18—Larry Allen, Totowa ....W 4
Sept. 26—Marciano Bernardi, Totowa ....L 6
Nov. 14—Ray Bryant, Totowa ....W 6
1979
Apr. 27—Andrew Coe, Newark ....KO 3
June 29—Kevin Perry, Jersey City ....KO by 1
Dec. 12—Ralph Mifka, Scranton ....K 6
1980
Feb. 22—Danny Long, Fall River ....KO by 4
May   22—Tommy Merola, Totowa ....L 6

ROGER STAFFORD
Philadelphia, Pa. Welterweight
1977
May   7—Newton Mc Swain, St. Louis ....KO 2
June 1—Bobby Hughes, Montreal ....W 4
Oct. 22—Richie Kronich, Las Vegas ....KO 1
1978
Feb. 11—Ron Turner, Las Vegas ....KO 1
Mar. 18—Gil Valdez, Las Vegas ....KO 4
Apr. 7—Enrique Silva, Los Angeles ....W 8
Dec. 15—Al Fletcher, White Plains ....L 6
1979
Feb. 16—Vincent Evans, Louisville ....KO 1
Mar. 14—Malik Muhammad, White Plains ....KO 2
June 20—Robert Davis, White Plains ....KO 8
Sept. 12—Dale Staley, White Plains ....W 10
1980
Feb. 18—Michael Herron, Upper Darby ....W 8
May   16—Bernard Peterson, Chester ....D 8
Aug. 7—Bernard Peterson, Atlantic City ....L 8
Sept. 4—Johnny Cooper, Atlantic City ....W 10
Dec. 4—Tony Suero, Atlantic City ....W 10

DALE STALEY
Hillcrest Hgts., Md. Welterweight
1977
Dec. 17—Frank Brimage, Lowell .... ,, W 4
1978
Jan. 5—Don Godrey, Portland, Me. ....KO 2
Jan. 28—Buddy Carr, Providence ....KO 2

Mar. 1—Don McCrea, White Plains ....KO 1
Mar. 23—Kevin Murphy, Portland, Me. ....KO 1
May   10—Ray Rosa, White Plains ....KO 1
July 20—Gene Ellington, Detroit ....KO 3
      —Conway Bollins, North Bergen ....KO 3
Aug. 8—Floyd Pittman, Baltimore ....KO 3
Aug. 13—Ralph Dumont, Portland ....KO 2
Sept. 21—Ron Pettigrew, Washington, D.C. ....L disq. 6
1979
Jan. 22—Marvin Ladson, Washington, D.C. ......L 6
Mar. 28—Alvin Anderson, Baltimore ....KO by 3
Aug. 7—Jessie Carter, Baltimore ....L 6
Sept. 12—Roger Stafford, White Plains ....L 10
1980
Feb. 27—Wilbert Thomas, Washington, D.C. ..W disq. 2
Apr. 10—Mike Picciotti, Atlantic City ....KO by 6

BOB STALLINGS
Long Island, N.Y., Heavyweight
Born: 1944, South Carolina
1965
Feb. 1—Rudy Pavesi, New York ....L 4
Feb. 28—Mel Turnbow, New York ....L 4
Mar. 23—Pat Louis, New York ....W 4
Apr. 21—Frank Rindgen, New York ....K 4
Apr. 30—Don McAteer, Paterson ....L 6
July 26—Devieny Washington, Freeport ....W 4
Aug. 23—Devieny Washington, Freeport ....W 4
Sept. 20—Pat Louis, Freeport ....W 4
Sept. 23—Buster Mathis, Grand Rapids ....L 6
Oct. 19—Chuck Wepner, New York ....W 6
1966
Feb. 3—Ossi Buttner, Frankfort ....W 8
Mar. 15—Henry Wallitsch, New York ....W 6
Aug. 10—Frank Fudge, Freeport ....W 6
Sept. 8—Louis Hicks, Freeport ....W 6
Sept. 15—Buster Mathis, Akron ....L 10
Oct. 10—Lee Carr, Walpole ....L 8
Dec. 13—Jack Bodell, Wolverhampton ....KO by 7
1967
May   2—Curtis Bruce, Boston ....L 8
Nov. 6—Lee Batts, Philadelphia ....L 6
Dec. 5—Al Jones, Miami Beach ....L 10
Dec. 12—Al Lewis, Buffalo ....KO 7
1968
Jan. 28—Piero Tomasoni, Milan ....L 10
Mar. 14—John Jordan, Baltimore ....L 8
Apr. 5—Eduardo Corletti, Goteberg ....L 10
Apr. 16—Vic Brown, Buffalo ....W 10
May   8—Al Lewis, McKeesport ....L 10
June 5—John Jordan, Norfolk ....L 10
Sept. 21—Al Lewis, Detroit ....KO by 2
Oct. 29—Roy Williams, Philadelphia ....L 8
1969
Apr. 14—Henry Clark, San Carlos ....KO by 8
June 30—Wendell Newton, Hempstead ....L 8
July 30—Willie McMillan, Indianapolis ....W 10
Oct. 3—Leweni Waqa, Papeete ....W 8
Dec. 4—Willie McMillan, Indianapolis ....L 10
1970-1971
(Inactive)
1972
Mar. 14—Willie Moore, New York ....KO by 7
Apr. 20—Martin Middleton, Baltimore ....KO by 6
Nov. 10—Billy Daniels, New York ....W 8
1973
Apr. 14—Ron Lyle, Missoula ....L 10
June 30—Mac Foster, Chicago ....W 10
Dec. 14—Charlie Green, New York ....KO 4
1974
May   4—James J. Woody, New York ....KO 6
Aug. 12—Bob Mashburn, New York ....W 10
Nov. 4—Earnie Shavers, New York ....W 10
1975
(Inactive)
1976
Aug. 13—Greg Johnson, New York ....KO 8
Nov. 26—Greg Johnson, New York ....L 12
1977
Apr. 15—Horace Robinson, New York ....L 8
1978
Feb. 6—Horst Geisler (Him), Edmonton ....KO 3
Apr. 14—Clarence Thomas, Ft. Lauderdale ......KO 1
May   18—Bobby Jordan, Virginia Beach ....L 8
June 10—Hubert Hilton, Brooklyn ....KO 4
Sept. 6—Tyrone Harlee, White Plains ....L 6
Oct. 12—Broderick Mason, Rahway ....W 4
Dec. 14—Don Spellman, Virginia Beach ....W 6
1979
Mar. 29—Greg Sorrentino, Cohoes ....L 8
May   20—Calvin Hardy, White Plains ....KO 1
June 12—Mike Tarasewich, Totowa ....KO 1
Nov. 13—Ernie Smith, Beaumont ....KO 3

1980
Feb. 19—Jerry McIntyre, Totowa .... KO 1
Apr. 24—Larry Alexander, Totowa .... KO by 8
Aug. 1—Alfredo Evangelista, Mallorca .... L disq. 6

RUBEN STAMULI
Argentine Junior Lightweight
1980
Mar. 7—Ruben Riani, Mar del Plata .... KO by 5
Apr. 25—Faustino Barrios, San Nicolas .... L 10
Aug. 8—Oscar Silva, Mar del Plata .... KO 6
Sept. 13—Faustino Barrios, Mar del Plata .... W 10
Dec. 12—Faustino Barrios, Bolivar .... TD 9

RON STANDER
Omaha, Neb. Heavyweight
1969
July 31—Bobby Street, Milwaukee .... KO 1
Aug. 15—Red Ferris, Sioux Falls .... KO 1
Sept. 29—Lee Estes, Milwaukee .... KO 2
Nov. 17—Willie Elbert, Omaha .... KO 1
Dec. 19—Joe Byrd, Omaha .... W 6
1970
Jan. 29—Roy Rodriguez, Waterloo .... W 6
Feb. —Lee Powell, Omaha .... KO 1
Mar. 23—Joe Harris, Milwaukee .... KO 4
Apr. 9—Woody Parks, Omaha .... KO 1
May 11—Earnie Shavers, Omaha .... KO 5
June 8—Eddie Dembry, Omaha .... W 8
July 17—Ray Ellis, Omaha .... KO 3
Aug. 28—Bill Hardney, Omaha .... KO 1
Sept. 17—Manuel Ramos, Omaha .... D 10
Nov. 3—Murphy Gordwin, Oklahoma City .... KO 1
1971
Mar. 30—Frank Bullard, Omaha .... KO 6
Apr. 23—Thad Spencer, Omaha .... W 10
May 24—Lee Carr, Omaha .... KO 6
July 29—Jack O'Halloran, Omaha .... W 10
Aug. 10—Manuel Ramos, Omaha .... W 10
Oct. 26—Jesse Crown, Omaha .... KO 3
Dec. 20—Clyde Brown, Elgin .... KO 3
1972
Jan. 22—Reco Brooks, Denver .... L 10
Feb. 14—Mike Boswell, Omaha .... W 10
Mar. 20—Johnny Mac, Council Bluffs .... W 10
May 25—Joe Frazier, Omaha .... KO by 5
(World Heavyweight Title)
1973
Mar. 29—John Jordan, Portland, Me. .... L 10
Sept. 10—Walker Smith, Providence .... KO 3
Nov. 28—Jeff Merritt, Cleveland .... KO by 3
1974
Feb. 19—Charlie James, Honolulu .... L 10
Mar. 22—Morris Jackson, Omaha .... D 10
July 31—Rodney Bobick, Bloomington .... L 10
1975
May 7—Fred Askew, Minneapolis .... L 10
Aug. 5—Bruce Scott, Oklahoma City .... KO 2
Sept. 4—Morris Jackson, Omaha .... KO 2
Nov. 20—Terry Daniels, Omaha .... KO 1
Dec. 10—Scott LeDoux, Minneapolis .... L 10
1976
Jan. 6—Willie Jackson, Oklahoma City .... KO 1
Apr. 30—Ken Norton, Landover .... KO by 5
June 1—Bo Williford, Oklahoma City .... KO 3
July 18—Gerrie Coetzee, Johannesburg ...... KO by 8
1977
July 19—Boone Kirkman, Seattle .... KO by 9
Nov. 15—Raul Hernandez, Oklahoma City .... KO 4
Nov. 30—Horace Robinson, White Plains ...... KO by 5
1978
Mar. 23—Clyde Mudgett, Omaha .... KO 4
July 26—Bill Jackson, Omaha .... KO 1
Oct. 25—Charley Polite, Omaha .... W 10
Nov. 29—Charles Atlas, Omaha .... KO 1
1979
Apr. 3—Rick Howe, Marshalltown .... KO 6
Apr. 28—James Dixon, Omaha .... L 10
June 25—James Dixon, Omaha .... L 12
Aug. 16—Jim Pearish, North Platte .... KO 5
Aug. 24—Tom Fischer, Cincinnati .... L 10
1980
Jan. 8—Scott Frank, Totowa .... KO by 1
Mar. 3—James Tillis, Chicago .... KO by 7
May 24—Jeff Shelburg, Salt Lake City .... L 10
July 27—Otis Hardy, Omaha .... D 10

LARRY STANTON
Merrick, N.Y. Junior Welterweight
1969
—Tulip Turnseed, Indianapolis .... KO
1970
Mar. 16—Tito Flores, New York .... W 4

Apr. 1—Jose Pagan (Rivera), New York .... KO 1
May 27—Roy Williams, Scranton .... ND
Aug. 10—Charles Scott, Freeport .... KO 2
Sept. 10—Oreste Lebron, New York .... L 4
1971-1975
(Inactive)
1976
Jan. 3—Ruben Grant, Philadelphia .... KO 2
Jan. 24—Paddy Dolan, Commack .... KO 4
Jan. 29—Jimmy McCloud, New York .... W 4
Feb. 25—Alphonse Joseph, Scranton .... KO 2
Feb. 28—George Fakaras, Commack .... W 6
Mar. 30—Jose Corra, Miami Beach .... KO 3
May 12—Lou Vega, Scranton .... W 6
May 23—Ruby Ortiz, Erie .... D 8
July 30—Morris Cronin, Indianapolis .... KO 2
Oct. 4—Quenton Blackman, Scranton .... KO 1
Oct. 22—Joe Grier, New York .... D 8
Oct. —Carlos Gonzalez, Albany .... W 8
1977
Jan. 21—Johnny Copeland, Cincinnati .... W 10
Mar. 25—Marcos Barahona, New York .... L 8
June 18—Angel Cintron, Commack .... KO 7
July 26—Charlie Nash, Derry .... L 10
Oct. 7—Claude Noel, Port of Spain .... L 10
Oct. 27—Johnny Turner, New York .... L 10
1978
Jan. 14—Rufus Miller, Hauppauge .... W 10
Mar. 2—Vilomar Fernandez, New York .... D 10
May 13—Howard Davis, Orlando .... L 10
July 9—Johnny Copeland, Indianapolis .... KO 5
July 26—Alfredo Escalera, New York .... KO by 3
Oct. 14—Ralph Racine, Commack .... L 10
Dec. 8—Johnny Lira, New York .... L 10
1979
May 11—George Fakaris, Commack .... KO 5
June 19—Jimmy Blevins, Orlando .... L 10
June 29—Marvin Edwards, Commack .... KO 8
Aug. 24—Jerry Strickland, Cincinnati .... KO 2
Sept. 14—Sammy Ayala, Houston .... W 10
Oct. 12—Fred Johnson, Nassau .... KO 3
Nov. 30—Tony Petronelli, Las Vegas .... W 10
1980
Feb. 29—Teo Ozuna, Commack .... L 10

MARCUS STARKS
Hartford, Conn. Junior Welterweight
1979
July 27—Mike Knox, Hartford .... W 4
Sept. 7—Mike Knox, Hartford .... KO 4
Sept. 27—Eddie Flores, Bristol .... D 4
Oct. 17—Benny Benitez, Hartford .... W 4
Nov. 15—Charlie Newell, Bristol .... W 4
Nov. 28—Benny Benitez, Hartford .... D 6
1980
Feb. 28—Jose Gonzales, Hartford .... KO 3
Apr. 8—Lloyd Jones, Hartford .... KO 3
June 20—Joshua King, Hartford .... W 6
Oct. 15—Jeff Passero, White Plains .... L 8
Nov. 3—Norberto Figueroa, Hartford .... L 6

MARLON (MOOCHIE) STARLING
Hartford, Conn. Welterweight
1979
July 27—Tim LaValley, Hartford .... KO 3
Sept. 7—Hubert Jackson, Hartford .... W 4
Sept. 27—Jerry Worth, Hartford .... W 4
Oct. 17—Hector Ortiz, Hartford .... W 6
Nov. 5—John Saxton, Hartford .... KO 4
1980
Jan. 9—Charlie Newell, Hartford .... KO 7
Feb. 28—Frank Minigan, Hartford .... KO 6
Apr. 8—Feliciano Cintron, Hartford .... KO 8
May 23—Eddie Campbell, Hartford .... W 8
June 20—Benji Goldstone, Hartford .... KO 5
Nov. 3—Dave Bolden, Hartford .... KO 3
Nov. 25—Curtis Taylor, Hartford .... W 10

WOODY STARR
Miami, Fla. Middleweight
1978
Feb. 17—Slick Boy, Nassau .... L 4
Apr. 29—William Young, Nassau .... KO by 4
1979
Jan. 13—Jean Claude LeClair, Miami Beach .. KO by 3
June 22—Clevez Williams, Nassau .... L 8
1980
Mar. 28—Pat Strachen, Nassau .... L 6
July 25—Dave Starkey, Miami .... KO by 3

HARVEY STEICHEN
Spokane, Wash. Heavyweight
1979
Feb. 14—Al Neumann, Spokane .... L 8

222

Mar. 31—Bennett White, Spokane .... W 8
July 3—Ken Austin, Gardnerville .... W 10
Sept. 18—Wilbert Albers, Reno .... KO 8
Oct. 3—Abdullah Muhammad, Spokane .... KO 5
Oct. 16—Ernie Smith, Sparks .... KO by 1
Nov. 20—Ken Austin, Sparks .... W 10
Dec. 11—Ken Arlt, Spokane .... W 10
1980
Jan. 23—Ken Arlt, Portland .... L 8
Feb. 9—Franco Thomas, Clarksburg .... L 10
Mar. 15—Jeff Shelburg, Denver .... L 10
Mar. 19—Jeff Podgurski, Las Vegas .... W 8
Apr. 15—Ernie Smith, Sparks .... KO 5
Apr. 24—Ken Arlt, Portland .... L 12
May 28—George O'Mara, Las Vegas .... L 10
June 21—Franco Thomas, Las Vegas .... L 10
July 3—Joe Garcia, Gardnerville .... KO 3
Aug. 23—Jeff Shelburg, Salt Lake City .... KO by 1
Oct. 11—Gord Racette, Nanaimo .... KO by 5
Dec. 17—Bruce Scott, Crystal Bay .... KO 3

GREG STEPHENS
San Diego, Calif. Welterweight
1977
Apr. 29—Bert Lee, San Diego .... KO 2
May 13—Ken Sheppard, San Diego .... KO 2
May 20—Larry Myers, San Diego .... KO 3
June 10—Ricky Gibbs, San Diego .... KO 2
June 24—Ted Sanders, San Diego .... KO 3
Aug. 19—Ken Crooms, San Diego .... L 6
Nov. 4—Vince Delgado, San Diego .... KO by 5
Dec. 16—Vince Delgado, San Diego .... W 6
1978
Mar. 18—Zeferino Gonzalez, Los Angeles .... L 6
Apr. 19—Fred Lorona, San Francisco .... W 10
May 17—David Oropeza, Las Vegas .... KO 4
June 7—Ramon Reyes, Las Vegas .... KO 2
June 21—Victor Martinez, Concord .... KO by 7
Sept. 8—Manny Lopez, Los Angeles .... KO 2
Dec. 8—Hector Thompson, Brisbane .... W 10
1979
Feb. 24—Neil Pattel, Brisbane .... KO 9
Sept. 25—Bruce Curry, Las Vegas .... L 10
Oct. 30—Pepe Dominguez, Las Vegas .... W 10
1980
June 3—Bruce Curry, Las Vegas .... KO 11
(NABF Welterweight Title)
July 8—Pepe Dominguez, Las Vegas .... W 12
Nov. 11—Pepe Dominguez, Las Vegas .... L 12
(NABF Welterweight Title)

PAUL STEPHENS
Houston, Tex. Middleweight
1977
Oct. 22—Macaro Estoga, Lubbock .... KO 2
Oct. 26—David Kuykendall, Dallas .... KO 2
1978
Mar. 22—Dennis Haggerty, Dallas .... W 4
June 20—Ignacio Lopez, Houston .... W 6
June 27—Marcus Dorsey, Odessa .... KO 3
Aug. 22—Robert Perry, Odessa .... KO 8
Nov. 14—Freddy Johnson, New Orleans .... L 10
1979
Mar. 20—Robert Powell, Houston .... L 8
1980
July 18—Chato Ramos, Houston .... L 8
Aug. 16—Marcario Estorga, Odessa .... KO 1
Sept. 9—Ed Temple, Warren .... KO 3
Sept. 23—Ignacio Lopez, Houston .... L 8
Oct. 28—Jesse Clark, Warren .... KO 1
Dec. 9—Ted Hamilton, Warren .... KO 1
Dec. 17—Henry Patterson, Youngstown .... W 10

GREG STEVENS
Washington, D.C. Junior Welterweight
1977
Nov. 25—Earl Stringer, Detroit .... W 4
1978
Mar. 15—Robert Brumfield, Washington, D.C. ..... W 4
Apr. 5—Ditman Becton, Washington, D.C. ...... L 4
Apr. 19—Ernest Gladney, Washington, D.C. ..... W 4
May 24—Otis Hooper, Washington, D.C. .... W 6
Nov. 21—Al Hughes, Washington .... W 5
1980
Feb. 27—James Lee, Washington, D.C. .... KO 1
Mar. 12—Otis Hooper, Washington, D.C. .... W 6
Sept. 11—Ronnie Green, Washington, D.C. .... L 6

ROCKY STEVENS
Jacksonville, Fla. Light Heavyweight
1977
Nov. 17—Irving Gifford, Gainesville .... W 4

1978
Feb. 25—Olomon Brown, Jacksonville .... KO 5
Apr. 10—Willie Stevens, Jacksonville .... KO 5
May 11—Chris Lange, Palatka .... L 6
Aug. 22—Dennis Riggs, Jacksonville .... KO by 7
Sept. 19—Jimmy Salerno, Orlando .... KO by 2
Nov. 6—Willie Goodwin, Jacksonville .... KO 3
Dec. 5—Chris Lange, Jacksonville .... L 6
1979
Jan. 8—Solomon Howard, Jacksonville .... KO 2
Jan. 17—John Symonette, Orlando .... KO by 1
Jan. 29—Marcus Davis, Jacksonville .... W 6
Feb. 12—James Crocker, Jacksonville .... KO 7
Mar. 21—A. W. Muhammad, Alachua .... L 8
May 9—Slick Mitchell, Fernanina .... L 6
—Kenny Klingman, Fort Lauderdale ... KO by 1
1980
Apr. 26—Demetrius Edwards, Greenville ...... KO by 1
July 24—Marvin Pearish, Savannah .... KO by 9

ROBERT STEVENSON
Atlantic City, N.J. Featherweight
1979
July 31—Ron Aurit, Atlantic City .... KO by 5
1980
Aug. 9—Kevin Renshaw, Atlantic City .... D 4
Sept. 27—Ken Bogner, Trenton .... KO by 1

TOM STEVENSON
Indianapolis, Ind. Heavyweight
1980
May 9—Jimmy Flynn, Chicago .... W 6
Aug. 13—Ric Ennis, Indianapolis .... KO 1
Sept. 6—Jerry Hunter, Jenkins .... W 6

J. W. STEWART
California Middleweight
1980
June 13—Marcos Garcia, San Diego .... D 4
June 19—Jeff McCracken, Tacoma .... TD 4
July 1—Scott Wilson, San Bernardino W-5
July 16—Marcos Garcia, San Diego .... KO by 2
Aug. 2—Jeff McCracken, Cincinnati .... KO by 2

MARVIN STINSON
Philadelphia, Pa. Heavyweight
Born: May 4, 1952
1977
July 20—Charles Boston, Virginia Beach .... KO 2
Aug. 26—Will Payne, Allentown .... KO 2
Sept. 17—Rocky Bently, Richmond .... KO 1
Oct. 6—Al Surafail, Philadelphia .... W 8
Nov. 1—Fred Jones, Philadelphia .... KO 3
Dec. 6—Mike Montgomery, Philadelphia .... KO 6
1978
Jan. 6—Johnny Warr, Philadelphia .... W 8
Mar. 14—Leroy Diggs, Philadelphia .... W 8
May 15—Pedro Soto, New York .... W 8
Dec. 5—Randy Mack, Philadelphia .... D 8
1979
July 10—Tyrone Harlee, Atlantic City .... W 8
Dec. 4—Larry Alexander, Upper Darby .... D 8
1980
Mar. 31—Eddie Wilson, Las Vegas .... KO 3
May 25—Randy Mack, Atlantic City .... D 10
Oct. 23—Jeff Shelburg, Las Vegas .... W 10

WILLIE STOGLIN
Odessa, Texas Heavyweight
1978
July 31—Alvin Dominey, Odessa .... KO by 1
Sept. 19—Ernie Smith, Odessa .... L 4
Nov. 18—Jimmy Pearish, Joplin .... KO 4
Dec. 15—Lou Bailey, Omaha .... L 6
1979
May 22—Larry Montgomery, Beaumont .... L 4
June 19—Tom Trim, Houston .... KO by 3
July 2—Pinklon Thomas, Washington .... KO by 2
1980
June 24—George Graham, Honolulu .... KO by 1
Aug. 31—Mark Lee, Carson City .... KO by 3

JEFF STOUDEMIRE
Cleveland, Ohio Middleweight
Born: September 24, 1957. Height: 6 ft. 2 in.
1980
Sept. 18—Mike Sacchetti, Cleveland .... L 4
Oct. 28—Felix Siefrentes, Warren .... KO 1
Nov. 25—Ron Ayers, Hartford .... KO 1
Dec. 5—Kevin Cheatim, Versailles .... KO 3
Dec. 11—Elvis Parks, Chicago .... KO 5
Dec. 16—Steve Woods, Cleveland .... KO 2

DARRELL STOVALL
Phoenix, Ariz. Lightweight
1979
July	25—Ricardo Jiminez, Phoenix	L	4
Aug.	15—Rudy Matta, Tucson	W	4
Aug.	22—Rudy Matta, Phoenix	W	4

1980
Jan.	11—Robert Anderson, Phoenix	L	6
July	24—Eliu Hernandez, Las Vegas	W	4
Sept.	25—Rosendo Caldez, Las Vegas	KO	1
Oct.	22—Raymond Grant, Las Vegas	KO	1
Nov.	5—Ricardo Jiminez, Phoenix	L	8
Dec.	16—Mauro Fuentes, Phoenix	KO	3

KEVIN STRAUGHTER
Columbus, Ohio Welterweight
1979
Sept.	18—Greg Nutter, Columbus	L	4
Nov.	27—Tony Johnson, Columbus	L	4

1980
June	1—Greg Netter, Columbus	KO by	5
July	6—Steve Johnson, Columbus	W	6
July	17—Rodney Kennebrew, Maumee	KO	4
Aug.	20—Mike Napolitano, Warren	L	6
Aug.	23—Willie Brown, Alliance	W	6
Sept.	10—Milton McCrory, Detroit	KO by	1
Sept.	27—Andre Williams, Detroit	KO by	1

BRUCE (THE MOUSE) STRAUSS
(AKA RUBEN BARDOT)
Omaha, Nebr. Welterweight
Born: February 6, 1952
1976
June	1—Gary Maiza, Oklahoma City	W	4
June	2—Tony McMinn, Topeka	KO	3
Aug.	26—Hank Gregory, Kansas City	L	6

1977
Nov.	15—Clyde Spencer, Oklahoma City	KO	3

1978
Sept.	21—Nino Cosmo, Jersey City	W	6
Nov.	29—Bill Thompson, Council Bluffs	KO	3

1979
Jan.	10—Mauricio Aldana, Las Vegas	KO by	1
Jan.	19—Ivy Brown, Overland Park	KO by	1
Feb.	14—Ossie Quast, St. Paul	W	6
Feb.	28—Dave Grant, St. Paul	KO	5
Mar.	8—Roy Taylor, Wichita	W	4
Mar.	14—Nick Miller, Marshalltown	KO	4
Mar.	16—Steve Kruger, St. Paul	L	5
Apr.	3—Nick Miller, Marshalltown	KO	3
Apr.	20—Ossie Quast, Winnipeg	W	6
Apr.	28—Clyde Spencer, Omaha	KO	6
May	4—Larry Putka, St. Paul	W	5
May	12—Larry Mayes, Wichita	KO	6
May	31—Ali Ayub, Brandon	KO	8
June	11—Floyd Pearson, Chicago	W	6
June	14—Terry Jesmer, Winnipeg	D	6
June	25—Cisero Blake, Omaha	KO	6
July	18—Charlie Peterson, Indianapolis	L	8
Sept.	18—Pat Hallacy, Wichita	L	10
Oct.	9—Bill Thompson, Council Bluffs	KO	3
Oct.	27—Tim Mullens, Regina	KO	5
Nov.	1—Tim Mulhurn, Wichita	KO	4
Nov.	16—Eddie Marcelle, Trinidad	KO by	7
Dec.	2—Billy Evans, Muncie	KO	3
Dec.	8—Dave Reynolds, Winnipeg	KO	3
Dec.	14—Tim Ellis, Evansville	KO	2
Dec.	20—Frank Patterson, Wichita	KO	4

1980
Feb.	9—Charlie Weir, Johannesburg	KO by	1
Feb.	29—Dave Simmonds, Nanaimo	L	10
Mar.	7—Odell Willis, Kansas City	W	6
Mar.	16—Ralph Jackson, Omaha	KO	1
Mar.	29—Juan Jose Giminez, Rome	KO by	5
Apr.	1—Nino Gonzales, Totowa	KO by	8
Apr.	19—Deryl Springer, Council Bluffs	KO	4
Apr.	24—Ralph Racine, Winnipeg	KO by	5
Apr.	26—Ron Madsap, Hastings	KO	3
May	13—Rodney Foster, Indianapolis	KO	3
June	6—Dave Bolden, Kansas City	W	8
June	14—Charles LeCour, Nanaimo	L	8
June	18—Nick Wills, Struthers	KO	3
June	20—Billy Evans, Ft. Wayne	KO	3
June	28—Billy Turner, Rapid City	KO	5
July	17—Bobby Czyz, Totowa	KO by	4
July	18—Nick Milner, Grand Island	KO	4
July	24—Dave Grant, Winnipeg	KO	5
Aug.	29—Dave Gordon, Grand Island	KO	5
Aug.	30—Dave Holmgren, N. Platte	KO	6
Sept.	6—Charlie Keller, Sious Falls	KO	10
Sept.	23—Johnny Compo, Edmonton	L	8
Oct.	28—Malcolm Gordon, Indianapolis	KO	2
Oct.	30—Rocky Trampler, Louisville	KO	5

Nov.	1—Charlie Susens, Wichita	KO	6
Dec.	11—Ernie Davis, Kansas City	W	8

JERRY STRICKLAND
Columbus, Ohio Welterweight
1976
July	24—Bob Plegge, Kalamazoo	L	4
Sept.	22—Gary Pope, Cleveland	KO by	2
Nov.	3—Albert Collazo, Cleveland	KO by	2
Nov.	27—Steve Adams, Lincoln	L	6

1977
Feb.	1—Aundra Love, Indianapolis	KO by	2
Feb.	15—Louis Self, Toledo	L	4
Mar.	15—Danny Stokes, Toronto	KO by	3
Apr.	27—Wilfredo Vasquez, Lorain	L	4
May	11—Tony Johnson, Cleveland	L	4
May	17—Eddie Graves, Mentor	L	6
June	11—Bob Plegge, Jackson	L	4
June	22—Forest Winchester, Columbus	KO by	4
Sept.	20—Jimmy Heair, Memphis	KO by	1
Oct.	5—Anthony Daniels, Elkins	L	8
Oct.	15—Bobby Plegge, Salem	L	10
Nov.	11—Juan LaPort, Cincinnati	L	4
Dec.	7—Tommy Hearns, Mt. Clemens	KO by	3

1978
Mar.	10—Roedell Stephens, Cincinnati	L	4
Mar.	16—Eddie Graves, Cleveland	KO by	3
May	13—Tommy Rose, Boston	KO by	3
June	3—Paul Stewart, Pikeville	KO	1
Aug.	28—Floyd Pearson, Chicago	KO by	3
Nov.	18—Warren Thunder, DePaul	KO	2

1979
May	21—Tom Crowley, Belleville	L	8
Aug.	24—Larry Stanton, Cincinnati	KO by	2
Nov.	8—Charlie Brown, Indianapolis	KO by	2

1980
Feb.	1—Tyrone Moore, Louisville	L	6
Mar.	28—Louie Mateo, Chicago	KO by	2
July	17—Robert Rucker, Maumee	KO by	2
Nov.	1—Andre Wynn, Detroit	L	4
Dec.	12—Gene Stevens, Louisville	L	10

EARL STRINGER
Detroit, Mich. Lightweight
1977
Nov.	25—Craig Stevens, Detroit	L	4
Dec.	16—Hilmer Kenty, Detroit	KO by	3

1978
Nov.	3—Ron Flores, Detroit	KO by	2

1979
May	24—LeVant Williams, Detroit	W	6
June	28—Benny Ray Trusel, Detroit	L	4
July	12—LeVant Williams, Detroit	KO	5
Aug.	23—Cecil Fernandez, Detroit	KO by	6

1980
May	23—Andre Wynn, Pontiac	KO by	1
Oct.	18—Andre Wynn, Pontiac	KO by	4

RONALD STRODE
Honolulu, Hawaii Welterweight
1979
Apr.	24—Eduardo Acuna, Hilo	KO	3
June	5—Virgilio Legaspi, Hilo	W	5
July	3—Ful Sumagaysay, Hilo	W	5
Aug.	21—Ful Sumagaysay, Honolulu	W	6
Dec.	18—Angel Salinas, Honolulu	KO	3

1980
Feb.	20—Paul Morales, Hilo	L	6
Apr.	1—Freddie Mensah, Honolulu	L	8

LARRY STROGEN
Shreveport, La. Light Heavyweight
1980
June	3—Adolfo Rivas, Houston	KO	3
July	29—Eddie Gonzales, Houston	L	8

MIKE STUART
Los Angeles, Calif. Flyweight
1974
Sept.	19—Mario Rojellio, Los Angeles	W	4
Oct.	10—Caeser Kee, Los Angeles	KO by	1
Dec.	4—Johnny Meza, Las Vegas	W	4

1975
(Inactive)
1976
Mar.	19—Jorge Flores, Los Angeles	KO	4
Apr.	7—Shuji Kambara, Los Angeles	KO	1
May	13—Alfonso Delgadillo, Los Angeles	T.D.	1
June	10—Alfonso Delgadillo, Los Angeles	KO	2
July	8—Santiago Hernandez, Los Angeles	KO	4
Aug.	19—Arnulfo Martinez, Los Angeles	W	5
Oct.	2—Matias Marin, Los Angeles	L	8

1977

Mar. 3—Carlos Alcivar, Los Angeles .... W 10
May 27—Raul Pacheco, San Diego .... W 10
Sept. 20—Candy Iglecias, Phoenix .... KO 2
Oct. 20—Raul O'Choa, Los Angeles .... KO 3
Nov. 17—Anthony Kiriz, Los Angeles .... L 10

1978

Jan. 18—Raul Pacheco, Anchorage .... W 12
Jan. 30—Rafal Rubio, Tijuana .... L 10
Mar. 16—Santos Nunez, Anchorage .... KO 5
July 18—Rafal Rubio, Pico Rivera .... W 12

1979

Jan. 23—Charlie Magri, London .... KO by 3
June 3—Adelaido Galindo, Las Vegas .... TL 6

1980

Mar. 3—Carlos Alcivar, Los Angeles .... W 10

AL STYLES, JR.

Philadelphia, Pa. Middleweight
Born: May 22, 1955, Height: 6 ft.

1974

Jan. 16—Sylvester Moore, Baltimore .... KO 4
Mar. 20—Ray Moncrief, Scranton .... W 6
May 29—Skipper Jones, Philadelphia .... D 4
June 27—Bobby Golson, Baltimore .... KO 3
July 18—Zack Page, Baltimore .... KO 1
Aug. 19—Tyrone Freeman, Philadelphia .... D 6
Oct. 13—Lester Camp, Wilmington .... W 6
Oct. 24—Jose Elias, Wilmington .... W 6

1975

Jan. 9—Lester Camper, Wilmington .... KO 6
Apr. 17—Bob Payton, Upper Darby .... L 8
Aug. 15—Tyrone Freeman, Atlantic City .... W 8
Dec. 10—Mike Rossman, Scranton .... L 10

1976-1977

(In Military Service)

1978

Nov. 16—Willie Classen, New York .... W 8
Nov. 24—Titus Burgess, Atlantic City .... W 8

1979

May 31—Odell Leonard, Philadelphia .... W 8
July 16—Jesus (Pecho) Castro, New York .... W 8
Oct. 18—Ernie Singletary, Philadelphia .... L 10

1980

Mar. 7—Harry Fryer, Staten Island .... KO 2
Apr. 11—Carlton Swift, Staten Island .... L 8
May 3—Miguel Castellini, Buenos Aires .... L 10
Sept. 18—Mario Maldonado, Philadelphia .... W 8
Oct. 25—Ruben Pardo, Sun City, South Africa .... L 10
Nov. 20—Roy Gumbs, London .... KO by 2

TONY STYLES

Florida Featherweight

1979

Feb. 6—Ralph Berrios, Orlando .... L 6
Feb. 20—Earl Wilson, Orlando .... L 6
Mar. 5—Thomas Rodriguez, Miami Beach .... KO by 2
Nov. 27—Tommy Rodriguez, Miami Beach .... KO 4
Dec. 18—Danny Wilcox, Miami Beach .... L 4

1980

Jan. 29—Terry Pizzarro, Miami .... L 4
June 19—George Garcia, Los Angeles .... KO by 4

AMERICO SUAREZ

Argentine Flyweight

1980

Feb. 16—Raul Pared, Toay .... W 10
June 4—Jose Izquierdo, Quemu-Quemu .... KO 8
June 27—Luis Alvarez, Salta .... W 10
Aug. 8—Hugo Espinosa, T. Lauquem .... KO 6
Aug. 29—Esteban Bustos, Santa Rosa .... D 10
Oct. 10—Hector Rosa, S. Sal. de Jujuy .... D 10

ARCADIO (PEE WEE) SUAREZ

New York, N.Y. Welterweight

1976

Jan. 24—James Williams, Syracuse .... KO 2
Mar. 16—Richard Novick, New York .... KO 1
Apr. 14—Julio Cheualier, New York .... W 4
June —Willie Davis, Providence .... W 6
June 26—Seymour Sheppard, New York .... KO 2
Aug. 14—Neil Floyd, Utica .... W 6
Sept. 15—Jim Williams, Utica .... KO 2
Oct. 2—Tom McGillicott, Utica .... KO 1

1977

May 20—Willie Davis, Binghamton .... W 4
Sept. 27—Benito Jiminez, W. New York, N.J. .... KO 1
Nov. 9—Willie Davis, White Plains .... W 6
Nov. 18—Willie Davis, Commack .... KO 3
Nov. 25—Dave Bolden, Providence .... W 6

1978

Jan. 18—Jose Resto, White Plains .... W 6
Feb. 17—George Green, Commack .... KO 2
Apr. 5—Pete O'Keefe, White Plains .... KO 1
June 2—Angel Ortiz, Jersey City .... KO 6
June 29—D.C. Cunningham, North Bergen .... KO 1
Sept. 21—Dave Bolden, Jersey City .... KO 2
Oct. 27—Bobby Alexander, New York .... KO 8

1979

Jan. 27—Justice Ortiz, Jersey City .... W 10
May 11—Teo Ozuna, New York .... L 10
June 27—Justice Ortiz, Secaucus .... W 8

1980

Mar. 28—Dave Bolden, Tarrytown .... W 10
May 31—Derrik Cuttino, Elizabeth .... W 8
June 26—Jose Gonzales, New York .... W 10
Dec. 27—Benito Juarez, North Bergen .... KO 4

JUAN D. SUAREZ

Argentine Light Heavyweight

1980

Mar. 7—Candido Barrera, Cordoba .... KO 3
Apr. 5—Carlos Pouyannes, Buenos Aires .... KO 1
Apr. 25—Cesar Duarte, Buenos Aires .... KO by 4
July 18—Ramon Cerrezuela, Mar del Plata .... L 10
Aug. 15—Candido Barrera, Cordoba .... KO 9

LUIS ANGEL SUAREZ

Argentine Welterweight

1980

Oct. 17—Hector Sosa, Federal .... W 6
Dec. 20—Santos Medina, Federal .... KO 2

TONY SUERO

Upper Darby, Pa. Junior Middleweight

1979

May 14—John Bovenzi, Philadelphia .... W 4
July 16—Wallace Battles, Philadelphia .... KO 2
Aug. 18—Abel Santiago, Atlantic City .... W 4
Nov. 7—Tyronne Rackley, Las Vegas .... D 4

1980

Apr. 26—Ronald Jones, Atlantic City .... KO 2
July 31—Matador Loving, Atlantic City .... W 6
Aug. 21—Al Little, Totowa .... W 8
Sept. 18—Sean Mannion, Totowa .... KO 8
Dec. 4—Roger Stafford, Atlantic City .... L 10

FUL SUMAGAYSAY

Hawaii Lightweight

1979

Mar. 27—Terry Welch, Honolulu .... W 5
Apr. 24—Mitsuyuki Nakane, Hilo .... W 10
May 30—Mark Ibanez, Honolulu .... L 6
July 3—Ronald Strode, Hilo .... L 5
July 24—Rogelio Tulonghari, Honolulu .... W 4
July 31—Malo Fale, Honolulu .... KO by 1
Aug. 21—Ronald Strode, Honolulu .... L 6
Oct. 16—Malo Fale, Honolulu .... KO by 1

1980

Feb. 20—Reuben Dudoit, Honolulu .... L 4
Apr. 1—Reuben Dudoit, Honolulu .... L 5
June 17—Frank Cabanig, Honolulu .... W 4
July 19—Jale Fotu, Hilo .... L 6
Dec. 9—Tino Savea, Honolulu .... KO by 4

GARY SUMMERHAYS

Canadian Light Heavyweight

1970

Apr. 20—John Mason, Windsor .... W 4
May 28—Jim Davis, Windsor .... W 6
Sept. 14—Skip Gray, Windsor .... W 6
Sept. 29—Skip Gray, Buffalo .... KO 4
Oct. 21—Jim Davis, Detroit .... L 6
Dec. 18—Lambert McIntosh, Halifax .... KO 6

1971

Jan. 28—Ellis Poole, Toronto .... W 8
May 7—Johnny Mangum, Detroit .... L 6
June 7—Billy Parker, Windsor .... W 4
June 11—Stu Gray, Kitchener .... W 8
Sept. 27—Leo Richards, Quebec .... KO 3
Dec. 3—Casey Gacic, Akron .... D 6

1972

Jan. 21—Casey Gacic, Parma .... L 8
Feb. 18—Ted Paxton, Parma .... KO 2
Mar. 24—Harold Carter, Parma .... W 6
Apr. 14—Joey Ray, Parma .... W 6
May 17—Walter Osphinsky, Scranton .... KO 4
Sept. 25—Roy McMillian, Toronto .... W 6
Nov. 6—Ted Paxton, Toronto .... W 6
Nov. 29—Kenny Baker, McKeesport .... W 6

1973

Feb. 12—Al Sparks, Toronto .... W 12
(Canadian Light Heavyweight Title)
Apr. 11—Al Quinney, Toronto .... KO 10
June 10—Marion Connors, Toronto .... W 8
Sept. 27—Barry Morris, Halifax .... KO 3
Oct. 11—Casey Gacic, Toronto .... W 10

Nov. 20—Karl Zurheide, Milwaukee ....D 10
1974
Jan.   22—Karl Zurheide, Milwaukee.................L 10
Apr.   11—Mike Quarry, Orlando....................L 12
Aug. 20—Walter White, Orlando ....W 10
Oct.   25—Pedro Soto, New York ....L 8
1975
Jan.   29—Marvin Johnson, Indianapolis ....L 10
Mar.   3—Dennis Cochran, Calgary ....KO 3
       (Canadian Light Heavyweight Title)
July   3—Alvaro Lopez, Garnerville ....L 10
Dec. 15—Tracy Morrison, Hamilton ....W 10
1976
Feb. 19—Tracy Morrison, Kansas City............W 10
Apr.   13—Kosie Smith, Durban ....D 10
May   6—Billy Wagner, Cleveland ....KO 7
Sept. 15—Joe Smokey Middleton, Cleveland ....W 10
1977
Feb. 26—Tommy Hanna, Detroit ....KO 10
May   6—Marvin Camel, Missoula ....L 12
May 18—Edgar Wallace, Phoenix ....L 10
June 22—Vonzell Johnson, Columbus ....L 10
Sept. 29—Mike Rossman, New York ....L 10
Oct.   22—Michael Spinks, Las Vegas ....L 10
1978
Feb.   6—Bob Smith, Edmonton ....W 10
Feb. 27—Tony Mundine, Melbourne ....KO 11
       (British Commonwealth Light Heavyweight Title)
Apr.   1—Hal (TNT) Carroll, Halifax ....W 10
May 27—Gary Alexander, Brantford ....W 10
Sept. 29—Pat Cuillo, Hamilton ....W 10
Dec.   4—Pablo Ramos, Saginaw ....L 10
1979
Jan.   31—Bill Ratliff, Saginaw ....W 10
Mar.   3—Lotte Mwale, Lusaka ....KO by 5
       (Commonwealth Light Heavyweight Title)
July   17—Damiano Pellegrino, Ontario ....KO 6
       (Canadian Light Heavyweight Title)
Oct.   11—Ivy Brown, Kansas City ....L 10
Dec. 18—Jean-Claude LeClair, Montreal ....KO 9
1980
Mar.   —Eddie Melo, Montreal ....KO 11
       (Retained Canadian Light Heavyweight Title)
July 22—Roddy MacDonald, Halifax ....KO 7

JOHNNY SUMMERHAYS
Brantford, Canada Lightweight
1970
Apr. 20—Tulip Turnspeed, Windsor................W 4
May   4—Johnny Thomas, Toronto................W 4
May 28—Bobby Parnell, Windsor.................W 4
Sept. 14—Larry Rossi, Windsor ....KO 2
1971
Jan.   28—John Thomas, Toronto ....W 4
May   7—Andre Reed, Detroit ....KO 2
Sept. 27—Billy Poulton, Quebec ....W 4
Oct.   5—Sonny Oliver, Windsor..................W 6
Nov.   3—Sonny Oliver, Detroit...................KO 5
Dec.   3—Sonny Oliver, Akron....................KO 8
1972
Feb. 18—Andre Reed, Parma ....KO 7
Mar. 24—Mike Harris, Parma ....W 8
Apr. 14—Marion Thomas, Parma.................W 10
May 17—Willie Daniels, Scranton.................L 8
Nov.   6—Julio Mandell, Toronto..................W 6
Nov. 29—Mike Harris, McKeesport ....W 6
1973
Feb. 12—Willie Williams, Toronto ....W disq. 6
Aug. 30—Eddie Rivera, Halifax ....KO 4
Sept. 27—Johnny North, Halifax ....L 8
Dec.   8—Dennis Cochrane, Titusville ....KO 6
1974
Jan.   24—Bobby Crawford, Milwaukee ....W 6
May 26—Willie Williams, Brantford ....TD 8
Aug. 20—James Martinez, Orlando ....W 8
Sept. 7—Dennis Stokes, Toronto ....W 12
       (Canadian Lightweight Title)
Oct.   25—Frankie Benitez, New York ....KO by 6
1975
Mar.   3—Barry Sponagle, Calgary ....W 12
       (Canadian Lightweight Title)
Nov. 28—Al Ford, Edmonton....................W 12
       (Canadian Lightweight Title)
Dec. 15—Johnny Bay, Hamilton..................KO 6
       (Canadian Lightweight Title)
1976
Jan.   24—Dom Monaco, Commack ....L 10
June 3—Barry Sponagle, Halifax.................L 12
       (Canadian Lightweight Title)
Sept. 15—Ron Pettigrew, Cleveland.................L 6
Nov.   6—Vinnie DeBarrpos, Waterbury ....W 8
1977
Jan.   9—Barry Sponagle, New Glasgow ....D 12
Aug.   4—Greg Coverson, Wyoming ....L 10

Oct.   7—Aaron Pryor, Cincinnati ....L 8
1978
Jan.   17—Bobby Hughes, Toronto ....L 10
Feb.   2—Charles Buggs, Cleveland ....W disq. 3
Apr.   11—Lawerence Hafey, Halifax ....W 10
May 27—Harvey Wilson, Brantford ....W 10
July 26—Dale Hernandez, Omaha ....L 10
Nov.   9—Greg Coverson, Mt. Clemens ....L 10
Dec.   5—Gaetan Hart, Montreal ....L 12
       (Canadian Lightweight Title)
1979
Mar.   3—James Blevins, Detroit ....W 10
July 17—Danny Stokes, Toronto ....W 6
Oct.   11—Steve Homan, Kansas City ....L 10
Dec.   8—Pedro Acosta, Winnipeg ....W 10
1980
Mar. 17—Al Ford, Edmonton ....W 10
Sept. 7—Ray Mancini, Warren ....L 10

MURRAY SUTHERLAND
Bay City, Mich. Light Heavyweight
Managed by Arthur Dorr
1977
Aug.   —Kevin Downey, Hamilton ....W 6
1978
Jan.   17—Willie Featherstone, Toronto .... KO by 3
Feb.   2—Tony Curovic, Cleveland ....KO 3
Apr.   6—Gus Turner, Cleveland ....KO 4
Apr.   —Dwight Davison ....KO by 4
May   —Ivy Cory, Flint ....KO 2
May 27—Harold Riggins, Brantford ....KO 6
Sept. 29—Zack Page, Hamilton ....KO 3
Oct.   —Gary Alexander, Canton ....W 8
Dec.   4—Bill Hollis, Saginaw ....KO 3
1979
Jan.   —Rick Jester, Saginaw ....KO 1
Mar.   —Harold Riggins, Saginaw ....KO 2
July 21—Richie Kates, Pontiac ....L 10
Nov.   —Karl Zurheide, Saginaw ....KO 2
Dec.   —Al Bolden, Columbus ....W 10
1980
Jan.   2—Jose Gutierrez, Bay City ....KO 2
Jan. 15—Alex Bell, Pensacola ....KO 2
Jan. 26—Gus Turner, Lansing ....KO 5
Feb.   1—Julius Noble, Chicago ....KO 5
Mar.   8—Don Addison, Detroit ....KO 4
Apr.   11—Benny Mitchell, Grand Rapids ....KO 3
Apr. 13—Eddie Smith, Huntington, W. Virginia ..KO 4
May   —Michael Spinks, Kiamesha Lake ....L 10
July   —Greg Payne, Tampa ....KO 6
Aug. 1—Johnny Townsend, Council Bluffs ....KO 7
Aug. 15—Stanley Scott, Muskegon ....KO 2
Sept. 12—John Cox, Milwaukee ....KO 2
Sept. 13—Joey Butcher, Milwaukee ....KO 1
Oct.   4—Phil Wade, Des Moines ....KO 3
Oct.   25—Pablo Ramos, Pontiac ....W 12
Dec.   5—John Beveridge, Columbus ....KO 1

JIMMY SYKES
Philadelphia, Pa. Light Heavyweight
1975
May 29—Bill Sharkey, North Bergen ....KO by 1
1976
(Inactive)
1977
Oct.   25—Eddie Warren, Philadelphia ....W 4
Nov. 22—Lee Thomas, Chicago ....KO by 3
Dec. 21—Gerrie Cooney, New York ....KO by 1
1978
Feb. 20—Frankie Williams, Philadelphia ....KO 1
May 24—Mike Robinson, Philadelphia ....KO 2
June 29—Bill Cornell, North Bergen ....KO by 1
1979
July 10—Mario Maldonado, Atlantic City ....W 4
Aug. 14—Emmett Johnson, Atlantic City ....KO 6
Oct.   30—Guy Gargan, Upper Darby ....L 6
Dec.   4—Mario Maldonado, Philadelphia ....L 6
1980
May   8—Tony Tassone, Atlantic City ....KO 2
Nov. 12—James Macey, Philadelphia ....D 6

PAUL TALBOT
Halifax, Canada Middleweight
1980
Jan. 22—Pierre Savard, Halifax ....W 4

Apr. 29—Pierre Cormier, Halifax ....W 6

JORGE TALQUENCA
Argentine Lightweight
1980
Apr. 3—Abraham Valenzuela, Mendoza ....KO 10
May 23—Ramon Mirabal, Mendoza ....L 10
Sept. 5—Abraham Valenzuela, Gral Alvear ....L 12

NELSON CRUZ TAMARIZ
Dominican Republic Featherweight
1970
Oct. —Andres Rodriguez, San Juan ....W 4
1971
Jan. 27—Manuel Rivera, Mayaguez ....W 6
Feb. 4—Tomas Rivera, Ponce ....L 4
Mar. 13—Hiram Potrito Morales, San Juan ....W 8
Apr. 10—Luciano Santos, San Juan ....D 6
May 1—Willie Pastrano, Bayamon ....L ● 8
May 22—Andres Torres, San Juan ....KO by 2
1972
Sept. 27—Tony Trys, Santo Domingo ....W 6
1973
Feb. 19—Livio Nolasco, Santo Domingo...........W 10
Mar. 26—Jeriberto Olivera, Santo Domingo ....W 10
Nov. —Aurelio Birriel, Romana ....KO by 9
1974
Aug. 10—Tony Tris, Santo Domingo ....W 10
July 6—Emilio Hernandez, Santo Domingo ......KO 1
Nov. 25—Pedro Jose Diaz, Santo Domingo.........W 12
1975
Feb. 8—Livio Nolasco, Santo Domingo ....W 10
Apr. 28—Andres Torres, Santo Domingo ....W 10
June 9—Livio Nolasco, Santo Domingo...........W 10
Dec. 15—Benitin Estrela, Santo Domingo ....W 12
1976
Apr. 3—Rodolfo Francis, Panama City ....KO by 2
Aug. 16—Guillermo Almengot, Santo Domingo ....KO 8
Oct. 28—Pedro Jose Diaz, Santo Domingo.........W 12
1977
Mar. 14—Leo Cruz, Santo Domingo ....L 12
June 13—Leo Cruz, Santo Domingo ....L 12
Sept. 16—Nestor Jiminez, Cartagena ....L 12
Oct. 7—Nestor Jiminez, Cartagena ....L 10
Dec. 1—Jose Cervantes, Barranquilla ....L 10
1978
Jan. 12—Jose Cervantes, Barranquilla ....L 10
Apr. 24—Leo Lopez, Santo Domingo ....KO 3
Sept. 8—Roberto Bido, Santo Domingo ....KO 10
Dec. 14—Jacinto Herrera, Curacao ....KO 7
(Won WBA Latin American Featherweight Title)
1979
Apr. 6—Felix Rodrigues, Albany ....KO 4
May 21—Wilfredo Gomez, New York ....KO by 2
1980
Nov. 24—Juan Castro, Santo Domingo ....KO 6

JOSE LUIS TAPIA
1977
Feb. 26—Jorge Quintana, Cartagena ....KO
June 1—Jose Luis Lara, Mexico City ....KO 1
Aug. —Angel Mata, Mexico City ....KO 4
Sept. 21—Jesus Hernandez, Mexico City ....KO 2
Dec. 3—Roberto Madrid, Mexico City ....W 8
1978
Apr. 3—Hector Pinto, Mexico ....KO 3
May 24—Jesus Calante, Mexico City ....KO 3
Nov. 3—Tomas Maza, Monteria ....KO 5
(Colombian 112 Title)
Dec. 6—Chucho Ramirez, Mexico City ....D 10
1979
Feb. —Juan Sarmiento, Mexico City ....L 10
Mar. 30—Alfredo Thomas, Monteria ....KO 2
May 3—Maximo Rodriguez, Monteria ....KO 9
May 12—Jose Chucho Ramirez, Mexico City ......KO 4
June 23—Jose Luis Castillo, Mexico City ....L 10
Aug. 17—Jose Luis Soberanes, Culiacan ....KO 2
Sept. 21—Leo Chino Bermudez, Culiacan ....KO 2
1980
Feb. 17—Antonio Nava, Mexico City ....L 10

RAMON TAPIA
Argentine, Junior Middleweight
1980
Feb. 1—Miguel Arguello, Tucuman ....KO by 4
Apr. 18—Roberto Tapia, Catamarca ....L 6
July 4—Catalino Sosa, Concepcion ....D 10

TOM TARANTINO
Milwaukee, Wisc. Junior Welterweight
1971
Sept. 12 Ernie Witcher, Milwaukee ....W 4
Nov. 2—Bob Crawford, Green Bay.............KO 1

1972
Jan. 10—Bob Crawford, Milwaukee...........KO by 4
Mar. 8—Bobby Rodriguez, St. Paul...............D 6
Apr. 17—Ray Carrington, Chicago ....L 6
June 5—Bob Crawford, Chicago................W 6
Sept. 6—Dale Hernandez, Des Moines ....KO by 5
Nov. 16—Sam Black, Milwaukee ....KO 1
1973
Jan. 29—Sammy Maul, Milwaukee................L 4
1974
Jan. 24—Bruce Finch, Milwaukee ....L 6
May 23—Rueben Green, Milwaukee ....KO 2
Aug. 26—Bob Crawford, Chicago..................D 4
Nov. 20—Danny Starks, Milwaukee.............KO 4
1975
Jan. 25—Ray Carrington, Chicago ....L 6
Feb. 4—Fred Harris, Milwaukee ....L 6
July 16—George Anderson, St. Paul..............L 8
Aug. 19—Danny Starks, Chicago................KO 1
Sept. 17—Ron Pettigrew, Waukesha ....W 8
Dec. 3—Larry Moore, Waukesha ....KO 4
1976
Feb. 4—Manuel Torres, Waukesha ....W 10
Apr. 29—Jerry Strickland, Waukesha ....KO 5
July 14—Rick Folstad, Minneapolis ....L 6
Oct. 13—Marion Thomas, Milwaukee.............W 10
1977
Feb. 28—Charlie Nash, London ....KO by 1
Apr. 19—Luis Vegas, White Plains ....W 8
May 26—Harvey Wilson, Waukesha ....KO 2
May 31—Andrew Ganigan, Honolulu ....KO by 7
—Tony Johnson, Waukesha ....W 10
1978
Apr. 18—Ralph Racine, Winnipeg ....KO by 2
May 9—Luis Davila, Hartford ....L 10
Nov. 7—Frank Mills, Waukesha ....KO 3
Dec. 5—Al Ford, Winnipeg ....L 10
1979
Jan. 16—Jimmy Blevins, Waukesha ....L 8
Apr. 17—Jimmy Blevins, Waukesha ....W 10
Apr. 27—Johnny Lira, Chicago ....KO by 7
1980
Jan. 12—Saoul Mamby, Atlantic City ....KO by 1
Mar. 6—Carl Crowley, Winnipeg ....KO by 3

TONY (ROCKY) TASSONE
Philadelphia, Pa. Middleweight
1975
Aug. 15—Jackie Thornton, Atlantic City..........D 4
Oct. 21—Moses Robinson, Philadelphia..........W 4
1976
Jan. 13—James Macey, Philadelphia ....D 4
Apr. 6—Jesse Freeman, Philadelphia ....W 4
July 2—Sid Minott, Atlantic City................W 6
Aug. 6—Ray Davis, Atlantic City................W 6
Aug. 27—Nikita Tarhocker, Atlantic City ....W 6
1977
Mar. 7—Marvin Lee, Upper Darby ....KO 3
Apr. 7—Daryl Lampkin, Upper Darby ....W 6
May 9—Daryl Lampkin, Upper Darby ....W 6
July 26—Carlos Prigg, Philadelphia ....W 6
Sept. 15—Carlos Prigg, Upper Darby ....W 8
Oct. 20—Jerome Goodman, Upper Darby ....W 8
1978
Jan. 31—Lester Camper, Upper Darby ....KO 2
Mar. 14—Tyrone Freeman, Philadelphia ....KO 2
May 24—Oscar Balderas, Philadelphia ....KO 1
June 19—Archie Andrews, Philadelphia ....KO by 6
Aug. 24—Archie Andrews, Philadelphia ....W 10
Oct. 24—Ralph Godwin, Philadelphia ....KO 6
Nov. 21—Don Addison, Upper Darby ....L 8
1979
Feb. 5—Rudy Donato, Philadelphia ....KO 7
Aug. 7—Wilson Bell, Baltimore ....KO by 1
Nov. 14—Ted Mann, Philadelphia ....L 10
1980
May 9—Jimmy Sykes, Atlantic City ....KO by 2
Oct. 29—Ralph Mifka, Scranton ....KO by 5

LARRY TATMAN
Metairie, La. Junior Middleweight
1980
July 15—Louis Coleman, New Orleans ....KO 3
Aug. 9—Harold Pinkley, Lake Charles ....KO 3
Sept. 23—Johnson Cragton, New Orleans ....KO 3

CURTIS TAYLOR
Memphis, Tenn. Welterweight
1977
June 10—Dale Dennis, Brunswick ....W 6
Dec. 17—Dale Dennis, Atlanta ....KO 6
1978
Apr. 21—Dale Dennis, Atlanta ....KO 6

May   10—Dale Dennis, Vidella .... W   6
May   22—Spook Jackson, Vidella .... W   8
June 16—Spook Jackson, Atlanta .... KO   7
Aug.   3—James Wallace, Birmingham .... KO   3
Aug. 18—Arnell Thomas, Lesley .... KO   6
Sept. 21—Sammy Floyd, Birmingham .... W   10
Nov.   4—Sammy Ruckard, Atlanta .... W   10
1979
Feb. 16—Bruce Thompson, Louisville L   8
Mar.   6—Ed Montique, Memphis .... W   10
Apr. 12—Ed Montique, Memphis L   10
Nov. 16—Bruce Finch, Chicago .... KO by 8
1980
Apr. 26—Tyrone Demby, Atlantic City .... KO by 3
May   16—Manning Galloway, Lexington .... KO   2
June   6—Kirkland Laing, London .... KO by 7
Sept. 9—Mike Picciotti, Atlantic City L   10
Oct.   1—Buster Drayton, Atlantic City L   8
Nov. 25—Marlon Starling, Hartford L   10

MIKE TAYLOR
Texas Middleweight
1975
Nov.   4—Juan Garcia, Houston .... W
1976-1978
(Inactive)
1979
June 19—Carlos Black, Houston .... KO   1
1980
July 29—Anderson Harris, Jr., Houston .... KO   2
Aug. 26—Alfonso Aguirre, Houston .... KO   3

MYRON TAYLOR
Philadelphia, Pa. Featherweight
1980
Aug. 25—Mike Davis, Philadelphia .... KO   2
Sept. 9—Melvin Bethea, Atlantic City .... KO   1
Oct.   1—Bennie Baker, Atlantic City .... KO   1
Nov.   6—Jose Figueroa, Atlantic City .... KO   1
Dec.   4—Earl Wilson, Atlantic City .... KO   2

TONY TAYLOR
Muncie, Ind. Junior Welterweight
Born: September 12, 1956
1979
Aug.   2—Charley Evans, Omaha L   5
Aug. 23—Danny Jones, Detroit L   6
Dec.   2—Eric Tribeau, Muncie .... KO   4
1980
Jan. 22—Mark Lemerick, Indianapolis .... W   6
July 11—Ralph Twinning, Chicago .... KO by 3
Oct. 29—Gary Holmgren, St. Paul L   10
Nov.   1—Mike Bradley, Dayton L   4
Dec.   9—Bobby Joe Young, Warren .... KO by 2

ARTURO TEBAQUI
Tucson, Ariz. Flyweight
1978
Oct. 28—Tony Marino, Tucson .... KO   1
Nov. 25—Augustine Sanchez, Tucson .... KO   2
1979
Jan.   3—Pedro Marentes, Las Vegas .... KO   2
Jan. 24—Juan Banuelos, Las Vegas .... KO   6
1980
Feb.   3—Orlando Maldonado, Las Vegas ...... KO by 10
July 18—Jose Zavala, Los Mochis ....
Aug.   6—Olivaritos Olguin, Agua Prieta .... KO   3
Sept. 27—Candido Tellez, Mexico City .... KO by 3

RAFAEL TEJADA
Bantamweight
1979
June 27—Robert Anderson, Phoenix L   4
Aug. 22—Johnny Mesa, Tucson .... KO by 3
Oct. 18—Robert Anderson, Phoenix L   4
1980
Jan. 20—Bobby Krueger, Tucson .... KO by 2
Mar. 13—Francisco Rodriguez, Las Vegas .... KO   2
Mar. 20—Corky Polanos, Phoenix .... W   4
May   5—Bebe Martinez, Phoenix .... W   4

TONY TEJEDA
Lightweight
1979
Oct. 27—Johnny Sanchez, Albuquerque .... KO by 2
1980
Mar. 17—Gonzallo Montellano, Bakersfield .... KO by 1

ED TEMPLE
Columbus, Ohio Light Heavyweight
1980
June   1—Vernon Cunningham, Columbus ..... KO by 3
July   6—Bill Brown, Columbus .... KO   1

228

July 26—Al Fracker, Kalamazoo .... KO by 4
Aug. 21—Earl Caldwell, Columbus .... KO   3
Aug. 23—Gary Alexander, Alliance .... KO by 4
Sept. 9—Randy Stephens, Warren .... KO by 3
Sept. 27—Lemuel McLittle, Detroit .... KO by 2
Oct. 28—Jeff Lampkin, Warren .... KO by 1

ANDRES TENA
Bronx, N.Y. Junior Featherweight
Managed by Adonis Torres
Represented Santo Domingo in the 1980 Olympics
1980
Dec. 20—Ruben Mayet, Bronx .... KO   1

MARIO TENIO
Tucson, Ariz. Welterweight
1980
Feb. 20—Sammy Horne, Las Vegas L   6
July 17—Julio Alfonso, Tucson .... L disq. 4
Nov.   5—Packy Paulson, Phoenix .... W   6
Dec. 10—Joe Bahash, Las Vegas .... W   6
Dec. 26—Donald Curry, Las Vegas .... KO by 1

HARRY TERRELL
Cleveland, Ohio Heavyweight
1976
May   6—Gary Alexander, Cleveland.............. W   6
June 23—Al Bell, Mentor .... KO   6
Sept. 22—Joe Taylor, Cleveland................... W   6
1977
Jan.   5—Boom-Boom Moorer, Cleveland .... W   6
Mar. 22—Verbie Garland, Cleveland .... W   6
Apr. 27—Boom-Boom Moorer, Lorain .... KO   7
May   18—Frankie Williams, Lorain L   6
Sept. 29—Robert Yarborough, Cleveland .... W   6
Oct. 25—Walter Moore, Chicago .... KO by 3
Dec.   8—Bob Bozic, Toronto .... KO   2
1978
Apr. 28—Horst (Him) Geisler, Toronto .... KO   2
July 29—Earnie Shavers, Virginia Beach .... KO by 2
Nov. 29—Charlie Johnson, Richfield .... KO   8
1979
Mar. 14—Lynn Ball, Las Vegas .... W   10
Apr. 18—Terry Mims, Richfield .... W   10
May   12—Leroy Jones, Las Vegas L   10
Sept. 22—Mike Weaver, Los Angeles .... KO by 4
Nov. 20—James Tillis, Chicago .... KO by 1
1980
May   4—Johnny Blaine, Canton .... KO   3
June 14—Percell Davis, Cincinnati .... W   10
Sept. 30—Charley Jordan, Niles .... KO   5

ARNELL THOMAS
Houston, Texas Junior Middleweight
1976
Aug.   3—Joe Escalante, Memphis .... D   6
Sept. 1—Joe Escalante, Topeka .... D   6
Nov. 30—Juan Pina, Memphis .... KO   3
1977
Aug. 23—Daryl Brumley, Memphis .... W   8
Nov. 30—Joe Barrientos, Topeka .... W   8
1978
Feb. 16—Daryl Brumley, Houston L   10
June 28—Mike Wyant, Hamilton L   10
Aug. 18—Curtis Taylor, Lesley .... KO by 6
Sept. 27—Rafael Rodriguez, St. Paul .... KO by 8
Nov.   2—Tiger Hall, Orlando L   4
1979
Apr.   3—Curtis Parker, Philadelphia .... KO by 3
June 26—Wilford Scypion, Beaumont .... KO by 2
Oct. 16—Gary Giron, Sparks .... KO by 3
1980
May   9—Louie Mateo, Chicago .... KO by 1

BILLY JOE THOMAS
Lexa, Ark. Heavyweight
1979
Sept. 25—Steve Mormino, Belleville .... KO by 2
Oct. 30—John Lee, Memphis .... KO by
1980
Jan. 22—Ed (Too Tall) Jones, Indianapolis .... KO by 4
July 15—Phillip Brown, New Orleans L   5

CHARLIE THOMAS
Irvington, N.J. Welterweight
1979
Nov. 15—Ray Shelton, Dover .... KO   2
1980
Apr. 11—Victor Manuel, Staten Island L   6
May   9—Kevin Rooney, Staten Island .... KO by 3

DUANE THOMAS
Detroit, Mich. Junior Middleweight
1979
June	28—Ron Tillman, Detroit	KO	4
Aug.	2—Dave Myrick, Detroit	W	4
Oct.	18—Harvey Wilson, Detroit	KO	2
Nov.	19—Rodney Cummings, Detroit	W	6

1980
Jan.	24—Lenny Villers, Detroit	W	6
Feb.	22—Lamont Hopkins, Detroit	KO	3
Oct.	23—Randall Jackson, Detroit	KO	1
Dec.	2—Olan Avery, Toledo	KO	2
Dec.	12—Jerry Hall, Detroit	W disq.	1

GARY (TIGER) THOMAS
Evansville, Ind. Middleweight
1975
Nov.	13—Clifford Wills, Indianapolis	L	4

1976
Apr.	15—George Jacops, Indianapolis	D	4
July	14—Glenn Morgan, Rochester	L	6
Aug.	31—Milton Owens, Orlando	KO by	1

1977
(Inactive)
1978
May	13—Roy Dale, Dayton	L	8
July	12—C. J. Brown, Kansas City	KO by	3

1979
June	28—Clifford Wills, Ft. Mitchell	KO by	2
July	2—Chris Davis, Portland, Maine	KO by	
Aug.	10—Terry Jesmer, Evansville	KO	4
Nov.	3—Ken Heflin, Owensboro, Ky.	L	6
Dec.	14—Charley Peterson, Evansville	L	6

1980
Nov.	7—Ken Rankin, Clarksville	KO	3
Dec.	12—Lindell Holmes, Detroit	KO by	4

JAMIE THOMAS
Cincinnati, Ohio Middleweight
1976
Nov.	11—Ron Bosley, Cincinnati	KO	3

1977
Feb.	1—Joey Blair, Cincinnati	KO	3
Feb.	24—Herman Graham, Cincinnati	KO	4
Mar.	26—Zack Page, Cincinnati	W	4
May	7—Gary Alexander, Cincinnati	W	6
Sept.	24—Lloyd Richardson, Hamilton	L	8
Oct.	29—Don Ruckard, Hamilton	W	8
Nov.	12—Ron Bosley, Cincinnati	KO	3

1978
Mar.	1—Steve Gregory, Dayton	L	6
June	3—Chick Kelly, Pikeville	KO	3
June	28—Sammy Floyd, Hamilton	W	8
Sept.	5—Chuck Mince, New Orleans	L	10
Oct.	10—Chuck Mince, New Orleans	KO	4
Dec.	1—Tony Licata, New Orleans	L	10

1979
Feb.	17—Tommy Brooks, Indianapolis	W	6
Apr.	1—Fulgencio Obel, Caracas	KO by	5
May	26—Marvin Hagler, Portland, Me.	KO by	4
June	28—Fred Reed, Fort Mitchell	W	10

1980
Feb.	22—Dwight Davison, Detroit	KO by	6
May	2—Rocky Mattioli, Rome	KO by	4
Aug.	2—Ray Seales, Baton Rouge	L	10
Dec.	6—Caveman Lee, Detroit	KO by	2

LEE THOMAS
Memphis, Tenn. Middleweight
1977
Aug.	9—Edgar Ross, Orlando	KO by	3
July	27—Scott Clark, Orlando	KO by	4
Nov.	22—Jimmy Sykes, Chicago	KO by	1
Aug.	6—Max Hord, Fernando Beach	KO by	7
Dec.	19—Max Hord, Fernando Beach	KO by	10

1978
(Inactive)
1979
June	11—Roosevelt Green, Chicago	KO by	1
Dec.	19—Ralph Twinning, Rockford	KO by	4

1980
Oct.	9—John Collins, Chicago	KO by	4

MARION THOMAS
Indianapolis, Ind. Junior Welterweight
1968
Sept.	11—Rufus Holliday, Indianapolis	KO	2
Oct.	3—Howard Carney, Cincinnati	W	4
Oct.	14—Clay Evans, Indianapolis	KO	1

1969
Jan.	18—Arnold Bush, Indianapolis	W	
Feb.	2—John McCleod, Indianapolis	W	6
Feb.	14—Lyle Randolph, Indianapolis	L	4

Mar.	28—Bobby Parnell, Indianapolis	W	4
May	1—Saunders Crowe, Fort Wayne	W	4
July	18—Bobby Parnell, Indianapolis	W	10
July	30—Johnny McCleod, Indianapolis	W	6
Sept.	28—Jesus Nieves, Lorain	W	10
Nov.	8—Rufus Holliday, Lima	KO	2
Dec.	4—Junior Varney, Indianapolis	W	6

1970
Feb.	5—Jo Jo White, Indianapolis	W	8
Mar.	6—Bobby Parnell, Canton	W	8
Mar.	28—Wilson Yambo, San Juan	D	10
Apr.	27—Sonny Oliver, Akron	W	4
June	15—Sammy Goss, Philadelphia	L	10
May	22—Tommy Fix, Akron	W	8
Aug.	14—Willie Williams, Welch	KO	5
Aug.	17—Eddie Rivera, Lorain	KO	10
Nov.	25—Willie Williams, Covington	W	6

1971
Apr.	12—Bennie McCall, New Orleans	W	10
May	11—Angel Macias, San Antonio	KO by	3
Nov.	13—Sammy Ruckard, Brydstown	W	10
Dec.	14—Adelipos Munoz, Aruba	W	10

1972
Jan.	13—Jose Fernandez, New York	KO by	3
Jan.	15—Spider Black, Byrdstown	KO	4
Apr.	1—Rocky Kosakowski, Jamestown	KO	3
Apr.	14—Johnny Summerhays, Parma	L	10
Nov.	10—Johnny Copeland, Indianapolis	KO by	6

1973
Apr.	18—John Howard, Des Moines	W	8
Aug.	24—Harvey Wilson, Indianapolis	KO	4
Sept.	22—Danny Figueroa, Indianapolis	W	8
Oct.	27—Johnny Copeland, Indianapolis	KO by	1

1974
Feb.	16—Ron Pettigrew, New Castle	W	4
Apr.	13—Billy Holliday, New Castle	KO	2
Dec.	8—Ronnie Jones, Chicago	KO by	4

1975
Jan.	29—Donnie Starks, Indianapolis	KO	3
Apr.	12—Giancarlo Usai, Milan	KO by	3
May	14—Al Franklin, St. Paul	KO by	8
June	6—Clarence Jones, Indianapolis	KO	1
July	16—Termite Watkins, Houston	KO by	7
Nov.	15—Freddie Harris, Chicago	KO by	4

1976
Apr.	3—Larry Moore, Indianapolis	W	5
Apr.	15—Lou Bizzarro, Indianapolis	L	10
May	6—Jimmy Martinez, Indianapolis	W	6
Sept.	29—Tony Johnson, Cleveland	L	6
Oct.	13—Tom Tarantino, Milwaukee	L	10
Oct.	27—Paul Marcum, Cleveland	W	6
Nov.	17—Rick Folstad, St. Paul	L	8
Nov.	30—Norman Goins, Indianapolis	L	10

1977
Jan.	26—Tony Johnson, Cleveland	W	6
Feb.	1—Tony Johnson, Indianapolis	W	6
Mar.	22—Ralph Racine, Cleveland	KO by	7

1978
Apr.	3—Carlos Serrano, Indianapolis	KO	5

1979
July	8—Saoul Mamby, New York	KO by	4
Sept.	20—Phil Bowen, Indianapolis	KO	5

1980
Jan.	22—Danny Myers, Indianapolis	W	12
May	13—Billy Turner, Indianapolis	KO	3
June	30—Luis B. Rodriguez, Caracas	KO by	4
Dec.	11—Roberto Elizondo, Los Angeles	KO by	2

MIKE THOMAS
Springfield, Mass. Lightweight
1976
Oct.	30—Seymour Sheppard, East Hartford	KO	
Nov.	6—Marcelino Ortiz, Waterbury	KO	2

1977
Jan.	21—Eddie Campbell, Sunnyside	L	4
Mar.	1—Seymour Sheppard, Albany	KO	3
Mar.	11—Manuel Jiminez, Sunnyside	KO by	3
May	5—Eddie Campbell, Albany	KO by	3

1978
Jan.	28—Mike Ramalho, Providence	KO by	2
Nov.	16—Jose Pena, New York	L	8
Nov.	30—Teodoro Ozuna, New York	KO by	2

1979
Sept.	—Robert Rucker, White Plains	KO by	3

1980
Jan.	18—Richie Ciquin, Trenton	KO by	1

PINKLON THOMAS
Pontiac, Mich. Heavyweight
Born: February 10, 1958
1978
Aug.	00—Ken Arlt, Seattle	W	6
Oct.	31—Mustafa El Amin, Lacey	KO	3

1979

Jan.	8—Roger Braxton, Seattle	KO	7
Feb.	20—Lew Lockwood, Seattle	KO	4
Apr.	7—Elmo Henderson, Billings	KO	5
Apr.	26—Foma Leota, Seattle	KO	2
May	23—Lee Holloman, Las Vegas	KO	2
June	7—George Jerome, Portland	KO	2
July	2—Willie Stoglin, Sedro Wooley	KO	2
July	18—Leroy Caldwell, Las Vegas	KO	10
Dec.	14—Bobby Jordan, Atlantic City	KO	5

1980

Feb.	10—Jerry Williams, Miami	KO	5
Aug.	28—Jerry Williams, Las Vegas	W	10

ROBERT THOMAS
San Antonio, Texas Middleweight
1978

July	20—Mickey Goodwin, Detroit	KO by	1
Sept.	19—Tommy King, San Antonio	KO	1
Dec.	5—Mark Hughes, San Antonio	KO	1

1979
(Inactive)
1980

Nov.	13—John Collins, Chicago	KO by	2

ROBERT LEE THOMAS
Memphis, Tenn. Heavyweight
1977

June	13—Roger Wells, Memphis	W	4
July	9—Roger Wells, Memphis	W	6
Nov.	19—Anthony Daniels, Wheeling	KO by	4

1978

Jan.	25—Jim Claar, Indianapolis	KO by	2
Sept.	27—Henry Sims, Chicago	KO by	3
Nov.	11—Don Bester, Sterling	L	4

1979

Nov.	3—Tony Cook, Owensboro, Ky.	KO	2

1980

Mar.	22—Randy Nelson, N. Platte	KO	1
Aug.	2—Dan Kiser, Millington	KO by	8

TOMMY FRANCO THOMAS
Fairmont, W. Va. Heavyweight
1977

Sept.	18—Limmit Langley, Fairmont	W	6
Dec.	18—Dave Mounts, Fairmont	KO	3
Dec.	29—Amos Haines, Pittsburgh	KO	3

1978

Jan.	8—Baker Tinsley, Knoxville	KO	3
*Feb.	22—Bruce Hannon, Anchorage	KO	3
*Feb.	22—Travis Pickering, Anchorage	KO	3
Apr.	12—Victor Van Fleet, Anchorage	KO	6
May	10—Al Neuman, Anchorage	KO	9
Aug.	19—Oliver Phillips, Las Vegas	KO	10
Sept.	17—Elliott Bryant, Reno	W	10
*Both on the same card.			

1979
(Inactive)
1980

Feb.	9—Harvey Steichen, Clarksburg	W	10
May	10—Jerry Thompkins, Clarksburg	KO	6
June	21—Harvey Steichen, Las Vegas	W	10
Aug.	2—Henry Patterson, Clarksburg	KO	7
Dec.	5—Jim Ingram, Clarksburg	KO	5

JERRY THOMPKINS
Paterson, N.J. Heavyweight
1976

Feb.	11—Jaime DeLavega, Bayonne	KO	3
June	22—Dennis Jordan, Hartford	W	6
Aug.	12—Joe Stevens, Paterson	KO	2
Aug.	16—Doug Franklin, Newark	KO	1
Aug.	26—C. J. Brown, Allentown	KO	1
Sept.	28—Dennis Jordan, New York	KO by	1
Oct.	30—Bobby Walker, Hartford	L	8
Nov.	10—Ernie Lassiter, West Orange	W	8

1977

Jan.	22—Horace Robinson, Pensacola	L	10
May	7—John Tate, St. Louis	KO by	5
Oct.	18—Eugene Green, Elizabeth	L	8
Dec.	26—Dante Cane, Bologna	KO by	6

1978

Mar.	1—John Dennis, White Plains	L	10
Apr.	21—Jimmy Warr, New York	L	10
June	19—Mike Koranicki, Philadelphia	L	10
July	15—Randy Mack, Atlantic City	KO by	7
Aug.	16—Duane Bobick, Nanuet	KO by	2

1979

Mar.	28—George Chaplin, Baltimore	KO by	9
June	18—Grady Daniels, Highland Park	L	10
July	16—Marty Capasso, Philadelphia	L	8
Oct.	31—Chuck Gardner, Phoenix	L	4
Nov.	13—Jimmy Wallace, Phoenix	W	4

1980

Feb.	24—Larry Alexander, Atlantic City	KO by	2
May	10—Tommy Franco Thomas, Clarksburg	KO by	6

AL (BUBBA) THOMPSON
Tulsa, Okla. Lightweight

Dec.	16—Sean O'Grady, Oklahoma City	KO by	3

1976

Feb.	17—Rocky Smith, Oklahoma City	L	10
Oct.	16—Wendell Williams, Key	L	6

1977

June	30—Billy Pearish, Wichita	L	6

1979

Sept.	20—Frank Newton, Tulsa	KO by	3
Nov.	8—Alvin Fowler, Tulsa	W	8
Dec.	13—Simmie Black, Tulsa	W	8

1980

Mar.	16—Wardell Williams, Kansas City	KO	6
June	13—Simmie Black, Tulsa	W	8

BRUCE THOMPSON
Muncie, Ind. Welterweight
Born: Sept. 20, 1953
1975

July	8—Ruben Crosco, Chicago	KO	5

1976
(Inactive)
1977

Jan.	27—Ron Pettigrew, Indianapolis	W	4

1978

June	4—Sam Hailstock, Allentown	L disq.	4

1979

Feb.	16—Curtis Taylor, Louisville	W	8
Apr.	22—Jerry Strickland, Indianapolis	KO by	1

1980

Mar.	8—Don Morgan, Knoxville	W	10

WARREN THUNDER
Chicago Middleweight
1977

Nov.	22—Floyd Pearson, Chicago	KO by	2

1978

Apr.	10—Leonard Boyd, Chicago	KO	2
May	8—Billy Moreno, Chicago	KO	2
May	22—Bobby Crawford, Chicago	KO	3
June	30—Eddie Partee, Chicago	KO	1
Aug.	28—Bobby Orr, Chicago	L	6
Oct.	6—Franklin Wilson, Waukegan	KO	1
Nov.	18—Jerry Strickland, DePaul	KO	2

1979

Feb.	2—Roosevelt Green, Chicago	KO by	3
Mar.	17—Carl Crowley, Chicago	KO by	2
July	20—Elvis Parks, U. of Ill.	W	6
Dec.	15—Imara Epesi, Chicago	KO	6

1980

Feb.	18—Harlan Holden, Chicago	W	6
Apr.	17—Elvis Parks, Chicago	KO by	2
Sept.	22—Jack Torrance, Chicago	KO by	3

JOE TIBERI
Vineland, N.J. Middleweight
1977

Jan.	27—Nikita Tarhocker, Wilmington	KO	2
Feb.	24—Frank Sumter, Wilmington	KO	2
Mar.	26—Al Little, Bristol	W	4
Apr.	21—Billy Murphy, Wilmington	KO	1
Sept.	16—Ed Freeman, Wilmington	W	6
Oct.	6—George Sydnor, Philadelphia	KO	5

1978

Apr.	22—Jesse Barclay, Trenton	KO	4
June	1—Mike Picciotti, Upper Darby	KO By	3
Nov.	14—Marciano Bernardi, Totowa	KO	4
Dec.	29—Morris Grant, Vineland	KO	1

1979

Feb.	14—Charlie Benjamin, White Plains	KO	2
Mar.	13—Ray Rivera, Totowa	KO	2
May	23—Abdul Hassen, White Plains	KO	2
June	12—Jaime Rodriguez, Totowa	W	8

Jan.	12—Kevin Howard, Atlantic City	L	6
Mar.	26—Bob Patterson, Baltimore	KO by	7
Nov.	25—Fernando Fernandez, Boston	KO	5

JAMES (QUICK) TILLIS
Chicago, Ill. Heavyweight
1978

Nov.	18—Ron Stephany, DePaul	KO	1
Dec.	15—Al Bell, Chicago	KO	1

1979

Feb.	2—Dave Watkins, Chicago	KO	1
Feb.	28—Sylvester Wilder, Chicago	KO	3
Mar.	31—Rocky Lane, Chicago	KO	1

230

June	11—George Gofarth, Chicago	KO	5	

June   11—George Gofarth, Chicago .... KO 5
July   20—Henry Porter, Univ. of Ill. .... KO 6
July   30—Charles Atlas, Chicago .... KO 2
Sept.   7—Jimmy Cross, Chicago .... KO 2
Oct.   19—Bob Whaley, Chicago .... KO 1
Nov.   20—Harry Terrell, Chicago .... KO 1
Dec.   13—(Memphis) Al Jones, Tulsa .... KO 4
1980
Feb.   1—Cookie Wallace, Chicago .... W 10
Mar.   3—Ron Stander, Chicago .... KO 7
Apr.   17—Frank Schram, Chicago .... KO 2
May   15—Walter Santemore, Chicago .... W 10
June   12—Eric Sedillo, Chicago .... KO 3
Aug.   14—Mike Koranicki, Chicago .... W 10
Nov.   13—Domingo D'Elia, Chicago .... KO 4

BAKER TINSLEY
1980
Apr.   5—Tom Fischer, Louisville .... L 8
May   3—Gary Alexander, Canton .... L 6
Aug.   2—Mike Schiebelhood, Cincinnati .... L 6
Sept.   24—Amos Hayes, Struthers .... L 8
Oct.   28—Clyde Mudgett, Indianapolis .... W 8
Oct.   30—Pete Susens, Louisville .... KO 3
Nov.   7—Willard Dumas, Clarksville .... KO 2
Dec.   13—Clyde Mudgett, Louisville .... KO 6

NIUA TOFAEONO
Los Angeles, Calif. Light Heavyweight
1979
Mar.   9—Sylvester Green, San Diego .... KO 4
Apr.   4—Charles Roye, Las Vegas .... KO 1
Apr.   11—Gary Yeates, Las Vegas .... KO 3
May   20—Jesse Island, Las Vegas .... KO 4
Aug.   17—Jesse Island, San Diego .... KO 2
Sept.   30—Lee Lacy, Reno .... KO 4
Oct.   19—Leni Provo, San Diego .... KO 2
1980
Feb.   13—King David Smith, Las Vegas .... W 10
Apr.   9—James Williams, Las Vegas ...... W disq. 10
May   24—S.T. Gordon, Santa Monica .... KO by 2
Sept.   19—Clarence Geigger, Inglewood .... KO 1
Oct.   22—King David Smith, Santa Monica ...... D 10

ADONIS TORRES
1979
Oct.   4—Melvin Bethea, New York .... W 4
1980
Feb.   8—James Marshall, New York .... KO 3
May   2—Roberto Sanchez, New York .... KO 4
Nov.   12—Edwin Oquendo, New York .... KO by 2

ANDRES TORRES
Puerto Rican Bantamweight
1969
July   21—Santos Rivera, San Juan.............. L 4
Sept.   20—Benjamin Camacho, San Juan .... L 4
Oct.   25—Hector Vallee, San Juan .... W 4
1970
Feb.   28—Rivera Cintron, San Juan............. KO 3
Mar.   14—Modesto Escalera, San Juan........... W 6
Oct.   19—Tony Bezares, San Juan .... L 6
Oct.   24—Bennie Rivera, San Juan............. W 6
1971
Apr.   3—Danny Figueroa, San Juan............ W 6
May   5—Gregory Benitez, San Juan........... L 8
May   23—Nelson de la Cruz, San Juan .... W 8
1972
Feb.   19—Heriberto Oliveras, San Juan .... W 10
Feb.   —Hector McBride, Tampa............... W 8
Aug.   8—Francisco Villegas, San Juan .... L 10
1973
Apr.   28—Leo Cruz, Carolina .... D 10
1974
May   30—Francisco Villegas, San Juan .... L 10
July   15—Andres Hernandez, San Juan .... L 12
Aug.   19—Davey Vasquez, New York .... L 10
Oct.   27—Martin Corona, Mexicali .... L 10
1975
Apr.   28—Nelson Tamariz, Santo Domingo ...... L 10
Nov.   17—Enrique Solis, San Juan.............. D 10
1976
Aug.   16—Gerald Hayes, San Juan .... W 8
Oct.   11—Andres Hernandez, San Juan .... L 10
1977
July   11—Hector Carrasquilla, San Juan .... KO by 7
Aug.   20—Lupe Pintor, Los Angeles .... KO by 4
1978
June   3—Dennis Moran, San Juan .... W 10
Oct.   24—Jeff Chandler, Philadelphia .... L 10
1979
Jan.   27—Tony (Pee Wee) Stokes, San Juan ...... KO 5
Aug.   22—Juan LaPorte, New York .... KO by 6

1980
July   31—Jimmy Washington, Atlantic City .... L 6
Aug.   25—Enrique Sanchez, Santo Domingo .... KO by 2

HERIBERTO TORRES
Vineland, N.J. Featherweight
1979
Jan.   30—Pedro Lebron, Upper Darby .... W 4
Apr.   10—Pete Torres, Philadelphia .... KO 1
May   22—Ken Carpenter, Upper Darby .... KO by 1
June   29—Benny Llanos, Jersey City .... W 4
Sept.   30—Tim Daniels, Trenton .... D 4
Nov.   23—Tim Daniels, Trenton .... W 4
1980
Jan.   12—Pedro Lebron, Atlantic City .... D 6
Jan.   18—Santos Cruz, Trenton .... L 4

HUMBERTO TORRES
Argentine Featherweight
1980
Feb.   14—Jorge Martinez, Mendoza .... D 8
Mar.   8—Raul Pared, Buenos Aires .... W 6
Apr.   11—Pedro Burki, Just. Posse .... KO by 5
July   4—Jorge Martinez, Mendoza .... D 10
Oct.   10—Jose Antonio Gomez, Salta .... W 6

JOSE (PULGA) TORRES
Tucson, Ariz. Flyweight
1980
Jan.   20—Jose Luis Leos, Tucson .... KO 2
Feb.   20—Dennis Tenio, Las Vegas .... D 4
Mar.   8—Dennis Tenio, Las Vegas .... L 4
Mar.   26—Rafael Capristro, Las Vegas .... W 6
Apr.   14—Marcelo Camacho, Fresno .... W 6
May   5—Tito Arzate, Phoenix .... W 6
June   3—Frankie Granados, Phoenix .... W 8
June   19—Arturo Vasquez, Tucson .... KO 2
July   17—Tito Arzate, Tucson .... KO 8
Sept.   25—Luis Gonzales, Los Angeles .... KO 3
Nov.   5—Manuel Martinez, Las Vegas .... KO 2
Nov.   21—Franco Torregosa, Los Angeles .... W 10

JOSE TORRES
Mexico City, Mexico Featherweight
Born: Arandas, Jalisco, Mexico
1972
Jan.   29—Raul Gillen, Mexico City .... KO 3
Mar.   —Changa Moreno, Salinas Cruz .... KO 6
Mar.   29—Emilio Calleja, Mexico City .... KO 3
Apr.   —(Chamaco) Salazar, Culiacan, Sinaloa .. KO 2
May   17—Ramiro Flores, Mexico City .... KO 2
May   31—Antonio Torres, Mexico City .... KO 4
June   14—Armando Olivares, Culiacan, Sinaloa ... KO 4
July   5—Jose Pozos, Mexico City .... KO 4
Aug.   26—Leon Meza, Mexico City .... KO 6
Sept.   30—Memo Ortiz, Mexico City .... KO 8
Nov.   1—Nacho Lomeli, Mexico City .... W 10
1973
Jan.   17—Goyo Vargas, Mexico City .... L 10
Mar.   21—Juan Fabila, Mexico City .... KO 2
Apr.   4—Urbano Davila, Mexico City .... W 10
July   7—Tomas Frias, Mexico City .... L 10
Aug.   25—Modesto Concepcion, Mexico City .... KO 7
Oct.   20—Felipe (Cachorro) Ursua, Mexico City ... KO 5
1974
Feb.   13—Tomas Frias, Mexico City .... KO 10
Mar.   16—Frank Durango, Mexico City .... KO 8
May   4—Chanakiat Kiatmougyoum, Mexico City KO 1
June   29—Rafael Ortega, Guadalajara, Jalisco .. KO by 2
Oct.   26—Benjamin Ortiz, Mexico City .... KO 8
Nov.   29—Salvador Martinez Carrillo, Guadalajara KO 7
1975
Feb.   22—Enrique Garcia, Mexico City .... KO 5
Apr.   3—Carlos Becerril, Los Angeles .... KO 4
June   28—Alfonso Ibarra, Mexico City .... KO 4
Aug.   16—Saul Montana, Mexico City .... KO 3
1976
Feb.   1—Alexis Arguello, Mexicali, Baja California L 10
June   19—Abdul Bey, Los Angeles .... D 10
Oct.   29—Ney Gordillo, Reynosa, Tamaulipas .... KO 8
1977
Feb.   26—Rosalio Muro, Estado de Mexico .... KO 8
July   16—Francisco (Toro) Coronado, Managua .... L 10
Sept.   13—Danny Lopez, Los Angeles .... KO by 7
(For WBC Featherweight Title)
1978
Feb.   25—Jorge David Monzon, Mexico City ...... KO 9
(Won Mexican Featherweight Title)
Apr.   3—Fel Clemente, Stockton .... L 10
July   21—Norberto Cabrera, Ciudad Obregon,
Sonora .... KO 7
Oct.   7—Justo Garcia, Mexico City .... W 12
(Retained Mexican Featherweight Title)

1979

June 18—Bobby Chacon, Los Angeles .... L 10
July 24—Rolando Navarette, Honolulu .... L 10

1980

Oct. 28—Ruben Castillo, Bakersfield .... L 10

MILTON TORRES
Holyoke, Mass. Featherweight
1979

June 29—Jose Gonzales, Hartford .... W 4
Oct. 17—Felix Rodriguez, Hartford .... W 4

1980

July 17—Jesus Montanez, Rio Piedras .... D 4
Aug. 7—Noel Rivera, Rio Piedras .... W 4
Aug. 28—Edwin Salgado, Rio Piedras .... D 4

RAUL TORRES
Argentine Welterweight
1980

Jan. —Hugo Castellano, Coronel Pringles .... L 10
Mar. 13—Mario Arreguez, Bahia Blanca .... L 8
Apr. 24—Horacio Mendez, Bahia Blanca .... D 8

ROBERTO TORRES
Apatzinean, Mexico Featherweight
1979

May 5—Benny Marquez, Chicago .... W 10
Aug. 23—Refugio Rojas, Los Angeles .... L 10
Sept. 25—Ruben Castillo, Los Angeles .... KO by 3

1980

Aug. 7—Rocky Garcia, Los Angeles .... L 10
Sept. 11—Ricardo Jiminez, Los Angeles .... D 10

SALVADOR (NEGRO) TORRES
Mexican Flyweight
1974

—Jose Luis Lopez, Mexico City .... KO 5
—Francisco Durando, Mexico City .... W 10
Aug. 10—Ernie de la Cruz, Mexico City .... KO 4

1975

Mar. 1—Jose Martin Del Campo, Los Angeles .... KO 8
Mar. 16—Sanjio Takamori, Mexicali .... KO by 2
May 14—Jose Luis Lima, Mexico City .... KO 2
July 26—Rafael Rojas, Mexico City .... W 8
Aug. 30—Art Hafey, Anaheim .... L 10
Sept. 3—Fedrico F. Gonzalez, Mexico City ...... KO 2
Nov. 29—Rosalio Muro, Mexico City .... KO 4

1976

Apr. 21—Jesus Martinez, Mexico City .... KO 4
June 19—Alexis Arguello, Los Angeles .... KO by 3
(World Featherweight Title)
Oct. 9—Vosme Corcuera, Mexico City .... KO 6
Nov. 20—Jose Mendez, Mexico City .... W 10

1977

Feb. 12—Chuy Rodriguez, Manzanillo .... KO 10
Feb. 26—Ernesto Herrera, Estado De Mexico ...... L 12
Apr. —Chuy Rodriguez, Manzavilla .... KO 10
June 11—Ruben Garcia, Mexico City .... L 10
July 30—Gustavo Segura, Mexico City .... KO 3
Aug. 20—Raul Arroyo, Mexico City .... KO 8
Sept. 27—Rosario Gonzalez, Tijuana .... KO 5
Nov. 5—Clemente Mucino, Mexico City .... KO 9
Dec. 3—Jose Mo, Mexico City .... KO 8

1978

Jan. 1—Celso Limon, Manzanillo .... L 10
Apr. 5—Celso Limon, Mexico City .... D 10
June 28—Jesus Ramirez, Mexico City .... D 10
July 18—Robert Vasquez, San Antonio .... D 10
Nov. 25—Lupe Galindo, Mexico City .... KO 6

1979

Mar. 30—Rodolfo Chavez, Culiacan .... W 10
May 19—Salvador Sanchez, Mexico City ...... KO by 7
July 28—Brigido Martinez, Mexico City .... L 10
Sept. 14—Daniel Felizardo, Reynosa .... KO 1
Nov. 10—Rodolfo (Gato) Gonzales, Guadalajara KO by 1
Dec. 9—Guillermo (Lobo) Morales, Tuxtla
—Gutierrez .... L 10

1980

Oct. 7—Gonzallo Montellano, Bakersfield .... L 10

SANDY TORRES
Puerto Rican Junior Middleweight
1969

Aug. 9—Hector Matta, San Juan .... W 8
Sept. 20—Johnny Tutuska, San Juan.............. W 8
Oct. 11—Jose Peterson, San Diego .... KO by 2

1970

Jan. 31—David Aran, San Juan .... KO 2
Feb. 28—Rafael Jimenez, San Juan............... W 6
Mar. 21—Rufus Figaro, San Juan.............. KO by 3
May 6—Roberto Gomez, Ponce .... D 10
May 30—Rafael Jimenez, San Juan .... KO by 3
Oct. 12—Miguel Morales, San Juan .... W 6

1971

Apr. 10—Ruben Carmona, San Juan .... D 8

1972

Feb. 4—Walter Peters, St. Thomas .... W 10
Mar. 17—Walter Peters, St. Thomas .... W 10
May 13—Ernie Witcher, San Juan .... KO 1

1973

Jan. 26—Elisha Obed, Nassau .... KO by 8
Mar. 29—Angel Robinson Garcia, Tampa.......... W 10
May 28—Guacharaco Viera, San Juan .... KO 2
June 3—Bunny Grant, Kingston .... D 10
June 28—Ruben Arocha, San Juan .... W 10
July 14—Art Kettles, San Juan .... W 10
Sept. 15—Dario Hidalgo, San Juan............... W 10
Nov. 26—Fermin Guzman, San Juan .... KO 9

1974

Mar. 3—Al Moss, San Juan .... KO 2
July 15—Papo Melendez, San Juan............... W 12
July 31—Freytas Laban, Fajardo................. KO 7

1975

Jan. 18—Eduardo Trinidad, San Juan .... KO 2
Feb. 24—Jose Figueroa, San Juan............... W 10
Mar. 18—Dario Hidalgo, Miami Beach .... KO 8
Apr. 9—Jose Rodriguez, Houston, Texas .... W 10
Oct. 4—Miguel Castellini, Milan .... KO 6
Nov. 19—Pablo Rodriguez, New York .... W 8

1976

Oct. 22—Ronnie Harris, New York .... L 10

1977

Apr. 1—Pic Diamante, Manila .... KO by 10
Nov. 5—Karl Vinson, Camione d'Italia .... L 8

1978

Feb. 15—Alan Minter, Las Vegas .... KO by 5
May 1—Armin Marbella, Laguna .... KO 3
July 29—Fulgencio Obel, Caracas .... KO by 4
Sept. 23—Fighting Jim, St. Thomas .... KO 8
Nov. 5—Ken Bristol, Georgetown .... L 10

1979

Feb. 23—Jesus Castro, Santo Domingo .... KO by 6
Apr. 6—Jesus Castro, Santo Domingo .... KO 12
Aug. 25—Marifan Benes, Zenica .... KO 6
Dec. 14—Carlos Herrera, Buenos Aires .... KO by 5

1980

Feb. 5—Victor Gonzalez, Houston .... KO 3

WILLIE TORRES
So. Philadelphia, Pa. Middleweight
1979

Sept. 26—Emmett Johnson, Upper Darby .... KO 2
Dec. 4—Emmett Johnson, Upper Darby .... KO 4

1980

Feb. 1—Mario Maldonado, Philadelphia .... D 4
Apr. 26—Mickey Lewis, Lynchburg .... KO 2
May 3—Lindell Holmes, Detroit .... KO by 1

CARLOS TOTARO
Argentine Junior Featherweight
1980

Jan. —Carlos Villarruel, Tandil .... KO by 3
Mar. 14—Jorge Gomez, Gral Roca .... KO by 8
May 17—Sergio Palma, Mar del Plata .... L 10
Aug. 8—Carlos Russo, Mar del Plata .... W 10
Sept. 26—Luis Alvarez, Salta .... L 10

TOM TRIM
Texas Heavyweight
1979

June 19—Willie Stoglin, Houston .... KO 3
Aug. 15—Clarence Allen, Beaumont .... KO 3
Sept. 14—Larry Montgomery, Houston .... KO 1

1980

Jan. 8—Paul Lawson, Houston .... KO 3
Oct. 18—Henry Pamplin, Lake Charles .... KO by 1
Nov. 11—Henry Pamplin, Houston .... KO by 3

FELIX (DIABILLO) TRINIDAD
Puerto Rican Welterweight
1975

Mar. 31—Nick Ortiz, San Juan................. KO by 6
Apr. 28—Francisco Sullivan, San Juan............ KO 2
Nov. 3—Carlos Rodriguez, San Juan............. L 6
Nov. 6—Frankie Aponto, San Juan .... KO 4

1976

May 31—Jose A. Rosa, San Juan .... L 6

1977
(Inactive)

1978

Jan. 14—Fernando Rivera, Carolina .... L 6
Apr. 22—Manuel Quiles, San Juan .... KO 4
May 20—Ruben Adordo, Carolina .... KO 1
Sept. 18—Maelo Santana, Rio Piedras .... KO 4
Nov. 27—Fernando Rivera, San Juan .... W 12

1979
Aug. 7—Salvador Sanchez, Houston .... KO by 5
Dec. 18—Qui Que Solis, Rio Piedras .... KO by 9
1980
May 19—Jose Alexander, San Juan .... L 10
Aug. 18—Carlos Pinango, Caracas .... KO by 6

DWIGHT TRIPLETT
Philadelphia, Pa. Light Heavyweight
1980
Jan. 18—Bill Tuttle, Trenton .... ND 4
Mar. 14—Quadir Muntaquim, Trenton .... W 4
May 16—Quadir Muntaquim, Chester .... KO 5
Oct. 18—Reggie Patrick, Atlantic City .... KO by 1
Dec. 12—Everett Conklin, New York .... KO by 2

EARL TRIPP
Las Vegas, Nev. Heavyweight
1977
Dec. 24—Greg Johnson, St. Thomas .... W 10
1978
Apr. 26—I. Taylor, Las Vegas .... KO 1
May 24—Walter Cloud, Las Vegas .... KO 1
June 7—Godfrey White, Las Vegas .... KO 1
June 28—Lee Mitchell, Las Vegas .... KO 1
July 12—Rahman Muhammad, Las Vegas .... L 4
Aug. 2—Verlee Price, Las Vegas .... KO 2
Aug. 23—Toni Pulu, Las Vegas .... KO 1
Oct. 18—S. T. Gordon, Las Vegas .... W 10
Dec. 5—King David Smith, Las Vegas .... W 10
1979
Mar. 23—Kevin Isaac, Las Vegas .... L 10
May 18—Jimmy Ingram, Pico Rivera .... KO 2
June 6—S. T. Gordon, Las Vegas .... KO by 7
Sept. 12—Mustafa El Amin, Las Vegas .... KO 1
Oct. 31—Al Neumann, Las Vegas .... W 10
Nov. 28—Roberto Reynosa, Las Vegas .... KO 2
1980
Jan. 13—Mike Dokes, Las Vegas .... KO by 1
May 14—King David Smith, Las Vegas .... W 10
July 9—Leroy Caldwell, Las Vegas .... W 10
Aug. 29—John L. Johnson, W. Palm Beach ...... KO 2
Oct. 22—S.T. Gordon, Santa Monica .... KO by 4

ROGER TROUPE
Los Angeles, Calif. Heavywight
1978
Sept. 26—Roger Braxton, Pico Rivera .... W 4
Oct. 25—Walter Cloud, Las Vegas .... L 4
1979
Apr. 21—Steve Huntington, Las Vegas .... KO by 5
1980
Apr. 26—Robert Coley, Atlantic City .... KO by 5
May 25—Kerry Judge, Atlantic City .... L 4
June 27—Joe Vescio, New York .... D 4
July 29—Donnie Glover, Philadelphia .... W 4
Aug. 7—Lindsay Page, Atlantic City .... KO 1
Sept. 12—Marvis Frazier, New York .... KO by 3
Oct. 24—Broderick Mason, Philadelphia ...... KO by 1

HUGO TRUJILLO
Argentine Middleweight
1980
Feb. 1—Enrique Coronel, S. Sal. de Jujuy .... L 10
Mar. 28—Alfredo Lucero, Salta .... KO by 3
June 6—Luis Peralta, La Banda .... L 10
Aug. 29—Carlos Flores, Salta .... L 10
Oct. 3—Ricardo Cisneros, P.R.S. Pena .... KO by 9

BENNY RAY TRUSEL
Detroit, Mich. Junior Welterweight
1979
June 12—Leon Garner, Detroit .... W 6
June 28—Earl Stringer, Detroit .... W 4
1980
Nov. 8—Jeff Foster, Detroit .... KO 1

RODNEY TRUSEL
Detroit, Mich. Welterweight
1980
Feb. 7—John Allen, Detroit .... KO 1
Sept. 30—Robert Hensley, Niles .... KO 2
Oct. 23—Mike Senegal, Detroit .... W 4
Dec. 2—Greg Harper, Toledo .... W 6
Dec. 12—Mike Grant, Detroit .... KO 3

TONY TUBBS
Los Angeles, Calif. Heavyweight
1980
June 14—Bruce Scott, Cincinnati .... KO 1
Aug. 2—Jerry Hunter, Cincinnati .... KO 4
Nov. 7—Ron Draper, San Antonio .... W 10
Nov. 14—John L. Johnson, Miami .... KO 1

Nov. 22—Larry Simms, Cincinnati .... KO 3
Nov. 29—Mike Creel, Los Angeles .... KO 3

TONY TUCKER
Grand Rapids, Mich. Heavyweight
Managed by Shelly Finkel & Lou Duva
1980
Nov. 1—Chuck Gardner, Lake Tahoe .... KO 3
Dec. 2—Jesse Clark, Toledo .... KO 1
Dec. 11—Max Baer Smith, Chicago .... KO 5

ROGELIO (RUDY) TULONGHARI
Honolulu, Hawaii Junior Lightweight
1979
July 24—Ful Sumagaysay, Honolulu .... L 4
1980
Nov. 8—Jeff Foster, Detroit .... KO 1

ED (SAVAGE) TURNER
Orlando, Fla. Light Heavyweight
1975
May 19—Mike McKinney, Tampa .... KO 1
June 3—Clarence Morris, Orlando .... W 6
June 16—George Clark, Brunswick .... KO 3
June 24—Gene Idlette, Orlando................ KO by 1
July 8—Marc Hans, Orlando.................... KO 1
July 22—Enrique Rodriguez, Miami Beach .... D 6
Aug. 5—George Clark, Orlando.................. KO 4
Sept. 23—Roger Pinkney, Orlando................ KO 5
Nov. 11—Gene Idlette, Orlando.................. W 6
Dec. 9—Ray Collins, Orlando .... KO 2
Dec. 12—Bob Freeze, Nassau .... L 10
1976
Feb. 3—Jimmy Nixon, Orlando .... KO 2
Feb. 17—Nat Gates, Orlando .... L 6
Mar. 16—Tony Greene, Miami Beach .... L 6
Mar. 23—Ernie Barr, Orlando .... W 6
Mar. 26—Anthony Teran, Tuscaloosa .... KO 2
Apr. 13—Nat Gates, Orlando.................... W 6
May 11—Fred Sullivan, Orlando .... W 6
June 4—George Holden, Tuscaloosa............. W 6
July 17—Osvaldo Ocasio, San Juan .... L 8
Oct. 12—Sam Bowie, Orlando................... KO 4
1977
Jan. 14—Willie Goodman, Orlando .... KO 2
Feb. 1—Ernie Barr, Orlando .... KO by 8
Feb. 12—Osvaldo Ocasio, San Juan .... KO by 2
Apr. 10—Mike Dokes, Miami Beach .... L 6
May 6—Bobby Lloyd, Miami Beach .... L 8
May 17—Willie Goodman, Orlando .... W 4
June 23—Matt Franklin, Philadelphia .... KO by 6
July 15—Clarence Morris, Tampa .... W 6
1978
Jan. 19—Roberto Rockett, Memphis .... KO by 2
Apr. 18—James Dixon, Memphis .... W 4
May 23—Roberto Rockett, Greenville .... L 8
June 2—Ivy Brown, Kansas City .... L 8
June 14—Eddie Gregory, White Plains .... KO by 4
July 12—Ned Hallacy, Memphis .... W 10
Aug. 29—Roberto Rockett, Memphis .... L 8
Nov. 1—Conrad Tooker, St. Louis .... L 8
Nov. 14—Eugene Stimson, Memphis .... L 8
1979
Mar. 14—Tommy Evans, Oakland .... KO by 2
1980
Feb. 8—Domenico Adinolfi, Milan .... L 10

JOHNNY TURNER
Brooklyn, N.Y. Welterweight
1975
Feb. 20—Kenny Jones, North Bergen............ KO 1
Mar. 14—Pedro Acevedo, Elizabeth .... KO 1
Apr. 11—Jimmy Nieves, Stamford .... KO 2
Apr. 24—Tommy Smith, North Bergen.......... KO 4
June 28—Jimmy Nieves, Islip .... KO 2
Aug. 5—Pete Pagan, Elizabeth .... KO 3
Aug. 26—Randy Milton, Albany................... D 6
Sept. 30—Pete Pagan, New York................ W 6
Nov. 7—Steve Tooney, Latham .... KO 2
Nov. 21—Harvey Wilson, Kingston .... KO 5
1976
Jan. 22—Angel Cintron, Kingston.............. KO 2
Feb. 25—Ron Meaweather, New York .... W 6
May 14—Johnny Thompson, Albany .... KO 6
May 14—Juan Rosado, Weehawken .... KO 6
June 28—Angel Cintron, New York .... KO 2
Oct. 24—Celio Romero, New York............... W 8
1977
Mar. 1—Papo Melendez, Albany .... KO 4
Mar. 25—Tony Petronelli, Milwaukee .... L 10
May 3—Donnie Bennett, Albany .... W 6
July 14—Willie Davis, Dover .... KO 5

Aug.	3—Julio Garcia, New York	W 8
Sept.	9—Julio Garcia, Nanuet	W 10
Oct.	27—Larry Stanton, New York	L 10
Dec.	21—Ricky Craney, Brooklyn	KO 2

1978

Apr.	21—George Fakaris, Albany	W 8
May	15—Frankie Benitez, New York	KO 8
June	22—Pat Maloney, New York	KO 8
Aug.	16—Charlie Benjamin, Nanuet	KO 3
Sept.	20—Steve Michalerya, Scranton	KO 1
Oct.	25—Luis Vega, Scranton	KO 7
Nov.	22—Roland Pryor, Scranton	KO 7

1979

Jan.	26—Cemal Kamaci, New York	KO 6
Mar.	30—Randy Milton, Scranton	KO 3
June	14—Danny McAloon, New York	KO 2
Aug.	22—Santiago Valdez, New York	KO by 2
Oct.	4—Larry Peterson, New York	KO 4
Nov.	21—C. J. Faison, Scranton	KO 3
Dec.	12—Julio Garcia, Scranton	W 10

1980

Mar.	16—Wilfred Benitez, Miami	KO by 9
Apr.	30—Jaime Rodriguez, Scranton	W 10
June	30—Mike Michaud, New York	KO 4
Sept.	10—Alfonso Hayman, Scranton	KO 6
Oct.	2—Pat Hallacy, New York	D 10

ROBERT TURNER
San Diego, Calif. Welterweight
1976

Aug.	5—Juan Arcos, Los Angeles	L 4

1977

June	24—Bert Lee, San Diego	L 5,
Sept.	30—Bert Lee, San Diego	KO by 4
Nov.	10—Rocky Fukumoto, Los Angeles	L 5

1978

Jan.	28—Alejandro Rodriguez, Fresno	KO 5
Feb.	11—Roger Stafford, Las Vegas	KO by 1
Mar.	30—Genaro Gloria, Las Vegas	L 1
June	21—Jesse James Castleberry, Las Vegas	L 5

1979

Mar.	5—Jose Baquedano, Houston	KO 2
Apr.	4—Ken Crooms, Los Angeles	KO by 2
May	14—Armando Ramirez, Phoenix	L 6
Dec.	14—Armando Ramirez, Orange County	L 6

1980

Mar.	27—Rick Wynne, San Carlos	KO by 2
Sept.	17—Eric Bonilla, San Diego	KO 3
Sept.	19—Katsuhiro Okubo, Inglewood	KO 3

WILLIE TURNER
Kansas City, Mo. Junior Lightweight
1980

Mar.	7—Marshall Villa, Jr., Kansas City	KO 3
Apr.	13—C.B. Brown, Kansas City	W 4
June	6—James Buckley, Kansas City	KO by 4

BILL TUTTLE
Bowie, Md. Light Heavyweight
1979

Sept.	26—Willie (Caveman) Lee, Baltimore	KO 1
Oct.	11—Charles Brown, Richmond	KO 1
Oct.	24—Robert McFarland, Baltimore	KO 1
Nov.	14—Charlie Carey, Baltimore	W 6
Nov.	29—Carl Cherry, Richmond	KO 1
Dec.	12—Raymond Boykin, Washington, D.C.	KO 1

1980

Jan.	16—Mike Grant, Washington, D.C.	KO 3
Jan.	18—Dwight Triplett, Trenton	D 4
May	8—Charlie Smith, Atlantic City	L 8
Oct.	4—Junior Edmonds, McAfee, N.J.	L 6

RALPH TWINNING
Muskegon, Mich. Junior Welterweight
Managed by Jack Cowen
1979

Apr.	17—James Stamps, Milwaukee	KO 1
June	4—Pete Podgorski, Chicago	KO 3
June	13—George Hightower, Chicago	KO 1
July	18—Jamie Knox, Indianapolis	KO 4
Nov.	23—Howard Griffin, Kansas City	KO 3
Dec.	19—Lee Thomas, Rockford	KO 4

1980

Feb.	18—Simmie Black, Chicago	KO 3
Mar.	22—Norman Banner, Grand Rapids	KO 1
July	11—Tony Taylor, Chicago	KO 3
Aug.	8—C.B. Brown, Chicago	KO 3
Apr.	19—Chuck Spicer, Muskegon	KO 2
Oct.	31—Nino LaRocca, Rome	KO by 4
Dec.	8—Ronald Zenon, Paris	KO by 3

234

OSCARN UAGINES
Bantamweight
1980

Feb.	15—Arturo Hernandez, Guadalajara	KO 4
Apr.	27—Enrique Romero, Guadalajara	KO 1
May	23—Juan Zarate, Guadalajara	KO 2
Oct.	17—Victor Hernandez, Guadalajara	KO 1
Nov.	21—Rosenao Alonso, Guadalajara	KO 5

CARLOS URBANO
Lightweight
1977

Mar.	25—Jaime Carbajal, Acapulco	KO 5
Apr.	6—Jose Reyes, Mexico City	W 8
Apr.	25—Mario Simon, Mexico City	KO by 7

1978-1979
(Inactive)

1980

June	27—Antonio Maroues, Apatzingan	KO by 3

FELIPE URQUIZA
Mexican Lightweight
1979

May	25—Jorge Portela, San Diego	KO 7
July	20—Manuel Leon, San Diego	KO 4
Nov.	26—Ringo Lopez, Tijuana	KO 3
Dec.	11—Juan Villa, San Jose	KO by 7

1980

Sept.	17—Ignacio Campus, Tijuana	KO 6
Nov.	17—Antonio Perez, Tecate	KO 2

PORFIRIO URRUTIA
Bantamweight
1980

May	7—Elueterio Flores, Mexico City	KO 2
May	31—Ray De La Cruz, Mexico City	D 6
July	23—Salomon Urrutiam, Mexico City	KO 2
Nov.	12—Jose Franco, Mexico City	KO by 2

AMADO PANTORITA URSUA
Mexican Flyweight
1974

May	8—Alfonso Beasa, Mexico City	KO 2
June	15—Panchito Gayton, Mexico City	W 4

1975

Sept.	12—Nicolas Rivera, Mexico City	KO 3
Sept.	27—Punco, Mexico City	KO 2
Dec.	25—Pedro Flores, Mexico City	KO 3

1976

Jan.	31—Porfirio Perez, Mexico City	KO 1
Feb.	7—Gaspar Meza, Mexico City	KO 1
Mar.	10—Rodolfo Lopez, Mexico City	KO 7
Apr.	14—Lauro Garcia, Mexico City	KO 2
May	3—Romulio Rivera, Mexico City	KO 3
June	7—Jose Gallegos, Piedras Negro	L 10
Aug.	6—Juan Lopez, Matamoros	KO 3
Sept.	10—Anthony Sanchez, Mexico City	KO 4
Oct.	10—Rafael Gandarilla, Mexico City	KO by 9
Dec.	4—Juan Jose Guzman, Guadalajara	KO by 8

1977

Mar.	18—Juan Monito Diaz, Mexico City	W 10
June	12—Herman Prado, Managua	KO 4
July	30—Eusebio Urcuyo, Costa Rica	KO 1
Oct.	7—Alfonso Lopez, Panama	KO 6

1978

Feb.	19—Benny Cantera, Santa Resito	KO 3
May	13—Jose Sosa, Mexico City	KO 6

1979

May	26—Lupe Madora, Merida	KO by 6
Nov.	6—Juan Castellanos, Reynosa	KO 10

1980

Apr.	19—Jorge DeJesus, Mexico City	W 10
Oct.	25—Freddie Castillo, Mexico City	KO 3

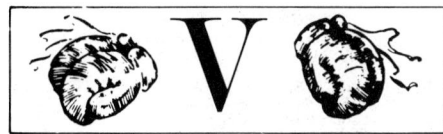

MIGUEL VALDERRAMA
1978
Nov. 22—Miguel Alvarez, Mexico City .... W 4
1979
Feb. 14—Gil Estrada, Mexico City .... W 6
Apr. 11—Rigobeto Herrera, Mexico City .... KO by 2
May 19—Rigoberto Herrera, Mexico City .... KO 3
June 23—Nacho Rivera, Mexico City .... KO by 6
Aug. 11—Chivo Molina, Mexico City .... L 6
1980
May 7—Rodolfo Morales, Mexico City .... KO by 5
Nov. 5—Raul Rosas, Mexico City .... KO 2

ELPIDIO VALDEZ
Mexican Junior Welterweight
1977
Mar. 11—Francisco Cruz, Guadalajara .... KO 5
May 15—Arturo Rodriguez, Guadalajara .... KO 7
1978
Dec. 11—Petronillo Velaaquez, Bakersfield .... L 8
1979
Jan. 30—Andy Ganigan, Honolulu .... KO by 2
Mar. 15—Irlesi Perez, Los Angeles .... KO by 1
1980
Mar. 14—Juan Hernandez, Merida .... KO 2
Nov. 14—Manuel Sanchez, Lapaz .... KO by 4

RUBEN VALDEZ
Colombian Bantamweight
Born: November 22, 1954, Guacamayal, Magdalena
1971
Dec. 22—Jacinto Herrera, Lo Amador .... W 4
1972
Apr. 28—Jaime Ramirez, Cartagena .... W 4
May 21—Donald Leon, Cartagena .... W 6
July 14—Nestor Rafael Herrera, Cartagena .... W 4
Aug. 18—Kid Avelino, Barranquilla .... KO 1
Sept. 8—Juan Zabaleta, Santa Marta .... KO 1
Oct. 11—Juan Martinez, Barranquilla .... KO 2
1973
Feb. 9—Luis Zuniga, Cartagena .... KO 3
Mar. 16—Mario de Leon, Cartagena .... KO 7
May 11—Pedro Moreno, Cartagena .... KO 2
June 8—(Tranquita) Brown, Cartagena .... KO 3
July 17—Antonio Barbosa, Cartagena .... W 10
Aug. 3—Juan Martinez, Monteria .... KO 2
Aug. 17—Enrique Martinez, Barranquilla .... W 10
Sept. 30—Eduardo Barragan, Cartagena .... KO 2
Nov. 2—Ismael Escobar, Cartagena .... KO 2
Dec. 2—Herbert Locke, Sincelejo .... W 10
1974
Jan. 20—Marcelino Beckles, Cartagena .... KO 5
Apr. 9—Lorenzo Gutierrez, Cartagena .... W 10
May 19—Javier (Pajaro) Guido, Cartagena .... KO 7
June 30—Catalino Flores, Cartagena .... KO 2
Aug. 31—Nestor (Baba) Jimenez, Cartagena ... KO by 4
Dec. 8—Francisco Villegas, Cartagena .... D 10
1975
Mar. 8—Gilberto Illueca, Panama City .... L 10
1976
Apr. 25—Pedro Diaz, Cartagena .... KO 9
June 17—Miguel Espinosa, Cartagena .... W 10
Aug. 29—John Cajina, Cartagena .... W 10
Nov. 13—Luis Ibanez, Cartagena .... W 10
1977
June 5—Guillermo Gomez, San Andres .... KO 7
Aug. 7—Livio Nolasco, Barranquilla .... W 15
(Panamanian Junior Featherweight Championship)
Nov. 28—Ulises Morales, Panama .... L 10
1978
Feb. 18—Nestor (Baba) Jimenez, Cartagena .... L 15
(For Central American & Caribbean
Junior Featherweight Title)
Apr. 22—Tarcisio (Famosito) Gomez, Cartagena ... KO 6
Sept. 2—Ricardo Cardona, Cartagena .... L 15
(For WBA Junior Featherweight Title)
Oct. 21—Gilberto Illueca, Cartagena .... W 10
1979
Feb. 25—Dennis Moran, Cartagena .... W 12
(Retained American Junior Featherweight Title)
Apr. 1—Rafael Gonzalez, Cartagena .... W 10
May 10—Remeo Amaya, Cartagena .... KO 7
Aug. 15—Freddie Perez, Cartagena .... KO 2

1980
Feb. 3—Wilfredo Gomez, Las Vegas .... KO by 6
(For World Junior Featherweight Title)
May 8—Enrique Chavez, Maicao .... KO 8
June 28—Jose Cervantes, Cartagena .... L 12
(Lost American Junior Featherweight Title)

RAUL VALDEZ
Mexican Bantamweight
1979
May 1—Carlos Cantu, Houston .... W 10
1980
June 4—Aureliano Sanchez, Mexico City .... KO 5
July 19—Jimmy Fernandez, Mexico City .... D 10

SALVANO VALENCIA
1978
Mar. 19—Fernando Gomez .... KO by 3
1979
(Inactive)
1980
July 4—Chamaco Casanova, Salinas Cruz .... KO 6
—Benny Arguelles, Salinas Cruz .... W 10
Oct. 10—Rafael Gonzales, Salinas Cruz .... KO 3

RODOLFO VALERO
Bantamweight
1978
May 4—Gregorio Rodriguez, Monterrey .... KO 5
June 16—Jorge Vaca, Monterrey .... KO 3
July 15—Francisco Famoso, Mexico City ...... KO by 1
Sept. 8—Ruby Mireles, Monterrey .... KO 2
1979
(Inactive)
1980
Feb. 29—Francisco Famoso, Guadalajara .... KO 3
July 11—Ernesto Caballero, Monterrey .... W 8

GUILLERMO VALLEJO
1980
Feb. 6—Arturo Manny Cano, Mexico City ...... KO 1
May 7—Ambrujio Luna, Mexico City .... KO 4
Mar. 8—Rosendo Alfonso, Mexico City .... KO 6
July 18—Manuel Luna, Mexico City .... KO 7
July 23—Raul Lopez, Mexico City .... L 10

MARTIN VARGAS
Chilean Flyweight
Born: January 24, 1955
1977
Jan. 28—Felix Madrigal, Santiago .... W 10
Mar. 19—Mauricio Buitrago, Santiago .... W disq. 6
Apr. 23—Angel Luis Fernandez, Santiago .... W 10
July 8—Carlos Escalante, Santiago .... KO 4
Sept. 17—Miguel Canto, Merida .... L 15
(For World Flyweight Title)
Nov. 30—Miguel Canto, Santiago .... L 15
(For World Flyweight Title)
1978
Mar. 23—Raul Perez, Punta Arenas .... W 10
Apr. 21—Alfonso Lopez, Santiago .... KO 1
(Retained South American Flyweight Title)
May 26—Alex Santana Guido, Santiago .... KO 2
(Retained South American Flyweight Title)
July 7—Jiro Takada, Santiago .... KO 6
Aug. 11—John Cajina, Santiago .... KO 2
Nov. 4—Betulio Gonzalez, Maracay .... KO by 12
(For WBA Flyweight Title)
1979
Apr. 27—Manuel Carrasco, Santiago .... W 10
May 25—Jose L. Lopez, Santiago .... KO 1
July 20—Reyes Arnal, Santiago .... KO 1
Aug. 10—Carlos Gutierrez, Santiago .... W 10
Sept. 5—Nestor Obregon, Santiago .... KO 4
Oct. 5—Nestor Obregon, Santiago .... KO 2
Oct. 26—Maximo Rodriguez, Santiago .... KO 2
Nov. 16—Joey Olivo, Santiago .... W 10
Dec. 14—Jose Ricardo, Valparaiso .... KO 8
1980
Jan. 18—Dagoberto Perinan, Valparaiso .... KO 1
Mar. 7—Orlando Rudas, Santiago .... KO 2
Apr. 10—Luis Sierra, Santiago .... W 10
June 1—Yoko Gushiken, Kochi .... KO by 8
(For WBA Junior Flyweight Title)

MEMO VARGAS
Heavyweight
1980
Mar. 22—Jorge Flores, Mexico City .... KO by 2
Sept. 12—Guillermo Soto, Gomez Palacio ...... KO by 4

DAVEY VASQUEZ
New York, N.Y. Bantamweight
1969
Nov. 21—Eulilio Garces, New York .... W 6
1970
Jan.   29—Lloyd Wilson, New York .... KO 3
Mar. 11—Blas Viera, New York .... W 6
June 10—Joe Torres, New York .... KO 5
July   15—Manuel Nieves, New York .... KO 4
Oct.   5—Ricardo Delgado, New York .... L 10
Nov. 12—Jesus Nieves, North Bergen .... W 10
Dec. 16—Carlos Zayas, New York .... W 10
1971
May   24—Arlindo Borges, New York .... KO 6
       (North American Bantamweight Title)
July   12—Ricardo Delgado, New York .... W 10
Aug. 19—Chuck Spencer, New York .... KO 7
       (North American Bantamweight Title)
Oct.   3—Enrique Pinder, New York .... L 12
       (North American Bantamweight Title)
Nov. 17—Enrique Pinder, New York .... L 12
       (North American Bantamweight Title)
1972
Mar. 14—Barry Sponagle, New York............ W 10
Apr.   17—Wilson Yambo, New York .... KO 9
June 26—Walter Seeley, New York .... L 8
Aug. 29—Famosito Gomez, Los Angeles........... L 10
1973
Mar. 13—Francisco Villegas, New York.......... W 10
1974
May   6—Natalio Jimenez, New York........... W 10
June   3—Benny Rodriguez, New York .... W 10
Aug. 19—Andres Torres, New York............. W 10
Oct.   28—Earl Large, New York .... W 10
1975
Feb.   18—Joe Guevara, Sacramento.............. L 12
June   9—Francisco Villegas, San Juan .... L 10
       (U.S. Bantamweight Title)
1976
Oct.   24—Luis Medrano, New York .... W 10
1977
Feb.   13—Richard Rozelle, Annapolis .... L 8
       (U.S. Championship Tournament)
June 22—Sean O'Grady, New York .... L 10
1978
Jan.   30—Guadalupe Pintor, San Antonio ...... KO by 2
Aug. 24—Jimmy Farrell, Boston .... W 10
1979
Apr.   3—Jeff Chandler, Philadelphia .... L 10
May   11—Jose Pena, New York .... W 10
Nov. 29—Johnny Owen, Ebbw Vale .... L 10
1980
June 20—Carmelo Negron, New York .... KO by 6

ENRIQUE VASQUEZ
Mexican Lightweight
1977
Aug. 31—Miguel Lopez, Mexico City .... KO 3
1978
Jan.   25—Romula Rocha, Mexico City .... L 4
Mar. 31—Chucho Ramirez, Mexico City .... KO by 4
May   3—Melesio Perez, Mexico City .... KO by 3
Aug.   9—Juan Trejo, Mexico City .... D 6
Nov. 29—Reyes Gonzalez, Mexico City .... L 6
1979
Jan.   20—Cayetano Correa, Mexico City .... W 4
Feb.   7—Juan Robles, Mexico City .... W 4
Feb.   28—Memo Miranda, Mexico City .... KO by 6
May   9—Chucho Ramirez, Mexico City .... L 5
June 10—Victor Vega, Tuxtla Gut............... L 5
Aug.   1—Sergio Sanchez, Mexico City .... KO by 1
1980
Jan.   20—Cayetano Correa, Mexico City .... W 4

MANUEL (TOPO GIGIO) VASQUEZ
Mexican Bantamweight
1979
    —Efraim Chacon, Culiacan .... KO by 4
    —Candelario Bobadilla .... W 10
    —Francisco Marquez, Guaymas .... KO 4
Dec.   7—Mauricio Beltran, Hermosillo .... KO 4
Dec. 29—Lupe Pintor, Hermosillo .... KO 6
1980
May   17—Jorge Ramirez, Mexico City .... L 10
July   30—Antonio Delapaz, Merida .... KO by 7

PEDRO VASQUEZ
Junior Featherweight
1980
June   4—Juan Gomez, Mexico City .... KO 1
Nov. 29—Ramon Jiminez, Mexico City .... KO by 2

ROBERT VASQUEZ
San Antonio, Texas Lightweight
1975 Texas GG Champion
1976
July   23—Mariano Serrano, San Antonio .... KO by 5
Sept.   9—Robert Tijerina, San Antonio .... W 4
Sept. 30—Lamar Baskins, Galveston .... KO 2
Nov.   4—Phillip Sotelo, Ft. Worth............... KO 2
Nov.   9—Phillip Reed, Memphis................. KO 5
Nov. 30—Simmie Black, Memphis............... KO 6
Dec.   7—Efren Gonzales, Galveston .... KO 3
1977
Jan.   4—Israel Garza, Corpus Christi .... KO 4
Feb.   1—Rodolfo Perez, Corpus Christi .... KO 4
Feb.   28—Oscar Balderas, Galveston .... KO 1
Mar. 25—Preciliano Castillo, San Antonio .... KO 6
Apr.   12—Cornelio Cordova, San Antonio .... KO 2
May   17—Augustin Estrada, San Antonio ...... KO by 9
June 28—Juan A. Villasana, San Antonio .... KO 6
July   21—Larry Brown, Laredo .... KO 7
Aug. 31—Jimmy Martinez, Austin .... KO 4
Nov.   8—Alvaro Alvarado, San Antonio .... KO 2
1978
Jan.   30—Paulino Garcia, San Antonio .... KO 7
Feb.   20—Gerardo Aceves, San Antonio ...... KO by 8
July   18—Salvatore Torres, San Antonio .... D 10
Sept. 19—Jesus Plata, San Antonio .... KO 3
Nov. 21—Arturo Garcia, San Antonio .... W 10
Dec. 19—Rafael Limon, Houston .... KO by 5
1979
June 28—Alex Oregel, Los Angeles .... D 10
July   16—Leoncio Meza, Bakersfield .... W 10
July   31—Andy Ganigan, Honolulu .... KO 7
Nov.   3—Jim Watt, Glasgow .... KO by 9
       (For WBC Lightweight Title)
1980
Feb.   19—Andrew Ganigan, Honolulu .... KO by 7
May   6—Ralph Aviles, Honolulu .... KO 7

ALEJANDRO VEGA
Bantamweight
1976
    —Pablo Ramirez, Mexico City .... W 6
Dec. 18—Pablo Ramirez, Mexico City .... L 6
1977
Mar. 11—Estieban Gonzalez, Coatzacoalcos .... L 10
Sept.   3—Alefandro Lopez, Mexico City .... L 8
1978
Aug. 28—Rosenburg Macias, Gut................ KO 9
1979
(Inactive)
1980
May   11—Lupe Ramirez, Monterrey .... KO 3
May   24—Chano Molina, Mexico City .... KO by 4

MARCELO VEGA
1980
Apr.   2—Hector Rodriguez, Mexico City .... D 4
Oct.   8—Goyo Moran, Mexico City .... D 6
Nov. 15—Roberto Arredondo, Mexico City .... D 6

VICTOR VEGA
1978
Feb.   8—Roserto Reyes, Mexico City .... KO 1
Mar.   4—Romulo Rocha, Mexico City .... KO 2
June 10—Melicon Perez, Mexico City .... L 8
July   28—Miguel Hernandez, Coatzacoalors ...... KO 3
Oct.   —Clodoaldo Barrera, Morelia .... KO 5
Nov.   4—Alberto Lopez, Mexico City .... L 8
Dec. 16—Francisco Tapia, Mexico City .... W 6
1979
June 10—Enrique Vasquez, Tuxtla .... W 5
1980
Apr.   16—Gilberto Montes, Mexico City .... KO by 1
May   24—Francijco Tapia, Mexico City .... KO 5
Aug. 22—Cheinoi Andrade, Salinas Cruz .... KO 3
Oct.   8—Julio Martinez, Mexico City .... KO 5
Nov. 12—Jacozo Fonseca, Mexico City .... KO 4
Dec.   3—Chuco Ramirez, Mexico City .... KO 2

JOHN VERDEROSA
Staten Island, N.Y. Lightweight
Born: October 28, 1957
Managed by Frank Sciacca
1979
June 28—Charley Brown, Staten Island .... KO 1
Oct.   3—Charles Brown, Brooklyn .... KO 2
Oct.   10—Ahmad Muhammad, White Plains ...... KO 1
Oct.   25—Ed Welcome, Staten Island .... KO 4
Nov. 24—Tomas Diaz, Staten Island .... W 6

1980

Jan.	19—Maximo Luciano, Hempstead	KO 5
Mar.	7—Jorge Diaz, Staten Island	KO 3
Apr.	11—Jose Gonzales, Staten Island	W 8
May	9—Willie Daniels, Staten Island	KO 2
June	11—Jorge Nina, Westchester	W disq. 6
June	20—Tim Daniels, New York	KO 5
Sept.	12—Louie Hubela, New York	KO 7
Oct.	15—Hilbert Sevenson, Westchester	W 10
Nov.	12—Felix Perez, New York	KO 7

CARLOS VILLACANO

1978

Mar.	17—Arturo Monsivais, Monterrey	KO 3
Dec.	1—Jose Cancho, Monterrey	KO 1

1979

Mar.	23—Jose Luis Solis, Monterrey	KO 3
Apr.	20—Juan Elizondo, Monterrey	KO by 9
June	29—Alfonso Hernandez, Monterrey	KO 2
Nov.	15—Teodoro Larios, Monterrey	W 10

1980

July	22—Ezzaro Charles, Houston	KO by 5

EMETERIO VILLANUEVA
Mexican Lightweight
(Complete Record Unavailable)

1974

Nov.	4—Ruben Pascon, Tijuana	KO 2
Dec.	14—Hugo Saavedra, Mexico City	KO 8

1975

Feb.	17—Manuel Fierro, Tijuana	TD 7
July	12—Renato Garcia, Mexico City	KO 6
Dec.	6—Manuel Fierro, Mexico City	KO by 3

1976

May	1—Nick Peoples, Mexico City	KO 4
July	17—Manuel Fierro, Mexicali	KO 8
Aug.	16—Bennie Briscoe, Philadelphia	KO by 5

1977

June	11—Alex Olguin, Mexico City	KO 7
Aug.	12—Manuel Elizondo, Coatzacoalcos	KO 4
Oct.	22—Marcos Geraldo, Mexico City	KO by 2

1978

Mar.	11—David Cabrera, Mexico City	KO 3
Apr.	24—Bobby Brown, Tijuana	KO 4
May	12—Mario Luna, Mazatlan	KO 4
July	29—David Cabera, Mexico City	KO by 3

1979

Mar.	28—Jim Ingram, Stockton	KO by 8

1980

Mar.	1—Carlos Marks, Birds Island	L 10
June	27—Jacobo Padilla, Obregon	KO 1
Aug.	15—David Cabrera, Ciudad Madero	KO 4
Oct.	12—David Cabrera, Mexico City	KO by 1
Dec.	20—David Cabrera, Mexico City	KO by 4

JUAN ANGEL VILLASANA
San Antonio, Texas Welterweight

1978

Aug.	4—Alejandro Agosto, Guadalajara	KO by 7

1979

Jan.	31—Tom Pinner, Laredo	KO by 4
Mar.	31—Alfredo Perez, San Antonio	L 6

1980

May	23—Guillermo Alvarez, Monterrey	KO by 7

MARCOS VILLASANA
Mexican Flyweight

1978

Jan.	11—Roberto Hernandez, Acapulco	KO 3
Jan.	20—Flavio Renteria, Acapulco	KO 1
Feb.	—Javier Jimenez, Acapulco	KO 4
Apr.	—David Perez, Acapulco	KO 1
May	—Victor Banos, Acapulco	D 10

1979

Mar.	23—Pedro Martinez, Acapulco	KO 4
June	9—Alfonso (Gato) Ramirez, Mexico City	W 10
July	14—Artemio Ramirez, Mexico City	KO by 7
	—Ambrosio Luna, Mexico City	L 10

1980

Jan.	25—Augustin Macias, Acapulco	W 10
July	5—Pablo Ramirez, Mexico City	KO 1
Oct.	18—Carlos Ibarra, Mexico City	KO 9
Dec.	3—Javier Barcenas, Mexico City	KO 8

ADOLFO VIRUET
Hoboken, N.J. Junior Welterweight

1969

Oct.	30—Raymond Morales, North Bergen	KO 2
Nov.	28—Marcelino Trinidad, Worcester	W 4

1970

May	7—Henry Ocasio, North Bergen	W 6
May	27—Teddy Pick, Scranton	KO 2
Sept.	24—Carlos Soto, North Bergen	W 6

Nov.	23—Benny James, Providence	KO 5

1971
(Inactive)

1972

Apr.	28—Marty Richardson, New York	W 4
May	26—Jose Candelerio, New York	W 4

1973

Mar.	15—Thomas Roane, North Bergen	W 6
Nov.	26—Oscar Piton, New York	KO 3

1974

July	22—Chris Fernandez, New York	W 10

1975

June	5—Roy Holloway, Los Angeles	KO 5
Aug.	29—Monroe Brooks, Las Vegas	W 12

(U.S. Junior Welterweight Title)

1976

Feb.	24—Pete Ranzany, Sacramento	L 10

1977

Feb.	15—Rudy Barro, Sacramento	L 10
May	6—Juan Hidalgo, Miami Beach	W 10

1978

Apr.	27—Roberto Duran, New York	L 10
Oct.	27—Bruce Curry, New York	W 10

1979

Apr.	21—Ray Leonard, Las Vegas	L 10

1980

Mar.	28—Luis Resto, New York	D 10
Aug.	27—Ruby Ortiz, Elizabeth	W 10

EDWIN VIRUET
New York, N.Y. Lightweight

1969

Apr.	28—Azael Curet, Secaucus	W 4
May	19—Otho Tyson, Secaucus	W 6
Nov.	19—Rafael Marquez, North Bergen	KO 4
Nov.	28—Lloyd Wilson, Worcester	W 4

1970

Jan.	15—Roy Williams, North Bergen	W 6
Jan.	26—Eddie Rivera, New York	W 4
Apr.	3—Carlos Santiago, New York	W 6
May	7—Eddie Rivera, North Bergen	KO 5
May	28—Danny Figueroa, North Bergen	KO 7
Aug.	10—Kid Lumumbra, Portland, Me.	W 8
Oct.	8—Angel Rivera, North Bergen	W 8

1971

Mar.	18—Henry Ocasio, North Bergen	W 8
Apr.	15—Bill Whittenberg, North Bergen	W 8
Sept.	23—Alfredo Escalera, Paterson	W 8
Dec.	3—Saoul Mamby, New York	D 10

1972

Apr.	6—Guilermo Taco, New York	KO 1
Apr.	28—Guelo Hernandez, New York	KO 5
May	26—Tommy Grant, New York	KO 7
July	21—Nestor Rojas, New York	D 8

1973

Mar.	13—Nestor Rojas, New York	W 10
Aug.	18—Sammy Goss, New York	L 10

1974

Mar.	8—Vilomar Fernandez, New York	W 10
Apr.	15—Felix Morales, New York	W 10

1975

June	12—Rogelio Castenada, Los Angeles	W 10
Sept.	30—Roberto Duran, Uniondale	L 10

1976

June	26—Billy Wade, Providence	KO 3
Oct.	2—Ricky Camona, Utica	W 10

1977

Feb.	13—Tommy Rose, Annapolis	KO 4

(U.S. Championship Tournament)

Sept.	17—Roberto Duran, Philadelphia	L 15

(World Lightweight Title)

1978

Apr.	8—Josue Marquez, San Juan	KO 10
Oct.	27—Esteban DeJesus, New York	L 10

1979

Aug.	25—Jimmy Brackett, San Juan	W 10
Oct.	13—Alfonso Perez, San Juan	KO 8

1980

Mar.	10—Antonio Cruz, San Juan	W 10

JOE WADE
Bellingham, Heavyweight Canada

1980

Feb.	29—Jesse Aldrich, Nanaimo	KO 3

237

May	17—Larry Puchta, Kelowna	KO 1
June	13—Mike Quinsey, Nanaimo	KO 2
June	26—Sofia Sefo, Bellingham	KO 3
Dec.	23—Ernie Goodwood, Tacoma	KO 3

BASHIR ALI WADUD
San Diego, Calif. Heavyweight
1978

June	1—Junior Albers, Sacramento	L 6
June	21—Charley Terrell, Concord	W 6
July	12—Jimmy Ingram, Oakland	L 6
July	28—Reggie Phillips, San Diego	L 5
Aug.	18—Robbie Bryant, San Diego	W 5
Aug.	29—Rick Mills, Pico Rivera	W 6
Oct.	5—Larry Frazier, Seattle	KO by 8
Dec.	6—Tony Stone, Stockton	W 6
	1979	
Feb.	6—Maryln Johnson, San Carlos	KO 2
Feb.	27—Greg McPhearson, San Carlos	L 10
Mar.	27—Bashiru Ali, San Carlos	L 6
Apr.	24—Omer Dokovic, San Carlos	W 4
June	19—Len Lawson, San Carlos	D 8
Dec.	7—Roger Braxton, San Diego	W 6
Dec.	—Ron Tucker, San Diego	KO 2
	1980	
Feb.	28—Pernall Fairley, Los Angeles	L 6
June	13—Alf Coffin, San Bernardino	W 6
July	16—Rick Mills, San Diego	W 8
Nov.	5—Lee Mitchell, San Diego	W 8
Dec.	10—Lee Mitchell, San Diego	W 8

JAMES WAIRE
Los Angeles, Calif. Middleweight
1977

Dec.	16—Hector Fernandez, San Diego	W 4
	1978	
Feb.	10—Ricky Weigel, San Diego	KO by 2
Apr.	15—John Vasquez, Los Angeles	W 5
May	18—Richard Abbott, Los Angeles	W 6
May	27—John Locicero, Los Angeles	L 6
June	21—Pat Coffey, Las Vegas	KO 3
July	20—Ted Sanders, Los Angeles	W 6
Aug.	1—Dave Meadows, Honolulu	KO 3
Aug.	30—C. J. Brown, Reno	KO 7
Nov.	16—Ted Sanders, Los Angeles	W 6
Nov.	28—Clifford Wills, Billings	W 10
	1979	
Feb.	14—Chris Black, Las Vegas	W 8
Mar.	7—Steve Delgado, Las Vegas	L 10
Apr.	24—Ted Sanders, San Carlos	W 4
May	23—Erwin Williams, Concord, Calif.	D 10
June	24—Keith Broom, Las Vegas	W 10
Oct.	17—Rudy Robles, Las Vegas	L 10
	1980	
Jan.	22—Tony Sibson, London	L 10
May	24—Rudy Robles, Santa Monica	W 10
Aug.	8—Leroy Green, Las Vegas	W 10
Nov.	28—Fulgencio Obelmejias	KO by 3

HENRY WALKER
San Bernardino, Calif. Junior Middleweight
1968

Oct.	4—Ted Liggett, San Bernardino	KO 3
Oct.	29—James Polk, San Bernardino	D 6
	1969	
Mar.	13—Rudy Escobedo, Los Angeles	W 4
Mar.	27—Nathanael Macias, Los Angeles	W 4
Apr.	3—Rudy Escobedo, Los Angeles	W 4
Apr.	18—Joe Cokes, Los Angeles	W 6
Apr.	24—Rodney Reed, Los Angeles	W 6
June	11—Tommy James, Los Angeles	W 10
July	1—Steve Gutierrez, Woodland Hills	W 6
July	29—Art Carrillo, Woodland Hills	W 6
Sept.	9—Denny Moyer, Woodland Hills	KO by 9
Nov.	19—Nate Williams, Las Vegas	L 10
	1970	
Mar.	23—Jose Rodriguez, San Francisco	W 10
Apr.	15—George Cooper, Sacramento	D 10
Oct.	1—Jean Claude Bouttier, Los Angeles	L 10
	1971	
May	14—Kim Booker, San Jose	L 10
	1972-1976	
	(Inactive)	
	1977	
Mar.	30—Vinnie Curto, Boston	L 10
	1978	
Mar.	22—Roy Jones, Las Vegas	KO 10
Apr.	19—Rudy Cruz, San Francisco	W 10
June	27—Rocky Mosley Jr., Las Vegas	L 12
Aug.	25—Raul Aguirre, Dallas	KO 9
Nov.	16—Stephen Delgado, Las Vegas	L 10
	1979	
Feb.	27—Babs McCarthy, Sacramento	L 10

May	14—Robbie Epps, Phoenix	W 10
June	24—Carlos Herrera, Las Vegas	KO by 6
Nov.	13—Robbie Epps, Phoenix	L 10
	1980	
June	13—Rick Weigel, San Diego	W 10
July	11—Steve Delgado, Phoenix	L 10

WAYNE WALKER
Los Angeles, California Welterweight

Sept.	17—Clarence Hayes, Las Vegas	W 4
Oct.	8—Hector Jiminez, Las Vegas	KO 2
Nov.	8—Rigoberto Lopez, Lake Tahoe	D 4
Nov.	29—Paul Gonzalez, Las Vegas	W 4

LARRY WARD
Spokane, Wash. Middleweight
1976

Feb.	2—Holandus Oliver, Milwaukee	KO 2
Sept.	25—Kenny Camel, Spokane	D 4
Oct.	12—J. Heard, Milwaukee	L 6
Oct.	23—Kenny Camel, Missoula	L 4
	1977	
Sept.	7—Ivy Brown, Kansas City	KO by 4
	1978	
	(Inactive)	
	1979	
July	26—Larry Martin, Overland Pk.	L 6
Nov.	9—Sammy Floyd, Saginaw	L 6
Dec.	9—Wayne Caplette, Winnipeg	L 6
	1980	
Dec.	10—Ellis Betts, Moline	D 6

STAN WARD
Sacramento, Calif. Heavyweight
1974

June	25—George Gray, Sacramento	KO 3
Dec.	7—John Robinson, San Jose	KO 2
	1975	
Jan.	18—John Boudreaux, Sacramento	D 8
Mar.	1—Les Miller, Melbourne	KO 8
May	7—Pat Duncan, Carson City	D 10
Dec.	18—Dwain Bonds, Stockton	W 10
	1976	
Feb.	26—Mac Foster, San Jose	W 10
Aug.	16—Jeff Merritt, Utica	KO 3
	1977	
Jan.	29—Jody Ballard, Miami Beach	W 10
Mar.	6—Kevin Isaac, Marion	W 8
	(U.S. Championship Tournament)	
Sept.	14—Ron Lyle, Las Vegas	L 10
	1978	
Jan.	24—Mike Weaver, Sacramento	W 12
Aug.	25—Randy Stephens, Dallas	L 10
Nov.	10—Mel Rush, Las Vegas	W 10
	1979	
Jan.	18—Mike Weaver, Las Vegas	KO by 9
	(U.S. Heavyweight Title)	
	1980	
Mar.	8—Leroy Caldwell, Las Vegas	W 10
May	3—Jimmy Ingram, San Carlos	KO 10
Aug.	22—Toni Pulu, Las Vegas	KO 6

JOHNNY WARR
New York, N.Y. Heavyweight
1977

Jan.	21—Mike Koranicki, Rochester	L 8
Mar.	16—Ron Drinkwater, Boston	L 8
May	20—Jerry Foley, Binghamton	W 6
June	10—Matt Robinson, Hartford	W 6
Sept.	16—C. J. Brown, New York	L 8
	1978	
Jan.	6—Marvin Stinson, Philadelphia	L 8
Mar.	30—Wendell Bailey, Baltimore	L 6
Apr.	21—Jerry Thompkins, New York	W 8
June	3—Wendell Bailey, Baltimore	L 6
Aug.	16—Greg Sorrentino, Newark	L 10
	1979	
Apr.	27—Joe Alexander, Newark	W 8
	—Marty Capasso, Scranton	L 8
	1980	
Feb.	23—Rochelle Norris, Atlantic City	L 6
Mar.	11—Trevor Berbick, Halifax	L 10
June	11—Renaldo Snipes, White Plains	L 8
Sept.	10—Jumbo Cummings, Cicero	L 10
Nov.	25—Steve Zouski, Boston	L 10

JIMMY WASHINGTON
So. Philadelphia, Pa. Featherweight
1977

Feb.	19—Mark Christian, Bristol	W 4
Mar.	1—Tom Brown, Philadelphia	KO 3
Mar.	8—Wayne King, Bristol	L 4

Mar.	26—Wayne King, Bristol	W 4
Apr.	21—Willie Green, Wilmington	W 4
June	23—Ray Hall, Philadelphia	W 6
Oct.	6—Mike Frazier, Philadelphia	W 8
1978		
Apr.	22—Johnny Glover, Trenton	D 6
May	26—John Glover, Lawrenceville	KO 2
1979		
Feb.	27—Bobby Everett, Philadelphia	KO 6
May	21—Jose Nieto, New York	L 6
Aug.	18—Nelson Diaz, Atlantic City	W 6
1980		
Feb.	1—Danny Daniels, Philadelphia	KO 4
July	31—Andres Torres, Atlantic City	W 6
Oct.	1—Santos Cruz, Atlantic City	W 8
Dec.	4—Chico Rodriguez, Atlantic City	KO 4

BILLY WATKINS JR.
Houston, Texas Junior Welterweight

1974		
July	16—Torito Rivas, Houston	KO 2
Aug.	27—Torito Rivas, Corpus Christi	KO 1
Sept.	17—Benny Smith, Corpus Christi	KO 1
1975		
July	24—Gil Lopez, Jacinto City	KO 1
Aug.	18—Lamar Baskin, Jacinto City	KO 4
Sept.	23—Juan Lopez, Jacinto City	KO 1
1976		
Sept.	21—Whitey McCullum, Corpus Christi	W 6
1977		
Sept.	1—Arturo Cirlos, Houston	W 4
Dec.	1—Arturo Cirlos, Houston	W 4
1978-1979		
(Inactive)		
1980		
Feb.	15—Chavis Arellano, Houston	KO 3
Mar.	1—Matine Jiminez, Beaumont	KO 3
Mar.	18—Eloy Armadaries, Houston	KO 2
Apr.	19—Phil Estie, Muskegon	KO 2
Apr.	29—Romiro Hernandez, Houston	KO 4
May	22—Frankie Mills, Holland	KO 3
June	3—James Wallace, Houston	KO 2
June	24—Simmie Black, Houston	KO 4
July	29—Freddie Harris, Houston	W 8
Aug.	19—Jose Angel Medina, Beaumont	KO 3
Aug.	26—Clyde Spencer, Houston	KO 2
Nov.	11—Jose Sota, Beaumont	KO 1

MAURICE (TERMITE) WATKINS
Houston, Texas Lightweight
1973 National Golden Gloves Lightweight Champion
Amateur record: 112-10-1, Born: Aug. 29, 1956

1974		
May	21—Cesar Cortez, Houston	KO 1
June	4—Lupe Cantu, Houston	KO 3
July	2—Art Cirillo, Houston	KO 3
July	16—Harvey Wilson, Houston	KO 6
Aug.	5—Art Cirillo, Corpus Christi	KO 3
Aug.	18—Nick Alfaro, Houston	W 8
Aug.	26—Ricky Ramos, Corpus Christi	KO 4
Oct.	13—Baby Rodriguez, Corpus Christi	KO 1
Dec.	17—Ray Sears, Orlando	W 6
1975		
Jan.	17—Vicente Hernandez, San Jose	W 10
Jan.	29—Dave Kibby, San Francisco	W 8
Feb.	17—Machete Galvan, Corpus Christi	W 10
Apr.	15—Mike Whyms, Orlando	W 8
Apr.	22—Otis Locklear, Orlando	KO 3
May	6—Rudy Gonzalez, San Jose	W 10
May	21—Leroy Walker, San Carlos	KO 8
June	17—Vic de la Cruz, San Jose	W 10
July	16—Marion Thomas, Houston	KO 7
July	29—Gene Prado, San Carlos	W 10
Aug.	19—Larry Peterson, Orlando	KO 5
Nov.	18—Bobby Flores, Houston	KO 6
1976		
Jan.	20—Juan Hidalgo, Miami Beach	W 10
Feb.	10—Chamaco Cuenca, Miami Beach	KO 5
Feb.	24—Lamar Baskin, Albuquerque	KO 2
Mar.	9—Valente Ramos, Orlando	KO 3
Mar.	16—Nani Marrero, Miami Beach	L 10
July	24—Rich Puentes, Biloxi	KO 6
Aug.	9—Augie Estrada, New Orleans	KO 7
Aug.	31—Rocky Ramon, Corpus Christi	W 12
Sept.	21—Art Leon, Corpus Christi	W 10
Oct.	26—Oliver Bolden, Orlando	KO 3
Nov.	17—Augie Estrada, San Antonio	L 10
1977		
Jan.	25—Terry Schrapnel, Corpus Christi	Exh. 4
Feb.	16—Jose Gonzalez, Orlando	W 10
Mar.	22—Norman Goins, Corpus Christi	ND 3
July	26—Ernesto Ortega, Orlando	KO 7
Sept.	22—Paul Garcia, Tampa	KO 3
Sept.	27—Cuyo Mendoza, Orlando	KO 3
Oct.	25—Stepper Harris, Orlando	W 10
Dec.	1—Steve Hulman, Houston	W 10
1978		
Jan.	19—Bennie Marquez, Houston	W 10
Apr.	11—Hilbert Stevenson, Orlando	W 10
Apr.	20—John Morgan, Houston	KO 4
May	16—Joe Medrano, Houston	KO 7
Aug.	15—Rick Craney, Houston	KO 1
Nov.	2—Gary Smith, Orlando	KO 5
Dec.	9—Arthur Clarke, Houston	KO 7
1979		
Jan.	16—Richard Roberts, Houston	KO 3
Mar.	9—Teodoro Ozuna, New York	D 10
Aug.	15—Robert Perez, Beaumont	KO 1
Sept.	14—Howard Davis, Jr., Houston	L 10
	—Robert Perez, Beaumont	KO 7
1980		
Jan.	9—Jimmy Martinez, Holland	KO 1
Mar.	22—Nathan Davis, Grand Rapids	KO 3
Apr.	6—Sammy Ruckard, Houston	KO 4
May	22—Larry Moore, Holland, Mich.	KO 3
Oct.	2—Saoul Mamby, Las Vegas	L 15
	(For WBC Junior Welterweight Title)	

BOBBY (BOOGALOO) WATTS
Philadelphia, Pa. Middleweight

1969		
Mar.	13—Teddy Cooper, Philadelphia	W 6
Mar.	28—Al Millan, Baltimore	KO 4
June	30—Carlos Byrd, Washington, D.C.	KO 2
Sept.	30—Ron Nesby, Philadelphia	W 6
Oct.	14—Leroy Roberts, Philadelphia	W 6
Nov.	11—Tommy Shaffer, Philadelphia	W 6
1970		
Mar.	25—Joe Greene, Las Vegas	KO 2
Apr.	25—Clarence Greigger, Las Vegas	KO by 6
Sept.	3—Armando Muniz, Los Angeles	L 6
Nov.	24—Ken Robbins, Philadelphia	KO 1
1971		
Feb.	9—Roy Edmonds, Philadelphia	W 6
Apr.	29—Perry Abney, Philadelphia	KO 7
June	7—Julio Figueroa, Philadelphia	W 8
Aug.	10—Junius Hinton, Philadelphia	KO 5
Sept.	21—Luis Vinales, Philadelphia	W 10
Oct.	9—Roy Edmonds, New York	KO 5
Dec.	1—Ralph Palladin, Scranton	W 10
1972		
Apr.	5—Ralph Palladin, Scranton	D 10
June	20—Ralph Palladin, Baltimore	KO 6
Oct.	20—Alvin Phillips, New York	W 10
Nov.	20—Don Cobbs, Philadelphia	KO by 2
1973		
Mar.	6—Willie Warren, Philadelphia	W 10
Apr.	10—Gary Broughton, Philadelphia	W 10
May	24—Don Cobbs, Philadelphia	KO 3
July	23—Manuel Gonzalez, Philadelphia	W 10
Oct.	8—Carlos Salinas, Philadelphia	KO 8
Dec.	17—Mario Rosa, New York	W 10
1974		
July	15—Eugene Hart, Philadelphia	KO 1
Nov.	12—Willie Monroe, Philadelphia	W 10
1975		
Sept.	16—James Marshall, Philadelphia	KO 9
1976		
Jan.	13—Marvin Hagler, Philadelphia	W 10
May	10—Ernie Burns, Philadelphia	KO 2
July	14—Casey Gacic, Philadelphia	KO 7
1977		
Jan.	22—Reggie Ford, Pensacola	W 10
Mar.	27—David Love, San Antonio	KO by 4
	(U.S. Championship Tournament)	
1978		
June	3—Johnny Heard, Baltimore	W 10
Sept.	21—Mustafa Hamsho, Jersey City	KO by 6
Dec.	2—Norberto Cabrera, Marsals	W 8
1979		
Oct.	30—Clifford Willis, Upper Darby	KO 3
1980		
Feb.	1—Fred Johnson, Philadelphia	KO 3
Apr.	20—Marvin Hagler, Portland	KO by 2

ALAN WEBB
Troutdale, Ore. Welterweight

1977		
July	30—Charles Wilson, Longview	KO 1
1978		
Mar.	30—Eugene White, Portland	W 6
May	4—Eugene White, Portland	W 6
Sept.	14—Stan Reed, Portland	KO 1
Oct.	19—Kid Hinestroza, Portland	W 6
Nov.	21—Eric Bonilla, Portland	W 6
1979		
Jan.	18—Curtis Ramsey, Portland	D 10

Feb. 22—Curtis Ramsey, Portland .... KO by 10
Sept. 27—Manny Gonzales, Portland .... W 10
1980
Jan. 23—Pepe Dominguez, Portland .... L 10

RICKY WEIGEL
Los Angeles, Calif. Junior Middleweight
1976
Sept. 23—Ron West, Los Angeles. .... W 5
Oct. 14—Armando Alatoore, Los Angeles .... W 5
Dec.   2—Frank Battaglia, Los Angeles .... KO 2
1977
Feb. 10—Armando Alatoore, Los Angeles .... TO 2
Apr. 21—Freddie Washington, Los Angeles .... KO by 4
1978
Jan. 19—Pasqual Ramirez, Los Angeles .... KO 3
Feb. 10—James Waire, San Diego .... KO 2
Mar.   3—Hector Fernandez, San Diego .... KO 2
Mar. 17—Richard Abbott, Anaheim .... KO 3
Apr. 28—Troy Vaughn, San Diego .... W 6
May   5—Steve Bentley, San Diego .... KO 5
June   8—Richard Abbott, Los Angeles .... W 6
June 29—Ted Sanders, Los Angeles .... W 6
Aug. 28—Agapito Ramirez, Bakersfield .... W 10
Sept. 9—Carlos Santos, San Juan .... L 8
1979
Feb. 23—Antonio Adame, San Diego .... KO 1
Mar.   9—Carmelo Garcia, San Diego .... KO 3
Apr.   8—Mike Baker, Las Vegas .... L 10
June   3—Paddy Wilson, Las Vegas .... KO 3
July 20—Renato Garcia, San Diego .... TD
1980
June 13—Henry Walker, San Diego .... L 10

ED (TWIST) WELCOME
Albany, N.Y. Junior Lightweight
1979
Mar. 29—Francisco Maldonado, Cohoes .... KO 4
May   24—Bob Ingras, Cohoes .... W 6
June 18—Felix Rodrigues, Cohoes .... W 6
Oct. 25—John Verderosa, Staten Island ...... KO by 4
        —Herman Ingram, Syracuse .... W 6
1980
June 19—Dave Ramalho, Lawrence .... KO by 1

SCOTTY WELSH
Vancouver, Canada, Heavyweight
1973
     —Larry Watts, Moncton .... KO 6
     —Tony Grazette, Fredericton .... KO 4
1974
     —Tony Pasco, St. John .... KO 7
1975
     —Ronnie Brothers, Halifax .... W 8
1976
Oct. —Bruce St. John, Seattle .... W 6
1977
June 10—Kenji Sabu, Parksville .... KO 2
Aug. 31—George Wells, Port Alberni .... KO 4
Nov. 24—Humberto Ghiotti, Parksville .... KO 5
1978
Apr.   8—Al Neumann, Everett .... L disq. 8
July   4—Kim Edwards, Vancouver .... Exh.
Sept. 2—Jean Pierre Coopman, Izegem .... L disq. 1
1979
July 26—Wayne Bobick, Anchorage .... KO by 2
1980
June 18—Fossie Schmidt, Honolulu .... KO by 1

BOB WHALEY
Columbus, Ohio Heavyweight
1979
Oct. 19—James (Quick) Tillis, Chicago .... KO by 1
Nov. 27—Ramon Scott, Columbus .... KO by 1
Dec. 28—Victor Wallace, Columbus .... KO by 4
1980
June   5—Harold Spellman, Columbus .... KO by 1
Aug. 25—George Mostardini, Chicago .... KO by 1
Sept. 12—Scott Huston, Columbus .... KO by 2

TERRY WHITAKER
Chicago, Ill. Junior Welterweight
1980
July 10—Evarista Rodriguez, Chicago .... W 4
Aug. 25—Tony Brown, Chicago .... KO 1
Sept. 22—Clint Harris, Chicago .... W 4
Nov. 13—Chuck Spicer, Chicago .... W 6
Dec. 11—Phil Batie, Chicago .... KO 1

JEFF WHITE
Detroit, Mich. Welterweight
1979
Nov.   1—Ken Dallas, Detroit .... KO by 2
1980
Jan. 24—Johnny Meyers, Detroit .... L 4

TEDDY WHITE
Paterson, N.J. Welterweight
1978
Oct.   8—Don Downey, Halifax .... L 4
1979
Dec. 12—Garland Wright, Scranton .... W 6
1980
Dec. 20—Davey Moore, Bronx .... L 6

HANK WHITMORE
Brooklyn, N.Y. Middleweight
1979
Oct.   4—Peter Pennello, North Bergen .... D 4
Oct. 24—Steve Arvin, Scranton .... KO by 1
1980
Jan. 24—Elijah Hamm, Dover .... KO by 3
Mar. 20—Peter Pennello, North Bergen .... D 4
Apr. 24—Bobby Czyz, Totowa .... KO by 1
Oct.   2—Bernard Taylor, Commack .... L 4
Oct. 16—Jose Cruz, Totowa .... KO by 1
Dec. 11—Ross D'Amico, New York .... L 4

CURTIS WHITNER
Heavyweight
1975
Feb. 17—Pete Chianchiano, Beaumont .... KO by 2
1976
Sept. 11—Eddie Phillips, Waterbury .... L 4
1977-1979
(Inactive)
1980
Aug. 21—Bruce Perry, Revere .... L 4
Oct. 16—Bruce Perry, Revere .... W 4
Dec. 15—Peter Bissonette .... W 4

JOHNNY WILBURN
Baltimore, Md. Light Heavyweight
Born: Nov. 11, 1955
1975
Apr. 11—Larry Washington, Baltimore .... KO 6
Apr. 29—Anthony Bryant, Largo .... KO 3
May   9—Roy Ingram, Baltimore .... KO 6
June 17—Dennis Roberts, Largo .... KO 3
July 23—Oliver Lewis, Largo .... KO 5
1976
Feb. 13—Sugar Moore, Owings Mill .... KO 5
Mar. 27—Ray Timmons, Owings Mill .... KO 2
July 29—Otis Gordon, Baltimore .... KO 4
Sept. 16—Jerry Martin, Baltimore .... L 6
Oct. 28—Roy Ingram, Baltimore .... KO 2
1977
Jan. 18—Eddie Gregory, New York .... KO by 3
Apr. 14—Jimmy McClain, Landover .... KO 3
1978
*Jan. 8—Joe Klutz, Knoxville .... KO 2
*Jan. 8—Ernie Wicher, Knoxville .... KO 1
Jan. 26—Dale Grant, Seattle .... L 10
Feb. 21—Ponce Ortiz, Kingsport .... KO 1
Mar. 30—Nate Dixon, Baltimore .... W 6
Aug.   8—Lou Butler, Baltimore .... W 6
Nov. 25—Irwin Hines, Kingsport .... L 6
*Both on the same card.
1979
Aug. 31—Eddie Gregory, Shirley .... KO by 1
Sept. 8—Obbie Garnett, Kingsport .... KO by 1
Nov. 14—Dwight Braxton, Baltimore .... L 8
Nov. 28—Cornell Chavis, Hauppauge .... KO 8
Dec. 14—Tony Mundine, Milan .... L 8
1980
Feb.   1—Michael Spinks, Louisville .... L 8
Feb. 29—Curtis Goins, Commack .... KO 8
May   9—Eddie Davis, Commack .... KO by 9

DANNY WILCOX
Florida Junior Lightweight
1979
Aug. 24—Terry Pizzaro, Sunrise .... KO by 4
Oct.   5—Terry Pizzarro, Ft. Lauderdale .... W 6
Dec. 14—Jorge Ortiz, Sunrise .... KO 3
Dec. 18—Tony Styles, Miami Beach .... W 4
1980
May   2—Frankie Wilcox, Miami .... KO 3

MIKE WILCOX
1980
Feb.	21—Max Hord, Gainesville	KO by	2
June	26—Max Hord, Gainesville	L	8
Oct.	11—E. McNeeley, Ft. Meyers	W	4
Sept.	2—Clay Cunningham, N. Miami	KO	1
Dec.	20—Tiger Hall, Ft. Meyers	KO	3

SYLVESTER WILDER
Cleveland, Ohio Heavyweight
1971
June	25—Morris Jordan, Dayton	L	4
July	13—Stanley Jackson, Washington, D.C.	W	4
Sept.	10—Bobby Haye, Toledo	L	4
	1972		
Mar.	24—Ray Timmons, Cincinnati	W	6
Mar.	27—John Taylor, Buffalo	KO by	4
June	17—John Taylor, Buffalo	L	4
Aug.	30—Paul Minor, Baltimore	L	4
Oct.	11—Howie Jones, Sharon	KO	1
Nov.	6—Aldo Carelli, Toronto	KO by	3
Nov.	16—John Girowski, Sharon	L	8
	1973		
Jan.	24—Bill Hardney, Baltimore	W disq.	4
May	23—Marvin Johnson, Indianapolis	KO by	2
June	26—Bill Hardney, Baltimore	KO by	6
July	27—Lee Martin, Toledo	KO by	3
Aug.	10—Tom Van Hoof, St. Cloud	L	10
Sept.	29—Charlie Johnson, Alliance	L	10
Oct.	6—John Dennis, Brockton	KO by	5
	1974		
Feb.	16—Jerry Evans, New Castle	L	8
Mar.	23—Lou Rogan, Weston	KO by	2
May	25—Charley Johnson, Alliance	L	8
Nov.	12—Vonzell Johnson, Indianapolis	L	4
Nov.	21—Johnny Baldwin, Highland Park	KO by	6
	1975		
May	10—John Girowski, Toledo	KO by	4
Aug.	26—Smokey Middleton, Largo	KO by	4
Oct.	4—Eddie Taylor, Chicago	KO by	2
	1976		
Mar.	27—Frank Schram, Weston	L	10
Apr.	2—Bill Hardney, Washington, D.C.	L	8
May	15—Lou Rogan, Parkesburg	L	8
June	22—Mike Quarry, Orlando	KO by	5
July	28—Hal Carroll, Utica	KO by	3
Oct.	27—Bill Radcliffe, Cleveland	L	6
Nov.	6—Gary Alexander, Alliance	L	8
Nov.	10—Boom Boom Moorer, Cleveland	KO by	3
	1977		
	(Inactive)		
	1978		
July	20—Bobby Jordan, Virginia Beach	KO by	1
Aug.	26—Frankie Williams, Dayton	KO by	4
Oct.	3—Scott LeDoux, Winnipeg	KO by	2
Dec.	15—George Mostardini, Chicago	KO by	1
	1979		
Feb.	28—James (Quick) Tillis, Chicago	KO by	3
May	9—Billy Douglas, Columbus	KO by	2
June	1—Baker Tinsley, Louisville	L	8
July	30—Ron Rousselle, Toronto	KO by	1
	1980		
Feb.	1—Jumbo Cummings, Chicago	KO by	2
Apr.	30—Charles Williams, Youngstown	KO by	1
Dec.	9—Curtis Isaac, Kalamazoo	KO by	2

HERBIE WILENS
Gaithersburg, Md. Middleweight
1979
Aug.	1—Al Bevier, Secaucus	KO	4
Aug.	28—Ben Serrano, Atlantic City	D	4
Nov.	28—Raul Sanchez, W. New York, N.J.	KO	2
	1980		
Mar.	28—Danny Perez, Tarrytown	KO	3
May	2—Charles Hecker, New York	L	6
Sept.	24—Mark Medel, Elizabeth	KO by	4

BUTCH WILKERSON
Cape Girardeau, Canada Heavyweight
1980
May	12—Greg Arnold, Cape Girardeau	KO	3
June	6—Paul Mauros, Kansas City	KO	1
Oct.	7—Carl Halburton, St. Charles	KO	1

SHELBY WILKERSON
Nashville, Tenn. Welterweight
1980
May	8—Charlie Peterson, Nashville	KO	3
May	9—Larry Mayes, Nashville	KO by	1
Sept.	25—Claude Samuels, Winston Salem	W	4
Oct.	30—Gary Brown, Louisville	W	6

BRUCE WILLIAMS
Lightweight
1978
Apr.	17—Richie Garland, Philadelphia	W	4
Dec.	12—Jorge Diaz, Philadelphia	W	4
	1979		
Jan.	9—Marvin Edwards, Philadelphia	KO	3
Feb.	27—Franny Gillen, Philadelphia	W	6
Sept.	11—Luis Isaac, Philadelphia	W	4
	1980		
Dec.	4—Livingston Bramble, Atlantic City	D	4

CHARLEY WILLIAMS
Mansfield, Ohio Light Heavyweight
1978
June	28—Henry Brunch, Washington, D.C.	L	4
	—Keith Broom, Washington, D.C.	L	
	1979		
Feb.	7—Michael Hardin, Richfield	W	4
Mar.	21—Willie Crawford, Richfield	W	4
Apr.	27—Willie Crawford, Dayton	KO	3
May	19—Gus Turner, Findley	W	4
Sept.	20—Sam Bryant, Richfield	KO	1
	1980		
Apr.	30—Sylvester Wilder, Youngstown	KO	1
May	17—Michael Harden, Dayton	D	6

DON WILLIAMS
North Vernon, Ind. Junior Welterweight
1978
July	22—Percy Hairston, Knoxville	W	4
Nov.	17—Ron Brown, Denver	KO by	4
	1979		
	(Inactive)		
	1980		
Sept.	23—Bryan Burnette, Indianapolis	KO by	1

GEORGE WILLIAMS
Washington, D.C. Heavyweight
1977
Sept.	8—Juan Sawbridge, Virginia Beach	L	4
	1978		
Jan.	25—Bob Podrich, Washington, D.C.	KO	2
Mar.	15—Richard Claiborne, Washington, D.C.	KO	1
May	24—David Johnson, Washington, D.C.	L	6
	1979		
May	23—Broderick Mason, Washington, D.C.	L	4
Dec.	12—Alf Coffin, Washington, D.C.	L	6
	1980		
Mar.	31—Ouinnie Lacklear, Landover	KO	2

GREG WILLIAMS
Teaneck, N.J. Junior Lightweight
1977
Mar.	24—Jimmy Nelson, Dover	KO by	2
May	26—Jose Ortiz, Dover	W	4
June	24—Benito Jiminez, Sunnyside	W	4
Sept.	28—Jimmy Nelson, Passaic	KO	1
	1978		
June	13—Benito Jiminez, Totowa	D	4
	1980		
June	18—Juan Dominguez, Las Vegas	KO by	3
Sept.	3—Daniel Cruz, Las Vegas	KO by	2
Dec.	9—Ben Carino, Honolulu	KO by	1

HAROLD WILLIAMS
1980
May	9—Pedro Rivera, Staten Island	KO by	3
Nov.	7—Donald Julian, Trenton	W	4
Dec.	12—Billy Gray, Felt Forum	KO	4

JAMES WILLIAMS
Portland, Ore. Middleweight
1979
June	14—Doug Demmings, Winnipeg	L	8
Oct.	25—Ralph Gidley, Portland	KO	2
Nov.	6—Mike Clark, Sparks	L	10
	1980		
Nov.	26—Chris Schwewice, Las Vegas	KO by	3
Dec.	23—Sugar Ray Seales, Tacoma	L	10

JERRY WILLIAMS
Fayetteville, N.C. Heavyweight
1979
Nov.	7—Henry Patterson, Spartanburg	W	6
Nov.	13—Horace Robinson, Orlando	W	6
	1980		
Feb.	10—Pinklon Thomas, Miami Beach	KO by	5
Aug.	0—Tom Davis, Las Vegas	L	8
Aug.	28—Pinklon Thomas, Las Vegas	L	10
July	26—Stanley Scott, Jenkins	KO	5

LEVANT WILLIAMS
Detroit, Mich. Lightweight
1978
Apr. 21—Carlos Amaya, Detroit .... W 4
Aug. 3—Freddie Figueroa, Detroit .... W 4
Aug. 17—Ken Dallas, Detroit .... L 4
Sept. 7—Robert Matos, Detroit .... KO by 1
Nov. 3—Andrew Hill, Detroit .... KO 2
1979
Jan. 11—Sanford Ricks, Detroit .... KO by 5
May 24—Earl Stringer, Detroit .... L 6
July 12—Earl Stringer, Detroit .... KO by 5
1980
Jan. 12—Kid Madison, Detroit .... L 4

MIKE TANK WILLIAMS
Gulport, Miss. Middleweight
1980
Apr. 3—Kevin Reidy, Oklahoma City .... KO 2
June 10—Jay Arbuckle, Oklahoma City .... KO 1
July 1—Lorenzo Jones, Oklahoma City .... L 4
Aug. 5—Virgil Moore, Oklahoma City .... W 4

SONNY WILLIAMS
Thunder, Heavyweight
1978
Oct. 13—Rodrigo Hernandez, Denver .... KO by 2
1979
Mar. 24—Gil Cardona, Denver .... KO by 3
Aug. 31—Rodrigo Hernandez, Denver .... KO by 2
1980
Feb. 23—Gary Miller, Greeley .... KO by 3

STANLEY WILLIAMS
Philadelphia, Pa. Welterweight
1979
Mar. 28—Chris Reeder, Baltimore .... KO by 3
May 12—Dan Snyder, Atlantic City .... KO by 1
Aug. 3—Malik Muhammad, Homestead .... KO 2
1980
Apr. 3—Bob Franchino, Tampa .... KO by 1

STEVE WILLIAMS
Chicago, Ill. Welterweight
1980
July 10—Robert Hughes, Chicago .... W 6
Sept. 22—Jeff Madison, Chicago .... W 6

SUGAR BEAR WILLIAMS
Chicago, Ill. Heavyweight
1978
Feb. 27—Farrokh Shanghai, Chicago .... KO 1
May 22—Derrick Harrison, Chicago .... KO 2
July 24—Jimmy Phillips. Bridgeview .... KO 2
Sept. 27—Jimmy Phillips, Chicago .... L 6
Oct. 6—Ronald Snipes, Waukegan .... Exh.
1979
Mar. 31—Bob Dodson, Chicago .... KO 1
1980
July 10—Chuck Gardner, Chicago .... KO by 2

T. C. WILLIAMS
Shreveport, La. Welterweight
1980
Aug. 9—Michael Senegal, Lakes Charles ..... KO by 3
Sept. 23—Anthony Releford, Odessa .... KO by 3
Dec. 9—Mike Hutchinson, Birmingham .... L 4

WARDELL WILLIAMS
Kansas City, Mo. Featherweight
1975
Oct. 1—Alonzo Plaiko, Topeka .... W 4
Nov. 4—Bob Clark, Topeka .... W 4
1976
Feb. 19—Tony Reed, Kansas City .... W 4
July 27—Allen Saenz, Topeka...................... W 4
Aug. 26—Allan Ray Sanchez, Kansas City .... W 6
Oct. 6—Bubba Thompson, Kansas City .... W 6
1977
Jan. 29—Peanuts Emerson, Kansas City .... W 6
Mar. 30—William Whipple, Cleveland .... KO by 4
Apr. 29—Shannon Williams, Wichita .... W 6
June 17—Leonard Boyd, Kansas City .... KO 2
June 30—Isaac Vega, Wichita .... W 6
Aug. 1—Robert Perez, Topeka .... KO 1
Oct. 13—Richard Rozelle, Columbus .... L 10
Oct. 25—Simmie Black, Kansas City .... KO 1
Dec. 15—Tony Reed, Kansas City .... W 6
1978
Jan. 19—Richard Rozelle, Houston .... KO by 5
June 2—Ernesto Gonzales, Kansas City .... W 4
June 12—Ken Sallee, Kansas City .... KO by 4

1979
Jan. 19—Ray Menefee, Overland Pk. .... W 6
Mar. 16—Alfonso Cirillo, Kansas City .... KO 3
Apr. 10—Jim Flint, London .... KO by 3
June 1—Ray Menefee, Kansas City .... W 4
Aug. 16—Juan LaPorte, Kansas City .... KO by 2
1980
Mar. 16—Bubba Thompson, Kansas City ...... KO by 6

J. B. WILLIAMSON
Indianapolis, Ind. Middleweight
1979
Nov. 27—Micha True Hickman, Los Angeles ...... KO 1
1980
Jan. 26—Ernest Rabotte, Los Angeles .... W 6
Mar. 9—Jose Martinez, St. Paul .... KO 2
Mar. 28—Dan Kirk, Tacoma .... KO 1
May 4—Lander Clark, Seattle .... KO 6
June 14—Jamie Thomas, Cincinnati .... W 10
July 16—Antonio Adamie, Tacoma .... W 10
Sept. 27—Antonio Adame, Los Angeles .... KO 5
Nov. 29—Ted Sanders, Los Angeles .... W 10

ODELL WILLIS
Wichita, Kan. Middleweight
1979
Sept. 18—Joe Acosta, Wichita .... KO 1
Nov. 1—Jim Reed, Wichita .... KO 1
Nov. 16—Rocky Mack, Kansas City .... L 6
Dec. 20—Dennis Horne, Wichita .... W 6
1980
Feb. 21—Pipino Garcia, Tulsa .... W 6
Mar. 7—Bruce Strauss, Kansas City .... L 6
Mar. 16—Randy Nelson, Omaha .... L 4

CLIFFORD WILLS
Hamilton, Ohio Middleweight
1975
Sept. 6—Joey Blair, Hamilton .... W 4
Nov. 13—Gary Thomas, Indianapolis .... W 4
1976
Feb. 21—Fred Reed, Chicago .... W 4
May 6—Alfonso Aguirre, Indianapolis .... W 4
May 15—Joey Blair, Parkersburg .... W 6
Nov. 12—Al Bell, Cincinnati .... D 6
1977
Feb. 1—Steve St. Charles, Cincinnati .... W 6
June 23—Ray Seales, Vancouver .... L 10
July 28—Doug Demmings, Bloomington .... L 6
Sept. 28—Ronnie Harris, Canton .... KO by 10
1978
Mar. 30—Mike Colbert, Portland .... L 10
Apr. 21—Tommy Hanna, Detroit .... L 10
Nov. 28—James Waire, Billings .... L 10
1979
Feb. 7—Don Cobbs, Richfield .... L 10
Feb. 22—Tommy Hanna, Saginaw .... L 10
Apr. 10—Jerome Jackson, Philadelphia .... L 8
June 28—Gary Thomas, Fort Mitchell .... W 10
Oct. 30—Bobby Watts, Upper Darby .... KO by 3
1980
May 2—Nicola Cirelli, Rome .... L 8
June 30—Fulgencio Obelmejias, Caracas .... KO by 3
Nov. 1—Bernard Mays, Detroit .... L 10

CARL WILSON
Bronx, N.Y. Middleweight
1980
Jan. 19—Jerry Clark, Hempstead .... W 4
Nov. 12—Mark McPherson, Felt Forum .... L 4

CLYDE WILSON
Featherweight
1978
Dec. 16—Kid Chocolate, Port of Spain .... W 6
1979
—Michael Drayton, Diego Martin ...... KO by 7
1980
May 2—Cleomaus James, Port of Spain .... L 6
Oct. 17—Terrence Ali, Port of Spain .... L 6

EARL WILSON
Memphis, Tenn. Featherweight
Managed by T. David Goodwin
1975
May 4—Simmie Black, Memphis .... W 4
1976
Nov. 9—Lupe Garcia, Little Rock .... KO 2
Nov. 30—Johnny Marino, Memphis .... KO 5
1977
Aug. 23—Gerald Bradley, Memphis .... KO 2
Sept. 20—Bobby Vascoco, Memphis .... KO 5

Feb. 28—Joe De La Rosa, Memphis .... KO 5
May —Simmie Black, Memphis .... L 6
June 6—Gabby Cantera, Hattisbury .... KO by 3
Oct. 12—Anthony Murray, Memphis .... KO by 4
1979
Jan. 16—Jesse Montemayor, Little Rock .... W 6
Feb. 20—Tony Styles, Orlando .... W 6
May 29—Jerry Strickland, Memphis .... KO 4
July 10—Ray Menefee, Memphis .... KO 8
Aug. 24—Hilberto Stevenson, Memphis .... W 8
1980
Oct. 21—Pat Cowdell, Wolverhampton .... L 10
Dec. 4—Myron Taylor, Atlantic City .... KO by 2

EDDIE WILSON
Los Angeles, Calif. Heavyweight
1978
Nov. 21—William Banks, Las Vegas .... KO 1
1979
Feb. 9—As-Saff Muhammad, San Diego .... KO 3
Feb. 14—Mike Creel, Las Vegas .... KO 1
Mar. 23—Henry Washington, Las Vegas .... KO 1
June 24—Roger Braxton, Las Vegas .... W 5
1980
Mar. 31—Marvin Stinson, Las Vegas .... KO by 2

JESSIE WILSON
Sommers, Conn. Light Heavyweight
1976
May 28—John D'Amore, Latham .... KO by 1
Sept. 11—Sanny Asani, Waterbury .... KO by 3
Sept. 15—Al Yasbech, Scranton .... KO by 2
Nov. 19—Jose Elias, Sunnyside .... KO by 1
1977
Nov. 27—Eddie Phillips, Waterbury .... KO by 2
1979
Feb. 3—Bushy Bester, Boston .... KO by 2
1980
May 29—Wilbur Henderson, West Hartford .... KO by 1

PADDY WILSON
Portland, Ore. Middleweight
Born: July 1950
1977
July 2—Bobby Howard, Salem, Ore. .... L 6
July 30—Alan Webb, Longview, Wash. .... KO by 1
Oct. 27—Eugene White, Portland .... W 6
Nov. 19—Eugene White, Hillsboro, Ore. .... KO 7
Dec. 13—Jose Peterson, Anchorage .... KO 5
1978
Jan. 25—Ken Camel, Las Vegas .... L 8
Mar. 15—Robby Epps, Incline Village .... KO by 6
May 4—Larry Smith, Portland .... L 8
May 27—Ken Camel, St. Ignatius .... L 8
June 25—Babs McCarthy, Stateline .... KO by 2
Aug. 9—Steve Moyer, Seattle .... L 6
Aug. 22—Ken Camel, Coeur d'Alene .... L 8
Sept. 14—C. J. Brown, Portland .... D 6
Oct. 19—Jimmy Carter, Portland .... KO 1
Nov. 21—Ken Martin, Portland .... KO 5
1979
Mar. 10—Dennis Mancini, Los Angeles .... W 4
Mar. 15—Robbie Epps, Lake Tahoe .... KO by 5
Mar. 22—Mike Lancaster, Portland .... KO by 6
Apr. 24—Dick Fisher, Missoula .... L 6
May 4—Steve Delgado, San Diego .... KO by 5
June 3—Ricky Weigel, Las Vegas .... KO by 3
Aug. 10—Steve Delgado, San Diego .... KO by 5
1980
Jan. 23—Abe Schwartz, Portland, Ore. .... W 4
May 28—Chris Lange, Portland, Ore. .... D 8
July 15—Byron Campbill, Reno .... L 10
Sept. 18—Jerry Reddick, Nanaimo .... KO by 5
Oct. 22—Lee Burkey, Crystal Bay .... KO by 2

SAM WILSON
San Diego, California Heavyweight
1972
July 14—Charlie Brooks, San Diego .... D 4
July 30—Billy Ryan, Watsonville .... KO by 3
Sept. 29—Larry Frazier, San Carlos .... KO by 1
1973
(Inactive)
1974
Feb. 15—Melvin Marshall, San Diego .... W 4
Mar. 8—Melvin Marshall, San Diego .... W 5
Mar. 15—Melvin Marshall, San Diego .... D 4
Aug. 23—Dave Harmon, San Diego .... L 4
Sept. 6—Bart Boyrsse, San Diego .... L 8
Sept. 20—Tommy Evans, Richmond .... KO by 2
Nov. 7—Reggie Flemming, Canton .... W 6

1975
Apr. 21—Maurice Quillens, New Orleans .... L 4
1976-1978
(Inactive)
1979
Nov. 23—George O'Mara, San Diego .... KO by 2
1980
July 15—Bruce Calloway, New Orleans .... KO by 2

ERIC WINBUSH
New York, N.Y. Light Heavyweight
1978
June 10—Luis Guzman, Brooklyn .... L 4
June 15—Gino Milano, Atlantic City .... W 4
June 30—Melvin Richardson, Newark .... L 8
Aug. 2—Johnny Kane, Bayonne .... KO 3
1979
Jan. —Ben Ferguson, Philadelphia .... KO 5
Apr. 20—Willie Stallings, New York .... W 6
June 20—Dave Dittman, White Plains .... W 6
Sept. 12—Dave Dittman, White Plains .... W 6
1980
Apr. 18—Joe Britt, Syracuse .... KO by 2
Sept. 17—Bobby Walker, White Plains .... L 6
Nov. 28—Ron Huston, New York .... L 8

FOREST WINCHESTER
Kalamazoo, Mich. Junior Lightweight
1977
June 11—Chuck Spicer, Jackson .... KO 2
June 22—Jerry Strickland, Columbus .... KO 4
Aug. 4—Bobby Plegge, Wyoming .... KO by 1
Oct. 13—Ray Greene, Columbus .... KO 2
Nov. 26—Al Carter, Columbus .... KO 5
1978
Mar. 17—Ernesto Gonzales, Kalamazoo .... KO 3
Aug. 25—Ezzard Charles Adams, Houston .... W 6
1979
May 17—Manning Galloway, Columbus .... W 6
June 28—Calvin Slaughter, Columbus .... KO 8
Sept. 30—Bobby Plegge, Canton .... W 8
1980
Aug. 8—Billy Parks, Las Vegas .... D 10
Dec. 6—Louis Self, Detroit .... KO 2

TYRONE WREN
Kansas City, Mo. Welterweight
1977
June 17—James Pixley, Kansas City, Mo. .... W 4
Aug. 1—Arturo Cirillo, Topeka, Kansas .... W 4
Sept. 7—Ken Sallee, Kansas City .... W 4
Oct. 3—Pete Seward, Columbus, Ohio .... L 6
Oct. 25—Ken Sallee, Kansas City .... L 4
Dec. 15—Steve Bowen, Kansas City .... W 4
1978
Mar. 31—Larry Mayes, Kansas City .... W 6
Apr. 25—Pat Hallacy, Wichita .... L 6
June 2—Michael Herron, Kansas City .... W 6
June 28—Gary Holmgren, Minneapolis .... W 6
July 28—Jerome Hill, Kansas City .... KO 3
Oct. 6—Pete Seward, Kansas City .... L 8
Dec. 2—Bobby Orr, Kansas City .... KO 5
1979
Jan. 19—James Hearn, Overland Pk. .... W 6
Mar. 16—Basil Buchanan, Kansas City .... W 6
May 17—Clarence Gilmore, Memphis .... L 8
July 26—Billy Goodwin, Overland Pk. .... KO 6
Oct. 11—Frankie Mills, Kansas City .... W 6
Oct. 30—Michael Herron, Memphis .... L 10
Nov. 23—Nicky Miller, Kansas City .... KO 3
Dec. 15—Don Masterson, Kansas City .... W 6
1980
Mar. 16—Willie Jackson, Kansas City .... KO 1
May 9—Don Morgan, Nashville .... KO by 9
Aug. 12—Mike Garcia, Wichita .... D 8
Sept. 10—Pat Hallacy, Wichita .... KO by 7

GARLAND WRIGHT
Scranton, Pa. Welterweight
1978
Sept. 20—Abel Santiago, Scranton .... W 4
Oct. 25—Mike Martinez, Scranton .... KO 2
Nov. 22—Ray Rosa, Scranton .... W 4
1979
Feb. 21—Dennis Dixon, Scranton .... D 4
Apr. 25—Mario Williams, Scranton .... W 4
Sept. 19—Jose Green, Scranton .... KO 3
Oct. 24—Ricky Johnson, Scranton .... D 4
Dec. 12—Teddy White, Scranton .... L 6
1980
Feb. 27—Ray Madera, Scranton .... W 6
Sept. 10—Kevin Rooney, Scranton .... L 6

JOE DEAN WRIGHT
Spartanburg, S.C. Heavyweight
1977
June 22—Hawthorn Davis, Spartanburg .... KO by 8
(South Carolina Light Heavyweight Championship)
1979
Apr. 5—Jo Jo Waddell, Spartanburg .... KO by 2
1980
July 19—Robert Hamler, Spartanburg .... KO 3
July 26—Ronnie Caldwell, Charlotte .... KO 2
Sept. 6—Jeremiah Jones, Lincolnton .... KO 2

OLIVER WRIGHT
Kingston, Jamaica Heavyweight
1973
Jan. 16—Tommy Howard, Miami Beach .... KO 6
Jan. 30—Robert Lloyd, Miami Beach .... KO 5
Feb. 20—Gil Escalera, Miami Beach .... KO 2
Feb. 27—Hydra Lacey, Miami Beach .... KO 3
Mar. 13—Larry Renaud, Miami Beach .... W 10
Apr. 3—Vicente Rondon, Miami Beach .... L 10
May 8—Johnny Hudgins, Miami Beach .... KO 2
June 15—Larry Renaud, Tampa .... W 10
June 23—Wendell Joseph, Kingston .... W 10
Aug. 7—Jimmy Summerville, Miami Beach .... KO 6
Aug. 21—Raul Gorosito, Miami Beach .... KO by 1
Sept. 13—Levi Forte, Orlando .... W 10
Sept. 25—Raul Gorosito, Miami Beach .... W 10
Oct. 13—Roy Williams, Miami Beach .... KO by 6
1974
Apr. 10—Larry Caldwell, Orlando .... L 10
Apr. 23—Johnny Boudreaux, Houston .... L 10
May 7—Lloyd Price, Houston .... KO 2
May 21—Bunny Johnson, London .... L 10
Aug. 16—Wendell Newton, Nassau .... L 10
Oct. 18—Oscar Bonavena, Rome .... KO by 9
1975
Apr. 10—Larry Holmes, Honolulu .... KO by 3
May 8—Earnie Shavers, Baltimore .... KO by 3
June 25—Duane Bobick, Bloomington .... KO by 10
Sept. 9—Tommy Howard, Miami Beach .... KO 6
Sept. 23—John L. Johnson, Miami Beach .... W 10
Oct. 28—Bobby Lloyd, Miami Beach .... W 10
1976
May 4—Randy Stephens, Miami Beach .... L 8
1977-1979
(Inactive)
1980
May 25—Eddie Gregg, Atlantic City .... D 6
Oct. 24—Tim Witherspoon, Philadelphia ...... KO by 2

MELVIN WYNN
Atlanta, Ga. Welterweight
1979
Oct. 23—Homer Jackson, Orlando .... W 4
1980
Mar. 25—Homer Jackson, Jacksonville .... W 6
Nov. 11—Steve Hearon, Beaumont .... KO by 5

RICHARD WYNNE
Welterweight
1979
Oct. 24—Dave Garza, Oakland .... D 5
Nov. 27—Tommy Greer, Stockton .... KO 2
1980
Jan. 22—Larry Batiste, Sacramento .... KO 1
Feb. 5—Pablo Gomez, Sacramento .... KO 5
Feb. 19—Joe Maldonado, Sacramento .... L 6
Mar. 27—Robert Turner, San Carlos .... KO 2

AL YASBICK
Philadelphia, Pa. Light Heavyweight
1975
Oct. 28—Robert Hill, Philadelphia .... W 4
Nov. 18—Johnny Wilderson, Philadelphia .... L 4
1976
Jan. 27—Emerito Morales, Philadelphia .... W 4
May 19—Charley Stern, Philadelphia .... W 4
Sept. 15—Jessie Wilson, Scranton .... KO 2
Oct. 5—Eddie Phillips, Scranton .... W 4
1977
Jan. 4—Charley Stern, Bristol .... KO 4
May 26—Robert Smith, Allentown .... D 6
June 15—Jasper Brisbane, Philadelphia .... KO 1

Oct. 18—Charlie Smith, Virginia Beach .... L 6
Nov. 3—Oscar Freeman, Virginia Beach .... KO 3
Dec. 1—Charlie Smith, Virginia Beach .... L 6
1978
Oct. 9—Stanley Scott, Norfolk .... W 6
1979
Apr. 26—Leonard Langley, Virginia Beach ..... W 6
May 17—Eddie Smith, Virginia Beach .... W 6
1980
Apr. 26—Jimmy McClain, Lynchburg .... KO by 6

GARY YEATS
Reno, Nev. Middleweight
1979
Jan. 24—Charlie Merritt, Las Vegas .... L 4
Feb. 28—Charles Roye, Las Vegas .... W 4
Mar. 14—Pascual Ramirez, Oakland .... KO by 4
Apr. 11—Niua Tofaeono, Las Vegas .... KO by 4
Aug. 1—Frank Dabrowski, Reno .... KO by 4
1980
Dec. 17—David Simpson, Crystal Bay .... KO 1

KEITH YORK
Paterson, N.J. Welterweight
1978
Aug. 6—Nino Gonzales, Bayonne .... KO by 1
Nov. 1—Pedro Odiot, White Plains .... KO by 4
1979
Feb. 14—Ken Fusco, White Plains .... KO by 1
Oct. 4—Martin Parham, N. Bergen .... KO by 3
1980
Feb. 8—Norberto Figueroa, New York .... KO by 2
Dec. 11—Jose Antonetti, New York .... KO by 2

BOBBY JOE YOUNG
Steubenville, Ohio Welterweight
Born: March 4, 1959
Managed by Carmen Castellano
1980
Aug. 29—Pedro Vilella, New York .... L 4
Sept. 9—Robert Buscombe, Warren .... KO 1
Oct. 10—Alfredo Doubouchet, New York .... KO 2
Dec. 9—Tony Taylor, Warren .... KO 2
Dec. 17—Eddie Campbell, Steubenville .... KO 3

CHARLES YOUNG
New York, N.Y. Middleweight
1979
June 28—Milton Hopkins, Staten Island .... KO 4
July 8—Ricky Johnson, New York .... L 4
1980
Jan. 19—Steve Arvin, Syracuse .... KO by 2
Mar. 8—Tom Merola, Great Gorge .... KO by 2
Dec. 17—Freddie Spry, White Plains .... KO by 3

EARL YOUNG
Lightweight
1976
Apr. 6—Jose Mendoza, Salt Lake City .... KO 1
Nov. 4—Harvey Arnold, Incline Village .... D 10
Dec. 1—Leroy Maley, Las Vegas .... L 10
1977
Apr. 2—Ramon Contreras, Ogden .... KO by 7
Nov. 1—Jose Hernandez, Incline Village .... W 10
1978
Feb. 4—Reynaldo Zaragoza, Salt Lake City ..... L 10
Feb. 14—Santos Moreno, Salt Lake City .... L 10
Mar. 24—Miguel Estrada, Ogden .... L 10
July 1—Manny Lopez, Salt Lake City .... L 12
(Utah Lightweight Title)
Nov. 11—Humberto Lara, Salt Lake City .... W
Dec. 9—Jose Hernandez, Incline Village ...... L 10
1979
(Inactive)
1980
Mar. 22—Santos Moreno, Salt Lake City .... KO by 4
Sept. 19—Roberto Elizondo, Los Angeles .... KO by 3

JIMMY YOUNG
Philadelphia, Pa. Heavyweight
Born: Nov. 14, 1948
1969
—Jim Gilmore, San Diego .... W 4
Oct. 28—Jim Jones, Philadelphia .... KO 1
Dec. 9—Johnny Gause, Philadelphia .... W 6
1970
Apr. 3—Clay Hodges, Los Angeles .... L 4
Nov. 24—Howard Darlington, Philadelphia .... W 6
1971
Feb. 22—Roy Williams, Philadelphia .... L 4
Sept. 27—Andy Geiger, Philadelphia .... KO 1
Oct. 21—Lou Hicks, Philadelphia .... W 8

                              1972
Feb.   11—Jasper Evans, New York .... W 6
Mar.   10—Randy Neumann, New York .... L 10
                              1973
Feb.   19—Earnie Shavers, Philadelphia .... KO by 1
Apr.   23—Obie English, Philadelphia .... W 6
Aug.   15—Mike Boswell, Philadelphia .... W 6
Oct.   22—Billy Aird, London .... D 8
                              1974
Feb.   11—Richard Dunn, London .... KO 8
Mar.   4—John Jordan, Washington, D.C. .... W 6
Apr.   22—Les Stevens, London .... W 10
July   6—Jose Luis Garcia, Caracas .... W 10
Nov.   26—Earnie Shavers, Landover, Md. .... D 10
                              1975
Feb.   11—Ron Lyle, Honolulu .... W 10
Aug.   16—Robert Lloyd, Scranton .... KO 7
Nov.   11—Al Jones, Philadelphia.................. KO 4
                              1976
Feb.   20—Jose Roman, San Juan.................... W 10
Apr.   30—Muhammad Ali, Landover................. L 15
                   (World Heavyweight Title)
Sept.   3—Lou Rogan, Philadelphia................. KO 2
Sept. 11—Mike Boswell, Utica..................... KO 4
Nov.   6—Ron Lyle, San Francisco .... W 12
                              1977
Mar.   17—George Foreman, San Juan .... W 12
Sept. 14—Jody Ballard, Las Vegas .... W 10
Nov.   5—Ken Norton, Las Vegas .... L 15
                              1978
June   9—Ossie Ocasio, Las Vegas .... L 10
                              1979
Jan.   27—Ossie Ocasio, San Juan .... L 10
June   22—Wendell Bailey, New York .... KO 3
Sept. 28—Michael Dokes, Las Vegas .... L 10
Dec.   4—John L. Gardner, Wembley .... W 10
                              1980
Mar.   8—Don Halpin, Great Gorge .... KO 2
May   25—Gerry Cooney, Atlantic City .... KO by 4

                       MELVIN YOUNG
              Little Rock, Ark. Welterweight
                              1977
Mar.   5—Bobby Vascocu, Marshall .... KO by 1
Aug.   20—Rocky Matthews, Oklahoma City .... KO by 3
Nov.   8—Donnie London, Memphis .... KO by 1
                              1978
Mar.   21—Phil Reed, Memphis .... KO by 2
Apr.   3—Danny Myers, Indianapolis .... KO by 1
June   2—Paul Gosland, Wichita .... KO by 1
Sept.   6—Ken Fusco, White Plains .... KO by 1
                              1980
Aug.   2—Eddie Freeman, Millington .... KO by 2

                       RAFAEL ZAMORA
              Los Angeles, Calif. Middleweight
                              1980
Mar.   5—Karl Hess, Las Vegas .... D 4
Apr.   2—Ted Bartimus, Las Vegas .... KO 1
Apr.   21—Sylvester Green, Bakersfield .... KO by 2
May   27—Mike Carrere, Honolulu .... KO by 1
Aug.   5—Tim Harris, Sacramento .... KO by 2

                       LEONARDO ZAPATA
                    Mexican Lightweight
                              1979
Aug.   28—Daniel Favela, San Antonio .... KO by 2
Dec.   11—Johnny Contreras, Corpus Christi .... KO by 5
                              1980
May   20—Juventino Gonzales, San Antonio .... KO by 4

                       RICKY ZARBATANY
                   Canadian Welterweight
                              1975
Nov.   7—Sylvain Gagnon, Granby .... KO 1
                              1976
Mar.   2—Avaadis Kassabian, Montreal .... D 6
May   7—Jean Avena, Granby .... KO 5
June   3—Andre Barrel, Granby .... KO 3
July   9—Christian Houle, Magaa .... KO 2
July   10—Ray Johnson, Quebec .... W 6
Aug.   2—Billy Duquette, Peabody .... L 6
Sept. 25—Sammy Loews, Boston .... KO 2
Nov.   19—Avaadis Kassabian, Ottawa .... D 8

                              1977
Jan.   18—Daniel Levesque, Montreal .... L 8
Feb.   9—Jean Guy Binette, Quebec .... W 6
Mar.   22—Jean Guy Binette, Quebec .... W 6
Apr.   26—Alain Turenne, Montreal .... KO by 6
June   1—Michel Doucet, Montreal .... KO 1
July   5—Avaadis Kassabian, Montreal .... W 8
Sept. 20—Billy Duquette, Boston .... W 8
Sept. 29—Manny Turgo, Mass. .... KO 7
Dec.   13—Daniel Levesque, Montreal .... L 8
                              1978
Jan.   24—Jean Guy Binette, Montreal .... W 8
Feb.   11—Michael Stokes, Mass. .... W 10
Feb.   24—Joe Houston, Chicoutimi .... W 8
Mar.   19—D. C. Walker, Chicoutimi .... W 8
June   6—Daniel Levesque, Montreal .... W 8
June   27—Jean Guy Binette, Montreal .... W 8
Sept. 26—Alain Turenne, Montreal .... W 8
Oct.   12—Jessie Oliver, Montreal .... L 8
Oct.   21—Kelly Oille, Halifax .... L 6
                              1979
June   1—Tony Chiaverini, Kansas City .... KO by 6
                              1980
July   25—Rocky Fratto, Rochester .... KO by 7

                       ZEKE ZELICHOWSKI
              Hamtramck, Mich. Light Heavyweight
                              1979
Sept. 20—Jose Gutierrez, Detroit .... W 4
Oct.   18—Gary Hunter, Detroit .... KO 4
Nov.   1—W. C. Honeycutt, Detroit .... KO 1
                              1980
Sept. 10—Darnell Hayes, Detroit .... KO by 2

                          BOB ZESSIN
                  Peoria, Illinois Featherweight
                              1980
Nov.   7—Fernando Garcia, Chicago .... W 6
Nov.   19—Joe Baker, Moline .... KO 1
Dec.   19—Jeff Gettemy, Peoria .... W 6

                         KID ZORRITA
                   Mexican Welterweight
                              1979
June   7—Robert Turner, Los Angeles .... KO 9
                              1980
Sept.   4—Andres Ramirez, Los Angeles .... W 10

                         STEVE ZOUSKI
                 Brockton, Mass. Heavyweight
                              1978
Aug.   3—Joe Maye, Boston .... W 4
Oct.   14—Johnny Blaine, New Haven .... KO 4
Nov.   11—Tom Landry, Boston .... KO 2
                              1979
Jan.   15—Joe Maye, Boston .... KO 8
Feb.   3—Joe Maye, Boston .... KO 6
Sept. 28—Bobby Jones, Taunton .... KO 2
                              1980
Feb.   27—Leroy Boone, Scranton .... L 10
Apr.   20—Don Halpin, Portland, Me. .... KO 7
June   20—Mike Boswell, Boston .... KO 1
Aug.   18—Greg Sorrentino, Boston .... KO 10
Sept.   5—Kid Samson, Dorchester .... W 10
Oct.   2—Rodell Dupree, Boston .... W 10
Nov.   25—Johnny Warr, Boston .... W 10
Dec.   12—Henry Patterson, Brockton .... KO 3

                        CAESAR ZULUETA
                 Honolulu, Hawaii Bantamweight
                              1979
Aug.   28—Noe Montano, Honolulu .... KO 3
Oct.   9—Frank Hesia, Honolulu .... KO by 2
Dec.   18—James Estrella, Honolulu .... KO 2
                              1980
Feb.   20—Frank Hesia, Hilo .... KO by 3
Aug.   19—Julio Rodrigues, Honolulu .... KO by 2
Nov.   19—Frank Hesia, Honolulu .... KO by 2

                        CARLOS ZUNIGA
                  Stockton, Calif. Bantamweight
                              1978
Apr.   19—George Maldonado, San Francisco .... KO 3
May   15—Darryl Jones, Stockton .... L 6
July   3—Roberto Lopez, Gardnerville .... W 4
July   22—Horacio Pintado, Truckee .... KO 5
Sept. 19—Juan Castro, Stockton .... KO 2
                              1979
Mar.   28—Lino Casillas, Stockton .... KO 1
Apr.   19—Catalino Flores, Stockton .... KO 1
June   10—Jose Villegas, Stockton .... W 10
Dec.   11—Lionel Hainey, Sparks .... KO 1

1980

Apr. 24—Rodolfo Perez, Stockton .... W 10
June 12—Frankie Granados, Stockton .... KO 8
Sept. 19—Adelaido Galindo, Los Angeles .... KO by 6

JORGE ZUNIGA
Houston, Texas Featherweight
1979

Feb. 13—Jesse Montemayor, Houston .... W 6

July 21—Victor Arguello, Houston .... KO 2
Nov. 27—Alberto Rivera, Houston .... KO 2

1980

Jan. 9—Gaby Cantera, Beaumont .... W 6
Apr. 6—Arturo Munoz, Houston .... W 4
Sept. 23—Rocky Montoya, Houston .... KO by 8
(For Texas Featherweight Title)

246

THE RING'S UPDATED RECORDS OF ACTIVE FIGHTERS OUTSIDE OF THE AMERICAS

DON AAGESEN
Birmingham, England Lightweight
Born: Sept. 16, 1950
1975
Oct.	27—Ginger Bell, London	W	6
Nov.	10—Kenny Matthews, London	L	6
Nov.	26—Frankie Wagstaff, Birmingham	W	6

1976
Jan.	14—Roger Doyle, Solihull	L	6
Jan.	28—Dave Connell, Birmingham	W	6
Feb.	16—Dave Wraxall, Manchester	D	6
Mar.	1—Wally Angliss, Walworth	W	6
Mar.	30—Danny Connolly, Hammersmith	L	6
June	14—Wally Angliss, Walworth	KO	6
Sept.	20—Danny Connolly, Walworth	L	6
Oct.	4—Alan Oag, Hanley	L	6
Oct.	25—Steve Butler, Mayfair	KO by	3
Nov.	20—Kevin Sheehan, Dudley	KO	1
Dec.	15—Steve Enright, Bradford	L	6

1977
Feb.	1—Graham Laybourn, London	W	6
Mar.	8—Kevin Docherty, Wolverhampton	L	6
Mar.	16—Paul Clemit, Solihull	L	6
Apr.	21—Steve Enwright, Liverpool	L	6
May	17—Paul Varden, Wolverhampton	W	6
May	30—Alan Robertson, Marton	KO by	3
Sept.	20—Paul Chance, Southend	KO by	2

1978
Apr.	12—Larry Richards, Evesham	L	6
Oct.	31—George Baily, Wolverhampton	W	6

1979
June	25—John Henry, Edgbaston	L	6
Sept.	24—Pat Devanney, Birmingham	D	6
Oct.	8—Jimmy Hancock, Nantwich	D	6
Nov.	21—Robert Hepburn, Eversham	L	6
Nov.	27—John Henry, Wolverhampton	L	6

1980
Jan.	28—John Henry, Edgbaston	KO	3
Feb.	5—Steve Topliss, Wolverhampton	L	6
Feb.	27—Doug Hill, Burslem	L	6
Apr.	21—Mike Redden, Edgbaston	KO	1
June	11—Alec Irvine, Edgbaston	W	8
Sept.	24—Doug Hill, Burslem	L	10
	(For Midland Area Featherweight Title)		
Oct.	18—Alec Irvine, Birmingham	L	8

JOHNNY ABA
Papua, New Guinea Featherweight
Born: 1956
1976
Apr.	10—Alan Hilt, Port Moresby	W	10
June	5—Guinea Hillier, Goroka	KO by	4
Aug.	26—John Kopi, Panguna	KO	9
	(Won Vacant New Guinea Featherweight Title)		
Nov.	—John Kopi, Panguna	KO	5
Dec.	18—Phillip Yang, Panguna	WF	4
	(Won Vacant New Guinea Lightweight Title)		

1977
Apr.	16—John Kopi, Panguna	KO	5
	(New Guinea Featherweight Title)		
June	2—Reg King, Boroko	W	8
July	2—Charlie Gergan, Panguna	KO	3
July	14—Guinea Hillier, Boroko	W	10
July	28—Guinea Hillier, Boroko	D	10
Aug.	11—Willie Leslie, Port Moresby	W	10
Dec.	1—Billy Moeller, Boroko	W	15
	(Won Commonwealth Junior Lightweight Title)		

1978
Feb.	2—Willie Leslie, Penguna	W	10
Feb.	27—Brian Roberts, Melbourne	W	12
Apr.	21—David Austin, Boroko	D	1
May	5—Brian Roberts, Port Moresby	KO	12
	(Commonwealth Junior Lightweight Title)		
May	25—Roger Henry, Panguna	W	10
June	30—Roger Henry, Rabaul	W	10
Aug.	11—Billy Moeller, Rabaul	KO	2
	(Commonwealth Junior Lightweight Title)		
Sept.	9—Paul Baker, Kundiawa	KO	7
Oct.	5—Paul Baker, Panguna	KO	9
Nov.	3—Paul Baker, Goroka	KO	3
Nov.	17—Flash Oliver, Goroka	W	10

1979
Feb.	16—Sandy Noora, Gordon	W	10

Apr.	20—Gary Rosen, Panguna	KO	7
June	1—Domingo Torres, Port Moresby	W	10
June	16—Paul Baker, Panguna	KO	8
July	14—Reg King, Goreka	KO	7
Oct.	20—Willie Tarika, Suva	W	15
	(Commonwealth Junior Lightweight Title)		
Nov.	17—Eusebio Pedroza, Port Moresby	KO by	11
	(WBA Featherweight Title)		

1980
Mar.	21—Willie Tarika, Boroko	W	15
	(Retained Commonwealth Junior Lightweight Title)		
Sept.	19—Buddy Clare, Rabaul	KO	3

BILLY ABATO
Filipino Featherweight
1978
Sept.	29—Rene Cruz, Cag. de Oro	W	10

1979
Jan.	27—Bob Caster, Davao City	KO	2
Mar.	17—Ric Diamale, Davao City	L	12
June	25—Raffy Saulong, Manila	W	10
	(Philippine Bantamweight Title)		
Sept.	1—San Sacrostan, Cag. de Oro City	D	10
Sept.	29—Ronald Sumalis, Devao City	W	12
	(Philippine Bantamweight Title)		
Nov.	24—Eddie Miral, Cag. de Oro City	W	10

1980
Mar.	15—Al Steat, De Oro City	W	10
Aug.	30—Arnel Arrozal, Angels City	L	10
Sept.	27—Dede Suaybaguio, Butan City	W	10
Oct.	25—Flash Jagdon, Gen. Santos City	D	10

ROBINSON ABATO
Filipino Flyweight
1980
Mar.	15—Julius Gonzaga, De Oro City	W	10
July	2—Dede Suaybaguio, Butan City	KO by	7
Sept.	27—Carlos Aradora, Butan City	KO by	6

JAMES (JIMMY) ABBOTT
South African Heavyweight
Born: May 11, 1959
1978
June	2—Frans Manyaniso, Bloemfontein	W	4
June	9—Jeffrey Ellis, Johannesburg	KO	1
July	1—Wiets De Beer, Pretoria	KO	3
Aug.	5—Robert Williams, Johannesburg	KO	5
Aug.	28—Fraser Memela, Durban	KO	2
Sept.	9—Terry O'Connor, Cape Town	W	6
Oct.	7—Tom Kiely, Johannesburg	W	8
Nov.	6—Caiphus Masondo, Durban	KO	1

1979
Mar.	10—Terry Mintus, Johannesburg	KO	4
Apr.	25—Robbie Williams, Durban	KO	4
June	2—Dave Johnson, Bophutatswana	KO	3
Aug.	27—Hennie Thoonan, Johannesburg	KO	1
Sept.	14—Eddie (Animal) Lopez, Durban	L	8
Oct.	20—Walter Santemore, Pretoria	KO	6
Nov.	12—Leon Shaw, Cape Town	KO	4

1980
Mar.	8—Kallie Knoetze, Johannesburg	KO	1
	(Won Transvaal Heavyweight Title)		
Apr.	14—Henry Porter, Cape Town	KO	4
May	10—George Chaplin, Johannesburg	D	10
Aug.	16—Robbie Williams, Johannesburg	D	6
Oct.	15—Robbie Williams, Cape Town	L	8
Dec.	19—Mike Koranicki, Welkom	L	10

RICKY CHARLES ABBOTT
South African Junior Middleweight
1980
Apr.	19—Cornelius de Beer, Rand Stadium	L	4

TITO ABELLA
Filipino Featherweight
1978
Feb.	18—Netrnoi Vorasing, Bangkok	KO by	5
Sept.	22—Peter Siscon, Manila	L	10

1979
Jan.	14—Tae-Shik Kim, Seoul	KO by	5
Mar.	26—Juan Fernandez, Quezon City	KO	4
Apr.	21—Jimmy Boy, Baguio City	KO	4
May	4—Peter Siscon, Manila	W	10
May	26—Johnny Castro, Queen City	KO	9
Oct.	28—Yoko Gushiken, Tokyo	KO by	7
	(WBA Junior Flyweight Title)		
Dec.	8—Guraman Ueda, Ohita	KO	3

1980
Jan.	22—Kap-Chul Shin, Pusan	L	10
Mar.	2—Chi-Bok Kim, Seoul	KO by	1
Apr.	29—Syuichi Hozumi, Tokyo	L	10
July	18—Rene Busayong, Manila	L	10
Nov.	29—Juanito Ablaca, Davao City	KO by	3

JUANITO ABLACA
Filipino Junior Flyweight
1980
May   23—Henry Balina, Manila .... W 10
July   27—Ver Libradilla, Cebu City .... W 10
Nov. 29—Tito Abella, Davao City .... KO 3

PETRUS ABRAHAMS
South African Junior Featherweight
1980
May   31—Samuel Wolf, Bethlehem .... L 4
Sept. 6—Michael Khuto, Ficksburg .... L 4

BILL ABROGAR
Filipino Bantamweight
1975
Aug. 28—Amelito Punat, Cagayan de Oro .... L 10
1976
(Inactive)
1977
June 22—Venice Borkorsor, Bankok .... KO by 6
1978
(Inactive)
1979
May   26—San Sacristan, Cagayan de Oro City ..... L 10
Nov. 3—Raffy Saulong, Cagayan de Oro City ..... W 10
1980
June 14—Rudy Patalinhug, De Oro City .... W 10
Aug. 31—Sammy Insular, Bukidnon .... W 10
Sept. 27—Ronald Sumalis, De Oro City .... L 10
Nov. 15—Dede Suaybaguio, Butan .... KO by 5

LOUIS ACARIES
French Welterweight
1975
Nov. 13—Jean-Pierre Moreau, Paris .... W 6
1976
Jan. 15—Gus Bleus, Paris .... W 5
Feb. 19—Jean Paul Seera, Paris .... W 6
Mar. 11—Andre Sainseaux, Paris .... KO 4
Apr. 8—Giovanni DeVita, Paris .... KO 2
Apr. 29—Mauricio Bittarelli, Paris .... KO 2
May 13—Jean Pierre Di Stefano, Paris .... KO 5
Oct. 1—Sreco Weiner, Marseille .... W 8
Nov. 20—Antonio Casado, Tarbes .... W 8
Dec. 2—Billy Waith, Paris .... W 10
1977
Apr. 1—Luciano Laffranchi, Tarbes .... KO 7
May 7—George Perrot, Tarbes .... KO 8
Oct. 6—Terry Petersen, Paris .... W 10
Nov. 3—Achille Mitchell, Marseille .... W 10
Nov. 18—Micky Ryce, Tarbes .... W 10
1978
Jan. 12—Pascal Zito, Paris .... KO 4
(French Welterweight Title)
Feb. 16—Aundra Love, Paris .... W 10
Apr. 21—Alain Ruocco, Toulon .... L 12
(French Welterweight Title)
Oct. 9—Randy Milton, Salle Wagram .... KO 3
Dec. 16—Alain Ruocco, Parris .... W 12
(French Welterweight Title)
1979
May 10—Everaldo Costa Azevedo, Paris .... L 10
June 15—Fred Coranson, Nice .... W 12
(French Welterweight Title)
Oct. 15—Des Morrison, Pravia .... KO by 1
Dec. 14—Richard Rodriguez, Nice .... W 12
(Retained French Welterweight Title)
1980
Feb. 15—Everaldo Costa Azevedo, Nice .... W 10
July 18—Djibril Bathily, Mont de Marsan .... KO 6
(Won Vacant French Junior Middleweight Title)
Oct. 6—Jose Hernandez, Paris .... KO 6
Dec. 18—Claude Martin, Paris .... KO 10
(Retained French Junior Middleweight Title)

ANTONIO ACEDO
Spanish Junior Welterweight
1979
Nov. 21—Juan Fernandez, Barcelona .... W 4
1980
Jan. 30—Juan Jose Fernandez, Madrid .... W 4

MANUEL ACIDO
Spanish Welterweight
1978
Mar. 3—Raul Anon, Lugo .... D 6
Apr. 1—Don Aisa Lugo .... D 8
1979
Oct. 19—Jose M. Domingo, Madrid .... D 8
Dec. 1—Angel Pedraza, Leon .... KO 3
1980
June 7—Domingo Gimenez Martinez, La Coruna ... D 8

July 4—Basila Betula, Madrid .... KO 4
Sept. 5—Julian Alonso, Palma de Mallorca .... D 6

NILO ACIDO
Filipino Junior Lightweight
1977
Nov. 19—Eddie Cajas, Davao City .... KO 5
1978
Nov. 11—Ric Quijano, Davao City .... W 10
1979
Jan. 21—Young Fely, Orquista City .... W 10
Mar. 3—Cris Boy Ptero, Davao City .... KO 6
Mar. 31—Dario Melida, Ozamis City .... W 10
May 12—Ben Basa, Davao City .... KO 2
June 2—Max Boy Toyogon, Davao City .... KO 9
June 30—Keystone Flash, Davao City .... W 10
Aug. 26—Al Rodrigo, Davao Del Norte .... KO 7
Nov. 17—Armand Bangoyyan, Davao City .... W 12
(Won Philippine Junior Lightweight Title)
1980
Feb. 1—Nen Jun, Manila .... L 10
(Lost Philippine Junior Lightweight Title)
May 17—Rey Tam, Baguio City .... L 10
June 25—Rod Sequenan, Quezon City .... L 10
July 30—Eddie Cejas, Manila .... W 10
Sept. 7—Pete Alferez, De Oro City .... KO 7
Oct. 26—Tony Flores, Cebu City .... KO 10
Dec. 18—Lito Pena, Manila .... L 10

STEVE ACZEL
Australian Light Heavyweight
1974
Feb. 25—Gerry Fanning, Melbourne .... KO 4
Apr. 18—Dragan Todorovic, Blacktown .... KO 4
May 9—Greg McNamara, Blacktown .... W 10
May 30—Steve Cansdell, Blacktown .... KO 8
June 25—Monty Betham, Melbourne .... KO 4
(Vacant Australian Light Heavyweight Title)
July 25—Tommy Mears, Blacktown .... KO 6
Aug. 22—Dragan Todorovic, Blacktown .... KO 8
Sept. 19—Steve Cansdell, Blacktown .... KO 4
(Won Australian Light Heavyweight Title)
Nov. 14—Kim Miller, Blacktown .... KO 3
Dec. 12—Greg McNamara, Blacktown .... KO 9
(Australian Light Heavyweight Title)
1975
Feb. 19—Maxie Smith, Manchester .... KO 3
(Won Vacant Commonwealth Light Heavyweight Title)
Mar. 25—Victor Attivor, Melbourne .... KO by 2
May 16—Peter Clay, Melbourne .... KO 2
June 26—Tommy Mears, Blacktown .... KO 4
(Won Vacant Australian Heavyweight Title)
Sept. 18—Senitiki Qata, Blacktown .... KO 7
Oct. 30—Tony Mundine, Blacktown .... KO by 12
(Commonwealth & Australian Light Heavyweight Titles)
1976
Feb. 11—Ted Gray, Marrickville .... KO 10
(Australian Heavyweight Title)
June 14—Joe Jackson, Auckland .... KO 8
Nov. 10—Maile Haumono, Marrickville .... KO by 9
(Australian Heavyweight Title)
1977
(Inactive)
1978
May 24—Ken Eldridge, Bankstown .... KO 4
July 14—Steve Cansdell, Brisbane .... KO 7
Sept. 20—Maile Haumono, Mount Pritchard ...... W 10
1979
Mar. 30—Fetiaki Namoa, Brisbane .... KO 9
May 18—Maile Havmona, Brisbane .... KO 8
Sept. 7—Victor Attivor, Brisbane .... KO 5
Oct. 19—Robert Smith, Brisbane .... KO 3
1980
May 16—Maile Havmona, Borokova .... D 10
July 28—Tony Mundine, Brisbane .... KO by 9
(Australian Heavyweight Title)
Nov. 6—Young Sekona, Auckland .... KO 12

CAMERON ADAMS
South African Middleweight
Born: Sept. 11, 1954
1978
Apr. 29—Thornton Oakes, Johannesburg .... KO 2
Sept. 8—Morgan Moledi, Johannesburg .... KO 6
Dec. 4—Philip Hlope, Durban .... KO 3
1979
Feb. 3—Joseph Hali, Johannesburg .... KO 2
Sept. 15—Daniel Mapanya, Johannesburg .... KO 2
Dec. 1—Bruce McIntyre, Johannesburg .... KO by 5
1980
Feb. 9—Lovisa Motya, East London .... L 8
Mar. 13—Ernie Singleury, Cape Town .... L 10
June 7—Samson Mohloai, Johannesburg .... KO 6
(Won Transvaal Middleweight Title)

DOMENICO ADINOLFI
Italian Heavyweight
Born: June 20, 1946, Ceccano, Italy

1969

Nov.	29—Pietro Disaro, Ceccano	W	6

1970

Mar.	6—Domenico Coppola, Rome	KO	5
Apr.	3—Carlo De Carli, Rome	KO	1
Apr.	30—Raffaele Maio, Latina	KO	4
May	15—Daniel Flahuat, Rome	KO	2
July	4—Arnaldo Patelli, Latrina	KO	6
Aug.	8—Adriano Rosati, Velletri	KO	7
Sept.	19—Vlado Blazatic, Velletri	W	8
Oct.	23—Giulio Rinaldi, Rome	KO	5
	(Won Italian Light Heavyweight Title)		
Dec.	18—Serge Cauver, Rome	KO	4
Dec.	26—Silvio Baroni, Rome	W	8

1971

Feb.	13—Gianfranco Macchia, Rome	W	12
	(Italian Light Heavyweight Title)		
Apr.	23—Jean Tshikuna, Bologna	W	8
July	3—Bernard Quellier, Ostia Lido	W	8
Sept.	15—Guerrino Scattolin, Enna	W	12
	(Retained Italian Light Heavyweight Title)		
Oct.	1—Wendell Joseph, Rome	W	8
Oct.	22—Kenny Warner, Rme	WF	5
Nov.	29—Roy John, Bologna	W	8
Dec.	26—Carl Baker, Bologna	KO	4

1972

Mar.	4—Gianfranco Macchia, Rome	L	12
	(Italian Light Heavyweight Title)		
July	5—Luigi Patruno, San Remo	KO	4
Aug.	4—Adonis Ray, Latina	W disq.	3
Oct.	27—Pierre Fourie, Vereeniging	L	10
Nov.	11—Chris Roos, Johannesburg	L	10

1973

Mar.	14—Renzo Grespan, Frosinone	W	12
	(Italian Light Heavyweight Title)		
Apr.	27—Eric Nussbaum, Geneva	D	10
Aug.	25—Aldo Traversar, Charivari	L	12
	(Italian Light Heavyweight Title)		

1974

Jan.	30—Jean Tshikuna, Palermo	W	8
Feb.	16—Raffaele Maio, Turin	KO	2
Mar.	8—Ba Sounkalo, Milan	KO	6
Apr.	26—Dino Tarocco, Milan	KO	4
June	3—Tom Bethea, Toronto	L	10
July	13—Karl Zurheide, Rome	KO	7
Sept.	21—Sergio Jannilli, Rome	KO	7
Oct.	18—Billy Lloyd, Rome	NC	
Dec.	4—Karl Heinz Klein, Compiegne	KO	1
	(European Light Heavyweight Title)		

1975

Jan.	24—Willie Taylor, Milan	L	8
Feb.	28—Jose Antonio Galvez, Torino	KO	4
Apr.	19—Freddy De Kerpel, Wieze	KO	11
	(European)		
July	19—Frankie Evans, Frosinone	KO	7
Oct.	31—Rudi Lubbers, Turin	KO	2
	(European Light Heavyweight Title)		
Nov.	7—Melvin Mott, Milan	KO	3

1976

Mar.	5—Victor Attivor, Turin	D	8
May	14—Leo Kakolewicz, Rome	KO	8
July	10—Mate Parlov, Belgrade	KO by	11
	(European Light Heavyweight Title)		
Nov.	27—Vasco Faustino, Latina	W	8

1977

May	27—Jose Gomez, Rome	W	8
Dec.	2—Lisimo Obutobe, Hamburg	W	10

1978

Oct.	13—Albert Syben, Ravenna	D	10
Dec.	23—Lucien Rodriguez, Liege	L	10

1979

May	19—Gilberto Acuna, Bruxelles	W	10
Dec.	8—T.C. Bowman	W	6

1980

Feb.	8—Ed Turner, Milan	W	10
Mar.	21—Charley Mudgett, Bologna	KO	2
May	22—Terry Mims, Bologna	KO	4
Aug.	17—Giovanni De Luca, Norcia	W	12
	(Won Italian Heavyweight Title)		
Oct.	31—Lee Rogers, Rome	W disq.	9
Dec.	26—Vincenzo Pesapane, Piacenza	KO	9
	(Retained Italian Heavyweight Title)		

NARDITO ADRAYAN
Philippine Lightweight

1977

Nov.	14—Arman Bangoyan, Cagayan de Oro	W	10

1978

Feb.	4—Nene Jun, Cagayan de Oro	L	12
	(For Philippines Featherweight Title)		
Apr.	1—Boy Oliva, Cagayan de Oro	W	10
May	6—Boy Oliva, Cebu City	W	10
Nov.	18—Romeo Olivetti, Cagayan de Oro	W	10
Dec.	2—Wonder Biy Bulfa, Cebu City	W	10

1979

Jan.	20—Johnny Sato, Santos City	KO by	5
June	22—Rey Tam, Manila	KO by	6
Nov.	24—Fred Basa, Cagayan de Oro	W	10

1980

Feb.	16—Ric Dolotallas, De Oro City	L	10
Mar.	15—Eddie Cejas, De Oro City	W	10
June	12—Rommy Cunanan, Angels City	L	10

GIUSEPPE AGATE
Italian Welterweight
Born: Sept. 29, 1949

1973

Feb.	8—Luigi Sorangelo, Milano	W	6
Feb.	23—Almo Quaini, Milano	W	4
Mar.	24—Sergio Emili, S. Elpidio	L	6
June	8—Abdelkader Bouguetaib, Milan	D	6
June	28—Pasqualino Morbidelli, Novara	W	5
Aug.	12—Bobby Guy, Parma	W	6
Sept.	2—Augusto Quadri, Cadorago	NC	5
Oct.	5—Natale Vezzoli, Milano	L	6
Oct.	19—Gianni Locci, Milano	W	6
Nov.	3—Roberto Franceschi, Perugia	W	5
Nov.	23—Nedo Fabbri, Milan	KO	4
Dec.	28—Paul Ikumapayi, Novara	W	8

1974

Jan.	19—Paul Ikumapayi, Como	W	6
Feb.	19—Amleto Restano, Como	KO by	4
Mar.	22—Paul Ikumapayi, Milan	W	6
Apr.	5—Renzo Battistelli, Milan	W	8
Apr.	30—Pasquale Morbidelli, Bologna	L	8
May	22—Nedo Fabbri, Stradella	D	8
Oct.	1—Franco Diana, Castelvetrano	KO by	4
Dec.	6—Vincenzo Quero, Milan	L	8
Dec.	26—Salvatore Dui, Milano	W	5

1975

Feb.	1—Giovanni Girgenti, Milan	L	12
	(Italian Junior Lightweight Title)		
Feb.	28—Vincenzo Quero, Rome	L	8
Mar.	28—Giancarlo Barabotti, Bologna	L	6
Apr.	18—Bruno Pierri, Milan	L	6
May	17—Giuseppe Mura, Porto Torres	L	8
June	15—Renzo Battistelli, Macerata	L	8
Sept.	13—Mario Redi, Pela	W	8
Oct.	6—Mario Redi, Zagreb	L	8
Nov.	13—Lionel Rose, Melbourne	KO by	3

1976

Feb.	6—Nevio Carbi, Trieste	L	4
Mar.	12—Biagio Pierri, Milan	L	8
Apr.	21—Valerio Fretta, Caserta	L	8
Apr.	30—Salvatore Liscapade, Rome	L	8
May	15—Valerio Fretta, Forli	W	8
June	12—Natale Vezzoli, Brescia	L	8
July	2—Natale, Credda, Cagliari	D	8
Aug.	11—Sergio Emili, Civitanova	L	8
Sept.	10—Rudi Haeck, Zele	L	8
Sept.	24—Aristide Pizzo, Milan	KO by	4
Oct.	25—Charlie Nash, London	L	10

1977

Jan.	8—Jean Van Torre, Zele	L	6
Feb.	12—Mario Oliveira, St. Maur	D	8
Feb.	26—Albert Amatler, Villeurbanne	L	8
Mar.	11—Vincenzo Quero, Milan	L	8
May	29—Salvatore Liscapede, Taurisano	KO by	2
	(Italian Junior Lightweight Title)		
Oct.	28—Aristide Pizzo, Milan	L	8
Nov.	12—Cosimo Lavino, Brindisi	L	6
Nov.	26—Elio Cotena, Scafati	L	10
Dec.	17—Vincenzo Quero, Pesaro	L	8

1978

Feb.	11—Gilberto Orsaldo, Voiron	L	8
Mar.	31—Franco Siddu, Florence	L	8
May	27—Natale Caredda, Oristano	L	8
July	2—Giovanni Vitillo, Calcinaia	L	7
July	30—Pellegrino Ventrone, Marcianise	L	8
Oct.	26—Nunziato Sanna, Lecco	W	6
Dec.	17—Aristede Pizzo, Lecco	L	8

1979

Jan.	6—Christian Garcia, Agen	L	8
Feb.	23—Luigi De Rosa, Capua	L	8
Mar.	10—Danny M'Putu, Dunkerque	L	8
Apr.	7—Bruno Demontis, Sassari	L	8
May	25—Annurizizto Sanna, Ravegnate	L	8
June	23—Joe Gibilisco, Cinisello Balsama	L	8

Sept. 30—Bruno Demontis, Oristane . . . . L 8
Oct. 10—Joe Gibilisco, Faenza . . . . L 8
Nov. 23—Aristede Pizzo, Pordenone . . . . LF 6
Dec. 21—Francesco Agate, Casalmonferrate . . . . L 8
1980
Mar. 29—Eupremio Epifani, Pesaro . . . . L 6
Apr. 11—Giovanni Chirra, Sassari . . . . W 6
June 28—Eupremio Epifani, Potenza . . . . L 6
Sept. 12—Francisco Gallo, Chivasso . . . . L 8
Nov. 21—Patrizio Burini, Figline . . . . L 8
Dec. 19—Bruno Simili, Lucca . . . . D 8

LITTLE AGUILAR
Filipino Junior Bantamweight
1979
Sept. 22—Salvador Perez, Quezon . . . . W 10
1980
Feb. 15—William Develos, Manila . . . . KO 1
Mar. 30—Yung-Shik Kim, Seoul . . . . L 10
(For Vacant OPBF Junior Bantamweight Title)
Nov. 19—Allan Jardenil, Quezon City . . . . KO by 4
Dec. 12—Larry Enriquez, Elorde . . . . W 10

BILLY AHEARNE
British Welterweight
1975
Nov. 17—Jimmy Pickard, Manchester . . . . W 6
Dec. 2—Joe Ward, Leeds . . . . D 6
1976
Feb. 9—Yotham Kunda, London . . . . L 5
June 8—Terry Schofield, Bradford . . . . D 6
Sept. 13—Terry Schofield, Manchester . . . . L 8
Sept. 20—Russ Shaw, Manchester . . . . W 6
1977
Sept. 14—Bertie Green, Sheffield . . . . W 6
Sept. 22—Russ Shaw, Birkinhead . . . . W 6
Oct. 24—Carl Bailey, Manchester . . . . L 8
1978
Jan. 18—Prince Rodney, Solihull . . . . L 8
Jan. 30—Tommy Joyce, Cleethorpes . . . . KO 2
1979
Sept. 12—Johnny Elliott, Liverpool . . . . D 6
Sept. 17—Phil Lewis, Manchester . . . . W 6
Oct. 15—Ady Allen, Manchester . . . . L 8
Oct. 27—Herol Graham, Barnsley . . . . KO by 6
1980
Apr. 9—Phil Lewis, Liverpool . . . . W 6
Apr. 29—Robert Armstrong, Stockport . . . . KO 1
May 7—Chris Glover, Liverpool . . . . KO by 3
June 16—Jeff Aspell, Manchester . . . . W 8
July 7—Neil Fannon, Middlesbrough . . . . KO by 1

GRAEME AHMED
British Welterweight
1980
Sept. 11—Paul Murray, Hartlepool . . . . W 6
Oct. 13—Kevin Walsh, Newcastle . . . . W 6

BILLY AIRD
Liverpool, England Heavyweight
Born: March 15, 1946
1969
June 1—Paul Cassidy, London. . . . . KO 4
June 23—George Dulaire, London. . . . . W 6
Sept. 8—John Cullen, London . . . . W 6
Sept. 29—Dennis Avoth, London . . . . W 6
Nov. 3—Dickie Dunn, Bedford . . . . L 3
1970
Feb. 23—Richard Dunn, London. . . . . W 8
Apr. 21—Del Phillips, London. . . . . W 6
Sept. 7—Richard Dunn, Manchester. . . . . KO 6
Nov. 11—Bunny Johnson, Solihull. . . . . L 8
Dec. 7—Foster Bibron, Melbourne . . . . L 10
1971
Jan. 11—Cliff Field, Bloomsbury . . . . KO 2
May 1—Arno Prick, Johannesburg . . . . W 10
July 5—Cliff Field, London . . . . KO 7
Oct. 28—Rocky Campbell, Bristol . . . . W 8
Dec. 7—Ted Gullick, London . . . . D 10
1972
May 9—Roger Tighe, London . . . . W 8
June 6—John Conteh, London . . . . KO by 8
Oct. 23—Bunny Johnson, London . . . . L 8
1973
Apr. 5—Brian Jewitt, Walworth . . . . W 8
Apr. 16—Rocky Campbell, London . . . . D 8
May 14—Richard Dunn, London . . . . L 10
July 9—Rocky Campbell, Liverpool . . . . KO 7
Sept. 21—Greg Field, Hamburg . . . . KO by 4
Oct. 22—Jimmy Young, London . . . . D 8
Nov. 12—Obie English, London . . . . L 10
1974
Apr. 28—Lloyd Walford, Southend . . . . W 8

June 21—Bernd August, Berlin . . . . D 8
1975
Feb. 4—Ngozika Ekwelum, Southend . . . . W 8
Mar. 11—Kevin Isaac, London . . . . W 8
June 6—Rady Neuman, London . . . . KO by 8
1976
Mar. 21—Bunny Johnson, Frimley Green . . . . D 10
Oct. 18—Denton Ruddock, Marylebone . . . . W 10
1977
Feb. 28—Avenamar Peralta, Luton . . . . L disq. 5
Oct. 11—Gilberto Acuna, Marylebon . . . . KO 6
1978
Mar. 3—Alfredo Evangelista, Leon . . . . L 15
(European Heavyweight Title)
Oct. 24—John Gardner, Kensington . . . . KO by 5
(British Heavyweight Title)
1979
May 21—Tommy Kiely, Walworth . . . . W 8
Oct. 1—Neil Malpass, Marylebone . . . . W 10
1980
Apr. 17—Gordon Ferris, Edgbaston . . . . L 10
Oct. 18—Tony Moore, Birmingham . . . . W 10

NAMIO AKAMINE
Japanese Featherweight
1978
Sept. 9—Hisao Sakurai, Okinawa-Naha City . . . . . . W 10
Nov. 26—Susumu Okabe, Tokyo . . . . KO 4
1979
Mar. 30—Kazuaki Hamada, Tokyo . . . . W 10
June 1—Spider Nemoto, Osaka . . . . L 10
(JBC Featherweight Title)
Nov. 27—Koichi Matsushima, Tokyo . . . . KO by 9
1980
Apr. 20—Johnny Fujimoto, Tokyo . . . . KO by 6

VERDAT AKOVA
Turkish Light Heavyweight
1977
May 20—Peter Baumgart, Hannover . . . . KO 3
Dec. 10—Antonis Rimasti, Berlin . . . . KO 3
1978
Mar. 18—Agamal Yildirim, Uestersen . . . . L 6
Apr. 7—Agamil Yildirim, Berlin . . . . L 6
Oct. 15—Gregory Downes, Hamburg . . . . D 6
Nov. 6—Jose Centa, Berlin . . . . KO 5
Dec. 7—Horst Lang, Luebeck . . . . W 6
1979
July 28—Miroslav Popovic, Munich . . . . L 6
Sept. 14—Teunis Kok, Durban . . . . KO by 6
1980
Apr. 18—Walter Nikkel, Berlin . . . . KO 2
Sept. 22—Hubert Zimmermann, Rotterdam . . . . KO 3

GEN AKUTSU
Japanese Junior Lightweight
1979
Mar. 19—Shuhei Takebe, Tokyo. . . . . D 8
Oct. 5—Hikaru Tomonari, Miyagi Ken . . . . KO by 3
1980
Jan. 28—Gen Tosa, Tokyo . . . . KO by 8
July 31—Gen Tosa, Tokyo . . . . L 10
Oct. 31—Kaneatsu Yamamoto, Tokyo . . . . KO by 3

NEPTALI ALAMAG
Filipino Junior Featherweight
1974
June 14—Boy Marino, Masbate . . . . KO 1
Nov. 24—Teody Vargas, Masbate . . . . KO 8
Dec. 21—Tony Marcdlo, Rizol . . . . W 8
1975
Jan. 6—Roger Garcia, Masbate . . . . W 10
Mar. 16—Lorrie Garcia, Masbate . . . . D 10
Aug. 1—Nono Ignacio, Rizal . . . . KO 2
Aug. 20—Jaime Pitalbo, Channel . . . . D 10
Oct. 18—Jun Sillbason, Masbate . . . . D 10
Nov. 21—Eduardo Ejandra, Inceros Rinc . . . . W 10
Dec. 20—Young Frankie, Pangasinan . . . . W 10
1976
Feb. 11—Jun Siilbason, Pasay City . . . . W 10
Apr. 7—Sandy Torres, R.m.c. Mla . . . . L 10
May 1—Arman Acta, Manila . . . . KO 1
Aug. 27—Rey Cellano, Manila . . . . KO 7
Dec. 31—Romy Roa, Cebu City . . . . KO 7
1977
Feb. 11—Rey Cellano, Manila . . . . W 10
Mar. 5—Benny Vargas, Cebu City . . . . W 10
Apr. 29—Ric Diamale, Manila . . . . KO 2
June 3—Arman Bangoyan, Manila . . . . W 10
Sept. 2—Choon-Ha Park, Rizal . . . . KO 7
Nov. 26—Teoruiz Dautiote, Masbate . . . . W 10
1978
Sept. 22—Ric Quijano, Manila . . . . W 10

Jan. 12—Sukothai Thanonchit, Manila .... W 10
Mar. 30—San Sacristan, Manila .... W 10
May 12—Gerron Porras, Davao City .... W 10
Aug. 10—Ric Diamale, Manila .... L 12
 (Philippine Junior Featherweight Title)
Oct. 5—San Sacristan, Manila .... W 10
Dec. 7—Venice Borkorsor, Manila .... W 10
1980
Feb. 10—Dommy Marolena, Cebu City .... L 10
Mar. 15—Ronald Sumalis, Davao City .... W 10
Dec. 20—Rey Naduma, Elorde .... KO 10

AZIZ ALAOUI
Belgian Welterweight
1980
Mar. 21—Marco Giuliani, Cheratte .... D 6
Sept. 19—Philippe Parent, Elouges .... L 6

BEN ALDEGUER
Filipino Flyweight
1975
—Naduma Junior, Cebu City .... W 10
—Francisco Cruz, Manila .... KO by 8
Sept. 30—Al Gutierrez, Manila .... W 10
1796
Feb. 28—Tanny Simbajon, Ormoc City .... W 10
—Julius Gozaga, Cebu City .... KO 6
Dec. 8—Franco Torregassa, Cagayan de Oro ...... L 10
1977
(Inactive)
1978
Feb. 11—Andy Balaba, Cebu City .... W 10
May 6—Siony Carupo, Cebu City .... D 12
 (For Filipino Junior Flyweight Title)
1979
Mar. 18—Demetrio Alferez, Cebu City .... W 10
Apr. 21—Melchor Dessi, Baguio City .... L 10
May 18—Mal Espanola, DiPolog City .... W 10
June 3—Demetrio Alferez, Cebu City .... W 10
July 15—Melchor Degsi, Cebu City.............. W 10
Sept. 8—Ric Barimbad, Santos City .... W 10
Nov. 17—Ver Libradilla, Santos City............ D 10
1980
Feb. 10—Andy Balaba, Cebu City .... D 10

PETE ALFEREZ
Filipino Lightweight
1978
Feb. 4—Joe Lim, Cebu City .... KO by 7
May 6—Winnie Guinieta, Cebu City .... KO 2
Aug. 5—Jimmy Abarca, Cebu City .... KO 3
Sept. 27—Jimmy Leonar, Iligan City............ KO 6
Nov. 4—Joe Lim, Cebu City...................... W 10
1979
Jan. 7—Rolando Navarette, Cebu City........ KO by 2
Mar. 30—Joe Lim, Manila..................... KO by 9
Oct. 5—Lito Pena, Manila.................... KO by 4
1980
Feb. 1—Star Lantapan, Manila .... KO by 4
Sept. 7—Nilo Acido, De Oro City .... KO by 4

MOHAMMED ALI
Ghanan Middleweight
Residing in England
1978
Oct. 9—Carl Bailey, Middlesborough .... KO 8
1979
Feb. 21—Jimmy Harrington, Cambridge .... KO 3
Apr. 23—Roger Ryder, Reading .... W 6
May 17—Roger Ryder, London .... W 6
June 28—Paul Baekgarrd, Randers .... L 6
Oct. 17—Gordon Stracey, London .... KO 6
Nov. 26—Art Brown, Birmingham .... W 6
Dec. 10—Art Brown, Birmingham .... KO 6
1980
Feb. 5—Jim Fenwick, Wolverhampton .... D 4
Feb. 20—Jim Fenwick, Evesham .... KO 4
Mar. 13—Redmond Everard, Birkenhead .... W 6
June 3—Mike Burton, Aylesbury .... KO by 3

ADEY ALLEN
British Junior Lightweight
1978
Mar. 6—George Metcalf, Manchester .... KO 3
Mar. 15—Gary Collins, Solihull .... W 6
Mar. 31—Brian Snagg, Liverpool .... KO 4
Apr. 12—George Metcalf, Evesham .... W 4
Apr. 17—Steve Ward, London .... W 6
May 8—Kevin Quinn, Manchester .... L 6
Sept. 11—Brian Snagg, Liverpool .... L 6
Sept. 18—George O'Neill, Wolverhampton ..... L disq. 3
Oct. 2—Granville Allen, Nantwich .... L 8
Nov. 27—Hugh Smith, Glasgow .... L 8

1979
Sept. 11—Chris Sanigar, London .... L 6
Oct. 15—Billy Aherne, Manchester............... W 8
Nov. 15—Kevin Quinn, Caister................... W 8
1980
Jan. 7—John Mount, Manchester .... W 8
Mar. 10—Jarvis Greenidge, Wolverhampton .... L 6
Apr. 21—Barry Price, Nottingham .... W 8
May 8—Granville Allen, Solihull .... L 8
July 8—Roger Guest, Wolverhampton .... W 8
Oct. 19—Roger Guest, Birmingham .... W 10
 (Won Midlands Area Junior Lightweight Title)

DAVE ALLEN
British Welterweight
1978
Sept. 27—Jimmy Smith, Rotherham .... W 4
Oct 2—Marty Jacobs, Liverpool .... KO 5
Oct. 31—Paul Clemit, Barnsley .... KO 5
Nov. 14—Dave Taylor, Birkenhead .... L 8
1979
Jan. 17—Lee Hartshorn, Stoke..................... L 6
Mar. 22—Terry Welch, Liverpool .... L 6
Mar. 28—Tommy Thomas, Kettering .... D 4
Apr. 9—Dai Davies, Nottingham .... KO 4
May 16—Derek Nelson, Sheffield .... D 8
May 21—Derek Nelson, Birmingham .... W 8
June 18—Jess Harper, Manchester................. KO 6
Sept. 26—Dave Douglas, Sheffield .... W 8
Nov. —Johnny Elliott, Southend................ W 8
Dec. 4—Les Wint, Southend .... W 8
1980
Jan. 6—Richard Avery, Burslem .... W 8
Feb. 5—Vic Jackson, Southend .... W 8
Mar. 11—Joe Oke, Southend .... D 8
Mar. 19—Tommy Wright, Doncaster .... W 8
May 14—Billy Waith, Burslem .... L 8
June 16—Dennis Pryce, Burslem .... KO 5

GRANVILLE ALLEN
British Junior Welterweight
1977
July 5—Ray Thomas, Wolverhampton .... KO 4
Sept. 20—Mickey Durkin, Southend .... L 6
Oct. 11—Mickey Bell, Coventry .... W 6
Oct. 31—Ian Pickersgill, Birmingham .... KO 2
Nov. 30—Tommy Glencross, Wolverhampton .. W disq. 6
Dec. 14—Tommy Glencross, Kingston .... W 8
1978
Jan. 23—Mickey Bell, London .... KO by 8
Mar. 6—Dill Collins, London .... W 8
Apr. 4—Marty Jacobs, London .... KO 2
Apr. 21—Davy Campbell, Enniskillen .... W 8
Oct. 2—Adey Allen, Nantwich .... W 8
Oct. 23—Eric Purkis .... D 8
Oct. 31—Tommy Dunn, Birmingham .... W 8
1979
Jan. 22—Dave McCabe, Wolverhampton .... LD 7
Jan. 29—Chris Sanigar, Glasgow .... KO by 3
Feb. 19—Tommy Dunn, Wolverhampton .... KO 7
Mar. 21—Jimmy Roberts, Stoke .... L 8
Oct. 15—Jeff Prichard, Wolverhampton........... W 8
1980
Feb. 20—Dennis Sullivan, Evesham .... W 8
Mar. 18—Roy Varden, Wolverhampton .... W 8
May 8—Adey Allen, Solihull .... W 8
July 14—Alan Lamb, London .... KO by 5

HARRY (POMPEY) ALLEN
British Heavyweight
1979
Dec. 3—Mick Chmilowskyz, Marylebone ...... KO by 2
1980
Jan. 28—Paul Newman, Hove .... KO by 2
Oct. 22—Glen Stevens, Doncaster .... KO 4

TONY ALLEN
British Light Heavyweight
1974
May 1—Dave Nelson, Birmingham .... W 6
May 6—Billy Brooks, London .... W 8
June 13—Terry Graham, Wolverhampton .... KO 4
Sept. 16—Steve Walker, Birmingham .... LF 5
Dec. 4—Dave Mullins, London .... L 6
Dec. 16—Carl Watson, London .... W 6
1975
Jan. 20—Tony Roberts, Manchester .... KO 4
Feb. 3—Pat Thopmpson, Mayfair .... W 8
Feb. 10—Alan Minter, Mayfair .... L 8
Feb. 17—Phil Martin, Manchester .... L 8
Mar. 12—Dave Parris, Solihull .... W 8
Mar. 24—Steve Foley, Bedford .... W 8
May 16—Steve Hill, Blackpool .... L 8

1976

Jan.	14—Steve Foley, Solihull	W	8
Jan.	28—George Gray,Birmingham	W	8
Feb.	16—Terry Armstrong, Manchester	LF	4
Feb.	25—Dave Parris, Birmingham	W	8
Mar.	13—Mukeba Apolosa, S. Brieuc	KO	6
Nov.	5—Steve Walker, Coventry	W	8
Dec.	12—Robert Amory, Chantilly	KO by	4

1977

Feb.	14—Rab Affleck, Birmingham	KO by	6
Apr.	24—Dave Mullings, Birmingham	W	5
May	4—Vernon Scott, Solihull	W	8
July	10—Eddy Fenton, Birmingham	W	8
Oct.	19—Pat McCann, Kingston	L	8

1978

May	23—Harry White, Leicester	W	8

1979

Feb.	21—Steve Fenton, Evesham	KO	•9
May	2—Eddie Fenton, Solihull	LF	7

1980

Apr.	28—Danny Lawford, Birmingham	L disq.	5

WINSTON ALLEN
British Heavyweight

1978

Apr.	20—Terry Chard, London	L	6
May	16—Terry Chard, Newport	KO	3
Sept.	11—Allan Bagley, Birmingham	W	6
Nov.	2—John DePledge, Ebbw Vale	W	8
Nov.	15—David Collins, Merthyr	KO	1
Nov.	15—John Depledge, Merthyr	W	3

1979

Jan.	17—Terry O'Connor, Solihull	L	8
*Jan.	22—Danny Miller, London	W	3
*Jan.	22—Bobby Hennessey, London	KO by	1
	*(Fought twice on same night — Mini-tourney)		
Mar.	16—Derek Simpkin, Bradford	W	8
Apr.	3—David Pearce, Caerphilly	L	6
June	18—Manny Gabriel, Windsor	KO by	1
Oct.	4—Bob Young, Ebbw Vale	L	6
Oct.	23—Andy Palmer, Londra	KO	2
Nov.	29—Glenn Adair, Ebbw Vale	L	8

1980

Feb.	7—Pete Holm, Randers	KO	3
Mar.	4—Stan McDermott, Wimbley	KO	1
May	1—Jean Pierre Coopmans, Izegem	KO	1
June	21—Alfredo Evangelista, Barcelona	L	8
Oct.	1—Neville Meade, Swansea	KO by	2
	(For Welsh Heavyweight Title)		

JOSE LUIS ALVAREZ
Spanish Middleweight

1976

Apr.	24—Daniel Bouleux, Argeteuil	L	6
May	14—Mushapata Kubangu, Ginevra	W	6
Nov.	2—Fred Coranson, Dunkerque	L	6

1977

Aug.	12—Emilio Garcia, Macotera	KO by	5
Nov.	12—Jose Silva, La Coruna	LF	6
Nov.	19—Jose Manuel Menendez, Aviles	L	6
Dec.	3—Juan Rubio, Lugo	L	5

1978

Feb.	4—Alberto Ramirez, Lugo	D	6
May	24—Jose Fernandez Punales, Lugo	W	8
July	14—Orlando De Jesus, Madrid	W	6
Sept.	3—Illuminado Diez, Villaba	W	8

1979

Nov.	3—Arnoldo Olivares, Lugo	W	8
Dec.	8—Ignacio Gorostidi, Lugo	W	8

1980

Jan.	12—Alfredo Naveiras, La Coruna	KO by	5
	(For Spanish Middleweight Title)		
June	20—Scassino Ferreira, Madrid	KO by	1

JOSE RAMON (CABANIN) ALVAREZ
Spanish Junior Middleweight
Record from, 1973-1976: Won 8 Lost 3 Draw 3

1977-1978
(Inactive)

1979

Oct.	12—Emilio Molero, Oviedo	D	6

1980

Mar.	8—Juan Melian, Leon	D	4

ADONI AMANA
Spanish Middleweight

1976

Nov.	13—Manuel Rico, Bilboa	KO	4
Dec.	3—Francisco Carmona, Madrid	KO	8

1977

Mar.	9—Tekyla Rodri, Bilboa	KO	2
Apr.	1—Juan Rubio Melero, Bilboa	KO	5
June	1—Daniel Makre, Bilboa	KO	2

July	15—Manuel Rico, Madrid	KO	2
Aug.	20—Jose Carlo Diaz, Jeres de la Fontera	W	8
Sept.	9—Jose Lozano, Madrid	KO	4
Oct.	7—Jose Hernandez, Barcelona	W	12
	(Spanish Junior Middleweight Title)		
Nov.	5—Tiger Quaye, Bilboa	W	8
Dec.	25—Aroldo Olivares, Bilboa	KO	1

1978

Jan.	14—Mushapata Kubangu, Eibar	W	8
Feb.	4—Joel Bonnetaz, Bilboa	KO	4
Apr.	14—Leon Galan, Bilbo	KO	4
	(Spanish Junior Middleweight Title)		
Mar.	11—Pascual Zito, Santander	W	8
May	31—Jacques Ghinon, Bilboa	KO	5
Sept.	9—Billy Waith, Bilboa	KO	6
Oct.	5—Pat Thomas, Bilboa	W	10
Nov.	11—Pat Thomas, Zele	W	8
Dec.	2—Joe Lally, Bilboa	KO	5

1979

Jan.	6—Ali Guechin, Bilboa	KO	4
Feb.	3—Tyrone Phelps, S. Sebastiano	W	8
Feb.	19—Angel Ortiz, Barcelona	KO	2
Mar.	3—Joseph Pires, Malaga	KO	1
Mar.	17—Johnny Davis, Barcelona	KO	5
May	5—Angel Ortiz, Eibar	KO	5
June	6—Marijan Benes, Bilboa	KO by	8
	(For European Junior Middleweight Title)		
July	24—Arnoldo Olivares, Villafranca	W	8
Aug.	11—Jose Melendez, S. Sebastiano	KO	6
Sept.	10—Young Griffo, Bilboa	KO	2
Oct.	13—Jose Ramirez, S. Sebastiano	W	8
Nov.	10—Jose Hernandez, Salamanca	L	10
Dec.	8—Manducai Ali, Salamanca	KO	1

1980

Jan.	6—George Lee, Bilboa	W	6
Feb.	14—Henry Rhiney, Bilboa	W	10
Apr.	25—Alfredo Naveiras, Barcelona	W	12
	(Won Spanish Middleweight Title)		
May	23—Johnny Lira, Palma di Mallorca	W	8
July	22—Dum Dum Pacheco, Bilboa	KO	9
Aug.	9—Frank Medina, San Sebastian	KO	4
Sept.	6—Scasino Ferreira, Bilboa	KO	5
Nov.	17—Seasak Muangsurin, Bilboa	W	10

ALBERT AMATLER
French Lightweight

1972

Jan.	15—Amar Arslane, S. Dizier	KO	6
Jan.	20—Jean Levasseur, Paris	KO	5
Feb.	3—Souleymahe Ba-Thierno, Paris	W	6
Feb.	12—Alain Laine, Valence	W	4
Feb.	24—Abdelkader Bouguetaib, Paris	L	6
Mar.	15—Sergio Emili, Lione	KO by	4
Apr.	11—Michele Siracusa, Milano	KO	5
Apr.	5—Ali Mebarki, Voiron	D	6
May	13—Boulem Blidi, Vienna	W	6
June	30—Manuel Alcala, Marsiglia	W	8
Dec.	3—Hamed Jelidi, Villeurbanne	KO	4
Dec.	10—Roger Jabeneau, S. Etienne	KO	1

1973

Jan.	14—Antoine Lasala, Villeurbanne	W	6
Feb.	1—Kesmane Larbi, Paris	KO	2
Feb.	8—Mohammed Alik, Paris	KO	5
Feb.	15—Tahar Azziz, Paris	W	6
Mar.	2—Franco Soro, Grenoble	W	6
Apr.	14—Soulemahe Ba-Thierno, Vienna	KO	5
May	22—Vernon Sollas, London	KO by	5
Oct.	7—Roland Cazeaux, Lione	KO	5
Nov.	22—Souleymahe Ba-Thierno, Paris	W	8

1974

Jan.	18—Helenio Ferrera, Milano	L	8
Feb.	16—Roland Cazeaux, Lione	KO	4
Mar.	1—Ugo Poli, Novara	LF	3
Apr.	26—Michel Jamet, Lione	KO	5
May	3—Natale Vezzoli, Milano	L	8
May	27—Leonard Tavarez, Paris	L	8
Oct.	4—Raymond Libbrecht, Lione	KO	4
Oct.	25—Jacky Bihin, Lione	KO	1
Dec.	7—Daniel Verdmandere, Lione	D	12
	(For French Featherweight Title)		

1975

Jan.	10—Helenio Ferreira, Milano	KO by	4
Jan.	24—Mario Oliveira, Annecy	W	8
Feb.	16—Miguel Araujo, Villeurbane	W	8
Apr.	25—Carlos Foldes, Annecy	D	10
Sept.	26—Ali Messaoud, Lione	KO	3
Oct.	24—Michele Siracusa, Marsiglia	L	10
Oct.	31—Jean Pierre Hainault, Villeurbane	KO	2
Dec.	27—Michel Lefebvre, Villeurbane	W	12
	(Won French Featherweight Title)		

1976

Mar.	6—Helenio Ferreira, Lione	L	10
Apr.	24—Guy Caudron, Chasse	KO	9
	(For French Featherweight Title)		

253

Dec.	3—Mario Oliveira, Lione....................	W 10
Dec.	20—Adolfo Osses, Nizza......................	L 10

1977

Feb.	12—Giovanni Cavazzini, Lione...............	W 8
Feb.	26—Giuseppe Agate, Nizza...................	W 8
Apr.	1—Natale Vezzoli, Brescia ....KO by 11	
	(For European Junior Lightweight Title)	
Nov.	12—Gerard Jacob, Lione....................	KO 11
	(For French Featherweight Title)	

1978

Feb.	18—Salvatore Fabrizio, Villeurbane	KO 5
Mar.	18—Sergio Emili, Villeurbane..............	KO 4
May	26—Michel Lefebvre, Berck	KO by 10
	(Lost French Featherweight Title)	
July	15—Roberto Castanon, La Coruna	KO by 5

1979

(Inactive)

1980

Feb.	15—Alain LeFol, Villeurbanne	W 10
Mar.	28—Gilbert Helluin, Villeurbanne	KO 4
Apr.	26—Joel Moulin, Villeurbanne..............	KO 4
July	12—Leopold Agbazo, Cotonou	KO by 2
Oct.	10—Georges Cotin, Villeurbanne	WF 4
Nov.	15—Dan M'Putu, Dunkirk	KO by 7

CESAR AMAZAN
Filipino Bantamweight
1977

July	15—Cesar Ligan, Manila	KO 10

1978

Mar.	10—Star Dayanan, Manila	KO 4
May	12—Didik Moeljadi, Manila	W 10
July	19—Teddy Galler, Araneta	L 10
Dec.	15—Danilo Berdida, Manila	W 10

1979

Mar.	10—Noe Canini, Manila	KO by 2
June	15—Eddie Miral, Manila	KO 10
Sept.	—Larry Enriquez, Manila	KO 7
Nov.	16—Rocky Constantino, Manila	KO 7
Nov.	24—Glen Orlano, Manila	KO by 2
Dec.	14—Ely Barrios, Manila	KO 7

1980

Jan.	25—Flash Gapasin, Manila	W 10
Mar.	21—Roger dela Rosa, Manila	KO 7
May	30—Ronald Sumalys, Manila	L 12
	(For Philippine Bantamweight Title)	
Sept.	26—Lito Molina, Quezon City	W 10

ROMAL AMBROSE
British Middleweight
1977

Mar.	24—Cyril Bishton, Leicester	W 4
May	2—Dave Cammis, Walworth	L 4
May	27—Dennis Price, Digbeth	L 4
Nov.	16—Roger Guest, London	L 4
Dec.	6—Mohammed Akran, Leeds	W 6

1978

Feb.	7—Tony Hill, Coventry	L 4
Apr.	10—Clifton Wallace, Nottingham	KO 2
Apr.	17—Dennis Powell, Reading	KO 1
Sept.	11—Joey Sauders, Liverpool	KO 5
Sept.	18—Richard Kenyon, Manchester	KO 5
Oct.	10—Mick Morris, Wolverhampton	KO by 3
Nov.	30—Richard Kenyon, Gaister	KO 8

1979

Feb.	21—Paul Schutt, Evesham	KO 7
Mar.	12—Dave Owens, Manchester	W 8
Nov.	29—Dave Davies, Liverpool	KO 5

1980

Feb.	5—Martin McEwan, Wolverhampton	W 10
	(Retained Midlands Area Middleweight Title)	
Mar.	19—Glen McEwan, Solihull ....KO by 10	
	(Lost Midlands Area Middleweight Title)	
Oct.	20—Glen McEwan, Birmingham	KO by 6
	(For Midlands Area Middleweight Title)	

EIJI AMINO
Japanese Junior Featherweight
1980

Mar.	13—Fumiharu Honma, Tokyo	L 6
Dec.	16—Naojiro Toda, Tokyo	W 8

ROBERT AMORY
French Light Heavyweight
Born: August 25, 1948
1971

Mar.	11—Claude Courteille, Paris	KO 2
Mar.	25—Joel Leguern, Paris	L 6
	—Jose Guillois, ...	KO 5
	—Titi Larbi, ...	KO 5

1972

Feb.	4—Casimir Duda, Compiegne	KO 2
Mar.	9—Jean Claude Genno, Paris	W 5
Mar.	23—Daniel Latartre, Paris	W 6

254

Apr.	6—Alain Riviere, Paris	W 6
Apr.	28—Christian Joan, Caompiegne	KO 5
Oct.	10—Christian Rubin, Paris	KO 7
Dec.	2—Angelo Ivkovic, Blois	W 6
Dec.	20—Robert Brunel, Throurotte	KO 6

1973

Jan.	27—Angelo Ivkovic, Compiegne	KO 5
Mar.	17—Lionel Mercier, Thourotte	KO 7
Apr.	14—William Poitrimol, Compiegne	KO 7
May	5—Abdel Memba, Thourotte............	W 8
Oct.	16—Jean Tshikuna, Paris................	W 8
Nov.	2—Pascal Di Benedetto, Compiegne	W 10
Dec.	8—Antonio Rinasti, Thourotte...........	KO 7

1974

Jan.	26—Jean-Claude Capitolin, Compiegne	W 12
Apr.	5—Erwin Josepha, Compiegne	KO 3
May	11—Christian Poncelet, St. Quentin	L 12
	(French Light Heavyweight Title)	
June	22—Pascal Di Benedetto, Compiegne	L 10
Dec.	20—Jose Maver, Compiegne	KO 1

1975

Jan.	25—Alain Riviere, Compiegne.............	W 10
Mar.	8—Serge Jagot, St. Brieuc................	L 10
Mar.	28—Vlado Blazetic, Compiegne............	KO 3
June	20—Mate Parlov, Milan.................	KO by 5
Oct.	11—Jean Tshikuna, Compiegne	W 10
Oct.	30—Frankie Evans, Paris..................	L 8
Dec.	6—Heinz Dieter Schwartz, Compiegne ...	KO 4

1976

Jan.	24—Arno Prick, Compiegne	W 10
Jan.	30—Arno Prick, Compiegne	W 10
Feb.	7—Onelio Grando, Pordenone	L 6
Mar.	20—Victor Attivor, Thourette...........	L 10
Oct.	16—Yannick Dufour, Compiegne	KO 9
Dec.	10—Tony Allen, Chantilly	KO 4

1977

Jan.	28—Christian Poncelot, Compiegne	W 12
	(French Light Heavyweight Title)	
Mar.	19—Freddie De Kerpel, Bruxelles	KO 6
Apr.	29—Ivan Matekovic, Morges	KO 8
June	18—Michel Dylbaytis, Fresnes sur Escaut ...	KO 11
	(French Light Heavyweight Title)	
Oct.	7—Ba Sounkala, Bamako	L 10

1978

Jan.	21—Gerald Bois, Compiene	KO 12
	(French Light Heavyweight Title)	
Mar.	16—Mustapha Wassaja, Copenhagen	L 8
Apr.	14—Gregory Downes, Essen	D 10
June	9—Hocine Tafer, Grenoble	KO by 12
	(French Light Heavyweight Title)	
Nov.	4—Hocine Tafer, Compiegne	KO by 7

1979

Jan.	27—Joze Centa, Compiegne	KO 1
Mar.	31—Laurent Zardi, Compiegne	KO 6
May	28—Rudi Koopmans, Netherland	KO by 10
	(European Light Heavyweight Title)	
Dec.	1—Ibelo Moano, Bonneovie	D 8

Jan.	28—Shaun Chalcraft, Rotterdam	L 8
Feb.	10—Andre Mongelema, Compiegne	KO by 2
Nov.	29—Gino Freo, Padova	L 8

KOSEI ANAN
Japanese Bantamweight
1976

May	25—Toshiaki Sato, Tokyo	KO 1
June	27—Tetsuo Matsumura, Tsuchiura	KO 1
Aug.	20—Seitaro Uehara, Tokyo	KO 1
Sept.	7—Eiji Amino, Tokyo	W 4
Sept.	30—Terauki Arai, Tokyo	KO 1
Oct.	24—Hirakur Kameo, Tokyo	KO 1
Nov.	15—Shuji Hirata, Tokyo	D 4
Dec.	23—Kazuhito Eikura, Tokyo	KO 2

1977

Feb.	21—Eiji Hamada, Tokyo	KO 1
Apr.	25—Katsuhiko Takuno, Tokyo	KO 7
May	13—Gosho Ofu, Nagoya	L 8
July	5—Uichiro Hayashida, Tokyo	KO 6
Sept.	10—Uichiro Hayashida, Mito City	L 10
Dec.	15—Hideo Kobayashi, Tokyo	D 10

1978

Feb.	12—Shiro Hiromori, Tokyo	W 10
May	19—Satoru Uehara, Tokyo	W 10
Aug.	1—Satoru Uehara, Tokyo	KO 4
Nov.	25—Joe Araki, Tokyo	W 10
	(Japanese Bantamweight Title)	

1979

Feb.	11—Futaro Tanaka, Tokyo	W 10
Mar.	24—Jo Araki, Tokyo.....................	W 10
May	21—Isao Okahashi, Tokyo	W 10
July	16—Hurricane Teru, Tokyo	KO by 2
	(JBC Bantamweight Title)	
Oct.	5—Hurricane Teru, Miyagi Ken.............	L 10
	(JBC Bantamweight Title)	

1980

Mar.   13—Bunji Ando, Tokyo .... L 10

BRIAN ANDERSON
British Welterweight
1980

Apr.   14—Jeff Stanley, Manchester .... W 6
May   7—Jeff Aspell, Liverpool .... W 6
May   28—Dave Ward, Cramlington .... L disq. 4
July   8—Cliff Gilpin, Wolverhampton .... L 8
Sept.   16—Dominic Bergonzi, Wembley .... D 6
Sept.   29—Kevin Walsh, Chesterfield .... D 8
Oct.   16—Dennis Sullivan, Bolton .... W 8
Oct.   29—Robbie Smith, Burslem .... W 6

TORBEN ANDERSON
Danish Middleweight
1978

Jan.   25—Johnny Elliott, Copenhagen .... W 4
Aug.   10—Joe Lally, Glyngore .... W 4
Sept.   14—Jimmy Pickard, Randers .... W 4
Nov.   11—Scott Burnett, Copenhagen .... KO 1
Dec.   7—Dave Owens, Copenhagen .... W 8
1979
Feb.   15—Oscar Angus, Randers .... L 6
Mar.   15—Idrissa Konate, Copenhagen............. W 6
May   24—Wolfgang Gans, Randers .... W 6
June   28—Billy Lauder, Randers .... W 6
Sept.   6—Mike Copp, Copenhagen .... W 8
Oct.   11—Marce Scane, Copenhagen .... KO 2
Dec.   6—Gerry Young, Copenhagen .... W 6
1980
Feb.   7—Albert Hillman, Randers .... KO 4
Feb.   29—Mimun Mohatar, Odense .... W 8
Apr.   17—Henry Rhiney, Copenhagen .... W 8
June   12—Gert Steyn, Randers .... KO by 8
Sept.   6—Dennis Price, Aarhus .... W 6
Oct.   17—Tony Britton, Copenhagen .... W 8

WELCOME ANDERSON
South African Welterweight
1980

Apr.   28—Johannes Gwala, Durban .... KO 4
May   19—Neil Walker, Durban .... L 4
Nov.   1—Bhekani Dludia, Stanger .... W 6
Nov.   10—Johannes Gwala, Durban .... KO 3

BUNJI ANDO
Japanese Junior Featherweight
1980

Mar.   13—Kosei Anan, Tokyo .... W 10
July   6—Hiroyuki Iwamoto, Tokyo .... W 10
        (Won Japanese Junior Featherweight Title)
Oct.   5—Hiroyuki Iwamoto, Tokyo .... L 10
        (Lost Japanese Junior Featherweight Title)

DENNIS ANDRIES
British Light Heavyweight
1978

May   16—Ray Pearce, Newport .... KO 1
June   1—Mark Cumber, Doncaster .... KO 1
June   20—Bonny McKenzie, Southend .... L 8
Sept.   18—Ken Jones, London .... W 6
Oct.   31—Neville Estaban, Barnsley .... W 6
Nov.   14—Les McAteer, Birkenhead .... D 8
Nov.   22—Garfield McEwan, Stoke .... KO 7
Dec.   4—Tom Collins, Southend .... W 8
1979
Jan.   22—Bunny Johnson, Wolverhampton .... L 10
Jan.   30—Tom Collins, London .... KO 6
Apr.   5—Francis Hand, Liverpool .... KO 8
June   6—Bonny McKenzie, Burslem .... W 8
Sept.   17—Johnny Waldron, Mayfair .... W 10
1980
Feb.   27—Bunny Johnson, Burslem .... L 15
        (For British Light Heavyweight Title)
Apr.   17—Mustafa Wasajja, Copenhagen .... L 8
June   18—Chris Lawson, Burslem .... KO 8

MARINO ANGELI
Italian Junior Lightweight
1978

Jan.   27—Augusto Quadri, Faenza .... D 6
Mar.   3—Antonio Germano, Lugo .... KO 5
July   8—Rosario Pomponi, Ostia .... D 6
Nov.   3—Gregorio Ciancaglioni, Forli .... WF 5
Dec.   26—Mario Ficano, Bologna .... W 6
1979
June   8—Abass Macauley, Ravenna .... WF 6
Dec.   30—Abass Macauley, Forli .... W 6
1980
Mar.   15—Franco Siddu, Forli .... W 6

Apr.   24—Eloy De Souza, Forli .... D 8
Oct.   4—Marco Boero, Cagliari .... D 6
Dec.   3—Mario Tiano, Forli .... W 8
Dec.   19—Alfredo Reininger, Latina .... KO 6

RUFFINO ANGULO
French Middleweight
1978

Nov.   24—Andre Genasi, Villanave .... KO 6
1979
Apr.   6—Rhida Hakimi, Villanave .... KO 2
Dec.   10—Daniel Hyvon, Paris................... KO 4
Dec.   21—Maurice Renaud, Agen .... D 6
1980
Feb.   15—Mauricio Da Cruz, Bordeoux .... W 6
Oct.   18—Maurice Renaud, Villeneuve .... W 8
Dec.   6—Idrissa Konate, Villeneuve .... KO 4

OSCAR ANGUS
Aylesbury, England Middleweight
Born: Feb. 4, 1953, Jamaica
1973

Sept.   5—Mick Lock, London..................... KO 2
Sept.   26—Dave Nelson, Solihull.................. W 6
Oct.   24—Henry Cooper, Stoke................... W 6
Nov.   6—Joey Gammon, Hemel Hempstead .... W 6
Nov.   26—Dave Nelson, London .... W 6
Dec.   10—Billy Brooks, London .... W 8
1974
Jan.   7—Jeff Burns, Piccadilly .... W 8
Mar.   11—Tim McHugh, Mayfair................. L 6
Mar.   27—Joe Gregory, Southend .... D 6
May   13—Joe Gregory, Mayfair .... W 8
Oct.   16—Lloyd Gardner, London................ D 6
Oct.   29—Colin Davies, London................. L 8
Dec.   5—Mick Hussey, London .... D 6
1975
Jan.   6—Joe Lally, Hemel Hempstead .... KO by 1
Feb.   18—Peter Cain, Bethnal Green .... KO by 7
Mar.   13—Trevor Francis, Southend .... L 8
July   8—Mike Manley, Caerphilly............... W 8
Oct.   25—Claude Martin, St. Malo .... L 8
Nov.   25—Kirkland Laing, London .... L 6
1976
Jan.   19—John Rushton, Mayfair .... W 8
Feb.   3—Mick Hussey, London................. KO 3
Feb.   20—Peter Wulf, Hamburg .... L 10
Mar.   15—Kevin Finnegan, London .... L 8
Apr.   5—Carl Thomas, London .... W 8
Apr.   12—Rudi Koopmans, Rotterdam .... LF 3
Apr.   26—Rudi Koopmans, Amsterdam .... L 8
May   17—Errol McKenzie, Manchester .... L 8
June   4—Elio Calcabrini, Milano .... L 8
June   21—Errol McKenzie, London .... L 8
Sept.   14—Billy Knight, London.................. L 8
Nov.   15—Kevin Finnegan, London .... L 8
1977
Feb.   1—Jean Claude Warusfel, Paris .... L 8
Oct.   6—Jan Magdziarz, Southsea .... KO by 8
Nov.   30—Tony Sibson, Wolverhampton ...... KO by 6
1978
Feb.   21—Young McEwan, London .... D 8
Feb.   28—Roy Gumbs, Atlesbury .... D 8
Mar.   20—Carl Speare, London .... KO 4
Apr.   3—Roy Gumbs, London .... KO by 3
Nov.   17—Keith Bussey, Wembley .... L 8
Dec.   11—Bonny McKenzie, London .... L 8
1979
Feb.   15—Torben Andersen, Randers .... W 6
Mar.   17—Franz Amping, Banja Luka .... W 8
Apr.   7—Raymond Langewouters, Bruxelles .. KO by 7
Sept.   18—Mike Copp, Lewisham .... W 8
Oct.   23—Robbie Davies, Blackpool .... L 8
1980
Feb.   23—Michel Stini, Moulinbeek .... L 8
Mar.   31—Alex Blanchard, Rotterdam .... KO by 2
Apr.   30—George Danahar, Aylesbury .... L 8

ROCKY ANOBLING
Filipino Welterweight
1978

Mar.   4—Fred Pastor, Angels City .... L 10
June   18—Rey Bustillos, Balawan .... KO by 2
Nov.   29—Young Dela Cruz, Clark Air Base ...... W 10
1979
Feb.   17—Mike De Guzman, Pampanga .... KO by 6
Mar.   24—Mar Alverio, Laguna .... KO by 8
Nov.   27—Erning Marin, Angels City............. D 10
1980
Jan.   5—Jun Sarana, Santos City .... KO 7
Feb.   10—Fernando Gloria, South Cotabato ...... KO 4
Feb.   17—Mike De Guzman, Manila .... KO by 6
Mar.   15—Boy Bernadas, Santos City .... KO by 6
June   12—Mike de Guzman, Angels City .... D 10

Aug. 30—Young dela Cruz, Angels City ...... KO by 1

MARTIN ANTICH
Spanish Flyweight
1976
Aug. 19—Raton Rodriquez, Madrid .... D 6
1977
July   2—Joseph Tiaba, Las Palmas .... D 6
Aug. 26—Valeriano Morales, Felantis .... W 6
Sept. 23—Jose L.R. Marquez, Palma Mallorca ...... L 8
Oct.   1—Valeriano Morales, Palma Mallorca ..... W 8
1978
Nov. 23—Luis de la Sarga, Barcelona .... L 6
1979
Feb. 25—German Yeste, Reus .... D 6
Mar. 16—Abdekader Esmain, Barcelona .... L 9
July   6—Raton Rodriguez, Palma de Mallorca .... D 8
Aug.   2—Raton Rodriguez, Mallorca .... W 6
Aug. 10—Jose A. Salinas, Luch .... L 8
Aug. 14—Vicente Rodriguez, Benidorm .... L 8
Sept. 15—Enrique Rodriguez, Cal Aviles .... L 12
        (Spanish Flyweight Title)
Oct. 13—German Yeste, Reus .... W 6
Oct. 27—Manuel Carrasco, La Coruna .... L 8
1980
Jan. 26—Angel Oliver, Zaragoza .... L 8
Feb. 29—Mike Irungi, Odense .... L 8

ANTONIO ANTINO
Italian Junior Welterweight
1978
Apr.   7—Patrizio Rubini, Milan.................. KO 3
July 14—Raimondo Riccio, Monte Morenzio .... W 6
Oct. 26—Alfonso Bonavita, Lecco .... W 6
Nov. 30—Franco Recupero, Calolziocorte .... W 4
1979
Feb. 23—Angelo Zanetti, Bolzano .... D 6
July   1—Antonio Germano, Merano .... W 6
July 27—Vincezo DiRuocco, Bolzano .... W 6
Dec. 15—Josia M. Da Sylva, Fabriano .... W 8
1980
May   31—Ignazio Fara, Lugano .... W 6

BERNARD ANTONE
German Light Heavyweight
1980
Apr.   4—Luc Gossens, Middelkerke .... KO by 5
May   5—Maik Krol, Rotterdam .... KO by 2
June 19—Robert Bosio, La Louviere .... L 8
July 27—Robert Desnouck, Bruxelles .... KO by 2

MARK APAI
New Guinea Welterweight
1977
June   2—Tony Aba, Port Moresby .... D 6
July 14—Phillip Sapak, Boroko .... KO 1
        (New Guinea Light Welterweight Title)
Oct.   6—Jeff Malcolm, Hoholo .... LF 4
        (Australian Light Welterweight Title)
Nov. 19—Martin Beni, Goroka .... KO 2
1978
Mar. 23—Steve Ayerst, Bougainville .... KO by 10
Sept. 8—Dave Sarago, Goroka .... W 10
Nov. 10—Dave Saraga, Townsville .... KO by 10
1979
June   1—Ceddy McGrady, Port Moresby .... KO 2
June 16—Francis Bale, Panguna .... W 10
Oct. 20—Joe Nitiva, Suva .... KO by 1
Nov. 17—Dave Agnew, Port Moresby .... W 10
1980
Feb.   9—Phil Cherrington, Panguna .... W 10
Apr. 26—Kerrt Bell, Goroka .... W 10
Nov. 28—Benny Tabua, Port Moresby .... KO 7

MAURICE APEANG
French Junior Lightweight
1973
May   26—Jose Cejudo, Papeete .... W 6
Oct. 31—Rimi Vaka, Papeete .... W 8
Nov. 24—Billy Graham, Papeete .... W 10
1974
(Inactive)
1975
May   14—Paul Blink, Papeete .... W 10
Oct. 31—Billy Mulholland, Papeete .... L 10
1976
May   28—Gilbert Orsaldo, Tahiti .... W 10
Dec. 18—Lionel Rose, Noumea .... KO 2
1977
Aug. 13—Billy Mulholland, Papeete .... W 10
1978
Feb.   4—Bingo Crooks, Grenoble .... W 10
Apr. 28—Alain LeFol, Grenoble .... W 8

June 30—Georges Cotin, Papeete .... KO 8
        (Won French Junior Lightweight Title)
Oct.   7—Domingo Gimenez, Papeete .... W 10
Nov. 17—Charles Jurietti, Papeete .... W 12
        (For French Junior Lightweight Title)
1979
Mar.   3—Cecilio Lastra, Papeete .... KO 4
May   13—Charles Jurietti, Valence .... L 12
        (Lost French Junior Lightweight Title)
Nov. 30—Charles Jurietti, Valence .... L 12
        (For French Junior Lightweight Title)
1980
Apr.   4—Samuel Meck, Papeete .... L 10
June 27—Samuel Meck, Papeete .... L 10

JEFFREY APHANE
S. African Junior Welterweight
1979
May   25—Terrence Molefe, Springs .... KO by 3
Sept. 7—Mankuna Mziwanele, Springs .... L 4
1980
Feb. 29—Frank Thobakgale, Springs .... D 4

GERMANO APOSTOLI
Italian Light Heavyweight
1978
June   9—Bruno Polloni, Brescia .... W 6
Aug.   2—Joze Centa, Maderno .... WF 5
Aug. 25—Noriano Bonacin, Orzinuovi .... W 6
Oct. 28—Drago Umicevich, Roncadelle .... KO 4
1979
Feb.   3—Ibelo Moano, Brescia .... KO 5
Aug.   3—Ray Opoka, Tuscolane .... KO 3
Sept. 21—Pier Paolo, Capezzone .... L 6
1980
Feb.   1—Gabriele Lazzari, Montova .... W 6
Mar. 17—Wilson Perez, Oslo .... D 6
Sept. 20—Ivan Simingia, Sebenico .... KO 3

YONICHI (YOHI) ARAI
Japanese Welterweight
1974
        —Arab Suga, Tokyo .... KO by 3
Nov. 17—Ichiro Izawa, Nara .... W 10
1975
Jan. 13—Kazuharu Arai, Osaka .... W 10
May   1—Ray Adio, Osaka .... KO 2
July 25—Hurber Watanabe, Tokyo .... KO by 8
Sept. 27—Ichiro Izawa, Osaka .... KO 3
1976
Jan. 16—Kazunori Shiratori, Osaka .... W 10
Apr. 15—Toshiharu Mori, Osaka .... KO 6
May   26—Wang Soo Lee, Osaka City .... KO 5
Oct.   1—Tetsuo Furuyama, Osaka .... L 10
        (Japanese Junior Welterweight Title)
1977
Jan. 13—Haruki Miyakawa, Osaka City .... KO 3
Apr. 10—Masahiro Kato, Tokyo .... L 10
Dec.   8—Ichiro Izawa, Osaka City .... KO 2
1978
Feb.   8—Missuo Kushikino, Osaka City .... L 10
Mar.   7—Chu Ho, Pusan .... L 12
June 21—Guts Ishimatsu, Tokyo .... W 10
Oct. 27—Ako Kameda, Tokyo .... L 10
        (Japanese Welterweight Title)
1979
(Inactive)
1980
Mar. 30—Mitsuo Kushikino, Osaka .... W 10
Sept. 9—Ryutaro Otsuki, Tokyo .... KO 4
Nov. 20—Kenzo Nishi, Hofu .... KO 2

JOE ARAKI
Japanese Bantamweight
1976
Aug.   8—Atomic Kurusu, Tokyo .... W 6
Sept. 26—Hayato Koito, Tokyo .... L 6
1977
Apr. 26—Eijiro Murata, Tokyo .... L 10
Aug. 26—Shuichi Isogami, Tokyo .... KO by 7
1978
Mar. 11—Tsuyoshi Okabe, Takamatsu City .... KO 1
May   7—Kenzo Takasugi, Hiroshima .... W 10
Aug. 25—Go Numata, Sendai City .... KO 6
        (Japanese Bantamweight Title)
Nov. 25—Kosei Anan, Tokyo .... L 10
        (Japanese Bantamweight Title)
1979
Mar. 24—Kosei Anan, Tokyo .... L 10
May   7—Takashi Uezu, Tokyo................. L 10
1980
Apr. 28—Hiroshi Fukui, Tokyo .... D 10
Oct. 21—Hurricane Teru, Tokyo .... KO by 3

BRUNO ARATI
Italian Light Heavyweight
1978
Nov.	9—Ignacio Gorostidi, Berne	W	6
Dec.	23—Noriano Bonacin, Berne	W	6

1979
Mar.	23—Gabriel Maillard, Berne	W	6
June	9—Helmut Ulka, Essen	D	6
Sept.	13—Luciano Bolis, Bern	W	6
Oct.	31—Jean Luc Lami, Berne	W	8
Dec.	14—Ibelo Moano, Berne	L	8

1980
June	14—Gabriele Lazzari, Bern	KO by	6

GAETANO ARDITO
French Middleweight
1980
Dec.	26—Cyrille Barbe, Firenze	KO	2

LUCIANO ARDIUNI
Italian Junior Welterweight
1979
May	12—Raffaele Di Lernia, Latina	KO by	6

1980
Feb.	29—Bruno Gubala, Rome	L	6

FRANCESCO ARESTI
Italian Welterweight
1978
Apr.	29—Giuseppe Juppa, Cagliari	W	6
May	27—Gerardo Scognamiglio, Oristano	KO	3
July	1—Augusto Quadri, Cagliari	W	2
Sept.	29—Gerardo Del Guacchio, Saniuri	KO	3
Dec.	1—Raimondo Riccio, Olbia	KO by	6

1979
June	9—Scipione Colaianni, Cagliari	W	6
July	28—Erwin Heiber, Munich	D	6
Sept.	5—Giovanni Maiorano, Fort Village	W	6
Dec.	21—Luigi Del Santo, Caglieri	KO	3

1980
Feb.	2—Vincenzo Bottigliero, Cagliari	KO	7
Mar.	8—Marco Francesco Gallo, Cagliari	W	8
Apr.	19—Jean Pierre Moreau, Cagliari	W	8
May	3—Luigi Martello, Cagliari	W	8
June	20—Ugo DiPietro, Cagliari	W	8
Aug.	15—Luiz Ribeiro, Portoscuso	W	8
Sept.	3—Claudio Pereyra, Santa Teresa	D	8
Oct.	31—Claudio Pereyra, Cagliari	D	8
Nov.	29—Benedito Santos, Cagliari	W	6
Dec.	27—Titmoteo Boizzoni, Cagliari	KO	7

OSAMU ARIMA
Japanese Flyweight
1980
Mar.	13—Yoji Asahina, Tokyo	KO	1
Oct.	16—Yoshiyuki Uchikoshi, Tokyo	KO by	3

DAVEY ARMSTRONG
British Middleweight
1977
Oct.	17—Billy Turkington, London	KO	1
Dec.	1—H.H. Thompson, London	KO by	3

1978
Nov.	27—Stan Thompson, Mayfair	W	6
Dec.	18—Owen Slue, London	W	6

1979
Feb.	26—Lloyd Gardner, London	KO	2
May	21—John Breen, Walworth	KO	2
June	26—Chris Coady, London	W	6
Dec.	4—Gordon George, Wembley	KO	2

1980
Apr.	1—Mick Morris, Wembley	KO	1
Oct.	14—Joe Jackson, London	L	6

ROBERT ARMSTRONG
British Welterweight
1980
Mar.	19—Kevin Walsh, Doncaster	KO	3
Apr.	29—Billy Ahearne, Stockport	KO by	1
June	11—Martin Bridge, Morecambe	W	8
July	30—Gerry White, Doncaster	L	6
Sept.	15—Kevin Walsh, Manchester	L	6
Oct.	22—Robert Thornton, Doncaster	KO	3

ARNEL ARROZAL
Filipino Flyweight
1976
	—Johnny Sato, Quezon City	W	10
June	19—Nene Jun, Davao City	W	10
	—Johnny Sato, Cebu City	W	10

1977
	—Danilo Berdida, Angeles City	W	10

June	24—Bernabe Villacampo, Manila	KO by	3
	(For Philippine Flyweight Title)		
	—George Pedroso, Angeles City	L	10

1978
Feb.	10—Tony Co, Manila	KO	5
Mar.	4—Oscar Gonzales, Angeles City	KO	5
Apr.	21—Chai-Yong Maungsurin, Manila	KO	10
June	30—Franco Torregozam, Manila	D	10
Oct.	14—Julius Gonzaga, Davao City	W	12
	(Philippine Flyweight Title)		

1979
Apr.	7—Bernabe Villacampo, Pampanga	KO	4
June	29—Siony Carupo, Manila	W	10
Oct.	19—William Develos, Quezon City	KO	6
	(Philippine Flyweight Title)		
Dec.	30—Danilo Inocian, Pampango	W	10

1980
Jan.	10—Chan-Hee Park, Seoul	L	15
	(For WBC Flyweight Title)		
May	16—Frank Cedeno, Manila	L	10
Aug.	30—Billy Abato, Angels City	W	10

STEVE ASEANG
Australian Featherweight
1978
Apr.	4—Steve Campbell, Kingsford	W	6
May	16—Theo James, Kingsford	W	6
May	31—Joey Collins, Brookvale	L	6
June	12—Wayne Berg, Cammeray	KO	6
June	27—Paul Barron, Kingsford	W	6
July	11—Paul Barron, Kingsford	W	8
July	26—Ezzard Charles, Brookvale	L	6
Aug.	7—Ezzard Charles, Cammeray	D	8
Oct.	31—Willie Leslie, Kingsford	W	8

1979
Jan.	30—Paul Barron, Kingsford	W	8
Sept.	1—Buddy Clare, Berkeley	W	6
Sept.	5—Buddy Clare, Brookvale	W	6
Sept.	25—Paul Baker, Kingsford	L	10

1980
Apr.	22—Paul Baker, Kingsford	L	6
May	21—Graham Bell, Mt. Pritchard	L	10
Oct.	16—Kirk Blair, Marrickville	L	8
Nov.	17—Ezzard Charles, Cronville	L	6

NIKONOR ASHIPALA
South African Welterweight
1980
Feb.	2—Johannes Modise, Kimberley	W	8
May	30—Zehonia Mlothshwa, Springs	W	4

JEFF ASPELL
British Welterweight
1979
Sept.	17—Wayne Barker, Manchester	L	6
Oct.	9—Mickey Mapp, Kensington	L	6
Oct.	16—Ricky Daniels, West Bremwich	KO	5
Oct.	29—Gary Newell, Wolverhampton	KO by	4
Nov.	28—Pat Smythe, Doncaster	WF	2
Dec.	3—Micky Mapp, Marylebone	L	6
Dec.	10—Dave Aspill, Piccadilly	KO	3

1980
Jan.	16—Ian Murray, Stoke	L	8
Jan.	22—Dave Sullivan, Caerphilly	L	6
Feb.	18—Dave Douglas, Birmingham	L	6
Apr.	23—Steve Henty, Hove	W	6
May	7—Brian Anderson, Liverpool	L	6
May	12—George Sutton, Reading	L	4
May	19—Dave Ward, Birmingham	KO	3
May	27—Gerry Young, Belfast	L	6
June	16—Billy Ahearne, Manchester	L	8
July	1—Dave Sullivan, Swindon	W	6
Aug.	12—Ian Murray, Gowerton	W	8
Sept.	15—Johnny Francis, Manchester	KO by	1
Oct.	20—Ian Murray, Birmingham	KO by	5

DAVE ASPILL
British Welterweight
1979
Oct.	17—Jeff Lee, Lewisham	L	6
Nov.	6—Micky Mapp, Kensington	L	6
Dec.	10—Jeff Aspel, Piccadilly	KO by	3

1980
Mar.	3—Lee Town, Hove	W	6
Mar.	11—Jimmy Smith, Southend	W	6
Mar.	24—Adrian Clamp, London	KO by	2
Apr.	29—Gary Petty, London	L	6

STAN ATHERTON
British Junior Welterweight
1979
Mar	2—Martin Bridge, Liverpool	W	6
Mar.	15—Steve Early, Solihull	L	6

Apr.	17—Martin Bridge, Bradford	D 6
May	18—Dave Taylor, Liverpool	W 6
Aug.	29—Eric Wood, Liverpool	L 6
Sept.	28—Eric Wood, Liverpool	W 6
Oct.	12—Najib Daho, Liverpool	W 6

1979

Feb.	12—Frank McCord, Manchester	W 6
Feb.	22—Tommy Wright, Liverpool	W 6
Mar.	15—Jesse Harper, Caister	W 6
Mar.	22—George Schofield, Liverpool	KO by 2
Apr.	30—Tommy Wright, Barnsley	L 8

1980

Mar.	27—Terry Welch, Liverpool	L 8

BERND AUGUST
German Heavyweight
Born: Feb. 22, 1952
1973

Mar.	2—Herbert Ficks, Berlin	KO 1
Mar.	30—Manfred Ackers, Oldenburg	KO 2
Apr.	27—Ray Adonis, Berlin	WF 2
May	11—Ferenc Christofcsak, Wiesbaden	KO 2
June	3—Arno Pryx, Berlin	KO 3
Aug.	31—Horst Lang, Lubeck	KO 1
Sept.	28—Billy Joyner, Berlin	W 8
Oct.	26—Jose Maria Echevarria, Hamburg	W 6
Nov.	9—Rocky Campbell, Berlin	W 8
Nov.	17—Brian Jewitt, Frankfurt	KO 1
Dec.	7—Hasse Thomsen, Hamburg	W 8

1974

Feb.	20—Vasco Faustinho, Berlin	W 10
Mar.	14—Pietro Zanola, Koeln	KO 4
Apr.	11—Alberto Lovell, Berlin	KO 8
May	16—Conny Velensek, Hamburg	W 12
	(Won German Heavyweight Title)	
June	21—Billy Aird, Berlin	D 8
Oct.	14—Jan Lubbers, Rotterdam	KO 2
Nov.	22—Jean-Pierre Coopman, Gand	L 10
Dec.	1—Reco Brooks, Muenchen	KO 5

1975

Mar.	18—Giuseppe Ros, Berlin	W 8
May	16—Kilani Romdani, Ludwigshafen	KO 2
June	24—Wendell Newton, Berlin	WF 3
Sept.	6—Avenemar Peralta, Berlin	KO by 3
Oct.	31—Lothar Stengel, Offenbach	KO 4

1976

Apr.	6—Richard Dunn, London	KO by 3
	(For European Heavyweight Title)	
Aug.	6—Hartmut Sasse, Berlin	KO 3
	(For German Heavyweight Title)	
Oct.	30—Ruediger Scmidtke, Frankfurt	KO 1

1977

Jan.	15—Karl Luedecke, Kiel	KO by 2
	(Heavyweight Championship of Germany)	
Apr.	4—Hennie Thoonen, Amsterdam	KO 3

1978

Apr.	14—Tony Moore, Berlin	D 8
Sept.	2—Kurt Luedecke, Berlin	KO 3
	(For German Heavyweight Title)	
Nov.	6—Ngozika Ekwelum, Berlin	KO by 5

1979
(Inactive)
1980

Feb.	6—Harry Friedel, Lubeck	KO 5
	(Retained German Heavyweight Title)	
June	13—Hennie Thoonen, Lubeck	KO by 2
Sept.	22—Al Syben, Differdingen	KO 7

JAN AUGUST
South African Flyweight
1979

June	29—Meshack Mazibuko, Natalspruit	W 4

1980

Nov.	22—Zollie Godwana, Queenstown	W 4

LAURIE LOCHE (BABY CASSIUS) AUSTIN
Australian Junior Welterweight
1971

Nov.	2—Delson Stokes, Nunawading	W 4
Nov.	23—Matt Ropis, Nunawading	W 4
Nov.	25—Matt De Palma, Brunswick	W 4
Dec.	14—Chris Constantino, Nunawading	W 4

1972

June	15—Kid Eugene, Leederville	W 6
July	4—Paddy Green, Leederville	KO 5
July	12—Jerry Nundle, Bast Fremantle	W 8
Dec.	14—Alan Hayden, East Perth	W 6

1973

June	22—Delson Stokes, Boulder	W 10
July	19—Gary Bennell, Perth	W 10
Aug.	16—Sid Dumbrell, Perth	L 10
Sept.	10—Austin Eades, Perth	W 10

1974

Jan.	28—Kid Eugene Eades, Mandurah	W 10
June	20—Michael Cassidy, Perth	W 10
Aug.	15—Kid Eugene Eades, Perth	W 8
Sept.	5—Shocker Myles, Perth	KO 4

1975

Feb.	7—Eddie Buttons, Bulli	L 10
Mar.	2—Martin Beni, St. Kilda	L 8
July	10—Lou Cruz, Blacktown	D 10
Oct.	15—Puth Lawlek, Bangkok	L 10

1976

July	23—Eugene Eades, Cannington	W 10
Sept.	8—Matt Ropis, Kewdale	W 15
	(Australian Lightweight Title)	

1977

Jan.	12—Alan Aldenhoven, North Perth	KO 10
Apr.	28—Hector Thompson, Perth	KO 15
	(Australian & Commonwealth Junior Welterweight Title)	
June	16—Hector Thompson, Perth	L 15
	(Australian & Commonwealth Junior Welterweight Title)	
Aug.	4—Joey Collins, Perth	KO 7
Sept.	15—Hector Thompson, Perth	W 15
	(Australian & Commonwealth Junior Welterweight Title)	

1978

Apr.	21—Tony Aba, Melbourne	KO 4
Sept.	24—Jeff Malcolm, Rockbank	L 15
	(Commonwealth Junior Welterweight Title)	
Dec.	15—Jeff Malcolm, Griffith	L 15
	(Won Commonwealth Junior Welterweight Title)	

1979

Nov.	14—Frank Ropis, Melbourne	D 10
Dec.	13—Steve Dennis, Melbourne	W 15
	(Won Australian Welterweight Title)	

1980

Feb.	16—Sakarai Ye, Suva	L 10
Apr.	16—Frank Ropis, Melbourne	L 15
	(Lost Australian Welterweight Title)	

SALVATORE AVELLA
Italian Junior Lightweight
1975

Jan.	31—Vicenzo Di Ruocco, Campi Bisenzio	KO 6
Apr.	18—Alvaro Checche, Scandicci	W 6
Sept.	26—Abu Arrow, Sesto F.	W 6
Nov.	22—Ritter Schofer, Basilea	KO 4

1976

Jan.	30—Gianni Garbo, Bologna	LF 6
May	21—Giuseppe Pappalardo, Catania	W 6
July	10—Lucio Vailati, Campi Bisenzio	WF 2
Sept.	18—Mario De Prosperis, Foggia	KO by 6

1977

Jan.	21—Salvatore Melluzzo, Pesaro	L 8
Oct.	7—Natale Caredda, Cagliari	L 8

1978

Feb.	25—Gianfranco Lalli, Campi Bisenzio	KO 3
Apr.	21—Pasqualino Morbidelli, Campi Bisenzio	KO by 3
Oct.	27—Rosario Mucaria, Chaux Fond	LF 5

1979

May	25—Salvatore Melluzzo, Pesaro	KO by 5

1980

Mar.	22—Salvatore Liscapade, Ostia	L 8

RICHARD AVERY
Newport, England Welterweight
1979

Apr.	24—Pat Smythe, Southend	W 6
Apr.	30—Tommy Thomas, London	D 6
May	10—Jess Harper, Pontypool	W 6
May	16—Jess Harper, Sheffield	W 6
June	18—Lee Hartshorn, Manchester	KO by 4
Nov.	28—Chris Christian, Solihull	W 6
Dec.	5—Dave Taylor, Liverpool	W 6
Dec.	10—Dennis Sullivan, Torquay	L 8

1980

Jan.	9—Dave Allen, Burslem	L 8
Mar.	18—Cliff Gilpin, Wolverhampton	L 6
Apr.	14—Chris Christian, London	L 8
May	27—Gary Pearce, Newport	W 10
	(Elimination, Welsh Welterweight Title)	
Aug.	12—Dennis Sullivan, Gowerton	W 8

JOE AWOME
British Heavyweight
1979

Feb.	6—Clive Beardsley, Wembley	KO 2
Feb.	19—Alan Bagley, Birmingham	KO 1
Apr.	4—Alan Bagley, Birmingham	KO 4
May	1—Ron McLean, London	KO by 2
May	23—Reg Long, Nottingham	KO 2
June	26—Ron McLean, London	KO 3
Sept.	11—Austin Okoye, London	KO 6
Oct.	9—Glen Adair, Kensington	KO 5
Oct.	23—Ricky James, London	KO 4

1980
Jan.　22—Manny Gabriel, Albert Hall ....KO　3
Feb.　19—Stan McDermott, Albert Hall ....KO by　3
Apr.　21—Neil Malpass, London ....KO by　8

YASUO AZATO
Japanese Bantamweight
1979
Apr.　17—Makoto Kumagaya, Tokyo ....W　6
1980
Feb.　19—Kikeaki Sawada, Tokyo ....W　8
Apr.　30—Fujimi Wada, Takasaki ....W　6
Oct.　16—Hirohisa Iino, Tokyo ....D　8

YOSHIMITSU AZATO
Japanese Featherweight
1980
Aug.　19—Johnny Fujimoto, Tokyo ....KO　2
Oct.　23—Katsuji Sano, Tokyo ....W　10

EVERALDO COSTA AZEVEDO
Italian Welterweight
Born: July 24, 1944, Jaciupe, Brazil, naturalized Argentinian, living in Pavia, Italy. Professional from 1966. From 1966 to 1969: 35 fights, Won 17 (4 by KO), Draw 14, Lost on points 4, last defeat Feb. '67, Lost points Carlos Aro.
1970
Mar.　11—Adan Gomez, Buenos Aires ....W　10
June　5—Adan Gomez, Neuquen ....W　10
June　19—Luis Bustabas, Neuquen..................W　10
Aug.　19—Carlos Peralta, Buenos Aires............W　10
Sept.　11—Carlos Chavez, Neuquen ....W　8
Dec.　9—Omar Gottifredi, Buenos Aires ....W　10
1971
Feb.　10—Antonio Romero, Buenos Aires ....W　10
Mar.　12—Carlos Peralta, Tucuman................D　10
May　28—Joao Dos Santos, Sao Paulo ....W　10
July　9—Pedro Parra, Sao Paulo ....KO　6
Aug.　20—Dorman Crawford, Sao Paulo............KO　6
Oct.　16—Luis Golepa Cebral, Santa Rosa..........D　10
Oct.　22—Jerry Wells, Sao Paulo ....KO　2
1972
Jan.　5—Pietro Ceru, Viareggio ....D　10
Jan.　28—Serafino Lucherini, Milano ....W　8
Feb.　18—Johnny White, Pavia ....W　8
Mar.　31—Johnny White, Reggio Emilia ....W　8
Apr.　20—Jonathan Dele, Milano ....W　10
July　5—David Pesenti, Sanremo ....NC　3
July　27—Johnny White, Viareggio ....W　10
Aug.　16—Sugar Ray, Lignano Sabbiadoro ....KO　4
Sept.　12—Carlos Capella, Grisignano di Zocco.......W　10
Dec.　2—Bruno Arcari, Turin ....L　15
　　　　(WBC Junior Welterweight Title)
1973
Apr.　4—Nicola D'Orazio, Cagliari ....KO　7
May　10—Jorgen Hansen, Copenhagen ....W　8
Sept.　6—Jorgen Hansen, Copenhagen ....L　12
Sept.　28—Pietro Ceru, Sarzana ....W　10
Dec.　14—Jose' Luis Pacheco, Barcelona ....KO　6
Dec.　28—Max Hebeisen, Zurich ....KO by　3
1974
Feb.　1—Otha Tyson, Milano ....W　10
Mar.　15—Pascal Zito, Milano......................W　10
May　7—Luciano De Luca, Terni.................KO　6
Nov.　30—Norman Sekgapane, Johannesburg ....L　10
Dec.　21—Jose Gonzalez Dopico, La Coruna ....W　8
1975
May　16—Nicola Sassanedi, Milano ....KO　6
May　31—Pietro Ceru', Opatija......................W　8
June　20—Giuseppe Martinese, Milan ....D　8
Aug.　22—Romualdo D'Alo', Spnato..................W　8
Sept.　13—Enzo Pizzoni, Pula ....KO　5
Oct.　6—Lorenzo Nardillo, Zagreb ....W　8
Nov.　22—Jorgen Hansen, Skopije..................KO　6
1976
Jan.　31—Ray Chavez, Caracas ....D　10
May　29—Musaphata Kabangu, Pavia..............W　8
July　18—Juan Gonzalez, Caracas ....KO　3
Sept.　11—Mario Molina, Zagreb ....W　10
Nov.　12—Mario Guillotti, Milan...................D　8
1977
Jan.　9—Mario Guillotti, Como ....W　10
Feb.　11—Billy Waith, Milan ....W　10
Mar.　5—Nicola Sassanelli, Velenje ....W　10
May　6—Aroldo Olivares, Milano ....W　8
July　24—Pedro Rojas, Caracas ....L　10
Aug.　29—Carlos Palomino, Los Angeles ....L　15
　　　　(WBC Welterweight Title)
Nov.　19—Billy Backus, Syracuse ....D　10
1978
Apr.　28—Efisio Pinna, Sarajevo ....W　10
May　14—Mario Guillot, Pescara ....L　8
June　15—Johnny Subunga, Oslo ....L　8
Nov.　18—Marijan Benes, Berlin ....L　10

Dec.　8—Rocky Fratto, Syracuse ....L　10
1979
Mar.　3—Alain Marion, Creil ....KO　9
May　10—Louis Acaries, Paris.....................W　10
1980
Feb.　15—Louis Acaries, Nice ....L　10
May　9—Andre Holyk, Villeurbanne ....W　10
Sept.　12—Salvatore Cascio, Lido ....KO by　1

MICHAEL BABALAAS
Filipino Junior Lightweight
1980
Mar.　28—Jay Nardo, Bulawayo ....L　8

STEVE BABBS
British Light Heavyweight
1979
Mar.　16—Peter Tidgwell, Bradford.................L　6
Apr.　4—Mark Bennett, Birmingham ....L　4
Apr.　30—Tom Jones, Barnsley ....WF　5
May　21—Peter Tidgwell, Bradford................W　8
June　6—Peter Les Read, Burslem................W　6
June　18—Liam Coleman, London ....L　6
Oct.　17—Billy Keen, Evesham ....L　6
1980
Feb.　3—Danny McLoughlin, Liverpool ....KO by　4
Mar.　3—Joe Jackson, London ....L　6
Oct.　1—John O'Neill, Swansea ....L　8
Oct.　18—Al Stevens, Birmingham ....KO by　2

PATRICK BABOURAM
French Junior Middleweight
1977
June　11—Jean Paul Coppyn, Creil ....W　6
Dec.　17—Rene Guillot, Creil ....KO　1
1978
Oct.　6—Jean Michel Iger, Amiens ....W　6
1979
Feb.　3—Jean Michel Iger, Creil ....W　6
Mar.　3—Serge Poulain, Laval ....W　6
June　15—Maurice Renaud, Creil ....D　6
Dec.　14—Jean Jacques Benchetrit, Nizza ....L　6
1980
Jan.　4—Kachama Musasa, Capri ....KO by　4
Feb.　15—Stephane Ferrara, Bordeaux ....L　6
Mar.　1—Johnny Cooper, Creil ....D　6
Oct.　6—Erwin Heiber, Paris ....D　6
Nov.　15—Stephene Ferrara, Criel ....L　6

POUL (ANDERSEN) BAEKGAARD
Danish Middleweight
1979
Mar.　15—Ignacic Gorostidi, Copenhagen............W　4
May　24—Corrado Sortino, Randers ....W　4
June　28—Muhammad, Randers ....W　4
Sept.　6—Roberto Manoni, Randers ....W　4
Oct.　11—Antonio Ceraude, Copenhagen............W　4
1980
Feb.　29—Ignacio Gorostidi, Odense ....W　4
Apr.　17—Tony Britton, Copenhagen ....KO by　2

CARL BAILEY
British Welterweight
1976
Oct.　11—Chris Walker, Manchester ....KO by　3
Nov.　3—Chris Glover, Caister ....L　6
Nov.　18—Dave Farrell, Liverpool ....W　6
Dec.　6—Chris Glover, Manchester ....L　8
Dec.　15—Terry Schofield, Bradford ....W　8
1977
Jan.　20—Tommy Joyce, Liverpool ....W　8
Mar.　3—Terry Schofield, Caister ....L　8
Mar.　24—Terry Schofield, Bradford ....W　8
Apr.　20—Colin Deans, Manchester ....D　8
May　16—Roysie Francis, Manchester ....W　8
June　13—Joey McIntosh, Manchester ....KO by　2
Sept.　26—Roysie Francis, Manchester ....W　8
Oct.　24—Billy Ahearne, Manchester ....W　8
Nov.　1—Colin Deans, Newcastle ....D　8
Nov.　10—Al Stewart, Liverpool ....W　8
Dec.　1—Roycie Francis, Caister ....KO　5
Dec.　19—Joe Hannaford, Bradford ....W　8
1978
Jan.　18—Bob Bravado, Solihull ....WF　7

259

Feb.	13—Horace McKenzie, Manchester	L 8
Mar.	2—Prince Rodney, Caister	L 8
Apr.	4—Prince Rodney, London	KO by 7
Apr.	27—Chris Glover, Doncaster	LF 6
June	19—Tony Kavanaugh, Manchester	W 8
Sept.	18—Sylvester Gordon, Manchester	L 8
Oct.	9—Ali Mohammad, Middlesbrough	KO 8
Oct.	18—Charley Malarkey, Glasgow	KO by 3
Nov.	15—Johnny Pincham, Solihill	L 8
Nov.	20—Roy Varden, Birmingham	W 8
Dec.	1—Billy Waith, Minster	L 8
Dec.	18—Prince Rodney, Bradford	W 8
	1979	
Jan.	17—Joey Mack, Solihull	KO by 8
Feb.	26—Roy Varden, Edgbaston	W 8
Mar.	5—Terry Petersen, Barnsley	W 8
Apr.	3—Joey Singleton, Hammersmith	L 8
May	29—Sylvester Mitee, Kensington	KO by 1
Sept.	24—Joey Singleton, Hammersmith	L 8
Oct.	15—Josef Nsubuga, Oslo	KO by 8
	1980	
Feb.	12—Mick Mills, Sheffield	KO by 5
Mar.	10—Jimmy Ellis, Manchester	L 8

GEORGE BAILEY
British Flyweight
1977

Sept.	29—Jackie Dinning, Newcastle	D 4
Oct.	10—Jackie Dinning, Marton	L 4
Nov.	8—Jackie Dinning, Darlington	W 4
	1978	
Jan.	23—Eddie Glencross, Bradford	L 4
Mar.	2—Jimmy Bott, Liverpool	W 6
Mar.	20—Jimmy Bott, Bradford	D 6
Apr.	17—Jimmy Bott, Bradford	L 8
July	12—Jackie Dinning, Newcastle	W 6
Sept.	8—Jimmy Bott, Wakefield	KO by 8
Oct.	2—Joey Spring, Nantwich	L 6
Oct.	31—Don Aageson, Wolverhampton	L 6
	1979	
Apr.	3—Joey Singleton, Hammersmith	L 8
June	14—Bryn Jones, Wolverhampton	D 8
Sept.	3—Eddie Glencross, Glasgow	L 8
Sept.	10—Kevin Smart, Birmingham	KO by 4
Oct.	9—Bryn Jones, Wolverhampton	D 8
Oct.	15—Bryn Jones, Dudley	W 6
Nov.	6—Robert Hepburn, Stafford	L 6
Nov.	21—John Griffiths, Evesham	L 6
	1980	
Apr.	28—Iggy Jano, Windsor	L 4
June	11—Peter Gabbitus, Morecambe	L 4
Sept.	4—Carl Cleasby, Morecambe	L 4
Sept.	16—Eddie McAllister, Southend	KO 4
Oct.	8—Pat Mallo, Stoke	W 8

FRANCIS BAILLEUL
French Junior Welterweight
1977

May	21—Laurent Crimbert, Arques	KO 4
Oct.	22—Jean Keirseblick, Calais	KO 3
Nov.	11—Abdel Ben Ameur, Bruges	L 6
	1978	
Jan.	7—Dibalu Mvuemba, Calais	KO by 3
Mar.	11—Phillipe Dumont, Louvroil	L 6
Mar.	25—Francois Poisot, Argues	W 6
Apr.	8—Patrick Drelon, Calais	W 6
Oct.	28—N'Toya Kilala, Calais	D 8
Nov.	18—Andre Blanco, Creil	W 6
	1979	
Jan.	13—Patrick Goblet, Calais	KO 2
Feb.	24—Mohamed Boundtka, Calais	KO by 7
Mar.	24—Potito Di Muro, Calais	D 8
June	15—Tusikoleta Nkalankete, Conde	L 6
July	14—Andre Blanc, Middlekerke	L 6
Oct.	19—Georges Lietaer, Calais	W 8
Oct.	30—Maurice Fice, Paris	KO by 6
Nov.	24—Sana Kabore, Calais	W 6
	1980	
Feb.	9—Lucien Campo, Calais	L 8
Mar.	8—Gilbert Helluin, Calais	W 8
May	10—Melquiades Da Silva, Calais	WF 6
May	23—Andre Blanco, Middelkerke	D 6
Oct.	3—Angelo Licata, Calais	W 8
Nov.	8—Guy Caudron, Calais	W 8

ERNIE BAISTER
British Light Heavyweight
1979

Nov.	12—Gary Jones, Marton	KO 5
	1980	
Feb.	25—Gary Jones, Glasgow	L 6
Mar.	27—Nigel Savory, Newcastle	KO by 4

MICKEY BAKER
British Lightweight
1979

Apr.	10—Selvin Bell, London	KO 3
July	2—Bill Smith, London	KO 1
Dec.	3—Tommy Thomas, Wolverhampton	KO 1
	1980	
Jan.	21—Dai Davies, Wolverhampton	W 6
Mar.	10—Tyrrel Wilson, Wolverhampton	W 8
May	29—Ian Kid Murray, Wolverhampton	W 6
July	8—Dave Taylor, Wolverhampton	KO 5
Sept.	22—Billy Vivian, Wolverhampton	W 8
Oct.	30—Eric Wood, Wolverhampton	L 6

PAUL BAKER
Australian Lightweight
1977

Feb.	22—Ezzard Charles, Kingsford	L 5
Mar.	8—Gabby Darmon, Kingsford	L 6
Mar.	22—Ezzard Charles, Kingsford	L 6
Apr.	26—Gabby Darmon, Kingsford	W 6
May	4—Mick Williams, Cammeray	KO 1
May	10—Gabby Darmon, Kingsford	L 6
May	11—Ezzard Charles, Marrickville	D 4
June	21—Ezzard Charles, Kingsford	L 6
June	29—Ezzard Charles, Brookvale	L 6
July	6—Steve Assang, Cammeray	L 6
July	13—Ezzard Charles, Marrickville	L 6
Aug.	10—Barry Bell, Marrickvale	L 6
Sept.	7—Ezzard Charles, Cammeray	L 4
Sept.	13—Mick Christopher, Kingsford	D 4
Sept.	21—Brian Schofield, Melbourne	KO by 3
Sept.	28—Gary Rosen, Brookvale	L 6
Oct.	26—Buddy Clare, Brookvale	W 5
Nov.	2—Ezzard Charles, Cammeray	L 6
Nov.	9—Buddy Clare, Marrickvale	L 6
Nov.	18—Ezzard Charles, Thirroul	L 6
Nov.	22—Buddy Clare, Kingsford	L 6
Nov.	30—Joey Collins, Brookvale	L 6
Dec.	6—Joey Collins, Brookvale	L 6
	1978	
Feb.	1—Ezzard Charles, Cammeray	L 6
Feb.	7—Gary Rosen, Kingsford	L 6
Feb.	22—Gary Rosen, Brookvale	L 8
May	31—Dick Bolton, Brookvale	L 6
June	7—David Sarago, Townsville	KO by 7
June	21—Ken Carmody, Brookvale	W 6
June	27—Steve Assang, Kingsford	L 6
July	2—David Tolls, Hexham	W 6
July	4—Ezzard Charles, Cardiff	W 6
July	11—Steve Assang, Kingsford	L 6
July	19—Ezzard Charles, Mt. Pritchard	L 6
July	25—Pepe French, Kingsford	L 6
July	26—Teddy Hopkins, Brookvale	D 6
Aug.	8—Joey Collins, Kingsford	W 8
Aug.	12—David Tolls, Conabarabran	KO 3
Aug.	16—Teddy Hopkins, Brookvale	L 8
Aug.	22—Gary Rosen, Kingsford	L 8
Aug.	29—Pepe French, Cardiff	L 6
Sept.	9—Johnny Aba, Kundiana	KO by 7
Oct.	5—Johnny Aba, Panguna	KO by 9
Nov.	3—Johnny Aba, Panguna	KO by 3
Nov.	15—Jeff Malcolm, Brisbane	KO by 9
Nov.	28—Gary Rosen, Kingsford	L 6
Dec.	2—Buddy Clare, Kingsford	W 6
Dec.	20—Sparrow Freeman, Mt. Pritchard	D 6
	1979	
Jan.	30—Steve Assang, Kingsford	L 6
Feb.	27—Brocky Crowe, Kingsford	L 6
Mar.	27—Joey Collins, Kingsford	W 6
Apr.	4—Dick Bolton, Brookvale	D 6
May	23—Amos Roberts, Brookvale	W 6
June	5—Ezzard Charles, Kingsford	W 6
June	6—Buddy Clare, Brookvale	KO 2
June	16—Johnny Aba, Panguna	KO by 8
July	3—Steve Campbell, Kingsford	W 5
July	4—Steve Campbell, Brookvale	W 6
July	17—Ezzard Charles, Kingsford	W 8
Aug.	15—Gary Rosen, Mt. Pritchard	D 10
Sept.	25—Steve Assang, Kingsford	W 10
Oct.	17—Joey Collins, Brookvale	W 6
	1980	
Feb.	20—Graham Bell, Mt. Pritchard	D 10
Apr.	22—Steve Assang, Kingsford	W 6
May	6—Buddy Nixon, Kingsford	D 6
May	7—Buddy Nixon, Kingsford	D 6
May	16—Peter Berrigan, Cardiff	L 10
June	24—Lindsay Roberts, Brookvale	KO 4
June	24—Willie Tarika, Brookvale	L 8
July	16—Willie Tarika, Mt. Pritchard	L 10
Aug.	13—Clint Brown, Brookvale	L 6
Sept.	3—Steve Campbell, Brookvale	W 6
Sept.	10—Willie Tarika, Gosford	L 10
Sept.	22—Kau Boi, Boroko	L 10

Oct. 19—Robert Namana, Boroko .... KO by 5
Nov. 5—Gary Rosen, Brookvale .... D 6

ANDY BALABA
Filipino Flyweight
1979
Feb. 17—Ric Barimbad, Davao City .... L 10
Mar. 31—Diego De Villa, Davao City .... L 10
May 26—Ver Libradilla, Santos City .... L 10
Nov. 24—Little Carupo, Santos City .... W 10
1980
Jan. 5—Rudy Magdasal, Santos City .... W 10
Feb. 10—Ben Aldeguer, Cebu City .... D 10

TERRY BALDWIN
British Welterweight
1979
Nov. 12—Chris Christian, Mayfair .... KO by 5
1980
Jan. 25—Colin Wake, Hull .... L 4
Oct. 13—Kirk Davis, Newcastle .... L 4

STEPHENE BALENE
South African Junior Welterweight
1979
Aug. 18—Lucas Sebego, Welkom .... W 4
Dec. 8—Simon Mxawe, Bloemfontein .... L 6
1980
Feb. 2—Joseph Molahloe, Virginia .... W 4
Mar. 8—Martin Jacobs, Bloemfontein .... L 6
Apr. 12—Jonas Tladi, Ficksburg .... L 10
(For OFS Junior Welterweight Title)
Aug. 23—Johannes Ramasimong, Bethlehem .... W 8
Sept. 13—Samuel Pule, Welkom .... KO by 3
Dec. 6—Jonas Tladi, Ficksburg .... L 10
(For OFS Junior Welterweight Title)

HENRY BALINA
Filipino Flyweight
1979
Feb. 16—Jun Falsario, Manila .... W 10
May 4—Tony Seas, Manila .... W 10
June 29—Lord Esmero, Manila.................... L 10
Sept. 15—Ver Libradilla, Ozamis City .... L 10
1980
Jan. 18—Lord Esmero, Manila .... L TD 2
May 23—Juanito Ablaca, Manila .... L 10
Aug. 16—Lennon Arcega, Manila .... KO 7
Sept. 13—Lord Esmero, Ormoc City .... L 10

GARY BALL
British Junior Welterweight
1978
Oct. 12—John Flynn, Wimbledon .... W 6
Oct. 18—Gerry O'Neill, Glasgow .... L 6
Nov. 7—Austin Owens, Wembley .... L 6
Nov. 20—Gary Lucas, Birmingham .... L 6
Dec. 11—Gary Lucas, Birmingham .... W 6
1979
Jan. 22—Carl Mullings, Birmingham .... W 6
Feb. 19—Jimmy Hancock, Birmingham........... KO 3
Mar. 19—Gary Nickels, Marylebone .... D 8
May 21—Billy O'Grady, Walworth .... D 8
Oct. 17—Alan Lamb, Lewisham................. KO by 6
Nov. 19—Billy O'Grady, Lewisham .... L 8
Dec. 13—Barry Price, Wimbleton .... L 8
1980
Sept. 15—Glen Rhodes, London .... D 6

EDDIE BALLARAN
Filipino Featherweight
1978
Sept. 10—Sandy Torres, Manila................. KO by 7
1979
Jan. 12—Willie Espinosa, Manila .... L 10
Apr. 27—Fel Viesea, Manila.................... KO by 7
Sept. 29—Sandy Torres, San Pablo City .... L 10
Nov. 16—Oscar Barola, Quezon City .... D 10
1980
Feb. 8—Jessie Dariagan, Manila .... W 10

GIUSEPPE BALLONE
Italian Junior Lightweight
1979
Sept. 8—Ignacio Fara, Alhero.................... W 4
Nov. 10—Abass Macauley, Alghero .... W 6
1980
Feb. 8—Vincenzo Di Ruocco, Sassari .... KO 5
Mar. 15—Francisco DeRosa, Alghero .... W 6
Apr. 11—Palmiro Pizzata, Modena .... W 6
Oct. 10—Fiovante Calce, Villeurbanne .... W 6

NITOY BANTILAN
Filipino Junior Lightweight
1979
Feb. 17—Primo Bulambao, Davao City .... D 10
Mar. 31—Arman Bangoyan, Santos City .... W 10
Apr. 21—Johnny Sato, Santos City .... KO by 7
Sept. 8—Boy Reyes, Cotobato City .... KO by 6
Oct. 20—Fred Basa, Pampanga .... W 10
Dec. 22—Boy Reyes, Zambales .... KO by 7
1980
Feb. 1—Roy Reyes, Manila .... KO by 6

ROCKY BANTLEMAN
British Featherweight
1980
Oct. 7—John Griffiths, London .... W 6
Nov. 3—Steve Pollard, London .... KO by 2

GIANCARLO BARABOTTI
Italian Welterweight
Born: Nov. 30, 1951, Pontedera
1974
July 13—Claudio Banco, Buti .... W disq. 4
Aug. 24—Aurelio Lai, Viareggio .... KO 6
Sept. 24—Salvatore Gennatiempo, KO 3
Oct. 10—Salvatore Gennatiempo, Monsummo ..... KO 3
Oct. 31—Giovanni Maiorano, Viareggio .... D 6
Dec. 6—Giovanni Maiorano, Reggio Emili. ...... W 6
Dec. 26—Giovanni Cavazzini, R. Emilia .... W 6
1975
Feb. 7—Nicolo Bennici, Empoli .... W 6
Mar. 14—Fernand Roelands, Bruges .... KO 5
Mar. 28—Giuseppe Agate, Bologna............... W 8
May 23—Abu Arrow, Empoli .... W 8
June 20—Rocco Zecca, Milan .... KO 2
Sept. 26—Pierre Petit, Milan .... KO by 4
Dec. 7—Giorgio Merlin, Buti .... W 8
1976
Jan. 16—Pierino Meraviglia, Empoli .... W 12
(Italian Lightweight Title)
Mar. 5—Giuseppe Minotti, Reggio Emilia .... D 8
Apr. 3—Hugo Barraza, Caracas .... KO by 1
July 2—Vincenzo Burgio, Empoli .... L 12
Aug. 28—Vincenzo Quero, Taranto .... L 10
Sept. 18—Luiz Ribero, Foggia .... W 8
Oct. 22—Giovanni Maiorano, Montecatini........ KO 6
Dec. 10—Fernand Roelands, Bruges .... L 8
1977
Feb. 12—Jean Baptiste Piedvache, Perigueux ...... L 10
May 13—Pierino Meraviglia, Sarzana .... W 8
July 2—Luciano Laffranchi, Buti .... W 8
Oct. 21—Giuseppe Martinese, Milan .... L 12
(Italian Junior Welterweight Title)
Dec. 17—Luciano Laffranchi, Cecina .... W 8
1978
Mar. 4—Efisio Pinna, Pesaro .... L 8
Apr. 7—Bruno Freschi, Udine .... KO 1
May 25—Jorgen Hansen, Copenhagen .... KO by 6
Aug. 18—Luciano Navarra, Massa .... KO by 3
1979
July 2—Boro Jovic, Buti...................... W 8
Sept. 9—Alois Carmeliet, Buggenhout .... L 8
Nov. 24—Perice Fernandez, Zarageza .... KO by 3
1980
Feb. 16—Zradvo Jovicic, Riccione .... KO 2
May 28—Giuseppe Di Padova, Mantova ...... KO by 7

BRANKO BARAKOVIC
Yugoslav Middleweight
1972
June 3—Young Griffo, Jesenice .... D 4
Sept. 16—Milos Todorovic, Kranj .... KO 3
Oct. 7—Jean Pierre Younsy, Dunkerque .... L 6
Nov. 4—Young Griffo, Kamnik .... L 8
Nov. 18—Predrag Petrovic, Kranj .... KO 4
(Won Yugoslav Welterweight Title)
1973
Feb. 10—Alain Giraudon, St Etienne .... L 6
Feb. 17—Luciano Bomben, Pordenone .... L 6
Apr. 14—Dusan Kukic, Lubiana .... D 6
May 12—Franjo Kovac, Lubiana .... KO 4
May 26—Sreco Weiner, Lubiana .... D 6
July 14—Nicola Sassanelli, Summonte .... L 6
Sept. 27—Dusan Kukic, Lubiana .... L 10
Oct. 13—Luciano Marchetti, Pesaro .... L 6
Oct. 27—Ali Bechir, Lubiana .... KO 2
Nov. 16—Young Griffo, Lubiana .... D 8
Dec. 8—Guy Vercoutter, Dunkerque .... L 8
1974
Feb. 2—Ile Krstanovic, Lubiana .... KO 1
Feb. 8—Germano Germani, Biterbo .... L 6
Apr. 6—Dusan Kukic, Lubiana .... D 10
Apr. 20—Sreco Weiner, Lubiana .... D 4

May   17—Benny Zwezerijnen, Utrecht ....KO by 6
June   8—Sreco Weiner, Lubiana ....D 6
July 26—Giancarlo Pedrinelli, Chiari ....L 6
Nov. 23—Young Griffo, Kamnik ....D 6
1975
Feb.   7—Biagio Violino, Montale ....L 6
May   24—Igor Barakovic, Kamnik ....D 4
Oct. 30—Antonio Cresenza, Rome ....L 6
Nov. 14—Vincenzo Pulcrano, Rome ....L 6
Dec. 21—Dusan Kukic, Lubiana ....D 4
Dec. 27—Frank Wissenbach, Berlin ....KO by 5
1976
Feb. 13—Young Griffo, Gorenji Logatec ....D 4
Mar. 28—Predrag Petrovic, Kamnik ....KO 3
May   28—Young Griffo, Postojna ....D 6
July 17—Biagio Violino Castiglion Fibocchi........L 6
Sept. 25—Joseph Pachler, Lienz ....L 10
Oct.   6—Joseph Pachler, Wolfsberg ....L 10
Nov. 26—Guido Corpotaux, Berne ....D 4
Dec. 12—Gilbert Cohen, Paris ....KO by 7
1977
Jan. 14—Nazif Biberovich, Bregenz ....W 6
Mar. 18—Jean Symos, Anversa ....KO by 5
Apr.   1—Christian Sittler, Bregenz ....D 4
Apr. 22—Pol Payen, La Louviere ....KO by 2
June   4—Clement Tshinza, Esch sur Alzette ....L 8
July   2—Ivan Zupan, Sobec ....LF 1
Aug. 24—Dario Vigini, Grado ....KO 1
Oct. 14—Eric Seys, Gits ....L 8
Nov. 11—Antonio Stocchino, Bologna ....KO by 4
1978
Feb.   1—Guido Corpataux, Berne ....L 6
Feb. 18—Wolfgang Gans, Kiel ....L 8
Mar. 10—Georges Lemmer, Esch ....L 8
Apr. 25—Sonny Kamunga, Domzale ....W 6
May   19—Karl Heinz Schulz, Essen ....KO by 5
Aug. 18—Franz Dorfer, Wien ....KO by 4
Dec.   8—Hendrick Seys, Gits ....L 8
1979
Apr. 21—Sreco Weiner, Hrastnik ....D 6
May   19—Vincenze De Camilles, Rome.............L 8
May   21—Boro Jovic, Lubiana ....D 4
June 30—Zdravko Jovicic, Kamnik ....D 4
July   7—Lino Lemma, Roccapriora ....KO by 5
July 28—Zoran Mijovic, Komenda ....W 6
Aug. 12—Nicola Cirelli, Morcone ....KO by 4
Sept. 1—Joze Centa, Hrastnik ....D 6
Sept. 30—Joze Centa, Toplice ....D 6
Nov. 17—Raymond Langwouters, Antwerp .....KO by 4
Nov. 25—Zahrudin Dacic, Trbovlje ....KO 5
(Won Yugoslav Middleweight Title)
1980
Apr. 11—Luciano Renzi, Chivasso ....L 6

DARKO BARAKOVIC
Yugoslavian Light Heavyweight
1972
Sept. 16—Ivan Matekovic, Kranj ....L 4
Sept. 30—Dusan Kukic, Kamnik ....D 6
1973
Feb. 17—Onelio Grando, Pordenone ....KO by 4
1974
Nov. 21—Francois Fiol, Ginerva ....KO by 2
Nov. 23—Martin Koller, Kamnik ....D 6
Dec.   6—Ezechiele Fanti, R. Emilia ....KO by 2
1975
Oct. 25—Gerald Bois, Sedan ....KO by 2
1976
May   28—Joze Centa, Postonja ....W 4
July 17—Giorgio Valeri, Castiglioni ....KO by 4
Sept. 8—Joze Centa, Moravce ....D 4
Oct. 23—Joze Centa, Moravce ....D 6
Nov. 20—Hocine Tafer, Grenoble ....KO by 3
1977
Jan. 22—Joze Centa, Kamnik ....W 4
Feb. 27—Joze Centa, Kranj ....L 4
Apr.   2—Eric Kopec, S. Quentin ....KO by 7
Apr. 16—Joze Centa, Hrastnik ....D 6
May   20—Uwe Meinicke, Hannover ....W 6
Oct.   1—Renzo Trevisan, Ponte Pattoli ....L 6
Oct. 23—Joze Centa, Lubiana ....L 10
(For Yugoslavian Light Heavyweight Title)
1978
Mar. 10—Fred Serres, Esch ....L 6
Apr. 25—Andrej Vestan, Domzale ....D 4
Sept. 2—Antimo Tescione, Casagiove ....L 6
Nov.   6—Stanislav Kubienic, Berlin ....L 4
Dec.   8—Salmin Boutera, Gits ....KO by 5
1979
July   7—Lino Lemma, Rocca Priora ....KO by 5
1980
Nov. 29—Walter Cevoli, Padova ....KO by 2

CYRILLE BARBE
French Junior Middleweight
1979
Nov. 24—Christian D'Helf, Sin le Nosle............L 6
1980
Feb.   8—Michel Moinard, Palaiseau ....KO by 1
Apr. 12—Jean Philippe Truchelut, Troylo ....L 6
Apr. 19—Frank Winstertein, St. Geneviere ....KO by 2
Dec. 26—Gaetano Ardito, Firenze ....KO by 2

EMILIO BARCALA
Spanish Junior Lightweight
1975
Aug. 21—Angel Oliver, Madrid ....D 6
Nov. 14—Jose Francico Artigao, Madrid ....KO 4
1976
Feb.   6—Pedro Coque, Madrid ....KO 3
Feb. 13—Jose Luis Rodriquez, Madrid ....L 6
Apr. 23—Jose Luis Rodriquez, Madrid.............D 8
July 23—Francisco Santaengracia, Madrid ....W 8
Aug.   7—Flamenco Rodriguez, Madrid............KO 1
Aug. 20—Jose Rodriguez, Madrid ....KO 1
1977
July   8—Pedro Pinto, Madrid ....KO 1
July 15—Dos Anjos, Madrid ....W 8
Sept. 9—Henry Lone, Madrid ....L 8
1978
Apr.   9—Jose Lopez, Madrid ....KO 3
May   12—Mariano Rodriguez, Valladolid ....L 10
Nov.   2—Abdelkader Esmain, Barcelona ....D 8
Dec. 16—Vicente Rodriguez, Leon ....L 10
1979
Feb.   2—Joaquin Garcia del Moral, Madrid ....W 8
Mar. 16—Manuel Masso, Barcelona...............L 8
May   4—Mohamed Jofre II, Madrid ....W 6
June   1—Ramon Garcia Marichal, Mallorca ....L 8
July   6—Juan Barros, Mallorca ....W 8
July 20—Francisco Garcia Herrera, Madrid ....W 8
Aug. 10—Nani Rodriguez, Madrid ....W 8
Aug. 24—Francisco Moya, Madrid ....W 6
Oct.   5—Francisco Garcia Herrera, Madrid ....W 6
1980
Jan.   5—Torito Gomez, Santander ....L 8
Mar.   8—Roberto Castanon, Leon ....L 12
(For European Junior Lightweight Title)
Aug.   1—Jose Luis Vicho, Palma de Mallorca ....L 8
Aug. 22—Jose Luis Vicho, Madrid ....L 8

RIC BARIMBAD
Filipino Junior Featherweight
1978
Oct. 14—Ronald Sumalis, Davao City ....L 10
Oct. 28—Willie Iao, Davao del Norte ....KO 3
1979
Feb.   3—Diego De Villa, Davao del Norte ....L 10
Feb. 17—Andy Balara, Davao City ....W 10
Mar. 31—Lord Esmero, Davao City ....W 10
June   2—Lino Boy Base, Davao City ....D 10
June 30—Ver Libradilla, Gen. Santos City ....D 11
Aug. 19—Little Carupe, Davao Del Sur ....W 10
Sept. 8—Ben Aldoguer, Santos City.............W 10
Oct. 27—Jun Resma, Davao City................W 10
1980
Jan. 19—Siony Carupo, Santos City ....D 12
May   4—Emmanuel Javar, Davao ....KO 3
May   31—Siony Carupo, Davao City ....W 10
July 30—Leo Pareno, Davao City ....KO 5
Nov. 29—Siony Carupo, Davao City ....L 12
(For Filipino Junior Featherweight Title)

WAYNE BARKER
British Junior Middleweight
1979
Sept. 17—Jeff Aspell, Manchester ....W 6
Oct. 15—Jimmy Ellis, Manchester.................W 6
Oct. 23—Tommy Baldwin, Blackpool ....KO 3
Oct. 27—Joey Saunders, Barnsley ....W 6
Nov. 15—Joey Sauders, Caister..................KO 4
Nov. 19—Schris Glover, Stockport ....W 8
Nov. 27—Jimmy Ellis, Sheffield ....W 8
Dec. 10—Chris Glover, Manchester ....W 8
1980
Jan.   7—Terry Matthews, Manchester ....D 8
Jan. 21—Dennis Pryce, Nottingham ....W 8
May   12—Leo Mulhearn, Manchester ....W 8
June   3—Jimmy Batten, Albert Hall ....L 4

MARTIN C. BARNARD
South African Light Heavyweight
Born: January 24, 1956
1977
June 27—Mark Melville, Durban ....L 4
Aug. 13—Dewald van den Berg, Johannesburg ...KO 1

Aug. 29—Mathinus Oosthuizen, Johannesburg ....KO 2
Sept. 10—Joseph Matjui, Johannesburg ....KO 4
Oct. 17—Peyrus Marx, Johannesburg ....W 4
Nov. 14—Jeffrey Ellis, London ....KO 5

1978

Mar. 4—Jeffrey Ellis, Ermelo ....KO 3
Aug. 26—Joseph Matjiu, Bophuthatswana ....W 6
Oct. 23—Mervin Smit, Ermelo ....L 6

1979

Mar. 24—Willem Giesing, Johannesburg ......KO by 2
Apr. 28—Willem Giesing, Johannesburg ....W 4
Sept. 3—Mervin Smit, Welkom ....L 6
Nov. 3—Harold Saaiman, Port Elizabeth ....L 6
Dec. 1—Theunis Kok, Johannesburg.........KO by 1

1980

Apr. 21—James Mathatho, Secunda ....W 10
(Retained Transvaal Light Heavyweight Title)
May 12—Sydney Hoho, Cape Town ....L 12
(For South African Light Heavyweight Title)
Aug. 29—Prince Tukane, East London ....W 8
Dec. 1—Temba Buthelezi, Durban ....KO 7

OSCAR BAROLA
Filipino Featherweight
1978

Nov. 24—Lito Pena, Manila ....D 10

1979

Mar. 10—Virgilio Berdefler, Manila ....W 10
Sept. 7—Jessie Dariagan, Manila.................KO 4
Nov. 16—Eddie Ballaran, Quezon City ....D 10

1980

Feb. 2—Lulu Villaverde, Dipolog City ....L 10

BRIAN BARONET
South African Lightweight
1980

Apr. 14—Paulus Shozi, Durban ....KO 2
May 19—Koos Mifuphi, Durban ....KO 3
July 2—Temba Tshabalala, Durban ....KO 1
Sept. 15—Moses Mthiyane, Durban ....KO 3
Nov. 2—Sipho Malinga, Durban ....KO 3

LIBER (DUQUE) BARRIOS
Spanish Lightweight
1979

July 24—Antonio Granados, S. Cugat ....L 4
Dec. 2—Antonio Granados, Barcelona ....W 6

1980

Jan. 12—Carlos Miguel Rodriguez, Lugo ....L 6
May 10—Jimmy Cruz, Tenerife ....L 8

JUAN BARROS
Spanish Lightweight
1972

Sept. 2—Conde, Salamarca ....L 6
Oct. 28—Jose Luis Otero, Ontoria ....L 8
Nov. 11—Pedro Molledo, Burgos ....L 8
Dec. 2—Perico Fernandez, Zaragoza ....LF 6

1973

Jan. 6—Luis Cristobal Diaz, Madrid ....D 6
Jan. 23—Jose Luis Otero, Madrid ....LF 4
Feb. 3—Perico Fernandez, Zaragoza ....L 8
Feb. 19—Ramon Garcia Marichal, S. Cruz ....L 8
May 12—Pedro Nino Jimenez, Madrid ....LF 4
July 28—Santiago Cebollada, Calatyud ....L 6
Aug. 18—Sebastian Gonzalez, Jativa ....L 8

1974

(Inactive)

1975

May 31—Francisco Santaengracia, Cuenca ....LF 5
July 2—Tito Blanco, Vallecas ....L 8
July 25—Rustan II, Madrid ....L 8
July 29—Franciso Santaengracia, Bilbao ....L 8
Aug. 6—Julio M. Rubio, Valencia ....L 8
Aug. 21—Juan Jose Hernandez Garcia, Almeria ....L 6
Sept. 19—Salim Mimoun, Villaverde ....D 6
Nov. 14—Faustino Blanco, Madrid ....KO by 5
Dec. 20—Cecilio Lastra, Santander ....L 6
Dec. 27—Esteban Eguia, Santander ....L 8

1976

Feb. 14—Roberto Castanon, Oviedo ....KO by 4
Apr. 24—Andres Ramos, Vigo ...•.................W 6
June 4—Francisco Leon, Badalona ....L 8
June 12—Agustin Plou, Zaragoza ....L 8
June 23—Paulino Garcia, Madrid ....L 8
Nov. 6—Luis F. Leon Mejias, S. Cruz ....L 8

1977

Feb. 4—Juan Francisco Rodriguez, Bilbao ....L 8
Apr. 23—Roberto Castanon, Leon ....KO by 5
June 8—Jose Luis Heredia, Malaga ....L 6
Aug. 23—Santiago Monzon, Galdar ....L 8
Aug. 27—Jose Luis Fleta, Tordomar ....KO 6
Nov. 4—Vicente Rodriguez, Madrid ....L 6

1978

Mar. 4—Serafin Dos Anjos, Mirando De Ebro .....W 8
July 14—Victoriano Solis, Madrid ....LF 5
Aug. 26—Garcia Herrera, Cuerva ....W 8
Sept. 3—Jaime Rodriguez Lozano, Villalba ....D 8
Sept. 8—Vicente Manzanares, Tarancon ....W 6
Oct. 7—Francisco Kiko Garcia, Lugo ....L 6
Nov. 11—Francisco Kiko Garcia, Gijon ....D 6
Dec. 9—Angel Ramirez, La Coruna ....KO 1

1979

Feb. 17—Esteban Eguia, Santander ....L 8
Mar. 30—Francisco Rodriguez Jeronimo, Las Palmas KO 1
Apr. 21—Francisco Moya, Valencia ....L 6
June 29—Francisco Moya, Torrente ....L 6
July 6—Emilio Barcala, Mallorca ....L 8
July 17—Jose Luis Vicho, Andraix ....L 6
July 21—Jose Luis Vicho, Mallorca ....L 6
Aug. 17—Mohamed Larbi, Madrid ....D 6

1980

Mar. 7—Jose Antonio Salinas, Barcelona ....D 6

MARIO BARUZZI
Italian Heavyweight
Born: July 12, 1946, Provaglio
1967 European Amateur Champion
1969

Jan. 24—Natale Solda, Rome ....KO 3
Feb. 14—Gianfranco Giannini, Rome ....KO 1
Mar. 7—Burghard Lembke, Genoa ....W 6
Apr. 4—Pietro Besi, Milan......................KO 4
Apr. 18—Paul Kraus, Rome.......................KO 4
May 17—Ermanno Festorazzi, Brescia ....KO 4
June 6—Francisco San Jose, Rome.................W 8
June 27—Jose Peyre, Rome ....KO 2
July 26—Vittorio Verrengia, Rome ....W 6
Sept. 19—Giancarlo Bacchini, Rome. ....KO 4
Oct. 13—Vasco Faustino, Milan ....W 8
Dec. 19—Jose Menno, Turin ....KO 6

1970

Jan. 31—Rocky Campbell, Rome ....KO 2
Mar. 20—Getulio Bueno, Rome....................KO 2
Apr. 10—Carl Gizzi, Rome.......................KO 4
May 29—Willie Moore, Rome ....W 8
July 10—Ireno Werlemann, Lignano...............KO 1
Oct. 8—Hugh Mercer, Rome ....KO 1
Nov. 18—Bepi Ros, Turin ....W 12
(Italian Heavyweight Title)
Dec. 26—Al Jones, Rome ....KO 8

1971

Mar. 6—Phil Smith, Rome ....KO 6
Apr. 23—Bepi Ros, Bologna.................KO by 12
(Italian Heavyweight Title)
Aug. 13—Eddie Land, Chiavai....................KO 7
Oct. 9—Tommy Sheehan, Genoa ....KO 4
Nov. 26—Carl Baker, Turin ....KO 8
Dec. 17—Eddie Bailey, Turin ....WF 4

1972

Feb. 16—Stanford Harris, S. Remo ....W 8
May 12—Vasco Faustino, Torino ....W 10
June 10—Expedit Montcho, Genova.................KO 2
Aug. 14—Jose Maria Echevarria, Chiavari ....W 10
Oct. 19—Charley Polite, Milano...................W 10
Dec. 26—Giuseppe Ros, Rome.................KO by 4
(For Italian Heavyweight Title)

1973

May 19—Mongol Ortiz, Udine....................W 10
July 25—Dante Cane, Rapallo ....W 12
(Won Italian Heavyweight Title)

1974

Feb. 16—Johnny Gause, Torino ....KO 1
May 29—Joe Bugner, Copenhagen ....KO by 10

1975

Apr. 24—Vasco Faustino, Brescia.............KO by 4
July 5—Amadeo Laurenti, Brescia ....KO 4
Sept. 26—Benito Penna, Milano ....KO 4

1976

Mar. 5—Domenico Scala, Salo ....KO 3
Apr. 9—Dante Cane, R. Emilia ....LF 6
(Lost Italian Heavyweight Title)
July 2—Alfredo Evangelista, Barcelona.......KO by 4
Aug. 7—Alfio Righetti, Rimini ....L 8

1977

May 7—Alfio Righetti, Rimini ....L 12
(For Italian Heavyweight Title)
Oct. 8—Jerry Tompkins, Rimini ....KO by 6

1978

Apr. 22—Jean Pierre Coopman, La Louveiere ..KO by 6

1979

(Inactive)

1980

Apr. 11—Vincenzo Pesapane, Piacenza ....KO by 6

FRED (BRUCE LEE) BASA

Filipino Flyweight

	1979		
Mar.	16—Rocky Genandizo, Angeles City	W	10
Apr.	24—Mar Agustin, Angeles City	W	10
May	21—Mar Agustin, Angeles City	W	10
July	13—Nene Jun, Manila	L	12
Oct.	20—Nitoy Bantilan, Pampanga	L	10
Nov.	24—Nardito Adrayan, Cag. de Oro City	L	10
	1980		
Feb.	23—Dony Soriano, Angeles City	L	10
May	17—Eddie Miral, Tariac	D	10
Dec.	20—Gener Cruz, Cabanatuan City	L	10

MANASEH BASE

Filipino Junior Flyweight

	1979		
Nov.	9—Cesar Kid Navarosa, Manila	W	10
	1980		
Feb.	15—Netrenoi S. Vorasing, Manila	KO by	11
Sept.	11—Jae-Hyun Kim, Cotabato	W	10

MARZIO BASEOTTI

Italian Junior Middleweight

	1980		
Feb.	1—Boro Jovic, San Dona	KO	5
Mar.	28—Pascal Maliba Kibassa, San Dona	KO by	6
May	9—Mauro Da Cruz, San Dona	W	6
Sept.	19—Claudio Pereyra, San Dona	D	6
Oct.	24—Mauro Da Cruz, San Dona	W	6
Nov.	29—Mauro Da Cruz, Padova	W	6

PETER BASSEY

British Middleweight

	1980		
Jan.	16—Tommy Williams, Liverpool	W	6
Jan.	21—Jerry Golden, Birmingham	W	4
Feb.	6—Terry Matthews, Liverpool	L	8
Feb.	11—Tony Britton, Manchester	W	6
Feb.	18—Joe Jackson, Stockport	W	6
Mar.	5—Henry Cooper, Liverpool	L	8
Mar.	24—Leo Mulhearn, Bradford	W	6
Mar.	31—Jimmy Ellis, Cleethorpes	L	8
Apr.	9—Winston Davis, Liverpool	L	8
Apr.	29—Leo Mulhearn, Stockport	W	6
May	7—Doug James, Liverpool	D	8
June	16—Henry Cooper, Manchester	W	8
Sept.	15—Leo Mulhearn, Manchester	W	8
Sept.	22—Martin McEwen, Birmingham	W	8
Oct.	16—Mick Morris, Bolton	L	8

STEVE BATEMAN

British Middleweight

	1980		
Sept.	24—Willie Wright, Evesham	L	6
Oct.	1—Mohammed Ben, Swansea	W	4
Oct.	13—Steve Goodwin, Manchester	D	6

DEBRIL BATHILI

South African Welterweight

	1978		
Jan.	7—Pal Payen, Grivegnee	L	8
Sept.	14—William Collet, Paris	W	6
	1979		
Sept.	15—Frank Decaestecker, Ostend	D	8
Oct.	13—Dirck Declerk, Antwerp	W	8
Nov.	3—Yannick Blandin, St. Malo	W	8
	1980		
Mar.	22—Scassino Ferreira, Santander	KO by	2

JIMMY BATTEN

English Junior Middleweight

Born: Nov. 7, 1955

	1974		
June	4—George Salmon, London	W	6
Oct.	1—Brian Gregory, London	W	6
Oct.	15—Rod Griffith, Shoreditch	KO	2
Oct.	21—Yotham Kunda, Bethnal Green	W	6
Nov.	12—Bob Langley, London	KO	2
Dec.	12—Brian Gregory, Bethnal	W	6
	1975		
Feb.	18—Joe Hannaford, Bethnal Green	KO	2
Mar.	25—Dave Davies, Kensington	W	8
Apr.	29—Victor Perez, London	W	8
Dec.	2—Peter Cain, Bethnal Green	L	8
	1976		
Jan.	20—John Smith, London	W	8
Mar.	2—Peter Cain, London	KO by	6
Apr.	20—Roy Commosioung, Bethnal Green	W	8
June	1—Jim Moore, London	KO	5
Sept.	14—Jeff Burns, London	KO	3
Oct.	26—Steve Angell, London	KO	6
Nov.	15—Liam White, London	KO	3
Dec.	7—Kevin White, London	W	8
	1977		
Feb.	1—Albert Hillman, London	KO	8
	(British Junior Middleweight Title)		
Feb.	22—Jimmy Savage, Kensington	KO	2
Mar.	29—Trevor Francis, London	W	10
Apr.	12—Michel Chapier, London	KO	9
June	14—Julio Garcia, Wembley	KO	6
Oct.	25—Larry Paul, London	KO	4
	1978		
Jan.	24—Clarence Howard, Kensington	KO	4
Apr.	25—Georges Warusfel, London	W	10
Sept.	12—Tony Poole, Wembley	KO	13
	(British Junior Middleweight Title)		
Nov.	21—Gilbert Cohen, Wembley	KO by	3
	1979		
Jan.	23—Aundra Love, London	W	8
Apr.	10—Dave Proud, Kensington	W	10
May	14—Colin Ward, Wembley	W	10
Sept.	9—Pat Thomas, London	KO by	9
	(Lost British Junior Middleweight Title)		
Dec.	4—George Walker, Wembley	W	8
	1980		
June	3—Wayne Barker, London	W	4
Sept.	16—Charlie Malarkey, London	W	4
Nov.	7—George Walker, London	L	4

ROLAND BAYENS

Belgian Middleweight

	1978		
May	4—Sabania, Kalken	W	6
Sept.	4—Rob Czabania, Rotterdam	L	6
Sept.	23—Antonio Rimasti, Lede	KO	5
Oct.	14—Salmin Boutera, Menin	KO by	6
Dec.	16—Jean Luc Lami, Kalken	W	6
	1979		
Feb.	3—Bernard Artone, Wetteren	W	6
Mar.	24—Roberto Bosio, Kalken	KO	3
Apr.	8—Bernard Artone, Geel	L	6
May	26—Maurice Trepant, Kalken	KO by	5
June	30—Maurice Trepant, Kalken	W	6
Sept.	28—Roberto Bosio, La Loviere	KO by	3
	1980		
Mar.	22—Michel Caron, Termonde	L	6

JOHNNY BEAUCHAMP

British Junior Welterweight

	1976		
Sept.	21—Delvin Whyte, Southend	W	6
	1977		
Apr.	5—Mick O'Mara, Hove	L	6
Apr.	18—Dave Taylor, Stafford	D	6
Apr.	24—Delvin Whyte, Birmingham	L	6
May	3—Delvin Whyte, Southend	W	6
May	16—Earl Noel, Hove	W	6
June	14—Eric Purkis, Southend	L	6
Sept.	5—George Daines, Hove	W	4
Sept.	14—John Kelly, Sheffield	L	6
Nov.	23—Bob Lewis, Stoke	D	6
	1978		
Feb.	28—Jimmy Smith, Athlesbury	L	4
Mar.	6—Nigel Thomas, London	L	4
Apr.	6—Nigel Thomas, Ebbw Vale	L	6
May	16—Nigel Thomas, Newport	L	6
Sept.	19—Terry Welch, Southend	L	6
Dec.	4—Jimmy Smith, London	KO by	2
	1979		
Apr.	9—Shaun Stewart, Nottingham	D	6
	1980		
Sept.	22—Rob Thornton, Birmingham	W	6
Nov.	3—Tommy Thomas, Hammersmith	L	6

RICKY BEAUMONT

British Lightweight

	1976		
Nov.	30—Tommy Davitt, Leeds	W	6
Dec.	7—Tommy Davitt, London	KO by	4
	1977		
Feb.	1—Barry Price, Kensington	KO	3
Feb.	22—Jeff Pritchard, Kensington	KO	3
Dec.	13—Steve Holdsworth, Slough	L	6
	1978		
Jan.	24—Tony Zeni, London	KO	2
Feb.	27—Ray Ross, Sheffield	W	8
Apr.	11—Eric Purkis, Sheffiled	KO by	2
Sept.	13—Eric Wood, Cambridge	W	6
Dec.	11—Bingo Crooks, Birmingham	L	8
	1979		
Dec.	3—Bingo Crooks, Hull	KO	1
	1980		
Jan.	25—Tommy Wright, Hull	W	8
Feb.	18—Tommy Davitt, London	W	8
Feb.	28—Des Gwilliam, Hull	KO	7
Mar.	17—Sylvester Gordon, London	W	8

Apr. 21—Willie Booth, Glasgow ....KO 4
June 2—Jeff Pritchard, London ....W 6
Oct. 2—George Feeney, Hull ....W 10
(Elimination, British Lightweight Title)

COENRAAD BEKKER
South African Welterweight
1976
Aug. 8—Louis Fourie, Durban ....L 4
Dec. 13—Mattheus A. Ludick, Durban ....W 4
1977
Feb. 28—Zacharia Thabethe, Durban ....W 4
May 30—Willie Phillips, Goodwood ....KO 1
July 6—Neil Lang, Cape Town ....W 6
Aug. 9—Charlie Weir, Goodwood ....KO by 5
1978
Feb. 22—Livingstone Luphondo, Cape Town ......W 4
Mar. 20—Johnny Sham, Cape Town ....W 8
July 17—Bushy Bester, Goodwood ....KO by 7
Nov. 15—Joseph Hali, Cape Town ....W 6
Dec. 18—James Abrahams, Goodwood ....KO 4
1979
Feb. 3—Phalo Tahume, Port Elizabeth ....KO 1
Mar. 10—Robbie Kleynhans, Oudtshoorn ....KO 2
June 21—Tom Ellis, Cape Town ....W 8
Sept. 27—Jack Jim, Cape Town ....W 10
Nov. 13—Jesse Carter, Cape Town ....W 8
Dec. 19—Gert Craemer, Cape Town ....W 6
1980
Mar. 29—David Kambule, Johannesburg ....W 6
May 12—Horace McKenzie, Cape Town ....W 10
Oct. 25—Harold Volbrecht, Sun City ....L 12
(For South African Welterweight Title)
Dec. 20—Mzwandile Biyana, East London ....L 10
(For Cape Welterweight Title)

GRAHAM BELL
Australian Junior Welterweight
1969
July 9—Nooky Davis, Cammeray ....W 4
Nov. 24—Carl Rowland, South Melbourne ....L 3
1970
May 6—Sam Bracken, Cammeray ....W 4
May 20—Sam Bracken, Brookvale ....W 6
May 28—Billy Moeller, Redfern ....L 3
Aug. 28—John Cullen, Brisbane ....L 3
Sept. 4—Marv Maddison, Brisbane ....L 3
Oct. 2—Ian Looker, Brisbane ....L 3
Nov. 6—Stephen Dale, North Albury ....D 6
1971
Jan. 21—Peter Vafeas, White City ....W 4
Feb. 3—Kevin Chester, Brookvale ....W 10
1972
Nov. 9—Col Connors, Redfern ....W 4
1973-1978
(Inactive)
1979
May 16—Stumpy Whitmore, Mt. Pritchard ....KO 2
Aug. 15—Ceddy McGrady, Mt. Pritchard ....W 8
Sept. 19—Buddy Clare, Mt. Pritchard ....W 6
Dec. 19—Greg Weston, Mt. Pritchard ....KO 4
1980
Feb. 20—Paul Baker, Mt. Pritchard ....D 10
May 21—Steve Assang, Mt. Pritchard ....W 10
(New South Wales Junior Welterweight Title)
July 18—Jeff Malcolm, Dapto ....L 12
(Lost New South Wales Junior Welterweight Title)
Sept. 17—Barry Micheal, Mt. Pritchard ....KO by 6
(For Australian Lightweight Title)

KERRY BELL
Australian Welterweight
1974
Oct. 25—Rocky Morelli, Brisbane ....KO 2
Dec. 6—Alby Roberts, Brisbane ....W 6
1975
Feb. 28—Gus Spina, Brisbane ....W 8
Mar. 14—Speedy Duke, Brisbane ....W 6
May 2—Gus Spina, Brisbane ....KO 7
May 19—Speedy Duke, Brisbane ....KO 5
July 7—Darcy Richie, Brisbane ....L 8
Aug. 4—Alby Roberts, Brisbane ....KO 6
Sept. 29—Leroy King, Tweed Heads ....KO 5
Nov. 17—Sid Dumbrell, Tweed Heads ....W 10
1976
Mar. 15—Speedy Duke, Tweed Heads ....W 8
Mar. 20—Martin Beni, Goroka ....KO 4
May 3—Steve Dennis, Tweed Heads ....KO by 7
(For Vacant Australian Welterweight Title)
Sept. 13—Phil Davies, Tweed Heads ....W 8
Nov. 3—Mark Bennett, Cammeray ....W 10
1977
Apr. 15—Ross Eadie, Boondall ....KO by 6
July 8—Speedy Duke, Brisbane ....W 8

Aug. 10—Jeff Malcolm, Marrickvale ....W 10
Sept. 30—Neil Pattel, Brisbane ....KO by 9
1978
Apr. 3—Gus Spina, Zillmere ....W 10
1979
(Inactive)
1980
Apr. 26—Mark Apai, Goroka ....L 10
May 25—Ali Afakasi, Wellington ....KO by 9
June 28—Gary Tomlinson, Nanango ....KO 6
July 7—Robert Colley, Brisbane ....W 10

SELWYN (SELVIN) BELL
British Featherweight
1977
Nov. 8—Rodney Collinson, Darlington ....W 4
Nov. 29—Brian Snagg, Birkenhead ....L 6
Dec. 5—Brian Snagg, Manchester ....L 6
Dec. 12—Rodney Collinson, Barnsley ....W 6
1978
Jan. 23—Steve Early, London ....KO by 2
Apr. 11—Bobby Baker, Sheffield ....KO 6
Apr. 18—John Cooper, London ....W 6
May 11—Benny Purdy, Belfast ....KO by 6
June 19—Kevin Quinn, Manchester ....L 6
June 29—Doug Gregory, Wolverhampton ....L 6
Sept. 4—Tony Vernon, Wakefield ....KO 2
Sept. 12—Terry Welch, Stoke ....L 6
Sept. 27—Doug Hill, Stoke ....L 6
Oct. 2—George Metcalf, Liverpool ....L 6
Oct. 9—Derek Nelson, Middlesbrough ....L 6
Oct. 16—George Metcalf, London ....L 6
Oct. 24—Nagib Daho, Blackpool ....L 6
Nov. 15—Lawrence Williams, Solihull ....KO by 6
Dec. 11—Dai Davies, Plymouth ....L 6
Dec. 18—Young Chezz, Bradford ....W 6
1979
Jan. 18—Gary Lucas, Liverpool ....W 6
Feb. 6—Austin Owens, Wembley ....L 6
Feb. 26—Larry Richards, Edgbaston ....L 6
Mar. 15—Larry Richards, Caister ....L 6
Mar. 22—Gary Lucas, Liverpool ....L 6
Apr. 3—Kenny Matthews, Hammersmith ....L 6
Apr. 10—Mickey Baker, Wolverhampton ......KO by 3
May 16—Johnny Burns, Wolverhampton ....L 5
May 23—Steve Parker, Nottingham ....KO 1
June 6—Doug Hill, Burslem ....L 8
June 18—Sammy Simms, Manchester ....L 6
Sept. 11—Austin Owens, London ....KO by 4
Oct. 15—Steve Cleak, Windsor ....L 6
Oct. 22—Donald George, Nottingham ....L 6
Nov. 15—Alec Irvine, Caister ....L 6
Nov. 26—Alan Storey, Birmingham ....L 6
Dec. 17—Paul Keers, Bradford ....W 8
1980
Jan. 8—Jim McKeown, Windsor ....L 6
Jan. 16—Terry McKeown, Solihull ....L 8
Feb. 25—Dave George, Bradford ....L 8
Mar. 3—Alan Storey, Marton ....D 6
Mar. 10—Dave Ramsden, Manchester ....L 6
Mar. 17—Dave Ramsden, Doncaster ....W 6
Mar. 24—Dave Ramsden, Bradford ....W 6
Mar. 31—Dave Ramsden, Cleethorpes ....KO 3
Apr. 21—Doug Hill, London ....KO by 5
May 28—Norman Morton, Cramlington ....L 6
July 7—Mick Mason, Middlesbrough ....L 6
Sept. 9—Steve Farnsworth, Sheffield ....L 6
Oct. 13—Mick Mason, Newcastle ....L 6
Oct. 23—Mick Mason, Middlesbrough ....L 8

STEVE BELL
Australian Flyweight
Turned Pro 1970. Through 1975 had 29 fights.
Won 25, Lost 4
1970
July 16—Steve Gibson, Redfern ....W 3
Aug. 6—Wayne Wallace, Redfern ....KO 3
Aug. 11—Buddy Clare, Bondi Junction ....KO by 1
Sept. 10—Eddie Attard, Redfern ....KO 3
Sept. 16—Steve Gibson, Fairfield ....W 4
Oct. 1—Wayne Wallace, Redfern ....KO 3
Oct. 7—Eddie Attard, Brookvale ....W 4
Oct. 14—Steve Gibson, Riverwood ....W 4
Nov. 11—Eddie Attard, Riverwood ....KO 6
Nov. 26—Wayne Wallace, Redfern ....W 3
Dec. 3—Greg Haggart, Richmond ....W 6
1971
Jan. 13—Stan Treffery, Riverwood ....KO 2
Jan. 24—Steve Gibson, Redfern ....W 3
Jan. 28—Wayne Wallace, Redfern ....W 4
Feb. 11—Wayne Wallace, White City ....W 4
Apr. 7—Wayne Wallace, Riverwood ....W 10
(Won New South Wales Flyweight Title)
June 17—Big Jim West, Redfern ....W 6

June	23—Wayne Wallace, Cammeray	W	10
July	7—Big Jim West, Riverwood	W	10
Aug.	11—Wayne Wallace, Cammeray	W	10
Aug.	17—Big Jim West, Penrith	W	10
Aug.	24—Harry Hayes, Nunawading	L	10
Sept.	15—Big Jim West, Cammeray	W	10
Oct.	18—Wayne Wallace, Marrickvale	W	10
Dec.	1—Wayne Watson, Riverwood	W	10
Dec.	13—Henry Hayes, Marrickvale	L	10

1972

May	3—Robert Eggleton, Cardiff	W	10
	(Retained New South Wales Flyweight Title)		
Aug.	15—Robert Eggleton, Cardiff	L	10
	(Retained New South Wales Flyweight Title)		

1973-1974
(Inactive)

1975

Oct.	30—Steve Walker, Blacktown	W	10

1976

Mar.	11—Steve Walker, Blacktown	D	8
May	4—Charlie Brown, Cardiff	D	15
	(For Australian Flyweight Title)		
Oct.	13—Steve Walker, Marrickvale	W	8
Dec.	13—Steve Walker, Bankstown	KO by	4
	(For Vacant New South Wales Flyweight Title)		

1977

Apr.	26—Charlie Brown, Cardiff	W	15
	(Won Australian Flyweight title)		
June	28—Roger Richens, Bankstown	KO	8
	(Australian Flyweight Title)		

1979
(Inactive)

1980

June	1—Pedro Solo, Revesby	W	15
	(For Australian Flyweight Title)		
Sept.	12—Junior Thompson, Auburn	KO	6
	(For Australian Flyweight Title)		
Oct.	10—Pedro Solo, Lidcombe	KO	13
	(For Australian Flyweight Title)		

MOHAMMED BEN
British Middleweight
1980

Sept.	22—Peter Morris, Lewisham	L	6
Oct.	1—Steve Bateman, Swansea	L	4

JEAN JACQUES BENCHETRIT
French Junior Middleweight
1978

Oct.	13—Tony Francisque, Nice	W	6

1979

Mar.	15—Rhida Hakimi, Nizza	KO	2
Apr.	14—Pierre Konig, Nice	KO	6
June	15—Jean Paul Coppyn, Nizza	W	6
Oct.	6—Ben Ouada, Marseille	KO	4
Nov.	9—Jose Luis Ribero, Nice	W	6
Dec.	1—Lucien Campo, Nice	KO	4
Dec.	14—Patrick Babouram, Nizza	W	6

1980

May	9—Sergio D'Angelo, Nice	KO	5
May	24—Cachama (Zhora) Musasa, Nice	W	6
Oct.	4—Claudio Pereyra, Nice	W	8
Dec.	6—Dragan Tadic, Nice	W	6

JAN BENEKE
South African Junior Middleweight
Born: May 21, 1952
1977

Mar.	4—Timotheus Modise, Pretoria	KO	1
Mar.	19—Gerhardus Koekemoer, Johannesburg	KO	4
May	6—Timothy Lerefole, Pretoria	KO	2
June	4—Joseph Mohlala, Johannesburg	KO	4
Aug.	13—Leslie Baker, Johannesburg	KO	1
Sept.	10—Emmanuel Gumede, Johannesburg	W	4

1978

Feb.	4—David Kgotsane, Johannesburg	W	4
June	9—Johnny Sham, Johannesburg	KO	2
	(South African Welterweight Title)		
July	1—David Kgotsane, Pretoria	KO	3
Aug.	26—Luis Lara Acosta, Bophuthatswana	L	6
Nov.	11—David Kambule, Johannesburg	KO by	2

1979

Nov.	12—David Kalako, Welkom	KO	2
Dec.	3—David Motlengwa, Welkom	KO by	5

1980

Apr.	21—Joseph Matthysen, Secunda	KO by	2

MARIJAN BENES
Yugoslav Junior Middleweight
Born: June 11, 1951
1977

Aug.	6—Clement Tshinza, Berlin	W	4
Sept.	8—Palscal Zito, Vienna	W	6

Oct.	1—Ridha Hakini, Vienna	KO	2
Oct.	10—John Smith, Rotterdam	W	8
Oct.	31—Mick Minter, Rotterdam	KO	2
Nov.	18—Alain Ruocco, Vienna	W	8
Dec.	10—Steve Angell, Berlin	KO	4
Dec.	16—Wa Bukasa, Vienna	KO	3

1978

Jan.	11—Pat Thomas, Rotterdam	W	8
Mar.	1—Tiger Quye, Rotterdam	KO by	3
Apr.	7—Tiger Quaye, Berlin	KO	1
May	6—Peter Neal, Frankfurt	KO	5
May	29—Tiger Quaye, Rotterdam	W	6
Sept.	2—Elisha Obed, Berlin	W	8
Nov.	18—Everaldo Costa Azevedo,Berlin	W	10

1979

Mar.	17—Gilbert Cohan, Banja Luca	KO	4
	(European Junior Middleweight Title)		
Apr.	29—Pricillano Castillo, Belgrade	KO	1
June	6—Andoni Amana, Bilabao	KO	8
	(EBU Junior Middleweight Title)		
Aug.	25—Sandy Torres, Belgrade	KO by	6
Nov.	5—Andre Huussen, Rotterdam	KO	3
	(EBU Junior Middleweight Title)		

1980

Feb.	13—Damiano Lassandro, Pesaro	D	12
	(Retained European Junior Middleweight Title)		
Mar.	29—Freddie Boynton, Berlin	KO	3
	(Retained European Junior Middleweight Title)		
June	12—Ayub Kalule, Randers	L	15
	(For WBA Junior Middleweight Title)		
Oct.	6—Georges Warfusel, Paris	KO	5
Dec.	19—Sandy Torres, Spalato	W	10

MIKE BENITEZ
Filipino Lightweight
1978

Nov.	10—Winnie Guineta, Cavite City	D	10

1979

Feb.	20—Rey Bustillos, Capiz	D	10
Mar.	29—Orlando Cruz, Olongapo	W	10
May	4—Mar Simbajon, Manila	D	10
June	23—Tony Flores, Cebu City	KO by	3
Aug.	26—Alex Infante, Cag. de Oro City	W	10
Nov.	24—San Mo Koo, Teku City	KO by	3

1980

Jan.	18—Leo Viajedos, Manila	W	10

JAMEL BENMEZIANE
French Junior Lightweight
1980

Feb.	9—Vincent Cipolla, Uigneux	W	6
Dec.	20—Patrick Drelon, Chateau Neuf	L	6

CARLTON BENOIT
Goeseinon, England Light Heavyweight
1976

May	10—Len Brittain, London	KO by	5
	(Pro debut)		
Sept.	21—Roy Gumms, Southend	W	6
Oct.	12—Johnny Wadron, Wembley	KO by	3
Dec.	2—Bob Pollard, Southend	D	6

1977

Jan.	17—Johnny Cox, London	W	6
Feb.	14—Reg Long, Bedford	W	6
Mar.	16—Johnny Cox, Stoke	W	8
Sept.	14—Danny McLoughlin, Sheffield	W	8
Sept.	20—Johnny Cox, Southend	W	8
Sept.	26—Winston Cousins, Manchester	L	8
Dec.	5—Brian Paul, London	W	8

1978

Feb.	15—Paul Kinsella, Cambridge	KO	6
Mar.	14—George Gray, Southend	W	6
Mar.	20—Billy Knight, Mayfair	W disq.	6
May	3—Tim Wood, Solihull	W	8
Nov.	21—Steve Taylor, Cambridge	KO	5
Nov.	28—Tom Collins, Sheffield	KO by	1

1979

Feb.	28—Eddy Fenton, Burslem	KO by	5
Apr.	27—Ken Jones, Newcastle	W	8
May	13—Chris Lawson, Plymouth	KO	2
Oct.	23—Frankie Hands, Blackpool	KO	7
Oct.	31—Karl Canwell, Burslem	L	8
Nov.	27—Alex Penarski, Sheffield	L	8

1980

Apr.	28—Pat McCann, Windsor	W	8
Sept.	22—Shaun Chalcraft, Lewisham	L	10
	(For Vacant Southern Area Light Heavyweight Title)		

DOMINIC BERGONZI
Italian Welterweight
1980

June	3—George McGurk, London	KO	2
July	12—Paul Wetter, London	W	6

Sept. 16—Brian Anderson, London .... D 6

LINO BERNADAS
Filipino Lightweight
1979
Dec. 22—Erning Marin, Davao Del North .... W 10
1980
Jan. 5—Greg Clarin, Santos City .... W 10
Feb. 9—Vincent Mawas, Santos City .... L 10
Dec. 13—Moises Cantoja, Manila .... KO by 9

PETER BERRIGAN
Australian Junior Welterweight
1976
Oct. 26—John Bowen, Cardiff .... W 4
Nov. 3—Steve Assang, Cammeray .... W 6
1977
Feb. 22—Dawsie Kelly, Cardiff .... W 8
Sept. 29—Cal Hickling, Shortland .... W 6
Oct. 7—Dawsie Kelly, Beresfield .... W 8
1978-1979
(Inactive)
1980
Mar. 11—Kirk Blair, Kingsford .... W 6
Mar. 29—Kelly Thompson, Tighes Hill .... W 8
Apr. 12—Speedy Duke, Tamworth .... W 8
May 16—Paul Baker, Cardiff .... W 10
(Won New South Wales Junior Welterweight Title)
Aug. 22—Speedy Duke, Cardiff .... KO 5
(For New South Wales Junior Welterweight Title)
Nov. 12—Rex Cannon, Belmont .... W 10

SOLOMON (BUSHY) BESTER
South African Junior Middleweight
1977
Jan. 29—Lemuel Nkumane, Johannesburg .... W 4
Mar. 4—Daniel Mphuthi, Pretoria .... W 4
Mar. 19—Philippus van As, Johannesburg .... KO 2
May 21—Jerry Molefe, Johannesburg .... W 4
Aug. 29—Charles Weir, Johannesburg .... KO by 1
1978
Apr. 3—Wentzel Marais, Pretoria .... KO 3
May 20—Louis Fourie, Tzaneen .... L 10
July 17—Coenraad Bekker, Goodwood ..... KO 7
Aug. 5—Johannes Mthembu, Bloemfontein ..... KO 5
Sept. 23—Louis Fourie, Booysens .... KO 4
Oct. 23—Neson Bosso, Johannesburg .... KO 7
Nov. 11—Johannes Mpesi, Johannesburg .... KO 3
1979
Apr. 28—Patrick Tshababla, Johannesburg .... KO 1
Aug. 27—Gert Craemer, Johannesburg .... KO 3
Dec. 1—Gert Steyn, Johannesburg .... W 10
1980
Feb. 9—Pat Hallacy, Johannesburg .... W 8
Mar. 1—Maxwell Malinga, Ermelo .... KO 6
Mar. 29—Gert Steyn, Johannesburg .... KO 10
(Retained South African Junior Middleweight Title)
May 10—Alvin Anderson, Johannesburg .... KO 2
Sept. 6—Ayub Kalule, Aarhus .... L 15
(For WBA Junior Middleweight Title)
Nov. 28—Steve Delgado, Johannesburg .... W 10

MONTY BETHAM
New Zealand Middleweight
Born: Sept. 27, 1952, West Samoa
1973
Feb. 19—Billy Fruen, Auckland .... KO 3
Mar. 12—Red Durange, Auckland .... W 6
Apr. 2—Leo Pua, Auckland .... KO 1
May —Rocky Taitin, Apia .... W 8
June 28—Dave Clarke, Wellington.............. W 10
July 9—Barry Asekona, Auckland .... KO 1
July 26—Dennis Cutmore, Wellington .... KO 1
Oct. 1—Kahu Mahanga, Auckland .... W 10
Oct. 22—Peter Clay, Auckland.................. W 10
Nov. 19—Peter Clay, Auckland .... W 10
1974
Feb. 19—Ray McGrady, Auckland................ KO 4
Apr. 4—Eddie Tavui, Wellington............... KO 3
Apr. 16—Ruben Arocha, Auckland .... W 10
May 6—Jone Mataitini Papeete .... W 10
June 25—Steve Aczel, Melbourne .... KO by 4
(Vacant Australian Light Heavyweight Title)
July 17—Aseri Namua, Auckland .... W 10
Sept. 11—Ted Gray, Auckland.................... KO 7
Oct. 14—Seva Mocasui, Auckland .... KO 1
Oct. 31—Semi Bula, Wellington.................. KO 8
Nov. 15—Renie Pinder, Auckland .... WF 7
1975
Feb. 3—Carlos Mark, Auckland................. L 10
Feb. 19—Greg McNamara, Auckland .... W 10
Mar. 19—Ricky Patterson, Wellington .... KO 9
May 1—Tony Dowling, Auckland.............. KO 5

May 30—James Marshall, Brisbane........... KO by 3
July 24—Carlos Mark, Wellington................. W 15
(Won Vacant Commonwealth Middleweight Title)
Aug. 27—Manuel Fierro, Auckland .... W 10
1976
Feb. 19—Semi Bula, Port Kembla................ KO 9
(British Empire Title)
Mar. 11—Alipate Korovou, Wellington........... W 15
(Commonwealth Middleweight Championship)
June 5—Jone Mataitini, Suva Fugi .... KO 7
(Commonwealth Middleweight Title)
July 12—Wally Carr, Wellington .... KO by 6
July 30—Carlos Mark, Trinidad................... W 15
(Commonwealth Middleweight Championship)
Sept. 23—Wally Carr, Wellington................. KO 11
(Commonwealth Middleweight Title)
1977
Mar 26—Roy Dale, Cincinnati .... L 10
May 9—Gert Steyn, Durban .... L 10
1978
Mar. 17—Al Korovou, Suva .... KO by 12
(Commonwealth Middleweight Title)
June 29—Benny Holt, Napier .... KO 4
1979
Feb. 1—Wally Carr, Auckland .... W 12
(Australian Middleweight Title)
Mar. 15—Ayub Kalule, Copenhagen .... KO by 4
June 26—Alan Minter, London .... KO by 2
1980
Apr. 13—Lance Revill, Auckland .... KO 11
(Won New Zealand Light Heavyweight Title)
June 30—Ross Eadie, Auckland .... W 12
Nov. 14—Gordie Lawson, Auckland .... KO 5
Dec. 15—Tony Mundine, Auckland .... KO by 5
(For Vacant Australian Light Heavyweight Title)

ALEX BEYNAERT
French Welterweight
1979
Sept. 8—Jo Bollue, Lierre .... L 6
Nov. 10—Dominique Fortemps, Montaigu .... L 6
1980
Jan. 25—Dominique Fortemps, Cheratte .... L 6
Mar. 8—Rafael Salamone, Montaigne .... D 6
Mar. 22—Phillipe Parent, Vilaverde .... KO by 5
Sept. 12—Marco Guiliani, Louvain .... D 6

SIPHIWE BHENGU
South African Bantamweight
1973
Apr. 14—Jerry Gumede, Durban .... KO 2
June 16—Johannes Phathi, Port Elizabeth .... W 6
June 22—Johannes Masehla, Springs .... W 4
July 14—Joe Mthiyame, Durban .... W 4
1974
Feb. 2—Anthony Sithole, Durban .... KO by 7
Apr. 6—John Frazier Mkhize, Durban .... W 4
July 19—Bassie Modise, Durban .... KO by 1
Sept. 14—William Matlokotsi .... L 6
1975
(Inactive)
1976
Dec. 18—John Ngwenya, Durban .... W 6
1977
Jan. 29—Christopher Dlamini, Port Elizabeth KO by 2
Nov. 12—Vincent Ngcobo, Durban .... W 6
1978
Mar. 18—Richard Modise, Durban .... KO 4
Aug. 12—Vincent Ngcobo, Durban .... L 10
(For Natal Black Bantamweight Title)
Sept. 30—Sikweyiya, Transkei .... KO by 2
1980
Mar. 1—Robert Makhoba, Durban .... KO by 4
(For Vacant South African Bantamweight Title)
Sept. 5—Wellie Nkosinkulu, Springs .... KO by 4

NAZIF BIBEROVIC
Yugoslavian Middleweight
1976
Dec. 2—Hans-Joachim Trautwein, Vienna .... W 6
1977
Jan. 14—Branco Barakovic, Bregenz .... L 6
Aug. 13—Alfredo Rossi, Zeltweg .... W 6
1979
Jan. 19—Drago Umicevich, Wien .... KO 2
Mar. 17—Mike Coy, Koblenz .... KO 4
Mar. 24—Haci Yildiz, Neustadt .... KO 3
July 6—Giampaolo Piras, Waidhofen .... KO 4
July 14—Luciano Casali, Lignano .... L 6
Sept. 8—Josef Kossman, Waidhofen .... D 8
Oct. 5—Cosimo Carbone, Firenze .... L 8
Nov. 15—Kurt Oerter, Eggenburg .... W 6
1980
Feb. 6—Frank Wissenbach, Lubeck .... KO by 8

Feb. 22—George Steinberr, Dusseldorf .... KO by 2
Sept. 26—Gino Freo, Abano .... L 8
Oct. 11—Mauricio Da Cruz, Wien .... L 8

PHAROAH BISH
British Middleweight
1980
Sept. 22—Paddy Ryan, London .... L 6
Oct. 13—Paddy Ryan, London .... L 6
Oct. 20—Winston Burnett, Birmingham .... L 6
Nov. 3—Owen Stafford, Hammersmith .... W 6

MARIO BITETTO
Italian Flyweight
1978
Nov. 25—Michele De Marco, Seregno .... W 6
Dec. 26—Gavino Luciano, Seregno .... W 6
1979
Feb. 2—Luigi Paravati, Milano .... KO 4
June 15—Corrado Infanti, Lissone .... W 6
July 6—Antonio Galletta, Seregno .... KO 2
Dec. 14—Filippo Belvedere, Milano .... W 6
1980
Feb. 29—Salvatore Laconi, Seregno .... W 8

RUDIGER BITTERLING
German Middleweight
1979
Jan. 26—Mi Whan Ki, Dusseldorf .... W 4
Apr. 22—Giampoalo Piras, Hamburg .... W 6
May 28—Etienne Bayadikilla, Amsterdam .... KO 5
June 16—Mike McCoy, Koblenz .... W 8
Sept. 16—Josef Kossmann, Koeblenz .... W 8
Sept. 28—Brahim Ferizovia, Munich .... KO 6
1980
Feb. 6—Klaus Hein, Lubeck .... KO 2
Feb. 22—Josef Kossman, Dusseldorf .... W 6
May 14—Mauro Valentini, Munich .... W 6
Sept. 26—Claude Kalanda, Koln .... KO 3
Dec. 5—Eddie Chileshe, Koln .... W 8

MZWANDILE BIYANA
South African Junior Welterweight/Welterweight
1978
Oct. 28—Leonard Silwana, East London .... KO 2
Dec. 15—Ntsola Songongo, East London .... L 6
1979
Mar. 10—Kenneth Moyi, East London .... W 6
Apr. 28—Fungile Buti, East London .... W 6
June 8—Stricker Studdard, East London .... KO 5
July 14—Tamie Spampool, East London .... W 8
Aug. 4—Empraim Mabena, East London .... W 6
Sept. 29—Justus Josephs, East London .... W 6
Nov. 10—Fungile Buti, King Williamstown .... KO 7
Dec. 8—Bramley Whiteboy, East London .... W 10
1980
Mar. 1—Simon Dladla, East London .... NC 3
Apr. 5—Jack Jim, East London .... W 8
May 31—Hardy Mileham, East London .... W 6
Aug. 16—Norman Sekgapane, East London .... KO 7
(Retained South African Junior Welterweight Title)
Sept. 6—Jorge Mojuia, East London .... W 8
Dec. 20—Coenraad Bekker, East London .... W 10
(Retained Cape Welterweight Title)

ALFRED BIYELA
South African Lightweight
1980
Nov. 1—Alfred Ndlovu, Stanger .... L 4

ANGELO BIZZARRO
Italian Lightweight
1978
Dec. 9—Palmiro Pizzata, Caserta .... KO 5
Dec. 28—Antonino Sandrin, Marcianise .... W 6
1979
Feb. 17—Abass Macauley, Caserta .... W 6
June 23—Josia Malquides Da Sylva, Marcianise .... W 8
Aug. 3—Angelo Zanetti, Tuscolano .... L 6
Dec. 29—Masu Mapanzi, Agerola .... W 6
1980
Mar. 29—Carlo Frassinetti, Nocera .... WF 8
June 28—Cosimo Lavino, Caserta .... W 8

KIRK (KID) BLAIR
Australian Featherweight
1977
Apr. 13—Roger Richens, Marrickville .... L 4
Apr. 26—Johnny Hipwell, Cardiff .... L 6
May 4—Bobby Williams, Cammeray .... KO 5
May 24—Steve Saxon, Kingsford .... W 6
June 8—Roger Richens, Marrickvale .... L 6
Aug. 16—Kirk Davis, Kingsford .... W 4

Sept. 13—Hank Leonard, Kingsford .... L 6
Sept. 27—Hank Leonard, Kingsford .... KO 4
Nov. 30—Kid Avery, Brookvale .... W 4
1978
Feb. 1—Gavin Kennedy, Cammeray .... KO 3
Apr. 18—Sparrow Freeman, Kingsford .... W 4
Apr. 26—Sparrow Freeman, Brookvale .... W 6
May 2—Sparrow Freeman, Kingsford .... W 8
May 17—David Carriage, Mt. Pritchard .... KO 5
May 31—Sparrow Freeman, Brookvale .... W 8
July 4—Charlie Brown, Cardiff .... W 8
July 26—Patrick Burns, Bankstown .... W 8
Sept. 27—Roger Richens, Bankstown .... W 10
Oct. 24—Charlie Brown, Cardiff .... W 8
Nov. 15—Jeff Smith, Paihatoa .... KO by 2
1979
Mar. 1—Tom Roberts, Blacktown .... W 6
Mar. 27—Clint Brown, Kingsford .... KO 4
Apr. 18—Steve Pike, Mt. Pritchard .... L 10
Aug. 7—Chris Bennett, Cardiff .... L 6
Oct. 17—Dennis Talbot, Mt. Pritchard .... D 8
Nov. 7—Lucky Campbell, Brookvale .... W 8
Dec. 8—John Fimec, Berkeley .... KO 3
1980
Feb. 26—Gary Rosen, Kingsford .... D 6
Mar. 5—Reg King, Brookvale .... L 6
Mar. 11—Peter Berrigan, Kingsford .... L 6
Mar. 30—Dennis Talbot, Ingleburn .... W 10
Apr. 26—Bimbo Morris, Berkeley .... KO 6
May 19—Sammy Misale, Kingsford .... W 8
June 29—Garry Williams, Rozelle .... L 8
July 11—Dennis Talbot, Auburn .... L 10
Aug. 11—Greg Leisegang, Brisbane .... KO by 9
Sept. 17—Barry Bell, Mt. Pritchard .... W 8
Nov. 15—Saiyad Hassan, Nandifiji .... KO by 10

ALEX BLANCHARD
Dutch Middleweight
1979
Jan. 8—Klaus Hein, Rotterdam .... KO 2
Mar. 7—Rainer Gutekunst, Rotterdam .... KO 3
Mar. 26—Sonny Kamunga, Groningen .... W 6
May 28—Jean Luc Lami, Amsterdam .... KO 2
Nov. 5—Etienne Bayadikilla, Rotterdam .... KO 4
Nov. 26—Josef Kossman, Rotterdam .... KO 1
1980
Jan. 28—Mike McCoy, Rotterdam .... KO 2
Mar. 31—Oscar Angus, Rotterdam .... KO 2
May 5—Billy Lauder, Rotterdam .... KO 4
May 19—Michel Chapier, Rotterdam .... KO 6
June 13—Gregory Marshall, Lubeck .... KO 2
Oct. 20—Michel Pagani, Rotterdam .... KO 1

ANDRE BLANCO
Dutch Junior Welterweight
1977
Sept. 23—N'Toya Kilala, Braine .... D 6
Nov. 26—Gilbert Helluin, Auxi .... L 6
1978
Jan. 7—Paul Croigny, Calais .... L 6
Feb. 23—N'Toya Killala, Louvain .... L 6
May 6—Jean Pierre Meganck, Kalken .... D 6
Sept. 23—Jean Pierre Meganck, Lede .... W 6
Nov. 3—Jo Bollue, Braine .... L 6
Nov. 18—Francis Bailleul, Creil .... L 6
Dec. 2—Gilbert Bayens, Zele .... D 6
1979
Jan. 9—Angelo Licata, St. Servais .... D 6
Feb. 6—Dave Williams, Zele .... KO by 4
Apr. 6—Kader Ben Mimoun, S. Tround .... W 6
July 13—Francis Bailleul, Middelkerke .... W 6
Sept. 15—Georges Lietaer, Ostend .... D 6
Oct. 6—Rudy Haeck, St. Amand .... D 8
Oct. 20—Jose Garcia, Liege .... L 8
Nov. 10—Gilbert Bayens, Zele .... D 6
1980
Feb. 16—Patrick Drelon, Middelkerke .... D 6
May 23—Francis Bailleul, Middelkerke .... D 6
Sept. 1—Anton Verrips, Rotterdam .... D 6
Oct. 20—Anton Verrips, Rotterdam .... L 6
Nov. 7—Angelo Licata, Middelkerke .... L 8

RAPHAEL BLANCO
Belgian Bantamweight
1978
May 4—Jean Pierre Meganck, Kalken .... D 6
Sept. 23—Jean Pierre Meganck, Lede .... W 6
Nov. 3—Jean Pierre Meganck, Braine .... W 6
Nov. 27—Roy Somer, L'Aja .... L 6
Dec. 15—Angelo Licata, La Louviere .... L 6
1979
Mar. 26—Georges Lieater, Louvain .... L 6
Sept. 14—Georges Lieater, Molenbeek .... D 6
Dec. 21—Patrick Drelon, Ostenda .... L 6

Feb.   8—Mohammed Maalen, Gentbrugge ....L 6

CHARLES BOIAS
South African Featherweight
Born: July 11, 1955, Johannesburg
1975
July   11—Howard Motumi, Orlando West 4
1976-1977
(Inactive)
1978
July   3—Cornelius Swanepoel, Fedfordview ......KO 4
Sept. 8—Willie McGeer, Johannesburg ....W 4
1979
Feb.   3—Norman Bromfield, Johannesburg ....L 4
Aug.   4—Guy Ratazayo, East London ....L 6
1980
Mar.   13—Chris Whiteboy, Cape Town ....L 6

JAFTA BOHOPE
South African Flyweight
1980
Oct.   11—Meshack Dhlamini, Odendaalsrust ....W 4
Nov.   29—Elias Gwamanda, Odendaalsrust ....W 4

FREDERIC BOISSY
French Junior Welterweight
1979
Apr.   13—Maurice Renaud, Nizza ....W 6
Sept. 29—Justin M'Foudi, Villerbaune ....W 6
Nov.   3—Daniel Huyon, Le Mans ....L 6
1980
Feb.   1—Dominique Delorme, Paris ....W 6
Feb.   15—Pax Kibassa, Villeurbanne ....W 6
Oct.   10—Michel Moinard, Villeurbanne ....W 6

JO BOLLUE
French Welterweight
1978
Oct.   14—Charles Restivo, Leval ....KO 3
Nov.   3—Andre Blanco, Braine ....W 6
Dec.   22—Aziz Balhasanne, Leval ....W 6
1979
Sept. 8—Alex Baynaerts, Lierre ....W 6
Oct.   5—Mohamed Bouziani, Binche ....D 6
Dec.   8—Philippe Parent, La Louviere ....W 6
1980
Apr.   5—Lucien Campo, La Louviere ....W 6
May   31—Mohamed Bouziani, Binche ....D 6
June   28—Philippe Parent, Gembloux ....W 6
Oct.   21—Marco Giuliani, Poinche ....W 6
Nov.   22—Dominique Fortempts, La Louviere ......W 6

MARTIN BOLTON
British Lightweight
1980
Oct.   2—Paul Wake, Hull ....W 6

LUCIANO BOMBEN
Italian Middleweight
1973
Feb.   17—Branko Barakovic, Pordenone ....W 6
May   5—Ahmed Bouchara, Pordenone ....W 6
May   26—Lawrence Ekpeli, S. Maria Fel. ....W 6
July   4—Mario Favotto, Lignano ....W 6
Nov.   10—Lawrence Ekpeli, Pordenone ....W 6
1974
Mar.   8—Guerino Cipriani, Pordenone ....W 8
Apr.   19—Giuseppi Panunzio, Pordenone ....W 6
July   25—Giuseppe Borghi, Cantu ....KO by 5
Aug.   17—Bortolo Cogoli, Jesolo ....W 6
Oct.   5—Mario Coiro, Pordenone ....W 6
1975
Feb.   15—Gabriele Lazzari, Pordenone ....L 8
Mar.   28—Gabriele Lazzari, Udine ....KO by 6
Oct.   24—Cristiano Cavina, Bologna ....L 8
Nov.   29—Elia Bettinzoli, Vincenza ....D 8
1976
Jan.   30—Otello Natale, Bologna ....W 6
Apr.   9—Mariano Salamone, R. Emilia ....W 6
Nov.   6—Adriano Rodriguez, Pordenone ....W 6
1977
Jan.   22—Mariano Salamone, Pordenone ....W 8
Feb.   18—Mariano Salamone, Lucca ....W 8
Sept. 30—Giuseppi Borghi, Lucca ....KO by 3
1978
June   28—Mario Pagani, Bologna ....D 6
1979
(Inactive)
1980
Mar.   22—Luciano Di Giacomo, Pordenone ....W 0
July   5—Mauricio Da Cruz, Taiedo ....W 6
Oct.   25—Aldo Polesel, Pordenone ....W 8

JANUARY BONGO
South African Featherweight
1978
Sept. 2—Alexis Khaeeane, Ficksburg ....W 4
Oct.   7—Alexis Khaeeane, Virginia ....W 6
1979
May   5—David Motaung, Ficksburg ....KO by 3
1980
June   7—David Majoe, Odenaalsrust ....L 4

TIMOTEO BONIZZONI
Italian Lightweight
1976
Sept. 25—Angelo D'Isidoro, Cremona ....KO 4
Oct.   29—Augusto Lauri, Novara ....W 6
Nov.   26—Mario Favotto, Milano ....W 6
Dec.   17—Vittorio Tamburini, Novara ....W 6
1977
Feb.   19—Giancarlo Serangeli, Milano ....W 6
Apr.   1—Jose Luis Ribeiro, Milano ....W 6
Mar.   20—Mario Martiliano, Milano ....W 8
June   24—Luigi Martello, Fontanella ....D 8
Aug.   26—Giancarlo Serangeli, Orzinuovi ....W 6
Oct.   21—Guido Galletti, Milano ....W 6
1978
Mar.   17—Giampaolo Piras, Mantova ....W 8
May   26—Augusto Lauri, Crema ....KO 5
Aug.   2—Boro Jovic, Maderno ....W 8
Aug.   25—Edson Lima, Orinuovi ....W 8
Nov.   11—Alois Carmeliet, Zele ....L 10
1979
Feb.   3—Italo Venturi, Brescia ....D 10
Apr.   20—Joel Leprodhomme, Milano ....D 8
May   19—Ernesto Ros, Crema ....W 8
Sept. 8—Antonio Torsello, Offanengo ....KO 5
1980
Dec.   27—Guiseppe Tidu, Cagliari ....KO by 7

JOEL BONNETAZ
French Middleweight
1974
Feb.   21—Jean Paul Serra, Paris.................KO 4
Mar.   14—Leocadie Calcul, Paris ....W 6
June   21—Frank Wissenback, Berlin ....L 6
Nov.   7—Jean Claude Midoux, Paris.............W 8
Nov.   22—Adriano Rodriguez, Perigueux..........KO 8
1975
Feb.   22—Robert Mathieu, Perigueux ....W 8
Mar.   8—Stan Van Der Driessche, The Hague .....W 8
Apr.   10—Francis Vermandere, Perigueux ....W 10
Nov.   6—Chedli Tebourski, Perigueux ....W 6
Nov.   29—Francis Vermandere, Bethune..........KO 3
Dec.   13—Vincent Parra, Paris...................W 8
1976
Jan.   22—Jimmy Savage, Paris ....W 10
Feb.   26—Daniel Martin, Paris ....W 10
Mar.   27—Salam Ouedraogo, Abidjan Ivory Coast KO by 4
Apr.   22—Jean Claude Warusfel, Paris ....W 12
(French Junior Middleweight Title)
Nov.   18—Kevin White, Paris....................W 10
Dec.   11—Claude Martin, Saint Malo.............KO 3
1977
Jan.   28—Michel Chapier, Perigueux ....W 12
Apr.   15—Emile Griffith, Perigueux ....W 10
Oct.   7—Roy Kaba, Lyon ....W 10
Nov.   8—Maurice Hope, London ....KO by 5
(European Junior Middleweight Title)
1978
Feb.   4—Adoni Amana, Bilbao ....KO by 4
Apr.   15—Claude Martin, St. Malo ....L 12
(French Junior Middleweight Title)
Nov.   4—Gerard Breton, Perigueux ....KO 1
Nov.   18—Michel Chapier, Tarbes ....W 10
1979
Jan.   12—Gerard Nosley, Perigueux ....L 10
May   18—Georg Steinherr, Munich ....L 10
Nov.   9—Mustaphata Kabunga, Nice ....W 6
1980
Mar.   28—Roberto Felicioni, Rome ....L 8
July   16—Nicola Cirelli, Lignano ....KO by 5

WILLIE BOOTH
Scottish Lightweight
Born: Sept. 5, 1956
1976
Feb.   9—Delvin White, London.................W 6
Feb.   23—Kenny Matthews, Glasgow ....W 6
Mar.   11—Ginger Bell, Hamilton ....KO 4
Mar.   22—Dave Tuohey, Glasgow ....W 6
Apr.   5—Steve Elliston, London................W 6
Apr.   26—Ian Doherty, London ....W 6
June   24—Dill Collins, London ....W 8
Nov.   15—Ian Pickersgill, Glasgow ....KO 7

Nov.   22—Billy Vivian, London .... L 8
1977
Mar.   18—Don Burgin, Holytown .... W 8
May   2—Von Reid, Holytown .... KO 3
Oct.   10—Bingo Crooks, Glasgow .... W 8
Nov.   14—Tommy Glencross, Glasgow .... W 10
        (Scottish Lightweight Title)
1978
Jan.   9—Billy Vivian, London .... W 8
Jan.   16—Jeff. Pritchard, Birmingham .... D 8
May   8—Tommy Dunn, Glasgow .... KO 5
Oct.   31—Johnny Claydon, Hammersmith .... L 10
Nov.   27—Mick Bell, Glasgow, ... KO 8
        (Scottish Junior Welterweight Title)
1979
Jan.   29—Tommy Davitt, Glasgow .... KO by 3
Apr.   17—Sylvester Gordon, Glasgow .... W 8
June   18—George Peacock, Glasgow .... L 10
        (Scottish Junior Welterweight Title)
Oct.   8—Bingo Crooks, Glasgow .... KO by 6
1980
Mar.   10—Paul Chance, Wolverhampton .... L 10
Apr.   21—Ricky Beaumont, Glasgow .... KO by 4
June   7—Duncan Hamilton, Glasgow .... W 10
        (Retained Scottish Lightweight Title)
Sept.   6—Langton Tinango, Salisburg .... L 10

CLAUDIO BOSIO
Belgian Middleweight
1980
Jan.   25—Carl Daly, La Louviere .... KO by 5
Apr.   19—Jean Luc Lami, Belgium .... W 6
Sept.   27—Chaed Ringo, Santander .... L 6
Nov.   8—Jean Luc Lami, St. Truiden .... D 6

ROBERTO BOSIO
Belgian Heavyweight
1978
Feb.   11—Lassine Niare, Liege .... L 6
Mar.   18—Maurice Trepant, La Louviere .... L 6
May   27—Claudio Cassanelli, Crevalcore .... KO by 4
1979
June   9—Ahmed Galloul, La Louviere .... KO by 2
Sept.   28—Roland Bayens, La Louviere .... KO 3
1980
Jan.   25—Joey Williams, La Louviere .... KO by 5
Apr.   19—Horst Lang, Belgium .... KO 4
June   19—Bernard Antone, La Louviere .... W 8
June   27—Luc Gossens, Bruxelles .... D 6
Oct.   24—Abdel Qissi, Moulinbeck .... KO by 5

SERGIO BOSIO
Belgian Light Heavyweight
1980
Jan.   25—Jean Luc Lami, La Louviere .... W 6
Apr.   19—Nedja Memeti, Belgium .... W 6
Sept.   27—Nedja Memeti, La Louviere .... D 6
Nov.   22—Mustapha Kabangu, La Louviere .... KO 4

RONALD (RODNEY) BOTHA
South African Lightweight
1979
Dec.   19—Alfred Mcilizeli, Cape Town .... KO 3
1980
Jan.   14—Patrick Majada, Cape Town .... W 4
June   4—Sazi Xamalashe, Cape Town .... KO 4
Dec.   22—Manny de Paiva, Cape Town .... W 6

WILLIAM BOTHA
South African Featherweight
1980
Nov.   22—Andile Xhotyeni, Queenstown .... W 4
Dec.   13—Andile Xhotyeni, Queenstown .... W 4

PETRUS (PEET) BOTHMA
South African Lightweight
Born: April 27, 1955
1974
June   15—Robert Donaldson, Turffontein .... D 4
June   28—Eddie Mileham, Welkom .... L 4
July   20—Abraham Smith, Pretoria .... WF 2
Aug.   30—Mike Botes, Kroonstad .... KO 3
Oct.   26—Abraham Smith, Johannesburg .... KO 6
1975
Feb.   17—Harry Barbaries, Durban .... KO 4
Mar.   24—Les Baker, Durban...................,....D 8
May   3—Alec McMillan, Johannesburg .... W 6
May   26—Ronnie du Preez, Durban .... L 8
Aug.   16—Leslie Baker, Durban.................... KO 4
1976
Jan.   31—Kokkie Olivier, Durban .... W 8
Aug.   16—Johnny Sham, Westridge .... L 6

1977
Jan.   29—Thuso Mapela, Johannesburg .... W 6
May   21—Eddie Mileham, Johannesburg .... L 12
        (For Vacant South African National Lightweight Title)
Sept.   26—Eddie Mileham, Johannesburg .... W 12
        (Won South African National Lightweight Title)
Dec.   3—Simon Zondo, Johannesburg .... W 6
1978
Feb.   2—Tadios Fisher, Salisbury .... W 10
Apr.   10—Leslie Baker, Johannesburg .... W 6
Apr.   14—Jimmy Ellis, Bulawayo .... W 6
Apr.   28—Jose Rios, Salisbury .... W 6
May   26—Gordon Mopufa, Salisbury .... KO 5
June   1—Leslie Baker, Goodwood .... KO 4
Aug.   26—Anthony Morodi, Mmabatho .... KO 1
Nov.   11—Ephraim Mabena, Johannesburg .... L 6
1979
Jan.   16—Bramley Whiteboy, Cape Town .... L 8
Feb.   23—Langton Tinago, Bulawayo .... KO 6
Mar.   24—Justus Josephs, Johannesburg .... W 6
Apr.   28—Rolly Xipu, Johannesburg .... W 12
        (Won Vacant South African National Lightweight Title)
July   9—Elias Diraditsile, Welkom .... W 6
Sept.   27—Bowell Zono, Capetown .... W 12
        (Won South African Lightweight Title)
Nov.   12—Bramley Whiteboy, Cape Town .... L 8
         —Goodwin Phofu, Bulawayo .... KO 4
         —Tadios Fisher, Bulawayo .... W 8
         —Langton Tinago, Bulawayo .... L 8
         —Langton Tinago, Bulawayo .... W 8
1980
Feb.   9—Simon Dhladla, Johannesburg .... W 6
Mar.   1—Alfred Sibisi, Ermelo .... L 6
May   10—Johnny Copeland, Johannesburg .... KO 2
May   26—Rolly Xipu, Johannesburg .... W disq. 7

JIMMY BOTT
British Bantamweight
1976
Oct.   26—Gary Davidson, Kensington .... KO by 3
1977
Jan.   10—Dave Smith, Walworth .... L 8
Feb.   14—Ian Murray, Manchester .... W 6
Feb.   22—Dave Smith, Kensington .... L 6
Mar.   3—Ian Murray, Caister .... W 6
Mar.   29—Noel Evans, Ebbw Vale .... D 6
May   11—Noel Evans, Swansea .... KO by 3
June   13—Ian Murray, Manchester .... L 6
July   30—Davy Larmour, Derry .... KO by 1
Sept.   22—Trevor Bromby, Birkenhead .... KO 4
Oct.   10—John Feeny, Maton .... KO by 6
1978
Mar.   2—George Bailey, Liverpool .... L 6
Mar.   20—George Bailey, Bradford .... D 6
Apr.   6—Bryn Griffiths, Ebbw Vale .... L 8
Apr.   17—George Bailey, Bradford .... W 8
Apr.   24—Eddie Glencross, Glasgow .... D 8
Sept.   8—George Bailey, Wakefield .... KO 8
Oct.   23—Ian Murray, Manchester .... L 6
Nov.   20—Alan Storey, Birmingham .... D 6
1979
Feb.   21—Pip Coleman, Evesham .... L 6
Mar.   15—Mohammed Younis, Dudley .... KO by 2
May   21—Bryn Jones, London .... W 6
June   18—Billy Straub, Glasgow .... L 6
Oct.   31—Eddie Glencross, Burslem .... W 8
1980
Feb.   28—Joey Wainwright, Hull .... D 6
Mar.   24—Steve Enwright, Bradford .... L 10
        (For Vacant Central Area Bantamweight Title)
Apr.   28—Dave Smith, Walworth .... L 8
Oct.   14—Dave George, Nantwich .... L 8
Oct.   29—Dave George, Burslem .... L 8

VINCENZO BOTTIGLIERO
Italian Welterweight
1978
June   5—Francesco Sanna, Villaricca .... W 6
July   14—Salvatore Cascio, Lido di Ostia .... L 6
Oct.   13—Giuseppe Di Padova, Mantova .... KO by 3
Nov.   25—Salah Ben Saad, Ascoli .... LF 2
Dec.   15—Donato Romano, Lugo di Romagna .... L 6
1979
Mar.   31—Antonio Stocchino, Cagliari .... D 6
May   12—Filiberto Zaccheo, Latina .... L 6
June   9—Francesco Morrone, Taranto .... L 6
July   27—Luigi Marini, S. Elpidio .... L 8
Sept.   21—Salvatore Cascio, Rome .... L 8
Oct.   6—Francesco Sanna, Aversa .... KO 5
1980
Feb.   9—Franco Aresti, Cagliari .... KO by 7
Apr.   25—Ugo Di Pietro, Cisterna .... L 6
Aug.   10—Luciano Navarra, Siderno .... L 6

270

MOHAMED BOUMEDIEN
(JOFRE II)
Spanish Junior Lightweight
1980
Feb. 16—Modesto Torito Gomez, Oviedo ....W 8
Apr. 19—Isidoro Cabeza, Palma de Mallorca ....W 10
Aug. 30—Hugo Carrizo, Cuenea ....D 8

BECHIR BOUNDKA
French Welterweight
1976
Dec. 10—Jean Pierre Moreau, Blois ....L 8
Dec. 18—Jean Claude Sider, S. Amand ....W 8
1977
Apr. 2—Jean Pierre Moreau, Nemours ....KO 3
Nov. 25—Alain Ruocco, Tolone ....KO by 7
1978
Jan. 7—Laurent Grimbert, Crepy en Valois ....L 8
Mar. 11—William Collet, Nemours ....W 8
May 27—Alain Marion, Creil ....KO by 7
June 23—Joseph Bessala, Younde-Cameroun ......L 15
(African Welterweight Title)
1979
Nov. 1—Frank De Caessecker, Izegem ....L 8
Nov. 26—Gerard Bok, Rotterdam ....D 6
Dec. 8—Alois Carmeliet, Zele ....L 8
1980
Apr. 5—Luigi Martello, Tunis ....KO 10
Nov. 27—Ronald Zenon, Paris ....L 10

JULIAN BOUSTEAD
British Lightweight
1979
May 21—Tommy Burling, Walworth ....W 4
Oct. 15—Terry Parkinson, Mayfair ....KO 3
Nov. 10—Joe Mills, Birmingham ....D 4
Dec. 10—Walter Clayton, Torquay ....W 4
1980
June 2—Mike Clemow, Plymouth ....W 6
Oct. 2—Colin Wake, Hull ....KO by 4

SALMIN BOUTERA
Belgian Light Heavyweight
1977
Sept. 9—Leander Pante, Izegem ....W 6
1978
Oct. 14—Roland Bayens, Menin ....KO 6
Nov. 1—Nedza Memeti, Izegem ....W 6
Dec. 8—Darko Barakovic, Gits ....KO 5
Dec. 25—Pierre Kabassu, Esch ....L 6
1979
Jan. 19—Esad Memeti, Brussels ....KO by 3
July 2—Fred Serres, Esch ....KO by 6
Oct. 31—Nedza Memeti, Duffel ....L 6
1980
Apr. 12—Walter Cevoli, Rimini ....KO by 4

MOHAMED BOUZIANI
Belgian Welterweight
1977
Dec. 16—N'Toya Kilala, Grivgnee ....W 6
1978
Jan. 20—William Collet, Grivgnee ....D 6
Mar. 24—Charles Testivo, Tubize ....W 6
Apr. 14—N'Toya Kilala, La Louviere ....W 6
June 5—Lucien Campo, Paris ....W 6
Oct. 14—Abdallah Salah Kaci, Pepinster ....W 6
1979
Jan. 13—Leandre Luigiery, Braine Le Chateau .....L 6
Mar. 2—Fredo Roelands, Bruges ....L 6
Apr. 14—Jean Marie Touati, Lieges ....L 6
Oct. 5—Jo Bollue, Binche ....D 6
Nov. 1—Cor Eversteijn, Rotterdam ....L 6
Nov. 24—Pierre Koenig, St. Trond ....W 6
1980
Feb. 23—Philippe Parent, Pepinster ....KO 3
Mar. 21—Dominique Fortemps, Cheratte ....W 6
Apr. 19—Philippe Parent, Belgium ....L 6
May 31—Jo Hollue, Binche ....D 6
Oct. 6—Gilles Elbilia, Paris ....L 6
Nov. 8—Philippe Parent, St. Truiden ....D 6

JIMMY BOWEN
Australian Bantamweight
1978
Nov. 1—Steve Freeman, Brookvale ....W 8
1979
May 8—Sparrow Freeman, Kingsford ....W 6
1980
Feb. 26—Chris Bennett, Kingsford ....W 8
Mar. 0—Glenn Wallace, Revesby ....KO 10
May 2—Glenn Walsh, Melton ....W 10
June 1—Dennis Talbot, Revesby ....L 6

July 22—Sparrow Freeman, Sutherland ....KO 10
Aug. 19—Chris Bennett, Sutherland ....D 10
Sept. 18—Patrick Burns, Marrickvale ....L 8
Oct. 20—Bimbo Morris, Cronulla ....W 8
Nov. 20—Fred Carlson, Marrickvale ....L 8

JIMMY BOY
Filipino Bantamweight
1978
Nov. 25—Al Norris, La Union ....W 10
1979
Jan. 27—Rodrigo Saomoy, Benguet ....W 10
Apr. 21—Tito Abella, Baguio City ....KO by 4
1980
Mar. 29—Allan Jarnenil, Baguio City ....L 10
July 4—William Develos, Manila ....KO by 7

CORNELIUS BOZA-EDWARDS
Ugandan Lightweight
Living in England
1976
Dec. 12—Barry Price, Mayfair ....KO 6
Dec. 20—Paul Clemit, Walworth ....KO 3
1977
Jan. 25—Tommy Wright, Bethnal ....KO 1
Feb. 1—Danny Connally, Kensington ....KO 2
Feb. 15—George McGurk, Mayfair ....KO 2
Mar. 16—Godfrey Butler, Solihull ....KO 2
Apr. 18—Billy Vivian, Mayfair ....KO 1
May 31—Tommy Glencross, Kensington ....KO 2
June 14—Mario Oliveira, London ....KO 2
Sept. 27—Des Gwilliam, London ....KO by 6
Nov. 8—Bingo Crooks, London ....W 8
Dec. 6—Dilwyn Collins, Kensington ....KO 5
1978
Feb. 21—Carlos Foldes, London ....KO disq. 5
July 19—Ethem Oezekalin, Bellaria ....KO 3
Sept. 26—George Feeney, Wembley ....W 8
Nov. 4—Godfrey Mwamba, Lusaka ....KO 3
Dec. 18—Georges Cotin, London ....KO 1
1979
Jan. 13—Frankie Moultrie, Miami Beach ....W 8
Mar. 4—Nino Jimenez, San Remo ....W 8
Mar. 31—Godfrey Mwamba, Lusaka ....KO 3
June 24—Fernando Jimenez, Monte Carlo ....KO 5
Nov. 3—Jose Gonzalez, Glasgow ....KO 3
1980
Mar. 16—Fili Ramirez, Las Vegas ....KO 7
Apr. 1—Jimmy Washington, London ....KO 2
Apr. 22—Benny Marques, London ....KO 4
June 7—Jerome Artis, Glasgow ....KO 3
June 28—Ron Green, London ....KO 6
July 12—Manuel Velasquez, London ....KO 3
Aug. 9—Alexis Arguello, Atlantic City ....KO by 8
Oct. 14—Roberto Torres, London ....KO 2

KEITH ALLAN BRADFORD
South African Middleweight
Born: Nov. 2, 1951
1977
June 4—Neil Lang, Bloemfontein ....L 4
Aug. 19—Andrie van Greunen, Bloemfontein .....KO 3
Sept. 8—Billy Jooste, Goodwood ....KO 2
Nov. 14—Frederick Smit, Johannesburg ....KO 2
1978
Mar. 4—Cornelius de Beer, Ermelo ....L 4
Apr. 3—Cornelius de Beer, Pretoria ....KO 3
Oct. 28—Brian Smit, Ermelo ....W 4
1979
Mar. 24—Basie Gouws, Johannesburg ....L 4
Sept. 3—Michael Motsoane, Welkom ....L 4
1980
Mar. 1—Johannes Mpesi, Ermelo ....D 4

BOBBY BREEN
British Bantamweight
1978
Sept. 11—Pip Coleman, Birmingham ....W 6
Sept. 18—Terry McKeown, Glasgow ....L 6
Oct. 18—Terry McKeown, Glasgow ....L 6
1979
Mar. 20—Terry Hanna, Glasgow ....W 6
Nov. 19—Alan Storey, Glasgow ....L 6
1980
Jan. 21—Billy Straub, Glasgow ....L 8

MARTIN BRIDGE
British Junior Welterweight
1977
May 9—Delvin Whyte, London ....W 6
May 16—Kevin Webber, Nottingham ....L 6
May 26—Dave Farell, Bradford ....W 6
June 20—George Kidd, Glasgow ....W 6

271

Aug.	5—Don Hughes, Glasgow	W 6
Sept.	'5—Trevor Roomes, Hove	L 6
Oct.	10—Don Hughes, Glasgow	D 6
Oct.	17—Frank McCord, Bedford	KO 5
Oct.	24—Sylvester Gordon, London	W 6
Nov.	24—Barton McAllister, Doncaster	W 6
Dec.	1—Colin Jones, Heathrow	KO by 4

1978

Feb.	20—Eric Purkis, London	L 6
Mar.	2—Stan Atherton, Liverpool	L 6
Mar.	13—Dave McCabe, Birmingham	L 8
Apr.	10—Frank McCord, Birmigham	W 6
Apr.	17—Stan Atherton, Bradford	D 6
May	8—Eric Purkis, Nottingham	L 8
June	19—Hugh Smith, Glasgow	KO 3
Sept.	12—Dave Taylor, Birkenhead	W 6
Sept.	28—Al Stewart, Liverpool	L 8
Nov.	13—John Gilling, Glasgow	D 8
Dec.	4—Dai Davies, Manchester	D 6

1979

Feb.	26—George Peacock, Glasgow	L 8
Mar.	19—Dave McCabe, Glasgow	L 8
Apr.	23—Dave Taylor, Bradford	W 10
July	14—Frank DeCaesteecker, Middlekerke	L 8
Sept.	24—George Peacock, London	L 8

1980

Jan.	24—Derek Nelson, Hartlepool	KO by 4
June	11—Robert Armstrong, Morecambe	L 8

KEITH BRISTOL
British Light Heavyweight
1980

Sept.	16—Clint Jones, Southend	L 6
Oct.	6—Lee White, Southwark	W 6
Oct.	20—Tommy Jones, Birmingham	W 6

TONY BRITTON
British Junior Middleweight
1979

June	4—Terry Matthews, London	W 6
July	30—Ronald Pearce, London	W 6
Sept.	17—Terry Matthews, Mayfair	W 8
Oct.	29—Steve Henty, Hove	W 6
Nov.	12—Dennis Pryce, Mayfair	W 6
Dec.	4—John Ridgman, Southend	L 6

1980

Feb.	4—Alan Cable, Hammersmith	W 8
Feb.	11—Peter Bassey, Manchester	L 6
Mar.	10—Martin McEwan, Liverpool	KO by 6
Apr.	17—Paul Baekgaard, Copenhagen	KO by 2
May	20—Leo Mulhearn, Southend	W 6
Sept.	22—Chris Glover, Liverpool	D 8
Oct.	6—Mickey Mapp, Southwark	L 6
Oct.	17—Torben Andersen, Copenhagen	L 6

NORMAN BROMFIELD
South African Featherweight
1978

Feb.	27—Rocky Meyer, Durban	KO 3
Aug.	5—Amon Ndlovu, Empangeni	KO 3
Aug.	28—Jacob Moyeye, Durban	W 4

1979

Feb.	3—Charles Boias, Johannesburg	W 4
Feb.	12—Alexander Sibiya, Durban	W 4
Mar.	10—Viyisile Ntunzi, Johannesburg	KO 2
Sept.	14—Alex Venter, Durban	W 4
Dec.	1—Thomas Sithebe, Johannesburg	L 10

1980

Feb.	1—Smart Thompson, Salisbury	KO 2
Apr.	7—Jay Nardo, Salisbury	L 8
May	24—Joshua Nhlapo, Orlando	L 6
Sept.	20—Stricker Studdard, Johannesburg	KO 4
Nov.	10—John Xaba, Durban	KO 2
Dec.	1—Anthony Dlamini, Durban	W 4

GARY BROOKS
British Welterweight
1980

June	12—Tony Stanton, Cambridge	L 6
Sept.	22—Paul Wetter, Liverpool	KO 6
Oct.	14—Alan Hardiman, Nantwich	KO 1
Nov.	4—Gerry McGrath, Southend	KO by 3

ANDY BROOME
Australian Lightweight
1971

Jan.	18—Mick Hatzell, Melbourne	W 3
Feb.	1—Tony Ryder, Melbourne	W 4
Feb.	22—Daryl Kane, Melbourne	KO 3
Aug.	16—Eddie Downes, Melbourne	W 4
Aug.	30—Tony Ryder, Melbourne	W 4
Sept.	13—Louis Grech, Melbourne	W 6
Sept.	27—Michael Cassidy, Melbourne	W 4

Oct.	4—Billy O'Connor, Melbourne	D 6
Nov.	15—Colin Cassidy, Melbourne	D 6

1972

May	15—Steve Chester, Melbourne	W 8
May	29—David Poison, Melbourne	W 8
June	19—Miguel Araujo, Melbourne	W 8
July	3—Tony Cunningham, Melbourne	W 8
Aug.	14—Alan Pressnell, Melbourne	D 8
Sept.	4—Alan Pressnell, Melbourne	W 10

(Vacant Victoria State Junior Lightweight Title)

Sept.	18—Colin Cassidy, Melbourne	KO by 8
Dec.	4—Hilary Connolly, Melbourne	W 10

(Victoria State Lightweight Title)

1973

June	4—Toro George, Melbourne	L 10
June	14—Sonny Bell, Blacktown	W 10
July	19—Paul Bink, Blacktown	KO 6
Nov.	19—Bobby Cotterill, Melbourne	KO 4

1974

Feb.	18—Colin Cassidy, Melbourne	L 10
April	19—Matt Ropis, Melbourne	KO 8
June	7—Gilbert Biondi, Melbourne	L 10
June	13—Wally Carr, Blacktown	KO 3
Aug.	1—Billy Moeller, Blacktown	D 10
Dec.	12—Martin Beni, Port Moresby	KO 5

1975

Feb.	13—Blakeney Matthews, Blacktown	KO by 8

(Australian Lightweight Championship)

Nov.	20—Barry Michael, Melbourne	L 10

1976

Feb.	19—Jim West, Blacktown	W 10
Mar.	11—Matt Ropis, Blacktown	W 10
May	21—Dally Law, South Melbourne	KO 4

(Vacant Victoria State Lightweight Title)

July	30—Blakeney Matthews, Melbourne	KO 9
Aug.	16—Hector Thompson, Tweed Heads	KO by 6
Oct.	29—Primo Bandini, Melbourne	W 10
Nov.	19—Blakeney Matthews, Melbourne	KO 9
Dec.	8—Jeff Malcolm, Marrickville	L 10

1977

Sept.	22—Martin Beni, Boroko	KO 10
Nov.	11—Frank Ropis, Heidelberg	L 10
Dec.	5—Colin Cassidy, Melbourne	KO 10

1978

Feb.	27—Frank Ropis, Melbourne	L 10
Apr.	28—Hector Thompson, Melbourne	L 12

1979

Mar.	30—Frank Ropis, Ravesby	L 12
Sept.	28—Darryl Carrick, Melton	W 10
Oct.	17—Eddie Buttons, Melbourne	L 10

1980

Mar.	7—Frank Ropis, Melbourne	KO by 4
July	28—Eugene Eades, Belmont	D 10
Oct.	10—Manny Benson, Preston	KO 5

ABEL BROWN
South African Welterweight
1976

Apr.	10—Alpheus Mshali, Stanger	L 4

1977

Aug.	1—Wentzel Marais, Durban	D 4
Nov.	28—Wentzel Marais, Durban	L 4

1978

Aug.	5—Sipho Malinga, Malinga	KO 3
Aug.	28—Wentzel Marais, Durban	KO 4
Oct.	10—Clements Smith, Durban	KO 1

1979

Feb.	12—Gregory Schmidt, Durban	L 4
June	9—Johannes Mthembu, Durban	D 4
Sept.	15—Hardy Mileham, Johannesburg	L 4

1980

Apr.	14—Gregory Clark, Durban	L 4
May	19—Johannes Mthembu, Durban	W 10

(Retained Natal Welterweight Title)

June	7—Ernest Moledi, Johannesburg	KO by 5
July	4—Hardy Mileham, Durban	L 6
Nov.	1—Peter Gumede, Stanger	L 6
Dec.	1—Gregory Clark, Durban	L 10

(Lost Natal Welterweight Title)

Dec.	20—Nkosana Mgwaji, East London	L 8

CHARLIE BROWN
Australian Featherweight
1973

June	5—Neil Docherty, New Lambton	D 4
June	12—Steve Wonder, Marrickville	KO by 2
Aug.	1—Gwynne Jones, Kingsford	L 5
Aug.	15—Gwynne Jones, Kingsford	L 5
Aug.	21—Gwynne Jones, New Lambton	L 10
Sept.	4—Fred Finneran, Brookvale	KO 2
Sept.	6—Mo Hamid, Blacktown	KO 2
Sept.	20—David Byrne, Blacktown	W 4
Dec.	4—Buddy Clare, Cardiff	W 6

	1974	
Feb.	28—Steve Wonder, Blacktown	L 4
Mar.	5—Donny Leslie, New Lambton	W 6
Mar.	21—Steve Wonder, Blacktown	KO 5
Apr.	4—Steve Walker, Blacktown	L 6
May	8—Steve Walker, Blacktown	L 6
May	14—Greg Morris, New Lambton	W 4
June	18—Steve Walker, New Lambton	L 10
July	23—Gwynne Jones, Brookvale	L 8
Oct.	10—Steve Walker, Blacktown	KO by 6
Dec.	10—Peter Luzinski, Cardiff	D 8
	1975	
Feb.	5—Peter Luzinski, Cammeray	D 8
Mar.	20—Steve Walker, Blacktown	KO by 4
May	20—Steve Walker, New Lambton	L 8
July	24—Steve Walker, New Lambton	D 10
	(Vacant N.S.W. State Flyweight Title)	
Sept.	2—Steve Walker, Wallsend	KO 9
	(Won Vacant Australian Flyweight Title)	
	1976	
Feb.	12—Steve Walker, Blacktown	W 8
May	4—Steve Bell, Cardiff	D 15
	(Australian Flyweight Title)	
Nov.	30—Gwyn Jones, Cardiff	KO 10
	(Australian Flyweight Title)	
	1977	
Apr.	6—Roger Richens, Cammeray	W 6
Apr.	26—Steve Bell, Cardiff	L 15
	(Australian Flyweight Title)	
July	6—Johnny Hipwell, Cammeray	L 6
Aug.	28—Chenrob Muangsurin, Bangkok	L 8
	1978	
Feb.	24—Glen Walsh, Melbourne	L 8
July	4—Kid Blair, Cardiff	L 8
Oct.	7—Paul Ferreri, Griffith	KO by 6
	(Australian Bantamweight Title)	
Oct.	24—Kid Blair, Cardiff	L 8
	1979	
Feb.	24—Steve Freeman, Kempsey	W 6
Apr.	3—Sparrow Freeman, Cardiff	W 10
Apr.	26—Patrick Burns, Revesby	KO 8
May	30—Brian Roberts, Revesby	L 10
	(Australian Junior Featherweight Title)	
Aug.	7—Brian Roberts, Cardiff	L 12
	(For Australian Junior Featherweight Title)	
Nov.	17—Tiger Mann, Port Moresby	D 10
	1980	
Sept.	8—Brian Roberts, Cronulla	L 12
	(For Australian Junior Featherweight Title	
Oct.	10—Patrick Burns, Cardiff	W 10
Nov.	16—Didik Mulyardi, Djkarta	L 10
Dec.	17—Steve Walker, Mt. Pritchard	KO 7
	(Won New South Wales Junior Featherweight Title)	

CHARLIE BROWN
British Junior Welterweight
1980

Jan.	21—Barry Price, London	L 8
Feb.	4—Barry Price, London	D 8
June	2—Colin Wake, London	L 8

CLINT BROWN
Australian Welterweight
1978

Sept.	6—Chris Sherd, Brookvale	W 4
Sept.	16—Joe Williams, Queanbeyan	W 4
Oct.	4—Saladine Allaf, Brookvale	L 4
Oct.	17—Andy Roberts, Kingsford	W 4
Oct.	31—Andy Roberts, Kingsford	W 6
Nov.	28—Doug Dixon, Kingsford	W 4
Dec.	4—Bob Lawrence, Blacktown	D 4
	1979	
Jan.	30—Fat Albert, Kingsford	W 4
Feb.	7—Fat Albert, Brookvale	W 4
Mar.	7—Andy Mann, Brookvale	D 6
Mr.	27—Kirk Blair, Kingsford	KO by 4
Apr.	24—Mick McLean, Kingsford	W 5
May	22—Jimmy Chico, Kingsford	L 5
June	5—Jimmy Chico, Kingsford	W 5
June	19—Alex Schaeffer, Kingsford	W 6
July	4—Andy Mann, Brookvale	W 8
Nov.	6—Carpa Jones, Kingsford	W 4
Nov.	20—Willie Nixon, Kingsford	KO 3
Dec.	4—Manuel Trikillis, Kingsford	W 5
Dec.	19—Tony Adcock, Mt. Pritchard	W 4
	1980	
Jan.	29—Kelly Thompson, Kingsford	D 6
Feb.	12—Tommy Roberts, Kingsford	W 8
Mar.	11—Andy Mann, Kingsford	W 6
Mar.	25—Billy Harrison, Kingsford	W 6
Apr.	2—Billy Harrison, Kingsford	W 8
Apr.	20—Gil McGrath, Jindera	W 8
May	6—Tommy Roberts, Kingsford	W 8
June	3—Buddy Nixon, Kingsford	L 6

June	17—Robbie Scott, Kingsford	W 8
July	2—Ceddy McGrady, Brookvale	W 6
July	15—Dawsie Kelly, Kingsford	W 8
Aug.	13—Paul Baker, Brookvale	W 6
Aug.	27—Andy Mann, Mt. Pritchard	W 10
Sept.	10—Willie Nixon, Gosford	W 6
Sept.	23—Kelly Thompson, Kingsford	KO 5
Oct.	7—Mick Thompson, Kingsford	W 8
Nov.	4—Lou Cruz, Kingsford	W 8

JIMMY BROWN
Australian Lightweight
1973

Feb.	12—Guinea Hillier, Melbourne	D 3
Mar.	5—Dominic Papaleo, Melbourne	W 3
Mar.	12—Frank Bernadino, Melbourne	W 3
Apr.	9—Steve Johnson, Melbourne	KO by 1
May	14—Domenic Papaleo, Melbourne	L 4
June	4—Brian Parkinson, Melbourne	W 4
July	2—Guinea Hillier, Melbourne	W 4
July	30—Mick Harley, Melbourne	W 4
Aug.	20—Mick McLean, Melbourne	W 4
Aug.	27—John Brancarto, Melbourne	W 6
Sept.	3—Barry Townsend, Brisbane	W 6
Oct.	1—Des Pearce, Melbourne	KO 3
Oct.	8—Wayne Wallace, Melbourne	D 6
Oct.	29—Brian Clout, Melbourne	KO 4
Nov.	19—Robert Green, Melbourne	W 4
	1974	
Feb.	18—Barry Michael, Melbourne	W 6
Mar.	8—Billy Mulholland, Albury	D 8
May	3—Dave Richards, Melbourne	KO 7
May	24—Darryl Hammond, Melbourne	KO 4
June	21—Lindsay Roberts, Melbourne	KO 1
June	28—Wayne Wallace, Melbourne	L 6
July	19—Glen Howard, Melbourne	W 6
July	26—Keith Ball, Melbourne	W 8
Sept.	27—Roger Bowyer, Melbourne	W 6
Oct.	18—Robbie Williams, Melbourne	KO 5
	1975	
Apr.	28—Billy Mulholland, Melbourne	KO 5
June	2—Dave Richards, Melbourne	W 10
Aug.	4—Tony Ryder, Brisbane	W 10
Oct.	10—Tony Ryder, Brisbane	KO by 12
	(For Australian Featherweight Title)	
	1976	
Mar.	19—Keith Ball, Moore Park	KO 4
	1977	
Apr.	6—Joey Gibilisco, Melbourne	KO by 7
June	1—Brian Clayton, Melbourne	W 10
July	27—Larry Valesini, Melbourne	KO 6
	1978	
Apr.	6—Steve Gossen, Melbourne	W 10
May	24—Willie Leslie, Preston	KO 6
June	30—Blakeney Matthews, Preston	KO by 4
Oct.	13—Glenn Howard, Preston	W 10
	1979	
Feb.	28—Billy Moeller, Preston	D 10
June	13—Speedy Duke, Preston	W 10
Sept.	19—Jeff Malcolm, Melbourne	L 10
Dec.	19—Barry Michael, Williamstown	D 10
	(For Australian Lightweight Title)	
	1980	
Mar.	19—Lindsay Roberts, Melbourne	KO 3
Dec.	17—Barry Michael, Melbourne	KO by 15
	(For Australian Lightweight Title)	

JIMMY BROWN
British Lightweight
1978

Jan.	18—Steve Engwright, Stoke	KO 3
Feb.	1—Mark Hill, Evesham	KO 1
Feb.	7—Gerry Howland, London	KO 1
Feb.	15—Eric Purkis, Cambridge	L 6
Mar.	20—Colin Miles, Aberavon	KO 1
May	11—Ray Heaney, Belfast	W 8
May	18—John Singlewood, Liverpool	KO 3
Oct.	27—Benny Purdy, Belfast	KO 1
	1979	
Feb.	7—Najib Daho, Manchester	W 8
Feb.	28—Billy Moeller, Preston	D 10
Mar.	1—Jeff Pritchard, Liverpool	W 8
June	13—Speedy Duke, Preston Town Hall	W 10
Dec.	5—Gerry O'Neill, Liverpool	W 8
	1980	
Feb.	18—Gerry O'Neill, Birmingham	W 8
June	7—Jim McKeown, Glasgow	W 8
Oct.	27—Lawrence Williams, Liverpool	KO by 7

NEIL BROWN
British Lightweight
1979

Oct.	24—John Henry, Norwich	W 4

273

Nov.   6—Ray Price, Stafford ....L 6
Nov. 21—Ray Price, Evesham ....L 6
Nov. 29—Phillip Morris ....D 6
Dec. 13—George White, Wimbledon ....KO by 5
1980
Feb. 18—Mick Redding, Birmingham ....L 4
Feb. 28—Tony Davis, London ....L 6
Apr.   8—Joe Mills, Norwich ....L 6
July 14—Mick Redding, Birmingham ....L 6

MAURICE BUFI
French Junior Middleweight
1976
Nov. 26—Jean Pierre Heirmann, Le Roeuix ....W 6
1977
Jan. 21—Fernand Banckaert, Le Roeuix ....W 6
Feb. 18—Leander Pante, La Louviere ....W 6
Mar.   4—Antonio Balletta, Le Roeuix ....W 6
May   20—Guido Beuselick, Le Roeuix ....KO 5
Oct.   7—Gilbert Cnudde, Le Roeuix ....W 6
Nov. 25—Michel Parent, Le Roeuix ....W 6
1978
Jan. 13—Chaed Ringo, Le Roeuix ....W 6
Jan. 30—Rob Czabania, Schiedam ....KO 5
Mar.   3—Lionel Alfred Lagasse, Le Roeux ....W 6
Mar. 24—Eric Seys, Tubize ....W 8
Apr. 14—Olton Beltchika, La Louviere ....D 8
June   3—Stephan Vertore, Le Roeuix ....W 8
Sept. 30—Hendrick Seys, Turnhout ....L 8
Oct. 20—Celestin Kanynda, La Louviere ....L 8
1979
Feb.   2—Paul Payen, La Louviere ....KO 3
Mar. 17—Michael Pigani, Calais ....KO by 5
Sept. 21—Giampaolo Piras, Le Roeuix ....KO 6
Nov. 10—Ringo Chaed, Bruxelles ....W 8
1980
May   23—Andre Mongalema, LeRoeulx ....L 8
Oct.   4—Ignacio Gorostidi, LeRoeulx ....W 6
Oct. 31—Yvon Segor, Marseilles ....KO by 5
Nov. 29—Christian D'Helft, Liege ....W 8

FRANCO BUGLIONE
Italian Bantamweight
Born: Jan. 14, 1948
1973
Mar. 10—Salvatore Laconi, Nocera ....W 6
Apr. 13—Rocco D'Ambrosio, Capua ....KO 5
May   5—Grazietto Soro, Nocera ....W 6
July 22—Antonio Galletta, Capua ....W 6
Aug. 12—Giancarlo Anibaldi, Gerola ....KO 5
Sept. 8—Mario De Prosperis, Priverno ....W 6
Nov. 11—Salvatore Laconi, Cagliari ....W 8
Nov. 20—Joe Latour, Capua ....W 8
Dec.   5—Salvatore Laconi, Cagliari ....W 6
Dec. 17—Frank Realinho, Napoli ....KO by 1
1974
May   4—Luigi Paravati, Capua ....KO 4
July 19—Tarcisio Boi, Capua ....W 8
Aug.   8—Salvatore Laconi, Terlizzi ....W 8
Aug. 18—Tarcisio Boi, Rocamonfina ....W 8
Oct. 15—Daniel Charvet, S. Maria ....W 10
Dec. 11—Franco Sperati, Caserta ....W 12
(Won Italian Flyweight Title)
1975-1977
(Inactive)
1978
Mar.   3—Teodoro Corallo, Milan ....W 8
Mar. 31—Claudio Tanda, Capua ....W 12
(Italian Bantamweight Title)
Aug. 20—Franco Zurlo, Rocco Monfina ....KO by 11
(European Bantamweight Title)
Dec. 13—Alfredo Mulas, Lugo Di Romagna ....L 8
1979
Jan. 13—Giovanni Camputaro, Piedimonte ....D 12
(Italian Flyweight Title)
Feb. 23—Raga Purphy, Capua ....D 8
Aug. 31—Franco Zurlo, Conca ....KO 8
1980
Apr. 24—Valerio Nati, Forli ....KO by 3
(For Italian Bantamweight Title)

JIMMY BUNCLARKE
British Lightweight
1980
Mar.   5—Kevin Sheehan, Liverpool ....KO 1
Mar. 10—Robert Wakefield, Manchester ....KO 4
May   19—Jackie Turner, Liverpool ....L 8
Sept. 18—Selvin Bell, Liverpool ....W 6
Oct. 30—Glen Rhodes, Liverpool ....KO 7
Nov. 10—Billy O'Grady, Southwark ....L 8

PATRIZIO BURINI
Italian Junior Welterweight
1978
Feb. 24—Gerardo Scognamiglio, Figline ....W 6
Apr.   7—Antonio Antino, Milano ....KO by 3
May   5—Francesco De Marco, Figline ....KO 1
July   6—Salvatore Morello, Pietraviva ....KO 1
July 22—Darko Covic, Roccatederighi ....KO 2
Nov.   3—Angelo Zanetti, Montevarchi ....KO 1
Nov. 18—Graziano Gusai, Vald'Elsa ....KO 3
Dec. 23—Palmiro Pizzata, Figline Valdarno ......KO 4
1979
Jan. 26—Guiseppe Monotti, Florence ....W 8
Mar.   3—Zdravko Jovicic, Figline Valdarno ....W 8
Apr. 20—Rocco Frasca, Figline Valdarno ....KO 2
May   25—Pascal Mlira, Florence ....W 8
June 15—Luigi Dal Santo, Figline Valdarno ......KO 1
July   6—Zdravko Jovicic, Pietrafifitta ....KO 5
Sept. 15—Giovanni Mairorano, Marciano ....KO 3
Dec. 14—Gregorio Ciancaglione, Florence ....D 8
1980
Oct. 18—Rosario Di Tommaso, Torino ....KO 1
Nov. 21—Guiseppe Agate, Figline ....W 8

EDDIE BURKE
Scottish Light Heavyweight
1976
Nov. 15—Tony Burnett, Glasgow ....KO 5
Dec. 13—Bonnie McKenzie, London ....W 6
1977
Jan. 24—Jim Moore, Glasgow ....KO 4
Feb.   7—Mickey Lock, London ....KO 1
Mar. 28—Joe Jackson, Glasgow ....KO 2
Apr. 18—Steve Walker, London ....KO 4
May   16—Carl Thomas, Glasgow ....KO 2
June 13—Tony Burnett, London ....KO 5
Sept. 19—Bonny McKenzie, Glasgow ....W 8
Oct. 17—Wayne Bennett, Glasgow ....L 8
Nov. 29—Bonny McKenzie, London ....W 8
1978
Jan. 30—Howard Mills, Glasgow ....KO by 7
Oct. 18—Trevor Kerr, Glasgow ....KO 2
1979
Mar. 20—Tony Monaghan, Glasgow ....KO 5
Nov.   3—Mick Morris, Glasgow ....KO 2
1980
Feb. 18—Eddie Smith, Stockport ....W 8
Nov.   1—Freddie Brown, Glasgow ....KO 1

WINSTON BURNETT
British Middleweight
1980
Feb. 12—Mike Burton, London ....L 4
Mar. 24—Mike Burton, London ....L 4
May   27—Ray Pearce, Newport ....L 6
Oct. 20—Pharoah Bish, Birmingham ....W 6
Oct. 27—Prince Wilmot, London ....W 6

JIM BURNS
British Heavyweight
1980
Sept. 22—Bob Young, Wolverhampton ....KO by 2
Oct. 19—Steve Gee, Birmingham ....KO by 3

JOHNNY BURNS
British Junior Welterweight
1979
Jan. 22—Brenden O'Donnell, Wolverhampton ......W 6
Mar.   5—Gene McGarrigale, Wolverhampton .....KO 1
Apr.   4—Mark Hill, Birmingham ....KO 3
May   16—Selwyn Bell, Wolverhampton ....WF 6
June   6—Barry Price, Bedworth ....D 4
July   2—Norman Morton, Wolverhampton ....KO by 4
Sept. 8—Dennis Sullivan, Wolverhampton ....L 6
Oct. 29—Mickey Baker, Wolverhampton ....D 8
1980
Jan. 21—Steve Ward, Wolverhampton ....W 6
Feb. 20—Ian Kid Murray, Evesham ....L 6
July   8—Steve Ward, Wolverhampton ....L 6
Oct. 30—Paul Chance, Wolverhampton ....L 8

PATRICK BURNS
Australian Bantamweight
1978
Feb. 22—Billy Trialanous, Bankstown ....W 4
Mar.   7—Steve Saxon, Kingsford ....W 4
Mar. 21—Steve Saxon, Kingsford ....W 6
Apr.   3—Steve Freeman, Cammeray ....KO by 4
May   16—Sparrow Freeman, Penrith ....W 6
June 28—Sparrow Freeman, Bankstown ....KO 6
July 26—Kirk Blair, Bankstown ....L 8
Sept. 29—Steve Freeman, Mt. Pritchard ....W 6

274

1979
Feb. 15—Gary Bice, Blacktown .... W 8
Mar. 28—Gary Bice, Revesby .... W 8
Apr. 26—Charlie Brown, Revesby .... KO by 4
Sept. 7—Glenn Walsh, Spring .... D 8
1980
Apr. 11—Wayne Mulholland, Wollongong .... L 10
May 24—Peter Thompson, Doyalson .... KO 4
June 27—Buddy Clare, Canley Vale .... W 6
June 29—Billy Doyles, Rozelle .... D 6
July 4—Billy Doyles, Wollongong .... W 8
Sept. 18—Jimmy Bowen, Marickvale .... W 8
Oct. 10—Charlie Brown, Cardiff .... L 10

MIKE BURTON
British Middleweight
1980
Feb. 12—Winston Burnett, London .... W 4
Feb. 18—Casey McAllum, London .... W 4
Mar. 24—Winston Burnett, London .... W 4
Apr. 28—Joe Dean, Southwark .... W 6
May 19—Prince Wilmot, London .... KO 3
June 3—Mohammed Ali, Aylesbury .... KO 3
Sept. 22—Gareth Tashy Jones, London .... W 4

ROCKY BURTON
British Heavyweight
1977
Oct. 18—Tony Bennett, Wolverhampton .... KO 1
Nov. 30—Joey Williams, Wolverhampton .... W 4
1978
Feb. 13—Eddie Vierling, Reading .... KO by 2
Mar. 6—Joey Williams, London .... L 6
Oct. 31—Reginald Squire, Wolverhampton ... KO by 2
Nov. 27—Manny Gabriel, Kettering .... L 6
1979
Jan. 31—Roy Skeldon, Stoke .... L 4
Mar. 15—Roy Skeldon, Dudley .... L 4
Mar. 21—Emmanuel Lucas, Stoke .... W 6
Mar. 28—Manny Gabriel, Kettering .... KO by 1
June 6—Emmanuel Lucas, Bedworth .... W 6
Sept. 26—Peter Les Reed, Stoke .... W 6
Dec. 17—John O'Neill, Wolverhampton .... W 6
1980
Jan. 28—George Lewis, Edgbaston .... KO 3
Feb. 18—Nigel Savory, Stockport .... W 6
Mar. 18—Gary Jones, Wolverhampton .... W 6
Mar. 27—Steve Carnall, Liverpool .... W 6
Apr. 21—Nigel Savory, Bradford .... KO 4
Sept. 29—Terry O'Conner, Bedworth .... L 6
(For Vacant Midlands Area Heavyweight Title)

THEMBA BUTHELEZI
South African Light Heavyweight
1978
Aug. 5—Isaac Dube, Empangeni .... KO 1
Aug. 28—David Montlengwa, Durban .... W 4
Oct. 10—Nels de Beer, Durban .... KO 1
1979
Feb. 12—Wentzel Marais, Durban .... KO 2
Mar. 10—Johanes Mpesi, Newcastle .... W 6
Aug. 27—Bruce McIntyre, Johannesburg ..... KO by 1
Sept. 29—Joseph Zikhali, Durban .... W 6
1980
Feb. 4—Bertie Potgieter, Durban .... KO 2
May 3—Cecil Sandow, Witsieshoek .... KO 2
July 19—Daniel Mapanya, Durban .... L 8
Oct. 6—Champion Mokone, Pietermaritzburg .... W 10
(Retained Natal Light Heavyweight Title)
Nov. 3—Mark Melville, Durban .... W 4
Dec. 1—Martin Bernard, Durban .... KO by 7

EDDIE BUTTONS
Australian Junior Middleweight
1972
May 21—Johnny Huvvoch, Kingsford............. L 4
June 7—Johnny Huvvoch, Kingsford .... W 4
June 14—Kim Wallace, Kingsford .... L 5
June 21—Frank Allen, Kingsford .... W 6
July 19—Johnny Russell, Kingsford .... L 5
July 26—Harry Odd, Kingsford .... L 6
Aug. 2—Bricky Squire, Kingsford .... L 6
Aug. 9—Benny Moss, Kingsford .... W 5
Aug. 15—Rappy Score, Austimmer .... L 6
Aug. 30—Sonno Fitzpatrick, Kingsford .... W 5
Sept. 6—Paul Donnelly, Kingsford .... W 6
Sept. 13—Paul Donnelly, Kingsford .... W 6
Sept. 27—Sonno Fitzpatrick, Kingsford .... W 6
Oct. 11—Lou Cruz, Kingsford .... W 5
Oct. 10 Jeff Fowler, Kingsford .... L 6
1973
Mar. 21—Don Ryan, Kingsford................... L 4
Mar. 28—Johnny Huvvoch, Brookvale .... D 6

Apr. 4—Steve Braid, Kingsford................ W 5
Apr. 18—Harry Odd, Kingsford................. W 6
May 2—Jimmy Metcalf, Kingsford .... L 8
Sept. 26—Dennis Bell, Kingsford.............. W 5
Oct. 10—Dennis Bell, Kingsford .... L 6
Oct. 24—Chilla Naismith, Kingsford .... W 6
Nov. 7—Craig Windle, Kingsford .... W 5
Nov. 20—Craig Windle, Brookvale............. L 8
1974
Mar. 27—Ross Eadie, Kingsford .... W 5
Apr. 3—Jimmy Metcalf, Kingsford .... D 6
Apr. 5—Graeme Merkel, Capto .... D 6
Apr. 10—Graeme Merkel, Brookvale............. W 6
Apr. 16—Warren Frewen, Brookvale............. W 5
Apr. 17—Warren Frewen, Kingsford .... W 6
May 8—Jimmy Metcalfe, Kingsford .... W 8
May 22—Lou Cruz, Kingsford .... W 6
June 19—Jimmy Metcalfe, Brookvale .... W 10
July 3—Ross Eadie, Kingsford .... W 8
Aug. 14—Ceddy McGrady, Kingsford .... W 5
Aug. 20—Joey Collins, Brookvale............. W 6
Aug. 21—Joey Collins, Kingsford .... W 6
Sept. 4—Ross Eadie, Kingsford .... D 8
Sept. 25—Mark Duffy, Kingsford .... W 8
Oct. 9—Binky Rominski, Kingsford .... W 8
Oct. 22—Joey Collins, Brookvale............. W 8
Oct. 30—Sid Dumbrell, Kingsford............. D 8
Nov. 20—Dally Law, Kingsford .... L 8
1975
Feb. 5—Speedie Duke, Kingsford............... W 6
Feb. 7—Lachie Austin, Woonona .... W 10
Feb. 18—Ross Eadie, Brookvale .... L 8
Apr. 23—Max Milan, Kingsford .... W 6
May 14—Max Milan, Kingsford .... KO 2
May 21—Mario Martinello, Kingsford .... KO 2
Aug. 26—Dally Law, Kingsford .... D 8
Sept. 23—Sonny Bathis, Kingsford .... D 8
Oct. 1—Seamus McGahon, Cammeray .... W 10
1976
June 29—Alex Vella, Kingsford .... W 5
July 20—Barry Benson, Brookvale............. W 4
Aug. 10—Frank Roberts, London .... W 8
Sept. 15—Steve Campbell, Brookvale.......... W 8
Nov. 2—Frank Allan, Kingsford .... KO 3
Nov. 24—Blinky Rominsky, Kingsford .... W 8
1977
May 25—Ceddy McGrady, Brookvale............. W 6
July 27—Eric King, Brookvale................. W 8
Aug. 16—Binky Rominsky, Kingsford .... W 10
Sept. 28—Ceddy McGrady, Brookvale........... W 10
Oct. 25—Colin Cassidy, Kingsford .... D 10
Nov. 22—Steve Ayerst, Kingsford .... W 10
1978
Feb. 22—Eric King, Brookvale................. W 6
Mar. 21—Laurie Mack, Kingsford .... W 10
Apr. 3—Laurie Mack, Kingsford .... D 6
Apr. 26—Steve Ayerst, Bankstown .... W 10
May 17—Steve Dennis, Mount Pritchard .... W 10
June 27—Speedie Duke, Kingsford .... W 10
Aug. 8—Gus Spina, Kingsford .... KO 9
Sept. 5—David Hill, Kingsford .... W 10
Oct. 17—Speedie Duke, Kingsford .... W 10
Nov. 10—Ross Eadie, Kingsford .... KO 8
1979
Apr. 10—Dawsie Kelly, Kingsford .... W 10
May 8—Eric King, Kingsford .... KO 3
June 5—Benny Tabua, Kingsford .... KO 8
(Won New South Wales Welterweight Title)
July 18—Jeff Sait, Mt. Pritchard .... KO 5
Aug. 15—Steve Dennis, Mt. Pritchard .....KO by 9
(Lost New South Wales Welterweight Title)
Oct. 17—Andy Broome, Melbourne .... W 10
1980
Apr. 8—Buddy Nixon, Kingsford .... KO 3
Apr. 19—Thomas Americo, Surabaya .... L 10

GEORGE BUTZBACH
German Heavyweight
1976
Oct. 30—Reinhard Seydock, Frankfurt .... KO 2
1977
Jan. 31—Detleff Naseband, Bremen .... KO 1
Mar. 25—Gerd Frings, Bremen .... KO 1
Apr. 1—Hartmut Sasse, Saarlouis .... KO 3
Apr. 22—Coulibaly Demba, Saarbruecken ...... KO 3
Apr. 28—Horst Lang, Muenchen .... W 6
June 11—Reinhard Seydock, Sittersswald ..... KO 4
Sept. 9—Vincenzo Pesapane, Muenchen .... KO 3
Sept. 21—Lisimo Obutobe, Frankfurt .... D 8
Sept. 30—Terry O'Connor, Hamburg............. D 8
Dec. 12—Kilani Ramdani, Kiel .... W 8
1978
May 6—Tony Moore, Frankfort .... D 8
Sept. 30—Terry O'Connor, Hamburg .... W 6

Dec.   7—Brian Huckfield, Lubeck .... KO 1
1979
Apr. 22—Tony Moore, Hamburg .... D 10
Sept. 14—Kallie Knoetze, Durban .... KO by 7
Nov.   1—Jean Pierre Coopman, Izegem .... W 10
1980
Sept. 19—Al Syben, Vise .... L 10

ALDO BUZZETTI
Italian Middleweight
1978
Mar.   9—Giancarlo Denti, Paderno .... W 6
Mar. 31—Kadir Youceler, Piacenza .... W 6
July   7—King Karimou, Podenzano .... KO 2
Nov. 10—Luciano Renzi, Piacenza .... KO 2
Dec. 26—Luciano Bolis, Piacenza .... KO 3
1979
July 21—Corrado Sortino, Piacenza .... W 6
Dec. 26—Aldo Polesel, Piacenza .... KO 2
1980
Mar.   7—Mustapha Kabangu, Piacenza .... KO 4
May   31—Ray Opoku, Piacenza .... LF 2
July   6—Clemente Gessi, Piacenza .... KO 3
Dec.   5—Sumbu Kalambay, Piacenza .... W 8

ISIDORO CABEZA
Spanish Junior Lightweight
Born: June 23, 1950
1972
Feb. 24—Mariano Gasco, Zargoza .... W 6
      —Francisco Rodriguez, Valencia .... W 6
1973
      —Francisco Rodriguez, Palma Maiorca .... KO 1
      —Martin Callero, ... KO 3
      —Francisco Santaengracia, Palma Maiorca KO 6
Aug.   3—Jose Antonio Donoso, Son Perriol .... W 6
Sept. 9—Juan Iglesias, Palma Maiorca .... W 6
Oct. 19—Jeronimo Lucas, Barcelona .... L 8
Nov. 16—Francisco Santaengracia, Palma Maiorca W 8
Dec. 29—Fernando Sanchez, Barcelona .... L 8
1974
May   19—Manuel Velazquez, Manacor .... W 6
June 13—Abadesalem Manan, Mallorca .... KO 1
July 12—Jose Antonio Donoso, Mallorca .... KO by 4
Aug.   2—Luis Cristobal Diaz, Madrid .... KO 5
Aug.   9—Pedro Nino Jimenez, Madrid .... D 8
Nov.   6—Santiago Cebollada, Madrid .... KO 3
      —Francisco Larxe, ... KO 5
1975
Jan. 10—Michel Lefebvre, Barcelona .... D 8
Feb.   7—Alessandro Bini, Barcelona .... KO 7
Feb. 21—Enzo Farnnelli, Madrid .... KO by 3
Apr.   5—Antonio Tenza, Palma .... KO 3
May   24—Luis Alisa, Azragoza ....L 8
Aug.   1—Lothar Abend, Palma de Mallorca ... W disq. 8
Nov. 28—Francisco Santaengracia, Brussels .... W 8
Dec. 13—Edouardo Tavares, Palma............... KO 6
1976
Feb. 27—Nino Jinenenz, Madrid .... L 8
Apr. 23—Heleno Ferreira, Madrid .... L 8
Aug.   7—Mario Oliveira, Santander .... L 8
Sept. 3—Tino Blanco, Madrid..................... W 8
1977
Mar. 12—Cecilio Lastra, Santander .... L 12
(Spanish Featherweight Title)
July 15—Mario Molina, Madrid .... D 8
Sept. 23—Miguel Molleda, Palma de Mallorca ..... W 12
(Spanish Junior Lightweight Title)
Nov. 18—Francisco Garcia, Palma Mallorca .... W 8
1978
Feb.   4—Carlos Hernandez, Valladolid .... KO 6
(Spanish Junior Lightweight Title)
May   20—Hector Molina, Palma Mallorca .... D 8
May   31—Leon Mejias, Bilbao ....KO 7
Aug. 11—Natale Vezzoli, Lepe .... L 15
Sept. 23—Ramon Garcia Marichal, Lepe .... D 12
1979
Mar. 10—Jesus Canut, Vallidolid .... KO 4
Mar. 30—Serafin Dos Anjos, Las Palmas .... W 8
Apr. 28—Cecilio Lastra, Santander .... L 8
June   1—Pedro Nino Jimenez, Mallorca .... D 10
July   6—Andres Torres, Mallorca .... W 8
Aug. 10—Cayetano Alcala, Lepe .... W 12
(Spanish Junior Lightweight Title)
Aug. 25—Malanga Torres, Mallorca .... W 8

Aug. 31—Tek Nkalznkete, Madrid .... D 8
Dec. 20—Ramon Marichal, Palma de Mallorca KO by 9
(Spanish Junior Lightweight Title)
1980
Feb. 15—Jose Luis Vicho, Palma de Mallorca ...... L 8
Mar. 28—Ramon Garcia, Palma de Mallorca ...... D 10
(For Spanish Junior Lightweight Title)
Apr. 19—Jofre II, Palma de Mallorca .... L 10
June 13—Angel Oliver, Palma de Mallorca .... W 8
Aug.   1—Juan Francisco Rodgriguez, Madrid ...... L 8

ALAN CABLE
British Middleweight
1975
Mar. 26—Terry Schofield, Stoke .... L 6
May   16—Achille Mitchell, Birmingham .... KO by 5
Sept. 29—Keith Bundy, London .... KO by 3
Oct. 27—Russ Shaw, Walworth .... W 6
Nov. 10—Martin Lewis, Croydon .... L 6
Nov. 24—Rock Munday, Walworth .... KO by 4
1976
Jan. 12—Mick Hampston, Walworth .... L 6
Jan. 26—Mick Hampston, Hammersmith .... L 6
1977
Jan. 19—George Salmon, Stoke .... KO by 4
1978
(Inactive)
1979
Jan. 18—Tommy Thomas, Wimbledon .... KO 4
Mar. 15—Gary Cooper, Wimbledon .... KO by 5
May   17—Tommy Thomas, Wimbledon .... KO 4
June 26—Roger Guest, Leicester .... L 6
Sept. 18—Ossie Musa, Lewisham .... W 8
Oct. 24—Joe Oke, Norwich .... L 8
Dec. 13—Johnny Pincham, Wimbledon .... L 8
1980
Feb.   4—Tony Britton, Hammersmith .... L 8

JAMES CALLAGHAN
Born: May 3, 1956, Yokohama, Japan
Japanese Middleweight Champion
Manager: Tetsuro Kawai
Amateur record: 24-1, 15 kayoes
Won British Amateur Middleweight Title in Liverpool
1978
Nov.   7—Eiji Tanaka, Yokohama .... KO 5
1979
June 28—Mohammet Matsumoto, Tokyo .... W 10
Oct. 23—Minoru Ono, Tokyo .... KO 9
Jan.   9—Tsutomu (Dynamite) Matsuo, Yokohama KO 8
(Won Japanese Middleweight Title)
May   25—Jong Sathiragym, Tokyo .... W 10
Aug. 17—Tsumoru Okamoto, Tokyo .... KO 8
(Retained Japanese Middleweight Title)

GIAMBATTISTA CALVIA
Italian Featherweight
1980
Apr. 11—Pietro Donati, Sassari .... L 6
Apr. 25—Leo Gomez, Mantova .... KO by 2
Dec. 27—Roberto Serrelli, Cagliari .... L 4

DAVE CAMPBELL
Irish Junior Welterweight
1977
Dec. 16—Gene McGarrigale, Enniskillen .... KO 3
1978
Feb.   3—Gordon Kidd, Enniskillen .... KO 4
Feb. 21—Granville Allen, Enniskillen .... L 8
Oct. 11—Benny Purdy, Belfast .... W 8
Dec.   1—Steve Early, Enniskillen .... KO by 2
1979
Oct. 11—Vernon Van Reil, Liverpool .... W 6
Oct. 29—Mike Clemow, Camborne .... W 6
Nov. 28—Hugh Smith, Solihull .... KO 7
1980
Feb. 25—Ray Heaney, Belfast .... KO 7
(Won Vacant North Ireland Junior Welterweight Title)
Mar.   4—Eddie Copeland, Wembley .... KO by 5

STEVE CAMPBELL
Australian Lightweight
1980
Sept. 3—Paul Baker, Brookvale .... L 6
Sept. 10—Calby Barkell, Gosford .... L 6
Sept. 16—Sam Parsons, Sutherland .... KO 6
Sept. 22—Calby Barkell, Rozelle .... L 6
Oct.   1—Calby Barkell, Brookvale .... L 6
Oct. 14—Calby Barkell, Sutherland .... L 6
Oct. 21—Elley Parker, Kingsford .... L 6
Oct. 29—Calby Barkell, Gosford .... L 6

Nov.   4—Ray Kelly, Kingsford .... W   4
Nov.   6—Eric King, Kingsford .... D   6

LUCIEN CAMPO
French Welterweight
1978
Jan. 16—Ronald Zenon, Paris .... KO by   2
Mar. 11—Serge Malpris, Sens .... W   6
June   5—Mohammed Bouziani, Paris L   6
Sept. 14—Mongi Khemeri, Paris .... KO   3
Oct. 28—Hugues Samo, Calais .... KO by   5
1979
Feb. 10—Jean Marie Touati, Arques L   6
Mar.   3—Maliba Kibassa, Creil .... D   6
Apr.   7—Serge Poulain, Argenteuil .... W   6
May   4—Angelo Licata, La Louviere L   6
May   12—Antoine Muadia Muita, Argenteuil ...... W   6
June   7—Claude Lancastra, Paris .... KO by   4
Sept. 22—Dave Williams, Zele .... KO by   5
Dec.   1—Jean Jacques Benchetrit, Nice .... KO by   4
1980
Jan. 19—Mutuawale Kibassa, Argenteuil .... W   6
Feb.   9—Francis Bailleul, Calais L   8
Mar.   8—Boro Jovic, Argenteuil .... KO   8
Apr.   5—Jo Bollue, La Louviere L   6

GIOVANNI CAMPUTARO
Italian Flyweight
1976
Oct.   3—Gavino Luciano, Piedimonte .... KO   6
Oct. 22—Sabatino DeFilippo, Milan L   6
Nov. 27—Luigi Parvati, Salerno .... W   6
Dec. 23—Filippo Belvedere, Piedimonte Matese .... W   8
1977
Feb. 12—Giuseppe Luciano, Piedimonte Matese .... W   4
Feb. 12—Santo Medici, Piedimonte Matese .... W   4
Feb. 25—Gavino Luciano, Milano .... W   6
Mar. 26—Tarcisio Boi, Piedimonte .... W   6
June 17—Arturo Menciassi, Milan L   6
Aug.   9—Nessim Zebelini, Piedimonte Matese ..... W   8
Oct. 14—Claudio Tanda, Milan .... KO 10
         (Italian Flyweight Title)
Dec.   3—Santo Medici, Piedmonte Matese .... W 12
         (Italian Flyweight Title)
1978
Feb. 11—Sabatino De Filippo, Piedimonte .... W 12
         (Italian Flyweight Title)
May   5—Filippo Belvedere, Milan .... W 12
July   1—Salvatore Laconi, Cagliari .... W 12
         (Italian Flyweight Title)
July 29—Emilio Pireddu, Piedimonte Matese ...... W 15
         (Italian Flyweight Title)
Oct. 28—Altero Marini, Piedimonte Matese .... W   8
1979
Jan. 13—Franco Buglione, Piedimonte Matese .... D 12
         (Italian Flyweight Title)
Apr. 18—Claudio Tanda, S. Lorenzello .... W   8
June 22—Sabatino De Filippo, Savona .... L 12
         (Italian Flyweight Title)
Sept. 26—Mariano Garcia, Piedimonte Matese ..... W 10
Nov. 16—Sabatino De Filippo, Piedimonte Matese KO   6
Dec. 28—Salvatore Laconi, Agerola .... WF   4
1980
Mar.   7—Sabatino De Filippo, Savona .... D 10
June 28—Charlie Magri, Glasgow .... KO by   3
         (For European Flyweight Title)
Dec. 28—Paolo Castrovilli, Torino .... KO by   5
         (For Italian Flyweight Title)

BRIGILDO CANADA
Filipino Flyweight
1978
Nov.   4—Frank Cedeno, Quezon .... KO by   7
1979
Oct. 20—Rodrigo Saomoy, Lucena City .... W 10
Nov. 24—Rodrigo Saomoy, Manila .... W 10
Dec. 19—Star Blijido, La Union .... W 10
Dec. 29—Teo Montejo, Lucena City .... W 10
1980
Feb.   3—Teo Montejo, Quezon city .... W 10
May   9—Oscar Gonzales Jr., Manila .... W 10
July   4—Netrenoi Vorasing, Manila .... L 10
Oct.   3—Netrenoi Vorsing, Quezon City .... D 10
Nov. 29—Frank Cedeno, Davao City .... L 10

FRANCO CANINI
Italian Junior Lightweight
1980
Mar. ?1—Mario Tiano, Bologna .... W   6
Apr. 12—Antonio Germano, Rimini .... W   6
Sept. 20—Pasquale Riboli, Sebenico .... W   8
Oct. 18—Aniello Ventrone, Rimini .... W   6
Nov. 28—Titi Larbi, Campione .... W   6

Dec. 26—Gregorio Ciancaglione, Bologna .... KO   4

NOE CANINO
Filipino Bantamweight
1977
Nov. 26—Rey Orbino, Masbate .... L 10
1978
Nov. 24—Eddie Galler, Manila .... L 10
1979
Jan. 12—Rey Orbino, Manila .... W 10
Mar. 10—Cesar Amazan, Manila .... KO   2
Apr.   8—Hadji Humanid, Cebu City .... D 10
May   18—Jaime Sanama, Manila .... KO   2
May   26—Reben Arevalo, Sorsogon .... L 10
Nov.   3—Rey Naduma Jr., Cag. De Oro City ... KO   8
Dec. 29—Rudy Garcia, Cabanturan City .... W 10
1980
Jan. 18—Tale Maguan, Manila .... L 10
Feb. 23—Rudy Garcia, Cabanatuan .... KO   3
Mar. 15—Danilo Inocian, Santos City .... L 10
May   31—Rene Cruz, Jr., Cabanatuan City .... D 10

JESUS CANUT
Spanish Junior Lightweight
1972
May   13—Luis Cristobal Diaz, Salmanca .... W   6
July 21—Jose Broncano, Madrid .... D   6
Sept. 2—Francisco Santaengracia, Salamanca .... WF   2
1973
Mar. 16—Jose Antonio Donoso, Madrid .... W   6
Apr. 13—Pedro Nino Jimenez, Madrid L   6
1974
Dec.   1—Jalifa Ahmed Mimoun, Salamanca ...... WF   6
1975
Mar.   1—Mohatar II, Salmanca .... W   6
1976-1977
(Inactive)
1978
July 28—Jose Antonio Parreno, Madrid .... D   6
Sept. 5—Salid Mimun Amar, Melilla L   8
Nov.   4—Carlos Hernandez, Valladolid L   8
1979
Mar. 10—Isidoro Cabeza, Valladolid .... KO by   4
May   5—Antonio Munoz Jurado, Salamanca ..... KO   2
May   26—Joaquin Garcia del Moral, Salamanca ... W   6
July 21—Manuel Velazquez, Guadalajara .... L 12
         (Spanish Lightweight Title)
Nov. 10—Mohamed El Kadoumni, Salmanca .... W   6
1980
Feb. 16—Mohamed El Coudoumi, Leon .... D   6
Nov. 22—Dave Williams, Zele .... KO by   4

KARL CANWELL
British Light Heavyweight
1977
Sept. 5—Len Brittain, Mayfair .... KO   4
Sept. 20—Wally Barnes, Southend .... W   6
Oct. 10—Joey Williams, London .... W   6
Oct. 19—Steve Taylor, London .... W   6
Dec. 13—Pat Thompson, Southgate .... W   8
1978
Jan. 24—Theo Josephs, Solihull .... KO   4
Feb.   6—Bonny McKenzie, London .... W   8
Feb. 27—Billy Knight, London L   8
May   15—Victor Attivor, London .... L disq.   6
July 17—Tom Collins, London .... KO   6
Sept. 18—Chris Lawson, Wolverhampton .... KO   5
Sept. 30—Patrick Lyampemshya, Wolverhampton   KO   3
Nov. 24—Tony Mundine, Brisbane .... KO by   3
1979
Feb. 27—Lloyd James, London .... KO   6
Mar.   1—Bonny McKenzie, London L   8
Mar. 12—Bonny McKenzie, London .... W   8
Mar. 31—Chisanda Mutti, Lusaka .... KO by   2
Sept. 10—Harald Skog, Oslo .... KO   2
Oct. 31—Carlton Benoit, Burslem .... W   8
1980
Oct. 17—Mustafa Wasajja, Copenhagen L   8

NICK CAPUTOL
Filipino Lightweight
1978
Sept. 29—Ric Dolotallas, Cag. De Oro City ...... L 10
1979
Mar. 31—Jun Moises, Santos City .... W 10
Apr. 21—Frankie Tayo, Santos City .... KO   4
June 16—Ding Villafuerte, Davao City .... W 10
Aug. 10—Willie Espinosa, Manila .... W 10
Oct. 26—Joe Francisco, Manila .... KO by   2
1980
Feb.   2—Joel Insular, Davao City .... W 10
Mar.   1—Roland Dante, Davao City .... W 10
May   31—Francis Camatagan, Baguio City .... W 10

277

Aug. 29—Eddie Cejas, Quezon City .... W 10

RICHARD CARAMANOIS
French Light Heavyweight
1980
Feb. 29—Bojan Sverzina, Marseille .... W 6
Apr. 18—Gabrielle Lazzari, Paris .... W 6
June 6—Jose Centa, Marseille .... KO 3
Oct. 4—Boyd Farrar, Marseille .... KO 7
Nov. 28—Maurice Trepant, Marseille .... W 6

ALEX CARDOZO
Spanish Light Heavyweight
1972
June 1—Antonio Dos Santos, Lisbon .... L 6
June 17—Manuel Carracelas, Tarrasa .... D 6
July 15—Manuel Carracelas, Reus .... D 6
Oct. 20—Manuel Carracelas, Barcelona .... L 6
Nov. 3—Emile Okee, Marsiglia .... L 6
Dec. 7—Cirillo Jareno, Tarrasa .... L 6
Dec. 26—Gianni Franzolin, Milano .... KO by 6
1973
Feb. 8—Ennio Cometti, Milano .... KO by 2
July 14—Angel Andres, Villanueva .... KO 3
Oct. 11—Manuel Carracelas, Villanueva .... W 6
Nov. 3—Antonio Puente, Sabadell .... L 8
Nov. 16—Lino Finotti, Novara .... D 8
Dec. 1—Antonio Puente, Sabadell .... KO by 5
Dec. 28—Lino Finotti, Novara .... L 6
1974
Feb. 7—Tom Jensen, Copenhagen .... KO by 2
Mar. 16—Manuel Trujillo, S. Cruz .... KO 6
May 17—Aldo Traversaro, Genova.............. KO by 5
Sept. 14—Antonio Puente, Llagosta .... L 8
Oct. 3—Jose Antonio Vasquez, Bilbao .... KO by 6
1975
Feb. 7—Francisco Barrilado, Palma Mallorca..... NC 3
Mar. 1—Manuel Carrecelas, Mataro .... W 6
Mar. 18—Leo Kakolewicz, Berlin .... L 6
May 31—Jose Antonio Vasquez, Cuenca .... D 8
June 25—Jose Antonio Vasquez, Madrid .... D 8
Aug. 23—Manuel Trujillo, Cuenca .... KO by 6
1976
Mar. 13—Antonio Puente, Llagosta................ L 8
Apr. 2—Victor Varon, Bilbao................... KO by 3
May 6—Jose Antonio Galvez, Bilbao............ KO 8
June 5—Jose Antonio Galvez, Almeria .... L 8
July 2—Alberto Lovell, Barcelona .... W 8
July 21—Jose Iniguez, Barcelona .... KO by 7
Dec. 11—Giacinto Cattani, Montecchino .... KO 3
1977
June 1—Sugar Silex, Bilbao .... L 8
July 8—Gilberto Acuna, Madrid .... KO by 4
Dec. 25—Jose Iniguez, Bilbao .... KO 7
1978
Feb. 23—Francois Fiol, Chavannes .... D 8
Apr. 28—Hocine Tafer, Ginerva .... KO by 1
July 12—Rocky Perez, Bilbao .... KO 7
Sept. 16—Felipe Rodriguez, Vigo .... L 8
Oct. 28—Avenamar Peralta, La Coruna .... KO by 7
1979
(Inactive)
1980
May 10—Ali Lisaka, Zaragoza .... L 6
June 1—Juan Saavedra, Madrid .... W 6
July 4—Scassino Ferreira, Madrid .... W 8
Aug. 8—Avenemar Peralta, Madrid .... L 10
(For Spanish Light Heavyweight Title)
Aug. 29—Avenemar Peralta, Melilla .... L 10
(For Spanish Light Heavyweight Title)
Oct. 10—Alfredo Naveiras, Barcelona .... KO by 7
Nov. 21—Avenemar Peralta, Palma de Mallorca ....L 8

NATALE CAREDDA
Italian Junior Lightweight
Born: Dec. 24, 1945.
Turned pro 1969. Through 1971 had 15 fights,
Won 13, Lost 2.
1972
May 5—Lothar Abend, Hamburg .... KO by 9
July 29—Paul Ikumapayi, Carbonia .... D 8
1973
Jan. 10—Giovanni Girgenti, Enna .... KO by 9
June 9—Abu Arrow, Siena .... W disq. 3
June 20—Giuseppe Martucci, Carole................. D 8
June 28—Nicolo Bennici, Novara .... L 6
Sept. 23—Ugo Poli, Caspoggio .... L 8
Nov. 10—Ugo Di Pietro, Cagliari .... KO by 4
1974
May 1—Giuliano Lai, Cagliari .... D 5
June 7—Michele Siracusa, Rome .... KO by 5
Sept. 28—Paul Ikumapayi, Cabras .... W 6
Nov. 29—Rudi Voegl, Bern .... D 8

Dec. 28—Renzo Battistelli, Cagliari................ W 8
1975
Feb. 21—Rodolfo Sanchez, Madrid................ L 8
Mar. 8—Nevio Carbi, Trieste .... KO by 1
June 21—Dante Guarneri, Cantu................ L 8
July 26—Oscar Aparicio, Civitanova Marche ... KO by 3
Aug. 14—Pietro Candida, Portocuso............... W 6
Aug. 30—Domenico Condello, Laconi .... D 6
Nov. 29—Antonio Poccai, Cagliari .... W 6
Dec. 19—Salvatore Liscapade, Rome............. L 8
1976
Jan. 30—Luigi Zanghi, Bolonga.................. L 8
Mar. 5—Iganzio Fara, Sassari .... W 6
Mar. 26—Giovanni Cavazzini, Cagliari .... W 6
Apr. 30—Gianfranco Bulla, Cagliari .... D 6
May 21—Domenico Radiccioni, Cagliari.......... D 8
July 2—Giuseppe Agate, Cagliari .... W 8
Sept. 9—Giovanni Scarpati, Cagliari .... W 6
Oct. 15—Gabriel Lamperti, Cagliari .... W 8
Dec. 3—Sergio Emili, Cagliari .... W 12
(Italian Featherweight Title)
1977
Mar. 11—Carlo Frassinetti, Cagliari .... W 8
Apr. 8—Amrogio Mariani, Cagliari .... W 12
(Italian Featherweight Title)
June 17—Sergio Emili, Civitanova .... L 12
(Italian Featherweight Title)
Oct. 7—Salvatore Avella, Cagliari .... W 8
Dec. 2—Domenico Condello, Siniscola .... W 8
Dec. 23—Gianfranco Lalli, Gagliari .... D 8
1978
Jan. 27—Salvatore Liscapade, Milano .... L 8
May 27—Giuseppe Agate, Oristano .... W 8
July 1—Biaggio Pieri, Port Village .... W 8
1979
Feb. 10—Salvatore Melluzzo, Cagliari .... W 12
(Italian Featherweight Title)
June 9—Marco Gallo, Cagliari .... W 8
Sept. 5—Potito Di Muro, Fort Village .... L 12
(Italian Featherweight Title)
Sept. 30—Antonio Franca, Oristano .... W 8
Dec. 21—Annunzio Sanna, Cagliari .... D 8
1980
Feb. 8—Charles Jurietti, Valence .... KO by 3
May 30—Michele D'Amato, Rome .... W 6
July 5—Salvatore Melluzzo, Siracusa .... L 10
Aug. 15—Annuiziato Sanna, Portoscuso .... KO 3
Sept. 14—Michel D'Amato, Avezzano .... D 8
Oct. 11—Abass Macauley, Cagliari .... W 6
Oct. 31—Luigi DeRosa, Capua .... L 8

CEDRIC CARLSONS
South African Lightweight
1979
Mar. 2—Abel Rapulan, Bloemfontein .... L 4
Nov. 9—Enock Motsoane, Bloemfontein .... L 6
1980
Mar. 8—Teboho Lento, Bloemfontein .... KO by 2

ALOIS CARMELIET
Belgian Welterweight
1973
Dec. 15—Fernand Banckaert, Zele .... KO 1
1974
Jan. 25—Daniel Ringuet, Zele .... KO 1
Feb. 8—Daniel Ringuet, S. Amand .... W 6
Mar. 3—Henri Taillez, Zele .... W 6
Mar. 15—Ahmed Sareh, Bruges .... W 6
Mar. 30—Jean Pierre Hiermann, Kalken .... L 6
Apr. 13—Victor Thorel, Zele .... W 6
Sept. 21—Daniel Jacquin, Zele .... KO 3
Oct. 26—Alex Anglio, Zele .... WF 6
1975
Jan. 4—Victor Thorel, Zele .... KO by 5
Feb. 1—Jean Pierre Heirman, Zele .... L 6
Sept. 20—Jacky Peraire, Zele .... W 6
Oct. 4—Jacky Peraire, Hayange .... KO by 4
Dec. 6—Mohamed Mechlia, Zele .... W 6
1976
Jan. 22—Jean Claude Bodchon, Paris........... KO 4
Feb. 14—Jean Claude Sider, Zele Belgium .... W 6
Apr. 10—Jean Simos, Leige .... KO 6
May 1—Giampolo Piras, Zele .... W 8
Sept. 10—Angelo Tomasini, Zele .... KO 1
Oct. 16—Roy Commosioung, Zele............... W 8
Nov. 11—Augusto Lauri, Zele .... D 8
Dec. 4—Bobby Arthur, Zele................... KO 1
1977
Jan. 8—Italo Venrui, Zele .... W 8
Feb. 19—Terry Peterson, Zele .... KO 5
Apr. 16—Luciano Borraccia, Zele .... W 8
Oct. 8—Luciano Laffranchi, Zele .... W 10
Nov. 11—Augusto Lauri, Zele .... W 10

278

1978

Jan.	7—Justice Ortiz, Zele	W	10
Feb.	17—Jesse Lara, Zele	W	10
Mar.	24—Beau Jaynes, Zele	KO	3
Apr.	29—Jo Kimpuani, Zele	KO by	3
Sept.	16—Alain Salmon, Zele	W	8
Oct.	13—Remo Costa, Ravenna	W	10
Nov.	11—Timoteo Bonizzoni, Zele	W	10

1979

Feb.	10—Vittorio Conte, Zele	D	10
Feb.	17—Billy Waith, Zele	W	8
Mar.	31—Billy Waith, Zele	W	10
Apr.	21—Giuseppe Russi, Zele	D	8
Sept.	9—Giancarlo Barabotti, Buggenhout	W	8
Oct.	20—Johnny Barr, Liege	KO	5
Nov.	10—Danny Heath, Zele	KO	1
Dec.	8—Bechir Boundtka, Zele	W	8

1980

Feb.	2—Jorgen Hansen, Randers	KO by	5
	(Lost European Welterweight Title)		

STAN CARNELL
British Middleweight
1979

Sept.	26—Chris Devine, Sheffield	L	6
Oct.	8—Nigel Savory, Bradford	KO	2
Nov.	6—Jimmy Harrington, Kensington	KO by	2
Dec.	20—Joey Williams, Queensway	KO by	5

1980

Feb.	25—Trevor Kerr, Belfast	L	8
Mar.	27—Rocky Burton, Liverpool	L	6
Oct.	22—Ian Scotting, Doncaster	KO by	5

MICHEL CARON
Belgian Light Heavyweight
1975

Mar.	14—Walter Verschueren, Bruges	KO	3
June	13—Bernard Artone, Gand	W	6
Sept.	16—Gilbert Cnudde, Bruges	W	6
Oct.	4—Larbi Titi, Mouscron	KO by	3

1976

Feb.	6—Jacques Chinon, Bruges	W	6
May	17—Sonny Kamunga, Esch	D	6
Oct.	9—Bernard Artone, Anversa	KO	1
Dec.	10—Armando Lena, Bruges	W	6

1977

Jan.	8—Hocine Tafer, Grenoble	KO by	3
Nov.	21—Babo Kabassu, Esch	KO by	2

1978-1979
(Inactive)
1980

Mar.	22—Roland Bayens, Dendermonde	W	6
Nov.	1—Luc Gossens, Bruxelles	W	6
Nov.	17—Nadja Memeti, Bruxelles	W	6
Dec.	25—Robert Desnouck, Izegem	L	8

WALLY CARR
Australian Middleweight
1971

Aug.	26—Graham Murray, Redfern	D	3
Sept.	2—Graham Murray, Redfern	W	4
Sept.	9—Laurie Johnson, Redfern	L	4
Sept.	15—Graham Murray, Cammeray	W	4
Sept.	30—Frank Geebung, Redfern	L	4
Oct.	13—Dennis Cutmore, Cammeray	D	4
Oct.	18—Graham Murray, Marrickville	W	4
Nov.	4—Laurie Johnson, Redfern	KO	3
Nov.	15—Bob West, Marrickville	KO	3
Nov.	25—Elley Dennis, Redfern	W	4
Dec.	1—Elley Dennis, Cammeray	W	4
Dec.	7—Wayne Oldham, Penrith	KO	3
Dec.	9—Frank Geebung, Redfern	W	4
Dec.	16—Ern McNeill, Redfern	KO	2

1972

Jan.	11—Alan Scott, Marrickville	KO	5
Jan.	27—Jim Metcalf, Redfern	L	6
Feb.	3—Frank Geebung, Redfern	D	4
Feb.	8—Lance McConnell, Marrickville	L	6
Mar.	2—Lance McConnell, Redfern	L	6
May	25—Les Knox, Redfern	W	4
June	1—Les Knox, Redfern	W	4
June	7—Neville Williams, Redfern	KO by	3
June	15—Eric Larche, Redfern	W	3
June	22—Jim Metcalf, Redfern	L	4
July	11—Binky Rominsky, Corrimal	W	8
Aug.	10—Ross Armstrong, Redfern	W	4
Aug.	17—Ross Armstrong, Redfern	L	4
Sept.	20—Jeff Malcolm, Cammeray	D	4
Sept.	26—Rod Connors, Cronulla	W	4
Oct.	10—Jim Metcalf, Marrickville	L	8
Oct.	18—Bob West, Cammeray	W	6
Oct.	31—Matt Davis, Cronulla	W	8
Nov.	15—Binky Rominsky, Cammeray	KO	1
Nov.	30—Ceddy McGrady, Redfern	W	6

1973

Jan.	18—Ceddy McGrady, South Sydney	W	8
Feb.	7—Alan Mander, Cammeray	LF	8
Feb.	28—Rod Connors, Redfern	L	6
Apr.	19—Eric King, Blacktown	W	6
May	2—Binky Rominski, Brookvale	W	8
May	8—Mick Maher, Marrickville	W	6
May	17—Jim Metcalf, Blacktown	D	8
June	14—David Hill, Blacktown	L	6
June	19—Les Knox, Cronulla	W	8
Aug.	15—Colin Cassidy, Marrickville	KO by	6
Sept.	13—Bobby Cotterill, Blacktown	L	10
Nov.	12—Antoine Oke, Noumea	L	8

1974

Feb.	14—Martin Ross, Blacktown	KO	5
Mar.	15—Fred Pastor, Melbourne	W	8
Mar.	28—Barry Facer, Blacktown	KO	2
Apr.	4—Matt Ropis, Blacktown	W	8
May	8—Wayne Cullen, Cammeray	KO	1
May	17—Billy O'Connor, Melbourne	KO	5
June	13—Andy Broome, Blacktown	KO by	3
Aug.	14—Colin Cassidy, Marrickville	L	10
Aug.	18—Dennis Enright, Invercargill	L	10

1975

Feb.	27—Alan Aldenhoven, Blacktown	KO	4
Mar.	13—Martin Beni, Port Moresby	D	10
Apr.	3—Billy O'Donnell, Blacktown	KO	1
Apr.	19—Martin Beni, Melbourne	KO by	5
May	22—Ben Holt, Blacktown	L	10
June	5—Alex Burns, Blacktown	KO	9
July	10—Benny Holt, Blacktown	KO	9
Oct.	2—Joe Keresi, Blacktown	KO	5

1976

June	9—Eric King, Marrickville	W	8
July	1—Julius Leuipa, Chingola	KO by	4
July	12—Monty Betham, Wellington	KO	6
Aug.	4—Eric King, Cammeray	KO	6
Sept.	8—Neil Pattel, Marrickvelle	L	15
Sept.	23—Monty Betham, Wellington	KO by	11
Oct.	27—John Layton, Bankstown	D	10

1977

Sept.	11—Rudy Siregar, Surabaya	W	10
Oct.	12—John Layton, Marrickville	W	12
	(Australian Junior Middleweight Title)		
Dec.	14—Al Korovou, Marrickville	L	12
	(Australian Middleweight Title)		

1978

June	30—Neil Pattel, Brisbane	L	10
July	26—Al Korovou, Bankstown	KO	13
	(Australian Middleweight Title)		
Dec.	7—Benny Holt, Revesby	KO	3
	(Australian Middleweight Title)		
Dec.	15—Torkano Marcos, Suva	KO	11
	(Australian Middleweight Title)		

1979

Feb.	1—Monty Betham, Auckland	L	12
	(Australian Middleweight Title)		
Feb.	18—John Krishna, Moore Park	KO	3
	(For Australian Middleweight Title)		
June	16—Terry Fox, Victoria Park	W	12

1980

Apr.	12—Fossie Schmidt, Suva	KO	3
June	29—Terry Fox, Rozelle	KO	5
Aug.	2—Philip Kating, Laucaula Bay	L	10
Nov.	20—Ken Eldridge, Marrickville	KO	2

MANUEL CARRASCO
Spanish Flyweight
1975

Dec.	27—German Yeste, Irun	W	6

1976

Feb.	5—Raimon S. Sebastiano	W	6
Mar.	7—German Yestes, San Sebastian	W	6
Apr.	13—Valeriano Morales, San Sebastian	W	8
July	24—Miguel Montes, Villafranca	W	8
July	31—Eduardo Tabares, Tolosa	W	8
Aug.	22—Angel Oliver, S. Sebastiano	W	8
Sept.	18—Jose Cantero, San Sebastian	W	8
Oct.	2—Jose Castillejos, Bolbao	KO	3
Dec.	23—Mariano Garcia, S. Sebastiano	W	8

1977

Feb.	19—Nassim Zebillini, San Sebastien	W	10
Mar.	26—Jose Cantero, Huelva	L	12
	(Spanish Flyweight Title)		
Nov.	5—Pedro Molledo, Irun	W	8

1978

Feb.	18—Pedro Molledo, Irun	W	8
Mar.	11—Garcia Del Moral Tanio, Vegara	W	8
Apr.	25—Charlie Magri, London	L	8
May	27—Nessem Zebellini, San Sebastian	W	8
July	29—German Yeste, Elizondo	W	8
Sept	23—German Yeste, Azcoitia	W	8
Nov.	15—Franco Udella, Bellaria	L	15
	(European Flyweight Title)		

279

1979

Apr.	27—Martin Vargas, Santiago	L	10
May	26—Antonio Garcia del Moral, Salamanca	W	8'
July	21—Jose Hernandez Cornejo, Irun	W	8
Oct.	27—Martin Antich, La Coruna	W	8
Dec.	4—Charlie Magri, London	L	12

(European Flyweight Title)

1980

Apr.	17—Steve Muchoki, Copenhagen	L	8
May	17—Esteben Eguia, Leon	W	8

ALFONSO CARRILLO
Italian Lightweight
1977

Feb.	25—Giuseppe Corbo, Milano	L	4
Apr.	8—Franco Siddu, Ozieri	D	6
Apr.	22—Mario De Camillo, Rome	W	6
June	4—Sergio D'Angelo, Frosinone	KO by	2
Aug.	2—Gerardo Scognamiglio, Orsomarso	W	6
Aug.	13—Alfonso Bonavita, Civitavecchia	W	6
Aug.	23—Gerardo Scognamiglio, S. Anastasia	W	6
Oct.	7—Leonardo Pantaleo, Capua	KO	6
Oct.	18—Giovanni Maiorano, Mugnano	W	6
Nov.	18—Antonio Casamonica, Rome	W	6
Dec.	22—Abass Macauley, Capua	W	8

1978

Mar.	3—Giovanni Carrino, Milan	D	8
Mar/	17—Domenico Traini, Montecosaro	W	8
June	28—Wcio Cusme, Castelsanpietro	D	8
Aug.	20—Ugo Poli, Roccamonfina	WF	3
Sept.	23—Carlo Frassinetti, Pietramelara	KO	6
Oct.	27—Sergio Emili, Capua	W	8
Nov.	17—Giovanni Vitillo, Milan	L	8
Dec.	22—Eloy De Souza, Capua	KO	4

1979

Mar.	4—Joe Gibilisco, San Remo	L	8
May	6—Vicenzo Quero, Taranto	L	10
July	28—Rosario Di Tommaso, Terracina	KO by	7

1980

Jan.	25—Lucio Cusma, Bologna	KO by	3
Aug.	23—Giuseppe Russi, Capua	W	8
Dec.	23—Luigi Curcetti, Recanati	D	6

GIOVANNI CARRINO
Italian Junior Welterweight
1977

Feb.	11—Giuseppe Pappalardo, Milan	W	6
Mar.	4—Giovanni Cavazzini, Lugo Romagna	W	6
May	14—Raimondo Riccio, Grottaglie	W	6
June	25—Gerardo Scognamiglio, Taranto	KO	4
Aug.	12—Domenico Condello, Taranto	W	6
Oct.	14—Renzo Battistelli, Bologna	W	6
Dec.	2—Gianfranco Palazzi, Milano	WF	4

1978

Jan.	7—Ben Jelassie, Milan	W	6
Mar.	3—Alfonso Carrillo, Milan	D	8
May	5—Gerardo Del Guacchio, Milan	KO	6
May	26—Giovanni Mairorano, Taranto	W	8
July	20—Carlos Dos Santos, Taranto	W	8
Oct.	20—Giovanni Vitillo, Milan	LF	6
Nov.	4—Bernardo Ciramella, Caserta	L	8
Jan.	27—Lucio Cusma, Salerno	KO by	8
May	25—Palmiro Masala, Ravegnate	W	8
June	16—Annunziato Sanna, Rovagnate	ND	6
July	26—Annunziato Sanna, Taranto	KO	7
Oct.	7—Eloy De Souza, Taranto	W	8

1980

Mar.	6—Palmiro Masala, Taranto	KO by	7
Apr.	18—Lucio Cusma, Bologna	KO by	7

(For Italian Lightweight Title)

July	24—Biagio Pierri, Taranto	W	8

HUGO CARRIZO
Spanish Lightweight
1977

June	16—Cecilio Lastra, Santander	L	8
Aug.	2—Ramon Garcia Marichal, S. Cruz	L	8
Sept.	16—Antonio Guinaldo, Barcelona	L	8
Oct.	7—Rodolfo Sanchez, Madrid	W	8
Nov.	5—Nino Jimenez, Madrid	W	8
Dec.	25—Rodolfo Sanchez, Bilbao	D	8

1978

Feb.	17—Pedro Nino Jimenez, Madrid	L	8
May	6—Antonio Amaya, Madrid	D	8
June	30—Antonio Guinaldo, Barcelona	L	8
Aug.	19—Roberto Castanon, Gijon	L	8
Sept.	23—Jose Manuel Velazquez, Lepe	L	8
Dec.	26—Oscar Aparicio, Bologna	L	8

1979

July	27—Modesto Torito Gomez, Santander	W	8
Aug.	4—Chato Melillense, Vigo	W	8
Aug.	10—Rodolfo Sanchez, Santander	D	8

Aug.	26—Chato Mellillense, La Coruna	W	8
Aug.	31—Anjos Dos Santos, Madrid	W	8
Sept.	29—Carlos Hernandez, Santander	L	8
Oct.	26—Anjos Dos Santos, La Coruna	W	8
Oct.	27—Juan Carlos, La Coruna	W	8
Nov.	3—Serafin Dos Anjos, Lugo	W	8
Dec.	1—Antonio Reinoso, La Coruna	KO	7

1980

Jan.	12—Francisco Leon, La Coruna	L	8
Aug.	20—Mohamed Boumedian (Jofre II), Cuenca	D	8
Oct.	4—Jose Luis Vicho, Palma de Mallorca	L	10

TONY CARROLL
British Junior Welterweight
1977

Sept.	22—Eric Wood, Birkenhead	W	6
Oct.	6—Marty Jacobs, Liverpool	W	6
Nov.	10—Brian Sanagg, Liverpool	W	6
Nov.	29—Marty Jacobs, Birkenhead	KO	2
Dec.	12—Dave McCabe, London	L	6

1978

Mar.	31—Eric Wood, Liverpool	W	6
Nov.	14—Nigel Thomas, Birkenhead	W	6
Dec.	4—Nigel Thomas, Manchester	W	6

1979

Jan.	18—Jesse Harper, Liverpool	W	8
Feb.	12—Dai Davies, Manchester	W	8
Mar.	15—Brian Snagg, Caister	W	8
Apr.	2—Kevin Quinn, Manchester	W	8
Apr.	19—Tommy Wright, Birkenhead	L	8
May	21—George Schofield, Manchester	W	8
Sept.	20—Robbie Robinson, Liverpool	KO	4

1980

Jan.	28—James Cooke, Edgbaston	L	8
Apr.	22—Winston Spencer, London	W	8
May	31—Derek Nelson, Liverpool	W	8
Sept.	18—Robbie Robinson, Liverpool	L	8

SIONY (LITTLE) CARUPO
Filipino Junior Flyweight
1977

Nov.	19—Danilo Gonzaga, Davao City	L	10

1978

Oct.	28—Rudy Canasa, Davao Del Norte	W	10
Nov.	11—Diego De Villa, Davao City	KO	4
Nov.	25—Julius Gonzaga, Davao City	W	10

1979

Jan.	14—Diego De Villa, Davao City	W	10
Jan.	27—Rondald Sumalis, Davao City	W	10
Apr.	20—Ver Libradilla, Manila	W	12

(Philippine Junior Flyweight Title)

Apr.	22—Chris Maratas, Davao Del Norte	KO	6
June	29—Arnel Arrozal, Manila	L	10
July	28—Sung Jun-Kim, Seoul	L	15

(WBC Junior Flyweight Title)

Aug.	19—Ric Barimbad, Davao Del Sur	L	10
Nov.	24—Andy Balaba, Santos City	L	10

1980

Jan.	19—Ric Barimbad, Santos City	D	12
May	31—Ric Barimbad, Davao City	L	10
July	16—Frank Cedeno, Manila	L	12
Aug.	16—Danilo Inocian, De Oro City	W	10
Aug.	24—Antonio Baja, Butan City	D	10
Nov.	29—Ric Barimbad, Davao City	W	12

(Retained Filipino Junior Featherweight Title)

ANTONIO CASADO
Spanish Junior Middleweight
1974

Dec.	7—Kid Dongo, Sabadell	KO	3

1975

Feb.	15—Cipriano Garcia, Mataro	W	6
Mar.	15—Jose Carlo Diaz, Mataro	W	6
Apr.	26—Fernando Taveraz, Mataro	W	6

1976

Jan.	17—Antonio Perez, Cadiz	W	6
Mar.	13—Manual Rico, Sabadell	D	6
June	5—Jose Lopez Barillado, Almeria	L	6
July	2—Fernando Perez, Madrid	D	8
Sept.	18—Tony Ortiz, Jerez	L	12
Nov.	19—Luis Aaries, Tarbes	L	8

1977

Apr.	15—Mario Guilloti, Genova	KO by	7
Oct.	1—Josines, Leom	L	8
Nov.	12—Mimoun Mohatar, La Coruna	D	8
Dec.	10—Jose Ramon Gomez Fouz, Aviles	L	8

1978

Feb.	18—Dum Dum Pachecho, Logrono	D	8
May	6—Jose Ramon Gomez, Pravia	W	8
May	20—Jose Luis Fernandez Josines, Logrono	W	8
Sept.	30—Fernando Bermejo, Sabadell	KO	5
Nov.	9—Carlos Morales, Barcelona	D	8

1979
Mar. 17—Alain Ruocco, Arles .... KO by 9
May 18—Oswaldo Lopez, Valladolid .... D 8
Dec. 12—Jesus Rodriguez De La Rosa, Barcelona .. W 6
1980
Feb. 2—Cristobal Crepsi, St. Maria Barbera .... KO 3
Feb. 16—Frank Decaestecker, Middelkerke .... L 8
Mar. 7—Juan Manuel Domingo, Barcelona .... W 8
June 20—Luiz Riberiro, Barcelona .... W 8
Sept. 6—Francisco Gomez, Fuengirola .... W 10
(Won Spanish Welterweight Title)
Oct. 10—Mario Molina, Barcelona .... W 8
Dec. 19—Jose Ramon Gomez (Fouz), Barcelona ..... L 10
(Lost Spanish Welterweight Title)

ALESSANDRO CASANOVA
Italian Heavyweight
1979
Dec. 8—Miroslav Surla, Split .... L 4
1980
Feb. 14—Antimo Tescione, Modena .... W 6
Apr. 11—Claudio Cassanelli, Modena .... D 8
Apr. 25—Abdel Qissi, Bruxelles .... L 6
May 23—Augusto Dal Monte, Pesaro .... W 6
Sept. 24—Guido Frane, Fiuggi .... D 6
Dec. 27—Antimo Tescione, Cagliari .... KO 5

SALVATORE CASCIO
Italian Middleweight
1978
July 14—Vincenzo Bottoglieri, Lido di Ostia ...... W 6
Nov. 3—Biase Casoria, Rome .... W 4
Nov. 23—Pietro Callara, Rome .... L 5
Dec. 2—Serangeli, Marsala .... KO 3
Dec. 15—Spartaco Verna, Rome .... W 6
1979
Mar. 9—Luiz Ribeiro, Rome .... W 6
May 4—Franco Recupero, Rome .... KO 2
Sept. 21—Vincenzo Gottigliero, Rome .... W 8
Oct. 27—Guido Galletti, Rieti .... W 8
1980
Feb. 2—Nelson Gomez, Marsala .... W 8
May 30—Luciano Navarra, Rome .... KO 5
Sept. 12—Everaldo Costa Azevedo, Lido .... KO 1

CLAUDIO CASSANELLI
Italian Heavyweight
1978
Jan. 28—Antimo Tescione, Nonantola .... W 6
Mar. 31—Coulibaly Demba, Bologna .... KO 4
May 27—Roberto Bosio, Crevalcore .... KO 4
June 15—Angelo Visini, Imola .... W 6
July 6—Vasco Faustino, Lugo di Romagna ...... KO 2
Nov. 10—Antimo Tescione, Milano .... KO 4
1979
Feb. 23—Fausto Costantino, Modena .... W 6
June 24—Fausto Costantino, Monte Carl .... W 6
1980
Feb. 22—Horst Lang, Sassuolo .... KO 3
Apr. 11—Alessandro Casanova, Modena .... D 8
May 23—Mohammed Galloule, Castlenuevo ...... W 8
Dec. 5—Ralph Cuomo, Modena .... KO 4

ROBERTO CASTANON
Spanish Featherweight
1975
Nov. 29—A. Munoz Jurado, Leon .... KO 3
Dec. 6—J. Rodriguez Marquez, Oviedo .... W 6
Dec. 20—Miguel Montes, Leon .... KO 3
1976
Feb. 14—Juan Barros, Oviedo .... KO 4
Mar. 26—Miguel Montes, Castellon .... KO 5
May 1—A. Horacajo Moreno, Leon .... KO 2
June 19—Calrlos Hernandez, Leon .... W 8
Aug. 8—Luis Cabezas Sanchez, Madrid .... W 8
Nov. 20—Fernando Bernardez, Santander .... KO 8
Nov. 27—Francisco Larxe, Leon .... KO 4
1977
Jan. 6—Carlos Hernandez, Leon .... W 8
Feb. 5—Faustino Glanco, Santander .... KO 1
Mar. 12—Grancisco Larxe, Leon .... KO 4
Apr. 23—Juan Barros, Leon .... KO 5
May 14—Ramon Gavia Marichal, Leon .... W 8
May 28—Pedro Coque Martin, Panencia .... W 8
June 20—Enrique Sosa Felipe, Leon .... KO 3
Aug. 20—Cecilio Lastra, Santander .... KO 8
(Spanish Featherweight Title)
Sept. 1—Hector Modina, Leon .... W 8
Oct. 15—Abud Arrow, Leon .... W 10
Dec. 16—Manuel Masso, Paris .... KO 11
(European Featherweight Title)
1978
Feb. 4—Georges Cotin, Leon .... W 10
Mar. 3—Gerard Jacob, Leon .... KO 4

May 27—Roland Cazeaux, Leon .... KO 2
July 15—Albert Amatler, La Coruna .... KO 5
(European Featherweight Title)
Aug. 19—Hugo Carrizo, Gijon .... W 8
Dec. 16—Dave Needham, Leon .... KO 5
(European Featherweight Title)
1979
Feb. 3—Gerard Jacob, Creil .... KO 7
(European Featherweight Title)
Mar. 10—Danny Lopez, Salt Lake City .... KO by 2
(WBC Featherweight Title)
Apr. 21—Claudio Dos Santos, Valencia .... W 8
June 2—Carlos Foldes, Santander .... W 8
Sept. 29—Cecilio Lastra, Santander .... W 12
(European Featherweight Title)
Oct. 27—Hector Molina, La Coruna .... W 8
Dec. 22—Helenio Ferreira, Leon .... KO 3
1980
Feb. 16—Tek Kalenteke, Leon .... W 8
Mar. 8—Emilio Barcala, Leon .... W 12
(Retained European Featherweight Title)
Apr. 12—Modesto (Torito) Gomez, Santander ..... W 12
(Retained European Featherweight Title)
May 17—Salvatore Meluzzo, Leon .... W disq. 9
(Retained European Featherweight Title)
Aug. 22—Hector Molina, Madrid .... W 8
Oct. 10—Ethen Oezakalin, Barcelona .... KO 8
Nov. 29—Cecilio Lastra, Leon .... KO 4
(Retained European Featherweight Title)

PABLO CASTROVILLI
Italian Flyweight
1978
Apr. 9—Michele De Marco, Torino .... KO 2
May 27—Altero Marini, Fort Village .... W 6
June 9—Antonio Galletta, Fort Village .... KO 4
1979
Feb. 2—Antonio Galletta, Milano .... KO 2
Mar. 4—Salvatore Laconi, San Romeo .... KO 4
Apr. 18—Salvatore Laconi, Torino .... KO 2
Oct. 10—Dominique Piedeleu, Torino .... KO 2
Nov. 16—Mariano Garcia, Milan .... W 8
1980
Feb. 8—Antonio Franca, Milan .... W 6
Apr. 18—Antonio Franca, Torino .... W 6
May 22—Jean Jacques Saris, Bologna .... KO 4
July 6—Emilio Pireddu, Fort Village .... W 12
(Won Italian Flyweight Title)
Sept. 10—Dominique Cesari, San Remo .... W 8
Dec. 20—Giovanni Camputaro, Torino .... KO 5
(Retained Italian Flyweight Title)

RAY CATTOUSE
Balham, England Lightweight
Born: July 24, 1952
1975
Sept. 29—Bartom McAllister, Nottingham........... L 6
Oct. 29—Winston McKensie, Southend .... W disq. 6
Nov. 4—Winston McKenzie, London .... W 6
1976
Jan. 27—Willie Owen, Bethnal .... KO 5
Feb. 23—Paddy Moore, Nottingham .... KO 1
Mar. 2—Keith Bundy, London .... W 6
Mar. 15—Lawrence Devanney, Mayfair .... W 8
Apr. 6—Von Reid, London .... KO 4
May 18—Kevin Evans, Walworth................. W 8
Oct. 25—Godfrey Butler, London .... W 8
1977
Feb. 7—Dill Collins, London .... W 8
Apr. 4—Billy Vivian, Piccadilly .... W 8
June 21—Barry Price, London .... D 8
Aug. 5—Jackie McGill, Glasgow .... KO 3
Nov. 18—Jeff Pritchard, London .... W 8
1978
Jan. 31—Tommy Dunn, Marylebone .... W disq 3
Apr. 24—Cookie Roomes, Walworth .... KO 1
June 20—Sylvester Gordon, Piccadilly .... W 8
Nov. 27—Tommy Davitt, London .... W disq. 7
1979
Feb. 13—Johnny Claydon, Marylebone .... KO 10
Oct. 23—Georges Cotin, London .... KO 1
1980
Mar. 24—Dave McCabe, Glasgow .... KO 8
(Won Vacant British Lightweight Title)

TREVOR CATTOUSE
British Light Heavyweight
1977
Oct. 12—Pat Thompson, Stoke .... L 6
Oct. 19—Alan Tasby, Kipeston .... W 6
Nov. 10—Joey Williams, London .... W 6
1978
Feb. 28—Ken Jones, Heathrow .... L 8

281

Mar. 13—Theo Josephs, Hove .... W 8
Apr. 20—Eddie Vieling, London .... L 8
May 3—Joe Jackson, Solihull .... W 8
Sept. 18—Eddie Vieling, Reading .... KO 4
Oct. 12—Shaun Chalcraft, London .... L 8
Nov. 23—Dave Mullings, London .... KO 4
1979
Jan. 18—Clint Jones, London .... W 8
Mar. 16—Eddie Vieling, Thetford .... KO 5
Apr. 10—Steve Lewin, Kensington .... W 6
Dec. 3—Roy Skeldon, Wolverhampton .... L 8
1980
Jan. 16—Rey Skeldon, Stoke .... W 8
Jan. 21—Ken Jones, Mayfair .... L 8
Feb. 13—Steve Fenton, London .... KO 5
Mar. 24—Danny Lawford, London .... KO by 2
June 11—Rupert Christie, Edgbaston .... W 8

GUY CAUDRON
French Bantamweight
Born: September 30, 1946
1969
Jan. 25—Angelo D'Aleo, Lens.................... KO 2
Apr. 19—Dom Cesari, Avion .... W 6
Dec. 4—Hocine Mahammedi, Paris.............. D 6
Dec. 12—Jean-Louis DeSouza, Toulouse .... L 8
Dec. 26—Ben Salah Abdesselem, Marseilles .... W 8
1970
Apr. 11—Werner Blanquaert, Lens .... W 6
Dec. 5—Hocine Mahammedi, Lens............... W 6
1971
Feb. 7—Gerard Macrez, Dunkirk .... W 10
Feb. 20—Norbert Barriere, Lens................. W 8
May 8—Marc Vandomme, Bethune .... W 10
Aug. 15—Michel Jamet, Berck-sur-Mer .... W 10
Sept. 25—Claude Lapinte, Lens................... W 12
(French Bantamweight Title)
1972
Feb. 2—Augustin Senin, Barcelona .... L 15
(European Bantamweight Title)
Apr. 21—Norbert Barriere, La Rochelle........... W 12
(French Bantamweight Title)
July 19—Paddy Maguire, Dublin................. L 8
Oct. 14—Claude Lapinte, Avignon .... W 12
(French Bantamweight Title)
1973
Jan. 23—Franco Zurlo, Palermo .... L 12
Apr. 13—Antoine Porcel, Villeurbanne........... KO 5
(French Bantamweight Title)
May 26—Paul Ferreri, Papete .... L 10
Aug. 18—Rodolfo Martinez, Inglewood.......... L 10
Oct. 20—Ferdinando Ripamonti, Bethune....... KO 7
1974
Feb. 16—Arnold Taylor, Johannesburg .... L 10
Mar. 18—Heleno Ferreira, Paris .... W 8
Oct. 4—Bob Allottey, Madrid.................. L 15
(EBU Bantamweight Title)
1975
Mar. 8—Jacky Bihin, Vire.................... KO 4
(French Bantamweight Championship)
May 2—Luigi Tessarin, Lens................... KO 4
May 10—Ernesto Miranda, St. Nazaire .... KO 10
1976
Jan. 10—Isidore La Barbera, Douai .... KO 4
Jan. 30—Murphy Ragga, Dunkurke .... W 10
Mar. 19—Antonio Franca, Salaumines........... KO 6
Mar. 27—Jeff Pritchard, Dunkerke .... W 10
Apr. 24—Albert Amatler, Chasse sue Rhone.... KO by 9
(French Featherweight Title)
May 7—Armando Cornellio, Henin-Beaumont .... KO 6
May 29—Cecilio Lastra, Santander................ L 8
Oct. 9—Antonio Franca, Bethune .... KO 4
Dec. 18—Gitano Jiminez, Santander .... D 10
1977
Jan. 22—Adolfo Osses, Lens .... W 10
Apr. —Fernando Bernardez, Amentiers .... KO 3
Apr. 23—Ramon Garcia Marichal, Lille .... W 10
May 19—Heleno Ferreira, Lens .... W 10
Oct. 29—Jacky Bihin, Mericourt .... KO 5
1978
Jan. 28—Christian Martin, St. Ouen .... KO 9
(French Bantamweight Title)
Apr. 29—Melquiades Da Silva, Lievin .... KO 5
June 10—Cecilio Lastra, Santander .... L 8
Sept. 30—Laurent Grimbert, Crepy en Valois .... L 12
(French Bantamweight Title)
Nov. 18—Georges Lietaer, Mericourt .... KO 6
1979
Mar. 24—Mohammed Boundra, Mericourt .... W 8
May 13—Johnny Owen, Pontypool .... L 10
June 15—Jean Jacques Souris, Creil .... KO 9
(French Bantamweight Title)
Nov. 17—Dominique Cesari, Mericourt .... W 12
(French Bantamweight Title)

1980
Jan. 29—Mory Cisse, Abidjan .... L 10
Feb. 23—Laurent Grimbert, Mericourt .... L 12
(For French Bantamweight Title)
May 9—Manuel Masso, Barcelona .... L 8
June 12—Stephen Muchoki, Randers .... L 8
Nov. 8—Francis Bailleul, Calais .... L 8
Nov. 21—Jose Luis Vicho, Palma de Mallorca ..... L 10

CHRISTIANO CAVINA
Italian Light Heavyweight
1974
Sept. 13—Mario Favotto, Faenza................. W 6
Dec. 6—Vincenzo Nardillo, Reggio Emilia .... D 6
Dec. 26—Raffale Cotunga, R. Emilia .... W 4
Dec. 26—Claudio Moretti, R. Emilia .... KO 3
1975
Feb. 15—Gianni Mingardi, Faenza................ D 6
Mar. 1—Gianni Mingardi, Bologna .... L 6
June 6—Raffale Cotunga, Napoli .... D 6
Sept. 14—Giuseppe Panunzio, Faenza .... W 6
Oct. 10—Trento Facchiocchi, Bologna .... KO 3
Oct. 24—Luciano Bomben, Bologna.............. W 8
Nov. 29—Guerrino Cipriani, Trieste .... W 8
Dec. 26—Giovani Bertini, Bologna .... W 8
Dec. 26—Gino Freo, Bologna .... L 4
1976
Feb. 6—Pietropaolo Capezzone, Faenza .... NC 1
Mar. 5—Ezzechielo Fanti, Reggio Emilia .... L 6
Mar. 26—Gino Freo, Bologna .... W 4
July 11—Faustino Quinales, Caracas .... W 10
Sept. 11—Salvatore Russo, Zagreb .... L 8
Nov. 3—Gina Freo, Gardone Val Trompia .... W 8
Dec. 3—Ennio Commetti, Faenza .... L 10
1977
Jan. 28—Bruno Polloni, Faenza .... W 6
Apr. 29—Louis Pergaud, Munich .... L 6
June 11—Aldo Traversaro, Pordenone .... KO by 5
(Italian Light Heavyweight Title)
Dec. 16—Gino Freo, Romano Lombardo .... KO 8
1978
Jan. 7—Freddie De Kerpel, Zele .... KO 8
Jan. 26—Mushapata Kabangu, Faenza .... W 8
Apr. 7—Enio Cometti, Faenza .... KO by 2
(Italian Lightheavyweight Title)
July 21—Gregory Downes, Rosenheim .... L 6
Sept. 3—Harold Skog, Bergen .... KO by 6
1979
Oct. 12—Lino Lemma, Rome .... KO 10
1980
Mar. 26—Bonnie McKenzie, Lugo di Romagna ..... W 8
June 20—Lino Lemma, Cagliari .... KO 9
Sept. 3—Luciano Sordini, Santa Teresa .... W 12
(Won Italian Light Heavyweight Title)

FRANK CEDENO
Filipino Flyweight
1978
Sept. 30—Little Aguilar, Quezon City .... W 10
Nov. 4—Brigildo Canada, Quezon City .... KO 7
Nov. 30—Eric Blancia, Bukidnon .... L 10
1979
Apr. 20—Lino Boy Base, Manila .... W 10
May 26—William Develos, Quezon City .... L 10
June 15—Robinson Abata, Manila .... W 10
Oct. 5—Pablo Pepito, Manila .... W 10
Dec. 23—Flash Jagdon, Cedu City .... KO 5
1980
Mar. 29—Melchor Degsi, Baguio City .... W 10
May 16—Arnel Arrozal, Manila .... W 10
July 16—Siony Carupo, Manila .... W 12
Sept. 17—Monsyram H. Mahachai, Pasay City ... KO 7
Nov. 29—Brigildo Canada, Davao City .... W 10

CHRISTIAN CELE
South African Junior Lightweight
1980
Apr. 28—Joseph Zulu, Durban .... L 4
June 16—Moses Mthiyane, Durban .... W 4
Aug. 4—Elijah Cele, Durban .... L 4
Oct. 6—Themba Ntuli, Pietermaritzburg .... W 4
Dec. 15—Thomas Tsotsetsi, Pietermaritzburg ..... KO 2

ELIJAH CELE
South African Lightweight
1978
Aug. 12—Simon Mauvundla, Durban .... KO 4
1979
Mar. 10—Koos Mifuphi, Newcastle .... KO 3
July 28—Wonga Lawuse, King Williamstown ..... KO 3
Sept. 29—Jerome Gumede, Durban .... L 6
Nov. 3—Phindile Ndilele, Queenstown .... KO 4
1980
May 19—Alex Sibiya, Durban .... W 4

June 16—Jackie Colbeck, Durban .... W 4
Aug. 4—Christian Cele, Durban .... W 4
Oct. 6—Aladin Stevens, Pietermaritzburg .... L 6
Dec. 1—Jerome Gumede, Durban .... L 6

JOSE CENTA
Yugoslav Light Heavyweight
1976
May 28—Darko Barakovic, Postonja .... L 4
Sept. 8—Darko Barakovic, Medvode .... D 4
Oct. 23—Darko Barakovic, Moravce .... D 6
Dec. 18—Gerald Bois, Sedan .... KO by 5
1977
Jan. 22—Darko Barakovic, Jamnik ....L 4
Feb. 27—Darko Barakovic, Kranj .... W 4
Apr. 16—Darko Barakovic, Hrastnik .... D 6
Apr. 30—Martin Koller, Lubiana .... W 4
May 27—Renzo Travisani, Montecchio .... L 4
Oct. 23—Darko Barakovic, Lubiana .... W 10
Nov. 26—Gerald Bois .... KO by 4
Nov. 29—Mladin Ruske, Hrastnik .... W 4
Dec. 28—Andrej Vestan, Lubiana .... D 4
1978
Jan. 27—Andrej Vestan, Lubiana .... D 6
Feb. 25—Drago Umicevic, Lubiana .... D 4
Mar. 18—Salko Brkic, Hrastnik .... L 8
Mar. 31—Mladin Ruske, Lubiana .... D 4
Apr. 25—Mladin Ruske, Domzale .... W 4
June 1—Andrej Vestan, Lubiana .... D 4
July 2—Leopoldo Centorrino, Messina .... L 8
Aug. 2—Germano Apostoli, Toscolano .... KO by 5
Sept. 24—Bojan Zverzina, Dolenjske ....D 4
Nov. 6—Vedat Akova, Berlin .... KO by 5
Dec. 9—Valentino Nardini, Udine .... L 6
1979
Jan. 27—Robert Amory, Compiegne .... KO by 1
Feb. 16—Bojan Zverzina, Menges ....D 4
Mar. 23—Lino Lemma, Rome .... L 4
Apr. 18—Gianni Filippetto, Torino .... KO by 4
Aug. 11—Lino Lemma, Roccapriera .... KO by 1
Sept. 1—Branko Barakovic, Hrastnik .... D 6
Sept. 30—Branko Barakovic, Toplice .... D 6
Oct. 27—Fred Serres, Differdange .... KO by 4
Nov. 25—Mladen Ruske, Trbovlje .... W 4
1980
Mar. 18—Jean Louis Martin, Argenteuil ...... KO by 9
June 6—Richard Caramanolis, Marseile ...... KO by 3
June 27—Gino Freo, Padova .... L 8
Oct. 18—Walter Cevoli, Rimini .... L 8
Nov. 29—Mondini Lutshadi, Padova .... KO by 4

DOMINIQUE CESARI
French Flyweight
Began Professional Career in 1969
1972
Feb. 5—Gerard Macrez, Dunkirk .... L 12
May 19—Fritz Chervet, Neuchatel .... KO by 5
June 30—Gerard Macrez, Marsiglia .... W 12
(Won French Flyweight Title)
Aug. 19—Dionisio Bisbal, Ajaccio .... W 10
Dec. 21—Altero Marini, Ajaccio .... W 8
1973
Mar. 10—Franco Sperti, Como .... L 8
June 28—Fernando Atzorti, Novara .... KO by 12
(European Flyweight Title)
Oct. 19—Franco Udella, Milano .... L 8
1974
Feb. 16—Christian Martin, Troyes .... D 12
Oct. 4—Abu Arrow, Marsiglia .... W 10
Nov. 17—Christian Martin, Bastia .... W 12
Dec. 26—Fritz Chervet, Berne .... L 10
1975
Oct. 25—Daniel Chervet, Voiron .... L 12
(Lost French Flyweight Title)
1976
Apr. 6—Franco Buglione, Capua .... L 8
Oct. 29—Franco Udella, Cagliari .... L 8
1977
Mar. 5—Salvatore Laconi, Aix .... W 8
Apr. 22—Nesim Zebellini, Antibes .... L 10
Oct. 29—Christian Martin, Troyes .... W 12
(Won French Flyweight Title)
1978
Mar. 29—Abu Arrow, Marseille .... W 8
Apr. 4—Charlie Magri, London .... KO by 3
Oct. 14—Patrick Goblet, Troyes .... W 10
Nov. 21—Frank Realinho, Marsiglia .... W 10
1979
Jan. 27—Laurent Grimbert, Compiegne ...... KO by 6
Nov. 17—Guy Caudron, Mericourt .... L 12
(French Bantamweight Title)
1980
Apr. 10—Dominique Pideleu, Caen .... W 10
Sept. 10—Paolo Castrovilli, San Remo .... L 8

WALTER CEVOLI
Italian Light Heavyweight
1980
Mar. 21—Aldo Tramentozzi, Bologna ....KO 6
Apr. 12—Salmin Boutera, Rimini .... KO 4
May 22—Nedjat Mameti, Bologna .... W 6
June 27—Giuseppe Cortesi, St. Arcangelo .... KO 3
Aug. 14—Bonnie McKenzie, Rimini .... L 6
Sept. 6—Antonio Cresenza, Riccione .... KO 4
Oct. 18—Jose Centa, Rimini .... W 8
Nov. 29—Darko Barakovic, Padova ....KO 2
Dec. 26—Gabrielle Lazzari, Bologna .... W 6

SHAUN CHALCRAFT
British Light Heavyweight
1978
Jan. 16—Tony Burnett, Hove .... W 6
Feb. 13—Joey Williams, Walworth .... W 6
Apr. 17—Manny Gabriel, Hove .... W 8
Apr. 24—Joey Williams, Walworth .... D 6
July 17—Ken Jones, London .... L 6
Oct. 12—Trevor Cattouse, Wimbledon .... W 8
Nov. 23—Eddie Vierling, Wimbledon ....KO 7
1979
Jan. 18—Bonny McKenzie, Wimbledon .... L 8
Feb. 6—Johnny Waldron, Wembley .... W 8
Feb. 27—Danny Miller, London .... L 8
Mar. 15—Bob Young, Wimbledon ....KO 3
Apr. 24—Steve Taylor, London ....KO 7
May 29—Alex Thompkins, London .... L 8
Sept. 18—Joey Williams, Lewisham .... W 8
Oct. 29—Lloyd James, Hove ....KO 5
Nov. 19—Alex Thompkins, Lewisham .... W 8
1980
Jan. 28—Robert Amory, Rotterdam .... W 8
Apr. 24—Ken Jones, Queensway .... W 8
Sept. 22—Carlton Benoit, Lewisham .... W 10
(Won Vacant Southern Area Light Heavyweight Title)
Oct. 17—Joh Odihambo, Copenhagen .... L 8

PAUL CHANCE
British Lightweight
1977
July 5—Malcolm McHugh, Wolverhampton ......KO 3
Sept. 20—Don Aagesen, Southend ....KO 2
Oct. 18—Paul Clemit, Wolverhampton .... W 6
Oct. 31—Kenny Matthews, Birmingham .... W 6
Nov. 30—Tony Kerr, London .... W 6
1978
Jan. 23—Gerry O'Neill, London .... W 6
Feb. 13—Kenny Matthews, Birmingham ....KO 4
Mar. 6—Steve Henderson, London ....KO 7
Apr. 4—Gene McGarrigale, London ....KO 1
Apr. 18—Jeff Pritchard, London .... W 8
Sept. 18—Mark Bliss, Wolverhampton .... W 8
Oct. 31—George Sutton, Wolverhampton .... W 8
1979
Jan. 22—Tommy Wright, Wolverhampton .... W 8
Mar. 5—Billy Rabbit, Wolverhampton ....KO 4
Apr. 10—Najib Daho, Wolverhampton .... W 8
May 16—Mohamed Boundtka, Wolverhampton ... W 8
Sept. 8—Bingo Crooks, Wolverhampton .... W 8
Oct. 29—Des Gwilliam, Wolverhampton .... W 10
1980
Jan. 21—Kevin Quinn, Wolverhampton .... W 8
Mar. 10—Willie Booth, Wolverhampton .... W 10
May 29—Bingo Crooks, Wolverhampton .... KO by 9
(Lost Midlands Area Lightweight Title)
Sept. 27—Winston Spencer, Wembley .... KO by 1
Oct. 30—Johnny Burns, Wolverhampton .... W 8

MICHEL CHAPIER
French Middleweight
Born: January 30, 1946
1970
Jan. 26—Georges Danin, Paris ....D 6
Feb. 16—Jean Ramon, Paris ....KO 6
Apr. 4—Lionel Mercier, Chalons ....KO 3
Apr. 25—Victor Caloc, Soissons ....KO 3
May 11—Zenin Nebot, Paris ....KO 3
Sept. 26—Beaute Ouaffouny, Rheims...............KO 3
Dec. 14—Gerard Cola, Paris .... L 6
1971
Mar. 5—Guido Praloran, Ancona .... W 6
Apr. 17—Mohamed Touatti, Epernay ....KO 6
May 15—Pierre Lambert, Rheims .... W 8
Sept. 18—Lionel Mercier, Rheims...............KO 5
Oct. 23—Epifanio Collado, Rheims .... W 8
1972
Feb. 5—Lionel Mercier, Epernay ....KO 5
Feb. 8—Vincent Para, Paris ....L 8
Apr. 15—William Poitrimol, Epernay ....KO 4
Oct. 6—Jose Duran, Madrid .... L 8

Dec. 2—Cerra Cheraka, Epernay .... KO 9
Dec. 18—Jules Bellaiche, Paris .... D 8
1973
Feb. 3—Abdendi Baali, Epernay .... D 10
Mar. 8—Chris Larsen, Copenhagen .... L 8
Apr. 28—Fabio Bettini, Epernay .... D 12
(French Middleweight Title)
June 16—Joel LeGuern, Rouen .... KO by 4
Dec. 1—Eusebio Qnani, Epernay .... W disq. 5
Dec. 28—Jose Duran, Barcelona.................. L 8
1974
Feb. 9—Daniel Cabrera, Paris .... L 6
May 10—Jules Bellaiche, Marseilles............. L 8
June 1—Flash Patterson, St. Nazaire .... KO 2
July 26—Jose Duran, Madrid .... L 8
Dec. 12—Phillipe Jacques, Paris .... KO by 6
1975
Feb. 15—Marcel Giordanella, Epernay .... WF 7
Oct. 30—Jean-Claude, Warusfel.................. D 10
Dec. 6—Jean Grandjean, Reims .... KO 9
1976
Jan. 31—Jurgan Voss, Reims .... W 10
Feb. 23—Claude Martin, Paris.................. L 10
Apr. 24—Gerard Breton, Epernay .... W 10
July 3—Loucif Hamani, Algiers .... KO by 3
Oct. 4—Stan Van den Driessche, Rotterdam .... L 8
1977
Jan. 2—Peter Assandoh, Marseille .... W 10
Jan. 28—Joe Bonnetaz, Perigueux .... L 12
(French Junior Middleweight Title)
Mar. 16—Charlie Cooper, Reims .... W 10
Mar. 31—Gilbert Cohen, Paris .... L 8
Apr. 12—Jimmy Batten, London .... KO by 9
1978
Jan. 27—Yvon Segor, Marsiglia .... KO 8
Feb. 27—Gerard Nosley, Paris .... D 8
May 9—Georg Steinherr, Lubeck .... KO by 3
Sept. 5—Stan Van Der Driesche, Rotterdam .... L 8
Oct. 14—Michel Stini, Pepinster .... L 10
Nov. 18—Joel Bonnetaz, Tarbes .... L 10
1979
Jan. 27—Claude Martin, St. Malo .... L 10
Feb. 10—Luigi Minchillo, Havange .... KO by 5
Apr. 20—Jacques Ghinon, Epernay .... W 8
June 21—Georges Warusfel, Alfrotville .... KO by 11
(French Junior Middleweight Title)
Oct. 19—Michel Pagani, Calais .... L 10
1980
Mar. 29—Celestin Kanynda, Rotterdam .... D 8
May 19—Alex Blanchard, Rotterdam .... KO by 6

DON CHARLES
British Heavyweight
1980
Apr. 29—Steve Gee, London .... KO by 2
June 11—Mike Creasy, Morecambe .... KO by 2
July 14—Andre Olley, London .... KO by 2

CHRISTIAN CHESINI
French Junior Middleweight
1977
Nov. 19—Jean Luc Lami, Vandoeuvre .... W 6
Dec. 24—Jean pierre Fuches, Lupeville .... W 6
1978
(Inactive)
1979
Dec. 9—Maurice Flot, Vitry .... L 6
Dec. 15—Jean Truchelut, Vandoeuvre .... W 6
1980
Jan. 4—Mauricio Da Cruz, Carpi .... D 6
Mar. 8—James Dovin, Nice .... NC 3
Apr. 11—Johnny Cooper, Villeurbanne .... W 6
Apr. 26—Andre Mongalema, Luneville .... KO by 3
May 17—Michel Moinard, Vandeuvre .... W 6
July 2—Mario Morelli, Annecy .... W 6

MOHAMED CHINO
(MOHAMED EL CAUDOUMI)
(MOHAMED EL KADOUMI)
Spanish Lightweight
1979
Mar. 30—Jose Luis Vicho, Mallorca .... L 4
Apr. 21—Carlos Montesinos, Valencia .... L 4
June 2—Pedro Calero, Mataro .... L 4
June 16—Antonio Reinoso, Santander .... L 6
June 29—Julio Garcia, Madrid .... L 4
July 6—Francisco Cabello, Madrid .... W 4
July 13—Rodrigo Garcia, Malaga .... L 4
July 27—Emilio Molero, Madrid................. L 6
Aug. 4—Julio Garcia, Vigo .... W 6
Aug. 10—Manuel Garcia Requena, S. Cruz .... L 6
Aug. 17—Julio Garcia, Madrid .... W 4
Aug. 24—Basilio Roman, Madrid .... D 4

Aug. 30—Manuel Garcia Requena, Puerto Cruz ....L 6
Oct. 13—Jose Luis Vicho, Pravia .... L 6
Nov. 10—Jesus Canut, Salamanca .... L 6
Dec. 1—Pedro Morales, Pamplona .... L 8
Dec. 21—Jose Maria Llorente, Vallidolid .... D 6
1980
Jan. 6—Young Marin, Bilbao .... D 6
Jan. 12—Morales II, Zaragoza .... L 6
Feb. 2—Julio Barcina, Fuengirola .... W 6
Feb. 16—Jesus Canut, Leon .... D 6
Aug. 29—Tanyo II, Palma de Mallorca .... D 8
Oct. 10—Julio Barcina, Madrid .... W 6
Dec. 26—Patrizio Olivia, Bologna .... L 6

JACQUES CHINON
Luxembourg Middleweight
1975
Oct. 6—Fernand Backaert, Esch .... W 6
Nov. 1—Michel Stini, Verviers .... KO by 5
Nov. 17—Maioli, Esch .... KO 5
1976
Jan. 19—Bernard Artone, Luxembourg .... KO 2
Feb. 6—Michel Caron, Bruges .... L 6
Apr. 2—Idrissa Konate, Dakar .... KO by 4
Apr. 19—Mustapha Kabangu, Esch .... L 6
May 15—Eric Kopec, Bethune .... KO by 1
Oct. 16—Marcel Giordanella, Dijon .... L 8
Nov. 6—Alfredo Naveiras, St. Servais .... L 8
Nov. 27—Eric Seys, Gits .... L 6
1977
Jan. 15—Alfredo Naveiras, Izegem .... W 8
Feb. 12—Daniel Martin, Differdange .... W 8
Mar. 15—Mehmet Besli, Berlin .... L 4
Mar. 18—Gerard Nosley, Annecy .... LF 7
May 17—Peter Scheibner, Altona .... L 8
June 10—Eric Seys, Esch sur Alzette .... D 8
1978
Jan. 21—Jean Luis Martin, Argenteuil .... L 6
Mar. 31—Matteo Salvemini, Milano .... KO by 7
May 31—Andoni Amana, Bilbao .... KO by 5
Sept. 23—Charley Schulz, Haiger .... W 6
Dec. 13—Vincenzo Ungaro, Brescia, ... L 8
1979
Jan. 26—Juergen Gries, Dusseldorf .... KO 5
Feb. 23—Jean Marie Amebe, Doula .... L 10
Apr. 6—Frank Wissenbach, Lubeck .... L 10
Apr. 20—Michel Chapier, Epernay .... L 8
Apr. 27—Nicola Cirelli, Rome .... KO by 4
May 18—Idrissa Konate, Perigueux .... KO 8
June 26—Tony Sibson, Leicester .... KO by 8
Oct. 15—Mario Romersi, Rome .... KO 8
Nov. 24—Michel Pagani, Calais .... KO 2
1980
Apr. 5—Michel Pagani, Calais .... KO 11
(Won French Middleweight Title)
June 12—Jose Hernandez, Paris .... D 8
Nov. 7—Gerard Nosley, Nice .... KO 5
(Retained French Middleweight Title)
Nov. 29—Manuel Lira, Cayenne .... W 10

GIOVANNI CHIRRA
Italian Welterweight
1979
Nov. 10—Francesco Morrone, Alghero .... W 6
Dec. 28—Roy Kaba, Sassari .... D 6
1980
Apr. 11—Guiseppe Agate, Sassari .... W 6
Oct. 26—Michel Moinard, Mulhouse .... D 6

BOBBY CHISALE
South African Middleweight
1980
June 7—Issac Mabuza, Johannesburg .... W 4
July 2—Issac Enslin, Welkom .... L 4
Dec. 15—Johannes Mthembu, Pietermaritzburg ....L 6

CHARM CHITEULE
Zambian Featherweight
(Living in England)
1978
Nov. 4—Lee Graham, Lusaka .... W 5
1979
Feb. 26—Terry McKeown, London .... KO 5
Dec. 29—Titus Sangwape, Lusaka .... W 15
(Won Zambian Featherweight Title)
1980
Mar. 14—Najib Daho, Glasgow .... L 6
May 4—Dave Needham, Lusaka .... KO 5
(Elimination Bout for Commonwealth Featherweight Title)
Sept. 26—Dieter Schantz, Cologne .... KO 4
Dec. 5—Gary O'Neill, Cologne .... KO 6

MICK CHMILOWSKYZ
British Heavyweight
1979
Dec.   3—Harry Pompey Allen, Marylebone .... KO 2
1980
Feb.   4—Kenny March, Hammersmith .... KO 2
Mar. 17—Colin Flute, London .... KO 2
Apr.   1—David Fry, London .... KO by 6

PRINCE CHOKO
South African Welterweight
1979
July 31—Alexandre Montshusi, Bloemfontein ..... KO 2
1980
Apr. 14—Petrus Mtonxa, Kimberley .... W 4
Sept. 6—Johannes Motsumi, Welkom .... L 4
Dec. 19—Deon Labuschagne, Welkom .... L 4

MICHAEL CHOPHISO
South African Lightweight
1980
July   5—Goodman Njova, East London .... W 4
Aug. 23—Mzwandile Mbaliso, East London .... W 4

CHRIS CHRISTIAN
British Middleweight
1979
Sept. 24—Paul Jones, Mayfair .... KO by 1
Oct. 29—Dave Douglas, Birmingham .... D 6
Nov. 12—Tony Baldwin, Mayfair .... KO 5
Nov. 28—Richard Avery, Solihull .... L 6
1980
Jan. 16—Mike Clemow, Solihull .... D 6
Jan. 21—Dave Douglas, Birmingham .... W 6
Feb. 19—Colin Derrick, Albert Hall .... W 6
Mar. 10—Frank McCord, Liverpool .... W 8
Apr. 14—Richard Avery, Liverpool .... W 8
Sept. 24—Johnny Francis, Solihull .... L 8
Nov.   4—Mick Mills, Southend .... W 8

RUPERT CHRISTIE
British Light Heavyweight
1980
Apr. 21—Gary Jones, Edgbaston .... KO 2
June 11—Trevor Cattouse, Edgbaston .... L 8
Sept. 24—Liam Coleman, Burslem .... W 8
Oct. 20—Chris Lawson, Birmingham .... L 8

JOE CHRISTLE
Dublin, Ireland Heavyweight
1980
Nov.   1—John Rafferty, Glasgow .... W 6

TERRY CHRISTLE
Dublin, Ireland Middleweight
1980
Nov.   1—Jerry Golden, Glasgow .... KO 2

SOON HYUNG CHUNG
Korean Junior Featherweight
Born: September 30, 1954
1975
July   8—Sung-Do Park, Seoul .... W 4
Nov. 23—Chang-Ok Choi, Pusan .... W 8
Dec.   7—Yong-Shul Choi, Chungjoo .... L 10
1976
Mar. 28—Il-Sung Choi, Inchon .... W 8
June 16—Chong-Tae Yuh, Pusan .... W 10
Oct.   8—Didik Morzadi, Seoul .... W 10
Nov.   6—Ik-Jae Yuh, Seoul .... W 10
1977
Apr. 15—Ric Quijano, Manila .... L 12
(For OPBF Junior Featherweight Title)
July 23—Duck-Hoon Ko, Chungjoo .... KO 9
Sept. 17—Eduardo Batista, Seoul .... KO 2
Dec. 11—Futaro Tanaka, Seoul .... KO 2
1978
Jan. 22—Bok-Soo Hwang, Seoul .... W 10
Apr.   2—Ric Quijano, Seoul .... W 12
(Won OPBF Junior Featherweight Title)
May   13—Hideo Kobayashi, Seoul .... KO 3
(Retained OPBF Junior Featherweight Title)
July 22—Yu Kasahara, Pusan .... KO 5
(Retained OPBF Junior Featherweight Title)
Nov. 12—Ricardo Cardona, Seoul .... L 15
(For WBA Junior Featherweight Title)
1979
Mar. 23—Satoru Hirata, Taegu .... KO 4
Apr.   1—Ric Quijano, Seoul ..... W 12
May   11—Thanomjit Sukhothai, Pusan .... W 12
(Retained OPBF Junior Featherweight Title)

June 23—Ricardo Cardona, Seoul .... L 15
(For WBA Junior Featherweight Title)
Sept. 23—Kanekatsu Daito, Seoul .... KO 5
Nov. 27—Sandy Torres, Teku City .... KO 2
1980
Feb.   1—Kanekatsu Daito, Osaka .... KO 4
(Retained OPBF Junior Featherweight Title)
July   5—Ric Diamale, Pusan .... KO 1
(Retained OPBF Junior Featherweight Title)
Oct.   4—Chong-Woo Baek, Pusan .... KO 4
(Retained OPBF Junior Featherweight Title)
Nov. 21—Willie Lucas, Seoul .... L 12
(Lost OPBF Junior Featherweight Title)

GREGORIO CIANCAGLIONE
Italian Lightweight
1976
Jan.   9—Fulvio Giacomini, Como .... LF 2
Oct. 10—Sabato Coppola, Pollenam .... D 6
Nov. 13—Angelo Capitani, Guidonia .... W 6
Dec. 10—Fulvio Giancomini, Falconara .... W 8
1977
Jan.   9—Fulvio Giancomini, Como .... LF 2
Feb. 19—Annunziato Sanna, Milano .... W 6
Mar. 11—Abass Macauley, Milano .... KO 3
Apr.   7—Pellegrino Ventrone, Forli .... L 8
May   6—Aristide Pizzo, Milano .... LF 5
May   20—Aristide Pizzo, Milano .... LF 5
Dec.   7—Annunziato Sanna, Caloziorcorte .... L 6
Dec. 26—Giovanni Vitillo, Pisa .... L 8
1978
Feb. 24—Domenico Train, Modena .... L 6
Mar. 31—Pellegrino Ventrone, Rome .... L 8
May   26—Luigi Dal Santo, Rome .... D 8
Aug.   5—Josia Malquides Da Sylva, Pogio Mirteto . D 8
Nov.   3—Marino Angeli, Forli .... L disq. 5
Dec. 23—Bruno Demontis, Sassari .... KO by 5
1979
May   4—Michele D'Amato, Rome .... D 6
May   19—Boro Jovic, Rome .... D 6
Dec. 14—Patrizio Burini, Florence .... D 8
1980
Mar. 28—Giovanni Vitillo, Pisa .... KO by 2
Nov.   7—Franco Siddu, Firenze .... KO by 5
Nov. 29—Guiseppe Tidu, Cagliari .... KO by 5
Dec. 26—Franco Canini, Bologna .... KO by 4

VINCENT CIPOLLA
Italian Junior Lightweight
1979
Feb.   2—Angelo Licata, La Louviere .... L 6
Mar.   2—Angelo Licata, Liegi .... L 6
Apr.   7—Alain Marchand, Vilvorde .... D 6
Apr. 27—Jean Pierre Meganck, Anversa .... W 6
Oct.   5—Haidar Mouredine, Binche .... W 6
1980
Feb.   9—Jamel Benmeziane, Uigneux .... L 6
Mar.   8—Claude Kessaci, Conde Sur Escant ... KO by 4

NICOLA CIRELLI
Italian Middleweight
1978
Jan. 27—Luciano Spina, Rome .... KO 6
Feb. 17—Mariano Solomone, Rome .... KO 2
Oct. 27—Mario Favotto, Rome .... KO 2
Dec.   1—Andre Genasi, Rome .... KO 3
Dec. 26—Ray Opoku, Rome .... KO 3
1979
Mar.   9—Hendryk Seys, Rome .... KO 3
Mar. 23—Marino Pagani, Rome .... KO 5
Apr. 27—Jacques Chinon, Rome .... KO 5
May   18—Sonny Kamunga, Rieti .... W 8
July 14—Gabriele Lazzari, Cerveteri .... KO 5
Aug. 12—Branko Barakovic, Morcone .... KO 5
Oct. 12—Matteo Salvemini, Rome .... KO by 11
(Italian Middleweight Title)
1980
Jan. 30—Mauricio Da Cruz, Viterbo .... W 8
Feb. 29—Manuel Lira, Rome .... W 8
Mar. 28—Idrissa Konate, Rome .... KO 7
May   2—Cliff Willis, Rome .... W 8
May   30—Lancelot Innes, Rome .... W 8
July 16—Joel Bonnetaz, Lignano .... KO 5
Sept. 5—Roberto Manoni, Vieste .... KO 2
(Won Italian Middleweight Title)
Oct. 31—Johnny Heard, Rome .... KO 2
Dec.   4—Fred Reed, Rome .... W 8

SIDNEY CLAASEN
South African Junior Middleweight
1979
Nov.   9—Zezile Makanda, Bloemfontein .... L 4

1980
Apr. 14—Jankie Thlapane, Kimberley .... W 4
May 5—G. Engelbrecht, Welkom .... KO 3

ADRIAN CLAMP
British Welterweight
1980
Mar. 24—Dave Aspill, London .... KO 2
Apr. 8—Sean Jones, Norwich .... KO 5
Apr. 28—Gerry McGrath, Windsor .... KO by 3
May 20—Steve Henty, Southend .... W disq. 6
Sept. 11—Neil Fannon, Hartlepool .... KO by 3

BUDDY CLARE
Australian Lightweight
1978
Oct. 4—Bimbo Morris, Cammeray .... KO 3
Oct. 25—Steve Pike, Cammeray .... L 8
Nov. 14—Paul Baker, Kingsford .... L 6
1979
June 1—Shane Rank, Epping .... L 8
June 6—Paul Baker, Brookvale .... KO by 2
July 17—Gary Rosen, Kingsford .... L 6
Sept. 1—Steve Assang, Berkeley .... L 6
Sept. 5—Steve Assang, Brookvale .... L 6
Sept. 7—Greg Grogan, Epping .... KO by 4
Sept. 25—Andy Roberts, Kingsford .... L 6
Oct. 14—Buddy Nixon, Revesby .... KO by 5
1980
Feb. 16—Arthur Bradley, Murgon .... KO by 4
Mar. 26—Calby Markell, Kingsford .... L 6
Mar. 30—Pablo Caan, Ingleburn .... L 4
Apr. 2—Calby Markell, Brookvale .... L 5
May 16—Wayne Mulholland, Wollongong ...... L 8
May 20—Calby Markell, Kingsford .... L 6

GREGORY CLARK
South African Welterweight
1979
Sept. 29—Alpheus Dlangisa, Durban .... KO 1
1980
Feb. 4—Ness Roux, Durban .... KO 2
Mar. 1—Nicholas Gumede, Durban .... KO 2
Apr. 14—Abel Brown, Durban .... W 4
Apr. 29—John da Paiva, Durban .... KO 2
May 19—Hardy Mileham, Durban .... W 4
July 2—Neil Walker, Durban .... W 6
Sept. 15—Neil Walker, Durban .... W 4
Oct. 6—Joseph Zikwali, Pietermaritzburg ..... W 6
Nov. 10—Fanie van Staden, Durban .... W 6
Dec. 1—Abel Brown, Durban .... W 10
(Won Natal Welterweight Title)

WALTER CLAYTON
British Lightweight
1979
Oct. 22—Wally Stocks, Nottingham .... KO 4
Oct. 27—Duncan Hamilton, Barnsley .... W 6
Dec. 10—Julian Boutead, Torquay .... L 4
1980
Jan. 9—Tyrrel Wilson, Burslem .... KO 1
Jan. 22—Wally Stocking, Piccadilly .... KO 5
Feb. 12—Norman Morton, Sheffield .... W 8
Mar. 13—Von Reid, Birkenhead .... KO 6
Apr. 9—Vernon Vanreil, Burslem .... W 8
Apr. 22—Mike Clemow, Sheffield .... KO 8
May 20—George Sutton, Southend .... KO 5
Sept. 29—Dave Taylor, Chesterfield .... W 8

STEVE CLEAK
British Featherweight
1978
Sept. 4—Pip Coleman, Barry .... L 6
Sept. 21—Ian Murray, Caerphilly .... W 6
Sept. 27—Alec Irvine, Evesam .... W 6
Nov. 15—Pip Coleman, Merthyr .... KO by 2
Dec. 11—Mick Whelan, London .... W 6
1979
Jan. 18—John Cooper, London .... D 6
Mar. 27—John Cooper, London .... L 8
May 13—Terry McKeown, Glasgow .... L 8
May 29—Gary Lucas, London .... L 8
June 4—John Cooper, London .... L 8
June 18—Gerry O'Neil, London .... L 8
Sept. 24—Gary Luas, London .... L 8
Oct. 15—Selvin Bell, London .... L 6
Nov. 5—Harry Henderson, London .... W 8
Nov. 29—Mike Pickett, Ebbw Vale .... W 6
Dec. 13—John Cooper, London .... W 8
1980
Feb. 28—Glyn Davies, Ebbw Vale .... W 8
Mar. 19—Alec Irvine, Solihull .... L 8
Apr. 17—Leo Graham, London .... W

June 16—Steve Henderson, London .... W 8
July 1—Glyn Davies, Swindon .... KO 5
Sept. 11—Paul Keers, Hartlepool .... KO by 4

CARL CLEASBY
British Bantamweight
1980
Sept. 4—George Bailey, Morecambe .... W 4
Oct. 20—Mark West, Hove .... L 6

MIKE CLEMOW
British Welterweight
1979
Oct. 8—Tim Maloney, London .... L 6
Oct. 29—Dave Campbell, Camborne .... L 6
Nov. 28—Steve Ward, Solihull .... L 6
Dec. 10—Glen Rhodes, Torquay .... W 6
1980
Jan. 16—Chris Christian, Solihull .... D 6
Jan. 22—Collin Derrick, Albert Hall .... KO by 4
Feb. 20—Jimmy Smith, Evesham .... W 6
Mar. 26—Paul Wetter, Evesham .... D 6
Apr. 22—Walter Clayton, Sheffield .... KO by 8
June 2—Julian Boustead, Plymouth .... L 6
July 1—Philip Morris, Swindon .... L 6

GERRIE COETZEE
(GERHARDUS CHRISTIAN GOETZEE)
South African Heavyweight
Born: April 8, 1955
1974
Sept. 14—Chris Roos, Johannesburg .... W 4
Oct. 26—Bert Nikkelen-Kuyper, Johannesburg ... KO 1
Nov. 2—Kosie Oosthuizen, Pretoria .... KO 1
1975
Feb. 22—Steve Foley, Johannesburg.............. KO 3
May 5—Hennie Thoonen, Johannesburg .... W 6
June 7—Amedio Lauret, Johannesburg.......... W 6
June 27—Hennie Thoonen, Johannesburg .... KO 3
Oct. 27—Chris Roos, Johannesburg .... KO 3
1976
Feb. 26—Jimmy Richards, Johannesburg.......... W 6
Mar. 22—Hartmut Sasse, Johannesburg........... W 8
Apr. 10—Jimmie Richards, Johannesburg......... KO 9
(Transvaal Heavyweight Title)
July 17—Ron Stander, Johannesburg .... KO 8
Aug. 16—Mike Schutte, Durban................... WF 6
(South African Heavyweight Title)
Oct. 30—Kallie Knoetze, Johannesburg........... W 10
Nov. 27—James Mathatho, Johannesburg......... KO 7
(South African Heavyweight Title)
1977
Mar. 19—Pierre Fourie, Johannesburg .... KO 3
(South African Heavyweight Title)
Apr. 16—Mike Schutte, Johannesburg........... W 12
(South African Heavywight Title)
Oct. 29—Tom Prater, Johannesburg .... KO 4
Dec. 3—Johnny Boudreaux, Johannesburg ...... KO 6
1978
May 26—Randy Stephens, Johannesburg .... W 10
Dec. 15—Ibar Arrington, Durban,................. W 10
1979
June 24—Leon Spinks, Monte Carlo .... KO 1
Oct. 20—John Tate, Pretoria .... L 15
(WBA Heavyweight Title)
1980
Apr. 19—Mike Koranicki, Johannesburg .... KO 1
Oct. 25—Mike Weaver .... KO by 13
(For WBA Heavyweight Title)

JACKIE COLBECK
South African Junior Lightweight
1972
Aug. 5—German Sicwa, Durban .... W 4
1973
Mar. 10—Absolom Mdlalose, Durban .... D 4
Apr. 14—Joseph Xulu, Durban .... L 4
July 28—Themba Hlabisa, Durban .... L 4
Nov. 3—William Radebe, Durban .... L 6
1974
Apr. 6—Bernard Zungu, Durban .... L 6
Sept. 7—Selby Shange, P.M. Burg .... W 6
1975
(Inactive)
1976
Nov. 10—Rocky Mabaso, Durban .... W 6
May 1—Stezy Buthelezi, Durban .... W 6
Dec. 18—Anthony Morodi, Durban .... L 8
1977
Nov. 12—Bernard Zungu, Durban .... L 10
1978
Mar. 18—Essau Dlamini, Durban .... L 6

1979)
(Inactive)
1980

June	16—Elijan Cele, Durban	L	4
Nov.	10—Thomas Msini, Durban	W	4

LIAM COLEMAN
British Light Heavyweight
1979

Feb.	28—Mick Fellingham, Harrogate	W	6
Apr.	23—Mick Fellingham, Glasgow	W	6
June	6—Joe Jackson, Bedweorth	W	4
June	18—Steve Babbs, London	W	6
Oct.	24—George Lewis, Norwich	W	8

1980

May	19—Roy Skeldon, Bradford	D	6
Sept.	24—Rupert Christie, Burslem	L	8
Oct.	16—Alec Penarski, Bolton	L	8

PIP COLEMAN
Welsh Bantamweight
1978

Sept.	4—Steve Cleak, Barry	W	6
Sept.	11—Bobby Breen, Birmingham	L	6
Oct.	9—Terry McKeown, London	L	6
Nov.	15—Steve Cleak, Merthyr	KO	2
Nov.	29—Mick Whelan, Swansea	W	6
Dec.	5—Gary Nickels, Kensington	L	6

1979

Jan.	18—Ian Murray, Liverpool	KO	8
Feb.	21—Jimmy Bott, Evesham	W	6
Feb.	26—Alan Storey, Middlesborough	L	4
Apr.	5—Neil McLaughlin, Belfast	KO by	6
May	14—Gary Davidson, London	L	8
June	18—Ian Murray, London	W	8
Oct.	8—Glyn Davies, Windsor	KO by	7

1980

Oct.	1—Glyn Davies, Swansea	W	10

ROBERT COLLEY
New Zealand Welterweight
1977

July	15—Dave Agnew, Prerirua	W	10
Sept.	8—Phil Khan, Wellington	W	8

1978

May	26—Buddy Nixon, Brisbane	W	8
June	30—Kevin Gibb, Brisbane	W	10
July	14—Gus Spina, Kingsford	W	10
July	26—Speedy Duke, Kingsford	W	8
Oct.	6—Gus Spina, Brisbane	W	8
Nov.	10—Terry Miller, Brisbane	KO	3
Nov.	24—Robert Hinkling, Brisbane	KO	7

1979

Feb.	9—Steve Dennis, Brisbane	L	10
Feb.	17—Eddie Tauvi, Lower Hutt	W	10
May	18—Andy Palermo, Brisbane	KO	4
June	1—Speedy Duke, Brisbane	W	10
July	27—Robert Hickling, Beaudeset	KO	8
Sept.	28—Graham Dicker, Brisbane	KO	8

1980

Feb.	28—Dennis Smith, Wellington	W	10
July	7—Kerry Bell, Brisbane	L	10

DILL COLLINS
Llantwit Major, Wales Welterweight
Born: May 24, 1955
1975

June	2—Steve Gaze, London	W	6
June	24—Pat Singer, London	W	6
Sept.	9—Keith Bundy, Taunton	W	6
Sept.	29—Joey Gilbert, Caerphilly	W	6
Nov.	10—Joey Gilbert, London	W	6
Nov.	26—Von Reid, Birmingham	L	6

1976

Feb.	2—Von Reid, Piccadilly	L	8
Feb.	9—Tony Mattia, Bedford	KO	4
Mar.	8—Ian Pickersgill, Birmingham	W	6
Apr.	5—Ian Pickergill, Piccadilly	D	8
May	10—Noel McIvor, Bedford	W	8
May	26—Kevin Evans, Wolverhampton	W	8
June	7—Ian Pickersgill, Piccadilly	L	8
June	24—Willie Booth, Piccadilly	L	8
Nov.	22—Godfrey Butler, Birmingham	KO	2
Dec.	13—Martin Galleozzie, London	L	10

(Vacant Welsh Lightweight Title)
1977

Jan.	17—Ian Pickersgill, Birmingham	L	8
Feb.	1—Ray Cattouse, London	L	8
Feb.	21—Gary Dunks, Piccadilly	W	8
May	16—Barry Price, Nottingham	W	8
June	10 Barry Price, London	KO by	6
July	18—Tommy Dunn, Mayfair	L	8
Oct.	3—Frank McCord, Aberavon	KO	6

Nov.	21—Johnny Wall, London	L	10

(Welsh Lightweight Title)

Dec.	6—Cornelius Boza-Edwards, London	KO by	5

1978

Mar.	6—Granville Allen, London	L	8
July	10—Billy Vivian, Aberavon	L	10

(Welsh Junior Welterweight Title)

Sept.	18—Tommy Dunn, Reading	L	8
Nov.	21—Chris Sanigar, Wolverhampton	KO by	7

1979

Apr.	4—Des Gwilliam, Birmingham	L	8
June	4—Jess Harper, Liverpool	W	6
July	2—Roy Varden, London	L	8
Sept.	24—Winston Spencer, Mayfair	KO by	3
Nov.	29—Gary Pearce, Ebbw Vale	L	8

1980

Feb.	28—Nigel Thomas, Ebbw Vale	L	8
Mar.	26—Des Gwilliam, Evesham	KO by	4
Oct.	23—Dave Douglas, Liverpool	L	8

KERRY COLLINS
British Lightweight
1977

Feb.	15—Alan Jones, Merthyr	W	6
Feb.	25—Wayne Floyd, Digbeth	KO by	5
June	16—Phillip Morris, Ebbw Vale	W	4
Oct.	11—Gerry Burns, Marylebone	KO	1
Nov.	21—Johnny Gwilliam, Birmingham	KO	3

1978

Jan.	9—Eric Wood, London	D	8
Feb.	13—Eric Wood, Birmingham	L	6
Apr.	3—Kevin Doherty, London	W	8
Apr.	10—Albert Coley, Birmingham	L	8
Apr.	20—Barry Price, Bradford	L	8
May	15—Dai Davies, London	W	6
Sept.	21—Dai Davies, Caerphilly	L	8
Nov.	6—Ian Pickersgill, London	W	8
Nov.	15—Brian Schofield, Merthyr	W	8

1979

Jan.	23—Toni Zeni, London	D	8
Feb.	28—George Metcalf, Harrogate	W	8
Apr.	2—George Metcalf, London	KO by	5
Sept.	10—James Cooke, Birmingham	KO by	8
Nov.	19—Norman Morton, Piccadilly	D	8

1980

Feb.	18—Lance Williams, Stockport	W	8
Mar.	3—Barry Price, Hove	D	8
June	11—Alan Lamb, Morecambe	L	6
Sept.	7—Glyn Rhodes, Liverpool	L	8

TOM COLLINS
British Light Heavyweight
1977

Jan.	17—Ginger McIntyre, Birmingham	W	6
May	16—Mick Dolan, Manchester	W	8
June	1—Johnny Cox, Dudley	KO	3
Nov.	23—George Gray, Stoke	KO	3

1978

Jan.	19—Clint Jones, Wimbledon	KO	3
Mar.	20—Joe Jackson, Luton	W	8
May	9—Harold Sog, Oslo	L	8
July	17—Carl Canwill, London	KO by	6
Nov.	28—Carlson Benoit, Sheffield	KO	1
Dec.	4—Dennis Andrews, Southern	L	8

1979

Jan.	30—Dennis Andries, London	KO by	6
Oct.	22—Danny Miller, Nottingham	KO	7
Nov.	28—Eddie Smith, Solihull	W	8

1980

Feb.	25—Greg Evans, Bradford	KO	1

(Won Vacant Central Area Light Heavyweight Title)

Apr.	15—Chris Lawson, Blackpool	KO	4
Dec.	4—Mustapha Wasajja, Randers	L	8

ENIO COMETTI
Italian Light Heavyweight
Born: January 29, 1951
1972

Nov.	25—Anglo Visini, Canegrate	KO	1
Dec.	7—Frajio Kovac, Milan	KO	1
Dec.	26—Salko Brkic, Milan	KO	3

1973

Jan.	25—Bruno Osca, Milan	KO	3
Feb.	8—Alejandro Cardoso, Milan	KO	2
Mar.	15—Miguel Cequer, Milan	KO	6
May	29—Gilert Montayne, Bergamo	KO	3
July	25—Dino Tarocco, Monza	W	5
Sept.	14—Luis Augusto, Milan	KO	3
Oct.	10—Vlado Blasetic, Rimini	KO	3

1974

Jan.	4—Paul Poirier, Milano	KO	3
Jan.	25—Kevin Isaac, Milano	D	8
Mar.	1—Jean Tshikuna, Milano	W	8

Apr.   5—Mario Almanzo, Milano .... W 8
May   10—Jose Antonio Glavez, Milan .... L 8
July   26—Aldo Traversaro, Sestri Levante ..... KO by 8
            (Italian Championship)
Dec.   12—Raffaele Maio, Milano .... KO 6
1975
Apr.   11—Lazari, Milan .... KO 6
May   26—Peter Asandoh, Milan.................... W 8
July   26—Jose Gomez, Pedrengo .... W 8
Oct.   8—Aldo Traversaro, Arma di Taggio..... KO by 11
Dec.   18—Jose Gomez, Milan .... W 8
1976
Feb.   27—Victor Varon, Milano .... KO 3
Apr.   30—Sergio Jannilli, Milano .... KO 5
July   10—Jose Gomez, Belgrade................... W 8
Oct.   15—Jose Gomez, Milan .... W 8
Oct.   30—Leo Kakolewicz, Frankfurt............. KO 6
Dec.   3—Cristiano Cavina, Faienza .... W 10
1977
Apr.   29—Avenemar Peralta, Munich .... D 10
Aug.   6—Kassongo Mukandjo, Romano L. .... KO 6
Dec.   16—Onelio Grando, Romano Lombardo ...... KO 11
            (Italian Light Heavyweight Title)
1978
Jan.   7—Phil Martin, Milan .... KO 7
Mar.   3—Eddie Fenton, Milan .... KO 8
Apr.   7—Cristiano Cavina, Faenza .... KO 2
            (Italian Light Heavyweight Title)
June   17—Francisco Fiol, Beograd .... W 8
Nov   4—Lottie Lusaka .... KO by 5
Dec.   26—Gino Free, Piove De Sacco .... KO 10
            (Italian Light Heavyweight Title)
1979
Aug.   26—James Scott, Rahway .... KO by 6
Nov.   30—Tony Mundine, Trieste .... KO by 9
1980
Jan.   28—Rudi Koopmans, Rotterdam .... L 12

GIANCARLO COMPIANI
Italian Junior Lightweight
1979
Dec.   26—Ignazio Fara, Cremona .... W 6
1980
Feb.   29—Antonio Pocai, Cremona .... W 6
Mar.   14—Antonio Franca, Milan .... D 6
Apr.   4—Francisco Dionisio (Leo) Gomez, Milan ....L 6
Oct.   11—Antonio Franca, Cremona .... W 6

DANNY CONNOLLY
British Lightweight
1976
Mar.   30—Don Aagesen, Hammersmith .... W 6
May   3—Roger Doyle, Walworth .... W 6
May   24—Steve Butler, Mayfair .... W 6
Sept. 20—Don Aagesen, Walworth .... W 6
Oct.   25—Dave Connell, Hammersmith .... D 6
Nov.   22—Andy Dane, Walworth .... KO 6
1977
Jan.   10—Barry Price, Walworth .... L 6
Feb.   1—Cornelius Boza-Edwards, Kensington KO by 2
1978-1979
(Inactive)
1980
Feb.   18—Tyrrel Wilson, London .... W 6
Mar.   24—Tyrrel Wilson, Liverpool .... W 6
Apr.   23—Tim Maloney, Hove .... L 8
June   12—Dave Laxen, Cambridge .... KO 7

DEL CONTADO
Filipino Junior Lightweight
1979
Sept. 15—Salvador Darlo, Rizal .... KO 6
Nov.   17—Henry Barcellano, Manila .... W 10
1980
Jan.   18—Willie Espinosa, Manila .... NC 4
May   9—Max Boy Toyogon, Manila .... KO 2
July   11—Nene Jun, Manila .... L 10
            (For Philippine Junior Lightweight Title)
Nov.   19—Francis Camatagan, Quezon City .... KO by 5

VITTORIO CONTE
Italian Welterweight
Born: Aug. 18, 1948
1972
Dec.   7—Vincenzo Petrillo, Pescia .... W 6
1973
Jan.   12—Celestino Uteh, Pescia .... W 6
June   28—Achille Fortuna, Pistoia .... W 6
Nov.   30—Emilio Zanotti, Buggiano .... W 6
Dec.   26—Armand Rindlisbacher, Zurigo .... W 6
1974
Mar.   22—Luciano Borracia, Milano .... KO by 2

1975
July   15—Libero Panella, Pistoria .... W 6
Aug.   22—Marcello D'Isidoro, Milan .... W 6
Sept. 26—Mario Calzone, Milan .... W 6
Oct.   10—Paolo Zanusso, Bologna .... W 6
Oct.   31—Giuseppe Martinese, Reggio Emilia ..... KO 3
Dec.   5—Jean Simos, Liege .... KO 4
1976
Jan.   16—Luigi Martello Empoli .... W 8
Feb.   20—Angelo Tomasini, Pistoia .... W 8
Mar.   19—Fredo Roelands, Gand .... D 8
Apr.   9—Tomaso Marocco, Empoli .... KO 4
June   11—Adriano Rodriguez, Pistoia .... KO 7
July   7—Nicola D'orazio, Pistoia .... W 8
Aug.   13—Italo Venturi, Rimini .... W 12
Oct.   22—Paolo Zanusso, Montecatini............. D 12
Dec.   3—Horacio Ruiz, Madrid .... KO by 6
1977
Feb.   2—Tommaso Morocco, Latina .... LF 2
May   7—Tommaso Marocco, Priverno .... KO by 6
Aug.   13—Joseph Pachler, Zeltweg .... L 10
1978
Feb.   11—Luciano Laffranci, Pescia .... W 8
Apr.   8—Antonio Torsello, Pistoia .... KO 10
July   12—Gianni Molesini, Pistoia .... D 12
            (Italian Welterweight Title)
Dec.   7—Jorgen Hansen, Copenhagen .... KO by 4
1979
Feb.   10—Alois Carmeliet, Zele .... D 10
Dec.   21—Omar Olivo, Lucca .... KO 6
1980
Jan.   16—Amar Olivio, Ancona .... KO 6
Sept. 26—Mauricio Da Cruz, Lucca .... W 8
Dec.   5—Claudio Pereyra, Massa .... L 8

ALAN COOPER
British Junior Welterweight
1980
Sept.   9—Steve McLeod, Sheffield .... W 6
Sept. 22—Tony Davis, Lewisham .... KO 1
Oct.   20—Wally Stockings, Hove .... W 6
Oct.   29—Dave Taylor, Burslem .... W 6

GARY COOPER
British Welterweight
1978
Nov.   21—Dennis Price, Wolverhampton .... D 6
1979
Jan.   22—Gary Newell, Wolverhampton .... KO 5
Feb.   12—Alan Hardiman, Reading .... D 6
Mar.   7—Kendrick Edwards, Solihull .... W 6
Mar.   15—Alan Cable, London .... KO 5
Apr.   2—Ian Cole, London .... KO 5
Apr.   23—Jess Harper, Reading .... W 6
Oct.   17—Lloyd Hibbert, Evesham .... KO 6
Dec.   17—Al Stewert, Wolverhampton .... W 8
1980
Jan.   16—Dennis Sullivan, Solihull .... W 6
Apr.   30—Cliff Gilpin, Wolverhampton .... L 8

HENRY COOPER
British Middleweight
1973
June   11—Dave Nelson, Glasgow .... W 6
July   18—Dave Nelson, Birmingham .... W 6
Sept. 17—Dave Nelson, Bedford .... W 6
Oct.   24—Oscar Angus, Stoke .... L 6
Nov.   14—Batman Austin, Solihull .... W 8
Dec.   5—Dave Nelson, Stoke .... KO 4
1974
Jan.   16—Mike Manley, Solihull .... W 8
Jan.   30—Peter Mullens, Stoke .... W 8
Feb.   11—Dave Mullings, Bedford .... W 8
May   6—Pat Brogan, Bradford .... W 8
Oct.   23—Joey Yekinn, Stoke .... KO by 1
Nov.   18—Peter Cain, Mayfair .... KO 2
1975
Jan.   20—Alan Minter, Mayfair .... KO by 1
1976
(Inactive)
1977
Feb.   14—Johnny Waldron, Mayfair .... KO by 5
Mar.   16—Johnny Breen, Solihull .... W 8
May   4—Steve Fenton, Solihull .... W 8
1978-1979
(Inactive)
1980
Jan.   21—Winston Davis, Birmingham .... W 6
Mar.   5—Petter Bassey, Liverpool .... W 8
Mar.   10—Winston Davis, Liverpool .... W 8
Mar.   17—Earl Edwards, Birmingham .... KO by 2
Apr.   14—Billy Lauder, Motherwell .... L 8
June   16—Peter Bassey, Manchester .... L 8

JOHN COOPER
British Featherweight
1980
Feb.	5—Glen Rhodes, Southend	L	6
Mar.	1—Patrick Babouram, Criel	D	6

JOHNNY COOPER
French Middleweight
1980
Feb.	7—Ignacio Gorostidu, Paris	L	6
Apr.	11—Christian Chesini, Villeurbanne	L	6

JEAN PIERRE COOPMAN
Belgian Heavyweight
Born: July 11, 1946
1972
Sept.	29—Eric Suehrig, Lauwe	KO	3
Nov.	1—Siegfried Ackers, Izegem	KO	2
Dec.	8—Antonio Rimasti, Tournai	KO	4
Dec.	25—Kilani Ramdani, Izegem	W	6

1973
Jan.	25—Harald Skog, Oslo	L	6
Feb.	16—Gino Martinis, Ingelmunster	W	6
Mar.	16—Ermanno Festorazzi, Inglemunster	W	8
May	5—Ray Phillipe, Ghent	KO	5
May	19—Ireno Werleman, Isegem	KO by	2
Sept.	8—Juan Rodriguez, Izegem	KO	2
Nov.	1—Elwin Josepha, Izegem	KO	3
Nov.	16—Horst Lang, Ghent	KO	3
Dec.	28—Jean Beval, Izegen	W	6

1974
Jan.	25—Ireno Werleman, Izegem	KO	1
Feb.	23—Ferenc Kristofczack, Roulers	WF	3
Apr.	27—Rudi Lubbers, Ghent	L	10
Sept.	8—Rocky Campbell, Turnhout	KO	6
Nov.	1—Ermelino Finotti, Gits	KO	4
Nov.	22—Berndt August, Ghent	W	10
Dec.	25—Vasco Faustinho, Izegem	KO	10

1975
Jan.	17—Charlie (Devil) Green, Ghent	KO	8
Feb.	21—Adriano Rosati, Izegem	KO	5
Mar.	14—Jan Lubbers, Bruges	W	10
Apr.	12—Karsten Honhold, Lavwe	KO	6
May	17—Terry Daniels, Antwerp	W disq.	7
Oct.	4—Domingo Silveria, Antwerp	W	10
Nov.	1—Lissoko Abibobele, Izegem	KO	7

1976
Feb.	20—Muhammad Ali, San Juan	KO by	5
	(World Heavyweight Title)		
May	31—Hennie Thoonan, Rotterdam	LF	5
Oct.	9—Hennie Thoonen, Antwerp	KO	6
Oct.	30—George Jerome, Brussells	KO	4
Nov.	20—Cookie Wallace, Liege	W	10
Dec.	26—Neville Meade, Izegem	W	10

1977
Jan.	15—Lucien Rodriguez, Izegem	L	10
Mar.	12—Jose Urtain, Belgium	KO	4
	(European Heavyweight Title)		
May	8—Lucien Rodriguez, Antwerp	L	15
	(European Heavyweight Title)		
Sept.	10—Kurt Luedecke, Izegem	W	10
Nov.	1—Tony Moore, Ezegem	D	10
Nov.	26—Alfredo Evangelista, Brussels	KO by	1
	(European Heavyweight Title)		

1978
Feb.	11—Santiago Albert Lovell, Liege	KO	3
Apr.	22—Mario Baruzzi, La Louviere	KO	6
Sept.	2—Scotty Welsh, Izegem	KO	1
Sept.	30—Rudy Gauwe, Turnhout	L	12

1979
(Inactive)
1980
Feb.	2—Denton Ruddock, Turnhout	W	10
May	1—Winston Allen, Izegem	KO by	1
June	27—Al Syben, Bruxelles	L	10
Dec.	25—Pierre Kabassu, Izegem	L	10

EDDIE COPELAND
British Junior Welterweight
1979
Nov.	19—Dai Davies, Stockport	KO	4

1980
Feb.	18—Tommy Wright, Stockport	W	8
Mar.	1—Dave Campbell, Wembley	KO	5
Apr.	29—Jeff Pritchard, Stockport	KO	2
June	28—Barry Price, Wembley	KO	3
Sept.	27—Eric Purkis, Wembley	W	6

MIKE COPP
British Middleweight
1070
Feb.	9—Mick Minter, Croydon	L	6
Mar.	1—Peter Neal, London	KO by	6

Mar.	29—Russ Shaw, Swansea	KO	3
June	21—Chester Couburn, Bedford	KO	3
Aug.	11—Terry Schofield, Cardiff	W	6
Sept.	30—Mick Barker, Pontypool	W	6
Oct.	11—Terry Schofield, Manchester	W	8
Nov.	23—Chris Davies, Treorchy	L	6
Dec.	6—Jimmy King, Manchester	W	8
Dec.	25—Dirk Declercq, Izegem	LF	4

1977
Feb.	2—Roysie Francis, Swansea	KO by	1
June	21—Mickey Morse, London	L	8
Oct.	3—Colin Jones, Aberavon	KO by	5
Dec.	14—Tommy Joyce, Swansea	W	8

1978
Jan.	16—Johnny Elliott, Hove	L	6
Feb.	23—Terry Petersen, Doncaster	D	8
Mar.	20—Steve Goodwin, Aberavon	W	8
July	10—Horace McKenzie, Aberavon	L	10

1979
Feb.	19—Terry Knight, Mayfair	W	6
Feb.	26—Mike Morris, Edgbaston	L	6
Mar.	8—Jimmy Roberts, Bangor	W	8
Mar.	19—Prince Rodney, Bradford	KO by	3
June	27—Trevor Kerr, Derry	W	8
July	30—Richard Kenyon, Mayfair	W	8
Sept.	6—Torben Anderson, Randers	L	8
Sept.	18—Oscar Angus, Lewisham	L	8
Oct.	1—Albert Hillman, Marylebone	L	8
Nov.	21—Clifton Wallace, Evesham	KO by	3

1980
Apr.	21—Mickey Kidd, London	L	6
Apr.	29—Mickey Kidd, London	L	6
July	30—Leo Mulhearn, Doncaster	L	8

JEAN PAUL COPPYN
French Welterweight
1976
Nov.	20—Joel Leprodhomme, Troyes	D	6
Dec.	16—Joel Leprodhomme, Paris	W	6

1977
June	10—Biase Casoria, Paris	L	6
June	11—Patrick Babouran, Creil	L	6
Oct.	7—Serge Sinelnikov, Lione	L	6
Dec.	15—Dragan Tadic, Paris	L	6

1978
Jan.	12—Jean Michel Iger, Paris	D	6
Feb.	16—Djibril Bathily, Paris	L	6
Mar.	18—Mongo Kemri, Dijon	L	6
Sept.	14—Tjani Sidibe, Paris	KO by	1
Oct.	27—Serge Lemoine, Rennes	D	6

1979
Feb.	3—Serge Poulain, Laval	KO by	4
Apr.	28—Jean Touati, Barlin	L	6
June	15—Jean Benchetrit, Nizza	L	6
Sept.	28—Maurice Renaud, Villers	L	6
Dec.	1—Jean Pierre Moreau, Dhuizon	KO by	1

1980
Apr.	19—Salah El Gharbi, Cormeilles en Parisis	L	6

JEAN LOUIS COQUIN
French Welterweight
1980
Mar.	10—Fred Bothy, Paris	KO	2
Nov.	27—Dominique Delorme, Paris	KO by	3

FRED CORANSON
French Junior Middleweight
1974
Dec.	13—Seissies, Fresnes	W	6

1975
Feb.	22—Bernard Dylbaitis, Fresnes	L	6
Oct.	11—Jean Marc Beaurain, Dunkirk	D	6
Nov.	1—Rene Deharchies, Petit Synthe	W	6
Nov.	21—Dominique Cella, Paris	W	6
Dec.	12—Wa Bukasa, Dunkirk	W	6

1976
Jan.	10—Christian Lancery, Dunkirk	KO	4
Jan.	31—Rene Deharchies, Florange	L	6
Mar.	6—Luigi Renda, Petit Synthe	W	6
Apr.	9—Georges Lemmer, Petit Synthe	W	6
Apr.	29—Jean Pierre Moreau, Paris	W	6
May	8—Dick Declerc, Izegem	W	6
Oct.	4—Jose Alvarez, Dunkerque	W	8

1977
Feb.	5—Antonio Capuano, Dunkirk	W	6
Mar.	27—Georges Perot, Maubeuge	D	10
Apr.	9—Fredo Roelands, Bruges	L	8
Apr.	23—Mick Minter, Lille	W	7
June	11—Fernando Roelands, Grande Synthe	KO	1
Oct.	15—Remo Costa, Petite Synthe	KO	8

1978
Jan.	7—Jose Louis Ribeiro, Coudekerque	W	10
Jan.	14—Anthony Martin, Dunkirk	W	10

Feb. 17—Peter Morris, Dunkirk .... KO 7
Mar. 11—Georges Warusfel, Grand Synthe .... W 12
Apr. 15—Terry Petersen, Dunkerque .... KO 8
May 26—Alain Ruocco, La Seyne .... L 12
       (French Welterweight Title)
Oct. 14—Horace McKenzie, Durkerque .... W 8
1979
Feb. 10—Yannick Blandin, Dunkerque .... KO 7
Mar. 10—Italo Venturi, Dunkerque .... W 8
May 18—Jacques Van Mellaerts, Dunkirk .... KO 3
June 15—Loui Acaries, Nice .... L 12
       (French Welterweight Title)
Oct. 19—Charley Malarky, Dunkerque .... W 10
Nov. 24—Achille Mitchell, Dunkirk .... W 10
Dec. 8—Lloyd Lee, Dunkerque .... KO 2
1980
Feb. 9—George Walker, Dunkirk .... W 8
June 15—Ronald Zenon, Dunkirk .... KO by 9
       (For Vacant French Welterweight Title)
Nov. 8—Thierry Samo, Calais .... KO by 5

ALBERTO CORDERO
Filipino Junior Welterweight
1978
Sept. 24—Edward Maneral, Manila .... KO by 7
1979
Mar. 30—Art Alcantara, Manila .... L 10
Sept. 7—Ruben Rabago, Manila .... W 12
       (Philippine Junior Welterweight Title)
Nov. 16—Willie Makitoki, Quezon City .... W 10
1980
Jan. 25—Danilo Limpahan, Manila .... L 10
June 27—Edward Heneral, Manila .... L 10
       (Lost Philippine Junior Welterweight Title)

GUISEPPE CORTESI
Italian Light Heavyweight
1980
May 1—Luc Goosens, Izegem .... D 6
June 27—Walter Cevoli, St. Arcangelo .... KO by 3

GEORGES COTIN
French Lightweight
Born: Apr. 2, 1951
1974
Jan. 10—Ben Kerrou, Paris .... D 6
Feb. 14—Boualem Tadjeddine, Paris............. KO 4
Mar. 14—Boualem Tadjeddine, Paris .... D 6
Mar. 28—Joseph Sossou, Paris..................... KO 5
May 24—Hamil Smail, Caen .... KO 5
Nov. 21—Ali Issaoui, Paris .... W 8
Dec. 7—Roland Cazeaux, S. Nazaire .... KO 4
1975
Mar. 13—Raymond Libbreht, Paris .... KO 7
Apr. 19—Fernand Roelands, Wieze .... L 8
Oct. 16—Mario Oliveira, Paris .... D 8
Dec. 13—Michele Siracusa, Paris .... D 8
1976
Feb. 5—Paul Rouree, Paris .... KO 6
Mar. 6—Carlos Foldes, Paris .... W 8
May 6—Daniel Vermandere, Paris .... KO 6
June 30—Nino Jiminez, Madrid .... L 8
Oct. 1—Mario Oliveira, Alfortville .... W 12
       (French Lightweight Title)
Oct. 3—Manuel Abedoy, Abidjan .... KO by 9
Dec. 11—Jean Pierre Hainault, Blois............. KO 11
1977
Jan. 2—Daniel Bellantonio, Marseille .... KO 11
       (French Junior Lightweight Title)
Jan. 15—Lothar Abend, Kiel .... KO 8
Feb. 26—Roland Cazeaux, St. Nazaire .... D 12
       (French Featherweight Title)
May 27—Natale Vezzoli, Brescia .... KO by 11
       (European Junior Lightweight Title)
1978
Feb. 4—Roberto Castanon, Leon .... L 10
Feb. 16—Rocky Orengo, Paris .... W 10
Mar. 30—Rene Martin, Paris .... KO 8
       (French Junior Lightweight Title)
June 30—Maurice Apeang, Papeete .... KO by 8
Oct. 9—Dave Bolden, Salle Wagram .... W 10
Dec. 18—Cornelius Boza-Edwards, London ..... KO by 1
1979
Jan. 23—Ralph Racine, Montreal .... KO 2
May 18—Samuel Meck, Perigueux .... L 10
Oct. 15—Bouchiba Messaoud, Paris .... KO 8
Oct. 23—Ray Cattouse, London .... KO by 1
Dec. 14—Didier Kowalski, St. Amand .... W 12
       (Won French Lightweight Title)
1980
Mar. 7—Antonio Guinaldo, Barcelona .... L 10
Apr. 26—Didier Kowalski, Lille .... KO by 5
       (For French Lightweight Title)
June 15—Francisco Leon, Barcelona .... KO by 1

Oct. 10—Albert Almatler, Villeurbanne .... LF 4
Dec. —Didier Kowalski, Paris .... KO by 9
       (For French Lightweight Title)

JEAN MARIE COTINAUT
French Junior Welterweight
1973
Nov. 29—Christian Lancery, Paris .... W 6
Dec. 13—Ernest Andalon, Paris .... W 6
Dec. 20—Yves Husson, Paris .... W 6
1974
Feb. 23—Antone Capuano, Paris .... W 6
Mar. 19—Gerardo Del Guacchio, Chaux Fonds ..... W 6
May 17—Saadi Saadii, Villeurbanne .... L 6
Sept. 30—Klaus Fuchs, Esch .... W 6
Oct. 12—Jean Lefarge, Amiens .... L 8
Nov. 22—Jean Bodchon, Longwy .... KO 5
Dec. 14—Antoine Capuano, Villerupt .... L 6
1975
Feb. 1—Pierre Petit, Dijon .... L 8
Feb. 15—Saadi Saadii, Villeurbanne .... L 8
Mar. 8—Jean Lefarge, Sens .... L 10
Apr. 5—Pierre Petit, Vandoeuvre .... D 8
Apr. 17—Claude Lormeau, Paris .... KO by 4
Oct. 11—Franco Soro, Joeuf .... W 6
Dec. 6—Jean Pierre Younsy, Conde .... L 8
1976
Jan 10—Jo Kimpuani, Dunkirk .... KO by 1
1977
Jan. 15—Patrick Christ, Creil .... KO 6
Feb. 5—Pietro Marselli, Vandoeuvre .... KO 7
Mar. 18—Pascal Real Martin, Annecy .... D 8
Apr. 16—Didier Kowalski, Noeux .... KO 3
Nov. 11—Freddy Roelands, Bruges .... L 8
Nov. 19—Jean Lefarge, Vandoeuvre .... W 8
1978
Apr. 14—Gianbattista Capretti, Milano .... L 8
1979
(Inactive)
1980
Jan. 4—Eloy De Souza, Capri .... W 8
Mar. 7—Francesco Marcello, Torino .... L 8
Apr. 19—Guiseppe Martinese, Senigallia .... L 8

PAT COWDELL
British Featherweight
1977
July 5—Albery Coley, Wolverhampton .... W 6
Sept 20—Paul Varden, Southend .... KO 5
Oct. 18—Henri Coni, Wolverhampton .... KO 6
Oct. 31—Lee Graham, Birmingham .... W 8
Dec. 14—Kevin Doherty, Kingston .... W 8
1978
Jan. 23—Alan Robertson, London .... KO by 3
June 29—Alan Buchanan, Wolverhampton .... W 8
Sept. 18—Jackie McGill, Wolverhampton .... W 8
Nov. 15—Paddy Graham, Solihull .... W 8
1979
Mar. 5—Les Pickett, Wolverhampton .... W 12
May 16—Jean Jacques Souris, Wolverhampton ...KO 6
Nov. 6—Dave Needham, Kensington .... W 15
       (Won British Featherweight Title)
1980
Jan. 21—Alain LeFol, Wolverhampton .... W 10
Feb. 19—Jimmy Flint, London .... KO by 12
       (Lost British Featherweight Title)

STUART CRABB
British Featherweight
1979
Sept. 25—Chris Moorcraft, Southend .... L 6
Oct. 24—Robert Hepburn, Norwich .... D 6
Nov. 19—Iver Jones, Lewisham .... KO by 3
1980
Mar. 6—John Griffiths, Wimbledon .... L 6
Apr. 10—Robert Hepburn, Norwich .... L 6
Apr. 23—Clyde Ruan, Hove .... L 6
Sept. 10—Jeff Smart, Lewisham .... L 4

MIKE CREASY
British Heavyweight
1980
Apr. 15—Steve Gee, Blackpool .... KO by 5
June 11—Don Charles, Morecambe .... KO 2

CRISTOBAL CREPSI
Spanish Welterweight
1979
Mar. 30—Jose Luis Fernandez, Las Palmas .... KO 2
Apr. 26—Jose Manuel Domingo, Las Palmas ...... W 4
June 27—Ali Mohamed Ches, Andraix .... D 4
Aug. 2—Jose Manuel Domingo, Mallorca .... W 6
Aug. 18—Illuminado Diez, Aviles .... KO 6

Aug.	31—Ignacio Gorostidi, Melilla	WF	3
Oct.	10—Francesco Alcala, Almeria	L	4
Oct.	26—Escasino Ferreira, La Coruna	KO by	3

1980

Feb.	2—Antonio Casado, St. Maria Barbera	KO by	3
Mar.	8—Jorge Sala, Mallorca	KO	1
Mar.	28—Juan Saavedra, Mallorca	KO by	3

ANTONIO CRESENZA
Italian Middleweight

1975

Feb.	28—Pietropaolo Capezzone, Rome	D	6
Oct.	30—Branko Barakovic, Rome	W	6

1976

Apr.	23—Young Griffo, Rome	KO	2

1977

Aug.	5—Gianni Filippetto, Fort Village	L	6
Dec.	3—Noriano Bonacin, Montecchio	D	6
Dec.	29—Giorgio Giana, Morbegno	KO by	1

1978

Jan.	14—Giovanni Marchesini, Castelforte	L	6
Apr.	15—Luciano Renzi, Chivasso	L	6
May	5—Franco Saputo, Latina	W	6
May	27—Valentino Nardini, Pordenone	L	6
June	26—Damiano Pellegrino, Forte Village	L	6

1979

Aug.	4—Giancarlo Serangei, Ladispeli	W	6
Aug.	14—Giancarlo Serangeli, Vivo	D	6
Sept.	2—Luciano Bolis, Sermoneta	W	8
Dec.	22—Luciano diGiancomo, Citsterna	L	8

1980

Mar.	14—Franco Recupero, Rome	WF	3
May	26—Mario Loreni, Travagliato	KO	4
Sept.	6—Walter Cevoli, Riccione	KO by	4
Nov.	7—Gaetano Ardito, Firenze	KO by	3

BINGO CROOKS
Wolverhampton, England Lightweight
Born: 1952

1971

Nov.	10—Brian Harding, Nottingham	W	6
Nov.	30—Bria Harding, London	L	6
Dec.	8—Brian Harding, London	D	6
Dec.	13—Alan Richardson, Manchester	L	6

1972

Jan.	10—Alan Richardson, Manchester	L	6
Jan.	26—Neil Gauci, Wolverhampton	L	6
Feb.	22—Mike Frampton, Lndon	W	6
Feb.	28—Sammy Vernon, Nottingham	D	6
Mar.	15—Dave Tuohey, Caerphilly	W	6
Mar.	29—Dave Granley, Wolverhampton	W	6
Apr.	18—Mike Frampton, Birmingham	KO	1
Apr.	25—John O'Rawe, Birmingham	W	8
July	12—Joey Lando, Wolverhampton	KO	8
Sept.	19—Tony Cunningham, Manchester	W	8
Nov.	20—Billy Hardacre, London	L	8
Dec.	11—John Mitchell, London	W	8

1973

Feb.	1—Tommy Glencross, Wolverhampton	W	8
May	9—Paddy Graham, Solihull	W	8
May	22—Evan Armstrong, London	L	8
Oct.	6—David Poison, Accra	KO by	6
Nov.	6—Jimmy Bell, Wolverhampton	D	8

1974

Feb.	1—Lothar Abend, Hamburg	L	10
Feb.	26—Jimmy Revie, Wolverhampton	L	8
Apr.	24—Tommy Glencross, Wolverhampton	KO	5
Aug.	31—Nkosana Mgxaji, E. London (Africa)	L	10

1975

Mar.	3—Clive Hogben, Hemel Hempstead	D	8
May	19—George Turpin, London	L	8

1976

Feb.	13—Benny Purdy, Birmingham	W	8
Mar.	4—Charlie Nash, Belfast	L	8
Apr.	12—Benny Purdy, Birmingham	W	8
May	10—Vernon Sollas, London	KO by	8

1977

Feb.	1—Jimmy Flint, London	W	8
Mar.	29—Jeff Pritchard, Ebbw Vale	L	8
Oct.	10—Willie Booth, Glasgow	L	8
Nov.	8—Cornelius Boza-Edwards, London	L	8
Nov.	22—Roy Varden, Wolverhampton	L	8
Nov.	30—Mark Bliss, Wolverhampton	W	8

1978

Feb.	4—Maurice Apeang, Grenoble	L	10
Mar.	13—Billy Vivian, Birmingham	W	8
Sept.	27—Des Gwilliam, Stoke	D	8
Oct.	18—Gerry Duffy, Glasgow	D	8
Oct.	31—Des Gwilliam, Wolverhampton	L	10
Dec.	11—Ricky Beaumont, Birmingham	L	8

1979

Feb.	28—George Feeney, Harrogate	W	8
Apr.	17—Dave McCabe, Glasgow	L	8
May	18—Dan M'Putu, Dunkirk	L	8
Sept.	8—Paul Chance, Wolverhampton	L	8
Sept.	26—George Feeney, Solihull	L	8
Oct.	8—Willie Booth, Glasgow	KO	6
Oct.	29—James Cooke, Wolverhampton	LF	7
Dec.	3—Ricky Beaumont, Hull	KO by	1

1980

Feb.	4—George Feeney, Hammersmith	L	8
Mar.	10—Maurice Fico, Paris	W	8
May	29—Paul Chance, Wolverhampton	KO	9
	(Won Midlands Area Lightweight Title)		
June	15—Dan M'Putu, Dunkirk	L	8
Oct.	14—Peter Harrison, Wolverhampton	W	8

MARK CROUCH
British Welterweight

1980

Oct.	18—Kevin Johnson, Birmingham	W	6

PETRUS (PIET) CROUS
South African Light Heavyweight

1977

Nov.	14—Barend Steyn, Johannesburg	KO	1

1978

Aug.	21—Brian Smit, Welkom	KO	4
Oct.	28—Gerhardus Joubert, Ermelo	KO	1

1980

Apr.	21—Petrus Espag, Secunda	KO	1
July	4—John Dhlamini, Durban	KO	1
Sept.	15—Solomon Dhladla, Durban	KO	1
Dec.	19—Mervin Smit, Welkom	KO	3

ALBERTO CRUZ
Filipino Middleweight

1978

Nov.	24—Neil Pattel, Brisbane	KO by	8

1979

Nov.	5—Dommy Cotacte, Manila	W	10

1980

Jan.	24—Tadashi Mihara, Tokyo	L	10
Aug.	1—Fred Pastor, Manila	W	10
Oct.	1—Armando Boniquit, Manila	W	10

JIMMY CRUZ
Spanish Lightweight

1973

May	17—Jesus Rodriguez, Las Palmas	KO by	3
Oct.	26—Juan M. Dominguez, Las Palmas	D	6
Nov.	29—Manuel Velazquez, S. Cruz	L	6

1974
(Inactive)

1975

July	17—Luis F.L. Mejias, S. Cruz	L	6
Aug.	5—Luis F.L. Mejias, S. Cruz	L	6
Sept.	13—Manuel R. Orteguita, S. Cruz	L	8
Dec.	5—Jose Del Pino Jimenez, S. Cruz	W	6

1976

Jan.	17—Cecilio Lastra, Santander	KO by	1
Aug.	7—Juan M. Sierra, S. Cruz	D	6
Oct.	11—Juan M. Sierra, S. Cruz	D	6

1977

Jan.	29—Luis Fernando Leon, S. Cruz	L	6
May	21—Antonio Vazquez, Las Palmas	W	6
July	16—Santiago Monzon, Las Palmas	KO by	4
Aug.	2—Juan Santana, S. Cruz	WF	6
Aug.	6—Gorrin, Las Palmas	LF	2

1978

Mar.	10—Santiago Gonzalez, Las Palmas	KO by	4
Apr.	15—Joaquin Garcia Del Moral, Utera	D	6

1979

Mar.	30—Manuel Hatero, Blanes	L	4
May	11—Antonio Granados, Barcelona	KO	4
June	15—Jose Manuel Padron, S. Cruz	L	6
Oct.	20—Juan Melian Sierra, S. Cruz	KO by	6
Dec.	8—Enrique Sosa, Ternerife	W	8

1980

May	10—Liber Barrios, St. Cruz de Tenerife	W	8

ORLANDO CRUZ
Filipino Lightweight

1979

Mar.	29—Mike Benitez, Olongapo City	L	10
Dec.	20—Young De La Cruz, Olongapo City	W	10

1980

Feb.	23—Boy Reyes, Angele City	L	10

RENE CRUZ, JR.
Filipino Bantamweight

1978

Sept.	2—Fred Ebon, Cabanatuan City	W	10
Sept.	29—Billy Abato, Cag. de Oro	L	10

1979

Jan.	20—Polly Boron, Cabantuan City	KO by	5
Apr.	27—Raffy Saulong, Angeles City	L	10

Dec. 29—Rene Sedayon, Cabantuan City .... W 10
1980
May 31—Noe Canino, Cabanatuan City .... D 10
July 30—Willie Lucas, Manila .... L 10
Sept. 13—Allan Baylon, Ormoc City .... KO 5

ROMMY CUNANAN
Filipino Featherweight
1980
Feb. 28—Fel Viesca, Jr., Angeles City .... L 10
June 12—Nardito Adrayan, Angeles City .... L 10
Aug. 1—Willie Espinosa, Manila .... W 10
Oct. 4—Boy Reyes, Angeles City 10
Nov. 30—Fel Viesca, Jr., Angeles City .... W 10

LUIGI CURCETTI
Italian Junior Welterweight
1978
Oct. 28—Roberto D'Elia, Riccione .... D 6
1979
Mar. 17—Francesco Marcello, Chivasso .... KO by 3
May 11—Antonio Sandrin, Senigallia .... W 6
July 7—Maurizio Condello, Roccapriora .... D 6
Aug. 14—Pasquale Zampano, Chiavari .... D 6
Aug. 29—Angelo Zanetti, Iseo .... D 6
Dec. 21—Roberto Masini, Savona .... L 6
1980
Mar. 14—Bechir Jelassi, Rome .... D 6
July 2—Scipione Colainni, Bitonto .... D 6
Aug. 10—Antonio Sandrin, Monte Cassiano ...... W 6
Aug. 27—Biase Casoria, Senigallia .... KO 4
Dec. 23—Alfonso Carrillo, Recanati .... D 6

CEMEL CURNACZAN
Dutch Light Heavyweight
1977
Sept. 21—Karl Heinz Schulz, Frankfurt .... KO by 3
1978
Mar. 18—Juergen Gries, Uetersen .... KO by 2
1979
(Inactive)
1980
Feb. 6—Walter Nickel, Lubeck .... KO 2

ALDO CURTI
Italian Welterweight
1980
Mar. 14—Francois Kaiuwa, Frejus .... W 6
Dec. 13—Serge Sinelnikow, Frejus .... W 6

ANTOINE CURTI
Italian Lightweight
1980
Mar. 14—Jean Noel Lohr, Frejus .... KO 5
Apr. 5—Francis Tripp, Nice .... L 6
Apr. 23—Bruno Dario, Antibes .... D 6
Dec. 13—Bruno Dario, Frejus .... W 6

LUCIO CUSMA
Italian Lightweight
1977
Apr. 1—Charles Jurietti, Bologna .... W 6
Apr. 29—Abass Macauley, Bologna .... KO 4
May 13—Gianfranco Cianconi, Imola .... KO 3
Oct. 14—Domenico Traini, Bologna .... L 6
Dec. 1—Giovanni Mura, Bologna .... WF 2
Dec. 15—Rocco Frisi, Bologna .... KO 2
1978
Jan. 27—Eloy De Souza, Faenza .... W 6
Feb. 9—Bechir Jelassi, Bologna .... W 6
Mar. 17—Giovanni Cavazzini, Bologna .... KO 4
Apr. 27—Eloy De Souza, Bologna .... D 8
June 28—Alfonso Carrillo, Castelsanpietro ..... D 8
Dec. 26—Domenico Traini, Bologna .... W 8
1979
Jan. 27—Giovanni carrino, Salerno .... KO 8
Mar. 17—Charles Jurietti, Valence .... L 8
July 11—Joe Gibilisco, Rimini .... D 8
Dec. 26—Melquiades Da Silva, Lugo di Romagna .. W 8
1980
Jan. 25—Alfonso Carrillo, Bologna .... KO 3
Mar. 21—Sergio Emili, Bologna .... KO 6
Apr. 18—Giovanni Carrino, Bologna .... KO 7
(Won Italian Lightweight Title)
Oct. 4—Giancarlo Usai, Cagliari .... W 12
(Retained Italian Lightweight Title)

MAURICIO DA CRUZ
Spanish Junior Middleweight
1979
Mar. 23—Luigi Marini, S. Elpidio .... L 8
Apr. 30—Alvaro Scarpelli, Forli .... L 8
May 18—Giorgio Giana, Rieta .... L 8
June 16—Cosimo Carbone, Pontedera .... L 6
July 20—Cosimo Carbone, Collenarino .... L 6
Aug. 10—Omar Olivo, Genova .... W 8
Sept. 8—Raymond Langewouters, Lirre .... L 8
Dec. 1—Roberto Manoni, Sondrio .... L 8
Dec. 21—Roberto Manoni, Citta di Castello ...... L 8
1980
Jan. 4—Christian Chesini, Carpi .... D 6
Jan. 30—Nicola Cirelli, Viterbo .... L 8
Feb. 15—Angulo Pufino, Bordeaux .... L 8
Feb. 29—Roberto Felicioni, Rome .... L 8
Mar. 14—Donato Romano, Milan .... L 8
Mar. 28—Roberto Manoni, Monzon .... L 8
Apr. 25—Cosimo Funto, Brundisi .... L 8
May 24—Libero Moi, Ostia .... KO by 5
July 5—Luciano Bomben, Taiedo .... L 6
July 26—Ray Opoku, Rapallo .... L 8
Aug. 10—Donato Romano, Siderno .... L 6
Sept. 5—Cosimo Carbone, Vieste .... L 6
Sept. 26—Vittorio Conte, Lucia .... L 8
Oct. 11—Nazif Biberovic, Wien .... W 8
Oct. 24—Luciano Sorgon, San Dona .... L 6

MAURO DA CRUZ
Spanish Junior Mddleweight
1980
Jan. 25—Daniele Zapaterra, Bologna .... KO by 4
Mar. 8—Michel Pagani, Calais .... KO by 5
Apr. 4—Raffaele Prette, Napoles .... L 6
May 9—Marzio Baseotti, San Dona .... L 6
Aug. 17—Pasquale Rippa, Cervester .... D 6
Oct. 11—Pasquale Rippa, Naples .... L 6
Oct. 24—Marzio Baseotti, San Dona .... L 6
Nov. 29—Marzio Baseotti, Padova .... L 6
Dec. 5—Corrado Sortino, Pesaro .... KO by 5

NAJIB DAHO
Morrocan Lightweight
(Fighting Out of England)
1977
May 17—Kevin Sheenan, Wolverhampton .... KO 2
May 31—Tony Zeni, Kensington .... L 4
June 13—Roy Varden, Manchester .... L 6
July 5—Winston Spencer, Wolverhampton .... KO by 5
Oct. 3—Paul Clemit, Barnsley .... W 8
Oct. 10—Don Burgin, Marton .... W 8
Oct. 24—Mick Bell, Manchester .... D 8
Nov. 2—George McGurk, Newcastle .... L 8
Dec. 5—Mickey Bell, Manchester .... W 8
1978
Jan. 18—Steve Early, Solihull .... L 6
Oct. 12—Stan Atherton, Liverpool .... L 6
Oct. 24—Selwyn Bell, Blackpool .... W 6
Nov. 2—Terry Welsch, Liverpool .... W 6
Nov. 30—Tommy Wright, Caister .... W 6
Dec. 11—Vernon Penprase, Plymouth .... W 8
Dec. 18—Tommy Wright, Bradford .... W 8
1979
Feb. 12—Jimmy Brown, Manchester .... L 8
Feb. 19—Martyn Galleozzie, London .... L 6
Mar. 1—Robbie Robinson, Liverpool .... KO by 8
Apr. 10—Paul Chance, Wolverhampton .... L 8
Apr. 17—Gerry Duffy, Glasgow .... W 8
June 18—Brian Snagg, Manchester .... W 10
July 5—Barry Michael, Aberavon .... W 8
Sept. 12—Jimmy Brown, Liverpool .... W 8
Sept. 20—Brian Snagg, Liverpool .... W 8
Oct. 29—Lawrence Williams, Birmingham .... L 8
Dec. 4—Chris Sanigar, London .... KO 1
1980
Feb. 9—Dan M'Putu, Dunkirk .... L 8
Mar. 14—Charm Chiteule, Glasgow .... W 6
Apr. 29—Billy Vivian, London .... W 6
May 15—Ken Buchanan, London .... KO by 7
Nov. 1—Winston Spencer, Glasgow .... KO by 5

KANEKATSU DAITO
Japanese Junior Featherweight
1980
Feb. 4—Soon-Hyun Chun, Osaka ....KO by 4
(For OPBF Junior Featherweight Title)
May 24—Hiroyuki Iwamoto, Tokyo ....L 10
(For Japanese Junior Featherweight Title)

LUIGI DAL SANTO
Italian Welterweight
1977
Dec. 26—Giampiero Bertuzzi, Piacenza ....KO by 3
1978
May 26—Gregorio Ciancaglioni ....D 6
Dec. 13—Serge Sinelnikow, Brescia ....KO 5
1979
Feb. 9—Francesco Morrone, Milano ....KO by 3
June 15—Patrizio Burini, Figline Valdarno ....KO by 1
1980
Apr. 24—Bachisio Mereu, Forli ....L 6

CARL DALY
British Middleweight
1979
Feb. 27—Curtis Marsh, London ....KO by 2
Nov. 19—Martin Francis, Lewisham ....W 6
Dec. 20—Earl Edwards, Queensway ....W 6
1980
Feb. 28—Earl Edwards, London ....KO by 5
Apr. 8—Joe Oke, Norwich ....KO 3
Apr. 21—Joe Lally, London ....D 8
Oct. 1—Ezeo Groubiza, Oslo ....KO 4

MICHELE D'AMATO
Italian Junior Lightweight
1969
Mar. 15—Altero Marini, Agropoli ....W 6
Apr. 11—Ernesto Sole, Rome ....D 6
May 16—Bruno Usai, Rome ....KO 5
June 27—Ernesto Sole, Rome ....W 6
Aug. 16—Paul Ikumapay, Oriolo ....W 6
Sept. 6—Mario Calandro, Monteporzio ....WF 4
Dec. 19—Edilio Montaldo, Monteporzio ......W 6
1970
Jan. 10—Abu Arrow, Agropoli ....W 6
Mar. 2—Sergio Mencarelli, Agropoli ....L 8
June 24—Luigi Sorangelo, Napoli ....W 6
Aug. 1—Franco Petrozzi, Salerno ....KO 6
Oct. 2—Salvatore Fabrizio, Genova ....LF 2
Oct. 30—Salvatore Fabrizio, Genova ....KO 5
Nov. 26—Sergio Mencarelli, Napoli ....W 10
1971
Feb. 22—Paul Ikumapayi, Palermo ....KO by 3
1972-1978
(Inactive)
1979
May 4—Gregorio Ciancaglione, Rome ....D 6
July 21—Antonio Franca, Salerno ....W 8
Nov. 14—Vincenzo Di Ruocco, Ascoli ....D 6
1980
Mar. 14—Carlo Frassinetti, Rome ....W 8
May 30—Natale Caredda, Rome ....L 6
Sept. 14—Natale Caredda, Avezzano ....D 8

GEORGE DANAHAR
British Middleweight
1979
Jan. 8—George Walker, London ....W 6
Apr. 2—Joe Jackson, London ....KO 3
Apr. 23—Gordon George, London ....W 6
Apr. 30—Russell Blanks, London ....KO 3
Oct. 8—Chris Coady, London ....W 8
Dec. 10—Peter Gorny, Piccadilly ....W 8
1980
Mar. 17—Doug James, London ....KO 6
Apr. 22—Herol Graham, Sheffield ....L 8
Apr. 30—Oscar Angus, Aylesbury ....W 8

ANTONY DA PAIVA
South African Welterweight
1979
Dec. 3—Chris Sampson, Welkom ....KO 2
Dec. 14—Michael Mohlabane, Welkom ....L 4
1980
Mar. 21—Martin Jacobs, Bloemfontein ....W 4

MANNY DA PAIVA
South African Junior Lightweight
1979
Mar. 5—Samuel Pule, Welkom ....L 4
1980
May 3—Kallie Swanepoel, Witsiehoek ....L 4

Dec. 22—Rodney Botha, Cape Town ....L 6

JESSIE DARIGAN
Filipino Featherweight
1979
Sept. 7—Oscar Barola, Manila ....KO by 4
1980
Feb. 8—Eddie Ballaran, Manila ....L 10

SALVAOR DARLO
Filipino Lightweight
1979
Aug. 6—Lito Pena, Quezon City ....KO by 4
Sept. 15—Del Contado, Rizal ....KO by 6
1980
Jan. 20—Dario Merida, De Oro City ....L 10

MELQUIADES DA SILVA
Spanish Junior Welterweight
1977
Nov. 26—Salvatore Fabrizio, Genova ....L 6
Dec. 23—Alfredo Mulas, Cagliari ....L 8
1978
Feb. 10—Heleno Ferreira, Lugo Romagna ....L 10
Mar. 4—Salvatore Malluzo, Pesaro ....L 8
Mar. 18—Gerard Jacob, Creil ....L 10
Mar. 31—Luigi Tessarin, Vegevano ....KO by 8
Apr. 14—Giuseppe Fossati, Milan ....L 8
Apr. 29—Guy Caudron, Lievin ....KO by 5
May 14—Heleno Ferreira, Pescara ....L 8
May 26—Giuseppe Fossati, Crema ....KO by 2
July 6—Lugi Tessarin, Lugo di Romagno ....L 8
Aug. 5—Gregorio Ciancaglione, Pogio Mirteto .....D 8
Sept. 14—Cosimo Lavino, Prato ....D 8
Nov. 3—Nevio Carbi, Monfalcone ....W 8
Dec. 9—Salvatore Liscapade, Isernia ....L 6
1979
Jan. 12—Heleno Ferreira, Milano ....NC 3
Feb. 10—Bruno Demontis, Cagliari ....KO by 5
Mar. 30—Heleno Ferreira, Pavia ....L 8
Apr. 14—Cosimo Lavino, Brindisi ....L 8
May 25—Franco Stolo, Florence ....L 8
June 23—Angelo Bizzaro, Marcianese ....L 8
July 27—Gianfrance Lalli, Chiesa Valmalcenca ....L 8
Sept. 30—Potite Di Muro, Oristano ....L 8
Nov. 9—Potite Di Muro, Torino ....L 8
Nov. 30—Patrick Goblet, Troyes ....L 8
Dec. 15—Antonio Antino, Fabriano ....L 8
Dec. 26—Lucio Cusma, Lugo di Romagna ....L 8
1980
Feb. 2—Salvatore Melluzo, Marsala ....L 8
Mar. 7—Alessandro Nardi, Rome ....L 8
Mar. 28—Gianfranco Lallim, Monza ....L 8
Apr. 18—Franco Zurlo, Fasano ....L 8
May 31—Valerio Nati, Sassari ....L 8
Sept. 3—Guiseppe Tidu, Santa Teresa ....L 6

TITO DASTILE
South African Bantamweight
1974
June 29—Mncdi Batyi, Queenstown ....W 4
1975
(Inactive)
1976
Nov. 6—Spokes Witbooi, King Williamstown ....KO 3
1977
May 7—Howard Xakava, Zwelitsha ....W 4
Nov. 19—Lennox Mtyongwe, East London ....L 6
Dec. 10—Phindile Gaika, East London ....L 6
1978
May 6—Daluxolo Tyekana, East London ....KO 1
Aug. 26—Siphiwo Gaika, East London ....W 4
Sept. 9—Welile Nkosenkulu, East London ...KO by 6
1979
Aug. 18—Nkosana Moss, King Williamstown ..KO by 7
1980
July 26—Siphiwo Fuma, King Williamstown ....W 6

ROBERTO D'AULA
Italian Flyweight
1979
Apr. 25—Corrado Infanti, Mantova ....W 6
June 29—Michele DiMarco, Empoli ....KO 3
July 21—Corrado Infanti, Buti ....D 6
1980
Mar. 21—Giampiero Pinna, Bologna ....KO by 1

CHRIS DAVIES
British Welterweight
1976
Sept. 27—Dave Massey, Mayfair ....KO 5
Oct. 25—Barton McAllister, Mayfair ....W 8
Nov. 23—Mike Copp, Treorchy ....W 6

293

Jan. 24—Ray Heaney, Mayfair .... KO 5
Mar. 5—Al Stewart, Liverpool .... KO 4
Mar. 21—Mickey Flynn, Caerphilly .... W 8
Apr. 2—Dan Mputu, Grande Synthe .... L 6
Apr. 25—Carlos Foldes, Mayfair .... W 8
Sept. 16—Perico Fernandez, Barcelona .... L 8
Oct. 7—Saadi Saadli, Lione .... KO 3
Nov. 14—Barton McAllister, Reading .... W 8

1978

Jan. 16—Clinton McKenzie, Nottingham .... L 12
Dec. 8—Obisia Nwakpa, Lagos .... L 10

1979

Apr. 9—Sylvester Mitee, Mayfair .... KO by 2
Sept. 28—Juan Jose Gimenez, Munich .... L 10
Nov. 6—Mick Bell, Stafford .... W 8

1980

Apr. 21—Steve Early, Edgbaston .... KO by 3
Sept. 6—Hans Henrik Palm, Aarhus .... L 8

DAI DAVIES
British Junior Welterweight

1972

Nov. 13—Joey Deriu, London .... W 6

1973

Feb. 13—Martin Galleozie, Haverfordwest ..... KO by 1
Nov. 27—Gary Dunks, Shoreditch .... L 6
Dec. 4—Kevin Evans, Southend .... L 6
Dec. 17—Jimmy Flint, Southend .... L 6

1974-1976
(Inactive)

1977

Apr. 26—Sylvester Gordon, London .... L 6
May 11—Philiph Morris, Swansea .... D 4
June 2—Sylvester Gordon, London .... L 6
Oct. 17—Gary Collins, Bedford .... W 6
Nov. 7—Sylvester Gordon, London .... L 6
Dec. 14—Eric Wood, Swansea .... W 6

1978

Jan. 30—Dave McCabe, Glasgow .... L 6
Feb. 6—Peter Snowsall, London .... W 6
Apr. 20—Robbie Robinson, London .... L 6
May 15—Ceri Collins, London .... L 6
June 29—Alan Burrows, Caerphilly .... L 6
July 10—Nigel Thomas, Aberavon .... W 6
Sept. 4—Roddy Evans, Barry .... L 8
Sept. 21—Ceri Collins, Caerphilly .... L 8
Sept. 27—Albert Coley, Evesham .... L 8
Oct. 2—Brian Snagg, Liverpool .... KO by 2
Nov. 2—Charlie Brown, Ebbw Vale .... L 6
Nov. 29—Brian Schofield, Swansea .... L 6
Dec. 4—Martin Bridge, Manchester .... D 6
Dec. 11—Sewin Bell, Plymouth .... W 6
Dec. 21—Dave Farrell, Liverpoos .... W 6

1979

Jan. 18—Dave Taylor, Liverpool .... L 8
Feb. 12—Tony Carroll, Manchester .... L 8
Feb. 26—Young Nelson, Middlesbrough .... W 8
Mar. 15—Sid Smith, Marylebone .... L 8
Apr. 5—Ray Heaney, Belfast .... L 8
Apr. 9—Dave Allen, Nottingham .... KO by 4
June 13—Pat Smythe, Caerphilly .... L 8
Oct. 16—Roger Guest, West Bromwich .... KO by 3
Nov. 19—Eddie Copeland, Stockport .... KO 4
Dec. 17—Ian Murray, Wolverhampton .... D 6

1980

Jan. 21—Mickey Baker, Wolverhampton .... L 6
Feb. 13—Jackie Turner, London .... L 6

GLYN DAVIES
British Bantamweight
Began professional career in 1962
Record from 1962-1975 Won 26 Lost 22 Drew 5

1976-1978
(Inactive)

1979

Mar. 5—John Cooper, London .... W 8
Mar. 19—Vernon Penprase, Haverfordwest ...... L 8
Apr. 19—John Cooper, London .... W 8
May 10—Paul Keers, Pontypool .... D 6
June 27—Damien McDermott, Derry .... KO by 3
Oct. 8—Pip Coleman, Windsor .... KO 7
Oct. 22—David Smith, London .... L 8

1980

Jan. 22—Johnny Owen, Piccadilly .... KO by 6
Feb. 28—Steve Cleak, Ebbw Vale .... L 8
July 1—Steve Cleak, Swindon .... KO by 5
Oct. 1—Pip Coleman, Swansea .... L 10
(Lost Welsh Bantamweight Title)
Nov. 3—Dave Smith, Hammersmith .... KO by 2

PHIL DAVIES
Australian Junior Middleweight

1975

June 17—Andy Marks, New Lambton .... KO 2
July 16—Des Ord, Kingsford .... KO 3
July 24—Ken Carmody, New Lambton .... W 4
Aug. 19—Merv Brown, New Lambton .... W 6
Sept. 15—Buddy Clare, New Lambton .... W 6
Oct. 24—Dick Bolton, St. Marys .... W 5

1976

Jan. 27—Dick Bolton, Kingsford .... W 6
Feb. 17—Dick Bolton, Brookvale .... W 8
Mar. 2—Dave Agnew, New Lambton .... W 8
Apr. 7—Cal Hickling, Cammeray .... W 8
May 18—Joey Collins, Brookvale .... W 8
July 13—Billy Mulholland, New Lambton ...... L 10
Sept. 7—Speedy Duke, Cardiff .... W 8
Sept. 13—Kerry Bell, Tweed Heads .... L 8
Nov. 2—Speedy Duke, Cardiff .... W 8
Nov. 24—Domenic Marano, Brookvale .... W 8

1977

Feb. 22—Big Jim West, Cardiff .... W 10
Apr. 7—Martin Beni, Port Moresby .... L 10
May 6—Ross Eadie, Wollongong .... KO by 3

1978

Feb. 7—Bob McQueenie, Kingsford .... KO 7
Apr. 3—Steve Ayerst, Cammeray .... W 8
July 4—Benny Tabua, Cardiff .... D 8
Aug. 29—Robert Hickling, Cardiff .... W 10

1979

Mar. 21—Benny Tabua, Blacktown .... W 10
May 30—Richie Roberts, Revesby .... W 10
July 11—Torkano Marcos, Kingsford .... KO 5
(Won New South Wales Middleweight Title)
Aug. 25—Sakarai Ve, Suva .... D 10

1980

Feb. 12—Billy Harrison, Cardiff .... KO 5
Mar. 9—Ross Eadie, Revesby .... KO by 8
Nov. 4—Chong-Pal Park, Seoul .... KO by 3
(For Orient & Pacific Middleweight Title)

STEVE DAVIES
British Welterweight

1980

Sept. 15—Kevin Johnson, Manchester .... W 4
Sept. 24—John Wiggins, Evesham .... W 6
Oct. 13—Kevin Dirkin, Manchester .... L 6
Oct. 20—Paul Murray, Birmingham .... D 6

TONY DAVIS
British Lightweight

1979

Oct. 1—Young John Daly, Marylebone .... L 4
Oct. 29—Tim Maloney, Hove .... L 4
Nov. 26—Terry Parkinson, Hammersmith .... L 6

1980

Feb. 18—Terry Parkinson, Birmingham .... W 6
Feb. 28—Neil Brown, London .... W 6
Mar. 17—Tim Maloney, London .... L 8
May 15—Philip Morris, London .... W 6
Sept. 15—Brian Lawrence, London .... KO 3
Sept. 22—Alan Cooper, Lewisham .... KO by 1

WINSTON DAVIS
British Middleweight

1979

Sept. 24—Emmanuel Lucas, Birmingham .... KO 2
Oct. 11—Paul Jones, Liverpool .... L 6
Oct. 22—Harry Watson, Nottingham .... W 8
Nov. 12—Harry Watson, Mayfair .... L 8

1980

Jan. 16—Earl Edwards, Solihull .... W 6
Jan. 21—Henry Cooper, Birmingham .... L 6
Feb. 13—Gordon George, Liverpool .... W 8
Mar. 10—Henry Cooper, Liverpool .... L 8
Apr. 9—Peter Bassey, Liverpool .... W 8
Apr. 22—Jimmy Harrington, Albert Hall ...... KO by 6
Sept. 9—Harry Watson, Mexcorough .... KO 7
Sept. 29—Joe Jackson, Bedworth .... KO by 2

AZZIZ DAWOOD
South African Bantamweight

1979

Sept. 29—Robert Makhoba, Durban .... KO by 2

1980

Mar. 1—Richard Mtobeni, Durban .... D 4
Apr. 4—Vicent Ngcobo, Durban .... D 4
July 4—Vicent Ngcobo, Durban .... D 4
Nov. 10—Paul Tshala, Durban .... L 4

STAR DAYANAN
Filipino Bantamweight
1978
Oct. 21—Eddie Miral, Pampanga ....D 10
1979
May 22—Eddie Miral, Angeles City ....D 10
June 26—Alex Bitong, Angeles City ....W 10
Sept. 22—Star Dan, Angeles City ....W 10
Oct. 30—Ali Jr., Angeles City ....KO 2
1980
Jan. 21—Eddie Miral, Clark Air Base ....L 10
Feb. 9—Jun Padinit, Santos City ....L 10
Feb. 27—Al Sicat, Clark Air Base ....TD 10
Apr. 14—Takashi Uezu, Tokyo ....L 10

JOE DEAN
British Light Heavyweight
1980
Apr. 21—Redmond Everard, Bradford ....KO 3
Apr. 28—Mike Burton, London ....L 6
May 28—Paul Heatley, London ....KO 4
June 16—Joe Frater, Manchester ....L 6
Sept. 10—Jerry Golden, Liverpool ....KO 3
Oct. 23—Brian Graham, Middlesbrough ....L 8

CORNELIUS ABRAHAM DE BEER
South African Middleweight
1977
Nov. 7—Pieter Gouws, Johannesburg ....W 4
1978
Mar. 4—Keith Bradford, Ermelo ....W 4
Apr. 3—Keith Bradford, Pretoria ....KO by 3
June 5—Jan Pienaar, Pretoria ....L 4
Sept. 23—Basil Meintjies, Johannesburg ....W 4
Oct. 10—Themba Buthelezi, Durban ....KO by 1
1979
(Inactive)
1980
Apr. 14—Ricky Abbott, Johannesburg ....W 4
May 25—Isaac Enslin, Johannesburg ....D 4

FRANKIE DE CAESSECKER
Belgian Junior Welterweight
1977
Sept. 30—Calogero Restivo, Ostenda ....W 6
Oct. 30—Kader Ben Mimoun, Duffel ....W 6
Dec. 2—Fernand Banckaert, Ostenda ....KO 4
Dec. 25—Richard Rodriguez, Izegem ....KO by 4
1978
Feb. 10—Tony Baletta, Ostend ....W 6
Apr. 14—Luigi Renda, S. Amand ....W 6
July 10—Colin Jones, Aberavon ....L 6
Sept. 2—Calogero Restivo, Izegem ....KO 4
Sept. 18—Franklin Manuela, Heerenveen ......KO by 2
Nov. 3—Fredo Roelands, Bruges ....KO 4
Dec. 25—Michel Luzolanu, Izegem ....W 8
1979
Jan. 19—Richard Rodriguez, Bruxelles ....L 8
Mar. 2—Dirck Declerck, Bruges ....W 8
July 14—Martin Bridge, Middelkerke ....W 8
Sept. 15—Djibali Bathily, Ostend ....D 8
Nov. 1—Bechir Boundtka, Izgem ....W 8
Dec. 21—Pean Claude Lafarge, Ostenda ....KO 7
1980
Feb. 2—Lee Hartshorn, Torhut ....W 8
Feb. 16—Antonio Casado, Middelkerke ....W 8
May 1—Luciano Navarra, Izegem ....W 8
May 23—Jean Pierre Moreau, Middelkerke ....KO 5
Nov. 29—Bonet, Middelkerke ....W 6

DIRCK DECLERCK
Belgian Junior Middleweight
1976
Jan. 3—Filippo Rocchi, Gits ....KO 4
Feb. 6—Rene Deharcies, Bruges ....KO by 4
Mar. 3—Jean Pierre Heirmann, Bavikhove ....W 6
May 8—Fred Cornansen, Izegem ....L 6
Oct. 1—Luigi Ruggierio, Lauwe ....WF 4
Oct. 8—Luigi Ruggiero, Lauwe ....W 4
Nov. 1—Michel Luzolanu, Izegem ....W 6
Nov. 20—Richard Rodriguez, Liege ....W 4
Dec. 25—Mike Copp, Izegem ....WF 4
1977
Jan. 15—Richard Rodriguez, Izegem ....D 6
Jan. 31—Frank Albertus, Amsterdam L
Mar. 5—Luigi Renda, Dunkirk ....KO by 5
Mar. 12—Manuel Acedo, Antwerp ....KO 3
Apr. 2—Guus Bleus, Ostenda L
Apr. 30—Giampaolo Piras, Lauwe ....W 8
Oct. 8—Jean Symos, Liege ....L 8
Nov. 1—Mickey Ryce, Izegem ....WF 8
Nov. 25—Franklin Manuela, Harelbeke ....KO 5
Dec. 25—Guus Bleus, Izegem ....W 6

1978
Jan. 11—Franklin Manuela, Rotterdam ....WF 5
Feb. 25—Jean Pierre Luzolanu, Osteanda .....KO by 8
Mar. 31—Casimir Kanynda, Grivegnee ....KO 5
Apr. 22—Eric Caposella, La Louviere ....D 8
May 20—Jean Pierre Luzolanu, Moelenbeeck ....D 8
Sept. 2—Stephane Vertpre, Izegem ....D 6
Sept. 30—Chaed Ringo, Turnhout ....KO by 5
Nov. 1—Steve Early, Izegem ....KO by 2
Dec. 25—Richard Rodriguez, Izegem ....L 8
1979
Mar. 2—Frankie De Caessecker, Bruges ....L 8
Apr. 6—Jean Luigieri, Bruxelles ....L 6
July 19—Jean Pierre Luzolanu, Kinshasa ....L 8
Oct. 13—Djibril Bathily, Antwerp ....L 8
Nov. 1—Fredo Roelands, Izegem ....KO 5
Dec. 25—Jean Pierre Moreau, Izegem ....KO 6
1980
Feb. 2—Chaed Ringo, Torhut ....KO by 6
Apr. 5—Paul Payen, La Louviere ....L 8
May 1—Corrado Cortino, Izegem ....L 6

SABATINO DE FILIPPO
Italian Flyweight
1972
Nov. 29—Frank Realinho, Genova ....KO 2
1973
Mar. 15—Filippo Belvedere, Milano ....LF 4
1974
Oct. 11—Paolo Mareddu, Milano ....KO 6
1975
(Inactive)
1976
Aug. 14—Sante Medici, Ospidaletti ....W 6
Oct. 22—Giovanni Camputaro, Milano ....W 6
Dec. 3—Claudio Tanda, Ozieri ....LF 10
1977
Mar. 7—Nassim Zebelini, Savona ....W 8
Apr. 8—Salvatore Laconi, Cagliari ....KO by 4
May 20—Filippo Belvedere, Savona ....W 8
Aug. 27—Claudio Tanda, Ozieri ....LF 10
Oct. 7—Tarcisio Boi, Savona ....KO 5
Feb. 11—Giovanni Camputero, Piedimonte ....L 12
(Italian Flyweight Title)
July 28—Altero Marini, Mondovi ....W 8
Sept. 12—Charlie Magri, London ....KO by 7
1979
Mar. 16—Nessim Zebelini, Savona ....W 8
June 22—Giovanni Camputaro, Savona ....W 12
(Italian Flyweight Title)
Nov. 16—Giovanni Camputaro, Piedimonte Matese KO by 6
(Italian Flyweight Title)
1980
Mar. 7—Giovanni Camputaro, Savona ....L 10
(For Italian Flyweight Title)

DAN DE GUZMAN
Filipino Welterweight
1979
July 20—Saensak Muangsurin, Manila ....W 10
Nov. 16—Lee Man Duk, Quezon City ....KO 6
(Won OPBF Welterweight Title)
1980
Jan. 25—Mana Premchai, Manila ....W 10
Feb. 29—Chung-Jae Hwang, Manila ....L 12
(Lost OPBF Welterweight Title)
June 27—Ramon Diosisio, Manila ....KO 4
Aug. 15—Kanichiro Takase, Quezon City ....KO 2
Sept. 26—Ching-Yul Lee, Quezon City ....W 10

MIKE DE GUZMAN
Filipino Welterweight
1979
Feb. 17—Rocky Anobling, Pampanga ....KO 6
Apr. 23—Fred Pastor, Tokyo ....W 10
Sept. 8—Erning Marin, Cotabato City ....W 10
Oct. 20—Felix Montanez, Pampanga ....KO 3
Dec. 30—Edito del Monte, Pampanga ....KO 6
1980
Feb. 17—Rocky Anobling, Manila ....KO 6
Mar. 21—Fred Pastor, Manila ....L 12
(Won Filipino Welterweight Title)
June 12—Rocky Anobling, Angeles City ....TD 10
Aug. 2—Erning Marin, Pampanga ....L 10
Sept. 30—Saensak Muangsurin, Nakhon Sawan KO by 5
Nov. 30—Rocky Anobling, Angeles City ....KO 2
(Retained Filipino Welterweight Title)

YOUNG DELA CRUZ
Filipino Lightweight
1980
June 20—Danny Soriano, Clark Air Base ....L 10
Aug. 30—Rocky Anobling, Angeles City ....KO 1

Nov. 21—Danilo Limpahan, Quezon City .... L 10

ROGER DELA ROSA
Filipino Bantamweight
1980
Jan. 12—Raffy Saulong, Santos City .... D 10
Mar. 21—Cesar Amazan, Manila .... KO by 7

LUIS DE LA SAGRA
Spanish Bantamweight
1978
Nov. 2—Valeriano Morales, Barcelona .... KO 2
Nov. 9—Jose Rodriguez Jeronimo, Barcelona .... KO 2
Nov. 23—Martin Antich, Barcelona .... W 6
1979
Mar. 2—Vicente Manzanares, Madrid .... D 6
Mar. 16—Jose Maria Gueros, Madrid .... KO 5
Apr. 6—Vicente Manzanares, Madrid .... W 6
Apr. 20—Mohamed Larbi, Madrid .... W 6
Apr. 28—Modesto Torito Gomez, Santander .... W 6
July 13—Francisco Moya, Madrid .... W 6
Aug. 3—Francisco Moya, Madrid .... W 6
Aug. 17—Basilio Roman, Madrid .... W 8
Sept. 8—Juan Francisco Rodriguez, Lepe .... D 8
Sept. 29—Francisco Garcia Herrera, Madrid .... W 6
Nov. 10—Francisco Kiko Garcia, Leganes .... W 6
1980
Mar. 22—Esteban Eguia, Santander .... L 12
(For Spanish Bantamweight Title)
Sept. 27—Modesto (Torito) Gomez, Santander ...... W 8
Oct. 7—Enrique Rodriguez Cal, Barcelona .... D 10
(For Spanish Flyweight Title)

ROBERT D'ELIA
Italian Junior Welterweight
1979
Dec. 15—Guiseppe Juppa, Rome .... D 6
1980
Oct. 31—Pellegrino Ventrone, Rome .... W 6
Dec. 4—Bruno Gumbala, Rome .... D 6

DOMINIQUE DELORME
French Junior Middleweight
1980
Feb. 1—Frederic Boissy, Paris .... L 6
Apr. 12—Sandro Jaconelli, Paris .... KO 1
Nov. 27—Jean Louis Coquin, Paris .... KO 3

ROD DE LOS SANTOS
Filipino Lightweight
1978
Nov. 25—Dario Melida, Misamis Oriental .... L 10
1979
Jan. 7—Al Espinosa, Cebu City .... W 10
Mar. 4—Tony Flores, Cebu City .... KO 9
June 3—Tony Flores, Cebu City .... KO by 7
Dec. 23—Al Espinosa, Cebu City .... W 10
1980
Feb. 23—Lito Pena, Angeles City .... L 10
Sept. 7—Willie Makitoki, De Oro City .... L 10
Dec. 13—Ric Dolotallas, Manila .... L disq. 10

GIOVANNI DE LUCA
Italian Heavyweight
1979
Feb. 2—Rinaldo Pelizzari, Milano .... W 12
(Italian Heavyweight Title)
Apr. 21—Vasco Faustino, Milano .... W 8
Aug. 3—Rinaldo Pelizzari, Tuscolano .... KO 9
(Italian Heavyweight Title)
Nov. 24—Vasco Faustino, Ascoli Piceno .... W 12
(Italian Heavyweight Title)
1980
May 18—Rinaldo Pelizzari, Naples .... W 12
(Won Italian Heavyweight Title)
Aug. 17—Domenico Adinolfi, Norcia .... L 12
(Lost Italian Heavyweight Title)

BRUNO DEMONTIS
Italian Lightweight
1977
Apr. 30—Giuseppe Pappalardo, Muoro .... KO 1
Aug. 14—Andrea Vittolazzi, Cagliari .... KO 5
1978
Apr. 29—Gabriele Peruzzi, Cagliari .... KO 2
May 24—Jofre II, Cagliari .... W 6
July 1—Antonio Germano, Cagliari .... KO 5
Aug. 5—Mario Ficano, Fort Village .... KO 6
Sept. 28—Vincenzo Di Ruocco, Milan .... KO 3
Nov. 20—Gerardo Scognamiglio, Milano .... WF 3
Dec. 23—Gregorio Ciancaglione, Sassari .... KO 5
1979
Feb. 10—Melquiades Da Silva, Cagliari .... KO 5

Apr. 7—Guiseppi Agato, Sassari .... W 8
Aug. 19—Gerardo Scognamiglio, Fort Village ..... KO 3
Sept. 30—Guiseppi Agato, Oristano .... W 8
Dec. 28—Carlo Frassinetti, Sassari .... W 8
1980
Mar. 28—Palmiro Masala, Cagliari .... KO 3

STEVE DENNIS
Australian Welterweight
1972
Apr. 20—Jim Sheridan, Redfern .... W 6
May 3—Bobby Dodds, Riverwood .... KO 2
1973
Dec. 5—Alex Burns, Riverwood .... KO 3
Dec. 19—Ricky Patterson, Marrickville .... KO 1
1974
Apr. 10—Ricky Patterson, Marrickville .... KO by 5
July 31—Maxie Milan, Kingsford .... KO 2
Aug. 7—Allan Hall, Kingsford .... KO 4
Sept. 25—Kevin Rose, Kingsford .... KO 1
Oct. 23—Paddy Green, Kingsford .... KO 8
Oct. 31—Les Knox, Blacktown .... KO 9
1975
Sept. 10—Ceddy McGrady, Marrickville .... W 8
Oct. 8—Dave Leon, Marrickville .... KO 5
Nov. 12—Ritchie Brown, Marrickville........... KO 6
Dec. 10—John Layton, Marrickville .... KO 7
1976
Jan. 24—Martin Beni, Panguana................. KO 8
Mar. 10—Dennis Enright, Marrickville .... KO 10
May 3—Kerry Bell, Tweed Heads .... KO 7
(Australian Welterweight Title)
1977
July 13—Colin Cassidy, Marrickville .... KO 8
Sept. 8—Ali Afakasi, Wellington .... KO by 8
(Australian Welterweight Title)
1978
Jan. 14—Sakaraia Ve, Suva .... KO by 10
Mar. 26—Eric King, Parkes .... KO 3
May 17—Eddie Buttons, Mount Pritchard .... L 10
May 26—Neil Pattel, Brisbane .... D 10
Sept. 26—Ross Eadie, Bankstown .... KO by 2
Dec. 7—Lou Hirst, Revesby .... W 8
1979
Feb. 9—Robert Colley, Brisbane .... W 10
Apr. 9—Neil Pattel, Brisbane .... KO 12
(Australian Welterweight Title)
June 16—Ceddy McGrady, Victoria Park .... W 8
Aug. 15—Eddie Buttons, Mt. Pritchard .... KO 9
(Australian Welterweight Title)
Dec. 13—Lachie Austin, Melbourne .... L 15
(Lost Australian Welterweight Title)
1980
Nov. 19—Ross Eadie, Mt. Pritchard .... W 10
Nov. 24—Hector Thompson, Brisbane .... KO 6

ARTURO DE PREZZO
Italian Featherweight
1978
Apr. 7—Leo Scorza, Milano .... L 6
July 7—Vincenzo Morana, Bassano .... KO 4
Dec. 12—Potito Di Muro, Piove di Sacco .... D 6
1979
Feb. 23—Giovanni Scarpati, Bolzano .... W 6
July 1—Vincenzo Morana, Merano .... KO 5
July 27—Lorenzo Paciullo, Bolzano .... W 8
Oct. 10—Potito Di Muro, Torino .... KO by 3

Apr. 19—Giancarlo Ravaioli, Ostia .... L 8

FRANCESCO DE ROSA
Italian Junior Lightweight
1979
Dec. 7—Fabrizio Saraullo, Chieti .... D 6
Dec. 28—Giovanni Pasca, Sassari .... L 6
1980
Mar. 15—Giuseppe Ballone, Alghero .... L 6
Apr. 19—Roberto Serreli, Cagliari .... L 4

LUIGI DE ROSA
Italian Lightweight
1976
Dec. 3—Giuseppe Pappalardo, Capua .... W 6
1977
May 14—Vincenzo Morana, Capua .... W 6
June 17—Franco Siddu, Milano .... KO by 5
Oct. 4—Gerardo Scognamiglio, Vitulazio .... WF 5
1978
Jan. 27—Salvatore Morello, Milano .... W 6
Mar. 3—Severino Picca, Piacenza .... KO by 5
May 26—Leo Scorza, Taranto .... L 6
Aug. 20—Antonio Franca, Roccamonfina .... W 8
Sept. 23—Domenico Traini, Pietramelara .... W 8

Oct. 27—Mario Ficano, Capua .... W 8
Nov. 18—Giovanni Mannu, Sassari .... KO 4
Dec. 22—Leo Scorza, Capua .... W 8
1979
Feb. 23—Guiseppe Agate, Capua .... W 8
Apr. 24—Leo Scorza, Pesaro .... L 6
July 14—Domenico Traini, Fabriano .... NC 8
1980
Apr. 5—Cosimo Lavino, Rimini .... D 8
May 30—Potito De Muro, Capua .... W 8
Oct. 31—Natale Carreda, Capua .... W 8

COLIN DERRICK
British Welterweight
1980
Jan. 22—Mike Clemow, London .... W 4
Feb. 19—Chris Christian, London .... L 6

ROBERT DESNOUCK
Belgian Heavyweight
1977
Sept. 9—Laurent Zardi, Izegem .... L 6
Sept. 30—Mohamed Galoul, Lauwe .... D 6
Oct. 15—Lassine Naire, Molenbeek .... W 6
Nov. 1—Fausto Costantino,Izegem .... L 6
Dec. 25—Reinhard Seydock, Izegem .... KO 2
1978
Jan. 7—Laurent Zardy, Barentin .... L 6
Feb. 11—Mohammed Galoul, Liegi .... W 6
Feb. 27—Vincent Kafoa, Paris .... KO 6
June 7—Daniel Laghi, Faenza .... L 6
Sept. 2—Jacques Martin, Izegem .... KO 2
Sept. 30—Bernard Artone, Turnhout .... KO 3
Nov. 1—Gordon Ferris, Izegem .... W 6
Dec. 26—Laurent Zardy, Izegem .... D 8
1979
Apr. 7—Terry O'Connor, Bruxelles .... L 8
Oct. 12—Albert Syben, Antwerp .... L 12
Dec. 15—Uwe Meinecke, Izegem .... W 6
1980
Feb. 2—Hendrik Seys, Torhout .... L 8
Apr. 18—Hendrik Seys, Llauwe .... L 12
(For Vacant Belgian Heavyweight Title)
July 27—Bernard Antone, Bruxelles .... KO 2
Sept. 1—Rudi Lubbers, Rotterdam .... L 10
Dec. 15—Michel Caron, Izegem .... W 8

ELOY DE SOUZA
Italian Lightweight
1977
May 5—Palmiro Masala, Civitanova Marcne ...... W 6
May 20—Palmiro Masala, Milano .... L 8
May 28—Rolf Kersten, Koln .... KO 6
June 2—Henry Palm, Randers .... L 6
June 25—Vincenzo Quero, Taranto .... L 6
Aug. 7—Sergio Emili, Macerata .... KO by 6
Sept. 16—Sergio Emili, Civitanova .... L 8
Oct. 14—Elio Cotena, Milan .... L 8
Oct. 28—Biagio Pierri, Milano .... L 8
Nov. 26—Angelo Provenzano, Genova .... L 8
Dec. 10—Pellegrino Ventrone, Maddaloni .... L 8
Dec. 26—Angelo Provenzano, Rimini .... L 6
1978
Jan. 7—Giuseppe Russi, Milan .... L 8
Jan. 27—Lucio Cusma, Faenza .... L 6
Feb. 18—Andre Holyk, Lyon .... L 10
Mar. 31—Angelo Fanciulli, Florence .... W 8
Apr. 15—Charles Jurietti, Valence .... L 10
Apr. 27—Lucio Cusma, Bologna .... D 8
May 31—Angelo Provenzano, Pescara .... L 8
June 2—Angelo Provenzano, Pescara .... L 6
June 15—Svein Paulsen, Oslo .... L 8
July 8—Sal Liscapade, Ostia .... L 8
Aug. 5—Abass Macauley, Ascoli Piceno .... W 8
Sept. 14—Angelo Fanciulli, Prato .... D 8
Oct. 27—Vicenzo Burgio, Florence .... L 8
1979
Feb. 4—Giancarlo Usai, Rimini .... L 8
Feb. 17—Christiaj Garcia, Agen .... L 8
Mar. 23—Robert Gambini, Marseilles .... KO by 10
Sept. 6—Ken Buchanan, Randers .... L 8
Oct. 7—Giovanni Carrino, Taranto .... L 8
Oct. 27—Eupremio Epifani, Pessary .... W 6
Nov. 9—Francesco Marcello, Torino .... L 8
Dec. 21—Giancarlo Usai, Savona .... L 10
1980
Jan. 4—Jean Marie Cotinaut, Carpi .... L 8
Mar. 28—Pellegino Ventrone, Monza .... L 8
Apr. 24—Marino Angeli, Forli .... D 8

WILLIAM DEVELOS
Filipino Bantamweight
1979
Jan. 12—Allan Jardemil, Manila .... W 10

Apr. 27—Diony Diaz, Manila .... W 10
May 26—Frank Cedeno, Quezon .... W 10
Oct. 19—Arnel Arrozal, Quezon City .... KO by 6
(Vacant Philippine Flyweight Title)
Dec. 7—Charngcheng Borkorser, Manila ...... KO 6
1980
Feb. 15—Little Aguilar, Manila .... KO by 1
June 6—Takenao Nakajima, Manila .... W 10
July 4—Jimmy Boy, Manila .... KO 7
Oct. 15—Yung-Sik Kim, Quezon City .... W 12
(Won OPBF Junior Bantamweight Title)
Dec. 20—Alibaba Looklongton, Manila .... KO 4
(Retained OPBF Junior Bantamweight Title)

DIEGO DE VILLA
Filipino Flyweight
1979
Jan. 14—Siony Carupo, Davao City .... D 10
Feb. 3—Ric Barimbad, Davao del Norte .... W 10
Mar. 31—Andy Balara, Davao City .... W 10
Apr. 20—Flash Jagdon, Manila .... D 10
Aug. 25—Danilo Inocian, Davao City .... D 10
Oct. 6—Jocie Cels, Davao City .... W 10
Dec. 1—Rudy Garcia, Davao City .... W 10
1980
Feb. 16—Al Sicat, Davao City .... W 12
(Won Vacant Junior Bantamweight Title)
May 17—Hak-Yung Kim, Davao City .... W 10
Aug. 9—Ric Diamale, Davao City .... L 10
Aug. 25—Flash Jagdon, De Oro City .... L 10
Dec. 29—Dede Suaybaguio, Butuan City ...... KO by 5

CHRIS DEVINE
British Heavyweight
1979
May 16—Peter Lythgoe, Sheffield .... KO 1
May 21—Bob Bleau, Bradford .... KO 1
Sept. 26—Stan Carnall, Sheffield .... W 6
Dec. 10—Glen Adair, Torquay .... L 8
1980
Sept. 29—Paul Newman, Chesterfield .... W 6

DEXTER DHLAMINI
South African Flyweight
1976
Apr. 2—Shadrack Mogupudi, Orlando West ...... W 4
Nov. 6—Philemon Mphomelo, Parys .... KO by 2
Nov. 20—Jama Qualinga, Bloemfontein .... W 4
Aug. 21—Benjamin Sebego, Kroonstad .... KO by 5
1977
Oct. 29—Charles McGeer, Johannesburg .... D 4
Dec. 3—Charles McGeer, Johannesburg .... W 4
1978
Apr. 15—Daluxolu Tyekana, Butterworth .... L 8
May 27—Monde Mpulampula, East London .... D 8
Sept. 30—Elliot Zonde, East London .... W 12
1979
Aug. 4—Monde Mpulampula, East London ...... L 6
Sept. 7—Freddie Masemola, Springs .... KO by 4
Dec. 3—Godfrey Nkate, Welkom .... KO by 5
(South African Junior Flyweight Title)
1980
Mar. 1—Cosmo Ziqu, East London .... D 6
Mar. 28—Norman Hlalele, Springs .... KO 5
Apr. 25—Johannes Miya, Sebokeng .... L 6
Nov. 21—Edison Ramagole, Sebokeng .... W 4

ESSAU DHLAMINI
South African Featherweight
1980
Apr. 14—Alex Sibiya, Durban .... KO by 9
(For Vacant Featherweight Title)
Oct. 6—Anton Dlamini, Pietermaritzburg ...... KO 4

MESHACK DHLAMINI
South African Flyweight
1980
Sept. 6—Lloyd Segapane, Welkom .... L 4
Sept. 13—Joseph Mokomatsili, Welkom .... L 6
Sept. 27—Godfrey Nkate, Welkom .... L 6
Oct. 11—Jophta Bohope, Odendaalsrust .... L 4
Dec. 1—Godfrey Nkate, Virginia .... L 4

RIC DIAMALE
Filipino Junior Featherweight
1979
Feb. 24—Gony Albar, Santos City .... KO 6
Mar. 17—Billy Abato, Davao City .... W 12
Apr. 21—Ric Quijano, Santos City .... KO 10
May 18—Ador Seguin, Manila .... W 12
June 16—Chito Adigue, Davao City .... W 10
July 15—Derule Oulis, Manila .... KO 11
Aug. 10—Neptali Alamag, Manila .... W 12

Oct.　26—Rudy Patalihug, Manila .... W 12
Dec.　15—Ronald Sumalis, Davao City .... L 10
1980
Mar.　1—Rey Naduma Jr., Davao City .... W 12
May　23—Ador Seguin, Manila .... W 12
(Retained Filipino Junior Featherweight Title)
Aug.　9—Diego de Villa, Davao City .... W 10
Aug.　29—Sandy Noora, Quezon City .... W 10
Oct.　29—Rey Naduma Jr., Manila .... KO by 9
(Lost Filipino Junior Featherweight Title)

ROCKY DIAMOND
Rhodesian Light Heavyweight
1980
Feb.　1—Ishmael Menemene, Salisbury .... KO by 7
Mar.　28—Black Tiger, Bulawayo .... L 4

DIONY DIAZ
Filipino Flyweight
1979
Apr.　27—William Develos, Manila .... L 10
1980
Feb.　8—Manny Sacey, Manila .... D 10
June　21—Cesar Kid Navarosa, Camarines Norte KO by 7
Nov.　14—Elmer Valenzuela, Panaraque .... D 10

VINCENZO DI BARI
Italian Lightweight
1977
May　29—Leo Scorza, Taurisano .... D 6
July　6—Silvio Mauro, Vieste .... W 6
Oct.　14—Cosimo Lavino, Milano .... L 6
Dec.　14—Michele De Mita, Taurisano .... W 6
1978
Mar.　3—Potito Di Muro, Torino .... D 6
Mar.　16—Darko Covic, Tripoli .... D 8
Apr.　22—Stefan Kobli, Graz .... D 6
May　12—Antonio Pisani, Imola .... D 6
Sept.　2—Vincenzo Di Ruocco, Teramo .... W 6
Nov.　4—Pietro Donati, Sassari .... L 6
Nov.　17—Michele De Mita, Milano .... W 4
Nov.　17—Potito Di Muro, Milano .... L 4
(Italian Tourney, 2 fights same night)
1979
Dec.　9—Giancarlo Ravaioli, Isernia .... L 6
July　11—Salvatore Fabrizio, Rimini .... L 8
Sept.　22—Luciano Frasca, Nettuno .... L 6
1980
Mar.　29—Andrea Ricci, Bitonto .... D 8
Apr.　18—Roberto Masini, Bologna .... L 6
May　3—Giuseppe Tiddu, Cagliari .... L 6

LUCIANO DI GIACOMO
Italian Middleweight
1978
Jan.　9—Luciano Spina, Penne .... W 6
Apr.　7—Lorenzo Nardillo, Senigalia .... D 6
May　5—Roberto Manoni, Milano .... L 6
Oct.　13—Georges Lemmer, Metz .... D 6
Nov.　24—Ray Opoku, Penne .... W 6
1979
June　29—Roberto Manoni, Sondrio .... L 6
July　25—Cosimo Funto, Rimini .... L 6
Dec.　22—Antonio Cresenza, Cisterna .... W 8
1980
Mar.　22—Luciano Bomben, Pordenone .... L 6

POTITO DI MURO
Italian Junior Lightweight
1977
May　20—Lorenzo Paciullo, Piacenza .... L 6
June　25—Gianfranco Lalli, Sondrio .... L 6
1978
Mar.　3—Vincenzo Di Bari, Torino .... D 6
May　11—Andrea Ricci, Caloiziocorte .... W 6
June　9—Andrea Ricci, Milano .... KO 2
July　12—Marco Gallo, Pistoia .... KO 7
Sept.　3—John B. Muwanga, Bergen .... L 6
Nov.　17—Pietro Donati, Milan .... KO 3
Nov.　17—Vincenzo Di Bari, Milan .... W 4
(Italian Tourney, 2 fights same night)
Dec.　26—Arturo De Prezzo, Piove di Sacco .... D 6
1979
Jan.　12—Antonio Franca, Milano .... W 8
Mar.　10—Patrick Goblet, Troyes .... D 8
Mar.　24—Francis Bailleul, Calais .... D 8
Apr.　6—Giovanni Scarpati, Barletta .... W 6
Sept.　5—Natale Caredda, Fort Village .... W 12
(Italian Featherweight Title)
Sept.　30—Melquiades Da Silva, Oristane .... W 8
Oct.　10—Arturo De Prezzo, Torino .... KO 3
Nov.　9—Melquiades Da Silva, Torino .... W 8

Dec.　26—Alfredo Mulas, Lugo di Romagna ....KO by 9
(Italian Featherweight Title)
1980
May　30—Luigi De Rosa, Capua .... L 8
Oct.　24—Helena Fererra, Basale .... D 10

RAMON DIONISIO
Filipino Junior Middleweight
1979
Mar.　10—Dan De Guzman, Manila .... KO by 4
Apr.　21—Dommy Cotacte, Remblon .... KO 7
Dec.　14—Aquilini Nicolas, Jr., Manila .... KO by 4
(Philippine Junior Middleweight Title)
1980
Feb.　23—Tadashi Mihara, Tokushima .... KO by 7
(For OPBF Junior Middleweight Title)
June　27—Dan de Guzman, Manila .... KO by 4

GIUSEPPE DI PADOVA
Italian Welterweight
1977
Feb.　18—Angelo Zanetti, Mantova .... KO 3
Apr.　22—Carmine Zollo, Mantova .... W 6
May　27—Augusto Lauri, Brescia .... D 6
June　11—Augusto Lauri, Mantova .... W 6
Aug.　9—Angelo Tomasini, Tuscolano .... W 6
1978
Feb.　25—Giovanni Mairorano, Mantova .... W 8
Mar.　20—Jose Ribeiro, Mantova .... W 8
June　9—Angelo Tomasini, Brescia .... W 8
Oct.　13—Vincenzo Bottigliero, Mantova .... KO 3
Nov.　24—Boro Jovic, Mantova .... KO 2
Dec.　26—Giuseppe Russi, Mantova .... KO 3
1979
Apr.　25—Vittorio Conte, Mantova .... WF 3
July　26—Giuseppi Corbo, Mantova .... W 8
Nov.　9—Jean Claude Lafarge, Marmirolo .... KO 4
1980
Apr.　25—Esperno Postl, Mantova .... KO 7
May　28—Giancarlo Barabotti, Mantova .... KO 7
Dec.　4—Jorgen Hansen, Randers .... L 12
(For European Welterweight Title)

ELIJAH DIPHAGWE
South African Flyweight
1980
July　5—Jacob Tauto, Kimberley .... KO 3
Aug.　23—Simon Mafere, Kimberley .... W 6

HUGO DI PIETRO
Italian Welterweight
1980
Apr.　25—Vincenzo Bottigliero, Cisterna .... W 6
June　20—Franco Aresti, Cagliari .... L 8

ELIAS DIRADITSILE
South African Lightweight
1976
June　5—Solomon Mthalane, Pietermaritzburg .....W 6
Dec.　4—Petrose Molefe, Welkom .... KO 3
1977
Mar.　19—Daniel Mokhema, Kroonstad .... KO 1
Apr.　30—Samuel Nhlapo, Kroonstad .... L 6
May　21—Paulus Twala, Kroonstad .... L 6
June　11—Elias Mphatsoe, Kroonstad .... KO 4
Oct.　8—Paulus Twala, Kroonstad .... W 8
Nov.　18—Michael Zim, Bloemfontein .... KO 3
1978
June　3—Joseph Tsotetsi, Bloemfontein .... L 8
1979
Mar.　9—Norman Sekgapane, Springs .... L 8
July　9—Peet Bothma, Welkom .... L 6
May　10—Jacob Motseki, Virginia .... KO 3
(Retained OFS Lightweight Title)
Sept.　27—Jacob Motseki, Welkom .... W 10
(Retained OFS Lightweight Title)
Dec.　19—Aladin Stevens, Welkom .... L 6

JACOB DIRADITSILE
South African Junior Featherweight
1973
May　5—Mathews Mokotsi, O.F.S. .... KO by 2
1974
Apr.　6—Sebego B., Welkom .... KO 4
Sept.　14—Jama Qalinga, Welkom .... KO 4
1975
(Inactive)
1976
Mar.　6—Paulus Twala, Kroonstad .... KO by 5
May　15—Samuel Nhlappo, Kroonstad .... KO 1
July　3—Mathews Shezi, Parys .... KO 2

Sept. 11—Samuel Nhlappo, Kroonstad .... W 10
(OFS Bantamweight Title)
Oct. 9—Spider Moeketsi, Kroonstad .... KO 4
Nov. 6—Daniel Mokhema, Parys .... W 6
Nov. 20—Richard Modise, Bloemfontein .... KO 3
1977
Apr. 30—Elias Mphatsoe, Kroonstad .... KO 6
May 21—Edwin Mokotso, Kroonstad .... KO 2
June 11—Spider Moeketsi, Kroonstad .... KO 4
Nov. 5—Lazarus Mofokeng, Viljoenskroon .... W 8
Nov. 18—Samuel Nhlapo, Bloemfontein .... W 10
1978
June 2—Jama Qalinga Bloemfontein .... KO 7
Dec. 4—Jacob Moyeye, Bloemfontein .... W 10
1979
Mar. 9—Gaybon Yekiso, Springs .... L 6
Mar. 30—Pieter Swanepool, Bloemfontein ...... KO 2
July 9—Jacob Moyeye, Welkom .... KO by 9
Sept. 3—Cecil Baatjies, Welkom .... KO 2
Dec. 14—Bashew Sibaca, Welkom .... L disq. 5
1980
May 24—Nkosnathi Silolo, Welkom .... KO 3
July 19—Welile Nkosinkulu, East London ..... KO by 2
Aug. 2—Israel Khonkhobe, Welkom .... W 10
(Retained OFS Junior Featherweight Title)
Dec. 6—Lazarus Mofokeng, Welkom .... L disq. 4

JOSEPH DIRADITSILE
South African Bantamweight
1978
June 3—Jacob Mokoneyane, Bloemfontein .... W 4
Sept. 2—Leslie Pikoli, Port Elizabeth .... L 12
1979
Feb. 5—Pieter Swanepool, Welkom .... KO by 1
Mar. 30—Abraham Safothelo, Bloemfontein ...... KO 3
1980
Apr. 12—Caiphus Khuto, Ficksburg .... L 6
July 19—Lucas Ncetezo, East London .... W 4
Aug. 2—Samuel Serekego, Welkom .... W 4
Sept. 6—David Majoe, Welkom .... KO 5
Oct. 4—Joshua Mahlangu, Welkom .... W 6

VINCENZO DI RUOCCO
Italian Lightweight
1972
Sept. 15—Graziotto Soro, Nettuno .... D 6
Dec. 8—Almo Quaini, Pavia .... L 6
1973
Jan. 25—Franco Diana, Milano .... KO by 5
June 2—Almo Quaina, Como .... L 6
July 13—Alessandro Bini, Nettuno .... KO by 3
1974
Feb. 8—Dante Guarnieri, Milano .... L 6
Mar. 9—Biagio Pierri, Cinisello .... KO by 2
May 17—Giuliano Lonzi, Livorno .... L 6
June 12—Salvatore Canu, Porto Torres .... KO 3
Oct. 4—Salvatore Liscapade, Rome .... KO by 3
1975
Jan. 31—Salvatore Avella, Campi Bisenzio ... KO by 6
1976
May 14—Guglielmo Cese, Rieti .... KO 3
July 23—Domenico Condello, Nettuno .... L 6
Oct. 8—Vincenzo Morano, Milano .... KO 1
Nov. 26—Nunziato Sanna, Milano .... KO by 1
1977
Feb. 2—Marc Ackerman, Ginerva .... KO by 6
Mar. 11—Giovanni Vitillo, Cascina .... KO by 3
Mar. 25—Cosimo Lavino, Brindisi .... KO by 6
Apr. 10—Vincenzo Morano, Mazara .... L 6
May 20—Andrea Vitolazzi, Rome .... L 6
June 12—Bernardo Ciaramella, Meleto .... KO by 3
Dec. 16—Franco Siddu, Firenze .... KO by 4
1978
Jan. 27—Pellegrino Ventrone, Rome .... KO by 3
Sept. 2—Vincenzo Di Bari, Teramo .... L 6
Sept. 29—Bruno De Montis, Milano .... KO by 2
1979
July 27—Antonio Antino, Bolzano .... L 6
Oct. 6—Francisco Pestorino, Aversa .... L 6
Nov. 26—Michele D'Amato, Ascoli .... D 6
Dec. 21—Alfredo Reininger, Savona .... L 6
1980
Oct. 24—Alessandro Scapecchi, Grosseto ..... KO by 2

ROSARIO DI TOMMASO
Italian Lightweight
1972
Aug. 12—Santino Reali, Priverno .... W 6
Nov. 18—Giovanni Lamusta, Latina .... D 6
1973
Jan. 10—Vincenzo Labella, Enna .... D 6
July 7—Italo Duranti, Terracina .... L 6

1974
Mar. 9—Enzo Saltarelli, Sabaudia .... D 6
Apr. P9—Enzo Saltarelli, Latina .... W 6
May 4—Giampiero Mereu, S. Nicola .... KO by 3
Sept. 16—Rocco Zecca, Foligno .... NC 2
Oct. 18—Olivero Pierleoni, Pesaro .... L 6
Dec. 20—Rocco Frasca, Milano .... KO by 3
1975
(Inactive)
1976
Mar. 26—Giuseppe Opedisano, Latina .... W 6
1977
Feb. 19—Mario Di Camillo, S. Felice Circeo .... L 6
Mar. 26—Giuseppe Corbo, Piedimonte .... L 6
Oct. 9—Giampiero Bertuzzi, Terracina .... W 6
1978
Jan. 14—Darko Covic, Latina .... W 6
Jan. 28—Gabriele Peruzzi, Veroli .... W 6
May 5—Vincenzo Castiello, Latina .... KO by 1
1979
Apr. 14—Darko Covic, Terracina .... W 6
July 28—Alfonso Carillo, Ro Ferrarese .... KO 7
1980
Apr. 30—Abass Macauley, Nepi .... D 6
Oct. 18—Patrizio Burini, Torino .... KO by 1

ANTHONY DLAMINI
South African Featherweight
1980
Apr. 28—Alfred Mapumulo, Durban .... W 4
Aug. 4—Alex Sibiya, Durban .... W 4
Oct. 6—Essau Dhlamini, Pietermaritzburg ... KO by 3
Dec. 1—Norman Bromfield, Durban .... L 4

JOHN DLAMINI
South African Middleweight
1980
Feb. 4—Solomon Khumalo, Durban .... KO by 2
July 2—Piet Crous, Durban .... KO by 1
Oct. 6—Joseph Thabethe, Pietermaritzburg ...... W 4

RIC DOLOTALLAS
Filipino Lightweight
(Previous Record Unavailable)
1978
Sept. 29—Nick Caputol, Cag. De Oro City .... W 10
Oct. 22—Roldan Jumuad, Zamboanga De Sur ..... W 10
Nov. 25—Rombo Sajonia, Misamis Oriental .... W 10
1979
Jan. 31—Romeo Sajondia, Agusan Del Morte ...... W 10
Mar. 31—Ding Villafuerte, Misamis .... KO 12
May 27—Roly Pugahan, Butuan City .... KO 4
1980
Feb. 16—Nardito Adrayan, De Oro City .... W 10
Mar. 1—Dario Melida, De Oro City .... KO 7
May 19—Rod de los Santos, Butuan City .... L 10
June 21—Gar Atayde, Santos City .... W 10
Dec. 13—Rod de los Santos, Manila .... W disq. 10

JOSE MANUEL DOMINGO
Spanish Welterweight
1973
July 13—Jose R. Alvarez, Madrid .... L 6
Aug. 10—Santiago Cebollada, Madrid .... D 6
Nov. 2—Francisco Gomez, Barcelona .... W 6
1974
Nov. 15—Manuel Velazquez, Las Palmas .... L 8
Nov. 29—Jesus Rodriguez, S. Cruz .... KO by 2
1975
Nov. 1—Tekyla Rodri, Iran .... L 6
Dec. 20—Josines, Santander .... L 6
1976
Jan. 24—Jose Diaz Carlo, Zaragoza .... L 8
Feb. 27—Juan Lopez Chamorro, Madrid .... L 8
Mar. 12—Raul Anon, Barcelona .... L 8
1977
Mar. 5—Antonio Leon, Jerez .... L 8
Mar. 26—Antonio M. Jurado, Huelva .... W 6
Apr. 16—Jose L. Barrilado, Almeria .... L 6
Dec. 9—Antonio Reinoso, Vallecas .... L 6
1978
Feb. 2—Jose Luis Fernandez, Leon .... L 6
1979
Mar. 30—Fernando Bermejo, Madrid .... W 6
Apr. 26—Cristobal Crespi, Las Palmas .... L 4
May 11—Manuel Hatero, Barcelona .... L 4
July 14—Enrico P. Tobio, Pontedera .... W 6
July 22—Juan Sierra, Logrono .... L 6
Aug. 2—Cristobal Crespi, Mallorca .... L 6
Oct. 10—Jesus Duran Sanchez, Pontevedra .... L 6
Oct. 19—Manuel Acedo, Madrid .... D 6
Dec. 1—Jose Luis Fernandez, Leon .... L 8

1980
Mar.   7—Antonio Casado, Barcelona L   8

PIETRO DONATI
Italian Featherweight
1978
Nov.   4—Vincenzo Di Bari, Sassari .... W   6
Nov.   17—Potito Di Muro, Milano .... KO by   3
Dec.   22—Vincenzo Morana, Ozieri .... W   6
1979
May   25—Fabio Mannai, Cagliari .... W   6
June   23—Fabio Mannai, Sassari .... W   6
Aug.   2—Luciano Frasca, Nettuno L   6
Nov.   10—Giorgio Pipia, Odolo L   6
1980
Mar.   28—Renzo Mannai, Cagliari .... LF   4

ANDREA DORE
Italian Flyweight
1979
Dec.   28—Antonio Galletta, Sassari .... WF   4
1980
Apr.   11—Salvatore Laconi, Sassari .... KO   1
May   31—Antonio Franca, Sassari .... KO by   4

FRANZ DORFER
Austrian Middleweight
1977
Mar.   22—Mehmet Besli, Vienna .... D   4
May   17—Klaus Hein, Vienna .... KO   4
Aug.   6—Lutz Walter, Berlin .... KO   2
Sept.   8—Gregory Marshall, Vienna .... W   4
Oct.   1—Antonio Rimasti, Vienna .... KO   2
Nov.   18—Mehmet Besli, Vienna .... D   8
Dec.   16—Horst Brinkmeyer, Vienna .... KO   1
1978
Apr.   22—Tomaso Marocco, Graz .... KO   2
Aug.   18—Branko Barakovic, Villach .... KO   4
Sept.   2—Agamali Yildirim, Berlin L   6
Dec.   2—Jacky Bauer, Dornbirn .... KO   6
1979
Mar.   17—Oscar Angus, Banja Luka L   8
Apr.   17—Sonny Kamunga, Belgrade .... KO by   4
July   13—Fritz Krenslehner, Greinsfurth .... KO   1
1980
June   13—Frank Wissenbach, Lubeck L   8

CHARLES DOUGLAS
British Welterweight
1980
Aug.   31—Kevin Dirkin, Glasgow .... KO by   4
Oct.   8—Kevin Johnson, Stocks .... D   6
Oct.   30—Ronnie Rathbone, Liverpool .... KO by   2

DAVE DOUGLAS
Scottish Welterweight
1978
Oct.   18—Chris Sanigar, Glasgow .... KO by   5
Nov.   13—Tony Bogle, Glasgow .... W   6
1979
Feb.   26—Pat Smythe, Glasgow .... W   6
Mar.   20—Gerry Maguire, Glasgow .... W   6
Apr.   23—Gerry Maguire, Glasgow .... KO   3
May   13—Peter Snowsall, Glasgow .... KO   4
Sept.   3—Derek Young Nelson, Glasgow L   8
Sept. 26—Dave Allen, Sheffield L   8
Oct.   29—Chris Christian, Birmingham .... D   6
Nov.   5—Jimmy Smith, London .... W   6
Dec.   6—Liam Linnen, Glasgow .... W   6
1980
Jan.   21—Chris Christian, Birmingham L   6
Feb.   18—Jeff Aspell, Birmingham .... W   6
Apr.   14—Tommy Wright, Motherwell .... W   6
Apr.   28—Neil Fannon, Birmingham .... D   6
June   2—Liam Linnen, Glasgow .... KO   9
(Won Vacant Scottish Welterweight Title)
Sept. 22—Gerry Young, Belfast .... KO by   3
Oct.   23—Dill Collins, London .... W   8
Oct.   30—Tony Sinnot, Liverpool L   8

EUGENE DOVIN
French Junior Middleweight
1979
June   8—Maurice Renaud, Salon .... W   6
Oct.   6—Daniel Hywon, Salon de Provence .... KO   4
1980
Mar.   8—Christian Chesini, Nice .... NC
Mar.   14—Stephane Ferrera, Limoges L   6
May   3—Pierre Frank Winsterstein, Paris .... KO by   1

PATRICK DRELON
French Lightweight
1978
Jan.   28—Jean Yves Julian, Waziers L   6
Feb.   3—Jean Pierre Del Torre, Avion .... W   6
Apr.   8—Francis Bailleul, Calais L   6
Oct.   30—Jacky Andre, Paris .... KO   5
Nov.   24—Angelo Licata, Liegi .... D   6
1979
Feb.   24—Robert Van Rompaey, Beaumont .... W   6
Apr.   21—Jean Yves Julien, Denain .... W   8
Apr.   30—Anthoine M. Muita, Fouquires .... W   6
May   12—Patrick Goblet, Troyes .... D   8
May   23—Djamel Ben Meziane, Epinay L   6
Nov.   15—Maurice Fico, Paris .... KO by   3
Nov.   24—Gilbert Helluin, Zix le Chateau .... D   8
Dec.   21—Raphael Blanco, Ostenda .... W   6
1980
Feb.   16—Andre Blanco, Middelkerke .... D   6
Apr.   5—Dave Williams, Zele .... KO by   3
May   30—Bruno Simili, Florence .... KO by   2
Dec.   20—Jamel Benmeziane, Chateau Neuf .... W   6

PHIL DUCKWORTH
British Welterweight
1980
May   19—Alex Gregal, Bradford .... W   4
June   2—Dave Sullivan, Plymouth .... KO   3

JOHNNY DUFFY
Australian Bantamweight
1979
Feb.   16—Billy Connelly, Walla Walla L   6
Mar.   1—Sparrow Freeman, Jindera .... W   8
Mar.   30—Paul Hansen, Jerilerie .... D   8
July   26—Greg Grogan, Springvale .... KO by   4
Nov.   23—Jeff Charles, Jerildene .... D   4
1980
Mar.   7—Mario Rizzeri, Dederang .... W   8
Apr.   20—Doc Rutton, Jindera L   6
June   1—Tony Noone, Walla Walla .... D   4
July   29—Jeff Perkins, Kingsford L   6
Oct.   31—Des Pearce, Parafield L   8

SPEEDY DUKE
Australian Junior Welterweight
1971
Jan.   27—Sam Bolt, Cammeray .... KO   3
Feb.   8—Matt Davis, Marrickville .... W   4
Mar.   18—Sam Testa, Redfern .... W   4
Mar.   24—Sam Testa, Cammeray L   4
Apr.   7—Tommy Roberts, Cammeray .... W   4
Apr.   22—Matt Davis, Redfern .... W   4
May   6—Ceddy McGrady, Redfern .... W   4
June   3—Steve Campbell, Redfern .... W   3
June   10—Matt Quinlivan, Redfern .... D   4
June   22—Billy Bungie, Kurri Kurri .... KO   2
June   24—Joe Thompson, Penrith .... W   4
July   13—Dennis Bell, New Lambton .... W   4
July   29—Sam Testa, Redfern .... W   4
Aug.   12—Sonny Bell, Redfern L   6
Aug.   26—Ceddy McGrady, Redfern .... W   6
1972-1973
(Inactive)
1974
Apr.   16—Reg Church, New Lambton .... KO by   4
May   14—Eric King, New Lambton .... D   6
July   31—Joey Collins, Kingsford .... W   5
Aug.   7—Seamus McGahon, Cammeray .... KO by   4
Oct.   2—Jade Emerald, Kingsford L   8
Oct.   16—Ross Eadie, Kingsford .... W   8
Oct.   22—Kim McCain, New Lambton .... W   6
Dec.   10—Ross Eadie, Cardiff .... W   6
1975
Feb.   5—Eddie Buttons, Kingsford L   5
Feb.   28—Alby Roberts, Brisbane .... W   6
Mar.   14—Kerry Bell, Brisbane L   6
May   7—Doug Pitt, Cammeray .... W   6
May   19—Kerry Bell, Brisbane .... KO by   5
Aug.   7—Robert Hinkling, Brisbane .... W   6
Oct.   1—Mario Martinelli, Cammeray .... KO   5
Oct.   23—Joey Gibilisco, Melbourne .... KO by   6
Nov.   5—Jimmy Greco, Cammeray L   6
Dec.   15—Robert Hinkling, Tweed Heads .... W   8
1976
Feb.   4—Jimmy Greco, Cammeray .... L 10
Feb.   23—Kevin Gibb, Tweed Heads .... L 10
Mar.   15—Kerry Bell, Tweed Heads L   8
May   4—Joey Collins, Cardiff .... W   6
July   26—Robert Hinkling, TGweed Heads .... W   4
Sept.   7—Phil Davies, Cardiff L   8
Sept. 13—Dawsie Kelly, Tweed Heads .... W   6
Oct.   8—Reno James, Tweed Heads .... KO   2

300

Oct.   26—Rex Carlson, Cardiff .... W   4
Nov.   2—Phil Davies, Cardiff L   8
1977
May   19—Martin Beni, Port Moresby .... L 10
July   5—Joey Collins, Kingsford .... W   8
July   8—Kerry Bell, Brisbane L   8
1978
Feb.   10—Nobby Clarke, Kempsey .... W   6
Apr.   19—Jimmy Greco, Mt. Pritchard .... L 10
May   16—George Reno, Kingsford .... L 10
June   27—Eddie Buttons, Kingsford .... L 10
Aug.   4—Robert Colley, Brisbane L   8
Oct.   17—Eddie Buttons, Kingsford .... L 10
Oct.   22—Ritchie Roberts, Bankstown .... L 10
Nov.   25—Paul Baker, Mt. Pritchard .... W   6
Nov.   28—Jeff Sait, Kingsford .... TD 5
1979
Feb.   24—Joey Collins, Kempsey .... W 10
Mar.   23—Robert Hinkling, Lismore .... W 10
Apr.   26—Frank Ropis, Revesby .... KO by 3
June   1—Robert Coley, Brisbane .... L 10
June   13—Jimmy Brown, Preston Town Hall L   8
Oct.   22—Dave Agnew, Cardiff .... L 10
(For New South Wales Junior Welterweight Title)
1980
Apr.   12—Peter Berrigan, Tmaworth L   8
July   4—Jeff Malcolm, Wollongong .... KO by 3
July   28—David Sarago, Brisbane L   8
Aug.   22—Peter Berrigan, Cardiff .... KO by 5

LES DUNN
British Heavyweight
1979
Oct.   3—Ken March, Reading .... W   6
Oct.   29—Stuart Lithgoe, Birmingham .... KO by 4
1980
Mar.   6—Martin Nee, Wimbledon L   6
Mar.   17—David Fry, NSC L   8
June   3—David Fry, Aylesburg .... KO by 5
(Announced Retirement)

KEVIN DURKIN
British Welterweight
1980
Aug.   31—Charlie Douglas, Glasgow .... KO   4
Sept.   9—Gary Petty, Mexborough .... KO   5
Oct.   13—Steve Davies, Manchester .... W   6

SHAUN DURKIN
British Lightweight
1978
May   15—Liam Linnen, Glasgow .... W   6
May   22—Billy O'Grady, Mayfair L   6
June   7—Alan Burrows, Cardiff L   8
Sept.   4—Charlie Brown, Barry .... KO by 3
Sept. 27—Lawrence Williams, Rotherham L   6
Oct.   16—Bonnet Bryan, Bradford .... W   6
Oct.   23—Liam Linnen, Glasgow .... D   6
Oct.   31—Shaun Stewart, Barnsley L   6
Nov.   21—Dave Hill, Cambridge L   6
1979
Nov.   28—Ray Price, Doncaster .... D   6
Dec.   3—Bill Smith, Hull L   4
Dec.   10—Wally Stocks, London L   6
1980
Jan.   25—Glyn Rhodes, Hull L   6

MBONELEGO DYANTJIES
South African Lightweight
1979
Nov.   10—Ngcambaza Madaduli, King Williamstown W 4
Dec.   1—Alfred Gcaza, King Williamstown .... W   4
1980
Nov.   8—Sazi Xamlashe, East London .... W   4

STEVE EARLY
British Junior Welterweight
1977
Oct.   11—Kevin Sheenan, Coventry .... KO   3
1978
Jan.   18—Najib Daho, Solihull .... W   6
Jan.   23—Selvin Bell, London .... KO   2
Feb.   7—Ian Pickersgill, Coventry .... KO   1
Mar.   6—Joey Saunders, London .... W   6

Mar.   15—Stan Atherton, Solihull .... W   6
Apr.   18—Paul Clemit, Coventry .... W   8
May   3—Padey McAleese, Solihull .... W   8
June   1—Eric Purkis, Coventry .... KO   2
Nov.   1—Dirck Declerk, Izegem .... KO   2
Nov.   20—George McGurk, Birmingham .... KO   5
Dec.   1—Dave Campbell, Ennisvillen .... KO   2
1979
Feb.   26—Frank Mcord, Edgbaston .... KO   1
No.   19—Roger Guest, Birmingham .... KO   1
1980
Jan.   28—Sylvester Gordon, Edgbaston .... W   6
Mar.   10—Billy Waith, Wolverhampton .... W   8
Apr.   17—Chris Davies, Edgbaston .... KO   3
June   11—Tony Martey, Edgbaston .... W   8
Oct.   19—Dan M'Putu, Birmingham .... W 10

FRED EBON
Filipino Bantamweight
1979
Sept.   2—Rene Cruz, Cabanaturan City .... L 10
Oct.   26—Boy Estrella, Manila .... KO   5
Nov.   3—Renato Paulino, Santos City .... W 10
1980
Feb.   1—Danilo Inocian, Manila .... W 10

MARC ECIMOVIC
Australian Heaveweight
1973
Feb.   12—Robert Franklin, Melbourne .... KO   2
Feb.   19—Robert Doyle, Melbourne .... W   3
Mar.   12—Martin O'Toole, Melbourne .... KO   3
May   14—Ron Robson, Melbourne L   3
June   4—Mick Gatto, Melbourne .... KO   1
Aug.   27—Ian Overhead, Melbourne .... KO   1
Oct.   15—Tommy Mears, Melbourne .... KO by 4
1974
Apr.   25—Tony Coyne, Melbourne .... W   4
May   17—Geoff Horne, Melbourne .... KO   1
July   19—Tony Coyne, Melbourne .... D   4
July   26—Tony Coyne, Melbourne .... W   3
Aug.   24—Tony Coyne, Ballarat .... KO   8
1975
May   19—Pat Hubble, Brisbane .... KO   1
Aug.   21—Les Miller, Blacktown L   8
Dec.   4—Maile Haumono, Blacktown .... KO by 5
1976
Mar.   19—Tommy Mears, Moore Park .... KO by 4
1977
Aug.   4—Maile Haumono, Melbourne .... KO by 7
1978
June   17—Ted Gray, Corio .... W 10
Oct.   24—Maile Haumono, Corio .... KO   4
1979
Mar.   31—Tony Mundine, Melbourne .... KO by 2
(Australian Heavyweight Title)
Dec.   15—Vicent Kafoa, Moumea .... L 10
1980
May   23—Henry Patterson, Melbourne .... KO   3
Aug.   23—Terry Denny, Melbourne .... KO   1

COLIN ECKFORD
Australian
1978
Nov.   14—Paul Kilgannon, Kingsford .... W   4
Dec.   20—Mick McCabe, Mt. Pritchard L   4
1979
Feb.   15—Mick McCabe, Blacktown .... D   4
June   6—Alex Schafer, Brookvale .... W   4
Nov.   21—Mick McCabe, Mt. Pritchard .... W   4
Dec.   19—Benny Tabua, Mt. Pritchard .... KO by 5
1980
Feb.   26—Spiros Otis, Kingsford L   4
Mar.   26—Young Corbett, Newcastle .... D   4
Apr.   22—Merv Crocker, Kingsford L   4
May   7—Con O'Connor, Brookvale L   8

EARL EDWARDS
British Middleweight
1979
Sept. 17—Doug James, Mayfair L   6
Oct.   24—Curtis March, Norwich .... W   8
Nov.   26—Peter Simon, Hammersmith .... W   6
Dec.   10—Billy Hill, Manchester L   8
Dec.   20—Carl Daley, Queensway L   6
1980
Jan.   16—Winston Davis, Solihull L   6
Feb.   5—Jimmy Ellis, Southend .... W   8
Feb.   12—Peter Simon, Southend .... D   8
Feb.   28—Carl Daly, Queensway .... KO   5
Mar.   11—Harry Watson, London .... KO   5
Mar.   17—Henry Cooper, Birmingham .... KO   2
Apr.   14—Joe Lally, Manchester .... W   8

301

Apr. 28—Vernon Scott, Windsor ....L 8
Oct. 13—Dave Owens, Windsor ....KO 3

KENDRICK EDWARDS
British Middleweight
1977
Oct. 6—Ian Tungett, Southsea ....KO 3
Nov. 8—Roger Guest, West Bromwich ....L 6
Nov. 22—Alan Copp, Hemel Hempstead ....L 4
Dec. 5—Tony Bogle, Luton ....W 6
Dec. 13—Mohammed Akram, Slough ....W 6
1978
Jan. 16—Mick Hampston, Hove ....W 6
Feb. 13—Jimmy Roberts Barnsley ....L 6
Feb. 28—Des Miller, Atlesbury ....W 4
Mar. 15—Tony Hague, Solihull ....L 4
Apr. 12—Dave Maloney, Hammersmith ....L 6
May 24—Des Miller, Southend ....W 6
May 15—Pat Singer, Aylesbury ....KO 4
June 20—Jesse Wells, London ....KO 5
Sept. 18—Dave Southwell, Reading ....KO by 3
Oct. 10—Martin McEwan, Wolverhampton ....L 4
Oct. 16—Richard Kenyon, Bradford ....L 8
Nov. 6—Martin McEwan, Stafford ....L 6
Nov. 11—Ian Cole, Marylebone ....KO by 2
1979
Mar. 7—Gary Cooper, Solihull ....L 6
Nov. 27—Mickey Kidd, Wolverhampton ....L 6
1980
Jan. 28—Casley McAllum, Hove ....L 6

ESTEBAN EGUIA
Spanish Bantamweight
1975
Dec. 27—Juan Barros, Santander ....W 6
1976
Jan. 10—Luis Cabeza, Cabezon ....W 6
Jan. 31—Jose Luis Rodriguez, Santander ....W 6
Mar. 6—Andres Ramos, Santander ....W 6
June 19—Miguel Montes, Santander ....W 6
July 17—Antonio Garcia del Moral, Santander .....W 6
Aug. 6—Jose Castillejos, Santander ....KO 1
Sept. 4—Pedro Robles, Santander ....KO 4
Nov. 5—Francisco R. Jeronimo II, Santander .....W 8
Nov. 27—Raimon, Santander ....KO 6
Dec. 4—Francisco R. Jeronimo II, Santander .....W 8
1977
Jan. 29—Pedro Pinto, Santander ....KO 4
Mar. 12—Antonio R. Moro, Santander ....W 8
Apr. 2—Pedro Molledo, Santander ....KO 8
(Spanish Bantamweight Title)
May 28—Tanio, Utrerea ....W 12
(Spanish Bantamweight Title)
July 23—Juan Francisco Rodriguez, Almeria ......W 7
(Spanish Bantamweight Title)
Sept. 24—Acene Saifi, Santander ....KO 2
Nov. 19—Jacky Bihin, Santander ....KO 8
Dec. 30—Nessim Zebelini, Santander ....W 8
1978
Jan. 6—Fernando Bernardez, Bilbao ....KO 4
Feb. 4—Tanyo, Bilbao ....KO 4
Mar. 11—Henry Kone, Santander ....W 8
Apr. 20—Franco Zurlo, Viarggio ....D 15
(European Bantamweight Title)
May 12—Antonio Rodriguez, Bilbao ....W 8
Dec. 30—Fernando Bernardez, Santander ....W 8
1979
Jan. 6—Ramon G. Marichal, Bilbao ....L 8
Feb. 3—Joseph Tabla, Santander ....KO 4
Feb. 17—Juan Barros, Santander ....W 8
Mar. 24—Kikko Garcia, Santander ....KO 5
May 5—Angel Oliver, Logrono ....W 8
June 15—Antonio G. del Moral ....L 8
Aug. 10—Cornejo Hernandez, Santander ....KO 6
Sept. 29—Angel Oliver, Santander ....W 8
1980
Jan. 5—Antonio Garcia, Santander ....KO 4
Jan. 19—Vicente Rodriguez, Santander ....KO 5
(Retained Spanish Bantamweight Title)
Mar. 22—Luis de la Sagra, Santander ....W 12
(Retained Spanish Bantamweight Title)
Apr. 17—(Trevino), Santander ....W 8
May 17—Manuel Carasco, Leon ....L 8
Sept. 6—Jose Calixto Rueda, Santander ....W 8
Sept. 27—Cecilio Lastra, Santander ....D 10
(Retained Spanish Bantamweight Title)
Nov. 29—Hector Molina, Leon ....W 8

NGOZIKA EKWELUM
Nigerian Heavyweight
(Residing in Germany)
Born: March 15, 1948
1973
Nov. 24—Armando Zanini, Brescia ....D 8

1974
Feb. 20—Avenamar Peralta, Berlin ....L 8
Mar. 15—Alberto Lovell, Cologne ....D 8
Apr. 9—Richard Dunn, Berlin...................KO 7
May 16—Kilani Damdani, Hamburg..............KO 2
July 12—Jose Antonio Galvez,
    Palma de Mallorca ....KO 8
Sept. 3—Conny Velensek, Berlin ....D 8
1975
Jan. 6—Eddie Neilson, Piccadilly............KO by 2
Feb. 4—Billy Aird, Southend ....L 8
Mar. 18—Francoisin ....KO 2
May 16—Ray Anderson, Ludwigshafen ....D 8
June 21—Ray Anderson, Berlin...............KO by 5
Oct. 10—Conny Velensek, Berlin...............KO 7
Dec. 27—Jerry Judge, Berlin....................KO 3
1976
May 25—Tony Moore, Munich ....W 8
Nov. 19—Raul Gorosito, Madrid................D 8
Dec. 12—Lucien Rodriguez, Berlin ....W 6
1977
Jan. 29—Kallie Knoetze, Johannesburg ....KO by 7
May 31—John L. Gardner, London ....KO by 6
1978
Nov. 6—Bernd August, Berlin ....KO 5
1979
(Inactive)
1980
Mar. 29—Paul Sykes, Lagos ....KO 1

GILLES ELBILIA
French Welterweight
1977
Dec. 15—Jean Michele Iger, Paris ....W 6
1978
Jan. 12—Serge Sinelnikov, Paris ....W 6
Mar. 30—Dragan Tadin, Paris ....W disq. 4
June 30—Manate Teritau, Papeete ....W 6
Oct. 9—Eric Caposella, Paris ....W 6
Oct. 30—Serge Sinelnikov, Paris ....W 6
Dec. 15—Jean Pierre Moreau, Paris ....W 6
1979
Feb. 16—Angel Carmona, Tarbes ....W 8
June 21—Claude Lancastre, Alfrotville ....KO by 5
Oct. 15—Jacky Peraire, Paris ....W 6
Nov. 15—Pax Maliba, Paris ....W 6
Dec. 10—Yannick Blandin, Paris ....W 8
1980
Mar. 10—Jean Marie Touati, Paris ....W 8
Nov. 13—Lichi Maudoze, Paris ....W 8

MOHAMED EL CAUDOUMI
(See MOHAMED CHINO)

MOHAMAD-SALAH EL GHARBI
Yugoslavian Welterweight
1979
Nov. 24—Serve Poulain, Laal ....KO 4
1980
Apr. 19—Jean Paul Coppyn, Cormeilles en Parisis W 6

JOHNNY ELLIOT
British Welterweight
1974
Dec. 3—Devlin White, Southampton ....W 6
1975
Jan. 27—Mick Hampston, Walworth ....KO 5
Apr. 21—Tom Howard, Southampton ....W 6
1976
June 29—Chris Walker, London ....D 6
Sept. 27—Les Wint, London ....W 6
Nov. 8—Chris Walker, London ....L 6
1977
Mar. 21—Kevin Webber, Caerphilly ....L 4
Apr. 5—Terry Knight, Hove ....L 8
May 2—Andy Braidwood, Walworth ....L 6
May 23—Mick Hampston, Hammersmith ....W 6
July 18—Kelvin Webber, London ....W 6
Aug. 1—Andy Braidwood, Hove ....L 6
Oct. 10—Mick Hampston, Walworth ....W 4
Oct. 17—Andy Braidwood, Hammersmith ....L 6
Nov. 14—Peter Neal, Reading ....L 8
1978
Jan. 16—Michael Copp, Hove ....W 6
Feb. 13—Dave Ward, Reading ....W 8
Feb. 23—Tommy Joyce, Doncaster ....L 8
Mar. 14—Jim Montague, Belfast ....KO by 4
Apr. 17—Alan Copp, Reading ....D 8
May 27—Torben Anderson, Copenhagen ....L 4
Sept. 11—Tony Kavanaugh, Birmingham ....L 8
Nov. 20—Tony Hague, Birmingham ....W 8
1979
Feb. 19—Gerry Maguire, Belfast ....KO 5

Feb. 27—Alan Hardiman, London .... KO by 2
Apr.   2—Roy Commosioung, Kettering .... W 8
Apr. 23—Lloyd Hibbert, Reading .... L 8
May   29—Colin Powers, London .... KO by 6
Sept. 12—Billy Aherne, Liverpool .... D 6
Nov.   1—David Allen, Southend .... L 8
1980
Jan. 12—Thierry Samo, Calais .... L 8

JIMMY ELLIS
British Middleweight
1979
Apr.   7—David Kambule, Vereeniging .... KO by 2
Oct. 15—Wayne Barker, Manchester .... L 6
Nov.   1—Gordon Stacey, Southend .... KO 4
Nov. 27—Wayne Barker, Shellfield .... L 8
Dec.   4—Roy Commosiung, Southend .... KO 4
1980
Jan.   9—Richard Kenyon, Burslem .... KO 4
Jan. 25—Malcolm Heath, Hull .... L 6
Feb.   5—Earl Edwards, Southend .... L 8
Mar.   5—Kenny Webber, Liverpool .... L 8
Mar. 10—Carl Bailey, Manchester .... W 8
Mar. 31—Peter Bassey, Cleethorpes .... W 8
Apr. 14—Kenny Webber, Manchester .... D 8
Apr. 22—Mick Mills, Sheffield .... KO 6
May   14—Joe Jackson, Burslem .... W 8

SERGIO EMILI
Italian Lightweight
Born: September 16, 1948
1972
Dec.   4—Natale Vezzoli, Bologne .... D 6
1973
Jan.   5—Natale Vezzoli, Forli .... D 6
Mar. 24—Giuseppe Agate, San Elpidio .... W 6
May   24—Almo Quaini, Port San Elpidio .... W 6
June 14—Gianmario Lumbricci, San Elipdio .... W 6
June 23—Body Guy, Givitanova .... KO 4
Aug. 28—Paul Ikumapayi, Penna.................. KO 3
Sept. 8—Body Guy, Mogliano...................... W 6
Oct.   6—Giovanni Cavazzini, Macerata............ W 8
Oct. 25—Arrow Abu, San Benedetto .... W 8
Dec. 21—Mario Siracusa, Rimini.................. L 8
1974
Mar. 17—Albert Amatler, Lyon.................. KO 4
Apr.   5—Ottavio Quaresmini, Civitanova Mache ... W 8
May   3—Giuseppe Fascella, Porto Sant' Elpidio .. KO 8
June   1—Palmiro Masala, Tolentino .... W 8
Aug. 30—Amleto Restano, Civitanova............. KO 2
Oct.   4—Blackney Matthews, Melbourne .... L 4
1975
Mar. 21—Renzo Battistelli, Civitanova .... W 8
Apr. 16—Abu Arrow, Monturano .... D 8
May   10—Lucio Vailati, Porte Dan Elipidio........ WF 3
July 26—Pasqualino Morbidelli, Civitanova
          Marche.................................. W 12
          (Italian Title)
Sept. 26—Paul Ikumapayi, Montegranaro.......... W 8
Oct. 24—Guiliano Martucci, Bologna............... D 8
Nov. 29—Nervio Carbi, Trieste .... L 12
          (Italian Featherweight Title)
1976
Feb.   6—Giuseppi Martucci, Civitanova .... W 8
Apr. 30—Ambrogio Mariani, Civitanova .... KO 1
June 11—Giuseppe Martucci, Civitanova .... KO 9
Aug. 11—Giuseppe Agate, Civitanova .... D 8
Oct.   6—Pasqualino Morbidelli, Civitanova........ W 12
          (Italian Title Fight)
Dec.   3—Natale Caredda, Civitanova............. L 12
          (Italian Featherweight Title)
1977
Feb. 18—Domenico Radicioni, Civitanova .... W 8
Apr. 15—Jose L. R. Marques, Civitanova .... W 10
June 17—Natale Caredda, Civitanova .... W 12
          (Italian Featherweight Title)
July 22—Mouldi Manai, Portorecanati .... W 8
Aug.   7—Eloy De Souza, Macerata .... KO 5
Sept. 16—Eloi Emiliano, Civitanova .... W 8
Nov. 18—Salvatore Melluzzo, Pesaro .... KO by 10
          (Italian Featherweight Title)
1978
Mar. 17—Albert Amatler, Villeurbanne .... KO by 4
Oct. 29—Alfonso Carillo, Capua .... L 8
1979
May   19—Salvatore Liscapade, Canepina .... L 12
          (Italian Junior Lightweight Title)
July   6—Marco Gallo, Pistoia .... L 8
1980
Mar. 21—Lucio Cusma, Bologna .... KO by 6

ISAK JOHANNES ENSLIN
South African Middleweight
Born: March 21, 1960
1980
Mar.   1—Basil Meintjies, Ermelo .... L 4
May   26—Cornelius de Beer, Johannesburg .... D 4
July   3—Bobby Chisale, Welkom .... W 4

STEVE ENWRIGHT
British Bantamweight
Born: Dec. 26, 1953
1974
Sept. 17—Ray Scott, Glasgow..................... W 6
Oct. 21—Billy Smart, Nottingham .... KO by 3
Dec.   3—Ray Scott, Leeds .... W 6
1975
Jan. 13—Gerry McBride, Nottingham.............. W 6
Jan. 29—Richard Scarth, Stoke.................... W 6
Mar.   6—Dave Tuohey, Bradford................... D 6
Mar. 26—Dave Connell, Stoke.................... L 6
Apr. 29—Dave Connell, Salford .... L 6
Sept. 22—Roger Doyle, Bedford.................... L 6
Nov.   3—Frank Wagstaff, Bedford .... W 6
Nov. 10—Dave Tuohey, Bradford................... D 6
Dec.   2—Dave Tuohey, Leeds .... L 6
Dec. 15—Frankie Wagstaff, Bedford .... W 6
1976
Apr. 26—Andy Dane, Nottingham................. KO 4
Dec. 15—Don Aagesen, Bradford .... W 6
1977
Jan. 10—Wally Angliss, Walworth ....
Feb.   2—George Sutton, London .... KO by 2
Mar. 21—Lee Graham, Birmingham .... KO by 5
Apr. 21—Don Aagesen, Liverpool .... W 6
Apr. 26—Tony Zeni, Northampton .... W 6
May   16—Dave Wraxall, Manchester .... W 6
May   26—Dave Waraxall, Bradford .... KO 6
June 14—Gary Davidson, Wembley .... KO by 6
Aug. 22—Alan Roberton, Stockton .... L 6
Nov.   2—Alan Roberton, Newcastle .... D 8
Dec.   1—Tony Whitmore, Caister .... W 6
1978
Jan. 18—Jimmy Brown, Stoke .... KO by 3
Feb. 13—Larry Richards, Manchester .... W 6
Feb. 20—Malcolm McHugh, Bradford .... W 6
Mar.   2—Larry Richards, Caister .... L 6
Mar. 20—Lawrence Devanney, Bradford .... L 8
Apr.   4—Larry Richards, Manchester .... W 6
Sept. 12—Gary Lucas, Manchester .... KO 6
Sept. 18—Larry Richards, Manchester .... D 6
Nov. 28—Doug Hill, Sheffield .... L 6
Dec. 18—Gary Lucas, Bradford .... W 6
1979
Sept. 10—Carl Gaynor, Bradford .... W 6
Sept. 20—Chris Moorcraft, Liverpool .... W 6
Oct.   8—Ian Murray, Bradford .... W 6
Oct. 23—Ian Murray, Blackpool .... L 6
Dec.   5—Chris Moorcroft, Liverpool .... W 6
Dec. 10—Ian Murray, Manchester .... W 6
Dec. 17—Dave George, Bradford .... L 6
1980
Jan. 24—John Feeney, Hartlepool .... L 8
Mar. 24—Jimmy Bott, Bradford .... W 10
          (Won Vacant Central Area Bantamweight Title)
Oct. 20—Ivor Jones, Birmingham .... W 8

EUPREMIO EPIFANI
Italian Junior Welterweight
1978
June 30—Graziano Gusai, Parma .... W 6
Dec. 16—Giuseppe Cola, Pesaro .... W disq. 6
1979
Jan. 19—Augusto Quadri, Pesaro .... W 6
Apr. 24—Antonio Moja, Pesaro .... W 6
May   6—Raimondo Riccio, Taranto .... W 6
May   25—Graziano Gusai, Pesaro .... W 6
July 26—Giovanni Mairano, Taranto .... KO 5
Oct. 27—Eloy De Souza, Pesaro .... L 6
Nov. 24—Filiberto Zaccheo, Latina .... D 6
Dec. 15—Angelo Zanetti, Pesaro .... KO 3
1980
Mar. 29—Giuseppe Agate, Pesaro .... W 6
June 28—Giuseppe Agate, Potenza .... W 6

KATSUO ESASHI
Japanese Middleweight
1978
May   22—Mashashi Kudo, Tokyo .... L 8
          (Japanese Middleweight Title)
1979
Mar.   6—Nessie Koriguichi, Yokohama...........KO 1
June   5—Osamu Daoahii, Yokohama ....KO by 5
Oct. 13—Tsutomu Matsuo, Aizuwakamatsu Shi KO by 3

1980
Jan. 27—Chong-Pal Park, Seoul .... KO by 3
(For OPBF Middleweight Title)

CELSO ESMERO
Filipino Lightweight
1979
Apr. 27—Myungkil Chun, Manila .... KO by 9
July 20—Willie Makitoki, Manila .... L 10
1980
Jan. 22—Ki-Hoon Kwak, Pusan .... KO by 3

LORD ESMERO
Filipino Flyweight
1978
Nov. 24—Teo Montejo, Manila .... W 10
1979
Mar. 10—Tony Seas, Manila .... KO by 5
Mar. 31—Ric Barimbad, Davao City .... L 10
June 29—Henry Balina, Manila .... W 10
Oct. 5—Lennon Arcega, Manila .... W 10
1980
Jan. 18—Henry Balina, Manila .... W TD 2

PETRUS JOHANNES ESPAG
South African Light Heavyweight
1979
Nov. 12—Cecil Sandow, Welkom .... KO by 3
1980
Apr. 21—Petrus Crous, Secunda .... KO by 1

WILLIE ESPINOSA
Filipino Junior Lightweight
1978
Nov. 19—Andy Pacayuan, Bauio City .... KO 3
1979
Jan. 12—Eddie Ballarand, Manila .... W 10
Mar. 19—Henry Barcello, Quezon City .... D 10
July 15—Baby Francisco, Cebu City .... W 10
Aug. 10—Nick Caputol, Manila .... W 10
Nov. 8—Chung Il Choi, Seoul .... KO by 5
1980
Jan. 18—Del Contado, Manila .... NC 3

ALFREDO EVANGELISTA
Spanish Heavyweight
Born: Dec. 4, 1954, Uruguay
1975
Oct. 10—Angelo Visini, Madrid .... KO 1
Dec. 25—Alberto Lovell, Bilbao .... KO 2
1976
Jan. 29—Adriano Rosati, Bilbao .... KO 3
Feb. 20—Jose A Galvez, Almeria .... D 8
Mar. 12—Neville Meade, Madrid................... W 8
Apr. 2—Bepi Ros, Madrid....................... W 8
Apr. 23—Benito Penna, Madrid .... KO 2
May 14—Jose Manuel Ibar Urtain, Madrid....... KO 5
June 2—Lucien Rodriguez, Bilbao .... KO 4
July 2—Mario Baruzzi, Barcelona .... KO 4
July 21—Tony Moore, Bilbao.................... KO 4
Aug. 7—Fermin Hernander, S. Cruz .... KO 4
Oct. 8—Rudi Lubbers, Madrid .... KO 3
Nov. 19—Lissoko Abibobele, Madrid .... KO 5
Dec. 3—Guillermo de La Cruz, Montevideo ...... KO 6
1977
Feb. 4—Lorenzo Zanon, Bilboa .... L 8
May 16—Muhammad Ali, Landover .... L 15
(World Heavyweight Title)
June 17—Christian Poncelet, Madrid .... KO 3
Sept. 9—Lucien Rodriguez, Madrid .... KO 11
(European Heavyweight Title)
Sept. 29—Pedro Soto, New York .... KO 8
Nov. 26—Jean Pierre Coopman, Brussels .... KO 1
(European Heavyweight Title)
1978
Mar. 3—Billy Aird, Leon .... W 15
(European Heavyweight Title)
May 27—William Joiner, Leon .... KO 1
June 9—Jody Ballard, Las Vegas .... W 10
Aug. 11—Jean Tchathunig, Leye .... W 8
Sept. 9—Joe Maye, Las Corogne .... KO 3
Nov. 10—Larry Holmes, Las Vegas .... KO by 7
(WBC Heavyweight Title)
Dec. 26—Dante Cane, Bologna .... KO 4
(European Heavyweight Title)
1979
Mar. 2—Lucien Rodriguez, Liege .... KO 2
Mar. 19—Guilleamo De La Cruz, Valencia .... KO 4
Apr. 18—Lorenzo Zanon, Turin .... L 12
(European Heavywight Title)
July 14—Felipe Rodriguez, Pontevedra .... D 12
(Spanish Heavyweight Title)
July 23—Johnny Blaine, Lograno .... KO 2

July 27—Ronnell Johnson, Santander .... KO 2
Aug. 7—Eliot Bryant, Vigo .... KO 3
Oct. 26—Tony Moore, La Coruna .... W 8
Nov. 8—Jacob Tschanchuing, La Coruna .... KO 2
Dec. 1—Calvin Langston, Pamplona ....'... KO 3
Dec. 9—Tony Moore, Lugo .... W 8
1980
Jan. 12—Leon Spinks, Atlantic City .... KO by 5
Mar. 17—Fetiche Kassongo, Barcelona .... KO 3
May 9—Tom Kiely, Barcelona .... W 8
June 21—Winston Allen, Barcelona .... W 8
July 17—Neil Malpass, Barcelona .... W 8
Aug. 1—Bob Stallings, Palma de Mallorca .... WF 6
Sept. 13—John Blaine, Malaga .... KO 4

GREG EVANS
British Light Heavyweight
1976
Oct. 12—Terry Armstrong, Wembley .... W 6
Nov. 9—George Gray, Wembley .... W 6
1977
Feb. 14—Bob Pollard, Manchester ....L 8
Mar. 13—Winston Cousins, Manchester .... W 8
Apr. 21—Brian Huckfield, Liverpool .... KO 1
June 14—Roy Gumbs, Wembley .... W 8
Sept. 5—Eddie Fenton, London .... KO 3
Nov. 8—Vernon Scott, London .... KO by 5
1978
Feb. 20—Harry White, Nottingham .... W 8
Sept. 11—Rab Alleck, Liverpool .... KO by 1
Oct. 30—Billy Knight, Nottingham .... KO 1
Nov. 27—Harry White, Kettering .... KO 6
Dec. 21—Roy Gumbs, Liverpoos .... KO by 6
1979
May 29—Johnny Waldron, Kensington .... KO by 4
Feb. 25—Tom Collins, Bradford .... KO by 1
(For Vacant Central Area Light Heavyweight Title)

WAYNE EVANS
British Featherweight
Born: May 13, 1955
1974
Oct. 17—Ray Scott, Southsea .... KO 5
1975
Mar. 4—Dave Connell, Portsmouth .... KO 6
June 2—Dave Connell, Manchester .... KO 6
Sept. 8—Tony Kerr, Glasgow .... KO 4
Oct. 1—Charlie Parvin, Hamilton .... W 8
Oct. 16—Dave Tuohey, Portsmouth .... KO 5
Dec. 4—John McCluskey, Hamilton .... KO 1
1976
May 3—Jules Piga, Southsea .... KO 5
June 14—Paddy Graham, Portsmouth............. W 12
1977
May 31—Lee Graham, Kensington .... W 8
1978
Feb. 13—Wally Angliss, Walworth .... KO 4
Apr. 6—Johnny Ownen, Ebbw Vale .... KO by 10
(British Bantamweight Title)
1979
Mar. 7—Lee Graham, Solihull .... KO 2
1980
Sept. 22—Paul Keers, Birmingham ....L 8

REDMOND EVERARD
British Middleweight
1979
Jan. 22—Tommy Baldwin, Bradford .... KO 4
Mar. 1—Alan Worthington, Liverpool ....L 6
Apr. 5—Alan Worthington, Liverpool .... W 6
May 13—Chris Coady, Edgbaston .... KO by 4
Sept. 20—Chris Coady, Liverpool .... KO by 4
Oct. 31—Martin McEwan, Burslem .... KO by 3
1980
Mar. 13—Mohammed Ali, Birkenhead ....L 6
Apr. 21—Joe Dean, Bradford .... KO by 3
(Announced Retirement)

COR EVERSTEJIN
Dutch Junior Welterweight
1979
Sept. 10—Andre Blanco, L'Aja .... W 6
Oct. 15—Kader Ben Mimoun, L'Aja .... KO 6
Nov. 5—Mohammed Bouziani, Rotterdam .... W 6
Nov. 26—Calogero Restivo, Rotterdam .... WF 5
1980
Jan. 28—Jean Michel Iger, Rotterdam .... W 6
Mar. 31—Herbert Trausmuth, Rotterdam .... KO 5

CHUNG-JAE EWANG
Korean Welterweight
1979

Apr.	1—Fred Pastor, Seoul	W	8
June	29—Tarzan Tobaru, Seoul	KO	2
Aug.	11—Ramon Dionisio, Seoul	KO	4
Sept.	23—Armando Boniquit, Seoul	KO	5
Nov.	9—Mitsuo Kushikino, Seoul	KO	9

1980

Jan.	1—Nessi Horiguchi, Seoul	KO	5
Feb.	29—Dan de Guzman, Manila	W	12
	(Won OPBF Welterweight Title)		
Apr.	7—Tsutomu Hagusa, Seoul	KO	3
May	30—Vicente Mawas, Seoul	KO	1
	(Retained OPBF Welterweight Title)		
July	12—Yohi Arai, Won Joo	KO	7
	(Retained OPBF Welterweight Title)		
Sept.	24—Eddie Ofosa, Seoul	KO	4
	(Retained OPBF Welterweight Title)		
Nov.	3—Dynamite Matsuo, Seoul	KO	5
	(Retained OPBF Welterweight Title)		

BILLY FACER
Australian Junior Lightweight
1979

Apr.	9—Greg Liesegang, Brisbane	KO by	8
July	21—Steve Buttons, Murgon	L	10
Dec.	8—Steve Buttons, Redcliffe	D	10

1980

Apr.	26—Tiger Mann, Papua	KO by	4
June	9—Greg Leisegang, Brisbane	KO by	2
June	27—Bullet Bradley, Gympie	KO	
June	18—Jim West, Mt. Pritchard	KO by	4
Sept.	29—Rex Cannon, Brisbane	L	8
Oct.	2—Jeff Smith, Wellington	L	10

NEIL FANNAN
British Junior Middleweight
1980

Mar.	27—Eric Hirchmann, Newcastle	KO	2
Apr.	28—Dave Douglas, Birmingham	D	6
May	19—Michael Miller, London	KO by	2
July	7—Billy Ahearne, Middlesbrough	KO	3
Sept.	11—Adrian Clamp, Liverpool	W	8
Sept.	16—Vic Jackson, Southend	W	8
Sept.	23—Casey McAllum, Middlesbrough	W	6

IGNAZIO FARA
Italian Lightweight
1975

Mar.	22—Beniamino Marzano, Sassari	W	6
May	2—Guido Luttazzi, Forli	W	6
May	24—Filippo Belvedere, Sassari	W	6
June	21—Lucio Vailoti, Sassari	D	6
Oct.	11—Ferdinando Ripamonti, Cantu	W	6
Nov.	28—Jules Piga, Forbach	L	6
Dec.	26—Gianni Garbo, Bologna	D	6

1976

Mar.	5—Natale Caredda, Sassari	L	6
Apr.	3—Salvatore Melluzzo, Milano	L	6
July	2—Salvatore Melluzzo, Siracusa	L	6
Aug.	12—Salvatore Laconi, Alghero	KO	2
Sept.	10—Salvatore Laconi, Cagliari	W	6
Oct.	7—Lucio Vailati, Sassati	D	6

1977

Mar.	26—Claudio Piccolo, Gorizia	L	6
June	25—Lucio Vailoti, Crema	KO by	6
Aug.	10—Alfredo Mulas, Rimini	L	8
Oct.	21—Giuseppe Fossati, Milano	L	6
Nov.	18—Alfredo Mulas, Forli	KO by	2

1978
(Inactive)

1979

June	23—Pietro Candidda, Sassari,	KO	3
Sept.	8—Giuseppe Ballone, Alhero	L	4
Nov.	16—Alfredo Raininger, Milan	L	6
Dec.	20—Giancarlo Compiani, Cremona	L	6

1980

Apr.	19—Giuseppe Tidu, Calgari	KO by	4
May	31—Antonio Antino, Lugano	L	6

STEVE FARNSWORTH
British Featherweight
1980

Sept.	9—Selvin Bell, Sheffield	W	6
Sept.	15—Paul Huggins, WSC	L	6
Sept.	29—Tony Manson, Chesterfield	W	6
Oct.	13—Andy Thomas, Manchester	L	6
Oct.	20—Peter Ewebanks, Hove	W	6

BOYD FARRAR
British Light Heavyweight
1975

May	12—Lloyd Gardner, Mayfair	L	6
Nov.	12—John Rushton, Bethanal	W	6
Dec.	1—Peter Lane, Mayfair	W	6

1976

Jan.	13—Clive Davidson, Hornsey	W	6
Feb.	25—Ritchie Smith, Bethanal	KO	3
Oct.	28—Winston Cousins, Mayfair	D	8

1977
(Inactive)

1978

Sept.	26—Steve Lewin, Wembley	L	6
Dec.	11—Peter Tedgwell, London	KO	4

1979

Feb.	5—Lloyd James, London	L	6
Mar.	5—Steve Fox, London	W	6
Mar.	19—Roger Rider, London	W	6
Apr.	6—Clint Jones, Norwich	W	8
May	17—Reginald Squire, Wimbledon	W	8
June	26—Keith Bussey, London	L	8
Oct.	15—Lloyd James, Windsor	W	8

1980

May	29—Steve Lewin, Wimbledon	L	8
Oct.	6—Richard Caramanolis	KO by	7

VASO (VASCO) FAUSTINO
Italian Heavyweight
Born: February 5, 1945
1969

June	16—Ray Patterson, Helsinki	L disq.	3
July	11—Giancarlo Bacchini, Ancona	W	6
Aug.	3—Giancarlo Bacchini, Arcevia	W	8
Sept.	5—Alfredo Vogrig, Udine	L	8
Oct.	10—Mario Baruzzi, Milan	L	8
Nov.	8—Antonio Zanini, Reggio Emilia	L	8
Nov.	29—Pietro Besi, San Croce	KO	1
Dec.	30—Jose Urtain, Barcelona	KO by	1

1970

Apr.	18—Giulio Rinaldi, Anzio	L	8
May	8—Ermanno Festorazzi, Ancona	KO	2
May	29—Armando Zanii, Rome	D	8
June	26—Vittorio Verrengia, Ancona	KO	4
Aug.	5—Ermanno Festorazzi, Ascoli	WF	1
Oct	2—Expedit Mountcho, Ancona	D	8
Dec.	11—Lucianno Ghiotti, Ancona	KO	1

1971

Jan.	11—Christian Poncelot, Paris	L	8
Feb.	6—Jurgen Blin, Frankfurt	L	10
Mar.	6—Expedit Mountcho, Ancona	W	8
Mar.	26—Steve Jones, Turin	KO	4
Apr.	3—Horst Lenedens, Duseldorf	L disq.	3
Apr.	23—Dante Cane, Bologna	L	8
May	19—Burghard Lembke, Ancona	KO	2
Sept.	17—Tommy Sheehan, Turin	KO by	3

1972

Feb.	18—Dante Cane, Reggio Emilia	L	10
Apr.	29—Bepi Ros, Schio	L	8
May	12—Mario Baruzzi, Torino	L	10
Dec.	2—Miguel Paez, Turin	L	8
Dec.	26—Miguel Angel Paez, Rome	D	8

1973

Mar.	12—Ba Sounkalo, Paris	L	8
May	11—Dante Cane, Ancona	KO by	6
June	30—Mongol Ortiz, Cordenons	L	8
July	22—Armando Zanini, Brescia	L	8
Oct.	11—Harold Skog, Oslo	L	6
Nov.	24—Pietro Zanola, Brescia	L	8
Dec.	3—Eddie Neilson, Bristol	KO	2
Dec.	26—Bepi Ros, Bologna	D	10

1974

Feb.	20—Bernd August, Berlin	L	10
Mar.	15—Mongol Ortiz, Ancona	W	8
Apr.	26—Pietro Zanola, Terni	D	8
May	17—Vasco Faustino, Milan	L	8
June	21—Vincenzo Sciarrone, Rome	L	8
Sept.	24—Eddie Neilson, Reading	KO by	4
Dec.	25—Jean Pierre Coopman, Izegem	L	10

1975

Feb.	14—Marcello Betti, Milan	L	6
Apr.	24—Piermario Baruzzi, Brescia	KO	4
May	16—Bjorn Rudi, Oslo	L	8
Sept.	20—Luis Faustino Pires, S. Paolo	KO by	6

Dec. 12—Alfio Righetti, Turin ....L 8
1976
Mar. 12—Abdul Fheti, Istanbul...................KO 2
Oct. 16—Giacinto Cattani, Castelfranco Veneto .....L 8
Nov. 27—Domenico Adinolfi, Latina ....L 8
1977
Mar. 5—Lorenzo Zanon, Velenje ....L 8
May 28—Horst Lan, Koln ....L 8
Oct. 7—Ferruccio Mazzardi, Ancona ....KO 2
1978
Jan. 7—Rudy Gauwe, Zele ....L 6
Apr. 14—Giovanni De Luca, Milan ....L 8
July 6—Claido Cassaneli, Lugo di Romagna ..KO by 2
Aug. 25—Romeo Malvarini, Orzinuovi ....KO 3
Nov. 25—Leopoldo Centorrino, Ascoli ....L 8
1979
Apr. 21—Giovanni De Luca, S. Sebastiano ....L 8
Nov. 24—Giovanni De Luca, Ascoli Picento ....L 12
(For Italian Heavyweight Title)
1980
Feb. 8—Vincenzo Pesapane, Piacenza ....L 8
Mar. 14—Romeo Malgarini, Milan ....L 8
Apr. 25—Al Syben, Bruxelles ....KO by 3

GEORGE FEENEY
British Lightweight
1977
Aug. 22—Eric Wood, Stockton ....KO 4
Sept. 29—Billy Vivian, Newcastle ....W 8
Nov. 2—Mick Bell, Newcastle ....W 8
1978
Feb. 7—Barry Price, Islington ....KO 3
Feb. 27—Hector Molina, Middlesborough ....W 8
Apr. 17—Tommy Davitt, London ....L 8
Sept. 26—Cornelius Boza-Edwards, Wembley ....L 8
Dec. 4—Eric Wood, Marton ....W 8
1979
Feb. 28—Bingo Crooks, Harrogate ....L 8
Sept. 26—Bingo Crooks, Solihull ....W 8
Nov. 3—George Peacock, Glasgow ....W 8
Nov. 19—Chris Walker, Glasgow ....KO 8
1980
Feb. 4—Bingo Crooks, London ....W 8
Apr. 1—Clinton McKenzie, London ....L 10
Oct. 2—Ricky Beaumont, Hull ....L 10
(Elimination Bout For British Lightweight Title)

JOHN FEENEY
British Bantamweight
1977
July 10—Larry Richards, Birmingham ....KO 2
Aug. 22—Paul Varden, Stockton ....W 8
Oct. 10—Jimmy Bott, Marton ....KO 6
Oct. 18—Mohammad Younis, Wolverhampton ....W 8
Dec. 5—Charlie Parvin, Marton ....W 8
1978
Jan. 24—George Sutton, London ....KO 6
Feb. 23—Dave Larmour, Walworth ....KO 4
Oct. 9—Mark Bliss, Middleborough ....W 8
Oct. 31—Alex McIntosh, Hammersmith ....KO 5
Nov. 11—Neil McLaughlin, Marylebone ....W 8
1979
Jan. 17—Mohammed Younis, Solihuss ....W 10
Feb. 5—Alan Robertson, Nottingham ....W 8
Feb. 20—Tony Kerr, London ....KO 6
May 2—George Sutton, Solihull ....KO 8
Sept. 24—Paddy Graham, Hammersmith ....W 8
Dec. 3—Lee Graham, Marylebone ....W 8
1980
Jan. 24—Steve Enwright, Hartlepool ....W 8
Mar. 4—Neil McLaughlin, London ....KO 3
June 28—Johnny Owen, Glasgow ....L 15
(For British Commonwealth Bantamweight Title)
Nov. 1—Terry McKeown, Glasgow ....W 8

REVERTO FELICIONI
Italian Middleweight
1977
Mar. 4—Salvano Bisonari, Rome ....KO 2
Apr. 22—Biagio Violino, Rome ....KO 3
May 27—Mushapata Kubangu, Rome ....W 6
July 22—Alfredo Rossi, Fiumicino ....KO 2
Sept. 24—Ali Yacoubi, Ostia ....KO 4
Oct. 22—Luciano Bolis, Ostia ....KO 4
Nov. 18—Lorenzo Nardillo, Rome ....W 8
Dec. 16—Mariano Salamone, Rome ....W 6
1978
Mar. 31—Gianni Mingardi, Rome ....W 8
May 26—Giuseppe Borghi, Rome ....KO 3
July 14—Nicola Sassenelli, Lido Di Ostia ....W 8
Dec. 1—Walter Guernieri, Rome ....W 8
1979
Feb. 23—Gabriele Lazzari, Rome ....W 8
Apr. 7—Sonny Kamunga, Bracciano ....W 8

306

May 18—Matteo Salvemini, Rieti ....L 12
(For Italian Middleweight Title)
1980
Feb. 1—Roy Kaba, Ostia ....W 8
Feb. 29—Mauricio Da Cruz, Rome ....W 8
Mar. 28—Joel Bonnetaz, Rome ....W 8
May 2—Ray Opuku, Rome ....L 8

MICK FELLINGHAM
British Light Heavyweight
1978
Nov. 21—Steve Lewin, Wembley ....KO by 2
1979
Feb. 28—Liam Coleman, Harrogate ....L 6
Apr. 23—Liam Coleman, Glasgow ....L 6
June 18—Keith Roberts, Glasgow ....KO 4
Sept. 3—Gary Jones, Glasgow ....D 6
Sept. 24—Wally Barnes, London ....D 6
Oct. 8—Gary Jones, Glasgow ....W 6
Oct. 15—Trevor Kerr, Glasgow ....W 6
Oct. 29—Roy Skeldon, Wolverhampton ....L 6
1980
Jan. 21—Danny McLoughlin, Glasgow ....L 2
Feb. 28—Nigel Savory, Hull ....L 6
May 5—Malcolm Heath, Glasgow ....KO by 4
Sept. 22—Trevor Kerr, Belfast ....KO by 7
(For Vacant Northern Ireland Light Heavyweight Title)

EDDY FENTON
Leicester, England Light Heavyweight
Born: Jan. 12, 1954
1974
Apr. 22—John Celebanski, Nottingham ....W 6
Apr. 29—John Depledge, Bristol ....L 8
May 6—David Fry, Bedford ....KO 4
May 13—Lloyd Stewart, Nottingham ....W 6
June 3—Lloyd Stewart, Manchester ....W 6
June 24—Lloyd Stewart, Bedford ....W 6
Sept. 9—Tony Moore, Bedford ....L 6
Sept. 16—Dave Parris, Birmingham ....KO 2
Oct. 7—Dave Fry, Bristol ....D 8
Oct. 14—John Celebanski, Bedford ....W disq. 5
Oct. 23—Guinea Roger, Stoke...................W 8
Nov. 13—Steve Foley, Solihull ....W 8
Nov. 18—Neville Meade, London ....KO by 5
1975
Feb. 17—Tony Moore, Mayfair...................L 6
Mar. 4—John Depledge, Portsmouth ....KO by 3
Apr. 28—John Depledge, Kensington ....W 8
May 14—Sid Paddock, Camberley ....KO 7
June 24—Denton Ruddock, London ....L 6
Sept. 2—David Fry, Solihull ....W 8
Oct. 10—Sid Falconer, Birmingham ....L 8
Nov. 10—Peter Freeman, Bradford ....W 8
Nov. 25—Eddie Neilson, London.............KO by 3
1976
Jan. 16—David Fry, Bournemouth..............W 8
Mar. 22—John DePledge, Nottingham ....WF 8
Apr. 9—Garfield McEwan, Digbeth ....L 10
Apr. 27—Paul Kinsella, Kensington ....KO 4
July 14—Danny McAlldin, Wolverhampton ...KO by 4
Sept. 7—Isaac Hussein, London ....L 8
Dec. 14—Brian Huckfield, W. Bromwich ....NC
1977
Feb. 10—Terry O'Connor, Coventry ....L 8
Feb. 23—Ishaq Hussien, Bradford ....KO by 4
May 4—Garfield McEwan, Solihull ....L 8
July 10—Tony Allen, Birmingham ....KO by 8
Sept. 5—Greg Evans, London ....KO by 3
Oct. 19—Roy John, Kington ....D 8
Dec. 12—Sid Falconer, London ....W 8
1978
Mar. 3—Enio Cometti, Milan ....KO by 6
May 23—Tim Wood, Leicester ....L 8
Oct. 11—Gordon Ferris, Belfast ....KO by 1
Nov. 29—Time Woo, Evesham ....L 8
1979
Feb. 28—Carlton Benoit, Burslem ....KO 5
Mar. 28—Tim Wood, Evesham ....W 8
May 2—Tony Allen, Solihull ....WF 7
June 26—Ken Jones, Leicester ....KO 8
Sept. 24—Danny Miller, Birmingham ....KO by 1
Nov. 27—Harry White, Wolverhampton ....L 10
1980
Mar. 19—Harry White, Solihull ....W 10
(For Midlands Area Light Heavyweight Title)
May 21—Howard Mills, Coventry ....KO by 2
July 8—Roy Skeldon, Wolverhampton .....KO by 6
(Lost Midlands Area Light Heavyweight Title)
(Announced Retirement)

STEVE FENTON
British Light Heavyweight
1976
Mar. 26—Owen Lotreit, Bournemouth ....KO 1
Mar. 31—Charlie Richardson, Birmingham........W 6
Apr. 27—Micky Lock, Kensington ....KO 3
July 14—Leroy Herriot, Wolverhampton ......KO by 4
Sept. 21—David Owens, Bethnel Green........KO by 3
Oct. 27—Randy Barrett, Wolverhampton ....W 6
Nov. 24—Winston Cousins, London ....KO by 4
1977
Mar.   1—Henry Johnson, Marylebone ....W 8
Mar. 15—Jim Moore, Leeds ....W 8
Mar. 21—Eddie Smith, Birmingham ....KO by 6
Apr. 18—Colin Breen, Bedford ....D 8
May   4—Henry Cooper, Solihull ....L 8
July 10—Malcolm Wortington, Birmingham .....KO 2
Oct. 12—Tony Burnett, Stoke ....KO 5
Nov.   2—Carlton Benoit, Southend ....KO 2
1978
Jan. 18—Danny McLaughlin, Solihull ....D 8
Feb.   7—Roger Barlow, Coventry ....KO 1
Apr. 24—Steve Taylor, Bradford ....KO by 3
June   1—Ricky James, Coventry ....W 6
1979
Feb. 21—Tony Allen, Evesham ....KO by 9
June 26—Colin Flute, Leicester ....W 8
Sept. 9—Tim Wood, Bradford ....KO by 6
1980
Feb. 13—Trevor Cattouse, London ....KO by 5
Apr.   9—Danny McLoughlin, Liverpool ....KO 1
Oct. 30—Cordwell Hylton, Wolverhampton ....KO by 2

JIM FENWICK
British Middleweight
1977
Nov.   2—Carl North, Newcastle ....KO by 2
Dec.   5—Jack Gilling, Marton ....KO by 3
1978
Feb. 23—Mohammed Akran, Doncaster ....L 4
Mar. 23—Derek Young Nelson, Sunderland ....KO by 1
1979
(Inactive)
1980
Feb.   5—Mohammed Ali, Wolverhampton ....D 4
Feb. 20—Mohammed Ali, Evesham ....KO by 4

BRAKIM FERIZOVIA
Yugoslav Middleweight
1978
Oct. 31—Roy Kaba, Munich ....D 4
1979
Sept. 28—Ruediger Bitterling, Munich ....KO by 6
1980
May   14—Wolfgang Leichner, Munich ....KO 3

JOSE LUIS (PUNALES) FERNANDEZ
Spanish Welterweight
1977
Aug. 20—Serafin Dos Anjos, Santander ....L 8
Oct. 15—Jose G. Jurado, Leon ....KO 4
1978
Feb.   4—Jose M. Domingo, Leon ....W 8
May   24—Jose Luis Alvarez, Lugo ....L 8
Aug. 19—Fernando Perez, Gijon ....KO by 5
Aug. 26—Jose Antonio Parrenco, Cuenca ...L disq. 6
1979
Feb. 26—Jesus Rodriguez De La Rosa, Barcelona ...L 8
Mar. 30—Cristobal Crespi, Mallorca ....KO by 2
May   19—Gorriti, S. Sebastiano ....L 4
Aug. 25—Raul Anon, La Coruna ....KO 2
Oct. 27—Ahmed Ben Aissa, Leon ....KO 6
Dec.   1—Jose Manuel Domingo, Leon ....W 8
Dec. 21—Manuel Alcala, Leon ....KO by 3
1980
Jan. 30—Antonio Acedo, Madrid ....L 4

STEPHANE FERRARA
French Junior Middleweight
1980
Feb. 15—Patrick Babouram, Bordaux ....W 6
Mar. 14—Eugene Dovin, Limoges ....W 6
May   5—Maurice Renaud, Paris ....W 6
June   6—Serge Sinelnikov, Massay ....KO 4
Oct. 17—Pierre Joly, Massay ....L 6
Nov. 15—Patrick Babouram, Criel ....W 6

ESCASSINO FERREIRA
Spanish Middleweight
1980
Jan.   5—Jorge Oulu, Santander ....KO 3
Jan. 19—Manuel Sanchez, Santander ....KO 2
Feb. 14—Jose Omedes, Bilbao ....KO 2

Mar. 22—Debril Bathili, Santanger ....KO 2
June 20—Jose Luis Alvarez, Madrid ....KO 1
July   4—Alex Cardoza, Madrid ....L 8
Sept. 6—Andoni Amana, Bilbao ....KO by 5

PAUL FERRERI
Australian Bantamweight and Featherweight
Born: Jan. 1, 1948, Sicily
1968
Aug.   2—Pietro Granata, Melbourne ....W 3
Aug.   5—Pietro Granata, Melbourne ....W 3
Sept. 13—Johnny Ell, Melbourne ....KO 4
Sept. 30—Geoff Marriett, Melbourne ....KO 1
Nov.   1—Mick Crombie, Melbourne ....W 3
Nov. 29—Barry Edwards, Melbourne ....W 3
Dec.   9—Bobby Edwards, Melbourne ....W 3
1969
Feb.   3—Danny Adams, Sth. Melbourne...........W 4
Mar.   3—David Atkins, Sth. Melbourne...........W 4
Mar. 17—Bob Sandys, Sth. Melbourne ....KO 2
May   5—Nev Maddison, Sth. Melbourne ....KO 2
May   30—Robbie Hayes, Melbourne ....W 6
June 30—John Gatti, Sth. Melbourne ....W 6
July 28—Roger Carroll, Sydney ....W 3
Aug.   8—Alan Pressnell, Melbourne ....W 8
Aug. 18—Alan Pressnell, Sth. Melbourne ....W 6
Sept. 22—Tony Caminiti, Sth. Melbourne.........KO 4
Oct. 17—Alan Pressnell, Melbourne ....W 15
(Won Vacant Australian Bantamweight Title)
1970
Feb.   2—Norm Britton, Sth. Melbourne...........W 6
Feb. 25—Reg King, Redfern......................W 8
Mar.   2—Carmelo Massa, Melbourne.........W disq. 5
May   11—Sid Vicera, Melbourne ....W disq. 10
July   6—Johnny Keelie, Melbourne ....W 10
Aug. 31—Tony Humm, Melbourne ....W 10
Oct. 19—Johnny McCluskey, Melbourne ....W 10
Nov. 16—Floro Ybanez, Melbourne ....W 10
1971
Feb.   8—Tony Moreno, Melbourne ....D 10
Feb. 22—Willie Cordova, Melbourne ....D 10
June   7—Willie Cordova, Melbourne ....L 10
Aug.   5—Harry Hayes, St. Kilda ....W 10
Aug. 26—Anthony Sithole, Melbourne ....W 10
Oct.   3—Willie Leslie, Melbourne Exh. Gr. ....W 15
(Retained Australian Bantamweight Title)
Nov.   4—Fernando Sotelo, Brunswick ....W 10
Dec. 17—Sam Chander, Brunswick ....KO 3
1972
Feb. 24—Harry Hayes, Thebarton ....KO 8
(Retained Australian Bantamweight Title)
Apr.   8—Fernando Sotelo, Richmond ....W 10
June   6—Jim Bowen, Marrickville................W 15
(Retained Australian Bantamweight Title)
Sept. 16—John Kellie, Frankston ....W 15
(Won Vacant Commonwealth Bantamweight Title)
1973
Feb.   7—Raul Noria, Sydney ....W 10
Apr. 26—Fred Burns, Carlton....................W 15
May   26—Guy Caudron, Papete ....D 10
Aug. 29—Big Jim West, Melbourne ....W 10
Oct. 22—Brian Roberts, Melbourne ....W 10
1974
Mar. 18—Arnold Taylor, Cape Town..............L 10
May   16—Big Jim West, Blacktown ....W 10
June   6—Brian Roberts, Blacktown ....W 10
Sept. 12—Brian Roberts, Blacktown ....D 10
Oct.   3—Big Jim West, Blacktown ....W 10
Nov. 29—Paddy Graham, Melbourne ....W 10
1975
Mar.   7—Paddy Maguire, Melbourne ....KO 8
(Retained Commonwealth Bantamweight Title)
May   14—Brian Roberts, Marrickville.............L 10
Oct. 31—Mouldi Manai, Turin ....KO 4
Dec. 12—Murphy Ragga, Turin...................W 8
1976
Jan. 30—Heleno Ferreira, Milan ....D 10
Mar. 25—Brian Roberts, Blacktown ....W 15
(Retained Commonwealth Bantamweight Title)
June 30—Rolando Navarrete, Cebu City ....W 10
Aug. 30—Carlos Zarate, Los Angeles ....KO by 12
(For WBC Bantamweight Title)
Nov.   2—Merv Wockner, Cardiff ....W 10
1977
Jan. 29—Sulley Shittu, Accra, Ghana ....L 15
(Lost British Commonwealth Bantamweight Title)
June   8—Brian Roberts, Marrickville ....KO 15
(Retained Australian Bantamweight Title)
Aug.   4—Guinea Hillier, Melbourne ....KO 4
Sept. 15—Brian Roberts, Perth ....KO 15
(Won Commonwealth Junior Featherweight Title)
Dec.   5—Roger Henry, Melbourne ....KO 8
(Won Australian Featherweight Title)

1978

Mar.	11—Brian Schofield, Melbourne	W	10
May	9—Venice Borkorsor, Melbourne	W	10
June	30—Neptali Alamag, Manila	L	10
Aug.	11—Billy Facer, Nambour	KO	2
Oct.	7—Charlie Brown, Griffith	KO	6

(Retained Australian Bantamweight Title)

Nov.	2—Johnny Owen, Ebbw Vale	L	15

(For Commonwealth Bantamweight Title)

1979

Feb.	18—Rocky Gattellari, Sydney	KO	3

(Won Australian Featherweight Title)

July	27—Brian Roberts, Reversby	W	12

(Retained Australian Featherweight Title)

1980

Feb.	10—Big Jim West, Revesby	W	15

(Won Australian Junior Lightweight Title)

Mar.	21—Roger Henry, Deniliquin	KO	8

(Retained Australian Featherweight Title)

Aug.	21—Dejuarin Hollywood, Perth	W	10
Sept.	19—Big Jim West, Lidcombe	KO	10

(Retained Australian Junior Lightweight Title)

Oct.	18—Dennis Talbot, Darwin	KO	6

(Retained Australian Junior Lightweight Title)

GORDON FERRIS
Irish Heavyweight
1977

Dec.	16—Keith Johnson, Enniskillen	KO	5

1978

Feb.	3—Tony Monaghan, Enniskillen	KO	2
Feb.	7—George Scott, Islington	KO by	3
Apr.	21—Terry O'Connor, Enniskillen	W	8
Oct.	11—Eddie Fenton, Belfast	KO	1
Nov.	1—Robert Desnovck, Izegem	L	6
Dec.	1—Martin Nee, Enniskillen	KO	4

1979

Jan.	26—Stan McDermott, London	L	8
Feb.	26—Austin Okoye, Edgasbaston	W	8
May	13—Bonnie McKenzie, Edgasbaston	W	8
May	29—Stan McDermott, Kensington	KO	1
Sept.	10—Ricky James, Birmingham	W	8
Sept.	25—Terry Mintus, London	KO	6
Nov.	19—Ricky James, Birmingham	KO	6
Dec.	3—Austin Okoye, Wolverhampton	KO	5

1980

Jan.	28—Mohammed Galoul, Edgbaston	KO	5
Feb.	25—Sylvain Watbled, Belfast	KO by	10
Apr.	21—Billy Aird, Edgbaston	W	10
Sept.	22—Tom Kiely, Belfast	W	12

(Won Vacant Irish Heavyweight Title)

MAURICE FICO
French Junior Lightweight
1977

Dec.	5—Tchambe Tchatchoua, Paris	W	4
Dec.	15—Christian Valentin, Paris	W	6

1978

Jan.	16—Mohammed Boundka, Paris	D	6
Feb.	2—Christian Valentin, Melun	D	6
May	11—Michel Lirola, Paris	LF	4
Nov.	24—Jose Garcia, Liegi	D	6
Dec.	16—Alan Marchand, Paris	KO	2

1979

Feb.	17—Jean Yves Julien, Neuville	KO	4
Mar.	26—Tusikoleta Nkalankete,Paris	L	
May	19—Georges Lietaer, Tourcoing	KO	8
Oct.	30—Francis Bailleol, Paris	KO	6
Nov.	15—Patrick Drelon, Paris	KO	3
Dec.	10—Alain Le Fol, Paris	W	8

1980

Jan.	16—Alain Le Fol, Bologna	L	12

(For French Junior Lightweight Title)

Feb.	1—Samuel Meck, Marseilles	L	8
Mar.	10—Bingo Crooks, Paris	L	8

DAVE FINIGAN
British Welterweight
1980

July	14—Peter Lock, London	L	6
Sept.	22—Steve Freeman, London	W	6
Oct.	6—Billy Bryce, Southwark	L	6

KEVIN FINNEGAN
British Middleweight
Brother of Chris Finnegan
Born: Apr. 18, 1948, Hayes, England
1970

Nov.	23—Bill Deasey, London	KO	4
Dec.	8—Maurice Thomas, London	KO	6

1971

Jan.	25—Gerald Gooding, London	W	6
Feb.	10—Dave Ivory, London	KO	4

Apr.	6—Clive Cook, London	W	8
Apr.	27—Dick Duffy, London	W	8
June	14—Ronnie Hough, London	KO by	2
Sept.	27—Mick O'Neill, London	KO	6
Nov.	16—Pat Dwyer, London	W	8

1972

Feb.	15—Harry Scott, London	W	10

(Elim British Middleweight Title)

Mar.	13—Tom Bell, London	W	8
Apr.	10—Eric Blake, London	W	10
May	24—Don McMillan, Bedford	KO by	5

(Final Eliminator British Middleweight Title)

Sept.	12—Dave Cranswick, London	KO	3
Oct.	17—Len Gibbs, London	KO	6
Nov.	14—Carlos Marks, Wembley	W	8

1973

Jan.	17—Pat McCann, London	W	12
Mar.	12—Leon Washington, London	KO	7
Mar.	27—Alvin Anderson, London	W	8
May	7—Ronnie Hough, London	KO	8
Oct.	23—Bob Murphy, London	KO	4
Dec.	3—Frank Young, London	W	8

1974

Feb.	11—Bunny Sterling, London	W	15

(British Title)

May	27—Jean Claude Bouttier, Paris	W	15

(European Middleweight Title)

Oct.	29—Eddie Mazon, London	KO	9
Nov.	12—Frank Reiche, London	W	10

1975

May	7—Gratien Tonna, Monte Carlo	L	15

(European Middleweight Title)

Nov.	4—Alan Minter, London	L	15

(British Middleweight Title)

1976

Feb.	25—Danny McCafferty, London	KO	4
Mar.	15—Oscar Angus, London	W	8
Apr.	10—Freddie DeKerpel, Zele	KO	9
Sept.	14—Alan Minter, London	L	15

(British Middleweight Title)

Nov.	15—Oscar Angus, Bethnal Green	W	8
Dec.	7—Alec Tompkins, Kensington	W	8

1977

May	31—Frankie Lucas, London	KO	11

(British Middleweight Title)

Sept.	30—Karl Vinson, London	W	10
Nov.	8—Alan Minter, London	L	15

(British Middleweight Title)

1978

Mar.	4—Marvin Hagler, Boston	KO by	8
May	13—Marvin Hagler, Boston	KO by	7
Sept.	26—Bobby Patterson, Wembley	W	8
Dec.	7—Ayub Kalule, Copenhagen	L	10

1979

Feb.	3—Charlie Weir, Johannesburg	KO by	7
May	29—Abel Cordova, Kensington	W	8
Nov.	6—Tony Sibson, Kensington	W	15

(Won British Middleweight Title)

1980

Feb.	7—Gratien Tonna, Paris	W	12

(Won Vacant European Middleweight Title)

May	14—George Steinherr, Munich	D	12

(Retained European Middleweight Title)

Sept.	10—Matteo Salvemini, San Remo	L	12

(Lost European Middleweight Title)
(Announced Retirement)

JIMMY FLINT
British Featherweight
1973

Dec.	17—Dai Davies, London	W	6

1974

Apr.	1—Alan Trumbath, London	W	6
Nov.	18—Devlin White, Mayfair	W	6

1975

Jan.	28—Dave Tuohey, Shoreditch	W	6
Mar.	18—Gerry McBride, Bethnal Green	W	6
Apr.	2—Lawrence Devanney, Hammersmith	W	6
Oct.	14—Delvin White, London	W	6

1976

June	22—Dave Tuohey, Wembley	KO	3
Sept.	14—Roger Doyle, Kensington	KO	8
Oct.	26—Kenny Matthews, London	KO	8
Dec.	7—Alan Oag, Kingsington	KO	1

1977

Feb.	1—Bingo Crooks, London	L	8
May	31—Mark Bliss, Kensington	KO	4

1978

Jan.	24—Danny Tratzinski, London	W	8
Apr.	25—Paddy Graham, London	KO	8
Nov.	11—Jean-Pierre Planque, Wembley	KO	2

1979

Feb.	20—Sam Meck, Kensington	KO	6
Apr.	10—Wardell Williams, London	KO	3

May	29—Gianfranco Lalli, Kensington	KO	2
Sept.	11—Pee Wee Stokes, London	KO	4
Oct.	9—Leo Lopez	KO	9
Nov.	6—Victor Diaz, Kensington	KO	1
1980			
Feb.	19—Pat Cowdell, London	KO	12
	(Won British Featherweight Title)		
June	28—Doug Hill, London	KO	1
Oct.	14—Cordobes Lopez, London	KO	2

TONY FLORES
Filipino Lightweight
1979

Mar.	4—Rod De Los Santos, Cebu City	KO by	9
June	3—Rod De Los Santos, Cebu City	KO	7
June	23—Mike Benitez, Cebu City	KO	3
Aug.	26—Joe Lim, Cebu City	KO	4
Dec.	21—Lito Pena, Quezon City	L	12
1980			
Mar.	16—Al Cordero, Cebu City	TD	10
June	22—Mar Sumbajon, Cebu City	W	10
July	16—Deuk-Koo Kim, Manila	KO by	8
Sept.	7—Petsayam Petcharern, De Oro City	KO	7
Oct.	26—Nilo Acido, Cebu City	KO by	10
	(Lost Phillipine Lightweight Title)		

COLIN FLUTE
British Heavyweight
1977

Oct.	18—Clive Beardsley, Wolverhampton	L	6
Nov.	8—Bob Young, West Bromwich	D	6
1978			
Apr.	17—Frank Caulfield, Walworth	D	6
June	29—Terry O'Connor, Wolverhampton	L	8
July	12—Neil Malpass, Newcastle	KO by	6
Sept.	27—Terry Chard, Evesham	KO by	5
Oct.	31—Roy Skeldon, Wolverhampton	KO	4
Nov.	20—Derek Simpkin, Birmingham	L	6
1979			
Mar.	28—Glenn Adair, Kettering	L	6
Apr.	10—Roy Skeldon, Wolverhampton	L	4
May	16—Roy Skeldon, Wolverhampton	KO by	4
June	26—Steve Fenton, Leicester	L	4
Sept.	26—Stuart Lithgoe, Solihull	KO by	4
Dec.	13—Martin Nee, Wimbledon	W	6
1980			
Mar.	17—Mick Chmilowskyz, London	KO by	2
May	14—Steve Gee, Burslem	L	6
Sept.	22—Steve Gee, Birmingham	L	6

ARTHUR FOGUEIRO
Italian Junior Welterweight
1976

Nov.	27—Michel Lecerf, Brive	W	6
1977			
Feb.	5—Fernand Gomar, Brive	W	6
Mar.	11—Michel Guiot, Marsiglia	KO	3
Oct.	15—Gilbert Helluin, Brive	W	6
Nov.	12—Lamjed Guizani, Brive	WF	3
1978			
Jan.	13—Christian Garcia, Tarbes	KO by	6
Jan.	28—Jean Michele Iger, Perigueux	D	6
Feb.	4—Philipe Dumont, Brive	W	6
Feb.	11—Pierre Koenig, Tolosa	W	6
Mar.	31—Salid Mimun Amar, Tarbes	W	8
Apr.	21—Claude Viard, Tolosa	W	8
Apr.	28—Martin P. Real, Grenoble	W	8
May	26—Salid Mimun Amar, Agen	D	8
Oct.	20—Joel Moulin, Agen	W	8
Oct.	27—Carlos Foldes, Brive	W	10
Nov.	4—Dider Kowalski, Marly	KO by	3
1979			
Jan.	13—Didier Kowalski, Lille	KO by	3
	(French Lightweight Title)		
Jan.	19—Carlos Foldes, Echirolles	D	8
Feb.	3—Joel Moulin, Limoges	L	8
Feb.	13—Juan Jose Jimenez, Pesaro	KO by	3
1980			
Feb.	13—Juan Jose Gimenez, Pesaro	KO by	2

DOMINIQUE FORTEMPS
Belgian Welterweight
1979

Apr.	6—Raphael Salamone, Bruxelles	L	6
Oct.	20—Eric Caposella, Liegi	W	6
Nov.	10—Alex Beynaert, Montaigu	W	6
Dec.	14—Raffaele Salamone, Bruxelles	W	6
1980			
Jan.	25—Alex Beynaerts, Cheratte	W	6
Feb.	??—Dennis Price, Molenbeek	L	6
Mar.	21—Mohamed Bouziani, Cheratte	L	6
Nov.	22—Jo Bollue, La Louviere	L	6

STEVE FOX
British Light Heavyweight
1977

May	16—Mickey Quinn, London	KO by	3
Nov.	22—Carl North, Wolverhampton	L	4
1978			
Feb.	13—Mohammad Akram, Birmingham	W	6
Apr.	4—Clifton Wallace, London	W	6
Apr.	21—Trevor Kerr, Enniskellen	W	8
May	8—Joe Hannaford, Birmingham	KO	4
June	19—Neville Estaban, Manchester	L	6
Oct.	23—Jimmy Pickard, Manchester	KO by	4
Nov.	22—Martin McEwan, Stove	L	6
1979			
Mar.	5—Boyd Farrar, London	L	6
Apr.	25—Russ Blanks, Burslem	W	6
June	14—Joe Jackson, Dudley	L	6
Nov.	14—Joe Jackson, Stoke	KO by	4
1980			
Oct.	8—Joe Frater, Stoke	KO by	4

ANTONIO FRANCA
Italian Featherweight
1975

May	1—Fritz Chervet, Frauenfeld	KO by	8
June	6—Franco Sperati, Milano	KO by	3
June	20—Emilio Pireddu, Milano	L	8
July	12—Franco Sperati, Arenzano	L	8
Aug.	2—Filippo Belvedere, Cingoli	W	8
Aug.	14—Heleno Ferreira, Portoscuso	KO by	6
Sept.	6—Teodoro Corallo, Brindisi	KO by	6
Dec.	6—Nessim Zebellini, Villeurbanne	L	8
1976			
Mar.	19—Guy Caudron, Sallaumines	KO by	6
May	8—Ali Messaoud, Algeri	L	8
Oct.	9—Guy Caudron, Bethune	KO by	4
Oct.	16—Gererd Jacob, Creil	L	8
Nov.	20—Christian Martin, Troyes	L	8
Dec.	4—Jean Jacques Souris, Creil	W	6
1977			
Jan.	29—Jose Luis Rodriguez II, Marsiglia	L	8
Apr.	1—Manuel Masso, Barcelona	KO by	3
May	6—Alfredo Mulas, Milano	L	6
May	20—Giuseppe Fossati, Milano	L	8
June	3—Jean Pierre Planque, Dijon	L	8
June	24—Alfredo Mulas, Lugo di Romagna	L	8
July	15—Cornejo Hernandez, Numana	D	8
Aug.	9—Franco Udella, Fort Village	L	8
Aug.	21—Franco Udella, Rijeka	L	8
Sept.	28—Franco Udella, Fort Village	L	8
Oct.	7—Elmilio Pireddu, Capua	D	8
Oct.	26—Luigi Tessarin, Vigevano	L	8
Nov.	10—Jose Cornejo Hernandez, Bologna	KO by	7
Dec.	14—Franco Zurlo, Taurisano	L	8
1978			
Mar.	10—Marco Gallo, Pistoia	L	8
Apr.	14—Heleno Ferreira, Milan	KO by	4
July	6—Valerio Nati, Lugo	L	8
Aug.	2—Giuseppe Fossati, Maderno del Garda	L	8
Aug.	20—Luigi De Rosa, Roccamonfina	L	8
Sept.	14—Michele De Mita, Prato	L	8
Sept.	30—Gianfranco Lalli, Sondrio	L	8
1979			
Jan.	12—Potito Di Muro, Milano	L	8
July	21—Michele D'Amato, Salerno	L	8
Aug.	3—Luigi Tessarin, Ariano Polesine	L	8
Sept.	30—Natale Caredda, Oristano	L	8
Dec.	8—Dominique Piedeleu, Calais	L	8
1980			
Feb.	8—Paolo Castrovilli, Milan	L	6
Mar.	14—Giancarlo Compiani, Milan	D	6
Mar.	28—Giancarlo Ravaioli, Rome	L	8
Apr.	18—Paolo Castrovilli, Torino	L	6
May	9—Alessandro Nardi, Rome	L	8
May	31—Andrea Dore, Sassari	KO	4
Oct.	11—Giancarlo Compiani, Cremona	L	6
Oct.	24—Giuseppe La Vite, Grosseto	L	6
Dec.	5—Romano Mugnai, Massa	W	6
Dec.	18—Pasquale Mazza, Milan	D	6

JOHNNY FRANCIS
British Welterweight
1980

May	12—Winston Ho-Shing, Manchester	W	6
May	21—Joe Mills, Coventry	W	6
June	16—Mick Redden, Manchester	W	6
July	30—Tommy Joyce, Doncaster	KO	5
Sept.	9—Steve Ward, Sheffield	KO	3
Sept.	15—Jeff Aspell, Manchester	KO	1
Sept.	24—Chris Christian, Solihull	W	8
Oct.	13—Al Stewart, Manchester	W	8

MARTIN FRANCIS
British Middleweight
1979
Oct. 22—Mick Lock, London ....KO 2
Nov. 19—Carl Daly, Lewisham ....L 6
1980
Feb. 4—Dai Woods, London ....D 6
Feb. 18—Malcolm Heath, London ....L 8
Oct. 2—Malcolm Heath, London ....L 6

BABY FRANCISCO
Filipino Featherweight
1978
Nov. 15—San Sacristan, Dumaguete City ....L 10
1979
Feb. 5—Sandy Torres, Manila ....L 10
July 15—Willie Espinosa, Cebu City ....L 10
1980
Feb. 10—Boy Dela Cruz, Cebu City ....W 10
Oct. 24—Joval de Rama, Quezon City ....KO by 7

JOE FRANCISCO
Filipino Junior Featherweight
1979
Oct. 26—Nick Caputol, Manila ....KO 2
Dec. 8—Boy Recodo, Mindoro ....KO 4
1980
Feb. 16—Rey Orbino, Mindoro ....KO 2
May 2—Somkiat Sukothai, Manila ....KO 7
June 6—Pedro Lipata, Mindoro ....KO 8
July 18—Suk-Tae Yun, Manila ....W disq. 12
Oct. 3—Gener Cruz, Quezon City ....L 10
Oct. 29—Dado Bersabal, Manila ....KO 5
Dec. 6—Mario Odias, Mindoro ....W 10

NACIAS FRANCISCO
Filipino Junior Featherweight
1979
June 25—Jaime Sanama, Manila ....D 10
Sept. 29—Geron Perros, Davao City ....W 10
Nov. 24—Rene Sedayon, Cag. de Oro City ....W 10
1980
Feb. 16—David Inocian, De Oro City ....L 10

CARLO FRASSINETTI
Italian Junior Welterweight
1971
Feb. 17—Luciano De Luca, P.S. Stefano ....L 6
June 8—Nicola Benici, Firenze ....L 6
Nov. 19—Giorgio Merlin, Frosinone ....KO by 6
Dec. 10—Vittorio Mole, Cisterna ....KO 2
1972
Apr. 27—Nedo Fabbri, Milano ....L 6
June 9—Vito Mazzoni, Pomezia ....W 6
Aug. 4—Antonio Casamonica, Albano ....L 6
Nov. 13—Vito Viola, Bologna ....L 6
1973
Jan. 25—Giancarlo Usai, Milano ....KO by 6
July 7—Mario Catena, Terracina ....D 6
Aug. 4—Raffaele Maria, Tor. S. Lorenzo ....KO 2
Oct. 6—Alfredo Di Silvio, Pomezia ....W 6
Oct. 26—Michele Siracusa, Rome ....L 8
Dec. 7—Franco Diana, Pomezia ....L 10
Dec. 17—Giovanni Maiorano, Napoli ....D 6
1974
Jan. 28—Franco Diana, Naples ....L 10
Mar. 15—Ottavio Quaresmini, Brescia ....W 6
Mar. 29—Palmiro Masala, Milan ....L 6
Apr. 26—Firmo Pasotti, Milan ....KO 4
June 28—Amleto Restano, Ardea ....W 8
Aug. 30—Giovanni Girgenti, Erice ....L 10
Oct. 24—Renzo Battistelli, Milan ....D 6
1975
Oct. 24—Renzo Battistelli, Milano ....D 6
Nov. 7—Alessandro Bini, Milan ....W 6
Dec. 27—Giancarlo Usai, Rimini ....LF 4
1976
May 21—Giovanni Girgenti, Catania ....L 8
Jun. 11—Alessandro Nardi, Roma ....D 8
Sept. 17—Giovanni Cavazzini, Colleferro ....W 8
Nov. 12—Vincenzo Burgio, Signa ....W 10
Mar. 11—Natale Caredda, Cagliari ....L 8
Oct. 8—Ugo Poli, Morbegna ....KO 8
(Italian Junior Lightweight Title)
1978
Jan. 21—Biagio Pierri, Cinciello Salsamo ......L 12
(Italian Super Featherweight Title)
Feb. 25—Cosimo Lavino, Brindisi ....L 8
Apr. 19—Giovanni Vitillo, Viareggio ....L 8
June 9—Aristede Pizzo, Milano ....KO by 2
July 7—Angelo Provenzano, Genova ....L 6
Sept. 23—Alfonso Carrillo, Pietramelara ...KO by 6

1979
Aug. 10—Giancarlo Usai, Santander ....KO by 4
Dec. 28—Bruno Demontis, Sassari ....L 8
1980
Mar. 14—Michele D'Amato, Rome ....L 8
Mar. 29—Angelo Bizzarro, Nocera ....LF 8
Dec. 26—Severino Picca, Piacenza ....L 8

JOE FRATER
British Light Heavyweight
1980
Feb. 6—Nigel Savory, Liverpool ....KO by 3
Mar. 31—John Stone, Cleethorpes ....KO 1
Apr. 14—Paul Heatley, Manchester ....KO 5
May 12—Chuck Hirschmann, Manchester ....D 4
June 16—Joe Dean, Manchester ....W 6
Sept. 9—Nigel Savory, Mexborough ....KO by 6
Oct. 8—Steve Fox, Stoke ....KO 4

SPARROW FREEMAN
Australian Bantamweight
1978
Feb. 9—David Carriage, Marrickville ....W 4
Feb. 21—Bobby Williams, Kingsford ....W 6
Mar. 7—Alan Ashby, Kingsford ....L 6
Mar. 23—Wayne Mulholland, Campbelltown ....L 6
Apr. 3—Patrick Burns, Cammerary ....KO 4
Apr. 18—Kirk Blair, Kingsford ....L 6
Apr. 26—Kirk Blair, Brookvale ....L 6
May 2—Kirk Blair, Kingsford ....D 6
May 16—Patrick Burns, Penrith ....L 6
May 31—Kirk Blair, Brookvale ....L 8
June 21—Victor Ward, Mt. Pritchard ....L 4
June 28—Patrick Burns, Bankstown ....KO by 6
July 19—Max Nabete, Mt. Pritchard ....W 6
July 20—David Carriage, Kogarah ....W 4
July 25—David Carriage, Kingsford ....L 6
July 26—David Carriage, Bankstown ....KO 6
Aug. 7—Saladine Allaf, Cammeray ....W 4
Aug. 8—Dick Hulzan, Kingsford ....KO 3
Aug. 16—Dick Hulzan, Brookvale ....W 4
Aug. 22—Dick Hulzan, Kingsford ....W 4
Sept. 5—Andy Roberts, Kingsford ....W 4
Sept. 19—Roy Hughes, Kingsford ....L 6
Sept. 20—Patrick Burns, Mt. Pritchard ....L 6
Sept. 27—Tom Roberts, Bankstown ....W 4
Oct. 4—Bobby Williams, Brookvale ....W 5
Oct. 17—David Carriage, Kingsford ....D 5
Oct. 25—Jimmy Bowen, Bankstown ....L 8
Dec. 2—Ron Christian, Hillston ....L 6
Dec. 14—Dick Hulzan, Kingsford ....KO 2
Dec. 20—Paul Baker, Mt. Pritchard ....D 6
1979
Feb. 7—Benny Bazz, Brookvale ....W 4
Feb. 13—David Carriage, Kingsford ....W 4
Feb. 24—Charlie Brown, Kempsey ....L 6
Mar. 1—Johnny Duff, Jindera ....L 8
Mar. 13—Wayne Mulholland, Kingsford ....L 6
Apr. 3—Charlie Brown, Cardiff ....L 10
May 8—Jimmy Bowen, Kingsford ....L 6
May 21—Chris Bingham, Booty Hill ....L 6
June 25—Gary Bice, Booty Hill ....L 6
June 27—Reg King, Revesby ....KO by 2
July 17—Bimbo Morris, Kingsford ....W 6
July 18—Gary Bice, Mt. Pritchard ....L 6
July 31—Bimbo Morris, Kingsford ....KO 4
Aug. 14—Idries Ali, Kingsford ....D 6
Aug. 15—Gavin Ridgway, Brookvale ....W 4
Aug. 28—Peter Thompson, Kingsford ....W 4
Sept. 11—Kirk Davis, Kingsford ....W 6
Sept. 25—Selby Pattel, Kingsford ....KO 3
Oct. 9—Selby Pattel, Kingsford ....W 4
Oct. 17—Selby Pattel, Brookvale ....D 4
Nov. 6—Charlie Brown, Kingsford ....L 8
(For New South Wales Junior Featherweight Title)
Dec. 14—Johnny Duff, Jindera ....L 8
Dec. 19—Kirk Davis, Mt. Pritchard ....W 3
1980
Jan. 29—Kirk Davis, Kingsford ....W 4
Feb. 6—Wayne Mulholland, Brookvale ....L 5
Mar. 5—Kirk Davis, Brookvale ....W 6
Mar. 11—Albert Singh, Kingsford ....W 6
Mar. 21—Tiger Mann, Port Moresby ....L 10
Apr. 8—Doc Rutton, Kingsford ....D 4
Apr. 22—Patrick Freeman, Kingsford ......KO by 4
May 6—Bimbo Morris, Kingsford ....KO by 4
June 4—Jeff Perkins, Brookvale ....L 6
June 17—Jeff Perkins, Kingsford ....L 6
July 2—Jeff Perkins, Brookvale ....L 6
July 15—Frank Carlson, Kingsford ....L 6
July 22—Jimmy Bowen, Sutherland ....KO by 10
Aug. 13—Joe Carriage, Brookvale ....W 6
Aug. 26—Joe Carriage, Kingsford ....W 4
Sept. 9—Joe Carriage, Kingsford ....W 4

Sept.	10—Joe Carriage, Gosford	D 6
Oct.	7—Patrick Young, Kingsford	D 6
Oct.	14—Patrick Young, Sutherland	KO 4
Oct.	21—Lou Williams, Kingsford	W 4
Nov.	4—Lou Williams, Kingsford	W 4
Nov.	5—Patrick Young, Brookvale	W 6
Nov.	14—Johnny Duff, Dederang	D 8
Dec.	2—Joe Carriage, Kingsford	W 5
Dec.	5—Johnny Duff, Berrigan	D 6
Dec.	9—Joe Carriage, Sutherland	W 6
Dec.	18—Bimbo Morris, Marrickville	W 6

STEVE FREEMAN
British Welterweight
1980

Sept.	22—Dave Finigan, London	L 6
Oct.	2—Bobby Welburn, Hull	L 6

VALERIO FRETTA
Italian Lightweight
1975

May	9—Aristide Pizzo, Milano	KO by 1
Aug.	24—Alfonso Bonavita, Marcianise	W 6
Sept.	28—Giuseppe Pappalardo, Marcianise	W 6
Oct.	31—Giovanni Maiorano, R. Emilia	KO 5
Nov.	28—Augusto Quadri, R. Emilia	KO 5
Dec.	20—Angelo Fanciulli, Tarquinia	L 6

1976

Jan.	30—Domenico Condello, Bologna	W 6
Mar.	13—Giuseppe Martucci, Latisana	L 8
Apr.	21—Giuseppe Agate, Caserta	W 8
May	15—Giuseppe Agate, Forli	L 8
Sept.	10—Antonio Puddu, Cagliari	KO by 5
Oct.	1—Bouchiba Messaoud, Lauwe	L 8
Nov.	12—Rosario Sanna, Milano	KO by 5

1977

Jan.	29—Santino Reali, Pavia	L 8
Apr.	1—Vincenzo Quero, Pesaro	KO by 5

1978
(Inactive)
1979

Sept.	22—Mario Tiano, Marcianise	KO by 5

1980

Apr.	5—Roberto Masini, Rimini	L 6
Dec.	26—Alessandro Scapecchi, Firenze	KO by 4

HARRY FRIEDEL
German Heavyweight
1978

Apr.	14—Ranier Saydok, Essen	W 4
May	6—Burghard Lembke, Luebeck	W 4

1979

Apr.	6—Gregory Downes, Luebeck	L 6
Dec.	7—Horst Lang, Luebeck	KO 1

1980

Feb.	6—Bernard August, Luebeck	KO by 5

(For German Heavyweight Title)

DAVID FRY
Irish Heavyweight
1973

Oct.	22—Kenny Burrell, Mayfair	D 6
Nov.	12—Kenny Burrell, Mayfair	KO by 5
Dec.	4—Kenny Burrell, London	KO by 4

1974

Feb.	5—Bruce Woodward, London	KO 3
Feb.	11—Dave Parris, Bedford	L 6
Feb.	18—Tony Mikulski, Mayfair	KO by 3
Apr.	29—Kenny Burrell, Kensington	D 6
May	6—Eddy Fenton, Bedford	KO by 4
June	19—Wally Pearce, Caerphilly	D 6
Sept.	23—Tony Moore, Kensington	L 6
Oct.	7—Eddy Fenton, Bristol	D 8
Oct.	29—Wally Pearce, Southsea	W 8
Dec.	3—Sid Paddock, Southhampton	KO by 7

1975

Jan.	6—Art Gibson, Hemel	W 8
Jan.	13—Sid Paddock, London	W 6
Jan.	29—Guinea Roger, Stoke	L 8
Feb.	17—Derek Simpkin, Mayfair	KO by 6
Mar.	13—Sid Paddock, London	L 8
Apr.	21—Tony Mikulski, Southhampton	KO by 1
Sept.	6—Tony Blackburn, Taunton	L 8
Sept.	24—Eddy Fenton, Solihull	L 8
Nov.	18—Paul Tucker, Hornsey	W 8
Dec.	2—Terry Mintus, Leeds	D 6

1976

Jan.	16—Eddy Fenton, Bournemouth	L 8
Feb.	3—Derek Simpkin, London	L 8
Mar.	9—Steve Carr, Hornsey	KO by 3
July	14—Brian Huckfield, Wolverhampton	KO by 7

1977

Mar.	1—Tommy Kiely, Hove	L 8

Oct.	4—Brian Paul, Southgate	L 8

1978
(Inactive)
1979

Nov.	26—Sean McKenna, Belfast	KO 4

1980

Feb.	19—Andy Palmer, London	KO by 3
Mar.	17—Les Dunn, London	W 8
Apr.	1—Mick Chmilowskyz, London	KO 6
Apr.	14—Clarence Hill, London	KO by 1
June	3—Les Dunn, London	W 8
Sept.	22—Danny McAlinden, Belfast	L 6

MASARU FUJI
Japanese Junior Lightweight
1977

Nov.	13—Tsutomu Igarashi, Tokyo	L 10

1978

Apr.	22—Bazca Shoji, Shoshi City	KO 2
Aug.	9—Nobuyuki Watanabe, Akita	KO by 8
Dec.	14—Masami Sekiyama, Tokyo	KO 5

1979

May	31—Koichi Maki, Nigata	L 10

(JBC Flyweight Title)

Oct.	22—Hiroyuki Tanaka, Tokyo	KO by 7

1980

Jan.	28—Tadao Yamane, Tokyo	KO by 4

JOHNNY FUJIMOTO
Japanese Featherweight
1980

Feb.	26—Yasuhide Takahashi, Tokyo	KO by 1
Apr.	20—Akio Akamine, Tokyo	KO 6

RYU FUKIDA
Japanese Junior Lightweight
Born: Nov. 8, 1950, Kurayoshi City, Tottori Prefecture
1973

Apr.	20—Yoshisuke Gonda, Osaka Prefectural Gym	KO 1
June	2—Masayuki Miyashita, Nishio	KO by 3
July	27—Toshimasa Nakai, Osaka	D 4
Sept.	26—Makoto Shigeki, Osaka	KO 1
Oct.	12—Takeo Kajimoto, Osaka	KO 1
Nov.	12—Kikuo Ita, Osaka	W 6
Dec.	19—Yoshio Yoshida, Nagoya	W 6

1974

Feb.	20—Hidemaru Sugawara, Osaka	W 6
May	10—Sakae Nakamura, Osaka	W 6
Sept.	5—Royal Kobayashi, Osaka	KO by 4

1975

Jan.	13—Junichi Okubo, Osaka	KO by 6
Apr.	18—Jumbo Nakatsuka, Tokuyama	L 10
July	15—Bargilio Amano, Honolulu	KO by 2
Sept.	23—Kid Pabanlag, Honolulu	KO 1
Oct.	14—Rudy Tolongali, Honolulu	KO 5

1976

July	23—Roger Moreno, Honolulu	W 4
Oct.	6—Virgilio Legaspi, Honolulu	KO 5

1977

Apr.	2—Masayuki Miyashita, Tokyo	KO 4
June	21—Masabumi Mochizuki, Tokyo	KO 5
Aug.	23—Chong Tae Yuh, Tokyo	W 10
Nov.	30—Lee Yidano, Tokyo	W 10

1978

Jan.	24—Mun-Suk Choi, Tokyo	KO by 4
Apr.	28—Yatsutsune Uehara, Tokyo	KO by 7

(Japanese Junior Lightweight Title)

Aug.	29—Koji Kunishege, Tokyo	KO 6

1979

Jan.	14—Mun-Suk Choi, Pusan	KO by 11

(OPBF Junior Lightweight Title)

June	22—Johnny Sato, Manila	L 12
Nov.	6—Mun-Suk Choi, Tokyo	KO 1

(Won OPBF Junior Lightweight Title)
1980

Apr.	25—Yang Il, Tokyo	W 12

(Retained OPBF Junior Lightweight Title)

EIICHI FUKUMOTO
Japanese Junior Welterweight
Amateur Record: 59-9 37 KOs
1977

Mar.	8—Shoji Ito, Tokyo	KO 4
May	15—Ko Kazagawa, Tokyo	KO 1
Oct.	13—Ruben Martinez, Los Angeles	KO 2
Oct.	27—Jose Mora, Los Angeles	KO 1
Nov.	10—Ron Turner, Los Angeles	W 6
Dec.	15—Jose Cota, Los Angeles	L 4

1978

Feb.	2—Pablo Baez, Los Angeles	KO by 3
June	27—Hiromi Nishida, Tokyo	KO 6
Aug.	15—Senju Yamaguchi, Tokyo	KO 6
Dec.	28—Harbar Watanabe, Tokyo	W 10

1979
Mar. 14—Toru Sugawara, Tokyo .... W 10
June 28—Akiyoshi Ogino, Tokyo .... W 10
Sept. 24—Noboru Hatakeyama, Tokyo .... KO 4
(Won JBC Junior Welterweight Title)
1980
Jan. 29—Gold Joe (Jyo), Tokyo .... KO 3
Mar. 17—Hayao Shiba, Tokyo .... KO 3
(Retained Japanese Junior Welterweight Title)
May 19—Minoru Sugiya, Tokyo .... L 10
(Lost Japanese Junior Welterweight Title)
Sept. 23—Minoru Sugiya, Tokyo .... KO 1
(Won Japanese Junior Welterweight Title)

SIPHIWO FUMA
South African Bantamweight
1978
July 29—Marva Malla, Queenstown .... KO 2
Oct. 21—Ntsikelelo Mona, Queenstown .... W 4
1979
Feb. 10—Tembile Sigetye, Queenstown .... KO 1
July 7—Lucas Ncetezo, Queenstown .... KO 4
Nov. 3—Joe Ngidi, Queenstown .... KO 6
Dec. 1—Nkosana Tolbert, King Williamstown .... W 6
1980
Feb. 9—Duluxolo Tyekana, East London .... KO 3
(Retained Cape Bantamweight Title)
Mar. 29—Vincent Ngcobo, Queenstown .... KO 5
May 31—Monde Mpulampula, East London ... W disq. 4
July 19—Gaybon Yekiso, East London .... L 8
July 26—Tito Dastile, King Williamstown .... L 6
Dec. 13—Nkosana Tolbert, Queenstown .... W 8

COSIMO FUNTO
Spanish Middleweight
1979
July 25—Luciano Di Giacomo, Rimini .... W 6
1980
Mar. 15—Raffaele Prete, Brindisi .... W 6
Apr. 25—Mauricio Da Cruz, Brundisi .... W 6

PETER GABBITUS
British Bantamweight
1980
May 20—Iggy Jano, Southend .... W 4
June 11—George Bailey, Morecambe .... W 4
July 30—Brindley Jones, Doncaster .... W 4
Oct. 22—Sammy Sims, Doncaster .... L 4

MANNY GABRIEL
British Heavyweight
1976
Oct. 11—Winston Cousins, Nottingham .... W 8
1977
Feb. 15—Davey Mullings, Northampton .... L 6
Mar. 21—Davey Mullings, Nottingham .... L 8
Apr. 18—Reg Long, Bedford .... NC 2
Apr. 27—Francis Hand, Bradford .... L 8
May 16—Reg Long, Glasgow .... W 6
June 9—Eddie Vierling, Portsmouth .... L 6
1978
Mar. 20—George Gray, Luton .... D 6
Apr. 17—Shaun Chalcraft, Hove .... L 8
Nov. 27—Rocky Burton, Kettering .... W 6
1979
Mar. 28—Rocky Burton, Kettering .... KO 1
June 18—Winston Allen, Windsor .... KO 1
Dec. 11—Reg Long, Bletchley .... KO 3
1980
Jan. 22—Joe Awome, London .... KO by 3
June 3—Larry McDonald, Aylesbury .... KO by 2
Oct. 20—Stuart Lithgow, Birmingham .... L 4
(Announced Retirement)

PHINDILE GAIKA
South African Flyweight
1975
Aug. 23—Fezile Mzalazala, Port Elizabeth .... L 6
Sept. 6—Peter Windvogel, Port Elizabeth .... W 6
Dec. 6—Ruben Matewu, Port Elizabeth .... W 6
1976
Mar. 13—Mcenizeli Stootman, Port Elizabeth .... W 6
May 22—Hendrik Koelman, Port Elizabeth .... W 6
July 17—Gilbert Makenete, Port Elizabeth .... W 6
Nov. 6—Ruben Matewu, King Williamstown ..... L 6

1977
Nov. 19—Andile Tywabi, East London .... W 10
Dec. 10—Tito Dasitile, East London .... L 6
1978
Feb. 18—Daluxolo Tyekana, East London .... W 6
Aug. 26—Peter Mathebula, East London .... KO by 5
Nov. 4—Monde Mpulampula, Port Elizabeth .... W 10
1979
Apr. 7—Peter Mathebula, Port Elizabeth ..... KO by 9
Nov. 3—Ruben Matewu, Port Elizabeth .... W 6
1980
July 19—Cosmo Zigu, East London .... D 6
Dec. 20—Sexon Ngqayimbana, East London ... KO by 5

MXOLISI GALADA
South African Bantamweight
1980
Mar. 1—Temba Gawula, East London .... L 4
May 3—Mbinasi Fuma, East London .... KO 3
May 31—Zola Mali, East London .... L 4
Nov. 8—Sexon Ngqayimbana, East London ... KO by 3

AMALIO GALAN
Spanish Junior Lightweight
1979
Apr. 7—Carlos M. Rodriguez, Mondragon .... W 4
May 12—Jose M. Llorente, Arechaveleta .... W 4
June 9—Vicente Manzanares, Logrono .... L 6
June 22—Antonio Vazquez, Mondragon .... W 4
July 14—Francisco Cabello, S. Sebastiano .... W 4
July 30—Julio Garcia, S. Sebastiano .... D 4
Oct. 6—Mohamed Larbi, Mondragon .... W 6
Dec. 8—Jose Maria Guevos, Orio .... KO 3
1980
Mar. 8—Vincente Hernando, Mondragon .... W 8

FERMIN GALLARDO
Spanish Lightweight
1979
Sept. 22—Jose A. Martin Mateos, Oviedo .... W 4
Oct. 20—Jose M. Guervos, Oviedo .... L 4
1980
Feb. 14—Jose Pacheco, Bilbao .... W 8
Feb. 16—Lorenzo Martinez, Oviedo .... W 4
Mar. 8—Miguel A. Rodriguez, Oviedo .... W 4

MARTIN GALLEOZZIE
Welch Lightweight
Born: March 12, 1954
1972
Nov. 20—Billy Belnavis, Caerphilly .... KO by 1
1973
Jan. 15—Dave Grantley, Caerphilly .... KO 2
Feb. 13—Dai Davies, Haverfordwest .... KO 1
Mar. 27—Vernon Sollas, Birmingham .... KO by 7
Apr. 30—Mario Stango, Bedford .... KO by 4
Aug. —Graham Murphy, Cardiff .... W 6
Dec. 4—Billy Belnavis, Merthyr .... W 8
1974
Mar. 26—Colin Miles, Caerphilly .... KO by 5
Apr. 23—Billy Taylor, Kensington .... KO by 6
1975
Oct. 13—Ian Pickersgill, London................. D 8
Nov. 12—Young Silky, Caerphilly .... W 8
Dec. 2—Alun Trembath, London .... W 8
Dec. 15—Young Silky, London .... W 8
1976
Jan. 14—Tommy Glencross, Solihull .... KO by 1
Mar. 1—Johnny Claydon, Walworth .... KO 5
Mar. 8—Barton McAllister, Birmingham ..... KO by 6
Sept. 27—Gary Dunks, London .... KO 6
Oct. 11—Jeff Pritchard, London.................. L 8
Nov. 23—Johnny Wall, Teorchu .... W 10
Dec. 13—Dill Collins, London .... W 10
(Vacant Welsh Lightweight Title)
1977
Feb. 15—Johnny Wall, Merthyr .... L 10
(Welsh Lightweight Title)
1978
Jan. 26—Omar Sahli, Oslo .... D 6
Mar. 2—Hans Henrik Palm, Vejle .... KO by 1
June 1—Eric Wood, Cardiff .... W 8
July 10—Kelvin Webber, Aberavon .... W 10
(Welsh Lightweight Title)
Sept. 21—Jeff Pritchard, Caerphilly .... W 10
(Welsh Lightweight Title)
1979
(Inactive)
1980
Jan. 8—Dave McCabe, Windsor .... L 12
(Elimination Bout For British Lightweight Title)
Sept. 15—George Metcalf, Windsor .... L 8
Oct. 6—Joey Singleton, Southwark .... KO by 5

GUIDO GALLETTI
Italian Welterweight
1972
Nov. 17—Vittorio Tamburini, Rome .... KO by 5
1973
Feb. 8—Emilio De Plano, Bergamo .... KOby 4
July 20—Giuseppe Maniccini, Fiuggi .... L 6
July 28—Piercarlo Pedrinelli, Trenzano .... KO by 4
1974
Jan. 25—Umberto Restanti, Nettuno .... KO by 3
Feb. 19—Alvaro Pegoli, Rome .... W 6
Apr. 30—Ali Kaya, Faenza .... L 6
May 23—Ali Kaya, Bologna .... L 6
Aug. 3—Giancarlo Serangeli, Bagni .... D 6
Dec. 6—Vincenzo Muruzzi, R. Emilia .... L 6
1975
June 27—Angelo Scaffeo, Valco Lucano .... W 6
Aug. 8—Paolo Zanusso, Jesolo .... KO by 5
Nov. 28—Clemente Gessi, Ferrera .... L 6
Dec. 27—Italo Venturi, Rimini .... LF 5
1976
Apr. 23—Luigi Martello, Rome .... D 6
May 21—Sejfudin Hozic, Rome .... KO 4
Oct. 15—Angelo D'Isidoro, Rome .... W 6
Nov. 14—Alvaro Pegoli, Magliano S. .... W 6
Dec. 18—Reynald Iten, Sierre .... W 6
1977
Feb. 23—Vittorio Tamburini, Fasano .... KO 5
Mar. 9—Vittorio Tamburini, Reiti .... KO 6
Apr. 1—Remo Costa, Rome .... KO by 2
June 15—Bernardo Bonizzoni, Milano .... KO 6
Aug. 13—Esperno Postl, Zeltweg .... L 8
Oct. 21—Timoteo Bonizzoni, Milano .... L 6
Dec. 14—Remo Costa, Taurisano .... L 6
1978
Mar. 16—Kadir Yuceler, Tripoli .... W 10
Sept. 5—Giuseppe Russi, Bibione .... KO by 3
Nov. 3—Pietro Callara, Rome .... L 4
Dec. 19—Kadir Yuceler, Istanbul .... L 10
1979
Apr. 12—Mehmet Cakal, Izmit .... KO by 3
Sept. 21—Giancarlo Marinelli, Rome .... KO 5
Oct. 27—Salvatore Cascio, Rieti .... L 8
1980
Apr. 11—Franz Hohl, Rome .... KO 1
May 15—Luis Ribeiro, Rome .... D 8

FRANCESCO GALLO
Italian Welterweight
1976
Aug. 27—Domenico Milone, Chivasso .... KO 4
Sept. 10—Carmine Zollo, Fort Village .... W 6
Oct. 29—Alfonso Bonavita, Novara .... KO 4
Dec. 17—Giuseppe Corbo, Novara .... L 6
1977
Mar. 4—Franco Canconi, Torino .... KO 1
Mar. 19—Fernandez Gualberto, Chivasso .... W 6
Apr. 22—Rocco Frasca, Milano .... KO 4
May 13—Domenico Radicioni, Turin .... KO 6
Aug. 5—Carmine Zollo, Forte Village .... W 6
Oct. 22—Giuseppe Corbo, Torino .... D 6
Nov. 19—Domenico Milone, Torino .... KO 6
Dec. 26—Luciano Navarra, Milano .... W 8
1978
Jan. 27—Giovanni Maiorano, Milano .... W 8
Mar. 3—Claude Virard, Torino .... KO 2
Apr. 15—Luiz Ribeiro, Biella .... D 8
July 21—Giuseppe Corbo, Ischia .... D 8
Oct. 20—Giuseppe Corbo, Milano .... L 10
1979
Jan. 12—Luciano Navarra, Milano .... KO 2
Feb. 3—Robert Gambini, Marseille .... KO by 2
May 11—Giuseppe Martinese, Senigallia ...... NC 6
(Italian Junior Welterweight Title)
July 13—Giuseppe Russi, San Severo .... L 8
Oct. 26—Giuseppe Martinese, Chivasso .... L 12
(Italian Junior Welterweight Title)
1980
Mar. 8—Franco Aresti, Calgari .... L 8
July 6—Giuseppe Russi, Fort Village .... W 8
Sept. 12—Giuseppe Agate, Chibasso .... W 8
Oct. 18—Roberto Masini, Rimini .... KO 1

MARCO GALLO
Italian Featherweight
1977
Nov. 11—Vincenzo Mrana, Pistoia .... KO 6
Dec. 1—Lorenzo Paciullo, Trieste .... W 6
Dec. 16—Domenico Condello, Pistoia .... KO 4
1978
Jan. 27—Lucio Vailoti, Pistoia .... W 8
Mar. 10—Antonio Franca, Pistoia .... W 8
Apr. 15—Mario Cappellotto, Montecatini .... KO 3

May 5—Pasqualino Morbidelli, Pistoia .... KO 7
July 12—Potito Di Muro, Pistoia .... KO by 7
1979
Mar. 9—Alessandro Nardi, Rome .... W 8
June 9—Natale Caredda, Cagliari .... L 8
July 6—Sergio Emili, Pistoia .... W 8
1980
Mar. 26—Alfredo Mulas, Lugo di Romagna .... KO 3
(Won Italian Featherweight Title)
May 23—Gerard Jacob, Pistoia .... KO 3
July 11—Gianfranco Lalli, Sondrio .... KO 3
(Retained Italian Featherweight Title)
Sept. 24—Salvatore Melluzzo, Giuggi .... L 12
(Lost Italian Featherweight Title)

MOHAMED GALOUL
French Heavyweight
1977
Sept. 30—Robert Desnouck, Lauwe .... D 6
Oct. 14—Rinaldo Pelizzari, Milano .... KO by 6
Nov. 26—Albert Syven, Bruxelles .... L 6
1978
Feb. 11—Robert Desnouck, Liegi .... L 6
Mar. 18—Albert Syben, Vivegnis .... L 8
July 15—Felipe Rodriguez, La Coruna .... L 8
Dec. 26—Giovanni De Luca, Milano .... L 8
1979
June 9—Roberto Bosio, La Louviere .... KO 2
Sept. 28—Albert Syben, Moelenbeek .... L 8
Dec. 26—Giovanni De Luca, Milan .... L 8
1980
Jan. 28—Gordon Ferris, Edgbaston .... KO by 5

LUNGILE GANGALA
South African Welterweight
1977
June 11—Tembile Piliso, East London .... KO 4
1978
July 29—Kho Tywakadi, Queenstown .... KO by 2
1979
July 14—Leonard Siliwane, East London .... W 4
1980
Feb. 9—Eric Ncedane, East London .... KO 1
Aug. 16—Aaron Somdaka, East London .... KO by 4

FLASH GAPASIN
Filipino Bantamweight
1979
Mar. 20—Eddie Miral, Angeles City .... L 10
Nov. 27—Al Sicat, Angeles City .... L 10
Dec. 22—Star Dayanan, Zambales .... L 10
1980
Jan. 25—Cesar Amazan, Manila .... L 10

ANTONIO GARCIA DEL MORAL
(TANIO I)
Spanish Featherweight
1980
Jan. 5—Esteban Eguia, Santander .... KO by 4
Apr. 19—Angel Oliver, Zaragoza .... KO 1
June 1—Diego Valero, Tarrasa .... W 8

JOAQUIN GARCIA (DEL MORAL)
(TANIO II)
Spanish Lightweight
1980
Mar. 26—Antonio Granados, Palma de Mallorca .... W 6
Apr. 19—Jose Luis Vicho, Palma de Mallorca ...... L 8
May 23—Francisco Moya, Palma de Mallorca ..... D 6
July 5—Jose Heredia, Malaga .... LF 8
(For Spanish Lightweight Title)

JOSE GARCIA
Belgian Junior Welterweight
1977
Dec. 23—Giovanni Mannu, Molenbeek .... KO 3
1978
Mar. 3—Jean Yves Julien, Chatelineau .... W 6
Mar. 17—Abdel Ben Ameur, La Louviere .... L 6
Apr. 28—Jooris Demeyer, Chatelineau .... KO 3
May 19—Tchambe Tchatchoua, Charleroi .... KO 3
Nov. 24—Maurice Fico, Liegi ....'........... D 6
1979
Jan. 6—Michel Lirola, St. Servais .... KO 5
Mar. 2—Abdel Ben Ameur, Liegi .... KO 2
May 19—Claude Viard, Bruxelles .... KO 1
June 9—Patrick Goblet, La Louviere .... W 6
Oct. 30—Andres Blanco, Liege .... W 8
Nov. 10—Alain LeFol, Bruxelles .... W 8
Dec. 14—Dave Williams, Bruxelles .... KO by 4
1980
Jan. 12—Mohamed Titi Larbi, Zaragoza .... W 8

Jan. 26—Joaquin Garcia del Moral, Zaragoza ......W 6
Aug. 30—Chato Melillense, Vitoria ....D 8

JULIO GARCIA (BARCINA)
Spanish Lightweight
1979
Aug. 4—Mohamed El Kodoumi, Vigo ....L 6
Nov. 16—Mohamed Chino, Madrid ....L 6
1980
Feb. 2—Mohamed El Kadoumi, Fuengirola ....L 6

MARIANO GARCIA
Spanish Flyweight
1972
Mar. 3—Antonio Tenza, Madrid ....KO 7
Mar. 17—Pedro de Latorre, Madrid ....W 8
Apr. 14—Jose Lopez Gallego, Madrid ....W 8
June 1—Gonzalo Aspron, Leon ....KO 8
July 14—Fernando Segura, Madrid ....KO 6
Aug. 4—Manuel Castro, Madrid ....W 8
Oct. 13—Fritz Chervet, Geneva ....L 15
(European Flyweight Title)
1973
Mar. 16—Pedro Molledo, Madrid ....W 8
May 12—Pedro De La Torre, Madrid ....W 8
July 20—Jose Luis Otero, Madrid ....KO 8
(Spanish Flyweight Title)
Oct. 19—Antonio Tenza, Barcelona ....W 8
1974
May 19—Jose Rodriguez, Monacor ....W 8
June 28—Pedro Molleda, Burgos ....L 12
(Spanish Flyweight Title)
Aug. 30—Jose Rodriguez, Madrid ....W 8
Nov. 15—Fritz Chervet, Geneva ....L 10
1975
July 26—Betulio Gonzelez, Caracas ....KO by 2
Dec. 5—Francisco Rodriguez, Madrid ....KO 6
1976
Jan. 10—Pedro Molledo, Alicante ....W 15
Apr. 2—Antonio Tenza, Catorroja ....W 8
Apr. 10—Angel Oliver, Oviedo ....W 8
Aug. 7—Jose Cantero, Lepe ....L 12
(Spanish Flyweight Title)
Nov. 26—Jose Cantero, Madrid ....W 8
Dec. 23—Manuel Carrasco, S. Sebastiano ....L 8
1977
Oct. 7—Jose Cantero, Malaga ....W 12
(Spanish Flyweight Title)
Dec. 2—Jose Herrera, Madrid ....L 10
1978
Feb. 4—Jaime Rodriguez, Lugo ....W 12
(Spanish Flyweight Title)
May 24—Franco Udella, Cagliari ....KO by 6
(European Flyweight Title)
Oct. 7—Jaime R. Lozano, Lugo ....KO 6
Oct. 28—Vicente Rodriguez, La Coruna ....L 8
Dec. 5—Charlie Magri, Kensington ....KO by 3
1979
Mar. 19—German Yestes, Valencia ....KO 5
(Spanish Flyweight Title)
Aug. 18—Enrique Rodriguez Cal, Aviles ....L 12
(Spanish Flyweight Title)
Sept. 26—Giovanni Camputaro, Piedimonte ....L 10
Nov. 16—Paolo Castrovilli, Milan ....L 8
1980
Feb. 29—Steve Muchoki, Odense ....L 8
Apr. 17—Mike Irungu, Copenhagen ....L 8
June 27—Enrique Rodriguez Cal, La Coruna ....L 10
(For Spanish Flyweight Title)

RAMON GARCIA (MARICHAL)
Spanish Junior Lightweight
1980
Jan. 11—Carlos Hernandez, Las Palmas ....D 8
Mar. 28—Isidoro Cabeza, Palma de Mallorca ....D 10
(For Spanish Junior Lightweight Title)
May 10—Mariano Rodriguez, Cruz Tenerife ....W 8
Sept. 6—Carlos Hernandez, Cruz Tenerife ....L 12
(For European Junior Lightweight Title)

JOHN L. GARDNER
British Heavyweight
Born: January 2, 1953
1973
Oct. 2—Brian Hall, London.....................KO 2
Oct. 30—Sid Paddock, London ....KO 3
Nov. 13—Gerald Gooding, London ....W 6
Dec. 11—Kenny Burrell, London ....KO 5
Dec. 18—Lloyd Stewart, Shoreditch ....KO 2
1974
Jan. 15—Barry Clough, London..................KO 2
Mar. 26—Les McGowan, London..................KO 5
May 7—John Celebanski, Shoreditch ....KO 7

May 21—Sid Poddock, Wembley..................KO 4
June 4—John Celebanski, London ....KO 3
Oct. 29—Toni Mikulski, London...................W 6
Dec. 3—Tony Blackburn, London................W 8
1975
Mar. 11—Peter Freeman, Wembley ....KO 6
Apr. 29—Tony Mikulski, London ....KO 3
Oct. 14—Jerry Huston, London ....KO 5
1976
Jan. 20—Lloyd Walford, London ....KO 2
Mar. 2—Bjorn Rudim, London..................KO 3
Apr. 6—Bobby Walker, London ....KO 8
Apr. 27—Tony Moore, Kensington................KO 6
June 1—Fred Askew, London ....WF 6
Oct. 12—Joe Gholson, Wembley.................W 8
Oct. 26—Neville Meade, Kensington ....KO 6
1977
Mar. 29—Brian O'Melia, London ....KO 2
May 31—Ngozika Ekwelum, London ....KO 6
Sept. 27—Ibar Arrington, London ....KO by 1
Dec. 6—Denton Ruddock, London ....KO 8
1978
Apr. 4—Dennis Jordan, London ....KO 3
Oct. 24—Billy Aird, London ....KO 5
(British Heavyweight Title)
Dec. 5—Greg Sorrentino, Kensington ....KO 7
1979
Feb. 20—Mike Koranicki, Kensington ....KO 9
June 26—Paul Sykes, London ....KO 6
(British Heavyweight Title)
Dec. 5—Jimmy Young, London ....L 10
1980
Apr. 22—Rudi Gauwe, London ....KO 9
(Won Vacant European Heavyweight Title)
Nov. 28—Lorenzo Zanon, Ostia ....KO 5
(Retained European Heavyweight Title)

RUDI GAUWE
Belgian Heavyweight
1976
Nov. 11—Maurice Trepant, Zele ....KO 3
1977
Jan. 8—Lassine Naire, Zele ....KO 2
Feb. 19—Fausto Constantino, Zele ....KO 5
Mar. 5—Jean Belval, Hamme ....D 6
Apr. 16—Ferruccio Mazzardi, Zele ....KO 2
Sept. 10—Horst Lang, Zele ....KO 4
Oct. 8—Jean Tshikuna, Zele ....KO 3
Nov. 11—Lissoko Abibobele, Zele ....D 6
1978
Jan. 7—Vasco Faustinho, Zele ....W 6
Mar. 24—Lissoko Abibole, Zele ....KO 4
May 20—Dave Wilson, Appelterre ....W 8
Sept. 30—Jean Pierre Coopman, Turnhout ....W 12
Nov. 11—Tony Moore, Zele ....KO by 2
Nov. 15—Alfonso Bonavita, Bellaria ....KO 1
1979
Apr. 21—Albert Syben, Zele ....KO by 4
Nov. 10—Tom Halpern, Zele ....KO 3
Dec. 14—Albert Syben, Bruxelles ....KO 8
(Won Belgian Heavyweight Title)
1980
Jan. 26—Christian Poncelet, Zele ....W 10
Apr. 22—John L. Gardner, London ....KO by 9
(For Vacant European Heavyweight Title)
Oct. 25—James Dixon, Herentals ....L 8
Nov. 22—Stuart Lithgoe, Zele ....L 8

TEMBU GAWULA
South African Bantamweight
1979
Dec. 8—Edward Williams, East London ....W 4
1980
Mar. 1—Mxolisi Galada, East London ....W 4
Aug. 23—Sexon Ngqayimbana, East London ......L 4

CARL GAYNOR
British Featherweight
1979
Sept. 10—Steve Enwright, Bradford ....L 6
Oct. 17—Ivor Jones, Lewisham ....KO by 3
Nov. 19—Kelvin Smart, Birmingham ....KO by 3
Dec. 10—Chris Moorcroft, Manchester ....KO by 2
1980
Sept. 10—Carl Mullings, Liverpool ....D 6
Oct. 20—Paul Huggins, Hove ....L 6

STEVE GEE
British Heavyweight
1980
Apr. 15—Mike Creasy, Blackpool ....KO 5
Apr. 29—Don Charles, London ....KO 2
May 14—Colin Flute, Burslem ....W 6

Sept. 22—Colin Flute, Birmingham .... KO 3
Oct. 30—Derek Simpkin, Wolverhampton .... D 6

EDWARD GENU
South African Featherweight
1978
Aug. 29—Zola Lawuse, Queenstown .... L 4
Oct. 21—Victor Mkohlakali, Queenstown .... L 4
1979
Feb. 10—Mbulelo Majaja, Queenstown .... L 4
1980
Mar. 29—Malungelo Ggola, Queenstown .... KO by 4

DAVE GEORGE
British Flyweight
1979
Oct. 3—Iggy Jano, Reading .... KO 4
Nov. 12—Alan Storey, Marton .... W 6
Dec. 17—Steve Enwright, Bradford .... W 6
1980
Feb. 25—Selvin Bell, Bradford .... W 8
Oct. 14—Jimmy Bott, Nantwich .... W 8
Oct. 29—Jimmy Bott, Burslem .... W 8

DON GEORGE
British Featherweight
1979
Sept. 12—Paul Keers, Liverpool .... L 6
Oct. 22—Selwyn Bell, Nottingham .... W 6
1980
Jan. 28—Terry McKeown, Glasgow .... D 6
Apr. 1—Austin Owens, Wembley .... L 8
May 12—Ian Murray, Reading .... KO 7
May 19—Alan Storey, London .... KO 7
Sept. 24—Gary Lucas, Brighton .... W 8
Oct. 14—Sammy Sims, Nantwich .... W 8

GORDON GEORGE
British Light Heavyweight
1978
Nov. 6—Lloyd James, London .... D 6
Nov. 20—Tony Hill, Birmingham .... KO 3
Nov. 27—Joe Hannaford, Liverpool .... W 6
Dec. 4—Steve Goodwin, London .... WF 5
1979
Apr. 23—George Danahar, London .... L 6
May 16—Herol Graham, Sheffield .... L 8
May 29—Stan Thompson, London .... KO by 4
June 18—Harry Watson, London .... L 6
Dec. 4—Dave Armstrong, London .... KO by 2
1980
Feb. 13—Winston Davis, London .... L 6
Feb. 18—Gary Jones, Birmingham .... D 6
Feb. 28—Tony Pearce, Queensway .... L 6
Mar. 17—John O'Neill, Birmingham .... D 8
Mar. 24—Gary Jones, Glasgow .... L 6
Mar. 31—Malcolm Heath, London .... W 6
Apr. 24—Clint Jones, Queensway .... W 8

ANTONIO GERMANO
Italian Lightweight
1977
May 7—Cosimo Lavino, Brindisi .... L 6
May 21—Antonio Pocai, Pisa .... L 6
June 6—Domenico Traini, Grotta Zolina .... L 6
June 24—Giovanni Vitillo, Viareggio .... KO by 2
July 23—Gianfranco Pallazzi, Senegal .... KO by 5
Aug. 28—Pasquale Arini, Marcianise .... L 6
Sept. 17—Nunziato Sanna, Calolziocorte ..... KO by 2
Dec. 30—Andrea Ricci, Lecco .... L 6
1978
Mar. 4—Angelo Marino, Lugo .... KO by 5
Mar. 18—Gabriele Peruzzi, Tarquinia .... L 6
Apr. 14—Vito Viola, Budrio .... L 6
Apr. 30—Raimondo Riccio, Luguano .... L 6
May 12—Severino Picca, Piancenza .... L 6
May 27—Gianfranco Lalli, Morbegno .... L 6
June 15—Leo Scorza, Imola .... L 6
July 1—Bruno Demontis, Cagliari .... KO by 5
July 28—Graziano Gusai, Mondovi .... KO by 3
1979
Oct. 20—Antonio Sandrin, Latisana .... L 6
1980
Mar. 21—Jose Sanchez, Rapallo .... L 6
Apr. 12—Franco Canini, Rimini .... L 6
May 18—Alfredo Reininger, Bosco .... KO by 4
Oct. 4—Angelo Ambrosio, San Michele .... L 6

CLIFF GILPIN
British Welterweight
1980
Mar. 18—Richard Aver, Wolverhampton .... W 6
Apr. 9—Dave Taylor, Burslem .... W 6

Apr. 30—Gary Cooper, Wolverhampton .... W 8
May 29—Tommy Wright, Wolverhampton .... KO 5
July 8—Brian Anderson, Wolverhampton .... W 8
Sept. 24—Nigel Thomas, Evesham .... W 8
Oct. 13—John Smith, Nottingham .... W 8

JUAN JOSE GIMENEZ
Spanish Junior Welterweight
1977
Mar. 5—Mohamed Salid Mimun, Velenje ...... KO 6
Apr. 7—Ceferino Morales, Lugo di Romagna ..... W 8
Apr. 22—Luiz Ribeiro, Faenza .... KO 7
May 7—Ernesto Bergamasco, Pesaro .... KO 7
May 28—Marcos Paperito, Pesaro .... KO 3
July 3—Wongso Suseno, Surabaya .... W 10
Aug. 8—Epifanio Pavon, Tandil .... KO 5
Aug. 16—Hector Caceres, Bahia Blanca .... W 10
Sept. 4—Barry Michael, Surabaya .... W 10
Oct. 4—Jae Ho Kim, Bali .... KO 7
Oct. 16—Benny Lerinsky, Surabaya .... KO 6
Dec. 17—Pascal Real Martin, Pesaro .... KO 5
1978
Jan. 28—Cererino Morales, Pesaro .... KO 4
Feb. 25—Oscar Aparicio, Riccione .... W 10
Apr. 15—Laurent Dejila, Pesaro .... KO 6
May 20—Mario Molina, Pesaro .... KO 4
June 9—Antonio Amaya, Milano .... KO 6
Oct. 21—Rufus Miller, Pesaro .... WF 4
Oct. 31—Ike Hooks, Munich .... KO 5
1979
Jan. 19—Oscar Aparicio, Pesaro .... W 10
Mar. 1—Floro Zarza, Bahia Blanca .... W 10
Mar. 16—Alfredo Coria, Cipoletti .... W 10
Apr. 7—Alfredo Coria, V. Dolores .... KO 4
May 18—Alain Salmon, Munich .... KO 8
Sept. 28—Chris Davies, Munich .... W 10
Oct. 27—Tommy Davitt, Pesaro .... W 8
1980
Feb. 13—Antonio Fogueiro, Pesaro .... KO 2
Mar. 28—Bruce Strauss, Rome .... KO 5
July 19—George Feeney, Castiglion .... W 8
Sept. 10—Alsenio Green, San Remo .... KO by 2

ABDEL GISSI
Dutch Heavyweight
1980
Mar. 28—Lassine Niare, Bruxelles .... W 6
Apr. 25—Alessandro Casanova, Molenbeek .... W 6

MARCO GIULIANI
Belgian Welterweight
1979
Oct. 13—Rafael Salamone, Cheratte .... W 6
1980
Mar. 21—Azziz Alaoui, Cheratte .... D 6
Sept. 12—Alex Beynaerts, Lovain .... D 6
Oct. 21—Jo Bollue, Poinche .... L 6

EDDIE GLASS
British Featherweight
1980
Sept. 11—Mark Mason, Hartlepool .... L 6
Sept. 24—John Griffiths, Solihull .... L 6
Oct. 2—Steve Pollard, Hull .... L 6
Oct. 13—Ian Murray, Newcastle .... L 6
Oct. 23—Andy Thomas, Middlesbrough .... L 6

IAN GLENN
British Heavyweight
1975
Mar. 5—Dennis Reynolds, Belfast .... KO by 3
Apr. 12—Roy Bailey, Belfast .... L 6
Oct. 2—Danny Friel, Derry .... KO 2
1976
Mar. 4—Roy Bailey, Belfast .... KO 2
(Irish Light Heavyweight Title)
Oct. 28—Tony Monoghan, Ballymena .... KO by 2
1977-1978
(Inactive)
1979
Nov. 26—Trevor Kerr, Belfast .... KO by 5
1980
July 28—Trevor Kerr, Belfast .... KO by 2

CHRIS GLOVER
British Junior Middleweight
1976
Nov. 3—Carl Bailey, Caister .... W 6
Nov. 18—Chester Coburn, Liverpool .... KO 2
Dec. 6—Carl Bailey, Manchester .... W 8
Dec. 14—Johnny Beauchamp, W. Bromwich ...... KO 4
1977
Jan. 20—Peter Beauvoisin, Liverpool .... KO 4

Feb.   2—Alan Copp, London ....L 8
Mar. 24—Von Reid, Bradford ....KO 4
Apr.   7—Des Gwilliam, Dudley ....D 6
Apr. 21—Jimmy King, Liverpool ....W 8
Apr. 27—Jimmy King, Bradford ....W 8
May   9—Kevin Davies, Liverpool ....L 8
Sept. 8—Dave Taylor, Liverpool ....W 8
Sept. 21—Hugh Smith, London ....KO 4
Dec.   6—Terry Peterson, Leeds ....L 12
1978
Mar.   2—Sabuya Victor, Osla ....KO by 6
Apr. 27—Carl Bailey, Doncaster ....KO 6
June 19—Chris Walker, Manchester ....W 8
Sept. 13—Des Morrison, Cambridge ......KO by 4
Dec.   5—Tony Kavanaugh, Manchester ....W 8
1979
Feb. 19—Terry Peterson, London ....KO by 6
Nov. 19—Wayne Barker, Stockport ....L 8
Dec. 10—Wayne Barker, Manchester ....L 8
1980
Jan. 21—Clifton Wallace, Wolverhampton .....W 6
Mar. 10—Kenny Webber, Manchester ....L 8
May   7—Billy Ahearne, Liverpool ....KO 3
May   12—Peter Bassey, Manchester ......KO by 7
Sept. 22—Tony Britton, Liverpool ....D 8

JERRY GOLDEN
British Middleweight
1979
Sept. 24—Peter Simon, Hammersmith ......KO by 2
1980
Jan. 16—Mickey Kidd, Stoke ....L 6
Jan. 21—Peter Bassey, Birmingham ....L 4
Mar. 31—Chuck Hirschmann, Cleethorpes ....D 4
Sept. 10—Joe Dean, Liverpool ....KO by 3
Oct. 16—John Stone, Bolton ....KO 5
Nov.   1—Terry Christle, Glasgow ....KO by 2

FRANCISCO DIONISIO (LEO) GOMEZ
Spanish Welterweight
1976
Nov. 20—Antonio Hermoso, Fuengirola ....WF 5
Dec. 11—Antonio Hermoso, Malaga ....W 6
1977
Jan. 15—Juan Morales, Malaga ....W 6
Mar.   5—Antonio Hermoso, Almeria ....L 6
Apr. 30—Serafino Bento, Malaga ....KO 2
May   28—Juan Jose Hermandez, Melilla ....D 6
June 11—Serafino Bemto, Malaga ....KO 5
July 23—Antonio Hermoso, Almeria ....KO 3
July 29—Juan Morales, Malaga ....KO 5
Aug. 27—Jose Ramon Fouz, Gijon ....KO by 7
Oct. 22—Juan Hermando, Malaga ....W 6
Oct. 30—Juan Escolar, Malaga ....W 6
Dec.   3—Juan Chammoro, Malaga ....D 8
1978
July 28—Osvaldo Lopez, Malaga ....KO by 6
Sept. 2—Osvaldo Lopez, Malaga ....W 8
Sept. 29—Primitivo Medina, Malaga ....W 8
Dec.   6—Jose M. Fernandez, Malaga ....W 6
1979
Apr. 21—Ahmed Ben Aissa, Malaga ....W 6
Dec.   8—Ahmed Ben Aissa, Fuengirola ....W 6
1980
Apr.   4—Giancarlo Compiani, Milan ....W 6
Apr. 25—Giambattista Calvia, Mantova ......KO 2
May   28—Pietro Donati, Mantova ....W 6
July 18—Angelo Quintavalle, Marnirolo .....KO 3
Sept. 12—Guilio Greco, Lido ....KO 4
Dec. 19—Gabrielle Di Stazio, Navara ....D 6

JOSE RAMON GOMEZ (FOUZ)
Spanish Welterweight
Born: January 27, 1952
1971
Nov. · 6—Fernando Jiminez, Oviedo...........W 6
Dec. 11—Luis Bautista, Oviedo..............W 6
1972
Jan. 22—Rodolfo Sanchez, Mirando de Ebro....L disq. 6
May   13—Rejon Gonzalez, Gijon ....KO 6
June 17—Guillermo Perez, Gijon ....W 8
Sept. 1—Jose Villalobos, Madrid............KO 7
Oct. 12—Luis Bautista, Gijon ....W 8
Nov.   4—Juan Iglesiad, Gijon ....W 8
Dec.   1—Horacio Ruiz, Madrid...............L 8
Dec. 30—Juan Iglesias, Madrid..............W 8
1973
Feb. 17—Kid Dongo, Almeria................KO 2
Mar.   3—Fernando Bermejo, Gijon...........W 8
Mar. 17—Enrique Levy, Gijon ....W 8
Mar. 31—Romero Valerio, Orense ....W 8
Apr. 28—Juan Pena, Zaragosa ....W 8
May   5—Valentin Loren, Zaragosa ....W 8
May   12—Abu Arrow, Gijon ....KO 5

June   1—Fernando Romeo, Madrid ....W 8
June   8—Juan Pena, Madrid ....W 8
July   6—Perico Fernandez, Madrid ....L 12
       (Spanish Lightweight Title)
July 27—Jeronimo Lucas, Madrid ....W 8
Aug. 24—Luis Aisa, Madrid.................W 8
Sept. 7—Horacio Ruiz, Madrid...............D 8
Sept. 22—Fernando Sanchez, Oviedo ....W 8
1974
Mar.   9—Juan Pena, Zaragosa ....KO 6
Mar. 29—Santino Reali, Barcelona ....KO 4
Apr. 17—Fernando Fermejo, Barcelona ....D 8
Apr. 30—Klaus Jacoby, Barcelona ....KO 4
May   22—Luciano Laffranchi, Madrid ....W 8
Aug. 10—Jesus Zarco, Norena...............KO 3
Aug. 23—Guillermo Perez, Norena............KO 3
Sept. 14—Ben Ademola, Norena ....KO 7
Oct. 17—Costa Rodriguez, Beron ....KO 4
Nov.   6—Roland Cazeaux, Madrid ....W 8
1975
Jan. 10—Nedo Fabbri, Barcelona.............KO 6
Feb.   7—Romano Fanale, Barcelona...........W 10
Mar.   8—Walter Blaser, Zurich ....W 15
       (European Junior Welterweight Championship)
Apr. 19—Tommaso Maroccoo, Barcelona ......KO 1
June 18—Romano Fanalli, Barcelona ....W 15
       (European Junior Welterweight Title)
July 23—Miguel Velazquez, Madrid ....W 8
Aug.   6—Miguel Araujo, Valencia ....W 8
Oct. 31—Cemal Kamaci, Cologne ....KO by 7
       (European Junior Welterweight Title)
Dec. 20—Fierrito Fernandez, Oviedo..........KO 3
1976
Jan. 30—Perico Fernandez, Barcelona.........D 10
Mar. 12—Toni Ortez, Madrid ....D 8
July 30—Mario Molina, Madrid ....W 8
1977
Apr.   1—Manuel Masso, Barcelona ....KO by 3
May   6—Alfredo Mulas, Milano ....L 6
June 24—Alfredo Mulas, Lugo di Romagna ......L 8
July 15—Cornejo Hernandez, Numana ....D 8
Aug. 21—Franco Udella, Rijeka ....L 8
Sept. 28—Franco Udella, Fort Village ....L 8
Oct.   7—Elmilio Pireddu, Capua ....D 8
1978
Jan.   7—Jose Lopez Barrillado, Gijon ....W 8
Feb.   4—Joe Carlos, Gijon ....KO 4
Apr.   4—Osvaldo Lopez, Gijon ....KO 7
June 10—Josines, Gijon ....W 8
Aug. 19—Billy Waith, Gijon ....D 8
1979
Aug. 18—Oswaldo Lopez, Aviles ....W 8
Nov. 10—Jose Ramirez, Aviles ....W 8
Dec. 14—Iluminado Diez Castelanos, Madrid ....WF 5
1980
Feb.   1—Osvaldo Lopez, Madrid ....W 8
Feb. 16—Carlos Morales, Oviedo ....KO 8
       (Won Spanish Welterweight Title)
Dec. 19—Antonio Casado, Barcelona ....W 10
       (Retained Spanish Welterweight Title)

MODESTO (TORITO) GOMEZ
Spanish Featherweight
1979
June   2—Mohatar II, Santander ....W 8
June 16—Juan Francisco Rodriguez, Santander ...KO 6
July 27—Garrido, Santander ....W 8
Aug. 31—Daniel Figueroa, Madrid ....KO by 4
Nov.   8—Nani Rodriguez, La Coruna ....D 8
1980
Jan.   5—Emilio Barcala, Santander ....W 8
Jan. 19—Francisco Garcia Herrara, Santander ..KO 6
Feb. 16—Mohamed Jofre II, Oviedo ....L 8
Apr. 12—Roberto Castanon, Santander ....L 12
       (For European Featherweight Title)
June   7—Jose Rueda, La Coruna ....D 8
Sept. 27—Jose Luis Dela Sagra, Santander .....L 8

NELSON GOMEZ
Spanish Welterweight
1977
May   13—Remo Costa, Sarzana ....D 8
May   28—Kadir Yuceler, Koeln ....D 6
June   2—Erkki Meronen, Randers ....KO by 6
June 18—Mario Guilloti, Rome ....L 6
July   9—Angelo Faniciulli, Viterbo ....W 8
July 22—Vincenzo Moruzzi, Fiumicino .....KO by 3
Oct. 14—Georges Warusfel, Tarbers ....L 10
Oct. 28—Giuseppe Russi, Milano ....L 8
Nov. 12—Andre Holyk, Lione ....L 10
Dec. 22—Bruno Arari, Gallipoli ....KO by 7
1978
       (Inactive)

Dec.   8—Jo Kimpuani, Dunkerque .... KO by 3
1980
Feb.   2—Salvatore Casio, Marsala .... L 8
Feb. 13—Luigi Minchillo, Pesaro .... KO by 3
May   2—Ben Saad Salah, Rome .... W 6
May 31—Gianfranco Rosi, Spoleto .... KO 7
June 27—Tidjani Sidibe, Palermo .... KO by 5
Sept. 6—Roberto Masini, Riccione .... L 6
Aug. 20—Bruno Gumbala, Cerveteri .... L 6
Oct. 11—Patrizio Oliva, Naples .... L 6
Oct. 18—Claude Martin, St. Malo .... KO by 7

STEVE GOODWIN
British Junior Welterweight
1977
Nov. 29—David Roberts, Birkenhead .... KO 5
Dec.   8—Prince Rodney, Liverpool .... W 6
Dec. 13—Mattin Coracchio, London .... KO 2
1978
Jan. 18—Steve Hopkin, Stoke .... W 6
Feb.   1—Tony Kavanaugh, Evesham .... KO by 4
Mar.   6—Vince Baxter, Manchester .... KO 3
Mar. 20—Michael Copp, Aberavon .... L 8
Apr. 11—Steve Hopkin, Sheffield .... KO by 6
May 18—Jimmy Roberts, Liverpool .... D 6
May 24—Ron Pilgrim, Southend .... KO 4
June 20—Viv Jackson, Southend .... L 6
Nov. 21—Vivian Waite, Cambridge .... W disq. 5
1979
(Inactive)
1980
Oct. 13—Steve Bateman, Manchester .... D 6
Oct. 22—Leo Mulhearn, Doncaster .... W 8

SYLVESTER GORDON
British Junior Welterweight
1977
Apr. 18—Wayne Floyd, London .... L 6
Apr. 26—Dai Davies, London .... W 6
May 23—Wayne Floyd, Hammersmith .... L 6
June   2—Dai Davies, London .... W 6
Oct. 10—Steve Holdsworth, Walworth .... L 6
Oct. 24—Martin Bridge, London .... L 6
Nov.   7—Dai Davies, London .... W 6
Nov. 15—Mick O'Mara, London .... D 6
Dec. 12—Dave Taylor, London .... W 8
1978
Jan. 16—George Peacock, Birmingham .... L 6
Jan. 31—Cookie Roomes, Marylebone .... W 6
Feb. 21—Sylvester Mittee, London .... KO by 5
Mar. 20—Paddy McAleese, London .... D 8
May 23—Mick Bell, Leicester .... KO 6
June 20—Ray Cattouse, London .... L 6
Sept. 11—Chris Walker, Birmingham .... L 6
Sept. 18—Carl Bailey, Manchester .... W 6
Sept. 25—Tommy Davitt, London .... D 8
Nov. 15—Tony Martey, Solihull .... KO by 7
1979
Jan. 15—Joey Singleton, Nottingham .... L 8
Feb.   5—Tommy Davitt, London .... W 8
Mar. 19—George Peacock, London .... L 8
Apr. 17—Willie Booth, Glasgow .... L 8
May 21—Joey Singleton, Walworth .... L 8
Oct. 17—Gary Pearce, London .... D 8
Oct. 30—Gary Pearce, Caerphilly .... L 8
Dec.   3—Sid Smith, Marylebone .... KO by 5
1980
Jan. 28—Steve Early, Edgbaston .... KO by 4
Feb. 25—Herbie McLean, Glasgow .... W 8
Mar. 17—Ricky Beaumont, London .... L 8
Oct.   1—Erling Engh, Oslo .... L 6

IGNACIO GOROSTIDI
Spanish Middleweight
1975
Oct. 10—Roberto Marques, Tolosa .... KO 2
1976
July   2—Manuel Rico, Tolosa .... KO 3
1977
Sept. 11—Ali Yacoubi, S. Sebastiano .... W 6
Nov.   5—Jean Luc Lami, Bilbao .... D 6
Dec. 15—Gabriel Maillard, Paris .... W 6
1978
Mar. 31—Bader Ouakhai, Marsiglia .... D 6
Apr. 28—Bader Ouakhai, Tolosa .... D 6
Nov.   9—Bruno Arati, Bern .... D 6
Nov. 17—Pierre Joly, Tolosa .... D 6
Dec. 15—Gerard Breton, Paris .... L 6
Dec. 23—Tekyla Rodri, Hernani .... D 8
1979
Mar. 15—Paul Baekgaard, Copenhagen .... L 4
May   5—Jose M. Omedas, Eibar .... KO 3
June   6—Perez Azuwache, Bilbao .... L 8

July 14—Alberto Ramirez, San Sebastian .... W 8
Aug. 11—Manuel Sanchez, S. Sebastiano .... D 6
Aug. 31—Cristobal Crespi, Melilla .... KO by 3
Nov.   5—Erwin Heiber, Paris .... D 6
Dec.   8—Jose Luis Alvarez, Lugo .... L 8
Dec. 15—Marcial T. Vega, S. Cruz .... KO by 1
1980
Feb.   7—Johnny Cooper, Paris .... W 6
Feb. 17—Paul Payon, Maubeuge .... KO 3
Feb. 29—Poul Baekgaard, Odense .... L 4
Apr. 18—Bader Houaki, Paris .... W 6
Oct.   4—Maurice Bufi, Roeulx .... L 6

LUC GOSSENS
German Light Heavyweight
1980
Apr.   4—Bernard Antone, Middelkerke .... KO 5
May   1—Guiseppe Cortesi, Izegem .... D 6
June 27—Roberto Bosio, Bruxelles .... D 6
Nov.   1—Michel Caron, Bruxelles .... L 6

MALUNGELO GQOLA
South African Flyweight
1976
May 22—Johannes Shwana, Port Elizabeth .... W 4
Nov.   6—King Williamstown .... W 4
1977
Sept. 3—Nkosomzi Moss, Queenstown .... L 6
1978-1979
(Inactive)
1980
Mar. 29—Edward Genu, Queenstown .... KO 4

BRIAN GRAHAM
British Middleweight
1980
July   7—Paul Heatley, Middlesbrough .... KO 2
Sept. 11—Peter Lock, Hartlepool .... KO 3
Oct. 23—Joe Dean, Middlesbrough .... W 8

HEROL GRAHAM
British Junior Middleweight
1978
Nov. 28—Viwan Waite, Sheffield .... W 6
Dec.   4—Curtis Marsh, London .... KO 1
1979
Jan. 22—Jimmy Roberts, Bradford .... KO 2
Feb. 12—Dave Southwell, Reading .... W 8
Feb. 28—Dave Southwell, Burslem .... W 8
Mar. 27—George Walker, London .... W 8
Apr. 27—Mac Nicholson, Newcastle .... W 8
May 16—Gordon George, Sheffield .... W 8
Sept. 26—Lloyd James, Sheffield .... W 8
Oct.   7—Billy Ahearne, Barnsley .... KO 3
Nov. 27—Errol McKenzie, Sheffield .... W 8
1980
Feb. 12—Glen McEwan, Sheffield .... W 8
Apr. 22—George Danahar, Sheffield .... W 8
Sept. 9—Joey Mack, Sheffield .... W 8
Oct. 30—Larry Mayes, Liverpool .... KO 4

LEE GRAHAM
Scottish Featherweight
1976
Nov. 15—Tommy Davitt, Kensington .... L 6
Nov. 22—Michael La Grange, Southampton .... D 4
1977
Feb.   7—Kevin Docherty, London .... D 6
Feb. 22—Gary Davidson, Kensington .... L 6
Mar. 21—Steve Enwright, Birmingham .... KO 5
Mar. 29—Wally Angliss, London .... KO 5
Apr. 12—Mark Bliss, London .... W 8
May 31—Wayne Evans, Kensington .... L 8
Sept. 19—Alan Oag, Glasgow .... KO 1
Oct. 10—Kenny Matthews, London .... L 8
Oct. 31—Pat Cowdell, Birmingham .... L 8
Nov. 29—Alan Buchanan, London .... D 8
1978
Jan. 16—Eric Wood, Nottingham .... L 8
Jan. 24—Gerry Duffy, Solihull .... KO by 2
Feb. 28—Tony Whitmore, Heathrow .... D 6
Mar.   6—Jeff Pritchard, London .... L 8
May 15—Tony Whitmore, London .... KO 3
May 23—Vernon Penprasz, London .... L 6
June 29—George Sutton, Caerphilly .... D 8
Nov.   4—Char Chiteule, Lusaka .... L disq. 5
1979
Jan. 29—Terry McKeown, Glasgow .... L 6
Feb.   5—John Cooper, London .... W 8
Mar.   7—Wayne Evans, Solihull .... KO by 2
Apr.   3—Vernon Penprase, Caerphilly .... L 8
Apr. 18—Johnny Owen, London .... L 8
May 13—Vernon Penprase, Plymouth .... L 8

Oct.	15—Vernon Penprase, Mayfair .... KO by	6
Nov.	19—Jimmy Brown, Liverpool L	8
Dec.	3—John Feeney, Marylebone L	8
	1980	
Mar.	31—Jim McKeown, London L	8
Apr.	17—Steve Cleak, London L	8

ANTONIO GRANADOS
Spanish Junior Welterweight
1979

Apr.	21—Manuel Hatero, Pineda ....D	6
May	5—Jimmy Cruz, Barcelona ....KO by	4
July	24—Liber Barrios, S. Cugat ....W	4
Sept.	1—Benito Murillo, S. Sebastiano L	4
Oct.	4—Benito Murillo, Leon L	4
Dec.	12—Liber Barrios, Barcelona L	6
	1980	
Mar.	28—Joaquin Garcia, Palma de Mallorca L	6
Aug.	1—Chato Melillense, Badalona L	8

GIULIO GRECO
Italian Featherweight
1978

Mar.	18—Silvio Mauro, Lignano ....KO	5
Apr.	7—Michele De Mita, Udine ....W	6
Apr.	21—Domenico Palumbo, Manzano ....D	6
Oct.	21—Valerio Nati, Pesaro ....KO by	5
	1979	
Feb.	16—Romano Mugnai, Massa L	6
Apr.	20—Domenico Palumbo, Udine ....W	6
May	11—Pasquale Mazza, Senegallia ....KO	2
Oct.	13—Andrea Ricci, Udine ....W	8
Nov.	3—Andrea Ricci, Prodenone ....W	6
	1980	
Feb.	8—Fabio Mannai, Milan L	6
Mar.	21—Giuseppe La Vite, Rapallo L	6
July	16—Lorenzo Paciullo, Lignano L	6
Aug.	12—Francisco (Leo) Gomez, Lido .... KO by	4

DAVE (BOY) GREEN
British Welterweight
Born: June, 2, 1953
1974

Dec.	10—Yotham Kunda, Nottingham ....KO	2
	1975	
Jan.	20—Dave Coombs, Mayfair..................KO	2
Feb.	12—Derek Simpson, Cambridge ....KO	7
Mar.	11—Barton McAllister, Wembley ....KO	2
Apr.	8—George Salmon, Cambridge ....W	8
May	12—Tommy Joyce, Mayfair ....KO	3
June	3—Angus McMillan, London ....W	8
Oct.	14—Al Stewart, London....................KO	2
Nov.	10—Brian Jones, Cambridge ....KO	2
Nov.	25—Alan Salter, London...................KO	1
	1976	
Jan.	20—George McGirk, London ....KO	2
Mar.	2—Billy Waith, London...................KO	11
Mar.	20—Giuseppe Minotti, London...............KO	4
Apr.	6—Jim Montague, London ....W	8
Apr.	27—Herbie McLean, Kensington ....KO	4
June	1—Joey Singleton, London.................KO	6
	(British Junior Welterweight Title)	
June	22—Ernesto Bergamesco, Wembley ....KO	5
Sept.	14—Jean Pierre Younsi, London..............KO	1
Oct.	12—Ugo Di Pietr, Wembley.................KO	1
Oct.	27—Ramiro Bolanos, London................KO	4
Nov.	9—Jimmy Heair, Wembley ....W	10
Dec.	7—Jean Baptiste Peidvache, Kensington .....KO	9
	(European Light Welterweight Title)	
	1977	
Feb.	22—Mario Guilloti, London ....W	10
Mar.	29—John Stracey, London ....KO	10
June	14—Carlos Palomino, London ....KO by	11
	(WBC Welterweight Title)	
Sept.	27—Andy Price, London ....W	10
	1978	
Feb.	21—Roy Johnson, London ....KO	4
Nov.	7—Aundra Love, London ....KO	8
Dec.	5—Sammy Masias, Kensington ....KO	1
	1979	
Jan.	23—Henry Rhiney, London ....KO	5
	(British and European Welterweight Titles)	
May	1—Lawrence Hafey, London ....KO	5
May	15—Rafael Rodriguez, Wembley ....KO	8
June	28—Jorgen Hansen, Randers .... KO by	3
	(Lost EBU Welterweight Title)	
Sept.	25—Steve Michalerya, London ....KO	3
Dec.	5—Dick Ecklund, London ....W	10
	1980	
Mar.	31—Sugar Ray Leonard, Landover .... KO by	4
	(For WBC Welterweight Title)	
Oct.	13—Mario Mendez, London ....KO	2

JARVIS GREENIDGE
British Lightweight
1979

Oct.	9—Pat Devanney, Wolverhampton ....W	6
Oct.	17—Steve Simms, Evesham ....W	6
Oct.	30—John Henry, Bedford ....KO	4
Nov.	20—Paddy Graham, Belfast L	8
Dec.	3—Steve Parker, Wolverhampton .... KO by	3
	1980	
Jan.	28—Paul Keers, Bradford L	8
Feb.	5—Steve Parker, Wolverhampton ....W	6
Feb.	21—Brian Snagg, Liverpool L	8
Mar.	10—Adey Allen, Wolverhampton ....W	6
Mar.	19—Sammy Sims, Stoke L	8
May	15—Tim Maloney, London L	6
Sept.	4—Glen Rhodes, Morecambe L	8
Oct.	13—Kevin Sheehan, Nottingham ....W	8

ALEX GREGAL
British Welterweight
1980

Apr.	14—Maduka Mirschmann, Motherwell ......KO	3
May	19—Phil Duckworth, Bradford L	4
June	2—Francis McLay, Glasgow ....KO	2
June	23—Joe McNamee, Glasgow ....W	4
Aug.	31—Francis McLay, Glasgow ....KO	1
Oct.	20—Bobby Welburn, Glasgow ....KO by	5

JOHN GRIFFITHS
British Featherweight
1979

Nov.	21—George Bailey, Evesham ....W	6
	1980	
Jan.	28—Jim McKeown, Glasgow ....KO by	4
Feb.	28—Brindley Jones, Ebbw Vale ....W	6
Mar.	6—Stuart Crabb, London ....W	6
Mar.	31—Joey Wainwright, London L	6
Apr.	29—Ivor Jones, London ....KO by	6
Sept.	24—Eddie Glass, Solihull ....W	6
Oct.	7—Rocky Bantleman, London L	6

LAURENT GRIMBERT
French Bantamweight
1976

May	8—Jean-Luc Fonroques, Villers ....W	6
Oct.	6—Mohamed Boundka, Compiegne ....D	6
Oct.	29—Jean Yves Julien, Denain L	6
Dec.	11—Patrick Goblet, Crepy ....W	6
	1977	
Jan.	29—Patrick Goblet, Troyes ....W	6
Feb.	12—Jacky Azil, Crepy ....KO	5
Feb.	19—Jean-Yves Julien, Bethune ....D	6
Mar.	5—Michel Lecerf, Crepy ....KO	4
Mar.	26—Michel Walbert, Villers ....W	6
Apr.	1—Juan F. Rodriguez, Madrid ....D	6
Apr.	8—Michel Walbert, Villers ....W	6
Apr.	16—Juan F. Rodriguez, Almeria L	8
May	21—Francis Bailleul, Arques .... KO by	6
Nov.	5—Jean Pierre Meganck, Schoonaare ....W	6
Nov.	12—Christian Valentin, Crepy ....W	8
Dec.	25—Abdel Ben Ameur, Izegem ....D	6
	1978	
Jan.	7—Bechir Boundka, Crepy en Valois ....W	8
Jan.	21—George Lietar, Campeigne ....W	6
Feb.	11—Henri Kone, Crepy ....W	8
Mar.	25—Michel Lefebvre, Berck Plage L	10
Mar.	31—Alfredo Mulas, Milan ....W	8
Apr.	15—Jacky Bihin, Crepy en Valois ....W	8
May	19—Alfredo Mulas, Milano ....LF	9
Sept.	30—Guy Caudron, Crepy ....W	12
	(Won French Bantamweight Title)	
Jan.	27—Dominique Cesari, Campeigne ....KO	6
Mar.	31—Abdel Hammi, Compiegne ....KO	4
Apr.	7—Raga Purphy, Meaux ....W	10
Apr.	21—Alain Le Fol, Crepy En Valois ....W	10
Aug.	10—Juan Francisco Rodriguez, Huelva L	10
	(EBU Bantamweight Title)	
	1980	
Feb.	23—Guy Caudron, Mericourt ....W	12
	(Won French Bantamweight Title)	
Apr.	12—Cecilio Lastra, Santander ....KO by	2
Oct.	17—Mike Irungu, Copenhagen ....KO by	7
Nov.	15—Gerard Jacob, Criel ....KO	4
	(Won French Featherweight Title)	

DEREK GROARKE
British Featherweight
1980

Mar.	24—Glyn Rhodes, Bradford ....KO by	4
May	7—Mick Mason, Liverpool ....D	4
Aug.	31—Chris McCallum, Glasgow L	6
Oct.	16—Steve Topliss, Bolton L	6

318

BRUNO GUMBALA
Italian Junior Welterweight
1979
Oct. 12—Giovannino Mannu, Rome .... W 4
1980
Feb. 29—Luciano Arduini, Rome .... W 6
May 2—Raimondo Riccio, Rome .... W 6
Aug. 20—Nelson Gomez, Cervanteri .... W 6
Sept. 24—Audry, Fiuggi .... KO 5
Dec. 4—Roberto D'Elia, Rome .... D 6

ROGER GUEST
British Junior Welterweight
1977
Oct. 11—Ronnie Pilgrim, Coventry .... KO by 4
Nov. 8—Kendrick Edwards, West Bromwich ..... W 6
Nov. 16—Romal Ambrose, London .... W 4
1978
Feb. 13—Prince Rodney, Manchester .... L 8
Feb. 21—Dennis Price, London .... L 4
Apr. 17—Sid Smith, Walworth .... KO by 2
Sept. 27—Shaun Stewart, Stoke .... KO 5
Oct. 30—Young Nelson, Nottingham .... W 6
Nov. 27—Bob Baker, London .... W 6
Dec. 11—Nigel Thomas, Birmingham .... D 6
1979
Jan. 22—Nigel Thomas, Birmingham .... D 6
Feb. 19—Nigel Thomas, Birmingham .... W 8
Mar. 7—Tommy Thomas, Solihull .... KO by 5
June 14—Barry Price, Dudley .... L 8
June 26—Alan Cable, Leicester .... W 6
Oct. 16—Dai Davies, West Bromwich .... KO 3
Oct. 22—Derek Young Nelson, London .... W 8
Nov. 19—Steve Early, Birmingham .... KO 1
Dec. 10—Clinton McKenzie, London .... L 8
1980
Feb. 19—Clinton McKenzie, London .... L 8
July 8—Adey Allen, Wolverhampton .... L 8
Sept. 19—Giuseppe Di Padova, Mantova .... KO by 5
Oct. 19—Giuseppe Di Padova, Birmingham .... L 10

ANTONIO GUINALDO
Spanish Lightweight
Born: February 21, 1953, Salamanca
1973
Dec. 14—Andres Ramos, Barcelona .... W 6
1974
Jan. 25—Santiago Cebolleda, Zaragoza .... W 6
Mar. 23—F. Santaengracia, Tarrasa.............. W 6
Mar. 29—Antonio Donoso, Feather............... W 6
May 18—Jose Antonio Donoso, Tarrasa .... W 6
June 1—Santiago Cebolleda, Tarrasa .... W 8
June 14—Antonio Donoso, Madrid .... W 8
June 28—Jesus Zarco, Madrid .... W 8
Aug. 9—Antonio Rejon, Madrid.............. W disq. 7
Aug. 30—Pedro Coque, Madrid .... W 8
Oct. 4—Pedro Coque, Madrid .... W 8
1975
Jan. 10—Roland Cazeaux, Barcelona .... W 8
Apr. 19—Sebastian Ruiz, Barcelona .... KO 3
June 18—Antonio Donoso, Barcelona............. W 8
July 23—Tinc Blanco, Madrid .... D 8
Sept. 25—Svein-Erik Paulsen, Oslo .... L 15
(European Junior Lightweight Title)
Dec. 5—Rodolfo Sanchez, Madrid................ W 12
(Spanish Junior Lightweight Title)
1976
Feb. 28—Antonio Donoso, Tarrasa................ W 12
May 21—Domingo Jiminez, Barcelona .... W 8
July 2—Rodolfo Sanchez, Barcelona .... W 12
(Spanish Junior Lightweight Title)
Sept. 4—Yata Ist, Santander .... WF 10
(Spanish Junior Lightweight Title)
Dec. 11—Fernando Bermejo, Mataro .... KO 6
Dec. 23—Francisco Santaengracia, Mataro .... W 8
1977
Apr. 1—Giancarlo Usai, Barcelona .... W 8
Aug. 12—Gitano Jimenez, Figueras .... W 8
Aug. 26—Adolfo Osses, Tarrasa .... W 8
Sept. 16—Hugo Carrizo, Barcelona .... W 8
Dec. 16—Hector Molina, Barcelona .... W 10
1978
May 31—Antonio Amaya, Barcelona .... W 8
June 30—Hugo Carrizo, Barcelona .... W 8
Oct. 18—Jim Watt, Glasgow .... KO by 5
(European Lightweight Title)
1979
Oct. 6—Fernando Sanchez, Bilbao .... W 8
Dec. 8—Paperito Jimenez, Salamanca .... KO 9
(Won Spanish Junior Welterweight Title)
1980
Mar. 7—Georges Cetin, Barcelona .... W 10
Apr. 25—Rene Martin, Barcelona .... W 8

July 10—Fernando (Kung-Fu) Sanchez, Barcelona W 10
(Retained Spanish Lightweight Title)
Aug. 1—Carlos Morales, Badalona .... KO 5
(Won Spanish Junior Welterweight Title)
Sept. 12—Juan Melian, Salamanca .... KO 3
(Retained Spanish Junior Welterweight Title)
Dec. 17—Guiseppe Martinese, Senigallia .... KO 3
(Retained Spanish Junior Welterweight Title)

ROY GUMBS
Tottenham, England Middleweight
1976
May 18—Vernon Shaw, Southend .... KO 6
June 7—Eddie Viering, London.................... L 6
June 29—Eddie Viering, Southampton .... L 6
Sept. 21—Carlton Benoit, Southend................ L 6
Oct. 13—Len Brittain, Stoke.................... KO 3
Nov. 22—Henry Johnson, Walworth .... W 6
Dec. 6—Johnny Cox, Luton..................... KO 1
1977
Jan. 19—Tony Sibson, Solihull .... L 8
Jan. 25—Peter Mullins, London .... KO 4
Feb. 14—Malcolm Heath, Bedford .... KO 4
Feb. 21—Bonny McKenzie, London .... W 8
Apr. 24—Wayne Bennett, Birmingham .... LF 8
June 14—Greg Evans, Wembley .... L 8
1978
Jan. 18—Eddie Smith, Solihull .... KO by 8
Feb. 28—Oscar Angus, Atlesbury .... D 8
Mar. 16—Per Mullertz, Copenhagen .... KO 4
Apr. 3—Oscar Angus, London .... KO 3
Apr. 29—Algredo Naveiras, Emines .... KO by 3
Sept. 27—Bonny McKenzie, Stoke .... W 8
Nov. 6—Keith Bussey, London .... D 8
Dec. 21—Greg Evans, Liverpool .... KO 6
1979
Feb. 19—Jan Magdziarz, London .... KO 7
Apr. 3—Errol McKenzie, Hammersmith .... KO 4
Apr. 24—Bonny McKenzie, London .... W 8
Oct. 15—Bonny McKenzie, Mayfair .... KO 3
Nov. 26—Victor Attivor, Hammersmith .... KO 5
1980
Feb. 18—Frankie Lucas, Birmingham .... W 10
(Won Southern Area Middleweight Title)

JEROME GUMEDE
South African Junior Lightweight
1978
Nov. 25—Stezi Buthelezi, Durban .... KO 2
1979
June 9—Stezi Buthelezi, Durban .... KO 6
Sept. 1—Essau Dlamini, Empangeni .... KO 6
Sept. 29—Elijah Cele, Durban .... W 6
1980
June 16—Bernard Zungu, Durban .... KO 10
(Retained Natal Junior Lightweight Title)
Sept. 5—Aladin Stevens, Springs .... W 6
Oct. 31—Evans Gwiji, Springs .... L 12
(For South African Junior Lightweight Title)
Dec. 1—Elijah Cele, Durban .... W 6

JOSEPH GUMEDE
South African Featherweight
Born: October 17, 1945
1969
May 17—Ben Lekohe, Sharpeville .... W 4
Sept. 7—Vincent Mthembu, Swaziland .... D 4
Sept. 13—Richard Ngidi, Orlando .... KO 1
1970
Feb. 7—Smuts Mokoena, Orlando .... W 4
Feb. 28—Blakeney Mathews, Durban .... W 6
June 12—William Oliphant, Mamelodi .... KO 5
Sept. 5—Alfred Buqwana, Jabulane .... D 6
Oct. 2—Lucas Sematle, Springs .... W 6
Nov. 11—Wallace v.d. Haar, New Clare .... KO 4
1971
Feb. 6—Isaac Nuku, Jabulani .... W 6
Feb. 20—Meschack Mncube, Natalspruit .... D 6
Mar. 12—Rafty Mngadi, Mamelodi .... L 8
June 5—Anthony Sithole, Jabulani .... KO 9
(Won South African Bantamweight Title)
July 17—Jacob Mokotong, Springs .... W 6
Aug. 14—Little Joe Mtiyane, Durban .... KO 3
Oct. 2—Isaac Nuku, Jabulani .... W 6
Nov. 27—Alfred Cele, Durban .... W 8
1972
Feb. 24—Bashew Sibaca, Langa .... KO 6
Mar. 25—Anthony Sithole, Jabulani .... KO 9
May 6—Meshack Mncube, Jabulani .... W 6
June 3—Solomon Ramafikeng, Jabulani .... W 12
June 9—Simon Monomodi, Atteridgev. .... W 8
July 21—Gideon Borias, Coronation............. W 8
Sept. 30—Rafty Mngadi, Jabulani .... KO 9
Oct. 21—Sipho Yaka, Port Elizabeth .... W 8

Dec.	2—Meshack Mncube, Jabulani	W 12

1973

Mar.	3—John Frazer Mkhize, Jabulani	KO 12
Apr.	13—Andries Moloi, Springs	KO 4
June	22—Simon Monodi, Springs	KO 3
June	30—Phillip Masiza, Port Elizabeth	W 8
July	28—Bashew Sibaca, Port Elizabeth	W 12
Aug.	17—Johannes Sithebe, Springs	W 6
Sept.	29—Aubrey Peta, Port Elizabeth	W 8
Oct.	20—Johannes Masehla, Port Elizabeth	KO 7
Nov.	10—Jacob Jobe, Port Elizabeth	W 12

1974-1975
(Inactive)
1976

Feb.	6—Rafty Mngadi, Kwa-Thema	W 6
Apr.	9—Johannes Sithebe, Springs	W 8
Mar.	27—Guy Ratazayo, East London	W 6
Apr.	24—Joseph Tsotetsi, Jabulani	W 8

1977

June	4—Victor Mpiyake, Johannesburg	L 8
Oct.	14—Paulus Mnisi, Krugersdorp	W 8
Nov.	18—Joseph Tsotetsi, Krugersdorp	L 6

1978

Mar.	3—Lazarus Mofokeng, Krugersdorp	W 8

1979

Mar.	10—Alexander Sibiya, Newcastle	W 6

1980

Feb.	29—Joshua Nhlapo, Springs	L 8
Apr.	5—Nkosana Moss, East London	L 6
May	31—Monwabisi Kana, East London	KO 4
Aug.	29—Lazarus Mofokeng, Sebokeng	KO 2
Sept.	20—Joseph Nhlapo, Johannesburg	KO by 5

NICHOLAS GUMEDE
South African Junior Welterweight
1978

Aug.	12—Moses Mthembu, Durban	W 6
Aug.	28—Andre Rheeders, Durban	KO by 1

1979

Apr.	25—Bennie Nortman, Durban	KO by 2
Aug.	18—Moses Mthembu, Durban	L 10

1980

Feb.	4—Alfred Ndhlovu, Durban	W 4
Mar.	1—Gregory Clark, Durban	KO by 2
Aug.	4—Moses Mthembu, Durban	W 10

(Won Natal Junior Welterweight Title)

PETER GUMEDE
South African Welterweight
1980

June	16—Nicholas Mhlaba, Durban	W 4
Nov.	1—Abel Brown, Stanger	W 6

JOE GUNUZA
South African Bantamweight
1980

July	26—Mncedi Masiza, KWT	D 4
Aug.	23—Ntsikelo Mona, East London	W 4
Nov.	8—Monde Sibaca, East London	W 6
Dec.	6—Sexon Ngqayimbana, East London	KO by 2

REINER GUTEKUNST
German Middleweight
1978

Nov.	18—Klaus Hein, Berlin	D 6

1979

Mar.	7—Alex Blanchard, Rotterdam	KO by 3
Apr.	28—Klaus Hein, Belgrade	W 4

1980

Mar.	28—Georges Lemmer, Berlin	L 6
June	7—Horst Brinkmeier, Cologne	KO by 6

JOHANNES FANO GWALA
South African Welterweight
1980

Apr.	28—Welcome Anderson, Durban	KO by 4
Nov.	10—Welcome Anderson, Durban	KO 3

EVANS GWIJI
South African Junior Lightweight
Born: December 9, 1954
1974

Aug.	30—Philemon Tshabalabala, Orlando West	KO 1
Nov.	8—Jacob Mphore	KO 2

1975

Feb.	21—Paulus Mnisi, Orlando West	L 4
Apr.	26—Moeketsi Simon Mahlasi, Sharpeville	KO 3
July	25—Jacob Hlanyane, Orlando	W 6

1976

Apr.	9—Jonas Skosana, Springs	KO 2
June	5—Jacob Morake, Jabulani	KO 1
July	17—Tsietsi Maretloane, Port Elizabeth	L 8
Nov.	13—Guy Ratazayo, East London	L 8

1977

Apr.	16—Thomas Mathibela, Johannesburg	W 4
June	3—Joseph Tsotetsi, Springs	L 10
Nov.	19—Nkosana Mgxaji, Port Elizabeth	D 8
Dec.	3—Eddie Mileham, Johannesburg	KO 5

1978

Apr.	29—Patrick Kohli, Cape Town	W 8
Aug.	12—Joseph Tsotetsi, Jabulani	KO 10

1979

Feb.	3—Johan Weyer, Johannesburg	L 6
Mar.	30—Simon Molahole, Springs	KO 2
May	4—Norman Sekapane, Springs	W 8
Aug.	4—Nkosana Mgxaji, East London	L 12
Sept.	15—Johan Weyer, Johannesburg	KO 3

1980

Feb.	1—Guy Ratazayo, Springs	W 12

(Retained South African Junior Lightweight Title)

May	24—Joseph Tsotetsi, Orlando	KO 9

(Retained South African Junior Lightweight Title)

Aug.	1—Simon Dhladhla, Springs	KO 6
Oct.	31—Jerome Gumede, Springs	W 12

(Retained South African Junior Lightweight Title)

DES GWILLIAM
British Lightweight
1977

Feb.	25—Marty Jacobs, Digbeth	KO 6
Apr.	7—Chris Glover, Dudley	D 6
May	27—Barton McAllister, Digbeth	KO by 5
Sept.	19—Barry Price, Walworth	D 6
Sept.	30—Cornelius Bosa-Edwards, London	KO 6

1978

Jan.	5—Hans Henrik Palm, Randers	L 6
Mar.	15—Joey Singleton, Solihull	L 8
Apr.	18—Roy Varden, Coventry	L 10
Sept.	27—Bingo Crooks, Stoke	D 8
Oct.	31—Bingo Crooks, Wolverhampton	W 10
Nov.	11—Dan M'Putu, Dunkirk	L 8

1979

Apr.	4—Dill Collins, Birmingham	W 8
July	2—Barry Price, London	W 8
Oct.	29—Paul Chance, Wolverhampton	L 10

1980

Feb.	28—Ricky Beaumont, Hull	KO by 7
Mar.	26—Dill Collins, Evesham	KO 4
Apr.	30—Dave Taylor, Wolverhampton	W 8
Oct.	20—Ken Buchanan, Birmingham	L 8
Dec.	1—John Muwanga, Oslo	L 6

LUC (RUDI) HAECK
German Junior Lightweight
1972

Sept.	22—Francesco Condello, Gand	KO 6
Oct.	20—Salvatore Caffieri, Gand	KO 1
Nov.	17—Albert Voisin, Gand	KO 3
Dec.	16—Franco Soro, Gand	W 6

1973

Feb.	9—Werner Blanquaert, Gand	KO 2
Mar.	10—Daniel Ringuet, Gand	KO by 3
May	5—Abdel Meziche, Gent	W 8
Aug.	25—Jose Gonzalez Carrera, Gand	KO 4
Sept.	15—Jean C. Vanderbreght, Zele	W 6
Sept.	21—Christian Levy, Gand	W 6
Oct.	19—Michel Lefebvre, Gand	L 8
Dec.	7—Christian Hardelin, Gand	KO 7

1974

Jan.	25—Gerard Bok, Zele	W 6
Feb.	4—Mario Oliveira, S. Armand	KO 7
Feb.	22—Fernand Roelands, Roulers	D 8
Sept.	21—Christian Levy, Zele	W 8
Oct.	26—Iwan Roessli, Zele	KO 2

1975

Jan.	4—Ernesto Miranda, Zele	W 10
Feb.	1—Roland Cazeaux, Zele	KO 10
Apr.	19—Iwan Roessli, Bruges	KO 4
Apr.	19—Renza Battistelli, Wieze	W 10
June	—Jean Pierre Hainault, Selzate	NC 4
Sept.	20—Ali Messaoud, Zele	W 8
Oct.	24—Ugo Poli, Zele	D 8
Dec.	6—Tommy Dunn, Zele	W 10

1976

Feb.	27—Roland Cazeaux, S. Nazaire	L 15

(European Junior Lightweight Title)

Apr.	30—Raymond Dauteuille, Zele	W 10
Sept.	11—Giuseppe Agate, S. Amand	W 8

Oct. 16—Ugo Poli, Zele .... W 8
Nov. 11—Mario Redi, Zele .... KO by 6
1977
Mar. 12—Miguel Molleda, Anversa .... KO by 1
Oct. 8—Pellegrino Ventrone, Zele .... NC 6
1978
(Inactive)
1979
Oct. 6—Andres Blanco, St. Amand .... D 8
1980
Apr. 5—Angelo Licata, La Louviere .... D 10

TSUTOMU HAGUSA
Japanese Junior Middleweight
1975
Aug. 30—Sanshiro Higo, Tsukumi .... KO by 6
1976
Aug. 23—Sumio Kai, Tokyo .... KO by 7
Nov. 20—Jael Keun Yim, Kitakyshi City .... W 12
1977
May 14—Armando Boniquit, Tokyo .... W 12
June 27—Hideo Kanazawa, Osaka City .... W 10
1978
Mar. 16—Ayub Kalule, Copenhagen .... KO by 3
Apr. 21—Jo Ho, Tokyo .... D 12
Oct. 14—Jae Kun Lim, Tokyo .... KO by 5
(OPBF Junior Middleweight Title)
Nov. 23—Tadashi Mihara, Tokyo .... KO by 6
1979
Mar. 19—Cassius Naito, Tokyo .... KO by 7
May 19—Hirofumi Sawada, Kumamote .... KO 6
Dec. 20—Caesar Sasaki, Tokyo .... KO by 2
1980
Apr. 7—Chung-Jae Hwang, Seoul .... KO by 3
(For OPBF Welterweight Title)

JOSEPH HALI
South African Middleweight
1971
Jan. 14—Pancho Radebe, Langa .... W 6
Mar. 4—Sydney Hoho, Langa .... L 10
Apr. 5—John Abrahams, Athlone .... W 8
June 19—Gordon Goba, Cape Town .... W 8
Sept. 30—Mike Ramagole, Cape Town .... KO 1
Dec. 7—Sydney Hoho, Cape Province .... L 10
1972
Feb. 24—Petrus Buhali, Langa .... KO 1
Sept. 23—Curtis Cokes, Port Elizabeth .... L 10
Oct. 31—Gordon Goba, Langa .... L 12
1973
Mar. 1—Moses Mkwanazi, Langa .... KO 7
Mar. 24—Sydney Hoho, Cape Town L
Oct. 20—Simon Mphuthi .... KO 2
1974
Jan. 17—Morgan Moledi, Langa .... W 8
Sept. 23—Elijh Makhathini, Cape Town .... L 10
1975
Jan. 23—Black Bullet Ndlovu, Cape Town .... KO 4
Feb. 8—Maxwell Malinga, East London .... L 10
Aug. 1—Gordon Goba, Kwa-Thema .... L 12
1976
Mar. 22—Morgan Moledi, Guguletu .... KO 2
1977
Jan. 29—Elijah Makathini, Port Elizabeth .... KO by 10
May 7—Loyisa Mtya, Zwelitsha .... L 10
Nov. 14—Doug Lumley, Cape Town .... L 10
Dec. 1—Charlie Weir, Cape Town .... KO 5
1978
Mar. 20—Gert Craemer, Cape Town .... L 6
Apr. 17—Charlie Weir, Johannesburg .... KO by 2
July 31—Stanley Maxebengula, Cape Town ...... KO 3
Nov. 15—Coenraad Bekker, Cape Town .... L 6
1979
Feb. 3—Cameron Adams, Johannesburg ...... KO by 2
June 2—Terrance Makaluza, Port Elizabeth ...... L 6
Nov. 12—Bruce McIntyre, Welkom .... KO by 3
1980
Mar. 13—Thornton Oakes, Cape Town .... W 4

TSUYOSHI HAMADA
Japanese Junior Lightweight
1980
Feb. 22—Kunio Tada, Tokyo .... KO 5
Apr. 29—Katsuo Kazama, Tokyo .... KO 1
Nov. 23—Takeshi Mine, Tokyo .... KO 1

JAMIL RODRIGUE HAMDOUCHE
Spanish Featherweight
1979
Oct. 29—Norbert Alcade, Paris .... KO 5
1980
Mar. 1—Antonio Secci, Carrieres Sur Seine ...... D 6
Apr. 12—Herve Lorant, LeMans .... W 6

Apr. 19—Shamedine Gardach, Lyon .... W 6
Apr. 26—Di Benedetto, Aix en Provence .... D 6

DUNCAN HAMILTON
British Lightweight
1979
Nov. 19—Thommy Thomas, Glasgow .... W 6
1980
Jan. 8—Kevin Walsh, Windsor .... W 6
Feb. 25—Norman Morton, Glasgow .... W 8
June 7—Willie Booth, Glasgow .... L 10
(For Scottish Lightweight Title)
Sept. 15—Colin Wake, Glasgow .... W 8
Sept. 24—Lance Williams, Solihull .... L 6

FUMIKI (WARRIOR) HANADA
Japanese Junior Middleweight
1979
Dec. 20—Mamoru Taira, Tokyo .... KO 8
1980
Feb. 18—Michihire Horiguchi, Tokyo .... KO by 4
(For Japanese Junior Middleweight Title)

JORGEN HANSEN
Danish Welterweight
Born: March 22, 1943
1969
Apr. 10—Daniel Vedani, Copenhagen .... W 4
June 6—Arenski Galon, Copenhagen .... KO 4
Sept. 11—Lakdor Boulaiche, Copenhagen .... KO 3
Nov. 6—Gerard Hedin, Copenhagen............. W 6
Dec. 7—Giovanni Murgia, Aarhus................. W 6
1970
Feb. 12—Mohammed Taif, Copenhagen .... KO 2
Apr. 2—Bobby Arthur, Aarhus.................... W 6
June 4—Barry Calderwood, Copenhagen........... W 6
Aug. 27—Roy Francis, Copenhagen .... W 6
Oct. 8—Gus Farrell, Copenhagen .... KO 7
Dec. 4—Aldo Mondora, Rome .... KO 6
1971
Jan. 24—Guy Vercoutter, Holestbro .... W 8
Feb. 11—Bernie Terrell, Copenhagen .... KO 5
Apr. 22—Romualdo D'Alo, Copenhagen .... W 8
July 1—Des Rea, Copenhagen .... W 8
Sept. 2—Johnny Cooke, Aarhus .... W 8
Sept. 15—Jesus Gonzalez, Copenhagen .... KO 5
Oct. 21—Yvon Mariolle, Copenhagen .... W 8
Nov. 21—Dave Wyatt, Nykoebing .... KO 2
1972
Jan. 27—Francisco Martin Figueroa, Copenhagen .. W 8
Mar. 2—Ricky Porter, Copenhagen .... W 10
Apr. 13—Rainer Muller, Copenhagen .... W 8
June 22—Rober Menetry, Copenhagen .... KO by 10
(European Welterweight Title)
Aug. 19—Johnny White, Copenhagen .... W 8
Nov. 19—Eddie Blay, Aarhus................... KO by 8
Dec. 7—Pat McCormack, Copenhagen .... KO 5
1973
Jan. 18—Pat McCormack, Copenhagen .... KO by 4
Mar. 1—Adriano Rodriguez, Oslo .... W 8
Mar. 8—Pat McCormack, Copenhagen .... KO 7
May 10—Everaldo Azevdo, Copenhagen .... L 8
June 14—Eddie Blay, Copenhagen .... W 10
Sept. 7—Everaldo Costa Azevedo, Copenhagen ...... W 12
Nov. 1—Bruno Arcari, Copenhagen .... KO by 5
(WBC Lightweight Title)
1974
Jan. 17—Pietro Ceru', Randers................... W 8
Feb. 7—Des Morrison, Copenhagen .... W 8
Mar. 14—Kurt Hombach, Randers .... KO 6
Apr. 4—Mickey Flynn, Copenhagen .... WF 5
Aug. 17—Norman (Pangaman) Sekgapane,
Johannesburg .... KO by 9
Oct. 10—Jim Montague, Copenhagen .... W 8
Nov. 21—Bruno Freschi, Copenhagen .... KO 6
Dec. 10—Jaroslaw Travnik, Offenbach .... W 8
1975
Feb. 15—Jurgen Voss, Randers................... W 8
Mar. 1—Horst Brinkmeier, Koln .... KO 3
Mar. 8—Marco Scano, Cagliari.................. LF 3
May 6—Jimmy Carter, Holstebro .... KO 3
June 19—Kristiam Hoydahl, Oslo................. KO 6
Oct. 24—Rocky Mattioli, Milan .... KO by 7
Nov. 22—Everaldo Azevedo, Skopije .... L 8
1976
Apr. 8—Billy Waith, Copenhagen .... W 8
June 3—Pat Thomas, Copenhagen .... KO 3
Oct. 9—Tiger Quaye, Copenhagen............... KO 1
Nov. 19—Luciano De Luca, Randers .... KO 6
Dec. 9—Augusto Lauri, Copenhagen............ W 8
1977
Jan. 20—Frank Albertus, Copenhagen .... KO by 3
Feb. 24—Mehmed Cacal, Copenhagen .... W 8

Mar.	31—Carlos Almeida, Copenhagen	KO 3
Apr.	28—Nicola Sassanelli, Copenhagen	KO 4
June	2—Marco Scano, Randers	KO 5
	(European Welterweight Title)	
Aug.	6—Jorg Eipel, Berlin	LF 13
	(European Welterweight Title)	
Sept.	8—Tony Hudson, Copenhagen	W 8
Nov.	3—Steve Angell, Randers	KO 6
Dec.	8—Paolo Zanusso, Copenhagen	WF 6

1978

Jan.	5—Juan Battista, Randers	KO 2
Feb.	9—Mike Everett, Copenhagen	KO by 1
Apr.	27—Alain Marion, Randers	KO 6
May	25—Giancarlo Barabotti, Copenhagen	KO 6
Aug.	18—Joseph Pachler, Wien	LF 8
	(European Welterweight Title)	
Sept.	14—Eddie Marcelle, Randers	W 8
Nov.	11—Johnny Copeland, Copenhagen	KO 7
Dec.	7—Vittorio Conte, Copenhagen	KO 4

1979

Feb.	15—Billy Waith, Randers	W 8
June	28—Dave Green, Randers	KO 3
	(EBU Welterweight Title)	
Sept.	6—Gert Steyn, Randers	W 8
Oct.	11—Remo Costa, Copenhagen	W 8
Dec.	6—Joseph Pachler, Copenhagen	KO 6

1980

Feb.	7—Alois Carmeliet, Randers	KO 5
	(Retained European Welterweight Title)	
Feb.	29—Jose Ramirez, Odense	KO 7
Apr.	17—Joey Singleton, Copenhagen	W 12
	(Retained European Welterweight Title)	
June	12—Ernesto Postl, Randers	KO 7
Oct.	17—Hans Erik Palm, Copenhagen	KO 9
	(Retained European Welterweight Title)	
Dec.	4—Giuseppe Di Padova, Randers	W 12
	(Retained European Welterweight Title)	

JIMMY HARRINGTON
British Light Heavyweight

1979

Feb.	6—John Breen, London	KO 2
Feb.	21—Mohammed Ali, Cambridge	KO 3
Nov.	6—Stan Carnell, Kensington	KO 2

1980

Apr.	22—Winston Davis, London	KO 3
June	12—Joe Lally, Cambridge	KO 3
July	12—Mick Morris, London	L 4
Sept.	16—Steve Lewin, London	KO by 3

PETER HARRISON
British Lightweight

1980

Feb.	28—Colin Wake, Hull	W 6
Mar.	14—John Lindo, Glasgow	W 6
Mar.	19—Steve Parker, Stoke	L 6
Mar.	24—Colin Wake, Glasgow	W 6
May	27—Tim Malonay, Glasgow	W 8
June	23—Norman Morton, Glasgow	W 8
Sept.	24—Jackie Turner, Solihull	KO 3
Oct.	14—Bingo Crooks, Wolverhampton	L 8

LEE HARTSHORN
Scottish Welterweight

1978

Nov.	27—Don Hughes, Glasgow	W 6

1979

Jan.	17—Dave Allen, Stoke	W 6
Jan.	22—John Chard, London	L 3
Mar.	12—Tommy Baldwin, Manchester	KO 2
Mar.	16—Jess Harper, Bradford	W 6
Apr.	2—Tony Hague, Manchester	W 6
Apr.	10—Gary Newell, Wolverhampton	W 6
Apr.	23—Carl North, Bradford	KO 3
May	2—John Kennedy, Solihull	L 8
May	21—Dennis Pryce, Manchester	W 8
June	18—Richard Avery, Manchester	KO 4
July	5—Nigel Thomas, Aberavon	L 8
Oct.	15—Lloyd Lee, Windsor	L 8
Oct.	23—Pat Smythe, Blackpool	W 8
Nov.	29—Al Stewart, Liverpool	W 8
Dec.	17—Terry Peterson, Bradford	W 8

1980

Feb.	2—Frank Decaestecker, Torhut	L 8
Feb.	11—Roy Varden, Manchester	KO by 2
Mar.	27—Derek Nelson, Newcastle	W 8
Apr.	28—Nigel Thomas, London	W 8
Sept.	22—Lloyd Hibbert, Wolverhampton	L 8
Oct.	13—Tony Martey, Windsor	L 8

NOBORU HATAKEYAMA
Japanese Junior Welterweight

1972

July	16—Akisumi Yamazaki, Tokyo	KO 2
Sept.	17—Itaru Yamauchi, Tokyo	W 4
Nov.	26—Sai Harako, Tokyo	L 4
Dec.	18—Sakae Takeyama, Tokyo	W 4

1973

May	20—Toru Kuroda, Tokyo	W 4
June	19—Toru Kuroda, Tokyo	W 4
July	12—Ken Kokubo, Tokyo	W 6
Aug.	26—Yasumasa Miura, Tokyo	D 6

1974

(Inactive)

1975

Nov.	17—Junji Onodera, Tokyo	KO 2
Dec.	22—M. Koichi Fukuda, Tokyo	L 8

1976

Feb.	1—Akiyoshi Ogino, Tokyo	W 8
June	24—Koji Nakada, Tokyo	W 10
Sept.	23—Huber Watanabe, Tokyo	W 10

1977

Jan.	17—Ken Kokubo, Tokyo	KO 3
June	27—Masahiro Kato, Tokyo	W 10
Oct.	27—Tetsuo Furuyama, Tokyo	W 10
	(Won Japanese Junior Welterweight Title)	
Dec.	4—Masahiro Kato, Tokyo	KO 7
	(Japanese Junior Welterweight Title)	

1978

Feb.	27—Huber Watanabe, Tokyo	W 10
June	26—Shigeru Goda, Tokyo	W 10
Sept.	28—Mashiro Yokai, Tokyo	L 10

1979

May	19—Tsutomu Matsuo, Shizueka	KO 8
	(Japanese Junior Welterweight Title)	
Aug.	3—San-Mo Koo, Pusan	L 12
	(OPBF Junior Welterweight Championship)	
Sept.	24—Eichi Fukumoto, Tokyo	KO by 4
	(JBC Junior Welterweight Title)	

1980

Apr.	28—Masahiro Yokai, Tokyo	W 10

BILL HAY
British Featherweight

1980

June	2—Jim Harvey, Glasgow	L 4
July	28—Glen Rhodes, Glasgow	D 6

RAY HEANEY
British Junior Welterweight

1976

Oct.	18—Tommy Duffy, Glasgow	D 6
Oct.	25—John Henry Wall, London	L 8

1977

Jan.	24—Chris Davies, London	KO by 5
Oct.	17—Barry Price, Mayfair	L 8

1978

Jan.	23—Billy Vivian, Aberavon	L 8
Mar.	14—Benny McQuade, Belfast	KO by 9
May	11—Jimmy Brown, Belfast	L 8

1979

Feb.	19—Gerry Burns, Belfast	KO 3
Mar.	19—Ian Pickersgill, Glasgow	KO 1
Apr.	5—Dai Davies, Belfast	W 8

1980

Feb.	25—Davy Campbell, Belfast	KO by 8
(For Vacant Northern Ireland Junior Welterweight Title)		

MALCOLM HEATH
British Middleweight

1977

Jan.	19—John Laine, Stoke	L 8
Feb.	14—John Laine, London	KO by 5
Mar.	8—Tony Kelsey, London	KO 6
Mar.	16—Mick Lock, Stoke	KO 4
May	3—Chris Williams, London	KO by 2

1978

(Inactive)

1979

Dec.	3—Joe Jackson, Hull	W 6

1980

Jan.	25—Jimmy Ellis, Hull	W 6
Feb.	18—Martin Francis, London	W 8
Mar.	31—Gordon George, London	L 6
Apr.	28—Joe Jackson, London	W 8
May	5—Mick Fellingham, Glasgow	KO 4
Oct.	2—Martin Francis, Hull	W 6
Oct.	20—Billy Lauder, Glasgow	L 6

PAUL HEATLEY
British Light Heavyweight

1980

Apr.	9—Chuck Hirschmann, Liverpool	L 4

Apr. 14—Joe Frater, Manchester .... KO by 5
May 28—Brian Graham, Middlesbrough .... KO by 2

ERWIN HEIBER
German Light Heavyweight
Born: March 1, 1956
1977
April 1—Joachim Trautwein, Cologne .... W 4
May 17—Wilhelm Ermen, Hamburg .... KO 2
Sept. 30—Giampaolo Piras, Hamburg .... W 4
1978
Feb. 17—Alfred Fries, Kiel .... W 6
June 30—Josef Kossmann, Morsbach .... W 6
Oct. 9—Djibril Bathily, Paris .... L 6
Oct. 31—Donato Romano, Munich .... D 6
1979
Apr. 6—Min Whan Ki, Luebeck .... KO 4
May 18—Roy Kaba, Munich .... W 6
July 28—Franco Aresti, Munich .... D 6
Nov. 5—Ignacio Gorostidi, Paris .... D 6
Dec. 7—Jose Luis Ribeiro, Luebeck .... W 8
1980
Feb. 6—Claude Kalanda, Luebeck .... KO 5
June 13—Fritz Krenstehner, Lubeck .... KO 3
Oct. 6—Patrick Babouram, Paris .... D 6

RANDY HENDERSON
British Welterweight
1980
Apr. 18—Dave Sullivan, Southend .... L 6
May 15—Sean Jones, London .... L 6
Sept. 16—Gerry White, Southend .... D 6
Nov. 4—Ronnie Rathbone, Southend .... L 6

STEVE HENDERSON
British Featherweight
1977
Oct. 19—Eric Wood, Kingston .... L 6
Nov. 10—Tony Whitmore, Wimbledon .... W 6
1978
Jan. 19—John Cooper, Wimbledon .... L 6
Mar. 6—Paul Chance, Wolverhampton .... KO by 7
Apr. 17—Walter Angliss, London .... KO 5
Apr. 24—Tony Whitmore, Walworth .... L 6
May 16—John Cooper, Aylesbury .... L 6
Oct. 11—Muhammad Younis, Stoke .... KO by 5
1979
Nov. 5—Steve Cleak, Piccadilly .... L 8
1980
Feb. 28—Ho-Shing Winston, Queensway ...... KO by 5
Apr. 24—Robert Hepburn, Queensway .... KO 6
May 15—Sean Jones, London .... L 6
June 16—Steve Cleak, London .... L 8

LOUIS HENDRIKS
South African Heavyweight
1978
Dec. 15—Joseph Sgudla, Durban .... KO 3
1979
Feb. 5—Sofonia Naile, Welkom .... W 4
Mar. 10—Joseph Sgudla, Johannesburg .... KO 2
Oct. 5—Timothy Zwane, Bloemfontein .... KO 2
Dec. 3—Wiets de Beer, Welkom .... KO 4
1980
Feb. 4—Caifas Masondo, Welkom .... W 6
Mar. 21—King Motsi, Bloemfontein .... KO 4
May 5—Jonas Malan, Welkom .... KO 3
July 2—Terry O'Connor, Welkom .... D 8

EDWARD HENERAL
Filipino Junior Welterweight
1979
Feb. 24—Danny Martarillas, Mindoro .... W 10
June 15—Tom Singthanonsak, Manila .... W 10
July 20—Pitsiam Petcharon, Manila .... KO by 9
Nov. 16—David Bernales, Quezon City .... W 10
Dec. 14—Willie Makitoki, Manila .... W 10
1980
Jan. 25—Jimmy Gonzales, Manila .... W 10
May 30—Romy Angels, Manila .... W 10
June 27—Al Cordero, Manila .... W 12
(Won Filipino Junior Welterweight Title)
Aug. 15—Petchsayarm Petcharern, Quezon City ...W 10

BOBBY HENNESSEY
British Heavyweight
1977
Oct. 10—Brian Paul, London .... W 6
Nov. 8—Alan Ward, London .... KO 4
Dec. 6—Clive Beardsley, London .... W 6
1070
Apr. 4—Stan McDermott, London .... KO by 1
May 23—George Scott, Ilsington .... W 8

Sept. 18—Rab Affleck, Glasgow .... L 8
Nov. 23—Tom Kiely, Wimbledon .... L 8
1979
*Jan. 22—John DePlege, London .... KO 2
*Jan. 22—Winston Allen, London .... KO 2
*Jan. 22—David Pearce, London .... KO by 2
May 27—Terry O'Connor, London .... WF 6
*Fought on same night (Mini-tourney)
1980
Sept. 11—Stewart Lithgo, Hartlepool .... L 6

JOHN HENRY
British Featherweight
1978
Nov. 29—Carl Mullings, Evesham .... D 4
1979
Feb. 20—Alec Irvine, Belfast .... KO by 4
Mar. 15—Jimmy Hancock, Dudley .... W 4
Mar. 28—Carl Mullings, Evesham .... D 4
Apr. 6—Robert Hepburn, Norwich .... L 4
May 21—Carl Mullings, Birmingham .... W 6
June 6—Jimmy Hancock, Bedworth .... W 8
June 25—Don Aagesen, Edgbaston .... W 6
Oct. 24—Neil Brown, Norwich .... L 4
Oct. 30—Marvis Greenidge, Bedford .... KO by 4
Nov. 27—Don Aagesen, Wolverhampton .... D 6
Dec. 17—Steve Simms, Wolverhampton .... KO by 1
1980
Jan. 28—Don Aagesen, Edgbaston .... L 3
Mar. 19—Joe McNamee, Stoke .... W 3
Apr. 21—Glyn Rhodes, Bradford .... L 5
May 19—Andy Thomas, Birmingham .... L 1
July 8—Gary Kittle, Wolverhampton .... L 1

STEVE HENTY
British Junior Middleweight
1979
Oct. 29—Tony Britton, Hove .... L 6
1980
Apr. 23—Jeff Aspell, Hove .... L 6
May 20—Adrian Clamp, Southend .... L 5
June 16—Bobby Welburn, NSC .... W 6
July 14—Michael Miller, WSC .... D 6

ROBERT HEPBURN
British Featherweight
1979
Apr. 6—John Henry, Norwich .... W 4
June 26—Alec Irvine, Leicester .... L 6
Oct. 24—Stuart Crabb, Norwich .... D 6
Nov. 6—George Bailey, Stafford .... W 6
Nov. 21—Don Aagesen, Evesham .... W 6
1980
Mar. 6—Ivor Jones, Wimbledon .... L 8
Mar. 17—Joey Wainwright, NSC .... L 6
Apr. 10—Stuart Crabb, Norwich .... W 6
Apr. 24—Steve Henderson, Queensway .... L 6
May 29—Garry Kittle, Wimbledon .... L 6
June 3—Clyde Ruan, Aylesbury .... KO by 2

JOSE LUIS HEREDIA
Spanish Lightweight
1977
May 14—Pedro Coque, Malaga .... W 6
June 8—Juan Barros, Malaga .... W 6
July 22—Ouali M. Bel Allal, Malaga .... W 6
Aug. 12—Antonio Navarro, Malaga .... W 6
Aug. 26—Antonio M. Jurado, Malaga .... W 6
Nov. 12—Nicolas Culebras, Malaga .... W 6
Dec. 3—Cayetano Alcala Cruz, Malaga .... W 8
1978
Jan. 14—Serafin Dos Anjos, Malaga .... W 8
July 28—Ahmed Ben Aissa, Malaga .... W 8
Aug. 26—Jose Godoy, Malaga .... W 8
Sept. 19—Mohatar II, Malaga .... W 8
Sept. 29—Jose M. I. Arenas, Malaga .... W 6
Oct. 14—Jeronimo Lucas, Malaga .... W 12
(Won Spanish Lightweight Title)
Nov. 11—Adolfo Osses, Malaga .... W 8
Dec. 16—Domingo Gimenez, Malaga .... KO 10
1979
Mar. 3—Fernando Sanchez, Malaga .... W 15
(Won European Junior Welterweight Title)
May 18—Jo Kimpuani, Dunkirk .... KO by 3
(EBU Junior Welterweight Title)
Aug. 31—Mohamed Jofre II, Melilla .... KO 8
Dec. 8—Mohatar II, Malaga .... W 8
Dec. 24—Hector Medina, Fuengirola .... W 8
1980
Mar. 29—Nino Jiminez, Malaga .... W 10
(Won Spanish Lightweight Title)

323

CARLOS HERNANDEZ
Spanish Junior Lightweight
1975
Nov.　8—Jose D. Labarga, Valladolid .... KO　4
Nov.　29—L. Montes Rodriguez, Valladolid .... W　6
1976
Jan.　7—Jose L. R. Marquez, Valladolid .... W　6
Apr.　3—Jose Artigao, Valladolid .... KO　3
May　21—Jose D. Labarga, Valladolid .... W　6
June　19—Roberto Castanon, Leon .... L　8
Aug.　14—Antonio A, Sanmiguel .... D　6
Sept.　3—Cecilio Lastra, Madrid .... W　8
Oct.　9—Rodolfo Sanchez, Valladolid .... L　8
Nov.　27—Francisco Santagracia, Valladolid .... W　8
1977
Jan.　6—Roberto Castanon, Leon .... L　8
Jan.　29—Manuel Llata, Santander .... KO　3
Mar.　5—Ramon G. Marichal, Valladolid .... W　8
Apr.　1—Alain Le Fol, Madrid .... W　8
May　7—Frank Realhino, Valladolid .... W　8
July　3—Adolfo Osses, Valladolid .... W　8
Dec.　30—Cayetano Alcala, Valladolid .... KO　1
1978
Feb.　4—Isidoro Cabezas, Valladolid .... KO by　6
(Spanish Junior Lightweight Title)
Mar.　11—Antonio Medina, Valladolid .... KO　4
Apr.　8—Ramiro Suarez, Valladolid .... KO　2
May　12—Hector Molina, Valladolid .... W　8
May　24—Antonio Puddu, Cagliari .... W　8
Oct.　7—Serafin Dos Anjos, Valladolid .... W　8
Nov.　4—Jesus Canut, Valladolid .... W　6
Dec.　25—Ramon G. Marichal, Bilbao .... W　8
1979
Mar.　10—Natale Vezzoli, Valladolid .... KO　4
Mar.　31—Jofre, Zamora .... W　8
May　5—Carlos Foldex, Valladolid .... W　8
June　3—Rodolfo Sanchez, Miranda de Ebro .... L 12
Aug.　10—Hector Molina, Lepe .... KO　7
Aug.　24—Ramon Garcia Marichal, Madrid .... KO　5
Sept.　29—Hugo Carrizo, Santander .... W　8
Dec.　22—Rodolfo Sanchez, Valladolid .... W 12
(Won EBU Junior Lightweight Title)
1980
Jan.　11—Ramon Garcia Marichal, Las Palmas ..... D　8
Feb.　16—Hector Molina, Zamora .... W　8
Apr.　30—Salvatore Liscapade, Nepi .... KO　6
(Won European Junior Lightweight Title)
Sept.　6—Ramon Garcia Marichal, Tenerife .... W 12
(Retained European Junior Lightweight Title)
Nov.　29—Aristide Pizzo, Marsales .... KO　7
(Retained European Junior Lightweight Title)

JOSE HERNANDEZ
Spanish Junior Middleweight
1966
Jan.　28—Pedro Tari, Barcelona .... W　8
Feb.　13—Pedro Tari, Elche .... W　8
Mar.　3—Antonio Valverde, Barcelona .... KO　4
Mar.　10—Pedro Tari, Barcelona .... W　8
Mar.　31—Javier Mayayo, Barcelona .... W　8
Apr.　17—Javier Mayayo, La Coruna .... W　8
May　7—Javier Mayayo, Barcelona .... W　8
June　28—Guadalupe Mancheno, Valencia .... W　8
July　17—Vicente Fernando, Valencia .... W　8
Aug.　6—Jose L. Fernandez, Valencia .... W　8
Sept.　3—Jose Grandio, Canet .... W　8
Sept.　22—Andres Navarro, Barcelona .... L 12
(Spanish Junior Middleweight Title)
Dec.　16—Antonio Torres, Barcelona .... L　8
1967
Jan.　14—Guadalupe Mancheno, Barcelona .... W　8
Feb.　2—Vicente Fernando, Barcelona .... W　8
Apr.　27—M. Cesareo Barrera, Barcelona .... NC 11
June　3—Joseph Gonzelez, Carcassonne .... KO by　6
Aug.　12—Fred Emi, Gijon .... KO　9
Sept.　21—Edoardo Batista, Barcelona .... W　8
Oct.　8—Golden Abdul, Barcelona .... KO　5
Oct.　26—Guadalupe Mancheno, Barcelona .... KO　4
(Won Spanish Junior Middleweight Title)
Nov.　9—Jose Galvez, Barcelona .... KO　6
Nov.　18—Souleymane Diallo, Nantes .... KO by　7
Dec.　16—Sergio Santana, Las Palmas .... W　8
1968
Feb.　15—Edoardo Batista, Barcelona .... KO　7
Mar.　7—Julio Rocha, Barcelona .... KO　4
Mar.　19—Francisco Ferri, Valencia .... KO by 12
(Lost Spanish Junior Middleweight Title)
Apr.　25—Augusto Ferreira, Barcelona .... KO　4
June　26—Mario Lamagna, Napoli .... KO by　3
Aug.　14—Jesus G. Dopico, Vigo .... W　8
Sept.　27—Luis Folledo, Barcelona .... KO by　5
Nov.　7—Angel Guinaldo, Barcelona .... L　8
1969
Mar.　7—Jerome Adje, Abidjan .... D 10

July　25—Giuseppe Muzio, Chiavari .... L　8
Nov.　13—Angel R. Garcia, Barcelona .... D 10
Nov.　27—Emile Okee, Barcelona .... W　8
Dec.　18—Remo Golfarini, Rieti .... W　8
1970
Mar.　7—Don McMillan, Vigo .... W　8
Apr.　3—Francisco Ferri, Madrid .... KO　5
May　21—Angel Robinson, Barcelona .... W　8
June　17—Edoardo Batista, Bilbao .... KO　4
Sept.　11—Gerhardt Piaskowy, Barcelona .... KO 14
(Won European Junior Middleweight Title)
Nov.　27—Peter Marklewitz, Berlin .... W 15
1971
Jan.　29—Roger Van Laere, Barcelona .... KO　4
Apr.　29—Carmelo Bossi, Madrid .... D 15
June　18—Domenico Tiberia, Barcelona .... W 15
July　18—Angel R. Garcia, La Coruna .... D 10
Aug.　10—Angel R. Garcia, Bilbao .... W 10
Oct.　15—Nojim Maiyegun, Berlin .... W 10
Nov.　5—Jose Duran, Madrid .... D 10
Nov.　17—Angel Guinaldo, Barcelona .... KO　7
Dec.　15—Antonio Torres, Barcelona .... W 10
1972
Feb.　17—Mohamed Sahib, Barcelona .... KO　5
Mar.　24—Jacques Kechichian, Barcelona .... D 15
July　5—Carlo Duran, S. Remo .... L 15
(Lost European Junior Middleweight Title)
July　24—Juvenal de Oliviera, Villafranca .... KO　3
Sept.　22—Antonio De Souza, Barcelona .... KO　2
Oct.　13—Silvano Bertini, Rome .... L 10
Dec.　12—Nojim Malyegun, Wien .... KO by　6
1973-1974
(Inactive)
1975
Feb.　15—Mimoun Mohatar, Barcelona .... W　8
Mar.　14—Mimoun Mohatar, Madrid .... W　8
Apr.　19—Jose M. Madrazo, Barcelona .... W 12
(Won Spanish Middleweight Title)
May　31—Jean Mateo, Bayonne .... KO by　2
Sept.　13—Carmelo Martin Cendon, Zaragoza ... KO by　1
1976
May　21—Antonino Ferreira, Barcelona .... KO　5
June　4—Jose Luis Palacios, Barcelona .... W　8
Aug.　21—Arnoldo Olivares, Sitges .... W　8
1977
Mar.　2—Abel Nessaoud, Mataro .... W　8
May　22—Edoardo Batista, Mataro .... W　8
July　16—Daniel Anekore, S. Coloma .... KO　7
Sept.　3—Mario Molina, St. Coloma de Gramenet ... W　8
Oct.　7—Adoni Amana, Barcelona .... L 12
(Spanish Junior Middleweight Title)
1978
Feb.　9—Ayub Kalule, Copenhagen .... KO by　5
Dec.　26—Josef Nsubuga, Basilea .... KO by　6
1979
Mar.　2—Jean Simos, Leige .... KO　4
Apr.　28—Claude Martin, S. Malo .... KO　6
Sept.　13—Arnoldo Olivares, Barcelona .... W　8
Nov.　10—Andoni Amana, Salamanca .... W 10
(Spanish Junior Middleweight Title)
Dec.　8—Clemente Tshinza, Zele .... L 10
1980
Feb.　15—Georges Warusfel, Nice .... L 10
Mar.　22—Manuel Lira Amaral, Santander .... W　8
Apr.　30—Clemente Tshinza, Abidjan .... KO by　7
June　12—Jacques Chinon, Paris .... D　8
June　20—Alfredo Navareiras, Barcelona .... D　8
Oct.　6—Louis Acaries, Paris .... KO by　4
Nov.　22—Clemente Tshinza, Zele .... W 10

LLOYD HIBBITT
British Welterweight
1979
Jan.　31—Tommy Wright, Stoke .... W　6
Feb.　26—Gary Pearce, Edgbaston .... W　6
Mar.　5—Peter Snowsall, Wolverhampton .... W　8
Apr.　23—Johnny Elliott, Reading .... W　8
May　16—Tommy Wright, Wolverhampton .... W　8
July　2—Vic Jackson, London .... W　8
Sept.　26—Al Stewart, Stoke .... W　8
Oct.　17—Gary Cooper, Evesham .... W　8
Dec.　3—Nigel Thomas, Wolverhampton .... W　8
1980
Sept.　22—Lee Hartshorn, Wolverhampton .... W　8

BILLY HILL
British Middleweight
1977
Feb.　14—Dave Merrel, Manchester .... D　6
Mar.　14—Jimmy Pickard, Manchester .... W　8
Apr.　20—David Owens, Manchester .... KO by　2
1978
(Inactive)

1979

Mar.	1—Joe Jackson, Liverpool	W	6
Mar.	12—Joe Hannaford, Manchester	W	6
Apr.	2—Peter Tidgwell, Manchester	W	8
May	21—Martin McEwan, Bradford	L	8
Dec.	10—Earl Edwards, Manchester	W	8

1980

Feb.	21—Mick Morris, Liverpool	W	8
Mar.	13—Joe Lally, Birkenhead	D	8

DOUG HILL
British Featherweight
1978

June	20—Bobby Baker, Southen	D	6
Sept.	27—Selvin Bell, Stoke	L	6
Nov.	8—John Singlewood, Stoke	KO	2
Nov.	21—Shaun Durkin, Cambridge	W	6
Nov.	28—Steve Enwright, Sheffield	W	6

1979

Jan.	30—Bobby Baker, London	KO	6
Feb.	28—Andy Dane, Burslem	W	6
Mar.	19—Shaun Stewart, London	W	6
Apr.	25—Eric Ragonisi, Burslem	D	6
June	6—Selvin Bell, Burslem	W	8
Sept.	12—Alec Irvine, Burslem	W	10

1980

Feb.	27—Don Aagesen, Burslem	W	8
Mar.	11—Billy Vivian, Nantwich	L	8
Apr.	21—Selvin Bell, NSC	W	5
June	28—Jimmy Flint, Wembley	KO	1
Sept.	24—Don Aagesen, Burslem	W	10

(For Midlands Area Featherweight Title Defense)

MARK HILL
British Lightweight
1977

Oct.	11—Larry Richards, Coventry	D	4
Oct.	31—Larry Richards, Birmingham	D	4
Nov.	22—Larry Richards, Wolverhampton	L	4
Nov.	30—Larry Richards, London	W	4

1978

Feb.	1—Jimmy Brown, Evesham	KO by	1
Mar.	6—Jimmy Cooke, London	KO by	2
Apr.	4—John Singlwood, London	KO	3
Apr.	18—Tony Whitmore, London	W	6
Apr.	24—Gary Lucas, Glasgow	W	4
June	29—Larry Richards, Wolverhampton	L	6
Oct.	11—Gary Collins, Stoke	KO by	1

1979

Apr.	4—Johnny Burns, Birmingham	KO by	3

1980

Oct.	8—Barry Winter, Stoke	L	3

STEVE HILL
British Heavyweight
1974

Mar.	7—Pat Thompson, Mayfair	W	6
Apr.	24—Pat Thompson, Blackpool	W	8

1975

May	16—Tony Allen, Blackpool	W	8
Sept.	22—Ralph Green, Manchester	W	8

1976-1977
(Inactive)
1978

Aug.	29—Reg Long, Liverpool	W	8
Sept.	29—Theo Josephs, Liverpool	KO	4
Nov.	2—Chris Lawson, Liverpool	KO by	2

1979

Nov.	29—Ken Jones, Liverpool	W	8

1980

Feb.	21—Danny McLoughlin, Liverpool	W	4

ALBERT HILLMAN
Orpington, England Junior Middleweight
1974

June	10—Ray Thorogood, Walworth	KO	2
Sept.	2—Allan Jones, Walworth	W	6
Dec.	3—Kimmy Corrigan, London	KO	2

1975

Feb.	11—Augustus Simms, Kensington	W	6
June	3—Roy Commosioung, London	W	6
Sept.	22—Liam White, Walworth	W	8
Oct.	27—Liam White, Walworth	KO	5
Nov.	18—Mickey Ryce, Reading	D	8
Dec.	15—Roy Commosioung, Walworth	W	8

1976

Jan.	12—Kevin White, London	W	8
Mar.	1—Jim Moore, Walworth	W	8
Mar.	29—Micky Ryce, Walworth	L	8
June	14—Micky Ryce, Walworth	W	10
Sept.	29—Achille Mitchell, Hammersmith	L	8
Nov.	22—Tony Poole, London	KO	7

1977

Feb.	1—Jimmy Batten, London	KO by	8

(British Junior Middleweight Title)

May	2—Tony Hudson, Walworth	L	10
Oct.	10—Mick Minter, Walworth	L	8
Dec.	13—Colin Ward, Walworth	L	8

1978

Apr.	17—Dennis Price, Walworth	W	8
Sept.	5—Andre Huussen, Rotterdam	L	8
Oct.	24—Billy English, Kensington	L	8

1979

Oct.	1—Mike Copp, Marylebone	W	8
Oct.	29—Terry Knight, Hove	L	8
Dec.	3—Johnny Pincham, Marylebone	W	8

1980

Jan.	28—Joe Oke, Hove	W	8
Feb.	7—Torben Andersen, Randers	L	4
Apr.	28—Kenny Webber, Walworth	L	8

YOSHITAKA HINENOYA
Japanese Junior Welterweight
1979

Dec.	9—Shizuo Tosaka, Osaka	D	6

1980

Mar.	24—Haruo Narita, Tokyo	KO by	1
June	1—Haruki Miyagawa, Kochi City	KO	4

CHUCK HIRSCHMANN
British Light Heavyweight
1980

Apr.	9—Paul Heatley, Liverpool	W	4
May	12—Joe Frater, Manchester	D	4

NORMAN HLALELE
South African Flyweight
1974

May	24—Freddie Maake, Tembisa	L	4
Sept.	27—Sidwell Mhlongo, Wattville	L	4

1975

Apr.	12—Simon Lehoko, Bloemfontein	L	4
June	20—John Thompson, Tembisa	D	4
Nov.	1—Petrus Makwanzi, Sasolburg	KO	6

1976

Sept.	11—Philemon Mpomeloa, Kroonstad	KO by	1

1977

Sept.	10—Lodewicus Pretorius, Johannesburg	L	4

1978

May	15—Lodewicus Pretorius, Johannesburg	W	4

1979

Mar.	10—Charles McGeer, Johannesburg	W	4

1980

Mar.	28—Dexter Dhlamini, Springs	KO by	5
May	30—Simon Moema, Springs	KO by	5

CHRISTOPHER HLONGWE
South African Middleweight
1980

Mar.	1—Dennis Masondo, Durban	D	4
June	16—Jack Ntuli, Durban	W	4
Aug.	4—Graham Mdinga, Durban	W	4
Dec.	15—Shadrack Sithole, Pietzumburg	D	4

SYDNEY HOHO
South African Light Heavyweight
1970

Oct.	6—Johnny Abrahams, Athlone	L	
Dec.	10—Wellington Semelane, Langa	W	6

1971

Jan.	14—Rodwell McKay, Langa	KO	5
Mar.	1—Joseph Hali, Langa	W	10
Sept.	22—Zollie Khonza, Cape Town	W	8
Sept.	30—Petrus Nkosi, Cape Town	W	8
Nov.	11—Morgan Moledi	W	8
Dec.	7—Joseph Hali, Cape Province	W	10

1972

Jan.	20—Ezra Mzinyane, Cape Town	W	10
Mar.	4—Gordon Goba, Jabulani	W	12

(Won South African Middleweight Title)

Apr.	26—Billy Douglas, Athlone	W	8
May	27—Elijah Makhatini, Durban	KO by	7
Aug.	26—Joseph Sishi, Durban	L	8
Oct.	4—Elijah Makhatini, Durban	W	12
Nov.	18—Zolile Khonza, Port Elizabeth	W	8

1973

Mar.	1—Gordon Goba, Langa	W	10
May	24—Joseph Hali, Cape Town	W	
Oct.	5—Ezra Mzinyane, Springs	W	8

1974

Jan.	17—Elijah Makhatani, Langa	KO	11
Sept.	23—Juarez De Lima, Cape Town	L	10

1975

Jan.	23—Gordon Goba, Cape Town	W	12

1976
Mar. 27—John Nyalunga, East London .... L 6
1978
Feb. 22—Mark Melville, Cape Town .... W 8
June 1—James Mathatho, Goodwood .... W 12
1979
Jan. 16—Kosie Smith, Cape Town .... W 12
(Won South African Light Heavyweight Title)
Apr. 2—Mervin Smit, Welkom .... L 8
Dec. 1—Gerrie Bodenstein, Port Elizabeth .... W 12
1980
Feb. 9—Ivy Brown, Johannesburg .... KO by 5
Apr. 14—Mervin Smit, Cape Town .... KO 8
May 12—Martin Barnard, Cape Town .... W 12
(Won South African Light Heavyweight Title)
Sept. 15—Doug Lumley, Durban .... KO by 11
(Lost South African Light Heavyweight Title)

ANDRE HOLYK
French Welterweight
Born: March 3, 1951, Lyons
1972
Oct. 10—Jean Claude Vanderbreght, Paris .... W 6
Nov. 16—Jesus Baro, Paris .... KO 4
Nov. 30—Jean Claude Vanderbreght, Paris .... W 6
Dec. 7—Antoine Capuano, Paris .... W 6
1973
Jan. 11—Jean Claude Vanderbreght, Paris .... W 6
Feb. 22—Said El Firoudi, Paris .... W 6
Mar. 2—Carlos Foldes, S. Leger .... D 6
Apr. 8—Andre Jordan, Lione .... W 6
Apr. 15—Andre Lopez, Paris .... W 6
May 11—Fernand Gomar, Lione .... W 6
June 8—Luciano Laffranchi, Milano .... KO 2
Oct. 19—Jacques Martucci, Lione .... KO 2
Nov. 9—Nicola D'Orazio, Lione .... KO 3
Nov. 19—Joseph Sossou, Paris .... D 8
Dec. 1—Fernand Gomar, Annecy .... W 8
1974
Feb. 16—Ali Issaoui, Lione .... KO 8
Mar. 15—Paul Rourre, Lione .... W 8
Apr. 26—Dominique Azzaro, Lione .... KO 5
May 17—Renzo Battistelli, Annecy .... KO 5
Oct. 4—Gualberto Fernandez, Lione .... KO 6
Oct. 25—Joseph Sossou, Lione .... W 10
1975
Jan. 17—Pierre Petit, Villeurbanne............. W 8
Feb. 15—Henri Nesi, Villeurbanne .... KO 7
(French Lightweight Championship)
Mar. 15—Carlos Foldes, Villeurbanne .... L 10
May 5—Esperno Postl, Vienne .... W 10
June 13—Raymond Dauteuille, Reims .... D 12
(Lightweight Championship of France)
Sept. 26—Joao Merencio, Lyons.................. W 8
Oct. 31—Jim Watt, Lyons .... W 12
1976
Feb. 6—Fernand Roelands, Bruges................ L 15
May 15—Theo Lemoine, Bethune .... KO 11
(French Lightweight Title)
Dec. 17—Gilbert Orsaldo, Noumea .... KO 11
1977
Feb. 12—Ernesto Bergamasco, Villeurbanne .... W 10
Mar. 5—Ceferino Morales, Villeurbanne .... W 10
Aug. 5—Jim Watt, Glasgow .... KO by 1
(European Lightweight Title)
Oct. 22—Raymond Dautheuille, Scissons .... KO 10
(French Lightweight Title)
Nov. 12—Nelson Gomes, Lyon .... W 10
1978
Feb. 18—Eloy De Souza, Lyon .... W 10
Apr. 28—Didier Kowalski, Villeurbanne .... KO 9
(French Lightweight Title)
1979
Feb. 17—Pascal Real Martin, Lione .... KO 4
Apr. 20—Efisic Pinna, Lyon .... W 10
June 27—Charlie Nash, Londonderry .... L 12
(EBU Lightweight Title)
1980
Mar. 14—Tek N'Kalankete, Villeurbanne .... L 10
May 9—Everaldo Costa Azevedo, Villeurbanne .... L 10
July 4—Jeff Sonny, Contonou .... KO 3
July 19—Aziza Bossou, Villeurbanne .... D 10
Oct. 10—Rene Martin, Villeurbanne .... KO 2
Nov. 12—Jo Kimpuani, Dunkirk .... L 12
(For French Welterweight Title)
Dec. 19—Andre Salmon, Villeurbanne .... W 8

STEVE HOPKINS
British Junior Middleweight
1977
Sept. 14—Eric Purkis, Cambridge .... W 6
Nov. 2—Ronnie Pilgrim, London .... W 6
Nov. 14—Dave Hamm, Cambridge .... W 8
Nov. 29—Billy English, London .... KO 5

1978
Jan. 18—Steve Goodwin, Stoke .... L 6
Feb. 15—Joe Oke, Cambridge .... D 8
Mar. 22—Salvo Nucifero, London .... W 8
Mar. 19—Jimmy Pickard, Stoke .... KO 6
Apr. 11—Steve Goodwin, Sheffield .... KO 6
Sept. 13—Curtis Marsh, Cambridge .... W 6
1979
Jan. 22—Mick Minter, London .... KO 7
Feb. 21—John Smith, Cambridge .... W 8
May 14—Paul Shutt, Wembley .... KO 2
Oct. 22—Billy Lauder, London .... KO 5
Dec. 4—Prince Rodney, Wembley .... W 8
1980
Jan. 26—Clemente Tshinza, Zele .... D 10
June 7—Charlie Malarkey, Glasgow .... W 5
(For Final Eliminator, British Junior Middleweight Title)
Sept. 16—Pat Thomas, Wembley .... L 15

MICHIHIRO HORIGUCHI
Japanese Junior Middleweight
1980
Feb. 18—Warrior Hanada, Tokyo .... KO 4
(Retained Japanese Junior Middleweight Title)
May 30—Tadashi Mihara, Tokyo .... L 12
(For OPBF Junior Middleweight Title)

HIDEYOSHI HORINAGA
Japanese Junior Lightweight
(Previous Record Unavailable)
1978
May 5—Ken Togawa, Tokyo .... W 6
Sept. 25—Hirofumi Mochizuki, Tokyo .... W 10
Nov. 25—Tasutsune Uehara, Tokyo .... KO by 2
(Japanese Junior Lightweight Title)
1979
Jan. 30—Kenichi Ito, Tokyo .... L 10
Feb. 19—Hirofumi Mochizuki, Tokyo .... L 10

SHUICHI HOZUMI
Japanese Flyweight
1977
Nov. 30—Isamu Machida, Tokyo .... W 4
1978
Apr. 27—Hitoshi Shibata, Tokyo .... W 4
Oct. 26—Hirobumi Ogawa, Tokyo .... W 4
Nov. 27—Naojiro Toda, Tokyo .... W 4
Dec. 28—Nobuyoshi Ohashi, Tokyo .... W 6
1979
Feb. 22—Masao Sugawara, Tokyo .... KO 5
Mar. 27—Toshihiro Okumoto, Tokyo .... W 6
May 21—Tsuguhiro Miyaoka, Tokyo .... W 8
Sept. 6—Hammer Yoshida, Hachinohe .... KO 7
Nov. 27—Ben Aldguer, Tokyo .... W 10
1980
Feb. 22—Keisuke Yuguchi, Tokyo .... KO 7
Apr. 29—Tito Abella, Tokyo .... W 10
Aug. —Tadashi Tomeri, Tokyo ....
(Won Japanese Junior Flyweight Title;
Relinquished Japanese Junior Flyweight Title)
Nov. 23—Hong-Soo Yang, Tokyo .... KO by 9
(For OPBF Flyweight Title)

PAUL HUGGINS
British Bantamweight
1980
Sept. 15—Steve Farnsworth, London .... W 6
Oct. 20—Carl Gaynor, Hove .... W 6

JOHN HUMPHREYS
British Middleweight
1980
Sept. 22—Clifton Wallace, Wolverhampton .... W 6
Oct. 13—Clifton Wallace, Nottingham .... W 6
Oct. 19—Willie Wright, Birmingham .... W 6

CHUNG-JAE HWANG
Korean Welterweight
1979
Apr. 1—Fred Pastor, Seoul .... W 10
June 29—Tarzan Tobaru, Seoul .... KO 2
Aug. 11—Ramon Dionisio, Seoul .... KO 5
Sept. 23—Armand Boniquit, Seoul .... KO 3
Nov. 9—Mitsuo Kushikino, Seoul .... KO 6
1980
Jan. 11—Nessie Horiguchi, Seoul .... KO 5
Feb. 29—Dan DeGuzman, Seoul .... W 12
(Won OPBF Welterweight Title)
Apr. 7—Tsutomu Hogusa, Seoul .... KO 3
(Retained OPBF Welterweight Title)

IN-WAN HWAN
Korean Junior Flyweight
(Previous Record Unavailable)
1980
Jan. 27—Song-Nam Kim, Seoul ....KO by 6
(For Vacant Korean Junior Flyweight Title)
Mar. 22—Yung-Hwan Cho, Inchon ....W 10

CORDWELL HYLTON
British Light Heavyweight
1980
Sept. 22—Nigel Savory, Wolverhampton ....W 6
Oct. 30—Steve Fenton, Wolverhampton ....KO 2

TSUTOMU (RIKI) IGARASHI
Japanese Flyweight
Born: June 7, 1951, Hokkaido
Weight: 112 lbs.; Height: 5 ft. 4½ in.
1971
Mar. 29—Shigeru Tajima, Tokyo ....KO by 3
May 20—Tomio Yamashita, Tokyo ....KO 2
June 14—Toshiyuki Hanafusa, Tokyo ....W 4
Sept. 19—Mamoru Ouchi, Tokyo ....L 4
Nov. 15—Tetsuo Kumada, Tokyo ....KO 2
1972
Feb. 10—Yasuo Nishiyama, Tokyo ....D 4
June 18—Yuichi Fujita, Tokyo ....L 4
July 13—Yukio Makino, Tokyo ....KO by 1
Sept. 28—Kazunori Tenryu, Tokyo ....L 4
Nov. 19—Kiyohide Toda, Tokyo ....W 4
1973
Feb. 20—Kimiyasu Ishikawa, Tokyo ....D 4
Apr. 26—Teruyuki Murasaki, Tokyo ....D 4
May 21—Hisami Numata, Tokyo ....W 4
June 26—Isao Watanabe, Tokyo ....L 4
July 30—Yasunobu Nitta, Tokyo ....L 4
Sept. 1—Fujio Matsuoka, Tokyo ....L 4
Sept. 24—Shigemitsu Izawa, Tokyo ....W 4
Oct. 22—Uichiro Hayashida, Tokyo ....D 4
1974
Feb. 3—Yasuo Nishiyama, Tokyo ....KO 3
Apr. 11—Hidemori Usuyama, Tokyo ....KO 4
June 28—Matsushi Yoshida, Tokyo ....W 8
Aug. 26—Takenobu Shimabukuro, Tokyo........W 10
Dec. 27—Jiro Takada, Tokyo ....L 10
(For Japanese Flyweight Title)
1975
June 1—Isao Watanabe, Tokyo ....W 10
Dec. 2—Hak Yung Kim, Tokyo...................D 12
1976
Feb. 13—Kenji Kato, Tokyo.......................W 10
(Won Japanese Flyweight Title)
June 6—Makdong Kim, Tokyo....................D 10
Aug. 19—Beaver Kajimoto, Tokyo..................D 10
(Retained Japanese Flyweight Title)
Nov. 19—Koichi Maki, Hirosaki City..............D 10
1977
Mar. 8—Tiro Takada, Tokyo ....L 10
June 27—Kenji Kato, Tokyo ....L 10
(Lost Japanese Flyweight Title)
Sept. 19—Kenji Kato, Tokyo ....D 10
(For Japanese Flyweight Title)
Nov. 13—Masaru Ruji, Tokyo ....W 10
1978
Jan. 15—Shigeo Maezawa, Tokyo ....KO 8
July 25—Hong Soo Yang, Tokyo ....W 12
(Won OPBF Flyweight Title)
Oct. 30—Koichi Maki, Tokyo ....W 10
1979
Mar. 6—Jiro Takada, Yokohoma ....D 12
May 19—Chan Hee Park, Seoul ....L 15
(For WBC Flyweight Title)
Aug. 8—Hwang-Soo Yang, Aomori ....:..L 12
(Lost OPBF Flyweight Title)
Nov. 18—Tae Shik Kim, Seoul ....KO by 4
Dec. 17—Shoji Oguma, Tokyo ....KO by 8
1980
Mar. 18—Hong-Soo Yang, Shige ....L 12
(For OPBF Flyweight Title)

JEAN MICHEL IGER
French Welterweight
1977
Nov. 25—Joel Leprodhomme, Le Havre ....L 6

Dec. 15—Gilles Elbilia, Paris ....L 6
1978
Jan. 12—Jean Paul Coppyn, Paris ....D 6
Jan. 28—Arthur Fogeiro, Perigueux ....D 6
Apr. 21—Andre Camonin, Le Havre ....W 6
Oct. 6—Patrick Babouram, Amiens ....L 6
Nov. 25—Pierre Koenig, Brest ....W 6
1979
Jan. 6—Maliba Kibassa, Barentin ....KO by 3
Feb. 3—Patrick Babouram, Creil ....L 6
Feb. 14—Jimmy Connally, Bern ....L 6
Apr. 7—Jean Marie Touati, Bethune ....L 6
Sept. 29—Francis Derebian, Villeurbanne ....L 6
Oct. 16—Francesco Marcello, Torino ....KO by 1
1980
Jan. 28—Cor Everstein, Rotterdam ....L 6
Mar. 15—Jean Pierre Moreau, Blois ....D 8

YOSHITAKA IKEHARA
Japanese Featherweight
1979
Apr. 22—Shigeyuki Otake, Tokyo ....L 10
July 12—Yasutsune Uehara, Tokyo ....L 10
(JBC Junior Lightweight Title)
1980
Mar. 13—Hikaru Tomonari, Tokyo ....L 10

YANG IL
Korean Featherweight
1979
Dec. 8—Dae-Whan Lee, Seoul ....L 10
(For Vacant Korean Featherweight Title)
1980
Apr. 15—Ryu Fukida, Tokyo ....L 12
(For OPBF Junior Lightweight Title)

MASAHARU INAMI
Japanese Flyweight
1977
July 19—Noboru Kimishima, Yokohama ....W 4
Aug. 24—Akiharu Oikawa, Tokyo ....KO 3
Oct. 20—Seishiro Kaneshiro, Tokyo ....W 4
Nov. 21—Shiggeru Okusa, Tokyo ....W 4
Dec. 21—Shigeru Soda, Tokyo ....KO 5
1978
Feb. 22—Kunio Inayoshi, Osaka ....W 6
Apr. 27—Tsugumasa Toma, Tokyo ....W 8
Nov. 11—Masaru Fuji, Tokyo ....D 10
1979
Mar. 23—Keisuke Youguchi, Tokyo ....KO 10
June 5—Nobuo Horigome, Yokohoma ....KO 3
July 11—Phenix Taniguchi, Tokyo ....W 10
Aug. 28—Kazunori Tenryu, Tokyo ....KO by 10
(Japanese Junior Flyweight Title)
1980
Jan. 29—Puma Koya, Tokyo ....W 10

DANILO INOCIAN
Filipino Bantamweight
1979
Apr. 28—Danila Gonzaga, Misamis Oriental ......KO 2
May 26—Flash Jagdon, Cag. de Oro City ....L 10
Aug. 25—Diego Da Villa, Davao City ....D 10
Nov. 11—Chris Espinosa, South Cotabato ....W 10
Nov. 24—Bernabe Villacampo, Santos City ....KO 5
Dec. 30—Arnel Arrozal, Pampanga ....L 10
1980
Feb. 1—Fred Ebon, Manila ....L 10
Feb. 22—Peter Siscon, Manila ....W 10
Mar. 1—Glen Orlanes, Davao City ....W 12
Mar. 15—Noe Canino, Santos City ....W 10
May 2—Hua-Cheng Chua, Manila ....KO 5
June 22—Glen Orlanes, Cebu City ....KO 5
Aug. 16—Siony Carupo, De Oro City ....L 10
Sept. 27—Elmer Valenzuela, Manila ....KO by 3
Nov. 19—Manny Sacay, Quezon City ....W 10

DAVINO INOCIAN
Filipino Junior Featherweight
1980
Feb. 16—Nacias Francisco, De Oro City ....W 10
May 16—Sandy Noora, Manila ....KO by 4
Aug. 16—Jun Escalera, De Oro City ....W 10

MANABU IREI
Japanese Junior Flyweight
1980
Jan. 10—Kiyomi Sato, Tokyo ....KO 4
Mar. 29—Toshikozu Kiga, Oyama ....W 8
Apr. 14—Torayuki Nanaska, Tokyo ....D 8

MICHAEL IRUNGU
Kenyan Bantamweight
1980
Feb.	7—Luigi Tessarin, Randers	KO	?
Feb.	29—Martin Antich, Odense	W	o
Apr.	17—Mariano Garcia, Copenhagen	W	8
June	12—Neil McLaughlin, Randers	KO	3
Oct.	17—Laurent Grimbert, Copenhagen	KO	7

ALEC IRVINE
British Lightweight
1978
Sept.	27—Steve Cleak, Evesham	L	6
Oct.	24—Gary Nickels, Kensington	L	6
Nov.	14—Gary Lucas, Birkenhead	L	4
1979
Feb.	20—Roger Hendry, Wolverhampton	KO	4
Mar.	15—John Cooper, Caister	L	6
Apr.	4—Jimmy Hancock, Birmingham	D	6
Apr.	17—Terry McKeown, Glasgow	L	8
May	17—John Cooper, London	L	8
May	21—Mick Whelan, Birmingham	W	6
June	26—Robert Hepburn, Leicester	W	6
Sept.	12—Doug Hill, Burslem	L	10
Nov.	15—Selvyn Bell, Caister	W	8
1980
Feb.	6—Dave Laxson, Southend	D	8
Mar.	19—Steve Cleak, Solihull	W	8
Apr.	2—Joey Wainwright, London	W	8
June	11—Don Aagesen, Edgbaston	L	8
Oct.	18—Don Aagesen, Birmingham	W	8

GERALD RODRICK ISAACS
South African Featherweight
1980
Mar.	22—Jafta Mkgosi, Jabulani	KO	2
June	7—Elias Nkabinde, Eldorado	W	4
Aug.	16—Welcome Jonas, East London	D	4
Oct.	4—Joshua Nhlapo, Johannesburg	D	6

SHUICHI ISOGAMI
Japanese Bantamweight
1975
May	3—Masashi Unten, Tokyo	KO	1
June	8—Hideaki Fukuura, Tokyo	KO	1
July	25—Seishi Ii, Tokyo	W	4
Sept.	18—Hikaru Naya, Tokyo	KO	1
Oct.	2—Ryuichi Kashima, Tokyo	KO	1
Oct.	23—Shuji Hirata, Tokyo	KO	1
Nov.	10—Ryuji Higashi, Tokyo	D	4
Dec.	28—Makoto Saito, Tokyo	KO	3
1976
Mar.	3—Makoto Kumagaya, Sakai City	W	6
	(Won All-Japan Shinjin-o Tournament)		
May	3—Yoshiki Ota, Tokyo	W	8
Sept.	14—Hisao Nishi, Tokyo	D	10
Dec.	9—Go Mifune, Tokyo	L	10
1977
Jan.	17—Hideo Kobayashi, Tokyo	KO	8
Mar.	19—Uchiro Hayashida, Tokyo	KO	10
June	26—Go Mifune, Osaka City	W	10
Aug.	28—Joe Araki, Tokyo	KO	6
Nov.	24—Hurricane Teru, Tokyo	W	10
1978
May	22—Seishi Ii, Tokyo	KO	5
Aug.	15—Yung Sik Kim, Tokyo	W	12
Oct.	24—Rey Orbino, Tokyo	KO	6
1979
Jan.	30—Yu Kasahara, Tokyo	KO	8
Apr.	17—Eddie Miral, Tokyo	KO	8
June	26—Hitoshi Ishigaki, Tokyo	KO	10
Oct.	16—Jiro Takada, Tokyo	D	10
1980
Apr.	2—Jorge Lujan, Tokyo	KO by	9
	(For WBA Bantamweight Title)		

KENICHI ITO
Japanese Junior Featherweight
1979
Jan.	30—Hideyoshi Horinaga, Tokyo	W	10
Aug.	23—Isao Okahashi, Tokyo	W	10
Dec.	17—Mitsuo Shima, Tokyo	L	10
1980
Apr.	2—Kiroyaiki Tanaka, Tokyo	KO	6

MASA ITO
Japanese Lightweight
1973
Oct.	3—Rocky Iwamoto, Yamaguchi	W	10
1974
Mar.	3—Takemi Suyama, Miyazski City	W	10
Apr.	11—Tony Amor, Honolulu	W	6
May	21—Sam Fraticelli, Honolulu	L	5

May	26—Ichiro Izawa, Hofu City	W	10
1975
Apr.	18—Shoji Uchida, Tokuyama City	D	10
Aug.	22—Ray Adio, Tokuyama	KO	7
Oct.	19—Yasutsune Uehara, Okinawa	KO	7
Oct.	19—Yasutsune Uehara, Okinawa	KO by	5
	(Japanese Junior Lightweight Title)		
1976
Apr.	21—Yujin Konno, Tokyo	L	6
Apr.	23—Yasutsune Uehara, Tokouyama City	W	10
	(Japan Junior Lightweight Champion)		
July	29—Yasutsune Uehara, Tokyo	L	10
	(Japanese Junior Lightweight Title)		
1977
Jan.	28—Tamio Negishi, Bofu City	W	10
	(Japanese Lightweight Title)		
Apr.	27—Tamio Negishi, Hofu City	L	10
	(Japanese Lightweight Title)		
July	27—Tadashi Akiyama, Chigasak City	W	10
Dec.	17—Hajime Momosaki, Bufu City	KO	7
1978
Jan.	12—Sanny Mensah Koga, Osaka City	L	10
Mar.	11—Mitsue Koide, Takamatsu City	KO	9
June	7—Tsutomu Matsuo, Yamaguichi City	W	10
Oct.	12—Shoichi Abe, Tokyo	KO by	6
1979
June	14—Tatsuya Moriyasu, Yamaguchi	W	10
Oct.	6—Choi Moonsuk, Bofu Shi	W	10
1980
Feb.	24—Royal Kobayshi, Yamaguchi	KO by	7

HIROYUKI IWAMOTE
Japanese Junior Featherweight
Born: Feb. 5, 1957, Odawara City, Japan
Height: 5'6"
1974
June	27—Kiyoshi Yamazaki, Tokyo	KO	2
July	15—Shinji Maehara, Tokyo	W	4
Oct.	27—Eiji Genga, Tokyo	W	4
Nov.	20—Shigenori Maki, Tokyo	D	4
Dec.	4—Hiroshi Higuchi, Tokyo	W	4
Dec.	26—Eiji Shimamura, Tokyo	L	4
1975
May	18—Katsuhiro Sato, Tokyo	W	4
Oct.	26—Kiyomitso Hoshina, Tokyo	W	4
Nov.	13—Kazuhiro Kitagaki, Tokyo	L	8
Dec.	28—Tadao Hatano, Tokyo	W	6
1976
Mar.	3—Masaji Nishi, Sakai City	D	6
July	12—Shiro Hiromori, Tokyo	KO	5
Sept.	17—Kazuhiro Kitagaki, Tokyo	L	8
1977
Mar.	19—Seishi Ii, Tokyo	W	10
May	22—Hisami Mizuno, Sapporo City	L	10
1978
Mar.	7—Seishi Ii, Tokyo	KO	8
July	11—Yung-Sik Kim, Seoul	L	10
Aug.	28—Futaro Tanaka, Tokyo	KO	9
Oct.	3—Keo-Sung Lee, Seoul	L	10
1979
Jan.	28—Satoru Hirata, Tokyo	W	10
June	12—Katsuji Sano, Tokyo	W	10
Sept.	4—Yu Kasahara, Tokyo	W	10
	(JBC Junior Featherweight Title)		
Dec.	18—Yu Kasahara, Tokyo	W	10
1980
May	24—Kanekatsu Daito, Tokyo	W	10
	(Retained Japanese Junior Featherweight Title)		

JOE JACKSON
British Middleweight
1975
Oct.	15—Albert Smith, Birmingham	W	6
Nov.	6—Albert Smith, Blackpool	W	6
Nov.	12—Patrick Mahoney, Caerphilly	W	6
Nov.	17—Francis Hands, Manchester	KO by	4
1976
Mar.	24—Ritchie Smith, Stoke	KO	2
Apr.	5—Charlie Richardson, Bradford	W	6
May	17—Henry Johnson, Nottingham	W	6
June	8—David Owens, Bradford	L	6
June	21—Keith Bussey, Bethnal	L	6
Sept.	21—Bunny McKenzie, London	L	6
Oct.	5—Owen Robinson, Coventry	KO	3
Oct.	11—Eddie Smith, Manchester	L	4

Oct. 25—Howard Mills, Birmingham .... KO by 2
1977
Feb. 14—Owen Lotriet, Birmingham .... W 6
Feb. 21—Dave Merrel, Nottingham .... W 6
Mar. 28—Eddie Burke, Glasgow .... KO by 2
Apr. 19—Geoff Horton, Mayfair .... W 6
Apr. 26—Owen Lotriet, London .... W 6
May 11—Colin Breen, Swansea .... D 8
May 30—Albert Smith, Barnsley .... L 8
Aug. 22—Tony Kelsey, Stockton .... L 8
Sept. 21—Johnny Breen, Solihull .... KO 1
Oct. 17—Clint Jones, Hove .... L 6
Nov. 7—Joe Gregory, London .... L 8
1978
Jan. 23—Roger Barlow, Wolverhampton .... L 8
Mar. 21—Tom Collins, Luton .... L 8
Apr. 4—Keith Bussey, Kensington .... LF 5
Apr. 18—Larry Paul, Wolverhampton .... L 8
May 3—Trevor Cattouse, Solihull .... L 8
Oct. 11—Peter Mullins, Stoke .... W 6
Nov. 6—Clifton Wallace, Stafford .... W 6
Nov. 29—Martin McEwan, Evesham .... L 6
1979
Mar. 3—Billy Hill, Liverpool .... L 6
Mar. 15—Alan Worthington, Dudley .... W 6
Mar. 21—Peter Morris, Stoke .... KO 4
Apr. 2—George Danahar, London .... KO by 3
June 6—Liam Coleman, Bedworth .... L 4
June 14—Steve Fox, Dudley .... W 6
June 26—Peter Morris, Leicester .... W 8
Oct. 30—Clifton Wallace, Bedford .... W 8
Nov. 6—Doug James, Stafford .... L 8
Nov. 14—Steve Fox, Stoke .... KO 4
Dec. 3—Malcolm Heath, Hull .... L 6
Dec. 10—Martin McEwan, Birmingham .... L 6
1980
Feb. 18—Peter Bassey, Stockport .... L 6
Mar. 3—Steve Babbs, London .... W 6
Mar. 27—Joe Lally, Liverpool .... L 8
Apr. 21—Peter Tidgewell, Bradford .... D 8
Apr. 28—Malcolm Heath, London .... L 8
May 14—Jimmy Ellis, Burslem .... L 8
Sept. 22—Al Stevens, Wolverhampton .... W 4
Sept. 29—Winston Davis, Bedworth .... KO 2
Oct. 8—Willie Wright, Stoke .... W 6
Oct. 14—Dave Armstrong, Albert Hall .... W 6

VIC JACKSON

British Welterweight
1977
July 20—Teddy Haines, Sheffield .... KO 1
Sept. 5—Salvo Nucifero, Hove .... KO by 4
Oct. 12—Dave Merrell, Stoke .... W 6
Oct. 17—Dave Merrell, Bedford .... L 8
Oct. 24—Billy Lauder, London .... L 8
1978
Feb. 20—Des Miller, London .... W 4
Mar. 6—Brian Gregory, London .... L 8
June 20—Steve Goodwin, Southend .... W 6
Sept. 13—Neville Estaban, Cambridge .... L 6
Nov. 8—Owen Robinson, Stone .... L 8
1979
July 2—Lloyd Hibbitt, London .... L 8
1980
Feb. 5—Dave Allen, Southend .... L 8
Feb. 27—Johnny Ridgeman, Burslem .... W 6
Apr. 18—Dennis Sullivan, Southend .... W 8
Sept. 16—Neil Fannon, Southend .... L 8

GERARD JACOB

French Featherweight
1974
Feb. 7—Christian Hardelin, Paris .... W 6
Feb. 25—Moussa Maldouche, Creil .... W 6
May 31—Michel Lecerf, Tours .... KO 3
1975
Apr. 26—Christian Valentin, Creil .... W 6
May 31—Michel Lecerf, Tours .... KO 3
June 7—Alain Le Fol, Creil .... D 6
Sept. 20—Rene Martin, Creil .... KO by 3
Nov. 3—Jean-Pierre Planque, Paris .... L 6
Dec. 6—Raymond Libbrecht, Boulogne .... W 6
Dec. 13—Paul Rourre, Creil .... W 6
1976
Jan. 17—Ali Messaoud, Creil .... W 6
Feb. 14—Christian Valentin, Meaux .... W 8
Mar. 7—Isidoro La Barbera, Creil .... KO 1
Apr. 3—Souleymane Ba, Creil .... KO 2
May 15—Abdelkader Bouguetaib, Creil .... W 8
June 12—Jose Manuel Padron, Zaragoza .... L 8
Oct. 16—Antonino DeFranca, Creil .... W 8
Dec. 4—Ali Issaoui, Creil .... KO 1
1977
Jan. 15—Samuel Meck, Creil .... KO 7
Feb. 26—Gabriel Lamperti, Creil .... KO 6
Mar. 26—Mario Oliviera, Creil .... W 10
Apr. 30—Mouldi Mani, Creil .... KO 3
May 4—Les Pickett, Merthryr .... KO by 2
June 11—Luis Rodriguez, Creil .... W 8
Sept. 24—Michele Siracusa, Creil .... KO by 10
(French Featherweight Title)
Nov. 12—Albert Amatler, Lyon .... L 11
(French Featherweight Title)
Dec. 17—Ambrogio Mariani, Creil .... KO 2
1978
Feb. 11—Rudi Vogel, Criel .... W 10
Mar. 3—Roberto, Castanon, Leon .... KO by 4
Mar. 18—Jose Malgueves, Criel .... W 10
May 26—Mohamed Boundka, Creil .... KO by 5
Oct. 6—Mike Brisette, Amiens .... KO 1
Oct. 27—Michel Levebvre, Creil .... KO 2
(French Featherweight Title)
Nov. 18—Adolfo Osses, Creil .... W 10
Dec. 22—Helenio Ferriera, Besancon .... W 10
1979
Feb. 3—Roberto Castanon, Creil .... KO by 7
(European Featherweight Title)
Apr. 21—Damien Dermotte, Creil .... KO 1
May 4—Maurice Cisse, Abidjan .... KO by 3
1980
Mar. 1—Raga Murphy, Criel .... W 8
Nov. 15—Laurent Grimbert, Criel .... KO by 4

MARTIN JACOBS

South African Junior Welterweight
1978
June 2—Willem Visser, Bloemfontein .... L 4
July 22—Simon Molahloe, Bloemfontein .... L 6
Aug. 5—Jopie Griessel, Bloemfontein .... W 4
1979
Feb. 5—Simon Mokwena, Welkom .... W 4
Mar. 5—Simon Molahloe, Welkom .... L 10
Sept. 1—Jonas Tladi, Ficksburg .... L 10
Oct. 5—Alfred Sibisi, Bloemfontein .... L 6
Nov. 9—Godfrey Manyaniso, Bloemfontein .... W 6
Dec. 14—Enock Motsoane, Welkom .... W 8
1980
Feb. 4—Naftaly Matthys, Welkom .... W 4
Mar. 8—Stephen Balene, Bloemfontein .... W 8
Apr. 21—Anthony Da Paiva, Bloemfontein .... L 4

SANDRO JACONELLI

Italian Junior Middleweight
1980
Apr. 5—Frank Winsterstein, Massay .... KO by 5
Apr. 12—Dominique Delorme, Paris .... KO by 1
June 7—Frank Winsterstein, Massay .... KO by 2

DOUG JAMES

British Middleweight
1979
Sept. 17—Earl Edwards, London .... W 6
Oct. 11—Joe Hannaford, Liverpool .... KO 2
Oct. 30—Keith Roberts, Bedford .... KO 5
Nov. 6—Joe Jackson, Stafford .... W 8
Nov. 27—Clifton Wallace, Wolverhampton .... W 6
1980
Feb. 4—Harry Watson, London .... KO 1
Mar. 17—George Danahar, London .... L 6
May 7—Peter Bassey, Liverpool .... D 8
Aug. 12—Dave Owens, Gowerton .... W 8

RICKY JAMES

British Heavyweight
1978
June 1—Steve Fenton, Coventry .... L 6
June 29—Roy Gregory, Wolverhampton .... KO 2
Sept. 27—Bob Young, Stoke .... KO 3
Oct. 24—Stan McDermott, Kensington .... KO 2
Nov. 20—Austin Okoye, Birmingham .... KO 6
1979
May 21—Danny Miller, Birmingham .... L 8
June 25—Terry Mintus, Edgbaston .... W 8
Sept. 10—Gordon Ferris, Birmingham .... L 8
Oct. 23—Joe Awpme, London .... KO by 4
Nov. 19—Gordon Ferris, Birmingham .... KO by 6
1980
Apr. 30—Larry McDonald, Aylesbury .... L 8
June 3—Stan McDermott, London .... KO by 4

IGGY JANO

British Flyweight
1979
Sept. 26—Eddie Glencross, Sheffield .... W 8
Oct. [illegible]—Dave George, Reading .... KO by 4
1980
Feb. 12—Kelvin Smart, London .... L 4

Mar. 11—Eddie McAllister, Southend .... W 6
Mar. 19—Kelvin Smart, Solihull .... L 8
Apr. 18—Eddie McAllister, Southend .... L 6
Apr. 28—George Bailey, Windsor .... W 8
May 20—Peter Gabbitus, Southend .... L 4
May 29—Ivor Jones, London .... L 8

JACK JIM
South African Junior Welterweight
1970
Dec. 10—Ngqika Tshume, Langa .... L 6
1971
June 26—Ngqika Tshume, King Williamstown ..... W 8
Aug. 14—Victor Kwaza, King Williamstown ...... KO 5
Dec. 4—P. Mbele, East London .... L 6
1972
Mar. 4—Acliff Stengile, East London .... W 10
Sept. 2—Maurice Mohlai, East London .... L 6
Dec. 15—Alesta Mahashe, Mdantsane .... W 6
1973
Mar. 3—Terence Makluza, King Williamstown .... W 10
May 12—Daniel Mkhize, Port Elizabeth .... L 10
July 14—Simon Nxawe, East London .... D 6
Dec. 22—Victor Tshabalala, Port Elizabeth .... L 8
1974
Mar. 30—Philip Hlophe, East London .... W 6
July 20—Isaac Rakhajane, East London .... D 6
Oct. 5—Simon Mpthuti, East London .... W 6
Nov. 9—Daniel Mkhize, Port Elizabeth .... W 10
Dec. 14—Louis Miya, East London .... W 6
1975
June 21—Phalo Tshume, East London .... W 10
Aug. 30—Isaac Rakhajane, East London .... W 8
1976
Jan. 31—Jeremiah Nzelwane, East London .... W 6
Apr. 10—Phalo Tshume, Port Elizabeth .... L 8
May 15—Norman Sekgapane, Jabulani .... L 12
July 10—Phalo Tshume, East London .... KO 5
Oct. 9—Emmanuel Gumede, East London .... L 6
1977
Apr. 2—Griffiths Mgijia, East London .... W 10
Oct. 15—Rolly Xipu, East London .... L 12
Dec. 1—Harold Volbrecht, Cape Town .... L 6
1978
Feb. 18—Welcome Mtyongwe, East London .... KO 5
Aug. 5—Simon Dhladhla, East London .... L 6
Sept. 8—Justus Josephs, Johannesburg .... L 4
Sept. 30—Hardy Mileham, East London .... W 6
1979
Apr. 14—Harold Volbrecht, Goodwood .... L 6
Sept. 27—Coenraad Bekker, Cape Town .... L 10
1980
Apr. 5—Mzwandile Biyane, East London .... L 8
May 3—Aaron Sondaka, East London .... W 6
May 24—David Kambule, Orlando .... KO by 1

NINO JIMINEZ
Spanish Lightweight
Born: May 29, 1953
1973
Jan. 6—Francisco Santaengracia, Madrid .... KO 5
Feb. 23—Jose Luis Madriles, Madrid .... W 8
Mar. 2—Antonio Munoz, Madrid................. KO 4
Mar. 23—Abdeselem Argaz-Hausi, Madrid .... KO 3
Mar. 30—Mohamed Ben Salah, Madrid .... KO 2
Apr. 13—Jesus Canut, Madrid .... W 8
May 11—Juan Barros, Madrid .... TKO 4
June 1—Francisco Larxe, Madrid .... KO by 2
July 6—Artigao II, Madrid .... KO 6
July 20—Antonio Rejon, Madrid.................. W 8
July 27—Valentine Loren, Madrid .... D 8
Sept. 28—Ringo Valeiro, Barcelona................ KO 6
Oct. 5—Jose Artigao, Barcelona.................. KO 8
Nov. 9—Cristobal Diaz, Madrid.................. W 8
Nov. 23—Ringo Valeiro, Madrid.................. KO 5
Dec. 14—Heriberto Marsarell, Madrid .... KO 7
Dec. 25—Luis Aisa, Bilbao .... D 8
1974
Feb. 15—Horacio Mascarell, Barcelona .... KO 6
Mar. 1—Rodolfo Suarez, Madrid .... W 8
Apr. 20—Ramiro Suarez, Las Palmas .... KO 3
May 22—Paul Ikumapayi, Madrid................. W 8
June 14—Francisco Santaengracia, Madrid .... KO 2
Aug. 2—Adolfo Osses, Madrid .... KO 3
Aug. 9—Isidoro Cabezas, Madrid................. W 8
Sept. 20—Ramon Garcia .... L disq. 12
(Spanish Featherweight Championship)
Oct. 4—Francisco Santaengracia, Bilbao........ KO 7
Nov. 7—Jesus Zarco, Bilbao...................... KO 3
1975
Jan. 6—Bruno Pieracci, Madrid................. W 8
Feb. 14—Sebastian Ruiz, Barcelona .... KO 3
Mar. 14—Dante Guarneri, Madrid .... W 8
July 17—Pedro Coque, Madrid .... KO 4

Aug. 16—Adolfo Osses, Madrid .... W 8
Sept. 20—Jose Bisbal, Almeria .... KO 8
(Spanish Featherweight Title)
1976
Feb. 27—Isidoro Cabezas, Madrid................. W 8
Mar. 12—Tino Blanco, Barcelona .... KO 10
Mar. 27—Isidoro Cabeza, Madrid .... W 10
May 14—Heleano Ferreira, Madrid .... W 8
June 30—Georges Cotin, Madrid.................. W 8
July 30—Adolfo Osses, Madrid .... W 8
Dec. 3—Elio Cotena, Madrid................... KO 12
(European Featherweight Title)
1977
Mar. 31—Henry Palm, Copenhagen .... L 6
Apr. 1—Michel Lefebvre, Madrid .... L 10
Apr. 16—Alfonso Osses, Almeria .... KO 4
May 13—Michele Siracusa, Madrid .... W 15
(European Featherweight Title)
Sept. 16—Manuel Masso, Barcelona .... KO by 10
(European Featherweight Title)
Nov. 5—Hugo Carrizo, Madrid .... L 8
Dec. 17—San Miguel, Torrelvega .... KO 4
1978
Jan. 28—Hector Molina, Oviedo .... W 8
Feb. 17—Hugo Carrizo, Madrid .... W 8
Apr. 15—Hector Carasquilla, Panama .... NC 6
May 31—Rodolfo Jimenez, Bilbao................. L 8
Sept. 2—Adolfo Osses, Guadalajara .... KO 4
Dec. 9—Adolfo Osses, La Coruna .... KO 7
1979
Mar. 4—Cornelius Boza-Edwards, San Remo ...... L 8
June 1—Isidoro Cabeza, Palma de Mallorca .... D 12
(Spanish Junior Lightweight Title)
June 16—Hector Molina, Santander .... W 8
Aug. 3—Jose Rueda, Madrid .... KO 2
Aug. 17—Samuel Meck, Madrid .... W 8
Dec. 7—Santiago Gonzalez, Las Palmas .... KO 5
Dec. 28—Luis F. L. Mejias, Las Palmas .... KO 6
1980
Mar. 29—Jose Luis Heredia, Malaga .... L 10
(For Spanish Lightweight Title)

BUNNY JOHNSON
Leicester, England Light Heavyweight
Born: May 10, 1947
1968
Feb. 8—Peter Thomas, Bristol .... KO 2
Feb. 20—Bernard Pollard, London................ KO 3
Mar. 6—Roy Ferguson, Solihull................. KO 3
Mar. 23—Paul Brown, London.................... W 6
Apr. 2—Billy Wynter, Wolverhampton........... KO 2
Apr. 29—Tommy Woods, Manchester .... KO 2
Aug. 12—Guinea Roger, Blackpool............ KO by 6
Sept. 16—George Dulaire, London .... KO 6
Oct. 1—Lloyd Walford, Wolverhampton .... W 8
Oct. 23—Lloyd Walford, London................. W 8
Nov. 20—Guinea Roger, London .... KO by 7
1969
Jan. 2—Roger Tighe, London .... KO by 6
Mar. 25—Peter Boddington, London............... W 8
Apr. 10—Hans-Jorgen Jacobsen, Copenhagen ... KO 2
May 7—Dennis Avoth, Solihull................. W 8
Aug. 27—Roger Tighe, Hull...................... L 10
Sept. 8—Billy Wynter, Bedford .... KO 1
Sept. 29—Terry Daly, London .... W 8
Oct. 27—Eddie Avoth, Nottingham............... L 8
1970
Jan. 14—Guinea Roger, Solihull................. KO 1
Mar. 24—Maxie Smith, Wembley................. KO 3
May 6—Rocky Campbell, Solihull.............. KO 4
Oct. 19—Dennis Avoth, Aberavon............... W 10
Nov. 11—Billy Aird, Solihull..................... W 8
1971
Feb. 24—Dick Hall, Wolverhampton............. W 10
Mar. 22—Jerry Judge, London .... KO 10
Apr. 13—Richard Dunn, Wolverhampton .... L 8
Sept. 22—Dennis Avoth, Solihull................. L 8
Oct. 20—Brian Jewett, Stoke .... KO 7
Nov. 9—Peter Boddington, Wolverhampton....... KO 4
1972
Jan. 26—Rocky Campbell, Wolverhampton........ W 8
Mar. 15—Eddie Avoth, Caerphilly................ KO 3
Apr. 25—Brian Jewitt, Birmingham .... W 8
June 27—Roger Tighe, Birmingham............... W 8
Oct. 11—Guinea Roger, Stoke................... W 8
Oct. 23—Billy Aird, London .... W 8
Nov. 20—Roger Russell, Wolverhampton .... KO 5
1973
Apr. 30—Guinea Roger, Bedford................. KO 6
June 5—Les Stevens, London .... W 10
July 2—Morrie Jackson, Earls Court .... KO 5
Oct. 11—Richard Dunn, Manchester .... KO 10
1974
Feb. 18—Roy Wallace, London .... KO 4

330

Mar.	11—Koli Vailea, London	KO	3
May	21—Oliver Wright, London	W	10

1975

Jan.	13—Danny McAlinden, London	KO	9

(British and Commonwealth Heavyweight Titles)

Feb.	19—Pedro Agosto, Manchester	W	10
Mar.	11—Angel Oquendo, Wembley	KO	15
May	12—Obie English, Mayfair	KO	3
June	19—Ray Anderson, Oslo	W	8
Sept.	30—Richard Dunn, London	L	15

(British and Commonwealth Heavyweight Titles)

Dec.	1—Young Sekona, Auckland	KO	2

1976

Jan.	13—Danny McAlinden, London	KO	9

(British and Commonwealth Heavyweight Titles)

Mar.	21—Billy Airdi, Frimley Green	D	10
May	25—Duane Bobick, Munich	KO by	8
Sept.	27—Peter Brisland, London	KO	7
Dec.	14—Phil Martin, West Bromwich	KO	10

1977

Mar.	8—Tim Wood, Wolverhampton	KO	1

(British Light Heavyweight Title)

May	17—Harry White, Wolverhampton	KO	9

(British Light Heavyweight Title)

June	1—Terry Mintus, Dudley	KO	1
Nov.	26—Aldo Traversaro, Genoa	KO by	11

(European Light Heavyweight Title)

1978

Feb.	7—Dave Conteh, Islington	KO by	3
Sept.	14—Sylvain Watl led, Paris	KO	6

1979

Jan.	22—Dennis Andries, Wolverhampton	W	10
Feb.	15—Mustapha Wassaja, Randers	KO by	7
May	13—Rab Affleck, Glasgow	KO	4

(British Light Heavyweight Title)

July	1—James Scott, Rahway	KO by	7
Oct.	23—Lotte Mwale, London	L	10
Dec.	10—Sylvain Watbled, Paris	L	10

1980

Feb.	27—Dennis Andries, Burslem	W	15

(Retained British Light Heavyweight Title)

June	12—John Odhiambo, Randers	L	6

KEVIN JOHNSON
British Welterweight
1980

Apr.	30—Casley McAllum, Wolverhampton	KO by	4
Sept.	15—Steve Davies, Manchester	KO by	4
Oct.	13—Charlie Douglas, Nottingham	D	6
Oct.	19—Mark Crouch, Birmingham	L	6

BILLY JOHNSTONE
Australian Middleweight
1977

July	22—Tony Hass, South Brisbane	W	3
July	22—Bernie Teys, South Brisbane	W	3
July	30—Paul Overton, Grange	KO	1
Sept.	30—Livi Huni, Brisbane	W	4
Nov.	18—Gary Roberts, Brisbane	W	4

1978

Oct.	6—Gary Tomlinson, Brisbane	W	6
Oct.	15—Vince Hopkins, Davies Park	KO	3
Oct.	15—Mark Grice, Davies Park	KO	1
Nov.	24—Cal Hickling, Brisbane	KO	5
Dec.	8—Lou Hirst, Brisbane	W	8

1979

Sept.	7—Alby Roberts, Brisbane	KO	3
Sept.	28—Gary Tolinson, Brisbane	W	10
Oct.	19—Buddy Nixon, Brisbane	KO	4
Dec.	15—Raymond Nebays, Noumea	L	6

1980

Mar.	31—Dave Edwards, Brisbane	KO	9
Nov.	14—Nu'u Tanuvasa, Auckland	KO	3

PIERRE JOLY
French Middleweight
1977

Oct.	15—Alain Servais, Tarbes	W	6
Nov.	25—Mushapata Kubangu, Tolosa	W	6

1978

Jan.	13—Andre Genasi, Tolosa	W	6
Oct.	13—Jean Luc Lami, Tolosa	W	6
Nov.	17—Ignacio Gorstidi, Tolosa	W	6

1979

Jan.	13—Rhida Hakimi, Auch	W	6
Apr.	7—Alain Bolzer, Auch	W	6
Apr.	20—Gerard Breton, Tolosa	W	8
May	4—Kassongo Mukandjo, Tarbes	W	8
Oct.	26—Etienne Bayadikilla, Limoges	W	8
Nov.	30—Aroldo Oliveras, Toulouse	W	8

1980

Jan.	11—Idrissa Konate, Tarbes	W	8
Feb.	2—Jose Lozano, Toloso	W	10

Mar.	15—Gerard Nosley, Toulouse	W	8
Oct.	17—Stephane Ferrara, Massay	W	8

(BRINLEY) BRYN JONES
Welsh Bantamweight
1979

May	21—Jimmy Bott, London	L	6
June	14—George Bailey, Dudley	L	6
Sept.	17—Billy Straub, Glasgow	L	6
Oct.	15—George Bailey, Wolverhampton	D	8
Oct.	30—Kelvin Smart, Caerphilly	L	6
Dec.	3—Alan Storey, Hull	KO by	3

1980

Jan.	22—Ivor Jones, NSC	L	6
Feb.	18—Joey Wainwright, NSC	L	6
Feb.	28—John Griffiths, Ebbw Vale	L	6
Mar.	11—Joey Wainwright, NSC	L	6
Apr.	22—Gary Nickels, Albert Hall	L	6
Apr.	28—Steve Pollard, NSC	L	6
May	12—Clyde Ruan, Reading	L	6
May	29—Steve Topliss, Wolverhampton	L	6
July	30—Peter Gabbitus, Doncaster	KO by	4

CLINT JONES
British Light Heavyweight
1977

Apr.	7—Owen Robinson, Dudley	L	6
May	2—Paul Bussette, Walworth	L	6
June	27—Wally Barnes, Hove	KO	5
Sept.	5—Paul Bussett, Hove	W	8
Oct.	17—Joe Jackson, Hove	W	6
Nov.	10—Pat Thompson, Wimbledon	W	6
Dec.	14—Alan Tashy, Kingston	W	8

1978

Jan.	19—Wimbledon	KO by	3
Mar.	13—Eddie Vierling, Hove	L	8
Jan.	18—Trevor Cattouse, London	L	8
Mar.	15—Reginald Squire, London	W	8
Mar.	27—Jimmy Pickard, Hemel Hempstead	L	8
Apr.	6—Boyd Farrar, Norwich	L	8

1979

Jan.	18—Trevor Cattouse, London	L	8
Mar.	15—Reginald Squire, London	W	8
Mar.	27—Jimmy Pickard, Hemel Hempstead	L	8
Apr.	6—Boyd Farrar, Norwich	L	8

1980

Apr.	24—Gordon George, Queensway	L	8
Sept.	16—Keith Bristol, Southend	W	6

COLIN JONES
British Welterweight
1977

Oct.	3—Mike Copp, Aberovon	KO	5
Dec.	1—Martin Bridges, Heathrow	KO	4

1978

Jan.	23—Alan Reid, Aberavon	KO	1
Feb.	7—Willie Turkington, Islington	KO	1
Mar.	20—Tony Matey, Aberavon	W	6
July	10—Frankie Decaesteker, Aberavon	KO	6
Oct.	3—Horace McKenzie, Aberavon	W	8
Dec.	11—Johnny Pincham, Plymouth	KO	4

1979

Apr.	3—Sam Hailstock, Caerphilly	KO	4
May	13—Salvo Nucifero, Plymouth	KO	4
July	5—Alain Salmon, Aberavon	KO	1
Oct.	30—Joey Mack, Caerphilly	KO	10

1980

Jan.	21—Billy Waith, Mayfair	KO	6
Apr.	1—Kirkland Laing, London	KO	9

(Won British Welterweight Title)

GARY JONES
British Light Heavyweight
1979

Sept.	3—Mick Fellingham, Glasgow	D	6
Sept.	10—Nigel Savory, Bradford	L	6
Oct.	8—Mick Fellingham, Glasgow	L	6
Nov.	12—Ernie Baister, Marton	KO by	5
Dec.	6—Nigel Savory, Glasgow	W	6

1980

Jan.	21—Nigel Savory, Glasgow	W	4
Feb.	18—Gordon George, Birmingham	D	6
Feb.	25—Ernie Baister, Glasgow	W	6
Mar.	18—Rocky Burton, Wolverhampton	L	6
Mar.	24—Gordon George, Glasgow	W	6
Apr.	21—Rupert Christie, Edgbaston	KO by	2
Aug.	31—Peter Tidgewell, Glasgow	L	8

IVOR JONES
British Bantamweight
1979

Oct.	17—Carl Gaynor, Lewisham	KO	3
Nov.	19—Stuart Crabb, Lewisham	KO	3

1980

Jan.	22—Vryn Jones, Piccadilly	W	6
Mar.	6—Robert Hepburn, London	W	8
Apr.	29—John Griffiths, London	W	6
May	29—Iggy Jano, London	W	8
Oct.	20—Steve Enwright, Birmingham	L	8

KEN JONES
British Light Heavyweight
1977

Nov.	2—Dai Woods, Cardiff	W	6

1978

Jan.	23—Billy Lauder, Aberavon	W	6
Feb.	28—Trevor Cattouse, Heathrow	W	8
May	16—Bonny McKenzie, Newport	W	8
July	17—Shaun Chalcraft, London	W	6
Sept.	18—Dennis Andries, London	L	6

1979

Mar.	19—Chris Lawson, Haverfordwest	L	10
Apr.	27—Carlton Benoit, Newcastle	L	8
June	13—Alex Tompkins, Caerphilly	W	8
June	26—Eddie Fenton, Leicester	KO by	8
Nov.	29—Steve Hill, Liverpool	L	8

1980

Jan.	21—Trevor Cattouse, Mayfair	W	8
Apr.	24—Shaun Chalcraft, London	L	8
Aug.	12—Chris Lawson, Gowerton	W	10
	(Won Welsh Light Heavyweight Title)		
Oct.	6—Steve Lewin, Southwark	D	8

(SEAN) SHAUN JONES
British Welterweight
1980

Apr.	8—Adrian Clamp, Norwich	KO by	5
May	15—Randy Henderson, London	W	6
May	29—Gerry McGrath, London	L	6

TOMMY JONES
British Light Heavyweight
1978

June	19—Stan Thompson, Hove	L	6
Sept.	19—Joey Williams, Southend	W	6

1979

Apr.	30—Steve Babbs, Barnsley	KO by	5

1980

Jan.	7—Nigel Savory, Manchester	W	6
June	16—Peter Tidgewell, Manchester	L	6
Oct.	20—Keith Bristol, Birmingham	L	6
Oct.	29—Liam Coleman, Burslem	L	6

JUSTUS JOSEPHS
South African Junior Welterweight
Born: August 6, 1957
1978

July	3—Solomon Bango, Befordview	W	4
Sept.	8—Jack Jim, Johannesburg	W	4
Oct.	7—Philipus Van As, Ellis Park	KO	1
Oct.	23—Gregory Schmidt, Johannesburg	D	4

1979

Feb.	3—Hardy Mileham, Johannesburg	KO	6
Mar.	24—Peet Bothma, Johannesburg	L	6
Aug.	3—Norman Sekgapane, Springs	KO by	8
Sept.	29—Mzwandile Biyane, East London	L	6

1980

Mar.	5—Isaac Yoto, Cape Town	L	4
Mar.	28—Simon Dhladhla, Springs	L	6
Apr.	25—Terrence Molefe, Sebokeng	D	6
Sept.	20—Fanie van Staden, Jabulani	D	6

THEO JOSEPHS
British Heavyweight
1977

Oct.	6—Richie Smith, Liverpool	KO	3
Oct.	24—Alan Tashy, London	W	6
Nov.	23—Pat Thompson, Stoke	L	8
Dec.	1—Danny McLoughlin, Caister	W	8
Dec.	19—Pat Thomspson, Bradford	L	8

1978

Jan.	18—George Gray, Stoke	W	8
Jan.	24—Carl Canwell, Solihull	KO by	4
Mar.	13—Trevor Cattouse, Hove	L	8
Mar.	23—Howard Mills, Sudnerland	L	8
Apr.	24—Reg Long, Middlesbrough	L	8
May	8—Ron Green, Nottingham	L	6
July	18—Ron Green, Wakefield	L	8
Sept.	18—Paul Bussette, Manchester	KO	6
Sept.	28—Steve Hill, Liverpool	KO by	4
Oct.	24—George Scott, Blackpool	L	6
Nov.	30—Derek Simpkin, Caister	W	6
Dec.	11—David Pearce, Plymouth	L	8

1979

Feb.	13—Reg Long, Wakefield	W	8
Feb.	22—Ron McLean, Liverpool	KO	5

Mar.	20—Terry Chard, London	L	6
July	5—David Pearce, Aberavon	KO by	3
Nov.	28—Tim Wood, Doncaster	W	8

1980

Mar.	3—Neil Malpass, Middlesbrough	L	8
Mar.	19—Neil Malpass, Middlesbrough	L	8

BORO JOVIC
Yugoslav Junior Welterweight
1978

May	26—Ivan Simungia, Monfalcone	L	4
June	1—Zdravko Jovicic, Lubiana	L	4
Aug.	2—Timoteo Bonizzoni, Toscolano	L	6
Sept.	24—Zdravko Jovicic, Toplice	L	10
	(Yugoslavian Junior Welterweight Title)		
Oct.	8—Roman Hirsch, Kamnik	D	6
Oct.	14—Zdravko Jovicic, Lubiana	D	
Nov.	24—Giuseppe Di Padova, Mantova	KO by	2

1979

Jan.	19—Esperno Postl, Wien	L	8
Feb.	16—Zdravko Jovicic, Menges	L	10
	(Won Yugoslavian Welterweight Title)		
Mar.	2—Patrizio Burini, Figline	L	8
Mar.	19—Zahrudin Sacic, Ljubljana	D	8
Apr.	28—Remo Costa, La Spezia	L	8
May	11—Branko Barakovic, Ljubljana	D	4
May	19—Gregorio Giancaglione, Rome	D	8
July	21—Giancarlo Barabotti, Buti	L	8
Aug.	25—Etham Oezakalin, Zenica	KO by	2
Oct.	12—Josip Latric, Ljubljana	D	6

1980

Feb.	1—Marzio Baseotti, San Dona	KO by	5
Mar.	8—Lucien Campo, Argenteuil	KO by	8
Apr.	18—Francesco Marcello, Torino	KO by	7

NENE JUN
Filipino Junior Lightweight
1979

Feb.	17—Donny Soriani, Pampanga	L	10
Mar.	31—Fernando Cabanela, Santos City	L	12
May	18—Dony Soriano, Manila	W	12
June	25—Romy Cunanan, Manila	W	12
	(Philippine Featherweight Title)		
July	13—Fred Basa, Manila	W	12
Oct.	20—Rey Tam, Manila	L	10
Dec.	21—Dommy Morolena, Quezon City	L	12
	(Philippine Featherweight Title)		

1980

Feb.	1—Nilo Acido, Davao City	W	10
Apr.	—Nilo Acido, Manila	W	12
	(Won Filipino Junior Lightweight Title)		
May	9—Woon-Chul Shin, Manila	KO	6
June	14—Ray Bansan, Davao City	KO	7
July	11—Del Contado, Manila	W	10
	(Retained Filipino Junior Lightweight Title)		
Aug.	29—Dorn Sornsakdisith, Quezon City	L	10
Sept.	19—Erning Grafe, Quezon City	W	10
Nov.	14—Dommy Morolena, Panaraque	L	10

CHARLES JURIETTI
French Junior Lightweight
1976

Jan.	16—Claude Viard, Cluses	W	6
Jan.	24—Christian Valentin, Grenoble	D	6
Feb.	21—Alain Le Fol, Maubege	L	6
Oct.	16—Alain Le Fol, Maubege	D	6
Nov.	19—Pietro Marselli, Annecy	W	6
Nov.	26—Pietro Marselli, Zurigo	D	6

1977

Feb.	11—Patrick Goblet, Valence	W	6
Apr.	1—Lucio Cusma, Bologna	L	6
May	6—Gilbert Hollouin, Valence	W	6
May	14—Christian Gracia, Pont Casse	KO	8
Oct.	22—Mario Oliveira, Antibes	KO	4
Nov.	5—Rene Martin, Boulogne	L	6
Nov.	18—Alain Le Fol, Valence	W	8

1978

Jan.	14—Rudy Vogel, Valence	KO	7
Mar.	18—Jean Pierre Hainault, Villerbanne	KO	7
Apr.	15—Eloy De Souza, Valence	W	10
May	13—Natale Vezzoli, Brescia	D	10
June	9—Carlos Dos Santos, Grenoble	W	8
July	21—Elio Cotena, Ischia	L	10
Oct.	5—Josias DaSilva, Vallence	KO	4
Nov.	18—Maurice Apeang, Papeete	L	10
Dec.	13—Naalee Vezzoli, Brescia	D	12
	(European Junior Lightweight Title)		

1979

Mar.	17—Lucio Cusma, Valence	W	8
May	13—Maurice Apeang, Valence	W	12
	(French Junior Lightweight Title)		
June	21—Palmiro Masala, Valence	KO	6

Oct.	6—Rodolfo Sanchez, Bilbao L	12

(EBU Junior Lightweight Title)

Nov.	30—Maurice Apeang, Valence .... W	12

(French Junior Lightweight Title)

1980

Feb.	8—Natale Carrede, Valence .... W disq.		3
Mar.	14—Samuel Meck, Villeurbanne .... W		10
Apr.	26—Michel Lefevbre, Rumilly .... KO		7

(Won French Junior Lightweight Title)

MUSHAPATU KABANGU
South African Light Heavyweight
(Based in Paris)
1980

Feb.	22—Pierre Kabassu, Luxembourg .... KO		5
Mar.	7—Aldo Buzzetti, Piacenza .... KO by		4
Nov.	22—Sergio Bosio, La Louviere .... KO by		4

KINJI KAJITA
Japanese Junior Lightweight
1980

Apr.	3—Takashi Asuka, Nara .... KO		1
June	1—Katsuo Kazama, Kochi City .... KO		4

DAVID KALAKO
South African Middleweight
1977

Oct.	6—Zenzile Makanda, Bloemfontein .... KO		3
Nov.	5—Johannes Tladi, Viljoenskroon .... W		4

1978

Mar.	31—Zacharia Makolomakoe, Bloemfontein .... W		6
May	1—George Slabbert, Welkom .... W		4
Aug.	12—Kenneth Maseko, Johannesburg .... KO		1
Aug.	21—Frederick Berry, Welkom .... W		4

1979

Mar.	9—Sydney Shezi, Springs .... D		4
June	11—Basie Gouws, Welkom L		4
July	9—Thornton Oakes, Welkom .... D		4
Nov.	12—Jan Beneke, Welkom .... KO by		2

1980

May	5—Joseph Lala, Welkom L		6

DAVID (BABY LUX) KAMBULE
South African Welterweight
1975

Apr.	25—Elias Maredi, Dobsonville .... W		4
May	9—Godfrey Simelane, Natalspruit .... KO		4
July	3—Petrus Mahlangu, Natalspruit .... W		4
Oct.	31—Daniel Makhudu, Natalspruit .... W		6

1976

Jan.	30—Simon Zondo, Orlando West L		6
Mar.	12—Sydney Tshabalala, Vereeniging .... W		6
July	3—Jacob Matseki, Parys .... KO		3
Aug.	21—Isaac Rakhajane, Kroomstad .... W		6
Nov.	6—Ben Molokeng, Parys .... KO		3

1977

Mar.	19—Emmanuel Gumede, Kroonstad .... W		8
Apr.	30—Jeremiah Nzelwane, Kroonstad .... KO		7
May	21—Louis Sibiya, Kroonstad .... W		8
July	9—Timothy Lerefolo, Parys .... W		6
Sept.	10—George Selebi, Kroonstad .... KO		3
Oct.	4—Sothoane Khoalelane, Kroonstad .... KO		2
Nov.	5—Samuel Pule, Parys .... KO		2

1978

Mar.	3—Simon Zondo, Krugersdorp .... KO		4
Apr.	22—Ernest Moledi, Vereeniging .... KO		1
Apr.	22—Ben Mutle, Vereeniging .... KO		2
June	10—Simon Zondo, Sharpville .... D		6
June	10—Emmanuel Gumede, Sharpville .... W		8
Sept.	30—Joseph Mohlala, Sharpville .... KO		1
Nov.	11—Jan Beneke, Johannesburg............. KO		2

1979

Feb.	16—Morris Mohloai, Springs .... W		10
Apr.	7—Jimmy Ellis, Vereeniging .... KO		2
May	25—Langton Tinago, Springs .... W		8
June	8—Griffiths Mgijima, East London .... W		6
Oct.	20—Harold Volbrecht, Pretoria L		12

(South African Welterweight Title)

1980

Mar.	29—Coenie Bekker, Johannesburg L		6
Apr.	25—George Selebi, Sebokeng .... KO		6

(Retained Transvaal Welterweight Title)

May	24—Jack Jim, Orlando .... KO		1
Aug.	29—Joseph Lala, Sebokeng .... W		10

AKIO KAMEDA
Japanese Welterweight
1977

Mar.	15—Edmond Goveyer, Hawaii .... KO		2
May	22—Shigeru Goda, Sapporo City .... KO		2
July	23—Senju Yamaguchi, Tokyo .... KO		5
Oct.	29—Kazunori Shiratori, Tokyo .... KO		5

1978

Jan.	23—Mamoru Taira, Nagoya .... KO		3
Mar.	3—Kyung Il Lee, Tokyo .... KO		6
Apr.	28—Shoji Tsujimoto, Tokyo .... KO		5

(Japanese Welterweight Title)

Oct.	27—Yohi Arai, Tokyo .... W		10

(Japanese Welterweight Title)

1979

Jan.	26—Yong Taek Kim, Tokyo .... KO		6
Apr.	12—Kazumi Nakao, Tokyo .... KO		2

(JBC Welterweight Title)

July	12—Hirofumi Sawada, Tokyo .... KO		2
Nov.	29—Tatsuo Ohara, Tokyo .... W		10

(Retained JBC Welterweight Title)

1980

Mar.	13—Kazunori Shiratori, Tokyo .... KO		8

(Retained Japanese Welterweight Title)

Nov.	12—Kazumi Nakao, Tokyo .... KO		4

(Retained Japanese Welterweight Title)

MONWABISI KANA
South African Bantamweight
1977

Apr.	2—Sipho Kema, East London .... KO		3
May	28—Spokes Witbooi, King Williamstown .... KO		3
May	31—Houlet Nohenda, Queenstown .... KO		3
June	11—Zola Lawuse, East London L		6

1978

Jan.	28—Elias Mphatsoe, East London .... W		4

1979

Feb.	10—Sonwabo Sigetye, Queenstown .... KO		3
Dec.	1—Nkosana Moss, King Williamstown ...... W		6

1980

Mar.	15—Lennox Mtyongwe, East London .... W		4
May	31—Joseph Gumede, East London .... KO by		4

PETER KANIE
South African Junior Welterweight
1979

May	26—Velile Klaas, King Williamstown .... W		4
Nov.	10—Alfred Gcaza, King Williamstown .... W		4

1980

Mar.	15—Hamilton Nyakatha, East London .... KO		3
May	17—Alfred Sibisi, East London .... KO		5
June	4—Bramley Whiteboy, Cape Town L		8
July	26—Tamie Spampool, K.W.T. .... W		6
Aug.	16—Bramley Whiteboy, East London .... W		6
Sept.	20—Ernest Moledi, Jabulani L		6
Oct.	11—Bramley Whiteboy, Elizabeth L		10

(For Cape Junior Welterweight Title)

Dec.	6—Ernest Moledi, East London L		6

KATSUO KAZAMA
Japanese Junior Lightweight
1979

	—Elniro Kuruma, Osaka L		6
Dec.	9—Jo Tatsuki, Osaka .... KO by		2

1980

Apr.	29—Tsuyoshi Hamada, Tokyo .... KO by		1
June	1—Kinji Kajita, Kochi City .... KO by		4

KUJOSHI (BATTLE HAWK) KAZAMA
Japanese Junior Lightweight
Born: Jan. 2, 1950 Narashino City Japan
Amateur Record: 123-9 104 KOs
1974

July	24—Sam Frachiseli, Hawaii .... W		5
Aug.	16—Sam Frachiseli, Hawaii .... W		5
Sept.	10—Jessie Villagonza, Hawaii .... KO		1
Oct.	1—Floro Ibanes, Hawaii .... W		6
Oct.	15—Mitsuaki Nakane, Tokyo .... W		6

1975

Jan.	5—Lion Furuyama, Tokyo .... D		10

(Japanese Junior Welterweight Championship)

Aug.	17—Chito Gonzaga, Macao .... W		10
Aug.	31—Lion Furuyama, Tokyo .... W		10
Sept.	30—Antonio Cervantes, Caracas .... KO by		6
Nov.	30—Bull Kato, Tokyo .... W		10

1976

Mar.	22—Yasuaki (Sinichi) Kadota, Tokyo .... W		10
May	9—Tae-Ho Kim, Seoul L		10
July	17—Yung-Ho Oh, Pusan L		12

(For Oriental Lightweight Title)

Sept.	26—Toku Oushi, Tokyo .... KO		7

1977

Jan.	4—Mashiro Yokai, Tokyo .... KO by		6

333

Mar.	9—Tae-Ho Kim, Seoul	L	10
May	7—Yung-Ho Oh, Pusan	D	10
Oct.	6—Hyung-Il Park, Seoul	W	10

1978

May	14—Shigeru Goda, Tokyo	W	10
Aug.	9—Shoichi Kumada, Akita City	KO	8
Nov.	15—Bossow Aziza, Tokyo	W	10

1979

Apr.	26—Katsuhiro Okubo, Tokyo	W	10
July	6—Mitsuo Ohashi, Nara City	KO	3
Sept.	27—Katsuhiro Okubo, Tokyo	KO	1

(For Japanese Lightweight Title)

1980

| Jan. | 6—Takeshi Mine, Nara City | KO | 3 |
| Apr. | 3—Samuel Serrano, Nara | KO by | 13 |

(For WBA Junior Lightweight Title)

PAUL KEERS
British Featherweight

1979

Apr.	5—Joey Spring, Liverpool	W	6
Apr.	26—Bobby Breen, Liverpool	W	6
May	1—Austin Owens, London	L	6
May	10—Glyn Davies, Pontypool	D	6
June	18—Alan Storey, Bradford	W	8
July	5—Vernon Penprase, Aberavon	L	8
Sept.	12—Donald George, Liverpool	W	6
Sept.	25—Gary Nickels, London	W	6
Oct.	8—Terry McKeown, Glasgow	L	8
Dec.	3—Mohammed Younis, Wolverhampton	W	8
Dec.	17—Selwyn Bell, Bradford	L	8

1980

Jan.	8—Mohammed Younis, Windsor	KO	6
Jan.	28—Jarvis Greenidge, Bradford	W	8
Mar.	3—Vernon Penprase, London	L	8
Mar.	27—Gary Lucas, Liverpool	L	8
May	12—Austin Owens, Reading	D	8
June	2—Vernon Penprase, Plymouth	L	10
July	7—Charlie Parvin, Middlesbrough	KO	5

JOHN KENNEDY
British Junior Middleweight

1979

Mar.	12—Casley McAllum, London	KO	3
May	2—Lee Hartshorn, Solihull	W	8
Sept.	25—Nigel Thomas, London	KO	2
Oct.	22—Manny Romain, London	W	8

1980

Feb.	12—Dave Southwell, London	KO	2
Mar.	3—Salvo Nuciforo, Nottingham	W	8
Apr.	14—Achille Mithcell, London	W	8

RICHARD KENYON
British Middleweight

1978

Apr.	17—Mohammed Akram, Bradford	KO	4
Apr.	27—Mick Morris, Doncaster	KO	5
May	8—John Parr, Manchester	KO	3
May	15—Dave Merrell, Bradford	W	6
June	19—Mick Morris, Manchester	D	6
July	18—Dave Merrell, Wakefield	W	8
Sept.	8—Brian Gregory, Wakefield	KO	5
Sept.	18—Romal Ambrose, Manchester	KO by	5
Oct.	16—Kendrick Edwards, Bradford	W	8
Nov.	2—Dave Davies, Liverpool	W	8
Nov.	30—Romal Ambrose, Caister	KO by	8

1979

| Apr. | 5—Dave Davies, Liverpool | L | 8 |
| July | 30—Mike Copp, London | L | 8 |

1980

| Jan. | 9—Jimmy Ellis, Burslem | KO by | 4 |

TREVOR KERR
British Light Heavyweight

1977

| Dec. | 16—Albert (Gypsy) Smith, Enniskillen | W | 8 |

1978

Feb.	3—John Breen, Enniskillen	W	0
Apr.	21—Steve Fox, Enniskillen	W	6
July	10—Chris Lawson, Aberavon	KO by	4
Oct.	11—John Breen, Belfast	KO	1
Oct.	18—Eddie Burke, Glasgow	KO by	2
Dec.	1—Peter Gorny, Enniskillen	L	8

1979

June	27—Mike Copp, Derry	L	8
Oct.	15—Nick Pauling, Glasgow	L	6
Nov.	26—Ian Glenn, Belfast	KO	5

1980

Feb.	25—Stan Carnall, Belfast	W	8
July	28—Ian Glenn, Fivemiletown	KO	2
Sept.	22—Mick Fellingham, Belfast	KO	7

(Won Vacant Northern Ireland Light Heavyweight Title)

DAVID KGOTSANE
South African Welterweight

1975

Jan.	23—Spunkie Ngubane, Cape Town	KO	1
Aug.	1—George Selebi, Kwa-Thema	KO by	2
Sept.	6—Petrus Motaung, Sharpeville	KO by	4

1976

| Apr. | 30—Kenneth Maseko, Springs | L | 6 |

1977

(Inactive)

1978

Feb.	4—Jan Beneke, Johannesburg	L	4
June	10—Thuso Mapela, Sharpeville	W	8
July	1—Jan Beneke, Pretoria	KO by	3

1979

| Feb. | 16—Joseph Lala, Springs | L | 6 |
| Apr. | 7—Ephraim Mabema, Vereeniging | L | 6 |

1980

| Apr. | 19—Fanie van Staden, Rand Stadium | L | 4 |

ISRAEL KHONKHOBE
South African Featherweight

1972

Feb.	5—Albert Khoadi, Bloemfontein	W	6
Apr.	22—Andile Tywabi, King Williamstown	D	6
Oct.	21—Leslie Pikoli, Port Elizabeth	W	6
Nov.	11—Andile Tywabi, King Williamstown	W	10

1973

Mar.	9—William Sefefe, Tembisa	W	6
Feb.	—William Molatudi, Port Elizabeth	W	8
Mar.	24—Chris Dlamini, Port Elizabeth	L	8
May	12—Chris Dlamini, Port Elizabeth	L	10
Oct.	13—Johannes Sithebe, Port Elizabeth	W	8
Nov.	9—Anthony Sithole, Springs	D	6

1974

Feb.	1—Thomas Mathibela, Springs	W	6
Apr.	5—Jacob Jobe, Kwa-Thema	W	6
Mar.	2—I. Peete, Welkom	KO	3
June	Anthony Sithole, Kwa-Thema	W	6
Mar.	23—Z. Mahaluba, Port Elizabeth	KO	6
Apr.	13—T. Yako, Port Elizabeth	W	6
Nov.	9—Leslie Pikoli, Port Elizabeth	L	8
Dec.	14—Mzukisi Skweyiya, East London	KO by	5

1975

Feb.	28—Johannes Sithebe, Kwa-Thema	W	6
Mar.	8—Mqondisi Ntshika, Port Elizabeth	L	6
June	20—Lucas Semtale, Tembisa	W	6
Sept.	6—Johannes Sithebe, Port Elizabeth	D	6

1976

| Jan. | 31—Boy April, East London | KO by | 3 |
| Apr. | 10—Mzukisi Skweyiya, Port Elizabeth | KO by | 7 |

1977-1978

(Inactive)

1979

June	23—Michael Moamogwa, Bloemfontein	W	8
Nov.	19—Samuel Motsabi, Kimberly	W	8
Dec.	8—Daniel Rammilli, Bloemfontein	KO	5

1980

Feb.	2—Samuel Mafere, Kimberley	W	6
Apr.	14—John Riet, Kimberley	KO	2
Aug.	2—Jacob Diraditsile, Welkom	L	10

(For OFS Junior Featherweight Title)

| Aug. | 23—Michael Moamogoa, Kimberley | L | 6 |
| Sept. | 13—Jacob Moyeye, Welkom | W | 8 |

JOHN KHOOE
South African Junior Middleweight

1978

| July | 22—Abraham Tlathe, Bloemfontein | KO | 4 |
| Mar. | 3—Elias Malefane, Virginia | W | 6 |

1979

| Oct. | 10—Joseph Lala, Bloemfontein | KO by | 3 |
| Nov. | 12—Bennie Nortman, Welkom | L | 4 |

1980

| Aug. | 23—Daniel Mkhize, Kimberley | L | 6 |
| Sept. | 6—Daniel Mkhize, Welkom | W | 10 |

(Won OFS Junior Middleweight Title)

| Dec. | 19—Michael Motsoane, Welkom | KO by | 2 |

CAIPHUS (CAIFAS) KHOTLE
South African Junior Featherweight

1977

| Dec. | 3—Alexis Khaeeane, Ficksburg | W | 4 |

1978

| July | 22—Jama Qualinga, Bloemfontein | W | 4 |
| Sept. | 2—Samuel Koalepe, Ficksburg | KO | 1 |

1979

Feb.	9—Elijah Siyaya, Bethlehem	W	4
Feb.	24—Jacob Peter, Bethlehem	D	4
Sept.	1—Amos Mpenga, Ficksburg	W	4

1980

| Feb. | 4—Elijah Siyaya, Bethlehem | W | 4 |
| Apr. | 12—Joseph Diraditsile, Ficksburg | W | 6 |

Sept. 6—Elijah Siyaya, Ficksburg .... W 6
Dec. 6—Samuel Wolf, Ficksburg .... W 6

EPHRAIM KHUTO
South African Junior Welterweight
1980
Apr. 12—Teboho Lento, Ficksburg .... W 6
Aug. 22—Johannes Nhlapo, Bethlehem .... KO by 1
Sept. 6—Daniel Mohoi, Ficksburg .... L 6
Dec. 6—Joseph Molahloe, Ficksburg .... D 6

MICHEL KHUTO
South African Junior Featherweight
1978
July 22—Sabata Moholo, Bloemfontein .... KO 4
Oct. 7—David Motaung, Virginia .... L 4
1979
(Inactive)
1980
Apr. 12—Elias Raliteng, Ficksburg .... W 6
Sept. 6—Petrus Abrahams, Ficksburg .... W 4
Dec. 6—Macholi Nqomfe, Ficksburg .... W 4

GEORGE KIDD
Scottish Welterweight
1976
May 17—Gordon Jennings, Glasgow .... W 4
Sept. 27—Chris Walker, Birmingham .... L 4
1977
Mar. 15—George Daines, Leeds .... W 4
Apr. 25—George Daines, Glasgow .... W 4
May 16—Peter Rushfirth, Glasgow .... L 6
June 20—Martin Bridge, Glasgow .... L 6
Aug. 5—George Daines, Glasgow .... W 4
1978
Feb. 3—Dave Campbell, Enniskellen .... KO by 4
1979
(Inactive)
1980
Mar. 19—Gary Newell, Stoke .... KO by 4

MICKEY KIDD
British Middleweight
1979
Sept. 26—Barry Oakes, Stoke .... KO 1
Oct. 30—Terry Matthews, Bedford .... L 6
Nov. 27—Kendrick Edwards, Wolverhampton ...... W 6
Dec. 17—Gary Newll, Wolverhampton .... W 6
1980
Jan. 16—Jerry Golden, Stoke .... W 6
Apr. 21—Mike Copp, London .... W 6
Apr. 29—Mike Copp, London .... W 6
Nov. 13—Al Neville, Stafford .... W 6
Nov. 25—Russell Humphreys, Bedworth .... W 6
Dec. 8—Russell Humphreys, Nottingham .... D 6

TOM KIELY
British Heavyweight
Born: Sept. 22, 1955
1976
Sept. 22—Terry Jones, Battersea.................. W 6
Oct. 18—Ken Burrell, Bedford .... KO 1
Oct. 18—Sean (Jumbo) McKenna, Bedford .... KO 2
Oct. 18—George Gray, Bedford................... W 3
(Final of Heavyweight Tournament)
Nov. 24—Keith Johnson, London .... W 6
1977
Feb. 15—Brian Paul, Walworth .... W 6
Mar. 1—David Fry, Hove .... W 8
Apr. 7—Keith Johnson, Hove .... W 8
May 23—Kris Smith, Walworth .... L 8
Oct. 17—Paul Kinsella, Hove, ... W 6
Nov. 8—Neil Malpass, London .... W 8
1978
Jan. 11—Hennie Thoonen, Rotterdam .... KO by 5
Feb. 13—Austin Okoye, Walworth .... KO 5
Mar. 16—Fleming Jensen, Copenhagen .... W 6
Apr. 17—Paul Sykes, Bradford .... L 8
May 23—Danny McAlinden, London .... KO 6
Oct. 7—Jimmy Abbott, Johannesburg .... L 8
Nov. 23—Bobby Hennessey, Wimbledon .... W 8
1979
(Inactive)
1980
Jan. 31—Sylvain Watbled, Paris .... L 10
Mar. 6—Tony Moore, London .... W 10
(Retained Southern Area Heavyweight Title)
May 3—Alfredo Evangelista, Barcelona .... KO by 3
Sept. 22—Gordon Ferris, Belfast .... L 12
(For Vacant All-Ireland Heavyweight Title)

WILLEM KILLIAN
South African Middleweight
1978
May 20—Gert Pienaar, Tzanenn .... W 4
July 17—Emil Brice, Goodwood .... KO 4
Sept. 23—Anton Retief, Johannesburg .... KO by 2
1979
(Inactive)
1980
Mar. 21—Willie Opperman, Bloemfontein ...... KO by 4
Apr. 21—Basil Meintjies, Secunda .... KO by 1

CHI-BOK KIM
Korean Junior Flyweight
1979
Dec. 8—Olds Calmeri, Seoul .... KO 9
1980
Mar. 2—Tito Abella, Seoul .... KO 1

CHUL-HO KIM
Korean Junior Bantamweight
Born: March 3, 1961, Ohsan, Korea
Amateur Career; 8 Wins (4 by KO), 1 Loss
Height: 5 ft. 6 in.
1978
Oct. 7—Jae-kyu Bae .... W 4
Oct. 29—Dong-Yong Kim .... KO 3
Dec. 7—Suk-Chol Bae .... W 4
Dec. 8—Hie-Won Chung .... W 4
Dec. 9—Kwang-Suk Lee .... W 4
Dec. 10—Kwan-Su Chung .... W 6
1979
Feb. 10—Hak-Dal Kim .... W 6
Apr. 1—Jae-Yong Song .... W 8
Aug. 25—Sington Sithmlong, Thailand .... KO 3
Sept. 29—Il-Song Choi .... W 10
Nov. 11—Yong-Hwan Kim .... L 10
1980
Feb. 23—Kyung-Ju Ha .... D 10
Mar. 30—Larry Enriquez, Philippines .... KO 6
Aug. 10—Il-Song Choi .... W 10
(Won Vacant Korean Junior Bantamweight Title)
Sept. 26—Jung-Kun Choi .... KO 2
(Retained Title)
Nov. 2—Ben Olivette, Philippines .... KO 3

HAK-YUNG KIM
Korean Flyweight
1980
May 17—Diego De Villa, Davao City .... L 10

HWAN-JIN KIM
Korean Junior Flyweight
1979
Nov. 24—Mario Kakika, Teku City .... W 10
1980
Mar. 2—Grumman Ueda, Seoul .... KO 6

KWANG-MIN KIM
Korean Lightweight
1977
—Mitsuyuki Nakane, Seoul .... W 10
1978
—Sang-Mo Koo, Pusan .... KO 1
—Rey Tam, Seoul .... W 10
—Abdul Bey, Pusan .... D 10
1979
—Tae-Ho Kim, Seoul .... W 10
Apr. 25—Young-Ho Oh, Seoul .... W 10
Aug. 25—Antonio Cervantes, Seoul .... L 15
(For WBA Junior Welterweight Title)
—Fitzroy Giuseppe, Seoul .... W 10
1980
May 3—Boy Reyes, Kwangjoo .... KO 6
July 14—Rod Sequenan, Seoul .... KO 2
Sept. 25—Sang-Hyun Kim, Seoul .... L 10

SA-WANG KIM
Korean Featherweight
1977
June 21—Oh-Boo Kwon, Seoul .... KO 3
July 30—Byung-Chul Lee, Seoul .... KO 2
Aug. 28—Hwang Ki, Seoul .... KO 1
Sept. 30—Dong-Rae Yim, Seoul .... KO 6
1978
Feb. 12—Go Mifune, Seoul .... W 10
1979
Jan. 14—Jong-Kil Chung, Pusan .... KO 4
Feb. 2—Eddie Vallidos, Seoul .... KO 2
Mar. 12—Elmer Elisondo, Seoul .... KO 2
June 2—De Juanin Hollywood, Seoul .... W 10
June 23—Juan Mayoral, Seoul .... KO 9
Sept. 13—Danilo Batista, Choon Chun .... KO 2

335

Oct. 20—Erning Grafe, Seoul ....KO 2
1980
Mar. 16—Koichi Matsushima, Seoul ....W 10
July 20—Eusebio Pedrosa, Seoul ....KO by 8
(For WBA Feaherweight Title)

SONG-NAM KIM
Korean Junior Flyweight
1980
Jan. 27—In-Wan Hwan, Seoul ....KO 6
(Won Vacant Korean Junior Flyweight Title)

YONG-HYUN KIM
Korean Junior Flyweight
1979
Nov. 27—Sang-Il Chung, Teku City ....KO 2
1980
Jan. 27—Yoko Gushiken, Osaka ....L 15
(For WBA Junior Flyweight Title)

YUNG-SHIK KIM
Korean Bantamweight
Born: November 15, 1950
1972
Sept. 9—Dae-Sung Ra, Taegu ....D 6
Dec. 23—Min-Chul Choi, Pusan ....KO 4
1973
Mar. 4—Sang-Il Kim, Seoul ....W 6
May 13—Toshio Nishi, Pusan ....W 10
Sept. 29—Young-Ho Choi, Pusan ....W 10
Nov. 25—Dae-Sung Ra, Pusan ....W 10
1974
Mar. 17—Bok-Soo Hwang, Pusan ....L 10
July 28—Jube-Yung Kim, Pusan ....KO 8
Dec. 14—Saeng-Ki Chung, Seoul ....W 10
1975
Feb. 24—Hisami Mizuno, Tokyo ....W 10
Mar. 9—Chun-Ha Park, Pusan ....W 10
Apr. 20—Bok-Soo Hwang, Pusan ....W 10
Aug. 10—Bae Hyung, Seoul ....KO 4
1976
Jan. 14—Il-Sung Choi, Seoul ....W 10
Apr. 11—Jung-Hoon Oh, Jinhas ....KO 6
July 30—Didik Nuljadi, Jakarta ....W 10
Oct. 12—Venice Borkorsor, Bangkok ....L 10
1977
Feb. 6—Chun-Ha Park, Kwangjoo ....W 10
Mar. 19—Chong-Han Kim, Seoul ....W 10
June 17—Rolando Navarette, Seoul ....W 12
(Won Vacant OPBF Bantamweight Title)
Aug. 18—Go Mifune, Pusan ....W 12
(Retained OPBF Bantamweight Title)
1978
Feb. 11—Chun-Ha Park, Seoul ....W 10
Mar. 26—Neptali Alamag, Seoul ....W 12
(Retained OPBF Bantamweight Title)
June 11—Hiroyuki Iwamoto, Seoul ....W 10
Aug. 15—Shuichi Isogami, Tokyo ....L 12
Dec. 14—Eijiro Murata, Tokyo ....L 12
(Lost OPBF Bantamweight Title)
1979
May 27—Chung-Chul Kim, Pusan ....W 10
Oct. 14—Isao Okahashi, Tokyo ....W 10
Nov. 19—Kazzuma Tamaki, Tokyo ....W 10
1980
Mar. 30—Little Aguilar, Seoul ....W 12
(Won Vacant OPBF Junior Bantamweight Title)
June 20—Il-Song Choi, Seoul ....W 10
Oct. 15—William Develos, Manila ....L 12
(Lost OPBF Junior Bantamweight Title)

JO KIMPUANI
French Junior Welterweight
Born: Oct. 10, 1949, Luzubi, Zaire
1971
Nov. 6—Saadi Saadli, Dunkirk ....W 6
Dec. 11—Oliviero Pierleoni, Dunkirk ....W disq. 4
1972
Jan. 8—Michel Briatte, Dunkirk ....KO 2
Feb. 5—Rolf Kestern, Dunkirk ....KO 3
Mar. 11—Franz Meganck, Dunkirk ....KO by 6
Apr. 8—Michel Danjou, Dunkirk ....KO 2
Apr. 15—Georges Perrot, Calais..................KO 3
May 13—Carlo Sanbnsiti, Dunkirk ....W 8
Oct. 1—Roy Chavez, Istanbul .`..................KO 3
1973
May 12—Carlos Almeida, Dunkirk ....W disq. 3
Oct. 14—Kid Silent, Dunkirk ....KO 1
Nov. 4—Nicola Sassanelli, Dunkirk ....W 10
Dec. 8—Srco Weiner, Dunkirk ....KO 1
1974
Jan. 5—Gerard Leteune, Dunkirk ....KO 4
Feb. 16—Aad Jansen, Dunkerque ....KO 3
Mar. 9—Jean Claude Delgove, Dunkerque........KO 2

Aug. 7—Flash Patterson, Dunkirk...............KO 2
May 7—Cemal Kamaci, Dunkerque ....W 10
Oct. 19—Luciano Laffranchi, Dunkerque..........W 8
Dec. 13—Nicola Doraz 10, Dunkirk...............KO 3
1975
Mar. 8—Giuseppe Minotti, Dunkerque ....W 10
Apr. 21—Luigi Martello, Dunkirk ....KO 8
Apr. 26—Pierre Petit, Dunkerque ....KO 3
June 28—Dan Patterson, Accra...................KO 6
(All-African Junior Welterweight Title)
Oct. 11—Enzo Pizzoni, Petit Synthe...............KO 5
Nov. 21—Lorenzo Trujillo, Paris.................W 10
Dec. 6—Tony Alfonso, Dunkerque ....KO 1
1976
Jan. 10—Jean Marie Cotinaut, Dunkerque.......KO 1
Mar. 6—(Irish) Beau Jaynes, Dunkerque.........KO 4
Apr. 10—Lorenzo Trujillo, Dunkirk...............WF 7
Oct. 1—Jeff Holmes, Dunkerque ....KO 4
Dec. 10—Benny Huertus, Dunkerque...............KO 2
1977
Jan. 15—Efisio Pinna, Grande Snythe ....W 10
Feb. 4—Jose Resto, Dunkirk ....W 10
Mar. 5—Billy Waith, Dunkerque ....W 10
Apr. 2—Jesse Lara, Dunkerque ....KO 3
Apr. 23—Jesus Rodriguez De La Rosa, Lille ......KO 1
Oct. 15—Pietro Ceru, Petite Synthe ....W 10
Nov. 12—Justice Ortiz, Dunkerque ....KO 6
Dec. 30—Saensak Muangsurin, Chantaburi ....KO by 14
(WBC Junior Welterweight Title)
1978
Jan. 14—Joey Mack, Dunkerque ....W 10
Mar. 17—Achille Mitchell, Grand Synthe..........W 10
Apr. 15—Steve Angell, Dunkerque ....KO 6
Apr. 29—Alois Carmeliet, Zele ....KO 3
May 11—Eddie Marcel, Paris ....KO 5
Oct. 14—Tiger Quaye, Dunkirk ....KO 1
Nov. 11—Speedy Mitchell, Kunkirk..............KO 2
1979
Feb. 10—Jimmy Rothwell, Dunkerque ....KO 7
Mar. 10—Oscar Aparicio, Dunkerque ....KO 3
May 18—Jose Luis Heredia, Dunkerque ....KO 3
(EBU Junior Welterweight Title)
Dec. 8—Nelson Gomes, Dunkerque ....KO 3
1980
Jan. 6—Perico Fernandez, Bilbao ....W 12
(Retained European Junior Welterweight Title)
Feb. 9—Eddie Campbell, Dunkirk ....KO 2
Mar. 15—Christian Garcia, Mont de Marsan ....W 12
(Retained European Junior Welterweight Title)
Dec. 13—Arwell Thomas, Aire ....KO 1

GARY KITTLE
British Featherweight
1980
May 29—Robert Hepburn, London ....W 6
July 8—John Henry, Wolverhampton ....KO 1

BAREND MATTHEUS (BENNIE) KNOETZE
South African Heavyweight
1980
Mar. 8—Timothy Zwane, Johannesburg ....W 4
Mar. 21—Sofonia Naile, Bloemfontein ....KO 2
Apr. 19—Timothy Zwane, Rand Stadium ....KO 1
Aug. 16—Caifas Masondo, Johannesburg ....W 4
Dec. 22—Caifas Masondo, Cape Town ....KO 3

KALLIE KNOETZE
(NIKOLAAS JACOBUS KNOETZE)
South African Heavyweight
Born: April 24, 1953
1976
Feb. 28—Jeff Ellis, Johannesburg ....KO 2
Mar. 20—Karsten Honhold, Johannesburg..........KO 1
Mar. 27—Horst Lang, Pretoria ....KO 3
May 21—Amedeo Laureti, Bloemfontein ....KO 3
June 19—Domingo Silvera, Pretoria ....KO 4
Aug. 13—Frankie Schram, Bloemfontein ....KO 3
Oct. 5—Raul Gorosito, Johannesburg ....LF 5
Oct. 30—Gerrie Coetzee, Johannesburg...........L 10
Dec. 6—Jerry Houston, Durban ....KO 4
1977
Jan. 29—Ngozika Kwelum, Johannesburg ....KO 7
Mar. 7—Raul Gorosito, Pretoria ....W 10
May 6—Ishaq Hussien, Pretoria ....KO 4
June 4—Neville Meade, Johannesburg ....KO 4
Aug. 13—Mike Schutte, Johannesburg ....KO 2
Sept. 10—Richard Dunn, Johannesburg ....KO 5
1978
Feb. 4—Duane Bobick, Johannesburg..............KO 3
July 1—Denton Ruddock, Pretoria...............KO 4
Aug. 26—G. G. Maldonado, Mmabatho............KO 4
1979
Jan. 13—Bill Sharkey, Miami Beach ....KO 4

336

June   2—John Tate, Mmbatho .... KO by 8
Sept. 14—George Butzbach, Durban .... KÖ 7
Oct. 20—Randy Stephens, Pretoria .... KO 3
Dec. 19—Mike Koranicki, Cape Town .... KO by 10
1980
Mar.   8—Jimmy Abbott, Johannesburg .... KO by 1

REINER KOBER
German Middleweight
1980
Feb. 22—Giampaolo Piras, Dusseldorf .... W 4
Mar. 22—Mike McCoy, Friedewald .... L 4
Dec.   5—Andre Wissenbach, Koln .... D 4

PIERRE KOENIG
French Junior Welterweight
1977
Mar. 26—Joel Leprodhomme, Argenteuil ...... KO by 5
May   13—Biase Casoria, Paris .... KO by 6
Oct.   8—Biase Casoria, Argenteuill .... D 6
Nov. 12—Jean Pierre Moreau, Blois .... D 6
Nov. 25—Christian Garcia, Mont Marson ...... KO by 4
1978
Jan. 21—Joel Moulin, Argenteuil .... L 6
Feb. 11—Arthur Fogeiro, Tolosa .... L 6
Mar. 11—Joel Leprodhomme, Troyes .... L 6
May   11—Claude Lancastre, Paris .... KO by 1
Nov. 25—Jean Michel Iger, Brest .... L 6
1979
Feb.   2—Eric Caposella, La Louviere .... L 6
Apr. 14—Jean Jacques Benchetrit, Nice ...... KO by 6
May   12—Jean Pierre Maoreau, Dhuizon .... L 8
June   7—William Collet, Paris .... L 6
Nov. 24—Mohamed Bouziani, St. Trond .... L 6
1980
Jan. 19—Sona Kabore, Argenteuil .... L 4
Mar. 15—Joel Moulin, Blois .... L 6

PATRICK KOHLI
South African Lightweight
1970
Oct. 16—Boyce Maleki, Athlone .... L 4
1971
Mar.   4—Dinah Radebe, Langa .... W
Mar.   5—May Jacobs, Athlone .... KO 6
June 19—Wallace v.d. Haar, Cape Town .... KO 1
Sept. 22—Victor Siko, Cape Town .... W 8
Sept. 30—Bashew Sibaca, Cape Town .... L 6
Dec.   7—L. Dukashe, Cape Town .... W 6
1972
Apr. 26—Victor Siko, Athlone .... KO 6
Oct. 31—James Jacobs, Langa .... W 8
1973
Mar.   3—Aubrey Peta, Port Elizabeth .... KO by 5
Oct. 20—Victor Mpiyakhe, Port Elizabeth .... W 6
1974
(Inactive)
1975
Nov.   3—Boswell Zono, Guguletu .... L 6
1976
Jan. 29—Welile Dyantyi, Guguletu .... W 8
Mar.   1—Xhanti Singaphi, Guguletu .... W 8
1977
Mar. 19—Vuyisile Ntunzi, Mbekweni .... W 8
Dec. 10—Tsietsi Maretloane, East London .... W 10
1978
Apr. 29—Evans Gwiji, Cape Town .... L 8
July 31—Cecil Baatjies, Cape Town .... L 6
Nov. 25—Chief Masemola, Paarl .... W 6
Dec. 18—Sazi Xamlashe, Goodwood .... W 6
1979
June 21—Tsietsie Maretloane, Cape Town .... L 6
Nov. 12—Guy Ratazayo, Cape Town .... KO by 3
Dec. 19—Sipho Mange, Cape Town .... KO by 4
1980
Oct. 15—Sam Williams, Cape Town .... L 6

THEUNIS KOK
South African Light Heavyweight
1978
Feb. 27—William Mandyu, Durban .... KO 3
Mar. 11—Johan Nel, Newcastle .... KO 1
Dec. 15—Jackson Hlongwane, Durban .... KO 2
1979
Apr. 25—Bruce McIntyre, Durban .... W 6
Sept. 1—Smiley Giesing, Empangeni .... KO 1
Sept. 14—Vedat Akova, Durban .... KO 6
Oct. 20—Mervin Smit, Pretoria .... KO 1
Dec.   1—Martin Barnard, Johannesburg .... KO 1
1980
Feb.   4—Dwight Braxton, Durban .... KO by 10

IDRISSA KONATE
French Middleweight
1975
Jan. 10—Maurice Renaut, Toul .... W 6
Jan. 25—Maurice Renaut, Metz .... D 6
Feb. 22—Christian Chesini, Toul .... W 6
Mar. 20—Serge Frambach, Paris .... KO 6
Apr. 17—Alfred Lagasse, Paris .... KO 4
May   17—Georges Lemmer, Toul .... W 6
Dec. 20—Jean Claude Genno, Reims .... KO 4
1976
Jan. 24—Alfred Lagasse, Reims .... KO 4
Feb.   7—King George Aidoo, Accra .... KO 12
(Won African Middleweight Title)
Apr.   2—Jacques Chinon, Dakar .... KO 4
June 12—Daniel Martin, Metz .... KO 3
Dec.   5—Pascal Zito, Metz .... L 10
Dec. 23—Shako Mamba, Kinshasa .... KO by 13
(Lost African Middleweight Title)
1977
Mar. 11—Chedk Tebourski, Metz .... KO 3
Oct.   1—Richard Ofosu, Accra .... KO by 3
1978
Jan. 12—Gerard Breton, Paris .... W 8
Apr. 27—Ayub Kalule, Randers .... KO by 7
July 21—Georg Steinherr, Rosenheim .... KO by 3
1979
Feb.   9—Romeo Malgarini, Milano .... KO 1
Mar. 15—Torben Anderson, Copenhagen .... L 6
May   5—Jean Marie Emebe, YaoUnde .... KO by 3
May   18—Jacques Chinon, Periguex .... KO by 8
1980
Jan. 11—Pierre Joly, Tarbes .... L 8
Mar. 28—Nicola Cirelli, Rome .... KO by 7
Dec.   6—Rufino Angulo, Villeneuve .... KO by 4

WINNERTON KONDILE
South African Bantamweight
1976
Apr. 28—Reuben Matewu, Guguletu .... L 6
1977
Mar. 19—Rothwell Matsha, Mbekweni .... W 4
May   30—Reginald Peters, Goodwood .... W 4
1978
June   1—Alfred Mangxola, Goodwood .... KO 3
Sept. 9—Dolly Bangiso, East London .... W 4
Nov. 25—Fundisile Kralo, Paarl .... W 4
Dec. 18—Pillay Duiker, Goodwood .... W 6
1979
Apr. 14—Daluxolo Tyekana, Goodwood .... D 4
1980
Jan. 14—Daniel Skalika, Cape Town .... W 4
Feb.   8—Monde Mpulampula, Cape Town .... D 6
Apr.   5—Monde Mpulampula, East London .... L 6
May   12—Matata Plaatjies, Cape Town .... L 4

RUDI KOOPMANS
Dutch Light Heavyweight
Born: January 30, 1948
1972
Dec.   8—Raffaele Massei, Koeln .... KO 1
1973
Feb.   2—Claude Clerget, Kiel .... KO 4
Feb. 16—Alfred Fries, Koeln .... KO 4
Mar.   9—Sule Adisa, Lubeck.................... KO 2
May   24—Burhan Yesilbag, Graz .... W 6
Oct. 26—Franklin Arrindel, Cologne .... KO 2
Nov.   9—Jojo Melis, Berlin .... KO 1
Nov. 17—Wilhelm Janco, Frankfurt .... KO 4
1974
Feb. 20—Daniel Makre, Berlin .... KO 8
May   14—Daniel Martin, Berlin................. W 8
1975
Jan. 31—Jaroslav Travnik, Hamburg............. KO 5
Mar. 18—Arpad Majai, Vienna .... KO 4
Oct. 31—Burhan Yesilbag, Cologne .... KO 1
Dec.   8—Peter Scheibner, The Hague .... W 10
1976
Feb. 18—Clement Tsinza, Scheveningen, Holland... W 10
Mar. 27—Daniel Martin, Amsterdam .... KO 2
Apr. 12—Oscar Angus, Rotterdam............... WF 3
Apr. 26—Oscar Angus, Amsterdam .... W 8
May   21—Jan Magdziarz, Rotterdam .... KO 2
Sept. 18—Carlos Marks, Berlin .... W 10
Oct. 30—Joe Oke, Groningen .... KO 4
Dec. 13—Frankie Lucas, Durban .... WF 7
1977
Feb. 20—Bunny Sterling, Rotterdam .... W 10
Sept. 10—Gregory Downes, Scheveningen .... KO 4
Oct. 10—Delime, Rotterdam .... W 10
1978
Jan. 12—Young McEwan, Rotterdam............. KO 2

Feb.	15—Aldo Traversaro, Rotterdam	D 15
	(European Light Heavyweight Title)	
May	29—Leo Kakolewicz, Rotterdam	KO 8
Sept.	16—Nat Gates, Heerenveen	KO 10
	1979	
Jan.	8—Melvin Mott, Rotterdam	W 8
Mar.	—Aldo Traversaro	W 12
	(European Light Heavyweight Title)	
May	28—Robert Amory, Netherlands	KO 10
	(European Light Heavyweight Title)	
Nov.	5—Hocine Tafer, Rotterdam	D 12
	(EBU Light Heavyweight Title)	
	1980	
Jan.	28—Ennio Cometti, Rotterdam	W 12
	(Retained European Light Heavyweight Title)	
Apr.	1—Tony Dowling, Rotterdam	KO 1
	(Retained European Light Heavyweight Title)	
July	12—Fred Serres, Luxembourg	W 12
	(Retained European Light Heavyweight Title)	

JOSEF KOSSMANN
German Junior Middleweight

	1976	
Dec.	10—Mehmet Cakal, Pahdule	KO by 3
	1977	
Mar.	25—Georg Steinherr, Bremen	KO by 3
June	11—Karl Heinz, Sitterswald	L 4
Sept.	21—Wolfgang Lueger, Frankfurt	D 6
Oct.	16—Juergen Gries, Hamburg	KO by 3
	1978	
Mar.	18—Alfred Fries, Uetersen	L 4
May	19—Helmuth Baumann, Essen	L 4
June	20—Erwin Heiber, Morsbach	L 6
Oct.	14—Giampaolo Piras, Koblenz	W 10
Nov.	4—Juergen Gries, Friedewald	L 8
Dec.	15—Giampaolo Piras, Asbach	W 10
Dec.	19—Georges Lemmer, Duesseldorf	D 6
	1979	
Jan.	27—Francisco Panos, Koblenz	W 6
Mar.	17—Claude Kalanda, Koblenz	D 8
Mar.	24—Fritz Krenslehner, Neustadt	L 8
Apr.	6—Fritz Krenslehner, Waldhofen	L 6
June	16—Giampaolo Piras, Koblenz	W 8
July	11—Rudy Robles, Las Vegas	KO by 4
Sept.	8—Nazif Biberovic, Waldhofen	D 8
Sept.	16—Rudgier Bitteeling, Koblenz	L 8
Oct.	20—Esperno Postl, Gansbacher	L 6
Nov.	15—Otto Zinoeder, Eggenburg	L 8
Nov.	26—Alex Blanchard, Rotterdam	KO by 1
	1980	
Feb.	22—Rudiger Bitterling, Dusseldorf	L 6
Mar.	22—Andre Mongelema, Friedewald	KO by 6

DIDIER KOWALSKI
French Lightweight

	1974	
Nov.	21—Claude Lormeau, Paris	W 6
	1975	
Feb.	13—Pascal Real Martin, Paris	KO by 4
Mar.	15—Frans Meganck, Conde sur Escant	W 6
May	25—Christian Lancery, Quievrechian	W 6
Dec.	6—Ali Messaoud, Conde	W 6
	1976	
Jan.	24—Pascal Real Martin, Grenoble	KO by 5
Feb.	7—Dominque Cella, Conde sue Escaut	KO 1
Feb.	19—Saladin Tebessi, Paris	KO 4
Feb.	28—Ali Messaoud, Joef France	W 8
Mar.	12—Hu Bong, Douai	KO 1
Apr.	1—Jean Parrie Barrie, Conde	L 6
Apr.	10—Jean Pierre Moreau, Blois	LF 4
Apr.	22—Paul Rourre, Fresnes	W 8
Oct.	10—Pietro Marselli, Geneva	D 6
Oct.	23—Pierre Petit, Conde	NC 7
	1977	
Jan.	8—Jean Michel Vantauraux, Conde.	KO 5
Feb.	12—Jean Claude Tellier, Conde	KO 3
Apr.	9—Claude Viard, St Etienne	W 8
Apr.	16—Jean Marie Cotinaut, Noux Les Mines	KO by 2
Apr.	23—Gerard Bok, Rotterdam	KO 6
Oct.	8—Carlos Foldes, Conde sur Escaut.	W 10
	1978	
Jan.	7—Daniel Leterme, Code Sur Escaut	W 8
Feb.	27—Christian Garcia, Paris	KO 3
Mar.	24—Alain Le Fol, Maubege	KO 9
Apr.	28—Andre Holyk, Villeurbanne	KO by 9
	(French Lightweight Title)	
Nov.	4—Arthur Fogeiro, Marly	KO 3
	1979	
Jan.	13—Arthur Fogueiro, Lille	KO 3
	(French Lightweight Title)	
Mar.	11—Rene Martin, Maubege	KO by 3
Apr.	21—Real Martin, Denain	KO 3
	(French Lightweight Title)	

June	15—Daniel Bellantonio, Valenciennes	KO 3
	(French Lightweight Title)	
Dec.	14—George Cotin, St. Amand	L 12
	(French Lightweight Title)	
	1980	
Mar.	8—Bouchiba Messaoud, Conde sur Escaut	KO 1
Apr.	26—Georges Cotin, Lille	KO 5
	(Won French Lightweight Title)	

PUMA KOYA
Japanese Flyweight

	1975	
May	19—Kimio Furesawa, Tokyo	L 10
Aug.	23—Kazunori Tenryu, Ito City	KO by 6
	1976	
Mar.	23—Yukimitsu Kondo, Nagoya	L 10
May	4—Shoji Warabino, Tokyo	W 10
Sept.	23—Ryuji Iwamoto, Tokyo	W 10
Nov.	23—Yukimitsu Kondo, Tokyo	KO 7
	1977	
May	15—Kenji Daruma, Tokyo	W 10
June	15—Kazunori Tenryu, Tokyo	L 10
	(Japanese Junior Flyweight Title)	
Aug.	29—Shoji Oguma, Tokyo	KO by 5
Nov.	16—Yoshinao Ohfu, Nagoya City	W 10
	1978	
Feb.	27—Kazunori Tenryu, Tokyo	L 10
	(Japanese Junior Flyweight Title)	
June	20—Shigeo Nakajima, Tokyo	L 10
Sept.	25—Shoji Oguma, Shizueka City	L 10
	1979	
Aug.	23—Keisuke Yuguchi, Tokyo	KO 2
	1980	
Jan.	29—Masaharu Inami, Tokyo	L 10
Apr.	20—Tadashi Tomori, Tokyo	L 10

MAIK KROL
Dutch Heavyweight

	1980	
May	5—Bernard Antone, Rotterdam	KO 2
May	19—Hans Michel, Rotterdam	KO 1

LAWRENCE KRUNE
South African Junior Flyweight

	1977	
May	31—Ntsikelela Kato, Queenstown	W 6
June	11—Monde Mpulampula, East London	L 6
Sept.	3—Thozamile Gxabeka, Queenstown	KO 2
Nov.	19—Dolly Bangiso, East London	W 4
	1978	
Mar.	4—Dolly Bangiso, King Williamstown	W 4
July	8—Elliot Zondi, East London	KO 9
Sept.	9—Thembisile Ngxingolo, East London	W 6
	1979	
May	26—Thembisile Ngxingole, King Williamstown	W disq. 1
July	7—Monde Mpulampula, East London	L 6
Sept.	3—Monde Mpulampula, Zwelitsha	KO by 3
	1980	
Feb.	2—Godfrey Nkate, Virginia	L 12
	(For South African Junior Flyweight Title)	
July	26—Reuben Matewu, King Williamstown	KO 2
	(Won Cape Junior Flyweight Title)	
Nov.	8—Tamsanga Sogcwe, East London	L 10
	(Lost Cape Junior Flyweight Title)	

KEIZO KUREBAYASHI
Japanese Junior Lightweight

	1980	
Jan.	24—Tenyu Maruki, Nagoya	KO by 6
Apr.	3—Yoshihiro Hattori, Nara	KO 1

EIJIRO KURUMA
Japanese Flyweight

	1979	
Nov.	22—Kazumi Sato, Tokyo	D 8
	1980	
Mar.	18—Shoji Okubo, Shiga	W 8
June	1—Ken Sogo, Kochi City	KO 8

MITSUO KUSHIKINO
Japanese Welterweight

	1979	
Jan.	8—Norboru Kokida, Osaka	KO 1
Feb.	26—Tarzan Tobaru, Tokyo	KO 8
Nov.	9—Chung-hae Hwang, Seoul	KO by 9
	1980	
Feb.	4—Hirofumi Sawada, Osaka	KO 4
Mar.	30—Yohi Arai, Osaka	L 10

338

DANIEL LABUSCHAGNE
South African Lightweight
1978

May	26—Phanuel Mosoane, Johannesburg	KO	2
Aug.	21—Victor Harris, Welkom	KO	1

1979

Apr.	7—Ernest Moledi, Vereeniging	L	4
Apr.	28—Aladin Stevens, Johannesburg	L	4

1980

Feb.	4—John Lutchanna, Johannesburg	D	6
Mar.	1—Thomas Tsotetsi, Ermelo	KO	1
Mar.	29—Aladin Stevens, Johannesburg	KO by	2
Dec.	19—Prince Choko, Welkom	W	4

SALVATORE LACONI
Italian Flyweight
Born: July 27, 1948, Cagliari
1972

July	14—Grazietto Soro, Arezo	KO by	5
Dec.	8—Filippo Belvedere, Pordenone	L	6

1973

Jan.	26—David Natta, Cantu	L	6
Mar.	10—Franco Buglione, Nocera	L	6
May	21—Mario De Prosperis, Cagliari	KO	4
June	28—Luigi Paravati, Novara	D	6
Nov.	11—Franco Buglione, Cagliari	L	6
Dec.	5—Franco Buglione, Cagliari	L	6

1974

Jan	11—Rino Ferrari, Milano	L	6
Apr	24—Angelo Spano, Alghero	L	6
Aug.	8—Franco Buglione, Terlizzi	L	8
Sept.	6—Angelo Spano, Thiesi	KO	1
Sept.	28—Luigi Paravati, Cabras	KO	2
Nov.	6—Guido Luttazzi, Cagliari	W	6
Dec.	7—Filippo Belvedere, Cagliari	W	8

1975

Apr.	4—Franco Sperati, Milan	L	8
June	21—Tarcisio Boi, Cagliari	D	8
July	25—Claudio Tanda, Cagliari	KO by	2
Nov.	8—Guido Luttazzi, Cagliari	W	6
Dec.	19—Claudio Tanda, Cagliari	L	4

1976

Jan.	30—Filippi Belvedere, Calairi	W	8
Mar.	5—Santo Medici, Sassari	D	8
May	7—Rino Ferrari, Cagiari	L	6
June	12—Filippo Belvedere, Santa Teresa	W	6
Aug.	13—Ignazio Fara, Alghero	LF	3
Sept.	10—Iganzio Fara, Cagliari	L	6
Nov.	26—Mario Oliva, Milano	L	6

1977

Feb.	12—Santo Medici, Piedimonte Matese	L	4
Mar.	6—Dominique Cesari, Aix	L	8
Apr.	22—Alfredo Mulas, Faenzo	L	6
Aug.	13—Santo Medici, Groseebo	W	8
Nov.	4—Gavino Luciano, Cagliari	W	6
Dec.	2—Luigi Paravati, Siniscola	D	6

1978

Apr.	27—Antonio Galletta, Bologna	L	6
July	1—Giovanni Camputaro, Cagliari	L	12
	(Italian Flyweight Title)		
Nov.	3—Valerio Nati, Flori	KO by	3

1979

Mar.	4—Pablo Castrovilli, San Remo	KO by	4
Apr.	18—Pablo Castrovilli, Torino	KO by	2
Dec.	28—Giovanni Camputaro, Agerela	LF	4

1980

Feb.	8—Dominique Piedeleu, Caen	L	4
Feb.	29—Mario Bitetto, Seregno	L	8
Apr.	11—Andrea Dore, Sassari	KO by	1
May	22—Giampiero Pinna, Bologna	ND	5

DANIELE LAGHI
Italian Heavyweight
1977

Oct.	28—Alfredo Mulas, Faenza	KO	6
Dec.	2—Tony Oudina, Lugo	KO	2

1978

Jan.	27—Jean Pierre Leseigneur, Faenza	W	6
Feb.	10—Antimo Tescione, Lugo Romagna	KO	5
Apr.	7—Leopoldo Centorrino, Faenza	D	6
June	7—Robert Desnouck, Faenza	W	6
Dec.	1—Bruno Polloni, Faenza	KO	1

1979

Feb.	23—Angelo Visini, Modena	KO	4
Apr.	13—Augusto Dal Monte, Forli	W	6
Oct.	11—Augusto Dal Monte, Faenza	KO	4
Nov.	30—Orazio Alexci, Forli	KO	2

1980

Mar.	15—Fausto Constantino, Forli	W	6

KIRKLAND LAING
British Welterweight
Born: June 20, 1954
1975

Apr.	14—Joe Hannaford, Nottingham	KO	2
May	12—Liam White, Nottingham	W	8
Sept.	29—Derek Simpson, Nottingham	W	8
Nov.	25—Oscar Angus, London	W	6

1976

Jan.	19—Terry Schofield, Nottingham	W	8
Mar.	2—Charlie Cooper, Southend	W	8
Apr.	13—Mike Manley, Southend	W	8
May	18—John Laine, Nottingham	KO	3
Sept.	22—Harry Watson, London	KO	5
Oct.	11—Jim Moore, Nottingham	KO	2
Nov.	22—Jim Montague, Birmingham	W disq.	7

1977

Jan.	11—John Smith, London	W	10
Mar.	8—Peter Morris, Wolverhampton	D	10
Nov.	16—Peter Morris, London	KO	5

1978

Sept.	27—Achille (Speedy) Mitchell, Solihull	W	12

1979

Apr.	4—Henry Rhiney, Birmingham	KO	10
	(British Welterweight Title)		
Nov.	6—Des Morrison, Kensington	W	8

1980

Jan.	22—Salvo Nucifero, Kensington	KO	6
Feb.	19—Colin Ward, London	KO	5
Apr.	1—Colin Jones, London	KO by	9
	(Lost British Welterweight Title)		
May	8—George Walker, Solihull	W	8
June	3—Curtis Taylor, London	KO	7

JOSEPH LALA
South African Welterweight
1977

Nov.	26—Ephraim Mabena, Bloemfontein	W	4

1978

Mar.	31—Samuel Motake, Bloemfontein	W	6
Aug.	12—Ben Mutle, Bloemfontein	KO	7

1979

Feb.	16—David Kgotsane, Springs	W	6
Mar.	5—Samuel Tshabalala, Welkom	W	6
Mar.	30—Morris Mohloai, Springs	L	8
Oct.	5—John Khooe, Bloemfontein	KO	3
Nov.	9—Simon Mokoena, Bloemfontein	KO	4

1980

May	5—David Kalako, Welkom	W	6
Aug.	29—David Kambule, Sebokeng	L	10
Nov.	21—Peter Mgojo, Sebokeng	L	6

JOE LALLY
British Middleweight
1974

Apr.	17—George Salmon, Manchester	W	6
May	9—George Salmon, Liverpool	L	8
Nov.	18—Tony La Cruz, Mayfair	KO	2

1975

Jan.	6—Oscar Angus, Hemel Hempstead	KO	1
Apr.	1—Mick Hussey, Liverpool	KO	4
May	13—Joe Gregory, Liverpool	KO	3
July	1—Batman Austin, Southend	L	8
July	14—Alec Tompkins, London	L	8

1976
(Inactive)

1977

Jan.	20—Carl Speare, Liverpool	L	8
June	14—Errol McKenzie, Southend	KO by	5
Sept.	8—Eddie Smith, Liverpool	L	8
Oct.	6—Brian Gregory, Liverpool	W	8
Oct.	31—Pat Brogan, Nantwich	L	8
Nov.	10—Dave Davies, Liverpool	D	8
Dec.	8—Charlie Malarkey, Liverpool	KO	8

1978

Feb.	1—Owen Robinson, Evesham	L	8
Apr.	27—Brian Gregory, Doncaster	KO	8
May	25—Per Mullertz, Copenhagen	W	6
Aug.	10—Torben Anderson, Glygore	L	4
Oct.	2—Billy Lauder, Liverpool	L	8
Oct.	24—Prince Rodney, Blackpool	KO by	5
Nov.	27—Dave Davies, Liverpool	KO	8
Dec.	2—Adoni Amana, Dilkar	KO by	5

1979

Mar.	1—Robbie Davies, Liverpool	KO by	4

339

1980
Mar. 13—Billy Hill, Birkenhead .... D 8
Mar. 27—Joe Jackson, Liverpool .... W 8
Apr. 14—Earl Edwards, Manchester .... L 8
Apr. 21—Carl Daly, London .... D 8
June 12—Jimmy Harrington, Cambridge ...... KO by 3

ALAN LAMB
British Junior Welterweight
1979
Oct. 17—Gary Ball, Lewisham .... KO 6
Nov. 19—Ray Ross, Lewisham .... KO 3
Dec. 20—Dave Taylor, Queensway .... KO 3
1980
Apr. 15—Frank McCord, Blackpool .... KO 1
June 11—Kerry Collins, Morecambe .... W 6
July 14—Granville Allen, London .... KO 5
Sept. 4—Messaoud Bouschiba, Morecambe ...... KO 1

JEAN LUC LAMI
French Middleweight
1977
Feb. 12—Daniel Bouleaux, Argenteuil .... L 6
Mar. 26—Justin M'Foudi, Argenteuil .... KO by 4
June 11—Marc Petit, Creil .... L 6
Nov. 5—Ignacio Gorostidi, Bilbao .... D 6
Nov. 19—Christian Chesini, Vandoeuvre .... L 8
Nov. 26—Michel Pagani, Calais .... KO by 4
1978
Feb. 4—Jean Claude Terlon, Villers .... D 6
Apr. 15—Jacky Bauer, Strasburgo .... D 6
May 20—Alfred Kohler, Bern .... D 6
Sept. 14—Andre Genasi, Paris .... D 4
Oct. 13—Pierre Joly, Tolosa .... L 6
Dec. 16—Roland Bayens, Kalken .... L 6
1979
May 28—Alex Blanchard, Amsterdam .... KO by 2
1980
Jan. 25—Sergio Bosio, La Louviere .... L 6
Feb. 17—Philippe Truchelut, Maubeuge .... W 6
Apr. 19—Claudio Bosio, Belgium .... L 6
Nov. 8—Claudio Bosio, St. Truiden .... D 6

CLAUDE LANCASTRE
French Welterweight
1977
Dec. 5—Ronald Zenon, Paris .... KO by 3
1978
Jan. 16—Dragon Tadic, Paris .... KO 2
May 11—Pierre Koenig, Paris .... KO 1
June 5—Serge Malapris, Paris .... KO 2
1979
Jan. 20—Jack Peraire, S. Maur .... KO 4
Feb. 22—Maurice Renaud, Paris .... KO 3
Mar. 26—Tijani Sidibe, Paris .... KO by 6
June 7—Lucien Gampo, Paris .... KO 3
June 21—Gilles Elbilia, Alfortville .... KO 5
Nov. 15—Hughes Samo, Paris .... W 8
1980
Mar. 8—Dennis Price, St. Maur .... W 8

HORST LANG
German Light Heavyweight
1972
Aug. 11—Manfred Ackers, Krefeld .... W 4
Nov. 3—Manfred Ackers, Krefeld .... D 4
Nov. 10—James Helwig, Koeln .... L 6
Dec. 8—Bert Nikkelen-Kuyper, Koeln .... KO 4
Dec. 12—Ferenc Kristofosak, Wien .... W 4
1973
Feb. 16—Arno Pryx, Koeln .... L 6
May 4—Manfred Ackers, Krefeld .... W 4
May 13—Karsten Honhold, Kiel .... KO by 4
Aug. 31—Bernard August, Lubeck .... KO by 1
Nov. 16—Jean Pierre Coopmans, Ghent .... KO by 3
Dec. 15—Christian Poncelet, Sedan .... L 10
1974
Feb. 2—Christian Mossoux, Eupen .... W 8
Mar. 15—Hartmut Sasse, Cologne .... KO by 2
Apr. 27—Gerrie Bodenstein, Port Elizabeth .... KO by 7
Nov. 9—Armand Xhonneux, Liegi .... W 8
1975
July 12—Mate Parlov, Arenzano .... KO by 1
Oct. 11—Christian Mossoux, Eupen .... D 8
Dec. 27—Arno Pryx, Bucholz .... KO by 7
1976
Mar. 27—Kallie Knoetze, Pretoria .... KO by 3
May 24—Arno Pryx, Munich .... D 8
Oct. 29—Avenamar Peralta, Cologne .... KO by 2
Dec. 12—Detleff Naseband, Berlin .... D 6
1977
Feb. 12—Freddy De Kerpel, Liegi .... L 10
Mar. 1—Gerald Bois, Sedan .... L 8

340

Apr. 29—Rudiger Schmidtke, Munich .... L 8
May 7—Fernand De Ruyter, Antwerp .... L 8
May 28—Vasco Faustino, Koln .... W 8
Sept. 10—Rudy Gauwe, Zele .... KO by 4
1978
Jan. 7—Albert Syben, Grivegnee .... KO by 3
Feb. 18—Gregory Downes, Kiel .... KO by 2
May 6—Karsten Honhold, Luebeck .... L 8
Oct. 15—Georg Butzbach, Hamburg .... KO by 9
Dec. 7—Vedat Akova, Luebeck .... L 6
Dec. 25—Fred Serres, Esch .... L 6
1979
Apr. 6—Ralf Hertling, Luebeck .... W 4
Apr. 22—Uwe Meinicke, Hamburg .... L 6
June 29—Pierre Kabussu, Esch sur Alzette .... L 6
Dec. 7—Harry Friedel Luebeck .... KO by 1
1980
Feb. 22—Claudio Cassanelli, Sassuolo .... KO by 3
Apr. 19—Roberto Bosio, Belgium .... KO by 4
Dec. 5—Hans Ginborn, Koln .... W 4

STAR LANTAPAN
Filipino Lightweight
1979
Sept. 29—Mar Simajen, San Pablo City .... D 10
Oct. 19—Dony Soriano, Quezon City .... D 10
1980
Feb. 1—Pete Alfrez, Manila .... KO 4
Mar. 14—George Tam, Manila .... D 10

MOHAMED TITI LARBI
Spanish Lightweight
1978
Apr. 8—Tony Martin, Gijon .... KO 3
1979
Jan. 6—Enrique R. Cal, Aviles .... L 6
Mar. 3—German Nunez, Aranda .... L 6
Apr. 7—German Nunez, Palencia .... D 6
Apr. 20—Luis de la Sagra, Madrid .... L 6
Apr. 28—Raton Rodriguez, Santander .... NC 4
May 5—Enrique R. Cal, Ribadebella .... L 4
June 15—Antonio Barreto, S. Cruz .... D 6
July 14—Carlos M. Rodriguez, Pontevedre .... L 6
Aug. 17—Juan Barros, Madrid .... D 6
Sept. 15—Jose Maria Guervos, Aviles .... D 6
Oct. 6—Amalio Galan, Mondragon .... L 6
Oct. 27—Jose A. M. Mateos, Leon .... L 4
Nov. 3—Vicente Hernando, Burgos .... L 4
Nov. 9—Francisco D. Pena, Las Palmas .... L 4
Dec. 15—Francisco D. Pena, Las Palmas .... L 4
1980
Jan. 12—Jose Garcia, Zaragoza .... L 8
Nov. 28—Franco Canini, Campione .... L 6

DAVY LARMOUR
Irish Bantamweight
1977
July 30—Jimmy Bott, Derry .... KO 1
1978
Feb. 13—John Feeney, Walwroth .... KO by 4
Mar. 14—George Sutton, Belfast .... KO by 6
May 11—Alan Oag Belfast .... W disq. 1
June 19—Johnny Owen, Caerphilly .... KO by 7
Oct. 27—Neil McLaughlin, Belfast .... W 10
1979
Feb. 19—George Sutton, Belfast .... W 8
Apr. 5—Larry Richards, Belfast .... KO 6
Nov. 26—Dave Smith, Belfast .... W 10
1980
Feb. 25—Gilbert Garza, Belfast .... W 8
May 27—Isaac Vega, Belfast .... W 10
Sept. 22—Sammy Sims, Belfast .... L 8

DAMIANO LASSANDRO
Spanish Junior Middleweight
Born: Dec. 18, 1947
1972
Nov. 25—Mario Petrillo, Pesaro .... KO 3
Dec. 16—Franco Indelicato, Lunano .... WF 2
1973
Jan. 12—Achille Fortuna, Pesaro................ W 6
Feb. 24—Celestino Uteh, Pesaro.................. W 6
Mar. 15—Lorenzo Nardillo, Milan .... KO 6
Apr. 7—Lorenzo Pontiroli, Pesaro .... KO 8
May 26—Mario Favotto, Bari .... KO 8
Aug. 4—Salah Arafa, Viareggio .... KO 2
Sept. 28—Dum Dum Pacheco, Sarzano .... KO 2
Oct. 13—Young Griffo, Pesaro .... KO 1
Nov. 10—Adriano Rodriguez, Pesaro .... W 8
1974
Jan. 4—Guerrino Cipriani, Milano .... KO 1
Feb. 8—Walter Guernieri, Milano............... D 8
Nov. 22—Armstrong Vasco, Pesaro .... W 8
Dec. 20—Pascal Zito, Ancona .... KO 3

1975

Mar.	1—Gabriele Lazzari, Pesaro	KO	5
Apr.	19—Mario Coiro, Pesaro	KO	3
June	6—Germano Valsecchi, Milan	KO	7
Aug.	14—Jose Luis Duran, Rimini	KO by	3
Nov.	5—Antonio Castelini, Pesaro	W disq.	4

(Italian Middleweight Title)

1976

Feb.	6—Gianni Mingard, Pesero	W	8
Apr.	21—Antonino Castellini, Palermo	KO by	4
Sept.	25—Mushapata Kubangu, Pesaro	KO	4
Nov.	3—Aldo Bentini, Pesaro	W	2

1977

| Jan. | 19—Ayb Kalule, Copenhagen | KO by | 4 |
| May | 28—Aldo Bentini, Pesaro | KO | 11 |

(For Italian Junior Middleweight Title)

| July | 8—Frank Reiche, Bremen | KO by | 5 |
| Oct. | 22—Walter Guernieri, Pesaro | W | 12 |

(Italian Junior Middleweight Title)

1978

| Mar. | 17—Roy Kaba, Milan | KO | 7 |
| June | 3—Clemente Gessi, Pesaro | KO | 2 |

(Italian Junior Middleweight Title)

July	21—Wolfgang Gans, Rosenheim	KO	2
Oct.	20—Nicola Sasenelli, Pesaro	KO	4
Dec.	16—Georges Warusfel, Pesaro	W	10

1979

| Oct. | 27—Glenn McEwan, Pesaro | KO | 2 |

1980

| Feb. | 13—Marijan Benes, Pesaro | D | 12 |
| May | 14—Frank Wissenbach, Munich | KO by | 2 |

BILLY LAUDER
Scottish Middleweight
1977

Sept.	19—Dave Merrell, Glasgow	W	6
Oct.	24—Vic Jackson, London	W	8
Nov.	24—Brian Gregory, Doncaster	W	8
Dec.	6—Joe Oke, Leeds	W	8

1978

Jan.	23—Ken Jones, Aberavon	L	6
Feb.	13—Kenny Feehan, Reading	KO	2
Feb.	27—Owen Robinson, Glasgow	W	8
Apr.	10—Joey Mack, Birmingham	KO by	2
May	8—Charlie Malarkey, Glasgow	W	10
June	20—Joe Oke, London	W	8
Oct.	2—Joe Lally, Liverpool	KO by	6

1979

Feb.	19—Gerry Young, Belfast	W	8
Mar.	19—Harry Watson, Glasgow	W	8
June	4—Chris Walker, London	W	8
June	28—Torben Anderson, Randers	L	6
Sept.	17—Harry Watson, Glasgow	W	8
Oct.	22—Steve Hopkins, Mayfair	KO by	5
Nov.	27—Gerry Young, Belfast	W	8

1980

Jan.	28—John Smith, Glasgow	W	8
Apr.	14—Henry Cooper, Motherwell	W	8
Apr.	28—Alex Blanchard, Amsterdam	KO by	4
Oct.	20—Malcolm Heath, Glasgow	W	6

AUGUSTO LAURI
Italian Junior Middleweight
1974

| Dec. | 26—Armin Rindlisbacher, Bern | L | 6 |

1975

Jan.	10—Guglielmo Caldera, Milan	W	4
Feb.	15—Paolo Zanusso, Pordenone	W	6
Feb.	28—Adriano Rosati, Novara	W	6
Apr.	12—Paolo Zanusso, Monfalcone	L	6
May	31—Remo Costa, Tolentino	W	6
June	20—Paolo Zanusso, Udine	L	6
July	25—Giovanni Caldera, Venegono	D	6
Sept.	5—Guglielmo Caldera, Robbio	L	6
Nov.	8—Mario Calzone, Macerata	KO by	4

1976

Mar.	5—Angelo D'Isidoro, Milan	KO by	4
Apr.	16—Frank Hohl, Udine	W	8
May	14—Angelo Tomasini, Brescia	KO	4
June	4—Remo Costa, La Spezia	L	6
July	9—Ciro Seta, Siano	L	6
July	24—Ali Kaja, Venegono	L	6
Oct.	1—Adriano Rosati, Foligno	L	6
Oct.	2—Timoteo Bonnizzoni, Novara	L	6
Nov.	11—Alois Carmeliet, Zele	D	6
Dec.	9—Jorgen Hansen, Copenhagen	L	8

1977

Jan.	9—Gaetano Sguazza, Como	KO	2
Feb.	4—Horacio Ruiz, Bilbao	L	6
Feb.	25—Pierino Meraviglia, Venegono	W	8
Mar	25—Vittorio Tamburini, Udine	D	6
Apr.	23—Pierangelo Pira, Rimini	L	6
May	27—Giuseppe Di Padova, Brescia	D	6
June	11—Giuseppe Di Padova, Padova	L	6

July	23—Giancarlo Serangeli, Venegono	W	8
Sept.	17—Vincenzo Moruzzi, Rome	L	8
Nov.	11—Alois Carmeliet, Zele	L	10

1978

Feb.	10—Daniele Zappaterra, Saletta	L	6
Feb.	24—Luigi Martello, Rome	L	8
May	14—Luciano De Luca, Pescara	D	6
May	16—Timoteo Bonizzoni, Crema	KO by	5
July	21—Giuseppe Russi, Rosenheim	D	6
Aug.	5—Edson Lima, Ascoli Piceno	L	8
Oct.	20—Alain Ruocco, Tolone	KO by	8

1979

(Inactive)

1980

| Feb. | 1—Ben Saad Salah, Ostia | L | 8 |

COSIMO LAVINO
Italian Junior Lightweight
1977

Feb.	23—Salvatore Morello, Faeano	KO	4
Mar.	25—Vincenzo Di Ruocco, Brindisi	KO	6
May	7—Antonio Germano, Brindisi	W	6
July	15—Domenico Condello, Sarzana	W	6
Oct.	14—Vincenzo Di Bari, Milano	W	6
Nov.	12—Giuseppe Agate, Brindisi	W	6

1978

Jan.	14—Fulvio Giacomini, Brindisi	KO	1
Feb.	25—Carlo Frassinetti, Brindisi	W	8
May	20—Jose Sanchez, Brindisi	KO by	6
July	22—Jose Sanchez, Brindisi	D	8
Sept.	14—Melquiades Da Silva, Prato	D	8

1979

| Feb. | 24—Salvatore Liscapade, Lisernia | L | 12 |

(Italian Junior Lightweight Title)

| Apr. | 14—Melquiades Da Silva, Brindisi | W | 8 |
| Dec. | 14—Aristide Pizzo, Milan | KO by | 6 |

(Italian Junior Lightweight Title)

1980

| Apr. | 6—Luigi De Rosa, Rimini | D | 8 |
| June | 28—Angelo Bizzarri, Caserta | L | 8 |

GIUSEPPE LA VITE
Italian Featherweight
1980

| Mar. | 21—Giulio Greco, Rapallo | W | 6 |
| Oct. | 24—Antonio Franca, Grosseto | W | 6 |

DANNY LAWFORD
British Light Heavyweight
1980

Jan.	21—Alek Penarski, Nottingham	KO	5
Feb.	13—Chris Lawson, London	D	8
Mar.	17—Chris Lawson, Birmingham	L	8
Mar.	24—Trevor Couttouse, London	KO	2
Apr.	28—Tony Allen, Birmingham	KO	5
Sept.	22—Bonny McKenzie, London	W	8

CHRIS LAWSON
(Previously known as DANNY MILLER)
Welsh Light Heavyweight
1978

Jan.	23—Malcolm Worthington, Aberavon	KO	2
Feb.	7—Ralph Green, Islington	KO	3
Mar.	20—Winston Cousins, Aberavon	KO	3
May	23—Bonny McKenzie, London	L	8
July	10—Trevor Kerr, Aberavon	KO	4
Sept.	18—Carl Canwell, Wolverhampton	KO by	5
Nov.	2—Steve Hill, Liverpool	KO	2
Nov.	29—Bonny McKenzie, Swansea	W	10

1979

Jan.	17—Eddie Lawson, Stoke	KO by	4
Mar.	19—Ken Jones, Haverfordwest	W	10
May	13—Carlton Benoit, Plymouth	KO by	2
Oct.	23—Alex Pernaski, Blackpool	KO	5

1980

Feb.	13—Danny Lawford, London	D	8
Mar.	17—Danny Lawford, Birmingham	W	8
Apr.	15—Tom Collins, Blackpool	KO by	4
June	18—Dennis Andries, Burslem	KO by	8
Aug.	12—Ken Jones, Gowerton	L	10

(Lost Welsh Light Heavyweight Title)

| Sept. | 22—Harry White, Wolverhampton | KO | 5 |
| Oct. | 20—Rupert Christie, Birmingham | W | 8 |

ZOLA LAWUSE
(AKA LAUSE)
South African Featherweight
1977

Apr.	2—Daluxolo Tyekana, East London	L	4
June	11—Monwabisi Kana, East London	W	6
Oct.	15—Daluxolo Tyekana, East London	L	4

1978

| Feb. | 18—Fezile Mzalazala, East London | W | 4 |

Mar.	4—Sipho Mtyeku, King Williamstown	...... W	4
July	29—Edward Genu, Queenstown	.... W	4
Oct.	21—Zandile Nukani, Queenstown	.... W	4

1979

Feb.	24—Nkosana Moss, King Williamstown	...... W	6
July	7—Mqondishi Ntshinka, East London	..... KO	3
Sept.	8—Welile Nkosinkulu, Zwelitsha	 L	6
Sept.	29—Welile Nkosinkulu, East London	..... KO by	2
Nov.	12—Joshua Plaatjies, Cape Town	 L	6

1980

Feb.	3—Herbert Plaatjies, Goodwood	 L	6
Feb.	8—Herbert Plaatjies, Cape Town	 L	6
Mar.	15—Nkosana Moss, East London	 L	10
	(For Cape Junior Featherweight Title)		
Apr.	5—Herbert Plaatjies, East London	.... W	10
	(Won Cape Featherweight Title)		

DAVE LAXEN
British Lightweight
1979

Apr.	9—Gerry Howland, Nottingham	.... W	6
Apr.	24—Steve Briers, London	.... D	6
May	13—Steve Briers, Plymouth	.... W	6
May	29—Joe Mills, London	.... KO	5
June	6—Eric Raonisi, Burslem	.... D	6
Sept.	12—Bonnet Bryan, Burslem	.... W	6
Sept.	25—Jeff Pritchard, London	 L	8
Oct.	29—Vernon Penprase, Camborne	 L	8
Dec.	4—Gary Lucas, Southend	.... D	8

1980

Jan.	28—Tim Moloney, Hove	 L	6
Feb.	5—Alec Irvine, Southend	.... D	8
Mar.	3—Steve Parker, Nottingham	.... W	6
Mar.	11—Gary Lucas, Nantwich	.... D	8
Apr.	18—Wally Stockings, Southend	 L	8
June	12—Danny Connolly, Cambridge	.... KO by	7

GABRIELE LAZZARI
Italian Light Heavyweight
Born: Feb. 2, 1951, Portomaggiore, Italy
1973

Jan.	19—Guerrino Cipriani, Milano	 L	6
Feb.	3—Daniel Letarte, Rimini	.... D	6
Mar.	17—Daniel Letarte, Rimini	.... W	6
Apr.	28—Giuseppe Panunzio, Rimini	.... D	6
May	25—Roberto Benacquista, Roma	 L	6
Oct.	4—Paul Knudsen, Randers	 L	6
Dec.	26—Ivan Matekovic, Milan	.... KO by	5

1974

Feb.	22—Giuseppe Borghi, Cantu	 L	6
Mar.	7—Thor Horngro, Oslo	.... D	4
May	22—Gino Freo, Reggio Emilia	.... N	6
June	28—Elia Bettinzoli, Lodrino	 L	8
July	19—Bortolo Cogoli, Brescia	.... N	6
Sept.	27—Paolo Vianini, Milan	.... KO	1
Nov.	8—Paolo Vianini, Milan	 L	6

1975

Jan.	24—Philo Bandu, Bruxelles	 L	8
Feb.	15—Luciano Bomben, Pordenone	.... W	8
Mar.	1—Damiano Lassandro, Pesaro	.... KO by	5
Mar.	14—Moises Fajardo, Madrid	 L	8
Mar.	28—Luciano Bomben, Udine	.... KO	5
Apr.	11—Raffaele Di Costanzo, Milan	.... D	8
May	26—Raffaele Di Costanzo, Milan	.... KO by	6
Aug.	14—Giuseppe Borghi, Asso	.... W	8
Oct.	6—Adriano Rodrigues, Zagreb	.... W	8
Nov.	21—Gianni Mingardi, Lugo Romagna	 L	8
Dec.	26—Elia Bettinzoli, Brescia	 L	8

1976

Jan.	31—Trento Facciocchi, Lucca	.... KO	8
Feb.	13—Jose Luis Duran, Milan	.... D	8
Mar.	12—Trento Facciocchi, Milan	.... D	8
Apr.	2—Trento Facciocchi, Milan	 L	8
Oct.	22—Mariano Salamone, Bologna	.... W	8
Dec.	10—Lorenzo Nardillo, Molinella	.... W	8

1977

Jan.	19—Jose Luis Duran, San Remo	.... KO by	2
Apr.	10—Angelo Jacopucci, Marsala	 L	8
May	13—Damiano Pellegrino, Turnin	.... KO by	4
Sept.	10—Gianni Mingardi, Ostia	.... KO	2
Sept.	21—Matteo Salvemini, Milan	.... KO by	5
Nov.	4—Trento Faciocchi, Piacenza	 L	8
Nov.	19—Gianni Filipetto, Torino	.... KO by	5

1978

Nov.	9—Guido Corpataux, Bern	 L	8

1979

Feb.	23—Roberto Felicioni, Rome	 L	8
Mar.	30—Kassongo Mukandjo, Geneve	.... KO by	6
May	4—Luciano Sordini, Rome	 L	8
June	29—Giorgio Giana, Sondrio	 L	8
July	14—Nicola Cirelli, Cerveteri	.... KO by	5
Nov.	23—Gino Freo, Pordenone	 L	6

1980

Feb.	1—Germano Apostoli, Mantova	 L	6
Mar.	14—Luciano Sordini, Rome	 L	8
Apr.	4—Andrea Sangaletti, Milan	.... W	6
Apr.	18—Richard Caramonolis, Paris	 L	6
June	14—Bruno Arati, Bern	.... KO	6
Dec.	4—Ceraro Mauriello, Rome	 L	6
Dec.	26—Walter Cevoli, Bologna	 L	6

STANLEY LEDIMO
South African Welterweight
1979

Aug.	29—Deon Van Der Poel, Bloemfontein	 L	4
Oct.	5—Godfrey Manyaniso, Bloemfontein	.... KO by	2
Dec.	8—Johannes Modise, Bloemfontein	.... W	6

1980

Mar.	8—Ezekiel Melupe, Bloemfontein	.... KO	2

JEFF LEE
British Welterweight
1979

Apr.	30—Jimmy Smith, London	.... W	6
Sept.	18—Jimmy Smith, Lewisham	.... KO	3
Oct.	17—Dave Aspil, Lewisham	.... W	6

1980

Feb.	18—Mickey Mapp, Lewisham	 L	8
Apr.	28—Mickey Mapp, Southwark	 L	8
June	11—Ian Kid Murray, Morecambe	.... W	8
Sept.	22—Ian Kid Murray, Lewisham	.... W	8

KANG-SAN LEE
Korean Bantamweight
1980

Mar.	30—Myung-An Moon, Seoul	.... D	10
	(For Korean Bantamweight Title)		

SANG-BONG LEE
Korean Bantamweight
1979

Oct.	21—Venice Borkorsor, Seoul	.... KO by	6

1980

Mar.	18—Ja-Ho Cho, Seoul	.... W	10

SEUNG-HOON LEE
Korean Flyweight
1977

July	30—Dong-Sung Park, Seoul	.... W	4
Sept.	30—Young-Shik Moon, Seoul	.... KO	1
Nov.	6—Hwan-Jin Kim, Seoul	 L	6
Dec.	20—Young-Shik Chong, Seoul	.... W	6

1978

Feb.	26—Jong-Ho Kim, Seoul	.... KO	3
Oct.	3—Man-Oh Kim, Seoul	.... W	8
Dec.	20—Young-Hwan Kim, Seoul	.... W	10
	(Won Korean Flyweight Title)		

1979

Feb.	10—Netrnoi Vorasingh, Bangkok	 L	10
Apr.	7—Peter Siscon, Pusan	.... W	10
May	15—Prudencio Cardona, Seoul	.... W	10
Sept.	29—Nari Endiguez, Seoul	.... W	10
Nov.	11—Chungcherng Borkorsor, Pusan	.... W	10
Nov.	30—Jose Tito, Seoul	.... W	10

1980

Feb.	2—Rafael Orono, Caracas	 L	15
	(For Vacant WBC Junior Bantamweight Title)		
May	9—Sung-Jun Kim, Seoul	.... W	10
July	19—Fred Ibon, Pusan	.... W	10

MICHEL LEFEBVRE
French Junior Lightweight
1971

Nov.	6—Roland Cazeaux, S. Nazaire	 L	6

1972

Jan.	20—Samuel Grunitzky, Paris	.... W	6
Feb.	3—Abdelkader Bouguetaib, Paris	 L	6
Feb.	20—Georges Fontaine, Berck	.... D	6
Mar.	25—Souleymahe Ba-Thierno, Douai	.... D	6
Apr.	1—William Turpin, Berck	.... W	6
June	2—Ahmed Touel, Berck	.... KO	2
Aug.	15—Daniel Ringuet, Berck	.... KO	2

1973

May	26—Tahar Azziz, Paris	.... W	6
Oct.	19—Luc Rudi Haeck, Gand	.... W	8

1974

Apr.	5—Souleymahe Ba-Thierno, Puteaux	.... W	8
Apr.	20—Gilbert Cohen, Crepy en Valois	.... D	6
June	1—Ernesto Miranda, St. Nazaire	.... W	8
June	22—Raymond Lebbrecht, Compiegne	 L	8

1975

Jan.	10—Isidoro Cabezas, Barcelona	.... D	8
Feb.	8—Jean Pierre Hainault, Puteaux	.... W	8
Mar.	9—Daniel Vermandere, St. Ouen	.... W	12
	(French Featherweight Championship)		

Oct. 22—Elio Cotena, Cefalu .... KO by 11
      (European Featherweight Title)
Dec. 27—Albert Amatler, Villeurbane........... L 12
      (French Featherweight Title)
1976
Mar. 12—Ramon Marichal, Madrid .... W 8
Mar. 27—Laurent Bazie, Abidjan Ivory Coast .... L 10
Apr.   2—Rodolfo Sanchez, Madrid................. L 8
May   1—Eder Jofre, Brasilia.................. KO by 3
Dec.   3—Michele Siracusa, Marseilles .... KO by 7
      (French Featherweight Title)
1977
Apr.   1—Nino Jimenez, Madrid .... W 10
Oct. 28—Roland Cazeaux, St. Nazaire.............. L 12
      (French Featherweight Title)
1978
Mar. 25—Laurent Grimbert, Berck Plage.......... W 10
May   26—Albert Amatler, Berch.................. KO 10
Oct. 27—Gerard Jacob, Creil.................. KO by 2
      (French Featherweight Title)
1979
Mar. 24—Alain Le Fol, Berck .... W 10
June   2—Cecilio Lastra, Santander .... KO by 2
Nov. 10—Patrick Goblet, Berch .... W 10
1980
Apr. 26—Charles Jurietti, Rumilly .... KO by 7
      (For French Junior Lightweight Title)

ALAIN LE FOL
French Featherweight
1975
Apr.   5—Christian Levy, Calais .... W 6
Apr. 26—Ali Issaoui Ben Moussa, Boulogne .... W 6
June   7—Gerard Jacob, Creil .... D 6
Nov. 18—Joel Moulin, Blois .... L 6
Dec. 20—Joel Moulin, Orleans .... W 6
1976
Jan. 15—Patrick Goblet, Paris .... WF 8
Feb.   5—Raymond Libbrecht, Paris .... KO 5
Feb. 21—Charles Juretti, Rumilly .... D 6
Mar. 20—Jean Pierre Meganck, Kalken .... KO 4
Apr.   3—Jean Pierre Planck, Dijon .... D 6
Apr. 23—Bouchiba Messaoud, Lokeren .... W 6
June 11—Raymond Libbrecht, Boulogne .... W 6
Oct. 16—Charles Juretti, Maubege .... L 6
1977
Jan. 22—Christian Valantine, Calais .... W 8
Mar. 12—Bouchiba Messaoud, Antwerp .... W 8
Apr.   1—Carlos Faralle, Madrid .... L 8
May   14—Alessandro Nardi, Bastia .... W 8
Nov. 12—Carlos Foldes, Boulogne sur Mer .... L 8
Nov. 18—Charles Juretti, Valence .... L 8
1978
Feb.   4—Mario Oliveira, Boulogne .... W 8
Mar. 24—Didier Kowalski, Maubege .... KO by 9
Apr. 28—Maurice Apeang, Grenoble .... L 8
May   26—Henri Kone, Berck .... L 8
July   7—Maurice Cisse, Abidjan .... KO by 6
1979
Jan. 13—Gilbert Heluin, Calais .... W 8
Mar. 24—Michel Lefebvre, Berck .... L 10
Apr. 21—Laurent Grimbert, Crepy en Valois ..... L 10
May   26—Cecilio Lastra, Santander .... L 8
      —Roland Cazeaux, St. Nazaire .... W 8
Sept. 8—Rodolfo Sanchez, Miranda del Ebro ...... L 8
Nov. 10—Jose Garcia, Bruxelles .... L 8
Dec. 10—Maurice Fico, Paris .... L 8
Dec. 26—Gianfranco Lalli, Sondrio .... L 8
1980
Jan. 21—Pat Cowdell, Wolverhampton .... L 10
Feb. 15—Albert Amatler, Villeurbanne .... L 10
Mar.   7—Natale Vezzoli, Brescia .... KO by 5
May   3—Dave Williams, St. Trond .... L 8

GEORGE LEMMER
German Middleweight
1972
Mar.   4—Daniel Jacquin, Moyeuvre .... W 6
Apr. 15—Rabah Hamdi, Moyeuvre .... L 6
June 18—Daniel Jacquin, Forseville .... W 6
1973-1974
(Inactive)
1975
May   17—Idrissa Konate, Toul .... L 6
1976
Feb. 28—Claude Worbel, Villerupt .... W 6
Apr.   9—Fred Coranson, Petit Synthe .... L 6
Apr. 24—Kader Ben Mimoun, Villerupt .... KO 4
Oct.   9—Jannick Blandin, Lannion .... L 6
Nov. 21—Jack Peraire, Villerupt .... L 6
1977
(Inactive)

1978
Feb.   4—Raymond Langewouters, Turnhout ... KO by 4
Mar. 10—Branko Barakovic, Esch .... W 8
Apr. 10—Rene Deharchies, Lalange .... D 6
Sept. 2—Olton Beltchika, Turnhout .... KO by 2
Oct. 13—Luciano DiGiacomo, Metz .... D 6
Nov.   4—Richard Rodriguez, Paris .... KO by 4
Nov. 25—Hughes Samo, Bruay .... KO by 4
Dec. 19—Joseph Kossmann, Dusseldorf .... D 6
1979
Jan. 20—Bernard Dylbaitis, Onnaing .... L 6
May   11—Kadir Yuceler, Istanbul .... L 10
1980
Mar. 28—Reiner Gutenkust, Berlin .... W 6
May   3—Roman Manziula, St. Trond .... KO by 4

TEBOHO LENTO
South African Junior Welterweight
1980
Feb.   2—Simon Nxane, Kimberley .... KO by 3
Mar.   8—Cedric Carson, Bloemfontein .... KO 2
Apr. 12—Ephraim Khuto, Ficksburg .... L 6
June 14—Joseph Molahloe, Welkom .... W 4
Aug. 23—Johannes Modise, Kimberley .... D 6

FRANCISCO LEON
(ANTONIO LEON GALAN)
Spanish Lightweight
1976
Apr. 11—J. Carabajal, Jerez .... W 6
Apr. 25—Mohamed Boumedien, Jerez............. W 6
June 12—A. Perez Velez, Jerez .... KO 5
July 31—Fernando Bermejo, Jerez .... W 6
Aug. 21—Joaquin Caravajal, Jerez.............. KO 5
Oct.   2—Juan de Dios Morales, Jerez........... W 6
Dec. 23—J. L. Fernandez Perez, Jerez.......... W 6
1977
Mar.   5—J. M. Domingo Delgado, Jerez .... W 8
Apr. 30—Julio Garcia Munox, Jerez .... KO 4
June   4—Tony Ortiz, Jerez................. KO by 7
Aug. 20—Horacio Ruiz, Jerez.................. W 12
      (Spanish Welterweight Title)
Oct.   1—Horacio Ruiz, Bilbao .... L 12
      (Spanish Welterweight Title)
1978
May   31—Juan Pena, Barcelona .... KO 5
1979
Feb. 26—Alcala Cruz, Barcelona .... W 8
1980
Jan. 12—Hugo Carrizo, La Coruna .... W 8
May   31—Giancarlo Usai, Tarrasa .... KO 9
      (Won Vacant European Lightweight Title)
June 15—Georges Cotin, Barcelona .... KO 1

JOHANNES LESIBO
South African Bantamweight
1979
Feb. 10—Samuel Serekego, Virginia .... W 4
June 16—Samuel Serekego, Virginia .... L 4
July 14—Michael Khuto, Virginia .... W 4
Dec.   1—Michael Moamogoa, Odenaalsrust .... L 10
1980
May   31—Samuel Mcina, Bethlehem .... W 4

STEVE LEWIN
British Light Heavyweight
1977
Sept. 15—Mohammed Akram, Bethnal Green...... KO 2
Oct. 19—Peter Mullins, London .... KO 1
Nov.   7—Dave Callen, Walworth .... KO 4
Nov. 15—Steve Walker, London .... W 6
Nov. 29—Clifton Wallace, Bethnal .... L 6
1978
Jan. 31—Joe Hannaford, Marylebone .... KO 3
Mar. 13—John Breen, Walworth .... W 6
Apr.   4—Lloyd Gardner, London .... W 6
Apr. 25—Tim McHugh, London................... W 6
Sept. 26—Boyd Farrar, Wembley................. W 6
Nov.   7—Joey Williams, Wembley............... W 6
Nov. 21—Mick Fellingham, Wembley............ KO 2
1979
Jan. 23—Reginald Squire, Kensington .... KO by 2
Feb. 20—Nick Morris, Kensington .... W 6
Apr. 10—Trevor Cattouse, Longon .... L 6
May   14—Keith Bussey, Wembley................. D 6
1980
Feb. 18—Joey Williams, Lewisham .... KO 4
Apr. 28—Bonny McKenzie, Southwark .... L 8
May   29—Boyd Formor, Wimbledon .... W 8
Sept. 16—Jimmy Harrington, London .... KO 3
Oct.   6—Ken Jones, Southwark .... D 8

PHIL LEWIS
British Junior Middleweight
1979
June	6—Ian Murray, Bedworth	L 6
June	18—Mark Osbourne, Manchester	KO 2
Sept.	17—Billy Ahearne, Manchester	L 6
Sept.	24—Charlie Brown,London	KO by 3
Oct.	15—Kevin Quinn, Manchester	L 8
Oct.	31—Derek Nelson, Burslem	KO by 1

1980
Mar.	27—Kevin Quinn, Liverpool	KO 3
Apr.	9—Billy Ahearne, Liverpool	L 6
May	31—Kevin Quinn, Liverpool	W 6

VER LIBRADILLA
Filipino Junior Flyweight
1979
Jan.	19—Jun Bobier, Manila	KO 6
Apr.	20—Siony Caruopo, Manila	L 12
	(Philippine Junior Flyweight Title)	
May	26—Andy Balaba, Gen. Santos City	W 10
June	30—Ric Barimbad, Gen. Santos City	D 10
Sept.	15—Henry Balina, Ozamis City	W 10
Nov.	17—Ben Aldeguer, Santos City	D 10
Dec.	8—Rodrigo Saomoy, Ozamis City	KO 2

1980
Jan.	20—Ed Clementes De Oro City	KO 9
May	23—Melchor Degsi, Manila	D 10
July	30—Juanito Ablaca, Cebu City	L 10
Sept.	17—Juanito Ablaca, Pasay City	L 10

ANGELO LICATA
Italian Junior Lightweight
1978
Oct.	20—Angelo D'Aleo, La Louviere	W 6
Nov.	24—Patrick Drelon, Liegi	D 6
Dec.	15—Raphael Blanco, La Louviere	W 6

1979
Jan.	6—Andres Blanco, St. Servais	D 6
Feb.	2—Vincent Cipolla, La Louviere	W 6
Mar.	2—Vincent Cipolla, Liegi	W 6
May	4—Lucien Campo, La Louviere	W 6
May	25—Jean Pierre Meganck, Bruges	KO 6
Nov.	17—Nourredine, Antwerp	W 6
Dec.	8—Gilbert Helluin, La Louviere	W 8

1980
Jan.	18—Bouchiba Messauod, La Louviere	W 8
Mar.	7—Joel Moulin, La Louviere	D 8
Apr.	5—Rudi Haeck, La Louviere	D 10
Nov.	—Andre Blanco, Belgium	W 8
Oct.	3—Francis Bailleul, Calais	L 8

GREG LIESEGANG
Australian Junior Lightweight
1978
Aug.	4—Glen Burgoyne, Brisbane	W 4
Oct.	6—Bert Hornery, Brisbane	WF 2
Nov.	10—Rex Cannon, Brisbane	KO 6
Nov.	25—Johnny Kemp, Maryborough	KO 7
Dec.	8—Bert Hornery, Brisbane	W 4

1979
Feb.	9—Noel Kelly, Brisbane	KO 3
Feb.	23—Fred Burns, Brisbane	KO 8
Apr.	9—Billy Facer, Brisbane	KO 8
Apr.	20—Fred Burns, Brisbane	KO 10
June	1—Steve Button, Brisbane	D 10
Sept.	7—Rex Cannon, Brisbane	W 10
Sept.	28—Rex Cannon, Brisbane	L 10
Oct.	17—Reg King, Mt. Pritchard	W 10

1980
Mar.	31—Rex Cannon, Brisbane	KO by 8
June	9—Billy Facer, Brisbane	KO 2
Aug.	11—Kirk Blair, Brisbane	KO 8

CESAR LIGAN
Filipino Featherweight
1980
June	14—Joe Moreno, Davao City	KO 10
Sept.	19—Lulu Villaverde, Quezon City	W 12
	(Won Filipino Featherweight Title)	
Dec.	18—Ernie Pinon, Manila	W 10

DANILO LIMPAHAN
Filipino Junior Welterweight
1979
Mar.	10—David Bernales, Manila	L 8
Dec.	28—Jun Gonzales, Mandaluyong	W 10

1980
Jan.	25—Al Cordero, Manila	W 10
June	25—Jimmy Gonzalez, Manila	W 10
Sept.	26—Romy Angels, Quezon City	W 10
Nov.	21—Young Dela Cruz, Quezon City	W 10

344

JOHN LINDO
British Lightweight
Oct.	29—Tyrrel Wilson, Birmingham	L 6
Nov.	19—Glen Rhodes, Liverpool	W 6
Dec.	17—Winston Ho-Shing, Bradford	D 6

1980
Jan.	24—Bill Smith, Hartlepool	W 4
Feb.	6—Ronnie Rathbone, Liverpool	D 6
Feb.	25—Kevin Sheehan, Bradford	D 6
Mar.	14—Peter Harrison, Glasgow	L 6
Apr.	22—Gary Lucas, Sheffield	W 6
May	19—Barry Winters, Bradford	KO by 3
Sept.	9—Eric Wood, Mexborough	L 6

LIAM LINNEN
British Welterweight
1978
May	8—Alan Burrows, Glasgow	L 6
May	15—Shaun Durkin, Glasgow	L 6
Oct.	9—Andy Dane, London	W 6
Oct.	23—Shaun Durkin, Glasgow	D 6
Nov.	27—Derek Young Nelson, Glasgow	L 6

1979
Jan.	29—Pat Smythe, Glasgow	L 6
Feb.	26—Tommy Thomas, Glasgow	D 6
Mar.	19—Pat Smythe, Glasgow	KO 1
Apr.	17—Young Nelson, Glasgow	KO by 5
Oct.	8—Hugh Smith, Glasgow	KO by 6
Dec.	6—Dave Douglas, Glasgow	L 6

1980
June	2—Dave Douglas, Glasgow	KO by 9
	(For Vacant Scottish Welterweight Title)	
July	28—Gerry Young, Fivemiletown	KO by 3
Nov.	3—Mickey Mapp, Hammersmith	L 8

MANUEL (AMARAL) LIRA
Spanish Middleweight
1979
Apr.	28—Pierangelo Pira, Rimini	L 8

1980
Feb.	29—Nicola Cirelli, Rome	L 8
June	6—Jose Luic Pacheco, Madrid	L 8
July	2—Matteo Salvemini, Bitonto	L 8
Nov.	29—Jacques Chinon, Cayenne	L 10

SALVATORE LISCAPADE
Italian Junior Lightweight
Born: May 5, 1952, Taurisano
1973
Oct.	20—Mario Catena, Civitacastellana	KO 5
Nov.	23—Raffaele Maria, Rome	KO 3
Dec.	21—Salvatore Gennatiempo, Viterbo	KO 6

1974
July	6—Fulvio Giacomini, Nepi	W 6
Oct.	4—Vincenzo Di Ruocco, Rome	KO 3
Nov.	29—Adriano Ubertini, Rome	D 8

1975
Feb.	28—Domenico Condello, Rome	KO 2
Mar.	28—Abu Arrow, Rome	W 8
June	6—Paul Ikumpay, Rome	W 8
June	21—Abu Arrow, Nepi	W 8
Dec.	19—Natale Caredda, Rome	W 8

1976
Jan.	16—Enzo Cavazzini, Civitcastellana	W 8
Mar.	26—Giovanni Mura, Rome	KO 3
Apr.	30—Giuseppe Agate, Roma	W 8
Sept.	11—Ugo Poli, Nepi	W 12
	(Italian Junior Lightweight Title)	
Nov.	14—Giovanni Girgenti, Magliano Sabina	W 12
	(Italian Junior Lightweight Title)	

1977
Jan.	15—Ugo Poli, Civita	W 8
Mar.	9—Biagio Pierri, Rieti	W 12
	(Italian Junior Lightweight Title)	
May	29—Giuseppe Agate, Taurisano	KO 2
	(Italian Junior Lightweight Title)	
July	23—Renzo Battistelli, Nepi	W 8
Dec.	14—Natale Vezzoli, Taurisano	L 15
	(European Junior Lightweight Title)	

1978
Jan.	27—Natale Credda, Milano	W 8
July	9—Eloy De Souza, Ostia	W 8
Sept.	28—Aristed Pizzo, Milan	KO by 3
	(Italian Junior Lightweight Title)	
Dec.	9—Josia Malquides Da Sylva, Isernia	W 10

1979
Feb.	24—Cosimo Lavino, Isernia	W 12
	(Italian Junior Lightweight Title)	
May	19—Sergio Emili, Canepina	W 12
	(Italian Junior Lightweight Title)	
Aug.	4—Salvatore Fabrizio, Tarquinia	W 12
	(Italian Junior Lightweight Title)	

Mar. 22—Salvatore Avella, Ostia .... W 8
Apr. 30—Carlos Hernandez, Nepi .... KO by 6
(For European Junior Lightweight Title)

STEWART LITHGOE
British Heavyweight
1979
Sept. 26—Colin Flute, Solihull .... KO 4
Nov. 12—Mal Tetley, Marten .... W 6
Nov. 26—Kenny March, Hammersmith .... W 6
1980
Jan. 24—Mal Tetley, Hartlepool .... W 6
July 7—Reg Long, Middlesbrough .... KO 3
Sept. 11—Bob Hennessey, Hartlepool .... W 6
Oct. 20—Manny Gabriel, Birmingham .... KO 4
Nov. 22—Rudi Gauwe, Zele .... L 8

ISAAC LITLHAKANYANE
South African Junior Welterweight
1974
Apr. 6—Petrus Motaung, Sharpeville .... L 4
1975
(Inactive)
1976
Nov. 20—Richard Ngidi, Bloemfontein .... W 6
July 3—John Masapo, Parys .... KO 2
1977
(Inactive)
1978
Sept. 30—Ephraim Mathenjwa, Sharpeville .... W 4
1979
Aug. 31—Elias Nkabinde, Natalspruit .... L 4
1980
June 7—Menase Potse, Odenaalsrust .... L 8

PETER LOCK
British Middleweight
1980
July 14—Dave Finigan, London .... W 6
Sept. 11—Brian Graham, Hartlepool .... L 4
Oct. 13—Owen Stafford, Windsor .... W 6
Nov. 4—Tony Walton, Southend .... W 6

REG LONG
British Heavyweight
1977
Jan. 24—John McCallum, Glasgow .... L 6
Feb. 14—Carlton Benoit, Bedford .... L 6
Mar. 18—John McCallum, Holytown .... KO 4
Apr. 18—Manny Gabriel, Bedford .... NC 2
Apr. 24—Glenroy Taylor, Birmingham .... KO 1
May 16—Manny Gabriel, Glasgow .... L 6
May 30—Len Brittain, Marton .... W 6
June 13—Winston Cousins, Manchester .... KO by 5
Aug. 22—Len Brittain, Stockton .... W 8
Sept. 29—Roy Gregory, Newcastle .... KO 5
Nov. 8—Ralph Green, Darlington............... W 10
Dec. 8—Francis Hands, Liverpool .... KO by 7
1978
Feb. 7—Steve Taylor, London .... L 6
Apr. 24—Theo Josephs, Middlesbrough.......... W 8
May 3—Bonny McKenzie, Solihull............. KO by 7
July 12—Paul Tucker, Newcastle .... W 6
Aug. 29—Steve Hill, Liverpool .... L 8
Dec. 4—George Scott, Marton .... D 8
1979
Feb. 13—Theo Josephs, Wakefield .... L 8
May 13—Terry Chard, Glasgow .... W 6
May 23—Joe Awome, Nottingham .... KO by 2
Nov. 12—George Scott, Marton .... L 10
Dec. 11—Manny Gabriel, Bletchley .... KO by 3
1980
July 7—Stewart Lithgo, Middlesbrough ...... KO by 3

MARIO LORENI
Italian Middleweight
1979
Nov. 18—Rasario Pacileo, Brescia .... D 8
Dec. 15—Corrado Sortino, Pesaro .... KO by 5
1980
Mar. 28—Aldo Polesel, Ponte Priula .... D 6
Apr. 12—Aldo Polesel, Sereguo .... W 6
May 26—Antonio Cresenza, Travagliato .... KO by 4

RANCHING LOUW
South African Bantamweight
1979
June 23—Jama Qalinga, Bloemfontein .... W 6
Nov. 19—Moses Moamogoa, Kimberley .... W 4
Dec. 8—Albert Kgwadi, Bloemfontein .... W 6
1980
Feb. 2—Gift Xaluva, Kimberley .... W 8

Mar. 8—Simon Mafere, Bethlehem .... W 6
July 5—Moses Moamogoa, Kimberley .... W 4
Aug. 2—Jacob Molefe, Welkom .... L 6
Aug. 23—Moses Moamogoa, Kimberley .... W 6
Oct. 4—Hendrick Koelman, Welkom .... W 4

JOSE LOZANO
Spanish Middleweight
1976
Nov. 25—Marc Petit, Beauvais .... L 6
1977
Jan. 10—Johnny Collet, Paris .... W 6
Jan. 19—Jean Claude Terlon, Compiegne .... W 6
Mar. 19—Johnny Collet, Amiens .... W 6
Apr. 30—Marc Petit, Creil .... W 6
June 4—Justin M'Foudi, Argenteuil .... L 6
Sept. 9—Antonio Saez Amana, Madrid .... KO by 4
Nov. 5—Jean Claude Terlon, Chantilly .... KO 5
1978
Jan. 7—Michel Pagani, Calais .... KO 4
Feb. 11—Dusan Kukic, S. Gregorio .... KO 6
Mar. 3—Gianni Filippetto, Torino............... W 6
Apr. 1—Langewouters, Bruxelles................. W 6
Apr. 27—Per Mullertz, Randers .... W 6
May 6—Avenamar Peralta, Madrid.......... KO by 4
Sept. 30—Eric Kopec, Crepy....................... KO 2
Dec. 1—Mario Romersi, Rome.................... W 8
1979
Feb. 24—Michel Pagani, Calais .... KO by 3
Apr. 7—Jean M. Emebe, Doula .... KO by 8
July 14—Alfredo Naveiras, Mataro .... D 12
(Spanish Middleweight Title)
1980
Jan. 6—Jean Marie Emebe, Lille .... KO 4
Feb. 2—Pierre Joly, Tolosa .... L 10
May 29—Manduka Kassongo, Grenoble .... W 8
Nov. 7—Christian D'Elft, Tarbes .... W 8

RUDI LUBBERS
Dutch Heavyweight
1970
Feb. 23—Jose Guillois, Rotterdam .... W 6
Feb. 28—Mohamed Sahib, Eindhoven .... KO 2
Mar. 11—Andre Haudrechy, Dordrecht .... KO 3
Mar. 16—Herbert Wick, Amsterdam .... W 6
Mar. 31—Henry Keraven, La Haye .... W 6
Apr. 27—Jose Guillois, Rotterdam .... KO 1
July 13—Horst Volpert, Nijmwegen .... KO 1
Sept. 14—Detleff Naseband, Rotterdam .... W 8
Sept. 28—Jean Tshikuna, La Haye .... W 8
Oct. 2—Willy Karall, Frankfurt .... KO 6
Dec. 7—Lloyd Walford, Amsterdam .... W 8
1971
Jan. 2—Detleff Naseband, Berlin .... W 8
Apr. 2—Mohammed Nassen, Koeln .... KO 6
Apr. 18—Manfred Ackers, Uithoon .... KO 8
May 17—Bos Van Duivenbode, Amsterdam ...... W 12
(Won Dutch Heavyweight Title)
May 27—Henry Ferjules, Koeln .... KO 4
Nov. 8—Bos Van Duivenbode, Rotterdam .... KO 5
(Retained Dutch Heavyweight Title)
1972
Jan. 31—Piero Del Papa, Rotterdam .... W 10
May 2—Expedit Momtcho, Amsterdam .... W 10
1973
Jan. 16—Joe Bugner, London .... L 15
(For European Heavyweight Title)
Oct. 20—Muhammad Ali, Jakarta .... L 10
1974
Apr. 27—Jean Pierre Coopman, Gand .... W 10
Sept. 23—Horace Hal Carrol, Rotterdam .... L 10
Oct. 14—Avenamar Peralta, Rotterdam .... WF 3
1975
Oct. 31—Domenico Adinolfi, Torino .... KO by 2
(For European Heavyweight Title)
1976
May 22—Mike Schutte, Johannesburgh .... KO by 3
Oct. 8—Alfredo Evangelista, Madrid .... KO by 3
1977-1979
(Inactive)
1980
Mar. 31—Terry O'Conners, Rotterdam .... W 10
May 19—Henny Thoonen, Rotterdam ....WF 7
(Won Dutch Heavyweight Title)
Sept. 1—Robert Desnouch, Rotterdam .... W 10

FRANK LUCAS
British Middleweight
1974
Oct. 16—Pat Brogan, Mayfair .... KO 5
Nov. 12—Mike Manley, London .... W 6
1975
Mar. 11—Joe Gregory, London .... W 6

Mar.	19—Phil Martin, London	KO by 4
Oct.	27—Jan Magdziarz, London	KO 7

1976

Mar.	29—Jan Magdziarz, Mayfair	KO by 6
Dec.	13—Rudd Koopmans, Amsterdam	LF 7

1977

Mar.	21—Wane Bennett, London	W 8
Apr.	12—Alec Tompkins, London	KO 6
May	31—Kevin Finnegan, London	KO by 11

(British Middleweight Title)

Nov.	19—Angelo Jacopucci, Turin	KO 2

1978

Jan.	7—Norberto Cabrera, Milan	W 8
Apr.	22—Willie Monroe, San Remo	KO by 9
Sept.	30—Chisanda Mutti, Lusaka	KO 9
Nov.	7—Dino Del Cid, Wembley	KO 1

1979

Apr.	10—Tony Sibson, Kensington	KO by 5

1980

Feb.	18—Roy Gumps, London	L 10

(For Southern Area Middleweight Title)

GARY LUCAS
British Featherweight
1978

Apr.	24—Mark Hill, Glasgow	L 4
Sept.	12—Steve Enright	KO by 6
Nov.	8—John Flynn, Stoke	L 4
Nov.	14—Alex Irvine, Birkenhead	W 4
Nov.	20—Gary Ball, Birmingham	W 6
Dec.	11—Gary Ball, Birmingham	L 6
Dec.	18—Steve Enright, Bradford	L 6

1979

Jan.	18—Selvin Bell, Liverpool	L 6
Feb.	22—Larry Richards, Liverpool	W 6
Mar.	22—Selvin Bell, Liverpool	L 6
Apr.	19—Carl Mullings, Birkenhead	W 6
May	21—Steve Cleak, London	W 6
June	18—Terry McKeown, Glasgow	KO by 4
Sept.	24—Steve Cleak, London	L 6
Oct.	8—Mohamed Younis, Nantwich	KO 5
Nov.	19—Gerry O'Neill, Glasgow	L 6
Dec.	4—Dave Laxen, Southend	D 8

1980

Jan.	21—Gerry O'Neill, Birmingham	L 8
Feb.	27—Dave Laxen, Burslem	L 8
Mar.	3—Jim McKeown, London	D 6
Mar.	11—Dave Laxen, Nantwich	D 8
Mar.	19—Jim McKeown, Stoke	L 8
Mar.	27—Paul Keers, Liverpool	W 8
Apr.	9—Steve Parker, Burslem	W 8
May	5—Jim McKeown, Glasgow	L 8

ALI LUKASA
Spanish Heavyweight
1979

June	16—Jose M. Menendez, Aviles	W 4
July	21—Jose M. Menendez, Aviles	W 4
Aug.	3—Joe Tarzan, Madrid	KO 3
Aug.	11—Marcial T. Vega, S. Sebastiano	KO 3
Sept.	1—Mary Konate, San Sebastian	KO 2
Nov.	8—Teo Vega, La Coruna	KO 5
Dec.	22—Francisco Macias, Logrono	KO 3

1980

Jan.	6—Lassine Niare, Bilbao	KO 5
May	10—Alex Cardoza, Zaragoza	W 6

DOUG LUMLEY
South African Middleweight
Born: July 14, 1955
1975

Oct.	27—Theunis Pretorious, Durban	KO 1
Dec.	17—Hendrik Ludick, Durban	KO 3

1976

Jan.	26—Esias Bosch, Durban	W 4
Mar.	15—Dave Koen, Durban	KO 2
May	4—Johnny Smith, Durban	W 8
Aug.	16—Sias Bosch, Durban	W 6
Nov.	1—Steven Els, Durban	KO 2
Dec.	7—Willem Giessing, Durban	KO 3

1977

Feb.	28—Maxwell Malinga, Durban	W 10
June	27—Jan Kies, Durban	KO 11

(Won South African White Middleweight Title)

Aug.	1—Elijah Makhatini, Durban	W 12

(Won Supreme South African Middleweight Title)

Oct.	3—Tom Howard, Durban	W 10
Nov.	14—Joseph Hali, Capetown	W 10
Nov.	28—Elijah Makhatini, Durban	W 12

1978

Feb.	27—Daniel Mapanya, Durban	KO by 1
May	29—Daniel Mapanya, Durban	KO by 3

(Lost Supreme South African Middleweight Title)

Oct.	7—Charlie Weir, Johannesburg	KO by 2

(For South African National Middleweight Title)

(Inactive)

1980

Feb.	4—Champion Mokone, Durban	W 6
Apr.	14—Solomon Dhladla, Durban	W 6
May	19—Elijah Makhatini, Durban	W 8
July	4—Robert McFarland, Durban	W 8
Sept.	15—Sydney Hoho, Durban	KO 11

(Won South African Light Heavyweight Title)

Dec.	22—Willie Opperman, Cape Town	W 12

(Retained South African Light Heavyweight Title)

JOHN LUTCHANA
South African Junior Welterweight
1978

Oct.	10—Henna Hawkey, Durban	D 4

1979

Feb.	12—Henna Hawkey, Durban	KO 3
Aug.	18—July Maduna, Durban	W 4

1980

Feb.	4—Deon Labuschagne, Durban	D 6
Mar.	1—Nicholas Mlaba, Durban	L 4

EDDIE McALLISTER
(Fought as EDDIE SMITH in the Amateurs)
British Bantamweight
1980

Mar.	11—Iggy Jano, Southend	L 6
Apr.	15—Iggy Jano, Southend	W 6
Apr.	24—Tony Manson, London	KO 1
Sept.	16—George Bailey, London	L 4

CASLEY McALLUM
British Junior Middleweight
1978

Sept.	25—Dave Southwell, Mayfair	KO by 1
Oct.	31—Les Foster, Hammersmith	W 4

1979

Mar.	12—John Kennedy, London	KO by 3

1980

Jan.	28—Kendrick Edwards, Hove	W 6
Feb.	18—Mike Barton, Lewisham	L 4
Apr.	8—Steve Pearson, Norwich	KO 3
Apr.	21—Willie Wright, Edgbaston	L 6
Apr.	30—Kevin Johnson, Wolverhampton	KO 4
May	29—Steve Pearson, Wimbledon	KO 2
Sept.	24—Neville Wilson, Evesham	L 6
Oct.	23—Neil Fannon, Middlesbrough	L 6

DAVE McCABE
Scottish Lightweight
1977

Oct.	17—Phillip Morris, Glasgow	W 4
Nov.	7—Gary Collins, Glasgow	KO 3
Nov.	14—Gene McGarrigle, Glasgow	KO 6
Nov.	24—Ian Pickersgill, Doncaster	W 6
Dec.	12—Tony Carroll, London	W 6

1978

Jan	9—Billy Jeram, London	W 6
Jan.	30—Dai Davies, Glasgow	W 6
Feb.	27—Albert Coley, Glasgow	W 6
Mar.	13—Martin Bridge, Birmingham	W 8
Mar.	20—Eric Wood, Glasgow	W 8
Sept.	18—George Peacock, Glasgow	W 8
Oct.	9—Tony Zeni, London	KO 7
Oct.	23—Eric Wood, Glasgow	W 8
Nov.	27—Eric Purkis, Glasgow	W 8

1979

Jan.	22—Granville Allen, Wolverhampton	W disq. 7
Mar.	17—Martin Bridge, Glasgow	W 8
Apr.	17—Bingo Crooks, Glasgow	W 8
Sept.	3—Joe Phillips, Glasgow	KO 9

1980

Jan.	8—Martyn Galeozzie, Windsor	W 12
Mar.	24—Ray Cattouse, Glasgow	KO by 9

(For Vacant British Lightweight Title)

June	23—Derek Nelson, Glasgow	W 8
Oct.	7—Chris Sanigar, London	W 8

CHRIS McCALLUM
British Lightweight
1980
Aug.	31—Derek Groarke, Glasgow	W	6
Sept.	15—John Sharkey,Glasgow	KO by	3

TOMMY McCALLUM
British Welterweight
1980
June	2—Paul Wetter, Plymouth	W	6
Oct.	13—Ronnie Rathbone, London	W	6

BRYAN McCONNELL
British Lightweight
1980
Apr.	21—Bobby Welburn, Glasgow	W	6
May	5—Colin Wake, Glasgow	W	6
May	27—Colin Wake, Glasgow	KO by	4

FRANK McCORD
British Welterweight
1977
Mar.	29—Phillip Morris, Ebbw Vale	W	4
Apr.	18—Roger Doyle, Bedford	W	6
May	2—George Daines, London	W	4
May	9—Winston Spencer, London	KO by	3
June	21—Eric Purkis, London	L	6
Oct.	3—Dil Collins, Aberavon	KO by	6
Oct.	17—Martin Bridge, Bedford	KO by	5
Nov.	22—Eddie Porter, Hemel Hempstead	KO	4
Dec.	14—Ian Pickersgill, Swansea	KO	1
	1978		
Mar.	13—Paddy McAleese, Birmingham	L	6
Apr.	6—Mick Barker, Ebbw Vale	KO	2
Apr.	10—Martin Bridge, Birmingham	L	6
Apr.	17—Eric Purkis, London	KO by	5
June	19—Billy O'Grady, Hove	D	6
June	27—Benny Purdy, Derry	KO	4
Sept.	18—Alan Burrows, Reading	L	6
Oct.	3—Lloyd Lee, Aberavon	L	8
Oct.	16—Harry Watson, London	W	6
Oct.	28—Omar Sahli, Oslo	L	6
Nov.	2—Al Stewart, Liverpool	KO	3
Dec.	5—Sid Smith, Kensington	W	6
Dec.	11—Tommy Wright, Plymouth	D	6
	1979		
Feb.	12—Stan Atherton, Manchester	L	8
Feb.	26—Steve Early, Edgbaston	KO by	1
Apr.	5—Hugh Kelly, Belfast	L	8
May	10—David Pearce, Pontypool	L	8
June	6—Roy Varden, Bedworth	L	8
July	30—Tony Martey, London	KO by	4
	1980		
Jan.	22—John Mount, London	W	8
Feb.	28—Jeff Pritchard, Ebbw Vale	L	8
Mar.	10—Chris Christian, London	L	8
Apr.	15—Alan Lamb, Blackpool	KO by	1

DAMIEN McDERMOTT
Irish Featherweight
1977
Apr.	26—Jim McAuley, Derry	KO	4
June	27—Jackie McGill, Derry	W	8
Oct.	18—Albert Coley, Belfast	L	8
	1978		
June	27—Jackie McGill, Derry	W	8
Oct.	11—Bryan Wilson, Belfast	KO	4
	1979		
Apr.	21—Gerard Jacob, Creil	KO by	1
June	27—Glyn Davies, Derry	KO	3
	1980		
May	27—Gerry O'Neill, Belfast	D	8

STAN McDERMOTT
British Heavyweight
1977
Sept.	27—Clive Beardsley, London	D	6
Oct.	25—Brian Paul, London	KO	3
Dec.	6—Terry O'Connor, London	KO	5
	1978		
Jan.	24—Guinea Roger, London	KO	2
Apr.	4—Bob Hennessey, London	KO	1
Sept.	26—George Scott, Wembley	KO	5
Oct.	24—Ricky James, Kensington	KO by	2
	1979		
Jan.	26—Gordon Ferris, London	W	8
May	29—Gordon Ferris, Kensington	KO by	1
	1980		
Feb.	19—Joe Awome, London	KO	4
Mar.	1—Winston Allen, London	KO by	1
June	3—Ricky James, London	W	4
July	12—Andy Palmer, London	KO	2
Sept.	16—Denton Ruddock, London	KO	3

LARRY McDONALD
British Heavyweight
1980
Feb.	5—Terry O'Connor, Wolverhampton	W	8
Apr.	30—Ricky James, Aylesbury	W	8
June	3—Manny Gabriel, Aylesbury	KO	3

GLENN (YOUNG) McEWAN
British Middleweight
1977
Oct.	11—Mickey Hinton, Coventry	KO	2
Oct.	17—Horace H. Thompson, Mayfair	KO	5
Nov.	21—Bunny McKenzie, Birmingham	W	8
	1978		
Jan.	12—Rudi Koopmans, Rotterdam	KO by	2
Jan.	15—Per Muellertz, Randers	W	6
Feb.	21—Oscar Angus, Wolverhampton	D	8
Apr.	4—Wayne Bennett, Wolverhampton	W	8
June	1—Paul Shutt, Coventry	KO	2
Sept.	4—David Owens, Wakefield	KO	1
Oct.	10—Mac Nicholson, Wolverhampton	KO	5
Nov.	22—Dennis Andries, Stoke	KO by	7
	1979		
June	25—Prince Rodney, Edgbaston	L	8
Sept.	24—Howard Mills, Mayfair	L	8
Oct.	27—Damiano Lassandro, Pesaro	KO by	2
	1980		
Feb.	12—Herol Graham, Sheffield	L	8
Mar.	19—Romal Ambrose, Birmingham	KO	10
	(Won Midlands Area Middleweight Title)		
Apr.	15—Robbie Davies, Blackpool	KO	6
Oct.	20—Romal Ambrose, Birmingham	KO	6
	(Retained Midlands Area Middleweight Title)		

MARTIN McEWAN
British Middleweight
1978
Feb.	21—Mick Morris, London	KO by	1
May	8—Dave Merrell, Nottingham	W	6
Sept.	18—Mick Morris, Wolverhampton	KO by	2
Oct.	10—Kendrick Edwards, Wolverhampton	W	4
Nov.	6—Kendrick Edwards, Stafford	W	6
Nov.	22—Steve Fox, Stoke	W	6
Nov.	29—Joe Jackson, Evesham	W	6
	1979		
Mar.	15—Ron Green, Dudley	W	6
Apr.	19—Joe Hannaford, Birkenhead	KO	2
May	21—Billy Hill, Bradford	W	8
June	25—Harry Watson, Edgbaston	W	6
Sept.	11—Jimmy Harrington, London	L	6
Oct.	31—Redmond Egerhard, Burslem	KO	3
Dec.	10—Joe Jackson, Birmingham	W	6
	1980		
Feb.	5—Romel Ambrose, Wolverhampton	L	10
Mar.	10—Tony Britton, London	KO	6
Sept.	22—Peter Bassey, Birmingham	L	8

GERRY McGRATH
British Welterweight
1980
Apr.	28—Adrian Clamp, Windsor	KO	3
May	29—Shaun Jones, Wimbledon	W	6
June	16—Gary Petty, London	KO	1
Oct.	13—Dave Dunn, Windsor	KO	3
Nov.	4—Gary Brooks, London	KO	3

GEORGE McGURK
British Junior Welterweight
Born: May 27, 1950
1970
May	18—Micky Vann, London	KO	4
Dec.	1—Al Hutcheon, Leeds	KO	2
Dec.	7—Noel McIvor, Bedford	L	6
	1971		
Jan.	11—Dave Touhy, Gasforth	KO	1
Jan.	20—Alan Salter, Wolverhampton	W	6
Feb.	4—Billy Belnevis, London	W	6
Mar.	24—Noel McIver, Stoke-On-Trent	L	8
May	17—Roger Howes, London	W	6
June	7—Freddie Williams, Nottingham	KO	4
Sept.	27—Simon Rawlings, London	W	8
Oct.	20—Barton McAlister, Stoke	W	6
Nov.	1—Jose Cascales, Bedford	W	8
Nov.	9—Freddie Williams, Wolverhampton	L	6
Dec.	9—Ron Clifford, Wolverhampton	W	8
	1972		
Jan.	26—Paul Bromely, Wolverhampton	KO	1
Apr.	11—Ron Clifford, Wolverhampton	KO	1
Apr.	24—Alan Salter, Nottingham	W	8
May	3—Sammy Lockhart, Solihull	D	8
July	12—George O'Neill, Wolverhampton	L	8
Sept.	20—Steve Cleaver, Solihull	W	8
Nov.	6—Don Burgin, Bedford	W	8

Dec. 6—Bob Langley, Stoke ....L 8
1973
Jan. 17—Danny Fearon, London ....L 8
Jan. 29—Brian McAlister, Bedford ....W 8
May 21—George McKay, London ....W disq. 7
July 2—Vernon Sollas, Earls Court............KO 6
Sept. 17—Jimmy Revie, Bedford ....L 8
Oct. 8—Noel McIvor, London....................D 8
Nov. 28—Noel McIvor, Southend ....L 8
1974
Jan. 30—Tony Cunningham, N. Staffordshire .....W 8
Feb. 4—Jimmy Revie, Mayfair ....L 8
May 8—Tony Cunningham, Solihull ....W 8
May 13—Billy Hardace, Nottingham...............W 8
June 3—Billy Hardace, Manchester ....KO 6
June 12—Billy Belnavis, Wolverhampton..........W 8
Nov. 13—Jimmy Revie, Solihull ....L 8
1975
Jan. 19—Jean-Baptiste Piedvache, St. Maur.... KO by 3
Mar. 10—Ray Holdcroft, Gosforth ....W 8
Apr. 7—Tommy Dunn, London ....KO 2
Apr. 14—Ray Holdcroft, Manchester ....W 8
May 5—Noel McIvor, Bedford ....D 8
Oct. 27—Jimmy Revie, Walworth ....KO by 9
1976
Jan. 20—Dave Green, London.................KO by 2
Apr. 27—Colin Powers, Kensington ....L 8
May 26—Billy Belnavis, Wolverhampton..........W 8
Sept. 22—Barton McAllister, Solihull ....KO 8
Nov. 9—Charlie Nash, Derry ....L 8
1977
Jan. 19—Johnny Wall, Solihull ....L 8
Feb. 1—Clinton McKenzie, Kensington ....L 8
Feb. 14—Cornelius Bosa-Edwards, London ..... KO by 1
Sept. 29—Godfrey Butler, Newcastle ....W 8
Nov. 2—Nagib Daho, Newcastle ....L 8
Dec. 5—Jeff Pritchard, Marton ....W 8
1978
Feb. 7—Roy Varden, Coventry ....L 8
Apr. 12—Joey Singleton, Hammersmith........ KO by 8
Nov. 20—Steve Early, Birmingham ....KO by 5
1979
Mar. 7—Schris Sanigar, Solihull ....KO 2
Mar. 19—Winston Spencer, London ....LF 2
Dec. 10—Lance Williams, Birmingham ....KO by 6
1980
Mar. 5—Terry Welsh, Liverpool ....L 6
Apr. 22—Ronnie Rathbone, Sheffield ....L 6
Apr. 29—Lawrence Williams, Stockport ....L 8
June 3—Dominic Bergonzi, London ....KO by 2

JOEY McINTOSH
(See JOEY MACK)

BRUCE McINTYRE
South African Middleweight
Born: April 26, 1954
1978
May 29—Aswan Simalane, Durban...............KO 1
July 3—Victor Ntloko, Johannesburg...........KO 1
Aug. 5—Willem Giesing, Johannesburg..........KO 1
Oct. 9—Albertus Opperman, Johannesburg ....W 4
Nov. 6—Solomon Dladla, Durban ....KO 3
1979
Feb. 3—Joseph Matjius, Johannesburg ....KO 1
Mar. 24—James Mathatho, Johannesburg ....KO 7
Apr. 25—Teunis Kok, Durban ....L 6
June 11—Mervin Smit, Welkom ....KO 7
July 28—Nelson Bosso, Bulawayo ....KO 2
Aug. 27—Themba Buthelezi, Johannesburg ....KO 1
Sept. 15—Elijah Makhatini, Johannesburg ....KO 6
Nov. 12—Joe Hali, Welkom ....KO 3
Dec. 1—Cameron Adams, Johannesburg ....KO 5
1980
Feb. 9—Mel Dennis, Johannesburg ....W 8
Mar. 8—Loyiso Mtya, Johannesburg ....KO 2
Mar. 29—Freddie Johnson, Johannesburg ....KO 5
May 26—Ruben Pardo, Johannesburg ....L 10
Aug. 16—David Love, Johannesburg ....KO 1
Sept. 15—Ralph Moncrief, Durban ....KO by 10

BONNY McKENZIE
British Light Heavyweight
1976
June 21—Joe Jackson, Piccadilly...................W 6
Aug. 11—Colin Breen, Cardiff.....................W 6
Sept. 10—Tony Sibson, Digbeth ....KO by 7
Nov. 24—Al Neville, London ....W 6
Dec. 1—Pat Brogan, Stoke........................L 8
Dec. 14—Eddie Burke, London....................L 6
1977
Feb. 11—Roy Gumbs, London ....L 8
Feb. 14—Jimmy Pickard, Bedford ....W 8

Mar. 21—Eddie Vieling, London ....KO 1
Mar. 24—Tony Sibson, Leicester ....KO by 7
Sept. 9—Eddie Burke, Glasgow ....L 8
Oct. 3—Wayne Bennett, Aberavon ....L 8
Nov. 2—Kenny Feehan, Cardiff ....KO 5
Nov. 21—Young McEwan, Birmingham...........L 8
Nov. 29—Eddie Burke, London..................L 8
1978
Feb. 6—Carl Canvell, London ....L 8
May 3—Reg Long, Solihull ....KO 7
May 16—Ken Jones, Newport....................L 8
May 23—Chris Lawson, London ....W 8
June 20—Dennis Andries, Southend ....W 8
July 18—Tony Sibson, Wakefield.................L 8
Sept. 27—Roy Gumbs, Stoke ....L 8
Nov. 29—Chris Lawson, Swansea ....L 10
Dec. 11—Oscar Angus, London ....W 8
1979
Jan. 18—Shaun Chalcraft, Wimbledon ....W 8
Feb. 19—David Pearce, London ....L 8
Mar. 1—Karl Canwell, London ....W 8
Mar. 12—Karl Canwell, London ....L 8
Mar. 19—Eddie Smith, London ....W 8
Apr. 24—Roy Gumbs, London ....L 8
May 13—Gordon Ferris, Edgbaston ....L 8
June 6—Dennis Andries, Burslem ....L 8
June 18—Alek Pernaski, Windsor ....D 8
Sept. 26—Eddie Smith, Solihull ....L 8
Oct. 15—Roy Gumbs, Mayfair ....KO by 3
1980
Mar. 26—Cristiano Cavina, Rome ....L 8
Apr. 28—Steve Lewin, Southwark ....W 8
May 10—Michel Pagini, Calais ....KO by 3
Aug. 14—Walter Cevoli, Rimini ....W 8
Sept. 6—John Odihambo, Aarhus ....L 6
Sept. 22—Danny Lawford, London ....L 8

CLINTON McKENZIE
British Junior Welterweight
1976
Oct. 21—Jimmy King, Bethnal Green ....W 8
Nov. 15—Barton McAllister, Kensington ....W 8
1977
Feb. 1—George McGurk, Kensington ....W 8
Feb. 14—Harry Watson, London ....KO 4
Mar. 21—Colin Powers, London ....KO by 2
Apr. 18—Al Stewart, Mayfair ....KO 3
May 7—Fernand Roeland, Antwerp ....W 8
June 11—Bouchiba Messaoud, S. Amand ....W 8
Sept. 5—Johnny Pincham, London ....L 8
Oct. 10—Kevin Davies, London ....W 8
Nov. 3—Erkki Meronen, Randers.................KO 5
1978
Jan. 16—Chris Davies, Nottingham ....W 12
Mar. 2—Mike Everett, Oslo......................W 10
May 23—Chris Walker, London ....W 8
Oct. 11—Jim Montague, Belfast ....KO 10
(British Junior Welterweight Title)
Dec. 18—Tony Martey, London..................W 8
1979
Feb. 6—Colin Powers, Wembley ....L 15
(British Junior Welterweight Title)
Feb. 24—Bruce Curry, Las Vegas ....L 10
Apr. 30—Des Morrison, London ....W 12
Sept. 11—Colin Powers, London ....W 15
(Won British Junior Welterweight Title)
Dec. 10—Roger Guest, Piccadilly ....W 8
1980
Feb. 19—Roger Guest, London ....W 8
Apr. 1—George Feeney, London ....W 10
Apr. 17—George Peacock, London ....KO 3
June 12—Hans Henrik Palm, Randers ....W 8
Aug. 27—Giuseppe Martinez, Senigallia .... KO by 11
(For European Junior Welterweight Title)

HORACE McKENZIE
British Welterweight
1977
Apr. 25—Ray Thomas, London ....KO 2
June 2—Peter Rushfirth, London ....KO 6
June 14—Mick Mills, Southend ....KO by 4
July 18—Alan Jones, Mayfair ....KO 7
Sept. 21—Al Stewart, London ....KO 7
Oct. 11—Peter Neal, Marylebone ....D 8
Nov. 2—Eric Purkis, Cardiff...................W 8
Dec. 6—Colin Deans, Leeds ....W 8
Dec. 15—Louis Acaries, Paris ....KO by 9
1978
Jan. 30—Tommy Davitt, Glasgow ....W 8
Feb. 13—Carl Bailey, Manchester ....W 8
Mar. 20—Tim McHugh, Aberavon ....W 8
May 22—Roy Commosioung, Mayfair ....W 8
July 10—Michael Copp, Aberavon ....W 10
(Welsh Welterweight Title)

July 18—Prince Rodney, Wakefield................L 8
Sept. 3—Josef Nusubuga, Bergen................L 8
Sept. 9—Raul Anon, Las Corogne...............W 8
Oct. 3—Colin Jones, Aberavon...................L 8
Oct. 14—Fred Coranson, Dunkerque.............L 8
Dec. 7—Hans Henrik Palm, Copenhagen.........L 8
1979
Jan. 8—Frank Albertus, Rotterdam..............W 8
Mar. 2—Clemente Tshinza, Bruges...............L 10
May 13—Lloyd Lee, Edgbaston...................L 8
June 18—Chris Walker, London..................W 8
Nov. 19—Prince Rodney, Stockport..............L 8
Dec. 10—Ronald Zenon, Paris....................L 10
1980
Mar. 11—Gary Pearce, London...................W 10
(Retained Welsh Welterweight Title)
May 12—Coenie Bekker, Cape Town..............L 10
June 16—Roy Varden, London....................L 8
Sept. 6—Jorgen Hansen, Aarhus.............KO by 7
Oct. 23—George Walker, London.................L 8

JIM McKEOWN
British Featherweight
1980
Jan. 8—Selvin Bell, Windsor....................W 6
Jan. 28—John Griffiths, Glasgow................KO 4
Feb. 25—Alan Storey, Glasgow...................W 6
Mar. 3—Gary Lucas, London.....................D 6
Mar. 19—Gary Lucas, Stoke......................W 8
Mar. 31—Leo Graham, London....................W 8
May 5—Gary Lucas, Glasgow....................W 6
June 7—Jimmy Brown, Glasgow..................L 8

TERRY McKEOWN
Scottish Featherweight
1978
Sept. 18—Bobby Breen, Glasgow..................W 6
Oct. 9—Pip Coleman, London....................W 6
Oct. 18—Bobby Breen, Glasgow..................W 6
Oct. 23—John Cooper, Glasgow..................W 6
Oct. 31—Larry Richards, Birmingham............W 6
Nov. 27—Lawrence Williams, Glasgow............W 6
1979
Jan. 29—Lee Graham, Glasgow...................W 6
Feb. 26—Charm Chiteule, London............KO by 5
Apr. 17—Alec Irvine, Glasgow...................W 8
May 13—Steve Cleak, Glasgow...................W 8
June 18—Gary Lucas, Glasgow...................KO 4
Oct. 8—Paul Keers, Glasgow....................W 8
Nov. 3—Louis Loy Junior, Glasgow..............KO 3
Dec. 10—Vernon Penprase, Torquay..............L 8
1980
Jan. 16—Selvin Bell, Solihull...................W 8
Jan. 28—Don George, Glasgow...................D 8
Mar. 14—Gerry O'Neill, Glasgow.................L 10
(For Vacant Scottish Featherweight Title)
Sept. 16—Austin Owens, London.................KO 2
Nov. 1—John Feeney, Glasgow...................L 8

NEIL McLAUGHLIN
British Flyweight
1976
Jan. 26—George Sutton, Glasgow.................L 8
Feb. 23—Tony Kerr, Glasgow.....................KO 4
Apr. 26—Tony Kerr, Glasgow.....................L 6
Nov. 9—Johnny Owen, Derry.....................D 8
1977
Jan. 28—Johnny Owen, West Bromwich...........L 8
Feb. 15—Johnny Owen, Merthyr..................L 8
Apr. 18—David Smith, Walworth..................D 8
May 23—David Smith, Walworth..................L 8
July 26—Terry Hanna, Derry.....................KO 5
Oct. 25—Charlie Magri, Kensington.........KO by 2
1978
June 27—Ian Murray, Derry......................W 8
Sept. 12—Gary Davidson, Wembley...............L 8
Oct. 27—Davy Larmour, Belfast..................L 10
Nov. 11—John Feeney, Marylebone...............L 8
1979
Feb. 19—Mohammad Younis, Belfast..............W 8
Apr. 5—Pip Coleman, Belfast....................KO 6
Apr. 21—Jean Jacques Souris, Creil.............L 8
Sept. 17—Johnny Owen, Glasgow.................L 10
Nov. 10—Enrique Rodriguez Cal, Aviles..........L 8
1980
Feb. 8—Ray Amoo, Lagos........................L 15
(For Vacant Commonwealth Flyweight Title)
Mar. 4—John Feeney, London...................IIO L 9
June 12—Mike Irungu, Randers..............KO by 3
Dec. 1—Dave George, Reading..................L 8

RON McLEAN
British Heavyweight
1979
Feb. 22—Theo Josephs, Liverpool...........KO by 5
Apr. 3—Kenny March, Hammersmith...........KO 1
May 1—Joe Awome, London.....................KO 1
June 26—Joe Awome, London................KO by 3
1980
Jan. 22—Andy Palmer, London..............KO by 2
Feb. 18—Martin Nee, Lewisham.............KO by 3
May 29—Martin Nee, Wimbledon.................L 8
Nov. 10—Andy Palmer, Southwark...........KO by 3

STEVE McLEOD
British Welterweight
1980
June 2—Shaun Bell, Glasgow....................KO 1
Sept. 9—Alan Cooper, Sheffield.................L 6
Oct. 14—Paul Murray, Wolverhampton............L 6

STIX McLEOD
Rhodesian Bantamweight
1980
Feb. 1—Paul Tshelba, Salisbury............KO by 2
Mar. 28—Joe Joburg, Bulawayo.............KO by 6
Apr. 7—Paul Tshelba, Salisbury................W 6
Sept. 9—Alan Cooper, Sheffield.................L 6

DANNY McLOUGHLIN
British Light Heavyweight
1975
Dec. 4—Len Brittain, Blackpool................KO 5
1976
Feb. 9—Pat Mahoney, London...................KO 6
Feb. 24—Tony Monoghan, Manchester...........W 6
Mar. 31—Len Brittain, Doncaster...............W 6
May 17—Winston Cousins, Manchester..........KO 1
June 7—Alex Penarski, Manchester.............L 8
Sept. 20—Tony Monoghan, Manchester..........W 8
Nov. 22—George Lewis, London.................W 6
1977
Mar. 24—Francis Hands, Bradford...............L 8
May 31—Johnny Waldron, Kensington........KO by 7
Sept. 14—Carlton Benoit, Sheffield.............L 8
Sept. 26—George Gray, Manchester..............KO 3
Dec. 1—Theo Josephs, Caister..................L 8
1978
Jan. 18—Steve Fenton, Solihull.................D 8
June 19—Ron Green, Manchester................L 8
June 29—Tony Sibson, Wolverhampton.......KO by 3
1979
(Inactive)
1980
Jan. 21—Mick Fellingham, Glasgow..............KO 2
Feb. 6—Steve Babbs, Liverpool.................KO 4
Feb. 21—Steve Hill, Liverpool.............KO by 4
Apr. 9—Steve Fenton, Liverpool...........KO by 1

JOE McNAMEE
British Lightweight
1980
Mar. 19—John Henry, Stoke................KO by 3
June 23—Alex Gregal, Glasgow.............KO by 4
Sept. 15—Bobby Welburn, Glasgow..........KO by 2

MOHAMMED MAALEN
Belgian Bantamweight
1980
Feb. 8—Rafael Blanco, Gentbrugge..............W 6
Apr. 18—Haidar Nourredine, Llauwe.............KO 3
May 1—Mohammed Knani, Tilerode..............

PHINEAS MABASO
South African Bantamweight
1979
July 26—George Seathlolo, Wattville............W 4
Oct. 18—Solomon Mokgesi, Tembisa.............KO 3
1980
May 3—Mncedisi Mbunje, East London..........L 4
July 3—Tenyson Molebeledi, Welkom............KO 4

EPHRAIM JABULANI MABENA
South African Junior Welterweight
1977
Nov. 26—Joseph Lala, Bloemfontein.............L 4
Dec. 14—Dumile Siko, Guguletu.................L 6
Mar. 31—Louis Sibiya, Natalspruit..............W 4
May 26—John Collins, Johannesburg.............KO 3
Sept. 30—Simon Zondo, Sharpeville.............W 8
Nov. 11—Peet Bothma, Johannesburg............W 6

1979
Apr.   7—David Kgotsane, Vereeniging .... W 6
May   4—Sydney Tshabalala, Springs .... W 6
Aug.   4—Mzwandile Biyane, East London .... L 6
Nov. 10—Simon Dhladhla, Jabulani .... W 6
1980
Mar. 22—Ernest Moledi, Soweto .... L 10
         (Transvaal Junior Welterweight Title)
May   30—Jonas Tladi, Springs .... W 6

ISAAC MABUZA
South African Junior Middleweight
1976
Apr.   2—Sophania Manyika, Orlando West .... W 4
1977
Oct. 14—Samson Mohloai, Krugersdorp .... L 6
Nov. 18—Kenneth Maseko, Krugersdorp .... W 4
1978
Nov. 27—Anton Retief, Johannesburg .... KO by 3
1979
         (Inactive)
1980
June   7—Johannes Chisale, Eldorado .... L 4

ABASS MACAULEY
Italian Lightweight
1976
Oct. 15—Augusto Quadri, Piacenza............... W 6
Nov. 19—Salvatore Morello, Piacenza............ KO 2
Dec. 10—Franco Benes, Monfalcone............... W 8
Dec. 26—Alvaro Checche, Piacenza.............. KO 2
1977
Mar. 11—Gregorio Ciancaglione, Milano .... KO by 3
Apr.   1—Luigi Zanghi, Bologna................... L 6
Apr. 29—Lucio Cusma, Bologna .... KO by 4
Sept. 17—Bernardo Ciaramella, Rome .... L 4
Oct. 21—Antonio Pocai, Piacenza................. W 8
Nov. 11—Jean Van Torre, Zele................... LF 3
Dec.   1—Vito Viola, Bologna .... L 6
Dec. 22—Alfonso Carillo, Capua .... L 8
1978
Feb.   3—Vincenzo Morano, Milan............... KO 3
May   19—Giovanni Vitillo, Viareggio .... L 6
June 15—John B. Muwanga, Oslo .... L 6
June 30—Ugo Polit, Sondrio..................... W 8
July 21—Vincenzo Quero, Rosenheim.............. L 6
Aug.   5—Eloy De Sooza, Ascol, Piceno........... L 8
Oct. 27—Mario Siddu, Florence .... L 8
Nov. 18—Ethem Oezakalin, Berlin .... L 8
Dec. 26—Andrea Ricci, Piacenza .... W 8
1979
Feb. 17—Angelo Bizzaro, Caserta .... L 6
Mar. 23—Domenico Traini, Porto S. Elpido .... L 8
Apr. 24—Nunziato Sanna, Calolziocorte .... L 8
May   25—Vincenzo Morana, Piacenza .... KO 5
June   8—Marino Angeli, Ravenna .... LF 4
June 23—Biagio Pierri, Cinisello Balsama .... L 8
July 21—Heleno Ferreira, Bellola .... D 8
Aug. 11—Vincenzo Quero, Ginosa .... L 8
Nov. 10—Giuseppe Ballone, Alghero .... L 6
Nov. 30—Marino Angeli, Forli .... L 6
Dec. 14—Bruno Simili, Pisa .... L 8
1980
Apr. 18—Fioravante Calce, Bologna .... W 6
Apr. 30—Rosario Di Tommaso, Nepi .... D 6
June 14—Mario Boero, Cagliari .... W 6
Oct. 11—Natale Carreda, Cagliari .... L 6

JOEY MACK
British Welterweight
1977
Apr.   7—Gerry Young, Belfast .... L 8
Apr. 18—Tommy Joyce, Nottingham .... L 8
May   17—Colin Ward, Wolverhampton .... W 8
June   1—Les Pearson, Dudley .... KO 1
June 13—Carlos Bailey, Manchester .... KO 2
Oct. 11—Henry Rhiney, Marylebone .... KO 7
Dec. 26—Mario Guilloti, Rimini................. L 8
1978
Jan.   3—Jo Kimpuani, Dunkerque................ L 10
Feb. 17—Clement Tshinza, Zele .... KO by 1
Apr. 10—Billy Lauder, Birmingham.............. KO 2
May   8—Billy Waith, Birmingham.............. L 8
Aug.   5—Gert Steyn, Empagnani................. L 8
Oct. 13—Rogelio Zarza, Ravenna................ L 8
Nov. 13—Giovanni Molesini, Milan .... KO by 4
1979
Jan. 17—Carl Bailey, Solihull .... KO 3
Feb.   6—Mick Mills, Wembley .... KO 3
May   2—Achille Mitchell, Solihull .... KO 4
Oct. 30—Colin Jones, Caerphilly .... KO by 10
1980
Jan. 16—Salvo Nuciforo, Solihull .... W 8

350

Sept. 9—Herol Graham, Sheffield .... L 8
Oct. 19—Roy Varden, Birmingham .... W 10
         (Retained Midlands Area Welterweight Title)

SIXULI MADONDILE
South African Flyweight
1978
May   27—Boy Mnyaka, East London .... L 4
1979
May   26—Boy Boy Mazaleni, King Williamstown ....L 4
July 14—Fernald Tilitwa, East London .... KO 3
Aug. 18—Sazi Tolbert, King Williamstown .... W 4
1980
May   3—Godfrey Mafanya, London .... W 4
Aug. 16—Honey Ndwanya, East London .... L 4
Dec. 13—Monde Mpulampula, Queenstown .... W 6

JULY MADUNA
South African Junior Welterweight
1978
Nov. 25—Isaac Khuzwayo, Durban .... W 4
1979
Aug. 18—Johnny Lutchanna, Durban .... L 4
Sept. 29—Joseph Nene, Durban .... L 4
1980
Mar. 28—Moses Mthembu, Durban .... KO by 6
         (Natal Lightweight Title)

SAMUEL MAFERE
South African Junior Featherweight
1979
Dec.   1—Israel Papane, Odendaalsrust .... L 4
1980
Feb.   2—Isreal Khonkhobe, Kimberley .... L 6
June   7—Samuel Motsumi, Welkom .... KO 2
Sept. 13—Samuel Wolf, Welkom .... KO by 1

SIMON MAFERE
South African Flyweight
1979
Feb. 10—Martin Nkokoto, Virginia .... W 4
Mar.   3—Johannes Phumo, Virginia .... KO 3
Mar. 24—Samuel Koalepe, Virginia .... L 4
Aug. 18—Jacob Mokonenyana, Welkom .... W 6
Dec.   1—Andrew Pietersen, Odendaalsrust .... L 6
1980
Feb.   2—Samuel Motsumi, Virginia .... W 4
Mar.   8—Ranching Louw, Odendaalsrust .... L 6
May   24—Gift Xaluva, Welkom .... L 6
Aug. 23—Elijah Diphagwe, Kimberley .... L 6

CHARLIE MAGRI
British Flyweight
Born: July 20, 1956
1977
Oct. 25—Neil McLaughlin, London............... KO 2
Nov. 15—Bryn Griffiths, London .... KO 2
Dec.   6—Dave Smith, London................... KO 7
         (British Flyweight Title)
1978
Feb. 21—Nessem Zebellini, London............... KO 3
Apr.   4—Dominique Cesari, London .... KO 3
Apr. 25—Manuel Carrasco, London............... W 8
Sept. 12—Sabatino De Filippo, London .... KO 7
Oct. 24—Claudio Tanda, Kensington .... KO 1
Dec.   5—Mariano Garcia, Kensington .... KO 3
1979
Jan. 23—Filipo Belvedere, London.............. KO 1
Feb. 20—Mike Stuart, London .... KO 3
May   1—Franco Udella, London .... W 12
         (European Flyweight Title)
May   29—Freddie Gonzalez Kensington .... KO 3
Sept. 25—Ray Pacheco, London .... KO 6
Oct. 23—Candy Iglesias, London .... KO 3
Dec.   5—Manuel Carrasco, London .... W 12
         (For EBU Flyweight Title)
1980
Jan. 22—Aniceto Vargas, London .... KO 3
June 28—Giovanni Camputaro, Glasgow .... KO 3
         (Retained European Flyweight Title)

MONSAYARM (MONSIAM) H. MAHACAI
Thai Bantamweight
1975
Mar. 31—Little Park, Bangkok .... KO 6
May   30—Dan Reyes, Bangkok .... W 12
         (Title)
Sept. 24—Ravee Sithchangsee, Bangkok.......... KO 6
         (Title)
1976
June   6—Chung Sang II, Seoul .... L 12
         (Orient Junior Flyweight Title)

1977
Apr. 29—Matuphum Siththumrong, Bangkok ..... KO 3
July 15—Seki Singthong, Bangkok .... W 10
Oct. 9—Yoko Gushiken, Beppu .... KO by 4
    (WBA Junior Flyweight Title)
1978
Oct. 12—Dan Pisalchai, Bangkok .... L 10
    (Thai Flyweight Title)
Dec. 7—Duen Esan Luklongjun, Bangkok .... D 6
1979
Nov. 16—Kingpetch Vachirasakdi, Bangkok ..... KO 1
1980
Feb. 5—Kongchai Sithgunpai, Bangkok .... KO 4
Mar. 18—Unmach Singhjinda, Bangkok .... KO 3

JOSHUA MAHLANGU
South African Bantamweight
1979
Mar. 3—Benjamin Sebego, Virginia .... KO 1
June 16—Jacob Molefe, Virginia .... L 4
1980
Apr. 25—Edward Twayl, Sebokeng .... W 4
Oct. 4—Joseph Diraditsile, Welkom .... L 6

DAVID MAJOE
South African Junior Featherweight
1979
Aug. 4—Martin Nkokoto, Odendaalsrust .... L 4
1980
June 7—January Bongo, Odenaalsrust .... W 4
Sept. 6—Joseph Diraditsile, Welkom ..... KO by 5

JONAS MAJORO
South African Welterweight
1980
Sept. 6—Klaas Dhlamini, Welkom .... KO 1
Sept. 13—Samuel Motake, Welkom .... W 6
Oct. 4—Johannes Modise, Welkom .... KO 4
Dec. 6—Johannes Tiadi, Welkom .... W 6

TERRENCE MAKALUZA
South African Junior Middleweight
Born: March 6, 1957
1970
Sept. 12—Z. Pule, King Williamstown .... KO 3
Dec. 20—Happy Boy Mgxaji, Langa .... KO by 3
1971
June 26—Aycliff Stengile, King Williamstown .... KO 5
Aug. 7—Victor Tshabalala, East London .... L 8
Nov. 20—Richard Borias, King Williamstown ..... W 6
1972
Feb. 19—Anthony Morodi, King Williamstown ..... D 8
Aug. 26—Gash Dlamini, ... W 8
Sept. 2—Cecil Kekana, East London .... D 6
Oct. 7—Jeremiah Nzelwane, East London .... L 8
1973
Feb. 3—Jerry Molefe, King Williamstown .... W 6
Mar. 3—Jack Jim, King Williamstown .... L 10
Aug. 4—Griffith Mgijima, King Williamstown .... L 6
Sept. 29—Zolile Khonza, Port Elizabeth .... W 10
Nov. 10—Griffith Mgijima, Port Elizabeth .... L 10
1974
Apr. 13—A. Ntuli, Port Elizabeth .... W 6
May 31—Philip Hlophe, Umtata .... W 6
1975
Apr. 5—Thusa Mapela, Port Elizabeth .... W 6
Aug. 9—Louis Miya, Port Elizabeth .... W 8
1976
Nov. 6—Loyisa Myta, King Williamstown .... D 8
1978
Mar. 19—Loyisa Mtya, Port Elizabeth .... KO by 10
Apr. 1—Volfart Rala, East London .... KO by 6
Nov. 4—Robert Kleynhans, Port Elizabeth .... W 6
1979
Feb. 3—Andre Nel, Port Elizabeth .... W 6
June 2—Joseph Hali, Port Elizabeth .... W 6
Nov. 3—Elijah Makhathini, Port Elizabeth .... W 8
1980
Mar. 29—Charlie Weir, Johannesburg .... KO by 4
Oct. 11—Volfart Rafa, Port Elizabeth .... W 10
    (Cape Middleweight Title)

ZENZILE MAKANDA
South African Lightweight
1977
Oct. 6—David Kalako, Bloemfontein .... KO by 3
Nov. 26—Daniel Mphuthi, Bloemfontein .... W 4
1978
Aug. 12—William Malefane, Bloemfontein .... D 6
Dec. 4—Robert Donaldson, Bloemfontein .... L 4
1979
Feb. 5—Michael Motsoane, Welkom .... L 4

May 30—Mannetjie Oliver, Bloemfontein .... D 4
Nov. 9—Sydney Classen, Bloemfontein .... W 4
Dec. 14—David Motlengwa, Welkom .... KO by 1
1980
Mar. 21—Thomas Taylor, Bloemfontein .... W 4
Aug. 28—Nathaniel Moloi, Sebokeng .... KO by 2

CHARLES MAKASI
South African Featherweight
Born: May 14, 1953
1975
May 30—Isaac Gwebu, Kwa-Thema .... KO 2
June 28—Jonas Skosana, Jabulani .... KO 4
1976
Apr. 17—Lennox Mtyongwe, East London ..... KO by 2
May 15—Koos Slaffa, Jabulani .... W 4
1977
(Inactive)
1978
Aug. 12—Paulus Mnisi, Johannesburg .... L 4
1979
Mar. 9—Joshua Nhlapo, Springs .... L 4
1980
Feb. 29—Howard Motumi, Springs .... D 4

ELIJAH (TAP TAP) MAKHATINI
South African Middleweight
1971
May 1—Derrick Mncwango, Durban .... KO 6
June 19—Maxwell Malinga, Durban .... KO 1
June 30—Joe Joker, Durban...................... W 6
Aug. 7—Jetros Luhungwana, Durban .... W 6
Aug. 14—Gordon Goba, Durban................... W 8
Sept. 18—John Fighter, Durban .... KO 4
1972
Jan. 22—Abraham Siberko, Durban .... KO 3
Apr. 8—Simon Sithole, Durban .... KO 2
May 6—Joe Sishi, Durban .... W 10
May 27—Sydney Hoho, Durban .... KO 7
Aug. 4—Gordon Goba, Springs .... W 10
Sept. 2—Curtis Cokes, Durban .... W 10
Sept. 23—Zolile Khonza, Port Elizabeth .... W 8
Oct. 5—Sydney Hoho, Cape Town................ L 12
Nov. 11—Abraham Sibeko, Durban .... KO 7
Dec. 2—Maxwell Milinga, Durban .... L 10
1973
Mar. 10—Joseph Sishi, Durban................... KO 7
May 24—Willie Warren, Cape Town .... W 10
June 16—Willie Warren, Durban .... W 10
Aug. 25—Gordon Goba, Durban .... W 10
Dec. 22—Billy Douglas, Durban................... W 10
1974
Jan. 17—Sydney Hoho, Cape Town............ KO by 11
Aug. 17—Juarez Lima, Johannesburg .... W 10
Sept. 14—Richard Ndlovu, Stanger............... W 6
Sept. 23—Joseph Hali, Cape Town .... W 10
1975
May 10—Joseph Sishi, Stanger................... W 10
June 21—Carl Speare, Stanger................... L 10
Aug. 9—Emile Griffith, Johannesburg .... W 10
Oct. 27—Manuel Fierro, Durban .... W 10
1976
Apr. 10—Victor Ntloko, Stanger................... KO 7
    (South African Non-White Middleweight Title)
June 5—David Love, Jabulani Amphiteature....... L 10
June 19—Gordon Goba, Port Elizabeth .... W 10
Nov. 27—Jan Kies, Johannesburg...............KO 3
    (South African Middleweight Title)
1977
Jan. 29—Joseph Hali, Port Elizabeth .... KO 10
    (South African Black Middleweight Title)
Feb. 28—Morgan Moledi, Durban .... KO 11
    (South African Black Middleweight Title)
July 9—Morgan Moledi, Stanger .... W 10
Aug. 1—Doug Lumley, Durban .... L 12
    (South African Middleweight Title)
Oct. 29—Nat King, Johannesburg .... W 10
Nov. 28—Doug Lumley, Durban................... L 12
    (South African Middleweight Title)
1978
Feb. 22—Jan Kies, Cape Town .... W 8
Mar. 18—Maxwell Malinga, Durban .... W 10
May 29—Morgan Moledi, Durban .... KO 8
Aug. 5—Howard Mills, Empangani .... KO 5
Aug. 28—Daniel Mapanya, Durban .... KO 7
Oct. 10—Bonifacio Avila, Durban .... W 10
Nov. 11—Tommy Howard, Johannesburg.......... KO 5
1979
Feb. 12—Gert Steyn, Durban .... L 10
Apr. 25—Charlie Weir, Johannesburg .... KO 8
June 2—Gary Guiden, Mmabatho .... KO 4
June 30—Alfredo Cabral, Monte Carlo .... KO by 1
Nov. 3—Terence Makaluza, Port Elizabeth .... L 8
Nov. 10—Terence Makaluza, Jabulani .... L 10

Dec.   1—Anton Retief, Empangeni .... W disq. 6
1980
Apr. 14—Daniel Mapanya, Durban ....L 10
May   19—Doug Lumley, Durban ....L 8

ROBERT MAKHOBA
South African Bantamweight
1977
Nov. 12—Leslie Bunting, Durban ....W 4
1978
Mar. 18—Roy Damon, Durban ....KO 2
Aug. 12—Alexander Sibiya, Durban ....KO 3
1979
Mar. 10—Paul Tshela, Newcastle ....L 4
July 28—Lundi Skepu, King Williamstown ....W 4
Aug. 18—Richard Mthombeni, King Williamstown KO 3
Sept. 29—Aziz Dawood, Durban ....KO 2
Nov.   3—Lundi Skepu, Queenstown ....D 4
1980
Mar.   1—Siphe Bhengu, Durban ....KO 4
(Won Vacant Natal Bantamweight Title)
Nov. 10—Joseph Ngubane, Durban ....KO by 10
(Lost Natal Bantamweight Title)

KOICHI MAKI
Japanese Flyweight
(Previous Record Unavailable)
1976
Jan. 30—Beaver Kajimoto, Nagoya ....L 10
Mar. 28—Isao Watanabe, Tokyo ....W 10
Nov. 19—Tsutomu Igarachi, Hirosaki City ....D 10
1977
Mar.   9—Dan Pisalchai, Bangkok ....L 10
Aug. 26—Gosho Ohfu, Nagoya City...............KO 9
Nov. 28—Bazooka Shoji, Tokyo...................W 10
1978
Mar. 27—Kenji Kato, Tokyo......................W 10
(Japanese Flyweight Title)
Sept. 13—Susumu Wakabayashi, Isawa ....W 10
Oct. 30—Tsutomu Igarashi, Tokyo ....L 10
1979
Feb. 22—Ryu Kaionji, Tokyo ....KO 8
(Japanese Flyweight Title)
   —Kazumasa Tamaki, Tokyo ....KO 8
(Japanese Flyweight Title)
May   31—Massuru Fuji, Nigata ....W 10
(JBC Flyweight Title)
Nov. 22—Nobuyuki Watanabe, Tokyo ....W 10
(Japanese Flyweight Title)
1980
Jan. 10—Kazumasa Tamaki, Tokyo ....L 10
(Lost Japanese Flyweight Title)
Apr. 24—Kazumasa Tamaki, Tokyo ....D 10
(For Japanese Flyweight Title)

WILLIE MAKITOKI
Filipino Lightweight
1979
July 20—Celso Esmero, Manila ....W 10
Sept. 7—Mar Alverio, Manila ....W 10
Nov. 16—Al Cordero, Quezon City ....L 10
Dec. 14—Edward Heneral, Manila ....L 10
1980
Feb.   8—Mar Simbajon, Manila ....L 10

JONAS MALAN
South African Heavyweight
1979
Apr.   2—Gary Webb, Welkom ....KO by 3
Sept. 15—Timothy Zwane, Johannesburg ....L 4
1980
Mar.   1—Robbie Williams, Durban ....KO by 3
May   5—Louis Hendriks, Welkom ....KO by 3
Aug.   4—Bertie Potgieter, Durban ....L 4
Oct.   6—Mark Melville, Pmburg ....W 4
Nov.   1—Marcus Ndhlovu, Stanger ....KO 4

CHARLEY MALARKY
Scottish Junior Middleweight
1977
Oct. 10—Albert Smith, Glasgow...................W 6
Nov. 14—Willie Turkington, Glasgow ....W 8
Dec.   8—Joe Lally, Liverpool ....KO by 8
1978
Jan. 23—Brian Gregory, Bradford..................L 8
Feb. 27—Terry Schofield, Middlesbrough..........W 8
Mar. 20—Tony Burnett, Glasgow ....W 8
May   8—Billy Lauder, Glasgow...................L 10
June 19—Slavo Nucigero, Glasgow ....L 8
Oct. 18—Carl Bailey, Glasgow...................KO 3
Nov. 13—Terry Petersen, Glasgow ....W 8
1979
Jan.   8—Roy Commosioung, London ....W 8

Feb. 26—Joe Oke, Glasgow ....W 8
Apr. 23—John Smith, Glasgow ....W 12
Oct.   8—Salvo Nuciforo, London ....W 8
Oct. 19—Fred Coranson, Dunkerque ....L 10
Nov.   5—George Walker, Piccadilly ....L 8
1980
Mar. 14—Prince Rodney, Glasgow ....W 10
May   5—Harry Watson, Glasgow ....W 8
(Retained Scottish Junior Middleweight Title)
June   7—Steve Hopkin, Glasgow ....KO by 5
(For Vacant British Junior Middleweight Title)
Sept. 16—Jimmy Batten, London ....KO by 4

JEFF MALCOLM
Australian Junior Welterweight
Born: May 9, 1956
1971
Sept. 22—John Cassidy, Guildford...................W 4
Oct. 20—Larry Saddler, Guildford...................L 4
1972
June 15—Brian Roberts, Redfern ....D 3
June 29—Brian Roberts, Redfern ....D 4
Aug.   8—Brian Roberts, Marrickville ....L 4
Aug. 16—Ian McNeil, Cammeray ....D 4
Sept. 12—Steve Walker, Marrickville ....W 4
Sept. 20—Wally Carr, Cammeray ....D 4
Oct.   5—Rod Connors, Redfern ....L 4
Oct. 10—Rod Connors, Marrickville ....D 4
Oct. 12—J. J. Finley, Redfern ....D 4
Oct. 19—Peter Knott, Redfern ....KO 3
Nov.   7—Neil Patel, Marrickville ....D 8
Nov. 23—Mick Mercedes, Redfern.................W 6
Dec. 12—Keith Ball, Marrickville ....W 6
1973
Jan. 17—Gwynn Jones, Kingsford ....W 4
Jan. 29—Greg Haggert, Melbourne ....D 4
Feb. 14—Alan Hedges, Redfern ....KO 5
Feb. 22—Nev. Short, Blacktown ....KO 3
Mar.   1—J. J. Finlay, Blacktown ....W 6
Apr.   5—J. J. Finlay, Blacktown ....W 6
Apr. 19—Tony McCoy, Blacktown ....W 6
July 12—Frank Geebung, Blacktown ....W 6
July 17—Kid George, Cronulla ....W 8
July 19—Jim Metcalf, Blacktown ....W 8
Aug. 23—Frank Geebung, Blacktown ....W 6
Aug. 29—Peter Knott, Cammeray ....W 8
Sept. 20—Danny Reilly, Blacktown ....W 8
Nov.   7—Neil Pattell, Marrickville.................D 8
1974
Feb. 13—Michael Cassidy, Marrickville ....L 10
Apr. 10—Billy Moeller, Marrickville..........L disq. 7
June   5—Danny Reilly, Cammeray ....W 8
June 12—Billy Moeller, Marrickville ....W 8
June 27—Shocker Myles, Blacktown ....KO 4
July   3—Merv Wockner, Cammeray ....L 10
Aug.   7—Jim Metcalfe, Cammeray ....W 8
Sept. 10—Binky Rominsky, New Lambton ....W 8
Oct. 24—Billy Moeller, Blacktown ....L 10
Dec.   5—Mick O'Brien, Blacktown ....KO 5
1975
Feb. 12—Shocker Myles, Marrickville ....W 10
Mar.   6—Dave Richards, Blacktown ....L 10
Mar. 25—Dade Emerald, New Lambton ....W 10
Apr.   9—Billy Moeller, Marrickville ....L 10
Apr. 22—Kim McCain, New Lambton ....KO 4
June 11—Billy Moeller, Marrickville ....W 10
Aug. 13—Billy Mulholland, Marrickville ....L 10
Oct. 10—Billy Mulholland, Wollongong ....L 10
Oct. 16—Ross Eadie, Blacktown ....L 10
Nov. 13—Kim McCain, Blacktown ....D 10
1976
Apr.   7—Jimmy Greco, Cammeray ....W 8
Apr. 14—Matt Ropis, Marrickville ....W 8
May   18—Ross Eadie, Kingsford ....L 10
Sept. 8—Buddy Nixon, Marrickville ....W 8
Oct. 13—Joey Gibilisco, Marrickville ....W 10
Nov.   5—Billy Mulholland, Port Kembla ....W 10
Dec.   8—Andy Broome, Marrickville ....W 10
1977
Apr. 27—Buddy Nixon, Albury ....W 6
July 30—Kevin Gibb, The Grange ....KO 10
Aug. 10—Kerry Bell, Marrickville ....L 10
Sept. 22—Tony Aba, Boroko.....................KO 5
Oct.   6—Mark Apai, Hoholo ....WF 4
(Australian Junior Welterweight Title)
1978
Feb. 16—Hector Thompson, Melbourne ....L 12
Mar. 26—Billy Moeller, Parks League ....W 12
Apr. 15—Sakaraia Ve, Suva ....W 10
Apr. 28—Barry Michael, Melbourne ....W 10
Sept. 24—Lachie Austin, Rockbank ....W 15
(Commonwealth Junior Welterweight Title)
Dec.   2—Paul Baker, Hillston ....KO 9
Dec. 15—Lachie Austin, Griffity ....W 15

1979

Mar. 3—Obisis Nwakpa, Lagos .... L 15
(Commonwealth Junior Welterweight Title)
Apr. 13—Tony Aba, Griffith .... KO 7
Sept. 19—Jimmy Brown, Melbourne .... W 10
Nov. 2—Frank Ropis, Griffith .... WF 3
(Retained Australian Junior Welterweight Title)
Nov. 13—Celso Esmero, Port Moresby .... W 10

1980

May 4—Wongso Suseno, Jakarta .... W 10
June 6—Binky Rominsky, Wollongong .... WF 9
(Retained Australian Junior Welterweight Title)
July 4—Speedy Duke, Wollongong .... KO 3
(Retained Australian Junior Welterweight Title)
July 18—Graham Bell, Dapto .... W 12
(Retained Australian Junior Welterweight Title)
Oct. 4—Joe Nitiva, Suva .... W 8
Oct. 16—Joe Nitiva, Marrickville .... W 10

ELIAS MALEFANE
South African Junior Middleweight
Born: October 28, 1951

1973

May 5—Wilfred Twala, Sharpeville .... D 4
Oct. 6—Daniel Mokhema, Sharpeville .... KO 3

1974

Apr. 6—William Raserogeng, Sharpeville .... W 4

1975

Apr. 26—Abie Radebe, Sharpeville .... W 4
June 28—Alfred Sibisi, Jabulani .... L 4
Sept. 6—Daniel Makhudu, Sharpeville .... L 6

1976
(Inactive)

1977

July 9—Sidney Tshabalala, Parys .... L 4

1978
(Inactive)

1979

Mar. 3—John Kooe, Virginia .... L 6

1980

May 4—Leo Simelane, Orlando .... KO by 3

WILLIAM MALEFANE
South African Middleweight

1976

Nov. 6—David Mokhele, Parys .... L 4

1977

July 9—Samson Mohloai, Parys .... L 6
Nov. 5—David Mokhele, Parys .... L 4

1978

Aug. 12—Zenzile Makanda, Bloemfontein .... D 6

1979

Nov. 10—Samson Mohloai, Jabulani .... KO by 1
Dec. 3—Thomas Taylor, Welkom .... KO 2

1980

Mar. 21—Bollie Hendriks, Bloemfontein .... D 4

ZOLA MALI
South African Bantamweight

1979

Nov. 3—Zandile Nukani, Queenstown .... W 4

1980

May 31—Mxolisi Galada, East London .... W 4
Nov. 22—Edward Genue, Queenstown .... W 4
Dec. 13—Vuyani Xabanisa, Queenstown .... KO by 3

JEREMIA MALIKHETLA
South African Junior Lightweight

1977

Dec. 3—David Motaung, Ficksburg .... W 4

1978

Oct. 7—Samuel Motsabi, Virginia .... W 4

1979

Feb. 9—Joseph Ntela, Bethlehem .... KO
Feb. 24—David Motaung, Bethlehem .... L 6
Sept. 1—Manase Potse, Ficksburg .... KO 4
Nov. 17—Abel Rapulane, Ficksburg .... W 6

1980

Feb. 9—Joseph Ntela, Bethlehem .... KO 3
Apr. 12—Daniel Mkenku, Ficksburg .... W 6
Sept. 6—Daniel Mkenku, Ficksburg .... L 6
Dec. 6—Michael Mohiabane, Ficksburg .... L 6

DAVID MALINGA
South African Flyweight

1979

Feb. 9—James Mqeku, Bethlehem .... W 8
May 5—Martin Nkokoto, Ficksburg .... L 4
May 12—James Mqheku, Virginia .... L 4
Nov. 17—Alfred Sebala, Ficksburg .... W 6

1980

Feb. 9—James Mqeku, Bethlehem .... L 8

May 31—Martin Nkokoto, Bethlehem .... L 10
(OFS Junior Flyweight Title)
Aug. 23—Martin Nkokoto, Bethlehem .... W 8
Dec. 1—Lloyd Seghapane, Virginia .... L 8

MAXWELL MALINGA
South African Middleweight

1973

Feb. 9—Johannes Dladla, Springs .... W 8
Apr. 14—Cecil Kekane, Durban .... W disq. 7
June 16—McKeed Mofokeng, Port Elizabeth .... W 6
June 20—Gordon Goba, Springs................. W 8
Oct. 13—McKeed Mofokeng, Durban .... KO 10
Oct. 27—Abraham Sibeko, Durban................ W 10
Nov. 24—Thurman (Doc) Holliday, Johannesburg... W 10

1974

Feb. 2—Cecil Kekan, Ladysmith .... KO 7
June 7—Victor Tahabalala, Springs............... W 12
(South African Welterweight Title)
July 19—Alvin Anderson, Durban .... D 10
Aug. 31—Daniel Mkhize, Port Elizabeth........... W 8
Sept. 7—Cecil Kekana, Pietermaritzburg .... W 10
Oct. 26—Eddie Perkins, Johannesburg .... W 10
Dec. 14—Griffith Mgijima, Ladysmith .... KO 10
(South African Non-White Welterweight Title)

1975

Feb. 8—Joe Hali, East London .... W 10
May 3—Joe Hali, Durban....................... W 8
May 30—Moses Mohleai, Springs .... L 12
(South African Non-White Welterweight Title)
Nov. 28—Moses (Morris) Mohleai, Springs .... L 12

1976

Oct. 11—Richard Ndlovu, Durban................ KO 4
Dec. 18—Daniel Sereme, Durban................. W 10

1977

Feb. 28—Doug Lumley, Durban .... L 10
June 6—Victor Ntloko, Durban .... W 12

1978

Mar. 18—Elijah Makhathini, Durban.............. L 10
Apr. 29—Daniel Mapanya, Cape Town......... KO by 5

1979

Mar. 10—Morgan Moledi, Johannesburg .... W 6

1980

Mar. 1—Bushy Bester, Ermelo .... KO by 6

SIPHWE MALINGA
South African Lightweight

1978

Aug. 5—Abel Brown, Empangeni .... KO by 3

1979

Mar. 10—Moses Mthembu, Newcastle .... W 4

1980

Nov. 3—Brian Baronet, Durban .... KO by 3

PAT MALLON
British Bantamweight

1980

May 27—Steve Pollard, Glasgow .... L 6
June 23—Tony Manson, Glasgow .... W 2
Oct. 8—George Bailey, Stoke .... L 8

TIM MALONEY
British Lightweight

1979

Sept. 17—Ray Price, Mayfair .... W 6
Oct. 8—Mike Clemow, London .... W 6
Oct. 15—Wally Stocks, Mayfair .... W 6
Oct. 29—Tony Davis, Hove .... W 4
Dec. 3—Ray Price, Marylebone .... W 6

1980

Jan. 28—Dave Laxen, Hove .... W 6
Mar. 3—Wally Stockings, Hove .... W 6
Mar. 17—Tony Davis, London .... W 6
Apr. 23—Danny Connolly, Hove .... W 8
May 15—Jarvis Greenidge, London .... W 8
May 27—Peter Harrison, Glasgow .... L 8
June 3—Tommy Thomas, Aylesbury .... W 4
Oct. 20—Barry Price, Hove .... W 8

NEIL MALPASS
British Heavyweight

1977

Feb. 10—Roy Johnson, Coventry .... L 4
Feb. 23—Keith Johnson, Bradford .... KO 3
Feb. 28—Johnny Clark, Mayfair .... KO 3
Feb. 28—Henry Mears, Mayfair .... KO 3
Feb. 28—Brian Paul, London .... W 4
Mar. 24—Johnny Clark, Leicester .... KO 3
Apr. 4—Ward, Luton .... KO 3
May 9—Derek Simpkin, London .... W 6
July 18—Tony Blackburn, London .... KO 3
Sept. 19—Danny McAlinden, London .... KO 3
Oct. 25—Kris Smith, London .... KO 1

353

Nov.	8—Tommy Kiely, London	L	8
Dec.	12—Sean Reilly, Barnsley	KO	3

1978

Jan.	19—Austin Okoye, Wimbledon	KO by	4
Feb.	20—Peter Freeman, Bradford	KO	2
Feb.	27—Sean (Jumbo) McKenna, Sheffield	KO	2
Mar.	20—Paul Sykes, Bradford	W disq.	7
Apr.	24—George Scott, Middlesbrough	L	8
June	1—Bob Polard, Heathrow	L	8
July	12—Colin Flute, Newcastle	KO	6
July	18—Paul Sykes, Wakefield	D	10
Sept.	27—Bob Pollard, Rotterdam	W	8
Dec.	4—Christian Poncelet, Marton	KO	3

1979

June	16—Mike Schutte, Johannesburg	L	8
Oct.	1—Billy Aird, Marylebone	L	10
Nov.	28—Terry Mintus, Doncaster	L disq.	5

1980

Mar.	3—Theo Josephs, Marton	W	8
Mar.	19—Theo Josephs, Doncaster	W	8
Apr.	21—Joe Awome, London	KO	6
July	17—Alfredo Evangelista, Barcelona	L	8
Sept.	27—Clarence Hill, Wembley	KO by	2

SIPHO MANGE
South African Featherweight
1972

Nov.	18—Mongezi Ntshinka, Port Elizabeth	L	6

1973

Oct.	5—Thomas Sithebe, Springs	L	6

1974-1975
(Inactive)
1976

Jan.	29—Griffiths Jacobs, Guguletu	KO	4
Mar.	1—Fezile Mzalazala, Guguletu	W	6
Mar.	22—Bassie Modise, Guguletu	W	6
Apr.	28—Xolile Ngxabani, Guguletu	KO	6

1977

Mar.	15—Leslie Pikoli, Mbekweni	L	10
May	30—James Jacobs, Goodwood	W	4
Dec.	14—Cecil Baatjies, Guguletu	L	6

1978

Nov.	15—Freddie Rust, Cape Town	W	6
Dec.	18—Chris Dlamini, Goodwood	W	12

1979

Mar.	7—Alex Venter, Cape Town	W	12
	(South African Junior Featherweight Title)		
June	21—Ralph Barrios, Cape Town	W	8
Sept.	27—Bashew Sibaca, Cape Town	L	12
	(South African Featherweight Title)		
Dec.	19—Patrick Kohli, Cape Town	KO	4

1980

Feb.	4—Johan Putter, Welkom	KO	4
	(Regained Junior Featherweight Title)		
Mar.	1—Welile Nkosonkulu, East London	KO by	5
Sept.	5—Nkosana Moss, Springs	L	12
	(Lost Junior Featherweight Title)		
Oct.	15—Herbert Plaatjies, Cape Town	W	8

JEFFREY MANKUNE
South African Junior Welterweight
1980

June	7—David Louw, Johannesburg	KO	5
Oct.	4—Godfrey Mashaya, Johannesburg	KO	2

TIGER MANN
(KUSAK KAMENIAK)
Australian Featherweight
1979

June	29—John Kopi, Port Moresby	KO	6
Nov.	17—Charlie Brown, Port Moresby	D	10

1980

Mar.	21—Steve Freeman, Port Moresby	WF	5
Apr.	26—Billy Facer, Goroka	KO	4
Nov.	28—Patrick Young, Port Moresby	KO	6

FABIO MANNAI
Italian Welterweight
1979

Mar.	31—Silvio Ortiz, Cagliari	W	6
May	25—Pietro Donati, Cagliari	W	6
June	23—Pietro Donati, Sassari`	L	6
Oct.	19—Antonio Pisani, Cagliari	W	6
Dec.	28—Antonio Pocai, Cagliari	W	6

1980

Jan.	17—Antonio Pocai, Genova	W	6
Mar.	28—Vincenzo Morena, Cagliari	KO	3
May	22—Lorenzo Paciullo, Bologna	L	6

TONY MANSON
British Bantamweight
1980

Apr.	24—Eddie McAllister, Queensway	KO by	1

June	23—Pat Mallon, Glasgow	KO by	2
Sept.	29—Steve Farnsworth, Chesterfield	L	6

WILLIAM MANTSO
South African Lightweight
1976

Sept.	11—Michel Zim, Kroonstad	W	4

1977

Apr.	16—Michel Zim, Kroonstad	W	4
June	18—John Masapo, Parys	L	4
Oct.	8—Anthony Mohlala, Kroonstad	KO	1
Nov.	5—Moses Dabula, Viljoenskroon	W	6

1978

Jan.	28—Boy Boy Mtimkulu, East London	L	6
Nov.	28—Johannes Motsumi, Virginia	L	6

1979
(Inactive)
1980

Mar.	1—Enock Motsoane, Odenaalsrust	D	4

GODFREY MANYANISO
South African Junior Welterweight
1976

Oct.	9—Ernest Thibeli, Kroonstad	L	6

1977

June	11—Paulus Dichakane, Kroonstad	L	4
June	18—Allen Ferland, Parys	L	4

1978
(Inactive)
1979

May	12—Ezekiel Medupe, Virginia	W	4
Oct.	5—Stanley Ledimo, Bloemfontein	KO	2
Nov.	9—Martin Jacobs, Bloemfontein	L	6
Nov.	19—Daniel Mkhize, Kimberley	L	6
Dec.	8—Daniel Mkhize, Bloemfontein	W	6

1980

May	24—Mtutuzeli Ngqakayi, Welkom	L	6
Sept.	6—Johannes Modise, Welkom	W	6
Dec.	6—Sydney Tshabalala, Welkom	W	6

DANIEL MAPANYA
South African Middleweight
1975

Feb.	28—Petrus Kubheka, Kwa-Thema	W	4
Mar.	21—Sophania Manyika, Kwa-Thema	KO	1
June	28—George Motswalo, Jabulani	KO	4
Aug.	1—Johannes Dhladhla, Kwa-Thema	KO	2
Aug.	30—McKeed Mofokeng, Jabulani	L	6
Oct.	25—Gordon Goba, Jabulani	KO by	6
Nov.	28—Lemwell Nkumane, Kwa-Thema	W	4

1976

Feb.	6—Johannes Mlotshwa, Kwa-Thema	W	6
Mar.	27—Meshack Chlamini, Natalspruit	KO	3
Mar.	6—Charapane Mofokeng, Kroonstad	KO	1
Apr.	30—Joel Ndlovu, Springs	KO	3
Dec.	4—France Manyaniso, Welkom	W	8

1977

June	3—Gordon Goba, Springs	W	8

1978

Feb.	27—Doug Lumley, Durban	KO	1
Apr.	29—Maxwell Malinga, Cape Town	KO	5
May	29—Doug Lumley, Durban	KO	3
	(South African Middleweight Title)		
July	3—Mark Melville, Welkom	KO	6
July	31—Dan Snyder, Cape Town	W	10
Aug.	28—Elijah Makhatini, Durban	KO by	7

1979

Mar.	9—McDonald Shezi, Springs	KO	3
June	11—Stanley Maxembenqula, Welkom	KO	5
July	9—Joe Shishi, Welkom	KO	6
Sept.	15—Cameron Adams, Johannesburg	KO by	2

1980

Apr.	14—Elijah Makhatini, Durban	W	10
May	15—Themba Buthelezi, Durban	W	8
Nov.	21—Samson Mohioai, Sebokeng	KO by	7

MICKY MAPP
British Welterweight
1979

Sept.	17—Pat Smithe, Mayfair	W	6
Oct.	9—Jeff Aspel, Kensington	W	6
Nov.	6—Dave Aspel, Kensington	W	6
Dec.	3—Jeff Aspel, Marylebone	W	6

1980

Jan.	21—Kevin Walsh, London	W	6
Feb.	18—Jeff Lee, Lewisham	W	8
Mar.	10—Nigel Thomas, London	W	8
Apr.	28—Jeff Lee, Southwark	W	8
Oct.	6—Tony Britton, Southwark	W	6
Nov.	3—Liam Linnen, Hammersmith	W	8
Nov.	10—Achille Mitchell, Southwark	D	8

FRANCESCO MARCELLO
Italian Lightweight
1978
Apr. 8—Gabriele Peruzzi, Torino .... KO 4
May 27—Giovannino Mannu, Fort Village ..... KO by 1
July 8—Granco Cantu, Forte Village .... KO 2
1979
Mar. 17—Luigi Curcetti, Chivasso .... KO 3
Apr. 18—Luigi Del Santo, Torino .... KO 2
May 18—Raimondo Riccio, Torino .... KO 3
Sept. 28—Salvatore Morello, Torino .... KO 2
Oct. 10—Michel Iger, Torino .... KO 1
Nov. 9—Eloy De Souza, Torino .... W 8
Dec. 21—Giuseppe Agate, Casalmonferrato .... W 8
1980
Mar. 7—Jean Marie Cotinaut, Torino .... W 8
Apr. 18—Boro Jovic, Torino .... KO 7

KENNY MARCH
British Heavyweight
1979
Apr. 3—Ron McLean, Hammersmith .... KO by 1
Oct. 3—Les Dunn, Reading .... L 6
Oct. 17—Martin Nee, Lewisham .... W 6
Nov. 26—Stuart Lithgoe, Hammersmith .... L 6
1980
Feb. 4—Mick Chmilowskyz, Hammersmith ... KO by 2
(Announced Retirement)

TORKANO MARCOS
Australian Middleweight
1976
Jan. 20—Pierin Mingon, Brookvale .... L 5
Feb. 24—Artie Bronson, Kingsford ... W 4
Apr. 6—John Rogers, Kingsford .... KO 3
Apr. 7—Ray Hovendon, Cammeray .... KO 2
Apr. 20—Frank Atkins, Kingsford .... W 6
May 4—Johnny Compain, Kingsford .... W 6
June 1—Jeff Sait, Kingsford .... W 6
Aug. 18—Steve Campbell, Brookvale .... W 5
Dec. 2—Bobby Wayne, Hillsdale .... D 4
1977
Jan. 25—Phil Khan, Kingsford .... KO 2
Mar. 8—John Layton, Kingsford .... KO by 9
(For Vacant Australian Junior Middleweight Title)
1978
Mar. 7—Charles Dando, Kingsford .... KO 7
Apr. 4—Ben Holt, Kingsford .... W 8
May 30—Junior Alberts, Kingsford .... KO 3
Dec. 16—Wally Carr, Suva .... KO by 11
(For Australian Middleweight Title)
1979
Feb. 24—Ruby Steele, Mt. Pritchard .... W 10
Mar. 27—Eric King, Kingsford .... KO 6
Apr. 24—Ruby Steele, Kingsford .... D 10
June 13—Ruby Steele, Preston Town Hall .... KO 6
June 20—Garry Hubbie, Preston Town Hall .... W 8
July 31—Phil Davies, Kingsford .... KO by 5
1980
July 12—Buddy Nixon, Wollongong .... KO 4
Aug. 16—Willie Nixon, Wollongong .... KO 2
Aug. 30—George Saxon, Kanwal .... KO 4
Sept. 24—Chong-Pal park, Seoul .... KO by 5
(For Orient & Pacific Middleweight Title)
Oct. 27—Roy Bernadas, Manila .... KO 7

TSIETSI MARETLOANE
South African Lightweight
1973
Nov. 24—Mandila Ketile, Port Elizabeth .... L 6
1974
June 1—Ben Kekalake, East London .... KO by 6
July 20—Fred Baker, East London .... W 6
Oct. 5—Guy Ratazayo, East London .... W 6
Dec. 14—William Mlambo, East London .... W 6
1975
Mar. 29—Alfred Buqwane, East London .... W 6
June 21—Paulos Twala, East London .... W 6
Aug. 30—Khanti Singapi, East London .... W 6
Oct. 4—Aubrey Peta, East London .... W 10
Dec. 13—Joseph Tsotetsi, East London .... W 8
1976
Mar. 27—Paulos Twala, East London .... W 4
Apr. 10—Vuyisile Ntunzi, Port Elizabeth .... W 6
May 8—Victor Mpiyakhe, East London .... W 12
(Won South African National N.E. Featherweight Title)
July 17—Evans Gwiji, Port Elizabeth .... W 8
Oct. 9—Bashew Sibaca, East London .... W 12
1977
Sept. 17—Derrick Phetoe, East London .... W 8
Nov. 14—Freddie Rust, Cape Town .... KO 11
(Won Supreme South African Featherweight Title)
Dec. 10—Patrick Kohli, East London .... W 10

1978
May 6—Guy Ratazayo, East London .... L 10
Oct. 28—Bashew Sibaca, East London .... KO by 11
(Lost Supreme South African Featherweight Title)
1979
Feb. 12—Andries Steyn, Durban .... D 6
Mar. 7—Bowell Zono, Cape Town .... KO 5
June 8—Nkosana Mgxaji, East London .... W 8
June 21—Patrick Kohli, Cape Town .... W 6
Sept. 5—Bramley Whiteboy, Cape Town .... D 10
Sept. 29—Norman Sekgapane, East London .... W 10
Dec. 8—Alfred Sibisi, East London .... W 8
1980
Mar. 15—Nkosana Mgxaji, East London .... L 10

YOUNG MARIN
Spanish Junior Welterweight
1979
Oct. 6—Francisco Cabello, Bilbao .... KO 2
1980
Jan. 6—Mohammed Chino, Bilbao .... D 6
Feb. 2—Julio Garcia, Logrono .... W 6

CALBY MARKELL
Australian Welterweight
1980
Feb. 6—Albert Singh, Brookvale .... W 6
Mar. 11—John Lawrie, Kingsford .... W 4
Mar. 25—Buddy Clare, Kingsford .... W 6
Apr. 2—Buddy Clare, Brookvale .... W 5
Apr. 22—Steve Hanson, Kingsford .... KO 2
May 7—Ray Kelly, Brookvale .... W 6
May 20—Buddy Clare, Kingsford .... W 6
June 3—Alex Schafer, Kingsford .... KO 2
July 15—Andy Mann, Kingsford .... KO 6
July 22—Willie Nixon, Sutherland .... KO 3
Aug. 12—Ezzard Charles, Kingsford .... W 6
Aug. 19—Ezzard Charles, Sutherland .... W 6

DOMMY MAROLENA
Filipino Featherweight
1979
Feb. 3—Rey Naduma, Butuan City .... KO 3
Mar. 18—Sandy Torres, Cebu City .... D 10
May 27—Al Rizo, Manaue City .... W 10
June 23—Anthony Jamid, Cebu City .... KO 7
Oct. 5—Fel Viesca Jr., Manila .... W 12
Dec. 21—Nene Jun, Quezon City .... W 12
(Filipino Featherweight Title)
1980
Feb. 10—Neptali Alamag, Cebu City .... W 10
May 23—Lulu Villaverde, Manila .... L 12
(Lost Filipino Featherweight Title)

CURTIS MARSH
British Middleweight
1978
Sept. 13—Steve Hopkin, Cambridge .... L 6
Nov. 21—Peter Mullins, Wolverhampton .... KO 1
Dec. 4—Herol Graham, London .... KO by 1
1979
Jan. 30—Alan Hardiman, London .... W 4
Feb. 21—Vivian Waite, Cambridge .... W 6
Feb. 27—Carl Daly, London .... KO 2
Mar. 7—Mac Nicholson, Solihull .... W 6
Oct. 24—Earl Edwards, Norwich .... L 8
Dec. 11—Terry Mathews, Bletchley .... L 6
1980
Apr. 9—Mick Mills, Burslem .... W 8

LUIGI MARTELLO
Italian Welterweight
1972
Aug. 10—Giovanni Maiorano, Zaragolo .... KO 5
Nov. 17—Rocco Zecca, Rome .... L 6
Dec. 16—Pierre Petit, Rome .... D 6
1973
Feb. 23—Nicola Sassanelli, Rome .... D 6
Apr. 14—Santino Reali, Milan .... D 6
May 4—Giancarlo Usai, Milan .... L 6
June 28—Roberto Franceschi, Rome .... D 6
Oct. 12—Pietro Mereu, Rome .... W 6
1974
Jan. 4—Bruno Freschi, Milan .... L 6
Apr. 11—Giovambattista Capretti, Milan .... L 8
June 21—Osvaldo Cittadoni, Rome .... W 6
Dec. 6—Italo Venturi, Bologna .... D 8
1975
Feb. 8—Italo Venturi, Bologna .... L 8
Apr. 12—Jo Kimpuani, Dunkirk .... KO by 8
Dec. 16—Abdul Al Kaya, R. Emilia .... L 4
1976
Jan. 16—Vittorio Conte, Empoli .... L 8

Apr. 23—Guido Galletti, Rome .... D 6
June 11—Joseph Pachler, Wolfsburg .... L 8
Aug. 12—Tommaso Marocco, Priverno ....LF 7
Oct. 22—Gianni Molesini, Cremona .... L 8
1977
Jan. 28—Pierangelo Pira, Faenza .... L 6
Mar. 4—Vincenzo Moruzzi, Rome .... L 8
June 24—Timoteo Bomizzoni, Fontanella ....D 8
Jan. 18—Luciano Giorgi, Rome .... W 6
Feb. 24—Augusto Lauri, Rome .... L 8
May 25—Cosimo Del Guacchio, Catania ....KO 1
1979
Aug. 6—Vittorio Costa, Montecatini .... NC 7
1980
Apr. 5—Bechir Boundtka, Tunis .... KO by 10
May 3—Franco Aresti, Cagliari .... L 8

TONY MARTEY
British Welterweight
(Ghanan Based in London, England)
1978
Jan. 16—Fred Corensen, Rennes..................... L 8
Mar. 20—Colin Jones, Aberavon .... L 8
Apr. 10—Des Morrison, Sheffield .... KO by 6
Aug. 10—Hans Henrik Palm, Glyngore .... L 8
Nov. 15—Sylvester Gordon, Solihull ....KO 7
Dec. 18—Clinton McKenzie, London................ L 8
1979
Feb. 10—Perico Fernandez, Zaragoza .... L 8
June 18—Billy Waith, Windor .... L 8
July 30—Frank McCord, London ....KO 4
Oct. 9—Sylvester Mittee, Kensington .... L 8
1980
June 11—Steve Early, Birmingham .... L 8
July 9—Nino LaRocca, Bellaria .... KO by 6
Oct. 3—Lee Hartshorn, Windsor .... W 8

CLAUDE MARTIN
French Junior Middleweight
1973
Sept. 15—Angelo Ivkovic, S. Brieuc .... KO 3
Oct. 20—Mohamed Alem, S. Malo .... KO 4
Nov. 3—Roger Lobjois, Brest .... W 6
Dec. 22—Jean Claude Genno, S. Malo .... W 6
1974
Feb. 21—Larbi Titi, Rennes .... W 6
Mar. 28—Hassen Feguiri, Paris ....KO 6
Apr. 20—Francois Tahi, Annecy .... KO by 3
Apr. 27—Francois Tahi, Annecy .... KO by 3
May 25—Gerard Breton, St. Malo ....KO 3
Oct. 26—Angelo Ivkovic, S. Malo ....KO 4
Nov. 23—Phillipe Girotti, Rennes .... KO 7
1975
Mar. 22—Eric Seys, Saint Malo .... W 8
Apr. 26—Joel Le Guern, S. Malo ....KO 7
Oct. 25—Oscar Angus, St. Malo .... W 8
Dec. 20—Henry Rhiney, Saint Malo ....D 10
Jan. 19—Alec Tompkins, Paris .... W 10
Feb. 23—Michel Chapier, Paris .... W 10
Apr. 3—Vincent Parra, St. Malo .... W 10
Apr. 24—Batman Austin, St. Malo .... W 10
Oct. 30—Marcel Giorndanella, St. Malo ....KO 8
Dec. 11—Joel Bonnetaz, St. Malo .... KO by 3
1977
Feb. 5—Mickey Ryce, St. Malo .... W 10
Apr. 2—John Smith, St. Malo .... W 10
May 13—Kevin White, Paris .... W disq. 6
Oct. 15—Marcel Giordanella, St. Malo ....KO 6
(French Junior Middleweight Title)
1978
Jan. 28—Walter Guernieri, St. Malo.............KO 3
Apr. 15—Joel Bonnetaz, St. Malo................ W 12
Sept. 23—Pat Thomas, St. Malo................. W 10
Oct. 27—Georges Warusfel, Rennes .... W 12
(French Junior Middleweight Title)
1979
Jan. 27—Michel Chapier, St. Malo .... W 10
Apr. 28—Jose Hernandez, S. Malo .... KO by 6
Oct. 6—Tiger Quaye, St. Malo ....KO 5
Dec. 15—Georges Warusfel, St. Malo ....D 12
(French Junior Middleweight Title)
1980
Oct. 18—Nelson Gomez, St. Malo ....KO 7
Dec. 18—Louis Acaries, Paris .... KO by 10

JEAN LOUIS MARTIN
French Light Heavyweight
1974
Mar. 21—Jean Marie Torchy, Paris .... W 6
Mar. 28—Hassen Feguiri, Paris ....KO 6
Apr. 27—Francis Tahi, Annecy .... KO by 3

1975-1976
(Inactive)
1977
Oct. 28—Maurice Trepant, S. Quentin ....W 6
1978
Jan. 21—Jacques Chinon, Argenteuil ....W 6
Feb. 11—Laurent Zardi, Darnetal ....W 6
May 11—Maurice Trepant, Paris ....W 6
Apr. 7—Mustapha Kabangu, Argenteuil ....W 8
May 12—Fred Kohler, Argenteuil ....W 8
Dec. 8—Eric Kopec, Argenteuil ....W 8
1980
Jan. 19—Sonny Kamunga, Argenteuil ....W 8
Mar. 8—Jose Centa, Argenteuil ....KO 9
Apr. 18—Hocine Tafer, Paris .... KO by 7
(For French Light Heavyweight Title)

RENE MARTIN
French Lightweight
1974
Nov. 23—Jean Claude Sider, Calais ....KO 6
Dec. 14—Jacky Robert, S. Malo ....L 6
Dec. 21—Lahoucine Safi, Boulogne ....KO 4
1975
Feb. 6—Robert Van Rompaey, Paris ....KO 4
Feb. 13—Joel Moulin, Paris ....L 6
Mar. 1—Jean Michael Vantoroux, Calais ....KO 4
Mar. 15—Jean Claude Sider, Conde ....W 6
Apr. 26—Joseph Sissaoui, Boulogne ....KO 2
Sept. 20—Gerard Jacob, Creil ....KO 3
Oct. 4—Patrick Christ, Calais ....KO 4
Oct. 10—Raymond Libbrecht, Compiegne ....W 6
Dec. 12—Charles Chenouf, Boulogne ....KO 5
1976
Apr. 3—Pierre Petit, Bethune ....W 8
Apr. 10—Barton McAllister, Calais ....KO 6
June 11—Jacques Mamane, Boulogne ....W 6
July 3—Ali Messaoud, Algiers ....KO 6
Oct. 16—Abdelkader Bouguetaib, Maubeuge ....KO 8
Dec. 4—Adolfo Osses, Calais .... KO by 7
1977
Feb. 12—Jean Claude Sider, Conde ....NC 4
Mar. 12—Jean Claude Sider, Louvroil ....W 8
Apr. 30—Bouchiba Messaoud, Lauwe ....L 10
Nov. 5—Charles Jurietti, Boulogne ....L 8
1978
Feb. 4—Roland Cazeaux, Boulogne ....KO 9
(French Junior Lightweight Title)
Mar. 30—Georges Cotin, Paris.............. KO by 8
(French Junior Lightweight Title)
May 20—Roland Cazeaux, S. Nazaire ....L 10
July 17—Charlie Nash, London .... KO by 7
1979
Mar. 11—Didier Kowalski, Maubege ....KO 3
Apr. 21—Didier Kowalski, Denain .... KO by 6
Nov. 3—Giuseppe Russi, San Severo .... KO by 5
1980
Apr. 25—Antonio Guinaldo, Barcelona ....L 8
Oct. 10—Andre Holyk, Villeurbanne .... KO by 2
Dec. 26—Franco Siddu, Firenze ....L 8

GIUSEPPE MARTINESE
Italian Junior Welterweight
1975
Jan. 31—Vincenzo Moruzzi, Milan ....L 6
May 1—Adriano Rosati, Milano ....KO 5
June 20—Everaldo Azevedo, Milan ....D 8
July 12—Remo Costa, Arenzano ....W 6
Oct. 31—Vittorio Conte, Reggio Emilia .... KO by 3
Nov. 28—Mohamed Arras, Forbach ....W 6
1976
Jan. 30—Jean Pierre Heirman, Forbach ....WG
Feb. 14—Italo Venturi, Forli.....................L 8
Apr. 16—Luciano Laffranchi, Ancona ....W 8
May 14—Rocco Frasca, Milano.....................D 8
June 4—Rocco Frasca, Civitona ....KO 2
June 4—Franco Recorpeo, Civitona ....KO 4
July 16—Domenico Milone, Civitanova ....WF 7
Aug. 13—Gaetano Sguzza, Senigallia ....KO 3
Oct. 31—Giuseppe Minotti, Pesaro ....W 8
Dec. 10—Ernesto Bergamasco, Falconara ....W 10
1977
Feb. 12—Jean Claude Laffarge, Forbach ....W 8
May 13—Giuseppe Minotti, Fana ....KO 1
June 31—Pierino Meraviglia, Senigallia ....KO 6
Aug. 24—Bruno Freschi, Grado ....KO 8
(Italian Junior Welterweight Title)
Oct. 21—Giancarlo Barabotti, Milan ....W 12
(Italian Junior Welterweight Title)
1978
Feb. 3—Ernesto Bergamasco, Milan ....KO 8
(Italian Junior Welterweight Title)
Apr. 7—Giuseppe Corbo, Senigallia..............KO 9

July 28—Efisio Pinna, Senigallia................KO 8
    (Italian Junior Welterweight Title)
Oct. 13—Alain Salmon, Metz....................W 10
Dec.   2—Fernando Sanchez, Bilbao............L 15
    (European Junior Welterweight Title)
1979
Feb.   9—Giuseppe Corbo, Milano..............KO 10
    (Italian Junior Welterweight Title)
May 11—Francesco Gallo, Senigallia............NC 6
    (Italian Junior Welterweight Title)
July 14—Luciano Navarra, Fabriano.............W 12
    (Italian Junior Welterweight Title)
Aug. 29—Giuseppe Russi, Iseo...................W 12
    (Italian Junior Welterweight Title)
Oct. 26—Francesco Gallo, Chivasso..............W 12
    (For Italian Junior Welterweight Title)
1980
Jan. 30—Luciano Navarea, Viterbo............KO 2
    (Retained Italian Junior Welterweight Title)
Apr. 19—Jean Marie Cotinaut, Senigallia........W 8
Aug. 27—Clinton McKenzie, Senigallia...........KO 11
    (Won European Junior Welterweight Title)

TAKAO MARUKI
Japanese Lightweight
1973
Apr.   4—Kozo Sato, Tokoname City...............W 10
Nov. 29—Sakae Makamura, Shizuoka.............W 10
Dec. 10—Hyun Kim, Tokoname...................W 10
1974
May 10—Susumu Okabe, Osaka...................L 10
July 19—Ben Villaflor, Manila................KO by 7
Sept. 28—Sakae Nakamura, Nagoya...............KO 4
Oct. 28—Sususmu Okabe, Aomori.................L 10
    (Japanese Junior Lightweight Championship)
1975
Mar.   3—Noriyasu Yoshimur, Nagoya............KO 1
May 28—Tamio Negishi, Nagoya...................L 10
Oct.   1—Susumu Okabe, Utsunomiva..............D 10
Dec. 16—Mitsuo Ohashi, Nagoya.................KO 3
1976
Jan. 31—Masashi Kamiyama, Nagoya............KO 1
Mar. 23—Hitoshi Takahashi, Nagoya.............W 10
June 1—Yoshihro Hattori, Nagoya...............W 10
July 24—Susumu Oakabe, Nagoya................W 10
1977
Jan. 29—Iwao Murakami, Nagoya...............KO 6
Dec. 17—Ryuya Moriyashu, Nagoaya.............KO 6
1978
Mar. 18—Tamio Negishi, Nagoya................KO 4
May   2—Ryuchi Narita, Nagoya..................W 10
June 24—Takeshi Mine, Handa...................KO 4
July 29—Yidano Lee, Nagoya.....................D 10
Nov. 29—Samuel Serrano, Nagoya..................L 15
    (WBA Junior Lightweight Title)
1979
Sept. 5—Shuzo Yoshida, Nagoya ....W 10
Nov.   6—Kensogo, Nagoya ....KO 4
1980
Feb.   4—Ryuya Moriyasu, Osaka ....W 10

JACKAL MARUYAMA
Japanese Bantamweight
1979
July 26—Seishi II, Tokyo ....W 10
Oct. 28—Ryu Takeshi, Aomori Ken ....L 10
1980
Apr. 26—Takanao Nakajima, Hachinohe...........D 10

KENNETH MASEKO
South African Welterweight
1975
Feb.   6—Louis Sibiya, Kwa-Thema ....W 4
1976
Apr. 30—David Kgotsane, Springs ....W 6
1977
Nov. 18—Isaac Mabuza, Krugersdorp ....L 4
1978
Aug. 12—David Kalako, Johannesburg ....KO by 1
1979
Mar.   9—Timothy Lerefolo, Springs ....L 4
1980
May 30—Peter Mgojo, Springs ....KO by 1

FREDDIE MASEMOLA
South African Flyweight
1977
Oct. 14—Daniel Sekgaolelo, Krugersdorp ....W 4
1978
Nov. 17—Bassie Motsei, Springs ....W 4
1979
Feb. 16—Isaac Seripe, Springs ....W 4
May 25—David Molefe, Springs ....KO 3

Sept. 7—Dexter Dhlamini, Springs ....KO 4
1980
Feb.   2—Johannes Sithebe, Springs ....KO by 10
    (Transvaal Flyweight Title)
Sept. 5—Jacob Molefe, Springs ....KO 4
Nov. 14—Simon Moema, Diepkloof ....KO by 3

CANNY MASHELE
South African Lightweight
1979
Mar. 10—Themba Maseko, Johannesburg ....W 4
July   9—Manuel Da Paiva, Welkom ....KO 1
Dec.   1—Aladin Stevens, Johannesburg ....L 4
1980
Apr.   7—Smart Thompson, Salisbury ....KO 2
May 26—Aladin Stevens, Johannesburg ....KO by 4
Nov. 10—Jeremiah Zulu, Durban ....W 4
Dec.   1—Arthur Mayisela, Durban ....KO by 1

RAYMOND MASHIFANE
South African Middleweight
1978
Nov. 17—Samson Mohloai, Springs ....L 6
1979
Mar. 10—Joseph Matthysen, Johannesburg ....KO 4
Apr.   7—David Mikhele, Vereeninging ....W 6
Aug. 27—Basil Meintjies, Johannesburg ....L 4
Nov. 10—Patrick Tshabalala, Jabulani ....L 6
1980
Feb.   9—Basil Meintjies, Johannesburg ......KO by 1
Apr. 25—Leo Simelane, Sebokeng ....L 6

ROBERTO MASINI
Italian Lightweight
1979
Nov. 14—Mario Tiano, Gualdo ....WF 6
Dec. 21—Luigi Curcetti, Savona ....W 6
1980
Jan. 25—Antonio Sandrin, Bologna ....W 6
Apr.   5—Valerio Fretta, Rimini ....W 6
Apr. 18—Vincenzo Di Bari, Bologna ....W 6
Sept. 6—Nelson Gomez, Riccione ....W 6

MNCEDI MASIZA
South African Junior Featherweight
1980
May   3—Lehlohonolo Nkaklo, East London ....KO by 3
July 26—Joe Gununza, King Williamstown ....D 4
Aug. 23—Zandisile Vamazonke, East London .....KO 3

MICK MASON
British Lightweight
1980
Apr. 28—Carl Mullings, Birmingham ....KO 3
May   7—Derek Groarke, Liverpool ....D 4
July   7—Selvin Bell, Middlesbrough ....W 6
Sept. 11—Eddie Glass, Hartlepool ....W 6
Oct. 13—Selvin Bell, Newcastle ....W 6
Oct. 23—Selvin Bell, Middlesbrough ....W 8

CAIFAS (KING KONG) MASONDO
South African Heavyweight
1976
Apr.   2—Louis Mngomezula, Orlando West ....KO 2
1977
    (Inactive)
1978
Oct.   7—Fraser Memela, Johannesburg ....W 4
Nov.   6—Jimmy Abbott, Durban ....KO by 1
1979
Apr.   2—Sophonia Naile, Welkom ....D 4
Aug. 27—James Neiring, Johannesburg ....KO 4
Nov. 12—Gary Webb, Welkom ....KO 3
1980
Feb.   4—Louis Hendriks, Welkom ....L 6
Apr. 19—Robbie Williams, Joburg ....KO by 2
Aug. 16—Bennie Knoetze, Joburg ....L 4
Dec. 22—Bennie Knoetze, Cape Town ....KO by 3

DENNIS LUCKY MASONDO
South African Middleweight
1979
Apr. 25—Basie Gouws, Durban ....L 4
Sept. 1—Isaac Dube, Empangeni ....W 4
Mar.   1—Christopher Hlongwe, Durban ....D 4
Mar.   8—Joseph Matthysen, Johannesburg ....L 4
Apr. 18—Albert Mklize, Durban ....KO 1
May   3—Michael Motsoane, Witsieshoek ......KO by 4

MANUEL MASSO
Spanish Featherweight
1973
Sept. 28—Francisco Santaengracis, Barcelona ......W 6
Oct. 10—Jose Luis Fleta, Barcelona ....KO 2
Oct. 25—Antonio Vasquez, Barcelona ....KO 4
Nov. 9—Jose A. Donoso, Barcelona ....KO 6
Nov. 23—Fernando Bernardez, Barcelona ....WF 5
1974
Jan. 25—Jose Luis Fleta, Zaragoza ....W 6
Mar. 23—Fernando Bernardez, Tarrasa ....WF 6
Mar. 29—Jose Del Pino Rodriguez, Barcelona .....KO 4
June 1—Antonio Martin, Tarrasa ....KO 2
June 14—Andres Ramos, Madrid ....KO 2
June 21—Fernando Gabino, Madrid ....W 8
Aug. 1—Frank Realinho, Madrid ....KO 1
Aug. 30—Francisco Rodriguez, Madrid ....KO 5
Oct. 4—Fernando Bernardez, Madrid ....W 8
1975
Jan. 10—Christian Levy, Barcelona ....KO 1
Feb. 7—Fernando Atzori, Barcelona ....KO 7
Feb. 21—Teodoro Corallo, Madrid ....KO 4
Apr. 19—Enzo Farinelli, Barcelona ....KO 4
June 18—Adolfo Osses, Barcelona ....W 8
1976
Jan. 3—Frank Realinho, Tarrasa ....W 8
Feb. 13—Agostino Pineiro, Figuras ....KO 1
1977
Jan. 31—Frank Realinho, Tarrasa ....KO 8
Mar. 5—Rodriguez Moro, Almeria ....W 8
Apr. 1—Antonio Franca, Barcelona ....KO 3
Aug. 12—Joseph Tlaba, Figueras ....KO 1
Sept. 16—Nino Jiminez, Barcelona ....KO 10
(European Featherweight Title)
Dec. 16—Roberto Castanon, Paris ....KO by 11
(European Featherweight Title)
1978
May 12—Dos Santos, Bilbao ....KO 2
June 30—Ramon Garcia Marichal, Barcelona ......W 8
Aug. 26—Mario Molina, Cuenca...................D 8
1979
Mar. 17—Emilio Barcala, Barcelona ....KO 8
May 4—Claudio Dos Santos, Barcelona ....KO 4
July 7—Angel Oliver, Zaragoza ....L 8
Sept. 1—Angel Oliver, San Sebastian ....W 8
Oct. 13—Mariano Rodriguez, S. Sebastiano ....W 8
Dec. 12—Angel Oliver, Barcelona ....W 8
1980
May 9—Guy Caudron, Barcelona ....W 8

REUBEN MATEWU (MATEYA)
South African Junior Flyweight
1971
Nov. 20—A. Kilimane, King Williamstown ....KO by 1
1972
Nov. 11—Boy Putye, King Williamstown ......KO by 3
1973
(Inactive)
1974
Feb. 2—Tembile Sgetye, East London ....L 4
1975
Feb. 8—Mngieda Batyi, East London ....W 4
Mar. 8—Fundisile Kralo, East London ....L 6
June 14—T. Sgetye, Port Elizabeth ....W 6
June 28—Andile Tywabi, Queenstown ....L 6
Aug. 9—Johannes Sithebe, Port Elizabeth..........L 6
Oct. 4—Tembile Sgetye, East London ....W 6
Dec. 6—Phindile Gaika, Port Elizabeth ....L 6
1976
Jan. 31—Andile Tywabi, East London..............L 10
(Cape Flyweight Title)
Apr. 17—Gilbert Makenete, East London ....W 4
Apr. 28—Winnerton Kondile, Guguletu ....W 6
July 10—Leslie Pikoli, East London................L 10
Oct. 9—Isaac Mazibuko, East London ....KO 2
Nov. 6—Pindile Gaika, King Williamstown.......W 6
1977
Mar. 5—Alfred Mphake, East London ....KO 5
May 7—Daluxolo Tyekana, Zwelitsha ....W 6
Oct. 15—Peter Mathebula, East London ....KO by 1
Nov. 19—Elliot Zondi, East London ....L 10
1978
Mar. 4—Monde Mpulampula, King Williamstown... L 8
July 8—Tembisile Ngxingolo, East London ....D 8
July 29—Monde Mpulampula, Queenstown ....L 8
Aug. 26—Simon Moema, East London ....L 6
1979
Feb. 24—Siphiwo Gaika, King Williamstown ......KO 2
Mar. 10—Monde Mpulampula, East London ....L 8
July 28—Daluxolo Tyekana, King Williamstown ...L 8
Aug. 4—Simon Moema, East London ....L 4
Nov. 3—Phindile Gaika, Port Elizabeth ....L 4
1980
July 26—Lawrence Krune, King Williamstown KO by 2

JAMES MATHATHO
South African Light Heavyweight
Born: June 14, 1943
1970
July 3—John Nyalunga, Springs ....L 6
1971
June 11—Joao Alfonso, Mamelodi ....KO by 5
Nov. 12—Dely Setiba, Thembisa ....KO 3
1972
Mar. 17—Paulus Hlatswayo, Thembisa ....KO 1
July 14—Ezra Mzinyane, Thembisa ....W 6
Aug. 25—Lucas Nxumalo, Springs ....KO 3
1973
Mar. 9—Ezra Mzinyane, Thembisa ....W 10
(Won Vacant Tvl. Light Heavyweight Title)
July 7—Sandy Kwazw, Bloemfontein ....W
Nov. 2—Frazer Memela, Thembisa ....D 8
1974
Feb. 9—Sandy Kwaza, Orange Free State ....KO 8
(Won Vacant South African NF Light Heavyweight Title)
May 24—Phuthuma Koboni, Thembisa ....KO 3
July 19—Richie Kates, Durban ....KO by 4
1975
(Inactive)
1976
Feb. 14—Frazer Memela, Alexandra ....KO 6
(South African Nat. NE Heavyweight Title)
Apr. 24—Joao Afonso, Jabulani ....KO 4
Nov. 27—Gerri Coetzee, Johannesburg ....KO by 7
(For Supreme South African Heavyweight Title)
1977
Feb. 19—Kosie Smith, Johannesburg ....KO by 5
(For Supreme South African Light Heavyweight Title)
Apr. 16—Kosie Smith, Johannesburg ....W 12
(Won Supreme South African Light Heavyweight Title)
Dec. 6—Kosie Smith, Port Elizabeth ....KO by 3
(Lost Supreme South African Light Heavyweight Title)
1978
June 1—Sydney Hoho, Goodwood ....L 12
(For Vacant South African Nat. NE Light Heavy Title)
Dec. 4—Mervin Smit, Bloemfontein ....L 8
Dec. 15—Gerrie Bodenstein, Durban ....KO 7
1979
Mar. 24—Bruce McIntyre, Johannesburg ....KO by 7
(For Vacant Transvaal Light Heavy Title)
June 2—Gerrie Bodenstein, Port Elizabeth ....L 8
1980
Apr. 21—Martin Barnard, Secunda ....L 10
(Transvaal Light Heavyweight Title)

BUKUWANE (ALFRED) MATINWANE
South African Lightweight
1977
May 31—Sibongya Zituma, Queenstown ....W 4
Sept. 3—Reginald Mpondo, Queenstown ....W 4
1978
Mar. 4—Kenneth Moyi, King Williamstown ....D 4
July 29—Phindile Ndilele, Queenstown ....KO by 4
Oct. 21—Solomon Nojanga, Queenstown ....W 6
1979
Feb. 10—Wonga Lawuse, Queenstown ....KO by 3
1980
Mar. 29—Mtutuzeli Ngqakayi, Queenstown ....W 4

JOHN MATSABU
South African Junior Flyweight
1979
Mar. 24—Martin Nkokoto, Virginia ....L 4
1980
Feb. 2—Jeffrey Nkate, Virginia ....L 4
Oct. 11—Johannes Phumo, Odendaalsrust ....L 6
Dec. 1—Martin Nkokoto, Virginia ....KO by 4

TSUTOMU (DYNAMITE) MATSUO
Japanese Middleweight
1978
June 7—Masa Ito, Yamaguchi ....L 10
Sept. 25—Senju Yamaguchi, Shizuoka ....KO 7
1979
Feb. 20—Tatsuo Ohara, Tokyo ....KO 7
May 19—Noboru Hatakeyama, Shizuoka .....KO by 8
(Japanese Junior Welterweight Title)
Oct. 13—Katsuo Esashi, Aizuwakamatshu Shi ...KO 3
(JBC Middleweight Title)
Nov. 30—Minoru Ono, Shizuoka ....KO 6
1980
Jan. 9—Jamese Callaghan, Yokohama ....KO by 8
(Lost Japanese Middleweight Title)
Apr. 29—Shigeo Takagi, Shimizu ....KO 2

KOICHI MATSUSHIMA
Japanese Featherweight
1978
Sept. 2—Leopardo Tsuruta, Tsuchiura City ......KO 7
Nov. 15—Kenoh Kashi, Tokyo ....W 10
1979
Mar. 22—Spider Nemoto, Tokyo ....KO 9
Nov. 27—Namio Akamine, Tokyo ....KO 9
1980
Mar. 16—Sa-Wang Kim, Seoul ....L 10

ILAND MATTHEWS
South African Featherweight
1980
Aug. 1—Enoch Mazibuku, Springs ....L 4
Oct. 4—Siphwe Sithole, Johannesburg ....KO 4
Nov. 14—Moses Sithebe, Diepkloof ....KO 3

TERRY MATTHEWS
British Junior Middleweight
1979
May 10—Ronald Pearce, Pontypool ....L 6
May 23—Joey Sounders, Nottingham ....KO 3
June 4—Tony Briton, London ....L 6
July 30—Owen Slue, London ....W 6
Sept. 17—Tony Brittom, Mayfair ....L 8
Oct. 30—Mickey Kidd, Bedford ....W 6
Nov. 29—Tommy Williams, Liverpool ....L 6
Dec. 11—Curtis Marsh, Bletchley ....W 6
1980
Jan. 7—Wayne Barker, Manchester ....D 8
Jan. 16—Gary Newell, Stoke ....W 6
Feb. 6—Peter Bassey, Liverpool ....W 8
Feb. 20—Clifton Wallace, Evesham ....W 6
Mar. 3—John Smith, London ....W 8
Mar. 17—Peter Simon, London ....W 8
Apr. 17—George Walker, London ....KO by 3

JOSEPH MATTHYSEN
South African Junior Middleweight
1979
Mar. 10—Raymond Mashifane, Johannesburg .. KO by 4
Nov. 12—Jaacobus Horn, Welkom ....KO 1
Dec. 1—Hubert Botha, Port Elizabeth ....W 4
1980
Mar. 8—Lucky Masondo, Johannesburg ....W 4
Apr. 21—Jan Beneke, Secunda ....KO 2
May 24—Patrick Tshabalala, Orlando ....KO by 5

LICHI MAUDOZE
Italian Welterweight
1980
Feb. 9—Yves Giroux, St. Malo ....KO 3
Nov. 13—Gilles Ebilia, Paris ....L 8

GENARO MAURIELO
Italian Light Heavyweight
1980
Feb. 2—Antimo Tescione, Mugnano ....W 6
Mar. 4—Gabriele Lazzari, Napoli ....D 6
Mar. 29—Antimo Tescione, Nocwra ....W 6
May 18—Andre Sangalletti, Naples ....W 6
Dec. 4—Gabrielle Lazzari, Rome ....W 6

ARTHUR MAYISELA
South African Junior Welterweight
1980
Mar. 22—Nkululeko Nkosi, Soweto ....KO 3
Aug. 4—Sipho Mzano, Durban ....KO 3
Aug. 29—Azael Lebitso, Sebokeng ....KO 2
Nov. 14—Matthews Ndlovu, Diepkloof ....KO 3
Dec. 1—Canny Mashele, Durban ....KO 1

BOY BOY MAZALENE
South African Flyweight
1979
May 26—Sixto Madondile, King Williamstown ...W 4
July 28—Lindile Yam, King Williamstown ....KO 3
Aug. 18—Pretty Petela, King Williamstown .....KO 1
Sept. 8—Cosmo Ziqu, Zwelitsha ....KO by 2
Nov. 10—Elliot Zondi, King Williamstown ....KO 5
Dec. 1—Dolly Bangiso, King Williamstown ....D 4
1980
Sept. 5—Cosmo Ziqu, East London ....W 6
Oct. 18—Mxolisi Nohenda, King Williamstown ...KO 3
Nov. 8—Ntsikelelo Mana, East London ....D 6

ENOCH MAZIBUKU
South African Featherweight
1970
Aug. 3—Moses Ditlopo, Springs ....W 4
Aug. 31—Patrick Hlomuka, Natalspruit ....KO 4

1980
Feb. 29—Lehlohonolo Nkaklo, Springs ....D 6
May 30—Joseph Moneoane, Springs ....W 4
Aug. 1—Iland Matthews, Springs ....W 4
Oct. 31—Kemmel Phele, Springs ....L 4

PASQUALE MAZZA
Italian Bantamweight
1979
May 11—Giulio Greco, Senigallia ....KO by 2
Dec. 29—Antonio Franca, Perugia ....W 6
1980
May 3—Roberto Serrelli, Cagliari ....W 6

NGCAMBAZA MBADULI
South African Lightweight
1979
Aug. 18—Ncedo Mpetsheni, King Williamstown ....D 4
Sept. 9—Goodman Njova, Zwelitsha ....W 4
1980
Oct. 11—Joseph Poyo, Port Elizabeth ....W 6
Oct. 18—Phindile Ndilele, King Williamstown .....W 6
Nov. 22—Wonga Lawuse, Queenstown ....W 8

DAVID MBOMAY
South African Lightweight
1980
Jan. 14—Sazi Xamlashe, Cape Town ....W 4
Feb. 8—Mutile Nkeli, Cape Town ....W 4
Apr. 14—Chris Whiteboy, Cape Town ....L 6

GRAHAM MDINGI
South African Junior Middleweight
1980
Aug. 4—Christopher Hiongwe, Durban ....L 4
Nov. 1—Joseph Zikhall, Stanger ....D 4
nov. 10—Bernard Sikakane, Durban ....W 4

NEVILLE MEADE
Welsh Heavyweight
1974
Sept. 9—Tony Mikulski, London ....L 6
Oct. 14—Riger Barlow, Swansea ....KO 3
Oct. 21—Geoff Hepplestone, London ....KO 1
Oct. 21—Les McGowan, London...................KO 1
Oct. 21—Harold James, London ....W 4
Nov. 18—Eddy Fenton, London ....KO 5
1975
Feb. 17—Richard Dunn, Mayfair ....KO by 4
Apr. 29—Tony Moore, Kensington ....KO by 5
June 5—Tony Moore, Hammersmith ....D 8
July 1—Lloyd Walford, Swansea ....KO 6
Aug. 6—Derek Simpkin, Cardiff.................KO 3
Sept. 1—John Depledge, Cardiff ....KO 5
Sept. 24—Tony Moore, Solihull ....W 8
Nov. 4—Lucien Rodriguez, Paris ....KO 3
1976
Mar. 12—Alfredo Evangelista, Madrid ....L 8
Mar. 29—Tony Blackburn, Swansea ....KO 4
May 26—Garfield McEwan, Wolverhampton ......KO 9
Aug. 11—Denton Ruddock, Cardiff...........KO by 7
Oct. 26—John L. Gardner, Kensington.........KO by 6
Dec. 20—Bjorn Rudi, Oslo ....KO 7
Dec. 26—Jean Pierre Coopman, Izegem.............L 10
1977
June 4—Kallie Knoetze, Johannesburg ....KO by 4
Dec. 8—Bruce Grandham, Liverpool.............KO 3
1978
Mar. 31—Bruce Grandham, Liverpool ....KO by 3
May 15—Paul Sykes, Bradford ....KO by 5
1979
Jan. 19—Albert Syben, Bruxelles ....KO by 4
1980
Jan. 22—David Pearce, Caerphilly ....KO 2
(Retained Welsh Heavyweight Title)
Oct. 1—Winston Allen, Swansea ....KO 2
(Welsh Heavyweight Title)

UWE MEINECKE
German Light Heavyweight
1974
May 10—Herbert Wick, Luebeck ....W 4
June 3—Hans Albert Theis, Luebeck ....KO 3
1975
June 24—Gregory Downes, Berlin ....L 4
Dec. 8—Sjoerd Tuininga, L'Aja ....L 6
1976
Apr. 26—Uwe Arrindel, Amsterdam ....KO 4
1977
Apr. 22—Louis Pergaud, Saarbruecken ....L 6
May 09—Darko Parakovic, Hanover ....W 6
Oct. 3—Franklin Arrindel, Scheveningen ....W 8
Oct. 16—Louis Pergaud, Hamburg ....KO by 6

359

Dec.	10—Gregory Downes, Kiel	L 8

1978

Mar.	11—Gerald Bois, Sedan	D 10
Sept.	7—Sidney Hoho, Cape Town	KO by 6

1979

Jan.	27—Pierre Kabassu, Esch Sur Alzette	L 8
Apr.	22—Horst Lang, Hamburg	W 6
June	7—Sylvain Watbled, Paris	KO by 1
Sept.	16—Kurt Oerter, Koblenz	W 4
Nov.	3—Gerald Bois, Sedan	KO 7
Dec.	15—Robert Desnouck, Izegem	L 6

1980

Apr.	18—Helmut Ulka, Berlin	KO 1

BASIL MEINTJIES
South African Light Heavyweight

1978

June	9—Gert Pienaar, Johannesburg	W 4
Sept.	23—Cornelius de Beer, Johannesburg	L 4
Nov.	27—Werner Kalin, Johannesburg	W 4

1979

June	18—Morgan Moledi, Johannesburg	L 4
Aug.	27—Raymond Mashifane, Johannesburg	W 4

1980

Feb.	9—Raymond Mashifane, Johannesburg	KO 1
Mar.	1—Isak Enslin, Ermelo	W 4
Apr.	21—Willem Kilian, Secunda	KO 1
Nov.	28—Abram Sello, Johannesburg	KO 4

CHATO MELILLENSE
Spanish Lightweight

1975

July	25—Jose Godoy, Madrid	KO 1
Aug.	7—Augustin Guemez, Vallecas	D 6
Sept.	19—Juan Barros, Villaverde	D 6
Nov.	15—Santiago Cebollada, Zaragoza	KO 4

1976

Jan.	24—Manuel Llata, Santander	L 6
Feb.	6—Jose Barillado, Madrid	L 6
Feb.	21—Josines, Cadiz	D 6
May	21—Francisco Leon, Badalona	L 8
Aug.	21—Jose Godoy, Cuenca	D 8
Oct.	11—Luis Mejias, S. Cruz	L 8
Oct.	23—Ungidos III, Santander	L 8

1977

June	16—Daniel Bellantoni, Salamanca	D 8
Aug.	28—Antonio Ibanez, Cuenca	KO 3
Nov.	12—Angel Quiles, Zaragoza	LF 2
Dec.	30—Antonio Ibanez, Santander	W 6

1978

Mar.	4—Fernando Bermejo, Caceres	KO 2
Mar.	31—Arthur Fogiero, Tarbes	L 8
Apr.	28—Christian Garcia, Agen	L 8
May	26—Arthur Fogiero, Agen	D 8
July	15—Eduardo Carreira, La Coruna	L 8
Sept.	5—Jesus Canut, Melilla	W 8
Nov.	2—Francisco Leon, Barcelona	L 8
Nov.	18—Domingo Gimenez, Casablanca	W 8
Dec.	23—Bossou Azizan, Casablanca	D 10

1979

Mar.	9—Rafael Gutierrez, Madrid	D 6
Apr.	7—Cecilio Lastra, Santander	L 8
May	5—Serafin dos Anjos, Casablanca	KO 5
June	16—Mimoun Mukasaf, Casablanca	D 8
July	27—Carlos Morales, Santander	LF 3
Aug.	4—Hugo Carrizo, Vigo	L 8
Aug.	26—Hugo Carrizo, La Coruna	L 8
Dec.	8—Manuel Garcia Requena, Tenerife	LF 4

1980

Feb.	8—Emilio Molero, Madrid	W 8
Apr.	18—Jose Garcia Barcina, Madrid	KO 6
May	2—Francisco Moya, Madrid	D 8

SALVATORE MELLUZZO
Italian Featherweight
Born: June 12, 1952, Siracusa, Italy

1975

May	9—Antonio Pocai, Milan	W 6
Oct.	10—Lucio Vailati, Milan	W 6
Oct.	24—Alvaro Checche', Milan	KO 2
Nov.	28—Filippo Loiacono, Milan	WF 5

1976

Feb.	5—Pasquale Arini, Milan	W 3
Mar.	18—Dante Guarnieri, Milano	KO 6
Apr.	2—Ignacio Fara, Milan	W 8
May	21—Luigi Zanghi, Milano	W 8
July	2—Ignacio Fara, Siracusa	W 8
Oct.	22—Mario De Prosperis, Bologna	KO 4
Dec.	3—Giovanni Scarpati, Milan	KO 3

1977

Jan.	21—Salvatore Avella, Pesaro	W 8
Feb.	25—Jean Pierre Planque, Pesaro	KO 6
Apr.	1—Domenico Condello, Pesaro	KO 4

May	13—Mouldi Manai, Siracusa	W 8
Aug.	21—Joseph Tlaba, Rijeka	KO 5
Nov.	18—Sergio Emili, Pesaro	KO 10
	(Italian Featherweight Title)	

1978

Mar.	3—Emiliano Da Silva, Pesaro	W 8
May	20—Salvatore Fabrizio, Pesaro	WF 1
	(Italian Featherweight Title)	

1979

Feb.	10—Natal Caredda, Cagliari	L 12
	(Italian Featherweight Title)	
Mar.	7—Bashew Sibaca, Capetown	L 10
May	25—Salvatore Avella, Pesaro	KO 5
July	25—Giancarlo Ravaili, Rimini	KO 4

1980

Feb.	2—Melquiades Da Silva, Marsala	W 8
Mar.	29—Raga Murphy, Pesaro	WF 7
May	17—Roberto Castanon, Leon	L disq. 9
	(For European Featherweight Title)	
July	5—Natale Carreda, Siracuisa	W 10
Sept.	24—Marco Gallo, Fiuggi	W 12
	(Won Italian Featherweight Title)	
Nov.	29—Helenio Ferreira, Marsala	D 8

MARK MELVILLE
South African Heavyweight

1978

Feb.	22—Sydney Hoho, Capetown	L 8
Mar.	11—Tienie Oosthuizen, Natal	KO 3
June	10—Gerrie Bodenstein, Port Elizabeth	L 8
Aug.	5—Albertus Opperman, Bloemfontein	L 6
Oct.	28—Gerrie Bodenstein, East London	KO by 6
Dec.	4—Pius Dladla, Durban	KO 3

1979
(Inactive)

1980

Oct.	6—Jonas Malan, Pmburg	L 4
Nov.	3—Temba Buthelezi, Durban	L 4
Dec.	1—Gerrie Schneiganz, Durban	L 4
Dec.	15—Champion Mokone, Pmburg	W 4

NEDJAD MEMETI
Belgian Light Heavyweight

1978

Nov.	1—Salmin Boutera, Izengem	L 6
Nov.	24—Roberto Bosio, La Louviere	L 6

1979

Jan.	19—Roberto Bosio, Brussels	D 6
Oct.	6—Henryk Seys, Lauwe	NC
Nov.	1—Salmin Bouteraa, Duffel	W 6

1980

Apr.	19—Sergio Bosio, Belgium	L 6
May	22—Walter Cevoli, Bologna	L 6
Sept.	27—Sergio Bosio, La Louviere	D 6
Nov.	17—Michel Caron, Buex	I 6

REGGIE MENONG
South African Welterweight

1976

May	15—Alfred Sibisi, Jabulani	KO by 3

1977-1978
(Inactive

1979

May	4—David Mohale, Springs	D 4
June	29—Zephania Mlotshwa, Natalspruit	W 4

1980

Mar.	28—Peter Mgojo, Springs	L 4
Oct.	31—John John Lukuleni, Springs	L 4

BOUCHIBA MESSAOUD
Belgian Lightweight

1975

Jan.	24—Francesco Musolino, Brussels	W 6
Feb.	7—Domenico Radicioni, Gand	W 6
Apr.	4—Jean Vantouroux, Ostenda	D 6
May	2—Franz Meganck, Ostenda	KO 5
May	17—Antoine La Sala, Liege	L 6
May	30—Jean Claude Sider, Heudsen-Lez-Gand	W disq. 3
June	13—Bung Ho Park, Mont St. Amand	KO 1
July	5—Fernand Roelandt, Kalken	KO by 6

1976

Mar.	11—Jean Pierre Barrie, Paris	L 6
Apr.	24—Alain Lefol, Lokeren	L 6
May	8—Lahcen Maghfouri, Izegem	KO 2
July	3—Mohamen Knani, Kalken	KO 3
Aug.	6—Etham Oezaklin, Berlin	W 6
Oct.	1—Valerio Fretta, Lauwe	L 8
Oct.	16—Patrick Christ, Gand	L 8
Nov.	1—Ali Issaoui, Izegem	W 8
Dec.	25—Fernand Roelands, Izegem	KO 3

1977

Mar.	12—Alain Le Fol, Antwerp	L 8

Apr.	2—Gerard Bok, Ostenda	D	8
Apr.	30—Rene Martin, Lauwe	W	10
June	6—Clinton McKenzie, S. Amand	L	8
Sept.	30—Gerard Bok, Rotterdam	W	10
Nov.	11—Mario Oliviera, Bruges	W	8
Nov.	26—Carlos Goldstein Foldes, Brussels	L	8
1978			
Feb.	25—Jean Pierre Hainalut, Ostenda	W	8
Mar.	10—Samuel Meck, Gand	L	8
Apr.	1—Carlos Foldes, Forest	D	8
Apr.	14—Batdabchi, S. Amand	KO	8
Sept.	4—Gerard Bok, Rotterdam	L	8
Nov.	3—Fernand Roelands, Bruges	KO	5
1979			
July	14—Perico Fernandez, San Sebastian	KO by	4
Oct.	15—Georges Cotin, Paris	KO by	2
1980			
Jan.	18—Angelo Licata, La Louviere	L	8
Mar.	18—Didier Kowalski, Conde Sur Escaut	KO by	1

GEORGE METCALF
British Lightweight
1978

Mar.	6—Adey Allen, Manchester	KO by	3
Apr.	12—Adey Allen, Evesham	L	4
May	15—Gary Collins, Aylesbury	W	6
May	24—Delvin Whyte, Southend	KO	6
Sept.	18—Charlie Tonna, London	KO	3
Oct.	2—Selvin Bell, Liverpool	W	6
Oct.	16—Selvin Bell, London	W	6
Nov.	20—Charlie Brown, London	L	8
1979			
Jan.	30—Kevin Doherty, London	KO	6
Feb.	28—Ceri Collins, Harrogate	L	8
Apr.	2—Ceri Collins, London	KO	5
Oct.	4—Charlie Brown, Ebbw Vale	KO	1
Oct.	15—John B. Muwanga, Oslo	KO by	8
1980			
Feb.	21—Robbie Robinson, Liverpool	KO	5
May	31—Robbie Robinson, Liverpool	L	6
Sept.	15—Martyh Galeozzie, London	W	8

ISAAC MFENE
South African Bantamweight
1979

May	25—Stephen Nkomo, Springs	L	4
1980			
June	7—Jeffrey Nkate, Odenaalsrust	KO	3
Aug.	29—Stephen Nkomo, Sebokeng	L	4
Sept.	27—Israel Papane, Welkom	L	6

PETER MGOJO
South African Welterweight
1980

Feb.	28—Terrence Molefe, Springs	L	4
Mar.	28—Reginald Menong, Springs	W	4
Apr.	19—Neil Walker, Johannesburg	W	4
May	10—Jeffrey Diodio, Virginia	KO	2
May	30—Kenneth Maseko, Springs	KO	1
Aug.	1—George Selebi, Springs	W	6
Oct.	4—Daniel Mkhize, Welkom	W	8
Nov.	21—Joseph Lala, Sebokeng	W	6

MLUNGWANA MGXAJI
South African Flyweight
1979

Sept.	29—Eric Mtana, East London	W	4
Dec.	8—Victor Tladi, East London	KO by	3
1980			
July	19—Stedy Tikolo, East London	W	6
Aug.	16—Tamsanqa Sogowe, East London	L	6

NKOSANA (HAPPY BOY) MGXAJI
South African Junior Welterweight
1969

May	10—Isaac Khoza, Port Elizabeth	W	6
June	7—Eric Mtamo, East London	W	6
Aug.	1—Torch Tant, Port Elizabeth	KO	2
Aug.	30—Joe Motsiri, Port Elizabeth	W	6
Sept.	20—Kulile Dolo, Port Elizabeth	KO	1
Oct.	25—Lefty Maselana, Uitengage	W	6
Nov.	8—Fisherman Njwabule, Port Elizabeth	W	6
Dec.	20—Jimmy Raolane, East London	KO	6
1970			
Feb.	7—Jeremiah Nzelwane, East London	W	6
Feb.	28—Isaac Boqwana, King Williamstown	KO	2
Mar.	28—Caswell Juqula, East London	W	6
May	16—Mongezi Twani, East London	KO	5
(Won Cape Junior Lightweight Title)			
June	6—Nqgika Tshume, King Williamstown	KO	3
July	4—Joe Africa, East London	W	10
(Won Cape Lightweight Title)			
Aug.	1—Phalo Tshume, East London	KO	3

Sept.	5—Abe Ncala, East London	W	8
Nov.	28—Mamiso Mtamo, Uitenhage	KO	5
Dec.	12—Terence Makaluza, Cape Town	KO	3
Dec.	19—Isaac Rakhajane, Port Elizabeth	W	8
1971			
Feb.	27—Terence Makaluza, King Williamstown	KO	6
Mar.	27—Nqgika Tshume, Port Elizabeth	KO	6
May	15—Levy Madi, King Williamstown	W	8
May	22—Isaac Rakhajane, East London	W	8
June	19—Blakney Matthews, Durban	W	8
July	3—Joe Zwane, East London	KO	5
Aug.	7—Louis Miya, East London	KO	5
Aug.	14—Joe Motsiri, King Williamstown	W	8
Sept.	18—Gideon Borias, King Williamstown	W	8
Oct.	23—Joe Archer, King Williamstown	W	8
Nov.	6—Andries Moloi, East London	W	8
1972			
Jan.	29—Philip Masiza, East London	KO	7
Mar.	4—Shole Mokoena, East London	W	8
May	27—Joseph Ngidi, East London	KO	3
June	24—Anthony Morodi, Johannesburg	L	12
(For S. Africa National NE Junior Lightweight Title)			
Aug.	5—Nqgika Tshume, King Williamstown	W	10
Sept.	2—Moses Mthembu, East London	W	8
Oct.	14—Isaac Rakhajane, King Williamstown	KO	7
Nov.	11—Alfred Cele, King Williamstown	W	8
Dec.	2—Cynet Tshabalala, Durban	KO	8
Dec.	9—Aubrey Peta, Port Elizabeth	W	10
1973			
Feb.	3—Vincent Mthembo, King Williamstown	KO	6
May	12—Solomon Ramafikeng, King Williamstown	W	8
June	9—Reginald Hilmer, King Williamstown	KO	8
June	30—Anthony Morodi, Johannesburg	W	12
July	28—Joe Archer, Port Elizabeth	W	8
Oct.	6—Jeremiah Nzelwane, Nzelwane	W	8
Nov.	17—Alfred Cele, Durban	W	8
Dec.	1—Alfred Buqwana, East London	W	12
Dec.	29—Phillip Masiza, Port Elizabeth	W	10
1974			
Mar.	9—Anthony Morodi, East London	W	10
Apr.	13—Ernest Phage, Fort Elizabeth	KO	7
June	1—Anthony Morodi, East London	KO	11
(South African Junior Lightweight Title)			
July	20—Gideon Borias, East London	W	8
Aug.	31—Bingo Crooks, East London	W	10
Oct.	2—Tadios Fisher, East London	W	10
Nov.	2—Sammy Goss, East London	W	10
Dec.	14—Rolly Xipu, East London	W	8
1975			
Mar.	29—Ben Lekalake, East London	W	12
June	21—Antonio Amaya, East London	W	10
Oct.	4—Ben Lekalake, East London	W	12
Dec.	13—Hyun Chi Kim, East London	W	10
1976			
Apr.	17—Norman Goins, East London	KO	10
May	8—Moses Mthembu, East London	W	8
July	10—Antonio Juma-Os, East London	W	10
Aug.	7—Norman Sekgapane, Port Elizabeth	D	6
Oct.	9—Thomas Sithebe, East London	KO	8
(Retained South African Junior Lightweight Title)			
Oct.	30—Norman Sekgapane, East London	W	10
1977			
Sept.	17—Joseph Tsotetsi, East London	KO	4
Nov.	14—Manuel de Paiva, Cape Town	KO	8
Nov.	19—Evans Gwiji, Port Elizabeth	D	8
1978			
Aug.	5—Langton Tinago, East London	D	10
Sept.	30—Eddie Mileham, East London	KO	3
Nov.	15—Willie Rodriquez, Cape Town	W	10
1979			
Apr.	14—Sam Serrano, Goodwood	KO by	8
(WBA Junior Lightweight Title)			
June	8—Tsietsi Maretloane, East London	L	8
Aug.	4—Evans Gwiji, East London	W	12
Nov.	10—Bowell Zono, King Williamstown	W	8
Dec.	8—Victor Mpiyakhe, East London	W	8
1980			
Mar.	1—Tsietsi Maretioane, East London	W	10
Mar.	29—Bernard Zungu, Queenstown	W	8
Dec.	6—Norman Sekgapane, East London	W	8
Dec.	20—Abel Brown, East London	W	8

JOHANNES MHLONGO
South African Lightweight
1980

June	16—Eugene Mthiyane, Durban	KO	2
Nov.	1—Enoch Jwara, Stranger	W	8

BARRY MICHAEL
Australian Lightweight
Born: June 2, 1955
1970

June	18—Mick McLean, Melbourne	W	3

June 25—Gary Leggett, Melbourne .... W 3
July 23—Mick McLean, Melbourne .... W 3
Aug. 6—Neil Hankin, Melbourne .... W 3
Oct. 15—Dale Doherty, Melbourne .... KO 2
Oct. 22—Glen Howard, Melbourne .... W 3
Nov. 19—Mick Maybury, Melbourne .... KO 3
1974
Feb. 4—Des Pearce, Melbourne................... W 4
Feb. 18—Jimmy Brown, Melbourne .... L 6
Apr. 19—Dally Law, Melbourne................... D 6
1975
Mar. 7—Mick OBrien, Melbourne............... KO 4
Apr. 11—Glen Howard, Melbourne .... W 6
Apr. 28—Willie Leslie, Melbourne .... W 6
June 2—Robbie Williams, Melbourne .... KO 3
Sept. 4—Glen Howard, North Melbourne .... W 10
Sept. 25—Keith Ball, North Melbourne.......... W 10
Nov. 20—Andy Broome, North Melbourne......... W 10
(Vacant Victorian State Lightweight Title)
1976
Feb. 26—Dave Richards, Blacktown .... W 10
Apr. 23—Dave Richards, South Melbourne .... W 12
(Vacant Victorian State Junior Lightweight Title)
Sept. 4—Nene Junior, Cebu City .... L 10
Nov. 26—Wongso Suseno, Surabaya .... W 10
Dec. 22—Billy Moeller, Orange .... L 15
(Commonwealth & Australian Junior Lightweight Titles)
1977
May 4—Joe Gibilisco, Melbourne................. W 10
Sept. 11—Jose Juan Gimenez, Surabaya .... L 10
Sept. 29—Spurling Pharangeburn, Djakarta .... W 10
Oct. 16—Fred Ramashie, Surabaya.............. W 10
1978
Jan. 24—Domenic Marano, Melbourne........... W 10
Apr. 28—Jeff Malcolm, Melbourne .... L 10
June 16—Kevin Franklin, West Heidelberg....... KO 3
Aug. 12—Billy Mulholland, Coonabarabran .... W 15
(Australian Lightweight Title)
Nov. 15—Billy Vivian, Merthyr .... W 10
Dec. 26—Lennox Blackmore, Georgetown ..... KO by 7
1979
Feb. 2—Blackeney Matthews, Williamstown .... KO 7
Feb. 18—Lucky Gattelaris, Sydney .... KO by 3
(Australian Lightweight Title)
July 5—Najib Daho, Aberavon .... L 8
Dec. 19—Jimmy Brown, Williamstown .... D 1
(For Australian Lightweight Title)
1980
Apr. 19—Manny Ysrael, Footscray .... W 10
Sept. 17—Graham Bell, Mt. Pritchard .... KO 6
(Won Australian Lightweight Title)
Dec. 17—Jimmy Brown, Melbourne .... KO 15
(Retained Australian Lightweight Title)

KOOS MIFUPHI
South African Junior Lightweight
1979
Mar. 10—Elijah Cele, Newcastle .... KO by 3
Apr. 25—Aubrey Lovett, Durban .... W 4
1980
May 19—Brian Baronet, Durban .... KO by 3

TADASHI MIHARA
Japanese Junior Middleweight
(Previous Record Unavailable)
1979
Feb. 22—Fil Robinson, Tokyo .... KO 1
Apr. 26—Jae-Keun Yim, Tokyo .... KO 5
(Won OPBF Junior Middleweight Title)
July 15—Armando Boniquit, Tokyo .... KO 5
(Retained OPBF Junior Middleweight Title)
Sept. 9—Nessie Horiguchi, Takasaki .... KO 4
Oct. 25—Ho Joo, Tokyo .... KO 3
1980
Jan. 24—Alberto Cruz, Tokyo .... W 10
Feb. 23—Ramon Dionisio, Tokushima .... KO 7
(Retained OPBF Junior Middleweight Title)
May 30—Michihiro Horihata, Tokyo .... W 12
(Retained OPBF Junior Middleweight Title)

HARDY MILEHAM
South African Welterweight
Born: July 19, 1956
1977
Mar. 19—Thornton Oakes, Johannesburg .... L 4
May 6—Johan Botes, Pretoria................... W 4
May 21—Gerrie Koekemoer, Johannesburg.......... W 4
Sept. 26—Phillipus van As, Johannesburg.......... D 4
Oct. 3—Peet van der Westhuizen, Johannesburg .. W 4
Nov. 14—Phillipus van As, London .... W 10
(Won Vacant Tvl. Junior Welterweight Title)
1978
Mar. 11—Peet van der Westhuizen, Johannesburg ... L 4

Apr. 10—Peet van der Westhuizen, Johannesburg ... L 10
(Lost Tvl. Junior Welterweight Title)
June 5—Peet van Der Westhuizen, Pretoria ...... KO 5
July 7—Richard Rova, Salisbury .... W 8
Sept. 30—Jack Jim, East London .... L 6
Oct. 28—Dirk van der Westhuizen, Ermelo .... W 12
1979
Feb. 3—Justus Josephs, Johannesburg .... KO by 6
Mar. 7—Bramley Whiteboy, Cape Town ...... KO by 6
Sept. 15—Abel Brown, Johannesburg .... W 4
Dec. 1—Phillip Maoara, Port Elizabeth .... L 4
1980
May 19—Gregory Clark, Durban .... L 4
May 31—Mzwandile Biyana, East London .... L 6
July 4—Abel Brown, Durban .... W 6
Aug. 16—Bennie Nortman, Johannesburg .... L 4
Sept. 15—Johannes Mthembu, Durban .... D 4
Oct. 11—Terrence Jonas, Elizabeth .... W 6

MICHAEL MILLER
British Junior Middleweight
1980
May 19—Neil Fannon, London .... KO 3
July 14—Steve Henty, London .... D 6

HOWARD MILLS
British Middleweight
1976
Sept. 13—Eddie Smith, Manchester .... L 4
Sept. 21—Al Neville, London .... L 6
Oct. 13—Dave Merrell, Stoke .... W 6
Oct. 25—Joe Jackson, Birmingham............... KO 2
1977
Jan. 25—Bob Mays, Bethnal .... L 6
Mar. 14—Eddie Smith, Manchester .... W 6
May 16—Dave Owens, Manchester .... KO by 8
Nov. 8—Tony Kelsey, Darlington .... D 8
Dec. 5—Tony Kelsey, Marton .... W 6
1978
Jan. 30—Eddie Burke, Glasgow .... KO 7
Feb. 27—Tony Kelsey, Middlesborough .... KO 4
Mar. 23—Theo Josephs, Sunderland............. W 8
May 8—Dave Owens, Nottingham............... KO 4
Aug. 7—Elijah Makhatini, Empangani........ KO by 5
1979
Sept. 24—Glen McEwan, Mayfair .... W 8
1980
May 21—Eddie Fenton, Coventry .... KO 2

JOE MILLS
British Junior Welterweight
1978
June 1—Derek Tew, Coventry................... KO 2
Sept. 27—Alan Burrows, Solihull .... KO by 6
Nov. 6—George Schofield, Stafford .... L 6
Nov. 27—Brendan O'Donnell, Liverpool .... W 6
Dec. 21—Terry Welsh, Liverpool .... W 6
1979
Mar. 5—Tommy Wright, Barnsley .... KO by 6
Apr. 4—Nigel Thomas, Birmingham .... L 6
May 29—Dave Laxen, London .... KO by 5
Oct. 17—George White, London .... W 6
Oct. 22—Steve Parker, London .... W 6
Nov. 12—George White, Mayfair .... KO 5
Nov. 26—Julian Boustead, Birmingham .... D 4
1980
Apr. 8—Neil Brown, Norwich .... W 6
May 21—Johnny Francis, Coventry .... L 6
June 2—Bobby Welburn, London .... D 6

MICK MILLS
British Junior Middleweight
1977
Mar. 21—Dave Taylor, Stoke .... W 6
Apr. 5—Earl Noel, Southend .... KO 2
Apr. 18—Bertie Green, Stafford .... KO 1
May 3—Johnny Hamm, Southend .... KO 6
June 14—Horace McKenzie, Southend .... KO 4
July 20—Johnny Breen, Sheffield .... KO 2
Sept. 14—Owen Robinson, Sheffield .... KO 8
Sept. 20—Rocky Butler, Southend .... KO 2
Nov. 2—Jim Moore, London.................... KO 1
Dec. 5—Tim McHugh, London .... KO 2
Dec. 13—Owen Robinson, London .... W 8
1978
Feb. 7—Henry Turkington, London............. KO 3
Feb. 27—Albert (Gypsy) Smith, Sheffield......... W 8
Mar. 14—Albert (Gypsy) Smith, Southend .... KO 2
Apr. 11—John Smith, Sheffield................. W 8
May 24—Joe Oke, Southend .... KO 1
Nov. 28—Esperno Postl, Sheffield................ KO 2
1979
Feb. 6—Joey Mack, Wembley .... KO by 3

Apr.	10—Salvo Nucifero, Kensington	KO by	5
May	16—Prince Rodney, Sheffield	KO by	4
	1980		
Feb.	12—Carl Bailey, Sheffield	KO	
Apr.	9—Curtis Marsh, Burslem	L	8
Apr.	22—Jimmy Ellis, Sheffield	KO by	6
Nov.	4—Chris Christian, Southend	L	8

LUIGI MINCHILLO
Italian Junior Middleweight
1977

Jan.	21—Silvano Bischeri, Pesaro	KO	5
Feb.	4—Ali Jacoubi, Milan	KO	3
Feb.	25—Mario Favotto, Pesaro	W	6
Apr.	1—Armando Lena, Pesaro	KO	3
May	7—Luciano Spina, Pesaro	W	6
May	28—Guglielmo Caldera, Pesaro	KO	3
Aug.	10—Murio Martillano, Rimini	W	8
Oct.	22—Roy Kaba, Pesaro	W	8
Nov.	18—Walter Guernieri, Pesaro	W	8
Dec.	17—Gerard Breton, Pesaro	KO	3
	1978		
Jan.	28—Mariano Salamone, Pesaro	W	8
Feb.	24—Jack Peraire, Milano	KO	4
Apr.	15—Wa Bukasa, Pesaro	W	8
May	20—Giancarlo Serangeli, S. Sevaro	KO	3
June	3—George Martins, Pesaro	KO	1
Sept.	29—Luigi Marini, Milano	KO	3
Nov.	10—Alvaro Scarpelli, Milano	KO by	4
Dec.	15—Roy Kaba, Pesaro	WF	6
	1979		
Feb.	10—Michel Chapier, Havange	KO	5
Apr.	21—Clemente Gessi, Pesaro	KO	1
	(Italian Junior Middleweight Title)		
June	12—Paolo Zanusso, San Paolo di Civitate	KO	5
	(Italian Junior Middleweight Title)		
June	30—Antonio Torsello, Monte Carlo	KO	6
Nov.	16—Joe Oke, Milan	KO	5
Dec.	15—Vincenzo Ungaro, Pesaro	KO	7
	(Italian Junior Middleweight Title)		
	1980		
Feb.	13—Nelson Gomez, Pesaro	KO	3
Mar.	29—Alvaro Scarpelli, Pesaro	KO	4
	(Retained Italian Junior Middleweight Title)		
Apr.	20—Celestine Kanynda, Hayange	W	8
May	23—Horace McKenzie, Resaro	W	8

TAKESHI MINE
Japanese Lightweight
1979

Oct.	23—Mitsuo Kobayashi, Tokyo	KO by	3
Dec.	1—Tatsuya Moriyasu, Okayama	W	10
	1980		
Jan.	6—Kujoshi (Battle Hawk) Kazama, Nara	KO by	3
Feb.	18—Shigeyuki Otake, Tokyo	L	10
Mar.	22—Chung-Il Choi, Inchon	KO by	1
Nov.	23—Tsuyoshi Hamada, Tokyo	KO by	1

TERRY MINTUS
British Heavyweight
1975

Apr.	28—Reg Smith, Kensington	KO	2
Sept.	8—Ishaq Hussein, London	W	6
Nov.	4—Paul Kinsella, London	L	6
Nov.	18—Isaac Hussen, Reading	L	6
Dec.	2—David Fry, Leeds	D	6
	1976		
Jan.	14—John DePledge, Bradford	W	6
Jan.	20—Denton Ruddock, London	L	6
Feb.	24—Sean Reilly, Manchester	D	8
Mar.	10—Brian Huckfield, Wolverhampton	D	8
Apr.	5—John DePledge, Bradford	W	6
May	5—Derek Simpkin, Solihull	KO	6
July	9—Aldo Rightetti, Rimini	KO by	5
Sept.	21—Paul Kinsella, London	KO	3
Oct.	25—Isaac Hussein, London	L	8
	1977		
Feb.	7—Derek Simpkin, London	L	8
June	1—Bunny Johnson, Dudley	KO by	1
Oct.	19—Tony Moore, Kingston	W	8
Nov.	14—Les Stevens, Reading	L	8
	1978		
Apr.	6—Bjorn Rudi, Oslo	W	6
Apr.	29—Rudy Gauwe, Zele	KO by	4
Oct.	12—Austin Okoye, Wimbledon	KO	8
Oct.	30—Sylvain Watbled, Paris	L	10
	1979		
Mar.	10—Jimmy Abbott, Johannesburg	KO by	4
June	25—Ricky James, Edgbaston	L	8
Sept.	25—Gordon Ferris, London	KO by	6
Nov.	28—Neil Malpass, Doncaster	W disq.	5
	1980		
May	28—George Scott, Cramlington	W	10
	(Eliminator, British Heavyweight Title)		

EDDIE MIRAL
Filipino Bantamweight
1979

Feb.	17—Pablo Gernandizo, Pampanga	W	10
Feb.	20—Flash Gapasin, Angeles City	W	10
May	22—Star Dayanan, Angeles City	D	10
June	15—Cesar Amazan, Manila	L	10
Nov.	24—Billy Abato, Cag. do Oro City	L	10
Dec.	20—Al Sicat, Olongapo City	D	10
	1980		
Jan.	21—Star Dayanan, Clark Air Base	W	10
Feb.	23—Ver Basa, Angeles City	W	10

ACHILLE (SPEEDY) MITCHELL
British Junior Middleweight
1975

May	16—Alan Cable, Birmingham	KO	5
June	27—John Sagar, Birmingham	KO	6
Oct.	29—Brian Gregory, Wolverhampton	W	6
	1976		
Jan.	13—Martin Lewis, Wolverhampton	W	8
Feb.	13—Derek McCarthy, Digbeth	KO	3
Mar.	10—Terry Schofield, Wolverhampton	W	8
Mar.	29—Paul Davis, Walworth	W	8
May	3—Paul Davis, Walworth	D	8
Sept.	29—Albert Hillmann, Hammersmith	W	8
Oct.	25—Billy Waith, Hammersmith	W	8
Dec.	14—Al Stewart, W. Bromwich	L	8
	1977		
Jan.	11—Johnny Pincham, London	KO by	7
Feb.	25—Paul Shutt, Digbeth	KO	6
Mar.	14—Johnny Pincham, Hammersmith	W	8
Oct.	24—Steve Angell, London	L	8
Nov.	3—Louis Acaries, Marseille	L	10
Nov.	22—Roy Commosioung, Hemel Hempstead	L	8
	1978		
Jan.	12—Frank Albertus, Rotterdam	W	8
Mar.	17—Jo Kimpuani, Grand Synthe	L	10
Apr.	29—Clement Tsinza, Zele	D	8
May	29—Frank Albertus, Rotterdam	D	8
Sept.	27—Kirkland Laing, Solihull	L	12
Oct.	9—Colin Ward, Marylebone	W	8
Nov.	11—Jo Kimpuani, Dunkirk	KO by	2
Dec.	2—Clement Tsinza, Zele	L	10
	1979		
Mar.	26—Ronald Zenon, Paris	L	8
May	2—Joey Mack, Solihull	KO by	4
Oct.	16—Joey Singleton, West Bromwich	L	8
Nov.	5—Georges Warusfel, Paris	L	10
Nov.	24—Fred Coranson, Dunkirk	L	10
	1980		
Feb.	7—Han Henrik Palm, Randers	KO by	6
Apr.	14—John F. Kennedy, London	L	8
Nov.	10—Mickey Mapp, Southwark	D	8

SYLVESTER MITTEE
British Junior Welterweight
1977

Oct.	25—Earl Noel, Kensington	KO	2
Nov.	15—Rocky Butler, Bethnal	KO	2
Nov.	29—Barton McAllister, Bethnal	KO	4
	1978		
Feb.	21—Sylvester Gordon, Kensington	KO	5
Dec.	5—Ray Ross, Kensington	KO	2
	1979		
Apr.	9—Chris Davies, Mayfair	KO	2
May	29—Carl Bailey, Kensington	KO	1
Oct.	9—Tony Martey, Kensington	W	8
Dec.	11—Mick Bell, Bletchley	KO	2
	1980		
Jan.	22—Colin Power, London	KO	7
Apr.	22—Des Morrison, London	L	12
Sept.	27—Derek Nelson, London	KO	2

JOHANNES MIYA
South African Junior Flyweight
1979

June	29—Edison Ramagole, Natalspruit	D	4
Aug.	31—Wilson Dhlamini, Natalspruit	W	4
	1980		
Mar.	22—Jacob Molefe, Soweto	D	6
Apr.	25—Dexter Dhlamini, Sebokeng	W	6
May	17—Honey Ndwanya, East London	KO	4
Aug.	29—Edison Ramagole, Sebokeng	W	6
Oct.	4—Simon Moema, Joburg	L	10
	(Transvaal Junior Flyweight Title)		
Nov.	28—Paul Tshala, Johannesburg	W	6

MASAO MIZUI
Japanese Bantamweight
1979

Apr.	17—Susumi Shinaba, Nagoya	D	10
	1980		
Feb.	1—Kazumi Sato, Osaka	L	10

DANIEL MKENKU
South African Featherweight
1980
Mar.	8—Victor Harris, Bloemfontein	KO 4
Apr.	12—Jeremiah Malikhetla, Ficksburg	L 6
June	14—Joseph Teteli, Welkom	L 4
Sept.	6—Jeremiah Malikhetia, Ficksburg	W 6

DANIEL MKIZE
South African Junior Middleweight
1971
June	26—Victor Tshabalala, New Clare	L 8
Nov.	12—Enoch Nhlapo, Thembisa	L 8

1972
Feb.	5—Jeremiah Mzakwana, Bloemfontein	L 6
Feb.	24—Petrus Sithebe, Langa	W 8
Mar.	4—S. Mphuti, Galeshewe	W 8
Mar.	25—Norman Sekgapane, Jabulani	L 6
Apr.	22—Aycliff Stengile, King Williamstown	KO 1
June	26—Richard Borias, Port Elizabeth	W 8
Oct.	21—Norman Sekgapane, Port Elizabeth	L 6
Nov.	3—Norman Sekgapane, Tembisa	L 6

1973
Feb.	—Phalo Tshume, Port Elizabeth	L 6
May	12—Jim Jack, Port Elizabeth	W 10
July	14—Griffiths Mgijima, East London	W 8
Oct.	13—Jeremiah Nzelwane, Port Elizabeth	L 8
Oct.	27—Victor Tshabalala, Jabulani	L 6

1974
Apr.	6—McK. Mofokeng, Welkom	L
Apr.	13—Victor Tshabalala, Port Elizabeth	L 8
Oct.	18—Petrus Sithebe, Tembisa	W 6
Nov.	9—Jack Jim, Port Elizabeth	L 10
Dec.	14—Victor Tshabalala, East London	L 8

1975
Feb.	28—Morris Mohloai, Kwa-Thema	KO by 6
Apr.	9—Ben Molokeng, Bloemfontein	W
June	14—Anthony Morodi, Port Elizabeth	W 8
Sept.	6—Rolly Xipu, Port Elizabeth	W 8
Dec.	6—Isaac Rakhajane, Port Elizabeth	W 8

1976
Jan.	31—Griffiths Mgijima, East London	KO by 4

1977-1978
(Inactive)
1979
Nov.	19—Godfrey Manyaniso, Kimberley	W 6
Dec.	8—Godfrey Manyaniso, Bloemfontein	L 8

1980
July	5—Jantjie Hiapane, Kimberley	W 4
Aug.	12—Jeffrey Diodio, Welkom	W 6
Aug.	23—John Khooe, Kimberley	W 6
Sept.	6—John Khooe, Welkom	L 10
	(For OFS Junior Middleweight Title)	
Oct.	4—Peter Mgojo, Welkom	L 8

VICTOR MKOHLAKALI
South African Featherweight
1977
Nov.	19—Nkosana Moss, East London	L 4

1978
July	8—Ndodomzi Witi, East London	D 4
Sept.	9—Moses Mahlangu, East London	W 4
Oct.	21—Edward Genu, Queenstown	W 4

1979
Apr.	28—Thobile Siyokwana, East London	W 4
July	7—Government Feleti, Queenstown	W 4

1980
July	5—Nkosana Moss, East London	W 8

NICHOLAS MLABA
South African Welterweight
1979
Mar.	10—John More, Newcastle	L 4
July	28—Alfred Gcaza, King Williamstown	KO by 2
Aug.	18—Alfred Ndlovu, King Williamstown	L 4

1980
Mar.	1—Johnny Lutchmanna, Durban	W 4
June	16—Peter Gumede, Durban	L 4
Nov.	3—Johnny Lutchmanna, Durban	KO 4

ZEPHANIA MLOTSHWA
South African Welterweight
1978
Sept.	30—Poloso Rubushe, East London	W 4

1979
Mar.	31—Petrus Moloi, Welkom	KO 2
June	29—Reginald Menong, Natalspruit	L 4

1980
May	30—Nikanor Ashipala, Springs	L 4

JOHN MOALUSI
(AKA CHAMPION MOKONE)
South African Light Heavyweight
1978
Oct.	10—Solomon Dladla, Durban	KO by 1

1979
Feb.	12—Willem van der Merwe, Durban	KO 3
Mar.	10—Joe Jatjiu, Newcastle	KO 3
Sept.	1—Solomon Dladla, Empangeni	KO 5

1980
Feb.	4—Doug Lumley, Durban	L 6
Oct.	6—Themba Buthelezi, Pmburg	L 10
Nov.	3—Willem van der Merwe, Durban	W 4
Dec.	15—Mark Melville, Pmburg	L 4

MICHAEL MOAMOGOA
South African Featherweight
1977
Nov.	26—Michael Mohlabane, Bloemfontein	W 4

1978
Mar.	31—Jacob Moyeye, Bloemfontein	L 6
June	3—Joshua Nhlapo, Bloemfontein	L 6
Aug.	12—Shadrak Mogupudi, Bloemfontein	W 6

1979
Feb.	5—Johan Putter, Welkom	L 6
Mar.	31—Hope Mambolo, Welkom	L 6
June	23—Israel Khonkhobe, Bloemfontein	L 8
Oct.	5—Gaybon Yekiso, Bloemfontein	L 6
Nov.	9—Hendrik Koelman, Bloemfontein	W 6
Dec.	1—Johannes Lebibo, Odendaalsrust	W 10

1980
Apr.	14—Gift Xaluva, Kimberley	D 6
July	5—P. J. Xhelishio Kimberley	L 6
Aug.	23—Israel Khonkhobe, Kimberley	W 8
Dec.	13—Israel Papane, Wesselsbron	L 8

MOSES MOAMOGOA
South African Bantamweight
1979
Nov.	19—Ranching Louw, Kimberley	L 4

1980
July	5—Ranching Louw, Kimberley	L 4
Aug.	23—Ranching Louw, Kimberley	L 6
Dec.	13—Frans Mphatsoe, Wesselsbron	L 6

HIROFUMI MOCHIZUKI
Japanese Lightweight
1979
Nov.	27—Katsutoshi Takaski, Tokyo	KO 4

1980
Feb.	19—Hideyoshi Horinaga, Tokyo	W 10

JACOB MODIPA
South African Welterweight
1979
Aug.	18—John Khooe, Welkom	W 4

1980
May	24—Dumishani Hokoma, Welkom	KO 3
Dec.	6—Allen Ferland, Welkom	W 6

JOHANNES MODISE
South African Welterweight
1979
June	23—John Khooe, Bloemfontein	L 6
Dec.	8—Stanley Ledimo, Bloemfontein	L 6

1980
Feb.	2—Nikonor Ashipala, Kimberley	L 8
Aug.	23—Teboho Lento, Kimberley	D 6
Sept.	6—Godfrey Manyaniso, Welkom	L 4
Oct.	4—Jonas Majoro, Welkom	KO by 3

RICHARD MODISE
South African Bantamweight
1974
Mar.	9—Guy Ratazayo, East London	KO by 5
June	29—Fred Baker, Jabulani	L 4
July	19—Siphiwe Bhengu, Durban	KO 1
Sept.	27—Johnny Dlamini, Wattville	L 6
Nov.	15—John Ngwenya, Orlando West	W 4

1975
July	25—Johannes Sithebe, Orlando	W 6

1976
Feb.	6—William Molatudi, Kwa-Thema	W 10
Mar.	22—Sipho Mange, Guguletu	L 6
June	5—Peter Mathebula, Jabulani	L 6
Nov.	20—Jacob Raditsile, Bloemfontein	KO by 3

1977
Mar.	5—Mzukisi Skweyiya, East London	L 12
May	30—Nkululeko Sandi, Port Elizabeth	L 8

1978
Mar.	18—Siphiwe Bhengu, Durban	KO by 4
Mar.	31—Daniel Hlahane, Natalspruit	L 10
May	15—Sybrand Oelofse, Johannesburg	KO 2

1979
Nov. 17—Daniel Hlahane, Springs ....L 10
1980
Apr. 21—Kallie Swanepoel, Secunda ....L 4
May 10—Samuel Serekego, Virginia ....L 6
Oct. 31—Simon Skosana, Springs ....L 6

SIMON MOEMA
South African Junior Flyweight
Born: March 19, 1956
1975
July 25—William Thompson, Orlando ....W 4
1976
Jan. 30—Philemon Mphomela, Orlando West ......W 4
1977
Sept. 17—Monde Mpulampula, East London ....L 4
Oct. 14—Paulus Tshehla, Krugersdorp ....W 6
Nov. 18—Gilbert Makenete, Krugersdorp ....W 6
1978
Apr. 15—Mxolisi Mpama, Butterworth ....D 6
May 27—Lucas Ncetezo, East London ....W 6
Aug. 26—Reuben Matewu, East London ....W 6
1979
Mar. 31—Jama Qalinge, Welkom ....W 8
Aug. 4—Reuben Matewu, East London ....W 4
Nov. 10—Johannes Sithebe, Jabulani ....L 4
1980
Mar. 22—Johannes Sithebe, Soweto ....W 10
(Won Vacant Transvaal Flyweight Title)
May 3—Cosmo Ziqu, East London ....W 8
May 30—Norman Hlalele, Springs ....KO 5
Aug. 1—Johannes Sithebe, Springs ....L 10
(Lost Transvaal Flyweight Title)
Oct. 4—Johannes Miya, Johannesburg ....W 10
Nov. 14—Freddie Masemola, Diepkloof ....KO 3

ROBERT MOEPI
South African Featherweight
1980
May 24—Naftaly Mathys, Welkom ....KO 1
June 7—Elias Mphatsoe, Odenaalsrust ....KO 1
Aug. 2—Joseph Monedane, Welkom ....KO 2
Dec. 6—Paulus Monewoang, Welkom ....KO 1

LAZARUS MOFEKENG
South African Featherweight
Born: January 29, 1951
1973
Oct. 13—S. Mokoka, Bethlehem ....KO
1974
(Inactive)
1975
Apr. 26—Lucas Tlala, Sharpeville ....W 4
1976
Oct. 9—Samuel Nhlapo, Kroonstad...............W 6
Nov. 6—Samuel Nhlapo, Parys ....W 6
Dec. 4—Isaac Gwebu, Welkom ....KO 4
1977
May 21—Spider Moeketsi, Bethlehem..............W 6
June 3—Paulus Mnisi, Springs...................D 6
Sept. 10—Abraham Mphatsoe, Kroonstad ....D 6
Oct. 8—Abraham Mphatsoe, Kroonstad ....W 6
Oct. 14—Thomas Mathibela, Krugersdorp..........W 8
Nov. 5—Jacob Diraditsile, Viljoenskroon ....L 8
1978
Mar. 3—Joseph Gumede, Krugersdorp ....L 8
1979
May 4—Joshua Nhlapo, Springs ....L 6
June 16—Elias Mphatsoe, Virginia ....W 6
Aug. 4—Jacob Motseki, Odendaalsrust ....L 8
1980
Aug. 29—Joe Gumede, Sebokeng ....KO by 2
Nov. 21—Stephen Nkomo, Sebokeng ....W 4
Dec. 6—Jacob Diraditsile, Welkom ....W 4

MICHAEL MOHLABANE
South African Lightweight
1976
Oct. 9—Elias Mphatsoe, Kroonstad ....L 4
1977
Aug. 27—Abraham Mphatsoe, Odendaalsrust .....W 6
Nov. 26—Michael Moanmogoa, Bloemfontein ......L 4
1978
Nov. 28—Abraham Mphatsoe, Virginia ....KO 6
1979
Feb. 10—Johannes Motsumi, Virginia ....W 6
Aug. 18—Elias Mphatsoe, Welkom ....KO by 1
Oct. 2—Stephen Nchee, Bloemfontein ....W 4
Dec. 14—Anthony De Paiva, Welkom ....W 4
1980
Mar. 6—Samuel Pule, Bloemfontein ....L 10
May 31—Daniel Moloi, Bethlehem ....D 4
June 14—Jacob Motseki, Welkom ....W 8

Sept. 13—David Mogape, Welkom ....KO 2
Sept. 27—Isaac Tshoane, Welkom ....W 4
Dec. 6—Jeremiah Maliketia, Ficksburg ....W 6

(MORRIS) MOSES MOHLOAI
South African Junior Middleweight
Born: June 17, 1950
1972
May 12—Meshack Nene, Kwa Thema ....W 4
July 28—Joseph Mphlala, Natalspruit ....KO by 2
Sept. 2—Jack Jim, East London ....W 6
Nov. 17—Gabriel Dlamini, Springs ....W 4
1973
Mar. 31—Phillip Hlophe, Durban ....KO by 5
May 26—Thuso Mapela, Jabulani ....W 4
June 22—Emmanuel Gumede, Springs ....W 6
Aug. 11—Jack Khoza, Jabulani ....KO 3
Aug. 17—Gordon Goba, Springs ....KO by 3
Nov. 9—Johannes Dladhla, Springs ....W 6
1974
Apr. 5—Jeremiah Nzelwane, Kwa-Thema ....W 6
May 3—McKeed Mofokeng, Katlehong...........W 6
July 20—Welcome Mtyongwe, East London ....W 6
Aug. 9—Cecil Kekana, Springs ....W 10
Sept. 6—Lawrence Mphuthi, Kwa-Thema ....KO 3
1975
Feb. 28—Daniel Mkize, Kwa-Thema ....KO 6
Mar. 21—Mike Ramagole, Springs ....W 6
Mar. 29—Griffithes Mgijima, East London ....W 6
May 30—Maxwell Malinga, Springs ....W 12
June 28—Jackson Diphofa, Johannesburg ....KO 3
Aug. 1—Jeremiah Nzelwane, Springs ....W 6
Aug. 30—Jeremiah Nzelwane, Johannesburg ......KO 4
Oct. 18—Griffiths Mgijima, Durban ....W 8
Oct. 25—Emmanuel Gumede, Johannesburg ....W 6
Nov. 11—Maxwell Malinga, Kwa-Themba.........W 12
1976
Apr. 24—Langton Tinago, Jabulani................W 8
May 1—Phillip Hlophe, Durban ....W 8
May 15—Griffiths Mgijima, Johannesburg ....W 12
Oct. 30—Mzwandile Mquanto, East London ....W 6
1977
Jan. 29—Gert Craemer, Johannesburg ....W 6
June 4—Thuso Mapela, Johannesburg ....KO 7
Dec. 1—Phillip Hlope, Cape Town ....W 12
1978
Apr. 29—Harold Volbrecht, Johannesburg ....KO by 2
(South African Welterweight Title)
Aug. 26—Gert Craemer, Bophuthatswana ....W 6
1979
Feb. 16—David Kambule, Springs ....L 10
Mar. 30—Joseph Lala, Springs ....W 8
Sept. 7—David Kambule, Springs ....L 10
1980
Apr. 6—Arturo Guzman, Houston ....KO 4
June 7—Zachariah Thebethe, Joburg ....KO 2
Oct. 4—Patrick Tshabalala, Joburg ....KO 1

SAMSON MOHLOAI
South African Middleweight
1977
July 9—William Malefane, Parys ....W 6
Oct. 14—Isaac Mabuza, Krugersdorp ....W 6
1978
Sept. 30—David Mohale, Sharpeville ....W 6
Nov. 17—Raymond Mashifane, Springs ....W 6
1979
Apr. 7—Johannes Mpesi, Vereeniging ....W 6
June 18—Anton Retief, Johannesburg ....KO 6
Nov. 10—William Malefane, Jabulani ....KO 1
1980
June 7—Cameron Adams, Joburg ....KO by 5
(Transvaal Middleweight Title)
Nov. 21—Daniel Mapanya, Sebokeng ....KO 7

MICHEL MOINARD
French Middleweight
1979
Dec. 8—Jean Pierre Trichelut, Epinaysous Senard L 6
1980
Feb. 8—Cyrille Barbe, Palaiseau ....KO 1
May 17—Chruistian Chesini, Vandoevre ....L 6
Oct. 10—Frederic Boissy, Villeurbanne ....L 6
Oct. 26—Giovanni Chirra, Mulhóuse ....D 6

JAFTA MOKGOSI
South African Junior Welterweight
1979
July 31—Samuel Pule, Bloemfontein ....W 6
1980
May 10—Joseph Teteli, Virginia ....W 4
Mar. 22—Gerald Isaacs, Jabulani ....KO by 2

SIMON MOKOENA
South African Welterweight
1974
Mar. 23—E. Mbayo, Virginia .... L disq. 1
1975
(Inactive)
1976
Mar. 6—Ben Mutle, Kroonzxd .... KO 5
May 15—Samuel Tshabalala, Kroonstad .... KO by 1
1977-1978
(Inactive)
1979
Feb. 5—Martin Jacobs, Welkom .... L 4
Mar. 2—Danie Jacobs, Bloemfontein .... W 4
June 11—Bennie Nortman, Welkom .... KO by 4
Nov. 9—Joseph Lala, Bloemfontein .... KO by 4
1980
Feb. 2—Samuel Visser, Kimberley .... KO 2

JOSEPH MOLAHLOE
South African Lightweight
1979
Feb. 10—Ediel Hlephudi, Virginia .... L 6
Feb. 24—Petrus Motaung, Bethlehem .... W disq. 4
Mar. 24—Johannes Ramasimong, Virginia .... W 4
May 12—Jacob Motseki, Virginia .... L 4
July 14—Jonas Tladi, Virginia .... L 8
Sept. 3—Johann Ronquest, Welkom .... L 4
Dec. 1—Manase Potse, Odendaalsrust .... L 6
1980
Feb. 2—Stephen Balene, Virginia .... L 4
June 14—Teboho Lento, Welkom .... L 4
Sept. 6—Motsie Tiadi, Ficksburg .... L 4
Dec. 6—Ephraim Khuto, Ficksburg .... D 6

SIMON MOLAHLOE
South African Lightweight
1978
June 3—Benard Dayel, Bloemfontein .... D 6
July 22—Martin Jacobs, Bloemfontein .... W 4
Aug. 12—Isaac Tsosane, Bloemfontein .... KO 1
1979
Mar. 5—Martin Jacobs, Welkom .... W 10
Mar. 30—Evans Gwiji, Springs .... KO by 2
Oct. 5—Samuel Pule, Bloemfontein .... W 10
Nov. 9—Petrus Rampoporo, Bloemfontein .... L 6
Dec. 1—Jacob Motseki, Odendaalsrust .... D 10
Dec. 14—Eddie Mileham, Welkom .... W 6
1980
Mar. 1—Jacob Motseki, Odendaalsrust .... L 10
(Lost Orange Free State Lightweight Title)
Oct. 11—Petrus Rampororo, Odendaalsrust .... KO by 9
Dec. 6—Notsi Tladi, Ficksburg .... KO by 5

TENYSON MOLEBELEDI
South African Junior Featherweight
1979
Aug. 29—Daniel Rammilli, Bloemfontein .... W 4
1980
May 3—Gift Xaluva, Witsieshoek .... D 4
July 3—Phineas Mabaso, Welkom .... KO by 4
Nov. 29—Samuel Mufamane, Odendaalsrust ...... KO 1

ERNEST MOLEDI
South African Junior Welterweight
1978
Mar. 3—Simon Dhladhla, Krugersdorp .... W 4
Apr. 15—Poloso Rubushe, Butterworth .... W 4
Apr. 22—David Kambule, Vereeniging .... KO by 1
Sept. 30—Jonathan Mabaso, Sharpeville .... KO 1
1979
Apr. 7—Deon Labuschagne, Vereeniging .... W 4
Apr. 28—Gregory Schmidt, Johannesburg .... W 4
Aug. 31—Terrence Molefe, Natalspruit .... D 6
1980
Mar. 22—Ephraim Mabena, Soweto .... W 10
(Transvaal Junior Welterweight Title)
June 7—Abel Brown, Johannesburg .... KO 5
Sept. 20—Peter Kanie, Jabulani .... W 6
Dec. 6—Peter Kanie, East London .... W 6

DAVID MOLEFE
South African Junior Flyweight
1976
May 15—Simon Sehloho, Kroonstad .... KO 2
July 3—Jacob Mokoneyane, Parys .... W 4
Aug. 21—Godfrey Nkale, Kroonstad .... W 6
1977
Apr. 16—Jama Qalinge, Kroonstad .... L 6
May 21—Joseph Ncheto, Kroonstad .... W 6
June 11—Godfrey Nkato, Kroonstad .... W 4
Oct. 8—Speedy Mahlatsa, Kroonstad .... W 4

1978
Jan. 28—Monde Mpulampula, East London .... KO by 6
1979
Mar. 5—Gift Xaluwa, Welkom .... L 4
Mar. 24—Godfrey Nkate, Virginia .... L 8
Apr. 2—Gift Xaluva, Welkom .... KO by 6
May 25—Freddie Masemola, Springs .... KO by 3
1980
Feb. 2—Martin Nkokoto, Virginia .... KO by 10
(OFS Junior Flyweight Title)

JACOB MOLEFE
South African Bantamweight
1979
June 16—Joshua Mahlangu, Virginia .... W 4
July 31—Gift Xaluva, Bloemfontein .... W 8
1980
Mar. 22—Johannes Miya, Soweto .... D 6
May 10—Andrew Peterson, Virginia .... W 6
Aug. 2—Ranching Masemola, Springs .... W 6
Sept. 5—Freddie Masemola, Springs .... KO by 4

TERRENCE MOLEFE
South African Welterweight
1979
Mar. 30—Frank Thobakgale, Springs .... KO 1
May 25—Jeffrey Aphane, Springs .... KO 3
June 29—Petrus Motaung, Natalspruit .... KO 2
Aug. 31—Ernest Moledi, Natalspruit .... D 6
Sept. 15—Bennie Nortman, Johannesburg .... L 4
1980
Feb. 29—Peter Mgojo, Springs .... W 4
Apr. 25—Justus Josephs, Sebokeng .... D 6
May 24—Fanie van Staden, Orlando .... D 6

EMILIO MOLERO
Spanish Welterweight
1979
June 6—Victor Lopen, Bilbao .... KO by 4
July 27—Mohammed El Kadoumi, Madrid .... W 4
Aug. 10—Jose M. Llorente, Madrid .... KO 3
Aug. 24—Ahmed Ben Aissa, Madrid .... L 6
Sept. 8—Jose G. Sanchez, Aranda .... W 6
Sept. 14—Jose Luis Vicho, Aviles .... L 6
Oct. 6—Mutil Nande, Bilbao .... D 6
Oct. 20—Jose Alvarez, Oviedo .... D 6
Nov. 2—Carlos Montesihos, Benetuset .... D 4
Dec. 1—Manuel Pena, Las Palmas .... KO 6
1980
Jan. 5—Melian Sierra, Santander .... KO 4
Feb. 8—Salid Mimun Armar, Madrid .... L 8

HECTOR MOLINA
Spanish Junior Lightweight
1977
July 15—Isidoro Cabeza, Madrid .... D 8
Aug. 12—Ramon Marichal, S. Cruz .... L 8
Oct. 1—Roberto Castanon, Leon .... L 10
Dec. 16—Antonio Guinaldo, Barcelona .... L 8
Dec. 30—Manuel Llata, Santander .... L 8
1978
Jan. 28—Nino Jimenez, Oviedo .... L 8
Feb. 27—George Feeney, Middlesbrough .... L 8
Apr. 17—Jose Antonio Jimenez, Aviles .... W 8
May 12—Carlos Hernandez, Valladolid .... L 8
May 20—Isidoro Cabeza, Palma Mallorca .... D 8
July 12—Rodolfo Sanchez, Bilbao .... L 8
Aug. 5—Mohammed Jofre I, Melilla .... L 8
Aug. 26—Manuel Masso, Cuenca .... D 8
Oct. 28—Cecilio Lastra, Santander .... KO by 4
1979
May 18—Manuel Masso, Barcelona .... L 8
June 1—Mohamed Jofre II, Mallorca .... D 8
June 16—Pedro Jimenez, Santander .... L 8
Aug. 10—Carlos Hernandez, Lepe .... KO by 7
Oct. 27—Roberto Castanon, La Coruna .... L 8
Dec. 24—Jose Luis Heredia, Fuengirola .... L 8
1980
Feb. 16—Carlos Hernandez, Zamora .... L 8
Aug. 22—Roberto Castanon, Madrid .... L 8
Oct. 4—Goichi Oshi, Palma de Mallorca .... D 8
Nov. 29—Esteban Eguia, Leon .... L 8

DANIEL MOLOI
South African Lightweight
1979
Feb. 9—Motsie Tladi, Bethlehem .... W 4
1980
May 5—George Parking, Welkom .... KO 1
May 31—Michael Mohlabane, Bethlehem .... D 4
Aug. 29—Zenslie Makanda, Sebokeng .... KO 2
Nov. 21—Leo Simelane, Sebokeng .... W 6
Dec. 19—David Kalako, Welkom .... L 6

NTSIKELOLO MONA
South African Bantamweight
1978
Oct. 21—Siphiwo Fuma, Queenstown ....L 4
1979
Aug. 18—Boy Boy Mgayi, King Williamstown .....L 4
1980
Aug. 23—Joe Gunuza, East London ....L 4
Nov. 8—Boy Boy Mazaleni, East London ....D 4

JOSEPH MONEOANE
South African Featherweight
1979
July 31—Samuel Motsabi, Bloemfontein ....L 6
1980
May 30—Enoch Mazibuku, Springs ....L 4
Aug. 2—Robert Moepi, Welkom ....KO by 2

PAULUS MONEOANG
South African Lightweight
1979
July 31—Abel Rapulane, Bloemfontein ....L 6
1980
May 10—Johannes Motsumi, Virginia ....W 4
Dec. 6—Robert Moepi, Welkom ....KO by 1

ANDRE MONGALEMA
German Junior Middleweight
1979
Nov. 30—Giampaolo Piras, Bonnevoie ....W 6
1980
Feb. 10—Robert Amory, Compiegne ....KO 2
Feb. 17—Maurice Renaud, Metz ....D 6
Mar. 22—Josef Kossmann, Friedewald ....KO 6
Apr. 26—Chruistian Chesini, Luneville ....KO 3
May 23—Maurice Bufi, Le Roeuex ....W 8

MYUNG-AN MOON
Korean Bantamweight
(Previous Record Unavailable)
1979
Nov. 9—Dong-Yul Oh, Seoul ....KO 5
(Won Vacant JBC Bantamweight Title)
1980
Mar. 30—Kang-San Lee, Seoul ....D 10
(Retained Korean Bantamweight Title)

TAE-JIN MOON
Korean Lightweight
1979
Dec. 29—So-Heang Lee, Buyo City ....W 10
1980
Mar. 1—Woon-Chul Shin, Raesan ....KO 5
(Retained Korean Lightweight Title)

CHRIS MOORCROFT
British Featherweight
1979
June 18—Jimmy Hancock, Manchester ....KO 1
Sept. 20—Steve Enwright, Liverpool ....L 6
Sept. 25—Stuart Crabb, Southend ....W 6
Nov. 1—John Cooper, Southend ....KO by 2
Nov. 28—Kelvin Smart, Solihull ....L 6
Dec. 5—Steve Enwright, Liverpool ....L 6
Dec. 10—Carl Gaynor, Manchester ....KO 2
1980
Jan. 16—Ian Murray, Liverpool ....L 6

TONY MOORE
British Heavyweight
1974
June 10—John Depledge, Walworth................W 6
July 8—John DePledge, Mayfair ....KO 4
Sept. 9—Eddie Fenton, Bedford..................W 6
Sept. 16—Derek Simpkin, Birmingham...........KO 5
Sept. 23—David Fry, London ....W 6
Oct. 21—Les McGowan, Mayfair ....KO by 3
Nov. 18—Tony Blackburn, Walworth ....W 8
Dec. 5—Les McGowan, London................KO 6
1975
Jan. 13—Toni Mikulski, Mayfair ....KO 2
Feb. 17—Eddy Fenton, Mayfair ....W 6
Mar. 24—Tony Blackburn, London ....W 8
Apr. 29—Neville Meade, Kensington ....KO 5
June 5—Neville Meade, Hammersmith ....D 8
Sept. 24—Neville Meade, Solihull....................L 8
Nov. 11—Garfield McEwan, Manchester ....KO 1
1976
Jan. 19—Sid Paddock, Mayfair ....KO 4
Feb. 16—Denton Ruddock, London ....L 10
Apr. 10—Miguel Angel Paez, Rimini ....D 8
Apr. 27—John L. Gardner, Kensington........KO by 8
May 25—Ngozika Ekwelum, Munich ....L 8

July 21—Alfredo Evangelista, Bilbao ....KO by 4
Nov. 30—Dan McAlinden, London ....KO 5
1977
Jan. 13—Ishaq Hussien, Reading ....L 8
Mar. 1—Denton Ruddock, Marylebone ....L 8
Apr. 7—Garfield McEwan, Dudley ....W 8
May 9—Young Sekona, Auckland ....W 10
May 26—Mani Vaka, Wellington ....W 10
Sept. 19—Kris Smith, Walworth ....W 8
Oct. 19—Terry Mintus, Kingston ....L 8
Nov. 1—Jean Pierre Coopman, Izegem ....D 10
Dec. 5—Lucien Rodriguez, Paris ....L 8
Dec. 26—Alfio Righetti, Rimini ....L 10
1978
Feb. 17—Avenamar Peralta, Madrid ....D 8
Apr. 14—Bernd August, Essen ....D 8
Apr. 17—Les Stevens, Reading ....L 8
May 6—George Butzbach, Frankfort ....D 8
June 27—Dante Cane, Derry ....D 10
Aug. 1—Trevor Berbick, Halifax ....KO by 6
Sept. 9—Gilberto Acuna, Las Corogne ....KO by 6
Nov. 11—Rudy Gauwe, Zele ....KO 2
1979
Apr. 7—Albert Syben, Bruxelles ....L 8
Apr. 22—Georg Butzbach, Hamburg ....D 10
June 16—Ngozika Ekwelum, Lagos ....KO by 6
Aug. 25—Avenamar Peralta, La Coruna ....W 8
Oct. 26—Alfredo Evangelista, La Coruna ....L 8
Dec. 1—Felipe Rodriguez, La Coruna ....L 8
Dec. 9—Alfredo Evangelista, Lugo ....L 8
1980
Mar. 6—Tommy Kiely, Wimbledon ....L 10
(For Southern Area Heavyweight Title and
Eliminator for British Heavyweight Title)
Oct. 19—Billy Aird, Birmingham ....L 10

JACOB MORAKE
South African Junior Lightweight
1974
Nov. 15—Johannes Seabelo, Orlando West ....W 4
1975
Mar. 21—Louis Mbogazi, Kwa-Thema ....L 4
July 11—Simon Thamae, Orlando West ....W 4
Aug. 30—Rafty Mngadi, Jabulani ....D 4
Nov. 28—Lucas Tlala, Kwa-Thema ....W 4
1976
Feb. 6—Herbert Gumede, Kwa-Thema ....D 6
Apr. 2—Paulus Mnisi, Orlando West ....L 6
Apr. 17—Boy April, East London ....KO 6
Apr. 30—Petrus Molefe, Springs ....W 6
June 5—Evans Gwiji, Jabulani ....KO by 1
Oct. 30—Bramley Whiteboy, East London ....W 6
1977
Mar. 5—Guy Ratazayo, East London ....L 8
Dec. 3—Johan Weyer, Johannesburg ....W 4
1978
Aug. 5—Guy Ratazayo, East London ....L 6
1979
Mar. 30—Charles Marule, Springs ....W 6
May 25—Elias Tshabalala, Springs ....KO 3
June 29—Joshua Nhlapo, Natalspruit ....W 6
Nov. 10—Joseph Tsotetsi, Jabulani ....W 8
1980
Feb. 29—Joseph Tsotetsi, Springs ....L 10
(Transvaal Junior Lightweight Title)

CARLOS MORALES
Spanish Welterweight
1977
Dec. 17—Fernando Bermejo, Logrono ....W 6
1978
May 27—Fernando Bermejo, S. Sebastiano ....W 6
Sept. 22—Fernando Bermejo, Zaragoza ....W 6
Oct. 7—Enrique Pino Tobia, Lugo ....D 6
Nov. 9—Antonio Casado, Barcelona ....D 8
1979
Mar. 10—Ahmed Ben Aissa, Logrono ....W 6
Apr. 7—Aureliano Guemez, Logrono ....D 8
May 18—Jose Luis Pacheco, Barcelona ....D 8
July 22—Bobby Hughes, Logrono ....W 8
Sept. 8—Jose Luis Pacheco, Lepe ....W 12
(Spanish Welterweight Title)
Oct. 6—Enrique Pino Tobia, Villava ....KO 3
Dec. 21—Jose Ramirez, Leon ....W 8
1980
Feb. 15—Jose Ramon Gomez, Oviedo ....KO by 8
(For Spanish Welterweight Title)

PEDRO MORALES
Spanish Lightweight
1979
Mar. 10—Serafin Dos Anjos, Logroño ....W 6
Apr. 7—Francisco Jeronimo, Logrono ....KO 2

367

June 9—Serafin Dos Anjos, Logrono .... W 6
July 21—Julio Garcia, Logrono .... W 4
July 27—Salid Mimun Amar, Santander .... KO 3
Oct. 14—Jose Martin Garzon, Villava ...... KO by 3
Dec. 1—Mohamed El Caudoumi, Pamplona ...... W 6
1980
Jan. 12—Mohamed El Caudoumi, Zaragoza .... W 6
Feb. 14—Garcia Marin, Bilbao .... KO by 5

VINCENZO MORANA
Italian Junior Lightweight
1976
Sept. 17—Salvatore Morello, Sondrio .... W 4
Oct. 8—Vincenzo Di Ruocco, Mazara .... KO by 1
1977
Apr. 10—Vincenzo Di Ruocco, Mazara .... W 6
May 14—Luigi De Rosa, Capua .... L 6
Oct. 28—Leo Scorza, Milano .... KO by 3
Nov. 11—Marco Gallo, Pistoia .... KO by 6
Dec. 26—Michele De Mita, Rimini .... KO by 5
1978
Feb. 3—Abass Macauley, Milano .... KO by 3
Feb. 16—Andrea Ricci, Calolziocorte .... L 4
Apr. 21—Lorenzo Paciullo, Genova .... L 6
May 12—Giancarlo Ravaioli, Torvaianica .... L 6
July 7—Arturo De Prezzo, Bassano .... KO by 4
Aug. 7—Giuseppe LaCorte, Martinico .... LF 6
Aug. 18—Leo Scorza, Massa .... L 6
Nov. 10—Silvio Ortiz, Milano .... KO by 5
Dec. 22—Pietro Donati, Ozieri .... L 6
1979
Feb. 10—Giancarlo Ravaioli, Marsala .... L 6
Apr. 6—Andrea Ricci, Bitono .... L 6
May 25—Abass Macauley, Piacenza .... KO by 5
July 1—Arturo De Prezzo, Merano .... KO by 4
July 29—Alfredo Raininger, Marzano .... KO by 4
Nov. 17—Giuseppe La Corte, Salemi .... NC 4
Dec. 26—Giorgio Pipia, Cremona .... L 6
1980
Jan. 16—Giorgio Pippia, Cremona .... L 6
Mar. 28—Fabio Mannai, Cagliari .... KO by 3

JEAN PIERRE MOREAU
French Welterweight
1974
Oct. 26—Christian Lancery, Blois .... KO 3
Dec. 13—Gerard Leterme, Chateaubriand .... L 6
1975
Jan. 16—Claude Wrobel, Paris .... W 6
Jan. 23—Jean Bodchon, Paris .... W 6
Jan. 30—Alain Salmon, Paris .... W 6
Mar. 1—Gerard Leterme, Blois .... W 6
Mar. 8—Serge Dupuis, Dijon .... W 6
Apr. 19—Jack Peraire, Metz .... L 6
Oct. 18—Rene Van Herreweghe, Blois .... W 6
Oct. 4—Alain Marion, Meaux .... L 6
Nov. 4—Richard Rodriguez, Paris .... L 6
Nov. 13—Louis Acaries, Paris .... L 6
1976
Feb. 5—Mohamed Mechlia, Blois .... WF 5
Feb. 7—Claude Lormeau, Luce .... KO by 7
Apr. 1—Roger Lobjois, Paris .... W 6
Apr. 10—Didier Kowalski, Blois .... WF 4
Apr. 29—Fred Coranson, Paris .... L 6
Oct. 2—Jean Dercle, Dunkirk .... KO 6
Oct. 16—Gerard Leterme, Blois .... W 8
Dec. 10—Bechir Boundka, Blois .... W 6
1977
Jan. 8—Jean Pierre Younsy, Conde .... KO by 5
Feb. 12—Alain Salmon, Argenteuil .... L 8
Mar. 11—Yvon Segor, Marsiglia .... L 6
Apr. 2—Bechir Boundka, Nemours .... KO by 3
Apr. 22—Andre Camonin, Blois .... W 6
Oct. 8—Alain Salmon, Argenteuil .... L 10
Nov. 12—Pierre Koenig, Blois .... D 6
Nov. 26—Biase Casoria, Dhuizon .... W 6
Dec. 5—Alain Ruocco, Paris .... L 8
1978
Jan. 28—Richard Rodriguez, S. Ouen .... KO by 5
Apr. 15—Gerard Leterme, S. Malo .... D 8
May 12—Pierangelo Pira, Rimini .... KO by 3
Oct. 27—Jannick Blandin, Rennes .... L 8
Dec. 15—Gilles Elbilia, Paris .... L 6
1979
Mar. 24—Michel Guiot, Aix Provence .... D 6
May 12—Pierre Koenig, Dhuizon .... W 8
June 10—Robert Gambini, Monte Carlo .... KO by 2
Oct. 19—Thierry Samo, Calais .... KO by 2
Dec. 1—Jean Paul Coppyn, Dhuizon .... KO 1
Dec. 26—Dirk Declercq, Izegem .... KO by 6
1980
Mar. 15—Jean Michel Iger, Blois .... D 8
Apr. 19—Franco Aresti, Calgari .... L 8
May 23—Frank Decaestecker, Middelkerke .... KO by 5

MICK MORRIS
British Middleweight
1978
Feb. 21—Martin McEwan, London .... KO 2
Apr. 18—Dave Hunt, London .... KO 2
Apr. 27—Richard Kenyon, Doncaster .... KO by 5
June 19—Richard Kenyon, Manchester .... D 6
Sept. 18—Martin McEwan, Wolverhampton .... KO 2
Oct. 2—Clifton Wallace, Nantwich .... D 4
Oct. 10—Romal Ambrose, Wolverhampton .... KO 3
Oct. 30—Dave Merrell, Nottingham .... KO 4
Nov. 15—Salco Nucifero, Solihull .... KO by 7
1979
Feb. 20—Steve Lewin, Kensington .... L 6
Feb. 26—Mike Copp, Edgbaston .... W 6
Mar. 5—Peter Gorny, London .... L 6
Apr. 9—Keith Bussey, London .... L 8
Apr. 19—Leslie McAteer, Birkenhead .... L 8
May 1—Jimmy Harrington, Wembley .... D 6
Nov. 3—Eddie Burke, Glasgow .... KO by 2
1980
Feb. 21—Billy Hill, Liverpool .... L 8
Mar. 18—Clifton Wallace, Wolverhampton .... W 6
July 12—Jimmy Harrington, Wembley .... W 4
Oct. 16—Peter Bassey, Bolton .... W 8

PETER MORRIS
British Middleweight
1975
Sept. 24—Bobby Unwin, Solihull .... KO 1
Oct. 10—Jimmy Corrigan, Birmingham .... W 6
Oct. 29—Joe Hannaford, Wolverhampton .... KO 2
Dec. 5—Al Stewart, Birmingham .... KO 3
1976
Jan. 13—Jim Moore, Wolverhampton .... KO 4
Feb. 13—Wayne Bennett, Birmingham .... D 8
Mar. 17—Micky Flynn, Solihull .... W 8
Apr. 9—Kenny Weber, Digbeth .... KO 5
May 6—Billy Waith, Birmingham .... L 8
Sept. 22—Steve Angell, Solihull .... W 8
Oct. 22—Larry Paul, Digbeth .... KO by 2
Dec. 13—James Vrig, Amsterdam .... L 8
1977
Mar. 8—Kirkland Laing, Wolverhampton .... D 10
Mar. 24—Billy Waith, Leicester .... KO by 7
Sept. 14—Andre Huussen, Schevenihgen .... D 8
Oct. 11—Joe Oke, Coventry .... W 8
Nov. 16—Kirkland Laing, London .... KO by 5
1978
Feb. 17—Fred Coranson, Dunkirk .... KO by 7
1979
Mar. 21—Joe Jackson, Stoke .... KO by 5
June 26—Joe Jackson, Leicester .... L 8
1980
Sept. 22—Mohammed Ben, Lewisham .... W 6
Oct. 14—Mark Kaylor, London .... KO by 5

PHILLIP MORRIS
British Junior Welterweight
1977
Mar. 29—Frank McCord, Ebbw Vale .... L 4
Apr. 18—Devlin White, Mayfair .... L 4
May 11—Dai Davies, Swansea .... D 4
June 16—Ceri Collins, Ebbw Vale .... L 4
July 4—Steve Holdsworth, Wales .... L 4
Oct. 3—Nigel Thomas, Aberavon .... L 4
Oct. 17—Dave McCabe, Glasgow .... L 4
1978
Feb. 7—James Cooke, Coventry .... KO by 5
June 29—Roddy Evans, Caerphilly .... L 6
1979
Apr. 23—Wally Stocks, London .... L 6
June 13—Tommy Burling, Caerphilly .... W 6
Oct. 4—Tyrrel Wilson, Ebbw Vale .... L 6
Oct. 30—Ray Price, Caerphilly .... D 6
Nov. 29—Neil Brown, Ebbw Vale .... D 6
1980
Apr. 28—Bobby Wellburn, London .... L 6
May 15—Tony Davis, London .... L 6
May 27—Steve Simms, Newport .... L 6
July 1—Mike Clemow, Swindon .... W 6

DES MORRISON
British Junior Welterweight
Born: Feb. 1, 1950
1970
Jan. 27—Pat Walsh, London .... KO 3
Feb. 24—Lex Wilson, London .... W 6
Mar. 9—Tony Burnett, London .... W 6
Mar. 17—Pat Walsh, London .... KO 4
May 4—Ray Fallone, Bedford .... W 6
May 19—Danny Turpin, London. .... W 6
Oct. 7—Leroy Mack, Maidstone .... W 6

Nov. 23—Tony Burnett, London .... W 6
Dec. 17—Harry Adams, London.................. D 6
1971
Feb. 10—Lex Wilson, London .... KO 2
Mar. 1—Dusty Smith, Bedford .... L 6
Apr. 16—Alan Reid, London .... KO 6
Oct. 28—Pat Marshall, Bristol .... W 6
Nov. 22—Ron Woods, London .... KO 6
1972
Feb. 1—Robin Polak, Nottingham .... KO 5
Feb. 7—Alan Reid, London .... W 8
Mar. 14—Phil Dykes, Shoreditch .... KO 2
Apr. 24—Mickey Flynn, Nottingham.............. W 8
Sept. 11—Ricky Porter, London .... L 12
Oct. 23—Frank Young, London .... KO 8
Dec. 11—Des Rea, Nottingham................... W 8
1973
Jan. 29—Tommy Joyce, Mayfair.................. W 8
Mar. 12—Des Rea, London .... W 8
July 2—Ricky Porter, Earls Court............... W 12
Oct. 29—Kevin White, Nottingham .... D 8
Nov. 27—Joe Tetteh, Shoreditch................. W 15
(Vacant British Junior Welterweight Title)
1974
Feb. 7—Jorgen Hansen, Copenhagen .... L 8
Mar. 26—Pat McCormack, London .... KO by 11
Sept. 2—Steve Angell, Walworth .... KO 8
1975
Mar. 24—Tony Poole, London .... L 12
Apr. 21—Billy Waith, Mayfair .... W 8
Nov. 11—Joey Singleton, Manchester............. L 15
(British Junior Welterweight Title)
1976
Feb. 13—Derek Simpson, Cambridge .... W 8
Feb. 18—Tom Imrie, London..................... KO 5
Mar. 20—Kenny Webber, London.................. KO 8
Sept. 22—Colin Powers, London .... KO 5
1977
Sept. 14—Barton McAllister, Cambridge .... KO 1
Oct. 19—Colin Powers, Bethnal .... KO by 10
(For British Junior Welterweight Title)
1978
Apr. 10—Tony Martey, Sheffield .... KO 6
Sept. 13—Chris Glover, Cambridge .... KO 4
Nov. 16—Joey Singleton, Liverpool .... KO 7
1979
Apr. 30—Clinton McKenzie, London .... L 12
Oct. 15—Lewis Acaries, Pravia .... KO 1
Nov. 6—Kirkland Laing, Kensington .... L 8
Dec. 11—Billy Waith, Bletchley .... W 8
1980
Mar. 31—Otis Hooper, Landover .... KO 3
Apr. 22—Sylvester Mittee, London .... W 12

NORMAN MORTON
British Lightweight
1978
Apr. 24—Derek Young, Middlesbrough .... D 4
May 8—George Peacock, Glasgow .... L 6
July 12—Derek Young Nelson, Newcastle .... W 6
Oct. 9—Sid Smith, Marylebone .... KO by 4
1979
Feb. 26—Steve Crocker, Middlesbrough .... W 6
Mar. 16—Wayne Floyd, Thetford .... L 8
Apr. 27—Derek Nelson, Newcastle .... L 8
June 18—Nigel Thomas, Bradford .... D 8
July 2—Johnny Burns, London.................. KO 2
Sept. 17—Jeff Pritchard, Glasgow .... W 8
Oct. 8—Terry Welch, Bradford .... L 8
Oct. 22—Vernon van Riel, Mayfair .... D 8
Nov. 19—Kerry Collins, London .... D 8
1980
Jan. 28—John Mount, Glasgow .... W 8
Feb. 12—Walter Clayton, Sheffield .... L 8
Feb. 25—Duncan Hamilton, Glasgow .... L 8
Mar. 11—Jeff Pritchard, London .... W 8
Apr. 21—Alan Oag, Glasgow .... KO 3
May 28—Selvin Bell, Cramlington .... W 6
June 23—Peter Harrison, Glasgow .... L 8
Oct. 13—Eric Wood, Newcastle .... W 8
Nov. 3—Chris Sanigar, London .... L 8

NKOSANA MOSS
South African Junior Featherweight
1977
May 31—Samson Majeke, Queenstown .... W 4
Nov. 19—Victor Mkohlakali, East London .... W 4
1978
Mar. 4—Daluxolo Tyekana, King Williamstown ...D 6
July 8—Sonwabo Soci, East London .... W 4
1979
Feb. 24—Zola Lawuse, King Williamstown .... L 6
Apr. 28—Welile Nkosenkulu, East London ... KO by 3
July 7—Nksona Tolbert, East London .... KO 4

July 28—Joe Ngidi, King Williamstown .... W 6
Aug. 18—Tito Dastile, King Williamstown .... KO 7
Nov. 10—Welile Nkosenkulu, King Williamstown ... L 6
Dec. 1—Monwabisi Kana, King Williamstown ..... L 6
1980
Mar. 15—Zola Lawuse, East London .... W 10
(Won Cape Junior Featherweight Title)
Apr. 5—Joe Gumede, East London .... W 6
July 5—Victor Mkhoklakli, East London .... L 8
Sept. 5—Sipho Mange, Springs .... W 12
(South African Junior Featherweight Title)
Nov. 8—Bashew Sibaca, East London .... KO by 10

SAMUEL MOTAKE
South African Welterweight
1971
Dec. 4—Johannes Modise, Bloemfontein .... W 6
1972-1973
(Inactive)
1974
Mar. 2—S. Nxawe, Welkom .... L 6
Apr. 6—B. Molokeng, Welkom .... L 6
Sept. 14—Martin Nooi, Welkom .... W 6
1975
(Inactive)
1976
May 15—Godfrey Mthimkulu, Kroonstad .... D 6
Nov. 6—Ben Mutle, Parys .... KO by 9
1977
May 21—Samuel Tshabalala, Kroonstad .... W 6
June 11—Samuel Tshabalala, Kroonstad .... L 4
June 18—Ben Mutle, Parys .... L 6
Oct. 6—Zacharia Makolomakoe, Bloemfontein ...W 8
Nov. 5—David Kambule, Parys .... KO by 3
1978
Mar. 31—Joseph Lala, Bloemfontein .... L 6
1979
Mar. 3—Petrus Motaung, Virginia .... L 6
Aug. 18—Samuel Tshabalala, Welkom .... KO 8
1980
Aug. 23—Simon Nxane, Kimberely .... L 6
Sept. 13—Jonas Majolo, Welkom .... W 6

DAVID MOTAUNG
South African Featherweight
1976
Nov. 20—Abraham Mphatsoe, Bethlehem ...... KO by 3
1977
May 21—Alexis Khaeeane, Bethlehem .... KO 3
July 9—Jacob Moyeye, Kroonstad .... W 6
Nov. 5—Samuel Nhlapo, Parys .... W 6
Dec. 3—Jeremiah Malikhetla, Ficksburg .... L 4
1978
Oct. 7—Michael Khuto, Virginia .... W 4
1979
Feb. 24—Jeremiah Malikhetla, Bethlehem .... W 6
May 5—January Bongo, Ficksburg .... KO 3
1980
May 31—Elias Mphatsoe, Bethlehem .... L 6

DAVID MOTLENGWA
South African Middleweight
1976
Dec. 4—Jacob Xaba, Welkom .... KO 1
1977
July 9—Petrus Motaung, Kroonstad .... KO 1
Aug. 29—Ernest Thibeli, Odendaalrust .... KO 1
1978
Mar. 4—Daniel Sereme, Durban .... L 8
May 1—Eben Marais, Welkom .... KO 4
May 27—Loyiso Mtya, East London .... KO 7
Aug. 12—Victor Ntloko, Johannesburg .... KO 1
Aug. 28—Themba Buthelezi, Durban.............. L 4
1979
July 9—Michael Motsoane, Welkom .... L 4
Dec. 3—Jan Beneke, Welkom .... KO 5
Dec. 14—Zenzile Makanda, Welkom .... KO 1
1980
Feb. 4—Michael Motsoane, Welkom .... KO by 7
(For Orange Free State Middleweight Title)

BASSIE SAMSON MOTSEI
South African Flyweight
1978
Nov. 17—Freddie Masemola, Springs .... L 4
1979
(Inactive)
1980
Mar. 28—James Sibeko, Springs .... L 4
Apr. 25—Edison Ramagole, Sebokeng .... L 4

JACOB MOTSEKI
South African Lightweight
1971
Apr.   24—Meschack Mncube, Natalspruit ...... KO by 5
1972
Sept.   1—Joseph Baloyi, Natalspruit .... KO by 8
1973
Oct.   6—Paulus Twala, Kroonstad L
1974
Mar.   2—B. Lekalake, Welkom .... KO by 6
Apr.   6—Paulus Twala, Welkom L
1975
(Inactive)
1976
Sept. 11—Paulus Twala, Kroonstad .... KO by 6
(For Vacant South African Junior Lightweight Title)
1977-1978
(Inactive)
1979
May   12—Joseph Molahloe, Virginia .... W 4
July   14—Samuel Koalepe, Virginia .... KO 2
Aug.   4—Lazarus Mofokeng, Odendaalsrust .... W 8
Aug.   29—Victor Harris, Bloemfontein .... KO 4
Dec.   1—Simon Molahloe, Odendaalsrust .... D 10
1980
Mar.   1—Simon Molahloe, Odenaalsrust .... KO 9
(Won Orange Free State Lightweight Title)
May   10—Elias Diraditsile, Virginia .... KO by 3
(For Orange Free State Lightweight Title)
June   14—Michael Mohlabane, Welkom .... L 8

ENOCK MOTSOANE
South African Junior Welterweight
1978
July   22—Victor Harris, Bloemfontein .... W 4
1979
Mar.   31—Joseph Tsotetsi, Welkom .... L 8
June   11—Samuel Phule, Welkom .... L 10
Nov.   9—Cedric Carson, Bloemfontein .... W 6
Dec.   14—Martin Jacobs, Welkom .... L 8
1980
Mar.   1—William Mantso, Odenaalsrust .... D 4

MICHAEL MOTSOANE
South African Middleweight
1979
Feb.   5—Zenzile Makanda, Welkom .... W 4
Mar.   2—Brian Smit, Bloemfontein .... KO 1
Apr.   2—April Speelman, Welkom .... KO 1
July   9—David Motlengwa, Welkom .... W 4
Sept.   3—Keith Bradford, Welkom .... W 4
1980
Feb.   4—David Motlengwa, Welkom .... KO 7
(Won Orange Free State Middleweight Title)
May   3—Lucky Masondo, Witsieshoek .... KO 4
July   2—Sydney Shezi, Welkom .... W 6
Nov.   29—Louis Sibiya, Odendaalsrust .... W 8
Dec.   19—John Khooe, Welkom .... KO 2

JOHANNES MOTSUMI
South African Junior Welterweight
1978
Sept.   2—Jonas Tlali, Ficksburg .... L 4
Oct.   7—Johannes Ramasimong, Virginia .... W 4
Nov.   28—William Mantso, Virginia .... W 6
1979
Feb.   10—Michael Mohlabane, Virginia .... L 6
Feb.   24—Japie Patala, Bethlehem .... KO 1
Mar.   24—Japie Patala, Virginia .... W 6
June   16—Ediel Hlephuli, Virginia .... W 6
1980
Feb.   2—David Paul, Virginia .... KO by 2
May   10—Paulus Monewoang, Virginia .... L 4
May   31—Johannes Ramasimong, Bethlehem .... L 6
Aug.   9—Joseph Teteli, Wesselsbron .... L 6
Sept.   6—Prince Choko, Welkom .... W 4

SAMUEL MOTSUMI
South African Featherweight
1980
Feb.   2—Simon Mafere, Virginia .... L 4
June   7—Simon Mafere, Welkom .... KO by 2
Aug.   9—Israel Papane, Wesselsbron .... L 6

JOEL MOULIN
French Welterweight
1975
Feb.   6—Tony Maulus, Paris .... W 6
Feb.   13—Rene Martin, Paris .... W 6
Mar.   1—Christian Lancery, Blois .... W 6
Oct.   18—Alain LeFol, Blois .... W 6
Oct.   31—Antoine Lasala, Villeurbanne .... L 6
Dec.   20—Alain LeFol, Orlean .... L 6

1976
(Inactive)
1977
Nov.   12—Serge Legros, Blois .... W 6
1978
Jan.   7—Gilbert Bayens, Zele .... D 6
Jan.   21—Pierre Koenig, Argenteuil .... W 6
Feb.   3—Serge Legros, Berlamont .... W 6
Feb.   18—Jean Michel Vantouroux, Blois .... W 6
Apr.   18—Hans Henrik Palm, Randers .... KO by 1
Oct.   20—Arthur Fogeiro, Agen .... L 8
Nov.   11—Gilbert Helluin, Berck .... W 8
1979
Jan.   27—Dave Williams, Zele .... KO by 1
Feb.   3—Arthur Mogueiro, Limoges .... W 8
1980
Mar.   8—Angelo Licata, Epinay Sous Senart ...... D 8
Mar.   15—Pierre Koenig, Elois .... W 6
Mar.   22—Daniele Zappaterra, Bologna .... L 6
Apr.   26—Albert Amatler, Villeurbanne ...... KO by 4

JOHNNY MOUNT
British Junior Welterweight
1975
Dec.   4—Yotham Kunda, Hamilton .... KO by 5
1976
Mar.   4—Joe Ward, Glasgow .... W 6
Mar.   11—Karl McCarthy, Hamilton .... W 6
Mar.   22—Karl McCarthey, Glasgow .... W 6
May   17—Jim Moore, Glasgow .... L 8
1977
Mar.   7—Gerry Young, Glasgow .... W 6
Apr.   5—Augustus Simms, Marylebone .... W 8
May   2—Terry Schofield, Holytown .... D 8
Oct.   10—Mickey Morse, London .... L 8
Oct.   18—Jim Montague, London .... L 8
1978
Apr.   21—Jim Montague, Enniskillen .... KO by 4
1979
Dec.   5—Terry Welch, Liverpool .... L 8
1980
Jan.   7—Adey Allen, Manchester .... L 8
Jan.   22—Frank McCord, London .... L 8
Jan.   28—Norman Morton, Glasgow .... L 8
Feb.   18—Dave Taylor, Birmingham .... KO by 4

FRANCISCO MOYA
Spanish Featherweight
1977
Oct.   8—Joaquin Garcia Del Moral, Utrera .... D 6
Nov.   19—Francisco Herrera, Utrera .... W 6
Dec.   3—Carlos Rodriguez, Lugo .... L 8
Dec.   22—Carlos Rodriguez, Cangas .... D 6
1978
Mar.   4—Nicolas Culebras, Sarria .... D 6
Mar.   31—Francisco Herrera, Lugo .... KO 6
Apr.   21—Juan Barros, Valencia .... W 6
June   29—Juan Barros, Torrente .... W 6
July   13—Luis De La Sagra, Madrid .... L 6
Aug.   3—Luis De La Sagra, Madrid .... L 6
Aug.   24—Emilio Barcala, Madrid .... L 6
Oct.   26—Jofre II, Madrid .... L 6
1980
Feb.   1—Jose Luis Vicho, Madrid .... L 6
Mar.   7—Jose Luis Vicho, Palma de Mallorca ..... L 8
May   2—Chato Melillense, Madrid .... D 8
May   23—Joaquin Garcia, Palma de Mallorca ...... D 6

JACOB MOYEYE
South African Featherweight
1976
Dec.   4—Moses Dabula, Welkom .... KO 3
1977
June   11—Alexis Khaeene, Kroonstad .... W 4
July   9—David Motaung, Kroonstad .... W 6
Nov.   5—Piet Shabangu, Viljoenskroon .... KO 3
1978
Mar.   9—Charles Mahole, Springs .... W 6
Mar.   31—Michael Moamogoa, Bloemfontein .... W 6
May   1—Pieter Swanepoel, Welkom .... L 4
Aug.   21—Wally van der Haar, Welkom .... L 4
Aug.   28—Norman Bromfield, Durban .... L 4
Dec.   4—Jacob Diraditsile, Bloemfontein .... L 10
1979
May   4—Thomas Sithebe, Springs .... L 6
July   9—Jacob Diraditsile, Welkom .... KO 9
Sept.   3—John Putter, Welkom .... L 10
1980
May   3—Johan Putter, Witsieshoek .... W 10
(Won Orange Free State Featherweight Title)
Sept. 13—Israel Khonkhobe, Welkom .... L 8
Oct.   31—Joshua Nhlapo, Springs .... L 6

MXOLISI MPAMA
South African Bantamweight
1976
July	10—Mxolisi Mgidi, East London .... W	4	
Oct.	30—Daluxolo Tyekana, East London L	4	

1977
Mar.	5—Daluxolo Tyekana, East London L	4	
May	31—Lucas Ncetezo, Queenstown L	6	
Dec.	17—Vincent Mgcobe, Butterworth .... W	8	

1978
Apr.	1—Monde Mpulampula, East London .... KO by	2	
Apr.	15—Simon Moema, Butterworth .... D	6	
May	27—Welile Nkosenkulu, East London .... KO by	2	

1979
(Inactive)
1980
May	3—L. Ncetezo, Transkei L	6	

JOHANNES MPESI
South African Middleweight
1977
Mar.	4—Wiets de Beer, Pretoria L	4	
Mar.	19—Timothy Lerefolo, Kroonstad L	4	

1978
Apr.	22—David Mokhele, Vereeniging .... W	6	
May	15—Gerhardus Gouws, Johannesburg .... W	4	
June	10—Mike Ramagole, Sharpeville .... KO	8	
Sept.	30—McDonald Shezi, Sharpeville ...... KO by	7	
Nov.	11—Bushy Bester, Johannesburg .... KO by	3	

1979
Mar.	10—Thema Buthelezi, Newcastle L	6	
Apr.	7—Samson Mohloai, Vereeniging L	6	

1980
Mar.	1—Keith Bradgord, Ermelo .... D	4	

NCEDO MPETSHENI
South African Lightweight
1978
May	6—Bukang Mollele, East London .... W	4	
Dec.	15—Solomon Nojanga, East London .... W	4	

1979
Apr.	28—Boy Boy Mtimkulu, East London .... W	6	
Aug.	18—Ncgambaza Mbaduli, King Williamstown	D	4
Sept.	29—Striker Studdard, East London L	4	

1980
Feb.	9—Phindile Ndilele, East London L	6	
May	17—Reginald Mpondo, East London L	6	

ELIAS MPHATSOE
South African Junior Lightweight
1976
Oct.	9—Michael Mohlabane, Kroonstad .... W	4	
Nov.	20—William Mantsho, Bethlehem .... KO	3	

1977
Apr.	30—Jacob Diraditsile, Kroonstad .... KO by	6	
June	11—Elias Diraditsile, Kroonstad .... KO by	4	
Aug.	27—Jacob Mokonenyane, Odenaalsrust .... W	4	

1978
Jan.	28—Monwabisi Kana, East London L	4	
Nov.	28—John Nhlapo, Virginia .... KO	3	

1979
June	16—Lazarus Mofokeng, Virginia L	6	
Aug.	18—Michael Mohlabane, Welkom .... KO	1	

1980
Mar.	1—Thebe Monyane, Odendaalsrust .... KO	5	
May	31—David Motaung, Bethlehem .... W	6	
June	7—Robert Moepi, Odendaalsrust .... KO by	1	
Nov.	29—Samuel Wolf, Odendaalsrust .... W	6	

FRANS MPHATSOE
South African Bantamweight
1980
Aug.	9—Hendrik Kowlman, Wesselsbron .... W	4	
Dec.	13—Moses Moamogoa, Wesselsbron .... W	6	

DANIEL MPHUTHI
South African Junior Middleweight
1977
Mar.	4—Bushy Bester, Pretoria L	4	
Nov.	26—Zenzile Makanda, Bloemfontein L	4	

1978
May	26—Werner Kalin, Johannesburg L	4	

1979
Apr.	28—Fred Berry, Johannesburg .... W	4	

1980
Mar.	22—Abeam Sello, Soweto .... W	4	
Aug.	1—Leo Simelane, Springs .... KO by	3	

VICTOR MPIYAKHE
South African Featherweight
1971
July	2—Aaron Nkala, Dobsonville .... W	4	

1972
Mar.	25—Richard Ngidi, Jabulani .... W	4	
June	9—Jack Methule, Atteridgev .... D	6	
July	21—Joseph Nhlapo, Coronationville .... W	6	
Sept.	30—Benjamin Molokeng, Jabulani .... W	4	
Oct.	21—Xhanti Singaphi, Port Elizabeth L	6	
Dec.	2—Petrus Molefe, Jabulani .... W	4	

1973
Mar.	3—Serame Molefe, Jabulani .... W	4	
June	30—Victor Siko, Port Elizabeth .... KO	4	
July	13—Jack Methule, Atteridgev. .... KO	5	
July	28—Reginald Mpondo, Port Elizabeth L	8	
Aug.	17—Daniel Makhudu, Springs .... W	4	
Sept.	29—Leslie Pikoli, Port Elizabeth .... W	8	
Oct.	20—Kid Kohli, Port Elizabeth L	6	

1974
Feb.	15—Alfred Buqwana, Rabasutho L	6	
Mar.	30—Cyril Adams, East London .... D	6	
June	29—Isaac Nuku, Jabulani .... KO	4	
Aug.	30—Joseph Tsotetsi, Orlando West .... W	10	

1975
Mar.	7—Thomas Sithebe, Natalspruit .... W	10	
Oct.	31—Gideon Borias, Natalspruit .... W	12	

1976
May	8—Tsietsi Maretloane, East London L	12	

1977
June	4—Joseph Gumede, Johannesburg .... W	8	

1978
Apr.	29—Bashew Sibaca, Cape Town .... W	12	
May	29—Bernard Zungu, Durban L	6	

1979
Mar.	10—Essau Dlamini, Newcastle .... W	8	
Apr.	14—Bashew Sibaca, Goodwood .... KO by	5	

(South African Featherweight Title)
Dec.	8—Nkosana Mgxaji, East London L	8	

1980
Feb.	1—Thomas Sithebe, Springs .... D	6	
Mar.	13—Herbert Plaatjies, Cape Town L	6	

REGINALD MPONDO
South African Lightweight
1973
Feb.	3—Tamie Dulaze, King Williamstown ... KO by	1	
July	28—Victor Mpiyakhe, Port Elizabeth .... W	6	

1974
June	29—Mwalaza Bunu, Queenstown .... KO	3	

1975
Feb.	8—Guy Ratzayo, East London L	4	
June	28—Lennox Mtyongwe, Queenstown .... W	6	

1976
(Inactive)
1977
Sept.	3—Alfred Matiwane, Queenstown L	4	
Nov.	19—Solomon Nojanga, East London ...... KO by	3	

1978
(Inactive)
1979
Sept.	8—Welile Klaas, Zwelitsha .... W	4	
Nov.	10—Boy Boy Mtimkulu, King Williamstown ... D	4	

1980
May	17—Ncedo Mpetsheni, East London .... W	6	
Oct.	18—Wonga Lawuse, King Williamstown ..... KO	1	

MONDE MPULAMPULA
South African Flyweight
1976
Nov.	13—Thembisile Ngxingolo, East London ...... W	4	

1977
Apr.	2—Balisa Molao, East London .... W	4	
May	28—Tembile Sigetye, King Williamstown ..... KO	5	
June	11—Lawrence Krune, East London .... W	6	
Sept.	17—Simon Moema, East London .... W	4	
Oct.	15—Isaac Mazibuko, East London .... KO	1	
Dec.	17—Joe Ngidi, Butterworth .... KO	4	

1978
Jan.	28—David Molefe, East London .... KO	6	
Feb.	18—Fundisile Kralo, East London .... W	6	
Mar.	4—Reuben Matewu, King Williamstown ..... W	8	
Apr.	1—Mxolisi Mpama, East London .... KO	2	
May	27—Dexter Dhlamini, East London .... D	8	
July	29—Reuben Matewu, Queenstown .... W	8	
Aug.	26—Johannes Sithebe, East London .... W	6	
Sept.	30—Charles McGeer, East London .... KO	2	
Nov.	4—Phindile Gaika, Port Elizabeth L	10	

1979
May	10—Reuben Matewu, East London .... W	8	
July	7—Lawrence Krune, East London .... W	6	
Aug.	4—Dexter Dhlamini, East London .... W	6	
Sept.	8—Lawrence Krune, Zwelitsha .... KO	3	
Sept.	29—Peter Mathebula, East London .... KO by	2	
Dec.	1—Thembisile Ngxingolo, King Williamstown W	6	

1980
Feb.	8—Winnerton Kondile, Cape Town .... D	6	
Apr.	5—Winnerton Kondile, East London .... W	6	

May	31—Siphwe Fuma, East London	L 4
Aug.	23—Cosmo Ziqu, East London	KO by 2
Nov.	22—Tembile Sigetye, Queenstown	W 8
Dec.	13—Sixuli Madondile, Queenstown	L 6

DAN M'PUTU
French Lightweight
1977

Jan.	15—Franco Soro, Grande Synthe	KO 2
Apr.	2—Chris Davies, Dunkerque	W 6
Oct.	15—Jean Claude Vanderbreght, St. Pol sur Mer	KO 2

1978

Jan.	7—Giuseppe Minotti, Coudekerque	W 8
Jan.	14—Jim Montague, Dunkerque	W 8
Feb.	17—Tommy Davitt, Dunkirk	L 8
Mar.	17—Kevin Davies, Grand Sythe	W 8
Nov.	11—Des Gwilliam, Dunkirk	W 8

1979

Feb.	10—Ethem Oezakalin, Dunkerque	KO 3
Mar.	10—Giuseppe Agate, Dunkerque	W 8
May	18—Bingo Crooks, Dunkerque	W 8
Oct.	19—Fred Mensah, Dunkerque	WF 4

1980

Feb.	2—Najib Daho, Dunkirk	W 8
June	15—Bingo Crooks, Dunkirk	W 6
Nov.	15—Albert Amatler, Dunkirk	KO 7

JAMES MQHEKU
South African Flyweight
1979

Feb.	9—David Malinga, Bethlehem	L 8
May	12—David Malinga, Virginia	W 4

1980

Feb.	4—David Malinga, Bethlehem	L 8
May	24—Tamasanqa Sogwe, Welkom	L 6
Aug.	2—Jeffrey Nkate, Welkom	KO by 2

JOHANNES MTHEMBU
South African Welterweight
1973

June	16—Maxwell Zondo, Durban	W 4
Nov.	17—Mike Mazibuko, Durban	KO by 1

1974

Oct.	26—Nicholas Gumede, Durban	KO 4

1975-1976
(Inactive)
1977

Nov.	28—Andre Rheeders, Durban	L 4

1978

Aug.	5—Bushy Bester, Bloemfontein	KO by 5
Oct.	10—Amos Gumede, Durban	KO 1

1979

June	9—Abel Brown, Durban	D 4
Sept.	14—Gregory Schmidt, Durban	L 4
Sept.	29—Phillip Hlope, Durban	KO 8

1980

May	19—Abel Brown, Durban	L 10

(Natal Welterweight Title)

Sept.	15—Hardy Mileham, Durban	D 4
Nov.	29—Joseph Zikhall, Durban	KO 2
Dec.	15—Bobby X. Chisale, Pmburg	W 6

MOSES MTHEMBU
South African Lightweight
Born: April, 1, 1937
1967

June	30—Elliott Kweyama, Durban	L 4

1968

Sept.	7—Norman Keshav, Durban	L 4

1969

Feb.	1—Alpheus Sikhosane, Durban	L 4
Mar.	15—David Mhlonge, Durban	D 4

1970

Mar.	15—Alpheus Sikhosane, Durban	KO by 9
June	6—Cynet Thabalala, Durban	D 6
July	4—Alpheus Sikhosane, Durban	W 6
Oct.	31—Mike Duma, Durban	L 6
Nov.	14—Eric Majola, Durban	W 6

1971

Jan.	30—Mike Duma, Durban	W 4
Mar.	6—Abe Ncala, Durban	W 4
Apr.	24—Cynet Thabalala, Durban	W 6
June	19—Wilfred Buhlalu, Durban	W 6
June	—Abram Mbonambi, Durban	W 10
Aug.	9—Solomon Ramafikeng, Durban	W 6
Sept.	18—Zakes Moahloli, Durban	W 6
Oct.	23—Phillip Peterson, Durban	D 6

1972

Jan.	29—Angel (Baby) Jake, Durban	W 6
Feb.	12—Victor Shabalala, Durban	W 8
Mar.	4—Anthony Morodi, Durban	KO by 11
May	27—Blakeney Mathews, Durban	L 8
Aug.	26—Phillip Hlope, Durban	W 10
Sept.	2—Maxwell Malinga, Durban	L 6

Sept.	—Nkosana Mgxaji, East London	L 8

1973

Feb.	3—Anthony Morodi, Durban	D 8
Mar.	31—Norman Sekgapane, Durban	W 10
June	16—Myinja Moloi, Port Elizabeth	L 8
June	30—Wally Van der Haar, Durban	W 6
Oct.	13—Alfred Cele, Durban	W 6
Oct.	27—Philip Hlope, Durban	KO by 3

1974

Feb.	1—Norman Sekgapane, Springs	KO by 8
June	29—Tadios Fisher, Durban	L 8
Oct.	26—Joseph Xulu, Durban	KO 3

1975

Aug.	9—Anthony Morodi, Johannesburg	L 6
Nov.	1—Philip Masiz, Port Elizabeth	W 6

1976

May	8—Nkosana Mgxaji, East London	L 6
Oct.	11—Bernard Zungu, Durban	L 6

1977

Oct.	3—Andreis Steyn, Durban	KO by 2

1978

Aug.	12—Nicholas Gumede, Durban	L 6

1979

Mar.	10—Sipho Malinga, Newcastle	L 4
June	9—Shadrack Zulu, Durban	W 10
Aug.	18—Nicolas Gumede, Durban	W 10

1980

Apr.	28—July Maduna, Durban	KO 6

(Natal Lightweight Title)

Aug.	4—Nicholas Gumede, Durban	L 10

(Natal Junior Lightweight Title)

Nov.	29—Eugene Mthiyane, Durban	W 6

RICHARD MTHOMBENI
South African Junior Featherweight
1978

Nov.	25—Aubrey Mazibuko, Durban	W 4

1979

Aug.	18—Robert Makhoba, Durban	KO by 3
Sept.	29—Joseph Ngubane, Durban	KO by 3
Nov.	25—Aubrey Mazibuko, Durban	W 4

1980

Mar.	1—Aziz Dawood, Durban	D 4
Nov.	1—Amos Ndwalane, Stanger	L 4

BOY BOY MTIMKULU
South African Lightweight
1977

June	11—Boy April, East London	W 4
July	30—Tinini Kwetane, East London	W 4

1978

Jan.	28—William Mantso, East London	W 6
Mar.	4—Chris Bente, King Williamstown	L 4
July	8—Tamie Spampool, East London	D 4
Dec.	15—David Kaptein, East London	W 4

1979

Feb.	24—Joseph Mnyabiso, King Williamstown	L 6
Apr.	28—Ncedo Mphetsheni, East London	L 6
July	14—Bogili Sovili, East London	W 6
Nov.	10—Reginald Mpondo, King Williamstown	D 4

1980

Feb.	9—Stricker Studdard, East London	W 6
May	17—Solomon Nojanga, East London	W 6
June	—Chris Whiteboy, Cape Town	L 6
Dec.	6—Lethohonolo, East London	L 4

BASIE MTSHAMBA
South African Featherweight
1979

Nov.	17—Motsie Tlali, Ficksburg	KO by 3

1980

June	14—Israel Papane, Welkom	D 6
Oct.	4—Elias Tshabalala, Welkom	KO by 3
Dec.	6—Emmanuel Mathibedi, Welkom	D 4

LOYISO MTYA
South African Welterweight
1974

Aug.	31—Mzwandile Mqanto, East London	W 4

1975

Feb.	8—Kenneth Moyi, East London	W 4
June	21—Godfrey Mtimkulu, East London	W 4
Dec.	13—Mzwandile Mqanto, East London	W 6

1976

Jan.	31—Mxolisi Mgidi, East London	W 4
Apr.	10—Sizwe Tshume, Port Elizabeth	KO 2
May	8—Enoch Hlongwane, East London	KO 1
July	17—Jerry Molefe, East London	W 6
Oct.	9—Gordon Goba, East London	W 6
Nov.	6—Terence Makaluza, King Williamstown	D 8

1977

Mar.	19—Terence Makaluza, Port Elizabeth	KO 10
May	7—Joseph Hali, Zwelitsha	W 10

372

Dec. 10—Morgan Moledi, East London .... KO 10
1978
May   27—David Motlengwa, East London ..... KO by 7
Sept. 8—Gert Steyn, Johannesburg .... KO by 5
1979
Feb. 10—Volfart Rala, Queenstown .... W 6
Nov.   3—David Klaas, Port Elizabeth .... W 10
1980
Feb.   9—Cameron Adams, East London .... W 8
Mar.   8—Bruce McIntyre, Johannesburg ...... KO by 2
May   31—Thornton Oakes, East London .... W 8

NYINGI MTYA
South African Featherweight
1980
July   5—Fudukile Mboyane, East London .... W 4
Aug. 23—Mxolisi Gawula, East London .... L 4
Oct. 18—Government Feleti, King Williamstown KO 1

LENNOX MTYONGWE
South African Featherweight
1973
July 14—Boy Putye, East London .... D 6
Aug.   —Winkie Yaka, East London .... L 6
Oct.   6—Boy Putye, East London .... KO by 4
1974
Mar.   9—Thomas Mathibela, East London .... L 6
June   1—Albert Kilimane, East London .... W 4
July 20—George Mabetu, East London .... KO 1
Aug. 31—Mqondisi Ntshinga, East London .... L 6
1975
Mar. 29—Guy Ratazayo, East London .... L 6
June 28—Reginald Mpondo, Queenstown .... L 6
1976
Mar. 27—Thomas Sithebe, East London .... L 6
Apr.   3—Tamganqa Mazaleni, East London ...... W 6
Apr. 17—Charles Makasi, East London .... KO 2
May   8—Steve Mtoba, East London .... W 4
Nov.   6—Xanti Singapi, King Williamstown .... L 8
Nov. 13—Bramley Whiteboy, East London ..... KO by 5
1977
June 11—Cecil Baatjies, East London .... L 6
Sept. 17—Simon Dhladla, East London .... L 6
Nov. 19—Tito Dastile, East London .... W 6
1978
May   6—Wonga Lawuse, East London .... KO by 4
1979
(Inactive)
1980
Mar. 15—Monwabisi Kana, East London .... L 4
July   5—Joe Jongile, Umtata .... L 8
July 19—Lethohonolo Nkatio, East London .... L 6

STEVE MUCHOKI
Kenyan Flyweight
(Based in Denmark)
1979
Dec.   6—Eddie Glencross, Copenhagen .... KO 2
1980
Feb.   7—Emilio Pireddu, Randers .... W 8
Feb. 29—Marciano Garcia, Odense .... W 8
Apr. 17—Manuel Carrasco, Copenhagen .... W 8
June 12—Guy Caudron, Randers .... W 8
Oct. 17—Ray Amoo, Copenhagen .... KO 12
(Retained European Flyweight Title)

WAYNE MULHOLLAND
Australian Junior Featherweight
1978
Mar. 23—Steve Freeman, Campbelltown .... W 6
1979
Mar. 13—Steve Freeman, Kingsford .... L 6
Apr. 10—Paul Hansen, Kingsford .... W 6
1980
Feb.   6—Steve Freeman, Brookvale .... W 5
Feb. 20—Bimbo Morris, Mt. Pritchard .... W 6
Mar. 19—Bimbo Morris, Mt. Pritchard .... W 10
Apr. 11—Patrick Burns, Wollongong .... W 10
(Won New South Wales Junior Featherweight Title)
May   16—Buddy Clare, Wollongong .... W 8
June   7—Buddy Clare, Wollongong .... W 8
July   4—Buddy Clare, Wollongong .... W 8
Oct. 20—Steve Walker, Cornulla .... W 8
Dec. 18—Brian Roberts, Marrickvale .... KO by 3
(For Australian Junior Featherweight Title)

CARL MULLINGS
British Featherweight
1978
Nov. 29—John Henry, Evesham .... D 4
1979
Jan. 22—Gary Ball, Birmingham .... L 6
Mar. 28—John Henry, Evesham .... D 4

Apr. 19—Gary Lucas, Birkenhead .... L 6
Apr. 26—Jimmy Hancock, Liverpool .... L 6
May   13—Jimmy Hancock, Egdbaston .... D 6
May   21—John Henry, Birmingham .... L 6
1980
Apr. 28—Mick Mason, Birmingham .... KO by 3
May   19—Larry Richards, Birmingham .... L 6
Sept. 10—Carl Gaynor, Liverpool .... D 6

TONY MUNDINE
Australian Light Heavyweight
Born: June 10, 1951
1969
Mar.   5—Frank Graham, Cammeray.............. W 4
Apr.   9—Frank Graham, Redfern .... KO 3
Apr. 16—Ted McKenzie, Brookvale .... W 10
May   7—Ted McKenzie, Redfern .... KO 5
May   28—Ray Wheatley, Brookvale .... KO 2
June 23—Ricky Datsun, South Melbourne .... W 8
July 28—Ted McKenzie, Sydney .... KO 3
Sept. 8—Sione Sani, South Melbourne .... W 8
Sept. 23—Lee Moto, Kogarah .... KO 5
Oct. 22—Les Dixon, Redfern .... KO 6
Nov. 10—Kahu Mahanga, Melbourne .... KO by 9
Dec. 12—Feleti Leone, Melbourne .... KO 2
Dec. 17—Billy Opetaia, Bondi Junction .... KO 7
1970
Feb.   9—Billy Choules, Melbourne .... KO 4
Mar. 10—Sione Sani, Bondi Junction .... KO 1
Mar. 19—Jeke Nagelebukia, Redfern .... KO 3
Apr. 23—Billy Choules, Redfern .... KO 4
(Australian Middleweight Title)
May   28—Ravuama Roko, Redfern .... KO 2
June   9—Filipino Rapalo, Sydney .... KO 2
July 16—Billy Marsh, Redfern .... KO 8
Aug. 25—Johnny Kramer, Bondi Junction....... KO 5
Dec. 10—Barry Calderwood, Richmond .... KO 5
1971
Jan. 21—Bunny Sterling, Sydney................ D 15
Feb. 18—Victor Basilio, Sydney .... KO 2
Apr.   7—Luis Rodriguez, Melbourne .... KO by 1
July   1—Alipata Korovou, Redfern .... KO 5
Sept. 5—Jackson McQuade, Milton............ KO 1
Sept. 23—Rod Kenny, Redfern .... KO 4
Oct. 22—Tommy Gray, Brisbane .... KO 7
Nov. 25—Eric Blake, Brisbane .... KO 3
Dec. 10—Charlie Austin, Brisbane .... KO 2
1972
Feb. 17—George Carter, Redfern .... KO 2
Feb. 25—Foster Bibron, Brisbane .... KO 11
(Bibron out-weighed Mundine by 46 pounds)
Apr. 14—Bunny Sterling, Milton............... KO 15
(Won Empire Middleweight Title)
May   31—Denny Moyer, Sydney .... KO 7
Aug. 21—Juarez De Lima, Brisbane .... KO 5
Sept. 26—Antonio Aguilar, Sydney............. KO 3
Nov.   7—Roy Lee, Noumea .... KO 2
Dec.   8—Lonnie Harris, Brisbane .... KO 5
1973
Feb.   7—Matt Donovan, Sydney .... KO 3
May   1—Luis Vinales, Brisbane .... KO 2
May   14—Max Cohen, Paris .... KO 4
Aug.   3—Carlos Marks, Brisbane .... KO 10
Aug. 20—Fred Etuati, Auckland.............. KO 1
(British Commonwealth Middleweight Title)
Sept. 28—Carlos Marks, Brisbane.............. W 15
(British Commonwealth Middleweight Title)
Nov. 19—Emile Griffith, Paris .... W 12
1974
Feb. 11—Manuel Fierro, Brisbane .... KO 6
Feb. 28—Benny Briscoe, Paris .... KO by 5
May   10—Don Cobbs, Brisbane .... KO 6
Aug.   9—Nate Collins, Brisbane............... KO 6
May   27—Lenny Harden, Paris .... KO 3
Oct.   5—Carlos Monzon, Buenos Aires........ KO by 7
(World Middleweight Title)
1975
Feb. 28—Rudy Robles, Brisbane .... L 10
May   2—James Marshall, Brisbane........... KO by 1
Sept. 4—Joe Jackson, Blacktown .... W 10
Oct. 30—Steve Aczel, Blacktown .... KO 12
(Commonwealth Light Heavyweight Title)
Dec.   4—Victor Attivor, Blacktown .... KO 2
(Commonwealth Light Heavyweight Title)
1976
Mar. 19—Karl Zurheide, Sydney............... KO 1
Mar. 26—Baby Boy Rolle, Brisbane........... KO 3
(Commonwealth Light Heavyweight Title)
May   14—Jesse Burnett, Brisbane .... KO by 6
Aug. 11—Mafile Maumoua, Marrickville .... W 10
Sept. 4—Victor Attivor, Accra .... KO 9
(Commonwealth Light Heavyweight Title)

1977

June	2—Maile Haumono, Port Moresby	KO	10

(Retained Australian Heavyweight Title)

July	8—Ernie Barr, Brisbane	W	15

(British & Commonwealth Light Heavyweight Title)

July	28—Lee Royster, Port Moresby	KO by	1
Sept.	9—Lee Royster, Brisbane	W	10
Oct.	21—Danny Brewer, Brisbane	KO	7
Dec.	5—Maile Haumono, Melbourne	KO	3

(Australian Heavyweight Title)

1978

Jan.	24—Ernie Barr, Melbourne	W	10
Feb.	27—Gary Summerhays, Melbourne	KO by	11

(Commonwealth Light Heavyweight Title)

July	15—Fossie Schmidt, Suva	KO	1
Nov.	24—Karl Canwell, Brisbane	KO	3

1979

Feb.	9—Ronnie Wilson, Brisbane	KO	7
Feb.	18—Ananai Curubera, Sydney	KO	2
Mar.	31—Marc Ecimovic, Melbourne	KO	2

(Australian Light Heavyweight Title)

Apr.	20—Tony Greene, Melbourne	KO	4
Aug.	3—Pete McIntyre, Sydney	KO	5
Sept.	26—Mate Parlov, Gorizia	L	12
Nov.	30—Enio Cometti, Trieste	KO	9
Dec.	14—Johnny Wilburn, Milan	W	8

1980

Apr.	4—Pat Cuillo, Milan	KO	5
Apr.	18—David Conteh, Bologna	W	10
May	30—King David Smith, Pirae	W	10
July	28—Steve Aczel, Brisbane	KO	9

(Retained Australian Heavyweight Title)

Sept.	20—Joe Fabiano, Noumea	KO	6
Dec.	15—Monty Betham, Auckland	KO	5

(Australasian Light Heavyweight Title)

EIJIRO MURATA
Japanese Bantamweight
1976

July	—Masaru Fuji, Tokyo	KO	1
Sept.	—Yoshiro Shakauchi, Tokyo	KO	3
Oct.	18—Go Numata, Nagoya	KO	8

1977

Jan.	17—Kiyotaka Mikami, Tokyo	KO	1
Feb.	—Kiyotaka Mikami, Tokyo	KO	1
Apr.	26—Joe Araki, Tokyo	W	10
July	5—Hurricane Teru, Tokyo	W	10
Oct.	22—Bunji Ando, Tsuname	KO	2
Nov.	18—Shiro Hiromori, Tokyo	KO	6

1978

Mar.	28—Hisami Mizuno, Tokyo	KO	8
May	5—Kosei Kawaguchi, Tokyo	W	10
June	30—Inkyu Park, Tokyo	D	10
Dec.	14—Yung Sik-Kim, Tokyo	W	12

(OBPF Bantamweight Title)

1979

Mar.	19—Moon Myung-An Tokyo	KO	2
June	19—Dong Yul Oh, Tokyo	KO	2

(OPBF Bantamweight Title)

Sept.	18—Raffy Saulong, Tokyo	W	12

(OPBF Bantamweight Title)

Dec.	11—Jiro Takada, Tokyo	W	12

(Retained OPBF Bantamweight Title)

1980

June	11—Lupe Pintor, Tokyo	D	15

(For WBC Bantamweight Title)

Oct.	27—Ronald Sumalis, Tokyo	W	12

(Retained OPBF Bantamweight Title)

RAGA MURPHY
Italian Featherweight
1979

Feb.	23—Franco Buglione, Capua	D	8
Apr.	7—Laurent Grimbert, Meaux	L	10
June	22—Heleno Ferreira, Monfaccone	D	8
July	28—Giuseppe Fossati, Mezzanica	L	8
Aug.	19—Heleno Ferreira, Fort Village	D	8
Sept.	5—Heleno Ferreira, Fort Village	D	8
Nov.	3—Heleno Ferreira, San Severo	D	6
Nov.	30—Heleno Ferreira, Forli	D	8

1980

Mar.	1—Gerard Jacab, Criel	L	8
Mar.	29—Salvatore Melluzzo, Resaro	LF	7
Apr.	11—Giovanni Pasca, Sassari	D	8

IAN MURRAY
British Featherweight
1975

June	11—Peter Scott, Bradford	KO	6
Sept.	22—Peter Scott, Manchester	KO	5
Nov.	10—John Chesters, Bradford	W	6
Dec.	2—George Sutton, London	L	6

1976

Jan.	5—George Sutton, London	KO by	3

Jan.	28—John Chesters, Stoke	W	6
Feb.	11—John Chesters, Bradford	W	6
Sept.	21—Gary Davidson, Bethnal Green	KO by	6
Nov.	15—Trevor Bromby, Nottingham	W	6
Nov.	23—John Owen, Teorchu	KO by	6
Dec.	20—David Smith, Walworth	L	6

1977

Feb.	14—Jimmy Bott, Manchester	L	6
Mar.	3—Jimmy Bott, Caister	L	6
Mar.	30—Trevor (Sticker) Bromby, Barnsley	W	8
Apr.	24—Paul Verden, Birmingham	W	6
May	10—Bryn Griffiths, Merthyr	D	8
June	13—Jimmy Bott, Manchester	W	6
Sept.	21—Mohammed Younis, London	KO by	3

1978

Apr.	12—Wally Angliss, Hammersmith	L	8
May	15—Dave Smith, London	L	8
June	27—Neil McLaughlin, Derry	L	8
Sept.	21—Steve Cleak, Caerphilly	L	6
Oct.	9—Gary Nickels, Middlesbrough	L	6
Oct.	23—Jimmy Bott, Manchester	W	8
Dec.	4—Alan Storey, Marton	D	4

1979

Jan.	18—Pip Coleman, Liverpool	KO by	8
June	18—Pip Coleman, Windsor	L	8
Oct.	8—Steve Enwright, Bradford	L	6
Oct.	23—Steve Enwright, Blackpool	W	6
Dec.	10—Steve Enwright, Manchester	L	8

1980

Jan.	16—Chris Moorcroft, Liverpool	W	6
Jan.	22—Kelvin Smart, Caerphilly	L	6
Mar.	14—Billy Straub, Glasgow	L	6
Apr.	14—Billy Straub, Motherwell	L	6
May	12—Don George, Reading	KO by	7
Oct.	13—Eddie Glass, Newcastle	W	6

IAN (KID) MURRAY
British Welterweight
1979

June	6—Phil Lewis, Bedworth	W	6
June	14—Wally Stockings, Dudley	W	6
Sept.	8—Steve Ward, Wolverhampton	L	8
Sept.	26—Barry Price, Stoke	L	8
Oct.	9—Tyrrel Wilson, Wolverhampton	W	6
Oct.	17—Jeff Pritchard, Evesham	L	6
Nov.	14—Nigel Thomas, Stoke	L	8
Nov.	21—Nigel Thomas, Evesham	L	8
Nov.	27—Jimmy Smith, Wolverhampton	W	6
Dec.	17—Dai Davies, Wolverhampton	D	8

1980

Jan.	16—Jeff Aspell, Stoke	W	8
Jan.	21—Dave Taylor, Wolverhampton	W	6
Feb.	20—Johnny Burns, Evesham	W	6
Mar.	10—Dave Taylor, Wolverhampton	L	6
Mar.	18—Paul Wetter, Wolverhampton	W	6
Mar.	26—Dennis Pryce, Evesham	L	8
Apr.	21—Roy Varden, Edgbaston	L	8
May	29—Mickey Baker, Wolverhampton	L	6
June	11—Jeff Lee, Morecambe	L	8
Aug.	12—Jeff Aspell, Gowerton	L	8
Sept.	4—Dave Taylor, Morecambe	W	8
Sept.	22—Jeff Lee, Lewisham	L	8
Oct.	20—Jeff Aspell, Birmingham	KO	5

PAUL MURRAY
British Welterweight
1980

Sept.	4—Gerry White, Morecambe	W	6
Sept.	11—Graeme Ahmed, Hartlepool	L	6
Sept.	29—Richard Wilson, Bedworth	L	6
Oct.	8—Carl North, Stoke	KO	2
Oct.	14—Steve McLeod, Wolverhampton	W	6
Oct.	30—John Wiggins, Wolverhampton	W	6

KACHAMA (ZHORA) MUSASA
Italian Junior Welterweight
1979

Dec.	21—Serge Sinlenikov, Ancona	W	6

1980

Jan.	4—Patrick Babouram, Capri	KO	4
Jan.	19—Maurice Prunier-Flot, Vitry	KO	3
Feb.	6—Antonio Stocchino, Falconara	KO	6
Mar.	8—Hugues Samo, Criel	W	8
Mar.	22—Tidjani Sidibe, Rome	L	8
May	24—Jean Jacques Benchetrit, Nice	L	6

CHISANDA MUTTI
British Light Heavyweight
1979

Dec.	29—George Chisenga, Lusaka	KO	1

(Won Zambian Middleweight Title)

1980

Mar.	4—Tony Sibson, London	L	1

(For Vacant Commonwealth Middleweight Title)

May	21—Eddie Smith, Coventry	W	

Sept. 26—Uwi Meicke, Cologne .... KO 3

LOTTE MWALE
Zambian Light Heavyweight
1977
—Fanwell Mwanza, Lusaka .... KO 6
—Julius Luipa, Lusaka .... KO 6
—Trosan Todorovic, Lusaka .... KO 6
—George Chisanta, Lusaka .... KO 4
—Fanwell Mwanza Kitwe .... KO 2
1978
Apr. 6—Bobby Lloyd, Oslo .... W 10
May 23—Tony Sibson, Leicester .... KO 1
June 17—Marvin Johnson, Belgrade .... W 8
Sept. 30—Lonnie Bennett, Lusaka .... KO 1
Nov. 4—Enio Commetti, Lusaka .... KO 5
Dec. 30—Bob Smith, Lusaka .... KO 4
1979
Feb. 26—Bill Ratliff, London .... KO 2
Mar. 3—Gary Summerhays, Lusaka .... KO 5
(Commonwealth Light Heavyweight Title)
June 4—Lee Royster, Liverpool .... KO 4
Sept. 30—Ba Sounkala, Lusaka .... KO 5
(African Light Heavyweight Title)
Oct. 9—Carlos Marks, London .... KO 2
Dec. 29—Freddie Brown, Lusaka .... KO 7
1980
Mar. 4—Jesse Burnett, London .... W 12
Nov. 28—Matthew Saad Muhammad, San Diego KO by 4
(For WBC Light Heavyweight Title)

REY NADUMA, JR.
Filipino Junior Featherweight
1979
Feb. 3—Domy Marolena, Butuan City .... KO by 3
Mar. 24—Gerron Porras, Surigao Del Sur .... L 10
Apr. 22—Jun Belemac, Davao Del Norte .... KO 7
Aug. 25—Gerron Porras, Davao City .... D 10
Oct. 27—Al Vargas, Davao City .... D 10
Nov. 3—Noe Canino, Cag. de Oro City .... KO by 9
Dec. 29—Gerron Porras, Davao Del Norte .... W 10
1980
Jan. 19—Ronald Sumalis, Davao City .... D 10
Dec. 20—Neptali Alamag, Elorde .... KO by 10

KIYOSHI NAGASHIMA
Japanese Junior Featherweight
1979
Nov. 27—Minoru Namjo, Tokyo .... L 10
1980
Mar. 29—Hideharu Nitsui, Oyama .... KO 7

TAKANAE NAKAJIMA
(Previously Fought Under SASUMA SHINBA)
Japanese Bantamweight
1980
Feb. 22—Katsuyuki Ohashi, Tokyo .... L 8
Apr. 26—Jackal Maruyama, Hachinohe .... D 10
June 6—William Develos, Manila .... L 10

TOMIO NAKAMURA
Japanese Featherweight
1979
Dec. 9—Gen Tosa, Osaka .... L 10
1980
Mar. 30—Spider Nemoto, Osaka .... KO by 9
(For Japanese Featherweight Title)

KAZUMI NAKAO
Japanese Welterweight
1979
Apr. 22—Akio Kameda, Tokyo .... KO by 2
(JBC Welterweight Title)
Oct. 28—Minoru Sugiya, Tokyo .... L 10
1980
Nov. 12—Akio Kameda, Tokyo .... KO by 4
(For Japanese Welterweight Title)

ALESSANDRO NARDI
Italian Junior Lightweight
1975
Mar. 8—Pietro Candidda, Cagliari .... W 4

Mar. 8—Antonio Pocai, Cagliari .... W 4
Mar. 28—Antonio Pocai, Rome .... W 6
May 24—Giovanni Mannu, Sassari .... W 6
June 6—Filippo Loiacono, Rome .... W 6
Oct. 3—Giovanni Cavazzini, Rome .... W 6
1976
May 7—Domenico Radiccioni, Rome .... W 8
June 11—Carlo Frascinetti, Rome .... D 8
Dec. 18—Gabriel Lamperti, Bastia .... D 8
1977
Feb. 11—Renzo Battistelli, Colleferri .... W 8
May 14—Alain Le Fol, Bastia .... L 8
Nov. 12—Fulvio Giocomin, Ostia .... W 8
1978
June 17—Salvatore Dui, Ladispoli .... W 6
1979
Mar. 9—Marco Gallo, Rome .... L 8
Nov. 24—Franco Siddu, Firenze .... L 8
1980
Mar. 7—Melquiades Da Silva, Rome .... W 8
May 9—Antonio Franca, Rome .... W 8

VALENTINO NARDINI
Italian Heavyweight
1978
May 5—Giancarlo Mezzadra, Udine .... W 6
May 27—Antonio Crescenza, Pordenone .... W 6
July 2—Pellegrino, Pordenone .... W 6
Dec. 9—Joze Centa, Udine .... W 6
1979
Nov. 18—Augusto Del Monte, Brescia .... W 6
1980
Feb. 8—Giulio Greco, Milan .... W 6
Mar. 17—Harold Skog, Oslo .... L 6

CHARLIE NASH
British Lightweight
Born: May 10, 1951
1975
Oct. 2—Ray Ross, Derry....................... W 10
1976
Jan. 26—Gordon Kirk, Glasgow .... W 8
Mar. 4—Bingo Crooks, Belfast................... W 8
Apr. 5—Tommy Glencross, London .... W 8
Apr. 26—Gordon Kirk, Glaskow .... W 8
May 24—Jimmy Revie, Mayfair................. KO 3
Sept. 22—Joe Singleton, London .... KO 9
Oct. 25—Guiseppe Agate, Mayfair .... W 10
Nov. 9—George McGurk, Derry................. W 8
1977
Jan. 24—Donny Sennett, London .... KO 5
Feb. 28—Tom Tarantino, London .... KO 1
Mar. 22—Benny Huertas, Derry .... KO 3
July 30—Larry Stanton, Derry .... W 10
Oct. 4—Adolfo Osses, Belfast .... KO by 5
1978
Feb. 28—Johnny Claydon, Derry .... KO 12
(For British Lightweight Title)
June 27—Adolfo Osses, Derry .... KO 3
July 17—Rene Martin, London .... KO 7
Sept. 18—Willie Rodriguez, London .... W 10
1979
Feb. 19—Luis Vega, London .... W 8
Mar. 20—Jerome Artis, London .... W 8
June 27—Andre Holyk, Londonderry .... W 12
(EBU Lightweight Title)
Dec. 7—Ken Buchanan, Copenhagen .... W 12
(EBU Lightweight Title)
1980
Mar. 14—Jim Watt, Glasgow .... KO by 4
(For WBC Lightweight Title)
May 27—Pedro Acosta, Belfast .... KO 7

VALERIO NATI
Italian Bantamweight
1978
Apr. 7—Domenico Palumbo, Faenza .... W 6
May 19—Luigi Paravati, Forli .... KO 2
July 6—Antonio Franca, Lugo .... KO 4
July 19—Domenico Palumbo, Bellaria .... KO 9
Oct. 21—Giulio Greco, Pesaro .... KO 5
Nov. 3—Salvatore Laconi, Forli .... KO 3
Dec. 26—Nessim Zebellini, Bologna .... W 8
1979
Apr. 13—Abdelkader Esmain, Forli .... W 8
June 8—Luigi Tessarin, Ravenna .... W 10
Oct. 11—Helenio Ferreira, Faenza .... W 8
Nov. 30—Giuseppe Fossati, Forli .... W 12
(Won Italian Bantamweight Title)
1980
Mar. 15—Claudio Tunda, Forli .... KO 1
Apr. 24—Franco Buglione, Forli .... KO 3
(Won Italian Bantamweight Title)

May	31—Melquiades Da Silva, Sassari	W 8
Dec.	3—Juan Francisco Rodriguez, Forli	W 12
	(Retained European Bantamweight Title)	

LUCIANO NAVARRA
Italian Junior Welterweight
1976

Oct.	1—Angelo Zanetti, Milano	W 6
Oct.	22—Luigi Ruggiero, Bologna	KO 4
Nov.	6—Carmine Zollo, Bari	W 6
Dec.	18—Domenico Milone, Gallarate	KO 2

1977
Feb.	11—Gualberto Fernandez, Milan	W 6
Apr.	29—Gualberto Fernandez, Bologna	W 6
June	10—Angelo Tomasini, Milan	KO 3
June	24—Luiz Ribeiro, Gallarate	W 6
Oct.	29—Giovanni Mairorano, Fagnano Olona	W 8
Dec.	2—Giuseppe Minotti, Milano	KO 6
Dec.	26—Francesco Gallo, Milano	L 8

1978
June	30—Giuseppe Minotti, Parma	W 8
Aug.	18—Giancarlo Barabotti, Massa	KO 3
Nov.	4—Giuseppe Minotti, Calolziocorte	KO 2

1979
Jan.	12—Francesco Gallo, Milano	KO 2
Apr.	6—Giuseppe Russi, Barletta	L 8
July	14—Giuseppe Martinese, Fabriano	L 12
	(Italian Junior Welterweight Title)	
Nov.	2—Richard Rodriguez, La Chaux de Fonds ...	L 10

1980
Jan.	30—Guiseppe Martinez, Viterbo	KO by 2
	(For Italian Junior Welterweight Title)	
Mar.	28—Giuseppe Russi, Bitonto	W 8
May	1—Fred Decaestecker, Izegem	L 8
May	30—Salvatore Cascio, Rome	KO by 5
Aug.	10—Vincenzo Bottigliero, Siderno	W 6

ROLANDO NAVARRETE
Junior Lightweight
Born: Feb. 14, 1957
1973

Feb.	17—Eddie C. Lementes, Gen Santos City	W 4
Mar.	24—Quirino Peligro, Gen Santos City	W 6
Apr.	14—Cris Espinosa, Gen Santos City	W 4
June	23—Abdul Maratan, Gen Santos City	W 8
Oct.	13—Cris Espinosa, Gen Santos City	W 8
Nov.	10—Jimi Verongue, Gen Santos City	D 8
Nov.	21—Fime Sun, Gen Santos City	KO 2
Dec.	22—Mar Belimar, Glan	KO 6

1974
June	12—Julius Gonzaga, Korondal	D 10
July	10—Roberto Cinco, Gen Santos City	L 10
Oct.	18—Willie Abenir, Rizal	W 10
Nov.	29—Dobo Quilario, Davo City	W 10

1975
Jan.	24—Rene Cruz Jr., Rizal	KO 10
Feb.	15—Courado Boy Vasquez, Gen Santos City ..	W 12

1976
Jan.	20—Bernabe Villacampo, Cebu City	KO 2
May	21—Paul Ferreri, Sydney	L 10
July	31—San Sacristan, Cebu City	KO 4
Aug.	21—Pol Ladeza, Deoro City	KO 1
Sept.	25—Rey Paulino, Cebu City	W 10
Nov.	13—Yungshik Kim, Cebu City	KO 7

1977
Jan.	29—Mario Odias, Cebu City	W 10
June	17—Yungshik Kim, Seoul	L 12
Sept.	12—Thanomchit Sukhothai, Rizal	KO by 9
Dec.	31—Johnny Sato, De Oro City	KO by 8

1978
May	28—Tony Jumaoas, Cebu City	KO 4
July	15—Nene Jun, Gen Santos City	W 12
Aug.	19—Fernando Cabanela, Gen Santos City	W 12
Sept.	30—Nene Jun, Dava City	W 12

1979
Jan.	7—Pete Alferez, Cebu City	KO 2
Feb.	16—Rey Tam, Manila	KO 4
Mar.	18—Sukothai Thanonchit, Cebu City	D 10
June	19—Frankie Duarte, Honolulu	W 10
July	24—Jose Torres, Honolulu	W 10
Aug.	28—Miguel Meza, Honolulu	KO 7
Oct.	9—Junichi Okubo, Honolulu	KO 3
Dec.	18—Abdul Bey, Honolulu	KO 7

1980
Jan.	16—Frankie Ahumada, Manila	W 10
Apr.	1—Jerome Artis, Honolulu	KO 7
Apr.	27—Alexis Arguello, San Juan	KO by 4
	(For WBC Junior Lightweight Title)	

ALFREDO NAVEIRAS
Spanish Middleweight
1973

Sept.	23—Titi Larbi, Gilly	W 6
Oct.	14—Dario Diamonte. Pietrabas	KO 5

Nov.	1—Fernand Banckaert, Izegem	KO 2
Nov.	16—Jean Grandjean, Gilly	KO 6
Dec.	1—Jean Pierre Steeland, Andenne	KO 1

1974
Jan.	12—Alfred Lagasse, Namur	KO 1
Jan.	25—Jannick Dufor, Gilly	LF 5
Mar.	8—Roger Lobjois, Gilly	W 6
Apr.	27—Gerard Brenton, Gembloux	W 6
May	11—Kijilali Koudier, Vigneux.............	L disq. 5
June	8—Giuseppe Panunzio, Vaux.............	KO 5
June	22—Jean Marie Tochy, Namur	KO 4
Sept.	13—Jean Claude Genno, Gand	KO 6
Sept.	27—Eric Seys, Turnhout	KO 3
Oct.	26—Daniel Letarte, Namur	W 8
Nov.	22—Stan Van den Driessche, Gand	KO 3
Nov.	30—Loucif Hamani, Paris	KO by 1

1975
Jan.	17—Gray Ibekwe, Gand	KO 3
Feb.	7—Valdir Silva, Gand	W 8
Mar.	8—Philippe Girotti, Namur	W 8
Apr.	19—Jean Bandu, Wieze	D 8
May	17—Mel Dennis, Liege	L 10
Oct.	11—Franklin Arrindel, Eupen	KO 6
Nov.	7—Joe Gregory, Cointe	L 8
Nov.	15—Joe Gregory, Liegi	L 8

1976
Jan.	30—Jose Luis Palacios, Barcelona	W 8
Feb.	13—Dino Fletas, Barcelona	KO 4
Feb.	27—Tony Perez, Madrid	W 8
Nov.	6—Jacques Chinon, St. Servais	W 8

1977
Jan.	15—Jacques Chinon, Brussels	W 8
Feb.	19—Sonny Kamunga, La Louviere	KO 7
Apr.	9—Clement Tshinza, St. Servais	L 8
Apr.	22—Francis Vermandere, Belgiu	KO 4
June	18—Michel Stini, Grivegnee	W 12
Oct.	8—Pablo Rodriguez, Liege	W 10
Nov.	26—Errol McKenzie, Brussels	KO 3

1978
Apr.	29—Roy Gumbs, Emines	KO 3
May	31—Jose Diogo, Barcelona	KO 2
June	30—Francisco Rodriguez, Barcelona	W 12
	(Spanish Middleweight Title)	

1979
Jan.	6—Robert Powell, St. Servais	W 10
Mar.	16—Angel Ortiz, Barcelona	W 8
May	4—Juarez De Lima, Barcelona	LF 1
May	18—Juarez de Lima, Barcelona	W 8
July	14—Jose Lozano, Mataro	D 12
	(Spanish Middleweight Title)	
Oct.	20—Aroldo Olivares, Oviedo	W 8
Dec.	20—Aroldo Olivares, Barcelona	W 8

1980
Jan.	11—Jose Luis Alvarez, La Coruna	KO 5
	(Retained Spanish Middleweight Title)	
Apr.	25—Andoni Amana, Barcelona	L 12
	(Lost Spanish Middleweight Title)	
June	20—Jose Hernandez, Barcelona	D 8
Oct.	20—Alex Cardoza, Barcelona	KO 7

LUCAS NCETEZO
South African Flyweight
1977

May	31—Mxolisi Mpama, Queenstown	W 6
Dec.	17—Mxolixi Nohenda, Butterworth	L 6

1978
Feb.	18—Mxolisi Nohenda, East London	D 4
Apr.	1—Fundisile Kralo, East London	W 6
May	27—Simon Moema, East London	L 6
Oct.	28—Thembisile Ngxingolo, East London	L 4

1979
July	7—Siphiwo Fuma, Queenstown	KO by 4

1980
Mar.	29—Nkosinathi Silolo, Queenstown	D 6
May	3—M. Mpama, Transkei	W 6
July	5—Edward Mtana, East London	KO 2
July	19—Joseph Diraditsile, East London	L 4
Nov.	8—Honey Ndwana, East London	L 4

VINCENT NCGOBO
South African Bantamweight
1980

Mar.	29—Siphwe Fuma, Queenstown	KO by 8
Apr.	14—Aziz Dawood, Durban	W 4
July	4—Aziz Dawood, Durban	D

VINCENT NCGOBO
South African Bantamweight
1980

Mar.	29—Siphwe Fuma, Queenstown	KO by
Apr.	14—Aziz Dawood, Durban	W
July	4—Aziz Dawood, Durban	D

PHINDILE NDILELE
South African Lightweight
1977

July	30—Walter Martins, East London	W	4
Sept.	17—Howard Motumi, East London	KO	3
Nov.	19—Kenneth Mooi, East London	W	6

1978

Jan.	28—Raymond Nombeko, East London	W	4
July	29—Alfred Matiwane, Queenstown	KO	4

1979

July	7—Joseph Mnyabiso, East London	KO	3
Nov.	3—Elijah Cele, Queenstown	KO by	4

1980

Feb.	9—Ncedo Mpetsheni, East London	W	6
Mar.	15—Louis Plaatjies, East London	W	6
June	6—Joshua Plaatjies, Cape Town	L	6
Aug.	16—Chris Whiteboy, East London	L	6
Oct.	18—Ngcambala Mbadull	L	6

HONEY NDYWANYA
South African Flyweight
1979

Dec.	1—Fernand Tilitwa, King Williamstown	W	4

1980

Mar.	22—Terry Tikolo, Queenstown	D	4
May	17—Johannes Miya, East London	KO by	4
Aug.	16—Sixuli Madondile, East London	W	4
Nov.	8—Manelisi Ncetozo, East London	W	4
Dec.	6—Victor Tiadi, East London	W	6

PETER NEAL
British Welterweight
1976

Mar.	1—Mike Copp, London	KO	6
Mar.	29—Mick Hampston, Walworth	D	6
Apr.	5—Johnny Pincham, London	L	6
Sept.	29—Barry Price, Hammersmith	L	6

1977

Jan.	25—Tommy Davitt, London	L	6
Mar.	16—Steve Laybourn, Solihull	KO	2
Mar.	21—George Kidd, London	W	6
May	2—Tommy Joyce, Walworth	KO	3
May	23—Dave Proud, Walworth	L	6
Oct.	11—Horace McKenzie, Marylebone	D	8
Nov.	14—Johnny Elliot, Reading	W	8
Dec.	12—Johnny Pincham, Walworth	W	8

1978

Jan.	31—Terry Petersen, Marylebone	W	8
Mar.	22—Steve Angell, London	W	10
May	5—Marijan Benes, Frankfurt	KO by	5

1979

Feb.	28—Chris Walker, Harrogate	KO	8
Apr.	23—Roy Commosioung, Reading	W	8
Oct.	3—Henry Rhiney, Reading	W	12

1980

July	1—Gary Pearce, Swindon	W	8
Aug.	12—Colin Jones, Gowergon	KO by	5
	(For British Welterweight Title)		

MARTIN NEE
British Heavyweight
1977

Feb.	28—Brian Paul, Mayfair	KO by	2
Oct.	24—Jim Evans, Hammersmith	D	4
Nov.	10—Johnny Clark, London	KO	4

1978

Jan.	19—Alan Ward, London	W	4
Apr.	3—Bob Young, London	L	6
Apr.	24—George Gray, Bradford	KO	3
Sept.	19—Bob Young, London	W	6
Nov.	20—Bob Young, London	W	8
Dec.	1—Gordon Ferris, Enniskillen	KO by	4

1979

Oct.	17—Kenny March, Lewisham	L	6
Dec.	13—Colin Flute, London	L	6

1980

Feb.	18—Ron McLean, Lewisham	KO	3
Mar.	6—Les Dunn, Wimbledon	W	6
May	29—Ron McLean, Wimbledon	W	8
Nov.	13—Derek Simpkin, London	W	8

DAVE (ARTFUL DODGER) NEEDHAM
British Featherweight
Born: Aug. 15, 1951
ABA Flyweight Champion in 1969 and 1970;
Commonwealth Games Flyweight Champion in 1970.
Won bronze medal as a bantamweight in 1970
European Youth Championships, in Hungary.
1971

Jan.	25—Jimmy Killeen, London	KO	3
Feb.	23—Sammy Abbey, London	KO	7
Apr.	6—Al Hutcheon, London	KO	3
Apr.	19—Roger Howes, London	W	8

May	4—Karim Young, London	W	8
Oct.	4—Dave Touhy, Nottingham	KO	4
Oct.	19—Billy Hardacre, London	W	8
Nov.	10—Michel Jamet, Nottingham	W	8
Nov.	24—John McCluskey, Nottingham	KO	8

1972

Feb.	1—Jean-Pierre Flambeau, Nottingham	KO	6
Feb.	22—Francis Payelle, Bethnal Green	KO	1
Mar.	27—Billy Hardacre, Nottingham	W	8
Apr.	18—Dionisio Bisbal, Nottingham	KO	4
June	19—Paddy Graham, Nottingham	W	8
Oct.	2—Billy Hardacre, Nottingham	W	8
Nov.	28—Colin Miles, Nottingham	W	12

1973

Jan.	15—Jesus Nieves, Nottingham	W	10
Mar.	26—Eddie Rivera, London	KO	3
Apr.	9—John Mitchell London	W	8
Apr.	30—John Kellie, London	W	8
Oct.	23—Hiro Hamada, Nottingham	W	10

1974

Mar.	7—Bashew Sibaca, Mayfair	WF	2
Dec.	10—Paddy Maguire, Nottingham	W	15
	(British Bantamweight Title)		

1975

Feb.	11—Earl Large, Kensington	W	10
Apr.	11—Daniel Trioulaire, Garentin	D	15
	(European Bantamweight Title)		
Oct.	20—Paddy Maguire, London	KO by	14

1976

May	8—Arnold Taylor, Johannesburg	L	10
Nov.	17—Alan Richardson, Solihull	KO by	3

1977

Jan.	17—Jeff Pritchard, London	KO by	5
July	5—Vernon Sollas, Wolverhampton	KO	7
Sept.	21—Pasqualino Morbidelli, Milan	W	8

1978

Apr.	20—Alan Richardson, London	W	15
	(British Featherweight Title)		
Oct.	9—Alan Robertson, Middlewbrough	W	8
Dec.	16—Roberto Castanon, Leon	KO by	5
	(European Featherweight Title)		

1979

Apr.	9—George Sutton, Nottingham	W	8
Sept.	18—Pat Cowdell, Wolverhampton	W	15
	(For British Featherweight Title)		
Nov.	6—Pat Cowdell, Kensington	L	15
	(Lost British Featherweight Title)		

1980

May	4—Charm Chiteule, Lusaka	KO by	5
May	29—Pat Cowdell, Wolverhampton	L	12
	(For British Featherweight Title)		

DEREK (YOUNG) NELSON
British Junior Welterweight
1978

Mar.	23—Jim Fenwick, Sunderland	KO	1
Apr.	17—Peter Snowsall, London	L	6
Apr.	24—Norman Morton, Middlesbrough	D	4
May	23—Peter Snowsall, London	W	6
July	12—Norman Morton, Newcastle	L	6
Oct.	9—Selvin Bell, Middlesbrough	W	6
Oct.	30—Roger Guest, Nottingham	L	6
Nov.	27—Liam Linnen, Glasgow	W	6
Dec.	4—Brendan O'Donnell, Marton	KO	4

1979

Jan.	15—Ian Pickersgill, Nottingham	W	6
Feb.	26—Dai Davies, Middlesbrough	L	8
Apr.	17—Liam Linner, Glasgow	KO	5
Apr.	27—Norman Morton, Newcastle	W	8
May	16—Dave Allen, Sheffield	D	8
May	21—Dave Allen, Birmingham	L	8
June	18—Tony Bogle, Bradford	W	8
Sept.	22—Gilbert Bayens, Zele	W	6
Oct.	31—Phil Lewis, Burslem	KO	1
Nov.	19—Eric Purkis, London	L	8

1980

Jan.	24—Martin Bridge, Hartlepool	KO	4
Feb.	4—Gary Pearce, London	L	8
Mar.	3—Kevin Quinn, Marton	W	8
Mar.	17—Lee Hartshorn, Newcastle	L	8
May	31—Tony Carroll, Liverpool	L	8
June	23—Dave McCabe, Glasgow	L	8
Sept.	27—Sylvester Mittee, London	KO by	2

SPIDER NEMOTO
Japanese Featherweight
Born: Nov. 17, 1950 Iwaki City, Japan Height: 5 ft. 1 in.
Real Name: Shigemitsu
1971

Mar.	1—Tetsunori Kunimura, Tokyo	L	4
Apr.	10—Akira Fujimoto, Tokyo	D	4
July	8—Noriyuki Hara, Tokyo	KO	3
Sept.	26—Masashi Nakamoto, Tokyo	W	4

Oct. 30—Joji Tanaka, Tokyo ....W 4
Nov. 28—Sanji Nemoto, Tokyo ....W 4
Dec. 26—Takemi Toyama, Tokyo ....W 6
1972
Jan. 28—Takenori Nakano, Osaka ....W 6
Mar. 28—Seiichi Eto, Tokyo ....W 6
Aug. 18—Ronito Cannones, Guam ....L 10
Sept. 28—Ushiwakamaru Harada, Tokyo ....W 10
1973
Mar. 16—Pepito Guirua, Guam ....L 10
Apr. 27—Hyun Kim, Nagoya ....W 10
July 19—Shunsaku Ikeda, Tokyo ....W 10
Sept. 8—Ernesto Marcel, Panama ....KO by 9
(For WBA Featherweight Title)
1974
Feb. 28—Shoji Okano, Tokyo ....W 10
Apr. 28—Fred Magarano, Tokyo ....W 10
May 23—Genzo Kurusawa, Tokyo ....W 10
Sept. 23—Sanjo Takemori, Tokyo ....W 10
Dec. 23—Noboru Konuma, Tokyo ....W 10
1975
Mar. 22—Woon-Chul Shin, Chunchon(Korea) .....KO 6
July 24—Jun Gallego, Tokyo ....W 10
Sept. 20—Bok-Soo Hwang, Inchon(Korea) ....L 10
Oct. 26—Masayuki Miyashita, Tokyo ....KO 6
Nov. 20—Moon-Suk Choi, Seoul ....W 10
1976
June 5—Tony Jumao, Cebu City ....D 10
July 10—Masayuki Miyashita, Tokyo ....W 10
Nov. 28—Norikazu Atomura, Tokyo ....KO 3
Dec. 26—Bomber Uchida, Tokyo ....W 10
1977
Feb. 15—Tatsunoshin Iwami, Tokyo ....KO 7
Apr. 17—Se-Keun Koh, Seoul ....L 10
June 26—Chongtae Yuh, Soka City ....W 10
Sept. 18—Shigeyoshi Adachi, Tokyo ....W 10
(Japanese Featherweight Title)
Dec. 4—Leopardo Tsurata, Tokyo ....W 10
(Japanese Featherweight Title)
1978
Feb. 23—Hirofumi Mochizuki, Tokyo ....KO 8
Mar. 23—Hector Cortez, Tokyo ....W 10
June 6—Yoshinori Kayama, Osaka City ....W 10
Aug. —Royal Kobayashi, Tokyo ....L 12
(OPBF Featherweight Title)
Oct. 16—Shigeyoshi Adachi, Osaka ....W 10
(Japanese Featherweight Title)
Nov. 25—Shinichi Aoki, Tokyo ....KO 8
1979
Mar. 22—Koichi Matsushima, Tokyo ....KO by 9
June 1—Namio Akamone, Osaka ....W 10
(JBC Featherweight Title)
1980
Jan. 22—Eusebio Pedroza, Tokyo ....L 15
(For WBA Featherweight Title)
Mar. 30—Tomio Nakamura, Tokyo ....KO 9
(Won Japanese Featherweight Title)

LOUIS NEVELING
South African Junior Welterweight
1971
Dec. 6—Henry Alley, Paarl ....KO 5
1972
Jan. 29—Harry Barbaries, Port Elizabeth ....W 8
Oct. 27—Kokkie Olivier, Vereeniging ....L 6
1973
Feb. 10—Jimmy Carrol, Port Elizabeth ....L 6
June 15—Dirk van der Westhuizen, Pt. Eliz. ...KO by 2
Aug. 13—Leslie Baker, Goodwood ....L 10
1974
Apr. 27—Gerald Oehley, Port Elizabeth ....L 4
May 4—Eddie Mileham, Brits ....W 6
May 31—Freddie Rust, Port Elizabeth ....W 10
June 15—Abraham Smith, Turffontein ....KO by 2
1975
May 30—Johnny Sham, Durban ....L 6
1976-1977
(Inactive)
1978
Feb. 3—Petrus Karstens, Port Elizabeth ....KO 4
June 10—Petrus Karstens, Port Elizabeth ....W 10
(Won Vacant Cape Province Lightweight Title)
Sept. 2—Pinki Dlale, Port Elizabeth ....W 6
Nov. 4—Michael Ndiyane, Port Elizabeth ....L 6
1979
Mar. 10—Stephen Naude, Oudtshoorn ....KO by 2
June 2—Bowell Zono, Port Elizabeth ....L 10
1980
Mar. 15—Phindile Ndilele, East London ....L 6

GARY NEWELL
British Welterweight
1978
June 29—Carl North, Wolverhampton ....W 6

378

Sept. 18—Jimmy Smith, Wolverhampton ....L 4
Oct. 2—Dennis Price, Nantwich ....L 6
Oct. 10—Dennis Price, Wolverhampton ....L 6
Oct. 31—Mick Tyson, Wolverhampton ....KO 3
Nov. 15—Jimmy Smith, Ipswich ....W 6
Nov. 22—Dave Farrell, Stoke ....W 6
1979
Jan. 22—Gary Cooper, Wolverhampton ....KO by 5
Feb. 19—Tommy Wright, Wolverhampton ......KO by 2
Mar. 21—Goodwin Josephs, Stoke ....L 8
Apr. 4—Von Reid, Birmingham ....W 4
Apr. 10—Lee Hartshorn, Wolverhampton ....L 6
Oct. 29—Jeff Aspel, Wolverhampton ....KO 4
Nov. 6—Nigel Thomas, Stafford ....W 6
Nov. 14—Al Stewart, Stoke ....KO by 1
Dec. 17—Mickey Kidd, Wolverhampton ....L 6
1980
Jan. 16—Terry Matthews, Stoke ....L 6
Mar. 10—Tommy Wright, Wolverhampton ....D 6
Mar. 19—George Kidd, Stoke ....KO 4
Apr. 30—Tommy Wright, Wolverhampton ....W 6
June 11—Jimmy Smith, Edgbaston ....L 6
Sept. 29—Roy Varden, Bedworth ....L 8

PAUL NEWMAN
British Light Heavyweight
1980
Jan. 28—Harry Pompey Allen, Hove ....KO 2
Mar. 3—John O'Neill, Hove ....D 6
May 19—John O'Neill, London ....KO by 6
Sept. 29—Chris Devine, Chesterfield ....L 6
Oct. 20—Gordon Stacey, Hove ....KO by 1

VINCENT NGCOBO
South African Bantamweight
1972
May 6—Ephraim Mnguni, Durban ....KO 2
1973
Aug. 25—Jerry Gumede, Durban ....W 6
1974
Apr. 6—Lemchion Mkhize, Durban ....W 4
June 29—John Frazer Mkhize, Durban ....L 6
Oct. 26—Jerry Gumede, Durban ....L 6
1975
(Inactive)
1976
Nov. 10—Joe Ngidi Jr., Durban ....W 6
1977
Nov. 12—Siphiwe Bhengu, Durban ....L 6
Dec. 17—Mxolisi Mpama, Butterworth ....L 8
1978
Aug. 12—Sephiwe Bhengu, Durban ....W 10
1979
Sept. 7—Peter Mathebula, Springs ....KO by 5
1980
Mar. 29—Siphiwo Fuma, Queenstown ....KO by 5
Apr. 14—Aziz Dawood, Durban ....W 4
July 4—Aziz Dawood, Durban ....D 4

MTUTUZELI NGQAKAYI
South African Junior Lightweight
1978
May 27—Howard Motumi, East London ....W 4
Aug. 26—Daniel Makhudu, East London ....W 4
1979
July 28—Fungile Buti, King Williamstown ....D 6
1980
Mar. 29—Bukwana Matiwane, Queenstown ....L 4
May 24—Godfrey Manyaniso, Welkom ....W 6

JOSEPH NGUBANE
South African Bantamweight
1979
Sept. 29—Richard Mthombeni, Durban ....KO 3
1980
Mar. 1—Anthony Hadebe, Durban ....W 4
Apr. 14—Raphael Miya, Durban ....KO 2
Apr. 28—Blessing Ndlela, Durban ....L 4
June 16—John Xaba, Durban ....KO 4
Aug. 4—Simon Zincube, Durban ....KO 4
Nov. 20—Robert Makhoba, Durban ....KO 10
Nov. 29—Joe Ngidi, Durban ....KO 5
Dec. 15—Johannes Sithebe, Pietermaritzburg .....W 6

TEMBISILE NGXINGOLO
South African Flyweight
1976
Nov. 13—Monde Mpulampula, East London ....L 4
1977
Oct. 15—Gaybon Yekiso, East London ....L 4
1978
Feb. 18—Boy Mnyaka, East London ....L 4
Apr. 1—Manduleli Sigam, East London ....W 4
May 5—Kato Ntsikelelo, East London ....W 4

May 27—Isaac Seripe, East London .... W 4
July 8—Reuben Matewu, East London .... D 8
Sept. 9—Lawrence Krune, East London .... L 6
Sept. 30—R. Makhaba, Transkei .... W
Oct. 28—Lucas Ncetezo, East London .... W 4
Dec. 15—Thomazile Yako, East London .... L 6
1979
May 26—Lawrence Krune, King Williamstown L disq. 3
Dec. 1—Monde Mpulampula, King Williamstown . . L 6
1980
Mar. 29—Tembisile Sigetye, Queenstown .... L 4
May 3—H. Dungwa, Monakali .... L 6

MTUTZELI NGZAKAYI
South African Lightweight
1980
Mar. 29—Bukwana Matiwane, Queenstown .... L 4
May 3—K. Tshaka, Mowakali .... W 4
May 24—Godfrey Manyaniso, Welkom .... W 6

SEXON NGZAYIMBANA
South African Bantamweight
1980
Mar. 29—Sipho Nongabe, Queenstown .... KO 3
July 19—Luyan Dwanga, East London .... KO 2
July 26—Ncethezo Manelisi, King Williamstown . . D 4
Aug. 23—Tembisile Gawula, East London .... W 4
Nov. 8—Mxolisi Galada, East London .... KO 3
Dec. 6—Joe Gunuza, East London .... KO 2
Dec. 20—Phindile Gaika, East London .... KO 5

JANUARY NHLAPO
South African Junior Welterweight
1979
Feb. 9—Eric Ndlebende, Bethlehem .... D 6
Sept. 1—Joseph Domkrag, Ficksburg .... W 4
1980
Feb. 9—Eric Ndiebende, Bethlehem .... D 6
Aug. 23—Ephraim Khuto, Bethlehem .... KO 1

JOSHUA NHLAPO
South African Featherweight
1977
Nov. 18—Simon Motloung, Krugersdorp .... KO 2
1978
Apr. 15—Nkosinathi Silolo, Butterworth .... W 4
June 3—Michael Moamogoa, Bloemfontein .... W 6
1979
Mar. 9—Charles Makasi, Springs .... W 4
May 4—Lazarus Mofokeng, Springs .... W 6
June 29—Jacob Morake, Natalspruit .... L 6
Aug. 3—Charles Marule, Springs .... W 6
1980
Feb. 29—Joseph Gumede, Springs .... W 8
May 24—Norman Bromfield, Orlando .... W 6

LASSINE NIARE
French Heavyweight
1976
Nov. 27—Laurent Zardy, Le Havre .... KO by 5
1977
Jan. 8—Rudy Gauwe, Zele .... KO by 2
Mar. 4—Albert Syben, Grivignee .... L 6
Oct. 15—Robert Desnouck, Molenbeek .... L 6
Nov. 11—Romeo Malgarini, Milan .... KO by 2
1978
Feb. 11—Robert Bosio, Liegi .... W 6
Feb. 18—Christian Poncelet, Charleville .... L 8
1979
(Inactive)
1980
Jan. 6—Ali Lukasa, Bilbao .... KO by 5
Mar. 28—Abdel Qissi, Bruxelles .... L 6
Apr. 19—Marco, Sombreffe .... KO by 1

GARY NICKELS
British Bantamweight
1978
Oct. 9—Ian Murray, Marylebone .... W 6
Oct. 24—Alec Irvine, Kensington .... W 6
Nov. 11—Terry Hanna, Marylebone .... KO 3
Dec. 5—Pip Coleman, Kensington .... W 6
1979
Feb. 13—John Cooper, Marylebone .... W 8
Mar. 19—Gary Ball, Marylebone .... D 8
Sept. 25—Paul Keers, London .... L 6
1980
Mar. 4—Mike Fickett, London .... W 6
Apr. 22—Brindley Jones, London .... W 6
Oct. 14—Billy Straub, London .... W 8

(TUSIKOLETA) TEK N'KALANKETE
French Welterweight
1979
June 7—Jimmy Kaute, Paris .... W 6
Aug. 31—Isidore Cabeza, Madrid .... D 8
1980
Feb. 16—Roberto Castanon, Leon .... L 8
Mar. 8—Jose Luis Pacheco, Palma de Mallorca .... L 8
Mar. 14—Andre Holyk, Villeurbanne .... W 10
Nov. 14—Jean Symos, Liege .... KO 8

GODFREY NKATE
South African Junior Flyweight
1976
Aug. 21—David Molefe, Kroonstad .... L 4
1977
Apr. 30—Benjamin Metsing, Kroonstad .... W 4
June 11—David Molefe, Kroonstad .... L 4
Nov. 5—Paul Masoane, Viljoenskroon .... L 6
Dec. 3—Edward Nzimande, Ficksburg .... KO 3
1978
Sept. 2—Michael Khuto, Ficksburg .... W 6
Oct. 7—Daniel Ramille, Virginia .... W 6
Nov. 28—Meshack Dhlamini, Virginia .... KO 4
1979
Feb. 10—Joseph Mokomaditsile, Virginia .... W 8
Mar. 24—David Molefe, Virginia .... W 8
June 16—Johannes Sithebe, Virginia .... W 8
July 14—Elias Raliting, Virginia .... KO 2
Aug. 29—Martin Nkokoto, Bloemfontein .... KO 5
Nov. 12—Martin Nkokoto, Welkom .... W 10
Dec. 3—Dexter Dhlamini, Welkom .... KO 5
(South African Flyweight Title)
1980
Feb. 2—Lawrence Krune, Virginia .... W 12
(South African Junior Flyweight Title)
Mar. 28—Peter Mathebula, Springs .... KO by 4
(For South African Flyweight Title)
Sept. 27—Meshack Dhlamini, Welkom .... W 6
Dec. 1—Meshack Dhlamini, Virginia .... W 6

JEFFREY NKATE
South African Junior Flyweight
1980
Feb. 2—John Matsabu, Virginia .... W 4
May 10—Joseph Malefetsi, Virginia .... KO 1
June 7—Isaac Mfene, Odenaalsrust .... KO by 3
Aug. 2—James Mqueku, Welkom .... KO 2

LEHLOHONOLO NKATLO
South African Featherweight
1979
Nov. 10—Peter Shakong, Jabulani .... KO 2
1980
Feb. 29—Enoch Mazibuku, Springs .... D 6
May 3—Mncedi Masiza, East London .... KO 3
May 10—Kallie Swanepoel, Johannesburg .... KO 1
July 19—Lennox Mtyongwe, East London .... W 6
Dec. 6—Boy Boy Mtimkulu, East London .... W 4

MARTIN NKOLOTO
South African Junior Flyweight
1978
Sept. 2—Edward Nzimande, Ficksburg .... L 4
Oct. 7—Johannes Phumo, Virginia .... W 4
Nov. 28—Abraham Moholo, Virginia .... L 4
1979
Feb. 10—Simon Mafere, Virginia .... L 4
Mar. 24—John Matsabu, Virginia .... W 4
May 5—David Malinga, Ficksburg .... W 4
July 14—Meshack Dhlamini, Virginia .... W 6
July 31—Wilson Dhlamini, Bloemfontein .... W 6
Aug. 4—David Majoe, Odendaalsrust .... W 4
Aug. 29—Godfrey Nkate, Bloemfontein .... KO by 5
Nov. 12—Godfrey Nkate, Welkom .... L 10
1980
Feb. 2—David Molefe, Virginia .... KO 10
(Won Vacant OFS Junior Flyweight Title)
May 31—David Malinga, Bethlehem .... L 8
(Lost OFS Junior Flyweight Title)
Aug. 23—David Malinga, Bethlehem .... L 8
Dec. 1—John Matsabu, Virginia .... KO 4

WELILE NKOSINKULU
South African Bantamweight
1977
Nov. 19—Nkosana Tolbert, East London .... KO by 1
Dec. 17—Mava Malla, Butterworth .... W 4
1978
May 6—Ndodomzi Witi, East London .... KO 2
May 27—Mxolisi Mpama, East London .... KO 2
July 8—Pretty Petela, East London .... W 1
Aug. 5—Khulile Radu, East London .... KO 4

379

Sept. 9—Tito Dastile, East London ....KO 6
Sept. 30—Guybon Yekiso, East London ....W 6
Oct. 28—Leku Sandi, East London ....KO 5
1979
Mar. 10—Thomazile Yako, East London ....KO 4
Apr. 28—Nkosana Moss, East London ....KO 3
June 8—Daniel Hlahane, East London ....W 6
Aug. 4—Shadrack Mogopudi, East London ......KO 1
Sept. 8—Zola Lawuse, Zwelitsha ....W 6
Sept. 29—Zola Lawuse, East London ....KO 2
Nov. 10—Nkosana Moss, King Williamstown .....W 6
Dec. 8—Peter Mathebula, East London ....KO 9
(Won South African Bantamweight Title)
1980
Feb. 9—David Smith, East London ....KO 5
Mar. 1—Sipho Mange, East London ....KO 5
Apr. 5—Johan Putter, East London ....KO 5
May 3—Gaybon Yekiso, East London ....KO 4
May 31—Julian Solis, East London ....L 10
July 19—Jacob Diraditsile, East London ....KO 2
Sept. 5—Siphwe Bhengu, Springs ....KO 4
Oct. 25—Ramon Soria, Sun City ....W 8
Dec. 6—Ruben Solorio, East London ....W 10

SOLOMON NOJANGA
South African Lightweight
1977
Nov. 19—Reginald Mpondo, East London ....KO 3
1978
Oct. 21—Alfred Matiwane, Queenstown ....L 6
Dec. 15—Ncedo Mpetsheni, East London ....L 4
1979
July 14—Welile Klaas, East London ....L 4
1980
May 17—Boy Boy Mtimkulu, East London ....L 6
Aug. 23—Spokes Witbooi, East London ....KO by 4

ERIC NOLEBENDE
South African Junior Welterweight
1979
Aug. 18—Joseph Mphlahoe, Welkom ....L 4
1980
Feb. 4—January Nhlapho, Bethlehem ....D 6
Mar. 1—Manasse Potse, Odendaalsrust ....L 6

BAREND HENDRIK (BENNIE) NORTMAN
South African Junior Welterweight
Born: Feb. 13, 1956
1979
Feb. 3—Solomon Bango, Johannesburg ....W 4
Apr. 25—Nicolas Gumede, Durban ....KO 2
June 11—Simon Mokoena, Welkom ....KO 4
July 28—Jimmy Ellis, Bulawayo ....W 3
Sept. 15—Terrence Molefe, Johannesburg ....W 4
Nov. 12—John Khooe, Welkom ....W 4
Dec. 1—Anton Weitzs, Port Elizabeth ....KO 3
1980
Mar. 8—Timotheus Modise, Johannesburg ....W 4
May 26—Norman Sekgapane, Johannesburg ....W 8
Aug. 16—Hardy Mileham, Joburg ....W 4
Dec. 22—Bramley Whiteboy, Cape Town ....W 6

GERARD NOSLEY
French Middleweight
Born: Oct. 5, 1948
1972
Mar. 25—Alfred Lagasse, S. Michel ....L 6
Apr. 8—Areski Galou, Troyes ....KO 4
May 6—Alain Riviere, Nemours ....L 6
Sept. 30—Robert Brunel, Troyes ....W 6
Oct. 21—Christian Joan, Calais ....W 8
Dec. 2—Mohamed Alem, Orleans ....W 6
Dec. 17—Jannick Dufour, Calais ....KO by 6
1973
Feb. 2—Jean Grandjean, Douai ....L 6
Feb. 28—Siovano Bischeri, Terni ....KO 2
Mar. 8—Kante Nangui, Paris ....W 6
Mar. 15—Regis Yapende, Paris ....W 6
Apr. 13—Ahmed Boucharra, Lione ....W 6
June 8—Nino Castellini, Milan ....KO by 6
July 11—Jean Genno, Perpignano ....D 8
Sept. 15—Vincent Parra, Martigues ....L 8
Oct. 6—Philippe Girotti, Le Harve ....L 6
Oct. 19—Ahmed Bouchara, Genova................W 6
Nov. 3—Shaco Mamba, Ville rut...............KO by 1
1974
Jan. 17—Jean Claude Warusfel, Paris..............L 8
Feb. 1—Eusebio Anani, Marseille................D 8
Feb. 23—Joel LeGuern, St. Etienne ....W 10
Mar. 17—Eusebio Anani, Lyons ....KO 5
Apr. 20—Gianfranco Meconi, Villeurbanne........KO 3
Sept. 27—Germano Valsecchi, Milan ....L 8
Oct. 5—Adriano Rodriguez, Villeurbanne.........W 8

1975
Jan. 17—Salah Arafa, Villeurbanne ....KO 6
Feb. 1—Loucif Hamani, Algiers ....KO by 4
May 21—Jean Claude Warusfel, Paris ....D 12
(French Junior Middleweight Title)
Oct. 24—Walter Guarnieri, Annecy................W 8
Nov. 14—Germano Valsecchi, Milan................D 8
1976
Jan. 16—Mustapha Kabangu, Clauses............KO 6
Apr. 2—Alfonso Fernandez, Madrid ....KO 7
Apr. 24—Nat King, Abidjan......................W 8
May 8—Daniel Martin, Vandoeuvre ....KO 8
May 21—Trento Facciocchi, Milan ....D 8
Nov. 19—Chedk Tebourski, Annecy ....WF 7
Dec. 17—Norberto Cabrera, Milan................KO 2
1977
Feb. 4—Angelo Jacopucci, Milan ....L 8
Mar. 18—Jacobs Chinon, Annecy ....W disq. 7
June 4—Marcel Giordanella, Dijon ....L 12
(French Junior Middleweight Title)
1978
Feb. 27—Michel Chapier, Paris ....D 8
Apr. 21—Norberto Cabrera, Genova ....L 8
Nov. 7—Tony Sibson, Wembley ....KO by 7
1979
Jan. 12—Joel Bonnetaz, Perigueux ....W 12
May 18—Gratien Tonna, Perigueux ....KO by 6
(For French Middleweight Title)
June 30—Ruben Pardo, Monte Carlo ....KO by 5
1980
Mar. 15—Pierre Joly, Toulouse ....L 8
Nov. 7—Jacques Chinon, Nice ....KO by 5
(For French Middleweight Title)

HAIDAR NOURREDINE
Belgian Junior Lightweight
1979
Oct. 5—Vincent Cipolla, Binche ....L 6
Nov. 17—Antonio Licata, Antwerp ....L 6
Dec. 23—Jean Pierr Meganck, Izegem ....D 6
1980
Feb. 2—Jean Pierre Meganck, Kalken ....W 6
Mar. 22—Jean Pierre Meganck, Termonde ....W 6
Apr. 18—Mohamed Maalem, Llauwe ....KO by 3

JOSEF NSUBUGA
Ugandan Welterweight
Based in Denmark
1975
May 30—Juergen Voss, Hamburg ....W 4
1976
Apr. 14—Trevor Francis, Helsinki ....L 6
July 7—Juergen Voss, Oulu ....KO 4
1977
Sept. 8—Per Muellertz, Copenhagen ....KO 3
1978
Mar. 2—Chris Glover, Oslo ....KO 2
Apr. 6—Johnny Pincham, Oslo ....KO 4
May 19—Mimoun Mohatar, Oslao ....W 8
June 15—Everaldo Costa Azevedo, Oslo ....W 8
Sept. 3—Horace McKenzie, Bergen ....W 8
Oct. 28—Billy Waith, Oslo ....W 8
Nov. 11—Steve Mechalerya, Copenhagen ....KO 4
Dec. 26—Jose Hernandez, Basilea ....KO 8
1979
Feb. 16—Johnny Cooper, Oslo ....KO 3
May 30—Alfonso Hayman, Oslo ....W 8
Sept. 10—Omar Olivo, Oslo ....W 8
Oct. 15—Carl Bailey, Oslo ....KO 8
1980
Jan. 13—Roberto Duran, Las Vegas ....KO by 4
Dec. 6—Joey Mack, Islip ....W 8

JOSEPH NTELA
South African Junior Lightweight
1979
Feb. 9—Jeremiah Malikhetla, Bethlehem ....KO by 3
1980
Feb. 4—Jeremiah Malikhetia, Bethlehem ....KO by 3
Sept. 6—Petrus Raleting, Ficksburg ....L 4

TEMBA JACK NTULI
South African Junior Lightweight
1979
Aug. 18—Dumisani Zondi, Durban ....W 4
1980
June 16—Christopher Hlongwe, Durban ....L 4
Oct. 6—Christian Cele, Pmburg ....L 4

SALVO NUCIFERO
British Junior Middleweight
1977
Sept. 5—Viv Jackson, Hove ....KO 4

380

Oct.	10—Earl Wallace, London ....KO 3
Nov.	18—Dave Hamm, London ....KO 6
Dec.	13—Clifton Wallace, Walworth ....KO 6

1978

Jan.	10—H. H. Thompson, Walworth ....KO by 3
Feb.	27—Lloyd Gardner, London ....W 8
Mar.	22—Steve Hopkins, London ....L 8
Apr.	20—Joe Oke, Bradford ....W 8
May	8—Joe Oke, Birmingham ....W 8
June	19—Charlie Malarkey, Glasgow ....W 8
July	19—Rogelio Zarza, Bellaria ....KO by 5
Nov.	15—Mick Morris, Solihull ....KO 7
Nov.	27—Pat Thomas, Kettering ....KO by 1

1979

Mar.	19—George Walker, London ....W 8
Apr.	10—Mick Mills, Kensington ....KO 5
May	13—Colin Jones, Plymouth ....KO by 4
Oct.	8—Charlie Malarky, London ....L 8
Oct.	29—Richard Kenyon, Camborne ....KO 5

1980

Jan.	16—Joey Mack, Solihull ....L 8
Jan.	22—Kirkland Laing, London ....KO by 6
Mar.	3—John F. Kennedy, Nottingham ....L 8

SIMON (PRIEST) NXAWE
South African Junior Welterweight
1972

Feb.	5—Abe Ncala, Bloemfontein ....W 6
Feb.	24—Anthony Morodi, Langa ....KO by 8
Apr.	22—Terence Makaluza, King Williamst'n KO by 4
May	12—Andries Moloi, Springs ....L 6
June	26—F. Majwabule, Port Elizabeth ....KO 4

1973

Mar.	9—Paulus Buthelezi, Tembisa ....W 6
May	12—Paulo Tshume, Port Elizabeth ....L 6
July	7—J. Masupye, Bloemfontein ....W
July	14—Jack Jim, East London ....D 6
Oct.	27—Anthony Morodi, Jabulani ....L 6

1974

Mar.	2—S. Motake, Bloemfontein ....W
Apr.	5—Norman Sekgapane, Kwa-Thema ....KO by 4
Nov.	9—Phalo Tshume, Port Elizabeth ....L 8

1975-1978
(Inactive)
1980

Feb.	2—Teboho Lento, Kimberley ....KO 3
Aug.	23—Samuel Motake, Kimberley ....W 6

ALAN OAG
British Lightweight
Born: May 9, 1951
1974

May	6—Ian Pickersgill, London....................L 6
June	10—Mickey Van Day, Glasgow ....W 6
Oct.	28—Hugh Smith, Glasgow ....W 6
Nov.	25—Hugh Smith, Glasgow ....L 6

1975

Dec.	2—Gary Dunks, Bethnal Green ....L 6

1976

Jan.	28—Graham Laybourn, Stoke ....WF 6
Feb.	9—Mario Stango, Bedford...............KO by 1
Sept.	20—Tommy Duffy, Glasgow...................L 6
Sept.	30—Gerry McBride, Liverpool..................L 8
Oct.	4—Don Aagesen, Hanley.....................W 6
Oct.	18—Jackie McGill, Glasgow ....KO by 8
Dec.	7—Jimmy Flint, Kensington ....KO by 1

1977

Apr.	27—Mickey Bell, Leicester ....D 6
May	16—Clive Hogben, Glasgow ....L 6
Sept.	19—Lee Graham, Glasgow ....KO by 1

1978

Jan.	23—Johnny Owen, Aberavon ....KO by 8
May	11—Day Larmour, Belfast..............L disq. 1
Oct.	3—Vernon Penprase, Aberavon ....KO by 5

1979
(Inactive)
1980

Jan.	25—Jackie Turner, Hull ....L 6
Apr.	21—Norman Morton, Glasgow ....KO by 3

THORNTON OAKES
South African Junior Middleweight
1977

Mar.	19—Hardy Mileham, Johannesburg ....W 4

Nov.	14—Eddie Scott, Johannesburg ....L 4

1978

Mar.	4—Eddie Scott, Ermelo ....W 6
Apr.	29—Cameron Adams, Johannesburg ......KO by 2

1979

July	9—David Kalako, Welkom ....D 4

1980

Mar.	3—Joseph Hali, Cape Town ....L 6
Mar.	13—Joseph Hali, Cape Town ....L 4
May	17—Loyiso Miya, East London ....L 8
May	31—Loyiso Miya, East London ....L 8

TERRY O'CONNER
British Heavyweight
Born: July 7, 1953
1976

Mar.	10—Barry Clough, Wolverhampton ....W 6
Mar.	17—Artist Gibson, London ....W 6
Mar.	29—Kenny Burrell, London ....W 6
Apr.	12—Kenny Burrell, Birmingham ....W 6
May	26—Artist Gibson, Wolverhampton ....W 6
June	28—John DePledge, Luton ....KO 6
July	14—Alan Ward, Wolverhampton ....KO 2
Aug.	29—Keith Johnson, Solihull ....W 6
Sept.	10—Brian Huckfield, Digbeth ....L 8
Oct.	27—Steve Carr, Wolverhampton ....W 8
Nov.	22—Kenny Burrell, Birmingham ....W 8
Dec.	20—Kris Smith, Walworth ....L 8

1977

Feb.	10—Eddie Fenton, Coventry ....W 8
Mar.	8—George Gray, Wolverhampton ....W 8
Apr.	7—Danny McAlinden, Dudley ....KO by 1
Sept.	19—Les Stevens, London ....L 8
Sept.	30—George Butzbach, Hamburg ....L 10
Oct.	6—Bruce Grandham, Liverpool ....KO by 4
Dec.	6—Stan McDermott, London ....KO by 5

1978

Axpr.	21—Gordon Ferris, Enniskillen ....L 8
June	29—Colin Flute, Wolverhampton ....W 8
July	12—George Scott, Newcastle ....D 8
Sept.	9—Jimmy Abbott, Capetown ....L 6
Nov.	6—Brian Huckfield, Stafford ....L 10
Nov.	22—Eddie Neilson, Stoke ....KO by 3

1979

Jan.	17—Winston Allen, Solihull ....W 8
Feb.	10—Benito Eschche, Zaragoza ....W 8
Mar.	5—Ishaq Hussein, Wolverhampton ....W 6
Apr.	7—Robert Desnouck, Bruxelles ....W 8
May	17—Bobby Hennessey, London ....LF 6
May	30—Thomas Blyth, Oslo ....W 6
Nov.	10—Hennie Thoonen, Eindhoven ....L 8
Dec.	13—Tommy Kiely, London ....L 8

1980

Feb.	5—Larry McDonald, Wolverhampton ....L 8
Mar.	31—Rudi Lubbers, Rotterdam ....L 8
July	2—Louis Hendricks, Welkom ....D 8
Sept.	29—Rocky Burton, Bedworth ....W 6

(Won Vacant Midlands Area Heavyweight Title)

Oct.	11—Felipe Rodriguez, Pontevedre ....

LOURENS SYBRAND OELOFSE
South African Junior Lightweight
1978

Apr.	17—Isaac Mazibuko, Johannesburg ....KO 2
May	15—Richard Modise, Johannesburg ....KO by 2
June	9—Barend Bester, Johannesburg ....W 4
Sept.	23—Barend Bester, Johannesburg ....KO 4
Nov.	27—Gaybon Yekiso, Johannesburg ....KO by 3

1980

Mar.	8—Anthony Wiese, Ermelo ....KO 1
Apr.	21—Joseph Nene, Secunda ....KO 3
Nov.	28—Mike Wessels, Joburg ....W 6

ETHAM OEZAKALIN
German Junior Welterweight
1975

May	16—Hu Bong Park, Ludwigshafen ....W 4
May	31—Giampaolo Piras, Koeln ....W 6
June	14—Boualem Belouard, Berlin ....W 4
Sept.	6—Jose Rios, Berlin ....KO 4
Sept.	12—Giampaolo Piras, Offenbach ....W 6
Sept.	26—Bong Hu Park, Ketsch ....KO 4
Oct.	31—Jules Piga, Koeln ....W 4

1976

May	7—Lothar Abend, Berlin ....W 8
June	5—Bong Hu Park, Istanbul ....KO 1
June	11—Mi Whan Ki, Berlin ....W 6
Aug.	6—Bouchiba Messaoud, Berlin ....W 6
Aug.	20—Boualem Belouard, Timmendorfer ....W 6
Oct.	21—Jan Arne Pederson, Oslo ....D 6
Dec.	21—Giampaolo Piras, Berlin ....W 6

1977

Jan.	20—Hans Henrik, Copenhagen ....KO by 3

Mar.	15—Vito Triassi, Berlin	W	4
July	6—Natale Vezzoli, Vieste	KO by	12
	(For European Junior Lightweight Title)		

1978

July	19—Cornelius Boza-Edwards, Bellaria	KO by	3
Sept.	2—Klaus Hein, Berlin	W	6
Nov.	18—Abass Macauley, Berlin	W	8

1979

Feb.	10—Danny M'Putu, Dunkerque	KO by	3
Apr.	28—Utker, Belgrade	KO	2
Aug.	25—Zdravko Jovicic, Zenica	KO	2
Nov.	5—Dieter Schantz, Rotterdam	KO	3

1980

Mar.	28—Cemal Kamaci, Berlin	W	10
May	14—Toni Habermayer, Munich	W	4
June	7—Rolf Kersten, Colgne	KO	4

YOUNG-HO OH
Korean Lightweight
Born: April 23, 1952

1971

Nov.	7—Hae-Eun Chung, Seoul	D	4
Dec.	12—Bvung-Hwa Min, Kwangjoo	W	8

1972

Sept.	23—Hwa-Nam Kim, Taegu	L	10
Dec.	2—Chang-Hyun Choi, Seoul	W	10

1973

Feb.	4—Koo-Min Ro, Taegu	KO	2
Apr.	1—Wang-Soon Lee, Taegu	D	8
Aug.	4—Cho-Hyun Choi, Seoul	W	8
Sept.	9—Hwang-Chi Kim, Seoul	L	10
Nov.	18—Victor Dounue, Seoul	W	10

1974

Jan.	27—Ichiro Isawa, Pusan	KO	8
Feb.	27—Victor Dounue, Seoul	KO	7
May	26—Wang-Soo Lee, Pusan	KO	2
July	14—Earnie Cruz, Guam	KO by	7
Sept.	14—Pu-Choi Lee, Taegu	KO	3
Oct.	3—Freddie Mason, Pusan	W	10
Oct.	23—Kazuyuki Iwagiri, Seoul	KO	5
Dec.	1—Baek Ho, Kwangjoo	KO	8
Dec.	22—Chong-Hoon Moon, Seoul	KO	1

1975

Jan.	25—Pu-Choi Lee, Kwangjoo	KO	9
Feb.	23—Arab Suga, Tokyo	KO	5
Mar.	29—Doh-Soo Lee, Kwangjoo	KO	7
Apr.	—Yasu Saigoh, Pusan	W	10
June	7—Narongsak Dejkajorn, Seoul	KO	3
Sept.	20—Romeo Tomagan, Seoul	KO	1
Oct.	19—Changchern Singthanong	KO	3
Nov.	29—Sakae Nakamura, Pusan	KO	5
Dec.	21—Boy Obreno, Pusan	KO	5

1976

Feb.	22—Many Ysrael, Pusan	W	10
Mar.	28—Shichamonsa Sakdi, Inchon	KO	4
Apr.	25—Jumao-As Tony, Taegu	W	12
	(Won OPBF Lightweight Title)		
June	24—Leo Viajedor, ...	W	10
July	17—Kiyoshi Kazama, Pusan	W	12
	(Retained OPBF Lightweight Title)		
Sept.	11—Jumao-As Tony, Bangkok	KO	4
	(Retained OPBF Lightweight Title)		
Oct.	5—Putt Laoleg, Pusan	L	10
Nov.	20—Sparling Bangariban, Pusan	KO	4
	(Retained OPBF Lightweight Title)		
Dec.	18—James Clavilas, Seoul	KO	6

1977

Mar.	27—Fred Pastor, Taegu	KO	1
	(Retained OPBF Lightweight Title)		
May	7—Kiyoshi Kazama, Pusan	D	10
Oct.	24—Toru Sugawara, Seoul	W	10
Nov.	20—Petchsyarm Petcharern, Bangkok	L	10

1978

Jan.	21—Joe Lim, Pusan	W	12
	(Retained OPBF Lightweight Title)		
Mar.	12—Dony Soriano, Seoul	W	10
Apr.	5—Fred Basa, Seoul	W	10
July	9—Samuel Serrano, San Juan	KO by	9
	(For WBA Junior Lightweight Title)		
Sept.	2—Boy Oliver, Pusan	W	10
Dec.	17—Mar Sinbajon, Seoul	KO	6
	(Retained OPBF Lightweight Title)		

1979

Mar.	4—Yidano Lee, Seoul	KO	3
Apr.	22—Kwang-Min Lee, Seoul	L	10

1980

Feb.	22—Yidano Lee, Seoul	KO	1
	(Retained OPBF Lightweight Title)		
Aug.	2—Hilmer Kenty, Detroit	KO by	9
	(For WBA Lightweight Title)		

KATSUYUKI OHASHI
Japanese Bantamweight

1980

Jan.	29—Hirohisa Iino, Tokyo	W	6
Feb.	22—Takenae Nakajima, Tokyo	W	8
Apr.	15—Hitoshi Ohashi, Tokyo	KO by	6

MITSUO OHASHI
Japanese Lightweight

1979

July	6—Hawk Kazama, Nara	KO by	3
	(JBC Lightweight Title)		

1980

Feb.	22—Tsunehiro Fuchiwaki, Tokyo	KO by	1

ISAO OKAHASHI
Japanese Flyweight

1978

Feb.	12—Tatsunoshin Iwami, Tokyo	KO	7
Aug.	1—Yasuhide Takahaski, Tokyo	KO	6
Sept.	8—Tasuhide Takahashi, Tokyo	L	10
Oct.	2—Abebe Yoshida, Tokyo	W	10
Nov.	4—Jose Caba, Nagoya	KO by	8

1979

Aug.	23—Kenichi Ito, Tokyo	L	10
Oct.	14—Yung Sik Kim, Tokyo	L	10

1980

Jan.	22—Katsuji Sano, Tokyo	L	10

JOE OKE
British Junior Middleweight

1973

Feb.	9—Abraham Tonil, Lagos	KO	9
Oct.	24—Jimmy Standpip, Accra	KO	4
Dec.	14—Osvaldo Smerilli, Kumasi	W	12

1974

Apr.	6—Charles Bocco, Accra, Ghana	KO	4
Aug.	6—Shaco Mamba, Lome	KO by	8
	(African Championship)		

1975

Apr.	12—King George Aidoo, Accra	KO by	12
Nov.	11—Roger Maxwell, Manchester	L	6
Nov.	17—Dave Mullings, London	W	8
Dec.	12—Armand Xhonneux, Eupen.............	W	10

1976

Jan.	12—Leroy Herriott, London	KO	7
Feb.	20—Ba Sounkalo, Hamburg	W	8
Mar.	10—Larry Paul, Wolverhampton............	KO by	7
May	6—Karl Vinson, Paris	L	8
July	3—Peter Assandon, Accra	D	10
Oct.	30—Rudi Koopmans, Groningen	KO by	4

1977

Sept.	26—Jim Moore, London	KO	6
Oct.	11—Peter Morris, Coventry	L	8
Nov.	7—John Smith, Glasgow	W	8
Dec.	6—Billy Lauder, Leeds	L	8

1978

Feb.	15—Steve Hopkin, Cambridge	D	8
Mar.	2—Dave Davies, Liverpool	KO by	6
Apr.	20—Salvo Nucifero, Bradford	L	8
May	8—Salvo Nucifero, Birmingham	L	8
May	24—Mick Mills, Southend	KO by	1
June	20—Billy Lauder, London	L	8
July	17—Terry Knight, London	KO	5
Sept.	14—Per Mullertz, Randers	W	6
Oct.	9—Bob Mayes, Middlesbrough	W	8
Nov.	15—Cliftn Wallace, Ipswich	KO	6

1979

Jan.	22—Prince Rodney, Bradford	L	8
Feb.	26—Charley Malarkey, Glasgow	L	8
Oct.	3—Dave Southwell, Reading	L	8
Oct.	24—Alan Cable, Norwich	W	8
Nov.	10—Luigi Minchillo, Milan	KO by	5

1980

Jan.	25—Albert Hillman, Hove	L	8
Mar.	11—Dave Allen, Southend	D	8
Apr.	8—Carl Daley, Norwich	KO by	3

AUSTIN OKOYE
British Heavyweight

1977

Sept.	19—Cliff Beardsley, London	W	6
Oct.	12—Dave Fry, Stoke	KO	4
Nov.	10—Guinea Roger, Wimbledon	KO	7
Dec.	11—Brian Paul, Kingston	KO	5

1978

Jan.	19—Neil Malpass, Wimbledon	KO	4
Feb.	13—Tom Kiely, Walworth	KO by	5
Apr.	24—Brian Huckfield, Walworth	KO	4
Oct.	12—Terry Mintus, Wimbledon	KO by	8
Nov.	20—Ricky James, Birmingham	KO by	6

1979

Feb.	26—Gordon Ferris, Edgebaston	L	8

Sept.	11—Joe Awome, London	KO by	6
Dec.	3—Gordon Ferris, Wolverhampton	KO by	5

1980

Mar.	6—Bob Young, Wimbledon	W	8
Apr.	29—Andy Palmer, London	KO by	5

BLAZER OKUBO
Japanese Junior Lightweight
1979

May	8—Hikari Tomorari, Osaka	L	10
Sept.	7—Kench Kashi, Osaka	W	10
Oct.	9—Rolando Navarete, Honolulu	KO by	3

1980

Mar.	13—Yasutsune Uehara, Tokyo	KO by	5

(For Japanese Junior Lightweight Title)

TOSHIHIRO OKUMOTO
Japanese Junior Flyweight
1979

Nov.	30—Goichi Oshi, Shimizu City	L	6

1980

Mar.	3—Ken Kesugai, Chigasaki	L	10
June	1—Kenji Sogaku, Kochi City	KO	4

PATRIZIO OLIVA
Italian Welterweight
1980

Oct.	11—Nelson Gomez, Naples	W	6
Dec.	6—Eloi Des Santos, Bologna	W	6
Dec.	26—Mohamed Chino, Bologna	W	6

ANGEL OLIVER
Spanish Featherweight
1973

Apr.	7—Jose Luis Fleta, Miranda	L	6
May	26—Fernando Bernardez, Vitoria	KO by	3
Aug.	24—Angel Cristobal Diaz, Madrid	L	6
Sept.	20—Heriberto Mascarell, Gijon	W	6

1974

Jan.	12—Jaime Rodriguez, La Coruna	L	6

1975

Feb.	22—Andres Ramos, Zaragoza	W	6
Apr.	12—Pedro Pinto, Matero	D	8
May	24—Andres Ramos, Zaragoza	W	8
May	31—Abdelkader Esmain, Tarrasa	D	8
Aug.	21—Emilio Barcala, Madrid	D	6
Sept.	4—Jose Antonio Donoso, Calatyud	W	6
Oct.	4—Zaragata, Zaragoza	L	6

1976

Feb.	13—Abdelkedar Esmain, Figureas	W	6
Feb.	20—Jose Luis Rodriguez, Madrid	L	6
Apr.	10—Marino Garcia, Oviedo	L	8
June	5—Pedro Molleda, Mirando del Ebro........	L	8
Aug.	22—Manuel Carrasco, S. Sebastiano	L	8
Sept.	18—Pedro Pinto, Mataro	L	8
Nov.	20—Pedro Molleda, Santander	L	8
Dec.	26—Pedro Molleda, Bilbao	L	8

1977

July	8—Faustino Blanco, Madrid	L	8
Sept.	9—Juan Francisco Rodriguez, Madrid	L	8
Dec.	3—Francisco Jeronimo, Logrono	W	8

1978

Feb.	4—Vicente Rodriguez, Leon	L	8
Feb.	18—Vicente Manzanares, Logrono	W	6
May	20—Vicente Manzanares, Logrono	W	8
May	31—Abdelkader Esmain, Barcelona	L	8
Sept.	22—Francisco Jeronimop, Zaragoza	W	6
Nov.	11—Francisco Jeronimo, Zaragoza	W	8
Dec.	2—Kiko Garcia, Zaragoza	W	6

1979

Feb.	24—Angel Ramirez, Zaragoza	W	8
May	5—Esteban Eguia, Logrono	L	8
July	7—Manuel Masso, Zaragoza	W	8
Sept.	1—Manuel Masso, San Sebastian	L	8
Sept.	29—Esteban Eguia, Santander	L	8
Nov.	17—Ramon Marichal, S. Cruz ....'..	L	8
Dec.	12—Manuel Masso, Barcelona	L	8

1980

Jan.	26—Martin Antich, Zaragoza	W	8
Apr.	19—Jose Antonio Garcia, Zaragoza	KO by	1
June	13—Isidoro Cabeza, Palma de Mallorca	L	8

AMAR OLIVO
Italian Welterweight
1979

Aug.	8—Mauricio Hernandez Da Cruz, Genova	L	8
Sept.	10—Joseph Nsubuga, Oslo	L	8
Oct.	11—Han Henrik Palm, Copenhagen	KO by	7
Dec.	21—Vittorio Conte, Lucca	KO by	6

1980

Jan.	16—Vittorio Conte, Ancona	KO by	6

GERRY O'NEILL
Scottish Featherweight
1977

Sept.	29—Alan Robertson, Newcastle	L	8
Nov.	7—Tony Kerr, Glasgow	L	6
Nov.	14—Paul Clemit, Glasgow	W	6

1978

Jan.	23—Paul Chance, London	L	6
Jan.	30—Robbie Robinson, Glasgow	L	6
Oct.	18—Garry Ball, Glasgow	W	6

1979

June	18—Steve Cleak, London	W	8
Sept.	26—Eric Ragonisi, Solihull	L	8
Oct.	16—Eric Ragonisi, West Bromwich	L	8
Nov.	10—Dave Williams, Zele	KO by	1
Nov.	19—Gary Lucas, Glasgow	W	8
Dec.	5—Jimmy Brown, Liverpool	L	8

1980

Jan.	21—Gary Lucas, Birmingham	W	8
Feb.	18—Jimmy Brown, Glasgow	L	8
Mar.	14—Terry McKeown, Glasgow	W	10

(Won Scottish Featherweight Title)

May	27—Damien McDermott, Belfast	D	8
Sept.	15—Vernon Vanreil, Glasgow	L	8
Oct.	13—Gary Lucas, London	W	8

(Relinquished Scottish Featherweight Title)

JOHN O'NEILL
British Light Heavyweight
1979

Dec.	17—Rocky Burton, Wolverhampton	L	6

1980

Feb.	18—Lenny Remice, Lewisham	KO	3
Mar.	3—Paul Newman, Hove	D	6
Mar.	17—Gordon George, Birmingham	D	6
Apr.	15—Nigel Savory, Blackpool	W	6
May	19—Paul Newman, London	KO	5
May	31—Nigel Savory, Liverpool	L	6
Oct.	1—Steve Babbs, Swansea	W	8

JOSE MARIA OMEDES
Spanish Middleweight
1978

June	3—Enrique Pino Tobbio, Pontevedra	KO by	4
Aug.	11—Manuel Sanchez, Lluchamayhor	L	6
Sept.	22—Genaro Tapia, Zaragoza	W	6
Dec.	23—Ahmed Matia, Casablanca	L	6

1979

Feb.	24—Alberto Ramirez, Zaragoza	L	6
Mar.	17—Fernando Bermejo, Guadalajara	W	6
Apr.	6—Salvador Perez, Bilbao	W	6
Apr.	26—Manuel Sanchez, Mallorca	L	6
May	5—Ignacio Gorostidi, Eibar	KO by	3
July	7—Pedro Calero, Zaragoza	D	6
Nov.	24—Jorge Sala, Zaragoza	L	4

1980

Feb.	14—Helenio Ferreira, Bilbao	KO by	2

RAY OPOKU
Ghianan Middleweight
(Residing in Italy)
1978

June	30—Roberto Manoni, Sondrio	L	4
July	14—Luciano Bolis, Monte Marenzio	KO by	5
Nov.	24—Luciano Di Giacomo, Penne	L	6
Dec.	9—Ivan Simimgia, Udine	KO	4
Dec.	21—Nicola Cirelli, Rome	KO by	3

1979

Aug.	3—Germano Apostoli, Toscolano	L	6
Oct.	12—Girogio Giana, Rome	KO	2

1980

May	3—Roberto Felicioni, Rome	W	8
May	31—Aldo Buzzetti, Piacenza	WF	2
July	26—Mariucio Da Cruz, Rapallo	W	8
Dec.	4—Roberto Manoni, Rome	KO by	2

WILLIE OPPERMAN
South African Light Heavyweight
1980

Feb.	4—Cecil Sandow, Welkom	L	4
Mar.	21—Willem Killian, Bloemfontein	KO	4
May	5—April Speelman, Welkom	W	10

(OFS Light Heavyweight Title)

July	3—McDonald Shezi, Welkom	W	6
Dec.	22—Doug Lumley, Cape Town	L	12

(South African Light Heavyweight Title)

GOICHI OSHI
Japanese Flyweight
1979

Nov.	30—Teshihiro Okumoto, Shimizu City	W	6

1980

Jan.	10—Yoshinobu Sasaki, Tokyo	W	8

383

Feb. 28—Funaki Kazuyoshi, Tokyo ....L 10
Oct. 4—Hector Molina, Palma de Mallorca ....D 8

SHIGEYUKI OTAKE
Japanese Junior Lightweight
1979
Apr. 22—Yoshitaka Ikehara, Tokyo ....W 10
1980
Feb. 18—Takeshi Mine, Tokyo ....W 10

JOHNNY OWEN
Welsh Bantamweight
1976
Sept. 30—George Sutton, Pontypool ....W 8
Nov. 9—Neil McLoughlin, Derry ....D 8
Nov. 23—Ian Murray, Teorchu ....KO 7
1977
Jan. 28—Neil McLaughlin, West Bromwich ....W 8
Feb. 15—Neil McLaughlin, Merthyr ....W 8
Mar. 29—George Sutton, Ebbw Vale ....W 10
(Welsh Bantamweight Title)
Apr. 25—John Kellie, Glasgow ....KO 6
June 16—Terry Hanna, Ebbw Vale ....KO 4
Sept. 21—George Sutton, London ....W 8
Nov. 29—Paddy Maguire, London ....KO 11
(British Bantamweight Title)
1978
Feb. 27—Antonio Medina, Middlesborough ....W 8
Apr. 6—Wayne Evans, Ebbw Vale ....KO 10
(British Bantamweight Title)
June 12—Dave Smith, London ....W 8
June 29—Davy Larmour, Caerphilly ....KO 7
Sept. 2—Klaus Hein, London ....KO 6
Sept. 25—Wally Angliss, London ....KO 3
Nov. 2—Paul Ferreri, Ebbw Vale ....W 15
(Commonwealth Bantamweight Title)
1979
Mar. 4—Juan Francisco Rodriguez, Almeria ....L 15
(European Bantamweight Title)
Apr. 19—Lee Graham, London ....W 8
May 13—Guy Caudron, Pontypool ....W 10
June 13—Dave Smith, Caerphilly ....KO 12
(Commonwealth Bantamweight Title)
Sept. 17—Neil McLaughlin, Glasgow ....W 10
Oct. 4—Jose Luis Garcia, Cardiff ....KO 5
Nov. 29—Davey Vasquez, Ebbw Vale ....W 10
1980
Jan. 22—Glyn Davies, Piccadilly ....KO 6
Feb. 28—Juan Francisco Rodriguez, Ebbw Vale ....W 12
(Won European Bantamweight Title)
June 28—John Feeney, Glasgow ....W 15
(Retained British Bantamweight Title)
—Lupe Pintor, Los Angeles ....KO by

AUSTIN OWENS
British Featherweight
1978
Sept. 12—John Flynn, Wembley ....KO 6
Sept. 26—Larry Richards, Wembley ....KO 2
Nov. 7—Gary Ball, Wembley ....W 6
1979
Feb. 6—Selvin Bell, Wembley ....W 6
Apr. 10—Kenny Matthews, London ....KO 3
May 1—Paul Keers, London ....W 6
Sept. 11—Selwyn Bell, London ....KO 4
1980
Apr. 1—Don George, London ....W 8
May 12—Paul Keers, Reading ....D 8
Sept. 16—Terry McKeown, London ....KO by 2

DAVE OWENS
British Middleweight
Born: December 11, 1954
1976
May 12—Steve Heavisides, Bradford..............KO 2
June 8—Joe Jackson, Bradford ....W 4
Sept. 10—Carl McCarthy, Digebth ....KO 2
Sept. 21—Stege Fenton, Bethnel Green...........KO 3
Sept. 27—Neville Estaban, Piccadilly ....D 6
Nov. 30—Owen Robertson, London...............W 6
1977
Apr. 20—Billy Hill, Manchester ....KO 2
Apr. 27—Jim Moore, Bradford ....W 8
May 16—Howard Mills, Manchester ....KO 8
July 10—Pat Brogan, Birmingham ....KO 9
1978
May 8—Howard Mills, Nottingham ....KO by 4
May 24—Paul Shutt, Nottingham ....KO 2
Sept. 4—Young McEwan, Wakefield ....KO by 1
Dec. 7—Torben Anderson, Copenhagen ....L 8
1979
Mar. 12—Romal Ambrose, Manchester ....L 8
Sept. 20—Dave Davies, Liverpool ....KO 3

Oct. 17—Jimmy Pickard, London ....KO 4
1980
Apr. 29—Eddie Smith, Stockport ....KO by 1
Aug. 12—Doug James, Gowerton ....L 8
Oct. 13—Earl Edwards, Windsor ....KO by 3

JOSE LUIS (DUM DUM) PACHECO
Spanish Welterweight
Born: August 22, 1949
1970
Oct. 4—Felipe Prada, Ardoz ....KO 2
Nov. 21—Antin II, Madrid ....KO 1
Dec. 4—Francisco Sevilla, Barcelona ....KO 2
Dec. 18—Juan Jose Pardo, Barcelona ....KO by 4
1971
Feb. 4—Andres Perez, Gomis, Barcelona ....KO 5
Feb. 19—Francisco Sevilla, Madrid ....KO 6
Apr. 15—Antonio Molina, Madrid ....KO 6
May 14—Francisco Larroya, Barcelona ....KO 6
May 21—Pablo Vallecillo, Barcelona ....L 8
June 8—Juan Pena, Zaragoza....................D 8
July 3—Armstrong Vasco, Zaragoza ....W 8
Nov. 7—Pablo Vallecillo, Barcelona.............KO 7
Dec. 17—Jesus Gonzalez Dopico, Madrid.......KO by 10
(Spanish Junior Welterweight Title)
1972
Feb. 18—Victor Marquez, Madrid ....KO 4
Mar. 14—Ait Ahmed, Barcelona ....W 8
June 28—Famoso Dongil, Madrid................KO 6
Aug. 2—Juan Kid Dongo, Ceuta.................KO 6
Sept. 22—Famoso Dongil, Barcelona ....D 8
Oct. 7—Mimoun Mohatar, La Coruna ....L 8
Oct. 27—Juan Pardo, Barcelona..................W 8
Nov. 26—Jose Maria, Madrazo, Zragoza ....W 8
1973
Mar. 9—Mimoun Mohatar, Madrid...............W 8
Mar. 14—Vasco Armstrong, Madrid ....W disq. 5
May 11—Mimoun Mohatar, Madrid.........KO by 4
June 23—Manuel Carrecelas, Valencia ....KO 3
July 6—Fernando Perez, Madrid.................D 8
July 20—Jose Madrazo, Madrid...................D 8
Aug. 10—Epifanio Collado, Madrid ....KO 6
Sept. 8—Bo Hogberg, Palma.....................KO 5
Sept. 28—Damanio Lassandro, Sarzana........KO by 2
Nov. 2—Epifanio Collado, Barcelona ....KO 6
Nov. 23—Jose Duran, Barcelona..................L 8
Dec. 14—Everaldo Costa Azevedo, Barcelona ...KO by 6
1974
Mar. 29—Flash Patterson, Barcelona ....KO 5
May 1—Marco Scano, Cagliari ....L 8
May 22—Mimoun Mohtar, Madrid ....W 8
July 12—Pascal Zito, Madrid ....L 8
July 26—Wolfgang Gans, Madrid ....D 8
Sept. 14—Gonzalez Dopico, La Coruna ....L 12
(Spanish Welterweight Title)
Oct. 5—Felix Romero, Las Palmas ....KO 5
Oct. 25—Toni Molina, Milan ....KO 3
Nov. 16—Canarian Francis, Santa Cruz...........KO 5
Dec. 14—Adriano Rodriguez, S. Cruz............W 8
1975
Jan. 18—Moises Fajardo, Santa Cruz Tenerife   KO by 5
(Spanish Light Middleweight Title)
Feb. 14—Frank Medina, Barcelona ....W disq. 4
Apr. 30—Domenico DiJorio, Naples ....L 8
June 5—Mario Molina, Bilbao ....D 8
July 2—Mimoun Mohatar, Madrid ....L 8
Aug. 16—Mario Molina, Madrid ....W 8
Oct. 10—Moises Fajardo, Madrid.................KO 4
(Spanish Junior Middleweight Title)
Nov. 6—Torres Arbizu, Huelva ....W 8
1976
Jan. 10—Moises Fajardo, Santa Cruz ....KO 2
Feb. 27—Perico Fernandez, Madrid ....NC 10
July 3—George Perrot, Zaragoza ....W 8
July 17—Jose Piras, Santander ....W 6
Aug. 20—Jose Luis Palacios, Zaragoza ....KO 4
Sept. 9—Juan Pena, Mellilla ....KO 8
(Spanish Junior Middleweight Title)
Nov. 6—Diaz Requena, Cadiz ....KO 2
Nov. 26—Floyd Ngomba, Madrid ....KO 1
1977
Apr. 1—Kevin White, Madrid ....D 8
June 11—Jose Piras, Malaga ....KO 2
June 17—Antonio Torsello, Madrid ....KO 3
Sept. 24—Abel Messaoud, Santander ....KO 5

Oct.	7—Antoine Oke, Madrid	W	8
Nov.	5—Tony Ortiz, Madrid	L	8
Dec.	31—Mario Molina, Torremolinas	W	10

1978

Jan.	1—Mario Molina, Torremolinos	W	8
Jan.	6—Jesus De La Rosa, Bilbao	KO	7
Feb.	18—Antonio Casado, Logrono	D	8
Apr.	14—Joe Carlos, Bilbao	D	8
May	12—Horacio Ruiz, Bilbao	W	12
	(Spanish Welterweight Title)		
June	17—Carlos Santos, Logrono	KO	2
July	14—Fernando Perez, Madrid	W	8
Aug.	25—Jose Piras, Gijon	KO	2
Nov.	11—Jose Ramon Garcia, Gijon	D	12
	(For Spanish Welterweight Title)		
Dec.	9—Raul Anon, La Coruna	KO	4
	(For Spanish Welterweight Title)		
Dec.	25—Fernando Perez, Bilbao	KO	6

1979

Feb.	26—Johnny Disla, Barcelona	KO	3
Apr.	7—Angel Ortiz, Santander	D	
May	18—Carlos Morales, Barcelona	W	8
July	6—Johnny Davis, Palma de Mallorca	KO	5
July	21—Jurgen Voss, Benidorm	KO	2
Aug.	14—Smelin Jimenez, Benidorm	KO	2
Sept.	8—Carlos Morales, Lepe	L	12
	(Spanish Welterweight Title)		
Dec.	8—Osvaldo Lopez, Malaga	KO	5

1980

Feb.	14—Fermin Gallardo, Bilbao	L	8
Mar.	8—Tek N'Kalankete, Palma de Mallorca	W	8
May	3—Pino Tobio, Seville	KO	2
June	6—Manuel Lira, Madrid	W	8
July	22—Andoni Amana, Bilbao	KO by	9

ROSARIO PACILEO
Spanish Junior Middleweight
1980

Mar.	14—Ben Saad Salah, Rome	L	6
Mar.	29—Corrado Sortino, Pesaro	W	6
May	3—Giuseppe Semilia, Palermo	D	6

LORENZO PACIULLO
Spanish Junior Lightweight
1977

Nov.	13—Emilio Chiloiro, Rimini	L	6

1978

Jan.	14—Leo Scorza, Brindisi	W	6
Apr.	21—Vincenzo Morando, Genoa	W	6

1979

July	1—Antonio Pisani, Merano	W	6
July	27—Arturo De Prezzo, Bolzano	L	8
Dec.	1—Gianfranco Lalli, Sondrio	L	8

1980

Mar.	15—Antonio Pocai, Brindisi	W	6
May	22—Fabio Mannai, Bologna	W	6
Dec.	6—Renzo Mannai, Bologna	W	6

JUN PADINIT
Philippine Bantamweight
1979

Nov.	17—Fel Aporto, Santos City	L	10

1980

Feb.	9—Star Dayanan, Santos City	W	10

MICHEL PAGANI
French Middleweight
1977

Apr.	23—Leander Panted, Calais	KO	3
Oct.	22—Daniel Boulex, Calais	W	6

1978

Jan.	7—Jose Lacano, Calais	KO by	4
Feb.	10—Andrej Vestan, Bologna	KO	2
Mar.	4—Etienne Bayadikila, Calais	W	6
June	28—Luciano Bomben, Bologna	D	6

1979

Feb.	24—Jose Lozano, Calais	KO	3
Mar.	23—Nicola Cirelli, Rome	KO by	5
Oct.	19—Michel Chapier, Calais	W	10
Nov.	24—Jacques Shinon, Calais	KO by	2

1980

Jan.	12—Errol McKenzie, Calais	W disq.	3
Feb.	9—Willie Taylor, Calais	KO	2
Mar.	8—Fernandez Cruz, Calais	KO	5
Apr.	5—Jacques Chinon, Calais	KO by	11
	(For French Middleweight Title)		
Oct.	20—Alex Blanchard, Rotterdam	KO by	1

HANS HENRIK PALM
Dutch Welterweight
1976

Oct.	9—Tommy Wright, Copenhagen	W	4
Oct.	21—Hu Bong Park, Oslo	KO	3

Nov.	19—Rocco Frasca, Randers	W	4

1977

Jan.	20—Ethem Ozekalin, Copenhagen	KO	3
Feb.	24—Lothar Abend, Copenhagen	KO	3
Mar.	31—Jose Antonio Jimenez, Copenhagen	W	6
Apr.	28—Jose Sanchez, Copenhagen	KO	6
June	2—Eloy De Souza, Randers	W	6
Sept.	8—George Turpin, Copenhagen	KO	3
Dec.	8—Giuseppe Russi, Copenhagen	W	6

1978

Jan.	5—Des Gwilliam, Randers	W	6
Feb.	9—Tommy Dunn, Copenhagen	L	6
Mar.	2—Martyn Galleozzie, Vejle	KO	1
Mar.	16—Tommy Davitt, Copenhagen	W	6
Apr.	27—Joel Moulin, Randers	KO	1
Aug.	10—Toney Marety, Glyngore	W	8
Sept.	14—Terry Petersen, Randers	W	8
Dec.	7—Horace McKenzie, Copenhagen	W	8

1979

Feb.	15—Joey Singleton, Randers	L	8
Mar.	15—Alain Salmon, Copenhagen	KO	4
Sept.	6—Roy Varden, Copenhagen	KO	7
Oct.	11—Clinton McKenzie, Copenhagen	KO	7
Dec.	6—Henry Rhiney, Copenhagen	W	8

1980

Feb.	7—Achille Mitchell, Randers	KO	6
June	12—Clinton McKenzie, Randers	W	6
Sept.	6—Chris Davies, Aarhus	W	8
Oct.	17—Jorgen Hansen, Copenhagen	KO by	9
	(For European Welterweight Title)		

ANDY PALMER
British Heavyweight
1979

Oct.	23—Winston Allen, London	KO by	2

1980

Jan.	22—Ron McClean, London	KO	2
Feb.	19—David Fry, London	KO	3
Apr.	29—Austin Okoye, London	KO	5
July	12—Stan McDermott, London	KO by	2
Nov.	10—Ron McLean, Southwark	KO	3

APRIL PAPANE
South African Featherweight
1979

Feb.	9—William Mosia, Bethlehem	KO	2
Aug.	4—Samuel Koalepe, Odendaalsrust	KO	4
Oct.	2—Abel Rapulan, Bloemfontein	L	4
Nov.	19—Simon Makole, Kimberley	D	4

1980

Feb.	4—William Mosia, Bethlehem	KO	2
Apr.	12—Motsie Tladi, Ficksburg	LF	6
June	14—Daniel Mtsanda, Welkom	D	6

ISRAEL PAPANE
South African Flyweight
1979

Dec.	1—Samuel Mafere, Odendaalsrust	W	4

1980

Feb.	1—Johannes Phumo, Odendaalsrust	W	6
Mar.	1—Johannes Phumo, Odendaalsrust	W	6
June	14—Daniel Mkenku, Welkom	D	4
Aug.	9—Samuel Motsumi, Wesselsbron	W	6
Sept.	27—Issac Mfone, Welkom	W	6
Dec.	13—Michael Moamogoa, Wesselsbron	W	8

PHILIPPE PARENT
French Welterweight
1979

Oct.	19—Charles Restivo, Mouscron	W	6
Nov.	17—Raphael Salamone, Pepinster	W	6
Dec.	8—Jo Bollue, Las Louviere	L	6

1980

Feb.	23—Mohamed Bouziani, Pepinster	KO by	3
Mar.	22—Alex Beynaerts, Vilvoorde	KO	5
Apr.	19—Mohamed Bouziani, Belgium	KO	6
June	28—Jo Bollue, Gembloux	L	6
Sept.	19—Aziz Alaoui, Elouges	W	6
Nov.	8—Mohamed Bouziani, St. Truiden	D	6

CHONG-PAL PARK
Korean Middleweight
1977

Nov.	26—Yong-Soo Chung, Pusan	KO	
Dec.	23—Kyung-Sik Kim, Seoul	KO	
Dec.	25—Seung-Hwan Kang, Seoul	W	8

1978

Mar.	25—Seung-Hwan Kang, Seoul	D	10
June	14—Hung-Won Kang, Seoul	L	10
Aug.	28—Kazuo Goshima, Tokyo	KO	1
Dec.	17—Chung-Duck Choi, Seoul	KO	9
	(Won Korean Middleweight Title)		

Feb. 3—Thomas Abarca, Seoul .... KO 2
Mar. 17—Alberto Cruz, Taegu .... KO
Apr. 22—Armanco boniquit, Seoul .... KO 3
June 2—Michihiro Horibata, Seoul .... KO 3
Aug. 22—Cassius Naito, Seoul .... KO 2
        (Won OPBF Middleweight Title)
1980
Jan. 27—Katsuo Esashi, Seoul .... KO 3
        (Retained OPBF Middleweight Title)
Mar. 18—Kenji Shibata, Seoul .... KO 12
        (Retained OPBF Middleweight Title)
Apr. 26—Rocky Joe, Jakarta .... KO 8
        (Retained OPBF Middleweight Title)
June 21—Fred Pastor, Seoul .... KO 4
        (Retained OPBF Middleweight Title)
Aug. 8—Peter Piamonte, Seoul .... KO 4
        (Retained OPBF Middleweight Title)
Sept. 24—Torkano Marcos, Seoul .... KO 5
        (Retained OPBF Middleweight Title)
Nov. 3—Phil Davies, Seoul .... KO 3
        (Retained OPBF Middleweight Title)

STEVE PARKER
British Lightweight
1979
May 23—Selvin Bell, Nottingham .... KO by 1
Sept. 24—Tyrrell Wilson, Birmingham .... W 6
Oct. 22—Joe Mills, London .... L 6
Dec. 3—Jarvis Greenidge, Wolverhampton ..... KO 3
1980
Feb. 5—Jarvis Greenidge, Wolverhampton .... L 6
Mar. 3—Dave Laxen, Nottingham .... L 6
Mar. 19—Peter Harrison, Stoke .... W 6
Apr. 9—Gary Lucas, Burslem .... L 8

TERRY PARKINSON
British Lightweight
1979
Sept. 25—Wally Stockings, London .... L 6
Oct. 15—Julian Beaustead, Mayfair .... KO by 3
Nov. 26—Tony Davis, Hammersmith .... W 6
1980
Jan. 28—Mick Redden, Hove .... W 4
Feb. 18—Tony Davis, London .... L 6
Mar. 3—Tommy Thomas, Hove .... KO 4
Mar. 17—Ray Price, London .... L 6

CHARLIE PARVIN
Scottish Bantamweight
Born: Jan. 15, 1951
1972
Mar. 2—John McKnight, Glasgow .... KO 5
Mar. 14—Jimmy Killeen, Wolverhampton .... KO 1
Sept. 25—Clive Hogben, London .... W 6
Dec. 11—John O'Rawe, London.................... W 8
1973
Mar. 20—Mickey Piner, London .... L 8
Oct. 23—Clive Hogben, Nottingham............... L 8
Nov. 14—Paddy Graham, Solihull .... L 8
1974
Feb. 25—John Mitchell, Glasgow................... L 8
1975
May 26—Tony Kerr, Glasgow .... KO 5
Oct. 1—Wayne Evans, Hamilton .... KO by 5
Nov. 12—Jeff Pritchard, Solihull .... KO by 4
Dec. 4—John McKnight, Hamilton .... W 10
1976
May 18—Paddy Maguire, Walworth .... KO by 3
Oct. 18—John Kellie, Glasgow................... L 10
        (Scottish Bantamweight Title)
1977
Dec. 5—John Feeney, Maton .... L 8
1978
Oct. 23—Tony Kerr, Glasgow .... W 10
        (Scottish Bantamweight Title)
1979
(Inactive)
1980
Apr. 21—Alan Storey, Nottingham .... W 8
Apr. 28—Alan Storey, Birmingham .... W disq. 6
May 19—Mohammed Younis, Bradford .... NC 3
July 7—Paul Keers, Middlesbrough .... KO by 5

GIOVANNI PASCA
Italian Featherweight
1979
Oct. 17—Corrado Infanti, Sassari .... W 6
Nov. 17—Mario De Prosperis, Sassari .... KO 2
Dec. 7—Domenico Palumbo, Ozieri .... W 6
Dec. 28—Francesco De Rosa, Sassari .... W 6
1980
Apr. 11—Raga Murphy, Sassari .... D 8

NEIL PATTEL
Australian Welterweight
1973
Sept. 25—Martin Richards, St. Marys .... L 4
Sept. 27—Martin Ross, Blacktown .... L 4
Oct. 3—Carl Carlson, Riverwood .... W 3
Oct. 10—Ross Eadie, Kingsford .... W 5
Oct. 16—Eric King, Brookvale .... W 6
Oct. 19—Chris Ward, Woonona .... W 6
Oct. 24—Paul Hayward, Cammeray .... D 4
Nov. 7—Jeff Malcolm, Marrickville .... D 8
Nov. 14—Ross Eadie, Kingsford .... W 5
1974-1975
(Inactive)
1976
Feb. 12—John Layton, Blacktown .... W 6
Mar. 3—Ceddy McGrady, Cammeray.............. W 6
Mar 18—Steve Campbell, Blacktown .... W 6
Mar. 26—Calvin Hinkling, Wollongong........... W 6
Apr. 7—Mark Barnett, Cammeray .... D 8
May 5—Ross Eadie, Cammeray .... W 10
June 2—John Layton, Marrickville .... W 10
July 14—John Layton, Marrickville .... W 10
Aug. 4—Johnny Holt, Cammeray .... L 10
Sept. 8—Wally Carr, Marrickville .... W 15
Oct. 8—Hector Thompson, Tweed Heads ...... KO by 8
1977
July 8—Phil Khan, Brisbane .... KO 8
Sept. 30—Kerry Bell, Brisbane .... KO 9
    (Vacant Queensland State Welterweight Title)
Oct. 21—Jack Delaney, Brisbane .... KO 3
Nov. 18—Ross Eadie, Brisbane .... KO 10
1978
Feb. 10—Steve Ayerst, Brisbane .... W 10
Mar. 11—Mark Bennet, Melbourne .... W 10
May 9—Leroy King, Melbourne .... KO 10
May 26—Steve Dennis, Brisbane .... D 10
June 30—Wally Carr, Brisbane .... W 10
Aug. 4—Ross Eadie, Brisbane .... W 10
Oct. 6—Hector Thompson, Brisbane .... L 10
Nov. 24—Alberto Cruz, Brisbane .... KO 8
1979
Feb. 23—Greg Stephens, Brisbane .... KO by 9
Apr. 9—Steve Dennis, Brisbane .... KO by 12
        (Australian Welterweight Title)
1980
June 15—Silio Tiko, Laucaula Bay .... L 10
Oct. 27—Dave Edwards, Brisbane .... L 10

PAUL (POL) PAYON
Belgian Junior Middleweight
1976
Apr. 2—Fernando Bankaert, Charleroi.......... KO 2
Apr. 24—Jean Pierre Heirman, Charleroi .... KO 4
May 14—Gilbert Cnudde, Maurage .... KO 6
Sept. 18—Michel Parent, Marchienne .... KO 4
Oct. 2—Antonio Baletta, La Louviere .... KO 5
Nov. 6—Giampaolo Piras, Marchienne .... W 6
Nov. 20—Leander Pante, La Louviere............. KO 3
Dec. 3—Floyd Ngoba, Marchienne .... KO 2
Dec. 17—Eric Seys, La Louviere .... W 8
1977
Jan. 15—Eric Seys, Izegem .... W 6
Feb. 12—Julien Van Damme, Liegi .... W 8
Feb. 26—Gerard Breton, Marchienne .... W 8
Apr. 2—Alan Salmon, Nivelles .... KO 6
Apr. 22—Branko Barakovic, La Louviere .... KO 2
May 7—Stan Van Der Driessche, Antwerp ....
Dec. 9—Francisco Panos, La Louviere .... W 10
1978
Jan. 7—Bathily, Grivegnee .... W 8
Jan. 21—Beltichika, La Louviere .... W 8
Feb. 25—Angel Robinson Garcia, La Louviere ..... W 10
Apr. 1—Mohamed Mechlia, Bruxelles .... KO 7
May 20—Michel Stini, Charleroi .... KO by 9
        (Belgium Middleweight Title)
1979
Feb. 2—Maurice Bufi, La Louviere .... KO by 3
1980
Jan. 18—Giampaolo Piras, La Louviere .... D 6
Feb. 17—Ignacio Gorostidi, Maubeuge .... KO by 3
Apr. 5—Dirck Declerck, La Louviere .... W 8

GEORGE PEACOCK
Scottish Junior Welterweight
1976
Feb. 23—Kevin Doherty, Glasgow .... W 6
Mar. 4—Tony Mattia, Glasgow .... W 6
Sept. 20—Kevin Quinn, Glasgow .... L 6
Sept. 27—Jimmy King, Birmingham .... D 6
1977
(Inactive)
1978
Jan. 16—Sylvester Gordon, Birmingham .... W 6

May   8—Norman Morton, Glasgow ....W 6
May   15—Cookie Roomes, Glasgow ....W 8
June 19—Mickey Dirkin, Glasgow ....L 8
Sept. 18—Dave McCabe, Glasgow ....L 8
Sept. 25—Tony Zeni, London ....KO 8
1979
Feb. 26—Martin Bridge, Glasgow ....W 8
Mar. 19—Sylvester Gordon, London ....W 8
Apr. 23—Hugh Kelly, Glasgow ....KO 5
June 18—Willie Booth, Glasgow ....W 10
(Scottish Junior Welterweight Title)
Sept. 24—Martin Bridge, London ....W 8
Nov.   3—George Feeney, Glasgow ....L 8
1980
Mar. 24—Hugh Smith, Glasgow ....KO 7
(Retained Scottish Junior Welterweight Title)
Apr. 17—Clinton McKenzie, London ....KO by 3

DAVID PEARCE
British Heavyweight
1978
Nov. 15—Oabourne Taylor, Merthyr ....KO 1
Dec.   1—Bob Bleau, Minster ....KO 2
Dec. 11—Theo Josephs, Plymouth ....W 8
1979
Jan. 22—Mal Tetley, London ....KO 1
Jan. 22—Bobby Hennessey, London ....KO 2
Feb. 19—Bonny McKenzie, London ....W 8
Apr.   3—Winston Allen, Caerphilly ....W 6
May   10—Frank McCord, Pontypool ....W 8
July   5—Theo Josephs, Aberavon ....KO 3
1980
Jan. 22—Neville Meade, Caerphilly ....KO by 2
(For Welsh Heavyweight Title)

GARY PEARCE
British Welterweight
1978
Sept. 25—Billy O'Grady, Piccadilly ....D 6
Nov.   2—Mel Jones, Ebbw Vale ....KO 2
Nov. 20—Jimmy Smith, Piccadilly ....W 6
1979
Feb. 26—Lloyd Hibbitt, Edgbaston ....L 6
Apr.   3—Allan Burrows, Caerphilly ....W 8
Nov. 29—Dill Collins, Ebbw Vale ....W 8
1980
Feb.   4—Derek Nelson, London ....W 8
Mar. 11—Horace McKenzie, London ....L 10
(For Welsh Welterweight Title)
Mar. 31—Roy Varden, London ....W 8
May   27—Richard Avery, Newport ....L 10
July   1—Peter Neal, Swindon ....L 8
July 28—Terry Welsh, Doncaster ....KO 4

RONALD PEARCE
British Welterweight
1979
May   10—Terry Matthews, Pontypool ....W 6
June   4—Chris Coady, Liverpool ....D 6
July 30—Tony Britton, London ....L 6
1980
May   27—Paul Wetter, Newport ....L 6
July   1—Jimmy Smith, Swindon ....W 6

TONY PEARCE
British Light Heavyweight
1979
Apr.   6—Wally Barnes, Norwich ....W 4
May   17—Billy Keen, Wimbledon ....W 4
Dec. 20—Wally Barnes, Queensway ....KO 2
1980
Feb. 28—Gordon George, Queensway ....W 6

STEVE PEARSON
British Junior Middleweight
1980
Mar.   6—Phil Pourou, Wimbledon ....L 6
Apr.   8—Casley McAllum, Norwich ....KO by 3
May   29—Casley McAllum, Wimbledon ....KO by 2

RINALDO PELLIZZARI
Italian Heavyweight
1976
Nov.   3—Gianfranco Giannini,
Gardone Val Trompia ....KO 4
Dec.   2—Antino Tescione, Gardone ....W 6
1977
Feb. 25—Coulibali Demba, Milano ....KO 1
Apr.   1—Giovanni De Luca, Brescia ....W 6
Apr. 22—Giacinto Cattani, Milan ....W 8
June   3—Bruno Polloni, Lumezzane ....KO 5
Oct. 14—Mohammed Galloui, Milan ....KO 8
Oct. 28—Antimo Tescione, Salo ....KO 6

Dec. 16—Domenico Scala, Gardone ....W 8
1978
Feb.   3—Laurent Zardi, Milan ....D 8
May   5—Giancinto Cattani, Milan ....W 8
Dec. 26—Leopoldo Cantorrino, Milan ....W 8
1979
Feb.   2—Giovanni De Luca, Milano ....L 12
(Italian Heavyweight Title)
May   5—Laurent zardy, Gardone ....KO 8
Aug.   3—Giovanni De Luca, Tuscolano ....KO by 9
(Italian Heavyweight Title)
1980
May   18—Giovanni De Luca, Naples ....L 12
Aug. 10—Lorenzo Zanon, Siderno ....L 8

LITO PENA
Filipino Lightweight
1978
Nov. 24—Oscar Barola, Manila ....D 10
1979
Feb. 16—Fel Viesca, Manila ....KO by 4
Apr. 30—Eddie Camero, Ilecos Sur ....W 10
June 29—Baby Art Alcantara, Manila ....W 10
Aug.   6—Salvador Darle, Quezon City ....KO 4
Oct.   5—Pete Alfferez, Manila ....KO 4
Dec. 21—Tony Flores, Quezon City ....W 12
1980
Feb. 23—Rod Delos Santos, Angeles City ....W 10

ALEK PENARSKI (PERNASKY)
British Light Heavyweight
1972
Dec.   4—Steve Foley, bedford ....KO by 3
1973
Mar. 27—Barry Clough, Birmingham ....W 6
Apr.   3—Nigel Williams, Blackpool ....L 6
Apr. 10—Johnny Wall, London................KO by 3
June   6—Lloyd Stewart, London..............KO by 4
Oct. 29—Pat Thompson, Walworth ....L 8
1974
Jan. 30—Gilly Baggott, Wolverhampton ....KO by 3
Mar. 19—Pat Thompson, Blackpool ....KO by 5
Oct. 29—Pat Thompson, London ....L 8
1975
Mar. 10—Len Britton, Nottingham...............W 6
Apr.   9—Len Britton, Bradford..................W 6
Oct. 15—Len Britton, Birmingham ....W 8
1976
Feb. 16—Francis Hands, Manchester ....L 6
Mar.   9—Randy Barratt, Bradford ....W 6
June   7—Danny McLoughlin, Manchester ....W 8
Oct. 25—Johnny Cox, Luton....................KO 7
1977
Jan. 31—Pat Thompson, London ....L 8
Feb.   7—Pat Thompson, Liverpool ....W 8
May   10—Bimbo Pearce, Merthyr ....W 8
Dec. 17—Freddie De Kerpel, Grivegnee ....L 10
1978
Jan. 30—Tim Wood, Cleethorpes ....W 8
Apr.   6—Harold Skog, Oslo ....L 8
Oct. 24—Francis Hands, Blackpool ....L 10
1979
Jan. 17—Hocine Tafer, Grenoble ....KO 5
June 18—Bonny McKenzie, Windsor ....D 8
Oct. 23—Chris Lawson, Blackpool ....KO by 5
Nov. 27—Carlton Benoit, Sheffield ....W 8
1980
Jan. 21—Danny Miller, Nottingham ....L disq. 5
Oct. 16—Liam Coleman, Bolton ....W 8

VERNON PENPRASE
British Featherweight
1978
May   23—Lee Graham, London ....W 6
July 10—Billy Rabbitt, Aberavon ....W 6
Sept. 18—Eric Wood, Mayfair ....L 6
Oct.   5—Alan Oag, Aberavon ....KO 5
Dec. 11—Najib Daho, Plymouth ....L 8
1979
Jan. 17—Lawrence Williams, Stoke ....W 6
Mar. 19—Glyn Davies, Haverfordwest ....W 8
Apr.   3—Lee Graham, Caerphilly ....W 8
May   13—Lee Graham, Plymouth ....W 8
June 13—Jeff Pritchard, Caerphilly ....W 8
July   5—Paul Keers, Aberavon ....W 8
Oct. 15—Lee Graham, Mayfair ....KO 6
Dec. 10—Terry McKeown, Torquay ....W 8
1980
Mar.   3—Paul Keers, London ....W 8
June   9—Paul Keers, Plymouth ....W 10
Aug. 12—George Sutton, Gowerton ....W 8

387

PABLO PEPITO
Filipino Junior Bantamweight
1979
July	13—Rolando Rosuento, Manila	W	10
Aug.	20—Salvador Perez, Quezon City	W	10
Oct.	5—Frank Cedeno, Manila	L	10
Dec.	21—Franco Torregosa, Quezon City	L	10

1980
Feb.	10—Peter Siscon, Quezon City	W	10

RAMON AVENAMAR PERALTA
Spanish Light Heavyweight
Born: Jan. 3, 1943, San Juan, Argentina
Residing in Spain
1965
June	5—Raul Diaz, Azul	KO	3
June	19—Angel Coria, Azul	KO	6
July	2—Rito Leiva, Azul	KO	3
Sept.	11—Nelson Valdez, Azul	KO	7
Oct.	9—Miguel Gonzalez, Azul	KO	6
Nov.	5—Marcos Bustos, Azul	KO	6
Nov.	20—Omar Peppi, Buenos Aires	KO	4
Dec.	4—Federal Magarinos, Azul	KO	6

1966
Feb.	4—Anibal Cordoba, Azul	W	10
Apr.	2—Marcelo Garnica, Azul	D	10
Apr.	23—Roberto Catabajal, Olavarria	KO	8
May	7—Natividad Orona, Azul	W	10
May	21—Gregorio Gomez, Azul	W	10
June	4—Omar Tisera, Azul	KO	8
June	18—Natividad Orona, Azul	KO	10
July	9—Ricardo Medina, Azul	KO	3
Aug.	6—Marcelo Garnica, Azul	W	10
Aug.	20—Anibal Cordoba, Tandil	W	10
Sept.	3—Gregorio Gomez, Azul	W	10
Sept.	17—Nelson Valdez, Dolores	KO	4
Oct.	8—Luis A. Pereyra, Azul	KO	4
Nov.	5—Rene Sosa, Azul	KO	5
Nov.	18—Gregorio Gomez, San Juan	KO	5
Dec.	16—Anibal Cordoba, San Juan	KO	7

1967
Mar.	4—Alberto Massi, Azul	KO	2
Mar.	17—Antonio Magaldi, San Nicolas	W disq.	8
May	6—Hugo Danielle, Azul	W	10
May	20—Marcelo Garnica, Tandil	W	10
July	12—Rafael Gargiulo, Buenos Aires	KO	8
Aug.	5—Bruno Segura, Azul	KO	3
Sept.	20—Marcelo Garnica, Buenos Aires	KO	4
Oct.	6—Bruno Segura, Paso de los Libres	KO	2
Oct.	21—Luiz Rosendo, Azul	KO	7
Nov.	4—Oscar Coria, Mar del Plata	KO	6

1968
Jan.	6—Jose Menno, Mar del Plata	D	10
Feb.	3—Jose Menno, Mar del Plata	D	10
Feb.	17—Roberto Veliz, Azul	KO	3
Apr.	3—Mario Tarsetti, Buenos Aires	KO	4
May	11—Igmacio Magallanes, Azul	KO	9
May	22—Santos Gimenez, Buenos Aires	L disq.	4
June	15—Miguel A. Paez, Mar del Plata	D	10
July	19—Henri Marquez, Mendoza	KO	4
Aug.	10—Renato Moares, Buenos Aires	KO	6
Sept.	14—Santos Gimenez, Buenos Aires	W disq.	3
Oct.	4—Jose Ferreyro, Trelew	KO	2
Oct.	30—Henri Marquez, Buenos Aires	KO	8
Nov.	23—Miguel Paez, Buenos Aires	W	12
Dec.	7—Oscar Wondrik, Azul	KO	5
Dec.	27—Enrique Mayo, La Plata	KO	4

1969
Feb.	1—Kurt Luedecke, Mar del Plata	KO	3
Mar.	3—Jose Menno, Mar del Plata	L	10
May	14—Jose Menno, Buenos Aires	W	12
July	17—Mario Loayza, Santa Rosa	KO	4
Aug.	1—Ramon Rocha, Rosario	D	10
Aug.	23—Luis Rozendo, Buenos Aires	KO	5
Sept.	12—Omar Woldrik, Cordoba	KO	3
Oct.	4—Ramon Rocha, Rivadavia	W	10
Oct.	8—Carlos Santagada, Olavarria	KO	4
Dec.	6—Vicente Ronbon, Buenos Aires	L	10

1970
Jan.	9—Angel Coria, Mar Plata	W	10
Mar.	28—Angel Coria, Mar Plata	KO	5
May	8—Juan Aguilar, Mendoza	KO	6
July	11—Eddie Jones, Buenos Aires	L	10
Aug.	22—Gabino Bay, Olavarria	KO	6
Oct.	9—Carlos Santagada, Cipoletti	KO	6
Nov.	28—Victor Galindez, Buenos Aires	W	15
	(Won Argentine Light Heavyweight Title)		

1971
Jan.	9—Victor Galindez, Buenos Aires	L	10
Mar.	20—Jorge Ahumada, Buenos Aires	L	10
June	11—Juan Aguilar, Mendoza	L	12
	(Lost Argentine Light Heavyweight Title)		
Aug.	25—Pedro Rimovski, Buenos Aires	KO	9

Sept.	11—Victor Galindez, Buenos Aires	KO	9
Oct.	20—Juan Aguilar, Buenos Aires	W	10
Dec.	18—Victor Galindez, Buenos Aires	W	10

1972
Jan.	15—Carlos Pouyannes, Tandil	NC	8
Apr.	1—Roberto Aguilar, Mar Plata	KO	6
Apr.	15—Eddie Jones, Mar Plata	W	10
Apr.	29—Juan Aguilar, Buenos Aires	W	12
	(Won Argentine Light Heavyweight Title)		
June	24—Jorge Ahumada, Buenos Aires	W	10
July	8—Ruben Gonzalez, Rosario	KO	6
Sept.	2—Victor Galindez, Buenos Aires	L	12
	(Lost Argentine Light Heavyweight Title)		
Oct.	7—Victor Galindez, Buenos Aires	L	12
	(For South American Light Heavyweight Title)		
Nov.	10—Jorge Ahumada, Mendoza	KO by	5

1973
Jan.	19—Raul Loyola, Buenos Aires	L	10
Mar.	2—Charlie Green, Berlin	W	10
Apr.	6—Eddie Patterson, Hamburg	KO	3
May	13—Christian Poncelet, Kiel	KO	5
Sept.	21—Ba Sounkalo, Hamburg	W	10
Oct.	26—Angel Paez, Koeln	KO	5
Nov.	9—Hartmut Sasse, Berlin	W	8

1974
Jan.	12—Billy Suze, Madrid	W	8
Feb.	8—Ba Sounkalo, Frankfurt	KO	3
Feb.	15—Carlo Clementi, Luebeck	KO	2
Feb.	20—Ngozika Ekwelum, Berlin	W	10
May	14—Jean Tshikuna, Graz	KO	2
Aug.	7—Maxie Smith, Wien	KO	3
Oct.	14—Rudi Lubbers, Rotterdam	LF	3
Dec.	10—Kilani Ramdani, Offenbach	KO	3

1975
Jan.	7—Kilani Ramdani, Wien	KO	5
Jan.	18—Ray Anderson, Hamburg	KO	8
Jan.	31—Ruediger Schmidtke, Hamburg	KO	4
Mar.	1—Conny Valensek, Koeln	KO	8
Mar.	18—Horace Hal Carrol, Wien	W	10
Apr.	4—Eddie Duncan, Hamburg	KO	7
May	30—Tom Bethea, Hamburg	KO by	3
Sept.	6—Bernd August, Berlin	KO	3
Sept.	12—Ray Anderson, Offenbach	D	10

1976
Jan.	16—Tom Bethea, Berlin	D	10
May	22—Pierre Fourie, Johannesburg	L	10
June	17—Tony Green, Berlin	D	8
Oct.	21—Harald Skog, Oslo	W	8
Oct.	29—Horst Lang, Koeln	KO	2

1977
Feb.	28—Billy Aird, Luton	WF	5
Apr.	1—Gregory Downes, Koeln	KO	7
Apr.	28—Ennio Cometti, Muenchen	D	8
May	20—Leo Kakolewicz, Hannover	D	10
June	2—Mustapha Wasajja, Randers	D	6
Oct.	31—Hennie Thoonen, Rotterdam	W	10

1978
Feb.	17—Tony Moore, Madrid	D	8
May	6—Negritillo Lozano, Madrid	KO	4
May	20—Sugar Silex, La Coruna	W	8
Sept.	5—Aldo Traversaro, Venice	D	15
	(European Light Heavyweight Title)		
Nov.	6—Alex Cardozo, La Coruna	KO	7
Dec.	2—Felipe Rodriguez, Pontevedra	KO by	4

1979
Mar.	4—Lorenzo Zanon, San Remo	L	8
Apr.	28—Alfio Righetti, Rimini	L	10
July	20—Jose Antonio Galvez, Benidorm	W	8
Aug.	25—Tony Moore, La Coruna	L	8
Oct.	6—Jose Antonio Galvez, Bilbao	W	8
Oct.	13—Faustino Quinales, S. Sebastiano	D	8
Dec.	25—Jean Pierre Coopman, Izegem	W	10

1980
Feb.	28—Mustapha Wassajja, Odense	L	8
Aug.	8—Alex Cardozo, Madrid	W	10
	(Retained Spanish Light Heavyweight Title)		
Aug.	29—Alex Cardozo, Melilla	W	10
	(Retained Spanish Light Heavyweight Title)		

CLAUDIO PEREYRA
French Welterweight
1980
Sept.	3—Franco Aresti, Santa Teresa	D	8
Sept.	19—Marzio Baseotti, San Dona	D	6
Oct.	4—Jacques Benchetrit, Nice	L	8
Oct.	31—Franco Aresti, Cagliari	D	8
Nov.	29—Spartaco Verna, Marsala	W	6
Dec.	5—Vittorio Conte, Massa	W	8

VINCENZO PESAPANE
Italian Heavyweight
1976
Oct.	15—Antimo Tescione, Piacenza	W	6
Oct.	28—Angelo Visini, Milan	KO	1

388

Nov. 19—Coulibaly Demba, Piacenza .... W 6
Dec. 3—Ferruccio Mazzardi, Milan .... KO 4
Dec. 25—Jean Belval, Piacenza .... KO 4
1977
Feb. 19—Ferruccio Mazzardi, Milan .... W 6
Mar. 11—Danny Machado, Milan .... KO 4
Apr. 29—Dominico Scala, Bologna .... W 8
June 24—Jose Antonio Galvez, Podenzano .... W 8
Sept. 9—Georg Butzbach, Muenchen .... KO by 3
1978
Mar. 3—Domenico Scala, Piacenza .... W 6
1979
Nov. 9—Fausto Costantino, Pianceza .... KO 2
1980
Feb. 8—Vasco Faustino, Piacenza .... W 8
Apr. 11—Piermario Baruzzi, Piacenza .... KO 6
Dec. 26—Domenico Adinolfi, Piacenza .... KO by 9

ANDREW PETERSON
South African Bantamweight
1979
Mar. 3—Samuel Serekego, Virginia .... W 4
May 12—Samuel Serekego, Virginia .... L 4
June 16—Johannes Phumo, Virginia .... W 4
Aug. 4—Johannes Phumo, Odendaalsrust .... W 4
Nov. 17—Edward Nzimande, Ficksburg .... KO 3
Dec. 1—Simon Mafere, Odenaalsrust .... W 6
1980
May 10—Jacob Molefe, Virginia .... L 6
June 7—Johannes Phumo, Odenaalsrust .... W 4

TERRY PETERSON
British Welterweight
Born: July 10, 1951
1975
May 5—Tom Howard, Piccadilly .... KO 2
May 19—Hughie Clarke, Piccadilly................ W 8
June 10—Barton McAllister, London.............. W 8
June 24—Hugh Clarke, London.................... W 8
Sept. 8—Johnny Wall, London.................... L 8
Oct. 20—Brian Jones, London .... L 8
Oct. 27—Barton McAllister, London .... W 6
Dec. 2—Jess Harper, Leeds...................... W 10
1976
Jan. 26—Hugh Smith, Glasgow .... W 8
Feb. 9—Gordon Kirk, London .... L 8
Apr. 12—Hugh Smith, Birmingham .... W 8
May 10—Jim Montague, London .... W 8
May 17—Billy Waith, Glasgow....................L 8
June 19—Dirk vander Westhuizen, Pretoria .... L 8
Sept. 27—Gordon Kirk, London .... L 12
Oct. 25—Jess Harper, London..................... KO 7
Nov. 2—Colin Powers, London................. KO by 4
Nov. 24—Jeff Gale, London .... W 12
1977
Feb. 19—Alois Carmeliet, Zele .... KO by 5
Apr. 4—Henry Rhiney, Luton .... KO by 7
June 13—Johnny Pincham, London .... W 8
June 16—John Smith, Glasgow .... D 8
Oct. 5—Louis Acaries, Paris .... L 10
Dec. 6—Chris Glover, Leeds .... W 12
1978
Jan. 31—Peter Neal, Marylebone .... L 8
Feb. 23—Mike Copp, Doncaster .... D 8
Apr. 15—Fred Coranson, Dunkerque .... KO by 8
Sept. 14—Hans Henrik Palm, Randers .... L 8
Nov. 13—Charley Malarkey, Galsgow .... L 8
1979
Jan. 23—Ray Varden, London .... KO by 8
Feb. 19—Chris Glover, London .... KO 6
Mar. 5—Carl Bailey, Barnsley .... L 8
Dec. 17—Lee Hartshorn, Bradford .... L 8
1980
Feb. 4—Joey Singleton, Hammersmith .... L 10
(Lost Central Area Welterweight Title)
June 1—Dennis Sullivan, Plymouth .... L 8

GARY PETTY
British Welterweight
1980
Apr. 21—Don Hughs, Glasgow .... KO 4
Apr. 29—Dave Aspill, London ....W 6
June 16—Gerry McGrath, London .... KO by 1
Sept. 9—Kevin Durkin, Mexborough .... KO by 5

KENNETH PHELE
South African Featherweight
1978
Mar. 3—Howard Motumi, Krugersdorp .... D 6
Apr. 15—Sibongya Zitumane, Butterworth .... W 6
May 26—Johannes Steyn, Johannesburg .... KO 2
1979
Mar. 5—Pieter Swanepoel, Welkom .... W 4

1980
Mar. 1—Bungili Sovili, East London .... W 6
Oct. 31—Enoch Mazibuku, Springs .... W 4

JOHANNES PHUMO
South African Junior Flyweight
1978
Oct. 7—Martin Nkokoto, Virginia ....L 4
1979
Feb. 10—Samuel Koalepe, Virginia .... D 4
Mar. 3—Simon Mafere, Virginia .... KO by 3
June 16—Andrew Peterson, Virginia .... L 4
Aug. 4—Andrew Peterson, Odendaalsrust .... L 4
Sept. 1—Michael Khuto, Ficksburg .... L 6
1980
Mar. 1—Israel Papane, Odendaalsrust .... L 6
June 7—Andrew Peterson, Odendaalsrust .... L 4
Oct. 11—John Matsabu, Odendaalsrust .... W 6

SEVERINO PICCA
Italian Junior Lightweight
1977
Oct. 21—Giovannino Mannu, Piacenza .... WF 4
Nov. 16—Gianfranco Cianconi, Piacenza .... KO 2
1978
Mar. 3—Luigi De Rosa, Piacenza .... KO 5
Mar. 31—Raimondo Riccio, Milan .... L 6
May 12—Antonio Germano, Piacenza .... W 6
1979
May 25—Andrea Ricci, Piacenza .... WF 4
Nov. 9—Antonio Sandrin, Piacenza .... W 6
1980
Apr. 11—Antonio Pocai, Piacenza .... KO 2
Dec. 26—Carlo Frassinetti, Piacenza .... W 8

MIKE PICKETT
British Featherweight
1977
Oct. 19—Walter Angliss, Kingston .... L 8
Dec. 14—Walter Angliss, Kingston .... L 8
1978
(Inactive)
1979
Nov. 19—Steve Cleak, Ebbw Vale .... L 6
Dec. 10—Alan Story, Birmingham .... L 6
1980
Mar. 4—Gary Nickels, London .... L 6
Mar. 11—Steve Topliss, Nantwich .... L 6

DOMINIQUE PIEDELEU
French Bantamweight
1978
Nov. 10—Robert Huylebroeck, Ouistream .... W 6
1979
Jan. 26—Georges Lietaer, Caen .... W 8
Mar. 2—Jean Jacques Souris, Coutances .... L 8
Apr. 20—Nessim Zebellini, Ouistream .... W 8
Oct. 10—Paolo Castrovilli, Torino .... KO by 2
Dec. 8—Antonio Franca, Calais .... W 8
1980
Jan. 28—Roy Somers, Rotterdam .... L 8
Feb. 8—Salvatore Laconi, Caen .... KO 4
Apr. 10—Dominique Cesari, Caen .... L 10

BIAGIO PIERRI
Italian Lightweight
1974
Mar. 9—Vincenzo Di Ruocco, Cinisello Balsamo... KO 1
May 4—Fulvio Giacomini, Cinisello Balsamo...... W 6
May 17—Salvatore Dui, Milan.................... WF 5
Oct. 29—Pasquale Arini, Cantu .... KO 2
Nov. 29—Prisco Rosetti, Milan .... KO 2
1975
Jan. 3—Domenico Radicioni, Milan .... D 6
Feb. 1—Enzo Saltrelli, Cinsello Balsamo.......... W 6
Apr. 18—Giuseppe Agate, Milano .... W 6
May 9—Jose Sanchez, Milan .... D 8
June 6—Vincenzo Quero, Milan.................. D 7
Aug. 13—Gianfranco Cianconi, Taranto .... WF 4
Nov. 14—Giuseppe Mura, Milan.................. L 8
1976
Mar. 12—Giuseppe Agate, Milan.................. W 8
June 11—Fulvio Giacomini, Milan................. W 8
Oct. 22—Palmiro Masala, Milan............... KO by 4
1977
Mar. 9—Salvatore Liscapade, Rieti ....L 12
(Italian Junior Lightweight Title)
Apr. 29—Renzo Battistelli, Cinicello .... W 8
July 2—Ugo Poli, Cinicello .... W 8
Oct. 28—Emiliano De Souza, Milan .... KO 8
1978
Jan. 21—Carlo Frassinetti, Ciniello Salsamo ...... W 12
(Italian Junior Lightweight Title)

389

Apr. 14—Aristide Pizzo, Milan .... KO by 8
       (Italian Junior Lightweight Title)
July 8—Natale Caredda, Forte Village .... L 8
Oct. 20—Brian Schofield, Milan .... KO by 6
1979
June 23—Abass Macauley, Ciniselle Balsama ..... W 8
1980
Feb. 9—Gregorio Ciancaglione, Cinisello .... W 8
July 24—Giovanni Carrino, Taranto .... L 8
Oct. 24—Giovanni Vitello, Grossetto .... KO 5

GIAMPIERO PINNA
Italian Flyweight
1980
Mar. 21—Roberto D'Aula, Bologna .... KO 1
May 22—Salvatore Laconi, Bologna .... ND 5

GIORGIO PIPIA
Italian Junior Lightweight
1979
Nov. 10—Pietro Donati, Odolo .... W 6
Dec. 26—Vincenzo Morana, Cremona .... W 6
1980
Jan. 16—Vicenzo Morana, Cremona .... W 6
Mar. 7—Pasquale Massa, Brescia .... L 6
Oct. 31—Guiseppe Tidu, Cagliari .... L 6

PIERANGELO PIRA
Italian Welterweight
1976
Nov. 3—Nicola D'Orazio, Pesaro .... W 6
Nov. 19—Giancarlo Serangeli, Milano .... KO 3
Dec. 18—Angelo Tomasini, Rimini .... W 6
1977
Jan. 28—Luigi Martello, Faenza .... W 6
Mar. 5—Nicola Marocco, Rimimi .... W 6
Apr. 1—Abdul Ali Kaya, Bologna .... KO 2
Apr. 23—Augusto Lauri, Rimini .... W 6
May 7—Piero Ceru, Rimini .... KO by 3
1978
May 5—Jean Pierre Moreau, Latina .... KO 2
July 19—Sergio D'Angelo, Bellaria .... KO 1
Sept. 5—Jose Luis Ribeiro, bibione .... W 8
Oct. 28—Giuseppe Russi, Riccione .... KO 4
Nov. 24—Remo Costa, rimini .... W 8
1979
Feb. 4—Luiz Ribeiro, Rimini .... W 6
Mar. 17—Angelo Fanciullo, Rimini .... KO 2
Apr. 28—Manuel Lira, Rimini .... W 8
July 25—Gianni Milesini, Rimini .... KO 5
       (Italian Welterweight Title)
Sept. 29—Antonio Torsello, Rimini .... KO 6
Nov. 14—Remo Costa, Gualdo Tadino .... WF 9
       (Italian Welterweight Title)
1980
Feb. 1—Giuseppe De Padova, Mantova .... KO 9
       (Retained Italian Welterweight Title)
Oct. 24—Antonio Torsello, Grosseto .... KO 3
       (Retained Italian Welterweight Title)
Dec. 26—Mario Redi, Piacenza .... L 6

GIAMPAOLO PIRAS
Dutch Middleweight
1972
Mar. 3—Karl Furcht, Koeln .... W 6
Mar. 23—Kurt Hombach, Offenbach .... L 6
Apr. 3—Randolph Hombach, Berlin .... L 6
July 7—Randolph Hombach, Fulda .... KO by 3
Sept. 9—Johann Orsolics, Lustenau .... KO by 1
Oct. 30—Tommy Van Hatten, Rotterdam ...... KO by 2
1973
Nov. 10—Joseph Pachler, Wien .... L 6
Dec. 11—Piercarlo Pedrinelli, Wien .... L 6
1974
Feb. 7—Lauritz Jensen, Copenhagen .... KO by 3
Apr. 12—Evariste Mukendi, La Louviere .... L 6
June 7—Klaus Fuchs, Wien .... KO 6
Oct. 4—Herbert Trausmith, Leoben .... L 6
Nov. 5—Cemal Kamaci, Berlin .... KO by 4
1975
Feb. 8—Jean Simos, Liege................... L 8
Mar. 1—Burhan Yelsibag, Koeln .... D 4
May 6—Herbert Trausmith, Vienna .... D 8
May 30—Ethem Ozakalin, Koln .... L 6
June 14—Dieter Klay, Berlin .... L 6
Sept. 6—Jorg Eipel, Berlin .... L 4
Sept. 12—Ethem Ozakalin, Offenbach .... L 6
Sept. 26—Joerg Eipel, Ketsch .... L 6
Dec. 14—Esperno Postl, Koeflach .... L 6
1976
Feb. 6—Fredo Roelands, Bruges.............. L 8
Mar. 6—Phillippe Girottix, Yvetot .... KO by 2
May 1—Fredo Roelands, Zele .... L 8

May 29—Franz Hohl, Lienz.................... L 8
June 11—Frank Albertus, Berlin .... KO by 1
Oct. 29—Mi Whan Ki, Cologne.................. W 4
Nov. 6—Pol Payen, Marchienne .... L 6
Nov. 29—Adrie Huussen, Nieuwegein .... L 8
Dec. 4—Georg Steinherr, Hamburg .... L 4
Dec. 12—Etham Oezakalin, berlin .... L 6
1977
Jan. 15—Mehmet Besli, Kiel .... D 4
Apr. 1—Mehmet Besli, Koeln .... L 8
Apr. 30—Dirk Declercq, Lauwe .... L 8
May 28—Jose Luis Ribeiro, Koeln .... D 8
July 9—Kassongo Mukandjo, Basel .... KO by 4
Sept. 30—Erwin Heiber, Hamburg .... L 4
Oct. 7—Kadir Yuceler, Istanbul .... D 10
Nov. 26—Hans Ermin, Hamburg .... D 6
1978
Feb. 25—Eric Caposella, La Louviere .... L 6
Mar. 20—Bernardo Bonizzonai, Mantova .... L 8
Mar. 24—Stephane Vert Pre, Waremme .... L 6
Apr. 14—Jirgen Gries, Essen .... L 6
July 7—Esperno Postl, Wels .... W 8
Sept. 23—Helmut Baumann, Haiger .... L 6
Oct. 14—Josef Kossman, Koblenz .... L 10
Dec. 15—Josef Kossman, Asbach .... L 10
Dec. 19—Klaus Fuchs, Dusseldorf .... L 8
Dec. 31—Esperno Postl, Seewalchen .... L 6
1979
Jan. 27—Mike McCoy, Koblenz .... D 6
Apr. 22—Ruediger Bitterling, Hamburg .... L 8
June 16—Josef Kossman, Koblenz .... L 8
July 6—Nazif Biberovic, Waidhofen .... KO by 4
Sept. 22—Maurice Bufi, Roeulx .... KO by 6
Dec. 1—Andre Monglema, Bonnevoie .... L 6
1980
Jan. 18—Paul Payen, La Louviere .... D 6
Feb. 22—Reiner Kober, Dusseldorf .... L 4
Mar. 22—Horst Schulze, Friedewald .... L 6
June 7—Agamil Yilderim, Cologne .... KO by 2

EMILIO PIREDDU
French Flyweight
Turned Pro 1970. Record to 1972—Total Bouts 5,
Won 3, Lost 0, Drew 2.
1972
June 9—Giovanni Mura, Pistoia .... L 6
July 29—Altero Marini, Carbonia .... W 8
Dec. 8—Giovanni Mura, Cagliari .... W 10
Dec. 29—Michele Spina, Cagliari .... W 8
1973
Apr. 4—Giancarlo Anibaldi, Cagliari .... KO 5
June 15—Luigi Paravati, Milan.................. W 6
Aug. 15—Franco Sperati, Sassari .... W 12
       (Italian Flyweight Title)
Nov. 25—Fritz Chervet, Zurich .... W 8
Dec. 28—Grazietto Soro, Cagliari............... KO 3
1974
Mar. 1—Waldino Lopez, Milano................. W 8
June 12—Antonio Tenza, Porto Torres .... KO 8
Aug. 31—Heriberto Mascarell, Alghero .... W 10
1975
Mar. 8—Altero Marini, Cagliari .... W 8
Apr. 19—Big Jim West, Melbourne.................. L 10
June 20—Antonio Franca, Milan.................. W 8
Sept. 13—Altero Marini, Pula.................. KO 6
Nov. 29—Adolfo Osses, Cagliari.................. L 8
1976
Aug. 13—Franco Buglione, Alhero .... KO 8
       (Italian Flyweight Title)
Oct. 15—Nessim Zebilini, Cagliari .... W 8
1977
July 30—Mario De Prosperis, Sassari .... KO 7
Aug. 13—Tarcisio Boi, Alghero .... W 8
Oct. 7—Antonio Franca, Capua .... D 8
Dec. 24—Franco Udella, Cagliari .... L 15
       (European Flyweight Title)
1978
July 29—Giovanni Camputaro, Piedimonte .... L 12
       (Lost Italian Flyweight Title)
1979
May 25—Claudio Tanda, Cagliari .... KO 5
1980
Feb. 7—Steve Muchoki, Randers .... L 8
July 6—Paolo Castrovilli, Fort Village .... L 12
       (For Italian Flyweight Title)

ANTONIO PISANI
Italian Flyweight
1978
May 12—Vincenzo DiBari, Imola .... D 6
June 23—Michele DeMita, Foggia .... L 6
Sept. 29—Pietro Candidda, Imola .... W 6
Nov. 30—Andrea Ricci, Calolziocorte .... L 6
Dec. 18—Giovanni Scarpati, Lecco .... W 4

Dec.   18—Pietro Candidda, Lecco ....KO   4
1979
July   1—Lorenzo Paciullo, Merano L   6
Oct.   19—Fabio Mannai, Caliari L   6
1980
Mar.   29—Fabrizio Saraullo, Chieti L   6
Apr.   18—Renzo Mannai, Bologna ....D   6

PALMIRO PIZZATA
Italian Lightweight
1978
Nov.   17—Bruno Simili, Val d'Elsa L   6
Dec.   9—Angelo Bizzara, Caserta ....KO by   5
1979
June   22—Alfredo Raininger, Savona L   6
1980
Mar.   8—Giuseppe Tidu, Calgari L   6
Apr.   11—Giuseppe Ballone, Modena L   6

ARISTIDE PIZZO
Italian Lightweight
1975
Jan.   3—Paul Ikumapayi, Milan ....KO by   3
Feb.   7—Almo Quaini, Milan...................KO   2
May   9—Valerio Fretta, Milan...................KO   1
June   6—Salvatore Mannu, Milan................KO   3
July   19—Fulvio Giacomini, Paullo.................W   6
Oct.   10—Giuseppe Pappalardo, Milan ....KO   1
Oct.   24—Abu Arrow, Milan.......................W   6
Dec.   12—Augusto Quadri, Milan ....W   6
Dec.   26—Giovanni Cavazzini, Milan ....W   6
1976
May   14—Gianfranco Bulla, Milano.................D   6
July   3—Giovanni Cavazzini, Paullo...............W   8
Sept. 24—Guiseppe Agate, Milan ....KO   4
Dec.   3—Giancafranco Cianconi, Milan ....KO   3
1977
Feb.   26—Renzo Battistelli, Caltagirone ....W   8
May   6—Gregorio Ciancaglioni, Milan ....WF   5
May   20—Gregorio Ciancaglione, Milano ....WF   5
June   10—Domenico Condello, Milan ....KO   4
Oct.   28—Giuseppe Agate, Milan ....W   8
Nov.   25—Ugo Poli, Milano ....KO   5
1978
Apr.   14—Biagio Pierri, Milan ....KO   8
       (Italian Junior Lightweight Title)
June   9—Carlo Frassinetti, Milan ....KO   2
July   6—Carlos Dos Santos, Lugo di Romagna ....KO   7
Sept. 28—Salvatore Liscapade, Milan ....KO   3
       (Italian Junior Lightweight Title)
Dec.   17—Giuseppe Agate, Lecco ....W   8
1979
Nov.   23—Giuseppe Agate, Perdenone ....WF   6
Dec.   14—Cesimo Lavino, Milan ....KO   6
       (Italian Junior Lightweight Title)
1980
Mar.   14—Jerome Artis, Milan ....L 10
May   30—Franco Siddu, Florence ....W 12
       (Won Italian Lightweight Title)
Nov.   29—Carlos Hernandez, Marsales ....KO by   7
       (For European Flyweight Title)

HERBERT PLAATJIES
South African Featherweight
1979
Sept.   5—Chris Whiteboy, Cape Town L   4
Nov.   12—Tertius Skalika, Cape Town ....W   4
Dec.   19—Sam Williams, Cape Town L   4
1980
Jan.   14—Monde Sibaca, Cape Town ....W   6
Feb.   8—Zola Lawuse, Cape Town ....W   6
Mar.   3—Victor Mpiyakhe, Cape Town ....W   6
Apr.   5—Zola Lawuse, East London ....L 10
       (For Cape Featherweight Title)
Oct.   15—Sipho Mange, Cape Town L   8

JOSHUA PLAATJIES
South African Lightweight
1976
Jan.   29—May Jacobs, Guguletu ....W   6
Mar.   1—Gladman Koni, Guguletu ....KO   3
Mar.   22—Daniel Makhudu, Guguletu ....W   8
1977
       (Inactive)
1978
Feb.   22—Bramley Whiteboy, Cape Town L   6
Apr.   17—Alfred Sibisi, Johannasburg ....D   4
July   31—Petrus Karsterns, Capetown ....KO   4
Nov.   15—Lucas Hickman, Capetown ....KO   2
1979
Nov.   1'—ZoLa Lawuse, Cape Town ....W   6
1980
Jan.   14—Bramley Whiteboy, Cape Town ....KO by   1
June   4—Phindile Ndilele, Goodwood ....W   6

ANTONIO POCAI
Italian Welterweight
1974
Dec.   20—Salvatore Canu, Sassari L   6
1975
Mar.   8—Alvaro Checche, Cagliari ....WF   4
Mar.   8—Alessandro Nardi, Cagliari L   4
Mar.   28—Alessandro Nardi Rome L   6
May   9—Salvatore Melluzo, Milano L   6
June   27—Alessandro Bini, Grassina ....D   6
July   15—Domenico Condello, Pistoia ....D   6
Nov.   29—Natale Caredda, Cagliari L   6
Dec.   26—Luigi zanghi, Lugo L   8
1976
Feb.   20—Giuseppe Pappalardo, Pistoia ....D   6
Mar.   19—Michele Luzolanu, Gand L   6
Apr.   30—Giuliano Lonzi, Livorno L   6
Nov.   27—Pellegrino Ventrone, Salerno ....KO by   4
1977
May   21—Antonio germano, Pisa ....W   6
June   10—Fulvio Giacomini, Senigallia L   8
July   8—Pasqualino Morbidelli, Viterbo L   6
Oct.   1—Franco benes, Monfalcone L   6
Oct.   21—Abass Macauley, Piacenza L   6
Nov.   12—Rosario Pomponi, Ostia L   6
Dec.   30—Nunzio Sanna, Lecco L   6
1978
       (Inactive)
1979
Oct.   4—Bruno Simili, Firenze ....KO by   5
Dec.   28—Fabio Mannai, Cagliari L   6
1980
Jan.   17—Fabio Mannai, Genova L   6
Feb.   15—Luciano Frasca, Nettuno L   6
Feb.   29—Giancarlo Compiani, Cremona L   6
Mar.   15—Lorenzo Paciullo, Brindisi L   6
Apr.   11—Severino Picca, Piacenza ....KO by   2

ALDO POLESEL
Italian Middleweight
1978
Nov.   24—Giuseppe Cola, Mantova ....KO   2
Dec.   26—Karimu Kijg, Mantova ....KO by   5
1979
May   12—Giancarlo Marinelli, Frosinone ......KO by   4
Dec.   26—Aldo Buzzetti, Piacenza ....KO by   2
1980
Mar.   28—Mario Loreni, Ponte Priula ....D   6
Apr.   12—Mario Loreni, Seregno L   6
Oct.   25—Luciano Bomben, Pordenone L   8

STEVE POLLARD
British Featherweight
1980
Apr.   28—Brindley Jones, London ....W   6
May   27—Pat Mallon, Glasgow ....W   6
June   2—Andy Thomas, London ....W   6
Oct.   2—Eddie Glass, Hull ....W   6
Nov.   3—Rocky Bantleman, London ....KO   2

BRUNO POLLONI
Italian Light Heavyweight
1973
Mar.   2—Ivan Matekovic, Cecina L   6
Apr.   14—Franco Feligioni, Ravenna L   6
Nov.   24—Ferruccio Mazzardi, Brescia ....KO by   4
1974
Mar.   1—Jose Maver, Udine ....W   6
Apr.   6—Christian Moussoux, Cointe L   8
May   11—Salko Brkic, Trieste ....D   6
Aug.   2—Ferruccio Mazzardi, Toscalano ....KO by   3
1975
Mar.   28—Ezechiele Fanti, Bologna L   6
Apr.   12—Raffaele Maio, Como L   6
May   31—Francois Fiol, Ginerva L   6
July   4—Salko Brkic, Trieste ....W   6
Oct.   30—Faustino Quinales, Milano ....KO by   6
1976
Sept. 30—Ezzechiello Fanti, R. Emilia L   6
1977
Jan.   28—Cristiano Cavina, Faenza L   6
May   6—Giuseppe Rizzo, Civitanova L   6
June   2—Rinaldo Pelizzari, Lumezzane ....KO by   5
Oct.   15—Gino Freo, Sottomarina L   6
Dec.   3—Renzo Trevisan, Montecchio ....KO by   3
1978
Jan.   28—Franco Saputo, Veroli ....D   6
Apr.   16—Lino Lemma, Palestrina L   8
June   8—Germano Apostoli, Brescia L   8
Nov.   18—Gino Freo, Rovigo L   8
Dec.   1—Daniele Laghi, Faenza ....KO by   1
1979
May   19—Andrea Sangalletti, Crema ....KO by   4

391

1980

May 18—Pasquale Rippa, Naples .... KO by 4

CHRISTIAN PONCELET
French Heavyweight
Born, June 16, 1947, Asfled
1969
Nov. 15—Alain Cherville, Sedan .... KO 3
1970
Jan. 3—Manfred Ackers, Sedan .... WF 3
Mar. 14—Burghard Lembke, Sedan .... W 8
Apr. 11—Manfred Ackers, Sedan .... W 6
June 13—Henri Ferjules, Sedan .... D 8
Nov. 16—Expedit Mountcho, Paris................ KO 7
Dec. 19—Henri Ferjules, Charleville.............. KO 3
(Won French Light Heavyweight Title)
1971
Jan. 11—Vasco Fausthino, Paris .... W 8
Feb. 22—Lloyd Walford, Paris .... KO 7
Mar. 6—Buíghard Lembke, Sedan .... W 8
Apr. 3—Ireno Verleman, Charleville .... KO 6
Oct. 16—Ba Sounkalo, Charleville .... KO by 4
Dec. 11—Jean Tshikuna, Charleville.............. D 10
1972
Jan. 8—John Roy, Charleville.................. KO by 3
Jan. 31—Jan Lubbers, Rotterdam................. L 10
Feb. 12—Kurt Ludecke, Charleville .... W 10
Mar. 3—Arno Prick, Hamburg .... L 8
Mar. 25—Ferenc Kristofcsak, Charleville.......... KO 7
May 19—Dante Cane, Reggio Emilia .... KO by 4
Dec. 4—James Helwig, Paris.................... KO by 1
Dec. 21—Getulio Bueno, Ajaccio................. W 10
1973
May 13—Avenamar Peralta, Kiel .... KO by 5
Sept. 29—Jean-Claude Capitolin, Paris .... L 12
(French Light Heavyweight Title)
Dec. 15—Horst Lang, Sedan .... W 10
1974
Jan. 12—Tino Rimasti, Sedan.................... KO 5
Feb. 16—Jean Tshikuna, Sedan.................. W 10
May 11—Robert Amory, St. Quentin.............. W 12
(French Light Heavyweight Title)
Sept. 21—Jean Claude Capitolin, St. Nazaire ...... KO 10
(French Light Heavyweight Title)
Nov. 22—Arno Pryx, Charlville .... W 10
1975
Jan. 4—Andre Bukasa, Charleville-Mezieres ..... KO 4
Apr. 5—Jannick Defour, Calais .... KO 6
May 31—Hans-Dieter Schwartz, Charleville .... KO 7
1976
Jan. 3—Sjimmy Verstappen, Charleville.......... W 10
Feb. 28—Jean Claude Capitolin, Charleville .... KO 1
Apr. 3—Arno Prick, Reims..................... W 8
May 15—Miguel Angel Paez, Charleville.......... W 10
Dec. 4—Jan Lubbers, Charleville................ W 10
1977
Jan. 28—Robert Amory, Compiegne .... L 12
(French Light Heavyweight Title)
Mar. 5—Mate Parlov, Velenje .... L 10
Apr. 2—Ivan Matekovic, St. Quentin .... L 10
June 17—Alfredo Evangelista, Madrid .... KO by 3
Oct. 15—Yannick Dufore, Charleville .... KO 9
(French Light Heavyweight Title)
Dec. 5—Sylvain Watbled, Paris .... KO by 3
1978
Jan. 14—Kassango, Charleville .... W 8
Feb. 18—Lassine Niare, Charleville .... W 8
Apr. 1—Albert Syben, Bruxelles .... L 8
Apr. 28—Lucien Rodriguez, Charleville........ KO by 7
(French Heavyweight Title)
Sept. 18—Lester Stevens, Reading .... L 8
Oct. 29—Felipe Rodriquez, Pontevedra .... W 8
Dec. 4—Neil Malpass, Marton .... KO by 3
1979
May 12—Gerald Bois, Vivier .... W 12
May 28—Henry Theonen, Amsterdam .... L 8
Nov. 5—Lucien Rodriguez, Paris .... L 12
(French Heavyweight Title)
1980
Jan. 26—Rudi Gauwe, Zele .... L 10
Mar. 29—Milo Popovic, Differdange .... L 8

ESPERNO POSTL
Austrian Welterweight
Born: Dec. 10, 1951
1971
Dec. 10—Angelo Tomasini, Vienna .... W 4
1972
July 22—Young Griffo, Gmunden .... KO by 3
Oct. 5—Hans Heukeshoven, Vienna .... W 6
Oct. 31—Horst Kelbassa, Vienna................. W 6
Nov. 24—Joachim Trautwein, Vienna.............. W 6
1973
July 7—Joachim Trautwein, Wels .... W 6

Sept. 12—Klaus Fuchs, Vienna.................... D 6
Nov. 6—Jaroslav Travnik, Vienna................ W 6
Dec. 14—Klaus Steinmetz, Vienna................ W 4
1974
Feb. 1—Kurt Hombach, Vienna .... W 6
Apr. 9—Klaus Jacoby, Graz.................... W 8
May 14—Jo Sossou, Graz .... W 8
June 7—Mickey Flynn, Vienna.................. KO 7
Oct. 10—Pietro Gasparri, Leoben................. W 8
Nov. 30—Frank Medina, Munich................. D 6
1975
Apr. 18—Mi Whan Ki, Vienna .... W 8
May 5—Andre Holyk, Vienna .... L 10
June 21—Miguel Velazquez, Berling.............. L 8
Dec. 14—Gianpaolo Piras, Koflach............... W 6
1976
Jan. 30—Young Griffo, Vienna.................. KO 7
Apr. 16—Bruno Freschi, Udine.............. KO by 9
Sept. 25—Hans Joachim Trautwein, Lienz.......... W 6
1977
Aug. 13—Guido Galleti, Zeltweg .... W 8
Oct. 7—Klaus Fuchs, Vienna .... W 6
Dec. 7—Pascal Zito, Dornbirn .... D 8
1978
Mar. 18—Alain Marion, Creil .... L 10
July 7—Gianpaolo Piras, Wels .... W 8
Oct. 29—Fritz Kremslehner, Vienna.............. W 6
Nov. 28—Mick Mills, Sheffield .... KO by 2
Dec. 31—Giampaolo Piras, Seewalchen .... W 6
1979
Jan. 19—Boro Jovic, Wien .... W 6
Apr. 7—Jose Luis Ribeiro, Waidhofen .... W 8
Apr. 21—Libero Moi, Ostia .... L 8
Oct. 20—Josef Kossmann, Gansbacher .... W 6
Oct. 29—Jose Luis Ribeiro, Wien .... W 8
Nov. 15—Claude Kalanda, Eggenburg .... KO 5
Nov. 30—Antonio Torsello, Chavannes .... L 10
Dec. 7—Frank Wissenbach, Lubeck .... L 8
1980
Apr. 25—Giuseppe Di Padova, Mantova .... KO by 7
June 12—Jorgen Hansen, Randers .... KO by 7

BERTIE POTGIETER
South African Light Heavyweight
1980
Feb. 4—Themba Buthelezi, Durban .... KO by 2
Apr. 28—Alfred Myandu, Durban .... KÖ 1
Aug. 4—Jonas Malan, Durban .... W 4

MANASE POTSE
South African Lightweight
1979
Aug. 4—Moses Dabula, Odendaalsrust .... W 6
Sept. 1—Jeremiah Malikhetla, Ficksburg ..... KO by 4
Dec. 1—Joseph Molahloe, Odendaalsrust .... W 6
1980
Mar. 1—Eric Nolebende, Odendaalsrust .... W 6
June 7—Isaac Litchakanyane, Odendaalsrust ..... W 8
Aug. 9—Abraham Mphatsoe, Wesselsbron ...... KO 5
Oct. 11—Samuel Rule, Odendaalsrust .... W 4
Nov. 29—Petrus Raleting, Odendaalsrust .... L 6
Dec. 13—Joseph Teteli, Wesselsbron .... L 8

COLIN POWER
British Junior Welterweight
Born: Feb. 2, 1956
1975
June 11—Kevin Quinn, Bradford .... KO 3
July 1—Hughie Clarke, Southend .... KO 4
Nov. 18—Barton McAllister, Hornsey .... W 8
Dec. 2—Winston McKensie, London .... KO 4
1976
Jan. 13—Willie Owen, Hornsey .... W 6
Feb. 23—Dannye Fearon, Nottingham .... W 8
Apr. 1—Tommy Dunn, Hornsey .... KO 8
Apr. 27—George McGurk, Kensington .... W 8
Sept. 22—Des Morrison, London .... KO by 5
Nov. 2—Terry Petersen, Southend .... KO 4
Dec. 6—Joey Singleton, Hammersmith.......... W 8
1977
Jan. 17—Barton McAllister, London .... KO 5
Jan. 25—Billy Vivian, Bethnal .... KO 4
Feb. 5—Claude Lormeau, Chartres .... KO 5
Mar. 1—Tommy Glencross, Marylebone .... KO 4
Mar. 21—Clinton McKensie, London .... KO 2
May 28—Fernando Sanchez, Miranda del Ebro ... D 8
Sept. 1—Efisio Pinna, Milan .... KO 6
Oct. 19—Des Morrison, Bethnal .... KO 10
(Won British Junior Welterweight Title)
Dec. 6—Rudy Barro, London .... W 10
1978
Feb. 27—Chris Walker, Sheffield .... KO 7
(British Junior Welterweight Title)

392

June 5—Jean Baptiste Piedvache, Paris .... KO 11
(European Junior Welterweight Title)
Sept. 10—Fernando Sanchez, Miranda de Ebro KO by 12
(European Junior Welterweight Title)
1979
Feb. 6—Clinton McKenzie, Wembley .... W 15
(For British Junior Welterweight Title)
May 29—Johnny Elliott, London .... KO 6
June 26—Jose Luis Ribero, London .... KO 6
Sept. 11—Clinton McKenzie, London .... L 15
(Lost British Junior Welterweight Title)
1980
Jan. 22—Sylvester Mittee, London .... KO by 7

KID PRESTON
Australian Welterweight
1979
Oct. 17—Eddie Nuri, Melbourne .... NC 5
Nov. 14—Eddie Nuri, Melbourne .... NC 2
Dec. 19—Joe Collins, Williamstown .... W 4
1980
Mar. 5—Rocky Villela, Melbourne .... L 6
Apr. 16—Dave Curran, Melbourne .... L 3
Apr. 18—Dave Curran, Footscray .... L 4
May 23—Gunner Stockholm, Melbourne .... W 4
Aug. 14—Hamza Okanla, Preston .... W 3
Oct. 31—Rocky Villela, Franksten .... L 10

RAFFAELE PRETE
French Middleweight
1979
Apr. 27—Giuseppe Cola, Rimini .... KO 3
1980
Feb. 8—Mohamed Ali, Sassari .... KO 1
Mar. 15—Cosimo Funto, Brindisi .... L 6
Apr. 4—Mauricio Da Cruz, Sassari .... W 6

BARRY PRICE
British Lightweight
1976
May 18—Eric Purkis, London...... D 6
June 14—Barry White, Portsmouth .... W 6
Sept. 20—T. Albert Coley, Walworth .... W 6
Sept. 29—Peter Neal, Hammersmith .... W 6
Oct. 4—Tommy Davitt, Kensington .... W 8
Oct. 27—Tommy Davitt, London .... W 8
Nov. 30—Von Reid, London...... D 8
Dec. 6—Billy Vivian, Hammersmith .... L 6
Dec. 13—Cornelius Bosa-Edwards, London .... KO by 6
1977
Jan. 10—Danny Connolly, Walworth .... W 6
Jan. 17—Von Reid, Birmingham .... W 6
Feb. 1—Ricky Beaumont, Kensington .... KO by 3
Mar. 1—Alan Jones, Hove .... W 6
Mar. 8—Don Burgin, London .... W 8
Mar. 21—Henry Jacobs, Stoke .... W 6
Apr. 5—Barton McAllister, Hove .... W 8
Apr. 18—Tommy Davitt, Walworth .... L 8
May 16—Dill Collins, Nottingham .... L 8
June 13—Dill Collins, London .... KO 6
June 23—Ray Cattouse, London .... D 6
Sept. 19—Des Gwilliam, Walworth .... D 6
Sept. 26—Tommy Davitt, London .... L 6
Oct. 10—Tommy Davitt, London .... L 8
Oct. 17—Sugar Ray Heaney, London .... W 6
Oct. 31—Chucho Zinnerman, Rotterdam .... W 6
Dec. 1—George Turpin, Heathrow .... D 8
1978
Feb. 7—George Feeney, Islington .... KO by 3
Mar. 22—Kevin Doherty, London .... D 8
Apr. 6—John B. Muwanga, Oslo .... L 4
Apr. 20—Kerry Collins, Bradford .... W 8
Apr. 25—Winston Spencer, London .... L 8
May 15—Robbie Robinson, London .... L 8
Oct. 14—Dan Mputu, Dunkirk .... KO by 1
Nov. 11—Billy O'Grady, Marylebone .... W 8
Dec. 18—Eric Wood, London .... W 8
1979
Jan. 8—Gerard Bok, Rotterdam .... D 8
Feb. 17—Jean Vantorre, Zele .... KO by 4
Mar. 15—Tommy Wright, Marylebone .... L 8
Apr. 24—Laurence Williams, London .... L 8
May 13—George Schofield, Edgbaston .... L 6
June 6—Johnny Burns, Bedworth ....D 4
June 14—Roger Guest, Dudley .... W 8
July 2—Des Gwilliam, London .... L 8
Sept. 18—Gary Ball, Lewisham .... W 8
Sept. 22—Ian Murray, Stoke .... W 8
Oct. 11—Lawrence Williams, Liverpool .... L 8
Nov. 19—Lawrence Williams, Stockport .... L 8
Dec. 3—Billy O'Grady, Marylebone ,,,,, W 8
Dec. 13—Gary Ball, Wimbledon .... W 8
1980
Jan. 21—Charlie Brown, London .... W 8

Feb. 4—Charlie Brown, London .... D 8
Mar. 3—Kerry Collins, Hove .... D 8
Apr. 21—Adey Allen, Nottingham .... L 8
June 28—Eddie Copeland, Wembley .... KO by 3
Oct. 20—Tim Moloney, Hove .... L 8
Nov. 3—Colin Wake, London .... KO by 2

RAY PRICE
British Lightweight
1979
Apr. 30—Gerry Howland, Barnsley .... D 4
Sept. 17—Tim Maloney, Mayfair .... L 6
Sept. 24—Bonnet Bryan, Mayfair .... W 4
Oct. 16—Kid Curtis, West Bromwich .... KO 2
Oct. 22—Bill Smith, Mayfair .... D 4
Oct. 30—Phillip Morris, Caerphilly .... D 6
Nov. 6—Neil Brown, Stafford .... W 6
Nov. 21—Neil Brown, Evesham .... W 6
Nov. 28—Shaun Dirken, Doncaster .... D 6
Dec. 3—Tim Maloney, Marylebone .... L 6
Dec. 11—John Dale, Bletchley .... L 6
1980
Mar. 17—Terry Parkinson, London .... W 6
Mar. 19—Colin Wake, London .... L 6

JEFF PRITCHARD
British Lightweight
1974
Oct. 14—Tony Fouweather, Swansea .... KO 2
Dec. 4—Billy Smart, Stoke.................... W 6
1975
Feb. 19—Lawrence Devanney, Manchester .... KO 6
Mar. 12—Brian Wilson, Solihull .... W 6
May 7—Billy Smart, Solihull .... W 8
July 2—Steve Gaze, Swansea .... KO 5
Aug. 6—Glyn Davies, Cardiff.................. W 8
Nov. 12—Charlie Parvin, Solihull .... KO 4
1976
Jan. 14—Mario Stango, London .... W 8
Mar. 27—Guy Caudron, Dunkerke .... L 10
May 5—Tommy Duffy, London .... W 8
Oct. 11—Martian Galleozzie, London .... W 8
Nov. 17—Less Pickett, London .... KO by 9
1977
Jan. 17—Dave Nedham, London .... KO 5
Jan. 25—Jackie McGill, London .... W 8
Feb. 22—Rocky Beaumont, London .... KO by 3
Mar. 29—Bingo Crooks, Ebbw Vale .... W 8
Apr. 25—Jackie McGill, Glasgow .... L 8
Nov. 18—Ray Cattouse, London .... L 8
Dec. 5—George McGurk, Marton .... L 8
Dec. 12—Roy Varden, Birmingham .... L 8
1978
Jan. 16—Willie Booth, Birmingham .... D 8
Jan. 23—Benny Purdy, Aberavon .... KO 4
Mar. 6—Lee Graham, London .... W 8
Apr. 6—Eric Wood, Ebbw Vale .... W 8
Apr. 18—Paul Chance, London .... L 8
May 15—Alan Buchanan, Glasgow .... L 8
May 23—James Cooke, Leicester .... L 8
Sept. 21—Maryn Galleozzie, Caerphilly .... L 10
(Welsh Lightweight Title)
Nov. 20—Winston Spencer, London .... KO by 6
1979
Jan. 8—Eric Wood, London .... W 8
Mar. 1—Jimmy Brown, Liverpool .... L 8
May 13—Jimmy Cooke, Edgbaston .... KO by 3
June 13—Vernon Penprase, Caerphilly .... L 8
Sept. 17—Norman Morton, Glasgow .... L 6
Sept. 25—Dave Laxen, London .... W 8
Oct. 15—Granville Allen, Wolverhampton .... L 8
Oct. 17—Ian Kid Murray, Evesham .... W 6
Oct. 29—Mick Bell, Wolverhampton .... LF 1
1980
Feb. 28—Frank McCord, Ebbw Vale .... W 8
Mar. 11—Norman Morton, London .... L 8
Mar. 24—Jackie Turner, London .... W 8
Apr. 29—Eddie Copeland, Stockport .... KO by 2
June 2—Ricky Beaumont, London .... KO by 2

DENNIS PRYCE
British Junior Middleweight
1977
May 27—Romal Ambrose, Digbeth .... W 4
Sept. 20—George Daines, Southend .... W 4
Oct. 19—Billy English, London .... L 6
Nov. 18—Andy Braidwood, London .... L 6
Nov. 22—Bertie Green, Wolverhampton .... L 8
Dec. 13—Andy Braidwood, Walworth .... L 6
1978
Feb. 13—Dave Maloney, Walworth .... W 6
Feb. 21—Roger Guest, London .... W 4
Apr. 17—Albert Hillman, Walworth .... L 8
Apr. 27—Dave Ward, Doncaster .... W 8

Sept. 12—Billy English Wembley ....L 6
Sept. 27—Johnny Chard, Evesham ....KO 4
Oct.   2—Gary Newel, Nantwich ....W 6
Oct. 10—Gary Newel, Wolverhampton ....W 6
Oct. 30—Des Spence, Nottingham ....W 6
Nov. 16—Des Spence, Liverpool ....W 6
Nov. 21—Gary Cooper, Wolverhampton ....D 6
Dec. 11—Harry Watson, Birmingham ....L 6
1979
Jan. 22—Colin Moore, Birmingham ....W 6
Jan. 31—Roy Varden, Stoke ....D 8
May   21—Lee Hartshorn, Manchester ....L 8
June   6—Johnny Burns, Bedworth ....D 6
Nov. 12—Tony Britton, Mayfair ....W 6
Nov. 20—John Breen, Belfast ....D 8
1980
Jan. 21—Wayne Parker, Nottingham ....L 8
Feb. 23—Dominique Fortemps, Moulinbeek ....W 6
Mar.   8—Claude Lancastre, St. Maur ....L 8
Mar. 26—Ian Kid Murray, Evesham ....W 8
June 18—Dave Allen, Burslem ....KO by 5
Sept. 6—Torben Andersen, Aarhus ....L 6
Oct.   4—Hugo Samo, Calais ....L 8

SAMUEL PULE
South African Junior Lightweight
1977
Nov.   5—David Kambule, Parys ....KO by 2
1978
June   3—Elias Nkabinde, Bloemfontein ....D 4
1979
Mar.   5—Manuel Da Paiva, Welkom ....W 4
Mar. 31—Bernard Dayel, Welkom ....W 6
June 11—Enock Motsoane, Welkom ....W 10
(Won OFS Junior Lightweight Title)
July 31—Jafta Mokgosi, Bloemfontein ....L 6
Oct.   5—Simon Molahloe, Bloemfontein ....L 10
1980
Feb.   4—Petrus Rampoporo, Welkom ....L 8
Mar.   6—Michael Mohlabane, Bloemfontein ......W 10
(For OFS Junior Lightweight Title)
May   3—Petrus Rampoporo, Witsieshoek ....L 8
(Lost OFS Junior Lightweight Title
by failing to make weight)
Sept. 13—Stephen Balene, Welkom ....KO 3
Oct. 11—Manasse Potse, Odendaalsrust ....L 4

PAULUS PULUMO
South African Featherweight
1979
June 29—Michel Shabane, Natalspruit ....W 4
Aug. 31—Joseph Mokiti, Natalspruit ....KO by 4
1980
Oct. 11—Samuel Wolf, Odendaalsrust ....W 6

JEFF PURKI
Australian Bantamweight
1979
Aug. 15—Jimmy Morris, Brookvale ....L 6
Aug. 28—Jimmy Morris, Kingsford ....L 4
1980
Mar.   5—Justin Skinner, Brookvale ....W 6
Apr.   2—Warren Lee, Brookvale ....W 6
May   7—Mick Thompson, Brookvale ....D 6
June   4—Sparrow Freeman, Brookvale ....W 6
June 17—Sparrow Freeman, Kingsford ....W 6
July   2—Sparrow Freeman, Brookvale ....W 8
July 29—Johnny Duff, Kingsford ....W 6

JOHAN PUTTER
South African Featherweight
1977
Nov. 18—Danie Erasmus, Bloemfontein ....KO 3
1978
Dec. 14—William Matlokotsi, Bloemfontein ....W 4
1979
Feb.   5—Michael Moamogoa, Welkom ....W 6
Mar.   2—Jama Qalinga, Bloemfontein ....W 10
Mar. 30—Samuel Motsabi, Bloemfontein ....W 6
Sept. 3—Jacob Moyeye, Welkom ....W 10
1980
Feb.   4—Sipho Mange, Welkom ....KO by 4
(For South African Junior Featherweight Title)
Apr.   5—Welile Nkosinkulu, East London .....KO by 5
May   3—Jacob Moyeye, Witieshoek ....L 10
(OFS Featherweight Title)

ABDEL QISSI
Belgian Heavyweight
1980
Mar. 28—Lassine Niare, Bruxelles ....W 6
Apr. 25—Alessandro Casanova, Bruxelles ....W 6
Oct. 24—Roberto Bosio, Moulinbeek ....KO 5
Nov. 15—Fred Voltine, Bruxelles ....W 6

KEVIN QUINN
British Junior Welterweight
1975
Apr. 14—Steve Gaze, Manchester ....KO 3
Apr. 24—Danny Fearon, Ramsey, Isle of Man ......D 6
May   5—Charlie Wallace, Manchester ....KO 4
May   13—Danny Fearon, Liverpool ....KO by 4
June 11—Colin Powers, Bradford ....KO by 3
Oct.   1—Hugh Smith, Hamilton ....L 6
Nov.   6—Jimmy McAllister, Blackpool...........KO 5
Nov. 13—Winston McKenzie, Caister ....W 6
Dec.   2—John Sagar, Leeds.....................W 8
1976
Jan. 12—Steve Laybourne, Manchester ....W 6
Jan. 19—Steve Laybourn, Nottingham...........KO 1
Jan. 27—John Sagar, Doncaster ....D 6
Sept. 20—George Peacock, Glasgow ....W 8
Sept. 30—Al Stewart, Liverpool................KO by 1
Nov.   3—Kevin Davies, Caister ....D 6
Nov. 15—Kevin Davies, Nottingham ....L 6
Nov. 22—Vernon Van Reill, Birmingham ......KO by 2
1977
(Inactive)
1978
May   8—Adey Allen, Manchester ....W 6
June 19—Selvin Bell, Manchester ....W 6
1979
Mar. 12—Shaun Stewart, Manchester ....D 6
Apr.   2—Tony Carroll, Manchester ....L 8
Apr. 17—Hugh Smith, Glasgow ....L 8
June 18—Shaun Stewart, Manchester ....L 8
Oct. 15—Phil Lewis, Manchester ....W 8
Nov. 15—Adey Allen, Caister ....L 8
1980
Jan. 21—Paul Chance, Wolverhampton ....L 8
Mar.   3—Derek Nelson, Marton ....L 8
Mar. 27—Phil Lewis, Liverpool ....KO by 3
May   31—Phil Lewis, Liverpool ....KO by 6

VOLFART RALA
South African Middleweight
1977
Apr.   2—Sinda Ndlovy, East London ....W 4
May   7—David Klaas, Zwelitsha ....W 4
1978
Jan. 28—Vuyisile Njaca, East London ....KO 2
Apr.   1—Terence Makaluza, East London ....KO 6
Aug.   5—Patrick Tshabalala, East London ....KO by 5
(Won Vacant Cape NE Junior Middleweight Title)
1979
Feb. 10—Loyiso Mtya, Queenstown ....L 8
Oct. 11—Terrence Makaluza, Elizabeth ....L 10
(For Cape Middleweight Title)

ELIAS RALETING
South African Junior Featherweight
1979
Mar.   2—Bredon Nelson, Bloemfontein ....KO 3
Mar. 30—Daniel Rammilli, Bloemfontein ....D 4
July 14—Godfrey Nkate, Virginia ....KO by 2
1980
Apr. 12—Michael Khuto, Ficksburg ....L 6
Nov. 29—Manasse Potse, Odendaalsrust ....W 6

EDISON RAMAGOLE
South African Flyweight
1979
June 29—Johannes Miya, Natalspruit .... D 4
1980
Apr. 25—Bassie Motsie, Sebokeng .... W 4
Aug. 29—Johannes Miya, Sebokeng .... L 6
Nov. 21—Dexter Dhlamini, Sebokeng .... L 4

JOHANNES RAMASIMONG
South African Junior Welterweight
1978
Oct. 7—Johannes Motsumi, Virginia .... L 4
1979
Feb. 9—Jonas Tladi, Bethlehem .... L 8
Feb. 24—Jonas Tladi, Bethlehem .... L 6
Mar. 24—Joseph Molahloe, Virginia .... L 4
1980
May 31—Johannes Motsumi, Bethlehem .... W 6

JOHANNES RAMMISMONG
South African Welterweight
1980
Feb. 4—Jonas Tiadi, Bethlehem .... L 8
May 31—Johannes Motsumi, Bethlehem .... W 6
Aug. 23—Stephen Balene, Bethlehem .... L 8

PETRUS RAMPOPORO
South African Junior Lightweight
1979
Sept. 3—Anton Weitz, Welkom .... W 4
Nov. 9—Simon Molahloe, Bloemfontein .... W 6
1980
Feb. 4—Samuel Pule, Welkom .... W 8
May 3—Samuel Pule, Witsieshoek .... W 8
June 7—Job Sissanga, Odendaalsrust .... W 8
Oct. 11—Simon Molahloe, Odendaalsrust .... KO 9
Oct. 31—Joseph Tsotetsi, Springs .... KO by 5

DAVE RAMSDEN
British Lightweight
1980
Jan. 7—Joey Gilbert, Manchester .... KO 4
Jan. 21—Kevin Sheehan, Nottingham .... KO by 1
Feb. 11—Winston Ho-Shing, Manchester .... L 6
Mar. 3—Winston Ho-Shing, Marton .... L 6
Mar. 10—Selvin Bell, Manchester .... W 6
Mar. 19—Selvin Bell, Doncaster .... L 6
Mar. 24—Selvin Bell, Bradford .... L 6
Mar. 31—Selvin Bell, Cleethorpes .... KO by 3
(Announced Retirement)

ABEL RAPULAN
South African Lightweight
1979
Mar. 2—Cedric Carlsons, Bloemfontein .... W 4
July 31—Paulus Moneang, Bloemfontein .... W 6
Oct. 2—April Papane, Bloemfontein .... W 4
Nov. 17—Jeremiah Malikhetla, Ficksburg .... L 6
1980
July 5—Samuel Taole, Kimberley .... W 4
Aug. 23—David Mogapi, Kimberly .... KO 4

GUY RATAZAYO
South African Junior Lightweight
1972
Nov. 18—Peter Ratazayo, Port Elizabeth .... L 4
Dec. 15—Lungisa Dukashe, Mdantsane .... L 6
1973
Mar. 24—Ben Lekalake, East London .... L 4
July 14—Petrus Makoloi, East London .... W 6
Oct. 6—Spider Moeketsi, East London .... W 6
Nov. 10—Ben Lekalake, Port Elizabeth .... L 6
1974
Mar. 9—Bassie Modise, East London .... KO 5
Mar. 30—Joseph Balovi, East London .... W 6
May 31—Chief Masemola, Umtata .... D 6
Oct. 5—Tsietsi Maretloane, East London .... L 6
1975
Feb. 8—Reginald Mpondo, East London .... W 4
Mar. 29—Lennox Mtyongwe, East London .... W 6
Aug. 30—Boy April, East London .... W 6
Oct. 18—Rocky Mabaso, Durban .... L 6
Dec. 13—Rafty Mngadi, East London .... W 6
1976
Mar. 13—Bashew Sibaca, Port Elizabeth............ L 10
(Cape Town Non-White Featherweight Title)
Mar. 27—Joe Gumede, East London .... L 6
Apr. 17—Derrick Photon, East London............. W 6
May 22—Wilton Mgwadleka, Port Elizabeth ...... IIO 0
June 19—Philip Masiza, Port Elizabeth .... W 6
Aug. 7—Vuyisile Ntunzi, Port Elizabeth .... W 8

Oct. 9—Ben Lekalake, East London .... L 8
(Junior Lightweight Title)
Nov. 13—Evans Gwiji, East London................ W 8
1977
Mar. 5—Jacob Morake, East London .... W 8
May 30—Bashew Sibaca, Port Elizabeth .... L 10
(For Cape NE Featherweight Title)
Oct. 15—Thomas Sithebe, East London .... W 6
1978
Feb. 18—Monde Mgwadleka, East London .... W disq. 3
May 6—Tsietsi Maretloane, East London .... W 10
(Won Cape NE Junior Lightweight Title)
Aug. 5—Jacob Morake, East London .... W 6
Sept. 30—Joseph Tsotetsi, East London .... W 6
1979
June 8—Johan Weyer, East London .... W 6
Aug. 4—Charles Boias, East London .... W 6
Nov. 15—Patrick Kohli, Cape Town .... KO 3
1980
May 17—Bramley Whiteboy, East London .... L 10
1980
Feb. 1—Evans Gwiji, Springs .... L 12
(For S.A. Junior Lightweight Title)
May 17—Bramley Whiteboy, East London .... L 10
(For Cape Lightweight Title)
Dec. 22—Chris Whiteboy, Cape Town .... L 10
(For Cape Junior Lightweight Title)

RONNIE RATHBONE
British Welterweight
1980
Feb. 6—John Lindo, Liverpool .... D 6
Feb. 12—Dave Sullivan, Sheffield .... W 6
Feb. 28—Jimmy Smith, Queensway .... D 6
Apr. 22—George McGurk, Sheffield .... W 6
May 14—Tony Stanton, Burslem .... D 6
Oct. 13—Tommy McCallum, London .... L 6
Oct. 22—Kevin Walsh, Doncaster .... W 6
Oct. 30—Charlie Douglas, Liverpool .... KO 2
Nov. 4—Randy Henderson, Southend .... W 2

GIANCARLO RAVAIOLI
Italian Bantamweight
1978
May 12—Vicenzo Morana, Torvaianica .... W 6
July 14—Mario Tiano, Ostia .... W 6
Nov. 17—Giovanni Scarpati, Torvaianica .... W 6
Dec. 9—Vincenzo di Bari, Isernia .... W 6
1979
Feb. 10—Vincenzo Morana, Marsala .... W 6
May 12—Domenico Palumbo, Torvaianica .... W 6
July 25—Salvatore Melluzo, Rimini .... KO by 4
Nov. 23—Luigi Tessarin, Pordenone .... W 8
1980
Mar. 28—Antonio Franca, Rome .... W 8
Apr. 19—Arturo DePrezzo, Ostia .... W 8
Dec. 3—Helenio Ferreira, Forli .... KO by 8

FRANCO RECUPERO
Italian Middleweight
1974
June 12—Domenico Milone, Monza .... WF 4
Sept. 6—Luigi Ruggiero, Castelpusterlengo .... W 6
Oct. 4—Pietro Marselli, Basilea .... L 6
Oct. 25—Giuseppe Russi, Milano .... KO by 2
Dec. 20—Aurelio Loi, Sassari .... KO 2
1975
Jan. 3—Luigi Mannarino, Milano .... KO by 6
May 1—Angelo Faniculli, Milano .... KO by 2
Oct. 11—Carmine Zollo, Summonte .... KO by 3
Dec. 19—Luigi Mannarino, Milano .... KO 4
1976
Mar. 5—Carmine Zollo, Torino .... W 6
June 4—Domenico Milone, Civitanova .... W 4
June 4—Giuseppe Martinese, Civitanova ...... KO by 4
July 9—Gaetano Sguzza, Portichetto .... KO by 1
Nov. 5—Mario Di Camillo, S. Remo .... L 6
1977
Jan. 19—Mario Di Camillo, S. Remo .... KO by 6
1978
Nov. 30—Antonio Antino, Caloiziocorte .... L 4
Dec. 26—Francesco Plate, Piacenza .... KO by 1
1979
Apr. 6—Francesco Sanna, Valenza .... LF 2
May 4—Salvatore Cascio, Rome .... KO by 2
Oct. 7—Francesco Morrone, Taranto .... KO by 1
1980
Mar. 14—Antonio Cresenza, Rome .... LF 3
Mar. 28—Donato Romano, Monza .... KO by 4

MICK REDDEN
British Lightweight
1980
Jan.	28—Terry Parkinson, Hove	L	4
Feb.	18—Neil Brown, London	W	4
Apr.	21—Don Aagesen, Edgbaston	KO by	1
June	16—Johnny Francis, Manchester	L	6
July	14—Neil Brown, London	W	6

MANDU REFRAID
Egyptian Light Heavyweight
(Based in Austria)
1980
Feb.	1—Kurt Oerter, Vienna	KO	4
Feb.	22—Fred Serres, Luxembourg	W	6
Mar.	29—Fred Serres, Differdange	KO by	4

VON REID
British Lightweight
1975
Oct.	15—Joey Gilbert, Birmingham	W	6
Nov.	17—Devlin White, Mayfair	KO	5
Nov.	26—Dilwyn Collins, Birmingham	W	6

1976
Jan.	14—Henry Jacobs, Solihull	WF	5
Feb.	2—Dilwyn Collins, London	W	8
Feb.	11—Henry Jacobs, Bradford	W	6
Feb.	25—Ray Murray, Birmingham	KO	1
Mar.	31—Kevin Evans, Birmingham	KO by	1
Apr.	6—Ray Cattouse, London	KO by	4
Oct.	13—Ian Pickersgill, Stoke	L	8
Oct.	22—Derrick Hollvoak, Digbeth	W	6
Oct.	27—Dick Goodman, Wolverhampton	W	6
Nov.	24—Barry Price, Battersea	D	8
Dec.	20—Billy Jeram, Walworth	L	6

1977
Jan.	17—Barry Price, Birmingham	L	8
Jan.	31—Ray Holdcroft, Bradford	KO	3
Feb.	22—Godfrey Butler, Wolverhampton	KO by	6
Mar.	24—Chris Glover, Bradford	KO by	4
May	2—Willie Booth, Holytown	KO by	3

1978
(Inactive)
1979
Apr.	4—Gary Newell, Birmingham	L	4

1980
Mar.	13—Walter Clayton, Birkenhead	KO by	6

MAURICE RENAUD
French Junior Middleweight
1977
Dec.	24—Serge Sinelnikov, Luneville	W	6

1978
(Inactive)
1979
Jan.	13—Hughes Samo, Arques	L	6
Feb.	22—Claude Lancaster, Paris	KO by	3
Apr.	7—Daniel Hyvon, Vandouevre	W	6
Apr.	13—Frederic Boisey, Nizza	L	6
May	26—Celestin Kanynda, Esch	L	6
June	8—Eugene Dovin, Salon	L	6
June	15—Patrick Babouram, Creil	D	6
June	27—Jimmy Connelly, Berne	D	6
Sept.	28—Jean Paul Coppyn, Viller Semeuse	W	6
Nov.	3—Thierry Samo, Louvril	L	6
Nov.	24—Gianfranco Rosi, Marsciano	L	6
Nov.	30—Mario Norelli, Annecy	L	6
Dec.	15—Celestin Kanynda, Vandouevre	W	6

1980
Feb.	17—Andre Mongalema, Metz	D	6
Mar.	8—Frank Winstertein, Epinay Sous Senart	L	6
Apr.	19—Romain Mianzuela, Liege	D	6
May	5—Stephane Ferrara, Paris	L	6
Oct.	6—Stephane Arnone, Paris	D	6
Oct.	18—Rufino Angulo, Villeneuve	L	8

LUCIANO RENZI
Italian Middleweight
1978
Apr.	15—Antonio Cresenza, Chivasso	W	6
July	22—Giancarlo Denti, Settimo M.	W	6
Nov.	10—Aldo Buzzetti, Piacenza	KO by	2

1979
Sept.	8—Roy Kaba, Montanaro	KO by	4

1980
Apr.	11—Branko Barakovic, Chivasso	W	6

MANUEL GARCIA REQUENA
Spanish Junior Welterweight
1979
Mar.	31—Ahmed Ben Aissa, Taco	W	6
Aug.	10—Mohamed El Kadoumi, S. Cruz	W	6
Aug.	30—Mohamed El Kadoumi, Puerto Cruz	W	6

Sept.	14—Santiago Gonzalez, Las Palmas	L	6
Dec.	8—Chato Melillense, Tenerife	WF	4

1980
Jan.	19—Gonzalez Monzon, Tenerife	KO	7

JUN RESMA
Filipino Bantamweight
1979
June	30—Tony Seas, Davao City	L	10
Aug.	19—Abdul Marajan, Davao Del Sur	KO	8
Oct.	27—Ric Barimbad, Davao	L	10
Dec.	30—Manuel Acuna, Davao City	KO	3

1980
Jan.	19—Eddie Amad, Santos City	KO	6
Mar.	15—Oscar Gonzales, Davao City	W	10
June	8—Danny Grey, South Cotabato	KO	5
June	22—Par Brancero, Davao Del Norte	KO	6
Sept.	27—Ric Barimbad, Manila	D	10
Dec.	20—Deo Mindoro, Manila	W	10

BOY REYES
Filipino Lightweight
1979
Feb.	17—Armand Bangoyan, Pampanga	W	10
Apr.	16—Alex Bitong, Angeles City	W	10
Sept.	8—Nitoy Bantillan, Cotabato City	KO	6
Oct.	20—Virgilio Berdeflor, Pampanga	KO	7
Dec.	7—Pedro Lipata, Tarlas	W	10
Dec.	22—Nitoy Bantilan, Zambales	W	10
Dec.	30—Pedro Lipata, Pampanga	W	10

1980
Feb.	2—Nitoy Bantilan, Tarlac	KO	6
Feb.	23—Orlando Cruz, Angeles City	W	10
Aug.	9—Max Boy, Angeles City	KO	6

HENRY RHINEY
British Welterweight
Born: November 28, 1951, Luton
1973
Apr.	5—Terry Davies, London	D	6
Apr.	16—Ray Thorogood, London	W	6
Apr.	30—Keith Nugent, Kensington	W	6
May	21—Mickey Evans, London	W	6
June	11—Derek Simpson, Glasgow	L	6
Nov.	6—Brian Gregory, Hemel Hempstead	W	8
Nov.	26—Jeff Gale, Mayfair	L	8
Dec.	3—Liam White, Bristol	W	6

1974
Jan.	7—Jim Devanney, London	W	6
Jan.	21—Liam White, London	W	8
Feb.	11—Tommy Joyce, Piccadilly	W	8
Mar.	4—John Smith, Piccadilly	W	8
Mar.	25—Alan Reid, Glasgow	W	8
Apr.	29—Les Pearson, Kensington	KO by	7
June	18—Jim Devanney, Southend	KO	7
June	25—Pat Thomas, London	L	8
Sept.	24—Trevor Francis, Reading	W	8
Oct.	31—Peter Cain, London	W disq.	3
Nov.	14—Mickey Flynn, Caister	D	8
Dec.	10—Pat Thomas, London	L	8

1975
Jan.	27—John Smith, Glasgow	W	8
Feb.	8—Germain Lemaitre, St. Nazaire	KO by	5
Mar.	3—John Smith, London	W	8
Mar.	12—Kevin White, Solihull	KO	2
Apr.	7—Trevor Francis, London	D	8
May	7—Kevin White, Solihull	KO	6
May	14—Trevor Francis, Camerley	D	8
June	16—Clement Tsinza, Luxembourg	D	10
Sept.	8—Kevin White, London	W	8
Oct.	11—Clemente Tsinza, Esch	L	10
Dec.	20—Claude Martin, Saint Malo	D	10

1976
Feb.	18—James Vrji, Scheveningen	L	8
Mar.	1—Mickey Flynn, London	W	8
Apr.	5—John Smith, Luton	W	8
June	28—Mickey Flynn, Luton	W	8
July	9—Josef Pachler, Klagenfurt	L	10
Oct.	25—Mickey Ryce, Luton	KO	8
Dec.	6—Pat Thomas, Luton	W	8

(British Welterweight Title)
1977
Mar.	16—Steve Angell, Solihull	L	8
Apr.	4—Terry Petersen, Luton	KO	7
Apr.	25—Mickey Flynn, Northampton	KO	6
June	14—Pat Thomas, Wembley	W	8
Oct.	11—Joe Mack, Marylebone	KO by	7
Nov.	22—Sinclair Christie, Hemel Hempstead	W	8
Dec.	5—Brian Gregory, Luton	KO	6

1978
Feb.	13—Billy Waith, Barnsley	W	15

(British Welterweight Title)
Apr.	20—Sinclaire Christie, London	W	8

May	15—Mickey Morse, Aylesbury	W	8
Aug.	5—Harold Volbrecht, Johannesburg	L	10
Oct.	16—Billy Waith, London	W	8
Dec.	2—Josef Pachler, Dornbirn	KO	10
	(European Welterweight Title)		
	1979		
Jan.	23—Dave Green, London	KO by	5
	(British and European Welterweight Title)		
Apr.	4—Kirkland Laing, Birmingham	KO by	10
Oct.	3—Peter Neal, Reading	L	12
Dec.	6—Hans Henrik Palm, Copenhagen	L	8
	1980		
Feb.	14—Andoni Amana, Bilbao	L	8
Apr.	17—Torben Anderson, Copenhagen	L	8
	(Announced Retirement)		

(GLYN) GLEN RHODES
British Lightweight

	1979		
Nov.	19—John Lindo, Liverpool	L	6
Nov.	28—Mark Osbourne, Doncaster	W	4
Dec.	10—Mike Clemow, Torquay	L	6
	1980		
Jan.	9—Steve Simms, Burslem	KO	6
Jan.	25—Shaun Dirkin, Hull	W	6
Feb.	5—John Cooper, Southend	W	6
Feb.	12—Bill Smith, Sheffield	W	4
Mar.	3—Kevin Sheehan, Nottingham	KO by	1
Mar.	24—Derek Groarke, Bradford	KO	4
Apr.	21—John Henry, Bradford	KO	5
Apr.	29—Jackie Turner, London	L	8
July	28—Billy Hay, Fivemiletown	D	6
Sept.	4—Jarvis Greenidge, Morecambe	KO	8
Sept.	15—Gary Ball, London	D	6
Oct.	7—Kerry Collins, London	KO	8
Oct.	30—Jimmy Bunclarke, Liverpool	KO by	7

LUIS RIBEIRO
Spanish Welterweight

	1975		
Apr.	24—Antonio Chiodoni, Brescia	KO by	6
May	10—Alain Ruocco, Tolone	KO by	10
June	6—Antonio Torsello, Losanna	W	10
June	21—Maurizio Bittarelli, Lausanne	L	10
Aug.	5—Luciano Laffranchi, Ascoli Piceno	W	8
Aug.	14—Nicola D'Orazio, Ariano Irpino	D	8
Sept.	12—Piero Meraviglia, Sondrio	D	8
Sept.	27—Saadi Saadi, Villeurbanne	L	8
Oct.	19—Rocco Frasca, Milan	L	8
Nov.	14—Romano Fanali, Livorno	L	8
Dec.	18—Prime Bandini, Forli	L	8
	1976		
Jan.	10—Bruno Freschi, Latina	L	8
Jan.	30—Antonio Puddu, Cagliari	L	8
Feb.	28—Ugo Di Pietro, Latina	D	8
Mar.	26—Efisio Pinna, Cagliari	L	8
Apr.	16—Giovanni Lamusta, Ancona	KO	8
Apr.	30—Efisio Pinna, Cagliari	L	8
May	26—Oscar Aparicio, Trieste	KO by	2
July	10—Bruno Freschi, Beograd	L	8
Sept.	18—Giancarlo Barabotti, Foggia	L	8
Oct.	2—Angelo Fanciulli, Viterbo	L	8
Oct.	23—Giuseppe Russi, San Severo	L	8
Nov.	10—Giuseppe Russi, Cagliari	L	8
Nov.	26—Italo Venturi, Lugo Romagna	D	8
Dec.	7—Oscar Aparicio, Civitanova	L disq.	5
	1977		
Jan.	21—Pascal Real Martin, Annedy	L	8
Feb.	24—Ould Maklufi, Oran	L	10
Apr.	1—Timoteo Bonizzoni, Milano	L	6
Apr.	22—Juan Jose Gimenez, Faenza	KO by	7
May	13—Eduardo Diana, Sarzana	L	8
May	28—Giampolo Piras, Koeln	D	8
June	24—Luciano Navarra, Gallarate	L	6
Aug.	12—Vincenzo Quero, Taranto	L	8
Aug.	24—Paolo Zanusso, Grado	L	8
Oct.	7—Jacques Van Maelerts, Nice	KO by	6
Nov.	4—Daniele Zappaterra, Ferrara	L	8
Dec.	3—Giuseppe Corbo, Piedimonte	L	8
Dec.	23—Luciano De Luca, Lanciano	L	8
	1978		
Jan.	7—Fred Coranson, Coudekerque	L	10
Jan.	30—George Warusfel, Perifueux	L	10
Mar.	20—Giuseppe Di Padova, Mantova	L	8
Mar.	31—Francesco Plate, Piacenza	KO	4
Apr.	15—Francesco Gallo, Biella	D	8
Apr.	28—Gianbattista Capretti, Sarajevo	D	8
May	29—Nicola Sassanelli, Catana	L	8
July	21—Ciro Seta, Salerno	L	8
Aug	13—Antonio Stocchino, Iglesias	L	6
Sept.	5—Pierangelo Fina, Diblan	L	8
Oct.	27—Antonio Torsello, Chavannes	L	10
Nov.	18—Libero Moi, Ostia	L	8
Dec.	12—Otto Zinoeder, Seewalchen	L	6

Dec.	16—Francesco Morrone, Pesaro	W	6
	1979		
Jan.	27—Dieter Schantz, Koblenz	D	6
Feb.	4—Pierangelo Pira, Rimini	L	6
Mar.	9—Salvatore Cascio, Rome	L	6
Apr.	7—Esperno Postl, Waidhofen	L	8
May	18—Dieter Schantz, Munich	W	6
June	26—Colin Powers, London	L	6
Sept.	8—Otto Zinoeder, Waidhofen	L	6
Oct.	20—Herbert Trausmuth, Gansbacher	LF	4
Oct.	29—Esperno Postl, Wien	L	8
Nov.	9—Jean Jacques Benchetrit, Nice	L	6
Dec.	7—Erwin Heiber, Lubeck	L	8
	1980		
May	15—Guildo Galletti, Rome	D	8
June	20—Antonio Casado, Barcelona	L	8
Aug.	15—Franco Aresti, Portoscuso	L	8

PASQUALE RIBOLI
Italian Junior Lightweight

	1979		
Sept.	8—Andrea Ricci, Offanengo	W	6
	1980		
Mar.	4—Alfredo Reininger, Napoli	L	6
Mar.	28—Bruno Simili, Pisa	LF	6
Sept.	20—Franco Canini, Sebenico	L	8

LARRY RICHARDS
British Featherweight

	1977		
June	1—Paul Clemit, Barnsley	L	4
July	10—John Feeney, Birmingham	KO by	2
Oct.	11—Mark Hill, Coventry	D	4
Oct.	31—Mark Hill, Birmingham	D	4
Nov.	22—Mark Hill, Wolverhampton	W	4
Nov.	30—Mark Hill, London	L	4
	1978		
Feb.	13—Steve Enright, Manchester	L	6
Mar.	2—Steve Enright, Caister	W	6
Apr.	4—Steve Enright, Manchester	L	6
Apr.	12—Don Aagesen, Evesham	W	6
Apr.	17—George Sutton, Reading	KO by	2
June	29—Mark Hill, Wolverhampton	L	6
Sept.	18—Steve Enright, Manchester	D	6
Sept.	26—Austin Owens, Wembley	KO by	2
Oct.	31—Terry McKeown, Birmingham	L	6
Nov.	—Bonnet Bryan, Caister	W	6
	1979		
Feb.	22—Gary Lucas, Liverpool	L	6
Feb.	26—Selvin Bell, Edgbaston	W	6
Mar.	15—Selvin Bell, Caister	L	6
Apr.	5—Davy Larmour, Belfast	KO by	6
	1980		
May	8—Clyde Ruan, Solihull	L	6
May	19—Carl Mullings, Birmingham	W	6
Oct.	23—Russell Jones, London	KO by	2

JOHN RIDGMAN
British Junior Middleweight

	1979		
Oct.	29—Dave Sullivan, Camborne	KO	3
Nov.	19—Phil Pourou, Lewisham	KO	5
Dec.	4—Tony Britton, Southend	W	6
	1980		
Feb.	27—Vic Jackson, Burslem	L	6

STEVEN RIET
South African Lightweight

	1980		
Apr.	14—P. J. Xhelishio, Kimberley	W	4

ALFIO RIGHETTI
Italian Heavyweight
Born: September 18, 1952, Montecdombo

	1974		
May	18—Domenico Scala, Rimini	KO	3
Aug.	13—Angelo Visini, Rimini	W disq.	4
Sept.	27—Pasquale Rizzardo, Rimini	KO	2
Nov.	15—Romano Peviani, Rimini	W	6
Dec.	20—Gino Martinis, Rimini	W	6
	1975		
Jan.	18—Francesco Piccinali, Rimini	KO	2
Feb.	22—Pietro Zanola, Rimini	W	8
Apr.	11—Larry Renaud, Bologna	W	8
July	19—Frankie Evans, Frosinone	KO	7
Aug.	14—Adriano Rosati, Rimini	KO	7
Oct.	3—Sergio Rodriguez, Milan	KO	4
Nov.	6—John L. Johnson, Milan	KO	6
Dec.	12—Vasco Faustino, Turin	W	8
	1976		
Feb.	5—Benito Penna, Milan	KO	7
Mar.	5—Armando Zanini, Turin	KO	1
Mar.	26—Bill Carson, Milano	KO	2

Apr. 10—Arno Prick, Rimini .... KO 2
June 4—Peter Freeman, Milano .... KO 3
July 9—Terry Mintus, Rimini.................. KO 5
Aug. 7—Piermario Baruzzi, Rimini .... W 10
Oct. 1—Cookie Wallace, Rome .... W 10
Dec. 17—Bepi Ros, Milan .... W 8
1977
Mar. 5—Dante Cane, Rimini .... W 12
(Italian Heavyweight Title)
May 7—Piermario Baruzzi, Rimini .... W 12
(Italian Heavyweight Title)
June 18—Cookie Wallace, Rome .... W 8
Sept. 17—Dennis Jordan, Rome .... KO 6
Oct. 8—Isaac Hussein, Nice .... W 8
Nov. 5—Leon Spinks, Las Vegas .... L 10
Dec. 26—Tony Moore, Rimini .... W 10
1978
Mar. 16—Joe Gholston, Bologna .... W 10
May 27—Joe Gholston, Genova .... W 10
July 19—Juan De La Garza, Bellaria .... KO 3
Oct. 21—Greg Johnson, Pesaro .... KO 5
Nov. 10—Joe Roman, Milano .... KO 2
1979
Feb. 4—Tom Prater, Rimini .... W 10
Mar. 17—Sam McGill, Rimini .... W 10
Apr. 28—Avenamar Peralta, Rimini .... W 10
July 14—Lorenzo Zanon, Rimini .... D 12
(EBU Heavyweight Title)
1980
Jan. 26—Terry Mims, Bologna .... KO by 1

CHAED RINGO
Belgian Junior Middleweight
1976
Mar. 19—Antonio Baletta, Gand .... W 6
Apr. 2—Luigi Renda, Charleroi .... W 6
May 20—Alain Salmon, Molenbeek .... W 6
July 3—Jean Heirmann, Kalken .... W 6
Oct. 26—Luigi Renda, Molenbeek .... W 6
Nov. 25—Antonio Balletta, Molenbeek .... W 8
Dec. 12—Wolfgang Lueger, Molenbeek .... KO 3
1977
Jan. 15—Alfred Fries, Brussels .... W 6
Feb. 19—Jean Heirmann, Montaign .... W 6
Mar. 4—Richard Rodriguez, Grivignee .... L 6
Mar. 18—Armin Rindlisbacher, Anderlecht .... W 8
Apr. 2—Dominique Cella, Nivelles .... W 8
Apr. 22—Jean Vanderbreght, Koekelberg ..... KO by 4
1978
Jan. 13—Maurice Bufi, Le Roeuix .... L 6
Feb. 25—Raymond Langewouters, Anversa .... KO by 2
Apr. 14—Daniel Dujardin, S. Amand .... KO 6
June 7—Alvaro Scarpelli, Faenza .... KO by 3
Sept. 30—Dirk Declercq, Turnhout .... KO 5
Dec. 23—Stephan Vertpre, Vivegnis .... D 8
1979
Nov. 10—Maurice Bufi, Brussels .... L 8
1980
Feb. 2—Dirck Declerick, Torhut .... KO 6
Sept. 27—Claudio Bosio, La Louviere .... W 6

PASQUALE RIPPA
Italian Middleweight
1980
May 18—Bruno Polloni, Naples .... KO 4
Aug. 17—Mauro Da Cruz, Cerveter .... D 6
Oct. 11—Mauro Da Cruz, Naples .... W 6

ANDY ROBERTS
Australian Lightweight
1979
Feb. 27—Max Nabete, Kingsford .... KO by 3
Apr. 13—Lachie Williams, Griffith .... L 6
Apr. 18—Elley Parker, Mt. Pritchard ...... KO by 3
June 16—Chris Bennett, Dubbo .... L 6
Sept. 1—Chris Bennett, Berkeley .... L 6
Sept. 11—Joe Collins, Kingsford .... W 6
Sept. 25—Buddy Clare, Kingsford .... W 6
Oct. 9—Lucky Campbell, Kingsford .... KO by 3
Oct. 17—Lucky Campbell, Brookvale .... KO by 3
1980
Feb. 12—Albert Singh, Kingsford .... W 6
Feb. 26—Doc Rutton, Kingsford .... L 6

BRIAN ROBERTS
Australian Junior Featherweight
Born: Sept. 17, 1953, Lismore, Australia
1972
May 2—Sabu, Cronulla .... KO 3
June 1—Buddy Clare, Redfern .... W 4
June 15—Jeff Malcolm, Redfern .... D 4
June 29—Jeff Malcolm, Redfern .... D 4
July 11—Winston Stokes, Marrickville .... W 4
July 20—Young Daylight, Redfern .... W 4

July 27—Terry Dixon, Redfern .... W 4
Aug. 8—Jeff Malcolm, Marrickville .... W 4
Aug. 29—Steve Walker, Cronulla................. L 4
Aug. 31—Young Daylight, Redfern .... L 4
Sept. 20—Larry Saddler, Cammeray .... KO 4
Sept. 26—Bob Taylor, Cronulla .... KO 5
Oct. 5—Wayne Hall, Redfern .... W 6
Oct. 31—Young Daylight, Cronulla............... W 8
Nov. 9—Young Daylight, Redfern................ W 6
Dec. 7—Dennis Talbot, Redfern .... W 8
1973
Feb. 28—Brian Clout, Cronulla .... L 4
Mar. 21—Brian Clout, Redfern .... L 8
Apr. 26—Steve Johnson, Blacktown............... W 8
June 7—Greg Hagart, Blacktown .... W 8
July 5—Tommy Strezos, Cammeray .... W 10
Aug. 29—Yoshiki Suda, Sydney .... W 10
Oct. 22—Paul Ferreri, Melbourne............... L 10
Nov. 21—Sharkey Hughes, Cammeray .... W 10
1974
Mar. 7—Dennis Talbot, Blacktown .... W 10
Mar. 22—Guinea Hillier, Melbourne .... D 8
Apr. 11—Big Jim West, Blacktown .... W 10
May 23—Guinea Hillier, Blacktown .... W 10
June 6—Paul Ferreri, Blacktown .... L 10
June 28—Henry Nissen, Melbourne .... L 10
Sept. 12—Paul Ferreri, Blacktown .... D 10
Oct. 9—Jimmy Slatter, Marrickville .... W 10
Nov. 13—Dennis Talbot, Marrickville............. W 10
1975
Mar. 12—Big Jim West, Merrickville .... L 10
May 14—Paul Ferreri, Sydney .... W 10
Aug. 21—Big Jim West, Blacktown .... W 12
(Australian Bantamweight Title)
Nov. 13—Luigi Tessarin, Melbourne .... KO 8
1976
Feb. 22—Guinea Hillier, Melbourne .... W 12
(Australian Bantamweight Title)
Mar. 25—Paul Ferreri, Blacktown .... L 15
(Commonwealth Bantamweight Title)
Oct. 7—Merv Wockner, Cammeray............. W 10
1977
Mar. 30—Noel Kelly, Bankstown .... KO 3
June 8—Paul Ferreri, Marrickville .... KO by 15
(Australian Bantamweight Title)
Sept. 15—Paul Ferreri, Perth .... KO by 15
(Commonwealth Junior Featherweight Title)
1978
Feb. 27—Johnny Aba, Melbourne .... L 12
(Commonwealth Featherweight Title)
Mar. 22—Guinea Hillier, Blacktown .... W 10
May 5—Johnny Aba, Port Moresby .... KO by 12
(Commonwealth Junior Lightweight Title)
1979
Feb. 18—Metat Balla, Sydney .... W 10
(Australian Super Bantamweight Title)
May 30—Charlie Brown, Revesby .... W 10
(Australian Junior Featherweight Title)
July 27—Paul Ferreri, Revesby .... L 12
(Australian Featherweight Title)
Aug. 7—Charlie Brown, Cardiff .... W 12
(Retained Australian Junior Featherweight Title)
1980
Sept. 8—Charlie Brown, Cronulla .... W 12
(Retained Australian Junior Featherweight Title)
Dec. 6—Sawani Raicebe, Suva .... W 10
Dec. 18—Wayne Mulholland, Marrickville .... KO 3
(Retained Australian Junior Featherweight Title)

RICHIE ROBERTS
Australian Welterweight
1977
Mar. 22—Sam Fizzari, Kingsford .... KO 1
Mar. 30—Wahdoo Miles, Bankstown .... KO 2
Apr. 26—David Blair, Cardiff .... W 4
May 4—John Bowen, Cammeray .... L 6
May 25—Wayne Berg, Brookvale .... W 5
June 7—Wayne Berg, Kingsford .... W 6
Sept. 16—Fred Repton, Doyalson .... W 6
Sept. 28—Mick Christopher, Brookvale .... W 6
Sept. 29—Dawsie Kelly, Shortland .... W 6
Oct. 12—Phil Kahn, Marrickville .... KO by 7
Nov. 9—Buddy Nixon, Marrickville .... W 6
Dec. 14—Benny Wayne, Marrickville .... L 8
1978
Feb. 9—Phil Kahn, Marrickville .... W 8
Apr. 26—Theo James, Brookvale .... W 6
June 12—Buddy Nixon, Cammeray .... W 8
July 26—Bob McQueenie, Bankstown .... W 10
Oct. 25—Speedy Duke, Bankstown .... W 10
Dec. 7—Kelly Thompson, Revesby .... W 8
1979
Feb. 4—Kelly Thompson, Newtown .... KO 8
May 30—Phil Davies, Revesby .... L 10

Aug.   3—David Hill, Sydney .... W 8
1980
Aug.   16—Sakarai Ve, Laucaula .... KO by 7
Oct.   16—Lou Cruz, Marrickville .... W 6
Nov.   27—Alex Temelkov, Melbourne .... W 10

TOMMY ROBERTS
Australian Bantamweight
1979
Feb.   4—Mick Clarke, Enmore .... KO 1
Mar.   1—Kid Blair, Blacktown .... L 6
Mar.   13—John Lawrie, Kingsford .... W 4
July   17—Elley Parker, Kingsford .... D 4
Aug.   7—Andy Mann, Cardiff .... W 6
Dec.   4—Ivan Terry, Kingsford .... KO 5
1980
Feb.   12—Clint Brown, Kingsford .... L 8
May   6—Clint Brown, Kingsford .... L 8
May   21—Kelly Thompson, Mt. Pritchard .... L 8
Sept.   8—Andy Mann, Cronulla .... D 6
Sept. 27—Sparrow Freeman, Bankstown .... L 4

ROBBIE ROBINSON
British Lightweight
1978
Jan.   24—Tony Whitmore, London .... W 6
Jan.   30—Gerry O'Neill, Glasgow .... W 6
Feb.   28—Steve Holdworth, Heathrow .... D 6
Apr.   3—Albert Coley, London .... L 6
Apr.   20—Dai Davies, London .... W 6
May   15—Barry Price, London .... W 8
May   18—Steve Ward, London .... KO 1
Sept. 25—Winston Spencer, London .... L 8
1979
Mar.   1—Najib Daho, Liverpool .... KO 3
Mar.   8—Andy Dane, Bangor .... KO 3
Apr.   5—Tommy Wright, Liverpool .... W 8
Apr.   26—Alan Burrows, Liverpool .... L 8
Sept. 20—Tony Carroll, Liverpool .... KO by 4
Nov.   29—George Schofield, Liverpool .... W 8
1980
Jan.   16—Lance Williams, Liverpool .... W 8
Feb.   21—George Metcalf, Liverpool .... KO by 5
May   31—George Metcalf, Liverpool .... KO 6
Sept. 18—Tony Carroll, Liverpool .... W 8

PRINCE RODNEY
British Junior Middleweight
1977
Oct.   24—Russ Shaw, Manchester .... KO 3
Nov.   8—Jack Gilling, Darlington .... L 6
Dec.   1—Paddy McAleese, Caister .... W 8
Dec.   8—Steve Goodwin, Liverpool .... L 6
Dec.   19—Steve Goodwin, Bradford .... D 6
1978
Jan.   18—Billy Ahearne, Solihull .... W 8
Jan.   30—Dave Moore, Cleethorpes .... KO 6
Feb.   13—Roger Guest, Manchester .... W 8
Mar.   2—Carl Bailey, Caister .... W 8
Apr.   4—Carl Bailey, London .... KO 7
July   18—Horace McKenzie, Wakefield .... W 8
Sept. 11—Johnny Pincham, Bradford .... KO 6
Oct.   16—Roy Commosioung, Bradford .... W 6
Oct.   24—Joe Lally, Blackpool .... WF 5
Dec.   18—Carl Bailey, Bradford .... L 8
1979
Jan.   22—Joe Oke, Bradford .... W 8
Feb.   13—Dave Davies, Wakefield .... KO 8
Feb.   26—John Smith, Middlesbrough .... W 8
Mar.   16—Mike Coup, Bradford .... KO 3
Apr.   28—Raymond Langewouters, Tamlise .... W 8
May   16—Mick Mills, Sheffield .... KO 4
June   25—Glen McEwan, Edgbaston .... W 8
Sept. 25—Dan Snyder, London .... W 10
Nov.   19—Horace McKenzie, Stockport .... W 8
Dec.   4—Steve Hopkin, Wembley .... L 8
1980
Mar.   14—Charlie Malarkey, Glasgow .... L 10
(Eliminator, British Junior Middleweight Title)

FELIPE (PANTERA) RODRIGUEZ
Spanish Heavyweight
1977
May   13—Francisco Barrilado, Madrid .... W 6
Aug.   20—Benito Escriche, Villagracia .... W 8
Oct.   8—Antonio Dos Santos, Grove .... KO 2
Nov.   20—Joaquin Rodriguez, La Linea .... KO 3
1978
Jan.   28—Sugar Silex, Oviedo .... KO 2
Apr.   1—Santiago Lovell, Pontevedra .... KO 2
June   3—Fermin Hernandez, Pontevedra .... KO 5
July   1—Sugar Silex, Villagracia .... KO 5
July   15—Mohammed Galoul, La Coruna .... W 8
Sept. 16—Alejandro Cardoso, Vigo .... W 8

Oct.   28—Christian Poncelet, Pontevedra .... W 8
Nov.   11—Benito Escriche, Zaragoza .... KO 6
(Won Spanish Heavyweight Title)
Dec.   2—Avenamar Peralta, Pontevedra .... KO 4
1979
Apr.   26—Francois Fiol, Las Palmas .... KO 9
(For Spanish Heavyweight Title)
July   14—Alfredo Evangelista, Pontevedra .... D 12
(Spanish Heavyweight Title)
Aug.   14—Tom Halpern, Pontevedra .... KO 4
Oct.   10—Lorenzo Zanon, Torino .... L 12
(EBU Heavyweight Title)
Nov.   10—Albert Syben, Forest .... L 10
Dec.   1—Tony Moore, La Coruna .... W 8
1980
Mar.   22—Ivan Popovich, Santander .... KO 6

JUAN FRANCISCO RODRIGUEZ
Spanish Bantamweight
1976
Oct.   29—L. Miguel Montes, Segovia .... KO 2
Nov.   6—Pedro Coque, Santander .... KO 6
Nov.   19—Antonio Tanio, Madrid .... W 8
1977
Feb.   4—Juan Barros, Bilbao .... W 8
Apr.   1—Laurent Grimbert, Madrid .... D 8
July   17—Daniel Trioulaire, Madrid .... KO 6
July   23—Esteban Eguia, Almeria .... L disq. 7
(Spanish Bantamweight Title)
Sept.   9—Angel Oliver, Madrid .... W 8
Dec.   2—Carlos Zarate, Madrid .... KO by 5
(WBC Bantamweight Title)
1978
Feb.   18—Daniel Figueroa, Dviedo .... KO 5
Sept. 16—Franco Zurlo, Vigo .... W 15
(European Bantweight Title)
1979
Mar.   4—Johnny Owens, Almeria .... W 15
(European Bantamweight Title)
Apr.   21—Patriota Lindarte, Valencia .... KO 4
May   4—Miguel Figueroa, Barcelona .... NC 7
June   16—Torito Gomez, Santander .... KO by 6
Aug.   10—Laurent Grimbert, Huelva .... W 10
(EBU Bantamweight Title)
Sept.   8—Luis de la Sagra, Lepe .... D 8
1980
Feb.   28—Johnny Owen, Ebbw Vale .... L 12
(Lost European Bantamweight Title)
Aug.   1—Isidoro Cabeza, Madrid .... W 8
Dec.   3—Valerio Nati, Forli .... L 12
(For European Bantamweight Title)

LUCIEN RODRIGUEZ
French Heavyweight
1973
Jan.   26—Bernard Varrenes, Paris .... W 6
Feb.   5—Jean-Pierre Younsi, Paris................ W 6
May   26—Francis Monnet, Japy .... KO 1
Dec.   17—Jean Pierre Leseigneur, Paris .... KO 4
1974
Feb.   25—Serge Jagot, Paris...................... WF 4
May   27—Jean Pierre Leseigneur, Paris .... KO 1
Nov.   30—Jean Belval, Paris...................... KO 1
Dec.   16—Lisimo Obutobe, Paris .... KO 2
1975
June   25—Henny Thoonen, Paris .... W 8
Nov.   4—Neville Meade, Paris .... KO by 3
1976
Mar.   28—Lorenzo Zanon, Paris .... W 8
Apr.   10—Sugar Silex, Irun...................... KO 5
Apr.   13—Sugar Silex, San Sebastian .... KO 5
Apr.   30—Lorenzo Zanon, Milano .... L 8
June   2—Alfredo Evangelista, Bilbao .... KO by 4
Dec.   25—Jose Antonio Galvez, Bilbao............ KO 1
1977
Jan.   15—Jean Pierre Coopman, Izegem .... W 10
Apr.   2—Arno Pryx, Ostend .... KO 2
May   8—Jean Pierre Coopman, Antwerp .... W 15
(European Heavyweight Title)
Sept.   9—Alfredo Evangelista .... KO by 11
(European Heavyweight Title)
Nov.   12—Ishaq Husein, Saint Quentin .... KO 4
Dec.   5—Tony Moore, Paris .... W 8
1978
Apr.   28—Christian Beneelet, Charleville .... KO 7
(French Heavyweight Title)
—Isaac Hussen, Saint Quentin .... KO 2
—Tony Moore, Paris .... W 8
Nov.   4—Laurent Zardy, Paris .... KO 5
(For French Heavyweight Title)
Dec.   23—Domenico Adinolfi, Liege .... W 10

399

	1979		
Mar.	2—Alfredo Evangelista, Liege .... KO by	2
	(European Heavyweight Title)	
May	12—Bob Hazelton, Wichita .... KO	3
June	24—Mahmoud Fadel, Monte Carlo .... KO	2
Nov.	5—Christian Poncelet, Paris .... W	12
	(French Heavyweight Title)	
	1980	
Jan.	29—Assane Moano, Abidjan .... KO	2

MANUEL (OLIVA) RODRIGUEZ
Spanish Lightweight
1980

Jan.	19—Cristobal Santana, St. Cruz .... W	6
Apr.	19—Cruz Holquin, Mataro .... KO by	2

MANUEL (RATON) RODRIGUEZ
Spanish Bantamweight
1976

Aug.	13—Antonio Tanio, Madrid L	6
Aug.	19—Martin Antich, Madrid .... D	6
	1977	
May	3—Juan Perez, S. Cruz L	6
May	14—Andres Rodriguez, Leon .... W	8
Sept.	10—Antonio Benitez, Gijon .... W	6
Oct.	1—Victoriano Solis, Gijon .... W	6
Nov.	8—Antonio Tanio, Utrera L	6
Dec.	3—Cristobal Santana, Las Palmas L	6
Dec.	23—Cristobal Santana, Las Palmas .... D	6
	1978	
May	31—Antonio Garcia del Moral, Utrera .... KO by	6
Dec.	2—Antonio Barreto, S. Cruz L	6
	1979	
Mar.	16—Cristobal Santana, Las Palmas .... W	6
Apr.	28—Mohamed Larbi, Santander .... NC	4
June	1—Jose R. Jeronimo, Mallorca L	6
June	15—Enrique Rodriguez Cal, Aviles L	6
July	6—Martin Antich, Mallorca .... D	6
Aug.	2—Martin Antich, Mallorca L	6
Aug.	12—Critobal Santana, Las Palmas .... W	6
Oct.	13—Enrique Rodriguez Cal, Pravia L	10
	(For Spanish Bantamweight Title)	
Nov.	10—German Yeste, Reus .... D	6
Dec.	1—Vicente Rodriguez, La Coruna .... KO by	2

MARIANO (NANI) RODRIGUEZ
Spanish Lightweight
1975

Dec.	20—Pedro Coque, Valladolid .... W	6
	1976	
Jan.	7—Francisco Garcia, Valladolid .... W	6
Apr.	3—Angel Oliver, Valladolid .... W	6
May	21—Mariano Gasco, Valladolid .... W	6
June	19—Pedro Coque, Leon .... D	6
Oct.	9—Jose Artigao, Valladolid .... W	6
Nov.	27—Emilio Barcala, Valladolid .... W	6
Dec.	11—A. Monteiro, Valladolid .... KO	7
	1977	
Mar.	5—Pedro Coque, Valladolid .... W	8
May	21—Angel Oliver, Valladolid .... W	8
July	2—Jose Ibanez, Valladolid .... W	8
Dec.	30—Adolfo Osses, Valladolid .... W	8
	1978	
Feb.	4—Antonio Medina, Valladolid .... W	10
Mar.	1—Adolfo Osses, Valladolid .... W	8
Apr.	8—Ramon Marichal, Valladolid .... W	12
	(Won Spanish Featherweight Title)	
May	12—Emilio Barcala, Valladolid .... W	10
June	17—Fernando Bermudez, Valladolid .... W	12
	(For Spanish Featherweight Title)	
Sept.	23—Roberto Castanon, Leon .... KO by	10
	(For European Featherweight Title)	
	1979	
Feb.	17—Cecilio Lastra, Santander .... KO by	5
	(Spanish Featherweight Title)	
Aug.	10—Emilio Barcala, Madrid L	8
Aug.	31—Modesto Gomez, Santander .... KO	4
Oct.	13—Manuel Masso, S. Sebastiano L	8
Nov.	8—Torito Gomez, La Coruna .... D	8
Dec.	21—Kiko Garcia, Valladolid .... W	8
	1980	
May	10—Ramon Garcia, St. Cruz L	8

MIGUEL ANGEL RODRIGUEZ
Spanish Lightweight
1980

Feb.	2—Jose A. Martin, Mateo .... KO by	4
Mar.	8—Fermin Gallardo, Santander L	4

RICHARD RODRIGUEZ
Spanish Welterweight
1975

Nov.	4—Jean Pierre Moreau, Paris .... W	6

	1976		
Feb.	7—Andre Camonin, Vandoeuvre .... W	6
Apr.	12—Alain Marion, Paris .... D	6
Oct.	17—Alain Salmon, S. Maur L	6
Nov.	20—Dirk Declercq, Liegi L	6
	1977	
Jan.	15—Dirk Declerq, Brussels .... D	6
Mar.	4—Chaed Ringo, Grivignee .... W	6
May	7—Yimaz Refik, Anversa .... W	6
Oct.	28—Gerard Leterme, S. Naizaire .... W	6
Dec.	5—William Collet, Paris .... W	6
Dec.	25—Frankie Decaestecker, Izegem .... KO	4
	1978	
Jan	28—Jean Pierre Moreau, S. Ouen .... KO	3
Mar.	18—Kader Ben Mimoun, Vivegnis .... LF	5
Mar.	31—Jean Symos, Grivignee L	8
Apr.	28—Mohamed Mechila, Charleville .... W	6
Nov.	4—Georges Lemmer, Paris .... KO	4
Dec.	25—Dirk Declercq, Izegem .... W	8
	1979	
Jan.	19—Frankie De Caessecker, Bruxelles .... W	8
Feb.	3—Alain Ruocco, Creil .... W	8
May	19—Alois Carmeliet, Brussels L	10
June	6—Fernando Sanchez, Bilbao .... W	8
Nov.	2—Luciano Navarra, La Chaux de Fonds .... W	10
Dec.	14—Louis Acaries, Nice L	12
	(French Welterweight Title)	
	1980	
Feb.	7—Ray Chavez, Paris .... W	8

VINCENTE RODRIGUEZ
Spanish Bantamweight
1977

Sept.	9—Antonio Munoz, Madrid .... KO	5
Oct.	7—Antonio Cabezas, Madrid .... KO	4
Nov.	4—Juan Barros, Madrid .... W	6
Dec.	10—Kiko Garcia, Benetesur .... W	8
Dec.	17—Kiko Garcia, Santander .... KO	5
	1978	
Feb.	4—Angel Oliver, Leon .... W	8
Feb.	18—Garcia Herrera Kiko, Oviedo .... W	8
May	6—Antonio Rodriguez, Madrid .... D	8
May	20—Fernando Bernardez, La Coruna .... W	8
May	27—Garcia del Moral, Leon .... KO	3
Oct.	28—Mariano Garcia, La Coruna .... W	8
Dec.	16—Emilio Barcala, Leon .... W	10
	(For Spanish Bantamweight Title)	
	1979	
Feb.	16—Kiko Garcia, Madrid .... W	6
Mar.	19—Antonio Garcia Del Moral, Valencia .... KO	8
	(Spanish Super Bantamweight Title)	
Apr.	21—Javan de Oliveira, Valencia .... KO	4
Aug.	10—Francisco Herrera, Madrid .... KO	6
Aug.	14—Martin Antich, Benidorm .... W	8
Dec.	1—Manuel Rodriguez, La Coruna .... KO	2
	1980	
Jan.	19—Esteban Eguia, Santander .... KO by	5
	(For Spanish Bantamweight Title)	

DONATO ROMANO
Italian Middleweight
1978

Mar.	31—Giancarlo Denti, Milano .... W	6
May	27—Bernardo Bonizzoni, Fort Village .... W	6
June	30—Giancarlo Serangeli, Parma, ... W	6
Oct.	20—Silvio Migale, Milan .... W	6
Oct.	31—Erwin Heiber, Munich .... D	6
Nov.	17—Serge Sinelnikow, Milan .... W	8
Dec.	15—Vincenzo Bottigliero, Lugo di Romagna ... W	6
	1979	
Feb.	9—Serge Sinelnikov, Milano .... W	6
Sept.	13—Mauro Favotte, Cesano Maderno .... KO	5
Nov.	16—Ernesto Ros, Milan .... W	6
	1980	
Mar.	14—Mauricio Da Cruz, Milan .... W	8
Mar.	28—Franco Recupero, Monza .... KO	4
Aug.	10—Mauricio Da Cruz, Siderno .... W	6

FRANK ROPIS
Australian Lightweight
1972

Sept.	13—Jim Arch, Essendon .... KO	2
Oct.	18—Wayne Smith, Essendon L	3
Nov.	27—Laurie Mack, Melbourne L	4
Dec.	11—Don Latella, Melbourne .... D	3
	1973	
Jan.	29—John Pisac, Melbourne .... W	3
Apr.	9—Reg Hudson, Melbourne L	4
Apr.	16—Ralph Henry, Melbourne .... W	4
Apr.	30—John Pisac, Melbourne .... W	3
May	7—Chris McKenzie, Melbourne .... W	4
May	28—Ralph Henry, Melbourne L	4
July	2—Frank Offa, Melbourne .... KO	2

400

Aug. 6—Mick McLean, Melbourne ... W 3
Aug. 13—Neil Hankin, Melbourne ... W 3
Aug. 20—Ron McLean, Melbourne ... W 3
Sept. 24—Ron McLean, Melbourne ... KO 6
Oct. 1—Ray Clark, Melbourne ... KO 2
Oct. 8—Glen Howard, Melbourne ... L 3
Oct. 29—Billy Mulholland, Melbourne ... W 3
Dec. 3—Laurie Mack, Melbourne ... KO 2

1974

June 7—Gary James, Melbourne ... W 3
June 21—Delson Stokes, Melbourne ... W 4
Sept. 27—Robert Green, Melbourne ... KO 6
Oct. 18—Dally Law, Melbourne ... L 6

1975

Sept. 25—Mick Heafey, North Melbourne ... W 6
Oct. 23—Glen Howard, North Melbourne ... KO 2

1976
(Inactive)

1977

Mar. 9—Joey Collins, Melbourne ... W 8
June 1—Billy Mulholland, Melbourne ... D 10
June 30—Martin Beni, Port Moresby ... D 10
Aug. 24—Alan Aldenhoven, Melbourne ... KO 6
Nov. 11—Andy Broome, West Heidelberg ... W 10

1978

Feb. 27—Andy Broome, Melbourne ... W 10
June 16—Steve Ayerst, West Heidelberg ... W 10
Aug. 11—Buddy Nixon, South Melbourne ... KO 7

1979

Mar. 30—Andy Broome, Revesby ... W 12
Apr. 26—Speedy Duke, Revesby ... KO 3
Nov. 2—Jeff Malcolm, Griffith ... KO by 3
Nov. 14—Lawrence Austin, Melbourne ... D 10

1980

Mar. 7—Andy Broome, Melbourne ... KO 4
Apr. 16—Lawrence Austin, Melbourne ... W 15
(Won Australian Welterweight Title)
Sept. 29—Hector Thompson, Brisbane ... KO 12

ERNESTO ROS
Italian Welterweight
1977

Jan. 29—Bernardo Bonizzoni, Longarone ... D 6
Mar. 17—Luciano Bolis, Milano ... KO by 5
July 3—Bernardo Bonizzoni, Trescore ... W 6
Oct. 29—Mario Favotto, Montebelluna ... D 6
Nov. 18—Giorgio Maggio, Livorno ... KO 2

1978

Feb. 4—Spartaco Verna, Ostia ... W 6
Feb. 24—Vincenzo Di Camillis, Modena ... D 6
Sept. 2—Mario Favotto, Crocetta ... D 6
Sept. 30—Roberto Manoni, Sondrio ... L 6
Dec. 26—Antonio Stocchino, Bologna ... WF 6

1979

May 19—Timoteo Bonizzoni, Crema ... L 8
Oct. 19—Antonio Stocchino, Cagliari ... D 8
Nov. 16—Donato Romano, Milan ... L 8
Dec. 14—Ciro Seta, Salerno ... L 8
Dec. 26—Gianni Molesini, Piacenza ... D 8

1980

Jan. 25—Antonio Stocchino, Bologna ... WF 6
Mar. 28—Paolo Zanusso, San Dona ... D 8

GARY ROSEN
Australian Lightweight
1979

Feb. 7—Joey Collins, Brookvale ... TD 4
Apr. 4—Mick McLean, Brookvale ... W 6
July 17—Buddy Clare, Kingsford ... W 6
Aug. 15—Paul Baker, Mt. Pritchard ... D 10
(For Vacant New South Wales Lightweight Title)

1980

Feb. 26—Kirk Blair, Kingsford ... D 6
July 29—Gil McGrath, Kingsford ... KO 3
Aug. 12—W. Leslie, Kingsford ... KO 5
Nov. 5—Paul Baker, Brookvale ... D 6

RAY ROSS
British Lightweight
1975

Mar. 5—Billy Boyd, Belfast ... KO 1
Apr. 12—Pat Campbell, Belfast ... KO 4
Apr. 28—Herbie McLean, Glasgow ... L 6
May 21—Benny Purdy, Belfast ... KO 5
Oct. 2—Charlie Nash, Derry ... L 10
Nov. 17—Hugh Smith, Glasgow ... KO by 6

1976

Mar. 4—Billy Surgeoner, Belfast ... KO 3
Mar. 22—Herbie McLean, Glasgow ... L 8
Apr. 5—Tommy Dunn, London ... KO by 7
May 24—Alan Richardson, London ... KO by 5
Nov. 9—Billy Vivian, Derry ... L 6

1977

Jan. 28—Godfrey Butler, West Bromwich ... W 8
Mar. 24—Kevin Davies, Leicester ... L 8
Apr. 26—Jim Montague, Derry ... L 10
July 30—Pat Campbell, Derry ... W 6
Aug. 5—Hogan Jimoh, Lagos ... KO by 6
Oct. 4—Benny Purdy, Belfast ... KO by 4

1978

Feb. 3—Gene McGarrigle, Enniskillen ... W 6
Feb. 27—Rocky Beaumont, Sheffield ... L 8
Oct. 11—Billy Rabbitt, Belfast ... KO 5
Nov. 11—Sid Smith, Marylebone ... KO by 7
Dec. 5—Sylvester Mittee, Kensington ... KO by 2

1979

June 27—Nigel Thomas, Derry ... KO by 5
Nov. 3—Hugh Smith, Glasgow ... L 6
Nov. 19—Alan Lamb, Lewisham ... KO by 3

1980

Feb. 28—Jackie Turner, Hull ... KO by 4

NESS ROUX
South African Junior Middleweight
1979

Sept. 1—Joseph Zikhala, Empangeni ... KO by 4

1980

Feb. 4—Gregory Clark, Durban ... KO by 2
Mar. 1—Zacharia Yhabethe, Durban ... W 4
Apr. 28—Jabulani Sithole, Durban ... KO 2
June 16—Bernard Sekhakane, Durban ... KO by 2

CLYDE RUAN
British Featherweight
1980

Apr. 23—Stuart Crabb, Hove ... W 6
Apr. 30—Andy Thomas, Aylesbury ... W 4
May 8—Larry Richards, Solihull ... W 6
May 12—Brindley Jones, Reading ... W 6
June 3—Robert Hepburn, Aylesbury ... KO 2
June 18—Steve Simms, Burslem ... W 6

DENTON RUDDOCK
British Heavyweight
1975

June 2—Tony Blackburn, London ... W 6
June 24—Eddy Fenton, London ... W 6

1976

Jan. 20—Terry Mintus, Kensington ... W 6
Feb. 16—Tony Moore, Mayfair ... W 10
May 10—Syd Falconer, Bournemouth ... KO 2
Aug. 11—Neville Meade, Cardiff ... KO 7
Oct. 18—Billy Aird, Marylebone ... KO by 10

1977

Mar. 1—Tony Moore, Marylebone ... W 8
Apr. 5—Ishaq Hussein, Marylebone ... W 10
Dec. 6—John L. Gardner, Kensington ... KO by 8

1978

July 1—Kallie Knoetze, Pretoria ... KO by 3

1979

Oct. 30—David Pearce, Caerphilly ... KO by 7

1980

Feb. 2—Jean-Pierre Coopmans, Torhout ... L 10
Mar. 29—Sylvain Watbled, Lyons ... L 10
Sept. 16—Stan McDermott, London ... KO by 3

GIUSEPPE RUSSI
Italian Junior Welterweight
Born: March 11, 1953, San Severo
1974

Oct. 25—Franco Recupero, Milano ... KO 2
Nov. 22—Paolo Russo, Milano ... KO 2
Dec. 6—Antonio Navarro, Milano ... KO 2
Dec. 26—Salvatore Gennatiempo, Milano ... KO 3

1975

Jan. 17—Jean Pierre Di Stefano, Milan ... W 6
Feb. 1—Paolo Russo, Cinisello Balsamo ... KO 4
Feb. 21—Giovanni Maiorano, Milan ... W 8
Mar. 7—Jacques Mamane, Milan ... KO 6
Apr. 4—Antonio Benz, Milan ... KO 4
Apr. 18—Rocco Zecca, Milan ... KO 3
May 26—Andre Jordan, Milan ... W 8
June 13—Augusto Quadri, Milan ... KO 3
June 29—Vasco Armstrong, San Severo ... W 8
Aug. 12—Giuseppe Juppa, Foggia ... KO 3
Oct. 10—Piero Ceru, Milan ... W 8
Nov. 28—Ernesto Bergamasco, Milan ... L 4
Dec. 20—Giovanni Majorano, Milan ... W 8

1976

Aug. 21—Nicola D'Orazio, Fort Village ... W 8
Oct. 23—Luiz Ribeiro, San Severo ... W 8
Nov. 10—Luiz Ribeiro, Cagliari ... W 8

1977

Aug. 19—Mario Martiliano, Termoli ... W 8
Oct. 28—Nelson Gomez, Milan ... L 8

Dec.   8—Henry Palm, Copenhagen L   6

1978
Jan.   7—Eloy De Souza, Milan .... W   8
Feb.   24—Giuseppe Corbo, Milan L   8
May   20—Giuseppe Minotti, San Severo .... W   8
July   21—Augusto Lauri, Rosenheim .... D   6
Sept.   5—Guido Galletti, Bibione .... KO   3
Oct.   28—Pierangelo Pira, Riccione .... KO by   4
Dec.   26—Giuseppe Di Padova, Mantova .... KO by   3
1979
Apr.   6—Luciano Navarra, Barletta .... W   8
Apr.   21—Alois Carmeliet, Zele .... D   8
July   13—Francesco Gallo, San Severo .... W   8
Aug.   29—Giuseppe Martinese, Iseo .... L 12
             (Italian Junior Welterweight Title)
Nov.   3—Rene Martin, San Severo .... KO   5
1980
Mar.   29—Luciano Navarra, Bitonto L   8
May   23—Jean Symos, Liege L   8
Aug.   23—Alfonso Carrillo, Capua L   8

PADDY RYAN
British Middleweight
1980
Sept.   22—Pharoah Bish, London .... W   6
Oct.   13—Pharoah Bish, London .... W   6

JUAN SAAVEDRA
Spanish Light Heavyweight
1979
Oct.   31—Francisco Macias, Madrid .... W   4
Nov.   21—Juan Holgado, Barcelona L   6
1980
Jan.   26—Jorge Perez, Lorongo .... D   6
Mar.   28—Cristobal Crepsi, Palma de Mallorca .... KO   3
June   1—Alex Cardozo, Tarrasa L   6

BONGANI SABATANA
South African Junior Flyweight
1980
Mar.   29—Alfred Nelani, Queenstown .... W   4
Aug.   23—Sikhumbozo, King Williamstown .... KO   3

MANNY SACAY
Philippine Bantamweight
1979
Feb.   3—Rey Orbino, Leyte .... W 10
Mar.   4—Romy Roa, Cebu City .... W 10
Sept.   1—Rene Sedayon, Manila .... W 10
Nov.   17—Ruben Arevalo, Manila .... L 10
1980
Feb.   8—Diony Diaz, Manila .... D 10
July   4—Jaime Sanama, Manila .... KO   3
Aug.   29—Flor Tampos, Quezon City .... W 10
Sept.   19—Glen Orlanes, Quezon City .... W 10
Nov.   19—Danilo Inocian, Quezon City .... L 10
Dec.   19—Rey Naduma Jr., Manila .... L 10

JORGE SALA
Spanish Middleweight
1979
Oct.   24—Diego Valero, Madrid .... W   4
Nov.   24—Jose M. Omedas, Zaragoza .... W   4
1980
Jan.   5—Scassino Ferreira, Santander .... KO by   1
Mar.   8—Cristobal Crepsi, Palma de Mallorca   KO by   1

BEN SAAD SALAH
Spanish Junior Middleweight
1980
Feb.   1—Augusto Lauri, Ostia .... W   8
Mar.   14—Rosario Pacileo, Rome .... W   6
May   2—Nelson Gomez, Rome L   8

KEN SALISBURY
Australian Middleweight
1979
June   25—Jim Gillon, Rooty Hill .... W   6
July   3—Benny Mack, Kingsford .... W   6
July   26—Joe Mario, Springvale .... KO   2
Aug.   28—Darryl Carrick, Springvale .... W   8
Oct.   23—Ken Morris, Kingsford .... W   8
Nov.   20—Ian Looker, Kingsford .... WF   5

1980
Mar.   25—Buddy Nixon, Kingsford .... W   8
Apr.   22—Bob McQueenie, Kingsford .... KO   6
June   3—Joe Mario, Kingsford .... KO   4
July   1—Buddy Nixon, Kingsford .... W   5
July   29—Laurie Mack, Kingsford .... KO   7
Aug.   26—Tony Martello, Kingsford .... KO   4
Sept.   16—Ross Eadie, Sutherland .... W 10
Nov.   11—Benny Tabua, Sutherland .... KO   9

MATTEO SALVEMINI
Italian Middleweight
1977
Feb.   4—Mashapata Kabangu, Milan .... KO   5
Feb.   19—Luciano Bolis, Milano .... W   6
Mar.   11—Giuseppe Panunzio, Milano .... W   6
June   10—Luciano Spina, Milan .... KO   5
June   24—Alberto Ramirez, Podenzano .... KO   2
Sept.   21—Gabrielle Lazzari, Milan .... KO   5
Oct.   14—Mariano Salomone, Bologna .... KO   2
Dec.   2—Ridha Hakimi, Milan .... KO   4
1978
Mar.   31—Jacques Chinon, Milan .... KO   7
Apr.   22—Jean Claude Warusfel, San Remo .... W   6
May   14—Aroldo Olivares, Pescara .... KO   3
June   7—Eric Seys, Faenza .... KO   4
July   7—Eric Seys, Podenzano .... KO   4
Sept.   28—Trento Facciocchi, Milan .... KO   7
             (Italian Middleweight Title)
Dec.   2—Giuseppe Martinese, Bilbao .... W 15
             (European Junior Welterweight Title)
1979
Jan.   12—Freddie Boynton, Milano .... KO   2
Apr.   6—Jimmy Pickard, Barletta .... KO   7
May   18—Roberto Felicioni, Reiti .... W 12
             (Italian Middleweight Title)
Oct.   12—Nicola Cirelli, Rome .... KO 11
             (Italian Middleweight Title)
1980
Feb.   29—Dan Snyder, Rome .... KO   4
May   2—Al Clay, Rome .... KO   2
July   1—Manuel Lira, Bitonto .... KO   6
Sept.   10—Kevin Finnegan, San Remo .... W 12
             (Retained European Middleweight Title)

HUGAES SAMO
French Welterweight
1978
Oct.   28—Lucien Campo, Calais .... KO   5
Nov.   18—Joel Leprodhomme, Calais .... D   6
Nov.   25—Georges Lemmer, Bruay .... KO   4
1979
Jan   6—Dragan Tadic, Aire .... W   6
Jan.   13—Maurice Renaud, Arques .... W   6
Feb.   17—Jean Claude Mabillard, Calonne .... KO   3
Apr.   28—Mutuawle Kibassa, Calais .... W   6
Oct.   19—Jean Pierre Moreau, Calais .... KO   2
Nov.   3—Maurice Renaud, Louvril .... W   6
Nov.   15—Claude Lancastre, Paris L   8
Nov.   24—Jackie Peraire, Calais .... KO   4
1980
Jan.   12—Johnny Elliott, Calais .... W   8
Mar.   8—Kachama Musasa, Calais L   8
Mar.   2—Sannlation, Calais .... KO   1
Oct.   3—Dennis Pryce, Calais .... W   8
Nov.   8—Fred Coranson, Calais .... KO   5

JOSE SANCHEZ
Spanish Junior Lightweight
1974
Mar.   8—Grazietto Soro, Milan .... W   6
Mar.   22—Lucio Vailati, Milan .... D   6
Apr.   17—Alessandro Bini, La Spezia .... KO   4
Apr.   28—Grazietto Soro, Palermo .... KO   1
May   17—Almo Quaini, Genova .... WF   4
June   12—Daniel Figuroa, Albenga .... W   8
July   26—Abu Arrow, Sestri Levante .... W   8
Oct.   11—Dante Guarnieri, Milan .... W   6
Nov.   29—Salvatore Dui, Milan L   6
Dec.   13—Carlo Bonfanto, Milan .... KO   1
1975
May   9—Biagio Pierri, Milan .... D   8
June   13—Domenico Radiccioni, Milan .... KO   6
July   18—Prisco Rossetti, Desenzano .... KO   3
1976
May   14—Fulvio Giacomini, Milan .... D   8
1977
Jan.   14—Giovanni Cavazzini, Genova .... W   8
Apr.   28—Hans Henrik Palm, Copenhagen .... KO by   6
1978
May   19—Cosimo Lavino, Brindisi .... KO   6
June   9—Vincenzo Quero, Milan .... KO   6
July   22—Cosimo Lavino, Brindisi .... D   8

402

1979
(Inactive)
1980
Mar. 21—Antonio Germano, Rapallo ....W 6
May 9—Natale Vezzoli, Brescia ....L 8

MANUEL SANCHEZ
Spanish Middleweight
1977
Nov. 3—Jose G. Juardo, Palma Mallorca ....W 6
1978
May 20—Alberto Ramirez, Mallorca ....W 6
Aug. 11—Jose M. Omedas, Lluchamayor ....W 6
Aug. 25—Osvaldo Lopez, Calvia ....D 8
1979
Apr. 26—Jose M. Omedas, Mallorca ....W 6
June 15—Aureliano Guemez, Mallorca ....L 6
Aug. 11—Ignacio Gorostidi, S. Sebastiano ....D 6
1980
Jan. 19—Scassino Ferreira, Santander ....KO by 2

CECIL SANDOW
South African Light Heavyweight
1979
Mar. 5—April Speelman, Welkom ....W 4
Mar. 30—Henk Devenier, Bloemfontein ....L 4
Nov. 12—Petrus Espag, Welkom ....KO 3
1980
Feb. 4—Willie Opperman, Welkom ....W 4
May 3—Themba Buthelezi, Witsieshoek ......KO by 2

ANTONIO SANDRIN
Italian Junior Welterweight
1978
Dec. 9—Gerardo Scognamiglio, Udine ....D 6
Dec. 28—Angelo Bizzaro, Marcianise ....L 6
1979
Mar. 17—Bruno Simili, Pisa ....D 6
May 11—Luigi Curcetti, Senigallia ....L 6
June 15—Bruno Simili, Figline Valdarno ....L 6
Oct. 20—Antonio Germano, Latisana ....W 6
Nov. 9—Severino Picca, Piacneza ....L 6
1980
Jan. 25—Robert Masini, Bologna ....L 6
Mar. 7—Luciano Gestri, Torino ....L 6
Aug. 10—Luigi Curcetti, Monte Cassiano ....L 6

ANDREA SANGALLETTI
Italian Light Heavyweight
1979
May 19—Bruno Polloni, Crema ....KO 4
July 28—Luciano Bolis, Mezzanica ....D 6
Sept. 21—Antonio Salatino, Rome ....KO 2
Oct. 27—Aldo Tramentozzi, Rieti ....KO 2
1980
Apr. 4—Gabrielle Lazzari, Milan ....L 6
May 18—Gennaro Mauriello, Naples ....L 6

CHRIS SANIGAR
British Junior Welterweight
1978
Sept. 19—Eric Purkis, Southend ....W 6
Sept. 25—Bob Bravado, London ....KO 5
Oct. 18—Dave Douglas, Glasgow ....KO 5
Nov. 4—Yotham Kunda, Lusaka ....W 8
Nov. 21—Dill Collins, Wolverhampton ....KO 7
1979
Jan. 29—Granville Allen, Glasgow ....KO 3
Feb. 20—Benny Purdy, Kensington ....KO 3
Mar. 7—George McGurk, Solihull ....KO by 2
Mar. 31—Paysom Choolwe, Lusaka ....L 8
Apr. 23—Roy Vard, London ....D 8
June 26—Lawrence Williams, London ....W 6
Dec. 4—Najib Daho, Wembley ....KO by 1
1980
Feb. 19—Winston Spencer, London ....L 8
Oct. 7—Dave McCabe, London ....L 8

CARLOS SANTOS
Spanish Junior Middleweight
1980
Apr. 4—Charley Peterson, Milan ....KO 2
May 30—Celestin Kanynda, Rome ....KO 3

CEASER SASAKI
Japanese Light Heavyweight
1979
June 5—Katsuo Esashi, Yokohama ....KO 5
Dec. 20—Tsutomu Haguno, Tokyo ....KO 2
1980
Feb. 25—Tsumoru Okamoto, Tokyo ....KO 5
Mar. 13—Super Riki, Tokyo ....KO 3

KOJIRO SASAKI
Japanese Junior Lightweight
1978
Sept. 24—Keizo Kurebayashi, Hamamatsu ....L 10
1979
Nov. 10—Yasutsune Uehara, Okonawa ....KO by 10
1980
Apr. 14—Yasuhide Takahashi, Tokyo ....L 10

YOSHINOBU SASAKI
Japanese Flyweight
1979
Mar. 18—Nubuo Horigome, Tokyo ....L 6
1980
Jan. 10—Goichi Oshi, Tokyo ....L 8
Apr. 29—Koki Ishii, Tokyo ....KO by 5

KAZUMI SATO
Japanese Bantamweight
1979
May 4—Yu Kasahara, Tokyo ....L 10
(JBC Junior Featherweight Title)
Nov. 22—Eijiro Kurauma, Tokyo ....D 8
1980
Feb. 4—Masao Mizui, Osaka ....W 10
May 25—Yuji Oka, Tokyo ....KO by 7

NIGEL SAVORY
British Light Heavyweight
1979
June 18—Peter Tidgwell, Bradford ....L 6
Sept. 10—Gary Jones, Bradford ....W 6
Oct. 8—Stan Cranell, Bradford ....KO by 2
Dec. 6—Gary Jones, Glasgow ....L 6
1980
Jan. 7—Tommy Jones, Manchester ....L 6
Jan. 21—Gary Jones, Glasgow ....L 6
Feb. 6—Joe Frater, Liverpool ....KO 3
Feb. 18—Rocky Burton, Stockport ....L 6
Feb. 28—Mick Fellingham, Hull ....W 6
Mar. 27—Ernie Baister, Newcastle ....KO 4
Apr. 15—John O'Neil, Blackpool ....L 6
Apr. 21—Rocky Burton, Bradford ....KO by 4
May 31—John O'Neil, Liverpool ....W 6
Sept. 9—Joe Frater, Mexborough ....KO 6
Sept. 22—Gordwell Hylton, Wolverhampton ....L 6
Oct. 23—Lee White, Middlesbrough ....L 6

STEVE SAXON
Australian
1980
July 2—Roger Walker, Brookvale ....KO 5
July 22—Rocky Warren, Sutherland ....D 4
July 29—Rocky Warren, Kingsford ....W 6
Aug. 13—Gary Tempest, Brookvale ....L 8

GEORGE SAXTON
Australian Middleweight
1979
Apr. 4—Robert Devlin, Springvale ....D 6
May 10—Shane Styles, Preston ....L 6
June 13—Robert Devlin, Preston ....W 6
1980
Apr. 18—T. Edwards, Footscray ....W 6
May 16—J. J. Mario, Melbourne ....L 6
May 23—J. J. Mario, Melbourne ....L 4
Aug. 30—Torkano Marcos, Kanwall ....KO by 4
Sept. 20—Rocky Ward, Lavington ....W 6
Oct. 31—Peter Lund, Frankton ....KO by 6

ALESSANDRO SCARECCHI
Italian Lightweight
1980
Oct. 24—Vincenzo Di Ruocco, Grosseto ....KO 2
Dec. 26—Valerio Fretta, Firenze ....KO 4

ALVARO SCARPELLI
Italian Junior Middleweight
1976
Sept. 24—Mario Favotto, Lugo ....W 6
Dec. 18—Luciano Bolis, R. Emilia ....W 4
Dec. 26—Roy Kaba, R. Emilia ....W 6
1977
Jan. 28—Alfredo Rossi, Faenza ....KO 4
Mar. 4—Lorenzo Nardillo, Lugo ....W 8
Apr. 22—Luciano Spina, Faenza ....D 8
Dec. 26—Luigi Marini, Bologna ....L 6
1978
Jan. 27—Guglielmo Caldera, Faenza ....W 8
Apr. 7—Bernardo Bonizzoni, Faenza ....KO 3
June 7—Chaed Ringo, Faenza ....KO 3
Nov. 10—Luigi Minchillo, Milano ....KO 4

403

Dec. 1—Luigi Marini, Faenza ....W 8
1979
Apr. 13—Mauricio Fernandez Cruz, Forli ....W 8
June 8—Roy Kaba, Ravenna ....KO 8
Oct. 11—Mario Favotto, Faenza ....L 6
Nov. 10—Luigi Minchillo, Milano ....KO 4
1980
Mar. 29—Luigi Minchillo, Pesaro ....KO by 4
(For Italian Junior Middleweight Title)

ALEX SCHAAER
Australian Welterweight
1979
Jan. 30—John Lawrie, Kingsford ....W 4
Mar. 13—Hamis Mouche, Kingsford ....L 4
Mar. 27—Tommy Woodward, Kingsford ....D 4
June 6—Col Eckford, Brookvale ....W 4
June 19—Clint Brown, Kingsford ....L 6
July 4—Elley Parker, Brookvale ....KO by 3
Sept. 5—Ray Smith, Brookvale ....KO by 4
1980
June 3—Calby Barkell, Kingsford ....KO by 2
Oct. 7—Glen Norman, Kingsford ....KO by 3

HORST SCHULZE
German Middleweight
1980
Feb. 22—Mauro Valentino, Dusseldorf ....L 4
Mar. 22—Giampaolo Piras, Friedewald ....W 6
June 13—Uwe Wissenbach, Luebeck ....KO 2

IAN SCORTING
British Heavyweight
1980
July 30—John Vaughan, Doncaster ....KO 4
Oct. 22—Stan Carnall, Doncaster ....KO 5

GEORGE SCOTT
British Heavyweight
1977
Sept. 29—Alan Ward, Newcastle ....W 6
Oct. 10—Alan Ward, Marton ....W 6
Nov. 2—Clive Beardsley, Newcastle ....D 6
Dec. 5—Bob Young, Marton ....KO 3
1978
Feb. 7—Gordon Ferris, Islington ....KO 3
Mar. 23—Alan Ward, Suderland ....KO 2
Apr. 24—Neil Malpass, Middlesbrough ....W 8
May 23—Bobby Hennessey, Islington ....L 8
July 12—Terry O'Connor, Newcastle ....D 8
Sept. 26—Stan McDermott, Wembley ....KO 5
Oct. 24—Theo Josephs, Blackpool ....W 6
Dec. 4—Reg Long, Marton ....D 8
1979
Feb. 26—Mal Tetley, Middlesbrough ....KO 6
May 19—Al Syben, Brussels ....W 10
Nov. 12—Reg Long, Marton ....W 10
Nov. 20—Danny McAlinden, Belfast ....W 8
1980
Jan. 2—Hennie Thoonen, Rotterdam ....W 8
May 28—Terry Mintus, Cramlington ....L 10
(Eliminator, British Heavyweight Title)
Oct. 27—Clarence Hill, London ....KO by 5

VERNON SCOTT
British Light Heavyweight
1974
Oct. 15—Harry White, Shoreditch ....KO by 4
Nov. 14—Paul Stocks, Caister ....KO 6
Dec. 11—Carl Watson, Reading ....L 6
1975
Feb. 3—Billy Baggott, Mayfair ....D 6
Feb. 10—Len Britton, Bedford ....KO 6
Feb. 19—Billy Baggott, Manchester ....W 6
Oct. 28—George Gray, London ....W 8
Nov. 10—Peter Brisland, Cambridge ....D 8
Nov. 17—Steve Foley, London ....KO 6
Dec. 2—Lloyd Gardner, London ....W 8
Dec. 8—Leroy Herriott, Merthyr ....KO by 6
1976
Feb. 3—Alan Butters, London ....W 8
Feb. 18—George Gray, London ....KO 6
Feb. 23—Alec Tompkins, London ....W 8
Mar. 15—Carl Watson, London ....L 8
Sept. 25—Gerald Bois, Sedan ....KO by 2
Oct. 22—Wayne Bennett, Digbeth................L 8
1977
May 4—Tony Allen, Solihull ....L 8
Sept. 26—Eddie Vieling, London ....KO 6
Nov. 8—Greg Evans, London ....KO 5
1978
May 18—Francis Hands, Liverpool ....L 8
Oct. 16—Errol McKenzie, London ....KO by 6

Nov. 21—Johnny Waldron, Wembley ....L disq. 3
1979
Nov. 26—Danny Miller, Birmingham ....KO by 5
1980
Feb. 28—Alex Tompkins, Queensway ......KO by 5
Apr. 28—Earl Edwards, Windsor ....W 8

YUKIO SEGAWA
Japanese Junior Featherweight
(Previous Record Unavailable)
1978
June 6—Keji Kunishige, Tokyo ....KO by 10
Aug. 15—Mukordum Muangsurin, Tokyo ....W 10
Oct. 26—Sandy Noora, Tokyo ....W 10
Dec. 28—Somkiat Sukothai, Tokyo ....KO 8
1979
Sept. 6—Ricardo Cardona, Rachinohe ....L 15
(WBA Junior Featherweight Title)
Nov. 27—Larry Enriquez, Tokyo ....W 10
1980
Apr. 26—Kenzo Takasugi, Hachinoche ....W 10

YVON SEGOR
French Welterweight
1976
Jan. 23—Jean Pierre Di Stefano, Marseille ....W 6
Apr. 8—Roger Lobjois, Paris ....W 6
Sept. 17—Mushapata Kubangu, Marseille ....KO 3
Oct. 1—Sejfudin Hozic, Marseille ....KO 2
1977
Mar. 11—Jean Pierre Moreau, Marseille ....KO 3
1977
Mar. 11—Jean Pierre Moreau, Marseille ....W 6
Sept. 11—Tekila Rodri, S. Sebastiano ....KO 5
Oct. 7—Alfred Lagasse Marseille ....KO 1
Nov. 4—Gerard Breton, Marseille ....W 8
1978
Jan. 27—Michel Chapier, Marseille ....KO by 8
1979
(Inactive)
1980
Apr. 18—Serge Sinelnikov, Paris ....W 6
Oct. 31—Maurice Bufi, Marseilles ....KO 5

ADOR SEGUIN
Filipino Junior Featherweight
1980
Feb. 8—Rudy Patalinhug, Manila ....W 10
May 23—Ric Diamale, Manila ....L 12
(For Philippino Junior Featherweight Title)
Aug. 1—Fel Viesca, Manila ....L 10

NORMAN SEKGAPANE
South African Junior Welterweight
Born: March 2, 1948
1970
Apr. 4—Lloyd Zulu, Natalspruit ....W 4
May 30—Joe Mosiere, Springs ....W 4
1971
Feb. 6—Jake Sennakgomo, Jabulani ....KO 2
May 1—Ernest Phage, Jabulani ....KO 1
June 11—Vincent Mthembu, Mamelodi ....W 6
Aug. 13—Reginald Hilmer, Natalspruit ....W 6
Sept. 4—Richard Borias, Barberton ....L 8
Oct. 2—Shole Mokoena, Jabulani ....W 8
Nov. 12—Petrus Khavumba, Thembisa ....KO 3
Dec. 4—Sparara Qubele, Thembisa ....KO 5
1972
Feb. 11—Jeremiah Nzelwane, Dobsonville ....W 8
Feb. 25—Petrus Mokoena, Kwa-Thema ....W 10
Mar. 17—Anthony Morodi, Thembisa ....W 8
Mar. 25—Daniel Mkize, Jabulani ....KO 6
May 12—Moses Mashigo, Springs ....KO 4
June 2—Norman Mabakane, Daveyton ....KO 6
June 24—Joe Archer, Jabulani ....W 10
July 28—Victor Tshabalala, Natalspruit ....KO 2
Aug. 25—Andries Moloi, Springs ....KO 5
Sept. 30—Gabriel Dlamini, Jabulani ....W 4
Oct. 21—Dan Mkhize, Port Elizabeth ....W 8
Nov. 3—Daniel Mkhize, Tembisa ....W 6
Nov. 17—Petrus Mokoena, Springs ....W 10
1973
Feb. 17—Joseph Baloyi, Orlando ....KO 8
Mar. 3—Johannes Zwane, Jabulani ....KO
Mar. 31—Moses Mthembu, Durban ....L 10
Apr. 13—Jeremiah Nzelwane, Springs L
May 26—Anthony Morodi, Jabulani ....W
(Won South African NE Lightweight Title)
June 22—Joe Archer, Springs ....W
Aug. 11—Joe Tetteh, Jabulani....................KO
Aug. 17—Abraham Lekhelebane, Springs ....KO
Oct. 6—Isaac Rakhajane, Kroonstad ....W
Oct. 27—Jonathan Bamidele, Jabulani ....W 1

Nov. 9—Jeremiah Nzelwane, Springs ....W 12
(Won Vacant South African NE Junior Welterweight Title)
1974
Feb. 1—Moses Mthembu, Springs ....KO 10
Apr. 5—Simon Nxawe, Springs..................KO 4
June 21—Anthony Morodi, Springs ....W 10
Aug. 17—Jorgen Hansen, Johannesburg..........KO 9
Sept. 6—Anthony Morodi, Springs ....W 12
(South African Lightweight Title)
Nov. 30—Everaldo Azevedo, Johannesburg.........W 10
1975
Feb. 28—Victor (Black Eagle) Tshabalala, Springs ....W 12
Apr. 21—Carlos Giminez, Cape Town ....L 10
June 28—Tadios Fisher, Jabulani.................KO 3
Aug. 30—Adriano Marrero, Jabulani...............W 10
Oct. 25—Anthony Morodi, Jabulani ....W 12
(South African Lightweight Title)
1976
Mar. 27—Rolly Xipu, Natalspruit..................W 12
(South African Non White Lightweight Title)
Apr. 24—Wally van der Haar, Jabulani...........KO 3
May 15—Jack Jim, Jabulani.....................W 12
June 5—Ben Lekalake, Jabulani.................W 10
Aug. 7—Nkosana (Happy Boy) Mgxaji,
Port Elizabeth ....D 6
Oct. 30—Nkosana Mgxaji, East London ....L 10
1977
Jan. 29—Dirk van der Westhuizen, Johannesburg ...WF 4
(South African Junior Welterweight Title)
May 6—Langton Tinago, Pretoria ....W 10
Sept. 8—Harold Volbrecht, Johannesburg ....L 10
Dec. 5—Rolly Xipu, Port Elizabeth ....D 10
1978
Apr. 29—Andries Steyn, Johannesburg ....W 12
(South African Lightweight Title)
Aug. 27—Antonio Cervantes, Mabatho ....KO by 9
(WBA Junior Welterweight Title)
Nov. 11—Andries Steyn, Johannesburg............L 12
(South African Lightweight Title)
1979
Mar. 9—Elias Diraditsile, Springs ....W 8
May 4—Evans Gwiji, Springs ....L 8
Aug. 3—Justus Josephs, Springs ....KO 8
Sept. 28—Tsietsi Meretloane, East London ....L 10
1980
Mar. 3—Bramley Whiteboy, Cape Town ....L 8
May 26—Bennie Nortman, Johannesburg ....L 8
Aug. 16—Mzwandile Biyana, East London .....KO by 7
(South African Junior Welterweight Title)

GEORGE SELEBI
South African Junior Middleweight
Born: May 16, 1953
1974
May 17—De Villiers Gongxeka, Orlando ....W 4
Aug. 30—Bethuel Mahlangu, Orlando West ......KO 2
Sept. 27—Simon Ramakgoakgoa, Wattville ....KO 2
Oct. 18—Jackson Masango, Tembisa ....W 4
1975
Feb. 21—Jeremiah Nzelwane, Orlando West ....L 6
July 25—Thuso Mapela, Orlando ....L 6
Aug. 1—David Kgotsane, Kwa-Thema ....KO 2
1976
Jan. 30—Emmanuel Gumede, Orlando West ....D 6
Apr. 2—Benjamin Molokeng, Orlando West .....KO 2
June 19—Emmanuel Gumede, Port Elizabeth ......W 8
1977
Sept. 10—David Kambule, Kroonstad ....KO by 3
Nov. 19—Gordon Mpehlo, Port Elizabeth ....KO 2
1978
(Inactive)
1979
Aug. 4—Mzwandile Mqanto, East London ....KO 3
1980
Apr. 25—David Kambule, Sebokeng ....KO by 6
(For Transvaal Welterweight Title)
Aug. 1—Peter Mjogo, Springs ....L 6

KULI ABRAM SELLO
South African Middleweight
1980
Mar. 22—Daniel Mphuthi, Soweto ....W 4
Nov. 28—Basil Meintjies, Johannesburg ......KO by 4

GUISEPPE SEMILIA
Italian Welterweight
1980
Jan. 17—Filiberto Bachiuo, Cremona ....KO 4
Mar. 28—Massimo Cini, Pisa ....D 6
May 3—Rosario Pacileo, Palermo ....D 6
June 28—Massimo Cini, Palermo ....W 6

ROD SEQUENAN
Filipino Welterweight
1980
June 25—Nilo Acido, Quezon City ....W 10
Aug. 23—Francis Camatagan, Baguio City ....D 10
Sept. 28—Agustin Llagos, Manila ....KO 6

SAMUEL SEREKEGO
South African Bantamweight
1976
May 15—Benjamin Sebego, Kroonstad ....KO by 2
1977
June 11—William Matlokotsi, Kroonstad ....L 4
Dec. 3—Michael Khuto, Ficksburg ....W 4
1978
(Inactive)
1979
Feb. 10—Johannes Lesibo, Virginia ....L 4
Mar. 3—Andrew Peterson, Virginia ....D 4
Mar. 24—Michael Khuto, Virginia ....L 4
May 12—Andrew Peterson, Virginia ....W 4
June 16—Johannes Lesibo, Virginia ....W 4
1980
May 10—Richard Modise, Virginia ....W 6
Aug. 2—Joseph Diraditsile, Welkom ....L 4
Oct. 11—Samuel Mofumane, Odendaalsrust ......KO 1
Dec. 1—Paul Masooane, Virginia ....W 6

ROBERTO SERRELI
Italian Featherweight
1980
Apr. 19—Francesco De Rosa, Calgari ....W 4
May 3—Pasquala Mazza, Calgari ....L 6
Dec. 27—Battista Calvia, Calgari ....W 4

FREDDY SERRES
German Light Heavyweight
1978
Mar. 10—Darko Barakovic, Esch ....W 6
Apr. 10—Mohammed Torch, Esch ....W 6
May 9—Eric Seys, Esch Sur Alzette ....W 6
Dec. 15—Hans Michel, Asbach ....KO 1
Dec. 25—Horst Lang, Esch ....W 6
1979
Jan. 27—Karl Heinz Schulz, Esch Sur Alzette ....KO 1
Mar. 3—Etienne Bayidkla, Differdange ....W 6
June 29—Salmin Bouteraa, Esch sur Alzette ......KO 3
Oct. 12—Louis Pergaud, Rome ....KO by 2
Oct. 27—Jose Centa, Differdange ....KO 6
1980
Feb. 22—Mandu Refraid, Luxembourg ....L 6
Mar. 29—Mandu Refraid, Differdange ....KO 4
July 12—Rudi Koopmans, Luxembourg ....L 12

HENDRYK SEYS
Belgian Heavyweight
1975
Oct. 4—Jean Pierre Heirman, Antwerp ....W 6
Nov. 1—Mohammed Arras, Izegem ....W 6
1976
Jan. 3—Sonny Kamunga, Gits ....W 6
Feb. 6—Mohammid Arras, Bruges ....W 6
Feb. 28—Antonino Baletta, Gits.................W 6
Apr. 23—Tito Larbe, Gits.....................KO by 3
Sept. 4—Gilbert Cnudde, Gistel ....KO 4
Oct. 9—Michel Parent, Anversa ....KO 6
Oct. 26—Michel Parent, Molenbeck ....KO 6
Nov. 27—Majoli, Gits..........................KO 5
1977
Mar. 12—Guss Bleus, Antwerp ....W 6
Apr. 2—Guido Beuselinck, Ostenda ....KO 3
Apr. 16—Bernard Artone, Zele ....WF 4
Sept. 9—Guss Bleus, Izegem ....KO by 6
1978
Feb. 25—Odon Beltchika, La Louviere ....W 8
June 7—Piermarino Pagani, Faenza ....KO 4
Sept. 4—Fighting Walcott, Rotterdam ....KO 2
Sept. 30—Maurice Bufi, Turnhout ....W 8
Nov. 1—Jose Lozano, Izegem ....KO by 8
Dec. 8—Branko Barokovic, Gits ....W 8
1979
Jan. 8—Stan Van Der Driessche, Rotterdam ..KO by 5
Mar. 9—Nicola Cirelli, Rome ....KO by 3
Apr. 28—Agamil Yildirim, Belgrade ....KO by 3
Oct. 6—Nedjad Memetti, Lauwe ....NC
1980
Feb. 8—Robert Desnouck, Torhout ....W 8
Apr. 18—Robert Desnouck, Lauwe ....W 12
(Won Vacant Belgian Heavyweight Title)

JOHN SHARKEY
British Lightweight
1980

Sept. 15—Chris McCallum, Glasgow .... KO 3
Oct. 14—Gerry Beard, Wolverhampton .... KO 3

KEVIN SHEEHAN
British Lightweight
1976

Oct. 25—Young Daly, Luton .... W 4
Nov. 30—Don Aagesen, Dudley .... KO by 1
1977
Mar. 3—Malcolm McHugh, Caister .... KO 3
Mar. 15—Albert Coley, Leeds .... D 4
Apr. 20—Cleveland Irvine, Manchester .... W 6
May 17—Nagib Daho, Wolverhampton .... KO by 2
Oct. 11—Steve Early, Coventry .... KO by 3
1978
Oct. 12—Tony Vernon, Liverpool .... L 6
Oct. 23—George Schofield, Manchester .... KO by 4
1979
(Inactive)
1980
Jan. 21—Dave Ramsden, Nottingham .... KO 1
Jan. 28—Robert Wakerfield, Bradford .... KO 4
Feb. 25—John Lindo, Bradford .... D 6
Mar. 3—Glen Rhodes, Nottingham .... KO 1
Mar. 5—Jimmy Bunclarke, Liverpool .... KO by 1
Oct. 13—Jarvis Greenidge, Nottingham .... L 8

McDONALD MANDLA SHEZI
South African Light Heavyweight
1973

Apr. 27—Augustus Motaung, Natalspruit .... KO 2
July 27—Abner Ngwenya, Natalspruit .... KO 2
Sept. 7—Abram Hlatshwayo, Orlando .... KO 2
1974
Feb. 15—Victor Ntloko, Rabasutho .... KO by 4
Sept. 20—Golden Mlotywa, Natalspruit .... KO by 5
1975-1977
(Inactive)
1978
Mar. 31—Sophania Manyika, Natalspruit .... W 4
May 15—Morgan Moledi, Johannesburg .... D 4
Sept. 30—Johannes Mpesi, Sharpville .... KO 7
1979
Mar. 9—Daniel Mapanya, Springs .... KO by 3
June 18—Sidney Bensch, Johannesburg .... L 6
1980
May 17—Prince Tukane, East London .... KO by 3
July 2—Willie Opperman, Welkom .... L 6

SYDNEY SIPHIWE SHEZI
South African Junior Middleweight
1978

Mar. 31—Abram Nthupi, Natalspruit .... W 4
1979
Mar. 9—David Kalako, Springs .... D 4
June 29—Simon Motlhabane, Natalspruit .... KO 2
Aug. 31—Morgan Moledi, Natalspruit .... W 6
1980
July 2—Michael Motsoane, Welkom .... L 6

KENJI SHIBATA
Japanese Middleweight
(Previous Record Unavailable)
1974

Jan. 15—Nobuyoshi Ozaki, Tokyo .... W 10
May 10—Hitosh Nakagawa, Osaka .... W 10
(Japanese Junior Middleweight Title)
July 21—Masami Yoshinaga, Tokyo .... KO 5
Nov. 11—Hideo Kanazawa, Nagoya .... KO 4
1975
Jan. 27—Hiroshi Hikichi, Tokyo .... D 10
(Japanese Junior Middleweight Title)
Mar. 30—Isamu Kondo, Tokyo .... KO 3
Apr. 28—In Choul Cho, Tokyo .... W 10
July 13—Jae Keun Yim, Inchon .... KO by 10
(Orient Junior Middleweight Title)
Aug. 9—Shoichi Yanagawa, Toyoda City .... KO 6
1976
Jan. 31—Takeshi Yamato, Nagoya .... KO 3
Mar. 6—Im JeaKeun, Seoul .... KO by 7
Apr. 14—Peter Noble, Hamamatsu City .... W 10
July 27—Hiroshi Hikichi, Tokyo .... W 10
(Japanese Junior Middleweight Title)
Oct. 25—Sumio Kai, Tokyo .... KO 9
(Japanese Junior Middleweight Title)
1977
Jan. 4—Michihiro Horihata, Tokyo .... W 10
Mar. 5—Sanshiro Higo, Kumamoto City .... KO 2
(Japanese Junior Middleweight Title)
June 5—Tazan Tobaru, Tokyo .... W 10

Sept. 13—Eddie Gazo, Tokyo .... L 15
(WBA Junior Middleweight Title)
Dec. 3—Sumid Kai, Tokyo .... KO 3
(Japanese Junior Middleweight Title)
1978
Apr. 11—Minoru Ono, Tokyo .... KO 5
(Japanese Junior Middleweight Title)
June 24—Mamoru Taira, Handa City .... KO 2
Sept. 9—Michihiro Horihata, Fujisawa City .... W 10
(Japanese Junior Middleweight Title)
Nov. 19—Yim Jae-Keun, Pusan .... D 12
1979
July 11—Michihiro Horihata, Yokohama ...... KO by 10
Oct. 18—Michihiro Horihata, Fujisawa Shi .... D 10
(JBC Junior Middleweight Title)
1980
Mar. 18—Chong-Pal Park, Seoul .... KO by 5
(For OPBF Middleweight Title)

WOON-CHUL SHIN
Korean Junior Lightweight
1980

Mar. 1—Tae-Jin Moon, Raesan .... KO by 5
(For Korean Lightweight Title)
May 9—Nene Jun, Manila .... KO by 6

KAZUNORI SHIRATORI
Japanese Welterweight
1975

Sept. 28—Masatoshi Ogasaware, Tokyo .... KO by 6
1976
Jan. 16—Yohi Arai, Osaka .... L 10
May 26—Hidemori Tsujimoto, Osaka City .... W 10
Dec. 19—Masahiro Misako, Tokyo .... KO by 9
1977
Feb. 25—Buffalo Susuki, Tokyo .... KO by 2
Mar. 26—Shoji Tsujimoto, Hamamatsu City .... L 10
(Japanese Welterweight Title)
Sept. 9—Ryuichi Narita, Nagoya City .... L 10
Dec. 3—Sumio Kai, Tokyo .... KO 3
(Japanese Junior Middleweight Title)
1978
Jan. 29—Ryuchi Narita, Nagoya City .... L 10
Apr. 11—Hiro Inada, Osaka .... KO 6
1979
June 19—Vito Meredith, Honolulu .... KO by 5
1980
Mar. 13—Akio Kameda, Tokyo .... KO by 8
(For Japanese Welterweight Title)

PAULOS SHOZI
South African Featherweight
1978

Nov. 25—Antony Hadebe, Durban .... D 4
1979
(Inactive)
1980
Mar. 2—Dan Veeran, Durban .... D 4
Apr. 14—Brian Baronet, Durban .... KO by 2

BASHEW SIBACA
South African Featherweight
1970

Dec. 10—Tabo Loko, Langa .... W 8
1971
Sept. 30—Patrick Khali, Cape Town .... W 6
Dec. 7—C. Adams, Cape Province .... W 8
1972
Feb. 24—Joseph Gumede, Langa .... KO by 6
Apr. 26—Chris Dlamini, Athlone .... W 10
May 27—John Fraser Mkhize, Durban .... D 8
Sept. 23—Chris Dlamini, Port Elizabeth .... L 8
Oct. 5—Jacob Jobe, Cape Town .... W 8
Oct. 31—Isaac Nuku, Langa .... W 8
1973
Mar. 3—Johannes Sithebe, Port Elizabeth .... D 8
May 24—Paulos Shozi, Cape Town .... W 8
July 28—Joseph Gumede, Port Elizabeth .... L 12
(For South African Bantmweight Title)
1974
Sept. 23—William Mahlokotsi, Cape Town .... W 8
1975
Feb. 8—Mzukisi Skweyiya, East London .... L 8
(For Cape Bantamweight Title)
June 14—Aurbrey Peta, Port Elizabeth .... W 8
Oct. 4—Chris Dlamini, East London .... L 8
1976
Mar. 13—Guy Ratazayo, Port Elizabeth .... W 10
(Won Vacant Cape NE Featherweight Title)
Oct. 9—Tsietsi Maretloane, East London .... L 12
(For South African Nat NE Featherweight Title)
1977
May 30—Guy Ratazayo, Port Elizabeth .... W 10

Nov. 14—Hansie van Rooyen, Cape Town ....W 8
Dec. 1—Alex Venter, Cape Town ....W 4
1978
Feb. 22—Thomas Sithebe, Cape Town ....W 12
(Won Vacant South African NE Featherweight Title)
Mar. 20—Freddie Rust, Cape Town ....KO 3
Apr. 29—Victor Mpiyakhe, Cape Town ....L 12
(Lost South African National NE Featherweight Title)
Oct. 28—Tsietsi Maretloane, East London ....KO 11
(Won Supreme South African Featherweight Title)
Nov. 15—Cecil Baatjies, Cape Town ....KO 2
1979
Mar. 7—Salvatore Melluzzo, Cape Town ....W 10
Apr. 14—Victor Mpiyake, Goodwood ....KO 5
(South African Featherweight Title)
Sept. 27—Sipho Mange, Cape Town ....W 12
(South African Featherweight Title)
Oct. 20—Jay Nardo, Pretoria ....W 6
Dec. 14—Jacob Diraditsile, Welkom ....W disq. 5
1980
June 4—Gerald Hayes, Cape Town ....L 10
Sept. 6—Andries Hernandez, East London ....W 10
Nov. 8—Nkosana Moss, East London ....KO 10
(For South African Featherweight Title)

ALFRED SIBISI
South African Junior Welterweight
1973
June 15—Moses Khoni, Orlando West ....L 4
Oct. 6—J. Masapo, Kroonstad ....W 4
1974
Feb. 22—Bethuel Mahlangu, Dobsonville ....W 4
1975
June 28—Elias Malefane, Jabulani ....W 4
Oct. 18—Absolom Ndhlosi, Durban ....KO 3
Nov. 28—Stefaans Phala, Kwa-Thema ....W 4
1976
Mar. 27—Alpheus Kgapola, Natalspruit ....KO 3
May 15—Reginald Menong, Jabulani ....KO 3
July 17—Michael Dala, Port Elizabeth ....D 6
Oct. 30—Tamie Spampool, East London ....W 4
1977
Mar. 4—Peet van der Westhuizen, Pretoria ......KO 3
Nov. 28—Andries Steyn, Durban ....L 6
1978
Apr. 17—Joshua Plaatjies, Johannesburg ....D 4
Nov. 17—Simon Dhladhla, Springs ....W 10
(Won Vacant Transvaal NE Lightweight Title)
1979
Oct. 5—Martin Jacobs, Bloemfontein ....W 6
Dec. 8—Tsietsi Maretloane, East London ....L 8
1980
Mar. 1—Peet Bothma, Ermelo ....L 6
May 17—Peter Kanie, East London ....KO by 5

ALEXANDER SIBIYA
South African Featherweight
1978
Feb. 27—Robert Baronet, Durban ....L 4
Aug. 12—Robert Makhoba, Durban ....KO by 3
Aug. 28—Robert Baronet, Durban ....W 4
Oct. 10—Jacob Mpanza, Durban ....KO 2
1979
Feb. 12—Norman Bromfield, Durban ....L 4
Mar. 10—Joseph Gumede, Newcastle ....L 6
1980
Apr. 14—Essau Dhlamini, Durban ....KO 9
(For Natal Featherweight Title)
May 19—Elijah Cele, Durban ....L 4
Aug. 4—Anthony Dhlamini, Durban ....L 4
Dec. 15—Essau Dhlamini, Pmburg ....L 10
(For Natal Featherweight Title)

LOUIS SIBIYA
South African Junior Middleweight
1975
Feb. 6—Kenneth Maseko, Kwa-Thema ....L 4
Mar. 7—Stefaan Mfaba, Natalspruit ....W 4
May 9—Sothoane Khoaelane, Natalspruit ....L 4
Oct. 31—Edward Moloi, Natalspruit ....W 4
1976
Mar. 27—Petrus Sikhosana, Natalspruit ....D 4
1977
May 21—David Kambule, Kroonstad ....L 8
1978
Mar. 31—Ephraim Mabena, Natalspruit ....L 4
1979
June 29—Aaron Somdaka, Natalspruit ....KO by 2
Aug. 01—Banginkosi Buthelezi, Natalspruit ....W 4
1980
Mar. 28—Leo Simelane, Springs ....KO by 1
Nov. 29—Michael Motsoane, Odendaalsrust ....L 8

TONY SIBSON
British Middleweight
1976
Apr. 9—Charlie Richardson, Digbeth ....KO 2
May 6—John Breen, Birmingham ....W 6
May 26—Liam White, Wolverhampton...........W 6
July 14—Jimmy Pickard, Wolverhampton..........W 6
Sept. 10—Bonnie McKensie, Digbeth ....KO 7
Oct. 22—Clive Davidson, Digbeth ....W 8
Nov. 3—Neville Esteban, Caister ....W 8
Nov. 24—John Breen, London ....KO 5
Dec. 14—Tim McHugh, West Bromwich...........KO 4
1977
Jan. 11—Tony Burnett, Wolverhampton ....W 8
Jan. 19—Roy Gumbs, Solihull ....W 8
Feb. 10—Arthur Winfield, Coventry ....KO 2
Feb. 25—Gareth Jones, Digbeth ....KO 1
Mar. 23—Bunny McKenzie, Leicester ....KO 7
Apr. 7—Steve Walker, Dudley ....W 8
Apr. 21—Tony Burnett, Liverpool ....W 8
Apr. 27—Sonny Kamunga, Leicester ....W 8
Oct. 18—Pat Thomas, Wolverhampton ....D 8
Nov. 8—Wayne Bennett, West Bromwich ....W 8
Nov. 30—Oscar Angus, Wolverhampton ....KO 6
1978
Jan. 23—John Smith, London ....KO 5
Mar. 6—Errol McKenzie, London ....KO 2
Mar. 31—Mac Nicholson, Liverpool ....KO 7
Apr. 4—Steve Walker, London ....KO 5
Apr. 25—Mac Nicholson, London ....KO 1
May 23—Lotte Mwale, Leicester ....KO by 1
June 29—Danny McLoughlin, Wolverhampton ...KO 3
July 18—Bonny McKenzie, Wakefield ....W 8
Sept. 12—Keith Bussey, Wembley ....KO 8
Oct. 24—Eddie Smith, Kensington ....L 8
Nov. 7—Gerard Nosely, Wembley ....KO 7
1979
Mar. 5—Eddie Smith, Wolverhampton ....W 10
Apr. 10—Frankie Lucas, Kensington ....KO 5
May 14—Al Clay, Wembley ....KO 7
June 26—Jacques Chinon, Leicester ....KO 8
Oct. 9—Willie Classen, London ....KO 2
Nov. 6—Kevin Finnegan, Kensington ....L 15
(British Middleweight Title)
Nov. 29—Robert Powell, Liverpool ....KO 1
1980
Jan. 22—James Waire, London ....W 10
Mar. 4—Chisanda Mutti, London ....W 15
(Won Vacant British Commonwealth Middleweight Title)
Dec. 8—Matteo Salvemini, London ....KO 7
(Retained European Middleweight Title)

AL SICAT
Filipino Flyweight
1979
Nov. 27—Flash Gapasin, Angeles City ....W 10
Dec. 20—Eddie Miral, Olongapo City ....D 10
1980
Feb. 16—Diego De Villa, Davao City ....L 12
(For Vacant Filipino Junior Bantamweight Title)
Feb. 27—Star Dayanan, Clark Air Base ....TD 10
Mar. 15—Billy Abato, De Oro City ....L 10

FRANCO SIDDU
Italian Junior Lightweight
1976
July 2—Alvaro Chece, Empoliq ....KO 2
Oct. 7—Giuseppe Pappalardo, Sassari ....W 6
Nov. 26—Marco Zanetti, Firenze ....KO 2
1977
Apr. 8—Alfonso Carillo, Ozieri ....D 6
June 17—Luigi De Rosa, Milano ....KO 5
Dec. 16—Vincenzo Di Ruocco, Firenze ....KO 4
Dec. 26—Renzo Battistelli, Firenze ....KO 3
1978
Mar. 31—Giuseppe Agate, Florence ....D 8
May 6—Salvatore Sui, Lido Camaiore ....D 8
Oct. 27—Abass Macauley, Florence ....W 8
1979
May 25—Melquiades Da Silva, Florence ....W 8
Nov. 24—Alessandro Nardi, Firenze ....W 8
1980
Mar. 15—Mario Angeli, Forli ....L 6
May 30—Aristide Pizzo, Florence ....L 12
(For Italian Lightweight Title)
Dec. 26—Rene Martin, Firenze ....W 8

TIDJANI SIDIBE
(NINO LA ROCCA)
Italian Welterweight
1978
Sept. 14—Jean Paul Coppyn, Paris ....KO 1

407

1979
Mar. 26—Claude Lancastre, Paris .... KO 6
Nov. 14—Giuseppe Minotti, Gualdo Tadino .... KO 2
1980
Jan. 24—Sammy Rookard, Genova .... KO 3
Feb. 6—Sinclair Chirstie, Falconara .... W 8
Feb. 29—Don Morgan, Rome .... KO 4
Mar. 28—Kachama Musassa, Rome .... W 8
May 2—Floyd Pearson, Rome .... KO 2
May 30—Larry McCall, Rome .... KO 5
June 27—Nelson Gomez, Palermo .... KO 5
July 9—Tony Martez, Bellaria .... KO 6
July 26—Billy Waith, Rapallo .... KO 3
Aug. 20—Carlos Pereyra, Cerveter .... KO 7
Aug. 30—Benedito Santos, Mali .... KO 4
Oct. 31—Ralph Twinning, Rome .... KO 5
Dec. 4—Santiago Valdez, Rome .... KO 5
Dec. 19—Frank Medina, Latina .... KO 6

TEMBISILE SIGETYE
South African Bantamweight
1973
June 9—Mzukisi Skewyiya, King Williamstown .... L 4
1974
Mar. 9—Joel Bochele, East London .... W 4
June 29—Leku Sandi, Queenstown .... W 8
Oct. 5—Manciedo Ntenjane, East London .... W 4
Nov. 2—Reuben Matewu, East London .... W 4
Nov. 9—Andile Tywabi, Port Elizabeth .... W 4
1975
June 14—Reuben Matewu, Port Elizabeth .... L 6
Oct. 4—Reuben Matewu, East London .... L 6
1976
Jan. 31—Kotikoti Sophila, East London .... W 4
May 22—Fundisile Kralo, Port Elizabeth .... W 6
Oct. 30—Lucas Nkoane, East London .... W 4
1977
May 7—Samson Majeke, Zwelitsha .... W 4
May 28—Monde Mpulampula, K. Wmstown ... KO by 5
1978
(Inactive)
1979
Feb. 10—Siphiwo Fuma, Queenstown .... KO by 1
1980
Mar. 29—Tembisile Nxingolo, Queenstown .... W 4
Nov. 22—Monde Mpulampula, Queenstown .... L 8

MAR SIMBAJON
Filipino Lightweight
1978
Sept. 22—Chun Mun Chin, Manila .... W 10
Nov. 5—Al Espinosa, Cebu City .... L 10
1979
Feb. 16—Leo Viajeder, Manila .... W 10
May 4—Mike Benitez, Manila .... D 10
June 25—Mashiro Yokai, Tokyo .... L 10
Sept. 15—Jun Gonzales, Manila .... KO 3
Sept. 29—Star Lantapan, San Pablo City .... D 10
Dec. 29—Max Boy Toyogon, Lucena City .... KO 5
1980
Feb. 8—Willie Makitoki, Manila .... W 10
May 23—Star Lantapan, Manila .... W 10

LEO SIMELANE
South African Junior Middleweight
1979
May 25—Bonginkosi Buthelezi, Springs .... KO 1
1980
Feb. 1—Johannes Hobbs, Springs .... KO 2
Mar. 12—Louis Sibiya, Springs .... KO 1
Apr. 25—Raymond Mashifane, Sebokeng .... W 6
May 14—Elias Malefane, Orlando .... KO 3
Aug. 1—Daniel Mphuthi, Springs .... KO 3
Oct. 4—David Kalako, Springs .... KO 3
Nov. 21—Nat Moloi, Sebokeng .... L 6

BRUNO SIMILI
Italian Lightweight
1978
Sept. 9—Gerardo Scognamiglio, Laitico .... W 6
Oct. 28—Giovanni Mannu, Pisa .... W 6
Nov. 17—Palmior Pizzata, Val d'Elsa .... W 6
1979
Jan. 26—Adriano Ubertini, Pisa .... KO 6
Mar. 17—Antonino Sandrin, Pisa .... D 6
June 15—Antonio Sandrin, Figline Valdarno .... W 6
Oct. 4—Antonio Pocai, Firenze .... KO 5
Dec. 14—Abass Macauley, Pisa .... W 8
1980
Mar. 28—Pasquale Riboli, Pisa .... WF 6
May 30—Patrick Drelon, Florence .... KO 2
Oct. 24—Mario Tiano, Grosseto .... W 8
Dec. 19—Guiseppe Agate, Lucca .... D 8

408

DUMILE SIKO
South African Welterweight
1976
Mar. 22—William Phillips, Guguletu .... W 4
Apr. 28—Prince Sithela, Guguletu .... W 6
1977
Dec. 14—Ephraim Mabena, Guguletu .... W 6
1978
June 1—James Abrahams, Goodwood .... W 4
1979
Jan. 16—Isaac Yoto, Cape Town .... L 6
June 21—Gordon Adams, Cape Town .... L 4
Sept. 5—Gordon Adams, Cape Town .... W 4
1980
Feb. 8—Isaac Yoto, Cape Town .... L 4

PETER SIMON
British Middleweight
1979
Sept. 24—Jerry Golden, Hammersmith .... KO 2
Oct. 29—Mickey Walker, Hove .... KO 4
Nov. 26—Earl Edwards, Hammersmith .... L 6
1980
Feb. 12—Earl Edwards, London .... D 8
Mar. 17—Terry Matthews, London .... L 8

DEREK SIMPKIN
British Heavyweight
1974
June 24—John DePledge, Bedford .... L 6
Sept. 9—Barry Clough, Bedford .... KO 3
Sept. 16—Tony Moore, Birmingham .... KO by 4
Oct. 23—Barry Clough, Stoke .... D 6
Dec. 4—Bruce Woodward, Stoke .... KO 4
Dec. 10—John DePledge, Blackpool .... W 6
1975
Jan. 13—Art Gibson, Mayfair .... KO 2
Feb. 17—Dave Fry, Mayfair .... KO 6
Feb. 26—Sid Paddock, Camberley .... W 6
Mar. 12—John DePledge, Solihull .... W 8
Mar. 24—Syd Paddock, Mayfair .... L 6
Apr. 9—John DePledge, Bradford .... W 6
Apr. 24—Bjorn Rudi, Ramsey .... W 8
May 13—Zambian Yotham Kunda, Southend ...... W 8
Aug. 6—Neville Meade, Cardiff .... KO by 3
Nov. 25—Paul Kinsella, London .... L 6
Dec. 12—Bjorn Rudi, Oslo .... L 8
1976
Jan. 13—Garfield McEwan, Wolverhampton .... L 8
Feb. 3—David Fry, London .... L 8
Mar. 29—Brian Huckfield, Bournemouth .... L 8
Apr. 6—Paul Kinsella, Kensington .... D 6
May 5—Terry Mintus, London .... KO by 6
Oct. 5—Brian Huckfield, Coventry .... KO by 5
1977
Feb. 7—Terry Mintus, London .... L 8
Feb. 22—Peter Freeman, Wolverhampton .... L 8
Mar. 1—Kris Smith, Marylebone .... L 8
Apr. 18—Paul Kinsella, Mayfair .... KO 4
May 9—Neil Malpass, London .... L 6
May 26—John DePledge, Bradford .... W 8
Sept. 8—Bruce Brandham, Liverpool .... KO by 5
1978
Nov. 20—Colin Flute, Birmingham .... W 6
Nov. 30—Theo Josephs, Caister .... L 6
1979
Mar. 16—Winston Allen, Bradford .... L 8
Oct. 16—Brian Huckfield, West Bromwich .... L disq. 7
1980
Oct. 30—Steve Gee, Wolverhampton .... D 6
Nov. 13—Martin Nee, Queensway .... L 8

ERROL SIMPSON
Australian
1979
Jan. 12—Red Christian, Urangan .... W 10
July 21—Arnold Murray, Murgon .... L 8
Aug. 31—Chris Murray, Redcliff .... D 8
Dec. 8—Col Thompson, Redcliff .... KO 9
1980
Apr. 25—Kevin Wagstaff, Mt. Granatt .... W 8
June 9—Red Christian, Brisbane .... D 8
June 28—Arnold Murray, Nanango .... L 10

SANDY SIMS
British Featherweight
1980
Jan. 9—Glyn Rhodes, Burslem .... KO by 8
Mar. 19—Jarvis Greenidge, Stoke .... L 8
Apr. 21—Barry Winter, Nottingham .... W 8
May 27—Philip Morris, Newport .... W 8
June 18—Clyde Ruan, Burslem .... L 8
Sept. 22—Davy Larmour, Belfast .... W 8

Oct.   14—Don George, Nantwich ....L 8
Oct.   22—Peter Gabbitus, Doncaster ....W 4

IVAN SIMUNGIA
Yugoslavian Middleweight
1979
Dec.   8—Roy Kaba, Split ....W 4
Dec.   26—Giorgio Giana, Sondrio ....NC 5
1980
Mar.   14—Roberto Manoni, Tirano ....KO by 6
Sept. 20—Germano Apostoli, Sebenico ....KO by 3

SERGE SINELNIKOV
French Middleweight
1977
Oct.   7—Jean Paul Coppyn, Lione ....W 6
Dec.   24—Maurice Renaud, Luneville ....L 6
1978
Jan.   12—Gilles Elbilia, Paris ....L 6
Feb.   4—Roland Perfetti, Grenoble ....L 6
Apr.   7—Moussa Mukandjo, Annecy ....KO by 3
Oct.   30—Gilles Elibia, Paris ....L 6
Nov.   17—Donato Romano, Milan ....L 8
Dec.   13—Luigi Dal Santo, Brescia ....KO by 5
1979
Feb.   9—Donato Romano, Milano ....L 6
Dec.   15—Jean Marie Touti, Bethune ....L 6
Dec.   21—Musasa Zhora, Ancana ....L 6
1980
Feb.   9—Jean Philippe Truchelut, Troyes ....L 6
Apr.   18—Yvon Segor, Paris ....L 6
June   7—Stephane Ferrara, Massay ....KO by 4

ALBERT SINGH
Australian Welterweight
1979
Dec.   4—Greg Weston, Kingsford ....L 4
1980
Jan.   29—Doc Rutton, Kingsford ....L 4
Feb.   6—Calby Markell, Brookvale ....L 6
Feb.   12—Andy Roberts, Kingsford ....L 6
Feb.   26—Alan Ashby, Kingsford ....KO by 5
Mar.   5—Colin Green, Brookvale ....D 6
Mar.   11—Sparrow Freeman, Kingsford ....L 4
Mar.   25—Mark Vallance, Kingsford ....KO by 3

JOEY SINGLETON
British Welterweight
1973
May   7—Angus McMillan, London ....W 8
May   27—Barton McAllister, London ....W 8
Sept. 20—Jess Harper, Liverpool.................W 10
Nov.   1—Jimmy Fairweather, Liverpool ....W 10
Nov.   26—Jim Montague, Nottingham ....KO by 8
Dec.   18—Noel McIvor, Blackpool ....W 8
1974
Sept.   5—Jim Melrose, Liverpool ....KO 2
Nov.   21—Pat McCormack, Liverpool ....W 15
(British Junior Welterweight Title)
1975
June   3—Alan Salter, London......................W 10
Sept. 30—Alan Salter, London......................KO 9
(British Junior Welterweight Title)
Nov.   11—Des Morrison, Manchester ....W 15
(British Junior Welterweight Title)
1976
Apr.   12—Carlos Foldes, Paris......................D 8
June   1—Dave Green, London.................KO by 6
(British Junior Welterweight Title)
Sept. 22—Charlie Nash, Solihull ....KO by 9
Nov.   18—George Turpin, Liverpool ....L 8
Dec.   6—Colin Powers, Manchester ....L 8
1977
(Inactive)
1978
Jan.   31—Tommy Glencross, Marylebone ....KO 4
Mar.   15—Des Gwilliam, Solihull ....W 8
Apr.   12—George McGurk, Hammersmith ....KO 8
Apr.   24—Kevin Davies, Walworth ....KO 6
Oct.   12—Mickey Bell, Liverpool ....W 8
Nov.   16—Des Morrison, Liverpool ....KO by 7
1979
Jan.   15—Sylvester Gordon, Nottingham ....W 8
Feb.   15—Hans Henrich Palm, Randers ....W 8
Apr.   3—Carl Bailey, Hammersmith ....W 8
May   21—Sylvester Gordon, Walworth ....W 8
Sept. 24—Carl Bailey, Hammersmith ....W 8
Oct.   16—Achille Mitchell, West Bromwich ....W 8
1980
Feb.   4—Terry Petersen, Hammersmith ....W 10
(Won Central Area Welterweight Title)
Apr.   17—Jorgen Hansen, Copenhagen ....L 12
(European Welterweight Title)

TONY SINNOTT
British Welterweight
1980
Sept. 18—Dave Sullivan, Liverpool ....KO 5
Oct.   30—Dave Douglas, Liverpool ....W 8

JOSEPH SISHI
South African Middleweight
1972
June   5—Elijah Makhatini, Durban ....L 10
Aug.   5—Enoch Nhlapo, Durban ....L 10
Aug.   26—Sydney Hoho, Durban ....W 8
1973
Mar.   10—Elijah Makhatini, Durban ....KO by 7
Oct.   13—Gordon Goba, Durban ....L 6
Nov.   3—Cecil Kekane, Durban ....L 8
1974
Apr.   6—Photuma Khuboni, Durban ....W 8
Oct.   26—Oscar Nyuswa, Durban ....W 6
1975
May   10—Elijah Makhatini, Stanger ....L 10
1976
(Inactive)
1977
Dec.   28—Mark Melville, Durban ....L 4
1978
Aug.   12—Zacharia Thabethe, Durban ....KO 8
Nov.   25—Richard Ndlovu, Durban ....W disq. 8
Dec.   4—Jan Kies, Durban ....W 6
1979
July   9—Daniel Mapanya, Welkom ....KO by 6
Aug.   18—Jabulani Sithole, Durban ....W 6
1980
Apr.   24—Charlie Weir, Secunda ....KO by 1

JOE SISSANGA
South African Junior Middleweight
1980
Mar.   28—Joseph Nene, Springs ....L 4
Apr.   25—Elias Tshabalala, Springs ....D 4
June   7—Petrus Rampoporo, Odendaalsrust ....L 8
Nov.   21—Samuel Nkejane, Sebokeng ....L 4

JOHANNES SITHEBE
South African Flyweight
Born: Nov. 11, 1943
1966
May   13—Johannes Mongale, Springs ....D 4
May   28—Kenneth Segola, Pretoria ....KO 3
Aug.   26—Andries Moloi, Johannesburg ....W 4
Sept. 10—Lambert Dukashe, East London ....W 6
Sept. 24—Ishmael Mokebe, Sharpeville ....KO 6
Nov.   12—Edmund Mayola, Johannesburg ....W 6
Dec.   21—Ace Nkwentsha, Johannesburg ....L 6
1967
June   11—Lucas Matseke, Springs ....W 6
Aug.   5—Johannes Motokeli, Pretoria ....KO 6
Nov.   25—Steve Khotle, Johannesburg ....KO by 4
1968
Apr.   20—Ace Nwentsha, Johannesburg ....L 6
May   11—Kid Mnqina, Port Elizabeth ....W 6
June   9—Rocky Sekhoalele, Johannesburg ....W 10
June   7—Ernest Mokalane, Springs ....W 6
Aug.   9—Jacob Mokotong, Johannesburg ....W 10
Sept. 28—Ishmael Mokebe, Sharpeville ....KO 6
Nov.   16—Sydney Mbanxa, Port Elizabeth ....W 6
Dec.   14—Stephen Khotle, Johannesburg .....KO by 5
(For South African Flyweight Title)
1969
Feb.   28—Ace Nkwentsha, Springs ....L 6
June   27—Tiny Sekgoalele, Johannesburg ....KO 10
1970
Feb.   7—Paulus Shozi, Durban ....L 10
Aug.   1—S. Mbangza, East London ....L 6
1971
Mar.   6—William Lolatudi, Alexandra ....W 4
June   12—Daniel Molutsi, Alexandra ....W 6
July   3—Walter Baepi, Daveyton ....KO 2
Dec.   18—Joe Ngidi, East London ....W 6
1972
Mar.   24—Ace Nkwentsha, Kwa-Thema ....W 6
Apr.   21—Rafty Mngadi, Mamelodi ....L 8
July   14—William Matlokotsi, Thembisa ....W 8
Sept.   2—Joe Ngidi, Jr., Durban ....KO by 3
1973
Feb.   17—Simon Monobi, Orlando................W 6
Feb.   23—William Sefefe, Dobsonville ....W 8
Mar.   3—Bashew Sibaca, Port Elizabeth ....D 8
Apr.   28—Fundisilo Kralo, Port Elizabeth ....D 8
June   16—Joe Ngidi, Jr., Port Elizabeth ....W 12
July   12—Daniel Hlahane, Atteridgeville ....W 8
Aug.   17—Joe Gumede, Springs....................L 6
Oct.   5—Rafty Mngadi, Springs..................W 6

Oct.   13—Israel Khonkobe, Port Elizabeth..........L 8
Dec.   22—Joe Ngidi, Jr., Durban....................L 6

1974

Feb.   23—Chris Dlamini, Port Elizabeth.......KO by 10
Apr.   5—Dennis Mashego, Kwa-Thema ....W 6
May   18—Chris Dlamini, Port Elizabeth ....L 10
Sept. 20—Jacob Jobe, Natalspruit ....L 10
Oct.   19—Fundisile Kralo, Port Elizabeth ......W 8

1975

Feb.   28—Israel Khonkhobe, Kwa-Thema ....L 6
Apr.   25—Peter Mathebula, Dobsonville............L 10
July   25—Richard Modise, Orlando ....L 6
Aug.   16—Ruben Mateya, Port Elizabeth..........W 6
Sept.   9—Israel Khonkhobe, Port Elizabeth ....D 6
Oct.   27—Joe Ngidi, Durban......................W 6
Nov.   7—Peter Mathebula, Dobsonville ....L 10
Dec.   13—Mzukisi Skweyiya, Port Elizabeth ....L 6

1976

Feb.   6—Denis Mashigo, Springs................W 6
Mar.   27—Andile Tywabi, East London ....W 6
Apr.   9—Joe Gumede, Springs..................L 8
Nov.   13—Andile Tywabi, East London ....W 6

1977

Mar.   4—Peter Mathebula, Pretoria ....L 12
June   3—Philemon Mphomela, Springs ....W 10
Sept. 17—Daluxolo Tyekana, East London ....W 6
Nov.   28—Peter Mathebula, Durban ....L 12

1978

Mar.   31—Jama Qalinga, Bloemfontein ....W 8
Apr.   29—Peter Mathebula, Johannesburg ....L 12
         (South African Flyweight Title)
Aug.   12—Derrick Phetoe, Johannesburg ....KO 10
Aug.   26—Monde Mpulampula, East London ....L 6
Dec.   4—Peter Mathebula, Durban ....L 6

1979

Apr.   7—Vicky Pretorius, Vereeniging ....KO 2
May   4—Gaybon Yekiso, Springs ....L 6
June 16—Godfrey Nkate, Virginia ....L 8
Nov.   10—Simon Moema, Jabulani ....W 10

1980

Feb.   1—Freddie Masemola, Springs ....KO 10
         (For Transvaal Flyweight Title)
Mar.   22—Simon Moema, Soweto ....L 10
         (For Transvaal Flyweight Title)
Aug.   1—Simon Moema, Springs ....W 10
         (For Transvaal Flyweight Title)
Sept. 20—Peter Mathebula, Jabulani ....KO by 9
Dec.   15—Joseph Ngubane, Pmburg ....L 6

JABULANI SITHOLE
South African Middleweight

1978

Nov.   25—Joseph Thabethe, Durban ....W 4

1979

Aug.   18—Joseph Sishi, Durban ....L 6

1980

Apr.   28—Nessie Roux, Durban ....KO by 2
Nov.   3—Johan Harburn, Durban ....L 4

SHADRACK SITHOLE
South African Middleweight

1980

Nov.   1—Dennis Masondo, Stanger ....W 4
Dec.   15—Chris Hiongwa, Pmburg ....D 4

NUMCHOK SITHSANEH
Thai Bantamweight

1980

Feb.   1—Charnek U. Yuthanakarn, Bangkok ..KO by 2
Mar.   7—Phaktai Bunset, Bangkok ....L 6

ELIJAH SIYAYA
South African Junior Featherweight

1979

Feb.   9—Caiphus Khotle, Bethlehem ....L 4
May   12—Jacob Molipa, Virginia ....L 4

1980

Feb.   4—Caphus Khotle, Bethlehem ....L 4
Aug.   23—Hendrik Koelman, Bethlehem ....W 6
Sept.   6—Caphus Khotle, Ficksburg ....L 6

ROY SKELDON
British Light Heavyweight

1972

Sept. 20—Dave Parris, Solihull ....D 6
Nov.   6—Steve Foley, Bedford ....KO by 2

1973-1977
(Inactive)

1978

Oct.   31—Colin Flute, Wolverhampton ....KO by 4

1979

Jan.   31—Rocky Burton, Stoke ....W 4
Mar.   15—Rocky Burton, Dudley ....W 4

410

Mar.   28—Ron Green, Evesham ....W 4
Apr.   10—Colin Flute, Wolverhampton ....W 4
May   16—Colin Flute, Wolverhampton ....KO 4
July   2—Wally Barnes, London ....KO 4
Sept.   8—Clive Beardsley, Wolverhampton ......KO 3
Oct.   29—Mick Fellingham, Wolverhampton ....W 6
Dec.   3—Trevor Catthouse, Wolverhampton ......W 8

1980

Jan.   16—Trevor Cattouse, Stoke ....L 8
May   19—Liam Coleman, Bradford ....D 6
July   8—Eddie Fenton, Wolverhampton ....KO 6
    (Won Midlands Area Light Heavyweight Title)

SIMON SKOSANA
South African Bantamweight

1979

May   4—Victor Tladi, Springs ....W 4
Aug.   3—Benjamin Thusi, Springs ....KO by 1

1980

Mar.   30—Lucas Nkoana, Springs ....W 4
Aug.   1—James Sibeko, Springs ....W 4
Oct.   31—Richard Modise, Springs ....W 6

GEOFF SMART
British Featherweight

1980

Sept. 22—Stuart Crabb, Lewisham ....KO 4
Oct.   27—Andy Thomas, London ....KO by 6

KELVIN SMART
British Flyweight

1979

Sept. 10—George Baley, Birmingham ....KO 4
Sept. 26—Billy Straub, Solihull ....W 6
Oct.   30—Bryn Jones, Caerphilly ....W 6
Nov.   19—Carl Gaynor, Birmingham ....KO 3
Nov.   28—Chris Moorcroft, Solihull ....W 6

1980

Jan.   22—Ian Murray, Caerphilly ....W 6
Feb.   12—Iggy Jano, London ....W 6
Mar.   19—Iggy Jano, Solihull ....W 8
Apr.   1—Mohammed Younis, London ....W 8
May   8—Mohammed younis, Solihull ....D 8

MERVIN SMIT
South African Light Heavyweight

1978

July   17—Johan van Watsleben, Goodwood ....KO 2
Aug.   5—Esau Mokotso, Bloemfontein ....KO 1
Aug.   21—Meshack Khoza, Welkom ....KO 1
Oct.   28—Martin Barnard, Ermelo ....W 6
Dec.   4—James Mathatho, Bloemfontein ....W 8

1979

Feb.   5—Gerrie Bodenstein, Welkom ....KO by 5
    (South African Light Heavyweight Title)
Apr.   2—Sidney Hoho, Welkom ....W 8
June 11—Bruce McIntyre, Welkom ....KO by 7
Sept.   3—Martin Barnard, Welkom ....W 6
Oct.   20—Theunis Kok, Pretoria ....KO by 1

1980

Apr.   14—Sydney Hoho, Cape Town ....KO by 5
Dec.   19—Piet Crous, Welkom ....KO by 3

BILL SMITH
British Lightweight

1979

July   2—Mickey Baker, London ....KO by 1
Oct.   22—Ray Price, Mayfair ....D
Nov.   19—Wally Stocking, Piccadilly ....W
Nov.   —Jimmy McEwan, Liverpool L
Dec.   3—Shaun Dirken, Hull ....W

1980

Jan.   24—John Lindo, Harlepool L
Feb.   12—Glyn Rhodes, Sheffield L

DAVE SMITH
British Bantamweight

1976

Nov.   22—Roy Dodd, Walworth ....KO
Dec.   20—Ian Murray, Walworth ....W

1977

Jan.   10—Jimmy Bott, Walworth ....W
Feb.   22—Jimmy Bott, London ....W
Apr.   18—Neil McLaughlin, Walworth ....D
May   23—Neil McLaughlin, Hammersmith ....KO
Sept. 19—Bryn Griffiths, Walworth ....W
Oct.   24—Terry Hanna, Hammersmith ....KO
Dec.   6—Charlie Magri, London ....KO by
    (British Flyweight Title)

1978

Mar.   13—Bryn Griffiths, Walworth ....W
Apr.   4—Gary Davidson, London L
May   15—Ian Murray, London ....W

June 12—Johnny Owen, London ....L 8
Nov. 21—Gary Davidson, Wembley ....KO 6
1979
June 13—Johnny Owen, Caerphilly ....KO by 12
(British and Commonwealth Title)
Oct. 22—Glyn Davies, London ....W 8
Nov. 26—Davy Larmour, Belfast ....L 10
1980
Feb. 10—Welile Nkosinkule, East London ....W disq. 4
Mar. 31—Roy Somer, Rotterdam ....KO 4
Apr. 28—Jimmy Bott, Walworth ....W 8
Nov. 3—Glyn Davies, Hammersmith ....KO 2

EDDIE SMITH
British Light Heavyweight
1976
Apr. 1—Cyril Bishton, Liverpool ....W 4
May 3—Peter Whittle, Southsea ....W 4
June 7—Steve Heavysides, Manchester ....KO 2
Sept. 13—Howard Mills, Manchester ....W 4
Oct. 11—Joe Jackson, Manchester ....W 4
Oct. 28—Al Neville, Mayfair ....L 4
Nov. 15—George Salmon, Nottingham ....W 4
Dec. 6—Owen Robinson, Manchester ....W 6
1977
Jan. 17—Steve Paul Stocks, Nottingham ....KO 5
Mar. 14—Howard Mills, Manchester ....L 6
Mar. 21—Steve Fenton, Birmingham ....KO 6
Apr. 20—Dave Merrell, Manchester ....KO 1
May 9—Jimmy Pickard, Liverpool ....D 8
June 13—Jimmy Pickard, Manchester ....L 8
Sept. 8—Joe Lally, Liverpool ....W 8
Oct. 24—Bob Tuckett, Manchester ....W 8
Dec. 5—Jimmy Pickard, Manchester ....W 8
1978
Jan. 18—Roy Gumbs, Solihull ....KO 8
Feb. 20—Joe Gregory, Nottingham ....W 8
Mar. 6—George Salmon, Manchester ....W 8
Apr. 24—H.H. Thompson, Middlesbrough ....KO 8
May 8—Jimmy Pickard, Manchester ....L 8
Oct. 24—Tony Sibson, Kensington ....W 8
1979
Jan. 17—Chris Lawson, Stoke ....KO 4
Mar. 5—Tony Sibson, Wolverhampton ....L 10
Mar. 19—Bonny McKenzie, London ....L 8
Sept. 26—Bonnie McKenzie, Solihull ....W 8
Nov. 28—Tom Collins, Solihull ....L 8
1980
Feb. 18—Eddie Burke, Stockport ....L 8
Mar. 27—Johnny Heard, Liverpool ....KO by 5
Apr. 29—Dave Owens, Stockport ....KO 1
May 21—Chisanda Mutti, Coventry ....L 8
Sept. 26—Frank Wissenbach, Cologne ....L disq. 4

HUGH SMITH
British Junior Welterweight
Born: Nov. 19, 1950
1974
Sept. 17—Tommy Naylor, Glasgow.................KO 3
Oct. 28—Alan Oag, Glasgow......................L 6
Nov. 25—Alan Oag, Glasgow.....................W 6
Dec. 3—John Sagar, Leeds......................W 6
1975
Jan. 27—Delvin White, Glasgow ....W 6
Feb. 3—Eric Williams, Piccadilly..............W 6
Feb. 24—Roger Aldis, Glasgow..................W 6
Mar. 17—Ray Fallone, London ....W 8
Apr. 7—John Sagar, London....................W 6
Apr. 28—Jimmy Corrigan, Glasgow................W 8
May 26—John Sagar, Glasgow...................KO 3
June 30—Barton McAllister, Glasgow ....D 8
Sept. 8—Dave Massey, Glasgow ....KO 3
Oct. 1—Kevin Quinn, Hamilton.................W 6
Oct. 20—Jim Montague, Glasgow.................W 8
Nov. 17—Ray Ross, Glasgow ....KO 6
Dec. 4—Jim Montague, Hamilton ....W 8
1976
Jan. 5—Barton McAllister, London.............KO 6
Jan. 26—Terry Petersen, Glasgow................L 8
Mar. 11—Gordon Kirk, Hamilton ....W 8
Apr. 12—Terry Petersen, Birmingham.............L 8
June 24—Ian Pickersgill, London ....KO 4
Sept. 20—Jess Harper, Glasgow..................W 8
Nov. 15—Billy Waith, Glasgow ....L 8
1977
Jan. 10—Barton McAllister, London .... W 8
Mar. 18—Jimmy King, Holytown ....WF 5
Mar. 31—Claude Lormeau, Paris ....KO by 4
Sept. 21—Chris Glover, London ....KO by 4
1978
Feb. 6—Trevor Rooms, London ....L 8
June 19—Martin Bridge, Glasgow ....KO by 3
Nov. 27—Adey Allen, Glasgow ....W 8

1979
Apr. 17—Kevin Quinn, Glasgow ....W 8
Oct. 8—Liam Linnen, Glasgow ....KO 6
Nov. 3—Ray Ross, Glasgow ....W 6
Nov. 19—Terry Welch, Liverpool ....W 8
Nov. 28—Dave Campbell, Solihull ....KO by 7
1980
Mar. 24—George Peacock, Glasgow ....KO by 7
(Scottish Junior Welterweight Title)
Oct. 20—Colin Wake, Glasgow ....W 8

JEFF SMITH
Australian Junior Lightweight
1978
May 25—Metat Balla, Wellington ....W 10
July 20—Alan Hilt, Wellington ....KO 6
Nov. 14—Kirk Blair, Paihatua ....KO 2
1979
Feb. 17—Larry Valesini, Lower Hutt ....KO by 8
Apr. 8—Mick McLean, Wainuiomata ....KO 7
Apr. 29—Guinea Hillier, Wainuiomata ....KO 6
Oct. 11—Willie Leslie, Wellington ....W 10
Oct. 28—Brian Everhard, Dunedin ....KO 6
1980
Feb. 28—Steve Button, Wellington ....KO 2
Mar. 27—Billy Facer, Wellington ....L 10
Apr. 17—Reg King, Wellington ....KO 9
May 25—Steve Button, Wellington ....KO 5
July 3—Chris Bennett, Wellington ....KO 4
July 17—Rex Cannon, Wellington ....W 10
Sept. 4—Roger Henry, Wellington ....KO 5
Oct. 2—Billy Facer, Wellington ....W 10
Oct. 10—Garry Williams, Auckland ....L 10
Nov. 14—Dennis Talbot, Auburn ....L 12
(For Vacant Australian Junior Lightweight Title)

JIMMY SMITH
British Welterweight
1977
Nov. 21—Tony Bogle, London ....KO by 2
1978
Feb. 13—Paul Clemit, Barnsley ....W 4
Feb. 28—Johnny Beauchamp, Atlesbury ....W 4
Apr. 12—Bob Lewis, Evesham ....KO 3
June 1—Johnny Chard, Cardiff ....L 6
Sept. 18—Gary Newell, Wolverhampton ....W 4
Sept. 27—Dave Allen, Rotherham ....L 4
Oct. 11—Bob Lewis, Stoke ....KO 2
Oct. 31—Colin Moore, Hammersmith ....L 4
Nov. 15—Gary Newell, Ipswich ....L 6
Nov. 20—Gary Pearce, Piccadilly ....L 6
Dec. 4—Johnny Beauchamp, London ....KO 2
Dec. 21—Mark Osbourne, Liverpool ....W 4
1979
Feb. 19—Pat Smythe, London ....L 6
Mar. 5—Shaun Stewart, Barnsley ....W 6
Mar. 19—Tony Laing, London ....KO by 4
Apr. 30—Jeff Lee, London ....L 6
Sept. 18—Jeff Lee, Lewisham ....KO by 3
Nov. 5—Dave Douglas, Piccadilly ....L 6
Nov. 19—Ricky Daniels, Birmingham ....KO 1
Nov. 27—Ian Murray, Wolverhampton ....L 6
1980
Feb. 20—Mike Clemow, Evesham ....L 6
Feb. 28—Ronnie Rathbone, Queensway ....D 6
Mar. 11—Dave Aspill, Southend ....L 6
Apr. 23—Lee Town, Hove ....D 6
Apr. 30—Lee Town, Aylesbury ....W 6
May 8—Steve Ward, Solihull ....L 6
June 11—Gary Newell, Edgbaston ....W 6
July 1—Ronald Pearce, Swindon ....L 6

JOHN SMITH
Scottish Junior Middleweight
Born: Oct. 19, 1950
1970
June 1—Dusty Smith, London...................L 6
Oct. 12—Bill Deasy, London ....W 6
Nov. 2—Tony Bagshaw, Hull ....W 6
Nov. 16—Billy Arne, Nottingham................W 6
Dec. 14—Johnny Shields, Manchester............W 6
Dec. 30—Johnny Shields, Douglas...............L 6
1971
Mar. 29—Billy May, Manchester ....L 6
Apr. 5—Rodney Brown, Manchester ....KO by 2
Nov. 1—Johnny Parr, Cleethorpes ....KO 1
Nov. 3—Rod Griffiths, Carlisle ....L 6
1972
Apr. 24—Rodney Brown, Manchester ....KO 2
May 24—Peter Mullens, Nottingham ....KO 1
June 12—Chuck Jones, Swansea.................KO by 1
Nov. 29—Dusty Smith, London ....W 8

411

1973

Jan.	8—Kevin White, Bristol	L 8
Jan.	29—Jim Moore, Glasgow	W 8
Feb.	5—Dennis Brannigan, Streatham	L 8
Feb.	26—Dennis Brannigan, London	KO 3
Mar.	26—Mike Manley, Glasgow	KO 3
Apr.	2—Dennis Brannigan, London	KO 3
Apr.	9—Liam White, Nottingham	W 8
Apr.	16—Liam White, London	L 8
May	9—Liam White, London	L 8
May	21—Peter Blake, London	W 8
June	7—Tony Bagshaw, Glasgow	L 8
June	18—Maurice Hope, Nottingham	L 8
June	26—Trevor Francis, Piccadilly	L 8
Dec.	14—Dave Davies, Liverpool	L 8

1974

Jan.	7—Alan Hardiman, London	W 8
Jan.	28—Derek Simpson, Glasgow	W 8
Mar.	4—Henry Rhiney, Piccadilly	L 8
Mar.	18—Pat Thomas, Piccadilly	L 8
Mar.	25—Liam White, Glasgow	L 8
Apr.	17—Maurice Hope, Manchester	KO by 2
June	10—Jim Devanney, Glasgow	D 8

1975

Jan.	27—Henry Rhiney, Glasgow	L 8
Feb.	3—Liam White, Piccadilly	KO 2
Feb.	17—Dave Mullings, Piccadilly	KO 7
Feb.	24—Bobby Arthur, Glasgow	L 8
Mar.	3—Henry Rhiney, London	L 8
Mar.	24—Derek Simpson, Glasgow	W 10
May	16—Bobby Arthur, Birmingham	L 8
Nov.	3—Loucif Hamani, Paris	KO by 3

1976

Jan.	20—Jimmy Batten, London	L 8
Feb.	2—Charlie Cooper, London	D 8
Feb.	9—John Rushton, London	KO by 5
Feb.	16—Carl Thomas, Birmingham	KO by 2
Mar.	8—Errol McKenzie, Birmingham	L 8
Mar.	22—Derek Simpson, Glasgow	W 10
Apr.	5—Henry Rhiney, Luton	L 8
Apr.	13—Johnny Sham, Durban	L 8
May	4—Doug Lumley, Durban	L 8
Oct.	26—Tony Poole, Kensington	KO 2
Nov.	24—Billy Knight, London	KO by 4

1977

Jan.	11—Kirkland Laing, London	L 10
Jan.	24—Steve Angell, Glasgow	L 8
Feb.	14—Carl Thomas, London	W 8
Mar.	21—Kenny Webber, Birmingham	L 8
Apr.	2—Claude Matin, St. Malo	L 10
June	16—Terry Petersen, Glasgow	D 8
Oct.	10—Marijan Benes, Rotterdam	L 8
Nov.	7—Joe Oke, Glasgow	L 8

1978

Jan.	23—Tony Sibson, London	KO by 5
Apr.	11—Mick Mills, Sheffield	L 8
May	18—Robbie Davies, Liverpool	KO by 1

1979

Feb.	21—Steve Hopkin, Cambridge	L 8
Feb.	26—Prince Rodney, Middlesbrough	L 8
Apr.	23—Charlie Malarkey, Glasgow	L 12

1980

Jan.	28—Billy Lauder, Glasgow	L 8
Mar.	3—Terry Matthews, London	L 8
Sept.	22—Billy Waith, London	L 8
Oct.	13—Cliff Gilpin, Nottingham	L 8

PAT SMYTHE
British Welterweight
1979

Jan.	15—Mark Osbourne, Nottingham	W 4
Jan.	29—Liam Linnen, Glasgow	W 6
Feb.	5—Bob Bravado, Nottingham	KO 6
Feb.	19—Jimmy Smith, London	W 6
Feb.	26—Dave Douglas, Glasgow	L 6
Mar.	5—Bob Bravado, Barnsley	KO 5
Mar.	19—Liam Linnen, Glasgow	KO by 1
Apr.	19—Tommy Thomas, London	W 8
Apr.	24—Richard Avery, London	L 6
June	4—Les Wint, London	L 6
June	13—Dai Davies, Caerphilly	W 8
Sept.	17—Mickey Mapp, Mayfair	L 6
Oct.	23—Lee Hartshorn, Blackpool	L 6
Nov.	28—Jeff Aspel, Doncaster	KO by 2

1980

Feb.	11—Dave Taylor, Manchester	L 6

BRIAN SNAGG
British Lightweight
1977

Nov.	10—Tony Carroll, Liverpool	L 6
Nov.	29—Selvin Bell, Birkenhead	W 6
Dec.	5—Selvin Bell, Manchester	W 6
Dec.	12—Billy Jeram, London	L 8

1978

Mar.	2—Don Burgin, Liverpool	KO 3
Mar.	31—Adey Allen, Liverpool	KO by 4
May	18—Eric Wood, Liverpool	W 8
June	19—Charlie Tonna, Hove	KO 5
Aug.	29—Ian Pickersgill, Liverpool	W 6
Sept.	11—Adey Allen, Liverpool	W 6
Oct.	2—Dai Davies, Liverpool	KO 2
Oct.	12—Ian Pickersgill, Liverpool	KO 5
Nov.	2—Dave Taylor, Liverpool	D 8

Jan.	22—Jimmy Cooke, Wolverhampton	L 8
Mar.	15—Tony Carroll, Caister	L 8
June	18—Najib Daho, Manchester	L 10
Sept.	20—Nagib Daho, Liverpool	L 8
Oct.	23—Charm Chiteule, London	L 6

1980

Feb.	21—Jarvis Greenidge, Liverpool	W 8

TAMSANQA SOGWE
South African Junior Flyweight
1979

Nov.	3—Phindile Nqompoyi, Queenstown	W 4
Dec.	1—Eric Mtana, King Williamstown	W 4

Mar.	29—Sitomama Vumendlini, Queenstown	W 4
Apr.	5—Fikile Ngubelanga, East London	KO 3
May	3—K. Matabese, Monakai	L 6
May	24—James Mqueku, Welkom	W 6
July	19—Ntsikelo Kato, East London	W 6
July	26—Sitomama Vumendlini, K. Wmstown	W 6
Aug.	16—Mlungwava Mgxaji, East London	W 6
Nov.	8—Lawrence Krune, East London	W 10
	(For Cape Junior Flyweight Title)	
Dec.	20—Thamie Tiyo, East London	W 6

PEDRO SOLO
Australian Flyweight
1973

Oct.	15—Peter Marmo, Melbourne	W 3
Oct.	22—Tony Gallo, Melbourne	L 3
Nov.	12—Peter Marmo, Melbourne	W 3

1974

Feb.	4—Frank Bernardini, Melbourne	W 3
Feb.	18—Frank Bernardini, Melbourne	W 4
Mar.	4—Peter Marmo, Melbourne	W 4
May	23—Steve Walker, Blacktown	L 6
June	6—Steve Walker, Blacktown	L 6
Oct.	4—Neville Dando, Melbourne	L 4

1975

Aug.	22—Bruce Pope, Melbourne	KO 3
Sept.	19—Sam Tezer, Melbourne	D 4
Nov.	5—Bruno Monti, Cammeray	L 6

1976
(Inactive)
1977

Feb.	16—Domenic Amoruso, Melbourne	W 6
Apr.	20—Mick Coates, Melbourne	W 6
Nov.	—Chan Hee-Park, Seoul	L 10

1978

Feb.	14—Nobuyuki Watanabe, Yokohama	KO by 6
May	9—Glen Walsh, Melbourne	KO 8
Oct.	4—Kriengkrai Yingsak, Melbourne	W 10

1979
(Inactive)
1980

June	1—Steve Bell, Revesby	L 15
	(For Australian Flyweight Title)	
Oct.	10—Steve Bell, Lidcombe	KO by 13
	(For Australian Flyweight Title)	

AARON SOMDAKA
South African Welterweight
1979

June	29—Louis Sibiya, Natalspruit	KO 2

1980

May	3—Jack Jim, East London	L 6
Aug.	16—Lungile Gangala, East London	KO 4

LUCIANO SORDINI
Italian Light Heavyweight
1975

Oct.	24—Biagio Violino, Montale	W 6
Nov.	14—Vittorio Tamburini, Rome	KO 5

1976

Mar.	5—Giuseppe Panunzio, Turin	LF 2
May	14—Silvano Bischeri, Rome	KO 4
June	12—Giuseppe Panunzio, Rome	W 8
July	28—Lorenzo Nardillo, Rome	W 6
Oct.	1—Lorenzo Nardillo, Rome	W 8
Dec.	18—Salvatore Russo, Civitavecchia	W 8

1977

Mar.	4—Mariano Salomone, Rome	D 8

Apr. 22—Mariano Salomone, Rome .... KO 3
1978
Mar. 31—Salvatore Russo, Rome .... KO 5
May 26—Rida Hakimi, Rome .... KO 5
1979
May 4—Gabriele Lazzari, Rome .... W 6
Nov. 8—Gino Freo, Hotel Colombo .... D 8
1980
Mar. 14—Gabrielle Lazzari, Rome .... W 8
Sept. 3—Cristiano Cavina, St. Teresa .... L 12
(For Italian Light Heavyweight Title)

DONY SORIANO
Filipino Lightweight
1978
Nov. 21—Resty Boniquit, Clark Air Base .... W 10
1979
Feb. 17—Nene Jun, Pampanga .... W 10
Mar. 2—Fred Pastor, Angeles City .... D 10
Apr. 24—Mar Marin, Angeles City .... L 10
May 18—Nene Jun, Manila .... L 12
June 20—Al Del Rosario, Angeles City .... W 10
Sept. 8—Max Toyogon, Cotabato City .... W 12
Oct. 19—Stan Lantapan, Quezon City .... D 10
1980
Jan. 28—Young Dela Cruz, Clark Air Base .... W 10
Feb. 23—Fred (Bruce Lee) Basa, Angeles City ..... W 10
Aug. 9—Fred Pastor, Angeles City .... W 10
Oct. 4—Lito Pena, Angeles City .... KO by 5
Nov. 16—Erning Grafe, Paranaque .... KO by 5

KOMLEG SORTHANIKUL
Thai Junior Flyweight
1979
Oct. 17—Srithuncha Sithsanae, Bangkok .... L 6
Nov. 14—Daibiu Sithsaneh, Bangkok .... L 6
1980
Mar. 12—Surija Pratumvadee, Bangkok .... KO 2

CORRADO SORTINO
Italian Junior Middleweight
1979
Apr. 20—Silvio Migale, Milano .... L 6
May 11—Jimmy Connelly, Bern .... L 6
May 24—Poul Baekgaard, Randers .... L 4
June 12—Antonio Ceraudo, San Paolo di Civitate ... L 6
July 7—Francesco Plate, Perino .... KO 5
July 21—Aldo Buzzetti, Piacenza .... L 6
Sept. 26—Dario Vigini, Gorizia .... KO 4
Nov. 16—Silvio Migale, Milan .... KO 3
Dec. 15—Mario Loreni, Pesaro .... KO 5
1980
Mar. 29—Rosario Pacileo, Pesaro ....L 6
May 1—Dirck Declerck, Ixegem .... W 6
Dec. 6—Mauro Da Cruz, Pesaro .... KO 5

DAVE SOUTHWELL
British Welterweight
1978
Sept. 18—Kendrick Edwards, Reading .... KO 3
Sept. 25—Casley McAllum, Mayfair .... KO 1
Nov. 20—Lloyd Lee, Birmingham .... L 8
1979
Feb. 12—Herol Graham, Reading .... L 8
Feb. 28—Herol Graham, Burslem .... L 8
Oct. 3—Joe Oke, Reading .... W 6
Oct. 15—Paul Jones, Mayfair .... KO by 3
1980
Feb. 12—John F. Kennedy, London .... KO by 2

TAMIE SPAMPOOL
South African Junior Welterweight
1972
Sept. 2—Enoch Nkwnyane, East London .... W 4
1973
Feb. 15—Thabo Seoka, Mdantsane .... KO by 2
July 14—Thabo Seoka, East London .... L 6
Aug. 4—Welile Dyantyi, King Williamstown ...... W 6
Nov. 24—Ben Lelelake, Port Elizabeth .... L 6
1974
Dec. 14—Timothy Sedise, East London .... W 4
1975
June 21—Shiran Dywili, East London .... W 4
1976
Oct. 30—Alfred Sibisi, East London .... L 4
1977
May 28—David Kaptein, King Williamstown ...... W 6
Sept. 3—Fungile Buti, Queenstown .... L 6
Oct. 10 Mpolisi Mgidi, East London .... W 4
Dec. 17—Sizwe Tutu, Butterworth .... W 4
1978
July 8—Boy Boy Mtimkulu, East London .... D 4

1979
July 14—Mzwandile Biyane, East London .... L 8
1980
July 5—Leonard Siliwane, East London .... W 6
July 26—Peter Kanie, King Williamstown .... L 6

APRIL SPEELMAN
South African Light Heavyweight
1979
Mar. 5—Cecil Sandow, Welkom .... L 4
Apr. 2—Michael Motsoane, Welkom .... KO by 1
July 9—Chris Volschenk, Welkom .... W 4
Sept. 3—Willie Marais, Welkom .... W 4
1980
May 5—Willie Opperman, Welkom .... L 10
(For OFS Light Heavyweight Title)

WINSTON SPENCER
British Lightweight
1977
Feb. 15—Charlie Wallace, Walworth ....KO 2
Feb. 21—Albert Coley, Nottingham ....L 6
Apr. 18—Pat Campbell, Walworth .... W 6
May 9—Frank McCord, London ....KO 3
May 23—Pat Campbell, Hammersmith ....KO 3
July 5—Nagib Daho, Wolverhampton ....KO 5
Oct. 10—Jimmy Gwillian, London ....KO 2
Nov. 15—Wayne Floyd, London ....KO 7
1978
Apr. 25—Barry Price, London .... W 8
Sept. 25—Robbie Robinson, London .... W 8
Nov. 20—Jeff Pritchard, London................KO 6
1979
Feb. 20—Eric Wood, Kensington ....KO 3
Mar. 19—George McGurk, London ....WF 2
Sept. 24—Dilwyn Collins, Mayfair ....KO 3
Nov. 12—Tommy Davitt, Mayfair .... W 8
1980
Feb. 19—Chris Sanigar, London .... W 8
Apr. 22—Tony Carroll, London .... L 8
June 28—Willie Booth, London .... W 8
Sept. 27—Paul Chance, London ....KO 1
Nov. 1—Najib Daho, Glasgow ....KO 5

TONY STANTON
British Welterweight
1980
May 14—Ronnie Rathbone, Burslem ....D 6
June 12—Gary Brooks, Cambridge .... W 6
June 18—Paul Wetter, Burslem .... W 6

GEORG STEINHERR
German Middleweight
1976
Dec. 4—Ciampaolo Piras, Hamburg .... W 4
1977
Mar. 25—Joseph Kossman, Bremen ....KO 3
Apr. 1—Arpat Maydar, Saarlouis ....KO 3
Apr. 24—Mehmet Besli, Munich ....KO 6
June 7—Mehmet Cakal, Hamburg ....KO 6
Aug. 17—Peter Scheibner, Timmendorfer .... W 6
Sept. 9—Frank Reiche, Munich ....L 6
Dec. 12—Domenico Tiberia, Hamburg ....KO 7
1978
Jan. 28—Eric Seys, Esch ....KO 6
May 6—Michel Chapier, Luebeck ....KO 3
May 19—Francisco Ramon Roguez Francis, Essen KO 6
June 9—Gianni Mingardi, Milan ....KO 6
July 21—Idrissa Konate, Rosenheim ....KO 3
Oct. 31—Elisha Obed, Munich .... W 10
1979
May 18—Joel Bonnetaz, Munich .... W 10
July 28—Pablo Rodriguez, Munich ....KO 5
Sept. 28—Frank Wissenback, Munich ....D 10
1980
Feb. 22—Josef Biberovic, Dusseldorf ....KO 2
May 14—Kevin Finnegan, Munich ....D 12
(For European Middleweight Title)

AL STEVENS
British Light Heavyweight
1980
May 29—Danny Cope, Wolverhampton ....KO by 1
Sept. 22—Joe Jackson, Wolverhampton ....L 4
Oct. 18—Steve Babbs, Birmingham ....KO 2

ALADIN STEVENS
South African Lightweight
1979
Apr. 28—Deon Labuschagne, Johannesburg ....W 4
Dec. 1—Canny Mashele, Johannesburg ....W 4
1980
Mar. 29—Deon Labuschagne, Joburg ....KO 2

May	26—Canny Mashele, Joburg	KO	3
July	2—Johan Weyers, Welkom	W	6
Aug.	16—Johan Weyers, Joburg	W	6
Sept.	5—Jerome Gumede, Springs	L	6
Oct.	6—Elijah Cele, Pmburg	W	6
Nov.	3—Koos Mifuphi, Durban	KO	4
Nov.	28—Elias Nkabinde, Joburg	KO	4
Dec.	19—Elias Diraditsile, Welkom	W	6

AL STEWART
British Welterweight
Born: Sept. 10, 1949
1974
Feb.	19—Dave Dunn, Blackpool	KO	1
Feb.	26—George Salmon, St. Helens	D	8
Apr.	23—Allan Jones, Kensington	KO	1
Apr.	29—Jimmy Fairweather, Bristol	W	10
June	3—Alan Hardiman, Manchester	K	3
Sept.	3—Jim Montague, Liverpool	W	8
Nov.	21—Jimmy Fairweather, Liverpool	KO	7
Dec.	11—Derek Simpson, Mayfair	KO by	5
1975
Oct.	14—Dave Green, London	KO by	2
Dec.	5—Peter Morris, Birmingham	KO by	3
1976
June	14—Johnny Pincham, Portsmouth	L	6
Sept.	30—Kevin Quinn, Liverpool	KO	1
Nov.	18—Chris Walker, Liverpool	KO by	7
Dec.	14—Achille Mitchell, W. Bromwich	W	8
1977
Mar.	5—Chris Davies, Liverpool	KO by	4
Apr.	18—Clinton McKenzie, Mayfair	KO by	3
Sept.	21—Horace McKenzie, London	KO by	7
Nov.	10—Carl Bailey, Liverpool	L	8
Nov.	29—Mickey Durkin, Birkenhead	L	6
1978
Apr.	4—Tony Kavanaugh London	KO by	3
Aug.	29—John Gilling, Liverpool	L	6
Sept.	11—John Gilling, Bradford	L	8
Sept.	28—Martin Bridge, Liverpool	W	8
Nov.	2—Frank McCord, Liverpool	KO by	3
1979
Sept.	26—Lloyd Hibbert, Stoke	L	8
Nov.	14—Gary Newell, Stoke	KO	1
Nov.	29—Lee Hartshorn, Liverpool	L	8
Dec.	17—Gary Cooper, Wolverhampton	L	8
1980
Sept.	18—Dennis Sullivan, Liverpool	KO by	7
Oct.	13—Johnny Francis, Manchester	L	8

GERHARDUS J. (GERT) STEYN
South African Junior Middleweight
Born: Feb. 12, 1951
1970
Dec.	28—Alfie Pitout, Durban	KO	1
1971
Feb.	5—Michel Le Roux, Durban	KO	4
May	1—Michel Le Roux, Durban	W	10
July	2—Tony Riley, Durban	W	10
July	17—Rockie Small, Johannesburg	KO	3
Oct.	18—Spider Kelly, Johannesburg	W	12
	(South African Welterweight Title)		
1972
Jan.	29—Aldo Mondora, Johannesburg	KO	2
Mar.	27—Pat McCormack, Johannesburg	D	8
May	13—Ronnie du Preez, Johannesburg	KO	1
Aug.	12—Tommy Joyce, Johannesburg	KO	1
Oct.	7—Shoji Tsujimoto, Johannesburg	D	10
1973
Jan.	29—Mickey Flynn, Cape Town	W	8
Mar.	17—Gielie Buitendag, Johannesburg	KO by	7
	(South African Welterweight Title)		
July	30—Chris du Plessis, Durban	KO	7
Nov.	3—Gielie Buitendag, Johannesburg	W	12
	(South African Welterweight Title)		
1974
Apr.	26—Spider Kelly, Koonstad	KO	8
July	20—Gert Craemer, Pretoria	W	12
	(South African Welterweight Title)		
1975
Feb.	22—Mickey Flynn, Johannesburg	W	10
Aug.	23—Gert Craemer, Johannesburg	W	12
	(South African Junior Middleweight Title)		
1976
Mar.	22—Peter Scheibner, Johannesburg	KO	5
May	8—Rene Emmerich, Johannesburg	W	8
July	17—Tony Gardner, Johannesburg	KO	1
Nov.	1—Victor Perez, Durban	KO	1
Dec.	13—Mike Nixon, Durban	KO by	1
1977
Feb.	28—Gordon Goba, Durban	KO	11
May	9—Monty Betham, Durban	W	10
June	27—Daniel Sereme, Durban	W	8

Aug.	1—Juarez de Lima, Durban	KO	9
Oct.	3—Angel Ortiz, Durban	W	10
1978
Feb.	27—Ralph Palladin, Durban	W	10
Aug.	5—Joey Mack, Empangeni	W	8
Sept.	8—Loyiso Mtya, Johannesburg	KO	5
1979
Feb.	12—Elijah Makhathini, Durban	W	10
Sept.	6—Jorgen Hansen, Randers	L	8
Oct.	20—Ruben Pardo, Pretoria	KO by	5
Dec.	1—Bushy Bester, Johannesburg	L	10
1980
Mar.	29—Bushy Bester, Joburg	KO by	10
	(For South African Junior Middleweight Title)		
June	12—Torben Anderson, Randers	KO	8
Nov.	3—Ralph Moncrief, Durban	KO by	7

MICHEL STINI
Belgian Junior Middleweight
1974
Sept.	27—Walter Verschueren, Grivignee	KO	5
Nov.	9—Harry Kobles, Liege	KO	1
Dec.	7—Larbi Titi, Eupen	W	6
1975
Feb.	1—Eric Seys, Eupen	W	8
Mar.	8—Alfred Fries, Cointe	W	6
Apr.	5—Jean Pierre Heirmann, Eupen	KO	5
Apr.	25—Jean Claude Midoux, Grivignee	KO	5
May	31—Eric Seys, Stockay	W	6
Oct.	6—Stan Van Den Driessche, L'Aja	KO	4
Nov.	1—Jacques Chinon, Verviers	KO	5
Nov.	15—Eric Seys, Stockay	W	6
Nov.	29—Jean Claude Genno, Verviers	KO	7
1976
May	21—Titi Larbi, Mouscron	KO	3
Oct.	1—Mariano Salamone, Lauwe	KO	7
Nov.	6—Salvatore Russo, Verviers	W	8
Nov.	20—Dino Walker, Liege	W	8
Dec.	18—Francis Vermandere, Verviers	KO	4
1977
Feb.	12—Gilbert Cohen, Liege	L	10
Apr.	1—Shako Mamba, Verviers	KO by	6
June	18—Alfredo Naveiras, Grivignee	L	12
Nov.	12—Jean Claude Warusfel, Verviers	W	10
1978
May	19—Paul Payen, Charleroi	KO	9
	(Won Belgian Middleweight Title)		
Oct.	14—Michel Chapier, Pepinster	W	10
Nov.	18—Bader Ouakhal, Casablanca	KO	7
Dec.	23—Arnoldo Olivares, Casablanca	KO	9
1979
May	16—Pierre Kabassu, Casablanca	W	10
May	19—Rogelio Zarza, Brussels	L	8
1980
Feb.	22—Oscar Angus, Molenbeek	W	8

ANTONIO STOCCHINO
Italian Welterweight
1977
Nov.	10—Branko Barakovic, Bologna	KO	4
Nov.	25—Giancarlo Serengeli, Cagliari	KO	2
Dec.	15—Giuseppe Casamonica, Bologna	KO by	1
1978
Feb.	11—Vittorio Tamburrini, Cagliari	KO	3
Mar.	17—Luciano Giorgi, Bologna	W	6
Apr.	15—Angelo Tomasini, Cagliari	W	6
June	28—Edson Lima, Castel San Pietro	L	6
Aug.	13—Jose Luis Ribiero, Iglesias	W	6
Nov.	18—Antonio Casamonica, Cagliari	W	6
Dec.	27—Ernesto Res, Bologna	LF	6
1979
Mar.	11—Vincenzo Bottigliero, Cagliari	D	8
Sept.	29—Mario Favotto, Cagliari	D	8
Oct.	19—Ernesto Ros, Cagliari	D	8
Dec.	28—Sergio D'Angelo, Cagliari	D	8
1980
Jan.	25—Ernesto Ros, Bologna	LF	8
Feb.	6—Kachama Musasa, Falconara	KO by	6
Mar.	28—Ciancarlo Serangeli, Cagliari	KO	

WALLY (STOCKS) STOCKING
British Lightweight
1979
Mar.	12—Steve Briers, London	W	
Mar.	15—Tommy Burling, Marylebone	D	
Apr.	2—Julian Balstead, London	L	
Apr.	23—Phillip Morris, London	L	
June	14—Ian Murray, Dudley	L	
Sept.	25—Terry Parkinson, Southend	L	
Oct.	15—Tim Moloney, Mayfair	L	
Oct.	22—Walter Clayton, Nottingham	KO by	
Nov.	19—Bill Smith, Piccadilly	L	
Nov.	27—Winston Ho-Sing, Sheffield	L	

Dec. 10—Shaun Dirken, Piccadilly .... W 6
Dec. 20—Tyrrel Wilson, Queensway .... D 6
1980
Jan. 22—Walter Clayton, London .... KO by 5
Mar. 3—Tim Moloney, Hove .... L 6
Mar. 17—Colin Wake, London .... L 6
Apr. 18—Dave Laxen, Southend .... KO 6
Oct. 20—Alan Cooper, Hove .... L 6

ALAN STOREY
British Featherweight
1978
Oct. 9—Jackie Dinning, Middlesbrough .... KO 3
Nov. 20—Jimmy Bott, Birmingham .... D 6
Dec. 4—Ian Murray, Marton .... D 4
1979
Feb. 26—Pip Colemena, Middlesbrough .... W 4
June 18—Paul Keers, Bradford .... L 6
Nov. 12—Dave George, Marton .... L 6
Nov. 19—Bobby Breen, Glasgow .... W 6
Nov. 26—Selvin Bell, Birmingham .... W 6
Dec. 3—Bryn Jones, Hull .... KO 3
Dec. 10—Mike Pickett, Birmingham .... W 6
1980
Feb. 25—Jim McKeown, Glasgow .... L 6
Mar. 3—Selvin Bell, Marton .... D 6
Apr. 21—Charlie Parvin, Nottingham .... L 8
Apr. 28—Charlie Parvin, Birmingham .... L disq. 6
May 19—Don George, London .... KO by 7

BILLY STRAUB
Scottish Bantamweight
1979
June 18—Jimmy Bott, Glasgow .... W 6
Sept. 17—Brinley Jones, Glasgow .... W 6
Sept. 26—Kelvin Smart, Solihull .... L 6
Oct. 15—George Bailey, Glasgow .... W 8
1980
Jan. 21—Bobby Breen, Glasgow .... W 8
Mar. 14—Ian Murray, Glasgow .... W 6
Apr. 14—Ian Murray, Motherwell .... W 8
June 7—Mohammed Younis, Glasgow .... KO by 1
Oct. 14—Gary Nickels, London .... L 8

STRIKER STUDDARD
South African Lightweight
Born: March 31, 1956
1978
Oct. 23—Theo Smit, Johannesburg .... KO 3
1979
June 8—Mzwandile Biyane, East London ..... KO by 5
Sept. 15—Anthony Wiese, Johannesburg .... W 4
Nov. 10—Ncedo Mpetsheni, East London .... W 4
1980
Feb. 9—Boy Boy Mtimkulu, East London .... L 6
Sept. 20—Norman Bromfield, Jabulani .... KO by 4

DED SUAYBAGUIO
Filipino Bantamweight
1980
July 5—Robinson Abato, Butan City .... KO 7
Aug. 24—Renato Paulino, Butan City .... KO 4
Sept. 27—Billy Abato, Butan City .... L 10
Nov. 15—Bill Abrogar, Butan City .... KO 5
Dec. 29—Diego de Villa, Butan City .... KO 5

MINORU SUGIYA
Japanese Junior Welterweight
1978
Jan. 26—Bruce Curry, Tokyo .... KO by 3
May 30—Alfredo Kid Logan, Honolulu .... W 6
Sept. 29—Choi Nak-Yung, Hakodate City .... W 10
Nov. 21—Huber Watanabe, Tokyo .... W 10
1979
June 5—Tatsuo Ohara, Aomori .... KO 3
Oct. 28—Kazumi Nakao, Tokyo .... W 10
1980
Jan. 24—Shigeo Takagi, Tokyo .... KO 3
May 19—Eiichi Fukumoto, Tokyo .... W 10
(Won Japanese Junior Welterweight Title)
Sept. 23—Eiichi Fukumoto, Tokyo .... KO by 1
(Lost Japanese Junior Welterweight Title)

DAVE SULLIVAN
British Welterweight
1979
Oct. 29—John Ridgman, Cambourne .... KO by 3
1980
Jan. 22—Jeff Aspell, Caerphilly .... W 6
Feb. 12—Ronnie Rathbone, Sheffield .... L 6
Mar. 3—Steve Ward, Nottingham .... L 6
Apr. 18—Randy Henerson, Southend .... W 6
June 2—Phil Duckworth, Plymouth .... KO by 3

July 1—Jeff Aspell, Swindon .... L 6
Sept. 18—Tony Sinnott, Liverpool .... KO by 5

DENNIS SULLIVAN
Irish Welterweight
1979
Sept. 8—Johnny Burns, Wolverhampton .... W 6
Oct. 8—Tommy Thomas, London .... KO 6
Oct. 29—Terry Welch, Cambourne .... W 6
Dec. 10—Richard Avery, Torquay .... W 8
1980
Jan. 16—Gary Cooper, Solihull .... L 6
Feb. 20—Granville Allen, Evesham .... L 8
Apr. 18—Vic Jackson, Southend .... L 8
June 2—Terry Petersen, Plymouth .... W 8
Aug. 12—Richard Avery, Gowerton .... L 6
Sept. 18—Al Stewart, Liverpool .... KO 7
Oct. 16—Brian Anderson, Bolton .... L 8

RONALD SUMALYS (SUMALIS)
Philippine Bantamweight
1978
Oct. 14—Ric Barimbad, Davao City .... W 10
Oct. 28—Bonnie Cajes, Davao Del Norte .... KO 3
1979
Jan. 27—Siony Carupo, Davao City .... L 10
Mar. 3—Robinson Abato, Davao City .... W 10
Apr. 20—Noe Canino, Manila .... W 10
May 12—Roy Arcillas, Davao City .... KO 8
June 2—Jaime Enriquez, Davao City .... W 10
Sept. 29—Billy Abato, Davao City .... L 12
(Philippine Bantamweight Title)
Nov. 17—Rudy Garcia, Davao City .... W 10
Dec. 15—Ric Diamale, Davao City .... W 10
1980
Jan. 19—Rey Naduma, Davao City .... D 10
Mar. 15—Neptali Alamag, Davao City .... L 15
May 30—Cesar Amazan, Manila .... W 12
(Retained Philippine Bantamweight Title)
Aug. 16—Bill Abrogar, Davao City .... W 10
Sept. 27—Bill Abrogar, De Oro City .... W 10
Dec. 29—Ali Granada, Butuan City .... KO 6

GEORGE SUTTON
British Bantamweight
1975
Dec. 2—Jan Murray, London .... W 6
1976
Jan. 5—Jan Murray, London .... KO 3
Jan. 26—Neil McLaughlin, Glasgow .... W 8
May 3—Dave Connell, Southsea .... W 8
May 24—Kenny Matthews, London .... L 8
Aug. 11—Dave Tuohey, Cardiff .... KO 3
Sept. 30—Johnny Owen, Pontypool .... L 8
1977
Feb. 2—Steve Enwright, London .... KO 2
Feb. 22—Paddy Maguire, Kensington .... KO by 4
Mar. 29—John Owen, Ebbw Vale .... L 10
(Welsh Bantamweight Title)
Sept. 21—John Owen, London .... L 8
Nov. 29—Roland Dakin, London .... L 8
Dec. 14—Mohammed Younis, Kingston .... D 8
1978
Jan. 24—John Feeney, London .... KO by 6
Mar. 14—Davy Larmour, Belfast .... KO 4
Apr. 17—Larry Richards, Reading .... KO 2
June 29—Lee Graham, Caerphilly .... D 8
Oct. 23—Muhammad Younis, London .... W 8
Oct. 31—Paul Chance, Wolverhampton .... L 8
1979
Feb. 19—Davy Larmour, Belfast .... L 8
Mar. 26—Roy Somers, Groningen .... W 8
Apr. 9—Dave Needham, Nottingham .... L 8
May 2—John Feeney, Solihull .... KO by 8
1980
May 12—Jeff Aspell, Reading .... W 4
May 20—Walter Clayton, Southend .... KO by 5
Aug. 12—Vernon Penprase, Gowerton .... L 8

CORNELIUS (KALLIE) SWANEPOEL
South African Featherweight
1978
Mar. 11—Pieter Swanepoel, Johannesburg ......KO 2
July 3—Charles Boias, Johannesburg .... KO by 4
Aug. 5—Gaybon Yekiso, Johannesburg .... L 4
1979
(Inactive)
1980
Apr. 21—Richard Modise, Secunda .... W 4
May 0—Manuel de Paiva, Witwisoonk .... W 4
May 10—Benedict Nkatlo, Johannesburg ...... KO by 1

415

ALBERT SYBEN
Belgian Heavyweight
1977
Jan.	15—Richard Dellerc, Brussels	D	6
Mar.	4—Lassine Naire, Grivignee	W	6
Apr.	22—Jean Belvai, Wandre	KO	2
June	18—Tony Oudina, Grivignee	KO	2
Oct.	8—Lisimo Obutobe, Liegi	W	4
Oct.	15—Fausto Constantino, Molenbeek	W	6
Oct.	28—Reinhard Seydock, Ougree	KO	3
Nov.	12—Laurent Zardy, Verviers	W	6
Nov.	26—Mohamed Galoul, Brussels	W	6
Dec.	10—Fernand Deruyter, La Loviere	KO	3
Dec.	23—Feruccio Mazzardi, Molenbeek	KO	6

1978
Jan.	7—Horst Lang, Grivignee	KO	3
Feb.	11—Jean Pierre Leseigneur, Liege	KO	2
Feb.	23—Ishaq Hussien, Antwerp	KO	4
Mar.	18—Ahmed Galloul, Liege	W	8
Apr.	1—Christian Poncelet, Brussels	W	8
May	20—Hennie Thoonen, Molenbeek	KO	4
June	24—Yannick Dufour, Grivignee	KO	3
Oct.	13—Domenico Adinolfi, Ravenna	D	10
Nov.	24—Dean Cooke Wallace, Liegi	W	10

1979
Jan.	19—Neville Meade, Bruxelles	KO	4
Apr.	7—Tony Moore, Bruxelles	W	8
Apr.	21—Rudi Gauwe, Zele	KO	4
	(Belgian Heavyweight Title)		
May	19—George Scott, Brussels	L	10
Sept.	28—Ahmed Galloul, Molenbeek	W	8
Oct.	12—Robert Desnouck, Antwerp	W	12
	(Belgian Heavyweight Title)		
Nov.	10—Felipe Rodriguez, Forest	W	10
Dec.	12—Rudi Gauwe, Bruxelles	KO by	8
	(Belgium Heavyweight Title)		

1980
Apr.	25—Vasco Faustino, Bruxelles	KO	3
June	27—Jean Pierre Coopman, Bruxelles	W	10
Sept.	19—George Butzbach, Vise	W	10

PAUL SYKES
British Heavyweight
1978
Feb.	20—Keith Johnson, Bradford	KO	1
Mar.	20—Neil Malpass, Bradford	L disq.	7
Apr.	17—Tommy Kiely, Bradford	W	8
May	15—Neville Meade, Bradford	KO	5
July	18—Neil Malpass, Wakefield	D	10
Sept.	8—Dave Wilson, Wakefield	KO	3
Oct.	24—Lisimo Obutobe, Blackpool	KO	6

1979
Feb.	13—Conrad Tooker, Wakefield	W	10
June	26—John L. Gardner, London	KO by	6
	(British Heavyweight Title)		

1980
Mar.	29—Ngozika Ekwelum, Lagos	KO by	1

JEAN SYMOS
Belgian Welterweight
1973
Sept.	14—Francesco Condello, Grivignee	W	6
Nov.	1—Francesco Condello, Duffel	KO	6

1974
Jan.	25—Kader Ben Mimoun, Gilly	KO	4
Mar.	8—Guido Beuselinck, Gilly	KO	2
Apr.	20—Lucchesi Sylvain, Hollogne	KO	5
May	10—Jean Pierre Heirmann, Grivignee	KO	2
June	8—Franco Contu, Vaux	KO	5
Sept.	27—Victor Thorel, Grivignee	W	6
Oct.	26—Jack Peraire, Grivignee	KO	5
Nov.	11—Jean Dercle, Charleroi	KO	6

1975
Jan.	17—Klaus Fuchs, Gand	KO	3
Feb.	7—Giampaolo Piras, Liegi	W	8
Feb.	21—Salah Arafa, Waremme	W	8
Apr.	25—Gerard Leterme, Grivignee	KO	5
May	16—Pietro Gasparri, Grivignee	W	10
Sept.	27—Rolf Kestern, Awirs	KO	3
Nov.	15—Giovanni De Vita, Stockay	KO	6
Dec.	5—Vittorio Conde, Grivignee	KO by	4

1976
Apr.	10—Alois Carmeliet, Liegi	KO by	7
May	21—Mario Calzone, Seraing	KO	4
Oct.	22—Johnny Pincham, Grivignee	W	8
Nov.	29—Mohammed Mechila, Liegi	W	8

1977
Feb.	12—Freddy Roelands, Liegi	W	10
Mar.	4—Alfred Fries, Grivignee	KO	8
Mar.	18—Branko Barakovic, Anversa	KO	5
Apr.	29—Abel Messaoud, Bomal	W	8
June	18—Ali Guechin, Grivignee	W	8
Oct.	8—Dirk Declercq, Liegi	W	8

1978
Dec.	16—Laurent Degila, Grivignee	W	8

1978
Jan.	6—Angel Garcia, Grivignee	W	10
Mar.	31—Richard Rodriguez, Grivignee	W	8
Apr.	29—Jean Vantorre, Zele	KO	2
June	24—Stephan Vertpre, Grivignee	W	8
Oct.	13—Mongo Kemiri, Molenbeek	KO	4
Nov.	24—Robert Powell, Liegi	KO by	9

1979
Mar.	2—Jose Hernandez, Liegi	KO by	4
May	4—Fredo Roelands, La Louviere	KO	3

1980
May	23—Giuseppe Russi, Liege	W	8
Sept.	19—Mohamed El Gharbi, Argenteau	KO	3
Nov.	4—Tek N'Kalankete, Liege	KO by	8

BENNY TABUA
(BENNY WAYNE)
Australian Junior Middleweight
1979
Mar.	21—Phil Davies, Blacktown	L	10
Apr.	28—Peter Yavala, Suva	KO	4
June	5—Eddie Buttons, Kingsford	KO by	8
	(For New South Wales Welterweight Title)		
Dec.	19—Colin Eckford, Mt. Pritchard	KO	5

1980
June	7—Alex Temelkov, Wollongong	KO by	4
Aug.	5—Merv Croaker, Kingsford	KO	5
Sept.	22—Buddy Nixon, Rozelle	KO	3
Nov.	11—Ken Salisbury, Sutherland	KO by	9

HOCINE TAFER
French Light Heavyweight
1976
Oct.	30—Francis Dupuy, Voiron	KO	2
Nov.	20—Darko Barakovic, Grenoble	KO	3

1977
Jan.	8—Mick Caron, Grenoble	KO	3
Jan.	21—Jose Gomez, Annecy	W	6
Feb.	19—Gino Freo, Grenoble	W	6
Mar.	18—Jean Tshikuna, Annecy	KO	4
Apr.	23—Jose Gomez, Grenoble	W	8
May	14—Tony Oudina, Annecy	KO	4
Oct.	15—Laurent Zardy, Grenoble	W	8
Nov.	5—Tony Monohan, Marseille	KO	2
Nov.	25—Jannick Dufour, Grenoble	KO	2

1978
Mar.	30—Michel Dylbaytis, Paris	KO	4
Apr.	27—Alex Cardozo, Geneva	KO	1
June	9—Robert Amory, Grenoble	KO	12
	(French Light Heavyweight Title)		
Sept.	30—Victor Attivor, Grenoble	KO	8
Nov.	4—Robert Amory, Compiegne	KO	7

1979
Jan.	17—Alek Penarski, Grenoble	KO by	5
Mar.	11—Michel Dylbaitis, Maubege	KO	11
	(Won French Light Heavyweight Title)		
Nov.	5—Rudi Koopmans, Rotterdam	D	12
	(EBU Light Heavyweight Title)		

1980
Feb.	7—Fausto Quinales, Paris	KO	2
Apr.	18—Jean Louis Martin, Paris	KO	7
	(Won French Light Heavyweight Title)		
May	29—Freddy Brown, Grenoble	W	10
Oct.	10—Dave Conteh, Paris	W	10

SHIGEO TAKAGI
Japanese Welterweight
1979
Oct.	22—Naoshito Suzuki, Tokyo	KO by	5
Nov.	29—Masasue Yoshikawa, Tokyo	KO	3

1980
Jan.	24—Minoru Sugiya, Tokyo	KO by	3

YASUHIDE TAKAHASHI
Japanese Featherweight
Aug.	1—Isao Okahaski, Tokyo	KO by	6
Sept.	8—Isao Okahaski, Tokyo	W	10

1979
Feb.	27—Yasutsune Uehara, Tokyo	KO by	6

1980
Feb.	26—Jonny Fujimoto, Tokyo	KO	1

416

Apr. 14—Kojiro Sasaki, Tokyo .... W 10

KENZO TAKASUGI
Japanese Bantamweight
1978
May 7—Joe Araki, Hiroshima .... L 10
Sept. 21—Yuji Keguchi, Kumamoto .... L 10
1979
(Inactive)
1980
Feb. 24—Mitsuo Shimokawa, Hofu City .... KO 3
Apr. 26—Yukio Segawa, Hachinohe .... L 10

DENNIS TALBOT
Australian Junior Lightweight
1972
Oct. 11—Larry Saddler, Woonona .... KO 2
Oct. 25—Big Jim West, Redfern .... KO by 8
Dec. 7—Brian Roberts, Redfern .... L 8
1973
Oct. 20—Neville Williams, Wellington .... KO 2
Nov. 24—Billy Mulholland, Mudgee .... L 8
1974
Feb. 6—Steve Walker, Riverwood .... KO 4
Feb. 13—Roger Henry, Marrickville .... KO 3
Mar. 7—Brian Roberts, Blacktown .... L 10
Apr. 19—Guinea Hillier, Melbourne .... KO by 4
June 20—Wayne Wallace, Blacktown .... W 8
July 11—Brian Clout, Blacktown .... L 8
Aug. 1—Jim Slatter, Blacktown .... L 10
Aug. 9—Billy Mulholland, Woonona .... L 10
Aug. 24—Brian Clout, Woonona .... W 8
Sept. 6—Brian Clout, Woonona .... KO by 9
(For New South Wales Bantamweight Title)
Oct. 9—Wayne Wallace, Marrickville .... W 8
Nov. 13—Brian Roberts, Marrickville .... L 10
1975
Feb. 6—Brian Clout, Blacktown .... L 10
Feb. 28—Billy Mulholland, Corrimal .... L 8
1976-1978
(Inactive)
1979
July 31—Chris Bennett, Kingsford .... W 6
Sept. 7—Shane Rank, Epping .... W 6
Oct. 17—Kirk Blair, Mt. Pritchard .... D 8
1980
Mar. 30—Kirk Blair, Ingleburn .... L 10
(For Vacant New South Wales Junior Lightweight Title)
May 9—Pablo Cann, Merrylands .... W 6
June 1—Jim Bowen, Revesby .... W 6
July 11—Kirk Blair, Auburn .... W 10
(Won New South Wales Junior Lightweight Title)
Aug. 8—Garry Williams, Merrylands .... L 6
Sept. 18—Garry Williams, Marrickville .... :.. W 10
Oct. 18—Paul Ferreri, Darwin .... KO by 6
(For Australian Junior Lightweight Title)
Nov. 14—Jeff Smith, Auburn .... W 12
(Won Vacant Australian Junior Lightweight Title)

KAZUMASA TAMAKI
Japanese Flyweight
1975
Mar. 2—Teruo Yamamoto, Tokyo .... L 4
June 23—Kenji Saka, Tokyo .... W 4
Aug. 23—Masao Shimosaka, Tokyo .... W 4
Sept. 18—Fumio Arai, Tokyo .... D 4
Oct. 31—Masanori Seki, Tokyo .... W 4
Dec. 17—Morio Yamazato, Okinawa .... W 4
1976
Jan. 3—Sadao Mitsunari, Kagoshima .... W 4
June 28—Ryuji Higashi, Tokyo .... KO by 5
Aug. 24—Masao Imai, Tokyo .... KO 2
Dec. 9—Mario Ishii, Tokyo .... D 6
1977
Jan. 24—Hiroyuki Tanaka, Tokyo .... KO by 6
Apr. 19—Yoshio Kimi, Tokyo .... W 6
Aug. 28—Atom Suzuki, Tokyo .... W 6
Nov. 5—Bazooka Shoji, Morioka .... KO 7
1978
Jan. 2—Luis Garcia, Tokyo .... W 10
June 22—Phenix Taniguchi, Okinawa .... D 10
Aug. 19—Chi-Bok Kim, Seoul .... KO 5
1979
Jan. 4—Guraman Udea, Tokyo .... KO 8
Mar. 11—Shinji Suga, Tokyo .... D 10
May 29—Ryu Kaionji, Tokyo .... KO 2
Aug. 27—Koichi Maki, Tokyo .... KO 8
Nov. 19—Yung Sik Kim, Tokyo .... L 10
1980
Jan. 10—Koichi Maki, Tokyo .... W 10
(Won Japanese Flyweight Title)
Apr. 24—Koichi Maki, Tokyo .... D 10
(Retained Japanese Flyweight Title)

HIROYUKI TANAKA
Japanese Bantamweight
1979
Oct. 22—Masaru Fuji, Tokyo .... KO 7
1980
Jan. 10—Takeshi Ryu, Tokyo .... KO by 2
Apr. 2—Kenichi Ito, Tokyo .... KO by 6

CLAUDIO TANDA
Italian Bantamweight
1975
June 20—Luigi Paravati, Florence .... KO 3
July 25—Salvatore Laconi, Cagliari .... KO 2
Dec. 1—Filippo Belvedere, Cagliari .... L 4
Dec. 19—Salvatore Laconi, Cagliari .... W 4
1976
Mar. 5—Tarcisio Boi, Torino .... L 6
May 7—Franco Sperati, Cagliari................. D 8
Aug. 21—Heleno Ferreira, Fort Village .... KO by 4
Oct. 29—Tarcisio Boi, Cagliari .... D 8
Nov. 10—Filippo Belvedere, Cagliari.............. W 8
Dec. 3—Sabatino De Fillipo, Cagliari .... KO by 4
1977
Apr. 8—Franco Buglione, Ozieri .... W 12
(Italian Flyweight Title)
June 10—Luigi Tessarin, Vigevano .... L 12
(Italian Bantamweight Title)
July 22—Tarcisio Boi, Florence .... KO 5
Aug. 27—Sabatino De Fillipo, Ozieri .... WF 7
Oct. 14—Giovanni Camputaro, Milan .... KO by 10
(Italian Flyweight Title)
1978
Mar. 31—Franco Buglione, Capua .... L 12
(Italian Bantamweight Title)
Oct. 24—Charlie Magri, Kensington .... KO by 1
1979
Apr. 18—Giovanni Camputaro, S. Lorenzello .... L 8
May 25—Emilio Pireddu, Cagliari .... KO by 5
1980
Mar. 15—Valerio Nati, Forli .... KO by 1

PHENIX TANIGUCHI
Japanese Junior Flyweight
1978
June 22—Kazumasa Tamashiro, Okinawa City ..... D 10
Aug. 24—Kazunori Tenryu, Sendai City .... L 10
(Japanese Junior Flyweight Title)
1979
July 11—Masaharu Inami, Tokyo .... L 10
1980
Feb. 19—Koki Ishii, Tokyo .... KO by 6
Mar. 26—Tsutomu Kawakami, Nagoya .... W 8

WILLIE TARIKA
Fijian Junior Lightweight
1978
Dec. 16—Sawani Raicebe, Suva .... L 8
1979
Feb. 17—Gary Rosen, Suva .... KO 6
Apr. 28—Paul Baker, Suva .... W 10
Oct. 20—John Aba, Suva .... L 15
(For Commonwealth Junior Lightweight Title)
1980
Feb. 28—Maurice Apeang, Papeete .... L 10
Mar. 21—Johnny Aba, Brookvale .... L 15
(For Commonwealth Junior Lightweight Title)
May 6—Mark Vallance, Kingsford .... Exb. 3
June 4—Paul Barrow, Brookvale .... W 8
July 16—Paul Baker, Mt. Pritchard .... W 10
Sept. 10—Paul Baker, Gosforth .... W 10
Oct. 29—Mick Binney, Gosforth .... W 10
Dec. 9—Kirk Blair, Sutherland .... W 10

DAVE TAYLOR
British Junior Welterweight
1972
Dec. 6—Bob Brown, Manchester .... KO 2
1973
Jan. 8—Jess Harper, Manchester .... L 6
Feb. 19—Jess Harper, Manchester .... L 6
Mar. 14—Alan Hardiman, Stoke .... KO by 4
1974-1975
(Inactive)
1976
June 7—Freddie Mills, Manchester .... KO by 3
Aug. 29—Barry White, Solihull .... KO 3
1977
Mar. 21—Mick Mills, Stoke .... D 6
Apr. 5—Delvin Whyte, Southend .... D 6
Apr. 18—Johnny Beauchamp, Stafford .... D 6
Apr. 27—Johnny Gwilliam, Leicester .... W 4
May 3—Rocky Butler, Southend .... L 6
June 1—Roy Varden, Dudley .... L 6

417

July   5—Roy Varden, Wolverhampton .... L 8
July 20—John Kelly, Sheffield .... L 6
Sept. 8—Chris Gover, Liverpool .... L 8
Oct.   4—Tony Zeni, Southgate .... L 6
Oct. 31—Steve Holdsworth, Nantwich .... W 6
Nov. 14—Tony Zeni, Cambridge .... KO by 3
Dec.   5—John Kelly, London .... W 6
Dec. 12—Sylvester Gordon, London .... L 8
1978
Jan. 18—John Kelly, Stoke .... D 8
Jan. 30—Eric Wood, Cleethorpes .... L 6
Feb. 27—John Kelly, Sheffield .... L 8
Mar.   6—Mickey Bell, Manchester .... L 8
Apr. 27—Ian Pickersgill, Doncaster .... KO 1
May   8—Charlie Tonna, Birmingham .... KO 3
May 18—Stan Atherton, Liverpool .... L 6
Sept. 7—Tony Hague, Liverpool .... D 6
Sept. 12—Martin Bridge, Birkenhead .... L 6
Nov.   2—Brian Snagg, Liverpool .... D 8
Nov. 14—Dave Allen, Birkenhead .... W 8
Nov. 27—Vernon Vanriel, London .... L 8
1979
Jan. 18—Dai Davies, Liverpool .... W 8
Feb. 22—Jess Harper, Liverpool .... D 8
Apr. 23—Martin Bridge, Bradford .... L 10
Sept. 17—Lee Hartshorn, Manchester .... L 8
Oct. 30—Roy Varden, Bedford .... L 8
Dec.   5—Richard Avery, Liverpool .... L 6
Dec. 20—Alan Lamb, Queensway .... KO by 3
1980
Jan. 21—Ian Kid Murray, Wolverhampton .... L 6
Jan. 28—Kevin Walsh, Bradford .... W 6
Feb. 11—Pat Smythe, London .... W 6
Feb. 18—John Mount, Birmingham .... KO 4
Mar. 10—Ian Kid Murray, Wolverhampton .... W 6
Apr.   9—Cliff Gilpin, Burslem .... L 6
Apr. 30—Des Gwilliam, Wolverhampton .... L 8
July   8—Mickey Baker, Wolverhampton ...... KO by 5

ALEX TEMELKOV
1977
Oct.   7—Tony Adcock, Thirroul .... D 4
1978
Sept. 5—Arthur Matey, Kingsford .... KO 2
Nov.   1—Goerge Weight, Brookvale .... D 6
1979
Jan. 30—Bernie Alexander, Kingsford .... W 6
Feb. 13—Bernie Alexander, Kingsford .... W 6
May   8—Dick Bolton, Kingsford .... KO by 4
Sept. 1—Ken Morris, Berkeley .... KO 7
Nov.   7—Ken Morris, Brookvale .... KO 4
Dec.   8—Buddy Nixon, Berkeley .... KO 3
1980
Feb. 20—Ben Holt, Mt. Pritchard .... W 8
Apr. 26—Eric King, Berkeley .... KO 4
June   7—Benny Tabua, Wollongong .... KO 4
July 12—Joe Mario, Wollongong .... KO 7
Aug. 16—Ross Eadie, Wollongong .... KO 7
(Won Australian Junior Middleweight Title)
Nov. 27—Richie Roberts, Melbourne .... L 10

KAZUNORI TENRYU
Japanese Junior Flyweight
1975
Mar.   2—Isao Watanabe, Tokyo .... W 10
(Japanese Junior Flyweight Title)
May 17—Jaime Rios, Panama City .... KO by 4
June 23—Issei Sukamoto, Tokyo .... KO 7
(Japanese Junior Flyweight Title)
Aug. 23—Koya Urasaki, Ito City .... KO 6
Oct. 24—Isao Watanabe, Tokyo .... W 10
(Japanese Junior Flyweight Title)
1976
Jan.   3—Jaime Rios, Kagoshima City.............. L 15
(WBA Junior Flyweight Title)
Apr.   6—Kenji Daruma, Tokyo.................. KO 2
(Japanese Junior Flyweight Title)
June   5—Shoji Warabino, Sendai .... W 10
(Japanese Junior Flyweight Title)
Aug. 24—Yukimitsu Kondo, Tokyo .... KO 6
(Japanese Junior Flyweight Title)
Nov. 15—Kenji Daruma, Nagoya City .... W 10
(Japanese Junior Flyweight Title)
1977
Apr. 19—Sungjoon Kim, Tokyo .... W 10
June 15—Puma Koya, Tokyo .... W 10
(Japanese Junior Flyweight Title)
Aug. 23—Shigeo Nakajima, Tokyo .... KO by 3
    —Sueo Taniguchi, Tokyo .... W 10
(Japanese Junior Flyweight Title)
1978
Feb. 27—Puma Koya, Tokyo .... W 10
(Japanese Junior Flyweight Title)
Mar. 27—Sungjum Kim, Seoul .... KO by 3

July 20—Yukimitsu Kondo, Kagoshima City ..... KO 4
Aug. 24—Phenix Taniguchi, Sendai City .... W 10
(Japanese Junior Flyweight Title)
Nov. 25—Okihiro Kiyokawa, Tokyo ....KO 4
(Japanese Junior Flyweight Title)
1979
Nov. 19—Tadashi Tomori, Tokyo .... W 10
(Retained JBC Junior Flyweight Title)
1980
Feb. 28—Tadashi Tomori, Tokyo .... KO by 1
(Won Japanese Junior Flyweight Title)

HURRICANE TERU
(Shunzo Terukina)
Japanese Bantamweight
1970
Sept. 23—Toshiaki Nishizawa, Tokyo .... W 4
Oct. 16—George Mizoo, Tokyo .... D 4
Nov. 15—Hiroyuki Masai, Tokyo .... W 4
Dec. 30—Hiroshi Nemoto, Tokyo .... KO 4
1971
Jan. 28—George Mizoo, Tokyo .... W 4
Mar.   5—Shiro Ito, Tokyo .... KO 2
Mar. 20—Mashahiro Nagashima, Tokyo .... W 4
Apr. 16—Susumu Inoue, Tokyo .... W 4
June   4—Masakazu Kobayashi, Tokyo .... D 6
Aug.   5—Shigeo Taniguchi, Tokyo .... W 6
Sept. 9—Joichi Hirakawa, Tokyo .... L 6
Oct. 14—Sakae Honma, Tokyo .... KO 5
Nov.   4—Joichi Hirakawa, Tokyo .... L 6
1972
Jan.   6—Shigeki Uehara, Tokyo .... W 6
Mar. 23—Matsushi Yoshida, Tokyo .... W 6
Apr. 14—Mitsuyoshi Hosokawa, Sendai .... KO 5
June 27—Kunio Takeuchi, Tokyo .... W 8
Sept. 15—Taku Tojo, Tokyo .... KO 7
Oct. 19—Shintaro Uchiyama, Tokyo .... L 10
Dec. 14—Kunio Takeuchi, Tokyo .... W 10
1973
Feb. 20—Shigenobu Fukazawa, Tokyo .... W 8
May 20—Masaji Sakugawa, Tokyo .... W 8
June 26—Sadao Fukumura, Tokyo .... KO 9
Aug. 26—Hisami Mizuno, Tokyo .... W 10
Nov. 23—Go Mifune, Tokyo .... L 10
1974
Jan. 20—Go Mifune, Tokyo .... L 10
1975
(Inactive)
1976
Dec. 14—Shinobu Tomeoka, Tokyo .... W 6
1977
Feb. 15—Kazuhiro Kitagaki, Tokyo .... KO 5
May   8—Seishi Ii, Tokyo .... D 10
July   5—Eijiro Numata, Tokyo .... L 10
Sept. 13—Kosei Kawaguchi, Tokyo .... W 10
Nov. 24—Shuichi Isogami, Tokyo .... L 10
Jan.   4—Uichiro Hayashida, Koriyama City ...... KO 6
Nov. 26—Futaro Tanaka, Tokyo .... KO 7
1979
Jan.   9—Susumu Shinba, Tokyo .... W 10
Mar. 11—Johnny Sato, Tokyo .... W 10
May 24—Masaru Yamamoto, Tokyo .... KO 4
July 16—Kosei Anan, Tokyo .... KO 2
(JBC Bantamweight Title)
Oct.   5—Kosei Anan, Miyagi Ken .... W 10
(JBC Bantamweight Title)
1980
Jan. 28—Hitoshi Ishigaki, Tokyo .... L 10
(Lost Japanese Bantamweight Title)
May   3—Hitoshi Ishigaki, Yamagata .... KO 9
(Won Japanese Bantamweight Title)

ANTIMO TESCIONE
Italian Heavyweight
1980
Feb.   2—Gennaro Mauriello, Mugnano .... L 6
Feb. 14—Alessandro Casanova, Calozicorte .... L 6
Mar. 29—Gennaro Mauriello, Nocera .... L 6
May 24—Peter Mulindwa Kozza, Ostia .... KO by 2
Dec. 27—Alessandro Casanova, Cagliari .... KO by 5

LUIGI TESSARIN
Italian Bantamweight
Born: June 13, 1948
Turned pro 1970. Record to 1972: Total Bouts: 5,
Won 3, Lost 0, Drew 2.
1972
Jan.   5—Pedro De Latorre, Viareggio .... W 6
May 12—Giovanni Mura, Arezzo ....D 6
June   9—Guiseppe Fascella, Vigevano .... W 8
June 23—Salvatore Fabrizio, Genova .... L 8
July 21—Maria Pinna, Vigevano .... W 8
Dec.   9—Francis Payelle, Dunkirk ....LF 4

1973

Jan.	19—Jean-Pierre Flambeau, Vigevano	W	8
Mar.	30—Domenico Chiloiro, Milan	L	6
Apr.	20—Abu Arrow, Vigevano	W	8
May	2—Heleno Ferreira, Cagliari	KO	5
June	22—Franco Petrozzi, Vigevano	W	10
Nov.	3—Joe Latour, Milan	KO	5
Nov.	23—Antonio Verdiani, Torino	W	10

1974

Feb.	15—Ambrogio Mariani, Milan	KO by	6
Apr.	30—Lucio Vailati, Bologna	D	8
May	16—Johnny Clark, London	L	10
June	21—Gianni Garbo, Vigevano	W	8
Oct.	18—Lucio Vailati, Vigevano	W	10
Nov.	8—Paul Ikumpayi, Milan	KO by	4
Nov.	22—Dante Guarneri, Milan	W	6
Dec.	6—Ray Alava, Milan	KO	4

1975

Jan.	23—Salvatore Fabrizio, Palermo	L	8
Feb.	7—Lucio Vailati, Milan	KO	3
Feb.	21—Salvatore Fabrizio, Vigevano	W	8
May	2—Guy Caudron, Lens	KO by	4
Sept.	5—Abu Arrow, Robbio	W	8
Nov.	13—Brian Roberts, Melbourne	KO by	8

1976

Jan.	14—Lucio Vailati, Campione	KO by	5
Mar.	5—Daniel Trioulaire, Nice	L	10
Apr.	16—Lucio Vailati, Vigevano	W	8
Nov.	19—Ambrogio Mariani, Vigevano	W	8

1977

Feb.	25—Teodoro Corallo, Vigevano	W	12
	(Italian Bantamweight Title)		
June	10—Claudio Tanda, Vigevano	W	12
	(Italian Bantamweight Title)		
Aug.	7—Freddie Moran, Caracas	W	10
Oct.	7—Franco Buglione, Capua	L	12
	(Italian Bantamweight Title)		
Oct.	26—Antonio Franca, Vigevano	W	8

1978

Mar.	31—Melquidades Da Silva, Vigevano	KO	8
July	6—Melquidades Da Silva, Lugo di Romagna	W	8
Oct.	13—Alfredo Mulas, Ravenna	L	12
	(European Bantamweight Title)		

1979

Apr.	20—Giuseppe Fossati, Milan	L	12
	(Italian Bantamweight Title)		
June	8—Valerio Nati, Ravenna	L	10
Aug.	3—Antonio Franca, Ariano Polesine	W	8
Nov.	23—Giancarlo Ravaioli, Pordonone	L	8

1980

Feb.	7—Michael Irungu, Randers	KO by	2

JOSEPH TETELI
South African Lightweight
1980

May	10—Jafta Mogotsi, Virginia	L	4
June	14—Basie Mtshamba, Welkom	W	4
Aug.	9—Johannes Motsumi, Wesselsbron	W	6
Sept.	27—Joe Sefanga, Welkom	W	6
Dec.	13—Manasse Potse, Wesselsbron	W	8

JOSEPH THABETHE
South African Middleweight
1978

Nov.	25—Jabulani Sithole, Durban	L	4

1979

Aug.	18—Graham Mningi, Durban	D	4

1980

Sept.	15—Mike Toweel, Durban	W	4
Oct.	6—John Dhlamini, Pmburg	L	4
Nov.	3—Bang Bang Makhatini, Durban	L	4

ZACHARIA THABETHE
South African Welterweight
1973

July	14—Joel Ndlovu, Durban	W	4

1974
(Inactive)

1975

June	21—Aswan Simelene, Stanger	W	4

1976

Dec.	18—Alfred Maduna, Durban	KO	1

1977

Feb.	28—Coenraad Bekker, Durban	L	4
Aug.	1—Charlie Weir, Durban	KO by	1

1978

Aug.	12—Joseph Sishi, Durban	KO by	8

1979
(Inactive)

1980

Mar.	1—Ness Roux, Durban	L	4
June	7—Morris Mohloai, Eldorado	KO by	2

FRANK THOBAKGALE
South African Junior Welterweight
1978

May	15—Renier de Beer, Johannesburg	KO	1

1979

Mar.	30—Terrence Molefe, Springs	KO by	1

1980

Feb.	29—Jeffrey Aphane, Springs	D	4
Aug.	1—Matthew Ndlovu, Springs	L	4

ANDY THOMAS
British Featherweight
1980

May	19—John Henry, Birmingham	KO	1
Apr.	30—Clyde Ruan, Aylesbury	L	4
June	2—Steve Pollard, London	L	6
Oct.	13—Steve Farnsworth, Manchester	W	6
Oct.	23—Eddie Glass, Middlesbrough	W	6
Oct.	27—Jeff Smart, London	KO	6

NIGEL THOMAS
British Welterweight
1977

Oct.	3—Phillip Morris, Aberavon	W	4
Oct.	17—Eddie Avoth, Bedford	KO by	2
Nov.	21—Derek Tew, Birmingham	L	4

1978

Jan.	16—Martin Crane, Birmingham	KO	1
Jan.	24—Peter Snowsall, London	L	4
Mar.	6—Johnny Beauchamp, London	W	4
Apr.	6—Johnny Beauchamp, Ebbw Vale	W	6
Apr.	20—Gary Collins, Bradford	L	6
May	16—Johnny Beauchamp	W	6
July	10—Dai Davies, Aberavon	L	6
Oct.	3—Steve Powell, Aberavon	W	6
Nov.	2—Brendan O'Donnell, Liverpool	W	6
Nov.	14—Tony Carroll, Birkenhead	L	6
Nov.	29—Johnny Chard, Swansea	KO	7
Dec.	4—Tony Carroll, Manchester	L	6
Dec.	11—Roger Guest, Birmingham	D	6

1979

Jan.	17—Shaun Stewart, Solihull	W	6
Jan.	22—Roger Guest, Birmingham	D	6
Feb.	12—Jesse Harper, Manchester	W	6
Feb.	19—Roger Guest, Birmingham	L	8
Apr.	4—Joe Mills, Birmingham	W	8
May	23—Mark Osborne, Nottingham	L	4
June	18—Norman Morton, Bradford	D	8
June	27—Ray Ross, Derry	KO	5
July	5—Lee Hartshorn, Aberavon	W	8
Sept.	25—John F. Kennedy, London	KO by	2
Nov.	6—Gary Newell, Stafford	L	6
Nov.	14—Ian Murray, Stoke	W	8
Nov.	21—Ian Murray, Evesham	W	8
Dec.	3—Lloyd Hibbitt, Wolverhampton	L	8

1980

Feb.	28—Dill Collins, Ebbw Vale	W	8
Mar.	10—Mickey Mapp, London	L	8
Mar.	31—Kenny Webber, Cleethropes	L	8
Apr.	28—Lee Hartshorn, London	L	4
May	19—Roy Varden, Birmingham	KO by	6
June	16—Dave Ward, Manchester	L	8
Sept.	24—Cliff Gilpin, Evesham	L	8

TOMMY THOMAS
British Junior Welterweight
1978

May	22—Brendan Devine, Mayfair	D	4
July	17—Brendan Devine, London	KO	2

1979

Jan.	18—Alan Cable, Wimbledon	KO by	4
Feb.	26—Liam Linnen, Glasgow	D	6
Mar.	7—Roger Guest, Solihull	KO	5
Mar.	28—Dave Allen, Kettering	D	4
Apr.	19—Pat Smythe, London	L	8
Apr.	30—Richard Avery, London	D	6
May	17—Alan Cable, Wimbledon	KO by	6
Oct.	8—Dennis Sullivan, London	KO by	6
Nov.	19—Duncan Hamilton, Glasgow	L	6
Dec.	3—Mickey Baker, Wolverhampton	KO by	1

1980

Mar.	3—Terry Parkinson, Hove	KO by	4
Apr.	30—Paul Wetter, Aylesbury	L	6
May	21—Eric Hirschmann, Coventry	L	4
June	3—Tim Moloney, Aylesbury	L	4
Nov.	3—Johnny Beauchamp, Hammersmith	W	6

GERALD (JUNIOR) THOMPSON
Australian Flyweight
1979

June	7—Cec Broome, Townsville	KO	3

Dec. 15—Bobby Williams, Townsville .... W 10
      (Won Vacant Australian Light Flyweight Title)
1979
      (Inactive)
1980
Sept. 12—Steve Bell, Auburn .... KO by 6
      (For Australian Flyweight Title)

HECTOR THOMPSON
Australian Welterweight
Born: June 28, 1949, Kempsey, N.S.W., Australia
1970
Mar. 11—Paul Pappas, Redfern .... D 4
Mar. 19—Ricky Donnelly, Redfern .... W 4
Apr.   6—Billy Murphy, Melbourne .... W 4
Apr.   9—Des Jackson, Redfern.................... W 4
July 13—Terry Ellis, Cardiff.....................KO 3
July 16—Steve Olds, Auburn....................... W 6
July 20—Ron Boyd, Toronto........................ W 4
July 28—Ricky Martin, Wallsend.................. W 4
July 30—Paul Craigie, South Newcastle .... W 6
Aug. 10—Stephen Dale, Melbourne .... W 8
Aug. 17—Peter Lord, Melbourne .... W 8
Sept. 4—Sid Capewell, Brisbane .... W 10
Sept. 28—Ricky Day, Melbourne .... W 8
Oct.   6—Roko Spanja, Wallsend .... KO 10
Oct. 16—Paul Craigie, Toukley .... W 8
Nov.   5—Ted Bonner, Redfern .... L 10
1971
Jan. 15—Ricky Johnson, Kurri Kurri .... L 10
Jan. 20—Ray Cannon, Maitland.................... W 10
Mar. 12—Alan Tunney, Kurri Kurri .... W 10
Mar. 19—Bobby Cotterill, Maitland............... W 10
Apr.   5—Johnny Phillips, Cardiff................. W 8
Apr. 26—Michele Vitale, Melbourne .... W 10
May   31—Hilary Connolly, Melbourne.............. W 10
July   5—Red Durange, Cardiff....................KO 10
July 12—Leo Young, Melbourne.................... W 10
Aug.   9—Michael Vitale, Melbourne .... W 10
Aug. 16—Johnny Cheshire, Melbourne .... KO 7
Sept. 28—Dave Rudkin, Cardiff.................... W 10
Oct. 25—Jimmy Noel, Melbourne .... W 10
Dec. 13—Leo Young, Melbourne....................KO 7
1972
Feb.   8—Rex Downward, Perth .... W 10
Mar. 10—Hilary Connolly, Brisbane .... W 10
Apr. 21—Rex Downward, Brisbane .... KO 7
May   19—Hernani Apatan, Brisbane................KO 10
June 16—Joe Tetteh, Brisbane .... W 10
June 30—Ali Afakasi, Brisbane ....KO 10
Sept. 1—Jeff White, Brisbane .... W 15
      (Australian Junior Welterweight Title)
Sept. 11—Hilary Connolly, Melbourne.............. W 10
Oct. 16—Manny Santos, Brisbane .... D 12
      (Vacant Australian Lightweight Title)
Oct. 30—Dave Rudken, Narrabri................... W 8
Dec.   8—Renaldo Victoria, Milton................KO 4
1973
Feb. 26—Manny Santos, Brisbane .... W 15
      (Vacant Australian Lightweight Title)
Mar. 26—Joe Tetteh, Brisbane .... W 15
      (Commonwealth Junior Welterweight Title)
June   2—Roberto Duran, Panama City........ KO by 8
      (WBA Lightweight Title)
July 16—Joe Tetteh, Brisbane .... W 15
Sept. 10—Pat McCormick, Melbourne ....KO 4
Nov.   5—Jouse Marquez, Brisbane .... W 10
Dec.   9—Raul Montoya, Brisbane .... W 10
1974
Mar. 29—Gerardo Ferrat, Brisbane ....KO 4
Apr. 26—Johnny Grant, Brisbane .... W 10
June 14—Carlos Giminez, Brisbane .... W 10
Aug.   2—Carlos Giminez, Brisbane ....KO 9
Aug. 30—Jimmy Heair, Brisbane .... W 10
Oct. 25—Peppermint Frazer, Brisbane............KO 8
Dec.   6—Javier Ayala, Brisbane .... KO by 3
1975
Apr.   4—Lion Furuyama, Brisbane .... W 10
May   19—Ali Afakasi, Brisbane ....KO 10
      (Commonwealth Light Welterweight Title)
July   7—Rudy Barro, Brisbane ....KO 6
July 17—Pedro Adrigue, Port Moresby............ W 10
Aug.   4—Shinichi Kadota, Brisbane ....KO 5
Oct. 10—Adriano Marrero, Brisbane .... W 10
Nov. 15—Antonio Cervantes, Panama City ..... KO by 7
      (WBA Junior Welterweight Title)
1976
Mar. 12—Alfonso Hayman, Brisbane................ W 10
Apr.   1—Chuck Wilburn, Blacktown ....KO 10
June 25—Charles Giminez, Brisbane............... W 10
July 15—Ali Afakasi, Auckland ....KO 6
      (Australian Welterweight Title)
Aug. 16—Andy Broome, Tweed Heads ....KO 6
Oct.   8—Neil Pattel, Tweed Heads................KO 8

Dec.   3—Ross Eadie, Wollongong .... KO 15
      (Commonwealth & Australian Junior Welterweight Titles)
Dec. 16—Martin Beni, Broadmeadow.............. KO 10
      (Commonwealth Light Welterweight Title)
1977
Apr. 28—Laurie Austin, Perth .... KO by 15
      (Commonwealth & Australian Junior Welterweight Titles)
May   20—Ross Eadie, Boondall .... KO 12
      (Vacant Australian Welterweight Title)
June 16—Laurie Austin, Perth .... W 15
      (Commonwealth and Australian Junior Welterweight Titles)
July   4—Jong Sathiayim, Bangkok .... W 10
Aug. 25—Ross Eadie, Penrith .... KO 7
      (Australian Welterweight Title)
Sept. 15—Laurie Austin, Perth .... L 15
      (Commonwealth and Australian Junior Welterweight Titles)
1978
Feb. 16—Jeff Malcolm, Melbourne .... W 12
Mar. 10—Dan De Guzman, Manila .... L 10
Apr. 28—Andy Broome, Melbourne .... W 10
Oct.   6—Neil Pattel, Brisbane .... W 10
Nov. 10—Ruben Rabago, Brisbane .... W 10
Dec.   8—Greg Stephens, Brisbane .... L 10
1979
Feb. 17—Sakaraia Ve, Suva ....KO 8
Nov. 24—Sakaraia Ve, Kingsford .... KO by 11
1980
Aug. 21—Ramon Dionisio, Perth ....KO 6
Sept. 29—Frank Ropis, Brisbane .... KO by 12
      (For Australian Welterweight Title)
Nov. 24—Steve Dennis, Brisbane .... KO by 6

KELLY THOMPSON
Australian Junior Welterweight
1978
Sept. 6—Ken Carmody, Brookvale ....KO 3
Sept. 14—Vinnie Edwards, Blacktown .... W 6
Sept. 20—Vinnie Edwards, Mt. Pritchard .... W 6
Sept. 27—Eric King, Bankstown .... W 8
Oct.   4—Eric King, Bankstown .... W 6
Oct. 12—Harry Vale, Blacktown .... W 6
Oct. 18—Dawsie Kelly, Mt. Pritchard .... L 8
Oct. 25—Dawsey Kelly, Bankstown .... W 8
Dec.   7—Ritchie Roberts, Revesby .... L 8
1979
Feb.   4—Ritchie Roberts, Enmore .... KO by 8
Apr.   9—Rocky Maguire, Blacktown ....KO 4
Apr. 26—George Reno, Revesby .... L 8
May   21—George Reno, Rooty Hill .... KO by 6
1980
Jan. 29—Clint Brown, Kingsford .... D 6
Feb. 10—Jamie Lewis, Revesby .... W 6
Mar. 29—Peter Berrigan, Newcastle .... L 6
May   9—Jamie Lewis, Merrylands ....KO 3
May   21—Tommy Roberts, Mt. Pritchard .... W 8
June 18—Andrew Palermo, Mt. Pritchard ...... KO by 8

MICK THOMPSON
Australian Welterweight
1979
Feb. 10—Simon Kirkness, Kingsford ....KO 5
June 20—Dawsey Kelly, Pritchard .... L 10
1980
May   9—Sam Parsons, Merrylands .... D 6
May   24—Sam Parsons, Blacktown ....KO 6
June 27—F. Gauci, Canley Vale .... D 6
Aug.   8—Dawsie Kelly, Merrylands .... W 10
Sept. 6—Buddy Nixon, Auburn .... W 6
Sept. 18—Buddy Nixon, Marrickville .... W 6
Oct.   7—Clint Brown, Kingsford .... L 8

PETER THOMPSON
Australian Bantamweight
1979
May   16—Gavin Rodgway, Mt. Pritchard ....KO 2
May   23—Jimmy Morris, Brookvale ....KO 4
June 20—Paul Roberts, Mt. Pritchard .... KO by 13
Aug. 28—Sparrow Freeman, Kingsford .... L 4
Sept. 6—Kirk Davis, Brookvale .... W 6
Sept. 25—Idries Ali, Kingsford .... W 6
1980
Feb.   6—Kirk Davis, Brookvale .... W 5
Apr. 16—Mario DeMarco, Mt. Pritchard .... KO by 4

HENNIE THOONEN
Dutch Heavyweight
Born: July 6, 1942, Eindhoven
1973
Sept. 9—Manfred Ackers, Amsterdam ....KO 2
Sept. 19—Ireno Werleman, Arnhem ....KO 4
1974
Feb. 18—Jean Belval, Rotterdam ....KO 4
Sept. 23—Ferenc Kristofcsak, Rotterdam ....KO 3

420

Nov. 21—Tim Ahola, Helsinki .... L 6
1975
May   5—Gerrie Coetzee, Johannesburg .... L 6
May   26—Ireno Werleman, Rotterdam .... KO 7
June 25—Lucien Rodriquez, Paris .... L 8
June 29—Gerrie Coetzee, Johannesburg .... KO by 5
1976
Feb. 16—Lisimo Obutobe, Scheveningen .... KO 3
Apr. 12—Jan Lubbers, Schidam .... KO 10
(Dutch Heavyweight Title)
May   31—Jean Pierre Coopman, Rotterdam .... WF 5
Oct.   9—Jean Pierre Coopman, Antwerp ...... KO by 6
1977
Apr.   4—Bernd August, Amsterdam .... KO by 3
Oct. 17—Arno Prick, Rotterdam .... KO 7
Oct. 31—Avenamar Peralta, Rotterdam .... L 10
1978
Jan. 11—Tom Keely, Rotterdam .... KO 5
May   19—Albert Syben, Brussels .... KO by 4
Sept. 4—George Jerome, Rotterdam .... KO 3
Sept. 16—Ekwelum, Heerenveen .... W disq. 3
1979
May   28—Christian Poncelet, Amsterdam .... W 8
Aug. 27—Jimmy Abbott, Johannesburg .... KO by 1
Nov. 10—Terry O'Connor, Eindhoven .... W 8
1980
Jan. 28—George Scott, Rotterdam .... L 8
May   19—Rudi Lubbers, Rotterdam .... LF 7
June 13—Bernard August, Luebeck .... KO 2

ROBERT THRONTON
British Junior Welterweight
1980
Sept. 22—Johnny Beauchamp, Birmingham .... L 6
Oct. 14—Barry Oliver, Nantwich .... D 4
Oct. 22—Robert Armstrong, Doncaster .... KO by 3

MARIO TIANO
Italian Junior Lightweight
1978
July 14—Giancarlo Ravioli, Lido di Ostia .... L 6
Dec. 21—Gerardo Scognamilgio, Rome .... KO 4
1979
Aug. 11—Domenico Condello, Rocca Prioria .... D 6
Sept. 22—Valerio Fretta, Marcianise .... KO 5
Nov. 14—Roberto Masini, Gualdo .... LF 6
1980
Mar. 21—Franco Canini, Bologna .... L 6
Oct. 24—Bruno Simili, Grosseto .... L 8

PETER TIDGEWELL
British Light Heavyweight
1978
Oct. 16—Dave Merrell, Bradford .... W 6
Oct. 23—Joey Saunders, Manchester .... KO 5
Nov. 16—Paul Bussette, Liverpool .... KO 4
Dec. 11—Boyd Farrar, London .... KO by 4
1979
Jan. 22—Dave Merrell, Bradford .... KO 5
Mar. 16—Steve Babbs, Bradford .... W 6
Apr.   2—Billy Hill, Manchester .... L 8
Apr. 23—Mick Dolan, Bradford .... W 8
May   21—Steve Babbs, Bradford .... L 8
June 18—Nigel Savory, Bradford .... W 8
1980
Apr. 21—Joe Jackson, Bradford .... D 8
June 16—Tommy Jones, Manchester .... W 8
Aug. 31—Gary Jones, Glasgow .... W 8

GUISEPPE TIDU
Italian Lightweight
1980
Feb.   9—Francisco Pestorino, Cagliari .... W 6
Mar.   8—Palmiro Pizzata, Cagliari .... W 6
Apr. 19—Ignazio Fara, Calgari .... KO 4
May   3—Vincenzo Di Bari, Cagliari .... W 6
June 20—Aniello Ventrone, Cagliari .... WF 4
Sept. 3—Melquiades Da Silva, St. Teresa .... W 6
Oct. 31—Giorgio Pipia, Cagliari .... W 6
Nov. 29—Gregorio Ciancaglione, Cagliari .... KO 5
Dec. 27—Timoteo Bonizzoni, Cagliari .... KO 7

STEDY TIKOLO
South African Flyweight
1979
Feb. 10—Godfrey Mafanya, Queenstown .... L 4
July   7—Edward Mtana, Queenstown .... W 4
Nov.   3—Lindile Yam, Queenstown .... W 4
1980
Mar. 29—Honey Ndwanya, Queenstown .... W 4

JONAS TLADI
South African Junior Welterweight
1978
Sept. 2—Johannes Motsumi, Ficksburg .... W 4
Oct.   7—Joseph Molatlhwe, Virginia .... W 4
1979
Mar.   3—Daniel Mantsi, Virginia .... D 4
May   5—Jeremiah Nzelwane, Ficksburg .... W 8
July 14—Joseph Molahloe, Virginia .... W 8
Sept. 1—Martin Jacobs, Ficksburg .... W 10
Oct.   2—Stephene Balene, Bloemfontein .... L 6
Nov. 17—Paulus Lechakane, Ficksburg .... W 8
1980
Feb.   9—Johannes Rammisong, Bethlehem .... W 8
Apr. 13—Stephen Balene, Ficksburg .... W 10
(Retained OFS Junior Welterweight Title)
May   30—Ephraim Mabena, Springs .... L 6
Dec.   6—Stephen Balene, Ficksburg .... W 10
(Retained OFS Junior Welterweight Title)

MOTSIE TLADI
South African Lightweight
1979
Feb.   9—Daniel Moloi, Bethlehem .... L 4
May   5—Lucas Sebego, Ficksburg .... W 4
Sept. 1—Samuel Wolf, Ficksburg .... KO 3
Oct.   2—Samule Motsabi, Bloemfontein .... L 6
Nov. 17—Basie Mtsamba, Ficksburg .... KO 3
1980
Feb.   4—Daniel Moloi, Bethlehem .... L 4
Apr. 12—April Papane, Ficksburg .... W 6
Sept. 6—Joseph Molahioe, Ficksburg .... W 4
Dec.   6—Simon Molahioe, Ficksburg .... KO 5

TARZAN TOBARU
Japanese Welterweight
1978
May   5—Sumio Kai, Tokyo .... KO 1
1979
Feb. 26—Mitsuo Kushikino, Tokyo .... KO by 8
1980
Feb. 25—Mamoru Taira, Tokyo .... KO 2

TADASHI TOMORI
Japanese Junior Flyweight
1979
Nov. 19—Kazunori Tenryu, Tokyo .... L 10
(JBC Junior Flyweight Title)
Dec. 24—Keisuke Yuguchi, Tokyo .... KO 2
1980
Feb. 28—Kazunori Tenryu, Tokyo .... KO 1
(Won Japanese Junior Flyweight Title)
Apr. 20—Puma Koya, Tokyo .... W 10

ALEC TOMPKINS
British Light Heavyweight
Born: Dec. 12, 1954
1974
Mar. 11—Joey Cammon, Kensington............. KO 5
Apr. 28—Kevin Paddock, Southend .... W 8
May   16—Mick Lock, Walworth................. KO 2
June 10—Alan Bursey, Walworth................ KO 2
Sept. 16—Bob Murphy, Southampton............. L 6
Nov. 13—Randy Barrett, Solihull .... KO 2
Dec.   5—Augustus Simms, London.............. KO 2
1975
Feb. 10—Charlie Richardson, Kensington ...... KO by 5
Feb. 18—Pat Brogan, Bethnal Green .... W 6
May   5—Batman Austin, Bedford .... L 8
July 14—Joe Lally, London .... L 8
Sept. 16—Batman Austin, London .... L 8
Sept. 22—Augustus Sims, Walworth .... KO 4
Nov. 24—Joe Yekinni, Walworth................. W 8
Dec.   1—Trevor Francis, London................ L 8
1976
Jan. 19—Claude Martin, Paris.................. L 10
Feb. 23—Vernon Scott, London .... L 8
May   3—Leroy Herriot, Walworth.............. KO 5
Oct. 18—Pat Brogan, Seymour Hall .... KO 5
Oct. 25—Gareth Tashy Jones, London .... KO 1
Dec.   7—Kevin Finnegan, Kensington........... L 8
1977
Feb.   1—Billy Knight, London .... KO 4
Feb. 22—Peter Cain, London .... KO 1
Apr. 12—Frankie Lucas, London .... KO by 6
July 18—Jan Magdziarz, London .... KO by 5
Oct.   8—Piermanio Baruzzi, Nice .... KO 6
Nov.   7—Keith Bussey, Walworth .... L 8
1978
(Inactive)
1979
May   00—Shaun Chalcroft, London .... W 8
June 13—Ken Jones, Caerphilly .... L 8

421

Oct.	17—Keith Bussey, Lewisham	KO 8
Nov.	19—Shaun Chalcraft, Lewisham	L 8

1980

Feb.	28—Vernon Scott. Queensway	KO 5

GRATIEN TONNA
French Middleweight
Born: Jan. 18, 1949, Tunis

1970

Dec.	4—Georges Danin, Marseille	KO 4

1971

Jan.	8—Jean Claude Courteille, Marseille	KO 2
Jan.	29—Christian Rubins, Marseille	KO 3
Mar.	19—Charley Kacem, Marseille	KO 1
Apr.	30—Victor Caloc, Marseille	KO 2
May	8—Epifanio Collado, Monaco	KO 2
June	4—Pablo Sanchez, Marseille	KO 1
Sept.	3—Kid Monte, Marseille	KO 2
Oct.	1—John Tiger, Marseille	KO 2
Oct.	29—Steyner Cassius, Marseille	KO 3
Nov.	8—Roberto Biscotti, Paris	KO 2
Nov.	29—Lloyd Duncan, Paris	KO 5
Dec.	12—Ralph Correa, Marseille	KO 3

1972

Jan.	3—Max Cohen, Paris	L 10
Jan.	15—Jose Maria Madrazo, Marsella	W disq. 5
Feb.	21—Mario Lamagna, Paris	W 10
Mar.	27—Vincent Parra, Paris	KO 2
Apr.	14—Howard Freeman, Marseille	KO 2
Apr.	29—Remo Golfarini, Cannes	KO 2
June	9—Fabio Bettini, Marseille	KO by 9
Aug.	14—Mataitini, Papeete	KO 9
Sept.	2—Pago Kid, Papeete	KO 4
Nov.	3—Jorge Fernandez, Marseille	LF 4
Nov.	25—Mario Lamagna, Cannes	W 10
Dec.	18—Manuel Gonzalez, Paris	W 10

1973

Jan.	3—Domenico Tiberia, Cannes	KO 5
Feb.	3—Domenico Tiberia, Cannes	KO 5
Mar.	12—Luis Vinales, Paris	KO 5
Apr.	7—Miguel Chequer, Marseille	KO 4
May	14—Tommy Hanna, Paris	KO 4
June	2—Thurman (Doc) Holliday, Monte Carlo	W 8
June	13—Nico Alosery, Frejus	KO 3
Oct.	5—Luciano Sarti, Marseille	KO 1
Nov.	12—Alipate Korovov Novmea	W 10

1974

Feb.	1—Fabio Bettini, Marseille	W 12
Mar.	17—Dave Wyatt, Lyon	KO 1
Mar.	29—Matt Donovan, Rome	KO 1
May	10—Fabio Bettini, Marseille	KO 7
	(French Middleweight Title)	
Oct.	18—Juan Botta, Rome	KO 1
Nov.	30—Rodrigo Valdes, Paris	KO by 11
	(WBC Middleweight Title)	

1975

May	7—Kevin Finnegan, Monte Carlo	W 15
	(European Middleweight Title)	
Dec.	13—Carlos Monzon, Paris	KO by 5
	(WBA Middleweight Title)	

1976

Mar.	12—Jules Bellaiche, Marseille	KO 6
	(French Middleweight Title)	
May	6—Jean Mateo, Paris	KO 2
Oct.	1—D. C. Walker, Marseille	KO 2
Dec.	3—Bob Payton, Marseille	KO 7

1977

Feb.	19—John Harris, Bastia	KO 4
Mar.	5—Pablo Rodriguez, St. Quentin	KO 1
Sept.	21—Alan Minter, Milan	KO 8
	(European Middleweight Title)	

1978

Feb.	25—Ronnie Harris, Las Vegas	L 12
Nov.	7—Alan Minter, London	KO by 6
	(European Middleweight Title)	

1979

May	18—Gerard Nosley, Perigueux	KO 6
	(French Middleweight Title)	

1980

Feb.	7—Kevin Finnegan, Paris	L 12
	(For European Middleweight Title)	

STEVE TOPLISS
British Featherweight

1980

Feb.	5—Don Aagesen, Wolverhampton	W 6
Mar.	11—Mike Pickett, Nantwich	W 6
May	29—Bryn Jones, Wolverhampton	W 6
Oct.	16—Derek Groarke, Bolton	W 6

ANTONIO TORSELLO
Italian Welterweight

1973

Oct.	19—Armin Rindlisbacher, Geneva	KO 5
Nov.	16—Alain Giraudon, Lusanne	W 6

1974

Feb.	1—Gianfranco Meconi, Geneva	W 6
Feb.	16—Rene Chanez, Chaux de Fonds	KO 6
Apr.	19—Chedik Tebourski, Chavennes	KO 5
May	3—Allah Krimm, Renens	KO 6
May	27—Georges Warusfel, Paris	L 6
Oct.	25—Mohamed Mechlia, Geneva	W 8
Nov.	18—Jack Peraire, Chaux de Fonds	L 6
Dec.	10—Zoubir Sadouchi, Dornbirn	W 8

1975

Jan.	31—Giancarlo Serangeli, Fibourg	W 8
Mar.	7—Luciano Borracia, Milan	L 8
Mar.	28—Italo Venturi, Turin	KO 3
Apr.	26—Sulah Arafa, Fribourg	KO 5
June	6—Ribeiro Luis, Lusanne	L 10
Aug.	2—Giovanni Molesini, Lusanne	KO by 6

1976

Jan.	10—Jean Dercle, Dunkerque	KO 4
Feb.	6—Sreco Weiner, Chavannes	KO 2
Oct.	23—Philippe Girotti, LeHarve	KO 2
Dec.	3—Bruno Freschi, Trieste	KO 2

1977

Jan.	14—Joseph Pachler, Bregenz	L 10
Feb.	4—Georges Warusfel, Geneva	KO by 3
Apr.	29—Alain Ruocco, Morges	W 10
June	17—Jose Luis Pacheco, Madrid	KO by 3
Oct.	22—Mario Guilloti, Turin	KO by 7

1978

Apr.	8—Victorrio Conte, Pistoia	KO by 10
May	12—Cemal Kamaci, Bregenz	L 8
Oct.	27—Jose Luis Ribiero, Chavannes	W 10

1979

Jan.	27—Alain Ruocco, Toulon	KO by 10
June	30—Luigi Minchillo, Monte Carlo	KO by 2
Sept.	8—Timoteo Bonizzoni, Offanengo	KO by 5
Sept.	29—Pirangelo Pira, Rimini	KO by 6
Nov.	30—Esperno Postl, Chavannes	W 10

1980

Mar.	7—Ciro Seta, Chavannes	W 8
Oct.	24—Pierangelo Pira, Grossetto	KO by 3
	(For Italian Welterweight Title)	

NKOSANA TOLBERT
South African Junior Featherweight

1977

Nov.	19—Welile Nkosenkulu, East London	KO 1

1978

Apr.	15—Ntutu Mazwana, Butterworth	L 4

1979

Feb.	24—Simthembile Mkhalipi, King Williamstown	W 6
July	7—Nkosana Moss, East London	KO by 4
Nov.	3—Ndodomzi Witi, Queenstown	KO 4
Dec.	1—Siphiwo Fuma, King Williamstown	L 6

1980

June	4—Matata Plaatjies, Goodwood	L 6
Sept.	5—Welcome Jonas, East London	L 4
Dec.	13—Siphiwe Fuma, Queenstown	L 8

HIKARU TOMONARI
Japanese Featherweight

1978

Jan.	26—Bomber Uchida, Tokyo	L 10

1979

May	8—Blazer Okubo, Osaka	W 10
July	26—Royal Kobayashi, Tokyo	W 10
Oct.	5—Gen Akutsu, Miyagi Ken	KO 3
Nov.	24—Koji Kunishige, Tokyo	KO 5

1980

Jan.	6—Royal Umeno, Nara	KO 3
Mar.	13—Yoshitaka Ikehara, Tokyo	W 10

GEN TOSA
Japanese Junior Lightweight

1979

Dec.	9—Tomio Nakamura, Osaka	W 10

1980

Jan.	28—Gen Akutsu, Tokyo	KO 8

JEAN MARIE TOUATI
Belgian Welterweight

1978

Oct.	14—Dragan Tadic, Bethune	W 6
Nov.	18—Abdullah Salah Kaci, Mericourt	KO 4

1979

Feb.	10—Lucien Campo, Arques	W 6
Apr.	7—Michel Iger, Bethune	L 6
Apr.	14—Mohamed Bouziani, Lieges	W 6
Apr.	28—Jean Paul Coppyn, Berlin	L 6

Nov. 17—Serge Poulain, Labeuvriere .... KO 5
Dec. 15—Serge Sinelnikov, Bethune .... W 6
1980
Mar. 10—Gilles Elbilia, Paris .... L 8
Nov. 13—Jeff Lee, Dunkirk .... KO 4

LEE TOWN
British Welterweight
1980
Mar. 3—Dave Aspill, Hove .... L 6
Mar. 11—Steve Ward, Southend .... W 6
Apr. 23—Jimmy Smith, Hove .... : .... D 6
Apr. 30—Jimmy Smith, Aylesbury .... L 6

ALDO TRAMENTOZZI
Italian Light Heavyweight
1979
Apr. 20—Luciano Casali, Udine .... KO by 2
Oct. 27—Andrea Sangalletti, Rieti .... KO by 2
1980
Mar. 21—Walter Cevoli, Bologna .... KO by 6

HERBERT TRAUSMUTH
Austrian Junior Middleweight
1973
Dec. 11—Natala Vezzoli, Italy .... W 4
1974
Apr. 9—Angelo Tomasini, Italy .... KO by 4
May 14—Dijiemai Belhadi, Algeria .... W 6
June 8—Dijiemai Belhadi, Algeria .... KO 1
Oct. 4—Gianpaolo Piras, Italy .... W 6
Dec. 14—Lothar Abend, W. Germany .... KO by 4
1975
May 2—Giampaolo Piras, Wien .... D 6
May 6—Gianpaolo Pedersen, Norway .... KO by 3
1976-1977
(Inactive)
1978
Aug. 18—Claude Kalanda, Zaire .... KO 1
Nov. 12—Darko Covic, Wien .... KO 3
1979
Jan. 19—Zdravko Jovicic, Wien .... KO 2
Mar. 17—Dieter Schantz, Koblenz .... KO by 2
Apr. 21—Rosario Pomponi, Ostia .... KO by 4
July 13—Otto Zinoeder, Greinsfurth .... L 8
Oct. 20—Jose Luis Ribiero, Gansbacher .... WF 4
Dec. 7—Alfred Fries, Lubeck .... W 6
1980
Feb. 1—Franz Hohl, Vienna .... KO 2
Mar. 31—Cor Everstein, Rotterdam .... KO by 5
June 13—Andre Wissenbach, Lubeck .... L 3

FRANCIS TRIPP
French Welterweight
1980
Apr. 5—Antoine Curti, Nice .... W 6
Apr. 19—Jean Michel Iger, Pontarlier .... KO 3
Apr. 26—Frederic Geoffroy, Ajaicio .... W 6
Nov. 7—Dario Bruno, Nice .... W 6

JEAN PHILIPPE TRUCHELUT
French Middleweight
1979
Sept. 29—Rida Hakima, Troyes .... KO 3
Dec. 7—Michel Moinard, Epinay .... W 6
1980
Feb. 9—Serge Sinelnikov, Troyes .... W 6
Feb. 17—Jean Luc Lami, Maubeuge .... L 6
Apr. 12—Cyrille Barbe, Troylo .... W 6
Apr. 26—Pierre Frank Winstertein, Le Grande KO by 4

ELIAS TSHABALALA
South African Junior Lightweight
1974
Apr. 6—Simon Mahlasi, Sharpeville .... W 4
1975
Mar. 7—Solomon Ramafikeng, Natalspruit .... W 6
May 9—Fred Baker, Natalspruit .... L 6
1976
Mar. 27—Fred Baker, Natalspruit .... L 6
1977
(Inactive)
1978
Apr. 22—Isaac Tshoane, Vereeniging .... W 4
1979
May 25—Jacob Morake, Springs .... KO by 3
1980
Apr. 25—Joe Sissanga, Sebokeng .... D 4
Oct. 4—Bogie Mtshembo, Welkom .... KO 3
Nov. 21—Sydney Padi, Sebokeng .... KO 2

PATRICK TSHABALALA
South African Junior Middleweight
1978
July 3—Morgan Moledi, Bedfordview .... W 4
Aug. 5—Volfart Rala, East London .... KO 5
Nov. 17—Morgan Moledi, Springs .... W 10
1979
Feb. 16—Lemuel Nkumane, Springs .... D 6
Mar. 30—Lemuel Nkumane, Springs .... KO 4
Apr. 28—Bushy Bester, Johannesburg .... KO by 1
Nov. 10—Raymond Mashifane, Jabulani .... W 6
1980
May 24—Joseph Matthysen, Orlando .... KO 5

PAUL TSHAKA
South African Bantamweight
1980
Feb. 1—Stix McLeod, Salisbury .... KO 2
Apr. 7—Stix McLeod, Salisbury .... L 6
Nov. 11—Aziz Dawood, Durban .... W 4
Nov. 28—Johannes Miya, Joburg .... L 6

PAULUS TSHEHLA
South African Flyweight
1974
May 10—Peter Mathebula, Mamelodi .... L 4
1975-1976
(Inactive)
1977
Apr. 16—Meshack Dlamini, Kroonstad .... L 8
Oct. 14—Simon Moema, Krugersdorp .... L 6
1978
Mar. 3—Gilbert Makanete, Krugersdorp .... W 6
1979
Mar. 10—Robert Makhoba, Newcastle .... W 4
Dec. 1—Johannes Shwana, Port Elizabeth .... W 4
1980
Feb. 1—Stix McLeod, Salisbury .... W 4
Apr. 7—Stix McLeod, Salisbury .... L 6

CLEMENT TSHINZA
South African Junior Middleweight
*Based in Belgium
Born: Jan. 21, 1948, Belgian Congo
1971
Apr. 19—Salvatore Enne, Esch................... W 6
Apr. 24—Daniel Martin, Villerupt .... L 6
May 17—Joachin Trautwein, Esch .... KO 4
June 13—Daniel Vadani, Guise .... KO 5
Oct. 30—Antoine Oke, Kinshasa .... KO 5
Dec. 18—Daniel Martin, Luxembourg .... D 6
1972
Mar. 18—Daniel Martin, Differdange .... W 8
Mar. 23—Horst Brinkmeyer, Offenbach .... KO 6
Apr. 24—Fernando Tavares, Differdange.......... KO 4
May 7—Wolfgang Lueger, Luxembourg.......... KO 3
May 10—Robert Brunel, Esch................... KO 4
Oct. 10—Francis Vermandere, Paris .... L 10
Oct. 23—Jean Heirmann, Esch.................. KO 1
Dec. 8—Francis Vermandere, Tournai .... D 10
1973
Jan. 13—Pierre Lambert, Villerupt .... W 8
Feb. 2—Klaus Tombers, Kiel .... KO 4
Feb. 23—Freddy Roelands, Esch .... KO 5
Apr. 2—Joop Kruis, Rotterdam .... D 8
May 4—Gerarr Cola, Liege .... W 8
May 25—Jorge Fernandez, Gratz .... W 8
Sept 11—Jose Duran, Terni .... W 8
Oct. 26—Randolph Hobach, Cologne .... W 8
Nov. 3—Helen Mack, Worms .... W 8
Dec. 7—Jean Emmerich, Hamburg .... W 8
1974
Feb. 1—Pascal Zito, Tunis .... W 12
Feb. 16—Roger Menetrey, Lyon .... KO by 2
Mar. 30—Kenny Webber, Luxembourg............ KO 3
May 14—Frank Reiche, Berlin .... L 8
July 20—Joseph Bessala, Yaounde .... L 15
1975
Mar. 2—Adriano Rodriguez, Kinshasa .... KO 5
May 5—Jacques Van Mellaerts, Luxembourg..... KO 5
June 16—Henry Rhiney, Luxembourg .... D 10
July 4—Sea Robinson, Tunis .... D 10
Oct. 11—Henry Rhiney, Esch .... W 10
Nov. 28—Frank Reiche, Hamburg .... KO by 1
1976
Feb. 18—Rudi Koopmans, Scheveningen .... L 10
Apr. 16—Aldo Bentini, Luxembourg.............. KO 10
May 17—Micky Flynn, Luxembourg.............. W 10
June 18—Frans Csandl, Berlin .... W 10
Oct. 6—Joseph Pachler, Wien .... L 10
1977
Jan. 15—Regis Yepende, Esch sur Alzette .... KO 3
Mar. 15—Jorg Eipel, Berlin .... W 8

423

Apr.   9—Alfredo Naveiras, St. Servais ....W 8
Apr.   29—Wolfgang Gans, Munich ....W 8
May   20—Joerg Eipel, Hannover ....L 8
June   4—Branko Barakovic, Esch sur Alzette ......W 8
Aug.   6—Marijan Benes, Berlin ....L 4
Sept.   9—Juergen Voss, Muenchen ....KO 2
Sept. 21—Jean Emmerich, Frankfurt ....W 8
1978
Feb.   17—Joey Mack, Zele ....KO 1
Mar.   24—Melendez, Zele ....KO 3
Apr.   29—Speedy Mitchell, Zele ....D 8
July   9—Sea Robinson, Abidjan ....KO 7
Sept. 30—Justice Ortiz, Turnhout ....KO 5
Oct.   13—Italo Venturi, Ravenna ....W 10
Dec.   2—Speedy Mitchell, Zele ....W 10
1979
Feb.   10—Billy Waith, Zele ....W 8
Mar.   2—Horace McKenzie, Bruges ....W 10
Apr.   21—Rogelio Zarza, Zele ....L 8
May   25—Raymond Langewouters, Bruges ....W 8
Oct.   20—Bennie Briscoe, Liege ....W 10
Dec.   8—Jose Hernandez, Zele ....W 10
1980
Jan.   26—Steve Hopkins, Zele ....D 10
Apr.   30—Jose Hernandez, Abidjan ....KO 7
Nov.   22—Jose Hernandez, Zele ....L 10

JOSEPH (SKITIMA) TSOTETSI
South African Junior Lightweight
Born: July 7, 1951
1972
Apr.   21—Piet Buys, Mamelodi ....W 6
May   26—Solly Hlatshwayo, Natalspruit ....W 4
June   3—Trueman Mnguni, Jabulani ....W 4
1973
Feb.   23—Simon Motloung, Dobsonville ....KO 3
Mar.   9—Ben Lekelake, Tembisa ....W· 4
June   15—Patrick Tshabalala, Orlando West ....W 4
Sept.   7—Isaac Nuku, Orlando ....W 6
Nov.   2—Anthony Sithole, Tembisa ....W 6
1974
Feb.   22—Alfred Buqwana, Dobsonville ....D 6
May   17—Paulus Twala, Orlando West ....W 8
Aug.   30—Victor Mpiyake, Orlando West ....L 10
1975
Feb.   21—Derrick Phetoe, Orlando West ....D 8
May   3—Thomas Sithebe, Orlando ....W 6
July   25—Fred Baker, Orlando ....L 8
Oct.   31—Rafty Mngadi, Natalspruit ....W 6
Dec.   13—Tsietsi Maretloane, East London ....L 8
1976
Apr.   24—Joseph Gumede, Jabulani ....L 8
1977
June   3—Evans Gwiji, Springs ....W 10
Sept. 17—Nkosana Mgxaji, East London ....KO by 4
Nov.   12—Rocky Mabaso, Durban ....W 8
Nov.   18—Joseph Gumede, Krugersdorp ....W 6
1978
Mar.   18—Barnard Zungu, Durban ....D 8
June   3—Elias Diraditsile, Bloemfontein ....W 8
Aug.   12—Evans Gwiji, Jabulani ....KO by 10
Sept. 30—Guy Ratazayo, East London ....L 6
1979
Feb.   16—Thomas Sithebe, Springs ....L 6
Mar.   31—Enoch Motsoane, Welkom ....W 6
Aug.   3—Paulus Mnisi, Springs ....W· 6
Nov.   10—Jacob Morake, Jabulani ....L 8
1980
Feb.   29—Jacob Morake, Springs ....W 10
        (For Transvaal Junior Lightweight Title)
May   24—Evans Gwiji, Orlando ....KO by 9
        (For S A Junior Lightweight Title)
Oct.   31—Petrus Rampoporo, Springs ....KO 5

THOMAS TSOTETSI
South African Junior Lightweight
1975
June   20—Paulus Mnisi, Tembisa ....L 4
1976
Feb.   14—Simon Thamae, Alexandra ....L 4
1977-1978
(Inactive)
1979
June   18—Sydney Padi, Johannesburg ....W 4
1980
Jan.   14—Chris Whiteboy, Cape Town ....L 6
Mar.   1—Deon Labuschagne, Ermelo ....KO by 1

PRINCE TUKANE
South African Light Heavyweight
1979
Apr.   14—Dan Dearham, Goodwood ....KO 2

1980
Mar.   15—Harold Saaiman, East London ....KO 6
May   17—McDonald Shezi, East London ....KO 3
Sept.   5—Martin Barnard, East London ....L 8
Oct.   11—Smiley Giesing, Port Elizabeth ....W 6

JACKIE TURNER
British Lightweight
1980
Jan.   25—Alan Oag, Hull ....W 6
Feb.   13—Dai Davies, London ....W 6
Feb.   28—Ray Ross, Hull ....KO 4
Mar.   24—Jeff Pritchard, London ....L 8
Apr.   29—Glyn Rhodes, London ....W 8
May   19—Jimmy Bunclark, London ....W 8
Sept. 22—Jeff Pritchard, London ....KO 2
Sept. 24—Peter Harrison, Solihull ....KO by 3

EDWARD TWAYI
South African Bantamweight
1976
June   5—Joseph Mokomatsidi, Jabulani ....W 4
1977
Mar.   19—Michael Mantsho, Kroonstad ....W 6
1978
Apr.   22—Lazarus Kwapeng, Vereeniging ....W 4
1979
Feb.   16—Shadrack Mogopudi, Springs ....KO by 3
1980
Apr.   30—Joshua Mahlungu, Sebokeng ....L 4

DALUXOLO TYEKANA
South African Bantamweight
1976
Oct.   30—Mxolisi Mpama, East London ....W 4
Nov.   13—Johannas Shwana, East London ....W 4
1977
Mar.   5—Mxolisi Mpama, East London ....W 4
Apr.   2—Zola Lawuse, East London ....W 4
May   7—Reuben Matewu, Zwelitsha ....L 4
May   31—Joe Ngidi, Queenstown ....W 8
Sept. 17—Johannes Sithebe, East London ....L 6
Oct.   15—Zola Lawuse, East London ....W 4
1978
Jan.   28—Joshia Dhlamini, East London ....KO 5
Feb.   18—Phindile Gaika, East London ....L 8
Mar.   4—Nkosana Moss, King Williamstown ......D 6
Apr.   15—Dexter Dhlamini, Butterworth ....W 6
May   6—Tito Dastile, East London ....KO by 1
1979
Apr.   14—Winnerton Kondile, Goodwood ....D 4
July   28—Reuben Matewu, King Williamstown .....W 8
Sept.   8—Leslie Pikoli, Zwelitsha ....W 8
Nov.   3—Mxolisi Nohenda, Queenstown ....D 8
1980
Feb.   9—Siphwe Fuma, East London ....KO by 3
        (For Cape Bantamweight Title)
May   3—N. Siloio, Mokacai ....KO 2

GRUMMAN UEDA
Japanese Junior Flyweight
1979
Jan.   4—Kazamasa Tamaki, Tokyo ....KO by 8
June   24—Mak Dong Kim, Kokura ....W 10
Dec.   8—Tito Abella, Ohita ....KO by 3
1980
Mar.   2—Hwang-Jin Kim, Seoul ....KO by 6

TAKASHI UEZU
Japanese Bantamweight
1978
Oct.   2—Tomio Takenouchi, Tokyo ....W 6
1979
Mar.   23—Shigeru Sasaki, Tokyo ....KO 7
May   7—Joe Araki, Tokyo ....W 10·
July   27—Danilo Batista, Tokyo ....KO 6
Nov.   20—Shogo Tabata, Tokyo ....KO 6
1980
Apr.   14—Star Dayanan, Tokyo ....W 10

424

ROYAL UMENO
Japanese Featherweight
1979
July   6—Ichiro Izawa, Nara ....D 8
Nov. 24—Norio Maruuchi, Osaka ....KO by 5
Nov. 30—Heung-Sok Yuh, Tokyo ....KO by 1
1980
Jan.   6—Nikaru Tomonari, Nara ....KO by 3
Mar. 18—Koji Kunishige, Shiga ....D 10

GIANCARLO USAI
Italian Lightweight
Born: June 14, 1950
1972
Nov.   3—Antonio Molina, Genoa ....KO 1
Nov. 29—Body Guy, Genoa........................W 6
1973
Jan. 25—Carlo Frassinetti, Milan ....KO 6
Feb.   7—Paolo Russo, Genoa.....................KO 3
Mar. 15—Alfredo Di Silvio, Milan.................W 6
May   4—Luigi Martello, Milan...................W 6
June   9—Jacques Mamane, Genova.............KO 6
July 25—Guiseppe Minotti, Rapallo.............W 8
Aug. 10—Amleto Restano, Sarzana ....KO 4
Aug. 25—Enrico Barlatti, Chiavari ....KO 8
Oct.   6—Mohamed Ben Said, Palermo...........KO 5
Oct. 26—Antonio Casamonica, Rome ....W 8
Nov. 23—Romualdo D'Alo, Milan ....W 8
Dec. 14—Giuseppe Minotti, Milan ....W 8
1974
Feb.   1—Sardi Saadli, Rimini.....................W 8
Mar.   1—Costa Rodriguez, Genova ....KO 3
Mar. 29—Henri Nesi, Rimini......................KO 9
Apr. 26—Enzo Pizzoni, Milan ....W 8
May 17—Nicolo' Bennici, Genova.................W 8
July 13—Amleto Restano, Rome.................KO 4
Aug. 14—Piero Meraviglia, Cefalu...........L disq. 7
Sept. 20—Gerardo Esposito, Milan ....W 5
Nov.   6—Enzo Pizzoni, Foligno...............L disq. 1
    (Italian Lightweight Title)
Dec. 26—Enzo Pizzoni, Milano ....KO 1
    (For Italian Lightweight Title)
1975
Jan. 18—Tommy Wright, Rimini ....W 8
Feb. 14—Jean-Pierre Younsi, Milan ....W 8
Apr. 11—Marion Thomas, Bologna ....KO 1
May   3—Giuseppe Minotti, Sassari ....W 8
June 21—Giovanni Lamusta, Cagliari............W 10
July 25—Ken Buchanan, Sardinia.............KO by 12
    (European Lightweight Title)
Dec. 12—Luciano Laffranchi, Turin...............W 8
Dec. 27—Carlo Frassinetti, Rimini ..............W.F. 4
1976
Jan. 16—Giuseppe Minotti, Milan ....W 8
Feb.   5—Ali Issaqui, Turin ....W 1
Apr. 21—Giovanni Maiorano, Palermo ....W 8
May 21—Luciano Laffranchi, Cagliari ....W 8
Aug. 21—Domenico Condello, Chiavari...........KO 7
Oct. 15—Luciano Laffranchi, Milan ....W 8
Nov. 13—Perico Fernandez, Bilbao ....L 15
    (For European Lightweight Title)
1977
Apr.   1—Antonio Guinaldo, Barcelona ....L 8
Apr. 22—Jean Claude Sider, Milan ....KO 2
June 12—Vincenzo Burgio, Castiglion Florentino ..KO 7
    (Italian Lightweight Title)
Nov. 13—Vicenzo Quero, Rimini...................W 12
    (Italian Lightweight Title)
1978
Jan. 18—Santino Reali, Rome.....................W 12
    (Italian Lightweight Title)
May 31—Rosario Sanna, Pescaro ....W 12
    (Italian Lightweight Title)
1979
Feb.   4—Eloy De Souza, Rimini ....W 8
Mar. 17—Giovanni Vitillo, Rimini ....W 12
    (Italian Lightweight Title)
Apr. 20—Howard Davis, Jr., New York ....KO by 3
Aug. 10—Carlo Frassinetti, Santander ....KO 4
Oct.   7—Vincenzo Quero, Taranto ....KO 10
    (Italian Lightweight Title)
Dec. 21—Eloy De Souza, Savona ....W 10
1980
June   1—Francisco León, Tarrasa ....KO by 9
Oct.   4—Lucio Cusma, Cagliari ....L 12
    (For Italian Lightweight Title)

MAURO VALENTINO
Italian Middleweight
1979
July 28—Zeljiko Sersek, Munich ....W 6
Sept. 10—Kristian Hoydahl, Oslo ....W 8
1980
Feb. 22—Horst Shulz, Dusseldorf ....W 4
May 14—Rudiger Bitterling, Munich ....L 6

DIEGO VALERO
Spanish Middleweight
1979
Oct. 24—Jorge Sala, Madrid ....L 4
1980
Mar.   1—Juan Munoz, Malgrat ....L 4
June   1—Antonio Garcia, Tarrasa ....L 8

MARK VALLANCE
Australian Welterweight
1980
Feb. 12—Andy Mann, Cardiff ....L 4
Mar. 25—Albert Singh, Kingsford ....KO 3
Apr.   8—Ray Kelly, Kingsford ....KO 3
May   6—Willie Tarika, Kingsford ....Exh. 3
May 21—Andy Grigor, Mt. Pritchard ....W 6
June   1—Pablo Caan, Revesby ....KO 2
Nov. 19—Saladine Allaf, Mt. Pritchard ....W 4
June 18—Barry Simons, Mt. Pritchard ....W 4
Aug. 22—Al Halletti, Cardiff ....KO by 5
Sept. 17—Richard Kumar, Mt. Pritchard ....KO 1

DEWALD VAN DEN BERG
South African Light Heavyweight
1977
Mar. 28—John Adriansen, Sea Point ....KO 2
May 30—Stanley Maxembenqula, Goodwood ....L 4
July   6—Clifford Manuel, Cape Town ....L disq. 4
Aug. 13—Martin Barnard, Johannesburg ......KO by 1
1978
Feb. 22—Stanley Maxembenqula, Cape Town ..KO by 4
1979
Jan. 16—Dan Dearham, Cape Town ....L 4
1980
Oct. 15—Fjaan Van Rooyen, Cape Town ....KO 1

WILLEM VAN DER MERWE
South African Light Heavyweight
1978
Dec. 15—Aswan Similane, Durban ....KO 1
1979
Feb. 12—John Champion Moalusi, Durban ....KO by 3
1980
Feb.   4—Solomon Dladla, Durban ....D 4
Nov.   3—Champion Mokone, Durban ....L 4

STEPHANUS (FANIE) VAN STADEN
South African Welterweight
1978
July   1—Tiger Wilson, Pretoria ....W 4
1979
Mar. 10—Johannes Bubb, Johannesburg ....KO 5
1980
Feb.   1—Richard Rova, Salisbury ....W 6
Apr. 19—David Kgotsane, Joburg ....W 4
May 24—Terrence Molefe, Orlando ....D 6
Sept. 20—Justus Joseph, Jabulani ....D 6
Nov. 10—Gregory Clark, Durban ....L 6

JOHAN VAN ZYL
South African Heavyweight
1979
Dec.   3—Churchill Williams, Welkom ....KO 2
1980
Mar. 21—William Matseo, Bloemfontein ....KO 2
May   5—Welcome Manda, Witsieshoek ....W 4

ROY VARDEN
British Welterweight
Born: Jan. 19, 1958
1976
Mar.   3—Dave Wenrell, Bradford ....W 6
Mar. 31—Steve Laybourn, Doncaster ....KO 4

Apr. 9—Godfrey Butler, Digbeth .... KO by 1
May 17—Dick Goodman, Nottingham .... W 6
June 8—Tommy Singleton, Bradford .... L 6
Sept. 27—Kevin Doherty, London .... W 6
Oct. 5—Albert Coley, Coventry .... W 6
Oct. 25—Tony Mattia, Birmingham .... KO 3
Nov. 24—Tony Vernon, London .... W 6
1977
Jan. 11—Vernon Vanriel, London .... L 6
Feb. 10—Dalvin White, Coventry .... W 6
Feb. 28—Young John Daly, Luton .... W 4
Mar. 8—Charlie Wallace, Wolverhampton .... KO 5
Apr. 7—Albert Coley, Dudley .... KO 5
May 17—Steve Butler, Wolverhampton .... W 6
June 1—Dave Taylor, Dudley .... W 6
June 13—Nagib Daho, Manchester .... W 6
July 5—Dave Taylor, Wolverhampton .... W 8
Aug. 22—Don Burgin, Stockton .... L 8
Sept. 20—Godfrey Butler, London .... W 8
Nov. 2—Kelvin Webber, Cardiff .... W 8
Nov. 22—Bingo Crooks, Wolverhampton .... W 8
Dec. 12—Jeff Pritchard, Birmingham .... W 8
1978
Feb. 7—George McGurk, Coventry .... W 8
Mar. 15—Tommy Dunn, Solihull .... W 8
Apr. 18—Des Gwilliam, Coventry .... W 10
June 1—Cookie Roomes, Coventry .... KO 8
Nov. 20—Carl Bailey, Birmingham .... L 8
1979
Jan. 23—Terry Peterson, London .... KO 8
Jan. 31—Dennis Price, Stoke .... D 8
Feb. 26—Carl Bailey, Edgbaston .... L 8
June 6—Frank McCord, Bedworth .... W 8
July 2—Dill Collins, London .... W 8
Sept. 6—Hans Henrick Palm, Copenhagen .... KO by 7
Oct. 30—Dave Taylor, Bedford .... W 8
1980
Feb. 11—Lee Hartshorn, Manchester .... KO 2
Mar. 18—Granville Allen, Wolverhampton .... L 8
Mar. 31—Gary Pearce, London .... L 8
Apr. 21—Ian Murray, Edgbaston .... W 8
May 19—Nigel Thomas, Birmingham .... KO 6
June 16—Horace McKenzie, London .... W 8
Sept. 29—Gary Newell, Bedworth .... W 8
Oct. 18—Joey Mack, Birmingham .... L 10
(Midlands Area Middleweight Title)

SAKARIA VE
Fijian Welterweight
1975
Nov. —Ramesh Chand, Suva .... W 6
Dec. —Tevita Varani, Suva .... KO 5
1976
Jan. —Dava Nand, Suva .... KO 3
Mar. —Sher Gul, Suva .... KO 5
Apr. —Bulwat Singh, Suva .... WF 6
June —Ramesh Chand, Suva .... KO 6
Aug. —Joe Vucago, Suva .... KO 4
Oct. —Bulwat Singh, Suva .... KO 4
Nov. —Ramesh Chand, Suva .... KO 2
Nov. —Bas Deo, Suva .... L 10
Dec. —Bas Deo, Suva .... W 10
1977
Jan. —Sakarai Qoro, Suva .... KO 6
Feb. —Bas Deo, Suva .... KO 13
Apr. —Inia Cataroga, Suva .... KO 4
(Won Fijian Welterweight Title)
June —Gilbert Orsaldo, Suva .... KO 8
Aug. —Rupeni Vutevute, Suva .... KO 8
Sept. —Ambika Prasad, Suva .... KO 8
Oct. —Peni Rauga, Suva .... KO 2
Nov. 12—Ali Afaksi, Suva .... KO 5
Dec. 9—Steve Ayerst, Suva .... KO 10
1978
Jan. 14—Steve Dennis, Suva .... KO 10
Feb. —Jone Mataitini, Suva .... KO 14
Apr. 15—Jeff Malcolm, Suva .... W 10
June 17—Ross Eadie, Suva .... W 10
Aug. 19—Clyde Gray, Suva .... KO by 8
(British Commonwealth Welterweight Title)
Oct. 14—Mark Bennett, Suva .... KO 4
Dec. 2—Clyde Gray, Lautoka .... KO by 8
(British Commonwealth Welterweight Title)
1979
Feb. 17—Hector Thompson, Suva .... KO by 8
Apr. —Paula Namosi, Suva .... KO 4
(Retained Fijian Welterweight Title)
June —Sammy Masias, Suva .... KO 2
Aug. 25—Phil Davies, Suva .... D 10
Nov. 24—Hector Thompson, Kingsford .... KO 11
1980
Feb. 16—Lachie Austin Suva .... W 10
Apr. 7—Eric King, Labaster .... KO 2
Aug. 16—Richie Roberts, Laucaula Bay .... KO 7

Oct. 4—Juan A. Merlo, Suva .... W 10
Dec. 6—Pablo Baez, Suva .... W 10
Dec. 20—Joe Nitiva, Suva .... KO 10

DAN VEERAN
South African Featherweight
1968
Sept. 20—Johannes Dlamini, Durban .... KO by 3
1969
(Inactive)
1970
Feb. 28—Henry Shozi, Durban .... W 4
June 27—Bethwell Xaba, Durban .... W disq. 2
Aug. 15—Lemchion Mkize, Durban .... KO by 4
Oct. 3—Joseph Mkhize, Durban .... L 4
1971
(Inactive)
1972
Feb. 12—Jerry Guude, Durban .... KO by 1
1973
Mar. 10—Mfakeni Mnguni, Natal .... D 4
1974
(Inactive)
1975
May 10—Edward Peterson, Stanger .... L disq. 4
1976
May 1—Ephraim Mnguni, Durban .... W 4
Nov. 10—Roy Damon, Durban .... L 4
1977
(Inactive)
1978
Oct. 10—Koos Mofiphu, Durban .... L 4
1979
Aug. 18—Simon Zincube, Durban .... L 4
1980
Mar. 1—Paulos Shozi, Durban .... D 4

ALEX JOHN VENTER
South African Featherweight
1977
Aug. 29—Johan Weyer, Johannesburg .... L 4
Sept. 26—Jan Blignaut, Johannesburg .... W 4
Oct. 17—Johan Weyer, Johannesburg .... KO by 3
Nov. 7—Sarel Stroebel, Johannesburg .... KO 1
Dec. 1—Bashew Sibaca, Cape Town .... L 4
1978
Mar. 4—Graham Jackson, Ermelo .... KO 3
Apr. 3—William McGeer, Pretoria .... W 4
Apr. 10—Johannes Jooste, Johannesburg .... KO 1
Aug. 21—Pieter Swanepoel, Welkom .... KO 3
Oct. 28—William McGeer, Ermelo .... KO 1
1979
Mar. 7—Sipho Mange, Cape Town .... L 12
Sept. 14—Norman Bromfield, Durban .... L 4
1980
Mar. 1—Gaybon Yekiso, Ermelo .... KO by 1
(For Transvaal Junior Featherweight Title)

PELLIGRINO VENTRONE
Italian Lightweight
1976
Aug. 24—Alfonso Bonavita, S. Anastasia .... W 6
Sept. 25—Marco Zanetti, Boscotrecase .... W 6
Oct. 22—Giovanni Cavazzini, Milano .... W 6
Nov. 27—Antonio Pocai, Salerno .... KO 4
1977
Mar. 12—Enzo Saltarelli, Maddaloni .... KO 5
Apr. 7—Gregorio Ciancaglione, Forli .... W 8
June 17—Giovanni Mura, Civitanova .... W 6
Oct. 8—Rudi Haeck, Zele .... NC
Dec. 10—Eloi De Souza, Maddaloni .... W 8
1978
Jan. 27—Vincenzo Di Ruocco, Rome .... KO 3
Mar. 31—Gregorio Ciancaglioni, Rome .... W 8
June 30—Gerardo Del Guacchio, Lugano .... KO 7
July 30—Giuseppe Agate, Marcianise .... W 8
1979
July 22—Angelo Fanciulli, Fort Village .... KO 4
1980
Mar. 28—Eloy De Souza, Monza .... W 8
Oct. 31—Roberto D'Ella, Rome .... L 6

ANTON VERRUPS
Dutch Junior Welterweight
1980
May 19—Friedhelm Manns, Rotterdam .... KO 1
Sept. 1—Andres Blanco, Rotterdam .... D 6
Oct. 20—Andres Blanco, Rotterdam .... W 6

NATALE VEZZOLI
Italian Junior Lightweight
Born: Oct. 5, 1950
1972
Sept. 27—Giovanni Scarpati, La Spezia ....L 6
Oct. 23—Vito Viola, Bologna ....L 6
Dec. 4—Sergio Emili, Bologna ....D 6
Dec. 26—Augusto Quadri, Reggio Emilia ....D 6
1973
Jan. 5—Sergio Emili, Forli ....D 6
Mar. 3—Domenico Angeli, Rimini ....W 6
Mar. 23—Enzo Saltarelli, R. Emilia ....D 6
Apr. 28—Enzo Saltarelli, Rimini ....W 6
May 11—Rocco Zecca, Anocna ....W 6
June 1—Jose Martin, Serle ....W 6
Aug. 4—Giovanni Maiorano, Tuscalano ....KO 4
Sept. 25—Arrow Abu, Lumezzane ....W 6
Oct. 5—Giuseppe Agate, Milano ....W 6
Nov. 3—Jose Carrera, Grivignee ....KO 5
Dec. 11—Herbert Trausmuth, Vienna ....L 4
1974
Mar. 8—Franco Diaha, Milano ....W 8
Mar. 29—Giuseppe Martucci, Milan ....KO by 8
May 3—Albert Amatler, Milan ....W 8
June 7—Klaus Jacobi, Vienna ....W 8
July 19—Giovanni Cabazzini, Brescia ....W 8
Oct. 18—Renzo Battistelli, Milan ....W 8
Dec. 3—Giovanni Girgenti, Marsala ....L 12
(Italian Junior Lightweight Title)
1975
Jan. 31—Enzo Farinelli, Bologna ....D 8
Feb. 28—Salvatore Dui, Milan ....W 8
Mar. 13—Svein Erik Paulsen, Oslo ....L 10
May 9—Giuseppe Martucci, Sirmoine ....W 8
June 13—Luis Aisa, Milan ....D 8
Dec. 26—Giuseppe Mura, Brescia ....KO 10
(Italian Junior Lightweight Title)
1976
May 14—Renzo Battistelli, Brescia ....W 12
June 12—Giuseppe Agate, Brescia ....W 8
Sept. 24—Roland Cazeaux, Milan ....KO 11
(European Junior Lightweight Title)
Nov. 12—Domingo Gimenez, Milan ....KO 13
(European Junior Lightweight Title)
1977
Apr. 1—Albert Amatler, Brescia ....KO 11
(European Junior Lightweight Title)
May 27—Georges Cotin, Brescia ....KO 11
(European Junior Lightweight Title)
July 7—Ethem Ozalin, Vieste ....KO 11
(European Junior Lightweight Title)
Oct. 21—Daniel Tratzinsky, Milan ....W 10
Dec. 14—Salvatore Liscapade, Taurisano ....W 15
(European Junior Lightweight Title)
1978
Mar. 8—Elio Cotena, Brescia ....W 15
(European Junior Lightweight Title)
May 13—Charles Jurietti, Brescia ....D 10
Aug. 11—Isodoro Cabeza, Lepe ....W 15
(European Junior Lightweight Title)
Dec. 13—Charles Jurietti, Brescia ....D 12
(European Junior Lightweight Title)
1979
Mar. 10—Carlos Hernandez, Valladolid ....KO by 4
(European Junior Lightweight Title)
1980
Mar. 7—Alain LeFol, Brescia ....KO 5
May 9—Jose Sanchez, Brescia ....W 8

JOSE LUIS VICHO
Spanish Featherweight
1979
Mar. 30—Mohamed El Kadoumi, Mallorca ....W 4
Apr. 26—Angel Ramirez, Las Palmas ....KO 1
June 15—Joaquin Moral, Mallorca ....W 4
June 27—Francisco Jeronimo, Mallorca ....KO 5
July 17—Juan Barros, Andraix ....W 6
July 21—Juan Barros, Mallorca ....W 6
Sept. 14—Emilio Molero, Aviles ....W 6
Oct. 13—Mohamed El Kadoumi, Pravia ....W 6
Nov. 10—Jofre II, Aviles ....W 8
Dec. 20—Serafin Dos Anjos, Mallorca ....W 8
1980
Feb. 1—Francisco Moya, Madrid ....W 6
Feb. 15—Isidoro Cabeza, Palma de Mallorca ....W 8
Mar. 7—Francisco Moya, Palma de Mallorca .....W 8
Apr. 19—Joaquin Garcia, Palma de Mallorca ......W 8
May 23—Cecilio Lastra, Palma de Mallorca ... KO by 1
Aug. 1—Emilio Barcala, Palma de Mallorca .....W 8
Aug. 22—Emilio Barcala, Madrid ....W 8
Oct. 4—Hugo Carrizo, Palma de Mallorca ....W 10
Nov. 21—Guy Caudron, Palma de Mallorca ....W 10

LULU VILLAVERDE
Filipino Featherweight
1980
Feb. 3—Oscar Barola, Quezon City ....W 10
May 23—Dommy Marolena, Manila ....W 12
(Won Filipino Featherweight Title)
Sept. 19—Cesar Ligan, Quezon City ....L 12
(Lost Filipino Featherweight Title)
Dec. 19—Ador Sequin, Manila ....KO 4

ROCCO VILLELA
Australian Welterweight
1979
Feb. 2—Eddie Muri, Williamston ....D 4
Feb. 28—Dennis Mizzi, Preston ....D 4
Mar. 31—Eddie Muri, Melbourne ....L 4
Apr. 20—Eddie Muri, Melbourne ....W 4
May 14—Tony Noon, Chelsea ....L 4
Sept. 19—Eddie Muri, Melbourne ....L 3
Sept. 28—Eddie Muri, Melton ....W 4
1980
Mar. 7—Kid Preston, Melbourne ....W 6
Mar. 19—Manny Benson, Melbourne ....KO 5
Apr. 18—Greg Grogan, Footscray ....L 10
Aug. 14—Johnny Sacco, Preston ....L 10
Oct. 31—Kid Preston, Frankston ....W 10

GIOVANNI VITILLO
Italian Lightweight
1977
Mar. 11—Vincenzo Di Ruocco, Cascina ....KO 3
June 25—Antonio Germano, Viareggio ....KO 4
July 8—Giovannino Mannu, Pistoia ....W 6
Oct. 22—Bernardo Ciaramella, Torino ....L 6
Nov. 13—Pietgro Marselli, Rimini ....W 6
Dec. 26—Gregorio Ciancaglione, Pisa ....W 8
1978
Mar. 19—Carlo Frassinetti, Viareggio ....W 8
Apr. 19—Carlo Frassinetti, Viareggio ....W 8
May 19—Abass Macauley, Viareggio ....W 8
July 2—Giuseppe Agate, Calcinaia ....KO 7
July 22—Renzo Battistelli, San Frediano ....KO 5
Oct. 20—Giovanni Carrino, Milan ....WF 8
Nov. 17—Alfonso Carrillo, Milan ....W 8
1979
Mar. 17—Giancarlo Usai, Rimini ....L 12
(Italian Lightweight Title)
July 25—Joe Gibilisco, Rimini ....L 8
1980
Mar. 28—Gregorio Ciancaglione, Pisa ....KO 2
Oct. 24—Biagio Pierri, Grosseto ....KO by 5

BILLY VIVIAN
Welsh Junior Welterweight
1976
Oct. 5—Godfrey Butler, Coventry ....W 6
Nov. 9—Ray Ross, Derry ....W 6
Nov. 22—Willie Booth, London ....W 8
Dec. 6—Barry Price, Hammersmith ....W 8
Dec. 13—Baton McAllister, London ....D 8
1977
Jan. 25—Colin Peters, Bethnal Green ....KO by 4
Feb. 15—Barton McAllister, Merthyr ....W 8
Mar. 29—Benny McQuade Purdy, Ebbw Vale .....KO 1
Apr. 4—Ray Cattouse, London ....L 8
Apr. 18—Cornelius Boza-Edwards, Mayfair ....KO by 1
June 16—Johnny Wall, Ebbw Vale ....L 10
Sept. 29—George Feeney, New Castle ....L 8
Nov. 7—Tommy Davitt, London ....L 8
Nov. 18—Tommy Davitt, London ....L 8
1978
Jan. 9—Willie Booth, London ....L 8
Jan. 23—Sugar Ray Heaney, Aberavon ....W 8
Mar. 13—Bingo Crooks, Birmingham ....L 8
Apr. 17—Eric Wood, London ....W 8
June 12—Jim Watt, London ....L 8
July 10—Dill Collins, Aberavon ....W 10
(Welsh Junior Welterweight Title)
Nov. 15—Barry Michael, Merthyr ....L 10
1980
Nov. 1—Eric Purkis, Southend ....L 8
Mar. 11—Doug Hill, Nantwich ....W 8
Apr. 29—Najib Daho, London ....KO by 5
Sept. 22—Mickey Baker, Wolverhampton ....L 8

HAROLD VOLBRECHT
South African Welterweight
1975
Nov. 29—Johnny Nel, Johannesburg ....KO 1
1976
Jan. 26—Boesman Potgieter, Durban.............KO 1

Feb. 28—Apie Smith, Johannesburg .... KO 2
Mar. 27—Gert Craemer, Pretoria .... W 4
May 8—Gert Craemer, Johannesburg........ KO by 4
May 21—Ronnie du Preez, Bloemfontein .... W 6
June 19—Gert Craemer, Pretoria .... W 12
(Vacant South African Welterweight Title)
Oct. 30—Gert Craemer, Johannesburg............D 6
Nov. 27—Johnny Sham, Johannesburg............ W 12
1977
Feb. 19—Johnny Sham, Johannesburg .... W 12
May 21—Rolly Xipu, Johannesburg .... W 8
May 30—Langton Tinago, Goodwood .... W 10
Sept. 10—Norman Sekapane, Johannesburg .... W 10
Oct. 17—Juan Orengo, Johannesburg .... W 8
Nov. 7—Gert Craemer, Johannesburg .... W 12
(South African Welterweight Title)
Dec. 1—Jack Jim, Cape Town .... W 6
1978
Apr. 29—Morris Mohloai, Johannesburg .... KO 2
(South African Welterweight Title)
July 7—Langton Schoolboy, Salisbury .... L 10
Aug. 5—Henry Rhiney, Johannesburg .... W 10
Nov. 6—Phillip Hlophe, Durban .... W 8
1979
Apr. 14—Jack Jim, Goodwood .... W 6
Apr. 28—Griffiths Mgijma, Johannesburg .... W 8
June 7—Johnny Gant, Bophuthatswanana .... W 10
Oct. 20—David Kambule, Pretoria .... W 12
1980
Apr. 6—Pipino Cuevas, Houston, Texas ...... KO by 5
(For WBA World Welterweight Title)
May 10—Pat Hallacy, Joburg .... W 8
Oct. 25—Coenie Bekker, Sun City .... W 12
(For South African Welterweight Title)

JOEY WAINWRIGHT
British Featherweight
1980
Feb. 18—Brindley Jones, London .... W 6
Feb. 28—Jimmy Bott, Hull .... D 6
Mar. 11—Brindley Jones, London .... W 6
Mar. 17—Robert Hepburn, London .... W 6
Mar. 21—John Griffiths, London .... W 6
Apr. 29—Alec Irvine, London .... L 8

BILLY WAITH
British Welterweight
Born: August 30, 1950
1970
Oct. 19—Mickey Vann, Aberavon .... W 6
Nov. 23—Alan Salter, London .... W 6
1971
Jan. 25—Mickey Lynch, London.................. W 6
Feb. 22—Nick Kennedy, Aberavon .... W 6
Apr. 5—Nero Luthman, London .... KO 3
Apr. 26—Arrow Abu, Aberavon .... L 6
May 12—Arrow Abu, Caerphilly .... KO 5
June 7—Malcolm Lowe, Nottingham .... W 6
June 14—Dave Tuohey, London .... L 6
June 22—Mickey Van Day, London .... W 6
July 5—Dave Grantley, Stockport .... W 6
Sept. 27—Gerry McBride, London................. KO 4
Oct. 11—Young Silky, London.................... W 8
Nov. 1—Roger Howes, London.................. KO 4
Nov. 8—Marcel Clolus, London................. KO 4
Nov. 30—Young Silky, Leeds..................... W 8
1972
Jan. 24—Billy Hardacre, London................. W 8
Feb. 21—Ali Messaoud, London.................. W 8
Mar. 28—Dennis Flynn, London.................. D 8
Apr. 10—Marius Cordier, London................ KO 7
June 10—Andries Steyn, Johannesburg............ L 10
Oct. 24—Howard Hayes, London................. L 10
(Elim British Featherweight Title)
Dec. 5—Alan Richardson, Leeds .... D 8
1973
Jan. 22—Jimmy Bell, Piccadilly .... D 8
Mar. 26—Tommy Glencross, Swansea .... W 8
May 14—Paul Bromley, Swansea .... W 8
June 16—Arnold Taylor, Johannesburg .... L 10
Oct. 5—Tony Cunningham, Cardiff.............. W 8
Nov. 19—Tony Cunningham, Glasgow .... W 8
1974
Jan. 16—Angus McMillan, Solihull .... W 8
May 7—Erik Nikkinan, Oslo .... L 8

June 19—Jim Watt, Caerphilly .... L 12
Nov. 25—Jim Montague, Glasgow .... W 8
Dec. 16—Jim Melrose, London .... KO 6
1975
Mar. 19—Jim Watt, London .... L 10
Apr. 21—Des Morrison, London .... L 8
Aug. 6—Dave Massey, Cardiff .... KO 5
Sept. 22—Pat McCormack, Walworth .... L 8
Nov. 24—Jimmy Revie, Walworth .... W 8
1976
Mar. 2—Dave Green, London............... KO by 11
Apr. 8—Jorgen Hansen, Copenhagen .... L 8
May 6—Peter Morris, Birmingham .... W 8
May 17—Terry Petersen, Glasgow .... W 8
June 24—Barton McAllister, London .... W 8
June 29—Jim DeVanney, London .... KO 3
Oct. 25—Achille (Speedy) Mitchell, Hammersmith . . L 8
Nov. 15—Hugh Smith, Glasgow .... W 8
Dec. 2—Louis Acaries, Paris..................... L 10
1977
Feb. 11—Everaldo Costa Azevedo, Milan .... L 10
Mar. 5—Jo Kimpuani, Dunkerque .... L 8
Mar. 15—Chris Walker, Leeds .... W 8
Mar. 24—Peter Morris, Leicester .... KO 7
July 4—Steve Angell, Wales .... L 8
July 30—Daniel Gonzalez, Monte Carlo ... KO by 7
Feb. 13—Henry Rhiney, Barnsley .... L 15
(British Welterweight Title)
May 8—Joey Mack, Birmingham .... W 8
June 1—Roy Commosioung, Cardiff .... W 8
June 28—Chris Clarke, Halifax .... L 10
Aug. 19—Ramon Fouz, Gijon .... D 8
Oct. 16—Henry Rhiney, London .... L 8
Oct. 28—Josef Nsubauga, Oslo .... L 8
Nov. 9—Hans Henrik Palm, Copenhagen .... L 8
Dec. 1—Carl Bailey, Minster .... W 8
1979
Jan. 22—Chris Walker, Birmingham .... L 8
Feb. 10—Clemente Tzina, Zele .... L 8
Feb. 15—Jorgen Hansen, Randers .... L 8
Feb. 17—Alois Carmeliet, Zele .... L 8
Mar. 31—Alois Carmeliet, Zele .... L 10
June 18—Tony Matey, Windsor .... W 8
Dec. 11—Des Morrison, Bletchley .... L 8
1980
Jan. 21—Colin Jones, London .... KO by 6
Mar. 10—Steve Early, Wolverhampton .... L 8
Apr. 18—Roland Zenon, Paris .... L 8
May 5—Richard Rodriguez, Paris .... L 8
May 14—Dave Allen, Burslem .... W 8
July 26—Tidjani Sidibe, Rapallo .... KO by 3
Sept. 22—John Smith, London .... W 8
Oct. 20—Fighting Mack, Rotterdam .... L 8

COLIN WAKE
British Junior Welterweight
1980
Jan. 25—Terry Baldwin, Hull .... W 4
Feb. 18—Michael LeGrange, London .... KO 4
Feb. 28—Peter Harrison, Hull....................L 6
Mar. 17—Wally Stocking, London .... W 6
Mar. 24—Peter Harrison, Glasgow .... L 6
May 5—Bryan McConnel, Glasgow .... L 6
May 19—Ray Price, London .... W 6
May 27—Bryan McConnel, Glasgow .... KO 4
June 2—Charlie Brown, London .... KO 8
Sept. 15—Duncan Hamilton, Glasgow .... L 8
Oct. 2—Julian Boustead, Hull .... KO 4
Oct. 20—Hugh Smith, Glasgow .... L 8
Nov. 3—Barry Price, London .... KO 2

GEORGE WALKER
British Junior Middleweight
1978
Nov. 21—Alan Worthington, Wolverhampton ...... W 6
1979
Jan. 8—George Danahar, London .... L 6
Jan. 23—Harry Watson, London .... D 6
Feb. 5—Harry Watson, Nottingham .... W 6
Mar. 12—Billy English, London .... L 8
Mar. 19—Salvo Nucifero, London .... L 8
Mar. 27—Herol Graham, London .... L 8
Apr. 23—Harry Watson, London .... W 8
Sept. 25—Richard Kenyon, London .... W 8
Nov. 5—Charlie Malarkey, Piccadilly .... W 8
Dec. 4—Jimmy Batten, Wembley .... L 8
Feb. 9—Fred Coransen, Dunkirk .... L 8
Apr. 17—Terry Matthews, London .... KO 3
May 8—Kirkland Laing, Solihull .... L 8
Oct. 23—Horace McKenzie, London .... W 8

NEIL NICHOLAS WALKER
South African Junior Middleweight
1980
Mar.	29—Jacobus Nell, Johannesburg	KO	2
Apr.	19—Peter Mgojo, Rand Stadium	L	4
May	19—Welcome Anderson, Durban	W	4
July	2—Gregory Clark, Durban	L	6
Sept.	15—Gregory Clark, Durban	L	4

KEVIN WALSH
British Welterweight
1979
Sept.	10—Duncan Hamilton, Bradford	L	6
Sept.	17—Johnny Koo, Manchester	KO	6
Oct.	15—Steve Ward, Manchester	L	6
Nov.	15—Steve Ward, Caister	W	6

1980
Jan.	8—Duncan Hamilton, Windsor	L	6
Jan.	16—Johnny Koo, Liverpool	KO	1
Jan.	21—Mickey Mapp, London	L	6
Jan.	28—Dave Taylor, Bradford	L	6
Mar.	19—Robert Armstrong, Doncaster	KO by	3
Sept.	15—Robert Armstrong, Manchester	W	6
Sept.	24—Carl North, Solihull	D	6
Sept.	29—Brian Anderson, Chesterfield	D	8
Oct.	13—Graeme Ahmed, Newcastle	L	6
Oct.	22—Ronnie Rathbone, Doncaster	L	6

COLIN WARD
British Junior Middleweight
1976
June	28—Les Wint, Luton	D	6
Sept.	15—Sinclair Christie, Luton	L	8
Sept.	22—Terry Knight, Battersea	L	6
Oct.	25—Chris Walker, Luton	W	6
Nov.	22—Malcolm Howard, Southampton	W	6

1977
Jan.	13—Malcolm Howard, Reading	W	6
Feb.	15—Nicky Bevans, Northampton	W	6
Mar.	16—Tommy Joyce, Stoke	L	8
Apr.	25—Brian Gregory, Northampton	W	8
May	17—Joey McIntosh, Wolverhampton	L	8
Sept.	5—Mick Minter, Hove	L	8
Nov.	7—Tim McHugh, London	W	8
Dec.	13—Albert Hillman, Walworth	W	8

1978
Jan.	16—Terry Knight, Hove	KO by	2
Mar.	19—Brian Gregory, Northampton	W	8
Oct.	9—Speedy Mitchell, Marylebone	L	8

1979
Jan.	23—Dave Proud, Kensington	L	8
Mar.	19—Dave Proud, Marylebone	KO	7
May	14—Jimmy Batten, Wembley	L	10
Oct.	1—Bob Mays, Marylebone	L	8

1980
Feb.	19—Kirkland Laing, London	KO by	5

DAVE WARD
British Welterweight
1980
May	28—Brian Anderson, Cramlington	W disq.	4
June	16—Nigel Thomas, Manchester	W	8
Sept.	10—Gordon Kirk, Liverpool	KO	4

STEVE WARD
British Welterweight
1977
Sept.	14—Peter Snowsall, Cambridge	W	6
Sept.	20—Steve Holdsworth, Southend	L	6

1978
Mar.	20—Tony Laing, London	KO by	2
Apr.	10—Gary Collins, Nottingham	L	6
Apr.	17—Adey Allen, London	L	6
Apr.	25—Sid Smith, London	L	6
May	18—Robbie Robinson, London	KO by	1

1979
Sept.	8—Ian Murray, Wolverhampton	L	6
Oct.	15—Kevin Walsh, Manchester	W	6
Nov.	15—Kevin Walsh, Caister	L	6
Nov.	28—Bryan Clemow, Solihull	W	6

1980
Jan.	21—Johnny Burns, Wolverhampton	L	6
Mar.	3—Dave Sullivan, Nottingham	W	6
Mar.	11—Lee Town, Southend	L	6
Apr.	7—Paul Wetter, London	W	6
Apr.	21—Paul Wetter, Nottingham	W	6
May	8—Jimmy Smith, Solihull	W	6
May	19—Geoff Aspell, Birmingham	KO by	3
June	12—Adrian Clamp, Cambridge	L	6
July	1—Johnny Burns, Wolverhampton	W	6
Sept.	9—Johnny Francis, Sheffield	KO by	3

ROCKY WARREN
Australian
1980
May	20—Justin Skinner, Kingsford	D	6
June	18—Peter Mills, Mt. Pritchard	L	3
July	11—Brett Dunn, Auburn	W	4
July	16—Paul Talbot, Mt. Pritchard	L	6
July	22—Steve Saxon, Sutherland	D	4
July	29—Steve Saxon, Kingsford	L	6
Sept.	12—Brett Dunn, Auburn	D	4
Sept.	16—T. Skruse, Kingsford	D	4
Sept.	23—T. Skruse, Sutherland	W	4
Nov.	14—Mark Aquilina, Auburn	KO by	

GEORGES WARUSFEL
French Junior Middleweight
1972
Feb.	10—Christian Zimini, Paris	W	6
Mar.	13—Gabriel Colombelle, Douai	D	6
Mar.	23—Gabriel Colombelle, Paris	W	6
Apr.	6—Jean Pierre Younsy, Paris	W	6
May	9—Mohamed Mechlia, Paris	W	6
Dec.	9—Emilio De Plano, Dunkirk	KO	5
Dec.	17—Robert Bavent, Somain	D	6

1973
Jan.	6—Michel Briatte, Dunkirk	KO	2
Feb.	3—Robert Bavent, Douai	D	6
Mar.	2—Christian Zimini, Lione	W	6
Sept.	8—Gerard Leterme, Graignes	W	8

1974
Jan.	24—Andre Sainseaux, Paris	W	6
Feb.	9—Freddy Roelands, Douai	W	8
Mar.	2—Klaus Fuchs, Paris	W	6
Mar.	22—Mongi Lahdhilli, Alfortville	D	8
May	18—Robert Bavent, Aniche	W	10
May	27—Antonio Torsello, Paris	W	6
Nov.	7—Salah Arafa, Paris	W	8
Nov.	21—Luciano Laffranchi, Paris	W	8

1975
Mar.	8—Joseph Gninion, Douai	KO	7
Mar.	20—Bobby Arthur, Paris	W	8
Oct.	18—Salah Arafa, Douai	KO	5
Oct.	25—Cipriano Garcia, Bayonne	KO	8
Nov.	27—Georges Perrot, Paris	KO	3
Dec.	18—Jimmy Savage, Paris	W	10

1976
Jan.	30—Nicola D'Orazio, Ginerva	KO	3
Mar.	6—Eddie Davis, Paris	KO	9
Apr.	4—Alain Ruocco, Paris	KO by	9
Dec.	2—Tony Alfonso, Paris	KO	2
Dec.	17—Vincennzo Ungaro, Ginerva	W	10

1977
Jan.	14—Wa Bukasa, Tarbes	L	8
Feb.	4—Antonio Torsello, Ginerva	KO	3
May	13—Pascal Real Martin, Annecy	KO	7
June	11—Alain Marion, Creil	L	12
	(For French Welterweight Title)		
Oct.	14—Nelson Gomez, Tarbes	W	10
Nov.	4—Jim Montague, Annecy	W	10
Nov.	25—Mickey Ryce, Le Harve	KO	4

1978
Jan.	30—Luiz Ribeiro, Periguex	W	10
Feb.	11—Oscar Aparicio, Annecy	W	10
Mar.	11—Fred Coranson, Grand Synthe		
Apr.	8—Italo Venturi, Annecy	W	10
Apr.	25—Jimmy Batten, London	L	10
May	23—John Stracey, Islington	KO by	9
Oct.	27—Glaude Martin, Rennes	L	12
	(French Junior Middleweight Title)		
Dec.	16—Damiano Lassandro, Pesaro	L	10

1979
May	12—Daniel Bouleux, Alfortville	W	8
June	21—Michel Chapier, Alfortville	KO	11
	(French Junior Middleweight Title)		
Nov.	5—Achille Mitchell, Paris	W	10
Dec.	15—Claude Martin, St. Malo	D	12
	(Retained French Junior Middleweight Title)		

1980
Feb.	15—Jose Hernandez, Nice	W	10
Oct.	6—Marijan Benes, Paris	KO by	5

MUSTAPHA WASSAJA
Ugandan Light Heavyweight
(Based in Denmark)
1977
Mar.	31—Juan Hildalgo, Copenhagen	KO	2
Apr.	28—Giancarlo Mezzadra, Copenhagen	KO	2
June	2—Avenamar Peralta, Randers	D	6
Sept.	8—Garfield McEwans, Copenhagen	W	6
Oct.	6—Rab Affleck, Copenhagen	W	6
Nov.	3—Bunny Sterling, Randers	W	8
Dec.	8—Tom Bethea, Copenhagen	W	8

429

Jan.	5—Roy John, Randers	KO	5
Jan.	26—Bobby Lloyd, Oslo	W	8
Feb.	9—Bob Foster, Copenhagen	W disq.	5
Mar.	2—Ernie Barr, Vejle	W	8
Mar.	16—Robert Amory, Copenhagen	W	8
Apr.	27—Victor Attivor, Randers	W	8
May	25—Jessie Burnett, Copenhagen	W	10

1979

Feb.	15—Bunny Johnnson, Randers	KO	7
Mar.	15—Jerry Celestine, Copenhagen	W	10

1980

Feb.	28—Avenamar Peralta, Odense	W	8
Apr.	17—Dennis Andries, Copenhagen	W	8
Oct.	17—Carl Candwell, Copenhagen	W	8

JIRO WATANABE
Japanese Flyweight
1980

Sept.	2—Chukthep Chuvatana, Tokyo	W	10
Dec.	15—Pactai Lipoviatan, Osaka	W	10

SYLVAIN WATBLED
French Heavyweight
1975

Oct.	20—Eric Seys, Paris	W	6
Nov.	3—Christian Pericat, Paris	KO	3
Dec.	8—Jean Pierre Lesigneur, Paris	KO	4

1976

Jan.	19—Maurice Trepant, Paris	W	6
Feb.	23—Jean Tshikuna, Paris	W	6
Mar.	29—Joop Kruys, Amsterdam	KO	3
Apr.	22—Alain Riviere, Paris	KO	3

1977

Nov.	19—Darko Covic, St. Brieuc	KO	3
Dec.	5—Christian Poncelet, Paris	KO	3

1978

Jan.	16—Rab Affleck, Paris	KO	1
Feb.	17—Francis Hands, Bethune	KO	3
Feb.	27—Juan De La Garza, Paris	KO	3
Sept.	14—Bunny Johnson, Paris	KO by	6
Oct.	30—Terry Mintus, Paris	W	10

1979

Feb.	22—Victor Attivor, Paris	W	10
Mar.	24—Leopoldo Centorrino, Paris	KO	5
May	24—Joe Maye, Paris	KO	3
June	7—Uwe Meinecke, Paris	KO	1
June	24—Jerry Foley, Monte Carlo	KO	6
Oct.	30—Matty Ross, Paris	KO	2
Nov.	15—Henry Patterson, Paris	KO	2
Dec.	10—Bunny Johnson, Paris	W	10

1980

Jan.	31—Tom Kiely, Paris	W	10
Feb.	25—Gordon Ferris, Belfast	KO	10
Mar.	28—Denton Ruddock, Villeurbanne	W	10

HARRY WATSON
British Middleweight
1976

May	10—Vernon van Riel, Mayfair	W	6
June	1—Johnny Pincham, London	W	6
Sept.	22—Kirkland Laing, London	KO by	5
Nov.	2—Barton McAllister, Cambridge	W	8

1977

Feb.	14—Clinton McKenzie, Mayfair	KO by	4

1978

Feb.	15—Bob Bravado, Cambridge	KO	1
Oct.	16—Frank McCord, Mayfair	L	6
Dec.	11—Dennis Price, Birmingham	W	6

1979

Jan.	15—Joey Saunders, Nottingham	W	6
Jan.	23—George Walker, London	D	8
Feb.	5—George Walker, London	L	6
Mar.	19—Billy Lauder, Glasgow	L	8
Apr.	23—George Walker, London	D	8
June	18—Gordon George, London	W	6
June	25—Martin McEwan, Edgbaston	L	6
Sept.	17—Billy Lauder, Glasgow	L	6
Oct.	22—Winston Davis, Nottingham	L	6
Nov.	5—Peter Gorney, Piccadilly	L	6
Nov.	12—Winston Davis, Mayfair	W	8

1980

Feb.	4—Doug James, London	KO by	1
Mar.	11—Earl Edwards, London	KO by	5
May	5—Charlie Malarkey, Glasgow	KO by	8
Sept.	9—Winston Davis, Mexborough	KO by	7

GARY WEBB
South African Heavyweight
1979

Mar.	2—Sofonia Naile, Bloemfontein	D	4
Apr.	2—Jonas Malan, Welkom	KO	3
Aug.	29—Sofonia Naile, Bloemfontein	W	6

Nov.	12—Caifus Masondo, Welkom	KO	3

1980

Mar.	21—Welcome Manda, Bloemfontein	KO	3

KENNY WEBBER
British Junior Middleweight
1972

Apr.	24—Bobby Ruffe, Swansea	W	6
May	3—Bob Langley, Caerphilly	W	6
Sept.	19—Derek Simpson, Manchester	W	8
Nov.	20—Rod Griffiths, Mayfair	L	8

1973

Jan.	15—Marty Dowd, Mayfair	KO	3
Jan.	23—Bob Langley, Birmingham	KO	7
Feb.	13—George O'Neill, Haverfordwest	KO	3
Feb.	19—Trevor Francis, Mayfair	L	8
Mar.	12—Phil Dykes, Caerphilly	KO	5
May	30—Des Rea, Caerphilly	D	8
Sept.	17—Tommy Joyce, Mayfair	KO	1

1974

Jan.	16—Kevin White, Solihull	L	8
Jan.	30—Trevor Francis, Wolverhampton	D	8
Feb.	26—Joe Yekinn, Wolverhampton	W	8
Mar.	30—Clement Tshinza, Esch	KO by	3
June	13—Trevor Francis, Wolverhampton	W	8
Sept.	25—Pat Thomas, Solihull	D	10

1975

Mar.	15—Germain Lemaitre, S. Nazaire	L	10

1976

Jan.	12—Les Pearson, Manchester	KO	6
Mar.	20—Des Morrison, London	KO by	8
Apr.	9—Peter Morris, Digbeth	KO by	5

1977

Mar.	21—John Smith, Birmingham	W	8
Oct.	3—Jimmy Devanney, Barnsley	W	10
Oct.	15—Jannick Blandin, S. Malo	L	8

1978-1979
(Inactive)
1980

Jan.	21—Chris Glover, Wolverhampton	L	6
Feb.	20—Terry Matthews, Evesham	L	6
Mar.	5—Jimmy Ellis, Liverpool	W	8
Mar.	10—Chris Glover, Manchester	W	8
Mar.	18—Mick Morris, Wolverhampton	L	6
Mar.	31—Nigel Thomas, Cleethorpe	W	8
Apr.	14—Jimmy Ellis, Manchester	D	8
Apr.	28—Albert Hillman, Walworth	W	8
Sept.	22—John Humphreys, Wolverhampton	L	6
Oct.	13—John Humphreys, Nottingham	L	6
Oct.	19—Vince Gajny, Birmingham	L	6

CHARLES HENRY (CHARLIE) WEIR
South African Junior Middleweight
Born: Nov. 26, 1956
1977

Aug.	1—Zacharia Thabethe, Durban	KO	1
Aug.	13—Esias Bosch, Johannesburg	KO	1
Aug.	29—Bushy Bester, Johannesburg	KO	1
Sept.	8—Coenraad Bekker, Goodwood	KO	5
Oct.	17—Kevin White, Johannesburg	KO	4
Nov.	7—Danny McAloon, Johannesburg	KO	2
Nov.	18—Eben Marais, Bloemfontein	KO	4
Dec.	1—Joseph Hali, Cape Town	KO by	5

1978

Mar.	11—Wolfgang Gans, Johannesburg	W	8
Apr.	17—Joseph Hali, Johannesburg	KO	2
May	15—Sidney Bensch, Johannesburg	KO	2
	(South African Middleweight Title)		
July	3—Mike Hallacy, Bedfordview	KO	7
Aug.	5—Steven Smith, Johannesburg	KO	2
Oct.	7—Doug Lumley, Johannesburg	KO	2
Nov.	6—Mike Baker, Durban	W disq.	6

1979

Feb.	3—Kevin Finnegan, Johannesburg	KO	7
Mar.	24—Mike Colbert, Johannesburg	W	10
Apr.	25—Elijah Makhathini, Durban	KO by	8

1980

Feb.	9—Bruce Strauss, Johannesburg	KO	1
Mar.	29—Terrance Makaluza, Johannesburg	KO	4
Apr.	21—Joseph Sishi, Secunda	KO	1
June	27—Carlos Betancourt, New York	KO	2
Aug.	16—Johnny Heard, Johannesburg	KO	1
Oct.	25—Ray Hammond, Sun City	KO	6

BOBBY WELBURN
British Lightweight
1980

Apr.	21—Bryan McConnel, Glasgow	L	6
Apr.	28—Phillip Morris, London	W	6
May	5—Barry Winter, Glasgow	KO by	2
June	2—Joe Mills, London	D	6
June	16—Steve Henty, London	L	6
Sept.	15—Joe McNamee, Glasgow	KO	2

Oct.	2—Steve Freeman, Hull	W 6
Oct.	20—Alex Gregal, Glasgow	KO 5
Nov.	3—Richard White, London	W 6

TERRY WELSH
British Junior Welterweight
1978

Sept.	12—Selvin Bell, Stoke	W 6
Sept.	19—Johnny Beauchamp, Southend	W 6
Oct.	27—Gerry Maguire, Belfast	KO 5
Nov.	2—Najib Daho, Liverpool	L 6
Nov.	21—Johnny Waring, Wolverhampton	L 6
Dec.	21—Joe Mills, Liverpool	L 6

1979

Jan.	17—Tony Zeni, Stoke	W 6
Feb.	13—Tommy Wright, Wakefield	L 8
Mar.	22—Dave Allen, Liverpool	W 6
Apr.	4—Martin McGough, Birmingham	L 8
May	21—Lawrence Williams, Manchester	L 8
Sept.	25—Peter Snowsall, London	KO 6
Oct.	8—Norman Bradford, Bradford	W 8
Oct.	29—Dennis Sullivan, Camborne	L 6
Nov.	19—Hugh Smith, Liverpool	L 8
Dec.	5—Johnny Mount, Liverpool	W 8

1980

Mar.	5—George McGurk, Liverpool	W 6
Mar.	27—Stan Atherton, Liverpool	W 8
July	28—Gary Pearce, Doncaster	KO by 4

MICHAEL WESSELS
South African Lightweight
1979

Mar.	30—Job Sisanga, Springs	W 4
Sept.	7—Christopher Sampson	W 4

1980

Nov.	28—Sybrand Oelofse, Johannesburg	L 6

(BIG) JIM WEST
Australian Junior Lightweight
1971

Feb.	24—Billy Pearce, Kingsford	W 4
Mar.	8—Carmen Cesario, Melbourne	D 3
Mar.	24—Billy Pearc, Kingsford	W 4
Apr.	5—Splinter Morris, Cardiff	W 4
Apr.	7—Splinter Morris, Kingsford	KO 3
Apr.	14—Billy Pearce, Guildford	W 4
Apr.	20—Frank Albisci, Nunawading	W 4
May	11—Greg Haggart, Nunawading	W 6
May	31—Steve Johnson, Melbourne	L 6
June	17—Steve Bell, Redfern	L 6
July	1—Steve Gossen, Redfern	L 6
July	7—Steve Bell, Riverwood	L 10
July	13—Wayne Wallace, New Lambton	D 10
July	22—Wayne Wallace, Redfern	L 10
Aug.	9—Wayne Wallace, Marrickville	D 6
Aug.	17—Steve Bell, Penrith	L 10
Sept.	17—Steve Bell, Cammeray	L 10
Sept.	21—Wayne Wallace, New Lambton	W 10
Oct.	5—John Keighly, Nunawading	D 6
Oct.	14—Robert Eggleton, Redfern	W 6
Nov.	11—Steve Johnson, Redfern	W 8
Nov.	15—Wayne Watson, Marrickville	W 8

1972

Mar.	23—Steve Gossen, Redfern	W 8
Apr.	11—Gwynne Jones, Marrickville	W 8
May	11—Wayne Hall, Redfern	KO 4
May	31—Willie Leslie, Moore Park	W 8
July	12—Fred Bruns, Kingsford	L 8
Aug.	8—Jim Bowen, Marrickville	W 8
Aug.	28—Steve Johnson, Melbourne	W 8
Sept.	14—Robert Eggleton, Redfern	D 10
Sept.	25—Steve Johnson, Melbourne	D 8
Oct.	12—Steve Johnson, Redfern	KO 5
Oct.	26—Dennis Talbot, Redfern	KO 8
Nov.	16—Brian Clout, Redfern	W 10
Dec.	12—Wayne Wallace, Marrickville	L 8

1973

Jan.	24—Wayne Wallace, Brookvale	W 10
Feb.	22—Steve Walker, Blacktown	KO 6
Mar.	22—Lorenzo Ramirez, Blacktown	W 10
Apr.	5—Robert Eggleton, Blacktown	KO 3
	(Won Vacant Australian Flyweight Title)	
May	17—Fred Burns, Blacktown	KO 7
July	5—Steve Johnson, Blacktown	KO 5
Aug.	9—Willie Leslie, Blacktown	KO 6
Aug.	29—Paul Ferreri, Moore Park	L 10

1974

Feb.	13—Hisao Adachi, Moore Park	W 10
Feb.	28—Keith Ball, Blacktown	W 10
Mar.	7—Steve Gossen, Blacktown	KO 9
Mar.	14—Henry Nissen, Ringwood	KO 4
	(Won Commonwealth Flyweight Title)	
Apr.	11—Brian Roberts, Blacktown	L 10

May	16—Paul Ferreri, Blacktown	L 10
June	20—Guinea Hillier, Blacktown	KO 9
July	18—Henry Nissen, Blacktown	W 10
Sept.	5—Jim Slatter, Blacktown	W 10
Oct.	3—Paul Ferreri, Blacktown	L 10
Oct.	17—Guinea Hillier, Blacktown	W 10
Nov.	28—Brian Clout, Blacktown	KO 6
	(Won New South Wales Bantamweight Title)	

1975

Mar.	2—Guinea Hillier, St. Kilda	KO 4
Mar.	12—Brian Roberts, Marrickville	D 10
	(Retained New South Wales Bantamweight Title)	
Apr.	19—Emilio Pireddu, Melbourne	W 10
June	12—Brian Clout, Blacktown	KO 7
	(Retained New South Wales Bantamweight Title)	
Aug.	21—Brian Roberts, Blacktown	L 12

1976

Feb.	19—Andy Broome, Blacktown	L 10
May	12—Matt Ropis, Marrickville	L 15
	(For Australian Lightweight Title)	

1977

Feb.	22—Phil Davies, Cardiff	L 10

1978
(Inactive)

1979

July	10—Robert Namana, Boroko	W 10
Aug.	1—Glenn Howard, Revesby	LF 9
Oct.	14—Larry Valesini, Revesby	KO 7
	(Won Australian Junior Lightweight Title)	
Dec.	19—Glenn Howard, Mt. Pritchard	KO 6
	(Retained Australian Junior Lightweight Title)	

1980

Feb.	10—Paul Ferreri, Revesby	L 15
	(Lost Australian Junior Lightweight Title)	
June	18—Billy Facer, Mt. Pritchard	KO 4
July	18—Roger Henry, Dapto	KO 6
Sept.	19—Paul Ferreri, Lidcombe	KO by 10
	(For Australian Junior Lightweight Title)	

PAUL WETTER
British Welterweight
1980

Mar.	18—Ian Kid Murray, Wolverhampton	L 6
Mar.	26—Mike Clemow, Evesham	D 6
Apr.	14—Steve Ward, London	L 6
Apr.	21—Steve Ward, Nottingham	L 6
Apr.	30—Tommy Thomas, Aylesbury	W 6
May	27—Ronald Pearce, Newport	W 6
June	2—Tommy McCallum, Plymouth	L 6
June	18—Tony Stanton, Burslem	L 6
July	12—Dominic Bergonzi, London	L 6
Sept.	22—Gary Brooks, London	KO by 5

JOHAN CHARLES WEYER
South African Junior Lightweight
Born: April 3, 1957
1977

June	26—Wally Brown, Durban	KO 3
Aug.	29—Alex Venter, Johannesburg	W 4
Oct.	17—Alex Venter, Johannesburg	KO 3
Oct.	29—Jan Hendrik Blignaut, Johannesburg	D 4
Dec.	3—Jacob Morake, Johannesburg	L 4

1978

Apr.	10—Eddie Mileham, Johannesburg	W 10
June	5—Eddie Mileham, Pretoria	D 6
Sept.	8—Eddie Mileham, Johannesburg	W 12
Oct.	23—Langton Tinago, Johannesburg	L 10
Dec.	4—Bernard Zungu, Durban	W 8

1979

Feb.	3—Evans Gwiji, Johannesburg	W 6
June	8—Guy Ratazayo, East London	L 6

1980

May	12—Chris Whiteboy, Cape Town	L 6
July	3—Aladin Stevens, Welkom	L 6
Aug.	16—Aladin Stevens, Johannesburg	L 6

GEORGE WHITE
British Welterweight
1979

Sept.	10—Tyrell Wilson, Birmingham	L 6
Oct.	17—Joe Mills, London	L 6
Nov.	12—Joe Mills, Mayfair	KO by 5
Dec.	13—Neil Brown, Wimbledon	KO 5

1980

July	30—Robert Armstrong, Doncaster	W 6
Sept.	4—Paul Murray, Morecambe	L 6
Sept.	16—Randy Henderson, Southend	D 6
Sept.	24—Mick H. Oliver, Burslem	KO 6

HARRY WHITE
British Light Heavyweight
1974

Sept.	24—Len Brittain, Nottingham	KO 3

Oct. 15—Vernon Scott, Shoreditch .... KO 4
Oct. 21—Johnny Cox, Nottingham .... W 6
1975
Jan. 6—Billy Brooks, Hemel Hempstead .... W 6
Jan. 13—Phil Martin, Nottingham .... W 6
Feb. 12—Carl Watson, Cambridge .... KO by 6
Apr. 2—George Gray, Hammersmith .... L 8
Apr. 7—George Gray, Mayfair .... W 8
Apr. 14—Dave Parris, Nottingham .... W 8
May 5—Terry Armstrong, Manchester .... KO 7
June 2—Ralph Green, Manchester .... L 8
Nov. 13—Ralph Green, Caister .... W 8
1976
Jan. 13—Peter Brisland, Hornsey .... KO by 8
Apr. 26—Ralph Green, Nottingham............... W 8
Oct. 27—Tim Wood, Wolverhampton .... KO 1
1977
May 17—Bunny Johnson, Wolverhampton ..... KO by 9
(British Light Heavyweight Title)
1978
Feb. 20—Greg Evans, Nottingham .... L 8
Mar. 20—Garfield McEwan, Luton .... KO 8
May 23—Tony Allen, Leicester .... L 8
Nov. 27—Greg Evans, Kettering .... KO by 6
1979
Nov. 27—Eddie Fenton, Wolverhampton .... W 10
1980
Mar. 19—Eddie Fenton, Solihull .... L 10
(Lost Midlands Area Light Heavyweight Title)
Sept. 22—Chris Lawson, Wolverhampton ..... KO by 5

BRAMLEY WHITEBOY
South African Lightweight and Junior Welterweight
Born: Oct. 26, 1956
1976
Aug. 7—Boy Boy Mpulampula, Port Elizabeth ...KO 1
Oct. 30—Jacob Morake, East London .... L 6
Nov. 6—Raymond Nombeko, King Williamstown ..W 4
Nov. 13—Lennox Mtyongwe, East London .... KO 5
1977
Mar. 5—Moses Mashigo, East London .... W 6
Apr. 2—Mbulelo Yoto, East London .... W 4
May 7—Raymond Nombeko, Zwelitsha .... W 6
May 30—Anthony Morodi, Port Elizabeth .... L 8
June 11—Fungile Buti, East London .... W 8
Nov. 19—Simon Dhladhla, Port Elizabeth .... L 6
Dec. 5—Tadios Fisher, Port Elizabeth .... W 8
Dec. 14—Simon Dladla, Guguletu .... W 8
1978
Feb. 22—Joshua Plaatjies, Cape Town .... W 6
Apr. 1—Xanti Singapi, Port Elizabeth .... KO 1
July 31—Philip van As, Cape Town .... W 8
Sept. 9—Rolly Xipu, East London .... L 12
Dec. 18—Bowell Zono, Goodwood .... W 8
1979
Jan. 16—Peet Bothma, Cape Town .... W 8
Mar. 7—Hardy Mileham, Cape Town .... KO 6
June 21—Arthur Clarke, Cape Town .... W 8
Sept. 5—Tsietsie Maretloane, Cape Town .... D 10
Nov. 12—Peet Bothma, Cape Town .... W 6
Dec. 8—Mzwandile Biyana, East London .... L 10
1980
Jan. 14—Joshua Plaatjies, Cape Town .... KO 1
Mar. 13—Norman Sekgapane, Cape Town .... W 8
May 17—Guy Ratazayo, East London .... W 10
(Won Vacant Cape Lightweight Title)
June 4—Peter Kanie, Goodwood .... W 8
Aug. 16—Peter Kanie, East London .... L 6
Oct. 11—Peter Kanie, Port Elizabeth .... W 10
(For Cape Junior Welterweight Title)
Dec. 22—Bennie Nortman, Cape Town .... L 6

CHRIS WHITEBOY
South African Junior Lightweight
1979
June 21—Sam Williams, Cape Town .... W 4
Sept. 5—Herbert Plaatjies, Cape Town .... W 4
Sept. 27—Sazi Xhamlashe, Cape Town .... W 4
1980
Jan. 14—Thomas Tsotetsi, Cape Town .... W 6
Feb. 3—Sam Williams, Goodwood .... W 6
Mar. 3—Charles Boais, Cape Town .... W 6
Apr. 14—David Mbomay, Cape Town .... W 6
May 12—Johan Weyer, Cape Town .... W 6
June 4—Boy Boy Mtimkulu, Goodwood .... W 6
Aug. 16—Phindile Ndilele, East London .... W 6
Dec. 22—Guy Ratazayo, Cape Town .... W 10
(For Cape Junior Lightweight Title)

ANTHONY JOHANNES WIESE
South African Lightweight
1978
May 20—Jacobus Nel, Tzaneen .... W 4

432

June 9—Willem Visser, Johannesburg .... L 4
Aug. 5—Richard Smit, Johannesburg .... W 4
Oct. 28—Jan Blignaut, Ermelo .... L 4
1979
June 18—Charles Marule, Johannesburg ...... KO by 1
Sept. 15—Stricker Studdard, Johannesburg .... L 4
1980
Mar. 1—Sybrand Oelofse, Ermelo .... KO by 1

JOHN WIGGINS
British Junior Welterweight
1980
Sept. 24—Steve Davies, Evesham .... L 6
Oct. 13—Barry Winters, Nottingham .... W 6
Oct. 30—Paul Murray, Wolverhampton .... L 6

GARY WILLIAMS
Australian
1980
June 29—Kirk Blair, Rozelle .... W 8
July 11—Reg King, Auburn .... W 6
Aug. 8—Dennis Talbot, Merrylands .... W 6
Aug. 27—Gary Temrest, Mt. Pritchard .... KO 3
Aug. 30—Willie Leblie, Kanwall .... KO 5
Sept. 18—Dennis Talbot, Marrickville .... L 10
Oct. 15—Barry Townsend, Mt. Pritchard .... KO 6

JOEY WILLIAMS
British Light Heavyweight
1977
Oct. 10—Carl Canwell, London .... L 6
Nov. 10—Trevor Cattouse, Wimbledon .... L 6
Nov. 30—Rocky Burton, London .... L 4
1978
Feb. 13—Shaun Chalcraft, Walworth .... L 6
Mar. 6—Rocky Burton, London .... W 6
Mar. 13—Kevin Felton, Walworth .... KO 3
Mar. 22—Wally Barnes, London .... W 6
Apr. 24—Shaun Shalcraft, Walworth .... D 6
Sept. 19—Tom Jones, Southend .... L 6
Oct. 11—Ramsey Khachik, Stoke .... KO 1
Nov. 7—Steve Lewin, Wembley .... L 6
1979
Mar. 27—Dave Mullings, Hemel Hempstead ...KO by 4
May 1—Johnny Wall, London .... L 6
Sept. 18—Shaun Chalcraft, Lewisham .... L 8
Dec. 6—Pete Holm, Copenhagen .... L 8
Dec. 20—Stan Carnell, Queensway .... KO 5
1980
Feb. 18—Steve Lewin, Lewisham .... KO by 4

LAWRENCE (LANCE) WILLIAMS
British Lightweight
1978
Sept. 19—John Cooper, Southend .... D 6
Sept. 27—Shaun Durkin, Rotherham .... W 6
Nov. 8—Eric Wood, Stoke .... D 8
Nov. 15—Selvyn Bell, Solihull .... KO 6
Nov. 27—Terry McKeown, Glasgow .... L 6
1979
Jan. 17—Vernon Penprase, Stoke .... L 6
Feb. 28—George Schofield, Burslem .... W 6
Mar. 27—Charlie Brown, London .... W 8
Apr. 23—Barry Price, Southend .... W 8
May 21—Terry Welch, Manchester .... W 8
June 26—Chris Sanigar, London .... L 6
Oct. 11—Barry Price, Liverpool .... W 8
Oct. 29—Nagib Daho, Birmgham .... W 8
Nov. 19—Barry Price, Stockport .... W 8
Dec. 10—George McGurk, Birmingham .... KO 6
1980
Jan. 16—Robbie Robinson, Liverpool .... L 8
Feb. 18—Kerry Collins, Stockport .... W 8
Apr. 29—George McGurk, Stockport .... W 8
Sept. 24—Duncan Hamilton, Solihull .... KO 6
Oct. 27—Jimmy Brown, London .... KO 7

ROBERT (ROBBIE) WILLIAMS
South African Heavyweight
1977
Aug. 19—Albertus Opperman, Bloemfontein ...... KO 3
Aug. 29—Jacobus Oosthuizen, Johannesburg ...... KO 1
Dec. 1—John Abrahams, Cape Town .... KO 1
1978
Aug. 5—Jimmy Abbott, Johannesburg .... KO by 5
Dec. 15—Fraser Memela, Durban .... KO 1
1979
Mar. 24—Kid Power, Johannesburg .... W 6
Apr. 25—Jimmy Abbott, Durban .... KO by 4
July 28—Ringo Starr, Bulawayo .... KO 1
Oct. 20—Dwain Bonds, Pretoria .... L 6
1980
Mar. 1—Jonas Malan, Durban .... KO 3

Apr. 19—Caifus Masondo, Rand Stadium .... KO 2
July 4—Freddie Brown, Durban .... L 8
Aug. 16—Jimmy Abbott, Joburg .... D 6
Oct. 15—Jimmy Abbott, Cape Town .... W 8
Oct. 25—Rahim Muhammad, Sun City .... L 4

SAM WILLIAMS
South African Junior Lightweight
1978
Nov. 25—Griffiths Matyum, Paarl .... W 4
1979
Jan. 16—Kevin MacKay, Cape Town .... W 4
Mar. 7—Kevin MacKay, Cape Town .... L 4
June 21—Chris Whiteboy, Cape Town .... L 4
Dec. 19—Herbert Plaatjies, Cape Town .... W 4
1980
Feb. 3—Chris Whiteboy, Goodwood .... L 6
Apr. 14—Boweel Zono, Cape Town .... W 4
Oct. 15—Patrick Kohil, Cape Town .... W 6

TOMMY WILLIAMS
British Middleweight
1975
Feb. 4—Steve Paul Stocks, Blackpool .... D 6
1976-1978
(Inactive)
1979
Nov. 29—Terry Matthews, Liverpool .... W 6
1980
Jan. 16—Peter Bassey, Liverpool .... L 6

TYRREL WILSON
British Lightweight
1979
Sept. 10—George White, Birmingham .... W 6
Sept. 24—Steve Parker, Birmingham .... L 6
Oct. 4—Phillip Morris, Ebbw Vale .... W 6
Oct. 15—Ian Murray, Wolverhampton .... L 6
Oct. 29—John Lindo, Birmingham .... W 6
Dec. 20—Wally Stocking, Queensway .... D 6
1980
Jan. 9—Walter Clayton, Burslem .... KO by 1
Feb. 18—Danny Connolly, London .... L 6
Mar. 10—Mickey Baker, Wolverhampton .... L 8
Mar. 24—Danny Connolly, London .... L 6

PIERRE FRANK WINSTERTEIN
French Junior Middleweight
1980
Jan. 19—Joachin Oliveira, Argenteil .... KO 2
Jan. 25—Christian D'Helft, Corbeil .... W 6
Mar. 8—Maurice Renaud, Epinay sous Senart ..... W 6
Apr. 5—Sandro Jaconelli, Massay .... KO 5
Apr. 19—Cyrille Barbe, St. Genevieve .... KO 2
Apr. 26—Jean Philippe Truchelut, LeGrand ...... KO 3
May 3—Eugene Dovin, Paris .... KO 1
June 7—Sandro Jaconelli, Massay .... KO 2
Oct. 6—Bader Ouakai, Paris .... KO 3
Oct. 27—Dragan Tadic, Paris .... KO 4
Nov. 27—Wenlenge N'Kongo, Paris .... KO 1

HO-SHING WINSTON
British Lightweight
1979
Oct. 27—Jim McEwan, Barnsley .... L 6
Nov. 27—Wally Stocks, Sheffield .... W 6
Dec. 17—John Lindo, Bradford .... D 6
1980
Feb. 11—Dave Ramsden, Manchester .... W 6
Feb. 28—Steve Henderson, Queensway .... KO 5
Mar. 3—Dave Ramsden, Marton .... W 6
May 12—Johnny Francis, Manchester .... L 6

BARRY WINTERS
Scottish Junior Welterweight
1980
Apr. 14—John Hadfield, Motherwell .... KO 1
Apr. 21—Sammy Sims, Nottingham .... L 6
May 5—Bobby Welburn, Glasgow .... KO 2
May 19—John Lindo, Bradford .... KO 3
Oct. 8—Mark Hill, Stoke .... KO 3
Oct. 13—Jimmy Wiggins, Nottingham .... L 6
Oct. 30—George Schofield, Liverpool .... D 8

ANDRE WISSENBACH
German Junior Middleweight
1980
Apr. 18—Klaus Klein, Berlin .... D 6
June 13—Herbert Trausmuth, Lubeck .... W 4
Sept. 26—Reiner Kober, Koln .... W 4
Dec. 5—Reiner Kober, Koln .... D 4

FRANK WISSENBACH
German Middleweight
Born: December 15, 1956
1974
May 14—Mustafa Demiroc, Berlin............... W 4
June 21—Joel Bonnetaz, Berlin................... W 4
Sept. 3—Alfred Fries, Berlin..................... W 6
Oct. 10—Gustav Rozovits, Berlin............... KO 6
Nov. 5—Mimoun Mohatar, Berlin............... W 6
Nov. 30—Carmelo Martin Cendon, Munich .... W 6
1975
Mar. 18—Titi Larbi, Berlin .... KO 2
May 30—Peter Scheibner, Hamburg .... KO by 2
Sept. 6—Klaus Fuchs, Berlin .... KO 2
Sept. 12—Sule Adisa, Offenbach .... KO 2
Sept. 26—Alfred Fries, Speier .... KO 3
Oct. 31—Arpad Majai, Offenbach .... KO 4
Nov. 4—Ludwig Kammerhofer, Vienna .... KO 2
Dec. 27—Branko Barakovic, Berlin.............. KO 5
1976
Jan. 16—Peter Schibner, Berlin................. W 8
Apr. 2—Reinhard Dampman, Keil................ W 8
May 7—Peter Tombers, Berlin................. W 8
June 18—Vito Antuofermo, Berlin............... W 8
Dec. 4—Jean Andre Emmerich, Hamburg........ W 12
(German Light Middleweight Title)
1977
Mar. 15—Juarez De Lima, Berlin .... W 8
May 7—Maurice Hope, Hamburg .... L 15
(European Junior Middleweight Title)
Aug. 6—Edwin Mack, Berlin .... W 8
Dec. 10—Larry Paul, Berlin .... KO 2
1978
Apr. 6—Dan Snyder, Berlin .... W 10
May 6—Tyrone Phelps, Berlin .... W 10
Nov. 6—Frank Reiche, Berlin .... W 10
(German Middleweight Title)
Dec. 2—Tiger Quaye, Lubeck .... W 8
1979
Apr. 6—Jacques Chinon, Lubeck .... W 10
Sept. 28—Georg Steinherr, Munich .... D 10
(German Middleweight Title)
Dec. 7—Esperno Postl, Lubeck .... W 8
1980
Feb. 6—Josef Biberovic, Lubeck .... KO 8
Apr. 18—Jim Richards, Copenhagen .... W 10
May 17—Damiano Lassandro, Munich .... KO 2
June 13—Franz Dorfer, Lubeck .... W 8
Sept. 26—Eddie Smith, Koln .... LF 4
Dec. 5—Eddie Smith, Koln .... KO by 8

SAMUEL WOLF
South African Featherweight
1979
May 5—Samuel Koalepe, Ficksburg .... KO 1
Aug. 4—Petrus Nyulewe, Odendaalsrust .... W 4
Sept. 1—Motsie Tladi, Ficksburg .... KO by 3
1980
May 31—Petrus Abrahams, Bethlehem .... W 4
Sept. 13—Samuel Mafere, Welkom .... KO 1
Oct. 11—Paulus Pulumo, Odendaalsrust .... L 6
Nov. 29—Elias Mphatsoe, Odendaalsrust .... L 6
Dec. 6—Caiphus Khotie, Ficksburg .... L 6

DAI WOOD
British Middleweight
1977
Oct. 17—Jimmy Thompson, Glasgow .... L 6
Nov. 2—Ken Jones, Cardiff .... L 6
1978
Nov. 20—Lloyd Gardner, Piccadilly .... D 6
1979
Jan. 8—Lloyd James, London .... KO by 3
1980
Feb. 4—Martin Francis, London .... D 6

ERIC WOOD
British Lightweight
1977
Aug. 22—George Feeney, Stockton .... KO by 4
Sept. 22—Tony Carroll, Birkenhead .... L 6
Oct. 3—Rodney Collinson, Barnsley .... W 4
Oct. 12—Steve Butler, Stoke .... W 6
Oct. 19—Steve Henderson, Kingston .... W 6
Nov. 24—Dai Davies, Doncaster .... W 6
Dec. 5—Gary Collins, Luton .... W 6
Dec. 14—Dai Davies, Swansea .... D 6
1978
Jan. 9—Ceri Collins, London .... L 6
Jan. 16—Lee Graham, Nottingham .... W 6
Jan. 30—Dave Taylor, Cleethorpes .... W 6
Feb. 13—Ceri Collins, Birmingham .... W 6
Feb. 23—Marty Jacobs, Doncaster .... W 8

Mar. 15—John Kelly, Stoke .... W 8
Mar. 20—Dave McCabe, Glasgow .... L 8
Mar. 31—Tony Carroll, Liverpool .... L 8
Apr. 6—Jeff Pritchard, Ebbw Vale .... L 8
Apr. 11—John Kelly, Sheffield .... L 6
Apr. 17—Billy Vivian, London .... L 8
May 3—Jimmy Cooke, Solihull .... L 8
May 18—Brian Snagg, Liverpool .... L 8
May 23—Tony Zeni, Islington .... L 8
June 1—Martin Galleozzie, Cardiff .... L 8
Aug. 29—Stan Atherton, Liverpool .... W 6
Sept. 8—Mickey Bell, Wakefield .... L 6
Sept. 13—Rocky Beaumont, Cambridge .... L 6
Sept. 18—Vernon Penprase, London .... W 6
Sept. 28—Stan Atherton, Liverpool .... L 6
Oct. 16—Peter Snowsall, London .... W 6
Oct. 31—Vernon Vanriel, Birmingham .... L 8
Nov. 8—Lawrence Willams, Stoke .... D 8
Dec. 4—George Feeney, Marton .... L 8
Dec. 18—Barry Price, London .... L 8
1979
Jan. 8—Jeff Pritchard, London .... L 8
Jan. 27—Gilbert Bayens, Zele .... W 6
Feb. 13—Sid Smith, Marylebone .... L 8
Feb. 20—Winston Spencer, Kensington .... KO by 3
Mar. 20—Charlie Brown, Mayfair .... KO by 5
1980
Sept. 9—John Lindo, Mexborough .... W 6
Sept. 18—George Schofield, Liverpool .... W 8
Oct. 13—Norman Morton, Newcastle .... L 8
Oct. 30—Mickey Baker, Wolverhampton ...... W disq. 6

TOMMY WRIGHT
British Welterweight
1973
Oct. 15—George McKay, London.................... D 8
Nov. 27—Mickey Piner, Shoreditch .... W 8
Dec. 17—George McKay, London.................... D 8
1974
Feb. 12—Vernon Sollas, Kensington............... L 8
Mar. 18—Danny Fearnon, Manchester .... KO 6
Apr. 4—Sven Paulsen, Copenhagen .... KO by 7
May 13—John Mitchell, London................... W 8
May 29—Sven Paulsen, Copenhagen .... L 8
June 10—John Kellie, Glasgow..................... L 8
Sept. 18—George Turpin, Manchester .... L 8
Oct. 21—Vernon Sollas, Bethnal Green .... D 8
1975
Jan. 18—Giancarlo Usai, Rimini................... L 8
Feb. 10—Noel McIvor, Nottingham .... W 8
Feb. 19—Billy Smart, Manchester .... W 6
Feb. 24—Barry Harris, Glasgow.................... KO 5
May 5—John Mitchell, Piccadilly .... L 8
June 30—Gerry Duffy, Glasgow............... KO by 3
Sept. 29—Colin Miles, London .... W 8
Oct. 28—Tommy Dunn, London .... KO by 3
Dec. 2—Billy Smart, London...................... L 8
Dec. 12—Jan Arne Pedersen, Oslo .... D 6
1976
Jan. 27—Mario Stango, Bethnal Green .... W 8
Mar. 4—Tommy Glencross, Glasgow.............. L 10
Mar. 28—Jan Arne Pedersen, Oslo .... D 6
June 26—Cecilo Lastra, Santander............. KO by 4
Sept. 14—Mark Bliss, London..................... L 10
Oct. 9—Hans Henrik Palm, Copenhagen .... L 4
Nov. 22—Jackie McGill, London.................... L 8
1977
Jan. 25—Cornelius Bosa-Edwards,
Bethnal Green .... KO by 1
Nov. 30—Najib Daho, Caister .... L 8
Dec. 11—Frank McCord, Plymouth .... D 6
Dec. 18—Najib Daho, Bradford .... L 8
1978
(Inactive)
1979
Jan. 22—Paul Chance, Wolverhampton .... L 8
Jan. 31—Lloyd Hibbitt, Stoke .... L 8
Feb. 13—Terry Welsh, Wakefield .... W 8
Feb. 19—Gary Newell, Wolverhampton .... KO 2
Feb. 22—Stan Atherton, Liverpool .... L 6
Mar. 5—Joe Mills, Barnsley .... KO 5
Mar. 15—Barry Price, Marylebone .... L 8
Apr. 5—Robbie Robinson, Liverpool .... L 8
Apr. 19—Tony Carroll, Birkenhead .... W 8
May 16—Lloyd Hibbitt, Wolverhampton .... L 8
1980
Jan. 25—Ricky Beaumont, Hull .... L 8
Feb. 18—Eddie Copeland, Stockport .... L 8
Mar. 10—Gary Newell, Wolverhampton .... D 6
Mar. 19—Dave Allen, Doncaster .... L 8
Apr. 14—Dave Douglas, Motherwell .... L 8
Apr. 30—Gary Newell, Wolverhampton .... L 6
May 29—Cliff Gilpin, Wolverhampton .... KO by 5
(Announced Retirement)

434

WILLIE WRIGHT
British Middleweight
1980
Mar. 26—Don Hughs, Evesham .... W 6
Apr. 21—Casley McAlum, Edgbaston .... W 6
Sept. 24—Steve Bateman, Evesham .... W 6
Sept. 29—Robert Smith, Bedworth .... W 6
Oct. 5—Joe Jackson, Stoke .... L 6
Oct. 14—Tommy Taylor, Wolverhampton .... L 6
Oct. 18—John Humphreys, Birmingham .... L 6

VUYANI XABANISA
South African Flyweight
1980
July 5—H.B. Dunjwa, Umtata .... L 6
July 26—Zamalake Losi, King Williamstown ..... W 4
Dec. 13—Zola Mali, Queenstown .... KO 3

GIFT XALUWA
South African Flyweight
1979
Mar. 5—David Molefe, Welkom .... W 4
Apr. 2—David Molefe, Welkom .... KO 6
July 31—Jacob Molefe, Bloemfontein .... L 8
1980
Feb. 2—Ranching Louw, Kimberley .... L 8
Mar. 8—Albert Kgwadi, Bloemfontein .... W 6
Apr. 14—Michael Moamogoa, Kimberley .... D 6
May 3—Tenyson Molebeledi, Witsieshoek .... D 4
May 24—Simon Mafere, Welkom .... W 6

SAZI XHAMLASHE
South African Lightweight
1976
Mar. 1—James Jacobs, Guguletu .... W 4
1977
May 11—David Scott, Guguletu .... KO 1
1978
June 1—Edward Turner, Goodwood .... KO 3
Nov. 25—David Nomoyi, Paarl .... KO 3
Dec. 18—Patrick Kohli, Goodwood .... L 6
1979
Sept. 27—Chris Whiteboy, Cape Town .... L 4
1980
Jan. 14—David Mboma, Cape Town .... W 4
June 1—Rodney Botha, Goodwood .... KO by 4
June 14—David Mbomay, Cape Town .... L 4
Nov. 8—Mboneleli Dyantijies, East London ...... L 4

ROLLY XIPU
South African Junior Welterweight
Born: Jan. 12, 1952
1972
July 14—Petrus Sithebe, Thembisa .... W 6
Sept. 29—Louis Miya, Kwa-Thema .... W 6
Nov. 17—Jackson Diphofa, Kwa-Thema .... W 4
1973
Mar. 3—Benjamin Molokeng, Jabulani .... W 4
Apr. 13—Michael Motloung, Springs .... KO 6
May 26—Daniel Makhudu, Jabulanik .... KO 3
June 22—Ernest Phage, Springs .... W 6
Aug. 17—Moses Mashego, Springs .... W 4
Oct. 27—Thuso Mapela, Jabulani .... W 6
Nov. 9—Serame Molefe, Springs .... KO 1
1974
Feb. 1—Petrus Mokoena, Springs................ W 6
Apr. 5—Petrus Mokoena, Kwa-Thema .... W 10
June 21—Joe Archer, Kwa-Thema .... W 6
Aug. 9—Petrus Sithebe, Kwa-Thema .... W 10
Spt. 6—Phillip Hlophe, Kwa-Thema .... W 6
Dec. 14—Nkosana Mgxaji, East London .... L 8
1975
May 9—Moses Khoni, Natalspruit .... KO
June 6—Temba Hlabisa, Kwa-Thema .... KO
Sept. 6—Daniel Mkize, Port Elizabeth L
Oct. 25—Victor Tshabalala, Jabulani .... W
Nov. 28—Jeremiah Nzelwane, Kwa-Thema ...... W
1976
Mar. 27—Norman Sekgapane, Natalspruit .... L 1
(South African Non-White Lightweight Title)
1977
May 21—Harold Volbrecht, Johannesburg L
Oct. 15—Jack Jim, East London .... W 1
Dec. 5—Norman Sekgapane, Port Elizabeth ...... D 1

Sept.   9—Bramley Whiteboy, East London ....W 12
Apr.   28—Peet Bothma, Johannesburg ....L 12
Apr.   19—Simon Dhladhla, Johannesburg ....W 6
May   20—Peet Bothma, Johannesburg ....L 7

HONG-SOO YANG
Korean Flyweight
(Previous Record Unavailable)
1977
Dec.   8—Jiro Takada, Osaka City ....W 12
(Won OPBF Flyweight Title)
1978
July   25—Tsutomu Igarashi, Tokyo ....L 12
(Lost OPBF Flyweight Title)
1979
Aug.   8—Tsutomu Igarashi, Aomori ....W 12
(Regained OPBF Flyweight Title)
Nov.   6—Shigeo Nakajima, Tokyo ....L 10
1980
Mar.   18—Riki Igarashi, Shiga ....W 12
(Retained OPBF Flyweight Title)
Nov.   23—Shuichi Hozumi, Tokyo ....KO 9
(Retained OPBF Flyweight Title)

GAYBON YEKISO
South African Junior Featherweight
1977
Oct.   15—Thembisile Ngxingolo, East London ......W 4
1978
Aug.   5—Kallie Swanepoel, Johannesburg ....W 4
Aug.   26—Khulile Radu, East London ....KO 3
Sept.   30—Welile Nkosenkulu, East London ....L 6
Nov.   27—Sybrand Oelofse, Johannesburg ....KO 3
1979
Mar.   9—Jacob Diraditsile, Springs ....W 6
May   4—Johannes Sithebe, Springs ....W 6
Aug.   3—Daniel Hlahane, Springs ....W 6
Oct.   5—Michael Moamagwa, Bloemfontein ......W 6
Dec.   1—Cecil Baatjies, Port Elizabeth ....KO 1
1980
Mar.   1—Alex Venter, Ermelo ....KO 1
May   3—Welile Nkosenkulu, East London ....KO 4
(For South African Bantamweight Title)
July   19—Siphwe Fuma, East London ....W 8
Dec.   6—Monwabisi Kana, East London ....KO 1

LEE YIDANO
Korean Lightweight
1979
Dec.   8—Ki-Hoon Kwak, Seoul ....W 10
(Won Korean Lightweight Title)
1980
Feb.   22—Yong-Ho Oh, Seoul ....KO by 1
(For OPBF Lightweight Title)

AGMIL YILDERIM
Turkish Middleweight
Born: May 1, 1957
1977
Dec.   10—G. Marshall, Berlin ....KO 2
1978
Feb.   15—Stephan Vertpre, Rotterdam ....KO 6
Mar.   18—Vedat Akova, Uestersen ....W 6
May   6—Mike McCoy, Frankfort ....W 4
May   29—Pat Thomas, Rotterdam ....L 8
Sept.   2—Franz Dorfer, Berlin ....W 6
1979
Mar.   7—Tiger Oquaye, Rotterdam ....KO 3
Mar.   17—Celestin Kanynda, Banja Luka ....W 8
Apr.   28—Hendrick Seys, Belgrade ....KO 3
Aug.   25—Sonny Kamunga, Zenica ....KO 6
Nov.   5—Antonio Garrido, Rotterdam ....W 8
1980
June   7—Giampaolo Piras, Cologne ....KO 2

MASAHIRO YOHAI
Japanese Junior Welterweight
1975
June   26—Yasushi Saigo, Tokyo......................W 10
Oct.   3—Tetsuo Uchiyama, Tokyo................KO 5
Dec.   22—Chung San Lee, Tokyo.................W 10

Apr.   11—Mitsuyuki Nakane, Tokyo............KO by 4
June   28—Hitoshi Takasashi, Tokyo................L 10
Aug.   23—Freddie Mensah, Kagoshima ....KO 7
Nov.   21—Tohru Sukarahar, Tokyo................KO 8
Jan.   4—Kiyoshi Kazama, Tokyo ....KO 6
Apr.   10—Mitsuyuki Nakane, Tokyo ....KO 10
June   25—Tamio Negishi, Tokyo ....KO 10
(Japanese Lightweight Title)
Dec.   3—Tamio Negishi, Tokyo ....KO 2
(Japanese Lightweight Title)
1978
Jan.   19—Mitsuhiro Nakane, Kita-Kyushu City ...KO 7
Apr.   11—Hiroshi Takahashi, Tokyo ....KO 2
(Japanese Lightweight Title)
July   27—Mitsuhiro Nakane, Tokyo ....W 10
(Japanese Lightweight Title)
Sept.   28—Noboru Hatakeyama, Tokyo ....W 10
Nov.   29—Ichiro Izawa, Nagoya ....KO 3
(Japanese Lightweight Title)
1979
Jan.   25—Kwang Sun Kim, Tokyo ....KO 8
Apr.   23—Fred Pastor, Tokyo ....KO 6
June   25—Mar Simbajon, Tokyo ....W 10
Oct.   4—Sang Hyun Kim, Tokyo ....KO by 11
(WBC Junior Welterweight Title)
1980
Apr.   28—Noboru Hatakeyama, Tokyo ....L 10

SHUZO YOSHIDA
Japanese Featherweight
(Previous Record Unavailable)
1978
Feb.   14—Arman Bangoyan, Yokohama City ......KO 8
July   25—Mitsuru Tomonari, Tokyo ....KO 3
Nov.   4—Elmer Arriesgado, Yokohama ....KO 7
1979
June   5—Juan A. Lopez, Yokohama ....KO by 9
Sept.   5—Takao Maruki, Nagoya ....L 10
Dec.   27—Sok-Kyu Park, Seoul ....KO by 10
1980
Mar.   25—Sok-Tae Yun, Tokyo ....KO by 8

ISAAC YOTO
South African Welterweight
1974
Sept.   23—Mandla Ketile, Cape Town ....W 4
1975
Jan.   23—Makatshana Luphondo, Cape Town ....D 4
Nov.   3—David Ngwenya, Guguletu ....KO 6
1976
Apr.   28—Mxolisi Mgidi, Guguletu ....W 8
1977
(Inactive)
1978
Feb.   27—Wentzel Marais, Durban ....L 4
1979
Jan.   16—Dumile Siko, Cape Town ....W 6
1980
Feb.   8—Dumile Siko, Cape Town ....W 4
Mar.   3—Justus Joseph, Cape Town ....W 6

BOB YOUNG
British Heavyweight
1977
July   20—Pat Thompson, Sheffield ....L 6
Sept.   5—Billy Warner, Hove ....D 6
Sept.   19—Billy Warner, London ....W 6
Nov.   8—Colin Flute, West Bromwich ....D 6
Dec.   5—George Scott, Marton ....KO by 3
1978
Feb.   7—Brian Paul, London ....W 6
Mar.   20—Guinea Roger, London ....W 6
Apr.   3—Martin Nee, London ....W 6
May   15—Paul Kinsella, Glasgow ....KO 3
Sept.   19—Martin Nee, Southend ....L 6
Sept.   27—Ricky James, Stoke ....KO by 3
Nov.   23—Martin Nee, Wimbledon ....W 6
1979
Feb.   21—Danny Miller, Cambridge ....KO by 3
Mar.   15—Shaun Chalcraft, Wimbledon ......KO by 3
Oct.   4—Winston Allen, Ebbw Vale ....W 6
1980
Mar.   6—Austin Okoye, Wimbledon ....L 8
Sept.   22—Jim Burns, Wolverhampton ....KO 2

GERRY YOUNG
Irish Welterweight
1977
Jan.   24—Mick Baker, Mayfair ....W 8
Mar.   7—John Mount, Glasgow ....
Apr.   7—Joey Mack, Belfast ....W 8

1978
June 27—Don Hughes, Derry .... KO 5
Oct. 27—Joe Hannaford, Belfast .... KO 3
1979
Feb. 19—Billy Lauder, Belfast .... L 8
Nov. 26—Billy Lauder, Belfast .... L 8
Dec. 6—Torben Anderson, Copenhagen .... L 6
1980
May 27—Jeff Aspell, Belfast .... W 6
July 28—Liam Linnen, Fivemiletown .... KO 3
Sept. 22—Dave Douglas, Belfast .... KO 3

PATRICK YOUNG
Australian Bantamweight
1980
Apr. 16—Kirk Davies, Mt. Pritchard .... KO 3
Apr. 22—Sparrow Freeman, Kingsford .... W 4
Oct. 7—Sparrow Freeman, Kingsford .... D 6
Oct. 14—Sparrow Freeman, Sutherland ...... KO by 4
Nov. 5—Sparrow Freeman, Brookvale .... L 6
Nov. 20—Bimbo Morris, Marrickville .... L 6

MOHAMMED YOUNIS
British Bantamweight
1977
Sept. 21—Ian Murray, London .... KO 3
Oct. 18—John Feeney, Wolverhampton .... L 8
Nov. 22—Lance Bantleman, Wolverhampton ...... W 6
Dec. 14—George Sutton, Kingston .... D 8
1978
Feb. 13—Tony Kerr, Birmingham .... L 8
Mar. 20—Tony Kerr, Glasgow .... KO 2
Apr. 12—Terry Hanna, Hammersmith .... KO 5
Oct. 11—Steve Henderson, Stoke .... KO 5
Oct. 23—George Sutton, London .... L 8
1979
Jan. 17—John Feeney, Solihull .... L 10
Feb. 19—Neil McLaughlin, Belfast .... L 8
Mar. 15—Jimmy Bott, Dudley .... KO 2
Oct. 8—Gary Lucas, Nantwich .... KO by 5
Nov. 14—John Cooper, Stoke .... W 8
Dec. 3—Paul Keers, Wolverhampton .... L 8
1980
Jan. 8—Paul Keers, Windsor .... KO by 6
Apr. 1—Kelvin Smart, London .... L 8
May 8—Kelvin Smart, Solihull .... D 8
May 19—Charlie Parvin, Bradford .... NC 6
June 7—Billy Straub, Glasgow .... KO 1

SOK-TAE YUN
Korean Featherweight
1979
July 3—Abdul Bey, Hilo .... L 10
Oct. 28—Royal Kobayashi, Aomori Ken .... L 12
1980
Mar. 25—Shuzo Yoshida, Tokyo .... KO 8

FILIBERTO ZACCHEO
Italian Welterweight
1977
Feb. 2—Giuseppe Oppedisano, Latino .... KO 5
Mar. 11—Giovanni Maiorano, Latina .... W 6
May 7—Sergio D'Angelo, Priverno .... W 6
1978
Jan. 28—Giancarlo Marinelli, Veroli .... KO by 2
May 5—Antonio Casamonica, Latina .... D 6
1979
May 12—Vincenzo Bottigliero, Latina .... W 6
Nov. 24—Eupremio Epifani, Latina .... D 6
1980
Jan. 17—Guiseppe Semilia, Genova .... KO by 4
Apr. 11—Bachisio Mereu, Sassari .... KO 3

LORENZO ZANON
Italian Heavyweight
Born: September 10, 1951
1973
July 26—Ermanno Festorazzi, Monza .... W 6
Sept. 13—Franco Giannini, Monza .... W 6
Sept. 28—Gino Martinis, Milan .... KO 3
Nov. 3—Angelo Visini, Milan .... KO 1
Nov. 30—Herbert Willems, Milan .... KO 1
Dec. 21—Alberto Lovell, Milan .... KO 1

1974
Jan. 4—Paul Simonetti, Milan .... W 6
Mar. 1—Lino Finotti, Milan .... W 6
May 4—Gianfranco Gianini, Ciniselo Balsamo ... KO 1
May 17—Vasco Faustino, Milan................. W 8
June 12—Jose Antonio Galvez, Monza........... W 8
Oct. 18—Reco Brooks, Milan................... W 8
1975
Feb. 21—Brian O'Melia, Milan................. W 8
Mar. 14—Randy Stevens, Milan................. D 8
May 26—Giuseppi Ros, Milan................... W 12
(Italian Heavyweight Title)
Oct. 24—Dante Cane, Milan .... KO by 8
(Italian Heavyweight Title)
1976
Mar. 28—Lucian Rodriguez, Paris .... L 8
Apr. 28—Lucian Rodriguez, Milan............... W 8
Oct. 22—Adriano Zanati, Bologna.............. KO 5
Dec. 3—Jose Galvez, Milan .... W 8
1977
Feb. 4—Alfredo Evangelista, Bilbao .... W 8
Mar. 5—Vasco Faustino, Velenje .... W 8
June 10—Manuel Quintana Trujillo, Milan .... KO 1
Sept. 14—Ken Norton, Las Vegas .... KO by 5
Nov. 5—Jerry Quarry, Las Vegas .... KO by 9
Dec. 26—Sugar Silex, Milan .... KO 2
1978
Dec. 26—Sugar Silex, Milan .... KO 2
1979
Mar. 4—Avenemar Peralta, San Remo .... W 8
Apr. 18—Alfredo Evangelista, Turin .... W 12
(European Heavyweight Title)
July 14—Alfio Righetti, Rimini .... D 12
(EBU Heavyweight Title)
Oct. 10—Felipe Panters Rodriguez, Torino ..... W 12
(EBU Heavyweight Title)
Dec. 14—Claman Parker, Milan .... KO 7
1980
Feb. 3—Larry Holmes, Las Vegas .... KO by 6
(For WBC Heavyweight Title)
Aug. 10—Renaldo Pelizzari, Siderno .... W 8
Oct. 31—Lupe Guerra, Gorizia .... KO 3
Nov. 28—John L. Gardner, Ostia .... KO by 5

PAOLO ZANUSSO
Italian Welterweight
Born: November 19, 1952
1974
May 10—Angelo Tomasini, Vicenza .... W 6
July 20—Angelo Tomasini, Lignana .... W 6
Aug. 17—Emilio Zanotti, Jesolo .... W 6
Dec. 6—Salah Arafa, S. Dona .... KO 3
1975
Feb. 15—Augusto Lauri, Pordenone .... W 6
Apr. 12—Augusto Lauri, Monfalcone............ W 8
June 20—Augusto Lauri, Udine................. W 8
Aug. 8—Guido Galletti, Jesolo................ KO 1
Sept. 12—Angelo Tomasini, Grisignano .... W 6
Oct. 10—Vittorio Conte, Bologna............... L 6
Oct. 31—Cira Seta, Reggio Emilia .... W 6
Nov. 21—Remo Costa, Bologna................. D 6
Dec. 5—Ali Kaja, Bologna.................... LF 3
1976
Mar. 5—Alfredo Rossi, Reggio Emilia .... KO 3
Apr. 1—Nicola Sassanelli, Pieve di Cadore ...... W 8
May 8—Antonino Chiodoni, Vicenza .... D 8
June 11—Luciano Borraccia, Salo .... KO by 8
Sept. 15—Nicolo Sassanelli, Mestre .... WF 5
Oct. 22—Vittorio Conte, Montecatini .... D 12
(Italian Welterweight Title)
1977
May 6—Giovanni Molesini, Cremona .... KO by 7
June 10—Remo Costa, Jesolo .... KO 3
Aug. 24—Luiz Ribeiro, Grado .... W 8
Dec. 8—Jorgen Hansen, Copenhagen .... LF 6
1978
Mar. 17—Giovanni Molesini, Milan .... L 12
(Italian Welterweight Title)
1979
Feb. 16—Giancarlo Serangelo, San Dena Piave .... W 8
June 12—Luigi Minchillo, San Paolo di Civitate .. KO by 5
(Italian Junior Middleweight Title)
1980
Mar. 28—Ernesto Ros, San Dona .... D 8

DANIELE ZAPPATERRA
Italian Welterweight
1977
Feb. 19—Giovanni Mairano, Milan .... W 6
Apr. 1—Gualberto Fernandez, Bologna .... W 6
Apr. 29—Angelo Tomasini, Bologna .... W 6
July 25—Domenico Milone, Bologna .... W 6
Nov. 4—Jose Luis Ribiero, Ferrera .... W 6

Feb. 10—Austo Lauri, Salletta .... W 6
Nov. 15—Angelo Fenu, Bellaria .... KO 4
1979
July 28—Scipione Colaianni, Re Ferrarese .... W 6
Dec. 14—Giovanni Lamusta, Milan .... KO 1
1980
Jan. 25—Mauro Da Cruz, Bologna .... KO 5
Feb. 22—Giovannino Mannu, Copparo .... KO 6
Mar. 22—Joel Moulin, Bologna .... W 6

RONALD ZENON
French Welterweight
1977
Oct. 8—Serge Malapris, Paris .... KO 4
Dec. 5—Claude Lancastre, Paris .... KO 3
1978
Jan. 16—Lucien Campo, Paris .... KO 2
May 20—Justin Foundi, Noisy .... KO 3
June 5—Dijbril Balhily, Paris .... KO 3
Oct. 30—Mohamed Benouadha, Paris .... KO 3
Dec. 15—Jack Peraire, Paris .... KO 3
1979
Feb. 3—Oswaldo Lopez, Creil .... KO 5
Feb. 22—Antoine Oke, Paris .... KO 6
Mar. 26—Achille Mitchell, Paris .... W 8
May 10—Ray Chavez, Paris .... KO by 3
Oct. 30—Roy Johnson, Paris .... W 10
Nov. 15—Sammy Rookard, Paris .... KO 2
Dec. 10—Horace McKenzie, Paris .... W 10
1980
Mar. 10—Joey Mack, Paris .... W 10
Apr. 18—Billy Waith, Paris .... W 10
June 15—Fred Coranson, Dunkirk .... KO 9
(Won Vacant French Welterweight Title)
Nov. 27—Bechir Boundka, Paris .... W 10

JOSEPH ZIKHALI
South African Junior Middleweight
1979
June 9—Albert Mkhize, Durban .... W 4
Sept. 1—Ness Roux, Empangeni .... KO 4
Sept. 29—Themba Buthelezi, Durban .... L 6
1980
Oct. 6—Gregory Clark, Pmburg .... L 6
Nov. 1—Graham Mdingi, Stanger .... D 4
Nov. 29—Johannes Mthembu, Durban .... KO by 2

COSMO ZIQU
South African Flyweight
1978
Dec. 15—Sazi Tokadi, East London .... KO 4
1979
Mar. 10—Mziwonke Jodwana, East London .... W 4
May 26—Godfrey Mafanya, King Williamstown .... W 4
June 8—Charles McGeer, East London .... W 4
July 7—Dolly Bangiso, East London .... W 4
Sept. 8—Boy Boy Mazaleni, Zwelitsah .... KO 2
Sept. 29—Nkenke Dunjwa, East London .... W 4
1980
Mar. 1—Dexter Dhlamini, East London .... D 6
May 3—Simon Moema, East London .... L 8
June 19—Phindile Gaika, East London .... D 6
Aug. 23—Monde Mpulampula, East London ...... KO 2
Sept. 5—Boy Boy Mazaleni, East London .... L 6

BOWELL ZONO
South African Lightweight
1974
Jan. 17—Daniel Makhudu, Cape Town .... D 4
1975
Nov. 3—Patrick Kohli, Guguletu .... W 6
1976
Mar. 1—Phillip Masemola, Guguletu .... W 6
Apr. 28—David Kaptein, Guguletu .... W 8
1977
Mar. 19—Michael Mana, Mbekweni .... W 8
May 11—Vuyisile Ntunzi, Guguletu .... KO 3
Dec. 14—Anthony Morodi, Guguletu .... L 10
1978
Sept. 9—Fungile Buti, East London .... KO 6
Nov. 25—Michael Mana, Paarl .... KO 3
Dec. 18—Bramley Whiteboy, Goodwood .... L 8
1979
Mar. 7—Tsietsie Maretloane, Cape Town ..... KO by 5
June 2—Louis Noveling, Port Elizabeth .... W 10
Sept. 27—Peet Bothma, Cape Town .... L 12
(South African Lightweight Title)
Nov. 10—Nkosana Mgxaji, King Williamstown ..... L 10
1980
Apr. 14—Sam Williams, Cape Town .... L 6

BERNARD ZUNGU
South African Junior Lightweight
1980
Mar. 29—Nkosana Mgxaji, Queenstown .... L 8
June 16—Jerome Gumede, Durban .... KO by 10
(For Natal Junior Lightweight Title)

FRANCO ZURLO
Italian Featherweight
1965
Jan. 27—Osvaldo Maffeis, Bari .... W 6
Mar. 19—Antonio Lopez, Bologna .... W 6
Apr. 2—Antonio Lopez, Rome .... W 6
June 26—Cataldo Jacca, Alghero .... KO 2
July 17—Benny Lee, Brindisi .... W 6
Oct. 30—Antonio Satta, Brindisi .... W 8
Dec. 17—Ray Devlees, Rome .... KO 2
1966
Jan. 19—Giuseppe Cali, Genova .... W 8
Mar. 4—Jacques Jacob, Rome .... W 8
June 5—Jose Robledo, Brindisi .... W 10
Aug. 14—Luigi Lucini, Maiolati .... KO 5
Nov. 23—Giancarlo Centa, Genova .... KO 7
Dec. 21—Tommaso Galli, Latina .... W 12
(Won Italian Bantamweight Title)
1967
Feb. 18—Michel Lamora, Brindisi .... KO 3
Apr. 7—Bob Allotey, Rome .... D 8
June 14—Antonio Sassarini, Subiaco .... W 12
(For Italian Bantamweight Title)
Aug. 15—Wellington Vilella, Pievetorina .... W 10
Nov. 3—Wellington Vilella, Brindisi .... KO 7
Dec. 7—Sean McCafferty, Rome .... KO 10
1968
Feb. 21—Antonio Sassarini, Brindisi .... W 12
(For Italian Bamtmweight Title)
June 7—Billy Brown, Rome .... W 8
July 31—Salvatore Burruni, S. Benedetto .... L 15
(For European Bantamweight Title)
Oct. 25—Messaud Boussaboua, Rome .... WF 2
Dec. 4—Carmelo Massa, Campobasso .... WF 6
(For Italian Bantamweight Title)
1969
Mar. 8—Enzo Farinelli, Bologna .... D 12
(For Italian Bantamweight Title)
Aug. 11—Glynn Davies, Fiuggi .... KO 3
Dec. 17—Mimoun Ben Ali, Taurianova .... W 15
(Won European Bantamweight Title)
1970
Mar. 11—Francisco Martinez, Caserta .... KO 4
(For European Bantamweight Title)
Apr. 4—John McCluskey, Zurigo .... W 15
(For European Bantamweight Title)
June 24—Enzo Farinelli, Napoli .... W 15
(For European Bantamweight Title)
1971
Feb. 16—Alan Rudkin, London .... KO by 12
(Lost European Bantamweight Title)
1972
Feb. 4—Bob Allotey, Torino .... D 8
Apr. 22—Romeo Annaya, Los Angeles .... L 10
Aug. 26—Antonio Tenza, S. Salvo .... W 8
1973
Jan. 24—Guy Caudron, Palermo .... W 12
Apr. 17—Johnny Clark, London .... L 15
(For European Bantamweight Title)
1974
Dec. 7—Paul Ikumapayi, Latiano .... W 8
1975
Mar. 14—Ambrogio Mariani, Milano .... KO 3
(For Italian Bantamweight Title)
1976
May 21—Lucio Vailati, Rome .... KO 2
July 9—Teodoro Corallo, Latina .... KO 10
1977
Feb. 23—Salvatore Fabrizion, Selva di Fasano ..... W 15
(For European Bantamweight Title)
June 15—Jacky Bihin, Forte Village .... KO 8
(For European Bantamweight Title)
Sept. 28—Paddy Maguire, Forte Village .... KO 8
(For European Bantamweight Title)
Dec. 14—Antonio Franca, Taurisano .... W 8
1978
Apr. 20—Esteban Eguia, Viareggio .... D 15
(European Bantamweight Title)
July 10—Alfredo Mulas, Ravenna .... D 15
(European Bantamweight Title)
Aug. 20—Franco Buglione, Rocco Monfina ...... KO 11
(European Bantamweight Title)
Sept. 16—Juan Francisco Rodriguez, Vigo .... L 15
(European Bantamweight Title)
1979
Aug. 31—Franco Buglione, Conca .... KO by 8

1980
Apr. 18—Melquiades Da Silva, Pasano .... W 8

TIMOTHY ZWANE
South African Heavyweight
1979
Sept. 15—Jonas Malan, Johannesburg .... W 4

Oct.   5—Lou Hendriks, Bloemfontein .... KO by 2
1980
Mar.   8—Bennie Knoetze, Johannesburg .... L 4
Apr. 19—Bennie Knoetze, Johannesburg ...... KO by 1
July   3—Gerrie Schneiganz, Welkom .... KO by 2

438

THE RING'S ALL-TIME ROLL CALL OF BOXING'S CHAMPIONS

Accavallo, Horacio
Flyweight Champion (WBA) 1966-1968

TB	KO	WD	WF	D	LD	LF	KO BY	ND	NC
84	33	43	0	6	1	0	1	0	0

Adigue, Pedro
Junior Welterweight Champion (WBC) 1968-1970

TB	KO	WD	WF	D	LD	LF	KO BY	ND	NC
52	13	21	0	4	12	0	2	0	0

Akins, Virgil
Welterweight Champion 1958

TB	KO	WD	WF	D	LD	LF	KO BY	ND	NC
92	34	25	0	2	29	0	2	0	0

Ali, Muhammad (A/K/A Cassius Clay)
Heavyweight Champion 1964-1970; 1974-1978; 1978-1979

TB	KO	WD	WF	D	LD	LF	KO BY	ND	NC
60	37	19	0	0	3	0	1	0	0

Allen, Terry
Flyweight Champion 1950

TB	KO	WD	WF	D	LD	LF	KO BY	ND	NC
76	18	42	2	1	10	0	3	0	0

Allen, Tom
Heavyweight Champion 1873-1876
Record Not Available

Albarado, Oscar
Junior Middleweight Champion 1974-1975

TB	KO	WD	WF	D	LD	LF	KO BY	ND	NC
60	39	12	1	1	6	0	1	0	0

Ambers, Lou
Lightweight Champion 1936-1938; 1939-1940

TB	KO	WD	WF	D	LD	LF	KO BY	ND	NC
102	29	59	0	6	6	0	2	0	0

Anaya, Romeo
Bantamweight Champion 1973

TB	KO	WD	WF	D	LD	LF	KO BY	ND	NC
66	37	8	0	1	6	0	14	0	0

Angelmann, Valentin
Flyweight Champion (IBU) 1937

TB	KO	WD	WF	D	LD	LF	KO BY	ND	NC
176	38	81	2	16	34	2	3	0	0

Angott, Sammy
Lightweight Champion (NBA) 1940; 1943-1944
Lightweight Champion 1941-1942

TB	KO	WD	WF	D	LD	LF	KO BY	ND	NC
125	22	72	0	8	22	0	1	0	0

Antuofermo, Vito
Middleweight Champion 1979-Present

TB	KO	WD	WF	D	LD	LF	KO BY	ND	NC
52	19	26	0	2	2	0	3	0	0

Apostoli, Fred
Middleweight Champion 1937-1939

TB	KO	WD	WF	D	LD	LF	KO BY	ND	NC
72	31	30	0	1	6	0	4	0	0

Arcari, Bruno
Junior Welterweight Champion (WBC) 1970-1974

TB	KO	WD	WF	D	LD	LF	KO BY	ND	NC
72	39	24	6	0	1	0	2	0	0

Archibald, Joey
Featherweight Champion 1939-1940; 1941

TB	KO	WD	WF	D	LD	LF	KO BY	ND	NC
106	28	32	0	5	32	1	8	0	0

Arguello, Alexis
Featherweight Champion (WBA) 1974-1977
Junior Lightweight Champion (WBC) 1978-1980

TB	KO	WD	WF	D	LD	LF	KO BY	ND	NC
73	56	13	0	0	3	0	1	0	0

Arizmendi, Alberto (Baby)
Featherweight Champion (Mexico-Calif.) 1934-1935

TB	KO	WD	WF	D	LD	LF	KO BY	ND	NC
99	11	49	0	13	23	0	3	0	0

Armstrong, Henry
Featherweight Champion 1937-1938
Lightweight Champion 1938-1939
Welterweight Champion 1938-1940

TB	KO	WD	WF	D	LD	LF	KO BY	ND	NC
174	97	47	0	8	18	1	2	1	0

Arrendondo, Ricardo
Junior Lightweight Champion 1971-1974

TB	KO	WD	WF	D	LD	LF	KO BY	ND	NC
90	50	16	1	1	17	2	3	0	0

Attell, Abe
Featherweight Champion 1901-1912

TB	KO	WD	WF	D	LD	LF	KO BY	ND	NC
169	48	43	1	1	7	0	3	50	0

Backus, Billy
Welterweight Champion 1970-1971

TB	KO	WD	WF	D	LD	LF	KO BY	ND	NC
73	22	26	0	5	15	0	5	0	0

Baer, Max
Heavyweight Champion 1934-1935

TB	KO	WD	WF	D	LD	LF	KO BY	ND	NC
83	52	18	0	0	8	2	3	0	0

Baldock, Teddy
Bantamweight Champion (GB) 1927

TB	KO	WD	WF	D	LD	LF	KO BY	ND	NC
80	37	33	2	3	3	1	1	0	0

Ballerino, Mike
Junior Lightweight Champion 1925

TB	KO	WD	WF	D	LD	LF	KO BY	ND	NC
96	8	32	0	14	19	0	5	18	0

Barrientos, Ireneo (Rene)
Junior Lightweight Champion (WBC) 1969-1970

TB	KO	WD	WF	D	LD	LF	KO BY	ND	NC
44	13	22	0	2	6	0	1	0	0

Barry, Jimmy
100 lb. Champion 1893
(claimed Bantamweight title 1894)
Won Bantamweight title 1897-1899

TB	KO	WD	WF	D	LD	LF	KO BY	ND	NC
70	39	20	0	9	0	0	0	0	2

Bartholomew, Jack
Heavyweight Champion 1797-1800
Record Not Available

Bartolo, Sal
Featherweight Champion (NBA) 1944-1946

TB	KO	WD	WF	D	LD	LF	KO BY	ND	NC
97	16	58	0	5	16	0	2	0	0

Basilio, Carmen
Welterweight Champion (NY) 1953
Welterweight Champion 1955-1957
Middleweight Champion 1957-1958

TB	KO	WD	WF	D	LD	LF	KO BY	ND	NC
79	27	29	0	7	14	0	2	0	0

Bass, Benny
Featherweight Champion 1927-1928
Junior Lightweight Champion 1929-1931

TB	KO	WD	WF	D	LD	LF	KO BY	ND	NC
197	59	79	2	6	16	10	2	22	1

Bassey, Hogan (Kid)
Featherweight Champion 1957-1959

TB	KO	WD	WF	D	LD	LF	KO BY	ND	NC
68	20	35	0	1	6	2	4	0	0

Battalino, Battling
Featherweight Champion 1929-1932

TB	KO	WD	WF	D	LD	LF	KO BY	ND	NC
87	24	33	0	3	24	1	1	0	1

Becerra, Joe
Bantamweight Champion 1959-1960

TB	KO	WD	WF	D	LD	LF	KO BY	ND	NC
78	42	29	0	2	3	0	2	0	0

Belanger, Albert (Frenchie)
Flyweight Champion (NBA) 1927-1928

TB	KO	WD	WF	D	LD	LF	KO BY	ND	NC
62	13	24	0	7	15	1	2	0	0

Belcher, Jim
Heavyweight Champion 1800-1803
Record Not Available

Belloise, Mike
Featherweight Champion (NY) 1936

TB	KO	WD	WF	D	LD	LF	KO BY	ND	NC
126	19	65	0	13	15	0	14	0	0

Benitez, Wilfred
Welterweight Champion (WBC) 1979

TB	KO	WD	WF	D	LD	LF	KO BY	ND	NC
42	25	15	0	1	0	0	1	0	0

Benvenuti, Nino
Junior Middleweight Champion 1965-1966
Middleweight Champion 1967; 1968-1970

TB	KO	WD	WF	D	LD	LF	KO BY	ND	NC
90	35	42	5	1	4	0	3	0	0

Berg, Jackie (Kid)
Junior Welterweight Champion 1930-1931

TB	KO	WD	WF	D	LD	LF	KO BY	ND	NC
197	59	89	14	9	18	0	8	0	0

Berlenbach, Paul
Light Heavyweight Champion 1925-1926

TB	KO	WD	WF	D	LD	LF	KO BY	ND	NC
50	30	7	0	3	4	0	4	1	1

Bernstein, Jack
Junior Lightweight Champion 1923

TB	KO	WD	WF	D	LD	LF	KO BY	ND	NC
107	17	48	0	7	22	0	1	12	0

Bettina, Melio
Light Heavyweight Champion (NY) 1939

TB	KO	WD	WF	D	LD	LF	KO BY	ND	NC
99	36	46	0	3	10	0	3	1	0

Borkorsor, Venice
Flyweight Champion (WBC) 1972-1973
Flyweight Champion 1973

TB	KO	WD	WF	D	LD	LF	KO BY	ND	NC
30	16	7	0	0	6	0	1	0	0

Bossi, Carmelo
Junior Middleweight Champion 1970-1971

TB	KO	WD	WF	D	LD	LF	KO BY	ND	NC
51	10	29	1	3	5	0	3	0	0

Bowker, Joe
Bantamweight Champion 1904-1905

TB	KO	WD	WF	D	LD	LF	KO BY	ND	NC
51	8	32	0	1	4	0	4	2	0

Boyle, Hughey
Bantamweight Champion 1887-1888
Record Not Available

Braddock, James J.
Heavyweight Champion 1935-1937

TB	KO	WD	WF	D	LD	LF	KO BY	ND	NC
85	27	17	0	5	19	1	2	12	2

Brain, Benjamin
Heavyweight Champion 1791-1794
Record Not Available

Bratton, Johnny
Welterweight Champion (NBA) 1951

TB	KO	WD	WF	D	LD	LF	KO BY	ND	NC
86	32	27	0	3	21	0	3	0	0

Britt, Jimmy
Lightweight Champion (Calif.) 1904-1905

TB	KO	WD	WF	D	LD	LF	KO BY	ND	NC
23	3	10	0	1	1	2	4	2	0

Britton, Jack
Welterweight Champion 1915; 1916-1917; 1919-1922

TB	KO	WD	WF	D	LD	LF	KO BY	ND	NC
325	21	77	1	20	25	2	1	177	1

Broome, Harry
Heavyweight Champion 1851-1856
Record Not Available

Broughton, Jack
Heavyweight Champion 1738-1750
Record Not Available

Brouillard, Lou
Welterweight Champion 1931-1932
Middleweight Champion (NY) 1933

TB	KO	WD	WF	D	LD	LF	KO BY	ND	NC
140	66	43	1	3	24	2	1	0	0

Brown, Alphonse (Panama Al)
Bantamweight Champion 1929-1935

TB	KO	WD	WF	D	LD	LF	KO BY	ND	NC
153	57	62	2	12	15	2	1	2	0

Brown, Jackie
Flyweight Champion 1932-1935

TB	KO	WD	WF	D	LD	LF	KO BY	ND	NC
129	36	58	3	7	17	4	4	0	0

Brown, Joe
Lightweight Champion 1956-1962

TB	KO	WD	WF	D	LD	LF	KO BY	ND	NC
160	48	56	0	12	32	1	9	0	2

Brown, Newsboy
Flyweight Champion (Calif.) 1928
Record Not Available

Buchanan, Ken
Lightweight Champion 1970-1972

TB	KO	WD	WF	D	LD	LF	KO BY	ND	NC
65	27	34	0	0	3	0	1	0	0

Buff, Johnny
Bantamweight Champion 1921-1922

TB	KO	WD	WF	D	LD	LF	KO BY	ND	NC
94	13	15	0	4	9	0	7	45	1

Burke, James (Deaf)
Heavyweight Champion 1833-1839
Record Not Available

Burns, Tommy
Heavyweight Champion 1906-1908

TB	KO	WD	WF	D	LD	LF	KO BY	ND	NC
57	35	8	0	8	3	0	2	1	0

Burruni, Salvatore
Flyweight Champion 1965-1966

TB	KO	WD	WF	D	LD	LF	KO BY	ND	NC
109	31	68	0	1	7	0	2	0	0

Callahan, Mushy
Junior Welterweight Champion 1926-1930

TB	KO	WD	WF	D	LD	LF	KO BY	ND	NC
60	18	25	0	4	10	0	2	1	0

Callura, Jackie
Featherweight Champion (NBA) 1943

TB	KO	WD	WF	D	LD	LF	KO BY	ND	NC
100	13	43	1	10	27	0	6	0	0

Cannon, Tom
Heavyweight Champion 1824-1825
Record Not Available

Canto, Miguel
Flyweight Champion (WBC) 1975-1979

TB	KO	WD	WF	D	LD	LF	KO BY	ND	NC
68	14	44	1	4	3	0	2	0	0

Canzoneri, Tony
Featherweight Champion 1928
Lightweight Champion 1930-1933; 1935-1936
Junior Welterweight Champion 1931-1932; 1933

TB	KO	WD	WF	D	LD	LF	KO BY	ND	NC
176	44	95	0	10	22	1	1	3	0

Cardona, Ricardo
Junior Featherweight Champion (WBA) 1978-Present

TB	KO	WD	WF	D	LD	LF	KO BY	ND	NC
28	11	11	0	1	4	0	1	0	0

Carmona, Chango
Lightweight Champion (WBC) 1972

TB	KO	WD	WF	D	LD	LF	KO BY	ND	NC
61	38	8	0	2	8	0	5	0	0

Carnera, Primo
Heavyweight Champion 1933-1934

TB	KO	WD	WF	D	LD	LF	KO BY	ND	NC
103	68	17	2	0	7	2	6	1	0

Carpentier, Georges
Light Heavyweight Champion 1920-1922

TB	KO	WD	WF	D	LD	LF	KO BY	ND	NC
109	56	28	4	6	4	2	8	1	0

Carrasco, Eduardo (Pedro)
Lightweight Champion (WBC) 1971

TB	KO	WD	WF	D	LD	LF	KO BY	ND	NC
110	66	35	3	2	3	0	0	0	0

Carruthers, Jimmy
Bantamweight Champion 1952-1954

TB	KO	WD	WF	D	LD	LF	KO BY	ND	NC
25	13	8	0	0	2	1	1	0	0

Carter, James
Lightweight Champion 1951-1952; 1952-1954; 1954-1955

TB	KO	WD	WF	D	LD	LF	KO BY	ND	NC
120	31	50	0	9	27	0	3	0	0

Castellini, Miguel
Junior Middleweight Champion 1976-1977

TB	KO	WD	WF	D	LD	LF	KO BY	ND	NC
93	49	24	0	12	2	0	6	0	0

Castillo, Jesus (Chucho)
Bantamweight Champion 1970-1971

TB	KO	WD	WF	D	LD	LF	KO BY	ND	NC
65	22	22	2	2	10	0	7	0	0

Castillo, Freddy
Junior Flyweight Champion (WBC) 1978

TB	KO	WD	WF	D	LD	LF	KO BY	ND	NC
45	21	10	1	3	6	1	3	0	0

Caunt, Ben
Heavyweight Champion 1840-1841; 1841-1845
Record Not Available

Cerdan, Marcel
Middleweight Champion 1948-1949

TB	KO	WD	WF	D	LD	LF	KO BY	ND	NC
123	74	45	0	0	1	2	1	0	0

Cervantes, Antonio
Junior Welterweight Champion (WBA) 1972-1976;
1977-1980

TB	KO	WD	WF	D	LD	LF	KO BY	ND	NC
97	41	43	0	3	8	0	2	0	0

Chacon, Bobby
Featherweight Champion (WBC) 1974-1975

TB	KO	WD	WF	D	LD	LF	KO BY	ND	NC
49	36	7	0	1	2	0	3	0	0

Chandler, Jeff
Bantamweight Champion 1980-Present

TB	KO	WD	WF	D	LD	LF	KO BY	ND	NC
25	12	12	0	1	0	0	0	0	0

Charles, Ezzard
Heavyweight Champion (NBA) 1949
Heavyweight Champion 1950-1951

TB	KO	WD	WF	D	LD	LF	KO BY	ND	NC
122	58	38	0	1	17	1	7	0	0

Chartvanchai, Berkerk
Flyweight Champion (WBA) 1970

TB	KO	WD	WF	D	LD	LF	KO BY	ND	NC
38	6	22	0	3	30	4	0	0	

Chionoi, Chartchai (Laemfapha)
Flyweight Champion 1966-1969; 1970
Flyweight Champion (WBA) 1973-1974

TB	KO	WD	WF	D	LD	LF	KO BY	ND	NC
82	36	23	0	3	15	0	5	0	0

Chip, George
Middleweight Champion 1913-1914

TB	KO	WD	WF	D	LD	LF	KO BY	ND	NC
155	34	3	1	3	10	3	3	97	1

Chocolate, Kid
Featherweight Champion (NY) 1932
Junior Lightweight Champion 1931-1933

TB	KO	WD	WF	D	LD	LF	KO BY	ND	NC
161	64	81	0	6	8	0	2	0	0

Christoforidis, Anton
Light Heavyweight Champion (NBA) 1941

TB	KO	WD	WF	D	LD	LF	KO BY	ND	NC
75	14	37	1	8	12	0	3	0	0

Clabby, Jimmy
Welterweight Champion 1910-1911

TB	KO	WD	WF	D	LD	LF	KO BY	ND	NC
155	40	37	2	20	16	1	4	34	1

Cochrane, Freddie (Red)
Welterweight Champion 1941-1946

TB	KO	WD	WF	D	LD	LF	KO BY	ND	NC
117	27	46	0	9	30	0	5	0	0

Cohen, Robert
Bantamweight Champion 1954-1956

TB	KO	WD	WF	D	LD	LF	KO BY	ND	NC
43	14	22	0	3	2	0	2	0	0

Cokes, Curtis
Welterweight Champion 1966-1969

TB	KO	WD	WF	D	LD	LF	KO BY	ND	NC
80	30	32	0	4	11	0	3	0	0

Conley, Frankie
Bantamweight Champion (Calif.) 1910-1911

TB	KO	WD	WF	D	LD	LF	KO BY	ND	NC
81	15	22	0	10	7	0	4	21	2

Conn, Billy
Light Heavyweight Champion (NY) 1939-1940

TB	KO	WD	WF	D	LD	LF	KO BY	ND	NC
74	14	49	0	1	8	0	2	0	0

Conteh, John
Light Heavyweight Champion (WBC)   1974-1977

TB	KO	WD	WF	D	LD	LF	KO BY	ND	NC
39	24	10	0	1	3	0	1	0	0

Corbett, James J.
Heavyweight Champion   1892-1897

TB	KO	WD	WF	D	LD	LF	KO BY	ND	NC
19	7	4	0	2	0	1	3	0	2

Corbett, Young II
Featherweight Champion   1901-1902

TB	KO	WD	WF	D	LD	LF	KO BY	ND	NC
104	34	19	0	12	6	0	8	25	0

Corbett, Young III
Welterweight Champion   1933-1933

TB	KO	WD	WF	D	LD	LF	KO BY	ND	NC
142	31	87	1	13	7	0	3	0	0

Corcoran, Peter
Heavyweight Champion   1771-1776
Record Not Available

Corro, Hugo
Middleweight Champion   1978-1979

TB	KO	WD	WF	D	LD	LF	KO BY	ND	NC
51	23	23	1	1	2	0	1	0	0

Cotton, Eddie
Light Heavyweight Champion (Mich.)   1963-1964

TB	KO	WD	WF	D	LD	LF	KO BY	ND	NC
83	34	23	1	2	19	0	4	0	0

Coulon, Johnny
Bantamweight Champion   1910-1914

TB	KO	WD	WF	D	LD	LF	KO BY	ND	NC
97	24	32	0	4	2	0	2	32	1

Crawley, Peter
Heavyweight Champion   1827
Record Not Available

Cribb, Tom
Heavyweight Champion   1808-1822
Record Not Available

Criqui, Eugene
Featherweight Champion   1923

TB	KO	WD	WF	D	LD	LF	KO BY	ND	NC
115	40	54	0	8	11	0	2	0	0

Cruz, Carlos Teo
Lightweight Champion   1968-1969

TB	KO	WD	WF	D	LD	LF	KO BY	ND	NC
57	13	28	0	2	11	1	2	0	0

Cruz, Roberto
Junior Welterweight Champion (WBA)   1963

TB	KO	WD	WF	D	LD	LF	KO BY	ND	NC
25	5	11	0	2	6	0	1	0	0

Cuello, Miguel Angel
Light Heavyweight Champion (WBC)   1977-1978

TB	KO	WD	WF	D	LD	LF	KO BY	ND	NC
22	20	1	0	0	0	0	1	0	0

Cuevas, Jose (Pipino)
Welterweight Champion (WBA)   1976-Present

TB	KO	WD	WF	D	LD	LF	KO BY	ND	NC
33	24	3	0	0	5	0	1	0	0

Dade, Harold
Bantamweight Champion   1947

TB	KO	WD	WF	D	LD	LF	KO BY	ND	NC
77	9	32	0	6	23	2	5	0	0

D'Agata, Mario
Bantamweight Champion   1956-1957

TB	KO	WD	WF	D	LD	LF	KO BY	ND	NC
67	23	27	4	3	8	1	1	0	0

Dagge, Eckhard
Junior Middleweight Champion (WBC)   1976-1977

TB	KO	WD	WF	D	LD	LF	KO BY	ND	NC
28	15	8	0	1	2	0	2	0	0

Darcy, Les
Middleweight Champion (Australia)   1915-1917

TB	KO	WD	WF	D	LD	LF	KO BY	ND	NC
50	29	16	1	0	2	2	0	0	0

Darts, William
Heavyweight Champion   1766-1769; 1769-1771
Record Not Available

DeJesus, Esteban
Lightweight Champion (WBC)   1976-1978

TB	KO	WD	WF	D	LD	LF	KO BY	ND	NC
62	32	25	0	0	2	0	3	0	0

Delaney, Jack
Light Heavyweight Champion   1926-1927

TB	KO	WD	WF	D	LD	LF	KO BY	ND	NC
86	42	27	1	3	7	0	3	2	1

DeMarco, Paddy
Lightweight Champion   1954

TB	KO	WD	WF	D	LD	LF	KO BY	ND	NC
104	8	67	0	3	19	0	7	0	0

DeMarco, Tony
Welterweight Champion   1955

TB	KO	WD	WF	D	LD	LF	KO BY	ND	NC
71	33	25	0	1	5	0	7	0	0

Dempsey, Jack
Heavyweight Champion   1919-1926

TB	KO	WD	WF	D	LD	LF	KO BY	ND	NC
80	49	10	1	7	6	0	1	5	1

Dempsey, Nonpareil Jack
Middleweight Champion   1884-1891

TB	KO	WD	WF	D	LD	LF	KO BY	ND	NC
68	25	23	0	7	0	0	3	7	3

DeOliveira, Miguel
Junior Middleweight Champion (WBC)   1975

TB	KO	WD	WF	D	LD	LF	KO BY	ND	NC
49	26	16	0	1	4	0	2	0	0

Dillon Jack
Light Heavyweight Champion   1916

TB	KO	WD	WF	D	LD	LF	KO BY	ND	NC
240	60	32	0	14	6	0	0	127	1

Dixie Kid, The
Welterweight Champion   1904

TB	KO	WD	WF	D	LD	LF	KO BY	ND	NC
126	63	13	2	6	13	2	3	23	1

Dixon, George
Bantamweight Champion   1890
Featherweight Champion   1891-1897; 1898-1900

TB	KO	WD	WF	D	LD	LF	KO BY	ND	NC
149	30	47	1	37	21	1	3	9	0

Downes, Terry
Middleweight Champion   1961-1962

TB	KO	WD	WF	D	LD	LF	KO BY	ND	NC
43	27	7	0	0	2	1	6	0	0

Downey, William Bryan
Middleweight Champion (Ohio)   1921

TB	KO	WD	WF	D	LD	LF	KO BY	ND	NC
119	18	19	0	14	9	1	0	57	1

Duane, Carl
Junior Featherweight Champion   1923

TB	KO	WD	WF	D	LD	LF	KO BY	ND	NC
63	14	28	1	5	10	1	1	3	0

Duffy, Paddy
Welterweight Champion   1888-1890

TB	KO	WD	WF	D	LD	LF	KO BY	ND	NC
36	14	9	1	11	0	0	1	0	0

Dundee, Joe
Welterweight Champion   1927-1929

TB	KO	WD	WF	D	LD	LF	KO BY	ND	NC
122	23	61	1	11	13	2	5	4	2

Dundee, Johnny
Featherweight Champion   1923-1924
Junior Lightweight Champion   1921-1923; 1923-1924

TB	KO	WD	WF	D	LD	LF	KO BY	ND	NC
322	19	93	1	18	29	0	2	160	0

Dundee, Vince
Middleweight Champion (NY)   1933-1934

TB	KO	WD	WF	D	LD	LF	KO BY	ND	NC
150	27	85	0	13	18	0	1	5	1

Dupas, Ralph
Junior Middleweight Champion   1963

TB	KO	WD	WF	D	LD	LF	KO BY	ND	NC
134	19	85	1	6	15	1	7	0	0

Duran, Jose
Junior Welterweight Champion (WBA)   1976

TB	KO	WD	WF	D	LD	LF	KO BY	ND	NC
78	23	38	2	9	4	0	2	0	0

Duran, Roberto
Lightweight Champion   1972-1979

TB	KO	WD	WF	D	LD	LF	KO BY	ND	NC
73	55	16	0	0	1	0	1	0	0

Ebihara, Hiroyuki
Flyweight Champion   1963-1964
Flyweight Champion (WBA)   1969

TB	KO	WD	WF	D	LD	LF	KO BY	ND	NC
69	34	29	0	1	5	0	0	0	0

Ellis, Jimmy
Heavyweight Champion (WBA)   1968-1970

TB	KO	WD	WF	D	LD	LF	KO BY	ND	NC
53	24	16	0	1	8	0	4	0	0

Elorde, Flash
Junior Lightweight Champion   1961-1964

TB	KO	WD	WF	D	LD	LF	KO BY	ND	NC
109	29	52	1	2	21	0	4	0	0

Erne, Frank
Lightweight Champion   1899-1902

TB	KO	WD	WF	D	LD	LF	KO BY	ND	NC
40	10	11	1	12	2	0	4	0	0

Ertle, Johnny (Kewpie)
Bantamweight Champion (claimant)   1915

TB	KO	WD	WF	D	LD	LF	KO BY	ND	NC
79	14	4	2	3	8	0	3	45	0

Escalera, Alfredo
Junior Lightweight Champion (WBC)   1975-1978

TB	KO	WD	WF	D	LD	LF	KO BY	ND	NC
54	26	14	1	3	7	0	3	0	0

Escober, Sixto
Bantamweight Champion (NBA)   1934-1935
Bantamweight Champion   1936-1937; 1938-1939

TB	KO	WD	WF	D	LD	LF	KO BY	ND	NC
64	21	21	0	4	18	0	0	0	0

Espada, Angel
Welterweight Champion (WBA)   1975-1976

TB	KO	WD	WF	D	LD	LF	KO BY	ND	NC
56	26	15	1	3	7	0	4	0	0

Espadas, Guty
Flyweight Champion (WBA)   1976-1978

TB	KO	WD	WF	D	LD	LF	KO BY	ND	NC
42	25	8	0	5	3	0	1	0	0

Espana, Ernesto
Lightweight Champion (WBA)   1979-1980

TB	KO	WD	WF	D	LD	LF	KO BY	ND	NC
29	23	3	0	0	1	0	2	0	0

Estaba, Luis
Junior Flyweight Champion (WBC)   1975-1978

TB	KO	WD	WF	D	LD	LF	KO BY	ND	NC
48	27	14	0	2	3	0	2	0	0

Famechon, Johnny
Featherweight Champion   1969-1970

TB	KO	WD	WF	D	LD	LF	KO BY	ND	NC
67	20	35	1	6	5	0	0	0	0

Fearns, Duggan
Heavyweight Champion   1780
Record Not Available

Fernandez, Perico
Junior Welterweight Champion (WBC)   1974-1975

TB	KO	WD	WF	D	LD	LF	KO BY	ND	NC
73	35	15	4	10	5	1	2	0	1

Ferns, Jim (Rube)
Welterweight Champion   1900; 1901

TB	KO	WD	WF	D	LD	LF	KO BY	ND	NC
53	31	9	1	1	8	0	3	0	0

Fields, Jackie
Welterweight Champion (NBA)   1929
Welterweight Champion   1929-1930; 1932-1933

TB	KO	WD	WF	D	LD	LF	KO BY	ND	NC
85	28	42	1	2	8	0	1	2	1

Figg, James
Heavyweight Champion   1719-1734
Record Not Available

Fitzsimmons, Bob
Middleweight Champion   1894-1897
Heavyweight Champion   1897-1899
Light Heavyweight Champion   1903-1905

TB	KO	WD	WF	D	LD	LF	KO BY	ND	NC
62	32	8	0	0	2	1	8	10	1

Flowers, Tiger
Middleweight Champion   1926

TB	KO	WD	WF	D	LD	LF	KO BY	ND	NC
149	49	61	5	6	3	2	8	14	1

Forbes, Harry
Bantamweight Champion   1901-1903

TB	KO	WD	WF	D	LD	LF	KO BY	ND	NC
130	30	47	3	23	4	0	11	12	0

Foreman, George
Heavyweight Champion   1973-1974

TB	KO	WD	WF	D	LD	LF	KO BY	ND	NC
47	42	3	0	0	1	0	1	0	0

Foster, Bob
Light Heavyweight Champion   1968-1974

TB	KO	WD	WF	D	LD	LF	KO BY	ND	NC
65	46	10	0	1	2	0	6	0	0

Frazer, Alfonso (Peppermint)
Junior Welterweight Champion   1972

TB	KO	WD	WF	D	LD	LF	KO BY	ND	NC
54	23	13	0	2	6	0	10	0	0

Frazier, Joe
Heavyweight Champion   1970-1973

TB	KO	WD	WF	D	LD	LF	KO BY	ND	NC
36	27	5	0	0	1	0	3	0	0

Freeman, Tommy
Welterweight Champion   1930-1931

TB	KO	WD	WF	D	LD	LF	KO BY	ND	NC
185	70	75	0	16	13	0	3	8	0

Fujii, Paul Takeshi
Junior Welterweight Champion 1967-1968

TB	KO	WD	WF	D	LD	LF	KO BY	ND	NC
36	27	5	0	1	1	0	2	0	0

Fullmer, Gene
Middleweight Champion 1957
Middleweight Champion (NBA) 1959-1962

TB	KO	WD	WF	D	LD	LF	KO BY	ND	NC
64	24	31	0	3	4	0	2	0	0

Galindez, Victor
Light Heavyweight Champion (WBA) 1974-1978; 1979

TB	KO	WD	WF	D	LD	LF	KO BY	ND	NC
70	34	21	0	4	7	0	2	0	2

Gans, Joe
Lightweight Champion 1902-1908

TB	KO	WD	WF	D	LD	LF	KO BY	ND	NC
156	55	60	5	10	3	0	5	18	0

Garcia, Ceferino
Middleweight Champion 1939-1940

TB	KO	WD	WF	D	LD	LF	KO BY	ND	NC
122	62	26	0	9	19	1	5	0	0

Gardner, George
Light Heavyweight Champion 1903

TB	KO	WD	WF	D	LD	LF	KO BY	ND	NC
65	19	20	2	10	5	1	5	2	1

Gardner, Jimmy
Welterweight Champion (claimant) 1908

TB	KO	WD	WF	D	LD	LF	KO BY	ND	NC
100	27	24	0	22	5	0	1	21	0

Gavilan, Kid
Welterweight Champion 1951-1955

TB	KO	WD	WF	D	LD	LF	KO BY	ND	NC
143	27	79	0	6	30	0	0	0	1

Gazo, Eddie
Junior Middleweight Champion 1977-1978

TB	KO	WD	WF	D	LD	LF	KO BY	ND	NC
48	21	18	0	2	3	0	4	0	0

Genaro, Frankie
Flyweight Champion (NBA) 1928-1929; 1929-1931

TB	KO	WD	WF	D	LD	LF	KO BY	ND	NC
129	19	59	5	9	16	2	4	15	0

Giardello, Joey
Middleweight Champion 1963-1965

TB	KO	WD	WF	D	LD	LF	KO BY	ND	NC
133	32	68	0	7	21	0	4	1	0

Glover, Mike
Welterweight Champion 1915

TB	KO	WD	WF	D	LD	LF	KO BY	ND	NC
95	18	12	1	4	4	0	0	56	0

Godwin, Bob
Light Heavyweight Champion (NBA) 1933

TB	KO	WD	WF	D	LD	LF	KO BY	ND	NC
130	44	51	0	16	6	0	10	3	0

Goldstein, Abe
Bantamweight Champion 1924

TB	KO	WD	WF	D	LD	LF	KO BY	ND	NC
130	30	55	0	5	10	0	4	26	0

Gomes, Harold
Junior Lightweight Champion (NBA) 1959-1960

TB	KO	WD	WF	D	LD	LF	KO BY	ND	NC
60	24	26	0	0	3	0	7	0	0

Gomez, Antonio
Featherweight Champion (WBA) 1971-1972

TB	KO	WD	WF	D	LD	LF	KO BY	ND	NC
46	19	21	0	1	3	0	2	0	0

Gomez, Wilfredo
Junior Featherweight Champion (WBC) 1977-Present

TB	KO	WD	WF	D	LD	LF	KO BY	ND	NC
32	31	0	0	1	0	0	0	0	0

Gonzalez, Betulio
Flyweight Champion (WBC) 1972; 1973-1974
Flyweight Champion (WBA) 1978-1979

TB	KO	WD	WF	D	LD	LF	KO BY	ND	NC
78	42	25	0	3	6	0	2	0	0

Gonzalez, Rodolfo
Lightweight Champion (WBC) 1972-1974

TB	KO	WD	WF	D	LD	LF	KO BY	ND	NC
66	43	13	1	1	4	0	4	0	0

Goodrich, Jimmy
Lightweight Champion 1925

TB	KO	WD	WF	D	LD	LF	KO BY	ND	NC
114	6	38	2	15	33	0	1	19	0

Goss, Joe
Heavyweight Champion 1876-1880
Record Not Available

Graham, Bushy
Bantamweight Champion (NY) 1928-1929

TB	KO	WD	WF	D	LD	LF	KO BY	ND	NC
128	37	63	1	6	12	1	2	6	0

Graves, Kid
Welterweight Champion (claimant) 1914

TB	KO	WD	WF	D	LD	LF	KO BY	ND	NC
157	35	24	3	28	3	1	1	62	0

Graziano, Rocky
Middleweight Champion 1947-1948

TB	KO	WD	WF	D	LD	LF	KO BY	ND	NC
83	52	14	1	6	7	0	3	0	0

Greb, Harry
Middleweight Champion 1923-1926

TB	KO	WD	WF	D	LD	LF	KO BY	ND	NC
294	47	64	1	3	5	1	2	170	1

Griffith, Emile
Welterweight Champion 1961; 1962-1963; 1963-1966
Middleweight Champion 1966-1967; 1967-1968

TB	KO	WD	WF	D	LD	LF	KO BY	ND	NC
112	23	62	0	2	21	1	2	0	0

Gully, John
Heavyweight Champion 1807-1808
Record Not Available

Gushiken, Yoko
Junior Flyweight Champion (WBA) 1976-1981

TB	KO	WD	WF	D	LD	LF	KO BY	ND	NC
23	15	8	0	0	0	0	0	0	0

Guzman, Juan Jose
Junior Flyweight Champion (WBA) 1976

TB	KO	WD	WF	D	LD	LF	KO BY	ND	NC
52	15	12	0	1	13	0	11	0	0

Hagler, Marvin
Middleweight Champion 1980-Present

TB	KO	WD	WF	D	LD	LF	KO BY	ND	NC
54	41	8	1	2	2	0	0	0	0

Halimi, Alphonse
Bantamweight Champion 1957-1959

TB	KO	WD	WF	D	LD	LF	KO BY	ND	NC
50	21	19	1	1	5	0	3	0	0

Hanagata, Susumu
Flyweight Champion (WBA) 1974-1975

TB	KO	WD	WF	D	LD	LF	KO BY	ND	NC
58	8	27	0	7	14	0	2	0	0

Harada, Masahiko (Fighting)

Flyweight Champion 1962-1963
Bantamweight Champion 1965-1968

TB	KO	WD	WF	D	LD	LF	KO BY	ND	NC
62	22	33	0	0	5	0	2	0	0

Harris, Harry

Bantamweight Champion 1901

TB	KO	WD	WF	D	LD	LF	KO BY	ND	NC
54	15	24	1	7	2	0	0	5	0

Hart, Marvin

Heavyweight Champion 1905-1906

TB	KO	WD	WF	D	LD	LF	KO BY	ND	NC
47	19	4	5	4	3	0	4	8	0

Harvey, Len

Light Heavyweight Champion (GB) 1939-1942

TB	KO	WD	WF	D	LD	LF	KO BY	ND	NC
133	51	54	6	9	11	0	2	0	0

Hearns, Thomas

Welterweight Champion (WBA) 1980-Present

TB	KO	WD	WF	D	LD	LF	KO BY	ND	NC
30	28	2	0	0	0	0	0	0	0

Herman, Pete

Bantamweight Champion 1917-1920; 1921

TB	KO	WD	WF	D	LD	LF	KO BY	ND	NC
149	19	50	0	8	1	9	1	61	0

Hernandez, Carlos

Junior Welterweight Champion 1965-1966

TB	KO	WD	WF	D	LD	LF	KO BY	ND	NC
71	39	17	0	4	6	0	5	0	0

Herrera, Rafael

Bantamweight Champion 1972
Bantamweight Champion (WBC) 1973-1974

TB	KO	WD	WF	D	LD	LF	KO BY	ND	NC
66	22	29	0	4	8	0	3	0	0

Heuser, Adolf

Light Heavyweight Champion (IBU) 1938

TB	KO	WD	WF	D	LD	LF	KO BY	ND	NC
125	43	43	0	16	7	1	13	0	2

Hill, Johnny

Flyweight Champion (GB) 1928-1929

TB	KO	WD	WF	D	LD	LF	KO BY	ND	NC
23	8	8	2	3	0	0	1	0	1

Holberg, Waldemar

Welterweight Champion 1914
Record Not Available

Holmes, Larry

Heavyweight Champion (WBC) 1978-Present

TB	KO	WD	WF	D	LD	LF	KO BY	ND	NC
36	27	9	0	0	0	0	0	0	0

Hong, Soo-Hwan

Bantamweight Champion 1974-1975
Junior Featherweight Champion (WBA) 1977-1978

TB	KO	WD	WF	D	LD	LF	KO BY	ND	NC
48	13	26	0	4	2	0	3	0	0

Hope, Maurice

Junior Middleweight Champion (WBC) 1979-Present

TB	KO	WD	WF	D	LD	LF	KO BY	ND	NC
32	23	6	0	1	1	0	1	0	0

Hostak, Al

Middleweight Champion (NBA) 1938; 1939-1940

TB	KO	WD	WF	D	LD	LF	KO BY	ND	NC
83	47	21	0	6	6	0	3	0	0

Ibarra, Luis

Flyweight Champion (WBA) 1979-1980

TB	KO	WD	WF	D	LD	LF	KO BY	ND	NC
23	8	12	1	0	1	0	1	0	0

Jack, Beau

Lightweight Champion (NY) 1942-1943; 1943-1944

TB	KO	WD	WF	D	LD	LF	KO BY	ND	NC
111	40	43	0	5	20	0	3	0	0

Jackling, Tom

Heavyweight Champion 1784-1791
Record Not Available

Jackson, John

Heavyweight Champion 1795
Record Not Available

Jadick, Johnny

Junior Welterweight Champion 1932-1933

TB	KO	WD	WF	D	LD	LF	KO BY	ND	NC
134	9	63	1	8	44	0	7	2	0

Jeby, Ben

Middleweight Champion (NY) 1932-1933

TB	KO	WD	WF	D	LD	LF	KO BY	ND	NC
73	22	32	0	4	12	0	2	0	1

Jeffra, Harry

Featherweight Champion 1937-1938; 1940-1941

TB	KO	WD	WF	D	LD	LF	KO BY	ND	NC
120	27	65	0	7	18	0	2	0	1

Jeffries, James J.

Heavyweight Champion 1899-1904

TB	KO	WD	WF	D	LD	LF	KO BY	ND	NC
21	15	3	0	2	0	0	1	0	0

Jenkins, Lew

Lightweight Champion 1940-1941

TB	KO	WD	WF	D	LD	LF	KO BY	ND	NC
109	47	18	0	5	27	0	12	0	0

Jofre, Eder

Bantamweight Champion (NBA) 1960
Bantamweight Champion 1961-1965
Featherweight Champion 1973-1974

TB	KO	WD	WF	D	LD	LF	KO BY	ND	NC
75	48	21	0	4	2	0	0	0	0

Johansson, Ingemar

Heavyweight Champion 1959-1960

TB	KO	WD	WF	D	LD	LF	KO BY	ND	NC
28	17	8	1	0	0	0	2	0	0

Johnson, Harold

Light Heavyweight Champion (NBA) 1961
Light Heavyweight Champion 1962-1963

TB	KO	WD	WF	D	LD	LF	KO BY	ND	NC
87	32	44	0	0	6	0	5	0	0

Johnson, Jack

Heavyweight Champion 1908-1915

TB	KO	WD	WF	D	LD	LF	KO BY	ND	NC
113	46	29	4	12	2	1	5	14	0

Johnson, Marvin

Light Heavyweight Champion (WBC) 1978-1979
Light Heavyweight Champion (WBA) 1979-1980

TB	KO	WD	WF	D	LD	LF	KO BY	ND	NC
29	19	6	0	0	1	0	3	0	0

Jones, Gorilla

Middleweight Champion 1931-1932
Middleweight Champion (NBA) 1933-1934

TB	KO	WD	WF	D	LD	LF	KO BY	ND	NC
141	53	44	0	13	21	2	0	5	3

Jones, Percy

Flyweight Champion (GB) 1914

TB	KO	WD	WF	D	LD	LF	KO BY	ND	NC
47	25	16	1	2	1	0	2	0	0

Jordan, Don

Welterweight Champion 1958-1960

TB	KO	WD	WF	D	LD	LF	KO BY	ND	NC
75	17	33	0	1	20	0	3	1	0

Jordon, Ben

Featherweight Champion (GB) 1898-1899

TB	KO	WD	WF	D	LD	LF	KO BY	ND	NC
36	22	10	0	1	0	0	2	1	0

Juchau, Tom

Heavyweight Champion 1765-1766
Record Not Available

Kalule, Ayub

Junior Middleweight Champion (WBA) 1979-Present

TB	KO	WD	WF	D	LD	LF	KO BY	ND	NC
35	18	17	0	0	0	0	0	0	0

Kane, Peter

Flyweight Champion 1938-1943

TB	KO	WD	WF	D	LD	LF	KO BY	ND	NC
95	51	33	1	2	3	0	4	0	1

Kansas, Rocky

Lightweight Champion 1925-1926

TB	KO	WD	WF	D	LD	LF	KO BY	ND	NC
164	32	32	0	7	8	2	2	81	0

Kaplan, Louis (Kid)

Featherweight Champion 1925-1927

TB	KO	WD	WF	D	LD	LF	KO BY	ND	NC
132	17	85	0	10	9	1	3	7	0

Kelly, Tommy (Spider)

Bantamweight Champion 1887; 1889; 1890-1892

TB	KO	WD	WF	D	LD	LF	KO BY	ND	NC
44	11	19	0	4	5	0	4	1	0

Kenty, Hilmer

Lightweight Champion (WBA) 1980-1981

TB	KO	WD	WF	D	LD	LF	KO BY	ND	NC
20	14	6	0	0	0	0	0	0	0

Ketchel, Stanley

Middleweight Champion 1907-1908; 1908-1910

TB	KO	WD	WF	D	LD	LF	KO BY	ND	NC
66	50	3	0	5	2	0	2	4	0

Kilbane, Johnny

Featherweight Champion 1912-1923

TB	KO	WD	WF	D	LD	LF	KO BY	ND	NC
140	21	25	1	8	2	0	2	80	1

Kim, Ki-Soo

Junior Middleweight Champion 1966-1968

TB	KO	WD	WF	D	LD	LF	KO BY	ND	NC
36	18	14	0	2	2	0	0	0	0

Kim, Sang-Hyun

Junior Welterweight Champion (WBC) 1978-1980

TB	KO	WD	WF	D	LD	LF	KO BY	ND	NC
36	19	11	1	2	2	0	1	0	0

Kim, Sung-Jun

Junior Flyweight Champion (WBC) 1978-1980

TB	KO	WD	WF	D	LD	LF	KO BY	ND	NC
41	11	15	0	6	9	0	0	0	0

Kim, Tae-Shik

Flyweight Champion (WBA) 1980

TB	KO	WD	WF	D	LD	LF	KO BY	ND	NC
16	11	3	0	0	1	0	1	0	0

King, Mick

Middleweight Champion (Australia) 1914
Record Not Available

King, Tom

Heavyweight Champion 1863
Record Not Available

Kingpetch, Pone

Flyweight Champion 1960-1962; 1963; 1964-1965

TB	KO	WD	WF	D	LD	LF	KO BY	ND	NC
40	11	20	1	0	5	0	3	0	0

Klaus, Frank

Middleweight Champion 1913

TB	KO	WD	WF	D	LD	LF	KO BY	ND	NC
90	27	20	4	2	2	0	2	33	0

Klick, Frankie

Junior Lightweight Champion 1933-1934

TB	KO	WD	WF	D	LD	LF	KO BY	ND	NC
118	24	54	1	12	22	0	4	0	1

Kobayashi, Hiroshi

Junior Lightweight Champion 1967-1971

TB	KO	WD	WF	D	LD	LF	KO BY	ND	NC
72	10	49	0	4	6	0	3	0	0

Kobayashi, Royal

Junior Featherweight Champion (WBC) 1976

TB	KO	WD	WF	D	LD	LF	KO BY	ND	NC
37	23	8	0	0	3	0	3	0	0

Kotey, David (Poison)

Featherweight Champion (WBC) 1975-1976

TB	KO	WD	WF	D	LD	LF	KO BY	ND	NC
44	23	15	0	1	4	0	1	0	0

Krieger, Solly

Middleweight Champion (NBA) 1938-1939

TB	KO	WD	WF	D	LD	LF	KO BY	ND	NC
111	53	27	0	7	21	0	3	0	0

Kudo, Masashi

Junior Middleweight Champion 1978-1979

TB	KO	WD	WF	D	LD	LF	KO BY	ND	NC
24	16	7	0	0	1	0	0	0	0

La Barba, Fidel

Flyweight Champion 1927

TB	KO	WD	WF	D	LD	LF	KO BY	ND	NC
97	15	57	0	8	15	0	0	2	0

La Blanche, George

Middleweight Champion (claimant) 1889

TB	KO	WD	WF	D	LD	LF	KO BY	ND	NC
69	17	18	0	6	10	2	14	1	1

Ladbury, Bill

Flyweight Champion (GB) 1913-1914

TB	KO	WD	WF	D	LD	LF	KO BY	ND	NC
50	10	20	0	5	5	0	10	0	0

Laguna, Ismael

Lightweight Champion 1965; 1970

TB	KO	WD	WF	D	LD	LF	KO BY	ND	NC
74	36	28	0	1	9	0	0	0	0

La Morte, Willie

Flyweight Champion (claimant) 1929

TB	KO	WD	WF	D	LD	LF	KO BY	ND	NC
56	13	23	0	6	6	0	2	6	0

LaMotta, Jake

Middleweight Champion 1949-1951

TB	KO	WD	WF	D	LD	LF	KO BY	ND	NC
106	30	53	0	4	15	0	4	0	0

Lane, Kenny

Lightweight Champion (Michigan) 1963-1964

TB	KO	WD	WF	D	LD	LF	KO BY	ND	NC
94	16	61	0	2	10	0	5	0	0

Larkin, Tippy

Junior Welterweight Champion 1946

TB	KO	WD	WF	D	LD	LF	KO BY	ND	NC
151	57	79	0	1	3	0	10	0	0

Lastra, Cecilio

Featherweight Champion (WBA) 1977-1978

TB	KO	WD	WF	D	LD	LF	KO BY	ND	NC
48	24	14	0	2	3	0	5	0	0

Latzo, Pete
Welterweight Champion 1926-1927

TB	KO	WD	WF	D	LD	LF	KO BY	ND	NC
151	25	35	4	3	29	0	2	52	1

Lavigne, George (Kid)
Lightweight Champion 1896-1899

TB	KO	WD	WF	D	LD	LF	KO BY	ND	NC
56	16	19	0	8	4	0	2	7	0

Ledoux, Charles
Bantamweight Champion (GB) 1912-1913

TB	KO	WD	WF	D	LD	LF	KO BY	ND	NC
133	79	14	3	4	19	0	3	11	0

Legra, Jose
Featherweight Champion (WBC) 1968-1969
Featherweight Champion 1972-1973

TB	KO	WD	WF	D	LD	LF	KO BY	ND	NC
153	50	87	0	4	9	0	3	0	0

Lemos, Richie
Featherweight Champion (NBA) 1941

TB	KO	WD	WF	D	LD	LF	KO BY	ND	NC
77	26	25	0	3	20	0	3	0	0

Leonard, Benny
Lightweight Champion 1917-1924

TB	KO	WD	WF	D	LD	LF	KO BY	ND	NC
210	71	18	0	1	0	1	4	115	0

Leonard, Sugar Ray
Welterweight Champion 1979-Present

TB	KO	WD	WF	D	LD	LF	KO BY	ND	NC
26	17	9	0	0	0	0	0	0	0

Lesnevich, Gus
Light Heavyweight Champion 1948-1950

TB	KO	WD	WF	D	LD	LF	KO BY	ND	NC
76	21	36	0	5	9	0	5	0	0

Levinsky, Battling
Light Heavyweight Champion 1916-1920

TB	KO	WD	WF	D	LD	LF	KO BY	ND	NC
274	23	42	1	13	13	2	4	176	0

Lewis, Harry
Welterweight Champion (Claimant) 1908-1911

TB	KO	WD	WF	D	LD	LF	KO BY	ND	NC
163	42	37	1	11	12	3	1	56	0

Lewis, Hedgemon
Welterweight Champion (NY) 1972-1973

TB	KO	WD	WF	D	LD	LF	KO BY	ND	NC
63	26	27	0	3	3	0	4	0	0

Lewis, John Henry
Light Heavyweight Champion 1935-1939

TB	KO	WD	WF	D	LD	LF	KO BY	ND	NC
105	54	38	0	5	7	0	1	0	0

Lewis, Ted (Kid)
Welterweight Champion 1915-1916; 1917-1919

TB	KO	WD	WF	D	LD	LF	KO BY	ND	NC
254	68	86	2	9	13	7	4	65	0

Limon, Rafael (Bazooka)
Junior Lightweight Champion (WBC) 1980-1981

TB	KO	WD	WF	D	LD	LF	KO BY	ND	NC
56	32	12	0	2	5	1	4	0	0

Liston, Sonny
Heavyweight Champion 1962-1964

TB	KO	WD	WF	D	LD	LF	KO BY	ND	NC
54	39	11	0	0	1	0	3	0	0

Little, Fred
Junior Middleweight Champion 1969-1970

TB	KO	WD	WF	D	LD	LF	KO BY	ND	NC
57	32	18	0	0	4	1	1	0	1

Loche, Nicolino
Junior Welterweight Champion 1969-1972

TB	KO	WD	WF	D	LD	LF	KO BY	ND	NC
136	14	104	0	14	3	0	1	0	0

Loi, Duilio
Junior Welterweight Champion 1960-1962

TB	KO	WD	WF	D	LD	LF	KO BY	ND	NC
126	25	90	1	7	3	0	0	0	0

Lopez, Alfonso
Flyweight Champion (WBA) 1976

TB	KO	WD	WF	D	LD	LF	KO BY	ND	NC
36	15	11	0	0	4	0	6	0	0

Lopez, Danny (Little Red)
Featherweight Champion (WBC) 1976-1980

TB	KO	WD	WF	D	LD	LF	KO BY	ND	NC
47	39	2	1	0	1	0	4	0	0

Lopopolo, Sandro
Junior Welterweight Champion 1966-1967

TB	KO	WD	WF	D	LD	LF	KO BY	ND	NC
76	20	36	2	7	8	0	2	0	1

Loughran, Tommy
Light Heavyweight Champion 1927-1929

TB	KO	WD	WF	D	LD	LF	KO BY	ND	NC
172	18	77	1	8	21	0	2	45	0

Louis, Joe
Heavyweight Champion 1937-1949

TB	KO	WD	WF	D	LD	LF	KO BY	ND	NC
71	54	13	1	0	1	0	2	0	0

Lujan, Jorge
Bantamweight Champion (WBA) 1977-Present

TB	KO	WD	WF	D	LD	LF	KO BY	ND	NC
25	14	8	0	0	3	0	0	0	0

Lynch, Benny
Flyweight Champion 1937-1938

TB	KO	WD	WF	D	LD	LF	KO BY	ND	NC
73	28	29	1	9	4	1	1	0	0

Lynch, Joe
Bantamweight Champion 1920-1921; 1922-1924

TB	KO	WD	WF	D	LD	LF	KO BY	ND	NC
133	29	13	0	15	13	0	0	63	0

Mace, Jem
Heavyweight Champion 1866-1871
Record Not Available

Macias, Raul (Raton)
Bantamweight Champion (NBA) 1955-1957

TB	KO	WD	WF	D	LD	LF	KO BY	ND	NC
38	22	14	0	0	1	0	1	0	0

Mamby, Saoul
Junior Welterweight Champion (WBC) 1980-Present

TB	KO	WD	WF	D	LD	LF	KO BY	ND	NC
46	14	15	0	5	12	0	0	0	0

Mandell, Sammy
Lightweight Champion 1926-1930

TB	KO	WD	WF	D	LD	LF	KO BY	ND	NC
168	28	53	1	8	11	1	5	61	1

Mantell, Frank
Middleweight Champion (Calif.) 1912

TB	KO	WD	WF	D	LD	LF	KO BY	ND	NC
101	23	14	1	18	13	1	5	25	1

Marcano, Alfredo
Junior Lightweight Champion 1971-1972

TB	KO	WD	WF	D	LD	LF	KO BY	ND	NC
62	29	14	0	5	8	0	5	0	1

450

Marcel, Ernesto

Featherweight Champion (WBA) 1972-1974

TB	KO	WD	WF	D	LD	LF	KO BY	ND	NC
47	24	17	0	2	3	0	1	0	0

Marciano, Rocky

Heavyweight Champion 1952-1956

TB	KO	WD	WF	D	LD	LF	KO BY	ND	NC
49	43	6	0	0	0	0	0	0	0

Marino, Salvador (Dado)

Flyweight Champion 1950-1952

TB	KO	WD	WF	D	LD	LF	KO BY	ND	NC
74	21	35	1	3	11	0	3	0	0

Marino, Tony

Bantamweight Champion 1936

TB	KO	WD	WF	D	LD	LF	KO BY	ND	NC
41	7	20	0	2	10	0	2	0	0

Martin, Eddie (Cannonball)

Bantamweight Champion 1924-1925

TB	KO	WD	WF	D	LD	LF	KO BY	ND	NC
90	27	45	0	3	8	0	3	3	1

Martinez, Rodolfo

Featherweight Champion (WBC) 1974-1976

TB	KO	WD	WF	D	LD	LF	KO BY	ND	NC
52	35	9	0	1	3	0	4	0	0

Mathebula, Peter

Flyweight Champion (WBA) 1980-1981

TB	KO	WD	WF	D	LD	LF	KO BY	ND	NC
36	15	16	0	0	3	0	2	0	0

Matthews, William R. (Matty)

Welterweight Champion 1900-1901

TB	KO	WD	WF	D	LD	LF	KO BY	ND	NC
85	15	31	2	17	9	1	3	7	0

Mattioli, Rocky

Junior Middleweight Champion 1977-1979

TB	KO	WD	WF	D	LD	LF	KO BY	ND	NC
66	45	13	0	2	3	0	3	0	0

Maxim, Joey

Light Heavyweight Champion 1950-1952

TB	KO	WD	WF	D	LD	LF	KO BY	ND	NC
115	21	61	0	4	27	1	1	0	0

Mazzinghi, Sandro

Junior Middleweight Champion 1963-1965; 1968

TB	KO	WD	WF	D	LD	LF	KO BY	ND	NC
69	42	21	1	0	2	0	1	0	2

McCormick, Tom

Welterweight Champion 1914

TB	KO	WD	WF	D	LD	LF	KO BY	ND	NC
40	17	11	3	2	4	0	3	0	0

McCoy, Al

Middleweight Champion 1914-1917

TB	KO	WD	WF	D	LD	LF	KO BY	ND	NC
144	28	22	0	7	3	0	2	82	0

McCoy, Johnny

Flyweight Champion (Calif.) 1927-1928
Record Not Available

McCoy, Kid

Middleweight Champion 1897

TB	KO	WD	WF	D	LD	LF	KO BY	ND	NC
105	55	24	2	6	2	0	4	9	3

McGovern, Terry

Bantamweight Champion 1899
Featherweight Champion 1900-1901

TB	KO	WD	WF	D	LD	LF	KO BY	ND	NC
77	34	24	1	4	1	1	2	10	0

McGowan, Walter

Flyweight Champion 1966

TB	KO	WD	WF	D	LD	LF	KO BY	ND	NC
40	14	18	0	1	3	0	4	0	0

McLarnin, Jimmy

Welterweight Champion 1933-1934; 1934-1935

TB	KO	WD	WF	D	LD	LF	KO BY	ND	NC
77	20	42	1	3	10	0	1	0	0

McTigue, Mike

Light Heavyweight Champion 1923-1925

TB	KO	WD	WF	D	LD	LF	KO BY	ND	NC
146	57	24	0	6	11	2	10	36	0

Meggs, George

Heavyweight Champion 1761-1762
Record Not Available

Mellody, Billy (Honey)

Welterweight Champion 1906-1907

TB	KO	WD	WF	D	LD	LF	KO BY	ND	NC
95	36	20	0	13	6	1	6	13	0

Mendoza, Daniel

Heavyweight Champion 1794-1795
Record Not Available

Miller, Freddie

Featherweight Champion (NBA) 1933
Featherweight Champion 1934-1936

TB	KO	WD	WF	D	LD	LF	KO BY	ND	NC
244	45	160	3	5	23	2	1	4	1

Mills, Freddie

Light Heavyweight Champion 1948-1950

TB	KO	WD	WF	D	LD	LF	KO BY	ND	NC
96	52	21	0	6	11	0	6	0	0

Millsom, George

Heavyweight Champion 1762-1765
Record Not Available

Minter, Alan

Middleweight Champion 1980

TB	KO	WD	WF	D	LD	LF	KO BY	ND	NC
36	18	12	0	0	0	0	5	0	1

Monaghan, Rinty

Flyweight Champion 1948-1950

TB	KO	WD	WF	D	LD	LF	KO BY	ND	NC
51	19	22	1	1	6	1	1	0	0

Montana, Small

Flyweight Champion (Calif.) 1935-1937

TB	KO	WD	WF	D	LD	LF	KO BY	ND	NC
111	10	70	0	6	20	0	1	21	1

Montgomery, Bob

Lightweight Champion (NY) 1943; 1944-1947

TB	KO	WD	WF	D	LD	LF	KO BY	ND	NC
97	37	38	0	3	16	0	3	0	0

Monzon, Carlos

Middleweight Champion 1970-1977

TB	KO	WD	WF	D	LD	LF	KO BY	ND	NC
102	61	28	0	9	3	0	0	1	0

Moore, Archie

Light Heavyweight Champion 1952-1962

TB	KO	WD	WF	D	LD	LF	KO BY	ND	NC
231	143	53	0	8	16	2	8	0	1

Moore, Davey

Featherweight Champion 1959-1963

TB	KO	WD	WF	D	LD	LF	KO BY	ND	NC
67	30	28	1	1	5	0	2	0	0

Moran, Chappie

Bantamweight Champion 1889-1890

TB	KO	WD	WF	D	LD	LF	KO BY	ND	NC
9	1	5	0	0	2	0	1	0	0

Morgan, Tod
Junior Lightweight Champion 1925-1929

TB	KO	WD	WF	D	LD	LF	KO BY	ND	NC
203	27	98	4	30	32	1	4	6	1

Moyer, Dennis
Junior Middleweight Champion 1962-1963

TB	KO	WD	WF	D	LD	LF	KO BY	ND	NC
140	25	73	0	4	30	0	7	0	1

Muangsurin, Saensak
Junior Welterweight Champion (WBC) 1975-1976; 1976-1978

TB	KO	WD	WF	D	LD	LF	KO BY	ND	NC
19	11	3	0	0	2	1	2	0	0

Muhammad, Eddie Mustafa (A/K/A Eddie Gregory)
Light Heavyweight Champion (WBA) 1980-Present

TB	KO	WD	WF	D	LD	LF	KO BY	ND	NC
43	32	6	0	1	4	0	0	0	0

Muhammad, Matthew Saad (A/K/A Matthew Franklin)
Light Heavyweight Champion (WBC) 1979-Present

TB	KO	WD	WF	D	LD	LF	KO BY	ND	NC
33	20	8	0	2	3	0	0	0	0

Murphy, Kid
Bantamweight Champion (claimant) 1907-1908

TB	KO	WD	WF	D	LD	LF	KO BY	ND	NC
70	24	14	0	10	4	1	3	14	0

Murphy, (Torpedo) Billy
Featherweight Champion 1890

TB	KO	WD	WF	D	LD	LF	KO BY	ND	NC
87	17	32	0	14	14	0	7	1	2

Nakajima, Shigeo
Junior Flyweight Champion (WBC) 1980

TB	KO	WD	WF	D	LD	LF	KO BY	ND	NC
18	7	6	0	1	2	0	2	0	0

Napoles, Jose
Welterweight Champion 1969-1970; 1971-1975

TB	KO	WD	WF	D	LD	LF	KO BY	ND	NC
84	54	21	1	0	4	0	4	0	0

Neil, Frankie
Bantamweight Champion 1903-1904

TB	KO	WD	WF	D	LD	LF	KO BY	ND	NC
56	24	1	1	4	9	0	4	13	0

Nelson, Battling
Lightweight Champion 1908-1910

TB	KO	WD	WF	D	LD	LF	KO BY	ND	NC
132	38	20	1	19	15	2	2	35	0

Nichols, George
Light Heavyweight Champion (NBA) 1932

TB	KO	WD	WF	D	LD	LF	KO BY	ND	NC
108	24	47	0	10	17	0	9	1	0

Norton, Ken
Heavyweight Champion (WBC) 1978

TB	KO	WD	WF	D	LD	LF	KO BY	ND	NC
49	33	9	0	1	3	0	3	0	0

Numata, Yoshiaki
Junior Lightweight Champion 1967
Junior Lightweight Champion (WBC) 1970-1971

TB	KO	WD	WF	D	LD	LF	KO BY	ND	NC
55	14	30	0	3	2	0	6	0	0

Obed, Elisha
Junior Middleweight Champion (WBC) 1976-1978

TB	KO	WD	WF	D	LD	LF	KO BY	ND	NC
97	56	24	0	4	6	0	5	0	2

O'Brien, (Philadelphia) Jack
Light Heavyweight Champion 1905-1912

TB	KO	WD	WF	D	LD	LF	KO BY	ND	NC
181	36	59	6	16	3	0	4	57	0

O'Dowd, Mike
Middleweight Champion 1917-1920

TB	KO	WD	WF	D	LD	LF	KO BY	ND	NC
115	35	16	1	3	7	0	1	52	0

Oguma, Shoji
Flyweight Champion (WBC) 1974-1975

TB	KO	WD	WF	D	LD	LF	KO BY	ND	NC
44	20	15	0	1	6	0	2	0	0

Ohba, Masao
Flyweight Champion (WBA) 1970-1973

TB	KO	WD	WF	D	LD	LF	KO BY	ND	NC
38	15	20	0	1	2	0	0	0	0

O'Leary, Artie
Lightweight Champion 1917-1919
Record Not Available

Olin, Bob
Light Heavyweight Champion 1934-1935

TB	KO	WD	WF	D	LD	LF	KO BY	ND	NC
85	25	27	1	5	23	0	4	0	0

Olivares, Ruben
Bantamweight Champion 1969-1970; 1971-1972
Featherweight Champion (WBA) 1974
Featherweight Champion (WBC) 1975

TB	KO	WD	WF	D	LD	LF	KO BY	ND	NC
100	77	9	1	2	3	0	8	0	0

Olson, Carl (Bobo)
Middleweight Champion 1953-1955

TB	KO	WD	WF	D	LD	LF	KO BY	ND	NC
109	42	49	0	2	9	0	7	0	0

Ortega, Rafael
Featherweight Champion (WBA) 1977

TB	KO	WD	WF	D	LD	LF	KO BY	ND	NC
26	6	13	0	4	3	0	0	0	0

Ortiz, Carlos
Junior Welterweight Champion 1959-1960
Lightweight Champion 1962-1965; 1965-1968

TB	KO	WD	WF	D	LD	LF	KO BY	ND	NC
70	30	31	0	1	6	0	1	0	1

Ortiz, Manuel
Bantamweight Champion 1942-1947; 1947-1950

TB	KO	WD	WF	D	LD	LF	KO BY	ND	NC
128	49	48	0	3	27	0	1	0	0

Overlin, Ken
Middleweight Champion (NY) 1940-1941

TB	KO	WD	WF	D	LD	LF	KO BY	ND	NC
148	23	104	0	7	12	0	1	0	1

Owen, Tom
Heavyweight Champion 1796-1797
Record Not Available

Pace, Georgie
Bantamweight Champion (NBA) 1940

TB	KO	WD	WF	D	LD	LF	KO BY	ND	NC
42	15	18	0	2	5	0	1	1	0

Paddock, Tom
Heavyweight Champion 1856-1858
Record Not Available

Palma, Sergio
Junior Featherweight Champion (WBA) 1980

TB	KO	WD	WF	D	LD	LF	KO BY	ND	NC
47	15	24	1	4	1	2	0	0	0

Palmer, Thomas (Pedlar)
Bantamweight Champion (GB) 1895-1899

TB	KO	WD	WF	D	LD	LF	KO BY	ND	NC
64	5	37	3	4	10	0	5	0	0

Palomino, Carlos

Welterweight Champion 1976-1979

TB	KO	WD	WF	D	LD	LF	KO BY	ND	NC
33	15	12	0	3	3	0	0	0	0

Papke, Billy

Middleweight Champion 1908; 1912-1913

TB	KO	WD	WF	D	LD	LF	KO BY	ND	NC
64	29	9	1	7	6	2	1	9	0

Paret, Benny (Kid)

Welterweight Champion 1960-1961; 1961-1962

TB	KO	WD	WF	D	LD	LF	KO BY	ND	NC
50	10	25	0	3	8	0	4	0	0

Park, Chan-Hee

Flyweight Champion (WBC) 1979-Present

TB	KO	WD	WF	D	LD	LF	KO BY	ND	NC
19	6	9	0	2	1	0	1	0	0

Parlov, Mate

Light Heavyweight Champion (WBC) 1978

TB	KO	WD	WF	D	LD	LF	KO BY	ND	NC
29	12	12	0	2	2	0	1	0	0

Pastrano, Willie

Light Heavyweight Champion 1963-1965

TB	KO	WD	WF	D	LD	LF	KO BY	ND	NC
84	14	49	0	8	11	0	2	0	0

Paterson, Jackie

Flyweight Champion 1943-1948

TB	KO	WD	WF	D	LD	LF	KO BY	ND	NC
91	41	21	1	3	14	1	10	0	0

Patterson, Floyd

Heavyweight Champion 1956-1959; 1960-1962

TB	KO	WD	WF	D	LD	LF	KO BY	ND	NC
64	40	15	0	1	3	0	5	0	0

Paul, Tommy

Featherweight Champion (NBA) 1932-1933

TB	KO	WD	WF	D	LD	LF	KO BY	ND	NC
114	28	48	2	10	20	3	2	1	0

Pearce, Henry

Heavyweight Champion 1803-1806
Record Not Available

Pedroza, Eusebio

Featherweight Champion (WBA) 1978-Present

TB	KO	WD	WF	D	LD	LF	KO BY	ND	NC
31	19	9	1	0	0	0	3	0	0

Pender, Paul

Middleweight Champion 1960-1961; 1962

TB	KO	WD	WF	D	LD	LF	KO BY	ND	NC
48	20	19	1	2	3	0	3	0	0

Pep, Willie

Featherweight Champion 1942-1948; 1949-1950

TB	KO	WD	WF	D	LD	LF	KO BY	ND	NC
241	65	164	0	1	5	0	6	0	0

Perez, Pascual

Flyweight Champion 1954-1960

TB	KO	WD	WF	D	LD	LF	KO BY	ND	NC
91	56	27	0	1	4	0	3	0	0

Perez, Victor (Young)

Flyweight Champion (IBU) 1931-1932

TB	KO	WD	WF	D	LD	LF	KO BY	ND	NC
131	26	62	1	16	19	0	7	0	0

Perkins, Eddie

Junior Welterweight Champion 1962; 1963-1965

TB	KO	WD	WF	D	LD	LF	KO BY	ND	NC
97	21	52	0	3	19	0	1	1	0

Perry, William

Heavyweight Champion 1850 1851
Record Not Available

Pinder, Enrique

Bantamweight Champion 1972-1973

TB	KO	WD	WF	D	LD	LF	KO BY	ND	NC
43	14	22	0	2	1	0	4	0	0

Pintor, Lupe

Bantamweight Champion 1979-Present

TB	KO	WD	WF	D	LD	LF	KO BY	ND	NC
50	35	9	0	1	3	1	1	0	0

Pladner, Emile (Spider)

Flyweight Champion 1929

TB	KO	WD	WF	D	LD	LF	KO BY	ND	NC
122	34	61	1	10	11	2	3	0	0

Plimmer, Billy

Bantamweight Champion (GB) 1892-1895

TB	KO	WD	WF	D	LD	LF	KO BY	ND	NC
46	15	18	0	5	1	1	3	3	0

Pryor, Aaron

Junior Welterweight Champion 1980-Present

TB	KO	WD	WF	D	LD	LF	KO BY	ND	NC
26	24	2	0	0	0	0	0	0	0

Ramos, Armando (Mando)

Lightweight Champion 1969-1970
Lightweight Champion (WBC) 1972

TB	KO	WD	WF	D	LD	LF	KO BY	ND	NC
49	23	14	0	1	4	1	6	0	0

Ramos, Ultiminio (Sugar)

Featherweight Champion 1963-1964

TB	KO	WD	WF	D	LD	LF	KO BY	ND	NC
65	39	14	1	4	2	1	4	0	0

Randolph, Leo

Junior Featherweight Champion (WBA) 1980

TB	KO	WD	WF	D	LD	LF	KO BY	ND	NC
19	9	8	0	1	0	0	1	0	0

Riasco, Rigoberto

Junior Featherweight Champion (WBC) 1976

TB	KO	WD	WF	D	LD	LF	KO BY	ND	NC
45	15	16	0	4	7	0	3	0	0

Rios, Jaime

Junior Flyweight Champion (WBA) 1975-1976

TB	KO	WD	WF	D	LD	LF	KO BY	ND	NC
25	10	10	0	1	3	0	1	0	0

Risko, Eddie (Babe)

Middleweight Champion (NY) 1935

TB	KO	WD	WF	D	LD	LF	KO BY	ND	NC
66	12	26	0	7	10	1	10	0	0

Ritchie, Willie

Lightweight Champion 1912-1914

TB	KO	WD	WF	D	LD	LF	KO BY	ND	NC
71	8	27	1	4	8	0	1	22	0

Robinson, Ray (Sugar)

Welterweight Champion 1946-1951
Middleweight Champion 1951; 1951-1952; 1955-1957; 1957-1958; 1958-1960

TB	KO	WD	WF	D	LD	LF	KO BY	ND	NC
201	109	65	0	6	18	0	1	1	1

Rodak, Leo

Featherweight Champion (NBA) 1938-1939

TB	KO	WD	WF	D	LD	LF	KO BY	ND	NC
117	6	74	0	10	22	0	5	0	0

Rodriguez, Luis

Welterweight Champion 1963-1964

TB	KO	WD	WF	D	LD	LF	KO BY	ND	NC
121	49	57	1	0	10	0	3	0	1

Rojas, Raul

Featherweight Champion (WBA) 1968

TB	KO	WD	WF	D	LD	LF	KO BY	ND	NC
46	24	14	0	2	4	0	2	0	0

Rondon, Vicente
Light Heavyweight Champion (WBA) 1971-1972

TB	KO	WD	WF	D	LD	LF	KO BY	ND	NC
55	22	16	0	1	8	0	7	0	1

Root, Jack
Light Heavyweight Champion 1903

TB	KO	WD	WF	D	LD	LF	KO BY	ND	NC
53	24	17	3	5	0	0	3	1	0

Rose, Lionel
Bantamweight Champion 1968-1969

TB	KO	WD	WF	D	LD	LF	KO BY	ND	NC
53	12	30	0	0	6	0	5	0	0

Rosenberg, Charley Phil
Bantamweight Champion 1925-1927

TB	KO	WD	WF	D	LD	LF	KO BY	ND	NC
65	7	28	1	6	15	1	0	7	0

Rosenberg, Dave
Middleweight Champion (NY) 1922

TB	KO	WD	WF	D	LD	LF	KO BY	ND	NC
65	10	26	0	5	8	3	0	13	0

Rosenbloom, Maxie
Light Heavyweight Champion 1930-1934

TB	KO	WD	WF	D	LD	LF	KO BY	ND	NC
289	18	187	5	23	33	0	2	19	2

Ross, Barney
Lightweight Champion 1933
Junior Welterweight Champion 1933
Welterweight Champion 1934; 1935-1938

TB	KO	WD	WF	D	LD	LF	KO BY	ND	NC
82	24	50	0	3	4	0	0	1	0

Rossman, Mike
Light Heavyweight Champion (WBA) 1978-1979

TB	KO	WD	WF	D	LD	LF	KO BY	ND	NC
48	24	15	0	3	3	0	3	0	0

Roth, Gustave
Light Heavyweight Champion (IBU) 1936-1938

TB	KO	WD	WF	D	LD	LF	KO BY	ND	NC
136	25	86	1	12	7	2	2	0	1

Routis, Andre
Featherweight Champion 1928-1929

TB	KO	WD	WF	D	LD	LF	KO BY	ND	NC
86	10	33	11	7	17	6	2	0	0

Ryan, Paddy
Heavyweight Champion 1880-1882
Record Not Available

Ryan, Tommy
Welterweight Champion 1894-1896
Middleweight Champion 1898-1907

TB	KO	WD	WF	D	LD	LF	KO BY	ND	NC
109	68	17	1	5	1	1	1	9	6

Saddler, Sandy
Featherweight Champion 1948-1949; 1950-1957

TB	KO	WD	WF	D	LD	LF	KO BY	ND	NC
162	103	41	0	2	14	1	1	0	0

Saijyo, Shozo
Featherweight Champion (WBA) 1968-1971

TB	KO	WD	WF	D	LD	LF	KO BY	ND	NC
38	8	21	0	2	6	0	1	0	0

Salas, Lauro
Lightweight Champion 1952

TB	KO	WD	WF	D	LD	LF	KO BY	ND	NC
148	39	44	0	12	44	1	7	1	0

Saldivar, Vicente
Featherweight Champion 1964-1967; 1970

TB	KO	WD	WF	D	LD	LF	KO BY	ND	NC
39	25	10	1	0	0	1	2	0	0

Salica, Lou
Bantamweight Champion (NBA) 1935
Bantamweight Champion 1941-1942

TB	KO	WD	WF	D	LD	LF	KO BY	ND	NC
90	13	49	0	11	16	0	1	0	0

Salvarria, Erbito
Flyweight Champion 1970-1973
Flyweight Champion (WBA) 1975-1976

TB	KO	WD	WF	D	LD	LF	KO BY	ND	NC
53	11	28	0	3	8	0	3	0	0

Sanchez, Clemente
Featherweight Champion 1972-1975

TB	KO	WD	WF	D	LD	LF	KO BY	ND	NC
58	30	14	1	3	9	0	1	0	0

Sanchez, Salvador
Featherweight Champion 1980-Present

TB	KO	WD	WF	D	LD	LF	KO BY	ND	NC
40	29	9	0	1	1	0	0	0	0

Sangchilli, Baltazar
Bantamweight Champion 1935-1936

TB	KO	WD	WF	D	LD	LF	KO BY	ND	NC
77	24	33	2	5	11	1	1	0	0

Santry, Eddie
Featherweight Champion (GB) 1899-1900

TB	KO	WD	WF	D	LD	LF	KO BY	ND	NC
78	33	15	2	15	4	0	9	0	0

Sarron, Petey
Featherweight Champion 1936-1937

TB	KO	WD	WF	D	LD	LF	KO BY	ND	NC
103	18	56	1	8	15	3	1	1	0

Saxton, Johnny
Welterweight Champion 1954-1955; 1956

TB	KO	WD	WF	D	LD	LF	KO BY	ND	NC
66	21	33	1	2	4	0	5	0	0

Sayers, Tom
Heavyweight Champion 1858-1860
Record Not Available

Scalzo, Pete
Featherweight Champion (NBA) 1940-1941

TB	KO	WD	WF	D	LD	LF	KO BY	ND	NC
111	46	44	0	5	12	0	3	1	0

Schmeling, Max
Heavyweight Champion 1930-1932

TB	KO	WD	WF	D	LD	LF	KO BY	ND	NC
70	38	15	3	4	5	0	5	0	0

Schwartz, Corporal Izzy
Flyweight Champion 1928-1929

TB	KO	WD	WF	D	LD	LF	KO BY	ND	NC
117	7	51	1	12	27	0	1	18	0

Sellers, Harry
Heavyweight Champion 1776-1780
Record Not Available

Serrano, Samuel
Junior Lightweight Champion 1976-Present

TB	KO	WD	WF	D	LD	LF	KO BY	ND	NC
43	15	23	0	1	3	0	2	0	0

Servo, Marty
Welterweight Champion 1946

TB	KO	WD	WF	D	LD	LF	KO BY	ND	NC
56	15	34	0	2	2	0	2	1	0

Sharkey, Jack
Heavyweight Champion 1932-1933

TB	KO	WD	WF	D	LD	LF	KO BY	ND	NC
55	15	20	3	3	8	1	4	1	0

Shaw, Battling

Junior Welterweight Champion 1933

TB	KO	WD	WF	D	LD	LF	KO BY	ND	NC
23	4	9	0	0	7	0	3	0	0

Shibata, Kuniaki

Featherweight Champion 1970-1972
Junior Lightweight Champion 1973
Junior Lightweight Champion (WBC) 1974-1975

TB	KO	WD	WF	D	LD	LF	KO BY	ND	NC
56	24	21	0	4	1	0	6	0	0

Shipes, Charlie

Welterweight Champion (Calif.) 1966-1967

TB	KO	WD	WF	D	LD	LF	KO BY	ND	NC
51	22	20	0	3	2	1	3	0	0

Shirai, Yoshio

Flyweight Champion 1952-1954

TB	KO	WD	WF	D	LD	LF	KO BY	ND	NC
56	20	25	1	2	4	1	3	0	0

Siki, Battling

Light Heavyweight Champion 1922-1923

TB	KO	WD	WF	D	LD	LF	KO BY	ND	NC
88	34	27	0	4	13	3	1	5	1

Singer, Al

Lightweight Champion 1930

TB	KO	WD	WF	D	LD	LF	KO BY	ND	NC
70	24	34	2	2	4	0	4	0	0

Slack, Jack

Heavyweight Champion 1750-1760
Record Not Available

Slattery, Jimmy

Light Heavyweight Champion (NBA) 1927
Light Heavyweight Champion 1930

TB	KO	WD	WF	D	LD	LF	KO BY	ND	NC
128	45	62	2	1	9	0	5	2	2

Smith, Jeff

Middleweight Champion (Australia) 1914; 1914-1915

TB	KO	WD	WF	D	LD	LF	KO BY	ND	NC
178	46	51	2	3	8	1	1	65	1

Smith, Mysterious Billy

Welterweight Champion 1892-1894; 1898-1900

TB	KO	WD	WF	D	LD	LF	KO BY	ND	NC
82	13	15	0	29	4	11	4	6	0

Smith, Sid

Flyweight Champion (GB) 1913

TB	KO	WD	WF	D	LD	LF	KO BY	ND	NC
99	10	65	1	5	8	0	9	1	0

Smith, Solly

Featherweight Champion 1897-1898

TB	KO	WD	WF	D	LD	LF	KO BY	ND	NC
45	6	13	1	17	3	2	1	2	0

Smith, Wallace (Bud)

Lightweight Champion 1955-1956

TB	KO	WD	WF	D	LD	LF	KO BY	ND	NC
60	18	13	0	6	16	0	7	0	0

Smith, Willie

Bantamweight Champion (GB) 1927-1928

TB	KO	WD	WF	D	LD	LF	KO BY	ND	NC
55	5	33	1	3	8	0	5	0	0

Solis, Julian

Bantamweight Champion 1980

TB	KO	WD	WF	D	LD	LF	KO BY	ND	NC
20	8	11	0	0	0	0	1	0	0

Soose, Billy

Middleweight Champion (NY) 1941

TB	KO	WD	WF	D	LD	LF	KO BY	ND	NC
41	13	21	0	1	6	0	0	0	0

Spinks, Leon

Heavyweight Champion 1978

TB	KO	WD	WF	D	LD	LF	KO BY	ND	NC
14	8	2	0	2	1	0	1	0	0

Spring, Tom

Heavyweight Champion 1823-1824
Record Not Available

Stanley, George (Digger)

Bantamweight Champion (GB) 1910-1912

TB	KO	WD	WF	D	LD	LF	KO BY	ND	NC
81	13	38	0	7	11	7	3	2	0

Steele, Freddie

Middleweight Champion (NY) 1936
Middleweight Champion (NBA) 1937

TB	KO	WD	WF	D	LD	LF	KO BY	ND	NC
139	62	62	0	8	2	0	4	0	1

Stevens, William

Heavyweight Champion 1760-1761
Record Not Available

Stracey, John H.

Welterweight Champion 1975-1976

TB	KO	WD	WF	D	LD	LF	KO BY	ND	NC
51	37	6	2	1	1	1	3	0	0

Sullivan, Dave

Featherweight Champion 1897-1898

TB	KO	WD	WF	D	LD	LF	KO BY	ND	NC
58	10	16	2	16	7	3	2	2	0

Sullivan, John L.

Heavyweight Champion 1882-1892

TB	KO	WD	WF	D	LD	LF	KO BY	ND	NC
46	33	8	0	3	0	0	1	1	0

Sullivan, Mike (Twin)

Welterweight Champion 1907-1908

TB	KO	WD	WF	D	LD	LF	KO BY	ND	NC
69	18	17	0	14	3	0	4	13	0

Sullivan, Steve (Kid)

Junior Lightweight Champion 1924-1925

TB	KO	WD	WF	D	LD	LF	KO BY	ND	NC
54	21	24	0	0	7	0	2	0	0

Suzuki, Yuji (Ishimatsu)

Lightweight Champion (WBC) 1974-1976

TB	KO	WD	WF	D	LD	LF	KO BY	ND	NC
48	16	12	0	6	9	0	5	0	0

Symonds, Joe

Flyweight Champion (GB) 1914-1916

TB	KO	WD	WF	D	LD	LF	KO BY	ND	NC
133	45	44	7	11	8	6	11	1	0

Tate, John

Heavyweight Champion (WBA) 1979-1980

TB	KO	WD	WF	D	LD	LF	KO BY	ND	NC
22	15	4	1	0	0	0	2	0	0

Taylor, Arnold

Bantamweight Champion 1973-1974

TB	KO	WD	WF	D	LD	LF	KO BY	ND	NC
49	17	21	2	1	5	0	3	0	0

Taylor, Charles (Bud)

Bantamweight Champion (NBA) 1927

TB	KO	WD	WF	D	LD	LF	KO BY	ND	NC
157	35	34	1	6	16	3	4	58	0

Taylor, George

Heavyweight Champion 1735-1738
Record Not Available

Terranova, Phil
Featherweight Champion (NBA)   1943-1944

TB	KO	WD	WF	D	LD	LF	KO BY	ND	NC
99	29	38	0	11	18	0	3	0	0

Terrell, Ernest
Heavyweight Champion (WBA)   1965-1967

TB	KO	WD	WF	D	LD	LF	KO BY	ND	NC
54	21	24	0	0	7	0	2	0	0

Thil, Marcel
Middleweight Champion   1932-1937

TB	KO	WD	WF	D	LD	LF	KO BY	ND	NC
96	34	40	4	4	12	0	2	0	0

Thompson, Young Jack
Welterweight Champion   1930; 1931

TB	KO	WD	WF	D	LD	LF	KO BY	ND	NC
74	33	16	0	6	18	1	0	0	0

Thompson, Cyclone Johnny
Middleweight Champion   1911-1914

TB	KO	WD	WF	D	LD	LF	KO BY	ND	NC
139	47	34	3	20	18	5	1	11	0

Thompson, William (Bendigo)
Heavyweight Champion   1839-1840; 1845-1850
Record Not Available

Tiger, Dick
Middleweight Champion (NBA)   1962-1963
Middleweight Champion   1965-1966
Light Heavyweight Champion   1966-1968

TB	KO	WD	WF	D	LD	LF	KO BY	ND	NC
81	26	35	0	3	16	0	1	0	0

Torres, Alcaran (Efren)
Flyweight Champion   1969-1970

TB	KO	WD	WF	D	LD	LF	KO BY	ND	NC
58	31	17	0	1	6	0	3	0	0

Torres, Jose
Light Heavyweight Champion   1965-1966

TB	KO	WD	WF	D	LD	LF	KO BY	ND	NC
45	29	12	0	1	2	0	1	0	0

Toweel, Vic
Bantamweight Champion   1950-1952

TB	KO	WD	WF	D	LD	LF	KO BY	ND	NC
32	14	13	1	1	1	0	2	0	0

Tunney, Gene
Heavyweight Champion   1926-1928

TB	KO	WD	WF	D	LD	LF	KO BY	ND	NC
77	42	14	1	1	1	0	0	17	1

Turpin, Randy
Middleweight Champion   1951

TB	KO	WD	WF	D	LD	LF	KO BY	ND	NC
75	45	17	4	1	3	0	5	0	0

Udella, Franco
Junior Flyweight Champion (WBC)   1975

TB	KO	WD	WF	D	LD	LF	KO BY	ND	NC
43	18	18	1	0	1	1	3	0	1

Uehara, Yasutsune
Junior Lightweight Champion   1980-1981

TB	KO	WD	WF	D	LD	LF	KO BY	ND	NC
31	21	6	0	0	3	0	1	0	0

Valdez, Rodrigo
Middleweight Champion (WBC)   1974-1976

TB	KO	WD	WF	D	LD	LF	KO BY	ND	NC
73	41	22	0	2	7	0	1	0	0

Velasquez, Miguel
Junior Middleweight Champion   1976

TB	KO	WD	WF	D	LD	LF	KO BY	ND	NC
73	33	30	3	2	2	0	1	0	0

Villa, Pancho
Flyweight Champion   1923-1925

TB	KO	WD	WF	D	LD	LF	KO BY	ND	NC
103	22	49	0	4	4	1	0	23	0

Villacampo, Bernabe
Flyweight Champion (WBA)   1969-1970

TB	KO	WD	WF	D	LD	LF	KO BY	ND	NC
42	13	9	1	2	12	0	5	0	0

Villaflor, Ben
Junior Lightweight Champion   1972-1973

TB	KO	WD	WF	D	LD	LF	KO BY	ND	NC
44	20	15	0	5	4	0	0	0	0

Vorasingh, Netrnoi Sor
Junior Flyweight Champion (WBC)   1978

TB	KO	WD	WF	D	LD	LF	KO BY	ND	NC
19	8	6	0	2	1	0	2	0	0

Wajima, Koichi
Junior Middleweight Champion (WBA)   1971-1974; 1975-1976

TB	KO	WD	WF	D	LD	LF	KO BY	ND	NC
38	25	6	0	1	1	0	5	0	0

Walcott, Joe (Barbados)
Welterweight Champion   1901-1904; 1906

TB	KO	WD	WF	D	LD	LF	KO BY	ND	NC
150	34	45	2	30	17	3	4	15	0

Walcott, (Jersey) Joe
Heavyweight Champion   1951-1952

TB	KO	WD	WF	D	LD	LF	KO BY	ND	NC
67	30	18	1	1	11	0	6	0	0

Walker, Mickey
Welterweight Champion   1922-1926
Middleweight Champion   1926-1931

TB	KO	WD	WF	D	LD	LF	KO BY	ND	NC
162	60	33	0	4	11	3	5	45	1

Walsh, Jimmy
Bantamweight Champion   1905-1906

TB	KO	WD	WF	D	LD	LF	KO BY	ND	NC
119	12	39	1	18	7	0	1	41	0

Ward, Jem
Heavyweight Champion   1825-1827; 1828-1832
Record Not Available

Ward, Nick
Heavyweight Champion   1841
Record Not Available

Watt, Jim
Junior Welterweight Champion   1979-Present

TB	KO	WD	WF	D	LD	LF	KO BY	ND	NC
45	28	11	0	0	4	0	2	0	0

Weaver, Mike
Heavyweight Champion (WBA)   1980-Present

TB	KO	WD	WF	D	LD	LF	KO BY	ND	NC
32	16	7	0	0	4	0	5	0	0

Wells, Matt
Welterweight Champion   1914-1915

TB	KO	WD	WF	D	LD	LF	KO BY	ND	NC
77	6	21	1	2	14	2	2	28	1

Welsh, Freddie
Lightweight Champion   1914-1917

TB	KO	WD	WF	D	LD	LF	KO BY	ND	NC
167	24	50	3	7	3	0	1	79	0

Wilde, Jimmy
Flyweight Champion   1916-1923

TB	KO	WD	WF	D	LD	LF	KO BY	ND	NC
140	77	48	1	2	1	0	3	8	0

Willard, Jess
Heavyweight Champion 1915-1919

TB	KO	WD	WF	D	LD	LF	KO BY	ND	NC
35	20	3	0	1	2	1	3	5	0

Williams, Ike
Lightweight Champion (NBA) 1945-1947
Lightweight Champion 1947-1951

TB	KO	WD	WF	D	LD	LF	KO BY	ND	NC
153	60	64	0	5	18	0	6	0	0

Williams, Kid
Bantamweight Champion 1914-1917

TB	KO	WD	WF	D	LD	LF	KO BY	ND	NC
204	48	53	6	8	8	5	3	73	0

Wilson, Jackie
Featherweight Champion (NBA) 1941-1943

TB	KO	WD	WF	D	LD	LF	KO BY	ND	NC
122	17	55	2	5	34	1	6	1	1

Wilson, Johnny
Middleweight Champion 1920-1923

TB	KO	WD	WF	D	LD	LF	KO BY	ND	NC
123	44	20	1	2	17	2	2	34	1

Winstone, Howard
Featherweight Champion (GB) 1968

TB	KO	WD	WF	D	LD	LF	KO BY	ND	NC
67	27	33	1	0	3	0	3	0	0

Wolfe, Jack (Kid)
Junior Featherweight Champion 1922-1923

TB	KO	WD	WF	D	LD	LF	KO BY	ND	NC
128	16	23	4	11	7	0	3	64	0

Wolgast, Ad
Lightweight Champion 1910-1912

TB	KO	WD	WF	D	LD	LF	KO BY	ND	NC
135	38	21	1	14	6	4	2	49	0

Wolgast, Midget
Flyweight Champion (NY) 1930-1935

TB	KO	WD	WF	D	LD	LF	KO BY	ND	NC
147	11	85	0	15	29	0	6	1	0

Wright, Chalky
Featherweight Champion 1941-1942

TB	KO	WD	WF	D	LD	LF	KO BY	ND	NC
198	73	70	0	15	32	0	7	0	1

Yarosz, Teddy
Middleweight Champion (NY) 1934-1935

TB	KO	WD	WF	D	LD	LF	KO BY	ND	NC
127	16	90	0	3	17	0	1	0	0

Yuh, Jae-Do
Junior Middleweight Champion 1975-1976

TB	KO	WD	WF	D	LD	LF	KO BY	ND	NC
44	24	15	0	2	0	0	3	0	0

Yum, Dong-Kyun
Junior Featherweight Champion (WBC) 1976-1977

TB	KO	WD	WF	D	LD	LF	KO BY	ND	NC
43	14	23	0	2	2	0	2	0	0

Zale, Tony
Middleweight Champion (NBA) 1940-1941
Middleweight Champion 1941-1947; 1948

TB	KO	WD	WF	D	LD	LF	KO BY	ND	NC
88	46	24	0	2	12	0	4	0	0

Zamora, Alfonso
Bantamweight Champion 1975-1976

TB	KO	WD	WF	D	LD	LF	KO BY	ND	NC
38	32	1	0	0	0	1	4	0	0

Zapata, Hilario
Junior Flyweight Champion (WBC) 1980-Present

TB	KO	WD	WF	D	LD	LF	KO BY	ND	NC
16	6	9	0	0	1	0	0	0	0

Zarate, Carlos
Bantamweight Champion (WBC) 1976-1979

TB	KO	WD	WF	D	LD	LF	KO BY	ND	NC
56	53	1	0	0	1	0	1	0	0

Zivic, Fritzie
Welterweight Champion 1940-1941

TB	KO	WD	WF	D	LD	LF	KO BY	ND	NC
230	80	74	1	10	61	0	4	0	0

Zurita, Juan
Lightweight Champion (NBA) 1945

TB	KO	WD	WF	D	LD	LF	KO BY	ND	NC
138	38	76	1	2	14	0	7	0	0

THE RING'S RECORDS OF ALL WORLD CHAMPIONS & CLAIMANTS IN EVERY WEIGHT DIVISION PAST & PRESENT

WORLD CHAMPIONS

HEAVYWEIGHTS

Bare Knuckle Champions *(London Prize Ring Rules)*	
JAMES FIGG	1719-1734
GEORGE TAYLOR	1735-1738
JACK BROUGHTON	1738-1750
JACK SLACK	1750-1760
WILLIAM STEVENS	1760-1761
GEORGE MEGGS	1761-1762
GEORGE MILLSOM	1762-1765
TOM JUCHAU	1765-1766
WILLIAM DARTS	1766-1769
TOM LYONS	1769
WILLIAM DARTS	1769-1771
PETER CORCORAN	1771-1776
HARRY SELLERS	1776-1780
DUGGAN FEARNS	1780
TOM JACKLING	1784-1791
BENJAMIN BRAIN	1791-1794
DANIEL MENDOZA	1794-1795
JOHN JACKSON	1795
TOM OWEN	1796-1797
JACK BARTHOLOMEW	1797-1800
JEM BELCHER	1800-1803
HENRY PEARCE	1803-1806
JOHN GULLY	1807-1808
TOM CRIBB	1808-1822
TOM SPRING	1823-1824
TOM CANNON	1824-1825
JEM WARD	1825-1827
PETER CRAWLEY	1827
JEM WARD	1828-1832
JAMES (DEAF) BURKE	1833-1839
WILLIAM (BENDIGO) THOMPSON	1839-1840
BEN CAUNT	1840-1841
NICK WARD	1841
BEN CAUNT	1841-1845
WILLIAM (BENDIGO) THOMPSON	1845-1850
WILLIAM PERRY	1850-1851
HARRY BROOME	1851-1856
TOM PADDOCK	1856-1858
TOM SAYERS	1858-1860
TOM KING	1863
JEM MACE	1866-1871

TOM ALLEN	1873-1876
JOE GOSS	1876-1880
PADDY RYAN	1880-1882
JOHN L. SULLIVAN	1882

Modern Champions
(Marquis of Queensberry Rules)

JOHN L. SULLIVAN	1885-1892
JAMES J. CORBETT	1892-1897
BOB FITZSIMMONS	1897-1899
JAMES J. JEFFRIES	1899-1905
MARVIN HART	1905-1906
TOMMY BURNS	1906-1908
JACK JOHNSON	1908-1915
JESS WILLARD	1915-1919
JACK DEMPSEY	1919-1926
GENE TUNNEY	1926-1928
MAX SCHMELING	1930-1932
JACK SHARKEY	1932-1933
PRIMO CARNERA	1933-1934
MAX BAER	1934-1935
JAMES J. BRADDOCK	1935-1937
JOE LOUIS	1937-1949
EZZARD CHARLES	1949-1951
JERSEY JOE WALCOTT	1951-1952
ROCKY MARCIANO	1952-1956
FLOYD PATTERSON	1956-1959
INGEMAR JOHANSSON	1959-1960
FLOYD PATTERSON	1960-1962
SONNY LISTON	1962-1964
CASSIUS CLAY (AKA MUHAMMAD ALI)	1964-1970
ERNEST TERRELL (WBA)	*1965-1967*
JOE FRAZIER (NEW YORK)	*1968-1970*
JIMMY ELLIS (WBA)	*1968-1970*
JOE FRAZIER	1970-1973
GEORGE FOREMAN	1973-1974
MUHAMMAD ALI	1974-1978
LEON SPINKS	1978
KEN NORTON (WBC)	*1978*
LARRY HOLMES (WBC)	*1978-*
MUHAMMAD ALI	1978-1979
JOHN TATE (WBA)	*1979-1980*
MIKE WEAVER (WBA)	*1980-*

Claimants not generally recognized are in *italics*.

WORLD HEAVYWEIGHT CHAMPIONSHIP BOUTS

Date	Winner	Weight	Loser	Weight	Result	Time KO	Site	Referee
9/ 7/92	James J. Corbett	178	John L. Sullivan	212	KO 21	1:30	Olympic Club, New Orleans	Prof. John Duffy
1/25/94	James J. Corbett	184	Charley Mitchell	158	KO 3		Duval A.C., Jacksonville	Honest John Kelly
3/17/97	Bob Fitzsimmons	167	James J. Corbett	183	KO 14	1:40	Carson City, Nevada	George Siler
6/ 9/99	James J. Jeffries	206	Bob Fitzsimmons	167	KO 11	1:32	Coney Island, New York	George Siler
11/ 3/99	James J. Jeffries	215	Sailor Tom Sharkey	183	ref 25	—	Coney Island, New York	George Siler
4/ 6/00	James J. Jeffries		Jack Finnegan		KO 1	0:55	Light Guard Armory, Detroit	George Siler
5/11/00	James J. Jeffries	218	James J. Corbett	188	KO 23		Coney Island, New York	Charley White
11/15/01	James J. Jeffries		Gus Ruhlin		TKO 6		Mechanics' Pavilion, San Fran.	Harry Corbett
7/25/02	James J. Jeffries	219	Bob Fitzsimmons	172	KO 8		San Francisco, California	Ed Graney
8/14/03	James J. Jeffries	220	James J. Corbett	190	KO 10		Mechanics' Pavilion, San Fran.	Ed Graney
8/25/04	James J. Jeffries	219	Jack Munroe	186	KO 2		Mechanics' Pavilion, San Fran.	Ed Graney
7/03/05	Marvin Hart	190	Jack Root	171	KO 12		Reno, Nevada	James J. Jeffries
2/23/06	Tommy Burns	180	Marvin Hart	188	ref 20	—	Naud Junction Pavilion, L.A.	Charles Eyton
10/ 2/06	Tommy Burns		Fireman Jim Flynn		KO 15		Naud Junction Pavilion, L.A.	Eddie Robinson
11/28/06	Tommy Burns	172	Philadelphia Jack O'Brien	163½	draw 20	—	Naud Junction Pavilion, L.A.	James J. Jeffries
5/ 8/07	Tommy Burns	180	Philadelphia Jack O'Brien	167	ref 20	—	Naud Junction Pavilion, L.A.	Charles Eyton
7/ 4/07	Tommy Burns	181	Bill Squires	180	KO 1	2:09	Colma, California	James J. Jeffries
12/ 2/07	Tommy Burns	177	Gunner Moir	204	KO 10	2:48	National Sporting Club, London	Eugene Corri
2/10/08	Tommy Burns		Jack Palmer		KO 4		Wonderland, London, England	Eugene Corri
3/17/08	Tommy Burns		Jem Roche		KO 1	1:28	Dublin, Ireland	R.P. Watson
4/18/08	Tommy Burns		Jewey Smith		KO 5		Paris, France	
6/13/08	Tommy Burns	184	Bill Squires	183	KO 8		Paris, France	
8/24/08	Tommy Burns	181	Bill Squires	184	KO 13		Rushcutter's Bay, Sydney	H.C. Nathan
9/ 2/08	Tommy Burns	183	Bill Lang	187	KO 6		Melbourne, Australia	Hugh McIntosh
12/26/08	Jack Johnson	192	Tommy Burns	168	TKO 14		Rushcutter's Bay, Sydney	Hugh McIntosh
3/10/09	Jack Johnson		Victor McLaglen		ND 6	—	Vancouver, B.C.	
5/19/09	Jack Johnson	205	Philadelphia Jack O'Brien	161	ND 6	—	Philadelphia, Pa.	
6/30/09	Jack Johnson	207	Tony Ross	214	ND 6	—	Pittsburgh, Pa.	
9/ 9/09	Jack Johnson	209	Al Kaufman	191	ND 10	—	San Francisco, California	Ed W. Smith
10/16/09	Jack Johnson	205½	Stanley Ketchel	170¼	KO 12		Colma, California	Jack Welch
7/ 4/10	Jack Johnson	208	James J. Jeffries	227	KO 15	2:20	Reno, Nevada	Tex Rickard
7/ 4/12	Jack Johnson	195½	Fireman Jim Flynn	175	TKO 9		Las Vegas, New Mexico	Ed W. Smith
12/19/13	Jack Johnson		Battling Jim Johnson		draw 10	—	Elysee Montmartre, Paris, France	Emil Maitrot
6/27/14	Jack Johnson	221	Frank Moran	203	ref 20	—	Velodrome d'Hiver, Paris, France	Georges Carpentier
12/15/14	Jack Johnson		Jack Murray		KO 3		Buenos Aires, Argentina	
4/ 5/15	Jess Willard	230	Jack Johnson	205½	KO 26	1:26	Mariano Race Track, Havana	Jack Welch
3/25/16	Jess Willard	225	Frank Moran	203	ND 10	—	Madison Sq. Garden	Charley White
7/ 4/19	Jack Dempsey	187	Jess Willard	245	TKO 4	*	Bay View Park Arena, Toledo	Ollie Pecord
9/ 6/20	Jack Dempsey	185	Billy Miske	187	KO 3	1:13	Benton Harbor, Michigan	James Dougherty
12/14/20	Jack Dempsey	188¼	Bill Brennan	197	KO 12	1:57	Madison Sq. Garden	Johnny Haukaup
7/ 2/21	Jack Dempsey	188	Georges Carpentier	172	KO 4	1:16	Jersey City, N.J.	Harry Ertle
7/ 4/23	Jack Dempsey	188	Tommy Gibbons	175½	ref 15	—	Shelby, Montana	James Dougherty
9/14/23	Jack Dempsey	192½	Luis Angel Firpo	216½	KO 2	0:57	Polo Grounds, New York	Jack Gallagher
9/23/26	Gene Tunney	189½	Jack Dempsey	190	unan 10	—	Sesquicentennial Stadium, Phila.	Pop Reilly
9/22/27	Gene Tunney	189½	Jack Dempsey	192½	unan 10	—	Soldiers' Field, Chicago	Dave Barry
7/26/28	Gene Tunney	192	Tom Heeney	203½	TKO 11	2:52	Yankee Stadium, New York	Ed Forbes
6/12/30	Max Schmeling	188	Jack Sharkey	197	WF 4	**	Yankee Stadium, New York	Jim Crowley
7/ 3/31	Max Schmeling	189	Young Stribling	186½	TKO 15	2:46	Municipal Stadium, Cleveland	George Blake
6/21/32	Jack Sharkey	205	Max Schmeling	18[illegible]	split 15	—	M.S.G. Bowl, L.I. City	Ed (Gunboat) Smith
6/29/33	Primo Carnera	260½	Jack Sharkey	201	KO 6	2:27	M.S.G. Bowl, L.I. City	Arthur Donovan
10/22/33	Primo Carnera	259½	Paulino Uzcudun	229¼	unan 15	—	Rome, Italy	Maurice Nicord
3/ 1/34	Primo Carnera	270	Tommy Loughran	184	unan 15	—	Miami, Florida	Leo Shea
6/14/34	Max Baer	209½	Primo Carnera	263¼	TKO 11	2:16	M.S.G. Bowl, L.I. City	Arthur Donovan
6/13/35	James J. Braddock	193¾	Max Baer	209½	unan 15	—	M.S.G. Bowl, L.I. City	Jack McAvoy
6/22/37	Joe Louis	197¼	James J. Braddock	197	KO 8	1:10	Comiskey Park, Chicago	Tommy Thomas
8/30/37	Joe Louis	197	Tommy Farr	204¼	unan 15	—	Yankee Stadium, New York	Arthur Donovan
2/23/38	Joe Louis	200	Nathan Mann	193½	KO 3	1:56	Madison Sq. Garden	Arthur Donovan
4/ 1/38	Joe Louis	202½	Harry Thomas	196	KO 5	2:50	Chicago Stadium	Dave Miller
6/22/38	Joe Louis	198¾	Max Schmeling	193	KO 1	2:04	Yankee Stadium, New York	Arthur Donovan
1/25/39	Joe Louis	200¼	John Henry Lewis	180¾	KO 1	2:29	Madison Sq. Garden	Arthur Donovan
4/17/39	Joe Louis	201¼	Jack Roper	204¾	KO 1	2:20	Wrigley Field, L.A.	George Blake
6/28/39	Joe Louis	200¾	Tony Galento	233¾	TKO 4	2:29	Yankee Stadium, New York	Arthur Donovan
9/20/39	Joe Louis	200	Bob Pastor	183	KO 11	0:38	Briggs Stadium, Detroit	Sam Hennessey
2/ 9/40	Joe Louis	203	Arturo Godoy	202	split 15	—	Madison Sq. Garden	Arthur Donovan
3/29/40	Joe Louis	201½	Johnny Paychek	187½	KO 2	0:44	Madison Sq. Garden	Arthur Donovan
6/20/40	Joe Louis	199	Arturo Godoy	201¼	TKO 8	1:24	Yankee Stadium, New York	Billy Cavanaugh
12/16/40	Joe Louis	202¼	Al McCoy	180¾	TKO 6	*	Boston Garden	Johnny Martin
1/31/41	Joe Louis	202½	Red Burman	188	KO 5	2:49	Madison Sq. Garden	Arthur Donovan
2/17/41	Joe Louis	203½	Gus Dorazio	193½	KO 2	1:30	Convention Hall, Philadelphia	Irvin Kutcher
3/21/41	Joe Louis	202	Abe Simon	254½	TKO 13	1:20	Olympia Arena, Detroit	Sam Hennessey
4/ 8/41	Joe Louis	203½	Tony Musto	199½	TKO 9	1:36	St. Louis Arena	Arthur Donovan
5/23/41	Joe Louis	201½	Buddy Baer	237½	W dis 7	**	Griffith Stadium, Wash., D.C.	Arthur Donovan
6/18/41	Joe Louis	199½	Billy Conn	174	KO 13	2:58	Polo Grounds, New York	Eddie Joseph
9/29/41	Joe Louis	202¼	Lou Nova	202½	TKO 6	2:59	Polo Grounds, New York	Arthur Donovan
1/ 9/42	Joe Louis	206¾	Buddy Baer	250	KO 1	2:56	Madison Sq. Garden	Frank Fullam

Date	Winner	Wt.	Loser	Wt.	Result	Rd.	Time	Venue	Referee
3/27/42	Joe Louis	207½	Abe Simon	255½	KO	6	0:16	Madison Sq. Garden	Eddie Joseph
6/ 9/46	Joe Louis	207	Billy Conn	187	KO	8	2:19	Yankee Stadium, New York	Eddie Joseph
9/18/46	Joe Louis	211	Tami Mauriello	198½	KO	1	2:09	Yankee Stadium, New York	Arthur Donovan
12/ 5/47	Joe Louis	211½	Jersey Joe Walcott	194½	split 15	—		Madison Sq. Garden	Ruby Goldstein
6/25/48	Joe Louis	213½	Jersey Joe Walcott	194¾	KO	11	2:56	Yankee Stadium, New York	Frank Fullam
† 6/22/49	Ezzard Charles	181¾	Jersey Joe Walcott	195½	unan 15	—		Comiskey Park, Chicago	Dave Miller
† 8/10/49	Ezzard Charles	180	Gus Lesnevich	182	TKO	8	*	Yankee Stadium, New York	Ruby Goldstein
†10/14/49	Ezzard Charles	182	Pat Valentino	188½	KO	8	0:35	Cow Palace, San Francisco	Jack Downey
† 8/15/50	Ezzard Charles	183¼	Freddie Beshore	184½	TKO	14	2:53	Memorial Auditorium, Buffalo	Barney Felix
9/27/50	Ezzard Charles	184½	Joe Louis	218	unan 15	—		Yankee Stadium, New York	Mark Conn
12/ 5/50	Ezzard Charles	185	Nick Barone	178½	KO	11	2:06	Cincinnati Gardens	Tommy Warndorf
1/12/51	Ezzard Charles	185	Lee Oma	193	TKO	10	1:19	Madison Sq. Garden	Ruby Goldstein
3/ 7/51	Ezzard Charles	186	Jersey Joe Walcott	193	unan 15	—		Olympia Arena, Detroit	Clarence Rosen
5/30/51	Ezzard Charles	182	Joey Maxim	181½	unan 15	—		Chicago Stadium	Frank Gilmer
7/18/51	Jersey Joe Walcott	194	Ezzard Charles	182	KO	7	0:55	Forbes Field, Pittsburgh	Buck McTiernan
6/ 5/52	Jersey Joe Walcott	196	Ezzard Charles	191½	unan 15	—		Municipal Stadium, Phila.	Zack Clayton
9/23/52	Rocky Marciano	184	Jersey Joe Walcott	196	KO	13	0:43	Philadelphia Stadium	Charley Daggert
5/15/53	Rocky Marciano	184½	Jersey Joe Walcott	197¾	KO	1	2:25	Chicago Stadium	Frank Sikora
9/24/53	Rocky Marciano	185	Roland LaStarza	184¾	TKO	11	1:31	Polo Grounds, New York	Ruby Goldstein
6/17/54	Rocky Marciano	187½	Ezzard Charles	185½	unan 15	—		Yankee Stadium, New York	Ruby Goldstein
9/17/54	Rocky Marciano	187	Ezzard Charles	192½	KO	8	2:36	Yankee Stadium, New York	Al Berl
5/16/55	Rocky Marciano	189	Don Cockell	205	TKO	9	0:59	Kezar Stadium, San Francisco	Frankie Brown
9/21/55	Rocky Marciano	188¼	Archie Moore	188	KO	9	1:19	Yankee Stadium, New York	Harry Kessler
11/30/56	Floyd Patterson	182¼	Archie Moore	187¾	KO	5	2:27	Chicago Stadium	Frank Sikora
7/29/57	Floyd Patterson	184	Tommy Jackson	192½	TKO	10	1:52	Polo Grounds, New York	Ruby Goldstein
8/22/57	Floyd Patterson	187¼	Pete Rademacher	202	KO	6	2:57	Sick's Stadium, Seattle	Tommy Loughran
8/18/58	Floyd Patterson	184½	Roy Harris	194	TKO	13	*	Wrigley Field, L.A.	Mushy Callahan
5/ 1/59	Floyd Patterson	182½	Brian London	206	KO	11	0:51	Fairgrounds Coliseum, Indianapolis	Frank Sikora
6/26/59	Ingemar Johansson	196	Floyd Patterson	182	TKO	3	2:03	Yankee Stadium, New York	Ruby Goldstein
6/20/60	Floyd Patterson	190	Ingemar Johansson	194¾	KO	5	1:51	Polo Grounds, New York	Arthur Mercante
3/13/61	Floyd Patterson	194¾	Ingemar Johansson	206½	KO	6	2:45	Convention Hall, Miami Beach	Billy Regan
12/ 4/61	Floyd Patterson	188½	Tom McNeeley	197	KO	4	2:51	Maple Leaf Gardens, Toronto	Jersey Joe Walcott
9/25/62	Sonny Liston	214	Floyd Patterson	189	KO	1	2:06	Comiskey Park, Chicago	Frank Sikora
7/22/63	Sonny Liston	215	Floyd Patterson	194½	KO	1	2:10	Convention Center, Las Vegas	Harry Krause
2/25/64	Cassius Clay	210½	Sonny Liston	218	TKO	7	*	Convention Hall, Miami Beach	Barney Felix
† 3/ 5/65	Ernest Terrell	199	Eddie Machen	192	unan 15	—		Int. Amphitheatre, Chicago	Bernard Weisman
5/25/65	Muhammad Ali	206	Sonny Liston	215¼	KO	1	1:52	St. Dominic's, Lewiston	Jersey Joe Walcott
†11/ 1/65	Ernest Terrell	206	George Chuvalo	209	unan 15	—		Maple Leaf Gardens, Toronto	Sammy Luftspring
11/22/65	Muhammad Ali	210	Floyd Patterson	196¾	TKO	12	2:18	Convention Center, Las Vegas	Harry Krause
3/29/66	Muhammad Ali	214½	George Chuvalo	216	unan 15	—		Maple Leaf Gardens, Toronto	Jackie Silvers
5/21/66	Muhammad Ali	201½	Henry Cooper	188	TKO	6	1:38	Arsenal Stadium, London	George Smith
† 6/28/66	Ernest Terrell	209½	Doug Jones	187½	unan 15	—		Sam Houston Coliseum, Houston	Ernie Taylor
8/ 6/66	Muhammad Ali	209½	Brian London	201½	KO	3	1:40	Earl's Court, London	Harry Gibbs
9/10/66	Muhammad Ali	203½	Karl Mildenberger	194¼	TKO	12	1:30	Frankfurt Walk Stadium	Teddy Waltham
11/14/66	Muhammad Ali	212¾	Cleveland Williams	210½	TKO	3	1:08	Houston Astrodome	Harry Kessler
2/ 6/67	Muhammad Ali	212¼	Ernest Terrell	212½	unan 15	—		Houston Astrodome	Harry Kessler
3/22/67	Muhammad Ali	211½	Zora Folley	202½	KO	7	1:48	Madison Sq. Garden	John LoBianco
§ 3/ 4/68	Joe Frazier	204½	Buster Mathis	243½	TKO	11	2:33	Madison Sq. Garden	Arthur Mercante
† 4/27/68	Jimmy Ellis	197	Jerry Quarry	195	maj 15	—		Oakland Coliseum	Elmer Costa
§ 6/24/68	Joe Frazier	203½	Manuel Ramos	208	TKO	2	3:00	Madison Sq. Garden	Arthur Mercante
† 9/14/68	Jimmy Ellis	198	Floyd Patterson	188	ref 15	—		Stockholm, Sweden	Harold Valan
§12/10/68	Joe Frazier	203	Oscar Bonavena	207	unan 15	—		Spectrum, Philadelphia	Joe Sweeney
§ 4/22/69	Joe Frazier	204½	Dave Zyglewicz	190½	KO	1	1:36	Houston Coliseum	Jimmy Webb
§ 6/23/69	Joe Frazier	203½	Jerry Quarry	198½	TKO	8	*	Madison Sq. Garden	Arthur Mercante
2/16/70	Joe Frazier	205	Jimmy Ellis	201	TKO	5	*	Madison Sq. Garden	Tony Perez
11/18/70	Joe Frazier	209	Bob Foster	188	KO	2	0:49	Cobo Hall, Detroit	Tom Briscoe
3/ 8/71	Joe Frazier	205½	Muhammad Ali	215	unan 15	—		Madison Sq. Garden	Arthur Mercante
1/15/72	Joe Frazier	215½	Terry Daniels	195	TKO	4	1:45	New Orleans, La.	Herman Dutreix
5/26/72	Joe Frazier	217½	Ron Stander	218	TKO	5	*	Omaha, Nebraska	Zack Clayton
1/22/73	George Foreman	217½	Joe Frazier	214	TKO	2	1:35	Kingston, Jamaica	Arthur Mercante
9/ 1/73	George Foreman	219½	Jose (King) Roman	196½	KO	1	2:00	Military Arts Hall, Tokyo	Jay Edson
3/26/74	George Foreman	224¾	Ken Norton	212¾	TKO	2	2:00	Caracas, Venezuela	Jimmy Rondeau
10/30/74	Muhammad Ali	216½	George Foreman	220	KO	8	2:58	20th of May Stadium, Kinshasa	Zack Clayton
3/24/75	Muhammad Ali	223½	Chuck Wepner	225	TKO	15	2:41	Coliseum, Cleveland, Ohio	Tony Perez
5/16/75	Muhammad Ali	224½	Ron Lyle	219	TKO	11	1:08	Convention Center, Las Vegas	Ferd Hernandez
7/ 1/75	Muhammad Ali	224½	Joe Bugner	230	unan 15	—		Kuala Lumpur, Malaysia	Takeo Ugo
10/ 1/75	Muhammad Ali	224½	Joe Frazier	215	TKO	15	*	Manila, Philippines	Carlos Padilla
2/20/76	Muhammad Ali	226	Jean Pierre Coopman	206	KO	5	2:46	Roberto Clemente Coliseum	Ismael Quinones Falu
4/30/76	Muhammad Ali	230	Jimmy Young	209	unan 15	—		Capital Centre, Landover	Tom Kelly
5/24/76	Muhammad Ali	220	Richard Dunn	206½	TKO	5	2:05	Munich, Germany	Herbert Thomser
9/28/76	Muhammad Ali	221	Ken Norton	217½	unan 15	—		Yankee Stadium, New York	Arthur Mercante
5/16/77	Muhammad Ali	221¼	Alfredo Evangelista	209¼	unan 15	—		Capital Centre, Landover	Harry Cecchini
9/29/77	Muhammad Ali	225	Earnie Shavers	211¼	unan 15	—		Madison Sq. Garden	John LoBianco
2/15/78	Leon Spinks	197¼	Muhammad Ali	224¼	split 15	—		Hilton Pavilion, Las Vegas	David Pearl
‡ 6/ 9/78	Larry Holmes	209	Ken Norton	220	split 15	—		Caesars Palace, Las Vegas	Mills Lane
9/15/78	Muhammad Ali	221	Leon Spinks	201	unan 15	—		Superdome, New Orleans	Lucien Joubert
‡11/10/78	Larry Holmes	214	Alfredo Evangelista	208¼	KO	7	2:14	Caesars Palace, Las Vegas	Richard Green
‡ 3/23/79	Larry Holmes	214	Osvaldo Ocasio	207	TKO	7	2:38	Caesars Palace, Las Vegas	Carlos Padilla
‡ 6/22/79	Larry Holmes	215	Mike Weaver	202	TKO	12	0:44	Madison Sq. Garden	Harold Valan
‡ 9/28/79	Larry Holmes	210	Earnie Shavers	211	TKO	11	2:00	Caesars Palace, Las Vegas	David Pearl

†10/20/79	John Tate	240	Gerrie Coetzee	222	unan 15		Loftus Versfeld Stadium. Pretoria	Carlos Berrocal
‡ 2/03/80	Larry Holmes	213½	Lorenzo Zanon	215	TKO 6	2:39	Caesars Palace. Las Vegas. Nev.	Raymundo Solis
† 3/31/80	Mike Weaver	232	John Tate	232	KO 15	2:15	Stokely A.C.. Knoxville. Tenn.	Ernesto Magana
3/31/80	Larry Holmes	211	Leroy Jones	254½	TKO 8	2:56	Caesars Palace. Las Vegas. Nev.	Richard Greene
7/07/80	Larry Holmes	214¼	Scott LeDoux	226	TKO 7	2:05	Metro Center, Minneapolis. Minn.	David Pearl
10/02/80	Larry Holmes	211½	Muhammad Ali	217½	TKO 11	*	Caesars Palace. Las Vegas. Nev.	Richard Greene
†10/25/80	Mike Weaver	210	Gerrie Coetzee	226½	KO 13	1:49	Sun City. Bophuthatswana	Jesus Celis

*Loser failed to answer bell for round indicated. **Loser was disqualified at end of round.

ref=referee's decision (sole arbiter)

†NBA (later WBA) world heavyweight title bout
‡WBC world heavyweight title bout
§New York State Athletic Commission world heavyweight title bout

The British Board of Boxing Control (BBBC) designated the June 6. 1950 bout between Bruce Woodcock (England) and Lee Savold (U.S.) as for the world heavyweight title. Savold stopped Woodcock in the fourth round at White City Stadium. London. and was recognized as world champion by the BBBC until knocked out by Joe Louis in six rounds in Madison Square Garden on June 15. 1951 The BBBC then acknowledged Ezzard Charles. who had defeated Louis on September 27. 1950. as world champion.

Muhammad Ali was known as Cassius Clay when he stopped Sonny Liston in Miami Beach on February 25, 1964.

The World Boxing Council (WBC) recognized Ken Norton as world champion when Leon Spinks declined to meet him before the latter's return bout with Muhammad Ali. Norton had won a fifteen round split decision over Jimmy Young at Caesars Palace in Las Vegas on November 5. 1977.

HEAVYWEIGHT DIVISION

JAMES FIGG
(First Heavyweight Champion)

Born, 1695, Thane, Oxfordshire, Eng. Weight, 185 lbs. Height, 6 ft.

James Figg came to the front as a fistic professor about 1719. Prior to that date he was known as a successful swordsman and cudgel expert, but when he opened an academy devoted principally to boxing, his fame spread, and it was not long before he was universally recognized as the champion of England. His academy was called Figg's Amphitheatre, and its proprietor was ready at all times to accomodate any challenger looking for a match.

Among those he defeated about 1720 were: Timothy Buck, Tom Stokes, Bill Flanders, and others.

In 1723 Figg defeated Chris Clarkson in a fierce battle of half an hour.

Other boxing academies sprung up in London and there was considerable rivalry between them.

Figg fought Ned Sutton three times, winning all three battles. In the first one the men fought with cudgels and then with their fists.

The first of the champions died in London on December 8, 1740.

Elected to Boxing Hall of Fame, 1954.

GEORGE TAYLOR

Born, 1718. Was known as George the Barber. Claimed title upon Figg's retirement. Lost to Jack Broughton, 1738, but became proprieter of Figg's Amphitheatre at the latter's death. He beat Jack Slack in 14 minutes on January 31, 1750, but was defeated by Tom Faulkner in an hour and 15 minutes in a contest of great skill and courage. Taylor, who was blind in one eye, lost complete sight in that fight and died three months later, in December, 1758.

JACK BROUGHTON

Born, 1704. Weight, 196 lbs. Height, 5 ft. 10½ in. Jack Broughton was the third recognized heavyweight champion of the prize ring. His name has come down in fistic history as the Father of Boxing, because it was he who first drew up and put into action a set of rules governing contests between the ropes, in 1743 rules which provided the foundation for those sponsored by the Marquis of Queensberry, when the bare knuckles gave way to gloves. Broughton reigned from 1729 to 1750, having won his title by defeating Tom Pipes and Bill Gretting. He was dethroned by Jack Slack, who beat him in fourteen minutes on April 10, 1750. Broughton then retired. He died in London at the age of eighty-five, during the third week of January, 1789. He left an estate of $35,000, a goodly sized fortune for that period.

Elected to Boxing Hall of Fame, 1954.

JACK SLACK

Jack Slack, fourth heavyweight champion of England. Born, Norfolk, Eng. Weight, 202 lbs. Height, 5 ft. 8½ in.

In 1744 he whipped Daniel Smith, and beat him again in less than 20 minutes on November 12 of the same year. He fought and won several bouts at the London Amphitheatre during that period, but suffered a reverse, when George Taylor knocked him out in 25 minutes, on January 31, 1750.

On October 12, 1748 Slack stopped Ned Hunt in 40 minutes.

On April 10, 1750, Slack won the heavyweight championship by defeating Jack Broughton in 14 minutes. Broughton's backer, the Duke of Cumberland, wagered and lost $250,000 on Broughton. On July 8, 1751, Slack beat a giant Frenchman, Monsieur Petit, in 25 minutes, and on March 13, 1755, he knocked out Cornelius Harris in 20 minutes. On October 20, 1759, the champion whipped Jack Moreton in 35 minutes. Slack lost the title on June 17, 1760, when he was decisively beaten by William Stevens, the "Nailer," and retired. He died in 1778.

BILL STEVENS

Born, 1736. Weight, 190 lbs. Height, 5 ft. 10 in. Bill Stevens, better known to the Fancy as "The Nailer," engaged in several minor contests of which no records are available. His first officially listed battle was with Jacob Taplin, at Marylebone Basin, which he won on a clean knockout in 30 minutes. Other battles were as follows:

1760

June 17—Stephens defeated Jack Slack for the title by a knockout in 17 mins.

1761

Mar. 2—Stevens lost to George Meggs in 17 mins.

In his next bout he was defeated by Turner. Later he was matched with John Maguire on July 4, 1769, and beat him in 20 mins. His last battle was with Harry Sellers in June, 1778, the latter winning in 10 mins.

Stevens died in London in 1781.

GEORGE MEGGS, THE COLLIER

Had little boxing skill. Won the championship by defeating Bill Stevens, "The Nailer," in London, March 2, 1761, in 17 minutes. That was Meggs' best fight. Was a fighter of inferior ability. Lost to Millson, "The Baker," at Calne, Wilshire, 40 minutes, July 2, 1762. He lost to Tom Tyne, 1787, twice and beat Joe Ward, 1790.

GEORGE MILLSOM

Millsom was a baker in Bath, England. In July, 1762, he won the title by defeating George Meggs in a stubbornly contested battle lasting 40 minutes in Calne, Wiltshire. Meggs demanded a return, but Millsom beat him easily the second time, that contest being fought the following month, in August, 1762.

Parfitt Meggs, a countryman, no relation to George, also challenged Millsom, but the baker gave him a severe beating.

Millsom successfully defended his title against all comers for the next three years. He lost his title to Tom Juchau, August 27, 1765.

TOM JUCHAU

Tom Juchau, known as "The Disher" or "The Paviour," came into prominence by beating Charles Cohant, a butcher, in a grueling battle held in Guildford, Surrey, lasting 50 minutes. He won the title by defeating Millsom in a hard-fought battle near St. Alban's.

Juchau subsequently lost his title to Bill Darts at Guildford, May, 1766.

BILL DARTS

(Champion of England 1764)

Born, 1741. Weight, 187 lbs. Height, 5 ft. 10 in. Fought Tom Jachau at Guildford, in May, 1766. The bout lasted forty minutes, Jachau being knocked out. Darts whipped Dogget, the Bargeman in 20 mins.

1767

Oct. 13—Darts beat Swansey, the Butcher, in 15 mins. at Epping Forest.

1769

June 27—Lyons, the Waterman, defeated Darts in 45 minutes and claimed the championship at Kingston.

1770

Mar. 25—Darts beat Death (Stephen) Oliver in 27 minutes.

1771

May 18—Darts lost to Peter Corcoran.

British sportsmen claimed that Capt. O'Kelly, famous turfman, bribed Darts with 100 pounds to lose the fight and Darts thereafter was ostracized by sportsmen.

TOM LYONS

A waterman from Kingston-upon-Thames, he

took the title from Bill Darts in Kingston on June 27, 1769. Lyons was really nothing more than a crude amateur, and Darts gave him a severe beating for the first 25 minutes of the battle. Lyons, however, had a tremendous capacity for punishment, and the tide soon turned. He vanquished Darts in a total of 45 minutes.

Lyons' face was badly cut in the fight, and when the cuts did not heal readily, he announced his retirement from the ring and "returned the championship" to Darts.

PETER CORCORAN

Corcoran, the first Irishman to win the title, beat four Englishmen (Turner, Dalton, Davis, and Smiler The Bricklayer) within a year and challenged Darts, the champion.

Corcoran defeated Darts on May 18, 1771 and defended the crown against a host of foes, including Sam Peters, whom he beat in June, 1774. He lost the title to Harry Sellers on October 10, 1776.

HARRY SELLERS
(Claimed Title of England in 1776)

Born Aug. 10, 1753. Weight, 178 lbs. Height 5 ft. 11½ in.

Sellers was a game fighter. His furst match of importance was with Peter Corcoran, October 10, 1776, at Staines, when Sellers won in 28 mins. Other fights follow:

1777

June 4—Sellers defeated Joe Hood in a hard battle of a little under an hour.

July 2—Sellers again defeated Joe Hood in 30 mins.

1778

June —Sellers beat Bill Stevens, the champion in 10 mins. Stevens was too old and never had a chance against the younger man, being merely a shell of his former self.

1780

Sept. 25—Sellers was beaten by Duggan Fearns (called Jack Fearns in some books) in one minute 30 seconds. Some of the boxing historians have referred to this battle as a "frame" but nothing more is known of it.

1785

June 7—Sellers was defeated by Wm. Harvey in 20 mins.

DUGGAN FEARNS

Also known as Jack Fearns. He was an Irish boatswain who won the title by defeating Harry Sellers in one minute and a half at the Crown, at Slough, September 25, 1780. The fight, it was charged, was a fix, and Fearns dropped out of sight. He was never heard from again, and the title was acknowledged to be vacant.

THOMAS JACKLING
(Tom Johnson)

Born, 1750, Derby. Weight, 202 lbs. Height, 5 ft. 10 in.

Thomas Jackling, the fourteenth heavyweight champion fought his first professional contest at Walworth in June, 1783, with Jack Jarvis. He defeated Jarvis in 15 minutes, winning in such spectacular fashion that the victory earned him widespread reputation as a youngster to be reckoned with. His other battles were as follows:

1784

Mar. —Johnson beat the "Croydon Drover" in 27 mins.

June —Beat Stephen (Death) Oliver in 35 mins. Oliver was blinded in both eyes and beaten severly.

1786

Feb. —Beat Jack Towers in less than 15 mins.

June —Beat a big fellow named Bill Fry in 30 mins.

June 11—Beat Bill Love in 4 mins.

1787

Jan. 18—Beat Bill Warr in 1 hour 40 mins. at Okingham.

Dec. 19—Johnson defeated Michael Ryan, the Irish champion in 30 mins.

1789

Feb. 11—Johnson defeated Michael Ryan in 33 mins. at Rickmansworth.

Nov. 22—Johnson beat Isaac Perrins in 62 rds., 1 hr. 15 mins., at Banbury for $1,250 a side.

1791

Jan. 17—Johnson lost to Ben Brain (Big Ben) in 18 rds. and the title went with it. It was Tom's last battle. Johnson died Jan. 21, 1791.

BENJAMIN BRAIN
(Big Ben, Champion of England)

Born, 1753, Bristol. Weight, 230 lbs. Height 6 ft. 4 in.

Brain was a coal miner and was matched with Jack Clayton, the champion of Kingswood, for his first battle, in 1774. He won after a hard fight and followed by beating Hob Harris.

1786

Oct. 31—Brain won from John Boone, "The Fighting Grenadier" at Bloomsbury. After 30 mins. of fighting, Brain's two eyes were almost closed when toughs broke into the ring. During the melee a surgeon lanced Brain's eyes and restored his vision. Inside of ten minutes Boone tossed the towel.

1788

Oct. 31—Brain defeated W. Corbally in 20 mins. at Navestock.

1789

Oct. 23—Ben defeated Jack Jacombs in 2 hrs. 5 mins. at Banbury.

Brain forfeited $500 to Tom Johnson on account of illness.

Brain defeated Tom Tring in 12 rds. at Dartford.

1796

Aug. 30—Brain fought draw with Wm. Hooper, the Tinman, of 3 hrs. 30 mins., 180 rounds, at Chapel Row Level, near Newbury.

1791

Jan. 17—Brain defeated Tom Johnson in 18 rds. for the title at Wrotham, in Kent, then announced his retirement due to lack of challengers. However, though the title was vacant after he abdicated, four years later he made a comeback, still claiming the title and was matched with Will Wood, February 24, 1794, but was taken ill and died on April 8, 1794, the undefeated, retired title holder.

DANIEL MENDOZA

Born, July 5, 1764, Aldgate, London. Nationality, Spanish-English-Jew. Weight, 160 lbs. Height, 5 ft. 7 in.

Daniel Mendoza was the first Jewish champion of the world and the sixteenth heavyweight champion of England. He was also the first fighter to cultivate and develop scientific boxing, and the adoption of his methods by contemporaries and later exponents of the fistic art, may be said to have revolutionized the prize ring. His first registered battle was with a big fellow known as Harry the Coalheaver, whom he defeated in 40 minutes. Other contests were as follows: Defeated Thomas Wilson, John Horn, Harry Davis, John Lloyd, Tom Monk, John Hand, Bill Move, John Williams, Richard Dennis, Geo. Cannon, Al Fuller, Tom Spencer, Wm. Taylor, John Knight, John Braintree, Wm. Bryant, John Matthews, Tom Tyne, Geo. Hoast, Geo. MacKenzie, John Hall, Wm. Cannon, Geo. Barry, Geo. Smith, Wm. Nelson.

1787

Apr. 17—Sam Martin, Barnet, Eng. .... W 10
—Wm. Warr .... W 23

1788

Jan. 9—Richard Humphries, Odiham, Eng. L 29 min.

1789

May 6—Richard Humphries, Stilton, Eng. ... W 52 min.

1790

Sept. 29—Richard Humphries, Doncaster, Eng. W 15 min.

465

1791

Laid claim to title after retirement of Benjamin Brain, the champion and was accepted as such due to his victories over Humphries, who at the time was England's best heavyweight. Bill Warr contested the claim of Mendoza and in 1792 got his chance and lost, thus tightening Mendoza's grip on the crown.

Aug.　2—Defeated Squire Fitzgerald in 26 minutes.
1792
May　14—Bill Warr, Croydon, Eng. ...... W　23 rds.
1794
Nov.　12—Bill Warr, Bexley Common ... W　15 min.
1795
Apr.　15—John Jackson, Hornchurch, Eng. KO by　9 rds.
1806
Mar.　21—Harry Lee, Grimsted Green ... W　53 rds.
1820
July　4—Tom Owen, Banstead Downs .... L　12

After retirement, Mendoza became London's most celebrated boxing instructor, operating a school-at-arms which was widely patronized by the nobility and sport patrons. He also toured England, Ireland and Scotland with Astley's Circus. He died in London, aged 72, on September 3, 1836.

Elected to Boxing Hall of Fame, 1954.

JOHN JACKSON

Born, September 25, 1769, London, England. Weight, 202 lbs. Height, 5 ft. 11 in.

Known as "Gentleman Jackson" because of his polished demeanour and charitable deeds, John Jackson was also an athlete of note outside of the prize ring, having won distinction as a jumper and sprinter, despite his bulk. Before turning professional he was noted as an exceptionally clever amateur boxer. His principal battles were:

1788
June　9—Jackson defeated Wm. Fewterell, who had never been beaten before, in 1 hr. 7 mins., at Smitham Bottom, Croydon.
1789
Mar.　12—Jackson gave up to George Ingelston in 20 mins. on account of breaking his leg in falling.
1795
Apr.　15—Jackson defeated Daniel Mendoza in 9 rds. at Hornchurch, Essex.

Jackson retired after his Mendoza match. Jackson died in London on October 7, 1845, and was buried in Brompton, where a handsome marble monument was erected to his memory.

Elected to Boxing Hall of Fame, 1954.

TOM OWEN

Born, December 21, 1768, Portsea, England. Weight, 168 lbs.

1796
Nov.　14—William Hooper, Harrow .... W　50
1797
Feb.　—William Hooper, near Harrow .... W
Aug.　20—Jack Bartholomew,
　　　　Sunbury Common .... L　30 min.
1799
Sept.　2—J. Houssa .... L　40 min.
Dec.　7—J. Davis, Depthford .... W　60 min.
1820
July　4—Dan Mendoza, Banstead Downs .... W　12

Died December 13, 1843, Plumstead, near Woolwich. Owen is credited with being the inventor of the dumbbell.

JACK BARTHOLOMEW

Bartholomew, who stood 5 ft. $9\frac{1}{2}$ in., was a first-rate scientific boxer and hard hitter. He won the right to challenge Tom Owen by defeating Fearby, the "Young Ruffian," on Hounslow Heath, June 8, 1795. Jack's next fight was with Bill Wood, to whom he lost on a foul.

Bartholomew won the title by beating Owen in 30 minutes on Sunbury Common, August 20, 1797, and

"enjoyed his honors uncontested" for two years before fighting a 51-round draw with Jem Belcher in Uxbridge, August 15, 1799. A rematch, held on Funchley Common on May 15, 1800, resulted in a victory for Belcher in 17 rounds.

Bartholomew died in July, 1803 in the Almonry, at Westminster.

JEM BELCHER

Born, April 15, 1781, Bristol, Eng. Nationality, British. Weight, 182 lbs. Height, 5 ft. $11\frac{1}{2}$ in. Twentieth heavyweight champion of the London Prize Ring.

1798
Mar.　16—Jack Britton, Bristol .... W　33 min.
1799
Apr.　15—Paddington Jones, Wormwood
　　　　Scrubbs .... W　33 min.
Aug.　15—Jack Bartholomew, Uxbridge ...... D　51
1800
May　15—Jack Bartholomew, Finchley .... W　17
Dec.　22—Andrew Gamble, Wimbledon ...... W　5
1801
Mar.　16—Joe Berks, Camberwell .... W　14
Nov.　25—Joe Berks, Hurley .... W　16
1802
Aug.　20—Joe Berks, London .... W　14
1803
Apr.　12—Jack Firley, Linton .... W　11
1805
Dec.　6—Henry Pearce, Near Doncaster ..... L　18
1807
Apr.　8—Tom Cribb, Moulsey Hurst .... L　41
1809
Feb.　1—Tom Cribb, Epsom Downs .... L　31
　　　　Died, July 30, 1811.

HENRY PEARCE

(The Game Chicken)

Born, 1777, Bristol, Eng. Weight, 175 lbs. Height, 5 ft. 9 in.

1803
June　3—Jack Firley, London .... W　10
Aug.　12—Joe Berks, London .... W　15
1804
Jan.　23—Joe Berks, Wimbledon .... W　24
1805
Mar.　11—Elias Spray, Hampton .... W　29
Apr.　27—Stephen Carte, Shepperton .... W　25
Oct.　8—John Gully, Hailsham .... W　64
Dec.　6—Jim Belcher, near Doncaster ...... W　18
　　　　Died April 30, 1809.

JOHN GULLY

(Champion Penciler and Member of Parliament)

Born, 1783, Bristol, England. Weight, 190 lbs. Height, 6 ft.

John Gully, son of a Bristol butcher, was in a debtor's prison, when Henry Pearce, twenty-first heavyweight champion, paid him a visit. Gully had some reputation as a boxer and Pearce sparred with him in his jail quarters.

Gully made such a good showing that the news went abroad, and a British sportsman named Fletcher Reid, paid Gully's debts, had him discharged from custody and pitted him against Pearce on October 8, 1805. Gully was beaten after a sixty-four round fight, lasting one hour and seventeen minutes, but the loser's reputation was greatly enhanced by the splendid fight he made.

When Pearce retired as a result of ill health, Gully was universally recognized as his successor to the title. Two years later, on October 14, 1807, Gully met Bob Gregson at Six Mile Bottom. Gully and Gregson fought a terrific battle of 36 rounds, Gully winning. They met again on May 10, 1808, at Woburn. Gully won in eight rounds.

He became wealthy and in 1832, as the result of a bet, he became a candidate for Parliament and was

466

elected. He served two terms and then resigned. He died March, 1863, at Durham.
Elected to Boxing Hall of Fame, 1959.

TOM CRIBB
Born, July 8, 1781, Hanaham, Eng. Weight, 196 lbs. Height, 5 ft. 10 in. One of England's most celebrated champions. His defeats of Tom Molineaux were his outstanding performances. Died May 11, 1848.
1805
Jan.	7—Geo. Maddox, Wood Green	W	76
Feb.	15—Tom Blake, Blackheath	W	20
May	21—Ikey Pig, London	W	11
July	20—Geo. Nichols, Blackwater	L	52
Oct.	8—Bill Richmond, Hailsham	W	90 min.

1807
Apr.	8—Jem Belcher, Moulsey Hurst	W	41

1808
May	1—George Horton, Woburn	W	25
Oct.	25—Bob Gregson, Moulsey Hurst	W	23

1809
Feb.	1—Jem Belcher, Epsom Downs	W	31

1810
Dec.	18—Tom Molineaux, Copthall Common	W	33

1811
Sept.	28—Tom Molineaux, Thistleton	W	11

1820
Feb. 1—Defeated Jack Carter.
Elected to Boxing Hall of Fame, 1954.

TOM SPRING
(Thomas Winter)
Born, February 22, 1795, Townhope, Herefordshire. Weight, 186 lbs. Height, 5 ft. 11½ in.
Tom Spring was the first holder of a world's heavyweight championship title to adopt a special fighting moniker. His real name was Thomas Winter. He might best be described as the Jim Corbett of his time, for he excelled in speed, grace and scientific boxing but never earned the reputation of a hard hitter. Like Mendoza, he did much toward eliminating the crude slugging methods of the ring. His first professional engagement was with John Hollands, a giant in size, whom he defeated quickly through sheer cleverness.
1814
June	12—Jack Henley	W	11

1817
Sept.	9—Jack Stringer, Moulsey	W	29

1818
Apr.	1—Ned Painter, Mickleham Downs	W	31
	1 hour 29 min.		
Aug.	7—Ned Painter, Russia Farm	L	42
Sept.	12—Bill Neat, won by forfeit.		

1819
May	4—Jack Carter, Crawley Downs	W	71
	Hard battling, 1 hr. 55 min.		

Spring then went on a sparring tour with Tom Cribb, the Champion, meeting all comers.
Dec.	20—Ben Burn	W	11

Another match was made with Ned Painter, but latter forfeited.
1820
May	16—Young Bob Burn, Epsom Downs	W	18
June	27—Josh Hudson, Moulsey Hurst	W	6

1821
Feb.	20—Tom Oliver, Arlington Corners	W	25

Tom Cribb retired in 1821 and handed the belt to Tom Spring.
1823
May	17—*Bill Neat, Hinckley Downs	W	8
	37 min.		

*Neat broke his arm in the 6th round.
1824
Jan.	7—Jack Langan, Worcester	W	77
	2 hrs. 29 min.		
June	8—Jack Langan, Warwick	W	76

Spring retired after his last battle with Langan, became an inn-keeper and died on August 20, 1851.
Elected to Boxing Hall of Fame, 1961.

TOM CANNON
(The Great Gun of Windsor)
Born, 1790. Weight, 166 lbs. Height, 5 ft. 9½ in.
1809
—Cannon defeated Tom Anslow, a soldier, in 39 minutes, knocking him out.
—Cannon whipped Dolly Smith in 1817 during a fair, which resulted in a match being made later.
1817
May 6—Cannon beat Dolly Smith in 60 rounds at Maidenhead, Eng.
Cannon was an expert cricketer and all-around athlete. He did not engage in any important bouts until 1824.
1824
Nov. 23—Cannon again defeated Josh Hudson in 16 rounds at Warwick. Cannon had backed himself and won over $5,000 besides the stake of $1,000.
1825
Cannon gave an exhibition to help Hudson and later made a tour during which he won a sprinting match for $200 a side.
Cannon then claimed the championship, but was immediately taken up by Jem Ward, and a match made. They met June 19, 1825, and Ward won in 10 rounds at Warwick.
1827
Feb. 20—Cannon beaten by Ned Neale in 22 hard fought rounds at Warwick.
Cannon retired after his Neale battle and for quite a time was seriously ill. He quit ring affairs entirely. On July 11, 1858, Cannon shot himself and died shortly after, aged 69 years.

JEM WARD
Champion from 1822-1831 — known as the "Black Diamond." Eldest of seven children. Born, December 26, 1800, the day known throughout the British Empire as "boxing day." Was adept in boxing and wrestling. Was a coal-whipper at sixteen. Received two championship belts. His hobby was painting. Had an inborn gift of artistic talent. Was also a devotee of music. He received the first championship belt ever awarded a boxer.
1816
May	6—Geo. Robinson, Stepney	W	45 min.
June	18—Bill Wall, Limehouse Fields	W	2 hrs.

1817
July	27—George Webb, Limehouse Fields	W	3 min.

1819
Feb.	12—Jack Murray, Shadwell Fields	W	45 min.
July	4—Nick Murphy, Barking	W	35 min.

1820
Sept.	29—Mike Hayes, Isle of Dogs	W	40 min.
Oct.	12—John Delaney, Bow Common	W	35 min.

1822
June	12—Dick Acton, Moulsey Hurst	W	6 rds.
Oct.	22—Bill Abbott, Moulsey Hurst	L	22 rds.

1823
July	4—Ned Baldwin, Wimbledon	W	20 rds.
July	—Joe Rickens, Bath	W	8 rds.
Nov.	11—Josh Hudson, Moulsey Hurst	L	15 rds.

1824
June	21—Phil Sampson, Colnbrook	W	26 rds.
Dec.	28—Phil Sampson, Stony Stratford	W	27 rds.

1825
July	19—Tom Cannon, Warwick	W	10 rds.

1827
Jan.	2—Peter Crawley, Royston	L	11 rds.

1828
May	27—Jack Carter, Shepperton	W	17 rds.

1831
July	12—Simon Byrne, Willeycutt	W	33 rds.

Died London, April 3, 1884 at age of 84.
Elected to Boxing Hall of Fame, 1963.

PETER CRAWLEY
(Champion of England for a Week)
Born, Dec. 5, 1800, in London. Weight, 185 lbs. Height, 6 ft. ½ in.
1819
—Defeated Pat Flannagan in 15 minutes.

1816
—Beat Bill Hunt in 10 minutes at Long Fields, Eng.
1816
—Beat Jack Bennett at Clara Market in 15 min. Peter also defeated Tom Price and Bill Coleman in short order. Next he defeated the "Clara Market Jehu" in 19 rounds.
1818
Aug. 7—Peter beat Ben Sutcliffe, in 50 minutes at Rushley Farm.
1819
March 16—Crawley was beaten by Tom Hickman in 13 rounds at Moulsey Hurst.
1822
May 7—Crawley defeated Bully Southerns in 50 minutes at Chester Races.
1823
May 6—Beat Dick Acton in 13 rounds at Blindlow Heath. Crawley had a few minor bouts, but of little importance.
1825
—Crawley tried to get backing to fight Jem Ward for the title, but failed.
1826
Oct. 17—Crawley and Ward signed articles for a finish battle.
1827
Jan. 2—Defeated Jem Ward in 11 rounds at Royston and was hailed as champion of England. It was a terrific battle while it lasted — 26 minutes.

Ward's friends immediately · challenged Crawley for a return battle for $5,000 a side. Peter, although he had fairly won the title, declined to hold it, declaring that he intended to go into business and would retire for good. This he did. Ward claimed the title again and defended it. Crawley died March 12, 1865.

JAMES (DEAF) BURKE
Born, December 8, 1809, St. Giles, London. Weight, 175 lbs. Height, 5 ft. 8½ in.

James Burke, later to be known as "the Deaf Un" in ring circles, was working as a waterman on the Thames River, when he made the acquaintance of a veteran fighter, Joe Parish, who taught him how to box and stirred the lad's ambition to become a star slugger. Parish put Burke against big Ned Murphy for a $70 purse. The contest lasted for fifty rounds, but darkness coming on, it was declared a draw and the stake divided. This was on February 4, 1828, and Burke's showing was so good that he was matched to fight Thomas (Bull) Hands. He whipped Hands in 12 rounds, on August 6 of the same year, and was fairly launched on his fighting career. Other battles were as follows:

1828
Aug. 20—Young Sambo .... W 15
1829
Mar. 10—Young Berridge, London .... W 11
June 9—Bill Fitzmaurice, Herpenden
Common .... W 166
Three hours
Aug. 25—Bill Cousens, Whetstone Commons L 111
2 hrs, 50 min.
Dec. 1—Young Girdler, Milford Bay .... W 17
1830
Oct. 4—Andrew Gow, Temple Mills .... W 22
$25 a side
Oct. 26—Bob Hompson, Hampden Common W 45
min.
Nov. 16—Tim Crawley, Whetstone .... W 6
1831
Feb. 22—Jack Davis, Shepperton Range ..... W 12
May 28—James Blissett, Near London ...... W 19
1832
May 8—*Jack Carter, Woolwich .... W 11
—Harry Macone, Lockington Bottom W 59
*Carter breaking his arm.
1833
Jan. 8—"Farmer" Macone .... W

May 30—Simon Byrne, near London .... W 99
3 hours, 16 min.

Byrne was so badly beaten that he died three days later, but Burke was exonerated from blame.

Burke then sailed for America and fought Samuel O'Rourke at New Orleans on May 6, 1836. O'Rourke's gang of thugs broke the ring in the third round when Burke was winning and the latter had to run to save his life. On Aug. 21, 1837, Burke beat Tom O'Connell in 10 rounds at Hart's Island, N.Y.

Burke returned to England soon after his battle with O'Connell.

Bendigo challenged Burke and a match was made for 1838, but didn't take place.
1839
Feb. 12—Bendigo, Heather, Leicestershire .... LF 10

Lack of condition is what beat Burke.

Bendigo thereupon claimed the championship.
1840
Sept. 22—Fought Nick Ward 17 rds., lasting two hours, in terribly cold weather and rain. Toughs broke up the fight to save Ward and claim of foul was made by Ward's seconds, which were allowed two days later.
1843
June 13—Bob Castles, Rainham Ferry ...... W 37

Burke died of tuberculosis on January 8, 1845.

Elected to Boxing Hall of Fame, 1966.

"BENDIGO"
(William Thompson)
Born, October 11, 1811, Nottingham, England. Weight, 165 lbs. Height, 5 ft. 9½ in.

One of England's most colorful fistic characters. He engaged in a number of tough battles, then retired and turned evangelist. Became a Methodist parson. Died on August 23, 1880, from a fall, in his 69th year.
1832
Oct. —Joe Hanley .... W 16
Oct. —Bill Fawkes .... W 11
1833
Mar. 17—Ned Smith .... W 5
Apr. 12—Charles Martin .... W 2
May 30—Lew Jackson .... W 3
June 14—Tom Cox .... W 9
Aug. 14—George Shelton .... W 3
Aug. 24—Tom Burton .... W 9
Sept. 4—Bill Mason .... W 3
Oct. 12—Bill Winterflood, Moulds .... W 1
Nov. 27—Bill Keyworth .... W 11
1834
Jan. 12—The Bingham Champ .... W —
1835
July 21—Ben Caunt, Appleby House,
Nottingham .... W 22
1836
May 24—Brassey (John Leachman),
Deepcar, near Sheffield .... WF 52
1837
Jan. 24—Young Charles Langan,
Newcastle-under-Lyme .... W 32
June 13—Bill Looney, Chapel-en-le-Frith .... W 99
1838
Apr. 3—Ben Caunt, Shepworth Common,
Shelby .... LF 75
June 24—A scheduled bout with Ben Caunt cancelled.
1839
Feb. 12—James "Deaf" Burke, Heather,
Leicestershire .... WF 10
Received the championship belt of England from Jem Ward.
1845
Sept. 9—Ben Caunt, Stoney Stratford ..... WF 93
Re-won championship he gave up upon retirement and purse of L400.
1850
June 5—Tom Paddock, Mildenham .... WF 49
The old time fighters were continually in jail for

468

breaking the peace following one of their battles, and Bendigo was no exception to the rule. When he was in prison for the twenty-eighth time Bendigo was strangely moved by a sermon delivered by the prison chaplain, and on his release embarked on a new career as an evangelist. His curious phraseology and quaint method of expressing himself drew vast crowds to his meetings in London and other big cities. He settled down to live at Nottingham, where he was greatly respected, and died there in 1880. On June 2, 1891 a memorial was set up at Nottingham.

A huge crowd of curiously assorted people who had known Bendigo as bruiser, saloon keeper and preacher, attended the unveiling ceremony. The memorial is in the form of a life size sleeping lion carved in stone, mounted on a pedestal. An inscription reads, "In Memory of William Thompson (Bendigo), who died Aug. 23, 1880, aged 69. In life always brave, fighting like a lion in death like a lamb, tranquil in Zion."

Died August 23, 1880.

Elected to Boxing Hall of Fame, 1955.

BEN CAUNT

Born, Hucknall Torkard, Eng. Weight, 210 lbs. Height, 6 ft. 2½ in.

Ben Caunt won several minor contests around the country hamlet where he lived and worked as a game keeper. His first regular ring battle was on July 21, 1835, with William Thompson, who later became famous as "Bendigo." Caunt lost in 22 rounds. On August 17, 1835, Caunt whipped William Butler in 14 rounds and on November 4 of the same year, beat Bill Boneford in 6 rounds.

1838
April   3—Caunt won from Bendigo on alleged foul in 75th round. Claim being made that Bendigo went down without being hit. Caunt was terribly punished. A riot followed the decision of the referee. Caunt afterwards claimed the championship.
1840
Oct.   26—Bill Brassey, Six Mile Bottom .... W 101
    (Caunt again claimed the championship.)
1841
Feb.   2—Nick Ward, London .... LF   7
May   11—Nick Ward, Long Marxden .... W   35
    Caunt then made a trip to America and challenged the world, but nothing came of it.
1845
Sept.   9—Bendigo, Stoney Stratford .... LF   93
1857
Sept.   22—Nat Langham .... D   60
    Ben Caunt died Sept. 10, 1861 from pneumonia.

NICK WARD

Was British Champion from 1835 to 1841. Was born on April 1, 1811. He had a successful career as a fighter. After retirement he became a publican in Liverpool, then in London. He died on February 17, 1850. Was a younger brother of Jem Ward.

WILLIAM PERRY
(The Tipton Slasher)
Born, March 21, 1819, Tipton, Eng. Weight, 185 lbs. Height, 6 ft. ½ in.
1835
Nov.   3—Barney Dougherty, Chelsea .... W   7
1836
Dec.   27—Ben Spilsbury, Oldbury .... W   7
1837
Nov.   22—Jem Scunner, Wolverhampton ..... W   31
1842
Dec.   10—Chas. Freeman, Sawbridgeworth
    .... Police stopped 70
Dec.   20—Chas. Freeman, Cliffe Marshes .... LF   37
1843
Dec.   19—Tass Parker, Dartford
    .... Police stopped 70
1844
Feb.   —Tass Parker, Holley .... W 133

1846
Aug.   4—Tass Parker, Linderick Common ... W   23
1850
Dec.   17—Tom Paddock, Woking Common .. WF   22
1851
Sept.   29—Harry Broome, Mild'nhall .... LF   33 rds.
1857
June   16—Tom Sayers, Down R. Thames L   10
    The police forced shifting places in the Freeman-Perry battles. Freeman weighed 276 pounds and stood 6 ft. 10½ inches. Perry lost last bout by going down without being hit.
    Died Wolverhampton, Jan. 18, 1881.

HARRY BROOME

Born, 1826, Birmingham. Weight, 165 lbs. Height, 5 ft. 9½ in.

Harry Broome began fighting professionally at the age of sixteen, starting his ring career by victories over Hal Mitchell and Bying Stocks. On October 11, 1843, he beat Fred Mason in 39 rounds. On December 10, 1845, the ring was broken into during the 81st round of his battle with Joe Rowe. Action was discontinued, and the battle was resumed on May 6 of the following year, according to ring custom of that time. Broome then finished his opponent in 27 rounds. Broome's battle with Ben Terry at Shrivenham on February 3, 1846, also wound up in a riot in the thirty-fifth round. The stakes were drawn and Terry refused to fight Broome again. On Sept. 29, 1851, he won on a foul from William Perry in 33rd round. On April 18, 1853, Broome beat Harry Orme in 31 rounds. During 1855, Broome forfeited to Tom Paddock. He then retired, but later agreed to meet Paddock; they fought at Stratford, December 12, 1855, Paddock winning in 51 rounds.

Harry Broome died November 2, 1865.

TOM PADDOCK

Born, 1824, Redditch, England. Weight, 175 lbs. Height, 5 ft. 9 in.

After winning several unimportant by-battles, young Tom Paddock forged to the front by decisively defeating a veteran, Elijah Parsons, on January 20, 1844. On January 27, 1846, Paddock beat Nobby Clarke in 42 rounds at Coleshill Castle, and defeated him again on April 6, 1847, at Stoney Stratford, in 35 rounds.
1850
June   5—Bendigo, Mildenham .... LF   49
Dec.   17—William Perry, the Tipton Slasher at Woking Common .... LF   27
1851
Sept.   23—Lost to Harry Poulson in 71 rounds at Sedgebrook.
Dec.   16—Defeated Harry Poulson in 86 rounds at Cross End, Derbyshire. Poulson was severly beaten. Police interfered and a riot resulted. Both Poulson and Paddock were arrested and given ten months in jail.
1854
Feb.   14—Paddock met Poulson for third time and beat him in 102 rounds, nearly three hours, in terrific battle, at point near East London.
July   18—Paddock beat Aaron Jones in 121 rounds at a point down the river from London. It was a hard fought battle and Jones was blind in both eyes at the finish.
Aug.   —Paddock issued challenges to both Wm. Perry and Harry Broome, claimants for the championship, but received no reply. Tom claimed the title and some recognized him, on condition that he meet Perry or Broome and also Jones again.
1855
June   26—Beat Aaron Jones in 61 rounds near London, both being badly bruised up.
1856
May   19—Paddock beat Harry Broome in 51 rounds at point near Condon.
    Paddock was taken ill and did not fight for a time, but got back in the ring in 1858.
1858
June   15—Lost to Tom Sayers in 21 rounds at Kent.

469

1860

—Lost to Sam Hurst, the giant, in 5 rounds.
Paddock retired soon after, appearing in only a few exhibitions.

His death occured June 30, 1863, after a long illness.

TOM SAYERS

(The Napoleon of the Prize Ring)
Born, May 25, 1826, Pimlico, Eng. Weight, 152 lbs. Height, 5 ft. 8½ in. Died Nov. 8, 1865.
One of England's most renowned Champions — famed for his fight with John C. Heenan, 1860, in first international white heavyweight, title bout.

1849
Mar. 19—Abe Couch, Greenhithe .... W 6
1850
Oct. 22—Fought Dan Collins to a draw, 9 rounds at Edenbridge when police stopped the fight after 27 minutes. They then went to Red Hill where the bout was continued for 39 rounds (1 hour 52 min.), when darkness caused a halt.
1851
Apr. 29—Dan Collins, Long Reach .... W 44
1852
June 29—Jack Grant, Mildenhall .... W 64
1853
Jan. 26—Jack Martin, Long Reach .... W 23
Oct. 18—Nat Langham, Lakenheath .... L 61
1854
Feb. 2—George Sims, Long Beach .... W 4
1856
Jan. 29—Harry Poulson, Appledore .... W 109
1857
Jan. 19—Aaron Jones, Canvey Island .... D 62
Feb. 10—Aaron Jones, Canvey Island .... W 85
June 16—Bill Perry, Down R. Thames ...... W 10
Sept. 21—Bob Brett, Leashford .... W 7
1858
Jan. 5—Bill Benjamin, Isle of Grain .... W 3
June 15—Tom Paddock, Kent .... W 21
1859
Apr. 5—Bill Benjamin, near Ashford .... W 11
1860
Apr. 17—J. C. Heenan, Farnborough .... D 42
Elected to Boxing Hall of Fame, 1954.

TOM KING

Born, August 11, 1835, Stepney, London. Weight, 175 lbs. Height, 6 ft. 2 in.
In his early youth Tom King joined the British Royal Navy and it was there that he became initiated into the mysteries of the fistic art, having many bouts with both gloves and bare knuckles, and making a reputation which finally resulted in his becoming a ring professional. His first officially recorded combat was with Bill Clamp, a Navy Dockyard champion, whom he knocked out in one round. His later battles were:
1860
Nov. 27—Tom Truckle, Kentish Marshes .... W 49
1861
Was matched with Harry Poulson, May 23, but later forfeited.
Oct. 21—Young Broome (Wm. Evans), Farnborough .... W 43
In 17th round police interfered and they moved to the next county, near by, where they finished it.
1862
Jan. 28—Jem Mace, Godstone .... L 43
Nov. 26—Jem Mace, Medway .... W 21
Won the championship.
1863
Dec. 8—John C. Heenan of America, Wadhurst, for world's title and $5,000 a side .... W 24
Tom King retired and became famous as an oarsman and also a noted character on the turf, having amassed a fortune estimated at $300,000. He died Oct. 3. 1888, at Stockbridge, England.
Elected to Boxing Hall of Fame, 1977

JEM MACE

(The Gypsy)
Born, April 8, 1831, Beeston, Norwich, Eng. Weight, 160 lbs. Height, 5 ft. 9½ in. Father of modern school of British scientific boxing.
1855
Oct. 2—Slasher Slack, Mildenhall .... W 9
1857
Feb. 17—Bill Thorpe, Medway .... W 18
1858
Sept. 21—Bob Brettle, Medway .... L 2
1859
Jan. 25—Posh Price, Surrey .... W 11
1860
Feb. 21—Bob Travers, P. I. .... W 6
Feb. 22—Bob Travers, London .... W 57
Sept. 19—Bob Brettle, Oxfordshire .... SP —
Sept. 20—Bob Brettle, Oxfordshire .... W 11
1861
June 18—Sam Hurst, Medway .... W 8
1862
Jan. 28—Tom King, Godstone .... W 43
Nov. 26—Tom King, Medway .... L 21
1863
Sept. 1—Joe Goss, London .... W 19
1 hr. 35 min.
1866
May 24—Joe Goss, Farningham .... D 1 hr. 5 min.
Aug. 6—Joe Goss, London .... W 21
1870
May 10—Tom Allen, Kennerville, La. .... W 10
1871
May 11—Joe Coburn, Port Ryeson, Canada
.... Police stopped 1 hr. 17 min.
Nov. 30—Joe Coburn, Bay St. Louis .... D 12
1882
—George Belcher, N.2 .... W 2
1890
Feb. 7—Charley Mitchell, 6 oz., Glasgow .... L 3
Two minute rounds, £1,000 and boxing championship of England.
1896
Dec. 14—Prof. Mike Donovan, Utica, N.Y.
Won championship from Sam Hurst in 1861. Lost to Tom King, 1862. Was awarded belt. King refused to meet him again, and Mace was acknowledged champion of the world by the British up to his retirement. He was the last champion of the world under London Prize Ring rules.
Mace died at Newcastle, March 3, 1910, and was buried in Liverpool.
Elected to Boxing Hall of Fame, 1954.

TOM ALLEN

Born, April, 1840, Birmingham, England. Weight, 175 lbs. Height, 5 ft. 11 in.
Won first professional fight from Posh Price, July 28, 1862, in fifty minutes. On January 28, 1864, he whipped Bingy Ross, defeated Jack Garkinson in 1865, and in a second encounter with Posh Price, won in two hours and five minutes. Lost to Bob Smith of USA, 50 rounds, 2 hours, 49 minutes.
Allen drew with Joe Goss in 34 rounds. March 6, 1867, went to America, and again met Goss, this time at Cincinnati, Ohio, on September 7, 1876, losing on a foul. On February 23, 1869 Allen lost in 3 minutes to Charley Gallagher. In June, 1869, Allen lost on a foul to Mike McCoole May 10, 1870. Allen was beaten in ten rounds by Jem Mace in a battle for the world's heavyweight title. On Mace's retirement, Allen claimed the title. His claim was disputed by Mike McCoole, who fought Allen on September 23, 1873, near St. Louis, the latter winning decisively in 7 rounds, lasting twenty minutes. Allen successfully defended his title against Joe Goss. In his last ring battle, with Joe Goss, Allen lost to Joe Goss in 21 rounds, on September 7, 1876, in Kentucky. On retiring he opened a saloon in St. Louis and died in that city on April 5, 1904, at the age of sixty-five years.

JOE GOSS
Born, November 5, 1838, Northampton, England.
Weight, 150 lbs. Height, 5 ft. 8½ in.
1859
Sept. 20—Jack Rooke, England .... W 64
Nov. 29—Won from Tom Price by forfeit.
1860
Feb. 10—Tom Price, England .... W 25 min.
July 17—Rodger Crutchley, Oxford, England W 120
1861
Sept. 24—Bill Ryall, England .... KO 37
2 hrs. 50 min.
1862
Feb. 20—Bill Ryall, England .... D 36
3 hrs. 18 min.
Nov. 25—Posh Price, England .... W 66
1863
Sept. 1—Jem Mace, London .... L 19
1 hr. 55 min.
Dec. 16—Ike Baker, London ...... W 1 hr. 20 min.
1866
May 24—Jem Mace, Farningham .... L 19
1 hr. 5 min.
Aug. 6—Jem Mace, London .... L 21
1867
Mar. 5—Tom Allen, Bristol, Eng. .... D 34
(Fought in 3 rings)
Sept. 7—Tom Allen, Cincinnati .... WF —
1868
Jan. 25—Joe Wormwald forfeited to Goss.
1876
Sept. 7—Tom Allen, Kentucky .... WF 21
(Fought 2 rings, Kenton and Boone counties)
1880
Apr. 6—J. L. Sullivan, Boston .... L 3
May 30—Paddy Ryan, Collier Station,
W. Va. .... KO by 87
1881
Apr. 6—J. L. Sullivan, Boston .... L 3
Died March 24, 1885, Boston, Mass.

PADDY RYAN
Born, March 15, 1853, Thurles, Tipperary,
Ireland. Weight, 200 lbs. Height, 5 ft. 11 in.
Early in his career he was beaten by Joe
McAuliffe, but on May 30, 1880, he won the American
heavyweight title by defeating Joe Goss in 87 rounds, at
Collier Station, W. Va., the fight lasting 1 hour and 24
minutes. He had the shortest record of the champions,
his only other listed battle being with John L. Sullivan,
who knocked him out at Mississippi City in 9 rounds, for
the title, for $5,000 a side. In 1885, police halted a glove
bout in New York City between Sullivan and Ryan in the
first round, to save the latter. On November 13, 1886,
Sullivan knocked out Ryan at San Francisco in three
rounds.
Died at Green Island, near Troy, N.Y., Dec. 14,
1900.
Elected to Boxing Hall of Fame, 1973.

JOHN L. SULLIVAN
(John Lawrence Sullivan)
(The Boston Strong Boy)
Born, October 15, 1858, Roxbury, Mass. Ancestry, Irish.
Weight, 190 lbs. Height, 5 ft. 10½ in.
1878
—Cockey Woods, Boston .... KO 5
1879
—Dan Dwyer, Boston .... KO 3
—Tommy Chandler, Boston .... W 4
—Jack (Patsy) Hogan, Boston .... W 4
1880
Feb. —Mike Donovan, Boston .... ND 3
Apr. 6—Joe Goss, Boston .... W 3
June 28—George Rooke, Boston .... KO 2
Dec —John Donaldson, Cincinnati .... KO 4
Dec. 24—John Donaldson, Cincinnati ...... KO 10
1881
Jan. 3—Jack Stewart, Boston .... KO 2
Mar. 31—Steve Taylor, New York .... KO 2
May 16—John Flood, New York .... KO 8

July 11—Fred Crossly, Philadelphia .... KO 1
July —Dan McCarty, Philadelphia .... KO 1
Sept. 14—James Dalton, Chicago .... KO 4
Sept. 27—Jack Burns, Chicago .... KO 1
1882
Feb. 7—Paddy Ryan, Mississippi City ...... KO 9
(Won Bare Knuckle World Heavyweight Title)
Mar. 27—Jack Douglas, New York .... KO 3
Apr. 20—John McDermott, Rochester .... KO 3
July 4—Jimmy Elliott, Brooklyn .... KO 3
July 17—Joe (Tug) Wilson, New York .... W 4
1883
May 14—Charley Mitchell, New York .... KO 3
Aug. 6—Herbert Slade, New York .... KO 3
Oct. 17—James McCoy, McKeesport, Pa. .... KO 1
Nov. 3—Jim Miles, East St. Louis .... KO 1
Nov. 25—Morris Hefey, St. Paul .... KO 1
Dec. 4—Mike Sheehan, Davenport .... KO 1
1884
Jan. 14—Fred Robinson, Butte .... KO 2
Mar. 6—George Robinson, San Francisco .... W 4
Apr. 10—Al Marks, Galveston .... KO 1
Apr. 28—William Fleming, Memphis .... KO 1
Apr. 29—Dan Henry, Hot Springs .... KO 1
May 2—Enos Phillips, Nashville .... KO 4
Nov. 10—John Laflin, New York .... KO 3
Nov. 17—Alf Greenfield, New York .... KO 2
1885
Jan. 12—Alf Greenfield, Boston .... W 4
Jan. 19—Paddy Ryan, New York .... KO 1
June 13—Jack Burke, Chicago .... W 5
Aug. 29—Dominick McCaffrey, Cincinnati .... W 6
(Won Queensberry World Heavyweight Title)
1886
Sept. 18—Frank Herald, Alleghany, Pa. ..... KO 1
Nov. 13—Paddy Ryan, San Francisco .... KO 3
Dec. 28—Duncan McDonald, Denver .... D 4
1887
Jan. 18—Patsy Cardiff, Minneapolis .... D 6
1888
Mar. 10—Charley Mitchell, Chantilly, France D 39
(Retained Bare Knuckle World Heavyweight Title)
1889
July 8—Jake Kilrain, Richburg, Miss. ..... KO 75
(Retained Bare Knuckle World Heavyweight Title)
1890-1891
(Inactive)
1892
Sept. 7—James J. Corbett, New Orleans   KO by 21
(Lost Queensberry World Heavyweight Title)
1893-1895
(Inactive)
1896
Aug. 31—Tom Sharkey, New York .... Exh. 3

TB	KO	WD	WF	D	LD	LF	KO BY	ND	NC
46	33	8	0	3	0	0	1	1	0

Died, February 2, 1918, Abingdon, Mass.
Elected to Boxing Hall of Fame, 1954

JAMES J. CORBETT
(James John Corbett)
(Gentleman Jim)
Born, September 1, 1866, San Francisco, Calif.
Weight, 178-190 lbs. Height, 6 ft. 1 in. Managed by
William A. Brady.
1884-1888
—Frank Smith, Salt Lake City ..... KO 2
—Duncan McDonald, Evanston, Wyom. D 8
1889
May 30—Joe Choynski, Fairfax, Cal. .... NC 4
June 5—Joe Choynski, Benecia, Cal. ...... KO 27
July 15—Joe Choynski, San Francisco ...... W 4
July 29—Dave Campbell, Portland, Ore. ..... D 10
1890
Feb. 18—Jake Kilrain, New Orleans ...... W 6
Mar. 20—Mike Donovan, New York .... Exh. 3
Apr. 14—Dominick McCaffrey, Brooklyn .... W 4
May 21—Peter Jackson, San Francisco ..... NC 61
June 26—John L. Sullivan, San Francisco Exh. 4

471

| Aug. | 5—Jim Hall, Chicago .... Exh. | 4 |
| Oct. | 8—Ed Kinney, Milwaukee .... W | 4 |

1892

Feb.	16—Bill Spilling .... KO	1
	—Bob Caffrey .... KO	1
	—Joe Lannon, New York .... Exh.	3
Sept.	7—John L. Sullivan, New Orleans ... KO	21

(Won World Heavyweight Title)

1893

(Inactive)

1894

| Jan. | 25—Charley Mitchell, Jacksonville, Fla. KO | 3 |

(Retained World Heavyweight Title)

| Sept. | 7—Peter Courtney, Orange, N.J. Exh. KO | 6 |

1895

| Jan. | 4—Jim McVey, New Orleans ... Exh. KO | 3 |

1896

| June | 24—Tom Sharkey, San Francisco .... Exh. | 4 |
| Dec. | 14—Jim McVey, New York .... Exh. | 3 |

1897

| Mar. | 17—Bob Fitzsimmons, Carson City   KO by | 14 |

(Lost World Heavyweight Title)

1898

| Nov. | 22—Tom Sharkey, New York ....,. LF | 9 |

1899

(Inactive)

1900

| May | 11—James J. Jeffries, Coney Island KO by | 23 |

(For World Heavyweight Title)

| Aug. | 30—Charles (Kid) McCoy, New York .. KO | 5 |

1901-1902

(Inactive)

1903

| Aug. | 14—James J. Jeffries, San Francisco KO by | 10 |

(For World Heavyweight Title)

TB	KO	WD	WF	D	LD	LF	KO BY	ND	NC
19	7	4	0	2	0	1	3	0	2

Died, February 18, 1933, Bayside, N.Y.
Elected to Boxing Hall of Fame, 1954.

BOB FITZSIMMONS

(Ruby Robert)
Born, May 26, 1863, Helston, Cornwall, England.
Weight, 150-175 lbs. Height, 5 ft. 11¾ in. Managed by
Martin Julian.

1883-1885

	—Jim Crawford, Sydney .... KO by	3
	—Pablo Fank, Sydney .... W	4
	—Joe Riddle, Sydney .... W	4
	—Alf Brinsmead, Sydney .... KO	2
	—Jack Greentree, Sydney .... KO	3
	—Jack Bonner, Sydney .... W	4
	—Dick Sandall, Sydney .... W	4

1886

May	15—Mick Dooley, Sydney .... KO by	4
June	2—Mick Dooley, Sydney L	4
June	5—Mick Dooley, Sydney L	4
July	10—Mick Dooley, Sydney .... KO	2
Aug.	7—McArdle, Sydney .... W	4
Oct.	7—Bill Smith, Sydney .... ND	4

1887

Mar.	—Bill Slavin, Sydney .... KO	5
	—George Eager, Sydney .... KO	2
	—Dave Conway, Sydney .... KO	2

1888

	—Jim Hall, Sydney .... ND	4
	—Paddy Slavin, Sydney .... ND	4
	—Jim Hall, Sydney .... ND	4
	—Billy McCarthy, Sydney .... ND	4
Dec.	1—McEwan, Sydney .... W	4

1889

(No Record)

1890

Feb.	4—E.W. (Starlight) Rollins, Sydney .. ND	4
Feb.	10—Jim Hall, Sydney .... KO	1
Feb.	12—Jim Hall, Sydney .... KO by	4

(For Australian Middleweight Title)

| Feb. | 22—E.W. (Starlight) Rollins, Sydney .. KO | 9 |
| Mar. | —Prof. West, Sydney .... KO | 1 |

May	17—Frank Allen, San Francisco ...... KO	1
May	29—Aus. Billy McCarthy, San Francisco KO	5
June	28—Arthur Upham, New Orleans ..... KO	9

1891

| Jan. | 14—Jack Dempsey, New Orleans ..... KO | 13 |

(Won World Middleweight Title)

| Apr. | 28—Abe Cougle, Chicago .... Exh. KO | 2 |
| May | 1—Black Pearl, Minneapolis .... Exh. | 4 |

1892

Mar.	2—Peter Maher, New Orleans ...... KO	12
Apr.	30—James Farrell, Newark .... KO	2
May	7—Joe Godfrey, Philadelphia .... KO	1
May	17—Jerry Slattery, New York .... KO	2
Sept.	3—Millard Zender, Anniston .... KO	1

1893

Mar.	8—Jim Hall, New Orleans .... KO	4
Mar.	25—Phil Mayo, Chicago .... KO	2
May	30—Jack Warner, Baltimore .... KO	1
Sept.	5—Jack Hickey, Newark .... W	4

1894

June	17—Joe Choynski, Boston .... NC	5
July	28—Frank Kellar, Buffalo .... KO	2
Sept.	26—Dan Creedon, New Orleans ...... KO	2

(Retained World Middleweight Title)

| Nov. | 19—Con Riordan, Syracuse ...... Exh. KO | 2 |
| Nov. | 19—Joe Dunfee, Syracuse .... Exh. | 1 |

1895

| Apr. | 16—Al Allich .... Exh. KO | 3 |
| Apr. | 19—Mike Connors, New York .... Exh. KO | 1 |

1896

Feb.	21—Peter Maher, Langtry .... KO	1
Feb.	29—Peter Maher, New York .... Exh.	3
Dec.	2—Tom Sharkey, San Francisco ...... LF	8

1897

| Jan. | 3—Ernest Roeber .... Exh. | 1 |
| Mar. | 17—James J. Corbett, Carson City .... KO | 14 |

(Won World Heavyweight Title)

| June | 5—Local Blacksmith, Leadville   Exh. KO | 2 |

1898

(Inactive)

1899

| June | 9—James J. Jeffries, Coney Island KO by | 11 |

(Lost World Heavyweight Title)

| Oct. | 28—Geoffrey Thorne, Chicago .... KO | 1 |

1900

Mar.	27—Jim Daly, Philadelphia .... KO	1
Apr.	30—Ed Dunkhorst, Brooklyn .... KO	2
Aug.	10—Gus Ruhlin, New York .... KO	6
Aug.	24—Tom Sharkey, Coney Island, N.Y. KO	2

1901

| Dec. | —Tom Sharkey, New York .... Exh. | 5 |

1902

| July | 25—James J. Jeffries, San Francisco KO by | 8 |

(For World Heavyweight Title)

| Dec. | 27—Mike Ranke, Bozeman ...... Exh. KO | 1 |

1903

Sept.	30—Con Coughlin, Philadelphia ...... KO	1
Oct.	14—Joe Grim, Philadelphia .... ND	6
Nov.	25—George Gardner, San Francisco .... W	20

(Won World Light Heavyweight Title)

1904

| July | 23—Phila. Jack O'Brien, Philadelphia ND | 6 |

(Retained World Light Heavyweight Title)

1905

| Dec. | 20—Phila. Jack O'Brien, San Fran. KO by | 13 |

(Lost World Light Heavyweight Title)

1906

(Inactive)

1907

| Mar. | 7—Tony Ross, Newcastle .... Exh. | 4 |
| July | 17—Jack Johnson, Philadelphia ... KO by | 2 |

1908

| Sept. | 21—Jim Paul, Benson Mines .... KO | 3 |

1909

| Dec. | 27—Bill Lang, Sydney .... KO by | 12 |

(For Australian Heavyweight Title)

1910-1913

(Inactive)

1914

Jan.	29—K.O. Sweeney, Williamsport ...... ND 6
Feb.	20—Jersey Bellew, Bethlehem .... ND 6

TB	KO	WD	WF	D	LD	LF	KO BY	ND	NC
62	32	8	0	0	2	1	8	10	1

Died, October 22, 1917, Chicago, Ill.
Elected to Boxing Hall of Fame, 1954.

JAMES J. JEFFRIES
(James Jackson Jeffries)
(The Boilermaker)
Born, April 15, 1875, Carroll, Ohio. Weight, 216 lbs. Height, 6 ft. 2½ in. Managed by William A. Brady.

1896
	—Hank Griffin, Los Angeles .... KO 14
	—Jim Barber, Los Angeles .... KO 2
July	2—Dan Long, San Francisco .... KO 2

1897
Apr.	9—T. Van Buskirk, San Francisco ... KO 2
May	19—Henry Baker, San Francisco ..... KO 9
July	17—Gus Ruhlin, San Francisco .... D 20
Nov.	30—Joe Choynski, San Francisco ...... D 20

1898
Feb.	28—Joe Goddard, Los Angeles .... KO 4
Mar.	22—Peter Jackson, San Francisco ..... KO 3
Apr.	22—Pete Everett, San Francisco ...... KO 3
May	6—Tom Sharkey, San Francisco ...... W 20
Aug.	5—Bob Armstrong, New York City .... W 10

1899
June	9—Bob Fitzsimmons, Coney Island ... KO 11
	(Won World Heavyweight Title)
Nov.	3—Tom Sharkey, Coney Island ...... W 25
	(Retained World Heavyweight Title)

1900
Apr.	6—Jack Finnegan, Detroit .... KO 1
	(Retained World Heavyweight Title)
May	11—James J. Corbett, Coney Island ... KO 23
	(Retained World Heavyweight Title)

1901
Sept.	17—Hank Griffin, Los Angeles ...... Exh. 4
Sept.	24—Joe Kennedy, Los Angeles .. Exh. KO 2
Nov.	15—Gus Ruhlin, San Francisco .... KO 5
	(Retained World Heavyweight Title)

1902
July	25—Bob Fitzsimmons, San Francisco .. KO 8
	(Retained World Heavyweight Title)

1903
Aug.	14—James J. Corbett, San Francisco .. KO 23
	(Retained World Heavyweight Title)
Dec.	19—Jack Munroe, Butte, Montana ... Exh. 4

1904
Aug.	26—Jack Munroe, San Francisco ...... KO 2
	(Retained World Heavyweight Title)

1905
May	13—Announced retirement.

1906-1909
(Inactive)

1910
July	4—Jack Johnson, Reno, Nevada .. KO by 15
	(For World Heavyweight Title)

1921
May	3—Jack Jeffries, Los Angeles .... Exh. 3

TB	KO	WD	WF	D	LD	LF	KO BY	ND	NC
21	15	3	0	2	0	0	1	0	0

Died, March 3, 1953, Burbank, Cal.
Elected to Boxing Hall of Fame, 1954.

MARVIN HART
Born, September 16, 1876, Jefferson County, Kentucky. Weight, 190 lbs. Height, 5 ft. 11¼ in. Managed by Tommy Ryan.

1899
Dec.	12—William Schiller, Louisville ...... KO 7

1900
Feb.	12—William Schiller, Louisville ...... KO 4
Apr.	2—Charles Meisner, Louisville ...... KO 1
May	10—Tommy Williams, Louisville ...... KO 2
June	12—Louis Seifker, Louisville .... KO 8
June	26—Harry Rogers, Louisville .... KO 14
Aug.	13—Kid Hubert, Louisville .... WF 7
Oct.	18—Kid Hubert, Louisville .... KO 6
Dec.	12—Peter Trainor, Louisville .... KO 17

1901
Jan.	14—Al Weinig, Louisville .... KO 11
Feb.	25—Jimmy Ryan, Louisville .... KO 8
Mar.	29—Tommy West, Louisville .... KO 16
May	24—Dan Creedon, Louisville .... KO 7
Nov.	1—Jack Beauscholte, Louisville ..... KO 10
Dec.	17—Billy Hanrahan, Louisville .... KO by 1

1902
Jan.	20—Billy Stift, Louisville .... KO 3
Apr.	7—Dick O'Brien, Louisville .... KO 4
May	3—Kid Carter, Louisville .... KO 9
Aug.	18—Billy Stift, Chicago .... W 6
Oct.	18—Kid Carter, Philadelphia .... ND 6
Nov.	10—Jack Root, Chicago .... L 6
Nov.	19—Phila. Jack O'Brien, Philadelphia ND 6

1903
Apr.	2—Jack Bonner, Louisville .... WF 4
May	5—Phila. Jack O'Brien, Philadelphia ND 6
May	13—George Gardner, Louisville .... L 12
Nov.	16—Joe Choynski, Philadelphia ...... ND 6
Dec.	1—Kid Carter, Boston .... W 15

1904
Jan.	5—George Gardner, Boston .... D 15
Jan.	25—John Willie, Chicago .... D 6
Mar.	16—Sandy Ferguson, Hot Springs ..... W 20
Apr.	20—Gus Ruhlin, Philadelphia .... ND 6
May	20—Gus Ruhlin, Baltimore .... D 12

1905
Mar.	28—Jack Johnson, San Francisco ...... W 20
May	8—John Willie, Philadelphia .... ND 6
July	3—Jack Root, Reno .... KO 12
	(Won World Heavyweight Title)

1906
Jan.	15—Pat Callahan, Butte .... Exh. KO 2
Feb.	23—Tommy Burns, Los Angeles .... L 20
	(Lost World Heavyweight Title)
May	3—Mike Schreck, New York .... ND 4

1907
Mar.	15—Harry Rogers, Hot Springs ...... KO 2
Apr.	1—Peter Maher, Hot Springs .... KO 2
May	30—Mike Schreck, Tonopah ...... KO by 21

1908
Mar.	17—John Willie, Hot Springs .... WF 4
Oct.	9—Kid Hubert, Lexington .... D 12
Oct.	20—Jack (Twin) Sullivan, Boston ..... WF 5
Nov.	14—John Willie, Philadelphia .... ND 6

1909
Mar.	12—Tony Ross, New Orleans .... WF 13
July	26—Mike Schreck, Terre Haute .... KO by 4

1910
Dec.	20—Carl Morris, Sapulpa, Ok. ..... KO by 3

TB	KO	WD	WF	D	LD	LF	KO BY	ND	NC
47	19	4	5	4	3	0	4	8	0

Died, September 17, 1931, Fern Creek, Ky.

TOMMY BURNS
(Noah Brusso)
Born, June 17, 1881, Chesley, Ontario, Canada. Nationality, German-Canadian. Weight, 175 lbs. Height, 5 ft. 7 in.

1900
	—Fred Thornton, Detroit .... KO 5
	—Fred Thornton, Delray .... KO 6

473

1901
—Billy Walsh, Detroit .... KO 5
—Archie Steele, Detroit .... KO 2
—Ed Sholtreau, Detroit .... KO 1
—Billy Walsh, Detroit .... KO 6
—Dick Smith, Mt. Clemens .... W 10
1902
—Dick Smith, Mt. Clemens .... KO 9
—Reddy Phillips, Lansing .... KO 9
Sept. 19—Jack O'Donnell, Butler, Ind. ...... KO 8
—Tom McCune, Detroit .... W 10
Nov. 29—Mike Schreck, Detroit .... L 10
1903
—Jim O'Brien, Delray .... W 10
Mar. 26—Dick Smith, Delray .... KO 2
Mar. 26—Reddy Phillips, Delray .... KO 3
—Harry Peppers, Detroit .... KO 2
—Tom McCune, Detroit .... KO 7
—Jimmy Duggan, Houghton .... KO 9
Oct. 25—Billy Moore, Houghton .... D 10
—Jack Hammond, Sault Ste. Marie KO 3
—Jack Butler, Sault Ste. Marie .... KO 2
—Jack O'Donnell, Evanston, Ill. .... KO 11
1904
—Ben O'Grady, Detroit .... KO 3
—George Shrosbee, Chicago ..... KO 5
Feb. 27—Mike Schreck, Milwaukee .... D 6
Mar. 3—Tony Caponi, Chicago .... D 6
Mar. —Tony Caponi, Chicago .... W 6
—Joe Wardinski, Salt Lake City .... KO 1
Aug. 20—Cyclone Kelly, Tacoma .... KO 4
Sept. 16—Billy Woods, Seattle .... D 15
Oct. 7—Phila. Jack O'Brien, Milwaukee ... L 6
Dec. —Indian Joe, Ballard, Wash. .... KO 6
1905
Mar. 7—Jack (Twin) Sullivan, Tacoma ...... D 20
May 3—Dave Barry, Tacoma .... W 20
June 7—Hugo Kelly, Detroit .... D 10
July 28—Hugo Kelly, Los Angeles .... D 20
Aug. 31—Dave Barry, San Francisco ...... KO 20
Oct. 17—Jack (Twin) Sullivan, Los Angeles .. L 20
1906
Feb. 23—Marvin Hart, Los Angeles .... W 20
(Won World Heavyweight Title)
Mar. 28—Jim O'Brien, San Diego ..... Exh. KO 1
Mar. 28—Jim Walker, San Diego ..... Exh. KO 1
Oct. 2—Fireman Jim Flynn, Los Angeles KO 15
(Retained World Heavyweight Title)
Nov. 28—Phila. Jack O'Brien, Los Angeles ... D 20
(Retained World Heavyweight Title)
1907
Jan. 10—Joe Grim, Philadelphia .... Exh. 3
May 8—Phila. Jack O'Brien, Los Angeles .. W 20
(Retained World Heavyweight Title)
July 4—Bill Squires, Colma, Calif. .... KO 1
(Retained World Heavyweight Title)
Dec. 2—Gunner Moir, London, England ... KO 10
(Retained World Heavyweight Title)
1908
Feb. 10—Jack Palmer, London, England ... KO 4
(Retained World Heavyweight Title)
Mar. 17—Jem Roche, Dublin, Ireland ...... KO 1
(Retained World Heavyweight Title)
Apr. 18—Jewey Smith, Paris, France .... KO 5
(Retained World Heavyweight Title)
June 13—Bill Squires, Paris, France .... KO 8
(Retained World Heavyweight Title)
Aug. 24—Bill Squires, Sydney, N.S.W. ..... KO 13
(Retained World Heavyweight Title)
Sept. 2—Bill Lang, Melbourne, Aus. .... KO 6
(Retained World Heavyweight Title)
Dec. 26—Jack Johnson, Sydney, N.S.W. KO by 14
(Lost World Heavyweight Title)
1909
(Inactive)
1910
Apr. 11—Bill Lang, Sydney, N.S.W. .... W 20
1911
(Inactive)
1912
Aug. 8—Bill Rickard, Saskatoon, Sask. ..... KO 6

1913
Apr. 2—Arthur Pelkey, Calgary, Alberta .. ND 6
1914
Jan. 26—Battling Brant, Taft, Cal. .... KO 4
1915-1917
(Inactive)
1918
Sept. 19—Tex Foster, Prince Rupert, B.C. .... KO 4
1919
(Inactive)
1920
July 16—Joe Beckett, London, England KO by 7

TB	KO	WD	WF	D	LD	LF	KO BY	ND	NC
57	35	8	0	8	3	0	2	1	0

Died, May 10, 1955, Vancouver, B.C.
Elected to Boxing Hall of Fame, 1960.

JACK JOHNSON
(John Arthur Johnson)
(The Galveston Giant)
Born, March 31, 1878, Galveston, Texas. Weight, 195 lbs. Height, 6 ft. 1¼ in. Managed by Morris Hart, Johnny Connors, Alec McLean, Sam Fitzpatrick, Abe Arends, George Little, Tom Flanagan, Sig Hart.
1897
—Jim Rocks, Galveston .... KO 4
—Sam Smith, Galveston .... W 10
1898
—Reddy Bremer, Galveston .... KO 3
—Jim Cole, Galveston .... W 4
—Henry Smith, Galveston .... D 15
1899
Feb. 11—Jim McCormick, Galveston .... NC 7
Mar. 17—Jim McCormick, Galveston .... WF 7
May 6—John (Klondike) Haynes,
Chicago .... KO by 5
Dec. 16—Pat Smith, Galveston .... D 12
1900
—Josh Mills, Memphis .... W 12
1901
Feb. 25—Joe Choynski, Galveston ...... KO by 3
Mar. 7—John Lee, Galveston .... W 15
Apr. 12—Charley Brooks, Galveston ...... KO 2
May 6—Jim McCormick, Galveston .... KO 2
May 28—Jim McCormick, Galveston .... KO 7
June 12—Horace Miles, Galveston .... KO 3
June 20—George Lawler, Galveston .... KO 10
June 28—John (Klondike) Haynes, Galveston D 20
—Willie McNeal .... KO 15
Nov. 4—Hank Griffin, Bakersfield .... L 20
Dec. 27—Hank Griffin, Oakland .... D 15
1902
Jan. 17—Frank Childs, Chicago .... D 6
Feb. 7—Dan Murphy, Waterbury .... KO 10
Feb. 22—Ed Johnson, Galveston : .... KO 4
Mar. 7—Joe Kennedy, Oakland .... KO 4
Apr. 6—Bob White .... W 15
May 1—Jim Scanlan .... KO 7
May 16—Jack Jeffries, Los Angeles .... KO 5
May 28—John (Klondike) Haynes, Memphis KO 13
June 4—Billy Stift, Denver .... D 10
June 20—Hank Griffin, Los Angeles .... D 20
Sept. 3—Mexican Pete Everett, Victor, Colo. W 20
Oct. 21—Frank Childs, Los Angeles .... W 12
Oct. 31—George Gardner, San Francisco .... W 20
Dec. 5—Fred Russell, Los Angeles .... WF 8
1903
Feb. 3—Denver Ed Martin, Los Angeles .... W 20
(Won Negro Heavyweight Title)
Feb. 27—Sam McVey, Los Angeles .... W 20
(Retained Negro Heavyweight Title)
Apr. 16—Sandy Ferguson, Boston .... W 10
May 11—Joe Butler, Philadelphia .... KO 3
July 31—Sandy Ferguson, Philadelphia .... ND 6
Oct. 27—Sam McVey, Los Angeles .... W 20
(Retained Negro Heavyweight Title)
Dec. 11—Sandy Ferguson, Colma, Calif. ..... W 20
1904
Feb. 16—Black Bill, Philadelphia .... ND 6

Apr.	22—Sam McVey, San Francisco	KO 20
	(Retained Negro Heavyweight Title)	
June	2—Frank Childs, Chicago	W 6
Oct.	18—Denver Ed Martin, Los Angeles	KO 2
	(Retained Negro Heavyweight Title)	

1905

Mar.	28—Marvin Hart, San Francisco	L 20
Apr.	25—Jim Jeffords, Philadelphia	KO 4
May	3—Black Bill, Philadelphia	KO 4
May	9—Walter Johnson, Philadelphia	KO 3
May	19—Jack Jeannette, Philadelphia	ND 6
June	26—Jack Monroe, Philadelphia	ND 6
July	13—Morris Harris, Philadelphia	KO 3
July	13—Black Bill, Philadelphia	ND 6
July	18—Sandy Ferguson, Chelsea, Mass.	WF 7
July	24—Joe Grim, Philadelphia	ND 6
Nov.	25—Joe Jeannette, Philadelphia	LF 2
Dec.	1—Young Peter Jackson, Baltimore	W 12
Dec.	2—Joe Jeannette, Philadelphia	ND 6

1906

Jan.	16—Joe Jeannette, New York	ND 3
Mar.	14—Joe Jeannette, Baltimore	W 15
Apr.	19—Black Bill, Wilkes-Barre	KO 7
Apr.	26—Sam Langford, Chelsea, Mass.	W 15
June	18—Charlie Haghey, Gloucester, Mass.	KO 2
Sept.	3—Billy Dunning, Millinocket, Me.	D 10
Sept.	20—Joe Jeannette, Philadelphia	ND 6
Nov.	8—Jim Jeffords, Lancaster, Pa.	W 6
Nov.	26—Joe Jeannette, Portland, Me.	D 10
Dec.	9—Joe Jeannette, New York	W 3

1907

Feb.	19—Peter Felix, Sydney	KO 1
Mar.	4—Jim Lang, Melbourne	KO 9
July	17—Bob Fitzsimmons, Philadelphia	KO 2
Aug.	28—Kid Cutler, Reading, Pa.	KO 1
Sept.	12—Sailor Burke, Bridgeport	W 6
Nov.	2—Fireman Jim Flynn, San Francisco	KO 11

1908

Jan.	3—Joe Jeannette, New York	D 3
June	11—Al McNamara, Plymouth, England	W 4
July	31—Ben Taylor, Plymouth, England	KO 8
Dec.	26—Tommy Burns, Sydney	KO 14
	(Won World Heavyweight Title)	

1909

Mar.	10—Victor McLaglen, Vancouver, B.C.	ND 6
	(Retained World Heavyweight Title)	
Apr.	—Frank Moran, Pittsburgh	Exh. 4
May	19—Phila. Jack O'Brien, Philadelphia	ND 6
	(Retained World Heavyweight Title)	
June	30—Tony Ross, Pittsburgh	ND 6
	(Retained World Heavyweight Title)	
Sept.	9—Al Kaufman, San Francisco	ND 10
	(Retained World Heavyweight Title)	
Oct.	16—Stanley Ketchel, Colma, Calif.	KO 12
	(Retained World Heavyweight Title)	

1910

July	4—James J. Jeffries, Reno	KO 15
	(Retained World Heavyweight Title)	

1911
(Inactive)

1912

July	4—Fireman Jim Flynn, Las Vegas, N.M.	KO 9
	(Retained World Heavyweight Title)	

1913

Dec.	19—Battling Jim Johnson, Paris, France	D 10
	(Retained World Heavyweight Title)	

1914

June	27—Frank Moran, Paris, France	W 20
	(Retained World Heavyweight Title)	
Dec.	15—Jack Murray, Buenos Aires	KO 3
	(Retained World Heavyweight Title)	

1915

Apr.	3—Sam McVey, Havana, Cuba	Exh. 6
Apr.	5—Jess Willard, Havana, Cuba	KO by 26
	(Lost World Heavyweight Title)	

1916

Mar.	10—Frank Crozier, Madrid, Spain	W 10
July	10—Arthur Craven, Barcelona, Spain	KO 1

1917
(Inactive)

1918

Apr.	3—Blink McCloskey, Madrid, Spain	W 4

1919

Feb.	12—Bill Flint, Madrid, Spain	KO 2
Apr.	7—Tom Cowler, Mexico City	D 10
June	2—Tom Cowler, Mexico City	KO 12
July	4—Paul Sampson, Mexico City	KO 6
Aug.	10—Marty Cutler, Mexico City	KO 4
Sept.	28—Capt. Bob Roper, Mexico City	W 10

1920

Apr.	18—Bob Wilson, Mexicali	KO 3
May	17—George Roberts, Tia Juana	KO 3
Nov.	25—Frank Owens, Leavenworth	KO 6
Nov.	25—Topeka Jack Johnson, Leavenworth	W 5
Nov.	30—George Owens, Leavenworth	KO 6

1921

Apr.	15—Jack Townsend, Leavenworth	KO 6
May	28—John Allen, Leavenworth	Exh. 2
May	28—Joe Boykin, Leavenworth	KO 5

1922
(Inactive)

1923

May	6—Farmer Lodge, Havana, Cuba	KO 4
May	20—Jack Thompson, Havana, Cuba	ND 15
Oct.	1—Battling Siki, Quebec	Exh. 6

1924

Feb.	22—Homer Smith, Montreal	W 10

1925
(Inactive)

1926

May	2—Pat Lester, Nogales, Mexico	W 15
May	30—Bob Lawson, Juarez, Mexico	WF 8

1927
(Inactive)

1928

Apr.	16—Bearcat Wright, Topeka, Kansas	KO by 5
May	15—Bill Hartwell, Kansas City, KS	KO by 7

TB	KO	WD	WF	D	LD	LF	KO BY	ND	NC
113	46	29	4	12	2	1	5	14	0

Died, June 10, 1946, Raleigh, N.C.
Elected to Boxing Hall of Fame, 1954.

JESS WILLARD
(The Pottawatomie Giant)

Born, December 29, 1881, Pottawatomie County, Kansas. Ancestry, English. Weight, 225-250 lbs. Height, 6 ft. 6¼ in. Managed by Tom Jones.

1911

Feb.	15—Louis Fink, Sapulpa, Ok.	LF 10
Mar.	7—Ed Burke, El Reno, Ok.	KO 3
Mar.	28—Louis Fink, Oklahoma City	KO 3
Apr.	14—Al Mendeno, Oklahoma City	KO 4
Apr.	29—Joe Cavanaugh, Oklahoma City	KO 11
June	8—Bill Shiller, Oklahoma City	KO 4
July	4—Frank Lyons, Elk City, Ok.	W 10
July	16—Mike Comiskey, Hammond, Ok.	W 10
Oct.	11—Joe Cox, Springfield, Mo.	KO by 5

1912

May	23—John Young, Fort Wayne	KO 6
June	29—Frank Bowers, St. Charles, Ill.	KO 3
July	2—John Young, South Chicago, Ill.	KO 5
July	29—Arthur Pelkey, New York	ND 10
Aug.	19—Luther McCarty, New York	ND 10
Dec.	2—Sailor White, Buffalo	KO 1
Dec.	27—Soldier Kearns, New York	KO 8

1913

Jan.	22—Frank Bauer, Fort Wayne	KO 5
Mar.	5—Jack Leon, Fort Wayne	KO 4
May	20—Ed (Gunboat) Smith, San Francisco	L 20
June	27—Charley Miller, San Francisco	D 4
July	4—Al William, Reno	W 8
Aug.	11—William (Bull) Young, Vernon	KO 11
Nov.	17—George (Boer) Rodel, Milwaukee	ND 10
Nov.	24—Jack Reed, Fort Wayne	KO 2
Dec.	3—Carl Morris, New York	ND 10
Dec.	12—George Davis, Buffalo	KO 2
Dec.	29—George (Boer) Rodel, New Haven	KO 0

1914

Mar.	27—Tom (Bearcat) MacMahon, Youngstown	L	12
Apr.	13—Dan Daily, Buffalo	KO	9
Apr.	28—George (Boer) Rodel, Atlanta	KO	6

1915

Apr.	5—Jack Johnson, Havana	KO	26
	(Won World Heavyweight Title)		

1916

Mar.	25—Frank Moran, New York	ND	10
	(Retained World Heavyweight Title)		
Aug.	8—Soldier Kearns, Plattsberg	Exh.	2

1917

(Inactive)

1918

July	4—Jim Golden, Ft. Riley, Kansas	Exh.	10
July	18—Tim Logan, Chester, Pa.	Exh.	10

1919

July	4—Jack Dempsey, Toledo	KO by	3
	(Lost World Heavyweight Title)		

1920-1921

(Inactive)

1922

Exhibitions: Tom Kennedy, 2; Joe Bonds, 2; Scotty Messer, 2; Tom Barnson, 2; Frank Farmer, 3; Alden Schumacher, 3.

1923

May	12—Floyd Johnson, New York	KO	11
July	12—Luis Firpo, Jersey City	KO by	8

TB	KO	WD	WF	D	LD	LF	KO BY	ND	NC
35	20	3	0	1	2	1	3	5	0

Died, December 15, 1968, Los Angeles, Calif.
Elected to Boxing Hall of Fame, 1977.

JACK DEMPSEY

(William Harrison Dempsey)
(The Manassa Mauler)
Born, June 24, 1895, Manassa, Colorado. Ancestry, Irish-Scotch-Cherokee. Weight, 187 lbs. Height, 6 ft. ¾ in. Managed by Frank Price, Jack Kearns.

1914

	—Fred Woods, Montrose, Colo.	KO	4
	—Andy Malloy, Durango, Colo.	L	10
	—Andy Malloy, Montrose, Colo.	KO	3
	—Andy Malloy, Durango, Colo.	NC	10
Aug.	17—Young Herman, Ramona, Colo.	D	6
	—George Copelin, Cripple Creek	KO	7
Nov.	2—Young Hancock, Salt Lake City	KO	1
Nov.	30—Bill Murphy, Salt Lake City	KO	1

1915

	—Battling Johnson	KO	1
	—Joe Lions	KO	9
Apr.	5—Jack Downey, Salt Lake City	L	4
Apr.	26—Anamas Campbell, Reno	KO	3
June	13—Johnny Sudenberg, Tonopah	W	10
July	3—Johnny Sudenberg, Goldfield	D	10
	—Johnny Person	KO	7
	—Chief Gordon	KO	6
Dec.	13—Jack Downey, Salt Lake City	D	4
Dec.	20—Two-Round Gillian, Salt Lake City	KO	1

1916

Feb.	—Johnny Sudenberg, Ely, Nevada	KO	2
Feb.	21—Jack Downey, Salt Lake City	KO	2
Feb.	23—Boston Bearcat, Ogden, Utah	KO	1
Mar.	9—Cyril Kohn, Provo, Utah	KO	4
Apr.	8—Joe Bonds, Ely, Nevada	W	10
May	3—Terry Kellar, Ogden, Utah	W	10
May	17—Dan Ketchell, Provo, Utah	KO	3
May	—George Christian, Price, Utah	KO	1
June	—Bob York, Price, Utah	KO	4
June	24—Andre Anderson, New York	ND	10
July	8—Wild Burt Kenny, New York	ND	10
July	14—John Lester Johnson, New York	ND	10
Sept.	28—Young Hector, Salida, Colo.	KO	3
Oct.	7—Terry Kellar, Ely, Nevada	W	10
Oct.	16—Fighting Dick Gilbert, Salt Lake City	W	10

1917

Feb.	13—Fireman Jim Flynn, Murray	KO by	1
Mar.	21—Al Norton, Oakland	D	4

Mar.	28—Willie Meehan, Oakland	L	4
Apr.	11—Al Norton, Oakland	D	4
July	25—Willie Meehan, Emeryville, Calif.	W	4
Aug.	1—Al Norton, Emeryville, Calif.	KO	1
Aug.	10—Willie Meehan, San Francisco	D	4
Sept.	7—Willie Meehan, San Francisco	D	4
Sept.	19—Charley Miller, Oakland	KO	1
Sept.	26—Bob McAllister, Emeryville, Calif.	W	4
Oct.	2—Ed (Gunboat) Smith, San Francisco	W	4
Nov.	2—Carl Morris, San Francisco	W	4

1918

Jan.	24—Homer Smith, Racine	KO	1
Feb.	4—Carl Morris, Buffalo	WF	6
Feb.	14—Fireman Jim Flynn, Ft. Sheridan	KO	1
Feb.	25—Bill Brennan, Milwaukee	KO	6
Mar.	16—Fred Saddy, Memphis	KO	1
Mar.	25—Tom Riley, Joplin	KO	1
May	3—Billy Miske, St. Paul	ND	10
May	22—Dan Ketchell, Excelsior Springs	KO	2
May	29—Arthur Pelkey, Denver	KO	1
July	1—Kid McCarthy, Tulsa	KO	1
July	6—Bob Devere, Joplin	KO	1
July	6—Dan (Porky) Flynn, Atlanta	KO	1
July	27—Fred Fulton, Harrison	KO	1
Aug.	17—Terry Kellar, Dayton	KO	5
Sept.	13—Willie Meehan, San Francisco	L	4
Sept.	14—Jack Moran, Reno	KO	1
Nov.	6—Battling Levinsky, Philadelphia	KO	3
Nov.	18—Dan (Porky) Flynn, Philadelphia	KO	1x
Nov.	28—Billy Miske, Philadelphia	ND	6
Dec.	16—Carl Morris, New Orleans	KO	1
Dec.	20—Clay Turner, Brooklyn	Exh.	4
Dec.	30—Ed (Gunboat) Smith, Buffalo	KO	2

1919

Jan.	20—Big Jack Hickey, Harrisburg	KO	1
Jan.	23—Kid Harris, Reading	KO	1
Jan.	29—Kid Henry, Easton	KO	1
Feb.	13—Eddie Smith, Altoona	KO	1
Mar.	1—Terry Kellar, Washington, D.C.	Exh.	3
Apr.	2—Tony Drake, New Haven	KO	1
July	4—Jess Willard, Toledo	KO	3
	(Won World Heavyweight Title)		
Aug.	24—One-Round Garrison, St. Louis	Exh.	4

1920

Mar.	5—Terry Kellar, Los Angeles	Exh.	3
Sept.	6—Billy Miske, Benton Harbor	KO	3
	(Retained World Heavyweight Title)		
Dec.	14—Bill Brennan, New York	KO	12
	(Retained World Heavyweight Title)		

1921

July	2—Georges Carpentier, Jersey City	KO	4
	(Retained World Heavyweight Title)		

1922

July	18—Elziar Rioux, Montreal	Exh. KO	1
July	18—Jack Renault, Montreal	Exh.	
July	18—Paul Lahaye, Montreal	Exh.	
July	19—Jack Renault, Ottawa	Exh.	3
Sept.	4—Jack Thompson, Michigan City	Exh.	2
Sept.	7—Andre Anderson, Michigan City	Exh.	2
Oct.	7—Jack Thompson, Boston	Exh.	2

1923

July	4—Tommy Gibbons, Shelby, Montana	W	15
	(Retained World Heavyweight Title)		
Sept.	14—Luis Firpo, New York	KO	2
	(Retained World Heavyweight Title)		

1924

Feb.	10—Dutch Seifert, Memphis	Exh. KO	1
Feb.	11—Martin Burke, New Orleans	Exh.	2
Feb.	11—Tommy Marvin, New Orleans	Exh. KO	2
June	3—Rock Stragmalia, Los Angeles	Exh. KO	2
June	3—Eli Stanton, Los Angeles	Exh. KO	1

1925

—Boxed eight exhibitions.

1926

Feb.	8—Boxed six opponents in exhibitions, knocking out four in the first round, Memphis.
Feb.	12—Boxed six opponents in exhibitions, knocking out four.
Sept.	23—Gene Tunney, Philadelphia	L	10
	(Lost World Heavyweight Title)		

1927

July	21—Jack Sharkey, New York .... KO	7
Sept.	22—Gene Tunney, Chicago L	10
	(For World Heavyweight Title)	

TB	KO	WD	WF	D	LD	LF	KO BY	ND	NC
80	49	10	1	7	6	0	1	5	1

Elected to Boxing Hall of Fame, 1954.

GENE TUNNEY
(James Joseph Tunney)
(The Fighting Marine)
Born, May 25, 1897, New York City, N.Y. Weight, 174-192 lbs. Height, 6 ft. ½ in. Managed by Sammy Kelly, Billy Roche, Frank (Doc) Bagley, Billy Gibson.

1915

July	2—Bobby Dawson, New York .... KO	7
Dec.	15—Young Sharkey, New York ...... KO	6
Dec.	29—Sailor Wolfe, New York .... KO	2

1916

	—Billy Rowe, New York .... ND	6
	—George Lahey, New York .... ND	6
Dec.	8—Young Guarini, New York .... WF	3
	—George Lahey, New York .... KO	3

1917

Feb.	9—Victor Dahl, New York .... ND	10
Oct.	2—K.O. Jaffe, New York .... ND	10
Dec.	21—Young Joe Borrell, New York .... KO	2

1918

Jan.	15—Hughey Weir, New York .... KO	2
May	2—Enlisted in U.S. Marine Corps.	
July	8—Young Guarini, Jersey City ...... KO	1
Dec.	—Tommy Gavigan, Romarantin ...... D	12
Dec.	—Howard Morrow, Romorantin ..... KO	6
Dec.	—Marchand, Paris, France .... KO	2

1919

Won A.E.F. light heavyweight championship in France, defeating K.O. Sullivan and Ted Jamieson in final rounds after defeating 20 opponents in elimination series staged throughout France. Also defeated A.E.F. heavyweight champion Fighting Bob Martin in special four-round bout.

Nov.	14—Dan Dowd, Bayonne .... ND	8
Dec.	15—Bob Pierce, Jersey City .... KO	2

1920

Jan.	1—Whitey Allen, Jersey City .... KO	2
Jan.	10—Bud Nelson, Bayonne .... KO	1
Jan.	26—Jim Monahan, Jersey City .... KO	1
Feb.	4—K.O. Sullivan, Newark .... KO	1
Mar.	4—Ed Kinley, Jersey City .... KO	5
Apr.	5—Al Roberts, Newark .... KO	7
June	7—Jeff Madden, Jersey City .... KO	2
June	28—Ole Anderson, Jersey City .... KO	3
Oct.	7—Paul Sampson, Paterson .... ND	8
Oct.	22—Sgt. Ray Smith, Camden .... KO	2
Nov.	25—Leo Houck, Philadelphia .... ND	6
Dec.	7—Leo Houck, Jersey City .... ND	8

1921

June	30—Young Ambrose, New York ...... KO	1
July	2—Soldier Jones, Jersey City .... KO	7
Aug.	16—Martin Burke, New York .... W	10
Aug.	29—Eddie Joseph, New York .... KO	12
Sept.	15—Herbert Crossley, New York ..... KO	7
Oct.	15—Jack Burke, New York .... KO	2
Nov.	22—Wolf Larsen, New York .... KO	7
Dec.	22—Eddie O'Hare, New York .... KO	6

1922

Jan.	13—Battling Levinsky, New York ...... W	12
	(Won American Light Heavyweight Title)	
Feb.	11—Jack Clifford, New York .... KO	6
Feb.	14—Whitey Wenzel, Philadelphia ..... KO	4
Mar.	3—Fay Kaiser, Grand Rapids .... ND	10
Apr.	10—Jack Burke, Pittsburgh .... KO	9
May	23—Harry Greb, New York L	15
	(Lost American Light Heavyweight Title)	
July	7—Fay Kaiser, Rockaway, New York	W 12
Aug.	1 Roy Thompson, Long Branch ..... KO	3
Aug.	17—Charley Weinert, Newark .... ND	12
Aug.	24—Tommy Loughran, Philadelphia .. ND	8
Oct.	25—Chuck Wiggins, Boston .... W	10

Nov.	3—Jack Hanlon, New York .... KO	1
Nov.	29—Charley Weinert, New York ...... KO	4

1923

Jan.	29—Jack Renault, Philadelphia .... NC	4
Feb.	3—Chuck Wiggins, New York .... W	12
Feb.	23—Harry Greb, New York .... W	15
	(Regained American Light Heavyweight Title)	
May	7—Jack Clifford, Detroit .... KO	8
May	16—Jimmy Delaney, Chicago .... ND	10
July	31—Dan O'Dowd, Long Island City ..... W	12
Dec.	10—Harry Greb, New York .... W	15
	(Retained American Light Heavyweight Title)	

1924

Jan.	15—Harry Foley, Grand Rapids .... ND	10
Jan.	24—Ray Thompson, Lake Worth, Fla.	KO 2
Feb.	15—Martin Burke, New Orleans .... W	15
Mar.	17—Jimmy Delaney, St. Paul .... ND	10
June	26—Erminio Spalla, New York .... KO	7
July	24—Georges Carpentier, New York ... KO	15
Aug.	18—Joe Lohman, Columbus .... W	8
Sept.	17—Harry Greb, Cleveland .... ND	10
Oct.	27—Harry Foley, Memphis .... KO	1
Nov.	10—Buddy McHale, Memphis .... KO	2
Dec.	8—Jeff Smith, New Orleans .... ND	15

1925

Mar.	27—Harry Greb, St. Paul .... ND	10
June	5—Tommy Gibbons, New York ...... KO	12
July	3—Italian Jack Herman, Kansas City	KO 2
Sept.	25—Bartley Madden, Minneapolis .... KO	3
Nov.	18—Johnny Risko, Cleveland .... W	12
Dec.	29—Dan O'Dowd, St. Petersburg ...... KO	2

1926

Sept.	23—Jack Dempsey, Philadelphia .... W	10
	(Won World Heavyweight Title)	

1927

Sept.	22—Jack Dempsey, Chicago .... W	10
	(Retained World Heavyweight Title)	

1928

July	26—Tom Heeney, New York .... KO	11
	(Retained World Heavyweight Title)	

TB	KO	WD	WF	D	LD	LF	KO BY	ND	NC
77	42	14	1	1	0	0	0	17	1

Elected to Boxing Hall of Fame, 1955.
Died, November 7, 1978, Greenwich, Conn.

MAX SCHMELING
(Maxmillian Adolph Otto Siegfried Schmeling)
(The Black Uhlan)
Born, September 28, 1905, Klein Luckaw (Brandenburg), Germany. Weight, 189 lbs. Height, 6 ft. 1 in. Managed by Arthur von Bulow in Germany, 1924-1928; by Joe Jacobs in the United States.

1924

Aug.	2—Hans Czapp, Dusseldorf .... KO	6
Sept.	20—Willy Louis, Duisburg .... KO	1
Sept.	22—Piet Van der Veer, Cologne ...... KO	3
Oct.	4—Rocky Knight, Cologne .... W	8
Oct.	10—Max Diekmann, Berlin .... KO by	4
Oct.	31—Fred Hammer, Cologne .... KO	3
Dec.	4—Hans Breuer, Cologne .... KO	2
Dec.	7—Battling Marthar, Dusseldorf ..... KO	3
Dec.	17—Helmuth Hartig, Berlin .... KO	1
Dec.	26—Jimmy Lyggett, Cologne .... WF	4

1925

Jan.	18—Johnny Kloudts, Cologne .... KO	2
Jan.	20—Joe Mehling, Berlin .... W	6
Mar.	1—Leon Randol, Cologne .... KO	4
Mar.	15—Alf Baker, Cologne .... W	8
Apr.	3—Jimmy Lyggett, Berlin .... D	8
Apr.	28—Fred Hammer, Bonn .... W	8
May	9—Jack Taylor, Cologne L	10
June	14—Leon Randol, Brussels .... D	10
Sept.	1—Larry Gains, Cologne .... KO by	2
Nov.	1—Rene Compere, Cologne .... W	8

1926

Feb.	12—Max Diekmann, Berlin .... D	8
Mar.	19—Willy Louis, Cologne .... KO	1
July	13—August Vongehr, Berlin .... KO	1

Aug.	24—Max Diekmann, Berlin	KO	1	

Aug. 24—Max Diekmann, Berlin .... KO 1
(Won German Light Heavyweight Title)
Oct. 1—Hermann Van't Hoff, Berlin ...... WF 8

1927
Jan. 13—Jack Stanley, Berlin .... KO 8
Jan. 23—Louis Wilms, Breslau .... KO 8
Feb. 4—Joe Mehling, Dresden .... KO 3
Mar. 12—Leon Sebilo, Dortmund .... KO 2
Apr. 8—Francis Charles, Berlin .... KO 8
Apr. 26—Stanley Glen, Hamburg .... KO 1
May 7—Robert Larsen, Frankfurt .... W 10
May 17—Raoul Paillaux, Frankfurt .... KO 3
June 19—Fernand Delarge, Dortmund ..... KO 14
(Won European Light Heavyweight Title)
July 13—Jack Taylor, Hamburg .... W 10
Aug. 7—Willem Westbroeck, Essen .... KO 1
Sept. 2—Robert Larsen, Berlin .... KO 3
Oct. 2—Louis Clement, Dortmund .... KO 6
Nov. 6—Hein Domogergen, Leipzig ...... KO 7
(Retained European Light Heavyweight Title)
Dec. 2—Gypsy Daniels, Berlin .... W 10

1928
Jan. 6—Michele Bonaglia, Berlin .... KO 1
(Retained European Light Heavyweight Title)
Feb. 25—Gypsy Daniels, Frankfurt ..... KO by 1
Mar. 11—Ted Moore, Dortmund .... W 10
Apr. 4—Franz Diener, Berlin .... W 15
(Won German Heavyweight Title)
Nov. 24—Joe Monte, New York .... KO 5

1929
Jan. 4—Joe Sekyra, New York .... W 10
Jan. 22—Pietro Corri, Newark .... KO 1
Feb. 1—Johnny Risko, New York .... KO 9
June 27—Paulino Uzcudun, New York ..... W 15

1930
June 12—Jack Sharkey, New York .... WF 4
(Won Vacant World Heavyweight Title)

1931
July 3—Young Stribling, Cleveland ..... KO 15
(Retained World Heavyweight Title)

1932
June 21—Jack Sharkey, Long Island City .... L 15
(Lost World Heavyweight Title)
Sept. 26—Mickey Walker, Long Island City KO 8

1933
June 8—Max Baer, New York .... KO by 10

1934
Feb. 13—Steve Hamas, Philadelphia .... L 12
May 13—Paulino Uzcudun, Barcelona .... D 12
Aug. 26—Walter Neusel, Hamburg .... KO 9

1935
Mar. 10—Steve Hamas, Hamburg .... KO 9
July 7—Paulino Uzcudun, Berlin .... W 12

1936
June 19—Joe Louis, New York .... KO 12

1937
Dec. 14—Harry Thomas, New York .... KO 8

1938
Jan. 30—Ben Foord, Hamburg .... W 12
Apr. 16—Steve Dudas, Hamburg .... KO 5
June 22—Joe Louis, New York .... KO by 1
(For World Heavyweight Title)

1939
July 2—Adolf Heuser, Stuttgart .... KO 1
(Won European Heavyweight Title)

1940-1946
(Inactive)

1947
Sept. 28—Werner Vollmer, Frankfurt ...... KO 7
Dec. 7—Hans Joachin Draegenstein,
Hamburg.......................... W 10

1948
May 23—Walter Neusel, Hamburg .... L 10
Oct. 2—Hans Joachin Draegenstein, Kiel KO 9
Oct. 31—Richard Vogt, Berlin .... L 10

TB	KO	WD	WF	D	LD	LF	KO BY	ND	NC
70	38	15	3	4	5	0	5	0	0

Elected to Boxing Hall of Fame, 1970.

478

JACK SHARKEY
(Joseph Paul Cukoschay)
(The Boston Gob)
Born, October 26, 1902, Binghamton, New York.
Weight, 196 lbs. Height, 6 ft. Managed by Johnny
Buckley.

1924
Jan. 29—Billy Muldoon, Boston .... KO 1
Feb. 8—Pat (Battling) Hance, Boston ..... KO 2
Feb. 26—Dan Lucas, Boston .... KO 2
Mar. 18—Eddie Record, Boston .... L 10
Apr. 25—Eddie Record, Boston .... KO 7
June 23—Floyd Johnson, Boston .... W 10
July 15—Homer Smith, Boston .... W 12
July 23—Al Roberts, Providence .... W 10
Aug. 20—Young Jack Johnson, Bangor ..... KO 6
Aug. 29—Quinton Romero Rojas, Boston KO by 9
Nov. 5—Jimmy Maloney, Boston .... L 10
Dec. 15—Charley Weinert, Newark .... ND 12

1925
Jan. 8—Jack DeMave, New York .... W 10
Jan. 20—Sully Montgomery, Boston .... W 10
Feb. 10—Charley Weinert, Boston .... L 10
Apr. 6—Jack Renault, Boston .... W 10
May 25—George Cook, Boston .... W 10
June 5—Jimmy Maloney, Boston .... WF 9
July 31—King Solomon, Boston .... W 10
Aug. 17—Bud Gorman, Boston .... L 10
Sept. 17—Johnny Risko, Boston .... W 10
Dec. 11—Jimmy Maloney, Boston .... W 10

1926
Jan. 18—Joe Lawson, Hartford .... KO 2
Feb. 12—Eddie Huffman, New York .... W 10
Apr. 1—King Solomon, Boston .... W 10
Apr. 19—Pat McCarthy, Boston .... W 10
June 25—Bud Gorman, Boston .... WF 2
Sept. 13—Orlando Riverberi, Newark ...... KO 3
Sept. 21—George Godfrey, Boston .... W 10
Oct. 12—Harry Wills, Brooklyn .... WF 13
Dec. 15—Homer Smith, Syracuse .... KO 7

1927
Mar. 3—Mike McTigue, New York .... KO 12
May 20—Jimmy Maloney, New York ...... KO 5
July 21—Jack Dempsey, New York ..... KO by 7

1928
Jan. 13—Tom Heeney, New York .... D 12
Mar. 12—Johnny Risko, New York .... L 15
Apr. 30—Jack Delaney, New York .... KO 1
June 21—Leo Gates, St. Louis .... KO 3
Dec. 6—Arthur DeKuh, Boston .... W 10

1929
Jan. 25—Meyer (K.O.) Christner, New York W 10
Feb. 27—Young Stribling, Miami .... W 10
Sept. 26—Tommy Loughran, New York ..... KO 3
(Won Vacant American Heavyweight Title)

1930
Feb. 27—Phil Scott, Miami .... KO 3
June 12—Max Schmeling, New York .... LF 4
(For Vacant World Heavyweight Title)

1931
July 22—Mickey Walker, Brooklyn .... D 15
Oct. 12—Primo Carnera, Brooklyn .... W 15

1932
June 21—Max Schmeling, Long Island City .. W 15
(Won World Heavyweight Title)

1933
June 29—Primo Carnera, Long Island City KO by 6
(Lost World Heavyweight Title)
Sept. 18—King Levinsky, Chicago .... L 10
Sept. 27—Tommy Loughran, Philadelphia .... L 15

1934
(Inactive)

1935
Nov. 22—Edward (Unknown) Winston,
Boston .... KO 2

1936
Feb. 7—Tony Shucco, Boston .... L 10
Apr. 14—Tony Shucco, Boston .... D 10

June 25—Phil Brubaker, Boston .... W 10
Aug. 18—Joe Louis, New York .... KO by 3

TB	KO	WD	WF	D	LD	LF	KO BY	ND	NC
55	15	20	3	3	8	1	4	1	0

Elected to Boxing Hall of Fame, 1980.

PRIMO CARNERA
(The Ambling Alp)
Born, October 26, 1906, Sequals, Italy. Weight, 260 lbs. Height, 6 ft. 5¾ in. Managed by Leon See in Europe; by Louis Soreci and Bill Duffy in United States.

1928
Sept. 12—Leon Sebilo, Paris .... KO 2
Sept. 25—Joe Thomas, Paris .... KO 3
Oct. 29—Salvatore Ruggirello, Paris .... KO 4
Nov. 25—Epifanio Islas, Milan .... W 10
Dec. 1—Constant Barrick, Paris .... KO 3

1929
Jan. 18—Ernst Roseman, Berlin .... W 8
Apr. 28—Franz Diener, Leipzig .... LF 1
May 22—Moise Bouquillon, Paris .... W 10
May 30—Marcel Nilles, Paris .... KO 3
June 26—Jack Humbeeck, Paris .... KO 6
Aug. 14—Jose Lete, St. Sebastian .... W 10
Aug. 25—Joe Thomas, Marseilles .... KO 4
Aug. 30—Nicolaieff, Dieppe .... KO 1
Sept. 18—Herman Jaspers, Paris .... KO 3
Oct. 17—Jack Stanley, London .... KO 1
Oct. 17—Pat Tarling, London .... Exh. KO 2
Nov. 18—Young Stribling, London .... WF 4
Dec. 7—Young Stribling, Paris .... LF 7
Dec. 17—Franz Diener, London .... KO 6

1930
Jan. 24—Big Boy Peterson, New York ..... KO 1
Jan. 31—Elziar Rioux, Chicago .... KO 1
Feb. 6—Cowboy Bill Owens, Newark ..... KO 2
Feb. 11—Buster Martin, St. Louis .... KO 2
Feb. 12—Billy Sigman, Memphis .... KO 1
Feb. 17—Man Mountain Erickson, Oklahoma City .... KO 2
Feb. 24—Farmer Lodge, New Orleans .... KO 2
Mar. 3—Roy (Ace) Clark, Philadelphia .... KO 6
Mar. 11—Sully Montgomery, Minneapolis .. KO 2
Mar. 17—Chuck Wiggins, St. Louis .... KO 2
Mar. 20—Frank Zavita, Jacksonville .... KO 1
Mar. 26—George Thayton, Kansas City .... KO 1
Mar. 28—Jack McAuliffe, Denver .... KO 1
Apr. 8—Neil Clisby, Los Angeles .... KO 2
Apr. 14—Leon Chevalier, Oakland .... KO 6
Apr. 28—Sam Baker, Portland, Ore. .... KO 1
June 5—Meyer (K.O.) Christner, Detroit .. KO 4
June 23—George Godfrey, Philadelphia .... WF 5
July 17—Bearcat Wright, Omaha .... KO 4
July 29—George Cook, Cleveland .... KO 2
Aug. 30—Ricardo Bertazzolo, Atlantic City KO 3
Sept. 8—Pat McCarthy, Newark .... KO 2
Sept. 18—Jack Gross, Chicago .... KO 2
Oct. 7—Jimmy Maloney, Boston .... L 10
Nov. 30—Paulino Uzcudun, Barcelona ...... W 10
Dec. 18—Reggie Meen, London .... KO 2

1931
Mar. 5—Jimmy Maloney, Miami .... W 10
June 15—Pat Redmond, Brooklyn .... KO 1
June 26—Umberto Torriani, Buffalo ...... KO 2
July 24—Knute Hansen, Rochester .... KO 1
Aug. 4—Roberto Riani, Newark .... KO 3
Aug. 6—Armando De Carlos, Wilmington KO 2
Oct. 12—Jack Sharkey, Brooklyn .... L 15
Nov. 19—King Levinsky, Chicago .... W 10
Nov. 27—Vittorio Campolo, New York ..... KO 2

1932
Jan. 25—Moise Bouquillon, Paris .... KO 2
Feb. 1—Ernest Guehring, Berlin .... KO 5
Feb. 29—Pierre Charles, Paris .... W 10
Mar. 23—George Cook, London .... KO 4
Apr. 7—Don McCorkindale, London ...... W 10
Apr. 29—Maurice Griselle, Paris .... W 10
May 15—Hans Schoenrath, Milan .... KO 4
May 30—Larry Gains, London .... L 10

July 20—Jack Gross, New York .... KO 7
July 28—Jerry Pavilec, W. New York, N.J. KO 3
Aug. 2—Hans Birkie, New York .... W 10
Aug. 16—Stanley Poreda, Newark .... L 10
Aug. 19—Jack Gagnon, Tiverton, R.I. ...... KO 1
Sept. 1—Art Lasky, St. Paul .... ND 10
Oct. 7—Ted Sandwina, Tampa .... KO 4
Oct. 13—Gene Stanton, Camden .... KO 6
Oct. 17—Jack Taylor, Louisville .... KO 2
Nov. 4—Les Kennedy, Boston .... KO 3
Nov. 18—Jose Santa, New York .... KO 6
Dec. 2—John Schwake, St. Louis .... KO 7
Dec. 9—King Levinsky, Chicago .... W 10
Dec. 13—Big Boy Peterson, Grand Rapids .. KO 2
Dec. 16—Meyer (K.O.) Christner, Omaha .. KO 4
Dec. 19—Jim Merriott, Tulsa .... KO 1
Dec. 29—Jack League, San Antonio .... W 6
Dec. 30—Jack Spence, Dallas .... KO 1

1933
Feb. 10—Ernie Schaaf, New York .... KO 13
June 29—Jack Sharkey, Long Island City .. KO 6
(Won World Heavyweight Title)
Oct. 22—Paulino Uzcudun, Rome .... W 15
(Retained World Heavyweight Title)

1934
Mar. 1—Tommy Loughran, Miami .... W 15
(Retained World Heavyweight Title)
June 14—Max Baer, New York .... KO by 11
(Lost World Heavyweight Title)
Dec. 1—Vittorio Campolo, Buenos Aires .... W 12

1935
Jan. 4—Cecil Harris, Montevideo .... Exh. 4
Jan. 4—Julia Pantega, Montevideo ...... Exh. 4
Jan. 13—Seal Harris, Sao Paulo .... KO 7
Jan. 22—Erwin Klausner, Rio de Janeiro .. KO 6
Mar. 15—Ray Impellitiere, New York ...... KO 9
June 25—Joe Louis, New York .... KO by 6
Nov. 1—Walter Neusel, New York .... KO 4
Nov. 24—Ford Smith, Philadelphia .... W 10
Dec. 9—Big Boy Brackley, Buffalo .... KO 4

1936
Mar. 6—Isidoro Gastanaga, New York .... KO 5
Mar. 16—Leroy Hanes, Philadelphia .... KO by 3
May 27—Leroy Hanes, Brooklyn .... KO by 9

1937
Nov. 18—Albert DiMeglio, Paris .... L 10
Dec. 4—Josef Zupan, Budapest .... KO by 2

1938-1944
(Inactive)

1945
July 22—Michel Blevens, Udine .... KO 3
Sept. 25—Sam Gardner, Trieste .... KO 1
Nov. 21—Luigi Musina, Milan .... KO by 7

1946
Mar. 19—Luigi Musina, Trieste .... L 8
May 12—Luigi Musina, Gorizia .... L 8

TB	KO	WD	WF	D	LD	LF	KO BY	ND	NC
103	68	17	2	0	7	2	6	1	0

Died, June 29, 1967, Sequals, Italy.

MAX BAER
(Maxmillian Adalbert Baer)
(The Livermore Larruper)
Born, February 11, 1909, Omaha, Nebraska. Ancestry, German-Scotch. Weight, 210 lbs. Height, 6 ft. 2½ in. Managed by Ancil Hoffman.

1929
May 16—Chief Cariboo, Stockton .... KO 2
June 6—Sailor Leeds, Stockton .... KO 1
July 4—Tillie Taverna, Stockton .... KO 1
July 18—Al Ledford, Stockton .... KO 1
July 24—Benny Hill, Oakland .... W 4
July 31—Benny Hill, Oakland .... W 4
Aug. 28—Al Ledford, Oakland .... KO 2
Sept. 4—Jack McCarthy, Oakland .... LF 3
Sept. 25—Frank Rujenski, Oakland .... KO 3
Oct. 2—George Carroll, Oakland .... KO 1
Oct. 16—Chief Cariboo, Oakland .... KO 1

Oct.	30—Alex Rowe, Oakland	KO	1
Nov.	6—Natie Brown, Oakland	W	6
Nov.	20—Tillie Taverna, Oakland	KO	2
Dec.	4—Chet Shandel, Oakland	KO	2
Dec.	30—Tony Fuente, Oakland	KO	1

1930

Jan.	15—Tiny Abbott, Oakland	LF	3
Jan.	29—Tiny Abbott, Oakland	KO	6
Apr.	9—Jack Stewart, Oakland	KO	2
Apr.	22—Ernie Owens, Los Angeles	W	10
May	7—Tom Toner, Oakland	KO	6
May	28—Jack Linkhorn, Oakland	KO	1
June	11—Buck Weaver, Oakland	KO	1
June	25—Ernie Owens, Oakland	KO	5
July	15—Les Kennedy, Los Angeles	L	10
Aug.	11—Meyer (K.O.) Christner, Oakland	KO	2
Aug.	25—Frankie Campbell, San Francisco	KO	5
Dec.	19—Ernie Schaaf, New York	L	10

1931

Jan.	16—Tom Heeney, New York	KO	3
Feb.	6—Tommy Loughran, New York	L	10
Apr.	7—Ernie Owens, Portland, Ore.	KO	2
May	5—Johnny Risko, Cleveland	L	10
July	4—Paulino Uzcudun, Reno	L	20
Sept.	23—Jack Van Noy, Oakland	KO	8
Oct.	21—Jose Santa, Oakland	KO	10
Nov.	9—Johnny Risko, San Francisco	W	10
Nov.	23—Les Kennedy, Oakland	KO	10
Dec.	30—Arthur DeKuh, Oakland	W	10

1932

Jan.	29—King Levinsky, New York	W	10
Feb.	22—Tom Heeney, San Francisco	W	10
Apr.	11—Walter Cobb, Oakland	KO	4
Apr.	26—Paul Swiderski, Los Angeles	KO	7
July	4—King Levinsky, Reno	W	20
Aug.	31—Ernie Schaaf, Chicago	W	10
Sept.	26—Tuffy Griffiths, Chicago	KO	10

1933

| June | 8—Max Schmeling, New York | KO | 10 |

1934

June	14—Primo Carnera, Long Island City	KO	11
	(Won World Heavyweight Title)		
Dec.	6—Johnny Miles, Des Moines	Exh.	4
Dec.	14—Les Kennedy, Kansas City	Exh.	4
Dec.	28—King Levinsky, Chicago	Exh. KO	2

1935

Jan.	4—Babe Hunt, Detroit	Exh.	4
Jan.	10—Dick Madden, Boston	Exh.	4
Jan.	21—Tony Cancela, Tampa	Exh.	4
Jan.	28—Jim Malone, Miami	Exh.	4
Feb.	15—Stanley Poreda, San Francisco	Exh.	4
Apr.	10—Ed Will, Grand Rapids	Exh.	4
Apr.	23—Eddie Simms, Cleveland	Exh.	4
June	13—James J. Braddock, Long Island City	L	15
	(Lost World Heavyweight Title)		
Sept.	24—Joe Louis, New York	KO by	4

1936

June	15—Tony Souza, Salt Lake City	W	6
June	17—Bob Frazier, Boise	KO	2
June	19—Millionaire Murphy, Pocatello	W	6
June	24—Wilson Dunn, San Antonio	W	6
	—George Brown	KO	3
July	2—Buck Rodgers, Dallas	KO	3
July	13—Jimmy Merriott, Oklahoma City	KO	2
July	16—Junior Munsell, Tulsa	KO	5
July	24—Bob Williams, Ogden	KO	1
Aug.	19—James J. Walsh, Vancouver	KO	1
Aug.	20—Nails Gorman, Marshfield, Ore.	KO	
Aug.	25—Cecil Myart, Portland, Ore.	W	6
Aug.	29—Al Franksco, Lewiston, Idaho	KO	2
Aug.	31—Don Baxter, Coeur d'Alene	KO	1
Sept.	2—Al Gaynor, Twin Falls	KO	1
Sept.	3—Eddie Franks, Provo	KO	3
Sept.	8—Sammy Evans, Casper	KO	4
Sept.	14—Bearcat Wright, Des Moines	W	6
Sept.	21—Andy (Kid) Miller, Sheldon	W	6
	—Cyclone Bench, Rock Springs	KO	
Oct.	6—Tim Charles, Evansville	KO	4
Oct.	8—Art Oliver, Platteville	L	6
Oct.	19—Dutch Weimer, Toronto	KO	2
	—Babe Davis, Keokuk, Iowa	W	6

1937

Apr.	15—Tommy Farr, London, England	L	12
May	27—Ben Foord, London, England	KO	9
July	30—Al Rovay, San Francisco	Exh.	4
Oct.	6—Nash Garrison, Oakland	Exh.	4

1938

| Mar. | 11—Tommy Farr, New York | W | 15 |
| Oct. | 27—Hank Hankinson, Honolulu | KO | 1 |

1939

Apr.	6—Nash Garrison, Oklahoma City	Exh.	4
June	1—Lou Nova, New York	KO by	11
Sept.	4—Ed Murphy, Silver Peak, Neb.	KO	1
Sept.	18—Babe Ritchie, Lubbock	KO	2

1940

| July | 2—Tony Galento, Jersey City | KO | 8 |
| Sept. | 26—Pat Comiskey, Jersey City | KO | 1 |

1941

| Apr. | 4—Lou Nova, New York | KO by | 8 |

TB	KO	WD	WF	D	LD	LF	KO BY	ND	NC
83	52	18	0	0	8	2	3	0	0

Died, November 21, 1959, Hollywood, Calif.
Elected to Boxing Hall of Fame, 1968.

JAMES J. BRADDOCK

(James Walter Braddock)
(The Cinderella Man)
Born, June 7, 1906, New York City, N.Y.
Ancestry, Irish. Weight, 162-197 lbs. Height, 6 ft. 3 in.
Managed by Joe Gould.

1926

Apr.	14—Al Settle, West Hoboken	ND	4
Apr.	22—George Deschner, Ridgefield Park	KO	2
June	18—Leo Dobson, Jersey City	KO	1
	—Walter Westman, Jersey City	KO	3
	—Jim Pearson	KO	2
	—Joe Hudson	ND	6
	—Al Settle	ND	6
	—Gene Travers	KO	1
	—Mick Rock	KO	1
Sept.	16—Ray Kennedy, New York	KO	1
	—Phil Weisberger	KO	1
Nov.	12—Lew Barba, New York	W	6
	—Carmine Caggiano	KO	1
	—Jack O'Day	KO	1

1927

Jan.	28—George LaRocco, New York	KO	1
	—Willie Daly, Wilkes-Barre	KO	1
	—Johnny Alberts, Wilkes-Barre	KO	3
	—Frankie Lennon, Wilkes-Barre	KO	3
Mar.	8—Nick Fadil, New York	W	6
	—Lew Barba	W	6
	—Tom McKiernan	KO	2
May	11—Jack Stone, West New York	ND	10
May	20—George LaRocco, New York	D	6
May	27—Paul Cavalier, Arcola Park	ND	10
June	8—Jimmy Francis, West New York	ND	10
July	1—Jimmy Francis, West New York	ND	10
July	23—George LaRocco, New York	W	10
Aug.	10—Vic McLaughlin, New York	W	10
	—Doc Conrad	ND	6
	—Stanley Simmons	KO	1
	—Joe Monte	D	10
	—Germany Heller	ND	10

1928

Jan.	6—Paul Swiderski, New York	W	10
May	7—Jack Darnell, Jersey City	KO	4
May	16—Jimmy Francis, West New York	ND	10
June	7—Joe Monte, New York	D	10
June	27—Billy Vidabeck, West New York	ND	10
July	25—Nando Tassi, New York	D	10
Aug.	8—Joe Sekyra, New York	L	10
Oct.	17—Pete Latzo, Newark	W	10
Nov.	30—Tuffy Griffiths, New York	KO	2

1929

Jan.	18—Leo Lomski, New York	L	10
Feb.	4—George Gemas, Newark	KO	1
Mar.	11—Jimmy Slattery, New York	KO	9
Apr.	22—Eddie Benson, Buffalo	KO	1
July	18—Tommy Loughran, New York	L	15
	(For World Light Heavyweight Title)		

Aug. 27—Yale Okun, Los Angeles .... L 10	**1935**
Nov. 15—Maxie Rosenbloom, New York ...... L 10	Jan. 4—Patsy Perroni, Detroit ....W 10
Dec. 7—Jake Warren, New York .... KO 2	Jan. 11—Hans Birkie, Pittsburgh.......KO 10

Aug. 27—Yale Okun, Los Angeles .... L 10
Nov. 15—Maxie Rosenbloom, New York ...... L 10
Dec. 7—Jake Warren, New York .... KO 2
1930
Jan. 17—Leo Lomski, Chicago .... L 10
Apr. 7—Billy Jones, Philadelphia .... L 10
June 5—Harold Mays, West New York .... ND 10
July 2—Joe Monte, Boston .... W 10
Aug. 12—Babe Hunt, Boston .... L 10
Sept. 19—Phil Mercurio, Boston .... KO 2
1931
Jan. 23—Ernie Schaaf, New York .... L 10
Mar. 5—Jack Roper, Miami .... KO 1
Mar. 30—Jack Kelly, Waterbury .... W 10
Sept. 3—Andy Mitchell, Detroit .... D 10
Oct. 9—Joe Sekyra, New York .... L 10
Nov. 10—Maxie Rosenbloom, Minneapolis .. NC 2
Dec. 4—Al Gainer, New Haven .... L 10
1932
Mar. 18—Baxter Calmes, Chicago .... L 10
May 13—Charley Retzlaff, Boston .... L 10
June 21—Vincent Parille, New York .... KO 5
July 25—Tony Shucco, New York .... L 8
Sept. 21—John Henry Lewis, San Francisco .. L 10
Sept. 30—Dynamite Jackson, San Diego ..... W 10
Oct. 21—Tom Patrick, Hollywood .... L 10
Nov. 9—Lou Scozza, San Francisco ..... KO by 6
1933
Jan. 13—Martin Levandowski, Chicago ..... W 10
Jan. 20—Hans Birkie, New York .... L 10
Mar. 1—Al Ettore, Philadelphia .... L disq. 4
Mar. 21—Al Stillman, St. Louis .... KO 10
Apr. 5—Martin Levandowski, St. Louis ..... L 10
May 19—Al Stillman, St. Louis .... L 10
June 21—Les Kennedy, Jersey City .... W 10
July 21—Chester Matan, West New York ... W 10
Sept. 25—Abe Feldman, Mt. Vernon .... NC 6
1934
June 14—Corn Griffin, New York .... KO 3
Nov. 16—John Henry Lewis, New York ..... W 10
1935
Mar. 22—Art Lasky, New York .... W 15
June 13—Max Baer, Long Island City .... W 15
(Won World Heavyweight Title)
July 18—Jack McCarthy, Columbus ...... Exh. 3
1936
(Inactive)
1937
June 22—Joe Louis, Chicago .... KO by 8
(Lost World Heavyweight Title)
1938
Jan. 21—Tommy Farr, New York .... W 10
1939-1940
(Inactive)
1941
Mar. 26—Red Burman, Charlotte .... Exh. 5

TB	KO	WD	WF	D	LD	LF	KO BY	ND	NC
85	27	17	0	5	19	1	2	12	2

Elected to Boxing Hall of Fame, 1964.
Died, November 29, 1974, North Bergen, N.J.

JOE LOUIS
(Joe Louis Barrow)
(Brown Bomber)
Born May 13, 1914, Lafayette, Alabama,
Nationality, American Negro. Weight, 200 lbs.,
Height, 6 ft. 1½ in. Managed by Julian Black and
John Roxborough, and later by Marshall Miles.
1934
July 4—Jack Kracken, Chicago ....KO 1
July 11—Willie Davis, Chicago ....KO 3
July 29—Larry Udell, Chicago ....KO 2
Aug. 13—Jack Kranz, Chicago ....W 8
Aug. 27—Buck Everett, Chicago ......KO 2
Sept. 11—Alex Borchuk, Detroit ......KO 4
Sept. 25—Adolph Wiater, Chicago ....W 10
Oct. 24—Art Sykes, Chicago ....KO 8
Oct. 30—Jack O'Dowd, Detroit ....KO 2
Nov. 14—Stanley Poreda, Chicago ......KO 1
Nov. 30—Charley Massera, Chicago .....KO 3
Dec. 14—Lee Ramage, Chicago ....KO 8

1935
Jan. 4—Patsy Perroni, Detroit ....W 10
Jan. 11—Hans Birkie, Pittsburgh.......KO 10
Feb. 21—Lee Ramage, Los Angeles.....KO 2
Mar. 8—Donald "Reds" Barry,
San Francisco ....KO 3
Mar. 28—Natie Brown, Detroit ....W 10
Apr. 12—Roy Lazer, Chicago ....KO 3
Apr. 22—Biff Benton, Dayton ....KO 2
Apr. 27—Roscoe Toles, Flint ....KO 6
May 3—Willie Davis, Peoria ....KO 2
May 7—Gene Stanton, Kalamazoo ....KO 3
June 25—Primo Carnera, N. Y. C. ......KO 6
Aug. 7—King Levinsky, Chicago ....KO 1
Sept. 24—Max Baer, N. Y. C...........KO 4
Dec. 13—Paolino Uzcudun, N. Y. C.....KO 4
1936
Jan. 17—Charley Retzlaff, Chicago ....KO 1
June 19—Max Schmeling, N. Y. C....KO by 12
Aug. 18—Jack Sharkey, N. Y. C. ......KO 3
Sept. 22—Al Ettore, Philadelphia ....KO 5
Oct. 9—Jorge Brescia, N. Y. C.........KO 3
Dec. 14—Eddie Simms, Cleveland ......KO 1
1937
Jan. 11—Steve Ketchel, Buffalo ....KO 2
Jan. 29—Bob Pastor, N. Y. C. ....W 10
Feb. 17—Natie Brown, Kansas City ....KO 4
June 22—James J. Braddock, Chicago ..KO 8
(Won the Heavyweight Championship
of the World)
Aug. 30—Tommy Farr, N. Y. C. ....W 15
(Title)
1938
Feb. 23—Nathan Mann, N. Y. C. ....KO 3
(Title)
Apr. 1—Harry Thomas, Chicago ......KO 5
(Title)
June 22—Max Schmeling, N. Y. C. ......KO 1
(Title)
1939
Jan. 25—John Henry Lewis, N. Y. C. ...KO 1
(Title)
Apr. 17—Jack Roper, Los Angeles .....KO 1
(Title)
June 28—Tony Galento, N. Y. C. ....KO 4
(Title)
Sept. 20—Bob Pastor, Detroit ....KO 11
(Title)
1940
Feb. 9—Arturo Godoy, N. Y. C. ....W 15
(Title)
Mar. 29—Johnny Paychek, N. Y. C. ....KO 2
(Title)
June 20—Arturo Godoy, N. Y. C. ......KO 8
(Title)
Dec. 16—Al McCoy, Boston ....KO 6
(Title)
1941
Jan. 31—Red Burman, N. Y. C. ....KO 5
(Title)
Feb. 17—Gus Dorazio, Philadelphia ....KO 2
(Title)
Mar. 21—Abe Simon, Detroit ....KO 13
(Title)
Apr. 8—Tony Musto, St. Louis ....KO 9
(Title)
May 23—Buddy Baer, Wash., D. C. . W disq. 7
(Title)
June 18—Billy Conn, N.Y.C............KO 13
(Title)
Sept. 29—Lou Nova, N. Y. C...........KO 6
(Title)
1942
Jan. 9—Buddy Baer, New York City ...KO 1
(Title)
(Donated Purse to Naval Relief Fund)
Mar. 27—Abe Simon, New York City ...KO 6
(Title)
(Donated Purse to Army Relief Fund)
Joined U. S. Army.
1946
June 19—Billy Conn, N. Y. C...........KO 8
(Title)
Sept. 18—Tami Mauriello, N. Y. C......KO 1
(Title)
1947
Dec. 5—Jersey Joe Walcott, N. Y. C.... W 15
(Title)
1948
June 25—Jersey Joe Walcott, New York KO 11
(World heavyweight title bout)

1949

Mar. 1—(Louis announced his retirement as undefeated world heavyweight·champion)

1950

Sept. 27—Ezzard Charles, New York ......L 15
(For the World Heavyweight Title)
Nov. 29—Cesar Brion, Chicago .... W 10

1951

Jan. 3—Freddie Beshore, Detroit .....KO 4
Feb. 7—Omelio Agramonte, Miami .... W 10
Feb. 23—Andy Walker, San Francisco ..KO 10
May 2—Omelio Agramonte, Detroit ... W 10
June 15—Lee Savold, New York .... KO 6
Aug. 1—Cesar Brion, San Francisco .... W 10
Aug. 15—Jimmy Bivins, Baltimore .... W 10
Oct. 26—Rocky Marciano, N. Y. .... KO by 8

TB	KO	WD	WF	D	LD	LF	KOBY	ND	NC
71	54	13	1	0	1	0	2	0	0

Elected to Boxing Hall of Fame 1954.

EZZARD CHARLES
(Ezzard Mack Charles)
Born, July 7, 1921, Lawrenceville, Ga. Negro. Weight, 182 lbs. Height, 6 ft. Managed by Jake Mintz and Tom Tannas.
Had 42 amateur bouts and won all.

1940

Mar. 15—Medley Johnson, Middletown .KO 3
Mar. 20—Jimmy Brown, Reading, Pa. ..KO 2
Mar. 27—John Reeves, Cincinatti ...... W 6
Apr. 2—Charley Banks, Cincinnati .... W 6
Apr. 10—Kid Ash, Portsmouth, O. .....KO 3
Apr. 16—Charley Banks, Cincinatti ...KO 2
Apr. 24—Remo Fernandez, Cincinnati .KO 6
May 10—Eddie Fowler, Portsmouth, O. KO 3
May 17—Pat Wright, Middletown .....KO 4
June 5—Frankie Williams, Cincinatti ..KO 7
June 12—John Reeves, Columbus, O. ...KO 4
June 24—Bradley Lewis, San Francisco .KO 3
Sept. 23—Marty Simmons, Cincinnati .... W 10
Oct. 3—Billy Hood, Cincinnati ......KO 2
Dec. 2—Charley Jerome, Cincinnati ...KO 2

1941

Feb. 10—Billy Bengal, Cincinnati ...... W 10
Feb. 22—Slak Carvick, Cincinnati .....KO 2
Mar. 10—Floyd Howard, Cincinnati ....KO 7
Mar. 31—Joe Sutka, Cincinnati .... W 10
May 12—Rudy Kezale, Cincinnati ...... W 10
June 9—Ken Overlin, Cincinnati ....L 10
July 21—Al Gilbert, Cincinnati ....KO 6
Oct. 13—Pat Mangini, Cincinnati ......KO 1
Nov. 17—Teddy Yarosz, Cincinnati ..... W 10

1942

Jan. 12—Anton Christoforidis, Cinn....KO 3
Mar. 2—Ken Overlin, Cincinnati .... D 10
Apr. 8—Billy Pryor, Cincinnati .... W 10
May 13—Kid Tunero, Cincinnati ....L 10
May 25—Charley Burley, Pittsburgh .... W 10
June 29—Charley Burley, Pittsburgh .... W 10
July 14—Steve Mamakos, Cincinnati ...KO 1
July 27—Booker Beckwith, Pittsburgh .KO 9
Aug. 17—Jose Basora, Pittsburgh ......KO 5
Sept. 15—Mose Brown, Pittsburgh ......KO 6
Oct. 27—Joey Maxim, Pittsburgh ...... W 10
Dec. 1—Joey Maxim, Cleveland .... W 10
In U. S. Army.

1943

Jan. 7—Jimmy Bivins, Cleveland ......L 10
Mar. 31—Lloyd Marshall, Cleveland .KO by 8
In U. S. Army. Boxed in Inter-Allied Tourneys in Italy and North Africa and won all bouts.

1946

Feb. 18—Al Sheridan, Cincinnati ......KO 2
Mar. 25—Tee Hubert, Cincinnati .... W 10
Apr. 1—Billy Duncan, Pittsburgh ....KO 4
Apr. 15—Georgie Parks, Pittsburgh ....KO 6
May 13—Tee Hubert, Cincinnati ......KO 4
May 20—Archie Moore, Pittsburgh .... W 10
June 13—Sheldon Bell, Youngstown ...KO 5
July 29—Lloyd Marshall, Cincinatti ...KO 6
Sept. 23—Billy Smith, Cincinnati .... W 10
Nov. 12—Jimmy Bivins, Pittsburgh ...... W 10

1947

Feb. 17—Billy Smith, Cleveland ......KO 5
Mar. 10—Jimmy Bivins, Cleveland .....KO 4
Apr. 14—Erv Sarlin, Pittsburgh .... W 10

May 5—Archie Moore, Cincinnati ...... W 10
July 14—Fitzie Fitzpatrick, Cincinnati .KO 5
July 25—Elmer Ray, N. Y. C. ....L 10
Sept. 16—Joe Matisi, Buffalo .... W 10
Sept. 29—Lloyd Marshall, Cincinnati ...KO 2
Oct. 16—Al Smith, Akron ....KO 4
Oct. 27—Clarence Jones, Huntington ..KO 1
Nov. 3—Teddy Randolph, Buffalo ... W 10
Dec. 2—Fitzie Fitzpatrick, Cleveland ..KO 4

1948

Jan. 13—Archie Moore, Cleveland .....KO 8
Feb. 20—Sam Baroudi, Chicago ....KO 10
May 7—Elmer Ray, Chicago ....KO 9
May 20—Erv Sarlin, Buffalo .... W 10
Sept. 13—Jimmy Bivins, Wash., D. C. .... W 10
Nov. 14—Walter Hafer, Cincinnati ....KO 7
Dec. 10—Joe Baksi, New York ....KO 11

1949

Feb. 7—Johnny Haynes, Philadelphia .KO 8
Feb. 28—Joey Maxim, Cincinnati ...... W 15
June 22—Joe Walcott, Chicago .... W 15
(Won vacant N. B. A. World Heavyweight Title.)
Aug. 10—Gus Lesnevich, New York ...KO 7
(N.B.A. Title Bout)
Oct. 14—Pat Valentino, San Francisco .KO 8
(N. B. A. Title Bout)

1950

Aug. 15—Freddy Beshore, Buffalo .....KO 14
(N. B. A. Title)
Sept. 27—Joe Louis, New York .... W 15
(N. B. A. and N. Y. title)
Dec. 5—Nick Barone, Cincinnati ......KO 11
(Title bout)

1951

Jan. 12—Lee Oma, New York ....KO 10
(Title bout)
Mar. 7—Joe Walcott, Detroit .... W 15
(Title bout)
May 30—Joey Maxim, Chicago .... W 15
(Title bout)
July 18—Joe Walcott, Pittsburgh ...KO by 7
(Lost world heavyweight title)
Oct. 10—Rex Layne, Pittsburgh ......KO 11
Dec. 12—Joey Maxim, San Francisco .... W 12
Dec. 21—Joe Kahut, Portland ....KO 8

1952

June 5—Joe Walcott, Philadelphia ......L 15
(title bout)
Aug. 8—Rex Layne, Ogden ....L 10
Oct. 8—Bernie Reynolds, Cincinnati ..KO 2
Oct. 24—Cesar Brion, New York .... W 10
Nov. 26—Jimmy Bivins, Chicago ...... W 10
Dec. 15—Frank Buford, Boston ....KO 7

1953

Jan. 14—Wes Bascom, St. Louis ....KO 9
Feb. 4—Tommy Harrison, Detroit ...KO 9
Apr. 1—Rex Layne, San Francisco ..... W 10
May 12—Bill Gilliam, Toledo ....KO 9
May 26—Larry Watson, Milwaukee ...KO 5
Aug. 11—Nino Valdes, Miami Beach .... W 10
Sept. 8—Harold Johnson, Philadelphia ...L 10
Dec. 16—Coley Wallace, San Francisco .KO 10

1954

Jan. 13—Bob Satterfield, Chicago ...KO 2
June 17—Rocky Marciano, New York ....L 15
(For the World Heavyweight Title)
Sept. 17—Rocky Marciano, N. Y. .....KO by 8
(For the World Heavyweight Title)

1955

Feb. 18—Charley Norkus, New York ... W 10
Apr. 11—Vern Escoe, Edmonton ......KO 3
Apr. 27—John Holman, Miami Beach KO by 9
June 8—John Holman, Cincinnati ...... W 10
July 13—Paul Andrews, Chicago ...... W 10
Aug. 3—Tommy Jackson, Syracuse ....L 10
Aug. 31—Tommy Jackson, Cleveland ...L 10
Nov. 14—Toxie Hall, Providence ....L 10
Dec. 6—Toxie Hall, Rochester ...... W 10
Dec. 22—Bob Albright, San Francisco ... W 10
Dec. 29—Young Jackson Johnson,
Los Angeles ....KO by 6

1956

Apr. 21—Don Jasper, Windsor ....KO 9
May 21—Wayne Bethea, New York .....L 10
June 19—Bob Albright, Phoenix ......KO 7
July 13—Pat McMurtry, Tacoma........L 10
Aug. 31—Harry Matthews, Seattle .....L 10
Oct. 2—Dick Richardson, London, L Disq. 2
Announced retirement December 1, 1956

1957
(inactive)
1958
Aug. 28—Johnny Harper, Fairmont,
W. Va. .... W 10
Sept. 30—Alfredo Zuany, Juarez ....L 10
Oct. 27—Donnie Fleeman, Dallas ...KO by 6
1959
July 3—Dave Ashley, Cincinnati ......KO 7
July 30—George Logan, Boise ......KO by 8
Sept. 1—Alvin Green, Oklahoma City ....L 10

TB	KO	WD	WF	D	LD	LF	KOBY	ND	NC
122	58	38	0	1	17	1	7	0	0

Elected Boxing Hall of Fame 1970.
Died May 27, 1975 in Chicago, Ill.

JERSEY JOE WALCOTT
(Arnold Raymond Cream)
Born, January 31, 1914, Merchantville, N. J. Weight, 194 pounds. Height 6 ft. Managed by Felix Bocchicchio. Previous record unavailable.

1930
Sept. 9—Cowboy Wallace, Vineland
N.J............................KO 1
1933
Bob Norris, Camden ....KO 1
—Henry Taylor, Camden ....KO 1
1934
—Pat Roland, Camden ....KO 5
—Louis LaPage, Camden ......KO 3
—Al King, Camden ....KO 4
1935
—Roxie Allen, Camden ....KO 7
—Al Lang, Camden ....KO 1
Sept. —Lew Alva, Camden ....KO 3
1936
Jan. 21—Al Ettore, Camden .... KO by 8
Mar. 16—Willie Reddish, Philadelphia ...... W 10
June 22—Phil Johnson, Philadelphia .... KO 3
June —Joe Colucci, Camden .... KO 4
July 1—Billy Ketchell, Camden .... D 10
—Yg. Carmen Passarella, Camden ... W 8
—Billy Ketchell, Camden .... W 10
Sept. 1—Billy Ketchell, Pensauken, N. J ..... L 10
1937
May 22—Tiger Jack Fox, N. Y. C. ...KO by 8
Sept. 3—Joe Lipps, Atlantic City ......KO 2
Sept. 25—Elmer Ray, N. Y. C. ....KO 3
Oct. 9—George Brothers, N. Y. C. ....L 8
1938
Jan. 10—Freddie Fiducia, Phila. .... W 8
Mar. 28—Art Sykes, Philadelphia ......KO 4
Apr. 12—Lorenzo Pack, Camden ......KO 4
May 10—Tiger Jack Fox, Camden ....L 10
June 14—Roy Lazer, Fairview, N. J. .....L 8
Dec. 13—Bob Tow, Camden .... W 8
1939
Aug. 14—Al Boros, Newark .... W 8
Nov. 18—Curtis Sheppard, N. Y. C. ...... W 8
1940
Jan. 19—Tiger Red Lewis, Phila. ....KO 6
Feb. 12—Abe Simon, Newark ......KO by 6
1941
June 27—Columbus Gant, Memphis ....KO 3
1944
June 7—Felix Del Paoli, Batesville, N.J. . W 8
June 28—Ellis Singleton, Batesville .....KO 3
1945
Jan. 11—Jackie Saunders, Camden .....KO 2
Jan. 25—Johnny Allen, Camden ....L 8
Feb. 22—Austin Johnson, Camden ...... W 6
Mar. 15—Johnny Allen, Camden .... W 8
Aug. 2—Joe Baksi, Camden ....W 10
Sept. 20—Johnny Denson, Camden ......KO 2
Oct. 23—Steve Dudas, Paterson ......KO 5
Nov. 12—Lee Q. Murray, Balt. ......W Dis. 9
Dec. 10—Curtis Sheppard, Baltimore ...KO 10
1946
Jan. 30—Johnny Allen, Camden ......KO 3
Feb. 25—Jimmy Bivins, Cleveland ...... W 10
Mar. 20—Al Blake, Camden ....KO 4
May 24—Lee Oma, N. Y. ....W 10
Aug. 16—Tommy Gomez, Garden .....KO 3
Aug. 28—Joey Maxim, Camden ....L 10
Nov. 15—Elmer Ray, Garden ....L 10

1947
Jan. 6—Joey Maxim, Philadelphia .....W 10
Mar. 4—Elmer Ray, Miami ....W 10
June 23—Joey Maxim, Los Angeles......W 10
Dec. 5—Joe Louis, N. Y. C. ....L 15
(For world heavyweight championship)
1948
June 25—Joe Louis, N. Y. C. ....KO by 11
(World Heavyweight title bout)
1949
June 22—Ezzard Charles, Chicago .....L 15
(For N. B. A. Heavyweight Title)
Aug. 14—Olle Tandberg, Stockholm ....KO 5
1950
Feb. 8—Harold Johnson, Philadelphia .KO 3
Mar. 3—Omelio Agramonte, New York KO 7
Mar. 13—Johnny Shkor, Philadelphia ..KO 1
May 28—Hein Ten Hoff, Mannhein .....W 10
Nov. 24—Rex Layne, New York ....L 10
1951
Mar. 7—Ezzard Charles, Detroit ....L 15
(For World Heavyweight Title)
July 18—Ezzard Charles, Pittsburgh....KO 7
(Won world heavyweight title)
1952
June 5—Ezzard Charles, Philadelphia ... W 15
(title bout)
Sept. 23—Rocky Marciano, Phila. ...KO by 13
(Lost World Heavyweight Title)
1953
May 15—Rocky Marciano, Chicago . KO by 1
(World Heavyweight Title Bout)

Elected to Hall of Fame 1969

TB	KO	WD	WF	D	LD	LF	KOBY	ND	NC
67	30	18	1	1	11	0	6	0	0

ROCKY MARCIANO
(Rocco Francis Marchegiano)
(Brockton Blockbuster)
Born, September 1, 1923, Brockton, Mass. Nationality, Italian-American. Weight 184 pounds. Height, 5 ft. 11 ins. Managed by Gene Caggiano. Later by Al Weill.
1947
Mar. 17—Lee Epperson, Holyoke ......KO 3
1948
July 12—Harry Balzerian, Providence ..KO 1
July 19—John Edwards, Providence ....KO 1
Aug. 9—Bobby Quinn, Providence ....KO 3
Aug. 23—Eddie Ross, Providence .....KO 1
Aug. 30—Jimmy Weeks, Providence ....KO 1
Sept. 13—Jerry Jackson, Providence ....KO 1
Sept. 20—Bill Hardeman, Providence ...KO 1
Sept. 30—Gil Cardione, Wash., D. C. ....KO 1
Oct. 4—Bob Jefferson, Providence ....KO 2
Nov. 29—Patrick Connolly, Providence .KO 1
Dec. 4—Gilley Ferron, Philadelphia ...KO 2
1949
Mar. 21—Johnny Pretzie, Providence ...KO 5
Mar. 28—Artie Donator, Providence ....KO 1
Apr. 11—James Walls, Providence .....KO 3
May 2—Jimmy Evans, Providence .....KO 3
May 23—Don Mogard, Providence ......W 10
July 18—Harry Haft, Providence ....KO 3
Aug. 16—Pete Louthis, New Bedford ....KO 3
Sept. 26—Tommy DiGiorgio, Providence KO 4
Oct. 10—Ted Lowry, Providence ...... W 10
Nov. 7—Joe Domonic, Providence ....KO 2
Dec. 2—Pat Richards, New York ......KO 2
Dec. 19—Phil Muscato, Providence ....KO 5
Dec. 30—Carmine Vingo, New York ....KO 6
1950
Mar. 24—Roland LaStarza, New York ... W 10
June 5—Eldridge Eatman, Providence .KO 3
July 10—Gino Buonvino, Boston ....KO 10
Sept. 18—Johnny Shkor, Providence....KO 6
Nov. 13—Ted Lowry, Providence ...... W 10
Dec. 18—Bill Wilson, Providence ....KO 1
1951
Jan. 29—Keene Simmons, Providence ..KO 8
Mar. 20—Harold Mitchell, Hartford ....KO 2
Mar. 26—Art Henri, Providence ....KO 9
Apr. 30—Red Applegate, Providence ...W 10
July 12—Rex Layne, N. Y. ....KO 6
Aug. 27—Freddie Beshore, Boston ......KO 4
Oct. 26—Joe Louis, N. Y. C. ....KO 8

483

1952

Feb. 13—Lee Savold, Philadelphia	KO	6
Apr. 21—Gino Buonvino, Providence	KO	2
May 12—Bernie Reynolds, Providence	KO	3
July 28—Harry Matthews, New York	KO	2
Sept. 23—Jersey Joe Walcott, Phila.	KO	13

(Won World Heavyweight Title)

1953

May 15—Jersey Joe Walcott, Chicago	KO	1

(Title Bout)

Sept. 24—Roland LaStarza, New York	KO	11

(Title Bout)

1954

June 17—Ezzard Charles, New York	W	15

(Title Bout)

Sept. 17—Ezzard Charles, New York	KO	8

(Title Bout)

1955

May 16—Don Cockell, San Francisco	KO	9

(Title Bout)

Sept. 21—Archie Moore, New York	KO	9

(Title Bout)

1956

Announced retirement as undefeated world heavyweight champion, April 27, 1956.

TB	KO	WD	WF	D	LD	LF	KOBY	ND	NC
49	43	6	0	0	0	0	0	0	0

Elected to Boxing Hall of Fame 1959.
Killed in an airplane accident in Newton, Iowa, August 31, 1969 the day before his 46th birthday.

FLOYD PATTERSON

Born, Jan. 4, 1935, Waco, N. C. Nationality, American Negro. Weight, 182 lbs. Height, 6 feet. Managed by Cus D'Amato.
1952 Olympic Middleweight Champion.

1952

Sept. 12—Eddie Godbold, New York	KO	4
Oct. 6—Sammy Walker, Brooklyn	KO	2
Oct. 21—Lester Jackson, New York	KO	3
Dec. 29—Lalu Sabotin, Brooklyn	KO	5

1953

Jan. 28—Chester Mieszala, Chicago	KO	5
Apr. 3—Dick Wagner, Brooklyn	W	8
June 1—Gordon Wallace, Brooklyn	KO	3
Oct. 19—Wes Bascom, Brooklyn	W	8
Dec. 14—Dick Wagner, Brooklyn	KO	5

1954

Feb. 15—Yvon Durelle, Brooklyn	W	8
Mar. 30—Sam Brown, Washington	KO	8
Apr. 19—Alvin Williams, Brooklyn	W	8
May 10—Jesse Turner, Brooklyn	W	8
June 7—Joe Maxim, Brooklyn	L	8
July 12—Jacques Royer-Crecy, N. Y.	KO	7
Aug. 2—Tommy Harrison, Brooklyn	KO	1
Oct. 11—Esau Ferdinand, Brooklyn	W	8
Oct. 22—Joe Gannon, New York	W	8
Nov. 19—Jimmy Slade, New York	W	8

1955

Jan. 7—Willie Troy, New York	KO	5
Jan. 17—Don Grant, Brooklyn	KO	5
Mar. 17—Esau Ferdinand, Oakland	KO	10
June 23—Yvon Durelle, Newcastle	KO	5
July 6—Archie McBride, New York	KO	7
Sept. 8—Alvin Williams, Moncton	KO	8
Sept. 29—Dave Whitlock, San Francisco	KO	3
Oct. 13—Calvin Brad, Los Angeles	KO	1
Dec. 8—Jimmy Slade, Los Angeles	KO	7

1956

Mar. 12—Jimmy Walls, New Britain	KO	2
Apr. 10—Alvin Williams, Kansas City	KO	3
*June 8—Tommy Jackson, New York	W	12
Nov. 30—Archie Moore, Chicago	KO	5

(Won vacant World Heavyweight Title)
*Elimination bout for heavyweight title.

1957

July 29—Tommy Jackson, New York	KO	10

(World Heavyweight Title)

Aug. 22—Pete Rademacher, Seattle	KO	6

(World Heavyweight Title)

1958

Aug. 18—Roy Harris, Los Angeles	KO	12

(World Heavyweight Title)

1959

May 1—Brian London, Indianapolis	KO	11

(World Heavyweight Title)

June 26—Ingemar Johansson, New York City	KO by	3

(Lost World Heavyweight Title)

1960

June 20—Ingemar Johansson, N. Y. C.	KO	5

(First Man to Regain Heavyweight Title)
Went to Europe and engaged in exhibitions in Sweden, Germany, England and Italy.

1961

Mar. 13—Ingemar Johansson, Miami Beach	KO	6

(World Heavyweight Title)

Dec. 4—Tom McNeeley, Toronto	KO	4

(World Heavyweight Title)

1962

Sept. 25—Sonny Liston, Chicago	KO by	1

(Lost World Heavyweight Title)

1963

July 22—Sonny Liston, Las Vegas	KO by	1

(For World Heavyweight Championship)

1964

Jan. 6—Sante Amonti, Stockholm	KO	8
July 5—Eddie Machen, Stockholm	W	12
Dec. 12—Charley Powell, San Juan	KO	6

1965

Feb. 1—George Chuvalo, N. Y. C.	W	12
May 14—Tod Herring, Stockholm, Sweden	KO	3
Nov. 22—Muhammad Ali, Las Vegas	KO by	12

(World Heavyweight Title)

1966

Sept. 20—Henry Cooper, London, Eng.	KO	4

1967

Feb. 13—Willie Johnson, Miami Beach	KO	3
Mar. 30—Bill McMurray, Pittsburgh	KO	1
June 9—Jerry Quarry, Los Angeles	D	10
Oct. 28—Jerry Quarry, Los Angeles	L	12

1968

Sept. 14—Jimmy Ellis, Stockholm	L	15

(W.B.A. Heavyweight Title)

1969

Inactive

1970

Sept. 15—Charlie Green, New York	KO	10

1971

Jan. 16—Levi Forte, Miami Beach	KO	2
Mar. 29—Roger Russell, Philadelphia	KO	9
May 26—Terry Daniels, Cleveland	W	10
July 17—Charlie Polite, Erie	W	10
Aug. 21—Vic Brown, Buffalo	W	10
Nov. 23—Charlie Harris, Portland	KO	6

1972

Feb. 11—Oscar Bonavena, New York	W	10
May 16—Charlie Harris, Washington, D.C.	Exh.	5
July 14—Pedro Agosto, New York	KO	6
Sept. 20—Muhammad Ali, New York	KO by	7

TB	KO	WD	WF	D	LD	LF	KO BY	ND	NC
64	40	15	0	1	3	0	5	0	0

Elected to Hall of Fame 1977

INGEMAR JOHANSSON

Born, Sweden, Sept. 22, 1932. 195 pounds, 6 ft. ½ in.
Represented Sweden in 1952 Olympics in Helsinki; reached final in heavyweight class, but lost on second-round disqualification to Ed Sanders of United States.
Amateur record 71 bouts-11 losses.

1952

Dec. 5—Robert Masson, Gothenburg	KO	4

1953

Feb. 6—Emile Bentz, Gothenburg	KO	2
Mar. 6—Lloyd Barnett, Gothenburg	W	8
Mar. 12—Erik Jensen, Copenhagen	W	6

(Scandinavian heavyweight title)

Dec. 4—Raymond Degl'Innocenti, Stockholm	KO	2

In Swedish Navy.

1954

Nov. 5—Werner Wiegand, Gothenburg	KO	5

1955

Jan. 6—Ansel Adams, Gothenburg	W	8
Feb. 13—Kurt Schiegl, Stockholm	KO	8
Mar. 5—Aldo Pellegrini, Gothenburg	WF	5
Apr. 3—Uber Bacilieri, Stockholm	W	8
June 12—Gunter Nurnberg, Dortmud	KO	7
Aug. 28—Hein ten Hoff, Gothenburg	KO	1

1956

Feb. 24—Joe Bygraves, Gothenburg	W	10
apr. 15—Hans Friedrich, Stockholm	W	10
Sept. 30—Franco Cavicchi, Milan	KO	13

(European heavyweight title)

Dec. 28—Peter Bates, Gothenburg	KO	2

1957

May 19—Henry Cooper, Stockholm ....KO 5
(European heavyweight title)
Dec. 13—Archie McBride, Gothenburg .. W 10

1958

Feb. 21—Joe Erskine, Gothenburg .....KO 13
(European heavyweight title)
July 13—Heinz Neuhaus, Gothenberg ..KO 4
Sept. 14—Eddie Machen, Gothenburg...KO 1

1959

June 26—Floyd Patterson, New York ...KO 3
(Won World Heavyweight Title)

1960

June 20—Floyd Patterson, N. Y. C. .. KO by 5
(Lost World Heavyweight Title)

1961

Mar. 13—Floyd Patterson, Miami
Beach ....KO by 6
(For World Heavyweight Title)

1962

Feb. 9—Joe Bygraves, Gothenburg ....KO 7
Apr. 15—Wim Snoek, Stockholm .....KO 5
June 17—Dick Richardson, Gothenburg KO 8
(Won European Heavyweight Title)

1963

Apr. 21—Brian London, Stockholm ..... W 12

TB	KO	WD	WF	D	LD	LF	KOBY	ND	NC
28	17	8	1	0	0	0	2	0	0

CHARLES (SONNY) LISTON

Born, May 8, 1932, St. Francis County, Arkansas.
Weight, 200-220 lbs. Height, 6 ft. 1 in.

1953

Sept. 2—Don Smith, St. Louis .... KO 1
Sept. 17—Ponce DeLeon, St. Louis .... W 4
Nov. 21—Ben Thomas, St. Louis .... KO 6

1954

Jan. 25—Martin Lee, St. Louis .... KO 6
Mar. 31—Stan Howlett, St. Louis .... W 6
June 29—John Summerlin, Detroit .... W 8
Aug. 10—John Summerlin, Detroit .... W 8
Sept. 7—Marty Marshall, Detroit .... L 8

1955

Mar. 1—Neil Welch, St. Louis .... W 8
Apr. 21—Marty Marshall, St. Louis .... KO 6
May 5—Emil Brtko, Pittsburgh .... KO 5
May 25—Calvin Butler, St. Louis .... KO 2
Sept. 13—Johnny Gray, Indianapolis .... KO 6
Dec. 13—Larry Watson, East St. Louis ..... KO 4

1956

Mar. 6—Marty Marshall, Pittsburgh .... W 10

1957

(Inactive)

1958

Jan. 29—Bill Hunter, Chicago............. KO 2
Mar. 11—Ben Wise, Chicago .... KO 4
Apr. 3—Bert Whitehurst, St. Louis .... W 10
May 14—Julio Mederos, Chicago .... KO 3
Aug. 6—Wayne Bethea, Chicago .... KO 1
Oct. 7—Frankie Daniels, Miami Beach ... KO 1
Oct. 24—Bert Whitehurst, St. Louis .... W 10
Nov. 18—Ernie Cab, Miami Beach .... KO 8

1959

Feb. 18—Mike DeJohn, Miami Beach ...... KO 6
Apr. 15—Cleveland Williams, Miami Beach KO 3
Aug. 5—Nino Valdes, Chicago .... KO 3
Dec. 9—Willi Besmanoff, Cleveland ...... KO 7

1960

Feb. 23—Howard King, Miami Beach ...... KO 8
Mar. 21—Cleveland Williams, Houston ..... KO 2
Apr. 25—Roy Harris, Houston .... KO 1
July 18—Zora Folley, Denver .... KO 3
Sept. 7—Eddie Machen, Seattle .... W 12

1961

Mar. 8—Howard King, Miami Beach ...... KO 3
Dec. 4—Albert Westphal, Philadelphia .... KO 1

1962

Sept. 25—Floyd Patterson, Chicago......... KO 1
(Won World Heavyweight Title)

1963

July 22—Floyd Patterson, Las Vegas ...... KO 1
(Retained World Heavyweight Title)
Aug.-Sept.—Exhibition tour in Europe.

1964

Feb. 25—Cassius Clay, Miami Beach ... KO by 7
(Lost World Heavyweight Title)

1965

May 25—Muhammad Ali, Lewiston, Me. KO by 1
(For World Heavyweight Title)

1966

June 29—Gerhard Zech, Stockholm .... KO 7
Aug. 19—Amos Johnson, Gothenburg ...... KO 3

1967

Mar. 30—Dave Bailey, Gothenburg .... KO 1
Apr. 28—Elmer Rush, Stockholm .... KO 6

1968

Mar. 16—Bill McMurray, Reno .... KO 4
May 23—Billy Joiner, Los Angeles .... KO 7
July 6—Henry Clark, San Francisco ...... KO 7
Oct. 14—Sonny Moore, Phoenix .... KO 3
Nov. 3—Willis Earls, Juarez .... KO 2
Nov. 12—Roger Rischer, Pittsburgh .... KO 3
Dec. 12—Amos Lincoln, Baltimore .... KO 2

1969

Mar. 28—Billy Joiner, St. Louis .... W 10
May 19—George Johnson, Las Vegas ...... KO 7
Sept. 23—Sonny Moore, Houston .... KO 3
Dec. 6—Leotis Martin, Las Vegas ..... KO by 9
(For Vacant NABF Heavyweight Title)

1970

June 29—Chuck Wepner, Jersey City ...... KO 10

TB	KO	WD	WF	D	LD	LF	KO BY	ND	NC
54	39	11	0	0	1	0	3	0	0

Died, December 30, 1970, Las Vegas, Nev.

MUHAMMAD ALI
(Cassius Marcellus Clay, Jr.)
(The Louisville Lip)

Born, January 17, 1942, Louisville, Ky. Weight, 186-230 lbs. Height, 6 ft. 3 in.
1959 Golden Gloves Tournament of Champions Light Heavyweight Winner. 1959 National AAU Light Heavyweight Champion. 1960 Golden Gloves Tournament of Champions Heavyweight Winner. 1960 National AAU Light Heavyweight Champion. 1960 Olympic Light Heavyweight Champion.

1960

Oct. 29—Tunney Hunsaker, Louisville ...... W 6
Dec. 27—Herb Siler, Miami Beach .... KO 4

1961

Jan. 17—Tony Esperti, Miami Beach ...... KO 3
Feb. 7—Jim Robinson, Miami Beach ...... KO 1
Feb. 21—Donnie Fleeman, Miami Beach ... KO 7
Apr. 19—Lamar Clark, Louisville .... KO 2
June 26—Duke Sabedong, Las Vegas .... W 10
July 22—Alonzo Johnson, Louisville ...... W 10
Oct. 7—Alex Miteff, Louisville .... KO 6
Nov. 29—Willi Besmanoff, Louisville .... KO 7

1962

Feb. 10—Sonny Banks, New York .... KO 4
Feb. 28—Don Warner, Miami Beach .... KO 4
Apr. 23—George Logan, Los Angeles ...... KO 4
May 19—Billy Daniels, New York .... KO 7
July 20—Alejandro Lavorante, Los Angeles KO 5
Nov. 15—Archie Moore, Los Angeles .... KO 4

1963

Jan. 24—Charlie Powell, Pittsburgh ...... KO 3
Mar. 13—Doug Jones, New York .... W 10
June 18—Henry Cooper, London .... KO 5

1964

Feb. 25—Sonny Liston, Miami Beach ...... KO 7
(Won World Heavyweight Title)

1965

May 25—Sonny Liston, Lewiston, Me. ..... KO 1
(Retained World Heavyweight Title)
July 31—Jimmy Ellis, San Juan, P.R. .... Exh. 3
July 31—Cody Jones, San Juan, P.R. ..... Exh. 3
Aug. 10—Cody Jones, Gothenburg .... Exh. 2
Aug. 16—Jimmy Ellis, Gothenburg .... Exh. 2

485

Aug.	20—Jimmy Ellis, London, England .. Exh.	4
Aug.	20—Cody Jones, Paisley, Scotland ... Exh.	4
Nov.	22—Floyd Patterson, Las Vegas ...... KO	12
	(Retained World Heavyweight Title)	

1966

Mar.	29—George Chuvalo, Toronto .... W	15
	(Retained World Heavyweight Title)	
May	21—Henry Cooper, London, England .. KO	6
	(Retained World Heavyweight Title)	
Aug.	6—Brian London, London, England .. KO	3
	(Retained World Heavyweight Title)	
Sept.	10—Karl Mildenberger, Frankfurt .... KO	12
	(Retained World Heavyweight Title)	
Nov.	14—Cleveland Williams, Houston ..... KO	3
	(Retained World Heavyweight Title)	

1967

Feb.	6—Ernest Terrell, Houston .... W	15
	(Retained World Heavyweight Title)	
Mar.	22—Zora Folley, New York .... KO	7
	(Retained World Heavyweight Title)	
June	15—Alvin (Blue) Lewis, Detroit ..... Exh.	3
June	15—Orvill Qualls, Detroit .... Exh.	3

1968-1969
(Inactive)
1970

Feb.	3—Announced retirement and offered his world heavyweight title belt to winner of Frazier-Ellis bout. Offer was turned down by Frazier.	
Sept.	10—Announced return to ring.	
Oct.	26—Jerry Quarry, Atlanta .... KO	3
Dec.	7—Oscar Bonavena, New York ...... KO	15

1971

Mar.	8—Joe Frazier, New York L	15
	(Lost World Heavyweight Title)	
June	25—J.D. McCauley, Dayton .... Exh.	2
June	25—Eddie Brooks, Dayton .... Exh.	3
June	25—Rufus Brassell, Dayton .... Exh.	3
June	30—Alex Mack, Charleston .... Exh.	3
June	30—Eddie Brooks, Charleston .... Exh.	4
July	26—Jimmy Ellis, Houston .... KO	12
	(Won Vacant NABF Heavyweight Title)	
Aug.	21—Lancer Johnson, Caracas .... Exh.	4
Aug.	21—Eddie Brooks, Caracas .... Exh.	4
Aug.	23—Lancer Johnson, Port of Spain ... Exh.	4
Aug.	23—Eddie Brooks, Port of Spain ..... Exh.	2
Nov.	6—James Summerville, Buenos Aires Exh.	5
Nov.	6—Miguel Angel Paez, Buenos Aires Exh.	5
Nov.	17—Buster Mathis, Houston .... W	12
	(Retained NABF Heavyweight Title)	
Dec.	26—Jurgen Blin, Zurich, Switzerland KO	7

1972

Apr.	1—Mac Foster, Tokyo, Japan .... W	15
May	1—George Chuvalo, Vancouver, B.C. .. W	12
	(Retained NABF Heavyweight Title)	
June	27—Jerry Quarry, Las Vegas .... KO	7
	(Retained NABF Heavyweight Title)	
July	1—Lonnie Bennett, Los Angeles .... Exh.	2
July	1—Eddie Jones, Los Angeles ...... Exh.	2
July	1—Billy Ryan, Los Angeles .... Exh.	2
July	1—Charley James, Los Angeles ...... Exh.	2
July	1—Rahaman Ali, Los Angeles ...... Exh.	2
July	19—Alvin (Blue) Lewis, Dublin .... KO	11
Aug.	24—Obie English, Baltimore .... Exh.	4
Aug.	24—Ray Anderson, Baltimore .... Exh.	2
Aug.	24—Alonzo Johnson, Baltimore ...... Exh.	2
Aug.	24—George Hill, Baltimore .... Exh.	2
Aug.	28—Alonzo Johnson, Cleveland ...... Exh.	2
Aug.	28—Amos Johnson, Cleveland .... Exh.	2
Sept.	20—Floyd Patterson, New York ...... KO	7
	(Retained NABF Heavyweight Title)	
Oct.	11—John (Dino) Denis, Boston ...... Exh.	2
Oct.	11—Cliff McDonald, Boston .... Exh.	2
Oct.	11—Doug Kirk, Boston .... Exh.	2
Oct.	11—Ray Anderson, Boston .... Exh.	2
Oct.	11—Paul Raymond, Boston .... Exh.	2
Nov.	21—Bob Foster, Stateline, Nev. .... KO	8
	(Retained NABF Heavyweight Title)	

1973

Feb.	14—Joe Bugner, Las Vegas .... W	12

486

Mar.	31—Ken Norton, San Diego L	12
	(Lost NABF Heavyweight Title)	
Sept.	10—Ken Norton, Los Angeles .... W	12
	(Regained NABF Heavyweight Title)	
Oct.	20—Rudi Lubbers, Jakarta .... W	12

1974

Jan.	28—Joe Frazier, New York .... W	12
	(Retained NABF Heavyweight Title)	
Oct.	30—George Foreman, Kinshasa, Zaire KO	8
	(Regained World Heavyweight Title)	

1975

Mar.	24—Chuck Wepner, Cleveland .... KO	15
	(Retained World Heavyweight Title)	
May	16—Ron Lyle, Las Vegas .... KO	11
	(Retained World Heavyweight Title)	
July	1—Joe Bugner, Kuala Lumpur .... W	15
	(Retained World Heavyweight Title)	
Oct.	1—Joe Frazier, Manila .... KO	14
	(Retained World Heavyweight Title)	

1976

Feb.	20—Jean Pierre Coopman, San Juan .. KO	5
	(Retained World Heavyweight Title)	
Apr.	30—Jimmy Young, Landover .... W	15
	(Retained World Heavyweight Title)	
May	24—Richard Dunn, Munich .... KO	5
	(Retained World Heavyweight Title)	
June	25—Antonio Inoki, Tokyo .... Exh. D	15
	(Above match was a boxer against a wrestler.)	
Sept.	28—Ken Norton, New York .... W	15
	(Retained World Heavyweight Title)	

1977

Jan.	29—Peter Fuller, Boston .... Exh.	4
Jan.	29—Walter Haines, Boston .... Exh.	1
Jan.	29—Jeyy Houston, Boston .... Exh.	2
Jan.	29—Ron Drinkwater, Boston .... Exh.	2
Jan.	29—Matt Ross, Boston .... Exh.	2
Jan.	29—Frank Smith, Boston .... Exh.	1
May	16—Alfredo Evangelista, Landover ..... W	15
	(Retained World Heavyweight Title)	
Sept.	29—Earnie Shavers, New York .... W	15
	(Retained World Heavyweight Title)	
Dec.	2—Scott LeDoux, Chicago .... Exh.	5

1978

Feb.	15—Leon Spinks, Las Vegas L	15
	(Lost World Heavyweight Title)	
Sept.	15—Leon Spinks, New Orleans .... W	15
	(Regained World Heavyweight Title)	

1979
—Announced retirement.
1980

Oct.	2—Larry Holmes, Las Vegas ..... KO by	11
	(For World Heavyweight Title)	

TB	KO	WD	WF	D	LD	LF	KO BY	ND	NC
60	37	19	0	0	3	0	1	0	0

ERNEST TERRELL
Born, April 4, 1939, Chicago, Ill. Weight, 200 lbs.
Height, 6 ft. 6 in. Managed by Julie Isaacson.
1957 Intercity Golden Gloves
Light Heavyweight Champion.

1957

May	15—Norman Bolden, Chicago .... W	4
June	26—Andy Bonds, Chicago .... KO	1
July	24—Ray Griggs, Chicago .... KO	1
Aug.	21—Neal Welch, Chicago .... W	6
Oct.	30—Ted Poole, Chicago .... KO	1

1958

Jan.	8—Cal Butler, Chicago .... W	6
Feb.	4—Emil Brtko, Chicago .... KO	2
Mar.	11—Johnny Harper, Chicago .... KO	1
Apr.	30—Johnny Gray, Chicago L	8
July	1—Bill Pickett, Chicago .... KO	2
Sept.	24—Joe Hemphill, Chicago .... KO	1
Oct.	7—John Hobart, East Chicago ...... KO	1
Nov.	3—Sid Peaks, Chicago .... W	8

1959

Jan.	14—Willie Coleman, Chicago .... W	8
Feb.	25—Johnny Gray, Chicago L	8
July	24—Tunney Hunsaker, Louisville ...... W	8
Nov.	11—Chuck Garrett, Chicago .... W	6

1960

Jan.	6—Clay Thomas, Chicago	KO	1
Mar.	30—Lee Williams, Chicago	W	10
May	18—Frankie Daniels, Chicago	KO	7
July	20—Joe Hemphill, Chicago	W	8
Dec.	5—Wayne Bethea, Chicago	L	10

1961

Feb.	6—Ernie Cab, Chicago	KO	8
Apr.	17—Willie Coleman, Chicago	KO	1
May	15—Chuck Garrett, Chicago	W	10
Dec.	4—Ernie Cab, Philadelphia	KO	3

1962

Feb.	28—Herb Siler, Miami Beach	W	10
Apr.	3—Cleveland Williams, Houston	KO by	7
June	9—Amos Lincoln, New York	W	6
Aug.	24—Eddie Jackson, Los Angeles	KO	2
Sept.	25—Ray Lopez, Chicago	KO	3
Dec.	14—Young Jack Johnson, Chicago	W	10

1963

Jan.	5—Young Jack Johnson, New York	W	10
Mar.	7—Herb Siler, Miami	KO	3
Apr.	13—Cleveland Williams, Philadelphia	W	10
July	27—Zore Folley, New York	W	10

1964

Mar.	6—Gerhard Zech, New York	W	10
June	17—Jeff Davis, Miami Beach	W	10
July	10—Bob Foster, New York	KO	7
Oct.	23—Henry Wallitsch, St. Louis	KO	5

1965

Mar.	5—Eddie Machen, Chicago	W	15
	(Won WBA Heavyweight Title)		
Nov.	1—George Chuvalo, Toronto	W	15
	(Retained WBA Heavyweight Title)		

1966

| June | 28—Doug Jones, Houston | W | 15 |
| | (Retained WBA Heavyweight Title) | | |

1967

Feb.	6—Muhammad Ali, Houston	L	15
	(For World Heavyweight Title)		
Aug.	5—Thad Spencer, Houston	L	12
	(WBA Heavyweight Elimination Tournament)		
Oct.	14—Manuel Ramos, Mexico City	L	10
Dec.	—Announced retirement.		

1968-1969

(Inactive)

1970

| Dec. | 15—Sonny Moore, Milwaukee | W | 10 |

1971

Apr.	3—Johnny Hudgins, Lake Geneva	KO	1
Apr.	28—Vic Brown, Cleveland	W	10
May	10—Luis Faustino Pires, Chicago	W	10
July	24—Roberto Davila, Lake Geneva	W	10

1972

| Oct. | 23—Jose Luis Garcia, Caracas | KO | 6 |

1973

Feb.	19—Bill Drover, Philadelphia	KO	1
June	23—Chuck Wepner, Atlantic City	L	12
	(For U.S. Heavyweight Title)		
Sept.	10—Jeff Merritt, New York	KO by	1

TB	KO	WD	WF	D	LD	LF	KO BY	ND	NC
55	21	25	0	0	7	0	2	0	0

JIMMY ELLIS

Born, February 24, 1940, Louisville, Ky. Weight, 145-205 lbs. Height, 6 ft. 1 in. Managed by Angelo Dundee.

1961

Apr.	19—Arley Seifer, Louisville	KO	3
May	6—Gene Leslie, Louisville	W	8
July	22—Johnny Morris, Louisville	W	6
Aug.	22—Wilf Greaves, Louisville	W	10
Oct.	7—Clarence Riley, Louisville	KO	2
Nov.	29—Holley Mims, Louisville	L	10

1962

Jan.	11—Rory Calhoun, Louisville	KO	1
Feb.	17—Johnny Alford, New York	W	6
May	4—Holley Mims, Louisville	W	10
June	7—Rudolph Bent, Louisville	KO	2
June	13—Charlie Glover, Lexington	W	4
June	13—Sammy Poe, Lexington	W	4

| Sept. | 1—Henry Hank, Louisville | L | 10 |
| Dec. | 3—Leroy Green, Louisville | W | 10 |

1963

| June | 18—Johnny Halifihi, London, England | KO | 1 |
| Sept. | 27—Lou Gutierrez, Louisville | W | 10 |

1964

Feb.	28—Ruben Carter, New York	L	10
Apr.	21—Joe Spencer, Lexington	KO	1
Oct.	21—Don Fullmer, Louisville	L	10
Nov.	30—George Benton, Philadelphia	L	10

1965

May	25—Joe Blackwood, Lewiston, Maine	KO	1
July	31—Muhammad Ali, San Juan, P.R.	Exh.	3
Aug.	16—Muhammad Ali, Gothenburg	Exh.	2
Aug.	20—Muhammad Ali, London, England	Exh.	4
Nov.	15—Chuck Leslie, Las Vegas	W	10

1966

Mar.	29—Hubert Hilton, Toronto	W	8
May	21—Lewina Waga, London, England	KO	1
Sept.	10—Billy Daniels, Frankfurt, Germany	W	6
Oct.	27—Eddie Dembry, Louisville	KO	1
Nov.	14—Tommy Sims, Houston	KO	1

1967

Mar.	22—Johnny Persol, New York	KO	1
Aug.	5—Leotis Martin, Houston	KO	9
	(WBA Heavyweight Elimination Tournament)		
Dec.	2—Oscar Bonavena, Louisville	W	12
	(WBA Heavyweight Elimination Tournament		

1968

Apr.	27—Jerry Quarry, Oakland	W	15
	(Won WBA Heavyweight Title)		
Sept.	14—Floyd Patterson, Stockholm	W	15
	(Retained WBA Heavyweight Title)		

1969

(Inactive)

1970

Feb.	16—Joe Frazier, New York	KO by	5
	(For Vacant World Heavyweight Title)		
Nov.	10—Roberto Davila, Miami Beach	KO	7

1971

Mar.	2—Tony Doyle, Miami Beach	KO	10
May	10—George Chuvalo, Toronto	W	10
July	26—Muhammad Ali, Houston	KO by	12
	(For Vacant NABF Heavyweight Title)		

1972

May	16—Richard Gosha, Seattle	KO	6
June	16—Reco Brooks, Miami Beach	KO	2
Sept.	21—Ollie Wilson, Parma	KO	5
Oct.	26—Harold Carter, Beckley	KO	7

1973

Feb.	21—Bob Felstein, Orlando	KO	2
Mar.	6—Charlie Harris, Miami Beach	KO	1
Apr.	15—Joe Harris, Huntington	KO	2
May	6—Reco Brooks, Phoenix	KO	5
June	18—Earnie Shavers, New York	KO by	1
Oct.	23—Memphis Al Jones, Atlanta	KO	7
Dec.	12—Boone Kirkman, Seattle	L	10

1974

| Mar. | 4—Larry Middleton, Largo | D | 10 |
| July | 16—Ron Lyle, Denver | L | 12 |

1975

| Mar. | 1—Joe Frazier, Melbourne, Aus. | KO by | 9 |
| May | 7—Carl Baker, Orlando | KO | 1 |

TB	KO	WD	WF	D	LD	LF	KO BY	ND	NC
53	24	16	0	1	8	0	4	0	0

JOE FRAZIER

Born, January 12, 1944, Beaufort, S.C. Weight, 205 lbs. Height, 5 ft. 11½ in.
1964 Olympic Heavyweight Champion.

1965

Aug.	16—Woody Goss, Philadelphia	KO	1
Sept.	20—Mike Bruce, Philadelphia	KO	3
Sept.	28—Ray Staples, Philadelphia	KO	2
Nov.	11—Abe Davis, Philadelphia	KO	1

1966

Jan.	17—Mel Turnbow, Philadelphia	KO	1
Mar.	4—Dick Wipperman, New York	KO	5
Apr.	4—Charley Polite, Philadelphia	KO	2
Apr.	28—Don (Toro) Smith, Pittsburgh	KO	3

May	19—Chuck Leslie, Los Angeles .... KO	3
May	26—Memphis Al Jones, Los Angeles .. KO	1
July	25—Billy Daniels, Philadelphia .... KO	6
Sept.	21—Oscar Bonavena, New York .... W	10
Nov.	21—Eddie Machen, Los Angeles ..... KO	10

1967

Feb.	21—Doug Jones, Philadelphia .... KO	6
Apr.	11—Jeff Davis, Miami Beach .... KO	5
May	4—George Johnson, Los Angeles .... W	10
July	19—George Chuvalo, New York ...... KO	4
Oct.	17—Tony Doyle, Philadelphia .... KO	2
Dec.	18—Marion Connors, Boston .... KO	3

1968

Mar.	4—Buster Mathis, New York .... KO	11
	(Won New York World Heavyweight Title)	
June	24—Manuel Ramos, New York .... KO	2
	(Retained New York World Heavyweight Title)	
Dec.	10—Oscar Bonavena, Philadelphia ..... W	15
	(Retained New York World Heavyweight Title)	

1969

Apr.	22—Dave Zyglewicz, Houston .... KO	1
	(Retained New York World Heavyweight Title)	
June	23—Jerry Quarry, New York .... KO	7
	(Retained New York World Heavyweight Title)	

1970

Feb.	16—Jimmy Ellis, New York .... KO	5
	(Won World Heavyweight Title)	
Nov.	18—Bob Foster, Detroit .... KO	2
	(Retained New York World Heavyweight Title)	

1971

Mar.	8—Muhammad Ali, New York .... W	15
	(Retained World Heavyweight Title)	
July	15—Cleveland Williams, Houston .... Exh.	3
July	15—James Helwig, Houston .... Exh.	3

1972

Jan.	15—Terry Daniels, New Orleans ...... KO	4
	(Retained World Heavyweight Title)	
May	25—Ron Stander, Omaha .... KO	5
	(Retained World Heavyweight Title)	

1973

Jan.	22—George Foreman, Kingston .... KO by	2
	(Lost World Heavyweight Title)	
July	2—Joe Bugner, London .... W	12

1974

Jan.	28—Muhammad Ali, New York L	12
	(For NABF Heavyweight Title)	
June	17—Jerry Quarry, New York .... KO	5

1975

Mar.	1—Jimmy Ellis, Melbourne .... KO	9
Oct.	1—Muhammad Ali, Manila ...... KO by	14
	(For World Heavyweight Title)	

1976

June	15—George Foreman, Uniondale. .. KO by	5

TB	KO	WD	WF	D	LD	LF	KO BY	ND	NC
36	27	5	0	0	1	0	3	0	0

Elected to Boxing Hall of Fame, 1980.

GEORGE FOREMAN

Born, January 22, 1948, Marshall, Texas. Weight,
220 lbs. Height, 6 ft. 3 in.
1968 Olympic Heavyweight Champion.

1969

June	23—Don Waldhelm, New York .... KO	3
July	1—Fred Askew, Houston .... KO	1
July	14—Sylvester Dullaire, Wash. D.C. .... KO	1
Aug.	18—Chuck Wepner, New York .... KO	3
Sept.	18—John Carroll, Seattle .... KO	1
Sept.	23—Cookie Wallace, Houston .... KO	2
Oct.	7—Vernon Clay, Houston .... KO	2
Oct.	31—Roberto Davila, New York .... W	8
Nov.	5—Leo Peterson, Scranton .... KO	4
Nov.	18—Max Martinez, Houston .... KO	2
Dec.	6—Bob Hazelton, Las Vegas .... KO	1
Dec.	16—Levi Forte, Miami Beach .... W	10
Dec.	18—Gary Wiler, Seattle .... KO	1

1970

Jan.	6—Charlie Polite, Houston .... KO	4
Jan.	26—Jack O'Halloran, New York ...... KO	5
Feb.	16—Gregorio Peralta, New York ...... W	10
Mar.	31—Rufus Brassell, Houston .... KO	1

Apr.	17—James J. Woody, New York ...... KO	3
Apr.	29—Aaron Easting, Cleveland .... KO	4
May	16—George Johnson, Los Angeles ..... KO	7
July	20—Roger Russell, Philadelphia ...... KO	1
Aug.	4—George Chuvalo, New York ...... KO	3
Nov.	3—Lou Bailey, Oklahoma City ...... KO	3
Nov.	18—Boone Kirkman, New York ...... KO	2
Dec.	19—Mel Turnbow, Seattle .... KO	1

1971

Feb.	8—Charlie Boston, St. Paul .... KO	1
Apr.	3—Stamford Harris, Lake Geneva ... KO	2
May	10—Gregorio Peralta, Oakland .... KO	10
Sept.	14—Vic Scott, El Paso .... KO	1
Sept.	21—Leroy Caldwell, Beaumont ...... KO	3
Oct.	7—Ollie Wilson, San Antonio .... KO	2
Oct.	29—Luis Faustino Pires, New York ... KO	4

1972

Feb.	29—Murphy Goodwin, Austin .... KO	2
Mar.	7—Clarence Boone, Beaumont .... KO	2
Apr.	10—Ted Gullick, Los Angeles .... KO	2
May	11—Miguel Angel Paez, Oakland ..... KO	2
Oct.	10—Terry Sorrels, Salt Lake City ..... KO	2

1973

Jan.	22—Joe Frazier, Kingston .... KO	2
	(Won World Heavyweight Title)	
Sept.	1—Jose (King) Roman, Tokyo .... KO	1
	(Retained World Heavyweight Title)	

1974

Mar.	26—Ken Norton, Caracas .... KO	2
	(Retained World Heavyweight Title)	
Oct.	30—Muhammad Ali, Kinshasa .... KO by	8
	(Lost World Heavyweight Title)	

1975

Apr.	26—Charley Polite, Toronto .... Exh.	3
Apr.	26—Boone Kirkman, Toronto .... Exh.	3
Apr.	26—Terry Daniels, Toronto .... Exh.	2
Apr.	26—Jerry Judge, Toronto .... Exh.	2
Apr.	26—Alonzo Johnson, Toronto .... Exh.	2
Nov.	26—Jody Ballard, Kianesha Lake ..... Exh.	2
Dec.	17—Eddie Brooks, San Francisco .... Exh.	4

1976

Jan.	24—Ron Lyle, Las Vegas .... KO	5
June	15—Joe Frazier, Uniondale .... KO	5
Aug.	14—Scott LeDoux, Utica .... KO	3
Oct.	15—John (Dino) Denis, Hollywood, Fla. KO	4

1977

Jan.	22—Pedro Agosta, Pensacola .... KO	4
Mar.	17—Jimmy Young, San Juan, P.R. L	12

TB	KO	WD	WF	D	LD	LF	KO BY	ND	NC
47	42	3	0	0	1	0	1	0	0

LEON SPINKS

Born, July 11, 1953, St. Louis, Mo. Weight, 200
lbs. Height, 6 ft. 2 in.
1976 Olympic Light Heavyweight Champion.

1977

Jan.	15—Bobby Smith, Las Vegas .... KO	5
Mar.	5—Peter Freeman, Liverpool .... KO	1
Mar.	20—Jerry McIntyre, Louisville .... KO	1
May	7—Pedro Agosto, St. Louis .... KO	1
June	1—Bruce Scott, Montreal .... KO	3
Oct.	22—Scott LeDoux, Las Vegas .... D	10
Nov.	18—Alfio Righetti, Las Vegas .... W	10

1978

Feb.	15—Muhammad Ali, Las Vegas .... W	15
	(Won World Heavyweight Title)	
Apr.	25—Leroy Diggs, Santo Domingo .... Exh.	4
June	30—George Mostardini, Chicago ..... Exh.	4
Sept.	15—Muhammad Ali, New Orleans L	15
	(Lost World Heavyweight Title)	

1979

June	24—Gerrie Coetzee, Monte Carlo ... KO by	1
Jan.	12—Alfredo Evangelista, Atlantic City KO	5
Mar.	8—Eddie (The Animal) Lopez, Las Vegas D	10
May	3—Kevin Isaac, Redwood City, Calif. KO	8
Oct.	2—Bernardo Mercado, Las Vegas .... KO	9

1980

TB	KO	WD	WF	D	LD	LF	KO BY	ND	NC
14	8	2	0	2	1	0	1	0	0

KEN NORTON
(Kenneth Howard Norton)
Born, August 9, 1945, Jacksonville, Ill. Weight, 210 lbs. Height, 6 ft. 3 in.

1967
Nov.	14—Grady Brazell, San Diego	KO	9

1968
Jan.	16—Sam Wyatt, San Diego	W	6
Feb.	6—Harold Dutra, Sacramento	KO	3
Mar.	26—Jimmy Gilmore, San Diego	KO	7
July	23—Wayne Kindred, San Diego	KO	6
Dec.	5—Cornell Nolan, Los Angeles	KO	6

1969
Feb.	11—Joe Hemphill, Wooded Hills	KO	3
Feb.	20—Wayne Kindred, Los Angeles	KO	9
Mar.	31—Pedro Sanchez, San Diego	KO	2
May	29—Bill McMurray, Los Angeles	KO	7
July	25—Gary Bates, San Diego	KO	8
Oct.	21—Julius Garcia, San Diego	KO	3

1970
Feb.	4—Aaron Eastling, Las Vegas	KO	2
Mar.	13—Stanford Harris, San Diego	KO	3
Apr.	7—Bob Mashburn, Cleveland	KO	4
May	8—Ray Ellis, San Diego	KO	2
July	2—Jose Luis Garcia, Los Angeles	KO by	8
Aug.	29—Cookie Wallace, San Diego	KO	4
Sept.	26—Chuck Leslie, Woodland Hills	W	10
Oct.	16—Ruby Harris, San Diego	KO	2

1971
Apr.	24—Steve Carter, Woodland Hills	KO	3
June	12—Vic Brown, Santa Monica	KO	5
Aug.	19—Chuck Haynes, Santa Monica	KO	10
Sept.	30—James J. Woody, San Diego	W	10

1972
Feb.	17—Charlie Harris, San Diego	KO	3
Mar.	17—Jack O'Halloran, San Diego	W	10
June	5—Herschel Jacobs, San Diego	W	10
June	30—James J. Woody, San Diego	KO	8
Nov.	21—Henry Clark, Stateline	KO	9
Dec.	13—Charlie Reno, San Diego	W	10

1973
Mar.	31—Muhammad Ali, San Diego	W	12
	(Won NABF Heavyweight Title)		
May	8—Mole Williams, Washington, D.C. Exh.		4
Sept.	10—Muhammad Ali, Los Angeles	L	12
	(Lost NABF Heavyweight Title)		

1974
Mar.	26—George Foreman, Caracas	KO by	2
	(For World Heavyweight Title)		
June	25—Boone Kirkman, Seattle	KO	8

1975
Mar.	4—Reed Brooks, Oklahoma City	KO	1
Mar.	24—Jerry Quarry, New York	KO	5
Aug.	14—Jose Luis Garcia, St. Paul	KO	5

1976
Jan.	3—Pedro Lovell, Las Vegas	KO	5
Apr.	30—Ron Stander, Lanover	KO	5
July	10—Larry Middleton, San Diego	KO	10
Sept.	28—Muhammad Ali, New York	L	15
	(For World Heavyweight Title)		

1977
May	11—Duane Bobick, New York	KO	1
Sept.	14—Lorenzo Zanon, Las Vegas	KO	5
Nov.	5—Jimmy Young, Las Vegas	W	15

1978
Mar.	29—Proclaimed World Heavyweight Champion by World Boxing Council.		
June	9—Larry Holmes, Las Vegas	L	15
	(Lost WBC Heavyweight Title)		
Nov.	10—Randy Stephens, Las Vegas	KO	4

1979
Mar.	23—Earnie Shavers, Las Vegas	KO by	1
Aug.	19—Scott LeDoux, Bloomington	D	10

1980
Nov.	7—Randall (Tex) Cobb, San Antonio	W	10

TB	KO	WD	WF	D	LD	LF	KO BY	ND	NC
49	33	9	0	1	3	0	3	0	0

LARRY HOLMES
Born, November 3, 1949, Cuthbert, Georgia. Weight, 215 lbs. Height, 6 ft. 4 in.

1973
Mar.	21—Rodell Dupree, Scranton	W	4
May	2—Art Savage, Scranton	KO	3
June	20—Curtis Whitner, Scranton	KO	1
Aug.	22—Don Branch, Scranton	W	6
Sept.	10—Bob Bozic, New York	W	6
Nov.	14—Jerry Judge, Scranton	W	6
Nov.	28—Kevin Isaac, Cleveland	KO	3

1974
Apr.	24—Howard Darlington, Scranton	KO	4
May	29—Bob Mashburn, Scranton	KO	7
Dec.	11—Joe Hathaway, Scranton	KO	1

1975
Mar.	24—Charley Green, Cleveland	KO	2
Apr.	10—Oliver Wright, Honolulu	KO	3
Apr.	26—Robert Yarborough, Toronto	KO	3
May	16—Ernie Smith, Las Vegas	KO	3
Aug.	16—Obie English, Scranton	KO	7
Aug.	26—Charlie James, Honolulu	W	10
Oct.	1—Rodney Bobick, Manila	KO	6
Dec.	9—Leon Shaw, Washington D.C.	KO	1
Dec.	20—Billy Joiner, San Juan	KO	3

1976
Jan.	29—Joe Gholston, Easton	KO	8
Apr.	5—Fred Askew, Landover	KO	2
Apr.	30—Roy Williams, Landover	W	10

1977
Jan.	16—Tom Prater, Pensacola	W	8
	(U.S. Championship Tournament)		
Mar.	17—Horacio Robinson, San Juan	KO	5
Sept.	14—Young Sanford Houpe, Las Vegas	KO	7
Nov.	5—Ibar Arrington, Las Vegas	KO	10

1978
Mar.	25—Earnie Shavers, Las Vegas	W	12
June	9—Ken Norton, Las Vegas	W	15
	(Won WBC Heavyweight Title)		
Nov.	10—Alfredo Evangelista, Las Vegas	KO	7
	(Retained WBC Heavyweight Title)		

1979
Mar.	23—Osvaldo Ocasio, Las Vegas	KO	7
	(Retained WBC Heavyweight Title)		
June	22—Mike Weaver, New York	KO	12
	(Retained WBC Heavyweight Title)		
Sept.	28—Earnie Shavers, Las Vegas	KO	11
	(Retained WBC Heavyweight Title)		

1980
Feb.	3—Lorenzo Zanon, Las Vegas	KO	6
	(Retained WBC Heavyweight Title)		
Mar.	31—Leroy Jones, Las Vegas	KO	8
	(Won Vacant World Heavyweight Title)		
July	7—Scott LeDoux, Bloomington	KO	7
	(Retained World Heavyweight Title)		
Oct.	2—Muhammad Ali, Las Vegas	KO	11
	(Retained World Heavyweight Title)		

TB	KO	WD	WF	D	LD	LF	KO BY	ND	NC
36	27	9	0	0	0	0	0	0	0

JOHN TATE
Born, January 29, 1955, Marion City, Arkansas. Weight, 240 lbs. Height, 6 ft. 4 in. Managed by Ace Miller.

1977
May	7—Jerry Thompkins, St. Louis	KO	5
June	1—Norm Kues, Montreal	KO	1
Aug.	20—Baker Tinsley, Pikesville	KO	2
Aug.	23—Walter Santemore, Memphis	W	8
Sept.	13—Eddie Lopez, Los Angeles	W	6
Oct.	22—Lou Esa, Las Vegas	KO	3
Nov.	18—Frank Schram, Las Vegas	KO	1
Dec.	3—Charlie Jordan, Knoxville	KO	1

1978
Jan.	29—James Dixon Knoxville	KO	3
Mar.	14—Leon Shaw, Orlando	KO	7
Apr.	25—Harold Carter, Orlando	W disq.	
May	13—Raul Gorosito, Orlando	KO	2
June	22—Bernardo Mercado, New York	KO	?

489

| July | 7—Walter Santemore, Orlando | ...... KO | 6 |

July   7—Walter Santemore, Orlando ...... KO 6
Aug.   25—Johnny Boudreaux, Houston .... W 10
Oct.   14—Cookie Wallace, Houston .... KO 9
Dec.   9—Ron Draper, Detroit .... KO 5
1979
Feb.   17—Duane Bobick, Indianapolis ...... KO 1
June   2—Kallie Knoetze, Mmabatho .... KO 8
Oct.   20—Gerrie Coetzee, Pretoria .... W 15
(Won Vacant WBA Heavyweight Title)
1980
Mar.   31—Mike Weaver, Knoxville ...... KO by 15
(Lost WBA Heavyweight Title)
June   20—Trevor Berbick, Montreal ..... KO by 9

TB	KO	WD	WF	D	LD	LF	KO BY	ND	NC
22	15	4	1	0	0	0	2	0	0

MIKE WEAVER

Born, June 14, 1952, Gatesville, Texas. Weight, 210 lbs. Height, 6 ft. 1 in. Managed by Don Manuel.
1972
Sept. 14—Howard Smith, Los Angeles ... KO by 3
Oct.   31—Howard Smith, Bakersfield .... L 5
1973
Feb.   2—Carlos Lopez, San Bernardino ..... W 5
Feb.   28—Billy Ryan, Fresno .... KO by 2
Sept. 10—Lynch Martin, Los Angeles .... KO 1
Oct.   11—Toni Pulu, Los Angeles .... KO 4
Nov.   9—Bob Swoopes, San Diego .... KO 1
Dec.   12—Larry Frazier, San Francisco .. KO by 2
1974
Feb.   21—Ellis McKinley, Los Angeles .... W 6
Mar.   22—Rod Bobick, Los Angeles .... L 10
May   31—Orville Qualls, San Diego .... KO 2
July   26—Duane Bobick, San Diego ..... KO by 7
Aug.   24—Mani Vaca, Honolulu .... W 10

1975
June   27—Tony Doyle, San Diego .... KO 9
1976
July   14—Jodie Ballard, Las Vegas .... W 10
Nov.   4—Fonomanu Sekona, San Carlos ... KO 6
1977
Jan.   19—Dwain Bonds, Las Vegas .... KO 9
Apr.   1—Bill Sharkey, New York .... W 10
Sept. 13—Dave Martinez, Anchorage .... KO 1
Nov.   15—Pedro Lovell, Anaheim .... W 10
1978
Jan.   24—Stan Ward, Sacramento .... L 12
(For Vacant California State Heavyweight Title)
Aug.   19—Leroy Jones, Las Vegas .... L 12
(For Vacant NABF Heavyweight Title)
Sept. 17—Mike Creel, Reno .... KO 2
Oct.   22—Bernardo Mercado, Reno .... KO 5
Dec.   5—Abdul Khan, Reno .... KO 2
1979
Jan.   18—Stan Ward, Las Vegas .... KO 9
(Won U.S. Heavyweight Title)
Mar.   2—Oliver Phillips, Las Vegas .... KO 4
June   22—Larry Holmes, New York ..... KO by 12
(For WBC Heavyweight Title)
Sept. 24—Harry Terrell, Los Angeles .... KO 4
Nov.   24—Scott LeDoux, Bloomington .... W 12
(Retained U.S. Heavyweight Title)

1980
Mar.   31—John Tate, Knoxville .... KO 15
(Won WBA Heavyweight Title)
Oct.   25—Gerrie Coetzee, Bophuthatswana   KO 13
(Retained WBA Heavyweight Title)

TB	KO	WD	WF	D	LD	LF	KO BY	ND	NC
32	16	7	0	0	4	0	5	0	0

LIGHT HEAVYWEIGHTS

JACK ROOT	1903	ANTON CHRISTOFORIDIS (NBA)	1941
GEORGE GARDNER	1903	GUS LESNEVICH	1941-1948
BOB FITZSIMMONS	1903-1905	*FREDDIE MILLS (GREAT BRITAIN)*	*1942-1946*
(PHILADELPHIA) JACK O'BRIEN	1905-1912	FREDDIE MILLS	1948-1950
JACK DILLON	1915-1916	JOEY MAXIM	1950-1952
BATTLING LEVINSKY	1916-1920	ARCHIE MOORE	1952-1962
GEORGES CARPENTIER	1920-1922	HAROLD JOHNSON	1961-1963
BATTLING SIKI	1922-1923	WILLIE PASTRANO	1963-1965
MIKE MC TIGUE	1923-1925	*EDDIE COTTON (MICHIGAN)*	*1963-1964*
PAUL BERLENBACH	1925-1926	JOSE TORRES	1965-1966
JACK DELANEY	1926-1927	DICK TIGER	1966-1968
JIMMY SLATTERY (NBA)	*1927*	BOB FOSTER	1968-1974
TOMMY LOUGHRAN	1927-1929	*VICENTE RONDON (WBA)*	*1971-1972*
JIMMY SLATTERY	1930	*JOHN CONTEH (WBC)*	*1974-1977*
MAXIE ROSENBLOOM	1930-1934	*VICTOR GALINDEZ (WBA)*	*1974-1978*
GEORGE NICHOLS (NBA)	*1932*	*MIGUEL CUELLO (WBC)*	*1977-1978*
BOB GODWIN (NBA)	*1933*	*MATE PARLOV (WBC)*	*1978*
BOB OLIN	1934-1935	*MIKE ROSSMAN (WBA)*	*1978-1979*
JOHN HENRY LEWIS	1935-1938	*MARVIN JOHNSON (WBC)*	*1978-1979*
GUSTAVE ROTH (IBU)	*1936-1938*	MATTHEW FRANKLIN (WBC)	
ADOLF HEUSER (IBU)	*1938*	(AKA MATTHEW SAAD MUHAMMAD)	1979-
MELIO BETTINA (NEW YORK)	1939	*MARVIN JOHNSON (WBA)*	*1979-*
LEN HARVEY (GREAT BRITAIN)	*1939-1942*	*EDDIE GREGORY (WBA)*	
BILLY CONN	1939-1940	*(AKA EDDIE MUSTAPHA MUHAMMAD)*	*1980-*

Claimants not generally recognized are in *italics*.

WORLD LIGHT HEAVYWEIGHT CHAMPIONSHIP BOUTS

Date	Winner	Weight	Loser	Weight	Result	Time KO	Site	Referee
4/22/1903	Jack Root	168	Charles (Kid) McCoy	173	ref 10		Light Guard Armory, Detroit	Bat Masterson
7/ 4/1903	George Gardner		Jack Root		TKO 12	2:20	International Athletic Club, Fort Erie, Ontario	······ McBride
11/25/1903	Bob Fitzsimmons	168	George Gardner	170	ref 20		Mechanic's Pavilion, San Francisco	Ed Graney
12/20/1905	Philadelphia Jack O'Brien	164	Bob Fitzsimmons	165	TKO 14		Mechanic's Pavilion, San Francisco	Ed Graney
4/25/1916	Jack Dillon		Battling Levinsky		ref 15		Kansas City, Mo.	
10/17/1916	Jack Dillon	173	Tim O'Neill	172	ND 10		Broadway Sporting Club, Brooklyn	
10/24/1916	Battling Levinsky		Jack Dillon		ref 12		Armory A. A., Boston	Larry Connolly
3/ 6/1917	Battling Levinsky		Jack Moran		ref 12		St. Louis, Mo.	
6/20/1917	Battling Levinsky		Johnny Howard		ref 12		Providence, R.I.	
12/25/1918	Battling Levinsky		Leo Houck		6		Lancaster, Pa.	
7/ 3/1919	Battling Levinsky		Billy Miske		ND 12	–	Toledo, Ohio	
8/11/1919	Battling Levinsky	173	Clay Turner	170	ND 8	–	Jersey City, N.J.	
5/ 3/1920	Battling Levinsky		Clay Turner		12	–	Portland, Maine	
5/21/1920	Battling Levinsky		Chuck Wiggins		draw 12	–	Dayton, Ohio	
10/12/1920	Georges Carpentier	170½	Battling Levinsky	175	KO 4	1:07	Int. League Park, Jersey City	Harry Ertle
6/11/1922	Georges Carpentier	175	Ted (Kid) Lewis	157	KO 1	2:15	Olympia Arena, London	Joe Palmer
9/24/1922	Battling Siki	174	Georges Carpentier	173½	KO 6	1:10	Velodrome Buffalo, Paris	Henri Bernstein
3/17/1923	Mike McTigue		Battling Siki		ref 20	–	Scala Opera House, Dublin	Jack Smith
6/25/1923	Mike McTigue	164½	Tommy Loughran	161	ND 8	–	Philadelphia, Pa.	
8/2/1923	Mike McTigue	163½	Tommy Loughran	166	ND 12	–	West New York Park, New Jersey	Eddie Dugan
10/4/1923	Mike McTigue		Young Stribling		draw 10	–	Columbus, Georgia	Harry Ertle
3/31/1924	Mike McTigue	166½	Young Stribling	165	ND 12	–	Newark Armory	Hank Lewis
1/7/1925	Mike McTigue	160	Mickey Walker	149¾	ND 12	–	Newark Armory	Hank Lewis
5/30/1925	Paul Berlenbach	170½	Mike McTigue	170½	unan 15	–	Yankee Stadium	Ed Purdy
9/11/1925	Paul Berlenbach	172	Jimmy Slattery	161½	TKO 11	1:28	Yankee Stadium	Patsy Haley
12/11/1925	Paul Berlenbach	173½	Jack Delaney	166	maj 15	–	Madison Sq. Garden	Ed Purdy
6/10/1926	Paul Berlenbach	174½	Young Stribling	171	unan 15	–	Yankee Stadium	Jim Crowley
7/16/1926	Jack Delaney	166½	Paul Berlenbach	174½	unan 15	–	Ebbets Field	Jim Crowley
10/7/1927	Tommy Loughran	175	Mike McTigue	172½	unan 15	–	Madison Sq. Garden	Lou Magnolia
12/12/1927	Tommy Loughran	173½	Jimmy Slattery	165½	unan 15	–	Madison Sq. Garden	Lou Magnolia
1/6/1928	Tommy Loughran	174½	Leo Lomski	171	unan 15	–	Madison Sq. Garden	Jack Denning
6/1/1928	Tommy Loughran	173¾	Pete Latzo	168	unan 15	–	Ebbets Field	Jed Gahan
7/16/1928	Tommy Loughran	172½	Pete Latzo	167½	unan 10	–	Artillery Park, Wilkes-Barre	Leo Houck
3/28/1929	Tommy Loughran	173¼	Mickey Walker	165	split 10	–	Chicago Stadium	Dave Miller
7/18/1929	Tommy Loughran	174	James J. Braddock	170	unan 15	–	Yankee Stadium	Eddie Forbes
2/10/1930	Jimmy Slattery	166¼	Lou Scozza	169½	maj 15	–	Buffalo Auditorium	Jim Crowley
6/25/1930	Maxie Rosenbloom	170½	Jimmy Slattery	166½	split 15	–	Bison Stadium, Buffalo	Patsy Haley
10/22/1930	Maxie Rosenbloom	174½	Abie Bain	171½	TKO 11	1:47	Madison Sq. Garden	Lou Magnolia
8/5/1931	Maxie Rosenbloom	171½	Jimmy Slattery	170½	unan 15	–	Ebbets Field	Kid McPartland
7/14/1932	Maxie Rosenbloom	175	Lou Scozza	173	maj 15	–	Bison Stadium, Buffalo	Gunboat Smith
3/10/1933	Maxie Rosenbloom	174	Adolf Heuser	172	unan 15	–	Madison Sq. Garden	Jed Gahan
3/24/1933	Maxie Rosenbloom	174¼	Bob Godwin	167¼	TKO 4	1:16	Madison Sq. Garden	Pete Hartley
11/3/1933	Maxie Rosenbloom	173¼	Mickey Walker	173½	split 15	–	Madison Sq. Garden	Eddie Forbes
2/5/1934	Maxie Rosenbloom	174	Joe Knight	173	draw 15	–	M.S.G. Stadium, Miami	Harry Graham
11/16/1934	Bob Olin	173	Maxie Rosenbloom	173½	split 15	–	Madison Sq. Garden	Arthur Donovan
10/31/1935	John Henry Lewis	174½	Bob Olin	173	unan 15	–	St. Louis Arena	Walter Heisner
3/13/1936	John Henry Lewis	172¼	Jock McAvoy	168¼	unan 15	–	Madison Sq. Garden	Arthur Donovan
11/9/1936	John Henry Lewis	173½	Len Harvey	172	ref 15	–	Empire Pool, Wembley	Jack Smith
6/3/1937	John Henry Lewis	174	Bob Olin	174¼	TKO 8	1:20	St. Louis Arena	Walter Heisner
4/25/1938	John Henry Lewis	174¼	Emilio Martinez	174	KO 4	0:54	Minneapolis Auditorium	Britt Gorman
10/28/1938	John Henry Lewis	174	Al Gainer	170	unan 15	–	New Haven Arena	Dave Fitzgerald
2/3/1939	Melio Bettina	172½	Tiger Jack Fox	174¼	TKO 9	1:22	Madison Sq. Garden	Eddie Joseph
7/13/1939	Billy Conn	170¼	Melio Bettina	173¼	unan 15	–	Madison Sq. Garden	Frank Fullam
9/25/1939	Billy Conn	172¼	Melio Bettina	174½	unan 15	–	Forbes Field, Pittsburgh	Red Robinson
11/17/1939	Billy Conn	171½	Gus Lesnevich	174¾	unan 15	–	Madison Sq. Garden	Johnny McAvoy
6/5/1940	Billy Conn	173½	Gus Lesnevich	173½	unan 15	–	Olympia, Detroit	Sam Hennessey
1/13/1941	Anton Christoforidis	168½	Melio Bettina	174	unan 15	–	Cleveland Arena	Joe Sedley
5/22/1941	Gus Lesnevich	175	Anton Christoforidis	166	unan 15	–	Madison Sq. Garden	Frank Fullam
8/26/1941	Gus Lesnevich	175	Tami Mauriello	170¾	split 15	–	Madison Sq. Garden	Eddie Joseph
11/14/1941	Gus Lesnevich	173¾	Tami Mauriello	173½	unan 15	–	Madison Sq. Garden	Arthur Donovan
5/14/1946	Gus Lesnevich	175	Freddie Mills	173⅞	TKO 10	2:56	Harringay Arena	Eugene Henderson
2/28/1947	Gus Lesnevich	174½	Billy Fox	172	TKO 10	2:19	Madison Sq. Garden	Johnny Burns
3/5/1948	Gus Lesnevich	175	Billy Fox	172¼	KO 1	1:58	Madison Sq. Garden	Frank Fullam
7/26/1948	Freddie Mills	171½	Gus Lesnevich	174¾	ref 15	–	White City Stadium	Teddy Waltham
1/24/1950	Joey Maxim	174¼	Freddie Mills	173	KO 10	1:54	Earl's Court	Andrew Smyth
8/22/1951	Joey Maxim	173½	Bob Murphy	174½	unan 15	–	Madison Sq. Garden	Ruby Goldstein
6/25/1952	Joey Maxim	173	Ray Robinson	157½	TKO 14	*	Yankee Stadium	Ruby Goldstein**
12/17/1952	Archie Moore	172½	Joey Maxim	174½	unan 15	–	St. Louis Arena	Harry Kessler
6/24/1953	Archie Moore	173¾	Joey Maxim	175	unan 15	–	Municipal Stadium, Ogden	Ray Miller
1/27/1954	Archie Moore	173	Joey Maxim	171¼	unan 15	–	Orange Bowl, Miami	Cy Gottfried
8/11/1954	Archie Moore	173	Harold Johnson	172½	TKO 14	0:56	Madison Sq. Garden	Ruby Goldstein

	6/22/1955	Archie Moore	175	Carl (Bobo) Olson	170¼	KO 3	1:19	Polo Grounds	Ruby Goldstein
	6/5/1956	Archie Moore	174½	Yolande Pompey	171¼	TKO 10	2:50	Harringay Arena	Jack Hart
	9/20/1957	Archie Moore	175	Tony Anthony	172	TKO 7	2:29	Olympic, L.A.	Mushy Callahan
	12/10/1958	Archie Moore	173¾	Yvon Durelle	172	KO 11	0:49	Forum, Montreal	Jack Sharkey
	8/12/1959	Archie Moore	174¼	Yvon Durelle	173	KO 3	2:52	Forum, Montreal	Jack Sharkey
	6/10/1961	Archie Moore	174½	Giulio Rinaldi	173¾	unan 15	—	Madison Sq. Garden	Ruby Goldstein
	5/12/1962	Harold Johnson	171½	Doug Jones	171½	unan 15	—	Philadelphia Arena	David Beloff
	6/23/1962	Harold Johnson	172½	Gustav Scholz	171	unan 15	—	Olympic Stadium, Berlin	Ike Powell
	6/1/1963	Willie Pastrano	174	Harold Johnson	173½	split 15	—	Convention Center, Las Vegas	Jim Olivas
	4/10/1964	Willie Pastrano	174¾	Gregorio Peralta	174¾	TKO 6	*	Municipal Auditorium, New Orleans	Peter Giarusso
	11/30/1964	Willie Pastrano	174¾	Terry Downes	171	TKO 11	1:17	Belle Vue Stadium, Manchester	Andrew Smyth
	3/30/1965	Jose Torres	171¼	Willie Pastrano	174½	TKO 10	*	Madison Sq. Garden	John LoBianco
	5/21/1966	Jose Torres	175	Wayne Thornton	174	unan 15	—	Shea Stadium	John LoBianco
	8/15/1966	Jose Torres	173	Eddie Cotton	173½	unan 15	—	Convention Center, Las Vegas	Nat Morgan
	10/15/1966	Jose Torres	175	Chic Calderwood	175	KO 2	2:06	Hiram Bithorn Stadium, San Juan	Teddy Martin
	12/16/1966	Dick Tiger	167	Jose Torres	175	unan 15	—	Madison Sq. Garden	John LoBianco
	2/5/1967	Dick Tiger	167	Jose Torres	175	split 15	—	Madison Sq. Garden	Harold Valan
	11/17/1967	Dick Tiger	168¼	Roger Rouse	174½	TKO 12	0:12	Convention Center, Las Vegas	Jim Olivas
	5/24/1968	Bob Foster	173½	Dick Tiger	168	KO 4	2:05	Madison Sq. Garden	Mark Conn
	1/23/1969	Bob Foster	171½	Frank DePaula	173	TKO 1	2:17	Madison Sq. Garden	John LoBianco
	5/24/1969	Bob Foster	174	Andy Kendall	175	TKO 4	1:15	Eastern States Coliseum, West Springfield, Mass.	Bill Connelly
	4/4/1970	Bob Foster	174	Roger Rouse	173½	TKO 4	*	University of Montana Fieldhouse, Missoula	Lee Sala
	6/27/1970	Bob Foster	173¼	Mark Tessman	170	KO 10	2:00	Civic Center, Baltimore	Terry Moore
	3/2/1971	Bob Foster	174	Hal Carroll	171½	KO 4	2:32	Catholic Youth Center, Scranton	Manny Gelb
	4/24/1971	Bob Foster	170¼	Ray Anderson	172½	unan 15	—	Curtis Hixon Hall, Tampa	Lee Sala
	10/29/1971	Bob Foster	174	Tommy Hicks	171	TKO 8	1:04	Catholic Youth Center, Scranton	Manny Gelb
	12/16/1971	Bob Foster	174	Brian Kelly	175	KO 3	1:56	Fairgrounds Arena, Oklahoma City	Earle Kell
	4/7/1972	Bob Foster	175	Vicente Rondon	175	KO 2	2:55	Convention Hall, Miami Beach	Cy Gottfried
	6/27/1972	Bob Foster	173½	Mike Quarry	175	KO 4	3:10	Convention Center, Las Vegas	Harry Krause
	9/26/1972	Bob Foster	174½	Chris Finnegan	173¾	KO 14	0:55	Empire Pool, Wembley	Roland Dakin
	8/21/1973	Bob Foster	173	Pierre Fourie	168	unan 15	—	University Arena, Albuquerque	Jim Cleary
	12/1/1973	Bob Foster	174	Pierre Fourie	167	unan 15	—	Rand Stadium, Johannesburg	Roland Dakin
	7/17/1974	Bob Foster	174	Jorge Ahumada	173½	draw 15	—	University Arena, Albuquerque	Jim Cleary
‡	10/01/74	**John Conteh**	174¼	**Jorge Ahumada**	174	ref 15		Empire Pool, Wembley, London	Harry Gibbs
†	12/07/74	**Victor Galindez**	174	**Len Hutchins**	172½	TKO 13	*	Luna Park Stadium, Buenos Aires	Jesus Celis
‡	3/11/75	**John Conteh**	174	**Lonnie Bennett**	172½	TKO 5	1:10	Empire Pool, Wembley, London	Roland Dakin
†	4/07/75	**Victor Galindez**	172	**Pierre Fourie**	168¾	unan 15		Ellis Park Stadium, Johannesburg	Waldemar Schmidt
†	6/30/75	**Victor Galindez**	174	**Jorge Ahumada**	175	unan 15		Madison Square Garden, New York	Jimmy Devlin
†	9/13/75	**Victor Galindez**	175	**Pierre Fourie**	174½	split 15		Rand Stadium, Johannesburg	Waldemar Schmidt
†	3/28/76	**Victor Galindez**	173½	**Harald Skog**	173½	TKO 3	1:45	Ekeberg Hall, Oslo, Norway	Tony Perez
†	5/22/76	**Victor Galindez**	174½	**Richie Kates**	173¾	KO 15	2:59	Rand Stadium, Johannesburg	Stan Christodoulou
†	10/05/76	**Victor Galindez**	175	**Kosie Smith**	174	unan 15		Rand Stadium, Johannesburg	Waldemar Schmidt
‡	10/09/76	**John Conteh**	174¼	**Yaqui Lopez**	173	unan 15		Forum, Copenhagen, Denmark	Rudolf Durst
‡	3/05/77	**John Conteh**	175	**Len Hutchins**	173¾	TKO 3	1:05	Liverpool Stadium, Liverpool	Sid Nathan
‡	5/21/77	**Miguel Angel Cuello**	173	**Jesse Burnett**	169	KO 9	2:49	Louis II Stadium, Monte Carlo	Ray Solis
†	6/18/77	**Victor Galindez**	174	**Richie Kates**	173¾	unan 15		Sports Palace, Rome, Italy	Waldemar Schmidt
†	9/17/77	**Victor Galindez**	174½	**Yaqui Lopez**	174½	unan 15		Sports Palace, Rome, Italy	Stan Christodoulou
†	11/20/77	**Victor Galindez**	173½	**Eddie Gregory**	174	unan 15		Sports Palace, Turin, Italy	Luis Sulbaran
‡	1/07/78	**Mate Parlov**	173½	**Miguel Angel Cuello**	174	KO 9	2:43	Sports Palace, Milan, Italy	Sid Nathan
†	5/06/78	**Victor Galindez**	174	**Yaqui Lopez**	172	unan 15		Sports Palace, Via Reggio, Italy	Mario Riva
‡	6/17/78	**Mate Parlov**	175	**John Conteh**	173	split 15		Red Star Stadium, Belgrade, Yug.	Rudy Ortega
†	9/15/78	**Mike Rossman**	173	**Victor Galindez**	174	TKO 13	0:55	Superdome, New Orleans, La.	Carlos Berrocal
‡	12/02/78	**Marvin Johnson**	175	**Mate Parlov**	174¾	TKO 10	2:33	Marsala, Sicily, Italy	Roland Dakin
†	12/05/78	**Mike Rossman**	171	**Aldo Traversaro**	173½	TKO 6	1:15	Spectrum, Philadelphia, Pa.	Jesus Celis
†	4/14/79	**Victor Galindez**	174½	**Mike Rossman**	174¼	TKO 10	*	Superdome, New Orleans, La.	Stan Christodoulou
‡	4/22/79	**Matthew Franklin**	175	**Marvin Johnson**	175	TKO 8	2:44	Market Square Arena, Indianapolis	George DeFabis
‡	8/18/79	**Matt. Saad Muhammad**	172½	**John Conteh**	175	unan 15		Resorts Int. Hotel, Atlantic City	Carlos Padilla
†	11/30/79	**Marvin Johnson**	173½	**Victor Galindez**	174¾	TKO 11	0:20	Superdome, New Orleans, La.	Jesus Celis
‡	3/29/80	**Matt. Saad Muhammad**	175	**John Conteh**	175	TKO 4	2:27	Resorts Int. Hotel, Atlantic City	Octavio Meyran
†	3/31/80	**Eddie Gregory**	174	**Marvin Johnson**	174½	TKO 11	2:43	Stokely Athletics Center, Knoxville	Carlos Berrocal
‡	5/11/80	**Matt. Saad Muhammad**	174½	**Louis Pergaud**	174½	TKO 5	1:19	Metro Center, Halifax, Nova Scotia	Rudy Ortega
‡	7/13/80	**Matt. Saad Muhammad**	174½	**Yaqui Lopez**	173¾	TKO 14	2:03	Great Gorge Playboy Club, McAfee	Waldemar Schmidt
†	7/20/80	**Ed. Mustafa Muhammad**	175	**Jerry Martin**	175	TKO 10	2:25	Great Gorge Playboy Club, McAfee	Tony Perez
‡	11/28/80	**Matt. Saad Muhammad**	175	**Lotte Mwale**	172½	KO 4	2:25	Sports Arena, San Diego, Calif	Tony Perez
†	11/29/80	**Ed. Mustafa Muhammad**	175	**Rudi Koopmans**	175	TKO 4	*	Olympic Auditorium, Los Angeles	Larry Rozadilla

*Loser failed to answer bell for round indicated.
**Goldstein victim of heat exhaustion after ten rounds; replaced by Ray Miller.
†NBA (later WBA) world light heavyweight title bout
‡WBC world light heavyweight title bout
††Michigan Athletic Board of Control world light heavyweight title bout
‡‡British Boxing Board of Control world light heavyweight title bout
§New York State Athletic Commission world light heavyweight title bout
Chart does not include Int. Boxing Union (Europe) world title bouts of 1936-1938.

LIGHT HEAVYWEIGHT DIVISION

JACK ROOT
(Janos Ruthaly)
Born, May 26, 1876, Austria. Nationality, Austrian-American. Weight, 165 lbs. Height, 5 ft. 10 in.

1897
Nov. 12—Charles Upton, Chicago ......KO 4
Dec. 24—Pat Brastand, Chicago ....KO 3
1898
Jan. 8—Charles Whitey, Chicago ......KO 2
Jan. 15—George Hipp, Chicago ....KO 1
Jan. 29—Mike Corrall, Chicago ....W 1
Feb. 12—Jack Hammond, Chicago .....KO 2
Feb. 26—Jack Moffatt, Chicago ....W 6
Mar. 10—Charles Withey, Green Bay ...KO 2
Mar. 27—Geo. Ryan,
Milwaukee .... Police Stpd. 1
May 14—Jack Moffatt, Chicago ....W 6
July 22—Tom Lansing, N. Y. C. ....W 6
Aug. 5—Jim Watts, N. Y. C. ....W 2
Aug. 19—Jack Murphy, Philadelphia ...KO 2
Nov. 15—Tom Lansing, Chicago ......KO 5
Dec. 30—Aus. Jim Ryan, Chicago ....W 6
1899
Jan. 21—Harry Peppers, Chicago ....W 6
Feb. 16—Billy Stift, Davenport ....WF 7
Apr. 29—Dick Moore, Chicago ....KO 2
May 15—Aus. Jim Ryan, Louisville ..... D 20
May 30—Tom Casey, Chicago ....KO 1
June 7—Tom Burke, Chicago ....KO 7
June 21—Jack Gorman, Chicago ......KO 2
July 7—Fred Grant, Chicago ....KO 3
Aug. 12—John Banks, Chicago ....KO 1
Aug. 21—Tom Casey, Chicago ....KO 1
Sept. 23—Bill Stift, Chicago ....W 6
Oct. 3—Frank Craig, Chicago ....W 6
Oct. 15—Frank Craig, Chicago ....W 6
Nov. 15—Alec Greggains, San Fran. ....KO 7
1900
Jan. 9—Tommy West, Chicago ....W 6
Feb. 5—Jack Hammond, Milwaukee ..KO 2
Feb. 20—Ed Denfass, Chicago ....KO 4
July 10—Dick O'Brien, Chicago ....W 6
July 24—Tommy Ryan, Chicago ....W 6
Oct. 4—Dan Creedon, Kansas City ....KO 1
Oct. 15—Dick O'Brien, Chicago ....KO 3
Nov. 16—Joe Ashley, Manistee ....KO 2
1901
Jan. 18—George Byers, San Francisco ..KO 9
June 28—Kid Carter, San Francisco ....WF 15
Oct. 30—Aus. Jim Ryan, Louisville ....KO 2
1902
Jan. 31—George Gardner, San Fran. ...WF 7
Apr. 26—Billy Stift, Chicago ....KO 2
Aug. 18—George Gardner, Salt Lake
City ....KO by 17
Oct. 27—Kid Carter, Chicago ....W 6
Nov. 10—Marvin Hart, Chicago ....W 6
1903
Apr. 22—Kid McCoy, Detroit ....W 10
(First Light Heavyweight Title Bout)
July 4—Geo. Gardner, Fort Erie ...KO by 12
(Lost Light Heavyweight Title)
Nov. 26—Jim Flynn, Pueblo, Colo. ......W 8
1904
Feb. 5—John Willie, Chicago .... D 6
Feb. 26—George Gardner, Chicago ..... D 6
May 2—George Gardner, Chicago ......W 6
Nov. 23—Tommy Ryan, Philadelphia ...ND 4
Dec. 5—John Willie, Chicago .... D 6
1905
July 3—Marvin Hart, Reno Nev. ...KO by 12
Listed by James J. Jeffries, who refereed as for his vacated heavyweight title.
1906
Feb. 26—Fred Russell, Kalamazoo ......W 10
Elected to Boxing Hall of Fame 1961.
Died Los Angeles, Calif. June 10. 1963.

TB	KO	WD	WF	D	LD	LF	KOBY	ND	NC
53	24	17	3	5	0	0	3	1	0

GEORGE GARDNER

Born, March 17, 1877, Lisdoonvarna, County Clare, Ireland. Nationality, Irish-American. Weight, 165 lbs. Height, 5 ft. 11¾ in.
1897
Knockouts: J. Young, 3 rds. J. Young, 2 rds. Tom Moore, 4 rds. Tom O'Brien, 1 rd. Emmett Johnson, 3 rds. Hugh Winters, 6 rds., all at Manchester, N. H.

1898
Nov. 20—Hugh Colgan, Manchester ....KO 3
Dec. 10—Prof. Evans, Manchester ....W 3
Dec. 25—Thunderbolt Smith, Montreal .KO 7
1899
Jan. 20—Bob Montgomery, Manchester . D 10
Mar. 24—Andy Moynahan, Manchester .KO 3
Apr. 9—John Butler, Lowell ....W 7
June 7—Young Sharkey, Lowell ....W 9
July 31—Bill Hanrahan, Lowell .... D 6
Aug. 5—Harry Fisher, Brooklyn ......W 17
Sept. 16—Jimmy Handler, Brooklyn .....L 18
Nov. 5—George Byers, Lynn .... D 15
Dec. 12—Jack Moffatt, N. Y. C. ....W 8
1900
Jan. 9—Harry Fisher, Lynn .... W 12
Jan. 16—George Byers, Lynn .... D 15
Feb. 12—Jimmy Handler, Brooklyn ....KO 3
Feb. 22—George Byers, Hartford .....WF 14
Mar. 14—Jack Burke, Lynn ....W 4
Apr. 7—J. Fitzpatrick, Portland ....W 9
Apr. 23—Dick Baker, Manchester .....KO 4
May 2—Charley Goff, Utica ....W 7
May 14—George Byers, Boston .... D 15
May 19—Kid Carter, Coney Island ....WF 19
Sept. 10—Frank Craig, England ....KO 4
Sept. 30—J. Scales, England ....W 3
1901
Apr. 18—Tim Hurley, Manchester ......W 5
July 4—Jack Moffatt, San Francisco ....W 3
Aug. 30—Kid Carter, San Francisco ...KO 18
Sept. 27—Joe Walcott, San Francisco ....L 20
Dec. 29—Kid Carter, San Francisco ...KO 8
1902
Jan. 31—Jack Root, San Francisco .....LF 7
Apr. 25—Joe Walcott, San Francisco ....W 20
Aug. 18—Jack Root, Salt Lake City ...KO 17
Oct. 31—Jack Johnson, San Francisco ...L 20
Dec. 11—Billy Stift, Chicago ....W 6
Dec. 29—Kid Carter, Chicago ....W 6
1903
Feb. 9—Bob Armstrong, Philadelphia .ND 4
Feb. 13—Al Weinig, Boston ....W 7
Apr. 6—Peter Maher, Boston ....KO 1
May 13—Marvin Hart, Louisville ......W 12
July 4—Jack Root, Fort Erie ....KO 12
(Won Light Heavyweight Title)
Nov. 25—Bob Fitzsimmons, San Fran. ....L 20
(Lost Light Heavyweight Title)
1904
Jan. 5—Marvin Hart, Boston .... D 15
Feb. 8—*Fred Cooley, Chicago ....W 6
Feb. 8—*Jim Driscoll, Chicago ....W 6
Feb. 19—Kid Carter, Milwaukee ....W 6
Feb. 26—Jack Root, Chicago .... D 6
May 2—Jack Root, Chicago ....L 6
July 1—John Willie, Chicago .... D 6
Aug. 15—Jim Jeffords, Butte, Mont.....KO 3
Sept. 16—Jim Flynn, Denver .... D 10
*Same night.
1905
Apr. 17—Mike Schreck, Salt Lake ...KO by 20
June 20—Billy Stift, Ogden ....KO 5
1906
Jan. 24—Jim Jeffords, Philadelphia ....ND 6
Apr. 19—Mike Schreck, Chelsea ....NC 2
Dec. 21—Al Kaufman, Los Ang. ....KO by 14
1907
Apr. 17—Jim Flynn, San Diego .....KO by 18
Oct. 12—Terry Mustain, San Diego ..... D 20
1908
Jan. 29—Terry Mustain, San Diego ..KO by 8
May 18—Tony Ross, New Castle, Pa. KO by 7

TB	KO	WD	WF	D	LD	LF	KOBY	ND	NC
65	19	20	2	10	5	1	5	2	1

Died, July 8, 1954, Chicago, Ill.

BOB FITZSIMMONS
(Record under Heavyweight Champions)

PHILADELPHIA JACK O'BRIEN
(Joseph Francis Hagen)
Born, January 17, 1878, Philadelphia, Nationality, Irish-American. Weight, 158 lbs. Height, 5 ft 10½ in.
1896
Dec. 12—Isador Strauss, Philadelphia .... D 6
Dec. 19—George Russell, Philadelphia ... W 6
Dec. 23—Bobby Dobbs, Chester .... D 4
1897
Jan. 11—Bobby Dobbs, Cohocton, Pa. ...L 4
Jan. 12—Martin Judge, Philadelphia ....D 6

Jan.	31—Isador Strauss, Philadelphia	W 6
Feb.	—Dan McConnell, Philadelphia ..	W 6
Feb.	—Leslie Pearce, Philadelphia.....	W 6
Mar.	—Billy Payne, Philadelphia	W 6
Apr.	—Young Smyrna, Chester	D 4
June	3—Bull McCarthy, Philadelphia ...	W 6
June	7—Barney Connors, Baltimore	D 15
June	9—Paddy Sheehan, Reading	D 4
June	25—Martin Judge, Reading	W 6
June	27—Jack Hanlon, Reading	W 6
Oct.	12—Joe Dougherty, Philadelphia ..KO	3

1898

Jan.	1—Isador Strauss, Philadelphia	W 6
Jan.	10—Barney Connors, Baltimore	W 8
Jan.	17—Paddy Sheehan, Reading	W 6
Jan.	31—Young Smyrna, Philadelphia ...	W 6
Feb.	4—Jack Daly, Philadelphia	D 6
Feb.	14—Jack McCann, Philadelphia	W 3
Apr.	—Bill Payne, Philadelphia	W 4
Apr.	—Dick Kelly, Philadelphia	W 4
Nov.	6—Kid Carter, Brooklyn	D 10
Dec.	19—Hugh McWinters, Brooklyn	W 20

1899

Jan.	—Tom Cavanaugh, Philadelphia ..	W 4
Jan.	—Fred Stricker, Philadelphia	W 6
Jan.	—Jack Collier, Philadelphia......	W 6
Feb.	—George Cole, Philadelphia	W 6
Mar.	20—George Cole, Trenton, ...	W 20
May	15—Tony Drew, Trenton ....KO	7
June	20—Kid Baxter, Chicago	W 6
June	27—Walter Nolan, Chicago ....KO	4
July	21—Shorty Ahearn, Chicago	W 6
Aug.	4—Tom McCune, Clinton ......KO	12
Sept.	15—Tom Tracey, Chicago	W 6

1900

Jan.	6—Al Neill, San Francisco	D 15
Feb.	14—Y'g. P. Jackson, San Fran. . KO by	13
Apr.	13—Bob Long, Chicago	W 6
May	23—Young Mahoney, Chicago	W 6
June	7—Charley Bell, Des Moines ....KO	6
June	14—Jack Lewis, Des Moines ......KO	7
June	21—Jim Adams, Des Moines	D 5
July	3—Jim Adams, Des Moines	D 6
Sept.	21—Andy Walsh, Philadelphia ...ND	6
Sept.	31—Jack Bonner, Philadelphia ...ND	6
Oct.	15—Tommy West, Philadelphia ...ND	6
Oct.	29—Jimmy Handler, Philadelphia .ND	6
Nov.	12—Jimmy Handler, Philadelphia .ND	6

1901

Feb.	25—Harry Smith, England	W 3
Mar.	20—Jack Thompson, England.....KO	2
May	20—George Crisp, England ......KO	11
June	25—Harry Newmier, England .....KO	6
Aug.	3—Jack Scales, England	W 6
Aug.	19—Dido Plumb, England ....KO	6
Sept.	3—Mike Lunch, England	W 6
Sept.	23—Jack McDonald, England	W 1
Sept.	23—Jasper White, England	W 2
Sept.	30—Harry Smith, England	W 3
Sept.	30—Cock Robin, England	W 3
Nov.	7—Jack Scales, England ....KO	1
Nov.	18—Frank Craig, England ....WF	7
Dec.	13—Yank Kenny, England ....WF	4

1902

Jan.	18—Frank Kelly, Scotland	W 4
Jan.	20—Pat McDonald, Scotland	W 2
Jan.	27—Chas. McKeever, England ....WF	3
Feb.	—Yank Kenny, England .... WF	5
Mar.	—Andy Walsh, Philadelphia ....KO	3
Mar.	10—Chas. McKeever, Philadelphia .ND	6
Mar.	19—Ed Denfass, Philadelphia ....KO	5
Mar.	20—Rufud Graham, Philadelphia ..ND	6
Mar.	26—Jack McCann, Reading ......KO	2
Mar.	26—Morris Mahoney, Reading	W 3
Apr.	—Chas. McKeever, Philadelphia .ND	6
Apr.	11—Joe Walcott, Philadelphia ....ND	6
Apr.	28—Yg. P. Jackson, Philadelphia ..ND	6
May	3—George Cole, Philadelphia ...ND	4
May	10—Lanahan, Philadelphia .....ND	2
May	10—Jack Williams, Philadelphia ...ND	6
May	23—Jack Bonner, Philadelphia ....ND	6
June	2—Chas. McKeever, Philadelphia .KO	1
June	6—Al Neill, Chicago ....KO	3
June	12—George Cole, Philadelphia ....ND	6
June	16—Jack Bonner, Paterson ....ND	6
June	21—Yank Kenny, Philadelphia ...KO	3
June	23—Joe Block, St. Louis..........ND	7
June	30—Jim Driscoll, Chicago	W 6
June	30—Jack Beauscholte, Chicago	W 6
July	?—Jack Lewis,Mt. Clemens	W 1
Sept.	12—Billy Stift, Chicago	W 6
Sept.	29—Joe Choynski, Chicago	W 6
Oct.	3—Peter Maher, Philadelphia ...ND	6
Oct.	23—Jim Jeffords, Philadelphia ....ND	6
Oct.	30—Peter Maher, Philadelphia ...ND	6
Nov.	19—Marvin Hart, Philadelphia ....ND	6

Dec.	15—Chas. McKeever, Philadelphia .ND	6
Dec.	18—Jim Watts, Philadelphia	W 4

1903

Jna.	1—Al Weinig, Fort Erie ....KO	12
Jan.	8—Joe Grimm, Philadelphia .....ND	6
Feb.	26—Al Weinig, Philadelphia.......	W 4
Mar.	5—Jack Butler, Lancaster	W 6
Mar.	9—Jim Jeffords, Pittsburgh	W 10
Mar	19—Billy Payne, Philadelphia	W 2
Mar.	30—Joe Choynski, Philadelphia ...ND	6
Apr.	20—Joe Walcott, Boston	D 10
May	5—Marvin Hart, Philadelphia ...ND	6
May	19—George Ester, Philadelphia ....KO	3
May	23—George Byers, Philadelphia ...ND	6
May	26—Jack Williams, Philadelphia ...ND	6
June	11—Al Limerick, Shenandoah . KO by	13
June	25—Jack Bonner, Mauch Chunk ...	W 10
July	1—Kid Carter, Philadelphia .....ND	6
July	11—Jim Jeffords, Philadelphia ....ND	6
July	21—Paddy Sheehan, Philadelphia .ND	6
Sept.	6—Charley Haghey, England .....KO	3
Oct.	12—Mullen, England	W 10
Oct.	26—Hevron, England ....KO	5
Nov.	18—Jack (Twin) Sullivan, Phila. ...ND	6
Dec.	5—Jack Williams, Philadelphia ...KO	3
Dec.	12—Mike Schreck, Chicago	W 6
Dec.	22—Jack (Twin) Sullivan, Boston ..	W 15
Dec.	24—Jim Jeffords, Philadelphia ....ND	6
Dec.	29—Hugh Kelly, Kansas City	D 10

1904

Jan.	27—Tommy Ryan, Philadelphia ...ND	6
Feb.	22—Chas. Mack, Chicago ....KO	3
Feb.	22—Jim Driscoll, Chicago	W 3
Mar.	10—Mike Schreck, St. Louis	W 15
Mar.	18—Hugo Kelly, Chicago	W 6
Apr.	14—Jack (Twin) Sullivan, St. L. ...KO	3
Apr.	28—Kid Carter, St. Louis	W 3
May	14—Kid McCoy, Philadelphia .....ND	6
May	25—Geo Cole, Philadelphia ....ND	6
July	23—B. Fitzsimmons, Philadelphia .ND	6
Sept.	14—Hugo Kelly, Philadelphia .....ND	6
Sept.	23—Billy Stift, Baltimore ....KO	2
Sept.	29—Joe Butler, Philadelphia .....KO	1
Oct.	7—Tommy Burns, Milwaukee	W
Oct.	21—Jim Jeffords, Baltimore ......KO	3
Nov.	9—John Willie, Philadelphia .....ND	6
Nov.	12—Dixie Kid, Philadelphia ......ND	6
Nov.	17—Black Bill, Philadelphia ......ND	6
Dec.	11—Larry Temple, Philadelphia ...ND	6
Dec.	19—Morris Harris, Philadelphia ...ND	6

1905

Feb.	1—John Willie, Philadelphia .....ND	6
Mar.	24—Yg. P. Jackson, Baltimore ....WF	2
Apr.	7—Yg. P. Jackson, Baltimore ...	W 10
Apr.	25—Hugo Kelly, Indianapolis L	10
July	4—Jack (Twin) Sullivan, Dawson ..	D 20
Aug.	28—Billy Bates, Dawson	W 10
Sept.	9—Billy Bates, Fairbanks ......WF	6
Oct.	27—Al Kaufman, San Fran.......KO	17
Dec.	20—Bob Fitzsimmons, San Fran...KO	13

(Won Light Heavyweight Title)

1906

July	16—Sam Berger, Philadelphia .....ND	6
Aug.	20—Mark Beecham, Newcastle ....KO	2
Oct.	16—Fred Cooley, Los Angeles ....KO	3
Oct.	16—Jim Trimble, Los Angeles ....KO	9
Nov.	28—Tommy Burns, Los Angeles....	D 20

(For World Heavyweight Title)

1907

Feb.	22—Abdul Malgan, Los Angeles ...WF	9
May	8—Tommy Burns, Los Angeles.....L	20

(For World Heavyweight Title)

Dec.	13—Bill Hevernon, Philadelphia ...KO	1

1908

Feb.	11—Bob Ward, Charleston, Va......	W 10
Mar.	2—Jack Bonner, Philadelphia ...ND	6
Apr.	4—A. J. D. Biddle, Philadelphia .Exh.	4
June	10—Jack Blackburn, Phila. ....ND	6
Aug.	29—Jack Rush, Clarksburg, Va. ...KO	7
Sept.	7—Larry Temple, Philadelphia ...ND	6
Sept.	23—A. J. D. Biddle, Philadelphia ..ND	4
Sept.	26—Tom Lenihan, Philadelphia ...KO	4
Nov.	9—George Cole, Philadelphia ....ND	6
Nov.	25—Al Kubiak, Phila. ....ND	6

1909

Jan.	4—Jack Reed, Philadelphia .....Exh.	2
Jan.	4—Fred Cooley, Philadelphia ...Exh.	2
Jan.	4—Jack Cooper, Philadelphia ...Exh.	2
Feb.	11—A. J. D. Biddle, Phila. ....Exh.	4
Mar.	26—*Stanley Ketchel, New York ..ND	10
May	19—Jack Johnson, Philadelphia ...ND	6
June	9—Stanley Ketchel, Phila. .... KO by	3
June	30—Jim Flynn, Denver, Col. ......ND	10
Nov.	25—Al Kubiak, Shamokin, Pa. ....ND	6
Nov.	29—Chas. Stevenson, Phila. ....ND	6

*O'Brien saved by bell.

1910
Jan. 19—Al Kaufman, Philadelphia ....ND 6
Apr. 21—Al Kaufman, Philadelphia ....ND 6
1911
Aug. 15—Sam Langford, New York . KO by 5
Nov. 27—Harry Ramsey, Philadelphia ..ND 6
1912
June 17—Ben Koch, Philadelphia ......ND 6
TB KO WD WF D LD LF KOBY ND NC
181 36 59 6 16 3 0 4 57 0
Died in New York City, Nov. 12, 1942.
Elected to Hall of Fame 1968

JACK DILLON
(Ernest Cutler Price)
(Jack the Giant Killer)
Born, February 2, 1891, Frankfort, Ind.
Nationality, Scotch-Irish-American. Weight, 158
lbs. Height, 5 ft. 7½ in. Managed by Sam
Marburger and Steve Harter.
1908
Apr. 18—Kid Brown, Indianapolis ...... D 6
July 20—Joe McAree, Indianapolis ..... W 6
Sept. 19—Jack Laffy, Indianapolis......KO 4
Oct. 27—Tom Delane, Indianapolis ...KO 4
Nov. 13—Pat Lark, Indianapolis........KO 4
Nov. 20—Teddy Malone, Dayton........ D 10
Dec. 19—Tommy Clark, Indianapolis .... W 10
1909
Jan. 22—Joe McAree, Indianapolis.....KO 5
Feb. 3—Kid Simms, Indianapolis .....KO 3
Feb. 20—Charles Humphries,
Indianapolis ....KO 2
Feb. 24—Kid Clark, Columbus.........KO 6
Mar. 3—Par Lark, Indianapolis.........W 6
Mar. 5—Kid Griffin, Indianapolis .....KO 4
Mar. 12—Ray Bronson, Hartford City ... D 6
Mar. 31—Bob Long, Indianapolis.......KO 5
Apr. 2—Kid Gray, Indianapolis ......KO 2
May 10—Young Connors, Indianapolis .KO 5
May 28—Kid Sullivan, Terre Haute ....KO 3
July 2—Tommy Scanlon, Terre Haute .KO 6
July 22—Everett Reeves, Anderson ....KO 5
Sept. 19—Kid Sparks, New Orleans .....KO 2
Dec. 21—Jimmy Cooley, Indianapolis ... W 6
1910
Jan. 31—Jap Roberts, Cincinnati ......KO 2
Feb. 8—Jimmy Cooley, Indianapolis ... D 6
Mar. 8—Ray Bronson, Anderson .... D 8
Apr. 2—Rube May, Anderson ....KO 5
Apr. 21—Dick Fitzpatrick, Anderson .... W 10
May 30—Howard Morrow, Anderson .... W , 8
June 20—Freddie Hicks, Newark, O..... W 15
July 28—Jack Ryan, Anderson ....KO 6
Sept. 17—Jim Perry, Pittsburgh ....ND 6
Oct. 3—Jack Herrick, Winnipeg.......ND 12
Oct. 21—George Chip, Pittsburgh .....ND 6
Oct. 29—Billy Berger, Pittsburgh .....ND 6
Nov. 11—Jack Herrick, Winnipeg.......ND 12
Nov. 28—Kid Brown, Springfield, O. .... W 20
Dec. 6—Eddie McGoorty, Anderson ....L 10
1911
Jan. 2—Harry Mansfield, Pittsburgh ..ND 6
Jan. 11—Eddie McGoorty, Winnipeg ...ND 12
Jan. 24—Geo. Chip, Dayton, O. ....W 15
Feb. 4—Mike Glover, Pittsburgh ......ND 6
Feb. 18—Young Loughrey, Pittsburgh ..ND 6
Feb. 22—Jimmie Gardner, Indianapolis .ND 10
Mar. 4—Billy Berger, Pittsburgh .....ND 6
Mar. 14—Jimmy Mellody, Brazil, Ind. ..KO 3
Mar. 15—Young Loughrey, Indianapolis ND 10
Mar. 17—Mike Twin Sullivan, Buffalo ..ND 10
Apr. 1—Billy Clarke, Pittsburgh .....KO 4
Apr. 4—Frank Mantell, Boston .... W 12
Apr. 12—Jack Stevens, Mt. Vernon, Ind. KO 1
Apr. 28—George Chip, Terre Haute ....ND 10
May 3—Bob Moha, Indianapolis ......ND 10
June 5—Ralph Erne, Muncie ....ND 10
June 21—Paddy Lavin, Indianapolis ...ND 10
July 3—Bob Mohan, Buffalo ....ND 10
Sept. 4—Eddie McGoorty, New Orleans ..L 4
Oct. 4—Jack Graham, Vincennes, Ind. KO 3
Oct. 20—Jack Herrick, So. Bend, Ind. .ND 10
Oct. 23—Barney Williams, Phila. ......ND 6
Oct. 28—Ralph Erne, Pittsburgh ......ND 6
Nov. 1—Eddie McGoorty, Indianapolis ND 10
Nov. 11—Geo. K. O. Brown, Pittsburgh .ND 6
Nov. 22—George Chip, Youngstown, O. ND 12
Dec. 6—Frank Klaus, Pittsburgh ......ND 6
1912
Jan. 1—Leo Houck, Indianapolis ......W 6
Jan. 20—Billy Griffith, Pittsburgh .....ND 6
Jan. 26—Howard Wiggen, Indianapolis .KO 2
Feb. 1—Billy Berger, Youngstown, O. .ND 12

Feb. 3—Jimmy Gardner, Pittsburgh ...ND 6
Feb. 8—Paddy Lavin, Buffalo ....ND 10
Feb. 10—Geo. Chip, Pittsburgh ....ND 6
Feb. 22—Kid Clark, Indianapolis.......ND 10
Mar. 7—Walter Coffey, Oakland, Cal.... W 10
Mar. 23—Frank Klaus, Daly City, Cal. ....L 20
May 3—Frank Klaus, N. Y. C. ....ND 10
May 28—Hugo Kelly, Indianapolis .....KO 3
(Dillon claimed world Light Heavyweight
Title)
June 11—Jack Twin Sullivan, Buffalo ...ND 10
June 27—Geo. K. O. Brown, Winnipeg,
Man.........................ND 12
July 4—Thomas, Terre Haute, Ind.....KO 8
July 22—Joe Gorman, Memphis, Tenn..KO 6
July 25—George Chip, Indianapolis ....ND 10
Aug. 12—Mike Donovan, Richmond, Ind.KO 4
Oct. 11—Harry Ramsey, Philadelphia ..ND 6
Oct. 17—Kid Wagner, Johnstown, Pa. ..ND 10
Oct. 19—George Chip, Pittsburgh .....ND 6
Oct. 23—Gus Christie, Dayton, O. ..... W 15
Oct. 25—Battling Conners, Indianapolis KO 7
Nov. 4—Jack Flynn, Wabash, Ind. .....KO 4
Nov. 8—Jimmy Howard, Memphis, Tenn.W 8
Nov. 11—George Chip, Columbus, O. ...ND 10
Nov. 22—Kid Clark, Indianapolis.......KO 2
Dec. 11—Gus Christie, Indianapolis ...ND 10
Dec. 19—Harry Ramsey, Cincinnati ....ND 10
1913
Jan. 1—Gus Christie, Indianapolis .....ND 10
Jan. 9—Frank Mantell, Thorton, R.I. .. W 15
Jan. 18—Al Rogers, Pittsburgh ....ND 6
Jan. 22—Leo Houck, Philadelphia .....ND 6
Jan. 24—Frank Logan, Philadelphia ...ND 6
Feb. 10—Bill McKinnon, Thornton, R.I. .. D 15
Feb. 19—Jack Denning, Indianapolis ...KO 2
Mar. 10—Al Rogers, Altoona, Pa. ......ND 6
Mar. 12—K. O. Brennan, Indianapolis ..ND 10
Apr. 10—Buck Crouse, Pittsburgh ......ND 6
Apr. 14—George Chip, Youngstown, O. ND 12
Apr. 17—Barney Williams, Rochester,
N. Y..........................ND 10
Apr. 28—Bob Moha, Milwaukee ....ND 10
May 29—Frank Klaus, Indianapolis ....ND 10
July 3—Bill McKinnon, Indianapolis ..KO 10
Aug. 8—George Ashe, Winnipeg.......ND 12
Aug. 11—Jack Williams, Peru, Ind. .....KO 3
Sept. 17—Tony Caponi, Winnipeg, Man.. KO 8
Oct. 9—Leo Houck, Lancaster, Pa. ....ND 6
Oct. 14—Walter Monaghan, Akron, O...KO 4
Nov. 3—Gus Christie, Milwaukee .....ND 10
1914
Jan. 1—Gus Christie, Indianapolis ....ND 10
Jan. 20—Vic Hanson, Denver, Colo...... W 12
Feb. 4—Freddy Hicks, Windsor, Can...ND 8
Feb. 9—Tommy Danforth, Memphis,
Tenn..........................KO 2
Feb. 17—Marshall Clairborne, Hot SpringsW 3
Mar. 3—Jim Flynn, Kansas City .... D 10
Mar. 11—Jack Lester, Hot Springs .....KO 10
Mar. 17—Dick Gilbert, Hot Springs...... W 10
Apr. 14—Battling Levinsky, Butte, Mont. W 12
Apr. 28—Al Norton, Kansas City .... W 10
(Won international recognition as Light
Heavyweight Title)
May 29—Battling Levinsky, Indiananp..ND 10
June 15—Bob Moha, Butte, Mont........ W 12
July 3—Sailor Ed. Petrosky, Kans. City . W 10
Sept. 7—Sailor Einert, Terre Haute ....ND 10
Sept. 15—Geo. K.O. Brown, Vincennes,
Ind............................ND 10
Sept. 28—Frank Mantell, Columbus, O. ..ND 12
Oct. 5—Jim Flynn, Kansas City .... W 10
Oct. 14—Geo. K.O. Brown, St. Louis ....NC 3
Nov. 9—Charlie Weinert, Philadelphia .KO 2
Nov. 24—Dick Gilbert, Denver .... W 15
1915
Jan. 1—Young Ahearn, Philadelphia ..ND 6
Jan. 16—Porky Flynn, Brooklyn ......ND 10
Jan. 22—Y'g Halstead, Christopher, Ill..KO 3
Jan. 25—Larry English, Memphis ......KO 10
Feb. 20—Frank Mantell, N.Y.C. ....ND 10
Feb. 23—Johnny Howard, Brooklyn ....ND 10
Mar. 2—Tom McCarty, Brooklyn .....ND 10
Mar. 16—Gunboat Smith, Milwaukee ...ND 10
Apr. 6—Billy Murray, Hudson, Wis. ...ND 10
Apr. 29—Marty Cutler, Lexington, Ky..KO 6
May 5—Andre Anderson, Lexington,
Ky............................KO 10
May 20—Jack Lester, Joplin, Mo. ...... W 15
June 7—Tom McMahon, Rochester ...ND 10
June 11—Frank Mantell, Cincinnati ....ND 10
July 5—George Chip, Kans. City, Mo. .. D 10
July 12—Johnny Howard, N. Y. C. .....ND 10
July 16—Zulu Kid, N. Y. C. ....ND 10

498

Aug.	17—Tom McCarty, Lewiston, Mont. D	10
Aug.	30—Sailor Grande, Philadelphia ...ND	6
Sept.	25—Tom McMahon, Pittsburgh ...ND	6
Oct.	5—Jim Savage, Brooklyn ....ND	10
Nov.	1—Charley Weinert, N. Y. C. .....ND	10
Nov.	18—Frank Farmer, Oshkosh, Wis. .KO	4
Nov.	29—Jim Flynn, Brooklyn ....ND	10
Dec.	7—Porky Flynn, Brooklyn ......ND	10
Dec.	17—Yankee Gilbert, Dayton, O....KO	4
Dec.	20—Al Norton, Memphis ....KO	4
Dec.	29—George Lewis, Toledo, O.....ND	8

1916

Jan.	10—Porky Flynn, Memphis ....W	8
Jan.	28—Billy Miske, Superior, Wis. ...ND	10
Feb.	1—Tom Cowler, N. Y. C. ....KO	2
Feb.	8—Battling Levinsky, Brooklyn ..ND	10
Feb.	14—Vic Hanson, Memphis ....W	8
Mar.	10—Jim Flynn, N. Y. C. ....ND	10
Mar.	14—Gunboat Smith, N. Y. C. .....ND	10
Mar.	17—Whitey Allen, Brooklyn .....KO	4
Mar.	28—Battling Levinsky, Brooklyn ..ND	10
Apr.	14—Billy Miske, St. Paul ....ND	10
Apr.	25—*Battling Levinsky, Kansas City W	15
May	23—Bob Devere, Buffalo ....ND	10
June	29—Frank Moran, Brooklyn .....ND	10
July	4—Jim Flynn, Dewey, Okla. .....KO	4
July	13—Battling Levinsky, Baltimore .ND	10
Sept.	12—Battling Levinsky, Memphis ...D	8
Oct.	10—Sailor Grande, Brooklyn .....KO	2
Oct.	17—*Tim O'Neill, Brooklyn ......ND	10
Oct.	23—Larry Williams, Philadelphia .ND	6
Oct.	24—Battling Levinsky, Boston L	12
	(Lost Light Heavyweight Title)	
Nov.	10—Mike Gibbons, St. Paul ......ND	10
Dec.	19—Billy Miske, B'klyn. ....ND	10
	*Title bout.	

1917

Jan.	1—Bob Moha, Dayton, O. ....ND	15
Jan.	16—Billy Miske, Brooklyn ....ND	10
Feb.	16—Gunboat Smith, New Orleans .. W	20
Feb.	26—Al McCoy, N.Y.C. ....ND	10
Mar.	19—Jack Moran, Memphis, Tenn. .KO	6
Mar.	30—Jack Barry, Hot Springs, Ark. .KO	3
May	15—Tommy McMahon, Dayton, O. .D	15
May	21—Jack McCarron, Toledo, O. ...D	10
May	29—George Chip, Cincinnati .....ND	10
June	25—Len Rowlands, Memphis, Tenn. W	8
July	4—Soldier Smith, Terre Haute, Ind. ....KO	1
July	10—Jack Clifford, Brooklyn .....ND	10
July	30—Harry Greb, Pittsburgh .....ND	10
Sept.	3—Mike Gibbons, Terre Haute, Ind. ....ND	10
Oct.	5—Hugh Walker, Ft. Riley, Kan. .ND	10
Oct.	15—Willie Meehan, Philadelphia ...ND	6
Oct.	17—Zulu Kid, Montreal, Can. .....ND	10
Nov.	3—Battling Stanley, Indianapolis.KO	2
Nov.	13—Billy Miske, Brooklyn ....ND	10

1918

Jan.	25—George Chip, Duluth ....ND	10
Feb.	22—Hugh Walker, Joplin ....D	12
Mar.	4—Harry Greb, Toledo ....ND	12
Mar.	22—Steamboat Bill Scott, Muncie ..D	10
Apr.	15—Hugh Walker, Memphis ....W	8
May	7—Frank Farmer, Tacoma L	6
May	29—Joe Walters, Connersville, Ind. KO	3
Je	17—Hugh Walker, Tulsa, Okla. L	12
July	1—Frank Hoe, Indianapolisis ....D	10
July	4—Al McCoy, Charleston ....ND	10
Aug.	8—Jack Daily, Valparaiso, Ind. ....ND	6
Aug.	20—Marty Cross, Columbus ......ND	15
Sept.	25—Billy Ryan, Charleston ....ND	10
Oct.	4—Jack Duffy, Cedar Rapids, Ia. .ND	10
Nov.	20—Harry Krohn, Chillicothe, O....W	6
Nov.	23—Gus Christie, Indianapolis ....ND	10
Nov.	29—Gus Christie, Indianapolis ...Exh.	3
Dec.	13—Ted Black, Detroit ....ND	6

1920

Feb.	9—Battling Halstead, Miami, Fla..ND	10
Mar.	21—Young Fitzsimmons, Hot Springs, Ark...........................ND	10
Mar.	28—Paul Roman, Dallas, Tex......ND	10
Apr.	2—Battling Halstead, Palm Beach, Fla. ....ND	10
May	8—Bob Sweeney, Kokomo, Ind. .KO	6
May	16—Jack Riley, Gary, Ind. ....KO	8
June	10—Young Fitzsimmons, scrammon, Kans. ....ND	10
July	4—Pat Weiss, El Reno, Okla. .....ND	10
Sept.	4—Bud Clancy, Cedar Rapids, Ia. .ND	10
Oct.	4—Jack Hall, Springfield, Mo.....ND	10
Oct.	9—Battling Logan, Okulkville, Ark............................ND	10
Nov.	2—Battling Halstead, Ft. Smith, Ark...............................ND	10
Nov.	25—Jack Moran, Shreveport, La. ..KO	2

Dec.	22—Harry Folly, Hot Springs, Ark. ND	4
Dec.	28—Young Fitzsimmons, San Antonio, Tex................................ND	12

1921

Jan.	25—Frisco Pete Brown, Louisville .KO	6
Feb.	11—Billy Edwards, Alexandria, La. KO	3
Feb.	15—Jack Denham, Atlanta, Ga. ...KO	6
Feb.	18—Ed. Warner, Helena, Ark. .....ND	10

1923

Jan.	12—Joe Walters, Bicknell, Ind. ....ND	10

Dillon was in no condition to box from 1921 and was urged by friends to quit the ring which he did.

Note—Barney Williams, named in this record, and Battling Levinsky, is the same person.

TB	KO	WD	WF	D	LD	LF	KOBY	ND	NC
240	60	32	0	14	6	0	0	127	1

Died Aug. 7, 1942, Chattahoochee, Fla.
Elected to Boxing Hall of Fame 1959.

BATTLING LEVINSKY
(Barney Lebrowitz)

Born June 10, 1891, Philadelphia, Pa. Nationality, Jewish-American. Weight, 175 lbs. Height, 5 ft. 11 in. Managed by Jack Hanlon and Dan Morgan. Started boxing under the name of Barney Williams. Changed his name in 1913. Started boxing 1906; early record unavailable.

1910

Knockouts: Marty McAndrews, 5; Jack Krause, 5; Fighting Dick, 4; Matt Ryan, 1; Joe Sandy, 1; Joe O'Neil, 4; Johnny Dogan, 2; Jack Ferry, 1. Won: Paddy Burns, 6. No decisions: Paddy Burns, 6; Leo Diamond, 6; Reddy Hogan, 6; Jimmy Dolan, 6; Kid Selby, 9; Paddy Burns, 6; Cropy Melley, 6; Joe Paige, 6; Kid Harris, 6; Jack Doyle, 6; Peck Miller, 6; Billy Burke, 6; Mickey McDonough, 6; Jack Fitzgerald, 6; Jimmy Glavin, 6; Jack Clarke, 6.

1911

	—Jack Doyle .... KO	6
Feb.	2—Leo Houck, Lancaster, Pa. .... ND	6
March	16—Leo Houck, Lancaster, Pa. .... ND	6
April	3—Mike Glover, Philadelphia, Pa. ... ND	6
	—Jack Fitzgerald .... ND	6
	—Johnny Howard .... ND	6
May	23—Al Kubiak, Philadelphia, Pa. ...... ND	6
June	26—Ralph Calloway, Albany, New York ND	10
July	12—Frank Mantell, New York City ... ND	10
	—Billy West .... ND	10
	—Jack Mitchell .... ND	10
	—Jumbo Welsh .... ND	6
Oct.	2—James J. Barry, Philadelphia, Pa. ND	6
Oct.	23—Jack Dillon, Philadelphia, Pa. .... ND	6
Oct.	24—Leo Houck, Boston, Mass. L	12
	—Jeff Clarke .... ND	10
	—Jeff Clarke L	15

1912

Jan.	3—Joe Grim, Philadelphia .....ND	6
Jan.	10—George Ash, Philadelphia ...ND	6
Jan.	21—George Ash, Baltimore, Md. .ND	13
Feb.	12—Eddie McGoorty, Pittsburgh .ND	6
Feb.	28—Eddie Palmer, Philadelphia ...ND	6
Mar.	6—Bill McKinnon, New York ...ND	10
Mar.	12—Eddie Palmer, Philadelphia ..ND	6
Mar.	18—Peck Miller, Allentown .....ND	10
Mar.	19—Bill McKinnon, New York ...ND	10
Apr.	2—Larry Williams, Philadelphia .ND	6
Apr.	14—Tony Caponi, Atlanta ....W	10
May	3—Eddie Palmer, Wilkes-Barre ..ND	10
May	24—Dick Gilbert, Jacksonville ....W	15
June	7—Dick Gilbert, Jacksonville ....W	15
June	14—Dick Gilbert, Jacksonville ....W	20
July	19—Harry Wuest, Jacksonville ...ND	15
Sept.	7—Kid Wagner, Wilkes-Barre ...ND	10
Sept.	22—Dave Smith, Philadelphia .....W	6
Sept.	28—Eddie McGoorty, Philadelphia ND	6
Oct.	8—Dave Smith, Philadelphia .....W	6
Nov.	12—Harry Ramsey, Philadelphia ..W	6
Nov.	28—Tom Kennedy, Philadelphia ..W	6
Dec.	20—Dick Gilbert, Jacksonville ...W	25

1913

Feb.	10—Tom McMahon, Buffalo ...ND	10
Mar.	8—One Round Davis, Buffalo ...ND	10
Apr.	17—Jack Dillon, Rochester, N. Y. ND	10
July	3—Jack Twin Sullivan, Buffalo .ND	10

July   30—Porky Flynn, New York ....ND 10
Aug.   19—Sailor White, Rockaway Bch. ND 10
Aug.   27—Nick Muller, New York .....KO 10
Sept. 10—Eddie McGoorty, New York .ND 10
Sept. 17—Whitey Allen, New York .....KO 5
Sept. 23—Frank McGuinness, New York KO 6
Sept. 27—Jack Twin Sullivan, N. Y. ...ND 10
Sept. 30—Jack Keating, New York .....ND 10
Nov.   18—Tim Logan, New York ......ND 10
Nov.   20—Ed Hagen, New York ......KO 7
Dec.   2—Charley Weinert, New York .ND 10
Dec.   9—Jim Flynn, New York ......ND 10
Dec.   22—Jim Coffey, New York .....ND 10
Dec.   25—Jack Driscoll, Brooklyn .....ND 10

1914
Jan.   1—Tom Daly, New York ....KO 2
Jan.   3—Jim Coffey, Philadelphia ....ND 6
Jan.   5—Bob McAllister, New York ..ND 10
Jan.   13—Porky Flynn, New York ....ND 10
Jan.   19—Jack Connors, New York ....ND 10
Jan.   20—Jack Keating, Bridgeport, Ct. ND 10
Jan.   22—Bob Kenny, Allentown, Pa. ..KO 3
Jan.   27—Soldier Kearns, New York ...ND 10
Jan.   31—Tony Ross, Philadelphia .....ND 6
Feb.   6—Tom McMahon, New York ..ND 10
Mar.   3—Fred McKay, Brooklyn .....ND 10
Mar.   7—Jack Keating, New York ....ND 10
Mar.   9—Jim Coffey, New York .....ND 10
Mar.   14—Tim O'Neill, Philadelphia ...ND 6
Mar.   17—Sailor Fritts, New York ....ND 10
Mar.   23—Bob Moha, Milwaukee ......ND 10
Apr.   14—Jack Dillon, Butte, Mont. ....L 12
May   19—Carl Lewis, Brooklyn .....ND 10
May   29—Jack Dillon, Indianapolis ....ND 10
June   6—Jack Davis, New York ......KO 7
June   26—Bert Kenny, New York .....ND 10
June   30—Charley Weinert, New York .ND 10
July   21—Porky Flynn, Brooklyn .....ND 10
July   31—Jack Driscoll, Far Rockaway .ND 10
Aug.   18—Sailor Fritts, New York ....ND 10
Aug.   19—Bartley Madden, New York ..ND 10
Aug.   31—Jack Nevins, New York .....KO 2
Sept. 18—One Round Davis, Buffalo ....ND 10
Oct.   9—Gunboat Smith, New York ..BD 10
Oct.   20—Jim Flynn, New York ......ND 10
Oct.   30—Sailor Fritts, New York ....ND 10
Oct.   31—Terry Keller, New York .....ND 10
Nov.   5—Frank Mantell, Providence ...D 12
Nov.   26—Tom McCarty, New York ...ND 10
Dec.   25—Porky Flynn, Brooklyn .....ND 10

1915
*Jan.   1—Bartley Madden, Brooklyn ..ND 10
*Jan.   1—Soldier Kearns, New York ...ND 10
*Jan.   1—Gunboat Smith, Waterbury ..ND 12
Jan.   6—Jack Keating, New York ....ND 10
Jan.   27—Gunboat Smith, New Orleans .L 20
Mar.   6—Sailor Fritts, New York ....ND 10
Mar.   8—George Ashe, Philadelphia ...ND 6
Mar.   19—Bill Ketchell, New York ....ND 10
Mar.   22—Jack Hanlon, New York ....ND 10
Mar.   26—Tom McCarthy, New York ...ND 10
Oct.   24—Jack Dillon, Boston ....W 12
Apr.   3—Zulu Kid, New York ....ND 10
May   14—Jack Connors, New York ....ND 10
May   28—George Ashe, New York .....ND 10
May   31—Porky Flynn, Brooklyn .....ND 10
July   9—Porky Flynn, Far Rockaway .ND 10
July   13—Lengthy Rosen, Philadelphia .ND 6
Aug.   6—Colin Bell, New York ......ND 10
Aug.   14—Sailor Carrol, Brooklyn .....ND 10
Aug.   28—Soldier Kearns, Brooklyn ...ND 10
Sept. 24—Sandy Ferguson, Boston .....W 12
Sept. 28—Soldier Kearns, Brooklyn ...ND 10
Oct.   25—Porky Flynn, Portland, Me. ..ND 6
Nov.   8—Jack Geyer, Shenandoah, Pa. .ND 6
Nov.   15—Tom Cowler, New York .....ND 10
Nov.   27—Porky Flynn, New York ....ND 10
Dec.   20—Jack Connors, New York ....ND 10
Dec.   25—Jim Flynn, Brooklyn ......ND 10

*All bouts same day; first in morning,
second in afternoon, third in evening.

1916
Jan.   1—Tom McMahon, Scranton ...ND 10
Jan.   11—Tom Cowler, Boston ....W 12
Jan.   14—Silas Green, New York .....ND 10
Jan.   21—Zulu Kid, Philadelphia ......ND 10
Jan.   25—Al Reich, Boston ....W 12
Feb.   8—Jack Dillon, Brooklyn .....ND 10
Feb.   28—Jack Driscoll, New York ....W   3
Mar.   3—Jack Hanlon, New York ...KO 3
Mar.   7—Bert Kenny, Bridgeport .....W 10
Mar.   9—Bob Carroll, New London ...ND 10
Mar.   16—Bob Devere, Syracuse .....ND 10
Mar.   20—Jack Keating, Schenectady ..ND 10
Mar.   25—Jim Savage, New York .....ND 6
Mar.   28—Jack Dillon, Brooklyn ......ND 10

Apr.   19—Mike Fitzgerald, Toronto ...KO 2
Apr.   25—Jack Dillon, Kansas City, Mo. .L 15
       (Light Heavyweight Title Bout)
May   15—Gunboat Smith, Philadelphia ND 6
May   30—Porky Flynn, Chattanooga ...D 8
June   30—Jim Barry, Syracuse ....ND 10
July   13—Jack Dillon, Baltimore .....ND 10
July   21—George Ashe, Rockaway ....ND 10
July   25—Tommy Burke, St. Louis ....ND 12
Sept.   4—K. O. Brown, Chicago .....ND 10
Sept. 12—Jack Dillon, Memphis ....D 8
Sept. 25—Battling Bradley, Columbus .ND 12
Oct.   3—Gus Christie, Memphis ......D 8
Oct.   10—Gunboat Smith, Boston ....W 12
Oct.   12—Billy Miske, Brooklyn ......ND 10
Oct.   24—Jack Dillon, Boston ....W 12

(Levinsky claimed Light Heavyweight
title as result of victory. Men did not make
weight, but each was below the class limit of
175 pounds.)

Oct.   30—Billy Miske, Brooklyn .....ND 10
Nov.   16—Carl Morris, Kansas City .....L 15
Dec.   8—Gus Christie, Dayton ....ND 10

1917
Jan.   1—Gunboat Smith, Brooklyn ...ND 10
Jan.   12—Jim Smith, New York .....ND 10
Jan.   17—Bob Moha, Youngstown ...ND 10
Feb.   27—Billy Miske, St. Paul .....ND 10
Mar.   6—Jack Moran, St. Louis .....W 12
Mar.   23—Tom Gibbons, St. Paul, Minn. ND 10
May   9—Bob McAllister, N. Y. C. ...ND 10
May   16—Leo Houck, York, Pa. ......ND 6
May   26—Bert Kenny, New York .....ND 10
June   1—Bartley Madden, Far Rocka'y .ND 10
June   20—Johnny Howard, Providence ...W 12
June   23—Al Benedict Brooklyn ......ND 10
July   16—Al Benedict, Brooklyn ......ND 10
Aug.   6—Jack London, Brooklyn .....W   4
Sept.   6—Harry Greb, Pittsburgh .....ND 10
Sept. 11—Jim Coffey, Boston ....D 12
Oct.   2—Bill Brennan, Boston ....D 12
Oct.   23—Bill Brennan, Boston ....L 12
Oct.   31—Zulu Kid, Montreal ......ND 10
Nov.   27—Bill Brennan, Boston ....W 12
Dec.   10—Johnny Jacobs, Boston .....D   3
Dec.   11—Bartley Madden, Boston ....D 12

1918
Jan.   15—Bill Brennan, Boston ....D 12
Mar.   10—Charley Seinert, Jersey City .ND 8
May   24—Jim Coffey, N. Y. C. ......ND 6
May   27—Bartley Madden, Bridgeport ...D 15
June   6—Jim Coffey, Buffalo ....ND 6
June   17—Charley Weinert, Jersey City .ND 8
July   22—Billy Madden, Atlantic City .ND 8
Aug.   6—Harry Greb, Philadelphia ...ND 6
Aug.   15—Billy Miske, Brooklyn .....Exh. 4
Aug.   26—Clay Turner, Jersey City ...ND 8
Nov.   6—Jack Dempsey, Phila. ...KO by 3
Dec.   25—Leo Houck, Lancaster ......W   6

1919
Feb.   13—Jim Coffey, Boston ....W 12
Feb.   17—Harry Greb, Buffalo ......ND 10
Apr.   28—Harry Greb, Canton, O. ...ND 10
July   3—Billy Miske, Toledo ......ND 12
July   14—Harry Greb, Philadelphia ...ND 6
Aug.   11—Clay Turner, Jersey City ...ND 8
Sept.   3—Harry Greb, Wheeling, W. Va. ND 10
Nov.   17—Bartley Madden, Montreal ...ND 10
Nov.   24—Clay Turner, Detroit ......ND 10
Dec.   3—Al Benedict, Philadelphia ..ND 8

1920
Jan.   1—Wild Burt Kenny, Toronto ...W   8
Jan.   23—Johnny Howard,
       perth Amboy ....ND 8
Feb.   16—Clay Turner, Detroit ......ND 10
Mar.   15—Al Benedict, W. Hoboken ...ND 8
Mar.   26—Clay Turner, Hartford, Ct. ..ND 10
Apr.   19—Silas Green, Montreal .....ND 10
Apr.   28—Tony Melchoir, Kenosha, Wis. ND 10
May   3—Clay Turner, Portland, Me. ...W 12
May   21—Chuck Wiggins, Dayton, O. ....D 12
June   28—Sergt. Ray Smith, Cleveland .ND 10
Oct.   12—Georges Carpentier, Jersey
       City ....KO by 4
       (Lost World's Light Heavyweight title)

Dec.   8—Boy McCormick, Portland ...LF 7
       —Jack Renault ....W 12
1921
Mar.   10—Homer Smith, N. Y. C. .....W 12

Mar.	18—Charley Weinert, Brooklyn ...	L	15
Apr.	15—Dan O'Dowd, Syracuse, N. Y..	W	12
Apr.	29—Wild Bill Reed, Syracuse, N. Y.	W	12
July	2—Carl Morris, Tulsa, Okla.	LF	6
July	20—Eddie Ricord, Montreal	ND	10
Sept.	14—Mike McTigue, Montreal	ND	10
Nov.	24—Bob Roper, Buffalo	D	12

1922

| Jan. | 13—Gene Tunney, N. Y. C. ...... | L | 12 |

(For the American Light Heavyweight Championship).

1926

Aug.	31—Tommy Madden, Reading ...	KO	1
Sept.	12—George Gemas, Philadelphia ..	W	10
Nov.	11—Young Stribling, Des Moines .	ND	10
Nov.	18—Jim Moran, Atlantic City ...	KO	1

1927

Jan.	1—George Gemas, Philadelphia ..	W	8
Feb.	7—Ray Newman, Philadelphia	W	10
Sept.	8—Matt Adgie, Philadelphia	L	10
Oct.	24—Ted Jackson, N. Bergen, N. J.	KO	4
Oct.	28—Willie Walker, Norristown, Pa. .	W	10
Nov.	2—George Gemas, Philadelphia ...	W	10
Nov.	17—Matt Adgie, Philadelphia	W	10
Nov.	28—Joe Lohman, Philadelphia	W	10

1928

Feb.	6—Sandy Seifert, Pittsburgh	D	10
Feb.	17—Homer Robertson, Boston ...	W	10
Feb.	27—Marcel de Rose, New Bedford	KO	2
Mar.	5—Earl Blue, New York City	W	6
Apr.	11—Tiny Roebuck, Kansas City ..	ND	10
Apr.	17—Jack McAuliffe, St. Louis ...	ND	10
Apr.	23—Jim Sigmund, Saginaw	ND	10
Apr.	30—Clem Johnson, Harrisburg	W	8
May	21—Benny Ross, Newark, N. J. ...	W	10
June	6—Emmett Rocco, Akron	ND	10
July	2—Tex McEwan, Dayton, Ky. ...	WF	4
July	13—Phil Mercurio, Long Branch ..	L	10
Aug.	21—Tony Youkonis, Allentown ...	L	10
Sept.	21—Herman Weiner, Baltimore ...	W	8
Oct.	28—Pietro Corri, Passaic, N.J.....	ND	8
Dec.	4—Marty Gallagher, Balt., Md.	L	12

1929

Jan.	4—Pietro Corri, Bridgeport	W	10
Jan.	11—Otto Von Porat, Grand Rapids	L. Disq.	5
Jan.	15—Herman Weiner, Hagerstown, Md.	Ko by	1

TB	KO	WD	WF	D	LD	LF	KO BY	ND	NC
274	23	42	1	13	13	2	4	176	0

Died, February 12, 1949, Philadelphia, Pa.
Elected to Boxing Hall of Fame, 1966.

GEORGES CARPENTIER
(The Orchid Man)

Born, January 12, 1894, Lens, France. Weight, 126-175 lbs. Height, 5 ft. 11½ in. Managed by Francois Descamps.

1908

Nov.	1—Ed Salmon, Mais-Laffitte	WF	13
Nov.	30—Ed Salmon, Mais-Laffitte	KO by	18
Dec.	4—Lepine, Paris	W	6
Dec.	4—Simon, Paris	W	6
Dec.	4—Charles Legrand, Bethune	D	6
Dec.	28—Charles Legrand, Lens	W	15

1909

Feb.	19—George Gloria, Paris	KO by	6
Feb.	25—Simon, Paris	W	10
Feb.	28—Charles Legrand, Lens	D	20
Mar.	18—Achalme, Lens	W	10
Apr.	6—Cheveau, Roubaix	W	6
May	11—Auguste Relinger, Maubeuge	KO	6
May	11—Lampin, Maubeuge	KO	8
June	26—E. Wetinck, Lille	KO	1
July	27—Lucien Dorgueille, Lille	KO	11
Oct.	15—Paul Til, Lille	D	10
Oct.	23—Lucien Dorgueille, Paris	W	10
Nov.	8—Lampin, Henin-Lietard	KO	7
Nov.	24—Charles Ledoux, Paris	W	15
Dec.	8—Georges Gaillard, Paris	W	6
Dec.	22—Paul Til, Paris	W	10

1910

Jan.	5—Young Warner, Paris	WF	7
Jan.	8—Georges Gaillard, Lens	W	10
Jan.	15—Wally Pickard, Brussels	KO	8
Jan.	22—Jean Audony, Brussels	D	10

Feb.	9—Lampin, Brussels	KO	8
Mar.	12—Buck Shine, Brussels	L	10
Mar.	26—Fernand Cuny, Lyons	W	10
Apr.	3—George Gloria, Lens	KO	8
Apr.	9—Young Snowball, Paris	KO by	4
Apr.	16—Fernand Cuny, Bordeaux	KO by	13
July	6—Paul Til, Paris	D	15
July	17—Hubert Baelen, Lille	KO	2
Aug.	13—Fernand Cuny, Cabourg	KO	8
Sept.	5—Achille, Cambrai	KO	5
Oct.	15—Percy Wilson, Paris	W	10
Oct.	22—Jim Campbell, Paris	KO	5
Nov.	6—Young Williams, Arras	KO	7
Nov.	19—George Randall, Paris	KO	10
Dec.	3—Henry Demlen, Brussels	W	10
Dec.	17—Jack Daniels, Paris	W	10

1911

Jan.	8—Ed Brochet, Lens	KO	7
Jan.	14—George Randall, Paris	KO	5
Jan.	27—Henry Piet, Paris	L	10
Feb.	17—Jack Daniels, Paris	W	10
Mar.	1—Young Nipper, Paris	W	8
Mar.	12—Harry Stassen, Lens	KO	1
Mar.	15—Henry Marchand, Liege	KO	6
Mar.	25—Jack Mookins, Paris	W	10
Apr.	1—Sid Stagg, Roubaix	W	10
Apr.	8—G. Colbourne, Brussels	W	10
Apr.	23—Henri Marchand, Arras	KO	7
May	20—Frank Loughrey, Paris	W	15
June	15—Robert Eustache, Paris	KO	16

(Won French Welterweight Title)

June	23—Jack Goldswain, Paris	KO	4
Aug.	14—Arthur Evernden, Cabourg	W	15
Aug.	29—Dixie Kid, Tourville	KO by	5
Oct.	2—Sid Burns, London	W	15
Oct.	23—Young Joseph, London	KO	10

(Won European Welterweight Title)

| Nov. | 17—Theo Clay, Boulogne .... | KO | 9 |
| Dec. | 13—Harry Lewis, Paris .... | W | 20 |

1912

Jan.	7—Battling Lacroix, Lille	KO	8
Jan.	14—Jim Taylor, Lille	KO	4
Jan.	20—Battling Lacroix, Rouen	KO	4
Jan.	27—Pat Bradley, Rouen	KO	2
Feb.	29—Jim Sullivan, Monte Carlo	KO	2

(Won Vacant European Middleweight Title)

| Apr. | 4—George Gunther, Paris .... | W | 20 |

(Retained European Middleweight Title)

| May | 10—Hubert Roc, Marseilles .... | KO | 6 |
| May | 23—Willie Lewis, Paris .... | W | 20 |

(Retained European Middleweight Title)

| June | 27—Frank Klaus, Dieppe .... | LF | 19 |
| Oct. | 23—Billy Papke, Paris .... | L disq. | 17 |

1913

| Jan. | 8—Marcel Moreau, Paris .... | KO | 8 |
| Feb. | 12—Bandsman Rice, Paris .... | KO | 2 |

(Won Vacant European Light Heavyweight Title)

Mar.	1—Cyclone Smith, Nice	KO	3
Mar.	17—George Gunther, Nice	W	15
June	1—Bombardier Billy Wells, Ghent ..	KO	4

(Won Vacant European Heavyweight Title)

June	29—Albert Lurie, Bordeaux	KO	3
Aug.	9—Ashley Williams, Vichy	KO	4
Aug.	10—O'Mara, Vichy	KO	2
Oct.	11—Jeff Smith, Paris	W	20
Oct.	31—M. Abott, Geneva	KO	2
Dec.	8—Bombardier Billy Wells, London ..	KO	1

(Retainded European Heavyweight Title)

1914

Jan.	19—Pat O'Keefe, Nice	KO	2
Mar.	21—Joe Jeannette, Paris	L	15
Apr.	13—O'Mara, Blois	KO	2
Apr.	14—George Mitchell, Paris	KO	1
June	2—Hubert Roc, Valenciennes	KO	2
June	14—Philippe Robinson, Beziers	KO	3
July	16—Gunboat Smith, London	WF	6

(Won White Heavyweight Title)

| July | 26—Kid Jackson, Bordeaux .... | WF | 4 |

1915 1919
(Inactive)

Jan. 27—Jean Bicot, Paris .... Exh. 4
1918
Jan. 1—Fernand Campagne, Paris ...... Exh. 4
Jan. 1—Jules Lanara, Paris .... Exh. 4
1919
July 19—Dick Smith, Paris .... KO 8
(Retained European Heavyweight Title)
Sept. 21—C. Croisilles, San Sebastian ...... KO 2
Dec. 4—Joe Beckett, London .... KO 1
(Retained European Heavyweight Title)
1920
Jan. 10—Blink McCloskey, Bordeaux ...... KO 2
Feb. 21—F. Grundhoven, Monte Carlo ..... KO 2
Oct. 12—Battling Levinsky, Jersey City .. KO 4
(Won World Light Heavyweight Title)
1921
July 2—Jack Dempsey, Jersey City .... KO by 4
(For World Heavyweight Title)
1922
Jan. 22—George Cook, London .... KO 4
May 11—Ted (Kid) Lewis, London .... KO 1
(Retained World Light Heavyweight Title)
Sept. 24—Battling Siki, Paris .... KO by 6
(Lost World Light Heavywieght Title)
1923
May 6—Marcel Nilles, Paris .... KO 1
(Won French Heavyweight Title)
Oct. 1—Joe Beckett, London .... KO 1
1924
May 1—Arthur Townley, Vienna .... KO 2
May 31—Tommy Gibbons, Michigan City .. ND 10
July 24—Gene Tunney, New York ...... KO by 15
1925
(Inactive)
1926
May 21—Eddie Huffman, New York .... D 10
June 17—Tommy Loughran, Philadelphia .... L 10
July 7—Jack Burke, Denver .... KO 2
Sept. 15—Rocco Stramaglia, Alan, Idaho .... KO 3
1927
Jan. 11—Jack Walker, Paris .... Exh. 4

TB	KO	WD	WF	D	LD	LF	KO BY	ND	NC
109	56	28	4	6	4	2	8	1	0

Elected to Boxing Hall of Fame, 1964.
Died, October 28, 1975, Paris, France.

BATTLING SIKI
(Louis Phal)
Born, September 16, 1897, St. Louis, Senegal.
Weight, 175 lbs. Height, 5 ft. 10¾ in. Managed by "Papa Bob" Levy in the United States.
1913
—Frank Roose .... W 10
—Frank Roose .... W 10
—Jules Perroud .... KO 8
—Pierre Nicolas .... KO 2
—Prat............................. D 8
—Servat .... L 8
—Henrys .... LF 3
1914
—Frank Roose .... W 10
—Pierre Nicolas .... KO 2
—Jules Perroud .... KO 8
—Jean Audony .... L 10
—Tajan .... LF 7
1915-1918
(Inactive)
1919
—Eugene Stuber .... KO 2
—Leonard .... D 10
1920
—Henrys .... W 10
—Lefevre .... W 10
—Jimmy Lyggett .... W 10
—Jeff de Paus .... W 10
—Jen Audony .... KO 4
—Derenzy .... KO 3

—Victor Marchand .... KO 8
—Nicol Simpson .... KO 1
Apr. 29—Rene Devos, Paris .... W 10
May 2—Willem Westbroeck, Rotterdam ... KO 7
June 15—Bertes Ahaus, Rotterdam .... W 10
June 24—Daan Holtkamp, Rotterdam .... KO 2
July 4—Willem Westbroeck, Rotterdam ... KO 3
July 17—Tom Berry, Rotterdam .... W 10
Aug. 30—Tom Berry, Rotterdam .... L 15
Dec. 6—Jeff de Paus, Rotterdam .... W 15
1921
Jan. 14—Hans Breitenstraeter, Berlin ...... W 15
Jan. 17—Herman Sjouwermann, Amsterdam W 10
Feb. 25—Giuseppe Spalla, Berlin .... KO 9
—Jeff de Paus .... W 10
—Billy Balzac .... W 10
—Jean Leroi .... KO 2
—Gabriel Pionnier .... KO 7
—Ercole Balzac .... KO 2
—Battling Marcot .... KO 5
—Jean Leroi .... KO 3
—Bertes Ahaus .... W 10
—Constant Barrick .... W 10
June 14—Harry Reeve, Rotterdam .... W 15
Nov. 24—Paul Journee, Paris .... W 15
—Jugo Podzuhn .... KO 10
1922
Jan. 17—Rogiers, Paris .... W 12
Feb. 3—Iter, Strassburg .... KO 2
Mar. 3—Jules Lenaers, Strassburg .... KO 2
Mar. 15—Rogiers, Brussels .... W 10
Mar. 31—Vige, Rotterdam .... KO 5
Apr. 16—Louis Piochelle, Algiers .... W 12
Apr. 26—Al Baker, Barcelona .... W 12
May 11—Harry Reeve, Amsterdam .... W 12
May 19—Harry Reeve, Antwerp .... D 10
June 23—Marcel Nilles, Paris .... W 15
July 24—Dressler, Amsterdam .... KO 6
July 28—Harry Reeve, Marseilles .... KO 6
Sept. 24—Georges Carpentier, Paris .... KO 6
(Won World Light Heavyweight Title)
1923
Mar. 17—Mike McTigue, Dublin .... L 20
(Lost World Light Heavyweight Title)
June 16—Emile Morelle, Paris .... LF 6
(For Vacant European Light Heavyweight Title)
July 8—Marcel Nilles, Paris .... KO 2
Aug. 5—Gaston Marmoguet, Bordeaux .... KO 3
Oct. 1—Jack Johnson, Quebec .... Exh. 6
Nov. 20—Kid Norfolk, New York .... L 15
Dec. 26—Jack Taylor, Philadelphia .... L 10
1924
Jan. 7—Tony Stabenau, Buffalo .... KO 2
Jan. 9—Young Ernie, Venice, Calif. ...... KO 2
Jan 14—Young Norfolk, Memphis .... W 10
Jan. 21—Battling Owens, New Orleans ...... L 15
Jan. 31—Joe Lohman, Minneapolis ...... ND 10
Feb. 8—Joe White, Rochester .... W 10
Feb. 12—Tut Jackson, Columbus .... ND 10
July 11—Ray Bennett, Bellaire, Ohio ...... ND 12
July 18—Blacksmith Russell, Manchester .. KO 7
Aug. 1—Jack Lynch, Providence .... L 10
Aug. 4—Dixie Kid, Allentown, Pa. ...... KO 3
Aug. 11—Homer Smith, Buffalo .... L 10
Aug. 20—Mike Conroy, Bellaire, Ohio ...... NC 8
Nov. 7—Young Roscoe, Passaic .... KO 5
Nov. 14—Tony Marullo, New York .... L 12
Nov. 27—Frank Kearns, Syracuse .... D 10
Dec. 4—Jack Burke, Brooklyn .... L 12
1925
Mar. 13—Paul Berlenbach, New York ... KO by 10
June 29—Art Weigand, Buffalo .... L 6
July 10—Chief Halbran, Rockaway, N.Y. ... KO 3
July 23—Jimmy Francis, W. New York, N.J. KO 2
Aug. 18—Billy Vidabeck, W. New York, N.J. ND 10
Sept. 8—Harold Mays, Newark .... ND 10
Nov. 13—Lee Anderson, Baltimore .... L 12

TB	KO	WD	WF	D	LD	LF	KO BY	ND	NC
88	34	27	0	4	13	3	1	5	1

Shot to death, December 15, 1925, New York City.

MIKE McTIGUE
(Michael Francis McTigue)
Born, November 26, 1892, County Clare, Ireland.
Nationality, Irish. Weight 165 lbs. Height, 5 ft. 9 in.
Managed by Joe Jacobs and Jimmy Johnston.
Started boxing 1909; early record unavailable.

1914
—Happy Howard . . . . LF 5

1915
Knockouts: Happy Davis, 3; Joe Marino, 1, Mike Greel, 3; Rube Howard, 5; K. O. Jaffie, 6; George Novick, 3; Paddy Sullivan, 3; Johnny Baker, 10; Young Al McCoy, 7; Tommy Teague, 6; Fred Kibler, 10; Jack Emmanen, 2; George Leahy, 3; Charles McGreevey, 1. No decisions: Walter McGirr, 10; Mike Farrell, 10; Walter McGirr, 10; Tex Kelly, 10; Joe Stein, 10; Happy Howard, 10.

1916
Knockout: Dan Tucker, 3; Billy Carter, 1; K. O. Jaffie, 6; Bell Tinkle, 10; Sailor J. Kelsey, 10; Harry Applegate, 7; Willie Langford, 4; Bat Monroe, 7; Battling Gans, 10; Bill Brown, 10; Young Al McCoy, 7. Won: K. O. Sweeney, 12; Al Rogers, 12. No decisions: Young Hickey, 10; Augie Ratner, 10; Jack Smith, 10; Tommy Robson, 10; Happy Howard, 10.
Aug. 28—Jim Healy, New York . . . KO by 1

1917
Won: Joe Eagan, 12; Hughey Ross, 15. No decisions: Johnny Kid Alberts, 10; Ed Kinley, 10.
Jan. 22—Jim Healy, New York . . . . . ND 10
Apr. 3—Bob McAllister, N. Y. C. . . . . . ND 10
June 18—Billy Kramer, Philadelphia . ND 6
Sept. 29—Augie Ratner, Brooklyn . . . . ND 10
Oct. 25—K. O. Sweeney, N. Y. C. . . . . ND 10
Nov. 1—Jeff Smith, Brooklyn . . . . . ND 10

1918
Mar. 11—Harry Greb, Cleveland . . . . . ND 10
June 14—Frank Carbone, Red Bank . . . ND 8
July 9—Frank Carbone,
W. Hoboken . . . . KO by 5

1919
Won: Battling Ortega, 12. No decision: Happy Howard, 6.
Oct. 23—Jackie Clark, Allentown . . . . ND 10
Dec. 13—Harry Greb, Binghamton . . . . ND 10

1920
Knockouts: Roddy McDonald, 11; Dan Ferguson, 8; Jack London, 2; Young O'Grady, 5; Billy Hurley, 3; Dan Ferguson, 2; Silent Martin, 7. Won: Sailor Petroskey, 4; Joe Eagan, 15; Jimmy O'Hagan, 10; Jack MaCarron, 10; Jackie Clark, 10 and 15.
—Harry Greb, Pittsburgh . . . . . ND 10
—Gene Brosseau, Montreal . . . . KO 5
—Jack Bloomfield, Montreal . . ND 10
Aug. 10—Jeff Smith, Halifax . . . . L 15
Dec. 10—Jack Bloomfield, Montreal . . ND 10

1921
—Tommy Madden, N. Y. C. . . . KO 1
—Tim Kelly, N. Y. C. . . . . KO 3
—Leo Leonard, Scranton . . . . . ND 10
—New Al McCoy, N. Y. C. . . . . . KO 2
July 25—Johnny Klesch, Scranton . . . KO 9
—Jack McKay, N. Y. C. . . . . KO 1
—George Robinson, Montreal . KO 4
Sept. 5—Panama Joe Gans, Jersey City ND 12
Sept. 14—Battling Levinsky, Montreal . ND 10
—Gus Platts, N. Y. C. . . . . W 12
Nov. 2—Buck Crouse, Montreal . . . . . KO 4
—Jack Stone, Montreal . . . . . KO 8
Dec. 1—Jeff Smith, N. Y. C. . . . . W 15
Dec. —Roddy McDonald, Quebec . . KO 10

1922
Jan. 27—Young Fisher, Syracuse . . . . . . L 15
Feb. 22—Young Fisher, N. Y. C. . . . . . . W 15
Mar. 11—Louis Bogash, New York . . . . . D 12
Mar. 16—Tommy Loughran, Scranton . ND 8
Apr. 7—Billy Beckett, Jersey City . . . KO 3
May 15—Tommy Bobson, Long Isl. City W 12
Oct. 23—Johnny Basham, Sheffld., Eng.KO 2
Nov. —Guardsman Penwill, Sheffield KO 1
Dec. 30—Harry Knight, Sheffield . . . . . KO 4

1923
Jan. 17—Harry Reeve, Liverpool . . . . KO 3
Mar. 17—Battling Siki, Dublin, Ire. . . . . W 90
(Won World Light Heavyweight Championship.)
June 25—Tommy Loughran, Philadelphia . . ND 8

Aug. 2—Tommy Loughran,
West New York, N. J. . . . . ND 12
Oct. 4—Young Stribling, Columbus, Ga. . . . . D 10

1924
Mar. 31—*Young Stribling, Newark . . . . ND 12
Oct. 29—Frank Carpenter, Providence . . . . . KO 6
Dec. 26—Johnny King, Atlanta . . . . KO 4
*Newspapers gave Stribling the point verdict.

1925
Jan. 7—Mickey Walker, Newark, N. J. . . . ND 12
May 30—Paul Berlenbach, N. Y. C. . . . . L 15
(Lost Light Heavyweight Title)
July 16—Frank Carpenter, Albany . . . . KO 7
Aug. 17—Art Weigand, Buffalo . . . . D 6
Aug. 22—Young Marullo, N. Y. C. . . . . W 12
Dec. 23—Tiger Flowers, N. Y. C. . . . . W 10

1926
Mar. 14—Jack Delaney, N. Y. C. . . . . KO by 4
May 7—Lou Scozza, N. Y. C. . . . . W 10
July 2—Johnny Risko, N. Y. C. . . . . W 10
Aug. 1—King Solomon, N. Y. C. . . . . KO 11
Aug. 31—King Solomon, N. Y. C. . . . . KO 11
Sept. 29—Roy Mitchell, Halifax, N. S. . . . . . . W 10
Nov. —Billy Vidabeck, N. Y. C. . . . . KO 3
Dec. 10—Soldier King, Grand Rapids . . . . . . KO 4

1927
Jan. 28—Paul Berlenbach, N. Y. C. . . . . KO 4
Mar. 3—Jack Sharkey, N. Y. C. . . . . KO by 12
May 9—Pat McCarthy, N. Y. C. . . . . . . W 10
Oct. 7 Tommy Loughran, N. Y. C. . . . . L 15
(For vacant Light Heavyweight Title)
Nov. 1—Mickey Walker, Chicago . KO by 1
Nov. 1—Larry Gains, Toronto, Ont. . . . D 10

1928
Feb. 3—Leo Lomski, N. Y. C. . . . . L 10
Mar. 26—Young Marullo, N. Y. C. . . . . . L 10
Apr. 23—Armand Emanuel, San Fran. . . D 10
May 8—Jack Willis, Los Angeles . . . . . D 10
June 7—Armand Emanuel, N. Y. C. . . . L 10
July 9—Matt Adgie, Philadelphia . . . . LF 2
Sept. 27—Jerry (Tuffy) Griffiths, Chi.KO by 1

1929
May 13—Paul Huffman, N. Y. C. . . . . W 10
May 27—George Hoffman, N. Y. C. KO by 2
Aug. 8—Steve Thompson, Manchester,
Va. . . . . KO 3
Sept. 9—Battling Bozo, Hambridge,
Birm. . . . . ND 10
Oct. 18—Jack Gagnon, Boston . . . KO by 1
Nov. 13—Emmett Curtis, Grand Rapids KO 5
Nov. 26—Big Jeff Carroll, W. Palm Beach L 10

1930
Feb. 7—Bob Godwin, Daytona Beach . L 10
Mar. 8—Isidoro Gastanaga, Havana KO by 1
Apr. 2—Bob Godwin, Miami . . . . L 10
June 20—George Neron, Schenectady . . L 10
Sept. 1—Patsy Perroni, Canton, O. . . . . L 10
Sept. 22—Garfield Johnson, Utica,
N. Y. . . . . KO by 4

TB	KO	WD	WF	D	LD	LF	KO BY	ND	NC
146	57	24	0	6	11	2	10	36	0

Died Aug. 12, 1966, Queens, N. Y.

PAUL BERLENBACH
(Astoria Assassin)
Born, February 18, 1901, New York, N. Y. Nationality, German-American. Weight, 170 lbs. Height, 5 ft. 10½ in. Managed by Dan Hickey. 1920—Won National A.A.U. Light Heavyweight Wrestling Championship.
Amateur Record: 1922
Won National amateur heavyweight championship of A. A. U. Knockouts scored as amateur: Ben Butler, 3; Charles Maisl, 2; Lou Ferguson, 2; Sam Singleton, 2; Joseph Pepperton, 1; Harry Fay, 1; Tom Calliland, 1; Geo. Rydel, 1; Sid Smith, 1; Matt Dunn, 1; Earl Fitzgibbons, 1; Charley Saint, 1; Tom Kirby, 1. Won: Ben Fehny, 3; Chas. Maisl, 3; Andy Zanboe, 3. Oct. 13, Freddie Krebs, N. Y. C. KO by 2
Berlenbach became a professional in 1923.

1923

Oct.	4—Jimmy Roberts, N. Y. C.	KO	1
Nov.	29—Charles Hoffman, N. Y. C.	KO	1
Dec.	13—Jerome Baird, N. Y. C.	KO	1

1924

Jan.	2—K. O. Jaffe, N. Y. C.	KO	7
Jan.	10—Bill Ryan, N. Y. C.	KO	1
Jan.	18—Lew Chester, N. Y. C.	KO	2
Jan.	28—Frank Carbone, N. Y. C.	KO	6
Feb.	15—Pat Walsh, N. Y. C.	KO	1
Feb.	28—Young Fisher, N. Y. C.	KO	6
Mar.	3—Jimmy Darcy, N. Y. C.	KO	3
Mar.	14—Jack Delaney, N. Y. C.	KO by	4
Mar.	31—Harry Krohn, Newark, N. J.	KO	4
Apr.	7—Jack Stone, Buffalo, N. Y.	KO	5
Apr.	29—Harold Abbott, N. Y. C.	KO	4
June	16—Chief Halbran, Freeport, L.I.	KO	3
July	7—Frank Carpenter, N. Y. C.	KO	7
July	24—Augie Ratner, N. Y. C.	D	8
Aug.	15—Joe Kelly, Boston, Mass.	KO	4
Aug.	27—Young Stribling, N. Y. C.	D	6
Sept.	19—Jack Reddick, N. Y. C.	KO	8
Oct.	1—Johnny Gill, Jersey City, N. J.	ND	10
Dec.	5—Tommy Burns, Detroit, Mich.	KO	5
Dec.	26—Larry Estridge, N. Y. C.	KO	2

1925

Jan.	14—Rocky Smith, Phila. Pa.	KO	4
Jan.	30—Tony Marullo, N. Y. C.	W	12
Feb.	9—Frankie Maguire, Phila. Pa.	KO	5
Mar.	13—Bat. Siki, N. Y. C.	KO	10
May	30—Mike McTigue, N. Y. C.	W	15

Won light heavyweight title.

July	13—Yg. Marullo, Newark	NC	9
Sept.	11—*Jimmy Slattery, N. Y. C.	KO	11
Oct.	12—King Solomon, N. Y. C.	KO	9
Dec.	11—*Jack Delaney, N. Y. C.	W	15

*Title bout.

1926

Mar.	19—Johnny Risko, N. Y. C.	L	10
Apr.	5—Ray Neuman, Hartford, Conn.	W	10
June	10—*Young Stribling, N. Y. C.	W	15
July	16—Jack Delaney, Brooklyn	L	15

Lost light heavyweight title.

Aug.	20—Francis Charles, N. Y. C.	W	10

*Title bout.

1927

Jan.	28—Mike McTigue, N. Y. C.	KO by	4
June	27—Chas. Rammel, N. Y. C.	KO	1
July	18—Billy Conley, N. Y. C.	W	10
July	20—Bob Lawson, N. Y. C.	KO	7
Oct.	13—Joe Lohman, Atlanta, Ga.	D	10
Nov.	25—Mickey Walker, Chicago, Ill.	L	10
Dec.	9—Jack Delaney, Chicago, Ill.	KO by	6

1928

Mar.	12—Babe Farmer, N. Y. C.	KO	1
May	22—Larry Estridge, N. Y. C.	KO	7

(Wrestling bouts)

On April 17, 1929 the New York State Athletic Commission granted Berlenbach a wrestler's license.

Apr.	22—Fred Grubmier, N. Y. C.	W	18 min., 27 sec.
May	1—George Zaharias, Brooklyn	W	22 min., 28 sec.
May	9—Farmer Bailey, Newark	W	30 min.
May	11—Pat McKay, Phila.	NC	

The referee stopped the contest. Berlenbach retired as a wrestler and tried a comeback as a boxer.

1931

Apr.	1—Eddie Clark, Brooklyn	KO	3
Apr.	13—Billy Henderson, Brooklyn	KO	1
July	22—Herman Weiner, Laurel, Md.	KO by	1

1933

Oct.	—Carl Knowles, Atlanta	L	10

TB	KO	WD	WF	D	LD	LF	KO BY	ND	NC
50	30	7	0	3	4	0	4	1	1

Elected to Boxing Hall of Fame, 1971.

JACK DELANEY
(Ovila Chapdelaine)

Born, St. Francis, Can., March 18, 1900. Nationality, French-Canadian. Weight, 175 pounds. Height, 5 ft. 11½ in. Managed by Al Jennings, Pete Reilly and Billy Prince.

1919-1920

Knockouts: Tom Nelson, 2; Jack Green, 6; Tom Spencer, 4; Art Griffin, 7; Bill Gorman, 3; Soldier Franz, 2; Battling Silveria, 9; Ted Marshall, 5; Jack Savage, 2. Won: Jim Hugo, 6; Mohawk Jimmy Coffey, 8. Draw: Steve August, 6; Jack McCarron, 12.

1921

Knockouts: Young Jack Johnson, 3; Bert Colima, 7. Won: Jack McClelland, 12; Jackie Mason (tkn.), 2; Happy Howard, 10; Joe Rivers, 12; George Robinson, 12; Steve Choynski, 12; Frank Carbone, 12. Lost: Tommy Robson, 12.

1922

Pat McCarthy, W., 12; Lou Bogash, W., 15; Augie Ratner, KO by 1; George Shade, KO 1; Frank Cavanaugh, KO 3; Young Fisher, KO by 3; Pal Reed, W., 12.

1923

Knockouts: Tommy Madden, 2 rds. Won: Augie Ratner, 12; Andy Palmer, 12.

Feb.	20—Italian Joe Gans, New York	W	12
Mar.	19—Jimmy O'Gatty, Providence	NC	5
Aug.	31—Jimmy Darcy, New York	W	10

1924

Jan.	4—Jackie Clark, Norwalk, Conn.	KO	2
Feb.	11—Sailor Martin, N. Y. C.	KO	1
Feb.	19—Tommy Loughran, Boston	W	10
Mar.	14—Paul Berlenbach, N. Y. C.	KO	4
Mar.	17—Jackie Clark, Newark, N. J.	ND	8
Mar.	31—Leo Leonard, Bridgeport	KO	3
Apr.	10—George Robinson, Boston	W	10
May	5—Bryan Downey, Columbus, O.	ND	12
Aug.	27—Frank Moody, Bridgeport	KO	5
Oct.	6—Jimmy Slattery, N. Y. C.	L	6
Oct.	27—*Pat McCarthy, Boston	W	8
Oct.	30—Jim Mulholland, Brooklyn	KO	8

*Referee disqualified McCarthy for not trying.

1925

Jan.	16—Tiger Flowers, N. Y. C.	KO	2
Jan.	19—Allentown Joe Gans, Wilkes-Barre	W	10
Feb.	13—Jimmy Slattery, N. Y. C.	L	6
Mar.	4—Tiger Flowers, N.Y.C.	KO	4
Mar.	9—Jamaica Kid, Buffalo	KO	2
Mar.	20—Soldier King, Grand Rapids	KO	4
May	31—Young Marullo, N. Y. C.	W	10
July	16—Tommy Loughran, Philadelphia	D	10
July	24—Jack Burke, N. Y. C.	KO	9
Dec.	11—†Paul Belenbach, N.Y.C.	L	15

†For light heavyweight title.

1926

Jan.	15—Bob Fitzsimmons, Jr., N. Y. C.	W	10
Jan.	25—Tom Roper, Canton, O.	KO	12
Feb.	5—Johnny Risko, N. Y. C.	W	10
Feb.	23—Quintin Rojas, Philadelphia	KO	4
Mar.	9—Joe Lohman, N. Y. C.	KO	10
Mar.	14—Mike McTigue, N. Y. C.	KO	4
Mar.	22—Maxie Rosenbloom, Phila.	W	10
Apr.	26—King Solomon, Hartford, Ct.	W	12
May	13—Martin O'Grady, Montreal	KO	7
June	3—Tommy Burns, N. Y. C.	KO	2
June	16—Bob Sage, Detroit	W	10
July	16—*Paul Berlenbach, Brooklyn	W	15
Dec.	12—Jamaica Kid, Waterbury	KO	3
Dec.	20—Bud Gorman, Jersey City	KO	2

*Won world light heavyweight title

1927

Feb.	18—Jimmy Maloney, N. Y. C.	L	10
Aug.	11—Paolino Uzcudun, N. Y. C.	WF	7
Sept.	14—Johnny Risko, Cleveland, O.	L	10
Oct.	14—Jack Renault, N. Y. C.	W	10
Dec.	9—Paul Berlenbach, Chicago	KO	6

1928

Jan.	16—Sully Montgomery, N. Y. C.	KO	1
Jan.	20—Jack Humbeck, Boston	KO	6
Feb.	13—Leo Gates, Rochester, N. Y.	KO	2
Mar.	1—Tom Heeney, N. Y. C.	L	15
Apr.	30—Jack Sharkey, N. Y. C.	KO by	1
Sept.	19—Nando Tassi, Brooklyn	KO	11

1932

Mar.	10—Phil Johnson, Bridgeport	KO	2
Mar.	29—Cowboy Willis, Stamford	KO	3
Apr.	21—Leo Williams, Hartford	KO	1

TB	KO	WD	WF	D	LD	LF	KO BY	ND	NC
86	42	27	1	3	7	0	3	2	1

Died, November 27, 1948, Katonah, N.Y.
Elected to Boxing Hall of Fame, 1973.

TOMMY LOUGHRAN

Born, Nov. 29, 1902, Philadelphia, Pa.
Nationality, Irish-American. Weight, 170-175 lbs. Height, 5 ft. 11 in. Managed by Joe Smith.

1919
Knockout: Eddie Carter, 2.

1920
Knockouts: Bill Clark, 3; Eddie Moran, 4; Tommy Coyle, 4; Kid Manual, 4; Joe Brock, 2; Jack Smith, 4. No decision: Jim McBride, 6; Jack Williams, 6; Joe Welling, 6; John Dougherty, 6; Ed Dougherty, 6; Bernie McLaughlin, 6; Rube Bennett, 8.

1921
Knockouts: Al Daly, 4; Hugh Blair, 3; Roy Hoist, 1; Vincent Lopez, 5. No decision: Lew Schupp, 8; Kid West, 8; Johnny Kelly, 8; Johnny McLaughlin, 8; Leo Dillon, 6; Charlie O'Neil, 8; Jack Reck, 8; Johnny Alex, 8; Jules Ritchie, 10; Frankie Britton, 6; Frankie Britton, 8; Al Miller, 8; Pat Bradley, 6; Len Rowlands, 6. Won: Al Nelson, 10; Young Remsey, 8; Ted Mitchell, 8.

1922
Jan.	24—Jimmy Darcy, Philadelphia	..ND	8
Feb.	7—Fay Kaiser, Philadelphia	....ND	8
Feb.	28—Bryan Downey, Philadelphia	.ND	8
Mar.	16—Mike McTigue, Scranton, Pa.	.ND	8
Mar.	21—Jackie Clark, Philadelphia	...ND	8
Apr.	6—Frank Carbone, Philadelphia	.ND	8
Apr.	28—Jimmy Darcy, Syracuse, N. Y.	W	12
May	12—Young Fisher, Syracuse, N. Y.	W	12
July	10—Harry Greb, Philadelphia	...ND	8
Aug.	24—Gene Tunney, Philadelphia	..ND	8
Sept.	25—George Shade, Philadelphia	..ND	8
Dec.	11—Lou Bogash, Philadelphia	...ND	8

1923
Jan.	8—Pal Reed, Newark, N. J.	...ND	12
Jan.	15—Harry Greb, Pittsburgh, Pa.	...ND	10
Jan.	30—Harry Greb, N. Y. C.	 L	15
	(American Light-Heavyweight Title)		
Mar.	8—Jeff Smith, Scranton, Pa.	...ND	10
June	18—Jeff Smith, Philadelphia	..ND	8
June	25—Mike McTigue, Philadelphia	.ND	8
Aug.	2—Mike McTigue, W. N. Y., N. J.	ND	8
Aug.	14—Teddy Taylor, Pottsville, Pa.	.KO	2
Sept.	14—Jim Delaney, Oklahoma City	ND	10
Oct.	11—Harry Greb, Boston	...... W	10
Nov.	14—Ted Moore, Boston	.... W	10
Dec.	10—Roland Todd, N. Y. C.	..... W	10
Dec.	26—Harry Greb, Pittsburgh, Pa.	... L	10

1924
Feb.	12—Johnny Wilson, Boston, Mass.	. W	10
Feb.	19—Jack Delaney, Boston, Mass.	.. L	10
Apr.	28—Charlie Nashert, Detroit, Mich.		
	....	ND	10
May	19—Ad Stone, Philadelphia, Pa.	...D	10
June	2—Jack Smith, Shamoken, Pa.	..KO	2
June	26—Young Stribling, N. Y. C.	 L	6
July	11—Joe Lohman, Erie, Pa.	... W	10
Oct.	13—Harry Greb, Philadelphia, Pa.	. D	10
Nov.	20—George Blake, Williamsport	..KO	2

1925
Jan.	1—Frankie McGuire, Williamsport	W	10
Feb.	4—Buck Holley, Oakland, Calif.	.. D	6
Feb.	7—Billy Freas, Culver City, Cal.	.. W	10
Feb.	18—Jack Reeves, Oakland, Calif.	.. W	10
Mar.	28—Young Stribling, San Fran.	...L,	10
June	11—Martin Burke, Brooklyn	..... W	12
July	16—Jack Delaney, Philadelphia	... D	10
Sept.	11—Tony Marullo, N. Y. C.	..... W	8
Sept.	23—Jack Burke, Philadelphia, Pa.	KO	6
Oct.	5—Benny Ross, Buffalo, N. Y.	... W	10
Oct.	26—Ad Stone, Philadelphia, Pa.	... L	10
Dec.	25—King Solomon, Philadelphia	.. W	10

1926
Jan.	1—Billy Freas, Grand Rapids	...ND	10
Jan.	6—Joe Packo, Grand Rapids	...ND	10
Feb.	8—Ad Stone, Philadelphia	..... W	10
Mar.	4—Yale Okun, Philadelphia	..... W	10
Apr.	5—Yale Okun, Philadelphia	..... W	10
May	28—Jack Ketchell, Ebensburg	..Exh.	6
June	17—Georges Carpentier, Phila.	...... W	10
July	2—George Manley, Omaha	......ND	10
July	30—Johnny Risko, Boston	...... W	10
Sept.	23—Jimmy Delaney, Philadelphia	.W	6
Oct.	8—Jimmy Burns, Allentown, Pa.	KO	2
Oct.	18—Martin Burke, Chicago	..... W	10
Oct.	29—Chuck Wiggins, Providence	..WF	5
Nov.	00—George Manley, Indianapolis	.ND	10

1927
Jan.	10—Tony Marullo, Philadelphia	.. W	10
Feb.	15—Johnny Risko, Wilkes-Barre	.. W	10

July	20—Tony Marullo, N. Y. C.	...... W	10
Aug.	8—Benny Ross, Buffalo, N. Y.	... W	12
Mar.	16—Joe Lohman, Philadelphia	.... W	10
Apr.	6—Tom Kirby, Philadelphia	..... W	10
May	3—Young Stribling, Brooklyn	... W	10
Oct.	7—Mike McTigue, N. Y. C.	...... W	15
	(Won Light Heavyweight title)		
Nov.	14—Pat McCarthy, Philadelphia	... W	10
Dec.	12—*Jimmy Slattery, N. Y. C.	.... W	15
	*Title bout.		

1928
Jan.	6—*Leo Lomski, N. Y. C.	......W	15
May	18—Joe Sekyra, Louisville	......ND	10
June	1—*Pete Latzo, Brooklyn	...... W	15
June	15—Roland Todd, London	...... W	10
June	28—Armand Emanuel, N. Y. C.	... W	10
July	16—*Pete Latzo, Wilkes-Barre	.... W	10
Oct.	1—Jack Gross, Philadelphia	..... W	10
Dec.	17—Big Boy Peterson, Chicago	..W	10
	*Title bout.		

1929
Feb.	5—Armand Emanuel, Los Angeles	W	10
Feb.	29—Joe Lohman, Tulsa, Okla.	.... W	10
Mar.	8—*Mickey Walker, Chicago	.... W	10
May	24—Ernie Schaaf, Boston, Mass.	.. W	10
July	18—*Jimmy Braddock, New York	. W	15
	(Vacated title to campaign as heavyweight)		
Sept.	36—Jack Sharkey, N.Y.C.	.....KO by	3
	*Title bout.		

1930
Feb.	28—Pierre Charles, Miami, Fla.	... W	10
Mar.	17—Jack Renault, Philadelphia	... W	10
Apr.	28—Ernie Schaaf, Philadelphia	.L	10
June	11—Ernie Schaaf, Philadelphia	L	10
Oct.	16—Dick Daniels, Minneapolis	...ND	10
Oct.	23—Dave Maier, Milwaukee, Wis.	.. W	10
Nov.	17—King Levinsky, Chicago, Ill.	.. W	10

1931
Jan.	26—Jack Gross, Philadelphia	..... W	10
Feb.	6—Max Baer, N. Y. C.	.... W	10
Mar.	13—Ernie Schaaf, N. Y. C.	...... W	10
Mar.	27—Tuffy Griffiths, Chicago	.... W	10
May	15—Vittorio Campolo, N. Y. C.	.... W	10
Sept.	9—Jack Gross, Philadelphia	.... W	10
Sept.	22—Joe Sekyra, N. Y. C.	...... W	10
Oct.	19—Johnny Risko, Philadelphia	.. W	10
Nov.	13—Paolino Uzcudun, N. Y. C.	... W	10
Dec.	18—King Levinsky, N. Y. C.	 L	10

1932
Jan.	15—Steve Hamas, N. Y. C.	... KO by	2
May	11—Steve Hamas, Philadelphia	 L	10
June	29—Steve Hamas, Philadelphia	... W	10
Oct.	17—Stanley Poreda, Philadelphia	.. L	10

1933
Jan.	10—King Levinsky, Philadelphia	.. W	10
Feb.	6—Walter Cobb, Philadelphia	.... W	10
Apr.	21—Isador Gastanaga, Chicago	.... W	10
June	21—Steve Hamas, N. Y. C.	...... W	10
July	26—Johnny Risko, Chicago, Ill.	... L	10
Sept.	27—Jack Sharkey, Philadelphia	.. W	15
Nov.	22—Ray Impellettiere, N. Y. C.	.. W	10

1934
Mar.	1—Primo Carnera, Miami	 L	15
	(World Heavyweight title)		
May	4—Walter Neusel, N. Y. C.	 L	10
July	31—Johnny Risko, Freeport	 L	10
Oct.	5—Jose Caratoli, Buenos Aires	.. L	12
Oct.	20—Arturo Godoy, Buenos Aires	.. D	12

1935
Jan.	5—Arturo Godoy, Buenos Aires	.. W	12
Feb.	2—Jose Caratoli, Buenos Aires	..D	10
Mar.	16—Arturo Godoy, Sanitago, Chile	L	12
Apr.	14—Vincent Parrille, Lima, Peru	.KO	9
May	20—Al Ettore, Philadelphia, Pa.	.. L	10
June	20—Ray Impellettiere, Philadelphia	W	10
July	29—Eddie Simms, Toronto, Can.	.. W	10
Aug.	22—Al Delaney, Buffalo, N. Y.	.. D	10
Nov.	13—Maurice Strickland, London	.. W	10
Dec.	9—Andre Lenglet, Paris, France	.. W	10

1936
Jan.	15—Tommy Farr, London	 L	10
Feb.	10—Ben Foord, Leicester, Eng.	.. L	12
Mar.	14—Jack London, Bristol	 L	10
July	30—Al McCoy, Montreal	.... D	12
July	6—Al McCoy, Montreal	 L	10
Sept.	16—Ray Impellettiere, Oakland	... W	10
Oct.	9—Tony Rossalia, Reno	.... KO	3
Nov.	12—Butch Rogers, San Diego	..... W	10
Dec.	3—Tom Beaupre, Dallas	.... W	10
Dec.	9—Sonny Walker, S. F.	 L	10

505

1937
Jan. 18—Sonny Walker, Philadelphia ... W 10
1942
Enlisted in U. S. Marines.

TB	KO	WD	WF	D	LD	LF	KOBY	ND	NC
172	18	77	1	8	21	0	2	45	0

Elected to Boxing Hall of Fame 1956.

JIMMY SLATTERY
Born, August 25, 1904, Buffalo, N. Y.
Nationality, Irish-American. Weight, 165 lbs.
Height, 5 ft. 11 in. Managed by Red Carr.
1921
Knockout: Joe Burns, 1. Won: Joe Carey, 4.
1922
Knockouts: Tommy Savage, 3; Joe Dietz, 2; Mike Peters, 4; Jimmy Morrison, 4; K. O. Kelly, 3; L. Linckner, 2; Sammy Weobert, 3. Won: Joe Morey, 4; Tommy Sayers, 4; Tommy Sayers, 4; Lee Bailey, 4; Joey Joynt, 5; Joey Joynt, 4; Buddy Merritt, 4; Joe Cauvel, 6; Jack Pry, 6; Sailor Hoffman, 6.
1923
Knockouts: Jimmy Bovo, 5; K. O. Loughlin, 1; Wally Hinckel, 3; Johnny Vascher, 2; Jim Lewis, 3. Won: Benny Rose, 6; Mixer Mitchell, 6; Tiger Smith, 6; Ray Graham, 6; Jack Pry, 6; Al Cross, 6; Tony Sarocco, 6; Soldier Bartfield, 6; Jimmy Sullivan, 6; Johnny Griffiths, 6; Jack Perry, 6; Jack McFarland, 8; Johnny Klesch, 6; Nick Vepelti, 6.
1924
Jan. 1—Joe Eagen, Buffalo .... L 6
Jan. 18—Al Cross, Syracuse ..... KO 3
Feb. 25—Young Stribling, Buffalo .... W 6
Mar. 21—Nick Vepelti, Syracuse .... KO 2
Mar. 31—Fay Kaiser, Buffalo .... KO 3
Apr. 14—Pat Walsh, Buffalo .... KO 2
Apr. 28—Harry Krohn, Buffalo ...... W 6
May 26—Jack Clark, Buffalo .... W 6
May 29—Young Fisher, Syracuse ..... W 6
June 11—Kid Numbers, Scranton ..... KO 2
June 19—Jack Lynch, N. Y. C. ...... W 6
Sept. 22—Jack Lynch, Buffalo .... W 6
Oct. 6—Jack Delaney, N. Y. C. ..... W 6
Oct. 27—Norman Genet, Buffalo ..... W 6
Nov. 24—Jack Clark, Rochester ...... W 6
Dec. 1—Vic McLaughlin, Buffalo .... W 6
Dec. 17—Jack Schoendorf, Buffalo ... KO 2
1925
Jan. 1—Joe Eagan, Buffalo .... KO 1
Jan. 21—Joe Lohman, Buffalo .... W 6
Feb. 2—Frankie Schoell, Buffalo ... KO 3
Feb. 13—Jack Delaney, N. Y. C. ..... W 6
Mar. 2—Mike Burke, Wilkes-Barre ... KO 2
Mar. 30—Augie Ratner, Boston ...... KO 2
Apr. 13—Jack Vascher, Ithaca ...... KO 5
Apr. 30—Billy McGowan, Buffalo .... KO 2
May 4—Jack McDonald, Buffalo .... KO 3
May 30—Jack Burke, N. Y. C. ...... KO 2
June 9—Johnny Gill, Boston .... W 10
July 2—Dave Shade, N. Y. C. ...... KO by 3
Aug. 22—Maxie Rosenbloom, Brooklyn . W 6
Sept. 4—Frank Carpenter, Buffalo .... KO 4
Sept. 11—Paul Berlenbach, N. Y. C. KO by 11
(For Light Heavyweight title)
Dec. 11—Patsy Motto, Syracuse ..... KO 3
Dec. 21—Boy McCormick, Buffalo ... W 10
Dec. 23—Joe Burke, Warren, Pa. ... KO 3
Sept. 4—Harry Greb, Buffalo .... L 6
1926
Jan. 1—Maxie Rosenbloom, Buffalo .. W 10
Jan. 13—Tommy Burn, Grand Rapids . ND 10
Jan. 16—Roland Todd, Boston ...... W 10
Feb. 1—Tommy Robson, Rochester .. W 10
Mar. 25—Young Stribling, N. Y. C. ... L 10
July 1—Jack Clark, W. N. York., N. J. ND 10
July 7—Bob Sage, N. Y. C. .... W 10
July 30—Billy Britton, Albany ..... KO 1
Sept. 27—Jack Schoendorf, Jamestown KO 7
Oct. 4—Tommy Burns, Buffalo ..... W 8
Oct. 25—Martin O'Grady, Buffalo ... KO 2
Dec. 13—Mike Wallace, Buffalo ..... W 10
1927
Feb. 21—Ray Fay, Buffalo .... W 6
Mar. 7—George Gemas, Buffalo ..... KO 3
Mar. 28—Johnny Risko, Buffalo ..... WF 5
Apr. 18—Lew Chester, Buffalo ...... W 10
Aug. 30—Maxie Rosenbloom, Hartford . W 10
(Won N. B. A. Light Heavyweight title)
Nov. 2—Murray Gitlitz, Buffalo ..... KO 6
Nov. 23—Pat McCarthy, Hartford .... W 6
Dec. 2—Joe Loaman, Akron .... W 10
Dec. 12—Tommy Loughran, N. Y. C. ... L 15
(Lost NBA Light-Heavyweight Title)
1928
Mar. 19—Frank Muskie, Buffalo ..... KO 3
Apr. 23—Billy Vidabeck, Buffalo ..... W 10
Apr. 30—Tony Marullo, Newark ..... W 10
May 9—Stanley Smith, Bradford, Pa.. KO 2
June 18—Tony Marullo, Buffalo ..... W 10
Oct. 8—Jack Lynch, Dayton, Ky..... KO 2
Oct. 29—Otis Gardner, Buffalo ..... KO 2
Nov. 5—Vic McLaughlin, Indianapolis KO 5
Dec. 10—Jimmy Mahoney, Buffalo ... W 10
Dec. 21—Jack Prybelic, Buffalo ..... D 6
1929
Jan. 21—Jimmy Mahoney, N. Y. C. ... KO 3
Mar. 4—Len Darcy, Buffalo .... W 6
Mar. 11—James J. Braddock, N. Y. C. KO by 9
July 2—Len Darcy, Steubenville, O. .. W 6
Sept. 30—Len Darcy, Buffalo .... W 6
Oct. 14—Maxie Rosenbloom, Phila.... L 10
Nov. 11—Johnny Haystack, Buffalo .. KO 1
Nov. 25—Maxie Rosenbloom, Buffalo .. W 10
1930
Feb. 10—Lou Scozza, Buffalo .... W 15
(Won N. Y. Commission Light Heavyweight title)
May 27—Pete Latzo, Boston .... NC 7
June 25—Maxie Rosenbloom, Buffalo .. L 15
(Lost N. Y. Light Heavyweight title)
Aug. 22—Pedro Lopez, Schenectady .. KO 2
Oct. 1—Len Darcy, Syracuse ...... NC 8
Nov. 6—King Levinsky, Chicago ..... L 10
1931
Jan. 14—King Levinsky, Chicago ..... W 10
Apr. 20—Tom Heeney, Buffalo ...... W 6
Aug. 5—Maxie Rosenbloom, Brooklyn . L 15
(For N. Y. Light-Heavyweight Title)
Oct. 30—King Levinsky, Detroit ..... L 10
1932
Aug. 22—Charley Belanger, Buffalo KO by 2
1934
May 21—Walter Kugel, Buffalo ..... KO 4
June 1—Gus Flugel, Buffalo .... KO 2
June 19—Eddie Kaminski, Buffalo .W Disq. 5
1935
Aug. 28—Jack Gibbons, Minot, N.D. KO by 4

TB	KO	WD	WF	D	LD	LF	KOBY	ND	NC
128	45	62	2	1	9	0	5	2	2

Died, August 30, 1960, Buffalo, N. Y.

MAXIE ROSENBLOOM
(Slapsie Maxie)
Born, September 6, 1904, New York, N. Y. Nationality, Jewish-American. Weight, 165-170 lbs. Height, 5 ft. 11 in. Managed by Frank Bachman.
1923
Knockout: Jack Rivers, 3 Won: Joe Scogny, 6; Kid Frankie, 6; Nick Scanlon, 6 and 6.
1924
Knockouts: Joe Magnante, 4; Frank Sweeney, 4; Won: Jimmy Roberts, 4; Jack Store, 6; Patsy Lodice, 6; Jack Lynch, 6; Jack Ford, 6; Jimmy Roberts, 6; Jimmy Amato, 6 and 6; Jack Fogarty, 6; Jimmy Amato, 6 and 6; Larry Mercedes, 6. No decisions: Bruno Frattini, 10; Joe McCarthy, 10 and 12; Lew Ferry, 10; Alex Kid Gibbons, 12; Tommy West, 8; Rocky Smith, 10. Draw: Joe Silvani, 4.
Dec. 16—Frankie Maxted, N. Y. C. .... W 6
1925
Jan. 1—Tommy West, Trenton, N. J.. ND 10
Jan. 19—Joe McCartney, Newark, N. J. KO 4
Jan. 27—Joe Silvani, N. Y. C. .... W 6
Feb. 13—Yale Okun, N. Y. C. .... D 6
Feb. 18—Carl Johnson, N. Y. C. ..... W 6
Mar. 3—Hambone Kelly, N. Y. C. .... W 6
Mar. 11—Carl Johnson, N. Y. C. ..... W 6
July 3—Jack De Mave, Long Branch . ND 10
July 16—Harry Greb, Cleveland .... ND 10
Aug. 14—George Courtney, Brooklyn . W 6
Aug. 22—Jimmy Slattery, Brooklyn ... L 6
Oct. 12—Tommy West, Trenton ... ND 10
Nov. 2—Joe Silvani, N. Y. C. .... KO 9
Nov. 11—Allentown Joe Gans, Syracuse .... WF 6
Nov. 23—Boy McCormick, N. Y. C. ... KO 8
1926
Jan. 1—Jimmy Slattery, Buffalo ..... L 10
Jan. 11—Art Weigand, Buffalo .... L 6

Jan. 18—Rocky Smith, Philadelphia ... W 10
Jan. 25—Frankie Schoell, Buffalo ..... D 10
Feb. 2—Frank Moody, N. Y. C. .... W 12
Feb. 22—Rock Smith, Trenton ......ND 10
Mar. 12—Willie Walker, Staten Island .. W 10
Mar. 22—Jack Delaney, Philadelphia ... L 10
Apr. 19—Frankie Schoell, Buffalo ..... W 10
Apr. 30—Tommy West, Camden ......ND 10
June 5—Dave Shade, L. I. City .... W 10
June 29—Dave Shade, L. I. City .... W 12
July 15—Lou Scozza, Buffalo .... W 10
July 23—Jamaica Kid, Atlantic City ..ND 8
Aug. 6—Jamaica Kid, Long Branch ..KO 6
Aug. 19—Chuck Burns, N. Y. C........ W 10
Aug. 27—Johnny Wilson, Brooklyn .... W 12
Sept. 14—Jimmy Francis, L. I. City .... W 10
Sept. 20—Frankie Schoell, Buffalo ..... L 12
Oct. 4—Johnny Wilson, Pittsburgh ... W 10
Oct. 15—Tiger Flowers, Boston ....WF 9
Dec. 12—Phil K. O. Kaplan, N. Y. C. .. W 10

1927
Jan. 26—Benny Ross, Buffalo .... W 10
Feb. 1—Jimmy Delaney, Cincinnati ..ND 10
Mar. 17—Young Stribling, Boston, Mass. L 10
Apr. 2—Willie Walker, N. Y. C. ...... W 12
Apr. 11—Frankie Schoell, Buffalo ..... W 15
June 21—Leo Lomski, Long Island City . L 12
July 3—Tiger Flowers, Chicago ...... D 10
July 26—Tony Marullo, N. Y. C. ...... W 10
Aug. 4—Bob Sage, Detroit .... W 10
Aug. 20—Lou Scozza, Buffalo .... W 10
Aug. 30—*Jimmy Slattery, Hartford ... L 10
Oct. 17—Homer Robertson, Pittsburgh . W 10
Nov. 9—Tiger Flowers, Detroit ...... D 10
Nov. 15—Jock Malone, St. Paul ......ND 10
Nov. 21—Pete Latzo, Philadelphia ..... W 10
Dec. 12—Joe Anderson, Cincinnati ....ND 10
*Advertised for light heavy title.

1928
Jan. 2—Frankie Schoell, Cincinnati ... W 10
Jan. 9—Godfrey Johnson, Pittsburgh . W 10
Jan. 20—Dick Evans, Rochester ...... W 10
Feb. 3—Phil Kaplan, N. Y. C. ...... W 8
Feb. 6—Pete Latzo, Wilkes-Barre ..... L 10
Feb. 17—Jack McVey, N. Y. C. .... W 8
Feb. 23—Willie Walker, Brooklyn ..... W 4
Mar. 5—Bobby Brown, Pittsburgh ... W 10
Mar. 20—Frankie Schoell, Wilkes-Barre . D 10
June 4—Tommy Milligan, London KO by 9
June 15—Roland Todd, London ...... W 15
July 27—Lou Scozza, Denver .... L 10
July 31—Ted Kid Lewis, Long Isl. City WF 6
Aug. 3—Harry Martone, Long Branch . W 8
Aug. 24—Leo Lomski, Long Branch .... D 10
Sept. 10—Homer Robertson, Springfield
Mass. ...... W 10
Oct. 11—Tiger Payne, N. Y. C. ...... W 10
Oct. 22—Garfield Johnson, Pittsburgh .. W 10
Nov. 22—Cuban Bobby Brown, Jer. City W 10
Nov. 27—Tiger Thomas, Williamsport .. W 10
Dec. 20—Osk Till, Buffalo .... W 10

1929
Jan. 28—Jack McVey, Rochester ..... W 10
Feb. 19—Greek Johnson, Wilkes-Barre .. W 10
Mar. 4—Greek Johnson, Buffalo ..... W 6
Mar. 11—Osk Till, N. Y. C. .... W 10
Mar. 18—Leo Lomski, Philadelphia ... W 10
Mar. 22—Bobby Brown, Syracuse ..... W 10
Apr. 3—Joe Anderson, Cincinnati ...W 10
Apr. 26—C. Belanger, Chicago ...... W 10
May 23—J. Anderson, Cincinnati ..... W 10
July 4—J. Anderson, Portland ...... W 10
July 12—W. Feldman, Aberdeen ..... W 8
July 19—Fred Lenhart, Allentown .... L 10
July 30—H. Dillon, Portland .... W 10
Aug. 16—L. Williams, Rockaway ....KO 9
Aug. 24—Tiger Payne, Coney Island .WF 8
Aug. 28—H. Martone, Bayonne ...... W 10
Aug. 29—B. Brown, Franklin .... W 10
Sept. 9—K. O. Brown, Pittsburgh .... W 10
Sept. 29—Tiger Payne, N. Y. C. ...... W 10
Oct. 14—J. Slattery, Philadelphia .... W 10
Oct. 21—Joe Sekyra, N. Y. C. .... W 10
Nov. 15—J. Braddock, N. Y. C. ...... W 10
Nov. 25—J. Slattery, Buffalo .... L 10
Nov. 30—L. Williams, N. Y. C. ...... W 10
Dec. 9—Yale Okun, N. Y. C. .... W 12

1930
Jan. 3—Leo Lomski, N. Y. C. ......, W 10
Feb. 14—Ace Hudkins, N. Y. C. ..... W 10
Mar. 10—Larry Johnson, N. Y. C. ....WF 6
Apl. 7 Harry Fuller, Buffalo ...... W 10
Apr. 30—Larry Johnson, N. Y. C. .... W 10

June 3—George Hoffman, N. Y. C. .... W 10
June 25—Jimmy Slattery, Buffalo ..... W 15
(Won New York Light Heavyweight title)
Aug. 4—Willard Dix, Oakland, Calif. .. W 10
Aug. 21—Leo Lomski, Aberdeen ...... D 8
Sept. 29—Battling Bozo, Birmingham ...D 10
Oct. 22—*Abie Bain, N. Y. C. ....KO 11
Nov. 24—Patsy Perroni, Canton, O. .... W 10
Dec. 2—Paul Swiderski, St. Louis .... NC 7
*Title bout.

1931
Jan. 27—Gene McCue, Stamford, Conn.KO 3
Feb. 9—Battling Bozo, Birmingham ..ND 10
Feb. 20—Tony Cancella, Tampa .... W 10
Mar. 5—Marty Gallagher, Miami .... W 8
Mar. 19—Joe Banovic, Scranton ...... W 10
Apr. 6—Billy Jones, Pittsburgh ..... L 10
Apr. 30—George Manley, Denver ...... L 10
May 6—Leo Lomski, Portland, Ore.... W 10
May 15—Don Petrin, Hollywood ..... W 10
June 2—Fred Lenhart, Coeur D'Alene,
Idaho ..... W 10
June 15—Charley Belanger, Toronto ... W 10
June 29—Billy Jones, Philadelphia .... W 10
July 9—Joe Banovic, Scranton ...... W 10
July 22—George Manley, Denver ...... L 10
Aug. 5—*Jimmy Slattery, Brooklyn ... W 15
Sept. 14—Owen Phelps, Des Moines .... W 10
Sept. 22—Battling Bozo, Atlanta, Ga.... D 10
Oct. 20—Dick Daniels, Minneapolis ...KO 7
Oct. 27—Russ Rowsey, Charleston, S. C. W 10
Nov. 2—Battling Bozo, Kansas City ... W 12
Nov. 10—James Braddock, Minneapolis NC 2
Dec. 17—Cyclone Smith, Savannah, Ga. W 10
*Title bout.

1932
Jan. 1—Dave Maier, Milwaukee ...... L 10
Jan. 15—Frankie Wine, Coral Gables ... W 10
Jan. 26—Gordon Fortenberry, W. Palm
Beach ..... W 10
Feb. 17—Bob Godwin, Daytona ...... D 10
Mar. 18—Joe Knight, Daytona .... L 10
Mar. 21—Willie Oster, Miami .... W 12
Apr. 15—Stanley Wellise, Grand Rapids . W 10
Apr. 21—Lou Scozza, Flint, Mich. .... W 10
May 11—Harry Fuller, Niagara Falls ... W 10
May 16—Harry Ebbets, Springfield .... W 10
May 23—Reds Barry Laurel, Md. ..... W 10
June 8—Larry Johnson, Pittsburgh ... W 10
June 14—Tony Shucco, W. Springfield .. L 10
June 20—Sam Weiss, Allentown, Pa. .. W 10
June 30—Martin Levandowski, Grand
Rapids ..... W 10
July 14—*Lou Scozza, Buffalo .... W 15
(Rosenbloom gained international
recognition as world champion)
Aug. 2—Joe Barlow, Boston .... W 10
Aug. 22—Bob Godwin, Laurel, Md. .... W 10
Aug. 30—Bob Godwin, Charlotte, N. C. .. D 10
Sept. 19—Jimmie Herman, Hazelton .... W 10
Sept. 29—Lou Scozza, Montreal ...... W 10
Oct. 13—Jack Redman, Brooklyn ..... W 10
Oct. 17—Jack Fox, Dayton, O. ...... W 10
Nov. 16—John Henry Lewis, San Fran. .. W 10
Nov. 23—Tony Poloni, Sacramento .... W 10
Dec. 1—Jack Silva, Stockton ...... W 10
Dec. 6—Tony Poloni, San Jose ...... W 10
Dec. 16—Leroy Haynes, San Fran..... W 10
Dec. 23—Jack Silva, Albuquerque .... W 10
Dec. 29—Billy Jones, Chicago ...... W 10
*Title bout.

1933
Jan. 20—Chuck Burns, Winston-Salem . W 10
Jan. 24—Al Stillman, St. Louis .... W 10
Feb. 22—*Al Stillman, St. Louis ...... W 10
Mar. 10—Ad Heuser, N. Y. C. .... W 15
Mar. 24—*Bob Godwin, N. Y. C. .....KO 4
Apr. 3—Lou Scozza, Buffalo .... L 10
Apr. 19—M. Levandowski, St. Louis ... W 10
Apr. 25—Al Stillman, Springfield, Ill. .. W 10
Apr. 28—Harold Murphy, Spring'd., Mo. W 10
May 5—Chas. Belanger, Jeffers'v., Ind. W 10
May 26—Frankie Ryan, Charleston .... W 10
June 2—Buddy McArthur, Clarksburg . W 10
June 20—Popper Stopper, Leiperville, Pa. W 10
July 12—J. H. Lewis, Frsico, Cal. .... L 10
July 20—Fred Lenhart, Tacoma, Wash. . D 10
July 31—J. H. Lewis, Frisco, Cal. .... W 10
Aug. 8—K. O. Christner, Los Angeles .KO 6
Aug. 15—Dynamite Jackson, Los Angeles W 10
Aug. 31—Leroy Haynes, Los Angeles ... W 10
Sept. 12—Joe Rice, Fort Worth ...... W 10

Sept. 19—Chuck Burns, San Antonio ... W 10
Sept. 22—Young Stribling, Houston, Tex. L 10
Sept. 28—Rosey Rosales, El Paso, Tex. .. W 10
Oct. 16—Clyde Chastain, Chattanooga . D 10
Nov. 3—*Mickey Walker, N. Y. C. .... W 15
Nov. 28—Clyde Chastain, Houston, Tex. D 10
Dec. 4—Nelson Dunn, Fort Worth .... W 10
Dec. 19—Charlie Massera, Brooklyn ... L 10
Dec. 21—Bob Godwin, W. Palm Beach .. D 10
*Title bout.

1934
Jan. 10—Bob Godwin, Palm Beach ... L 12
Feb. 5—*Joe Knight, Miami .... D 15
Mar. 12—G. Fortenberry, Orlando ..... W 10
Mar. 15—Cyclone Smith, Macon ...... W 10
Mar. 22—Leroy Brown, Charleston .... W 10
Apr. 9—Johnny Miler, New Orleans .. W 10
Apr. 16—Clyde Chastain, Okla. City ... L 10
Apr. 23—Al Gainer, New Haven .... D 10
May 8—Mickey Walker, Los Angeles .. L 10
June 1—Dutch Weiner, San Diego .... W 10
June 8—Young Langford, Phoenix .... W 10
June 12—Maxie Maxwell, Tucson ..... KO 4
June 15—Leo Kelly, Bakersfield .... W 10
June 26—Lee Ramage, Los Angeles ... D 10
July 10—Lee Ramage, Los Angeles ... L 10
July 31—Lee Ramage, Los Angeles ... L 10
Aug. 8—Pete Georgi, Oakland .... W 10
Oct. 8—Leo Kelly, San Francisco .... W 10
Oct. 22—Johnny Miller, Des Moines .. ND 10
Nov. 16—Bob Olin, N. Y. C. .... L 15
(Lost Light Heavyweight title)
Dec. 3—Al Gainer, New Haven .... W 12
Dec. 21—Tony Shucco, Boston .... W 10
*Title bout.

1935
Jan. 7—Al Stillman, St. Joseph ...... W 10
Jan. 14—Johnny Nelson, Syracuse .... W 10
Jan. 29—Frank Rowsey, Hollywood ... W 10
Feb. 5—Johnny Miler, Los Angeles .. W 10
Feb. 15—Bob Godwin, Hollywood .... W 10
Feb. 22—Rosey Rosales, Phoenix ....KO 2
Mar. 3—Homer Brandeis, Oakland ... W 10
Mar. 15—Frank Rowsey, Hollywood .. W 10
Apr. 19—Charlie Massera, Hollywood . W 10
May 2—Homer Brandeis, Oakland .... W 10
May 14—Oscar Rankins, Los Angeles . W 10
May 22—Harold Murphy, Wilmington .. W 6
June 7—Ford Smith, Hollywood ..... W 10
June 18—Abe Feldman, Los Angeles ... W 10
July 17—John Henry Lewis, Oakland .. W 10
July 19—Hank Hankinson, Hollywood . L 10
Aug. 12—Hank Hankinson, Oakland ... L 10
Aug. 16—Harold Murphy, Reno .... W 8
Aug. 21—Georgie Simpson, San Fran. . W 10
Sept. 6—Tiger Jack Fox, Spokane ..... D 10
Oct. 11—Tiger Jack Fox, Spokane .... W 10
Nov. 1—Frank Rowsey, Hollywood ... W 10
Nov. 15—Cannonball Green, Ventura ... D 6
Nov. 29—John Henry Lewis, San Fran. . W 10

1936
Jan. 15—Johnny Sykes, Las Vegas .... W 10
Jan. 28—Charley Coates, Los Angeles .. W 10
Feb. 7—Tuffy Dial, Phoenix .... W 10
Feb. 22—Johnny Sykes, Tonopah ..... W 10
June 20—George Simpson, Sydney ... KO 3
July 21—Leo Kelly, Sydney .... W 15
Aug. 14—Leo Kelly, Melbourne ...... D 15

1937
Jan. 5—King Levinsky, Los Angeles .. W 10
Feb. 9—Jack Kranz, Modesto ...... W 8
Mar. 11—Tom Beaupre, Dallas .... W 10
Mar. 29—Roscoe Toles, Detroit ...... W 10
Apr. 27—Alberto Lovell, Los Angeles .. L 10
June 8—Lee Ramage, Los Angeles ... W 10
July 20—Johnny Erjavac, Hollywood .. W 10
Sept. 17—Jimmy Adamick, Detroit .... W 10
Sept. 29—Nash Garrison, Oakland ..... W 10
Oct. 12—Bob Nestell, Los Angeles ..... W 10
Nov. 19—Jimmy Adamick, Detroit KO by 2
Dec. 7—Big Boy Bray, Los Angeles ... W 10

1938
May 20—O'Dell Pollee, San Diego .... KO 5
June 3—Lou Nova, Hollywood .... W 10
Aug. 5—Bob Pastor, Hollywood ...... D 10

1939
June 26—Al Ettore, Hollywood ...... KO 3
Elected to Hall of Fame in 1972

TB	KO	WD	WF	D	LD	LF	KOBY		ND	NC
289	18	187	5	23	33	0	2		19	2

Died March 6, 1976, in Los Angeles, Calif.

508

GEORGE NICHOLS
Born, July 9, 1908, Sandusky, Ohio.
Nationality, Italian-American. Height, 5 ft. 10½
in. Managed by Jack Singer.

1927
Knockouts: Johnny Fisher, 3; Frank
Rockey, 1; Jim Craig, 1; Joe Midway, 2. Won:
Joe Sharkey, 6; Harry Miller, 4; Joe Koppel, 6;
Larry Posen, 6; Paul Brown, 4; Ray Wolford, 6;
Art Ftizsimmons, 6 and 4; Charley Sherer, 10;
Charley Eck, 6. Lost: Harry Fuller, 4; Joe
Zuppko, 6. Draw: Frank Kearns, 6; Stanley
Simmons, 6. Knockout by: Garry Leach, 3.

1928
Knockouts: Ernie Burns, 2; Jack Golden,
1; Terry McMullen, 2; Johnny Brown, 1; Cliff
Becker, 2. Won: Dixie Kid, 6; Phil Jackson, 6;
Freeman Peoper, 10; Norm Genet, 10. Lost: Jack
McVey, 10. Draw: Geo. Perrato, 6. Knockout
by: Jack McVey, 10.

1929
Knockouts: Tubby Noble, 3; Ted
Esterbrook, 3; Art Cross, 7; Charley Sherer, 3;
Norm Wilson, 1. Won: Joe Banovic, 6; Nick
Martin, 6; Ben Stanley, 10; Art Spence, 10;
Snowflake Wright, 6; Osk Till, 6. Lost: Henry
Firpo, 8. Draw: Garry Leach, 6. Knockout by:
Billy Jones 5.

1930
Jan. 13—Henry Firpo, New Castle, Pa. ...L 10
Feb. 10—Harry Fuller, Buffalo .... D 6
Mar. 7—Indian Tiger West, Franklin, Pa. W 10
Mar. 14—Indian Tiger West, Erie, Pa. .... W 10
Mar. 24—Henry Firpo, Oil City, Pa. ..... W 10
May 26—Jimmie Rogers, Boston.......KO 5
June 3—Tiger Thomas, Williamsport, Pa. W 10
June 3—Jimmie Rogers, Boston.......KO 5
June 25—Gene McCue, Buffalo ....KO 3
July 10—Johnny Freeman, Buffalo ...... W 6
July 25—Tiger Thomas, Sayre, Pa. ...... W 6
Aug. 26—Tiger Thomas, Leiperville, Pa... D 10
Sept. 2—Harry Allen, Boston .... W 10
Nov. 11—Sunny Jim Williams, Franklin .. W 10
Nov. 24—Garfield Johnson, Buffalo ....KO 9
Dec. 3—Charley Belanger, Buffalo ..... W 10
Dec. 15—Chuck Burns, Buffalo .... W 10

1931
Jan. 16—Billy Jones, Erie ....L 10
July 13—Leo Larivee, Boston .... W 10
Aug. 25—Jack McVey, Sandusky .... W 10
Sept. 18—Sam Bruce, Buffalo ....KO 5
Sept. 25—Snowflake Wright, Milwaukee . W 10
Nov. 2—Gorilla Jones, Milwaukee ......L 10
Nov. 27—Dave Maier, Buffalo ....KO by 8
Dec. 30—Don Petrin, Chicago ....KO 5

1932
Jan. 15—Charley Belanger, Chicago ..... W 10
Jan. 28—Lou Scozza, Chicago .... W 10
Feb. 18—Billy Jones, Chciago .... W 10
Mar. 18—Dave Maier, Chicago .... W 10
(Final elimination for vacant N.B.A. Light
Heavyweight Title).
May 31—Lou Scozza, Buffalo ....L 10
July 22—Red Fitzsimmons, Colo. Spgs. KO 5
July 29—Ham Jenkins, Denver .... W 10
Oct. 17—Joe Knight, Charleston, S. C.....L 10
Oct. 26—Adolph Heuser, Boston ....L 10

1933
Feb. 17—George Forester, Elizabeth ...KO 2
Mar. 6—Lou Scozza, Buffalo .... D 10
Mar. 13—Don Petrin, Newark ....W 10
Mar. 30—Lou Scozza, Buffalo ....KO by 5
May 15—Al Gainer, New Haven ....L 10
June 12—Frank O'Brien, Hartford ...... W 10
July 7—Sammy Slaughter, Chicago .....L 10
July 17—Norm Conrad, Manchester, N. H. L 10
Aug. 10—Martin Levandowski,
Muskegon ....KO 8
Aug. 24—Harry English, Muskegon .....ND 10
Nov. 8—Joe Knight, New York ....L 8
Nov. 20—Larry Johnson, Chicago ...... W 10
Dec. 18—Harry English, Toledo .... D 10

1934
Jan. 11—Al Gainer, New Haven ....L 10
Feb. 5—George Manley, Miami .... W 5
Apr. 17—Mickey Dugan, Cleveland ..... W 10

1935
Oct. 18—Al Delaney, Buffalo .... D 6

1936
Apr. 7—John Henry Lewis, Buffalo .... D 10
Apr. 20—Al Gainer, Pittsburgh .....KO by 9
July 9—Allan Matthews, Chciago ...... W 10

Aug. 12—John Henry Lewis, St. Louis ....L 10
Dec. 26—Fanis Tzanatopoulous, BuffaloKO 1
1937
Jan. 8—Dominic Ceccarelli, Buffalo ... W 8
Mar. 2—Stanley Evans, Detroit .... W 8
May 18—Charlie Killer Coats, Los AngelesW 10
June 15—Alabama Kid, Denver ..... KO by 4
Sept. 27—Eddie Saxon, Buffalo .... W 6
Oct. 18—Ralph DeJohn, Buffalo .... KO by 1
1938
(Inactive)
1939
Feb. 17—Fred Apostoli, Houston ... KO by 2

TB	KO	WD	WF	D	LD	LF	KOBY	ND	NC
108	24	47	0	10	17	0	9	1	0

BOB GODWIN

NBA World Light Heavyweight Champion, 1933
Born: May 5, 1911, Moultrie, Ga.
Weight: 166 lbs., Height: 5 ft. 11½ in.
1927
—Allen Wood .... KO 2
—Tony Carroll .... KO 1
—Kid Roberts .... KO 1
—Burt Hamilton .... KO 3
—Roy Taylor .... KO 1
—Red Sea Boyette .... KO 1
—Walker .... KO 2
—Taylor .... KO 8
—Battling Fisk .... KO 5
—Nutter Wilcox .... W 4
—Nutter Wilcox .... W 4
—Leary Levette .... W 10
—Leary Levette .... W 10
—Leary Levette .... D 6
—Leary Levette .... D 8
—Bobby Cox .... N.D. 10
—Brady O'Hara .... N.D. 10
1928
—Skeeter Barwick .... KO 4
—Skeeter Barwick .... KO 2
—Red Hancock .... KO 5
—Vega Rubin .... KO 4
—Jack O'Mally .... KO 5
—Happy Finnegan .... KO 3
—Ted Taylor .... KO 4
—Johnny Garaden .... KO 6
—Monroe Porter .... KO 4
—Burnt Balchem .... W 8
—Red Sea Boyette .... W 10
—Red Hancock .... W 10
—Kid Williams .... W 10
—Kid Williams .... W 10
—Jack Staricka .... W 10
—Earl Hudson .... W 10
—Red Hancock .... D 8
—Willie Potomney .... D 10
—Spike Webb .... D 10
—Jim Beasley .... KO by 3
1929
—Puddy Hinkus .... KO 4
—Ollie Joyner .... KO 9
—Spike Kelly .... KO 5
—Antonio Diaz .... KO 4
—Billy Shell .... KO 3
—Kid Bombara .... KO 2
—Cyclone Williams .... KO 4
—Billy Shell .... KO 3
—Spike Kelly .... KO 4
—Red Reilly .... KO 6
—Bobby O'Hara .... KO 7
—Earl Hudson .... KO 3
—Jimmy Decapua .... KO 10
—Jimmy Decapua .... W 10
—Brady O'Hara .... W 10
—Kid Williams .... W 10
—Kid Williams .... W 10
—Alex Hart .... W 10
—Battling Bozo .... W 10
—Ernest Saguies .... W 10
—Battling Bozo .... D 10
—Jimmy Decapua .... L 10
—Alex Hart .... L 10
1930
Jan. 5—Battling Bozo, Birmingham .... D 10
Jan. 16—Lou Carpenter, Daytona Beach .... KO 6
Jan. 30—Ernest Saguies, Miami .... W 10
Feb. 7—Mike McTigue, Daytona Beach .... W 10
Feb. 13—Jimmy Sullivan, Miami .... W 10
Apr. 7—Mike McTigue, Miami .... W 10
Apr. 17—Jess Akers, Birmingham .... W 10

Apr. 22—Eddie Mack, Orlando .... KO 2
Apr. 29—Monroe Portet, Palatka, Fla. .... KO 4
May 3—K. O. Joe King, Jacksonville .... KO 3
May 6—Ollie Ollief, Savannah .... W 10
June 24—Paul Rojas, Jacksonville .... KO 9
July 1—Ernest Saguies, Jacksonville .... W 10
July 15—Ernest Saguies, Jacksonville .... W 10
Aug. 1—Ratels Kitchkline, Portsmouth, Va. ...... W 8
Aug. 8—Eric Lawson, Portsmouth .... W 10
Aug. 22—Joe Knight, Waycross, Ga. .... W 10
Sept. 5—Eric Lawson, Portsmouth .... W 10
Sept. 19—Sammy Weiss, Portsmouth .... W 8
Sept. 26—Jack Denning, Portsmouth .... W 8
Oct. 9—Earl Johnson, Palatka .... KO 4
Oct. 25—Buster Newberry, Savannah .... KO 4
Oct. 30—Mario Campi, Portsmouth .... W 8
Nov. 11—Jack Denning, Durham, N.C. .... W 10
Nov. 21—George Giacchino, Portsmouth .... W 8
1931
Apr. 9—Joe Knight, Daytona Beach .... W 10
Apr. 30—Joe Knight, Daytona Beach .... KO by 8
June 5—Doc Conrad .... D 8
July 6—Arthur Huttick .... W 6
Aug. 24—Jack Cotey .... KO 1
Sept. 28—Jimmy McDuffie .... KO 4
Oct. 8—Battling Bozo, Jacksonville .... W 10
1932
Jan. 4—Owen Phelps .... N.D. 10
Jan. 23—Joe Knight, Miami .... W 10
Jan. 29—Don Petrin .... D 10
Feb. 17—Maxie Rosenbloom, Daytona Beach .... D 10
Apr. 12—Willie Oster .... W 10
May 16—Joe Banovic, Alexandria, Va. .... D 8
July 1—Joe Knight, Daytona Beach .... L 10
Aug. 22—Maxie Rosenbloom, Laurel, Md. .... L 10
Aug. 30—Maxie Rosenbloom, Charlotte .... D 10
Sept. 26—Donald (Reds) Barry .... W 6
1933
Jan. 9—Eric Lawson, Charleston .... W 10
Jan. 23—Russ Rowsey, Charleston .... W 10
Feb. 14—Johnny Miles, West Palm Beach .... KO 6
Mar. 1—Joe Knight, West Palm Beach .... W 10
(Won NBA World Light Heavyweight Title)
Mar. 24—Maxie Rosenbloom, N. Y. C. .... KO by 4
(For World Light Heavyweight Title)
June 26—Charley (Trader) Horn, Laurel .... KO 2
July 10—Donald (Reds) Barry, Alexandria .... W 10
Aug. 30—Joe Knight, Laurel .... W 10
Oct. 10—Joe Knight, Miami .... KO by 5
Nov. 28—Henry Firpo, West Palm Beach .... W 10
Dec. 21—Maxie Rosenbloom, West Palm Beach ... D 10
1934
Jan. 10—Maxie Rosenbloom, West Palm Beach .... W 12
Jan. 29—Mickey Walker, West Palm Beach .... D 10
Mar. 22—Johnny Risko, Daytona Beach .... W 10
Apr. 13—Mickey Walker, San Francisco .... D 10
Apr. 20—Don Conn, Hollywood .... KO 10
May 4—Benny Miller, Hollywood .... W 10
May 25—Bob Olin, Hollywood .... KO by 1
June 22—Bob Olin, Hollywood .... KO 10
Aug. 31—Wesley Ketchell, Hollywood .... KO by 8
Sept. 28—Abe Feldman, Hollywood .... W 10
Oct. 26—Fred Lenhart, Hollywood .... KO by 7
1935
Feb. 15—Maxie Rosenbloom, Hollywood .... L 10
Feb. 26—Tony Shucco, Daytona Beach .... D 10
Mar. 22—Al McCoy, Boston .... KO by 8
Mar. 27—Leroy Brown, Charleston .... KO by 1
Sept. 30—Buck Everett, Washington, D.C. .... W 10
Dec. 9—Al Delaney, Washington, D.C. .... W by 2

TB	KO	WD	WF	D	LD	LF	KO BY	ND	NC
130	44	51	0	16	6	0	10	3	0

BOB OLIN

Born, July 4, 1908, New York City.
Weight, 175 lbs. Height, 6 ft. Managed by
Harold Scadron.
1928
Al Braddock, KO, 2.
1929
Frank Morris, d, 6; Jimmy Roberts, W, 6;
Larry Hogan, KO, 1; Jim Griffin, KO, 1; Jack
Finklea, KO, 1; Herman Riegals, KO, 4; Joe
Johnson, KO, 1; Eric Holmberg, KO, 5; Jim
Morris, KO, 3; Dave King, W, 8; Felix Milano,
KO, 1; Bruno Sala, W, 8; Amendeo Grillo, KO, 3;
George La Rocco, W, 10; Joe Banovic, L, 10; Olaf
Huset, KO, 1; Willie Lancaster, KO, 1; Jack
Marsling, KO, 1

509

1930

One Punch Williams, W, 10; Italian Jack Herman, W, 6; George La Rocco, W, 6; Ray Wallace, W (foul) 2; Ralph Ficucello, W, 8; Joe Sekyra, L, 10; Pat Wash, KO, 3; Bremen Eddie, W, 6; Willard Dix, W, 10; Joe Banovic, D, 10.

1931

Feb.	24—Tony Ferrante, N. Y. C.	W 10
Mar.	30—Joe Banovic, N. Y. C.	L 10
June	6—Tony Ferrante, N. Y. C.	KO 5
June	22—Willard Dix, N. Y. C.	KO 1
July	27—Al Gainer, New Haven, Conn.	W 10
Aug.	14—Willie Bush, New Haven, Ct.	L 10
Sept.	1—Al Gainer, New Haven, Conn.	L 10
Nov.	23—Don Petrin, N. Y. C.	KO 6
Dec.	18—Tait Littman, Chicago, Ill.	KO 4
Dec.	30—Clyde Chastain, Chicago	W 10

1932

Jan.	15—Baxter Calmes, Chicago, Ill.	L 10
Feb.	15—Art Huttick, Chicago, Ill.	L 10
June	1—Dick Fullam, N. Y. C.	W 8
July	20—Muggs Kerr, N. Y. C.	W 8
Sept.	1—Al Gainer, New Haven	L 10
Nov.	18—Tommy Welsh, N. Y. C.	W 6
Dec.	29—Martin Levandowski, Chicago	KO by 6

1933

Jan.	20—Paul Marque, N. Y. C.	W 6
Mar.	10—Chas. Massera, N. Y. C.	L 6
June	19—Tony Shucco, Albany, N. Y.	L 10
July	5—Chas. Massera, Brooklyn	D 10
July	26—Sam Portney, Brooklyn	W 10
Aug.	17—Al Gainer, N. Y. C.	D 6
Oct.	9—Unknown Winston, N. Y. C.	W 6
Nov.	17—Chas. Massera, N. Y. C.	W 8
Dec.	22—Al Gainer, New Haven	W 10

1934

Jan.	19—Lou Brouillard, N. Y. C.	L 10
Apr.	5—Lou Brouillard, New Haven	L 10
May	25—Bob Godwin, Hollywood	KO 1
June	22—Bob Godwin, Hollywood	W 10
July	20—Abe Feldman, Hollywood	D 10
Nov.	16—Maxie Rosenbloom, N. Y. C.	W 15

(Win Light Heavyweight Championship)

1935

Jan.	11—Fanis Tzanetopoulos, Boston	W 10
Feb.	26—Dutch Weimer, Detroit	L 10
Mar.	25—Mickey Dugan, Cleveland	W 8
Apr.	12—John Henry Lewis, San Fran.	L 10
Sept.	20—Henry Firpo, Arbury Park	KO 3
Oct.	31—John Henry Lewis, St. Louis	L 15

(Lost Light Heavyweight title)

Dec.	10—Al McCoy, Montreal	L 10

1936

Apr.	2—Tommy Farr, London	L 10
Aug.	4—Jimmy DeSola, Brooklyn	W 8
Aug.	17—Red Bruce, Pittsburgh	L 10
Nov.	2—Buck Everett, Wash.	KO 4

1937

Jan.	15—Tiger Jack Fox, Spokane	KO by 2
Mar.	10—Gunnar Barlund, N. Y. C.	W 10
May	4—Leonard Bostick, St. Louis	KO 1
June	3—John Henry Lewis, St. Louis	

(For Light-Heavy Title) KO by 8

Sept.	13—Patsy Perroni, Toledo	KO 4
Sept.	28—Leroy Haynes, Phila.	KO by 6
Nov.	17—Johnny Risko, Cleveland	L 10

1938

Jan.	8—Tiger Hairston, N. Y. C.	KO 2
Jan.	24—Steve Dudas, Philadelphia	L 10
Sept.	1—Buddy Knox, Montreal, Can.	L 10
Nov.	9—Al McCoy, Montreal, Can.	L 10

1939

Feb.	2—Gus Lesnevich, Sydney, Aust.	L 12
Feb.	22—Young Campbell, Newcastle, Australia	KO 4

1942

In U. S. Coast Guard.

TB	KO	WD	WF	D	LD	LF	KOBY	ND	NC
85	25	27	1	5	23	0	4	0	0

Died, December 16, 1956, New York, N.Y.

JOHN HENRY LEWIS

Born, May 1, 1914, Los Angeles, Calif. Nationality, American Negro. Height, 5 ft. 11 in. Managed by Gus Greenlee.

1931

Knockouts: Tommy Cadena, 1; Pietro Georgi, 1; Roy Gunn, 3; Kid Valdone, 3; Sammy Bass, 1; Jake Henderson, 4; Roy Imm,

4; Tiger Flowers, 6; Sam Terrain, Prescott, Ariz., KO, 4—Terrain died after the knockout.

	—Lloyd Phelps, Mesa, Ariz.	W 8

1932

Apr.	22—Yale Okun, San Francisco	W 10
Sept.	21—James J. Braddock, San Fran.	W 10
Oct.	5—Fred Lenhardt, San Francisco	KO 4
Oct.	26—Lou Scozza, San Francisco	W 10
Nov.	16—Maxie Rosenbloom, San Fran.	L 10
Nov.	27—Jimmy Hanna, San Francisco	KO 6
Dec.	12—Tuffy Dial, San Francisco	KO 4

1933

Feb.	7—Terris Hill, San Francisco	KO 4
Mar.	3—Tom Patrick, San Francisco	W 10
Apr.	7—Emmett Rocco, San Francisco	KO 7
June	16—Fred Lenhardt, San Francisco	D 10
July	12—Maxie Rosenbloom, San Fran.	W 10
July	31—Maxie Rosenbloom, San Fran.	W 10
Nov.	10—Frank Rowsey, San Francisco	W 10
	—Emmet Rocco	KO 7

1934

June	6—Sandy Casanova, Ft. Huachuca	KO 3
July	12—Bobby Brown, Tucson	KO 3
Sept.	3—Tony Poloni, Reno	KO 1
Sept.	1—Norman Conrad, Oakland	W 10
Sept.	20—Young Firpo, Portland	D 10
Oct.	3—Red Barry, San Francisco	D 10
Oct.	17—Pietro Georgi, Oakland	KO 2
Oct.	31—Earl Wise, Oakland	KO 3
Nov.	16—Jim Braddock, N. Y. C.	L 10
Nov.	23—Yale Okun, N. Y. C.	KO 3
Dec.	14—Tony Shucco, N. Y. C.	W 10

1935

Jan.	29—Don Petrin, Pittsburgh	KO 7
Feb.	25—Frank Wotanski, Syracuse	KO 3
Mar.	4—Terry Mitchell, Syracuse	KO 6
Mar.	13—Emilio Martinez, Denver	W 10
Apr.	12—Bob Olin, San Francisco	W 10
May	10—Frank Rowsey, San Francisco	W 10
June	3—Tommy Patrick, Pittsburgh	KO 1
June	24—Izzy Singer, Paterson	KO 1
July	8—Lou Poster, Cleveland	KO 5
July	17—Maxie Rosenbloom, Oakland	L 10
July	24—Abe Feldman, N.Y.C.	L 10
Oct.	31—Bob Olin, St. Louis	W 15

(Won Light Heavyweight Title)

Nov.	29—Maxie Rosenbloom, San Fran.	L 10
Dec.	11—Georgie Simpson, Oakland	KO 2
Dec.	19—Coleman Johns, Phoenix	KO 2
Dec.	20—Dutch Weimer, Tucson	W 10

1936

Jan.	10—Tiger Jack Fox, Spokane	KO 3
Jan.	17—Al Stillman, St. Louis, Mo.	KO 4
Jan.	29—Emilio Martinez, Denver	L 10
Jan.	31—Cyclone Lynch, Walsenburg	KO 1
Mar.	6—Eddies Simms, St. Louis, Mo.	W 10
Mar.	13—Jock McAvoy, N. Y. C.	W 15

(Title)

Apr.	7—George Nichols, Buffalo	D 10
Apr.	12—Izzy Singer, Chicago, Ill.	W 10
May	27—Charlie Massera, Pittsburgh	W 10
May	29—Bob Godwin, N. Y. C.	KO 1
June	8—John Anderson, N. Y. C.	W 10
June	12—Dutch Weiner, York, Pa.	KO 4
June	17—Tony Shucco, St. Louis, Mo.	KO 8
June	22—Jimmy Merriott, Peoria, Ill.	KO 3
July	10—Max Marek, Chicago, Ill.	W 10
July	30—Al Gainer, Pittsburgh, Pa.	W 12
Aug.	12—George Nichols, St. Louis	W 10
Sept.	17—Tiger Hairston, Charleston	KO 1
Oct.	2—Red Burman, Chicago, Ill	KO 2
Nov.	9—Len Harvey, London, Eng.	W 15

(Title)

Jan.	4—Al Ettore, Philadelphia	D 10
Jan.	11—Art Sykes, Pittsburgh	KO 6
Jan.	28—Chester Palutis, Scranton	KO 7
Feb.	8—Al Ettore, Philadelphia	W 15
Mar.	15—Hans Birkie, Philadelphia	W 10
Apr.	2—Donald Barry, St. Louis	KO 5
Apr.	12—Babe Davis, Indianapolis	KO 3
Apr.	13—Harold Murphy, Omaha	KO 4
Apr.	19—Pret Farrar, Des Moines	KO 6
May	4—Emilio Martinez, St. Louis	W 10
May	14—Patsy Perroni, N. Y. C.	W 10
May	21—Jack Kranz, Kansas City	KO 3
June	3—*Bob Olin, St. Louis	KO 8
June	15—Al Ettore, Philadelphia	W 10
June	28—Willie Reddish, Washington	W 10
Aug.	19—Italo Colonello, Pittsburgh	W 12
Oct.	15—Isadore Gastanaga, Detroit	L 10
Nov.	26—Salvadore Ruggierello	KO 4
Dec.	12—Isadore Gastanaga, St. Louis	KO 9
Dec.	17—Johnny Risko, Cleveland	W 10

510

1938

Jan.	10—Leonard Neblitt, Nashville	..KO	8
Jan.	18—Marty Gallagher, St. Louis	..KO	3
Jan.	31—Emil Scholz, Pittsburgh	.....W	10
Feb.	11—Fred Lenhart, St. Louis	...KO	3
Mar.	25—Bud Mignault, St. Paul	.....W	10
Apr.	4—Bud Tow, Philadelphia	....W	10
Apr.	25—*Emilio Martinez, MinneapolisKO		4
May	5—Domenic Ceccarelli, Baltimore	W	10
May	19—Elmer Ray, Atlanta	....KO	12
Aug.	25—Domenic Ceccarelli, Nutley	..KO	3
Sept.	15—Jimmy Adamick, Philadelphia	. W	10
Oct.	28—*Al Gainer, New Haven	.....W	15

*Title bout.

1939

Jan.   25—Joe Louis, N. Y. C. ..... KO by 1

(For the Heavyweight Championship
of the World)

(Lewis announced retirement as
undefeated champion)

TB	KO	WD	WF	D	LD	LF	KOBY	ND	NC
105	54	38	0	5	7	0	1	0	0

Died April 18, 1974 in Berkeley, Calif.

GUSTAVE ROTH

(Gustave Scillie)
Born, March 12, 1909, Antwerp, Belgium. Weight,
147-175 lbs. Height, 5 ft. 8 in.

1927

Sept.	14—Georges Covent, Brussels	.... W	6
Sept.	28—Molls, Brussels	.... W	6
Oct.	8—Van Outryve, Brussels	.... W	6
Oct.	26—Alexis Marin, Brussels	.... W	6
Nov.	22—Andre Reby, Pris	.... LF	2
Nov.	30—Henri Dupont, Brussels	.... W	10
Dec.	21—Henri Mouha, Brussels	.... W	10

1928

Jan.	12—Joe Ralph, Antwerp	.... W	10
Jan.	31—Van Diependael, Paris	.... W	8
Mar.	14—Tuns, Brussels	.... W	10
Mar.	23—Walter Libert, Limoges	.... D	10
May	9—Blommaert, Brussels	.... KO	6
Sept.	12—Camille Desmedt, Brussels	.... D	10
Sept.	26—Arie Van Vliet, Brussels	.... W	10
Nov.	9—Paul Franko, Ghent	.... W	10
Dec.	4—Georges Covent, Ghent	.... W	10

1929

Jan.	15—Camille Desmedt, Charleroi	 L	10
Jan.	23—Alf Genon, Brussels	.... W	10
Mar.	6—Joe Ralph, Brussels	.... W	10
Mar.	29—Franz Deconninck, Verviers	.... KO	6
Apr.	12—Nick Clausen, Copenhagen	.... W	10
May	15—Fritz Ensel, Brussels	.... KO	4
July	2—Edouard Baudry, Antwerp	.... W	10
Sept.	11—Leo Darton, Brussels	.... W	10
Oct.	9—Alf Genon, Brussels	.... W	15

(Won European Welterweight Title)

Dec.   17—Leo Darton, Charleroi .... D 15

(Retained European Welterweight Title)

1930

Feb.   5—Camille Desmedt, Charleroi .... W 15

(Retained European Welterweight Title)

Mar.	19—Francois Sybille, Brussels	.... W	12
Apr.	2—Adrien Anneet, Brussels	.... W	10
May	11—Vittorio Venturi, Rome	.... D	15

(Retained European Welterweight Title)

July	20—Piet Hobin, Antwerp	.... W	10
Nov.	4—Frantisek Dykast, Prague	.... D	10
Oct.	15—Aime Raphael, Brussels	.... W	15

(Retained European Welterweight Title)

Dec.   3—Gustav Eder, Frankfurt .... W 15

(Retained European Welterweight Title)

1931

Jan.   14—Hans Holdt, Copenhagen .... W 15

(Retained European Welterweight Title)

Jan.	30—Alf Berry, Paris	.... W	10
Feb.	26—Alf Howard, Liverpool	.... W	15
Mar.	16—Franta Nekolny, Prague	.... D	15

(Retained European Welterweight Title)

Apr.	17—Gunnar Anderson, Gothenburg	.... D	10
June	27—Vittorio Venturi, Brussels	.... W	15

(Retained European Welterweight Title)

Aug.   30—Gustav Eder, Berlin .... W 15

(Retained European Welterweight Title)

Sept.   18—Huib Huizenaar, Brussels .... W 15

(Retained European Welterweight Title)

Dec.   1—Francois Stevens, Antwerp .... W 10

1932

Feb.	17—Rene Devos, Antwerp	.... D	10
Mar.	3—Fritz Ensel, Verviers	.... KO	3
Apr.	5—Leone Jacovacci, Antwerp	.... WF	3

Apr.	26—Camille Desmedt, Charleroi	.... W	15

(Retained European Welterweight Title)

June   24—Gheorghe Axiotti, Bucharest .... W 15

(Retained European Welterweight Title)

Sept.	7—Rene Devos, Brussels	.... W	10
Oct.	26—Adrien Anneet, Brussels	.... LF	6
Nov.	25—Georges Delfanne, Namur	.... KO	6

1933

Feb.	2—Eddie Maguire, Liverpool	.... W	15
Feb.	17—Arthur Vermaut, Ghent	.... KO	4
Feb.	25—Hein Domgoergen, Brussels	.... W	10
Mar.	28—Amedee Dubus, Malines	.... W	10
Apr.	20—Claude Bassin, Ghent	.... W	10
May	16—Heinrich Trollmann, Antwerp	.... W	10
Aug.	5—Hein Domgoergen, Cologne	.... D	10
Sept.	15—Carmelo Candel, Paris	.... W	10
Oct.	6—Claude Bassin, Paris	.... W	10
Nov.	8—Piet Brandt, Brussels	.... W	10
Nov.	19—Kid Tunero, Brussels	.... W	10
Dec.	6—Jimmy Tarante, Brussels	.... W	10
Dec.	10—Roger Besneux, Antwerp	.... W	10

1934

Jan.	12—Tino Rolando, Paris	.... W	10
Jan.	20—Roger Lefebvre, Charleroi	.... KO	6
Feb.	3—Karl Neubauer, Brussels	.... W	10
Feb.	17—Claude Bassin, Limoges	.... W	10
Mar.	17—Eric Seelig, Brussels	.... W	15

(Won European Middleweight Title)

May   3—Marcel Thil, Paris .... L 15

(Lost European Middleweight Title)
(For IBU World Middleweight Title)

July	29—Rene Devos, Brussels	.... KO	8
Sept.	1—Beb Donnars, Antwerp	.... W	10
Sept.	19—Clemente Meroni, Brussels	.... W	12
Oct.	31—Eric Seelig, Brussels	.... W	10
Dec.	12—Tino Rolando, Brussels	.... W	10

1935

Feb.	20—Giacomo Ventrella, Brussels	.... KO	4
Mar.	2—Carmelo Candel, Brussels	.... W	10
Mar.	13—Joe Zeeman, Brussels	.... W	10
Apr.	24—Charles Sys, Ostend	.... W	15

(Won Belgian Middleweight Title)

June	22—Jean Burton, Limoges	.... KO	5
July	3—Emil Lebrize, Brussels	.... W	10
Aug.	7—Rienus de Boer, Brussels	.... W	10
Nov.	14—Jerome Wagner, Antwerp	.... KO	6
Dec.	20—Lou Brouillard, Paris	 L	15

1936

Feb.	28—Gustav Eder, Berlin	 L	12
Mar.	11—Victor (Kid) Janas, Brussels	.... W	10
June	28—Nestor Charlier	.... W	15

(Retained Belgian Middleweight Title)

Sept.   1—Heinz Lazek, Vienna .... W 15

(Won European Light Heavyweight Title)
(Won IBU World Light Heavyweight Title)

Oct.	6—Ercole Buratti, Antwerp	.... KO	5
Oct.	29—Adolph Witt, Berlin	.... W	15

(Retained European Light Heavyweight Title)
(Retained IBU World Light Heavyweight Title)

Nov.   24—Charles Sys, Antwerp .... W 10

1937

Jan.   12—Antonio Rodriguez, Rio de Janeiro ...... D 15

(Retained IBU World Light Heavyweight Title)

Mar.   24—Merlo Preciso, Brussels .... W 15

(Retained European Light Heavyweight Title)
(Retained IBU World Light Heavyweight Title)

Apr.	6—John Simmons, Antwerp	.... W	10
May	1—John Anderson, Antwerp	.... W	15

(Retained European Light Heavyweight Title)
(Retained IBU World Light Heavyweight Title)

July	10—Emil Ollive, Ostend	.... W	10
Dec.	1—Charles Sys, Brussels	.... D	15

(Retained European Light Heavyweight Title)
(Retained IBU World Light Heavyweight Title)

1938

Jan.   21—Jupp Besselmann, Berlin .... W 15

(Retained European Light Heavyweight Title)
(Retained IBU World Light Heavyweight Title)

Feb.   2—Walter Von Bueren, Zurich .... W 10

Mar.   25—Adolph Heuser, Berlin .... KO by 7

(Lost European Light Heavyweight Title)
(Lost IBU World Light Heavyweight Title)

1939

Feb.	4—Charles Rutz, Brussels	.... W	10
Apr.	11—Jerome Wegner, Antwerp	.... KO	8

(Won Belgian Light Heavyweight Title)

Aug.   6—Jean Simon, Brussels .... KO 11

(Retained Belgian Light Heavyweight Title)

1940

Jan.	16—Gaston Bridou, Antwerp	.... KO	7
Apr.	2—Vittorio Zanetti, Antwerp	.... KO	9
Apr.	16—Dorus Elten, Antwerp	.... W	10
Dec.	18—Vittorio Buratti, Brussels	.... KO	14

(Retained Belgian Light Heavyweight Title)

511

1941

Jan.	4—Vittorio Zanetti, Antwerp	W	10
Feb.	11—Jean Simon, Antwerp	KO	6
Mar.	20—Al Gerard, Antwerp	W	10
Apr.	9—Jean Motte, Brussels	KO	5
July	2—Charles Sys, Brussels	KO by	3
	(For Belgian Heavyweight Title)		
Oct.	25—Gaston Bridou, Brussels	KO	4
Nov.	12—Pierre Van Deuren, Brussels	KO	8
Dec.	4—Gerard Selhorst, Antwerp	KO	6
Dec.	23—Pol Goffaux, Antwerp	W	10

1942

Feb.	25—Georges Levasseur, Brussels	W	10
Mar.	10—Emil Ollive, Antwerp	KO	9
Apr.	1—Gerard Selhorst, Brussels	W	10
Apr.	14—Rienus de Boer, Antwerp	W	10
May	25—Charles Sys, Antwerp	W	12
	(Won Belgian Heavyweight Title)		
July	5—Oscar Menozzi, Paris	W	10
Oct.	14—Pol Goffaux, Brussels	L	12
	(Lost Belgian Light Heavyweight Title)		
Dec.	13—Pol Goffaux, Antwerp	L	12
	(For Belgian Light Heavyweight Title)		

1943

Mar.	11—Henri Lagrou, Ghent	KO	3
Mar.	15—Luis Potier, Ghent	NC	4
May	9—Henri Gaillard, Brussels	W	10
July	1—Maurice Robbensijn, Ghent	W	10
July	18—Assane Diouf, Brussels	L	10
Oct.	15—Jean Luis, Antwerp	KO	1
Oct.	21—Pierre Van Deuren, Antwerp	W	10
Oct.	28—Gerard Selhorst, Antwerp	W	10
Nov.	11—Gerard Selhorst, Brussels	W	10
Dec.	9—Marc Noben, Ghent	W	10

1944

Jan.	30—Pol Goffaux, Brussels	W	12
	(Regained Belgian Light Heavyweight Title)		

1945

Feb.	7—Pol Goffaux, Brussels	D	10

TB	KO	WD	WF	D	LD	LF	KO BY	ND	NC
136	25	86	1	12	7	2	2	0	1

ADOLF HEUSER

Born, October 3, 1907, Bonn, Germany.

1929

Aug.	2—Fernand Delarge, Dusseldorf	W	6
Sept.	7—Otto Hoelzl, Iserlohn	D	6
Sept.	20—Emil Scholz, Cologne	W	6
Nov.	2—Hein Heuser, Cologne	KO	4
Nov.	23—Debarbieux, Cologne	D	8

1930

Jan.	3—Louis Wuestenraedt, Cologne	D	8
Feb.	2—Otto Hoelzl, Dortmund	D	8
Apr.	11—Otto Hoelzl, Cologne	W	8
Oct.	10—Sewewers, Mainz	KO	3
Oct.	31—Helmuth Hartkopf, Cologne	KO	3
Nov.	30—Piet Brandt, Mainz	KO	2

1931

Jan.	9—Ernst Pistulla, Cologne	D	12
	(For German Light Heavyweight Title)		
Feb.	17—Moise Bouquillon, Berlin	W	8
Mar.	8—Jack Etienne, Cologne	KO	6
Mar.	27—Rienus De Boer, Hamburg	W	10
Apr.	17—Josef Hampacher, Berlin	W	8
June	5—Gustav Limousin, Hamburg	W	8
July	5—Emilio Bernasconi, Hamburg	KO	1
July	31—George Slack, Altona	W	10
Sept.	5—Ernst Pistulla, Hamburg	D	15
	(For European Light Heavyweight Title)		
Dec.	4—Patsy Perroni, Chicago	L	8

1932

Jan.	23—Tony Ferente, N.Y.C.	KO	2
Jan.	27—Pietro Corti, Portland, Me.	KO	3
Feb.	6—Al Rodriguez, Boston	KO	1
Feb.	11—George Manley, Cleveland	KO	5
Feb.	18—Nick Palmer, Brooklyn	KO	8
Mar.	5—Rosy Rosales, Boston	W	8
June	25—Martinez de Alfara, Valencia	KO	1
	(Won European Light Heavyweight Title)		
Oct.	5—Leo Williams, Portland	KO	2
Oct.	22—Norman Conrad, Holyoke, Mass.	W	10
Oct.	28—George Nichols, Boston	W	10
Dec.	6—Eddie Simms, Cleveland	W	10
	(Stripped of European Light Heavyweight Title by the IBU December 28.)		

1933

Feb.	10—Harry Ebbets, N.Y.C.	W	10
Mar.	10—Maxie Rosenbloom, N.Y.C.	L	15
	(For World Light Heavyweight Title)		
Apr.	1—Harry Ebbets, N.Y.C.	W	10
June	21—Abe Feldman, N.Y.C.	KO by	4
July	26—Ed (Unknown) Winston, N.Y.C.	KO by	12
Sept.	22—Lou Brouillard, Boston	KO by	6

1934

Mar.	26—J. Czihos, Berlin	W	10
May	14—G. Brown, Berlin	KO	7
June	15—Auguste Langagne, Magdebourg	KO	1
July	8—Alexis Marin, Berlin	KO	2
Aug.	26—Adolf Witt, Hamburg	D	12
	(For German Light Heavyweight Title)		
Sept.	28—Marcel Lauriot, Berlin	W	10
Oct.	26—Luigi Sciutto, Munich	KO	5
Nov.	23—Louis Vauclard, Berlin	KO	1
Dec.	9—Barrere, Munich	W	10
Dec.	14—A. Leidmann, Munich	W	10

1935

Jan.	21—Angel Cleville, Berlin	W	10
Feb.	8—Roger Royer, Cologne	KO	3
Feb.	25—Domenico Ceccarelli, Berlin	W	10
Mar.	10—Bob Carvill, Hamburg	KO	6
Apr.	12—Merlo Preciso, Berlin	LF	1
May	10—Len Steyaert, Munich	KO	6
May	23—Merlo Preciso, Berlin	W	10
June	21—Kunter, Berlin	W	10
Aug.	31—Vittorio Livan, Berlin	W	10
Sept.	12—Edgar Normann, Oslo	W	10
Oct.	7—Tino Rolando, Berlin	KO	3

1936

Jan.	11—Hans Schoenrath, Cologne	W	10
Mar.	27—Arno Koelbin, Berlin	W	10
May	8—Norman Tomasullo, Berlin	KO	1
June	6—Erwin Klein, Bonn	W	10
Sept.	4—Joe Zeeman, Stuttgart	W	10
Sept.	11—Dave Carstens, Berlin	KO	5
Oct.	3—Sante de Leo, Cologne	KO	5
Oct.	23—Emil Lebrize, Berlin	KO	1
Oct.	31—Emil Ollive, Cologne	KO	2
Nov.	4—Frank Hough, Berlin	W	10
Nov.	15—Gene Stanley, Frankfurt	KO	4
Nov.	25—Primo Bassi, Berlin	KO	5
Dec.	11—Vittorio Livan, Munich	KO	7

1937

Jan.	22—Karel Sys, Berlin	L	10
Feb.	3—Marcel Bazin, Frankfurt	KO	6
Mar.	25—Mario Liani, Berlin	KO	7
Apr.	30—Sandu Petrescu, Berlin	W	10
Aug.	22—Adolf Witt, Berlin	KO	8
	(Won German Light Heavyweight Title)		
Nov.	18—John Anderson, Berlin	KO	8

1938

Feb.	10—Karel Sys, Berlin	W	12
Mar.	25—Gustave Roth, Berlin	KO	7
	(Regained European Light Heavyweight Title)		
	(Won IBU World Light Heavyweight Title)		
Apr.	8—Vittorio Livan, Cologne	KO	1
Sept.	9—Merlo Preciso, Berlin	W	15
	(Retained European Light Heavyweight Title)		
Sept.	25—Bob Scalley, Dusseldorf	W	10
Oct.	7—Tony Shucco, Berlin	NC	5
Dec.	9—Joe Quigley, Berlin	W	12

1939

Mar.	17—Heinz Lazek, Berlin	KO	5
	(Won European Heavyweight Title)		
July	2—Max Schmeling, Stuttgart	KO by	1
	(Lost European Heavyweight Title)		
Aug.	11—Merlo Preciso, Berlin	KO	2
Dec.	15—Mario Casadei, Berlin	KO	7

1940

Feb.	4—Basile Serbanesco, Koenisberg	KO	3
Mar.	30—Jean Kreitz, Berlin	NC	12
	(For German Light Heavyweight Title)		
Sept.	8—Jean Kreitz, Berlin	KO by	8
	(For German Light Heavyweight Title)		

1941

Jan.	26—Walter Neusel, Berlin	KO by	9
Mar.	23—Heinz Lazek, Berlin	D	10
July	7—Arno Koelblin, Berlin	W	10

1942

Feb.	3—Heinz Lazek, Berlin	KO	3
May	19—Gerd Van Loon, Hanover	W	8
June	27—Walter Neusel, Hamburg	D	12
	(For German Heavyweight Title)		
Sept.	6—Walter Neusel, Berlin	KO by	8
	(For German Heavyweight Title)		

1943

Feb.	7—Harry Staal, Stuttgart	W	10
Dec.	12—Al Gerard, Breslau	KO	2
Dec.	19—Mathias Robensyn, Wien	KO by	4

1944

June	25—Robert Quentemeyer, Berlin	KO	6
Dec.	26—Jean Kreitz, Hamburg	KO by	7

1946

May	5—Zoschke, Wiesbaden	L	8
June	9—Erwin Klein, Mainz	W	8
July	13—Hans Baumann, Cologne	D	8
Sept.	15—Guenther Bola, Braunschweig	KO by	4

512

1947

May	18—Steinbrecher, Darmstadt	W 8
June	22—Polchar, Nuremberg	W 8
Aug.	1—Reinhold Balthasar, Munich	D 8
Sept.	21—Erich Alt, Berlin	W 6
Oct.	26—Adolf Witt, Berlin	W 8
Dec.	7—Hans Borowski, Berlin	D 8
Dec.	26—Hans Baumann, Berlin	L 8

1948

Mar.	7—Hans Borowski, Halle	L 8
Mar.	14—Willi Pietsch, Querfurt	D 8
Apr.	17—Bormann, Darmstadt	W 8
May	9—N. Nettekoven, Cologne .... KO by	5
June	20—W. Simon, Chemnitz	L 8
Oct.	3—Rudi Oremek, Cologne	D 6
Oct.	17—Jacob Schoenrath, Krefeld	D 6
Dec.	5—Walter Kadduck, Hamburg .... KO by	4
Dec.	26—Bormann, Darmstadt	D 8

1949

Feb.	13—Helmuth Janke, Dusseldorf .... KO by	5

TB	KO	WD	WF	D	LD	LF	KO BY	ND	NC
125	43	43	0	16	7	1	13	0	2

MELIO BETTINA

Born, November 18, 1916, Bridgeport, Conn. Nationality, Italian-American. Weight, 180 lbs. Height, 5 ft. 10 in. Managed by James V. Grippo.

1934

Oct.	6—Joe Gargiso, New York City .	KO 1
Oct.	27—John Dario, New York City .	KO 2
Nov.	10—Terry Mitchell, New York City	W 4
Dec.	1—Julius Vigh, New York City .	KO 3

1935

Mar.	15—Jimmy Varrelli, New York City	W 6
Apr.	4—Vinnie Funk, paterson	KO 2
Apr.	11—Babe Marshall, Paterson	W 6
Apr.	22—Ray Miller, Paterson	L 6
May	2—Charlie Mautz, Paterson	W 8
June	3—Lou LaPage, Paterson	W 10
June	25—Alfie Williams, Elmira	KO 3
Sept.	10—Mark Hough, Poughkeepsie ...	D 8
Nov.	13—"Tiger" Smith, New Haven ...	W 6

1936

Jan.	9—Joe Tinsley, White Plains	W 6
Feb.	17—Babe Childers, Miami Beach .	KO 2
Mar.	10—Tony Celli, W. Palm Beach ..	W 10
Mar.	31—Charlie Weiss, W. Palm Beach .	L 10
Apr.	14—Charlie Weiss, W. Palm Beach .	W 10
June	1—Bud Mignault, Poughkeepsie ..	W 10
July	13—Charlie Loughran, Washington	W 6
July	27—Buddy Ryan, Newark	ND 6
Aug.	24—Fred Caruso, Newark	L 10
Sept.	14—Frank Zamoris, Newark . KO by	6
Sept.	28—Frank Zamoris, Newark	W 8
Nov.	16—Buddy Ryan, Newark	W 8
Dec.	8—Steve Carr, West Palm Beach .	KO 6

1937

Jan.	12—Carl Knowles, W. Palm Beach	KO 2
Jan.	26—Leroy Brown, W. Palm Beach .	D 10
Mar.	2—Tony Celli, W. Palm Beach ...	W 10
Mar.	30—Barney Brock, Miami	W 10
June	18—Joe Knight, Miami	W 10
July	10—Jimmy Mendes, Bridgeport ..	KO 5
July	24—Joe Lipps, Bridgeport	KO 5
Aug.	7—Johnny Duarte, Bridgeport ...	W 8
Aug.	20—Buck Everett, Miami Beach ...	L 10
Sept.	28—Art Johnson, Los Angeles ...	KO 4
Nov.	5—Swede Berglund, Hollywood ..	W 10
Dec.	10—Swede Berglund, Hollywood .	KO 3

1938

Feb.	4—Bob Godwin, W. Palm Beach .	KO 7
Mar.	11—Tony Celli, W. Palm Beach ..	KO 2
Mar.	25—Pat McDuff, W. Palm Beach .	W 10
May	5—James J. Johnson, N. Y. C. ...	KO 7
May	20—Dominic Ceccarelli, N. Y. C. ..	W 6
June	17—Phil Sommese, Brooklyn	W 10
July	2—John Lasinski, Milford	KO 5
July	26—Gene Bonin, Poughkeepsie ...	KO 2
Aug.	18—Buck Everett, Poughkeepsie .	KO 1
Oct.	10—Basher Dean, Plainfield	W 8

1939

Jan.	3—Bud Mignault, New York City	KO 10
Jan.	20—Henry Cooper, New York City	W 8
Feb.	3—Tiger Jack Fox, N. Y. C.	KO 0

(New York State recognized Bettina lightweight champion)

May	15—Italo Colonello, Pittsburgh ..	KO 3
July	13—Billy Conn, New York City ...	L 15

(Lost Light Heavyweight title)

Aug.	8—Hobo Williams, Poughkeepsie .	W 8
Sept.	25—Billy Conn, Pittsburgh	L 15

(For Ligh Heavyweight title)

Nov.	28—Willie Pavlovich, Jersey City ..	W 8
Dec.	15—Mario Liani, Kingston	KO 4

1940

Jan.	5—Fred Apostoli, New York City	L 12
Feb.	2—Fred Apostoli, New York City	KO 12
June	7—Al McCoy, Boston	L 10
Aug.	7—Joe O'Gatty, Amsterdam	W 10
Sept.	10—Gunnar Barlund, N. Y. C. ...	W 10
Dec.	17—Solly Krieger, Brooklyn	W 10

1941

Jan.	13—Anton Christoforidis, Cleveland	L 15

(For vacant N. B. A. Light Heavyweight title)

Feb.	21—Herbie Katz, New York City .	KO 9
Mar.	9—Buddy Knox, Miami	KO 5
Mar.	25—Jack Marshall, Tampa, Fla. ..	KO 9
July	22—Red Burman, Brooklyn	W 10
Aug.	25—Pat Valentino, San Francisco .	W 10
Oct.	7—Sonny Boy Walker, Los Angeles	W 10
Nov.	17—Jimmy Bivins, Cleveland	W 10
Dec.	1—Harry Bobo, Pittsburgh	W 10

1942

Jan.	12—Mose Brown, Pittsburgh	W 10
Mar.	31—Gus Dorazio, Philadelphia ...	W 10
Apr.	10—Booker Beckwith, Chicago ...	W 10
June	12—Altus Allen, Chicago	W 10
June	23—Harry Bobo, Cleveland	W 10

In U. S. Army.

1943

June	14—Lou Brooks, Philadelphia ...	KO 1
Sept.	15—Jimmy Bivins, Cleveland	L 10

1944

May	22—Johnny Vorce, Pittsburgh ...	KO 5
June	12—Buddy Walker, Pittsburgh	W 10
July	18—Curtis Sheppard, Pittsburgh ..	W 10
Oct.	16—Saint Thomas, Philadelphia ..	KO 3
Dec.	11—George Parks, Washington, D. C.	W 10

1945

Mar.	16—Jimmy Bivins, N. Y. C.	D 10

1946

July	11—Eddie Blunt, Hartford	W 10
Aug.	19—Larry Bouchard, Troy	KO 2
Sept.	25—Eldridge Eatman, Norwalk ...	W 10
Nov.	19—Bill Weinberg, Buffalo	W 10
Dec.	10—Joe Muscato, Buffalo	KO 3

1947

May	23—Gus Lesnevich, N. Y. City	KO by 1

1948

May	12—Jackie Fisher, Bangor, Me. ..	KO 5
May	24—Ross Strickland, Newburgh ..	KO 5
June	16—Angel Sotillo, N. Y. C.	KO 3
July	6—Austin Johnson, Elizabeth ..	KO 2
July	27—Shamus O'Brien, N. Y. C. ...	KO 4
Nov.	8—Sandy McPherson, Providence .	W 10
Nov.	19—Enrique Felipi, New York	W 10
Dec.	21—Johnny Flynn, Rochester ..	KO by 6

TB	KO	WD	WF	D	LD	LF	KOBY	ND	NC
99	36	46	0	3	10	0	3	1	0

LEN HARVEY

(Leonard Austin Harvey)

Born, July 11, 1907, Stoke Climsland, Cornwall, England, Weight, 132-184 lbs. Height, 6 ft. Managed by Dan Sullivan.

1920

Jan.	2—Young King, Plymouth	W 6
Jan.	16—Young Fern, Plymouth	L 6
Apr.	9—Stanley's Nipper, Plymouth	W 6
July	30—Kid Roberts, Plymouth	W 6
Aug.	6—Young Mac, Plymouth	KO 1
Sept.	17—Young Paul, Plymouth	D 6

1921

Feb.	4—Young Jinks, Plymouth	W 6
Mar.	18—Young Jinks, Plymouth	W 6
Apr.	15—Young Jinks, Plymouth	W 8
May	6—Young Jinks, Plymouth	W 6
June	17—Young Richards, Plymouth	KO 1
June	24—Young Jinks, Plymouth	W 6
Sept.	9—Callicott's Nipper, Plymouth	W 6
Nov.	25—Johnny Cotter, Plymouth	W 6

513

1922

Feb.	4—Young O'Neill, Plymouth	KO 2
Mar.	17—Johnny Cotter, Plymouth	KO 3
Mar.	31—Bill Williams, Plymouth	KO 3
June	30—Young Callicott, Plymouth	L 8
Sept.	29—Young Callicott, Plymouth	W 8
Nov.	17—Jack Palmer, Plymouth	W 8

1923

Jan.	2—Bill Lewis, London	W 10
Apr.	27—Young Callicott, Plymouth	D 8
June	22—Fred Bicknell, Plymouth	W 8
July	28—Young Jinks, Plymouth	W 6
Sept.	21—George (Kid) Socks, Plymouth	W 15
Oct.	22—Pop Humphries, London	W 15
Nov.	30—Bill Riley, Plymouth	W 15

1924

Feb.	11—Pop Humphries, London	W 20
Mar.	10—Matt George, London	KO 3
Apr.	12—Bill Riley, London	W 15
Apr.	24—Bill Davies, London	W 15
May	17—Young Clancy, London	W 15
June	2—Ernie Jarvis, London	W 15
June	21—Young Fred Welsh, London	W 15
July	3—Wal Jordan, London	KO 1
July	17—Albert Hicks, London	W 15
Aug.	11—Billy Streets, London	W 12
Sept.	1—Tim Rowley, London	KO 2
Sept.	20—Bert Saunders, London	W 12
Oct.	4—Young Dando, London	D 15
Oct.	20—Young Dando, London	KO 4
Dec.	8—Sid Cannon, London	W 12

1925

Jan.	1—Seaman Harrod, London	KO 5
Jan.	26—Harry Kent, London	KO 4
Feb.	19—Laurie Guard, London	KO 5
Mar.	30—Walter Maloney, London	KO 1
Apr.	18—Johnny Thomas, London	KO 1
Apr.	30—Karel Veldt, London	W 15
May	14—Paul Leukemanns, London	W 15
June	13—Peter Bianchi, London	KO 6
June	22—Fred Bullions, London	KO 10
July	2—Terry Donlan, London	KO 2
July	20—Paul Leukemanns, London	W 15
Aug	22—Harry Gent, London	KO 2
Sept.	2—Bill Handley, Plymouth	KO 8
Sept.	26—Glyn Davies, London	KO 2
Oct.	29—Henri Dupont, London	KO 2
Nov.	19—Edouard Baudry, London	W 15

1926

Jan.	4—Alf Mancini, London	D 20
Feb.	2—Billy Bird, London	KO 7
Mar.	1—Johnny Sullivan, London	L 20
Apr.	29—Harry Mason, London	D 20
	(For British Welterweight Title)	
June	14—Billy Mattick, London	KO 7
July	4—Nol Steenhorst, London	KO 15
Sept.	13—Johnny Brown, London	D 20
Nov.	23—Nol Steenhorst, London	W 15
Dec.	13—Andrew Newton, London	KO 8

1927

Jan.	3—Len Johnson, London	L 20
Mar.	14—Maurice Prunier, London	W 15
Apr.	4—Joe Bloomfield, London	WF 12
Apr.	25—Joe Rolfe, London	KO 10
June	5—Piet Brand, London	WF 6
July	7—Emile Egrel, London	KO 13
Aug.	11—Charles Screve, London	KO 2
Sept.	1—Billy Farmer, London	KO 2
Sept.	22—Primo Ubaldo, London	KO 2
Oct.	16—Piet Brand, London	W 14
Oct.	31—Jack Etienne, London	KO 13
Dec.	12—Marcel Thil, London	W 15

1928

Jan.	19—Kid Nitram, London	WF 14
Mar.	5—Antoine Forr, London	KO 7
Apr.	24—Auguste Lengagne, London	KO 10
July	30—Emile Egrel, London	W 15
Sept.	2—George West, London	WF 4
Oct.	1—Auguste Lengagne, London	KO 9
Oct.	29—Johnny Sullivan, London	KO 6
Dec.	3—Leo Frick, London	KO 2

Dec.	17—Antoine Dubois, Birmingham	KO 1

1929

Feb.	21—Frank Moody, London	KO 6
May	16—Alex Ireland, London	KO 7
	(Won British Middleweight Title)	
Oct.	21—Jack Hood, London	W 15
	(Retained British Middleweight Title)	
Dec.	18—Jack Hood, London	D 15
	(Retained British Middleweight Title)	

1930

Mar.	24—Francis Stevens, London	KO 3
May	22—Steve McCall, London	KO 9
	(Retained British Middleweight Title)	
June	15—Charlie McDonald, London	KO 2
July	6—Henri Vandevever, London	KO 1
Sept.	29—Dave Shade, London	W 15
Dec.	14—George Slack, Leeds	W 12

1931

Jan.	9—Vince Dundee, New York	L 12
Jan.	13—Vince Dundee, New York	L 12
Mar.	20—Ben Jeby, New York	L 12
June	1—Rene Devos, London	KO 1
June	22—Jack Hood, London	W 15
	(Retained British Middleweight Title)	
July	1—Jerry Daley, Bristol	KO 3
Nov.	30—Fred Shaw, Manchester	KO 3

1932

Jan.	17—George Slack, London	W 15
Feb.	8—Jack Casey, Newcastle	W 15
Mar.	21—Jock McAvoy, Manchester	W 15
	(Retained British Middleweight Title)	
May	11—Len Johnson, London	W 15
	(Retained British Middleweight Title)	
July	4—Marcel Thil, London	L 15
	(For World Middleweight Title)	
Nov.	14—Theo Sass, Bradford	KO 1
Nov.	21—Seaman Harvey, Leicester	W 10
Dec.	2—Glen Moody, Plymouth	KO 6
Dec.	12—Jack Casey, Newcastle	W 15
	(Retained British Middleweight Title)	

1933

Mar.	13—Eddie Phillips, London	D 12
Apr.	10—Jock McAvoy, Manchester	L 15
	(Lost British Middleweight Title)	
June	12—Eddie Phillips, London	W 15
	(Won Vacant British Light Heavyweight Title)	
Oct.	16—Carmelo Candel, Paris	KO 5
Nov.	30—Jack Petersen, London	W 15
	(Won British Heavyweight Title)	

1934

Feb.	8—Larry Gains, London	W 15
	(Won British Empire Heavyweight Title)	
Apr.	12—Jimmy Tarante, London	WF 5
June	4—Jack Petersen, London	KO by 12
	(Lost British and Empire Heavyweight Titles)	
Nov.	26—Walter Neusel, London	D 12

1935

Apr.	29—Marcel Lauriot, London	W 10
Oct.	26—Eddie Phillips, Plymouth	W 15

1936

Jan.	29—Jack Petersen, London	L 15
	(For British and Empire Heavyweight Titles)	
Nov.	9—John Henry Lewis, London	L 15
	(For World Light Heavyweight Title)	

1937

Sept.	15—Manuel Abrew, Glasgow	KO 15

1938

Apr.	7—Jock McAvoy, London	W 15
	(Regained British Light Heavyweight Title)	
Dec.	1—Eddie Phillips, London	WF 4
	(Regained Vacant British Heavyweight Title)	

1939

Mar.	16—Larry Gains, London	KO 13
	(Regained Vacant British Empire Heavyweight Title)	
July	10—Jock McAvoy, London	W 15
	(Retained British Light Heavyweight Title)	
	(Won Vacant British Empire Light Heavyweight Title)	
	(Won Vacant British World Light Heavyweight Title)	

1940

(Inactive)

514

1941
Dec. 22—George Davis, London .... Exh. 2
Dec. 22—Corp. Hobson, London .... Exh. 2
1942
June 20—Freddie Mills, London .... KO by 2
(Lost British and Empire Light Heavyweight Titles)
(Lost British World Light Heavyweight Title)
Nov. 22—Relinquished British and Empire
heavyweight titles and announced retirement.

TB	KO	WD	WF	D	LD	LF	KO BY	ND	NC
133	51	54	6	9	11	0	2	0	0

Died, November 28, 1976, London, England.

BILLY CONN
(The Pittsburgh Kid)
Born, October 8, 1917, Pittsburgh, Pa.
Nationality, Irish-American. Heavyweight. Managed by Johnny Ray.
1935
—Dick Woodwer, Fairmont,
W. Va. .... L 4
—John Lewis, Charleston ..... KO 3
—Paddy Gray, Pittsburgh ..... W 4
—Bob Dorman, Clarksburg,
West Va. .... W 6
—Johnny Birek, Pittsburgh .. W 6
—Stan Nagey, Wheeling, W. Va. . W 4
Apr. 8—George Schley, Pittsburgh ... KO 6
Apr. 25—Ralph Gizzy, Pittsburgh ..... L 4
June 3—Ray Eberle, Pittsburgh ..... W 6
June 10—Ralph Gizzy, Pittsburgh .... L 6
July 9—Teddy Movan, Pittsburgh .... L 6
July 29—Ray Eberle, Pittsburgh ..... W 4
Aug. 19—Teddy Movan, Pittsburgh ... L 6
Sept. 9—Georgie Leggins, Pittsburgh .. W 4
Oct. 7—Johnny Yurcini, Johnstn., Pa. . W 6
Oct. 14—Teddy Movan, Pittsburgh ... D 6
Nov. 18—Steve Walters, Pittsburgh ..... W 6
1936
Jan. —Johnny Yurcini, Wash., Pa. ... W 6
Jan. 27—Johnny Yurcini, Pittsburgh .. KO 4
Feb. 3—Louis Kid Cook, Pittsburgh ... W 6
Feb. 17—Louis Kid Cook, Pittsburgh ... W 8
Mar. 16—Steve Nickleash, Pittsburgh ... W 6
Apr. 13—Steve Nickleash, Pittsburgh ... W 6
Apr. 27—General Burrows, Pittsburgh .. W 6
May 19—Dick Ambrose, Pittsburgh ... W 6
May 27—Honeyboy Jones, Pittsburgh .. W 8
June 3—Honeyboy Jones, Pittsburgh .. W 10
June 15—General Burrows, Pittsburgh .. W 8
July 30—Teddy Movan, Pittsburgh .... W 8
Aug. 10—Teddy Movan, Pittsburgh .... W 8
Sept. 8—Honeyboy Jones, Pittsburgh .. W 10
Sept. 21—Roscoe Manning, Pittsburgh ..KO 5
Oct. 19—Charlie Weise, Pittsburgh ..... W 10
Oct. 22—Ralph Chong, Pittsburgh .... W 10
Dec. 2—Jimmy Brown, Pittsburgh ...KO 9
Dec. 28—Fritzie Zivic, Pittsburgh ..... W 10
1937
Mar. 11—Babe Risko, Pittsburgh ...... W 10
May 3—Vince Dundee, Pittsburgh .... W 10
May 27—Oscar Rankins, Pittsburgh ... W 10
June 30—Teddy Yarosz, Pittsburgh .... W 12
Aug. 13—Young Corbett, San Francisco L 10
Sept. 30—Teddy Yarosz, Pittsburgh .... W 15
Nov. 8—Young Corbett, Pittsburgh ... W 10
Dec. 16—Solly Krieger, Pittsburgh ..... L 12
1938
Jan. 24—Honeyboy Jones, Pittsburgh .. W 12
Apr. 4—Domenic Ceccarelli, Pittsburgh W 10
May 10—Eric Seelig, Pittsburgh ...... W 10
July 25—Teddy Yarosz, Pittsburgh .... L 12
Sept. 14—Ray Actis, San Francisco ..KO 8
Oct. 27—Honeyboy Jones, Pittsburgh .. W 10
Nov. 28—Solly Krieger, Pittsburgh ..... W 12
1939
Jan. 6—Fred Apostoli, N. Y. C. ...... W 10
Feb. 10—Fred Apostoli, N. Y. C. ...... W 15
May 12—Solly Krieger, N. Y. C. ...... W 12
July 13—Melio Bettina, N. Y. C. ...... W 15
(Won New York State Light-heavyweight
Championship)
Aug. 14—Gus Dorazio, Philadelphia ...KO 8
Sept. 25—Melio Bettina, Pittsburgh .... W 15
(Title)
Nov. 17 Gus Lesnevich, N. Y. C. ..... W 15
Title)

1940
Jan. 10—Henry Cooper, N. Y. C. ...... W 12
June 5—Gus Lesnevich, Detroit ...... W 15
(Title)
Gave up his light heavyweight crown to
compete as a heavyweight.
Sept. 6—Bob Pastor, N. Y. C. .... KO 13
Oct. 18—Al McCoy, Boston .... W 10
Nov. 29—Lee Savold, N. Y. C. .... W 12
1941
Feb. 27—Ira Hughes, Clarksburg, W. Va.KO 4
Mar. 6—Dan Hassett, Wash., D. C. ... KO 5
Apr. 4—Gunnar Barlund, Chicago ...KO 8
May 26—Buddy Knox, Pittsburgh ....KO 8
June 18—Joe Louis, N. Y. C. ..... KO by 13
(For Heavyweight title)
1942
Jan. 12—Henry Cooper, Toledo ...... W 12
Jan. 28—James D. Turner, St. Louis ... W 10
Feb. 13—Tony Zale, N. Y. C. .... W 12
In U. S. Army.
1944
Exhibition bouts for the Service Men
Overseas, in European Theatre of Operations.
1945
Oct. 29—Bearcat Jones, Cleveland ... Exh. 3
Nov. 7—Bearcat Jones, Kansas City . Exh. 3
1946
June 19—Joe Louis, N. Y. C. ..... KO by 8
(For Heavyweight title)
1948
Nov. 15—Mike O'Dowd, Macon, Ga. ..KO 9
Nov. 25—Jackie Lyons, Dallas .... KO 9
Dec. 10—Joe Louis, Chicago .... Exh. 6

TB	KO	WD	WF	D	LD	LF	KOBY	ND	NC
74	14	49	0	1	8	0	2	0	0

Elected to Hall of Fame in 1965

ANTON CHRISTOFORIDIS
Born, Messina, Greece, May 26, 1918.
Nationality, Greek. Light Heavyweight. Height,
5 ft. 10 in. Managed by Lew Burston and Eddie
Mead.
1934
Knockouts: Taddei, 4; Korenyi, 2; Al
Mankini, 5; Jinie Sala, 7. Won: Thouvenin, 6;
Reis, 10; Blaise, 6; Hallart, 6; Damaguez, 10.
Draw: Jancellene.
1935
Mar. 6—Garcia Lluch, Paris .... W 10
Apr. 6—Georges Noche, Montlucon ... W 10
May 5—Paul Jeancenella, Paris ...... W 6
July —Jany Ambreski, Athens, Greece W 10
Aug. 6—Assane Diouf, Paris .... W 10
Aug. 20—Georges Noche, Paris .... W 10
Sept. 3—Kid Tunero, Paris .... D 10
Sept. 20—Vilda Jaks, Paris .... L 10
Oct. 15—Marcel Foulon, Paris .... KO 6
Oct. 28—Julien Faes, Paris .... W 10
Nov. 22—Vilda Jaks, Paris .... W 10
Dec. 9—Kid Janas, Paris .... W 10
1936
Jan. 6—Kid Tunero, Paris .... L 10
Feb. 7—Carmelo Candel, Paris ...... L 10
Mar. 6—Adrien Anneet, Paris .... W 10
Apr. 2—Vilda Jaks, Paris .... W 12
Apr. 19—Carmelo Candel, Marseille ...KO 8
May 2—Kid Janas, Algiers .... L 10
Oct. 2—Carmelo Candel, Oran ...... W 10
Nov. 5—Edouard Tenet, Paris .... L 10
Dec. 7—Mario Casadel, Paris .... WF 10
1937
Jan. 18—Edouard Tenet, Paris .... D 10
Feb. 4—Kid Janas, Paris .... W 10
Mar. 1—Martinez Alfara, Paris ...... D 10
Apr. 3—Martinez Alfara, Paris ...... D 10
June 13—Kid Tunero, Chantilly ...... L 10
Aug. 8—Kid Janas, Algiers .... W 10
Aug. 22—Martinez Alfara, Oran ...... D 10
Oct. 30—Tokulesco, Athens .... KO 1
Nov. 8—Costa Vassis, Athens .... W 15
1938
Jan. 14—Gustav Eder, Berlin .... W 12
May 6—Gustav Eder, Berlin .... D 12
May 23—Bep Van Klaveren, Rotterdam L 10
Nov. 14—Bep Van Klaveren, Rotterdam W 15
1939
Jan. 10—Edouard Tenet, Paris .... L 15
Apr. 5—Lou Brouillard, Paris .... W 10
May 12—Solly Krieger, N. Y. C. ...... W 12

1940

Jan.	5—Willie Pavlovich, N. Y. C.	W	8
Mar.	29—Frank Zamoris, N. Y. C.	W	6
Apr.	5—George Burnette, Detroit	W	8
June	5—Jimmy Burns, Chicago	KO	5
July	9—Joey Sutka, Detroit	W	10
Aug.	21—Tony Bruno, Chicago	W	10
Oct.	22—Jimmy Reeves, Cleveland	KO	2
Nov.	18—Jimmy Bivins, Cleveland	L	10
Dec.	2—Jimmy Bivins, Cleveland	W	10

1941

Jan.	13—Melio Bettina, Cleveland	W	15
	(Won vacant N.B.A. Light Heavyweight title)		
Apr.	7—Italo Colonello, Baltimore	KO	5
Apr.	30—Johnny Romero, St. Louis	KO	2
May	22—Gus Lesnevich, N. Y. C.	L	15
	(Lost Light Heavyweight title)		
Dec.	1—Ceferino Garcia, Cleveland	W	10

1942

Jan.	2—George Burnette, Detroit	W	10
Jan.	12—Ezzard Charles, Cincinnati	KO by	3
Apr.	17—Jimmy Reeves, Cleveland	W	10
Apr.	29—Paulie Mahoney, Buffalo	KO	9
May	20—Johnny Colan, Chicago	W	10
June	22—Johnny Colan, Cleveland	W	10
July	27—Mose Brown, Pittsburgh	W	10
Aug.	10—Nate Bolden, Chicago	D	10

1943

Feb.	23—Jimmy Bivins, Cleveland	L	15
Apr.	21—Lloyd Marshall, Cleveland	L	10
	In U. S. Navy.		

1946

July	8—Joe Lynch, Cleveland	KO	3
Aug.	19—Augie Fleishauer, Cleveland	KO	7
Nov.	22—Steve Belloise, Detroit	KO by	10

1947

Feb.	18—Anton Raadik, Chicago	KO by	8

TB	KO	WD	WF	D	LD	LF	KOBY	ND	NC
75	14	37	1	8	12	0	3	0	0

GUS LESNEVICH

Born, Feb. 22, 1915, Cliffside park, N. J. Nationality, Russian-American. Light-heavyweight. Height, 5 ft. 9 in. Managed by Joe Vella.

1934

Golden Gloves Inter-City Champion

May	5—Justin Hoffman, Brooklyn	KO	2
May	19—Sid Cohen, Brooklyn	KO	3
May	29—Jimmy Calabrese, Ft. Lee	KO	1
June	9—Willie Klein, Brooklyn	W	6
June	16—Roy Frisco, Brooklyn	W	8
July	23—Tony Kalb, Jersey City	KO	2
Sept.	13—Nicky Williams, Teterboro, N. J.	W	6
Sept.	22—Charlie Weisse, Brooklyn	W	6
Oct.	3—Mark Hough, Brooklyn	W	6
Nov.	3—Tom Chester, Brooklyn	W	6
Nov.	24—Jackie Aldare, Brooklyn	L	6
Dec.	8—San Willardon, Brooklyn	W	6
Dec.	29—Jackie Aldare, Brooklyn	W	8

1935

Jan.	12—Bucky Lawless, Brooklyn	KO	2
Feb.	2—Jackie Aldare, Brooklyn	W	8
Mar.	2—John Anderson, Brooklyn	W	8
Mar.	22—John Anderson, N. Y.	D	8
Apr.	12—Mark Hough, Brooklyn	W	8
May	2—Charley Weise, Brooklyn	W	8
May	25—Tony Celli, Brooklyn	W	8
Dec.	17—Butch Lynch, Newark	W	10

1936

Feb.	4—Eddie Kid Whalen, N. J.	KO	5
Mar.	16—Frankie Caris, Newark	D	10
Apr.	13—Frankie Caris, Newark	W	10
May	12—Sammy Christian, Los Angeles	W	6
May	30—Lou Rogers, Hollywood	KO	1
Aug.	21—Ray Actis, Hollywood	W	10
Oct.	9—Carmen Barth, Hollywood	W	10
Oct.	23—Marty Simmons, Hollywood	D	10
Nov.	4—Young Stubley, San Francisco	W	9
Nov.	17—Freddie Steele, Los Ang.	KO by	2

1937

Feb.	20—Tony Celli, N. Y.	W	8
Mar.	12—Young Corbett, San Fran.	KO by	5
June	22—Young Stuhley, Los Angeles	W	10
Aug.	24—Attilio Sabatino, San Francisco	W	10
Sept.	3—Alabama Kid, San Francisco	W	10

Oct.	5—Allan Matthews, Seattle	D	10
Nov.	19—Herbie Katz, N. Y.	W	10

1938

Jan.	7—Joey Parks, St. Louis	D	10
Feb.	8—Ben Brown, Miami Beach	W	10
Feb.	24—Jack Kirkland, Miami Beach	KO	1
Mar.	23—Lou Brouillard, N. Y. C.	W	10
June	1—Buddy Ryan, West N. Y.	W	10
June	16—Stanley Hasrato, West N. Y.	KO	1
Oct.	27—Ron Richards, Sydney, Aust.	L	12
Dec.	8—Ambrose Palmer, Sydney, Aust.	W	12

1939

Jan.	19—Alabama Kid, Sydney, Aust.	KO	9
Feb.	2—Bob Olin, Sydney, Aust.	W	12
May	15—Larry Lane, Trenton, N. J.	W	10
June	22—Dave Clark, Nutley, N. J.	KO	1
Nov.	17—Billy Conn, N. Y. C.	L	15
	(For World Light-heavyweight Title)		

1940

Jan.	1—Dave Clark, Cleveland	W	10
June	5—Billy Conn, Detroit	L	15
	(For World Light-heavyweight Title)		
July	22—Wally Sears, Garfield, N. J.	W	10
Sept.	5—Henry Cooper, Garfield, N. J.	KO	5
Nov.	23—Al Delaney, Brooklyn	L	5
Dec.	16—Jack Marshall, Newark	KO	4

Feb.	27—Nathan Mann, Detroit	W	10
May	22—Ant. Christoforidis, N. Y. C.	W	15
	(For N. B. A. Light Heavyweight title)		
Aug.	26—Tami Mauriello, N. Y. C.	W	15
	(Won International recognition as world light-heavyweight champion)		
Nov.	14—Tami Mauriello, N. Y. C.	W	15
	(Title bout)		

1942

Jan.	30—Bob Pastor, N. Y. C.	L	10
Mar.	11—Jimmy Bivins, Cleveland	L	10
	In U. S. Coast Guard.		

1943

Oct.	22—Joe Thomas, Wilmington Exh.	KO	3

1946

Jan.	11—Joe Kahut, Portland	KO	2
Feb.	15—Paul Cros.y, Danbury	Exh.	5
Feb.	22—Lee Oma, N. Y. C.	KO by	6
May	14—Freddie Mills, London	KO	10
	(World Light Heavyweight Title)		
Sept.	17—Bruce Woodcock, London	KO by	8

1947

Feb.	28—Billy Fox, N. Y. C.	KO	10
	(World Light-heavyweight Title)		
May	23—Melio Bettina, N. Y. C.	KO	1
July	30—Tami Mauriello, Brooklyn	W	10
Oct.	31—Tami Mauriello, N. Y. C.	KO	7

1948

Mar.	5—Billy Fox, N. Y. C.	KO	1
	(World Light Heavyweight Title)		
July	26—Freddie Mills, London	L	15
	(Lost World Light Heavyweight Title)		

1949

Mar.	3—Eldridge Eatman, Newark	KO	1
May	23—Joey Maxim, Cincinnati	L	15
	(For vacant American Light Heavyweight Title)		
Aug.	10—Ezzard Charles, New York	KO by	7
	(For World Heavyweight Title)		

TB	KO	WD	WF	D	LD	LF	KOBY	ND	NC
76	21	36	0	5	9	0	5	0	0

Died, February 28, 1964, Cliffside Park, N.J.
Elected to Boxing Hall of Fame, 1973.

FREDDIE MILLS

Born in Parkstone, Dorset, Eng., June 26, 1919. Weight, 175 lbs. Height, 5 feet, 10 in. Managed by Ted Broadribb.

1935

Was a booth fighter.

1936

Mar.	25—Reg Davis, Bournemouth	KO	2
Apr.	20—Stan Nelson, Bournemouth	D	6
May	—F. Lennington, Bournemouth	KO	4
Oct.	14—Jack Scott, Bournemouth	KO	1
Oct.	28—Stan Nelson, Bournemouth	KO	2
Nov.	—George Heskett, Weymouth	D	6
Dec.	9—George Bradby, Bournemouth	KO	1

1937

Jan.	6—Billy Brown, Bournemouth	..KO 1
Jan.	20—Terry Warren, Bournemouth	.KO 2
Feb.	3—Harry Frolic, Bournemouth	.KO 7
Feb.	17—Jack McKnight, Bournemouth	W 12
Mar.	3—Red Pullen, Bournemouth	.... W 12
Mar.	17—Jack McKnight, Bournemouth	W 12
Apr.	14—Jack Alder, Bournemouth	... W 12
Apr.	28—Harry Lister, Bournemouth	... W 12
May	5—Albert Johnson, Bournemouth	W 12
Aug.	14—George Davis, Poole	.... KO by 8
Oct.	8—Harold Kid Anthony, Paignt.	KO 1
Oct.	20—George Davis, Bournemouth	.. L 12
Nov.	3—Billy Fuller, Bournemouth	..KO 7
Nov.	17—Jim Greaves, Bournemouth	.. D 12
Dec.	1—Fred Clements, Bournemouth	KO 6
Dec.	15—Jack Lewis, Bournemouth	.... L 10
Dec.	17—Ginger Dawkins, Paignton	.... D 12

1938

Jan.	5—Ginger Dawkins, Bournem'th.	KO 8
Jan.	19—Jim Greaves, Bournemouth	... W 12
Feb.	2—Billy James, Bournemouth	...KO 2
Feb.	16—Ted Barter, Bournemouth	...KO 6
Mar.	2—Harry Vine, Bournemouth	..KO 9
Mar.	16—Tommy Taylor, Bournemouth	W 12
Mar.	30—Jack Lewis, Bournemouth	.... W 12
Apr.	13—Charley Parkin, Bournemouth	KO 3
Apr.	27—Charley Parkin, Bournemouth	. W 12
Aug.	1—Moe Moss, Bournemouth	...KO 5
Oct.	7—Fred Clements, Portsmouth	.KO 6
Nov.	9—Seaman Long, Bournemouth	.KO 3
Nov.	14—Tom Curran, Brighton	.... KO 10
Nov.	23—Yorkie Bentley, Bournemouth	KO 3
Dec.	7—Butcher Gascoigne, Bo'nem'th.	W 12
Dec.	14—Dave McCleave, Bournemouth	L 12

1939

Jan.	4—Yorkie Bentley, Bournemouth	KO 1
Jan.	18—Paul Schaeffer, Bournemouth	.W 10
Feb.	1—Johnny Blake, Bournemouth	KO 6
Feb.	20—Butcher Gascoigne, Yarmouth	L 12
Mar.	1—Eddie Maguire, Bournemouth	.W 10
Mar.	13—Nat Franks, Plymouth	.... D 12
Apr.	12—Elfryn Morris, Bournemouth	.. L 10
Apr.	26—Charley Parkin, Bournemouth	KO 1
June	14—Ginger Sadd, Bournemouth	... L 10
May	3—Dave McCleave, Bournemouth	KO 1
July	21—Charley Parkin, Plymouth	...KO 1
Oct.	28—Dave McCleave, Southampton	KO 3
Nov.	7—Eddie Maguire, Southampton	. L 10
Nov.	27—Eddie Maguire, Southampton	. D 10
Dec.	26—Elfryn Morris, Bournemouth	.KO 4

1940

Mar.	17—Jim Barry, Coventry	.... W 10
Apr.	10—Ginger Sadd, Eastbourne	..... W 10
Apr.	18—Stafford Barton, Walthamstow	KO 7
May	22—Ben Valentine, Bournemouth	KO 3
Aug.	8—Jock McAvoy, Liverpool	..... W 10
Sept.	7—Ernie Simmons, Newcastle	..KO 6

1941

May	26—Ginger Sadd, Leicester	..... KO 9
May	31—Trevor Burt, Pontypool	..... KO 1
June	6—Jack Hyams, Liverpool	....KO 4
June	30—Jack Powell, Reading	..... KO 1
Aug.	5—Tom Reddington, Leicester	... W 10
Sept.	1—Jack Hyams, Leicester	...... L 3
Sept.	29—Tommy Martin, London	.... KO 5
Nov.	3—Jim Wilde, London	.... KO 3
Nov.	28—Tom Reddington, Manchester	. L 10
Dec.	8—Jack London, London	.... W 10

1942

Jan.	26—Tom Reddington, London	..KO 9
Feb.	23—Jock McAvoy, London	.....KO 1
June	20—Len Harvey, London	.......KO 2

(Won the British Empire Light
Heavyweight title)

Oct.	23—Al Robinson, Manchester	...KO 6

1943

May	22—Al Robinson, Leeds	.... KO 2

1944

Feb.	16—Bert Gilroy, London	.... KO 8
May	25—Al Delaney, London	.... KO 5
Sept.	15—Jack London, Manchester	.... L 15

(For British Empire Heavyweight title)

1945

Feb.	7—Ken Shaw, London	.... KO 7

1946

May	14—Gus Lesnevich, London	.. KO by 10

(World Light Heavyweight title)

June	4—Bruce Woodcock, London	.... L 12
Aug.	13—John Nilsson, Brighton	.....KO 5
Nov.	5—Joe Baksi, London	..... KO by 6

1947

Jan.	20—Willi Quentemeier, London	.HO 2
Feb.	17—Enrico Bertola, London	....KO 5

Apr.	29—Nick Wolmarans, Johannesburg	
	....	KO 5
June	3—Lloyd Marshall, London	. KO by 5
Sept.	8—Pol Goffaux, Harringay	.....KO 4

(For vacant European light-heavy
title)

Nov.	28—Stephane Olek, Manchester	... W 10

1948

Feb.	17—Paco Bueno, Harringay	.....KO 2

(For European Light Heavy Title)

Apr.	20—Ken Shaw, London	........KO 1
July	26—Gus Lesnevich, London	...... W 15

(Won World Light Heavyweight title)

Nov.	6—Johnny Ralph, Johannesburg	KO 8

1949

June	2—Bruce Woodcock, London	KO by 14

(For European Heavy Title)

1950

Jan.	24—Joey Maxim, London	... KO by 10

(Lost world light-heavyweight title)

Retired to engage in television and later
opened a night club.

TB	KO	WD	WF	D	LD	LF	KOBY	ND	NC
96	52	21	0	6	11	0	6	0	0

Died from gunshot wound on July 25,
1965 in London.

JOEY MAXIM

(Guiseppe Antonio Berardinelli)
Born, March 28, 1922, Cleveland, Ohio.
Nationality, Italian-American. Light Heavy-
weight. Height, 6 ft. 1 in. Managed by Jack
Kearns.

1941

Jan.	13—Bob Perry, Cleveland	.... W 4
Jan.	27—Frank McBride, Chicago	..... W 8
Feb.	17—Orlando Trotter, Chicago	..... L 8
Apr.	29—Bob Berry, Cleveland	.... W 6
July	11—Tony Paoli, Cleveland	...... W 10
July	28—Johnny Trotter, Chicago	..... W 8
Sept.	13—Lee Oma, Youngstown, Ohio	. W 8
Sept.	15—Nate Bolden, Chicago	...... W 10
Oct.	6—Bill Peterson, Chicago	...... W 10
Oct.	27—Oliver Shanks, Chicago	...KO 5
Dec.	1—Clarence Red Burman, Cleve.	. W 10

1942

Jan.	16—Booker Beckwith, Chicago	.. L 10
Mar.	11—Herbie Katz, Cleveland	....KO 6
Mar.	23—Lou Brooks, Baltimore	..... W 10
Apr.	20—Frank Green, Chicago	......KO 2
May	11—Charles Roth, Chicago	.......LF 2
June	1—Charles Roth, Chicago	......KO 4
June	22—Jimmy Bivins, Cleveland	... L 10
July	10—Lou Brooks, Wilmington	..... W 10
July	27—Curtis Sheppard, Pittsburgh	.. W 10
Aug.	10—Altus Allen, Chicago	.... L 10
Aug.	27—Jack Marshall, Chicago	...KO 8
Sept.	22—Shelton Bell, Pittsburgh	.... W 10
Oct.	5—Hubert Hood, Chicago	...... W 10
Oct.	13—Larry Lane, Akron	.... W 10
Oct.	27—Ezzard Charles, Pittsburgh	.. L 10
Dec.	1—Ezzard Charles, Cleveland	.... L 10

1943

Jan.	18—Clarence Brown, Chicago	.... W 10
Feb.	15—Clarence Brown, Chicago	.... W 10
Mar.	10—Curtis Sheppard, Cleve.	... KO by 1
Mar.	31—Curtis Sheppard, Cleveland	... W 10
Apr.	26—Al Jordan, Chicago	.... W 10
Aug.	9—Nate Bolden, Chicago	...... W 10
Oct.	29—Buddy Scott, Chicago	...... W 10
Dec.	1—Claudio Villar, Cleveland	....KO 6

In U. S. Army.
(Physical Instructor, Army Air Force)
Won 14 out of 15 service bouts.

1944

Jan.	31—Georgie Parks, Washington	... W 10
Apr.	28—John (Buddy) Walker, Detroit	. W 10
May	29—Bob Garner, Chicago	...... W 10
June	26—Frank Androff, Chicago	.... W 10
July	27—Lloyd Marshall, Cleveland	... L 10
Dec.	19—Johnny Flynn, Cleveland	.... L 10

1945

Feb.	2—Johnny Flanagan, Chicago	... W 8
Apr.	16—Clarence Brown, Detroit	..... W 10
Nov.	26—Cleo Everett, Detroit	.... W 10

1946

Mar.	4—Howard Williams, Detroit	.... W 10
Mar.	11—John Thomas, N. Y. C.	...... L 10
Mar.	27—Ralph De John, Buffalo	....KO 1

517

Apr. 1—Buddy Walker, Baltimore .... W 10
Apr. 9—Phil Muscato, Buffalo .... L 10
May 7—Charley Eagle, Buffalo ...... D 10
May 14—Phil Muscato, Buffalo ...... W 12
Aug. 2—Phil Muscato, Rochester ..... W 10
Aug. 14—Henry Cooper, Chicago ..... W 10
Aug. 28—Jersey Joe Walcott, Camden .. W 10
Oct. 10—Clarence Jones, Akron ...... W 10
Oct. 16—Bearcat Jones, Toledo ...... KO 5
Nov. 12—Jim Ritchie, St. Louis .... D 10
Dec. 3—Jimmy Webb, Houston ..... KO 6
Dec. 12—Alvelez, El Paso .... W 10
Dec. 17—Jack Marshall, Houston ...... W 10

1947

Jan. 6—Jersey Joe Walcott, Phila. .... L 10
Jan. 28—Marty Clark, Miami .... KO 7
May 12—Charlie Roth, Louisville .... KO 4
June 23—Jersey Joe Walcott, Los Angeles L 10
Sept. 8—Clarence Jones, Wheeling ... KO 5
Sept. 17—John Thomas, Cleveland ..... W 10
Nov. 12—Bob Foxworth, Chicago ..... W 10
Dec. 8—Billy Thompson, Philadelphia .. W 10

1948

Jan. 9—Olle Tandberg, N. Y. C. ...... W 10
Feb. 2—Bob Sikes, Little Rock ...... W 10
Feb. 13—Tony Bosnich, San Francisco . W 10
Mar. 22—Pat Valentino, San Francisco . D 10
Apr. 27—Louis Berlier, Houston ...... W 10
May 7—Francisco de la Cruz, El Paso . W 10
May 27—Roy Hawkins, Tacoma ..... W 10
June 7—Pat Valentino, San Francisco . D 10
June 22—Joe Kahut, Portland, Ore. .... W 10
June 29—Bill Peterson, Seattle .... W 10
Sept. 28—Bill Peterson, Portland, Ore. .. W 10
Oct. 19—Joe Kahut, Portland, Ore. .... L 15
Nov. 12—Bob Satterfield, Chicago ..... W 10
Dec. 7—Jimmy Bivins, Cleveland ..... W 10

1949

Feb. 28—Ezzard Charles, Cincinnati ... L 15
May 23—Gus Lesnevich, Cincinnati ... W 15
    (For vacant American Light
    Heavyweight Title)
Oct. 25—Joe Kahut, Cincinnati ...... KO 5
Nov. 30—Pat McCafferty, Wichita .... KO 4
Dec. 9—Bill Petersen, Grand Rapids .. W 10

1950

Jan. 24—Freddie Mills, London ...... KO 10
    Won light heavyweight title)
Apr. 19—Joe Dawson, Omaha .... KO 2
Apr. 27—Jack Marshall, Dallas ...... Exh. 4
May 12—Bill Petersen, Memphis ..... KO 6
Sept. 25—Johnny Swanson, Hunt'gton . KO 3
Oct. 10—Bill Petersen, Salt Lake City .. W 10
Nov. 22—Big Boy Brown, Moline, Ill. .... W 10
Dec. 11—Dave Whitlock, San Francisco KO 4

1951

Jan. 27—Hubert Hood, Indianapolis .. KO 3
May 30—Ezzard Charles, Chicago ..... L 15
    (heavyweight title bout)
Aug. 22—Bob Murphy, New York .... W 15
    (Light heavyweight title bout)
Dec. 12—Ezzard Charles, San Francisco . L 12

1952

Mar. 6—Ted Lowry, St. Paul .... W 10
June 25—Ray Robinson, New York ... KO 14
    (Light Heavyweight Title)
Dec. 17—Archie Moore, St. Louis .... L 15
    (Lost Light Heavyweight Title)

1953

Mar. 4—Danny Nardico, Miami ...... W 10
June 24—Archie Moore, Ogden ...... L 15
    (For World Light Heavyweight Title)

1954

Jan. 27—Archie Moore, Miami .... L 15
    (For World Light Heavyweight Title)
June 7—Floyd Patterson, Brooklyn ... W 8
Nov. 24—Paul Andrews, Chicago ..... W 10

1955

Apr. 13—Bobo Olson, San Francisco .. L 10
June 28—Willie Pastrano, New Orleans .. L 10

1956

Sept. 29—Edgardo Romero, Vancouver . W 10

1957

Jan. 25—Eddie Machen, Miami Beach .. L 10
May 3—Eddie Machen, Louisville .... L 10
June 18—Bobo Olson, Portland, Ore. ... L 10

1958

Apr. 11—Heinz Neuhaus, Stuttgart .... L 10
Apr. 27—Mino Bozzano, Milan ...... L 10
May 17—Ulli Ritter, Mannheim ...... L 10

518

1959

Announced Retirement.

TB	KO	WD	WF	D	LD	LF	KOBY	ND	NC
115	21	61	0	4	27	1	1	0	0

Elected to Boxing Hall of Fame, 1975.

ARCHIE MOORE
(Archibald Lee Wright)
(The Old Mongoose)

Born, December 13, 1913, Benoit, Mississippi.
Weight, 147-192 lbs. Height, 5 ft. 11 in. Managed by Kid
Bandy, George Wilsman, Cal Thompson, Felix Thurman,
Jack Richardson Jimmy Johnston, Charley Johnston,
and Jack Kearns.

1936

Jan. 31—Poco Kid, Hot Springs ...... KO 2
Feb. 7—Dale Richards, Poplar Bluffs . KO 1
Feb. 18—Ray Halford, St. Louis ..... KO 3
Feb. 20—Willie Harper, St. Louis ..... KO 3
Feb. 21—Courtland Sheppard, St. Louis L 6
    —Kneibert Davidson .... KO 2
    —Ray Brewster .... KO 3
    —Billy Simms .... KO 2
    —Johnny Leggs .... KO 1
Apr. 15—Peter Urban, Cleveland .... KO 6
Apr. 16—Frankie Nelson, Cleveland .... L 6
May 4—Tiger Brown, St. Louis ..... L 6
May 18—Thurman Martin, St. Louis ... W 5
    —Ferman Burton .... KO 1
    —Billy Simms .... KO 1
July 14—Murray Allen, Quincy, Ill. ... KO 6
    —Julius Kemp .... KO 3
    —Four H. Posey .... KO 6
Oct. 9—Sammy Jackson, St. Louis ... W 6
    —Dick Putnam .... KO 3
Dec. 8—Sammy Jackson, St. Louis ... D 6
    —Sammy Christian, St. Louis . KO 6

1937

Jan. 5—Dynamite Payne, St. Louis ... KO 1
Jan. 18—Johnny Davis, Quincy, Ill. .... KO 3
Feb. 2—Joe Huff, St. Louis .... KO 2
    —Murray Allen, Keokuk, Ia. .. KO 2
Apr. 9—Charley Dawson, Indianapolis KO 5
Apr. 23—Karl Martin, Indianapolis ... KO 1
    —Frank Hatfield .... KO 1
    —Al Dublinsky .... KO 1
Aug. 19—Deacon Logan, St. Louis .... KO 3
Sept. 9—Sammy Slaughter, Indianapolis W 10
Nov. 16—Sammy Christian, St. Louis ... W 5
    —Sammy Jackson .... KO 8

1938

Jan. 7—Carl Lautenschlager, St. Louis ... KO 2
May 20—Jimmy Brent, San Diego .... KO 1
May 27—Ray Vargas, San Diego .... KO 3
June 24—Johnny Romero, San Diego .... L 10
July 22—Johnny Sykes, San Diego .... KO 1
Aug. 5—Lorenzo Pedro, San Diego .... W 10
Sept. 2—Johnny Romero, San Diego .... KO 8
Sept. 16—Frank Rowsey, San Diego .... KO 3
Sept. 27—Tom Henry, Los Angeles .... KO 4
    —Bobby Yannes .... KO 2
Nov. 22—Ray Lyle, St. Louis .... KO 2
Dec. 8—"Irish" Bob Turner, St. Louis .... KO 2

1939

Jan. 20—Jack Moran, St. Louis .... KO 1
Mar. 2—Domenic Ceccarelli, St. Louis ..... KO 1
Mar. 16—Marty Simmons, St. Louis .... W 10
Apr. 20—Teddy Yarosz, St. Louis .... L 10
July 21—Jack Coggins, San Diego .... NC 8
Sept. 1—Jack Coggins, San Diego .... W 10
Sept. 22—Bobby Seaman, San Diego .... KO 7
Dec. 7—Honeyboy Jones, St. Louis .... W 10
Dec. 29—Shorty Hogue, San Diego .... L 6

1940

Mar. 30—Jack McNamee, Melbourne .... KO 4
Apr. 18—Ron Richards, Sydney .... KO 10
May 9—Atilio Sabatino, Sydney .... KO 5
May 12—Joe Delaney, Adelaide .... KO 7
June 2—Frank Lindsay, Tasmania .... KO 4
June 27—Fred Henneberry, Sydney .... KO 7
July 11—Ron Richards, Sydney .... W 12
Oct. 18—Pancho Ramirez, San Diego ..... KO 5

<table>
<tr><td>

1941

Jan.	17—Clay Rowan, San Diego	KO	1
Jan.	31—Shorty Hogue, San Diego	L	10
Feb.	21—Eddie Booker, San Diego	D	10
	—Bobbie Birch, Shreveport	KO by	5

1942

Jan	28—Bobby Britton, Phoenix	KO	3
Feb.	27—Guero Martinez, San Diego	KO	2
Mar.	17—Jimmy Casino, Oakland	KO	5
Oct.	30—Shorty Hogue, San Diego	KO	2
Nov.	6—Tabby Romero, San Diego	KO	2
Nov.	27—Jack Chase, San Diego	W	10
Dec.	11—Eddie Booker, San Diego	D	12

1943

May	8—Jack Chase, San Diego	W	15
	(Won California Middleweight Title)		
July	22—Big Boy Hogue, San Diego	KO	5
July	28—Eddie Cerda, San Diego	KO	3
Aug.	2—Jack Chase, San Francisco	L	15
	(Lost California Middleweight Title)		
Aug.	16—Aaron (Tiger) Wade, San Francisco	L	10
Nov.	5—Kid Hermosillo, San Diego	KO	5
Nov.	26—Jack Chase, Hollywood	W	10

1944

Jan.	7—Amado Rodriguez, San Diego	KO	1
Jan.	21—Eddie Booker, Hollywood	KO by	8
Mar.	24—Roman Starr, Hollywood	KO	2
Apr.	21—Charley Burley, Hollywood	L	10
May	19—Kenny LaSalle, San Diego	W	10
Aug.	11—Louie Mays, San Diego	KO	3
Aug.	18—Jimmy Hayden, San Diego	KO	5
Sept.	1—Battling Monroe, San Diego	KO	6
Dec.	18—Nate Bolden, New York	W	10

1945

Jan.	11—Joey Jones, Boston	KO	1
Jan.	29—Bob Jacobs, New York	KO	9
Feb.	12—Nap Mitchell, Boston	KO	6
Apr.	2—Nate Bolden, Baltimore	KO	10
Apr.	23—Teddy Randolph, Baltimore	KO	9
May	21—Lloyd Marshall, Baltimore	W	10
June	18—George Kochan, Baltimore	KO	6
June	26—Lloyd Marshall, Cleveland	KO	10
Aug.	22—Jimmy Bivins, Cleveland	KO by	6
Sept.	17—Cocoa Kid, Baltimore	KO	8
Oct.	22—Holman Williams, Baltimore	L	10
Nov.	12—Odell Riley, Detroit	KO	6
Nov.	26—Holman Williams, Baltimore	KO	11
Dec.	13—Colion Chaney, St. Louis	KO	5

1946

Jan.	28—Curtis Sheppard, Baltimore	W	12
Feb.	5—Georgie Parks, Washington, D.C.	KO	1
May	2—Verne Escoe, Orange, N.J.	KO	7
May	20—Ezzard Charles, Pittsburgh	L	10
Aug.	19—Buddy Walker, Baltimore	KO	4
Sept.	9—Shamus O'Brien, Baltimore	KO	2
Oct.	23—Billy Smith, Oakland	D	12
Nov.	6—Jack Chase, Oakland	D	10

1947

Mar.	18—Jack Chase, Los Angeles	KO	9
Apr.	11—Rusty Payne, San Diego	W	10
May	5—Ezzard Charles, Cincinnati	L	10
June	16—Curtis Sheppard, Washington, D.C.	W	10
July	14—Bert Lytell, Baltimore	W	10
July	30—Bobby Zander, Oakland	W	12
Sept.	8—Jimmy Bivins, Baltimore	KO	9
Nov.	10—George Fitch, Baltimore	KO	6

1948

Jan.	13—Ezzard Charles, Cleveland	KO by	8
Apr.	12—Dusty Wilkerson, Baltimore	KO	7
Apr.	19—Doc Williams, Newark	KO	7
May	5—Billy Smith, Cincinnati	W	10
June	2—Leonard Morrow, Oakland	KO by	1
June	28—Jimmy Bivins, Baltimore	W	10
Aug.	2—Ted Lowry, Baltimore	W	10
Sept.	20—Billy Smith, Baltimore	KO	4
Oct.	15—Henry Hall, New Orleans	L	10
Nov.	1—Lloyd Gibson, Washington, D.C. ...	LF	4
Nov.	15—Henry Hall, Baltimore	W	10
Dec.	6—Bob Amos, Washington, D.C.	W	10
Dec.	27—Charley Williams, Baltimore	KO	7

</td><td>

1949

Jan.	10—Alabama Kid, Toledo	KO	4
Jan.	31—Bob Satterfield, Toledo	KO	3
Mar.	4—Alabama Kid, Columbus	KO	3
Mar.	23—Dusty Wilkerson, Philadelphia ..	KO	6
Apr.	11—Jimmy Bivins, Toledo	KO	8
Apr.	26—Harold Johnson, Philadelphia	W	10
June	13—Clinton Bacon, Indianapolis	LF	6
June	27—Bob Sikes, Indianapolis	KO	3
July	29—Esco Greenwood, North Adams ...	KO	2
Oct.	4—Bob Amos, Toledo	W	10
Oct.	24—Phil Muscato, Toledo	KO	6
Dec.	6—Doc Williams, Hartford	KO	8
Dec.	13—Leonard Morrow, Toledo	KO	10

1950

Jan.	31—Bert Lytell, Toledo	W	10
July	31—Vernon Williams, Chicago	KO	2

1951

Jan.	2—Billy Smith, Portland	KO	8
Jan.	28—John Thomas, Panama City	KO	1
Feb.	21—Jimmy Bivins, New York	KO	9
Mar.	13—Abel Cestac, Toledo	W	10
Apr.	11—Herman Harris, Flint	KO	4
May	14—Art Henri, Baltimore	KO	4
June	9—Abel Cestac, Buenos Aires	KO	10
June	23—Karel Sys, Buenos Aires	D	10
July	8—Alberto Lovell, Buenos Aires	KO	1
July	15—Vicente Quiroz, Montevideo	KO	6
July	26—Victor Carabajal, Cordoba	KO	3
July	28—Americo Capitanelli, Tucuman ...	KO	3
Aug.	5—Rafael Miranda, Argentine	KO	4
Aug.	17—Alfredo Lagay, Bahia Blanca	KO	3
Sept.	5—Embrell Davison, Detroit	KO	1
Sept.	24—Harold Johnson, Philadelphia	W	10
Oct.	29—Chubby Wright, St. Louis	KO	7
Dec.	10—Harold Johnson, Milwaukee	L	10

1952

Jan.	29—Harold Johnson, Toledo	W	10
Feb.	27—Jimmy Slade, St. Louis	W	10
May	19—Bob Dunlap, San Francisco	KO	6
June	26—Clarence Henry, Baltimore	W	10
July	25—Clint Bacon, Denver	KO	4
Dec.	17—Joey Maxim, St. Louis	W	15
	(Won World Light Heavyweight Title)		

1953

Jan.	27—Toxie Hall, Toledo	KO	4
Feb.	16—Leonard Dugan, San Francisco ...	KO	8
Mar.	3—Sonny Andrews, Sacramento	KO	5
Mar.	11—Nino Valdes, St. Louis	W	10
Mar.	17—Al Spaulding, Spokane	KO	3
Mar.	30—Frank Buford, San Diego	KO	9
June	24—Joey Maxim, Ogden, Utah	W	15
	(Retained World Light Heavyweight Title)		
Aug.	22—Reinaldo Ansaloni, Buenos Aires	KO	4
Sept.	12—Dogomar Martinez, Buenos Aires ..	W	10

1954

Jan.	27—Joey Maxim, Miami	W	15
	(Retained World Light Heavyweight Title)		
Mar.	9—Bob Baker, Miami Beach	KO	9
June	7—Bert Whitehurst, New York	KO	6
Aug.	11—Harold Johnson New York	KO	14
	(Retained World Light Heavyweight Title)		

1955

May	2—Nino Valdes, Las Vegas	W	15
June	22—Bobo Olson, New York	KO	3
	(Retained World Light Heavyweight Title)		
Sept.	21—Rocky Marciano, New York ...	KO by	9
	(For World Heavyweight Title)		

1956

Feb.	2—Dale Hall, Fresno, Calif.	Exh.	4
Feb.	20—Howard King, San Francisco	W	10
Feb.	27—Bob Dunlap, San Diego	KO	1
Mar.	17—Frankie Daniels, Hollywood	W	10
Mar.	27—Howard King, Sacramento	W	10
Apr.	10—Willie Bean, Richmond, Calif.	KO	5
Apr.	16—George Parmentier, Seattle	KO	4
Apr.	26—Sonny Andrews, Edmonton	KO	4
Apr.	30—Gene Thompson, Tucson	KO	3
June	5—Yolande Pompey, London	KO	10
	(Retained World Light Heavyweight Title)		

</td></tr>
</table>

July   25—James J. Parker, Toronto .... KO   9
Sept.   8—Roy Shire, Ogden, Utah .... KO   3
Nov.   30—Floyd Patterson, Chicago ...... KO by   5
         (For Vacant World Heavyweight Title)
1957
May   1—Hans Kalbfell, Essen, Germany .... W   10
June   2—Alain Cherville, Stuttgart .... KO   6
Sept.   20—Tony Anthony, Los Angeles ...... KO   7
         (Retained World Light Heavyweight Title)
Oct.   31—Bob Mitchell, Vancouver .... KO   5
Nov.   5—Eddie Cotton, Seattle .... W   10
Nov.   29—Roger Rischer, Portland .... KO   4
1958
Jan.   18—Luis Ignacio, Sao Paulo .... W   10
Feb.   1—Julio Neves, Rio de Janeiro ...... KO   3
Mar.   4—Bert Whitehurst, San Bernardino KO   10
Mar.   10—Bob Albright, Vancouver .... KO   7
May   2—Willi Besmanoff, Louisville .... W   10
May   17—Howard King, San Diego .... W   10
May   26—Charlie Norkus, San Francisco .... W   10
June   9—Howard King, Sacramento .... W   10
Aug.   4—Howard King, Reno, Nevada ...... D   10
Dec.   10—Yvon Durelle, Montreal .... KO   11
         (Retained World Light Heavyweight Title)
1959
Feb.   5—Eddie Cotton, Victoria, B.C. ..... Exh.   5
Mar.   9—Sterling Davis, Odessa, Texas .... KO   3
Aug.   12—Yvon Durelle, Montreal .... KO   3
         (Retained World Light Heavyweight Title)
1960
May   25—Willi Besmanoff, Indianapolis .... KO   10
Sept.   13—George Abinet, Dallas .... KO   4
Oct.   25—NBA withdrew recognition as world light
         heavyweight champion from Moore.
Oct.   29—Giulio Rinaldi, Rome, Italy L   10
Nov.   28—Buddy Turman, Dallas .... W   10
1961
Mar.   25—Buddy Turman, Manila .... W   10
May   8—Dave Furch, Tucson .... Exh.   4
May   12—Cliff Gray, Nogales, Ariz. .... KO   4
June   10—Giulio Rinaldi, New York .... W   15
         (Retained World Light Heavyweight Title)
Oct.   23—Pete Rademacher, Baltimore ..... KO   6
1962
Feb.   10—NYSAC and EBU withdrew recognition as
         world light heavyweight champion from Moore.
Mar.   30—Alejandro Lavorante, Los Angeles KO   10
May   7—Howard King, Tijuana .... KO   1
May   28—Willie Pastrano, Los Angeles .... D   10
Nov.   15—Cassius Clay, Los Angeles ..... KO by   4
1963
Mar.   15—Mike DiBiase, Phoenix .... KO   3
1964
         (Inactive)
1965
Aug.   27—Nap Mitchell, Michigan City Exh. KO   3

TB   KO WD WF   D   LD LF KO BY ND NC
231 143 53   0   8   16   2   8   0   1
Elected to Boxing Hall of Fame, 1966.

HAROLD JOHNSON
Born, Aug. 9, 1928, Manyunk, Pa. Height.
5 ft. 10 in.
1946
        —Joe Riley, Wilmington .... KO   2
        —Charley Lester, Wilmington ...... KO   2
        —Jack Simon, Allentown .... KO   4
Oct.   25—Randy Ingram, Philadelphia ..... KO   4
1947
Jan.   10—Frank Lowry, Philadelphia .. KO   2
Jan.   24—Chappie Manning, Reading ... W   6
Feb.   10—Jimmy Holden, Allentown .. KO   4
Feb.   17—Joe Van Loan, Philadelphia .. KO   2
Mar.   10—Tony Gillo, Philadelphia ..... W   6
Apr.   28—Leon Szymurski, Phila. .... KO   3
May   26—Fred Lester, Philadelphia .. KO   8
July   8—Tommy Ruth, Philadelphia .. KO   6
Aug.   4—Al Pinel, Philadelphia .... W   6
Oct.   6—Eddie Beazley, Philadelphia . KO   1

520

Nov.   6—Jimmy Moore, Atlantic City . KO   5
Nov.   24—Herbie Katz, Philadelphia ... KO   1
Dec.   11—Kid Wolfe, Atlantic City ..... W   8
1948
Mar.   1—Kenny Harris, Philadelphia ... W   8
Mar.   29—Kenny Harris, Philadelphia ... W   10
May   13—Vernon Williams, Atlantic City W   8
Sept.   28—Augustino Guedes, Phila. ... KO   3
Nov.   9—Jim Holden, Allentown ...... W   8
Dec.   14—Willie Brown, Philadelphia .. KO   7
1949
Feb.   23—Arturo Godoy, Philadelphia .. W   10
Apr.   26—Archie Moore, Philadelphia ... L   10
June   16—Henry Hall, Milwaukee ...... W   10
July   25—Henry Hall, Milwaukee ...... W   10
Oct.   26—Jimmy Bivins, Philadelphia .. W   10
Dec.   7—Bert Lytell, Dayton .... W   10
1950
Feb.   8—Joe Walcott, Philadelphia KO by   3
Dec.   18—Harry Daniels, Philadelphia .. KO   2
1951
Jan.   22—Dusty Wilkerson, Phila. ..... KO   4
Feb.   9—Chuck Hunter, New York .... W   8
June   18—Elkins Brothers, Philadelphia KO   10
July   23—Chubby Wright, Philadelphia .. W   10
Sept.   24—Archie Moore, Philadelphia ... L   10
Dec.   10—Archie Moore, Philadelphia .. W   10
1952
Jan.   29—Archie Moore, Toledo L   10
Mar.   17—Clarence Henry, Phila. .... W   10
Aug.   6—Bob Satterfield, Chicago L   10
Sept.   16—Leonard Morrow, Toledo ... KO   3
Oct.   6—Bob Satterfield, Phila. .... KO   2
Nov.   24—Nino Valdes, Brooklyn ...... W   10
1953
Jan.   16—Jimmy Slade, New York ..... W   10
Mar.   21—Bill Gilliam, Toledo .... W   10
May   11—Toxie Hall, Miami .... W   10
Sept.   8—Ezzard Charles, Philadelphia .. W   10
Nov.   7—Henry Hall, Milwaukee ...... W   10
Nov.   19—Chubby Wright, Hershey ..... W   10
1954
Jan.   29—Jimmy Slade, New York ..... W   10
Feb.   15—Charlie (Doc) Williams,
         Miami .... KO   8
Mar.   17—Paul Andrews, Chicago ...... W   10
Aug.   11—Archie Moore, New York KO by   14
         (World Light Heavyweight Title)
Oct.   8—Billy Smith, Philadelphia . KO by   2
Dec.   7—Julio Mederos, Miami Beach .. W   10
Dec.   22—Marty Marshall, Detroit ..... W   10
1955
Feb.   11—Paul Andrews, New York ... KO   6
May   6—Julio Mederos,
         Philadelphia .... KO by   2
1956
Dec.   8—Bert Whitehurst, Portland .... W   10
1957
Mar.   12—Bob Satterfield, Miami Beach . W   10
May   31—Clarence Hinnant, New York KO   1
Sept.   20—Wayne Bethea, Philadelphia .. W   10
Dec.   17—Sid Peaks, Toledo .... KO   5
1958
Jan.   17—Bert Whitehurst, Syracuse .... W   10
Apr.   15—Oliver Wilson, Hartford ..... KO   2
Dec.   3—Howard King, Chicago ...... W   10
Dec.   15—Rudy Watkins, Philadelphia . KO   6
1969
Aug.   4—Johnny Yorke, Pittsfield .... KO   6
Nov.   11—Sonny Ray, Chicago .... KO   10
1960
May   4—Clarence Floyd, Philadelphia .. W   10
1961
Feb.   7—Jesse Bowdry, Miami Beach . KO   9
         (Won vacant N.B.A. Light Heavyweight
         title)
Apr.   24—Von Clay, Philadelphia ..... KO   2
         (title bout)
July   1—Eddie Machen, Atlantic City .. W   10
Aug.   29—Eddie Cotton, Seattle .... W   15
         (title bout)
1962
May   12—Doug Jones, Philadelphia .... W   15
         (Won vacant World Lightheavyweight
         Title)
June   23—Gustav Scholz, Berlin .... W   15
         (Title Bout)
Mar.   19—Tommy Merrill, Scranton ... KO   9
June   1—Willie Pastrano, Las Vegas ... L   15
         (Lost World Light Heavyweight
         Championship)
Dec.   6—Henry Hank, Philadelphia .... W   10

1964
Apr. 20—Hank Casey, Santa Monica ..KO 8
1965
Inactive
1966
Jan. 7—Johnny Persol, New York .... L 10
Dec. 6—Pekka Kokkonen, Vienna .... W 10
1967
May 1—Herschel Jacobs, New Orleans . W 10
Aug. 7—Eddie Jones, New Orleans .... W 10
1968
Feb. 3—Lothar Stengel, Frankfurt .... W 10
June 11—Johnny Alford, Miami Beach . W 10
Johnson announced his retirement
1969-1970
Retired
1971
Mar. 30—Herschel Jacobs, N. Y. .... KO by 3

TB	KO	WD	WF	D	LD	LF	KO BY	ND	NC
87	32	44	0	0	6	0	5	0	0

WILLIE PASTRANO
(Wilfred Raleigh Pastrano)
Miami, Fla., Light Heavyweight
Born, November 27, 1935
Height, 5 ft., 11¾ Ins.
1951
Sept. 10—Domingo Rivera, New Orleans W 4
Sept. 17—Frank Speed, New Orleans ... W 4
Oct. 1—Jimmy Connino, New Orleans . W 4
Oct. 22—Domingo Rivera, New Orleans W 4
1952
Apr. 1—Alvin Boudreaux, New Orleans W 4
Apr. 21—Alvin Pellegrini, New Orl. .... D 4
July 1—Buzz Brown, Miami Beach ..KO 2
July 8—John Chaney, Miami Beach ...W 6
July 22—Al McCoy, Miami Beach ....KO 2
July 28—Jim Carter, Pensacola ......KO 4
Aug. 5—Sonny Luciano, Miami Beach . W 8
Aug. 19—Sonny Luciano, Miami Beach . W 8
Sept. 8—Johnny Capitano, New Orleans W 6
Oct. 6—Alvin Pellegrini, New Orleans . L 6
Oct. 14—Lonnie Rylant, New Orleans . KO 3
Nov. 17—Alvin Pellegrini, New Orleans . W 6
Nov. 24—Alvin Boudreaux, New Orl. ...KO 2
Dec. 15—Al Pelligrini, New Orleans .... D 8
1953
Jan. 26—Alfredo LaGrutta, New Orleans .... W 8
Feb. 24—Emerson Butcher, New Orleans W 8
Mar. 3—Chic Boucher, Miami Beach . KO 3
Mar. 16—Roger Trevino, New Orleans .. W 8
Apr. 6—Chato Hernandez, New Orleans W 8
May 25—Johnny Cesario, New Orleans . L 8
July 14—Del Flanagan, Miami Beach ... L 8
Sept. 22—Elmer Beltz, Miami Beach .... D 10
Oct. 5—Elmer Beltz, New Orleans .... W 8
Nov. 30—Italo Scortichini, New Orleans L 10
1954
Mar. 29—Jimmy Martinez, New Orleans . W 10
Apr. 12—Jacques Royer-Crecy, New Orl. W 10
June 18—Tommy Hatcher, Mobile ....KO 1
Aug. 9—Tommy Bazzano, New OrleansKO 8
Aug. 24—Jimmy Martinez, Miami Beach W 10
Sept. 14—Jackie LaBua, Miami Beach ... W 10
Nov. 23—Bobby Dykes, Miami Beach .. W 10
1955
Mar. 1—Tony Johnson, Miami Beach .. W 10
Mar. 23—Al Andrews, Chicago .... W 10
Apr. 22—Willie Troy, Chicago .... D 10
June 28—Joey Maxim, New Orleans .... W 10
July 27—Chuck Spieser, Chicago ...... W 10
Oct. 3—Paddy Young, New Orleans ... W 10
Nov. 18—Joey Rowan, New York .... W 10
Dec. 19—Rex Layne, New Orleans .... W 10
1956
Jan. 27—Chuck Spieser, Miami Beach .. D 10
Apr. 4—Johnny Arthur, New Orleans . W 10
May 30—Chuck Spieser, New Orleans .. W 10
Aug. 24—Pat McMurtry, Tacoma ...... W 10
Dec. 26—Charlie Norkus, Miami Beach . W 10
1957
Feb. 20—John Holman, Louisville ..... W 10
May 14—Neal Welch, Miami Beach .... W 10
June 11—Roy Harris, Houston .... L 10
Sept. 10—George Peyton, Miami Beach KO 8
Oct. 22—Dick Richardson, London .... W 10
Nov. 27—Willi Besmanoff, Miami Beach . W 10

1958
Feb. 25—Brian London, London ...... W 10
Apr. 21—Joe Bygraves, Leicester ...... W 10
June 15—Franco Cavicchi, Bologna .... W 10
Aug. 25—Tommy Thompson, Columbus .... KO 4
Sept. 30—Brian London, London .. KO by 5
1959
Feb. 24—Joe Erskine, London .... L 10
July 24—Alonzo Johnson, Louisville ... L 10
Aug. 30—Tom Davis, Knoxville ......KO 4
Dec. 7—Charley Pavlis, Tampa .... W 10
1960
Jan. 20—Jerry Luedee, Miami Beach ...W 10
Apr. 9—George Kartalian, Augusta ..KO 6
May 6—Alonzo Johnson, Louisville ...W 10
June 1—Sonny Ray, Chicago .... W 10
Sept. 16—Chic Calderwood, Glasgow ... L 10
Dec. 27—Jesse Bowdry, Miami Beach .. L 10
1961
Aug. 6—Lennart Risberg, Stockholm .. D 12
1962
May 1—Tom McNeeley, Boston ...... W 10
May 28—Archie Moore, Los Angeles .. D 10
June 25—Billy Ryan, New Orleans .... W 10
Sept. 8—Rodolfo Diaz, Miami Beach .. W 10
1963
Feb. 9—Wayne Thornton, New York .. L 10
Mar. 23—Wayne Thornton, New York .. D 10
May 4—Wayne Thornton, Las Vegas .. W 10
June 1—Harold Johnson, Las Vegas ... W 15
(Won World Light Heavyweight Championship)
Aug. 31—Ollie Wilson, Jacksonville ... W 10
Sept. 20—Gregorio Peralta, Miami Beach L 10
Nov. 30—Mike Holt, Johannsburg ..... W 10
1964
Apr. 10—Gregorio Peralta, New Orleans ....KO 6
(Retained World Light Heavyweight Title)
Nov. 30—Terry Downes, Manchester .. KO 11
(Retained World Light Heavyweight Title)
1965
Mar. 30—Jose Torres, New York City .... KO by 9
(Lost Light Heavyweight Title)

TB	KO	WD	WF	D	LD	LF	KOBY	ND	NC
84	14	49	0	8	11	0	2	0	0

EDDIE COTTON
Seattle, Wash. Light Heavyweight
Michigan World Light Heavyweight Champion, 1963-1964
1947
May 3—Bobby Roberts, Seattle ....KO 1
July 18—Billy Corbett, Seattle ....KO 3
Sept. 12—Alex Boode, Seattle ....L 6
1948
Jan. 6—Eddie Halliger, Seattle ....D 6
Feb. 21—Paul Kennedy, Seattle ....W 6
Apr. 6—Joe Albina, Seattle ....W 8
May 4—George Cote, Seattle ....KO 1
June 11—Frankie Gimbel, Butte ....KO 3
June 29—Roy Wouters, Seattle ....KO 5
Aug. 24—Van Holland, Seattle ....KO 3
Oct. 27—Mel Brown, Vancouver..................L 8
Nov. 18—Roy Wouters, Vancouver ....KO 8
1949
Jan. 7—Phil Sampson, Seattle ....KO 6
June 3—Roy Kennedy, Seattle ....KO 3
Oct. 6—Bob Murphy, Seattle ....KO by 6
Dec. 6—John L. Sullivan, Seattle ....KO 1
1950
Mar. 28—Pedro Jiminez, Seattle ....KO 1
Apr. 18—Don Lee, Seattle ....W 10
Sept. 8—Clinton Bacon, Denver ....L 10
1951
Apr. 14—Rusty Payne, Eureka ....L 10
Nov. 15—Joe Kahut, Seattle ....W 10
Dec. 2—Joe Kahut, Vancouver, B.C. ....W 10
Dec. 10—Ron Whittle, Vancouver ....KO 9
1952
Feb. 7—Bobby Wise, Vancouver ....KO 4
Mar. 18—Abel Fernandez, Seattle ....KO 4
Oct. 30—Frankie Crane, Vancouver ....KO 9
Nov. 12—Jimmy Ingram, Tacoma ....KO 2
1953
Feb. 5—Ron Whittle, Tacoma ....KO 8
Mar. 12—Lonnie Malone, Vancouver ....KO 3
July 14—Frankie Daniels, Tacoma ....L 10
Aug. 25—Rusty Payne, Tacoma ....W 10

1954

Mar.	6—Bill Boatsman, Longview	W	10
Mar.	29—Bill Boatsman, Portland	W	10
July	22—Henry Hall, Vancouver	W	10
Nov.	30—Murray Bennett, Seattle	W	8

1955

Jan.	11—Frankie Daniels, Seattle	W disq.	5
Feb.	10—Larry Watson, Seattle	W	8
Feb.	17—Bill Boatsman, Vancouver	KO	6
Mar.	8—Doug Harper, Calgary	KO	5
Apr.	27—Gene Brixon, Calgary	KO	5
June	13—Dave Whitlock, San Francisco	L	10

1956
(Inactive)

1957

May	23—Al Hogan, Vancouver	KO	5
Nov.	5—Archie Moore, Seattle	L	10

1958

Oct.	8—Sonny Ray, Louisville	L	10
Dec.	11—Rogue Maravilla, Boise	W	10

1959

Feb.	2—Archie Moore, Vancouver	Exh.	4
Feb.	5—Archie Moore, Victoria	Exh.	4
Sept.	15—Sixto Rodriguez, Richmond	L	10
Oct.	15—Hank Casey, Spokane	L	10

1960

Jan.	21—George Mahoni, Auckland	W	12
Nov.	—George Mahoni, Auckland	KO	11

1961

Feb.	9—Johnny Halifihi, Auckland	W	12
Feb.	27—Mike Holt, Auckland	W	10
Apr.	12—Rory Calhoun, Seattle	W	10
May	24—Neal Rivers, Bellingham	KO	6
Aug.	29—Harold Johnson, Seattle	L	15

(For NBA Light Heavyweight Title)

1962

May	11—Joey Bowman, Aberdeen	KO	2
June	3—Pekka Kokkonen, Stockholm	W	10
Aug.	17—Pekka Kokkonen, Helsinki	W	10
Oct.	17—Mauro Mina, Lima	L	10
Dec.	5—Von Clay, Seattle	W	10

1963

Jan.	18—Mauro Mina, Lima	L	12
May	29—Honey Peterson, Seattle	KO	3
June	18—Bob McKinney, Bremerton	W	10
June	27—Chic Calderwood, Glasgow	W	10
Oct.	29—Henry Hank, Flint	W	15

(Recognized in Michigan for
World Light Heavyweight Title)

Dec.	11—Don Bale, Bellingham	KO	2

1964

Feb.	21—Johnny Persol, New York	L	10
Mar.	13—Johnny Persol, New York	KO	4
July	3—Wayne Thornton, New York	L	10
Dec.	16—Wayne Thornton, Seattle	KO by	9

1965

May	11—Wayne Thornton, Seattle	L	12
July	30—Piero Del Papa, Pisa	L	10
Aug.	12—Roger Rouse, Butte	D	10
Sept.	30—Andy Kendall, Seattle	KO	10
Oct.	23—Roger Rouse, Butte	KO by	7

1966

Feb.	21—Sipa Fine, Auckland	KO	7
Apr.	21—Emil Umek, Vancouver	W	10
Aug.	15—Jose Torres, Las Vegas	L	15

(World Light Heavyweight Title)

Nov.	3—Roger Rouse, Seattle	L	12
Dec.	13—Charley Hall, Tacoma	KO	1

1967

Jan.	10—Bobby Rascon, Tacoma	KO	5
Mar.	22—Bobby Stininato, Auckland	KO	9
May	8—Bobby Foster, Washington, D.C.	KO by	3
Aug.	2—Ernie Gipson, Anchorage	KO	1

TB	KO	WD	WF	D	LD	LF	KO BY	ND	NC
83	34	23	1	2	19	0	4	0	0

JOSE TORRES
(Jose Luis Torres)
Puerto Rico Light Heavyweight
Born, May 3, 1936, Playa Ponce, Puerto Rico. Member 1956 U.S. Olympic Team. 1958 Inter-City Golden Glove Champion. Height, 5 ft. 10 in.

1958

May	24—Gene Hamilton, Brooklyn	KO	1
June	7—Walter Irby, Brooklyn	W	6
June	21—Joe Salvato, Brooklyn	KO	4
July	5—Wes Lowery, Brooklyn	W	6
Aug.	18—Benny Doyle, Los Angeles	KO	1

Sept.	29—Otis Woodard, New York	KO	5
Oct.	13—Frankie Anslem, New York	KO	9
Nov.	3—Burke Emery, New York	KO	5
Dec.	4—Ike Jenkins, New York	KO	5

1959

Feb.	26—Eddie Wright, New York	KO	5
Mar.	19—Leroy Oliphant, New York	KO	3
Apr.	23—Joe Shaw, New York	KO	5
June	27—Al Andrews, New York	KO	6
Sept.	26—Benny Paret, San Juan	D	10

1960

Jan.	30—Randy Sandy, Elizabeth	W	10
Mar.	15—Tony Dupas, Buffalo	W	10
June	11—Randy Sandy, New York	W	10

1961

Feb.	17—Gene Hamilton, San Juan	KO	4
Apr.	1—Bobby Barnes, Paterson	KO	3
May	23—Bob Young, Boston	KO	5
June	5—Mel Collins, Boston	KO	7
June	27—Ike White, Boston	KO	3
Oct.	31—Georgie Price, Houston	KO	2
Nov.	28—Tony Montano, Houston	KO	4

1962

Apr.	10—Jimmy Watkins, Utica	KO	7
July	27—Duilio Nunez, San Juan	KO	2
Dec.	14—Al Hauser, Boston	KO	3

1963

May	26—Florentino Fernandez, San Juan	KO by	5
Oct.	9—Don Fullmer, Teaneck	W	10

1964

Jan.	3—Jose Gonzalez, New York	W	10
Apr.	21—Walker Simmons, New York	KO	8
May	15—Wilbert McClure, New York	W	10
June	22—Frankie Olivera, New Bedford	KO	5
July	20—Walker Simmons, N. Bedford	KO	6
Sept.	4—Gomeo Brennan, Miami Beach	W	10
Nov.	27—Bobo Olson, New York	KO	1

1965

Mar.	30—Willie Pastrano, New York	KO	9

(Won World Light-Heavyweight Title)

July	31—Tom McNeeley, San Juan	W	10

1966

May	21—Wayne Thornton, Flushing, L.I.	W	15

(Retained World Light Heavyweight Title)

Aug.	15—Eddie Cotton, Las Vegas	W	15

(Retained World Light Heavyweight Title)

Oct.	15—Chic Calderwood, San Juan	KO	2

(Retained World Light Heavyweight Title)

Dec.	16—Dick Tiger, New York	L	15

(Lost World Light Heavyweight Title)

1967

May	16—Dick Tiger, New York	L	15

(World Light-Heavyweight Title)

1968

Apr.	1—Bob Dunlop, Sydney	KO	6

1969

July	14—Charlie Green, New York	KO	2

TB	KO	WD	WF	D	LD	LF	KOBY	ND	NC
45	29	12	0	1	2	0	1	0	0

DICK TIGER
(Dick Ihetu)

Born, August 14, 1929, Amaigbo, Orlu, Nigeria. After brief career as amateur, turned professional in 1952.

1952-1955

In Nigeria: Simon Eme, KO 2; Easy Dynamite, KO 1; Mighty Joe, W 8; Lion Ring, KO 6; Simon Eme, W 8; Koko Kid, W 8. Black Power, W 8; Tommy West, L 10; Bolaji Johnson, W 8. Robert Nuanne, KO 2; Tommy West, W 12. (Nigerian middleweight title); Roy Fargbemy, W 8; Peter Okptra, KO 8; Koko Kid, KO 6; Super Human Power, W 8; John Ama, KO 2.

In England:

Dec.	8, 1955—Alan Dean, Liverpool	L	6

1956

Jan.	27—Gerry McNally, Blackpool	L	8
Mar.	2—Jimmy Lynas, Blackpool	L	8
Mar.	22—George Roe, Liverpool	L	8
May	3—Dennis Rowley, Liverpool	KO	1
May	10—Alan Dean, Liverpool	W	8
May	28—Wally Scott, W. Hartlepool	KO	4
July	2—Jimmy Lynas, W. Hartlepool	W	8
Oct.	18—Alan Dean, Liverpool	L	6
Nov.	9—Alan Dean, Blackpool	W	8

1957

Apr. 29—Johnny Read, London ..... KO 2
May 14—Terry Downes, London ..... KO 5
June 4—Marius Dori, London .... KO 7
July 15—Willie Armstrong,
    W. Hartlepool .... L 8
July 25—Alan Dean, Liverpool .... W 8
Sept. 9—Phil Edwards, Cardiff .... W 10
Oct. 21—Jean-Claude Poisson, Cardiff .. W 10
Nov. 11—Pat McAteer, Cardiff .... D 10
Nov. 29—Paddy Delargy, Birmingham . KO 6

1958

Jan. 13—Jean Ruellet, Hull .... W 8
Feb. 3—Jimmy Lynas, Manchester ... KO 7
Feb. 25—Johnny Read, London ..... KO 6
Mar. 27—Pat McAteer, Liverpool .... KO 9
    (British Empire middleweight title)
May 1—Billy Ellaway, Liverpool .... KO 2
June 24—Spider Webb, London .... L 10
Oct. 14—Yolande Pompey, London ... W 10

1959

Mar. 19—Randy Sandy, Liverpool ..... L 10
May 12—Randy Sandy, London ...... W 10
June 5—Rory Calhoun, New York .... D 10
July 17—Rory Calhoun, Syracuse .... L 10
Sept. 2—Gene Ace Armstrong, Camden W 10
Sept. 30—Joey Giardello, Chicago ..... W 10
Nov. 4—Joey Giardello, Cleveland .... L 10
Dec. 30—Holly Mims, Chicago .... W 10

1960

Feb. 24—Gene Armstrong, Chicago .... W 10
Apr. 1—Victor Zalazar, Boston ...... W 10
June 22—Wilf Greaves, Edmonton ..... L 15
    (Lost British Empire Middleweight Title)
Nov. 30—Wilf Greaves, Edmonton .... KO 9
    (Regained British Empire Middleweight
    Title)

1961

Feb. 18—Gene Armstrong, New York . KO 9
Apr. 15—Spider Webb, New York .... KO 6
May 15—Hank Casey, New Orleans .... W 10
Dec. 16—Bill Pickett, New York ..... W 10

1962

Jan. 20—Florentino Fernandez,
    Miami Beach .... KO 6
Mar. 31—Henry Hank, New York ..... W 10
Oct. 23—Gene Fullmer, San Francisco . W 15
    (Won WBA Middleweight Title)
Nov. 9—Recognized by New York, European
    Boxing Union and British Board
    of Boxing Control as world champion.

1963

Feb. 23—Gene Fullmer, Las Vegas ..... D 15
    (Retained W.B.A. Middleweight Title)
May 7—With Paul Pender's retirement Tiger
    was given world-wide recognition as
    champion.
Aug. 10—Gene Fullmer, Ibadan ...... KO 7
    (World Middleweight Title Bout)
Dec. 7—Joe Giardello, Atlantic City .. L 15
    (Lost World Middleweight Title)

1964

July 31—Joe Gonzalez, New York .... KO 6
Sept. 11—Don Fullmer, Cleveland ..... W 10
Oct. 16—Joe Archer, New York ..... L 10

1965

Mar. 12—Rocky Rivero, New York City KO 6
May 20—Rubin Carter, New York City . W 10
Oct. 21—Joey Giardello, New York ..... W 15
    (Regained World Middleweight Title)

1966

Feb. 18—Peter Muller, Dortmund,
    Germany .... KO 3
Apr. 25—Emile Griffith, New York .... L 15
    (Lost world middleweight title)
Dec. 16—Jose Torres, New York ...... W 15
    (Won World Light Heavyweight Title)

1967

Feb. 5—Abraham Tomica, Port
    Harcourt .... W 10
May 16—Jose Torres, New York ...... W 15
    (Retained World Light-Heavyweight Title)
Nov. 17—Roger Rouse, Las Vegas .... KO 12
    (Retained World Light Heavyweight Title)

1968

May 24—Bob Foster, New York .. KO by 4
    (Lost World Light Heavyweight
    Championship)
Oct. 25—Frank DePaula, New York ... W 10

1969

May 26—Nino Benvenuti, New York ... W 10
Nov. 14—Andy Kendall, New York .... W 10

1970

July 15—Emile Griffith, New York .... L 10

1971

July 19 Retired.
Dec. 14—Died of Cancer in Nigeria.

TB	KO	WD	WF	D	LD	LF	KOBY	ND	NC
81	26	35	0	3	16	0	1	0	0

Elected Hall of Fame 1974

BOB FOSTER

Born, December 15, 1938, Albuquerque, New
Mexico. Weight, 173 lbs. Height, 6 ft. 3 in.

1961

Mar. 27—Duke Williams, Washington, D.C. KO 2
Apr. 3—Clarence Ryan, New York .... W 4
May 8—Billy Johnson, New York .... W 4
June 22—Ray Bryan, Montreal .... KO 2
Aug. 8—Floyd McCoy, Montreal .... W 6
Nov. 22—Ernie Knoxton, Norfolk .... KO 4
Dec. 4—Clarence Floyd, Toronto .... KO 4

1962

May 19—Billy Tisdale, New York .... KO 2
June 27—Bert Whitehurst, New York .... W 8
Oct. 20—Doug Jones, New York .... KO by 8

1963

Feb. 18—Richard Benjamin, Washington ... KO 1
Apr. 29—Curtis Bruce, Washington, D.C. .. KO 4
Nov. 6—Mauro Mina, Lima, Peru .... L 10
Dec. 11—Willi Besmanoff, Norfolk .... KO 3

1964

Feb. 25—Dave Bailey, Miami Beach .... KO 1
May 8—Allen Thomas, Chicago .... KO 1
July 10—Ernest Terrell, New York ..... KO by 7
Nov. 12—Don Quinn, Norfolk .... KO 1
Nov. 23—Norm Letcher, San Francisco ..... KO 1
Dec. 11—Henry Hank, Norfolk .... KO 10

1965

Feb. 15—Roberto Rascon, Albuquerque .... KO 2
Mar. 21—Dave Russell, Norfolk .... KO 6
May 24—Chuck Leslie, New Orleans .... KO 3
July 26—Henry Hank, New Orleans .... W 12
Dec. 6—Zora Folley, New Orleans .... L 10

1966

Dec. 6—Leroy Green, Norfolk .... KO 2

1967

Jan. 16—Jim Robinson, Washington, D.C. .. KO 1
Feb. 27—Andres Selpa, Washington, D.C. .. KO 2
May 8—Eddie Cotton, Washington, D.C. .. KO 3
June 9—Henry Mathews, Roanoke, Va. ... KO 2
Oct. 25—Levan Roundtree, Washington .... KO 8
Nov. 20—Eddie Vick, Providence .... W 10
Dec. 5—Sonny Moore, Washington, D.C. .. KO 2

1968

May 24—Dick Tiger, New York .... KO 4
    (Won World Light Heavyweight Title)
July 29—Charley Polite, West Springfield .. KO 3
Aug. 26—Eddie Vick, Albuquerque .... KO 9
Sept. 9—Roger Rouse, Washington, D.C. ... KO 5

1969

Jan. 22—Frank DePaula, New York .... KO 1
    (Retained World Light Heavyweight Title)
May 24—Andy Kendall, West Springfield .. KO 4
    (Retained World Light Heavyweight Title)
June 19—Levan Roundtree, Atlanta .... KO 4
Nov. 2—Chuck Leslie, New Orleans ...... KO 5

1970

Feb. 24—Bill Hardney, Orlando .... KO 4
Mar. 9—Cookie Wallace, Tampa .... KO 6
Apr. 4—Roger Rouse, Missoula .... KO 4
    (Retained World Light Heavyweight Title)
June 27—Mark Tessman, Baltimore .... KO 10
    (Retained World Light Heavyweight Title)
Nov. 18—Joe Frazier, Detroit .... KO by 2
    (For World Heavyweight Title)

1971

Mar. 2—Hal Carroll, Scranton .... KO 4
    (Retained World Light Heavyweight Title)
Apr. 24—Ray Anderson, Tampa .... W 15
    (Retained World Light Heavyweight Title)

523

Aug.   17—Vernon McIntosh, Miami Beach .. KO   3
Oct.   29—Tommy Hicks, Scranton .... KO   8
       (Retained World Light Heavyweight Title)
Dec.   16—Brian Kelly, Oklahoma City ..... KO   3
       (Retained World Light Heavyweight Title)
1972
Apr.   7—Vicente Rondon, Miami Beach .... KO   2
       (Retained World Light Heavyweight Title)
June   27—Mike Quarry, Las Vegas .... KO   4
       (Retained World Light Heavyweight Title)
Sept. 26—Chris Finnegan, London .... KO 14
       (Retained World Light Heavyweight Title)
Nov.   21—Muhammad Ali, Stateline ..... KO by 8
1973
Aug.   21—Pierre Fourie, Albuquerque .... W 15
       (Retained World Light Heavyweight Title)
Dec.   1—Pierre Fourie, Johannesburg ...... W 15
       (Retained World Light Heavyweight Title)
1974
June   17—Jorge Ahumada, Albuquerque ...... D 15
       (Retained World Light Heavyweight Title)
Sept. 16—Announced retirement.
1975
June   28—Bill Hardney, Santa Fe .... KO   3
1976
May   8—Al Boldon, Missoula .... KO   3
Aug.   28—Harold Carter, Missoula .... W 10
Sept. 25—Al Bolden, Spokane .... KO   6
1977
Sept.   2—Bob Hazelton, Curacao .... KO 10
1978
Feb.   9—Mustapha Wassaja, Copenhagen KO by   5
June   3—Bob Hazelton, Wichita .... KO by   2

TB	KO	WD	WF	D	LD	LF	KO BY	ND	NC
65	46	10	0	1	2	0	6	0	0

VICENTE PAUL RONDON
Born, July 29, 1938, San Jose de Rio, Chico, Venezuela. Weight, 175 lbs.
1965
June   28—Jose Caraballo, Caracas .... KO   3
July   26—Luis Toconis, Caracas .... KO   1
Oct.   29—Pedro Vanegas, Barranquilla ..... KO   4
Nov.   5—Pedro Vanegas, Cartagena .... KO   6
1966
June   25—Marco T. Polanco, Caracas ...... KO   3
Sept. 16—Melville Benuett, Caracas .... KO   2
Nov.   14—Marcos Pirela, Caracas .... KO   2
Dec.   4—Marco T. Polanco, Caracas ...... KO   2
1967
Mar.   20—Danny Machado, Caracas .... KO   3
June   12—Marco T. Polanco, Caracas ...... KO   3
Sept.   9—Tony Smith, San Juan .... KO   3
Oct.   14—Pedro Miranda, San Juan .... KO 10
Nov.   10—Harold Richardson, San Juan ...... D 10
1968
Jan.   12—Bobby Warthem, New York .... L 10
Apr.   19—Jose Gonzalez, New York ..... KO by   8
June   3—Luis Rodriguez, San Juan .... W 10
July   18—Luis Rodriguez, San Juan .... L 10
Sept. 23—Benny Briscoe, San Juan .... W 10
Nov.   3—Juarez de Lima, San Juan .... L 10
Nov.   12—Charlie Jordan, Miami Beach ...... W 10
Nov.   26—Charlie Jordan, Miami Beach ...... W 10
1969
Jan.   26—Benny Briscoe, San Juan ...... KO by   8
Apr.   1—Allen Thomas, Chicago .... W 10
May   3—Jose Garcia, Caracas .... W 12
May   6—Karl Zurheide, Chicago .... W 10
July   5—Eddie Talhami, San Juan .... W 10
Aug.   9—Stan Johnson, San Juan .... NC   7
Oct.   26—Angel Oquendo, San Juan .... KO   6
Nov.   29—Randy Stevens, San Juan .... KO   5
Dec.   6—Avenamar Peralta, Buenos Aires .. W 10
1970
Apr.   —Freddie Williams, San Juan ...... KO   4
May   —Levan Roundtree, San Juan ...... W 10
Aug.   11—Hydra Lacey, Miami Beach ...... KO   2
Oct.   6—Willie Johnson, Miami Beach ..... KO   4
Nov.   8—Roger Rouse, San Juan .... W 10

1971
Feb.   27—Jimmy Dupree, Caracas .... KO   6
       (Won Vacant WBA Light Heavyweight Title)
June   7—Piero Del Papa, Caracas .... KO   1
       (Retained WBA Light Heavyweight Title)
July   11—John Griffin, Valencia .... W 10
Aug.   21—Eddie Jones, Caracas .... W 15
       (Retained WBA Light Heavyweight Title)
Oct.   14—Conny Velensek, Berlin .... W 10
Oct.   26—Gomeo Brennan, Miami Beach ... KO 13
       (Retained WBA Light Heavyweight Title)
Dec.   15—Doyle Baird, Cleveland .... KO   8
       (Retained WBA Light Heavyweight Title)
1972
Apr.   7—Bob Foster, Miami Beach ..... KO by   2
       (For World Light Heavyweight Title)
July   11—Ron Lyle, Denver .... KO by   2
Aug.   26—Earnie Shavers, Canton .... L 10
Dec.   1—Jose Urtain, Madrid .... L 10
1973
Feb.   15—Larry Beilfuss, San Juan .... W 10
Apr.   3—Oliver Wright, Miami Beach ...... W 10
May   19—Len Hutchins, Detroit .... L 10
June   14—Tom Bogs, Oslo .... L 10
Aug.   24—Mike Boswell, Indianapolis .... KO   4
Sept. 10—John Conteh, London .... KO by   9
Nov.   17—Rudiger Schmidtke, Frankfurt ..... L 10
1974
Feb.   19—Rodney Bobick, Miami Beach .. KO by   3
June   6—Jose (King) Roman, Tampa .... KO by   2

TB	KO	WD	WF	D	LD	LF	KO BY	ND	NC
55	22	16	0	1	8	0	7	0	1

JOHN CONTEH
Born, May 27, 1951, Liverpool, England. Weight, 175-185 lbs. Height, 6 ft.
1971
Oct.   18—Okacha Boubekeur, London ...... KO   1
Nov.   8—Pierre Minier, London .... KO   5
Nov.   16—Frank Bullard, London .... KO   5
Nov.   24—Tony Burwell, Nottingham .... W   8
Dec.   7—Emile Okee Griffith, London ..... KO   5
1972
Jan.   25—Wilhelm Jankow, London .... KO   1
Feb.   15—Larry Sykes, London .... KO   1
Mar.   28—Ruben Figueroa, London .... KO   2
Apr.   25—Joe Gholston, London .... KO   6
June   6—Billy Aird, London .... KO   8
July   19—Johnny Mac, Dublin .... KO   2
Sept. 26—Eddie Duncan, London .... L 10
Oct.   18—Ferenc Cristofczak, London ..... KO   1
Oct.   31—Bill Drover, London .... KO   7
Nov.   14—Johnny Hudgins, London .... KO   3
Dec.   5—Sam McGill, London .... KO   9
1973
Jan.   15—Dave Matthews, Nottingham ...... W 10
Feb.   14—Terry Daniels, Las Vegas .... KO   6
Mar.   13—Rudiger Schmidtke, London ..... KO 12
       (Won European Light Heavyweight Title)
May   22—Chris Finnegan, London .... W 15
       (British, Commonwealth and European Titles)
Sept. 10—Vicente Rondon, London .... KO   9
Oct.   23—Baby Boy Rolle, Nottingham ..... W 15
       (Retained Commonwealth Light Heavyweight Title)
Dec.   14—Fred Lewis, Liverpool .... KO   3
1974
Feb.   12—Les Stevens, London .... W 10
Mar.   12—Tom Bogs, London .... KO   6
       (Retained European Light Heavyweight Title)
May   21—Chris Finnegan, London .... KO   6
       (British, Commonwealth and European Titles)
Oct.   1—Jorge Ahumada, London .... W 15
       (Won Vacant WBC Light Heavyweight Title)
1975
Mar.   11—Lonnie Bennet, London .... KO   5
       (Retained WBC Light Heavyweight Title)
Aug.   16—Willie Taylor, Scranton .... W 10
1976
Oct.   9—Yaqui Lopez, Copenhagen .... W 15
       (Retained WBC Light Heavyweight Title)

1977
Mar. 5—Len Hutchins, Liverpool .... KO 3
(Retained WBC Light Heavyweight Title)
May —WBC withdrew recognition as world light
heavyweight champion from Conteh.
1978
Feb. 7—Joe Cokes, Ilslington .... W 10
June 17—Mate Parlov, Belgrade .... L 15
(For WBC Light Heavyweight Title)
Sept. 26—Leo Rodgers, Wembley .... KO 7
1979
Apr. 9—Jesse Burnett, London .... D 10
June 4—Ivy Brown, Liverpool .... W 10
Aug. 18—Matthew Saad Muhammad,
Atlantic City .... L 15
(For WBC Light Heavyweight Title)
1980
Mar. 29—Matthew Saad Muhammad,
Atlantic City .... KO by 4
(For WBC Light Heavyweight Title)
May 31—James Dixon, Liverpool .... KO 5

TB	KO	WD	WF	D	LD	LF	KO BY	ND	NC
39	24	10	0	1	3	0	1	0	0

VICTOR GALINDEZ
Born, November 2, 1948, Vedia, Buenos Aires,
Argentina. Weight, 175 lbs. Height, 5 ft. 10 in.
1969
May 10—Ramon Ruiz, Buenos Aires .... KO 4
June 28—Ruperto Robledo, Buenos Aires ... KO 3
Aug. 16—Adolfo Cejas, Azul .... D 10
1970
Jan. 17—Adolfo Cardozo, Buenos Aires .... KO 5
Mar. 13—Ramon Rocha, Rosario .... KO 9
Apr. 8—Juan Aguilar, Buenos Aires .... L 10
May 9—Ramon Cerrezuela, Lujan .... KO 6
May 20—Alfredo Segura, Buenos Aires ... KO 3
June 24—Juan Aguilar, Buenos Aires .... D 10
July 22—Jorge Ahumada, Buenos Aires .... KO 5
Aug. 14—Juan Aguilar, Mendoza .... NC 1
Sept. 18—Juan Aguilar, Mendoza .... L 10
Nov. 28—Avenamar Peralta, Buenos Aires ... L 12
(For Argentine Light Heavyweight Title)
1971
Jan. 9—Avenamar Peralta, Buenos Aires .. W 10
Apr. 7—Pedro Rimovsky, Buenos Aires ... NC 1
May 24—Jorge Ahumada, Mendoza .... L 10
June 12—Pedro Rimovsky, Buenos Aires ..... D 10
July 31—Jorge Ahumada, Buenos Aires .... KO 9
Sept. 11—Avenamar Peralta, Buenos Aires .. TL 9
Oct. 30—Jorge Ahumada, Buenos Aires .... KO 6
Nov. 20—Juan Aguilar, Buenos Aires .... W 10
Dec. 18—Avenamar Peralta, Buenos Aires ... L 10
1972
Jan. 22—Carlos Santagda, De Julio .... KO 9
May 6—Eddie Jones, Buenos Aires .... W 10
July 22—Juan Aguilar, Buenos Aires .... W 12
(Won Argentine Light Heavyweight Title)
Aug. 18—Adolfo Cardozo, Rosario .... KO 4
Sept. 2—Avenamar Peralta, Buenos Aires .. W 12
(Retained Argentine Light Heavyweight Title)
Oct. 7—Avenamar Peralta, Buenos Aires .. W 12
(Won South American Light Heavyweight Title)
Nov. 10—Oscar Wondryk, Venado Tuerto .. KO 7
Dec. 15—Juan Aguilar, Mendoza .... D 10
1973
Jan. 29—Ruben Gonzalez, Salta .... KO 3
Apr. 4—Juan Aguilar, Buenos Aires .... W 12
May 12—Eddie Owens, Buenos Aires ..... KO 3
July 14—Karl Zurheide, Buenos Aires ..... KO 2
Aug. 10—Juan Aguilar, Tucuman .... KO 6
Sept. 7—Raul Loyola, Buenos Aires .... W 12
(Retained Argentine Light Heavyweight Title)
Nov. 10—Raul Loyola, Buenos Aires .... KO 8
Dec. 15—Eddie Duncan, Buenos Aires ..... KO 2
1974
Feb. 16—Ray Anderson, Balcarce .... KO 2
Apr. 5—Ruben Gonzalez, Rio Cuarto ..... KO 3
June 8—Jose Gonzalez, Buenos Aires .... W 10

1974
July 12—Domingo Silveira, Jujuy .... KO 4
Sept. 1—Domingo Silveira, San Juan ...... KO 5
Sept. 14—Angel Oquendo, Buenos Aires ..... W 10
Oct. 5—Domingo Silveira, Parana .... KO 4
Dec. 7—Len Hutchins, Buenos Aires ..... KO 13
(Won Vacant WBA Light Heavyweight Title)
1975
Feb. 15—John Griffin, Balcarce .... KO 6
Apr. 7—Pierre Fourie, Johannesburg ...... W 15
(Retained WBA Light Heavyweight Title)
May 16—Ray Elson, Las Vegas .... KO 8
June 30—Jorge Ahumada, New York .... W 15
(Retained WBA Light Heavyweight Title)
Sept. 13—Pierre Fourie, Johannesburg ...... W 15
(Retained WBA Light Heavyweight Title)
1976
Mar. 28—Harald Skog, Oslo .... KO 3
(Retained WBA Light Heavyweight Title)
Apr. 8—Jesse Burnett, Oslo .... W 10
May 22—Richie Kates, Johannesburg ...... KO 15
(Retained WBA Light Heavyweight Title)
Aug. 21—Bill Douglas, Buenos Aires .... W 10
Oct. 5—Kosie Smith, Johannesburg .... W 15
(Retained WBA Light Heavyweight Title)
1977
Apr. 6—Guillermo Aguirrezabla, Mendoza KO 4
June 18—Richie Kates, Rome .... W 15
(Retained WBA Light Heavyweight Title)
Sept. 17—Yaqui Lopez, Rome .... W 15
(Retained WBA Light Heavyweight Title)
Nov. 20—Eddie Gregory, Turin .... W 15
(Retained WBA Light Heavyweight Title)
1978
Apr. 8—Ramon Cerrezuela, Buenos Aires .. W 10
May 6—Yaqui Lopez, Lido Di Camaiore .... W 15
(Retained WBA Light Heavyweight Title)
June 16—Antonio Musladino, Mendoza ..... KO 9
July 18—Valdemar Raulino, Buenos Aires KO 9
Aug. 19—Marcos Tosto, General Pico .... KO 6
Sept. 15—Mike Rossman, New Orleans .. KO by 13
(Lost WBA Light Heavyweight Title)
1979
Mar. 10—Roberto Aguilar, San Miguel ..... KO 7
Apr. 14—Mike Rossman, New Orleans ..... KO 10
(Regained WBA Light Heavyweight Title)
Nov. 30—Marvin Johnson, New Orleans KO by 11
(Lost WBA Light Heavyweight Title)
1980
June 14—Jesse Burnett, Anaheim .... L 12

TB	KO	WD	WF	D	LD	LF	KO BY	ND	NC
70	34	21	0	4	7	0	2	0	2

Died, October 26, 1980, De Mayo, Argentina.

MIGUEL ANGEL CUELLO
Born, February 27, 1946, Elortondo, Santa Fe,
Argentina. Weight, 175 lbs. Height, 5 ft. 9 in.
1973
July 25—Ivan Rojas, Venado Tuerto .... KO 2
Aug. 25—Adolfo Cardozo, Buenos Aires .... KO 2
Oct. 20—Carlos Santagada, Venado Tuerto KO 2
Nov. 10—Simeon Gallardo, Buenos Aires ... KO 2
Nov. 24—Juan Aguilar, Buenos Aires .... W 10
Dec. 12—Simeon Gallardo, Salta .... KO 2
1974
Apr. 19—Ivan Rojas, Venado Tuerto .... KO 2
June 7—Luis Colen, San Juan .... KO 1
July 10—Roberto Aguilar, Buenos Aires ... KO 5
Sept. 27—Roberto Aguilar, San Juan .... KO 2
Dec. 11—Guillermo Aguirrezabala.
Buenos Aires .... KO 1
1975
Mar. 7—Raul Loyola, Cordoba .... KO 4
(Won Vacant Argentine Light Heavyweight Title)
June 13—Roberto Aguilar, Venado Tuerto .. KO 3
(Retained Argentine Light Heavyweight Title)
Oct. 10—Ivan Rojas, Rosario .... KO 4
(Retained Argentine Light Heavyweight Title)
Dec. 13—Charles Freeman, Paris .... KO 2

525

1976

Feb.	2—Phil Matthews, Paris	KO	2
Feb.	20—Ray Anderson, Hamburg	KO	6
Apr.	2—Mario Almanzo, Kiel	KO	2
Oct.	1—Wayne Magee, Milan	KO	4
Oct.	28—Kurt Ludecke, Milan	KO	1

1977

May	21—Jesse Burnett, Monte Carlo	KO	9

(Won Vacant WBC Light Heavyweight Title)

1978

Jan.	7—Mate Parlov, Milan	KO by	9

(Lost WBC Light Heavyweight Title)

TB	KO	WD	WF	D	LD	LF	KO BY	ND	NC
22	20	1	0	0	0	0	1	0	0

MATE PARLOV

Born, November 16, 1948, Split, Yugoslavia.
Weight, 175-180 lbs. Height, 6 ft. 2 in. Southpaw.
Managed by Boris Kramarsic.
1972 Olympic Light Heavyweight Gold Medalist

1975

May	31—Dante Lazzari, Abbazia	KO	3
June	20—Robert Amory, Milan	KO	5
July	12—Horst Lang, Arenzano	KO	1
Aug.	22—Jose Galvez, Split	W	8
Sept.	14—Jose Gomez, Pola	W	8
Oct.	7—Johnny Griffin, Azgrebb	KO	5
Oct.	31—Karl Zurheide, Milan	KO	1
Nov.	22—Billy Freeman, Skopje	W	10
Dec.	26—Onelio Grando, Reggio Emilia	W	8

1976

Feb.	6—Macka Foley, Trieste	KO	2
Mar.	6—Senitiki Qata, Alexander	W	10
Mar.	20—Maile Haumona, Melbourne	W	10
May	21—Matt Franklin, Milano	L	8
July	10—Domenico Adinolfi, Belgrade	KO	11

(Won European Light Heavyweight Title)

Sept.	11—Al Bolden, Zagreb	KO	9
Oct.	15—Aldo Traversaro, Milan	W	15

(Retained European Light Heavyweight Title)

Dec.	3—Matt Franklin, Trieste	D	10

1977

Mar.	5—Christian Poncelet, Velenje	W	10
Apr.	29—Francisco Fiol, Morges	W	15

(Retained European Light Heavyweight Title)

July	9—Harald Skog, Basle	W	15

(Retained European Light Heavyweight Title)

Aug.	20—Lalo Kakolewicz, Rijeka	KO	6

1978

Jan.	7—Miguel Angel Cuello, Milan	KO	9

(Won WBC Light Heavyweight Title)

Apr.	28—Tony Greene, Sarajevo	KO	6
June	17—John Conteh, Belgrade	W	15

(Retained WBC Light Heavyweight Title)

Dec.	2—Marvin Johnson, Warsala	KO by	10

(Lost WBC Light Heavyweight Title)

1979

July	28—Joe Maye, Munich	KO	5
Sept.	26—Tony Mundine, Gorizia	W	12
Dec.	8—Marvin Camel, Yugoslavia	D	15

(For Vacant WBC Cruiserweight Title)

1980

Mar.	31—Marvin Camel, Las Vegas	L	15

(For Vacant WBC Cruiserweight Title)

TB	KO	WD	WF	D	LD	LF	KO BY	ND	NC
29	12	12	0	2	2	0	1	0	0

MIKE ROSSMAN

Born, July 1, 1956, Turnersville, N.J. Weight, 175 lbs. Height, 6 ft.

1973

Aug.	10—Stanley Dawson, Atlantic City	KO	2
Sept.	24—Robert Ziegler, Philadelphia	KO	3
Oct.	22—Herman Nance, Philadelphia	KO	1
Oct.	31—Larry Parker, Baltimore	KO	1
Nov.	14—Nat Dixon, Scranton	KO	3
Dec.	8—Lester Camper, Atlantic City	KO	6
Dec.	15—Ed Townsend, Scranton	KO	2

1974

Feb.	9—Maximo Pierret, Scranton	W	6
Feb.	18—Greg Burch, Philadelphia	W	6
Mar.	20—Joey Blair, Scranton	KO	6
Apr.	29—Tyrone Freeman, Philadelphia	W	6
May	29—Walter Riley, Scranton	KO	1
June	17—Ray Hernandez, New York	W	6
July	15—Nat Dixon, Philadelphia	D	8
July	29—Mike Baker, New York	W	8
Sept.	9—Nat Dixon, New York	KO	4
Oct.	25—Mike Morgan, New York	W	8
Nov.	22—John Pinney, New York	KO	5
Dec.	11—Harold Richardson, Scranton	KO	3

1975

Jan.	21—Matt Donovan, Largo	W	10
Feb.	17—Matt Donovan, Philadelphia	W	10
Apr.	29—Dave Adkins, Largo	W	10
May	19—Mike Nixon, Binghamton	L	10
Aug.	1—Mike Nixon, Las Vegas	KO	7
Sept.	30—Mike Quarry, New York	L	10
Dec.	10—Al Styles, Scranton	W	10

1976

Feb.	13—Casey Gacic, Owings Mill	D	10
Mar.	8—Gene Wells, New York	W	10
May	14—Jose Anglada, Weehawken	KO	9
June	12—Tony Licata, New Orleans	L	10
Aug.	6—Steve Smith, Atlantic City	KO	6
Sept.	28—Christy Elliott, New York	KO	3
Nov.	4—Christy Elliott, West Orange	D	10
Dec.	11—Mike Quarry, Las Vegas	W	10

1977

Mar.	2—Ray Anderson, New York	KO	4
May	11—Mike Quarry, New York	KO	6
July	17—Marcel Clay, Miami Beach	KO	1
Sept.	29—Gary Summerhays, New York	W	10

1978

Mar.	2—Yaqui Lopez, New York	KO by	6
May	24—Lonnie Bennett, Philadelphia	KO	2
July	15—Matt Ross, Atlantic City	KO	2
Sept.	15—Victor Galindez, New Orleans	KO	13

(Won WBA Light Heavyweight Title)

Dec.	5—Aldo Traversaro, Philadelphia	KO	6

(Retained WBA Light Heavyweight Title)

1979

Apr.	14—Victor Galindez, New Orleans	KO by	10

(Lost WBA Light Heavyweight Title)

Sept.	18—Ramon Ronquillo, Meadowlands	KO by	6

1980

July	12—Don Addison, Atlantic City	W	10
Sept.	9—Al Bolden, Atlantic City	KO	10
Nov.	13—Luke Capuano, Chicago	W	10

TB	KO	WD	WF	D	LD	LF	KO BY	ND	NC
48	24	15	0	3	3	0	3	0	0

MARVIN JOHNSON

Born, April 12, 1954, Indianapolis, Indiana.
Weight, 175 lbs. Southpaw. Managed by Arnold Weiss.
1972 National Golden Gloves
Light Heavyweight Champion
1972 Olympic Middleweight Bronze Medalist

1973

May	23—Sylvester Wilder, Indianapolis	KO	2
Sept.	17—Al Byrd, Fort Wayne	KO	1
Oct.	30—Slugger Warfield, Ft. Wayne	KO	5

1974

July	17—Ted Paxton, Chicago	KO	2
Nov.	12—Johnny Words, Indianapolis	KO	6
Dec.	11—Jim Adams, Indianapolis	KO	1

1975

Jan.	29—Gary Summerhayes, Indianapolis	W	10
Apr.	17—Paul Cardoza, Indianapolis	KO	4
Nov.	13—Eddie Owens, Indianapolis	KO	3

1976

Apr.	3—Ray Anderson, Indianapolis	KO	6
Apr.	15—Harold Carter, Indianapolis	KO	2
Sept.	14—Wayne Magee, Philadelphia	KO	1
Nov.	30—Vandell Woods, Philadelphia	W	10

1977

Date	Opponent	Result	
Feb.	21—Johnny Townsend, Philadelphia	W	10
Apr.	22—Tom Bethea, Indianapolis	KO	4
July	26—Matthew Franklin, Philadelphia	KO by	12
	(For Vacant NABF Light Heavyweight Title)		
Sept.	28—Johnny Fields, Cleveland	KO	1
Nov.	1—Billy Douglas, Philadelphia	KO	5

1978

Date	Opponent	Result	
Jan.	25—Roberto Reynosa, Indianapolis	KO	1
Apr.	3—Eddie Davis, Indianapolis	KO	7
May	24—Johnny Baldwin, Philadelphia	W	10
June	17—Lotte Mwale, Belgrade	L	8
Sept.	15—Jerry Celestine, New Orleans	W	10
Dec.	2—Mate Parlov, Marsala	KO	10
	(Won WBC Light Heavyweight Title)		

1979

Date	Opponent	Result	
Apr.	22—Matt Franklin, Indianapolis	KO by	8
	(Lost WBC Light Heavyweight Title)		
Sept.	20—Carlos Marks, Indianapolis	W	10
Nov.	30—Victor Galindez, New Orleans	KO	11
	(Won WBA Light Heavyweight Title)		

1980

Date	Opponent	Result	
Mar.	31—Eddie Gregory, Knoxville	KO by	11
	(Lost WBA Light Heavyweight Title)		
Sept.	9—Lee Royster, Atlantic City	KO	4

TB	KO	WD	WF	D	LD	LF	KO BY	ND	NC
29	19	6	0	0	1	0	3	0	0

MATTHEW SAAD MUHAMMAD
(AKA Matthew Franklin)

Born, June 16, 1954, Philadelphia, Pa. Weight, 175 lbs. Height, 5 ft. 11 in.

1974

Date	Opponent	Result	
Jan.	14—Billy Early, Philadelphia	KO	2
Feb.	25—Bele Apolosa, Paris	W	4
Mar.	11—Roy Ingram, Philadelphia	W	4
May	22—Joe Middleton, Philadelphia	KO	5
July	15—Joe Jones, Philadelphia	KO	3
Sept.	10—Lloyd Richardson, Philadelphia	KO	4
Oct.	22—Joe Middleton, Alexandria, Va.	KO	2
Dec.	10—Wayne McGee, Philadelphia	L	6

1975

Date	Opponent	Result	
Feb.	25—Vandell Woods, Philadelphia	KO	6
July	24—Roosevelt Brown, Philadelphia	KO	4
Oct.	21—Wayne McGee, Philadelphia	D	6

1976

Date	Opponent	Result	
Feb.	13—Harold Carter, Baltimore	W	10
May	21—Mate Parlov, Milan	W	8
July	17—Marvin Camel, Stockton	W	10
Sept.	15—Bobby Walker, Scranton	KO	4
Oct.	23—Marvin Camel, Missoula	L	10
Dec.	3—Mate Parlov, Trieste	D	10

1977

Date	Opponent	Result	
Mar.	11—Eddie Gregory, Philadelphia	L	10
Apr.	21—Joe Maye, Wilmington	W	10
June	23—Ed Turner, Philadelphia	KO	6
July	26—Marvin Johnson, Philadelphia	KO	12
	(Won Vacant NABF Light Heavyweight Title)		
Sept.	17—Billy Douglas, Philadelphia	KO	6
	(Retained NABF Light Heavyweight Title)		
Nov.	1—Lee Royster, Philadelphia	W	10

1978

Date	Opponent	Result	
Feb.	10—Richie Kates, Philadelphia	KO	6
	(Retained NABF Light Heavyweight Title)		
June	19—Dale Grant, Philadelphia	KO	5
Aug.	16—Freddie Bright, Newark	KO	8
Oct.	24—Yaqui Lopez, Philadelphia	KO	11
	(Retained NABF Light Heavyweight Title)		

1979

Date	Opponent	Result	
Apr.	22—Marvin Johnson, Indianapolis	KO	8
	(Won WBC Light Heavyweight Title)		
Aug.	18—John Conteh, Atlantic City	W	15
	(Retained WBC Light Heavyweight Title)		

1980

Date	Opponent	Result	
Mar.	29—John Conteh, Atlantic City	KO	4
	(Retained WBC Light Heavyweight Title)		
May	13—Louis Pergaud, Halifax, N.S.	KO	5
	(Retained WBC Light Heavyweight Title)		
July	13—Yaqui Lopez, McAfee, N.J.	KO	14
	(Retained WBC Light Heavyweight Title)		
Nov.	28—Lotte Mwale, San Diego	KO	4
	(Retained WBC Light Heavyweight Title)		

TB	KO	WD	WF	D	LD	LF	KO BY	ND	NC
33	20	8	0	2	3	0	0	0	0

EDDIE MUSTAFA MUHAMMAD
(AKA Eddie Gregory)

Born, April 30, 1952, Brooklyn, New York. Weight, 175 lbs. Height, 6 ft. $\frac{1}{2}$ in. Managed by Ben Muhammad.

1972

Date	Opponent	Result	
Sept.	15—Dave Wyatt, New York	KO	4
Sept.	16—Jose Pagon, Boston	KO	1
Sept.	29—Pete Pagon, New York	KO	3

1973

Date	Opponent	Result	
Feb.	1—Percy Halsey, North Bergen	KO	1
May	17—Billy Wilson, North Bergen	W	6
July	9—Jose Anglada, New York	W	8
Sept.	24—Elwood Townsend, Philadelphia	KO	1
Dec.	3—Radames Cabrera, New York	L	10

1974

Date	Opponent	Result	
Apr.	8—Willie Classen, New York	W	8
May	10—Nessim Cohen, Marseilles	D	10
Aug.	26—Eugene Hart, New York	KO	4
Nov.	25—Mario Rosa, New York	KO	8

1975

Date	Opponent	Result	
Jan.	14—Steve Smith, Philadelphia	KO	4
Apr.	28—Don Cobbs, Philadelphia	KO	6
June	16—Lenny Harden, Philadelphia	KO	10
Aug.	18—Bennie Briscoe, Philadelphia	L	10

1976

Date	Opponent	Result	
Mar.	8—Hildo Silva, New York	KO	7
Apr.	29—D.C. Walker, Kingston, N.Y.	KO	6
June	28—Otis Gordon, New York	KO	4
July	14—Lee Barber, Philadelphia	KO	4
Oct.	1—Jimmy Owens, New York	KO	10
Oct.	29—Frank Davila, New York	KO	2

1977

Date	Opponent	Result	
Jan.	18—John Wilburn, New York	KO	3
Mar.	11—Matthew Franklin, Philadelphia	W	10
Sept.	16—Eddie Phillips, Wilmington	KO	4
Nov.	20—Victor Galindez, Turin	L	15
	(For WBA Light Heavyweight Title)		

1978

Date	Opponent	Result	
Feb.	15—Jesse Burnett, Las Vegas	KO	10
Mar.	22—Bo Soukalo, Mali	W	10
Apr.	14—Nat Gates, Orlando	KO	7
June	2—Ray Elson, Jersey City	KO	2
June	14—Ed Turner, White Plains	KO	4
Aug.	16—Chuck Warfield, Newark	KO	1
Sept.	6—James Dixon, White Plains	KO	1
Oct.	12—James Scott, Rahway	L	12

1979

Date	Opponent	Result	
Jan.	26—Dave Conteh, New York	KO	8
Feb.	26—Pat Cuillo, New York	W	10
July	10—Lee Royster, Atlantic City	KO	5
July	16—Fred Brown, New York	KO	3
Aug.	1—Johnny Wilburn, New York	KO	1
Nov.	28—Kid Samson, Hauppauge	KO	4

1980

Date	Opponent	Result	
Mar.	31—Marvin Johnson, Knoxville	KO	11
	(Won WBA Light Heavyweight Title)		
July	20—Jerry Martin, McAfee, N.J.	KO	10
	(Retained WBA Light Heavyweight Title)		
Nov.	29—Rudi Koopmans, Los Angeles	KO	3
	(Retained WBA Light Heavyweight Title)		

TB	KO	WD	WF	D	LD	LF	KO BY	ND	NC
43	32	6	0	1	4	0	0	0	0

MIDDLEWEIGHTS

JACK (NONPAREIL) DEMPSEY	1884-1891	**CEFERINO GARCIA**	1939-1940
GEORGE LA BLANCHE (CLAIMANT)	*1889*	**KEN OVERLIN**	1940-1941
BOB FITZSIMMONS	1891-1897	*TONY ZALE (NBA)*	*1940-1941*
CHARLES (KID) MC COY	1897-1898	**BILLY SOOSE**	1941
TOMMY RYAN	1898-1907	**TONY ZALE**	1941-1947
STANLEY KETCHEL	1907-1908	**ROCKY GRAZIANO**	1947-1948
BILLY PAPKE	1908	**TONY ZALE**	1948
STANLEY KETCHEL	1908-1910	**MARCEL CERDAN**	1948-1949
CYCLONE JOHNNY THOMPSON	1911	**JAKE LA MOTTA**	1949-1951
FRANK MANTELL (CALIF.)	*1912*	**SUGAR RAY ROBINSON**	1951
BILLY PAPKE	1912-1913	**RANDY TURPIN**	1951
FRANK KLAUS	1913	**SUGAR RAY ROBINSON**	1951-1952
GEORGE CHIP	1913-1914	**CARL (BOBO) OLSON**	1953-1955
AL MC COY	1914-1917	**SUGAR RAY ROBINSON**	1955-1957
JEFF SMITH (AUSTRALIA)	*1914*	**GENE FULLMER**	1957
MICK KING (AUSTRALIA)	*1914*	**SUGAR RAY ROBINSON**	1957
JEFF SMITH (AUSTRALIA)	*1914-1915*	**CARMEN BASILIO**	1957-1958
LES DARCY (AUSTRALIA)	*1915-1917*	**SUGAR RAY ROBINSON**	1958-1960
MIKE O'DOWD	1917-1920	*GENE FULLMER (NBA)*	*1959-1962*
JOHNNY WILSON	1920-1923	**PAUL PENDER**	1960-1961
WM. BRYAN DOWNEY (CLEVELAND)	*1921*	**TERRY DOWNES**	1961-1962
DAVE ROSENBERG (NEW YORK)	*1922*	**PAUL PENDER**	1962-1963
MIKE O'DOWD (NEW YORK)	*1922*	*DICK TIGER (WBA)*	*1962-1963*
HARRY GREB	1923-1926	**DICK TIGER**	1963
TIGER FLOWERS	1926	**JOEY GIARDELLO**	1963-1965
MICKEY WALKER	1926-1931	**DICK TIGER**	1965-1966
GORILLA JONES	1931-1932	**EMILE GRIFFITH**	1966-1967
MARCEL THIL	1932-1937	**NINO BENVENUTI**	1967
BEN JEBY (NEW YORK)	*1932-1933*	**EMILE GRIFFITH**	1967-1968
LOU BROUILLARD (NBA-NEW YORK)	*1933*	**NINO BENVENUTI**	1968-1970
VINCE DUNDEE (NBA-NEW YORK)	*1933-1934*	**CARLOS MONZON**	1970-1977
TEDDY YAROSZ (NBA-NEW YORK)	*1934-1935*	*RODRIGO VALDEZ (WBC)*	*1974-1976*
BABE RISKO (NBA-NEW YORK)	*1935-1936*	**RODRIGO VALDEZ**	1977-1978
FREDDIE STEELE (NBA-NEW YORK)	*1936-1938*	**HUGO CORRO**	1978-1979
FRED APOSTOLI	1937-1939	**VITO ANTUOFERMO**	1979-1980
AL HOSTAK (NBA)	*1938*	**ALAN MINTER**	1980
SOLLY KRIEGER (NBA)	*1938-1939*	**MARVIN HAGLER**	1980-
AL HOSTAK (NBA)	*1939-1940*		

Claimants not generally recognized are in *italics*.

WORLD MIDDLEWEIGHT CHAMPIONSHIP BOUTS

Date	Winner	Weight	Loser	Weight	Result	KO	Time	Site	Referee
7/30/84	Jack DEMPSEY	140	George FULLJAMES	156	KO 22			Great Kills, Staten Island, N.Y.	E.F. Mallahan
2/03/86	Jack DEMPSEY		Jack FOGARTY		KO 27			New York City, New York	
3/04/86	Jack DEMPSEY		George LaBLANCHE		KO 13			Larchmont, New York	
12/13/87	Jack DEMPSEY		Johnny REAGAN		TKO 45			Manhasset, Long Island, New York	Frank Stevenson
2/18/90	Jack DEMPSEY	147½	Aus. Billy McCARTHY	152½	TKO 28			California A.C., San Francisco	Hiram Cook
1/14/91	Bob FITZSIMMONS	150½	Jack DEMPSEY	147½	KO 13			Olympic Club, New Orleans, La.	Alex. Brewster
9/26/94	Bob FITZSIMMONS	156	Dan CREEDON	157	KO 2	1:40		Olympic Club, New Orleans, La.	Prof. John Duffy
12/17/97	Charles (Kid) McCOY		Dan CREEDON		TKO 16	*		Long Island City A.C., L.I.C.	
10/24/98	Tommy RYAN	149	Jack BONNER	158	ref 20			Greater New York A.C., Brooklyn	Alexander Brown
9/18/99	Tommy RYAN		Frank CRAIG		TKO 10			Greater New York A.C., Brooklyn	George Siler
3/04/01	Tommy RYAN		Tommy WEST		TKO 17			Southern A.C., Louisville, Ky.	Tim Hurst
9/15/02	Tommy RYAN		Kid CARTER		KO 6			International A.C., Fort Erie	George Siler
9/02/07	Stanley KETCHEL		Joe THOMAS		KO 32			Mission Street Arena, Colma, Cal.	Billy Roche
2/22/08	Stanley KETCHEL		Mike (Twin) SULLIVAN		KO 1	1:18		Mission Street Arena, Colma, Cal.	Billy Roche
5/09/08	Stanley KETCHEL		Jack (Twin) SULLIVAN		KO 20			Mission Street Arena, Colma, Cal.	Billy Roche
6/04/08	Stanley KETCHEL		Billy PAPKE		ref 10			Hippodrome, Milwaukee, Wisc.	Jack McGuigan
7/31/08	Stanley KETCHEL		Hugo KELLY		KO 3			Coliseum, San Francisco, Calif.	Jack Welsh
8/18/08	Stanley KETCHEL		Joe THOMAS		KO 2			Coliseum, San Francisco, Calif.	Ed. W. Smith
9/07/08	Billy PAPKE		Stanley KETCHEL		TKO 12			Arena, Vernon, California	James J. Jeffries
11/26/08	Stanley KETCHEL		Billy PAPKE		KO 11			Mission Street Arena, Colma, Cal.	Jack Welsh
3/26/09	Stanley KETCHEL	160	Phila. Jack O'BRIEN	160	ND 10			National A.C., New York, N.Y.	Tim Hurst
6/02/09	Stanley KETCHEL		Tony CAPONI		KO 4			American A.C., Schnectady, N.Y.	
6/09/09	Stanley KETCHEL		Phila. Jack O'BRIEN		TKO 3	0:40		National A.C., Philadelphia, Pa.	Jack McGuigan
7/05/09	Stanley KETCHEL		Billy PAPKE		ref 20			Mission Street Arena, Colma, Cal.	Billy Roche
3/23/10	Stanley KETCHEL	159½	Frank KLAUS	157	ND 6			Duquesne Garden, Pittsburgh, Pa	Jack McGuigan
5/27/10	Stanley KETCHEL	158	Willie LEWIS	148	KO 2			National Sporting Club, New York	Tom O'Rourke
6/10/10	Stanley KETCHEL		Jim SMITH		KO 5			National Sporting Club, New York	Tom O'Rourke
2/11/11	Cyclone J. THOMPSON		Billy PAPKE		ref 20			Baker's Stadium, Sydney, NSW	
4/28/11	Cyclone J. THOMPSON		Hugo KELLY		ND 10			Racine, Wisconsin	
7/27/11	Cyclone J. THOMPSON		Willie LEWIS		ND 10			National Sporting Club, New York	
8/17/11	Frank KLAUS		Cyclone J. THOMPSON		ND 10			National Sporting Club, New York	
2/22/12	Frank KLAUS		Sailor PETROSKEY		ref 20			Auditorium Pavilion, San Francisco	Jack Welsh
2/22/12	Frank MANTELL		Billy PAPKE		ref 20			Buffalo Park, Sacramento, Calif.	Sol Levinson
2/29/12	Georges CARPENTIER		Jim SULLIVAN		KO 2			Monte Carlo, Monaco	*
3/23/12	Frank KLAUS		Jack DILLON		ref 20			Mission Street Arena, Colma, Cal.	Jack Welsh
3/30/12	Frank MANTELL		Jack HERRICK		ref 20			Arena, Vernon, California	Charles Eyton
4/03/12	Georges CARPENTIER		George GUNTHER		ref 20			Cirque de Paris, Paris	
5/10/12	Georges CARPENTIER		Herbert ROC		KO 6			Marseilles, France	
5/22/12	Georges CARPENTIER		Willie LEWIS		ref 20			Cirque de Paris, Paris	
6/24/12	Frank KLAUS	161	Georges CARPENTIER		WF 19			Dieppe, France	
6/29/12	Billy PAPKE		Marcel MOREAU		TKO 16			Cirque de Paris, Paris, France	
7/01/12	Frank KLAUS		Jimmy GARDNER		KO 3			Armory A.A., Boston, Mass	
9/09/12	Frank KLAUS		Marcel MOREAU		WF 4			Aix-Les-Bains, France	
10/23/12	Billy PAPKE		Georges CARPENTIER		TKO 10	*		Cirque de Paris, Paris, France	
12/04/12	Billy PAPKE		George BERNARD		KO 7			Cirque de Paris, Paris, France	
3/05/13	Frank KLAUS		Billy PAPKE		WF 15			Cirque de Paris, Paris, France	
5/24/13	Frank KLAUS	158	Eddie McGOORTY	158	ND 6			Exposition Park, Pittsburgh, Pa.	... Henninger
9/29/13	Frank KLAUS		Eddie McGOORTY		ND 10			Elite Rink, Milwaukee, Wisconsin	Harry Stout
10/11/13	George CHIP	161½	Frank KLAUS	163	KO 6			Old City Hall, Pittsburgh, Pa.	Tom Bodkins
11/15/13	George CHIP		Leo HOUCK		ND 6			Philadelphia, Pa.	
11/25/13	George CHIP		Tim O'NEILL		ND 10			Racine, Wisconsin	
12/23/13	George CHIP	160½	Frank KLAUS	159	KO 5			Duquesne Garden, Pittsburgh, Pa.	Jack Dillion
1/12/14	George CHIP		Gus CHRISTIE		ND 10			Milwaukee, Wisconsin	
1/19/14	George CHIP		Tim O'NEILL		KO 2			Grand Rapids, Michigan	
1/26/14	George CHIP		Joe BORRELL		ND 6			Philadelphia, Pa.	
4/06/14	Al McCOY	156	George CHIP	162½	KO 1	1:55		Broadway Sporting Club, Brooklyn	Johnny Haukaup
5/08/14	Al McCOY		George PEARSALL		KO 1			South Norwalk, Connecticut	
5/21/14	Al McCOY	154½	Billy MURRAY	157	ND 10			St. Nicholas Arena, New York	Billy Joh
††6/06/14	Jeff SMITH		Jimmy CLABBY		ref 20			Baker's Stadium, Sydney, NSW	Harald Baker
6/11/14	Al McCOY		Billy MURRAY		ND 10			Broadway Sporting Club, Brooklyn	
7/09/14	Al McCOY		Soldier BARTFIELD		ND 10			Broadway, Sporting Club, Brooklyn	
8/06/14	Al McCOY		Soldier BARTFIELD		ND 10			Broadway Sporting Club, Brooklyn	
10/13/14	Al McCOY	157½	Willie LEWIS	157¼	KO 5			Broadway Sporting Club, Brooklyn	
10/19/14	Al McCOY	158	Willie (K.O.) BRENNAN	157	ND 10			Buffalo, New York	
††11/28/14	Mick KING		Jeff SMITH		ref 20			Baker's Stadium, Sydney, NSW	Harald Baker
††12/26/14	Jeff SMITH		Mick KING		ref 20			Baker's Stadium, Sydney, NSW	Harald Baker
††1/23/15	Jeff SMITH	160	Les DARCY	155	W dis 5	**		Baker's Stadium, Sydney, NSW	Harald Baker
1/23/15	Al McCOY		Billy GRUPP		ND 10			Federal A.C., New York, N.Y.	
1/25/15	Al McCOY		Joe BORRELL	.	ND 6			Philadelphia, Pa.	
2/16/15	Al McCOY	158½	Al THIEL	160¼	ND 10			Broadway Sporting Club, Brooklyn	
††2/20/15	Jeff SMITH		Mick KING		ref 20			Melbourne, Victoria, Australia	
3/23/15	Al McCOY		Silent MARTIN		ND 10			Broadway Sporting Club, Brooklyn	
4/06/15	Al McCOY		George CHIP		ND 10			Broadway Sporting Club, Brooklyn	
5/04/15	Al McCOY		Jimmy CLABBY		ND 10			Broadway Sporting Club, Brooklyn	
††5/23/15	Les DARCY	159	Jeff SMITH	159	WF 2			Baker's Stadium, Sydney, NSW	Harald Baker
5/31/15	Al McCOY		Silent MARTIN		ND 10			Ebbets Field, Brooklyn, New York	
††6/12/15	Les DARCY	159	Mick KING	159	TKO 10			Baker's Stadium, Sydney, NSW	Harald Baker
††7/31/15	Les DARCY	159¼	Eddie McGOORTY	159½	TKO 15			Baker's Stadium, Sydney, NSW	Harald Baker
††9/04/15	Les DARCY	159	Billy MURRAY	160	ref 20			Baker's Stadium, Sydney, NSW	Harald Baker
9/08/15	Al McCOY		Young AHEARN		ND 10			Ebbets Field, Brooklyn, New York	
††10/09/15	Les DARCY	159	Fred DYER	150	TKO 5			Baker's Stadium, Sydney, NSW	Harald Baker
††10/23/15	Les DARCY		Jimmy CLABBY		ref 20			Baker's Stadium, Sydney, NSW	Harald Baker

529

10/23/15	**Al McCOY**		**Soldier BARTFIELD**		ND 10		Clermont Sporting Club, Brooklyn	
11/13/15	**Al McCOY**	161	**Zulu KID**	157	ND 10		Clermont Sporting Club, Brooklyn	
11/25/15	**Al McCOY**		**Silent MARTIN**		ND 15		Waterbury, Connecticut	
1/01/16	**Al McCOY**	162	**Young AHEARN**	156	ND 10		Broadway Sporting Club, Brooklyn	
1/20/16	**Al McCOY**	159¾	**George CHIP**	157¾	ND 10		Broadway Sporting Club, Brooklyn	
4/17/16	**Al McCOY**		**Al THIEL**		ND 10		Military A.C., Brooklyn, New York	
‡‡5/13/16	**Les DARCY**	158	**Alex COSTICA**	154¼	TKO 5		Baker's Stadium, Sydney, NSW	Harald Baker
6/26/16	**Al McCOY**		**Hugh ROSS**		ref 15		Bridgeport, Connecticut	
‡‡9/09/16	**Les DARCY**	159¼	**Jimmy CLABBY**	153¾	ref 20		Baker's Stadium, Sydney, NSW	Arthur Scott
‡‡9/30/16	**Les DARCY**	159½	**George CHIP**	159½	KO 9		Baker's Stadium, Sydney, NSW	
4/30/17	**Al McCOY**		**Harry GREB**		ND 10		Exposition Hall, Pittsburgh, Pa.	Jimmy McAvoy
11/14/17	**Mike O'DOWD**	157	**Al McCOY**	162	KO 6		Clermont Sporting Club, Brooklyn	Johnny McAvoy
2/25/18	**Mike O'DOWD**		**Harry GREB**		ND 10		St. Paul, Minnesota	
7/17/19	**Mike O'DOWD**		**Al McCOY**		KO 3		St. Paul, Minnesota	
8/11/19	**Mike O'DOWD**		**Jackie CLARK**		ND 10		Syracuse, New York	
8/22/19	**Mike O'DOWD**	155	**Jack BRITTON**	146	ND 8		Armory, Newark, New Jersey	
9/01/19	**Mike O'DOWD**		**Ted (Kid) LEWIS**		ND 10		Syracuse, New York	
9/19/19	**Mike O'DOWD**		**Soldier BARTFIELD**		ND 10		St. Paul, Minnesota	
9/29/19	**Mike O'DOWD**	164	**Augie RATNER**	154	ND 8		Armory, Jersey City, New Jersey	
11/06/19	**Mike O'DOWD**		**Billy KRAMER**		KO 2		Lyceum Theatre, Paterson, N.J.	
11/21/19	**Mike O'DOWD**		**Mike GIBBONS**		ND 10		St. Paul, Minnesota	Curley Ulrich
3/01/20	**Mike O'DOWD**		**Jack McCARRON**		TKO 2	1:08	Olympia A.A., Philadelphia, Pa.	
3/30/20	**Mike O'DOWD**		**Joe EAGAN**		KO 5		Armory A.A., Boston, Mass.	
5/06/20	**Johnny WILSON**	158	**Mike O'DOWD**	159½	ref 12		Armory A.A., Boston, Mass.	Hector McInnis
7/01/20	**Johnny WILSON**		**Soldier BARTFIELD**		ND 12		Sportsman's Club, Newark, N.J.	
1/17/21	**Johnny WILSON**		**George CHIP**		ND 10		Motor Square Garden, Pittsburgh, Pa.	
3/17/21	**Johnny WILSON**	158	**Mike O'DOWD**	159¾	split 15		Madison Square Garden, New York	Johnny McAvoy
5/25/21	**Johnny WILSON**	158	**Joe CHIP**	158	ND 10		Roller Rink, Detroit, Michigan	
7/27/21	**Johnny WILSON**		**Wm. Bryan DOWNEY**		WF 7		Dunn Park, Cleveland, Ohio	Jimmy Gardner
9/05/21	**Johnny WILSON**	159	**Wm. Bryan DOWNEY**	154½	ND 12		Boyle's Thirty Acres, Jersey City	Jim Savage
§8/14/22	**Dave ROSENBERG**	160	**Phil KRUG**	155	unan 15		Velodrome, Bronx, New York	Kid McPartland
§11/30/22	**Mike O'DOWD**	159	**Dave ROSENBERG**	156	WF 8	2:10	Clermont Sporting Club, Brooklyn	Patsy Haley
8/31/23	**Harry GREB**	158	**Johnny WILSON**	158	unan 15		Polo Grounds, New York City, N.Y.	Jock O'Sullivan
10/04/23	**Harry GREB**		**Jimmy DARCY**		ND 10		Forbes Field, Pittsburgh, Pa.	Joe Keally
12/03/23	**Harry GREB**	161	**Wm. Bryan DOWNEY**	158½	unan 10		Motor Square Garden, Pittsburgh, Pa.	Joe Keally
1/18/24	**Harry GREB**	158	**Johnny WILSON**	159	unan 15		Madison Square Garden, New York	Ed Purdy
3/24/24	**Harry GREB**		**Fay KAISER**		TKO 12		Armory, Baltimore, Maryland	Benny Franklin
6/26/24	**Harry GREB**	159½	**Ted MOORE**	160	unan 15		Yankee Stadium, Bronx, New York	Ed Purdy
7/02/25	**Harry GREB**	159	**Mickey WALKER**	152	unan 15		Polo Grounds, New York City, N.Y.	Ed Purdy
11/13/25	**Harry GREB**	169	**Tony MARULLO**	168	unan 15		Coliseum Arena, New Orleans, La.	Jimmy Moran
2/26/26	**Tiger FLOWERS**	158½	**Harry GREB**	159½	split 15		Madison Square Garden, New York	Ed (Gunboat) Smith
8/19/26	**Tiger FLOWERS**	159¼	**Harry GREB**	159	unan 15		Madison Square Garden, New York	Jim Crowley
12/03/26	**Mickey WALKER**	154	**Tiger FLOWERS**	159	ref 10		Coliseum, Chicago, Illinois	Benny Yanger
6/30/27	**Mickey WALKER**	159½	**Tommy MILLIGAN**	159¼	KO 10		Olympia, London, England	Eugene Corri
6/21/28	**Mickey WALKER**	158	**Ace HUDKINS**	155	split 10		Comiskey Park, Chicago, Illinois	Ed Purdy
10/29/29	**Mickey WALKER**	159½	**Ace HUDKINS**	156	ref 10		Wrigley Field, Los Angeles, Cal.	Lt. Jack Kennedy
1/25/32	**Gorilla JONES**	152½	**Oddone PIAZZA**	153¾	TKO 6		Auditorium, Milwaukee, Wisc.	Julius Fidler
4/26/32	**Gorilla JONES**	151	**Young TERRY**	158	unan 12		Armory, Trenton, N.J.	Hank Lewis
6/11/32	**Marcel THIL**		**Gorilla JONES**		W dis 11		Parc des Princes, Paris, France	
7/04/32	**Marcel THIL**		**Len HARVEY**		ref 15		White City Stadium, London, Eng.	. . . . Devernaz
§1/13/33	**Ben JEBY**	158¾	**Frank BATTAGLIA**	159¼	TKO 12	1:46	Madison Square Garden, New York	Jack Britton
§3/17/33	**Ben JEBY**	159½	**Vince DUNDEE**	159¾	D 15		Madison Square Garden, New York	Eddie Forbes
§7/10/33	**Ben JEBY**	158¼	**Young TERRY**	157	ref 15		Dreamland Park, Newark, N.J.	John (Whitey) Healey
§8/09/33	**Lou BROUILLARD**	158½	**Ben JEBY**	159	KO 7	2:21	Polo Grounds, New York, N.Y.	Pete Hartley
10/02/33	**Marcel THIL**		**Kid TUNERO**		unan 15		Palais des Sports, Paris, France	
†§10/30/33	**Vince DUNDEE**	160	**Lou BROUILLARD**	159	unan 15		Boston Garden, Boston, Mass.	Johnny Martin
†§12/08/33	**Vince DUNDEE**	158½	**Andy CALLAHAN**	152½	split 15		Boston Garden, Boston, Mass.	Jack Decker
2/26/34	**Marcel THIL**		**Ignacio ARA**		unan 15		Palais des Sports, Paris, France	
†§5/01/34	**Vince DUNDEE**	157	**Al DIAMOND**	156½	ref 15		State Armory, Paterson, N.J.	Phil Ehrhardt
5/03/34	**Marcel THIL**		**Gustave ROTH**		unan 15		Palais des Sports, Paris, France	
†§9/11/34	**Teddy YAROSZ**	157¼	**Vince DUNDEE**	158½	split 15		Forbes Field, Pittsburgh, Pa.	Al Grayber
10/15/34	**Marcel THIL**	157	**Carmelo CANDEL**	158	D 15		Palis des Sports, Paris France	
5/04/35	**Marcel THIL**	159	**Vilda JAKS**	158½	TKO 14		Palais des Sports, Paris, France	
6/03/35	**Marcel THIL**	158½	**Ignacio ARA**	159¼	15		Madrid, Spain	
†§9/19/35	**Babe RISKO**	158¼	**Teddy YAROSZ**	158½	unan 15		Forbes Field, Pittsburgh, Pa.	Red Robinson
1/20/36	**Marcel THIL**	158¾	**Lou BROUILLARD**	154½	W dis 4		Palais des Sports, Paris, France	
†§2/10/36	**Babe RISKO**	159¾	**Tony FISHER**	159¾	ref 10		Laurel Gardens, Newark, N.J.	John (Whitey) Healey
†§7/11/36	**Freddie STEELE**	156¾	**Babe RISKO**	158	unan 15		Civic Stadium, Seattle, Wash.	Tommy McCarthy
†§1/01/37	**Freddie STEELE**	157	**Gorilla JONES**	153	unan 10		Auditorium, Milwaukee, Wisconson	Jim Keefe
2/15/37	**Marcel THIL**	159	**Lou BROUILLARD**	157¼	W dis 6		Palais des Sports, Paris, France	A. Falony
†§2/19/37	**Freddie STEELE**	157	**Babe RISKO**	158	unan 15		Madison Square Garden, New York	Arthur Donovan
†§5/11/37	**Freddie STEELE**	156	**Frank BATTAGLIA**	159¾	KO 3	0:34	Civic Auditorium, Seattle, Wash.	Tommy Clark
†§9/11/37	**Freddie STEELE**	157¼	**Ken OVERLIN**	160	KO 4		Civic Auditorium, Seattle, Wash.	Tommy Clark
9/23/37	**Fred APOSTOLI**	159¼	**Marcel THIL**	159	TKO 10	0:44	Polo Grounds, New York, N.Y.	Arthur Donovan
†§2/19/38	**Freddie STEELE**	159	**Carmen BARTH**	159¼	TKO 7		Auditorium, Cleveland, Ohio	James J. Braddock
4/01/38	**Fred APOSTOLI**	160¾	**Glenn LEE**	156¾	unan 15		Madison Square Garden, New York	Eddie Joseph
† 7/26/38	**Al HOSTAK**	158¼	**Freddie STEELE**	159	KO 1	1:43	Civic Stadium, Seattle, Wash.	Jack Dempsey
† 11/01/38	**Solly KREIGER**		**Al HOSTAK**		maj 15		Civic Auditorium, Seattle, Wash.	Rod Murphy
11/18/38	**Fred APOSTOIL**	159	**Young CORBETT**	159½	TKO 8	2:01	Madison Square Garden, New York	Eddie Joseph
† 6/27/39	**Al HOSTAK**		**Solly KREIGER**	160	KO 4	0:46	Civic Stadium, Seattle, Wash.	James J. Braddock
10/02/39	**Ceferino GARCIA**	153¾	**Fred APOSTOLI**	160	KO 7	2:07	Madison Square Garden, New York	Billy Cavanaugh
† 12/11/39	**Al HOSTAK**	159	**Eric SEELIG**	160	KO 1	1:21	Arena, Cleveland, Ohio	Tony LaBranche
12/23/39	**Ceferino GARCIA**	152½	**Glenn LEE**	156	TKO 13		Rizal Stadium, Manila, P.I.	Jack Dempsey
3/01/40	**Ceferino GARCIA**	153½	**Henry ARMSTRONG**	142	draw 10		Gilmore Stadium, Los Angeles	George Blake
5/23/40	**Ken OVERLIN**	159	**Ceferino GARCIA**	154½	unan 15		Madison Square Garden, New York	Arthur Donovan
† 7/19/40	**Tony ZALE**	158	**Al HOSTAK**	159¾	TKO 13	1:20	Civic Stadium, Seattle, Wash.	Benny Leonard
11/01/40	**Ken OVERLIN**	158	**Steve BELLOIS**	153	maj 15		Madison Square Garden, New York	George Walsh
12/13/40	**Ken OVERLIN**	159	**Steve BELLOISE**	154	split 15		Madison Square Garden, New York	Arthur Donovan

† 2/21/41	**Tony ZALE**	159	**Steve MAMAKOS**	157½	KO	14	0:26	Chicago Stadium, Chicago, Ill.	Tommy Gilmore
5/09/41	**Billy SOOSE**	157¾	**Ken OVERLIN**	159½	unan	15		Madison Square Garden, New York	Arthur Donovan
† 5/28/41	**Tony ZALE**	158¾	**Al HOSTAK**	158¼	KO	2	2:32	Chicago Stadium, Chicago, Ill.	Johnny Behr
11/28/41	**Tony ZALE**	158¼	**Georgie ABRAMS**	159	unan	15		Madison Square Garden, New York	Billy Cavanaugh
9/27/46	**Tony ZALE**	160	**Rocky GRAZIANO**	154	KO	6	1:43	Yankee Stadium, Bronx, New York	Ruby Goldstein
7/16/47	**Rocky GRAZIANO**	155¼	**Tony ZALE**	159	TKO	6	2:10	Chicago Stadium, Chicago, Ill.	Johnny Behr
6/10/48	**Tony ZALE**	158¾	**Rocky GRAZIANO**	158½	KO	3	1:08	Ruppert Stadium, Newark, N.J.	Paul Cavalier
9/21/48	**Marcel CERDAN**	158	**Tony ZALE**	159	TKO	12		Roosevelt Stadium, Jersey City	Paul Cavalier
6/16/49	**Jake LaMOTTA**	158½	**Marcel CERDAN**	159½	TKO	10		Briggs Stadium, Detroit, Mich.	Johnny Weber
††6/05/50	**Sugar Ray ROBINSON**	155	**Robert VILLEMAIN**	159½	unan	15		Municipal Stadium, Philadelphia	Charles Daggert
7/12/50	**Jake LaMOTTA**	159	**Tiberio MITRI**	159	unan	15		Madison Square Garden, New York	Mark Conn
††8/25/50	**Sugar Ray ROBINSON**	154¾	**Jose BASORA**	159¾	KO	1	0:52	Scranton Stadium, Scranton, Pa.	Johnny Kelly
9/13/50	**Jake LaMOTTA**	159½	**Laurent DAUTHUILLE**	160	KO	15	2:47	Olympia, Detroit, Michigan	Lou Handler
††10/26/50	**Sugar Ray ROBINSON**	158	**Carl (Bobo) OLSON**	159	KO	12	1:19	Convention Hall, Philadelphia	Charles Daggert
2/14/51	**Sugar Ray ROBINSON**	155½	**Jake LaMOTTA**	160	TKO	13	2:04	Chicago Stadium, Chicago, Ill.	Frank Sikora
7/10/51	**Randy TURPIN**	158¾	**Sugar Ray ROBINSON**	154½	ref	15		Earl's Court, London, England	Eugene Henderson
9/12/51	**Sugar Ray ROBINSON**	157½	**Randy TURPIN**	159	TKO	10	2:52	Polo Grounds, New York, N.Y.	Ruby Goldstein
3/13/52	**Sugar Ray ROBINSON**	157½	**Carl (Bobo) OLSON**	159½	unan	15		Civic Auditorium, San Francisco	Jack Downey
4/16/52	**Sugar Ray ROBINSON**	157¼	**Rocky GRAZIANO**	159¾	KO	3	1:53	Chicago Stadium, Chicago, Ill.	Tommy Gilmore
10/21/53	**Carl (Bobo) OLSON**	159½	**Randy TURPIN**	157	unan	15		Madison Square Garden, New York	Al Berl
4/02/54	**Carl (Bobo) OLSON**	159½	**Kid GAVILAN**	155	maj	15		Chicago Stadium, Chicago, Ill.	Bernard Weissman
8/20/54	**Carl (Bobo) OLSON**	160	**Rocky CASTELLANI**	160	unan	15		Cow Palace, San Francisco, Calif.	Ray Flores
12/15/54	**Carl (Bobo) OLSON**	159½	**Pierre LANGLOIS**	157¾	TKO	11	0:58	Cow Palace, San Francisco, Calif.	Ray Flores
12/09/55	**Sugar Ray ROBINSON**	159¾	**Carl (Bobo) OLSON**	159¼	KO	2	2:51	Chicago Stadium, Chicago, Ill.	Frank Sikora
5/18/56	**Sugar Ray ROBINSON**	159½	**Carl (Bobo) OLSON**	160	KO	4	2:51	Wrigley Field, Los Angeles, Calif.	Mushy Callahan
1/02/57	**Gene FULLMER**	157¼	**Sugar Ray ROBINSON**	160	unan	15		Madison Square Garden, New York	Ruby Goldstein
5/01/57	**Sugar Ray ROBINSON**	159½	**Gene FULLMER**	159¼	KO	5	1:27	Chicago Stadium, Chicago, Ill.	Frank Sikora
9/23/57	**Carmen BASILIO**	153½	**Sugar Ray ROBINSON**	160	split	15		Yankee Stadium, Bronx, New York	Al Berl
3/25/58	**Sugar Ray ROBINSON**	159¾	**Carmen BASILIO**	153	split	15		Chicago Stadium, Chicago, Ill.	Frank Sikora
† 8/28/59	**Gene FULLMER**	159½	**Carmen BASILIO**	156	TKO	14	0:39	Cow Palace, S. Francisco	Jack Downey
† 12/04/59	**Gene FULLMER**	159¾	**Spider WEBB**	157¾	unan	15		George Nelson Field House, Logan	Ken Shulsen
1/22/60	**Paul PENDER**	159¾	**Sugar Ray ROBINSON**	159¼	split	15		Boston, Garden, Boston, Mass.	Joe Zapustas
† 4/20/60	**Gene FULLMER**	160	**Joey GIARDELLO**	158¼	draw	15		Montana State College Field House	Harry Kessler
6/10/60	**Paul PENDER**	160	**Sugar Ray ROBINSON**	158½	split	15		Boston Garden, Boston, Mass	Jimmy McCarron
† 6/29/60	**Gene FULLMER**	159¼	**Carmen BASILIO**	156½	TKO	12	2:54	Derks Field, Salt Lake City, Utah	Pete Giacoma
† 12/03/60	**Gene FULLMER**	159	**Sugar Ray ROBINSON**	158¾	draw	15		Sports Arena, Los Angeles, Calif.	Tommy Hart
1/14/61	**Paul PENDER**	160	**Terry DOWNES**	160	TKO	7	0:57	Arena, Boston, Massachusetts	Bill Connelly
† 3/04/61	**Gene FULLMER**	159¾	**Sugar Ray ROBINSON**	159¾	unan	15		Convention Center, Las Vegas	Frank Carter
4/22/61	**Paul PENDER**	160	**Carmen BASILIO**	159	unan	15		Boston Garden, Boston, Mass.	Ed Bradley
7/11/61	**Terry DOWNES**	158¾	**Paul PENDER**	159	TKO	10		Wembly Pool, London, England	Ike Powell
† 8/15/61	**Gene FULLMER**	159¾	**Florentino FERNANDEZ**	157¼	split	15		Ogden Stadium, Ogden, Utah	Ken Shulsen
† 12/09/61	**Gene FULLMER**	159¾	**Benny PARET**	156¾	KO	10	2:30	Convention Center, Las Vegas	Harry Krause
4/07/62	**Paul PENDER**	159	**Terry DOWNES**	159	unan	15		Boston Garde, Boston, Mass.	Jimmy McCarron
† 10/23/62	**Dick TIGER**	159	**Gene FULLMER**	160	unan	15		Candlestick Park, San Francisco	Frank Carter
† 2/23/63	**Dick TIGER**	160	**Gene FULLMER**	160	draw	15		Convention Center, Las Vegas	Vern Bybee
8/10/63	**Dick TIGER**	159¾	**Gene FULLMER**	160	TKO	8		Liberty Stadium, Ibadan, Nigeria	Jack Hart
12/07/63	**Joey GIARDELLO**	158	**Dick TIGER**	159	ref	15		Convention Hall, Atlantic City	Paul Cavalier
12/14/64	**Joey GIARDELLO**	160	**Ruben CARTER**	158½	unan	15		Convention Hall, Philadelphia	Bob Polis
10/21/65	**Dick TIGER**	158½	**Joey GIARDELLO**	160	unan	15		Madison Square Garden, New York	John LoBianco
4/25/66	**Emile GRIFFITH**	150½	**Dick TIGER**	160	unan	15		Madison Square Garden, New York	Arthur Mercante
7/13/66	**Emile GRIFFITH**	152	**Joey ARCHER**	159½	maj	15		Madison Square Garden, New York	John LoBianco
1/23/67	**Emile GRIFFITH**	152	**Joey ARCHER**	160	unan	15		Madison Square Garden, New York	Arthur Mercante
4/17/67	**Nino BENVENUTI**	159	**Emile GRIFFITH**	153½	unan	15		Madison Square Garden, New York	Mark Conn
9/29/67	**Emile GRIFFITH**	154	**Nino BENVENUTI**	159¾	maj	15		Shea Stadium, Flushing, New York	Tommy Walsh
3/04/68	**Nino BENVENUTI**	160	**Emile GRIFFITH**	154½	unan	15		Madison Square Garden, New York	John LoBianco
12/14/68	**Nino BENVENUTI**	160	**Don FULLMER**	159	unan	15		Ariston Theatre, San Remo, Italy	Piero Brambille
10/04/69	**Nino BENVENUTI**	160	**Fraser SCOTT**	158	W dis	7	1:40	San Paolo Stadium Naples, Italy	Tonci Gilardi
11/22/69	**Nino BENVENUTI**	159½	**Luis RODRIGUEZ**	156	KO	11	1:08	Palazzo dello Sport, Rome, Italy	Mario Carrabellese
5/23/70	**Nino BENVENUTI**	160	**Tom BETHEA**	160	KO	8	2:43	Umag, Yugoslavia	Georges Gondre
11/07/70	**Carlos MONZON**	159¼	**Nino BENVENUTI**	159¾	KO	12	2:00	Palazzo dello Sport, Rome, Italy	Rudolf Durst
5/09/71	**Carlos MONZON**	159½	**Nino BENVENUTI**	160	TKO	3	1:05	Louis II Stadium, Monte Carlo	Victor Avendano
9/25/71	**Carlos MONZON**	159	**Emile GRIFFITH**	154	TKO	14	2:49	Luna Park Stadium, Buenos Aires	Ramon Berumen
3/04/72	**Carlos MONZON**	159	**Dennis MOYER**	158¾	TKO	5	1:50	Palazzo dello Sport, Rome, Italy	Lorenzo Fortunato
6/17/72	**Carlos MONZON**	159¼	**Jean-Claude BOUTTIER**	159	TKO	13		Colombes Stadium, Colombes	Rudolf Durst
8/19/72	**Carlos MONZON**	159	**Tom BOGS**	159½	TKO	5	2:30	Idraets Park Stadium, Copenhagen	Harry Gibbs
11/11/72	**Carlos MONZON**	158	**Bennie BRISCOE**	157	unan	15		Luna Park Stadium, Buenos Aires	Victor Avendano
6/02/73	**Carlos MONZON**	159	**Emile GRIFFITH**	157	unan	15		Louis II Stadium, Monte Carlo	Pierrot Brenbilla
9/29/73	**Carlos MONZON**	159¾	**Jean-Claude BOUTTIER**	159	unan	15		Roland Garros Stadium, Paris	Harry Gibbs
2/09/74	**Carlos MONZON**	159	**Jose NAPOLES**	153	TKO	7		Paris, France	Raymond Baldeyrou
‡ 5/25/74	**Rodrigo VALDEZ**	156¾	**Bennie BRISCOE**	156½	KO	7		Louis II Stadium, Monte Carlo	Harry Gibbs
10/05/74	**Carlos MONZON**	160	**Tony MUNDINE**	159¼	KO	7	1:20	Luna Park Stadium, Buenos Aires	Issac Herrera
‡ 11/13/74	**Rodrigo VALDEZ**	160	**Gratien TONNA**	159	KO	11		Parc des Expositions, Paris	Jean Deswert
‡ 5/31/75	**Rodrigo VALDEZ**	160	**Ramon MENDEZ**	159	TKO	8		Cali, Colombia	Humberto Caceres
6/30/75	**Carlos MONZON**	159¾	**Tony LICATA**	160	TKO	10	2:43	Madison Square Garden, New York	Tony Perez
‡ 8/16/75	**Rodrigo VALDEZ**	159½	**Rudy ROBLES**	159½	unan	15		Cartagena de Indias Bull Ring	Victor Amor
12/13/75	**Carlos MONZON**	160	**Gratien TONNA**	159	KO	5		Nouvel Hippodrome, Paris, France	Waldemar Schmidt
‡ 3/28/76	**Rodrigo VALDEZ**	159½	**Nessim COHEN**	158¼	TKO	4	2:45	Pavillon de Paris, Paris, France	Marcello Bertini
6/26/76	**Carlos MONZON**	159½	**Rodrigo VALDEZ**	160	unan	15		Louis II Stadium, Monte Carlo	Raymond Baldeyrou
7/30/77	**Carlos MONZON**	159	**Rodrigo VALDEZ**	158	unan	15		Louis II Stadium, Monte Carlo	Roland Dakin
11/05/77	**Rodrigo VALDEZ**	160	**Bennie BRISCOE**	160	unan	15		Campione d'Italia, Switzerland	Wally Thom
4/22/78	**Hugo CORRO**	159¾	**Rodrigo VALDEZ**	159¼	unan	15		San Remo, Italy	Angelo Poletti
8/05/78	**Hugo CORRO**	159	**Ronnie HARRIS**	159½	unan	15		Luna Park Stadium, Buenos Aires	Waldemar Schmidt
11/11/78	**Hugo CORRO**	159¼	**Rodrigo VALDEZ**	158¾	unan	15		Luna Park Stadium, Buenos Aires	Stan Christodoulou
6/30/79	**Vito ANTUOFERMO**	159¼	**Hugo CORRO**	158¾	split	15		Monte Carlo, Monaco	Ernesto Magana
11/30/79	**Vito ANTUOFERMO**	158½	**Marvin HAGLER**	158½	draw	15		Caesars Palace, Las Vegas, Nev.	Mills Lane
[illegible]	**Alan MINTER**	159¾	**Vito ANTUOFERMO**	158¾	split	15		Caesars Palace, Las Vegas, Nev.	Carlos Padilla
6/28/80	**Alan MINTER**	160	**Vito ANTUOFERMO**	[illegible]	TKO	[illegible]		Wembley Pool, London, England	Octavio Meyran
9/27/80	**Marvin HAGLER**	160	**Alan MINTER**	159¾	TKO	3	1:45	Wembley Pool, London, England	Carlos Berrocal

MIDDLEWEIGHT DIVISION

JACK DEMPSEY
(John Kelly)
("The Nonpareil")
Born, December 15, 1862, County Kildare,
Ireland. Weight, 140-148 lbs. Height, 5 ft. 8 in.

1883
Apr.	7—Ed McDonald, Long Island	KO	21
Aug.	14—Jack Boylan, Flushing, New York	KO	23
Sept.	3—Harry Force, Coney Island	NC	11
Oct.	15—Jack Boylan, New York	ND	6
Nov.	25—Bob Turnbull, New York	D	8

1884
Jan.	—Will Mahoney, New York	KO	3
Feb.	10—Joe Heiser, Williamsburg	D	8
Feb.	14—Jim Fell, New York	KO	2
Feb.	28—Jim Barry, New York	KO	3
Mar.	2—Joe Hennessey, New York	KO	4
Mar.	4—Tom Sullivan, New York	KO	2
Mar.	6—Bill Dacey, Coney Island	KO	9
Apr.	25—Joe Hayes, New York	D	6
July	9—Tom Henry, Rockaway	NC	3
July	30—George Fulljames, Great Kill	KO	22
	(Won World Middleweight Title)		
Sept.	4—Mike Dempsey, Rockaway	KO	7
Sept.	15—Jimmy Ryan, Philadelphia	NC	7
Oct.	8—Bob Turnbull, New York	W	8
Oct.	24—Tom Henry, New York	W	6
Nov.	6—Tom Ferguson, New York	W	4
Nov.	30—Mike Malone, Philadelphia	KO	2
Dec.	15—George Wilson, Philadelphia	ND	4

1885
Jan.	12—Billy Frazier, New York	ND	4
Jan.	12—Jimmy Ryan, New York	ND	4
Jan.	22—Jim Fell, New York	W	4
Mar.	19—Charles Bixamos, New Orleans	KO	5
May	4—Tom Barry, San Francisco	KO	5
May	11—Tom Cleary, San Francisco	KO	5
June	5—Jim Carr, San Francisco	KO	9
July	20—Jack Keenan, San Francisco	KO	2
Aug.	29—Billy Manning, Los Angeles	KO	7
Sept.	12—Tom Norton, Sacramento	KO	4
Nov.	2—Dave Campbell, Wash. Territory	KO	3
Dec.	16—Tom Barry, Portland, Ore.	W	6

1886
Jan.	15—Jimmy Murray, New York	W	4
Jan.	15—Tom Henry, New York	W	4
Feb.	3—Jack Fogarty, New York	KO	27
	(Retained World Middleweight Title)		
Feb.	24—Pete McCoy, Jersey City	W	6
Mar.	4—George LaBlanche, Larchmont	KO	13
	(Retained World Middleweight Title)		
Apr.	26—Ned Cook, Philadelphia	KO	4
Apr.	28—Charles McCarthy, Philadelphia	ND	4
Apr.	30—Jimmy Ryan, Philadelphia	W	4
May	20—Paddy Norton, St. Paul	W	4
Nov.	12—Jack Burke, San Francisco	D	10

1887
Jan.	31—Mike Boden, Philadelphia	W	4
Feb.	2—Jack Langdon, Philadelphia	W	4
Feb.	5—Danny Killian, Philadelphia	W	4
Apr.	9—Biddy Baker, Buffalo	ND	4
May	2—Reddy Gallagher, Cleveland	D	6
Oct.	10—Eddie Reede, Hoboken	W	4
Oct.	13—Jim McHugh, Hoboken	W	4
Oct.	15—Billy Dacey, Hoboken	W	4
Oct.	31—Ed McCann, Wilmington	W	4
Nov.	1—Frank Bosworth, Wilmington	W	4
Nov.	3—Denny Kelleher, Wilmington	W	4
Nov.	5—Bill Gabig, Wilmington	W	4
Dec.	13—Johnny Reagan, Long Island	KO	45
	(Retained World Middleweight Title)		

1888
Jan.	23—Denny Kelleher, Boston	Exh.	3
Jan.	31—Dominick McCaffrey, Jersey City	W	10
Feb.	18—Billy Maker, Buffalo	ND	1
Apr.	23—James Stevens, Williamsburg	W	4
Nov.	15—Mike Donovan, Brooklyn	D	6

1889
Aug.	22—Mike Dempsey, San Francisco	KO	7
Aug.	27—George LaBlanche, San Fran.	KO by	32
	(Declared a non-title bout when LaBlanche		
	weighed in at 161 lbs. LaBlanche still claimed title,		
	though he also used illegal "pivot blow" to kayo		
	Dempsey.)		

1890
Feb.	18—Aus. Billy McCarthy, San Francisco	KO	28
	(Retained World Middleweight Title)		

1891
Jan.	14—Bob Fitzsimmons, New Orleans	KO by	13
	(Lost World Middleweight Title)		

1892
(Inactive)

1893
Mar.	2—Mike Keogh, Portland	W	4

1894
Sept.	6—Aus. Billy McCarthy, New Orleans	D	20

1895
Jan.	18—Tommy Ryan, Coney Island	KO by	3
	(For World Welterweight Title)		

TB	KO	WD	WF	D	LD	LF	KO BY	ND	NC
68	25	23	0	7	0	0	3	7	3

Died, November 2, 1895, Portland, Oregon.
Elected to Boxing Hall of Fame, 1954.

GEORGE LaBLANCHE
(George Blais)
(The Marine)
Born, Dec. 17, 1856. Point Levi, Quebec,
Canada. Heighit, 5 ft. 6½ in. Weight, 140-158 lbs.
First known appearances in ring were in
Citadel, Quebec, where he defeated J. Putnam
and lost to T. Preston.

1883
Sept.	18—L. Witzell Brown, Lewiston, Me.	LF	
Oct.	19—Mike Barry, Lewiston	W	
Dec.	11—Enlisted in U. S. Marine Corps.		

1884
Jan.	28—George Smith, Boston	W	6
Feb.	28—Tommy McManus, Boston	W	6
Mar.	21—Tom Bates, Boston	W	5
May	7—Jimmy Hurst, Cambridgeport, Mass.	L	5
June	11—Discharged from U. S. Marine Corps.		
June	13—Jimmy Hurst, Boston	W	4
June	24—Ned Harnetty, Boston	KO	3
	Undated bouts: Won: C. Randall, 2; Tom		
	Henry, 2; Danny Kelleher, 6.		

1885
Apr.	17—Pete McCoy, Boston	D	8
Aug.	6—Pete McCoy, Fall River	KO	4
Sept.	15—Pete McCoy, Saugus Center, Mass.	D	6
	Undated bouts: Knockout: Frank Bosworth, 1; Won: Danny Kelleher, 3.		

1886
Jan.	8—Jack Burgess, Boston	LF	
Mar.	14—Jack Dempsey, Larchmont, N.Y.	KO by	13
	(World Middleweight Title)		
Apr.	7—Matt Cunningham, Manchester, N. H.	KO	
July	20—W. L. Leighton, Bradford, Pa.	W	4
Aug.	28—Sam Brittle, Denver	KO	1

1887
Feb.	14—J. W. Curtis, Eau Claire, Wis.	D	2
Feb.	23—T. Hanley, Omaha	D	6
Mar.	25—T. Hunter, St. Paul	KO	7
Oct.	18—Ed Buchanan, Boston	KO	5
Oct.	24—M. Gillespie, Hoboken, N. J.	KO	4
Oct.	26—H. Larydon, Hoboken	KO	2
Oct.	29—Bill Farnan, Hoboken	W	3
Nov.	9—Danny Kelleher, Wilmington, Del.	KO	2
Nov.	10—W. Gabig, Wilmington	D	4
Nov.	12—Mike Roden, Wilmington	W	4

1888

Jan.	19—M. Burns, Waterbury, Conn. ...	W	3
Feb.	24—Con Riley, Dayton, O.	W	2
Mar.	22—J. Peters, Detroit	KO	2
Apr.	19—John Martin, Newark, N.J.	W	3
Aug.	18—Jack Varley, Yonkers, N.Y. ..	KO	3

1889

Feb.	2—Dan Lynch, Buffalo	KO	2
Mar.	2—Ed Smith, Denver	Stpd.	2
Mar.	6—Murdy Buchanan, Butte, Mont.	KO	1
Aug.	27—Jack Dempsey, San Francisco .	KO	32

(LeBlanche claimed world middleweight title, but claim was not recognized as he used illegal "pivot blow" to knock Dempsey out.)

Sept.	19—Jack Burke, Seattle	D	9
Nov.	17—George Kessler, Butte	KO by	13

1890

May	28—Mike Lucie, San Francisco .	KO by	13

1891

Feb.	20—Young Mitchell, San Francsico	KO by	12
May	18—Billy McCarthy, New Orleans	KO by	16
May	30—Ed Gorman, Salt Lake City ...	KO	10
Nov.	26—Jim Williams, San Francisco	L	17
Dec.	14—Alex Greggains, Salt Lake City ..	L	3

1892

Feb.	19—Jim Lawson, Los Angeles ..	KO by	7
Mar.	8—Frank Childs, Los Angeles	L	8

1893

May	18—Billy McCarthy, New Orl ..	KO by	10
July	11—Bob Manning, Jackson, Mich. .	NC	8

(Stopped by police)

July	21—Dick O'Brien, Lewiston ...	KO by	3
Aug.	2—D. Dwyer, Goshen, Ind.	KO	3
Aug.	11—Tom O'Donnell, Grand Rapids .	L	8
Sept.	21—Billy Maber, Minneapolis ..	KO by	2
Oct.	23—Billy Layton, Des Moines ..	KO by	7

(Fought in an improvised ring, 15 miles out of Des Moines, for a $500 purse, winner take all.)

1894

Mar.	16—Charles Wickey, Muskegon	KO by	5
May	28—Buffalo Costello, Montreal	L	6

1895

Jan.	21—Jack Slavin, Montreal	L	6

(LeBlanche automatic loser when he failed to stop Slavin per agreement.)

Nov.	25—W. Hennessey, Lynn, Mass.	KO by	1

1896

Jan.	17—Joe Dunfee, Syracuse	L	5
Jan.	30—George Kessler, Chicago	ND	6
July	4—F. Moyniham, Jamestown, N.Y.	L	2

1897

Jan.	18—John Yowpers, Cleveland	W	6
Nov.	12—Kid McCoy, Dayton, O. ...	KO by	2

1898

Apr.	10—Bert Woods, Toledo	KO by	4

TB	KO	WD	WF	D	LD	LF	KOBY	ND	NC
69	17	18	0	6	10	2	14	1	1

Died, Lawrence, Mass., May 3, 1918.

BOB FITZSIMMONS
(Record under Heavyweight Champions)

CHARLES (KID) McCOY
(Norman Selby)

Born, October 13, 1873, Rush County, Indiana.
Weight, 160 lbs. Height, 5 ft. 11 in.

1891

June	2—Pete Jenkins, St. Paul	W	4

1892

June	6—Billy Barlow, Indianapolis	W	6
Sept.	14—Bob Lewis, Indianapolis	KO	1
Sept.	29—Herb Hall, Columbus	D	8

1893

Jan.	11—Jim Dickson, Hot Springs	KO	5
Jan.	27—Jim Connors, Hot Springs	KO	3
Feb.	12—"Unknown" boxer, Milen, Tenn. ..	KO	2
Feb.	22—Frank Lamode, New Orleans	KO	3
May	4—Frank Murray, Indianapolis	KO	2
June	14—Kid McCarthy, Muncie	KO	3
July	23—Ike Boone, Muncie, Ind.	NC	22
July	30—Dick Harris, Marion, Ind.	KO	1

Aug.	15—Frank Merritt, Indianapolis	KO	2
Sept.	26—George Bennett, Akron, Ohio	D	8
Oct.	13—Jack Welsh, Wheeling	NC	9
Oct.	22—"Deaf Mute," Pittsburgh	KO	4

1894

Jan.	8—Pat Hayden, Providence	KO	2
Feb.	12—Joe Burke, Fall River, Mass.	KO	2
Mar.	16—Jim Scully, New Bedford, Mass. ...	W	6
May	10—Billy Steffers, Cleveland	KO by	1
May	18—Aus. Jim Barron, Minneapolis	D	10
June	1—Charles Maxwell, Akron	W	6
July	2—Harry O'Connor, Cleveland	KO	3
Aug.	12—Jack Grace, Cleveland	KO	7
Aug.	29—Billy Steffers, Cleveland	W	10
Oct.	12—Al Roberts, Cincinnati	D	10

1895

Jan.	19—Al Roberts, Cincinnati	KO	5
Mar.	13—Shadow Maber, Memphis	W	10
Apr.	19—Jack Wilkes, Boston	KO	2
May	20—Dick O'Brien, Boston	D	25
Aug.	—Charles Siefert, Louisville	W	3
Aug.	—Joe Sheers, Louisville	W	3
Aug.	—Joe Sheers, Louisville	W	3
Aug.	—Charles Siefert, Louisville	W	3
Sept.	2—Dick Moore, Louisville	KO	6
Oct.	7—Abe Ullman, Baltimore	KO	13
Oct.	13—Arthur Walker, Jersey City	ND	3
Nov.	25—Ted White, London, England	L	10

1896

Jan.	31—Tommy West, New York	KO	2
Mar.	2—Tommy Ryan, Maspeth, N.Y.	KO	15
Mar.	21—Joe Choynski, New York	ND	4
Apr.	22—Frank Bosworth, Memphis	KO	2
May	7—Jim Daly, New York	W	3
May	18—Mys. Billy Smith, Boston	WF	6
May	30—Dick Moore, Brooklyn	KO	9
Dec.	26—Billy Doherty, Johannesburg	KO	9

1897

May	26—Dick O'Brien, New York	W	10
May	31—Jack Bonner, Philadelphia	W	6
July	21—Dick Moore, Buffalo	KO	2
Sept.	8—Tommy Ryan, Syracuse	NC	5
Oct.	18—Jim Hall, Philadelphia	ND	6
Nov.	12—George LaBlanche, Dayton	KO	1
Nov.	12—Beach Ruble, Dayton	KO	1
Nov.	15—Texas Billy Smith, Chicago	KO	2
Dec.	17—Dan Creedon, Long Island City ...	KO	15

(Won Vacant World Middleweight Title)

1898

Jan.	10—Doc Payne, Louisville	KO	4
Feb.	15—H. Long, Dayton	KO	2
Mar.	4—Nick Burley, Hot Springs	KO	2
Mar.	7—James Blackwell, Indianapolis	KO	2
Mar.	7—John Tierney, Indianapolis	KO	3
Mar.	11—Jim Bates, Fort Wayne, Ind.	KO	1
Mar.	18—Bert Bolby, Springfield, Ill.	KO	1
Apr.	1—Dan Molson, Indianapolis	KO	1
Apr.	5—Tom Shea, Dayton	KO	2
May	20—Gus Ruhlin, Syracuse	W	20
Dec.	16—Joe Goddard, Philadelphia	WF	5

1899

Jan.	10—Tom Sharkey, New York	KO by	10
Mar.	24—Joe Choynski, San Francisco	W	20
Aug.	10—Tom Dugan, Dubuque	KO	2
Aug.	10—Jack Graham, Dubuque, Iowa	KO	4
Aug.	14—Jim Carter, Joplin, Mo.	KO	2
Aug.	18—Jack McCormick, Chicago	KO by	1
Sept.	5—Geoffrey Thorne, New York	KO	3
Sept.	19—Steve O'Donnell, New York	KO	6
Sept.	27—Jack McCormick, New York	W	8
Oct.	6—Joe Choynski, Chicago	D	8
Oct.	27—Billy Stift, St. Louis	KO	13
Nov.	9—Jack McDonough, Buffalo	KO	4

1900

Jan.	1—Peter Maher, Coney Island	KO	5
Jan.	12—Joe Choynski, New York	KO	4
May	18—Dan Creedon, New York	W	6
May	29—Tommy Ryan, Chicago	W	6
June	1—Jack Bonner, New York	KO	13
Aug.	30—James J. Corbett, New York ...	KO by	5

1901

Dec.	2—Dave Barry, London, England	.... KO	2
Dec.	2—Jack Scales, London, England	.... KO	2
Dec.	2—Jack Madden, London, England	.. KO	2

1902

May	2—Fred Russell, Philadelphia	.... ND	6
May	19—Kid Carter, Philadelphia	.... ND	6

1903

Feb.	23—Jack McCormick, Philadelphia	... ND	6
Apr.	22—Jack Root, Detroit	 L	10
	(For World Light Heavyweight Title)		

1904

Apr.	5—Herr Placke, Philadelphia	.... KO	2
May	14—Phila. Jack O'Brien, Philadelphia	ND	6
Sept.	27—Jack (Twin) Sullivan, Los Angeles	W	20

1905

Mar.	8—Jack Crawford, Hot Springs	...... KO	1

1906-1907
(Inactive)

1908

July	25—Peter Maher, New York	.... KO	2
Oct.	16—Jim Stewart, New York	.... ND	6

1909-1910
(Inactive)

1911

Mar.	20—Jack Fitzgerald, Philadelphia	.... ND	6
Sept.	5—Bob Day, Toronto	.... KO	1
Sept.	22—Kid Ely, New York	.... KO	1
Oct.	6—Jim Savage, New York	.... KO	4
Nov.	23—Hubert Roe, Paris, France	.... W	10

1912

Jan.	18—George Gunther, Paris, France	.... W	10
Feb.	21—P.O. Curran, Nice, France	.... W	10

1913-1915
(Inactive)

1916

Aug.	4—Artie Sheridan, Mission, Texas	.... W	4

TB	KO	WD	WF	D	LD	LF	KO BY	ND	NC
105	55	24	2	6	2	0	4	9	3

Committed suicide, April 18, 1940, Detroit, Mich.
Elected to Boxing Hall of Fame, 1957.

TOMMY RYAN
(Joseph Youngs)

Born, March 31, 1870, Redwood, New York.
Ancestry, French-English. Weight, 142-158 lbs. Height,
5 ft. 7¾ in.

1887

	—John Case	.... KO	5
	—Jack Conway, Rock Island	.... KO	3
	—Chris Christopher, Grand Rapids	KO	8

1888

July	20—Joe Johnson, Marion, Mich.	...... KO	5
Dec.	21—Dick England, Lake City	.... KO	33

1889

April	30—M. Shaughnessy, Detroit	.... KO	23
May	29—Mike Dunn, Detroit	.... KO	9
June	18—M. Shaughnessy, Detroit	.... KO	46
Aug.	10—Jimmy Murphy, Grand Rapids	.... NC	57
Sept.	3—Henry Baker, Grand Rapids	...... KO	3
Nov.	20—Jimmy Murphy, Grand Rapids	.. Exh.	8

1890

July	20—John McInerssey, Chicago	.... KO	5
Aug.	4—Bob Harper, Chicago	.... KO	4
Aug.	28—Prof. Maguire, Chicago	.... KO	3
Sept.	6—Con Doyle, Shelby, Ind.	.... KO	28
Nov.	23—Ed Bartlett, Sheffield, Ind.	.... KO	3

1891

Feb.	16—Danny Needham, Minneapolis	.... KO	76
Aug.	9—Billy McMillan, Richardson	...... KO	3
Sept.	28—Jim Hall, Chicago	.... Exh.	5
Dec.	15—Frank Howson, Chicago	.... KO	14

1892

Apr.	8—Con Doyle, Dubuque, Iowa	.... W	8
May	6—Reddy Brennan, Dubuque	.... W	10
July	30—Jack Wilkes, South Omaha	...... KO	17
Nov.	24—Jack Collins, Detroit	.... D	8

1893

Apr.	18—George Dawson, Chicago	.... ND	6
Aug.	29—Mys. Billy Smith, Coney Island	.... D	6

Nov.	2—Harry Jamieson, Naugatuck	..... KO	2
Dec.	11—Dick Guthrie, Naugatuck	.... NC	3

1894

Jan.	9—Mys. Billy Smith, Boston	.... D	6
Apr.	10—Morris Lane, West Haven	.... KO	3
Apr.	22—Jack Wilkes	.... NC	5
May	22—Jack Falvey, Hartford	.... KO	8
June	1—Jack Pitts, Minneapolis	.... KO	3
July	26—Mys. Billy Smith, Minneapolis	... W	20
	(Won World Welterweight Title)		
Sept.	13—Billy Layton, St. Joseph	.... KO	4

1895

Jan.	18—Jack Dempsey, Coney Island	..... KO	3
	(Retained World Welterweight Title)		
Feb.	25—Shorty Ahearn, Chicago	.... W	4
Mar.	11—Emmett Mellody, Kansas City	..... W	4
Mar.	20—Tom Tracey, Chicago	.... ND	8
May	27—Mys. Billy Smith, Coney Island	... NC	18
	(Retained World Welterweight Title)		
June	26—Tom Crawford, Syracuse	.... ND	4
Nov.	18—Joe Dunfee, Buffalo	.... ND	3

1896

Jan.	9—George (Kid) Lavigne, New York	Exh.	4
Mar.	2—Charles (Kid) McCoy, Maspeth	KO by	15
Mar.	6—Mys. Billy Smith, Syracuse	.... ND	6
Mar.	18—Joe Dunfee, Buffalo	.... KO	5
June	22—Shadow Maber, Buffalo	.... KO	9
Aug.	20—Dick Moore, Buffalo	.... W	20
Nov.	25—Mys. Billy Smith, Maspeth, N.Y.	WF	9
	(Retained World Welterweight Title)		
Dec.	21—Billy McCarthy, Buffalo	.... KO	7
Dec.	23—Bill Payne, Syracuse	.... KO	4
	(Retained World Welterweight Title)		

1897

Feb.	24—Tom Tracy, Syracuse	.... KO	9
	(Retained World Welterweight Title)		
Mar.	17—Patsy Raedy, Rochester	.... KO	18
May	10—Paddy Gorman, Rochester	.... KO	3
May	21—Patsy Raedy, Rochester	.... KO	6
June	21—Tom Williams, Syracuse	.... KO	2
Sept.	8—Charles (Kid) McCoy, Syracuse	... NC	5
Nov.	25—Australian Jim Ryan, Elmira	.... KO	5
Nov.	30—Billy Stift, Chicago	.... W	6
Dec.	20—Bill Hefferman, Buffalo	.... KO	3

1898

Feb.	25—George Green, San Francisco	.... KO	18
June	13—Tommy West, New York	.... KO	14
	(Retained World Welterweight Title)		
Oct.	24—Jack Bonner, Coney Island	.... W	20
	(Won Vacant World Middleweight Title)		
Nov.	8—Jack Bonner, Philadelphia	.... ND	6
Nov.	28—Johnny Gorman, Syracuse	.... W	8
Dec.	2—Tommy West, Philadelphia	.... ND	6

1899

Jan.	23—Dick O'Brien, Hartford	.... KO	14
Feb.	1—Tom Sharkey, Syracuse	.... Exh.	6
Feb.	22—Tom McCarthy, Hot Springs	...... KO	12
Mar.	1—Charles Johnson, Hot Springs	.... KO	8
Mar.	5—C. Johnson, Hot Springs	.... KO	8
Mar.	13—Paddy Purtell, Cincinnati	.... KO	4
Mar.	18—Bob Douglass, St. Louis	.... ND	4
Apr.	6—Dutch Neal, Dubuque	.... W	6
Apr.	17—Billy Stift, Davenport	.... W	20
Aug.	31—Jack Moffatt, Dubuque	.... W	20
Sept.	18—Frank Craig, Coney Island	...... KO	10
	(Retained World Middleweight Title)		

1900

Feb.	2—George Lawlor, Hot Springs	...... KO	13
May	29—Charles (Kid) McCoy, Chicago	 L	6
June	29—Young Mahoney, Chicago	.... W	6
July	24—Jack Root, Chicago	.... D	6
Nov.	10—Jeff Thorne, Chicago	.... KO	3
Nov.	27—Kid Carter, Chicago	.... W	6

1901

Jan.	17—Jack Beauscholte, Springfield	.... KO	3
Jan.	31—Martin Judge, Minneapolis	...... KO	4
Mar.	4—Tommy West, Louisville	.... KO	17
	(Retained World Middleweight Title)		
Aug.	22—Bob Douglass, Kansas City	.... KO	7
Oct.	10—George Green, Kansas City	.... LF	6

534

1902

Jan.	30—George Green, Kansas City	KO	7
Feb.	16—Jack Beauscholte, Chicago	W	6
Feb.	25—Tim Murphy, Kansas City	KO	9
Mar.	14—Mys. Billy Smith, Kansas City	KO	4
Apr.	3—Billy Stift, Kansas City	W	10
May	26—Jim Handler, Kansas City	KO	4
June	24—Johnny Gorman, London, England	KO	3
Sept.	15—Kid Carter, Fort Erie, Ontario	KO	6
	(Retained World Middleweight Title)		
Oct.	3—Barney Walsh, Kansas City	KO	2
Oct.	3—Jack Beauscholte, Kansas City	KO	5

1903

Jan.	15—Billy Stift, Kansas City	KO	8
Feb.	3—Cyclone Kelly, Hot Springs	KO	7
June	1—James Walker, Battle Creek	KO	5
June	15—Jack Hickey, Battle Creek	KO	4
June	30—John Willie, Butte, Montana	KO	4

1904

Jan.	27—Phila. Jack O'Brien, Philadelphia	ND	6
Feb.	24—Jack Beauscholte, Indianapolis	W	6
Sept.	10—Frank Girard, Chicago	KO	3
Oct.	10—Bob Douglass, St. Louis	KO	4
Oct.	26—Tom Wallace, Benton Harbor	KO	5
Nov.	15—Jack Graham, South Bend	KO	4
Nov.	23—Jack Root, Philadelphia	NC	4
Dec.	29—Billy Stift, Benton Harbor	KO	4

1905-1906
(Inactive)

1907

Feb.	5—Dave Barry, Hot Springs	KO	5
Mar.	4—Hugo Kelly, Rochester	D	6
Aug.	4—Battling Nelson, South Bend	Exh.	6

TB	KO	WD	WF	D	LD	LF	KO BY	ND	NC
109	68	17	1	5	1	1	1	9	6

Died, August 3, 1948, Van Nuys, Calif.
Elected to Boxing Hall of Fame, 1958.

STANLEY KETCHEL
(Stanislaus Kiecal)
(The Michigan Assassin)
Born, September 14, 1886, Grand Rapids, Mich.
Ancestry, Polish. Weight, 154 lbs. Height, 5 ft. 9 in.
Managed by Willus Britt and Joe O'Connor.

1903

May	2—Kid Tracy, Butte, Montana	KO	1
Aug.	8—Mose LaFontise, Butte	KO	24

1904

Apr.	19—Rudolph Hinz, Miles City, Montana	D	20
May	11—Maurice Thompson, Butte	L	6
June	20—Jimmy Quinn, Butte	KO	3
July	7—Kid McGuire, Butte	KO	1
July	15—Kid LeRoy, Butte	KO	1
July	17—Young Gilsey, Butte	KO	4
Sept.	8—Bob Merrywell, Butte	KO	4
Sept.	15—Jimmy Murray, Butte	KO	3
Oct.	15—Bob Merrywell, Butte	KO	3
Oct.	21—Maurice Thompson, Butte	L	10
Oct.	29—Jimmy Kelly, Miles City	KO	1
Nov.	8—Kid Lee, Lewistown, Montana	KO	8
Nov.	10—Joe Mudro, Butte	KO	4
Dec.	16—Jack Grimes, Butte	KO	10
Dec.	29—Maurice Thompson, Butte	D	10

1905

Jan.	4—Kid Thomas, Butte	KO	1
Jan.	20—Jack Bennett, Butte	KO	5
Mar.	25—Sid LaFontise, Butte	KO	24
Apr.	19—Rudolph Hinz, Miles City	D	20
May	18—Sid LaFontise, Butte	KO	7
June	4—Curley Rue, Gregson Springs	KO	11
June	13—Kid Pecor, Butte	KO	5
June	16—Kid Lee, Helena, Montana	KO	17
July	4—Young Kelly, Butte	KO	8
July	15—Bob Sennate, Miles City	KO	17
Aug.	19—Roy Hart, Miles City	KO	1
Sept.	16—Bob Sennate, Miles City	KO	11
Dec.	1—Jerry McCarthy, Great Falls, Mont.	KO	12
Dec.	2—Marysville Kid, Butte	KO	3
Dec.	8—Kid Herrick, Butte	KO	7
Dec.	16—Jack Bennett, Butte	KO	5

Dec.	19—Jerry McCarthy, Great Falls	KO	11
Dec.	24—Kid Foley, Butte	KO	4

1906

Feb.	12—Montana Jack Sullivan, Butte	D	20
Mar.	19—Warren Zubrick, Great Falls	KO	2
May	11—Paddy Hall, Gregson Springs	KO	1
May	18—Mike Tierney, Butte	KO	7
June	16—Kid Lee, Helena	KO	17
Aug.	29—Kid Fredericks, Butte	KO	7
Sept.	2—Tom Kingsley, Butte	Exh.	6
Sept.	10—Kid Foley, Miles City	KO	11

1907

Mar.	23—Mike McClure, Redding, Calif.	KO	7
May	3—Benny Hart, Marysville, Calif.	KO	4
May	23—George Brown, Sacramento	KO	3
July	4—Joe Thomas, Marysville	D	20
Sept.	2—Joe Thomas, Colma, Calif.	KO	32
Dec.	12—Joe Thomas, San Francisco	W	20

1908

Feb.	22—Mike (Twin) Sullivan, Colma	KO	1
May	9—Jack (Twin) Sullivan, Colma	KO	20
	(Won Vacant World Middleweight Title)		
June	4—Billy Papke, Milwaukee	W	10
	(Retained World Middleweight Title)		
July	31—Hugo Kelly, San Francisco	KO	3
	(Retained World Middleweight Title)		
Aug.	18—Joe Thomas, San Francisco	KO	2
	(Retained World Middleweight Title)		
Sept.	7—Billy Papke, Vernon, Calif.	KO by	12
	(Lost World Middleweight Title)		
Nov.	26—Billy Papke, Colma	KO	11
	(Regained World Middleweight Title)		

1909

Jan.	15—Tony Caponi, Grand Rapids	Exh.	3
Mar.	26—Phila. Jack O'Brien, New York	ND	10
	(Retained World Middleweight Title)		
May	18—Kid Hubert, Pittsburgh	ND	6
June	2—Tony Caponi, Schenectady	KO	4
	(Retained World Middleweight Title)		
June	9—Phila. Jack O'Brien, Philadelphia	KO	3
	(Retained World Middleweight Title)		
July	5—Billy Papke, Colma	W	20
	(Retained World Middleweight Title)		
Oct.	16—Jack Johnson, Colma	KO by	12
	(For World Heavyweight Title)		

1910

Mar.	23—Frank Klaus, Pittsburgh	ND	6
	(Retained World Middleweight Title)		
Apr.	27—Sam Langford, Philadelphia	ND	6
May	17—Porky Flynn, Boston	KO	3
May	27—Willie Lewis, New York	KO	2
	(Retained World Middleweight Title)		
June	10—Jim Smith, New York	KO	5
	(Retained World Middleweight Title)		

TB	KO	WD	WF	D	LD	LF	KO BY	ND	NC
66	50	3	0	5	2	0	2	4	0

Shot and killed by Walter A. Dipley, October 15, 1910, Conway, Missouri.
Elected to Boxing Hall of Fame, 1954.

BILLY PAPKE
(William Herman Papke)
Born, September 17, 1886, Spring Valley, Ill. Nationality, German-American. Weight, 158-160 lbs. Height, 5 ft. 8¾ in. Managed by Tom Jones and Al Lippe.

1905

Nov.	6—Battling Hurley, New York	D	6
Nov.	20—Dave Deshler, Boston	D	12

1906

Mar.	24—Mexican Wonder, LaSalle, Ill.	W	4
Apr.	30—Red Morrissey, LaSalle	KO	3
May	30—Buster Tegan, LaSalle	KO	3
June	1—Jack Denny, Peru, Ill	KO	1
July	4—Carl Purdy, LaSalle	W	10
Nov.	27—Milt Kenney, Peoria, Ill.	KO	3
Dec.	17—Orig. Kid Farmer, Peoria	KO	6

1907

Jan.	15—Tom Wallace, Peoria	KO 4
Jan.	29—Dick Fitzpatrick, Peoria	W 10
Feb.	14—Carl Anderson, Spring Valley	KO 1
Mar.	6—Billy Rhodes, Peoria	W 10
Mar.	26—Billy Rhodes, Davenport, Ia.	D 15
Apr.	30—Johnny Carroll, Peoria	KO 4
May	29—Tony Caponi, Davenport, Ia.	D 15
June	6—Jack Morgan, Peoria	KO 7
June	14—Foster Walker, Detroit	KO 2
June	20—Tony Caponi, Spring Valley	D 10
Sept.	2—Tommy Sullivan, Lawrence	KO 1
Sept.	14—Terry Martin, Philadelphia	KO 3
Oct.	30—Sy Flynn, Brazil, Ind.	KO 3
Nov.	9—Pat O'Keefe, Philadelphia	W 6
Nov.	14—Tony Caponi, Peoria, Ill	KO 2
Nov.	22—Charles Haghey, Boston	KO 1
Nov.	22—Bartley Connolly, Boston	KO 4
Dec.	30—Hugo Kelly, Milwaukee	D 10

1908

Jan.	21—Walter Stanton, Boston	KO 4
Mar.	16—Hugo Kelly, Milwaukee	W 10
May	31—Eddie McGoorty, Kenosha	Exh. 6
June	4—Stanley Ketchel, Milwaukee	L 10
July	4—Rudy Unholz, Kewanee, Ill.	Exh. 6
Aug.	13—Johnnie Carroll, Boston	KO 2
Aug.	13—Frank Mantell, Boston	KO 1
Aug.	18—Sailor Burke, New York	ND 6
Sept.	7—Stanley Ketchel, Los Angeles	KO 12
	(Won World Middleweight Title)	
Nov.	26—Stanley Ketchel, San.Fran.	KO by 11
	(Lost World Middleweight Title)	
Dec.	15—Hugo Kelly, Los Angeles	D 25

1909

Mar.	19—Jim Flynn, Los Angeles	ND 10
May	15—Hugo Kelly, Colma, Cal.	KO 1
July	5—Stanley Ketchel, Colma, Cal.	L 20
	(For Middleweight Title)	
July	14—Jim Flynn, Los Angeles	ND 10
Oct.	8—Willie Lewis, Philadelphia	ND 6
Nov.	11—Frank Klaus, Pittsburgh	ND 6

1910

Mar.	19—Willie Lewis, Paris, France	KO 3
May	19—Joe Thomas, San Francisco	KO 16
June	14—Al Goodale, Kansas City	KO 2
June	21—J. Twin Sullivan, Boston	W 12
Oct.	25—Ed Williams, Sydney, N.S.W.	KO 6
Dec.	26—Dave Smith, Sydney, N.S.W.	LF 10

(Claimed middleweight title after Ketchel's death.)

1911

Feb.	11—Cyc. Johnny Thompson, Sydney, N.S.W.	L 20
	(Lost middleweight title)	
Mar.	11—Dave Smith, Sydney, N.S.W.	KO 7
June	8—Jim Sullivan, London	KO 9
Aug.	22—Sailor Burke, New York	ND 10
Oct.	31—Bob Moha, Boston	L 12

(Thompson vacated title; Papke claimed same.)

1912

Feb.	22—Frank Mantell, Sacramento	L 20

(Mantell claimed title, but was not recognized outside of California)

May	2—Billy Leitch, New York	KO 2
June	29—*Marcel Moreau, Paris	W 16
Sept.	25—Jack Denning, New York	ND 10
Sept.	27—Leo Houck, Philadelphia	ND 6
Oct.	23—*Georges Carpentier, Paris	WF 17
Dec.	4—*Geo. Bernard, Paris	KO 7

*Title bout.

1913

Mar.	5—Frank Klaus, Paris	LF 15
	(Lost Middleweight title)	
June	16—Irish Jack Smith, N. Y. C.	L 10
Oct.	14—Marty Rowan, St. Louis, Mo.	ND 8

1919

Apr.	8—Soldier Bartfield, San Fran.	W 4

TB	KO	WD	WF	D	LD	LF	KOBY	ND	NC
64	29	9	1	7	6	2	1	9	0

Died Nov. 26, 1936—killed himself and wife at Newport, Cal.

Elected to Hall of Fame in 1972

JOHNNY (CYCLONE) THOMPSON

Born, June 20, 1876, Ogle County, Illinois. Nationality, Danish-American. Weight, 146 lbs. Height, 5 ft. 4 in.

Started professional career 1892 (early record unavailable).

1900-1901

Knockouts: E. J. Price, 1; Kid Weimer, 3; Billy Alms, 5; Orville Thorne, 4; Jim Balwick, 2; Kid Green, 2; Joe Percente, 4; Chas. Conway, 3; Jack Calmers, 3; Orville Thorne, 2; Kid Weimer, 1; Harry Fields, 2; Hank Mansfield, 2; Harry Little, 3; Kid Green, 4; Rocky Swanson, 2; Jack Culp, 1; Sandy Nelson, 3; Kid Sanderson, 1; Henry Erns, 3; Kid Weimer, 5; Kid Ryan, 5; Jack Rock, 5. Won: Kid Weimer, 6; Henry Erns, 6; Billy Mott, 6; Billy Malcolm, 10; Jimmy Kileen, 6; Bob Porter, 6. Kid Goodwin, 6; Orville Thorne, 6; Henry Fagin, 10; Red Morrissey, 10; Kid Munzie, 3; Kid Black, 4; Jimmy Kileen, 4; Bob Porter, 4; Frankie Baker, 4; Young Kenny, 6; Frank Clancy, 10; Freckley O'Brien, 6; Jack Reed, 6; Jack Galligan, 6; Frank Jordan, 6; Kid Black, 10. Draw: Ole Oleson, 6; Harry Griffin, 6; Otto Sieloff, 15; Billy Moore, 15; Jack Dougherty, 5; Otto Sieloff, 10. Lost: Adam Ryan, 6; Emil Sanchez, 6. Lost, Foul: Shine Reed, 4; Harry Griffin, 3.

1902

Mar.	21—Battling Nelson, Chicago	L 6
Nov.	7—Paddy Norton, Milwaukee	KO 4
Dec.	5—Mickey Riley, Milwaukee	D 6

1903

Apr.	9—Charlie Neary, Milwaukee	KO by 6
Apr.	24—Battling Nelson, Milwaukee	L 6
June	29—Curley Ulrich, De Kalb	L 4
July	16—Curley Ulrich, De Kalb	W 6
Aug.	6—Harry Fails, Houghton	D 10
Aug.	11—Curley Ulrich, Sycamore	W 3
Aug.	18—Mickey Riley, Sycamore	D 10
Aug.	23—Curley Ulrich, De Kalb	LF 5

1904

Feb.	5—George Memsic, Chicago	L 6
Feb.	28—Kid Farmer, Chicago	L 6
Mar.	23—Mickey Riley, Green Bay	L 6
Apr.	21—Harry Fails, Racine	D 6
Oct.	12—Harry Griffin, Aurora, Ill	W 6
Oct.	24—Henry Fagin, Dubuque	D 10

1905

Apr.	14—Jimmy Potts, Milwaukee	L 6
June	16—Young Scotty, Duluth	W 6
Oct.	12—Kid Farmer, Peoria	D 10

1906

Jan.	19—Frank Jordan, La Salle	D 10
Feb.	20—Kid Herrick, Janesville	LF 6
Feb.	23—Frank Jordan, Janesville	D 8
Apr.	5—Otto Sieloff, New Orleans	KO 8
May	2—Edward Purdy, La Salle	W 10
May	17—Billy Mayfield, Peoria	W 10
June	21—Kid Black, Peoria	KO 2
June	29—Harry Griffin, Davenport	WF 3
July	19—Walter Parker, Burke, Idaho	W 6
July	7—Montana Kid, Los Angeles	D 10
Aug.	28—Dick Hyland, Los Angeles	WF 9
Nov.	15—Dick Hyland, Ogden, Utah	L 20
Nov.	28—Lew Powell, Colma, Cal.	LF 10
Dec.	11—Fred Ward, Vallejo, Cal.	KO 6
Dec.	15—Jack Clifford, Marysville	KO 5

1907

Jan.	8—Maurice Thompson, Ogden	KO 15
Feb.	22—Rufe Turner, Marysville	KO 11
Mar.	26—Dick Hyland, San Francisco	D 20
July	24—Peter Sullivan, Ogden	L 20
Sept.	2—Rudolph Unholz, Ogden	WF 9
Sept.	27—Charlie Neary, Milwaukee	L 10
Nov.	2—Freddie Welsh, Philadelphia	ND 6
Nov.	11—Kid Goodman, Chelsea	D 12

1908

Mar.	14—Johnny Murphy, San Fran.	KO 8
May	5—Mickey Gannon, Boston	D 12
June	29—Pete Sullivan, Salt Lake	KO 12
July	28—Kid Dalton, Ogden	KO 5
Oct.	29—Rudy Unholz, San Francisco	KO 11
Nov.	26—Kid Dalton, Marysville	KO 16

1909

Jan.	15—Peter Sullivan, Pocatello, Idaho	L 20
Mar.	5—Mickey Gannon, N. Y. C.	ND 10
Mar.	22—Adam Ryan, Philadelphia	ND 6
May	25—Ray Bronson, Columbus, O.	ND 6
July	5—Danny Goodman, Hammond	W 10
Nov.	8—Packey McFarland, Kans. City	L 10
Dec.	17—Dick Hyland, Kansas City	W 10

1910

Jan.	20—Tom McCarthy, San Francisco	D 20
Mar.	24—Charlies Norval, Oakland	W 10
Apr.	27—Chick Hudson, Oakland	KO 7
May	13—Pete Sullivan, Salt Lake City	KO 9
June	15—Birdlegs Collins, Salt Lake C.	KO 17
July	4—Pete Sullivan, Pocatello	KO 9

Aug. 18—Geo. Leatham, Aurora, Ill. ..KO 3
Nov. 9—Rudy Unholz, Sydney, N. S. W.W 6
Dec. 3—Hughie Mehegan, Sydney ..KO 5
Dec. 28—Tim Land, Sydney, N. S. W. .KO 20
1911
Jan. 11—Jerry Jerome, Brisbane, Aus..KO 3
Jan. 21—Tim Land, Sydney, N. S. W..KO 2
Feb. 6—Dave Smith, Sydney, N. S. W.. L 20
Feb. 11—Billy Papke, Sydney, N. S. W..W 20
(Won Middleweight Title)
Apr. 28—Hugo Kelly, Racine, Wis.....ND 10
July 27—Willie Lewis, N. Y. C. ......ND 10
Aug. 17—Frank Klaus, N. Y. C. ......ND 10
Oct. —Thompson vacated title.
Dec. 16—Bandsman Rice, Sydney .....L 20
1912
Jan. 26—Dave Smith, Sydney, N. S. W.. L 20
Feb. 17—Jack Lester, Sydney ....KO 20
Mar. 23—Jack Lester, Sydney ....L 20
July 3—Frank Mantell, Sacramento ..D 20
Sept. 16—Geo. K. O. Brown, Peoria ..KO 5
Sept. 16—Eddie McGoorty, Cincinnati .ND 10
Oct. 10—Art Godfrey, Fond du Lac .KO 8
1913
Feb. 17—Bob Moha, Milwaukee ......ND 10
Apr. 7—Young Mahoney, Superior ..ND 10
1914
Sept. 28—Gunboat Smith, Pittsburgh ..ND 6

TB	KO	WD	WF	D	LD	LF	KOBY	ND	NC
139	47	34	3	20	18	5	1	11	0

Died, Sycamore, Ill., May 28, 1951.

FRANK MANTELL
(Frank Otto Mintell)
Born, June 25 1886, Brandenburg, Germany. Nationality, German. Of Pawtucket, R. I. Weight, 154-158 lbs. Height, 5 ft. 9½ ins.
1906
Feb. 26—George Perry, Providence.....KO 2
Mar. 12—Jack Winters, Val. Falls, R. I...W 8
Mar. 25—Billy Smith, Providence......KO 2
May 17—Eddie Pendergast, Val. Falls ..KO 4
May 29—Hayward Briggs, Brockton....D 6
June 12—Jack Winters, Providence.....KO 3
Sept. 13—Bogudas Hyde, Val. Falls ....W 10
Oct. 29—Billy Yourall, Valley Falls ....D 10
Dec. 10—Billy Yourall, Providence.....KO 2
Dec. 28—Joe Ryan, Philadelphia.......KO 5
1907
Jan. 10—Jack Williams, Philadelphia ...ND 6
Jan. 14—Peck Lafavor, Valley Falls ....KO 5
Feb. 22—Kid Williams, Providence ......D 15
Mar. 14—Jack Robinson, Philadelphia ..ND 6
Apr. —Eddie Haney, Philadelphia ....ND 6
May 31—Russel Van Horn, Dayton .....D 8
July 4—Martin Judge, Salt Lake City ..D 15
Aug. 19—Rube Smith, Ogden, Utah ......L 20
Sept. 16—Andy Malloy, Helper, Utah ...KO 12
Oct. 16—Jack Rogers, Helper, Utah ....KO 9
Nov. 1—Honey Mellody, Dayton, O...KO 15
1908
Jan. 23—Harry Lewis, New Haven ..KO by 3
Feb. 27—Kid Farmer, Marysville, Cal. ...W 20
May 1—Mike Donovan, Dayton, O. ....D 20
Aug. 13—Billy Papke, Boston ....KO by 1
Sept. 7—Tommy Sullivan, New York ..ND 6
Dec. 4—Johnny O'Keefe, Los Angeles ..W 10
1909
Jan. 14—Jack Gardner, Sacramento....KO 8
Feb. 9—Rube Smith, Sacramento .....KO 12
May 21—Frank Mayfield, Sacramento..KO 13
Mar. 26—Kid Williams, Sacramento ....WF 13
Apr. 30—Rube Smith, Sacramento .....KO 16
July 5—Jack Twin Sullivan, Sacram...W 20
Sept. 6—Jack Twin Sullivan, San Fran...D 10
Nov. 19—Al Neill, Sacramento ....KO 11
Dec. 12—Bill McKinnon, Woonsocket ..D 12
1910
Feb. 2—Tom Sawyer, Thornton, R. I...KO 2
Mar. 2—Harry Mansfield, Thornton ....W 15
Mar. 29—Frank Klaus, Boston .....KO by 9
May. 19—Denver Jno. O'Keefe, Sacram...D 20
Aug. 1—Dixie Kid, N. Y. C. ....ND 10
Aug. 16 Jimmy Howard, Albany ....ND 10
Sept. 5—Bill McKinnon, Manchester ....L 16
Sept. 28—Frank Klaus, Pittsburgh ......ND 6
Oct. 25—Jim Smith, N. Y. C. ....KO 7
Nov. 11—Leo Houck, Thornton.........L 15

Nov. 24—Dixie Kid, Waterbury ....NC 5
Dec. 2—Sailor Burke, New York ......ND 10
1911
*Feb. 7—Joe Thomas, Augusta ....ND 6
*Feb. 7—Joe Thomas, Augusta ....ND 6
Feb. 22—Jeff Clak, New Bedford ....D 12
Mar. 13—Steve Smith, N. Y. C..........W 10
Mar. 15—Harry Mansfield, Columbus....W 12
Apr. 4—Jack Dillon, Boston ....L 12
Apr. 19—Bill McKinnon, Manchester ....D 15
May 8—Jack Herrick, Dayton ....D 15
June 19—Tom McMahon, New Castle ...ND 10
July 12—Barney Williams, N. Y. C.....ND 10
July 21—Ted Nelson, N. Y. C..........KO 5
Aug. 4—Connie Schmidt, N. Y. C......KO 8
Sept. 21—Leo Houck, N. Y. C..........ND 10
Oct. 17—Mont. Dan Sullivan, N. Y. C...ND 10
Oct. 23—Larry English, Troy, N. Y. ....ND 10
Nov. 20—Kid George, Sacramento ......W 20
Nov. 27—Frank Perron, Providence, R. I. W 15
*Same night.
1912
Feb. 22—Billy Papke, Sacramento ......W 20
*(Claimed world championship)
*Mar. 30—Jack Henrick, Vernon, Cal. ....W 20
*(Advertised as world title bout by the promoter)
Apr. 9—Russel Kane, Marysville, Cal...KO 8
June 4—Dan Sullivan, Sacramento ....W 20
July 3—Cy. John Thompson, Sacram...D 20
Sept. 4—Frank Perron, Thornton......KO 7
Sept. 25—Billy Glover, Thornton.......KO 3
1913
Jan. 19—Jack Dillon, Thornton ....L 15
Jan. 14—Tommy Gavigan, Youngstown ..L 12
Feb. 19—Jeff Smith, Paris ....D 20
Apr. 7—Pat O'Keefe, London ....L 20
May 26—Larry English, N. Y. C. ......ND 10
June 7—Fred Gunther, Staten Isl. .....KO 3
May 31—Tommy Bergen, Brooklyn.....ND 10
June 9—Fighting Kennedy, N. Y. C. ...ND 10
June 30—Sailor Grande, Sacramento ....L 20
July 15—Willie Meehan, Oakland ....L 10
Sept. 17—Harry Krantz, Sacramento ....D 20
Sept. 26—Roy Taylor, Reno ....D 20
1914
Jan. 1—Billy Weeks, Vancouver, B. C...W 15
May 11—Bob Moha, Milwaukee ....ND
Sept. 28—Jack Dillon, Columbus, O. ....ND 12
Oct. 12—K. O. Brennan, Buffalo .....LF 7
Nov. 5—Battling Levinsky, Providence .D 12
Dec. 25—Joe Borrell, Philadelphia .....ND 6
1915
Feb. 20—Jack Dillon, New York ....ND 10
May 19—Leo Houck, Providence ....L 12
June 11—Jack Dillon, Cincinnati ....ND 10
1916
Apr. 26—Jack McCarron, Dayton, O.....L 15
Aug. 3—Jack McCarron, Dayton ......D 15
Aug. 18—Gus Christie, Springfield, O. ...L 15
Oct. 4—Jack McCarron, Allentown ...ND 10
1917
Jan. 1—Jeff Smith, Baltimore ....L 15
Feb. 26—Jack McCarron, Toledo ....ND 12
June 14—Harry Greb, Uniontwn., Pa. KO by 1
Oct. 12—Mike Gibbons, St. Paul ....KO by 3

TB	KO	WD	WF	D	LD	LF	KOBY	ND	NC
101	23	14	1	18	13	1	5	25	1

Died on October 9, 1951, Phoenix, Arizona.

FRANK KLAUS
Born, December 30, 1887, Pittsburgh, Pa. Nationality, German-American. Weight, 158-160 lbs. Height, 5 ft. 7½ in. Managed by George Engel.
1904
Knockouts: Joe Morgan, 2; Cady Miller, 1; Frank Walton, 2. Won: Jack Simboe, 4; Frank Clarke, 4.
1905
—Pat Hogan, Pittsburgh ....W 4
—Andy Diamond, Pittsburgh ..KO 1
—George Decker, Pittsburgh ...W 6
Mar. 26—Ned Charnoff, Pittsburgh ....W 6
June 25—Dick Given, Pittsburgh .....W 6
Aug. 24—George Frazier, Ohio ....D 33
Oct. 29—Tom Broderick, Pittsburgh ..KO 2
Nov. 12—Jimmy Frazier, Pittsburgh ....W 6
Dec. 14—Mike Ward, Pittsburgh .....KO 4
1906
May 8—Jac Bruce, Pittsburgh ....W 6

Oct. 28—Dick Given, Pittsburgh ......W 6
Dec. 6—Paul Moore, Pittsburgh ......W 6
1907
Jan. 10—Paul Moore, Pittsburgh ......W 6
Dec. 10—Paul Moore, Pittsburgh ......W 6
1908
Mar. 16—Alex Laird, Latrobe, Pa. ....KO 2
Mar. 28—Billy Clarke, Philadelphia ...ND 6
May 4—Cub White, Philadelphia ....ND 6
Sept. 7—Jack Fitzgerald, Philadelphia .ND 6
Sept. 8—Dutch Zimmerman, N. Y. C. ..KO 3
Sept. 11—Jack Robinson, N. Y. C. ....ND 6
Sept. 12—Billy Clark, Philadelphia ....ND 6
Sept. 16—Jack Robinson, N. Y. C. ....ND 6
Sept. 25—Johnny Carroll, N. Y. C. ....ND 6
Oct. 24—Jim Donovan, N. Y. C. .....KO 6
Oct. 30—Kid Williams, N. Y. C. ......KO 4
Nov. 16—Jack Fitzgerald, Philadelphia .ND 6
Nov. 28—Billy Clarke, Philadelphia ...KO 2
Dec. 22—Paul Moore, Pittsburgh .....ND 6
1909
Jan. 16—Tommy Crawford, Pittsburgh KO 1
Feb. 8—Jim Donovan, Pittsburgh ....ND 6
Feb. 11—Pat Carney, Pittsburgh ....KO 1
Feb. 18—Harry Mansfield, Pittsburgh .ND 6
Mar. 4—Cy Flynn, Pittsburgh ....KO 3
Mar. 18—Kid Silbe, Pittsburgh ....KO 2
Apr. 24—Harry Lewis, Philadelphia ...WF 6
Apr. 31—Jack Fitzgerald, Philadelphia .ND 6
May 15—Jim Smith, Philadelphia ....KO 1
May 15—Harry Mansfield, Philadelphia KO 2
June 25—Hugo Kelly, Pittsburgh .....ND 6
Sept. 17—H. McGann, Pittsb., (Police) .WF 3
Oct. 26—Jack Rowan, Pittsburgh ....KO 2
Nov. 11—Billy Papke, Pittsburgh ....ND 6
Nov. 27—Harry Lewis, Philadelphia ...ND 6
Dec. 18—Joe Thomas, Philadelphia ...ND 6
Dec. 21—Porky Flynn, Boston ....W 12
1910
Jan. 7—Billy Berger, Pittsburgh ....ND 6
Jan. 18—J. (Twin) Sullivan, Boston ....W 12
Mar. 23—Stanley Ketchell, Pittsburgh .ND 6
Mar. 29—Frank Mantell, Boston ....KO 9
Apr. 12—Jimmy Gardner, Boston .....W 12
Sept. 28—Frank Mantell, Pittsburgh ..ND 6
Oct. 29—Leo Houck, Philadelphia ....ND 6
Nov. 24—Jimmy Goodman, Boston ...KO 8
Nov. 29—Jimmy Gardner, Boston .....L 12
1911
Jan. 11—Billy Berger, Pittsburgh ....ND 6
Jan. 31—Jimmy Gardner, Boston .....D 12
Feb. 14—Leo Houck, Boston ....W 12
Feb. 7—Willie Lewis, N.Y.C. ....KO 6
Mar. 28—Mont. Jack Sullivan, N.Y.C. ..KO 3
Apr. 11—Jimmy Gardner, Pittsburgh ...ND 6
May 6—Bill McKinnon, Philadelphia ..KO 6
June 15—*Mont. Dan Sullivan, Oakland .W 3
July 1—Vic Hansen, Coalinga, Cal. ..KO 8
Aug. 17—Cy. Johnny Thompson,
N.Y.C. ....ND 10
Oct. 12—Tommy Sullivan, Boston ....KO 2
Oct. 18—Leo Houck, Philadelphia ....ND 6
Dec. 6—Jack Dillon, Pittsburgh ....ND 6
*Sullivan claimed foul.
Dec. 20—Hugo Kelly, Boston ....L 10
1912
Jan. 15—Jimmy Howard, Pittsburgh ..ND 6
Jan. 29—K. O. Brown, Pittsburgh ....KO 6
Feb. 22—Geo. Sailor Petroskey, San Fran.W 20
Mar. 23—Jack Dillon, Daly City, Cal. ...W 20
May 3—Jack Dillon, N. Y. C. ....ND 10
June 24—Geo. Carpentier, Dieppe, Fr. .WF 19
(For vacant Middleweight Title as
recognized in Europe. Klaus 3 pounds
overweight.)
July 1—Jimmy Gardner, Boston ....KO 3
Sept. 9—Marcel Moreau, Vichy, Fr. ...W 4
Sept. 21—M. Boine, Lyons, France ....KO 3
Nov. 28—Jimmy Goodman, Boston ...KO 8
1913
Mar. 5—Billy Papke, Paris ....WF 15
(Won Middleweight Title)
May 24—Eddie McGoorty, Pittsburgh .ND 6
May 29—Jack Dillon, Indianapolis ....ND 10
Sept. 29—Eddie McGoorty, Milwaukee .ND 10
Oct. 11—George Chip, Pittsburgh .KO by 6
(Lost Middleweight Title)
Dec. 23—George Chip, Pittsburgh .KO by 5
(For Middleweight Title)
1918
Feb. 7—Harry Greb, Pittsburgh .....ND 6

TB	KO	WD	WF	D	LD	LF	KOBY	ND	NC
90	27	20	4	2	2	0	2	33	0

Died February 8, 1948, Pittsburgh, Pa.
Elected Hall of Fame 1974

GEORGE CHIP
(George Chipulonis)
Born, August 25, 1888, Scranton, Pa.
Nationality, Lithuanian-American. Weight, 158
lbs. Height, 5 ft. 8 in. Managed by Jimmy
Dime.
1909
Knockout: George Gill, 2; John Chew, 1;
Battling Connors, 4; Thunder Boltless, 3;
Punched Eagle, 3. Won (foul): Billy Manfredo,
2. No decision: Billy Manfredo (three times), 6;
Jack Abbott, 6; Jimmy Perry, 6; Battling
Simpson, 6; Billy Manfredo, 10.
1910
Knockout: Billy Manfredo, 5. No
decision: Tom McMahon, 6; Battling Connors,
6; Buck Crouse (twice), 6; Jimmy Perry (twice),
6; Billy Berger (twice), 6; Jack Dillon, 6;
Battling Simpson, 15; Cy Flynn, 10. Knockout
by: Buck Crouse, 3.
1911
Jan. 24—Jack Dillon, Dayton, O. .....L 15
Feb. 10—Jack Morgan, Indianapolis ...KO 10
Mar. 14—Jack Fitzgerald, Pittsburgh ..ND 6
Apr. 13—Geo. Jackson, New Castle, Pa. KO 3
Apr. 28—Jack Dillon, Terre Haute ....ND 10
May 15—Leo Houck, Philadelphia ....ND 6
Sept. 16—Jack Abbott, McKeesport, Pa. ND 6
Oct. 21—Jack Abbott, Pittsburgh ....KO 6
Nov. 22—Jack Dillon, Youngstown, O. .ND 12
Dec. 2—Geo K. O. Brown, Pittsburgh ND 6
Dec. 18—Joe Gorman, Akron, O. .....KO 5
1912
Jan. 1—Buck Crouse, Pittsburgh ....ND 6
Jan. 22—Buck Crouse, Pittsburgh ....ND 6
Feb. 10—Jack Dillon, Pittsburgh ......ND 6
Feb. 13—Walter Coffey, Rochester ....KO 3
Feb. 20—Jeff Smith, Thornton, R. I. ..L 15
Feb. 28—Battling Simpson, Johnstown ND 10
Mar. 18—Billy Berger, Pittsburgh ....ND 6
Mar. 25—Jimmie Howard, Akron ....ND 12
Apr. 18—Buck Crouse, Pittsburgh ....ND 6
Apr. 22—Kid Wagner, Easton, Pa. ....ND 10
May 16—Kid Clark, Columbus, O. ....ND 10
June 13—Leo Houck, Lancaster, Pa. ..ND 6
July 25—Jack Dillon, Indianapolis ....ND 10
Aug. 8—Tim O'Neill, Pittsburgh ....ND 6
Sept. 21—Tim O'Neill, Pittsburgh ....ND 6
Oct. 4—Geo. (Kid) Clark, Pittsburgh .KO 6
Oct. 19—Jack Dillon, Pittsburgh ....ND 6
Oct. 28—Geo. K. O. Brown, Syracuse .ND 10
Nov. 11—Jack Dillon, Columbus, O. ..ND 10
Nov. 18—Howard Morrow, Syracuse ..ND 10
Dec. 2—Paddy Lavin, Youngstown, O..KO 7
Dec. 4—K. O. Brennan, Buffalo, N. Y. ND 10
1913
Jan. 4—Tommy Gavigan, Pittsburgh .ND 6
Jan. 20—Howard Morrow, Syracuse ..ND 10
Feb. 11—Peck Miller, Altoona, Pa. ....ND 6
Feb. 17—Tommy Connors, Scranton ..ND 6
Feb. 24—Tommy Gavigan, YoungstownND 2
Mar. 17—Walter Monoghan, Pittsburgh ND 6
Apr. 14—Jack Dillon, Youngstown ...ND 12
May 14—Dick Gilbert, Pittsburgh ....ND 6
Sept. 30—Tommy Gavigan, Akron, O. ..KO 11
Oct. 11—Frank Klaus, Pittsburgh ....KO 6
(Won Middleweight Title)
Nov. 15—Leo Houck, Philadelphia ....ND 6
Nov. 25—Tim O'Neill, Racine, Wis. ...ND 10
Dec. 23—*Frank Klaus, Pittsburgh ...KO 5
*Title bout.
1914
Jan. 12—Gus Christie, Milwaukee ....ND 10
Jan. 19—Tim O'Neill, Grand Rapids ..KO 2
Jan. 26—Joe Borrell, Philadelphia ....ND 6
Apr. 6—Al McCoy, Brooklyn ....KO by 1
(Lost Middleweight Title)
Apr. 14—Geo. K. O. Brown, Akron ...ND 12
Apr. 21—Leo Houck, Youngstown ....L 12
May 26—Sailor Petroskey, Vernon, Cal.KO 12
July 4—Billy Murray, San Francisco .KO 15
Sept. 30—Billy Murray, San Francisco .KO 4
Nov. 6—Jimmy Clabby, Daly City, Cal. L 20
1915
Feb. 20—Jack McCarron, Philadelphia .ND 6
Feb. 22—Buck Crouse, Pittsburgh ....ND 6

Mar. 15—Sailor Szarmanski, Cincinnati KO   8
Mar. 22—Jimmy Clabby, Grand Rapids ND   6
Apr.   6—Al. McCoy, New York ......ND 10
Apr. 27—Jim Clabby, Marinette, Wis. ..ND 10
May 12—*Jimmy Clabby, New York .. NC   8
June 14—Sailor Grande, Philadelphia ..ND   6
June 21—Jack McCarron, Albany, N. Y.ND 10
July   5—Jack Dillon, Kansas City, Mo. .. D 10
Oct. 18—Harry Greb, Pittsburgh .....ND   6
Oct. 29—Jackie Clark, Scranton, Pa. ..ND 10
Dec.   7—Jeff Smith, Boston ....L-F   7
Dec. 16—Knockout Baker, Scranton ..KO   3
Dec. 21—Frank Loughrey, Boston ..... W   9
*Stopped by referee, declared no contest.
1916
Jan.   8—Silent Martin, Brooklyn ....ND 10
Jan. 20—Al. McCoy, Brooklyn ......ND 10
Feb. 12—Frankie Notter, Brooklyn ...KO   4
Feb. 22—Young Ahearn, Brooklyn ...L-F   5
Mar. 13—Gus Christie, Memphis ......D   8
Mar. 23—Johnny Howard, Bridgeport .KO   6
May 15—Sailor Grande, Bridgeport ..KO 14
June 26—Harry Greb, New Castle ....ND 10
Sept. 30—Les Darcy, Sydney ..... KO by   9
Nov.   6—Art Magirl, Melbourne ......KO 14
1917
Feb. 19—Geo. K.O.Brown, YoungstownND 12
Feb. 26—Sailor Einert, Cincinnati ....KO   2
Mar. 12—Bob Moha, Youngstown .....KO   4
Apr.   9—K. O. Loughlin, Philadelphia .ND   6
Apr. 23—Val Sontag, Bridgeport .....KO   2
May 22—Harry Greb, Pittsburgh .....ND 10
May 29—Jack Dillon, Cincinnati .....ND 10
June   8—Knockout Brown, Racine, Wis.ND 10
July   4—Mike Gibbons, Youngstown .ND 12
July 24—Johnny Howard, Providence ... W 12
Aug. 22—Tom Gibbons, St. Paul, Minn. ND 10
Nov.   9—Al Rogers, Duluth, Minn. ...KO   4
Nov. 19—Harry Greb, Cincinnati .....ND 10
1918
Jan. 25—Jack Dillon, Duluth ....ND 10
Feb.   4—Tommy Gibbons, Pittsburgh .ND 10
Mar.   7—Tommy Gibbons, Scranton ..ND 10
Mar. 10—Young Joe Borrell, Phila. ...ND 10
Apr. 24—Clay Turner, Bridgeport ....L-F 15
May   3—Tommy Gibbons, Des Moines . L 12
June 25—Eddie McGoorty, Racine .....ND 10
July   4—Leo Bens, Butte, Mont. ...... L 10
Sept. 27—Butch O'Hagen, Philadelphia .ND   6
1919
Jan. 31—Mike Gibbons, Duluth ......ND 10
Mar. 10—Tommy Robson, Syracuse ..ND 10
Mar. 31—Young Fisher, Syracuse .....ND 10
Apr. 11—Tommy Gibbons, Denver .... L 10
May 10—Jeff Smith, Baltimore .... L 12
June 10—Mike Gibbons, Terre Haute ..ND 10
June 17—Bud Clancy, St. Louis ......KO   2
July 22—K. O. Loughlin, Buffalo ....ND 10
Oct.   1—K. O. Brown, Detroit ......ND 10
Oct. 20—Tommy Robson, Jersey City .ND   8
Oct. 27—Russell Maneri, New Orleans .KO   2
Nov. 11—Eugene Brosseau, Portl'd., Me.ND 12
Nov. 28—Martin Burke, New Orleans ..ND 10
Dec. 13—George K. O. Brown, New Orl. D 15
1920
Apr. 19—Geo. K.O. Brown, New Orleans W 20
June 13—Frank Carbone, Youngstown ND 12
July 11—Happy Littleton, New Orleans L 15
Aug. 25—Johnny Howard, Montreal ..ND 10
Sept. 17—Paul Roman, Dallas, Texas ..ND 10
Nov.   8—Ted Block, Detroit, Mich. ...ND 10
Dec.   6—Eddie McGoorty, La Salle, Ill. ND 10
1921
Jan.   7—Bryan Downey, Cleveland, O. ND 10
Jan. 17—Johnny Wilson, Pittsburgh ..ND 10
(Middleweight Title Bout)
Feb. 21—Battling Ortega, New York ... L 15
Apr.   4—Whitey Wenzel, Pittsburgh ..ND 10
1922
Apr. 24—Frankie Maguire, Lancaster ..ND   8

TB KO WD WF D LD LF KOBY ND NC
155 34   3   1   3 10 3   3   97 1
Died, November 6, 1960, New Castle, Pa.

AL McCOY
(Al Rudolph)
Born, Oct. 23, 1894, Rosenhayn, N. J.
Nationality,   German-American.   Weight,
158-160 lbs. Height, 5 ft. 8 in. Managed by T.
Brennan, Jack Daugherty and Dan Morgan.
1908
Knockout: Unknown, 2.

1909
Knockouts: Dave Seide, 6; Kid Ryan, 2.
No decision: Willy Scott, 4; Joe Gilbert, 10;
Gus Murphy, 6; Benny Burke, 4; Chester
Walcott, 6; Spike O'Neil, 6; Young Cote, 6;
Young Hugo Kelly, 6; Kid Parsons, 6; Jim
Rippin, 6; Mickey Flynn, 6; Billy Shea, 6.
1910
Knockout: Buffalo Kid Ryan, 3. Won:
Johnny Glover, 12; Cliff Cote, 6; Tommy
Riley, 6. Draw: Johnny Gallant, 6; Jimmy
McGuiness, 12. No decision: Terry Brooks, 6;
Arthur Cote, 6; Spike O'Neil, 6; Shadow
McCormick, 6.
1911
Knockouts: Jack Ryan, 3; Jim Mc-
Guiness, 1; Jim McGuiness, 6; Eddy Hamburg,
2. Won: George Niedoff, 6; Billy Shea, 12;
Johnny Fraser, 6; Billy O'Brien, 6; Chester
Walcott, 6; Jack Langdon, 12; Henry Hall, 6;
Billy Shea, 12; George Niedoff, 12; Young Hugo
Kelly, 12; Kid Parsons, 6; Tommy Riley, 6;
Wild Bill Fleming, 6; Spike O'Neil, 6; George
Niedoff, 15. Draw: Young Hugo Kelly, 6;
Johnny Stewart, 6.
1912
Mar. 29—Young Otto, New York ....ND 10
Apr. 19—Johnny Waltz, Brooklyn ....KO   2
July 19—Mickey Farrell, Rockaway . .ND 10
Oct. 16—Johnny Shaw, Brooklyn ....KO   3
Nov.   9—Young Erne, Philadelphia ...ND   6
Dec.   4—Gus Christie, Dayton, O. ....ND 15
Dec. 25—Joe White, Brooklyn ......KO   8
Knockouts: Dick   Grant,   3;   Jack
Beckman, 2; Jack Smith, 2; Sailor Maher, 3;
Eddy Hanlon, 2; Battling Jack Nelson, 4; Billy
Sherman, 2; Jack Howard, 10; Charley Seiger,
3. Won: Bill Fleming, 6. No decision: Terry
McGraw,   10;   Rudolph   Heinz, 10; Young
Hickey, 10; Dave Kurtz, 10; Joe Stein, 10;
Marty Brown, 10.
1913
Jan.   1—Young McCartney, Phila. ...ND   6
Jan.   8—Harry Price, Brooklyn ......ND 10
Jan. 23—Wildcat Ferns, Dayton, O. ...D 15
Feb. 14—Al Thiel, Brooklyn ....ND 10
Mar. 14—Bud Anderson, Brooklyn ...ND 10
Apr. 28—Larry Ryan, Brooklyn .....ND 10
May 14—Young Ahearn, N. Y. C. ...ND 10
May 16—Eddie Mack, Brooklyn .....KO   4
May 28—Wildcat Ferns, Dayton .....D 20
June   6—Terry Mitchell, Brooklyn ....D 10
June 27—Billy Sherman, Rockaway ...KO   2
July 11—Soldier Bartfield, Brooklyn ..ND 10
July 12—Billy Grupp, N. Y. C. ......ND 10
July 22—Mike Farrell, Rockaway ....ND 10
July 26—Bill Fleming, Bangor, Me. ...ND   6
Aug.   9—Bill Anderson, Brooklyn ....ND 10
Sept. 9—Johnny Stewart, Bangor, Me. ND   6
Sept. 26—Noah Brusso, Boston ....W 12
Oct. 22—KO Brennan, Brooklyn .....ND 10
Nov.   1—Freddie Kiebler, N. Y. C. ...ND 10
Nov.   7—Mike Farrell, Brooklyn .....ND 10
Nov. 19—Billy Anderson, Brooklyn ...ND 10
Dec. 19—Zulu Kid, Brooklyn ....ND 10
1914
Jan. 31—Johnny Shaw, W. Brighton ..KO   3
Feb. 23—Mike Gibbons, Brooklyn ...ND 10
Apr.   6—George Chip, Brooklyn .....KO   1
(Won middleweight championship of world)
May 21—Billy Murray, Brooklyn ....ND 10
June 11—Billy Murray, Brooklyn ....ND 10
July   9—Soldier Bartfield, Brooklyn ..ND 10
Aug.   6—Soldier Bartfield, Brooklyn ..ND 10
Oct. 19—K. O. Brennan, Buffalo ....ND 10
Knockouts: George Pearsall, 1; Willie
Lewis, 4. No decision: Irish Jack Smith, 10; Joe
Chip, 10; Tommy Teague, 10.
1915
Jan. 24—Billy Grupp, N. Y. C. ......ND 10
Jan. 25—Joe Borrell, Philadelphia ....ND   6
Feb. 16—New Al McCoy, N. Y. C. ...ND 10
Apr.   6—George Chip, Brooklyn .....ND 10
May   4—Jimmy Clabby, Brooklyn ...ND 10
May 31—Silent Martin, Brooklyn ....ND 10
June 11—Soldier Bartfield, Brooklyn ..ND 10
Sept. 9—Young Ahearn, Brooklyn ...ND 10
Oct.   4—Soldier Bartfield, Brooklyn ..ND 10
Nov. 25—Jack McCarron, Philadelphia .ND   6
No decision: Zulu Kid, 10; K. O.
Brennan, 10; Italian Joe Gans, 10; Silent
Martin, 10; Kid Wagner, 10; Silent Martin, 15;
Tommy Madden, 10; Tex Kelly, 10.

539

1916

Jan.	1—Young Ahearn, Brooklyn	...ND 10
Jan.	20—George Chip, Brooklyn	.....ND 10
Mar.	21—Leo Benz, N. Y. C.	......ND 10
Apr.	8—Jack Hammond, N. Y. C.	...KO 2
Apr.	17—Al Thiel McCoy, N. Y. C.	...ND 10
May	9—Young Ahearn, N. Y. C.	....ND 10
June	26—Hugh Ross, Bridgeport, Conn.	..W 15
July	4—Dave Kurtz, N. Y. C.	........ND 10
Sept.	25—Jack Hanlon, Brooklyn	.....KO 3
Sept.	28—Jackie Clark, Scranton, Pa.	...ND 10

1917

Feb.	26—Jack Dillon, N. Y. C.	.......ND 10
Apr.	30—Harry Greb, Pittsburgh	.....ND 10
July	4—Jackie Clark, Lonaconing, Md.	ND 10
Nov.	8—Montana Dan Sullivan, Adams	W 12
Nov.	14—Mike O'Dowd, Brooklyn . KO by	6

(Lost middleweight championship of world)

1918

Jan.	9—Battling Ortega, Oakland	..... L 4
Mar.	2—K. O. Kruvosky, Oakland	.... L 4
May	13—Harry Greb, Cincinnati	....ND 10
July	4—Jack Dillon, Charleston, W. V.	ND 10
Aug.	10—Stkyds. T. Murphy, N. Y. C. Exh.	4
Oct.	11—Stkyds. T. Murphy, Brooklyn, N. Y.	.... L 10

1919

July	17—Mike O'Dowd, St. Paul .. KO by	3

(Middleweight Title Bout)

TB	KO	WD	WF	D	LD	LF	KOBY	ND	NC
144	28	22	0	7	3	0	2	82	0

Died in Los Angeles, Cal., August 22, 1966

JEFF SMITH
(Jerome Jeffords)

Born, April 23, 1891, New York. Nationality, American. Weight, 158 lbs. Height, 5 ft. 9 in. Managed by Al Lippe.

1910

Mar.	7—Ray Hatfield, Newark	.... W 4
Apr.	18—Tony Bender, Newark	.... W 4
May	4—Ray Hatfield, Newark	.......KO 3
May	23—Cyclone Flynn, Newark	......KO 2
Aug.	3—Yg. Joe Grimm, N. Y. C.	......KO 4
Aug.	22—Ben Duglass, Newark	.........W 4
Oct.	25—*Jack Zinn, N. Y. C.	.........KO 1
Oct.	25—*Al Rose, N. Y. C.	..........KO 3
Nov.	7—Ray Hatfield, Newark	.... W 4
Nov.	11—Battling Ryan, N. Y. C.	.......ND 6
Nov.	23—Batt. S. Ryan, N. Y. C.	.......ND 6
Nov.	25—Bill Lynch, N. Y. C.	........KO 2
Dec.	2—Jack Wade, N. Y. C.	........KO 1
Dec.	10—Sammy Delmont, Bayonne	....W 4
Dec.	23—Jack Denning, N. Y. C.	.......ND 6

*Same night.

1911

Jan.	5—Eddie Rector, N. Y. C.	.......KO 1
Jan.	19—Charlie Seiger, N. Y. C.	......KO 2
Jan.	30—Charlie Lawrence, Newark	.....W 4
Feb.	2—Jim Heywood, N. Y. C.	.......KO 2
Feb.	14—Kid Henry, Albany	.........ND 10
Mar.	28—Johnny Carroll, N. Y. C.	.....ND 10
Apr.	18—Paddy Lavin, N. Y. C.	......ND 10
May	1—Al McCloskey, Perth	........KO 2
May	16—Ftg. Dick Nelson, N. Y. C.	...ND 10
June	22—Jimmy Clabby, N. Y. C.	.....ND 10
Aug.	29—Jack Denning, N. Y. C.	......ND 10
Sept.	30—Ted Nelson, Albany	.........KO 4
Oct.	12—Willie Lewis, N. Y. C.	......ND 10

1912

Feb.	1—Young Loughrey, N. Y. C.	....KO 9
Feb.	20—George Chip, Thornton	......W 15
Feb.	26—Eddie Palmer, Philadelphia	...ND 6
Feb.	27—Billy West, N. Y. C.	........ND 10
Apr.	11—Mike Gibbons, N. Y. C.	........ND 10
June	6—Mike Glover, N. Y. C.	......ND 10
June	25—Jimmy Howard, N. Y. C.	.....ND 10
Sept.	24—Larry English, Albany	.......ND 10
Oct.	30—Tom Leary, Paris	..........W 10
Nov.	16—Harry Mansfield, Paris	.......W 3
Dec.	21—Jim O'Brien, Paris	..........KO 3

1913

Jan.	25—Bernard De Balzac, Paris	..... W 10
Feb.	19—Frank Mantell, Paris	.........D 20
Apr.	2—Adrian Hogan, Paris	.........KO 11
Oct.	11—Georges Carpentier, Paris	....L 20
Nov.	15—Bernard De Balzac, Paris	.....W 20

1914

Mar.	14—Eddie McGoorty, Sydney	......L 20
Apr.	13—Pat Bradley, Sidney	..........KO 16
June	6—Jimmy Clabby, Sydney	.... W 20
Nov.	28—Mick King, Sydney	...........L 20
Dec.	26—Mick King, Sydney	.... W 20

1915

Jan.	23—Les Darcy, Sydney	.... W 5

(Darcy refused to continue, claiming foul.)

Feb.	20—Mick King, Melbourne	.... W 20
May	1—Harold Hardwick, Sydney	..... W 20
May	23—Les Darcy, Sydney	...........LF 2
Dec.	7—George Chip, Boston	.........WF 7

1916

Mar.	16—Mike Gibbons, St. Paul	.......ND 10
Mar.	28—Zulu Kid, Albany	...........ND 10
June	23—Gus Christie, Rochester	......ND 10
July	4—Jack McCarron, Allentown	...ND 10
Nov.	6—Herman Miller, Baltimore	....KO 3
Nov.	10—Joe Herrick, Milwaukee	.....KO 3
Nov.	30—Kid Henry, Albany	..........KO 7
Dec.	13—Joe Eagan, Boston	...........W 12

1917

Jan.	1—Frank Mantell, Baltimore	......W 15
Jan.	25—Jack Clark, Utica	............ND 10
Jan.	30—Leo Lavin, Albany	...........KO 4
Feb.	2—Joe Borrell, Albany	..........KO 4
Apr.	23—Young Ahearn, New Orleans	..KO 5
May	19—Harry Greb, Buffalo	.........ND 10
June	15—Len Rowlands, Cincinnati	.....W 15
July	21—Zulu Kid, Baltimore	.........W 15
Sept.	11—Harry Greb, Milwaukee	......ND 10
Nov.	1—Mike McTigue, Brooklyn	.....ND 10
Dec.	20—Kid Sheeler, Ardmore, Md.	...KO 1

Boxing instructor, U. S. Army, Camp Dix, N. J.

1918

May	3—George Robinson, Boston	.....W 12
July	4—Leo Houck, Lancaster	........ND 6
Aug.	23—Johnny Howard, Jersey City	..ND 8
Nov.	30—Jack Hanlon, Philadelphia	....KO 1

1919

Jan.	1—Billy Kramer, Philadelphia	....KO 3
Feb.	3—Johnny Howard, Jersey City	..ND 3
Feb.	8—Dick Gilbert, Philadelphia	....KO 2
Mar.	13—Jim Booker, Atlantic City	....KO 3
Mar.	27—Frankie Carbone, Atlantic Cy.	ND 8
May	10—George Chip, Baltimore	.....W 12
June	24—Eugene Brosseau, Montreal	...ND 10
July	4—Mike Gibbons, Kansas City	..ND 10
July	9—Panama Joe Gans, Atlantic Cy.	ND 8
Aug.	12—Johnny Howard, Bayonne	.....ND 8
Sept.	1—Harry Greb, Youngstown, O.	..ND 12
Oct.	8—Jackie Clark, Syracuse	.......ND 10
Oct.	13—Frankie Mayo, Trenton	......KO 1
	—Jamaica Kid, Atlantic City	....ND 8
Oct.	17—K. O. Sampson, Trenton	.....ND 3
Oct.	22—Jack McCarron, Toledo	......ND 6
Nov.	6—Frankie Carbone, Scranton	...ND 3
Nov.	13—Jamaica Kid, Atlantic City	....ND 8
Nov.	17—Harry Sampson, Trenton	.....ND 8
Dec.	11—Jamaica Kid, Binghamton	....ND 10
Dec.	29—Jack Coyne, Jersey City	...... W 2

1920

Jan.	1—Arthur Magirl, Philadelphia	.... W 3
Jan.	7—Yg. Jack Johnson, Lewiston	..ND 12
Jan.	24—Herman Miller, York, Pa.	.....ND 6
Mar.	5—Paul DePaus, Paris	...........W 2
Apr.	22—Bandsman Rice, London	.....KO 2
	—Johnny Howard, Jersey City	... W 6
May	8—Ercole Balzac, Paris	.........KO 3
July	5—George Robinson, Lewiston, Me.	W 12
Aug.	10—Mike McTigue, Halifax, N.S.	... W 12
Aug.	24—Frankie Carbone, Youngstown	. W 12
Oct.	25—Jamaica Kid, Trenton	........ND 10
Nov.	9—Mike O'Dowd, N.Y.C.	.........L 15
Nov.	29—George Robinson, Montreal	..ND 10

1921

	—Pat McCarthy, Worcester	......W 10
Feb.	25—Harry Greb, Boston	...........L 10
Mar.	15—Cliff Jordan, Worcester	......W 10
May	20—Harry Greb, New Orleans	... D 15
Aug.	9—Mike Gibbons, Jersey City	..ND 12
Aug.	15—Harry Foley, New Orleans	... W 15
Oct.	7—Jimmy Darcy, New Orleans	... W 15
	—Jack White, Montreal	........KO 2
Dec.	1—Mike McTigue, N. Y. C.	......L 15

1922

Jan.	4—Andy Kid Palmer, Tulsa	.....W 15
Jan.	16—Frankie Fleming, Staten Isl.	..KO 2
Feb.	20—Harry Greb, Cincinnati	......ND 10

Feb. 27—K. O. Jaffe, Troy .... KO 2
May 3—Bob Moha, Youngstown, O. ...KO 7
May 10—Otto Hughes, Indianapolis ....KO 3
May 15—Pat McCarthy, Marlesville ..... W 12
May 22—Glenn Clickner, Tulsa .... KO 9
June 19—Bob Moha, Milwaukee .... ND 10
July 25—Roy Benson, Averne, L. I. ....KO 1
Aug. 21—Jamaica Kid, Dayton .... W 12
Sept. 4—Jackie Clark, Tulsa .... W 12
Oct. 3—Harry Krohn, Erie, Pa. .... ND 12
Oct. 12—George Robinson, Portld., Me. . W 12
Oct. 18—Bob Roper, New Orleans ...... W 15
Dec. 1—Martin Burke, New Orleans .... W 15
Dec. 13—Bob Roper, New Orleans ..... W 15
Dec. 18—Clay Turner, Canton .... KO 2
Dec. 25—Harry Greb, Pittsburgh .... ND 10
Dec. 29—Billy Britton, Atchison .... W 12
—Johnny Murphy .... KO 1
1923
Jan. 1—Fay Keiser, Dayton .... ND 12
Jan. 8—Jackie Clark, Tulsa .... ND 12
Jan. 10—Eddie Trembly, Portland, Me. .KO 5
Feb. 22—Jamaica Kid, Portland, Me. ....ND 12
Feb. 26—Jamaica Kid, Buffalo, N. Y. ...W 10
Mar. 2—Jimmy Darcy, Yngstwn., O. ..ND 12
Mar. 8—Tommy Loughran, Scranton ..ND 10
Mar. 20—Bob Roper, Portland, Me. ....ND 12
Apr. 4—Dan Dowd, Lewiston, Me. ....ND 12
May 15—Harry Krohn, Halifax ....KO 6
June 18—Tommy Loughran, Phila .....ND 8
Aug. 13—Kid Palmer, Philadelphia ....ND 8
Sept. 24—Lee Anderson, Juarez, Mex. ... W 15
Oct. 1—Chuck Wiggins, New Orleans ... W 15
Nov. 12—Young Fisher, Portland, Me. ..KO 10
1924
Feb. 18—Jamaica Kid, N. Y. C. .... W 12
Mar. 7—Joe Lohman, Atlanta, Ga. ....KO 9
Apr. 28—Ray Newman, Trenton ....ND 12
May 23—K. O. Samson, Mt. Holly......KO 2
May 30—Joe Lohman, Indianapolis ....ND 10
June 30—George Robinson, Troy ......KO 10
July 29—Ray Newman, Brooklyn......WF 3
Sept. 11—Yg. Narullo, New Orleans ... W 15
Oct. 2—Ray Pelky, Oakland .... D 4
Oct. 20—Billy Britton, Indianapolis ...ND 10
Oct. 27—Happy Howard, New Orleans ..W 15
Nov. 11—Frank Moody, Portland .....ND 12
Dec. 8—Gene Tunney, New Orleans ...ND 15
1925
Mar. 9—Buck Ashton, Lancaster ...... W 8
June 19—Bob Lawson, Portland, Me. ....NC 11
Aug. 3—Yg. Marullo, New Orleans . KO by 11
1927
Feb. 8—Lew Chester, Denver, Colo. .... W 6
Mar. 11—Chuck Burns, Savannah ...... W 15
Mar. —Henry LaMar, Washington ....ND 7
(Stopped by police because of anti-prize
fight law in D.C.)
Mar. 31—Terry Roberts, Charlotte .....KO 5
Apr. 18—Fred Cullen, El Paso ....L 10
June 11—George Manley, Denver, Colo. ..L 10

TB	KO	WD	WF	D	LD	LF	KOBY	ND	NC
178	46	51	2	3	8	1		65	1

Died, February 3, 1962, Levittown, N.J.
Elected to Boxing Hall of Fame, 1969.

MICK KING
(Record Not Available)

LES DARCY
(James Leslie Darcy)
Born, October 31, 1895, Woodville, N.S.W.
Nationality, Australian. Weight, 147-165 lbs. Height, 5
ft. 6 in. Managed by Tim O'Sullivan.
1910
—"Guv'nor" Balsa, Thornton .... W 11
(Scheduled for 10 rounds, but referee Evans was
unable to determine winner, so, by mutual agreement, an
extra round was fought.)
—Sid Pasco, Maitland .... KO 2
1911
July 26—Tom Donohue, Maitland .... W 4
1912
Mar. 20—R. Fairbairn, Newcastle .... KO 4
Apr. 6—Rhymer, Newcastle .... KO 6

Apr. 27—Harry Emery, Newcastle .... W 8
May 4—Tom Page, Newcastle .... W 10
Aug. 24—Jim Burns, Newcastle .... W 4
Sept. 14—Harry Richards, Newcastle .... W 8
Sept. 21—Peter Devon, Newcastle .... KO 6
Sept. 28—P. Barnes, Newcastle .... KO 9
Nov. 4—Dave Depena, Newcastle .... KO 9
Dec. 14—Jim Burns, Maitland .... KO 11
1913
Mar. 15—Billy Hannan, Maitland .... KO 18
July 19—Reg Delaney, Maitland .... KO 8
Sept. 27—Joe Shakespeare, Maitland .... KO 7
Oct. 25—Billy McNabb, Maitland .... W 20
Nov. 3—Bob Whitelaw, Newcastle .... L 20
(For Australian Welterweight Title)
1914
Jan. 5—Jack Clare, Newton .... KO 9
Jan. 30—Young Hanley, Newton .... KO 5
Mar. 21—Bob Whitelaw, Maitland .... KO 5
Apr. 23—Billy McNabb, Maitland .... KO 4
July 18—Fritz Holland, Sydney .... L 20
Sept. 12—Fritz Holland, Sydney .... LF 18
Oct. 5—Henri (K.O.) Marchand, Sydney .. KO 5
Nov. 17—Gus Christie, Sydney .... W 20
Dec. 26—Fred Dyer, Brisbane .... W 20
1915
Jan. 23—Jeff Smith, Sydney .... L disq. 5
(For Australian World Middleweight Title)
Feb. 27—Frank Loughrey, Sydney .... W 20
Mar. 13—Fritz Holland, Sydney .... W 20
Apr. 3—Henri Demlin, Sydney .... KO 5
May 1—Fritz Holland, Melbourne .... KO 13
May 22—Jeff Smith, Sydney .... WF 2
(Won Australian World Middleweight Title)
June 12—Mick King, Sydney .... KO 10
(Retained Australian World Middleweight Title)
July 31—Eddie McGoorty, Sydney .... KO 15
(Retained Australian World Middleweight Title)
Sept. 4—Billy Murray, Sydney .... W 20
(Retained Australian World Middleweight Title)
Oct. 9—Fred Dyer, Sydney .... KO 6
(Retained Australian World Middleweight Title)
Oct. 23—Jimmy Clabby, Sydney .... W 20
(Retained Australian World Middleweight Title)
Nov. 1—Billy Murray, Melbourne .... KO 6
Dec. 27—Eddie McGoorty, Sydney .... KO 8
1916
Jan. 15—George (K.O.) Brown, Sydney ..... W 20
Feb. 19—Harold Hardwick, Sydney .... KO 7
(Won Australian Heavyweight Title)
Mar. 25—Les O'Donnell, Sydney .... KO 7
(Retained Australian Heavyweight Title)
Apr. 8—George (K.O.) Brown, Sydney ..... W 20
(Retained Australian Heavyweight Title)
May 13—Alex Costica, Sydney .... KO 4
(Retained Australian World Middleweight Title)
June 3—Albert (Buck) Crouse, Sydney .... KO 2
(Retained Australian World Middleweight Title)
June 24—Dave Smith, Sydney .... KO 12
(Retained Australian Heavyweight Title)
Aug. 16—Dave Smith, Brisbane .... KO 11
(Retained Australian Heavyweight Title)
Sept. 9—Jimmy Clabby, Sydney .... W 20
(Retained Australian World Middleweight Title)
Sept. 30—George Chip, Sydney .... KO 9
(Retained Australian World Middleweight Title)

TB	KO	WD	WF	D	LD	LF	KOBY	ND	NC
50	29	16	1	0	2	2	0	0	0

Died, May 24, 1917, Memphis, Tennessee.
Elected to Boxing Hall of Fame, 1957.

MIKE O'DOWD
(St. Paul Cyclone)
Born, April 5, 1895, St. Paul, Minn.
Nationality, Irish-American. Weight, 154 lbs.
Height, 5 ft. 9 in. Managed by Mike McNulty,
Jack Reddy and Paddy Mullins.
1913
Knockouts: Henry Olson, 1; Henry
Gardner, 4; Pleabush, 2. Won: Al Johnson, 6;
Chas. Fuhrman, 6; Mike Brown, 1; Al Johnson,
4.

1914
Knockouts: Harold Jensen, 3; Cyclone Smith, 4; Labe Safo, 4; Mike Graham, 9; Young Pinkey, 1. No decision: Chas. Fuhrman, 6; Billy Perkins, 10; Dannie Hayes, 8.

1915
Feb.	3—Willy Shaffer, Hudson, Wis.	...ND 10
Mar.	2—Wally Monaghan, Hudson, Wis.	ND 10
Mar.	23—Stkyd. Tom Murphy, Hudson, Wis.	KO 10
Apr.	6—Billy Miske, Hudson, Wis.	...ND 10
May	21—Billy Miske, Hudson, Wis.	...ND 10
June	4—Billy Perkins, Eau Claire, Wis.	KO 3
July	12—Willy Schaefer, St. Paul	....ND 10
Aug.	20—Freddy Gilmore, St. Paul	...KO 5
Sept.	23—Walter Monaghan, Duluth	...ND 10
Oct.	22—Silent Martin, Minneapolis	..ND 10
Nov.	12—Soldier Bartfield, Hudson, Wis.	ND 10
Nov.	29—Billy Kramer, Milwaukee	....ND 10
Dec.	3—Franky Brennan, Minneapolis	ND 10
Dec.	21—Kid Graves, St. Paul	....ND 10

1916
Mar.	13—Willie Schaefer, Kansas City	..D 10
Mar.	18—Young Erne, Philadelphia	...ND 6
Mar.	25—Terry Mitchell, Brooklyn	...KO 8
Apr.	6—Jack Toland, Brooklyn	....ND 10
Apr.	25—Joe Egan, Boston	........KO 9
June	6—Jack Britton, Boston	........L 12
June	15—Willie Adams, N. Y. C.	....KO 4
Aug.	18—Mickey Sheridan, St. Paul	...ND 10
Oct.	23—Frank Barrieau, Denver	....KO 6

1917
Jan.	1—Kid Alberts, Brooklyn	......ND 10
Jan.	25—Jack Britton, St. Paul	......ND 10
Mar.	21—Joe Egan, Boston	..........L 12
Mar.	31—Frank Carbone, Brooklyn	...ND 10
June	28—Soldier Bartfield, Brooklyn	..ND 10
Apr.	17—Frank Carbone, Boston	......W 12
May	4—Silent Martin, Providence	....W 15
May	8—Jack Britton, Brooklyn	.....ND 10
May	17—Italian Joe Gans, Brooklyn	..ND 10
May	22—Silent Martin, N. Y. C.	....ND 10
May	24—Ted Lewis, N. Y. C.	.........ND 10
June	16—Zulu Kid, N. Y. C.	........ND 10
June	28—Soldier Bartfield, N. Y. C.	.ND 10
Aug.	9—Tommy Madden, Brooklyn	..KO 3
Aug.	11—Frank Carbone, Brooklyn	...ND 10
Aug.	17—Ted Lewis, N. Y. C.	.........ND 10
Aug.	28—Ted Lewis, Boston	........W 12
Sept.	6—Italian Joe Gans, N. Y. C.	...ND 10
Sept.	25—Joe Connolly, Boston	......KO 4
Oct.	4—Willie Laughlin, Brooklyn	...KO 2
Oct.	27—Jerry Cole, Brooklyn	......ND 10
Nov.	1—Frank Carbone, N. Y. C.	....ND 10
Nov.	14—Al McCoy, Brooklyn	.......KO 6
	(Won Middleweight Title)	
Nov.	24—Jack McCarron, Philadelphia	.ND 6
Dec.	15—Billy Kramer, Philadelphia	..ND 6
Dec.	19—Joe Welsh, Philadelphia	.....ND 6

1918
Feb.	25—Harry Greb, St. Paul	.......ND 10

Enlisted in U. S. Army and served with A. E. F. in Europe.
Dec.	12—Harold Ralph, London	......W 4
Dec.	12—Sergt. Ring, London	........W 4

1919
June	7—Al Norton, Rome, Italy	.....KO 1
July	17—*Al McCoy, St. Paul	........KO 3
July	21—Young Fisher, Syracuse, N. Y.	KO 5
Aug.	11—Jackie Clark, Syracuse	......ND 10
Aug.	22—Jack Britton, Newark	......ND 8
Sept.	1—Ted Lewis, Syracuse	......ND 10
Sept.	19—Soldier Bartfield, St. Paul	...ND 10
Sept.	29—Augie Ratner, Newark	......ND 8
Oct.	18—Steve Latzo, Philadelphia	..ND 6
Oct.	26—Jack Connors, Providence	...KO 2
Nov.	6—Billy Kramer, Paterson, N. J.	.KO 2
Nov.	10—Jimmy O'Hagen, Detroit	....KO 2
Nov.	21—Mike Gibbons, St. Paul	.....ND 10

*Title bout.

1920
Jan.	14—Frank Carbone, Detroit	.....ND 10
Jan.	20—Tommy Murphy, Boston	....KO 3
Jan.	26—Young Fisher, Syracuse	.....KO 3
Mar.	1—Jack McCarron, Philadelphia	.KO 2
Mar.	5—Tommy Murphy, Atlanta, Ga.	KO 9
Mar.	12—Tommy Madden, Denver	....KO 4
Mar.	17—Augie Ratner, St. Paul	....ND 10
Mar.	31—Joe Eagan, Boston	........KO 5
Apr.	3—Frankie Maphre, Phila.	.....ND 6
Apr.	14—Walter Laurette, Bridgeport	.KO 6
Apr.	26—Paul Sampson, Philadelphia	..KO 4

542

May	6—Johnny Wilson, Boston	......L 12
	(Lost Middleweight Title)	
May	11—Jackie Clark, Camden, N. J.	.ND 10
May	17—Jack Britton, Canton, O.	.....W 12
May	19—Geo. K. O. Brown, Phila.	....KO 6
June	24—Battling Ortega, Portland, Ore.	.D 12
July	5—Gordon McKay, Pocatello, Ida.	W 12
Aug.	21—Tommy Robson, Lawrence	...W 12
Sept.	15—Sailor Petrosky, Philadelphia	.ND 8
Sept.	23—Ted Lewis, Jersey City	.....ND 12
Oct.	22—Frank Carbone, Camden, N. J.	ND 10
Nov.	9—Jeff Smith, N. Y. C.	........W 15
Dec.	6—Len Rowlands, Philadelphia	.ND 8

1921
Mar.	17—Johnny Wilson, N. Y. C.	.....L 15
	(Middleweight Title Bout)	
Aug.	20—Silent Martin, N. Y. C.	......KO 9
Aug.	26—Young Fisher, Syracuse, N. Y.	L 12
Nov.	14—John Paske, Buffalo	........W 12
Dec.	6—Lou Bogash, N. Y. C.	........D 12
Dec.	16—Mike Gibbons, St. Paul	.....ND 10

1922
Mar.	18—Soldier Bartfield, Brooklyn	...W 12
May	6—Mike Gibbons, N. Y. C.	......W 12
May	15—Bryan Downey, Columbus	...L 12
Nov.	27—Lou Janita, Columbus, O.	...L 12
Nov.	30—Dave Rosenberg, N. Y. C.	..WF 8

(Won N. Y. Commission Middleweight Title)

1923
Mar.	16—Jock Malone, St. Paul	...KO by 1

TB	O	WD	WF	D	LD	LF	KOBY	ND	NC
115	35	16	1	3	7	0	1	52	0

Died, July 28, 1957, St. Paul, Minn.

JOHNNY WILSON
(John Panica)
Born, March 23, 1893, New York City. Nationality, Italian-American. Weight, 158 lbs. Managed by Frankie Marlowe and Martin Killilea.

1911
Knockout: George Cunningham, 2.

1912
Knockouts: Red O'Keefe (twice), 2; Frankie Farley, 3; Frankie Young, 4; Young Sally, 2; Jimmie Riley, 3; Frankie McGarry, 7; Charlie (Kid) Albert, 1; Tommy O'Keefe, 2; Willie Colins, 7; Eddie Smith, 2; Billy McGrave, 1; Red Gleary, 4; Young Sally, 1. Lost: Johnnie (Kid) Alberts, 7. No decisions: Al King, 4; Steve Callahan, 6; Dodo Maher, 6; Kid Bolt, 6; Joe Fox, 6; Heinie Ferino, 6; Freddy Gunther, 6; Charlie Smith, 10.

1913
Knockouts: Freddie Walsh, 3; Mike Farrell, 1; Joe Marto, 6; Sailor Donahue, 2. No decisions: Young Victor, 6; Fighting Kennedy, 10; Young McCartney, 10; Battling Nelson, 10; Fighting Kennedy, 10.

1914
Knockouts: Walter McGirr, 4; Fox, 3. Lost: Jimmy Fryer, 4. No decisions: Fighting Kennedy, 10; Jimmy Fryer, 10; Frank Carbone, 10.

1915
Knockouts: Red (Kid) Tucker, 1; Kid Broad, 5. Lost: Battling McFarland, 12. No decisions: K. O. Sweeney, 10; Chick Nelson, 10; Billy Bush, 10; Mike Mazie, 10; K. O. Sweeney, 10.

1916
Knockouts: Young Jasper, 2; Jack Donnelly, 8; Battling McFarland, 9; Roddy McDonald, 12. Won: K. O. Sweeney, 12; Johnny Mello, 8; Roddy McDonald, 12; Jack Savage, 12. Lost: Wild Bill Fleming, 12; Joe White, 10; Tommy Robson, 12; Silent Martin, 12. No decisions: Frankie Notter, 12; Al Rogers, 12.

1917
Knockouts: Al Nelson, 1; Art Magirl, 3. Won: Jack Savage, 12; Carl Herz, 12; Victor Dahl, 12; Jack Savage (twice), 12. Lost: George Robinson, 12; Roddy McDonald, 15. Lost (foul): Joe White, 4. No decision: Al Nelson, 12. Knocked out by: Italian Joe Gans, 4.
May	30—Frank Notter, Pittsfield	......L 12

1918
Knockouts: Victor Dahl, 1; Pinkie

Crosby, 3. Won: Leo Houck, 12; Augie Ratner, 12. Lost: Leo Houck, 12. Lost (foul): Frank Carbone, 3.

1919
Knockouts: Scotty Coyne, 3; Mathew Danielson, 1; Battling Carroll, 2; Cyclone Scottie, 4; Young Jake Ahearn, 6; Young Jake Ahearn, 1. Won: Pat McCarthy, 10; Young Fisher, 12. Draw: Pat McCarthy, 10; Young Jake Ahearn, 12. No decision: George Robinson, 12.

1920
Mar.	9—Billy Murray, Lynn	KO	2
Apr.	7—Pal Reed, Boston	W	12
May	6—Mike O'Dowd, Boston	W	12
	(Won Middleweight Title)		
July	1—Soldier Bartfield, Newark	ND	12
July	20—Young Fisher, Syracuse	ND	10
Aug.	2—Steve Choynski, Buffalo	KO	5
Dec.	9—Geo. Robinson, Montreal	ND	10

1921
Jan.	17—*George Chip, Pittsburgh	ND	10
Feb.	10—Navy Rostan, Kenosha, Wis.	KO	2
Mar.	17—*Mike O'Dowd, New York	W	15
May	25—Joe Chip, Detroit	ND	10
July	15—George Robinson, Boston	W	10
July	27—Bryan Downey, Cleveland	WF	7
	Cleveland boxing commission refused to		
abide by referee, claimed Wilson lost by K.O.			
Sept.	5—*Bryan Downey, Jersey City	ND	12
*Title bouts.			

1922
Apr.	21—*K. O. Jaffee, Hazelton, Pa.	NC	4
July	4—Al Demarest, Rutland, Va.	KO	
*Stopped by referee.			

1923
May	22—Jimmy Montgomery	ND	10
June	22—Eddie Carter	ND	12
Aug.	31—Harry Greb, New York	L	15
	(Lost world middleweight title.)		
Oct.	19—George Robinson, Boston	W	10
Nov.	16—Pal Reed, Boston	W	10
Dec.	18—Pat McCarthy, Boston	KO	3

1924
Jan.	18—Harry Greb, New York	L	15
	(For World Middleweight Title)		
Jan.	29—Pal Reed, Boston	W	10
Feb.	12—Tommy Loughran, Boston	L	10
July	29—Jock Malone, Boston	KO	6
Sept.	17—Jock Malone, St. Paul	ND	10
Dec.	9—Tiger Flowers, N. Y. C.	KO by	3

1925
Apr.	17—Harry Greb, Boston, Mass.	L	10

1926
Aug.	27—Maxie Rosenbloom, Brooklyn	L	12
Oct.	4—Maxie Rosenbloom, Pittsburgh	L	10

TB	KO	WD	WF	D	LD	LF	KOBY	ND	NC
123	44	20	1	2	17	2	2	34	1

WILLIAM BRYAN DOWNEY
(Claimant World Middleweight Title)
Born, September 7, 1896, Columbus, Ohio. Nationality, Irish-German-American. Weight, 165 lbs. Height 5 ft 6¼ in. Managed by Jimmy Dunn.

1914
Feb.	2—Jimmy Albright, Columbus	KO	2
Feb.	14—George Watson, Columbus	ND	4
Mar.	16—Eddy Erb, Columbus	KO	2
Mar.	30—Ted Hatch, Columbus	KO	3
Apr.	14—Jack Sullivan, Columbus	KO	2
May	18—Matty Califf, Columbus	KO	1
June	15—Jack Frambes, Cincinnati	ND	4
July	20—Willy Jennings, Columbus	KO	1
Aug.	31—Willy Jones, Columbus	KO	12
Nov.	5—Richie Mitchell, Columbus	ND	12
Dec.	8—Young Goldie, Columbus	ND	12

1915
Jan.	18—Patsy Cline, Columbus, O.	ND	12
Feb.	22—Peanuts Schieberl, Columbus	KO	1
Mar.	29—Cal Delaney, Columbus	ND	12
June	14—Joe Dailey, Columbus	ND	12
Aug.	2—Patsy McMahon, Columbus	ND	12
Sept.	6—Cal Delaney, Columbus	ND	12
Oct.	5—Franky Dailey, Columbus	KO	6

1916
Jan.	10—Johnny Griffiths, Columbus	ND	12
May	11—Jack Perry, Columbus	KO	11
May	29—Willie Beecher, Columbus	ND	12
July	3—Jimmy Duffy, Columbus	ND	12
Oct.	16—Johnny Griffiths, Columbus	ND	12
Nov.	14—Spike Kelly, Kenosha, Wis.	ND	10
Nov.	29—Frankey Murphy, Toledo	ND	12

Dec.	11—Johnny Harvey, Columbus	ND	12

1917
Jan.	1—Jack Perry, Columbus	KO	9
Jan.	10—J. McCarty, Windsor, Ont.	NC	6
Jan.	18—Frankey Murphy, Toledo, O.	ND	12
Jan.	29—Johnny Tillman, Columbus	ND	12
Mar.	5—Jack Britton, Columbus	ND	12
Mar.	16—Jimmy Duffy, Buffalo	ND	10
Apr.	2—Willie Beecher, Columbus	ND	12
July	4—Eddie Moha, Racine, Wis.	ND	10
July	9—Johnny Riley, Rochester, N.Y.	ND	10
July	23—Fred Dyer, Rochester	ND	10
Aug.	27—Matt Wells, Rochester	ND	10
Sept.	3—Vic Moran, Columbus	KO	5
Sept.	17—Matt Wells, Columbus	ND	12
Sept.	26—Goats Doig, La Salle, Ill.	D	10
Oct.	8—Young Denny, Columbus	ND	12
Oct.	20—Johnny Griffiths, Columbus	ND	12
Nov.	12—Young Denny, Columbus	ND	12
Dec.	17—Ted Kid Lewis, Columbus	ND	12

1918
Jan.	1—Johnny Griffiths, Akron	D	12
Jan.	7—Joe Eagan, Milwaukee	ND	10
Apr.	4—Jock Malone, Ft. Sheridan	W	10
Apr.	10—Tommy Robson, Boston	W	10
June	11—Jack Britton, Boston	L	12
June	22—Marty Cross, Dayton	D	15
July	3—Soldier Bartfield, Columbus	ND	12
Sept.	12—Jock Malone, St. Paul	ND	10
Dec.	16—Johnny Tillman, Columbus	ND	12

1919
Jan.	1—Ted Lewis, Columbus	ND	12
Jan.	29—K. O. Loughlin, Tulsa, Okla.	D	15
Feb.	17—K. O. Loughlin, Tulsa, Okla.	D	15
Mar.	20—Jock Malone, Columbus	L	15
Apr.	8—Jack Britton, Canton, O.	ND	12
May	26—K. O. Loughlin, Canton	ND	12
June	19—Jock Malone, Canton	ND	12
July	2—K. O. Loughlin, Columbus	W	15
Aug.	4—Jock Malone, Columbus	D	15
Sept.	26—K. O. Loughlin, Dayton, O.	D	15
Nov.	17—Goats Doig, Peoria, Ill.	D	10
Dec.	17—Navy Rostan, Columbus	W	15

1920
Jan.	12—Nip Howell, Dayton	KO	9
Jan.	19—Joe Chip, Canton	ND	10
Jan.	26—Steve Latzo, Dayton	W	12
Jan.	31—Len Rowlands, Wheeling, Va.	ND	10
Feb.	6—Navy Rostan, Milwaukee	ND	10
Mar.	10—Hope Mullen, Cincinnati	KO	4
Mar.	26—Jack Britton, Cleveland	ND	12
Mar.	28—Billy Weeks, Columbus	ND	12
Apr.	12—Tommy Robson, Dayton	W	10
May	5—Frankie Brennan, Cincinnati	KO	6
May	24—Joe Chip, Columbus	W	12
May	31—Marty Cross, Cincinnati	ND	10
July	14—Soldier Bartfield, Detroit	ND	10
July	21—Ralph Schappert, Dayton	D	12
Aug.	7—Walter Caldwell, Cincinnati	KO	3
Aug.	18—Soldier Bartfield, Detroit	ND	10
Oct.	25—Ralph Chappert, Dayton	ND	12
Nov.	15—Augie Ratner, Philadelphia	ND	8

1921
Jan.	1—Augie Ratner, Columbus	W	12
Jan.	7—George Chip, Cleveland	ND	15
Jan.	17—Augie Ratner, Rochester, N.Y.	W	15
Feb.	14—Augie Ratner, Rochester, N.Y.	W	15
Mar.	11—Young Fisher, Syracuse	D	5
May	11—Johnny Klesch, Toledo	W	12
May	23—Johnny Paske, Buffalo	w	15
May	28—Young Fisher, Cleveland	W	12
June	16—Frank Carbone, Columbus	W	12
July	4—Johnny Klesch, Canton	W	12
July	27—Johnny Wilson, Cleveland	*LF	7
Sept.	5—Johnny Wilson, Jersey City	ND	12
	(World Middleweight Title)		
Dec.	12—Happy Littleton, New Orleans	KO	2
*Cleveland boxing commission refused to			
abide by referee, claimed Wilson lost by KO.			
Downey claimed title.			

1922
Feb.	10—Young Fisher, Syracuse	D	15
Feb.	22—Frank Carbone, Canton	W	12
Feb.	28—Tommy Loughran, Phila.	ND	8
Mar.	13—Frank Carbone, Indianapolis	ND	10
May	15—Mike O'Dowd, Columbus	W	12
May	31—Harry Krohn, Akron	ND	12
June	13—Jock Malone, Aurora, Ill.	ND	10
Sept.	18—Jock Malone, Columbus	L	12
Oct.	16—Nate Siegel, Boston	W	10
Nov.	13—Frankie Schoell, Omaha	ND	10
Nov.	20—Lou Bogash, Boston	L	10
Dec.	5—Jock Malone, Louisville	ND	12

543

Dec. 15—Happy Littleton, New Orleans . D 15

1923

Jan. 8—Bob Sage, Detroit ....ND 10
Mar. 15—Phil Krug, Orange, N. J. ......ND 12
Apr. 2—Lou Bogash, Rochester, N. Y...D 12
Apr. 26—George Shade, Yngstwn., O. ..KO 2
May 25—Lou Bogash, Syracuse, N. Y. ...... L 12
July 24—Jock Malone, Columbus .... L 12
Dec. 3—Harry Greb, Pittsburgh, Pa........ L 10
(For Middleweight Title)

1924

July 7—Ted Moore, Columbus ....L 10
May 5—Jack Delaney, Columbus .....ND 12

1926

June 8—Augie Ratner, Cleveland......ND 10
—Joe Anderson, Columbus......L 10
Sept. 6—Ted Moore, Canton ....ND 10

TB	KO	WD	WF	D	LD	LF	KO BY	ND	NC
119	18	19	0	14	9	1	0	57	1

Died March 28, 1970 in Wadsworth, California.

DAVE ROSENBERG

Born, May 15, 1901, New York City, N.Y. Ancestry, Hebraic. Weight, 156-160 lbs. Height, 5 ft. 8½ in.

1919 New York State and National AAU Welterweight Champion. Turned professional, October, 1919.

1919-1921

—K.O. Bill Thompson .... W 3
—Frankie Fleming .... W 3
—Bill Thompson .... W 6
—Chief Halftown .... ND 6
—Babe Sullivan .... W 8
—Joe Lundy .... KO 3
—Frank Carpenter .... W 10
—Gus Platts .... ND 12
—Marty Summers .... ND 12
—Billy Bush .... KO 12
—Dan Lynch .... KO 7
—Tommy McAleer .... ND 12
—Italian Joe Gans .... D 12
—Italian Joe Gans .... L 12
—Charley Beck .... ND 12
—Red Allen .... W 15
—Irish Paddy Flynn .... D 15
—Farmer Sullivan .... D 15
—Johnny Smith .... ND 12

1920

Jan. 15—Young Jack Sheldon, Jersey City ND 8
May 15—Jimmy Kelly, Jersey City .... ND 6
July 9—Walter Laurette, Bayonne ...... ND 12
Aug. 3—Sailor McFarland, Bayonne ...... ND 15

1921

Mar. 24—Frankie Fields, New York .... KO 5
Apr. 19—Farmer Sullivan, New York ...... D 15
May 2—Young Ahearn, New York .... W 12
May 30—Mike Gibbons, New York .... L 12
June 17—Farmer Sullivan, New York ...... W 10
July 15—Buddy Sprague, New York .... W 12
July 16—Jackie Mason, New York .... KO 6
Sept. 17—Zulu Kid, New York .... W 12
Oct. 17—Phil Bloom, New York .... W 12
Nov. 25—Bert Colima .... W 12
Dec. 13—Jimmy O'Gatty, New York ...... KO 4
Dec. 22—Jimmy Darcy, New York .... W 8

1922

Jan. 3—Jack Stone, New York .... W 12
Jan. 14—Mike Donovan, New York .... W 12
Jan. 23—Soldier Bartfield, New York ... D 12
Feb. 20—Augie Ratner, New York .... W 10
Feb. 27—Marty Cross, New York .... W 12
May 4—Frankie Britton, Philadelphia ....ND 8
May 8—Zulu Kid, New York .... KO 3
May 13—Tommy McAleer, New York .... W 10
May 19—Tommy Robson, New York .... W 6
May 30—Tommy Robson, New York .... W 12
June 1—Phil Krug, Newark .... ND 12
June 19—Italian Joe Gans, New York ...... W 12
Aug. 14—Phil Krug, New York .... W 15
(Won New York World Middleweight Title)

Sept. 1—Jack Stone, New York .... W 12
Nov. 30—Mike O'Dowd, Brooklyn .... LF 8
(Lost New York World Middleweight Title)

1923

Aug. 27—Billy Naylor, New York .... KO 4
Sept. 26—Mike Morley, Albany .... W 12
Oct. 4—Soldier Bartfield, Brooklyn .... KO 4
Nov. 6—Pat Walsh, New York .... LF 5

1924

Jan. 1—Young Stribling, Newark .... ND 12
June 16—Georgie West, Brooklyn .... W 12
July 7—Tommy McAleer, New York .... L 10
Oct. 2—Lou Chester, New York .... W 12
Oct. 9—Johnny McGinty, Yonkers .... LF 7
Oct. 17—Pat Walsh, Providence .... KO 3
Nov. 22—Larry Estridge, New York .... L 12

1925

Jan. 5—Lou Chester, Brooklyn .... L 10
Feb. 12—Lou Bogash, New York .... L 6
Apr. 24—Pat McCarthy, Fall River .... L 10

1926

(Inactive)

1927

Nov. 12—Max Damsey, New York L

TB	KO	WD	WF	D	LD	LF	KO BY	ND	NC
65	10	26	0	5	8	3	0	13	0

HARRY GREB
(Edward Henry Greb)
(Human Windmill)

Born—June 6, 1894, Pittsburgh, Pa. Nationality, Irish-German-American. Weight, 158 lbs. Height, 5 ft. 8 in. Managed by James M. (Red) Mason and George Engel.

1913

Knockouts: Lloyd Crutcher, Punxsutawney, Pa., 1; Red Cumpston, 2; Battling Murphy, 2; Terry Nelson, 3. Knockout by: Joe Chip, 2. Won: Buck Miller, 3; Al Store, 4; Red Chumpston, 4; George Koch, 4. No decisions: Red Cumpston, 6; K. O. Kirkwood, 6; Hooks Evans, 6; Mike Milko, 6; Mike Milko, 6; Young Sherbine, 6.

1914

Jan. 1—Whitey Wenzel, Pittsburgh . *ND 6
Jan. 7—Whitey Wenzel, Pittsburgh . *ND 6
Mar. 2—Mickey Rodgers, Steubenville, Ohio ....WF 5
Apr. 14—Fay Kaiser, Pittsburgh, Pa. . *ND 6
May 13—Fay Kaiser, Pittsburgh, Pa. . *ND 6
May 25—George Lewis, Pittsburgh ..*ND 6
May 29—Whitey Wenzel, Pittsburgh .*ND 6
June 8—Walter Monoghan, Pittsburgh*ND 6
June 27—Irish Gargas, Pittsburgh, Pa. .ND 6
July 20—John Foley, Pittsburgh, Pa. .*ND 6
July 27—George Lewis, Steubenville . *ND 10
Aug. 10—Irish Gargas, Pittsburgh, Pa. *ND 6
Aug. 24—Whitey Wenzel, Pittsburgh .*ND 6
Aug. 31—John Foley, Pittsburgh, Pa. .*ND 6
Sept. 26—Jack Fink, Philadelphia, Pa. *ND 6
Nov. 14—Terry Martin, Philadelphia .*ND 6
Dec. 7—Joe Borrell, Philadelphia ...*ND 6

1915

Jan. 1—Bill Donovan, Philadelphia .*ND 6
Jan. 8—Howard Truesdale, Phila. ...ND 6
Jan. 12—Bill Miske, Philadelphia, Pa. *ND 6
Jan. 25—Jack Blackburn, Pittsburgh .*ND 6
Feb. 10—K. O. Baker, Pittsburgh, Pa. *ND 6
Mar. 4—Whitey, Wenzel, Pittsburgh .*ND 6
Mar. 6—Tommy Mack, Washington, Pa. ....*ND 6
Mar. 13—Jack Lavin, McKeesport, Pa. *ND 6
Mar. 25—Harry Baker, Pittsburgh ...*ND 6
Apr. 15—Whitey Wenzel, Pittsburgh .*ND 6
Apr. 22—Joe Borrell, Pittsburgh, Pa. .*ND 6
May 24—Whitey Wenzel, Pittsburgh .*ND 6
May 31—Fay Kaiser, Connellsville ...*ND 6
June 25—Fay Kaiser, Cumberland, Md.*ND 10
July 12—Tommy Gavigan, Pittsburgh *ND 6
July 21—George Hauser, Elwyn, Pa. ..KO 6
July 22—Fay Kaiser, Cumberland, Md.*ND 10
Aug. 23—Al Rogers, Pittsburgh, Pa. ..ND 6
Sept. 13—Al Rogers, Pittsburgh, Pa. ..ND 6
Oct. 18—George Chip, Pittsburgh ...ND 6
Nov. 16—Tommy Gibbons, St. Paul, Minn. ....ND 10
Dec. 16—Kid Graves, Pittsburgh .. KO by 2
(Greb broke arm)

1916

Feb. 26—Walter Monoghan, Pittsburgh ND 6
Apr. 1—Kid Manuel, Pittsburgh, Pa. . .ND 6
Apr. 27—Grant (Kid) Clark, Johnstown, Pa. ....KO 7
May 6—Whitey Wenzel, Charleroi, Pa. ND 6
June 3—Kid Manuel, Pittsburgh, Pa. . . .KO 1
June 17—Whitey Wenzel, New Kensgtn., Pa. ....ND 10
June 26—George Chip, New Castle, Pa. ND 10
Aug. 7—Al Grayber, Pittsburgh, Pa. . . .ND 6
Aug. 28—Jerry Cole, Pittsburgh, Pa. . . .ND 6
Sept. 4—Fay Kaiser, Cumberland, Md. . W 10
Oct. 16—Jackie Clarke, Lonaconing, Md. W 10
Oct. 21—Knockout Baker, Pittsburgh . ND 6
Nov. 4—K. O. Sweeney, Pittsburgh . .ND 6
Nov. 8—Knockout Brennan, Erie, Pa. . ND 10
Nov. 14—Jackie Clarke, Lonaconing, Md. ....KO 3
Nov. 17—K. O. Brennan, Buffalo, N. Y. ND 10
Nov. 24—Tommy Burke, Buffalo, N. Y. KO 10
Nov. 27—K. O. Brown, Pittsburgh, Pa. . ND 6
Dec. 26—Bob Moha, Buffalo, N. Y. . . .ND 10

1917

Jan. 1—Joe Borrell, Pittsburgh . . . . .ND 6
Jan. 13—Eddie Coleman, Charleroi, Pa. KO 2
Jan. 20—Jules Ritchie, Philadelphia . .KO 4
Jan. 29—Fay Kaiser, Lonaconing, Md. . W 20
Feb. 10—Mike Gibbons, Philadelphia . .ND 6
Feb. 12—K. O. Brennan, Buffalo . . . . .ND 10
Mar. 5—Frank Brennan, Pittsburgh . .ND 6
Mar. 20—Tommy Gavigan, McKeesport KO 5
Mar. 23—Young Herman Miller, Johnstown, Pa. . . . . .KO 5
Apr. 2—Young Ahearn, Pittsburgh . . .KO 1
Apr. 15—Zulu Kid, Pittsburgh . . . . . .ND 6
Apr. 16—Al Rogers, Charleroi, Pa. . . . .ND 10
Apr. 30—Al McCoy, Pittsburgh . . . . . .ND 10
May 5—Jackie Clark, Cumberland, Md. D 20
May 9—K. O. Baker, Uniontown, Pa. . KO 5
May 19—Jeff Smith, Buffalo . . . . .ND 10
May 22—George Chip, Pittsburgh . . .ND 10
June 14—Frank Mantell, Uniontown, Pa.KO 1
July 2—Buck Crouse, Pittsburgh . . .KO 6
July 30—Jack Dillon, Pittsburgh . . . .ND 10
Sept. 6—Battling Levinsky, Pittsburgh ND 10
Sept. 11—Jeff Smith, Milwaukee, Wis. .ND 10
Sept. 14—Jack London, New York . . . .KO 9
Sept. 17—Knockout Brown, Dayton . . . . .KO 9
Sept. 22—*Battling Kopin, Charleroi . . . . KO 3
Sept. 25—Johnny Howard, New York . . . . . . KO 9
Oct. 5—Billy Kramer, Philadelphia . .ND 6
Oct. 11—Gus Christie, Buffalo, N. Y. . .ND 10
Oct. 19—Len Rowlands, Milwaukee . . .ND 10
Oct. 23—Gus Christie, Chattanooga . . . .W 8
Nov. 2—Soldier Bartfield, Buffalo . . .ND 10
Nov. 19—George Chip, Cincinnati . . .ND 10
*Kopin claimed broken wrist.

1918

Jan. 4—Terry Kellar, Pittsburgh . . . .ND 10
Jan. 14—Battling Kopin, Charleroi, Pa. KO 1
Jan. 21—Augie Ratner, New Orleans . . . W 20
Jan. 29—Zulu Kid, Bridgeport, Conn. . .W 13
Feb. 4—Jack Hubbard, Lonaconing . .KO 3
Feb. 7—Frank Klaus, Pittsburgh . . .ND 6
Feb. 16—Bob Moha, Cincinnati . . . . . .ND 10
Feb. 25—Mike O'Dowd, St. Paul . . . . .ND 10
Mar. 4—Jack Dillon, Toledo, O. . . . . .ND 12
Mar. 11—Mike McTigue, Cleveland, O. .ND 10
Mar. 18—Willie Langford, Buffalo . . . .ND 6
May 13—Al McCoy, Cincinnati, O. . . . .ND 10
May 20—Soldier Bartfield, Pittsburgh .ND 10
May 29—Soldier Bartfield, Toledo, O. .ND 15
May 24—Gunboat Smith, New York . .ND 6
June 20—Zulu Kid, New York . . . . .Exh. 5
June 24—Frank Carbone, Bridgeport . . .W 15
July 4—Bob Moha, Rock Island, Ill. .ND 10
July 6—Harry Anderson, Cleveland .Exh. 4
July 16—Soldier Bartfield, Philadelphia ND 6
July 27—Eddy McGoorty, Ft. Sheridan ND 10
Aug. 6—Battling Levinsky, Phila. . . . .ND 6
Aug. 9—Clay Turner, Jersey City . . . .ND 8
Sept. 21—Billy Miske, Pittsburgh . . . .ND 10
Dec. 11—Sgt. Baker, London . . . . .W 4
Dec. 12—Pvt. Ring, London . . . . .W 4

1919

Jan. 4—Bob Moha, Buffalo . . . . .ND 10
Jan. 15—Leo Houck, Boston . . . . .W 12
Jan. 20—Young Fisher, Syracuse . . .ND 10
Jan. 23—Paul Sampson, Pittsburgh . . .ND 10
Jan. 27—Soldier Bartfield, Columbus . .ND 10
Jan. 31—Tommy Robson, Cleveland . .ND 10

Feb. 3—Len Rowlands, Pittsburgh . . .KO 3
Feb. 10—Bill Brennan, Syracuse . . . . .ND 10
Feb. 17—Battling Levinsky, Buffalo . .ND 10
Feb. 28—Chuck Wiggins, Toledo . . . . .ND 10
Mar. 3—Chuck Wiggins, Detroit . . . . .ND 8
Mar. 6—Leo Houck, Lancaster, Pa. . .ND 6
Mar. 13—George K. O. Brown, Canton, O. .ND 12
Mar. 17—Bill Brennan, Pittsburgh . . . .ND 10
Mar. 31—Billy Miske, Pittsburgh . . . . .ND 10
Apr. 8—One Round Davis, Buffalo . .ND 10
Apr. 25—Leo Houck, Erie, Pa. . . . . . . .ND 10
Apr. 28—Battling Levinsky, Canton, O. ND 10
May 6—Clay Turner, Boston . . . . .W 12
May 8—Willie Meehan, Pittsburgh . . .ND 10
May 14—Bartley Madden, Phila. . . . .ND 10
June 16—Joe Borrell, Philadelphia . . . .KO 5
June 23—Mike Gibbons, Pittsburgh . . .ND 10
July 4—Bill Brennan, Tulsa, Okla. . . .W 15
July 14—Battling Levinsky, Phila. . . . .ND 6
July 16—K. O. Brown, Wheeling, W.Va. W 10
July 21—Yankee Gilbert, Wheeling, W. Va. . . . . .KO 3
July 24—Joe Chip, Youngstown, O. . . .W 12
Aug. 11—Terry Kellar, Dayton, O. . . . .W 15
Aug. 23—Bill Brennan, Pittsburgh . . .ND 10
Sept. 1—Jeff Smith, Youngstown . . . .ND 12
Sept. 3—Battling Levinsky, Wheeling .ND 10
Sept. 18—Silent Martin, St. Louis . . . . .ND 8
Oct. 13—Sailor Petroskey, Phila. . . . . .ND 6
Nov. 17—George Brown, Canton, O. . .ND 12
Nov. 24—Larry Williams, Pittsburgh . .ND 10
Nov. 27—Zulu Kid, Beaver Falls . . . .ND 10
Nov. 29—Soldier Jones, Buffalo . . . . .KO 5
Dec. 10—Clay Turner, Buffalo . . . . . . .ND 10
Dec. 11—Clay Turner, Buffalo . . . . . . .ND 10
Dec. 13—Mike McTigue, Binghamton .ND 10
—Happy Howard . . . . .ND 10
Dec. 15—Billy Kramer, Pittsburgh . . .ND 10
Dec. 22—Clay Turner, Philadelphia . . .ND 6

1920

Feb. 6—Mike Lemair, Kalamazoo, Mich. . . . . .ND 10
Feb. 21—Bob Roper, Pittsburgh . . . . .ND 10
Mar. 6—C. Chapman, New York . . . . .W 4
Mar. 9—Clay Turner, Akron, O. . . . . .ND 12
Mar. 15—Larry Williams, Pittsburgh . .ND 10
Mar. 17—Tommy Robson, Dayton . . . .W 12
Mar. 25—K. O. Brown, Denver . . . . . . .W 12
Apr. 5—Bob Roper, Denver . . . . .W 12
May 15—Tommy Gibbons, Pittsburgh .ND 10
June 2—Clay Turner, Philadelphia . .ND 8
July 5—Bob Moha, Canton, O. . . . . .ND 12
July 8—Larry Williams, Buffalo . . . . .ND 10
July 31—Tom Gibbons, Pittsburgh . . .ND 10
Aug. 14—Bob Moha, Cedar Point . . .ND 10
Aug. 20—Chuck Wiggins, Kalamazoo .ND 10
Aug. 28—Ted Jamison, Grand Rapids .ND 10
Sept. 6—Chuck Wiggins, Benton Harbor .ND 6
Sept. 22—Ted Jamison, Milwaukee . . .KO 6
Oct. 21—Gunboat Smith, South Bend .KO 1
Oct. 28—Mickey Shannon, Pittsburgh .ND 10
Nov. 10—Bartley Madden, Kalamazoo .ND 10
Nov. 22—Bob Moha, Milwaukee . . . . .ND 10
Dec. 11—Jack Duffy, Pittsburgh . . . . .KO 6
Dec. 21—Bob Roper, Boston . . . . .W 10
Dec. —Mike McTigue, Pittsburgh . . .ND 10

1921

Jan. 20—Johnny Celmars, Dallas . . . . . .W 10
Jan. 29—Pal Reed, Boston . . . . .W 10
Feb. 25—Jeff Smith, Boston . . . . .W 10
Mar. 16—Jack Renault, Pittsburgh . . .ND 10
Apr. 11—Soldier Jones, Toronto, Can. .KO 4
May 5—Bartley Madden, Pittsburgh . .ND 10
May 13—Jimmy Darcy, Boston . . . . . .W 10
May 20—Jeff Smith, New Orleans . . .D 15
May 29—Chuck Wiggins, South Bend .ND 10
Aug. 29—Kid Norfolk, Pittsburgh . . . .ND 10
Sept. 20—Joe Cox, New York . . . . . . .W 10
Nov. 4—Charles Weinert, New York .W 15
Nov. 11—Billy Shade, Pittsburgh . . . .ND 10
Nov. 25—Homer Smith, Newark, N. J. .KO 5
Dec. 6—Fay Kaiser, Philadelphia . . . .ND 8

1922

Jan. 2—Chuck Wiggins, Cincinnati . . .ND 12
Feb. 1—Hugh Walker, Grand Rapids .ND 10
Feb. 20—Jeff Smith, Cincinnati . . . . . .ND 10
Mar. 13—Tommy Gibbons, New York . .W 15
May 12—Al Roberts, Boston . . . . .KO 6
May 23—Gene Tunney, New York . . .W 15
(Won vacant American Light Heavyweight Title)
June 26—Hughey Walker, Pittsburgh . .ND 10

July   10—Tommy Loughran, Phila. ...ND   8
Sept.   26—Al Benedict, Toronto, Can. ..KO   2
Sept.   29—Bob Roper, Grand Rapids ...ND   10
Oct.   25—Larry Williams, Mariesville,
            R. I. ....KO
Nov.   10—Capt. Bob Roper, Buffalo ....W   12
Dec.   25—Jeff Smith, Pittsburgh ......ND   10
1923
Jan.   1—Bob Roper, Pittsburgh .....ND   10
Jan.   15—Tommy Loughran, Pitts. ....ND   10
Jan.   22—Billy Shade, Jersey City ...ND   12
Jan.   30—Tommy Loughran, New York . W   15
        (For American Light Heavyweight Title)
Feb.   5—Pal Reed, Newark, N. J. ....ND   12
Feb.   16—Young Fisher, Syracuse, N. Y. W   12
Feb.   23—Gene Tunney, New York L   15
        (For American Light Heavyweight Title)
Aug.   31—Johnny Wilson, New York ...W   15
            (Won world middleweight title.)
Oct.   4—Jimmy Darcy, Pittsburgh ...ND   10
Oct.   11—Tommy Loughran, Boston ...L   10
Oct.   22—Lou Bogash, Jersey City ....ND   12
Nov.   5—Soldier Jones, Pittsburgh ...ND   10
Nov.   15—Chuck Wiggins, Grand Rapids ND   10
Dec.   3—Bryan Downey, Pittsburgh ...W   10
            (Middleweight Title Bout)
Dec.   10—Gene Tunney, New York L   15
        (For American Light Heavyweight Title)
Dec.   26—Tommy Loughran, Pittsburgh . W   10
1924
jan.   18—*Johnny Wilson, New York ..W   15
Feb.   2—Jack Reeves, Oakland, Cal. ...W   4
Mar.   24—*Fay Kaiser, Baltimore .....KO   12
Apr.   19—Kid Norfolk, Boston ....LF   6
May   5—Jackie Clark, Kenilworth, Md. KO   2
May   12—Pal Reed, Pittsburgh ....W   10
June   12—Martin Burke, Cleveland ....ND   6
June   16—Frank Moody, Waterbury ...KO   6
June   26—*Ted Moore, New York .....W   15
Aug.   21—Tiger Flowers, Fremont, O. ...ND   10
Sept.   4—Jimmy Slattery, Buffalo ....W   6
Sept.   15—Billy Hirsch, Steubenville, O. KO   2
Sept.   17—Gene Tunney, Cleveland ....ND   10
Oct.   13—Tommy Loughran, Philadelphia D   10
Nov.   17—Jimmy Delaney, Pittsburgh ...W   10
Nov.   25—Frankie Ritz, Wheeling ....KO   2
        *Title bout.
1925
Jan.   1—Augie Ratner, Pittsburgh .....W   10
Jan.   9—Bob Sage, Detroit ....W   10
Jan.   19—Johnny Papke, Zanesville, O. W   7
Jan.   22—Kid Lewis, Pittsburgh ......KO   1
Jan.   30—Jimmy Delaney, St. Paul ...ND   10
Feb.   17—Billy Britton, Allentown, Pa. ..W   10
Feb.   23—Young Fisher, Scranton, Pa. ..NC   6
Mar.   27—Gene Tunney, St. Paul .....ND   10
Apr.   17—Johnny Wilson, Boston ......W   10
Apr.   24—Jack Reddick, Toronto .....W   10
May   1—Quintin Rojas, Detroit .....W   10
May   6—Billy Britton, Columbus, O. .W   12
May   29—Tommy Burns, Indianapolis .ND   10
June   1—Soldier Buck, Louisville .....W   10
June   5—Jimmy Nuss, Marquette,
            Mich. ....KO   4
July   2—*Mickey Walker, New York ..W   15
July   16—Max Rosenbloom, Cleveland .ND   10
July   23—Billy Britton, Columbus ....ND   10
July   27—Ralph Bruucks, Wichita ....ND   10
July   31—Otis Bryant, Tulsa, Okla. ....KO   3
Aug.   5—Ed K. O. Smith, Kansas City .KO   4
Aug.   12—Pat Walsh, Atlantic City ....KO   2
Aug.   17—Tommy Burns, Detroit ......W   10
Oct.   12—Tony Marullo, Pittsburgh ....W   10
Nov.   13—*Tony Marullo, New Orleans . W   15
Dec.   14—Soldier Buck, Nashville, Tenn. W   8
        *Title bout.
1926
Jan.   11—Roland Todd, Toronto, Can. ...W   12
Jan.   19—Joe Lohman, Omaha, Neb. ...W   10
Jan.   26—Ted Moore, Los Angeles .....W   10
Jan.   29—Buck Holly, Hollywood, Calif.KO   5
Feb.   3—Jimmy Delaney, Oakland, Cal. W   10
Feb.   12—Owen Phelps, Prescott, Ariz. ..W   10
Feb.   26—Tiger Flowers, N. Y. C. L   15
        (Lost middleweight championship of world)
June   2—Art Wiegand, Buffalo, N. Y. ..W   10
June   15—Allen. Joe Gans, Wilkes Barre . W   10
Aug.   19—Tiger Flowers, N. Y. C. L   15
            (For World Middleweight Title)

TB	KO	WD	WF	D	LD	LF	KO BY	ND	NC
294	47	64	1	3	5	1	2	170	1

546

Greb died Oct. 22, 1926, following operation on
eye.

Elected to Boxing Hall of Fame 1955.

TIGER FLOWERS
(Theo Flowers—The Georgia Deacon)
Born, Aug. 5, 1895, Camille, Ga. Weight,
160 lbs. Height, 5 ft. 10 in. American Negro.
Managed by Walk Miller.
1918
    Knockouts: Billy Hooper, 11; Kid Fox, 2;
Batt Hazel, 8. Won: Batt Henry Williams, 20;
Rufus Cameron, 10; Batt Mims, 15.
1919
    Knockout: Rough House Baker, 3. Won:
Batt Mims, 10; Bill Hooper, 20.
1920
    Knockouts: Tiger Moore, 2; Kid Palmer,
3. Won: Sailor Darden, 15; Batt Mims, 10.
1921
    Knockouts: Kid Brown, 8; Batt Troupe,
3; Kid Brown, 3; Whitey Black, 1; Kid Williams,
3; Gorilla Jones, 4; Jim Barry, 5; Mexican Kid
Brown, 1. Won: Billy Hooper, 10; Batt Mims,
10; Batt Mims, 10; Batt Gahee, 10; Batt Gahee,
8; Whitey Black, 8; Jim Barry, 15. Knockout
by: Panama Joe Gans, 5.
1922
    Knockouts: Jack Ray, 2; Kid Brown, 2;
Kid Paddy, 1; Kid Davis, 1; Eddie Palmer, 10.
Won: Billy Britton, 15; Battling Gahee, 8;
Frankie Murphy, 10; Andy Kid Palmer, 15;
Frankie Carbone, 10; (foul) Eddie Palmer, 8.
Knocked out by: Kid Norfolk, 3; Sam
Langford, 2; Lee Anderson, 7; Jamaica Kid, 2.
Draw: Battling Norfolk, 8.
1923
Feb.   21—Bob Lawson, Nashville ......W   8
Feb.   28—Batt Mims, Nashville ....W   8
Mar.   10—Evansville Jack Ray,
            Nashville ....KO   3
Apr.   20—Jamaica Kid, Toledo ....ND   12
May   8—Kid Norfolk, Springfield,
            O. ....KO by   1
May   15—Tom King, Juarez, Mexico ...W   15
May   25—Panama Joe Gans, Toledo ...ND   12
July   3—Tut Jackson, Atlanta ....W   12
July   30—Whitey Black, Detroit ......ND   10
Sept.   3—Jamaica Kid, Atlanta ......W   12
Sept.   16—Jim Flynn, Mexico City ....W   5
Nov.   7—George Robinson, Atlanta ....D   12
Dec.   6—Rufus Cameron, Albany ....KO   4
1924
Jan.   23—Herbert Moore, Nashville ...KO   1
Jan.   30—Sam Goodrich, San Antonio ..W   12
Feb.   18—Bob Lawson, Toledo, O. .....KO   10
Feb.   25—Battling Gahee, Barberton, O. .W   12
Mar.   3—Jamaica Kid, Fremont, O. ...ND   10
Mar.   19—Bob Lawson, Nashville .....KO   5
Mar.   29—Lee Anderson, N. Y. C. .....W   12
Apr.   9—Dave Thorton, Nashville ....KO   2
Apr.   19—Jimmy Darcy, N. Y. C. .....W   10
Apr.   29—Geo. Robinson, Atlanta, Ga. ..W   10
May   3—Ted Jamieson, N. Y. C. .....W   12
May   14—Willie Walker, N. Y. C. .....KO   7
June   14—Joe Lohman, N. Y. C. ......W   12
June   20—Batt. Gahee, Freemont .....ND   10
June   27—Jamaica Kid, Grand Rapids ..WF   6
July   3—Lee Anderson, Atlanta .....WF   6
July   22—Jamaica Kid, Covington ....WF   5
Aug.   2—Jack Townsend, N. Y. C. ...KO   11
Aug.   12—Oscar Mortimer, San Antonio KO   4
Aug.   21—Harry Greb, Fremont, O. ...ND   10
Sept.   1—Tut Jackson, Martins Ferry ..ND   10
Sept.   15—Jamaica Kid, Columbus, O. ..W   12
Sept.   22—Lee Anderson, Columbus, O. ..W   12
Sept.   28—Battling Gahee, Zanesville, O. KO   4
Sept.   29—Tut Jackson, Canton, O. ....KO   1
Oct.   11—Jamaica Kid, N. Y. C. ......KO   7
Oct.   21—Cleve Hawkins, Atlanta .....KO   3
Oct.   23—Joe Lohman, Hamilton, O. ...WF   4
Nov.   1—George Robinson, N. Y. C. ...W   12
Nov.   10—*Jerry Hayes, Philadelphia ..KO   2
Nov.   10—*Hughie Clemons, Phila. ...KO   2
Nov.   27—Clem Johnson, Canton, O. ..ND   12
Dec.   1—Battling Gahee, Columbus, O. KO   3
Dec.   9—Johnny Wilson, N. Y. C. ....KO   3
Dec.   15—Jack Townsend, Phila. ....KO   3
Dec.   26—Frankie Schoell, Buffalo ....D   8
        *Both in same night.

1925

Jan.	1—Joe Lohman, Brooklyn ..... KO	3
Jan.	5—Billy Britton, Boston ...... KO	4
Jan.	7—Dan Dowd, Providence ..... KO	6
Jan.	16—Jack Delaney, N. Y. C. .. KO by	2
Jan.	28—Tommy Robson, Boston .... KO	8
Feb.	2—Ted Moore, Newark .... ND	12
Feb.	5—Jamaica Kid, Dayton .... KO	10
Feb.	14—Jackie Clarke, N. Y. C. ..... KO	5
Feb.	16—Lou Bogash, Boston ...... LF	3
Mar.	4—Jack Delaney, N. Y. C. .. KO by	4
Mar.	16—Sailor Darden, Toledo .... W	12
Mar.	20—Lou Bogash, Boston ...... W	10
Apr.	29—Sailor Darden, Savannah .... KO	5
May	18—Pal Reed, Boston .... W	10
May	26—Lou Bogash, Bridgeport .... W	12
June	4—Jock Malone, E. Chicago .....ND	10
June	8—Lee Anderson, Philadelphia ... W	10
July	24—Lou Bogash, Aurora .... ND	10
July	20—Pat McCarthy, Boston ...... W	10
Aug.	28—Jock Malone, Boston ...... W	10
Sept.	7—*Ted Moore, Cleveland ..... NC	6
Oct.	23—Jock Malone, St. Paul ..... ND	10
Oct.	28—Chuck Wiggins, E. Chicago ..ND	10
Dec.	10—Frank Moody, Boston ...... W	10
Dec.	23—Mike McTigue, N. Y. C...... L	10

*Referee stopped fight.

1926

Feb.	26—Harry Greb, N. Y. C........ W	15

(Won World Middleweight Title)

Apr.	16—Panama Joe Gans, Wilkes-Barre .... W	10
June	18—Young Bob Fitzsimmons, Jersey City .... ND	10
June	28—Ray Neuman, Boston ...... W	10
July	11—Lee Anderson, Juarez, Mex. .KO	2
July	24—Eddie Huffman, Los Angeles .. W	10
Aug.	10—Batt. McCreary, Atlanta .... WF	2
Aug.	19—*Harry Greb, N. Y. C....... W	15
Sept.	16—Happy Hunter, Memphis ...KO	3
Oct.	15—Maxie Rosenbloom, Boston . LF	9
Nov.	22—Eddie Huffman, Chicago ..... W	10
Dec.	3—Mickey Walker, Chicago L	10

(Lost World Middleweight Title)
*Title bout.

1927

Jan.	7—Tut Jackson, Grand Rapids ..KO	2
Jan.	22—Leo Lomski, Los Angeles L	10
Feb.	18—Lou Bogash, Boston .... W	10
Mar.	29—Soldier Geo. Jones, Atlanta ..KO	1
Apr.	29—Chuck Wiggins, Buffalo ..... W	10
May	13—Chuck Wiggins, Grand Rapids . W	10
May	27—Eddie Huffman, Boston .... W	10
June	6—Bob Sage, Detroit, Mich..... W	10
July	3—Maxie Rosenbloom, Chicago .. D	10
July	28—Bing Conley, Norwalk, Conn. . W	10
Aug.	3—Chuck Wiggins, Cleveland, O. . D	10
Aug.	11—Harry Dillon, Portland, Ore. .. W	10
Aug.	16—Jock Malone, Seattle, Wash. .. W	6
Sept.	1—Joe Anderson, N. Y. C....... W	10
Sept.	30—Pete Latzo, Wilkes-Barre, Pa... W	10
Oct.	17—Joe Lohman, Canton, O...... W	10
Nov.	9—Maxie Rosenbloom, Detroit .. D	10
Nov.	12—Leo Gates, N. Y. C......... KO	4

TB	KO	WD	WF	D	LD	LF	KOBY	ND	NC
149	49	61	5	6	3	2	8	14	1

Tiger Flowers died in New York, Nov. 16,
1927, from effects of an operation.
Elected Hall of Fame 1971

MICKEY WALKER
(Edward Patrick Walker)
(The Toy Bulldog)
Born, July 13, 1901, Elizabeth, N. J. Ancestry,
Irish. Weight, 147-170 lbs. Height, 5 ft. 7 in. Managed by
Johnny Anthes, Jack Bulger, and Jack Kearns.

1919

Feb.	10—Young Orsini, Elizabeth .... ND	4
Feb.	24—Jimmy McCrann, Elizabeth ...... KO	2
Mar.	3—Sailor Kirch, Elizabeth .... KO	2
Mar.	17—Young Frenchy, Elizabeth .... ND	6
Apr.	7—Eddie Summers, Elizabeth ...... ND	6
Apr.	14—Johnny Saas, Elizabeth .... KO	1
Apr.	21—Charley Hance, Elizabeth .... ND	6
Apr.	29—K.O. Phil Delmont, Elizabeth .. KO by	1
May	7—Young Dempsey, Elizabeth ...... ND	6
May	16—Young Frenchy, Elizabeth .... KO	3
May	31—Young Orsini, Elizabeth .... KO	6

June	13—George Adams, Elizabeth .... ND	6
Sept.	12—Mickey Sullivan, Elizabeth .... KO	1
	—Willie Herman, Elizabeth .... ND	6
Oct.	24—Young Dempsey, Elizabeth .... KO	7
Nov.	13—Harry Anthony, Elizabeth .... ND	8
Dec.	12—Jimmy Vallon, Elizabeth .... KO	6
Dec.	19—Young Thompson, Newark .... KO	5

1920

Jan.	2—Tommy Speno, Elizabeth .... ND	8
Jan.	20—Benny Cohen, Newark .... ND	8
Feb.	20—Joe Gannon, Elizabeth .... ND	8
Apr.	16—Willie Condon, Elizabeth .... KO	3
Apr.	30—Willie Gradwell, Elizabeth .... ND	8
May	18—Tommy Speno, Newark .... ND	8
Sept.	15—Shamus O'Brien, Newark .... ND	12
Sept.	21—Banty Lewis, Newark .... KO	8
Oct.	8—Jimmy Sullivan, Elizabeth ...... ND	8
Oct.	25—Shamus O'Brien, Elizabeth .... ND	12
Nov.	12—Mickey Donley, Elizabeth .... ND	12
Nov.	26—Jimmy Sullivan, Elizabeth .... ND	12

1921

Jan.	2—Charley Beck, Elizabeth .... KO	2
Feb.	3—Marcel Thomas, Newark .... ND	12
Feb.	24—Harlem Eddie Kelly, Newark ..... KO	5
Mar.	8—Charley Pitts, Newark .... ND	12
Mar.	29—Marty Summers, Newark .... ND	12
Apr.	6—Joe Stefanik, Providence .... LF	3
Apr.	12—Terry Brooks, Newark .... ND	12
Apr.	20—Kid Green, Providence .... ND	12
May	3—Marcel Thomas, Newark .... KO	4
May	26—Johnny Summers, Newark .... ND	10
July	18—Jack Britton, Newark .... ND	12

(For World Welterweight Title)

Aug.	19—Shamus O'Brien, Long Branch ... ND	12
Aug.	25—Wildcat Nelson, Newark .... ND	12
Nov.	21—Dave Shade, Newark .... KO	8
Dec.	21—Dave Shade, Newark .... ND	12
Dec.	30—Nate Siegal, Boston .... W	10

1922

Jan.	9—Johnny Griffiths, Jersey City ..... ND	12
Jan.	11—Soldier Bartfield, Philadelphia ... ND	8
Jan.	28—Georgie Ward, Newark .... ND	12
Jan.	31—Soldier Bartfield, Philadelphia .... ND	8
Feb.	10—Johnny Griffiths, Boston .... KO	9
Feb.	28—Soldier Bartfield, Newark .... ND	12
Mar.	14—Jack Palmer, Philadelphia ...... LF	5
May	30—Pal Reed, Boston .... KO	4
June	26—Lou Bogash, Boston L	12
June	29—Georgie Ward, Newark .... ND	12
Aug.	2—Jock Malone, Boston L	10
Aug.	25—Wildcat Nelson, Long Branch ..... LF	2
Sept.	14—Artie Bird, New York .... KO	8
Nov.	1—Jack Britton, New York .... W	15

(Won World Welterweight Title)

Dec.	18—Phil Krug, Newark .... ND	12

1923

Jan.	15—Steve Latzo, Philadelphia .... KO	3
Feb.	23—Johnny Griffiths, Scranton .... ND	10
Mar.	5—Johnny Gill, Philadelphia .... ND	8
Mar.	14—Charlie Fitzsimmons, Buffalo ...... W	12
Mar.	22—Pete Latzo, Newark .... ND	12

(Retained World Welterweight Title)

Apr.	5—Johnny Riley, Wilkes-Barre ...... KO	2
May	3—Morrie Schlaifer, Chicago .... KO	6
May	16—Cowboy Padgett, Chicago .... ND	10
July	2—Cowboy Padgett, Newark .... KO	11
July	16—Nate Siegal, Newark .... KO	10
Sept.	20—Bobby Green, Davenport .... KO	8
Oct.	8—Jimmy Jones, Newark .... NC	9

(Retained World Welterweight Title)

Dec.	23—Moe Herskovitz, Toronto .... KO	6

1924

Feb.	15—Wildcat Nelson, Norfolk .... KO	4
Mar.	3—Eddie Billings, Detroit .... KO	5
Mar.	10—Mike Dempsey, Pittsburgh .... KO	4
Apr.	21—Johnny Gill, Philadelphia .... W	10
June	2—Lew Tendler, Philadelphia .... W	10

(Retained World Welterweight Title)

Oct.	1—Bobby Barrett, Philadelphia ...... KO	6

(Retained World Welterweight Title)

Oct.	29—Jock Malone, Newark	ND	12
Dec.	8—Jock Malone, Milwaukee	ND	10

1925

Jan.	7—Mike McTigue, Newark	ND	12
	(For World Light Heavyweight Title)		
Feb.	24—Bert Colima, Los Angeles	KO	7
May	16—Lefty Cooper, San Francisco	KO	1
July	2—Harry Greb, New York	L	15
	(For World Middleweight Title)		
Aug.	24—Sailor Friedman, Chicago	ND	10
Sept.	21—Dave Shade, New York	W	15
	(Retained World Welterweight Title)		
Nov.	25—Sailor Friedman, Newark	ND	12
	(Retained World Welterweight Title)		

1926

May	20—Pete Latzo, Scranton	L	10
	(Lost World Welterweight Title)		
June	24—Joe Dundee, New York	KO by	8
Oct.	4—Shuffles Callahan, Chicago	KO	8
Nov.	1—Joe Simonich, Philadelphia	W	10
Nov.	22—Jock Malone, Boston	W	10
Dec.	3—Tiger Flowers, Chicago	W	10
	(Won World Middleweight Title)		

1927

Feb.	1—Mickey Wallace, Fresno, Calif. ...	KO	3
June	30—Tommy Milligan, London, England	KO	10
	(Retained World Middleweight Title)		
Aug.	24—Wilson Yarbo, Cleveland	W	12
Nov.	1—Mike McTigue, Chicago	KO	1
Nov.	25—Paul Berlenbach, Chicago	W	10

1928

Feb.	22—Cowboy Jack Willis, San Francisco	W	10
May	21—Georgie Smith, Elizabeth	KO	4
May	28—Tony Marullo, Cleveland	W	10
June	5—Jock Malone, St. Paul	W	10
June	21—Ace Hudkins, Chicago	W	10
	(Retained World Middleweight Title)		
Aug.	27—Armand Emanuel, San Francisco	KO	7

1929

Feb.	22—Cowboy Jack Willis, San Francisco	W	10
Mar.	28—Tommy Loughran, Chicago	L	10
	(For World Light Heavyweight Title)		
Aug.	19—Leo Lomski, Philadelphia	W	10
Oct.	29—Ace Hudkins, Los Angeles	W	10
	(Retained World Middleweight Title)		

1930

Feb.	14—Leo Lomski, Detroit	W	10
Mar.	17—Jim Mahoney, Chicago	KO	2
Mar.	24—Charley Arthurs, Flint	KO	4
Mar.	28—Kayo White, Davenport	KO	2
May	16—Paul Swiderski, Louisville	ND	10
May	23—Charley Belanger, Detroit	W	10
July	30—Willie Oster, Newark	KO	3
Aug.	20—Vincent Forgione, Newark	W	10
Sept.	24—Paul Swiderski, Newark	W	10
Oct.	3—Del Fontaine, St. Paul	KO	4
Oct.	13—Mike Mandell, Des Moines	KO	1
Oct.	17—Tiger Johnny Cline, St. Louis	KO	2
Oct.	22—Homer Sheridan, Wichita	KO	1
Nov.	7—Johnny Risko, Detroit	W	10
Nov.	28—K.O. Christner, Chicago	KO	1
Dec.	8—Chief Wilbur, Little Rock	Exh.	5

1931

Jan.	12—Matt Adgi, Philadelphia	KO	1
Jan.	19—Herman Weiner, Baltimore	KO	1
Jan.	23—Joe Lohman, Grand Rapids	KO	6
Feb.	25—Johnny Risko, Miami	W	10
Apr.	10—Bearcat Wright, Omaha	W	10
June	19—Relinquished world middleweight title.		
July	22—Jack Sharkey, Brooklyn	D	15
Aug.	17—Jack Gagnon, Buffalo	KO	1

1932

Mar.	8—Jackie Williams, Denver	KO	2
Mar.	11—Jim Mahoney, Salt Lake City ...	KO	2
Apr.	29—King Levinsky, Chicago	W	10
May	26—Paulino Uzcudun, New York	W	10
June	24—Johnny Risko, Cleveland	L	12
July	25—Salvatore Ruggirello, Newark	KO	1
Sept.	26—Max Schmeling,		
	Long Island City	KO by	8

548

Dec.	6—Arthur DeKuh, Los Angeles	KO	1

1933

Apr.	24—George Manley, San Francisco	W	10
July	6—Lou Brouillard, Boston	L	10
Nov.	3—Maxie Rosenbloom, New York	L	15
	(For World Light Heavyweight Title)		
Dec.	4—Les Kennedy, Newark	KO	2

1934

Jan.	29—Bob Godwin, West Palm Beach	D	10
Mar.	30—Tom Patrick, Hollywood	W	10
Apr.	6—Max Maxwell, San Diego	KO	5
Apr.	13—Bob Godwin, San Francisco	D	10
May	8—Maxie Rosenbloom, Los Angeles ...	W	10
Aug.	14—Young Corbett III, San Francisco ..	L	10
Oct.	24—Natie Brown, Washington, D.C.	D	10
Nov.	12—Paul Pirrone, Philadelphia	L	10
Nov.	26—Tait Littman, Pittsburgh	W	10
Dec.	3—Paul Pirrone, Philadelphia	KO by	11

1935

July	29—John Anderson, New York	L	8
Aug.	12—Lou Poster, Philadelphia	KO	2
Aug.	29—Thyrs Menger, New York	KO	2
Sept.	12—Joe Gorman, New York	W	8
Sept.	20—Charley Weise, New York	W	6
Sept.	26—Irish Eddie Whalen, Albany	KO	3
Oct.	25—Mickey McAvoy, Binghamton ...	KO	2
Nov.	29—Eric Seelig, New York	KO by	7

TB	KO	WD	WF	D	LD	LF	KO BY	ND	NC
162	60	33	0	4	11	3	5	45	1

Elected to Boxing Hall of Fame, 1955.

WILLIAM (GORILLA) JONES

Born, May 12, 1906, Memphis, Tenn. Nationality,
American-Negro. Weight, 158 lbs. Height, 5 ft. 6 in.
Managed by Suey Welch.

1924

	—Sunny Jim Williams	L	4

1925-1927

(Inactive)

1928

Jan.	27—George Moore, Akron ......KO		5
Feb.	23—Black Fitz, Barberton ......KO		3
Mar.	1—Sailor Maxwell, Canton ....KO		4
Mar.	29—K. O. Kelly, Akron ....W		10
Apr.	10—Joe Feldman, Cleveland ....KO		1
Apr.	27—Ben Spively, Marietta ......KO		4
May	4—Alvin Spence, Cleveland ....KO		1
May	17—Young Savlor, Marietta ....ND		10
May	29—Allan Beatty, McKeesport ..KO		10
June	1—Bobby Brown, Cleveland	L	10
June	18—Mickey Fedor, Akron ......KO		5
July	18—Jim Williams, Akron ......KO		3
July	25—Bobby Brown, Cleveland ....KO		3
Aug.	14—Billy Algers, Akron ....W		10
Aug.	29—Sammy Baker, Cleveland ...ND		10
Sept.	13—Tommy Freeman, Cleveland .ND		10
Oct.	2—Billy Leonard, Akron ......KO		1
Oct.	11—Heavy Andrews, Erie ......W		10
Oct.	19—Bucky Lawless, Erie ......ND		10
Oct.	25—Bucky Lawless, Cleveland ..W		10
Nov.	2—Jimmy Finley, Akron ......W		10
Nov.	16—Pal Silvers, N. Y. C. ......W		8
Dec.	28—Tony Vaccarelli, N. Y. C. ..D		10
	—Bobby La Salle, Cleveland ....W		10

1929

Jan.	8—Arturo Shackels, Cleveland ..KO		1
Jan.	14—Arturo Shackels, Buffalo .....W		10
Feb.	15—Jack Murphy, Erie ....KO		4
Feb.	18—Buckey Lawless, Buffalo	L	10
Feb.	25—Nick Testo, Holyoke ......LF		2
Mar.	11—Joe Zelinsky, Springfield ..KO		1
Apr.	2—George Fifield, Akron ......KO		1
Apr.	9—Tommy Freeman, Cleveland ..D		12
May	3—Al Mello, N. Y. C. ......KO		6
May	17—Izzy Grove, N. Y. C. ......KO		6
June	3—Al Mello, Boston ....KO		6
June	14—Jack Palmer, Chicago ......KO		6
June	25—Jack McVey, Boston ......KO		12
July	16—Bucky Lawless, Cleveland	L	10
Aug.	1—Battling Groves, Memphis ..KO		3
Aug.	12—Pete Meyers, San Francisco .KO		5
Aug.	20—Dummy Mahan, Los Angeles .KO		6
Oct.	9—Jack Horner, Akron ....KO		2

Oct. 21—Jackie Fields, San Francisco . . L 10
Nov.   8—Jack Sparr, San Diego . . . . . . W 10
Dec.   4—Nick Testo, Akron . . . . KO 6
Dec. 13—Jackie Fields, Boston . . . . . . NC 7
1930
Jan.   1—Billy Angelo, Philadelphia . . . . W 10
Jan. 17—Floyd Hybert, Holyoke . . . . . KO 3
Jan. 27—Izzy Grove, N. Y. C. . . . . . . KO 6
Feb.   7—Eddie Roberts, San Francisco . D 10
Feb. 14—Wesley Ketchell, San Fran. . . . W 10
Mar. 14—Meyer Grace, Akron . . . . . . KO 4
Mar. 17—Jock Malone, St. Paul . . . . . ND 10
Apr. 14—Gene Cardi, Wheeling . . . . . . KO 7
Apr. 22—Roy (Tiger) Williams, Dayton . . L 12
May   12—Bucky Lawless, Holyoke . . . . . L 10
May   26—Vincent Forgione, Pittsburgh . W 10
June   2—Henry Goldberg, W. Springfield W 10
June 25—Vincent Forgione, Cleveland . . W 10
July 18—Bucky Lawless, San Francisco KO 9
Aug.   8—Manuel Quintero, San Fran. . . . D 10
Aug. 15—Ham Jenkins, Denver . . . . W 10
Sept. 4—Harry Smith, L. I. City . . . . . NC 9
Sept. 15—Cowboy Jack Willis, Canton . . W 10
Oct. 23—Harry Smith, N. Y. C. . . . . . . L 10
Nov. 10—Abe Lichtenstein, Rochester . . W 10
Nov. 28—Jackie Brady, Erie . . . . L 10
1931
Jan. 13—Johnny Burns, Oakland . . . . . KO 7
Jan. 28—Chick Devlin, San Francisco . . D 10
Jan. 30—Mike Hector, Stockton . . . . . . W 10
Feb.   6—Frank Rowsey, San Francisco KO 8
Feb. 11—Herman Ratzleff, Portland . . . W 10
Mar. 11—Bud Gorman, Oakland . . . . . . W 10
Apr. 14—Paul Pirrone, Cleveland . . . . . W 10
Apr. 28—Ham Jenkins, Kansas City . . . W 10
May   25—Bucky Lawless, Chicago . . . . . L 10
Aug. 25—Tiger Thomas, Milwaukee . . . W 10
(Won Vacant N.B.A. Middleweight title)
Sept. 17—Clyde Chastain, Milwaukee . . KO 6
Oct. 21—Johnny Roberts, Akron . . . . KO 3
Nov.   3—Geo. Nichols, Milwaukee . . . . W 10
Nov. 19—Frankie O'Brien, Milwaukee . . W 10
Dec. 11—Henry Firpo, Milwaukee . . . . W 10
Jan. 25—Oddone Piazzo, Milwaukee . . . . . . KO 6
(NBA Middleweight Title)
Mar. 14—Frankie O'Brien, Holyoke . . . . L 4
(Jones was disqualified for not trying.)
Mar. 31—Chuck Burns, Akron . . . . KO 3
Apr.   7—Bud Saltis, Green Bay, Wis. . . . . . . W 4
Apr. 26—Young Terry, Trenton, N. J. . . . . . . W 12
(Title Bout)
June 11—Marcel Thil, Paris . . . . LF 11
(Lost NBA Middleweight Title)
Aug.   9—Jack December, Cleveland . . . . . . KO 2
Aug. 29—Kid Leonard, Davenport . . . . W 10
Oct.   3—Johnny Peppe, Atlantic City . . . . . . W 8
Nov. 24—Joe Purvis, Akron . . . . KO 3
Dec.   1—Willie Oster, Davenport . . . . W 10
Dec.   5—Manny Davis, Manche, Nev. . . . . . . W 6
Dec. 26—Tommy Freeman, Pittsburgh . . . . . . D 10
1933
Jan. 13—Young Stuhley, Clinton, Ia. . KO 4
Jan. 30—Sammy Slaughter, Cleveland . KO 7
(Won NBA Middleweight Title)
Feb. 21—Kid Baker, Indianapolis, Ind. . . W 10
Feb. 28—Willie Oster, Toledo, Ohio . . . KO 3
Apr. 19—Ben Jeby, Cleveland, O. . . . . NC 6
June   3—Babe Marino, San Francisco . KO 10
July 18—Wesley Ketchell, Los Angeles . W 10
July 28—Vere Whitehead, Los Angeles . L 10
Aug.   9—Vere Whitehead, Los Angeles . D 10
Aug. 25—Harold Hoxwood,
         Salt Lake City . . . . D 10
Sept. 2—Manuel Viccorio, Tijuana . . . KO 7
Sept. 15—John Romero, San Diego, Cal. KO 3
Sept. 21—Billy Papke, Pasadena, Cal. . . KO 8
Oct.   6—Mike Payan, San Diego, Cal. . . W 10
Oct. 15—Lou Bertman, Phoenix, Ariz. KO 2
Oct. 27—Ed Murdock, San Diego, Cal. KO 10
Dec.   5—Frank Remus, Seattle, Wash. . KO 6
1934
Jan. 16—Tony Poloni, Los Angeles . . . . W 10
Feb.   9—Max Maxwell, San Diego . . . . . D 10
Feb. 23—Dutch Weimer, San Diego . . . . L 10
May   22—Freddie Steele, Seattle . . . . . . D 10
June 19—Emilio Martinez, Denver . . . . . L 10
Aug. 21—Oscar Rankin, Los Angeles . . . L 10
(Vacated NBA Middleweight Title)
1935
Sept. 17 Freddie Steele, Seattle . . . . . . L 10

1936
Jan.   1—Tait Littman, Milwaukee . . . . KO 1
Jan. 27—Tait Littman, Milwaukee . . . . KO 10
Aug.   5—Art Taylor, Phoenix . . . . D 10
Dec.   4—Mickey Bottone, Milwaukee . KO 1
1937
Jan.   1—Freddie Steele, Milwaukee . . . L 10
(For N.B.A. Middleweight Title)
Jan. 29—Frankie Battaglia, Milwaukee . . D 10
Apr. 13—Battling Nelson, Omaha . . . . KO 4
July   —Frankie Misko, Sioux City . . KO 5
Aug.   9—Tommy Freeman, C'ncil Bluffs W 10
Oct. 27—Andy Miller, Sioux City . . . . . W 8
Nov. 23—Alabama Kid, Springfield, O. . L 10
Dec. 15—Bob Turner, Akron . . . . W 10
1938
Jan. 12—Frankie Hughes, Akron, O. . . . W 10
Jan. 19—Tiger Carsonia, Louisville, Ky. KO 2
Feb. 16—Johnny Davis, Akron . . . . . . KO 8
Feb. 23—Jack Moran, Akron . . . . W 10
Apr.   4—King Wyatt, Fort Wayne, Ind. . D 10
May   10—Babe Risko, Akron . . . . L 10
1939
Jan. 24—Angelo Puglisi, Seattle . . . . . . W 10
1940
May   29—Vern Earling, Kellogg, Idaho . . L 10

TB	KO	WD	WF	D	LD	LF	KO BY	ND	NC
140	53	44	0	13	20	2	0	5	3

MARCEL THIL

Born,   May   4,   1904,   Saint-Dizier.
Nationality, French. Weight, 160 lbs. Height, 5
ft. 10 in. Managed by Alex Taitard.
1925
Nov.   8—Klauss, Cherbourg . . . . W 1
1926
Jan.   9—Dussart, Calais . . . . W 10
Feb. 12—Gaston Lafont, Cannes . . . . . . L 10
Apr.   7—Gaston Lafont, Cherbourg . . . L 10
Apr. 12—Citony, Cannes . . . . W 8
Aug.   4—Kid Nitram, Marseilles . . . . . . L 10
Oct. 17—Kid Nomo, Paris . . . . L 10
Oct. 23—Forr, Paris . . . . D 10
Nov.   6—Raoul Dumondin, Paris . . . . . . L 10
Nov. 18—Leone Jacovacci, Nancy . . . . . L 10
Dec. 22—Gabiola, Barcelona . . . . KO 9
1927
Jan. 25—Christy, Paris . . . . W 10
Jan. 31—Battling Mathar, Paris . . . . . . W 10
Feb. 13—Maurice Forgeon, Paris . . . . . . D 10
May   3—Andrew Newton, London . . . KO 9
June 13—Billy Farmer, London . . . . L 15
July 28—Forgeon Jeune, Paris . . . . KO 7
Aug. 29—Joe Bloomfield, London . . . . . W 15
Sept. 19—Bob Youseff, Marseilles . . . . . W 10
Oct.   3—Joe Bloomfield, London . . . . . . L 12
Oct.   —Leone Jacovacci, Rome . . KO by 10
Nov.   3—George West, London . . . . D 15
Nov. 18—Jack Hood, London . . . . L 15
Dec. 12—Len Harvey, London . . . . L 15
1928
Apr. 21—Daniel Arnaud, St. Etienne . . KO 2
May   8—Kid Nomo, Paris . . . . KO 3
May   20—Andrew Newton, London . . . KO 9
June 10—Aden Raitori, Edmonton . . . . KO 8
June 11—Lauri Raitori, London . . . . . . KO 10
July   9—Orlando Leopardi, Tunis . . . . W 12
July 24—George West, London . . . . . . KO 5
Sept. —Ted Moore, London . . . . KO 8
Sept. 19—Pierre Gandon, Paris . . . . . . KO 5
Oct. 12—Marcel Thuru, Paris . . . . KO 1
(Middleweight Championship of France)
Nov.   2—Joe Bloomfield, Paris . . . . . . KO 2
Nov. 17—Orlando Leopardi, Paris . . . . KO 3
Dec.   5—Billy Farmer, Paris . . . . KO 1
1929
Jan.   8—Ivan Laffineur, Paris . . . . W 12
Mar. 12—Ivan Laffineur, Paris . . . . KO 2
Mar. 27—Leone Jacovacci, Paris . . . . . W 15
(Middleweight Championship of Europe)
May   15—Alexis Marin, Paris . . . . KO 4
Oct. 16—Alfred Pegazzano, Paris . . . . . W 12
Nov.   5—Fred Shaw, Manchester . . . . . L 15
Dec. 27—Charles Krauchi, Paris . . . . . KO 8
1930
Jan. 29—Alexis Marin, Paris . . . . W 12
Mar. 12—Alfred Pegazzano, Paris . . . . . W 12
July 27—Ali Sadek, Reims . . . . KO 6
Sept. 6—Emile Romerio, Paris . . . . . . W 10
Nov.   1—Motzi Spakow, Bucharest . . KO 7

549

Nov. 23—Mario Bosisio, Milan .... L 15
(Middleweight Championship of Europe)
Dec. 10—Pierre Gandon, Paris .... W 12
1931
Jan. 11—Andre Dhainaut, Lille ...... KO 8
Feb. 14—Alexis Marin, Beausoleil ..... W 12
Apr. 15—Emile Lebrize, Paris .... KO 5
June 18—Felix Sportiello, Paris ..... KO 8
July 10—Vince Dundee, Paris .... W 12
Sept. 5—Gh. Axiotti, Bucharest ...... W 10
Sept. 24—Tom Benjamin, Paris .... KO 8
Oct. 26—Herman Klintz, Paris ...... KO 4
Nov. 9—Jack Casey, London ' .... W 10
Dec. 1—Piero Toscani, Lyon .... KO 3
Dec. 12—Amedee Dubus, Basle ..... KO 4
1932
Jan. 20—Franz Boja, Paris .... KO 1
Feb. 22—Jimmy Tarante, Paris ..... W 10
Mar. 21—Jack Hood, Paris .... KO 7
June 11—Gorilla Jones, Paris .... WF 11
(Won N.B.A. & E.B.U. Middleweight
Championships of World)
July 4—*Len Harvey, London ...... W 15
Oct. 31—Len Johnson, Paris .... KO 7
Dec. 5—Ignacio Ara, Paris .... W 10
Dec. 25—Ch. Van Haecke, Cannes .... KO 2
*Title bout.
1933
Jan. 16—Kid Tunero, Paris .... L 12
Feb. 25—Jack Etienne, Bruxelles ..... W 10
Mar. 8—Louis Vauclard, Troyes ..... KO 6
May 23—Erich Seelig, Paris .... W 12
Sept. 15—Jack Etienne, Paris .... W 10
Oct. 2—*Kid Tunero, Paris .... W 15
*Title bout.
1934
Jan. 29—Erich Seelig, Paris .... W 12
Feb. 26—*Ignacio Ara, Paris .... W 15
Mar. 26—Martinez Alfara, Paris ..... WF 13
(Light Heavy Championship of Europe)
May 3—Gustave Roth, Paris .... W 15
June 11—Adolf Witt, Paris .... KO 8
June 27—Oddone Piazza, Paris ..... W 10
July 16—Rene Devos, Anvers .... W 10
Aug. 5—Clemente Meroni, Marseilles .. W 10
Oct. 15—*Carmelo Candel, Paris ..... D 15
Nov. 12—Tino Rolando, Paris .... W 10
*Title bout.
1935
Jan. 14—Jock MacAvoy, Paris .... W 15
(Light Heavy title of Europe)
May 4—Vilda Jaks, Paris .... KO 14
June 2—*Ignacio Ara, Madrid ...... W 15
June 28—*Carmelo Candel, Paris ..... W 10
July 13—Kid Tunero, Marseilles ..... W 12
Oct. 28—Al Diamond, Paris .... W 10
Nov. 25—Lou Brouillard, Paris .... W 12
*Title bout.
1936
Jan. 20—*Lou Brouillard, Paris ..... WF 4
*Title bout.
1937
Feb. 15—*Lou Brouillard, Paris ..... WF 6
Sept. 23—Fred Apostoli, N. Y. C. .. KO by 10
(Thil Vacated Title)
*Title bout.

TB	KO	WD	WF	D	LD	LF	KOBY	ND	NC
96	34	40	4	4	12	0	2	0	0

Died, August 14, 1968 in Cannes, France,
following two automobile accidents.

BEN JEBY
(Morris Jebaltowski)
Born, December 27, 1909, New York City, N.Y.
Weight, 158 lbs. Height, 5 ft. 10 in. Managed by Hymie
Caplin.
1928
—Benny Bonvita .... KO 3
—Joe Spatala .... KO 4
—Sammy Schneider .... W 4
—Young Frankie .... W 4
—Frankie Buchanan .... W 4
—Howard Reddy .... W 4
—Jack Kiernan .... W 6
—Justus Hoffman .... W 4
—Jimmy O'Hara .... D 4
—George Daggett .... L 4

1929
—Cecil Harper .... KO 1
—Cecil Harper .... KO 2
—Jackie Horner .... W 8
—Joe Salina .... W 10
—Joey LaGrey .... W 6
—Alf Ros, New York .... L 10
—Jackie Horner .... W 10
—Elky Miller .... KO 2
—Nick Palmer .... KO 8
—Charlie Rosen .... W 10
Oct. 11—Alf Ros, New York .... W 10
—Tony Vacarelli .... W 10
1930
Jan. 17—Billy Franklin, New York .... W 10
Mar. 8—Floyd Hybert, New York ...... W 6
Mar. 22—Floyd Hybert, New York .... KO 1
Apr. 4—Vince Dundee, New York ...... L 10
Aug. 1—Dennis Golden, New York .... KO 6
Aug. 19—Joey LaGrey, New York ..... W 8
Sept. 11—Joe Dundee, New York ..... W 8
Sept. 30—Babe McCorgary, New York .. W 6
Nov. 14—Harry Ebbets, New York ..... W 10
1931
Feb. 2—Battling Tracey, New York .... W 8
Mar. 20—Len Harvey, New York ...... W 12
Apr. 10—Laddie Lee, New York ...... KO 5
Apr. 24—Johnny Pilc, New York ..... W 10
June 4—Vince Dundee, New York ..... L 10
June 29—Young Terry, Newark ...... L 10
July 23—Ignacio Ara, New York ..... W 10
Aug. 24—Pete August, Newark .... D 10
Sept. 8—Dave Shade, New York ...... D 10
Sept. 26—Carley Horn, New York .... KO 6
Oct. 2—Dave Shade, New York ...... L 12
Nov. 10—Buck McTiernan, Pittsburgh .. KO 7
Dec. 2—Jackie Aldare, New York .... W 8
Dec. 29—Eddie (Kid) Whalen, New York ... KO 3
1932
Jan. 4—Al Delmont, New York ...... KO 2
Feb. 22—Babe Marshall, Newark ..... KO 6
Feb. 26—My Sullivan, Chicago ...... KO 9
Mar. 18—Frank Battaglia, Chicago ... KO by 1
July 15—Billy Kohut, New York ...... KO 3
July 21—Roscoe Maning, Garfield, N.J. ..... W 10
Aug. 4—Leo Larrivee, New York ..... KO 1
Aug. 19—Nick Palmer, New York .... KO 4
Oct. 13—Paul Pirrone, New York .... KO 6
Nov. 21—Chick Devlin, New York .... W 15
1933
Jan. 13—Frank Battaglia, New York ..... KO 12
(Won New York World Middleweight Title)
Jan. 30—Paul Pirrone, Cleveland .... KO 6
Mar. 17—Vince Dundee, New York .... D 15
(Retained New York World Middleweight Title)
Apr. 19—Gorilla Jones, Cleveland ..... NC 6
June 2—Al Rossi, New York .... W 12
July 10—Young Terry, Newark ...... W 15
(Retained New York World Middleweight Title)
Aug. 9—Lou Brouillard, New York ..... KO by 7
(Lost New York World Middleweight Title)
Sept. 5—Joey LaGrey, Newark ...... W 10
Nov. 9—Al Rossi, New Haven ...... W 10
Nov. 17—Joey LaGrey, New York ..... W 10
1934
Jan. 3—Young Terry, Trenton ...... L 10
Feb. 1—Vince Dundee, Chicago ..... L 10
Feb. 8—Al Diamond, Paterson ...... L 10
Apr. 6—Teddy Yarosz, Pittsburgh .... L 12
Apr. 27—Anson Green, Pittsburgh ... W 10
June 20—Swede Berglund, San Francisco .... L 10
1935
(Inactive)
1936
July 1—Al Cocozza, Long Island City ..... KO 2
July 14—Jackie Aldare, Brooklyn .... W 8

TB	KO	WD	WF	D	LD	LF	KO BY	ND	NC
73	22	32	0	4	12	0	2	0	1

550

LOU (LUCIEN) BROUILLARD

Born, May 23, 1911, St. Eugene, Que., Canada. Nationality, Canadian-French. Managed by Johnny Buckley.

(Early record unavailable; started professional career in 1928 and up through 1930 engaged in 64 bouts, scoring 44 knockouts, winning 16 decisions and losing 4 decisions.)

1931
Jan.	30—Al Palladino, Worcester	KO	1
Jan.	—Gaby Bagdad, Boston	W	10
Feb.	—Larry Brignolia, Boston	KO	3
Feb.	12—Canada Lee, Worcester	W	10
Mar.	13—Alf. Ros, Boston	KO	5
Mar.	6—Baby Joe Gans, Worcester	W	10
Mar.	27—Canada Lee, Worcester	W	10
May	1—Eddie Moore, Worcester	KO	2
May	15—Al Mello, Boston	KO	8
June	9—Paul Pirrone, Boston	KO	8
July	23—Yg. Jack Thompson, Boston	W	10
Aug.	25—Jackie Brady, Providence	W	10
Oct.	23—Yng. Jack Thompson, Boston	W	15

(Won World Welterweight Title)

Dec.	2—Bucky Lawless, Boston	KO	3
Dec.	10—Paul Pirrone, Cleveland	WF	7
Dec.	15—Baby Joe Gans, Montreal, Can.	D	10

1932
Jan.	28—Jackie Fields, Chicago	L	10

(Lost Welterweight Title)

Apr.	8—Johnny Indrisano, Boston	W	10
Apr.	29—Johnny Indrisano, Boston	L	10
June	15—Harry Wallace, Worcester	KO	2
Aug.	4—Jimmy McLarin, N. Y. C.	W	10
Sept.	9—Ad Zachow, Boston	W	10
Oct.	7—Andy Callahan, Boston	L	10
Dec.	19—Jimmy Smith, Philadelphia	L	10

1933
Jan.	9—Horatio Valha, Holyoke	W	10
Feb.	24—Johnny Indrisano, Boston	L	10
May	16—Sammy Slaughter, Boston	W	10
July	6—Mickey Walker, Boston	W	10
Aug.	9—Ben Jeby, N. Y. C.	KO	7

(Brouillard won recognition in New York as Middleweight Champion)

Sept.	22—Adolph Heuser, Boston	KO	8
Oct.	30—Vince Dundee, Boston	L	15

(Lost American Middleweight Title)

Nov.	24—Tony Shucco, Boston	L	10

1934
Jan.	19—Bob Olin, N. Y. C.	W	10
Feb.	16—Tommy Rios, Worcester	KO	5
Mar.	5—Al Gainer, New Haven	W	10
Apr.	5—Bob Olin, New Haven	W	10
May	11—Norman Conrad, Worcester	W	10
June	11—Henry Firpo, Providence	KO	6
July	12—Al Gainer, New Haven	L	10
Aug.	20—Anson Green, Pittsburgh	KO	8
Sept.	7—Solly Dukelsky, Chicago	KO	7
Oct.	8—Tait Littman, Pittsburgh	L	10
Nov.	23—Al Gainer, N. Y. C.	W	10
Dec.	25—Sammy Slaughter, Pittsburgh	KO	4

1935
Jan.	28—Oscar Rankins, Los Angeles	KO	4
Feb.	5—Indian Joe Rivers, Los Ang.	KO	4
Mar.	15—Babe Marino, San Francisco	KO	7
Mar.	22—Swede Berglund, San Fran.	W	10
Apr.	17—Marty Simmons, Pittsburgh	W	10
July	4—Yng. Corbet III, San Francisco	W	10
Sept.	20—Al McCoy, Boston	L	10
Nov.	25—Marcel Thil, Paris, France	L	12
Dec.	20—Gustave Roth, Paris, France	W	15

1936
Jan.	20—Marcel Thil, Paris	LF	4

(For Middleweight Title)

June	26—Jack Ennis, Worcester	KO	8
Oct.	9—Fred Apostoli, San Francisco	L	10
Dec.	4—Carl Knowles, New Haven	W	10

1937
Feb.	15—Marcel Thil, Paris	LF	6

(For Middleweight Title)

May	7—Teddy Yarosz, Boston	L	10
Sept.	9—Roy Williams, Portland	KO	2
Oct.	22—Roy Kelly, Boston	W	12
Dec.	10—Dick Maloney, Boston	W	12

1938
Feb.	18—Tiger Jack Fox, Boston	KO by	7
Mar.	23—Gus Lesnevich, N. Y. C.	L	10
Sept.	23—Joe Glaskow, Boston	KO	6
Nov.	7—Ray Miller, Newark	L	10
Dec.	30—Johnny Rossie, Worcester	KO	10

1939
Mar.	17—Edouard Tenet, Paris	D	10
Apr.	5—Antoine Christoforidis, Paris	L	10
June	2—Henry Chmielewski, Worcester	W	10
June	20—Georgie Abrams, Washington	L	10
July	13—Babe Verila, Portland	D	10
Aug.	17—Al Sinibaldi, Portland	W	10
Sept.	29—Howell King, Worcester	L	10
Nov.	9—Frankie Britt, Fall River	L	12

1940
Jan.	12—Henry Chmielewski, Worcester	L	10

TB	KO	WD	WF	D	LD	LF	KOBY	ND	NC
140	66	43	1	3	24	2	1	0	0

VINCE DUNDEE
(Vincent Lazzaro)

Born, 1904, Italy. Nationality, Italian-American. Weight, 147 lbs. Height, 5 ft. 8 in. Managed by Max Waxman.

1923
Sept.	19—Mickey White, Baltimore	W	4
Sept.	26—Pete Kelly, Baltimore	W	4
Oct.	17—Phil Herman, Baltimore	W	4
Nov.	2—Danny Rogers, Baltimore	D	4
Nov.	14—Pete Kelly, Baltimore	W	4
Nov.	21—Young Kilbane, Baltimore	KO	2

1924
Jan.	9—Lew McCarthy, Baltimore	W	6
Feb.	1—Lew McCarthy, Baltimore	KO	3
Feb.	15—Charlie Barber, Baltimore	D	6
Feb.	27—Charlie Barber, Baltimore	D	6
Mar.	14—Kid Buckey, Baltimore	W	6
Apr.	9—Charlie Barber, Baltimore	D	8
Apr.	23—Charlie Barber, Baltimore	KO	5
May	26—Lou Guggliemini, Kenilworth, Md.	W	6
June	4—Willie Patterson, Baltimore	D	6
June	13—Johnny Conroy, Baltimore	KO	3
June	25—Jackie Ryan, Baltimore	W	8
Aug.	13—Kid Buckey, Baltimore	KO	4
Sept.	3—Willie Patterson, Baltimore	W	8
Oct.	1—Jack Gallagher, Baltimore	W	6
Oct.	29—Frankie Ferro, Baltimore	W	6
Dec.	1—Young Mickey, Baltimore	KO	1
Dec.	29—George Leslie, Baltimore	D	6

1925
Feb.	2—Tony Cortez, Baltimore	W	6
Mar.	18—Young Willard, Baltimore	W	6
Apr.	2—Danny Gordon, Baltimore	D	6
Apr.	27—Joe Welling, Baltimore	W	6
June	8—Danny Gordon, Baltimore	W	6
Aug.	3—Nick Bass, Baltimore	W	10
Sept.	28—Tony Cortez, Baltimore	W	8
Oct.	12—Tony Cortez, Baltimore	W	8
Dec.	5—Johnny Hayes, N. Y. C.	W	8

1926
Feb.	8—Harry Kid Brown, Balt.	NC	5
Mar.	8—Lenny Mahoney, Baltimore	KO	3
June	8—Willie Wiggins, Kenilworth, Md.	KO	5
June	24—Carl Courtney, N. Y. C.	W	4
July	7—Battling Willard, Kenilworth, Md.	KO	9
Aug.	30—Alex Hart, Baltimore	W	12
Sept.	9—Charley Satko, N. Y. C.	W	4
Sept.	24—Patsy Haley, Phila.	W	10
Oct.	15—Andy DiVodi, N. Y. C.	L	6

1927
Feb.	14—Paul Dempsky, Baltimore	W	12
Mar.	7—Eddie Burnbrook, Balt.	KO	11
Apr.	4—Al Conway, Newark, N. J.	W	10
Apr.	11—George Russell, Baltimore	KO	3
	—Danny Cooney, Boston	W	10
	—Joe Reno, Long Beach	ND	8
July	21—Jackie Kiernan, Long Branch, N. J.	W	10
Aug.	1—Willie Harmon, Baltimore	W	10
Oct.	3—Joe Reno, Trenton, N. J.	ND	10
Nov.	3—Eddie Mahoney, Los Ang.	KO	2
Dec.	6—Baby Joe Gans, Los Angeles	W	10
Dec.	16—Tommy O'Brien, Hollywood	W	10
Dec.	23—Joe Vargas, San Francisco	D	10

1928
Feb.	15—Jackie Fields, Los Angeles	L	10
Feb.	22—Bobby La Salle, Wilmington	W	10
Mar.	16—Pete August, Hollywood	W	10
Apr.	17—Jackie Fields, Los Angeles	L	10
May	11—Jimmy Finley, Baltimore	W	12

551

May   21—Jimmy Finley, Baltimore   ....W 12
Aug.   13—Irish Fagan, Newark ....ND 10
Oct.   29—Billy Algers, Newark ....ND 10
Nov.   30—Izzy Grove, N. Y. C. ....W 10
Dec.   15—Canada Lee, N. Y. C. ....D 10
Dec.   20—Al Mello, Boston ....L 10
1929
Jan.   14—Billy Angelo, Philadelphia ....W 10
Jan.   21—Young Ketchell, Philadelphia . W 10
Feb.   18—Billy Angelo, Philadelphia ....L 10
Apr.   8—Izzie Grove, N. Y. C. ....L 10
Apr.   19—Joe LeGray, N. Y. C. ....W 10
May   22—Pal Silvers, Newark ....W 10
May   27—Bucky Lawless, Cleveland, O. . W 10
June   10—Izzie Grove, Newark ....W 10
July   1—Freddy Polo, Newark ....W 10
Aug.   19—Abie Bain, Newark ....D 10
Sept. 16—Abie Bain, Newark ....D 10
Oct.   2—Jackie Fields, Chicago ....L 10
Oct.   24—Young Ketchell, Newark .....W 10
Nov.   15—My Sullivan, Chicago ....W 10
1930
Jan.   13—Billy Leonard, Newark .....KO 1
Jan.   24—Jackie Fields, Chicago ......L 10
Feb.   21—Bucky Lawless, N. Y. C. .....W 10
Mar.   17—Alf Ros, Newark ....W 10
Mar.   21—Johnny Indrisano, Boston ....L 10
Ap.   4—Ben Jeby, New York ....W 10
June   19—Young Ketchell, Lieperville ...W 10
July   22—My Sullivan, St. Paul, Minn. ..ND 10
Aug.   27—Abie Bain, Newark ....W 10
Nov.   10—Joe Reno, Newark ....W 10
Dec.   2—Johnny Reppe, Reading .....W 8
Dec.   15—Denis Golden, Newark ....KO 7
Dec.   25—Buck McTiernan, Pittsburgh .. W 10
1931
Jan.   8—Len Harvey, New York ......W 12
Feb.   13—Len Harvey, New York ......W 12
May   7—Johnny Kerr, Paterson, N. J. ..KO 6
June   4—Ben Jeby, New York ....W 10
July   10—Marcel Thil, Paris, France ....L 12
July   26—Jack Hood, London, Eng. ....D 10
Oct.   12—Johnny Peppe, Philadelphia .. W 10
Oct.   16—Solly Kreiger, New York ....KO 8
Nov.   5—Jack Kiernan, Paterson .....KO 2
Dec.   8—Johnny Peppe, Plainsfield ....W 8
Dec.   14—Ernesto Sagues, Miami, Fla. .KO 9
1932
Jan.   18—Jimmy Smith, Philadelphia ...W 10
Mar.   7—Billy Angelo, Philadelphia ....W 10
Mar.   14—Vincent Forgione, Baltimore .KO 4
Mar.   18—Johnny Ketchell, Wilkes-Barre W 10
Apr.   4—Johnny Oakey, Trenton .....W 10
May   23—Bucky Lawless, Newark ....W 10
June   9—Matt Rice, Wilkes-Barre .....W 10
June   15—Abe Bain, Newark ....W 10
July   11—Joe Smallwood, Lieperville ...W 10
July   18—Young Terry, Newark ......W 10
Aug.   10—Ken Overlin, Virginia Beach ..W 10
Sept.   2—Billy Angelo, Asbury Park ....W 10
Sept. 15—Tiger Sullivan, Paterson ......W 10
Oct.   4—Cowboy Owen Phelps,
          Alexandria, Va. ....W 10
Dec.   12—Johnny Peppe, Trenton .....W 10
1933
Jan.   2—Franta Nekolny, N. Y. C. ....W 10
Mar.   6—Jimmie Rhodes, Atlantic City KO 6
Mar.   17—Ben Jeby, N. Y. C. ....D 15
          (N. Y. middleweight title bout)
May   25—Neil Kilbane, Brooklyn .....KO 6
June   8—Frank Goosby, Pittsburgh ....KO 5
Aug.   11—Danny Devlin, Patterson ....KO 5
Aug.   21—Ted Yarosz, Pittsburgh .....L 10
Sept. 18—Ted Yarosz, Newark ....L 10
Oct.   30—Lou Brouillard, Boston .....W 15
          (Won American middleweight title)
Dec.   8—Andy Callahan, Boston .....W 15
          (title bout)
1934
Feb.   1—Ben Jeby, Chicago ....W 10
Mar.   12—Joe Kaminsky, Holyoke ....W 10
Mar.   22—Al McCoy, Boston ....W 10
Apr.   10—Matt Rice, Pottsville ....KO 8
May   1—Al Dimaond, Paterson .....W 15
          title bout)
June   26—Young Stuhley, Chicago .....L 10
Aug.   9—Tommy Rios, Leiperville .....L 10
Aug.   17—Tony Brescia, Brooklyn ....W 10
Sept. 11—Teddy Yarosz, Pittsburgh ....L 15
          (Lost American middleweight title)
1935
Jan.   2—Vince Troiano, N. Y. C. ....KO 5
Jan.   14—Paul Pirrone, Philadelphia ....W 10

Jan.   25—Babe Risko, N. Y. C. ....W 10
Apr.   22—Joe Smallwood, Lancaster ....L 10
May   20—Anson Green, Pittsburgh .....W 10
July   30—Freddie Steele, Seattle .. KO by 3
1937
Mar.   1—Joe Duca, Newark ....W 10
Apr.   2—Johnny Duca, Philadelphia ...W 10
Apr.   12—Willie Murphy, Plainfield ....KO 3
Apr.   19—Red Finnegan, Trenton ....KO 3
May   3—Billy Conn, Pittsburgh ....L 10
May   17—Thys Menger, Newark ....W 8
June   15—Honeyboy Jones, Pittsburgh .. L 10

TB	KO	WD	WF	D	LD	LF	KOBY	ND	NC
150	27	85	0	13	18	0	1	5	1

Died July 27, 1949, Glendale, Calif.

TEDDY YAROSZ
Born, June 24, 1910, Pittsburgh, Pa.
Nationality, Polish-American. Weight, 158 lbs.
Height, 5 ft. 10 in. Managed by Ray Foutts.
1929
Knockouts: Jack McCarthy, 2; Johnny
Judd, 4; Carl Patron, 5; Johnny Dill, 5. Won:
Jackie King, 4; Johnny Brown, 6; Young Joe
Wolcott, 6; Georgie Bretch, 6; Bob Collura, 6;
Billy Yeltz, 6; Johnny Brown, 6; Billy Holt, 6.
1930
Knockouts: Billy Burke, 2; Jimmie
Herman, 3; Jack Murphy, 8; Benny Burns, 5.
Won: Johnny Ponoic, 6; Jackie Herman, 8;
Jimmie McGraw, 6; Hans Roberts, 10; Young
Joe Wolcott, 8; Paul Ogre, 10; Young Rudy, 10;
Joe Corelli, 8; Paul Ogre, 6; Young Rudy, 10;
Jackie Herman, 10; Roger Brooks, 10; Joe
Randall, 10; Jimmie Neal, 10; Young Billy
Holt, 10; Johnny Rich, 10; Tiger Rudy, 10.
1931
Jan.   13—Jimmie Moinette, Alliance, O. . W 10
Jan.   20—Jimmie Belmont, Oil City, Pa. .. W 10
Jan.   30—Mickey Fedor, E. Liverpool, O. W 10
Feb.   6—Larry Madge, Franklin, Pa. ....W 8
Feb.   21—Tiger Joe Randall, Pittsburgh . W 10
Mar.   16—Joe Trippe, Oil City, Pa. .....W 10
Mar.   23—Eddie Kaufman, Canton, O. . KO 4
Apr.   8—Larry Madge, Oil City, Pa. .... W 10
Apr.   16—Tiger Joe Randall, McKeesport,
          Pa. ....W 10
June   2—Tommy Rios, E. Liverpool, O. W 10
July   9—Buck McTiernan, Pittsburgh .. W 10
July   16—Marty McHale, Parkersburg,
          W. Va. ....W 10
July   27—Bucky Lawless, Pittsburgh ... W 10
Aug.   20—Tiger Joe Randall, Pittsburgh W 10
Dec.   10—Jimmie Moinette, East Liverpool
          Ohio ....W 10
Dec.   25—Jimmy Belmont, Pittsburgh .. W 10
1932
Jan.   22—Jimmy Hill, Detroit ....W 10
Apr.   11—Vincent Hambright, Pittsburgh W 10
June   30—Johnny Hayes, Pittsburgh ...KO 8
July   22—Lope Tenorio, Pittsburgh ....W 10
Aug.   12—Eddie Kid Wolfe, Detroit ....W 10
Aug.   30—Jimmy Belmont, Pittsburgh ...W 10
Oct.   7—Eddie Kid Wolfe, N. Y. C. ....D 10
Oct.   14—Abe Lichtenstein, Pittsburgh .. W 10
Nov.   18—Jack King, Pittsburgh ....W 10
Dec.   9—Jack King, Pittsburgh ....W 10
1933
Jan.   23—Eddie Kid Wolfe, Pittsburgh .. L 10
Feb.   27—Eddie Kid Wolfe, Pittsburgh .. D 10
Mar.   10—Eddie Ran, Detroit ....W 10
Mar.   24—Paulie Walker, Pittsburgh ....W 10
Apr.   10—Andy Divodi, Pittsburgh ....KO 5
May   22—Tommy Freeman, Pittsburgh .. W 10
June   20—Sammy Slaughter, Cleveland .. W 10
July   24—Freddie Polo, Newark ......KO 5
Aug.   1—Al Rossi, Newark ....W 10
Aug.   21—Vince Dundee, Pittsburgh ....W 10
Sept. 18—Vince Dundee, Newark .....W 10
Oct.   25—Young Terry, Newark ....L 10
Dec.   2—Paul Pirrone, Cleveland .....W 10
Dec.   11—Tony D'Alesandro, Holyoke .. W 10
1934
Feb.   12—Jimmy Smith, Pittsburgh ....W 15
Apr.   6—Ben Jeby, Pittsburgh ....W 12
Apr.   16—Tommy Rios, Canton ....W 10
May   18—Freddie Heinz, Clarksburg ...W 10
June   5—Pete Latzo, Pittsburgh ......KO 4

July 18—Tait Littman, Chicago ...... W 10
Aug. 13—Bud Saltis, E. Liverpool .... W 10
Sept. 11—Vince Dundee, Pittsburgh .... W 15
(Won American Middleweight Title)
Oct. 29—Johnny Phagan, Milwaukee ... W 10
Dec. 14—Kid Leonard, Chicago ...... W 10
1935
Jan. 1—Babe Risko, Scranton ... KO by 7
July 30—Fred Sallus, Steubenville .... KO 2
Sept. 2—Oscar Schmeling, Louisville .. KO 3
Sept. 19—Babe Risko, Pittsburgh ...... L 15
(Lost American Middleweight Title)
1936
May 19—Bob Turner, Pittsburgh ...... W 10
Aug. 13—Young Terry, Youngstown ..KO 10
Sept. 21—Babe Risko, Pittsburgh ...... W 10
Nov. 4—Ken Overlin, Pittsburgh ...... W 10
Dec. 17—Eddie Maguire, Pittsburgh .... W 10
1937
Jan. 13—Solly Krieger, N. Y. C. ...... W 10
May 7—Lou Brouillard, Boston ...... W 10
June 30—Billy Conn, Pittsburgh ...... L 12
Sept. 30—Billy Conn, Pittsburgh ...... L 15
Dec. 9—Carmelo Candel, Paris ...... L 10
1938
Feb. 7—Paulie Mahoney, Buffalo ...... W 10
Mar. 28—Carmen Barth, Cleveland .... L 10
Apr. 26—George Black, Milwaukee .... W 10
May 18—Al Quaill, Pittsburgh ...... W 10
June 6—Georgie Abrams, Wash., D. C. L 10
July 25—Billy Conn, Pittsburgh ...... W 12
Sept. 13—Jimmy Clark, Rochester .... W 10
Oct. 21—Oscar Rankins, Pittsburgh .... W 10
Nov. 1—Ralph DeJohn, Rochester ... W 10
Nov. 11—Ralph DeJohn, Rochester .... L 10
Dec. 12—Ralph DeJohn, Rochester .... W 10
1939
Feb. 3—Eric Seelig, N. Y. C. .... D 8
Mar. 27—Ken Overlin, Houston ...... W 10
Apr. 20—Archie Moore, St. Louis ..... W 10
July 17—Al Gainer, Pittsburgh ...... W 10
Aug. 9—Ben Brown, Atlanta .... L 10
Sept. 11—Ben Brown, Atlanta .... L 10
Sept. 29—Lloyd Marshall, San Francisco L 10
1940
Jan. 8—Nate Bolden, Pittsburgh .... W 10
Feb. 29—Willie Muldoon, Cleveland ... W 10
Mar. 26—Turkey Thompson, Los Ang. . L 10
Apr. 15—Jimmy Reeves, Cleveland ... W 10
June 27—Bud Mignault, E. Liverpool ... W 10
Oct. 21—Lloyd Marshall, Pittsburgh ... W 10
1941
Mar. 5—Jimmy Bivins, Cleveland .... L 10
Mar. 26—Bob Berry, Akron .... L 10
June 16—Tommy Gomez, Tampa ..... L 10
June 30—Jimmy Young, Johnstown ... W 10
Nov. 17—Ezzard Charles, Cincinnati ... L 10
1942
Feb. 12—Joe Muscato, Rochester ..... L 8

TB	KO	WD	WF	D	LD	LF	KOBY	ND	NC
127	16	90	0	3	17	0	1	0	0

Died March 30, 1974 in Moxaca, Pa.

EDDIE (BABE) RISKO
(Henry L. Pylkowski)
Born, July 14, 1911, Syracuse, N.Y. Ancestry, Polish-Lithuanian. Weight, 160 lbs. Height, 5 ft. 10 in. Managed by Gabe Genovese.
Fought as "Henry Pulaski," 1932-34.
1932
Apr. 14—Joe Smallwood, Philadelphia ...... W 6
Sept. 16—Harry Walton, San Diego .... D 4
Nov. 4—Tony Pena, San Diego .... W 4
1933
Jan. 13—Jack O'Neil, San Diego .... W 6
Mar. 3—Guy McKinney, San Diego .... W 6
Mar. 10—Grant Wildarson, San Diego ..... LF 3
May 19—Guy McKinney, San Diego ...... KO 5
June 15—Miles Murphy, Tacoma .... KO 6
Aug. 4—Fay Griffiths, San Diego .... KO 3
Aug. 18—Johnny Carvos, San Diego ...... KO 6
Sept. 3—Dutch Weimer, Tijuana .... L 4
Sept. 22—Leo Kelly, San Diego .... W 6
Oct. 20—Johnny (Bandit) Romero, San Diego W 10
Dec. 8—Nick Urez, San Diego .... KO 3
1934
Jan. 12—Swede Berglund, San Diego ... KO by 4
Mar. 16—Steve Wolanin, Utica .... W 8

May 7—Jackie Flowers, Syracuse .... W 6
May 15—Bucky Lawless, Syracuse .... W 6
June 12—Bucky Lawless, Binghamton ..... KO 5
July 18—Paulie Sykes, Oswego .... D 6
July 29—Joe Desmond, Saratoga .... W 6
Aug. 9—Larry Wagner, Johnson City .... D 6
Sept. 10—Werner Wilsch, Syracuse .... KO 2
Sept. 17—Pete Suskey, Syracuse .... W 6
Oct. 15—Freddie Sallus, Syracuse .... D 8
Oct. 29—Werner Wilsch, Binghamton ... KO 3
Nov. 5—Freddie Sallus, Syracuse .... KO 8
Nov. 19—Al Sabano, Syracuse .... W 10
Nov. 26—Chester Palutis, Scranton .... W 6
Dec. 12—Pete Suskey, Scranton .... W 6
1935
Jan. 1—Teddy Yarosz, Scranton .... KO 7
Jan. 25—Vince Dundee, New York .... L 10
Jan. 29—Solly Dukelsky, Chicago .... D 10
Feb. 25—Paul Pirrone, Philadelphia .... W 10
Mar. 11—Benny Levine, Syracuse .... KO 2
Mar. 18—Sammy Slaughter, Philadelphia ... W 10
Mar. 25—Jimmy Belmont, Cleveland .... L 8
May 22—Frank Battaglia, Pittsburgh .... W 10
July 8—Paul Pirrone, Cleveland .... L 10
Sept. 19—Teddy Yarosz, Pittsburgh .... W 15
(Won NBA-New York World Middleweight Title)
Oct. 4—Jackie Aldare, Syracuse .... W 10
Oct. 21—Chester Palutis, Scranton .... W 10
Dec. 9—Frank Battaglia, Philadelphia .... W 10
Dec. 20—Jock McAvoy, New York ...... KO by 1
1936
Feb. 10—Tony Fisher, Newark .... W 15
(Retained NBA-New York World Middleweight Title)
Mar. 24—Freddie Steele, Seattle .... L 10
Apr. 9—Mike Payan, San Diego .... W 10
May 8—Fred Apostoli, San Francisco ...... L 10
July 11—Freddie Steele, Seattle .... L 15
(Lost NBA-New York World Middleweight Title)
Sept. 21—Teddy Yarosz, Pittsburgh .... L 10
Oct. 28—Harry Balsamo, New York .... W 10
Nov. 27—Tony Tozzo, Buffalo .... W 10
Dec. 18—Joe (Butch) Lynch, Syracuse ..... KO 8
1937
Feb. 19—Freddie Steele, New York .... L 15
(For NBA-New York World Middleweight Title)
Mar. 11—Billy Conn, Pittsburgh .... L 10
July 13—Al Hostak, Seattle .... KO by 7
Aug. 17—George Black, Milwaukee ..... KO by 5
1938
May 10—Gorilla Jones, Akron .... W 10
June 6—Al Quaill, Pittsburgh .... D 10
June 27—Ralph DeJohn, Syracuse ...... KO by 7
July 18—Ben Brown, Atlanta .... D 10
Sept. 17—Larry Lane, Trenton .... KO by 2
Sept. 26—Ben Brown, Atlanta .... KO by 9
Oct. 5—Billy Soose, Pittsburgh .... KO by 3
1939
Feb. 7—Walter Franklin, New York ... KO by 6
May 17—Lloyd Marshall, Sacramento ... KO by 5

TB	KO	WD	WF	D	LD	LF	KO BY	ND	NC
66	12	26	0	7	10	1	10	0	0

Died, March 7, 1957, Syracuse, N.Y.

FREDDIE STEELE
Born, December 18, 1912, Tacoma, Washington. Weight, 158 lbs. Height, 5 ft. 10½ in. Managed by Dave Miller.
1928
Mar. 1—Billy Edwards, Tacoma .... KO 4
Mar. 15—Bud Weaver, Tacoma .... KO 4
1929
Jan. 1—Jimmy Parolic, Tacoma .... D 4
May 9—Eddie Foster, Tacoma .... KO 2
June 27—Ralph Smith, Tacoma .... W 4
Aug. 5—Arnold Smith, Tacoma .... KO 1
Career totals to October, 1929: 28 bouts, 15 kayoes, nine wins on points, four draws.
Nov. 14—Harry Davis, Tacoma .... KO 0

Date	Opponent	Result	Rds
Nov. 21	Paddy Ryan, Tacoma	KO	1
Dec. 19	Jimmy Parolic, Tacoma	W	6

1930

Date	Opponent	Result	Rds
Jan. 9	Frankie Monroe, Tacoma	W	6
Jan. 23	Joe Nash, Tacoma	KO	2
	—Jack Rondeaux	KO	3
	—Joe Coffman	W	6
Mar. 6	Jimmy Britt, Tacoma	D	6
May 8	Joe Townsend, Tacoma	W	6
May 22	Joe Townsend, Tacoma	W	6
June 26	Tommy Fielding, Tacoma	W	6
July 10	Tommy Fielding, Tacoma	W	6
Sept. 11	Jimmy Farrar, Seattle	KO	3
Oct. 2	Leslie Carter, Tacoma	KO	5
Oct. 16	Al Gracio, Tacoma	KO	6
Dec. 11	Tony Portillo, Tacoma	D	6
Dec. 17	Tony Portillo, Seattle	L	6

1931

Date	Opponent	Result	Rds
Jan. 1	Tony Portillo, Tacoma	W	6
Feb. 13	Mickey Trad, Tacoma	W	6
Feb. 18	Joe Townsend, Seattle	D	6
	—Al Gracio	W	6
Mar. 26	Nels Ferguson, Tacoma	W	6
Apr. 8	Nels Ferguson, Seattle	KO	2
Apr. 16	Richie King, Tacoma	KO	1
Apr. 22	Teddy Palacios, Seattle	KO	1
May 7	Esten Hunter, Tacoma	W	6
May 13	Joe Townsend, Seattle	KO	2
May 27	Jimmy Owens, Seattle	W	6
June 10	Jimmy Owens, Seattle	W	6
	—Don Fraser, Spokane	W	6
July 16	Al Gracio, Spokane	KO	3
Aug. 20	Johnny Woods, Spokane	KO	3
Sept. 23	Cowboy Sammy Evans, Seattle	W	6
	—Tommy Fielding	W	8

1932

Date	Opponent	Result	Rds
Mar. 3	Freddie Goldstein, Tacoma	W	6
Mar. 16	Lee Page, Seattle	W	6
Mar. 24	Matt Calo, Tacoma	W	6
Apr. 7	Bobby Vincent, Tacoma	W	6
Apr. 27	Tony Portillo, Seattle	W	6
May 18	Ceferino Garcia, Seattle	KO	2
May 24	Frankie Stetson, Portland	W	6
June 1	Alfonso Gonzales, Seattle	W	6
June 30	Larry Murphy, Spokane	W	6
July 20	Ralph Chong, Seattle	KO	6
Aug. 3	Lee Page, Spokane	W	6
Aug. 11	Alfonso Gonzales, Tacoma	W	6
Aug. 26	Billy Townsend, Seattle	W	6
Sept. 7	David Velasco, Seattle	W	6
Sept. 20	Ceferino Garcia, Los Angeles	KO	2
Sept. 27	Tommy Herman, Los Angeles	L	4
Oct. 26	Tommy Herman, Seattle	W	6
Nov. 2	Millio Millitti, Tacoma	W	6
Nov. 17	Battling Dozier, Tacoma	W	6

1933

Date	Opponent	Result	Rds
Jan. 17	Leonard Bennett, Seattle	W	6
May 18	Gilbert Attell, Tacoma	KO	3
June 6	Al Lewis, Seattle	KO	3
June 22	Joe Glick, Spokane	W	8
June 27	Eddie Ran, Seattle	W	6
Aug. 8	Frankie Petrolle, Seattle	KO	3
Oct. 1	Petey Mike, Tacoma	W	10
Nov. 22	Nash Garrison, San Jose	KO by	1

1934

Date	Opponent	Result	Rds
Feb. 15	Leonard Bennett, Tacoma	W	8
Feb. 27	Johnny (Bandit) Romero, Seattle	KO	2
Mar. 8	Vivenicio (Al) Alcante, Tacoma	KO	2
Apr. 10	Eddie Murdock, Seattle	KO	4
Apr. 26	Joe Cardoza, Tacoma	KO	2
May 22	Gorilla Jones, Seattle	D	10
June 8	Babe Marino, San Francisco	W	10
June 22	Sammy Slaughter, San Francisco	NC	1
June 29	Bucky Lawless, Seattle	KO	2
Oct. 25	Joe Glick, Yakima	KO	1
Nov. 1	Andy DiVodi, Tacoma	W	10
Nov. 13	Jimmy Evans, Seattle	KO	4
Dec. 5	Jack Hibbard, Walla Walla	KO	4
Dec. 20	Andy DiVodi, Tacoma	KO	6

1935

Date	Opponent	Result	Rds
Jan. 10	Tommy Rios, Tacoma	W	10
Jan. 24	Baby Joe Gans, Tacoma	KO	3
Feb. 21	Jimmy Rivers, Tacoma	KO	9
Apr. 1	Fred Apostoli, San Francisco	KO	10
Apr. 23	Sammy O'Dell, Seattle	KO	1
May 16	Mike Payan, Tacoma	W	10
June 11	Al Rossi, Seattle	KO	2
July 30	Vince Dundee, Seattle	KO	3
Sept. 17	Gorilla Jones, Seattle	W	10
Oct. 18	Swede Berglund, Hollywood	KO	6
Oct. 25	Mike Payan, San Diego	KO	5
Nov. 19	Young Stuhley, Seattle	W	10

1936

Date	Opponent	Result	Rds
Jan. 23	Meyer Grace, Tacoma	KO	1
Feb. 4	Henry Firpo, Seattle	KO	2
Feb. 25	Young Stuhley, Los Angeles	W	10
Mar. 24	Babe Risko, Seattle	W	10
Apr. 28	Tony Fisher, Seattle	W	10
July 11	Babe Risko, Seattle	W	15
(Won NBA-New York World Middleweight Title)			
Aug. 20	Jackie Aldare, Tacoma	KO	2
Sept. 3	Young Stuhley, Spokane	W	10
Oct. 21	Allen Matthews, Seattle	W	10
Nov. 17	Gus Lesnevich, Los Angeles	KO	2
Nov. 27	Al Rossi, San Diego	W	1
Dec. 8	Young Stuhley, Los Angeles	W	10

1937

Date	Opponent	Result	Rds
Jan. 1	Gorilla Jones, Milwaukee	W	10
(Retained NBA-New York World Middleweight Title)			
Feb. 10	Babe Risko, New York	W	15
(Retained NBA-New York World Middleweight Title)			
Mar. 2	Paul Pirrone, Philadelphia	KO	1
May 11	Frankie Battaglia, Seattle	KO	3
(Retained NBA-New York World Middleweight Title)			
July 21	Hobo Williams, Washington, D.C.	KO	8
Aug. 7	Chalky Wright, Seattle	Exh.	3
Sept. 11	Ken Overlin, Seattle	KO	4
(Retained NBA-New York World Middleweight Title)			

1938

Date	Opponent	Result	Rds
Jan. 7	Fred Apostoli, New York	KO by	9
Feb. 8	Bob Turner, Rochester	KO	1
Feb. 19	Carmen Barth, Cleveland	KO	7
(Retained NBA-New York World Middleweight Title)			

—New York State Athletic Commission withdrew recognition from Steele as world middleweight champion.

Date	Opponent	Result	Rds
June 14	Solly Kreiger, Seattle	W	10
July 28	Al Hostak, Seattle	KO by	1
(Lost NBA World Middleweight Title)			

1939-1940
(Inactive)

1941

Date	Opponent	Result	Rds
May 23	Jimmy Casino, Hollywood	KO by	5

TB	KO	WD	WF	D	LD	LF	KO BY	ND	NC
139	62	62	0	8	2	0	4	0	1

FRED APOSTOLI

Born, February 2, 1913. Ancestry, Italian. Weight, 160 lbs. Height, 5 ft. 7 in. Managed by Harold Seadron.

1934

Date	Opponent	Result	Rds
Oct. 8	Gilbert Attell, San Francisco	KO	3
Nov. 12	Jack Riley, San Francisco	KO	1
Nov. 30	Eddie Daniels, San Francisco	KO	2

1935

Date	Opponent	Result	Rds
Jan. 7	Eddie Fox, San Francisco	KO	5
Jan. 28	Andy DiVodi, San Francisco	W	6
Feb. 22	Newsboy Millich, San Francisco	KO	4
Apr. 1	Freddie Steele, San Francisco	KO by	10
May 31	Mike Payan, San Francisco	W	10
July 17	Eddie Schneider, San Francisco	KO	1
July 31	Dick Foster, San Francisco	KO	6
Aug. 14	Rudy Mendez, San Francisco	W	8
Oct. 4	Young Stuhley, San Francisco	W	10
Oct. 25	Babe Marino, San Francisco	W	10
Nov. 27	Swede Berglund, San Francisco	W	10

1936

Date	Opponent	Result	Rds
Jan. 20	Frankie Britt, San Francisco	W	10
Feb. 28	Paul Pirrone, San Francisco	KO	7

Apr. 6—Young Stuhley, San Francisco ..... W 10
May 8—Babe Risko, San Francisco .... W 10
Aug. 21—Marty Simmons, San Francisco .... W 10
Oct. 9—Lou Brouillard, San Francisco ..... W 10
Dec. 14—Babe Marino, San Francisco .... W 10
1937
Jan. 27—Ken Overlin, New York .... L 10
Feb. 17—Solly Krieger, New York .... W 10
Mar. 15—Joe (Butch) Lynch, Newark ...... KO 9
Apr. 14—Solly Krieger, New York .... KO 5
June 11—Dale Sparr, San Francisco .... W 10
June 22—Tommy Jones, Portland, Ore. ..... KO 2
Sept. 23—Marcel Thil, New York .... KO 10
    (Won World Middleweight Title)
Oct. 25—Tony Celli, Philadelphia .... KO 2
1938
Jan. 7—Freddie Steele, New York .... KO 9
Feb. 4—Glen Lee, New York .... W 12
Feb. 22—Young Corbett III, San Francisco ... L 10
Apr. 1—Glen Lee, New York .... W 15
    (Retained World Middleweight Title)
Sept. 6—Mike Payan, San Jose, Calif. ..... KO 10
Sept. 16—Joe (Butch) Lynch, San Francisco KO 2
Nov. 18—Young Corbett III, New York ..... KO 8
    (Retained World Middleweight Title)
Dec. 20—Al Cocozza, New Haven .... KO 4
1939
Jan. 6—Billy Conn, New York .... L 10
Feb. 10—Billy Conn, New York .... L 15
Apr. 17—George Nichols, Houston .... KO 2
May 11—Eric Seelig, Cleveland .... W 10
Aug. 7—Mohammed Fahmy, Springfield .. KO 3
Aug. 28—Glen Lee, Pittsburgh .... W 10
Oct. 2—Ceferino Garcia, New York .... KO by 7
    (Lost World Middleweight Title)
1940
Jan. 5—Melio Bettina, New York .... W 12
Feb. 2—Melio Bettina, New York ..... KO by 12
    —Freddie Graham, San Francisco Exh. 4
July 22—Dale Sparr, San Francisco .... KO 2
Aug. 19—Big Boy Hogue, San Francisco .... W 10
Sept. 16—Bobby Pacho, San Francisco ...... W 10
Nov. 19—Tony Zale, Seattle .... L 10
1941
Aug. 21—Bill McDowell, Norfolk, Va. ...... KO 2
Sept. 15—Joey Spangler, Norfolk, Va. ...... KO 5
Oct. 14—Ed Brookman, Washington, D.C. KO 6
1942
Mar. 7—Augie Arellano, Brooklyn .... KO 5
Apr. 4—Joe Mulli, Brooklyn .... KO 1
June 26—Ken Overlin, Norfolk, Va. .... D 10
Aug. 24—Saverio Turiello, Norfolk, Va. ..... W 10
1943
(Inactive)
1944
May 26—Vic Grupico, San Francisco ...... Exh. 4
1945
(Inactive)
1946
Aug. 12—Pedro Jiminez, San Francisco .... KO 4
Aug. 27—Sheik Rangel, Sacramento .... W 10
Sept. 9—Dencio Cabanella, San Francisco KO 7
Sept. 20—George Duke, San Francisco ...... KO 9
Oct. 21—Tommy Egan, San Francisco ..... W 10
Nov. 18—Frank Angustain, San Francisco ... W 10
Dec. 11—Paul Lewis, Oakland, Calif. .... W 10
1947
Feb. 28—Bobby Volk, San Francisco .... KO by 1
Apr. 7—Bobby Volk, San Francisco .... KO 3
May 2—George Duke, Los Manos, Calif. .... W 10
May 21—Earl Turner, Oakland, Calif. ...... W 10
July 14—Reuben Shank, San Francisco .... KO 8
Aug. 25—Reuben Shank, San Francisco ..... W 10
Nov. 17—Georgie Abrams, San Francisco .... W 10
1948
Dec. 1—Earl Turner, Oakland, Calif. .... L 10

TB	KO	WD	WF	D	LD	LF	KO BY	ND	NC
72	31	30	0	1	6	0	4	0	0

Died, November 29, 1973, San Francisco, Calif.
Elected to Boxing Hall of Fame, 1978.

AL HOSTAK

Born, January 7, 1916, Minneapolis, Minn. Nationality, Czechko-Slovakian. Middleweight. Managed by Eddie Marino.
1934
Knockouts: Jimmie Smith, 3; Frankie Dat, 1; Bob Wilson, 2; Joe Williams, 4; Willie Smith, 2; Harry Wharton, 3; Al Brown, 1; Phil Gleason, 2; Eddie Umbertus, 2; Bob Jeffries, 4; Kid Webb, 3; Eddie Foster, 3; Jimmie Ireland, 2. Won: Vern Moen, Allen Franks, Heinie Roberts, Alec Weber, Heinie Roberts, Phil Beck, Willis Over.
1935
Jack Hibbard, D; Dick Johnson, W; Allen Foster, W; Jack Hibbard, W; Jimmie Best, L; Sydney Brent, W; Willie Walker, W; Eddie Ivory, KO 2; Billie Lancaster, W. Billie Lancaster, KO 5.
1936
Cecil Gordon, W; Baby Joe Gans, W; Billie Lancaster, W; Jimmie Best, D; Jerome Lewis, W; Don La Rue, W; Jim Nealey, KO 1; Don La Rue, W; Johnny Smith, KO 2; Eddie Bradley, D; Mike Bazzone, KO 5.
1937
Jan. 12—Tony Fisher, Seattle ...... KO 2
Feb. 16—Leonard Bennett, Seattle ... KO 8
Mar. 9—Johnny Sikes, Seattle ...... KO 2
Apr. 13—Young Terry, Seattle .... KO 2
July 13—Babe Risko, Seattle .... KO 7
Aug. 10—Allen Matthews, Seattle .... KO 9
Oct. 14—Otto Blackwell, Tacoma .... KO 3
Nov. 2—Bob Turner, Seattle........ KO 2
Dec. 2—Don La Rue, Tacoma ...... KO 2
1938
Jan. 11—Jack Hibbard, Seattle ...... KO 1
Mar. 1—Swede Berglund, Seattle .... KO 2
Apr. 12—Chief Paris, Seattle .... KO 4
July 26—Freddie Steele, Seattle ...... KO 1
    (Won N. B. A. Middleweight Title)
Sept. 17—Young Stuhley, Seattle ..... KO 8
Nov. 1—Solly Kreiger, Seattle .... L 15
    (Lost N. B. A. Middleweight Title)
1939
Mar. 7—Johnny Erjavec, Seattle ..... KO 3
June 27—Solly Kreiger, Seattle ...... KO 4
    (Won N. B. A. Middleweight Title)
Oct. 26—Charley Killer Coates, Tacoma .... KO 3
Dec. 11—*Eric Seelig, Cleveland ..... KO 3
*Title bout.
1940
Jan. 29—Tony Zale, Chicago .... L 10
July 19—Tony Zale, Seattle ...... KO by 13
    (Lost N. B. A. Middleweight Title)
1941
Feb. 21—George Burnette, Chicago ... KO 1
Apr. 1—Ben Brown, Seattle .... KO 3
May 6—Atilio Sabatino, Seattle ..... KO 1
May 28—Tony Zale, Chicago ..... KO by 2
    (Middleweight Title Bout)
Nov. 21—Ken Overlin, N. Y. C. .... L 10
1942
Sept. 29—Harry Matthews, Seattle, Wash. L 10
Nov. 6—Harry Matthews, Seattle, Wash. D 10
In U. S. Army.
1944
Apr. 4—George Baratko, Houston ... KO 5
June 21—Glen Lee, Houston .... KO 3
1946
June 4—Roman Starr, Seattle .... KO 4
Oct. 22—George Evans, Seattle ...... KO 1
Nov. 12—Sam Hughes, Seattle ...... KO 1
1947
Jan. 7—Benny Droll, Seattle .... KO 2
Jan. 22—Steve Belloise, Houston .. KO by 3
June 6—Anton Raadik, Chicago .... KO 5
Aug. 26—Steve Belloise, Seattle ..... W 10
Oct. 7—George Duke, Seattle .... D 10
1948
Mar. 1—Jack Snapp, Portland .... L 10
Nov. 26—Paulie Perkins, Bellingham .. D 10
Dec. 9—Paulie Perkins, Tacoma ..... W 10
1949
Jan. 7—Jack Snapp, Seattle .... KO 9

TB	KO	WD	WF	D	LD	LF	KOBY	ND	NC
83	47	21	0	6	6	0	3	0	0

SOLLY KRIEGER

Born, March 28, 1909, New York, N. Y.
Nationality, Hebrew-American. Weight, 175 lbs.
Height, 5 ft. 8 in. Managed by Hymie Caplan.

1928
Knockouts: Duffy Moore, 3; Artie Carr, 4. Won: Lee Page, 4; Con Cordero, 4; Eddie McLaughlin, 6; Joe Gorman, 6. Draw: Manny Davis, 6; Jose Radriquez, 6.

1929
Knockouts: Rosen Brito, 4; Willie Young, 2; Eddie Foster, 3. Won: Pete Horton, 6.

1930
Knockouts: Freddie Kelly, 1; Steve Gotch, 3; Billy Drako, 1; Billy Di James, 2. Won: Mario Appicello, 4; Billy Tosk, 4. Lost: Joey La Gray, 6.

1931
July	13—Joey LaGray, N. Y. C.	W	8
Aug.	7—Larry Marrinucci, N. Y. C.	W	6
Aug.	27—Hans Mueller, N. Y. C.	W	8
Sept.	17—My Sullivan, N. Y. C.	D	10
Oct.	16—Vince Dundee, N. Y. C.	KO by	8

1932
Mickey Marino, N. Y. C., W 8; George Cheribuni, N. Y. C., KO 2; Red Gregory, Calif., W 6; Jimmy Evans, Calif., W 10; Ray Acosta, Calif., KO 1; Joe Gorman, N. Y. C., D 6; Walter Braun, N. Y. C., KO 2.

1933
Larry Marrinucci, N. Y. C., W 8; Connie Josenoi, N. Y. C., KO 2; Jay Macedon, Newark, KO 7; Pete Susky, Newark, W 10; Jackie Aldare, N. Y. C., L 6; Al Rossi, Newark, L 10; Al Diamond, Newark, W 10; Eddie Kid Whalen, N. Y. C., KO 2; Frank Fullam, N. Y. C., W 6; Vincent Serici, N. Y. C., D 8.

1934
Swede Berglund, Calif., L 10; Ray Acosta, Calif., KO 3.

1935
June	20—Tony Celli, N. Y. C.	KO	2
July	4—Eddie Kid Whalen, N. Y. C.	KO	1
July	24—Al Rossi, N. Y. C.	KO	6
Aug.	12—Tony Fisher, Newark	W	10
Sept.	30—Ray Miller, Newark	KO	6
Oct.	8—Charley Weisse, N. Y. C.	KO	6
Oct.	21—Young Terry, Newark	L	10
Nov.	19—Tom Chester, N. Y. C.	KO	6
Dec.	20—Jackie Ennis, N. Y. C.	KO	1

1936
Jan.	7—Jackie Aldare, N. Y. C.	KO	5
Jan.	17—Oscar Rankins, N. Y. C.	L	8
Mar.	3—Mickey Bottone, N. Y. C.	KO	1
Mar.	9—Young Terry, Newark	KO	7
Mar.	30—Roscoe Manning, Newark	D	10
Apr.	21—Jose Pimental, N. Y. C.	KO	4
Apr.	27—Anson Green, Pittsburgh	KO	8
May	25—Al Quaill, Pittsburgh	L	10
June	15—Joe Spiegel, Pittsburgh	KO	6
June	22—Johnny Rossi, Pittsburgh	KO	5
Sept.	8—Ralph Chong, N. Y. C.	KO	7
Sept.	21—Frank Battaglia, Pittsburgh	W	10
Oct.	6—John Anderson, N. Y. S.	W	10
Oct.	22—Oscar Rankins, Pittsburgh	W	12
Dec.	16—Harry Balsamo, N. Y. C.	KO	7

1937
Jan.	13—Teddy Yarosz, N. Y. C.	L	10
Feb.	2—Bob Turner, N. Y. C.	KO	7
Feb.	17—Fred Apostoli, N. Y. C.	L	10
Mar.	18—Oscar Rankins, Pittsburgh	L	10
Apr.	4—Eddie McGuire, N. Y. C.	KO	4
Apr.	14—Fred Apostoli, New Jersey	KO by	5
Aug.	12—Walter Woods, N. Y. C.	KO	8
Aug.	21—Joe Ducca, Brooklyn	KO	6
Oct.	3—Walter Woods, N. Y. C.	L	10
Oct.	27—Eddie Maguire, N. Y. C.	KO	7
Nov.	17—Frank Battaglia, N. Y. C.	W	10
Dec.	16—Billy Conn, Pittsburgh	W	12

1938
Jan.	1—George Black, Wisconsin	KO	3
Jan.	25—Al Diamond, Brooklyn	KO	1
Feb.	9—Johnny Rossi, N. Y. C.	KO	4
Mar.	8—Stanley Hasrato, N. Y. C.	KO	7
Apr.	6—Izzy Jannazzo, N. Y. C.	KO	11
May	20—Glen Lee, N. Y. C.	L	10
June	14—Freddie Steele, Seattle	L	10
July	15—Swede Berglund, Hollywood	KO	6
Aug.	10—Ace of Spades, Oakland	KO	4
Aug.	24—Dale Sparr, Oakland	KO	6
Nov.	1—Al Hostak, Seattle	W	15

(Won N. B. A. middleweight title)

Nov.	28—Billy Conn, Pittsburgh	L	12
Dec.	5—Carmen Barth, Cleveland	W	10
Dec.	16—Red Farmer, San Francisco	KO	8

1939
Jan.	2—Marty Simmons, Milwaukee	D	10
Feb.	23—Ben Brown, Miami	KO	9
Apr.	5—Allen Matthews, Seattle	W	10
May	12—Billy Conn, N. Y. C.	L	12
June	27—Al Hostak, Seattle	KO by	4

(Lost N. B. A. middleweight title)

1940
Feb.	3—Texas Joe Dundee, Brooklyn	KO	3
Feb.	17—Mario Liani, Brooklyn	KO	5
Apr.	23—Herbie Katz, Brooklyn	KO	4
May	16—Jimmy Reeves, Cleveland	L	10
July	1—Al McCoy, Woodhaven	W	10
July	18—Carl Johnson, Brooklyn	KO	4
Aug.	12—Wally Sears, Woodhaven	KO	3
Nov.	1—Tommy Tucker, N. Y. C.	L	8
Dec.	17—Melio Bettina, Brooklyn	L	10

1941
Mar.	10—Pat Valentino, San Francisco	L	10
May	13—Dan Gill, Los Angeles	KO	6
May	28—Booker Beckwith, Chicago	L	10
July	22—Lee Savold, Brooklyn	L	10

TB	KO	WD	WF	D	LD	LF	KOBY	ND	NC
111	53	27	0	7	21	0	3	0	0

CEFERINO GARCIA

Born, August 26, 1910, Manila, Philippines. Weight, 147 lbs. Height, 5 ft. 7 in. Managed by Jesus Cortez, George Parnassus.

1927
Feb.	—Ignacio Fernandez, Manila	D	12

1928-1931
(Records Unavailable)

1932
Jan.	19—Alfredo Ganoa, Los Angeles	KO	4
Jan.	26—David Velasco, Los Angeles	W	10
Feb.	19—Vearl Whitehead, Hollywood	KO	7
Mar.	11—Tommy Herman, Stockton	KO by	10
Apr.	1—Joe Saldivar, Pismo Beach	KO	1
Apr.	12—Young Corbett III, Los Angeles	L	10
May	6—David Velasco, Pismo Beach	W	10
May	18—Freddie Steele, Seattle	KO by	2
May	24—Joey Goodman, Los Angeles	L	10
June	22—Jimmy Duffy, San Francisco	KO	7
	—Jimmy Britt	D	6
Sept.	2—Tommy King, Hollywood	W	10
Sept.	20—Freddie Steele, Los Angeles	KO by	2
Oct.	10—Tommy King, San Francisco	D	10
Oct.	25—Young Corbett III, Fresno	L	10
Nov.	22—Andy DiVodi, Fresno	KO	2

1933
Jan.	20—Tommy King, San Francisco	L	10
Jan.	27—Charlie Cobb, San Diego	KO	5
Feb.	10—Johnny Romero, San Diego	KO	8

(Won California State Welterweight Title)

Mar.	3—Frankie Diaz, San Diego	KO	2
Mar.	10—Johnny Romero, San Diego	W	10
Mar.	24—Mike Payan, San Diego	D	10
	—Tommy Huffman	W	10
Apr.	12—Ray (Wildman) Macias, Wilmington	KO	1
Apr.	28—Howard Fritz, San Diego	KO	8
May	9—Leonard Bennett, Seattle	W	6
May	20—Eddie Ran, Los Angeles	L disq.	3
July	11—Kid Azteca, Los Angeles	L	10
July	18—Lloyd Smith, Stockton	KO	4
July	25—Kid Azteca, Los Angeles	KO by	8
Aug.	25—Eddie Frisco, Hollywood	KO	7
Sept.	23—Meyer Grace, Hollywood	W	10
Oct.	13—King Tut, Hollywood	KO	7
Oct.	27—Andy Callahan, San Francisco	L	10
Nov.	25—Vincent Martinez, Los Angeles	W	6
Dec.	12—Baby Joe Gans, Los Angeles	W	10
Dec.	22—Mike Payan, San Diego	W	10

1934
Jan.	16—Bobby Pacho, Los Angeles	KO	3
Feb.	9—Paulie Walker, Hollywood	W	10
Mar.	6—Eddie Cerda, Los Angeles	KO	6
Mar.	23—Tommy Herman, Pismo Beach	KO	2

Apr. 10—Yg. Peter Jackson, Los Ang. ... KO by 3
Apr. 20—Baby Sal Sorio, Watsonville ...... KO 4
May 18—Johnny Martinez, Watsonville .... KO 3
June 1—Billy Boggs, Hollywood .... KO 5
June 14—Tommy Herman, Sacramento ..... KO 3
July 7—Andy DiVodi, Stockton .... KO 1
July 27—Mike Payan, Hollywood .... KO 1
Aug. 9—Jimmy Evans, Sacramento .... W 10
Sept. 2—Joe Glick, Pismo Beach .... KO 2
Oct. 30—Bep Van Klaveran, Los Angeles ... W 10
Nov. 16—Manuel Victoria, Watsonville .... KO 3
Dec. 7—Bep Van Klaveran, Hollywood ..... L 10
1935
Mar. 26—Baby Joe Gans, Stockton .... KO 1
—Guy McKinney .... KO 1
Apr. 18—Al Manfredo, Sacramento .... L 10
May 17—Al Manfredo, Hollywood .... W 10
May 31—Meyer Grace, Watsonville .... KO 1
June 21—Al Romero, Hollywood .... W 0
July 4—Sammy O'Dell, Stockton .... KO 5
July 19—Baby Joe Gans, Pismo Beach ..... KO 3
Aug. 20—Sammy Brown, Fresno .... KO 3
Sept. 13—Barney Ross, San Francisco .... L 10
Oct. 18—Joe Bernal, San Francisco .... W 10
Oct. 23—Gordon Wallace, Vancouver .... D 10
Nov. 12—Otto Blackwell, Portland .... W 10
Nov. 20—Gordon Wallace, Vancouver ...... W 12
Nov. 29—Barney Ross, Chicago .... L 10
1936
Jan. 13—Al Manfredo, Oakland .... L 10
Feb. 7—Gordon Wallace, Hollywood ...... W 10
Mar. 2—Jackie Burke, Ogden, Utah .... D 10
Mar. 27—Lou Halper, Hollywood .... KO 6
May 8—Jackie Burke, Hollywood .... KO 8
June 9—Young Peter Jackson, Los Angeles W 10
July 17—Kid Azteca, Hollywood .... KO 5
Aug. 11—Leon Zoritta, Los Angeles .... KO 5
Sept. 11—Cleto Locatelli, New York .... W 10
Oct. 30—Izzy Janazzo, New York .... D 15
Dec. 18—Ray Acosta, Stockton .... KO 1
1937
Jan. 12—Otto Blackwell, Stockton .... KO 1
Feb. 5—Chief Paris, Hollywood .... KO 4
Feb. 23—Glen Lee, Los Angeles .... L 10
Mar. 23—Jack Wade, San Jose .... KO 1
May 7—Phil McQuillan, Watsonville ..... KO 2
May 21—George Salvatore, Hollywood ...... W 10
June 11—Phil Furr, Hollywood .... W 10
July 22—Bobby Pacho, New York .... KO 9
Sept. 23—Barney Ross, New York .... L 15
(For World Welterweight Title)
1938
Jan. 1—Otto Blackwell, Pismo Beach ..... KO 2
Jan. 28—Mickey Serrain, Hollywood .... KO 2
Feb. 18—Manuel Victoria, San Diego ...... KO 4
Mar. 12—Otto Blackwell, Honolulu .... KO 7
Mar. 25—Tony Roccaforte, Honolulu ...... KO 1
May 6—Glen Lee, Hollywood .... W 10
June 17—Frankie Blair, Hollywood .... KO 3
July 4—Jackie Burke, Stockton .... KO 4
July 25—Jackie Burke, Ogden, Utah ...... KO 2
Nov. 25—Henry Armstrong, New York .... L 15
(For World Welterweight Title)
1939
Jan. 27—Dick Foster, Hollywood .... KO 8
Feb. 7—Al Trulman, San Jose .... KO 2
Feb. 22—Lloyd Marshall, San Francisco ..... W 10
Mar. 17—Lloyd Marshall, San Francisco ... KO 5
Mar. 27—Chief Paris, Stockton .... KO 3
Apr. 21—Al Romero, Los Angeles .... KO 10
June 14—Walter Woods, New York .... KO 4
July 1—Bobby Pacho, Stockton .... W 10
Aug. 8—Bobby Pacho, Los Angeles .... KO 5
Oct. 2—Fred Apostoli, New York .... KO 7
(Won World Middleweight Title)
Dec. 23—Glen Lee, Manila .... KO 13
(Retained World Middleweight Title)
1940
Mar. 1—Henry Armstrong, Los Angeles ..... D 10
(Retained World Middleweight Title)

Apr. 24—Allan Matthews, Kansas City .... KO 4
May 23—Ken Overlin, New York .... L 15
(Lost World Middleweight Title)
Sept. 12—Steve Belloise, New York .... L 10
1941
July 11—Jimmy Casino, Los Angeles ...... KO 8
Sept. 15—Billy Soose, Los Angeles .... TD 8
Dec. 1—Anton Christoforidis, Cleveland .... L 10
1942
Feb. 24—Jackie Wilson, Los Angeles .... L 10
1943
(Inactive)
1944
Sept. 25—Willie Johnson, Ocean Park, Calif. KO 10
Oct. 6—Kid Azteca, Mexico City .... W 10
Oct. 16—PFC George Baratko, Houston .... KO 3
1945
Jan. 15—Wild Bill McDowell, Houston .... L 10

TB	KO	WD	WF	D	LD	LF	KO BY	ND	NC
122	62	26	0	9	19	1	5	0	0

Elected to Boxing Hall of Fame, 1977.
Died, January 2, 1981, San Diego, Calif.

KEN OVERLIN
Born, 1910, Decatur, Ill. Nationality, Irish-American. Weight, 160 pounds. Height, 5 ft. 8½ in. Managed by Chris Dundee.
1932
Won: Bill Brennan, 6 rds.; Sailor Johnny Skrinan, 6 rds.; Johnny Skrinan, 6 rds.; Red Journee, 8 rds.; Eric Lawson, 8 rds.; Tony D'Allessandro, 8 rds.; Joe Raymond, 8 rds.; Joe Smallwood, 8 rds. Lost: Vince Dundee, 10 rds.
1933
Jan. 24—Billy Brennan, Portsmouth ... W 4
Apr. 12—Walter Kirkwood, Norfolk ... W 4
Apr. 25—Joe Finnazzo, Wash. .... KO 4
May 3—Johnny Mays, Norfolk ...... W 8
—Red Journee, Norfolk ...... W 8
May 16—Walter Kirkwood, Wash. ...... W 6
May 17—Johnny Vermillion, Norfolk .. W 4
May 23—Henry Irving, Wash., D. C. .... W 8
July 19—Joe Lipps, Va. Beach, Va. .... W 8
Aug. 7—Billy Strickler, Wash. ...... W 8
—Roy Bailey, Charleston, S. C. . W 10
—Billy Shell, Charleston ..... W 10
Sept. 6—Art Sykes, Norfolk, Va. .....KO 5
Nov. 10—Johnny Bates, New York ...... W 8
Nov. 15—Tommy Rios, Norfolk ...... W 8
—Roxie Allen, Washington ... W 8
Dec. 8—Rudy Marshall, New York .... W 10
Dec. 29—Tommy Rios, Norfolk ...... W 8
1934
Jan. 2—Red Burman, Washington ... W 8
Jan. 26—Wiener Wilsh, Philadelphia ... W 10
Feb. 2—Andy Di Vodi, Norfolk ...... W 8
Mar. 2—Joe Kaminski, Philadelphia ... W 10
Mar. 8—Roxie Allen, Philadelphia ... W 10
Mar. 16—Dan Hassett, Philadelphia ... W 10
Apr. 6—Billy Ketchell, Philadelphia ... W 10
Apr. 20—Tommy Rios, Philadelphia ... W 10
Apr. 30—Paul Pirrone, Philadelphia ... L 10
June 4—Paul Pirrone, Norfolk ...... W 10
July 2—Jimmy Smith, Philadelphia ... L 10
Aug. 22—Henry Irving, Richmond ....KO 7
Sept. 8—Frankie Remus, Richmond . KO 8
Sept. 21—Pat Flaherty, Norfolk ......KO 6
Oct. 5—Al Diamond, Philadelphia ... W 10
Oct. 15—Dan Hassett, Philadelphia .... W 10
1935
Feb. 6—Charley Weise, Norfolk ...... W 10
July 9—Johnny Duca, Richmond ....KO 4
Aug. 9—Henry Firpo, Atlantic City ... W 10
Aug. 19—Joe Smallwood, Washington ... W 10
Aug. 26—Tommy Romano, Richmond . W 10
Sept. 19—Anson Green, Pittsburgh ..... W 8
Oct. 5—George Black, Chicago ...... W 8
Oct. 14—Al Quaill, Pittsburgh .... W 10
Nov. 18—Mooky Goldman, Norfolk ... W 10
Nov. 25—Carmen Barth, Richmond ... W 10
Dec. 9—Al Quaill, Pittsburgh ...... W 11
Dec. 20—Tony Brescia, Richmond .... W 10
1936
Feb. 10—Mickey Bottone, Richmond .. KO 4
Feb. 21—Roxie Allen, Baltimore ....KO 2

Mar. 2—Tony Fisher, Pittsburgh .....W 10
Mar. 20—Johnny Rossi, Boston ....W 10
Mar. 30—Ralph Chong, Baltimore ....W 10
Apr. 20—Jack Ennis, Richmond .....W 10
Apr. 27—Ralph Chong, Wash., D. C. ...W 10
June 16—Jimmie Jones, Baltimore .....W 10
June 22—Jackie Aldare, Richmond ....W 10
July 1—Georgie Black, Milwaukee ....W 10
July 19—Billy Hood, Ashville ....KO 3
Aug. 20—Al Quaill, Johnstown ......W 10
Aug. 31—Oscar Rankins, Pittsburgh ....W 10
Oct. 12—Ralph Chong, Norfolk ....W 10
Nov. 4—Teddy Yarosz, Pittsburgh ....L 10
Nov. 23—Ben Brown, Richmond ......W 10
Dec. 21—Kid Tunero, Paris ....L 10

1937

Jan. 27—Fred Apostoli, N. Y. C. ......W 10
Feb. 15—John Zawackie, Newpt. News KO 2
July 30—Young Stuhley, Hollywood ...W 10
Sept. 11—Freddy Steele, Seattle ...KO by 4
(Middleweight title bout)
Oct. 18—Roy Williams, White Plains ..KO 4
Oct. 25—Joe Butch Lynch, Albany ...KO 7
Nov. 15—Bobby Birch, Albany ....W 8

1938

Jan. 26—Walter Woods, N. Y. C. ......L 10
Mar. 16—Dick Foster, San Francisco ...W 10
Mar. 30—Fred Henneberry, Sydney ....L 12
June 23—Atilio Sabatino, Sydney ......D 12
July 15—Atilio Sabatino, Melbourne ..NC 7
Sept. 1—Lloyd Marshall, San Francisco L 10
Sept. 19—Billy Celebron, Chicago ......W 10
Oct. 7—Jimmy Clark, Chicago ......KO 4
Oct. 17—Jack Moran, Peoria, Ill. .....KO 6
Nov. 4—Nate Bolden, Chicago ....W 10
Nov. 16—Milt Shivers, Chicago ....W 10
Dec. 2—Nate Bolden, Chicago ....W 10
Dec. 17—Jack Moran, Akron, Ohio ....W 10
Dec. 20—Eric Seelig, N. Y. C. ....L 10

1939

Jan. 2—Al Quaill, Chicago ....W 10
Jan. 16—Billy Celebron, Chicago ......W 10
Feb. 14—Al Bernard, Houston ....W 10
Mar. 27—Teddy Yarosz, Houston ....L 10
Apr. 17—Jack Riley, Houston ....KO 2
May 1—Jimmy Webb, Houston ......W 10
May 18—Harvey Massey, Baltimore ....W 10
June 8—Eric Seelig, Chicago ....W 10
June 26—Honey Boy Jones, Pittsburgh .W 10
July 7—Irish Eddie Pierce, Lg. Branch .W 10
Aug. 28—Al Wardlow, Pittsburgh .....W 10
Oct. 18—Allen Matthews, St. Louis ....W 10
Oct. 23—Ben Brown, Atlanta ....D 10
Nov. 21—Honey Boy Jones, St. Louis ....W 10
Nov. 27—Ben Brown, Miami ....W 10
Dec. 4—Babe Orgovan, Wash., D. C. ...D 10
Dec. 11—Ben Brown, Atlanta ....D 10

1940

Feb. 21—Enzo Iannozzi, Raleigh, N. C. ..W 10
Mar. 15—Joe Butch Lynch, Cumb., Md.KO 8
Mar. 28—Jerry Maloni, Chicopee, Mass. ..W 10
Apr. 15—Frankie Nelson, Portland, Me. ..W 10
Apr. 25—Steve Wilkerson, Mem.,Tenn. KO 9
May 23—Ceferino Garcia, N. Y. C. ....W 15
(Won Middleweight Championship)
(N. Y. Version)
June 13—Ralph DeJohn, Syracuse .....W 10
June 28—Ben Brown, Richmond, Va. ...W 10
July 9—Harry Balsamo, N. Y. C. ...:KO 9
July 24—Billy Soose, Scranton ....L 10
Aug. 8—Ben Brown, Atlanta ....W 12
Sept. 18—Eddie Pierce, Norfolk ......W 10
Sept. 30—Larry Lane, Trenton ....W 10
Nov. 1—*Steve Belloise, N. Y. C. .....W 15
Dec. 13—*Steve Belloise, N. Y. C. .....W 15
*Title bout.

1941

jan. 21—Tony Cisco, Wash., D. C. .....W 10
Feb. 3—Jackie Munley, Allentown ....W 10
Feb. 10—Paulie Walker, Trenton ......D 10
Mar. 10—Mose Brown, Pittsburgh .....W 10
Mar. 27—Larry Kellum, Barre, Vt. ....KO 4
Mar. 31—Harvey Massey, Lancaster ....W 10
May 9—Billy Soose, N. Y. C. ....L 15
(Lost N. Y. Middleweight Title)
June 9—Ezzard Charles, Cincinnati ...W 10
Aug. 18—Jimmy Marmon, Augusta ...KO 3
Aug. 27—Jimmy Young, Bridgeport ...KO 8
Sept. 8—Young Crawford, Winst.-Sale. KO 3
Sept. 30—Bill McDowell, Jersey City ...W 10
Nov. 3—Al Gilbert, Norfolk ....W 10
Nov. 21—Al Hostak, N. Y. C. ....W 10
Dec. 15—Mose Brown, Pittsburgh .....W 10

558

1942

In U. S. Navy.
Feb. 23—Wild Bill McDowell, Newark ..D 10
Mar. 2—Ezzard Charles, Cincinnati ...D 10
Mar. 10—Paulie Mahoney, Buffalo .....W 10
June 26—Fred Apostoli, Norfolk ......D 10

1944

Aug. 31—John Donnelly, Santa Rosa ...W 10
Sept. 12—Al Labos, San Jose ....KO 6
Sept. 20—Paul Hartnek, Oakland ......W 10
Sept. 26—R. J. Lewis, Denver ....W 10

TB	KO	WD	WF	D	LD	LF	KOBY	ND	NC
148	23	104	0	7	12	0	1	0	1

Died July 24, 1969, Reno, Nev.

BILLY SOOSE

Born, August 2, 1915, Farrell, Pennsylvania.
Ancestry, Hungarian. Weight, 160 lbs. Height, 6 ft. $\frac{1}{2}$ in.
Managed by Paul Moss.

1938

Mar. 15—Johnny Dean, Los Angeles ....KO 4
Mar. 29—Jimmy Brent, Los Angeles ....W 4
Apr. 5—Hippo Hipps, Los Angeles ....KO 3
June 6—Joe Lugan, Long Beach ....KO 3
June 19—Johnny Foster, Hollywood ....W 6
July 25—Al Quaill, Pittsburgh ....W 10
Aug. 2—Eric Lawson, Clearfield, Pa. ......KO 6
Aug. 29—Freddy Lenn, Pittsburgh ....W 10
Sept. 13—Charley Weise, Farrell, Pa. ......KO 2
Oct. 5—Babe Risko, Pittsburgh ....KO 3
Oct. 13—Johnny Duca, Lancaster, Pa. ......L 10
Nov. 22—Charley Burley, Pittsburgh ......L 10

1939

Feb. 20—Johnny Duca, Youngstown ....W 10
Sept. 13—Joe Fedz, Rochester, Pa. ....KO 1
Sept. 25—Georgie Abrams, Pittsburgh ....L 8
Oct. 18—Jack Munley, Scranton ....KO 5
Nov. 15—Johnny Duca, Scranton ....W 10
Nov. 29—Joe (Butch) Lynch, Wilkes-Barre KO 4
Dec. 11—Paul Pirrone, Cleveland ....W 6
Dec. 19—Jimmy Jones, Philadelphia ....KO 5

1940

Jan. 15—Vincent Pimpinella, Cleveland .....W 8
Jan. 22—Jimmy Clark, Scranton ....KO 3
Jan. 29—Bud Mignault, Philadelphia ....W 10
Feb. 12—Georgie Abrams, Pittsburgh ....L 10
Mar. 15—Enzo Iannozzi, Scranton ....KO 4
Mar. 25—Frankie Nelson, Youngstown ......W 10
May 7—Eddie Peirce, Scranton ....W 10
May 30—Jack Ennis, Williamsport, Pa. .....W 10
July 24—Ken Overlin, Scranton ....W 10
Aug. 21—Tony Zale, Chicago ....W 10
Nov. 27—Vincent Pimpinella, Wilkes-Barre W 10
Dec. 13—Jimmy Casino, Hollywood ....W 10

1941

Jan. 3—Tami Mauriello, New York ......W 10
Feb. 7—Ernie Vigh, New York ....W 10
Mar. 7—Ernie Vigh, New York ....W 12
May 9—Ken Overlin, New York ....W 15
(Won World Middleweight Title)
July 11—Tony Celli, Cleveland ....KO 2
July 30—Georgie Abrams, New York ....L 10
Sept. 15—Ceferino Garcia, Los Angeles .....TD 8
Nov. —Relinquished world middleweight title.
Dec. 18—Jimmy Reeves, Cleveland ....W 10

1942

Jan. 13—Jimmy Bivins, Cleveland ....L 10

TB	KO	WD	WF	D	LD	LF	KO BY	ND	NC
41	13	21	0	1	6	0	0	0	0

TONY ZALE

(Anthony Florian Zaleski)
(Man of Steel)
Born, May 29, 1913, Gary, Ind.
Middleweight. Nationality, Polish-American.
Height, 5 ft. 8 in. Managed by Sam Pian and
Art Winch.

1934

June	11—Eddie Allen, Chicago .... W	4
June	15—Johnny Simpson, Chicago .... W	4
June	21—Bobby Millsap, Chicago ..... KO	1
June	25—Johnny Liston, Chicago .... KO	3
July	2—Ossie Jefferson, Chicago ... KO	3
July	9—Lou Bartell, Chicago .... W	4
July	16—Einar Headquist, Chicago ... KO	4
July	30—Bobby Millsap, Chicago ..... W	4
Aug.	6—Bruce Wade, Peoria .... KO	2
Aug.	13—Billy Hood, Chicago L	6
Aug.	20—Billy Black, Chicago L	6
Aug.	27—Wilbur Stokes, Chicago ..... W	8
Sept.	3—Mickey Misko, Chicago L	8
Sept.	17—Mickey Misko, Chicago ..... KO	8
Oct.	8—Jack Blackburn, Chicago .... W	8
Oct.	19—Jackie Schwartz, Milwaukee . KO	4
Oct.	22—Frankie Misko, Chicago ..... KO	6
Oct.	28—Jackie Schwartz, Milwaukee . KO	4
Nov.	5—Jack Charvez, Chicago ...... W	8
Nov.	26—Kid Leonard, Peoria L	10
Dec.	17—Jack Gibbons, Chicago L	10
Dec.	28—Joey Bazzione L	6

1935

Jan.	7—Max Elling, Chicago .... W	8
Feb.	4—Joe Bazzione, Chicago L	6
Feb.	11—Roughhouse Glover, Cincin. KO	9
Feb.	25—Jack Blackburn, Chicago ..... W	6
Mar.	11—Max Elling, Chicago .... W	8
May	6—Johnny Phagan, Chicago . KO by	6
July	2—Dave Clark, Chicago L	6

1936

Apr.	13—Jack Moran, Chicago .... D	5
	(Worked in Gary Steel Mills part of 1935 and 1936)	

1937

July	26—Elby Johnson, Chicago ...... W	4
Sept.	17—Elby Johnson, Chicago ..... KO	3
Oct.	11—Billy Brown, Chicago ...... KO	2
Oct.	18—Boby Gerry, Chicago .... KO	1
Nov.	1—Nate Bolden, Chicago L	5
Nov.	22—Nate Bolden, Chicago ...... W	6
Dec.	2—Leon Jackson, Gary .... W	6

1938

Jan.	3—Nate Bolden, Chicago ...... W	8
Jan.	24—Henry Schaft, Chicago ...... W	8
Feb.	21—Jimmy Clark, Chicago ... KO by	1
Mar.	28—King Wyatt, Chicago .... W	8
May	16—Bobby LaMonte, Chicago .... W	5
June	13—Jimmy Clark, Chicago ..... KO	8
July	18—Billy Celebron, Chicago ..... D	10
Aug.	22—Billy Celebron, Chicago L	10
Oct.	10—Tony Cisco, Chicago .... W	10
Oct.	31—Jimmy Clark, Chicago ..... KO	2
Nov.	18—Enzo Iannozzi, Chicago ..... W	6

1939

Jan.	2—Nate Bolden, Chicago L	10
May	1—Johnny Shaw, Chicago ..... KO	5
May	23—Babe Orgovan, N. Y. C. ..... W	6
Aug.	14—Milton Shivers, Chicago .... KO	3
Oct.	6—Sherman Edwards, Chicago .. KO	3
Nov.	3—Al Wardlow, Youngstown ... KO	3
Nov.	11—Eddie Mileski, Chicago .... KO	1
Dec.	12—Babe Orgovan, Chicago ... KO	3

1940

Jan.	29—Al Hostak, Chicago .... W	10
Feb.	29—Enzo Iannozzi, Youngstowns KO	4
Mar.	29—Ben Brown, Chicago .... KO	3
June	12—Baby Kid Chocol'e, Youngstn.KO	4
July	19—Al Hostak, Seattle .... KO	13
	(Won N.B.A. Middleweight Championship)	
Aug.	21—Billy Soose, Chicago L	10
Nov.	19—Fred Apostoli, Seattle .... W	10

1941

Jan.	1—Tony Martin, Milwaukee ... KO	8
Jan.	10—Steve Mamakos, Chicago .... W	10
Feb.	21—*Steve Mamakos, Chicago ... KO	14
May	28—*Al Hostak, Chicago ...... KO	2
July	23—Ossie Harris, Chicago ...... KO	1
Aug.	16—Billy Pryor, Milwaukee .... KO	9
Nov.	28—Georgie Abrams, N. Y. C. .... W	15
	(For vacant World Middleweight Title) *NBA Title Bout.	

1942

Feb.	13—Billy Conn, New York City ... L	12
	In U. S. Navy.	

1946

Jan.	7—Bobby Giles, Kansas City ... KO	4
Jan.	17—Tony Gillo, Norfolk .... KO	5
Feb.	7—Oscar Boyd, Des Moines .... KO	3
Feb.	26—Bobby Claus, Houston ..... KO	4
Apr.	12—Ira Hughes, Houston .... KO	2

May	2—Eddie Rossi, Memphis ...... KO	4
Sept.	27—Rocky Graziano, New York ..KO	6
	(Middleweight Title Bout)	

1947

Feb.	3—Deacon Logan, Omaha ....KO	6
Feb.	12—Len Wadsworth, Wichita .... KO	3
Mar.	20—Tommy Charles, Memphis ... KO	4
Apr.	1—Al Timmons, Kansas City ... KO	5
May	8—Cliff Beckett, Youngstown ..KO	6
July	16—Rocky Graziano KO by	6
	(Lost World Middleweight Title)	

1948

Jan.	23—Al Turner, Grand Rapids .... KO	5
Mar.	8—Bobby Claus, Little Rock ... KO	4
Mar.	19—Lou Woods, Toledo .... KO	3
June	10—Rocky Graziano, Newark ... KO	3
	(Won World Middleweight Title)	
Sept.	21—Marcel Cerdan, Jersey C. . KO by	12
	(Lost World Middleweight Title)	

TB	KO	WD	WF	D	LD	LF	KO BY	ND	NC
89	46	24	0	2	13	0	4	0	0

Elected to Boxing Hall of Fame 1958.

ROCKY GRAZIANO

(Thomas Rocco Barbella)

Born, January 1, 1922, New York City, N.Y.
Ancestry, Italian. Weight, 154 lbs. Height, 5 ft. 7 in.
Managed by Irving Cohen, Jack Hurley.

1942

Mar.	31—Curtis Hightower, Brooklyn ...... KO	2
Apr.	6—Mike Mastandrea, New York ..... KO	3
Apr.	14—Kenny Blackmar, Brooklyn ...... KO	1
Apr.	20—Godfrey Howell, New York .... D	4
Apr.	28—Charley Ferguson, Brooklyn L	4
May	4—Ed Lee, New York .... KO	4
May	12—Godfrey Howell, Brooklyn ...... KO	4
May	25—Lou Miller, New York .... D	6

1943

June	11—Gilbert Vasquez, Brooklyn .... KO	1
June	16—Joe Curcio, Elizabeth .... KO	4
June	24—Frankie Falco, Brooklyn .... KO	5
July	8—Johnny Attelly, Brooklyn .... KO	2
July	22—Georgie Stevens, Brooklyn ...... KO	1
July	27—Randy Drew, Long Island City .... KO	1
Aug.	12—Charley McPherson, Brooklyn ..... W	6
Aug.	20—Ted Apostoli, New York .... W	4
Aug.	24—Tony Grey, Long Island City ..... KO	6
Sept.	10—Joe Agosta, New York L	6
Sept.	21—Sonny Wilson, Brooklyn .... W	8
Oct.	5—Freddie Graham, Brooklyn ...... KO	1
Oct.	13—Jimmy Williams, Elizabeth ...... KO	2
Oct.	27—Charley McPherson, Elizabeth ..... D	6
Nov.	12—Steve Ruggio, New York L	6
Nov.	30—Freddie Graham, Jersey City ...... W	8
Dec.	6—Charley McPherson, New York .... W	6
Dec.	27—Milo Theodorescu, Newark .... KO	1

1944

Jan.	4—Harry Gray, Jersey City .... W	8
Jan.	7—Baby Galento, New York .... KO	1
Jan.	18—Phil Enzenga, Brooklyn .... KO	5
Feb.	9—Steve Riggio, New York L	6
Feb.	24—Manny Morales, Highland Park .. KO	4
Mar.	4—Leon Anthony, Brooklyn .... KO	1
Mar.	8—Harry Gary, Elizabeth .... W	6
Mar.	14—Ray Rovelli, Brooklyn .... W	8
Apr.	10—Bobby Brown, Washington, D.C. .. KO	5
May	9—Freddie Graham, Washington, D.C. KO	3
May	29—Tommy Mollis, Washington, D.C. KO	7
June	7—Larney Moore, Brooklyn .... KO	2
June	27—Frankie Terry, Brooklyn .... KO	6
July	21—Tony Reno, Brooklyn .... W	8
Aug.	14—Jerry Fiorello, Long Island City ... W	8
Sept.	15—Frankie Terry, New York .... D	8
Oct.	6—Danny Kapilow, New York .... D	10
Oct.	24—Bernie Miller, Brooklyn .... KO	2
Nov.	3—Harold Green, New York L	10
Dec.	22—Harold Green, New York L	10

1945

Mar.	9—Billy Arnold, New York .... KO	3
Apr.	17—Solomon Stewart, Washington .... KO	4
May	25—Al Davis, New York .... KO	4

June 29—Freddie Cochrane, New York ..... KO 10
Aug. 24—Freddie Cochrane, New York ..... KO 10
Sept. 28—Harold Green, New York .... KO 3
1946
Jan. 18—Sonny Horne, New York .... W 10
Mar. 29—Marty Servo, New York .... KO 2
Sept. 27—Tony Zale, New York .... KO by 6
(For World Middleweight Title)
1947
June 10—Eddie Finazzo, Memphis .... KO 1
June 16—Jerry Fiorello, Toledo .... KO 5
July 16—Tony Zale, Chicago .... KO 6
(Won World Middleweight Title)
1948
Apr. 5—Sonny Horne, Washington, D.C. ... W 10
June 10—Tony Zale, Newark .... KO by 3
(Lost World Middleweight Title)
Oct. 10—Dom Youvella, Jersey City ...... Exh. 5
1949
June 21—Bobby Claus, Wilmington .... KO 2
July 18—Joey Agosta, W. Springfield ...... KO 2
Sept. 14—Charley Fusari, New York .... KO 10
Dec. 6—Sonny Horne, Cleveland .... W 10
1950
Mar. 6—Joe Curcio, Miami .... KO 1
Mar. 31—Tony Janiro, New York .... D 10
Apr. 24—Danny Williams, New Haven ..... KO 3
May 9—Vinnie Cidone, Milwaukee ...... KO 3
May 16—Henry Brimm, Buffalo .... KO 4
Oct. 4—Gene Burton, Chicago .... KO 7
Oct. 16—Pete Mead, Milwaukee .... KO 3
Oct. 27—Tony Janiro, New York .... W 10
Nov. 27—Honey Johnson, Philadelphia ..... KO 4
1951
Mar. 19—Reuben Jones, Miami .... KO 3
May 21—Johnny Greco, Montreal .... KO 3
June 18—Freddy Lott, Baltimore .... KO 5
July 10—Cecil Hudson, Kansas City ...... KO 3
Aug. 6—Chuck Hunter, Boston .... W disq. 2
Sept. 19—Tony Janiro, Detroit .... KO 10
1952
Feb. 18—Eddie O'Neill, Louisville .... KO 4
Mar. 27—Roy Wouters, Minneapolis .... KO 1
Apr. 16—Ray Robinson, Chicago .... KO by 3
(For World Middleweight Title)
Sept. 17—Chuck Davey, Chicago .... L 10

TB	KO	WD	WF	D	LD	LF	KO BY	ND	NC
83	52	14	1	6	7	0	3	0	0

Elected to Boxing Hall of Fame, 1971.

MARCEL CERDAN
Born, July 22, 1916, Sidi Bel-Abbes, Algeria.
Weight, 147-160 lbs. Height, 5 ft. 8 in. Managed by
Lucien Roupp, Jo Longman.
1934
Nov. 4—Marcel Bucchianeri, Meknes .... W 6
Nov. 12—Benazra, Meknes .... KO 5
1935
Feb. 16—Perez III, Casablanca .... W 10
Mar. 20—Privat, Casablanca .... KO 5
Apr. 13—Benazra, Casablanca .... W 10
July 5—Mac Perez, Casablanca .... KO 2
July 19—Joseph Sarfati, Casablanca .... W 10
Aug. 8—Mestre, Casablanca .... W 10
Nov. 23—Mac Perez, Casablanca .... W 10
Dec. 14—Mac Perez, Casablanca .... W 10
1936
Mar. 4—Antoine Abad, Casablanca .... W 10
Apr. 7—M. Hergane, Casablanca .... W 10
Apr. 11—Joseph Martinez, Taza .... KO 9
May 23—M. Ricardo, Casablanca .... KO 5
May 27—Kid Abadie, Casablanca .... KO 3
June 6—M. Castillanos, Casablanca ...... W 10
July 19—Joseph Sarfati, Casablanca .... W 10
Aug. 2—Al Francis, Oran .... KO 6
Oct. 17—Primo Rubio, Casablanca .... W 10
Nov. 2—Aissa Attaf, Casablanca .... KO 1
Nov. 21—Jean Debeaumont, Casablanca ..... W 10

1937
Jan. 16—Aissa Attaf, Algiers .... KO 8
Jan. 30—Maurice Naudin, Algiers .... KO 3
Mar. 2—Omar Kouidri, Rabat .... W 10
Apr. 3—Omar Kouidri, Algiers .... W 10
July 3—Ali Omar, Algiers .... KO 5
Aug. 2—Kid Marcel, Oran .... W 10
Sept. 13—Eddy Rabak, Casablanca .... KO 6
Oct. 7—Louis Jampton, Paris .... W 10
Oct. 21—Jean Morin, Paris .... W 10
Dec. 18—Ifergane, Rabat .... W 10
1938
Jan. 6—Charles Feodorowich, Paris ...... KO 2
Jan. 13—Eddie Ran, Paris .... KO 2
Jan. 20—Jean Zides, Paris .... KO 9
Feb. 21—Omar Kouidri, Casablanca .... W 12
(Won French Welterweight Title)
Mar. 12—Charles Pernot, Algiers .... W 10
Apr. 13—Eddy Rabak, Paris .... W 10
May 5—Anacleto Locatelli, Paris .... KO 10
May 20—Gustave Humery, Paris .... KO 6
June 4—Jean Morin, Algiers .... W 10
July 3—Victor Deckmyn, Oran .... W 10
Sept. 15—Al Baker, Paris .... W 10
Oct. 27—Amedeo Deyana, Paris .... W 10
Nov. 10—Alfredo Katter, Paris .... KO 4
Nov. 24—Omar Kouidri, Paris .... W 12
(Retained French Welterweight Title)
1939
Jan. 9—Harry Craster, London .... LF 5
Jan. 21—Ercole Buratti, Algiers .... W 10
Feb. 4—Al Baker, Brussels .... KO 7
Feb. 20—Saverio Turiello, Paris .... W 12
Mar. 22—Felix Wouters, Brussels .... W 12
May 21—Roger Cadot, Marseilles .... KO 6
June 3—Saverio Turiello, Milan .... W 15
(Won European Welterweight Title)
June 18—Anacleto Locatelli, Marseilles ..... W 10
1940
(Inactive)
1941
Jan. 19—Young Raymond, Algiers .... KO 1
Jan. 26—Young Raymond, Casablanca ..... KO 6
Feb. 2—Victor Fortes, Algiers .... KO 7
Mar. 9—Victor (Kid) Janas, Casablanca .... W 10
Apr. 13—Victor Fortes, Oran .... KO 2
May 4—Omar Kouidri, Oran .... KO 6
June 22—Francois Blanchard, Marseilles ... KO 6
July 20—Joe Brun, Oran .... KO 2
Sept. 13—Roland Coureau, Algiers .... KO 9
Dec. 31—Robert Seidel, Vichy .... KO 3
1942
Feb. 21—Fred Flury, Nice .... KO 7
Apr. 26—Gustave Humery, Paris .... KO 1
May 17—Fernand Viez, Paris .... W 10
June 28—Gaspard de Ridder, Paris .... KO 1
July 25—Victor (Kid) Janas, Algiers .... KO 2
Aug. 2—Ben Frely, Marseilles .... KO 3
Aug. 15—Victor Buttin, Algiers .... LF 8
Sept. 30—Jose Ferrer, Paris .... KO 1
(Retained European Welterweight Title)
1943
Aug. 8—John McCoy, Oran .... KO 2
Sept. 12—Omar Kouidri, Algiers .... W 10
Oct. 13—Larry Cisneros, Oran .... KO 6
Oct. 31—Bulldog Milano, Casablanca ...... KO 2
Dec. 26—James Toney, Oran .... KO 2
Dec. 29—Larry Cisneros, Oran .... KO 2
1944
Jan. 30—Willie Sampson, Casablanca ...... KO 2
Feb. 15—Eugene Drouhin, Algiers .... KO 2
Feb. 17—Sammy Adragna, Algiers .... W 3
Feb. 20—Joe DiMartino, Algiers .... KO 2
(Won Inter-Allied Welterweight Tournament)
Oct. 21—Bouaya, Casablanca .... KO 1
Dec. 12—Clinton Perry, Rome .... KO 1
Dec. 14—Floyd Gibson, Rome .... KO 1
Dec. 16—Fred Burney, Rome .... KO 2
(Won Inter-Allied Welterweight Tournament)

1945

Mar. 9—Joe Brun, Paris .... KO 7
May 13—Jean Despeaux, Paris .... KO 5
June 3—Oscar Menozzi, Marseilles .... KO 3
June 24—Edouard Tenet, Croix de Berny .... W 10
Oct. 19—Tommy Davies, Paris .... KO 1
Nov. 30—Assane Diouf, Paris .... KO 3
   (Won French Middleweight Title)
Dec. 8—Victor Buttin, St. Etienne .... KO 3

1946

Jan. 13—Agustin Guedes, Lisbon .... KO 1
Jan. 18—Edouard Tenet, Paris .... W 12
   (Retained French Middleweight Title)
Feb. 24—Jose Ferrer, Barcelona .... KO 4
Apr. 14—Joe Brun, Nice .... KO 2
May 25—Robert Charron, Paris .... W 12
   (Retained French Middleweight Title)
July 7—Holman Williams, Paris .... W 10
Oct. 20—Jean Pankowiak, Paris .... KO 5
Dec. 6—Georgie Abrams, New York .... W 10

1947

Feb. 2—Leon Foquet, Paris .... KO 1
   (Won Vacant European Middleweight Title)
Feb. 11—Bert Gilroy, London .... KO 4
Mar. 28—Harold Green, New York .... KO 2
Oct. 7—Billy Walker, Montreal .... KO 1
Oct. 31—Anton Raadik, Chicago .... W 10

1948

Jan. 26—Giovanni Manca, Paris .... KO 2
   (Retained European Middleweight Title)
Feb. 9—Jean Walzack, Paris .... KO 4
   (Retained European Middleweight Title)
Mar. 12—Lavern Roach, New York .... KO 8
Mar. 25—Lucien Krawsyck, Paris .... W 10
May 23—Cyrille Delannoit, Brussels .... L 15
   (Lost European Middleweight Title)
July 10—Cyrille Delannoit, Brussels .... W 15
   (Regained European Middleweight Title)
Sept. 21—Tony Zale, Jersey City .... KO 12
   (Won World Middleweight Title)
Dec. 2—Dave Andrews, Lewiston, Me. ... Exh. 4
Dec. 10—Cosby Linson, New Orleans ..... Exh. 4

1949

Mar. 29—Dick Turpin, London .... KO 7
May 8—Lucien Krawsyck, Casablanca .... KO 4
June 16—Jake LaMotta, Detroit .... KO by 10
   (Lost World Middleweight Title)

TB KO WD WF D LD LF KO BY ND NC
123 74 45 0 0 1 2 1 0 0
Killed in airplane crash, October 27, 1949, Azores.
Elected to Boxing Hall of Fame, 1962.

JAKE (JACOB) LA MOTTA
(Bronx Bull)
Born, July 10, 1921, New York, N. Y.
Nationality, Italian-American. Middleweight.
Height, 5 ft. 8 in. Managed by Mike Capriano
and Joey LaMotta.

1941

Mar. 3—Charley Mackley, N. Y. C. ..... W 4
Mar. 14—Tony Gillon, Bridgeport, Ct. .. W 6
Apr. 1—Johnny Morris, Wh. Plains ... KO 4
Apr. 8—Joe Fredericks, Wh. Plains .... KO 1
Apr. 15—Stanley Goisz, Wh. Plains .... W 4
Apr. 22—Lorne McCarthy, Wh. Plains .. W 4
Apr. 26—Monroe Crewe, Brooklyn ..... W 4
May 20—Johnny Cihlar, Brooklyn ..... W 4
May 27—Johnny Morris, N. Y. C. ..... W 4
June 9—Lorenzo Strickland,
   Woodhaven, L. I. .... W 4
June 16—Lorenzo Strickland, N. Y. C. .. W 6
June 23—Johnny Morris, N. Y. C. ..... KO 3
July 15—Joe Baynes, L. I. C. .... W 6
Aug. 5—Joe Shikula, L. I. C. .... D 6
Aug. 11—Cliff Koerkle, N. Y. C. ...... W 6
Sept. 24—Jimmy Reeves, Cleve., O. .... L 10
Oct. 7—Lorenzo Strickland,
   White Plains, N. Y. .... W 8
Oct. 20—Jimmy Reeves, Cleve. O. .... L 10
Nov. 14—Jimmy Casa, N. Y. C. .... W 6
Dec. 22—Nate Bolden, Chicago .... L 10

1942

Jan. 27—Frankie Jamison, N. Y. C. .... W 8
Mar. 3—Frankie Jamison, N. Y. C. .... W 8
Mar. 18—Lorenzo Strickland, N. Y. C. ... W 10
Apr. 7—Lou Schwartz, N. Y. C. ...... KO 9
Apr. 21—Buddy O'Dell, N. Y. C. ...... W 10
May 12—Jose Basora, N. Y. C. .... D 10
June 2—Vic Dellicurti, N. Y. C. ...... W 10
June 16—Jose Basora, N. Y. C. .... L 10
July 28—Lorenzo Strickland, N. Y. C. .. W 8
Aug. 28—Jimmy Edgar, N. Y. C. ...... W 10
Sept. 8—Vic Dellicurti, N. Y. C. ...... W 10
Oct. 2—Ray Robinson, N. Y. C. ...... L 10
Oct. 20—Wild Bill McDowell, N. Y. C. .. KO 5
Nov. 6—Henry Chmielewski, Boston .. W 10

1943

Jan. 2—Jimmy Edgar, Detroit .... W 10
Jan. 15—Jackie Wilson, N. Y. C. ...... W 10
Jan. 22—Charley Hayes, Detroit ..... KO 6
Feb. 5—Ray Robinson, Detroit ...... W 10
Feb. 26—Ray Robinson, Detroit ...... L 10
Mar. 19—Jimmy Reeves, Detroit ..... KO 6
Mar. 30—Ossie Harris, Pitts., Pa. ..... W 10
May 12—Tony Ferrara, Cinc., O. .... KO 6
June 10—Fritzie Zivic, Pitts., Pa. ..... W 10
July 12—Fritzie Zivic, Pitts., Pa. ...... L 15
Sept. 17—Jose Basora, Detroit .... W 10
Oct. 11—Johnny Walker, Phila., Pa. ... KO 2
Nov. 12—Fritzie Zivic, N. Y. C. ...... W 10

1944

Jan. 14—Fritzie Zivic, Detroit .... W 10
Jan. 28—Ossie Harris, Detroit .... W 10
Feb. 25—Ossie Harris, Detroit .... W 10
Mar. 17—Coley Welch, Boston .... W 10
Mar. 31—Sgt. Lou Woods, Chicago ... W 10
Apr. 21—Lloyd Marshall, Cleveland .... L 10
Sept. 29—George Kochan, Detroit .... W 10
Nov. 3—George Kochan, Detroit ... KO 9

1945

Feb. 23—Ray Robinson, New York .... L 10
Mar. 19—Lou Schwartz, Norfolk .... KO 1
Mar. 28—George Costner, Chicago ... KO 6
Apr. 19—Vic Dellicurti, New York ... W 10
Apr. 27—Bert Lytell, Boston .... W 10
July 6—Tommy Bell, New York ...... W 10
Aug. 10—Jose Basora, New York ... KO 9
Sept. 17—George Kochan, New York .. KO 9
Sept. 26—Ray Robinson, Chicago .... L 12
Nov. 13—Coolidge Miller, Bronx, N. Y. KO 3
Nov. 23—Walter Woods, Boston ..... KO 8
Dec. 7—Charley Parham, Chicago ... KO 6

1946

Jan. 11—Tommy Bell, N. Y. C. ...... W 10
Mar. 29—Marcus Lockman, Boston .... W 10
May 24—Joe Reddick, Boston .... W 10
June 13—Jimmy Edgar, Detroit ...... D 10
Sept. 12—Bob Satterfield, Chicago .... KO 7
Aug. 7—Holman Williams, Detroit ... W 10
Oct. 25—O'Neill Bell, Detroit .... KO 2
Dec. 6—Anton Raadik, Chicago .... W 10

1947

Mar. 14—Tommy Bell, N. Y. C. ...... W 10
June 6—Tony Janiro, N. Y. C. ...... W 10
Sept. 3—Cecil Hudson, Chicago ..... W 10
Nov. 14—Billy Fox, N. Y. C. ..... KO by 4

1948

June 1—Ken Stribling, Wash., D. C. ..KO 5
Sept. 7—Burl Charity, N. Y. .... KO 6
Oct. 1—Johnny Colan, N. Y. .... KO 10
Oct. 18—Vern Lester, Brooklyn ...... W 10
Dec. 3—Tommy Yarosz, N. Y. C. ... W 10

1949

Feb. 21—Laurent Dauthuille, Montreal . L 10
Mar. 25—Robert Villemain, N. Y. ... W 12
Apr. 18—O'Neill Bell, Detroit .... KO 8
May 10—Joey DeJohn, Syracuse ..... KO 8
June 16—Marcel Cerdan, Detroit ..... KO 10
   (Won World Middleweight Title)
Dec. 9—Robert Villemain, New York . L 10

1950

Feb. 3—Dick Wagner, Detroit ...... KO 9
Mar. 28—Chuck Hunter, Cleveland ... KO 6
May 4—Joe Taylor, Syracuse ...... W 10
July 12—Tiberio Mitri, New York ..... W 15
   (title bout)
Sept. 13—Laurent Dauthuille, Detroit . KO 15
   (title bout)

1951

Feb. 14—Ray Robinson, Chicago .. KO by 13
   (Lost World Middleweight Title)
June 27—Bob Murphy, New York . KO by 7

1952

Jan.	28—Norman Hayes, Boston	L	10
Mar.	5—Eugene Hairston, Detroit	D	10
Apr.	9—Norman Hayes, Detroit	W	10
May	21—Eugene Hairston, Detroit	W	10
June	11—Bob Murphy, Detroit	W	10
Dec.	31—Danny Nardico, Coral Gables	KO by	8

1953
(Inactive)
1954

Mar.	11—Johnny Pretzie, W. Palm Bch.	KO	4
Apr.	3—Al McCoy, Charlotte	KO	1
Apr.	14—Billy Kilgore, Miami Beach ...	L	10

TB	KO	WD	WF	D	LD	LF	KOBY	ND	NC
106	30	53	0	4	15	0	4	0	0

RAY ROBINSON
(Walker Smith)
(Sugar Ray)
Born, May 3, 1920, Detroit, Mich. Height 5 ft. 11 in. Negro. Managed by George Gainford.

Won Golden Gloves featherweight title in 1939 and lightweight title in 1940 in New York and in intercity competition.

Engaged in 85 amateur bouts. Had 69 KO's (40 first round). Boxed as Walker Smith.

1940

Oct.	4—Joe Escheverria, N. Y. C.....	KO	2
Oct.	8—Silent Stefford, Savannah ...	KO	2
Oct.	22—Mistos Grispos, N. Y. C.	W	6
Nov.	11—Bobby Woods, Philadelphia . .	KO	1
Dec.	9—Norment Quarles, Phila.	KO	4
Dec.	12—Oliver White, N. Y. C.	KO	3

1941

Jan.	4—Henry La Barba, Brooklyn ..	KO	1
Jan.	13—Frankie Wallace, Philadelphia	KO	1
Jan.	31—George Zengaras, N. Y. C.....	W	6
Feb.	8—Benny Cartegena, Brooklyn .	KO	1
Feb.	21—Bobby McIntire, N. Y. C.	W	6
Feb.	27—Gene Spencer, Detroit	KO	5
Mar.	3—Jimmy Tygh, Philadelphia ...	KO	8
Apr.	14—Jimmy Tygh, Philadelphia ...	KO	1
Apr.	24—Charley Burns, Atlantic City .	KO	1
Apr.	30—Joe Ghnouly, Washington ...	KO	3
May	10—Vic Troise, Brooklyn, N. Y. .	KO	1
May	19—Nick Castiglione, Phila.	KO	1
June	16—Mike Evans, Phila..........	KO	2
July	2—Pete Lello, N. Y. C..........	KO	4
July	21—Sammy Angott, Philadelphia . .	W	10
Aug.	27—Carl Red Guggino, L. I. C....	KO	3
Aug.	29—Maurice Arnault, Atlantic Cy.	KO	1
Sept.	19—Maxie Shapiro, N. Y. C.	KO	3
Sept.	25—Marty Servo, Phila..........	W	10
Oct.	31—Fritzie Zivic, N. Y. C. ...... : .	W	10

1942

Jan.	16—Fritzie Zivic, N. Y. C.	KO	10
Feb.	20—Maxie Berger, N. Y. C.......	KO	2
Mar.	20—Norman Rubio, N. Y. C......	KO	7
Apr.	17—Harvey Dubs, Detroit	KO	6
Apr.	30—Dick Banner, Minneapolis ...	KO	2
May	28—Marty Servo, N. Y. C.	W	10
July	31—Sammy Angott, N. Y. C.	W	10
Aug.	21—Ruben Shank, N. Y. C.	KO	2
Aug.	27—Tony Motisi, Chicago	KO	1
Oct.	2—Jake La Motta, N. Y. C.	W	10
Oct.	19—Izzy Jannazzo, Philadelphia ..	W	10
Nov.	6—Vic Dellicurti, N. Y. C.	W	10
Dec.	1—Izzy Jannazzo, Cleveland ...	KO	8
Dec.	14—Al Nettlow, Philadelphia	KO	3

1943

Feb.	5—Jake LaMotta, Detroit	L	10
Feb.	19—Jackie Wilson, N. Y. C.	W	10
Feb.	26—Jake LaMotta, Detroit	W	10
Apr.	30—Freddie Cabral, Boston	KO	1
July	1—Ralph Zannelli, Boston	W	10
Aug.	27—Henry Armstrong, N. Y. C. ...	W	10

1944

Oct.	13—Izzy Jannazzo, Boston	KO	2
Oct.	27—Sgt. Lou Woods, Chicago ...	KO	9
Nov.	17—Vic Dellicurti, Detroit	W	10
Dec.	12—Sheik Rangel, Phila.	KO	2
Dec.	22—Georgie Martin, Boston	KO	7

In U. S. Army.

1945

Jan.	10—Billy Furrone, Washington ..	KO	2
Jan.	16—Tommy Bell, Cleveland	W	10
Feb.	14—George Costner, Chicago	KO	1
Feb.	24—Jake LaMotta, New York	W	10
May	14—Jose Basora, Philadelphia	D	10
June	15—Jimmy McDaniels, New York	KO	2
Sept.	18—Jimmy Mandell, Buffalo	KO	5
Sept.	26—Jake LaMotta, Chicago	W	12
Dec.	4—Vic Dellicurti, Boston	W	10

1946

Jan.	14—Dave Clark, Pittsburgh	KO	2
Feb.	5—Tony Riccio, Elizabeth	KO	4
Feb.	15—O'Neill Bell, Detroit	KO	2
Feb.	26—Cliff Beckett, St. Louis	KO	4
Mar.	4—Sammy Angott, Pittsburgh ...	W	10
Mar.	14—Izzy Jannazzo, Baltimore	W	10
Mar.	21—Freddy Flores, N. Y. C.....	KO	5
June	12—Freddy Wilson, Worcester ...	KO	2
June	25—Norman Rubio, Union City ...	W	10
July	12—Joe Curcio, N. Y. C.	KO	2
Aug.	15—Vinnie Vines, Albany	KO	6
Sept.	25—Sidney Miller, Elizabeth	KO	3
Oct.	7—Ossie Harris, Pittsburgh	W	10
Nov.	1—Cecil Hudson, Detroit	KO	6
Nov.	6—Artie Levine, Cleveland	KO	10
Dec.	20—Tommy Bell, N. Y. C.	W	15

(Won Vacant World Welterweight Championship)

1947

Mar.	27—Bernie Miller, Miami	KO	3
Apr.	3—Fred Wilson, Akron	KO	3
Apr.	8—Eddie Finazzo, Kansas City ..	KO	4
May	16—George Abrams, N. Y. C.....	W	10
June	24—Jimmy Doyle, Cleveland	KO	8

(Title)
Doyle died of injuries.

Aug.	21—Sammy Secreet, Akron	KO	1
Aug.	29—Flashy Sebastian, New York .	KO	1
Oct.	28—Jackie Wilson, Los Angeles .	KO	7
Dec.	10—Billy Nixon, Elizabeth	KO	6
Dec.	19—Chuck Taylor, Detroit	KO	6

(Title)

1948

Mar.	4—Ossie Harris, Toledo	W	10
Mar.	16—Henry Brimm, Buffalo	W	10
June	28—Bernard Docusen, Chicago ...	W	15

(Title Bout)

Sept.	23—Kid Gavilan, New York	W	10
Nov.	15—Bobby Lee, Philadelphia	W	10

1949

Feb.	10—Gene Buffalo, Wilkes-Barre ..	KO	1
Feb.	15—Henry Brimm, Buffalo	D	10
Mar.	25—Bobby Lee, Chicago	W	10
Apr.	11—Don Lee, Omaha............	W	10
Apr.	20—Earl Turner, Oakland	KO	8
May	16—Al Tribuani, Wilmington ...	Exh.	4
June	7—Freddie Flores, New Bedford	KO	3
June	20—Cecil Hudson, Providence ...	KO	5
July	11—Kid Gavilan, Philadelphia	W	15

(Title bout)

Aug.	24—Steve Belloise, N. Y. C.	KO	7
Sept.	2—Al Mobley, Chicago	Exh.	4
Sept.	9—Benny Evans, Omaha	KO	5
Sept.	12—Charley Dotson, Houston ...	KO	3
Nov.	9—Don Lee, Denver	W	10
Nov.	13—Vern Lester, New Orleans ...	KO	5
Nov.	15—Gene Burton, Shreveport ..	Exh.	6
Nov.	16—Gene Burton, Dallas	Exh.	6

1950

Jan.	30—George LaRover, New Haven	KO	4
Feb.	13—Al Mobley, Miami	KO	6
Feb.	22—Aaron Wade, Savannah	KO	3
Feb.	27—Jean Walzack, St. Louis	W	10
Mar.	22—George Costner, Philadelphia	KO	1
Apr.	21—Cliff Beckett, Columbus, O. .	KO	3
Apr.	28—Ray Barnes, Detroit	W	10
June	5—Robert Villemain, Philadelphia	W	15

(Won Pennsylvania middleweight title)

Aug.	9—Charley Fusari, Jersey City ...	W	15

(welterweight title bout)

Aug.	25—Jose Basora, Scranton	KO	1

(Pennsylvania middleweight title)

Sept.	4—Billy Brown, New York	W	10
Oct.	16—Joe Rindone, Boston	KO	6
Oct.	26—Carl Olson, Philadelphia	KO	12

(Pennsylvania middleweight title)

Nov.	8—Bobby Dykes, Chicago	W	10
Nov.	27—Jean Stock, Paris	KO	2
Dec.	9—Luc Van Dam, Brussels	KO	4
Dec.	16—Jean Walzack, Geneva	W	10
Dec.	22—Robert Villemain, Paris	KO	9
Dec.	25—Hans Stretz, Frankfort	KO	5

562

1951

Feb. 14—Jake LaMotta, Chicago .....KO 13
(Won world middleweight title)
Apr. 5—Holly Mims, Miami .... W 10
Apr. 9—Don Ellis, Oklahoma City ...KO 1
May 21—Kid Marcel, Paris ....KO 5
May 26—Jean Wanes, Zurich ....W 10
June 10—Jan deBruin, Antwerp ......KO 8
June 16—Jean Walzack, Liege ......KO 6
June 24—Gerhard Hecht, Berlin .....ND 2
(Robinson disqualified by Referee for kidney punch. Commission later reversed it to a no decision bout.)
July 1—Cyrille Delannoit, Turin ....KO 3
July 10—Randy Turpin, London ..... L 15
(Lost world middleweight title)
Sept. 12—Randy Turpin, N. Y. C. .....KO 10
(Regained world middleweight title)

1952

Mar. 13—Carl (Bobo) Olson, San Fran. . W 15
(Middleweight Title)
Apr. 16—Rocky Graziano, Chicago ...KO 3
(Middleweight Title)
June 25—Joey Maxim, New York . KO by 14
(For Light Heavyweight Title)
Announced Retirement December 18, 1952.

1954

Oct. 20—Announced return to ring.
Nov. 29—Gene Burton, Hamilton, Ont.Exh. 6

1955

Jan. 5—Joe Rindone, Detroit ......KO 6
Jan. 19—Ralph Jones, Chicago ....L 10
Mar. 29—Johnny Lombardo, Cincinnati W 10
Apr. 14—Ted Olla, Milwaukee ......KO 3
May 4—Garth Panter, Detroit ......W 10
July 22—Rocky Castellani, San Fran. . W 10
Dec. 9—Carl (Bobo) Olson, Chicago ..KO 2
(Won World Middleweight Title)

1956

May 18—Carl (Bobo) Olson, Los Ang. . KO 4
(Middleweight Title)
Nov. 10—Bob Provizzi, New Haven ....W 10

1957

Jan. 2—Gene Fullmer, New York .... L 15
(Lost World Middleweight Title)
May 1—Gene Fullmer, Chicago .....KO 5
(Re-won World Middleweight Title)
Sept. 10—Otis Woodard, Philadelphia . Exh. 2
Sept. 10—Lee Williams, Philadelphia . Exh. 2
Sept. 23—Carmen Basilio, New York ... L 15
(Lost World Middleweight Title)

1958

Mar. 25—Carmen Basilio, Chicago .....W 15
(Regained World Middleweight Title).

1959

Dec. 14—Bob Young, Boston ....KO 2

1960

Jan. 22—Paul Pender, Boston .... L 15
(Lost World Middleweight Title)
Apr. 2—Tony Baldoni, Baltimore ....KO 1
June 10—Paul Pender, Boston .... L 15
(For World Middleweight Title)
Dec. 3—Gene Fullmer, Los Angeles ... D 15
(For N.B.A. Middleweight Title)

1961

Mar. 4—Gene Fullmer, Las Vegas ..... L 15
(For N.B.A. Middleweight Title)
Sept. 25—Wilf Greaves, Detroit .... W 10
Oct. 21—Denny Moyer, New York .... W 10
Nov. 20—Al Hauser, Providence ......KO 6
Dec. 8—Wilf Greaves, Pittsburgh ....KO 8

1962

Feb. 17—Denny Moyer, New York .... L 10
Apr. 27—Bobby Lee, Port of Spain,
Trinidad ....KO 2
July 9—Phil Moyer, Los Angeles ... L 10
Sept. 25—Terry Downes, London ...... L 10
Oct. 17—Diego Infantes, Vienna ....KO 2
Nov. 10—Georges Estatoff, Lyons ....KO 6

1963

Jan. 30—Ralph Dupas, Miami Beach ... W 10
Feb. 25—Bernie Reynolds, Santo
Domingo ....KO 4
Mar. 11—Billy Thornton, Lewiston ..KO 3
May 5—Maurice Robnet, Sherbrooke KO 3
June 24—Joey Giardello, Philadelphia .. L 10
Oct. 14—Armand Vanucci, Paris ......W 10
Nov. 9—Fabio Bettini, Lyon ....D 10
Nov. 16—Emile Sarens, Brussels ......KO 8
Nov. 29—Andre Davier, Grenoble ..... W 10
Dec. 9—Armand Vanucci, Paris ......W 10

1964

May 19—Gaylord Barnes, Portland ....W 10
July 8—Clarence Riley, Pittsfield ....KO 6
July 27—Art Hernandez, Omaha ......D 10
Sept. 3—Mick Leahy, Paisley ....L 10
Sept. 28—Yolande Leveque, Paris ......W 10
Oct. 12—Johnny Angel, London ......KO 6
Oct. 24—Jackie Caillau, Nice ....W 10
Nov. 7—Baptiste Rolland, Calen ......W 10
Nov. 14—Jean Beltritti, Marseilles .....W 10
Nov. 27—Fabio Beltini, Rome ....D 10

1965

Mar. 6—Jimmy Beecham,
Kingston, Jamaica ....KO 2
Apr. 4—Ray Basting, Savannah ....KO 1
Apr. 28—Rocky Randell, Norfolk ....KO 3
May 24—Memo Ayon, Tijuana ....L 10
June 1—Stan Harrington, Honolulu ....L 10
June 24—Young Joe Walcott, Richmond .....W 10
July 12—Fred Hernandez, Las Vegas ....L 10
July 27—Young Joe Walcott, Richmond .....W 10
Aug. 10—Stan Harrington, Honolulu ....L 10
Sept. 15—Bill Henderson, Norfolk .... NC 2
Sept. 23—Young Joe Walcott, Phila. .... W 10
Oct. 1—Peter Schmidt, Germany ....W 10
Oct. 5—Neil Morrison, Richmond ....KO 2
Oct. 20—Rudolph Bent, Steubenville ......KO 3
Nov. 10—Joey Archer, Pittsburgh ....L 10

TB	KO	WD	WF	D	LD	LF	KO BY	ND	NC
201	109	65	0	6	18	0	1	1	1

Announced retirement — December 10, 1965 at farewell party.

Elected to Hall of Fame 1967.

RANDY TURPIN
(Randolph Adolphus Turpin)
Born, Leamington, England, June 7, 1928. 5 feet, 10 inches—middle and light-heavyweight. Managed by George Middleton.

Won 5 British amateur titles.

1946

Sept. 17—Gordon Griffiths, London ...KO 1
Nov. 9—Des Jones, London ....W 6
Dec. 26—Bill Blything, Birmingham ...KO 1

1947

Jan. 14—Jimmy Davis, London ......KO 4
Jan. 24—Dai James, Birmingham .....KO 3
Feb. 18—Johnny Best, London ......KO 1
Mar. 18—Bert Hyland, London ......KO 1
Apr. 1—Frank Dolan, London ......KO 2
Apr. 15—Tommy Davies, London ....KO 2
Apr. 28—Bert Saunders, Walthamstow . . W 6
May 12—Ron Cooper, Oxford ....KO 4
May 27—Jury VII, London ....W 6
June 3—Mark Hart, London ....W 6
June 23—Leon Fouquet, Coventry ....KO 1
Sept. 8—Jimmy Ingle, Coventry .....KO 3
Oct. 20—Mark Hart, London ....D 6

1948

Jan. 26—Freddie Price, Coventry .....KO 1
Feb. 17—Gerry McCready, London ...KO 1
Mar. 16—Vince Hawkins, London ......W 8
Apr. 26—Albert Finch, London .... L 8
June 28—Alby Hollister, Birmingham ...W 8
Sept. 21—Jean Stock, London ......KO by 5

1949

Feb. 7—Jackie Jones, Coventry ....KO 5
Feb. 21—Doug Miller, London ....W 8
Mar. 25—Mickey Laurent, Manchester . KO 3
May 3—Bill Poli, London ....WF 4
June 20—Cyrille Delannoit, Birmingham
..............................KO 8
Aug. 22—Jean Wanes, Manchester ....KO 3
Sept. 19—Roy Wouters, Coventry ......KO 5
Nov. 15—Pete Mead, London ....KO 4

1950

Jan. 31—Gilbert Stock, London ......W 8
Mar. 6—Richard Armah, London ....KO 6
Apr. 24—Gus Degouve, Nottingham ...W 8
Sept. 5—Eli Elandon, London ....KO 2
Oct. 17—Albert Finch, London ......KO 5
(British middleweight title)
Nov. 13—Jose Alamo, Abergavenny ...KO 0
Dec. 12—Tommy Yarosz, London ....WF 8

1951
Jan. 22—Eduardo Lopez, Birmingham KO 1
Feb. 27—Luc van Dam, London ..... KO 1
   (Vacant European Middleweight Title)
Mar. 19—Jean Stock, Leicester ...... KO 5
Apr. 16—Billy Brown, Birmingham ... KO 2
May 7—Jan de Bruin, Coventry ..... KO 6
June 5—Jackie Keough, London .... KO 7
July 10—Ray Robinson, London ...... W 15
   (Won world middleweight title)
Sept. 12—Ray Robinson, New York KO by 10
   (Lost World middleweight title)
1952
Feb. 12—Alex Buxton, London ...... KO 7
Apr. 22—Jacques Hairabedian, London KO 3
June 10—Don Cockell, London ...... KO 11
   (British and Empire light-heavyweight title)
Oct. 21—George Angelo, London ..... W 15
   (Vacant British Empire middleweight title.)
1953
Jan. 19—Victor d'Haes, Birmingham .. KO 6
Feb. 16—Duggie Miller, Leicester ...... W 10
Mar. 17—Walter Cartier, London ...W Dis. 2
June 9—Charley Humez, London ..... W 15
   (European Middleweight Title)
Oct. 21—Bobo Olson, New York City .. L 15
   (For vacant world middleweight title)
1954
Mar. 30—Olle Bengtsson, London ..... W 10
May 2—Tiberio Mitri, Rome .... KO by 1
   (European middleweight title)
1955
Feb. 15—Ray Schmidt, Birmingham ..WF 8
Mar. 8—Jose Gonzales, London ..... KO 7
Apr. 26—Alex Buxton, London ...... KO 2
   (British and Empire Light Heavyweight Titles)
Sept. 19—Ed Polly Smith, Birmingham ..W 10
Oct. 18—Gordon Wallace, London KO by 4
1956
Apr. 17—Alessandro D'Ottavio,
   Birmingham ...... KO 6
June 18—Jacques Bro, Birmingham ... KO 5
Sept. 21—Hans Stretz, Hamburg ...... L 10
Nov. 26—Alex Buxton, Leicester ..... KO 5
   (Vacant British light-heavy title)
1957
June 11—Arthur Howard, Leicester .... W 15
   (British Light-Heavyweight Title)
Sept. 17—Ahmed Boulgroune, London . KO 9
Oct. 28—Sergio Burchi, Birmingham .. KO 2
Nov. 25—Uwe Janssen, Leicester ..... KO 8
1958
Feb. 11—Wim Snoek, Birmingham ..... W 10
Apr. 21—Eddie Wright, Leicester ..... KO 7
July 22—Redvers Sangoe, Oswestry ... KO 4
Sept. 9—Yolande Pompey,
   Birmingham .... KO by 2
1963
Mar. 18—Eddie Marcano, Wisbech .... KO 6

1964
Aug. 22—Charles Seguna, Malta ...... KO 2

TB	KO	WD	WF	D	LD	LF	KOBY	ND	NC
75	45	17	4	1	3	0	5	0	0

Died, May 17, 1966 in Warwickshire, England.

CARL "BOBO" OLSON
Born, July 11, 1928, Honolulu, Hawaii, Height, 5 ft. 10½ in. Managed by Sid Flaherty.
1945
Nov. 23—Art Robinson, San Francisco KO 4
Dec. 10—Bobby Jones, San Francisco . KO 2
1946
Jan. 7—Obie Wooten, San Francisco . KO 1
Jan. 14—Vepe Watson, San Francisco . KO 1
Jan. 28—Pedro Jiminez, San Francisco .KO 4
Feb. 4—Chuck Ross, San Francisco ... W 6
Feb. 25—Delaware Bradby, San Fran. . KO 3
July 18—Trader Horne, Honolulu .... KO 2
Aug. 19—Johnny Boskie, Honolulu ... KO 3
Sept. 9—Jackie Ryan, Honolulu ..... KO 6
Dec. 2—Wayne Powell, Honolulu .... KO 4
1947
Jan. 28—Gil Mojica, Honolulu .... W 10
Mar. 21—Candy McDaniels, Honolulu .. W 10
May 2—Leroy Wade, Honolulu .... KO 4
June 20—Paul Lewis, Honolulu .... W 10

July 4—George Duke, Honolulu ..... L 10
Aug. 19—George Duke, Honolulu ..... W 10
Nov. 22—Boy Brooks, Manila .... L 10
Dec. 17—Nai Mayala, Manila .... KO 3
1948
Jan. 17—Boy Brooks, Manila .... W 12
Apr. 7—Flashy Sebastian, Manila .... KO 7
May 11—Bobby Castro, Honolulu .... W 8
July 20—Charley Cato, Honolulu ..... W 8
Oct. 12—Boy Brooks, Honolulu ..... KO 3
Oct. 26—Kenny Watkins, Honolulu .... W 10
Dec. 14—John Boski, Honolulu ...... KO 1
1949
Jan. 11—Paulie Perkins, Honolulu .... KO 2
Mar. 15—Anton Raadik, Honolulu .... KO 7
June 3—Tommy Yarosz, Honolulu .... W 10
July 26—Milo Savage, Honolulu ..... W 10
Aug. 23—Art Hardy, Honolulu .... KO 3
Nov. 22—Johnny Duke, Honolulu ..... W 10
Dec. 13—Earl Turner, Honolulu ...... W 10
1950
Feb. 22—Don Lee, Honolulu .... W 10
Mar. 7—Dave Sands, Sydney .... L 12
Apr. 25—Roy Miller, Honolulu ...... KO 5
May 22—Otis Graham, Honolulu ...... W 10
Sept. 5—Henry Brimm, Honolulu .... W 10
Oct. 26—Ray Robinson, Phila. ... KO by 12
   (Recognized by Pennsylvania as for middleweight title)
1951
Mar. 20—Art Soto, Honolulu .... W 10
May 7—Lloyd Marshall, Honolulu ... KO 5
July 9—Chuck Hunter, San Francisco . W 10
July 27—Charlie Cato, Richmond, Cal. KO 3
Aug. 27—Bobby Jones, San Francisco .. W 10
Oct. 3—Dave Sands, Chicago .... L 10
1952
Feb. 12—Woody Harper, Sacramento .. W 10
Feb. 15—Tommy Harrison, Hollywood . W 10
Mar. 13—Ray Robinson, San Francisco . L 15
   (For World Middleweight Title)
May 6—Woody Harper, Richmond .. KO 7
May 19—Walter Cartier, Brooklyn ... KO 5
June 6—Jimmy Beau, New York ..... W 10
July 12—Robert Villemain, San Fran. .. W 10
Aug. 27—Eugene Hairston, New York . KO 6
Nov. 20—Lee Sala, San Francisco ..... KO 2
Dec. 18—Norman Hayes, San Francisco . W 10
1953
Feb. 7—Norman Hayes, Boston ...... W 10
Mar. 16—Garth Panter, Butte .... W 10
June 19—Paddy Young, New York .... W 15
   (Won American Middleweight Title)
Oct. 21—Randy Turpin, New York .... W 15
   (For vacant world middleweight title)
1954
Jan. 23—Joe Rindone, San Francisco . KO 5
Apr. 2—Kid Gavilan, Chicago .... W 15
   (Title Bout)
June 15—Jesse Turner, Honolulu .... KO 8
July 7—Pedro Gonzales, Oakland .... KO 4
Aug. 20—Rocky Castellani, San Francisco W 15
   (Title Bout)
Nov. 3—Garth Panter, Richmond .... KO 8
Dec. 15—Pierre Langlois, San Francisco KO 11
   (Title Bout)
1955
Feb. 1—Benny Walker, Richmond ..Exh. 2
Feb. 1—Bull Halsey, Richmond ....Exh. 2
Feb. 16—Ralph Jones, Chicago ...... W 10
Mar. 12—Willie Vaughn, Hollywood ... W 10
Apr. 13—Joey Maxim, San Francisco .. W 10
June 22—Archie Moore, New York KO by 3
   (For World Light Heavyweight Title)
Aug. 13—Jimmy Martinez, Portland .... W 10
Aug. 26—Joey Giambra, San Francisco . W 10
Dec. 9—Ray Robinson, Chicago .. KO by 2
   (Lost World Middleweight Title)
1956
May 18—Ray Robinson, Los Ang. . KO by 4
   (For World Middleweight Title)
   Announced Retirement October 3, 1956, then made a comeback.
1957
June 18—Joey Maxim, Portland, Ore. .. W 10
Aug. 17—Pat McMurtry, Portland,
   Ore. .... KO by 2
1958
Oct. 28—Don Grant, Oakland .... KO 7
Nov. 25—Paddy Young, Oakland ..... KO 6
Dec. 16—Tommy Villa, Fresno ...... KO 5
1959
Mar. 30—Rory Calhoun, San Francisco . W 10
Aug. 25—George Kartalian, Fresno ... KO 5

1960
Apr.	7—Roque Maravilla, Portland ...	KO	7
May	5—Al Sparks, Vancouver	KO	5
June	6—Mike Holt, Johannesburg	W	10
Aug.	31—Doug Jones, Chicago	KO by	6

1961
Jan.	19—Bobby Daniels, Spokane	W	10
Feb.	16—Floyd Buchanan, Victoria ...	KO	3
Aug.	14—Roque Maravilla, Oakland	W	10
Sept.	11—Sixto Rodriguez, San Fran. ...	L	10
Oct.	23—Sixto Rodriguez, San Fran. ...	W	10
Nov.	14—Yancy D, Honolulu	KO	8

1962
Jan.	12—Al Williams, Honolulu	W	10
Jan.	19—Artie Dixon, Honolulu	W	10
Apr.	3—Pete Rademacher, Honolulu ..	L	10
June	3—Lennart Risberg, Stockholm .	KO	6
Dec.	14—Guilio Rinaldi, Rome	D	10

1963
Jan.	25—Al Williams, Eugene	KO	5
Apr.	30—Sonny Ray, Honolulu	KO	8
May	14—Jesse Bowdry, Honolulu ...	W	10
Oct.	21—Jose Menno, San Francisco ...	W	10
Dec.	9—Hank Casey, San Francisco ...	D	10

1964
Mar.	27—Wayne Thornton, San Francisco	W	10
June	19—Johnny Persol, New York	L	10
Aug.	28—Wayne Thornton, New York	W	10
Nov.	27—Jose Torres, New York ..	KO by	1

1965
June	24—Andy Kendall, Reno	W	10
Sept.	23—Fred Roots, Reno	KO	3

1966
July	11—Piero Del Papa, San Francisco, Cal.	W	10
Nov.	22—Don Fullmer, Oakland	L	10

TB	KO	WD	WF	D	LD	LF	KOBY	ND	NC
109	42	49	0	2	9	0	7	0	0

GENE FULLMER
Born, July 21, 1931, West Jordan, Utah.
Height, 5 feet 8 ins. Managed by Marv. Jenson.

1951
June	9—Glen Peck, Logan, Utah	KO	1
June	16—Andy Jackson, West Jordan .	KO	1
June	23—Gary Carr, Midvale, Utah ...	KO	3
July	2—Eddie Duffy, Vernal	KO	1
July	9—Eddie Duffy, Salt Lake City .	KO	2
July	16—Lamar Peterson, West Jordan	KO	1
Aug.	1—Carlos Martinez, San Francisco	KO	1
Aug.	24—Sam Healy, Hurricane	KO	1
Aug.	25—Buddy Sloane, Hurricane, Utah	KO	2
Sept.	7—Charley Cato, West Jordan ..	KO	4
Sept.	14—Sam Healy, Vernal, Utah ...	KO	4
Sept.	25—Garth Panter, Salt Lake City ..	W	10
Oct.	3—Gary Hanley, West Jordan ...	KO	1
Oct.	10—Rudy Zadell, Pittsburgh	W	6
Oct.	17—Ray Jones, Vernal	KO	1

1952
Aug.	8—Mickey Rhodes, Ogden	KO	6
Sept.	20—Armando Cotero, Hollywood .	W	6
	(Inactive—In U. S. Army)		

1954
Feb.	6—Kid Leon, West Jordan	KO	1
Apr.	26—Charley Cato, Salt Lake City .	KO	1
May	17—Andy Anderson, Salt Lake City	KO	7
June	5—Kid Rico, Salt Lake City ...	KO	1
July	12—Goven Small, Salt Lake City .	W	10
July	29—Reno Abellira, West Jordan ...	W	10
Aug.	16—Dick Wofe, West Jordan ...	KO	4
Nov.	8—Jackie LaBua, Brooklyn ...	W	10
Nov.	15—Peter Muller, Brooklyn	W	10

1955
Jan.	31—Marcel Assire, Brooklyn	W	10
Feb.	14—Paul Pender, Brooklyn	W	10
Mar.	21—Goven Small, Salt Lake City ..	W	10
Apr.	4—Gil Turner, Brooklyn	L	10
June	20—Gil Turner, Salt Lake City ...	W	10
July	26—Del Flanagan, Butte	W	10
Sept.	12—Al Andrews, Ogden	W	10
Sept.	28—Bobby Boyd, Chicago	L	10
Nov.	25—Eduardo Lausse, New York ...	L	10

1956
Jan.	4—Rocky Castellani, Cleveland ..	W	10
Feb.	17—Gil Turner, New York	W	10
Apr.	20—Ralph Tiger Jones, Cleveland .	W	10
May	25—Charley Humez, New York ...	W	10
Sept.	22—Moses Ward, West Jordan ...	KO	3

1957
Jan.	2—Ray Robinson, New York	W	15
	(Won World Middleweight Title)		
Jan.	28—Wilf Greaves, Salt Lake City ..	W	10
Feb.	18—Ernie Durando, Denver	W	10
May	1—Ray Robinson, Chicago ..	KO by	5
	(Lost World Middleweight Title)		
June	7—Ralph (Tiger) Jones, Chicago .	W	10
Sept.	4—Chico Vejar, West Jordan	W	10
Nov.	15—Neal Rivers, New York	W	10

1958
Mar.	3—Milo Savage, Salt Lake City ...	W	10
July	7—Jimmy Hegerle, West Jordan ..	W	10
Sept.	11—Spider Webb, Salt Lake City ..	W	10
Nov.	10—Joe Miceli, Salt Lake City ...	KO	2

1959
Jan.	9—Milo Savage, San Antonio ...	W	10
Feb.	20—Wilf Greaves, New York	W	10
Aug.	28—Carmen Basilio, San Fran. ...	KO	14
	(Won vacant N.B.A. Middleweight Title)		
Dec.	4—Spider Webb, Logan, Utah ...	W	15
	(N.B.A. Middleweight Title)		

1960
Apr.	20—Joey Giardello, Bozeman	D	15
	(N.B.A. Middleweight Title)		
June	29—Carmen Basilio, Salt Lake C. .	KO	12
	(N.B.A. Middleweight Title)		
Dec.	3—Ray Robinson, Los Angeles ..	D	15
	(N.B.A. Middleweight Title)		

1961
Mar.	4—Ray Robinson, Las Vegas	W	15
	(N.B.A. Middleweight Title)		
Aug.	5—Florentino Fernandez, Ogden .	W	15
	(N.B.A. Middleweight Title)		
Dec.	9—Benny Paret, Las Vegas	KO	10
	(N.B.A. Middleweight Title)		

1962
Oct.	23—Dick Tiger, San Francisco	L	15
	(Lost N.B.A. Middleweight Title)		

1963
Feb.	23—Dick Tiger, Las Vegas	D	15
	(W.B.A. Middleweight Title Bout)		
Aug.	28—Dick Tiger, Ibadan	KO by	7
	(Middleweight Title Bout)		

Announced retirement on July 23, 1964.

TB	KO	WD	WF	D	LD	LF	KOBY	ND	NC
64	24	31	0	3	4	0	2	0	0

Elected Hall of Fame 1974

CARMEN BASILIO
Born, April 2, 1927, Canastota, N. Y.
Height, 5 feet, 6½ ins. Managed by Johnny De John and Joe Netro.

1948
Nov.	24—Jimmy Evans, Binghamton ..	KO	3
Nov.	29—Bruce Walters, Syracuse	KO	1
Dec.	8—Eddie Thomas, Binghamton .	KO	2
Dec.	16—Rollie Johns, Syracuse	W	6

1949
Jan.	5—Johnny Cunningham, Binghamton	D	6
Jan.	19—Jay Parlin, Binghamton	D	6
Jan.	25—Ernie Hall, Syracuse	KO	2
Feb.	19—Luke Jordan, Rochester	W	6
Apr.	20—Elliott Throop, Syracuse	KO	1
May	2—Connie Thies, Rochester	L	6
May	8—Jerry Drain, Syracuse ...,..	KO	3
May	18—Johnny Clemmons, Syracuse .	KO	3
June	7—Johnny Cunningham, Syracuse	KO	2
July	12—Jesse Bradshaw, Syracuse ...	KO	2
July	25—Sammy Daniels, Utica	W	8
Aug.	2—Johnny Cunningham, Utica ...	L	8
Aug.	17—Johnny Cunningham, Syracuse	W	8
Sept.	7—Tony DiPelliho, Rochester	W	8
Sept.	30—Jackie Parker, Syracuse	KO	3

1950

Jan. 10—Sonny Hampton, Buffalo .... W 8
Jan. 24—Casse Tate, Buffalo .... W 8
Feb. 7—Adrien Mogart, Buffalo ..... KO 7
Mar. 6—Lew Jenkins, Syracuse ...... W 10
Mar. 27—Mike Koballa, Brooklyn ..... L 8
Apr. 12—Gaby Ferland, New Orleans .. D 10
May 5—Gaby Ferland, New Orleans . KO 1
June 21—Guillermo Giminez,
New Orleans .... KO 8
July 31—Guillermo Giminez,
New Orleans .... KO 9
Aug. 28—Eddie Giosa, New Orleans .... L 10
Dec. 15—Vic Cardell, New York ...... L 10

1951

Mar. 9—Flora Hita, Syracuse .... W 8
Apr. 12—Eddie Giosa, Syracuse ...... L 10
May 29—Lester Felton, Syracuse ..... L 10
June 18—Jonny Cesario, Utica .... L 10
Sept. 17—Shamus McCrae, Syracuse ..... W 8
Sept. 26—Ross Virgo, New Orleans ..... L 10

1952

Feb. 4—Emmett Norris, Wilkes-Barre .. W 10
Feb. 28—Jimmy Cousins, Akron ...... W 8
Mar. 31—Jackie O'Brien, Wilkes-Barre .. W 10
May 29—Chuck Davey, Syracuse ...... D 10
(Decision originally called a win then
was changed.)
July 16—Chuck Davey, Chicago ...... L 10
Aug. 20—Billy Graham, Chicago ...... L 10
Sept. 22—Baby Williams, Miami Beach .. W 10
Oct. 20—Sammy Giuliano, Syracuse .. KO 3
Nov. 18—Chuck Foster, Buffalo ...... KO 5

1953

Jan. 12—Ike Williams, Syracuse ...... W 10
Feb. 28—Vic Cardell, Toledo .... W 10
Apr. 11—Carmine Fiore, Syracuse .... KO 9
June 6—Billy Graham, Syracuse ...... W 12
(Won N. Y. State Welterweight Title)
July 25—Billy Graham, Syracuse ...... D 12
(For N. Y. State Welterweight Title)
Sept. 18—Kid Gavilan, Syracuse .... L 15
(For World Welterweight Title)
Nov. 28—Johnny Cunningham, Toledo KO 4
Dec. 19—Pierre Langlois, Syracuse .... D 10

1954

Jan. 16—Italo Scortichini, Miami ..... D 10
Apr. 17—Pierre Langlois, Syracuse ... W 10
May 15—Italo Scortichini, Syracuse ... W 10
June 26—Al Andrews, Syracuse ...... W 10
Aug. 17—Ronnie Harper, Ft. Wayne .. KO 2
Sept. 10—Carmine Fiore, New York ... W 10
Oct. 15—Allie Gronik, Syracuse ..... W 10
Dec. 16—Ronnie Harper, Akron .... KO 4

1955

Jan. 21—Peter Muller, Syracuse ...... W 10
June 10—Tony DeMarco, Syracuse .... KO 12
(Won World Welterweight title)
Aug. 10—Italo Scortichini, New York .. W 10
Sept. 7—Gil Turner, Syracuse ...... W 10
Nov. 30—Tony DeMarco, Boston ..... KO 12
(Title Bout)

1956

Mar. 14—Johnny Saxton, Chicago ..... L 15
(Lost World Welterweight Title)
Sept. 12—Johnny Saxton, Syracuse ... KO 9
(Re-won Welterweight Title)

1957

Feb. 22—Johnny Saxton, Cleveland ... KO 2
(World Welterweight Title)
May 13—Leo Owens, Longview, Ore. Exh. 3
May 14—Leo Owens, Spokane ...... Exh. 3
May 16—Harold Jones, Portland, Ore. . KO 4
June 27—Leo Owens, Jeannette, Pa. . Exh. 3
Sept. 23—Ray Robinson, New York ... W 15
(Won World Middleweight Title)
Basilio relinquished world welterweight
title.

1958

Mar. 25—Ray Robinson, Chicago ...... L 15
(Lost World Middleweight Title)
Sept. 5—Art Aragon, Los Angeles .... KO 8

1959

Apr. 1—Arley Selfer, Augusta ..... KO 3
Aug. 28—Gene Fullmer, San Fran. . KO by 14
(For vacant N.B.A. Middleweight Title)

1960

June 29—Gene Fullmer, Salt Lake City
.... KO by 12
(For N.B.A. Middleweight Title)

1961

Jan. 7—Gaspar Ortega, New York .... W 10
Mar. 11—Don Jordan, Syracuse ...... W 10
Apr. 22—Paul Pender, Boston .... L 15
(For World Middleweight Title)
Apr. 25 announced retirement.

TB	KO	WD	WF	D	LD	LF	KOBY	ND	NC
79	27	29	0	7	14	0	2	0	0

Elected Hall of Fame 1969

PAUL PENDER
Brookline, Mass., Middleweight
1949

Jan. 28—Paul Williams, Boston ...... KO 1
Feb. 17—Mickey Lane, Boston ...... KO 2
Mar. 3—Frank Theodore, Boston .... KO 2
Mar. 28—George Meyers, Boston ..... KO 3
Apr. 11—Jimmy Rice, Boston .... KO 1
May 2—Mike Saad, Boston .... W 6
June 9—Eddie Richardson, New Haven KO 1
Sept. 12—Ted Brassley, Boston .... KO 3
Sept. 26—Mike Gillo, New Haven ...... W 6
Oct. 5—Jose Contreras, Worcester ... KO 2
Oct. 21—Bill Daley, Boston .... W 10
Dec. 19—Bill Daley, Boston .... D 10

1950

Jan. 23—Sonny Horne, Boston .... W 10
Mar. 27—Leon Brown, Providence .... KO 5
May 3—Charley Dotson, Portland ... W 10
June 22—Al Couture, Portland .... KO 7
Sept. 25—Bobby James, Boston .... W 10
Oct. 9—Roy Wouters, Glace Bay ..... W 10
Oct. 23—Ernie Durando, Boston ...... W 10
Nov. 13—Norman Horton, Boston .... KO 2
Nov. 27—Harold Sampson, Boston .... KO 4
Dec. 11—Norman Hayes, Boston .... L 10

1951

Jan. 8—Norman Hayes, Boston .... KO 7
Jan. 22—Joe Rindone, Boston .... L 10
Mar. 12—Joe Rindone, Boston .... D 10
Apr. 30—Eugene Hairston, Boston . KO by 3
Oct. 1—Otis Graham, Boston .... W 10

1952

Mar. 31—Jimmy Beau, Boston .... KO by 5

1953
(Inactive)

1954

Aug. 3—Larry Villeneuve, Boston .... W 10
Dec. 20—Ted Olla, Brooklyn .... W 10

1955

Jan. 6—Freddy Mack, Boston ...... KO 4
Feb. 14—Gene Fullmer, Brooklyn ..... L 10

1956

Dec. 4—Jimmy Skinner, Boston ...... W 10

1958

Nov. 17—Jackson Brown, Boston .... KO 5
Dec. 15—Pete Adams, Boston .... KO 4
Dec. 22—Willie (Kid) Johnson,
Providence .... KO 3

1959

Jan. 5—Joe Gomes, Providence ..... KO 6
Feb. 9—Young Beau Jack,
Providence ....W Dis. 3
Feb. 16—Joe Shaw, Providence ...... KO 5
Mar. 17—Ralph Jones, Boston .... W 10
Aug. 17—Jackson Brown, Providence ... W 10
(Won New England Middleweight Title)
Dec. 14—Gene Hamilton, Boston ...... W 10

1960

Jan. 22—Ray Robinson, Boston ...... W 15
(Won World Middleweight Title)
June 10—Ray Robinson, Boston ...... W 15
(Retained World Middleweight Title)

1961

Jan. 14—Terry Downes, Boston ..... KO 7
(Title Bout)
Apr. 22—Carmen Basilio, Boston ...... W 15
(Title Bout)
July 11—Terry Downes, London .. KO by 9
(Lost World Middleweight Title)
(Pender quit at end of round)

1962

Apr. 7—Terry Downes, Boston ...... W 15
(Regained World Middleweight Title)
Nov. 9—Relieved of title by all boxing
associations except Mass.
Announced retirement May 7, 1963.

TB	KO	WD	WF	D	LD	LF	KOBY	ND	NC
48	20	19	1	2	3	0	3	0	0

TERRY DOWNES
British Middleweight Champion
Born, London (Paddington), England,
May 9, 1936.
Won various amateur and service
championships in United States while serving
with U. S. Marines, 1954, '55, '56.

1957
Apr.	9—Tony Longo, London	KO 1
Apr.	30—Jimmy Lynas, London	KO 3
May	14—Dick Tiger, London	KO by 5
June	4—Alan Dean, London	KO 4
June	25—John Woolard, London	KO 7
Sept.	17—Lew Lazar, London	W 8
Oct.	1—Derek Liversidge, London	KO 2
Oct.	28—Eddie Phillips, London	KO 3
Nov.	19—Les Allen, London	L 8
Dec.	10—George Lavery, London	KO 5
Dec.	19—Hamouda Bouraoui, London	KO 8

1958
Jan.	7—Serge Leveque, London	KO 4
Jan.	28—Freddie Cross, London	KO by 6
Feb.	25—Dennis Booty, London	KO 3
Mar.	17—Ben Salah Fahrat, London	KO 5
Apr.	16—Tuzo Portuguez, London	W 8
June	3—Pat McAteer, London	W 8
July	15—Constant Alcantara, London	KO 3
Sept.	30—Phil Edwards, London	KO 13
	(Vacant British middleweight title)	
Nov.	4—Mohamed Taibi, London	KO 3
Dec.	9—Spider Webb, London	KO by 8

1959
Feb.	24—Michel Diouf, London	KO by 5
July	7—Andre Davier, London	KO 7
Sept.	15—John McCormack, London	LF 8
	(British middleweight title)	
Nov.	2—John McCormack, London	KO 8
	(British middleweight title)	

1960
Mar.	8—Carlos Van Neste, London	KO 4
Mar.	24—Orlando DePietro, Liverpool	KO 4
June	9—Richard Bouchez, Manchester	KO 2
July	5—Phil Edwards, London	KO 12
	(British middleweight title)	
Oct.	11—Joey Giardello, London	W 10

1961
Jan.	14—Paul Pender, Boston	KO by 7
	(For World Middleweight Championship)	
Mar.	7—Willie Green, London	KO 3
May	2—Tony Montano, London	KO 5
July	11—Paul Pender, London	KO 9
	(Won World Middleweight Championship)	
	(Pender quit at end of round)	

1962
Apr.	7—Paul Pender, Boston	L 15
	(Lost World Middleweight Title)	
May	22—Don Fullmer, London	W 10
Sept.	25—Ray Robinson, London	W 10
Nov.	13—Phil Moyer, London	KO 9

1963
Mar.	5—Jimmy Beecham, London	KO 9
Oct.	8—Rudi Nehring, London	KO 3
Nov.	25—Mike Pusateri, Manchester	KO 5

1964
May	28—Ed Zaremba, Glasgow	W 10
Nov.	30—Willie Pastrano, Manchester	KO by 11
	(For World Light Heavyweight Title)	

TB	KO	WD	WF	D	LD	LF	KO BY	ND	NC
43	27	7	0	0	2	1	6	0	0

DICK TIGER
(Record Under Light Heavyweight Champions)

JOEY GIARDELLO
(Carmine Orlando Tilelli)
Philadelphia, Pa., Middleweight
Born, July 16, 1930, Brooklyn, N. Y.
Height, 5 ft. 10 in.

1948
Oct.	—Johnny Noel, Trenton	KO 2
Oct.	—Jimmy Larkin, Atlantic City	KO 1
Nov.	—Bobby Clark, Wilkes-Barre	W 4
Nov.	—Johnny Brown, Reading	KO 4
Dec.	16—Johnny Madison, Atlantic City	KO 1
Dec.	30—Willie Wigfall, Philadelphia	KO 1

1949
Feb.	24—Clyde Diggs, Philadelphia	D 6
Mar.	15—Don Ennis, Reading	KO 4
Apr.	7—Billy Montgomery, Phila.	KO 1
Apr.	25—Ray Morris, Wilkes-Barre	W 4
Apr.	28—Joe Aurillo, Philadelphia	W 6
May	2—Emerson Charles, Philadelphia	W 4
June	6—Henry Vonsavage, Phila.	KO 2
June	20—Ray Hass, Philadelphia	KO 3
July	13—Leroy Fleming, Washington	KO 1
Nov.	14—Mitchell Allen, Philadelphia	W 6
Dec.	5—Jim Dockery, Philadelphia	KO 2

1950
Jan.	5—Johnny Fry, Philadelphia	W 6
Jan.	16—Joe DiMartino, New Haven	L 8
Jan.	26—Johnny Bernardo, Phila.	W 8
Feb.	9—Johnny Bernardo, Phila.	W 8
Mar.	23—Armando Amanini, Brooklyn	W 8
Mar.	27—Steve Sabatino, Phila.	KO 1
Mar.	29—Johnny Brown, Allentown	W 6
Apr.	20—Tommy Varsos, Brooklyn	KO 1
May	4—Hurley Sanders, Brooklyn	W 8
Aug.	25—Al Berry, Scranton	KO 1
Sept.	26—Ted DiGiammo, Wilkes-Barre	KO 1
Oct.	16—Bruce Ubaldo, Wilkes-Barre	W 8
Oct.	26—Harold Green, Brooklyn	KO by 6
Nov.	27—Gene Roberts, Philadelphia	D 8
Dec.	18—Leroy Allen, Philadelphia	KO 5

1951
Jan.	6—Freddie Lott, Brooklyn	W 8
Feb.	10—Jan Henri, Philadelphia	W 8
Feb.	22—Hal Sampson, Brooklyn	W 8
Feb.	24—Tony Wolfe, Philadelphia	KO 3
Mar.	15—Ray Wouters, Philadelphia	L 8
Mar.	29—Primos Cutler, Philadelphia	W 8
Apr.	12—Roy Wouters, Philadelphia	W 8
Apr.	30—Ernie Durando, Scranton	W 10
May	25—Gus Rubicini, New York	L 8
Aug.	13—Otis Graham, Philadelphia	W 8
Aug.	27—Johnny Noel, Philadelphia	W 8
Sept.	14—Tommy Bazzano, N. Y.	W 6
Oct.	8—Tony Amato, N. Y.	KO 7
Nov.	13—Rocky Castellani, Scranton	L 10
Dec.	12—Bobby Dykes, Miami Beach	L 10

1952
Jan.	9—Sal Di Martino, Miami Beach	D 10
Mar.	28—Sammy Giuliani, New York	D 8
May	5—Joe Miceli, Scranton	D 10
June	5—Roy Wouters, Philadelphia	W 6
June	23—Pierre Langlois, Brooklyn	W 10
Aug.	5—Billy Graham, Brooklyn	W 10
Sept.	15—Georgie Small, Brooklyn	W 10
Oct.	13—Joe Giambra, Brooklyn	W 10
Nov.	11—Joe Giambra, Buffalo	L 10
Dec.	19—Billy Graham, New York	*W 10

*In the original official decision of the
referee and judges, Giardello was awarded the
verdict as follows: Judge Shortell, 7 rounds to 3
and 10 points to 4 for Graham; Judge Agnello,
6 rounds to 4 and 7 points to 4 for Giardello;
Referee Miller, 5 rounds to 4 for Giardello and
five points to each.

Commissioners Christenberry and Powell,
after the deicsion was rendered, changed Joe
Agnello's score card which resulted in awarding
the verdict to Graham. On Agnello's score card,
one point was awarded by the
Commissioners to Graham in round four and
the tenth round was taken from Giardello and
given to Graham who also received two points in
that round. Thus the score was changed to give
Graham the official split decision on the basis of
the revision of Agnello's card by the Commission
to read, five rounds each with Graham ahead in
points, 6o to 5, thereby reversing the original
majority decision of the judges and referee.

When the case came before the State
Supreme Court, Justice Botein ruled that the
New York State Athletic Commission had no
right to reverse the scorecard of the official and
decided the actual decision to be the one
originally given, in favor of Giardello.
Feb.	2—Harold Green, Brooklyn	W 10
Mar.	6—Billy Graham, New York	L 12
Apr.	7—Gil Turner, Philadelphia	W 10
May	30—Hurley Sanders, Newark	W 10
June	26—Ernie Durando, New York	W 10
Sept.	29—Johnny Saxton, Philadelphia	L 10
Oct.	26—Walter Cartier, Brooklyn	W 10
Nov.	23—Tuzo Portuguez, Brooklyn	W 10

567

1954

Jan.	8—Garth Panter, New York .... KO	5
Feb.	5—Walter Cartier, New York ... KO	1
Mar.	19—Willie Troy, New York ..... KO	7
May	21—Pierre Langlois, New York ... L	10
June	11—Bobby Jones, New York .... W	10
July	7—Billy Kilgore, Philadelphia .... W	10
Sept.	24—Ralph Jones, Philadelphia .... W	10

1955

Jan.	25—Al Andrews, Norfolk .... W	10
Feb.	15—Andy Mayfield, Miami Beach KO	8
Mar.	1—Peter Muller, Milwaukee .... KO	2

1956

Feb.	11—Tim Jones, Trenton .... KO	10
Mar.	10—Hurley Sanders, Paterson .... W	10
Mar.	27—Joe Shaw, Philadelphia ..... W	10
May	7—Charlie Cotton, New York ... L	10
May	28—Charlie Cotton, New York ... L	10
July	2—Tony Baldoni, New York .... KO	1
July	26—Franz Szuzina, Milwaukee .... W	10
Aug.	28—Georgie Kid, Miami Beach ... KO	9
Sept.	28—Bobby Boyd, Cleveland ..... KO	5
Nov.	15—Charlie Cotton, Milwaukee ... W	10
Dec.	14—Charlie Cotton, Cleveland ... W	10

1957

Feb.	6—Randy Sandy, Chicago ...... W	10
Mar.	27—Willie Vaughn, Kansas City .. ND	10

(Originally announced as split decision in
favor of Vaughn but the referee's card was
incorrectly marked and the decision was
changed by the Commission to No Decision.)

May	17—Rory Calhoun, Cleveland .... W	10
July	2—Joe Gray, Detroit .... KO	6
July	17—Chico Vejar, Louisville ..... W	10
Sept.	27—Bobby Lane, Cleveland .... KO	7
Nov.	5—Wilf Greaves, Denver .... W	10
Dec.	27—Ralph Jones, Miami Beach ... W	10

1958

Feb.	12—Franz Szuzina, Philadelphia .. W	10
May	5—Rory Calhoun, San Francisco . W	10
June	11—Franz Szuzina, Washington ... W	10
June	30—Joey Giambra, San Francisco . L	10
Nov.	19—Spider Webb, San Fran... KO by	7

1959

Jan.	28—Ralph Jones, Louisville L	10
May	6—Holly Mims, Washington .... W	10
June	16—Del Flanagan, St Paul ..... KO	1
Aug.	11—Chico Vejar, St. Paul ...... W	10
Sept.	30—Dick Tiger, Chicago L	10
Nov.	4—Dick Tiger, Cleveland ...... W	10

1960

Apr.	20—Gene Fullmer, Bozeman ..... D	15

(For N.B.A. Middleweight Title)

Sept.	27—Clarence Hinnant, Billings ... KO	3
Oct.	11—Terry Downes, London L	10
Dec.	1—Peter Muller, Cologne L	10

1961

Mar.	6—Ralph Dupas, New Orleans ... L	10
May	15—Wilf Greaves, Philadelphia .. KO	9
July	10—Henry Hank, Detroit L	10
Sept.	12—Jesse Smith, Philadelphia .... W	10
Nov.	6—Jesse Smith, Chicago .... W	10
Dec.	12—Joe DeNucci, Boston .... D	10

1962

Jan.	30—Henry Hank, Philadelphia .... W	10
July	9—Jimmy Beecham, St. Paul ... W	10
Aug.	6—George Benton, Philadelphia .. L	10
Nov.	12—Johnny Morris, Baltimore .... W	10

1963

Feb.	25—Wilf Greaves, Jacksonville .... W	10
Mar.	25—Ernie Burford, Philadelphia ... W	10
June	24—Ray Robinson, Philadelphia .. W	10
Dec.	7—Dick Tiger, Atlantic City ... W	15

(Won World Middleweight Title)

1964

Apr.	17—Rocky Rivero, Cleveland ..... W	10

(non-title)

May	22—Rocky Rivero, Cleveland ..... W	10

(non-title)

Dec.	14—Rubin Carter, Philadelphia .. W	15

(Retained World Middleweight Title)

1965

Apr.	23—Gil Diaz, Cherry Hill, N.J. .... W	10
Oct.	21—Dick Tiger, New York L	15

(Lost World Middleweight Title)

1966

Sept.	22—Cash White, Reading .... W	10
Dec.	5—Nate Collins, San Francisco ... KO by	8

1967

May	22—Jack Rodgers, Pittsburgh L	10
Nov.	6—Jack Rodgers, Philadelphia .... W	10

TB	KO	WD	WF	D	LD	LF	KO BY	ND	NC
133	32	68	0	7	21	0	4	1	0

568

EMILE GRIFFITH

(Emile Alphonse Griffith)
Born, February 3, 1938, St. Thomas, Virgin
Islands. Weight, 147-157 lbs. Height, 5 ft. 7½ in.

1958

June	2—Joe Parham, New York .... W	4
June	23—Bobby Gibson, New York .... W	4
July	21—Tommy Leak, New York .... W	4
Oct.	6—Art Cunningham, New York ...... W	6
Nov.	17—Sergio Rios, New York .... KO	3
Dec.	15—Larry Jones, New York .... KO	5

1959

Jan.	26—Gaylord Barnes, New York .... KO	5
Feb.	9—Willie Johnson, New York .... KO	5
Feb.	23—Barry Allison, New York .... KO	5
Mar.	23—Bobby Shell, New York .... W	10
Apr.	27—Mel Barker, New York .... W	10
May	25—Willie Stevenson, New York .... W	10
Aug.	7—Kid Fichique, New York .... W	10
Oct.	26—Randy Sandy, New York L	10
Nov.	23—Ray Lancaster, New York .... KO	7

1960

Jan.	8—Roberto Pena, New York .... W	10
Feb.	12—Gaspar Ortega, New York ...... W	10
Mar.	11—Denny Moyer, New York .... W	10
Apr.	26—Denny Moyer, Portland L	10
June	3—Jorge Fernandez, New York ..... W	10
July	25—Jorge Fernandez, New York ..... W	10
Aug.	25—Florentino Fernandez, New York .. W	10
Oct.	22—Willie Toweel, New York .... KO	8
Dec.	17—Luis Rodriguez, New York ...... W	10

1961

Apr.	1—Benny Paret, Miami Beach .... KO	13

(Won World Welterweight Title)

June	3—Gaspar Ortega, Los Angeles ...... KO	12

(Retained World Welterweight Title)

July	29—Yama Bahama, New York .... W	10
Sept.	30—Benny Paret, New York L	15

(Lost World Welterweight Title)

Nov.	4—Stanford Bulla, Hamilton .... KO	4
Dec.	23—Isaac Logart, New York .... W	10

1962

Feb.	3—Johnny Torres, St. Thomas ..... W	10
Mar.	24—Benny Paret, New York .... KO	12

(Regained World Welterweight Title)

July	13—Ralph Dupas, Las Vegas .... W	15

(Retained World Welterweight Title)

Aug.	18—Denny Moyer, Tacoma .... W	10
Oct.	6—Don Fullmer, New York .... W	10
Oct.	17—Ted Wright, Vienna .... W	15

(Advertised For World Junior Middleweight Title)

Dec.	8—Jorge Fernandez, Las Vegas ..... KO	9

(Retained World Welterweight Title)

1963

Feb.	3—Chris Christensen, Copenhagen .. KO	9

(Advertised For World Junior Middleweight Title)

Mar.	21—Luis Rodriguez, Los Angeles L	15

(Lost World Welterweight Title)

June	8—Luis Rodriguez, New York .... W	15

(Regained World Welterweight Title)

Aug.	10—Holley Mims, Saratoga Springs .... W	10
Oct.	5—Jose Gonzalez, San Juan .... W	10
Dec.	20—Ruben Carter, Pittsburgh ..... KO by	1

1964

Feb.	10—Ralph Dupas, Sydney .... KO	3
Mar.	11—Juan Carlos Duran, Rome .... NC	7
Apr.	14—Stan Harrington, Honolulu ...... KO	4
June	12—Luis Rodriguez, Las Vegas .... W	15

(Retained World Welterweight Title)

Sept.	22—Brian Curvis, London .... W	15

(Retained World Welterweight Title)

Dec.	1—Dave Charnley, London .... KO	9

1965

Jan.	26—Manuel Gonzalez, Houston L	10
Mar.	30—Jose Stable, New York .... W	15

(Retained World Welterweight Title)

June	14—Eddie Pace, Honolulu .... W	10
Aug.	20—Don Fullmer, Salt Lake City L	12

(For WBA American Middleweight Title)

Sept.	14—Gabe Terronez, Fresno .... KO	4
Oct.	4—Harry Scott, London .... KO	7

Dec. 10—Manuel Gonzalez, New York ...... W 15
    (Retained World Welterweight Title)

1966
Feb. 3—Johnny Brooks, Las Vegas .... W 10
Apr. 25—Dick Tiger, New York .... W 15
    (Won World Middleweight Title)
July 13—Joey Archer, New York .... W 15
    (Retained World Middleweight Title)

1967
Jan. 23—Joey Archer, New York .... W 15
    (Retained World Middleweight Title)
Apr. 17—Nino Benvenuti, New York .... L 15
    (Lost World Middleweight Title)
Sept. 29—Nino Benvenuti, Flushing .... W 15
    (Regained World Middleweight Title)
Dec. 15—Remo Golfarini, Rome .... KO 6

1968
Mar. 4—Nino Benvenuti, New York .... L 15
    (Lost World Middleweight Title)
June 11—Andy Heilman, Oakland .... W 12
Aug. 6—Gypsy Joe Harris, Philadelphia .... W 12
Oct. 29—Stan Hayward, Philadelphia .... L 10

1969
Feb. 3—Andy Heilman, New York .... W 10
May 12—Stan Hayward, New York .... W 12
July 11—Dick DiVeronica, Syracuse ...... KO 7
Aug. 15—Art Hernandez, Sioux Falls .... W 10
Oct. 18—Jose Napoles, Los Angeles .... L 15
    (For World Welterweight Title)

1970
Jan. 28—Doyle Baird, Cleveland .... W 10
Mar. 11—Carlos Marks, New York .... W 12
June 4—Tom Bogs, Copenhagen .... W 10
July 15—Dick Tiger, New York .... W 10
Oct. 17—Danny Perez, St. Thomas .... W 10
Nov. 10—Nate Collins, San Francisco ...... W 10

1971
Mar. 23—Rafael Gutierrez, San Francisco ... W 10
Apr. 10—Juan Ramos, St. Thomas .... KO 2
May 3—Ernie Lopez, Las Vegas .... W 10
July 26—Nessim Cohen, New York .... W 10
Sept. 25—Carlos Monzon, Buenos Aires .. KO by 14
    (For World Middleweight Title)
Dec. 10—Danny McAloon, New York ...... W 10

1972
Jan. 28—Arturo Muniz, Anaheim .... W 10
Feb. 21—Jacques Kechichian, Paris .... W 10
Mar. 30—Ernie Lopez, Los Angeles .... W 10
Sept. 16—Joe DeNucci, Boston .... W 10
Oct. 11—Joe DeNucci, Boston .... W 12
Dec. 18—Jean-Claude Bouttier, Paris ... L disq. 7

1973
Mar. 12—Nessim Cohen, Paris .... D 10
June 2—Carlos Monzon, Monte Carlo .... L 15
    (For World Middleweight Title)
Nov. 2—Manuel Gonzalez, Tampa .... W 10
Nov. 19—Tony Mundine, Paris .... L 10

1974
Feb. 5—Tony Licata, Boston .... L 12
    (For Vacant NABF Middleweight Title)
May 25—Renato Garcia, Monte Carlo .... W 10
Oct. 9—Bennie Briscoe, Philadelphia .... W 10
Nov. 22—Vito Antuofermo, New York ...... L 10
Dec. 10—Donato Paduano, Montreal .... W 10

1975
May 31—Juan Carlos Duran, Cali .... L 10
July 23—Leo Saenz, Landover .... W 10
Aug. 9—Elijah Makhatini, Johannesburg ... L 10
Nov. 7—Jose Chirino, Albany .... W 10

1976
Feb. 9—Loucif Hamani, Paris .... L 10
June 26—Bennie Briscoe, Monte Carlo .... D 10
Sept. 18—Eckhart Dagge, Berlin .... L 15
    (For WBC Junior Middleweight Title)
Oct. 24—Dino Del Cid, Cartagena .... KO 4
Dec. 4—Frank Reiche, Hamburg .... KO 10

1977
Feb. 2—Christy Elliott, New York .... W 10
Apr. 15—Joel Bonnetaz, Perigueux .... L 10
July 19—Mayfield Pennington, Louisville .... L 10
July 30—Alan Minter, Monte Carlo .... L 10

TB	KO	WD	WF	D	LD	LF	KO BY	ND	NC
112	23	62	0	2	21	1	2	0	1

GIOVANNI (NINO) BENVENUTI
Born, April 26, 1938, Trieste, Italy. Weight, 160 lbs. Height, 5 ft. 11 in. Managed by Bruno Amaduzzi.
1960 Olympic Welterweight Gold Medalist

1961
Jan. 20—Ben Ali Allala, Trieste .... W 6
Feb. 10—Nicola Sammartino, Rome .... KO 3
Feb. 27—Ben Ali Allala, Naples .... KO 1
Mar. 14—Sahib Mosri, Bologna .... KO 3
Apr. 7—Nick Maric, Milan .... W 6
Apr. 21—Pierre Mondino, Florence .... W 6
May 3—Daniel Brunet, Naples .... WF 3
May 16—Michel Francois, Turin .... KO 4
June 7—Henri Cabelduc, Bologna .... W 6
June 17—Marc Desforneaux, Trieste .... W 6
Oct. 2—Retmia Mahrez, Bologna .... KO 3
Nov. 1—Angelo Brisci, Trieste .... KO 1
Nov. 9—Jesse Jones, Rome .... WF 6
Dec. 20—Giuseppe Catalano, Rome .... W 8

1962
Jan. 19—George Aldridge, Rome .... KO 6
Feb. 19—Jose Riquelme, Bologna .... W 8
Mar. 8—Manfred Haas, Turin .... W 8
Mar. 17—Gianni Lommi, Milan .... KO 5
Apr. 1—Jim Hegerle, Rome .... KO 4
May 1—Hector Constance, Trieste .... W 10
June 2—Jean Ruellet, Cagliari .... W 8
June 22—Heini Freytag, Rome .... W 8
July 12—Gino Rossi, Trieste .... W 10
Aug. 2—Mahmout le Noir, Lignano .... W 8
Aug. 30—Giuseppe Gentiletti, Senigallia ... KO 2
Sept. 28—Diego Infantes, Rome .... W 8
Oct. 18—Daniel Leullier, Padua .... W 10
Nov. 30—Isaac Logart, Rome .... W 10
Dec. 26—Giampaolo Melis, Bologna .... KO 2

1963
Mar. 1—Tommaso Truppi, Rome .... KO 11
    (Won Vacant Italian Middleweight Title)
Apr. 5—Georges Estatoff, Turin .... KO 6
Apr. 24—Jean Ruellet, Alessandria .... W 10
May 23—Jimmy Beecham, Rome .... W 10
June 7—Tony Montano, Rome .... W 10
Aug. 31—Francesco Fiori, Priverno .... KO 3
    (Retained Italian Middleweight Title)
Sept. 16—Willy Niederau, Prato .... KO 6
Sept. 27—Victor Zalazar, Rome .... KO 2
Oct. 18—Gaspar Ortega, Rome .... W 10
Nov. 7—Jackie Cailleau, Prato .... W 10
Nov. 15—Lou Gutierrez, Rome .... KO 7
Dec. 13—Ted Wright, Rome .... W 10

1964
Feb. 28—Guillermo Ayon, Rome .... KO 5
Mar. 18—Michel Diouf, Bologna .... W 10
Apr. 10—Sugar Boy Nando, Rome .... W 10
May 28—Jimmy Beecham, Bologna .... KO 2
July 30—Fabio Bettini, San Remo .... W 12
    (Retained Italian Middleweight Title)
Sept. 18—Denny Moyer, Rome .... W 10
Oct. 9—Abrao De Souza, Rome .... WF 7
Nov. 27—Aristeo Chavarin, Rome .... KO 4
Dec. 19—Juan Carlos Duran, Milan .... W 10

1965
Jan. 22—Art Hernandez, Rome .... KO 3
Feb. 12—Tommaso Truppi, Bologna .... KO 5
    (Retained Italian Middleweight Title)
Feb. 26—Mick Leahy, Milan .... W 10
Mar. 18—Dick Knight, Bologna .... KO 6
Apr. 2—Rip Randall, Rome .... W 10
Apr. 30—Milo Calhoun, Genoa .... W 10
June 18—Sandro Mazzinghi, Milan .... W 6
    (Won World Junior Middleweight Title)
Aug. 15—Daniel Leullier, Senigallia .... KO 7
Oct. 15—Luis Folledo, Rome .... KO 6
    (Won Vacant European Middleweight Title)
Nov. 5—Johnny Torres, Turin .... WF 7

569

Nov.	15—James Shelton, Bologna	W	10
Dec.	17—Sandro Mazzinghi, Rome	W	15

(Retained World Junior Middleweight Title)

1966

Feb.	4—Don Fullmer, Rome	W	12
Mar.	11—Clarence James, Turin	W	10
May	14—Jupp Elze, Berlin	KO	14

(Retained European Middleweight Title)

June	25—Ki-Soo Kim, Seoul	L	15

(Lost World Junior Middleweight Title)

Sept.	23—Harry Scott, Rome	W	10
Oct.	21—Pascal DiBenedetto, Rome	KO	11

(Retained European Middleweight Title)

Dec.	2—Ferd Hernandez, Rome	W	10
Dec.	23—Renato Moares, Rome	KO	9

1967

Jan.	19—Manfred Graus, Bologna	KO	2
Mar.	3—Milo Calhoun, Rome	W	10
Apr.	17—Emile Griffith, New York	W	15

(Won World Middleweight Title)

Sept.	28—Emile Griffith, Flushing	L	15

(Lost World Middleweight Title)

1968

Jan.	19—Charley Austin, Rome	W	10
Mar.	4—Emile Griffith, New York	W	15

(Regained World Middleweight Title)

June	7—Yoshiaki Akasaka, Rome	KO	2
July	5—Jimmy Ramos, Turin	KO	4
Sept.	17—Art Hernandez, Toronto	W	10
Oct.	14—Doyle Baird, Akron	D	10
Dec.	14—Don Fullmer, San Remo	W	15

(Retained World Middleweight Title)

1969

May	26—Dick Tiger, New York	L	10
Oct.	4—Fraser Scott, Naples	W disq.	7

(Retained World Middleweight Title)

Nov.	22—Luis Rodriguez, Rome	KO	11

(Retained World Middleweight Title)

1970

Mar.	13—Tom Bethea, Melbourne	KO by	8
May	23—Tom Bethea, Umago	KO	8

(Retained World Middleweight Title)

Sept.	12—Doyle Baird, Bari	KO	10
Nov.	7—Carlos Monzon, Rome	KO by	12

(Lost World Middleweight Title)

1971

Mar.	17—Jose Chirino, Bologna	L	10
May	8—Carlos Monzon, Monte Carlo	KO by	3

(For World Middleweight Title)

TB	KO	WD	WF	D	LD	LF	KO BY	ND	NC
90	35	42	5	1	4	0	3	0	0

CARLOS MONZON

Born, August 7, 1942, Santa Fe, Argentina.
Weight, 158 lbs. Height, 5 ft. 11½ in.

1963

Feb.	6—Ramon Montenegro, Rafaela	KO	2
Mar.	13—Albino Veron, Vila	NC	1
Apr.	9—Albino Veron, Santa Fe	KO	2
Apr.	26—Mario Suarez, Posadas	KO	7
May	3—Raul Rivas, Posadas	KO	5
May	31—Juan Rodriguez, Parana	KO	5
July	17—Andres Cejas, Buenos Aires	KO	4
Aug.	9—Lisandro Guzman, Cordoba	KO	3
Aug.	28—Antonio Aguilar, Buenos Aires	L	10
Oct.	18—Benito Sanchez, Reconquista	KO	8
Dec.	6—Rene Sosa, Parana	KO	6

1964

Jan.	17—Roberto Carabajal, Parana	KO	8
June	13—Angel Coria, Mar del Plata	W	8
June	28—Felipe Cambeiro, Rio de Janeiro	L	8
July	10—Roberto Carabajal, Tostado	W	10
July	24—Walter Villa, Ceres	KO	9
Aug.	14—Juan C. Diaz, Villa Angela	KO	9
Sept.	4—Americo Vacca, Parana	KO	3
Sept.	25—Francisco Olea, Tostado	KO	9
Oct.	9—Alberto Massi, Cordoba	L	10

Oct.	28—Francisco Gelabert, Buenos Aires	KO	4
Nov.	18—Caledonio Lima, Buenos Aires	D	10

1965

Jan.	8—Andres Selpa, Mar del Plata	D	10
Mar.	11—Andres Selpa, Santa Fe	W	10
Apr.	9—Emilio Ale Ali, Tucuman	D	10
May	19—Anibal Cordoba, Buenos Aires	W	10
July	14—Alberto Rotondo, Buenos Aires	KO	8
Aug.	10—Felipe Cambeiro, San Pablo	W	8
Aug.	14—Manoel Severino, Rio de Janeiro	D	8
Aug.	28—Manoel Severino, Rio de Janeiro	D	8
Oct.	6—Gregorio Gomez, Buenos Aires	W	10
Nov.	17—Caledonio Lima, Buenos Aires	KO	5
Dec.	8—Antonio Aguilar, Buenos Aires	W	10
Dec.	29—Carlos Salinas, Buenos Aires	W	10

1966

Feb.	4—Ramon Rocha, Santa Fe	W	10
Feb.	17—Norberto Juncos, Santa Fe	KO	7
Apr.	29—Ismael Hamze, San Nicolas	KO	9
June	3—Marcos Bustos, Rio Gallegos	D	10
July	8—Benito Sanchez, S. Pereyra	KO	4
Sept.	3—Jorge Fernandez, Buenos Aires	W	12

(Won Argentine Middleweight Title)

Oct.	2—Angel Coria, Mar del Plata	W	10
Nov.	18—Luis A. Pereyra, Santa Fe	KO	2
Dec.	2—Alberto Massi, Santa Fe	KO	8
Dec.	23—Marcelo Farias	KO	3

1967

Jan.	13—Carlos Salinas, Santa Fe	KO	7
Jan.	27—Eudoro Robledo, Charata	KO	4
Feb.	15—Alberto Massi, San Francisco	W	10
Mar.	9—Osvaldo Marino, Santa Fe	KO	7
Mar.	18—Osvaldo Marino, Santa Fe	KO	7
Mar.	25—Angel Coria, Mar del Plata	KO	6
Apr.	9—Benito Sanchez, Santa Elena	KO	3
May	6—Bennie Briscoe, Buenos Aires	D	10
June	10—Jorge Fernandez, Buenos Aires	W	12

(Won South American Middleweight Title)

July	29—Antonio Aguilar, Buenos Aires	KO	9
Aug.	16—Tito Marshall, Buenos Aires	W	10
Sept.	8—Ramon Rocha, Rosario	W	10
Oct.	6—Carlos Estrada, Trelew	KO	7
Oct.	20—Ramon Rocha, San Juan	KO	7
Nov.	18—Tito Marshall, Buenos Aires	W	10

1968

Apr.	5—Juan Aguilar, Mendoza	D	10
May	17—Alberto Massi, Cordoba	W	10
June	19—Juan Aguilar, Buenos Aires	W	10
July	5—Benito Sanchez, Saenz Pena	KO	4
Aug.	14—Doug Huntley, Buenos Aires	KO	4
Oct.	23—Charlie Austin, Buenos Aires	W	10
Dec.	7—Johnny Brooks, Buenos Aires	W	10
Dec.	20—Emilio Ale Ali, Mendoza	W	10

1969

Jan.	10—Ruben Orrico, Santa Fe	KO	9

(Retained South American Middleweight Title)

Mar.	14—Mario Taborda, Saenz Pena	KO	3
Apr.	25—Carlos Salinas, Parana	D	10
June	6—Carlos Salinas, Parana	KO	7
July	5—Harold Richardson, Buenos Aires	KO	3
Aug.	10—Tom Bethea, Buenos Aires	W	10
Sept.	10—Emilio Ale Ali, Tucuman	KO	7
Oct.	27—Manuel Severino, Buenos Aires	KO	6

(Retained South American Middleweight Title)

Dec.	12—Carlos Estrada, Santa Fe	KO	2

1970

Feb.	11—Antonio Aguilar, Mar del Plata	KO	6
Mar.	7—Juan Aguilar, Rosario	KO	9
Apr.	17—Adolfo Cardoza, Santa Fe	KO	9
May	11—Ramon Rocha, Tucuman	KO	9
July	18—Eddie Pace, Buenos Aires	W	10
Sept.	19—Candy Rosa, Buenos Aires	KO	4
Nov.	7—Nino Benvenuti, Rome	KO	12

(Won World Middleweight Title)

Dec.	20—Charlie Austin, Buenos Aires	KO	2

1971

Feb.	19—Domingo Guerrero, Salta	KO	2
Mar.	5—Roy Lee, Santa Fe	KO	2
May	8—Nino Benvenuti, Monte Carlo	KO	3

(Retained World Middleweight Title)

Sept. 25—Emile Griffith, Buenos Aires ..... KO 14
 (Retained World Middleweight Title)
Dec. 5—Fraser Scott, Buenos Aires .... KO 3
1972
Mar. 4—Denny Moyer, Rome .... KO 5
 (Retained World Middleweight Title)
June 17—Jean-Claude Bouttier, Paris ..... KO 13
 (Retained World Middleweight Title)
Aug. 19—Tom Bogs, Copenhagen .... KO 5
 (Retained World Middleweight Title)
Nov. 11—Bennie Briscoe, Buenos Aires ..... W 15
 (Retained World Middleweight Title)
1973
May 5—Roy Dale, Rome .... KO 5
June 2—Emile Griffith, Monte Carlo ...... W 15
 (Retained World Middleweight Title)
Sept. 29—Jean-Claude Bouttier, Paris ..... W 15
 (Retained World Middleweight Title)
1974
Feb. 9—Jose Napoles, Paris .... KO 7
 (Retained World Middleweight Title)
Oct. 5—Tony Mundine, Buenos Aires ..... KO 7
 (Retained World Middleweight Title)
1975
June 30—Tony Licata, New York .... KO 10
 (Retained World Middleweight Title)
Dec. 13—Gratien Tonna, Paris .... KO 5
 (Retained World Middleweight Title)
1976
June 26—Rodrigo Valdez, Monte Carlo ..... W 15
 (Retained World Middleweight Title)
1977
July 30—Rodrigo Valdez, Monte Carlo ..... W 15
 (Retained World Middleweight Title)
Aug. 29—Announced retirement.

TB	KO	WD	WF	D	LD	LF	KO BY	ND	NC
102	61	28	0	9	3	0	0	0	1

RODRIGO VALDEZ
Born, December 22, 1946, Rocha, Colombia.
1963
Oct. 25—Orlando Pineda, Cartagena .... W 4
Nov. 6—Eliecer De Avila, Cartagena ...... KO 4
1964
Jan. 15—Alejandro Parra, Cartagena ...... KO 5
Feb. 6—Humberto Hurtado, Cartagena .... W 6
Feb. 28—Alejandro Parra, Barranquilla .... W 8
May 15—Fernando Alvarez, Barranquilla .. KO 8
Sept. 12—Manuel Jack Hernandez,
 Barranquilla .... W 10
1965
July 9—Elias Hidalgo, Barranquilla ...... KO 5
Oct. 2—Rudy Oscobar, Barranquilla ... KO by 6
1966
Mar. 13—Rafael Luna, Cartagena .... W 10
June —Rocky Ulloa, Cartagena .... W 10
June —Lucero Acary, Cartagena .... KO 2
July 29—Elias Lian, Cartagena .... W 10
Nov. 4—Alfonso Franco, Cartagena ...... KO 7
1967
Jan. 22—Julio Novella, Cartagena .... KO 2
Mar. 5—Eugenio Espinoza, Cartagena ..... W 10
Apr. 2—Mario Rosito, Cartagena .... D 10
June 10—Kid Revolledo, Sincelejo .... W 10
Aug. 12—Baby Mendez, El Carmen .... KO 3
Aug. 29—Kid Peche, Cartagena .... W 10
Oct. 1—Humberto Trottman, Cartagena ... W 10
Dec. 3—Ricard Morsles, Cartagena .... KO 2
1968
Jan. 21—German Castelbondi, Cartagena .... D 10
Apr. 15—Cartagenita Kid, Cartagena ...... KO 7
Aug. 6—Humberto Trottman, Bogota ...... W 10
1969
Feb. 16—Daniel Guanin, Quito .... L 10
June 4—Linfer Contreras, Cartagena ..... KO 2
Aug. 6—Peter Cobblah, Las Vegas .... W 10
Sept. 3—Mike LeFee, Las Vegas .... KO 1

Sept. 17—David Melendez, New York ...... KO 5
Oct. 18—Raul Rodriguez, Los Angeles .... KO 9
Dec. 11—Denny Stieletto, Las Vegas .... KO 1
1970
Feb. 14—David Oropeza, Los Angeles ...... KO 1
Mar. 2—Pete Toro, New York .... L 10
May 1—Cassius Green, New York .... W 10
May 11—Ralph Palladin, New York .... L 10
July 24—Juan Cordoba, Medellin .... KO 9
1971
Jan. 24—Juan Jimenez, Cartagena .... KO 2
Mar. 5—Arturo Lans, Barranquilla .... KO 5
Apr. 27—Marcos Tordoya, Barranquilla .... KO 4
June 28—Edmundo Leite, New York .... W 10
Aug. 9—Bobby Cassidy, New York .... KO 7
Oct. 19—Perry Abney, New York .... KO 1
Nov. 25—Doc Holliday, New York .... KO 4
1972
Apr. 2—Milton Mendez, Valledupar ...... KO 2
Aug. 10—Juan Cordoba, Barranquilla ...... KO 6
Aug. 28—Roy Edmonds, New York .... KO 2
Sept. 29—Lloyd Duncan, New York .... W 10
Dec. 18—Carlos Marks, Paris .... W 10
1973
Mar. 5—Jose Rodriguez, Cartagena ...... KO 5
Apr. 16—Kim Booker, New York .... KO 5
June 5—Leon Washington, Barranquilla .. KO 9
July 19—Antonio Aguilar, Bogota .... W 10
Sept. 1—Bennie Briscoe, Noumea .... W 12
Dec. 14—Joey Durelle, Bogota .... KO 2
1974
Mar. 16—Ernie Burns, Cartagena .... KO 2
May 25—Bennie Briscoe, Monte Carlo ..... KO 7
 (Won Vacant WBC Middleweight Title)
Sept. 7—Cuby Jackson, Cartagena .... KO 2
Oct. 25—Vinnie Curto, New York .... W 10
Nov. 13—Gratien Tonna, Paris .... KO 11
 (Retained WBC Middleweight Title)
1975
May 31—Ramon Mendez, Cali .... KO 8
 (Retained WBC Middleweight Title)
Aug. 16—Rudy Robles, Cartagena .... W 15
 (Retained WBC Middleweight Title)
1976
Mar. 28—Max Cohen, Paris .... KO 4
 (Retained WBC Middleweight Title)
June 26—Carlos Monzon, Monte Carlo ...... L 15
 (For World Middleweight Title)
Oct. 24—Ramon Veras, Cartagena .... KO 7
1977
Mar. 19—Oreste Lebron, Barranquilla ..... KO 5
July 30—Carlos Monzon, Monte Carlo ..... L 15
 (For World Middleweight Title)
Nov. 5—Bennie Briscoe, Campione .... W 15
 (Won Vacant World Middleweight Title)
1978
Apr. 22—Hugo Corro, San Remo .... L 15
 (Lost World Middleweight Title)
Sept. 29—Mayfield Pennington, Cartagena KO 7,
Nov. 11—Hugo Corro, Buenos Aires .... L 15
 (For World Middleweight Title)
1979
(Inactive)
1980
May 14—Charlie Heyward, Bogota .... KO 7
Nov. 28—Alberto Almonte, Bogota .... KO 1

TB	KO	WD	WF	D	LD	LF	KO BY	ND	NC
73	41	22	0	2	7	0	1	0	0

HUGO CORRO
Born, November 5, 1953, San Carlos, Mendoza, Argentina.
1973
Aug. 30—Gaston Dieff, Tunuyan .... W 6
Sept. 15—Pedro Bazan, Tunuyan .... D 6
Oct. 5—Juan Cantero, Tunuyan .... KO 4
Oct. 26—Raul Fleitas, Tunuyan .... KO 2
Nov. 23—Oscar Mercado, Tunuyan .... KO 7

Dec. 7—Pedro Bazan, Tunuyan ...... W disq. 4
Dec. 21—Rafael Lescano, Tunuyan .... KO 3
1974
Feb. 8—Ramon Robert, Tunuyan .... W 10
Apr. 14—Ruben Martinez, Tunuyan .... KO 5
June 19—Orlando Nasul, Tunuyan .... W 10
July 19—Juan Artaza, San Juan .... W 10
Sept. 8—Carlos Robledo, Tunuyan .... KO 7
Oct. 4—Ruben Martinez, San Juan .... KO 5
Nov. 8—Hugo Saavedra, Tunuyan ..... KO by 8
1975
Mar. 7—Hugo Obregon, Salta .... KO 7
Mar. 26—Eliseo Nieva, Mendoza .... KO 8
May 9—Orlando Nasul, Mendoza .... W 10
June 13—Norlberto Fleitas, Mendoza .... KO 4
July 4—Ramon Robert, Villas Merced .... KO 6
July 25—Octavio Escauriza, Mendoza ...... KO 3
Aug. 22—Camilo Gaitan, Mendoza .... KO 4
Sept. 27—Hugo Saavedra, Buenos Aires ..... W 10
Oct. 7—Norberto Cabrera, Tunuyan .... W 10
Dec. 19—Hugo Obregon, Cordoba .... W 10
1976
Feb. 2—Hugo Obregon, Salta .... W 10
Mar. 5—Hugo Saavedra, Cordoba .... W 10
Mar. 27—Roque Roldan, Buenos Aires .... W 10
May 21—Norberto Cabrera, Buenos Aires .... L 10
June 11—Gregorio Navarro, Tunuyan ...... KO 4
July 8—Roberto Marziali, Cordoba ...... KO 9
Aug. 6—Juan C. Bogado, Tunuyan ...... KO 10
Sept. 10—Juan C. Artaza, Mendoza .... KO 10
Oct. 8—F. Rodriguez Martin, Madrid ..... KO 2
Nov. 5—Raul A. Paez, Mendoza .... KO 2
Nov. 26—Pedro Acuna, Tunuyan .... KO 1
Dec. 10—Julio Medina, Mendoza .... KO 3
(Won Vacant Argentine Middleweight Title)
1977
Feb. 25—Rodolfo Rosales, Mendoza .... W 10
Apr. 6—Rodolfo Rosales, San Luis .... W 10
May 9—Marcelo Quinones, Lima .... W 12
(Won South American Middleweight Title)
July 2—Cesar Duarte, Buenos Aires .... W 12
(Retained Argentine Middleweight Title)
Sept. 2—Nolberto Fleitas, Mendoza .... KO 2
(Retained South American Middleweight Title)
Oct. 17—Roque Roldan, Carlos Paz .... W 10
Nov. 5—Robert Patterson, Buenos Aires ... KO 5
Nov. 19—Mario Romersi, Turin .... W 8
Dec. 20—Antonio Garrido, Godoy Cruz ..... W 12
(Retained South American Middleweight Title)
1978
Mar. 3—Juan Carlos Bogado, Buenos Aires W 10
Apr. 22—Rodrigo Valdez, San Remo .... W 15
(Won World Middleweight Title)
Aug. 5—Ronnie Harris, Buenos Aires ...... W 15
(Retained World Middleweight Title)
Oct. 6—Willie Warren, Mendoza .... W 10
Nov. 11—Rodrigo Valdez, Buenos Aires ..... W 15
(Retained World Middleweight Title)
1979
June 30—Vito Antuofermo, Monte Carlo ..... L 15
(Lost World Middleweight Title)

TB	KO	WD	WF	D	LD	LF	KO BY	ND	NC
51	23	23	1	1	2	0	1	0	0

VITO ANTUOFERMO
Born, February 9, 1953, Bari, Italy. Weight, 159 lbs. Height, 5 ft. 9 in. Managed by Tony Carione.
1971
Nov. 30—Ivelaw Eastman, New York .... W 4
1972
Jan. 17—Juan Rivera, White Plains .... W 6
Feb. 17—Charlie Hayward, North Bergen ... D 6
Mar. 1—Ivelaw Eastman, New York .... W 4
Apr. 11—John Presley, New York .... KO 1
May 26—Lenny Carter, New York .... KO 2
June 30—Don Sauls, New York .... W 6
July 21—Jerry Caballero, New York .... KO 4
Aug. 28—Gabe Bowens, New York .... W 4

Sept. 11—Charlie Hayward, New York ...... W 6
Oct. 10—Oresto Lebron, New York .... W 8
Nov. 23—Carlos Novotny, New York .... KO 3
Dec. 15—Al Sewell, New York .... KO 7
1973
Jan. 31—Skip Yeaton, Brooklyn .... KO 2
Mar. 9—Ray Villanueva, New York .... KO 4
Apr. 13—Luis Rivera, New York .... W 8
Apr. 30—Art Kettles, New York .... W 10
June 18—Tony Durango, New York .... KO 2
July 9—Harold Weston, New York .... KO by 5
Aug. 25—Danny McAloon, New York ...... W 10
Oct. 8—Tony Durango, New York .... W 10
Dec. 5—Buddy Boggs, Baltimore .... KO 6
1974
Jan. 14—Jessie Garcia, New York .... W 10
Mar. 9—John L. Sullivan, New York ...... W 10
May 3—Joey Durelle, Rome .... KO 1
June 3—Mel Dennis, Rome .... W 10
Sept. 9—Denny Moyer, New York .... W 10
Oct. 18—Paul Osborne, Baltimore .... KO 3
Nov. 22—Emile Griffith, New York .... W 10
1975
Jan. 24—Ramon Mendez, Milan .... W 10
Mar. 20—Dave Huckaby, Bristol .... W 10
June 6—Renalfo Oliveire, Naples .... KO 6
June 27—Antonio Castellini, Milan .... KO 5
Aug. 8—Vinnie Curto, Las Vegas .... W 10
Oct. 23—Ricky Ortiz, Binghamton .... KO 6
Nov. 28—Bruce Cantrell, Commack .... W 10
1976
Jan. 16—Eckhard Dagge, Berlin .... W 15
(Won EBU Junior Middleweight Title)
Mar. 26—Jean-Claude Warusfel, Milan ..... KO 14
(Retained EBU Junior Middleweight Title)
June 18—Frank Wissenbach, Berlin .... L 8
Oct. 1—Maurice Hope, Rome .... KO by 15
(Lost EBU Junior Middleweight Title)
Dec. 2—Pablo Rodriguez, New York ...... KO 4
1977
Mar. 11—Eugene Hart, Philadelphia .... KO 5
Aug. 30—Raymond Beras, Montreal .... KO 6
Oct. 27—Mike Nixon, New York .... KO 4
1978
Feb. 4—Bennie Briscoe, New York .... W 10
June 22—Willie Warren, New York .... W 10
Aug. 25—Willie Classen, New York .... W 10
Nov. 11—Mike Hallacy, Boston .... W 10
1979
June 30—Hugo Corro, Monte Carlo .... W 15
(Won World Middleweight Title)
Nov. 30—Marvin Hagler, Las Vegas .... D 15
(Retained World Middleweight Title)
1980
Mar. 16—Alan Minter, Las Vegas .... L 15
(Lost World Middleweight Title)
June 28—Alan Minter, London .... KO by 8
(For World Middleweight Title)

TB	KO	WD	WF	D	LD	LF	KO BY	ND	NC
52	19	26	0	2	2	0	3	0	0

ALAN MINTER
Born, August 17, 1951, Crawley, England. Weight, 160 lbs. Height, 5 ft. 9 in. Managed by Doug Bidwell.
1972
Oct. 31—Maurice Thomas, London .... KO 6
Nov. 14—John Lowe, Wembley .... KO 3
Dec. 5—Anton Schnedl, London .... KO 7
Dec. 11—Ron Hough, London .... KO 5
1973
Jan. 8—Mike McCluskie, Manchester ..... KO 5
Jan. 16—Pat Dwyer, London .... W 8
Jan. 30—Pat Brogan, London .... KO 7
Feb. 20—Gabe Bowens, London .... KO 7
Mar. 13—Harry Scott, London .... W 8
Mar. 27—Frank Young, Birmingham .... W 8
May 9—King George Aidoo, London ...... KO 5

June   5—Don McMillan, London .... W   8
Sept.   10—Octavio Romero, London .... W   8
Oct.   2—Ernie Burns, London .... KO   5
Oct.   30—Jan Magdziarz, London .... KO by   3
Dec.   11—Jan Magdziarz, London .... KO by   6
1974
Mar.   26—Tony Byrne, London .... W   8
May   21—Ricky Ortiz, London .... KO by   2
Oct.   29—Jan Magdziarz, Kensington ...... NC   2
Nov.   30—Shako Mamaba, Munich .... W   8
1975
Jan.   20—Henry Cooper, Mayfair .... KO   1
Feb.   10—Tony Allen, Mayfair .... W   8
Mar.   25—Larry Paul, London .... W   10
May   30—Peter Wulf, Hamburg .... KO   6
Nov.   4—Kevin Finnegin, London .... W   15
(British Middleweight Title)
1976
Jan.   20—Trevor Francis, London .... KO   8
Apr.   27—Billy Knight, London .... KO   2
(British Middleweight Title)
May   25—Frank Reiche, Munich .... KO   7
Sept.   14—Kevin Finnegan, London .... W   15
Nov.   9—Tony Licata, London .... KO   6
Dec.   12—Sugar Ray Seales, London .... KO   5
1977
Feb.   3—Germano Valeschi, Milan .... KO   5
(European Middleweight Title)
Apr.   12—Ronnie Harris, London .... KO by   8
July   30—Emile Griffith, Monte Carlo ...... W   10
Sept.   21—Gratien Tonna, Milan .... KO by   8
(European Middleweight Title)
1978
Feb.   15—Sandy Torres, Las Vegas .... KO   5
July   19—Angelo Jacopucci, Bellaria .... KO   12
(European Middleweight Title)
Nov.   7—Gratien Tonna, London .... KO   6
(European Middleweight Title)
1979
Feb.   6—Rudy Robles, London .... W   10
May   1—Renato Garcia, London .... KO   9
June   26—Monty Betham, London .... KO   2
Oct.   23—Doug Demmings, London .... W   10
1980
Mar.   16—Vito Antuofermo, Las Vegas .... W   15
(Won World Middleweight Title)
June   28—Vito Antuofermo, London .... KO   8
(Retained World Middleweight Title)
Sept.   27—Marvin Hagler, London .... KO by   3
(Lost World Middleweight Title)

TB	KO	WD	WF	D	LD	LF	KO BY	ND	NC
36	18	12	0	0	0	0	5	0	1

MARVIN HAGLER

Born, May 23, 1952, Newark, N.J. Weight, 160 lbs. Height, 5 ft. 9½ in. Southpaw. Managed by Goody and Pat Petronelli.

1973
May   18—Terry Ryan, Brockton .... KO   2
July   25—Sonny Williams, Boston .... W   6
Aug.   8—Muhammad Smith, Boston .... KO   2

Oct.   6—Don Wigfall, Brockton .... W   8
Oct.   26—Cove Green, Brockton .... KO   4
Nov.   18—Cocoa Kid, Brockton .... KO   2
Dec.   7—Manny Freitas, Portland, Me. .... KO   1
Dec.   18—James Redford, Boston .... KO   4
1974
Feb.   5—Bob Harrington, Boston .... KO   5
Apr.   5—Tracy Morrison, Boston .... KO   8
May   4—Jim Redford, Brockton .... KO   2
May   30—Curtis Phillips, Portland .... KO   5
July   16—Robert Williams, Boston .... KO   3
Aug.   13—Peachy Davis, New Bedford ...... KO   1
Aug.   30—Ray Seales, Boston .... W   10
Oct.   29—Morris Jordan, New Bedford ..... KO   4
Nov.   16—George Green, Brockton .... KO   1
Nov.   26—Ray Seales, Seattle .... D   10
Dec.   20—D. C. Walker, Boston .... KO   2
1975
Feb.   15—Don Wigfall, Brockton .... KO   5
Mar.   31—Joey Blair, Boston .... KO   2
Apr.   14—Jimmy Owens, Boston .... W   10
May   24—Jimmy Owens, Brockton ..... W disq.   6
Aug.   7—Jesse Bender, Portland .... KO   1
Sept.   30—Lamont Lovelady, Boston .... KO   7
Dec.   20—Johnny Baldwin, Boston .... W   10
1976
Jan.   13—Bobby Watts, Philadelphia L   10
Feb.   7—Matt Donovan, Boston .... KO   2
Mar.   9—Willie Monroe, Philadelphia L   10
June   2—Bob Smith, Taunton .... KO   5
Aug.   3—D. C. Walker, Providence .... KO   6
Sept.   14—Eugene Hart, Philadelphia ...... KO   8
Dec.   21—George Davis, Boston .... KO   6
1977
Feb.   15—Willie Monroe, Boston .... KO   12
Mar.   16—Reginald Ford, Boston .... KO   3
June   10—Roy Jones, Hartford .... KO   3
Aug.   23—Willie Monroe, Philadelphia ...... KO   2
Sept.   24—Ray Phillips, Boston .... KO   7
Oct.   15—Jim Henry, Providence .... W   10
Nov.   26—Mike Colbert, Boston .... KO   12
1978
Mar.   4—Kevin Finnegan, Boston .... KO   9
Apr.   7—Doug Demmings, Los Angeles .... KO   8
May   13—Kevin Finnegan, Boston .... KO   7
Aug.   24—Bennie Briscoe, Philadelphia ...... W   10
Nov.   11—Willie Warren, Boston .... KO   7
1979
Feb.   3—Ray Seales, Boston .... KO   1
Mar.   12—Bob Patterson, Providence .... KO   3
May   26—Jaime Thomas, Portland, Me. .... KO   3
June   30—Norberto Cabrera, Monte Carlo ... KO   8
Nov.   30—Vito Antuofermo, Las Vegas ...... D   15
(For World Middleweight Title)
1980
Feb.   16—Loucif Hamani, Portland .... KO   2
Apr.   19—Bobby Watts, Portland .... KO   2
May   17—Marcos Geraldo, Las Vegas .... W   10
Sept.   27—Alan Minter, London .... KO   3
(Won World Middleweight Title)

TB	KO	WD	WF	D	LD	LF	KO BY	ND	NC
54	41	8	1	2	2	0	0	0	0

JUNIOR MIDDLEWEIGHTS

DENNIS MOYER	1962-1963	**JAE-DO YUH**	1975-1976
RALPH DUPAS	1963	*ELISHA OBED (WBC)*	*1975-1976*
SANDRO MAZZINGHI	1963-1965	**KOICHI WAJIMA**	1976
NINO BENVENUTI	1965-1966	**JOSE DURAN**	1976
KI-SOO KIM	1966-1968	*ECKHARD DAGGE (WBC)*	*1976-1977*
SANDRO MAZZINGHI	1968	**MIGUEL ANGEL CASTELLINI**	1976-1977
FREDDIE LITTLE	1969-1970	**EDDIE GAZO**	1977-1978
CARMELO BOSSI	1970-1971	*ROCKY MATTIOLI (WBC)*	*1977-1979*
KOICHI WAJIMA	1971-1974	**MASASHI KUDO**	1978-1979
OSCAR ALBARADO	1974-1975	*MAURICE HOPE (WBC)*	*1979-*
KOICHI WAJIMA	1975	**AYUB KALULE**	1979-
MIGUEL DE OLIVEIRA (WBC)	*1975-1976*		

Claimants not generally recognized are in *italics*.

WORLD JUNIOR MIDDLEWEIGHT CHAMPIONSHIP BOUTS

Date	Winner	Weight	Loser	Weight	Result	Time KO	Site	Referee
10/20/62	**Dennis MOYER**	153¾	**Joey GIAMBRA**	154	unan 15		Memorial Coliseum, Portland, Ore.	Sonny Liston
2/19/63	**Dennis MOYER**	153½	**Stan HARRINGTON**	150¼	unan 15		Civic Auditorium, Honolulu, Oahu	Louis Freitas
4/29/63	**Ralph DUPAS**	151	**Dennis MOYER**	154	split 15		Municipal Auditorium, New Orleans	Peter Giarusso
6/17/63	**Ralph DUPAS**	150	**Dennis MOYER**	154	unan 15		Civic Center, Baltimore, Md.	Benny Goldstein
9/7/63	**Sandro MAZZINGHI**	153¼	**Ralph DUPAS**	152¼	KO 9	1:45	Vigorelli Velodrome, Milan, Italy	Rolf Neuhold
12/2/63	**Sandro MAZZINGHI**	153	**Ralph DUPAS**	150¼	KO 13	1:20	Sydney Stadium, Australia	Vic Patrick
10/3/64	**Sandro MAZZINGHI**	153¾	**Tony MONTANO**	156	KO 12	2:45	Sports Palace, Genoa, Italy	Rolf Neuhold
12/11/64	**Sandro MAZZINGHI**	154	**Fortunato MANCA**	153	ref 15		Sports Palace, Rome, Italy	Georgio Tinelli
6/18/65	**Nino BENVENUTI**	153	**Sandro MAZZINGHI**	153½	KO 6	2:40	San Siro Stadium, Milan, Italy	S. Brambilla
12/17/65	**Nino BENVENUTI**	153¾	**Sandro MAZZINGHI**	153¾	unan 15		Sports Palace, Rome, Italy	Giacinto Aniello
6/25/66	**Ki-Soo KIM**	152¼	**Nino BENVENUTI**	153	split 15		Changchung Gym., Seoul, Korea	Nick Pope
12/17/66	**Ki-Soo KIM**	153½	**Stan HARRINGTON**	154	unan 15		Changchung Gym., Seoul, Korea	Yung-Soo Chung
10/3/67	**Ki-Soo KIM**	154	**Freddie LITTLE**	152½	split 15		Baseball Stadium, Seoul, Korea	Yung-Soo Chung
5/25/68	**Sandro MAZZINGHI**	151½	**Ki-Soo KIM**	151¾	split 15		San Siro Stadium, Milan, Italy	Harold Valan
10/25/68	**Freddie LITTLE**	151¼	**Sandro MAZZINGHI**	151¼	TKO 9	*	Sports Palace, Rome, Italy	Herbert Tomser
3/17/69	**Freddie LITTLE**	153½	**Stan HAYWARD**	154	unan 15		Convention Center, Las Vegas, Nev.	Harry Krause
9/9/69	**Freddie LITTLE**	152¼	**Hisao MINAMI**	149⅞	KO 2	1:26	Prefectural Gymnasium, Osaka, Japan	Nick Pope
3/20/70	**Freddie LITTLE**	152¾	**Gerhard PIASKOWY**	153¼	ref 15		Sports Palace, Berlin, Germany	L. Sanchez Villard
7/9/70	**Carmelo BOSSI**	153	**Freddie LITTLE**	152	ref 15		Monza Stadium, Italy	Roland Dakin
4/29/71	**Carmelo BOSSI**	154	**Jose HERNANDEZ**	154	draw 15		Sports Palace, Madrid, Spain	Bernard Mascot
10/31/71	**Koichi WAJIMA**	152¾	**Carmelo BOSSI**	153¼	split 15		Nihon University Auditorium, Tokyo	Harold Valan
5/7/72	**Koichi WAJIMA**	153	**Domenico TIBERIA**	154	KO 1	1:49	Fukuoka Sports Centre, Tokyo	Yusaku Yoshida
10/21/72	**Koichi WAJIMA**	150½	**Matt DONOVAN**	151¾	KO 3	0:53	Nihon University Auditorium, Tokyo	Takeo Ugo
1/9/73	**Koichi WAJIMA**	152	**Miguel de OLIVIERA**	153½	draw 15		Municipal Gymnasium, Tokyo, Japan	Hiroyuki Tezaki
4/19/73	**Koichi WAJIMA**	154	**Ryu SORIMACHI**	151¼	maj 15		Prefectural Gymnasium, Osaka, Japan	Nobumitsu Inukai
8/14/73	**Koichi WAJIMA**	153¾	**Silvani BERTINI**	153	TKO 13	*	Makomanai Ice Arena, Sapporo	Takeo Ugo
2/5/74	**Koichi WAJIMA**	153	**Miguel de OLIVIERA**	153¾	maj 15		Metropolitan Gymnasium, Tokyo	Seiji Ebine
6/3/74	**Oscar ALVARADO**	151¾	**Koichi WAJIMA**	153¾	KO 15	:54	Nihon University Auditorium, Tokyo	Yusaku Yoshida
10/8/74	**Oscar ALVARADO**	154	**Ryu SORIMACHI**	152¾	TKO 7	2:17	Nihon University Auditorium, Tokyo	Dick Young
1/21/75	**Koichi WAJIMA**	153	**Oscar ALVARADO**	154	unan 15		Nihon University Auditorium, Tokyo	Dick Young
‡ 5/7/75	**Miguel de OLIVIERA**	154	**Jose DURAN**	154	unan 15		Louis II Stadium, Monte Carlo	Herbert Tomser
6/7/75	**Jae-Do YUH**	154	**Koichi WAJIMA**	154	TKO 7	2:00	Kitakyushu Municipal Gymnasium	Yusaku Yoshida
11/11/75	**Jae-Do YUH**	154	**Masahiro MISAKO**	153½	TKO 6	2:16	Sumpu Arena, Shizuoka, Japan	Takeo Ugo
‡11/13/75	**Elisha OBED**	154	**Miguel de OLIVIERA**	154	TKO 11	*	Nouveau Hippodrome, Paris, France	Kurt Halbach
2/17/76	**Koichi WAJIMA**	153	**Jae-Do YUH**	153	KO 15	1:47	Nihon University Auditorium, Tokyo	Jae-Duk Kim
‡ 2/28/76	**Elisha OBED**	154	**Tony GARDNER**	154	KO 2	2:55	Queen Elizabeth Centre, Nassau	Jay Edson
4/25/76	**Elisha OBED**	150	**Sea ROBINSON**	149½	split 15		Abidjan, Ivory Coast	Jay Edson
5/18/76	**Jose DURAN**	154	**Koichi WAJIMA**	154	KO 14	0:50	Nihon University Auditorium, Tokyo	Yusaku Yoshida
6/18/76	**Eckhard DAGGE**	154	**Elisha OBED**	154	TKO 10	1:47	Deutschlandhalle, Berlin, Germany	Jay Edson
‡ 9/18/76	**Eckhard DAGGE**	154	**Emile GRIFFITH**	151½	maj 15		Deutschlandhalle, Berlin, Germany	Angelo Poletti
10/8/76	**Miguel CASTELLINI**	153¼	**Jose DURAN**	153	split 15		Sports Palace, Madrid, Spain	Stan Christodoulou
3/5/77	**Eddie GAZO**	153	**Miguel CASTELLINI**	151	unan 15		National Baseball Stadium, Managua	Jay Edson
‡ 3/15/77	**Eckhard DAGGE**	153	**Maurice HOPE**	152	draw 15		Deutschlandhalle, Berlin, Germany	Dino Ambrosini
6/7/77	**Eddie GAZO**	152½	**Koichi WAJIMA**	154	TKO 11	0:45	Martial Arts Hall, Tokyo, Japan	Jay Edson
‡ 8/6/77	**Rocky MATTIOLI**	153⅞	**Eckhard DAGGE**	152	KO 5	2:20	Deutschlandhalle, Berlin, Germany	Richard Steele
9/13/77	**Eddie GAZO**	153¾	**Kenji SHIBATA**	153½	unan 15		Martial Arts Hall, Tokyo, Japan	Carlos Berrocal
12/18/77	**Eddie GAZO**	152½	**Chae-Keun LIM**	152½	split 15		Sunin Gymnasium, Inchon, Korea	Martin Denkin
‡ 3/11/78	**Rocky MATTIOLI**	151½	**Elisha OBED**	153	KO 7	1:07	Kooyong Tennis Stadium, Melbourne	Dick Young
‡ 5/14/78	**Rocky MATTIOLI**	152¾	**Jose DURAN**	153	KO 5	2:24	Adriatico Stadium, Pescara, Italy	Jean Deswert
8/9/78	**Masashi KUDO**	153¼	**Eddie GAZO**	152¼	split 15		City Gymnasium, Akita, Japan	Martin Denkin
12/13/78	**Masashi KUDO**	153½	**Ho-In JOO**	154	split 15		Prefectural Gymnasium, Osaka, Japan	Paul Field
‡ 3/4/79	**Maurice HOPE**	154	**Rocky MATTIOLI**	152	TKO 9	*	Sam Remo, Italy	Ray Solis
3/13/79	**Masashi KUDO**	154	**Manuel R. GONZALEZ**	153	maj 15		Korakuen Hall, Tokyo, Japan	Luis Sulbaran
6/20/79	**Masashi KUDO**	153¾	**Manuel R. GONZALEZ**	152	TKO 12	2:51	Yokkaichi City Gymnasium, Japan	Stan Christodoulou
‡ 9/25/79	**Maurice HOPE**	153½	**Mike BAKER**	152½	TKO 7	2:30	Wembley Pool, London, England	Ray Baldeyrou
10/24/79	**Ayub KALULE**	153¾	**Masashi KUDO**	154	unan 15		Prefectural Gymnasium, Akita, Japan	Robert Ferrara
12/6/79	**Ayub KALULE**	153	**Steve GREGORY**	152	unan 15		Brondbyhallen, Copenhagen, Denmark	Tony Perez
4/17/80	**Ayub KALULE**	153½	**Emiliano VILLA**	150¾	TKO 12	**	Brondbyhallen, Copenhagen, Denmark	Joe Santarpia
6/12/80	**Ayub KALULE**	153½	**Marijan BENES**	153	unan 15		Randers, Denmark	Max Strengfeld
‡ 7/12/80	**Maurice HOPE**	153	**Rocky MATTIOLI**	151¾	TKO 11	2:52	Wembley Conference Centre, London	Arthur Mercante
9/06/80	**Ayub KALULE**	153¼	**Bushy BESTER**	152½	unan 15		Aarhus Stadium, Aarhus, Denmark	David Pearl
‡11/25/80	**Maurice HOPE**	153½	**Carlos HERRERA**	151¾	unan 15		Wembley Conference Centre, London	Arthur Mercante

*Tony Montano was two pounds over the weight limit on October 3, 1964. *Loser failed to answer bell for round indicated. ref = referee's decision (sole arbiter)* ‡WBC world super welterweight title

JUNIOR MIDDLEWEIGHT DIVISION

DENNIS (DENNY) MOYER

Born, August 8, 1939, Portland, Oregon. Weight, 147-154 lbs. Height, 5 ft. 8½ in.
1957 National AAU Welterweight Champion

1957
Aug. 17—Jimmy McCoy, Portland .... W 4
Sept. 17—Buddy Ford, Portland .... W 8
Oct.. 8—John Medlock, Portland .... W 8
Oct. 22—Russell Davis, Portland .... W 8
Nov. 13—Doug Garrett, San Francisco ...... W 8
Nov. 26—Marvin Marcus, Portland .... KO 2
Dec. 17—Tommy Thomas, Portland .... W 8

1958
Jan. 16—Buddy McDonald, Portland .... W 10
Jan. 28—Jimmy McCoy, Portland .... W 8
Feb. 25—Howard Dixon, Portland .... KO 4
Apr. 9—Al Barbero, San Francisco .... KO 3
Apr. 22—Jim Hayes, Spokane .... W 8
July 1—Al Andrews, Portland .... W 10
Aug. 22—Chico Cerino, Anaconda .... KO 4
Sept. 17—Julian Valdez, Portland .... W 10
Oct. 2—Connie Citizen, Anchorage .... W 10
Oct. 21—Johnny Saxton, Portland .... W 10
Dec. 11—Tony Dupas, Portland .... W 10

1959
Jan. 2—Gaspar Ortega, New York .... W 10
Feb. 17—Vince Martinez, Portland .... W 10
July 10—Don Jordan, Portland .... L 15
(For World Welterweight Title)
Sept. 3—Paddy DeMarco, Portland .... KO 10
Dec. 10—Virgil Akins, Portland .... W 10

1960
Jan. 19—Pat Lowry, Seattle .... KO 3
Feb. 10—Tony DeMarco, Boston .... KO 2
Mar. 11—Emile Griffith, New York .... L 10
Apr. 26—Emile Griffith, New York .... W 10
Aug. 16—Benny Paret, New York .... W 10
Oct. 15—Jorge Fernandez, New York .... L 10

1961
Jan. 31—Willie Morton, San Jose .... W 10
Feb. 11—Charley Scott, New York .... W 10
Apr. 8—Jorge Fernandez, New York ...... L 10
May 19—Willie Jennings, Centralia .... KO 2
June 17—Dulio Nunez, New York .... L 10
Sept. 9—Dulio Nunez, Portland .... W 10
Oct. 21—Ray Robinson, New York .... L 10

1962
Feb. 17—Ray Robinson, New York .... W 10
June 9—Ted Wright, New York .... L 10
July 7—Ted Wright, New York .... W 10
Aug. 18—Emile Griffith, Tacoma .... L 10
Oct. 20—Joey Giambra, Portland .... W 15
(Won Vacant World Junior Middleweight Title)
Dec. 12—Gene Bryant, Billings .... W 10

1963
Jan. 5—Joey Archer, New York .... L 10
Feb. 19—Stan Harrington, Honolulu .... W 15
(Retained World Junior Middleweight Title)
Apr. 29—Ralph Dupas, New Orleans .... L 15
(Lost World Junior Middleweight Title)
June 17—Ralph Dupas, Baltimore .... L 15
(For World Junior Middleweight Title)
Aug. 19—Luis Rodriguez, Miami Beach KO by 9
Oct. 29—Memo Ayon, San Jose .... D 10
Dec. 3—Hurricane Kid, Honolulu .... W 10
Dec. 17—Stan Harrington, Honolulu .... L 10

1964
Apr. 13—Joe DeNucci, Boston .... L 10
Sept. 1—Manuel Gonzalez, Houston ...... L 10
Sept. 18—Nino Benvenuti, Rome .... L 10
Nov. 25—Memo Lopez, Boise .... W 10

1965
Jan. 5—Gene Bryant, Las Vegas .... L 10
Feb. 3—Rocky Montalvo, San Francisco .... W 10
Feb. 23—Fred Roots, Sacramento .... W 12
Mar. 21—Hilario Morales, Los Angeles .... W 10
Apr. 2—Jimmy Lester, San Francisco .... L 10
June 16—Ferd Hernandez, Las Vegas .... W 10

July 28—Jimmy Lester, San Francisco ...... W 10
Aug. 23—Ferd Hernandez, Las Vegas .... W 10
Oct. 14—Thell Torrence, Los Angeles .... D 10
Nov. 29—Johnny Brooks, Las Vegas .... W 12

1966
Jan. 3—Fred Little, Las Vegas .... KO by 4

1967
Dec. 9—Tony Montano, San Jose .... W 10

1968
Jan. 3—Danny Perez, Las Vegas .... KO 6
Jan. 31—Dub Huntley, Las Vegas .... W 10
Feb. 18—Rafael Gutierrez, Mexicali .... KO 4
Mar. 6—Eddie Coffey, Las Vegas .... KO 6
Apr. 8—Rafael Gutierrez, Tijuana .... D 10
Apr. 17—Gene Bryant, Las Vegas .... W 10
May 21—Lonnie Harris, San Diego .... W 10
July 22—Jesse Armentes, Tijuana .... KO 7
Aug. 10—Jesse Armentes, Hermosillo .... W 10
Oct. 4—Jorge Rosales, Laredo .... W 10
Oct. 30—Carl Moore, Las Vegas .... KO 9
Nov. 22—Bobby Harrington, St. Louis .... W 10
Dec. 17—Gene Bryant, Portland .... W 10

1969
Feb. 5—Frank Niblett, Las Vegas .... W 10
Feb. 20—Dave Reed, Portland .... KO 6
Mar. 27—Frank Niblett, Portland .... W 10
May 1—Fraser Scott, Seattle .... KO by 2
July 10—Rocky Hernandez, Las Vegas ...... W 10
Aug. 1—Jose Luis Rodriguez, San Diego ... KO 7
Sept. 9—Henry Walker, Woodland Hills ... KO 9
Sept. 18—Nat Macias, Portland .... KO 9
Oct. 17—Gerhard Piaskowy, Berlin .... W 10
Dec. 3—Art Alderete, Las Vegas .... KO 5

1970
Jan. 7—Dub Huntley, Las Vegas .... W 10
Jan. 28—Mike Pusateri, Las Vegas .... KO 2
Feb. 25—Eddie Pace, Las Vegas .... W 12
(Won Vacant NABF Middleweight Title)
Apr. 29—Nate Williams, Las Vegas ..... KO by 9
(Lost NABF Middleweight Title)
July 9—Fraser Scott, Seattle .... KO by 8
Aug. 11—Mike Seyler, Eugene .... KO 9
Sept. 30—Jesse Armentes, Las Vegas ...... KO 5
Nov. 4—Rafael Gutierrez, Las Vegas .... D 12
Dec. 16—Orlando de la Fuentes, Las Vegas .. W 10

1971
Jan. 1—Raul Soriano, San Luis .... W 10
Feb. 10—Art Hernandez, Las Vegas .... W 12
(Regained NABF Middleweight Title)
Mar. 5—Raul Soriano, Stateline .... W 12
Mar. 30—Jimmy Lester, Stateline .... W 12
(Retained NABF Middleweight Title)
Apr. 21—David Oropeza, Las Vegas .... KO 6
(Retained NABF Middleweight Title)
June 22—Jose Chirino, Stateline .... W 12
(Retained NABF Middleweight Title)
July 28—Mike Pusateri, Las Vegas .... KO 6
Sept. 7—Gene Bryant, Stateline .... W 10
Sept. 21—Eugene Hart, Philadelphia .... NC 6
Dec. 15—Aristeo Chavvarin, Las Vegas ..... W 10

1972
Feb. 15—Gene Bryant, Las Vegas .... W 12
(Retained NABF Middleweight Title)
Mar. 4—Carlos Monzon, Rome .... KO by 5
(For World Middleweight Title)
May 11—Carlos Salinas, Sacramento .... W 12
(Retained NABF Middleweight Title)
May 31—Tony Mundine, Melbourne .... KO by 7
July 5—Art Davis, Las Vegas .... W 10
July 26—Carlos Salinas, San Francisco .... W 12
(Retained NABF Middleweight Title)
Sept. 6—Art Hernandez, Des Moines ...... L 12
(Lost NABF Middleweight Title)
Dec. 13—Chu Chu Garcia, Las Vegas .... W 10

1973
Jan. 30—Nojim Maiyegun, Vienna .... L 10
Feb. 21—Walter Kelly, Las Vegas .... W 10
Mar. 7—George Davis, Las Vegas .... W 10

Mar.	23—Mario Marquez, Las Vegas	W	10
May	6—Manuel Fierro, Sonora	L	10
June	6—Pat O'Connor, Minneapolis	W	10
June	21—John L. Sullivan, Eugene	L	10
Aug.	24—Pat O'Connor, Rochester, Minn.....	W	10
Oct.	2—Tony Licata, New Orleans	L	10
Oct.	31—Mel Dennis, New Orleans	L	10
Dec.	14—Fighting Mack, Vienna	L	10

1974

Feb.	21—Eckhard Dagge, Berlin	L	10
Mar.	29—Renato Garcia, San Diego	L	10
Apr.	18—Jean Mateo, Portland	W	10
May	31—Battling Lavasa, Auckland	W	10
June	13—Mike Lancaster, Portland	KO	10
June	28—Vicente Medina, San Diego	W	10
Aug.	16—Rudy Cruz, Portland	W	10
Sept.	9—Vito Antuofermo, New York	L	10
Oct.	25—Vicente Medina, San Diego	W	10
Nov.	21—Paul Knudsen, Copenhagen	L	8
Dec.	12—Rocky DeFazio, Chicago	KO	10

1975

Feb.	3—Rafael Rodriguez, Minneapolis	L	10
Mar.	18—Franz Csandl, Vienna	L	10

TB	KO	WD	WF	D	LD	LF	KO BY	ND	NC
140	25	73	0	4	30	0	7	0	1

RALPH DUPAS

Born, October 14, 1935, New Orleans, La. Weight, 135-154 lbs. Height, 5 ft. 8½ in.

1950

Aug.	7—Jitterbug Smith, New Orleans	D	4
Aug.	16—Lawton Dioso, New Orleans	W	4
Aug.	28—Henry Loera, New Orleans	KO	4
Sept.	14—Ray Miranda, Tampa	KO	3
Oct.	3—Billy Hogan, Tampa	W	6
Oct.	11—Reuben Salazar, Galveston	W	4
Oct.	23—Lawton Disoso, New Orleans	W	6
Oct.	30—Kid Centella, New Orleans	KO by	2
Nov.	6—Val Lambert, New Orleans	W	4

1951

Feb.	26—John Capitano, New Orleans	D	4
Mar.	14—Johnny Longo, New Orleans	KO	2
Apr.	2—John Capitano, New Orleans	D	4
Apr.	24—Alex Vargas, Houston	W	8
June	4—Raoul Reyna, New Orleans	KO	2
June	18—Tommy Baker, New Orleans	W	6
June	25—Herb Fairris, New Orleans	KO	3
July	—George Easterling, New Orleans ..	KO	4
July	16—Bobby Brooks, New Orleans	W	6
Aug.	13—Alex Fimbres, New Orleans	W	8
Aug.	27—Pat Iacobucci, New Orleans	W	8
Sept.	10—Noel Humphries, New Orleans	W	8
Sept.	17—Freddie Monforte, New Orleans	L	8
Oct.	22—Noel Humphreys, New Orleans	W	8
Nov.	12—Fred Monforte, New Orleans	W	8

1952

Jan.	21—Johnny Capitano, New Orleans	W	6
Feb.	4—Bill Neri, New Orleans	W	6
Mar.	17—Kid Centella, New Orleans	W	6
Apr.	21—Juan Padilla, New Orleans	W	6
July	2—Sonny Luciano, Miami Beach	W	10
July	15—Diego Sosa, Miami Beach	W	10
July	29—Larry Mujica, Miami Beach	W	10
Aug.	12—Johnny Craven, Miami Beach	W	10
Aug.	26—Jose Vasquez, Miami Beach	L	10
Sept.	8—Larry Mujica, New Orleans	W	6
Oct.	14—Nelson Levering, New Orleans ...	KO	1
Nov.	17—Alfredo LaGrutta, New Orleans	W	8
Nov.	24—Jose (Baby) Vasquez, New Orleans	W	8
Dec.	8—Alfredo LaGrutta, New Orleans	W	8
Dec.	30—Jesse Underwood, Miami Beach	W	10

1953

Jan.	26—Basil Marie, New Orleans	W	8
Mar.	2—Baby Vasquez, Miami Beach	W	10
...	6—Voldo Fusaro, New Orleans	W	8
Apr.	20—Richie Howard, New Orleans	W	8
June	1—Tote Martinez, New Orleans	KO	6

June	15—Harold Jones, New Orleans	W	8
June	29—Armand Savoi, New Orleans	W	8
July	21—Brian Kelly, Miami Beach	L	8
Aug.	24—Brian Kelly, New Orleans	W	8
Sept.	14—Rocky Brisebois, New Orleans	W	8
Sept.	21—Johnny Gonsalves, New Orleans ...	W	8
Nov.	9—Phil Kim, New Orleans	D	8

1954

Jan.	2—Paddy DeMarco, New Orleans	L	10
Mar.	22—Santiago Esteban, New Orleans ...	W	10
Apr.	28—Dennis Pat Brady, New Orleans ...	W	10
May	24—Freddy Herman, New Orleans ...	W	10
July	20—Armand Savoi, New Orleans	W	10
Aug.	3—Bobby Woods, New Orleans	W	10
Sept.	13—Frankie Ryff, Brooklyn	L	8
Nov.	1—Carlos Chavez, New Orleans ...	KO	7

1955

Jan.	1—Cisco Andrade, New Orleans	W	10
Feb.	8—Richie Howard, New Orleans	W	10
Mar.	14—Kenny Lane, New Orleans	W	10
Mar.	28—Bobby Bickle, New Orleans	W	10
May	17—Frankie Ryff, New Orleans	W	10
July	11—Paddy DeMarco, New Orleans	W	10
Sept.	1—Leonard Gaines, Oakland	D	10
Sept.	17—Mickey Northrup, Hollywood	W	10
Dec.	16—Ludwig Lightburn, New York	L	10

1956

Feb.	20—Hoacine Khalfi, New Orleans	W	10
May	1—Johnny Digilio, Miami Beach	W	10
July	9—Kenny Lane, New Orleans	L	10
Sept.	10—Al Vargas, New Orleans	KO	5
Sept.	24—Hoacine Khalfi, New Orleans	KO	8
Nov.	26—Siegfried Burrow, New Orleans	W	10

1957

Feb.	11—Pat Mallane, New Orleans	KO	5
Mar.	4—Ray Portilla, New Orleans	W	10
Apr.	8—Vince Martinez, New Orleans	W	10
May	31—Seraphin Ferrer, Paris	D	10
Aug.	30—Johnny Busso, Miami Beach	W	10
Sept.	18—Joe Miceli, New Orleans	W	10
Nov.	25—Mickey Crawford, New Orleans	W	10

1958

Feb.	5—Gasper Ortega, Norfolk	W	10
Apr.	7—Ramon Fuentes, New Orleans	W	10
May	7—Joe Brown, Houston	KO by	8
	(For World Lightweight Title)		
Sept.	8—Johnny Gorman, New Orleans	W	10
Sept.	29—Ray Lancaster, New Orleans	W	10
Oct.	15—Gil Turner, Montreal	W	10
Nov.	10—Guy Sumlin, Mobile	W	10
Dec.	26—Sugar Hart, Miami Beach	L	10

1959

Feb.	4—Del Flanagan, St. Paul	L	10
Mar.	14—Gerald Gray, Kingston	W	10
May	13—Charley Scott, Chicago	L	10
July	20—Frankie Ryff, New Orleans	W	10
Aug.	24—Mel Barker, New Orleans	W	12
Oct.	7—Rudell Stitch, Louisville	L	10
Nov.	16—Pat Lowry, New Orleans	KO	6

1960

Jan.	13—Kenny Lane, Mobile	W	10
Mar.	23—Florentino Fernandez, Miami Beach	L	10
Apr.	11—George Barnes, Sydney	W	12
May	2—Rudell Stitch, Sydney	W	10
June	27—Eddie Jordan, New Orleans	W	10
Aug.	2—Charley Scott, Sydney	W	12
Sept.	5—Charley Scott, Sydney	W	12
Nov.	2—Gale Kerwin, New Orleans	KO	7

1961

Jan.	16—Antonio Marcilla, New Orleans	W disq.	9
Mar.	6—Joey Giardello, New Orleans	W	10
Apr.	7—Guy Sumlin, Mobile	L	10
June	2—Guy Sumlin, New Orleans	W	12
July	24—Guy Sumlin, Mobile	W	12
Oct.	9—Del Flanagan, New Orleans	W	10
Nov.	13—Hilario Morales, New Orleans	W	10
Dec.	27—Virgil Akins, Miami Beach	W	10

1962

Feb.	5—Charley Scott, New York	W	10
Apr.	23—Frank Ramirez, Los Angeles	W	10

July 13—Emile Griffith, Las Vegas .... L 15
    (For World Welterweight Title)
Aug. 21—Henry Watson, Beaumont .... W 10
Sept. 11—Brian Curvis, London .... LF 6
Oct. 2—Earl Citizen, Beaumont .... KO 4
Dec. 4—Henry Watson, Amarillo .... W 10

1963

Jan. 14—Rocky Randall, Harvey .... KO 6
Jan. 30—Ray Robinson, Miami Beach .... L 10
Apr. 29—Denny Moyer, New Orleans .... W 15
    (Won World Junior Middleweight Title)
June 17—Denny Moyer, Baltimore .... W 15
    (Retained World Junior Middleweight Title)
Sept. 7—Sandro Mazzinghi, Milan ...... KO by 9
    (Lost World Junior Middleweight Title)
Oct. 18—Gary Cowburn, Brisbane .... W 12
Dec. 2—Sandro Mazzinghi, Sydney .... KO by 13
    (For World Junior Middleweight Title)

1964

Feb. 10—Emile Griffith, Sydney .... KO by 3
June 18—Peter Schmidt, New Orleans ...... W 10
Sept. 12—Willie Ludwick, Johannesburg KO by 2
Sept. 18—Announced retirement.

1965

(Inactive)

1966

May 27—Steven Perez, Las Vegas .... KO 6
July 7—Eddie McGruden, Las Vegas .... W 10
Aug. 4—Joey Limas, Las Vegas .... KO 5
Sept. 7—Joe Clark, Las Vegas .... KO by 10

TB	KO	WD	WF	D	LD	LF	KO BY	ND	NC
134	19	85	1	6	15	1	7	0	0

SANDRO MAZZINGHI

Born, October 3, 1938, Pontedera, Italy. Weight, 154 lbs. Height, 5 ft. 8¼ in.

1961

Sept. 15—Severino Gagliardi, Florence ..... KO 2
Oct. 20—Mario Della Corte, Florence .... W 6
Nov. 9—Renato Ravasi, Rome .... KO 3
Dec. 15—Germano Cavalieri, Florence ..... KO 2
Dec. 26—Francesco Pondrelli, Bologna ..... KO 2

1962

Jan. 4—Guglielmo Paulon, Bologna ...... KO 3
Jan. 19—Claudio Buniva, Rome .... W 6
Feb. 5—Ben Hamida, Bologna .... KO 3
Feb. 16—Nick Maric, Milan .... W 6
Feb. 23—Gerhard Moll, Florence .... KO 5
Mar. 23—Mohamed Seba, Florence .... KO 5
Apr. 2—Teddy Schall, Bologna .... KO 4
June 6—Claude Canu, Prato .... KO 4
June 20—Jackie Cailleau, Florence .... W 8
June 30—Paolo Cottino, St. Vincent .... KO 3
July 18—Charley Kassem, Florence .... KO 1
July 27—Giampaolo Melis, Rome .... L 8
Aug. 19—Fabio Bettini, San Remo .... W 8
Sept. 24—Daniel Leullier, Bologna .... W 8
Oct. 15—Charley Attali, Paris .... KO 7
Nov. 9—Fabio Bettini, Milan .... W 8
Dec. 14—Francesco Fiori, Rome .... W 8

1963

Jan. 28—Hyppolite Annex, Paris .... KO 9
Mar. 1—Joseph N'Gan, Florence .... KO 4
Mar. 8—Rocky Randall, Milan .... KO 1
Apr. 5—Tony Montano, Rome .... W 10
May 5—Don Fullmer, Milan .... KO 5
June 7—Wilfie Greaves, Milan .... KO 5
July 13—Mohamed Sahib, Pontedera ...... KO 8
Sept. 7—Ralph Dupas, Milan .... KO 9
    (Won World Junior Middleweight Title)
Dec. 2—Ralph Dupas, Sydney .... KO 13
    (Retained World Junior Middleweight Title)

1964

Apr. 12—Hilario Morales, Milan .... KO 3
Apr. 24—Charley Austin, Rome .... KO 9
June 26—Charley Austin, Turin .... W disq. 7
Aug. 14—Cecil Mott, Terracina .... KO 5
Oct. 3—Tony Montano, Genoa .... KO 12
    (Retained World Junior Middleweight Title)

Nov. 6—Gaspar Ortega, Rome .... KO 7
Dec. 11—Fortunato Manca, Rome .... W 15
    (Retained World Junior Middleweight Title)

1965

Jan. 23—Isaac Logart, Milan .... KO 5
Apr. 2—Isaac Logart, Rome .... W 10
Apr. 30—Mel Ferguson, Genoa .... KO 3
June 18—Nino Benvenuti, Milan .... KO by 6
    (Lost World Junior Middleweight Title)
Oct. 15—Oscar Miranda, Turin .... KO 5
Dec. 17—Nino Benvenuti, Rome .... L 15
    (For World Junior Middleweight Title)

1966

Feb. 11—James Shelton, Bologna .... KO 5
Apr. 1—Sugar Cliff, Rome .... KO 4
May 6—Herman Dixon, Turin .... KO 2
June 17—Yoland Leveque, Rome .... KO 12
    (Won European Junior Middleweight Title)
Oct. 14—Tony Noriega, Teramo .... W 10
Nov. 11—Bo Hoberg, Stockholm .... KO 14
    (Retained European Junior Middleweight Title)

1967

Feb. 3—Jean Baptiste Roland, Milan ..... KO 10
    (Retained European Junior Middleweight Title)
Apr. 7—Henry Aldridge, Rome .... W 10
July 14—Gomeo Brennan, Rome .... W 10
Sept. 9—Wally Swift, Milan .... KO 6
    (Retained European Junior Middleweight Title)
Dec. 1—Jo Gonzales, Rome .... KO 4
    (Retained European Junior Middleweight Title)

1968

Feb. 9—Art Hernandez, Rome .... KO 4
Apr. 5—Bobby Cassidy, Rome .... KO 2
May 25—Ki-Soo Kim, Milan .... W 15
    (Regained World Junior Middleweight Title)
Sept. 14—Levi Campbell, Florence .... W 10
Oct. 25—Fred Little, Rome .... NC 8
    (Retained World Junior Middleweight Title)

1969

—Stripped of world junior middleweight title.
Mar. 28—Wilfredo Hurst, Rome .... NC 8
Dec. 18—Cipriano Hernandez, Las Vegas .. KO 2

1970

Apr. 18—Harry Scott, Bologna .... W 10
July 2—Harold Richardson, Milan .... KO 5
Sept. 10—Eddie Pace, Milan .... W 10
Oct. 31—Willie Warren, Bologna .... KO 9

1971-1976

(Inactive)

1977

Nov. 3—Dave Adkins, Castellanza .... W 10
Dec. 26—Gianni Mingardi, Florence .... W 8

1978

Mar. 4—Jean Claude Warusfel, Florence ... W 10

TB	KO	WD	WF	D	LD	LF	KO BY	ND	NC
69	42	21	1	0	2	0	1	0	2

NINO BENVENUTI

(Record Under Middleweight Champions)

KI-SOO KIM

Born, September 17, 1939, Buk-Chong, Hamkyongnamdo, Korea. Weight, 154 lbs.
Competed as welterweight in 1960 Olympic Games

1961

Aug. —Ansano Lee .... KO
    —Se-Chul Kang .... W 1
    (Won Korean Middleweight Title)
    —Se-Chul Kang .... KO
    (Retained Korean Middleweight Title)

1962

July 1—Makoto Watanabe, Tokyo ...... KO
    —Sakuji Shinozawa, Tokyo .... D

1963

May 18—Roberto Beniya, Seoul .... KO
May 24—Kyu-Soon Kang, Pusan .... W
July 2—Kyu-Soon Kang, Yeo-Soo .... W

1964

Jan.	22—George Carter, Tokyo	KO	6
Sept.	8—Kyu-Soon Kang, Seoul	KO	8
Oct.	10—Deuk-Bong Kim, Seoul	D	10
Nov.	21—Yoshiaki Akasaka, Seoul	KO	7
Dec.	22—Noboru Saito, Tokyo	KO	6

1965

Jan.	10—Fumio Kaizu, Tokyo	KO	6
	(Won Oriental Middleweight Title)		
Mar.	6—Katsuo Hujiyama, Seoul	KO	4
Mar.	28—Jung-Il Ham, Pusan	KO	4
Apr.	17—Masao Gondo, Seoul	W	10
June	19—Fumio Kaizu, Seoul	W	12
	(Retained Oriental Middleweight Title)		
Sept.	20—Masao Gondo, Tokyo	W	10
Oct.	30—Sakuji Shinozawa, Seoul	KO	7

1966

Jan.	4—Fumio Kaizu, Seoul	KO	7
	(Retained Oriental Middleweight Title)		
Jan.	23—Ben Argoncilo, Seoul	KO	9
Apr.	30—Hideaki Takada, Seoul	KO	10
	(Retained Oriental Middleweight Title)		
June	25—Nino Benvenuti, Seoul	W	15
	(Won World Junior Middleweight Title)		
Oct.	2—Sung-Kap Choi, Seoul	Exh.	4
Nov.	5—Yatsuo Sato, Seoul	KO	4
Dec.	17—Stan Harrington, Seoul	W	15
	(Retained World Junior Middleweight Title)		

1967

Mar.	25—George Carter, Seoul	KO	5
Sept.	7—Nakao Sasazaki, Tokyo	KO	6
	(Retained Oriental Middleweight Title)		
Oct.	3—Fred Little, Seoul	W	15
	(Retained World Junior Middleweight Title)		
Nov.	8—Apidej Sithiran, Bangkok	W	10

1968

Feb.	17—Manfredo Alipala, Seoul	W	12
	(Retained Oriental Middleweight Title)		
Mar.	11—Yoshiaki Akasaka, Tokyo	W	10
Apr.	4—Benkei Fujikura, Tokyo	W	10
May	25—Sandro Mazzinghi, Milan	L	15
	(Lost World Junior Middleweight Title)		
Nov.	20—Hisao Minami, Osaka	L	12
	(Lost Oriental Middleweight Title)		

1969

Mar.	1—Hisao Minami, Seoul	W	12
	(Regained Oriental Middleweight Title)		
Aug.	5—Announced retirement.		

TB	KO	WD	WF	D	LD	LF	KO BY	ND	NC
36	18	14	0	2	2	0	0	0	0

FRED LITTLE

Born, April 25, 1936, Picayune, Mississippi. Weight, 154 lbs. Managed by Whitey Esneault and James A. Stevenson.

1957

Apr.	5—Cal Campbell, New Orleans	KO	1
Apr.	22—Johnny Powell, New Orleans	KO	4
Apr.	25—James Glover, Mobile	KO	2
May	20—Earl Gray, New Orleans	W	6
June	3—Pero Bradley, New Orleans	KO	5
Aug.	31—Harold Redman, Bogalusa, La.	W	8
Dec.	2—George King, New Orleans	KO	1

1958

May	7—Al McCoy, Houston, Texas	KO	3
May	20—John Victor Penn, New Orleans	KO	3
May	29—Larry Osbey, Bogalusa, La.	KO	1
June	30—Ike Stewart, New Orleans	KO	4
July	7—Norris Burse, New Orleans	KO by	5
Aug.	4—Joey Gleason, New Orleans	KO	4
Oct.	10—Harold Redman, Franklinton	KO	2

1959

Jan.	13—George Price, Houston	KO	2
May	12—Norris Burse, Houston	KO	8
June	29—Billy Tisdale, New Orleans	W	10
Sept.	14—Ernie Burford, Bogalusa	W	10

1960

Apr.	5—Gene Hamilton, Bogalusa	KO	4
May	17—Mel Collins, Bogalusa	KO	6
June	6—Charlie Cotton, New Orleans	W	10
Aug.	15—Clive Stewart, Sydney	KO	4
Sept.	12—Billy Stanley, Sydney	KO	2
Oct.	18—George Benton, New Orleans	L	10

1961

Jan.	1—Charley Joseph, New Orleans	W	10
May	6—Larry Howard, Louisville	KO	1

1962
(Inactive)

1963

May	6—Tommy Sims, Bogalusa	KO	7

1964
(Inactive)

1965

June	1—Johnny Smith, Las Vegas	KO	3
Aug.	16—Milo Calhoun, Las Vegas	W	10
Sept.	13—Sonny Gill, Las Vegas	KO	2
Oct.	18—Charley Austin, Las Vegas	KO	7

1966

Jan.	3—Denny Moyer, Las Vegas	KO	4
Feb.	1—Eddie Pace, Las Vegas	L	12
Apr.	12—Ernie Burford, Las Vegas	KO	8
June	13—Eddie Pace, Las Vegas	W	10
Sept.	26—Johnny Gumbs, Las Vegas	W	10

1967

Feb.	16—Willard Wynn, Las Vegas	KO	8
Mar.	16—Fred McWilliams, Las Vegas	W	10
Apr.	10—Charley James, Las Vegas	W	10
July	17—Harold Richardson, New Orleans	W	10
Oct.	3—Ki-Soo Kim, Seoul, Korea	L	15
	(For World Junior Middleweight Title)		

1968

Jan.	17—Mel Collins, Las Vegas	W	10
June	19—Willard Wynn, Oakland	KO	3
Oct.	25—Sandro Mazzinghi, Rome	NC	8
	(For World Junior Middleweight Title)		
Nov.	30—Sugar Boy Nando, Rome	KO	4

1969

Mar.	17—Stan Hayward, Las Vegas	W	15
	(Won Vacant World Junior Middleweight Title)		
July	26—Joe Mzinyane, Johannesburg	W	10
Aug.	9—Joe N'Gidi, Benoni	KO	7
Sept.	9—Hisao Minami, Osaka	KO	2
	(Retained World Junior Middleweight Title)		
Oct.	31—Carmelo Bossi, Rome	KO	3

1970

Jan.	23—Eddie Pace, Rome	L disq.	8
Mar.	20—Gerhard Piaskowy	W	15
	(Retained World Junior Middleweight Title)		
July	9—Carmelo Bossi, Monza	L	15
	(Lost World Junior Middleweight Title)		
Nov.	25—Clarence Geigger, Las Vegas	W	10

1971

Dec.	23—Maurice Rice, Stateline	KO	5

1972

Apr.	13—Clarence Geigger, Stateline	W	10
July	6—Billy Walker, Stateline	KO	7

TB	KO	WD	WF	D	LD	LF	KO BY	ND	NC
57	32	18	0	0	4	1	1	0	1

CARMELO BOSSI

Born, October 15, 1939, Milan, Italy. Weight, 147-154 lbs.
1960 Olympic Light Middleweight Silver Medalist

1961

Mar.	4—Isidoro Princi, Milan	W disq.	3
Mar.	18—Henri Marchandau, Milan	W	6
Mar.	31—Dante Madella, Ancona	W*	6
May	21—Germano Cavalieri, Treviso	W	6

1962

May	4—Marcello Verziera, Rome	W	6
July	27—Carlo Sala, Rome	KO	9

1963

Apr.	19—Bruno Pomaro, Pavia	KO	4
May	24—Michel Francois, Milan	W	6
Sept.	13—Johnny Angelo, Rome	KO by	5
Nov.	4—Vicente Moktar, Ferrara	W	8
Nov.	22—Mirko Rossi, Milan	KO	6
Dec.	5—Jaconas Amorin, Milan	W	8
Dec.	26—Albert Alsinet, Milan	KO	2

1964

Feb.	7—Vicente Ferrando, Milan	W	8
Feb.	28—Sani Armstrong, Milan	W	8
Apr.	30—Julio Rocha, Milan	W	8
Nov.	4—Vicente Moktar, Ferrara	W	8
Nov.	12—Giuliano Nervino, Milan	W	8
Nov.	26—Fred Galiana, Barcelona	KO	10

1965

Feb.	4—Francisco Navarro Moreno, Barcelona	W	8
Feb.	26—Luciano Piazza, Milan	W	8
June	18—Alfredo Parmeggiani, Milan	W	10
Oct.	5—Domenico Tiberia, Naples	W	12
	(Won Italian Welterweight Title)		

1966

Mar.	11—Mario Landolfi, Rome	KO	8
Apr.	21—Angel Robinson Garcia, Barcelona	D	10
Aug.	18—James Shelton, San Remo	W	8
Sept.	14—Eduardo Batista, Arezzo	KO	5
Nov.	24—Teddy Meho, Barcelona	D	8

1967

Jan.	8—Domenico Tiberia, Aprilla	W	12
	(Retained Italian Welterweight Title)		
Feb.	24—Assane Fakyh, Turin	W	8
May	17—Jean Josselin, San Remo	W	15
	(Won European Welterweight Title)		
July	14—Angel Robinson Garcia, Rome	KO	5
Aug.	16—Johnny Cooke, San Remo	KO	12
	(Retained European Welterweight Title)		
Oct.	7—Willie Ludick, Johannesburg	L	15
Nov.	25—Willie Ludick, Johannesburg	L	15

1968

Jan.	27—Lennox Beckles, Milan	W	10
May	3—Jean Josselin, Rome	W	15
	(Retained European Welterweight Title)		
May	26—Abderamane Faradji, Milan	W	8
Aug.	14—Edwin (Fighting) Mack, Lignano	KO by	10
	(Lost European Welterweight Title)		

1969

Apr.	3—Klaus Klein, Milan	W	8
May	9—Fernand Ahumibe, Milan	W	8
June	20—Edwin (Fighting) Mack, Milan	W	10
July	11—John Tiger, Milan	W	8
Oct.	31—Fred Little, Rome	KO by	3

1970

Mar.	6—Guy Vercoutter, Milan	W	10
Apr.	9—Johann Orsolics, Vienna	L	15
	(For European Welterweight Title)		
July	9—Fred Little, Monza	W	15
	(Won World Junior Middleweight Title)		
Oct.	14—Aldo Battistutta, Udine	KO	5
Nov.	14—Pierre Fourie, Johannesburg	L	10

1971

Apr.	29—Jose Hernandez, Madrid	D	15
	(Retained World Junior Middleweight Title)		
Oct.	31—Koichi Wajima, Tokyo	L	15
	(Lost World Junior Middleweight Title)		

TB	KO	WD	WF	D	LD	LF	KO BY	ND	NC
51	10	29	1	3	5	0	3	0	0

KOICHI WAJIMA

Born, April 21, 1943, Nishisanjo, Tsuchida City, Hokkaido, Japan. Weight, 154 lbs. Height, 5 ft. 7¾ in. Managed by Hitoshi Misako.

1968

June	15—Akira Takegawa, Tokyo	KO	1
June	30—Koji Watanabe, Tokyo	KO	2
Aug.	8—Toshiaki Kaneko, Tokyo	KO	3
Aug.	31—Chuichi Sakai, Tokyo	KO	2
Oct.	6—Takao Higa, Tokyo	KO	3

| Oct. | 27—Sozo Yamamoto, Tokyo | KO | 1 |
| Dec. | 30—Masami Takechi, Tokyo | KO | 4 |

1969

Feb.	3—Masaki Nomoto, Tokyo	W	6
Mar.	27—Takemi Kato, Tokyo	KO	6
June	16—Hideo Kusanagi, Tokyo	KO	9
July	30—Rocky Alarde, Tokyo	KO	8
Sept.	4—Noriyasu Yoshimura, Nagoya	KO	4
	(Won Japanese Junior Middleweight Title)		
Oct.	30—Pedro Adigue, Tokyo	KO by	1
Dec.	18—Turtle Okabe, Tokyo	KO	7
	(Retained Japanese Junior Middleweight Title)		

1970

Feb.	2—George Carter, Tokyo	L	10
	(Lost Japanese Junior Middleweight Title)		
Apr.	9—George Carter, Tokyo	W	10
	(Regained Japanese Junior Middleweight Title)		
May	23—Ken Sato, Sapporo	KO	3
Aug.	8—Muneo Mizoguchi, Tokyo	KO	8
	(Retained Japanese Junior Middleweight Title)		
Sept.	10—Tetsuo Hoshino, Tokyo	KO	5
	(Retained Japanese Junior Middleweight Title)		
Oct.	30—Raizo Kajima, Tokyo	KO	3
	(Retained Japanese Junior Middleweight Title)		

1971

Jan.	8—Hisao Minami, Tokyo	KO	7
	(Retained Japanese Junior Middleweight Title)		
Feb.	18—Hideo Kanazawa, Osaka	KO	2
Mar.	26—Al Fuentes, Tokyo	KO	1
May	28—Tetsuo Hoshino, Tokyo	KO	2
	(Retained Japanese Junior Middleweight Title)		
Oct.	31—Carmelo Bossi, Tokyo	W	15
	(Won World Junior Middleweight Title)		

1972

Feb.	2—Cassius Naito, Tokyo	KO	7
May	7—Domenico Tiberia, Fukuoka City	KO	1
	(Retained World Junior Middleweight Title)		
Oct.	3—Matt Donovan, Tokyo	KO	3
	(Retained World Junior Middleweight Title)		

1973

Jan.	9—Miguel de Oliveira, Tokyo	D	15
	(Retained World Junior Middleweight Title)		
Apr.	20—Ryu Sorimachi, Osaka	W	15
	(Retained World Junior Middleweight Title)		
Aug.	14—Silvano Bertini, Sapporo	KO	13
	(Retained World Junior Middleweight Title)		

1974

Feb.	5—Miguel de Oliveira, Tokyo	W	15
	(Retained World Junior Middleweight Title)		
June	3—Oscar Alvarado, Tokyo	KO by	15
	(Lost World Junior Middleweight Title)		

1975

Jan.	21—Oscar Alvarado, Tokyo	W	15
	(Regained World Junior Middleweight Title)		
June	7—Jae-Do Yuh, Kokura	KO by	7
	(Lost World Junior Middleweight Title)		

1976

Feb.	17—Jae-Do Yuh, Tokyo	KO	15
	(Regained World Junior Middleweight Title)		
May	18—Jose Duran, Tokyo	KO by	14
	(Lost World Junior Middleweight Title)		

1977

| June | 7—Eddie Gazo, Tokyo | KO by | 11 |
| | (For World Junior Middleweight Title) | | |

TB	KO	WD	WF	D	LD	LF	KO BY	ND	NC
38	25	6	0	1	1	0	5	0	0

OSCAR ALBARADO

Born, September 15, 1948, Pecos, Texas. Weight, 154 lbs. Height, 5 ft. 7½ in.

1966

| Apr. | 12—Genaro Morones, San Antonio | KO | 4 |

1967

Mar.	11—Ramiro Hernandez, Rosita	KO	3
Apr.	—Jesse Lara, Rosita	KO	3
May	30—Freddie Burris, Corpus Christi	KO	2
July	16—Gary Pannell, Baton Rouge	KO	2
Aug.	8—Nat Jackson, New Orleans	W	6

Sept. 2—Piri Albarado, Rosita .... KO 6
Sept. 30—Lechero Gonzales, Rosita .... KO 1
Oct. 28—Chuy Andrade, Rosita .... KO 1
Nov. 14—Billy Strother, San Antonio ...... W 6
Dec. 12—Hector Ramirez, San Antonio ..... KO 2
1968
Jan. —Ruben Rivera, Piedras Negras .... KO 2
Feb. —Allen Moten, Piedras Negras ..... KO 1
Mar. 19—Gilbert Gutierrez, San Antonio .... W 8
Apr. 2—Gilbert Gutierrez, San Antonio ... KO 1
May 3—Gilbert de los Santos, San Antonio KO 6
July 17—Gilbert Gutierrez, Corpus Christi KO 3
Sept. 10—Cassius Greene, San Antonio ..... KO 1
Sept. 30—Lonnie Harris, San Antonio ...... KO 1
Oct. 29—Jerry Graci, San Antonio .... KO 9
1969
Jan. 9—Johnny Doyan, Los Angeles ...... KO 2
Jan. 23—Miguel Hernandez, Los Angeles ... W 10
Feb. 6—Jose Valenzuela, Los Angeles .... KO 6
Mar. 6—Miguel Aguilar, Los Angeles ..... KO 3
Apr. 10—Hedgemon Lewis, Los Angeles ..... L 10
June 3—Johnny Brooks, San Antonio ..... KO 7
Aug. 14—Thurman Durden, Los Angeles .... W 10
Oct. 7—L.C. Morgan, San Antonio .... W disq. 5
Oct. 28—L.C. Morgan, San Antonio ...... KO 5
Dec. 9—Robert Williams, San Antonio .... KO 7
1970
Jan. 27—Adolph Pruitt, Honolulu .... L 10
Mar. 30—Percy Pugh, New Orleans .... L 10
Apr. 14—Charlie Green, Corpus Christi .... KO 3
May 5—Roberto Amaya, Honolulu .... KO 9
June 2—Pedro Adigue, Honolulu .... W 10
Oct. 7—Larry Brasier, San Antonio ...... KO 3
Nov. 24—Raul Soriano, San Antonio .... W 10
1971
Mar. 30—Manuel Fierro, Honolulu .... L 10
Apr. 17—Frankie Lewis, San Antonio ...... W 10
May 6—Armando Muniz, Los Angeles ..... D 10
July 22—Freddie Jones, Los Angeles ...... KO 1
Aug. 7—Bobby Williams, Los Angeles ..... W 10
Oct. 4—Matt Roa, Los Angeles .... KO 4
Oct. 29—Ernie Lopez, Los Angeles .... L 10
1972
June 6—James Shelton, San Antonio ...... KO 3
July 11—Demetrio Salazar, San Antonio ... KO 4
Aug. 3—Ruben Arocha, Los Angeles ...... KO 9
Nov. 17—Ray Reyes, Los Angeles .... KO 1
1973
Jan. 4—Thurman Durden, Los Angeles .... W 10
Feb. 15—Rodolfo Martinez, Los Angeles .... KO 3
Mar. 29—Alex Olguin, Los Angeles .... KO 4
May 17—Dino Del Cid, Los Angeles .... KO by 1
June 28—Dino Del Cid, Los Angeles .... KO 2
Nov. 1—Eddie Mazon, Los Angeles .... W 10
1974
Apr. 26—Eddie Mazon, San Diego .... W 10
June 4—Koichi Wajima, Tokyo .... KO 15
(Won World Junior Middleweight Title)
Oct. 8—Ryu Sorimachi, Tokyo .... KO 7
(Retained World Junior Middleweight Title)
1975
Jan. 21—Koichi Wajima, Tokyo .... L 15
(Lost World Junior Middleweight Title)
1976-1979
(Inactive)
1980
Sept. 1—Jesse Lara, Laredo .... KO 6
Oct. 14—German Marquez, Laredo .... KO 2

TB	KO	WD	WF	D	LD	LF	KO BY	ND	NC
60	39	12	1	1	6	0	1	0	0

MIGUEL DE OLIVEIRA
Born, September 30, 1947, Sao Paulo, Brazil.
Weight, 154-160 lbs.
1968
June 16—Alvacir Doria, Sao Paulo .... W 4
Aug. 9—Oscar Michel, Sao Paulo .... KO 2
Sept. 5—Euclides Queiros, Sao Paulo ...... W 6

Oct. 30—Altecir Pereira, Sao Paulo .... KO 5
Dec. 3—Antonio Ferreira, Sao Paulo ...... KO 2
1969
Jan. 16—Victor Timoteo, Sao Paulo .... KO 2
Mar. 21—Adalberto Nascimento, Sao Paulo .. W 8
May 22—Alvacir Dora, Sao Paulo .... W 8
June 21—Martinez Larroys, Sao Paulo ..... KO 7
Dec. 11—Adalberto Nascimento, Sao Paulo KO 3
1970
Mar. 19—Alvacir Doria, Sao Paulo .... KO 7
May 29—Joe Inacio, Sao Paulo .... KO 2
June 3—Leonardo Peralta, Sao Paulo ..... KO 7
July 24—Armando Marchisio, Sao Paulo ... KO 6
Oct. 9—Robert Williams, Sao Paulo ...... KO 3
Dec. 9—Walter Kelly, Sao Paulo .... W 10
1971
Jan. 8—Walter Kelly, Sao Paulo .... W 10
Mar. 8—Antenor Santillan, Sao Paulo .... KO 8
June 4—Matt Donovan, Sao Paulo .... W 10
Aug. 6—Harold Richardson, Sao Paulo ... KO 2
Oct. 3—Roy Dale, Sao Paulo .... W 10
Nov. 26—Jorge Rosales, Sao Paulo .... W 10
1972
Jan. 22—Julio Calvetti, Sao Paulo .... KO 3
Mar. 17—Luis Vinales, Sao Paulo .... W 10
May 5—Eduardo Batista, Sao Paulo ...... KO 2
July 7—Francois Pano, Sao Paulo .... KO 7
Aug. 14—Roberto Carabajal, Sao Paulo ..... KO 4
Sept. 28—Gunter Valtinke, Sao Paulo ...... KO 4
Nov. 17—Doc Holliday, Sao Paulo .... KO 3
1973
Jan. 9—Koichi Wajima, Tokyo .... D 15
(For World Junior Middleweight Title)
Mar. 16—Nick Peoples, Sao Paulo .... KO 7
June 22—Carlos Marks, Sao Paulo .... W 10
Aug. 4—Roger Phillips, Brasilia .... KO 3
Sept. 28—Manoel Severino, Sao Paulo ...... KO 1
Dec. 8—Juan Artaza, Sao Paulo .... KO 3
1974
Feb. 5—Koichi Wajima, Tokyo .... L 15
(For World Junior Middleweight Title)
May 10—Anibal DiLella, Sao Paulo .... W 10
July 27—Dino Del Cid, Sao Paulo .... KO 2
Nov. 1—Rodolfo Rosalez, Sao Paulo ...... W 10
Dec. 6—Mario Delgado, Sao Paulo .... KO 3
1975
May 7—Jose Duran, Monte Carlo .... W 15
(Won Vacant WBC Junior Middleweight Title)
Aug. 9—Don Cobbs, Sao Paulo .... KO 5
Nov. 13—Elisha Obed, Paris .... KO by 11
(Lost WBC Junior Middleweight Title)
1976
Mar. —Juarez de Lima, Sao Paulo .... L 12
Aug. 20—Ramon Perez, Sao Paulo .... W 10
—Roque Roldan, Sao Paulo .... TL 8
1977
Sept. 16—Luis Fabre, Londrina .... L 12
(For Brazilian Middleweight Title)
1978-1979
(Inactive)
1980
Sept. 23—Edson Lima, Sao Paulo .... W 10
Nov. 4—Diogenes Pacheco, Sao Paulo .. KO by 9

TB	KO	WD	WF	D	LD	LF	KO BY	ND	NC
49	26	16	0	1	4	0	2	0	0

JAE-DO YUH
1969
Aug. 9—Byung-Mo Yim, Seoul .... KO by 7
Sept. 9—Armando Boniquit, Kwangju ..... W 10
Nov. 2—Jae-Chun Kim, Seoul .... KO 6
1970
Sept. 27—Ni-No Lee, Seoul .... W 10
Dec. 19—Hoshino Detsuo, Seoul .... KO 3
1971
Feb. 20—Hiraide Hiromichi, Seoul .... KO 10
Apr. 5—Ansano Lee, Seoul .... KO 1

581

May   22—Cho Park, Seoul .... KO   5
       (Won Korean Middleweight Title)
July   24—Cassius Naito, Seoul .... KO   6
       (Won Oriental Middleweight Title)
Sept. 30—Keum-Tae Lee, Seoul .... W   12
       (Retained Oriental Middleweight Title)
       —Turtle Okabe, Seoul .... W   10
Oct.   8—Steve Smith, Seoul .... KO   6
Dec.   14—Masakazu Taninobu, Seoul .... KO   2
       (Retained Oriental Middleweight Title)
1972
Jan.   29—Nakamura Kazua, Seoul .... KO   11
       (Retained Oriental Middleweight Title)
Mar.   11—Hideo Kanazawa, Seoul .... D   12
       (Retained Oriental Middleweight Title)
May   7—Hideo Kanazawa, Pusan .... W   12
       (Retained Oriental Middleweight Title)
June   25—Turtle Okabe, Pusan .... W   12
       (Retained Oriental Middleweight Title)
Sept. 9—Hiraide Hiromichi, Seoul .... KO   8
       (Retained Oriental Middleweight Title)
Oct.   1—Keum-Tae Lee, Seoul .... KO   3
       (Retained Oriental Middleweight Title)
Nov.   12—Cassius Naito, Taegu .... W   12
       (Retained Oriental Middleweight Title)
1973
Apr.   10—Cassius Naito, Seoul ..... KO   5
       (Retained Oriental Middleweight Title)
May   12—Ken Okita, Taegu .... W   12
       (Retained Oriental Middleweight Title)
June   16—Ken Okita, Pusan .... KO   3
July   14—Cassius Naito, Pusan .... W   12
       (Retained Oriental Middleweight Title)
Aug.   15—Han-Shik Kim, Taegu .... KO   10
1974
Mar.   31—Narong Phisanurachun, Pusan .... W   10
June   23—Hiroshi Nakagawa, Pusan .... KO   6
       (Retained Oriental Middleweight Title)
July   28—Nobuyoshi Ozaki, Pusan .... KO   8
       (Retained Oriental Middleweight Title)
Nov.   17—Yuji Miyagoshi, Tokyo .... W   12
       (Retained Oriental Middleweight Title)
1975
       —Isamu Kondo, Seoul .... KO   2
June   7—Koichi Wajima, Kitakyushu ..... KO   7
       (Won World Junior Middleweight Title)
Oct.   4—Nobuyoshi Ozaki, Pusan .... KO   4
       (Retained World Junior Middleweight Title)
Nov.   11—Masahiro Misako, Shizuoka ...... KO   6
       (Retained World Junior Middleweight Title)
1976
Jan.   17—Saburo Sakai, Pusan .... KO   8
Feb.   17—Koichi Wajima, Tokyo .... KO by 15
       (Lost World Junior Middleweight Title)
June   19—Peter Namboku, Seoul .... W   10
Sept. 26—Alberto Cruz, Seoul .... D   12
       (Retained Oriental Middleweight Title)
Dec.   12—Yuichiro Watanabe, Taegu .... W   12
       (Retained Oriental Middleweight Title)
1977
Apr.   9—Saburo Sakai, Kwangju .... KO   2
       (Retained Oriental Middleweight Title)
Aug.   26—Lim-Jae Keun, Kwangju .... KO   7
Oct.   9—Toshiaki Suzuki, Seoul .... W   12
       (Retained Oriental Middleweight Title)
1978
Jan.   21—Alberto Cruz, Pusan .... W   12
       (Retained Oriental Middleweight Title)
May   8—Frisco Montemayor, Seoul .... KO   6
July   16—Joo Ho, Seoul .... KO by 10

TB	KO	WD	WF	D	LD	LF	KO BY	ND	NC
44	24	15	0	2	0	0	3	0	0

ELISHA OBED
(Everett Oswald Ferguson)
Born, February 21, 1952, Nassau, Bahamas.
Weight, 154 lbs. Height, 5 ft. 10½ in.
1967
Aug. 10—Edison Stubbs, Nassau .... KO   2

Sept. 15—Taylor Ventura, Nassau .... KO   1
Oct.   13—Pino Romano, Nassau .... KO   3
Nov.   10—Taylor Ventura, Nassau .... D   4
Dec.   11—Kid Carew, Nassau .... KO by   2
1968
Feb.   16—Tony Mortimer, Nassau .... W   4
Aug.   10—Freddie Major, Nassau .... W   4
Nov.   22—Gypsy Mike Whymms, Nassau ... KO   3
Dec.   2—Taylor Ventura, Nassau .... KO   2
1969
Jan.   20—Gypsy Mike Whymms, Nassau ... KO   1
Feb.   7—Mighty Joe, Nassau .... KO   2
Feb.   21—Cornbread Rhamina, Nassau ..... KO   5
Mar.   14—Kid Joe, Nassau .... KO   6
July   11—Droopy Davis, Nassau .... W   8
Aug.   15—Sugarboy Monroe, Nassau .... KO   1
Sept. 26—Winston Greene, Nassau .... W   8
Oct.   31—Sandy Jeffries, Nassau .... W   8
Dec.   8—Don Frazer, Nassau .... W   8
1970
Apr.   3—Milton Hall, Nassau .... KO   2
May   15—Bert Woods, Nassau .... KO   3
Aug.   29—Droopy Davis, Nassau .... KO   6
Nov.   27—Buddy Taylor, Nassau .... W   10
Dec.   20—Don Fraser, Nassau .... KO   10
1971
June   5—Ray Minus, Nassau .... W   15
Sept. 25—Larry Adkins, Nassau .... W   10
1972
Apr.   8—Sugar Cliff, Nassau .... KO   6
May   26—Dorman Crawford, Nassau .... KO   10
July   15—Roscoe Bell, Nassau .... W   10
Aug.   26—Jimmy Hamm, Nassau .... KO   8
Nov.   17—Joe Hooks, Nassau .... KO   6
1973
Jan.   26—Sandy Torres, Nassau .... KO   8
Feb.   5—Terry Hayward, Nassau .... KO   1
Mar.   29—Al Cook, Nassau .... KO   6
Apr.   23—Roy Goss, Nassau .... W   10
May   30—Nat King, Nassau .... KO   8
July   19—Jimmy Williams, Nassau .... KO   1
Aug.   6—Doug Rogers, Nassau .... KO   4
Sept. 26—Bunny Grant, Nassau .... W   10
Oct.   19—Jose Melendez, Boca Raton ...... KO   8
Nov.   12—Dennis Riggs, Miami Beach ...... KO   4
Dec.   4—Mike Lancaster, Miami Beach .... KO   8
Dec.   14—Saoul Hernandez, Nassau .... KO   1
1974
Jan.   15—Tom Van Hatten, Miami Beach ... KO   2
Feb.   15—Wendell Spencer, Nassau .... KO   3
Feb.   26—Vicente Medina, Miami Beach .... KO   7
Mar.   15—Eddie Davis, Nassau .... KO   5
Apr.   9—Jessie Rios, Miami Beach .... KO   2
Apr.   26—Roy Lee, Nassau .... W   10
May   29—Jesus Garcia, Freeport .... W   10
June   11—Dario Hidalgo, Miami Beach ...... D   10
July   11—Carlos Marks, Nassau .... W   10
Aug.   16—Paco Flores, Tucson .... KO   5
Sept. 7—Guillermo Escalera, Freeport ..... KO   5
Sept. 27—Robert Williams, Nassau .... KO   5
Oct.   21—Johnny Rico, Tucson .... KO   2
Nov.   17—Renato Garcia, Tucson .... W   10
Dec.   25—Sammy Ruckard, Nassau .... W   10
1975
Jan.   21—Fernand Marcotte, Miami Beach .. KO   11
Feb.   22—Manuel Elizondo, Tucson .... KO   10
Apr.   29—Marcel Clay, Miami Beach .... KO   8
May   30—Nat King, Nassau .... KO   8
June   20—Chuchu Garcia, Freeport .... KO   5
July   22—Gene Wells, Miami Beach .... KO   5
Oct.   13—Nick Peoples, Nassau .... KO   6
Nov.   13—Miguel de Oliveire, Paris .... KO   11
       (Won WBC Junior Middleweight Title)
1976
Feb.   28—Tony Gardner, Nassau .... KO   2
       (Retained WBC Junior Middleweight Title)
Apr.   25—Sea Robinson, Abidjan .... W   15
       (Retained WBC Junior Middleweight Title)
June   18—Eckhard Dagge, Berlin .... KO by 10
       (Lost WBC Junior Middleweight Title)

582

Aug.	7—Larry Brasier, Freeport .... KO	1
Sept.	21—Victor Perez, Orlando .... W	10
Sept.	24—Sammy Barr, Nassau .... D	10
Nov.	19—Sammy Barr, Nassau .... W	10

1977

Jan.	18—Fernand Marcotte, Montreal .... W	10
Feb.	22—Jean-Claude LeClair, Montreal ..... D	10
June	2—Ayub Kalule, Randers L	10
Oct.	23—Henry Mitchel, Miami Beach ..... KO	3
Dec.	2—Joao Mendonca, Sao Paulo L	10

1978

Mar.	11—Rocky Mattioli, Melbourne .... KO by	7
	(For WBC Junior Middleweight Title)	
Apr.	28—Henry Hall, Nassau .... KO	7
Sept.	2—Marijan Benes, Berlin L	8
Oct.	31—Georg Steinherr, Munich L	10
Dec.	2—Tony Chiaverini, Kansas City L	10

1979

Jan.	13—Gary Smith, Miami Beach .... NC	2
Feb.	23—Lionel Cameron, Nassau .... KO	5
Mar.	30—Juan Serrano, Nassau .... W	10
Apr.	21—Pablo Rodriguez, Nassau .... KO	5
May	4—Terry Rondeau, Nassau .... KO	6
June	22—Hector Maldonado, Nassau .... KO	5
Aug.	17—Charlie Grimmit, Nassau .... KO	6
Sept.	11—Curtis Parker, Philadelphia ... KO by	7
Oct.	19—Richie Lee Roberts, Freeport ...... W	10
Nov.	23—Sammy Barr, Nassau .... NC	2
Dec.	26—Sammy Barr, Nassau .... KO	4

1980

Feb.	12—Willie Featherstone, Montreal ..... W	10
Mar.	3—Fulgencio Obel, Caracas ...... KO by	8
July	24—Steve Gregory, Columbus L	10
Oct.	7—Sammy Masias, Nassau .... KO	5

TB	KO	WD	WF	D	LD	LF	KO BY	ND	NC
97	56	24	0	4	6	0	5	0	2

JOSE DURAN

Born, October 9, 1945, Madrid, Spain. Weight, 147-154 lbs. Height, 5 ft. 9 in.

1968

Nov.	30—Ben Hamida, Barcelona .... KO	3
Dec.	17—Tony Ray, Barcelona .... KO	4

1969

Jan.	31—Jose Arnau, Madrid .... KO	4
Feb.	7—Mauricio Herman, Madrid .... W	8
Feb.	20—Jose Maria Riba, Barcelona ...... KO	3
Feb.	28—Pablo Vallecillo, Madrid .... W	8
Apr.	18—Canadas, Madrid .... W	8
Apr.	27—S. Adisa, Vittoria .... W	8
May	29—Quintano Soares, Barcelona ...... KO	2
June	20—Pablo Vallecillo, Barcelona .... W	8
July	24—Jo Martin, Madrid .... KO	4
Sept.	18—Jose Iturri, Barcelona .... KO	6
Oct.	2—Aldo Mondora, Barcelona .... KO	6
Oct.	9—Juan Antin, Barcelona .... W	10
Oct.	23—Giovanni Murgia, Barcelona ...... W	8
Oct.	30—Tomas Moktar, Vigo .... W	8
Nov.	13—D. Mahrez, Barcelona .... W disq.	3
Nov.	28—Thomas Moktar, Madrid .... W	8

1970

Feb.	6—Bob Cofie, Barcelona .... W	8
Mar.	20—Eduardo Batista, Madrid .... KO	7
Apr.	24—Johnny White, Madrid .... W	8
May	14—Ferdinand Ahumibe, Madrid ..... KO	6
June	22—Jean Josselin, Barcelona L	8
Aug.	1—Dante Pelaez, San Sebastian ...... W	8
Aug.	21—Angel Garcia, Madrid .... W	10
Sept.	12—Antonio Torres, Barcelona .... D	12
	(For Spanish Welterweight Title)	
Nov.	6—Eduardo Batista, Bilbao .... KO	4
Nov.	21—Bobby Arthur, Madrid .... W	8
Dec.	18—Antonio Torres, Madrid .... W	8

1971

Feb.	12—Frank Young, Barcelona .... W	8
May	21—Jean Josselin, Madrid .... W	8
July	7—Pablo Bethil, Valencia .... D	10
Oct.	15—Jimmy Carter, Barcelona .... W	8

Nov.	5—Jose Hernandez, Madrid .... D	10
Nov.	27—Epifanio Collada, Vigo .... D	10
Dec.	29—Jose Miguel Munoz, Barcelona ... KO	6

1972

Jan.	13—Francisco Ferri, Barcelona .... D	10
Feb.	2—Domenico Tiberia, Barcelona ...... W	10
Mar.	3—Dramane Ouedrago, Madrid ...... KO	8
May	3—Jean-Baptiste Rolland, Barcelona KO	4
June	15—Antonio Dos Santos, Bilbao ... W disq.	2
June	21—Dorman Crawford, Barcelona ..... KO	3
July	12—Angel Guinaldo, Barcelona L	8
Aug.	1—Jose Mario Madrazo, Barcelona .... W	12
	(Won Vacant Spanish Junior Middleweight Title)	
Aug.	25—Giancarlo Garbelli, Madrid .... KO	2
Sept.	29—Antonio Torres, Barcelona .... D	8
Oct.	6—Michel Chapier, Madrid .... W	8
Feb.	8—Juan Jose Pardo, Bilbao .... KO	6

1973

Feb.	8—Juan Jose Pardo, Bilbao .... KO	6
May	28—Fighting Mack, Rotterdam L	10
June	30—Jose Madrazo, Burgos .... W	12
Aug.	1—Bo Hoberg, Palma .... W	8
Oct.	11—Francis Vermandere, Madrid ...... W	10
Nov.	23—Jose Luis Pacheco, Barcelona ...... W	8
Dec.	14—Vincent Parra, Madrid .... W	10
Dec.	29—Michel Chapier, Barcelona .... W	8

1974

Apr.	5—Gray Ibegwe, Madrid .... W	8
Apr.	30—Gerard Cola, Barcelona .... W	10
June	7—Jacques Kechichian, Madrid .... W	15
	(Won European Junior Middleweight Title)	
July	12—Gray Ibekwe, Palma de Mallorca KO	6
July	26—Michel Chapier, Madrid .... W	8
Sept.	3—Eckhard Dagge, Berlin .... KO	11
	(Retained European Junior Middleweight Title)	
Nov.	5—Hans Orsolics, Berlin .... KO	14
	(Retained European Junior Middleweight Title)	

1975

Jan.	7—Frans Csandl, Vienna .... W	15
	(Retained European Junior Middleweight Title)	
Feb.	15—Peter Scheibner, Barcelona .... W	10
May	7—Miguel DeOliveira, Monte Carlo ... L	15
	(For WBC Junior Middleweight Title)	
June	24—Eckhard Dagge, Berlin .... KO by	9
	(Lost European Junior Middleweight Title)	
Oct.	17—Jules Bellaiche, Madrid .... D	8
Nov.	8—Mario Marina, Alicante .... W	8
Dec.	20—Dino Fleitas, Leon .... W	8

1976

Jan.	30—Jules Bellaiche, Barcelona .... D	8
Apr.	2—Arnoldo Olivares, Madrid .... W	8
May	18—Koichi Wajima, Tokyo .... KO	14
	(Won World Junior Middleweight Title)	
June	30—Juarez De Lima, Madrid .... W	10
Aug.	7—Peter Schreibner, Lepe .... W	8
Oct.	8—Miguel Angel Castellini, Madrid ... L	15
	(Lost World Junior Middleweight Title)	

1977

Oct.	1—Kassongo Mukandjo, Palma Mallorca .... KO	6

1978

May	14—Rocky Mattioli, Pescara .... KO by	5
	(For WBC Junior Middleweight Title)	

TB	KO	WD	WF	D	LD	LF	KO BY	ND	NC
78	23	38	2	9	4	0	2	0	0

ECKHARD DAGGE

Born, February 27, 1948, Berlin, Germany. Weight, 154-160 lbs. Height, 5 ft. 11½ in.

1973

Mar.	2—Hans Heukeshoven, Berlin .... KO	1
Mar.	9—Ferzi Ispir, Lubeck .... KO	1
Mar.	30—Waldi Clere, Oldenburg .... KO	1
Apr.	27—Anton Schendl, Berlin .... KO	4
May	11—Antonio Rimasti, Wiesbaden ..... KO	1
June	3—Klaus-Peter Tombers, Berlin ...... KO	5
	(Won German Middleweight Title)	

Aug.	31—Shaco Mamba, Lubeck	KO	8
Sept.	28—Matt Donovan, Berlin	KO	2
Oct.	26—Jose Madrazo, Hamburg	W	8
Nov.	9—Francis Vermandere, Berlin	KO	7

1974

Feb.	21—Denny Moyer, Berlin	W	10
May	14—Manny Gonzalez, Berlin	W	10
June	21—Billy Backus, Berlin	KO	3
Sept.	3—Jose Duran, Berlin	KO by	11

(For European Junior Middleweight Title)

| Nov. | 5—Jules Bellaiche, Berlin | W | 8 |
| Nov. | 30—Pascal Zito, Munich | W | 10 |

1975

| Mar. | 18—Carlos Marks, Berlin | L | 10 |
| June | 24—Jose Duran, Berlin | KO | 9 |

(Won European Junior Middleweight Title)

| Nov. | 4—Franz Csandl, Vienna | KO | 7 |

(Retained European Junior Middleweight Title)

1976

| Jan. | 16—Vito Antuofermo, Berlin | L | 15 |

(Lost European Junior Middleweight Title)

| Apr. | 2—Marcel Giordanella, Kiel | KO | 7 |
| June | 18—Elisha Obed, Berlin | KO | 10 |

(Won WBC Junior Middleweight Title)

| Sept. | 18—Emile Griffith, Berlin | W | 15 |

(Retained WBC Junior Middleweight Title)

1977

| Mar. | 15—Maurice Hope, Berlin | D | 15 |

(Retained WBC Junior Middleweight Title)

| Aug. | 6—Rocky Mattioli, Berlin | KO by | 5 |

(Lost WBC Junior Middleweight Title)

| Dec. | 9—Jimmy Savage, Berlin | KO | 8 |

1978

| Apr. | 7—Rene Pinder, West Berlin | KO | 4 |
| May | 6—Larry Davis, Frankfurt | W | 10 |

TB	KO	WD	WF	D	LD	LF	KO BY	ND	NC
28	15	8	0	1	2	0	2	0	0

MIGUEL ANGEL CASTELLINI

Born, January 26, 1947, Santa Rosa, La Pampa, Argentina. Weight, 154 lbs. Height, 5 ft. 11¼ in.

1965

May	28—Domingo Gerez, Tucuman	KO	2
June	18—Abelardo Rosales, Tucuman	W	6
Oct.	8—Juan C. Leiva, Tucuman	KO	1
Oct.	22—Rodolfo Varela, Concepcion	KO	5
Nov.	4—Jose Tula, Concepcion	D	10
Dec.	10—Amaro Vilar, Tucuman	W	8

1966

Jan.	19—Walter Romero, Tucuman	D	8
Feb.	18—Hector Paiva, Santa Rosa	KO	5
Mar.	11—Alfredo Paz, Santa Rosa	D	10
May	6—Angel Osuna, Santa Rosa	W	10
July	29—Luis Andrada, Tucuman	D	10
Aug.	26—Ramon Acosta, Tucuman	W	10
Sept.	9—Hermogenes Quintela, Ledesma	KO by	10
Oct.	7—Kid Roldan, Rio IV	W	10
Oct.	28—Jose Paredes, Rio IV	KO by	6
Dec.	7—Luis Barrios, Buenos Aires	KO	4
Dec.	29—Matias Colque, General Pico	KO	3

1967

Mar.	17—Tito Del Barco, Santa Rosa	L	10
Apr.	6—Luis Colman, La Rioja	KO	8
Apr.	21—Juan C. Quiroga, La Rioja	KO	3
May	12—Luis Andrada, La Rioja	W	10
May	26—Juan C. Velardez, La Rioja	KO	10
July	14—Ramon Pereyra, Rio IV	D	10
Aug.	23—Ramon Pereyra, Rio IV	D	10
Sept.	8—Ramon Silva, La Rioja	KO	3
Sept.	22—Armando Marchisio, La Rioja	W	10
Nov.	10—Leonardo Peralta, La Rioja	D	10
Nov.	29—Ramon Pereyra, Buenos Aires	D	10
Dec.	29—Moises Barbosa, La Rioja	KO	3

1968

June	15—Carlos Raimundo, Bariloche	KO	8
July	6—Ruben Orrico, Bariloche	KO	1
Aug.	7—Manuel Hernandez, Bariloche	KO	9
Sept.	21—Luis M. Pereyra, Bariloche	KO	1

1969

May	23—Osvaldo Marino, Santa Rosa	W	10
Sept.	12—Raul O. Pereyra, Rio IV	KO	2
Sept.	26—Enrique Orona, Rio IV	KO	9
Oct.	31—Carlos Estrada, Santa Rosa	KO by	5

1970

(Inactive)

1971

May	7—Ivan Rojas, La Rioja	KO	4
June	11—Domingo Guerrero, La Rioja	KO	8
July	8—Roberto Carabajal, La Rioja	KO	8
Sept.	17—Antenor Santillan, La Rioja	KO	6
Nov.	10—Hector Galvan, Buenos Aires	KO	4
Dec.	3—Alberto Massi, Buenos Aires	KO	5
Dec.	22—Ruben Martinez, Buenos Aires	KO	6

1972

Feb.	8—Ramon Pereyra, La Rioja	KO	9
Feb.	25—Edmundo Leite, Sao Paulo	KO	5
May	19—Miguel Chequer, La Plata	W	10
June	7—Ramon Pereyra, Buenos Aires	KO	3
Aug.	11—Miguel Chequer, La Plata	W	10
Sept.	23—Raul Pereyra, Buenos Aires	KO	3
Nov.	4—Hector Palleres, Buenos Aires	KO	1

(Won Argentine Junior Middleweight Title)

| Nov. | 25—Raul Soriano, Buenos Aires | KO | 2 |
| Dec. | 9—Matt Donovan, Buenos Aires | KO | 2 |

1973

Feb.	1—Ruben Martinez, Salta	KO	5
Mar.	23—Roberto Carabajal, La Rioja	KO	1
Apr.	10—Doc Holliday, Buenos Aires	W	10
June	10—Carlos Marks, Buenos Aires	W	10
Aug.	4—Ramon LaCruz, Buenos Aires	D	10
Oct.	31—Hector Galvan, Salta	KO	3
Nov.	15—Carlos Estrada, Bahia Blanca	KO	2
Dec.	4—Ramon LaCruz, Buenos Aires	W	12

(Retained Argentine Junior Middleweight Title)

1974

May	25—Carlos Salinas, Monte Carlo	KO	2
June	2—Roy McMillan, Rome	W	10
Oct.	10—Manuel Tapia, Bariloche	KO	6
Dec.	13—Manuel Fierro, Buenos Aires	KO	8

1975

Jan.	17—Mel Dennis, Balcarce	KO	2
Apr.	11—Norbert Cabrera, Salta	KO	3
May	3—Rodolfo Rosales, Buenos Aires	W	10
Sept.	19—Mimoun Mahatar, Milan	KO	9
Oct.	4—Sandy Torres, Milan	KO by	4
Dec.	8—James Marshall, Paris	KO	4

1976

Feb.	9—Jules Belaiche, Paris	KO	6
Feb.	23—Radames Cabrera, Paris	W	10
July	15—Juan C. Artaza, San Juan	W	10
Aug.	20—Octavio Escauriza, Rosario	D	10
Oct.	8—Jose Duran, Madrid	W	15

(Won World Junior Middleweight Title)

1977

| Mar. | 5—Eddie Gazo, Managua | L | 15 |

(Lost World Junior Middleweight Title)

| Nov. | 3—Ayub Kalule, Randers | KO by | 3 |

1978

Apr.	7—Alberto Almiron, Santa Rosa	W	10
Apr.	20—Roque Miranda, Posadas	KO	4
May	13—Camilo Gaitan, Buenos Aires	D	10

1979

Jan.	19—Manuel F. Gonzalez, Mar del Plata	W	10
May	17—Juan Mora, Villa Carlos Paz	KO	7
June	9—Alfredo Cabral, Buenos Aires	KO by	8
Dec.	21—Hugo Trujillo, Jujuy	KO	7

1980

Jan.	11—Julio Arancibia, Villa Carlos Paz	D	10
Feb.	15—Sixto Gomez, Mar del Plata	KO	2
Apr.	18—Raul Antonio Paez, Jujuy	KO	6
May	3—Al Styles, Buenos Aires	W	10
June	21—Alfredo Cicopiedi, Mar del Plata	W	10
July	4—Alfredo Cicopiedi, San Nicolas	KO	6
Aug.	22—Alfredo Cicopiedi, Bahia Blanca	KO	8
Sept.	20—Eddie Gazo, Buenos Aires	KO	9

TB	KO	WD	WF	D	LD	LF	KO BY	ND	NC
93	49	24	0	12	2	0	6	0	0

EDDIE GAZO

Born, September 12, 1950, San Lorenzo, Managua, Nicaragua. Weight, 147-154 lbs.

1971

Oct.	6—Carlos Espinosa, Leon	W	6
	—Sol Brillante Mitchel, Leon	KO	3
	—Carlos Sanchez, Managua	W	6
	—Carlos Ampie, Granada	KO	3

1972

	—Roberto Arias, Chinandega	W	10
	—Gerardo Sanders, Managua	KO	2
	—Monaco Valle, Jinotepe	KO	1
	—Frank Darce, Leon	W	10
	—Henry Thompson, Chinandega	KO	5
	—Freddy Menochal, Chinandega	W	10
	—Zapito Mora, Chinandega	W	10
	—Felix Bojorge, Chinandega	KO	5
	—Leo Campbell, Chinandega	W	10

1973

	—Tarzan Suazo, Esteli	KO	6
	—Julio Blanco, Managua	D	10
	—Pantera Negra, Managua	W	10
	—Carlos Espinosa, Managua	W	10
	—Omar Perez, Managua	L	10
	—Omar Perez, Managua	W	10
	—Frank Medina, Managua	W	10
	—Orlando Sinclair, Managua	KO	5
	—Carlos Espinosa, Managua	KO by	10
	—Gerardo Sanders, Managua	KO	6
	—Carlos Espinosa, Managua	W	12
	(Won Nicaraguan Welterweight Title)		
	—Gerardo Sanders, Masaya	KO	3

1974

Jan.	8—Roberto Arias, Masaya	KO	8
Feb.	4—Adalberto Vanegas, Cartagena	D	10
	—Hernan Grimaldi, Managua	KO	4
	(Won Central American Welterweight Title)		
	—Roberto Arias, Managua	W	10
	—Gerardo Sanders, Esteli	W	10
	—Rodolfo Contreras, Costa Rica	KO	10

1975

Feb.	7—Edmond Camayagua, Managua	KO	6
	(Retained Central American Welterweight Title)		
Apr.	18—Carlos Obregon, Bogota	KO by	6
	—Walter Zuniga, San Jose	W	10
	—Jose Scott, San Jose	L	10
	—Ezequiel Obando, Managua	KO	4

1976

Mar.	13—Rodrigo Delgado, Managua	KO	10
	(Won Central American Junior Middleweight Title)		
May	15—Rosalio Matute, Managua	KO	6
July	3—Dino Del Cid, Managua	KO	3
Sept.	4—Jorge de Avila, Managua	KO	7

1977

Mar.	5—Miguel Angel Castellini, Managua	W	15
	(Won World Junior Middleweight Title)		
June	7—Koichi Wajima, Tokyo	KO	11
	(Retained World Junior Middleweight Title)		
Sept.	13—Kenji Shibata, Tokyo	W	15
	(Retained World Junior Middleweight Title)		
Dec.	18—Chae-Keun Lim, Inchon, Korea	W	15
	(Retained World Junior Middleweight Title)		

1978

Aug.	9—Masashi Kudo, Akita, Japan	L	15
	(Lost World Junior Middleweight Title)		

1979

(Inactive)

1980

May	3—Thomas Hearns, Detroit	KO by	1
Sept.	5—Edgar Bravo, Managua	KO	1
Sept.	20—Miguel Angel Castellini, Buenos Aires	KO by	9

TB	KO	WD	WF	D	LD	LF	KO BY	ND	NC
48	21	18	0	2	3	0	4	0	0

ROCCO (ROCKY) MATTIOLI

Born, July 20, 1953, Ripa Teatine, Italy. Weight, 147-154 lbs. Height, 5 ft. 6½ in.

1970

Mar.	9—Tony Salta, South Melbourne	KO	2
Mar.	16—Glen Grinstead, Melbourne	W	4
Apr.	2—Tom Roberts, Redfern	KO	4
Apr.	23—Bernie Martin, Morwell	KO	5
May	4—Ricky Day, Melbourne	L	6
May	29—Billy Stewart, Morwell	KO	4
July	6—Billy Murphy, Melbourne	W	6
Aug.	3—Ray Cannon, Melbourne	KO	3
Oct.	5—Johnny Todd, Melbourne	KO	6
Oct.	19—Alby Roberts, Melbourne	KO	5
Nov.	9—George Kencheff, Melbourne	KO	5
Nov.	30—Bevan Minnett, Melbourne	KO	4

1971

Apr.	5—Red Durange, Melbourne	KO	4
Apr.	19—Doug Green, Melbourne	KO	3
May	10—Bill Fatu, Melbourne	D	8
June	7—Steve Ayerst, Melbourne	W	8
June	28—Si Nomura, Melbourne	W	8
July	26—Tiger Peni, Melbourne	KO	5
Aug.	30—Steve Hallcroft, Perth	KO	6
Sept.	23—Paul Moore, Brunswick	L	10
Nov.	25—Paul Moore, Brunswick	W	10
Dec.	17—Kahai Bauli, Brunswick	KO	6

1972

(Inactive)

1973

Apr.	19—Ted Gray, Blacktown	KO	4
Apr.	26—Eric King, Carlton, Victoria	KO	2
May	17—Jeff White, Carlton, Victoria	KO	12
	(Won Australian Welterweight Title)		
July	12—Pongi Lie, Carlton, Victoria	W	15
	(Retained Australian Welterweight Title)		
Aug.	24—Trevor Francis, Brisbane	KO	8

1974

Mar.	14—Billy O'Donnell, Ringwook	KO	3
Mar.	22—Dennis Enright, Melbourne	KO	3
Apr.	25—Jose Luis Baltazar, Melbourne	W	10
May	12—Jan Van Mellearts, Noumea	KO	10
June	25—David Oropeza, Melbourne	KO	6
June	26—Dommy Contacte, Melbourne	KO	4
Aug.	16—Eddie Perkins, Melbourne	W	10
Oct.	18—Ray Chavez, Melbourne	W	10

1975

Feb.	14—Ali Afakasi, Melbourne	KO by	12
Apr.	11—Billy Backus, Melbourne	KO	5
May	9—Chris Fernandez, Milan	KO	4
June	6—Mimoun Mahatar, Milan	W	10
Aug.	22—Fernand Marcotte, Melbourne	KO	9
Sept.	19—Harold Weston, Melbourne	L	10
Oct.	24—Jorgen Hansen, Milan	KO	7
Nov.	28—Domenico Di Jorio, Milan	KO	6

1976

Feb.	6—Cuby (Top Cat) Jackson, Milan	W	10
Apr.	2—Bruno Arcari, Milan	D	10
May	21—Chucho Garcia, Milan	KO	6
Oct.	1—Pablo Rodriguez, Milan	KO	2
Oct.	22—Ralph Palladin, Bologna	KO	7
Dec.	3—Alfonso Hayman, Milan	KO	10

1977

Jan.	28—Trevor Francis, Faenza	KO	6
Feb.	27—Aldo Olivares, Rimini	KO	5
June	18—Angel Ortiz, Rome	KO	3
Aug.	6—Eckhard Dagge, Berlin	KO	5
	(Won WBC Junior Middleweight Title)		
Dec.	3—Larry Paul, Milan	W	10

1978

Jan.	21—Jose Rodriquez, Las Vegas	W	10
Mar.	11—Elisha Obed, Melbourne	KO	7
	(Retained WBC Junior Middleweight Title)		
May	14—Jose Duran, Pescara	KO	5
	(Retained WBC Junior Middleweight Title)		
Sept.	20—Freddie Boynton, Milan	KO	7

1979

Mar.	4—Maurice Hope, San Remo	KO by	8
	(Lost WBC Junior Middleweight Title)		
Oct.	12—Leon McCullum, Rome	KO	5

585

Nov. 23—Roy Johnson, Pordenone .... KO 4
Dec. 14—Pat Murphy, Milano .... KO 2
1980
Mar. 21—Jesse Carter, Bologna .... KO 1
May   2—Jamie Thomas, Rome .... KO 2
May   30—Rafael Rodriguez, Rome .... KO 8
July 12—Maurice Hope, London .... KO by 11
    (For WBC Junior Middleweight Title)

TB	KO	WD	WF	D	LD	LF	KO BY	ND	NC
66	45	13	0	2	3	0	3	0	0

MASASHI KUDO
Born, August 24, 1951, Gojome-cho, Akita-Gun, Akita Prefecture, Japan. Weight, 154 lbs. Height, 5 ft. 8 in.
1973
May   18—Toshio Oki, Yokohama .... KO 3
Sept. 30—Keiji Miyawaki, Tokyo .... KO 3
Dec. 3—Hachiro Kuroichi, Tokyo .... KO 2
Dec. 27—Seiji Nagai, Tokyo .... KO 6
1974
July 29—Cassius Naito, Gifu .... W 10
1975
Mar. 2—Nobuyoshi Ozaki, Tokyo .... W 10
    (Won Vacant Japanese Middleweight Title)
June 1—Takeshi Watanebe, Tokyo .... W 10
July 18—Yuji Miyakoshi, Tokyo .... W 10
    (Retained Japanese Middleweight Title)
Nov. 30—Yuji Miyakoshi, Tokyo .... W 10
1976
Jan. 24—Takeshi Izumi, Tokyo .... KO 4
    (Retained Japanese Middleweight Title)
Mar. 28—Saburo Sakai, Tokyo .... KO 1
June 27—Yuichiro Watanabe, Tokyo .... KO 3
    (Retained Japanese Middleweight Title)
Sept. 26—Kazuhiro Horiguchi, Tokyo .... W 10
1977
Jan. 30—Saburo Sakai, Tokyo .... KO 9
    (Retained Japanese Middleweight Title)
May   3—Yuichiro Watanabe, Tokyo .... W 10
    (Retained Japanese Middleweight Title)
July 2—Saburo Sakai, Kumagaya City ... KO 7
Sept. 6—Peter Naboku, Tokyo .... KO 9
    (Retained Japanese Middleweight Title)
Oct. 31—Katsu Oezashi, Tokyo .... KO 3
1978
May   2—Katsuo Esashi, Tokyo .... W 10
    (Retained Japanese Middleweight Title)
Aug. 9—Eddie Gazo, Akita-Ken .... W 15
    (Won World Junior Middleweight Title)
Dec. 13—Joo Ho, Osaka .... W 15
    (Retained World Junior Middleweight Title)
1979
Mar. 13—Manuel R. Gonzalez, Tokyo .... W 15
    (Retained World Junior Middleweight Title)
June 20—Manuel R. Gonzalez, Yokaichi .... KO 12
    (Retained World Junior Middleweight Title)
Oct. 24—Ayub Kalule, Akita-Ken .... L 15
    (Lost World Junior Middleweight Title)

TB	KO	WD	WF	D	LD	LF	KO BY	ND	NC
24	16	7	0	0	1	0	0	0	0

MAURICE HOPE
Born, December 6, 1951, Antigua. Weight, 154 lbs. Managed by Terry Lawless.
1973
June 18—John Smith, Nottingham .... W 8
Sept. 25—Len Gibbs, Shoreditch .... KO 3
Oct. 1—Pat Brogan, Nottingham .... W 8
Oct. 23—Arthur Winfield, Nottingham .... KO 4
Nov. 21—Mickey Flynn, London .... L 8
1974
Jan. 28—Mike Manley, Nottingham .... W 8
Mar. 12—Mick Hussey, London .... KO 3
Apr. 17—John Smith, Manchester .... KO 2

586

May   13—Dave Davies, London .... KO 8
Nov. 5—Larry Paul, Wolverhampton ...... KO 8
    (Won British Light Middleweight Title)
Dec. 10—Cuby (Top Cat) Jackson, London .. KO 7
1975
Feb. 11—Don Cobbs, Kensington .... KO 4
Apr. 2—Jurgen Voss, Hammersmith ...... KO 3
June 10—Bunny Sterling, London .... KO by 8
Sept. 30—Larry Paul, London .... KO 4
    (Retained British Light Middleweight Title)
1976
Feb. 25—Carl Spear, London .... KO 4
Mar. 2—Mimoun Mohatar, London .... KO 2
Mar. 20—Kevin White Wembley, London ... KO 4
Apr. 20—Tony Poole, Bethnal Green ...... KO 12
    (Won Vacant British Commonwealth Light Middleweight Title)
June 1—Tim McHugh, London .... KO 4
Oct. 1—Vito Antouofermo, Rome .... KO 15
    (Won European Junior Middleweight Title)
1977
Mar. 15—Eckhard Dagge, Berlin .... D 15
    (For WBC Junior Middleweight Title)
May   7—Frank Wissenbach, Hamburg ...... W 15
    (Retained European Junior Middleweight Title)
Sept. 27—Tony Lopes, London ..,........ KO 6
Nov. 8—Joel Bonnetaz, London .... KO 5
    (Retained European Junior Middleweight Title)
1978
Jan. 24—Vincenzo Ungaro, London .... KO 5
Apr. 4—Melvin Dennies, London .... W 10
Sept. 26—Alphonso Hayman, London .... KO 5
Nov. 17—Relinquished European and British Titles.
1979
Mar. 4—Rocky Mattioli, San Remo .... KO 8
    (Won WBC Junior Middleweight Title)
Sept. 25—Mike Baker, London .... KO 7
    (Retained WBC Junior Middleweight Title)
1980
July 12—Rocky Mattioli, London .... KO 11
    (Retained WBC Junior Middleweight Title)
Nov. 25—Carlos Herrera, London .... W 15
    (Retained WBC Junior Middleweight Title)

TB	KO	WD	WF	D	LD	LF	KO BY	ND	NC
32	23	6	0	1	1	0	1	0	0

AYUB KALULE
Born, January 6, 1954, Kampala, Uganda. Weight, 154 lbs. Height, 5 ft. 8 in. Southpaw.
1976
Apr. 8—Kurt Hombach, Copenhagen .... W 4
June 3—Wayne Bennett, Copenhagen ..... KO 5
Oct. 9—Trevor Francis, Copenhagen ...... W 6
Nov. 19—Gualberto Fernandez, Randers ... KO 1
Dec. 9—Larry Paul, Copenhagen .... KO 2
1977
Jan. 19—Damiano Lassandro, Copenhagen KO 4
Feb. 24—Mimoun Mohatar, Copenhagen .... W 10
Mar. 31—Aroldo Olivares, Copenhagen ..... KO 7
Apr. 28—Jose Luis Duran, Copenhagen .... KO 7
June 2—Elisha Obed, Randers .... W 10
Sept. 8—Rudy Robles, Copenhagen .... W 10
Oct. 6—Alvin Anderson, Copenhagen .... KO 9
Nov. 3—Miguel Angel Castellini, Randers KO 4
Dec. 8—Ralph Palladin, Copenhagen ...... W 10
1978
Jan. 5—Bonifacio Avila, Randers .... KO 3
Jan. 26—Rene Pinder, Oslo .... W 10
Feb. 9—Jose Hernandez, Copenhagen ..... KO 5
Mar. 2—Johnny Baldwin, Vejle .... W 10
Mar. 16—Tsutomu Hagusa, Copenhagen ... KO 3
Apr. 27—Idrissa Konate, Randers .... KO 7
May   25—Al Korovou, Copenhagen .... KO 4
    (Won British Commonwealth Middleweight Title)
Aug. 10—Milton Owens, Glyngore .... KO 6
Sept. 14—Reggie Ford, Randers .... KO 5
    (Retained British Commonwealth Middleweight Title)

Nov.	9—Ray Seales, Copenhagen	W 10
Dec.	7—Kevin Finnegan, Copenhagen	W 10

1979

Feb.	15—Joo Ho, Randers	KO 2
Mar.	15—Monty Betham, Copenhagen	KO 4
May	27—Rogilio Zarza, Randers	W 10
June	28—Ray Hammond, Randers	W 8
Sept.	6—David Love, Randers	W 10
Oct.	24—Mashashi Kudo, Akita Ken	W 15
	(Won World Junior Middleweight Title)	
Dec.	6—Steve Gregory, Copenhagen	W 15
	(Retained World Junior Middleweight Title)	

1980

Apr.	16—Emiliano Villa, Copenhagen	KO 12
	(Retained World Junior Middleweight title)	
June	12—Marijan Benes, Randers	W 15
	(Retained World Junior Middleweight Title)	
Sept.	6—Bushy Bester, Aarhus, Denmark ...	W 15
	(Retained World Junior Middleweight Title)	

TB	KO	WD	WF	D	LD	LF	KO BY	ND	NC
35	18	17	0	0	0	0	0	0	0

587

WELTERWEIGHTS

PADDY DUFFY	1888-1890	BARNEY ROSS	1934
MYSTERIOUS BILLY SMITH	1892-1894	JIMMY MC LARNIN	1934-1935
TOMMY RYAN	1894-1898	BARNEY ROSS	1935-1938
MYSTERIOUS BILLY SMITH	1898-1900	HENRY ARMSTRONG	1938-1940
JAMES (RUBE) FERNS	1900	FRITZIE ZIVIC	1940-1941
MATTY MATTHEWS	1900-1901	FREDDIE (RED) COCHRANE	1941-1946
JAMES (RUBE) FERNS	1901	MARTY SERVO	1946
JOE WALCOTT	1901-1904	SUGAR RAY ROBINSON	1946-1951
THE DIXIE KID	1904	JOHNNY BRATTON (NBA)	1951
JOE WALCOTT	1905-1906	KID GAVILAN	1951-1954
HONEY MELLODY	1906-1907	JOHNNY SAXTON	1954-1955
MIKE (TWIN) SULLIVAN	1907-1908	TONY DE MARCO	1955
HARRY LEWIS (CLAIMANT)	*1908-1911*	CARMEN BASILIO	1955-1956
JIMMY GARDNER (CLAIMANT)	1908	JOHNNY SAXTON	1956
JIMMY CLABBY (CLAIMANT)	1910-1911	CARMEN BASILIO	1956-1957
WALDEMAR HOLBERG	1914	VIRGIL AKINS	1958
TOM MC CORMICK	1914	DON JORDAN	1958-1960
MATT WELLS	1914-1915	BENNY (KID) PARET	1960-1961
KID GRAVES (CLAIMANT)	*1914*	EMILE GRIFFITH	1961-1963
MIKE GLOVER	1915	LUIS RODRIGUEZ	1963
JACK BRITTON	1915	EMILE GRIFFITH	1963-1966
TED (KID) LEWIS	1915-1916	*CHARLIE SHIPES (CALIF.)*	*1966-1967*
JACK BRITTON	1916-1917	CURTIS COKES	1966-1969
TED (KID) LEWIS	1917-1919	JOSE NAPOLES	1969-1970
JACK BRITTON	1919-1922	BILLY BACKUS	1970-1971
MICKEY WALKER	1922-1926	JOSE NAPOLES	1971-1975
PETE LATZO	1926-1927	*HEDGEMON LEWIS (NEW YORK)*	*1972-1973*
JOE DUNDEE	1927-1929	*ANGEL ESPADA (WBA)*	*1975-1976*
JACKIE FIELDS	1929-1930	JOHN H. STRACEY	1975-1976
YOUNG JACK THOMPSON	1930	CARLOS PALOMINO	1976-1979
TOMMY FREEMAN	1930-1931	*JOSE (PIPINO) CUEVAS (WBA)*	*1976-1980*
YOUNG JACK THOMPSON	1931	WILFRED BENITEZ	1979
LOU BROUILLARD	1931-1932	SUGAR RAY LEONARD	1979-1980
JACKIE FIELDS	1932-1933	ROBERTO DURAN	1980
YOUNG CORBETT III	1933	*THOMAS HEARNS (WBA)*	*1980-*
JIMMY MC LARNIN	1933-1934	SUGAR RAY LEONARD	1980-

Claimants not generally recognized are in *italics*.

WORLD WELTERWEIGHT CHAMPIONSHIP BOUTS

Date	Winner	Weight	Loser	Weight	Result	Time KO	Site	Referee
10/30/88	Paddy DUFFY		William McMILLAN		KO 17		Fort Foote, Virginia	
3/29/89	Paddy DUFFY	140	Tom MEADOWS	142	WF 45		California A.C., San Francisco	Hiram Cook
12/14/92	Mys. Billy SMITH	142	Danny NEEDHAM	143	KO 14		Wigwam Theatre, San Francisco	Walter Watson
8/17/93	Mys. Billy SMITH		Tom WILLIAMS		KO 2		Coney Island A.C., Brooklyn, N.Y.	Johnny Eckhardt
7/26/94	Tommy RYAN		Mys. Billy SMITH		ref 20		Minneapolis, Minnesota	Joe Choynski
1/18/95	Tommy RYAN	145	Jack DEMPSEY	142	TKO 3		Coney Island A.C., Brooklyn, N.Y.	Tim Hurst
5/27/95	Tommy RYAN		Mys. Billy SMITH		NC 18		Coney Island A.C., Brooklyn, N.Y.	Tim Hurst
11/25/96	Tommy RYAN		Mys. Billy SMITH		WF 9		Empire A.C., Maspeth, New York	Tim Hurst
12/23/96	Tommy RYAN		Bill PAYNE		KO 4		Alhambra, Syracuse, New York	
2/24/97	Tommy RYAN		Tom TRACY		KO 9		Alhambra, Syracuse, New York	Yank Sullivan
6/13/98	Tommy RYAN	146	Tommy WEST	152	TKO 14	2:43	Lenox A.C., New York City, N.Y.	Charley White
7/29/98	Mys. Billy SMITH		George GREEN		ref 25		Lenox A.C., New York City, N.Y.	
8/25/98	Mys. Billy SMITH		Matty MATTHEWS		ref 25		Lenox A.C., New York City, N.Y.	Charley White
9/05/98	Mys. Billy SMITH		Andy WALSH		draw 25		Coney Island A.C., Brooklyn, N.Y.	
10/03/98	Mys. Billy SMITH		Jim JUDGE		KO 20	2:50	American Sporting Club, Scranton	Sam Austin
10/07/98	Mys. Billy SMITH		Charley McKEEVER		ref 25		Lenox A.C., New York City, N.Y.	Charley White
12/06/98	Mys. Billy SMITH		Joe WALCOTT		ref 20		Lenox A.C., New York City, N.Y.	Charley White
1/24/99	Mys. Billy SMITH		Billy EDWARDS		KO 14		Lenox A.C., New York City, N.Y.	
3/10/99	Mys. Billy SMITH	142	Kid LAVIGNE	139	TKO 14		Woodward's Pavilion, Colma, Calif.	Jim McDonald
6/29/99	Mys. Billy SMITH		Charley McKEEVER		D 20		Lenox A.C., New York City, N.Y.	
8/04/99	Mys. Billy SMITH		Andy WALSH		D 25		Broadway A.C., Brooklyn, New York	
11/08/99	Mys. Billy SMITH		Charley McKEEVER		ref 20		Lenox A.C., New York City, N.Y.	
1/15/00	Rube FERNS		Mys. Billy SMITH		WF 21		Buffalo, New York	. . . McBride
8/13/00	Rube FERNS		Eddie CONNOLLY		TKO 15		Buffalo, New York	. . . McBride
9/01/00	Rube FERNS		Matty MATTHEWS		ref 15		Detroit, Michigan	Malachy Hogan
10/16/00	Matty MATTHEWS		Rube FERNS		ref 15		Detroit, Michigan	
4/29/01	Matty MATTHEWS		Tom COUHIG		ref 20		Louisville, Kentucky	
5/24/01	Rube FERNS		Matty MATTHEWS		KO 10	2:10	Toronto, Ontario, Canada	Marvin Smith
9/23/01	Rube FERNS		Frank ERNE		KO 9		Int. A.C., Fort Erie, Ontario	
12/18/01	Joe WALCOTT		Rube FERNS		TKO 5		Int. A.C., Fort Erie, Ontario	. . . McBride
6/23/02	Joe WALCOTT		Tommy WEST		ref 15		London, England	
4/02/03	Joe WALCOTT		Billy WOODS		D 20		Century A.C., Los Angeles, Calif.	
4/29/04	Dixie KID		Joe WALCOTT		WF 20		Woodward's Pavilion, Colma, Calif.	James (Duck) Sullivan
9/30/04	Joe WALCOTT	141	Joe GANS	137	draw 20		Woodward's Pavilion, Colma, Calif.	Jack Welsh
10/16/06	Honey MELLODY		Joe WALCOTT		ref 15		Lincoln A.C., Chelsea, Mass.	Hector McInnis
11/29/06	Honey MELLODY		Joe WALCOTT		TKO 12		Lincoln A.C., Chelsea, Mass.	
4/23/07	Mike (Twin) SULLIVAN		Honey MELLODY		ref 20		Century A.C., Los Angeles, Calif.	
11/01/07	Mike (Twin) SULLIVAN		Frank FIELD		ref 20		Goldfield, Nevada	
11/27/07	Mike (Twin) SULLIVAN		Kid FARMER		KO 13		Century A.C., Los Angeles, Calif.	
4/23/08	Mike (Twin) SULLIVAN		Jimmy GARDNER		ref 25		Century A.C., Los Angeles, Calif.	James J. Jeffries
11/07/08	Jimmy GARDNER		Jimmy CLABBY		ref 15		New Orleans, Louisiana	
11/26/08	Jimmy GARDNER		Jimmy CLABBY		draw 20		New Orleans, Louisiana	
9/05/10	Jimmy CLABBY		Guy BUCKLES		KO 13		Sheridan, Wyoming	
11/02/10	Jimmy CLABBY		Bob BRYANT		TKO 7		Sydney, N.S.W., Australia	
12/26/10	Jimmy CLABBY		Gus DEVITT		KO 1		Brisbane, Queensland, Australia	
1/25/11	Harry LEWIS		Johnny SUMMERS		KO 4		Liverpool, England	
1/01/14	Waldemar HOLBERG		Ray BRONSON		ref 20		Melbourne, Victoria, Australia	
1/24/14	Tom McCORMICK		Waldemar HOLBERG		WF 6		Melbourne, Victoria, Australia	
3/21/14	Matt WELLS		Tom McCORMICK		ref 20		Sydney, N.S.W., Australia	
6/01/15	Mike GLOVER		Matt WELLS		ref 12		Armory A.A., Boston, Massachusetts	
6/22/15	Jack BRITTON		Mike GLOVER		ref 12		Armory A.A., Boston, Massachusetts	
8/31/15	Ted (Kid) LEWIS		Jack BRITTON		ref 12		Armory A.A., Boston, Massachusetts	Dan Lane
9/27/15	Ted (Kid) LEWIS		Jack BRITTON		ref 12		Armory A.A., Boston, Massachusetts	
10/26/15	Ted (Kid) LEWIS		Joe MANDOT		ref 12		Armory A.A., Boston, Massachusetts	
11/02/15	Ted (Kid) LEWIS		Milburn SAYLOR		ref 12		Armory A.A., Boston, Massachusetts	
11/23/15	Ted (Kid) LEWIS		Jimmy DUFFY		KO 1		Armory A.A., Boston, Massachusetts	
12/28/15	Ted (Kid) LEWIS		Willie RITCHIE		ND 10		New York City, New York	
1/17/16	Ted (Kid) LEWIS		Kid GRAVES		ND 10		Milwaukee, Wisconsin	
1/20/16	Ted (Kid) LEWIS	142	Jack BRITTON	144¾	ND 10		Broadway Auditorium, Buffalo, N.Y.	
2/15/16	Ted (Kid) LEWIS	141½	Jack BRITTON	143½	ND 10		Broadway Sporting Club, Brooklyn	
3/01/16	Ted (Kid) LEWIS		Harry STONE		ref 20		New Orleans, Louisiana	
4/24/16	Jack BRITTON	145	Ted (Kid) LEWIS	145	ref 20		New Orleans, Louisiana	Dick Burke
9/05/16	Jack BRITTON	147	Joe WELLING	134½	ND 10		Queensberry A.C., Buffalo, N.Y.	Joe Suttner
10/17/16	Jack BRITTON		Ted (Kid) LEWIS		ref 12		Armory A.A., Boston, Massachusetts	
11/14/16	Jack BRITTON		Ted (Kid) LEWIS		draw 12		Armory A.A., Boston, Massachusetts	
11/21/16	Jack BRITTON		Charley WHITE		ref 12		Armory A.A., Boston, Massachusetts	
3/26/17	Jack BRITTON		Ted (Kid) LEWIS		ND 10		Queen City A.C., Cincinnati, Ohio	
5/19/17	Jack BRITTON		Ted (Kid) LEWIS		ND 10		Toronto, Ontario, Canada	
6/06/17	Jack BRITTON		Ted (Kid) LEWIS		ND 10		St. Louis, Missouri	
6/14/17	Jack BRITTON		Ted (Kid) LEWIS		ND 10		New York City, New York	
6/25/17	Ted (Kid) LEWIS		Jack BRITTON		ref 20		Westwood Field, Dayton, Ohio	Lou Bauman
7/04/17	Ted (Kid) LEWIS		Johnny GRIFFITHS		ND 15		Akron, Ohio	
10/24/17	Ted (Kid) LEWIS		Battling ORTEGA		draw 4		Arena, Emeryville, California	Jim Griffin
11/13/17	Ted (Kid) LEWIS		Johnny McCARTHY		ref 4		Dreamland Arena, San Francisco	Harry Sullivan
5/17/18	Ted (Kid) LEWIS		Johnny TILLMAN		ref 20		Denver, Colorado	
7/04/18	Ted (Kid) LEWIS		Johnny GRIFFITHS		ND 20		Akron, Ohio	
9/23/18	Ted (Kid) LEWIS		Benny LEONARD		ND 8		Weidenmeyer's Park, Newark, N.J.	Patsy Kline
3/10/19	Ted (Kid) LEWIS		Johnny GRIFFITHS		ND 8		Memphis, Tennessee	
3/17/19	Jack BRITTON	144½	Ted (Kid) LEWIS		KO 9	2:10	Auditorium, Canton, Ohio	Matt Hinkel
3/08/19	Jack BRITTON		Johnny GRIFFITHS		ND 10		Broadway Auditorium, Buffalo	
5/19/19	Jack BRITTON		Joe WELLING		ND 10		Syracuse, New York	
7/04/19	Jack BRITTON		Johnny GRIFFITHS		ND 12		Auditorium, Canton, Ohio	
7/28/19	Jack BRITTON		Ted (Kid) LEWIS		ND 8		Jersey City, New Jersey	

589

	8/07/19	**Jack BRITTON**		**Johnny GRIFFITHS**		ND 12		Denver, Colorado	
	11/05/19	**Jack BRITTON**		**Johnny TILLMAN**		ND 10		Detroit, Michigan	
	12/01/19	**Jack BRITTON**		**Billy RYAN**		KO 11		Auditorium, Canton, Ohio	
	12/04/19	**Jack BRITTON**		**Steve LATZO**		ND 10		Wilkes-Barre, Pennsylvania	
	5/31/20	**Jack BRITTON**		**Johnny GRIFFITHS**		ref 15		Akron, Ohio	
	9/06/20	**Jack BRITTON**		**Ray BRONSON**		ref 10		Cedar Point, Iowa	
	9/13/20	**Jack BRITTON**		**Johnny TILLMAN**		ND 10		Cleveland, Ohio	
	12/06/20	**Jack BRITTON**		**Pinky MITCHELL**		ND 10		Milwaukee, Wisconsin	
	2/07/21	**Jack BRITTON**	145	**Ted (Kid) LEWIS**	145	unan 15		Madison Square Garden, New York	Dick Nugent
	3/07/21	**Jack BRITTON**		**Johnny TILLMAN**		ND 10		Des Moines, Iowa	
	5/25/21	**Jack BRITTON**		**Travis DAVIS**		draw 4		Seattle, Washington	
	6/03/21	**Jack BRITTON**		**Dave SHADE**		draw 10		Milwaukie Arena, Portland, Oregon	
	6/10/21	**Jack BRITTON**		**Frank BARRIEAU**		draw 10		Milwaukie Arena, Portland, Oregon	
	7/18/21	**Jack BRITTON**	149	**Mickey WALKER**	145	ND 12		Armory, Newark, New Jersey	Jimmy DeForest
	2/17/22	**Jack BRITTON**	146½	**Dave SHADE**	144¼	draw 15		Madison Square Garden, New York	Patsy Haley
	6/26/22	**Jack BRITTON**	146¼	**Benny LEONARD**	139¼	WF 13	2:42	Velodrome, Bronx, New York	Patsy Haley
	11/01/22	**Mickey WALKER**	144¼	**Jack BRITTON**	146	unan 15		Madison Square Garden, New York	Patsy Haley
	3/22/23	**Mickey WALKER**	146¼	**Pete LATZO**	144¼	ND 12		Armory, Newark, New Jersey	Harry Ertle
	10/08/23	**Mickey WALKER**	148	**Jimmy JONES**	145¾	NC 9	• •	Dreamland Park, Newark, N.J.	Danny Sullivan
	6/02/24	**Mickey WALKER**	147	**Lew TENDLER**	142¾	unan 10		Baker Bowl, Philadelphia, Pa.	Jim Brennan
	10/01/24	**Mickey WALKER**	146¾	**Bobby BARRETT**	147	KO 6	1:33	Baker Bowl, Philadelphia, Pa.	Dan Buckley
	9/21/25	**Mickey WALKER**	144½	**Dave SHADE**	147	split 15		Yankee Stadium, Bronx, New York	Patsy Haley
	11/25/25	**Mickey WALKER**	146½	**Sailor FRIEDMAN**	144	ND 12		Armory, Newark, New Jersey	Hank Lewis
	5/20/26	**Pete LATZO**	146	**Mickey WALKER**	144	maj 10		Armory, Scranton, Pennsylvania	Frank J. Floyd
	6/29/26	**Pete LATZO**	153	**Willie HARMON**	144¾	KO 5	2:50	Dreamland Park, Newark, N.J.	Hank Lewis
	7/09/26	**Pete LATZO**	147	**George LEVINE**	145½	WF 4	1:28	Polo Grounds, New York City	Ed Purdy
	6/03/27	**Joe DUNDEE**	143	**Pete LATZO**	146½	maj 15		Polo Grounds, New York City	Eddie Forbes
†	3/25/29	**Jackie FIELDS**	145¾	**Young Jack THOMPSON**	145	ref 10		Coliseum, Chicago, Illinois	Ed Purdy
	7/25/29	**Jackie FIELDS**	145	**Joe DUNDEE**	147	WF 2	1:55	Fair Grounds, Detroit, Michigan	Elmer McClelland
	5/09/30	**Young Jack THOMPSON**	142¾	**Jackie FIELDS**	145¾	ref 15		Olympia, Detroit, Michigan	Elmer McClelland
	9/05/30	**Tommy FREEMAN**	145¾	**Young Jack THOMPSON**	143¼	ref 15		League Park, Cleveland, Ohio	Patsy Haley
	4/14/31	**Young Jack THOMPSON**	145¼	**Tommy FREEMAN**	146¾	TKO 12		Public Hall, Cleveland, Ohio	Eddie Davis
	10/23/31	**Lou BROUILLARD**	146¾	**Young Jack THOMPSON**	146	unan 15		Boston Garden, Boston, Mass.	Johnny Brassil
	1/28/32	**Jackie FIELDS**	145½	**Lou BROUILLARD**	146	unan 10		Chicago Stadium, Chicago, Ill.	Dave Miller
	2/22/33	**Young CORBETT III**	146	**Jackie FIELDS**	146	ref 10		Seals Stadium, San Francisco	Lt. Jack Kennedy
	5/29/33	**Jimmy McLARNIN**	145¼	**Young CORBETT III**	146	KO 1	2:37	Wrigley Field, Los Angeles	George Blake
	5/28/34	**Barney ROSS**	137¾	**Jimmy McLARNIN**	142	split 15		M.S.G. Bowl, Long Island City	Eddie Forbes
	9/17/34	**Jimmy McLARNIN**	146¼	**Barney ROSS**	140¼	split 15		M.S.G. Bowl, Long Island City	Arthur Donovan
	5/28/35	**Barney ROSS**	141	**Jimmy McLARNIN**	144¾	unan 15		Polo Grounds, New York City	Jack Dempsey
	11/27/36	**Barney ROSS**	143¼	**Izzy JANNAZZO**	145¼	unan 15		Madison Square Garden, New York	Johnny McAvoy
	9/23/37	**Barney ROSS**	143	**Ceferino GARCIA**	145¾	unan 15		Polo Grounds, New York City	Billy Cavanaugh
	5/31/38	**Henry ARMSTRONG**	133½	**Barney ROSS**	142	unan 15		M.S.G. Bowl, Long Island City	Arthur Donovan
	11/25/38	**Henry ARMSTRONG**	134	**Ceferino GARCIA**	146½	unan 15		Madison Square Garden, New York	Arthur Donovan
	12/05/38	**Henry ARMSTRONG**	134¾	**Al MANFREDO**	146	TKO 3	1:45	Arena, Cleveland, Ohio	Tony LaBranche
	1/10/39	**Henry ARMSTRONG**	134½	**Baby ARIZMENDI**	136	ref 10		Olympic Auditorium, Los Angeles	George Blake
	3/04/39	**Henry ARMSTRONG**	134	**Bobby PACHO**	147	TKO 4	1:10	Tropical Stadium, Havana, Cuba	James J. Braddock
	3/16/39	**Henry ARMSTRONG**	135	**Lew FELDMAN**	134	KO 1	2:12	Municipal Auditorium, St. Louis	Walter Heisner
	3/31/39	**Henry ARMSTRONG**	135	**Davey DAY**	136	KO 12	2:49	Madison Square Garden, New York	Billy Cavanaugh
	5/25/39	**Henry ARMSTRONG**	135	**Ernie RODERICK**	145¾	ref 15		Harringay Arena, London, England	Wilfred Smith
	10/09/39	**Henry ARMSTRONG**	141½	**Al MANFREDO**	146¾	TKO 4	1:35	Riverview Park Arena, Des Moines	Alex Fidler
	10/13/39	**Henry ARMSTRONG**	141	**Howard SCOTT**	147	KO 2	1:38	Armory, Minneapolis, Minnesota	John de Otis
	10/20/39	**Henry ARMSTRONG**	139¾	**Ritchie FONTAINE**	141	KO 3	2:03	Civic Stadium, Seattle, Wash.	Tommy Clark
	10/24/39	**Henry ARMSTRONG**	138¼	**Jimmy GARRISON**	139½	ref 10		Olympic Auditorium, Los Angeles	George Blake
	10/30/39	**Henry ARMSTRONG**	140	**Bobby PACHO**	146	TKO 4		Municipal Auditorium, Denver	Jack Bloom
	12/11/39	**Henry ARMSTRONG**	138¾	**Jimmy GARRISON**	141	KO 7	1:19	Arena, Cleveland, Ohio	Benny Leonard
	1/04/40	**Henry ARMSTRONG**	136¾	**Joe GHNOULY**	135½	KO 5	1:34	Municipal Auditorium, St. Louis	Harry Cook
	1/24/40	**Henry ARMSTRONG**	139¾	**Pedro MONTANEZ**	144½	TKO 9	0:47	Madison Square Garden, New York	Billy Cavanaugh
	4/26/40	**Henry ARMSTRONG**	139½	**Paul JUNIOR**	141	TKO 7	1:05	Boston Garden, Boston, Mass.	Johnny Martin
	5/24/40	**Henry ARMSTRONG**	140½	**Ralph ZANELLI**	145½	TKO 5	1:30	Boston Garden, Boston, Mass.	Johnny Martin
	6/21/40	**Henry ARMSTRONG**	144	**Paul JUNIOR**	142½	TKO 3		Arena A.A., Portland, Maine	Johnny Martin
	9/23/40	**Henry ARMSTRONG**	146	**Phil FURR**	147	KO 4	1:45	Griffith Stadium, Washington, D.C.	Ray Powen
	10/04/40	**Fritzie ZIVIC**	145½	**Henry ARMSTRONG**	142	unan 15		Madison Square Garden, New York	Arthur Donovan
	1/17/41	**Fritzie ZIVIC**	145¾	**Henry ARMSTRONG**	140½	TKO 12	0:52	Madison Square Garden, New York	Arthur Donovan
	7/29/41	**Freddie COCHRANE**	142½	**Fritzie ZIVIC**	145	ref 15	2:54	Ruppert Stadium, Newark, N.J.	Joe Mangold
	2/01/46	**Marty SERVO**	143	**Freddie COCHRANE**	145	KO 4	2:54	Madison Square Garden, New York	Eddie Joseph
	12/20/46	**Sugar Ray ROBINSON**	146½	**Tommy BELL**	146	unan 15		Madison Square Garden, New York	Eddie Joseph
	6/24/47	**Sugar Ray ROBINSON**	146	**Jimmy DOYLE**	147	TKO 9	•	Arena, Cleveland, Ohio	Jackie Davis
	12/19/47	**Sugar Ray ROBINSON**	146½	**Chuck TAYLOR**	144¾	TKO 6	2:07	Olympia, Detroit, Michigan	Johnny Weber
	6/28/48	**Sugar Ray ROBINSON**	146½	**Bernard DOCUSEN**	145½	unan 15		Comiskey Park, Chicago, Illinois	Walter Brightmore
	7/11/49	**Sugar Ray ROBINSON**	147	**Kid GAVILAN**	144½	unan 15		Municipal Stadium, Philadelphia	Charles Daggert
	8/09/50	**Sugar Ray ROBINSON**	147	**Charley FUSARI**	145¼	ref 15		Roosevelt Stadium, Jersey City	Paul Cavalier
†	3/14/51	**Johnny BRATTON**	146¼	**Charley FUSARI**	146¼	split 15		Chicago Stadium, Chicago, Illinois	Tommy Gilmore
	5/18/51	**Kid GAVILAN**	145¼	**Johnny BRATTON**	147	unan 15		Madison Square Garden, New York	Ruby Goldstein
	8/29/51	**Kid GAVILAN**	145½	**Billy GRAHAM**	145	split 15		Madison Square Garden, New York	Mark Conn
	2/04/52	**Kid GAVILAN**	147	**Bobby DYKES**	146¾	split 15		Miami Stadium, Miami, Florida	Eddie Coachman
	7/07/52	**Kid GAVILAN**	146	**Gil TURNER**	144½	TKO 11	2:47	Municipal Stadium, Philadelphia	Pete Tomasco
	10/05/52	**Kid GAVILAN**	146½	**Billy GRAHAM**	146½	unan 15		Stadium Ball Park, Havana, Cuba	Mike Rojo
	2/11/53	**Kid GAVILAN**	146½	**Chuck DAVEY**	147	TKO 10	•	Chicago Stadium, Chicago, Illinois	Frank Gilmer
	9/18/53	**Kid GAVILAN**	146¾	**Carmen BASILIO**	147	split 15		War Memorial Auditorium, Syracuse	George Walsh
	11/13/53	**Kid GAVILAN**	146	**Johnny BRATTON**	145½	unan 15		Chicago Stadium, Chicago, Illinois	Frank Gilmer
	10/20/54	**Johnny SAXTON**	146¼	**Kid GAVILAN**	145½	unan 15		Convention Hall, Philadelphia, Pa.	Pete Pantaleo
	4/01/55	**Tony DeMARCO**	145	**Johnny SAXTON**	145½	TKO 14	2:20	Boston Garden, Boston, Mass.	Mel Manning
	6/10/55	**Carmen BASILIO**	145½	**Tony DeMARCO**	144¾	TKO 12	1:52	War Memorial Auditorium, Syracuse	Harry Kessler
	11/30/55	**Carmen BASILIO**	145½	**Tony DeMARCO**	145½	TKO 12	1:54	Boston Garden, Boston, Mass.	Mel Manning
	3/14/56	**Johnny SAXTON**	146	**Carmen BASILIO**	146¾	unan 15		Chicago Stadium, Chicago, Illinois	Frank Gilmer
	9/12/56	**Carmen BASILIO**	146¼	**Johnny SAXTON**	145¾	TKO 9	1:31	War Memorial Auditorium, Syracuse	Al Berl

2/22/57	**Carmen BASILIO**	147	**Johnny SAXTON**	147	KO	2	2:42	Arena, Cleveland, Ohio	Tony LaBranche
6/06/58	**Virgil AKINS**	146¾	**Vince MARTINEZ**	146¾	KO	4	0:52	Arena, St. Louis, Missouri	Harry Kessler
12/05/58	**Don JORDAN**	145	**Virgil AKINS**	145½	unan	15		Olympic Auditorium, Los Angeles	Lee Grossman
4/24/59	**Don JORDAN**	146¾	**Virgil AKINS**	147	unan	15		Kiel Auditorium, St. Louis, Mo.	Harry Kessler
7/10/59	**Don JORDAN**	147	**Dennis MOYER**	146½	unan	15		Meadows Race Track, Portland, Ore.	Harry Volk
5/27/60	**Benny (Kid) PARET**	146½	**Don JORDAN**	144½	unan	15		Convention Center, Las Vegas, Nev.	Charles Randolph
12/10/60	**Benny (Kid) PARET**	147	**Federico THOMPSON**	145½	unan	15		Madison Square Garden, New York	Arthur Mercante
4/01/60	**Emile GRIFFITH**	145½	**Benny (Kid) PARET**	146½	KO	13	1:11	Convention Hall, Miami Beach, Fla.	Jimmy Peerless
6/03/61	**Emile GRIFFITH**	145½	**Gaspar ORTEGA**	146	TKO	12	0:48	Olympic Auditorium, Los Angeles	Tommy Hart
9/30/61	**Benny (Kid) PARET**	146	**Emile GRIFFITH**	147	split	15		Madison Square Garden, New York	Al Berl
3/24/62	**Emile GRIFFITH**	144	**Benny (Kid) PARET**	146½	TKO	12	2:09	Madison Square Garden, New York	Ruby Goldstein
7/13/62	**Emile GRIFFITH**	145¼	**Ralph DUPAS**	145¾	unan	15		Convention Center, Las Vegas, Nev.	Frankie Van
12/08/62	**Emile GRIFFITH**	145	**Jorge FERNANDEZ**	147	TKO	9	1:34	Convention Center, Las Vegas, Nev.	Harry Krause
3/21/63	**Luis RODRIGUEZ**	146	**Emile GRIFFITH**	145½	unan	15		Dodger Stadium, Chavez Ravine	Tommy Hart
6/08/63	**Emile GRIFFITH**	146½	**Luis RODRIGUEZ**	146½	split	15		Madison Square Garden, New York	Jimmy Devlin
6/12/64	**Emile GRIFFITH**	146	**Luis RODRIGUEZ**	146½	split	15		Convention Center, Las Vegas, Nev.	Harry Krause
9/22/64	**Emile GRIFFITH**	145½	**Brian CURVIS**	145½	ref	15		Empire Pool, Wembley, London	Harry Gibbs
3/30/65	**Emile GRIFFITH**	146½	**Jose STABLE**	146	unan	15		Madison Square Garden, New York	Arthur Mercante
12/10/65	**Emile GRIFFITH**	146¼	**Manuel GONZALEZ**	146	unan	15		Madison Square Garden, New York	Arthur Mercante
† 8/24/66	**Curtis COKES**	145¾	**Manuel GONZALEZ**	147	unan	15		Municipal Auditorium, New Orleans	Pete Giarusso
11/28/66	**Curtis COKES**	145¾	**Jean JOSSELIN**	146¼	unan	15		Memorial Auditorium, Dallas, Texas	Dick Cole
‡ 12/07/66	**Charlie SHIPES**	146	**Percy MANNING**	146	TKO	10	2:49	High School Gymnasium, Hayward	Vern Bybee
5/19/67	**Curtis COKES**	145	**Francois PAVILLA**	146¾	TKO	10	2:50	Memorial Auditorium, Dallas, Texas	Pat Riley
10/02/67	**Curtis COKES**	145	**Charlie SHIPES**	145	TKO	8	1:37	Arena, Oakland, California	Jack Downey
4/16/68	**Curtis COKES**	145¾	**Willie Ludick**	146¼	TKO	5	0:34	Memorial Auditorium, Dallas, Texas	Lew Eskin
10/21/68	**Curtis COKES**	146½	**Ramon LaCRUZ**	147	unan	15		Municipal Auditorium, New Orleans	Herman Dutreix
4/18/69	**Jose NAPOLES**	143	**Curtis COKES**	145½	TKO	14	*	Forum, Inglewood, California	George Latka
6/29/69	**Jose NAPOLES**	145	**Curtis COKES**	146½	TKO	11	*	Monumental Plaza, Mexico City	Ramon Berumen
10/17/69	**Jose NAPOLES**	144¾	**Emile GRIFFITH**	144½	unan	15		Forum, Inglewood, California	Dick Young
2/15/70	**Jose NAPOLES**	145½	**Ernie LOPEZ**	146	TKO	15	2:38	Forum, Inglewood, California	Larry Rozadilla
12/03/70	**Billy BACKUS**	146½	**Jose NAPOLES**	144¼	TKO	4	0:55	War Memorial Auditorium, Syracuse	Jack Millicent
6/04/71	**Jose NAPOLES**	146	**Billy BACKUS**	145¼	TKO	4	1:53	Forum, Inglewood, California	Dick Young
12/14/71	**Jose NAPOLES**	145½	**Hedgemon LEWIS**	144¼	unan	15		Forum, Inglewood, California	Larry Rozadilla
3/28/72	**Jose NAPOLES**	146¼	**Ralph CHARLES**	147	KO	7	2:52	Empire Pool, Wembley, London	James Brimmell
6/10/72	**Jose NAPOLES**	146	**Adolph PRUITT**	143½	TKO	2	2:10	Memorial Plaza, Monterrey, Mexico	Octavio Meyran
§ 6/16/72	**Hedgemon LEWIS**	147	**Billy BACKUS**	147	unan	15		War Memorial Auditorium, Syracuse	Arthur Mercante
§ 12/08/72	**Hedgemon LEWIS**	145	**Billy BACKUS**	145	unan	15		War Memorial Auditorium, Syracuse	Tony Phillips
2/28/73	**Jose NAPOLES**	146½	**Ernie LOPEZ**	146½	KO	7	1:36	Forum, Inglewood, California	Dick Young
6/23/73	**Jose NAPOLES**	146	**Roger MENETRY**	145	unan	15		Sports Palace, Grenoble, France	Roland Dakin
9/22/73	**Jose NAPOLES**	147	**Clyde GRAY**	147	unan	15		Maple Leaf Gardens, Toronto	Jay Edson
8/03/74	**Jose NAPOLES**	145	**Hedgemon LEWIS**	141	TKO	9	2:34	Sports Palace, Mexico City	Ramon Berumen
12/14/74	**Jose NAPOLES**	146½	**Horacio SALDANO**	143	KO	3	1:55	Sports Palace, Mexico City	Ramon Berumen
3/30/75	**Jose NAPOLES**	147	**Armando MUNIZ**	145	TW	12	0:50	Convention Center, Acapulco	Ramon Berumen
6/28/75	**Angel ESPADA**	145¼	**Clyde GRAY**	144½	unan	15		Roberto Clemente Coliseum, San Juan	Isaac Herrera
7/12/75	**Jose NAPOLES**	146	**Armando MUNIZ**	146½	unan	15		Sports Palace, Mexico City	Octavio Meyran
† 10/11/75	**Angel ESPADA**	143½	**Johnny GANT**	144	unan	15		Roberto Clemente Coliseum, San Juan	Waldemar Schmidt
12/06/75	**John H. STRACEY**	145	**Jose NAPOLES**	147	TKO	6	2:30	Monumental Plaza, Mexico City	Octavio Meyran
3/20/76	**John H. STRACEY**	146¼	**Hedgemon LEWIS**	146¼	TKO	10	1:25	Empire Pool, Wembley, London	Harry Gibbs
† 4/27/76	**Angel ESPADA**	145½	**Alfonso HAYMAN**	147	TKO	8	1:37	Roberto Clemente Coliseum, San Juan	Ismael Quinones Falu
6/22/76	**Carlos PALOMINO**	145¼	**John H. STRACEY**	146	TKO	12	1:35	Empire Pool, Wembley, London	Sid Nathan
† 7/17/76	**Jose CUEVAS**	146	**Angel ESPADA**	145	TKO	2	1:00	Mexicali, Baja California, Mexico	Isidoro Rodriguez
† 10/27/76	**Jose CUEVAS**	145¾	**Shoji TSUJIMOTO**	146¼	KO	6	2:29	Jissen Rinri Stadium, Kanazawa	Carlos Berrocal
1/22/77	**Carlos PALOMINO**	146½	**Armando MUNIZ**	147	TKO	15	2:26	Olumpic Auditorium, Los Angeles	John Thomas
† 3/12/77	**Jose CUEVAS**	146½	**Miguel CAMPANINO**	146½	KO	2	2:05	Mexico City, Mexico	Isaac Herrera
6/14/77	**Carlos PALOMINO**	147	**Dave (Boy) GREEN**	146¼	KO	11	2:05	Empire Pool, Wembley, London	James Brimmell
† 8/06/77	**Jose CUEVAS**	145½	**Clyde GRAY**	147	KO	2	1:28	Olympic Auditorium, Los Angeles	Chuck Hassett
9/13/77	**Carlos PALOMINO**	147	**Everaldo AZEVEDO**	145½	unan	15		Olympic Auditorium, Los Angeles	Dick Young
† 11/19/77	**Jose CUEVAS**	147	**Angel ESPADA**	146½	TKO	12	*	Roberto Clemente Coliseum, San Juan	Jesus Celis
12/10/77	**Carlos PALOMINO**	147	**Jose PALACIOS**	146½	KO	13	0:49	Olympic Auditorium, Los Angeles	John Thomas
2/11/78	**Carlos PALOMINO**	147	**Ryu SORIMACHI**	147	KO	7	2:03	Hilton Sports Pavilion, Las Vegas	Ferd Hernandez
† 3/04/78	**Jose CUEVAS**	146¼	**Harold WESTON, Jr.**	146½	TKO	10	*	Olympic Auditorium, Los Angeles	Martin Denkin
3/18/78	**Carlos PALOMINO**	147	**Mimoun MOHATAR**	146¼	TKO	9	0:57	Aladdin Hotel, Las Vegas, Nev.	Charles Roth
† 5/20/78	**Jose CUEVAS**	146¾	**Billy BACKUS**	146¼	TKO	2	*	Forum, Inglewood, California	Carlos Berrocal
5/27/78	**Carlos PALOMINO**	147	**Armando MUNIZ**	146	unan	15		Olympic Auditorium, Los Angeles	Rudy Ortega
† 9/09/78	**Jose CUEVAS**	146¼	**Pete RANZANY**	146	TKO	2	1:57	Hughes Stadium, Sacramento	Isidoro Rodriguez
1/14/79	**Wilfred BENITIZ**	146	**Carlos PALOMINO**	146½	split	15		Hiram Bithorn Stadium, San Juan	Jay Edson
† 1/29/79	**Jose CUEVAS**	146	**Scott CLARK**	145½	TKO	2	2:15	Forum, Inglewood, California	Luis Sulbaran
3/25/79	**Wilfred BENITEZ**	147	**Harold WESTON, Jr.**	147	unan	15		Hiram Bithorn Stadium, San Juan	Richard Steele
† 7/30/79	**Jose CUEVAS**	146½	**Randy SHIELDS**	142½	unan	15		Int. Amphitheatre, Chicago	Luis Sulbaran
11/30/79	**Sugar Ray LEONARD**	146	**Wilfred BENITEZ**	144½	TKO	15	2:54	Caesars Palace, Las Vegas, Nev.	Carlos Padilla
† 12/08/79	**Jose CUEVAS**	146	**Angel ESPADA**	144½	TKO	10	2:03	Sports Arena, Los Angeles	Terry Smith
3/31/80	**Sugar Ray LEONARD**	147	**Dave (Boy) GREEN**	147	KO	4	2:27	Capital Centre, Landover, Md.	Arthur Mercante
† 4/06/80	**Jose CUEVAS**	146½	**Harold VOLBRECHT**	146¾	KO	5	1:19	Astro Arena, Houston, Texas	Carlos Berrocal
6/20/80	**Roberto DURAN**	145¼	**Sugar Ray LEONARD**	145	unan	15		Olympic Stadium, Montreal	Carlos Padilla
† 8/02/80	**Thomas HEARNS**	146½	**Pipino CUEVAS**	146	TKO	2	2:39	Joe Louis Arena, Detroit, Mich.	Stan Christodoulou
11/25/80	**Sugar Ray LEONARD**	146	**Roberto DURAN**	146	TKO	8	2:44	Superdome, New Orleans	Octavio Meyran
† 12/06/80	**Thomas HEARNS**	146½	**Luis PRIMERA**	146¾	KO	6	2:00	Joe Louis Arena, Detroit, Mich.	Ismael Fernandez

*Loser failed to answer bell for round indicated
**Bout declared "no contest" at end of round
ref = referee's decision (sole arbiter)
†NBA (later WBA) world welterweight title bout
‡California State Athletic Commission world welterweight title bout
§[illegible] State Athletic Commission world heavyweight title bout

WELTERWEIGHT DIVISION

PADDY DUFFY
Born, Boston, Mass. November 12, 1864.
Height, 5 feet, 7 inches. Weight, 135-140.

1884

Feb.	—Skin Doherty, Boston ....KO	3
Mar.	—Young Shannon, Boston .....W	4
Apr.	—Bob Lyons, Boston ....KO	11
May	15—Paddy Carey, Boston ....KO	4
May	—Paddy Sullivan, Gloucester ...D	6
June	—Paddy Sullivan, Lowell ......D	6
June	—Paddy Sullivan, Boston ......D	6
Oct.	31—Tug Collins, Boston ....D	4
Dec.	19—Jack McGee, Boston ....KO by	2

1885

Feb.	18—Dan Murphy, Boston ......KO	3
Oct.	27—Bill Rosamond, Boston ....KO	4

1886

Jan.	28—Bill Young, Baltimore ......D	6
Mar.	—Bill Young, Baltimore ......KO	2
Apr.	22—Billy Nally, Washington ....KO	4
Apr.	24—George Milton, Washington ..KO	2
	—Danny Shea, Baltimore ....KO	7
	—Charles Gleason, Phila. ......W	4
	—Walter Redmond, Phila. .....W	4
	—Pete Connolly, Phila. ....W	4
	—Butler's Unknown, Phila. ....W	4
	—Frank Brooks, Phila. ....W	4
	—Charley White, Phila. ....W	4
	—Charley McCarthy, Phila. ....W	4
	—Charley Hermon, Phila. .....KO	2
	—Tom Wall, Phila. ....D	4
	—Frank Burke, Phila. ....D	4
	—Charley Gleason, Phila. ......D	4
	—Billy Teese, Phila. ....D	4

1887

	—Pat Farley, Boston ....KO	3
	—Tom Murphy, Boston ......KO	4
	—Jack McGinty, Boston ......D	6
	—Jack McGinty, Boston ......D	6
	—Jack McGinty, Boston ......W	6

1888

Feb.	9—Jack McGinty, Boston .....KO	9
Aug.	26—Johnny Reagan, Brooklyn ..Exh.	3
Oct.	30—William McMillan,	
	Ft. Foote, Va. ....KO	17

(McMillan claimed English Title, Duffy,
the winner claimed world title)

1889

Mar.	29—Tom Meadows, San Fran. ..W.F.	45

(Meadows was Australian champion)
Duffy 140, Meadows 143, Referee Hiram
Cook.

TB	KO	WD	WF	D	LD	LF	KOBY	ND	NC
36	14	9	1	11	0	0	1	0	0

Died July 19, 1890 in Boston, Mass.

MYSTERIOUS BILLY SMITH
(Amos Smith)
Born, May 15, 1871, Eastport, Me.
Nationality, Irish-American, Height, 5 ft. 8½ in.
Won. "Spider Kelly, California Athletic
Club, 5; Draw: Ed Harvey, St. John, N. B., 10;
Fred Tebeau (stopped), 10. Bested by Frank
Purcell, California Athletic Club, 10.

1891

June	30—Jack Slavin, San Fran. ... KO by	49

1892

Feb.	16—Frank Kelly, Pacific Club, S.F.KO	7
Mar.	21—Billy Armstrong, Occidental,	
	San Francisco ....KO	13
Apr.	28—Tommy West, Portland, Ore...D	11
June	29—Charley Gleason, Portland, Ore.W	4
Sept.	21—"Shadow" Maber, Ptldn., Ore.KO	26
Dec.	14—Danny Needham, Pacific Club,	
	San Francisco ....KO	14

(For Welterweight Title)

1893

Apr.	17—*Tom Williams of Australia (140),	
	$4,500-500, Coney Island Athletic	
	Club......................KO	2
Aug.	29—Tommy Ryan, Coney Island	
	A.C.D. 6	
Sept.	20—Billy McCarthy, Australia,	
	Chicago ....D	6

*Title bout.

1894

Jan.	9—Tommy Ryan, Boston (gate) .. D	6
Feb.	19—Fletcher Robbins,	
	Streator, Ill. ....KO	4
May	15—Eddie Butler, Spring Valley, Ill. W	2

July	26—Tommy Ryan, purse, Minneapolis	
	L	20

(Lost Welterweight Title)
Referee Joe Choynski

Oct.	29—Dick O'Brien, Boston ....D	10
Nov.	19—Jack Powers, St. John, N.B. ..D	6

1895

Mar.	1—Joe Walcott, Boston ....D	15
May	27—Tommy Ryan, gate, Coney Isl. D	18

Police stopped in 11th and 18th rounds.
For welterweight championship. Matched
with Ryan, $4,500 and championship,
Dallas, Tex. Off.

Dec.	7—Tom Crawley, Syracuse .....ND	6
Dec.	11—Young Hagen ....W	4
Dec.	19—Harry Gallagher...........ND	4
Dec.	29—Jimmy Mann ....ND	4

1896

Jan.	15—Pat Kehoe, Hartford ....KO	1
Feb.	5—Dido Plumb, London ....W	3
Mar.	20—Bill Husbands, London ......W	8
May	6—Tommy Ryan, Syracuse ....ND	5
May	18—Kid McCoy, Boston ....LF	6
July	2—Billy Gallagher, San Fran. ....D	1

(Stopped by police)
(Ryan vacated title; Smith claimed it.)

Sept.	4—Jim Ryan, Astoria, Ore. ......LF	7
Nov.	25—Tommy Ryan, Maspeth,L.I. ..LF	9

1897

Jan.	9—Con Doyle, New York.......D	12
Mar.	17—Geo. Green, Carson, Nev. KO by	12
May	29—Abe Ullman, New York .....W	20
Aug.	23—Jack Power, St. John, N.B. ...D	8
Sept.	6—Mike Dempsey, Brooklyn ....KO	2
Dec.	6—Billy Mulligan, Yonkers ......W	2
Dec.	13—Johnny Gorman, Bridgeport ..W	5

1898

Jan.	28—Charley Johnson, Phila. .....LF	1
Feb.	18—Abe Ullman, Baltimore .....D	8
Apr.	4—Joe Walcott, Bridgeport ....D	25
May	23—Charley Johnson, Athens, Pa. .D	15
June	4—Billy Stift, Chicago ....LF	3
June	25—Andy Walsh, Coney Island ...D	20
July	29—George Green, New York ....D	25
Aug.	25—Matty Matthews, New York ..W	25

(World welterweight title)

Sept.	5—Andy Walsh, Coney Island ...D	25
Oct.	3—Jack Judge, Scranton, Pa. ...KO	20
Oct.	7—Charley McKeever, New York .W	25

(World welterweight title)

Nov.	14—Tommy West, Bridgeport ....D	20
Dec.	6—Joe Walcott, New York .....W	20

(World welterweight title)

1899

Jan.	24—Billy Edwards, New York ...KO	14
Mar.	10—Geo. Kid Lavigne, San Fran. ..W	14
June	30—Charley McKeever, New York .D	20

(World welterweight title)

July	28—Young Mahoney, Phila. .....ND	6
Aug.	4—Andy Walsh, New York .....D	25
Sept.	25—Bob Douglass, Denver ......KO	4
Sept.	29—Billy Stift, Chicago ....D	6
Oct.	—Charley McKeever, Phila. ....ND	6
Nov.	8—Charley McKeever, New York .W	20

1900

Jan.	15—Rube Ferns, Buffalo ....LF	21

(Lost Welterweight Title)

Jan.	26—Frank McConnell, N. Y. C. ..KO	22
Mar.	12—Young Mahoney, Brooklyn ...D	25
Apr.	17—Matty Matthews, N. Y. .. KO by	19
May	4—Joe Walcott, New York L	25
June	29—Jimmy Handler, N. Y. ....LF	15
Sept.	11—Young Jackson, Cleveland ...W	18
Sept.	24—Joe Walcott, Hartford ......LF	10
Nov.	14—Jim Judge, Savannah ....LF	11
Nov.	22—Mike Donovan, Wheeling ....D	10

1901

Feb.	12—Owen Ziegler, Erie ....D	10
Mar.	21—Tim Hurley, New London ...D	20
Aug.	19—George Yerkes, St. John ....D	15
Oct.	26—Tom Tracey, Portland ......D	20
Nov.	29—Al Neill, Portland ....D	20

1902

Jan.	23—Al Neill, Portland ....LF	10
Mar.	14—Tommy Ryan,	
	Kansas City ....KO by	4

1903

May	28—Joe Walcott, Portland L	4

1911

July	21—Jim Cameron, San Francisco .LF	3

Smith was running a hotel and Turkish bath at Tacoma, Wash.

TB	KO	WD	WF	D	LD	LF	KOBY	ND	NC
82	13	15	0	29	4	11	4	6	0

Died Oct. 15, 1937 at Portland, Ore.

TOMMY RYAN
(Record under Middleweight Champions)

JIM FERNS
(The Kansas Rube)

Born, January 20, 1874, Pittsburg. Kansas. Weight 145 lbs. Height, 5 ft. 8½ in. Welterweight.

1896
Knockout: Jack Dougherty, 2; Tom Mackey, 16; Harry Pigeon, 19; Fred Ross, 13; Cass Whitman, 3; Billy Mayhan, 6. Lost: Paddy Purtell, 3.

1897
Wor· Scaldy Billy Quinn, 6; Walter Montgomery, 10. Knockout: Billy Mayhan, 6; Louis de Montje, 8; Hugh McManus, 23. Draw: Kid Gardner, 6.

1898
Mar. 15—Billy Emerson .... KO 10
Apr. 1—Dutch Neal .... KO 6
June 8—Dutch Neal .... KO 7
July 12—George Fitzgerald .... KO 2
Oct. 6—Ben Smith .... W 12
Nov. 19—Paddy Purtell .... KO 5
Dec. 11—W. Montgomery .... KO 9
Dec. 23—Spot Robinson .... KO 2

1899
Feb. 7—Charles McKeever, Chicago ... L 6
Feb. 9—Shorty Ahearn, Chicago ..... W 6
Apr. 5—Otto Minke, Philadelphia ... KO 6
June 22—Shorty Ahearn, Chicago .... KO 6
July 18—Bert Young, Hartford ...... L 9
Sept. 29—Bobby Dobbs, Hartford .... W 20
Nov. 30—Sammy Callaghan, Detroit .. KO 1
Dec. 28—Walter Burgo, Chicago ..... KO 2

1900
Jan. 15—Mys. Billy Smith, Buffalo ... WF 21
(Won Welterweight Title)
Feb. 23—Mike Donovan, Buffalo ..... W 20
Mar. 20—Jack Hanly, Fort Erie ...... KO 6
May 24—Jack Bennett, Toronto ..... KO 1
June 19—Joe Reptie, Toronto ...... KO 2
June 19—Otto Knopp, Buffalo ...... KO 4
Aug. 13—E. Connolly, Buffalo ...... KO 15
Sept. 1—Matty Matthews, Detroit .... W 15
Oct. 16—Matty Matthews, Detroit .... L 15
(Lost Welterweight Title)

1901
May 24—Matty Matthews, Toronto ... KO 10
(Won Welterweight Title)
Sept. 23—*Frank Erne, Fort Erie ..... KO 9
Nov. 28—Chas. Thurston, Fort Erie ... W 15
Dec. 18—Joe Walcott, Fort Erie ... KO by 5
(Lost Welterweight Title)
*Title bout.

1902
Jan. 3—Jack Bennett, Philadelphia .. KO 2
Jan. 27—Tim Murphy, Chicago ...... W 6
Feb. 26—Tom Tracey, Portland ...... L 20
Mar. 21—Al Neill, San Francisco .. KO by 12
May 29—Owen Ziegler, Joplin, Mo. ... KO 3
Dec. 10—Hugo Kelly, Kansas City .... L 10
Dec. 22—Matty Matthews, Pittsburgh .. L 10

1903
Apr. 27—Matty Matthews, Fort Erie . KO 19
May 28—Martin Duffy, Louisville . KO by 13

1904
Feb. 26—Martin Duffy, Hot Springs ... L 20

1906
Feb. 22—Cal Delaney, Grand Rapids .. KO 3

TB	KO	WD	WF	D	LD	LF	KOBY	ND	NC
53	31	9	1	1	8	0	3	0	0

Died June 11, 1952, Pittsburg, Kan.

WILLIAM R. (MATTY) MATTHEWS
Born July 13, 1873, New York City. Nationality, Irish-American. Weight, 138 lbs. Height, 5 ft. 7½ in.

1891
—Johnny Bennis, New York ..KO 12

1894
Dec. 29—Joe Burke, M. A. C., New York D 6
1895
Nov. 16—Jack Gibbons, N. Y. C. .....W 4
Dec. 5—Tom Frazier, N. Y. C. ......KO 7
1896
Jan. 12—Billy Lee, N. Y. C. ....KO 3
Feb. 11—Nick Collins, N. Y. C. ......KO 7
Mar. 17—Johnny Laughlin, Buffalo ....D 15
May 2—Harry Peterson, N. Y. C. .....D 8
July 27—Mike Leonard, N. Y. C. .....D 8
Oct. 5—Jack Hanley, Buffalo ....W 8
Oct. 29—Stanton Abbott, Buffalo .....KO 7
Nov. 7—Sam Tonkins, N. Y. C. ......W 10
1897
Jan. 25—Jack Everhardt, N. Y. C. ....D 15
Feb. 6—John A. Sullivan, N. Y. C. ...KO 4
Apr. 10—Mike Farragher, N. Y. C. ....KO 2
May 5—Jack Daly, Syracuse ....L 2
Aug. 4—Frank Garrard, Jamestown ... D 20
Sept. 27—Frank Garrard, Buffalo ......W 20
Dec. 13—Charles McKeever, Athens, Pa. D 15
Dec. 21—Mike Leonard, Rochester ....W 20
Dec. 27—Owen Ziegler, Philadelphia ..ND 6
1898
Jan. 22—Charley Johnson, Phila......ND 4
Jan. 31—Dan McConnell, Trenton ....LF 7
Mar. 31—Austin Gibbons, Paterson ....W 10
Apr. 12—Chas. McKeever, Cleveland ... L 20
Apr. 20—Tom Broderick, Yonkers .....W 20
May 9—Owen Ziegler, Paterson ......W 20
May 26—Tom Broderick, Yonkers .....W 4
June 18—Kid McPartland, Coney Island . D 20
Aug. 25—"Mys" Billy Smith, N. Y. C. ... L 25
(Welterweight Title Bout)
Oct. 21—Tom Ryan of Phila., N. Y. C. . W 13
Dec. 10—Owen Ziegler, Toronto ......D 15
Dec. 24—George Kerwin, Toronto .....W 20
1899
Jan. 2—Owen Ziegler, Brooklyn ....D 20
Jan. 19—Paddy Fenton, Yonkers .....W 20
Mar. 27—Tom Ryan of Phila.,
Youngstown ....W 20
May 8—Frank Bartley, Denver ....D 20
May 13—Owen Ziegler, Chicago ......D 6
June 21—Charley Burns, Cincinnati ...KO 6
June 27—Jack Bennett, Wheeling, W. Va. D 20
July 10—Otto Sieloff, Coney Island ... W 9
July 31—Eddie Connolly, Coney Island . W 25
Aug. 14—George Kerwin, Coney Island . W 16
Sept. 14—Bobby Dobbs, Coney Island .WF 25
Oct. 27—Eddie Connolly, N. Y. C. .... W 25
Nov. 17—"Kid" McPartland, Chicago ... D 6
Nov. 20—Charley Burns, Cinn. ......W 15
Dec. 16—Kid Carter, Brooklyn ....W 20
1900
Jan. 8—Isadore Strauss, Brooklyn ...KO 12
Jan. 15—Jack Bennett, Cincinnati ....KO 7
Jan. 29—Kid McPartland, Brooklyn ...KO 1
Feb. 16—Kid McPartland, N. Y. C. ....W 17
Mar. 19—Eddie Connolly, Brooklyn ...W 14
Mar. 26—Owen Ziegler, Youngstown ..KO 2
Apr. 6—Charley McKeever, Phila. ...ND 6
Apr. 9—Billy Payne, Niles ....W 6
Apr. 9—Dan McConnell, Niles ......KO 3
Apr. 17—Mys. Billy Smith, N. Y. C....KO 19
May 4—Kid Parker, Denver ....D 10
June 5—Eddie Connolly, Coney Island . L 25
Sept. 1—Jim Ferns, Detroit ....L 15
Oct. 8—Jack Bennett, Philadelphia ..ND 6
Oct. 16—Jim Ferns, Detroit ....W 15
(Won Welterweight Title)
Oct. 30—Charley Burns, Chicago .....W 6
Nov. 21—Owen Ziegler, Philadelphia ..ND 6
1901
Apr. 29—*Tom Couhig, Louisville .....W 20
May 24—Rube Ferns, Toronto ... KO by 10
(Lost Welterweight Title)
Sept. 2—Patsy Sweeney, Hartford .....W 20
Sept. 28—Ed. Kennedy, Toronto ......W 13
Oct. 28—Tom Couhig, Fort Erie .....WF 5
*Title bout.
1902
Mar. 6—Tom Couhig, Hot Springs .... L 20
Mar. 10—Martin Duffy, Chicago .. KO by 6
Sept. 11—Patsy Sweeney, New Britain .. L 5
Nov. 25—Ed. Kennedy, Allegheny .....W 10
Dec. 6—Owen Ziegler, Savannah .....W 6
Dec. 22—Jim Ferns, Pittsburgh .....W 10
1903
Feb. 23—Tom Couhig, Pittsburgh .....W 10
Apr. 27—Jim Ferns, Fort Erie .... KO by 19
Aug. 25—Martin Duffy, Port Huron ,... L 10
Dec. 29—Isidor Strauss, Phila. ....KO 0

1904

Jan.	1—Frankie Tyson, Norfolk	..... W	6
Jan.	13—Billy Mellody, Boston	 L	12
Jan.	16—Billy Devine, Philadelphia	...ND	6
Apr.	16—Joe Grim, Philadelphia	.....ND	6
Oct.	26—Ed Kennedy, Carnegie	...... D	10

TB	KO	WD	WF	D	LD	LF	KOBY	ND	NC
85	15	31	2	17	9	1	3	7	0

Died, December 6, 1948, at Brooklyn, N.Y.

JOE WALCOTT

Born, March 13, 1873, Barbados, West Indies. Nationality, West Indian. Weight, 145 lbs. Height, 5 ft. 1½ in. Managed by Tom O'Rourke. Came to America in 1887 and lived in Boston. Boxed and wrestled as amateur 1887-1889.

1890
Feb.	29—Tom Powers, So. Boston	.... KO	2

1891
Jan.	30—J. Barrett, Providence	...... KO	1
Mar.	26—Alex Clark, Cambridge	...... W	2
Dec.	12—G. V. Meakin, Boston	...... W	4
Dec.	12—Teddy Kelly, Boston	 L	3
Dec.	23—Alex. Clark, Boston	.... W	3

1892
Mar.	28—T. Warren, Boston	.... W	4
May	17—Tom Powers, Boston	.... W	3
Aug.	4—Frank Carey, Walpole	...... D	3
Aug.	29—J. J. Leahy, Cambridge	..... KO	3
Oct.	22—Fred Morris, Philadelphia	.... D	4

Oct.	22—Joe Larg, Philadelphia	.... W	3
Oct.	29—Andy Watson, Philadelphia	... D	4
Nov.	4—Harry Tracey, Boston	...... D	5
Nov.	11—Charley Jones, Philadelphia	... W	3
Nov.	12—Jack Lymon, Philadelphia	... KO	1
Dec.	5—Sam Boden	.... D	3
Dec.	5—Jack Connors, New York	... KO	1
Dec.	8—Billy Harris, New York	..... KO	2

1893
June	5—Paddy McGuiggan, Newark	... W	10
June	17—Mike Harris, New York	 L	4
Aug.	22—Jack Hall, New York	.... KO	1
Dec.	22—Harry Tracey, Boston	...... WF	1
Dec.	28—Danny Russell	.... KO	2

1894
Jan.	11—Tommy West, So. Boston	... KO	3
Feb.	26—Mike Welsh, Boston	.... KO	2
Apr.	19—Tom Tracey, Boston	.... KO	16
June	22—Mike Harris, Boston	...... KO	6
July	6—Dick O'Brien, Boston	...... KO	12
Oct.	15—Austin Gibbons, New York	.. KO	4
Nov.	1—Frank Carpenter, Chicago	... KO	3
Nov.	3—Frank Neill, Chicago	.... W	8
Nov.	3—Shorty Ahern, Chicago	..... KO	8
Nov.	14—George Thomas, Louisville	.. KO	1
Nov.	15—Billy Green, Louisville	..... KO	2

1895
Mar.	1—Billy Smith, Boston	.... D	15
Apr.	3—Mick Dunn, Coney Island	.... W	8
Aug.	28—O'Brien, Boston	.... KO	1
Dec.	2—Geo. Lavigne, Maspeth	 L	15

1896
Jan.	30—Jim Jackson, New York	..... W	4
Mar.	16—Scott Collins, L. I. C.	...... KO	7
May	10—Scaldy Bill Quinn, Woburn	.. W	20
Oct.	12—Scaldy Bill Quinn, Maspeth	... W	17
Dec.	9—*Tommy West, New York	.. D	19

*Timer's error ended bout in 19th round.
Referee Charley White called it a draw.

1897
Mar.	3—Tommy West, New York	 L	20
Apr.	20—Jim Watts, New York	...... D	4
June	14—Tom Tracey, Philadelphia	.... D	6
Sept.	16—George Green, San Francisco	. W	18
Oct.	29—Kid Lavigne, San Francisco	... L	12

(World Lightweight Title)
| Dec. | 27—Tom Tracey, Chicago | .... D | 6 |

1898
| Apr. | 4—Mysterious Billy Smith, Bridgeport | .... D | 25 |

(Welterweight Title Bout)
Apr.	22—Tommy West, Philadelphia	..ND	6
Apr.	28—Kid McPartland, Detroit	.... D	8
Dec.	6—Mysterious Billy Smith, N. Y. . L	20

(Welterweight Title Bout)

1899

Feb.	4—Australian Jimmy Ryan, Cincinnati	.... KO	14
Mar.	16—Billy Edwards, New York	...KO	13
Apr.	8—Jim Judge, Toronto	........KO	11
Apr.	25—Dan Creedon, New York	....KO	1
May	8—Charley Johnson, Athens	....W	11
May	19—Dick O'Brien, New York	....KO	14
May	30—Jim Watts, Louisville	.......KO	8
June	12—Harry Fisher, Baltimore	.....W	11
June	23—Dan Creedon, New York	.....W	20
Nov.	25—Dan Creedon, Chicago	......W	6
Nov.	29—Dan Creedon, Utica	.........W	20
Dec.	5—Bobby Dobbs, New York	...KO	6

1900
Feb.	23—Joe Choynski, New York	...KO	7
Mar.	16—Andy Walsh, New York	......W	20
Apr.	10—Dick Moore, Baltimore	....KO	4
May	4—Mysterious Billy Smith, N. Y. . W	25
May	11—Jack Bonner, Philadelphia	...ND	6
Aug.	27—*Tommy West, New York KO by	11
Sept.	24—Mysterious Billy Smith, Hartford	.................WF	10
Dec.	13—Billy Hanrahan, Hartford	...KO	12

*Walcott quit at end of 11th round.
1901
Jan.	17—Kid Carter, Harford	........LF	10
Mar.	21—Chas. McKeever, Waterbury	. KO	6
July	26—Jack Bonner, Bridgeport	.....W	15
Sept.	27—George Gardner, San Fran.	... W	20
Oct.	15—Kid Carter, San Fran. ... KO by	7
Nov.	28—Young Jackson, Baltimore	... W	20
Dec.	18—Jim Rube Ferns, Fort Erie	..KO	5

(Won Welterweight Title)
1902
Jan.	13—Young Peter, Jackson, Phila. . ND	6
Feb.	13—Jimmy Handler, Philadelphia KO	2
Mar.	13—Young Peter, Jackson, Balti. . D	10
Mar.	15—Billy Stift, Chicago	.........W	6
Apr.	4—Fred Russell, Chicago	.......D	6
Apr.	11—Phil. Jack O'Brien, Phila.	...ND	6
Apr.	25—George Gardner, San Fran.	.. L	20
June	23—*Tommy West, London	.....W	15
Oct.	7—George Cole, Philadelphia	...ND	6
Oct.	9—Frank Childs, Chicago	L	3

*Title bout.
1903
Mar.	9—Mike Donovan, Pittsburgh	....W	10
Mar.	11—Charley Haghey, Boston	...KO	5
Mar.	18—George Cole, Pittsburgh	...KO	4
Apr.	2—Billy Woods, Los Angeles	... D	20
Apr.	15—Mike Donovan, Boston	.....W	10
Apr.	20—Phil. Jack O'Brien, Boston	. D	10
May	28—Mysterious Billy Smith, Portland	.... W	4
June	18—Young Peter Jackson, Portland D	20
July	3—Mose La Fontise, Butte	.....KO	3
Aug.	3—Tom Carey, Boston	........KO	8
Sept.	11—Joe Grimm, Philadelphia	....ND	6
Sept.	21—Tom Carey, Boston	........KO	5
Oct.	13—Kid Carter, Boston	.........W	15
Nov.	3—Kid Carter, Boston	.........W	15
Nov.	10—Sandy Ferguson, Boston	... L	15
Dec.	29—Larry Temple, Boston	.... D	15

1904
Jan.	18—Chas. Haghey, New Bedford	KO	3
Feb.	26—Black Bill, Philadelphia	....ND	6
Apr.	30—Dixie Kid, San Francisco	....LF	20

(Lost welterweight title)
| May | 12—Dixie Kid, San Francisco | ..... D | 20 |

(Welterweight title bout)
May	23—Sandy Ferguson, Portland	... D	10
June	10—Young Peter Jackson, Baltimore	.... KO by	4
June	24—Mike Donovan, Baltimore	...W	5
July	1—Larry Temple, Baltimore . ..... D	10
Sept.	5—Sam Langford, Manchester	. D	15
Sept.	15—Dave Holly, Philadelphia	....ND	6
Sept.	30—Joe Gans, San Francisco	... D	20

(World Welterweight Title)
(Dixie Kid outgrew class; Walcott claimed title)
1906
July	10—Jack Dougherty, Chelsea	....KO	8
Sept.	30—Billy Rhodes, Kansas City	.... D	20
Oct.	16—Honey Mellody, Chelsea	 L	15

(Lost welterweight title)
| Nov. | 29—Honey Mellody, Chelsea | ..... L | 12 |

1907
Jan.	15—Mike Donovan, Providence	... L	10
June	18—Mike Donovan, Brazil, Ind.	... D	10
Oct.	17—Billy Payne, Rockland, Me.	..KO	6
Oct.	25—Mike Donovan, Providence	... D	15
Dec.	26—George Cole, Philadelphia	...ND	6

1908

Jan.	7—Jimmy Gardner, Boston	 L	12
Jan.	14—George Cole, Troy, N. Y.	...ND	6
Jan.	15—Mike Donovan, Montreal	..... D	10
Mar.	3—Mike Donovan, Canadagua, N. Y.		
		.... D	10
Apr.	3—Charlie Hitte, Schenectady	... L	6
June	11—Charles Kemp, Springfield, O.	KO	5
June	16—Mike Lansing, Rochester, N. Y.	W	6
June	18—Russell Van Horne, Columbus	. W	6
June	29—Billy Hurley, Schenectady	...ND	6
July	5—Jack Robinson, New York	..ND	6
Sept.	8—Bartley Connelly, Portland, Me.	L	6
Nov.	17—Larry Temple, Boston	... KO by	10
Nov.	18—Jack Robinson, Easton, Pa.	.... W	10

1909

May	10—Ed Smith, Columbus, O.	......ND	6
Sept.	6—Tom Sawyer, Portland, Me.	...ND	6
Dec.	3—Young Jack Johnson, Haverhill, Mass.	.... D	6

1910

Mar.	7—Jimmy Potts, Minneapolis	..... D	10
Apr.	25—Bill McKinnon, Brockton, Mass.		
		...... LF	6
May	13—Kyle Whitney, Brockton	L	6

1911

Oct.	17—Bob Lee, Boston	.............KO	2
Nov.	2—Tom Sawyer, Lowell, Mass.	L	3
Nov.	13—Henry Hall, Eastport, Me.	....ND	6

TB	KO	WD	WF	D	LD	LF	KOBY	ND	NC
150	34	45	2	30	17	3	4	15	0

Killed in automobile accident near Massillon, Ohio, October, 1935.

Elected to Boxing Hall of Fame 1955.

DIXIE KID
(Aaron L. Brown)
Born, Dec. 23, 1883, Fulton, Mo. Weight, 145 lbs. Height 5 ft. 8 in.

1899
Knockouts: Tony Rivers, 1; Dan Ranger, 3; Clyde Burnham, 8. Draw: Kid Williams, 20; Billy Woods, 10.

1900
Knockouts: Mike McCure, 2; Tim Leonard, 4; Black Sharkey, 4; Bobby Dobbs, 4; Frank Dougherty, 2; Jack Dean, 10.

1901
Knockouts: Fresno Pete, 4; John Phillips, 2; Kid Ruggles, 6.

1902
Knockouts: Ben Hart, 4; Young McConnell, 4; Medal Dukelow, 1; Henry Lewis, 11; Guy Boros, 1; Medal Dukelow, 6. Won: Chas. Thurston, 20.

1903
Knockouts: Fred Mueller, 8; Soldier Green, 6; Eddie Cain, 2; Chas. Thurston, 1; Al Neil, 20; Mose La Fontise, 10.

1904
Apr.	30—Joe Walcott, San Francisco	...WF	20
	(Won Welterweight Title)		
May	12—Joe Walcott, San Francisco	.... D	20
	(Title Bout)		
Sept.	21—Joe Grim, Saginaw	.... W	10
Oct.	3—Joe Grim, Mt. Clemens, Mich.	... W	6

(Dixie Kid outgrew class and gave up title)
Nov.	12—Philadelphia Jack O'Brien Philadelphia	..................ND	6

Knockouts: Al Neil, 1; John Salomon, 11; Joe Mills, 9; John Dancer, 4; Chas. Thurston, 20; Young Peter Jackson, Draw, 15. No decisions: Dave Holly, 6; Larry Temple, 6; Dave Holly, 6.

1905
Jan.	2—Larry Temple, Baltimore	...... D	15

Won: Joe Grim, 6. No decision: Geo. Cole, 6.

1908
Knockout: Fighting Ghost, 2. No decision: Cub White, 6; Fighting Ghost, 6; Geo. Cole, 6; Tommy Coleman, 6.

1909
Knockouts: Sailor Cunningham, 5; Bert Whirlwind, 3; Kid Williams, 4; Yg. Sam Langford, 1; Battling Johnson, 6; Sam Bolen, 6; Mike McDonough, 10; Al Grey, 6; Fighting Ghost, 8, twice. Knocked out by: Sam Langford, 5.

1910

Jan.	3—Chris Williams, Memphis	.....KO	3
Jan.	10—Sam Langford, Memphis	.. KO by	3
Jan.	26—Jack Ferrole, N. Y. C.	.......KO	9
Mar.	2—Jack Fitzgerald, N. Y. C.	....ND	10
Mar.	14—Bill Hurley, Troy, N. Y.	......KO	4
Mar.	15—Kyle Whitney, Boston	L	8
Mar.	21—Kid Henry, Troy, N. Y.	......ND	8
Apr.	2—George Cole, N. Y. C.	......KO	4
Apr.	6—Bill Hurley, Glen Falls, N.Y.C.	ND	10
May	5—Jimmy Clabby, N. Y. C.	....ND	10
May	12—Fighting Kennedy, N. Y. C.	..KO	8
July	16—Fighting Kennedy, N. Y. C.	..ND	10
Aug.	1—Frank Mantell, N. Y. C.	......ND	10
Sept.	9—Willie Lewis, N. Y. C.	......ND	10
Sept.	19—Fightg. Dick Nelson, N. Y. C.	..ND	10
Aug.	19—Billy West, N. Y. C.	.......KO	4
Oct.	2—Dennis Tighe, N. Y. C.	.......ND	10
Nov.	17—Willie Lewis, N. Y. C.	........ND	10
Nov.	24—Frank Mantell, Waterbury	....NC	5

1911

Jan.	17—Mike Twin Sullivan, Buffalo	..ND	10
Jan.	29—Joe Gaynor, N. Y. C.	..........KO	3
Feb.	10—Bob Moha, Buffalo	..........ND	10
Feb.	13—Kid Wilson, Harrison, N. J.	.....ND	10
Feb.	17—Bill Hurley, Glens Fls., N. Y.	... W	8
Apr.	29—*Willie Lewis, Paris, France	L	20
May	20—Young Laughrey, Paris, Fr.	....WF	10
June	14—Fred Stuber, Reims, Fr.	......KO	3
July	3—Blink McCloskey, London	.... LF	3
July	10—Harry Duncan, Dublin, Ire.	...ND	6
Aug.	29—Georges Carpentier, Tourville	.KO	5
Sept.	22—Seaman Brown, Plymouth, England	......................KO	6
Nov.	9—Johnny Summers, Liverpool, England	......................KO	2

*Referee's decision was reversed by jury of Parisian sportsmen in favor of Dixie.

1912

Jan.	18—Harry Lewis, Liverpool	.... KO by	8
May	5—Dan Flynn, Glasgow, Scot.	L	10
June	1—Jack Morris, London, England	..L	10
Oct.	4—Marcel Thomas, Paris, France	...L	15
Oct.	12—Johnny Mathieson, Birmingham, England	L	20
Nov.	18—Johnny Mathieson, London	... D	10
Dec.	8—Bob Retson, London	.........KO	3
Dec.	20—Arthur Harman, London	.....KO	9
Dec.	21—Arthur Evernden, Liverpool	..KO	7

1913

Jan.	1—Arthur Harman, London	.....KO	9
Jan.	2—Arthur Evernden, Liverpool	..KO	9
Jan.	13—Johnny Mathieson, Birmingham		
Feb.	13—Jack Morris, Liverpool	.......KO	4
Mar.	1—Seaman Hulls, Plymouth	.....KO	3
Mar.	17—Louis Verger, London	.... W	20
Mar.	26—Johnny Mathieson, Leicester, England	.... LF	12
Apr.	10—Jerry Thomson, Liverpool	L	1
Sept.	22—Private Harris, London	L	10
Oct.	11—Jack Goldswain, London	.....KO	4
Oct.	27—Albert Scanlon, London	.......W	20
Nov.	2—"Bat." Dick Nelson, London	...KO	5
Nov.	29—Demlen, Paris	L	15
Dec.	—Dick Nelson, London	.... W	20
Dec.	22—Fireman Anderson, London	... W	10

1914

Jan.	1—Bandsman Blake, London	L	20
Jan.	12—Fireman Anderson, Birkenhead	......................KO	2
Jan.	28—Con. Pluyette, Yarmouth	......W	4
Feb.	28—Tom Stokes, London	.... W	10
Mar.	3—Fred Drummond, London	.....KO	5
Mar.	9—Jim Rideout, London	..........KO	8
Mar.	16—Bill Bristowe, London	L	20
Mar.	28—Dick Nelson, London	L	20
Mar.	30—Bill Bristowe, London	.......KO	2
Dec.	12—Nicol Simpson, London	L	20
Dec.	14—Dick Nelson, London	.... W	20

TB	KO	WD	WF	D	LD	LF	KO BY	ND	NC
126	63	13	2	6	13	2	3	23	1

Died, October 3, 1935, Los Angeles, Calif.
Elected to Boxing Hall of Fame, 1975.

BILLY (HONEY) MELLODY
Born, January 15, 1884, Charlestown, Mass. Nationality, Irish-American. Weight, 145 lbs. Height, 5 ft. 7 in.

1901
Mar.	20—Jack Kearns, Boston	.........KO	2
Apr.	17—Joe Reilly, Boston	........KO	
Apr.	20—Austin Maguire, Boston	......KO	1

595

Oct. 23—Joe Warner, Boston ....KO 2
Oct. 26—Jack Casey, Boston ....KO 2
Oct. 26—Joe Donohue, Boston ....KO 3
Nov. 30—Johnny Fitzgerald, Boston ...KO 3

1902

Jan.   8—A. Keefe, Boston ....KO 2
Jan. 11—Jim O'Hare, Boston ....KO 2
Jan. 14—Joe Mooney, Boston ....KO 2
Apr. 29—Martin Canole, Boston .... D 6
Nov.   3—Joe Nelson, Boston .... W 6

1903

Feb.   9—Young Sidney, Boston .... W 6
Feb. 17—Pete Ring, Boston ....KO 3
Feb. 23—Young Sidney, Boston .... W 6
Mar. 16—Billy Griffen, Boston..........KO 1
Mar. 24—Fred Dinsdale, Boston ....KO 2
Mar. 31—Mose King, Boston .... W 8
Apr. 17—Charles Sullivan, Cambridge ..KO 3
Apr. 20—Jimmy Dommineau, Boston ..KO 3
Apr. 29—Jerry Callahan, Boston ......KO 2
May 25—Jig Stone, Boston .... KO by 13
June 30—Joe Nelson, Boston ....KO 6
Sept. 25—Jig Stone, Boston .... D 12
Oct.   9—Billy Gardner, Boston ......KO 11
Nov.   9—George Ashley, Fall River ....KO 2
Nov. 18—Belfield, Wolcott, Boston...... W 12
Nov. 27—Jig Stone, Boston .... D 15
Dec. 25—Patsy Sweeney, Lawrence ..... W 12

1904

Jan. 13—Matty Matthews, Boston ...... W 12
Jan. 15—Eddie Connolly, Boston ......KO 1
Jan. 21—Patsy Sweeney, Lawrence .... W 12
Feb. 12—Buddy Ryan, Boston ....L 6
Feb. 19—Otto Sieloff, Chicago ....KO 4
Feb. 27—Dick Fitzpatrick, Chicago ..... D 6
Mar.   4—Buddy Ryan, Chicago ....LF 5
Mar. 24—Patsy Sweeney, Portland, Me..KO 9
Apr. 11—Jack O'Keefe, Chicago ....L 4
Apr. 22—Martin Duffy, Chicago ......KO 4
May   7—George Memsic, Chicago ...... W 6
June 13—Jack O'Keefe, Butte, Mont. .... D 20
Oct. 24—Jack O'Keefe, Chicago .... W 10
Nov.   5—Dick Fitzpatrick, Chicago .... D 6
Nov. 14—Buddy Ryan, Chicago ..... KO by 1

1905

Jan. 21—Fred Douglass, Marlboro ..... W 7
Jan. 28—Tommy Sullivan, Lawrence .... D 12
Mar. 17—Jerry McCarthy, Butte, Mont. .KO 15
Apr. 18—Jerry McCarthy, Spokane ....KO 11
May 12—Martin Duffy, Spokane ....KO 1
Oct.   7—Dick Fitzpatrick, Chicago ..... D 6
Oct. 27—George Peterson, Spokane ....KO 3
Nov. 24—Jack O'Keefe, Spokane ......KO 14

1906

Feb. 20—Terry Martin, Chelsea ....KO 12
Mar.   5—Terry Martin, Chelsea ....KO 11
Mar. 27—Charlie McKeever, Chelsea ...KO 11
Apr. 16—Charlie McKeever, Chelsea ...KO 6
Apr. 20—Jack Dougherty, Milwaukee ... D 8
July   4—Willie Lewis, Chelsea ....KO 3
Sept. 3—Joe Thomas, Chelsea ...... KO by 11
Oct. 16—Joe Walcott, Chelsea .... W 15
      (Won welterweight title)
Nov. 29—Joe Walcott, Chelsea .... W 12

1907

Jan.   8—Terry Martin, Augusta, Me..... W 15
Feb. 11—Willie Lewis, Val'y Fls, R. I....KO 4
Mar.   6—Joe Thomas, Philadelphia ...ND 6
Apr. 23—M. (Twin) Sullivan, Los Ang.....L 20
      (Lost welterweight title)
July   4—Jim Donovan, N. Y. C. ....KO 7
Nov.   1—Frank Mantell, Dayton, O.. KO by 15

1908

Apr.   4—Unk Russell, Philadelphia ...ND 6
Apr. 20—Harry Lewis, Boston ...... KO by 4

1909

May   8—Willie Lewis, Paris, Fr...... KO by 4
June   —Corley Watson, Paris, Fr......KO 4
Aug. 24—Billy Rolfe, Boston .... D 12
Oct. 15—Terry Martin, Manchester, N.H. .L 15
Nov. 25—Billy Rolfe, Boston .... W 12

1910

Jan. 14—Kyle Whitney, Boston.........L 10
Feb.   1—Frank Perron, Boston .... W 10
Feb. 25—Y. J. Johnson, Brockton, Mass.. W 12
Mar.   1—Jim Moriarty, Lowell, Mass. ... D 12
Mar.   8—Unk Russell, Boston .... W 8
Mar. 22—Jim Moriarty, Boston .... W 8
Apr. 19—Young Loughrey, Boston.......L 10
July   4—Kid Shea, Houlton, Me. ......ND 6

1911

May 30—Joe Stein, N. Y. C. ....ND 10
June 19—Willie Brennan, Toronto, Can. ND 10

June 28—Joe Stein, N. Y. C. ....ND 10
July 31—Joe Stein, N. Y. C. ....ND 10
Aug. 16—Chas. Lawrence, White Plains .ND 10
Sept. 25—Young Griffo, Philadelphia ...ND 6
Oct. 12—Terry Martin, Portland, Me....ND 6
Nov. 16—Young Nitchie, Adams, Mass. .. D 8
Dec. 25—Joe Hefferman, Philadelphia ..ND 6

1912

July 17—Johnny Waltz, Newark, N. J...ND 4
Aug. 27—Terry Mitchell, N. Y. C. ......ND 10

1913

Jan. 14—Noah Brusso, Putnam, Ct. ..... D 12
Jan. 30—Dave Powers, Lawrence, Mass. . W 10

TB	KO	WD	WF	D	LD	LF	KOBY	ND	NC
95	36	20	0	13	6	1	6	13	0

Died March 15, 1919, Charlestown, Mass.

MIKE (TWIN) SULLIVAN

Born, Sept. 23, 1878, Cambridge, Mass.
Nationality, Irish-American. Weight, 133 lbs.
Height, 5 ft. 10 in.

1901

Knockouts: Billy Thrower, 5; Frank
McLean, 2; Frank Scott, 3; Jack Mumford, 4.
Won: Tom Devine, 6; Jack Dwyer, 10; Belfield
Wolcott, 10. Lost: Billy Bergley, 4.

1902

Jan. 20—Joe Flaherty, Boston........... W 6
Jan. 21—Jack McKeever, Bath, Me. ....KO 14
Apr. 17—Arthur Cote, Lewiston .... W 15
Apr. 19—Tim Kearns, Boston .... D 6
May   5—Billy Gardner, Boston .... D 6
May   9—Arthur Cote, Biddeford .... W 15
June 25—Dan Littlejohn, St. John ......KO 9
July   3—Jack Carrig, Cambridge .... D 6
Sept. 16—Belfield Walcott, Bath, Me. ... W 15
Dec. 18—Jimmy Gardner, Bellows Falls . D 15

1903

Jan. 27—Jimmy Gardner, Boston ...... D 5
Feb.   6—Belfield Wolcott, Boston ...... D 10
Mar. 24—Geo. McFadden, Boston ...... D 12
Nov. 14—Willie Fitzgerald, Phila.......ND 6
Dec. 31—Jack Blackburn, Chelsea....... D 15

1904

Mar. 26—Dick Fitzpatrick, Chicago ..... W 6
Apr.   8—Billy Moore, Chicago .... W 6
Jan.   2—Young Loughrey, Boston .....ND 10
May 12—Sammy Phillips, St. Louis ....KO 5
May 16—Gus Gardner, Toledo, O. ..... W 8
Sept. 30—Joe Angell, San Francisco ....KO 7

1905

Mar. 24—Sieloff Allen, Lewiston, Me. ..KO 5
Apr. 27—Cor. Gormerly, Portland, Me. .KO 4
June 19—Beth McLeod, St. John ....KO 6
Sept. 16—Joe Gans, Baltimore .... D 15
Nov. 24—Jimmy Gardner, San Fran...... W 20

1906

Jan. 19—Joe Gans, San Fran........ KO by 15
Mar. 17—Joe Gans, Los Angeles..... KO by 10
Apr. 18—Rube Smith, Pueblo ....KO 18
July   3—Rube Smith, Pueblo .... D 10
Aug. 15—Rube Smith, Denver .... D 20
Sept. 3—Jack Dougherty, Butte, Mont. KO 19

1907

Feb. 21—Harry Lewis, Denver ....L 10
Apr. 23—Honey Mellody, Los Angeles... W 20
      (Won Welterweight Title)
Nov.   1—Frank Field, Goldfield, Nev. ... W 20
Nov. 27—Or. Kid Farmer, Los Angeles ..KO 13

1908

Feb. 22—Stan. Ketchel, Colma, Cal. . KO by 1
Apr. 23—Jimmy Gardner, Los Angeles .. W 25
Nov.   5—Young Allen, Halifax, N. S. .... W 8
      Gave up title due to eye injury.

1909

May 26—Kyle Whitney, San Francisco .. D 20
July 13—Kid Krantz, Oakland .... D 6
Sept. 21—Terry Martin, Boston .... W 12
Nov. 29—Jimmy Gardner, New Haven ..ND 12

1910

Feb.   4—Jimmy Clabby, Milwaukee ...ND 10

1911

Jan. 17—Dixie Kid, Buffalo ....ND 10
Feb.   1—Young Loughrey, Buffalo .....ND 10
Mar. 10—Bob Moha, Milwaukee ....ND 10
Mar. 17—Jack Dillon, Buffalo ....ND 10
June   3—Jimmy Clabby, Buffalo ....ND 10
June 12—*Kid Henry, Albany ....ND 2
Aug. 25—Sailor Tighe, Scranton .... D 10
Sept. 1—Paddy Lavin, Buffalo ....ND 10

Oct. 6—Paddy Lavin, Buffalo ....ND 10
*Sullivan quit, claiming foul.

1912
Apr. 29—Harry Wuest, Cincinnati ...... W 10
Dec. 20—Joe Baker, St. Johns, N.B. ....KO 1

1913
Jan. 15—Jim Kince, St. Johns, N.B. ....KO 5
Jan. 22—Dick Tresser, St.Johns,N.B....KO 4
Nov. 14—Joe Geary, Portland, Me. .....ND 6
Dec. 15—Paddy Lavin, Dover, N.H. ....KO 2

1914
Jan. 1—Roddie MacDonald, Canada ....L 12
Feb. 14—Roddie MacDonald,
Canada .... KO by 4

TB	KO	WD	WF	D	LD	LF	KOBY	ND	NC
69	18	17	0	14	3	0	4	13	0

Died 1937.

HARRY LEWIS
(Henry Besterman)

Born, September 16, 1886, New York City. Nationality, Jewish-American. Weight, 142 lbs. Height, 5 ft 7 in. Managed by E. W. Dickerson, Jacob Besterman and Al Lippe.

1904
—Mexican Jim, Chester, Pa. ....KO 4
—Mexican Jim, Chester, Pa. ..... W 6
—Mexican Jim, Chester, Pa. ..... W 6
—Young Mock, Chester, Pa. ..... D 6
—Young Mock, Chester, Pa. ..... W 6
—Young Mock, Chester, Pa. ..... D 6
—Fighting Mahoney, Chester ...KO 4
—Billy Manning, Chester, Pa. .... W 6
—Billy Manning, Chester, Pa. .... D 6
—Griff Jones, Chester, Pa. .... W 6
—Billy Keaton, Chester, Pa. ..... W 6
—Billy Boden, Chester, Pa. ..... W 6
—Young Joe Grim, Chester, Pa. .KO 4
—Jimmy Kohler, Chester, Pa. ...KO 4
—Kid Allen, Chester, Pa. .... W 6
—Kid Allen, Chester, Pa. .... D 6
—Kid Feltman, Chester, Pa. ..... W 6
—Mickey Telly, Chester, Pa. ....KO 4
—Jimmy Devine, Chester, Pa. .... W 6
—Bert Keyes, Chester, Pa. .... W 6
—Joe Jackson, Chester, Pa. ..... W 6
—Jack Durane, Chester, Pa. ..... W 6
—Frank Dillon, Chester, Pa. ..... W 6
—Frank Dillon, Chester, Pa. ..... W 6
—Geo. Walker, Chester, Pa. ..... W 6
Dec. 10—John Dehen, Chester, Pa. .... W 6
—Johnny Allen, Chester, Pa. ..... W 6
—Kid Tyler, Chester, Pa. .... W 6
—Kid Tyler, Chester, Pa. ....KO 1
—Kid Locke, Readings, Pa. ..... W 10
—Eddie Cody, Philadelphia ....KO 4
—Ch't'r Goodwin, Philadelphia .ND 6
—Jimmy Barnes, Philadelphia ...ND 6
—Buffalo Sunflower, Phila .....ND 6

1905
Jan. 2—Tommy Lowe, Washington .... D 15
Jan. 7—Jack Cardiff, Philadelphia ...ND 6
Jan. 25—Eddie Hanlon, Philadelphia ...ND 6
Jan. 31—Geo. Decker, Philadelphia ...ND 6
Feb. 13—Tim Callahan, Philadelphia ...ND 6
Feb. 17—Tony Moran, Philadelphia ...ND 6
Feb. 22—Jim Bonner, Pottsville, Pa. .. W 15
Mar. 13—Kid Sullivan, Philadelphia ...ND 6
Mar. 17—Tommy Love, Philadelphia ...ND 6
Apr. 28—Kid Herman, Baltimore .... D 15
May 6—Aurelia Herrera, Philadelphia .ND 6
May 19—Benny Yanger, Baltimore ..... W 1
May 27—Young Erne, Philadelphia ....ND 6
June 2—Willie Fitzgerald, Phila. ......ND 6
June 21—Young Ernie, Chester, Pa. ... D 10
July 7—Kid Goodman, Chelsea ....L 15
Aug. 7—Young Erne, Chester, Pa. ..... D 10
July 7—Kid Goodman, Chelsea ....L 15
Aug. 7—Young Erne, Chester, Pa. .....L 15
Aug. 21—Yng. Donahue, Philadelphia ..ND 6
Aug. 24—Kid Locke, Philadelphia .....ND 6
Aug. 28—Sammy Smith, Philadelphia ..ND 6
Sept. 7—Young Erne, Philadelphia ....ND 6
Sept. 22—Kid Sullivan, Baltimore ....L 15
Sept. 29—Jack Roller, Chelsea ....KO 6
Oct. 31—Yng. Donahue, Philadelphia .ND 6
Nov. 9—Unk Russell, Philadelphia ...ND 6
Dec. 4—Arthur Cote, Philadelphia ....ND 6
Dec. 6—Tommy Connely, Reading, Pa. .. W 10
Dec. 25—Maurice Sayers, Philadelphia .ND 6

1906
Jan. 13—Harry Edels, Philadelphia .....ND 6
Jan. 19—Amby McGarry, N. Y. C. .....ND 3
Jan. 26—Willie Lewis, New York ......ND 3
Feb. 10—Jimmy Gardner, Philadelphia .ND 6
Feb. 24—Adam Ryan, Philadelphia ....ND 6
Mar. 10—Jimmy Gardner, Philadelphia .ND 6
Mar. 31—Willie Fitzgerald, Phila ....ND 6
May 11—Willie Fitzgerald, Phila........ND 6
June 15—Joe Gans, Philadelphia ....ND 6
June 28—T. Prendergast, Grand Rapids .KO 4
July 12—Jimmy Briggs, Grand Rapids ... W 10
Aug. 9—Maurice Sayers, Grand Rapids LF 6
Sept. 3—Jimmy Briggs, Saginaw .... W 15
Sept. 13—Kid Herrick, Grand Rapid ...KO 3
Sept. 29—Joe Thomas, Philadelphia ....ND 6
Oct. 13—Willie Fitzgerald, Phila........KO 2
Oct. 19—Jack Dougherty, Milwaukee ..ND 6
Nov. 3—Willie Fitzgerald, Phila........ND 6
Nov. 15—Mike Ward, Grand Rapids ....KO 9

1907
Jan. 22—Rube Smith, Denver ....KO 8
Feb. 21—M. (Twin) Sullivan, Denver ....W 10
Feb. 28—Jim Perry, Pueblo, Colo......KO 6
May 21—Jimmy Gardner, Denver ....L 10
June 8—Tommy Sullivan, Phila.........ND 6
June 13—Jack Roller, Philadelphia .....KO 4
June 20—Billy Griffiths, Philadelphia ...ND 6
June 22—Dave Deshler, Philadelphia ...KO 2
July 1—Billy Griffiths, Phila ....KO 2
July 16—Jack Goldswain, Philadelphia .KO 5
July 25—Kid Locke, Philadelphia ......ND 3
July 25—Boxer Kelly, Philadelphia .....ND 3
Sept. 4—Cub White, Philadelphia ......ND 6
Oct. 17—Cub White, Philadelphia .....ND 6
Nov. 1—Mike Donovan, Philadelphia ..ND 6
Nov. 20—Jack Blackburn, Philadelphia .ND 6

1908
Jan. 23—Frank Mantell, New Haven ...KO 3
Feb. 15—Terry Martin, Philadelphia ...ND 6
Mar. 26—Terry Martin, Baltimore ...... W 15
Apr. 20—Honey Mellody, Boston ......KO 4
Harry Lewis claimed vacant world welterweight title.
Apr. 27—Larry Conley, Augusta, Me....KO 3
May 9—Unk Russell, Philadelphia ....ND 6
May 19—Charlie Hitte, New York .....ND 6
May 23—Unk Russell, Philadelphia ....ND 6
June 9—Willie Lewis, New York ......ND 6
June 23—Larry Temple, Boston .... W 12
June 29—Jim Donovan, Boston .... W 6
July 15—Unk Russell, Bangor, Me. .... W 6
Sept. 7—Unk Russell, Boston .... W 12
Sept. 25—Terry Martin, New York .....ND 5
Oct. 1—Unk Russell, Pittsburgh .....ND 6
Dec. 14—Willie Lewis, New Haven ...... D 12

1909
Jan. 5—Harry Mansfield, Philadelphia .ND 6
Feb. 2—Bill McKinnon, Boston ....L 12
Mar. 6—Tommy Sullivan, Phila. ......ND 6
Mar. 19—Johnny Dugan, Philadelphia ..KO 3
Mar. 19—George Krall, Philadelphia ...KO 1
Mar. 26—Terry Martin, Philadelphia ...ND 6
Apr. 24—Frank Klaus, Philadelphia ...LF 6
June 24—Harry Mansfield, Phila ......ND 6
July 26—Tommy Crawford, Williamsport
Pa. ....KO 2
Sept. 3—Harry Mansfield, Williamsport . W 10
Oct. 6—Harry Mansfield, Phila. ......ND 6
Oct. 13—Eddie Chambers, Phila.......KO 1
Oct. 19—Dan Sullivan, Boston ....KO 1
Nov. 27—Frank Klaus, Philadelphia ...ND 6

1910
Jan. 11—Howard Baker, Denver .... W 10
Feb. 19—Willie Lewis, Paris, Fr......... D 25
Mar. 12—Charlie Hitte, Paris ....LF 4
Apr. 23—Willie Lewis, Paris ....D 25
May 4—Peter Brown, Paris ....KO 3
May 18—*Bert Ropert, Paris ....KO 1
May 18—*Bill Davies, Paris ....KO 2
May 18—*Bob Scanlon, Paris ....WF 2
June 11—Sam Harris, Paris ....KO 2
June 27—Young Joseph, London, Eng. .. W 7
Aug. 23—Leo Houck, Boston ....L 12
Sept. 5—Harry Mansfield, New York ...ND 10
Sept. 17—Leo Houck, Philadelphia .....ND 6
Oct. 21—Billy Glover, New York ......KO 3
Oct. 28—Young Loughrey, New York .ND 6
Nov. 7—Dick Nelson, Schenectady ....KO 2
Dec. 14—Jeff Thorne, Paris, Fr........KO 1
*Same night.

1911
Jan. 25—Johnny Summers, London ...KO 4

Feb. 1—Blink McCloskey, Paris, Fr. .... W 3
Feb. 13—Private Harris, London ...... KO 5
Feb. 18—Seaman Hull, Plymouth, Eng. . KO 5
Feb. 22—Blink McCloskey, Paris, Fr. .... W 25
May 3—Leo Houck, Paris, Fr. .... L 20
Mar. 13—Jimmy Horman, London ..... KO 2
May 27—George Gunther, Paris, Fr. ..... L 20
Oct. 9—Geo. (K.O.) Brown, Memphis .. D 8
Dec. 13—Georges Carpentier, Paris .... L 20

1912
Jan. 18—Dixie Kid, Liverpool .... KO 8
Mar. 28—Harry Mansfield, Liverpool .... W 20
May 13—Pvt. Palmer, Liverpool .... L 20
June 10—Johnny Mathieson, Birmingham L 20
June 27—Johnny Mathieson, Liverpool ... L 20
Dec. 26—Johnny Mathieson, Liverpool . KO 3

1913
Jan. 30—Jerry Thompson, Liverpool ... KO 14
Mar. 17—Jack Harrison, London .... KO 3
Oct. 13—*Joe Borrell, Philadelphia . KO by 5
*Lewis collapsed and announced his retirement.

TB	KO	WD	WF	D	LD	LF	KOBY	ND	NC
163	42	37	1	11	12	3	1	56	0

Died, February 22, 1956, Philadelphia, Pa.

JIMMY GARDNER
Born, December 25, 1885, Lisdoonvarna, County Claire, Ireland. Weight, 135 lbs. Height, 5 ft. 7¾ in.

1900
Nov. 29—Kid Brady, Lowell, Mass. .... W 4
Dec. 11—Patsy McKenna, Boston .... L 4

1901
(Inactive)

1902
Jan. 1—George Dart, Boston .... D 6
Jan. 22—Johnny Sheehan, Boston .... D 6
Mar. 14—Kid Sheehan, Boston .... KO 2
Apr. 28—Monk Cronson, Boston .... W 6
Apr. 30—Johnny Taylor, Boston .... W 3
May 8—Kid Hessel, Boston .... D 6
May 12—Jimmy Sullivan, Boston .... D 6
July 3—Johnny Glynn, Cambridge .... KO 2
Aug. 13—Young Kelly, Wrentham .... D 6
Sept. 23—Ned Maher, Boston .... KO 3
Oct. 1—Billy Ryan, Boston .... KO 4
Oct. 22—Johnny Saxe, Bellows Falls .... KO 2
Oct. 29—Luther Manuel, Boston .... W 6
Oct. 30—Jimmy Kelly, Scituate, R.I. .... D 20
Nov. 14—Jimmy Kelly, Scituate, R.I. .... D 20
Dec. 18—Mike (Twin) Sullivan, Bellows Falls D 15
Dec. 30—Arthur Cote, Lewiston, Me. ...... KO 5

1903
Jan. 8—Belfield Wolcott, Boston .... D 8
Jan. 27—Mike (Twin) Sullivan, Boston .... ND 5
Feb. 18—Belfield Wolcott, Boston .... D 8
Feb. 19—Jimmy Kelly, Fall River .... D 10
Feb. 23—Patsy Sweeney, Boston .... D 15
Mar. 31—Belfield Wolcott, Boston .... W 15
Apr. 9—Jack Carrig, Boston .... KO 3
Apr. 20—Johnny Burns, Boston .... W 15
June 15—Tommy Devine, Boston .... KO 4
June ⸺Martin Reilly, Fall River .... KO 2
June 30—Jimmy Kelly, Scituate .... W 8
July 2—George McFadden, Boston .... D 10
July 20—Kid Coffey, Fall River .... W 15
Aug. 10—Patsy Sweeney, Manchester .... D 15
Sept. 1—Tom McInerney, Boston .... KO 1
Sept. 2—Spike Sullivan, Fall River .... D 15
Sept. 18—Kid Griffo, Boston .... W 12
Oct. 12—Kid Griffo, Boston .... W 12
Oct. 16—Kid Griffo, Boston .... W 12
Dec. 9—Jimmy Kelly, Boston .... KO 3

1904
Jan. 2—Jack Blackburn, Boston .... L 12
Jan. 22—Kid Griffo, Marlboro .... KO 4
Mar. 17—Mike Ward, Chicago .... W 6
Apr. 8—Buddy Ryan, Chicago .... D 6
May 20—Mike Memsic, Chicago .... KO 3

June 3—Buddy Ryan, Chicago .... W 6
July 4—Patsy Sweeney, Manchester ...... KO 4
July 22—Willie Fitzgerald, Butte, Mont. ... KO 5
Aug. 26—Guy Ashley, Cambridge .... KO 3
Sept. 5—Martin Canole, New Bedford .... D 10
Nov. 18—Rube Smith, Denver .... KO 5

1905
Mar. 21—Charlie Sieger, Boston .... W 15
June 13—Jack O'Keefe, Salt Lake .... D 20
Aug. 4—Rufe Turner, Colma. Calif. .... KO 11
Aug. 25—Buddy Ryan, Colma, Calif. .... W 15
Nov. 24—Mike (Twin) Sullivan, San Francisco L 20

1906
Feb. 5—Young Erne, Philadelphia .... ND 6
Feb. 12—Harry Lewis, Philadelphia .... ND 3
Feb. 22—Willie Lewis, New York .... ND 3
Mar. 10—Harry Lewis, Philadelphia .... ND 6
Mar. 27—Jack Dougherty, Milwaukee ...... D 8
Apr. 18—Willie Fitzgerald, Philadelphia ... ND 6
Apr. 28—Jack O'Keefe, Kalamazoo .... ND 10
May 23—Jack O'Keefe, Indianapolis .... KO 5
Nov. 15—Jack Dougherty, Davenport ...... KO 9
Nov. 29—Otto Sieloff, Fort Wayne .... KO 3
Dec. 11—Rube Smith, Denver .... W 10

1907
Jan. 29—Jeff Doherty, Lowell, Mass. .... W 3
Apr. 27—Jack Reed, Chicago .... W 6
May 21—Harry Lewis, Denver .... W 10
July 19—Clarence English, Fort Wayne ..... W 10
Sept. 2—Dick Fitzpatrick, Fort Wayne ...... KO 2
Nov. 8—Unk Russell, Philadelphia .... ND 6

1908
Jan. 7—Joe Walcott, Boston .... W 12
Apr. 23—Mike (Twin) Sullivan, Los Angeles L 25
(For World Welterweight Title)
June 26—Kyle Witney, San Franciso .... KO 13
Nov. 7—Jimmy Clabby, New Orleans ...... W 15
(Won Claim to World Welterweight Title)
Nov. 26—Jimmy Clabby, New Orleans ...... D 20

1909
Jan. 25—Harry Mansfield, Philadelphia ... KO 1
Feb. 5—Jack Fitzgerald, Philadelphia .... ND 6
Mar. 2—Bill McKinnon, Boston .... W 12
May 11—Bill McKinnon, Boston .... W 12
June 8—Tommy Quill, Boston .... D 12
Sept. 15—Clarence English, Omaha .... ND 10
Oct. 2—Young Loughrey, Philadelphia ... ND 6
Oct. 26—Bill McKinnon, Boston .... KO 4
Nov. 29—Mike (Twin) Sullivan, New Haven ND 12

1910
Mar. 11—Jimmy Clabby, Milwaukee .... ND 10
Apr. 12—Frank Klaus, Boston .... L 12
Aug. 9—Bill McKinnon, Portland .... ND 6
Oct. 17—Leo Houck, Philadelphia .... ND 6

1911
Jan. 18—Terry Martin, Fall River .... KO 3
Jan. 31—Frank Klaus, Boston .... D 12
Feb. 22—Jack Dillon, Indianapolis .... ND 10
Mar. 17—Johnny O'Keefe, Boston .... ND 6
Apr. 11—Frank Klaus, Pittsburgh .... ND 6
Apr. 22—Jack Dillon, Pittsburgh .... ND 6

1912
Feb. 3—Jack Dillon, Pittsburgh .... ND 6
May 1—Howard Baker, Denver .... ND 10

1913
June 17—Fighting Kennedy, Manchester .... KO 8
July 1—Frank Klaus, Boston .... KO by 3

TB	KO	WD	WF	D	LD	LF	KO BY	ND	NC
100	27	24	0	22	5	0	1	21	0

JIMMY CLABBY
Born, July 14, 1890, Norwich, Conn. Nationality, Irish-American. Weight, 158 lbs. Height, 5 ft 8½ in. Managed by Emil Theiry.

1906
Knockouts: Billy Smith, 2; Battling Hill, 3; Eddy Ryan, 2; Young Papke, 7; Kid Hogan, 2. Won: Jack Redmond, 6; Billy Moorehead, 1; Billy Moorehead, 6; Young Morris, 6; Young

Todd, 6. Draw: Mike McCarthy (twice), 6; Young Hankey, 6; Eddy Kenney, 6; Billy Moorehead, 4; Barney Cinnamon, 6. No decision: Eddy Wagner, 6; Kid Herrick, 6. Lost: Dick Hart, 4. Knockout by: Jack O'Leary, 4. (Police) Young Todd, 9.

1907
Knockouts: Young Connors, 3; Young Edwards, 1; Young Schultz, 1; Red Fredriksen, 2; Young Goegel, 1. Won: Red Halligan, 6; Gus Wendt (foul), 4. Draw: Kid Ducca, 8; Pat McMahon, 10. Lost: Matty Baldwin (foul), 4.

1908
Jan.	17—Mike Pooso, Milwaukee	KO	3
Feb.	1—Kid Leonard, Milwaukee	KO	2
Mar.	28—Kid Yanger, Milwaukee	W	6
Mar.	30—Dirus Cook, Milwaukee	W	6
Apr.	—Walt Bauman, Eagle, Wis.	W	6
Apr.	—Walt Bauman, Milwaukee	ND	6
Apr.	—George Newton, Milwaukee	KO	5
Apr.	25—Battling Kelley, Milwaukee	W	3
May	6—Jack Ward, Milwaukee	KO	2
June	4—Eddie Tancel, Milwaukee	W	8
Aug.	—Joe Clement, Minneapolis	KO	3
Aug.	26—Young Sullivan, Racine	KO	1
Sept.	4—Charles King, Milwaukee	KO	2
Sept.	24—Steve Kinney, Milwaukee	KO	2
Nov.	7—Jimmy Gardner, New Orleans	L	15
Nov.	26—Jimmy Gardner, New Orleans	D	20

1909
Jan.	12—Ralph Erne, Philadelphia	ND	6
Jan.	15—Mark Anderson, Dayton	D	20
Feb.	16—Dick Fitzpatrick, Hammond	W	10
Mar.	3—Fred Gilmore, Hammond	W	10
Mar.	20—Bob Salvin, New Orleans	KO	3
Apr.	3—Dave Barry, New Orleans	KO	1
Apr.	5—Dick Fitzpatrick, Memphis	D	8
Apr.	24—Bill Griffith, New Orleans	KO	4
May	18—Tom Quill, Boston	L	12
May	28—Jack Morgan, Dayton	ND	10
June	18—Dick Fitzpatrick Hammond	KO	8
Nov.	2—H. Morrow, Benton Harbor	*KO	10
	Jack Robson	KO	4
	*Referee later awarded decision to Clabby.		

1910
Jan.	17—Jimmy Howard, Memphis	D	8
Feb.	4—Mike Twin Sullivan, Milwaukee	ND	10
Feb.	8—Paddy Lavin, Buffalo	ND	10
Mar.	11—Jimmy Gardner, Milwaukee	ND	10
Mar.	12—Mike Gibbons, St. Paul, Minn.	W	10
Apr.	26—Paddy Lavin, Buffalo	D	10
May	5—Dixie Kid, N. Y. C.	ND	10
May	21—Young Loughrey, Philadelphia	ND	6
May	27—Tom Coleman, Philadelphia	ND	6
June	2—Bob Moha, Milwaukee	ND	10
July	4—Jack Fitzpatrick, North Platte	W	10
Sept.	5—Guy Buckles, Sheridan, Wyo.	KO	13
Nov.	2—Bob Bryant, Sydney, N. S. W.	W	7
Dec.	7—Mark Higgins, Sydney	KO	8
Dec.	21—Ed. Williams, Sydney	W	11
Dec.	26—Gus Devitt, Brisbane, Aus.	KO	1

1911
Jan.	17—Dave Smith, Sydney, N. S. W.	L	20
Jan.	23—W. Sanderson, Melbourne	KO	2
Mar.	22—Harry Duncan, London	W	20
May	29—*Paddy Lavin, Indianapolis	ND	1
June	3—Mike Twin Sullivan, Buffalo	ND	10
June	8—Geo. K. O. Brown, Hammond	ND	10
June	22—Jeff Smith, N. Y. C.	ND	10
Sept.	1—Mike Gibbons, Milwaukee	ND	10
Sept.	20—Mike Gibbons, Winnipeg	ND	15
Nov.	18—Arthur Cripp, Sydney	W	15
Nov.	20—Tim Land, Sydney	KO	10
Dec.	9—Dave Smith, Sydney	D	20
Dec.	28—Ted Whiting, Perth, W. Aus.	W	20
	*Called off—dispute.		

1912
Jan.	29—Jack Howard, Melbourne	KO	7
Feb.	24—Dave Smith, Sydney	D	20
Apr.	3—Hughie Mehegan, Sydney	W	20
May	31—Hughie Mehegan, Melbourne	KO	12
Oct.	8—Knockout Brennan, Buffalo	ND	10
Oct.	11—Tom Monahan, Gary, Ind.	KO	4

1913
Jan.	7—Roy Parker, Fond du Lac	KO	2
Jan.	24—Howard Baker, Denver	W	10
Feb.	3—Geo. K. O. Brown, Milwaukee	ND	10
Feb.	27—Freddy Hicks, Hammond	ND	10
May	9—Eddie McGoorty, Denver, Colo.	D	10
June	13—Eddie McGoorty, Butte, Mont.	W	12
Aug.	2—Freddy Hicks, Butte, Mont.	D	12
Sept.	1—Sailor Grande, San Francisco	W	20

Oct.	3—Sailor Petroskey, San Francisco	W	20	
Nov.	27—Frank Logan, San Francisco	KO	14	

1914
Feb.	12—Sailor Petroskey, Los Angeles	W	20
Apr.	3—Billy Murray, San Francisco	D	20
June	6—Jeff Smith, Sydney	L	20
July	4—Eddie McGoorty, Sydney	WF	8
Aug.	1—Dave Smith, Sydney	KO	1
Aug.	12—Dave Smith, Brisbane	L	20
Nov.	6—George Chip, Daly City, Cal.	W	20

1915
Jan.	21—Mike Gibbons, Milwaukee	ND	10
Mar.	17—Young Ahearn, Philadelphia	ND	6
Mar.	22—George Chip, Grand Rapids	ND	6
Apr.	27—George Chip, Marinette	ND	10
May	4—Al McCoy, Brooklyn	ND	10
May	12—George Chip, N. Y. C.	NC	8
July	12—Frank Farmer, Oshkosh	ND	10
Oct.	22—Les Darcy, Sydney	L	20

1916
Jan.	1—Mick King, Sydney	W	20
Mar.	4—Fritz Holland, Sydney	W	20
May	20—Dave Smith, Sydney	W	20
July	8—Fritz Holland, Melbourne	KO	6
Sept.	9—Les Darcy, Sydney	L	20
Oct.	28—Fred Kay, Sydney	L	2

1917
Feb.	17—Tommy Uren, Sydney	L	20
Apr.	28—Tommy Uren, Sydney	W	20
	(For Australian title)		
May	26—Dave Smith, Sydney	KO	10
June	6—Tommy Uren, Sydney	KO	10
July	14—Tommy Uren, Melbourne	L	20
Aug.	4—Albert Lloyd, Sydney	D	20

1918
Feb.	6—Albert Lloyd, Sydney	L	20

1919
Jan.	26—Albert Pooley, Sydney	KO	6
Feb.	21—Fritz Holland, Sydney	W	20
Sept.	3—George Cook, Sydney	W	20
	—Tommy Uren	L	15
	—Tommy Uren	L	20

1920
Jan.	2—Tommy Uren, Hastings, N. Z.	W	15
Feb.	8—Jim Tracey, Hamilton, N. Z.	W	15
Apr.	19—*Albert Lloyd, Auckland, N. Z.	W	10
July	16—Les Gleason, Poverty Bay, N. Z.	W	15
Aug.	26—George Cook, Dannevirke, N. Z.	W	15
	—Tommy Uren	L	15
	*Lloyd broke hand.		

1921
Feb.	27—Billy Shade, Seattle	L	20
Mar.	4—Frank Burns, Seattle	KO by	15

1922
June	9—Joe Egan, Vancouver	D	10
July	4—Gordon McKay, Seattle	ND	4
Sept.	4—Jimmy Darcy, Michigan City	ND	10
Oct.	2—Frank Carbone, Detroit	ND	10
Nov.	3—Dennis O'Keefe, Ind'a Harbor	ND	10
Nov.	24—Tommy Comiskey, Denver	ND	12
Dec.	18—Patsy Rocco, Indiana Harbor	ND	10

1923
Feb.	28—Joe Bello, Hammond, Ind.	KO	6
July	31—Morrie Schaifer, E. Chic.	KO by	2

TB	KO	WD	WF	D	LD	LF	KOBY	ND	NC
155	40	37	2	20	16	1	4	34	1

Died Jan. 18, 1934 at Calumet City, Ind.

WALDEMAR HOLBERG
World Welterweight Champion, 1914
(Record Not Available)

TOM McCORMICK
Born, August 8, 1890, Dundalk, Louth, Ireland.
Weight, 145 lbs.

1912
Jan.	15—Bill Mansell, London	KO	3
Jan.	20—Pte. Hutton, London	KO	6
	—Pte. Walker	KO	1
Mar.	4—Albert Bayton, London	KO	10
May	20—Albert Bayton, Sheffield	KO	2
June	21—Pte. Marks, Plymouth	KO	1
July	5—Battling Taylor, Plymouth	KO	6
July	26—Jack Meekins, Plymouth	KO	4
Aug.	16—Dick Knock, Plymouth	KO	5

599

Aug.	23—Boss Edwards, Plymouth .... KO	2
Aug.	28—Pte. Ponsford, Exeter .... W	15
Sept.	20—Harry Duncan, Plymouth .... WF	7
Oct.	3—Eddie Beattie, Liverpool .... W	20
Oct.	18—Jack Goldswain, Plymouth .... D	15
Nov.	8—Jack Goldswain, Plymouth .... W	20
Nov.	29—Young Joseph, Plymouth .... W	15
Dec.	20—Joe Goodwin, Plymouth .... KO	3

1913

Jan.	17—Sid Burns, Plymouth .... KO	7
Feb.	8—Albert Badoud, Paris .... W	15
Mar.	3—Arthur Evernden, London .... W	15
Apr.	21—Gus Platts, London .... W	20
May	31—Albert Badoud, Devonport .... W	15
June	27—Tom Tees, Plymouth .... WF	3
July	18—Eddie Elton, Plymouth .... KO	5
July	31—Johnny Basham, Liverpool .... D	15
Aug.	15—Eddie Beattie, Plymouth .... W	15
Sept.	5—Alf Goodwin, Plymouth .... KO	6
Sept.	8—Gus Platts, Sheffield L	20
Oct.	3—Sgt. Baker, Plymouth .... KO	1

1914

Jan.	10—Johnny Summers, Sydney .... W	20

(Won British and Empire Welterweight Titles)

Jan.	24—Waldemar Holberg, Melbourne ... WF	6

(Won World Welterweight Title)

Feb.	14—Johnny Summers, Sydney .... KO	1
Mar.	21—Matt Wells, Sydney L	20

(Lost British and Empire Welterweight Titles)
(Lost World Welterweight Title)

Mar.	28—Fritz Holland, Melbourne L	20
Apr.	18—Milburn Saylor, Sydney .... KO by	10

1915

May	10—Johnny Basham, London ...... KO by	13

(For British Welterweight Title)

Aug.	2—Harry Paddon, London .... KO	9
Aug.	20—Henri Tyncke, Plymouth .... W	15
Sept.	2—Albert Badoud, Liverpool L	15
Nov.	22—Eddie Beattie, Newcastle ...... KO by	14

TB	KO	WD	WF	D	LD	LF	KO BY	ND	NC
40	17	11	3	2	4	0	3	0	0

Killed in action, June, 1916, France.

MATT WELLS

Born, December 14, 1886, Walworth, London, England. Weight, 133-147 lbs.
1905-06-07 British Amateur Lightweight Champion
Competed as lightweight in 1908 Olympic Games

1909

Nov.	4—Battling LaCroix, London .... W	10
Dec.	20—Bob Russell, London .... W	10

1910

Jan.	3—Gunner Hart, London .... KO	6
Jan.	10—Dick Lee, London .... W	6
Feb.	19—Sid Stagg, London .... W	10
Mar.	14—Jack Turner, London .... D	20
Apr.	14—Young Nipper, London .... D	6
May	5—Smiling Kelley, Yonkers .... ND	8
June	28—Charley Lawrence, New York .... ND	10
July	19—Johnny Dohan, New York .... ND	10
Aug.	8—Paddy Sullivan, New York ...... ND	10
Sept.	14—Jimmy Howard, New York .... WF	9
	—Eddie McMahon, Yonkers .... ND	8
	—Dick Miller, Yonkers .... ND	8
	—Bill Leary, New York .... ND	10

1911

Feb.	27—Freddie Welsh, London .... W	20

(Won British Lightweight Title)

June	2—Leach Cross, New York .... ND	10
June	13—Pal Moore, Boston .... W	12
July	19—Dick Hyland, Albany .... ND	10
July	28—Willie Moody, Philadelphia ...... ND	6
Aug.	30—Knockout Brown, New York ...... ND	10
Sept.	20—Abe Attell, New York .... ND	10
Oct.	5—Billy Donovan, Toronto .... KO	5

1912

Apr.	26—Packey McFarland, New York .... ND	10
June	5—Young Brown, New York .... ND	10
June	7—Bobby Wilson, Utica .... ND	10
Sept.	16—Hughie Mehegan, London .... LF	14

Nov.	11—Freddie Welsh, London L	20

(Lost British Lightweight Title)

Dec.	26—Johnny Basham, Swansea .... KO	7

1913

Feb.	24—Hughie Mehegan, London .... W	20
Aug.	9—Hughie Mehegan, Sydney .... W	20
Sept.	27—Owen Moran, Sydney .... W	20
Nov.	8—Hughie Mehegan, Melbourne ...... W	20
Nov.	29—Harry Stone, Sydney L	20

1914

Jan.	17—Herb McCoy, Sydney L	20
Feb.	28—Ray Bronson, Sydney .... KO	7
Mar.	21—Tom McCormick, Sydney .... W	20

(Won British and Empire Welterweight Titles)
(Won World Welterweight Title)

Oct.	12—Young Nipper, London .... W	15

1915

Jan.	21—Gus Platts, Liverpool .... W	15
Mar.	22—Johnny Basham, London L	15
June	1—Mike Glover, Boston L	12

(Lost World Welterweight Title)

July	13—Young Neil, Allentown .... ND	6
Aug.	7—Willie Schaeffer, New York ..... ND	10
Oct.	29—Charley White, Milwaukee ...... ND	10
Nov.	12—Johnny Griffiths, Columbus ...... ND	12
Nov.	19—Young Brown, New York .... ND	10
Dec.	10—Johnny Dundee, New Haven L	6

1916

Jan.	4—Charley White, Boston .... W	12
Feb.	4—Young Brown, New York .... ND	10
Feb.	29—Johnny Griffiths, Columbus ...... ND	12
Mar.	20—Charley White, Cincinnati .... ND	10
Apr.	6—Charley White, Kansas City L	15
Apr.	18—Eddie Murphy, Boston .... W	12
May	16—Johnny Dundee, Boston L	12
June	9—Frankie Mack, Rochester .... ND	10
July	11—Charley White, Boston .... KO by	5

1917

June	16—Phil Bloom, Brooklyn .... ND	10
Aug.	27—Bryan Downey, Rochester .... ND	10
Sept.	9—Phil Bloom, New York .... ND	10
Sept.	17—Bryan Downey, Columbus .... ND	12
Oct.	5—Charley White, Syracuse .... NC	9

1918

(Inactive)

1919

Oct.	20—Kid Carter, London .... W	20
Nov.	13—Johnny Basham, London L	20
Dec.	26—Ted (Kid) Lewis, London ...... KO by	12

1920

Mar.	18—Phil Bloom, London L	15
Apr.	24—Ted Moore, Plymouth L	20
May	8—Bermondsey Billy Wells, London ... W	15
June	4—Fred Newberry, London .... W	20
June	20—Gus Platts, Sheffield .... W	20
Aug.	7—Ted Moore, London .... LF	13
Nov.	27—Kid Plested, Wallsend .... KO	6
Dec.	11—Joe Davis, Brighton .... W	10

1921

Sept.	2—Seaman James Hall, Plymouth L	15
Oct.	31—Carlos, London .... KO	13
Dec.	29—Ted Moore, London L	15

1922

Apr.	17—Stanley Glen, London .... W	15
May	12—Jack Hart, London .... W	15

TB	KO	WD	WF	D	LD	LF	KO BY.	ND	NC
77	6	21	1	2	14	2	2	28	1

Died, June 27, 1953, London, England.

KID GRAVES

(Perry Ivia Graves)
Claimant World Welterweight Championship
Born Plattsmouth, Neb., July 11, 1892.
Height, 5 ft. 7 in. Weight, 142-145 lbs.

1906

Knockouts: George Williams, 4; Joe Allen, 2; Hal Smith, 8; Young Joe Grim, 5 and 3; Kid Jordan, 4; Dave Rocks, 1; Slugger Dobbins, 5; Kid Aspinall, 5; Tom Scuudder, 6; Jack Smith, 3

and 4. Won: Gene McGovern, 6; Billy Roche, 6; Kid Jordan, 3 and 6; Jack Smith, 10 and 6; Fighting Al, 5. Draw: George Williams, 6; Young Joe Grim, 6; Slugger Dobbins, 6; Jack Smith, 6; Fighting Al, 6.

1907

Knockouts: Frank Carr, 2; Willie Crane, 4; Joe Allen, 5; Frank Simms, 4; Kid Abbott, 5 and 2; Henry Burr, 4; Kid Aspinall, 3; Tommy Scudder, 3; Slats McDonough, 4. Won: Fighting Al, 6; Kid Abbott 6; Red Lynch, 3; Bill Henning, 6; Butch Webber, 6; Battling Sully, 3; Kid Victor, 3. Won (foul): Fighting Al, 4. Draw: Fighting Al, 6 (twice); Willie Crane, 6; Frank Simms, 6; Kid Abbott, 6; Henry Burr, 6; Kid Booth, 6. Knocked out by: Willie Schumacher, 2.

1908

Knockout: Kid Mason, 8. Won (foul): Young White, 2. Draw: Kid Simon, 3; Kid Dalton, 6; Johnny Roth, 6.

1909

Knockouts: Kid Doll, 4; Dune Weir, 3; Kid Benn, 2. Won: Kid Little, 6; Kid Harris, 10; Kid Casper, 8. Draw: Johnny Coulon, 6; Kid Casper, 6; Jack White, 3; Johnny Dugan, 6.

1910

Knockouts: Posey Williams, 8; Mike Poozo, 2; The Black Prince, 3. Won: Jack McGraw, 10; Mickey Riley (foul), 4. Draw: Kid Dalton, 6; Young Deitz, 6; Kid LaMarche, 4; Joe Bartz, 10; Billy Morse, 8.

1911

Knockouts: Battling Dempsey, 2; Jack Lepper, 3. Won: George Watson, 8. Draw: Paul Sikora, 10; Jimmy Potts, 6. Lost: Paul Kohler, 10 (twice). No decision: Battling Hurley, 6 (twice) and 10; Maurice Sayres, 10 and 8; Danny Goodman, 8 (twice); Ray Temple, 10; Frank Whitney, 10; Greek Anton, 6; Eddie Wosinsky, 8.

1912

Knockouts: Dutch Zimmer, 2; Smoke Jones, 2; Frank Carson, 1. Won: Jack Lepper, 10; Paul Sikora, 12; Joe Grim, 12. Draw: Kid Alberts, 12. Lost: Leo Kelly, 12. No decision: Eddie McCloskey, 8; Rudy Unholz, 8; Billy Lewis, 10; Italian Joe Gans, 10; Battling Hurley, 10; Frank Loughrey, 10; Young Ahearn, 10 (twice); Kid Alberts, 10; Joe White, 10; Benny Franklin, 10.

1913

Jan.	1—Lee Barrett, Brooklyn	ND	10
Feb.	1—Lee Barrett, Brooklyn	ND	10
Feb.	18—You Ahearn, Brooklyn	ND	3
Mar.	22—Tommy Howell, Philadelphia	ND	6
Apr.	19—Young Erne, Philadelphia	ND	6
May	17—Jack Britton, Philadelphia	ND	6
July	26—Tommy Maloney, Philadelphia	ND	10
Oct.	13—Mike Glover, Brooklyn	ND	10
Oct.	20—Mike Glover, New York	ND	10
Dec.	4—Lee Barrett, Milwaukee	ND	10
Dec.	13—Jimmy Frier, Philadelphia	ND	6

1914

Jan.	1—Yg. Jack O'Brien, Phila.	ND	6
Feb.	16—Mike Gibbons, Philadelphia	ND	6
Mar.	10—Jack Britton, Brooklyn	ND	10
Apr.	25—Jack Britton, Philadelphia	ND	6
May	23—Soldier Bartfield, Brooklyn	ND	10
June	9—Soldier Bartfield, Brooklyn	ND	10
July	7—Mike Glover, New York	ND	10
July	18—Johnny Kid Alberts, N.Y.	KO	2

(Graves claimed welterweight title)

Sept.	29—Johnny Kid Alberts, N.Y.	ND	10
Nov.	28—Frankie Notter, Brooklyn	ND	10
Dec.	15—Jack Toland, Brooklyn	ND	10
Dec.	29—Soldier Bartfield, Brooklyn	ND	10

1915

Jan.	12—Johnny Kid Alberts, Albany	ND	10
Jan.	30—Jack Britton, Brooklyn	ND	10
Feb.	27—Terry Mitchell, Brooklyn	ND	10
Mar.	6—Walter Mohr, New York	ND	10
Apr.	3—Jimmy Capper, Brooklyn	ND	10
Apr.	20—Eddie Moran, New York	ND	10
Apr.	24—Harry Stone, Brooklyn	ND	10
Apr.	30—Frankie Notter, Brooklyn	ND	10
May	24—Italian Joe Gans, Brooklyn	ND	10
June	9—Ted Kid Lewis, New York	ND	10
June	29—Walter Mohr, Brooklyn	ND	10
Dec.	16—Harry Greb, Pittsburgh	KO	2

(Greb broke arm)

Dec.	21—Mike O'Dowd, St. Paul	ND	10

1916

Jan.	17—Ted Kid Lewis, Milwaukee	ND	10
Feb.	21—Eddie Moha, Dayton O.	LF	11

Feb.	28—Al Doty, Akron, O.	ND	12
Mar.	22—Jack Britton, Dayton	ND	15
Apr.	24—Eddie Melzer, Cincinnati	ND	10

1917

Feb.	6—Ted Kid Lewis, N.Y.C.	KO by	9

1920

	—Charley Neary, Milwaukee	ND	10
June	—Pete Scott, Omaha	W	8

1921

Apr.	4—Zip Webster, Albion, Ia.	ND	10
Dec.	15—Young Goldie, Omaha	D	10

TB	KO	WD	WF	D	LD	LF	KO BY	ND	NC
157	35	24	3	28	3	1	2	62	0

MIKE GLOVER

(Michael J. Cavanaugh)

Born, December 18, 1890, Lawrence, Mass. Weight, 145 lbs. Height, 5 ft. 9 in.

1908

—Red Shaw	KO	2
—Jack Gardner	KO	3
—Harry Phillips	KO	4
—Tom Murphy	KO	5
—Leach Cross	WF	5
—Frankie Madden	L	5
—Babe Cullen	ND	4
—George Hoey	ND	6
—Marty Rowan	ND	6
—Fred Dipples	ND	6
—Harry Lortz	ND	6
—Harry Powers	ND	6
—Jack Smith	ND	10
—Marty Rowan	ND	10
—Marty Rowan	ND	10

1909

—Willie Howard	KO	5
—Dodo Maher	KO	9
—Charley T. Miller	KO	5
—Harry Ferns	KO	7
—Jack Cardiff	KO	4
—Dick Nelson	W	15
—Jeff Doherty	W	15
—Billy Leary	ND	10
—Charley Sieger	ND	10
—Eddie Carter	ND	10
—Johnny Dohan	ND	10
—Willie Moody	ND	6
—Young Nitchie	ND	6
—Young Nitchie	ND	6
—Billy Donovan	ND	6
—Peck Miller	ND	6
—Ted Nelson	ND	10
—Tommy Murphy	ND	10
—Peck Miller	ND	6
—Harry Scroggs	ND	6
—Tony Bender	ND	6
—Tony Bender	ND	6
—Jack Curley	ND	10
—Billy Herman	ND	10

1910

—Fred Sidney	D	8
—Battling Levinsky	ND	6
—Young Erne	ND	6
—Frank Perrone	ND	6
—Freddie Corbett	ND	8
—Battling Levinsky	ND	6
—Billy Willis	ND	6
—Buck Crouse	ND	6
—Harry Ramsey	ND	6

1911

—Harry Duncan	KO	13
—Charley Victor	KO	7
—Jack Sincoe	KO	7
—Young Jackson	W	10
—Jack Dillon	ND	6
—Harry Mathewson	D	10

1912

—Joe Kostner	KO	1
—Pat Brislin	ND	10

—Fighting Zunner	ND	10
—Jeff Smith	ND	10
—Tommy Coleman	ND	10
—Tommy Coleman	ND	10
—Young Hickey	ND	10

1913

	—Tommy Malone, Brooklyn	ND	10
June	14—Paddy Sullivan, Rockaway	KO	7
July	4—Italian Joe Gans, Brooklyn	ND	10
July	10—Gus Platts, New York	ND	10
July	16—Young Hickey, New York	ND	10
Aug.	4—Young Denny, New Orleans	ND	10
Sept.	14—Jack Britton, Brooklyn	ND	10
Oct.	13—Kid Graves, Brooklyn	ND	10
Nov.	12—Bill Fleming, Brooklyn	ND	10
Nov.	27—Jack Britton, Brooklyn	ND	10

1914

Jan.	19—Jack Britton, New York	ND	10
May	23—Wild Bill Fleming, Chicopee, Mass	W	15
May	30—Howard Briggs, Cambridge	W	10
June	5—Al Britton, New York	ND	10
July	7—Kid Graves, N. Abington, Mass.	ND	12
July	23—Marcel Thomas, Boston	KO	4
Sept.	25—Bill Fleming, Oldtown, Me.	D	6
Oct.	29—K.O. Sweeney, Waterbury	W	10
	—Bill Flemming, Augusta, Ma.	ND	12
	—Bill Flemming, Brooklyn	ND	10

1915

Feb.	5—Howard Briggs, Abington	W	10
Feb.	22—Battling Downey, Boston	KO	3
June	1—Matt Wells, Boston	W	12
	(Won World Welterweight Title)		
June	22—Jack Britton, Boston	L	12
	(Lost World Welterweight Title)		
Aug.	3—Ted (Kid) Lewis, Boston	L	12
Aug.	28—Young Grady, North Adams, Mass.	KO	7
Sept.	23—Silent Martin, Boston	W	12
Nov.	30—Ted (Kid) Lewis, Boston	W	12
Dec.	14—Soldier Bartfield, Boston	W	12
Dec.	18—Bay Woods, Manchester	W	12

1916

Jan.	3—Joe Chick, Gloucester, Mass.	ND	12
Jan.	7—Billy Kramer, Milwaukee	KO	10
Mar.	21—Joe Egan, Boston	D	12
June	13—Ted (Kid) Lewis, Boston	L	12

TB	KO	WD	WF	D	LD	LF	KO BY	ND	NC
95	18	12	1	4	4	0	0	56	0

JACK BRITTON

(William J. Breslin)
Born, October 14, 1885, Clinton, N. Y.
Nationality, Irish-American. Weight, 144 lbs.
Height, 5 ft. 8 in. Managed by Dan Morgan.
Record incomplete.

1905

Won: Johnny Earle, 6; Eddie Wallace, 6.
No decisions: Young Loughrey, 6; Tommy Herman, 6; Tod Moran, 6; Eddie Carter, 6; Eddie Fay, 6; Young Kary, 6; Young Farrell, 6; Joe Smith, 6; Kid Hagan, 6.

Oct.	20—Steve Kinney	KO by	1

1906

Knockout: Johnny Reagan, 2. No decisions: Phil Griffin, 6; Bobby O'Neal, 6; Toney Haney, 6; Young Loughrey, 6; Reddy Moore, 6; Mississippi, 10; Terry Young, 6; Eddie O'Neal, 6.

Oct.	8—Leo Houck, Lancaster	L	6

1907

Knockout: Kid Gilbert, 2. Won: Kid Beebe, 6; Battling Stinger, 10. No decisions: Lew Sheppard, 6; Art Edmonds, 6; Percy Cove, 6; Percy Cove, 6; Young Pierce, 6; Mike Fleming, 6; Johnny Johnson, 6; Dimp O'Donnell, 6; Kid Haney, 6; Phil Griffin, 6; Reddy Moore, 6; Al Grander, 6.

1908

Knockouts: Young Bechtel, 2; Jim Holland, 4; Jimmy Dasher, 6. Won: Kid Burns, 10; Toney Haney, 6; Tommy Love, 6; Willie Lucas, 6. No decisions: Rouse O'Brien, 6; Tommy Carey, 6; Willie Riley, 6; Billy Glover, 6; Joe Seiger, 10; Johnny Dwyer, 6. Draw: Leo Houck, 6.

602

1909

Jan.	10—Kid Broad, Philadelphia	ND	6
Jan.	18—Harry Stone, Phila.	D	6
Feb.	2—Reddy Moore, Philadelphia	ND	6
Feb.	4—Leo Houck, Lancaster	L	6
Mar.	18—Leo Houck, Lancaster	L	6
Apr.	17—Joe Hurst, Philadelphia	ND	6
July	12—Chas. (Twin) Miller, Phila.	ND	6
Aug.	5—Joe Theel, Philadelphia	ND	6
Sept.	14—Leo Houck, Lancaster	ND	6
Oct.	6—Leo Houck, Lancaster	ND	6
Nov.	8—Johnny Hogan, Reading	W	6
Nov.	22—Jack Curley, Savannah	W	15
Dec.	3—Kid Farmer, Savannah	LF	3
Dec.	10—Kid Farmer, Savannah	KO	7
Dec.	17—Patsey Hogan, Savannah	KO	14
Dec.	28—Jimmy Dasher, Savannah	W	15

1910

Jan.	4—Nathan Erlich, Philadelphia	ND	6
Jan.	24—Tommy O'Keefe, Phila.	ND	6
Feb.	7—Harry Stone, Philadelphia	ND	6
Feb.	22—Young Erne, Philadelphia	ND	6
Mar.	10—Harry Cutch, Philadelphia	ND	6
Mar.	22—Mike Memsic, Atlanta	W	10
Apr.	11—Dummy Decker, Savannah	D	15
Apr.	18—Dummy Decker, Savannah	W	15
May	25—Tommy Devlin, Savannah	D	10
June	30—Ray Bronson, New Orleans	L	10
Aug.	19—Jack McGuire, Savannah	KO	7
Nov.	12—Bert Keyes, Savannah	W	15
Nov.	14—Young Saylor, Memphis	D	8
Nov.	21—Kid Farmer, Memphis	W	8
Dec.	5—Frankie White, Atlanta	D	10
Dec.	12—Ray Temple, Memphis	D	8

1911

Jan.	30—Packey McFarland, Memphis	D	8
Apr.	21—Jake Barada, St. Joseph	W	15
May	9—Johnny Marto, N. Y. C.	ND	10
Sept.	8—Jerry Murphy, San Fran.	L	4
Sept.	22—Denny O'Brien, San Fran.	KO	1
Oct.	6—Willie Ritchie, San Fran.	L	4
Oct.	14—Johnny McCarthy, Sacramento	W	10

1912

Jan.	5—Al Rogers, San Fran.	W	10
Apr.	29—Pal Moore, San Fran.	W	20
July	17—Harry Stone, N. Y. C.	ND	10
Aug.	12—Eddie Smith, N. Y. C.	ND	10
Aug.	27—Eddie Murphy, Boston	W	11
Sept.	10—Willie Beecher, N. Y. C.	ND	10
Sept.	17—Young Saylor, Boston	W	6
Sept.	24—Jack Redmond, N. Y. C.	ND	10
Oct.	2—Joe Egan, N. Y. C.	KO	4
Oct.	7—Yng. McDonough, Thornton	ND	12
Oct.	11—Leach Cross, N. Y. C.	ND	10
Oct.	24—Leach Cross, N. Y. C.	ND	10
Nov.	28—Young Saylor, Dayton	KO	7
Dec.	5—Billy Bennett, Brooklyn	W	10
Dec.	6—Young Loughrey, Phila.	ND	6
Dec.	17—Frankie Nelson, N. Y. C.	ND	10
Dec.	23—Young Ahearn, Brooklyn	ND	10
Dec.	25—Tommy O'Keefe, Phila.	KO	2

1913

Jan.	10—Young Thomas, New Orleans	W	10
Jan.	18—Frankie Gage, New Orleans	KO	9
Jan.	27—Jimmy Evans, Memphis	W	7
Jan.	31—Eddie Hanlon, Savannah	W	7
Mar.	7—Packey McFarland, Phila.	ND	10
Mar.	17—Johnny Krause, Philadelphia	ND	6
Mar.	20—Young Brown, N. Y. C.	ND	10
Mar.	31—Kid Curley, Philadelphia	KO	3
Apr.	15—Marty Baldwin, N. Y. C.	ND	10
Apr.	21—Pal Moore, Philadelphia	ND	4
Apr.	22—Johnny Dohan, N. Y. C.	ND	10
May	17—Kid Graves, Philadelphia	ND	6
May	20—Eddie Murphy, Kenosha, Wis.	ND	10
May	29—Jimmy Duffy, Buffalo	LF	2
June	23—Jimmy Duffy, Buffalo	ND	10
July	4—Charlie White, New Orleans	W	18
Sept.	14—Mike Glover, Brooklyn	ND	10
Nov.	21—Battling Gates, Wilkes-Barre	KO	3
Nov.	27—Mike Glover, Brooklyn	ND	10
Dec.	8—Packey McFarland, Milw.	ND	10
Dec.	29—Al Dewey, Wilkes-Barre	ND	10

1914

Jan.	5—Phil Bloom, N. Y. C.	ND	10
Jan.	19—Mike Glover, N. Y. C.	ND	10
Jan.	31—Ray Campbell, Brooklyn	ND	10
Feb.	10—Johnny Dohan, Brooklyn	ND	10
Feb.	17—Gene Moriarty, Brooklyn	W	7
Mar.	7—Joe Hirst, Philadelphia	ND	6
Mar.	10—Kid Graves, Brooklyn	ND	10
Mar.	30—Leo Kelly, St. Louis	ND	8

Apr.   14—Billy Griffith, Cincinnati .....ND 10
Apr.   25—Kid Graves, Philadelphia .....ND 6
June   30—Joe Eagan, Boston ....W   4
July   4—Johnny Griffiths, Akron, O. ..ND 12
Sept. 26—Soldier Bartfield, Brooklyn ..ND 10
Oct.   9—Eddie Moran, Brooklyn ......ND 10
Nov.   2—Eddie Moran, New Britain ....W 12
Nov.   26—Soldier Bartfield, Brooklyn ...ND 10

1915
Jan.   9—Frankie Notter, Brooklyn ....ND 10
Jan.   30—Kid Graves, Brooklyn ....ND 10
Mar.   4—Sel O'Donnell, Philadelphia ..ND 6
Mar.   6—Jack Toland, Brooklyn ......ND 10
Mar.   13—Phil Bloom, Brooklyn ....ND 10
Mar.   26—Ted Lewis, N. Y. C. ....ND 10
May   17—Leo Kelley, Columbus ......ND 12
June   1—Young Denny, Cincinnati ...ND 10
June   22—Mike Glover, Boston ....W 12
(For Vacant Welterweight Title)
Aug.   31—Ted Kid Lewis, Boston ....L 12
Sept.   6—Johnny Griffiths, Canton.....ND 12
Sept. 27—Ted Lewis, Boston ....L 12
Oct.   30—Terry Mitchell, Brooklyn ....ND 10
Dec.   28—Johnny Griffiths, Akron .....ND 12

1916
Jan.   20—Ted Lewis, Buffalo ....ND 10
Feb.   5—Silent Martin, Brooklyn ......ND 10
Feb.   15—Ted Lewis, Brooklyn ....ND 10
Mar.   13—K. O. Brennan, Buffalo ......ND 10
Mar.   22—Kid Graves, Dayton ....ND 15
Apr.   24—Ted Lewis, New Orleans ......W 20
(Won Welterweight Title)
June   6—Mike O'Dowd, Boston ....W 12
June   23—Battling Kopen, Syracuse .....ND 10
Sept.   5—Joe Welling, Buffalo ....ND 10
Oct.   2—Jimmy Coffey, Schenectady ..ND 10
Oct.   17—Ted Lewis, Boston ....W 12
Nov.   14—Ted Lewis, Boston ....D 12
Nov.   21—Charley White, Boston ....W 10
Dec.   4—Steve Latzo, Wilkes-Barre ....ND 10
Dec.   8—Sam Robideau, Cleveland ...ND 10

1917
Jan.   1—Jimmy Duffy, Buffalo ....ND 10
Jan.   9—Albert Badoud, New York ....ND 10
Jan.   25—Mike O'Dowd, St. Paul ....ND 10
Jan.   29—Johnny Griffiths, Cincinnati ..ND 10
Feb.   28—Tommy Robson, Lawrence ....D 12
Mar.   5—Bryan Downey, Columbus ....ND 12
Mar.   26—Ted Lewis, Cincinnati ......ND 10
May   8—Mike O'Dowd, Brooklyn .....ND 10
May   19—Ted Lewis, Toronto ....ND 10
June   6—Ted Lewis, St. Louis ....ND 10
June   14—Ted Lewis, N. Y. C. ....ND 10
June   25—*Ted Lewis, Dayton ....L 20
July   25—Johnny Griffiths, Boston ......D 10
Sept. 14—Marty Cross, N. Y. C. ....ND 10
Oct.   3—Eddie Kid Billings, Superior ..ND 10
Oct.   19—Benny Leonard, N. Y. C. .....ND 10
Nov.   12—Johnny Tillman, Philadelphia .ND 6
Nov.   13—Soldier Bartfield, Buffalo ....ND 10
Dec.   4—Johnny Tillman, Boston ....W 12
*Lost Welterweight title, Lou Bauman, referee.

1918
Jan.   1—Jimmy Duffy, Buffalo ....ND 10
Jan.   16—Tommy Robson, Providence ...W 12
Feb.   11—Marty Cross, Providence ....W 12
Mar.   6—Ted Lewis, Atlanta ....ND 10
Mar.   20—Vic Moran, Chattanooga ....KO 6
Mar.   27—Jimmy Duffy, Atlanta ....W 8
May   2—Ted Lewis, Scranton ....ND 10
May   24—Ted Lewis, New York ....ND 6
June   11—Bryan Downey, Boston ....W 12
June   20—Ted Lewis, New York ....ND 6
June   25—Benny Leonard, Philadelphia ND 6
July   9—Tommy Ferguson, Scranton ..ND 10
July   17—K. O. Laughlin, Camden .....ND 8
Aug.   6—Soldier Bartfield, Phila. ......ND 6
Aug.   14—Eddie Shevlin, Boston ....W 10
Aug.   25—Johnny Griffiths, Camp Bowie,
          Texas ....ND 6
Sept. 16—Tommy Robson, Boston ......W 10
Sept. 30—Willie Ryan, Jersey City .....ND 8
Nov.   11—Soldier Bartfield, Phila. ......ND 6
Nov.   16—Soldier Bartfield, New York ..ND 10
Dec.   8—Silent Martin, Jersey City .....ND 8
Dec.   17—Soldier Bartfield, Buffalo .....ND 10

1919
Feb.   3—Al Doty, Canton, O. ....ND 12
Feb.   10—Willie Ryan, Trenton, N. J. ...ND 8
Mar.   17—Ted Lewis, Canton, O. ....KO 9
(Regained World Welterweight Title)

Mar.   24—Jack Perry, Pittsburgh........ND 10
Apr.   8—Bryan Downey, Canton, O. ...ND 12
Apr.   28—Jock Malone, St. Paul, Minn. ..ND 10
May   5—Johnny Griffiths, Buffalo ....ND 10
(For Title)
May   12—Johnny Tillman, Baltimore ...ND 12
May   19—Joe Welling, Syracuse, N. Y. ..ND 10
May   24—Jimmy McCabe, Philadelphia .ND 6
June   13—Walter Mohr, Montreal ......ND 10
June   26—Jack Perry, Cumerland, Md. ..ND 12
July   4—Johnny Griffiths, Canton .....ND 12
July   10—Al Doty, Connellsville, Pa. .....KO 2
July   28—Ted Lewis, Jersey City ......ND 8
Aug.   7—Johnny Griffiths, Denver .....ND 12
Aug.   22—Mike O'Dowd, Newark ....ND 8
Nov.   5—Johnny Tillman, Detroit .....ND 10
Nov.   7—Goats Doig, La Salle, Ill. .....ND 10
Nov.   25—Harvey Thorpe, Buffalo .....ND 10
Dec.   1—Billy Ryan, Canton ....KO 11
Dec.   4—Steve Latzo, Wilkes-Barre ....ND 10

1920
Jan.   1—Johnny Gill, Steelton, Pa. .....W 10
Jan.   30—Jimmy Conway, Savannah .....W 10
Mar.   17—Kid Abberts, Bayonne, N. J. ..ND 8
Mar.   8—Dave Palttz, Hartford, Conn. ..ND 10
Mar.   17—Jack Perry, Canton, O. ....ND 12
Mar.   26—Bryan Downey, Cleveland ....ND 10
Apr.   7—Dennis O'Keefe, Kenosha,
          Wis. ....ND 10
Apr.   26—Jock Malone, Canton, O. ......W 12
May   17—Mike O'Dowd, Canton, O. .....L 12
May   31—Johnny Griffiths, Akron, O. ...W 8
June   2—Young Joe Borrell, Phila. .....ND 8
June   7—Len Rowlands, Phila. ....ND 8
June   26—Marcel Thomas, Newark, N.J. ..KO 10
Aug.   23—Lou Bogash, Bridgeport ....D 12
Sept.   6—Ray Bronson, Cedar Point .....W 10
Sept. 13—Johnny Tillman, Cleveland ...ND 10
Oct.   7—Jack Perry, Toledo ....D 12
Nov.   18—Morris Lux, Kansas City, Mo. .ND 10
Nov.   23—Bud Logan, San Antonio, Tex. ND 10
Nov.   29—Jake Abel, Atlanta, Ga. ......W 10
Dec.   6—Pinky Mitchell, Milwaukee ...ND 10
        —Johnny Gill ....ND 10
        —Frankie Maguire ....ND 6

1921
Feb.   7—Ted Lewis, N. Y. C. ....W 15
Mar.   7—Johnny Tillman, Des Moines ..ND 10
May   25—Travie Davis, Seattle ....D 4
June   3—Dave Shade, Portland, Ore. ....D 10
June   10—Frank Barrieau, Portland ......D 10
July   18—Mickey Walker, Newark, N.J. ..ND 12

1922
Feb.   17—*Dave Shade, N. Y. C. ....D 15
May   —Cowboy Padgett, Omaha, Neb.ND 10
May   16—Morrie Lux, Tulsa, Okla. .....KO 5
May   26—Ray Long, Oklahoma City .....D 12
June   26—*Benny Leonard, N. Y. C. .....WF 13
Oct.   10—Jimmy Kelly, Havana ....W 12
Nov.   1—†Mickey Walker, N. Y. C. .....L 15
*For welterweight title.
†Lost world welterweight title.

1923
May   —Joe O'Hara, Chicago ....ND 10
June   14—Soldier Bartfield, N. Y. C. ...W 10
Nov.   20—Frankie Schoell, Boston ....L 10
        —Phil Kaplan ....W 10

1924
Jan.   21—Fred Archer, Canton, Ohio ...ND 10
Feb.   11—Johnny Karr, Canton, Ohio ...ND 10
Aug.   28—Jack Rappaport, Newark, N.J. ND 10
Oct.   1—K. O. Phil Kaplan, Jersey City,
          N. J. ....ND 10
Oct.   13—Phil Krug, Newark, N. J. ......ND 10
Nov.   19—Jimmy Duffy, Oakland, Calif....L 4
Dec.   2—Sailor Billy Vincent, Los Ang... W 4

1925
Jan.   16—Norman Genet, San Fran. .....W 8
Jan.   22—Izy Tanner, Portland, Ore. .....W 10
Feb.   20—Billy Wells, San Francisco ......L 10
Mar.   20—Morrie Schlaifer, Omaha, Nebr. ..L 10
May   16—Ted Krache, Seattle ....D 6
May   20—Ray Moore, Los Angeles ......W 10
June   3—Harry Ritzer, Wilmington,Calif. W 10
June   26—Dave Forbes, Kans.City,Kans. ND 10

1926
Aug.   2—Red McLaughlin, Miami ....W 10

1927
Apr.   2—Arturo Shekels, Pompano, Fla.. W 10
Aug.   29—George Levine, N. Y. C. ....W 10
Sept. 12—Irish Tommy Jordan, N. Y. C... W 10
Sept. 19—Joey Knapp, N. Y. C. ....W 10
Oct.   17—Hilario Martinez, N. Y. C. ......L 10
Nov.   14—Jimmy Jones, Canton, O........L 10

1928

Jan.	4—Lloyd Hybert, Cleveland .....NC 5
	(Stopped by referee)
Aug.	15—Tony Vaccarelli, N.Y.C. ......W 10
Aug.	28—Pal Silvers, N.Y.C. ....L 10
Sept.	24—Mickey Sears, Lynn, Mass. .....W 10
Oct.	1—Pete Pacheco, Boston ....W 10
Oct.	16—Laddie Lee, Portland, Me. .....W 10
Oct.	22—Meyer Cohen, Holyoke, Mass... W 10
Nov.	1—Danny Sears, Portsmouth, N.H. W 10
Nov.	14—Larry Brignolia, Boston ......W 10
Dec.	7—Frankie O'Brien, Boston ......L 10
Dec.	20—Canada Lee, Boston ....W 10

1929

Mar.	22—Farmer Joe Cooper, N.Orleans .W 10
Apr.	8—Grover Mallini, Mobile, Ala. ...W 10
Apr.	12—Tot Wilson, Macon, Ga. ....W 10
Apr.	22—"Rebel" Red Herring, Memphis, Tenn. ....L 8
Apr.	30—Ted Goodrich, Atlanta, Ga. .....W 10
June	10—Bill Brown, New Orleans ......W 12
June	23—Patsy Pollock, Chicago ....W 10
July	9—"Ham" Jenkins, Denver ....L 10
Aug.	19—Morrie Sherman, Grand Rapids .L 10
Aug.	21—Henry Firpo, Zanesville, O. .....L 10
Sept.	3—T.N.T. Gibbons, Kenton, O. ... D 10
Sept.	30—Johnny Roberts, Portsmouth,O. L 10
Dec.	17—Farmer J. Cooper, Charlotte, N. C. ....L 10

1930

Mar.	6—Al Schell, Hartford, Conn. .....W 10
May	8—Yng. Bobby Ruffalo, Buffalo .. W 8

Retired in 1930 to become boxing instructor.

TB	KO	WD	WF	D	LD	LF	KOBY	ND	NC
325	21	77	1	20	25	2	1	177	1

Elected to Boxing Hall of Fame, 1960.
Died, March 27, 1962, Miami, Florida.

TED (KID) LEWIS
(Gershon Mendeloff)

Born, October 24, 1894, St. George's-in-the-East, London. Weight, 126-170. Height, 5 ft. 5½ in. Manged by Freeman Bernstein, Jimmy Johnston and Charley Harvey.

1909

Sept.	13—Johnny Sharpe, London ....L 6
Oct.	9—Joe Lipman, London ....W 6
Dec.	6—Dick Hart, London ....D 6
Dec.	18—Jack (Kid) Levene, London ...KO 3

1910

Knockouts: Young Sullivan, 3; George Powell, 2; Joe Madden, 3; Young Smith, 3; Ted O'Neil, 5; Kid Levene, 6. Won: Sid Venner, 6; Joe Lippan, 6; Alf Jacobs, 6; Curley Bume, 6.

1911

Knockouts: Jack Ginnion, 2; Jack Marks, 7; Bill Smith, 4; Charley Smith, 4; Jack Harbobur, 3; Young Klein, 3; Walt Marshall, 3; Jim Butler, 1; Billy Griggs, 2; Alf Small, 12. Won: Nat Brooks, 10; Dick Murray, 6; Eddie Foy, 6; George Marks, 6; Tom Perkins, 6; Bill Marsh, 6; Joe Madden, 6; Alf Jacobs, 6; Jack Marks, 10; Dick Murray, 6; Young Sullivan, 6; Jack Bunner, 10; Kid Levene, 6; Joe Jacobs, 6; Harry Ray, 6; Frank Warner, 6; Tom Perkins, 10; Kid Olds, 6. Draw: Young Greenstock, 6; Fred Halsband, 6.

1912

Knockouts: Jack Chinney, 5; Jack O'Neil, 3; Jack Harrison, 3; Alf Small, 5; Darkey Harris, 3; Jerry Murray, 1; Gus Venn, 7; Jim Shires, 2; Won: Jim Hales, 6; Jim Shires, 10; Tom Clifford, 6; Jack Chinney, 6; Fred Blake, 6; Billy Taylor, 8; Alf Mitchell, 10; Harry Wilson, 10; Duke Lynch, 10; Tom Mack, 10; Leon Truffler, 10; Leon Truffler, 10; George Buswell, 10; George Ruddick, 10; George Ruddick, 12; Sam Russell, 10; Allen Porter, 10; Fred Halsband, 10; Darkey Haley, 6; Seaman Hayes, 10; Harry Berry, 15; Jim Lloyd, 10. Lost: Fred Halsband, 10; Young Brooks, 15. Lost (foul): Con Houghton, 7. Knockout by: Duke Lynch, 1.

1913

Jan.	2—Jim Lloyd, Liverpool ....W 10
Jan.	4—George Buswell, London .....KO 14
Jan.	16—Nat Williams, Liverpool ....D 15
Jan.	27—Johnny Condon, Ring, Lond. .. W 20
Mar.	3—Johnny Condon, Ring, Lond. .. W 20
Apr.	7—Young Brooks, N.S.C., Lond. .. W 15
June	2—Joe Starmer, N.S.C., Lond. ... W 15
July	19—Harry Stirling, London ....KO 7
July	26—Duke Lynch, Ring, London .... W 20
Aug.	23—Harry Stirling, Ring, London .. W 20
Sept.	15—Fernand Quendreux, Ring, London ....KO 10
Oct.	6—Alec Lambert, N.S.C., Lond. .KO 17
	(Won British Featherweight Title)

1914

Jan.	14—George Buswell, London .....KO 2
Feb.	2—Paul Til, London ....WF 12
	(Won European Featherweight Title)
Mar.	15—Harry Berry, London ....KO 3
Mar.	18—Ted Saunders, Coventry ......KO 6
May	30—Herb McCoy, Sydney, NSW ... W 20
June	12—Hughie Mehegan, Syd., NSW . W 20
June	26—Young Shugrue, Syd., NSW .... W 20
July	11—Herb McCoy, Melbourne .....L 20
Aug.	1—Bobby Moore, Melbourne .....W 20
Nov.	2—Phil Bloom, N.Y.C. ....ND 10
Dec.	25—Yg. Jack O'Brien, Phila., Pa. ..ND 6

1915

Jan.	1—Willie Moore, Phila., Pa. ......ND 6
Mar.	10—Frankie Mack, Havana ....W 20
Mar.	26—Jack Britton, N.Y.C. ....ND 10
Apr.	6—Harry Lenny, New York ......ND 10
Apr.	16—Johnny Lore, Montreal ......ND 10
Apr.	30—Johnny Lustig, Montreal .....ND 10
June	9—Kid Graves, N.Y.C. ....ND 10
June	23—Johnny Marto, N.Y.C. ....ND 10
June	25—Mike Mazie, N.Y.C. ....ND 10
July	21—Charlie White, N.Y.C. ....ND 10
Aug.	3—Mike Glover, Boston ....W 12
Aug.	11—Kid Curley, Buffalo ....ND 10
Aug.	17—Fighting Zunner, Buffalo .....ND 10
Aug.	31—Jack Britton, Boston ....W 12
	(Won Vacant Welterweight Title)
Sept.	27—Jack Britton, Boston ....W 12
	(For World Welterweight Championship)
Oct.	18—Willie Moore, Phila., Pa. ......ND 6
Oct.	26—Joe Mandot, Boston ....W 12
Nov.	2—Milburn Saylor, Boston ....W 12
Nov.	23—Jimmy Duffy, Boston ....KO 1
Nov.	30—Mike Glover, Boston ....L 12
Dec.	28—Willie Ritchie, New York .....ND 10

1916

Jan.	1—Kayo Brennan, Buffalo ....ND 10
Jan.	17—Kid Graves, Milwaukee ......ND 10
Jan.	20—Jack Britton, Buffalo ....ND 10
Feb.	5—Marty Farrell, Phila. ....ND 6
Feb.	8—Soldier Bartfield, Buffalo .....ND 10
Feb.	15—Jack Britton, Brooklyn ......ND 10
Feb.	21—Jimmy Duffy, Buffalo ....ND 10
Feb.	24—Harry Trendall, St. Louis .....KO 7
Mar.	1—Harry Stone, New Orleans .....W 20
Apr.	19—Jake Abel, Chattanooga .....W 8
Apr.	24—Jack Britton, New Orleans .....L 20
	(Lost World Welterweight Title)
May	18—Mike Gibbons, N.Y.C. ....ND 10
May	24—Eddie Moha, Dayton, O. ......KO 13
June	13—Mike Glover, Boston ....W 12
Oct.	17—Jack Britton, Boston ....L 12
Oct.	24—Young Denny, St. Louis ......ND 12
Nov.	14—Jack Britton, Boston ....D 12
Nov.	23—Johnny Griffiths, Cleveland ..ND 10
Dec.	21—Johnny Griffiths, Cleveland ..ND 10

1917

Jan.	29—Willie Beecher, N.Y.C. ....ND 10
Jan.	31—Sam Robideau, Providence ....W 15
Feb.	2—Kid Graves, N.Y.C. ....KO 9
Feb.	26—Johnny Griffiths, Akron ......ND 12
Mar.	19—Willie Moore, N.Y.C. ....ND 1
Mar.	26—Jack Britton, Cincinnati ......ND 10
Apr.	2—Jim Coffey, N.Y.C. ....KO 1
Apr.	12—Billy Weeks, Springfield .....ND 12
Apr.	28—Johnny Griffiths, Columbus ..ND 12
May	4—Jimmy O'Hagen, N.Y.C. ......ND 2
May	19—Jack Britton, Toronto ....ND 10
May	22—Joe Egan, Boston ....W 12
May	24—Mike O'Dowd, N.Y.C. ....ND 10
June	6—Jack Britton, St. Louis ....ND 10
June	14—Jack Britton, N.Y.C. ....ND 10
June	25—Jack Britton, Dayton ....W 20
	(Re-won Welterweight Title)
July	4—*Johnny Griffiths, Akron ....ND 15
Aug.	7—Jimmy O'Hagen, Saratoga ....ND 10
Aug.	17—Mike O'Dowd, N.Y.C. ....ND 10
Aug.	28—Mike O'Dowd, Boston ....L 12
Aug.	31—*Albert Badoud, N.Y.C. ....L 1
Sept.	3—Soldier Bartfield, Buffalo .....ND 10
Sept.	11—Soldier Bartfield, Buffalo ....ND 10
Sept.	14—Jimmy O'Hagen, Brooklyn ..ND 10
Sept.	15—Italian Joe Gans, Brooklyn ...ND 10
Sept.	24—Frank Carbone, N.Y.C. ......ND 10
Oct.	24—Battling Ortega, Oakland ......D 4

Nov. 13—Johnny McCarthy, San Fran. ..W 4
Dec. 17—Bryan Downey, Columbus....ND 12
1918
Jan. 14—Soldier Bartfield, Columbus ..ND 12
Jan. 23—Soldier Bartfield, Toronto ....ND 10
Feb. 4—Johnny Tillman, Phila. ....ND 6
Feb. 18—Jimmy Duffy, Toledo ....KO 1
Feb. 25—Soldier Bartfield, Phila. ......ND 6
Feb. 26—Willie Langford, Buffalo .....ND 10
Mar. 6—Jack Britton, Atlanta ....ND 10
Apr. 16—Joe Egan, Milwaukee ....ND 10
May 2—Jack Britton, Scranton ....ND 10
May 17—*Johnny Tillman, Denver ......W 20
May 24—Jack Britton, N. Y. C. ....ND 6
June 20—Jack Britton, N. Y. City .....ND 6
June 25—Tommy Robson, Boston ......W 12
July 4—*Johnny Griffiths, Akron ....ND 20
Aug. 3—Tommy Robson, Boston ......W 12
Aug. 17—Walter Mohr, Jersey City .....ND 8
Sept. 23—Benny Leonard, Newark .....ND 8
*Title bout.
1919
Jan. 1—Bryan Downey, Columbus....ND 12
Jan. 15—George Rivet, Montreal ......ND 10
Mar. 10—Johnny Griffiths, Memphis ...ND 8
Mar. 17—Jack Britton, Canton, O. ..KO by 9
(Lost Welterweight Title)
July 14—Steve Latzo, Philadelphia .....ND 6
July 28—Jack Britton, Jersey City .....ND 8
Aug. 4—Steve Latzo, Philadelphia .....ND 6
Sept. 1—Mike O'Dowd, Syracuse, N.Y. ND 10
Oct. 11—K. O. Laughlin, Portl'd.Me. ...KO 1
Oct. 16—Jimmy McCabe, Atl. City .....KO 1
Oct. 29—Jake Abel, Atlanta ....W 10
Dec. 26—Matt Wells, Albert H., Lon. ...KO 12
1920
Jan. 13—Frank Moody, Manchester ....KO 1
Feb. 14—Prunier, Paris................KO 9
Feb. 28—Jerry Shea, Mountain Ash ....KO 1
Mar. 4—Gus Platts, Sheffield ....W 18
Mar. 11—Johnny Bee, London.........KO 4
(Middleweight Title)
Apr. 5—Kid Doyle, Liverpool ....W 11
Apr. 30—Kid Doyle, Holborn Std. ......W 5
June 9—Johnny Basham, Olympia ...KO 9
Sept. 23—Mike O'Dowd. Jersey City ...ND 12
Oct. 12—Marcel Thomas, Jersey City ...ND 6
Nov. 19—Johnny Basham, London .....KO 19
(British Empire Middleweight Championship)
1921
Feb. 7—Jack Britton, N. Y. C. ....L 15
(For World Welterweight Title)
Mar. 16—Jack Perry, Detroit ....ND 10
Apr. 8—Nate Siegel, Boston ....L 10
Apr. 13—Augie Ratner, N. Y. C. ....L 15
June 27—Jack Bloomfield, London ..... W 20
(British Middleweight Title)
Sept. 20—Ernie Barriean, Toronto ......KO 10
Oct. 14—Johnny Basham, London ......KO 12
(British Middleweight Title)
Nov. 17—Boy McCormick, London ..... W 14
1922
Feb. 17—Tom Gummer, Brighton......KO 1
May 11—George Carpentier, London KO by 1
(European heavyweight championship)
June 19—Frankie Burns, Holland Pk. ...KO 11
(British Empire Middleweight Championship)
Sept. 4—Marcel Thomas, London .....KO 4
Sept. 20—Roland Todd, London .... W 20
(British Middleweight Title)
1923
Feb. 15—*Roland Todd, London ....L 20
July 30—Augie Ratner, London ....L 20
Oct. 4—Frankie Burns, London .... W 20
Nov. 8—Fred Archer, London .... W 20
*For European Middleweight Title.
Dec. 26—Ted Davies, London .... W 20
1924
Jan. 29—Sid Pape, Bradford ....KO 2
Feb. 17—Bruno Frattini, Milan, Italy ...KO 17
Mar. 18—Francis Charles, Paris ....W 15
Apr. 5—Chic Nelson, Hamburg ....D 15
Apr. 12—Eric Milenz, Berlin ....KO 7
June 1—Piet Hobin, Paris..............D 20
July 3—Johnny Brown, London ...... W 20
Nov. 26—Tommy Milligan, Edinburgh ....L 20
(Lost British and European Welterweight Titles.)
1925
Jan. 22—Francis Charles, London ...... W 20
Mar. 19—Tommy Milligan, London ... LF 5
July 10—Bob Sage, Hollywood, Cal, ,,,, W 10
Oct. 8—Marcel Thuru, London ......LF 1

Nov. 8—Simmon Rossman, London ...LF 8
Nov. 27—Len Johnson, Manchester .KO by 9
1926
Mar. 7—Billy Pritchard, London ......KO 10
Mar. 21—Billy Mattick, London ....WF 5
1927
Aug. 4—Joe Green, Illford ....KO 6
Aug. 14—Jim Carr, London ....KO 3
Aug. 28—Noel Steenhurst, London ....KO 9
Sept. 11—Ted Coveney, London ....KO 6
Oct. 2—Amsenes, London ....KO 1
Oct. 16—Joe Rolfe, London ....KO 11
Dec. —Alex Storbeck, Johannesburg .....KO 1
1928
Jan. 7—Johnny Squires, Johannesburg .....D 15
July 23—Maxie Rosenbloom, L.I. City ......LF 6
Dec. 17—Charley Belanger, Toronto ..... L dis. 1
1929
Dec. 13—Johnny Basham, Hoxton .... KO 3

TB	KO	WD	WF	D	LD	LF	KO BY	ND	NC
254	68	86	2	9	13	7	4	65	0

Elected to Boxing Hall of Fame, 1964.
Died, October 20, 1970, London, England.

MICKEY WALKER
(Record under Middleweight Champions)

PETE LATZO
Born, Aug. 1, 1902, Coloraine, Pa. Nationality, Slav-American. Height, 5 ft. 8 in. Started boxing in 1919 under ring name of Young Clancy. Managed by Paddy Mullins and Jimmy Johnston.
1919
Knockouts: Red Ferguson, 3; Frankie Dehat, 5; Ed Milhelm, 2; K. O. Grant, 2. No decisions: Charley Warren, 3; Allen Crawley, 6; Jake Henry, 6; Joe Shugars, 6; Billy Gannon, 6; Joe Shugars, 6.
1920
Knockouts: Mickey Malloy, 3; Frankie McCarthy, 6; Ren Carlin, 6. No decisions: Joe O'Neil, 10; Al Reynolds, 8; Joe O'Neil, 10; Al Reynolds, 10; *Willie Ritchie, 10; Georgie Reynolds, 10; Al Murphy, 10; Johnny Maloney, 10; Georgie Reynolds, 10; *Willie Ritchie, 10; Frankie Venchall, 10; Jimmy Shevlin, 10.
*Not the lightweight champion.
1921
Knockouts: Jake Shuffer, 1; Harry Turner, 2; Nick "Kid" Moone, 6; Jimmy Sullivan, 7. Won: Jimmy Duffy, 12. No decisions: Al Dewey, 10; Georgie Reynolds, 10; Sammy Bernie, 10; Bud Logan, 8; Tim Dorney, 10; Johnny Herman, 10; Tim Droney, 10; Barney Adair, 10; Tim Droney, 10; Jack Palmer, 10.
1922
Jan. 26—Frankie Schoell, Buffalo ......W 10
Feb. 3—Jack Palmer, New York ....W 8
Mar. 7—Al Norton, Scranton ....ND 10
Apr. 1—Jack Palmer, Hazelton ....ND 10
Mar. 1—Al Norton, Scranton ....ND 10
Apr. 1—Jack Palmer, Hazelton ....ND 10
Apr. 6—Al Brown, Scranton ....ND 10
May 4—Marty Summers, Scranton ...ND 10
May 19—Dave Shade, Wilkes-Barre ....ND 10
June 8—Eddie Shevlin, Scranton .....ND 10
July 25—Paul Doyle, Scranton ....ND 10
Oct. 3—Frankie Schoell, Scranton ....ND 10
Oct. 16—Eddie Shevlin, Wilkes-Barre ...ND 10
Nov. 9—Georgie Ward, Scranton .....ND 10
Nov. 3—Tim Droney, Scranton ....ND 10
Dec. 11—Sailor Friedman, Phila. ......ND 10
Dec. 18—Billy Wells, Scranton ....ND 10
Dec. 26—Frankie Schoell, Buffalo ......L 12
1923
Jan. 16—Georgie Ward, Newark ......ND 10
Feb. 6—Paul Doyle, Boston ....L 10
Feb. 10—Johnny Nichols, New York ....W 12
Mar. 22—Mickey Walker, Newark .....ND 12
Mar. 29—Georgie Ward, Newark ......ND 12
Apr. 12—Jimmy Jones, Youngstown ...ND 12
June 5—Geo. Young Erne, Scranton...KO 6
June 13—K. O. Phil Kaplan, New York ...D 12
July 4—Frankie Schoell, Scranton ....ND 10
July 17—Wally Hinkle, Scranton ....KO 2
1924
Jan. 10—Georgie Ward, Boston ....W 10
Jan. 14—Frankie Schoell, Scranton .....L 10

Feb. 25—Billy Wells, Boston ....L 10
Mar. 4—Georgie Ward, Scranton ....W 10
Apr. 24—Harry Galfund, Scranton ......W 10
May 19—Dave Shade, Wilkes-Barre ......D 10
June 27—KO Phil Kaplan, Scranton .....W 12
July 21—Frankie Venchall, Wilkes-Barre W 10
Aug. 11—Frankie Quill, Scranton ......KO 3
Aug. 29—Frankie Venchall, Wilkes-Barre W 10
Sept. 8—Willie Harmon, Newark ......ND 12
Nov. 21—Morrie Schlaifer, Omaha ......W 10

1925
Jan. 1—Patsy Haley, Scranton.......KO 2
Jan. 19—Eddie Burnbrook, Scranton ..KO 2
Jan. 28—Billy Wells, Oakland ....L 10
Mar. 6—Jack Rappaport, Hollywood ...W 10
Apr. 27—Mannie Owens, Scranton .....KO 4
May 11—Willie Harmon, Scranton ....W 10
June 16—Georgie Levine, Brooklyn .....W 10,
June 23—Morrie Schlaifer,
    Wilkes-Barre ....KO by 3
Sept. 14—Italian Joe Gans, Scranton ...W 10
Oct. 12—Bobby Barrett, Scranton .....W 10
Dec. 21—Billy Wells, Newark ....ND 12

1926
Jan. 4—Italian Joe Gans, Brooklyn ....W 10
Jan. 25—Joe Carlo, Scranton ....KO 1
Feb. 12—Morrie Schlaifer, Phila........W 10
Mar. 22—George Russell, Wilkes-Barre ..KO 9
May 20—Mickey Walker, Scranton .....W 10
(Won world welterweight championship)
June 29—*Willie Harmon, Newark .....KO 5
July 9—*George Levine, N.Y.C.....WF 4
July 16—Sid Nelson, Steubenville.....KO 4
Dec. 8—Joe Simonich, Newark ......ND 10
    *Title bout.

1927
Jan. 14—Sergt. Sammy Baker,
    Wilkes-Barre ....W 10
Jan. 24—Jimmy Jones, Pittsburgh .....W 10
Feb. 18—Billy Piltz, Oklahoma City ...W 10
Feb. 21—Clyde Hull, Dallas, Tex. ......ND 10
Mar. 10—Joe Simonovich, Chicago .....W 10
May 9—Jack Rappaport, Scranton, Pa. KO 3
June 3—*Joe Dundee, New York ......L 15
Aug. 23—Allentown Joe Gans,
    Wilkes-Barre ....WF 8
Aug. 30—Jack McVey, Cleveland, O. ....D 12
Sept. 19—Dick Evans, Canton, O.........W 10
Sept. 30—Tiger Flowers, Wilkes-Barre ....L 10
Oct. 10—Wyoming Warner, Phila.......KO 2
Oct. 28—Frankie Schoell, Buffalo, N.Y. ..L 10
Nov. 21—Maxie Rosenbloom, Phila......L 10
    *Lost welterweight title.

1928
Feb. 6—Maxie Rosenbloom, Wilkes-B. .W 10
Feb. 23—Paul Swiderski, Syracuse ......W 10
Apr. 25—Tony Marullo, N.Y.C. ....W 10
May 14—Bing Conley, N.Y.C. ....W 10
June 1—Tommy Loughran, Brooklyn ...L 15
    (Light Heavyweight Title Bout)
June 12—Leo Lomski, Brooklyn......WF 6
July 16—Tommy Loughran, Wilkes-B. ...L 10
    (Light Heavyweight Title Bout)
Aug. 7—Tommy Dunn, New York .....W 10
Aug. 20—Matt Adgie, Philadelphia ......W 10
Sept. 7—Leo Lomski, Detroit, Mich......L 10
Oct. 5—Charlie Belanger, Detroit .....W 10
Oct. 17—James J. Braddock, Newark.....L 10

1929
Feb. 1—Louis Armand, New Orleans ..KO 3

1930
Jan. 16—Eddie Clark, Atlantic City ....KO 6
Jan. 27—Billy Jones, Philadelphia ....L 10
Feb. 21—Larry Johnson, N.Y.C. ......W 10
May 27—Jimmy Slattery, Boston ......NC 7
June 18—Larry Johnson, New York .....WF 6
July 31—Frankie Cawley, Wilkes-Barre ..L 10
Oct. 13—Tait Littman, Milwaukee ....L 10

1931
Jan. 22—Joe Banovic, Scranton ....L 10
Feb. 2—Johnnie Pilc, Newark ....L 10
Feb. 26—Sam Weiss, Allentown, Pa.......W 10
Mar. 12—Sam Weiss, Allentown, Pa......W 10
Mar. 26—Rattle Kichline, Bethlehem ....W 10
Apr. 22—Matt Adgie, Philadelphia ......W 10
May 18—Charley Belanger, Toronto .....L 8
June 9—Battling Bozo, Atlanta ....L 10
June 22—Battling Bozo, Birmingham ....L 10
June 29—Al Ettore, Philadelphia ....L 10
July 22—Sammy Weiss, Laurel ....L 10
Aug. 19—Jimmy Britt, Washington, N.J. ..L 10
Sept. 4—George Manley, Denver ....L 10

1932
Feb. 26—Joe Banovic, N.Y.C............L 10
1934
Jan. 18—Harry Fuller, Scranton, Pa. .....L 10
Apr. 27—Billy Ketchell, Philadelphia ....L 10
June 5—Teddy Yarosz, Pittsburgh .KO by 4

TB	KO	WD	WF	D	LD	LF	KOBY	ND	NC
151	25	35	4	3	29	0	2	52	1

Died 1968 in Atlantic City, N.J.

JOE DUNDEE
(Samuel Lazzaro)
Born, 1902, Italy. Nationality, Italian-American. Weight, 147 lbs. Height, 5 ft. 7 in.
Managed by Max Waxman.
1919
Mar. 14—Little Jeff, Baltimore ....L 4
May 9—Red Tendler, Baltimore ......L 4
June 2—Red Tendler, Baltimore ......KO 2
1920
Jan. 23—George Lewis, Baltimore .....KO 3
Feb. 7—Kid Richmond, Baltimore .....W 6
Feb. 13—Young Kilbane, Baltimore ....KO 3
Apr. 5—Battling Morgan, Balt..........L 6
Apr. 16—Goldie Ahearn, Baltimore ...D 6
Apr. 30—Battling Morgan, Balt........D 8
June 28—Goldie Ahearn, Baltimore .....W 8
Aug. 13—Mike Ertle, Baltimore ....W 8
Oct. 1—Young Leonard, Baltimore ...W 8
Dec. 22—Chick Kansas, Baltimore ......W 6
Dec. 29—Young Dempsey, Baltimore ...W 6
1921
Jan. 14—Eddie Kid Wagner, Balt. .....D 8
Feb. 5—Lenny Mahoney, Baltimore.....L 12
Oct. 12—Jack Hyman, Baltimore ......KO 5
Oct. 26—Harry Rice, Baltimore ....W 8
Nov. 21—Ralph Brady, Baltimore ......W 12
Dec. 5—Lenny Mahoney, Baltimore ..W 12
    Knockouts: Danny Duarte, 9; Speedy Lawrence, 4.
1922
Jan. 12—Freddie Jacks, Baltimore ......L 12
Apr. 18—Andy Chaney, Baltimore ..KO by 8
June 1—Joe McCabe, Baltimore ....W 8
July 24—Harry Rice, Baltimore ....W 8
Sept. 4—Kid Williams, Baltimore .....LF 10
Feb. 12—Tommy Cleary, Baltimore ....W 12
Oct. 24—Andy Tucker, Richmond, Va...W 12
Nov. 22—Matty Brooks, Baltimore .....W 10
    —Andy Bowen, Baltimore ....W 10
    —Gene Pointier, Baltimore .....W 10
    —Roddy McDonald, Baltimore ..W 12
1923
Jan. 3—Bob Robideau, Baltimore .....W 6
Feb. 5—Len Mahoney, Baltimore ......L 15
Apr. 11—Pedro Campo, Baltimore .....W 12
May 10—Johnny Reno, Berwyn, Md.....D 10
July 4—Andy Bowen, Washington ....W 10
July 19—Rod McDonald, Berwyn, Md. ...W 12
Aug. 30—Mel Coogan, Berwyn, Md. ...W 12
Sept. 12—Jack Zivic, Baltimore ....W 12
Oct. 3—Jack Darcy, Baltimore ....KO 2
Nov. 1—Ever Hammer, Baltimore ...W 12
Nov. 21—Joe Welling, Baltimore ....W 12
Dec. 19—Ted Marchant, Baltimore .....W 12
1924
Jan. 7—Ted Marchant, Philadelphia ....W 10
Jan. 16—Billy Angelo, Baltimore ......KO 8
Mar. 12—Alex Hart, Philadelphia ....L 12
Apr. 2—Andy Chaney, Baltimore ......W 12
Apr. 30—Johnny Donnelly, Baltimore ..KO 4
May 5—Jack Rappaport, Newark ......ND 12
June 13—Sailor Friedman, Baltimore ....W 12
June 27—Johnny Clinton, N.Y.C. ....W 12
July 3—Pedro Campo, Berwyn, Md.....W 12
Aug. 7—Joe Tiplitz, Philadelphia ....D 12
Aug. 26—Bud Christiano, Philadelphia ...W 10
Oct. 1—Red Cap Wilson, Baltimore ...W 12
Nov. 5—Joe Tiplitz, Baltimore ....WF 7
Nov. 11—Sailor Friedman, Newark ......D 12
Dec. 8—Alex Hart, Baltimore ....D 15
Dec. 25—Johnny Mosley, Philadelphia ..W 10
1925
Jan. 19—Nate Goldman, Philadelphia ..KO 4
Feb. 2—Cuddy DeMarco, Baltimore ...W 10
Feb. 11—Sailor Friedman, Philadelphia ..W 10
Feb. 25—Charlie O'Connell, N.Y.C. .....L 10
Mar. 16—Sid Barbarian, Baltimore .....W 12
Apr. 27—Alex Hart, Baltimore ....D 15
July 16—Lew Tendler, Philadelphia .....D 10

Aug.   10—Nate Goldman, Philadelphia ..KO   3
Aug.   17—Louis Vincenti, N. Y. C. ...... W 12
Sept. 24—Pinkey Mitchell, Philadelphia .. W 10
Oct.   12—Pep O'Brien, Baltimore ...... W 12
Dec.   5—Young Leonard, Phila. .... KO   3
Dec.   7—Harry Dudley, Newark, N. J. ...ND 12
1926
Jan.   15—Jack McVey, N. Y. C. .... W 10
Jan.   29—Joe Simonovich, N. Y. C. ...... W 10
Feb.   12—Jimmy Jones, N. Y. C......... W 10
Mar.   1—Tom Freeman, N. Y. C........ KO   4
May   7—Georgie Levine, N. Y. C. ...... W   8
May   28—Willie Harmon, N. Y. C. ...... W 10
June   24—Mickey Walker, N. Y. C. ..... KO   8
Sept.   9—Eddie Burnbrook, N. Y. C....KO   3
Oct.   15—Jack Zivic, N. Y. C. .... W 10
Nov.   —Billy Alger, San Francisco ..... W 10
Dec.   4—Eddie Roberts, San Fran. .. KO by 1
1927
Jan.   14—Eddie Roberts, N. Y. C. ...... W 10
May   11—Billy Drako, Annapolis, Md. ..ND 10
May   2—Johnny Mendelsohn, Balt. ....KO   4
June   3—Pete Latzo, N. Y. C. .... W 15
       (Won World's Welterweight Title)
July   13—Billy Drako, Cincinnati, O. ... W 10
Aug.   11—Pinky Mitchell, Milwaukee ...NC   6
Sept. 22—Johnny Indrisano, Boston ..... L 10
Dec.   9—Meyer Grace, Indianapolis ....ND 10
1928
Jan.   9—Joe Reno, Trenton, N. J. ...... W 10
Jan.   16—Jean Mangeot, Newark .... KO   9
Jan.   23—Joe Simonich, Philadelphia .... W 10
Feb.   13—Clyde Hull, Cleveland .... KO   8
Apr.   20—Julian Jim Moran, Tampa .....KO   9
Apr.   26—Billy Drako, St. Louis .... KO   3
May   17—George Levine, Detroit ...... NC   9
July   7—Hilario Martinez, Philadelphia KO   8
Aug.   30—Young Jack Thompson,
        Chicago .... KO by   2
Sept. 17—Johnny Roberts,
        Charlotte, N. C. .... W 10
Sept. 28—Jimmy Finley, Tampa .... D 10
Oct.   22—Walcott Langford, Phila. ...... W 10
1929
Jan.   14—Johnny Roberts, Portsmouth .. W 10
Jan.   25—Al Mello, Boston, Mass. .... L 10
Apr.   12—Al Mello, Boston, Mass. .... L 10
May   9—Jack Ketchell, Elaine, Ohio .... W 10
June   17—Billy Alger, Braddock, Pa. ....KO   8
July   25—Jackie Fields, Detroit .... LF   2
        (Lost Welterweight Title)
Oct.   13—Bert Colima, Mexico City ...... W 10
Nov.   4—Billy Angelo, Philadelphia ..... W 10
1930
Feb.   3—Paulie Walker, Philadelphia ....L 10
Mar.   3—Joe Trippe, Rochester, N. Y. .. W 10
Mar.   18—Ted Goodrich, Atlanta ....KO by   2
Apr.   14—Bucky Lawless, Rochester .....L 10
May   3—Charlie Rosen, New York ..... W   6
May   28—Harry Mason, N. Y. C. .... W 10
Aug.   11—Buck McTiernan, Pittsburgh ... D 10
Sept. 11—Ben Jeby, N. Y. C. L   8
Oct.   3—Peter Susky, Scranton ..... KO by   3
1931
Feb.   16—Mike Lichtenstein, Baltimore .. W 10

TB	KO	WD	WF	D	LD	LF	KOBY	ND	NC
122	23	61	1	11	13	2	5	4	2

JACKIE FIELDS
(Jacob Finkelstein)
Born, 1907, Chicago, Ill. Nationality,
Jewish-American. Weight, 130-145 lbs. Height, 5
ft. 7½ in. Manged by Willie Rooney.
  Fields started as an amateur and won 51
battles out of 54.
  In 1923 Harry Wallach beat Fields in 3 rds.
at Boston in semi-final of National tournament.
Joe Sallas beat Wallach in final for title. Fields
was sent to Olympic Games at Paris in 1924 as
alternate. In a tourney in Paris, Fields beat
Wallach. Later Fields and Sallas met in Olympic
finals and Fields won featherweight title of the
world as an amateur. Near the end of 1924 Fields
turned pro.
1924
Sept. 18—Joe Salas, Los Angeles .... W   4
Nov.   6—Al Leonard, Los Angeles ...... W   4
Dec.   10—Danny Woods, Alhambra ...... W   4

1925
   —Benny Pascal, Pasadena, Cal. ... W   6
   —Billy Young, Wilmington, C. ..KO   2
May   8—Joe Salas, Hollywood ....W 10
June   —Billy Young, Vernon, Cal. ....KO   1
Aug.   5—Johnny Lamar, Los Angeles ... D   6
Sept. 23—Frankie Fink, Los Angeles ..... W   6
Nov.   12—Jimmy McLorin, L.A. ..... KO by   2
1926
Feb.   24—Willie Buff, Wilmington ......KO   3
Mar.   13—Young Brown, Sacramento ...KO   5
Apr.   9—Phil Salvadore, Los Angeles .... W 10
Apr.   28—Johnny Lamar, Hollywood .... W 10
June   18—Johnny Lamar, Hollywood .... W 10
July   15—Roscoe Hall, Hollywood ...... W 10
Sept.   2—Sailor Ashmore, Pasadena ..... W 10
Sept. 24—Dick Hoppe, Hollywood ...... W 10
Dec.   7—King Tut, Los Angeles......... W 10
1927
Jan.   —Harry Kid Brown, Hollywood .. W 10
Jan.   14—Marty Mario, Hollywood ...... W 10
Mar.   10—Russ Whalen, Hollywood ..... W 10
Apr.   4—Sammy Mandell, Los Angeles .ND 12
June   2—Joey Kaufman, New York ..... W 10
June   15—Louis Kid Kaplan, New York ...L 10
July   4—Frankie Find, New York ...... W 10
Sept.   6—Baby Joe Gans, Los Angeles ... W 10
Nov.   3—Joey Silver, San Francisco ..... W 10
Nov.   22—Mushy Callahan, Los Angeles .. W 10
Dec.   2—Dick Ramies, Hollywood ....KO   2
Dec.   20—Buddy Saunders, Los Angeles .. W 10
1928
Jan.   13—Charley Feraci, San Diego ..... W 10
Feb.   15—Vince Dundee, Los Angeles .... W 10
Feb.   23—Sammy Mandell, Chicago .....L 10
Apr.   17—Vince Dundee, Los Angeles .... W 10
May   3—Don Frazer, Hollywood .....KO   1
June   8—Don Frazer, Hollywood .....KO   3
June   26—Jack Zivic, Los Angeles ......KO   7
July   13—Joe Cooper, San Francisco .... W 10
July   20—Joe Vargas, San Francisco ....KO   9
Aug.   10—Pete Meyers, San Francisco ...KO   4
Oct.   1—Young Jack Thompson, San
        Francisco .... W 10
Oct.   30—Sgt. Sammy Baker, Los
        Angeles........................KO   2
Nov.   30—Mike Payan, San Francisco ..KO   2
Dec.   27—Tommy Elks, Hollywood .....KO   7
1929
Jan.   28—Jack McCarthy, Chicago .... W 10
Feb.   15—Baby Joe Gans, New York ..... W 10
Mar.   8—Al Van Ryan, Detroit ....KO   5
Mar.   —Young Jack Thompson,
        Chicago .... W 10
        (Won NBA welterweight title)
May   24—Clyde Chastain, Chicago .... W 10
June   19—Jack Horner, St. Louis ....KO   4
June   28—Farmer Joe Cooper, Chicago ..KO   1
July   25—*Joe Dundee, Detroit ....WF   2
Oct.   2—Vince Dundee, Chicago .... W 10
Oct.   21—Gorilla Jones, San Francisco ... W 10
Nov.   5—Dummy Mahan, Kansas City,
        Mo..............................KO   2
Dec.   13—Gorilla Jones, Boston ....NC   7
        *For Welter Title.

1930
Jan.   6—Alf Ros, Philadelphia .... W 10
Jan.   10—Jimmy Owens, Chicago ......KO   2
Jan.   24—Vince Dundee, Chicago .... W 10
Feb.   22—Young Corbett, San Fran. ......L 10
Apr.   8—Tommy Freeman, Cleveland ..KO   5
Apr.   21—Meyer Grace, Kansas City ....KO   3
May   9—*Jg. Jack Thompson, Detroit ....L 15
        (Lost Welterweight championship of world)
Sept. 30—Jackie Horner, Rochester,
        N. Y............................... W 10
Oct.   7—Tommy Jordan, Indianapolis .KO   3
Nov.   24—Sam Bruce, Buffalo .... W 10
Dec.   9—Paul Pirrone, Cleveland .... W 10
Dec.   19—Bucky Lawless, Detroit ......KO   5
1931
Feb.   26—Jackie Brady, Syracuse, N. Y. ... W 10
Sept. 19—Young Terry, New York.......L 10
Oct.   8—King Tut, Detroit .... W 10
Nov.   16—Jimmy Belmont, Pittsburgh .. D 10
1932
Jan.   28—Lou Brouillard, Chicago .... W 10
        (Won welterweight title)
Feb.   29—Jimmy Belmont, Pittsburgh ..KO   8
Mar.   4—Johnny Indrisano, Boston .....L 10
Mar.   8—Patsy Pollock, Denver ....KO   2
Mar.   11—Izzy Kline, Salt Lake City ....KO   1

607

Apr. 1—Leslie Baker, Boston ....KO 5
Apr. 5—Peewee Jarrell, Dayton, O.....KO 4
May   6—Henry Firpo, Louisville, Ky....ND 10
Dec. 1—Tommy Herman, San Fran....KO 2
Dec. 30—Eddie Murdock, San Diego .....L 10
1933
Feb. 22—Young Corbett III, San
    Francisco ....L 10
    (Lost welterweight title)
May   2—Young Peter Jackson, Los
    Angeles ....W 10
    In U. S. Army.

TB	KO	WD	WF	D	LD	LF	KOBY	ND	NC
85	28	42	1	2	8	0	1	2	1

YOUNG JACK THOMPSON
(Cecil Lewis Thompson)
Born, 1904, Los Angeles, Calif. Weight, 145 lbs.
Height, 5 ft. 8 in. Managed by Clyde Hudkins, Ray Alvis.
1925
July 24—Young Harry Wills, San Diego ..... D 10
Oct. 7—Harry Scott, Oakland .... L 6
1926
Jan. 22—Baby Pete, San Diego .... W 6
Feb. 10—Bobby Ertle, Oakland .... KO 1
Mar. 9—Joe Layman, Vernon .... D 6
Mar. 31—Young Sam Langford, Los Angeles L
    —Billy Springfield .... D 6
May 18—Young Corbett III, Fresno .... L 6
May 21—Ad Ruiz, San Diego .... W 6
May 28—Buddy Bairie, San Diego .... W
June 18—Billy McCann, San Diego .... KO 8
July 24—Harry Whybrow, Los Angeles .... KO 2
Sept. 28—Jack Silver, Los Angeles .... KO 8
Oct. 15—Billy Adams, San Francisco ...... KO 5
Nov. 5—Billy Alger, San Francisco .... W 10
Nov. 14—Ted Makagon, San Francisco ...... D 10
Nov. 23—Russ Whalen, Los Angeles .... L 10
1927
Feb. 11—Tommy Cello, San Francisco ...... D 10
Feb. 18—Harry (Kid) Brown, San Francisco KO 5
Mar. 4—King Tut, San Francisco .... W 10
Mar. 11—Harry (Kid) Brown, San Francisco W 10
Apr. 8—Irineo Flores, San Francisco ...... KO 2
June 24—Young Corbett III, San Francisco ... D 10
July 22—Charley Feraci, San Francisco .... KO 5
    —Frankie Turner .... KO 8
    —Charley Pitts .... KO 4
1928
Jan. 17—Johnny Adams, Los Angeles ...... KO 4
Jan. 27—Don Fraser, San Francisco .... KO 3
Feb. 13—Young Corbett III, San Francisco ... L 10
Mar. 16—Johnny O'Donnell, San Francisco KO 8
Apr. 11—Jimmy Duffy, Oakland .... LF 9
June 8—Billy Light, Chicago .... W 8
July 11—Russie LeRoy, Chicago .... KO 5
Aug. 10—Eddie Dempsey, Chicago .... KO 4
Aug. 22—Gene Cardi, Cleveland .... KO 6
Aug. 30—Joe Dundee, Chicago .... KO 2
Oct. 1—Jackie Fields, San Francisco .... L 10
Oct. 31—Danny Gordon, Chicago .... KO 2
Dec. 7—Red Bragan, Buffalo .... KO 4
    —Sam Bruce, Buffalo .... KO 10
1929
Jan. 25—Red Herring, Buffalo .... KO 7
Jan. 30—Harry Dudley, Kansas City ...... KO 6
Feb. 18—Ham Jenkins, Kansas City .... W 10
Mar. 8—Heavy Andrews, Buffalo .... W 10
Mar. 25—Jackie Fields, Chicago .... L 10
    (For NBA Welterweight Title)
June 24—Jimmy Evans, San Francisco ..... KO 9
Aug. 7—Jimmy Duffy, Oakland .... W 10
Oct. 2—Jimmy Duffy, Oakland .... KO 10
Oct. 9—Freddie Fitzgerald, Oakland .... L 10
Nov. 18—Billy White, Pittsburgh .... KO 8
Dec. 10—Billy Wells, Minneapolis .... W 10
1930
Jan. 10—Tommy Freeman, Detroit .... L 10
Feb. 3—Bucky Lawless, Rochester .... L 10
Mar. 2—Freddie Fitzgerald, Chicago ...... W 10
Mar. 28—Jimmy McLarnin, New York ...... L 10

May   9—Jackie Fields, Detroit .... W 15
    (Won World Welterweight Title)
June 6—Billy Wells, Omaha .... KO 2
June 9—Jerry Dolan, Portland, Ore. ...... KO 3
June 17—Joe Cordoza, Los Angeles .... KO 3
July 4—Young Corbett III, San Francisco ... L 10
Sept. 5—Tommy Freeman, Cleveland .... L 15
    (Lost World Welterweight Title)
1931
Mar. 4—Babe Anderson, Oakland .... KO 9
Mar. 19—Larry (Kid) Kaufman, Moline, Ill. KO 3
Apr. 14—Tommy Freeman, Cleveland ...... KO 12
    (Regained World Welterweight Title)
May   8—Bucky Lawless, Chicago .... L 10
May 27—Pete August, Newark .... W 10
June 19—Speedball Turner, Little Rock .... KO 3
July 23—Lou Brouillard, Boston .... L 10
Oct. 23—Lou Brouillard, Boston .... L 15
    (Lost World Welterweight Title)
1932
Jan. 27—Jimmy Evans, Oakland .... L 10
Mar. 4—Billy Wells, Stockton .... KO 6
Mar. 11—Al Trulmans, San Diego .... W 10
Mar. 25—Charlie Cobb, San Diego .... L 10
May 25—Leonard Bennett, Seattle .... W 6

TB	KO	WD	WF	D	LD	LF	KO BY	ND	NC
74	33	16	0	6	18	1	0	0	0

Died, April 9, 1946, Los Angeles, Calif.

TOMMY FREEMAN
(Thomas H. Freeman)
Born, Jan. 22, 1904, Hot Springs, Ark.
Nationality, Irish-American. Weight, 150-156
lbs. Height, 5 ft. 7½ in. Managed by Tommy
McGinty.
1921
Kid Cuty, KO 3; Sammy Caldwell, KO 3;
Soldier Riley, KO 1; Voti Plymale, D 6; Frankie
Manilla, D 6; Cliff Foley, D 6; Bill Kennedy, D 4.
1922
Sammy Caldwell, KO 4; Jack Brennon, KO
3; Billy Ryan, KO 4; Kid Coster, D 6; Cliff Foley,
D 6; Frankie Jones, L 8; Jimmy Dunn, L 10; Al
Munroe, L 8; Dude Martinez, L 10.
1923
Dude Martinez, KO 7; Ray Maywood, KO
2; Al Thomas, KO 4; Herb Elders, KO 3; Dummy
McKinney, ND 8; Chuck Burns, ND 8; Doug Lee,
ND 8; Pat Burke, ND 15; Ray Rivers, W 10; Tom
Storey, W 10; Red Hill, W 15; Grady Franklin, W
15; Dummy McKinney, W 10; Billy Brown, W 10;
Johnny Tillman, W 15.
1924
Jan. 11—Jimmy Cox, New Orleans ...... W 15
Jan. 15—Frankie Murphy, Hot Spgs. .... W 10
Mar. 8—Jimmy Cox, Tampa .... W 10
Mar. 28—Ponce De Leon, Tampa .... W 10
Apr. 1—Jimmy Finley, Tampa .... W 10
June 2—Pinkey Mitchell, New Orleans .. W 15
Aug. 7—Johnny Shea, El Dorado, Ark. . KO 3
Sept. 18—Al Joachum, New Orleans ...... KO 9
Sept. 29—Jack Oakes, Erie, Pa. .... W 10
Oct. 13—Tansey Norton, Erie, Pa. .....KO 6
Nov. 17—Al Nowles, New Orleans ...... KO 4
Nov. 24—Hamp Brown, Memphis ...... W 8
Dec. 1—Humbert Brady, Memphis ..... W 8
1925
Jan. 8—Hamp Brown, Hot Springs ....KO 3
Jan. 30—Pat Corbett, Oklahoma City ... W 10
Feb. 17—Jack Willis, Hot Springs ...... W 10
Apr. 3—Billy Brown, Hot Springs .....KO 8
Apr. 17—Bennie Ross, Boston .... W 8
May   7—Panama Joe McGale, Boston ... W 8
June 12—Jimmy Jones, Erie, Pa. .... W 10
July 10—Floyd Hybert, Erie, Pa. .... W 10
Aug. 4—Dave Forbes, Cleveland ......KO 2
Aug. 18—Mike Dempsey, Cleveland ....KO 5
Sept. 1—Jimmy Jones, Cleveland ......KO 5
Sept. 16—Henry Shaw, Cleveland ...... KO 3
Sept. 30—Al Walther, Cleveland ....KO 6
Oct. 14—Let Philbin, Toledo .... W 6
Nov. 11—Ted Easterbrook, Toledo ......W 10
Nov. 18—Al Walther, Cleveland ....KO 4

608

1926

Jan.	1—Sammy Baker, New York	KO	7
Feb.	4—Norman Genet, Hot Springs	W	10
Feb.	19—Joe Simonich, N. Y. C.	W	10
Mar.	1—Joe Dundee, N. Y. C.	KO by	4
Apr.	6—Shuffle Callahan, Cleveland	KO	11
May	19—Joe Simonich, Cleveland	W	12
May	28—Paul Doyle, Brooklyn	W	10
June	22—Pinkey Mitchell, Cleveland	ND	10
July	22—Sgt. Sammy Baker, N. Y. C.	D	10
Sept.	29—Georgie Levine, Cleveland	ND	10
Oct.	25—Jack Zivic, Cleveland	D	12

1927

Feb.	4—Arturo Shekels, Tampa	KO	2
Feb.	25—Arturo Shekels, Tampa	KO	6
May	6—Mike Dempsey, Erie, Pa.	KO	4
June	1—Meyer Grace, Chicago	W	10
June	13—Joe Simonich, Boston	W	10
July	1—Sailor Darden, Erie, Pa.	W	10
Aug.	10—Billy Piltz, Toledo	KO	9
Aug.	18—Harry Mason, New York	W	10
Oct.	7—Johnny Indrisano, Boston	L	10
Nov.	25—My Sullivan, Chicago	W	10

1928

Feb.	29—Al Van Ryan, Milwaukee	ND	10
Mar.	29—Willie Harmon, Cleveland	KO	3
Sept.	15—Gorilla Jones, Cleveland	ND	10

1929

Feb.	18—Joe Simonich, Chicago	W	10
Mar.	1—Al Ros, New York	W	10
Mar.	22—Tilly Kid Herman, Erie	KO	2
Apr.	9—Gorilla Jones, Cleveland	D	12
Apr.	26—Andy Divodi, Chicago	D	10
July	26—Joe Schylocker, Erie, Pa.	KO	7
Sept.	30—Sam Bruce, Erie, Pa.	KO	9
Oct.	14—George Levine, Pittsburgh	W	10
Oct.	25—Bucky Lawless, Erie, Pa.	KO	7
Nov.	19—Joe Cooper, Cleveland	KO	1
Dec.	10—Clyde Hull, Hot Springs	W	10
Dec.	17—George Manley	KO	5
Dec.	23—Joe Reno	W	10
Dec.	29—Bucky Lawless	L	10

1930

Jan.	10—Yg. Jack Thompson, Detroit	W	10
Jan.	20—Paul Pirrone, Cleveland	D	10
Jan.	31—Bobby La Salle, Erie, Pa.	W	10
Mar.	10—Grover Mallini, Memphis	W	10
Mar.	25—Denny Burns, Hot Springs	W	10
Apr.	8—Jackie Fields, Cleveland	KO by	5
June	25—Billy Alger, Cleveland	W	10
Aug.	8—Canada Lee, Erie	W	10
Sept.	5—*Yg. Jack Thompson, Cleveland	W	15
Oct.	12—Len Andrews, Hot Springs	KO	7
Nov.	27—David Velasco, Hot Springs	KO	10

*Won World's Welterweight Championship.

1931

Jan.	9—*Pete August, Hot Springs	W	10
Jan.	26—*Eddie Murdock, Okla. City	W	10
Feb.	5—*Duke Trammel, Memphis	KO	5
Feb.	9—*Al (Kid) Kober, New Orleans	KO	5
Mar.	1—*Alfredo Gaona, Mexico City	W	10
Mar.	7—Ernie Sheldon, San Francisco	W	4
Apr.	14—Yg. Jack Thompson, Cleve.	KO by	12

(Lost welterweight title)

May	25—Buck McTiernan, Pittsburgh	W	10
June	20—Canada Lee, Erie, Pa.	D	10
Nov.	28—Spike Webb, Miami, Fla.	W	10
Dec.	18—Relampo Saguero, Tampa	W	10

*For title.

1932

Jan.	8—Billy Shell, Coral Gables, Fla.	KO	7
Feb.	2—Harry Wallach, Jacksonville	KO	4
Feb.	18—Owen Phelps, Miami	W	10
Feb.	29—Buster Mallini, Miami	KO	7
Apr.	11—Billy Shell, Miami	W	10
June	3—Buck McTiernan, Pittsburgh	W	10
June	23—Lee Sala, Pittsburgh	KO	1
June	24—Roy (Tiger) Williams, Cleve.	L	8
July	27—Tiger Joe Randall, Pittsburgh	KO	6
Nov.	11—Doc Conrad, Miami, Fla.	W	10
Nov.	18—Manuel Quintero, Tampa	L	10
Dec.	26—Gorilla Jones, Pittsburgh	D	10

1933

Feb.	22—Manuel Quintero, Hot Springs	W	10
Mar.	20—Jack King, Hot Springs	W	10
Apr.	10—Freddy Filer, Nashville	W	10
Apr.	28—Tony Havudo, Pine Bluff	KO	4
May	9—Jack King, Little Rock	W	10
May	22—Ted Yarosz, Pittsburgh	L	10
June	12—Alabama Kid, Pittsburgh	W	10
Sept.	7—Chas. Cogington, Jackson	KO	?
Sept.	14—Buster Mallini, Houston	KO	8

Nov.	20—Duke Trammel, Fort Worth	W	10
Dec.	4—Jack King	W	15

1934

Mar.	13—Tony Dominguez, St. Petersburg, Fla.	W	10
Apr.	10—Johnny Farrell, Dallas, Texas	KO	4
May	21—Gus Campbell, Houston	KO	8
June	15—Joe Dundee, Harlington, Tex.	W	10
June	22—Johnny Kerns, Harlington	KO	2
July	12—Ralph Chong, Dallas, Tex.	KO	6

1935

June	3—Earl Mason, Fort Smith	W	10
June	7—Babe Kaiser, Fort Smith	KO	6
June	21—Jimmy Carter, Hot Springs	KO	2
July	19—Johnny Hall, Little Rock	KO	2
July	26—Sid Scarlett, Little Rock	KO	3
July	30—Jimmy Carter, Waldron	KO	3
Sept.	30—Cap Harding, Fort Smith	W	10
Oct.	22—Billy Hood, Miami Beach	KO	6
Nov.	11—Paddy Creedon, Miami Beach	W	10
Nov.	13—Tommy Beck, Jacksonville	KO	6
Nov.	21—Texas Joe Dundee, Orlando	D	10
Dec.	5—Frankie Hughes, Miami	W	10
Dec.	10—Charley Weise, W. Palm Beach	W	10
Dec.	13—Joe Dundee, Tampa	D	10

1936

Jan.	13—Johnny Hull, Fort Smith	KO	4
Jan.	13—Bruce Brown, Kansas City	W	10
Feb.	21—Young (Cap) Harding, Hot Springs	KO	7
Mar.	3—Allen Matthews, Kansas City	L	10
Mar.	16—Karl Lautenschlager, Ft. Smith	KO	3
Mar.	27—Mickey O'Shea, Hot Springs	KO	4
May	18—Alabama Kid, Quincy	D	10
July	22—Johnny Phagan, Chicago	W	10
Oct.	16—Joey Parks, St. Louis	W	10
Dec.	4—Oscar Rankins, Milwaukee	L	10

1937

Mar.	1—Mickey Breen, Hot Springs	KO	4
Apr.	29—Kingfish Elling, Houston	KO	7
May	27—Charley Jerome, Little Rock	W	10
June	14—Earl Cox, Newark	KO	4
July	2—Al McCoy, Pine Bluff	D	10
July	16—Al McCoy, Pine Bluff	W	10
Aug.	9—Gorilla Jones, Council Bluffs	L	10

1938

Feb.	9—Irish Kennedy, Fort Smith	KO	3
Mar.	17—King Cole, Ft. Smith	KO	2
Mar.	28—Jimmy Francis, Hot Springs	KO	1
Apr.	25—Billy Hood, Hot Springs	KO	5
May	22—Ralph Chong, Ft. Smith	L	10

In U. S. Navy.

TB	KO	WD	WF	D	LD	LF	KOBY	ND	NC
185	70	75	0	16	13	0	3	8	0

LOU BROUILLARD
(Record under Middleweight Champions)

YOUNG CORBETT, III
(Ralph Capabianca Giordano)

Born May 27, 1905, Naples, Italy. Weight, 147 lbs. Height, 5 ft. 7½ in. Managed by Larry White.

Early record incomplete; started pro career Oct. 4, 1919.

1919

Sept.	28—Terry McGovern, Fresno	W	4
Oct.	3—Young Jeffries, Fresno	D	4
Oct.	28—Young Jeffries, Fresno	KO	2

1920

	—Eddie Morris, Marysville	KO	3
June	18—Terry Hogan, Fresno	D	4
July	1—Red Santos, Tulare	D	4
July	3—Kid Chris, Fresno	W	4
July	23—Kid Chris, Fresno	KO	2
Aug.	17—Eddie Mahoney, Fresno	W	4

1921

Jan.	10—Young Peters, Porterville	W	4
Feb.	5—Eddie Morris, Marysville	KO by	4
Sept.	27—Terry McGovern, Fresno	L	4
Dec.	15—Kid Hardy, Tulare	D	4

1922

Oct.	24—Terry Hogan, Fresno	W	4

1923

Jan.	9—Billy Jordan, Fresno	KO	2
Jan.	23—Billy Cole, Fresno	KO	2

Feb. 6—Jimmy Brady, Fresno .... W 4
Feb. 9—Eddie Mahoney, Hanford ...... W 4
May 10—Kid Hudson, Fresno .... W 4
May 22—Lee Weber, Tulare .... W 4
June 23—Billy Cole, Bakersfield ....KO 2
July 26—Ad Ramey, Visalia .... W 4
Sept. 14—Kid Ritchie, Bakersfield .... D 4
Sept. 18—Young Pardella, Fresno .... W 4
Oct. 16—Frank Vierra, Fresno .... W 4
Oct. 31—Georgie Lee, Fresno .... W 4
Nov. 9—Tommy O'Leary, Sacramento . W 4
Nov. 20—Eddie Haddon, Fresno .... W 4
Dec. 29—Trench King, Fresno ....L 4

1924
Mar. 4—Bennie Berries, Fresno .... D 4
Apr. 8—Bennie Berries, Fresno .... W 4
May 4—Sailor Ad Cadena, San Pedro ... L 4
—Jack Sparr, Hollywood .... D 4
June 5—Kid Swan, Bakersfield .... W 4
June 12—Kid Leoff, Bakersfield .... W 4
Nov. 18—Jimmy Shore, Fresno .... D 4
Dec. 16—Indian Mike Doyle, Fresno .... W 4

1925
Feb. 6—Jimmy Shore, Fresno .... W 6
Mar. 11—Gilbert Gallant, Hanford .....KO 2
Mar. 24—Dom. Jack McCarthy, Fresno ...L 10
Apr. 23—Sammy Robideau, San Pedro .. W 10
Apr. 28—Kid Kopecks, Fresno ....KO 6
June 19—Y. Sam Langford, Bakersfield .. D 10
July 7—Joe Powell, Fresno .... W 8
July 17—Billy Rayes, Fresno .... W 10
Sept. 24—Pete Francis, Hanford .... W 10
Oct. 27—Jack Garcia, Bakersfield ......KO 5

1926
Jan. 11—Sailor Carter, Fresno ....KO 6
Jan. 25—Battling Ward, Taft ....KO 10
Feb. —Dick Hoppe, Bakersfield ...... W 10
Feb. 23—Young Freeman, Fresno .....KO 3
May 18—Y. Jack Thompson, Fresno ... W 6
May 25—Young Burmay, Taft ....KO 3
May 10—Danny McCoy, Taft ....KO 4
June 15—Joe Schlocker, Fresno .... W 10
June 24—Jack Sparr, Fresno .... W 10
July 5—Billy Alger, Pismo Beach ...... D 10
July 13—Young Papke, Fresno .... W 10
Aug. 5—Billy Alger, San Diego .... W 10
June 29—Frankie Thomas, Fresno ...... W 6
July 26—Leo Claro, Taft ....KO 4
Aug. 26—Joe Layman, San Diego ...... W 10
Sept. 10—Sailor Ashmore, Taft ....KO 5
Sept. 24—Charlie Feraci, San Diego ..... W 10
Oct. 5—Jerry Carpenter, Fresno ......KO 5
Oct. 12—Joe Chaney, Fresno ....W 6
Nov. 23—Sailor Ashmore, Fresno ......KO 3
Nov. 3—Jack Sparr, Fresno ....KO 3

1927
Jan. 18—Phil Salvadore, Fresno ....KO 4
Mar. 1—Larry Murphy, Fresno .... W 10
Mar. 23—Billy Murphy, Oakland .... D 10
Apr. 13—Young Harry Wills, Oakland ..WF 10
May 25—Frank Tierney, Oakland ...... W 10
June 7—Jack Silver, Fresno .... W 10
June 24—Y. Jack Thompson, S. Fran. ... W 10
July 29—Tommy White, S. Francisco ... W 10
Aug. 5—Freddie Mack, San Francisco .. W 10
Sept. 20—Joe Vargas, Fresno .... W 10
Nov. 1—Dave Cook, Fresno .... W 10
Oct. 21—Charlie Ferarci, San Diego ..... W 10
Dec. 14—Gilbert Attell, San Francisco ..KO 3
Dec. 21—Y. Sam Langford, S. Francisco . W 10

1928
Feb. 13—Y. Jack Thompson, S. Fran. ... W 10
Mar. 12—K. O. Eddie Roberts, S. Fran. .KO 9
Apr. 20—Tony Azevedo, Hanford .... W 10
June 18—Jack Zivic, San Francisco ..... W 10
Aug. 17—Nick Testo, San Francisco ....KO 5
Sept. 13—Sgt. Sammy Baker, MSG, N.Y.. W 10
Sept. 26—Sgt. Sammy Baker, Ebbets Field,
New York ....L 10

1929
Jan. 11—Pete Meyers, San Francisco .... D 10
Feb. 12—Al Gracio, San Francisco .....KO 7
Mar. 15—Dummy Mahan, San Francisco . W 10
Apr. 22—Pete Meyers, San Francisco ... W 10
June 7—Al Van Ryan, San Francisco ... W 10
June 22—Clyde Chastain, San Francisco . W 10
Aug. 30—Buck Lawless, San Francisco ..KO 1
Dec. 13—Tommy Elks, San Francisco ... W 10

1930
Jan. 1—Babe Anderson, San Jose, Cal. . W 10
Feb. 22—Jackie Fields, San Francisco ... W 10
Apr. 25—Alf Ros, San Francisco .... W 10
May 16—Andy Divodi, San Francisco ..KO 4

July 4—Yg. Jack Thompson, San Fran.. W 10
Oct. 1—Sammy Jackson, Los Angeles .. W 10
Nov. 5—Farmer Joe Cooper, Oakland .KO 1

1931
Jan. 13—Paulie Walker, Los Angeles .... D 10
Aug. 14—Gaston Le Cadre, San Fran.....W 10
June 18—Meyer Grace, Hollywood ...... W 10
May 1—Tommy Herman, S. Francisco . W 10
Feb. 20—Paulie Walker, Los Angeles . W 10
Mar. 20—Paul Pirrone, San Francisco .... W 10

1932
Mar. 4—David Velasco, San Francisco .. W 10
Apr. 12—Ceferino Garcia, Los Angeles .. W 10
Apr. 21—Dave Velasco, Sacramento ..... W 10
May 16—Vearl Whitehead, San Fran.....W 10
Aug. 19—Babe Anderson, Stockton .....KO 9
Oct. 25—Ceferino Garcia, Fresno .... W 10
Dec. 19—Joe Glick, San Francisco ...... W 10

1933
Feb. 22—Jackie Fields, San Francisco ... W 10
(Won Welterweight Title)
May 29—Jimmy McLarnin, Los Ang. KO by 1
(Lost Welterweight Title)

1934
Feb. 5—Babe Marino, San Francisco ... W 10
Apr. 30—Young Terry, San Francisco ..KO 3
Aug. 14—Mickey Walker, San Francisco . W 10

1935
Jan. 20—Bep Van Klaveren, San Fran.... W 10
Feb. 22—Bep Van Klaveren, San Fran.... W 10
July 4—Lou Brouillard, San Francisco ..L 10

1936
July 1—Mike Bozzone, San Francisco .. W 10
July 10—Johnny Diaz, Oakland ....KO 7
Sept. 18—Joe Bernal, Fresno .... W 10

1937
Mar. 12—Gus Lesnevich, San Francisco .KO 5
Apr. 2—Dale Sparr, San Francisco ..... W 10
July 21—Joe Smallwood, Oakland ...... W 10
Aug. 13—Billy Conn, San Francisco ..... W 10
Nov. 8—Billy Conn, Pittsburgh ....L 10
Dec. 17—Dick Foster, San Francisco .... W 10

1938
Feb. 22—Fred Apostoli, San Francisco .. W 10
May 25—Jack Burke, Salt Lake City ..... W 10
July 19—Glen Lee, Fresno .... W 10
Nov. 18—Fred Apostoli, N. Y. C.......KO by 8
(Middleweight Title Bout)

1939
Dec. 14—Dick Foster, San Francisco ...KO 7

1940
Mar. 13—Dale Sparr, Oakland .... W 10
Apr. 15—Harry Cahill, San Francisco .... W 10
Aug. 20—Sheik, Rangel, Fresno .... W 10
Retired to join police force.

TB	KO	WD	WF	D	LD	LF	KOBY	ND	NC
142	31	87	1	13	7	0	3	0	0

JIMMY McLARNIN
(Baby Face)
Born, December 17, 1907, Belfast, Ireland.
Weight, 145 lbs. Height, 5 ft. 5½ in. Managed by Pop Foster.

1923
Won: George Ainsworth, 4; Mickey Gill, 4; Young Frye, 4; George Ainsworth, 4; Mickey Gill, 4; Hector McDonald, 4; Red Peterson, 4 and 4; Young Wallace, 4 and 4.

1924
Frankie Sands, W 4; Eddie Collins, KO 3; Joe Conde, KO 3; Frankie Sands, W 4; Sammy Lee, W 4; Jimmy Griffiths, KO 2; Frankie Grandetta, W 4; Jockey Lightener, W 4; Jockey Joe Dillon, W 4; Jimmy Griffiths, W 4; Abe Gordon, KO 2; Denny Diaz, W 4; Frankie Dollon, W 4; Young Nationalista, W 4; Fidel LaBarba, W 4; Fidel LaBarba, D 4; Pal Moore, D 4.

1925
Jan. 13—Fidel LaBarba, Los Angeles ....W 10
Mar. 25—Teddy Silva, Los Angeles ......W 10
Apr. 5—Young Farrell, Los Angeles .... W 6
Apr. 12—Spec Ramies, Los Angeles .... W 4
June —Bud Taylor, Vernon, Cal.......L 10
July 4—Pancho Villa, Oakland, Cal..... W 10
Aug. 10—Mickey Gill, Oakland, Cal..... W 10
Nov. 12—Jackie Fields, Los Angeles ....KO 2
Dec. 8—Bud Taylor, Vernon, Cal......WF 2

	1926		
Jan.	12—Bud Taylor, Vernon, Cal. L	10
Mar.	3—Joey Sangor, Los Angeles . . . . .KO	3
Mar.	17—Johnny Farr, Los Angeles L	10
Sept.	7—Sidney Glick, Vernon, Cal. . . . . W	10
Oct.	15—Doc Snell, Hollywood L	10

1927

Feb.	22—Tommy Cello, San Fran. . . . . . . D	10
Apr.	5—Tommy Cello, Los Angeles . . . . W	10
June	24—Tenario Pelkey, Hollywood . . . . W	10
Sept.	10—Charlie McBride, San Diego . . .KO	2
Oct.	18—Louis (Kid) Kaplan, Chicago . .KO	8
Nov.	23—Billy Wallace, Detroit, Mich. . . . W	10
	—Johnny LaMar, Hollywood . . . W	10
	—Frank Blach, San Diego, Cal. . .KO	2
	—Don Terror Long, San Diego . .KO	3

1928

Feb.	24—Sid Terris, N. Y. C. . . . . .KO	1
May	21—Sammy Mandell, N. Y. C. L	15
	(For World Lightweight Title)	
June	21—Phil McGraw, N. Y. C. . . . . .KO	1
July	23—Packy O'Gatty, Detroit . . . . .Exh.	3
Aug.	2—Stanislaus Loayza, Detroit . . . .KO	4
Nov.	30—Ray Miller, Detroit . . . . . . .KO by	8

1929

Jan.	11—Joe Glick, N.Y.C. . . . . W	10
Mar.	1—Joe Glick, N.Y.C. . . . . .KO	2
Mar.	22—Ray Miller, N. Y. C. . . . . W	10
Oct.	9—Sgt. Sammy Baker, N. Y. C. . . . .KO	1
Nov.	4—Sammy Mandell, Chicago . . . . . . W	10
Dec.	13—Ruby Goldstein, N. Y. C. . . . . .KO	2
	Receipts $87,760	

1930

Mar.	1—Sammy Mandell, Chicago, Ill. . . W	10
Mar.	28—Young Jack Thompson, N.Y.C. W	10
Sept.	11—Al Singer, N. Y. C. . . . . .KO	3
Nov.	21—Billy Petrolle, N. Y. C. L	10

1931

May	27—Billy Petrolle, N. Y. C. . . . . W	10
Aug.	20—Billy Petrolle, N. Y. C. . . . . W	10

1932

Aug.	4—Lou Brouillard, N. Y. C. L	10
Oct.	7—Benny Leonard, N. Y. C. . . . . .KO	6
Dec.	16—Sammy Fuller, N. Y. C. . . . . . . .KO	8

1933

May	29—Young Corbett, Los Angeles . .KO	1
	(Won World Welterweight Title)	

1934

May	28—Barney Ross, Long Island, N.Y. .L	15
	(Lost World Welterweight Title)	
Sept.	17—Barney Ross, N. Y. C.	
	L. I. Bowl . . . . W	15
	(Won World Welterweight Title)	

1935

May	28—Barney Ross, N. Y. C. L	15
	(Lost World Welterweight Title)	

1936

May	8—Tony Canzoneri, N. Y. C. L	10
Oct.	5—Tony Canzoneri, N. Y. C. . . . . . . W	10
Nov.	20—Lou Ambers, N. Y. C. . . . . W	10

TB	KO	WD	WF	D	LD	LF	KOBY	ND	NC
77	20	42	1	3	10	0	1	0	0

Elected to Boxing Hall of Fame 1956.

BARNEY ROSS
(Barnet Rosofsky)

Born, December 23, 1909, New York, N. Y. Nationality, Jewish-American. Weight, 145 lbs. Height, 5 ft. 7 in. Managed by Sam Pian and Art Winch.

Started as an amateur in 1926. Won Golden Gloves and Inter-City titles in 1929 and turned pro.

1929

Virgin Tobin, KO 2; Ray Lugo, W 6; Joe Borola, W 6 and 6; Joe Harth, W 5; Mickey Genaro, W 6; Al de Rose, W 6.

1930

Young Terry, KO 8; Harry Dublinsky, KO 8; Louis New, W 6; Johnny Andrews, W 4; Jiro Kumagay, W 4; Eddie Koppy, W 8; Young Terry, D 8; Harry Dublinsky, D 8; Carlos Garcia, L 6; Eddie Rojack, KO 2; Petey Mack, KO 1; Sammy Binder, KO 2; Louis Perez, KO 1.

1931

Jan.	14—Henry Faligano, Chicago . . . . . . W	8
Feb.	20—Young Terry, Chicago . . . . W	10
Mar.	20—Jackie Davis, Chicago . . . . W	6
Mar.	27—Roger Bernard, Chicago L	8

Apr.	8—Midget Mike O'Dowd, Moline . .W	8
Apr.	24—Lul Abella, Chicago . . . . .KO	2
May	1—Jackie Dugan, Moline . . . . .KO	2
May	13—Billy Shaw, Chicago . . . . W	10
July	15—Babe Ruth, Benton Harbor,	
	Mich. . . . . .KO	4
July	30—Jimmy Alvarado, Detroit . . . . . . W	8
Oct.	2—Glen Kamp, Chicago . . . . W	10
Nov.	4—Lou Jallos, Chicago . . . . W	8
Nov.	13—Young Terry, Moline . . . . W	8
Nov.	18—Jimmy Lundy, Kansas City . . . . W	8

1932

Feb.	8—Mickey O'Neill, Milwaukee . . . . W	6
Feb.	18—Billy Gladstone, Chicago . . . . . . W	6
Mar.	2—Nick Ellenwood, Muncie . . . . . . W	10
Apr.	5—Frankie Hughes, Indianapolis . .W	10
May	20—Dick Sisk, Chicago . . . . .KO	6
July	28—Henry Perlick, Chicago . . . . . . .KO	3
Aug.	26—Ray Miller, Chicago . . . . W	10
Sept.	15—Frankie Petrolle, Chicago . . . . .KO	2
Oct.	21—Battling Battalino, Chicago . . . . W	10
Nov.	11—Goldie Hess, Chicago . . . . W	10
Nov.	25—Johnny Farr, Milwaukee . . . . . . W	10

1933

Jan.	20—Johnny Dato, Pittsburgh . . . . .KO	2
Feb.	22—Tommy Grogan, Chicago . . . . . . W	10
Mar.	22—Billy Petrolle, Chicago . . . . W	10
May	4—Joe Ghnouly, St. Louis . . . . W	10
June	23—Tony Canzoneri, Chicago . . . . . . W	10
	(Won Lightweight & Jr.	
	Welterweight Titles)	
July	26—Johnny Farr, Kansas City . . . . .KO	6
Sept.	12—Tony Canzoneri, N. Y. C. . . . . . . W	15
	(Lightweight Title Bout)	
	Gave up lightweight title	
Nov.	17—Sammy Fuller, Chicago . . . . W	10
	(Jr. Welterweight Title Bout)	

1934

Jan.	24—Billy Petrolle, N. Y. C. . . . . W	10
Feb.	7—*Pete Nebo, Kansas City . . . . . . W	12
Mar.	5—*Frankie Klick, San Francisco . D	10
Mar.	14—Kid Morro, Oakland . . . . W	10
Mar.	27—Bobby Pacho, Los Angeles . . . . . W	10
May	28—Jimmy McLarnin, N. Y. C. . . . . . W	15
	(Won World Welter Title)	
Sept.	17—Jimmy McLarnin, N. Y. C. L	15
	(Lost World Welter Title)	
Dec.	10—*Bobby Pacho, Cleveland . . . . . W	12
	*Jr. Welterweight Title Bout.	

1935

Jan.	28—*Frankie Klick, Miami . . . . W	10
Apr.	9—*Henry Woods, Seattle . . . . W	12
May	28—Jimmy McLarnin, N. Y. C. . . . . . W	15
	(Re-won World Welterweight Championship)	
	Gave up Jr. Welterweight Title	
Sept.	6—Baby Joe Gans, Portland . . . . .KO	2
Sept.	13—Ceferino Garcia, San Francisco . W	10
Nov.	29—Ceferino Garcia, Chicago . . . . . . W	10
	*Jr. Welterweight Title Bout.	

1936

Jan.	27—Lou Halper, Philadelphia . . . . .KO	8
Mar.	11—Gordon Wallace, Vancouver . . . W	10
May	1—Chuck Woods, Louisville . . . . .KO	5
June	10—Laddie Tonelli, Milwaukee . . .KO	5
June	22—Morrie Sherman, Omaha . . . . .KO	2
July	22—Phil Furr, Washington, D. C. . . . W	10
Nov.	27—Izzy Janazzo, N. Y. C. . . . . W	15
	(Welterweight Title Bout)	

1937

Jan.	29—Al Manfredo, Detroit . . . . W	10
June	17—Chuck Woods, Indianapolis . . .KO	4
June	27—Jackie Burke, New Orleans . . . .KO	5
Aug.	19—Al Manfredo, Des Moines . . . . .ND	10
Sept.	23—Ceferino Garcia, N. Y. C. . . . . . . W	15
	(Welterweight Title Bout)	

1938

Apr.	4—Henry Schaft, Minneapolis . . .KO	4
Apr.	25—Bobby Venner, Des Moines . . .KO	7
May	31—Henry Armstrong, Long Island	
	City Bowl L	15
	(Lost World Welterweight Title)	

1942

Joined U. S. Marines. Wounded at Guadalcanal.

TB	KO	WD	WF	D	LD	LF	KOBY	ND	NC
82	24	50	0	3	4	0	0	1	0

Elected to Boxing Hall of Fame 1956.
Died January 17, 1967 in Chicago after a long illness. Death was caused by cancer.

611

HENRY ARMSTRONG
(Henry Jackson)
(Homicide Hank)
Born, December 12, 1912, Columbus,
Miss. American Negro. Weight, 145 pounds.
Managed by Eddie Mead and Wirt Ross.
(Fought early in career as Melody Jackson)
Won 58 out of 62 amateur bouts.

1931
July 27—Al Iovino, No. Braddock,
Pa. ....KO by 3
Aug. —Sammy Burns, Millville, Pa. .... W 6

1932
Won: Gene Espinoza, 4; Max Tarley, 4;
Mickey Ryan, 6; Georgie Dundee, 6; Perfecto
Lopez, 6; Steve Harky, 6; Perfecto Lopez, 8;
Young Corpus, 6. Knockouts: Bobby Calmes, 3;
Young Bud Taylor, 2; Vincente Torres, 3;
Johnny De Foe, 4; Vince Trujillo, 2. Draw:
Perfecto Lopez, 4; Perfecto Lopez, 4; Perfecto
Lopez, 6. Lost: Eddie Trujillo, 4; Al Greenfield,
4; Baby Manuel, 6. No decision: Hoyt Jones, 4.

1933
Won: Kid Moro, 10; Baby Manuel, 10;
Davey Abad, 10. Knockouts: Johnny Granone,
5; Gene Espinoza, 7; Max Tarley, 3; Joe Conde,
7; Ventura Arana, 5. Draw: Kid Moro, 10. Lost:
Baby Arizmendi, 10.

1934
Won: Varias Milling, 10; Mark Diaz, 8;
Midget Wolgast, 10. Knockouts: Sal Hernandez,
2; Baby Casanova, 3; Lester Marston, 7; Leo
Lomelli, 6. Draw: Perfecto Lopez, 8. Lost: Baby
Arizmendi, 12; Baby Manuel, 10.

1935
Won: Davey Abad, 10; Frankie Covelli, 8.
Knockouts: Tully Corvo, 7; Alton Black, 7. Lost:
Davey Abad, 10; Baby Arizmendi, 12.
Nov. 27—Midget Wolgast, Oakland ...... W 10

1936
Jan.   1—Joe Conde, Mexico City ....L 10
Feb. 26—Ritchie Fontaine, Oakland ....L 10
Mar. 31—Ritchie Fontaine, Los Angeles W 10
Apr. 17—Alton Black, Reno ....KO 8
May 19—Pancho Leyvas, Los Angeles ..KO 4
June 22—Johnny De Foe, Butte ....W 10
Aug.   4—Baby Arizmendi, Los Angeles .. W 10
Aug. 28—Juan Zurita, Los Angeles ....KO 4
Sept.   3—Buzz Brown, Portland ....W 10
Sept.   8—Dommy Ganzon, Sacramento ..W 10
Oct. 27—Mike Belloise, Los Angeles ..... W 10
Nov.   2—Gene Espinoza, Los Angeles ..KO 1
Nov. 17—Joey Alcanter, St. Louis ......KO 6
Dec.   3—Tony Chavez, St. Louis ...... LF 8

1937
Jan.   1—Baby Casanova, Mexico City ..KO 3
Jan. 19—Tony Chavez, Los Angeles ...KO 10
Feb.   2—Moon Mullins, Los Angeles ...KO 2
Feb. 19—Varias Milling, Hollywood ...KO 4
Mar.   2—Joe Rivers, Los Angeles ......KO 4
Mar. 12—Mike Belloise, Los Angeles .KO 4
Mar. 19—Aldo Spoldi, New York City ... W 10
Apr.   6—Pete De Grasse, Los Angeles ..KO 10
May   4—Frankie Klick, Los Angeles ....KO 4
May 28—Wally Hally, Los Angeles .....KO 4
June   9—Mark Diaz, Pasadena ....KO 4
June 15—Jackie Carter, Los Angeles ....KO 4
July   8—Alf Blatch, New York City ....KO 3
July 19—Lew Massey, Brooklyn ....KO 4
July 27—Benny Bass, Philadelphia .....KO 4
Aug. 13—Eddie Brink, New York City ..KO 3
Aug. 16—Johnny Cabello, Wash.,D.C. ..KO 2
Aug. 31—Orville Drouillard, Detroit ...KO 5
Sept.   9—Charley Burns, Pittsburgh ....KO 4
Sept. 16—Johnny De Foe, N. Y. C. ....KO 4
Sept. 21—Bobby Dean, Youngstown ...KO 1
Oct. 18—Joe Marcienti, Philadelphia ...KO 3
Oct. 29—Petey Sarron, New York City .KO 6
(World's Featherweight Championship)
Nov. 19—Billy Beautiful, N. Y. C. ......KO 5
Nov. 23—Joey Brown, Buffalo ....KO 2
Dec.   6—Tony Chavez, Cleveland ......KO 1
Dec. 12—Johnny Jones, New Orleans ...KO 2

1938
Jan. 12—Enrico Venturi, N. Y. C. ......KO 6
Jan. 21—Frankie Castillo, Phoenix .....KO 3
Jan. 22—Tommy Brown, Tucson ....KO 2
Feb.   1—Chalky Wright, Los Angeles ...KO 3
Feb.   9—Al Citrino, San Francisco .....KO 4
Feb. 25—Everett Rightmire, Chicago ...KO 4
Feb. 28—Charley Burns, Minneapolis ...KO 2

Mar. 15—Baby Arizmendi, Los Angeles .. W 10
Mar. 25—Eddie Zivic, Detroit ....KO 4
Mar. 30—Lew Feldman, N. Y. C. ....KO 5
May 31—Barney Ross, L.I. City, N.Y. ... W 15
(World's Welterweight Championship)
Aug. 17—Lou Ambers, New York City ... W 15
(World's Lightweight Championship)
Nov. 25—*Ceferino Garcia, N. Y. C. ..... W 15
Dec.   5—*Al Manfredo, Cleveland .....KO 3
(Armstrong relinquished Featherweight
Championship)
*Welterweight Title Bout.

1939
Jan. 10—*Baby Arizmendi, Los Angeles . W 10
Mar.   4—*Bobby Pacho, Havana ....KO 4
Mar. 16—*Lew Feldman, St. Louis ......KO 1
Mar. 31—*Davey Day, New York City ..KO 12
May 25—*Ernie Roderick, London .....W 15
Aug. 22—Lou Ambers, New York City ....L 15
(Lost World's Lightweight Championship)
Oct.   9—*Al Manfredo, Des Moines ....KO 4
Oct. 13—*Howard Scott, Minneapolis ..KO 2
Oct. 20—*Ritchie Fontaine, Seattle ....KO 3
Oct. 24—*Jimmy Garrison, Los Angeles . W 10
Oct. 30—*Bobby Pacho, Denver ....KO 4
Dec. 11—*Jimmy Garrison, Cleveland ..KO 7
*Welterweight Title Bout.

1940
Jan.   4—*Joe Ghnouly, St. Louis ......KO 5
Jan. 24—*Pedro Montanez, N. Y. C. ...KO 9
Mar.   1—Ceferino Garcia, Los Angeles .. D 10
(Middleweight Title Bout)
Apr. 26—*Paul Junior, Boston ....KO 7
May 24—*Ralph Zanelli, Boston ....KO 5
June 21—*Paul Junior, Portland ....KO 3
July 17—Lew Jenkins, N. Y. C. ....KO 6
Sept. 23—*Phil Furr, Washington, D.C. .KO 4
Oct.   4—Fritzie Zivic, New York City ....L 15
(Lost World's Welterweight Championship)
*Welterweight Title Bout.

1941
Jan. 17—Fritzie Zivic, N. Y. C. ..... KO by 12
(World Welterweight Championship)
Oct.   1—Knocked out two men in two rounds
each at Oklahoma City, Okla. in
exhibition bouts.
Oct. 12—Tried a comeback and knocked out
two opponents in 2 rounds each
(Exhibitions).

1942
June   1—Johnny Taylor, San Jose .....KO 4
June 24—Sheik Rangel, Oakland ...... W 10
July   3—Reuben Shank, Denver ....L 10
July 20—Joe Ybarra, Sacramento ......KO 3
Aug.   3—Aldo Spoldi, San Francisco ...KO 4
Aug. 13—Jackie Burke, Ogden, Utah ...KO 10
Aug. 26—Rudolfo Ramirez, Oakland ...KO 8
Sept.   7—Johnny Taylor, Pittman, Nev..KO 3
Sept.   4—Leo Rodak, San Francisco ....KO 8
Sept. 30—Earl Turner, Oakland ....KO 4
Oct. 13—Juan Zurita, Los Angeles ....KO 2
Oct. 26—Fritzie Zivic, San Francisco ... W 10
Dec.   4—Lew Jenkins, Portland, Ore. ...KO 8
Dec. 14—Saverio Turiello, San Fran. ...KO 4

1943
Jan.   5—Jimmy McDaniels, Los Ang. ... W 10
Mar.   2—Willie Joyce, Los Angeles ....L 10
Mar.   8—Tippy Larkin, San Francisco ..KO 2
Mar. 22—Al Tribuani, Phila., Pa. ...... W 10
Apr.   2—Beau Jack, N. Y. C. ....L 10
Apr. 30—Saverio Turiello, Wash., D. C. .KO 5
May   7—Tommy Jessup, Boston ....KO 1
May 24—Maxie Shapiro, Phila., Pa. .....KO 7
June 11—Sammy Angott, N. Y. C. ...... W 10
July 24—Willie Joyce, Hollywood ...... W 10
Aug.   6—Jimmy Garrison, Portl., Ore. ... W 10
Aug. 14—Joey Silva, Spokane .... W 10
Aug. 27—Ray Robinson, N. Y. C. ....L 10

1944
Jan. 14—Aldo Spoldi, Portland, Ore. ....KO 3
Jan. 26—Saverio Turiello, Kansas C. ... W 10
Feb.   7—Lew Hanbury, Wash., D. C. ....KO 3
Feb. 23—Jimmy Garrison, Kansas City .KO 10
Feb. 29—Jackie Byrd, Des Moines ......KO 4
Mar. 14—Johnny Jones, Miami ....KO 5
Mar. 20—Frankie Wills, Wash., D. C. ... W 10
Mar. 24—Ralph Zanelli, Boston .... W 10
Apr. 25—John Thomas, Los Angeles ... W 10
May 16—Ralph Zanelli, Boston .... W 10
May 22—Aaron Perry, Wash., D. C. ....KO 6
June   2—Willie Joyce, Chicago ....L 10
June 15—Al Davis, New York City .....KO 2

June	21—Nick Latsios, Wash., D.C.	W 10
July	4—John Thomas, Los Angeles	L 10
July	14—Slugger White, Hollywood	D 10
Aug.	21—Willie Joyce, San Francisco	W 10
Sept.	15—Aldo Spoldi, St. Louis	KO 2
Nov.	4—Mike Belloise, Portland, Ore.	KO 4

1945

Jan.	17—Chester Slider, Oakland	D 10
Feb.	6—Genaro Rojo, Los Angeles	W 10
Feb.	14—Chester Slider, Oakland	L 10

TB	KO	WD	WF	D	LD	LF	KOBY	ND	NC
174	97	47	0	8	18	1	2	1	0

Elected to Boxing Hall of Fame 1954.

FRITZIE ZIVIC

Born, May 8, 1913, Pittsburgh. Nationality, Croatian-American. Height, 5 ft. 9 in. Managed by Luke Carney.

1931
Knockouts: Al Reddinger, 1. Lost: Steve Senich, 6.

1932
Knockouts: Pat Gilmore, 1; Elmer Kozack, 4; Jimmy Dorsey, 4; Terry Waner, 3. Won: Young Lowsteter, 6; Eddie Cregan, 4. Lost: Steve Senich, 6; Jerry Clements, 6.

1933

Jan.	30—Georgie Schley, Pittsburgh	KO 2
Feb.	8—Steve Senich, Pittsburgh	KO 2
Mar.	24—U. S. Carpentier, Pittsburgh	KO 4
Apr.	10—Eddie Brannon, Pittsburgh	KO 6
Apr.	28—Patsy Henningan, Pittsburgh	W 6
June	26—Don Asto, Pittsburgh	W 6
July	10—Don Asto, Pittsburgh	KO 3
Aug.	7—Joey Greb, Millsdale, Pa.	W 10
Oct.	12—Joe Pimenthal, Pasadena	KO 4
Nov.	3—Gus Vagas, San Francisco	KO 2
Nov.	23—Don Miller, Pasadena	KO 3
Dec.	4—Homer Foster, Pico, Cal.	D 4
Dec.	15—Vincent Martinez, Hollywood	W 4
Dec.	27—Rudy Ayon, Pico, Cal.	W 4

1934

Jan.	5—Louis Carranza, Los Angeles	W 6
Jan.	30—Lloyd Smith, Los Angeles	D 6
Feb.	22—Perfecto Lopez, Los Angeles	W 6
Mar.	5—Lloyd Smith, Los Angeles	D 6
July	2—Eddie Ran, Pittsburgh	W 10
July	25—Young Joe Firpo
	Conneaut Lake, Pa.	W 8
Sept.	2—Harry Carlton, Pittsburgh	W 10
Oct.	25—Laddie Tonelli, Chicago	KO by 3

1935

Feb.	4—Jimmy Leto, Holyoke	L 10
Feb.	18—Johnny Jadick, Washington	L 10
Mar.	10—Kayo Castillo, Holyoke	W 10
Mar.	25—Dom Mancini, Pittsburgh	D 10
Apr.	2—Dom Mancini, Pittsburgh	KO 11
Apr.	16—Marty Gornick, Steubenville	KO 5
May	15—Freddy Chenowyth, Chicago	W 8
May	30—Eddie Adams, Kent	KO 6
June	4—Sammy Chivas, Chicago	KO 3
July	1—Lou Ambers, Pittsburgh	L 10
July	15—Jackie McFarland, Millvale	W 10
Aug.	1—Mike Barto, Millvale	W 12
Aug.	8—Joey Ferrando, Jersey City	L 10
Sept.	30—Tony Herrera, Pittsburgh	L 10
Oct.	4—George Salvadore, N. Y. C.	L 6
Dec.	16—Billy Celebron, Chicago	L 10

1936

Jan.	13—Eddie Cool, Pittsburgh	L 10
Jan.	27—Joey Ferando, N. Y.	L 8
Feb.	24—Chuck Woods, Pittsburgh	L 10
Apr.	15—Joe Flocco, Harrisburg	Exh. 10
Apr.	27—Gene Buffalo, Atlantic City	L 10
May	22—Billy Celebron, St. Louis	KO 1
June	9—Tony Falco, Pittsburgh	KO 8
June	27—Al Manfredo, St. Louis	W 10
July	2—Lou Jallos, Steubenville	KO 10
July	6—Laddie Tonelli, Pittsburgh	KO 4
July	22—Mickey Duris, Johnstown	W 12
July	30—Laddie Tonelli, Pittsburgh	KO 6
Aug.	12—Cleto Locatelli, Brooklyn	L 10
Sept.	28—Jackie McFarland, Canton	W 10
Oct.	5—Johnny Durso, Pittsburgh	KO 2
Oct.	16—Chuck Woods, St. Louis	KO 6
Nov.	9—Gaston LeCadre, Pittsburgh	W 10
Dec.	2—Harry Dublinsky, Pittsburgh	KO 6
Dec.	28—Billy Conn, Pittsburgh	L 10

1937

Feb.	11—Johnny Jadick, Pittsburgh	KO 6
Mar.	1—Bobby Pacho, Pittsburgh	W 10
Apr.	6—Chuck Woods, Detroit	W 10
May	21—Tony Petrowski, Muskegon	W 10
Oct.	29—Frankie Portland,
	Clarksb'h, W. Va.	KO 2
Nov.	18—Jimmy Reilly, McKeespt., Pa.	KO 1
Dec.	25—Tommy Bland, Pittsburgh	L 10

1938

Jan.	7—Harold Brown, Chicago	W 10
Feb.	14—Frankie Blair, Pittsburgh	W 10
Mar.	7—Tommy Bland, Pittsburgh	KO 8
Mar.	21—Charlie Burley, Pittsburgh	W 10
Apr.	12—Remo Fernandez, Detroit	W 10
May	29—Petey Mike, Brooklyn	KO 1
June	13—Charlie Burley, Pittsburgh	L 10
June	20—Ercole Buratti, Pittsburgh	KO 4
July	9—Eddie Connley, Walnut Beach	KO 6
July	12—Phil Furr, Pittsburgh	KO 3
Aug.	2—Joe Lemieux, Newark	KO 4
Aug.	12—Joe Pennino, Coney Island	W 8
Aug.	22—Steve Kahley, Newark	KO 3
Aug.	26—Mickey Paul, Lg. Beach, L.I.	KO 3
Sept.	13—Bobby Pacho, Newark	W 10
Oct.	3—Paul Cortlyn, Newark	KO 4
Oct.	10—Jay Macedon, Newark	KO 5
Oct.	27—Salvy Sabin, Pittsburgh	W 10
Nov.	5—Frankie Blair, N. Y. C.	W 8
Nov.	21—Al Hamilton, Columbus	KO 5
Dec.	7—Vincent Pimpinella, Pittsburgh	W 10
Dec.	26—Howell King, Toledo	D 10

1939

Jan.	—Al Costello, Columbus, Ohio	KO 2
Jan.	20—Jackie Burke, St. Louis	W 10
Feb.	10—Eddie Booker, N. Y. C.	W 8
Feb.	15—Charlie Bell, Columbus	KO 3
Mar.	20—Nick Pastore, Miami	KO 3
Mar.	29—Bobby Britton, Miami	W 10
Apr.	20—Tiger Walker, St. Louis	KO 1
May	9—Kenny La Salle, Houston	L 10
May	16—Al Traino, Rochester	W 10
June	5—Kenny La Salle, Pittsburgh	W 10
July	11—Jackie Burke, St. Louis	W 10
July	17—Charley Burley, Pittsburgh	L 10
Sept.	5—Pete De Ruzza, Pittsburgh	KO 6
Sept.	12—Ralph Gizzy, McKeesport, Pa.	KO 2
Oct.	24—Kid Azteca, Houston	W 10
Oct.	30—Milo Theodorescu, Pittsburgh	W 10
Nov.	18—Billy Lancaster, Brooklyn	KO 7
Dec.	9—Wicky Harkins, Philadelphia	KO 6
Dec.	27—Milt Aron, Chicago	KO by 8

1940

Jan.	22—Mike Kaplan, Philadelphia	W 10
Mar.	1—Saverio Turiello, Philadelphia	L 10
Mar.	7—Remo Fernandez, Cleveland	KO 7
Mar.	14—Johnny Barbara, Chicago	W 10
Apr.	8—Johnny Barbara, Philadelphia	L 10
May	3—Mansfield Driskell, Detroit	W 10
May	7—Johnny Barbara, Philadelphia	L 10
May	21—Ossie Harris, Pittsburgh	KO 3
June	24—Johnny Rinaldi, Pittsburgh	KO 1
July	8—Ossie Harris, Pittsburgh	W 10
July	22—Leonard Bennett, Chicago	KO 4
Aug.	5—Kenny La Salle, Pittsburgh	W 10
Aug.	28—Sammy Angott, Pittsburgh	W 10
Oct.	4—Henry Armstrong, N. Y. C.	W 15
	(Won Welterweight Title)
Nov.	15—Al Davis, N. Y. C.	W Disq. 2
Nov.	26—Ronnie Beaudin, Buffalo	KO 2
Dec.	20—Lew Jenkins, N. Y. C.	D 10

1941

Jan.	17—Henry Armstrong, N. Y. C.	KO 12
	(Title Match)
Mar.	17—Saverio Turiello, Pittsburgh	W 10
Mar.	20—Felix Garcia, Baltimore	KO 2
Apr.	4—Dick Demeray, Minneapolis	KO 5
Apr.	18—Mike Kaplan, Boston	L 10
May	2—Tony Marteliano, N. Y. C.	W 10
July	2—Al Davis, N. Y. C.	KO 10
July	14—Johnny Barbara, Philadelphia	W 12
July	29—Freddie Red Cochrane, Newark	L 15
	(Lost Welterweight Championship)
Sept.	15—Milt Aron, Pittsburgh	KO 5
Oct.	31—Ray Robinson, N. Y. C.	L 10
Nov.	26—Phil Furr, Wash., D. C.	W 10
Dec.	1—Harry Weekly, Cleveland	KO 9
Dec.	12—Young Kid McCoy, N. Y. C.	D 10

1942

Jan.	16—Ray Robinson, N. Y. C.	KO by 10
Feb.	2—Raul Carrabantes, Pittsburgh	W 10
Feb.	27—Tony Motisi, Chicago	L 10
Mar.	9—Tony Iannazzo, Pittsburgh	KO 5

Mar. 30—Wild Bill McDowell, Newark ..KO 6
Apr. 13—Maxie Berger, Pittsburgh ...... W 10
Apr. 23—Ruben Shank, Minneapolis .....L 10
May 25—Lew Jenkins, Pittsburgh ......KO 10
June 4—Reuben Shank, Minneapolis ... W 10
June 22—Bobby Dutton, Wilkes-Barre ..KO 4
June 29—Norman Rubio, Newark ....L 10
July 27—Norman Rubio, Pittsburgh ....KO 9
Aug. 13—Garvey Young, N. Y. C. ......KO 6
Sept. 10—Freddie Cochrane, N. Y. C. .... W 10
Sept. 21—Johnny Walker, Philadelphia ... W 10
Oct. 13—Tito Taylor, Milwaukee .... W 10
Oct. 26—Henry Armstrong, San Fran. ....L 10
Nov. 16—Sheik Rangel, San Fran. ....L 10
Dec. 15—Carmen Notch, Pittsburgh ..... W 10

1943
Feb. 5—Beau Jack, N. Y. C. ....L 10
Feb. 16—Mayon Padlo, Pittsburgh ...... W 10
Mar. 5—Beau Jack, N. Y. C. ....L 12
Apr. 30—Johnny Roszina, Milwaukee ..KO 8
June 10—Jake LaMotta, Pittsburgh ......L 10
July 12—Jake LaMotta, Pittsburgh ...... W 15
Aug. 9—Kid McCoy, Pittsburgh ....KO 4
Aug. 23—Bob Montgomery, Philadelphia .L 10
Sept. 10—Vinnie Vines, N. Y. C. ....KO 1
Oct. 15—Jose Basora, Detroit ....L 10
Oct. 29—Bobby Richardson, Chicago ... W 10
Nov. 12—Jake LaMotta, N. Y. C. ....L 10
Dec. 20—Ralph Zanelli, Boston ....L 10

1944
Jan. 3—Ossie Harris, Pittsburgh ......KO 10
Jan. 14—Jake LaMotta, Detroit ....L 10
Mar. 27—Harry Teaney, Milwaukee ..... W 10
Mar. 29—Freddie Archer, Elizabeth ......L 10
June 26—Tommy Bell, Pittsburgh ....L 10
In U. S. Army.
Aug. 1—Pete DeRuzza, Houston .....KO 8
Sept. 12—Felix Morales, San Antonio ..KO 2
Sept. 26—Artie Dorrell, Galveston .....KO 7
Oct. 16—Tommy Roman, Shreveport ....L 10
Oct. 18—Pete Saia, Dallas ....KO 8
Nov. 14—PFC Chuck Hirst, Houston ...KO 5
Nov. 29—Manuel Villa, Dallas ....KO 6
Dec. 12—Kid Azteca, San Antonio ...... W 10

1945
Jan. 5—Billy Arnold, New York ...... W 8
Feb. 22—Kid Astrada, Camp Maxey ....KO 2
Mar. 6—Bill McDowell, Galveston ..... W 10
Mar. 22—Ben Evans, Galveston ....KO 8
Apr. 3—Manuel Villa, San Antonio ...KO 8
May 7—Kid Azteca, San Antonio ...... W 10
May 8—Pat Saia, Beaumont ....W 10
June 12—Baby Zavala, San Antonio ...KO 4
June 22—Harold Green, New York ......L 10
July 3—Ruben Shank, Pittsburgh ......L 10
July 10—Ossie Harris, Pittsburgh ......L 10
July 16—Bill McDowell, New Orleans ...L 10
Sept. 12—Paul Altman, Houston ....L 10
Sept. 18—Billy Deeg, Oklahoma City .... W 10
Oct. 20—Joe Reddick, New York ......L 10
Nov. 2—Freddie Archer, New York ....L 10
Nov. 13—Joe Curcio, Elizabeth ....L 10
Dec. 10—Cecil Hudson, New York .....L 10

1946
Jan. 15—Al (Red) Priest, Boston ....L 10
Feb. 1—O'Neill Bell, Detroit ....L 10
Feb. 25—Aaron Perry, Wash., D. C. ....L 10
Mar. 19—Levi Southall, Kansas City ... W 10
Mar. 26—Tony Elizondo, San Antonio ...L 10
Apr. 5—Manuel Villa, El Paso .... D 10
Apr. 12—Lincoln Stanley, Portland, Ore. W 10
Apr. 18—Don Lee, Hollywood .... W 10
Apr. 29—Howard Blyhl, Omaha ....L 10
May 1—Joey Martinez, Wichita ....KO 10
May 14—Jackie Wilson, Los Angeles ...L 10
May 27—Tommy Lemmon, Milwaukee ...L 10
Oct. 29—Russell Wilhite, Memphis ....KO 5
Nov. 12—Al Mobley, Trenton ....L 8
Nov. 18—Jimmy McGriff, Wash. .... D 10
Dec. 2—Ralph Zannelli, Providence ....L 10
Dec. 6—Pete Mead, Grand Rapids ......L 10
Dec. 10—Bobby Britton, Memphis ..... W 10

1947
Jan. 8—Clyde Gordon, Miami ....L 10
Feb. 15—Kid Azteca, Mexico City ..KO by 5

1948
Oct. 28—Eddie Steele, Macon, Ga. ...... D 10

1949
Jan. 12—Al Reid, Macon, Ga. .... W 10
Jan. 17—Eddie Steele, Augusta .... W 10

TB	KO	WD	WF	D	LD	LF	KOBY	ND	NC
230	80	74	1	10	61	0	4	0	0

Elected to Hall of Fame in 1972

FREDDIE "RED" COCHRANE
Born, May 6, 1915, Elizabeth, N. J.
Nationality, Irish-American. Weight, 145 lbs.
Height, 5 ft. 7½ in. Managed by Willie Gilzenberg
and Larry Corbett.

1933
June 4—Steve Petronick, Eliza., N.J. ... W 4
July 19—Dinny Boyle, Eliza., N.J. .....KO 2
July 26—Tommy Mack, Eliza., N.J. ...KO 1
Sept. 1—Frank Orlando, Eliza., N.J. .... D 6
Nov. 10—Johnny Riccaduli, Eliza., N. J. . D 6

1934
Feb. 7—Johnny Riccaduli, Elizabeth, N. J. W 6
July 7—Marvin Hart, Elizabeth, N. J. .... W 6
July 14—Jackie Corcoran, Elizabeth, N. J. .. W 6
July 21—Jackie Corcoran, Elizabeth, N. J. .. W 6
Aug. 12—Paddy Gordon, Elizabeth, N. J. .... W 6
Aug. 19—Ernie Tackett, Elizabeth, N. J. .... W 6
Sept. 26—Lew Greenberg, Newark, N. J. ... KO 4
Oct. 8—Joe Ardito, Newark, N. J. .... W 6
Dec. 20—Emil Calcagni, Teterboro, N. J. ... L 6

1935
Jan. 7—Chang Collura, Newark, N. J. .. L 6
Jan. 22—Chang Collura, Elizabeth, N. J. .. KO 3
Feb. 5—Johnny Riccaduli, Elizabeth, N. J. W 6
Feb. 18—Joe Vacchiano, Newark, N. J. .. W 6
Mar. 3—Joe Ardito, Elizabeth, N. J. .... D 6
Mar. 25—Julie Katz, Newark, N. J. .... W 8
May 14—Al Roth, Newark, N. J. .... W 8
May 29—Mickey Greb, Elizabeth, N. J. .. W 6
June 11—Mickey Cohen, Nutley, N. J. ... KO 2
July 25—Lou Monte, Elizabeth, N. J. .... L 6
Sept. 9—Frankie Warno, Trenton, N. J. .. KO 8
Sept. 16—Lew Massey, Newark, N. J. ...... L 10
Oct. 7—Mickey Page, Newark, N. J. .... D 10
Oct. 28—Max Fisher, Newark, N. J. ...... L 10
Nov. 8—Aldo Spoldi, Chicago, Ill. .... L 8
Dec. 9—Max Fisher, Newark, N. J. ...... W 10

1936
Jan. 17—Georgie Levy, Newark, N. J. ... W 10
Feb. 24—Johnny Jadick, Newark, N. J. ... W 10
Apr. 9—Lew Feldman, N. Y. C. ....L 8
May 9—Al Gillette, Newark, N. J. ...... W 10
June 29—Al Roth, Newark, N. J. ...... W 10
July 21—Maxie Fisher, Newark, N. J. ....L 10
Sept. 1—Enrico Venturi, Jersey City .....L 10
Sept. 29—Phil Baker, Jersey City ....L 10
Oct. 19—Pete Mascia, Newark, N. J. ... W 10
Nov. 3—Charley Gomer, N. Y. C. ....L 8

1937
Jan. 22—Benny Bass, Phila., Pa. ....L 10
Feb. 19—Eddie Cool, Philadelphia, Pa. ...L 10
Mar. 22—Tippy Larkin, Newark, N. J. ...L 9
May 18—Irving Eldridge, N. Y. C. ....L 8
May 24—Tippy Larkin, Newark, N. J. ...L 10
June 7—Freddie Miller, Woodhaven .....L 8
June 15—Johnny Alba, Eliza., N. J. .....KO 3
June 28—Tony Morgano, Newark, N. J. ...L 10
July 2—Tippy Larkin, Lg. Branch ......L 10
Aug. 3—Ralph Vona, Eliza., N. J. ...... W 6
Aug. 10—Ralph Vona, Eliza., N. J. ...... W 6
Aug. 16—Pedro Montanez, Jer. City . KO by 2
Sept. 21—Buckey Keyes, Eliza., N. J. ...KO 2
Sept. 28—Mike Piskin, Newark, N. J. .... W 8
Oct. 4—Tommy Spiegel, Richmond, Va. D 10
Oct. 25—Tommy Spiegel, Richmond, Va. W 10
Nov. 8—Norment Quarles, Richmond ....L 10
Nov. 30—Tommy Spiegel, Coral Gables .. W 10
Dec. 28—Nat Litfin, New York .... D 6

1938
Feb. 17—Mickey Duca, Wilm., Del. ...... D 8
Feb. 24—Johnny Rohrig, Passaic, N. J. .. W 8
Mar. 1—Mickey Duca, Wilm., Del. ...... W 10
Apr. 4—Maxie Fisher, Newark, N. J. ... W 8
Apr. 18—Stumpy Jacobs, Wilm., Del. ... W 10
May 9—Eddie Alzek, Garfield, N. J. ...... D 8
June 6—Larry Mangine, Trenton, N. J. . KO 1
July 5—Tippy Larkin, Newark, N. J. .... W 10
July 25—Jack Kid Berg, Newark, N. J. ... W 10
Aug. 9—Phil Baker, Newark, N. J. .... W 8
Aug. 23—Pete Mascia, Eliza., N. J. .....KO 3
Aug. 29—Tippy Larkin, Newark, N. J. ....L 15
Oct. 10—*Paulie Walker, Trenton ..... KO by 5
Dec. 26—Lou Lombardi, Newark, N. J. .. W 8
*Cochrane's eye cut—bout stopped.

1939
Feb. 6—Ray Napolitano, Newark .....KO 4
Feb. 27—Billy Beauhuld, Newark ....L 10

Mar. 27—Tony Maglione, Trenton ..... W 8
Apr. 10—Mike Piskin, Newark .... L 10
Apr. 24—Eddie Brink, Newark .... W 10
May 8—Lou Fortuna, Newark .... W 8
June 26—Lou Fortuna, Newark .... W 10
July 31—Tony Martin, Newark .... W 10
Oct. 9—Julio Gonzales, Newark ...... W 10
1940
Jan. 15—Norman Hurdman, Baltimore .. W 8
Feb. 23—Mike Kaplan, N. Y. C. .... L 8
Mar. 11—Larry Mangine, Trenton ...... KO 3
Mar. 18—Billy Beauhuld, Newark .... D 10
Apr. 12—Dave Chacon, Elizabeth .... W 10
May 3—Dave Chacon, Elizabeth .... W 10
June 25—Maurice Arnault, Newark ..... KO 5
July 8—Mickey Makar, Newark ...... KO 4
Sept. 16—Bobby Masters, Newark ...... KO 5
Oct. 21—Norman Rubio, Newark ...... W 10
Nov. 25—Norman Rubio, Newark .... L 10
Dec. 16—Vince DeLia, Trenton .... KO 3
Dec. 30—Joe DeJesus, Newark .... W 8
1941
Jan. 13—Norman Rubio, Newark .... W 10
Feb. 5—Norman Hurdman, Perth Amb. W 8
Feb. 27—Ray Powell, Atlantic City .... KO 2
Mar. 5—Joe DeJesus, Perth Amboy ... KO 1
Mar. 20—Oscar Poindexter, Atl. City ... KO 3
Apr. 23—Rego Dell, Perth Amboy ...... W 8
June 27—Frankie Fariello, Long Br. .... KO 3
July 29—Fritzie Zivic, Newark .... W 15
(Won World's Welterweight Championship)
Oct. 6—Lew Jenkins, N. Y. C. ...... W 10
(Nontitle fight between two champions)
Dec. 19—Bobby Britton, Miami .... W 10
1942
May 8—Garvey Young, Boston .... L 10
Sept. 10—Fritzie Zivic, New York City .... L 10
Enlisted in U. S. Navy.
1945
June 1—Pete Lello, Jacksonville ...... KO 2
June 8—Jimmy Mazzio, Charlotte ..... KO 2
June 9—Al Stanley, Augusta .... KO 2
June 11—Eddie Miller, Atlanta .... KO 2
June 13—Alex Doyle, Wilmington ...... KO 2
June 29—Rocky Graziano, N. Y. C. ... KO by 10
July 17—Lou Miller, Knoxville .... KO 3
Aug. 24—Rocky Graziano, N. Y. C. ...... KO by 10
1946
Feb. 1—Marty Servo, N. Y. C. .... KO by 4
(Lost Welterweight Title)

TB	KO	WD	WF	D	LD	LF	KO BY	ND	NC
117	27	46	0	9	30	0	5	0	0

MARTY SERVO

Born, November 9, 1919, Schenectady, N. Y. Nationality, Italian-American. Managed by Al Weill.
1938
Jan. 8—George Hall, Washington ...... W 6
Feb. 12—Eddy Voccia, Brooklyn ...... KO 2
Feb. 29—Joe Coskey, Amsterdam ...... KO 4
Apr. 17—Monty Pignatore, N. Y. C. ..... W 6
May 27—Eddy Voccia, Brooklyn ...... KO 1
June 29—Al Ragone, N. Y. C. ...... W 6
Aug. 12—Tommy Fontana, N. Y. C. ..... W 6
1939
Jan. 3—Vince DeMarco, N. Y. C. ..... KO 3
Jan. 10—Eddie Barton, N. Y. C. .... W 6
Jan. 16—Joe Sole, Washington ...... KO 4
Feb. 6—Martin Riley, Providence ...... W 6
Feb. 14—Tommy Fontana, N. Y. C. ..... W 6
Feb. 21—Frankie Parcia, N. Y. C. ...... W 6
Mar. 14—Joe Garvey, N. Y. C. .... W 6
Mar. 24—Tony Giello, N. Y. C. .... W 6
Apr. 20—Lloyd Lasky, N. Y. C. ...... W 6
Apr. 25—Lloyd Lasky, Queens, N. Y. ... KO 1
May 2—Al Gillette, Hartford ...... KO 2
May 8—Frankie Rayo, Brooklyn ...... W 6
May 12—Frankie Rayo, Brooklyn ...... W 6
May 16—Mike Angieri, Hartford ...... KO 6
July 7—Larry Esposito, Kingston ..... W 6
July 11—Geo. Dusty Brown, Hartford ... W 6
July 25—Young Chappie, Hartford .... W 6
Aug. 8—George Salamone, Hartford .... W 8
Aug. 15—Martin Reilly, Hartford ...... W 8
Sept. 12—Bobby Ivy, Hartford .... W 8
Oct. 10—Jerry Zulu, Hartford .... W
Dec. 1—Joe Torre, Madison Sq. Garden. D 6

1940
Jan. 16—Joe Marciente, Hartford ...... KO 3
Jan. 24—Lenny Mancini, Garden .... D 6
Apr. 15—Willie Andrews, Holyoke ...... W 8
Apr. 26—Don De Santis, Boston ...... W 6
May 10—Maurice Arnault, Garden ...... W 6
July 25—Eddie Zivic, Hartford .... KO 6
Sept. 16—Lou Fontana, Philadelphia .... W 8
Oct. 21—Billy Maher, Philadelphia ...... W 10
1941
Feb. 14—Mitsos Grispos, Hartford ...... W 10
Feb. 28—Freddie Archer, Garden ...... W 6
Mar. 3—Billy Bullock, Philadelphia ... KO 4
Apr. 14—Danny Falco, Philadelphia ..... W 8
Apr. 22—Bill Duffy, Hartford .... W 8
May 29—Billy Davis, Philadelphia ...... W 10
June 17—Wishy Jones, Garfield .... W 10
July 15—Bobby Britton, Hartford ...... W 10
Sept. 25—Ray Robinson, Philadelphia ... L 10
Dec. 19—Larry Doros, Hoffman Island,
New York .... Exh. 4
1942
Feb. 17—Lew Jenkins, Philadelphia ..... W 10
May 28—Ray Robinson, N. Y. C. .... L 10
In U. S. Coast Guard.
1945
Dec. 10—Freddie Camuso, Providence .. KO 5
1946
Jan. 10—Stanley (Baby) Sims,
Schenectady .... W 10
Feb. 1—Freddie Cochrane, N. Y. C. ... KO 4
(Won Welterweight Crown)
Mar. 29—Rocky Graziano, N. Y. C. ... KO by 2
Aug. 1—Jimmy Anest, Halloran Hospital
(Exh. for Wounded Vets) .... KO 5
Aug. 15—Bobby Lakin, Fort Dix .... ND 10
(Exh. for Wounded Vets)
Sept. 25—(Announced retirement, nose injury)
1947
July 21—Benny Singleton, Albany ..... KO 2
Aug. 5—Joe DiMartino, Bridgeport . KO by 1

TB	KO	WD	WF	D	LD	LF	KO BY	ND	NC
56	15	34	0	2	2	0	2	1	0

Died in Pueblo, Colorado, February 9, 1969, after a long illness.

RAY ROBINSON
(Record under Middleweight Champions)

JOHNNY BRATTON
Born, Sept. 9, 1927, Little Rock, Ark. Managed by Howard Frazier and Hymie Wallman.
1944
June 12—Doyle Hirt, Chicago .... W 4
June 26—Larry Wright, Chicago ...... KO 3
July 7—Al Jordan, Chicago ...... KO 4
July 24—Walter Halba, Chicago .... KO 3
Aug. 7—Ted Christie, Chicago ...... W 8
Sept. 25—Gene Spencer, Chicago ...... L 8
Oct. 9—Gene Spencer, Chicago ...... W 8
Nov. 24—Gene Spencer, Chicago ...... W 8
Dec. 4—Ace Miller, Chicago .... L 8
Dec. 18—Ted Christie, Chicago .... KO 2
1945
Jan. 19—Robert Earl, Chicago .... KO 3
Feb. 1—Jimmy Anest, Chicago ...... W 6
Mar. 26—Patsy Spataro, Chicago ...... W 8
May 14—Melvin Bartholomew, Chi. .... KO 4
May 20—Melvin Johnson, Chicago ...... W 8
July 30—Joey Barnum, Chicago .... L 8
Aug. 10—Dave Castilloux, Milwaukee ... L 10
Nov. 2—Cleo Shans, New Orleans ...... D 10
Nov. 5—Cleo Shans, New Orleans ...... W 10
Dec. 14—Chalky Wright, New Orleans ... L 10
1946
Jan. 20—Ike Williams, New Orleans ... L 10
Apr. 12—Freddie Dawson, Chicago ..... W 10
May 3—Pedro Firpo, New Orleans ... KO 1
Aug. 1—Bill Eddy, Chicago .... W 10
Aug. 13—Roy Cadle, Chicago .... KO 5
Sept. 23—Eddie Lander, Chicago ...... W 10
Oct. 18—Richard Polite, New Orleans .. KO 3
Oct. 31—Willie Joyce, Chicago .... W 10
Dec. 20—Willie Joyce, Chicago ...... W 10
1947
Jan. 24—Morris Reif, Chicago .... W 10
Feb. 14—Danny Kapilow, Chicago ...... W 10
May 16—Sammy Angott, Chicago ...... L 10
June 6—Gene Burton, Chicago ..... L 10

Aug.	4—Herbie Biff Jones, Washington	KO	8
Oct.	6—Gene Burton, Chicago	L	10
Nov.	12—Phil Palmer, Chicago	KO	10

1948

Jan.	5—Livio Minelli, Philadelphia	L	10
Jan.	23—Beau Jack, Chicago	KO by	8
July	6—Jack Solomons, Chicago	KO	1
July	19—Frankie Abrams, Chicago	W	8
Sept.	15—Luigi Valentini, Chicago	KO	7
Oct.	29—Bernard Docusen, Chicago	L	10
Nov.	29—Bobby Lee, Philadelphia	D	10
Dec.	3—Joe Brown, New Orleans	KO	4

1949

Jan.	7—Melvin Bartholomew, New Orl.	W	10
Jan.	17—Ike Williams, Philadelphia	L	10
Feb.	25—Chester Rico, Chicago	KO	5
Mar.	29—Frankie Vigeant, Seattle	KO	4
Apr.	8—Roman Alvarez, Chicago	KO	5
Sept.	15—Chuck Taylor, Chicago	KO	2
Nov.	18—Gaby Ferland, Chicago	KO	2

1950

Jan.	4—Gene Hairston, New York	KO	2
Jan.	20—Ike Williams, Chicago	KO by	9
Nov.	6—Holly Mims, Baltimore	L	10
Nov.	22—Johnny Cesario, New York	KO	3
Nov.	27—Holly Mims, Baltimore	L	10
Dec.	13—Lester Felton, Chicago	KO	3

1951

Jan.	9—Sammy Mastrean, Chicago	KO	3
Jan.	24—Bobby Dykes, Chicago	KO	1
Mar.	14—Charley Fusari, Chicago	W	15
	(For vacant N. B. A. welterweight title)		
Apr.	18—Don Williams, Detroit	KO	4
May	18—Kid Gavilan, New York City	L	15
	(For American welterweight title)		
Oct.	15—Wilbur Wilson, Holyoke	W	8
Nov.	28—Kid Gavilan, Chicago	D	10
Dec.	27—Livio Minelli, Milwaukee	W	10

1952

Jan.	28—Bobby Rosado, Providence	KO	8
Feb.	20—Vic Cardell, Chicago	W	10
Mar.	28—Rocky Castellani, New York	L	10
May	1—Pierre Langlois, Montreal	KO	4
May	23—Del Flanagan, New York	W	10
June	18—Rocky Castellani, Chicago	L	10
July	28—Laurent Dauthuille, Montreal	KO	3
Aug.	25—Irwin Steen, Brooklyn	KO	3
Sept.	10—Ralph Zanelli, Detroit	W	10
Oct.	31—Joe Miceli, New York	KO	8
Dec.	5—Ralph Jones, New York	L	10

1953

Feb.	23—Tuzo Portuguez, Brooklyn	KO	5
Mar.	20—Bobby Jones, New York	KO	5
Apr.	14—Al Wilson, Brooklyn	W	10
May	6—Livio Minelli, Cleveland	W	10
June	9—Danny Womber, Montreal	W	10
Sept.	30—Al Wilson, Baltimore	W	10
Nov.	13—Kid Gavilan, Chicago	L	15
	(For World Welterweight Title)		

1954

| Feb. | 24—Johnny Saxton, Philadelphia | L | 10 |
| Oct. | 25—Chico Varona, New York | L | 10 |

1955

| Mar. | 17—Del Flanagan, St. Paul | KO by | 9 |

TB	KO	WD	WF	D	LD	LF	KOBY	ND	NC
86	32	27	0	3	21	0	3	0	0

KID GAVILAN
(Gerardo Gonzalez)
(The Hawk)

Born, January 6, 1926, Camaguey, Cuba.
Managed by Fernando Balido, Angel Lopez and
later by Yamil Chade. Height—5 feet 10½ in.

1943

June	5—Antonio Diaz, Havana	W	4
June	12—Bartolo Molina, Havana	W	4
Aug.	7—Nanito Kid, Havana	D	6
Sept.	11—Sergio Prieto, Havana	KO	5

1944

Oct.	1—Juan Villalba, Havana	KO	9
Nov.	25—Kid Bombon, Havana	W	10
Dec.	23—Miguel Acevedo, Havana	W	10
Feb.	10—Kid Bombon, Havana	W	10
Mar.	10—Jose Pedroso, Havana	W	10
Apr.	21—Santiago Sosa, Havana	KO	9
May	13—Kid Bebo, Cienfugos	KO	4
May	26—Julio Cesar Jiminez, Havana	W	10
June	23—Pedro Ortega, Havana	W	10
July	7—Jose Pedroso, Havana	KO	4
Aug.	4—Julio Cesar Jiminez, Mexico	W	10

Aug.	26—Pedro Ortega, Mexico	KO	6
Sept.	22—Carlos Malacara, Mexico	L	10
Nov.	3—Carlos Malacara, Havana	W	10
Nov.	17—Johnny Suarez, Havana	W	10

1946

Jan.	26—Kid Bururu, Havana	W	10
Feb.	9—Kid Bururu, Havana	W	10
Mar.	2—Jose R. Zorrilla, Bayamo	KO	4
Mar.	9—Santiago Sosa, Havana	W	10
Apr.	5—Tony Mar, Mexico	L	10
June	22—Jesus Varona, Havana	W	10
Aug.	4—Hankin Barrow, Havana	KO	7
Aug.	24—Jack Larrimore, Havana	KO	3
Sept.	7—Hankin Barrow, Havana	W	10
Nov.	1—Johnny Ryan, N. Y. C.	KO	5
Dec.	2—Johnny Williams, N. Y. C.	W	10
Dec.	13—Johnny Williams, N. Y. C.	W	10

1947

Jan.	28—Julio Pedroso, Havana	W	10
Feb.	8—Jose Garcia, Alvarez, Havana	W	10
Feb.	22—Baby Coullimber, Havana	W	10
Mar.	12—Nick Moran, Havana	W	10
Apr.	26—Vince Gambill, Havana	KO	2
Aug.	11—Charlie Williams, Newark	W	10
Aug.	18—Bobby Lee, Baltimore	W	10
Sept.	2—Doug Ratford, Newark	L	10
Sept.	15—Charley Millan, Baltimore	KO	1
Sept.	18—Billy Justine, Philadelphia	W	8
Oct.	23—Billy Nixon, Philadelphia	W	8
Nov.	3—Bee Bee Wright, Baltimore	KO	10
Dec.	29—Buster Tyler, New York	D	10

1948

Jan.	12—Gene Burton, New York	D	10
Jan.	23—Joe Curcio, New York	KO	2
Feb.	13—Vinnie Rossano, New York	W	10
Feb.	27—Ike Williams, New York	L	10
Apr.	13—Doug Ratford, Brooklyn	L	10
Apr.	26—Tommy Bell, Philadelphia	W	10
May	28—Rocco Rossano, New York	KO	1
July	22—Roman Alvarez, New York	W	10
Aug.	5—Buster Tyler, New York	W	10
Sept.	23—Ray Robinson, New York	L	10
Oct.	21—Vinnie Rossano, Wash., D. C.	KO	6
Nov.	12—Tony Pellone, N. Y. City	W	10
Dec.	11—Ben Buker, Havana	W	10

1949

Jan.	28—Ike Williams, N. Y. C.	W	10
Apr.	1—Ike Williams, N. Y. C.	W	10
May	2—Al Priest, Boston	W	10
June	7—Cliff Hart, Syracuse	KO	2
July	11—Ray Robinson, Philadelphia	L	15
	(World Welterweight Title Bout)		
Sept.	9—Rocky Castellani, N. Y. C.	W	10
Oct.	14—Beau Jack, Chicago	W	10
Oct.	15—Lester Felton, Detroit	L	10
Nov.	21—Laurent Dauthuille, Montreal	W	10
Dec.	17—Bobby Lee, Havana	W	10

1950

Feb.	10—Billy Graham, New York	L	10
Mar.	6—Otis Graham, Philadelphia	W	10
Mar.	20—Robert Villemain, Montreal	L	10
May	8—George Costner, Philadelphia	L	10
May	26—George Small, New York	W	10
June	5—Mike Koballa, Brooklyn	W	10
June	19—Bobby Mann, Hartford	W	10
July	2—Sonny Horne, Brooklyn	W	10
July	13—Phil Burton, Omaha	W	10
Aug.	15—Johnny Greco, Montreal	KO	6
Oct.	23—Tommy Ciarlo, New Haven	D	10
Oct.	30—Eugene Hairston, Scranton	L	10
Nov.	7—Billy Graham, New York	W	10
Dec.	4—Tony Janiro, Cleveland	W	10
Dec.	22—Joe Miceli, New York	W	10

1951

Jan.	26—Paddy Young, New York City	W	10
Feb.	7—Tommy Ciarlo, Caracas	W	10
Mar.	10—Tommy Ciarlo, Havana	KO	8
Mar.	30—Gene Hairston, New York City	W	10
Apr.	26—Aldo Minelli, New York City	W	10
May	18—Johnny Bratton, N. Y. C.	W	15
	(For American welterweight title)		
July	16—Fitzie Pruden, Milwaukee	W	10
Aug.	29—Billy Graham, New York City	W	15
	(Gavilan gained international recognition)		
Oct.	4—Bobby Rosado, Havana	KO	7
Nov.	7—Tony Janiro, Detroit	KO	4
Nov.	28—Johnny Bratton, Chicago	D	10
Dec.	14—Walter Cartier, New York	KO	10

1952

Feb.	4—Bobby Dykes, Miami	W	15
	(World welterweight title)		
Feb.	11—Don Williams, Boston	W	10
May	19—Ralph Zanelli, Providence	W	10
May	28—Fitzie Pruden, Indianapolis	KO	6

July 7—Gil Turner, Philadelphia ......KO 11
(World Title)
Aug. 16—Mario Diaz, Buenos Aires ......W 10
Sept. 6—Rafael Merentino,
Buenos Aires ....KO 9
Sept. 13—Eduardo Lausse, Buenos Aires .W 10
Oct. 5—Billy Graham, Havana ....W 15
(World Title)
1953
Jan. 13—Aman Peck, Tampa ....W 10
Jan. 21—Vic Cardell, Washington ....W 10
Feb. 11—Chuck Davey, Chicago ....KO 10
(Title Bout)
Apr. 14—Livio Minelli, Cleveland ....W 10
May 2—Danny Womber, Syracuse .....L 10
June 10—Italo Scortichini, Detroit ......W 10
July 15—Ramon Fuentes, Milwauke ...W 10
Aug. 26—Ralph Jones, New York ......W 10
Sept. 18—Carmen Basilio, Syracuse ......W 15
(Title Bout)
Nov. 13—Johnny Bratton, Chicago ......W 15
(Title Bout)
1954
Feb. 23—Johnny Cunningham, Miami
Beach ....W 10
Mar. 8—Livio Minelli, Boston ....W 10
Apr. 2—Carl (Bobo) Olson, Chicago .....L 15
(World Middleweight Title Bout)
Oct. 20—Johnny Saxton, Philadelphia ...L 15
(Lost World Welterweight Title)
1955
Feb. 4—Ernie Durando, New York ......W 10
Feb. 23—Hector Constance, Miami Beach .L 10
Mar. 16—Bobby Dykes, Miami ....L 10
June 2—Luigi Cemulini, Santa Clara ...NC 3
July 23—Cirilo Gil, Buenos Aires ....W 10
Aug. 13—Juan Bautista Burgues,
Montevideo ....KO 7
Sept. 3—Eduardo Lausse, Buenos Aires ..L 12
Dec. 3—Dogomar Martinez, Montivedeo .L 10
1956
Feb. 7—Peter Waterman, London ......L 10
Mar. 29—Germinal Ballarin, Paris ....L 10
Apr. 24—Peter Waterman, London ......W 10
May 13—Louis Trochon, Marseilles .....D 10
Aug. 18—Jimmy Beecham, Havana .....W 10
Oct. 13—Tony DeMarco, Boston ....L 10
Nov. 13—Chico Vejar, Los Angeles ......W 10
Dec. 4—Walter Byars, Boston ....L 10
Dec. 20—Ramon Fuentes, Los Angeles ...L 10
1957
Feb. 26—Vince Martinez, Newark.......L 10
Apr. 24—Del Flanagan, St. Paul ....L 10
June 17—Vince Martinez, Jersey City ....L 10
July 31—Gaspar Ortega, Miami Beach ...W 10
Oct. 22—Gaspar Ortega, Los Angeles ....L 12
Nov. 20—Walter Byars, Chicago ....W 10
1958
Feb. 19—Ralph (Tiger) Jones,
Miami Beach ....L 10
Apr. 4—Ralph (Tiger) Jones, Phila......W 10
June 18—Yama Bahama, Miami Beach ....L 10
Announced retirement from boxing, Sept. 11, 1958.

TB	KO	WD	WF	D	LD	LF	KOBY	ND	NC
143	27	79	0	6	30	0	0	0	1

JOHNNY SAXTON
Born, July 4, 1930, Newark, N. J. Height, 5 feet 9 ins. Managed by Frankie Palermo.
In 1947 won N. Y. City Golden Gloves title and 147 pound National AAU crown. In 1949 won National 147 pound title. Won total of 31 out of 33 amateur fights.
1949
May 9—Jimmy Swan, Philadelphia ....KO 3
July 20—Georgia Dixon, New York ....KO 1
Aug. 17—Dave Andrews, New York ....W 8
Sept. 6—George Hunter, Allentown ....KO 2
Oct. 24—Horace Bailey, Trenton ......W 6
Dec. 5—Bucky Slocum, Philadelphia ...W 4
Dec. 21—Adrian Morgart, New York ...KO 4
1950
Jan. 13—Mario Marino, New York ....KO 2
Feb. 10—Charley Salas, New York .....W 8
Mar. 15—Aldo Minelli, New York ......W 8
Mar. 22—John Bowman, Philadelphia ..KO 5
Apr. 21—Joe Miceli, New York ....W 10

May 17—Bert Linam, New York ....KO 1
June 5—Lionel Isadore, Philadelphia ...W 6
June 26—Mike Koballa, Elizabeth ....W 8
Aug. 28—Sonny Bunn, Brooklyn ......W 10
Sept. 22—Tony Pellone, New York ......W 10
1951
July 2—Lloyd Tate, Philadelphia .....KO 3
July 30—Gaby Ferland, Allentown ...KO 7
Aug. 6—Joey Carkido, Philadelphia ...KO 6
Aug. 20—Tommy Ciarlo, Allentown....KO 5
Oct. 4—Honeychile Johnson, Phila ...W 10
Nov. 5—Marshall Clayton,
Washington ....KO 7
Nov. 19—Charley Salas, Philadelphia ....W 10
1952
Jan. 25—Livio Minelli, New York City .KO 7
Mar. 14—Lester Felton, New York
City ....W. Dis. 6
Apr. 17—Charlie Thompson, Fall River ..W 10
Apr. 30—Bobby Lee, Baltimore ....KO 7
June 4—Luther Rawlings, Chicago .....W 10
July 17—Bobby Lee, Coatesville, Pa.....W 10
July 30—Virgil Akins, Chicago ....W 10
Oct. 3—Ralph Jones, New York City ...W 10
Oct. 28—Mario Trigo, Milwaukee ......KO 4
Dec. 12—Raoul Perez, New York City ..KO 1
Dec. 29—Danny Womber, Milwaukee ...W 10
1953
Feb. 10—Freddy Dawson, Philadelphia ..W 10
Feb. 24—Charlie Williams, Miami Beach .W 10
Mar. 10—Wallace Smith, Miami Beach ...D 10
Mar. 31—Charlie Williams, Brooklyn ....W 10
May 26—Joe Miceli, Detroit ....W 10
June 15—Gil Turner, Philadelphia ....L 10
Sept. 15—Charlie Williams, Allentown ...KO 2
Sept. 29—Joe Giardello, Philadelphia ....W 10
Dec. 3—Herman McCray, Fall River ...KO 3
Dec. 30—Del Flanagan, Minneapolis.....L 10
1954
Feb. 1—Mickey Laurent, Brooklyn ...KO 7
Feb. 24—Johnny Bratton, Philadelphia ..W 10
Aug. 4—Johnny Lombardo, Mt. Carmel D 10
Oct. 20—Kid Gavilan, Philadelphia ......W 15
(Won World Welterweight Title)
Dec. 2—Ramon Fuentes, Los Angeles ..W 10
1955
Feb. 11—Ronnie Delaney, Akron ....L 10
Apr. 1—Tony DeMarco, Boston ....KO by 14
(Lost World Welterweight Title)
June 20—Jimmy Fuller, Brockton ......KO 6
Sept. 15—Joe Shaw, Portland ....W 10
Oct. 25—Jackie O'Brien, Holyoke ......W 10
Nov. 9—Ralph Jones, Oakland ....W 10
1956
Mar. 14—Carmen Basilio, Chicago ......W 15
(Re-won World Welterweight Title)
May 16—Gil Turner, Chicago ....KO 10
Aug. 7—Barry Allison, Boston ....W 10
Aug. 23—Don Williams, Worcester ......W 10
Sept. 12—Carmen Basilio, Syracuse ...KO by 9
(Lost World Welterweight Title)
1957
Feb. 22—Carmen Basilio, Cleveland .KO by 2
(World Welterweight Title)
Sept. 6—Joe Miceli, Washington ....KO by 4
1958
Oct. 7—Barry Allison, Holyoke........W 10
Oct. 21—Denny Moyer, Portland ....L 10
Dec. 15—Willie Green, Providence ..KO by 3

TB	KO	WD	WF	D	LD	LF	KOBY	ND	NC
66	21	33	1	2	4	0	5	0	0

TONY DeMARCO
(Leonard Liotta)
Born, January 14, 1932. Height, 5 feet, 5½ in. Managed by Bobby Agrippino.
1948
Oct. 21—Meetor Jones, Boston ....KO 1
Nov. 16—Meetor Jones, Salem ....KO 2
Dec. 10—Billy Shea, Boston ....KO 3
Dec. 14—George Silva, Salem ....W 6
1949
Jan. 14—Joe Palaza, Boston ....KO 2
Feb. 17—Ray Dulmaine, Boston ....KO 2
Sept. 14—Roger Lessard, Boston ....KO 5
Oct. 7—Edward White, Providence.....L 6
Oct. 21—Vic Young, Boston ....KO 1
Nov. 14—Frankie Steele, Boston ....W 4
Dec. 19—Frankie Steele, Boston ....KO 3

1950

Jan.	9—Art Suffolatta, New Haven KO by	5
Feb.	20—Bobby Veal, Boston ....KO	2
July	10—Roger Ringuette, Boston .....KO	1
Sept.	19—Ricky Ferreira, New Bedford ..W	6
Sept.	25—Bobby Weaver, Holyoke ......KO	3
Oct.	9—Des Shanley, Holyoke........W	4
Oct.	20—Joe Wright, Boston ....W	6
Dec.	11—Ken Murray, Boston ....W	6

1951

Jan.	11—Ken Murray, Portland ....KO	2
Jan.	18—Larry Griffin, Portland, Me. ...W	8
Feb.	19—Reggie Martina, Boston ......KO	1
Mar.	12—Chick Boucher, Boston ....KO by	4
Oct.	1—Ferman King, Boston ....W	6
Nov.	27—Stanley Hilliard, Newark ......KO	4
Dec.	7—Joe Torrens, New York ....W	4
Dec.	17—Manny Santos, Trenton ......KO	2

1952

Jan.	15—Lewelyn Richardson, N. Y. ....W	6
Jan.	26—Julie Colon, Brooklyn........KO	3
Feb.	18—Ferman King, Providence .....W	8
Feb.	26—Abdul Ali, Newark...........KO	2
Mar.	1—Jackie O'Brien, Brooklyn.....W	8
Mar.	6—Puggy Brown, Newark ....KO	4
May	1—Bryan Kelly, Montreal L	8
May	15—Gene Poirer, Montreal.........L	8

1953

June	13—Ken Parsley, Boston ....KO	6
June	25—Jimmy Redding, Boston......KO	2
July	18—Pat Demers, Boston ....KO	7
Aug.	3—Terry Young, Boston ....KO	5
Sept.	10—Bertie Conn, Boston ....KO	1
Sept.	29—Chic Boucher, Boston ....KO	6
Oct.	10—Paddy DeMarco, Boston ......W	10
Dec.	12—Teddy Davis, Boston ....W	10

1954

Jan.	18—Wilbur Wilson, Boston ......W	10
Mar.	15—Wilbur Wilson, Boston ......KO	2
Apr.	24—Carlos Chavez, Boston ......W	10
May	22—Johnny Cesario, Boston ....W	10
July	12—George Araujo, Boston ....KO	5
Sept.	6—Chris Christensen, Boston ....KO	6
Nov.	6—Pat Manzi, Boston ....KO	1

1955

Feb.	11—Jimmy Carter, Boston........D	10
Apr.	1—Johnny Saxton, Boston .....KO	14
	(Won World Welterweight Title)	
June	10—Carmen Basilio, Syracuse .. KO by	12
	(Lost World Welterweight Title)	
Sept.	14—Chico Vejar, Boston ....KO	1
Nov.	30—Carmen Basilio, Boston ... KO by	12
	(For World Welterweight Title)	

1956

Mar.	5—Wallace (Bud) Smith, Boston .KO	9
Apr.	28—Arthur Persley, Boston ....W	10
June	16—Vince Martinez, Boston ....W	10
Oct.	13—Kid Gavilan, Boston ....W	10
Nov.	23—Gaspar Ortega, New York L	10
Dec.	21—Gaspar Ortega, New York L	10

1957

Feb.	9—Gaspar Ortega, Boston ....W	10
Mar.	30—Larry Boardman, Boston ......W	10
May	25—Walter Byars, Boston ....W	10
Oct.	29—Virgil Akins, Boston ......KO by	14

1958

Jan.	21—Virgil Akins, Boston ......KO by	12

1959

Mar.	11—George Monroe, Boston ......KO	8
Apr.	20—Eddie Connors, Boston........W	10

1960

Feb.	10—Denny Moyer, Boston .....KO by	2

1961

Dec.	19—Don Jordan, Boston ....KO	2

1962

Feb.	6—Stefan Redl, Boston .... W	10
Mar.	1—DeMarco announced retirement	

TB	KO	WD	WF	D	LD	LF	KOBY	ND	NC
71	33	25	0	1	5	0	7	0	0

CARMEN BASILIO
(Record under Middleweight Champions)

VIRGIL AKINS
St. Louis, Mo., Welterweight
Born, March 10, 1928. Height, 5 feet 9
inches. Won 14 out of 15 amateur bouts.

1948

Mar.	11—Albert Adams, St. Louis ...... W	6

Apr.	5—Charles Baxter, St. Louis ..KO by	3
Apr.	21—Charles Baxter, St. Louis ......W	6
Nov.	23—Danny Robinson, St. Louis ....W	6

1949

Jan.	17—Joe Henderson, St. Louis .....KO	3
Mar.	8—Willie Cheatum, St. Louis......W	8
Feb.	15—Russ Moore, Wichita ....KO	2
Mar.	30—Clem Custer, St. Louis ....W	8
Sept.	29—Art Persley, New York L	6

1950

July	6—Nelson Levering, Cheyenne L	6
July	15—Joe Fisher, Denver.............L	8
Oct.	5—Art Edmunson, St. Louis ......W	8
Oct.	24—Nelson Levering, St. Louis ....KO	2
Nov.	1—Rudy Zadell, St. Louis ....KO	3
Dec.	6—Joe Sgro, St. Louis ....W	10

1951

Jan.	18—Gene Parker, Minneapolis L	6
Mar.	7—Bill Neri, New York ....KO	8
Apr.	4—Bud Smith, St. Louis ....W	10
Apr.	17—Bud Smith, St. Louis ....W	10
May	25—Joe Brown, New Orleans L	10
June	8—Tommy Campbell, New Orleans W	10
July	6—Joe Brown, New Orleans L	10
Sept.	26—Freddie Dawson, St. Louis.....W	10
Oct.	17—Luther Rawlings, St. Louis ...W	10
Dec.	6—Joe Brown, St. Louis ....W	10
Dec.	14—Luther Rawlings, New York L	8

1952

Feb.	8—Baby Le Roy, Hollywood ....KO	4
Feb.	19—Joe Gilmer, Los Angeles .....KO	9
Feb.	29—Henry Davis, Hollywood .....KO	9
May	2—Jay Watkins, Chicago ....KO	2
July	30—Johnny Saxton, Chicago L	10
Sept.	30—Joe Miceli, Milwaukee.........L	10

1953

Apr.	4—Johnny Gonsalves, Chicago L	10
Aug.	29—Phil Kim, Chicago ....KO by	10

1954

June	2—Joey Greenwood, St. Louis ...KO	8
Oct.	16—Andy Brown, New Orleans L	10
Oct.	26—Henry Hank, Detroit ....W	8

1955

Mar.	2—Johnny Brown, Miami ....KO	10
Mar.	15—Tommy Maddox, Chicago ....KO	4
Apr.	8—Johnny Brown, St. Louis ......D	8
May	2—Ronnie Delaney, New York ...KO	8
May	23—Joe Miceli, New York ....KO	1
June	21—Billy Suddeth, Chicago ....KO	8
Aug.	8—Isaac Logart, New York ......W	10
Sept.	13—Harold Jones, Indianapolis ....W	10
Dec.	2—Isaac Logart, New York L	10

1956

Jan.	3—Rudolph Bent, Holyoke ......KO	5
Jan.	19—Clarence Cook, Dallas ....KO	4
Jan.	26—Mel Barker, E. St. Louis ......KO	8
Mar.	8—Andy Watkins, E. St. Louis ...W	10
Mar.	21—Hector Constance, St. Louis ...W	10
June	21—Don Jose, Monroe ....KO	4
Sept.	15—Charlie Sawyer, Hollywood L	10
Oct.	22—Pat Lowry, Miami ....KO	2

1957

Jan.	8—Sammy Walker, Buffalo ......W	10
Jan.	31—Al Andrews, St. Louis ....KO	6
Mar.	4—Franz Szuzina, St. Louis ......W	10
May	24—Jimmy Beecham, Washington .KO	3
June	12—Walter Byars, Norfolk ....W	10
July	8—Franz Szuzina, St. Louis ......KO	10
Aug.	9—Sugar Hart, Cleveland ....KO	8
Sept.	18—Gil Turner, Atlantic City L	10
Oct.	29—Tony DeMarco, Boston ......KO	14

1958

Jan.	21—Tony DeMarco, Boston ......KO	12
Mar.	21—Isaac Logart, New York ......KO	6
	(Welterweight Elimination bout)	
June	6—Vince Martinez, St. Louis ....KO	4
	(Won Vacant World Welterweight Title)	
Aug.	20—Charlie (Tombstone) Smith, Chicago ....KO	10
Sept.	18—Del Flanagan, St. Paul L	10
Dec.	5—Don Jordan, Los Angeles L	15
	(Lost World Welterweight Title)	

1959

Apr.	24—Don Jordan, St. Louis L	15
	(For World Welterweight Title)	
June	17—Luis Rodriguez, Miami Beach ..L	10
Aug.	4—Stan Harrington, Honolulu L	10
Oct.	28—Kenny Lane, Washington L	10
Dec.	10—Denny Moyer, Portland L	10

1960

Jan.	28—Don Fullmer, St. Louis L	10
Mar.	8—Wally Swift, London L	10
Apr.	1—Fernando Barreto, Sao Paulo ..W	10

May 20—Charley Scott, St. Louis .... W 10
July 6—Luis Rodriguez, Louisville ......L 10
Nov. 21—Carl Hubbard, Chicago ....KO 5
Dec. 6—Candy McFarland, Philadelphia .L 10
1961
Jan. 16—T. J. Jones, Chicago ....KO 10
Mar. 4—Gerald Gray, Kingston .... W 10
May 15—Billy Collins, Chicago .... W 10
July 10—Cecil Shorts, Chicago ....KO 8
Sept. 5—Henry White, Chicago ....L 10
Sept. 22—Kenny Lane, Annapolis ....L 10
Oct. 16—Jose Burgos, Caracas ....KO 10
Nov. 17—Stefan Redl, Totowa .... D 10
Dec. 13—Vince Bonomo, Miami Beach .KO 4
Dec. 27—Ralph Dupas, Miami Beach .....L 10
1962
Mar. 20—Rip Randall, Houston ....L 10
Mar. 21—Akins announced retirement due to eye injury.

TB	KO	WD	WF	D	LD	LF	KOBY	ND	NC
92	34	25	0	0	29	0	2	0	0

DON JORDAN
Los Angeles, Calif. Welterweight
Born, June 22, 1934. Height, 5 ft. 9 ins.
Managed by Don Nesseth and Jack McCoy.
1953
Apr. 27—Ray Serna, South Gate .... W 4
May 18—Al Barbero, South Gate .... W 4
July 4—ChiChi Martinez, Hollywood .. W 6
Aug. 9—ChiChi Martinez, Hollywood .. W 4
Sept. 26—George Macias, Hollywood ....KO 5
Oct. 17—Marvin Smith, Hollywood ....KO 5
Nov. 7—Marvin Smith, Hollywood ....KO 5
Dec. 16—Dave Cervantes, Hollywood ... W 5
1954
Jan. 16—Andy Escobar, Hollywood .... W 10
Mar. 20—Andy Escobar, Hollywood ....L 10
Apr. 17—Manuel Montes, Hollywood ...KO 2
May 31—Dickie Wong, Los Angeles .....L 10
June 28—Freddy Herman, Los Angeles .. W 10
Aug. 30—Art Ramponi, Los Angeles..... W 10
Sept. 20—Billy Hartman, Los Angeles...KO 4
Oct. 4—Art Ramponi, Los Angeles..... W 12
(California Welterweight Title)
Nov. 29—Manny Renteria, Los Angeles .KO 7
1955
Jan. 13—Lauro Salas, Los Angeles ...... W 12
Feb. 15—Jorge Macias, Sacramento ..... W 10
Mar. 3—Frankie Cockrell, Los Angeles . W 10
Mar. 31—Lauro Salas, Los Angeles ...... W 12
June 2—Art Aragon, Los Angeles ....L 10
Aug. 18—Joe Miceli, Los Angeles ...... W 10
Sept. 3—Woody Winslow, Hollywood... W 10
Oct. 20—Frankie Skidmore, San Fran. .. W 10
Dec. 15—Art Aragon, Los Angeles ......L 10
1956
Feb. 2—Paddy DeMarco, Los Angeles .KO 5
Mar. 29—Jimmy Carter, Los Angeles .....L 10
May 8—Joe Lopes, Sacramento ....L 12
June 7—Timmie Jefferson, Los Angeles . W 10
June 28—Frankie Skidmore,
Los Angeles ....KO 7
Oct. 16—Orlando Zulueta, Los Angeles...L 10
Nov. 18—Enrique Esqueda, Mexicali ...KO 1
Dec. 27—Archie Whitewater, Los Ang. .. W 10
1957
Jan. 1—Al Nevarez, Mexicali ....L 10
Jan. 24—Charley Tombstone Smith,
Los Angeles ....L 12
(California State Welterweight Title)
Mar. 19—Chico Uribe, Mexico City .... W 10
May 11—Jesse Morgan, Hollywood ....KO 1
June 15—L. C. Morgan, Hollywood......L 10
July 12—Arnoldo Gil, Mexicali ....KO 2
July 23—Alfredo Cota, Tijuana ....KO 1
Aug. 12—Juan Padilla, Tijuana .... W 10
Oct. 12—Orlando Zulueta, Hollywood .. W 10
Nov. 29—Ray Portilla, San Diego ......KO 6
1958
Jan. 4—Willie Morton, Hollywood .... W 10
Jan. 28—Dave Charnley, London ....L 10
Feb. 15—Karl-Heinz Guder, Hollywood . W 10
Apr. 15—Francisco Echevarria,
Mexicali ....KO 3
May 5—Kid Centella, Tijuana ....KO 2
May 18—Alfredo Cota, Mexicali .... W 10
July 2—Isaac Logart, Hollywood ...... W 10
Aug. 29—Lahouari Godih, New York .... W 10

Sept. 17—Gaspar Ortega, Portland .... W 10
Oct. 22—Gaspar Ortega, Long Beach .... W 12
Dec. 5—Virgil Akins, Los Angeles ...... W 15
(Won World Welterweight Title)
1959
Jan. 22—Alvaro Gutierrez, Los Angeles KO 3
Apr. 24—Virgil Akins, St. Louis .... W 15
(Title Bout)
July 10—Denny Moyer, Portland .... W 15
(Title Bout)
Dec. 5—Fernando Barreto, Sao Paulo .. W 10
Dec. 12—Federico Thompson,
Buenos Aires .... KO by 4
May 16—Candy McFarland, Baltimore ...L 10
May 27—Benny Paret, Las Vegas ....L 15
(Lost world Welterweight Title)
July 15—Phil Moyer, Portland ....L 10
Aug. 6—Jess Bogart, Nogales ....KO 1
Aug. 16—Julian Valdez, Tucson .... W 10
Oct. 16—Alfredo Cota, Mexicali .... D 10
Nov. 26—Ludwig Lightburn,
Guadalajaria ....L 10
1961
Mar. 11—Carmen Basilio, Syracuse ....L 10
Aug. 1—Ben Medina, Fresno ....L 10
Aug. 15—Hilario Morales, Juarez .... KO by 7
Nov. 14—Chivo Diaz, Sacramento ....L 10
Dec. 19—Tony DeMarco, Boston ... KO by 2
1962
Apr. 27—Giancarlo Garbelli, Rome ......L 10
July 26—Joey Limas, Albuquerque ......L 10
Oct. 5—Battling Torres, Los Angeles ..ND 7

TB	KO	WD	WF	D	LD	LF	KOBY	ND	NC
75	17	33	0	1	20	0	3	1	0

BERNARDO (BENNY) PARET
Cuban Welterweight
Born, March 14, 1937, Santa Clara, Las Villas.
As an amateur won 28 bouts and lost 1.
1955
Aug. 11—Esmerido Moya, Santa Clara ..KO 1
Sept. 8—Joel Morales, Santa Clara ...... W 4
Oct. 22—Miguel Cutino, Havana .... W 4
Oct. 26—Sandalio Santana, Santa Clara ... W 6
Dec. 2—Jose Delgado, Santa Clara ... W 6
Dec. 23—Joaquin Castillo, Santa Clara ... W 6
1956
Jan. 27—Jose Delgado, Santa Clara ....KO 4
Mar. 16—Reinaldo Caballero,
Santa Clara ....KO 3
Apr. 16—Oscar Campos, Santa Clara ... W 8
May 4—Carlos Chivas, Santa Clara ....KO 2
June 6—Tony Caspita, Santa Clara .... W 8
July 21—Carlos Chivas, Havana .... W 8
Aug. 9—Leo Villafanas, Santa Clara ...KO 3
Oct. 22—Rolando Rodriguez, Santa Clara
........................KO by 2
1957
Feb. 1—Oscar Campos, Santa Clara ... W 10
Mar. 9—Oscar Campos, Havana .... W 8
Mar. 23—Rolando Rodriguez, Havana ... W 8
Apr. 6—Guillermo Diaz, Havana ....L 8
May 4—Carlos Chivas, Havana .... W 8
May 25—Rolando Rodriguez, Havana ..KO 5
1958
Jan. 4—Regino Bravo, Havana ....KO 3
Jan. 25—Rolando Rodriguez, Havana .... W 8
Feb. 8—Luis Rodriguez, Havana ....L 10
Mar. 8—Tony Armenteros, Havana .... W 10
May 19—Bobby Shell, New York .... D 6
June 9—Eddie Armstrong, New York .. W 10
June 24—Agustin Rosales, Havana ....KO 8
Aug. 9—Luis Rodriguez, Havana ....L 10
Nov. 10—Andy Figaro, New York ......KO 1
Nov. 24—Barry Allison, New York ..... W 10
Dec. 15—Victor Zalazar, New York .... W 10
1959
Jan. 19—Victor Zalazar, New York .... W 10
Mar. 2—Cecil Shorts, New York ....L 10
Apr. 20—Eddie Thompson, New York ...L 10
June 1—Rudy Sawyer, New York ...... W 10
Aug. 7—Gaspar Ortega, New York .....L 10
Sept. 26—Jose Torres, San Juan .... D 10
Nov. 16—Bob Provizzi, New York ...... W 10
Dec. 18—Charley Scott, New York ..... W 10
1960
Jan. 29—Charley Scott, New York ...... W 10

Mar. 25—Federico Thompson, New York D 12
May 27—Don Jordan, Las Vegas .... W 15
(Won World Welterweight Title)
July 12—Sugar Hart, New York ....KO 6
Aug. 16—Denny Moyer, New York ......L 10
Dec. 10—Federico Thompson, New York W 15
(Retained World Welterweight Title)
1961
Feb. 25—Gaspar Ortega, Los Angeles . ..L 10
Apr. 1—Emile Griffith, Miami
Beach ....KO by 13
(Lost world welterweight title)
Sept. 30—Emile Griffith, New York ..... W 15
(Regained World Welterweight Title)
Dec. 9—Gene Fullmer, Las Vegas ..KO by 10
(For N.B.A. Middleweight Title)
1962
Mar. 24—Emile Griffith, New York .KO by 12
(Lost World welterweight title)
(Paret died on April 3, 1962, of injuries
suffered in the fight).

TB	KO	WD	WF	D	LD	LF	KOBY	ND	NC
50	10	25	0	3	8	0	4	0	0

EMILE GRIFFITH
(Record under Middleweight Champions)

LUIS RODRIGUEZ
Miami, Fla., Welterweight. Born, Cam-
aguez, Cuba, June 17, 1937. Height 5 ft. 7½ in.
1956
June 2—Lazaro Hernandez Kessell,
Havana ....KO 3
July 21—Vicente Reyes, Havana .... W 4
Oct. 20—Julian Yanes, Havana .... W 4
Nov. 28—Pablo Cardenas, Havana ......KO 2
Dec. 15—Jose Hernandez, Havana ......NC 2
(Bout Stopped By Rain)
1957
Jan. 12—Jose Hernandez, Havana ......KO 5
Feb. 16—Guillermo Diaz, Havana ...... W 6
Mar. 23—Vicente Reyes, Havana .... W 6
May 18—Vicente Reyes, Havana .... W 4
June 22—Antonio Salas, Havana .... W 8
July 20—Guillermo Diaz, Havana ...W. Dis. 6
Sept. 28—Gomeo Brennan, Havana ...... W 8
Nov. 15—Rolando Rodriguez, Havana ... W 8
1958
Feb. 8—Nardo Parets, Havana .... W 10
Mar. 29—Rolando Rodriguez, Havana ..KO 4
Apr. 19—Tony Armenteros, Havana..... W 10
July 26—Charley Scott, Havana ......KO 9
Aug. 9—Nardo Parets, Havana .... W 10
Sept. 20—Kid Fichique, Havana .... W 12
(Won Cuban Welterweight Title)
Nov. 22—Juan Padilla, Havana .... W 10

1959
Feb. 21—Joe Miceli, Havana ....KO 5
May 9—Cecil Shorts, Havana ....KO 9
June 17—Virgil Akins, Miami Beach ..... W 10
Aug. 26—Rudell Stitch, Louisville .... W 10
Oct. 3—Larry Baker, Havana .... W 10
Oct. 21—Isaac Logart, Miami Beach ..... W 10
Dec. 23—Sugar Hart, Miami Beach ...... W 10
1960
Feb. 10—Carl Hubbard, Miami Beach ...KO 4
Mar. 2—Chico Vejar, Miami Beach ..... W 10
Apr. 7—Alvaro Gutierrez,
Los Angeles ....KO 4
May 26—Alfredo Cota, Los Angeles ....KO 2
July 6—Virgil Akins, Louisville .... W 10
Aug. 17—Basil Campbell, Havana ......KO 5
Oct. 24—Mel Collins, Tampa .... W 10
Nov. 16—Yama Bahama, Miami Beach ...W 10
Nov. 28—Johnny Gonsalves, Oakland ... W 10
Dec. 27—Emile Griffith, New York ......L 10
1961
Feb. 21—Lyle Mackin, Oakland ....KO 5
Mar. 22—Johnny Gonsalves, Oakland ... W 10
Apr. 15—Alvaro Gutierrez, Mexico City KO 5
May 13—Alfredo Cota, Guadalajara ....KO 4
Aug. 3—Curtis Cokes, Dallas ....L 10
Sept. 13—Guy Sumlin, Miami Beach ....KO 6
Oct. 24—Joe Gonzalez, Miami Beach ...KO 6
Dec. 2—Curtis Cokes, Miami Beach ... W 10
1962
Jan. 27—Federico Thompson,
New York .... W 10
Mar. 17—Ricardo Falech, Miami Beach .KO 3

May 4—Yama Bahama, New York ....KO 3
June 30—Gene Armstrong, New York ..KO 8
Aug. 29—Ernie Burford, Miami Beach ..KO 7
Nov. 6—Santiago Gutierrez,
San Antonio ....KO 3
Dec. 12—Mel Collins, Miami Beach ...... W 10
1963
Jan. 19—Joey Giambra, Miami Beach ...W 10
Mar. 21—Emile Griffith, Los Angeles .... W 15
(Won World Welterweight Championship)
June 8—Emile Griffith, New York ......L 15
(Lost World Welterweight Championship)
Aug. 17—Denny Moyer, Miami Beach ..KO 9
Oct. 18—Wilbert McClure, New York ... W 10
Dec. 27—Wilbert McClure, Miami Beach . W 10
1964
Mar. 20—Holly Mims, New York .... W 10
Apr. 3—Jesse Smith, Miami Beach ..... W 10
June 12—Emile Griffith, Las Vegas ....L 15
(For World Welterweight Title)
Nov. 14—L. C. Morgan, Mexico City ....KO 2
1965
Feb. 12—Ruben Carter, New York .... W 10
Mar. 26—Johnny Smith, Los Angeles ...KO 10
Apr. 21—Garland Randall, Tampa ...... W 10
July 16—Memo Ayon, Los Angeles ....KO 3
July 26—Jose Assumption, Las Vegas ... W 10
Aug. 3—Charley Austin, Phoenix ...... W 10
Aug. 26—Ruben Carter, Los Angeles .... W 10
Oct. 4—Johnny Morris, Philadelphia ..KO 2
Nov. 16—Cecil Mott, Miami Beach .....KO 4
Dec. 2—Eddie Pace, Los Angeles .... W 10
Dec. 21—Joe Louis Murphy,
Albuquerque ....KO 4
1966
Jan. 18—Fred McWilliams, Phoenix ....KO 9
Jan. 25—Joey Lemas, Albuquerque ....KO 4
Mar. 7—George Benton, Albuquerque .KO 9
Apr. 11—Percy Manning, Phila. .... L 10
May 7—Tommy Caldwell, San Juan ...KO 2
July 6—Curtis Cokes, N. Orleans ...KO by 15
Sept. 9—Juarez de Lima, Rosario .....KO 3
Sept. 24—Ruben Orrico, Rosario ....KO 4
1967
Jan. 21—Manuel Alvarez, Mardel Plata .KO 8
Feb. 7—Esteban Osuna, Rosario ...... W 10
Mar. 20—Benny Briscoe, Philadelphia ... W 10
June 4—Rocky Rivero, San Juan ...... W 10
June 17—Jimmy Lester, Oakland ...... W 10
Sept. 7—Fred Hernandez, Oakland ..... W 10
Sept. 29—Phil Robinson, Caracas ...... W 10
Oct. 21—Candy McFarland, Caracas .... W 10
Nov. 6—Percy Manning, Caracas ......KO 1
Dec. 15—Benny Briscoe, New York ..... W 10
1968
Feb. 6—Charlie Austin, Miami Beach ..KO 6
Mar. 26—Carl Moore, Miami Beach ..... W 10
May 7—Ted Wright, Miami Beach ..... W 10
June 3—Vicente Rondon, San Juan .....L 10
July 18—Vicente Rondon, San Juan ..... W 10
Sept. 4—Rudy Rodriguez, Key West ...KO 4
Nov. 15—Joe Shaw, New York .... W 10
1969
Jan. 21—Dub Huntley, Miami Beach ... W 10
Feb. 20—Robert Williams, Tampa ......KO 7
Mar. 31—Rafael Gutierrez, San Diego ..KO 6
July 8—Eddie Owens, Miami Beach ...KO 7
Aug. 12—David Beckles, Miami Beach ..KO 2
Sept. 23—Tom Bethea, Miami Beach ..... W 10
Nov. 22—Nino Benvenuti, Rome ....KO by 11
(World Middleweight Title)
1970
Feb. 10—Porter Rolle, Miami Beach ....KO 4
Mar. 17—Joe Cokes, Miami Beach .....KO 4
Apr. 14—Willie Warren, Miami Beach ... W 10
June 16—Baby Boy Rolle, Miami ....KO 5
Aug. 20—Fraser Scott, Seattle .... W 10
July 31—Jose Gonzalez, San Juan ....L 10
Sept. 24—Jose Gonzalez, Miami Beach ... W 10
Dec. 1—J. C. Ponder, Miami Beach ....KO 5
1971
Jan. 26—Bobby Cassidy, Miami Beach ..W 10
Apr. 7—Tony Mundine, Melbourne ...KO 1
May 25—Bunny Sterling, London ....L 10
Aug. 3—Rafael Gutierrez,
San Francisco ....KO by 6
Nov. 1—Mike Padgett, Greenwood ....KO 2
Nov. 30—Dave Hilton, Miami Beach ..... W 10
1972
Mar. 16—Mike Lancaster, Seattle ....L 10
Apr. 12—Donato Paduano, Montreal ....L 10

TB	KO	WD	WF	D	LD	LF	KOBY	ND	NC
121	49	57	1	0	10	0	3	0	1

CURTIS COKES
Dallas, Texas, Welterweight, Born, June 15, 1937.

1958
Mar. 24—Manuel Gonzalez, Midland .... W 6
Apr. 8—Gil Tapia, Callas .... W 4
Apr. 28—Jimmy Leach, Dallas .... W 6
May 12—Babe Vance, Waco .... W 6
May 26—Cecil Courtney, Dallas .... W 6
June 30—Sammy Williams, Dallas .....KO 6
Oct. 27—Elmo Henderson, Dallas .... W 6
Nov. 22—Manuel Gonzales, Lubbock .... W 8
Dec. 1—Ruben Flores, Dallas .... W 6

1959
Jan. 20—George Carron, Lubbock .....KO 3
Apr. 1—Henry Watson, Dallas .... W 4
Apr. 27—Manuel Gonzales, Dallas ....L 10
May 18—Rip Randall, Dallas ....TD 3
July 27—Rip Randall, Dallas ....KO 1
Aug. 27—Reggie Williams, Baton Rouge KO 5
Sept. 14—Mel Ferguson, Dallas .... W 8
Dec. 2—Frankie Davis, Houston ....L 6
Dec. 14—Aman Peck, Dallas ....KO 5

1960
Mar. 1—Lovell Jenkins, Amarillo ...... W 8
July 29—Pedro Ruiz, El Paso ....KO 3
Sept. 13—Joe Louis Hargrove, Dallas ....KO 1
Oct. 24—Stefan Redl, Dallas ....KO 8

1961
Jan. 16—Joe Miceli, Dallas .... W 10
Feb. 13—Charlie Smith, Dallas.......... W 10
Apr. 4—Hilario Morales, Juarez ....L 10
June 8—Kenny Lane, Dallas .... D 10
Aug. 3—Luis Rodriguez, Dallas .... W 10
Sept. 14—Manuel Gonzales, Dallas ...... W 10
Dec. 2—Luis Rodriguez, Miami Beach ...L 10

1962
Jan. 23—Carlos Macias, Houston .....KO 4
Feb. 13—Kid Rayo, San Antonio .... W 10
Apr. 6—Hilario Morales, Dallas ......KO 5
May 11—Rudolph Bent, Dallas ....KO 8
Aug. 22—Joey Limas, Albuquerque ..... W 10
Sept. 8—Manuel Alvarez, Monterrey ....L 10
Nov. 15—Hubert Jackson, Dallas ......KO 1
Dec. 10—Puno de Oro, Dallas ....KO 2

1963
Feb. 11—Johnny Newman, Hollywood .KO 2
Feb. 25—Joey Parks, Wichita Falls .....KO 5
Apr. 20—Joe Stable, New York ....L 10
May 21—Stan Harrington, Honolulu .... W 10
May 30—Flory Olguin, Albuquerque ...KO 5

1964
May 1—Stan Hayward, Phila........ KO by 4
May 12—Tony Montano, Los Angeles ... W 10
June 9—Al Andrews, Las Vegas .... W 10
Aug. 10—Al Andrews, Fresno .... W 10
Aug. 27—Eddie Pace, Los Angeles ....L 10

1965
Mar. 15—Marshall Wells, Dallas ....KO 12
Apr. 23—Fortunato Manca, Rome ...... W 10
Dec. 13—Billy Collins, New Orleans .... W 12

1966
July 6—Luis Rodriguez, New Orleans .KO 15
Aug. 24—Manuel Gonzalez, New Orleans W 15
Won W.B.A. Welterweight Title
Sept. 27—Enrique Cruz, Corpus Christi .KO 7
Nov. 28—Jean Josselin, Dallas .... W 15
(Won Vacant World Welterweight Title)

1967
Jan. 24—Francois Pavilla, Paris .... D 10
Feb. 20—Ted Whitfield, Dallas.........KO 3
Mar. 31—Joe Harris, New York ....L 10
May 19—Francois Pavilla, Dallas ......KO 10
(Retained World Welterweight Title)
Oct. 2—Charlie Shipes, Oakland ......KO 8
(Retained World Welterweight Title)

1968
Feb. 5—Jean Josselin, Paris .... W 10
Mar. 15—Jimmy Lester, Oakland .... W 10
Apr. 16—Willie Ludick, Dallas ....KO 5
(Retained World Welterweight Title)
June 15—Joe Ngidi, Johannesburg .....KO 4
June 28—Willie Ludick,
Lourence Marques ....KO 3
July 5—Joseph Sishi, Durban ....KO 5
Oct. 21—Ramon LaCruz, New Orleans .. W 15
(Retained World Welterweight Title)

1969
Feb. 10—Don Cobbs, St. Louis ....KO 1
Apr. 18—Jose Napoles, Los Angeles . KO by 13
(Lost World Welterweight Title)
June 29—Jose Napoles, Mexico City . KO by 10
(World Welterweight Title)

1970
Jan. 28—Roberto Pena, Fort Worth ....KO 5
Mar. 3—Retired from the ring.
Aug. 11—Returned to ring as middleweight.
Aug. 11—Danny Perez, Dallas ....KO 7
Sept. 11—Fate Davis, Fort Worth .... W 10
Sept. 29—Harold Richardson, Dallas ..... W 10
Nov. 3—Billy Braggs, Milwaukee ......KO 6

1971
Mar. 17—Fate Davis, Akron .... D 10
May 24—Rafael Gutierrez, San Francisco .L 10
Dec. 2—Carlos Salinas, Sacramento ....L 10

1972
Sept. 2—Tap Tap Makathini, Durban ....L 10
Sept. 23—Joseph Hali, Port Elizabeth .... W 10
Oct. 5—Ezra Mzinyane, Capetown ....W 10

TB	KO	WD	WF	D	LD	LF	KOBY	ND	NC
80	30	32	0	4	11	0	3	0	0

CHARLIE SHIPES
Born, October 15, 1941, Jackson, Mississippi. Weight, 141-147 lbs. Height, 5 ft. 7 in. Managed by Dick Sadler.

1960
Oct. 11—Red Cunningham, Richmond, Calif. KO 1
Nov. 21—Charley Robinson, San Francisco .. W 4

1961
Jan. 9—Henry Berrera, San Francisco ..... W 4
May 2—Louis Uribe, Sacramento .... KO 1
June 26—Dorsey Williams, San Francisco ... W 4
July 25—Ed Hickman, Richmond, Calif. ..... W 6
Sept. 13—Bill Burk, Phoenix, Arizona ...... W 6
Sept. 21—Jose de la Rosa, Richmond .... KO 2
Oct. 23—Bobby Hurtt, Baltimore .... W 5
Nov. 28—Steve Mendoza, Santa Cruz ...... KO 4

1962
Jan. 16—Oscar Ortegon, Santa Cruz .... TD 1
May 22—Kid Rayo, Santa Rosa, Calif. ...... W 10
Aug. 7—Oscar Ortegon, Richmond .... KO 6

1963
Feb. 26—Mel Ferguson, Oakland, Calif. KO by 7
Apr. 26—Hachiro Ito, Tokyo, Japan .... KO 6
May 24—Sakuji Shinozawa, Tokyo, Japan .. KO 10
June 7—Noboru Saito, Tokyo, Japan ...... KO 4

1964
Oct. 28—Silky Shelton, Richmond .... W 12
(Won Vacant California State Welterweight Title)

1965
Mar. 2—Memo Lopez, Oakland, Calif. ..... KO 6
(Retained California State Welterweight Title)
Apr. 13—Silky Shelton, Richmond .... KO 7
July 26—Roberto Pena, Auckland, N.Z. ..... W 12
Aug. 16—Earl Nikora, Auckland, N.Z. .... W 12
Sept. 9—Gaspar Ortega, Modesto, Calif. .... W 10
Oct. 30—Al Andrews, Modesto, Calif. .... W 10

1966
Mar. 1—Al Andrews, Hayward, Calif. ...... W 12
(Retained California State Welterweight Title)
Apr. 14—Henry Aldridge, San Francisco ... KO 11
(Retained California State Welterweight Title)
May 13—Mauro Galvan, San Francisco ..... W 10
Sept. 23—Peter Schmidt, Sacramento .... KO 2
Oct. 26—Polo Corona, Modesto, Calif. ..... KO 7
Dec. 8—Percy Manning, Hayward .... KO 10
(Won California World Welterweight Title)

1967
Mar. 7—Jimmy Lester, Oakland .... D 10
May 10—Chico Santos, Reno, Nevada ..... KO 3
May 29—Andy Heilman, Oakland .... W 10
Oct. 2—Curtis Cokes, Oakland .... KO by 8
(For World Welterweight Title)
Dec. 13—Brad Silas, Oakland, Calif. .... W 10

1968
Jan. 24—Pulga Serrano, Oakland .... KO 1
Feb. 6—Manuel Gonzalez, Houston .... L 10
June 19—Jose Valenzuela, Oakland .... KO 6
Aug. 28—Mike Pusateri, Oakland .... TD 5
Oct. 14—Polo Corna, Phoenix, Arizona ...... W 10
Dec. 22—Mauricio Gazcon, Mexico City .... KO 9

621

1969

Mar.	28—Cassius Green, St. Louis	W	10
Apr.	2—Arnie Cota-Robles, Phoenix	KO	1
June	3—Raul Montoya, Juarez, Mexico	KO	1
July	1—Jess (Chucho) Garcia, Houston	W	10
Aug.	20—Johnny Brooks, Las Vegas	KO	1
Sept.	29—Alvin Phillips, New Orleans	L	10
Oct.	7—Johnny Brooks, Houston	KO	2
Oct.	22—Cipriano Hernandez, Las Vegas	W	10
Nov.	7—Mackeed Mofokeng, Johannesburg	L disq.	4

1970

June	17—Adolph Pruitt, Honolulu	KO by	5

TB	KO	WD	WF	D	LD	LF	KO BY	ND	NC
51	22	20	0	3	2	1	3	0	0

JOSE NAPOLES

Born, April 13, 1940, Santiago de Cuba, Oriente, Cuba.

1958

Aug.	2—Julio Rojas, Havana	KO	1
Oct.	11—Eurispides Guerra, Havana	KO	4
Nov.	29—Felix Pomares, Havana	KO	2

1959

Feb.	21—Armando Castillo, Havana	W	4
May	16—Juan Bacallao, Havana	KO	4
July	11—Cloroaldo Hernandez, Havana	KO	3
July	25—Cristobal Gonzalez, Havana	W	8
Aug.	22—Hilton Smith, Havana	L	10
Oct.	3—Chris Gonzalez, Havana	W	8

1960

Jan.	2—Isaac Espinosa, Havana	W	10
Feb.	20—Diwaldo Ventosa, Havana	L	10
May	21—Angel Garcia, Havana	W	10
July	2—Leslie Grant, Havana	W	10
Oct.	15—Tony Pardon, Havana	W	10
Nov.	26—Chico Morales, Havana	W	10

1961

Jan.	28—Guillermo Valdez, Havana	W	10
Mar.	19—Chico Morales, Havana	W	10
Mar.	29—Enrique Carabeo, Havana	KO	9

1962

July	21—Enrique Camarena, Mexico City	KO	2
Aug.	25—Kid Anahuac, Mexico City	KO	9
Sept.	29—Bobby Cervantes, Mexico City	KO	1
Nov.	10—Tony Perez, Los Mochis	W	10

1963

Jan.	5—Tony Perez, Hermosillo	L	10
Feb.	9—Jorge Gutierrez, Mexico City	KO	7
Mar.	30—Baby Vasquez, Mexico City	W	10
Apr.	27—Alfredo Urbina, Mexico City	L	10
May	27—Raul Soriano, Tijuana	KO	4
Aug.	19—Pulga Serrano, Tijuana	KO	10
Oct.	23—Francisco Cancio, Mexico City	KO	1
Nov.	16—Tony Perez, Mexico City	KO	3
Nov.	30—L. C. Morgan, Caracas	KO	7

1964

Mar.	1—Taketeru Yoshimoto, Tokyo	KO	1
Apr.	25—Alfredo Urbina, Mexico City	KO	1
June	22—Carlos Hernandez, Caracas	KO	7
Aug.	15—Eduardo Moreno, Culiacan	KO	5
Nov.	14—Alfredo Urbina, Mexico City	KO	3

1965

Jan.	1—Carlos Rios, Laguna	KO	7
Feb.	28—L. C. Morgan, Monterrey	KO	3
Mar.	25—Giordano Campari, Caracas	KO	2
Aug.	3—Eddie Perkins, Juarez	W	10
Dec.	11—Adolph Pruitt, Mexico City	KO	3

1966

Feb.	12—Johnny Santos, Mexico City	KO	3
Apr.	17—Al Grant, Reynosa	KO	4
July	27—Humberto Trottman, Juarez	KO	2
Aug.	22—L. C. Morgan, Reynosa	KO by	4
Oct.	30—Jimmy Fields, San Luis	KO	10
Dec.	17—Eugenio Espinoza, Mexico City	KO	6

1967

June	4—Johnny Brooks, Merida	KO	7
July	10—L. C. Morgan, Tijuana	KO	2
Sept.	11—Johnny DePeiza, Ciudad	KO	10
Dec.	3—Charlie Watson, Merida	KO	5

1968

Feb.	18—Mike Cruz, Tampico	KO	4
Apr.	29—Herbie Lee, Tijuana	KO	4
June	2—Peter Cobblah, Mexico City	W	10
June	14—Leroy Roberts, Los Angeles	KO	1
July	15—Eddie Pace, Tijuana	W	10
Nov.	5—Des Rea, Los Angeles	KO	5
Dec.	23—Lennox Beckles, Mexico City	KO	1

1969

Feb.	15—Fate Davis, Mexico City	KO	7
Apr.	18—Curtis Cokes, Los Angeles	KO	13
	(Won World Welterweight Title)		
June	29—Curtis Cokes, Mexico City	KO	10
	(Retained World Welterweight Title)		
Oct.	12—Emile Griffith, Los Angeles	W	15
	(Retained World Welterweight Title)		

1970

Feb.	15—Ernie Lopez, Los Angeles	KO	15
	(Retained World Welterweight Title)		
Aug.	14—Fighting Mack, Los Angeles	KO	3
Oct.	5—Pete Toro, New York	KO	9
Dec.	3—Billy Backus, Syracuse	KO by	4
	(Lost World Welterweight Title)		

1971

Mar.	27—Manuel Gonzalez, Mexico City	KO	6
June	4—Billy Backus, Los Angeles	KO	4
	(Regained World Welterweight Title)		
July	2—David Melendez, Mexico City	KO	5
Aug.	23—Jean Josselin, Los Angeles	KO	5
Oct.	17—Esteban Osuna, Mexico City	W	10
Dec.	14—Hedgemon Lewis, Los Angeles	W	15
	(Retained World Welterweight Title)		

1972

Mar.	28—Ralph Charles, London	KO	7
	(Retained World Welterweight Title)		
June	10—Adolph Pruitt, Monterrey	KO	2
	(Retained World Welterweight Title)		
Aug.	5—Edmundo Leite, Mexico City	KO	2

1973

Feb.	28—Ernie Lopez, Los Angeles	KO	7
	(Retained World Welterweight Title)		
June	23—Roger Menetrey, Grenoble	W	15
	(Retained World Welterweight Title)		
Sept.	22—Clyde Gray, Toronto	W	15
	(Retained World Welterweight Title)		

1974

Feb.	9—Carlos Monzon, Paris	KO by	7
	(World Middleweight Title)		
Aug.	3—Hedgemon Lewis, Mexico City	KO	9
	(Retained World Welterweight Title)		
Dec.	14—Horacio Saldano, Mexico City	KO	3
	(Retained World Welterweight Title)		

1975

Mar.	30—Armando Muniz, Acapulco	TW	12
	(Retained World Welterweight Title)		
July	12—Armando Muniz, Mexico City	W	15
	(Retained World Welterweight Title)		
Dec.	6—John Stracey, Mexico City	KO by	6
	(Lost World Welterweight Title)		

TB	KO	WD	WF	D	LD	LF	KO BY	ND	NC
84	54	21	1	0	4	0	4	0	0

BILLY BACKUS

Born, March 5, 1943, Canastota, New York. Weight, 146 lbs. Managed by Tony Graziano.

1962

Mar.	9—Randy Sanders, Totowa	W	4
Apr.	27—Sugar Lawson, Totowa	D	4
June	6—Steve Gellis, St. Jerome	W	6
June	22—Barney Garnez, Totowa	W	4
Nov.	24—Louis Ortiz Aponte, Totowa	L	4
Dec.	22—Mike Cortez, New York	D	4

1963

Jan.	23—Marcel Bizien, Paterson .... D	8
Feb.	27—Dick French, Worcester L	8
Aug.	2—Fernand Chretien, New Castle L	10
Dec.	19—Billy Anderson, Worcester L	8

1964

Feb.	1—Colin Fraser, Syracuse .... KO	6
Feb.	29—Dave Hilton, Syracuse .... KO	7
Apr.	18—Lou Anderson, Syracuse .... KO	5
May	19—Colin Fraser, Utica .... W	10
July	17—Genaro Soto, New York L	6
Oct.	30—Billy Anderson, Syracuse L	10

1965

Mar.	5—Rudy Richardson, Johnstown L	8

1966
(Inactive)

1967

Oct.	16—Tod Purtell, Worcester .... KO	1
Oct.	23—Ernie Robbins, Worcester .... KO	3
Nov.	24—Curtis Phillips, Syracuse .... KO	6
Nov.	30—Gene Herrick, Portland, Me. ..... KO	6

1968

Feb.	10—Juan Ramos, Syracuse .... W	10
Apr.	6—Danny Andrews, Syracuse .... W	10
May	19—Dick French, Syracuse .... KO	6
June	3—Percy Pugh, New Orleans L	10
July	30—Jerry Pellegrini, New Orleans ..... W	10
Sept.	14—Curtis Phillips, Syracuse .... KO	7
Oct.	7—Johnny Brooks, New Orleans ...... W	10
Nov.	12—Vince Shomo, Syracuse .... KO	8
Dec.	14—Freddie Cobb, Syracuse .... KO	5

1969

Jan.	24—Percy Pugh, Syracuse .... W	12
Mar.	17—C. L. Lewis, Syracuse .... KO	9
Apr.	25—Percy Pugh, Syracuse .... W	12
June	16—Percy Pugh, New Orleans L	15
July	21—Jerry Pellegrini, New Orleans L	10
Sept.	19—Jerry Pellegrini, Syracuse .... W	10
Oct.	31—Ricky Ortiz, Syracuse .... D	10

1970

Jan.	30—Ricky Ortiz, Syracuse .... KO	8
Mar.	24—Manny Burgo, Syracuse .... W	10
June	15—Frankie Steele, Syracuse .... W	10
July	22—Manuel Gonzalez, Syracuse .... W	10
Oct.	3—Denny Stiletto, Syracuse .... KO	8
Dec.	3—Jose Napoles, Syracuse .... KO	4
	(Won World Welterweight Title)	

1971

Jan.	24—Robert Williams, Syracuse .... W	10
Mar.	15—Robert Gallois, Paris .... W	10
June	4—Jose Napoles, Los Angeles ..... KO by	4
	(Lost World Welterweight Title)	
Dec.	10—Jose Gabino, Utica .... W	10

1972

Feb.	12—Pat Murphy, Syracuse .... KO	7
Apr.	14—Danny McAloon, Syracuse .... W	12
June	16—Hedgemon Lewis, Syracuse L	15
	(For New York State World Welterweight Title)	
Sept.	23—Dorman Crawford, Syracuse ...... KO	8
Dec.	8—Hedgemon Lewis, Syracuse L	15
	(For New York State World Welterweight Title)	

1973

Feb.	14—Jack Tillman, Baltimore L	12
Aug.	4—Miguel Barreto, New York L	12
Oct.	12—Al Romano, Syracuse .... KO	3
Dec.	9—Zovek Barajas, Los Angeles ... KO by	3

1974

Jan.	21—Roger Zami, Paris .... KO	9
Mar.	18—Roger Menetrey, Paris L	10
May	1—Jacques Kechichian, Paris .... KO	5
June	21—Eckhart Dagge, Berlin .... KO by	4

1975

Apr.	11—Rocky Mattioli, Melbourne .... KO by	5
Aug.	23—Marc Gervais, Binghamton .... KO	10

1976

Jan.	24—Pablo Rodriguez, Syracuse .... W	10
Apr.	3—Angel Garcia, Utica .... W	10
May	28—Jose Melendez, Latham .... W	10
Sept.	11—Pablo Rodriguez, Utica .... W	10
Oct.	—Tony Lopes, Utica .... KO	9

1977

Jan.	27—Justice Ortiz, Syracuse .... W	10
Apr.	8—Roy Barrientes, Syracuse .... W	10
June	3—Rafael Rodriguez, Syracuse .... W	12
Aug.	25—Joe Grier, Syracuse .... W	10
Nov.	19—Everaldo Costa Acevedo, Syracuse .. D	10

1978

May	20—Jose Cuevas, Los Angeles ..... KO by	1
	(For WBA Welterweight Title)	
July	30—Announced retirement.	

TB	KO	WD	WF	D	LD	LF	KO BY	ND	NC
73	22	26	0	5	15	0	5	0	0

HEDGEMON LEWIS

1966

May	13—Arnold Bush, Cincinnati .... KO	3
July	11—Larry Youngblood, Detroit .... W	4
Aug.	5—Larry Youngblood, Detroit .... KO	2
Aug.	29—Mike Belski, Detroit .... KO	1
Sept.	13—Arnold Blush, Detroit .... KO	3
Oct.	26—Calves DeJarenente, Akron ...... KO	1
Nov.	1—Charley Lewis, Grand Rapids ...... W	6
Nov.	20—Dawson Smith, Detroit .... W	6
Dec.	2—Phil Garcia, Los Angeles .... KO	3

1967

Jan.	29—Primus Williams, Newark, Ohio ... W	6
Mar.	18—Sam Ivory, Newark .... KO	5
Mar.	23—Charley Lewis, Louisville .... W	6
May	12—Primus Williams, Detroit .... W	8
Apr.	13—Melvin Fields, Los Angeles .... KO	3
June	15—Gary Broughton, Detroit .... W	8
June	26—Colin Fraser, Toronto .... W	8
Sept.	18—Carl Jordan, Detroit .... W	9
Oct.	19—Miguel Aguilar, Los Angeles ..... W	10

1968

Apr.	4—Ruben Rivers, Los Angeles .... KO	2
Apr.	25—Jose Valenzuela, Los Angeles .... KO	5
May	16—Bob Murray, Los Angeles .... W	10
June	13—Doug McLeod, Los Angeles ...... KO	2
July	18—Ernie Lopez, Los Angeles .... KO by	9
Sept.	3—Shelly Lyons, San Diego .... W	10
Sept.	19—Miguel Aguilar, Los Angeles ...... W	10
Oct.	31—Celso Olivas, Los Angeles .... KO	1

1969

Mar.	20—Miguel Hernandez, Los Angeles .. KO	1
Apr.	10—Oscar Alvarado, Los Angeles ..... W	10
July	10—Ernie Lopez, Los Angeles .... W	10
Oct.	4—Ernie Lopez, Los Angeles ..... KO by	10
Dec.	18—Don Cobbs, Detroit .... W	10

1970

May	13—Gustavo Garcia, Tijuana .... KO	5
May	26—Ricky Ortiz, Woodland Hills ...... KO	3
June	19—Servio Balboa, Woodland Hills ... KO	3
July	7—Raul Rodriguez, Tijuana .... TW	2
Aug.	13—Chucho Almazan, Los Angeles ... KO	8
Oct.	8—Raul Soriano, Los Angeles .... W	10
Oct.	31—Manuel Avitia, Woodland Hills ... KO	8

1971

Jan.	12—Adolph Pruitt, Honolulu L	10
Apr.	10—Pepper Romero, Pocatello .... TD	3
May	17—Percy Pugh, New Orleans .... KO	8
June	28—Arturo Lomeli, Tijuana .... KO	6
July	31—Ariel Green, Santa Monica ...... KO	6
Sept.	22—Jose Gabino, Anaheim .... KO	6
Dec.	14—Jose Napoles, Los Angeles L	15
	(For World Welterweight Title)	

1972

May	8—Ruben Vasquez, Los Angeles ...... W	10
June	16—Billy Backus, Syracuse .... W	15
	(Won New York World Welterweight Title)	
July	21—Mario Marquez, San Diego .... KO	2
Oct.	13—Jose Luis Baltazar, San Diego ..... W	10
Dec.	8—Billy Backus, Syracuse .... W	15
	(Retained New York World Welterweight Title)	

1973

Mar.	31—Ruben Vasquez, San Diego	KO	6
Oct.	13—Chucho Garcia, Los Angeles	W	10
Nov.	7—Rudy Barro, Sacramento	KO	3
Dec.	10—Johnny Gant, New York	W	10

1974

Mar.	2—Jose Miranda, San Diego	W	10
Apr.	28—Felipe Vaca, Mexicali	KO	4
Aug.	3—Jose Napoles, Mexico City	KO by	9

(For World Welterweight Title)

| Dec. | 3—Armando Muniz, Los Angeles | L | 10 |

1975

Mar.	19—Rafael Rodriguez, Minneapolis	W	10
May	7—Rafael Rodriguez, Minneapolis	W	10
Nov.	22—Carlos Palomino, Los Angeles	D	10
Dec.	12—Harold Weston, New York	D	10

1976

| Mar. | 20—John Stracey, London | KO by | 10 |

(For World Welterweight Title)

TB	KO	WD	WF	D	LD	LF	KO BY	ND	NC
63	26	27	0	3	3	0	4	0	0

ANGEL ESPADA

Born, February 2, 1948, Salinas, Puerto Rico.
Weight, 147 lbs. Height, 5 ft. 9 in.

1967

Mar.	11—Jose Markquez, San Juan	L	6
Apr.	8—Luis Vinales, Bayamen	D	6
June	4—Luis Vinales, San Juan	D	6
July	10—Chris Fernandez, San Juan	L	6

1968

Jan.	10—Chris Fernandez, San Juan	D	10
Apr.	1—Linford Contreras, San Juan	KO	1
Apr.	15—Embijao Carrion, San Juan	KO	3
Sept.	27—Jimmy Robertson, Los Angeles	L	6

1969

Apr.	19—Bobby Hughes, San Juan	W disq.	6
June	7—Enrique Paz, San Juan	KO	5
July	21—Roscoe Bell, San Juan	KO	2
Aug.	2—Ingemar Jones, San Juan	KO	4
Sept.	27—KO Kid, San Juan	W	8
Nov.	1—Roland Pryor, San Juan	W	10
Nov.	—Jerry Graci, San Juan	W	10
Dec.	12—Faye Davis, San Juan	W	10

1970

Feb.	27—Frankie Lewis, San Juan	W	10
Mar.	21—Raul Rodriguez, Mexico City	KO	2
Mar.	28—Juan Ramos, Ponce	KO	5
May	10—Frank Lewis, Ponce	KO	6
Aug.	5—Julio Cruz, San Juan	KO	2
Oct.	10—Pollo Gabino, San Juan	KO	3
Nov.	7—Matt Donovan, San Juan	L	10

1971

Apr.	12—Edmundo Leite, New York	W	10
July	10—Dino del Cid, San Juan	KO	3
Aug.	29—Manny Gonzalez, San Juan	W	10
Oct.	18—Eddie Perkins, San Juan	L	10

1972

June	12—Dario Hidalgo, New York	L	10
Oct.	24—Alfonso Aguirre, San Antonio	KO	3
Dec.	12—Luis Cariaco, San Juan	KO	9

1973

Jan.	17—Roscoe Bell, Miami Beach	KO	2
Mar.	10—Dario Hidalgo, San Juan	W	10
May	29—Jack Tillman, Baltimore	KO	8
July	14—Al Cook, San Juan	KO	2
Sept.	8—Jimmy Hamm, Panama City	KO	1
Nov.	9—Mario Saurennann, San Juan	W	10

1974

Apr.	15—Alvin Anderson, San Juan	KO	2
May	10—David Oropeza, San Juan	KO	4
July	29—Armando Muniz, San Juan	W	10
Nov.	15—Hector Rivas, San Juan	KO	2

1975

Mar.	15—Luis Acosta, Caracas	L	10
Apr.	13—Luis Acosta, San Juan	W	10

624

June	28—Clyde Gray, San Juan	W	15

(Won Vacant WBA Welterweight Title)

| Oct. | 11—Johnny Gant, Ponce | W | 15 |

(Retained WBA Welterweight Title)

1976

Apr.	27—Alfonso Hayman, San Juan	KO	8
July	17—Pipino Cuevas, Mexicali	KO by	2

(Lost WBA Welterweight Title)

| Sept. | 10—Augustin Estrada, San Juan | KO | 4 |

1977

May	21—John Morgan, San Juan	KO	2
Aug.	27—Ray Hammond, San Juan	W	10
Nov.	19—Pipino Cuevas, San Juan	KO by	11

(For WBA Welterweight Title)

1978

Sept.	9—Al Hocker, San Juan	KO	2
Oct.	28—Kevin Moefield, San Juan	KO	4

1979

Feb.	18—Sam Hailstock, San Juan	KO	9
June	16—Fitzroy Edward, San Juan	KO	5
Dec.	8—Pipino Cuevas, Los Angeles	KO by	10

(For WBA Welterweight Title)

1980

| Mar. | 2—Thomas Hearns, Detroit | KO by | 4 |

(For Vacant USBA Welterweight Title)

TB	KO	WD	WF	D	LD	LF	KO BY	ND	NC
56	26	15	1	3	7	0	4	0	

JOHN STRACEY

Born, September 22, 1950, Bethnal Green, London.
Competed as lightweight in 1968 Olympic Games
1969 British ABA Light Welterweight Champion

1969

Sept.	17—Santos Martins, London	KO	2
Oct.	2—Ron Clifford, London	KO	2
Nov.	18—Ray Opoku, London	KO	3
Dec.	9—Bryn Lewis, London	KO	6

1970

Jan.	20—Tommy Carson, London	KO	7
Feb.	10—Tei Dovie, London	KO	3
Mar.	17—Bernard Martin, London	KO	3
Apr.	21—Harri Pittulainen, London	KO	6
May	12—David Pesenti, London	W	8
Sept.	29—Billy Seasman, London	KO	5
Oct.	6—Willie Rea, London	KO	3
Dec.	8—Ferdinand Ahumibe, London	KO	4

1971

Jan.	19—Teddy Cooper, London	WF	5
Feb.	23—Yvon Mariolle, London	KO	6
Mar.	16—Dante Pelaez, London	W	8
May	4—Ait Bouzid Elmenceur, London	W	8
Oct.	5—Frankie Lewis, London	D	8
Oct.	27—Dave Wyatt, London	KO	3
Nov.	16—Guy Vercoutter, London	KO	7

1972

Jan.	25—Yvan Mariolle, London	KO	4
Feb.	15—Bernie Terrell, London	KO	2
Mar.	7—Des Rea, London	KO	2
Apr.	4—Ricky Porter, London	W	8
Apr.	25—Marshall Butler, London	L	8
May	22—Antonio Torres, Manchester	KO	6
June	6—Joe Yekinni, London	KO	2
Oct.	10—Les Pearson, London	KO	2

(Final Elim., British Welterweight Title)

| Oct. | 31—Bobby Arthur, London | LF | 7 |

(For Vacant British Welterweight Title)

| Dec. | 5—David Melendez, London | KO | 7 |

1973

Jan.	15—Otha Tyson, Nottingham	KO	3
Feb.	14—Danny McAloon, Las Vegas	W	10
Mar.	13—Jose Peterson, London	W	8
May	9—Irish Pat Murphy, London	KO	5
June	5—Bobby Arthur, London	KO	4
Sept.	10—Jose Melendez, London	KO	3
Oct.	30—Urban Baptiste, London	KO	4

Nov. 12—Marc Gervais, London .... KO 4
Dec. 11—Cubby Jackson, London .... KO by 3
1974
Mar. 26—Jackie Tillman, London .... KO 4
Apr. 23—Vern Mason, London .... KO 4
May 27—Roger Menetrey, Paris .... KO 8
(Won European Welterweight Title)
Oct. 1—Tony Garcia, London .... KO 2
Oct. 29—Ernie Lopez, London .... KO 7
1975
Apr. 29—Max Hebeisen, London .... KO 6
(Retained European Welterweight Title)
June 3—Ruben Vasquez, London .... KO 8
Sept. 30—Keith Averette, London ..... W disq. 8
Dec. 6—Jose Napoles, Mexico City .... KO 6
(Won World Welterweight Title)
1976
Mar. 20—Hedgemon Lewis, London .... KO 10
(Retained World Welterweight Title)
June 22—Carlos Palomino, London ...... KO by 12
(Lost World Welterweight Title)
1977
Mar. 29—Dave Green, London .... KO by 10
1978
May 23—George Warusfel, Islington .... KO 9

TB	KO	WD	WF	D	LD	LF	KO BY	ND	NC
51	37	6	2	1	1	1	3	0	0

CARLOS PALOMINO
Born, August 10, 1949, San Luis, Mexico.
1972
Sept. 14—Javier Martinez, Los Angeles ...... W 4
Oct. 5—Javier Martinez, Los Angeles ...... W 4
Nov. 16—Ted Liggett, Los Angeles .... D 4
1973
Jan. 19—Tim Walker, San Bernardino ..... W 6
Feb. 1—Ramon Solitario, Los Angeles .... KO 3
Mar. 1—Rosario Zavala, Los Angeles ..... W 6
Mar. 29—Lao Barriente, Los Angeles .... W 6
Apr. 2—Tommy Coulson, Los Angeles ..... W 6
1974
May 3—David Arrellano, San Diego .... W 8
May 23—Juan Garza, Los Angeles .... KO 3
June 14—Andy Price, San Diego .... L 10
Oct. 10—Nelson Ruiz, Los Angeles .... KO 6
Oct. 24—Jose Miranda, Los Angeles .... KO 6
Dec. 10—Tommy Howard, Los Angeles ..... W 10
1975
Feb. 13—Zovek Barajas, Los Angeles .... D 10
Mar. 27—Zovek Barajas, Los Angeles .... KO 9
May 23—Roger Buckskin, Los Angeles ..... W 10
July 19—Johnny Pinedo, Los Angeles ...... KO 2
Oct. 25—Eddie Alexander, Los Angeles .... KO 5
Nov. 22—Hedgemon Lewis, Los Angeles ..... D 10
1976
Feb. 12—Mike Avans, Los Angeles .... W 10
Apr. 29—Tosh Nambu, Los Angeles .... KO 2
June 22—John Stracey, London .... KO 12
(Won World Welterweight Title)
1977
Jan. 22—Armando Muniz, Los Angeles .... KO 15
(Retained World Welterweight Title)
June 14—David Green, London .... KO 11
(Retained World Welterweight Title)
Sept. 13—Everaldo Costa Azevedo, Los Angeles W 15
(Retained WBC Welterweight Title)
Dec. 10—Jose Palacios, Los Angeles .... KO 13
(Retained World Welterweight Title)
1978
Feb. 11—Ryu Sorimachi, Las Vegas .... KO 7
(Retained World Welterweight Title)
Mar. 18—Mimoun Mohatar, Las Vegas ..... KO 9
(Retained World Welterweight Title)
May 27—Armando Muniz, Los Angeles ...... W 15
(Retained World Welterweight Title)

1979
Jan. 14—Wilfred Benitez, San Juan .... L 15
June 22—Roberto Duran, New York .... L 10

TB	KO	WD	WF	D	LD	LF	KO BY	ND	NC
33	15	12	0	3	3	0	0	0	0

PIPINO CUEVAS
(Isidro Pipino Cuevas Gonzalez)
Born, December 27, 1957, Mexico City, Mexico.
1972
Jan. 1—Jose Arias, Mexico City .... KO 4
Mar. 4—Mario Roman, Mexico City .... L 6
May 24—Rielero Rodriguez, Mexico City ... KO 2
July 22—Paco Tapia, Mexico City .... KO 2
Aug. 19—Juan Pablo Oropeza, Mexico City ... L 8
Dec. 6—Raul Martinez, Mexico City ...... KO 1
1973
Feb. 28—Sergio Alego, Mexico City .... KO 4
May 11—Memo Cruz, Mexico City .... L 10
Aug. 3—Jose Figueroa, Mexico City .... KO 3
Oct. 6—Octavio Amparan, Mexico City ... KO 7
Nov. 24—Eleazar Delgado, Mexico City ...... L 10
1974
May 11—Salvador Ruvalcaba, Mexico City KO 1
June 12—Sugar Sanders, Mexico City ..... KO 1
Aug. 21—Jose Luis Pena, Mexico City ..... KO 1
Oct. 26—Samuel Garcia, Mexico City ...... KO 3
1975
Jan. 25—Ruben Vasquez, Mexico City ..... W 10
July 12—Carlos Obregon, Mexico City ..... W 10
Sept. 27—Jose Palacios, Mexico City ...... KO 10
(Won Mexican Welterweight Title)
1976
Apr. 3—Rafael Piamonte, Mexico City .... KO 1
Apr. 13—Relinquished Mexican welterweight title.
June 2—Andy Price, Los Angeles .... L 10
July 17—Angel Espada, Mexicali .... KO 2
(Won WBA Welterweight Title)
Oct. 27—Shoji Tsujimoto, Kanazawa, Japan KO 6
(Retained WBA Welterweight Title)
1977
Mar. 12—Miguel Campanino, Mexico City .. KO 2
(Retained WBA Welterweight Title)
Aug. 6—Clyde Gray, Los Angeles .... KO 2
(Retained WBA Welterweight Title)
Nov. 19—Angel Espada, San Juan .... KO 11
(Retained WBA Welterweight Title)
1978
Mar. 4—Harold Weston, Los Angeles ...... KO 9
(Retained WBA Welterweight Title)
May 20—Billy Backus, Los Angeles .... KO 1
(Retained WBA Welterweight Title)
Sept. 9—Pete Ranzany, Sacramento .... KO 2
(Retained WBA Welterweight Title)
1979
Jan. 29—Scott Clark, Los Angeles .... KO 2
(Retained WBA Welterweight Title)
July 30—Randy Shields, Chicago .... W 15
(Retained WBA Welterweight Title)
Dec. 8—Angel Espada, Los Angeles .... KO 10
(Retained WBA Welterweight Title)
1980
Apr. 6—Harold Volbrecht, Houston .... KO 5
(Retained WBA Welterweight Title)
Aug. 2—Thomas Hearns, Detroit .... KO by 2
(Lost WBA Welterweight Title)

TB	KO	WD	WF	D	LD	LF	KO BY	ND	NC
33	24	3	0	0	5	0	1	0	0

WILFRED BENITEZ
Born, September 12, 1958, Bronx, New York.
1973
Nov. 22—Hiram Santiago, San Juan .... KO 1
Nov. 30—Jesse Torres, St. Martin .... KO 2

625

1974

Jan.	7—Hector Amadis, San Juan	KO	4
Jan.	26—Joe "Hawk" York, St. Martin	KO	2
Feb.	18—Roberto Flanders, San Juan	KO	4
Apr.	1—Victor Mangual, San Juan	W	8
Apr.	30—Juan Disla, San Juan	KO	2
May	11—Sonny Lake, St. Martin	KO	1
June	21—Ives St. Jean, St. Martin	KO	1
June	26—Carlos Crispin, San Juan	KO	3
Aug.	31—"Easy Boy" Lake, St. Martin	KO	5
Sept.	16—Al Hughes, New York	W	8
Oct.	25—Terry Summerhays, New York	KO	6
Dec.	2—Lawrence Hafey, New York	W	8

1975

Jan.	4—Francisco Rodriguez, San Juan	KO	7
Feb.	8—Santiago Rosa, San Juan	KO	4
Mar.	31—Wilbur Seales, San Juan	KO	4
May	5—Santos Solis, San Juan	W	10
June	9—Angel Robinson Garcia, San Juan	W	10
June	28—Joe Henry, San Juan	KO	8
Aug.	1—Eyue Jeudy, St. Martin	KO	4
Sept.	1—Marcelino Alicia, San Juan	KO	2
Oct.	20—Omar Piton, New York	KO	6
Dec.	13—Chris Fernandez, San Juan	W	10

1976

Mar.	6—Antonio Cervantes, San Juan	W	15
	(Won World Junior Welterweight Title)		
May	31—Emiliano Villa, San Juan	W	15
	(Retained World Junior Welterweight Title)		
Oct.	16—Tony Petronelli, San Juan	KO	3
	(Retained World Junior Welterweight Title)		

1977

Feb.	2—Harold Weston, New York	D	10
Mar.	6—Mel Dennis, Marion	W	8
	(U.S. Championship Tournament)		
June	2—Roberto Gonzalez, St. Thomas	KO	1
July	1—"Easy Boy" Lake, St. Thomas	KO	1
Aug.	3—Guerrero Chavez, New York	KO	15
	(Retained World Junior Welterweight Title)		
Nov.	18—Bruce Curry, New York	W	10

1978

Feb.	4—Bruce Curry, New York	W	10
Aug.	25—Randy Shields, New York	KO	6
Dec.	5—Vernon Lewis, New York	W	10

1979

Jan.	14—Carlos Palomino, San Juan	W	15
	(Won World Welterweight Title)		
Mar.	25—Harold Weston, San Juan	W	15
	(Retained World Welterweight Title)		
Nov.	30—Ray Leonard, Las Vegas	KO by	15
	(Lost World Welterweight Title)		

1980

Mar.	9—Johnny Turner, Miami Beach	KO	9
Aug.	1—Tony Chiaverini, Las Vegas	KO	8
Dec.	12—Pete Ranzany, Sacramento	W	10

TB	KO	WD	WF	D	LD	LF	KO BY	ND	NC
42	25	15	0	1	0	0	1	0	0

(SUGAR) RAY LEONARD

Born, May 17, 1956, Wilmington, N.C. 1976
Olympic Games Light Welterweight Gold Medalist.

1977

Feb.	5—Luis Vega, Baltimore	W	6
May	14—Willie Rodriguez, Baltimore	W	6
June	10—Vinnie DeBarros, Hartford	KO	3
Sept.	24—Frank Santore, Baltimore	KO	5
Nov.	5—Augustin Estrada, Las Vegas	KO	5
Dec.	17—Hector Diaz, Washington D.C.	KO	2

1978

Feb.	4—Rocky Ramon, Baltimore	W	8
Mar.	1—Art McKnight, Dayton	KO	7
Mar.	19—Javier Muniz, New Haven	KO	1
Apr.	13—Bobby Haymon, Landover	KO	3
May	13—Randy Milton, Utica	KO	8
June	3—Rafael Rodriguez, Baltimore	W	10
July	18—Dick Eckland, Boston	W	10
Sept.	9—Floyd Mayweather, Providence	KO	9

Oct.	6—Randy Shields, Baltimore	W	10
Nov.	3—Bernardo Prada, Portland, Me.	W	10
Dec.	9—Armando Muniz, Springfield	KO	6

1979

Jan.	11—Johnny Gant, Landover	KO	8
Feb.	11—Fernand Marcotte, Miami Beach	KO	8
Mar.	24—Daniel Gonzales, Tucson	KO	1
Apr.	21—Adolfo Viruet, Las Vegas	W	10
May	20—Marcos Geraldo, New Orleans	W	10
June	24—Tony Chiaverini, Las Vegas	KO	4
Aug.	12—Pete Ranzany, Las Vegas	KO	4
	(Won NABF Welterweight Title)		
Sept.	28—Andy Price, Las Vegas	KO	1
	(Retained NABF Welterweight Title)		
Nov.	30—Wilfred Benitez, Las Vegas	KO	15
	(Won World Welterweight Title)		

1980

Mar.	31—Dave (Boy) Green, Landover	KO	4
	(Retained World Welterweight Title)		
June	20—Roberto Duran, Montreal	L	15
	(Lost World Welterweight Title)		
Nov.	25—Roberto Duran, New Orleans	KO	8
	(Regained World Welterweight Title)		

TB	KO	WD	WF	D	LD	LF	KO BY	ND	NC
29	19	9	0	0	1	0	0	0	0

ROBERTO DURAN

Born, June 16, 1951, Guarare, Panama. Weight,
124-147 lbs. Height, 5 ft. 7 in. Managed by Carlos Eleta.

1967

Mar.	8—Carlos Mendoza, Colon	W	4
Apr.	4—Manuel Jimenez, Colon	KO	1
May	14—Juan Gondola, Colon	KO	1
May	30—Eduardo Morales, Panama City	KO	1
Aug.	10—Enrique Jacobo, Panama City	KO	1

1968

Jan.	12—Uche De Leon, Panama City	KO	2
Feb.	8—Leroy Cargill, Panama City	KO	2
Mar.	16—Cafe Howard, Panama City	KO	1
Apr.	2—Alberto Brands, Panama City	KO	4
Sept.	4—Eduardo Fruto, Panama City	W	8

1969

Mar.	12—Jacinto Garcia, Panama City	KO	5
May	3—Adolfo Osses, Panama City	KO	7
July	16—Serafin Garcia, Panama City	KO	5
Aug.	15—Luis Patino, Panama City	KO	7

1970

Apr.	5—Felipe Torres, Mexico City	W	10
May	16—Ernesto Marcel, Panama City	W	10
July	10—Clemente Mucino, Colon	KO	6
Sept.	5—Marvin Castanedas, Puerto Armuelles	KO	1

1971

Jan.	10—Nacho Castanedas, Panama City	KO	4
Mar.	5—Jose Angel Herrera, Mexico City	KO	6
Apr.	4—Jose Acosta, Panama City	KO	1
May	29—Lloyd Marshall, Panama City	KO	6
July	18—Fermin Soto, Monterrey	KO	3
Sept.	13—Benny Huertas, New York	KO	1
Oct.	1—Hiroshi Kokayashi, Panama City	KO	7

1972

Jan.	15—Angel Robinson Garcia, Panama City	W	10
Mar.	10—Francisco Munoz, Panama City	KO	1
June	26—Ken Buchanan, New York	KO	13
	(Won World Lightweight Title)		
Sept.	2—Greg Potter, Panama City	KO	1
Oct.	29—Lupe Ramirez, Panama City	KO	1
Nov.	17—Esteban DeJesus, New York	L	10

1973

Jan.	20—Jimmy Robertson, Panama City	KO	5
	(Retained World Lightweight Title)		
Feb.	23—Juan Medina, Los Angeles	KO	7
Mar.	17—Javier Ayala, Los Angeles	W	10
Apr.	14—Gerardo Ferrat, Panama City	KO	2
June	2—Hector Thompson, Panama City	KO	8
	(Retained World Lightweight Title)		

Aug.	4—Doc McClendon, San Juan .... W	10
Sept.	8—Ishimatsu Suzuki, Panama City .. KO	10
	(Retained World Lightweight Title)	
Dec.	1—Tony Garcia, Santiago .... KO	2

1974

Jan.	21—Leonard Tavarez, Paris .... KO	4
Feb.	16—Armando Mendoza, Panama City KO	3
Mar.	16—Esteban DeJesus, Panama City ... KO	11
	(Retained World Lightweight Title)	
July	6—Flash Gallego, Panama City ...... KO	5
Sept.	2—Hector Matta, San Juan .... W	10
Oct.	10—Alberto Vanegas, Panama City ... KO	1
Oct.	31—Jose Vasquez, San Jose .... KO	2
Dec.	21—Masataka Takayama, San Jose ... KO	1
	(Retained World Lightweight Title)	

1975

Feb.	15—Andres Salgado, Panama City .... KO	1
Mar.	2—Ray Lampkin, Panama City ...... KO	14
	(Retained World Lightweight Title)	
June	3—Jose Peterson, Miami Beach ..... KO	1
Aug.	2—Pedro Mendoza, Managua .... KO	1
Sept.	13—Alirio Acuna, Chitre .... KO	3
Sept.	30—Edwin Viruet, Uniondale .... W	10
Dec.	14—Leonico Ortiz, San Juan .... KO	15
	(Retained World Lightweight Title)	

1976

May	4—Saoul Mamby, Miami Beach .... W	10
May	22—Lou Bizzarro, Erie .... KO	14
	(Retained World Lightweight Title)	
July	31—Emilliano Villa, Panama City .... KO	9
Oct.	15—Alvaro Rojas, Hollywood, Fla. .... KO	1
	(Retained World Lightweight Title)	

1977

Jan.	29—Vilomar Fernandez, Miami Beach KO	13
	(Retained World Lightweight Title)	
May	16—Javier Muniz, Landover .... W	10
Aug.	6—Bernandro Diaz, Panama City .... KO	1
Sept.	17—Edwin Viruet, Philadelphia .... W	15
	(Retained World Lightweight Title)	

1978

Jan.	21—Esteban DeJesus, Las Vegas .. KO	12
	(Retained World Lightweight Title)	
Apr.	27—Adolph Viruet, New York ...... W	10
Sept.	1—Ezequiel Obando, Panama City KO	2
Dec.	8—Monroe Brooks, New York .... KO	8

1979

Apr.	8—Jimmy Heair, Las Vegas .... W	10
June	22—Carlos Palomino, New York ......W	10
Sept.	28—Zeferino Gonzalez, Las Vegas ...... W	10

1980

Jan.	13—Josef Nsubuga, Las Vegas .... KO	4
Feb.	24—Wellington Wheatley, Las Vegas KO	6
June	20—Ray Leonard, Montreal .... W	15
	(Won World Welterweight Title)	

Nov.	25—Ray Leonard, New Orleans .... KO by	8
	(Lost World Welterweight Title)	

TB	KO	WD	WF	D	LD	LF	KO BY	ND	NC
73	55	16	0	0	1	0	1	0	0

THOMAS (HIT MAN) HEARNS
(The Motor City Cobra)
Born, October 18, 1958, Memphis, Tenn. Weight, 147 lbs. Height, 6 ft. 2½ in. Managed by Emanuel Steward.

1977

Nov.	25—Jerome Hill, Detroit .... KO	2
Dec.	7—Jerry Strickland, Mt. Clemens .... KO	3
Dec.	16—Willie Wren, Detroit .... KO	3

1978

Jan.	29—Anthony House, Detroit .... KO	2
Feb.	10—Robert Adams, Detroit .... KO	3
Feb.	17—Billy Goodman, Detroit .... KO	2
Mar.	17—Ray Fields, Detroit .... KO	2
Mar.	31—Tyrone Phelps, Saginaw .... KO	3
June	8—Jimmy Rothwell, Detroit .... KO	1
July	20—Raul Aguirre, Detroit .... KO	3
Aug.	3—Eddie Marcelle, Detroit .... KO	2
Sept.	7—Bruce Finch, Detroit .... KO	3
Oct.	26—Pedro Rojas, Detroit .... KO	1
Dec.	9—Rudy Barro, Detroit .... KO	4

1979

Jan.	13—Clyde Gray, Detroit .... KO	10
Jan.	31—Sammy Ruckard, Detroit .... KO	8
Mar.	3—Segundo Murillo, Detroit .... KO	8
Apr.	3—Alfonso Hayman, Philadelphia ..... W	10
May	20—Harold Weston Jr., Las Vegas .... KO	6
June	28—Bruce Curry, Detroit .... KO	3
Aug.	23—Mao DeLa Rosa, Detroit .... KO	2
Sept.	22—Jose Figueroa, Los Angeles .... KO	3
Oct.	18—Saensak Muangsurin, Detroit .... KO	3
Nov.	30—Mike Colbert, New Orleans .... W	10

1980

Feb.	3—Fighting Jim Richards, Las Vegas KO	3
Mar.	2—Angel Espada, Detroit .... KO	4
	(Won Vacant USBA Welterweight Title)	
Mar.	31—Santiago Valdez, Las Vegas ...... KO	1
May	3—Eddie Gazo, Detroit .... KO	1
Aug.	2—Pipino Cuevas, Detroit .... KO	2
	(Won WBA Welterweight Title)	
Nov.	29—William (Caveman) Lee, Los Angeles .... Exh.	
Dec.	6—Luis Primera, Detroit .... KO	6
	(Retained WBA Welterweight Title)	

TB	KO	WD	WF	D	LD	LF	KO BY	ND	NC
30	28	2	0	0	0	0	0	0	0

JUNIOR WELTERWEIGHTS

MYRON (PINKEY) MITCHELL	1922-1926	PAUL FUJII	1967-1968
MUSHY CALLAHAN	1926-1930	NICOLINO LOCHE	1968-1972
JACK (KID) BERG	1930-1931	*PEDRO ADIGUE (WBC)*	*1968-1970*
TONY CANZONERI	1931-1932	*BRUNO ARCARI (WBC)*	*1970-1974*
JOHNNY JADICK	1932-1933	ALFONSO FRAZER	1972
BATTLING SHAW	1933	ANTONIO CERVANTES	1972-1976
TONY CANZONERI	1933	*PERICO FERNANDEZ (WBC)*	*1974-1975*
BARNEY ROSS	1933-1935	*SAENSAK MUANGSURIN (WBC)*	*1975-1976*
TIPPY LARKIN	1946	WILFRED BENITEZ	1976-1979
CARLOS ORTIZ	1959-1960	*MIGUEL VELASQUEZ (WBC)*	*1976*
DUILIO LOI	1960-1962	*SAENSAK MUANGSURIN (WBC)*	*1976-1978*
EDDIE PERKINS	1962	*ANTONIO CERVANTES (WBA)*	*1977-1979*
DUILIO LOI	1962-1963	*SANG-HYUN KIM (WBC)*	*1978-1980*
ROBERTO CRUZ (WBA)	*1963*	ANTONIO CERVANTES	1979-1980
EDDIE PERKINS	1963-1965	*SAOUL MAMBY (WBC)*	*1980-*
CARLOS HERNANDEZ	1965-1966	AARON PRYOR	1980
SANDRO LOPOPOLO	1966-1967		

Claimants not generally recognized are in *italics*.

WORLD JUNIOR WELTERWEIGHT CHAMPIONSHIP BOUTS

Date	Winner	Weight	Loser	Weight	Result	Time KO	Site	Referee
7/9/23	**Pinkey MITCHELL**	139	**Nate GOLDMAN**	140	ND 10		Baker Bowl, Philadelphia, Pa.	
9/21/26	**Mushy CALLAHAN**		**Pinkey MITCHELL**		10		Arena, Vernon, California	
3/14/27	**Mushy CALLAHAN**	138½	**Andy DiVODI**	139½	KO 2	2:13	Madison Square Garden, New York	Jim Crowley
5/31/27	**Mushy CALLAHAN**	139½	**Spug MYERS**	137½	10		Wrigley Field, Chicago, Ill.	Jim Gardner
5/28/29	**Mushy CALLAHAN**	139¼	**Fred MAHAN**	140	KO 3		Olympic Auditorium, Los Angeles	
2/18/30	**Jack (Kid) BERG**	137¼	**Mushy CALLAHAN**	137¾	TKO 11		Royal Albert Hall, London	Ted Broadribb
4/4/30	**Jack (Kid) BERG**	139¼	**Joe GLICK**	137¼	unan 10		Madison Square Garden, New York	Jack Dorman
5/29/30	**Jack (Kid) BERG**	139	**Al DELMONT**	136	TKO 4		Dreamland Park, Newark, N.J.	
6/11/30	**Jack (Kid) BERG**	138¼	**Herman PERLICK**	138½	10		Queensboro Stadium, New York	Johnny McAvoy
9/3/30	**Jack (Kid) BERG**	136	**Buster BROWN**	134	10		Dreamland Park, Newark, N.J.	John Healy
9/18/30	**Jack (Kid) BERG**	136	**Joe GLICK**	139	10		Queensboro Stadium, New York	Arthur Donovan
10/10/30	**Jack (Kid) BERG**	135¾	**Billy PETROLLE**	137	10		Madison Square Garden, New York	Arthur Donovan
1/23/31	**Jack (Kid) BERG**	138¼	**Goldie HESS**	137¾	unan 10		Chicago Stadium, Illinois	
1/30/31	**Jack (Kid) BERG**	138½	**Herman PERLICK**	139	unan 10		Madison Square Garden, New York	Johnny McAvoy
4/10/31	**Jack (Kid) BERG**	138	**Billy WALLACE**	137	unan 10		Olympia, Detroit, Michigan	Elmer McClelland
4/24/31	**Tony CANZONERI**	132	**Jack (Kid) BERG**	134¼	KO 3	2:23	Chicago Stadium, Illinois	Phil Collins
7/13/31	**Tony CANZONERI**		**Cecil PAYNE**		10		Wrigley Field, Los Angeles	Abe Roth
9/10/31	**Tony CANZONERI**	131¾	**Jack (Kid) BERG**	134½	unan 15		Polo Grounds, New York, N.Y.	Patsy Haley
10/29/31	**Tony CANZONERI**	132	**Phillie GRIFFIN**	138¾	unan 10		Armory, Newark, New Jersey	John Healy
11/20/31	**Tony CANZONERI**	132	**Kid CHOCOLATE**	127½	split 15		Madison Square Garden, New York	Willie Lewis
1/18/32	**Johnny JADICK**	136½	**Tony CANZONERI**	132½	10		Arena, Philadelphia, Pa.	Leo Houck
7/18/32	**Johnny JADICK**	135¼	**Tony CANZONERI**	133	10		Baker Bowl, Philadelphia, Pa.	Joe McGuigan
2/20/33	**Battling SHAW**	136	**Johnny JADICK**	135	maj 10		Coliseum Arena, New Orleans, La.	Jimmy Moran
5/21/33	**Tony CANZONERI**	133	**Battling SHAW**	136½	unan 10		Heinemann Park, New Orleans, La.	Jimmy Moran
6/23/33	**Barney ROSS**	134¾	**Tony CANZONERI**	133½	maj 10		Chicago Stadium, Ilinois	Tommy Gilmore
7/26/33	**Barney ROSS**		**Johnny FARR**		TKO 6		Convention Hall, Kansas City	
9/12/33	**Barney ROSS**	135	**Tony CANZONERI**	133¼	split 15		Polo Grounds, New York, N.Y.	Arthur Donovan
11/17/33	**Barney ROSS**	135½	**Sammy FULLER**	139	maj 10		Chicago Stadium, Illinois	Joe McNamara
2/7/34	**Barney ROSS**	135½	**Pete NEBO**	139	unan 12		Convention Hall, New Orleans	
3/5/34	**Barney ROSS**	137½	**Frankie KLICK**	138	draw 10		Civic Auditorium, San Francisco	Toby Irwin
3/27/34	**Barney ROSS**	138½	**Bobby PACHO**	139½	10		Olympic Auditorium, Los Angeles	George Blake
12/10/34	**Barney ROSS**	138	**Bobby PACHO**	138¾	unan 12		Public Hall, Cleveland, Ohio	
1/28/35	**Barney ROSS**	136	**Frankie KLICK**	137	unan 10		Municipal Stadium, Miami, Fla.	Leo Shea
4/9/35	**Barney ROSS**	136½	**Harry WOODS**	137¼	12		Civic Auditorium, Seattle, Wash.	Tommy McCarthy
4/29/46	**Tippy LARKIN**	139½	**Willie JOYCE**	138¼	unan 12		Boston Garden, Massachusetts	Johnny Martin
9/13/46	**Tippy LARKIN**	139¼	**Willie JOYCE**	139	unan 12		Madison Square Garden, New York	Frank Fullam
6/12/59	**Carlos ORTIZ**	139¼	**Kenny LANE**	140	TKO 3		Madison Square Garden	Harry Kessler
2/4/60	**Carlos ORTIZ**	137	**Battling TORRES**	138	KO 10	2:56	Los Angeles Coliseum	Mushy Callahan
6/15/60	**Carlos ORTIZ**	137½	**Duilio LOI**	140	split 15		Cow Palace, San Francisco	Vern Bybee
9/1/60	**Duilio LOI**	139½	**Carlos ORTIZ**	138½	maj 15		San Siro Stadium, Milan	Andre Esparraguera
5/10/61	**Duilio LOI**	138	**Carlos ORTIZ**	136¾	unan 15		San Siro Stadium, Milan	Frank Carter
10/21/61	**Duilio LOI**	138	**Eddie PERKINS**	139	draw 15		Sports Palace, Milan, Italy	Nello Barrovecchio
9/14/62	**Eddie PERKINS**	140	**Duilio LOI**	140	unan 15		Vigorelli Stadium, Milan	Pierre Verriers
12/15/62	**Duilio LOI**	137¾	**Eddie PERKINS**	138¾	ref 15		Sports Palace, Milan, Italy	Georges Gondre
† 3/21/63	**Roberto CRUZ**	138¼	**Battling TORRES**	140	KO 1	2:07	Chavez Ravine, Los Angeles	Lee Grossman
6/15/63	**Eddie PERKINS**	138¼	**Roberto CRUZ**	140	unan 15		Rizal Coliseum, Manila	Teodorico Reyes
1/4/64	**Eddie PERKINS**	138¾	**Yoshinori TAKAHASHI**	139¼	KO 13	1:35	Kuramae Arena, Tokyo	Nick Pope
4/18/64	**Eddie PERKINS**	139	**Bunny GRANT**	137½	unan 15		National Stadium, Kingston	Willie Pep
1/18/65	**Carlos HERNANDEZ**	139¼	**Eddie PERKINS**	140	split 15		Caracas, Venezuela	Henry Armstrong
5/15/65	**Carlos HERNANDEZ**	134½	**Mario ROSSITO**	137½	TKO 5	*	Maracaibo, Venezuela	
7/10/65	**Carlos HERNANDEZ**	137½	**Percy HAYLES**	136½	KO 3	2:53	National Stadium, Kingston	Willie Pep
4/30/66	**Sandro LOPOPOLO**	139½	**Carlos HERNANDEZ**	139½	maj 15		Sports Palace, Rome, Italy	Manuel Risoto
10/21/66	**Sandro LOPOPOLO**	139¾	**Vicente RIVAS**	140	TKO 8	*	Sports Palace, Rome, Italy	
4/30/67	**Paul FUJII**	140	**Sandro LOPOPOLO**	139	TKO 2	2:33	Kuramae Arena, Tokyo	Jay Edson
11/16/67	**Paul FUJII**	140	**Willie QUATOUR**	139¼	KO 4	2:30	Kuramae Arena, Tokyo	Jay Edson
12/12/68	**Nicolino LOCHE**	138½	**Paul FUJII**	139¾	TKO 10	*	Kuramae Arena, Tokyo	Nick Pope
‡12/14/68	**Pedro ADIQUE**	140	**Adolph PRUITT**	140	unan 15		Araneta Coliseum, Quezon	Pempe Padilla
5/3/69	**Nicolino LOCHE**	139	**Carlos HERNANDEZ**	137	unan 15		Luna Park, Buenos Aires	Victor Avendano
10/11/69	**Nicolino LOCHE**	139¾	**Joao HENRIQUE**	138¼	unan 15		Luna Park Stadium, Buenos Aires	Alfonso Araujo
‡ 2/1/70	**Bruno ARCARI**	138½	**Pedro Adigue**	139½	ref 15		Sports Palace, Rome, Italy	Teddy Waltham
5/16/70	**Nicolino LOCHE**	139¼	**Adolph PRUITT**	138	unan 15		Luna Park Stadium, Buenos Aires	Joaquin Arvas
‡ 7/10/70	**Bruno ARCARI**	138¾	**Rene ROQUE**	139	W dis 6	1:29	Lignano Sabbiadoro, Italy	G. Martinelli
‡10/30/70	**Bruno ARCARI**	139	**Raymundo DIAS**	137½	KO 3	1:45	Sports Palace, Genoa, Italy	Domenico Carabellese
‡ 3/6/71	**Bruno ARCARI**	139¼	**Joao HENRIQUE**	138⅜	ref 15		Sports Palace, Rome, Italy	Teddy Waltham
4/3/71	**Nicolino LOCHE**		**Domingo BARRERA**	138	split 15		Luna Park Stadium, Buenos Aires	Antonio Guzman
‡ 6/26/71	**Bruno ARCARI**	139½	**Enrique JANA**	137¾	TKO 9	0:45	Palermo, Sicily, Italy	Georges Gondre
‡10/10/71	**Bruno ARCARI**		**Domingo CORPAS**		KO 10		Sports Palace, Genoa, Italy	Teddy Waltham
12/11/71	**Nicolino LOCHE**	139	**Antonio CERVANTES**	138	unan 15		Luna Park Stadium, Buenos Aires	Jose Gomez
3/10/72	**Alfonso FRAZER**	137	**Nicolino LOCHE**	139	unan 15		Panama City, Panama	Jesus Celis
‡ 6/10/72	**Bruno ARCARI**	139½	**Joao HENRIQUE**	139½	KO 12	2:15	Sports Palace, Genoa, Italy	Harry Gibbs
6/17/72	**Alfonso FRAZER**		**Al FORD**		KO 5		Panama City, Panama	
10/28/72	**Antonio CERVANTES**	138½	**Alfonso FRAZER**	138	KO 10		Panama City, Panama	Waldemar Schmidt
‡12/02/72	**Bruno ARCARI**	140	**E. Costa AZEVEDO**	139	15		Palasport di Barcoruffini, Turin	Jean Deswert
2/16/73	**Antonio CERVANTES**		**Josua MARQUEZ**		split 15		Roberto Clemente Stad., San Juan	
3/17/73	**Antonio CERVANTES**	139	**Nicolino LOCHE**	140	TKO 10	*	Maracay, Venezuela	Luis Sulbaran
5/19/73	**Antonio CERVANTES**	140	**Alfonso FRAZER**	140	TKO 5		Panama City, Panama	Luis Sulbaran
9/08/73	**Antonio CERVANTES**	139	**Carlos GIMINEZ**	140	TKO 5	1:45	El Campin Stadium, Bogota, Col.	Isaac Herrera
‡11/01/73	**Bruno ARCARI**	139	**Jorgen HANSEN**	141	KO 5		K.B. Hall, Copenhagen, Denmark	Raymond Baldeyrou
12/4/73	**Antonio CERVANTES**	139	**Lion FURUYAMA**	139	unan 15		Panama City, Panama	
‡ 2/16/74	**Bruno ARCARI**	[illegible]	**Tony ORTIZ**	136½	W dis 8		Palasport di Barcoruffini, Turin	Rudolf Drust
3/02/74	**Antonio CERVANTES**	140	**Chang-Kil LEE**	139	KO 8		[illegible]	
7/28/74	**Antonio CERVANTES**	139	**Victor ORTIZ**	140	KO 2	1:35	Cartagena, Colombia	Ray Solis

‡ 9/21/74	**Perico FERNANDEZ**		**Lion FURUYAMA**		split	15		Sports Stadium, Rome, Italy	
10/26/74	**Antonio CERVANTES**	140	**Shinchi KADOTO**	138½	KO	8	1:42	Nihon University Auditorium, Tokyo	Luis Sulbaran
‡ 4/19/75	**Perico FERNANDEZ**	139	**Joao HENRIQUE**	140	KO	9	1:00	Sports Stadium, Barcelona	
5/17/75	**Antonio CERVANTES**	139	**Esteban DeJESUS**	139	unan	15		Panama City, Panama	
7/15/75	**Saensak MUANGSURIN**	140	**Perico FERNANDEZ**	140	TKO	8	*	Huan Mark Stadium, Bangkok	Ernesto Magana
11/15/75	**Antonio CERVANTES**		**Hector THOMPSON**		TKO	8	*	Panama City, Panama	
‡ 1/25/76	**Saensak MUANGSURIN**	139½	**Lion FURUYAMA**	140	unan	15		Nihon University Auditorium, Tokyo	Enrique Jimenez
3/6/76	**Wilfred BENITEZ**		**Antonio CERVANTES**		split	15		Hiram Bithorn Stadium, San Juan	Isaac Herrera
5/31/76	**Wilfred BENITEZ**		**Emiliano VILLA**		unan	15		Roberto Clemente Coliseum	Ismael Quinones Falu
‡ 6/30/76	**Miguel VELASQUEZ**	140	**Saensak MUANGSURIN**	140	W dis	5	**	Sports Palace, Madrid, Spain	Abraham Echavarria
10/16/76	**Wilfred BENITEZ**		**Tony PETRONELLI**		TKO	3	0:53	Hiram Bithorn Stadium, San Juan	Ismael Quinones Falu
‡10/29/76	**Saensak MUANGSURIN**	139	**Miguel VELASQUEZ**	139	TKO	2		Segovia, Spain	Dick Young
‡ 1/15/77	**Saensak MUANGSURIN**	139½	**Monroe BROOKS**	139½	TKO	15	1:55	Chiang Mai, Thailand	Marcello Bertini
‡ 4/2/77	**Saensak MUANGSURIN**	139	**Ishimatsu SUZUKI**	140	KO	6	1:56	Kuramae Arena, Tokyo, Japan	Larry Nadayai
‡ 6/17/77	**Saensak MUANGSURIN**	140	**Perico FERNANDEZ**	135	unan	15		Sports Palace, Madrid, Spain	Jay Edson
‡ 6/25/77	**Antonio CERVANTES**	139¼	**Carlos M. GIMINEZ**	139¼	TKO	6	*	Maracaibo, Venezuela	Martin Denkin
8/3/77	**Wilfred BENITEZ**	139½	**Guerrero CHAVEZ**	139½	TKO	15	1:41	Madison Square Garden, New York	* Arthur Mercante
‡ 8/20/77	**Saensak MUANGSURIN**	140	**Mike EVERETT**	136	TKO	6	2:50	Roi-et, Thailand	Larry Nadayai
‡10/22/77	**Saensak MUANGSURIN**	139½	**Saoul MAMBY**	138	split	15		Korat, Thailand	Abraham Echavarria
†11/5/77	**Antonio CERVANTES**	139	**Adriano MARRERO**	139½	unan	15		Maracay, Venezuela	Luis Sulbaran
‡12/29/77	**Saensak MUANGSURIN**	138	**Jo KUMPUANI**	136½	TKO	14	*	Chanthaburi, Thailand	Marcelo Bertini
‡ 4/8/78	**Saensak MUANGSURIN**	140	**Francisco MORENO**	139	KO	13	2:40	Hat Yai, Thailand	Jay Edson
† 4/28/78	**Antonio CERVANTES**	140	**Tonga KIATVAYUPAKDI**	140	KO	6	2:40	Udon Thani, Thailand	Jesus Celis
† 8/26/78	**Antonio CERVANTES**	139	**Norman SEKGAPANE**	139¼	TKO	9	1:52	Independence Stadium, Mmabatho	Luis Sulbaran
‡12/30/78	**Sang-Hyun KIM**	140	**Saensak MUANGSURIN**	139½	KO	13	2:05	Munhwa Stadium, Seoul, Korea	Carlos Padilla
1/18/79	**Antonio CERVANTES**	140	**Miguel MONTILLA**	138	unan	15		Madison Square Garden, New York	Stan Christodoulou
‡ 6/3/79	**Sang-Hyun KIM**	139½	**Fitzroy GUISSEPPI**	139½	unan	15		Changchung Gymnasium, Seoul	Abraham Echavarria
8/25/79	**Antonio CERVANTES**	139¼	**Kwang-Min KIM**	139½	split	15		Changchung Gymnasium, Seoul	Stan Christodoulou
‡12/31/79	**Sang-Hyun KIM**	139½	**Masahiro YOKAI**	140	KO	11	2:01	Korakuen Hall, Tokyo, Japan	Ray Solis
‡ 2/23/80	**Saoul MAMBY**	139	**Sang-Hyun KIM**	140	KO	14	1:44	Changchung Gymnasium, Seoul	Harry Gibbs
3/29/80	**Antonio CERVANTES**	139¾	**Miguel MONTILLA**	139½	TKO	7	1:28	Cartagena de Indias Bull Ring	Waldemar Schmidt
‡ 7/07/80	**Saoul MAMBY**	139½	**Esteban DeJESUS**	140	TKO	13	1:13	Metro Center, Bloomington, Minn.	Rudy Ortega
8/02/80	**Aaron PRYOR**	138½	**Antonio CERVANTES**	139½	KO	4	1:47	Riverfront Coliseum, Cincinnati	Larry Rozadilla
‡ 10/02/80	**Saoul MAMBY**	138½	**Maurice WATKINS**	140	unan,	15		Caesars Palace, Las Vegas, Nev.	Mills Lane
11/22/80	**Aaron PRYOR**	138½	**Gaetan HART**	138¼	TKO	6	2:09	Riverfront Coliseum, Cincinnati	Roberto Ramirez

Jorgen Hansen was one pound over the weight limit on November 1, 1973.

* Loser failed to answer bell for round indicated.

** Loser was disqualified at end of round

†WBA world junior welterweight title

‡WBC world super lightweight title bout

ref = referee's decision (sole arbiter)

JUNIOR WELTERWEIGHT DIVISION

PINKEY MITCHELL
(Myron Mitchell)
Junior Welterweight Champion)
Born, 1899, Milwaukee, Wis. Nationality,
Irish-American. Weight, 135 lbs. Height, 5 ft. 11
in. First junior welterweight champion.
1917
Knockout: Joe Homeland, 3.
1918
No decisions: Johnny Mendelsohn, 10;
Clint Flynn, 10; Al Thomas, 10; Otto Wallace, 4.
1919

Jan.	1—Otto Wallace, Milwaukee	KO 10
Jan.	27—Eddy May, Milwaukee	ND 10
Mar.	5—Johnny Noye, Milwaukee	ND 10
Apr.	11—Heinie Schuman, Seattle	D 4
May	2—George Engle, Butte	D 12
June	6—Charley O'Connell, Detroit	ND 10
Sept.	21—Ever Hammer, Milwaukee	ND 10
Oct.	3—Charley McCarty, Milwaukee	KO 7
Oct.	23—Mickey Donley, Milwaukee	ND 10
Nov.	13—Sailor Friedman, Racine	ND 10
Nov.	24—Mel Coogan, Milwaukee	ND 10
Dec.	15—Mike Paulsen, Milwaukee	ND 10

1920

Feb.	6—Cal Delaney, St. Paul	ND 10
Feb.	16—Joe Welling, Minneapolis	ND 10
Mar.	8—Barney Adair, Milwaukee	ND 10
Apr.	17—Frankie Schoell, Milwaukee	ND 10
May	19—Lew Tendler, Milwaukee	ND 10
June	30—Rocky Kansas, Detroit	ND 10
Sept.	27—Johnny Noye, Peoria, Ill.	KO 4
Dec.	6—Jack Britton, Milwaukee	ND 10
Dec.	17—Clonie Tait, Minneapolis	ND 10

1921

Jan.	7—Willie Jackson, N. Y. C.	D 15
Apr.	8—Irish Patsy Cline, Milwaukee	ND 10
May	7—Neal Allison, Milwaukee	KO 9
June	14—Eddie Ftizsimmons, N. Y. C.	L 10
July	4—Dennis O'Keefe, Milwaukee	ND 10
Aug.	7—Cal Delaney, Milwaukee	ND 10
Sept.	3—Jack Josephs, Milwaukee	ND 10
Nov.	3—Tommy Neary, Milwaukee	ND 10

*1922

Mar.	2—Sid Barbarian, Milwaukee	ND 10
Mar.	20—Willie Doyle, Muskegon, Mich.	ND 10
Mar.	27—Dave Shade, Milwaukee	KO by 4
Apr.	7—Pal Moran, Milwaukee	ND 10
May	15—Frankie Welch, Peoria, Ill.	KO 10
June	30—Billy Burns, Peoria, Ill.	KO 5
July	21—Billy Burns, Peoria, Ill.	KO 5
Aug.	15—Joe Jawson, Milwaukee	ND 10
Aug.	28—Johnny Tillman, Madison, Wis.	ND 10
Sept.	11—Tommy O'Brien, Milwaukee	ND 10

*Proclaimed junior welterweight champion by popular vote.
1923

Jan.	30—Bud Logan, Milwaukee	ND 10
Feb.	13—Johnny Tillman, Milwaukee	ND 10
Apr.	2—Bobby Barrett, Philadelphia	KO 3
Apr.	13—Harvey Thorpe, Milwaukee	ND 10
May	29—Benny Leonard, Chicago	KO by 10
July	9—Nate Goodman, Philadelphia	ND 8
Oct.	11—Joe Simonovich, Milwaukee	ND 10
Nov.	6—Sid Barbarian, Detroit	ND 10

1924

Feb.	18—Lew Tendler, Milwaukee	ND 10
Apr.	8—Bobby Harper, Portland, Ore.	W 10
Apr.	16—Jimmy Duffy, Oakland, Cal.	L 4
Apr.	25—Joe Simonovich, Portland, Ore.	D 10
June	2—*Tommy Freeman, New Orleans	L 15
June	10—Al Van Ryan, Sioux City, Ia.	ND 10
July	21—†Joe Anderson, Cincinnati	KO by 8

*Title not at stake.
†Mitchell broke arm. Title not at stake.
1925

Mar.	27—Red Herring, Detroit, Mich.	LF 6
Apr.	27—Willie Harmon, Newark, N. J.	L 12
Aug.	14—Willie Harmon, Milwaukee	ND 10
Sept.	24—Joe Dundee, Philadelphia	L 10
Sept.	30—Oak. Jimmy Duffy, Los Ang.	L 10
Nov.	26—Billy Wells, Minneapolis	ND 10

1926

Jan.	14—Russie Leroy, Fargo, N. D.	ND 10
May	5—Jimmy Gill, Janesville, Wis.	W 10
May	31—Jimmy Finley, Cedar Rapids.	ND 10
June	22—Tommy Freeman, Cleveland	ND 10
July	18—Tommy White, Juarez	L 10
Aug.	12—Tommy White, Milwaukee	ND 10
Aug.	20—Georgie Ward, Jersey City	WF 2

Aug.	27—Jimmy Finley, Milwaukee	ND 10
Sept.	2—Georgie Levine, Youngstown	ND 10
Sept.	21—Mushy Callahan, Vernon, Cal.	L 10
	(Lost Junior Welterweight Title)	
Nov.	5—Shuffle Callahan, Chicago	KO by 3
Nov.	28—Tommy White, Mexico City	ND 12
Dec.	6—Clyde Hull, Ft. Worth	ND 10

1927

Aug.	11—Joe Dundee, Milwaukee	NC 6

TB	KO	WD	WF	D	LD	LF	KOBY	ND	NC
79	9	2	1	4	7	1	4	50	1

"MUSHY CALLAHAN"
(Vincent Morris Scheer)
(Junior Welterweight Champion)

Born, Nov. 3, 1905, New York City.
Nationality, Jewish-American. Weight, 140 lbs.
Height, 5 ft. 8½ in. Managed by Eddie Sears.
Started boxing as a newsboy.
1924
Davey Barnes, San Pedro, Cal, KO 1; Sailor
Bluell, Vernon, Cal, KO 2; Frankie Herman,
Vernon, Cal., KO 2; George Law, Hollywood,
Cal., W 4; Joe Summers, San Fernando, Cal., KO
3; Young Belol, Hollywood, Cal., W 4; Billy
Wallace, Hollywood, Cal., W 4; Frankie McCann,
Hollywood, Cal., W 4; Johnny Adams,
Hollywood, Cal., L 4; Joe McGovern, San
Fernando, Cal., KO 1; Batting Ward, San
Fernando, Cal., KO 2; Richie King, San Pedro,
Cal., W 4; Johnny Adams, Hollywood, Cal., D 4;
Roy Morrell, San Fernando, Cal., W 4; Battling
Ward, Los Angeles W 4; Sailor Britt, San Pedro,
Cal., W 4; Johnny Reno, San Pedro, Cal., W 4;
Young Burns, Hollywood, Cal., KO 2; Joe
Medina, Ventura, Cal., W 4.
1925
Knockouts: Russell Leroy, 3; Pal Moran, 3;
Won: Joe Layman, 10; Dode Bercot, 10; Spug
Meyers, 10; Johnny O'Donnell, 10; Red Herring,
10; Ace Hudkins, 10. Draw: Ace Hudkins, 10.

1926

Feb.	12—Frankie Schaiffer, Hollywood	W 10
Mar.	1—Archie Walker, N. Y. C.	D 10
Arp.	20—Jimmy Goodrich, Los Angeles	W 10
May	18—Jimmy Goodrich, Vernon, Cal.	W 10
July	5—Jack Silver, San Francisco	L 10
Aug.	24—Baby Joe Gans, Vernon, Cal.	L 10
Sept.	21—Pinkey Mitchell, Vernon, Cal.	W 10
	(Won junior welter title)	
Oct.	22—Charley Pitts, Hollywood	KO 2
Nov.	3—Joe Tiplitz, Vernon, Cal.	KO 2

1927

Jan.	11—Joe Jawson, Vernon, Cal.	W 10
Feb.	10—Spug Meyers, Chcago	L 10
Mar.	14—Andy Divodi, New York	KO 2
June	1—Spug Meyers, Chicago	W 10
July	12—Sergt. Sammy Baker, Chic.	KO by 9
Nov.	10—Dick Hoppe, Hollywood	L 10
Nov.	22—Jackie Fields, Los Angeles	L 10

1928

Mar.	27—Dick Hoppe, Los Angeles	W 7
Apr.	6—Dick Ramies, San Diego, Cal.	W 10
June	1—Jimmy Cottrell, Hollywood	KO 10
June	22—Jackie Carr, Hollywood	L 10
Oct.	12—Jimmy Owens, Fort Worth, Tex.	L 10
Oct.	23—Bobby Tracey, Chicago	D 10

1929

Feb.	19—Frankie Fuente, Fresno, Cal.	KO 4
Mar.	8—Joe Rivers, Hollywood	KO 9
Mar.	28—Jackie Carr, Hollywood	KO 4
Apr.	23—Spug Meyers, Los Angeles	W 10
May	28—Dummy Mahan, Los Angeles	KO 3
June	17—Jimmy Goodrich, Buffalo	L 15
July	11—Joey Harrison, Newark	ND 10
July	24—Jack Kid Berg, Brooklyn	L 10
Dec.	3—Alfonso Gonzales, Wilmington, Cal.	KO 5

1930

Feb.	18—Jack Kid Berg, London	KO by 10

(Lost Junior Welterweight Title)
In U. S. Army.

TB	KO	WD	WF	D	LD	LF	KOBY	ND	NC
60	18	25	0	4	10	0	2	1	0

JACK (Kid) BERG
(Judah Bergman)
(Junior Welterweight Champion)
(Whitechapel Whirlwind)
Born, June 28, 1909, London, Eng.
Nationality, British-Hebrew. Weight, 145 lbs.
Height, 5 ft. 9 in. Managed by Harry Levene in
Europe; Frankie Jacobs and Sol Gold, America.

1924

June	8—Yg. Johnny Gordon, London .KO	8
July	7—Charley Harwood, London ...KO	7
July	20—Syd Lyons, London..........KO	3
Aug.	3—Billy Clarke, London.........D	10
Sept.	21—Teddy Pullen, London ....KO	1
Oct.	2—Jimmy Wooder, London ......D	10
Oct.	16—Albert Hinks, London........W	10
Nov.	3—Young Clancy, London ....W	15
Nov.	10—Jimmy Wooder, London ......W	10
Nov.	20—Harry Miller, London ....KO	6
Nov.	27—Fred Patten, London.........W	15
Dec.	7—Teddy Shepard, London .....KO	9
Dec.	11—Bert Saunders, London......KO	14
Dec.	15—Arthur Lloyd, London ....W	10
Dec.	26—Billy Colebourne, London ...KO	6

1925

Jan.	8—Albert Colcombe, London ...KO	13
Jan.	26—Billy Streets, London ....W	15
Feb.	9—Arthur Lloyd, London ....W	15
Feb.	26—Billy Streets, London ....KO	9
Mar.	12—Johnny Cuthbert, London L	15
Apr.	6—Sid Carter, London ....W	15
Apr.	19—George Davis, London ......WF	6
May	21—Kid Lewis, London ....KO	10
June	7—Billy Sehpherd, London .....KO	13
June	18—Johnny Cuthbert, London.....L	15
June	28—Jack Slattery, London ......KO	9
July	16—Joe Samuels, London ....KO	15
July	26—George Green, London ......KO	11
Aug.	6—Fred Green, London ....W	15
Aug.	20—Fred Green, London ....W	15
Aug.	30—Johnny Britton, London .....W	15
Sept.	10—Norman Radford, London ....KO	14
Oct.	15—Johnny Cuthbert, London....KO	11
Oct.	29—Johnny Curley, London ....W	15
Nov.	12—Ernie Swash, London ....WF	2
Nov.	26—Van Dyke, London ....W	15

1926

Feb.	11—Harry Corbett, London L	15
Mar.	18—Andre Routis, London ....W	15
Apr.	26—Harry Corbett, London ....D	15
May	16—Mick Hill, London ....W	15
June	21—Andre Routis, London ...W (dis.)	3
July	8—Henri Hebrans, London .....KO	5
July	29—Paul Gay, London ....KO	6
Aug.	29—Harry Corbett, London ......W	15
Oct.	10—Phil Bond, London ....W	15
Nov.	21—Billy Gilmore, London .....KO	8
Dec.	19—Emil Saerens, London ....WF	9

1927

Jan.	13—Walter Wright, London ......KO	2
Jan.	23—Joe Claes, London ....W	15
Feb.	27—Paul Fritsch, London ....KO	8
Apr.	21—Alf Simmons, London ....WE	8
May	29—Bob Miller, London ....KO	6
Sept.	18—Robert Servain, London .....KO	6
Sept.	29—Jack Kirk, London ....KO	13
Oct.	11—Raymond Jansen, London ....WF	7
Nov.	7—Vittorio Venturi, London .....W	10
Dec.	4—Lucien Vinez, London ....W	15

1928

Jan.	6—Andre Routis, London ....WF	3
Feb.	11—Harry Corbett, London .....W	15
Feb.	27—Jack Donn, London ....WF	10
Mar.	7—Johnny Curley, London ......W	15
Mar.	24—Jack Don, London ....KO	7
May	12—Pedro Amador, Chicago ......W	10
May	28—Mike Gamiere, Ocean Park ...KO	6
May	30—Freddie Mueller, Chicago ....W	10
June	14—Johnny Mellow, Detroit ......W	8
July	4—Mike Watters, Chicago ......KO	8
July	26—Billy Petrolle, Chicago ......D	10
Aug.	24—Billy Petrolle, Chicago ....KO by	5
Sept.	6—Spug Meyers, Chicago ....WF	3
Dec.	6—Alf Mancini, London ....W	15

1929

Jan.	12—Lucien Vinez, London ....W	15
Feb.	8—Alf Mancini, London ....W	15
May	10—Bruce Flowers, New York ....W	10
May	23—Bruce Flowers, New York ....W	10
June	11—Stanislaus Loayza, New York .. D	10
July	12—Herman Perlick, Chicago	
July	24—Mushy Callahan, Brooklyn ....W	10
Aug.	5—Joe Trabon, New York ....KO	5

Aug.	19—Harry Wallach, New York ....KO	9
Aug.	29—Spug Myers, New York ....W	10
Sept.	16—Georgie Balduc, Brooklyn ...WF	2
Sept.	30—Phil McGraw, New York......W	10
Oct.	21—Bruce Flowers, New York ....W	10
Nov.	2—Tommy Gervel, New York....KO	2
Nov.	18—Eddie Elkins, New York .....W	10
Nov.	30—Artie De Luca, New York .....W	6
Dec.	18—Tony Caragliano, New York ..WF	2

1930

Jan.	16—Tony Canzoneri, New York ....W	10
Feb.	18—Mushy Callahan, London, Eng.KO	10
	(Won Junior Welterweight Title)	
Apr.	4—Joe Glick, New York ....W	10
Apr.	7—Jackie Philips, Toronto, Can. ..W	10
May	29—Al Delmont, Newark, N.J.....KO	6
June	11—Herman Perlick, New York ....W	10
July	10—Henry Perlick, Newark, N.J....W	10
Aug.	7—Kid Chocolate, New York ....W	10
Sept.	3—Buster Brown, Newark, N.J....W	10
Sept.	18—Joe Glick, New York ....W	10
Oct.	10—Billy Petrolle, New York .....W	10

1931

Jan.	23—Goldie Hess, Chicago.........W	10
Jan.	30—Herman Perlick, N.Y.........W	10
Apr.	10—Billy Wallace, Detroit ....W	10
Apr.	21—Berg was presented with the National Boxing Association Belt, emblematic of the Junior Welterweight title.	
Apr.	24—Tony Canzoneri, Chciago ..KO by	3
	(For World Lightweight Title)	
May	8—Tony Herrera, New York .....W	10
May	18—Ray Kiser, Pittsburgh ....W	10
June	22—Tony Lambert, Newark ......KO	8
July	24—Teddy Watson, Jersey City ..KO	7
July	27—Philly Griffin, Newark ....W	10
Aug.	4—Jimmy McNamara, N.Y. ...... w	10
Sept.	10—Tony Canzoneri, N.Y. L	15
	(For World Lightweight Title)	
Dec.	14—M. Baudry, London ....KO	5

1932

Mar.	21—Buster Brown, N.Y.C. ....W	10
Apr.	1—Sammy Fuller, N.Y.C. ....D	10
May	20—Sammy Fuller, N.Y.C.........L	12
June	29—Mike Sarko, N.Y.C. ....W	6
July	18—Kid Chocolate, N.Y.C. ....W	15

1933

Apr.	27—Cleto Locatelli, London L	10
May	28—Louis Saerens, London ......KO	4
July	8—George Rose, Cardiff ....KO	5
July	14—Eugene Drouhin, London ....KO	8
Sept.	30—Harry Wallace, New York ....KO	4
Oct.	19—Tony Falco, New York........L	10

1934

Jan.	12—Cleto Locatelli, New York L	10
Mar.	19—Joe Kerr, Liverpool ....KO	6
Apr.	14—Jackie Flynn, London ....W	10
May	12—Len Wickmar, Leicester .....KO	6
June	16—Jimmy Stewart, Liverpool . KO by	3
Aug.	19—Nicholas Wilke, London .....KO	9
Oct.	29—Harry Mizler, London, Eng....KO	10
	(British Lightweight Title)	
Dec.	2—Alfred Bastin, London ....KO	4

1935

Jan.	21—"Tiger" Gustave Humery, London, England ....KO	8
Feb.	25—"Tiger" Gustave Humery, Paris, France L	10
Apr.	1—"Tiger" Gustave Humery, London, Eng. L	10
May	19—Harry Brown, London ....KO	3
Oct.	21—Peter McKinley, London .....W	10
Nov.	14—Pat Butler, London ....KO	4

1936

Jan.	11—Laurie Stevens, Johannesburg ...L	12
	(British Empire Lightweight Title)	
Apr.	24—Jimmy Walsh, Liverpool ... KO by	9
	(British Lightweight Title)	
July	22—Aldo Spoldi, Brooklyn ....KO by	2

1937

Jan.	24—Ivor Pikens, "The Ring" ....W	10
Feb.	7—Pat Haley, "The Ring" ....WF	10
Feb.	11—Panther Purchase, West Ham ....W (rtd.)	12
Feb.	21—Harry Mason, "The Ring" W (rtd.)	10
Mar.	22—Louis Saerens, Bristol ....D	10
Apr.	11—Pat Haley, Cricklewood ..W (rtd.)	10
May	6—Alby Day, Harringay ....W	10
Aug.	14—Jack Lewis, Poole ....D	10
Oct.	4—Jake Kilrain, Earl's Court ....W (stpd.)	10
Nov.	1—George Odwell, Earl's Court ....L (rtd.)	10

633

Dec. 6—Charlie Chetwin,
Manchester ....W (stpd.) 10
Dec. 13—Leo Phillips, Birmingham......W 10

1938

Feb. 10—Silvio Zangrillo, Brooklyn ....KO 8
Mar. 5—Larry Anzalone, Brooklyn.....W 8
Mar. 15—Vincent Pimpinella, Brooklyn . W 10
Mar. 29—Frankie Wallace, Brooklyn ....W 8
Apr. 9—Johnny Horstman, Brooklyn ..W 8
May 3—Ray Napolitano, Brooklyn ....W 8
June 7—Johnny McHale, Brooklyn.....W 8
June 15—Augie Arellano, Long Island ...D 8
June 30—Johnny Horstman, Brooklyn....W 8
July 12—Johnny McHale, Brooklyn.....W 8
July 25—Red Cochran, Newark..........L 10
Aug. 5—Pete Cara, Brooklyn..........W 8
Oct. 11—Johnny McHale, Brooklyn.....W 8
Oct. 25—Joey Greb, New York.........W 8
Nov. 22—Frankie Cavanna, Brooklyn....W 8

1939

Feb. 3—Baby Breese, Hollywood.......L 10
Mar. 10—Pedro Montanez, N. Y. C...KO by 5
Apr. 4—Pete Galiano, Brooklyn......W 8
Apr. 11—Marine Bunker, Bermuda....KO 8
June 6—Tippy Larkin, Garfield........W 10
June 26—Milt Aron, Chicago......KO by 6
June 30—Mike Piskin, Lg. Branch, N. J...L 10
July 11—Johnny Rohrig, Garfield......W 10
Aug. 1—Joey Greb, Garfield...........W 8
Oct. 12—Paddy Roche, Southampton...W 10
Nov. 30—Paddy Roche, Nottingham...KO 5

1940

Jan. 25—Harry Davis, Hackney.........W 10
Feb. 5—George Reynolds, Bristol......W 10
Feb. 29—Eddie Ryan, London.........WF 6
Mar. 8—Garry Roche, Dublin.......KO 4
Mar. 10—Dick Bradshaw, Hackney.....KO 3
Apr. 4—Harry Davis, Hackney........KO 8

1941

Jan. 20—Harry Craster, London.......W 10
Feb. 5—Arthur Danaher, London..KO by 6
Feb. 20—Harry Charman, London......W 6
Feb. 27—Harry Muzler, London........W 10
Apr. 21—Eric Boon, London..........WF 2
May 30—Ernie Roderick, London.......L 10
In British Army.
Nov. 2—George Odwell, Stoke New'gton L 10
Nov. 24—Joe Connolly, Leeds.........KO 8

1942

Feb. 5—Paddy Roche, Newcastle....KO 4
Mar. 12—Joe Connolly, Glasgow.......KO 4

1943

May 22—Gordon Woodhouse, Handcross .L 6
In R.A.F.

1945

Mar. 1—Eric Dolby, London ....KO 4
Mar. 8—Jimmy Brunt, London........W 8
May 19—Johnny McDonald, Coventry .KO 5

TB	KO	WD	WF	D	LD	LF	KOBY	ND	NC
197	59	89	14	9	18	0	8	0	0

TONY CANZONERI
(Record Under Lightweight Champions)

JOHNNY JADICK
(John Jadick)
(Junior Welterweight Champion)
Born, June 16, 1908, Philadelphia, Pa.
Nationality, Ukrainian-American. Weight,
135-140 lbs. Height, 5 ft. 8½ in. Managed by
Tommy White.

1925

Harry Kid Decker (3), W 8; Charlie Mack,
ND 8; Jack Hindle, W 8; Tommy Murray, W 10;
Steve Nitchie, KO 4.

1926

Nick Quarrelli, W 8; Freddy Welsh (2), W 8;
Tommy Burns, W 8; Harry Scott (2), W 8; Lew
Skymer, W 8; Pedro Aquinaldo, KO 3; Len
Brenner, KO 2; Georgie Amblard, W 10; Pete
Nebo, ND 8; Ralph Repman, KO 2; Georgie
Siddons (2), W 10; Wilbur Cohen, W 10.

634

1927

Eddie Ochs, KO 1; Joey Hadfield, W 10;
Joey Williams (2), W 10; Johnny Sheppard, W 10;
Tim O'Dowd, W 10; Billy Humphries, W 10;
Eddie Anderson, L 10; Hubert Gillis, W 10; Joe
Bush, W 10.

1928

—Henri De Wanker, Philadelphia . W 10
—Joe Glick, Philadelphia.........L 10
—Chick Liadell, Wilmington.....W 8
—Buckeye Boyle, Philadelphia... W 10
Mar. 12—Pete Nebo, Philadelphia.....L 10
—Al Winkler, Philadelphia.......W 10
—Al Foreman, N. Y. C...........W 8
June 18—Honeyboy Finnegan, Phila.....W 10
Aug. 8—Honeyboy Finnegan, Boston ...L 10
Nov. 22—Steve Smith, Allentown, Pa. ...W 10
Dec. 7—Bruce Flowers, Boston........W 10

1929

Jan. 11—Louis Kid Kaplan, Boston .KO by 7
Mar. 14—Joey Kaufman, Allentown....WF 2
—Eddie Reed..............KO by 1
—Eddie Reed...................W 10
June 18—Tommy Grogan, Allentown....L 10
July 24—Billy Wallace, Philadelphia.....L 10
Sept. 17—Lope Tenorio, Philadelphia ...W 10
Nov. 17—Luis Vicentini, Philadelphia ...W 10
Nov. 25—King Tut, Philadelphia.......KO 7

1930

Feb. 3—Gaston Lecadre, Philadelphia .. D 10
June 16—Pat Igo, Allentown...........W 10
Oct. 4—King Tut, Milwaukee........W 10
Nov. 17—Tommy Grogan, Philadelphia .. W 10
Dec. 8—Benny Bass, Philadelphia.......L 10

1931

Feb. 20—Ray Miller, Detroit..........KO 1
Mar. 6—Ray Collins, Detroit.........KO 6
May 25—Wes Ramey, Chicago, Ill........L 8
June 2—Tommy Liberto, Wilmington ..W 8
July 13—Tony Herrera, Pittsburgh......W 10
Aug. 11—Sammy Dorfman, Pittsburgh...L 10
Oct. 5—Lew Massey, Philadelphia.....D 10
Oct. 26—Lew Massey, Philadelphia....KO 8
Nov. 30—Tony Herrera, Pittsburgh .. KO by 6

1932

Jan. 18—Tony Canzoneri, Philadelphia.. W 10
(Won Junior welterweight title)
Jan. 26—Wildcat O'Connor, W. Barre ...W 10
Feb. 8—Harry Dublinsky, Philadelphia ..L 10
Feb. 24—Wildcat O'Connor, W. Barre ....W 10
Mar. 9—Pat Igo, Wilkes-Barre...........W 10
May 26—Herman Folins, Pittsburgh.....W 10
June 28—Pat Igo, Waterbury, Conn......W 10
July 18—*Tony Canzoneri, Philadelphia ..W 10
Oct. 4—Lew Raymond, Reading, Pa.....W 8
Oct. 20—Joey Harrison, Paterson........W 10
Nov. 18—Lew Raymond, Philadelphia ..KO 5
*For Junior Welterweight title.

1933

Feb. 3—Johnny Lucas, Philadelphia....D 10
Feb. 20—Batt. Shaw, New Orleans......L 10
(Lost Junior welterweight title)
Mar. 3—Wesley Ramey, Grand Rapids...L 10
Apr. 3—Eddie Cool, Philadelphia.......L 10
Apr. 17—Cocoa Kid, New Haven, Conn. ..L 10
Oct. 13—Stumpy Jacobs, Philadelphia...W 10
Nov. 17—Pete Nebo, Philadelphia.......W 10
Dec. 8—Tony Falco, Philadelphia......W 10

1934

Jan. 12—Joe Glick, Philadelphia, Pa.....W 10
Feb. 5—Jimmy Leto, Holyoke, Mass.....L 10
Feb. 10—Ray Napolitano, N. Y. C.......D 6
Feb. 23—Harry Serody, Philadelphia....D 10
Feb. 26—Mickey Serrian, Syracuse......W 10
Mar. 12—Tony Falco, Philadelphia......W 10
Mar. 19—Lou Ambers, Holyoke, Mass. ...L 10
Apr. 16—Charlie Bedami, Holyoke......W 10
June 20—Eddie Cool, Philadelphia.......L 10
July 31—Benny Bass, Philadelphia......L 10
Sept. 21—Bucky Jones, Philadelphia.....D 10
Oct. 19—Mickey Serrian, Philadelphia ...W 10
Nov. 30—Sammy Fuller, N. Y. C.....KO by 4

1935

Jan. 11—Phil Baker, Philadelphia......W 10
Jan. 21—Phil Furr, Washington, D. C. ...W 10
Feb. 18—Fritzie Zivic, Washington ......W 10
Mar. 15—George Gibbs, Philadelphia....L 10
May 9—Max Strub, Erie, Pa.............L 10
June 10—Bucky Jones, Plainfield ....L 10
July 1—Joe Vignali, Albany, N. Y......W 10
July 16—Teddy Loder, N. Y. C............L 10
July 26—George Gibbs, Atlantic City ....L 10
Aug. 6—Bucky Jones, Plainfield, N. J....L 8

Sept. 20—George Gibbs, Philadelphia .... D 10
Sept. 27—Eddie Cool, Philadelphia ...... D 10
Oct. 2—Willie Pal, Albany, N.Y. ....L 10
Oct. 8—Tony Falco, Atlantic City ......L 10
Oct. 14—Jack Portney, Baltimore ......L 10
Oct. 21—Billy McHahon, Holyoke ..... W 10
Nov. 4—Billy McMahon, Holyoke ..... W 10
Nov. 22—Tony Falco, Philadelphia ......L 10
Dec. 9—Six-Second Powell, Plainfield ...L 8

1936
Jan. 16—Tony Morgano, Philadelphia ....L 10
Feb. 24—Freddy Cochrane, Newark ......L 10
Mar. 3—Sonny Jones, Holyoke ....L 10
Apr. 9—Tony Canzoneri, N.Y.C. ......L 10
May 11—Chino Alvarez, Tampa ....KO by 7
June 15—Bushy Graham, Utica ....L 8
July 22—Izzy Jannazzo, N.Y.C. ......L 10
Oct. 19—Jimmy Leto, Wash., D.C. ......L 10
Oct. 26—Mickey O'Brien, Lancaster .... W 8
Nov. 20—Johnny Clinton, Philadelphia ...L 10

1937
Jan. 1—Mickey Sherrian, Scranton .....L 10
Jan. 22—Wesley Ramey, Syracuse ......L 10
Feb. 3—Sammy Luftspring, Toronto ....L 8
Feb. 11—Fritzie Zivic, Pittsburgh ...KO by 6
Mar. 29—Ralph Zannelli, Providence .....L 8
Apr. 19—Saverio Turiello, Holyoke ......L 10
Aug. 27—Mike Piskin, Long Branch .....L 8

TB	KO	WD	WF	D	LD	LF	KOBY	ND	NC
134	9	63	1	8	44	0	7	2	0

BATTLING SHAW
(Junior Welterweight Champion)
Born October, 1910, Laredo, Mexico.
Height, 5 ft. 8½ in. Weight, 135-138 lbs.
Mexican. Manager, Emile Bruneau.

1932
Feb. 22—Ray Kiser ....L 10
Mar. 7—Lou Avery ....W 10
Apr. 18—Ervin Berlier, New Orleans ....KO 8
May 23—Matt Brock ....KO 9
June 6—Davey Abad ....L 10
June 13—Johnny Cook ....W 10
July 11—Joe Ghnouly, New Orleans ....KO 9
July 25—Davey Abad .... W 10
Aug. 15—Ray Kiser .... W 10
Aug. 29—Joe Ghnouly, New Orleans .... W 10
Oct. 3—Lou Terry ....L 10
Nov. 28—Lou Terry .... W 10
Dec. 19—Ervin Berlier, New Orleans .... W 10

1933
Feb. 7—Joe Ghnouly, St. Louis, Mo. ....L 10
Feb. 20—Johnny Jadick, New Orl., La. .. W 10
(Won Jr. Welterweight Title)
Apr. 17—Tommy Grogan, New Orl., La. .W 10
Apr. 10—Gabe Chamblain, N. Orl., La. ..KO 5
May 21—Tony Canzoneri, New Orl., La. ..L 10
(Lost Jr. Welterweight Title)
June 11—Willard Brown, New Orl., ..KO by 10
July 31—Ray Kiser, New Orl., La. ......L 10
Sept. 6—Tracey Cox, Galveston, Tex. ....L 10
Sept. 21—Willard Brown, Dallas,
Tex. .... KO by 4
Dec. 19—Yg. Peter Jackson, Los Ang.,
Cal. .... KO by 7

TB	KO	WD	WF	D	LD	LF	KOBY	ND	NC
23	4	9	0	0	7	0	3	0	0

BARNEY ROSS
(Record Under Welterweight Champions)

TIPPY LARKIN
(Tony Pilleteri)
(Junior Welterweight Champion)
(Garfield Gunner)
Born, November 11, 1917, Garfield, N.J.
Nationality, Italian - American Welterweight,
Height, 5 ft. 7 in.

1935
Mar. 14—Ed McGillick, Paterson .... L 3
Mar. 21—Johnny Fiore, Paterson .... KO 2
—Johnny Schibelli .... KO 1
—Johnny Gaja .... KO 3
—Pete Flash .... KO 3
—Dom Pasculli .... W 4
—Dom Pasculli .... W 4
—Tony Capria .... W 4
Nov. 7—Al Gianetti, Paterson .... KO 1
Dec. 16—Al (Nunzio) Bisagno, Newark .... KO 1
Dec. 23—Ed Capano, Newark .... KO 2

1936
Jan. 6—Lew Fascio, Newark .... W 4
—Ed Capano .... KO 2
—Phil Bafuto .... KO 1
March 9—Pete Stewart, Newark .... KO 2
—Ed Capano .... W 4
Apr. 13—Lew Fascio, Newark .... W 6
May 4—Dom Pasculli, Newark .... KO 2
—Ed Capano .... KO 3
—Tommy Mankin, Jr. .... KO 1
—Jimmy Donato .... KO 2
—Ted Adams .... KO 2
—Willie Chapman .... KO 4
—Johnny Schibelli .... W 6
—Jackie Corcoran .... W 6
—Al Simmons .... W 6
—Andre Sarilla .... W 6
—Dick McClintic .... KO 1
—Young Buckey .... W 4
—Jimmy Quinn .... W 6
—Chang Collura .... W 6
—Georgie Carlo .... W 8
—Meyer Alper .... W 8
—Jimmy Cogman .... W 8
—Chang Collura .... L 6

1937
Jan. 18—Chang Collura, Newark .... W 6
Feb. 8—Tony Morengo, Newark .....KO 4
Mar. 15—Jimmy Cogman, Plainfield ..... W 8
Mar. 22—Red Cochrane, Newark .... W 9
May 24—Red Cochrane, Newark .... W 10
July 2—Red Cochrane, Long Branch ... W 10
July 13—Maxie Fisher, Newark .... W 10
Sept. 3—Johnny Mason, Long Branch ..KO 3
Sept. 13—Jimmy Cogman, Long Branch .KO 4
Oct. 25—Maxie Fisher, Newark .... W 10
Nov. 15—Maxie Fisher, Newark .... W 10
Dec. 14—Lew Massey, Newark .... W 10
Dec. 28—Mickey Duca, Newark ....L 8

1938
Jan. 31—Mickey Duca, Newark .... W 8
Feb. 10—Jackie Stewart, Passaic .....KO 6
Mar. 10—Pete Mascia, Passaic .... W 8
Mar. 15—Charley Bedami, N.Y.C. ...... W 8
Mar. 24—Pedro Nieves, Passaic ....KO 5
May 5—Tommy Grady, Passaic ....KO 3
May 23—Julio Gonzales, Newark ...... W 8
June 8—Johnny Rohrig, Clifton ...... W 10
July 5—Red Cochrane, Newark ...... W 10
Aug. 2—Eddie Zivic, Newark ....KO 1
Aug. 15—Frankie Wallace, Newark ..... W 10
Aug. 29—Red Cochrane, Newark ...... W 15
Dec. 19—Charlie Burns, Newark .... W 8
Dec. 26—Jackie Savino, Newark ....KO 3

1939
Jan. 6—Billy Beauhuld, N.Y.C. ....KO 10
Feb. 3—Georgie Zengaras, N.Y.C. ..... W 8
Apr. 10—Billy Beauhuld, Newark .... W 10
June 6—Jack Kid Berg, Garfield ....L 10
Nov. 27—Steve Halaiko, Passaic ....KO 2
Dec. 7—Joey Greb, Paterson .... W 8
Dec. 15—Al Davis, N.Y.C. ....KO by 5

1940
Mar. 8—Lew Jenkins, N.Y.C ......KO by 1
May 7—Jimmy Lancaster, Jersey City .KO 3
June 3—Frankie Wallace, Garfield ....KO 4
June 25—Johnny Rohrig, Garfield ..... W 10
Aug. 12—Maxie Fisher, Newark .... W 10

1941
Mar. 13—Joey Silva, Jersey City ....KO 4
Mar. 24—Norman Rahn, Newark ....KO 3
May 5—Abie Cohen, Perth Amboy ....KO 2
June 16—Freddie Archer, Newark ......KO 1
July 18—Ray Bonti, Lodi, N.J. ....KO 1
Aug. 8—George Zengaras, Asbury Park.. W 10

Sept. 16—Joey Zodda, Garfield, N. J. ...KO 4
Dec. 16—Tommy Spiegel, Jersey City ... W 8
Dec. 22—Carmine Fatta, Newark .... W 10
1942
Jan. 12—Tommy Cross, Newark ......KO 6
Jan. 30—Chester Rico, N. Y. C.......... W 8
Apr. 13—Jerry Moore, Holyoke .... W 10
June 3—Leo Rodak, Newark .... W 10
June 9—Carmine Fatta, N. Y. C. .... W 8
June 23—Billy Davis, Newark .... W 10
Oct. 5—Charley Davis, Newark .... W 10
Oct. 13—Charley Davis, N. Y. C. ......KO 7
Oct. 26—Abe Denner, Newark ....KO 2
Nov. 16—Freddie Archer, Newark .... W 10
Dec. 18—Beau Jack, N. Y. C. .... KO by 3
1943
Mar. 8—Henry Armstrong, San Frn. KO by 2
June 17—Joe De Jesus, Richmond, Va. ...KO 5
June 23—Bobby McIntyre, Eliza., N. J. .KO 5
July 25—Johnny Jones, Eliza., N. J..... W 8
Aug. 17—Ruby Garcia, Bklyn., N. Y. .... W 8
Aug. 20—Harry Teaney, N. Y. C. .... W 10
Sept. 15—Patsy Spatora, Elizabeth ...... W 10
Oct. 16—Johnny Jones, Bklyn. .... W 8
Oct. 29—George (Red) Doty, Boston ...KO 4
Nov. 15—Al Costa, Providence .... W 10
Dec. 10—Doll Rafferty, Boston ....KO 2
Dec. 20—Gene Ward, Providence ....KO 4
1944
Jan. 14—Bobby Ruffin, New York City . D 10
Feb. 9—Luly Costantino, N. Y. C....... W 10
Mar. 23—Allie Stolz, New York City ...KO 3
June 2—Freddie Archer, N. Y. C.......KO 8
1945
June 29—Jackie Peters, Erie, Pa. ....KO 2
July 17—Joey Gambaro, New Bedford .KO 2
Aug. 3—Willie Joyce, New York .... W 10
Nov. 16—Nick Moran, New York .... W 10
1946
Feb. 20—Solomon Stewart, Akron .....KO 3
Mar. 6—Bobby McIntyre, Akron ...... W 10
Mar. 22—Nick Moran, New York ...... W 10
Apr. 29—Willie Joyce, Boston .... W 12
(Junior Welter Title)
Aug. 1—Bobby Claus, Akron ....KO 5
Aug. 21—Bobby McIntyre, Providence .. W 10
Sept. 13—Willie Joyce, New York .... W 12
(Title)
Nov. 5—Johnny Jones, Manchester .... NC 1
Nov. 21—Tommy Mills, Akron ....KO 4
1947
Feb. 14—Charley Fusari, N. Y. C. ... KO by 9
Mar. 21—Billy Graham, N. Y. C. .... W 10
June 4—Lou Fortuna, Providence .....KO 6
June 20—Ike Willimas, N. Y. C. ..... KO by 4
Dec. 18—Ernie Petrone, Worcester ....KO 5
Dec. 29—Pete Manchio, Boston .... W 10
1948
Jan. 26—Joe Di Martino, Boston .... W 10
Apr. 13—Billy Kearns, Salem .... W 10
Apr. 20—Joe Lucignano, Jersey City .... W 10
May 10—Ruby Kessler, Brooklyn ...... W 10
July 26—Joe Lucignano, N. Y. C. ...... W 10
Aug. 5—Willie Beltram, N. Y. C.......KO 5
Aug. 31—Ruby Kessler, Elizabeth .... W 8
Oct. 21—Charley Fusari, Jersey C. .. KO by 6
1949
May 2—Jack Boderone, Trenton ......KO 4
June 13—Al Guido, Newark .... W 10
June 27—Aldo Minelli, Newark .... W 8
Aug. 22—Al Evans, Newark .... W 8
Sept. 26—Hy Melzer, Brooklyn ....KO 2
Oct. 24—Aldo Minelli, Toledo .... W 10
Dec. 7—Bernard Docusen,
New Orleans .... KO by 6

1951
Oct. 16—Humberto Sierra, Newark ..... W 8
Nov. 6—Manouk Markarain, Newark ... W 8
Nov. 29—Alfredo La Grutta, Brooklyn .. W 8

1952
Mar. 6—Joey Lupo, Newark .... KO by 2
Oct. 23—Maurice Jenkins, Fall River ... W 10
Dec. 11—Maurice Jenkins, Fall River ... W 10
Dec. 29—Steve Marcello, Providence KO by 4

TB	KO	WD	WF	D	LD	LF	KO BY	ND	NC
152	57	79	0	1	4	0	10	0	1

636

CARLOS ORTIZ
(Record Under Lightweight Champions)

DUILIO LOI
World Junior Welterweight and European
Welterweight Champion
Born, Trieste, April 4, 1929.
1948
Nov. 1—Frangioni, Genoa .... W 6
1949
Feb. 12—Georgescu, Genoa .... W 6
Mar. 12—G. DeLucia, Genoa .... W 6
Apr. 12—Grilli, Milan .... W 6
Apr. 24—G. DiRocco, Genoa ... . W 6
Oct. 5—B. Bisterzo, Milan .... W 8
Nov. 23—Berthelier, Milan .... W 8
Nov. 30—Brioschi, Cagliari ....KO 3
Dec. 16—R. Robert, LaChaux de F. ..... W 10
1950
Jan. 31—Costa, Cagliari .... W 8
Mar. 4—Costa, Bologna .... W 8
Mar. 15—Martinez, Milan ....KO 2
Mar. 22—Nicola Funari, Milan .... W 8
Apr. 15—Jan Nicolaas, Milan .... W 10
May 8—Djilali Bouaziz, Gallarate ...... W 8
May 17—De Joanni, Milan .... W 8
July 14—Gianni Luigi Uboldi, Milan ... W 8
Sept. 13—Allan Tanner, Bologna .... W 10
Nov. 8—Luigi Male, Milano .... D 12
(Italian lightweight title)
Dec. 14—Frank Hermal, Milan .... W 10
1951
Feb. 21—Karl Machart, Milan .... W 10
Mar. 7—Juan Castellanos, Monza ...... W 10
Mar. 14—Paul Guillaume, Milan ....KO 5
Mar. 31—Roland Guilbert, Modena .... W 10
Apr. 14—Leon Bourlet, Milan .... W 8
June 9—Morlay Kamara, Cagliari ...... W 10
July 6—Ray Lewis, Genoa .... W 10
July 18—Gianluigi Uboldi, Milan .... W 12
(vacant Italian lightweight title)
Sept. 1—Leyton Lewis, Varese ....KO 2
Oct. 9—Ray Lewis, Cagliari ....KO 2
Oct. 26—Svend Wad, Geneva .... W 10
Dec. 10—Tommy Barnum, London .... W 10
Dec. 26—Emilio Orozco, Milan ....KO 6
1952
Jan. 14—Karl Pinsdorf, Genoa .... W 10
Apr. 2—Emilio Marconi, Cagliari ...... W 12
(Italian lightweight title)
Apr. 11—Charles Colpin, Genoa ......KO 6
June 4—Augustin Argote, Milan ...... W 10
Aug. 18—Jorgen Johansen, Copenhagen ..L 15
(European lightweight title)
Nov. 11—Alois Brandt, Cagliari .... W 10
Nov. 26—Serge Ceustermans, Milan ..... W 10
Dec. 17—Francis Bonnardel, Milan ..... W 10
1953
Jan. 29—Ernesto Formenti, Milan ....KO 9
(Italian lightweight title)
Feb. 20—Pepe DiJoanni, Genoa .... W 10
Apr. 2—Allan Tanner, Milan .... W 10
May 8—Jean Labalette, Geneva .... W 10
June 20—Ernesto Formenti, Milan .....KO 10
June 27—Franco Antonini, Foligno ..... D 10
July 11—Mario Rosellini, LaSpezia .....KO 2
Sept. 13—Emilio Marconi, Grosseto ..... D 12
(Italian lightweight title)
Oct. 21—Valde Fusaro, Milan .... W 10
Nov. 4—Sandy Manuel, Milan .... W 10
Nov. 15—Jo Janssens, Milan .... W 10
1954
Feb. 6—Jorgen Johansen, Milan .... W 15
(European lightweight title)
Mar. 3—Franco Antonini, Genoa ...... W 10
Mar. 18—Beppe DiJoanni, Rome .... W 10
May 13—Bruno Visintin, Milan .... W 15
(European and Italian lightweight titles)
June 23—Mario Ciccarelli, Milan .... W 10
July 16—Jacques Herbillon, Milan ..... W 10
(European lightweight title)
Sept. 10—Ivor Germain, Milan ....KO 9
Oct. 1—Mario Trigo, Melbourne ...... W 12
Nov. 8—Augustin Argote, Sydney ..... W 12
1955
Jan. 14—Glen Flanagan, Miami Beach ... W 10
Feb. 19—Ray Famechon, Milan .... W 10
Mar. 30—Guy Gracia, Milan .... W 10
Apr. 30—Alby Tissong, Trieste .... W 10
May 22—Louis Carrara, Milan .... W 10
June 8—Morlay Kamara, Florence ..... W 10

July   2—Giancarlo Garbelli, Milan ...... W 15
        (European and Italian lightweight titles)
July   30—Frank Hermal, St. Vincent .... KO 3
Sept. 13—Boswell St. Louis, Milan ...... KO 4
Oct.   15—Joe Lucy, Milan .... W 10
Oct.   29—Werner Handke, Milan .... W 10
Nov.   26—Seraphin Ferrer, Milan .... W 15
        (European lightweight title)
Dec.   26—Gordon Goodman, Milan ..... KO 6
1956
Jan.   21—Orlando Zulueta, Milan .... W 10
Apr.   7—Manolo Garcia, Milan .... W 10
Apr.   21—Abd ben Buker II, Tunis ...... W 10
May   12—Jose Hernandez, Milan .... D 15
        (European lightweight title)
June   23—Fred Galiana, Milan .... KO 6
July   11—Piet van Klaveren, Milan ..... KO 6
July   21—Karl-Heinz Friedrich, Bologna . W 10
Sept. 15—Fernand Nollet, Milan .... W 10
Sept. 23—Albert Muller, Forli .... KO 3
Oct.   13—Maurice Auzel, Milan .... W 10
Nov.   10—Sauveur Chiocca, Milan ...... W 10
Dec.   3—Felix Choicca, Paris .... W 10
Dec.   26—Jose Hernandez, Milan .... W 15
        (European lightweight title)
1957
Feb.   2—Bobby Ros, Milan .... WF 5
Apr.   3—Karl Heinz Bick, Milan .... KO 10
Apr.   27—Hoacine Khalfi, Milan .... W 10
May   29—Rudi Langer, Milan .... W 10
June   2—Chico Santos, Lecco .... KO 6
June   8—Ahcene Attar, Cagliari .... W 10
June   26—Piet van Klaveren, Milan ...... W 10
July   12—Ernst Zetzmann, Milan .... W 10
July   27—Jack Subero, Genoa .... W 10
Sept.   7—Stefano Bellotti, Rome .... W 10
Sept. 25—Idrissa Dione, Milan .... W 10
Oct.   29—Marcel Dupre, Milan .... W 10
Dec.   26—Felix Chiocca, Milan .... W 15
        (European lightweight title)
1958
Feb.   8—Manfred Neuke, Basle .... D 10
Mar.   1—Wallace Bud Smith, Milan .... KO 9
Apr.   27—Al Navarez, Milan .... W 10
July   7—Charley Douglas, Naples ...... W 10
Sept.   5—Mario Vecchiato, Milan ...... D 15
        (European lightweight title)
Dec.   13—Conny Rudhoff, Turin .... W 10
1959
Apr.   19—Emilio Marconi, Milan .... W 15
        (European welterweight title)
Relinquished European lightweight cham-
pionship.
1960
Feb.   13—Bruno Visintin, Milan .... W 15
        (European welterweight title)
Mar.   16—Tommy Molloy, Milan .... KO 4
Mar.   31—Giacomo Nervi, Rome .... W 10
June   15—Carlos Ortiz, San Francisco .... L 15
        (World junior welterweight title)
Sept.   1—Carlos Ortiz, Milan .... W 15
        (World junior welterweight title)
Nov.   25—Maurice Anzel, Rome .... W 15
        (European Welterweight Title)

1961
May   10—Carlos Ortiz, Milan .... W 15
        (retained Junior welterweight title)
Aug.   —Chris Christensen, St. Vincent . W 15
        (Retained European Welterweight Title)
Oct.   21—Eddie Perkins, Milan .... D 15
        (Retained NBA Junior Welterweight Title)
Dec.   6—Epiphane Akono, Rome ...... KO 8
Dec.   20—Gale Kerwin, Milan .... KO 7
1962
Feb.   9—J. D. Ellis, Rome .... W 10
Mar.   27—Billy Collins, Milan .... W 10
Apr.   13—Willie Stevenson, Rome ...... W 10
Apr.   29—Roger Harvey, Milan .... KO 8
May   26—Ike Vaughn, Milan .... KO 5
July   15—Fortunato Manca, Cagliari ..... W 15
        (Retained European Welterweight Title)
Sept. 14—Eddie Perkins, Milan .... L 15
        (Lost Junior Welterweight Title)
Dec.   15—Eddie Perkins, Milan .... W 15
        (Regained World Junior Welterweight Title)
        Announced retirement on January 23,
1963.

TB	KO	WD	WF	D	LD	LF	KOBY	ND	NU
126	25	90	1	7	3	0	0	0	0

EDDIE PERKINS
Chicago, Ill. Junior Welterweight
Born, Clarksdale, Miss., March 3, 1937.
Height 5 ft. 5 in.
1956
Dec.   27—Norm Johnson, Milwaukee ..... L 6
1957
Jan.   23—Jerry Jordan, Chicago .... L 4
Apr.   17—Jerry Jordan, Chicago .... W 4
May   3—Billy Williams, Louisville ...... W 4
Aug.   9—Solomon Boysaw, Cleveland .... L 6
Sept. 11—Jim McCoy, Chicago .... W 6
Oct.   30—Carlo Sario, Chicago .... W 6
Dec.   18—Don Ward, Chicago .... W 6
1958
Jan.   14—Chuck Adkins, Chicago ...... KO 1
Jan.   29—Alan Kennedy, Chicago ...... W 6
Mar.   4—Willie Dillon, Chicago .... KO 5
Apr.   15—Joe Reynolds, Chicago .... W 6
May   14—Cecil Shorts, Chicago .... L 8
June   25—Candy McFarland, Chicago .... W 8
Sept. 24—Cecil Shorts, Chicago .... KO 2
Nov.   12—Frankie Ryff, Chicago .... W 10
Dec.   17—Baby Vazquez, Washington ... KO 7
1959
Jan.   21—Lahouari Godih, Washington ... L 10
Apr.   8—Paul Armstead, Chicago ...... W 10
June   4—Hilario Morales, Los Angeles ... W 10
Sept. 24—Carl Hubbard, Philadelphia ..... L 10
Nov.   28—Al Urbina, Mexico City .... KO by 7
1960
Jan.   12—Larry Boardman, Miami Beach . W 10
Mar.   30—Chico Rollins, Chicago .... W 10
May   18—Paolo Rosi, Chicago .... W 10
Aug.   10—Joe Lopes, Chicago .... KO 7
Sept. 28—Gene Gresham, Chicago ...... W 10
Nov.   18—Chico Santos, Sacramento ..... W 10
1961
Jan.   12—L. C. Morgan, Los Angeles ..... L 10
Feb.   27—Chuck Taylor, Chicago .... W 10
May   6—Baby Vasquez, Monterrey ..... W 10
June   12—Carlos Hernandez, Caracas ..... W 10
July   10—Mauro Vazquez, Tijuana ...... W 10
Oct.   21—Duilio Loi, Milan .... D 15
        (For N.B.A. Junior Welterweight Title)
1962
Mar.   26—Mel Middleton, Philadelphia .. KO 8
June   8—Dick Gilford, Ft. Wayne .... W 10
Sept. 14—Duilio Loi, Milan .... W 15
        (Won World Junior Welterweight Title)
Dec.   15—Duilio Loi, Milan .... L 15
        (Lost World Junior Welterweight Title)
1963
Jan.   14—Omrane Sadok, Paris .... KO 6
Feb.   15—Angel Garcia, Paris .... W 10
June   15—Roberto Cruz, Manila .... W 15
        (Won Vacant World Junior
        Welterweight Title)
Aug.   27—Bobby Scanlon, Sacramento ... W 10
Oct.   1—Joey Limas, Albuquerque .... KO 10
1964
Jan.   4—Yoshinori Takahashi, Tokyo .. KO 13
        (Retained Junior Welterweight Title)
Apr.   18—Bunny Grant, Kingston .... W 15
        Retained Junior Welterweight Title)
June   24—Les Sprague, Regina .... W 10
Sept.   6—Mauro Vasquez, Monterrey ... KO 8
Sept. 18—Mario Rositto, Bogota .... W 10
1965
Jan.   18—Carlos Hernandez, Caracas ..... L 15
        (Lost Junior Welterweight Title)
May   28—Johnny De Pieza,
        Port-of-Spain .... W 10
Aug.   2—Jose Napoles, Juarez .... L 10
Oct.   25—Kenny Lane, New Orleans ..... W 10
1966
May   2—Mel Ferguson, Las Vegas ..... KO 8
Aug.   10—Lennox Beckles, Georgetown ... L 10
Sept. 25—Eugenio Espinosa, Quito ..... ND 3
1967
Feb.   14—Vic Andreeti, London .... KO 8
Mar.   3—Joe N'Gidi, Johannesburg .... W 10
Apr.   3—Adolph Pruitt, Las Vegas ..... W 10
May   29—Paul Armstead, Las Vegas ..... W 10
Aug.   19—Nicolino Loche, Buenos Aires .. L 10
Oct.   2—Adolph Pruitt, Las Vegas ..... W 10
Dec.   5—Angel Robinson Garcia, Milan . W 10
Dec.   19—Joao Henrique, Sao Paulo .... D 10
1968
Sept. 30—Fernand Simard, Quebec ..... KO 5
Oct.   19—NacKeed Mofokeng,
        Johannesburg .... W 10

1969

Jan.	2—Borge Krogh, Copenhagen	W	10
Mar.	15—Richard Boras, Durban	W	10
Mar.	29—Joseph Sishi, Durban	W	10
June	5—Maurice Cullen, Copenhagen	W	8
July	12—Joao Henrique, Sao Paula	L	10

1970

Feb.	16—Dino Del Cid, Chicago	W	10
Mar.	25—Lion Furuyama, Tokyo	W	10
Apr.	27—Clyde Gray, Chicago	W	10
July	21—Pedro Adigue, Honolulu	KO	5
July	26—Bunny Brant, Kingston	L	10
Aug.	8—Hidemori Tsujimoto, Tokyo	KO	10
Sept.	2—Johann Orsolics, Vienna	KO	4
Sept.	20—Raul Rodriguez, Chicago	TD	5
Nov.	20—Don Davis, Vienna	W	10
Dec.	19—Domingo Rubio, Santiago	KO	6

1971

Mar.	10—Dorman Crawford, San Jose	KO	10
Oct.	18—Angel Espada, San Juan	W	10

1972

Apr.	8—Paco Flores, Tucson	W	10
Apr.	17—Jesse Avalos, Niles	W	10
May	11—Frankie Lewis, Chicago	W	10
July	8—Victor Ortiz, San Juan	L	10

1973

Jan.	—Nelson Ruiz, Caracas	KO	10
Jan.	31—Armando Muniz, Denver	W	12
	(North American Welterweight Title)		
Mar.	24—Aristeo Castro, Tucson	KO	2
May	25—Eddie Blay, Vienna	W	10

1974

Mar.	14—Armando Muniz, Tucson	W	10
Apr.	29—Angel Robinson Garcia, Tucson	W	10
May	13—Ryu Sorimachi, Tokyo	W	10
Aug.	16—Rocky Mattiolli, Melbourne	L	10
Oct.	26—Maxwell Malinga, Johannesburg	L	10
Nov.	11—Shoji Tsujimoto, Tokyo	L	10

1975

May	30—Frans Csandl, Koln	L	8

TB	KO	WD	WF	D	LD	LF	KOBY	ND	N
97	21	52	0	3	19	0	1	1	0

ROBERTO CRUZ

Filipino Welterweight
WBA World Junior Welterweight Champion, 1963
Born: November 21, 1941, Baguio City

1958

Sept.	19—Larry Fernandez, Manila	W	8

1959

Feb.	21—Tanny Campo, Manila	W	10
June	5—Gil Flores, Manila	KO	8
July	26—Flashy Panio, Manila	L	8
Oct.	1—Leo Espinosa, Manila	W	12
	(Filipino Featherweight Title)		
Dec.	6—Paulito Escarlan, Manila	W	10
Dec.	19—Flashy Panio, Baguio City	W	8

1960

Jan.	23—Young Terror, Zamboanga	L	10
Apr.	2—Sompong Pitaksamut, Manila	KO	5
June	4—Solomon Boysaw, Manila	L	10
July	9—Solomon Boysaw, Manila	L	10
Nov.	19—J. D. Ellis, Manila	D	10

1961

Apr.	26—Rocky Kalingo, Manila	W	12
	(Filipino Welterweight Title)		
Aug.	5—Gary Cowburn, Manila	W	10
Oct.	21—Johnny Gonsalves, Manila	L	10

1962

Jan.	10—T. R. O. Manchai, Quezon City	W	10
Apr.	7—Shigemasa Kawakami, Manila	KO by	3
Sept.	15—Terry Flores, Manila	KO	6
	(Filipino Welterweight Title)		

1963

Mar.	21—Battling Torres, Los Angeles	KO	1
	(Vacant WBA Junior Welterweight Title)		
June	15—Eddie Perkins, Manila	L	15
	(WBA Junior Welterweight Title)		

1964

(Record Not Available)

1965

Jan.	23—Peter Cobblah, Rizal	L	10
Sept.	18—Rocky Montante, Luzon City	KO	5

1966

July	10—Carl Penalosa, Cebu City	W	10
Oct.	29—Carl Penalosa, Cebu City	D	10

TB	KO	WD	WF	D	LD	LF	KO BY	ND	NC
24	5	9	0	2	7	0	1	0	0

CARLOS HERNANDEZ

Venezuelan Junior Welterweight
Born, April 21, 1940

1959

Jan.	25—Felix Gil, Caracas	KO	3
Mar.	7—Armando Castillo, Havana	KO	2
Mar.	21—Ray Marquez, Havana	KO	2
Apr.	4—Isaac Espinosa, Havana	KO	6
Apr.	17—Angel Chapman, Santa Clara	KO	1
May	2—Frank Serrano, Havana	KO	6
May	16—Pedro Labarrere, Havana	KO	4
June	6—Isidro Rodiguez, Maracaibo	KO	7
June	19—Luke Easter, New York	W	8
Aug.	15—Angel Garcia, Havana	D	10
Aug.	31—Rodolfo Francis, Caracas	W	10
Nov.	2—Doug Vaillant, Caracas	D	10

1960

Jan.	25—Baby Vasuez, Caracas	KO	3
Mar.	14—Davey Moore, Caracas	KO	7
Apr.	1—Gil Cadilli, Caracas	W	10
Apr.	21—Alfredo Urbina, Los Angeles	W	12
July	5—Vicente Rivas, Caracas	KO	8
	(Won Venezuelan Lightweight Title)		
Aug.	31—Bobby Ros, Caracas	KO	6
Oct.	18—Angel Garcia, Caracas	W	10
Oct.	31—Angel Garcia, Caracas	W	10

1961

Feb.	20—Kenny Lane, Caracas	D	10
Mar.	27—Len Matthews, Caracas	W	10
June	12—Eddie Perkins, Caracas	L	10
Aug.	2—Sebastiao Nascimento, Caracas	KO	6
Nov.	2—Jethro Cason, Philadelphia	W	10
Dec.	11—Alfredo Urbina, Philadelphia	W	10

1962

Feb.	5—Tito Marshall, Caracas	KO	7
Mar.	30—Doug Vaillant, Caracas	W	10
May	21—Gene Gresham, Caracas	W	10
June	16—Paolo Rosio, New York	KO	1
July	14—Kenny Lane, New York	L	10
Sept.	17—Doug Vaillant, Caracas	W	10
Nov.	26—Paul Armstead, Caracas	L	10
Dec.	21—Eloy Henry, Caracas	KO	2

1963

May	27—Bunny Grant, Caracas	KO	2
Nov.	11—Joe Brown, Maracaibo	KO	3

1964

June	1—Carlos T. Cruz, Caracas	KO	2
June	22—Jose Napoles, Caracas	KO by	7
Oct.	5—Kenny Lane, Maracaibo	KO	2

1965

Jan.	18—Eddie Perkins, Caracas	W	15
	(Won Junior Welterweight Title)		
May	15—Mario Rossito, Maracaibo	KO	4
	(Retained World Junior Welterweight Title)		
July	10—Percy Hayles, Kinston, Jamaica, BWI	KO	3
	(Retained World Junior Welterweight Title)		

1966

Feb.	6—Humberto Trottman, Balboa	KO	?
Feb.	19—Ismael Laguna, Panama City	KO by	8
Apr.	29—Sandro Lopopolo, Rome	L	15
July	21—Vicente Derado, San Juan	L	10
Oct.	1—Hogan Kid Bassey II, San Juan	KO	3
Nov.	22—L. C. Morgan, Maracaibo	KO	2
Dec.	13—L. C. Morgan, Maracaibo	KO by	4

1967

Jan.	20—Lennox Beckles, San Cristobal	KO	4
June	10—Daniel Guanin, Caracas	KO	2
Sept.	2—Alfredo Urbina, Caracas	D	10
Sept.	29—Curly Aguirre, Caracas	KO	4
Nov.	6—Curly Aguirre, Caracas	KO by	1

1968

Feb.	6—Curly Aguirre, Caracas	KO	2
Apr.	1—Johnny Brooks, Caracas	W	10
July	5—Lalo Moreno, Caracas	KO	3
Aug.	16—Agustin Chavez, Caracas	KO	5
Oct.	6—Herbie Lee, Caracas	KO	7
Nov.	25—German Gastelbondo, Caracas	KO	6
Dec.	20—Ray Adigun, Caracas	KO	6

1969

Jan.	27—Grady Ponder, Caracas	KO	2
Mar.	31—Alfredo Urbina, Maracaibo	KO	2
May	4—Nicolino Locche, Buenos Aires	L	15
	(World Jr. Welter title bout)		
July	15—Jesus Almazzan, Maracaibo	KO	3
June	27—Jose Luis Cruz, Caracas	KO	3
Oct.	10—Eugenio Espinoza, Caracas	W	10

Dec. 8—George Foster, Caracas ......KO 1
Dec. 19—Raimondo Dias, Caracas ....KO 9
1970
Apr. 17—Lloyd Marshall Caracas.......KO 4
June 15—Jaguar Kakizawa, Caracas ..... W 10
1971
May 11—Ken Buchanan, London ...KO by 8
May 13—Retired from Ring.

TB	KO	WD	WF	D	LD	LF	KOBY	ND	NC
71	39	17	0	4	6	0	5	0	0

SANDRO LOPOPOLO
Italian Light Welterweight Champion
Born Milan, December 18, 1939.
Competed for Italy in 1960 Rome Olympiad; lost in final round of lightweight series to Kazimierz Pazdzior of Poland.

1961
Mar. 4—Fernando Favia, Milan ....KO 2
Mar. 18—Robert Misin, Milan...........D 6
Mar. 31—Luigi Lombardi, Ancona .....NC 3
May 31—Antonio DiPaoli, Rome .....WF 5
June 23—Milow Bulat, Milan ....KO 6
July 22—Renato Messori, Saronno ....KO 5
Aug. 5—Mario Pallavera, St. Vincent ...W 8
Sept. 26—Guiliano Tarquini, Turpin ....KO 2
Oct. 6—Nedo Stampi, Pesaro ....D 8
Oct. 21—Ahcene Attar, Milan ....KO 7
Nov. 24—Jamie Aparici, Milan ....W 8
Dec. 26—Giuseppe Fanfoni, Milan .....KO 1
1962
Jan. 19—Bobby Ros, Milan ....W 8
Feb. 27—Sesto Righeschi, Ascoli Piceno . W 8
Mar. 22—Jacky Chauveau, Milan ....KO 7
Apr. 10—Mohamed ben Said, Turin ....KO 6
Apr. 18—Aime Devisch, Milan ....W 8
May 25—Roger Younsi, Milan ....W 8
June 16—Miguel Lopez, Reggio Emilia ..KO 1
June 30—Belaid Meslem, St. Vincent .....W 8
July 22—Romolo Spila, Civitanova .....W 8
Sept. 14—Lucien Moreau, Milan ....W 8
Sept. 28—Franco Caruso, Rome ....W 8
Oct. 25—Jean Dantas, Salsomaggiore..... W 10
Dec. 15—Rene Barriere, Milan ....KO 4
1963
Jan. 25—J. D. Ellis, Milan ....W 10
Mar. 8—Tommy O'Connor, Milan.....KO 1
May 5—Mario Vecchiatto, Milan.......D 1C
Oct. 4—Michele Gullotti, Milan........W 10
Nov. 8—Karl Furcht, Milan...........KO 6
Nov. 28—Franco Caruso, Mestre ....W 12
Dec. 19—Doug Vaillant, Milan ....W 10
1964
Apr. 22—Valerio Nunez, Milan .... D 10
June 28—Giordano Campari, St. Vincent W 12
1965
Feb. 5—Cayetano DeJesus, Piacensa ...W 10
Mar. 12—Piero Brandi, Genoa ....KO 8
(Italian light-welterweight title)
June 18—Antonio de Jesus, Verona .....W 10
July 17—Juan Sombrita, Santa Cruz .....L 15
(European light-welterweight title)
Aug. 22—Franco Caruso, Francavilla .... D 10
Dec. 14—Romano Bianchi, Ascoli Piceno W 12
(Italian light-welterweight title)
1966
Apr. 30—Carlos Hernandez, Rome ......W 15
(Won World Junior Welterweight Title)
July 9—Vicente Rivas, Caracas ....L 10
Aug. 10—Klaus Klein, Senegalia.........W 10
Sept. 10—Nicolino Loche, Buenos Aires...L 10
Oct. 21—Vicente Rivas, Rome..........KO 7
(Retained World Junior Welterweight Title)
Nov. 25—Joe Africa, Torino ....W 10
1967
Apr. 30—Paul Fujii, Tokyo ....KO by 2
(World Junior Welterweight Title)
Oct. 8—Massimo Cosolati, Belgrade ...KO 2
1968
Mar. 23—Conny Rudhof, Belgrado ......W 10
May 25—Lennox Beckles, Milan ....L 8
1969
Mar. 4—Quintano Soarez, Pavia.......KO 2
Apr. 3—Sylvain Lucchesi, Milan ....W 8
May 0—El Harizi, Milan..............W 8
July 11—Olli Maki, Milan.............W 10
Sept. 6—Eddie Machen, Jr., Prato .....KO 1
Oct. 13—Larry Flaviano, Milan ....KO 8

Nov. 8—Miloud N'Diaye, Novara.......W 10
Dec. 19—Lennox Beckles, Milan ....KO 1
1970
Jan. 17—Miloud N'Diaye, Cagliari .....W 10
Apr. 22—Rene Roque, Montecatini ......L 15
(European Jr. Welterweight Title)
May 29—Georges Fabbri, Aosta ....W 10
July 2—Darmon Crawford, Milan ......D 10
Oct. 30—David Pesenti, Genoa ....W 10
1971
Jan. 25—Marcel Cerdan Jr., Paris ....D 10
Mar. 22—Roger Menetrey, Paris.........W 10
May 14—Dorman Crawford, Milan . W Disq. 5
June 9—Robert Gallois, Paris..........L 10
July 29—Jean Van Torre, Monza.......KO 1
Nov. 12—Percy Pugh, Milano ....W 10
1972
Feb. 28—Roger Zami, Paris..............L 15
(Vacant European Junior-Welterweight Title)
Apr. 20—Carlos Cappella, Milan ....W 10
Dec. 9—Roger Menetrey, Grenoble KO by 13
(European welter title)
1973
Mar. 30—Pietro Gasparri, Novara .... W 10

TB	KO	WD	WF	D	LD	LF	KOBY	ND	NC
76	20	36	2	7	8	0	2	0	1

PAUL TAKESHI FUJII
Born, July 6, 1940, Honolulu, Oahu, Hawaiian Islands. Ancestry, Japanese. Weight, 140 lbs. Height, 5 ft. 6½ in..

1964
Apr. 14—Minoru Goto, Tokyo ....KO 2
May 26—Kunio Yoshida, Tokyo ....W 6
June 30—Akio Matsunaga, Tokyo ....KO 3
July 18—Fujio Mikami, Tokyo ....KO 4
Oct. 3—Noriyasu Yoshimura, Tokyo ......KO 2
1965
Jan. 26—Bernie Magallanes, Honolulu.....KO 3
Feb. 16—Manuel Lugo, Honolulu ....KO 3
Feb. 23—Arnie Cotarobles, Honolulu .....KO 8
Mar. 9—Leopoldo Corona, Honolulu .... W 10
Apr. 6—Neto Villareal, Honolulu ....W 8
June 18—Nakao Sasazki, Tokyo ....KO 1
Sept. 9—Fuji Tsukuba, Tokyo ....KO 8
Nov. 16—Johnny Santos, Honolulu ....L 10
1966
Jan. 20—Duk-Bong Kim, Tokyo ....KO 2
Mar. 21—Ador Plaza, Tokyo ....KO 4
May 5—Rudy Gonzales, Tokyo ....W 10
June 5—Fel Pedranza, Tokyo ....KO by 8
June 27—Al Fuentes, Akita ....KO 4
July 7—Ryang-Oh Chang, Yamagata .....KO 2
Aug. 25—Shigeru Hagihara, Kitakyushu ...KO 2
Sept. 29—Rocky Alarde, Tokyo ....KO 3
(Won Oriental Junior Welterweight Title)
Nov. 10—Larry Flaviano, Tokyo ....KO 2
Nov. 15—Luis Molina, Honolulu ....KO 4
Dec. 6—Kid Bassey II, Honolulu ....W 10
1967
Jan. 5—Jesse Cortez, Tokyo ....KO 3
Feb. 12—Carl Penalosa, Tokyo ....KO 2
(Retained Oriental Junior Welterweight Title)
Apr. 30—Sandro Lopopolo, Tokyo ....KO 2
(Won World Junior Welterweight Title)
Aug. 29—Fel Pedranza, Honolulu ....KO 2
Nov. 16—Willi Quatour, Tokyo ....KO 4
(Retained World Junior Welterweight Title)
1968
Feb. 15—Johnny Williams, Tokyo ....KO 2
Apr. 2—Roberto Cruz, Sapporo ....KO 2
Dec. 12—Nicolino Loche, Tokyo .... KO by 10
(Lost World Junior Welterweight Title)
1969
July 24—Manfredo Alipala, Tokyo ....KO 10
Sept. 25—Byong-Mo Yim, Shizuoka City .., D 10

1970

Mar.	5—Pat-Sok Kyu, Tokyo .... KO	3
May	3—Benito Juarez, Tokyo .... KO	3
July	24—Announced retirement.	

TB	KO	WD	WF	D	LD	LF	KO BY	ND	NC
36	27	5	0	1	1	0	2	0	0

NICOLINO LOCHE
Born, September 2, 1939, Mendoza, Argentina.

1958
Dec. 11—Luis Garcia, Mendoza ....KO 2
1959
Jan. 9—Rodolfo Cattalini, Mendoza ... W 8
Jan. 30—Eduardo Zalazar, Mendoza .... W 10
Feb. 27—Leandro Ahumada, Mendoza .. D 9
Mar. 6—Rodolfo Cattalini, Mendoza ..KO 4
Apr. 3—Leandro Ahumada, Mendoza .. W 10
July 29—Juan C. Ramirez, Buenos Aires . W 8
Aug. 8—Pedro Videla, Buenos Aires .... W 8
Oct. 16—Juan Campos, Mendoza .... W 10
Nov. 6—Vicente Derado, Mendoza .....L 10
Dec. 11—Ricardo Joffre, Mendoza ..... D 10
1960
Jan. 8—Hector Tula, Mendoza ......KO 5
Jan. 22—Vincente Derado, Mendoza .... D 10
Feb. 26—Jaime Gine, Mendoza .... W 10
Mar. 25—Juan Campos, Mendoza ...... W 10
June 11—Jaime Gine, Buenos Aires ...... D 10
July 30—Pedro Bennelli, Buenos Aires .. W 10
Sept. 17—Manuel Alvarez, Buenos Aires.. D 10
Nov. 4—Rogelio Andre, Mendoza ...... W 10
1961
Jan. 20—Vicente Derado, Mendoza ..... W 10
Jan. 27—Juan Campos, Cordoba .... D 10
Mar. 10—Antonio Repollo, Mendoza .... W 10
May 12—Julio Cattalini, Mendoza .....KO 10
June 9—Guillermo Cano, Mendoza ..... W 12
Sept. 1—Juan Lujan Flores, Mendoza ..KO 5
Sept. 29—Ubaldino Escobar, Mendoza ... W 10
Oct. 10—Ubaldino Escobar, Mendoza ... W 10
Nov. 4—Jaime Gine, Buenos Aires .....W 12
(Won Lightweight Argentine Title)
Dec. 1—Pedro Benelli, Mendoza .... W 10
Dec. 16—Vicente Derado, Buenos Aires . W 10
1962
Jan. 25—Nuncio Canistra, Palmira .....KO 9
Mar. 30—Fernando Azocar, Mendoza ... W 10
Apr. 24—Abelardo Sire, Mendoza ...... W 10
May 16—Horacio Rivero, Mendoza ....KO 2
June 5—Eulogio Caballero, Mendoza ... W 10
July 6—Heuberto Barbato, Mendoza ... W 10
Aug. 24—Hugo Juarez, Mendoza .... W 10
Sept. 29—Pedro Benelli, Buenos Aires .... W 10
Oct. 20—Manel Alvarez, Buenos Aires .. W 12
(Retained Argentine Lightweight Title)
Dec. 14—Tirstan Falfan, Cordoba ......KO 6
Dec. 28—Tony Padron, Mendoza .... W 10
1963
Feb. 1—Pedro Benelli, Mendoza ...... W 10
Feb. 22—Gregorio Cintas, Salta .... D 10
Mar. 23—Javier Gomez, Buenos Aires ... W 10
Apr. 26—Rodolfo Cattalini, Mendoza ... W 10
May 24—Gregorio Cintas, Mendoza ..... W 10
June 8—Eulogio Caballero, Montevideo W 10
June 29—Sebastino Nascimento,
Buenos Aires .... W 15
(Won South American Lightweight Title)
July 20—Rodolfo Espinosa, M. del Plata . W 10
Aug. 10—Joe Brown, Buenos Aires ...... W 10
Sept. 13—Adan Gomez, Mendoza .... W 10
Sept. 27—Carolos Cappella, Tucuman.... D 10
Oct. 11—Tristan Falfan, Cordoba .... D 10
Dec. 14—Raul Villalba, Buenos Aires .... W 10
1964
Jan. 31—Pedro Benelli, Tucuman .... W 10
Feb. 14—Roberto Palavecino,
Mar Del Plata .... D 10
Mar. 6—Raul Villalba, Mar Del Plata .... W 10
Apr. 18—Roberto Palavecino,
Buenos Aires .... W 10
June 19—Carolos Cappella, Mendoza .... W 10
July 10—Carlos Clemente, Mendoza .... W 10
Aug. 8—Abel Laudonio, Buenos Aires .. W 10
Aug. 21—Diolidio Sosa, Rosario .... W 10
Sept. 4—Roberto Palavecino, Mendoza . W 10
Sept. 19—Gualberto Gutierrez,
Montevideo .... D 10

Oct. 9—Humberto Barbatto,
Bahia Blanca .... W 10
Nov. 14—Abel Lauvonio, Buenos Aires ...L 12
(Lost Argentine Lightweight Title)
Dec. 18—Pedro Beneli, Cordoba .... W 10
1965
Jan. 26—Adam Gomez, Sante Fe .... W 10
Mar. 23—Hugo Rambaldi, Buenos Aires . W 10
Apr. 10—Abel Laudonio, Buenos Aires .. W 12
(Retained South American Heavyweight Title)
Apr. 30—Juan Salinas, Rio Cuarto .....KO 8
July 17—Ismale Laguna, Buenos Aires ... D 10
Aug. 6—Leonardo Peralta, Resistencia .. W 10
Sept. 17—Raul Villalba, Mendoza .... W 10
Dec. 18—Hugo Rambaldi, Buenos Aires . W 12
(Argentina Lightweight Title)
1966
Jan. 22—Omar Gottifredi, Mendoza ..... W 10
Apr. 7—Carlos Ortiz, Buenos Aires ..... D 10
Aug. 19—Omar Salvo, Rio Gallegos ...... W 10
Sept. 10—Sandro Lopopolo,
Buenos Aires .... W 10
Oct. 7—Omar Gottifredi, Mendoza .... W 10
Dec. 30—Omar Salco, Mendoza .... W 10
1967
Jan. 13—Everaldo Costa, Mendoza ...... W 10
Apr. 8—Ubaldino Escobar, Mendoza ... W 10
Apr. 28—Ruben Estanislao, Mendoza ... W 10
May 2—Adan Gomez, Bahia Blanca ... W 10
May 13—L. C. Morgan, Buenos Aires ... W 10
June 2—Adam Gomez, Bahia Blanca ... W 10
July 10—Jose Acha Paz, Mendoza ......KO 7
July 22—Carlos Clemente, Tandil .... W 10
Aug. 4—Osvaldo Piazza, Cipolletti ..... W 10
Aug. 19—Eddie Perkins, Buenos Aires ... W 10
Sept. 1—Lalo Gomez, Bahia Blanca ...KO 10
Sept. 15—Osvaldo Piazza, Cordoba ...... W 10
Oct. 18—Leonardo Peralta, San Rafael .. W 10
Nov. 10—Abel Cachazu, Buenos Aires ... W 10
Nov. 24—Adan Gomez, San Juan .... W 10
Dec. 2—Vicente Derado, Buenos Aires KO 6
1968
Apr. 10—Al Urbina, Buenos Aires ...... W 10
Apr. 20—Juan Gomez, Mar del Plata .... W 10
May 11—Al Urbina, Buenos Aires ...... W 10
June 8—Abel Cachazu, Buenos Aires ... W 10
July 12—Juan Aranda, Mendoza .... W 10
Aug. 2—Tito del Barco, Cordoba .... W 10
Aug. 16—Hilario Suarez,
San Francisco, ... W 10
Sept. 13—Orlando Ribeiro, Mendoza .... W 10
Oct. 12—Anibal Di Lella,
Mar del Plata .... D 8
Dec. 12—Paul Fujii, Tokyo ....KO 10
(Won World Junior Welterweight Title)
1969
Apr. 3—Manuel Hernandez, Mendoza .. W 10
May 4—Carlos Hernandez,
Buenos Aires .... W 15
(World Junior Welterweight Title)
Aug. 2—German Gastelbondo,
Buenos Aires .... W 10
Aug. 20—Angel Roman, Cordoba ...... W 10
Oct. 12—Joao Henrique, Buenos Aires .. W 15
(Retained World Junior Welterweight Title)
1970
Apr. 3—Martin Luaros, Rosario .... W 10
Apr. 17—Marcelino Acevedo, Tandil ...KO 9
May 16—Adolph Pruitt, Buenos Aires ... W 15
(World Junior Welterweight Title)
1971
Feb. 13—Carlos Perlata, Tucuman ...... W 10
Mar. 3—Adan Gomez, La Falda .... W 10
Apr. 3—Domingo Barrera, Buenos Aires W 15
(Retained World Junior Welterweight Title)
Oct. 29—Angel Roman, Salta .... W 10
Nov. 13—Toni Ortiz, Buenos Aires ...... W 10
Dec. 12—Antonio Cervantes, Buenos AiresW 15
(Retained World Junior Welterweight Title)
1972
Feb. 4—Carlos Peralta, San Juan .... W 10
Feb. 16—Nicolas Arcuszyn, Cruz del Eje, W 10
Mar. 12—Alfonso Frazier, Panama City ...L 15
(Lost World Junior Welterweight Title)
Nov. 18—Gerardo Ferratt, Buenos Aires . W 10
Dec. 16—Rey Mercado, Buenos Aires ... W 10
1973
Jan. 25—Pedro Adigue, Buenos Aires ... W 10
Feb. 9—Benny Huertas, Mendoza ..... W 10
Mar. 17—Antonio Cervantes, MaracayKO by 9
(World Junior Welterweight Title)

1953

Mar.	10—Johnny Saxton, Miami Beach .. D	10
Mar.	23—Orlando Zulueta, Brooklyn L	10
May	5—Orlando Zulueta, Cincinnati ... W	10
May	19—Luther Rawlings, Miami Beach . D	10
June	26—Johnny Williams, New York ..KO	1
Aug.	3—Carl Coates, Brooklyn ....KO	6
Aug.	24—Charley Spicer, Brooklyn ....KO	6
Sept.	14—Arthur King, Brooklyn ....KO	5
Nov.	5—Billy Hazel, Newark ....KO	1
Dec.	11—Orlando Zulueta, N. Y. City ... W	10

1954

Feb.	20—Joe Miceli, Cincinnati ..... KO by	5
May	1—Johnny Gonsalves, Cincinnati ... W	10
July	27—Rafael Lastre, Miami Beach ...KO	9
Aug.	31—Rafael Lastre, Miami Beach ...KO	7
Sept.	11—Joe Miceli, Cincinnati L	10
Nov.	20—Arthur Persley, Miami ....KO	9

1955

Jan.	8—Johnny Gonsalves, Miami ..... D	10
June	29—Jimmy Carter, Boston .... W	15
	(Won World Lightweight Title)	
Oct.	19—Jimmy Carter, Cincinnati ...... W	15
	(Title Bout)	

1956

Feb.	7—Larry Boardman, Boston L	10
Mar.	5—Tony DeMarco, Boston ...KO by	9
May	2—Joe Brown, Houston L	10
Aug.	24—Joe Brown, New Orleans L	15
	(Lost World Lightweight Title)	

1957

Feb.	13—Joe Brown, Miami Beach .. KO by	11
	(For World Lightweight Title)	
May	23—Mickey Crawford, Flint L	10
July	25—Cisco Andrade, Los Ang. ..KO by	9
Oct.	31—Bobby Scanlon, San Fran. . KO by	10

1958

Feb.	11—Al Nevarez, Juarez L	10
Mar.	1—Duilio Loi, Milan .... KO by	9
Apr.	1—Gomeo Brennan,	
	Miami Beach ....KO by	5
	Retired in 1959.	

TB	KO	WD	WF	D	LD	LF	KOBY	ND	NC
60	18	13	0	6	16	0	7	0	0

Died. July 11, 1973, Cincinnati, Ohio.

JOE BROWN
(Old Bones)

Born, May 18, 1926, New Orleans, La.
Height, 5 feet, 7½ ins. Managed by Lou Viscusi.
(All Service Lightweight Champion)

1946

Jan.	13—Leoanrd Ceaser, New Orleans ...L	5
Jan.	20—Johnny Monroe, New Orleans .. W	6
Mar.	22—Leonard Ceaser, New Orleans .. D	6
Mar.	29—Leonard Ceaser, New Orleans .. W	8
Apr.	5—Frankie Adams, New Orleans .. W	6
June	28—Herbert Jones, New Orleans ... W	8
July	26—Buster Tyler, New Orleans L	10
Oct.	18—Robert Weatherly, New Orl'ns . W	8

1947

Mar.	7—Buster Tyler, New Orleans .... D	10
Mar.	28—Melvin Bartholomew, N. Orl. ...L	10
Apr.	18—James Carter, New Orleans .... W	10
May	2—Sandy Saddler, New Orl. ..KO by	3
July	4—Melvin Bartholomew, New Orl, W	10
July	23—Freddie Latson, Norwalk, Conn. W	6
Aug.	6—Danny Webb, Montreal ...... W	10
Sept.	24—Dan Robinson, Jersey City ... W	8
Oct.	6—Ernie Butler, Newark ....KO	5
Oct.	21—Arthur King, Toronto .... W	8
Nov.	10—Arthur King, Toronto L	8
Dec.	15—Joey Bagnato, Toronto ....KO	1

1948

Feb.	28—Bobby McQuillar, New Orleans D	10
May	7—Bobby McQuillar, New Orleans .L	10
July	25—Luther Burgess, New Orleans .. D	10
Oct.	1—Freddie Dawson, New Orleans ..L	10
Oct.	26—Frank Crockwell, San	
	Antonio ....KO	5
Nov.	18—Arthur Persley, New Orleans .. W	10
Dec.	3—Johnny Bratton, New Orl. . KO by	4

1949

Mar.	22—Booker Ellis, St. Paul .... W	6
Mar.	28—Luther Rawlings, Chicago ..... W	10
Apr.	25—Joe Sgro, Chicago .... W	8
May	10—Hugh Sublett, So. Bend .... W	8
May	23—John LaBroi, Chicago .... D	8
May	27—Leroy Willis, New Orleans ..... W	10

June	6—Willie Russell, Cincinnati ...... W	10
Dec.	5—Ike Jenkins, Philadelphia ...... W	6

1950

Jan.	20—Milton Scott, Chicago ....KO	2
Feb.	6—Danny Womber, Chicago ..... W	8
Feb.	23—Dave Marsh, Chicago .... W	4
June	16—John L. Davis, Hollywood L	10
Sept.	22—Jack Hassen, Melbourne ......KO	8
Oct.	30—Charley Williams, Sydney ....KO	1
Nov.	27—Irvin Steen, Sydney ....NC	10
Dec.	11—Bernie Hall, Broken Hill ......KO	11

1951

Feb.	20—Tommy Campbell, Los Angeles .L	10
Mar.	10—Baby Ortiz, Ocean Park ......KO	2
Apr.	13—Ted Davis, New Orleans .... W	10
Apr.	27—Lester Felton, New Orleans ... W	10
May	11—Honey Johnson, New Orleans .. W	10
May	25—Virgil Akins, New Orleans ..... W	10
July	6—Virgil Akins, New Orleans ..... W	10
July	22—K.O. Kelly, New Orleans .....KO	5
Aug.	31—Tommy Campbell,	
	New Orleans ....KO	1
Sept.	28—Stonewall Jackson,	
	New Orleans ....KO	5
Dec.	6—Virgil Akins, St. Louis L	10

1952

Feb.	4—Walter Haines, Miami .... D	6
Mar.	14—Walter Hines, New Orleans..... W	10
Mar.	28—Calvin Smith, New Orleans ...KO	7
June	10—Jerry Turner, Tampa ....KO	5
July	11—Melvin Bartholomew, New Orl. W	10
July	18—Marshall Clayton, New Orl. ...KO	9
Aug.	22—Jimmy (Bud) Taylor, New Orl. . W	10
Oct.	10—Georgie Araujo, New York KO by	7
Oct.	17—Dave Cheatum, New Orleans .Exh.	4
Dec.	10—Don Bowman, Cleveland ......KO	1

1953

Jan.	7—Joey Greenwood, Cleveland ... W	8
Apr.	22—Orlando Zulueta, Baltimore ... D	10
June	9—Luther Rawlings, Miami Bch. .. D	10
Dec.	29—Cliff Dyes, Miami Beach ......KO	9

1954

Feb.	8—Charlie Smith, Providence ....NC	6
Mar.	24—Isaac Logart, Miami Beach ..... W	10
June	20—Federico Plummer, Colon ....KO	8
July	25—Wilfredo Brown, Colon ......KO	4
Aug.	31—Nate Jackson, New Orleans ...KO	4
Sept.	28—Carl Coates, New Orleans L	10
Dec.	29—Tony Armenteros, Miami L	6

1955

Jan.	18—Tony Armenteros, New Orl. ..KO	7
Jan.	31—Tito Despaigne, Colon ....KO	4
Mar.	1—Bobby Rosado, Colon .... W	10
Mar.	20—Tony Armenteros, Colon ...... W	10
June	16—Junius West, Colon ....KO	3
Aug.	1—Arthur Persley, New Orleans ...L	12
Oct.	31—Jimmy Hackney, New Orleans. W	10
Nov.	8—Ray Riojas, Houston ....KO	7
Dec.	13—Ray Portilla, Houston ....KO	5

1956

Feb.	6—Arthur Persley, New Orleans ..KO	9
May	2—Wallace (Bud) Smith, Houston . W	10
June	4—Eddie Brant, Beaumont ......KO	3
Aug.	24—Wallace (Bud) Smith, N. Orl. ... W	15
	(Won World Lightweight Title)	

1957

Feb.	13—Wallace (Bud) Smith,	
	Miami Beach ....KO	11
	(World Lightweight Title)	
Mar.	12—Armand Savoie, Houston ..... W	10
June	19—Orlando Zulueta, Denver ....KO	15
	(World Lightweight Title)	
July	30—Gilberto Holguin, San Antonio . W	10
Aug.	21—Joe Lopes, Chicago .... D	10
Nov.	12—Kid Centella, Houston .... W	10
Dec.	4—Joe Lopes, Chicago ....KO	11
	(World Lightweight Title)	

1958

Jan.	24—Ernie Williams, Washington ...KO	5
Feb.	26—Orlando Echevarria, Havana ...KO	1
Apr.	7—Joe Cook, New Orleans ......Exh.	3
May	7—Ralph Dupas, Houston ......KO	8
	(World Lightweight Title)	
July	23—Kenny Lane, Houston .... W	15
	(World Lightweight Title)	
Nov.	5—Johnny Busso, Miami Beach L	10

1959

Feb.	11—Johnny Busso, Houston .... W	15
	(Title Bout)	
June	3—Paolo Rosi, Washington ...KO	8
	(Title Bout)	
Aug.	27—Santiago Ramirez,	
	Baton Rouge ....KO	8

Sept. 9—Gale Kerwin, Columbus ...... KO 4
Sept. 26—Joey Parks, Albuquerque ..... D 10
Dec. 2—Dave Charnley, Houston .....KO 5
   (Title Bout)
Dec. 14—Joey Parks, New Orleans ...... W 10
1960
Mar. 21—Ray Portilla, San Antonio . KO by 6
   (non-title)
Aug. 25—Harlow Irwin, Minneapolis ...KO 5
   (non-title)
Oct. 4—Battling Torres, Houston .....KO 4
Oct. 28—Cisco Andrade, Los Angeles ... W 15
   (World Lightweight Title)
Dec. 7—Giordano Campari, Rome ......L 10
   (non-title)
1961
Mar. 7—Joey Parks, Houston .... W 10
   (non-title)
Apr. 18—Dave Charnley, London .... W 15
   (World Lightweight Title)
Oct. 28—Bert Somodio, Quezon City ... W 15
   (World Lightweight Title)
1962
Apr. 21—Carlos Ortiz, Las Vegas ....L 15
   (Lost World Lightweight Title)
Aug. 24—Louis Molina, San Jose ....L 10
1963
Jan. 22—Tony Noriega, Houston .....KO 6
Feb. 25—Dave Charnley,
   Manchester .... KO by 6
Apr. 20—Manuel Alvarez, Monterrey ...KO 8
May 21—Joe Lopes, Sacramento.......KO 8
June 22—Alfredo Urbina, Monterrey .....L 10
Aug. 10—Nicolino Loche, Buenos Aires...L 10
Sept. 14—Pedro Galasso, Rio de Janeiro .KO 5
Nov. 14—Carlos Hernandez,
   Maracaibo .... KO by 3
1964
Apr. 2—Manuel Gonzales, Odessa ......L 10
Apr. 28—Paul Armstead, Sacramento ...L 10
May 5—Tony Perez, San Jose ...... W 10
May 25—Paul Armstead, San Francisco ...L 10
June 21—Esteban Santamaria, Colon .... L 10
Aug. 25—Richie Mederano, Austin ...L Dis. 10
Sept. 14—Chino Diaz, Omaha ....KO 8
Oct. 3—Percy Hayles, Kingston.......L 10
Nov. 21—Levi Madi, Johannesburg ...... W 10
Dec. 19—Joas Maote, Johannesburg ....KO 6
1965
Feb. 9—Levy Madi,
   Cape Town, S. Africa .... W 10
Feb. 27—Joe Ngidi, Asheshov,
   Johannesburg, S. Africa ....L 10
Mar. 9—Vic Andretti, London, Eng. KO by 5
May 18—Joey Olguin, Sacramento.......L 10
June 29—Blackie Zamora, Corpus Chirsti W 10
Aug. 27—Antonio Mochila,
   Herrera, Cali, Colombia ....L 10
Oct. 2—Mario Rossito, Barranquilla.....L 10
Nov. 13—Frankie Narvaez, San Juan......L 10
1966
Mar. 11—Bruno Arcari, Turin............L 10
Apr. 6—Enoch Nhlapo, Johannesburg .. W 10
Apr. 15—Jarmo Bergloef, Helsinki ...... D 10
May 14—Josiak Nakedi, Bloemfontein .KO 9
June 25—Joe N'Gidi, Durban ....L 10
July 30—Joe N'Gidi, Johannesburg .....L 10
Aug. 30—Rodwell Lekay, Marques ...... W 10
1967
June 16—Blackie Zamora, Baton Rouge KO 8
June 26—Joe Barrientes, New Orleans ... W 10
Aug. 1—Percy Pugh, New Orleans ......L 10
Sept. 11—Benito Juarez, New Orleans.... W 10
Dec. 13—Nathaniel Jackson, Pensacola .KO 5
1968
Apr. 23—Vic Graffio, Beaumont ....KO 8
June 9—Erubey Carmona,
   Mexico City ....KO by 4
Sept. 11—Ricardo Medrano, Beaumont ...L 10
Nov. 6—Jose Garcia, Beaumont ....KO by 9
1969
Aug. 12—Steve Freeman, Houston ...... D 10
1970
Apr. 24—Ramon Flores, Tucson .... W 10

TB	KO	WD	WF	D	LD	LF	KOBY	ND	NC
160	48	56	0	12	32	1	9	0	2

674

CARLOS ORTIZ
Born, September 9, 1936, Ponce, Puerto Rico.
Weight, 135 lbs. Height, 5 ft. 7½ in.
1955
Feb. 14—Harry Bell, New York .... KO 1
Feb. 28—Morris Hodnett, New York .... KO 1
May 13—Danny Roberts, New York ...... KO 3
May 30—Juan Pacheco, New York .... KO 2
June 24—Jimmy DeMura, Syracuse .... W 6
Aug. 10—Tony DeCola, New York .... W 6
Aug. 22—Armand Bush, New York .... W 6
Sept. 19—Hector Rodriguez, New York ..... KO 2
Oct. 3—Leroy Graham, New York .... KO 2
Oct. 29—Al Duarte, Boston .... KO 4
Nov. 12—Lem Miller, Boston .... W 8
Dec. 10—Charley Titone, Paterson .... KO 2
1956
Jan. 9—Ray Portilla, New York .... W 8
Feb. 17—Ray Portilla, New York .... W 8
May 25—Johnny Gorman, New York .... W 6
July 30—Tommy Salem, New York .... W 10
Oct. 27—Mickey Northrup, Hollywood ..... W 10
Dec. 15—Phil Kim, Hollywood .... KO 9
Dec. 31—Gale Kerwin, New York .... W 10
1957
Jan. 23—Bobby Rogers, Chicago .... W 10
Mar. 2—Lou Filippo, Hollywood .... NC 9
Apr. 9—Lou Filippo, Hollywood .... KO 7
May 7—Ike Vaughn, Miami Beach .... W 10
May 29—Felix Chiocca, Chicago .... W 10
Sept. 23—Harry Bell, New York .... W 10
1958
Feb. 28—Tommy Tibbs, New York .... W 10
May 9—Joe Lopes, Hollywood .... W 10
June 27—Johnny Busso, New York .... L 10
Sept. 19—Johnny Busso, New York .... W 10
Oct. 28—Dave Charnley, London .... W 10
Dec. 31—Kenny Lane, Miami Beach ...... L 10
1959
Apr. 13—Len Matthews, Philadelphia ...... KO 6
June 12—Kenny Lane, New York .... KO 2
   (Won Vacant World Junior Welterweight Title)
1960
Feb. 4—Battling Torres, Los Angeles ..... KO 10
   (Retained World Junior Welterweight Title)
June 15—Duilio Loi, San Francisco .... W 15
   (Retained World Junior Welterweight Title)
Sept. 1—Duilio Loi, Milan .... L 15
   (Lost World Junior Welterweight Title)
1961
Feb. 2—Cisco Andrade, Los Angeles .... W 10
May 10—Duilio Loi, Milan .... L 15
   (For World Junior Welterweight Title)
Sept. 2—Doug Vaillant, Miami Beach ..... W 10
Nov. 18—Paolo Rosi, New York .... W 10
1962
Apr. 21—Joe Brown, Las Vegas .... W 15
   (Won World Lightweight Title)
Aug. 1—Arthur Persley, Manila .... W 10
Nov. 7—Kazuo Takayama, Tokyo .... W 10
Dec. 3—Teruo Kosaka, Tokyo .... KO 5
   (Retained World Lightweight Title)
1963
Apr. 7—Doug Vaillant, San Juan .... KO 13
   (Retained World Lightweight Title)
Sept. 18—Pete Juarez, Honolulu .... KO 7
Oct. 22—Maurice Cullen, London .... W 10
1964
Feb. 15—Flash Elorde, Manila .... KO 14
   (Retained World Lightweight Title)
Apr. 11—Kenny Lane, San Juan .... W 15
   (Retained World Lightweight Title)
Dec. 14—Dick Divola, Boston .... KO 1
1965
Apr. 10—Ismael Laguna, Panama City ...... L 15
   (Lost World Lightweight Title)
Nov. 13—Ismael Laguna, San Juan .... W 15
   (Regained World Lightweight Title)
1966
Apr. 7—Nicolino Loche, Buenos Aires ...... D 10

June 20—Johnny Bizzarro, Pittsburgh ...... KO 12
(Retained World Lightweight Title)
Oct. 22—Sugar Ramos, Mexico City .... KO 5
(Retained World Lightweight Title)
Nov. 28—Flash Elorde, New York .... KO 14
(Retained World Lightweight Title)
1967
July 1—Sugar Ramos, San Juan .... KO 4
(Retained World Lightweight Title)
Aug. 16—Ismael Laguna, New York .... W 15
(Retained World Lightweight Title)
1968
June 29—Carlos Teo Cruz, Santo Domingo ... L 15
(Lost World Lightweight Title)
1969
Nov. 21—Edmundo Leite, New York .... W 10
1970
(Inactive)
1971
Dec. 1—Jimmy Ligon, Las Vegas .... KO 3
1972
Jan. 8—Bill Whittenburg, Miami .... KO 7
Jan. 20—Terry Rondeau, Portland, Me. .... KO 4
Jan. 31—Ivelaw Eastman, Waltham .... KO 2
Feb. 19—Leo DiFiore, San Juan .... KO 2
Mar. 20—Junior Varney, Ponce .... KO 2
May 1—Greg Potter, Los Angeles .... W 10
June 3—Gerardo Ferrat, Chicago .... KO 3
Aug. 1—Johnny Copeland, Oklahoma City KO 3
Sept. 20—Ken Buchanan, New York .... KO by 6

TB	KO	WD	WF	D	LD	LF	KO BY	ND	NC
70	30	31	0	1	6	0	1	0	1

KENNY LANE
Born, April 9, 1932, Big Rapids, Michigan.
Weight, 135-140 lbs. Height, 5 ft. 7 in. Southpaw.
Managed by Jack Kearns and Pete Petroskey.
1953
Apr. 9—Clinton McDade, Grand Rapids .... W 4
Apr. 16—Jimmy DeMura, Detroit .... W 4
Apr. 30—Jimmy DeMura, Detroit .... W 4
May 11—John Walls, Chicago .... W 4
May 23—Milton Scott, Chicago .... W 4
June 15—Benny Uhl, Chicago .... W 5
June 18—Johnny Valentine, Detroit .... W 4
July 16—Frank O'Neal, Detroit .... KO 3
July 23—Ron McGilvery, Detroit .... W 4
Aug. 6—Dick Holling, Detroit .... KO 2
Aug. 20—Don Grinton, Detroit .... KO 4
Sept. 10—Eddie Crawford, Detroit .... W 6
Sept. 14—Ralph Cervantes, Saginaw ...... W 6
Sept. 29—Ken Hohner, Grand Rapids ...... W 8
Oct. 20—Ron Stribling, Lansing .... KO by 2
Dec. 1—Ron Stribling, Grand Rapids ...... W 8
1954
Jan. 2—Mike Turcotte, New Orleans ...... W 6
Jan. 14—Jesse Underwood, Saginaw ...... W 10
Feb. 1—John Barnes, Detroit .... KO by 1
Mar. 22—John Barnes, Detroit .... L 8
May 27—Sammy Rodgers, Muskegon ...... W 10
June 22—Elmer Lakatos, Detroit .... W 10
Aug. 12—John Barnes, Muskegon .... W 10
Oct. 4—Georgie Collins, New York .... W 10
Nov. 8—Orlando Zulueta, New York ...... W 10
Dec. 13—Danny Jo Perez, New York ...... W 10
1955
Feb. 14—Jackie Blair, New York .... W 10
Mar. 14—Ralph Dupas, New Orleans .... L 10
Mar. 29—Armand Savole, Grand Rapids ..... W 10
May 31—Richie Howard, Halifax .... W 10
June 7—Eli Leggett, Detroit .... W 10
June 21—Larry Boardman, Miami Beach .... W 10
June 28—Richie Howard, Halifax .... W 10
July 12—Jimmy Ford, Miami Beach .... W 10
July 28—Elmer Lakatos, Milwaukee ...... KO 8
Aug. 3—Noel Humphreys, Mt. Pleasant .... W 10
Aug. 16—Hoacine Khalfi, Miami Beach ..... W 10
Oct. 3—Paddy DeMarco, New York ...... L 10
Nov. 7—Kid Centella, New Orleans ...... W 10

Dec. 6—Don Mason, Milwaukee .... W 10
1956
Feb. 25—Isaac Vaughn, Lansing .... W 10
Mar. 25—Enrique Esqueda, Mexico .... W 10
May 10—Danny Davis, St. Paul .... W 10
July 9—Ralph Dupas, New Orleans .... W 10
Aug. 2—Glen Flanagan, Minneapolis ...... W 10
Aug. 30—Ralph Capone, Muskegon ...... KO 5
Sept. 19—Ludwig Lightburn, Miami .... W 10
Nov. 14—Frankie Ryff, Miami .... W 10
1957
Jan. 30—Frankie Ryff, Norfolk .... KO 6
Apr. 6—Danny Davis, Muskegon .... KO 4
May 22—Henry Brown, Detroit .... KO 6
Aug. 3—Teddy Davis, Muskegon .... W 10
Aug. 20—Johnny Gonsalves, Oakland ...... W 10
Oct. 30—Orlando Zulueta, Chicago .... W 10
Dec. 9—Luke Easter, San Francisco ...... KO 8
1958
Jan. 9—Johnny Gonsalves, Oakland ...... W 10
May 26—Dave Dupas, Dallas .... KO 6
July 23—Joe Brown, Houston .... L 15
(For World Lightweight Title)
Sept. 6—Orlando Zulueta, Muskegon ...... W 10
Nov. 7—Lahouari Godih, Syracuse .... W 10
Dec. 31—Carlos Ortiz, Miami Beach ...... W 10
1959
Apr. 17—Johnny Busso, Hollywood .... KO 6
June 12—Carlos Ortiz, New York .... KO by 2
(For Vacant World Junior Welterweight Title)
Oct. 28—Virgil Akins, Washington .... W 10
Dec. 29—Ray Lancaster, St. Paul .... KO 3
1960
Jan. 13—Ralph Dupas, Mobile .... L 10
Apr. 25—Jerry Black, Philadelphia .... W 10
Aug. 16—Doug Vaillant, Miami Beach ...... W 10
Sept. 27—Sid Adams, Philadelphia .... KO 1
Oct. 8—Len Matthews, Los Angeles ... KO by 3
Dec. 6—Lahouari Godih, Philadelphia .... W 10
1961
Jan. 23—Jose Stable, New York .... L 10
Feb. 20—Carlos Hernandez, Caracas .... D 10
May 1—Rip Randell, Dallas .... W 10
May 16—Manuel Gonzales, Odessa .... W 10
June 8—Curtis Cokes, Dallas .... D 10
June 16—Ray Portilla, San Antonio .... KO 6
June 30—Wilbert Robertson, Muskegon .... W 6
Aug. 14—T. J. Jones, Chicago .... W 10
Sept. 22—Virgil Akins, Annapolis .... W 10
Oct. 16—Aissa Hashas, Paris .... W 10
1962
Jan. 23—Rip Randall, Houston .... L 10
Apr. 14—Louis Molina, San Jose .... W 10
June 11—Tommy Tibbs, Boston .... W 10
July 14—Carlos Hernandez, New York ...... W 10
Sept. 15—Len Matthews, Philadelphia ...... KO 9
1963
Mar. 2—Vicente Derado, New York .... W 10
Aug. 19—Paul Armstead, Saginaw .... W 15
(Won Vacant Michigan World Lightweight Title)
1964
Feb. 19—Johnny Bizzarro, Erie .... W 10
Apr. 11—Carlos Ortiz, San Juan .... L 15
(For World Lightweight Title)
May 9—Stoffel Steyn, Johannesburg ...... KO 9
June 2—Dave Charnley, London .... L 10
Oct. 1—Carlos Hernandez, Maracaibo KO by 2
1965
Oct. 25—Eddie Perkins, New Orleans ...... L 10

TB	KO	WD	WF	D	LD	LF	KO BY	ND	NC
94	16	61	0	2	10	0	5	0	0

ISMAEL LAGUNA
Born, June 28, 1943, Colon, Panama. Weight, 135 lbs. Height, 5 ft. 9 in. Managed by Hector (Tato) Valdes.
1961
Jan. 8—Al Morgan, Colon .... KO 2
Jan ??—Eduardo Frutos, Colon .... W 4
Mar. 5—Javier Valle, Panama City .... W 4

Mar.	26—Carlos Real, Panama City	W	4
Apr.	16—Jose Pacheco, Panama City	KO	3
Apr.	30—Ernest Campbell, Panama City	W	6
May	21—Battling Escudero, Colon	KO	2
June	4—Killer Solomon, Colon	KO	7
June	25—Claudio Martinez, Colon	KO	4
Aug.	27—Enrique Hitchman, Panama City	W	10
Oct.	15—Euro Partides, Panama City	KO	4
Dec.	1—Hector Hicks, Colon	KO	5

1962

Jan.	14—Eloy Sanchez, Colon	KO	3
Mar.	2—Castor Castillo, Maracaibo	W	10
Apr.	15—Nelson Estrada, Panama City	KO	7
June	3—Jorge Uzcategui, Colon	KO	2
June	10—Agustin Carmona, Panama City	KO	6
June	24—Carlos Celis, Panama City	KO	3
July	29—Jorge Salazar, Panama City	KO	6
Sept.	16—Pedro Ortiz, Panama City	KO	7
	(Won Panamanian Featherweight Title)		
Oct.	28—Beresford Francis, Colon	KO	5
Nov.	18—Enrique Hitchman, Colon	KO	2
Dec.	16—Tony Herrera, Panama City	KO	2

1963

Jan.	20—Bobby Gray, Colon	KO	9
Feb.	22—Juan Ramirez, Panama City	W	10
Mar.	17—Auburn Copeland, Panama City	W	10
May	21—Fili Nava, Panama City	KO	3
June	8—Antonio Herrera, Bogota	L	10
July	21—Don Johnson, Panama City	KO	3
Aug.	24—Lalo Guerrero, Panama City	W	10
Sept.	15—Antonio Herrera, Panama City	KO	7
Nov.	18—Rafiu King, Paris, France	W	10

1964

Jan.	26—Pedro Miranda, Colon	KO	4
Feb.	21—Orispo Dos Santos, Sao Paulo	KO	7
Mar.	9—Angel Robinson Garcia, Paris	W	10
June	1—Vicente Saldivar, Tijuana	L	10
July	6—Kid Anahuac, Los Angeles	KO	8
Aug.	2—Vicente Derado, Panama City	W	10
Oct.	25—Percy Hayles, Panama City	KO	7
Dec.	19—Sebastiano Mascimento, Panama City	W	10

1965

Apr.	10—Carlos Ortiz, Panama City	W	15
	(Won World Lightweight Title)		
June	20—Raul Soriano, Panama City	KO	8
July	17—Nicolino Loche, Buenos Aires	D	10
Nov.	13—Carlos Ortiz, San Juan	L	15
	(Lost World Lightweight Title)		

1966

Feb.	19—Carlos Hernandez, Panama City	KO	8
Mar.	19—Flash Elorde, Manila	L	10
July	28—Al Grant, Los Angeles	W	10
Oct.	2—Percy Hayles, Kingston	KO	6
Dec.	3—Daniel Guanin, Panama City	KO	8

1967

Mar.	10—Frankie Narvaez, New York	W	10
Apr.	2—Vicente Rivas, Panama City	KO	5
June	3—Alfredo Urbina, Panama City	W	10
Aug.	16—Carlos Ortiz, New York	L	15
	(For World Lightweight Title)		
Oct.	28—Paul Armstead, Panama City	W	10

1968

Feb.	26—Ray Adigun, Paris, France	W	10
Apr.	15—Bud Anderson, Philadelphia	KO	10
Apr.	29—Frankie Narvaez, San Juan	W	10
July	17—Victor Melendez, New York	W	10
Aug.	20—Lloyd Marshall, New York	KO	9
Oct.	7—Gabe LaMarca, Portland, Me.	KO	7
Oct.	22—Grady Ponder, Miami Beach	W	10
Nov.	15—Ramon Blanco, New York	W	10

1969

Mar.	1—Curley Aguirre, Panama City	KO	4
Mar.	31—Maurice Tavant, Lyons	W	10
May	24—Eugenio Espinoza, Quito	L	10
July	5—Eugenio Espinoza, Panama City	W	10
July	14—Genaro Soto, New York	W	10

1970

Mar.	3—Mando Ramos, Los Angeles	KO	9
	(Regained World Lightweight Title)		

June	7—Ishimatsu Suzuki, Panama City	KO	13
	(Retained World Lightweight Title)		
Sept.	26—Ken Buchanan, San Juan, P.R.	L	15
	(Lost World Lightweight Title)		

1971

Mar.	6—Lloyd Marshall, Panama City	W	10
Apr.	3—Chango Carmona, Panama City	W	10
June	22—Eddie Linder, Miami Beach	L	10
Sept.	13—Ken Buchanan, New York	L	15
	(For World Lightweight Title)		

1972

Apr.	15—Announced retirement.	

TB	KO	WD	WF	D	LD	LF	KO BY	ND	NC
74	36	28	0	1	9	0	0	0	0

CARLOS TEO CRUZ
(Carlos Teofilo Rosario Cruz)

Born, November 4, 1937, Santiago de los Caballeros, Dominican Republic. Weight, 135 lbs. Managed by Pete Martinez.

1959

Oct.	23—Juan Jose Jiminez, Santo Domingo	L	8
Dec.	3—Rafael Acevedo, Santo Domingo	W	10

1960

Mar.	26—Jesus Serrano, Santo Domingo	W	6
May	6—Daniel Berrios, San Juan	L	10
May	29—Eutaqui Gonzalez, San Juan	KO	5
June	11—Bob Ashford, San Juan	KO	3
July	5—Marcos Morales, San Juan	L	10
Sept.	2—Lionel Rivera, San Juan	KO	10
Sept.	15—Daniel Berrios, San Juan	L	10
Nov.	25—Gerardo Clemente, San Juan	KO	10

1961

Feb.	24—Daniel Berrios, San Juan	L disq.	2
May	26—Vernon Lynch, San Juan	L	10
Aug.	20—Daniel Berrios, San Juan	L	4
Aug.	26—Gerardo Clemente, San Juan	W	8
Oct.	17—Lionel Rivera, San Juan	KO	4

1962

Jan.	15—Jose Aneiro, San Juan	KO	8
Feb.	17—Rafael Acevedo, Santo Domingo	W	12
June	1—Alejandro Gonzalez, San Juan	W	6
Sept.	14—Sammy Burgess, San Juan	W	10
Nov.	24—Freddy Jackson, Totowa	D	6
Dec.	18—Candy Padilla, New York	W	6

1963

Jan.	12—Calvin Woodland, New York	W	6
Feb.	5—Roland Kellem, New York	W	8
Mar.	2—George Foster, New York	W	6
July	6—Johnny Bean, San Juan	W	10
Nov.	1—Vicente Derado, New York	L	10

1964

Feb.	14—Graham Dickers, Brisbane	L	12
Mar.	2—Guizani Rezgui, Sydney	KO	11
Mar.	6—Gilberto Biondi, Melbourne	W	12
June	1—Carlos Hernandez, Caracas	KO by	2
June	14—Tony Publico, Manila	L	10
Sept.	20—Julio Ruiz, Balboa	L	10
Dec.	12—Marcos Morales, Santo Domingo	KO	2

1965

Feb.	3—Cresencio Fernandez, St. Croix	KO	3
Apr.	3—Alejandro Parra, Santo Domingo	KO	4
June	18—Daniel Berrios, Caguas, P.R.	KO	1
July	6—Frankie Taylor, London	W	10
Aug.	14—Chico Veliz, Mayaguez, P.R.	W	10
Sept.	4—Vicente Derado, San Juan	W	10

1966

Feb.	12—Paul Armstead, San Juan	W	10
Apr.	2—Jaime Valladares, Quito	D	10
May	7—Bunny Grant, San Juan	W	10
Aug.	13—Vicente Derado, San Juan	W	10
Oct.	1—Fernand Simard, San Juan	KO	5
Dec.	12—Frankie Narvaez, San Juan	L	10

1967

May	6—Frankie Narvaez, San Juan	W	10
June	23—Grady Ponder, San Juan	W	10
Dec.	11—Kennedy Clark, San Juan	W	10

1968

Mar.	3—Johnny Bean, Santo Domingo	KO	2

Apr.   15—Julio Viera, San Juan .... W 10
June   29—Carlos Ortiz, Santo Domingo ...... W 15
       (Won World Lightweight Title)
Sept. 28—Mando Ramos, Los Angeles .... W 15
       (Retained World Lightweight Title)
1969
Feb.   18—Mando Ramos, Los Angeles ... KO by 11
       (Lost World Lightweight Title)
Aug.   9—Grady Ponder, San Juan .... W 10
Sept. 20—Len Kesey, San Juan .... KO   4
Oct.   20—Victor Melendez, New York .... W 10
1970
Jan.   17—Benito Juarez, San Juan .... W 10

TB	KO	WD	WF	D	LD	LF	KO BY	ND	NC
57	13	28	0	2	11	1	2	0	0

Died, February 15, 1970, with his wife and two children in an airplane crash off the coast of the Dominican Republic.

ARMANDO (MANDO) RAMOS

Born, November 15, 1948, Long Beach, California. Weight, 135 lbs. Managed by Jackie McCoy and Lee Prlia.

1965
Nov.   17—Berlin Roberts, Los Angeles .... W   4
Dec.   2—Chuey Loera, Los Angeles .... KO   2
1966
Jan.   27—Berlin Roberts, Los Angeles ...... KO   1
Mar.   3—Fidel Cruz, Los Angeles .... KO   3
Mar.   17—Jose Barrera, Los Angeles .... KO   2
May   12—Bosco Basillo, Los Angeles .... KO   6
June   23—Jerry Stevens, Los Angeles .... KO   1
July   7—Joey Aguilar, Los Angeles .... KO   8
July   22—Ray Coleman, Los Angeles .... KO   6
Aug.   11—Manny Linson, Los Angeles .... KO   2
Sept.   8—Baby Salazar, Los Angeles .... W 10
Oct.   13—Allen Syres, Los Angeles .... KO   5
Nov.   17—Al Franklin, Los Angeles .... W 10
Nov.   28—Al Franklin, Oakland .... KO   4
1967
Jan.   17—Ray Echevarria, Los Angeles ...... W 10
Mar.   30—Pete Gonzalez, Los Angeles .... W 10
June   22—Len Kesey, Los Angeles .... KO   5
July   6—Suh-Il Kang, Los Angeles .... L 10
Aug.   15—Alex Luna, Sacramento .... KO   2
Sept. 14—Eliseo Estrada, Los Angeles ...... KO   5
Oct.   5—Frankie Crawford, Los Angeles ..... L 10
1968
Feb.   1—Frankie Crawford, Los Angeles .... W 10
May   2—Phil Garcia, Los Angeles .... KO   9
June   20—Hiroshi Kobayashi, Los Angeles ... W 10
Sept. 28—Carlos Teo Cruz, Los Angeles ...... L 15
       (For World Lightweight Title)
Oct.   29—Billy Coleman, San Antonio ...... KO   3
Dec.   12—Beau Jaynes, Los Angeles .... KO   2
1969
Feb.   18—Carlos Teo Cruz, Los Angeles .... KO 11
       (Won World Lightweight Title)
May   21—Jerry Graci, Honolulu .... KO   7
Oct.   4—Yoshiaki Numata, Los Angeles ... KO   6
       (Retained World Lightweight Title)
1970
Jan.   13—Leonardo Aquero, San Antonio .... W 10
Mar.   3—Ismael Laguna, Los Angeles ... KO by   9
       (Lost World Lightweight Title)
Aug.   7—Sugar Ramos, Los Angeles .... W 10
Dec.   10—Raul Rojas, Los Angeles .... KO   6
1971
Sept. 30—Ruben Navarro, Los Angeles ...... W 10
Nov.   5—Pedro Carrasco, Madrid .... L disq. 11
       (For Vacant WBC Lightweight Title)
1972
Feb.   19—Pedro Carrasco, Los Angeles ...... W 15
       (Won WBC Lightweight Title)
June   28—Pedro Carrasco, Madrid .... W 15
       (Retained WBC Lightweight Title)
Sept. 15—Chango Carmona, Los Angeles KO by   8
       (Lost WBC Lightweight Title)

1973
Aug.   9—Arturo Pineda, Los Angeles ... KO by   5
1974
May   3—Jaroslav Travnik, Vienna .... D   8
May   10—Whan-Ki Min, Lubeck .... KO   2
May   16—Arpad Majai, Hamburg .... KO   4
June   3—Wolfgang Gans, Lubeck .... KO by   2
July   12—Wolfgang Gans, Palma .... KO by   6
1975
July   30—Tony Martinez, Las Vegas .... L 10
Sept.   2—Al Franklin, Oklahoma City .... W 10
Oct.   15—Antonio Leyva, Las Vegas .... KO   7
Oct.   29—Wayne Beale, Las Vegas ..... KO by   2

TB	KO	WD	WF	D	LD	LF	KO BY	ND	NC
49	23	14	0	1	4	1	6	0	0

KEN BUCHANAN

Born, June 28, 1945, Edinburgh, Scotland. Weight, 135 lbs. Height, 5 ft. 7½ in.

1965
Sept. 20—Brian Tonks, London .... KO   2
Oct.   18—Vic Woodhall, Manchester .... KO   2
Nov.   1—Billy Williams, London .... KO   2
Nov.   22—Joe Okezie, London .... KO   3
Dec.   13—Junior Cassidy, London .... W   8
1966
Jan.   24—Tommy Tiger, London .... W   8
Mar.   7—Manley Brown, London .... KO   4
Apr.   4—Tommy Tiger, London .... W   8
Apr.   19—Chris Elliott, London .... W   8
May   11—Junior Cassidy, Manchester ...... W   8
July   12—Brian Smyth, Aberavon .... KO   1
Aug.   6—Ivan Whiter, London .... W   8
Sept.   6—Mick Laud, London .... W   8
Oct.   17—Antonio Paiva, London .... W 10
Nov.   29—Al Keen, Leeds .... W   8
Dec.   19—Phil Lundgren, London .... W 10
1967
Jan.   23—John McMillan, Glasgow .... W 10
       (Won Vacant Scottish Lightweight Title)
Feb.   14—Tommy Garrison, London .... W 10
May   11—Franco Brondi, Paisley .... KO   3
June   3—Winston Laud, London .... W   8
July   26—Rene Roque, Aberavon .... W 10
Sept. 14—Al Rocca, London .... KO   7
Oct.   30—Spike McCormack, London ...... W 12
1968
Feb.   19—Maurice Cullen, London .... KO 11
       (Won British Lightweight Title)
Apr.   22—Leonard Tavarez, London .... W   8
June   10—Ivan Whiter, London .... W   8
Oct.   23—Angel Robinson Garcia, London .... W 10
Dec.   11—Ameur Lamine, Hamilton .... KO   3
1969
Jan.   2—Frankie Narvaez, London .... W 10
Feb.   17—Mike Cruz, London .... KO   4
Mar.   5—Jose Luis Torcida, Solihull .... W   8
July   14—Jerry Graci, Nottingham .... KO   1
Nov.   11—Vincenzo Pitardi, London .... KO   2
1970
Jan.   29—Miguel Velasquez, Madrid .... L 15
       (For Vacant European Lightweight Title)
Feb.   23—Leonard Tavarez, London .... W 10
Apr.   6—Chris Fernandez, Nottingham ..... W 10
May   12—Brian Hudson, London .... KO   5
       (Retained British Lightweight Title)
Sept. 26—Ismael Laguna, San Juan .... W 15
       (Won World Lightweight Title)
Dec.   7—Donato Paduano, New York .... W 10
1971
Feb.   12—Ruben Navarro, Los Angeles ...... W 15
       (Retained World Lightweight Title)
May   11—Carlos Hernandez, London ...... KO   8
Sept. 13—Ismael Laguna, New York .... W 15
       (Retained World Lightweight Title)
1972
Mar.   28—Al Ford, London .... W 10
Apr.   29—Andries Steyn, Johannesburg .... KO   3

June 26—Roberto Duran, New York ..... KO by 13
(Lost World Lightweight Title)
Sept. 20—Carlos Ortiz, New York .... KO 6
Dec. 4—Chang-Kil Lee, New York .... KO 2
1973
Jan. 29—Jim Watt, Glasgow .... W 15
(Regained British Lightweight Title)
Mar. 28—Hector Matta, London .... W 10
May 31—Frankie Otero, Miami Beach ..... W 10
Sept. 1—Chu Chu Malave, New York ..... KO 7
Oct. 11—Frankie Otero, Toronto .... KO 6
Dec. 6—Miguel Araujo, Copenhagen ...... KO 1
1974
Feb. 7—Jose Peterson, Copenhagen .... W 10
Apr. 4—Joe Tetteh, Copenhagen .... KO 3
May 1—Antonio Puddu, Cagliari .... KO 6
(Won European Lightweight Title)
Sept. —Relinquished British lighweight title.
Nov. 21—Winston Noel, Copenhagen ...... KO 2
Dec. 16—Leonard Tavarez, Copenhagen ... KO 14
(Retained European Lightweight Title)
1975
Feb. 27—Ishimatsu Suzuki, Tokyo .... L 15
(For WBC Lightweight Title)
July 25—Giancarlo Usai, Cagliari .... KO 12
(Retained European Lightweight Title)
1976-1978
(Inactive)
1979
June 28—Benny Benitez, Randers .... W 8
Sept. 6—Eloi de Souza, Randers .... W 8
Dec. 6—Charlie Nash, Copenhagen ...... L 12
(For European Lightweight Title)
1980
May 15—Najib Daho, London .... KO 7
Oct. 20—Des Gwilliam, Birmingham .... W 8

TB	KO	WD	WF	D	LD	LF	KO BY	ND	NC
65	27	34	0	0	3	0	1	0	0

EDUARDO (PEDRO) CARRASCO

Born, July 11, 1943, Huelva, Spain. Weight, 135 lbs. Height, 5 ft. 8½ in. Managed by Umberto Branchini.
1962
Oct. 24—Carlo Leggenda, Imola .... KO 2
Nov. 27—Domenico Pillon, Turin .... KO 4
1963
Jan. 9—Franco Rosini, Milan .... W 6
Jan. 30—Tristano Tartarini, Milan .... W 6
Feb. 22—Emilio Riccetti, Milan .... W 6
Mar. 29—Pietro Ziino, Milan .... W 4
Mar. 29—Luciano Lambertini, Milan .... W 4
(Won European Lightweight Prospects Tournament)
May 10—Franco Rosini, Turin .... D 6
May 27—Franco Rosini, Modena .... W 6
Aug. 2—Juan Carbajal, Barcelona .... W 6
Aug. 24—Juan Pinto, Barcelona .... W 6
1964
Feb. 7—Giuseppe Amante, Milan .... W 8
Mar. 11—Aldo Pravisani, Rome .... L 8
Apr. 22—Giuliano Scatolini, Milan ...... KO 4
May 16—Teresito Colombo, Gallarate .... W 6
June 28—Serafino Lucherini, St. Vincent .... W 8
July 6—Fortunato Munzone, St. Angelo
Lodigiano .... KO 6
July 18—Giancarlo Stelluti, Falconara ..... KO 5
Aug. 14—Tristano Tartarini, Falconara ..... W 6
Sept. 19—Cosimo Lacirignola, Milan .... W 8
Oct. 6—Aldo Pravisani, Turin .... W 8
Nov. 26—Pedro Gomez Acebo, Barcelona ... W 8
Dec. 10—Mohamed Laroussi, Basel .... KO 3
Dec. 23—Miguel Kimbo, Barcelona .... W 8
1965
Feb. 4—Juan Pinto, Barcelona .... W 8
Feb. 17—Vincenzo Pitardi, Turin .... W 8
June 28—Lat Shonibare, Naples .... KO 4
July 9—Cosimo Lacirignola, Bergamo .... KO 4
Aug. 28—Serfafino Lucherini, Gubbio ...... KO 7
Sept. 18—Mario Oberti, Varese .... KO 7
Oct. 30—Pedro Gomez Acebo, Como .... W 8

Dec. 13—Rene Roque, Milan .... W 8
1966
Jan. 20—Roger Younsy, Barcelona .... KO 1
Feb. 3—Serafino Lucherini, Barcelona ..... W 8
Feb. 17—Georges Payen, Barcelona .... KO 8
Mar. 3—Pierre Tirlo, Barcelona .... KO 8
Mar. 12—Ameur Lamine, Barcelona .... W 8
Mar. 31—Mario Oberti, Barcelona .... W 8
May 13—Emilio Riccetti, Madrid .... W 10
May 26—Quintino Soarez, Barcelona ...... KO 6
June 2—Victor Alves, Madrid .... KO 3
June 10—Dris Ben Amar, Madrid .... KO 3
June 17—Karl Furcht, Barcelona .... KO 3
June 28—Waldir Derceira, Valencia .... KO 5
July 8—Ricardo Navarro, Madrid .... KO 3
July 17—Manuel Prieto, Valencia .... W 10
Aug. 5—Pedro Gomez Acebo, Madrid ...... KO 3
Aug. 13—Joao Martin, Valencia .... KO 5
Sept. 2—Tony Falcon, Madrid .... KO 2
Sept. 9—Boaulem Belouard, Madrid ...... KO 3
Sept. 22—Daniel Deneux, Barcelona .... KO 6
Oct. 7—Roy Ate, Madrid .... KO 3
1967
Apr. 8—Yanclo II, Salamanca .... KO 5
Apr. 29—Abdel Bachir, Seville .... KO 3
May 13—Angel Neches, Salamanca .... W 8
June 2—Jesse Green, Madrid .... KO 3
June 30—Borge Krogh, Madrid .... KO 8
(Won European Lightweight Title)
Dec. 1—Aldo Pravisani, Madrid .... W 10
Dec. 16—Omar Oliva, Bilbao .... KO 4
Dec. 22—Franco Brondi, Madrid .,........ KO 4
1968
Feb. 3—Paul Rourre, Las Palmas .... KO 4
Mar. 9—Edoardo Batista, Tenerife .... KO 4
Mar. 19—Giampiero Salami, Valencia ...... KO 4
Apr. 7—Enrique Levy, Huelva .... KO 4
May 10—Kid Tano, Madrid .... KO 8
(Retained European Lightweight Title)
July 20—Jose Luis Penteado, Vigo .... KO 3
July 31—Serafino Lucherini, Valencia ...... W 10
Aug. 10—Valerio Nunez, Valladolid .... KO 3
Sept. 13—Bruno Melissano, Barcelona ...... KO 3
(Retained European Lightweight Title)
Oct. 19—Olli Maeki, Valencia .... W 15
(Retained European Lightweight Title)
Nov. 16—Kid Rainbow, Vigo .... KO 3
Dec. 6—Al Rocca, Barcelona .... KO 3
1969
Jan. 2—Jose Luis Penteado,
Copenhagen .... W disq. 4
Mar. 6—Tore Magnussen, Barcelona ...... KO 3
(Retained European Lightweight Title)
Mar. 29—Ould Makloufi, Malaga .... KO 6
Apr. 30—Klaus Jacobi, Barcelona .... KO 2
June 13—Miguel Velasquez, Madrid .... W 15
(Retained European Lightweight Title)
July 24—Paul Rourre, Villafranca .... KO 6
Aug. 6—Massimo Consolati, Bilbao .... KO 5
Sept. 11—Angel Robinson Garcia, Bilbao .... W 10
Sept. 27—Paul Rourre, Valencia .... KO 9
Oct. —Relinquished European lightweight title.
Oct. 24—Victor Baerga, Vigo .... KO 4
Nov. 6—Bill Whittenburg, Madrid .... KO 5
Nov. 22—Giampiero Salami, Rome .... KO 6
Dec. 20—Vic Andretti, Madrid .... KO 5
Dec. 30—Dino Del Cid, Barcelona ...... W disq. 2
1970
Jan. 15—Massimo Consolati, Las Palmas .. KO 3
Jan. 29—Giacomo Gulino, Madrid .... KO 6
Feb. 19—Dave Wyatt, Barcelona .... KO 3
Mar. 5—Luis Vallejo, Bilbao .... KO 2
Mar. 18—Lakdar El Harizi, Valencia ...... KO 6
May 23—Jaime Marquez, Madrid .... KO 2
June 13—Carlos Almeida, Almeria .... KO 5
June 26—Jean Pierre Le Jaouen, Madrid ... KO 2
Aug. 22—Olli Maeki, Valencia .... W 10
Sept. —Matthew Thomas, Madrid .... KO 2
Nov. 21—Joe Tetteh, Barcelona .... D 10
Dec. 26—Joe Tetteh, Madrid .... W 10

678

1971

Feb.	19—Pietro Vargellini, Madrid	KO	5
Apr.	17—Giacomo Gulino, Milan	KO	9
May	21—Rene Roque, Madrid	W	15

(Won European Junior Welterweight Title)

June	18—David Pesenti, Barcelona	W disq.	10
July	8—Klaus Jacobi, Zaragoza	KO	3
July	30—Bruno Meggiolaro, Madrid	W	10
Sept.	10—Jerry Wells, Bilbao	KO	5
Nov.	5—Mando Ramos, Madrid	W disq.	11

(Won Vacant WBC Lightweight Title)

1972

Feb.	18—Mando Ramos, Los Angeles	L	15

(Lost WBC Lightweight Title)

June	28—Mando Ramos, Madrid	L	15

(For WBC Lightweight Title)

Sept.	22—Enrico Barlatti, Barcelona	KO	4
Dec.	1—Beau Jaynes, Madrid	KO	6

TB	KO	WD	WF	D	LD	LF	KO BY	ND	NC
110	66	35	4	2	3	0	0	0	0

ROBERTO DURAN
(Record Under Welterweight Champions)

ERUBEY (CHANGO) CARMONA
(Eudibiel Guillen Chapin)
Born, September 29, 1944, Mexico City, Mexico.

1964

Jan.	18—Tony Lopez, Monterrey	W	6
Apr.	22—Joel Osorio, Mexico City	KO	2
Aug.	1—Arturo Salas, Mexico City	W	6
Aug.	15—Kid Chocolate, Acapulco	KO	6
Sept.	19—Jesus Gonzales, Mexico City	KO	2
Oct.	7—Jorge Jimenez, Mexico City	L	8
Oct.	24—Gustavo Garcia, Oaxaca	KO	8
Nov.	11—Joaquin Velazquez, Mexico City	KO	6

1965

Feb.	3—Gustavo Garcia, Mexico City	KO	5
Apr.	17—Lupe Ramirez, Mexico City	W	8
May	4—Rogelio Reyes, Juarez	D	10
July	24—Jorge Jimenez, Mexico City	KO	8
Aug.	28—Manuel Andrade, Mexico City	KO	5
Oct.	23—Arturo Morales, Mexico City	L	10

1966

Jan.	26—Arturo Morales, Mexico City	L	10
Mar.	19—Marcos Gomez, Guadalajara	KO	5
June	15—Nicolas Sanchez, Mexico City	KO	6
July	6—Battling Kid, Leon	KO	5
Aug.	10—Lupe Ramirez, Mexico City	W	10
Oct.	17—Juan Ortiz, Mexico City	KO	5
Nov.	5—Charro Gomez, Mexico City	KO	3

1967

Feb.	11—Lalo Moreno, Mexico City	KO	4
Mar.	11—Bernabe Vazquez, Mexico City	W	10
May	6—Alfredo Urbina, Mexico City	L	10
July	1—Chucho Garcia, Mexico City	W	10
Sept.	4—Arturo Lomeli, Tijuana	W	12

(Won Mexican Lightweight Title)

Oct.	21—Alfredo Urbina, Mexico City	L	12

(Lost Mexican Lightweight Title)

1968

Feb.	24—Javier Ayala, Mexico City	KO	3
June	9—Joe Brown, Mexico City	KO	4
Aug.	10—Renaldo Victoria, Mexico City	KO	3
Sept.	21—Norio Endo, Mexico City	KO	2
Nov.	13—Percy Hayles, San Antonio	KO	4
Dec.	21—Hugo Rambaldi, Mexico City	KO by	1

1969

Mar.	2—Frankie Narvaez, San Antonio	L	10
Mar.	7—Juan Escobar, Acapulco	KO	5
May	19—Ramon Blanco, San Diego	KO	8
June	20—Genato Soto, San Antonio	D	10
July	26—Alfonso Frazer, Mexico City	KO	3
Sept.	9—Doug Agin, San Antonio	KO	2
Sept.	30—Sugar Ramos, Tijuana	KO by	7

1970

Mar.	22—Jose Luis Herrera, Monterrey	KO	5

Apr.	11—Orlando Ribeiro, Mexico City	KO	4
July	13—Ray Adigun, Tijuana	KO	4
Aug.	22—Fermin Soto, Mexico City	KO	9
Oct.	10—Jaguar Kakizawa, Mexico City	KO	10
Nov.	17—Arturo Lomeli, Tijuana	KO	8

1971

Jan.	10—Gerardo Ferrat, Mexico City	KO	3
Feb.	13—Fermin Soto, Mexico City	W	12
Apr.	3—Ismael Laguna, Panama City	L	10
June	19—Antonio Amaya, Monterrey	KO	7
Aug.	6—Ismael Rivera, Acapulco	KO	4
Aug.	31—Raimundo Diaz, Juarez	KO by	5

1972

Feb.	12—Lalo Moreno, Mexico City	KO	7
Apr.	4—Raimundo Diaz, Tijuana	KO	8
May	18—Masataka Takayama, Los Angeles	KO	3
July	6—Jimmy Robertson, Los Angeles	KO	8
Sept.	15—Mando Ramos, Los Angeles	KO	8

(Won WBC Lightweight Title)

Nov.	10—Rodolfo Gonzalez, Los Angeles	KO by	13

(Lost WBC Lightweight Title)

1973

Mar.	17—Jimmy Heair, Los Angeles	L	10
July	31—Shinichi Kadota, Honolulu	KO by	7

1974-1978
(Inactive)

1979

Dec.	20—Francisco Candela, Acapulco	KO	2

TB	KO	WD	WF	D	LD	LF	KO BY	ND	NC
61	38	8	0	2	8	0	5	0	0

RODRIGO GONZALEZ
Born, 1945, Mexico. Weight, 117-135 lbs.

1960

Dec.	16—Javier Garcia, Jiquilpan	KO	2

1961

Jan.	15—Juan Arias, Leon, Guanajuato	KO	1
	—Jose Munoz, Atemaja	KO	1
	—Javier Garcia, Jiquilpan	KO	1
	—Roberto Nuno, Atemaja	KO	2
	—Tony G. Perez, Atemaja	KO	2
	—Jose Luis Castillo, Guadalajara	KO	3
	—Roberto Nuno, Guadalajara	KO	3
	—Jose Vargas, Atontonilco	KO	1
	—Serafino Sanchez, Jiquilpan	KO	4
	—Kid Irapuato, Jiquilpan	KO	8
	—Gregorio Lopez, Guadalajara	KO	2
	—Vaquero Montoya, Guadalajara	KO	4
	—Guadalupe Barrajas, Guadalajara	KO	3
	—Salvador Banvelos, Guadalajara	KO	3
	—Alfredo Sanchez, Guadalajara	W	10
	—Antonio Luna, Guadalajara	KO	7
	—Ruben Ramirez, Guadalajara	KO	4
	—Diablito Campos, Mazatlan	KO	5
	—Paco Gomez, Mazatlan	W	10
	—Ramon Cabiedes, Atotonilco	W	10
	—Jose Luis Castillo, Guadalajara	W	10
	—Evaristo Perez, Guadalajara	KO	8
	—Generalito Nunez, Autlan de la Grana	KO	4
	—Jose Luis Castillo, Guadalajara	L	8

1962

May	12—Babe Lopez, Guadalajara	W	8
June	23—Evaristo Perez, Guadalajara	KO	3
Sept.	1—Babe Lopez, Guadalajara	KO	2

1963

Feb.	15—Lecho Guerrero, Los Angeles	L	10

1964
(Inactive)

1965

Nov.	16—Bobby Valdez, Los Angeles	L	10
Dec.	20—Bobby Valdez, Los Angeles	D	10

1966

May	20—Bobby Valdez, San Bernardino	KO by	9
July	7—Ray Coleman, Las Vegas	W	6
Aug.	11—Raul Carreon, Las Vegas	W	8
Sept.	1—Raul Carreon, Las Vegas	KO	4
Oct.	13—Alton Colter, Las Vegas	L	10
Nov.	10—Daniel Valdez, Los Angeles	W	10

1967

Feb.	9—Marcelo Cid, Los Angeles	KO	4
May	10—Ram Sarmiento, Long Beach	KO	1
July	19—Claude Adams, Long Beach	KO	8

1968

Oct.	3—Ray Adigun, Los Angeles	KO	10
Dec.	19—Rene Macias, Los Angeles	KO	9

1969

Apr.	17—Pete Gonzales, Los Angeles	KO	4
May	15—Juan Collado, Los Angeles	KO	9
July	3—Julio Viera, Los Angeles	KO	2
Aug.	28—Steve Freeman, Los Angeles	KO	5
Nov.	11—Javier Jimenez, San Antonio	KO	6

1970

May	7—Fermin Soto, Los Angeles	KO	7
Dec.	17—Antonio Cervantes, Los Angeles	KO by	8

1971

Apr.	26—Ernesto Villaflor, Honolulu	KO	2
May	26—Beto Gonzalez, Sacramento	W	10
Oct.	2—Juan Collado, Northridge	W	10
Dec.	11—Nick Aghai, Long Beach	W	10

1972

Feb.	24—Manny Leal, Los Angeles	KO	7
Mar.	16—Chun-Kyo Shin, Los Angeles	KO	7
Apr.	27—Jimmy Robertson, Los Angeles	W	10
July	31—Ruben Navarro, Anaheim	W	10
Nov.	10—Chango Carmona, Los Angeles ...	KO	13
	(Won WBC Lightweight Title)		
Dec.	16—Jose Acosta, Monterrey	KO	1

1973

Mar.	17—Ruben Navarro, Los Angeles	KO	9
	(Retained WBC Lightweight Title)		
Aug.	31—Don Sennett, Los Angeles	KO	3
Oct.	27—Antonio Puddu, Los Angeles	KO	10
	(Retained WBC Lightweight Title)		

1974

Apr.	11—Ishimatsu Suzuki, Toky	KO by	8
	(Lost WBC Lightweight Title)		
Aug.	26—Clemente Mucino, Tijuana ...	W disq.	2
Nov.	28—Ishimatsu Suzuki, Osaka	KO by	13
	(For WBC Lightweight Title)		
Dec.	16—Javier Garcia, Jiquilpan	KO	2

TB	KO	WD	WF	D	LD	LF	KO BY	ND	NC
66	43	13	1	1	4	0	4	0	0

YUJI (ISHIMATSU) SUZUKI

Born, June 5, 1949, Tochigi Prefecture, Japan.
Weight, 135 lbs. Height, 5 ft. 8 in.

1966

Dec.	11—Masao Fujiwara, Tokyo	KO	1

1967

Jan.	9—Yoichi Ichikawa, Tokyo	KO	1
Feb.	12—Akio Fujita, Tokyo	W	4
Mar.	5—Toru Kimura, Tokyo	KO	3
May	17—Hajime Kagawa, Tokyo	L	4
June	12—Hajime Kagawa, Tokyo	D	4
Aug.	9—Keji Murabayashi, Tokyo	KO by	1
Oct.	6—Kazuo Yashiro, Tokyo	L	4
Nov.	8—Tadao Nakemura, Tokyo	KO	1
Dec.	5—Tetsuji Okamoto, Tokyo	W	4

1968

Jan.	17—Haruo Kikumoto, Tokyo	KO	3
Jan.	31—Toshio Araguchi, Tokyo	W	4
Apr.	2—Noboru Nakamoto, Tokyo	KO	2
June	15—Koichi Otomaru, Tokyo	L	4
July	15—Hitoshi Komase, Tokyo	D	4
Oct.	13—Tsunehisa Ninomiya, Tokyo	KO	2
Nov.	17—Makoto Yumi, Tokyo	KO	1

1969

Feb.	13—Tsuyoshi Yamamoto, Tokyo	KO	2
Mar.	3—Haruo Kikumoto, Tokyo	D	8
May	6—Hitoshi Komase, Tokyo	D	8
July	23—Isao Shuya, Tokyo	L	8
Sept.	10—Haruo Kikumoto, Tokyo	W	10
Oct.	9—Kenichiro Date, Tokyo	W	10
Dec.	10—Isao Ichihara, Tokyo	KO	6

1970

Jan.	25—Jaguar Kaizawa, Tokyo	L	10

June	7—Ismael Laguna, Panama City	KO by	13
	(For World Lightweight Title)		
Oct.	10—Lionel Rose, Melbourne	L	10
Oct.	30—Rene Barrientos, Honolulu	L	10

1971

Mar.	3—Masataka Takayama, Tokyo	D	10
	(For Japanese Lightweight Title)		
Apr.	7—Hitoshi Komase, Tokyo	W	10
Aug.	13—Shinichi Kadota, Tokyo	KO by	8
Jan.	16—Shinichi Kadota, Tokyo	W	12
	(Won Oriental Lightweight Title)		
Apr.	6—Hiroyuki Murakami, Tokyo	W	10
May	19—Rudy Gonzales, Tokyo	W	12
	(Retained Oriental Lightweight Title)		
Dec.	18—Kenji Iwata, Tokyo	KO	1

1973

Apr.	23—Fred Pastor, Tokyo	W	12
	(Retained Oriental Lightweight Title)		
July	30—Hiroshi Tonooka, Tokyo	KO	3
Sept.	8—Roberto Duran, Panama City ..	KO by	10

1974

Feb.	28—Jinny Cruz, Tokyo	KO	4
Apr.	11—Rodolfo Gonzalez, Tokyo	KO	8
	(Won WBC Lightweight Title)		
Sept.	12—Tury Pineda, Nagaya	D	15
	(Retained WBC Lightweight Title)		
Nov.	28—Rodolfo Gonzalez, Osaka	KO	13
	(Retained WBC Lightweight Title)		

1975

Feb.	27—Ken Buchanan, Tokyo	W	15
	(Retained WBC Lightweight Title)		
June	5—Tury Pineda, Osaka	W	15
	(Retained WBC Lightweight Title)		
Dec.	4—Alvaro Rojas, Tokyo	KO	14
	(Retained WBC Lightweight Title)		

1976

May	8—Esteban De Jesus, Puerto Rico	L	15
	(Retained WBC Lightweight Title)		

1977

Apr.	2—Saensak Muangsurin, Tokyo ..	KO by	6
	(For WBC Junior Welterweight Title)		

1978

June	20—Yohi Arai, Tokyo	L	10

TB	KO	WD	WF	D	LD	LF	KO BY	ND	NC
48	16	12	0	6	9	0	5	0	0

ESTEBAN DE JESUS

Born, August 2, 1951, Carolina, Puerto Rico.
Weight, 135-140 lbs. Height, 5 ft. 5½ in.

1969

Feb.	10—El Tarita, San Juan	KO	2
July	21—Braulio Rodriguez, San Juan	KO	4
Aug.	2—Francisco Maldonado, San Juan ..	KO	3
Aug.	23—Johnny Sandoval, San Juan	W	6
Sept.	27—Ramon Montes, San Juan	KO	3
Oct.	18—Kid Sheffield, San Juan	KO	2
Nov.	22—Ivelaw Eastman, San Juan	KO	5

1970

Jan.	24—Martin Cuello, San Juan	KO	2
Feb.	14—Chino Guerrero, San Juan	KO	3
Feb.	28—Braulio Rodriguez, San Juan	KO	8
Mar.	28—Bobby Parnell, San Juan	KO	1
Apr.	6—Ike Estrada, San Juan	KO	5
Apr.	30—Chino Jimenez, Ponce	W	10
May	12—Coverly Daniels, San Juan	KO	8
July	9—Tommy Shaffer, San Juan	KO	8
Sept.	30—Johnny Sandoval, San Juan	W	10
Oct.	3—Jose Llano, San Juan	KO	9

1971

Apr.	12—Johnny Harp, San Juan	W	10
May	5—Gustavo Briceno, San Juan	W	10
July	24—Josue Marquez, San Juan	W	12
Aug.	7—Victor Ortiz, San Juan	KO	4
Sept.	4—Josue Marquez, San Juan	W	12
Oct.	6—Lionel Hernandez, Caracas	W	10
Oct.	20—Frank LeRoy, Caracas	KO	7
Oct.	30—Milton Mendez, Caracas	KO	5
Dec.	10—Antonio Gomez, Caracas	L	10

1972

Feb.	14—Percy Hayles, San Juan	W	10
Apr.	10—George Foster, New York	KO	8
May	1—Josue Marquez, New York	KO	12
July	8—Angel Robinson, San Juan	W	10
July	28—Chuck Wilburn, New York	W	10
Sept.	18—Raymundo Dias, San Juan	W	10
Oct.	30—Doc McClendon, San Juan	W	10
Nov.	17—Roberto Duran, New York	W	10

1973

Feb.	16—Ray Lampkin, San Juan	W	12
	(Won Vacant NABF Lightweight Title)		
Apr.	16—Johnny Gant, San Juan	W	10
May	21—Raul Montoya, San Juan	W	10
July	14—Ray Lampkin, New York	W	12
	(Retained NABF Lightweight Title)		
Sept.	8—Radamas Checo, Panama City	KO	1
Oct.	29—Mike Mavon, San Juan	W	10
Nov.	22—Al Foster, San Juan	KO	1

1974

Jan.	7—Alfonso Frazer, San Juan	KO	10
Mar.	16—Roberto Duran, Panama City	KO by	11
	(For World Lightweight Title)		
June	10—Gerardo Ferratt, San Juan	KO	5
Sept.	2—Javier Ayala, San Juan	W	10

1975

Mar.	15—Jesse Lara, Caracas	KO	3
May	17—Antonio Cervantes, Panama City	L	15
	(For World Junior Welterweight Title)		
Oct.	11—Rudy Barros, Ponce	KO	5

1976

Mar.	6—Valentin Ramos, San Juan	KO	2
May	8—Ishimatsu Suzuki, San Juan	W	15
	(Won WBC Lightweight Title)		
Sept.	10—Hector Medina, San Juan	KO	7
	(Retained WBC Lightweight Title)		

1977

Feb.	12—Buzzsaw Yamabe, San Juan	KO	6
	(Retained WBC Lightweight Title)		
June	24—Vicente Saldivar, San Juan	KO	11
	(Retained WBC Lightweight Title)		
Sept.	10—James Brackett, San Juan	W	10

1978

Jan.	21—Roberto Duran, Las Vegas	KO by	12
	(For World Lightweight Title)		
June	3—Joe Baez, San Juan	KO	3
July	8—Chuchu Hernandez, San Juan	KO	2
Oct.	27—Edwin Viruet, New York	W	10

1979

Oct.	4—Jimmy Blevins, New York	W	10
Nov.	9—Ruby Ortiz, New York	W	10

1980

May	10—Jose Vallejo, San Juan	KO	7
July	7—Saoul Mamby, Bloomington	KO by	13
	(For WBC Junior Welterweight Title)		

TB	KO	WD	WF	D	LD	LF	KO BY	ND	NC
62	32	25	0	0	2	0	3	0	0

JIM WATT

Born, July 18, 1948, Glasgow, Scotland. Weight, 135 lbs. Southpaw. Managed by Terry Lawless.

1968

Oct.	30—Santos Martin, Hamilton	KO	4
Dec.	11—Alex Gibson, Hamilton	KO	2

1969

Apr.	10—Victor Paul, Glasgow	W	8
Sept.	15—Winston Thomas, London	KO	6
Nov.	24—Tommy Tiger, London	W	8

1970

Feb.	16—Victor Paul, London	KO by	6
June	1—Victor Paul, London	KO	5
June	15—Bryn Lewis, Nottingham	KO	6
Oct.	20—Sammy Lockhart, Belfast	KO	2
Dec.	1—Ron Clifford, Leeds	KO	4

1971

Jan.	11—David Pesenti, Nottingham	W	8
Mar.	22—Henri Nesi, London	KO	6
Sept.	27—Willie Reilly, London	KO	7
Nov.	1—Leonard Tavarez, London	KO	9

1972

Feb.	1—Willie Reilly, Nottingham	KO	10
	(Won British Lightweight Title)		
May	3—Tony Riley, Solihull	KO	12
	(Retained British Lightweight Title)		
Dec.	11—Novel McIvor, London	KO	3

1973

Jan.	29—Ken Buchanan, Glasgow	L	15
	(Lost British Lightweight Title)		
May	9—Johnny Cheshire, Solihull	W	8
June	7—Noel NcIvor, Glasgow	KO	4
Oct.	5—Angus McMillan, Glasgow	W	8

1974

Feb.	16—Andries Steyn, Johannesburg	KO	7
Mar.	2—Kokkie Olivier, Johannesburg	W	10
June	19—Billy Waith, Caerphilly	W	12
Oct.	26—Anthony Morodi, Johannesburg	L	10

1975

Jan.	27—Johnny Cheshire, Glasgow	KO	7
	(Regained Vacant British Lightweight Title)		
Mar.	19—Billy Waith, London	W	10
May	3—Jonathan Dale, Lagos	L	15
Oct.	31—Andre Holyk, Lyons	L	12

1976

Mar.	2—George Turpin, London	KO	4
Mar.	30—Jimmie Revie, Hammersmith	KO	7
May	10—Hector Diaz, London	KO	4
June	22—Johnny Claydon, London	KO by	3
Oct.	12—Franco Diana, London	KO	6

1977

Feb.	21—Johnny Claydon, London	KO	10
	(Retained British Lightweight Title)		
Aug.	5—Andre Holyk, Glasgow	KO	1
	(Won Vacant European Lightweight Title)		
Nov.	16—Jeronimo Lucas, Solihull	KO	10
	(Retained European Lightweight Title)		

1978

Feb.	17—Perico Ferndandez, Madrid	W	15
	(Retained European Lightweight Title)		
June	12—Billy Vivian, London	W	8
Oct.	18—Antonio Guinaldo, Glasgow	KO	5
	(Retained European Lightweight Title)		

1979

Apr.	17—Alfredo Pitalua, Glasgow	KO	12
	(Won Vacant WBC Lightweight Title)		
Nov.	3—Robert Vasquez, Glasgow	KO	9
	(Retained WBC Lightweight Title)		

1980

Mar.	14—Charlie Nash, Glasgow	KO	4
	(Retained WBC Lightweight Title)		
June	7—Howard Davis, Glasgow	W	15
	(Retained WBC Lightweight Title)		
Nov.	1—Sean O'Grady, Glasgow	KO	12
	(Retained WBC Lightweight Title)		

TB	KO	WD	WF	D	LD	LF	KO BY	ND	NC
45	28	11	0	0	4	0	2	0	0

ERNESTO ESPANA

Born, 1954, Venezuela. Weight, 135 lbs. Height, 5 ft. 11 in. Managed by Pepi Cordero.

1975

Mar.	17—Hernan Rodriguez, Caracas	KO	1
July	14—Jose Figuerero, Caracas	W	1
Aug.	8—Freddy Briceno, Caracas	KO	3
Aug.	25—Luis Beltran Rodriguez, Caracas	L	6
Oct.	4—Luis Romero, Caracas	KO	2
Nov.	17—Ruben Arias, Santo Domingo	KO	1

1976

Feb.	18—Cesar Chavez, Maturin	KO	2
Feb.	28—Danton Morillo, Caracas	KO	2
Mar.	6—Luis Beltran Rodriguez, Caracas	W	10
June	13—Juan Sarmiento, Caracas	KO	3
July	11—Julio Pena, Caracas	KO	1
Aug.	20—Clemente Mucino, Caracas	KO	1
Aug.	29—Rolando Martinez, Caracas	KO	1
Oct.	16—Andrew Fernandez, Caracas	KO	1
Nov.	14—Ricardo Arrendondo, Caracas	W	10

1977

Jan.	30—Isaac Martin, Caracas	KO	5

May	15—Milton Mendez, Caracas .... KO	1
July	3—Salvador Torres, Caracas .... KO	1
Aug.	27—Angel Rosas, San Juan .... KO	5

1978

Apr.	22—Geraldo Aceves, San Juan .... KO	2
July	8—Teo Ozuna, San Juan .... KO	1
Sept.	9—Bienvenido Quinto, San Juan .... KO	1
Oct.	28—Johnny Barr, San Juan .... KO	1

1979

Feb.	19—Fernando Jiminez, San Juan ..... KO	6
Mar.	25—Ed Bracetty, San Juan .... KO	1
June	16—Claude Noel, San Juan .... KO	13
	(Won Vacant WBA Lightweight Title)	
Aug.	4—Johnny Lira, Chicago .... KO	10
	(Retained WBA Lightweight Title)	

1980

Mar.	2—Hilmer Kenty, Detroit .... KO by	9
	(Lost WBA Lightweight Title)	
Sept.	20—Hilmer Kenty, San Juan ...... KO by	4
	(For WBA Lightweight Title)	

TB	KO	WD	WF	D	LD	LF	KO BY	ND	NC
29	23	3	0	0	1	0	2	0	0

HILMER KENTY
(James Hilmer Kenty)
Born, July 30, 1955, Austin, Texas. Weight, 135 lbs. Height, 5 ft 11 in. Managed by Emanuel Steward.

1977

Oct.	13—Steve Homan, Columbus .... W	6
Nov.	26—Ray Carrington, Columbus .... W	6
Dec.	16—Earl Stringer, Detroit .... KO	3

1978

Apr.	17—Mike Gray, Columbus .... KO	2
July	27—Ron Pettigrew, Canton .... W	6
Oct.	26—Jessie Rogers, Detroit .... KO	1
Dec.	9—Eddie Murray, Detroit .... KO	3

1979

Jan.	11—Jose Pena, Detroit .... KO	3
Jan.	25—Jose Gonzales, Detroit .... KO	7
Mar.	3—Alberto Herrera, Detroit .... KO	4
May	8—Danny Benitez, Detroit .... KO	4
June	28—Arturo Leon, Detroit .... W	10
Aug.	2—Ralph Racine, Detroit .... W	10
Aug.	23—Bobby Flores, Detroit .... KO	1
Oct.	18—Sebastian Mosquiera, Detroit ..... KO	4
Nov.	30—Scotty Foreman, New Orleans .... KO	3

1980

Mar.	2—Ernesto Espana, Detroit .... KO	9
	(Won WBA Lightweight Title)	
Aug.	2—Young-Ho Oh, Detroit .... KO	9
	(Retained WBA Lightweight Title)	
Sept.	20—Ernesto Espana, San Juan .... KO	4
	(Retained WBA Lightweight Title)	
Nov.	8—Vilomar Fernandez, Detroit .... W	15
	(Retained WBA Lightweight Title)	

TB	KO	WD	WF	D	LD	LF	KO BY	ND	NC
20	14	6	0	0	0	0	0	0	0

682

JUNIOR LIGHTWEIGHTS

ARTIE O'LEARY	*1917-1919*	**HIROSHI KOBAYASHI**	1967-1971
JOHNNY DUNDEE	1921-1923	*RENE BARRIENTOS (WBC)*	*1969-1970*
JACK BERNSTEIN	1923	*YOSHIAKI NUMATA (WBC)*	*1970-1971*
JOHNNY DUNDEE	1923-1924	**ALFREDO MARCANO**	1971-1972
STEVE (KID) SULLIVAN	1924-1925	*RICARDO ARRENDONDO (WBC)*	*1971-1974*
MIKE BALLERINO	1925	**BEN VILLAFLOR**	1972-1973
TOD MORGAN	1925-1929	**KUNIAKI SHIBATA**	1973
BENNY BASS	1929-1931	**BEN VILLAFLOR**	1973-1976
KID CHOCOLATE	1931-1933	*KUNIAKI SHIBATA (WBC)*	*1974-1975*
FRANKIE KLICK	1933-1934	*ALFREDO ESCALERA (WBC)*	*1975-1978*
SANDY SADDLER	1949-1950	**SAMUEL SERRANO**	1976-1980
HAROLD GOMES	1959-1960	*ALEXIS ARGUELLO (WBC)*	*1978-1980*
GABRIEL (FLASH) ELORDE	1960-1967	**YASUTSUNE UEHARA**	1980-
YOSHIAKI NUMATA	1967	*RAFAEL (BAZOOKA) LIMON (WBC)*	*1980-*

Claimants not generally recognized are in *italics*.

WORLD JUNIOR LIGHTWEIGHT CHAMPIONSHIP BOUTS

Date	Winner	Weight	Loser	Weight		Time KO	Site	Referee
11/18/21	Johnny DUNDEE	128¼	George K.O. CHANEY	130	WF 5	1:07	Madison Square Garden, New York	Kid McPartland
7/6/22	Johnny DUNDEE	129	Jack SHARKEY	127	unan 15		Ebbets Field, Brooklyn, N.Y.	Kid McPartland
8/28/22	Johnny DUNDEE	124¾	Pepper MARTIN	130	unan 15		Velodrome, New York City, N.Y.	Patsy Haley
2/2/23	Johnny DUNDEE	129¾	Elino FLORES	129½	unan 15		Madison Square Garden, New York	Patsy Haley
5/30/23	Jack BERNSTEIN	128	Johnny DUNDEE	128½	unan 15		Velodrome, New York City, N.Y.	Patsy Haley
6/25/23	Jack BERNSTEIN	129	Freddy JACKS	130	KO 5		Shetzline Park, Philadelphia, Pa.	Pop O'Brien
12/17/23	Johnny DUNDEE	127½	Jack BERNSTEIN	129	15		Madison Square Garden, New York	Jock O'Sullivan
6/20/24	Kid SULLIVAN	129½	Johnny DUNDEE	129	10		Henderson's Bowl, Brooklyn, N.Y.	Jock O'Sullivan
8/18/24	Kid SULLIVAN	129	Pepper MARTIN	130	unan 15		Queensboro Stadium, New York	Tommy Sheridan
10/15/24	Kid SULLIVAN	129½	Mike BALLERINO	129	KO 5	0:38	Madison Square Garden, New York	Tommy Sheridan
4/1/25	Mike BALLERINO	129½	Kid SULLIVAN	129½	unan 10		Armory A.A., Philadelphia, Pa.	Pop O'Brien
7/6/25	Mike BALLERINO	129¾	Pepper MARTIN	239¾	unan 15		Queensboro Stadium, New York	Johnny McAvoy
12/2/25	Tod MORGAN	128	Mike BALLERINO	129¾	TKO 10		Olympic Auditorium, Los Angeles	
6/3/26	Tod MORGAN	127½	Kid SULLIVAN	128½	TKO 6	2:05	Ebbets Field, Brooklyn, New York	Jim Crowley
9/30/26	Tod MORGAN	128½	Joe GLICK	129½	unan 15		Madison Square Garden, New York	Patsy Haley
10/19/26	Tod MORGAN	128½	Johnny DUNDEE	126¼	unan 10		Recreation Park, San Francisco	Harry Ertle
11/19/26	Tod MORGAN	127½	Carl DUANE	129	unan 15		Madison Square Garden, New York	Lou Magnolia
5/28/27	Tod MORGAN	129¾	Vic FOLEY	125½	ref 12		Arena, Vancouver, B.C.	Joe Waterman
2/16/27	Tod MORGAN	128¾	Joe GLICK	129½	WF 14	2:09	Madison Square Garden, New York	Eddie Forbes
5/24/28	Tod MORGAN	129¾	Eddie MARTIN	130	15		Madison Square Garden, New York	Lou Magnolia
7/18/28	Tod MORGAN	128	Eddie MARTIN	128	unan 15		Ebbets Field, Brooklyn, New York	Eddie Forbes
12/3/28	Tod MORGAN	130	Santiago ZORILLA	127¼	draw 10		State Armory, San Francisco	Toby Irwin
1/1/29	Tod MORGAN	128½	Joey SANGOR	128	ND 10		Milwaukee Auditorium, Wisconsin	Walter Houlehen
4/5/29	Tod MORGAN	128	Santiago ZORILLA	129	10		Olympic Auditorium, Los Angeles	Lt. Jack Kennedy
5/20/29	Tod MORGAN	129	Baby Sal SORIO	128¾	10		Wrigley Field, Los Angeles	Benny Whitman
12/20/29	Benny BASS	127	Tod MORGAN	128	KO 2	0:51	Madison Square Garden, New York	Jim Crowley
3/28/30	Benny BASS	128	Eddie SHEA	126½	ND 10		Arena, St. Louis, Missouri	Harry Ertle
1/5/31	Benny BASS	127½	Lew MASSEY	128	unan 10		Philadelphia Arena, Pa.	Leo Houck
7/15/31	Kid CHOCOLATE	125½	Benny BASS	128½	TKO 7	2:58	Baker Bowl, Philadelphia, Pa.	Leo Houck
4/10/32	Kid CHOCOLATE	128½	Davey ABAD	129¾	15		Polar Stadium, Havana, Cuba	
8/4/32	Kid CHOCOLATE	127½	Eddie SHEA	128	unan 10		Chicago Stadium, Illinois	Phil Collins
10/13/32	Kid CHOCOLATE	125¾	Lew FELDMAN	125½	TKO 12	2:45	Madison Square Garden, New York	Patsy Haley
12/9/32	Kid CHOCOLATE	125½	Fidel LA BARBA	124	maj 15		Madison Square Garden, New York	Willie Lewis
5/1/33	Kid CHOCOLATE	124	Johnny FARR	130	unan 10		Arena, Philadelphia, Pa.	Joe McGuigan
5/19/33	Kid CHOCOLATE	123½	Seaman Tom WATSON	125½	unan 15		Madison Square Garden, New York	Pete Hartley
12/4/33	Kid CHOCOLATE	130	Frankie WALLACE	130	unan 10		Public Hall, Cleveland, Ohio	Tommy Mulgrew
12/25/33	Frankie KLICK	127¾	Kid CHOCOLATE	130	TKO 7	2:58	Arena, Philadelphia, Pa.	Spud Murphy
12/6/49	Sandy SADDLER	127½	Orlando ZULUETA	129½	split 10		Arena, Cleveland Ohio	Vito Mazzeo
4/18/50	Sandy SADDLER	130	Lauro SALAS	130	TKO 9	2:51	Arena, Cleveland Ohio	Jackie Davis
7/20/59	Harold GOMES	127½	Paul JORGENSEN	129½	unan 15		Pierce Field, Providence	Sharkey Buonanno
3/16/60	Flash ELORDE	130	Harold GOMES	128½	KO 7	1:50	Araneta Coliseum, Quezon	Barney Ross
8/17/60	Flash ELORDE	130	Harold GOMES	130	KO 1	1:20	Cow Palace, San Francisco	Matt Zidich
3/19/61	Flash ELORDE	130	Joey LOPES	130	unan 15		Rizal Coliseum, Manila	Felipe Hernandez
12/16/61	Flash ELORDE	130	Sergio CAPRARI	129½	TKO 1	2:22	Rizal Coliseum, Manila	Felipe Hernandez
6/23/62	Flash ELORDE	130	Auburn COPELAND	129½	maj 15		Rizal Coliseum, Manila	Felipe Hernandez
2/16/63	Flash ELORDE	130	Johnny BIZZARO	129½	unan 15		Rizal Coliseum, Manila	Irineo Gallego
11/16/63	Flash ELORDE	130	Love ALLOTEY	128	W dis 11	0:36	Areneta Coliseum, Quezon	Jamie Valencia
7/27/64	Flash ELORDE	130	Teruo KOSAKA	129½	TKO 12	1:45	Kuramae Arena, Tokyo	Pempe Padilla
6/5/65	Flash ELORDE	130	Teruo KOSAKA	127½	KO 15	2:14	Araneta Coliseum, Quezon	Totoy Reyes
12/4/65	Flash ELORDE	130	Kang-Il SUH	129¾	unan 15		Araneta Coliseum, Quezon	Alex Villacampa
10/22/66	Flash ELORDE	130	Vicente DERADO	128	maj 15		Araneta Coliseum, Quezon	Toti Cayetano
6/15/67	Yoshiaki NUMATA	129½	Flash ELORDE	130	maj 15		Kuramae Arena, Tokyo	Alex Villacampa
12/14/67	Hiroshi KOBAYASHI	129	Yoshiaki NUMATA	129½	KO 12	1:56	Kuramae Arena, Tokyo	Ko Toyama
3/30/68	Hiroshi KOBAYASHI	129	Rene BARRIENTOS	130	draw 15		Martial Arts Hall, Tokyo	Ko Toyama
10/6/68	Hiroshi KOBAYSHI	129	Jaime VALLADARES	129½	unan 15		Martial Arts Hall, Tokyo	Nick Pope
2/15/69	Rene BARRIENTOS	129½	Ruben NAVARRO	129½	unan 15		Araneta Coliseum, Quezon	
4/6/69	Hiroshi KOBAYASHI	128¾	Antonio AMAYA	127½	split 15		Kuramae Arena, Tokyo	Ko Toyama
11/9/69	Hiroshi KOBAYASHI	128¼	Carlos CANETE	129	unan 15		Nihon University Auditorium, Tokyo	Nick Pope
‡ 4/5/70	Yoshiaki NUMATA	130	Rene BARRIENTOS	129	split 15		Municipal Gymnasium, Tokyo	Dick Young
8/23/70	Hiroshi KOBAYASHI	128¾	Antonio AMAYA	129½	unan 15		Korakuen Hall, Tokyo	Nick Pope
‡ 9/27/70	Yoshiaki NUMATA	130	Raul ROJAS	130	KO 5	2:47	Nihon University Auditorium, Tokyo	Hiroyuki Tezaki
‡ 1/3/71	Yoshiaki NUMATA	130	Rene BARRIENTOS	130	split 15		Sumpu Kaikan, Shizuaka, Japan	John Crowder
3/3/71	Hiroshi KOBAYASHI	129¼	Ricardo ARRENDONDO	128½	unan 15		Nihon University Auditorium, Tokyo	Yusaku Yoshida
‡ 5/30/71	Yoshiaki NUMATA	129¾	Lionel ROSE	130	unan 15		Hiroshima Prefectural Gym	Hiroyuki Tezaki
7/29/71	Alfredo MARCANO	128¾	Hiroshi KOBAYASHI	129¼	KO 10	1:25	Prefectural Gymnasium, Aomori, Japan	Yusaku Yoshida
‡10/10/71	Ricard ARRENDONDO	130	Yoshiaki NUMATA	130	KO 10	2:17	Miyagi Center, Sendai	Hiroyuki Tezaki
11/7/71	Alfredo MARCANO	128¼	Kenji IWATA	129¾	TKO 4	1:50	Nuevo Circo Ring, Caracas	Luis Sulbaran
‡ 1/29/72	Ricardo ARRENDONDO	129	Jose Issac MARIN	128½	unan 15		San Jose, Costa Rica	Jay Edson
4/22/72	Ricardo ARRENDONDO	129	William MARTINEZ	129	KO 5	2:35	Mexico City, Mexico	
4/25/72	Ben VILLAFLOR	128¾	Alfredo MARCANO	128	unan 15		Blaisdell Cntr, Honolulu	James Scaramozi
9/5/72	Ben VILLAFLOR	128¾	Victor ECHEGARAY	130	draw 15		Blaisdell Cntr, Honolulu	Wilbert Minn
‡ 9/15/72	Ricardo ARRENDONDO	129¾	Susumu OKABE	129¾	KO 12	1:39	Nihon University Auditorium, Tokyo	John Crowder
‡ 3/6/73	Ricardo ARRENDONDO	129¼	Apollo YOSHIO	129¼	unan 15		Kyuden Gym, Fukuoka City	Jim Rondeau
3/12/73	Kuniaki SHIBATA	130	Ben VILLAFLOR	130	unan 15		Blaisdell Cntr, Honolulu	Walter Cho
6/19/73	Kuniaki SHIBATA	129½	Victor ECHEGARAY	128½	unan 15		Nihon University Auditorium, Tokyo	Yusaku Yoshida
‡ 9/1/73	Ricardo ARRENDONDO	129¼	Morito KASHIWABA	129¾	KO 6	1:26	Martial Arts Hall, Tokyo	Jim Rondeau
10/18/73	Ben VILLAFLOR	129½	Kuniaki SHIBATA	130	KO 1	1:56	Blaisdell Center, Honolulu	
‡ 2/28/74	Kuniaki SHIBATA	129½	Ricardo ARRENDONDO	29½	unan 15		Nihon University Auditorium, Tokyo	Ray Solis
3/14/74	Ben VILLAFLOR	127¾	Apollo YOSHIO	130	draw 15		City Gymnasium, Toyama, Japan	Shoichi Kato
‡ 6/27/74	Kuniaki SHIBATA	[illegible]	A[illegible] AMAYA	128¾	maj 15		Nihon University Auditorium, Tokyo	Yusaku Yoshida
‡ 8/3/74	Kuniaki SHIBATA	130	Ramiro BOLANOS	128½	TKO 15	2:29	Nihon University Auditorium, Tokyo	Anselmo Perez

	Date	Winner	Wt	Opponent	Wt	Result	Rd	Time	Location	Referee
	8/24/74	Ben VILLAFLOR	129¾	Yasutsune UEHARA	129½	KO	2	1:17	Blaisdell Center, Honolulu	Walter Cho
	3/13/75	Ben VILLAFLOR	129¾	Hyun-Chi KIM	128½	split	15		Araneta Coliseum, Quezon	Herbert Minn
‡	3/27/75	Kuniaki SHIBATA	129½	Ould MAKLOUFI	129	unan	15		Kyuden Gym, Fukuoka City	Yusaku Yoshida
‡	7/5/75	Alfredo ESCALERA	128¾	Kuniaki SHIBATA	129¾	KO	2	2:56	Kasamatsu Gymnasium, Mito	Ken Morita
‡	9/20/75	Alfredo ESCALERA	129	Lionel HERNANDEZ	130	draw	15		Nuevo Circo Ring, Caracas	Ray Solis
‡	12/12/75	Alfredo ESCALERA	128	Sven-Erik PAULSEN	129	TKO	9		Oslo, Norway	Harry Gibbs
	1/12/76	Ben VILLAFLOR	128	Morito KASHIWABA	130	TKO	13	1:29	Korakuen Hall, Tokyo	Carlos Padilla
‡	2/20/76	Alfredo ESCALERA	130	Jose FERNANDEZ	130	TKO	13	2:13	Roberto Clemente Stadium	Waldemar Schmidt
‡	4/1/76	Alfredo ESCALERA	128½	Buzzsaw YAMABE	130	TKO	6	2:39	Kashiwara Gym, Nara	Ismael Quinones Falu
	4/13/76	Ben VILLAFLOR	129	Samuel SERRANO	130	draw	15		Blaisdell Center, Honolulu	Wilbert Minn
‡	7/1/76	Alfredo ESCALERA	130	Buzzsaw YAMABE	130	unan	15		Kashiwara Gymnasium, Nara	Rudy Ortega
‡	9/18/76	Alfredo ESCALERA	130	Ray LUNNY III	130	TKO	13		Roberto Clemente Stadium	Waldemar Schmidt
	10/16/76	Samuel SERRANO	130	Ben VILLAFLOR	129½	unan	15		Hiram Bithorn Stadium	Stan Christodoulou
‡	11/30/76	Alfredo ESCALERA	130	Tyrone EVERETT	130	split	15		Spectrum, Philadelphia	Ray Solis
	1/15/77	Samuel SERRANO	129½	Alberto HERRERA	128½	TKO	11	2:17	Guayaquil, Ecuador	Martin Denkin
‡	3/17/77	Alfredo ESCALERA	130	Ronnie McGARVEY	127	TKO	6	2:03	Roberto Clemente Stadium	Abraham Echavarria
‡	5/16/77	Alfredo ESCALERA	128½	Carlos BECERRIL	127¾	KO	8	0:38	Capital Centre, Landover	Larry Barnett
	6/26/77	Samuel SERRANO	129	Lionel HERNANDEZ	128	unan	15		Puerto la Cruz, Venezuela	Larry Rozadilla
	8/27/77	Samuel SERRANO	129	Apollo YOSHIO	129¼	unan	15		Roberto Clemente Stadium	Waldemar Schmidt
‡	9/10/77	Alfredo ESCALERA	127	Sigfredo RODRIGUEZ	125	unan	15		Roberto Clemente Stadium	Arthur Mercante
	11/19/77	Samuel SERRANO	130	Tae-Ho KIM	130	TKO	10	1:50	Roberto Clemente Stadium	Larry Rozadilla
‡	1/28/78	Alexis ARGUELLO	129½	Alfredo ESCALERA	130	TKO	13	2:24	Loubriel Stadium, Bayamon	Arthur Mercante
	2/18/78	Samuel SERRANO	129½	Mario MARTINEZ	130	unan	15		Roberto Clemente Stadium	Roberto Ramirez
‡	4/29/78	Alexis ARGUELLO	129½	Rey TAM	129¾	TKO	5	1:54	Forum, Inglewood, Calif.	Rudy Jordan
‡	6/3/78	Alexis ARGUELLO	129	Diego ALCALA	130	KO	1	1:55	Roberto Clemente Stadium	Roberto Ramirez
	7/8/78	Samuel SERRANO	130	Oh-Young HO	129¼	unan	15		Roberto Clemente Stadium	Luis Sulbaran
‡	11/10/78	Alexis ARGUELLO	130	Arturo LEON	128¼	unan	15		Caesars Palace, Las Vegas	David Pearl
	11/29/78	Samuel SERRANO	129	Takao MARUKI	129¼	unan	15		Aichi Gymnasium, Nagoya	Larry Rozadilla
‡	2/4/79	Alexis ARGUELLO	129	Alfredo ESCALERA	129¾	KO	13	1:24	Rimini, Italy	Angelo Poletti
	2/18/79	Samuel SERRANO	129½	Julio VALDEZ	130	unan	15		Hiram Bithorn Stadium, San Juan	Larry Rozadilla
	4/14/79	Samuel SERRANO	128¾	Nkosana MGXAJI	127¾	TKO	8	1:34	Good Hope Centre, Cape Town	Larry Rozadilla
‡	7/8/79	Alexis ARGUELLO	130	Rafael LIMON	129	TKO	11	1:40	Felt Forum, New York, N.Y.	Tony Perez
‡	11/16/79	Alexis ARGUELLO	129¾	Bobby CHACON	129½	TKO	8	*	Forum, Inglewood, Calif.	John Thomas
‡	1/12/80	Alexis ARGUELLO	130	Ruben CASTILLO	129½	TKO	11	2:03	Community Center, Tucson, Arizona	Octavio Meyran
	4/3/80	Samuel SERRANO	129½	Battle Hawk KAZAMA	129¾	TKO	13	0:45	Central Gymnasium, Nara, Japan	Stan Christodoulou
‡	4/27/80	Alexis ARGUELLO	130	Rolando NAVARETTE	130	TKO	5	*	Hiram Bithorn Stadium, San Juan	Roberto Ramirez
	8/02/80	Yasutsune UEHARA	129¼	Samuel SERRANO	130	KO	6	2:59	Joe Louis Arena, Detroit, Mich.	Luis Sulbaran
	11/20/80	Yasutsune UEHARA	129¼	Leonel HERNANDEZ	129¼	split	15		Kuramae Arena, Tokyo, Japan	Chin-Kook Kim
‡	12/11/80	Rafael LIMON	129¼	Ildefonso BETHELMY	129¼	TKO	15	1:21	Olympic Auditorium, Los Angeles	Larry Rozadilla

* Loser failed to answer bell for round indicated   † WBA world junior lightweight title bout   ‡ WBC world super featherweight title bout

686

JUNIOR LIGHTWEIGHT DIVISION

ARTIE O'LEARY
(Arthur Lieberman)
(Record Not Available))

JOHNNY DUNDEE
(Record Under Featherweight Champions)

JACK BERNSTEIN
(John Dodick)
(Junior Lightweight Champion)
Born, November 5, 1899, New York City.
Nationality, Jewish-American. Weight, 130 lbs.
Height, 5 ft. 4½ in. Managed by "Doc" Hirsch.

1914
No decisions: Young West, 4; Young Philips, 4; Benny Leonard, 6; Young Fulton, 6; Willie Beecher, 6.

1915
No decisions: Young West, 4; Young Phillips, 4; Willie Astey, 6; Titchie Ryan, 8.

1917
Knockout: John Sillo, 4. Won: Young Hockey, 6.

1918
Knockout: L. McCarthy, 3. Won: Red Margolis, 5. Lost: Mick Sunday, 4.

1919
Won: Red Margolis, 4; Kid Parr, 8; Joe Neil, 6; Joe Neil, 8; Nick Gundy, 20. Lost: Nick Gundy, 10.

1920
Knockouts: J. Moore, 2; Kid Speero, 3; Kid Marcel, 4; Soldier Shaw, 1; Joe Lyons, 5. Won: Sol Friedman, 10; Sol Friedman, 8; Young Schrabe, 6.

1921
Knockouts: Willie Mack, 4; Red Wilke, 2. Won: Eddie Gorman, 10; Young Britton, 10; Young Britton, 12. Lost: Red Monroe, 12; Billy Fitzsimmons, 12; Benny Valgar, 12.

1922
Feb. 23—Jimmy Cooney, Yonkers ...... W 12
Mar. 7—Johnny Darcy, N. Y. C. .... W 12
Apr. 6—Young Eddy, Yonkers ....KO 9
Apr. 22—Bert Spencer, N. Y. C. .... W 12
May 14—Archie Walker, Brooklyn ....L 12
June 21—Jimmy Carroll, N.Y.C. ....KO 10
June 28—Archie Walker, Yonkers ...... W 12
July 8—Solly Seeman, N. Y. C. .... W 12
July 20—Fred Jacks, N. Y. C. .... W 12
Sept. 7—Tony Caponi, Yonkers .... KO 9
Sept. 16—Johnny Conney, N. Y. C. .....KO 6
Oct. 14—Pal Moran, N. Y. C. .... W 12
Oct. 20—Joe Mandell, Yonkers, N. Y. ..KO 5
Nov. 16—Elino Flores, N. Y. C. .... D 12
Nov. 28—Babe Herman, N. Y. C. .... W 12
Dec. 11—Kid Wagner, N. Y. C. .... W 10

1923
Jan. 5—Pepper Martin, N. Y. C. .... W 12
Feb. 13—Gene Delmont, N. Y. C. .... W 12
Feb. 22—Earl Baird, N. Y. C. .... W 12
Mar. 17—Eddie Brady, N. Y. C. .... W 12
Mar. 27—Sammy Greene, N. Y. C. ...... W 4
Apr. 6—Tommy Noble, N. Y. C. .... W 12
May 8—Elino Flores, N. Y. C. .... W 15
May 30—Johnny Dundee, N. Y. C. ..... W 15
(Won Junior Lightweight title)
June 25—Freddie Jacks, Philadelphia ...KO 5
July 31—H. Kid Brown, Philadelphia ...ND 8
Aug. 9—Jimmy Goodrich, N. Y. C. ..... D 10
Oct. 12—Rocky Kansas, N. Y. C. .... W 15
Nov. 3—Billy Defoe, N. Y. C. .... D 12
Nov. 27—Harry Kabakoff, St. Louis ....ND 10
Dec. 17—Johnny Dundee, N. Y. C. .....L 15
(Lost Junior Lightweight title)

1924
Jan. 11—Sammy Mandell, N. Y. C. ...... D 15
Feb. 18—Rocky Kansas, Buffalo .... W 10
Mar. 24—Teddy Myers, Buffalo .... W 10
Apr. 12—Jack Hausner, New York ...... W 12
May 5—Sammy Mandell, Louisville ...ND 12
June 4—Sid Barbarian, New York ......L 12
June 23—Cuddy DeMarco, New Haven ..L 12
July 23—Jack Zivic, Brooklyn .... W 12
Aug. 14—Luis Vincentini, Brooklyn ..... W 15
Sept. 15—Johnny Dundee, N. Y. C. ..... W 15
Nov. 7—Sammy Mandell, New York ....L 12
Nov. 26—Rocky Kansas, Buffalo .... L 12
Dec. 16—Tony Russo, Buffalo .... W 6

1925
Jan. 9—Tommy O'Brien, N. Y. C. .... W 10
Apr. 22—Tony Palmer, N. Y. C. .... W 10
May 7—Earl Baird, Yonkers .... W 6
May 18—Harry Cook, Albany, N. Y. .... D 6
Aug. 31—Sid Terris, N. Y. C. ....L 12
Oct. 12—Sid Terris, N. Y. C. ....L 10

1926
Feb. 15—Ray Romney, Buffalo, N. Y. ... D 10
Mar. 6—Bobby Burns, N. Y. C. ....KO 4
Apr. 12—Tony Vaccarelli, N. Y. C. ...... W 10
May 3—Johnny Rocco, N. Y. C. ....KO 8
June 17—Stanislaus Loayza, N. Y. C. .....L 10
Oct. 11—Cuddy De Marco, Pittsburgh ... W 10
Dec. 12—Ray Miller, New York .... W 12

1927
Feb. 21—Jimmy Goodrich, N. Y. C. ..... W 10
Mar. 1—Lee Murray, N. Y. C. .... W 10
Apr. 1—Jimmy Goodrich, Buffalo ..... W 10
Apr. 25—Bobby Tracey, N. Y. C. .... W 10
May 13—Bruce Flowers, N. Y. C. ....L 10
Aug. 2—Bruce Flowers, N. Y. C. ....L 10
Aug. 15—Freddie Mueller, N. Y. C. ......L 10
Nov. 14—Joe Glick, N. Y. C. .... W 10

1928
July 3—Armand Schackels, New York ..L 10
Dec. 1—Bruce Flowers, New York . KO by 6

1929
Feb. 21—Al Tripoli, Yonkers, New York . W 6
—Harry Carlton, New York ....L 10
—Frankie LaFay .... D 6

1931
Nov. 10—Johnny Gaito, Yonkers ....L 6

TB KO WD WF D LD LF KOBY ND NC
107 17 48 0 7 22 0 1 12 0

Died. Yonkers, N. Y., December 26, 1945.

STEVE (KID) SULLIVAN
(Stephen J. Tricamo)
(Junior Lightweight, Champion)
Born, May 21, 1897, Brooklyn, N. Y.
Nationality, Italian-American. Weight, 130 lbs.
Height, 5 ft. 5 in.

1911
Knockout: Young Kenny, 3. No decisions: Andy Griffin, 4; Tommy Hynes, 4; Dick Lewis, 6; Young Cirina, 4; Jerry Clifford, 4.

1912
June 14—Charley Goldman, N. Y. C. ...ND 6
No decision: Young (Charlie) Marlow, 10.

1913
Knockouts: Willie Smith, 4; Young Alberts, 2. No decisions: Young (Charlie) Marlow, 10; Bobby Gair, 10; Young Neiman, 10; Young Jersey, 10; Mike Clancy, 10; Walter Nelson, 10; Young Mundy, 10; "Dutch" Brandt, 10; Battling Lahn, 10; Young Rector, 10. Exhibition: Battling Levinsky, 3.

1914
Knockouts: Eddie Brooks, 1; Eddie Lennon, 3. Won: Bobby Burns, 8. Draw: Young Rector, 10; Young Limbo, 10; "Dutch" Brandt, 10; Willie Doyle, 10. No decisions: Eddie Moran, 10; Battling Lahn, 10; Eddie Moran, 10; Nick Nelson, 10; Johnny Solsberg, 10; Young O'Leary, 10; Jim Kendrick, 10; Young Marino, 10; Jimmy Murray, 10; Joe Mooney, 10; Mickey Donnelly, 10; Kid Murphy, 10; Kid Taylor, 10; Frankie Mason, 10. Lost: Monk Fowler, 8. Exhibitions: Young Zulu Kid, 3; Harry Thomas, 3.

1915
Feb. 23—Eddie Campi, Brooklyn ......ND 10
Mar. 26—Red Dolan, New Orleans .... D 20
Apr. 19—Red Dolan, New Orleans .....L 20
June 24—Eddie Wallace, Brooklyn ....ND 10
Draw: Johnny Solsberg, 8. No decisions: Walter Nelson, 10; Young Limbo 10; K.O. Joe Daly, 10. Exhibition: John Murray, 3.

1916
Jan. 23—Frankie Callahan, Brooklyn ..ND 10
Jan. 26—Kid Wilson, New Orleans ..KO by 5
Feb. 14—Eddie Campi, Brooklyn ......ND 10
Apr. 1—Young Martin, Brooklyn .....KO 1
Won: K. O. Joe Daly, 2; Johnny Donovan, 8; Gus Lewis, 6. No decisions: Willie Jones, 10; Harry Glenn, 10; Walter Nelson, 10; Young Cardell, 10; Walter Nelson, 10; Marty Allen, 10. Draw: K.O. Eggers, 10.

1917
Won: Young Steele, 10. No decisions: Battling Lahan, 10; Young Al Kale, 10.
1918
Knockout: Vincent Pepper Martin, 4. No decision: Joe Garry, 10.
(Joined U. S. Navy during World War I, 1918. Discharged in 1919.)
1920
Dec. 11—Willie Kohler, Woodhaven . KO by 4
1921
Mar. 12—Young Limbo, Woodhaven .... W 10
Apr. 9—Terry Davis, Jamaica, N. Y. .... W 10
Apr. 23—Willie Daney, Woodhaven ..... W 10
Apr. 26—Irish Kid Williams, Brooklyn ... W 15
May 14—Silent Regan, Woodhaven ......L 12
Aug. 15—Stockings Conroy, Freeport.......................KO 7
Aug. 29—Eddie Gorman, Freeport ...... KO 4
Sept. 26—Dutch Brandt, Freeport .... W 12
Oct. 31—Bobby Michaels, Freeport ....WF 3
Dec. 19—Irish Patsy Philbin, Freeport........................ D 10
Knockouts: Pete McDonald, 2. Won: Lew McFarland, 7.
1922
Jan. 19—Pepper Martin, Brooklyn ....L 12
Feb. 6—Harvey Bright, Brooklyn ..... D 12
Feb. 26—Sammy Sieger, Brooklyn ...... W 12
Apr. 17—Harvey Bright, Brooklyn ...... W 12
Apr. 28—Joe King Leopold, Brooklyn ..WF 9
May 19—Joe King Leopold, New York ...L 4
June 1—Battling Reddy, New Yrok ... W 12
July 9—Eddie Brady, Coney Island .....L 12
Aug. 1—Pepper Martin, Brooklyn .....L 12
Sept. 11—Sammy Sieger, New York ....KO 3
Sept. 26—Pepper Martin, Brooklyn .....L 12
Nov. 24—Louis Kid Kaplan, New York ...L 12
1923
Jan. 22—Sammy Sieger, Brooklyn .....L 12
Mar. 8—Dutch Brandt, Brooklyn ..... W 12
Aug. 7—Pepper Martin, N. Y. ....LF 8
Dec. 17—Babe Herman, N. Y. C. ......KO 8
—Jimmy Mars, Brooklyn ....L 12
1924
May 30—Mike Ballerino, Brooklyn.......L 12
June 20—Johnny Dundee, Brooklyn .... W 10
(Won junior lightweight title)
Aug. 18—Pepper Martin, L. I. City .... W 15
Oct. 15—Mike Ballerino, N. Y. C. ......KO 5
(Retained junior lightweight title)
Dec. 15—Mike Ballerino, Milwaukee ...ND 10
1925
Mar. 23—Willie Ames, Canton, O. ......ND 12
Apr. 1—Mike Ballerino, Philadelphia ....L 10
(Lost junior lightweight title)
May 22—Louis Kid Kaplan, Wat'b'y . KO by 5
1926
Feb. 1—Georgie Balduc, N. Y. C........ W 10
Feb. 13—Frankie Brown, N. Y. C......... D
June 3—Tod Morgan Brooklyn .....KO by

TB	KO	WD	WF	D	LD	LF	KOBY	ND	NC
111	13	18	2	10	13	1	4	50	0

1923
Jan. 5—Frankie Jerome, New York .... D 12
Jan. 19—Carl Tremaine, New York . KO by 3
Dec. 28—Mickey Brown, New York ..... W 10
Won: Joe Nelson, 10; B. Fitzsimmons, 10.
No Decision: Bobby Wolgast, 8; Cuddy De Marco, 10; Cuddy De Marco, 8; Joe O'Donnell, 8.
Lost: Harvey Bright, 12.
1924
Apr. 10—Joe Souza, N. Y. C. .... W 10
Apr. 22—Joe Celmars, Bayonne, N. J. ..ND 12
May 30—Kid Sullivan, N.Y.C. .... W 10
June 24—Vincent Pepper Martin, N.Y.C. .... W 12
July 15—Johnny Leonard, N.Y.C. ...... W 10
Aug. 5—Johnny Leonard, N.Y.C. ...... W 12
Sept. 9—Tony Vaccarelli, N.Y.C. .... W 10
Oct. 15—Kid Sullivan, N.Y.C. ......KO by 5
Dec. 15—Kid Sullivan, Milwaukee .....ND 12
1925
Jan. 1—Frankie Monroe, Milwaukee ..ND 10
Feb. 5—Vincent Martin, Brooklyn ....KO 11
Apr. 1—Steve Kid Sullivan, Phila. ..... W 12
(Won Junior Lightweight title)
May 15—Mickey Brown, Bayonne .....ND 12
May 30—Frankie Callahan, Colum., O. .ND 10
June 12—Frankie Schaffer, Aurora, Ill. .ND 10
June 16—Billy Henry, Kansas City .....ND 10
June 23—Babe Ruth, Philadelphia, Pa. ... D 10
July 6—Pepper Martin, Brooklyn .....W 15
Aug. 14—Billy Henry, Bayonne, N. J. ...ND 10
Oct. 21—Ace Hudkins, Los Angeles ......L 10
Dec. 2—Tod Morgan, Los Angeles . KO by 10
(Lost Junior Lightweight title)
1928
June 6—Johnny Leonard, N. Y. C. ......L 10
June 25—Petey Mack, Bayonne, N. J. ..ND 10
July 9—Augie Pisano, Lg. Beach, N. Y. ..L 6
July 21—Johnny Leonard, Bayonne ...ND 10
Aug. 30—George Day, New Haven, Conn. .L 10
Sept. 15—Johnny Kochansky, Bayonne .ND 10
Sept. 30—Eddie Lord, N. Haven, Conn. ... W 10
Nov. 8—Tommy Herman, Philadelphia ..L 10
Nov. 13—Joe Glick, Brooklyn, N. Y...... D 10
Nov. 29—Georgie Balduc, N.Y.C. ...... W 10
Dec. 20—Joe Glick, N.Y.C. .... D 10
1927
Jan. 24—Al Foreman, Philadelphia ..... W 10
Feb. 2—Maxie Holub, Akron, Ohio .....L 10
Mar. 5—Martie Silvers, Brooklyn....... D 6
Mar. 19—Nat Kawler, Schenectady ......L 10
Apr. 19—Jack Duffy, Arkon, Ohio .....ND 10
Apr. 26—King Tut, St. Paul, Minn. ....L 10
Oct. 17—Benny Bass, Philadelphia .....L 10
Nov. 11—Joey Medill, Chicago, Ill. ......L 10
Nov. 21—Mike Dundee, Dayton, O. . KO by 10
1928
Jan. 20—Tommy Grogan, Omaha ... KO by 4
1929
—Murray Fuchs .... W 10

TB	KO	WD	WF	D	LD	LF	KOBY	ND	NC
96	8	32	0	14	19	0	5	18	0

Died April 4, 1965 in Tampa, Florida.

MIKE BALLERINO
(Junior Lightweight Champion)
Born, 1901, Bayonne, N. J. Nationality, Italian American. Weight, 126 lbs. Height, 5 ft. 4 in. Managed by Frank Churchill.
1920
Knockouts: Kid Ponso, 3; Young Gilbert, 3. Won: Kid Aguilar, 4; Kid Saunders, 4; Kid Ponso, 4; Kid Taylor, 4; Leoncio Bernabe, 6; Eddie More, 10. Draw: Ireno Flores, 4. Lost: Syd Keenan, 8; Pancho Villa, 6; Pancho Villa, 6. No decision: Pancho Villa, 6; Pancho Villa, 6.
1921
Knockouts: Kid Garcia, 11; Kid Tango, 3; Young Givinni, 1. Won: Tip O'Neill, 8. Draw: Pancho Villa, 15; Cowboy Reyes, 10; Pancho Villa, 15; Peter Sarmiento, 8. Lost: Pancho Villa, 15; Pancho Villa, 10; Pancho Villa, 20; Pancho Villa, 20.
1922
Knockouts: Joe Loth, 3; Tom Shea, 3. Won: Eddie More, 6; Mike Mitchell, 6; Jimmy Cole, 4; Kid La Rose, 4; Frankie Pantley, 6; Mike De Pinto, 6; Mike De Pinto, 6; Sam Gordon, 4; Sam Gordon, 4; Ernie Dailey, 6. Draw: Frankie Britt, 6; Vic Foley, 4; Vic Foley, 10, Bud Ridley, 10. Lost: Sam Gordon, 4.

TOD MORGAN
(Bert Pilkington)
Born, December 25, 1902, Sequim, Washington. Ancestry, English-Scotch. Weight, 130 lbs. Height, 5 ft. 7½ in. Managed by Frank Churchill.
1920
Won: George Green, 4; George Green, 4; Young Mike Gibbons, 4; Young Mike Gibbons, 4.
1921
Knockouts: Lou Hogan, 2; Bud Miller, 2. Won: Joe Bell, 4; Sammy Girsch, 4; Frankie Novey, 4; Alex McDonald, 4; Alex McDonald, 4; Trench King, 4; Young Carpenter, 4; Young Carpenter, 4; Willie Shyrock, 4; Willie Shyrock, 4; Jimmy Hackley, 4; Willie Shyrock, 4. Draw: Alex McDonald, 4; Frankie Nell, 4; Trench King, 4; Trench King, 4; Ad Remy, 4; Willie Shyrock, 4; Alex McDonald, 4.
1922
Won: Young Russ Pierce, 4; Johnny MacManus, 4; Calif. Joe Lynch, 4; Georgie Sollis, 4; Dynamite Murphy, 4; Al Roubideux, 4; Trench King, 4; Dynamite Murphy, 4; Johnny MacManus, 4; Spec. Ramies, 4; Vic Moran, 4; Jimmy Mendo, 4. Draw: Georgie Thompson, 4; Georgie Thompson, 4; Joe Lynch, 4; Young

Farrell, 4; Jimmie Mendo, 4. Lost: Calif. Joe Lynch, 4; Eddie Macy, 4; George Thompson, 4. Knockouts: Sailor Victrolia, 2.

1923

Won: Joe Lynch, 4; Dandy Dillon, 4; Jimmy Rackley, 4; Joe Coffeyn, 4; Frankie McCann, 4; Willie O'Brien, 4; Frankie McCann, 4; Bud Ridley, 6; Bud Ridley, 6; Dandy Dillon, 4; George Sollis, 6. Draw: Dandy Dillon, 6.

1924

Knockouts: Frankie Britt, 3; Dandy Edwards, 5. Won: Dandy Munce, 6; John Bedent, 4; Stewart McLean, 4; Georgie Spencer, 4; Al Walker, 4; Joe Gorman, 6; Georgie Spencer, 6; Ad Mackie, 6; Doc Snell, 6. Draw: Frankie Britt, 6; Joe Gorman, 6; Doc Snell, 6.

1925

Mar.	13—Gene Delmont, Hollywood	W	10
Apr.	22—Stewart McLean, Oakland	D	10
June	10—Joe Gorman, Oakland	W	10
June	19—Stewart McLean, Hollywood	W	10
Sept.	9—Harry Wallach, Los Angeles	W	10
Dec.	2—Mike Ballerino, Los Angeles	KO	10
	(Won World Junior Lightweight Title)		

1926

Jan.	7—Sammy Campagno, Portland	KO	7
Jan.	13—Stewart McLean, Oakland	W	10
Feb.	22—Jimmy Goodrich, Milwaukee	ND	10
Feb.	26—Don Davis, East Chicago	ND	10
Mar.	17—Charlie O'Connell, Cleveland	D	12
Mar.	29—Eddie Brady, Youngstown	W	12
June	3—Steve (Kid) Sullivan, Brooklyn	KO	6
	(Retained World Junior Lightweight Title)		
June	24—Babe Herman, Revere Beach	L	10
July	6—Ted Blatt, Cleveland	W	10
July	9—John Kochansky, Jersey City	ND	10
Aug.	4—Tommy O'Brien, Los Angeles	W	10
Sept.	30—Joe Glick, New York	W	15
	(Retained World Junior Lightweight Title)		
Oct.	19—Johnny Dundee, San Francisco	W	10
	(Retained World Junior Lightweight Title)		
Nov.	19—Carl Duane, New York	W	15
	(Retained World Junior Lightweight Title)		

1927

Jan.	7—Phil McGraw, New York	L	10
May	28—Vic Foley, Vancouver	W	12
	(Retained World Junior Lightweight Title)		
June	29—Doc Snell, Seattle	L	6
Sept.	20—Stanislaus Loayza, Chicago	LF	9
Dec.	2—Honeyboy Finnegan, Boston	L	10
Dec.	16—Joe Glick, New York	WF	14
	(Retained World Junior Lightweight Title)		

1928

Feb.	24—Ritchie King, Vancouver	W	10
Apr.	3—Jimmy Duffy, Toledo	ND	10
May	24—Eddie Martin, New York	W	15
	(Retained World Junior Lightweight Title)		
July	18—Eddie Martin, Brooklyn	W	15
	(Retained World Junior Lightweight Title)		
Sept.	3—Leslie (Wildcat) Carter, Vancouver	D	10
Oct.	2—King Tut, Minneapolis	ND	10
Dec.	3—Santiago Zorilla, San Francisco	D	10
	(Retained World Junior Lightweight Title)		

1929

Jan.	1—Joey Sangor, Milwaukee	ND	10
	(Retained World Junior Lightweight Title)		
Jan.	8—Eddie Mack, Denver	L	10
Apr.	5—Santiago Zorilla, Los Angeles	W	10
	(Retained World Junior Lightweight Title)		
Apr.	24—Eddie Mack, Denver	D	10
May	20—Baby Sal Sorio, Los Angeles	W	10
	(Retained World Junior Lightweight Title)		
July	9—Goldie Hess, Los Angeles	L	10
Nov.	1—Billy Townsend, Vancouver	D	10
Nov.	26—Eddie Mack, Los Angeles	L	10
Dec.	20—Benny Bass, New York	KO by	2
	(Lost World Junior Lightweight Title)		

1930

June	6—Santiago Zorilla, Vancouver	D	15'
July	23—Don Fraser, Spokane	W	6
July	25—Joey Coffman, Tacoma	W	6
Aug.	14—Leslie (Wildcat) Carter, Seattle	W	6

Aug.	29—Eddie Mack, Seattle	W	6
Sept.	23—Santiago Zorilla, Seattle	W	8
Oct.	31—Hector McDonald, Los Angeles	W	10

1931

Feb.	17—Billy Townsend, Los Angeles	L	10
Mar.	24—Goldie Hess, Los Angeles	W	10
Apr.	10—Ramon Ortega, San Francisco	KO	2
May	12—Cecil Payne, Los Angeles	L	10
July	1—Goldie Hess, Seattle	W	8
Aug.	11—Bobby Pacho, Los Angeles	L	10
Aug.	18—Frankie Stetson, Oakland	W	10
Sept.	3—Cecil Payne, Sacramento	W	10
Sept.	23—Eddie Thomas, Portland	W	10
Sept.	30—Sammy Santos, Seattle	W	6
Oct.	13—Sammy Santos, Seattle	W	8
Nov.	10—Bobby Pacho, Los Angeles	KO by	7

1932

Jan.	1—Eddie Volk, Portland	W	6
Jan.	21—Don Fraser, Tacoma	L	6
May	6—Mushy Callahan, Hollywood	L	10
June	23—Don Fraser, Spokane	L	6
July	8—Sammy Mandell, Hollywood	W	10
Aug.	19—Baby Sal Sorio, Hollywood	WF	8
Sept.	9—Kenneth LaSalle, Hollywood	L	10
Dec.	6—Harry Woods, Seattle	D	6

1933

Sept.	4—Bobby Blay, Sydney	W	15
Sept.	25—Nel Tarleton, Sydney	D	15
Oct.	9—Jack Carroll, Sydney	L	15
Oct.	30—Jimmy Kelso, Sydney	L	15
Nov.	11—Jimmy Kelso, Melbourne	W	15
Nov.	20—Jimmy Kelso, Sydney	D	15

1934

Apr.	30—Joe Ghnouly, Sydney	L	15
July	2—Jimmy Kelso, Sydney	KO	8
July	16—Tom Johns, Sydney	KO	1
July	30—Herb Bishop, Sydney	W	15
Aug.	8—Reg Hickey, Brisbane	D	15
Aug.	27—Jack Carroll, Sydney	L	15
Oct.	15—Herb Bishop, Sydney	NC	5
Nov.	5—Herb Bishop, Sydney	L	10
Nov.	12—Jack Portney, Sydney	D	15
Dec.	3—Jack Portney, Sydney	L	15
Dec.	10—Reg Hickey, Sydney	KO	8

1935

Feb.	4—Willard Brown, Sydney	L	15
	—Kid Moro, Honolulu	W	

1936

Feb.	3—Saverio Turiello, Sydney	L	15

1937

Mar.	20—Mick Leonard, Broken Hill	KO	2
Apr.	23—Sid Clarke, Wollongong	KO	5
May	19—Herb Bishop, Sydney	W	15
June	9—Bert Osborne, Leichhardt	W	15
June	30—Clever Henry, Leichhardt	W	15
Sept.	21—Jimmy Dundee, Leichhardt	KO	4
Oct.	5—Herb Bishop, Leichhardt	W	12

1938

Mar.	5—Manuel Cuzzolino, Newcastle	KO	4
Mar.	12—Jimmy Dundee, Newcastle	KO	6
Apr.	29—Jimmy Dundee, Lithgow	KO	6
May	11—Ron McLaughlin, Leichhardt	KO	10
June	7—Herb Bishop, Kalgoorlie	W	15
July	22—Mick Leonard, Perth	KO	8
Sept.	12—Herb Bishop, Kalgoorlie	L	12
Dec.	9—Bob King, Perth	KO	6
Dec.	26—Herb Bishop, Perth	W	15

1939

Feb.	24—Graham Evans, Perth	KO	9
May	12—Johnny Hutchinson, Brisbane	L	12
June	30—Paddy Boxall, Perth	L	15
Oct.	6—Danny LaVerne, Perth	L	12
Nov.	10—Danny LaVerne, Perth	W	12
Dec.	26—Paddy Boxall, Perth	KO by	5

1940

Jan.	26—Claude Varner, Perth	W	12
Feb.	15—Claude Varner, Perth	KO	8
Feb.	23—Herb Bishop, Perth	W	12
Mar.	26—Fighting Carlos, Sydney	KO	12
Apr.	13—Clever Henry, Melbourne	L	12

690

Apr. 24—Johnny Hutchinson, Melbourne .... W 12
Oct. 29—Tiger Parkes, Kalgoorlie .... KO 4
Nov. 25—Len Fay, Adelaide .... W 12
Dec. 14—Tiger Parkes, Broken Hill .... WF 3
Dec. 26—Joe Hall, North Sydney .... KO 11
1941
Jan. 18—Ron McLaughlin, Newcastle .... D 12
Feb. 1—Alan Westbury, Newcastle .... W 12
Feb. 8—Alan Westbury, Newcastle .... L 12
Mar. 15—Ron McLaughlin, Melbourne ..... W 12
June 5—Vic Patrick, Sydney .... WF 5
July 3—Vic Patrick, Sydney .... L 15
Sept. 11—Vic Patrick, Sydney .... L 15
1942
Mar. 9—Vic Patrick, Sydney .... KO by 11
July 18—Lew Edwards, Melbourne .... W 12

TB	KO	WD	WF	D	LD	LF	KO BY	ND	NC
203	27	98	4	30	32	1	4	6	1

Died, August 3, 1953, Seattle, Washington.

BENNY BASS
(Record Under Featherweight Champions)

KID CHOCOLATE
(Record Under Featherweight Champions)

FRANKIE KLICK
Born, May 5, 1909, San Francisco, California.
Ancestry, Polish-French. Weight, 120-140 lbs. Height, 5
ft. 6 in. Managed by Joe Doran in California, 1924-1932;
by Ray Carlin in New York.
1924
Oct. 29—Young Manila, San Francisco ...... W 4
Nov. 12—Tony Baroni, San Francisco .... W 4
Nov. 26—Dick Cruz, San Francisco .... W 4
Dec. 10—Frankie Wilson, San Francisco .... W 4
1925
Jan. 8—Jimmy Barry, San Francisco ...... W 4
Jan. 14—Phil Doro, San Francisco .... KO 3
Feb. 20—Jack Flynn, San Francisco .... W 4
Mar. 4—Kid Magsambol, San Francisco ... W 4
Dec. 2—Jimmy Briggs, San Francisco ..... W 4
Dec. 9—Fred Bindon, San Francisco ...... W 4
Dec. 30—Pal Bayardo, San Francisco ..... KO 1
1926
Jan. 13—Jimmy Dwyer, San Francisco ..... W 6
Feb. 5—Fred Bindon, San Francisco .... W 4
Feb. 12—Johnny Lawson, San Francisco ... KO 3
Feb. 19—Johnny Fiske, San Francisco ..... KO 4
Mar. 23—Jimmy Briggs, San Rafael .... KO 8
Apr. 30—Sydney White, San Francisco .... W 6
May 12—Sydney White, San Francisco ..... D 10
Nov. 12—Sydney White, San Francisco ..... W 6
Nov. 26—Davie Flash, San Francisco ..... KO 4
Dec. 17—Lou Richards, San Francisco ..... KO 5
Dec. 21—Joe French, San Francisco .... W 6
1927
Jan. 7—Leonardo Garcia, San Francisco ... W 6
Jan. 28—California Joe Lynch, San Francisco W 6
Apr. 1—Ollie Bartlett, San Francisco ...... W 6
Apr. 22—Billy Evans, San Francisco ...... KO 9
May 25—Joe Pimenthal, San Francisco ..... W 10
June 1—Dynamite Murphy, Oakland ... KO by 4
July 4—Georgie Lee, Reno, Nev. .... W 6
Aug. 26—Santiago Zorilla, San Francisco .... D 10
Sept. 23—Tommy O'Brien, San Francisco ... KO 7
1928
Jan. 17—Vic Foley, Seattle, Wash. ....L 6
Feb. 3—Charley Miller, San Francisco .... KO 3
Feb. 10—Midget Mike O'Dowd, San Fran. KO by 3
Mar. 23—California Joe Lynch, San Francisco W 4
Apr. 19—California Joe Lynch, Stockton ..... D 10
June 4—Ignacio Fernandez, San Francisco .. W 10
June 20—Bobby Herman, San Francisco ..... KO 6
Aug. 1—Charley Miller, San Francisco .... KO 4
Sept. 6—Sydney White, El Cerrito .... W 10

Oct. 2—Willie Gordon, Portland, Oregon ... W 10
Oct. 17—California Joe Lynch, San Francisco D 10
Dec. 14—Bobby Herman, San Francisco ..... W 6
1929
Jan. 30—Battling Bullahan, San Francisco .. W 10
Mar. 14—Bert Foster, Sacramento .... W 10
Mar. 27—Charley Miller, Reno, Nev. .... D 10
Apr. 24—Charley Miller, San Francisco .... KO 8
May 24—Bert Foster, San Francisco .... KO 3
June 14—Red Humphries, San Francisco .... W 10
July 5—Tommy Fielding, San Francisco .... W 10
Nov. 22—Huerta Evans, San Francisco ..... W 10
Nov. 29—Ignacio Fernandez, Los Angeles .... W 10
1930
Jan. 3—Maurice Holtzer, Hollywood .... L 10
Mar. 6—Ward Sparks, San Francisco .... W 10
June 13—Eddie Graham, San Francisco ..... KO 6
Sept. 3—Jackie Spencer, Reno, Nev. .... NC 10
Nov. 4—Bobby Gray, San Jose .... KO 7
Nov. 18—Joe Noto, San Jose .... KO 8
Nov. 23—Harry Wallace, Eureka .... KO 1
Dec. 14—Joe Noto, Eureka .... W 6
Dec. 19—Santiago Zorilla, San Francisco ... D 4
1931
Jan. 16—Santiago Zorilla, San Francisco .... D 10
Jan. 24—Ramon Montoya, Hollywood ...... W 6
Feb. 20—Ramon Montoya, Los Angeles ..... W 10
Mar. 13—Bobby Pacho, Hollywood .... W 10
May 14—Pierre Pothier, Klamath Falls ..... W 8
June —Johnny Christmas, Santa Rosa ... KO 8
July 14—Benny Gallup, Santa Rosa .... W 10
Aug. 20—Joe Noto, San Rafael .... W 10
Sept. 3—Joe Noto, Vallejo .... W 10
Sept. 11—Varias Milling, Hollywood .... W 10
Nov. 25—Buddy Ryan, San Francisco .... W 10
1932
Feb. 4—Hymie Miller, Sacramento .... WF 7
May 18—Young Peter Jackson, San Francisco L 10
July 18—Tony Falco, New York .... D 8
Oct. 7—Bobby Pacho, New York .... D 8
1933
Jan. 10—Paolo Villa, New York .... W 10
Jan. 13—Lou Jallos, New York .... W 5
Feb. 3—Tony Melore, New York .... KO 6
Mar. 2—Tony Scarpati, Brooklyn .... W 6
Mar. 25—Patsy Rubinetti, Brooklyn .... W 6
Apr. 8—Pete Gullotta, Brooklyn .... L 6
May 19—Tony Scarpati, New York .... KO 3
May 27—Johnny Bonito, Brooklyn .... W 6
June 1—Ernie Tedesco, Brooklyn .... KO 5
June 5—Pedro Nieves, Jersey City .... KO 4
Aug. 12—Joey Kaufman, Brooklyn .... W 6
Aug. 29—Al Cuillo, Brooklyn .... D 6
Sept. 8—Eddie Cool, Baltimore .... W 10
Sept. 18—Tony Falco, Baltimore .... W 10
Oct. 28—Tony Canzoneri, Brooklyn .... L 10
Nov. 13—Jimmy Leto, Holyoke .... L 10
Nov. 27—Eddie Cool, Philadelphia .... L 10
Dec. 25—Kid Chocolate, Philadelphia ...... KO 7
(Won World Junior Lightweight Title)
1934
Jan. 22—Frankie Wallace, Cleveland .... L 10
Mar. 5—Barney Ross, San Francisco .... D 10
(For World Junior Welterweight Title)
June 28—Tony Canzoneri, Brooklyn ..... KO by 9
July 31—Cleto Locatelli, Philadelphia ...... L 10
Nov. 2—Harry Dublinsky, New York ..... W 10
1935
Jan. 28—Barney Ross, Miami .... L 10
(For World Junior Welterweight Title)
June 10—Tony Canzoneri, Washington .... L 12
Aug. 19—Tony Canzoneri, San Francisco .... L 10
Nov. 22—Al Roth, New York .... W 10
1936
Jan. 3—Lou Ambers, New York .... L 10
Apr. 30—Indian Hurtado, New York .... W 10
June 8—Pedro Montanez, New York ...... L 10
July 20—Jimmy Vaughn, Louisville .... L 10
Aug. 3—Howard Scott, Washington .... L 10
Aug. 24—Eddie Zivic, Pittsburgh .... W 10

| Sept. | 1—Jimmy Garrison, Kansas City | L | 10 |
| Nov. | 13—Enrico Venturi, New York | L | 10 |

1937

| May | 4—Henry Armstrong, Los Angeles | KO by | 4 |
| Sept. | 27—Billy Beauhold, New York | L | 10 |

1938

| Jan. | 17—Felix Garcia, New York | W | 8 |
| Mar. | 17—Johnny Bellus, New Haven | L | 10 |

1939

| Jan. | 13—Clever Henry, Honolulu | L | 10 |

1940-1942
(Inactive)

1943

| Feb. | 19—Al Citrino, San Francisco | D | 8 |
| Apr. | 16—Al Citrino, San Francisco | L | 8 |

TB	KO	WD	WF	D	LD	LF	KO BY	ND	NC
118	24	54	1	12	22	0	4	0	1

SANDY SADDLER
(Record Under Featherweight Champions)

HAROLD GOMES
(Harold James Gomes)
Born, August 22, 1933, Providence, R.I. Weight, 126-130 lbs. Height, 5 ft. 5 in. Ancestry, Portuguese-Greek. Managed by Sammy Richman and Frank Travis.

1951

Sept.	17—Kobilly Pierre, Providence	KO	2
Oct.	15—Paul Hallie, Providence	KO	2
Nov.	5—Manuel Baptista, Providence	KO	2
Nov.	26—Al Duarte, Providence	W	4
Dec.	10—Billy Cruz, Providence	KO	3

1952

Feb.	4—Al Duarte, Providence	KO	2
Mar.	3—Don Nelson, Providence	W	4
Mar.	10—Don Nelson, Providence	W	4
Mar.	31—Manuel Baptista, Providence	W	6
Apr.	21—Tommy Tibbs, Providence	W	6
May	7—George Araujo, Providence	Exh.	
May	12—Tommy Tibbs, Providence	W	6
Dec.	1—Manuel Baptista, Providence	W	6
Dec.	29—Mickey Devano, Providence	KO	2

1953

Feb.	2—Tommy Tibbs, Providence	W	8
Apr.	6—Bob Davis, Providence	KO	3
May	6—Filberto Osario, Fall River	W	10
June	12—Art Mullin, New York	W	4
Sept.	10—George Allen, Boston	KO	2
Sept.	28—Art Mullin, Providence	W	6
Nov.	5—Bobby Chabot, Fall River	KO	5
Dec.	10—Stony Gaudette, Fall River	KO	1

1954

Jan.	28—Tommy Tibbs, Fall River	L	10
Mar.	1—Young Saint, Boston	KO	3
Mar.	15—Johnny O'Brien, Boston	W	12

(Won New England Featherweight Title)

Apr.	10—Black Pico, Boston	KO	10
May	11—Bill Bossio, Boston	W	10
June	12—Tommy Tibbs, Boston	KO by	10
July	12—Joe Wilkinson, Boston	W	10
Oct.	5—Tommy Tibbs, Boston	KO by	9

1955

Mar.	28—Art Mullin, Brockton	W	8
Oct.	24—Jimmy Ithia, Providence	KO	7
Nov.	7—Sergio Penalver, Providence	KO	2
Nov.	28—Carlo Fusco, Providence	W	10

1956

Jan.	9—Joe Wilkinson, Providence	KO	5
Feb.	6—Pat Marcune, Providence	KO	9
Mar.	12—Johnny O'Brien, Providence	W	12
Apr.	16—Dom Sacco, Providence	KO	4
Oct.	29—Charley McGarrity, Providence	KO	10
Nov.	12—Segundo Perez, New Britain	KO	3

1957

Apr.	24—Bobby Rogers, Providence	KO	9
July	12—Lulu Perez, Cleveland	KO	6
Aug.	28—Isidro Martinez, Boston	L	10

1958

Jan.	20—Harold Smith, New York	KO	7
Mar.	7—Ike Chestnut, New York	W	10
Oct.	14—Johnny Bean, Holyoke	W	10
Oct.	28—Louis Carmona, Holyoke	W	10

1959

Mar.	27—Paul Jorgensen, Miami Beach	W	10
June	29—Jimmy Kelly, Providence	KO	3
July	20—Paul Jorgensen, Providence	W	15

(Won Vacant World Junior Lightweight Title)

| Oct. | 2—Jay Fullmer, Providence | W | 10 |

1960

| Mar. | 16—Flash Elorde, Manila | KO by | 7 |

(Lost World Junior Lightweight Title)

| Aug. | 17—Flash Elorde, San Francisco | KO by | 1 |

(For World Junior Lightweight Title)

1961
(Inactive)

1962

Feb.	27—Paul Alba, Houston	KO	2
May	25—Lalo Guerrero, Los Angeles	W	10
July	10—Johnny Bean, New Bedford	W	10
Sept.	19—Daniel Berrios, Miami Beach	W	10
Oct.	18—Johnny Bizzarro, Erie	L	10

1963

Apr.	19—Valerio Nunez, Milan	KO by	5
Oct.	8—Frankie Taylor, London	KO by	9
Oct.	29—Dave Coventry, London	KO by	1

TB	KO	WD	WF	D	LD	LF	KO BY	ND	NC
60	24	26	0	0	3	0	7	0	0

GABRIEL (FLASH) ELORDE
Born, March 22, 1935, Bogo, Cebu, Philippines. Weight, 118-135 lbs. Height, 5 ft. 6 in. Southpaw. Managed by Lope Sarreal.

1951

June	16—Kid Gonzaga, Cebu City	KO	4
June	23—Young Basilian, Cebu City	KO	3
June	30—Mike Sanchez, Cebu City	W	5
July	14—Kid Santos, Cebu City	KO	5
July	28—Star Mercado, Cebu City	KO	1
Aug.	11—Fighting Echaves, Cebu City	KO	1
Sept.	8—Little Patilla, Cebu City	KO	6
Sept.	15—Star Flores, Cebu City	W	10
Oct.	31—Kid Independence, Cebu City	KO by	10
Dec.	1—Lucky Strike, Cebu City	KO	5

1952

Jan.	30—Tenejeros Boy, Davao City	W	8
Feb.	24—Little Dundee, Davao City	L	8
Mar.	16—Tommy Romulo, Davao City	D	10
May	3—Benny Escobar, Caloocan	W	8
May	10—Paulito Escarlan, Caloocan	W	8
May	31—Tanny Campo, Caloocan	W	10
July	26—Tanny Campo, Manila	W	12

(Won Filipino Bantamweight Title)

| Aug. | 12—Little Dundee, Davao City | KO | 4 |

(Retained Filipino Bantamweight Title)

| Oct. | 18—Horishi Hiroguchi, Tokyo | W | 12 |

(Won Oriental Bantamweight Title)

| Nov. | 18—Akiyoshi Akanuma, Tokyo | D | 12 |

(Retained Oriental Bantamweight Title)

1953

Feb.	18—Willie Brown, Manila	KO	4
Mar.	15—Al Cruz, Manila	W	10
May	20—Larry Bataan, Manila	L	12

(For Oriental Featherweight Title)

| July | 6—Akiyoshi Akanuma, Tokyo | W | 12 |

(Retained Oriental Bantamweight Title)

| Oct. | 8—Noboru Tanaka, Tokyo | W | 10 |
| Nov. | 25—Masashi Akiyama, Tokyo | L | 10 |

1954

Jan.	21—Kiyoaki Nakanishi, Tokyo	W	10
Apr.	21—Hiroshi Okawa, Tokyo	W	10
June	—Relinquished Oriental bantamweight title.		
June	29—Shigeji Kaneko, Tokyo	L	12

(For Oriental Featherweight Title)

| Aug. | 5—Roy Higa, Tokyo | W | 10 |
| Aug. | 18—Tommy Romulo, Manila | W | 12 |

(Won Filipino Lightweight Title)

Nov.	20—Katsumi Kosaka, Manila .... KO	8

1955

Jan.	12—Masashi Akiyama, Tokyo L	10
Apr.	15—Severo Fuentes, Manila .... W	10
June	15—Leo Alonzo, Manila L	12
	(Lost Filipino Lightweight Title)	
July	20—Sandy Saddler, Manila .... W	10
Oct.	3—Shigeji Kaneko, Tokyo L	10

1956

Jan.	18—Sandy Saddler, San Francisco KO by	13
	(For World Featherweight Title)	
Apr.	23—Cleo Lane, San Francisco .... KO	1
May	8—Chico Rosa, Stockton, Calif. ...... W	10
June	11—Gil Velarde, San Francisco ...... KO	7
June	26—Cecil Schoonmaker, Stockton ..... KO	9
July	24—Dave Gallardo, San Jose .... W	10
Aug.	22—Miguel Berrios, San Francisco L	10
Oct.	16—Luke Sandovan, San Jose .... KO	2
Nov.	9—Miguel Berrios, New York L	10

1957

Feb.	5—Hidemi Wade, Osaka .... KO	5
Mar.	16—Tommy Romulo, Manila .... W	12
	(Regained Filipino Lightweight Title)	
Apr.	27—Hideto Kobayashi, Nagoya .... W	12
	(Won Vacant Oriental Lightweight Title)	
June	23—Omsap Laempapha, Bangkok L	12
	(Lost Oriental Lightweight Title)	
Aug.	4—Salika Yontrakit, Bangkok .... KO	3
Sept.	24—Shigeji Kaneko, Tokyo L	10
Oct.	23—Leo Alonzo, Manila .... W	12
	(Regained Filipino Lightweight Title)	

1958

Mar.	2—Hiroshi Okawa, Tokyo .... W	12
	(Regained Oriental Lightweight Title)	
May	3—Javellana Kid, Manila .... W	12
	(Retained Oriental Lightweight Title)	
May	17—Paulito Escarlan, Manila .... Exh.	6
June	10—Ike Chestnut, Honolulu .... W	10
Sept.	2—Hisao Kobayashi, Tokyo .... W	12
	(Retained Oriental Lightweight Title)	
Nov.	15—Keiichi Ishikawa, Manila .... KO	6
	(Retained Oriental Lightweight Title)	
Dec.	27—Seichiro Nakaniski, Manila ...... KO	4

1959

Feb.	6—Takeo Sugimori, Tokyo .... W	12
	(Retained Oriental Lightweight Title)	
Feb.	23—Paolo Rosi, San Francisco L	10
Mar.	31—Teddy Davis, Stockton .... W	10
May	25—Sonny Leon, Caracas .... W	10
June	15—Vicente Rivas, Caracas L	10
July	29—Solomon Boysaw, Cleveland L	10
Oct.	7—Hisao Kobayashi, Tokyo .... W	12
	(Retained Oriental Lightweight Title)	
Dec.	15—Nursery Kid, Manila .... W	10

1960

Mar.	16—Harold Gomes, Quezon City ...... KO	7
	(Won World Junior Lightweight Title)	
July	9—Hachiro Ito, Manila .... KO	5
Aug.	17—Harold Gomes, San Francisco .... KO	1
	(Retained World Junior Lightweight Title)	
Oct.	17—Sakuji Shinozawa, Manila .... W	12
	(Retained Oriental Lightweight Title)	
Dec.	16—Vicente Rivas, Manila .... W	10

1961

Mar.	19—Joey Lopes, Manila .... W	15
	(Retained World Junior Lightweight Title)	
May	31—Giordano Campari, Manila .... W	10
Dec.	16—Sergio Caprari, Manila .... KO	1
	(Retained World Junior Lightweight Title)	

1962

Mar.	10—Somkiat Katmuangyon, Manila .. KO	2
	(Retained Oriental Lightweight Title)	
Apr.	30—Teruo Kosaka, Tokyo L	12
	(Lost Oriental Lightweight Title)	
June	23—Auburn Copeland, Manila .... W	15
	(Retained World Junior Lightweight Title)	
Aug	4—Teruo Kosaka, Cebu City .... W	12
	(Regained Oriental Lightweight Title)	
Nov.	17—Isarasak Puntainorasing, Manila KO	3
Dec.	21—Solomon Boysaw, Manila .... W	10

1963

Feb.	16—Johnny Bizzarro, Manila .... W	15
	(Retained World Junior Lightweight Title)	
June	1—Tsunstomi Miyamoto, Manila .... KO	9
	(Retained Oriental Lightweight Title)	
Aug.	3—Love Allotey, Manila .... W	10
Nov.	16—Love Allotey, Quezon City .... W disq.	11
	(Retained World Junior Lightweight Title)	

1964

Feb.	15—Carlos Ortiz, Manila .... KO by	14
	(For World Lightweight Title)	
May	8—Tawashi Maisumoto, Manila ...... W	12
	(Retained Oriental Lightweight Title)	
July	27—Teruo Kosaka, Tokyo .... KO	12
	(Retained World Junior Lightweight Title)	
Nov.	21—Kang-Il Suh, Manila .... W	12
	(Retained Oriental Lightweight Title)	

1965

Feb.	27—Rene Barrientos, Manila .... W	12
	(Retained Oriental Lightweight Title)	
June	5—Teruo Kosaka, Quezon City ...... KO	15
	(Retained World Junior Lightweight Title)	
Aug.	5—Frankie Narvaez, New York .... W	10
Dec.	4—Kang-Il Suh, Quezon City .... W	15
	(Retained World Junior Lightweight Title)	

1966

Mar.	19—Ismael Laguna, Tokyo .... W	10
June	9—Yoshiaki Numata, Tokyo L	12
	(Lost Oriental Lightweight Title)	
Aug.	7—Percy Hayles, Quezon City .... W	10
Oct.	22—Vicente Derado, Quezon City ..... W	15
	(Retained World Junior Lightweight Title)	
Nov.	14—Carlos Ortiz, New York .... KO by	14
	(For World Lightweight Title)	

1967

Feb.	2—Kang-Il Suh, Manila .... W	10
Apr.	25—Fujio Mikami, Honolulu .... W	10
June	15—Yoshiaki Numata, Tokyo L	15
	(Lost World Junior Lightweight Title)	
Oct.	28—Akihisa Someya, Manila L	10

1968

(Inactive)

1969

Feb.	15—Eugenio Espinosa, Quito, Ecuador .. L	10
Apr.	26—Jaguar Kakizama, Quezon City L	10

1970

June	27—Kenji Iwata, Manila .... W	10
Aug.	28—Chico Andrade, Manila .... KO	5
Oct.	31—Tatsunao Mitsuyama, Quezon City W	10

1971

Feb.	14—Isao Ichihara, Quezon City .... KO	6
May	20—Hiroyuki Murakami, Tokyo L	10

TB	KO	WD	WF	D	LD	LF	KO BY	ND	NC
109	29	52	1	2	21	0	4	0	0

YOSHIAKI NUMATA

Born, April 19, 1945, Tomikawa-cho, Sara-Gun, Hokkaido, Japan. Weight, 126-135 lbs. Height, 5 ft. 7½ in. Managed by Iwao Kodaka.

1962

July	26—Toshio Aida, Tokyo .... KO	3
Aug.	22—Kaoru Narita, Tokyo .... W	4
Oct.	18—Kazuji Toji, Tokyo .... KO	1
Nov.	8—Nabuyoshi Nagasaki, Tokyo ...... KO	2
Nov.	24—Tadao Abe, Tokyo .... W	4

1963

Jan.	4—Hiroshi Kaneko, Tokyo .... KO	1
Feb.	5—Susumu Akimoto, Tokyo .... W	4
Mar.	7—Yasushi Matsuzoe, Tokyo .... W	4
Apr.	11—Tatsuo Hokkai, Tokyo .... W	4
May	9—Kuniaki Masuda, Tokyo .... KO	2
May	30—Katsuhiro Sugawara, Tokyo ...... KO	6
July	11—Noriyoshi Toyoshima, Tokyo ..... W	4
Sept.	12—Kenzo Shimakura, Tokyo .... KO	3
Nov.	7—Katsuzo Nakamura, Tokyo .... W	10
Dec.	19—Yasuyuki Orito, Tokyo .... W	10

1964

Mar.	12—Pedro Adigue, Tokyo .... W	10

Apr. 23—Byang Chun, Tokyo .... W 10
May 28—Lennie Campos, Tokyo .... W 10,
July 30—Larry Fernando, Sapporo .... W 10
Sept. 3—Katsuo Yabe, Tokyo .... KO 4
Nov. 5—Atom Harai, Tokyo .... KO 4,
Dec. 3—Takeo Sugimori, Tokyo .... W 10
1965
Jan. 28—Young-Pal Lee, Tokyo .... W 10
Apr. 1—Larry Flaviano, Sapporo .... W 12
(Won Oriental Junior Lightweight Title)
May 20—Hidemori Tsujimoto, Tokyo .... W 10
July 29—Yuji Amashima, Tokyo .... KO by 4
Nov. 11—Antonio Paiva, Tokyo .... W 10
Dec. 23—Love Allotey, Tokyo .... KO by 4
1966
Feb. 10—Kang-Il Suh, Tokyo .... L 10
Mar. 24—Chong-Tae Lim, Oita .... KO 2
(Retained Oriental Junior Lightweight Title)
June 9—Flash Elorde, Tokyo .... W 12
(Won Oriental Lightweight Title)
July 4—Relinquished Oriental lightweight title.
Aug. 11—Kid Rosario, Tokyo .... L 10
Oct. 10—Kid Rosario, Tokyo .... W 12
(Retained Oriental Junior Lightweight Title)
1967
Jan. 12—Ju-Yi Kwang, Tokyo .... W 10
Mar. 23—Chokchai Krischai, Oita .... W 10
June 15—Flash Elorde, Tokyo .... W 15
(Won World Junior Lightweight Title)
Oct. 5—Yi-Sae Chung, Sapporo .... W 10
Dec. 14—Hiroshi Kobayashi, Tokyo ..... KO by 12
(Lost World Junior Lightweight Title)
1968
Mar. 21—Hajime Iwata, Tokyo .... W 10
June 13—Kang-Il Suh, Tokyo .... KO 7
(Retained Oriental Junior Lightweight Title)
Sept. 12—Rosalava Kid, Tokyo .... W 10
Dec. 5—Ruben Navarro, Tokyo .... D 10
1969
Apr. 2—Relinquished Oriental junior lightweight title.
Apr. 24—Jun Koiwa, Tokyo .... D 10
July 17—Ricardo Bermisa, Tokyo .... W 10
Oct. 4—Mando Ramos, Los Angeles ... KO by 6
(For World Lightweight Title)
Nov. 27—Jun Koiwa, Kumamoto City ...... KO 2
1970
Jan. 1—Sumio Nobata, Tokyo .... D 10
Apr. 5—Rene Barrientos, Tokyo .... W 15
(Won WBC Junior Lightweight Title)
June 13—Jung-Bok Lee, Tomakomai .... W 10
Aug. 16—Raymond Rivera, Tokyo .... W 10
Sept. 27—Raul Rojas, Tokyo .... KO 5
(Retained WBC Junior Lightweight Title)
1971
Jan. 3—Rene Barrientos, Shizuoka .... W 15
(Retained WBC Junior Lightweight Title)
May 30—Lionel Rose, Hiroshima .... W 15
(Retained WBC Junior Lightweight Title)
Oct. 10—Ricardo Arrendondo, Sendai ... KO by 10
(Lost WBC Junior Lightweight Title)
1972
Mar. 2—Kenji Iwata, Tokyo .... KO by 3

TB	KO	WD	WF	D	LD	LF	KO BY	ND	NC
55	14	30	0	3	2	0	6	0	0

HIROSHI KOBAYASHI

Born, August 23, 1944. Isesaki, Gumma, Japan. Weight, 125-130 lbs. Height, 5 ft. 6½ in. Managed by Shinichi Nakamura.
1962
July 2—Hisatsugu Kyoya, Tokyo .... W 4
July 13—Michio Ishii, Tokyo .... KO 2
July 30—Yuji Takase, Tokyo .... W 4
Aug. 20—Saburo Yanagi, Tokyo .... W 4
Sept. 11—Kiyokazu Komura, Tokyo .... W 4
Sept. 25—Kazuyoshi Ohashi, Tokyo .... W 4
Oct. 16—Masayoshi Otake, Tokyo .... W 4

Nov. 7—Kazuo Hayaseko, Tokyo .... W 4
Nov. 29—Saburo Yanagi, Tokyo .... W 4
Dec. 15—Hisao Omori, Tokyo .... W 4
Dec. 31—Noriyoshi Toyoshima, Tokyo ...... W 6
1963
Jan. 28—Tsutomu Yoshida, Tokyo .... W 6
Feb. 19—Isamu Kato, Tokyo .... W 6
Mar. 18—Hideo Fukuchi, Tokyo .... W 6
Apr. 4—Kazuhiro Furuya, Tokyo .... W 6
May 2—Teruo Hino, Tokyo .... W 8
May 13—Yuji Masuko, Tokyo .... KO 2
June 24—Tommy Barahaja, Tokyo .... W 10
Aug. 19—Manzo Kikuchi, Tokyo .... L 10
Nov. 2—Johnny Jamito, Manila .... KO by 6
1964
Jan. 25—Kang-Il Suh, Tokyo .... L 10
Feb. 20—Lalo Guerrero, Tokyo .... L 10
Apr. 6—Porte Villa, Tokyo .... W 10
Apr. 25—Mitsunori Seki, Tokyo .... W 10
July —Dong-Chun Lee, Tokyo .... W 10
Sept. 28—Yugi Masuko, Tokyo .... W 10
(Won Japanese Featherweight Title)
Nov. 9—Atsushi Gunzi, Tokyo .... W 10
Dec. 12—Hyon Kim, Maebashi .... W 10
1965
Jan. 18—Yugi Masuko, Tokyo .... W 10
(Retained Japanese Featherweight Title)
Mar. 1—Soo-Bok Kwan, Tokyo .... KO 7
May 9—Shigeo Shioyama, Tokyo .... W 10
(Retained Japanese Featherweight Title)
June 27—Chong-Tai Lim, Tokyo .... W 10
July 18—Kunio Sakata, Tokyo .... W 10
Aug. 30—Atsushi Gunzi, Tokyo .... W 10
Sept. 23—Hyon Kim, Tokyo .... W 10
Oct. 29—Sugar Carreon, Tokyo .... W 10
Dec. 9—Orlando Medina, Tokyo .... W 10
1966
Jan. 27—Katsutoshi Aoki, Tokyo .... W 10
Feb. 28—Shigeo Shioyama, Fukuoka City ... W 10
(Retained Japanese Featherweight Title)
Mar. 31—Hiroshi Mori, Tokyo .... W 10
May 14—Jaime Valladares, Quito .... D 10
May 30—Freddy Rengifo, Caracas .... L 10
June 25—Pedro Gomez, Caracas .... KO by 7
July 3—Fino Rasales, Culiacan .... KO 9
July 10—Aurelio Cazares, Sinaloa .... D 10
Aug. 18—Bobby Valdez, Los Angeles .... KO 7
Oct. 10—Nobuo Chiba, Tokyo .... W 10
Nov. 10—Sumio Nobata, Nagoya .... W 10
(Retained Japanese Featherweight Title)
Nov. 28—Del Rosario Kid, Tokyo .... W 10
1967
Jan. 17—Chun-Kyo Shin, Tokyo .... W 10
Feb. 2—Kang-Il Suh, Tokyo .... W 10
Feb. 27—Vicente Derado, Tokyo .... W 10
May 8—Takao Mihashi, Tokyo .... W 10
(Retained Japanese Featherweight Title)
June 26—Dony Tesorio, Fukushima .... W 10
Sept. 4—Soo-Yun Chang, Tokyo .... KO 7
Oct. 16—Ki-Chin Song, Tokyo .... KO 8
Dec. 14—Yoshiaki Numata, Tokyo .... KO 12
(Won World Junior Lightweight Title)
1968
Mar. 30—Rene Barrientos, Tokyo .... D 15
(Retained World Junior Lightweight Title)
June 20—Mando Ramos, Los Angeles .... L 10
July 21—Ulysses Botero, Tokyo .... KO 6
Aug. 26—Ruben Navarro, Tokyo .... L 10
Oct. 6—Jaime Valladares, Tokyo .... W 15
(Retained World Junior Lightweight Title)
1969
Jan. 27—Toro George, Tokyo .... W 10
Apr. 6—Antonio Amaya, Tokyo .... W 15
(Retained World Junior Lightweight Title)
July 7—Victor Ramos, Tokyo .... KO 2
Nov. 9—Carlos Canete, Tokyo .... W 15
(Retained World Junior Lightweight Title)
1970
Feb. 15—Hiroshi Shoji, Tokushima .... D 10
June 21—Ray Adigun, Tokyo .... W 10

694

Aug. 23—Antonio Amaya, Tokyo .... W 15
    (Retained World Junior Lightweight Title)
Dec. 3—Shozo Saijyo, Tokyo .... W 10
1971
Mar. 3—Ricardo Arrendondo, Tokyo .... W 15
    (Retained World Junior Lightweight Title)
July 29—Alfredo Marcano, Aomori ..... KO by 10
    (Lost World Junior Lightweight Title)

TB	KO	WD	WF	D	LD	LF	KO BY	ND	NC
72	10	49	0	4	6	0	3	0	0

IRENEO (RENE) BARRIENTOS
Born. February. 1942. Balite. Aklan. Philippines.
Weight. 130-135 lbs. Southpaw.
1962
Oct. 2—Charlie Kid. Tupi. Cotabato ..... KO 2
1963
    (Record Not Available)
1964
Jan. 25—Arthur Fuego. Cagayan de Oro ... KO 3
Mar. 28—Sampandh Laemfapha.
    Cagayan de Oro .... L 10
May 3—Rudy Perucho. Davao City .... KO 8
June 27—Koshiro Shimoji. Davao City ..... W 10
Aug. 25—Arthur Fuego. Cagayan de Oro ... KO 3
Sept. 19—Young Terror. Cagayan de Oro .... W 12
    (Won Filipino Junior Lightweight Title)
Oct. 31—Joe Flash Juezan. Cebu .... W 10
1965
Jan. 16—Francisco Balug. Cebu .... W 10
Feb. 27—Flash Elorde. Manila .... L 12
    (For Oriental Lightweight Title)
May 15—Carl Penalosa. Cebu .... KO 4
June 19—Carl Penalosa. Cebu .... W 10
Aug. 2—Larry Flaviano. Manila .... KO 7
Oct. 2—Noriyoshi Toyoshima. Luzon City .. W 10
Nov. 20—Love Allotey. Manila............ W 10
1966
Jan. 1—Ric Penalos. Manila.............. W 3
Jan. 1—Baby Paramount. Manila .... W 3
Jan. 1—Ely Yares. Manila .... W 3
Feb. 19—Young Terror. Quezon City .... KO 9
Aug. 26—Raymond Rivera. Cagayan de Oro W 12
    (Retained Filipino Junior Lightweight Title)
Oct. 1—Kang-Il Suh. Manila .... W 10
1967
Jan. 21—Pedro Adigue. Manila .... L 12
    (For Oriental Lightweight Title)
Feb. 17—Pedro Adigue. Manila .... D 10
Apr. 29—Raymond Rivera. Davao City ..... W 12
    (Retained Filipino Junior Lightweight Title)
June 19—Francisco Bolivar. Caracas .... W 10
July 22—Antonio Amaya. Panama City ..... L 10
Oct. 23—Koji Okana. Chiba City .... W 10
Nov. 13—Sumio Nobata. Tokyo .... KO 6
1968
Jan. 14—Herbert Kang. Manila .... W 10
Mar. 30—Hiroshi Kobayashi. Tokyo .... D 15
    (For World Junior Lightweight Title)
June 22—Antonio Amaya. Manila .... W 10
1969
Feb. 15—Ruben Navarro. Manila .... W 15
    (Won Vacant WBC Junior Lightweight Title)
Apr. 16—Len Kesey. Honolulu .... KO 9
July 29—Adolph Pruitt. Honolulu ...... KO by 8
Dec. 20—Eugenio Espinosa. Manila .... W 10
1970
Apr. 5—Yoshiaki Numata. Tokyo .... L 15
    (Lost WBC Junior Lightweight Title)
June 6—Shinichi Kodota. Manila .... W 10
Aug. 14—Saleman Ithianuchit. Manila ..... KO 8
    (Won Oriental Junior Lightweight Title)
Sept. 30—Roger Zami. Honolulu .... KO 8
Oct. 30—Ishimatsu Suzuki. Honolulu ...... W 10
1971
Jan. 3—Yoshiaki Numata. Shizuoka .... L 15
    (For WBC Junior Lightweight Title)
June 4—Tatenao Mitsuyama. Manila ..... KO 4

1972
June 7—Armando Zerqua, Honolulu ...... KO 9
July 25—Javier Ayala, Honolulu .... W 10

TB	KO	WD	WF	D	LD	LF	KO BY	ND	NC
44	13	22	0	2	6	0	1	0	0

ALFREDO MARCANO
Born. January 17. 1947. Sucre. Venezuela.
1966
Mar. 4—Pedro Chirinos, Caracas .... W 4
Apr. 2—Jose Ramon Arias, Caracas ...... KO 1
Apr. 29—Abraham Veliz, Caracas .... D 4
May 9—Abraham Veliz, Caracas .... D 4
May 30—Pedro Chirinos, Caracas .... W 6
July 23—Carlos Rojas, Caracas .... W 6
Aug. 19—Francisco Escalona. Caracas ...... L 6
Oct. 3—Pedro Escalona. Caracas .... W 6
Nov. 11—Martin Rivas. Caracas .... W 8
1967
Jan. 14—Aristidas Garcia. Cumana .... KO 2
Mar. 17—Nestor Rojas. Maracay .... L 8
May 12—Victor Palencia. Caracas .... KO 1
June 19—Nestor Rojas. Caracas .... D 8
July 18—Juan Conception. Maracay .... KO 1
Sept. 9—Claudio Lopez. Cumana .... KO 2
Nov. 18—Emiliano Marron. Cumana .... W 8
Nov. 30—Jose Ramon Arias. Caracas ...... KO 2
Dec. 11—Frank Leroy. Caracas .... KO 5
1968
Jan. 22—Arnaldo Lujan. Caracas .... KO 1
Apr. 5—Nestor Rojas. Caracas .... KO 3
June 7—Benny McCall. Caracas .... KO 3
July 19—Raymundo Vera. Caracas .... KO 2
Aug. 2—Jaime Perez. Caracas .... KO 7
Aug. 16—Francisco Bolivar. Caracas ...... KO 7
Sept. 14—Bernardo Caraballo. Caracas ..... KO 7
Oct. 4—Enrique Higgins. Caracas .... KO 6
Oct. 28—Antonio Herrera. Caracas .... W 10
Nov. 25—Calvin Woodland. Caracas .... KO 1
1969
Jan. 20—Miguel Botta. Caracas .... KO 10
Feb. 14—Miguel Herrera. Caracas .... KO 10
Mar. 7—Fernando Sotelo. Caracas .... KO by 5
May 3—Rocky Orengo. Caracas .... W 10
June 13—Richard Sue. Caracas .... W 10
July 21—Ken Nagamine. Caracas .... KO 1
Aug. 15—Cruz Marcano. Caracas .... D 10
Sept. 29—Joel Gomez. Caracas .... W 10
Dec. 8—Ricardo Arredondo. Tijuana ...... L 10
1970
Jan. 1—Ricardo Arredondo. Mexicali ...... W 10
Feb. 23—Raul Cruz. Tijuana .... KO by 7
June 25—Ray Vega. Los Angeles .... L 10
Sept. 17—Ray Vega. Los Angeles .... W 10
Oct. 31—Ernesto Marcel. Panama City ..... L 10
1971
Mar. —Nobuo Chiba. Caracas .... KO 6
Apr. —Memo Morales. Caracas .... KO 3
May 4—Ernesto Marcel. Caracas .... L 10
July 29—Hiroshi Kobayashi. Aomori ...... KO 10
July 29—Hiroshi Kobayashi. Aomori ...... KO 10
    (Won World Junior Lightweight Title)
Nov. 7—Kenji Iwata. Caracas .... KO 4
    (Retained World Junior Lightweight Title)
1972
Apr. 25—Ben Villaflor. Honolulu .... L 15
    (Lost World Junior Lightweight Title)
June 3—Flash Gallego. Caracas .... KO 4
Dec. 12—Raul Martinez Mora. Monterrey .. KO 3
1973
Jan. 31—Sumio Nabata. Caracas .... W 10
Aug. 4—Jose Salas. Maracaibo .... KO 3
Sept. 1—Herman Torres. Bogota .... NC 5
Sept. 3—Enrique Garcia. Caracas .... L 10
Sept. 29—Hernan Torres. Caracas .... KO 5
Nov. 17—Lupe Mendez. Caracas .... KO 1
1974
Feb. 9—Vicente Blanco. Caracas .... D 10

Mar. 15—Octavio Gomez, Maracaibo .... W 10
Sept. 7—Bobby Chacon, Los Angeles ... KO by 9
   (For Vacant WBC Featherweight Title)
Dec. 12—Ben Ortiz, Caracas .... KO by 7
1975
Mar. 22—Art Hafey, Caracas .... KO by 4

TB	KO	WD	WF	D	LD	LF	KO BY	ND	NC
62	29	14	0	5	8	0	5	0	1

RICARDO ARRENDONDO
Born, 1951, Apatzingan, Michoacan, Mexico.
1966
Aug. 10—Manuel Justo, Mexico City .... W 6
Sept. —Ray Garcia, Tuxtla Gutierrez ..... KO 9
Oct. 3—Raul Anaya, Tuxtla Gutierrez .... KO 3
Nov. —Pichon Contreras, Mexico City W disq. 6
1967
Feb. —Paul Mora, Mexico City .... W 8
Mar. —Pedro Torres, Mexico City .... W 8
Apr. 22—Kid Clay, Mexico City .... W 10
June —Tino Anguiano, Apatzingan ...... KO 7
July —Raul Anaya, Tuxtla Gutierrez .... KO 2
Aug. 4—Clemente Sanchez, Nuevo Laredo ... L 10
Aug. —Manuel Flores, Nuevo Laredo .... KO 5
Sept. —Sugar Pino, Guamuchil .... KO 4
Oct. —Jose Garcia, Tuxtla Gutierrez .... KO 4
Nov. 22—Emilio Olvera, Mexico City ...... KO 4
1968
Jan. 6—Raul Cruz, Mexico City .... L disq. 10
Feb. 18—Gustavo Sosa, Puebla .... KO 5
Mar. 18—Luis Barrios, Managua .... KO 6
Mar. 28—Kid Clay, Managua .... KO 5
Apr. 20—Chuy Rocha, Monterrey .... KO 3
May 18—Chucho Hernandez, Mexico City .. KO 8
June 22—Alfredo Meneses, Mexico City ..... W 10
July 13—Chiquis Rosales, Mexico City ..... KO 8
July 27—Enrique Garcia, Mexico City ...... W 10
Sept. 7—Jose Luis Lopez, Mexico City ...... L 10
Oct. 10—Roberto San Martin, Obregon .... KO 2
Nov. 7—Billy Brown, Los Angeles .... KO 5
Nov. 30—Memo Tellez, Mexico City .... W 10
1969
Jan. 19—Felipe Gonzalez, Mexicali .... W 10
Feb. 21—Johnny Sandoval, Mexicali .... KO 7
Mar. 10—Juan Baez, Tijuana .... KO 4
Mar. 23—Esteban Favela, Mexicali .... KO 3
Apr. 22—Flash Besande, Honolulu .... W 10
May 26—Roberto Andrade, Tijuana ...... KO 6
June 14—Jalapa Montes, Apatzingan ...... KO 3
Aug. 16—Jorge Villanueva, Mexico City .... KO 10
Sept. 13—Felipe Torres, Mexico City .... W 10
Oct. 14—Curly Dequino, Honolulu .... W 10
Nov. 20—Jet Parker, Obregon .... W 10
Dec. 8—Alfredo Marcano, Tijuana :....... W 10
1970
Jan. 1—Alfredo Marcano, Mexicali .... L 10
Mar. 7—Roberto Santana, Mexico City ... KO 2
Apr. 16—Ruben Ruiz, Torreon .... KO 3
May 9—Joel Gomez, Mexico City .... KO 4
July 18—Victor Echegaray, Mexico City ... KO 1
Sept. 19—Enrique Garcia, Mexico City .... KO 10
Oct. 24—Miguel Riasco, Mexico City ...... KO 6
Nov. 17—Sammy Goss, Philadelphia ...... KO 5
Dec. 2—Huracan Sanchez, Oaxaca .... KO 1
Dec. 12—David Duran, Apatzingan .... KO 4
1971
Jan. 18—Augie Pantellas, Philadelphia .... KO 10
Mar. 3—Hiroshi Kobayashi, Tokyo .... L 15
   (For World Junior Lightweight Title)
May 9—Sigfrido Rodriguez, Aguascalientes D 10
May 27—Pedro Valverde, Chihuahua ...... KO 4
June 20—Samuel Reyes, Jiquilpan de Juarez KO 3
June 26—Gato Fajardo, Los Reyes .... KO 2
July 9—Lenny Brown, Obregon .... KO 2
Aug. 19—David Duran, Chihuahua ...... KO 4
Aug. 29—Enrique Pinto, Morelia .... KO 2
Oct. 10—Yoshiaki Numata, Sendai, Japan KO 10
   (Won WBC Junior Lightweight Title)

1972
Jan. 29—Jose Issac Marin, San Jose, C.R. ... W 15
   (Retained WBC Junior Lightweight Title)
Apr. 22—William Martinez, Mexico City ... KO 5
   (Retained WBC Junior Lightweight Title)
Aug. 5—Jesus Alonso, Mexico City .... KO 7
Sept. 15—Susumu Okabe, Tokyo .... KO 12
   (Retained WBC Junior Lightweight Title)
1973
Mar. 6—Apollo Yoshio, Fukuoka City ...... W 15
   (Retained WBC Junior Lightweight Title)
May 28—Andres Steyn, Johannesburg .... L 10
July 21—Jesus Alonso, Monterrey .... L 10
Sept. 1—Morito Kashiwaba, Tokyo .... KO 6
   (Retained WBC Junior Lightweight Title)
Nov. 29—Yasutsune Uehara, Naha, Okinawa L 10
1974
Feb. 28—Kuniaki Shibata, Tokyo .... L 15
   (Lost WBC Junior Lightweight Title)
Aug. 3—Alfredo Escalera, San Juan ... L disq. 8
1975
Feb. 15—Johnny Martinez, Morelia .... KO 7
May 9—Miguel Aceves, Puebla .... KO 2
May 30—Jose Luis Soberanes, Culiacan ..... W 10
July 19—Gil Becerra, La Paz .... KO 6
Nov. 28—Ramiro Bolanos, Guataquil .... L 10
1976
Jan. 25—Eleuterio Hernandez, Taqachula .. KO 5
Feb. 23—Jean Baptiste Piedvache, Paris ..... L 10
Apr. 23—Jorge Martinez, Reynosa .... KO 7
May 8—Ould Makhloufi, Algiers .... L 10
June 26—Beto Gutierrez, Los Mochis ...... L 10
Aug. 22—Juan Rodriguez, Tuxpan .... KO 3
Oct. 1—Leonardo Bermudez, Apatzingan ... L 10
Nov. 14—Ernesto Espana, Caracas .... L 10
1977
Mar. 24—Ramiro Bolanos, Los Angeles .... L 10
June 10—Rogelio Castaneda, San Diego ..... L 10
Sept. 16—Miguel Montilla, Santo Domingo ... L 10
Nov. 25—Carlos Gil, Santo Domingo .... KO by 10
1978
May 26—Hans Henrik Palm, Copenhagen KO by 5
1979
Feb. 26—Robert Perez, Houston .... KO 4
Mar. 17—Sang-Hyun Kim, Seoul .... KO by 10

TB	KO	WD	WF	D	LD	LF	KO BY	ND	NC
90	50	16	1	1	17	2	3	0	0

BEN VILLAFLOR
Born, November 10, 1952, Negros, Philippines.
Weight, 130 lbs. Southpaw.
1968
Feb. —Rod Sario, Manila .... W 4
May —George Arindidon, Manila .... D 4
1969
July 7—Willy Cangas, Quezon City ...... W 10
Aug. —Marcial Macatangay, Manila ..... KO 7
Oct. 4—Fil Del Mundo, Manila .... W 10
Dec. 20—Arturo Eracho, Manila .... W 10
1970
Feb. 28—Tony Jumao-as, Manila .... TD
Mar. 7—Pedro Martinez, Manila .... L 10
May —Alfredo Avila, Manila .... L 10
June 6—Ernie Cruz, Quezon City .... W 10
July 12—Willie Asuncion, Manila .... W 10
July 25—Tony Jumao-as, Quezon City ..... W 10
Sept. 19—Don Johnson, Manila .... KO 7
Nov. —Baby Lorona, Quezon City .... W 10
1971
Apr. 13—Rafael Lopez, Honolulu .... KO 1
Apr. 26—Memo Morales, Honolulu .... KO 6
May 19—Jose Luis Martinez, Honolulu ... KO 5
June —Delfino Camacho, Honolulu ...... KO 2
June 22—Jesus Mariscal, Honolulu .... KO 4
July 6—Memin Hernandez, Honolulu ..... KO 1
Aug. 10—Manuel Mendoza, Honolulu .... W 10

Sept.	14—Tad Okamoto, Honolulu .... KO	1
Oct.	5—Ricardo Garcia, Honolulu .... W	10
Nov.	16—Raul Cruz, Honolulu .... KO	10
Dec.	14—Ray Vega, Inglewood .... KO	7

1972

Jan.	26—Frankie Crawford, Honolulu ..... KO	1
Mar.	7—Jose Luis Lopez, Honolulu ...... KO	2
Apr.	25—Alfredo Marcano, Honolulu .... W	15
	(Won World Junior Lightweight Title)	
July	5—Carlos Fernandez, Honolulu ...... KO	3
Sept.	5—Victor Echegaray, Honolulu .... D	15
	(Retained World Junior Lightweight Title)	
Nov.	15—Jimmy Robertson, Honolulu .... W	10

1973

Jan.	31—Juan Collado, Honolulu .... W	10
Mar.	12—Kuniaki Shibata, Honolulu L	15
	(Lost World Junior Lightweight Title)	
July	18—Kenji Iwata, Honolulu .... KO	1
Aug.	21—Akhiro Kawaski, Honolulu .... KO	3
Oct.	17—Kuniaki Shibata, Honolulu .... KO	1
	(Regained World Junior Lightweight Title)	

1974

Mar.	14—Apollo Yoshio, Tokyo .... D	15
	(Retained World Junior Lightweight Title)	
July	19—Takao Maruki, Manila .... KO	7
Aug.	24—Yasutsune Uehara, Honolulu ..... KO	2
	(Retained World Junior Lightweight Title)	

1975

Mar.	10—Hyun-Chi Kim, Quezon City .... W	15
	(Retained World Junior Lightweight Title)	

1976

Jan.	12—Morito Kashiwaba, Tokyo .... KO	13
	(Retained World Junior Lightweight Title)	
Apr.	13—Samuel Serrano, Honolulu .... D	15
	(Retained World Junior Lightweight Title)	
Aug.	31—Rogelio Castaneda, Honolulu ...... W	10
Oct.	16—Samuel Serrano, San Juan L	15
	(Lost World Junior Lightweight Title)	

TB	KO	WD	WF	D	LD	LF	KO BY	ND	NC
44	20	15	0	5	4	0	0	0	0

KUNIAKI SHIBATA
(Record Under Featherweight Champions)

ALFREDO ESCALERA
Born, November 21, 1952, Carolina, Puerto Rico.

1970

Sept.	24—Bob Paysant, Portland, Me. ...... KO	3
Dec.	1—Rod Walsh, Scranton .... W	4

1971

Jan.	26—Don McClendon, New York L	6
Mar.	20—Willie Lugo, New York .... W	6
Mar.	24—Jimmy Jaynes, Boston .... W	6
July	26—Henry Ocasio, New York .... W	6
Sept.	2—Eddie James, Baltimore .... W	6
Sept.	7—Reynald Cantin, Sorel .... W	10
Sept.	23—Edwin Viruet, Paterson L	8
Oct.	25—Henry Ocasio, New York .... W	6

1972

Feb.	15—Diego Alcala, New York L	10
June	13—Alejandro Falcon, San Juan .... KO	7
July	14—Carlos Penso, Ponce .... KO	1
Sept.	18—Miguel Morales, San Juan .... W	10

1973

Mar.	17—Miguel Montilla, Carolina L	10
Mar.	31—Rocky Orengo, Carolina .... W	10
Apr.	28—Gino Febus, Carolina L	10
July	14—Miguel Montilla, Caguas .... KO	8
July	21—Leo Randolph, San Juan .... KO	2
Aug.	21—Frankie Otero, San Juan .... KO	5
Sept.	15—Jose Luis Lopez, San Juan ...... KO	6
Nov.	12—Antonio Amaya, San Juan .... W	10
Nov.	30—Mike Mayan, San Juan .... KO	4
Dec.	17—Johnny Copeland, San Juan ...... KO	5

1974

Feb.	4—Stanley Yanecheck, San Juan ... KO	2
Mar.	3—Sigfredo Rodriguez, San Juan .... KO	1

Apr.	1—Jorge Ramos, San Juan .... KO	3
May	30—Carlos Mendoza, San Juan .... KO	8
Aug.	3—Ricardo Arredondo, San Juan W disq.	8
Sept.	9—Oscar Pitton, San Juan .... KO	5
Oct.	18—Eleuterio Hernandez, Pueblo ..... KO	8
Oct.	30—Memo Cruz, Oaxaca L	10
Nov.	15—Rodriguez Valdez, Pueblo .... KO	1
Dec.	14—Mario Roman, Mexico City .... KO by	2

1975

Feb.	24—Mario Roman, San Juan .... KO	3
Mar.	31—Francisco Villegas, San Juan ...... D	10
July	5—Kuniaki Shibata, Tokyo .... KO	5
	(Won WBC Junior Lightweight Title)	
Sept.	20—Lionel Hernandez, Caracas .... D	15
	(Retained WBC Junior Lightweight Title)	
Nov.	17—Gaetan Hart, San Juan .... KO	6
Dec.	12—Sven-Erik Paulsen, Oslo .... KO	9
	(Retained WBC Junior Lightweight Title)	

1976

Feb.	20—Jose Fernandez, San Juan .... KO	13
	(Retained WBC Junior Lightweight Title)	
Apr.	1—Buzzsaw Yamabe, Nara .... KO	6
	(Retained WBC Junior Lightweight Title)	
July	1—Buzzsaw Yamabe, Nara .... W	15
	(Retained WBC Junior Lightweight Title)	
Sept.	18—Ray Lunny, San Juan .... KO	12
	(Retained WBC Junior Lightweight Title)	
Nov.	30—Tyrone Everett, Philadelphia ...... W	15
	(Retained WBC Junior Lightweight Title)	

1977

Mar.	17—Ronnie McGarvey, San Juan ..... KO	6
	(Retained WBC Junior Lightweight Title)	
May	16—Carlos Becerril, Landover .... KO	8
	(Retained WBC Junior Lightweight Title)	
Sept.	10—Sigfredo Rodriguez, San Juan ...... W	15
	(Retained WBC Junior Lightweight Title)	

1978

Jan.	28—Alexis Arguello, San Juan .... KO by	13
	(Lost WBC Junior Lightweight Title)	
June	3—Rogelio Castaneda, San Juan .... W	10
July	26—Larry Stanton, New York .... KO	3
Oct.	27—Julio Valdez, New York L	10

1979

Feb.	4—Alexis Arguello, Rimini .... KO by	13
	(For WBC Junior Lightweight Title)	
Oct.	13—Antonio Cruz, San Juan .... D	10

TB	KO	WD	WF	D	LD	LF	KO BY	ND	NC
54	26	14	1	3	7	0	3	0	0

SAMUEL SERRANO
Born, November 7, 1952, Toa Alta, Puerto Rico.
Weight, 126-130 lbs. Height, 5 ft. 8½ in.

1969

Nov.	1—Ramon Laureano, San Juan ...... KO	4
Nov.	13—Radames Pizarro, San Juan ...... W	4

1970

Jan.	17—Sammy Correa, San Juan .... KO	3
Feb.	14—Modesto Escalera, San Juan ...... W	6
Mar.	14—Ramon Montes, San Juan .... W	6
Mar.	30—Francisco Villegas, San Juan ...... W	12
	(Won Puerto Rican Featherweight Title)	
Apr.	11—Roberto Guerrero, San Juan ...... W	6
Apr.	15—Francisco Villegas, San Juan L	12
	(Lost Puerto Rican Featherweight Title)	
Nov.	1—Modesto Concepcion, San Juan ... W	8

1971

Jan.	27—Wilson Yambo, Ponce .... W	8
July	3—Braulio Rodriguez, San Juan ..... W	10
Dec.	4—Angel Rivera, San Juan .... W	10

1972

Apr.	8—Francisco Villegas, San Juan L	12
	(For Puerto Rican Featherweight Title)	

1973

Feb.	16—Nestor Rojas, San Juan .... W	10
Apr.	14—Terry Rondeau, Carolina .... KO	2
June	9—Freddie Mayan, San Juan .... KO	2
July	21—Jose Marin, San Juan .... W	10
Dec.	8—Ernesto Marcel, Panama City L	10

1974

Apr.	15—Lorenzo Trujillo, San Juan .... W		10
July	15—Gustavo Briceno, San Juan ...... KO		10
July	24—Cocoa Sanchez, San Juan .... W		10
Nov.	15—Memo Cruz, San Juan .... W		10

1975

Apr.	13—Jose Pena, San Juan .... W		10
June	28—Victor Echegaray, San Juan ...... W		10
Sept.	1—Ahmet Tosci, San Juan .... KO		2
Oct.	11—Diego Alcala, Ponce .... W		10
Dec.	13—Manuel Rodriguez, San Juan ..... KO		3

1976

Apr.	13—Ben Villaflor, Honolulu .... D		15
	(For World Junior Lightweight Title)		
May	8—Mar Bassa, San Juan .... KO		9
Sept.	10—Adrian Villanueva, San Juan .... KO		3
Oct.	16—Ben Villaflor, San Juan .... W		15
	(Won World Junior Lightweight Title)		

1977

Jan.	15—Alberto Herrera, Guayaquil ...... KO		11
	(Retained World Junior Lightweight Title)		
June	26—Leonel Hernandez, Puerto La Cruz	W	15
	(Retained World Junior Lightweight Title)		
Aug.	27—Apollo Yoshio, San Juan .... W		15
	(Retained World Junior Lightweight Title)		
Nov.	19—Tae-Ho Kim, San Juan .... KO		10
	(Retained World Junior Lightweight Title)		

1978

Feb.	18—Mario Martinez, San Juan .... W		15
	(Retained World Junior Lightweight Title)		
July	8—Young-Ho Oh, San Juan .... KO		9
	(Retained World Junior Lightweight Title)		
Nov.	29—Takao Maruki, Nagoya .... W		15
	(Retained World Junior Lightweight Title)		

1979

Feb.	18—Julio Valdez, San Juan .... W		15
	(Retained World Junior Lightweight Title)		
Apr.	14—Nkosana Mgxaji, Capetown ...... KO		8
	(Retained World Junior Lightweight Title)		

1980

Apr.	3—Kiyoshi Kazama, Nara, Japan .... KO		13
	(Retained World Junior Lightweight Title)		
Aug.	2—Yasutsune Uehara, Detroit .... KO by		6
	(Lost World Junior Lightweight Title)		
Sept.	20—Jesus Delgado, San Juan .... KO		2

TB	KO	WD	WF	D	LD	LF	KO BY	ND	NC
43	15	23	0	1	3	0	1	0	0

ALEXIS ARGUELLO
(Record Under Featherweight Champions)

YASUTSUNE UEHARA
Born, October 12, 1949, Naha, Okinawa, Japan. Weight, 130 lbs. Height, 5 ft. 6½ in. Managed by Masaki Kanehira.

1972

Nov.	14—Sam Furachiseli, Honolulu .... KO		4
Nov.	21—Mar Yuzon, Honolulu L		6
Dec.	12—Shichiro Saito, Honolulu .... W		6

1973

Feb.	13—Rudy Tolongari, Honolulu .... KO		1
Mar.	12—Danny Campos, Honolulu .... KO		6
June	14—Noriaki Yoshimura, Tokyo .... KO		5
Aug.	4—Rocky Sawa, Naha, Okinawa ..... KO		6
Oct.	28—Tokichi Uehara, Tokyo .... KO		3
Nov.	29—Ricardo Arrendondo, Naha, Okinawa	W	10

1974

Mar.	26—Kae-Shik Yua, Nagoya .... KO		6
May	28—Hasaharu Tsuchiya, Tokyo .... KO		1
Aug.	24—Ben Villaflor, Honolulu .... KO by		2
	(For World Junior Lightweight Title)		
Nov.	30—Freddy Mason, Akita City .... W		10

1975

July	21—Susumu Okabe, Tokyo .... KO		1
	(Won Japanese Junior Lightweight Title)		

Oct.	19—Masa Ito, Naha, Okinawa .... KO		5
	(Retained Japanese Junior Lightweight Title)		
Dec.	9—Susumu Okabe, Tokyo .... KO		8
	(Retained Japanese Junior Lightweight Title)		

1976

Apr.	23—Masa Ito, Tokuyama L		10
	(Lost Japanese Junior Lightweight Title)		
July	29—Masa Ito, Tokyo .... W		10
	(Regained Japanese Junior Lightweight Title)		
Dec.	7—Joe Lim, Manila L		10

1977

May	29—Shoji Okano, Naha, Okinawa ..... KO		2
	(Retained Japanese Junior Lightweight Title)		
Sept.	9—Suketoshi Maruyama, Nagoya .... KO		6
Dec.	4—Tadashi Akiyama, Tokyo .... KO		7
	(Retained Japanese Junior Lightweight Title)		

1978

Apr.	28—Ryu Fukida, Tokyo .... KO		7
	(Retained Japanese Junior Lightweight Title)		
Aug.	9—Tatsuya Moriyasu, Omiya .... KO		2
Nov.	25—Hideyoshi Horinaga, Tokyo ...... KO		2
	(Retained Japanese Junior Lightweight Title)		

1979

Feb.	27—Yosuhide Takahashi, Tokyo ...... KO		6
July	12—Yoshitaka Ikehara, Tokyo .... W		10
	(Retained Japanese Junior Lightweight Title)		
Nov.	10—Kojiro Sasaki, Naha, Okinawa ... KO		10
	(Retained Japanese Junior Lightweight Title)		

1980

Mar.	13—Junichi (Blazer) Okubo, Tokyo ... KO		5
	(Retained Japanese Junior Lightweight Title)		
Aug.	2—Samuel Serrano, Detroit .... KO		6
	(Won World Junior Lightweight Title)		
Nov.	20—Leonel Hernandez, Tokyo .... W		15
	(Retained World Junior Lightweight Title)		

TB	KO	WD	WF	D	LD	LF	KO BY	ND	NC
31	21	6	0	0	3	0	1	0	0

RAFAEL (BAZOOKA) LIMON
Born, January 13, 1954, Mexico City, Mexico. Weight, 130 lbs. Southpaw.

1972

Dec.	5—Jose Garcia, Mexico City .... KO		1

1973

Feb.	3—Raul Juarez, Mexico City .... KO		5
Feb.	24—Joel Carmona, Mexico City ...... KO		1
Mar.	21—Magdaleno Andrette, Mexico City	KO	4
June	20—Carlos Mimila, Mexico City ... KO by		2
Sept.	1—Ventura Perez, Mexico City ..... KO		1
Sept.	20—Juan Ordanez, Mexico City .... KO by		4
Oct.	31—Canelo Salinas, Mexico City L		8

1974

Jan.	19—Armando Estavez, Mexico City ... KO		3
Mar.	9—Chamaco Casanova, Mexico City	KO	7
Apr.	7—Antonio Nava, Mexico City .... KO by		3
June	1—Canelo Salinas, Mexico City ...... KO		3
July	20—Gaby Morgan, Mexico City L		10
Sept.	14—Jose Pesos, Mexico City .... KO		1
Sept.	29—Alejandro Perez, Mexico City ..... KO		4
Oct.	28—Salvador Medina, Mexico City ... KO		3
Dec.	4—Memo Ramirez, Mexico City ..... KO		3
Dec.	17—Edel Burunda, Juarez .... KO		3

1975

Feb.	8—Chuy Rodriguez, Mexico City .... KO		4
Mar.	15—Tomas Frias, Mexico City .... W		10
May	4—Memo Rodriguez, Tuxtla Gutierrez	L	10
June	11—Victor Ramirez, Mexico City ..... W		10
July	12—Jose Luis Meza, Mexico City ...... W		10
Sept.	13—Victor Ramirez, Mexico City L		10
Nov.	15—Juan Pablo Oropeza, Mexico City .. W		10
Dec.	7—Bobby Chacon, Mexicali .... W		10

1976

Feb.	1—Yambito Blanco, Mexicali .... W		10
June	7—Saul Montana, Tijuana .... W		10
July	10—Ray Thomas, Juarez .... KO		1
Aug.	6—Ruben Coria, Inglewood .... KO		4
Aug.	28—Lionel Rose, Inglewood .... KO		3
Oct.	2—Teruyoshi Nohi, Los Angeles ..... KO		2

698

Nov.	13—Chuy Rodriguez, Culiacan .... KO	5

Nov. 13—Chuy Rodriguez, Culiacan .... KO 5
1977
Mar. 13—Leonardo Bermudez, Culiacan ...... D 10
May 31—Augustin Estrada, San Antonio .... W 10
Aug. 6—Mar Basa, Los Angeles .... KO 3
Sept. 2—Antonio Llamas, Coatzacoalcos ... KO 3
Sept. 15—Hector Munoz, Reynosa .... KO 3
Oct. 8—Ray Saldivar, Los Angeles .... KO 3
Oct. 22—Aurelio Muniz, Obregon Mante L disq. 6
Oct. 29—Ben Ortiz, Los Angeles .... W 10
1978
Mar. 4—Ernest Bing, Los Angeles .... KO 10
(Won Vacant NABF Junior Lightweight Title)
Apr. 15—Jose Marin, Los Angeles .... KO 1
June 10—Rocky Ramon, Oklahoma City ..... W 10
Aug. 6—Juan Villa, Stockton .... KO 7
Aug. 26—Jaime Nava, Fresno .... KO 10
Dec. 4—Abe Perez, Tijuana .... KO 6

Dec. 19—Robert Vasquez, Houston .... KO 5
1979
Feb. 26—Miguel Estrada, Houston .... KO 5
Apr. 9—Bobby Chacon, Inglewood .... TD 7
(Retained NABF Junior Lightweight Title)
July 8—Alexis Arguello, New York .... KO by 11
(For WBC Junior Lightweight Title)
Nov. 27—Faustino Pena, Houston .... W 10
1980
Mar. 21—Bobby Chacon, Los Angeles .... L 10
Apr. 25—Frank Ahumada, Los Angeles ..... W 10
July 24—Frankie Baltazar, Los Angeles ... KO 4
(Retained NABF Junior Lightweight Title)
Dec. 11—Ildefonso Bethelmy, Los Angeles .. KO 15
(Won Vacant WBC Junior Lightweight Title)

TB	KO	WD	WF	D	LD	LF	KO BY	ND	NC
56	32	12	0	2	5	1	4	0	0

FEATHERWEIGHTS

TORPEDO BILLY MURPHY	1890	*JACKIE WILSON (NBA)*	*1941-1943*
YOUNG GRIFFO	1890-1891	WILLIE PEP	1942-1948
GEORGE DIXON	1891-1897	*JACKIE CALLURA (NBA)*	*1943*
SOLLY SMITH	1897-1898	*PHIL TERRANOVA (NBA)*	*1943-1944*
BEN JORDAN (GREAT BRITAIN)	*1898-1899*	*SAL BARTOLO (NBA)*	*1944-1946*
EDDIE SANTRY (GREAT BRITAIN)	*1899-1900*	SANDY SADDLER	1948-1949
DAVE SULLIVAN	1898	WILLIE PEP	1949-1950
GEORGE DIXON	1898-1900	SANDY SADDLER	1950-1957
TERRY MC GOVERN	1900-1901	HOGAN (KID) BASSEY	1957-1959
YOUNG CORBETT II	1901-1902	DAVEY MOORE	1959-1963
ABE ATTELL	1901-1912	ULTIMINIO (SUGAR) RAMOS	1963-1964
JOHNNY KILBANE	1912-1923	VICENTE SALDIVAR	1964-1967
EUGENE CRIQUI	1923	*HOWARD WINSTONE*	
JOHNNY DUNDEE	1923-1924	*(GREAT BRITAIN)*	*1968*
LOUIS (KID) KAPLAN	1925-1927	*RAUL ROJAS (WBA)*	*1968*
BENNY BASS	1927-1928	*JOSE LEGRA (WBC)*	*1968-1969*
TONY CANZONERI	1928	*SHOZO SAIJYO (WBA)*	*1968-1971*
ANDRE ROUTIS	1928-1929	JOHNNY FAMECHON (WBC)	1969-1970
BATTLING BATTALINO	1929-1932	VICENTE SALDIVAR (WBC)	1970
TOMMY PAUL (NBA)	*1932-1933*	KUNIAKI SHIBATA (WBC)	1970-1972
KID CHOCOLATE (NEW YORK)	*1932-1933*	*ANTONIO GOMEZ (WBA)*	*1971-1972*
FREDDIE MILLER (NBA)	*1933-1936*	CLEMENTE SANCHEZ (WBC)	1972
ALBERTO (BABY)		*ERNESTO MARCEL (WBA)*	*1972-1974*
ARIZMENDI (CALIF.-MEXICAN)	*1935-1936*	*JOSE LEGRA (WBC)*	*1972-1973*
MIKE BELLOISE (NEW YORK)	*1936-1937*	*EDER JOFRE (WBC)*	*1973-1974*
PETEY SARRON (NBA)	*1936-1937*	*RUBEN OLIVARES (WBA)*	*1974*
HENRY ARMSTRONG	1937-1938	*BOBBY CHACON (WBC)*	*1974-1975*
JOEY ARCHIBALD (NEW YORK)	*1938-1939*	ALEXIS ARGUELLO (WBA)	1974-1976
LEO RODAK (NBA)	*1938-1939*	*RUBEN OLIVARES (WBC)*	*1975*
JOEY ARCHIBALD	1939-1940	*DAVID (POISON) KOTEY (WBC)*	*1975-1976*
PETEY SCALZO (NBA)	*1940-1941*	DANNY LOPEZ (WBC)	1976-1980
HARRY JEFFRA	1940-1941	*RAFAEL ORTEGA (WBA)*	*1977*
JOEY ARCHIBALD	1941	*CECILIO LASTRA (WBA)*	*1977-1978*
RICHIE LEMOS (NBA)	*1941*	*EUSEBIO PEDROZA (WBA)*	*1978-*
CHALKY WRIGHT	1941-1942	SALVADOR SANCHEZ (WBC)	1980-

Claimants not generally recognized are in *italics*.

HISTORY OF THE FEATHERWEIGHT CLASS

John Keating claimed the featherweight championship of America in the early 1860's, but he declined to meet Nobby Clark of England in a fight for world honors. Jimmy Elliott, later American Heavyweight Champion, was substituted, but lost to Clark.

May 28, 1860, Nobby Clark beat Jimmy Elliott, 34 rounds, 1 hour and 2 minutes at Palisades, New Jersey. Nobby Clark was never beaten in America, and he returned to England and retired from the game.

Dick Hollywood and John Keating then claimed the title, but Hollywood gave Keating several terrific beatings in championship fights in the early 1860's. Hollywood then retired, and the title was claimed by Tommy Kelly (the original Tommy Kelly, not the one who boxed George Dixon in 1888).

Oct. 7, 1868, George Seddons beat Tommy Kelly, 96 rounds, lasting 1 hour and 39 minutes, at Portmouth, N. H., for the championship.

George Seddons outgrew the class, and eventually boxed Arthur Chambers for the lightweight championship. After being beaten, Seddons retired. In the early 1870's the championship was claimed by Tommy Kelly, and later by John Keating and Long Tom Ryan.

In the early 1880's the featherweight championship was claimed by Jack Keenan, until 1885, when he was beaten by Young Mitchell (John Herget). Mitchell outgrew the class, and Harry Gilmore of Canada, claimed the title in 1887, but he, too, outgrew the class after a time. Then came the era in which Ike Weir, Dal Hawkins, Cal McCarthy and George Dixon contended for the title.

On June 3, 1889, Dal Hawkins and Fred Bogan engaged in what was advertised as a featherweight title bout and at the end of the 75th round the bout was halted due to darkness and called a draw. It took place in San Francisco. The next day the bout was resumed and Hawkins was stopped by Bogan in the 15th round.

Bogan returned to Australia and Hawkins claimed the title, but both had by then outgrown the class which then had a limit of 118 pounds.

March 31, 1889—Ike Weir and Frank Murphy fought to a draw, at Kouts, Ind., 80 rounds. (Designated as world title bout.)

On July 30, Billy Murphy and Frank Murphy fought a draw of 27 rounds and then Frank returned to England, refusing to fight Weir again for the right to meet Billy Murphy. Hence the Police Gazette arranged for a championship match between Australian Billy and Weir which the latter lost.

January 13, 1890—Billy Murphy, New Zealand, knocked out Ike Weir, Ireland, at San Francisco, in 14 rounds.

The American contention was that neither Weir nor Murphy had a right to a world title claim but only to the British Empire title.

In America, George Dixon, of Boston, and Cal McCarthy, of Troy, N. Y., each of whom had graduated from the bantamweight class which at the time was recognized at 110 pounds, were the leading contenders. When Dixon stopped McCarthy at Troy in 22 rounds the ringside weight was 115 pounds and he gained recognition as the American titleholder.

April 25, 1891—Ike Weir and Johnny Griffin fought at Nantucket, Mass. The bout was stopped by police in round 4. (Griffin had claimed title during Billy Murphy's absence in Australia.)

Dixon, on July 28, 1891, knocked out Abe Willis, featherweight champion of England, in five rounds, and thus became the world champion of the class.

Sept. 6, 1892—George Dixon knocked out Jack Skelly at New Orleans, in 8 rounds, for the world featherweight championship.

Tom O'Rourke, Dixon's manager, then gradually raised the weight limit and stipulated 120 pounds for a title match between Dixon and Solly Smith at San Francisco, October 4, 1897, Smith getting the referee's decision at the end of 20 rounds.

Smith then made a match with Dave Sullivan which was fought at Coney Island, N. Y., September 26, 1898, Smith breaking his arm and being compelled to quit in the fifth round.

Dixon challenged Sullivan and they met in the Lenox A. C., New York, November 11, 1898, and Dixon regained his title by stopping Sullivan in the tenth round, Sullivan's seconds entering the ring to prevent a knockout.

Dixon retained the title until January 9, 1900, when he was knocked out by Terry McGovern at the Broadway A. C., New York, in the eighth round. The weight was 118 pounds.

Nov. 28, 1901—Young Corbett knocked out Terry McGovern at Hartford, Conn., in 2 rounds.

(The weight was 126 pounds, nevertheless, the bout was billed as being for the featherweight championship. Corbett could never make the feather limit, and did not attempt to do so. When he and McGovern both competed in the lightweight class, Abe Attell claimed the featherweight championship.)

Attell gained the vacant title in matches with George Dixon, having drawn with him, 20 rounds, on Oct. 20, 1901, at Cripple Creek, Colo., and decisioning him, 15 rounds, Oct. 28, 1901, at St. rounds, Oct. 28, 1901, at St. Louis.

April 30, 1908—Abe Attell knocked out Brooklyn Tommy Sullivan at San Francisco, in 4 rounds in a non-title bout.

February 22, 1912—Johnny Kilbane outpointed Abe Attell at Vernon, Cal., in 20 rounds.

June 2, 1923—Eugene Criqui knocked out Johnny Kilbane at Polo Grounds, New York City, 6 rounds.

July 26, 1923—Johnny Dundee outpointed Eugene Criqui at Polo Grounds, New York City, in 15 rounds.

(In 1925, when Dundee outgrew featherweight class, an elimination tourney to determine his successor was won by Louis (Kid) Kaplan.)

Jan. 2, 1925—Louis (Kid) Kaplan knocked out Danny Kramer, in Madison Square Garden, New York City, in 9 rounds.

(By 1927 Kaplan outgrew the class. An elimination tourney made Benny Bass the leading contender.)

Sept. 12, 1927—Benny Bass outpointed Red Chapman at Philadelphia, Pa., in 10 rounds, Chapman being the N. B. A. champion.

Feb. 10, 1928—Tony Canzoneri outpointed Benny Bass in Madison Square Garden. New York City, in 15 rounds, to clinch world title.

Sept. 28, 1928—Andre Routis outpointed Tony Canzoneri at N. Y. C., in 15 rounds.

Sept. 23, 1929—Battling Battalino outpointed Andre Routis at Hartford, Conn., in 15 rounds.

(By 1932 Battalino outgrew the class. An N.B.A. elimination tournament was won by Tommy Paul of Buffalo.)

May 26, 1932—Tommy Paul outpointed Johnny Pena at Detroit, Mich., in 15 rounds. for N.B.A. title.

Oct. 13, 1932—Kid Chocolate knocked out Lew Feldman at New York, N.Y. in 12 rounds. This bout was recognized by the New York Commission as for the featherweight championship because Paul had previously lost to Feldman. The N.B.A. had not sanctioned the Feldman-Paul fight as for the crown. Chocolate later relinquished his claim to the title.

Jan. 13, 1933—Freddie Miller outpointed Tommy Paul at Chicago, Ill., in 10 rounds in an N.B.A. championship fight which New York refused to recognize.

Miller proceeded to clean up the cream of the world's contenders. He traveled all over Europe and beat all rivals, losing only two fights out of 34 and engaged in two draws. He lost only to one outstanding champion in Europe, Maurice Holtzer of France, in an overweight bout.

May 11, 1936—Miller lost to Petey Sarron, Washington, D. C., in 15 rounds.

October 29, 1937—Henry Armstrong knocked out Sarron, Madison Square Garden, in 6 rounds, to win world title.

1938—Henry Armstrong resigned as featherweight champion.

The New York State Commission, recognizing Mike Belloise of New York and Joey Archibald of Pawtucket, R. I., as the outstanding contenders, arranged a match for the St. Nicholas A. C. of New York and Archibald won the fight and recognition.

Oct. 17, 1938—Joey Archibald won decision from Mike Belloise, 15 rounds.

May 20, 1940—Joey Archibald lost to Harry Jeffra, 15 rounds, Baltimore, Md.

May 12, 1941—Joey Archibald beat Harry Jeffra, 15 rounds, Washington, D. C.

Sept. 11, 1941—Chalky Wright knocked out Joey Archibald, Washington, D.C., 11 rounds.

Petey Scalzo, on Dec. 5, 1938, knocked out Archibald in 2 rounds in an overweight match, and thereafter, tried desperately to meet Archibald in a title bout but was unsuccessful. When he refused to meet Scalzo, the N.B.A. declared Scalzo the champion and vacated Archibald's title on May 1, 1940. When Archibald fought Jeffra in Baltimore, only New York and Maryland recognized it as for the crown. But there could be no doubt that Archibald was champion and Jeffra, when he won, became successor to the crown.

As a result of this dispute, the N.B.A. had Scalzo as its champion and when Scalzo was knocked out by Richie Lemos at Los Angeles, in 5 rounds, July 1, 1941, Lemos received N.B.A. recognition. On Nov. 18, Lemos lost the N.B.A. title to Jackie Wilson. However, in 1941 Chalky Wright was the world champion.

Nov. 20, 1942—Willie Pep defeated Chalky Wright, Madison Square Garden, 15 rounds, decision. On January 18, 1943, Wilson lost the N.B.A. crown to Jackie Callura of Canada. The N.B.A. crown passed from Callura to Phil Terranova, by a knockout in 8 rounds on August 16, 1943, and Terranova lost it to Sal Bartolo on March 10, 1944 in 15 rounds at Boston.

Willie Pep, who was recognized as the international champion, joined the Navy on June 16, 1943, and was honorably discharged on February 15, 1944. He defended his title against Chalky Wright in the Garden on September 29, 1944 and won in 15 rounds. He then joined the Army. Thereafter Pep successfully defended the crown against Sal Bartolo (twice), Chalky Wright and Phil Terranova.

Oct. 29, 1948—Sandy Saddler scored a four-round knockout over Willie Pep at Madison Square Garden, New York, to win the world title.

Feb. 11, 1949—Willie Pep regained the title by winning a 15 round decision over Sandy Saddler at Madison Square Garden, New York.

September 8, 1950—Sandy Saddler regained the title by halting Willie Pep at Yankee Stadium, New York, N. Y., Pep being unable to answer the bell for the eighth round due to injury.

Saddler was inducted into the Army in 1952 and the N.B.A. recognized Percy Bassett as "Interim Champion."

Following an auto accident in which he was injured in 1956, Saddler relinquished the title in 1957.

After an elimination tournament, with Hogan (Kid) Bassey and Cherif Hamia as finalists, Bassey won the vacant title by stopping Hamia, 10 rounds, on June 24, 1957, at Paris, France.

March 18, 1959—Davey Moore won the title by knocking out Hogan (Kid) Bassey at the end of the 13th round, at Los Angeles, Calif.

March 21, 1963—Sugar Ramos won the title by stopping Davey Moore in the 11th round at Los Angeles, Calif.

September 26, 1964—Vicente Saldivar won the title by stopping Sugar Ramos in the 12th round at Mexico City, Mexico.

Feb. 12, 1966—Vicente Saldivar, Mexico City, knocked out Floyd Robertson, Ghana, in 2:29 of the second round in Mexico City. Saldivar, 125¾; Robertson, 124¼.

Aug. 7, 1966—Vicente Saldivar, Mexico City, defeated Mitsunori Seki, Japan, in Mexico City in 15 rounds by a decision. Saldivar, 124½; Seki, 124.

Jan. 29, 1967—Vicente Saldivar, Mexico City, 125, retained his crown by knocking out Mitsunori Seki, Japan, 126, in Mexico City, in the seventh round. Referee—Ramon Beruman.

June 15, 1967—Vicente Saldivar, Mexico City, 126, retained his title, defeating Howard Winstone, Wales, 125¼ by a decision in 15 rounds, in Cardiff, Wales. Referee—Wally Thom.

Oct. 14, 1967—Vicente Saldivar, Mexico City, 125, retained his crown, stopping Howard Winstone, Wales, 125¼, in 12 rounds in the Aztec Arena of Mexico City. Winstone's second tossed in the towel. Saldivar announced his retirement following his victory.

Jan. 23, 1969—Johnny Famechon, 125, Australia, decisioned Jose Legra, 124, Spain over 15 rounds to win the vacant world title. The bout was awarded to Famechon by referee George Smith by the score of 74½ to 73½. Bout held in London, England.

May 9, 1970—Vicente Saldivar of Mexico regained the world featherweight championship, defeating Johnny Fam-echon of Australia, winning the decision at the end of 15 rounds. Famechon announced his retirement after the loss.

Famechon scaled 124½ and Saldivar 126.

Dec. 11, 1970—Kuniaki Shibata, 126, Japan, halted Vicente Saldivar, 125, Mexico. in the 13th round to win world title. Bout was held in Tijuana, Mexico.

May 19, 1972—Clemente Sanchez, Mexico knocked out Kuniaki Shibata, Japan, at 2:26 of the third round to win the title. Weights, Shibata and Sanchez 126. Bout held in Tokyo, Japan.

Dec. 16, 1972—Clemente Sanchez vacated his title. He no longer could make the weight. W.B.A. recognition given to Ernesto Marcel, Panama: W.B.C. awarded Spain's Jose Legra its crown.

May 31, 1975—Alexis Arguello, Nicaragua won the vacant world title via a TKO at 2:00 of the second round over Panama's Rigoberto Riasco. Arguello also holds a win over the W.B.C. champion Ruben Olivares. Arguello and Riasco weight 126. Referee Ferly Carpentier. Contest was held in Managua, Nicaragua.

June 20, 1977—Alexis Arguello, Nicaragua, give up his title and retired as undefeated champion to move up to the lightweight division. He no longer could make the featherweight limit. See W.B.A. and W.B.C. for their champions. The Ring has the title vacant.

November 5, 1976—Danny Lopez, 124, Los Angeles, Cal., outpointed David (Poison) Kotey, 126, Ghana, over 15 rounds to win the WBC title. Site: Accra, Ghana.

April 15, 1978—Eusebio Pedroza, 126, Panama, TKO'd Cecilio Lastra, 126, Spain, in the 13th round to win the WBA title. Bout held in Panama City. Referee: Larry Rozadilla.

February 2, 1980—Salvador Sanchez, 125¼, Mexico, TKO'd Danny Lopez, 125¾, Los Angeles, Calif., at 0:51 of round 13 in Phoenix, Arizona, to win the WBC title. Waldemar Schmidt, referee.

FEATHERWEIGHT DIVISION

"TORPEDO" BILLY MURPHY
(Thomas W. Murphy)
Born, 1863, Auckland, N. Z. Height, 5 ft.
6½ in. Reach, 69½ in.

1887-1888
Won: Jack O'Meagher, 45 m; Frank Burns, KO 6; M. O'Brien, W4; J. Guller, KO 12; W. Burt, W 3; Charles Carter, W 3; J. Gardner, W 3; Walter Evans, W 3; Fuller, (twice) W 13; Sam Stewart, W 17; B. Johnson, W 3; F. King, W 3; bested by Young Mitchell, 5; Charlie Taylor, W 12; F. Bruce, W 7; C. Allen, W 7; Harry Laing, D 3; J. Fadders, KO 2; Bill Mitchell, W 4; Ike Fake, 3; Brooks, KO 1 and Parker, KO 3, in same night; J. Ford, W 11; Saxon, W 4; Jack Hall, D 8; Jerry Marshall, W 1; Basket, W 3; Smith, W 8, Eugene Donovan, L 11; Young Griffo, D 4.

1888
Nov. 20—Ben Seth, of Eng., Melbourne
.... Ko by   6

1889
June   7—Arrived in San Fran. on Zelandia.
July 12—Johnny Griffin (117-120), Cal.
A.C. ....KO   3
July 30—Frank Murphy, Eng. (119), Cal.
A. C. $1,250 each .... D 27

1890
Jan. 13—Ike Weir, (118-124), $2,250,
Calif. A. C., San Francisco ....KO 14
For R. K. Fox, belt and featherweight championship of the world.
Mar. 14—Tommy Warren, (116-118), $1,800, Occidental club, San Fran........... W   4
Apr. 21—Bested Tommy White, Chicaco   4
May   29—Eddie Greaney, Cal. A. C........ W   4
June 28—Returned to Auckland, N. Z.
Sept. 3—*Young Griffo, $1,500, Sydney .L 15
Murphy took off gloves.

*For featherweight championship of Australia.
  —Nipper Peakes, Melbourne ..... D 19
Nov. 10—Dummy Mace, (117-143), Melb. W   8
Dec. 17—Pat Carroll, (117-146) .... W   4

1891
Jan. 19—Jim Burge, $750, Broken Hill
.............................KO by 30
May   4—Artie Tully, Melbourne L   8
July 22—Young Griffo, Sydney, $750 ....L 22
Oct.   2—Spider Kelly, Guttenberg,
N. J.............................KO by   3
Oct. 19—Bill Jennings, Sydney, £25....KO   2
Nov. 23—Jim Burge, Sydney ....NC 29
Dec. 20—Spider Kelly, Hoboken,
N. J.............................KO by   2
Dec. 26—Chris Cunningham, Newcastle KO   2

1892
Jan. 23—Young Griffo failed to meet him, Melbourne
Feb. 16—Jim Barron, (136), Sydney KO by   3
May   31—Johnny Murphy, Boston ..... D 40
$1,250, Pacific club, S. F. Johnny Murphy gave Billy Half of purse.
July 25—Spider Kelly, New York City L   6
      —Jack Downey .... D   4
Dec. 28—Tommy White ....D NC 32
Pacific A. C., San Fran. White received $200, Murphy nothing.

1893
Feb.   6—Johnny Griffin, (122) $3,500-$500, C.I.A.C. ....KO by   7
Apr. 29—Bested by Jerry Barnett, N. Y. 4
May   30—Johnny Van Heest, Phil. .....ND   4
July 17—Ed Listman, Newark, N. J. ..... W   3
Sept. 13—Jack Collins, Brooklyn ....KO   2
Sept. 22—Jack Grace, Brooklyn, police .. W   2
Nov.   2—Ike Weir, (120), $650-$100, Bos-
ton ....KO by   6
Dec. 15—George Dixon, Paterson, N. J.
(row) L   3
Dec. 23—Jack Woods, Boston ....KO   2

1894
Feb. 19—Johnny Breslin, Boston ......KO   2
May   7—Young Griffo, Boston, Gate.
Referee, Capt. Bill Daly ....L 20
Nov.   6—Jack McCabe, Cincinnati .....KO   2
Nov. 12—Anthony Lefevre, Cincinnati .. W   2
Nov. 19—Jerry Barnett, $250, Atl. A. C.,
New York .... D 10
Dec.   8—Bested Kentucky Rosebud, Phila. .. 4

1895
Jan.   3—Frank Machiewski, Phila. police 4
Feb.   6—"Kid" McGraw, Cincinnati ...KO   4

Feb. 26—"Kid" Hogan, Cincinnati ....L 10
May   6—Jack Dougherty, Cincinnati .... D 10
May   30—Jack Dougherty, Cincinnati .... D   6
July 11—Tommy White, Columbus, O. .. D 20
Aug.   6—Harry Sheldon, Louisville .... W   5
Aug. 22—Harry Sheldon, Louisville ....KO   3
Nov. 13—Jack Doherty, Lexington, Ky. . W 10
Dec. 23—Sol Smith, New Orleans ....L 14

1896
Jan. 21—Mike Crotty, KO 1; Harry Dally, W 4; Joe Slink, W 4; Cincinnati,
Ohio ....Exh.   1
Feb. 11—Jimmy Devers, Jackson, Miss. .. W 10
Mar. 17—Paddy Smith, Cincinnati ..... D 10
Apr. 29—James Connors, Jackson, Mich.KO   4
Oct.   8—Johnny Lavack, Lexington, Ky. D 20

1897
Jan. 22—George Dixon, Broadway A. C.,
New York ....KO by   6
Jan. 30—Jack Delaney, Polo A. C., N. Y...L   5
Feb.   6—Dave Wall, Polo A. C., N. Y. .... D 10
Feb.   8—Danny McMahon, Philadelphia ..L   6

1899
Jan. 16—Casper Leon, Cincinnati ....L 10
Apr. 29—Harry Forbes, Chicago L   4

1904
Returned to Sydney.
Knocked out by: Tim Hegarty, 3. Lost: Peter Toohey, 2.

1906
Knockout: Tom Toohey, 1, New Plymouth, and fought draw with Jim Ross Auckland, 4.

TB	KO	WD	WF	D	LD	LF	KOBY	ND	NC
90	17	32	0	14	15	0	9	1	2

Died July 26, 1939, Auckland, N. Z.

YOUNG GRIFFO
(Albert Griffiths)
N.S.W. Nationality, Australian. Height 5 ft. 4 in.
Born, March 31, 1871, Miller's Point, Sydney.
(Claimant World Featherweight Title)

Prior to 1889
Won: Bob O'Neil, 15; Francis (bare knuckles), 7; Sam Matthews, 140 lb. competition; Chappie, Adelaide, 3; Smith, Adelaide, 4; Young O'Brien (twice) 8; Kiama Pet, 2; Sandy Ross, 4; Lewis, 3; Lane, 2; Sullivan, 4; Holden, 12; Draw: Young Pluto, 8, 6, 23 and 13; McShane, 8; Michie, 8; Lawrence, 8; Billy Murphy, 4; Ambrose Taylor, 8.

1889
June 15—Unknown, Sydney, Aust......KO   2
July 27—Abe Willis, Sydney, Aust...... D 20
Aug.   7—Doss Patterson, Sydney, Aust.. W   4
Nov. 19—Jem Dempsey, Sydney, Aust. .. W 12
Dec. 12—Young Pluto, Melbourne, Aust. D 70
Dec. 31—Nipper Peakes, Melbourne ..... W   8

1830
Jan. 11—Abe Willis, Sydney .... W   3
Feb.   —George McKenzie, Sydney .. W 15
June   —Young Patterson, Sydney ...... W   2
June 12—McLeod, Sydney ....KO   2
Sept. 13—Billy Murphy, Sydney .... W   7
Nov. 14—Paddy Moran, Sydney ....KO 13

1891
Mar. 12—George Powell, Sydney .....WF 20
July 22—Billy Murphy, Sydney .... W 22
Dec. 15—Billy Williams, Melbourne ..... W   8

1892
Jan. 23—Failed to meet Billy Murphy, $750; Melbourne.
Mar. 22—Mick McCarthy, $500 .... W   4
May   17—Mick Ryan, Sydney .... W   8
July 25—Jem Bavion, Sydney .... D 22
Nov.   8—Martin Denny, Sydney .... D 25
Dec. 24—Jerry Marshall, Sydney ...... W 12

1893
Feb. 28—Jerry Marshall, Sydney ....WF   4
Nov. 13—Young Scotty, Chicago .... W   6
Dec. 18—Tommy White, Chicago .... D   8
Dec. 28—Al Jansen, Chicago .... W   6

1894
Jan.   3—Solly Smith, Chicago .... D   6
Jan. 23—Johnny Van Heest, Chicago ....D   8

1953
Mar. 10—Johnny Saxton, Miami Beach .. D 10
Mar. 23—Orlando Zulueta, Brooklyn .....L 10
May 5—Orlando Zulueta, Cincinnati ... W 10
May 19—Luther Rawlings, Miami Beach . D 10
June 26—Johnny Williams, New York ..KO 1
Aug. 3—Carl Coates, Brooklyn .... KO 6
Aug. 24—Charley Spicer, Brooklyn .....KO 6
Sept. 14—Arthur King, Brooklyn .... KO 5
Nov. 5—Billy Hazel, Newark .... KO 1
Dec. 11—Orlando Zulueta, N. Y. City ... W 10

1954
Feb. 20—Joe Miceli, Cincinnati ..... KO by 5
May 1—Johnny Gonsalves, Cincinnati ...L 10
July 27—Rafael Lastre, Miami Beach ...KO 9
Aug. 31—Rafael Lastre, Miami Beach ...KO 7
Sept. 11—Joe Miceli, Cincinnati ....L 10
Nov. 20—Arthur Persley, Miami ....KO 9

1955
Jan. 8—Johnny Gonsalves, Miami ..... D 10
June 29—Jimmy Carter, Boston .... W 15
(Won World Lightweight Title)
Oct. 19—Jimmy Carter, Cincinnati ...... W 15
(Title Bout)

1956
Feb. 7—Larry Boardman, Boston ....L 10
Mar. 5—Tony DeMarco, Boston ...KO by 9
May 2—Joe Brown, Houston ....L 10
Aug. 24—Joe Brown, New Orleans ....L 15
(Lost World Lightweight Title)

1957
Feb. 13—Joe Brown, Miami Beach ..KO by 11
(For World Lightweight Title)
May 23—Mickey Crawford, Flint ....L 10
July 25—Cisco Andrade, Los Ang. ..KO by 9
Oct. 31—Bobby Scanlon, San Fran. .KO by 10

1958
Feb. 11—Al Nevarez, Juarez ....L 10
Mar. 1—Duilio Loi, Milan ....KO by 9
Apr. 1—Gomeo Brennan,
Miami Beach .... KO by 5
Retired in 1959.

TB	KO	WD	WF	D	LD	LF	KOBY	ND	NC
60	18	13	0	6	16	0	7	0	0

Died, July 11, 1973, Cincinnati, Ohio.

JOE BROWN
(Old Bones)
Born, May 18, 1926, New Orleans, La.
Height, 5 feet, 7½ ins. Managed by Lou Viscusi.
(All Service Lightweight Champion)
1946
Jan. 13—Leoanrd Ceaser, New Orleans ...L 5
Jan. 20—Johnny Monroe, New Orleans .. W 6
Mar. 22—Leonard Ceaser, New Orleans .. D 6
Mar. 29—Leonard Ceaser, New Orleans .. W 8
Apr. 5—Frankie Adams, New Orleans .. W 6
June 28—Herbert Jones, New Orleans .. W 8
July 26—Buster Tyler, New Orleans .....L 10
Oct. 18—Robert Weatherly, New Orl'ns . W 8
1947
Mar. 7—Buster Tyler, New Orleans ... D 10
Mar. 28—Melvin Bartholomew, N. Orl. ...L 10
Apr. 18—James Carter, New Orleans ... W 10
May 2—Sandy Saddler, New Orl. ..KO by 3
July 4—Melvin Bartholomew, New Orl, W 6
July 23—Freddie Latson, Norwalk, Conn. W 6
Aug. 6—Danny Webb, Montreal .... W 10
Sept. 24—Dan Robinson, Jersey City .... W 8
Oct. 6—Ernie Butler, Newark ....KO 5
Oct. 21—Arthur King, Toronto .... W 8
Nov. 10—Arthur King, Toronto ....L 8
Dec. 15—Joey Bagnato, Toronto ....KO 1
1948
Feb. 28—Bobby McQuillar, New Orleans D 10
May 7—Bobby McQuillar, New Orleans .L 10
July 25—Luther Burgess, New Orleans .. D 10
Oct. 1—Freddie Dawson, New Orleans ..L 10
Oct. 26—Frank Crockwell, San
Antonio .... KO 5
Nov. 18—Arthur Persley, New Orleans .. W 10
Dec. 3—Johnny Bratton, New Orl. . KO by 4
1949
Mar. 22—Booker Ellis, St. Paul .... W 6
Mar. 28—Luther Rawlings, Chicago ..... W 10
Apr. 25—Joe Sgro, Chicago .... W 8
May 10—Hugh Sublett, So. Bend ..... W 8
May 23—John LaBroi, Chicago .... D 8
May 27—Leroy Willis, New Orleans ..... W 10

June 6—Willie Russell, Cincinnati ...... W 10
Dec. 5—Ike Jenkins, Philadelphia ...... W 6
1950
Jan. 20—Milton Scott, Chicago ....KO 2
Feb. 6—Danny Womber, Chicago ...... W 8
Feb. 22—Dave Marsh, Chicago .... W 4
June 16—John L. Davis, Hollywood ......L 10
Sept. 22—Jack Hassen, Melbourne ......KO 8
Oct. 30—Charley Williams, Sydney ...KO 1
Nov. 27—Irvin Steen, Sydney ....NC 10
Dec. 11—Bernie Hall, Broken Hill ......KO 11
1951
Feb. 20—Tommy Campbell, Los Angeles .L 10
Mar. 10—Baby Ortiz, Ocean Park ......KO 2
Apr. 13—Ted Davis, New Orleans .... W 10
Apr. 27—Lester Felton, New Orleans .... W 10
May 11—Honey Johnson, New Orleans .. W 10
May 25—Virgil Akins, New Orleans ..... W 10
July 6—Virgil Akins, New Orleans ..... W 10
July 22—K.O. Kelly, New Orleans ....KO 5
Aug. 31—Tommy Campbell,
New Orleans ....KO 1
Sept. 28—Stonewall Jackson,
New Orleans ....KO 5
Dec. 6—Virgil Akins, St. Louis ....L 10
1952
Feb. 4—Walter Haines, Miami .... D 6
Mar. 14—Walter Hines, New Orleans..... W 10
Mar. 28—Calvin Smith, New Orleans ...KO 7
June 10—Jerry Turner, Tampa ....KO 5
July 11—Melvin Bartholomew, New Orl. W 10
July 18—Marshall Clayton, New Orl. ...KO 9
Aug. 22—Jimmy (Bud) Taylor, New Orl.. W 10
Oct. 10—Georgie Araujo, New York KO by 7
Oct. 17—Dave Cheatum, New Orleans .Exh. 4
Dec. 10—Don Bowman, Cleveland ....KO 1
1953
Jan. 7—Joey Greenwood, Cleveland ... W 8
Apr. 22—Orlando Zulueta, Baltimore ... D 10
June 9—Luther Rawlings, Miami Bch. .. D 10
Dec. 29—Cliff Dyes, Miami Beach ......KO 9
1954
Feb. 8—Charlie Smith, Providence ....NC 6
Mar. 24—Isaac Logart, Miami Beach ... W 10
June 20—Federico Plummer, Colon ....KO 8
July 25—Wilfredo Brown, Colon ......KO 4
Aug. 31—Nate Jackson, New Orleans ...KO 4
Sept. 28—Carl Coates, New Orleans ....L 10
Dec. 29—Tony Armenteros, Miami ....L 6
1955
Jan. 18—Tony Armenteros, New Orl. ..KO 7
Jan. 31—Tito Despaigne, Colon ......KO 4
Mar. 6—Bobby Rosado, Colon .... W 10
Mar. 20—Tony Armenteros, Colon ...... W 10
June 16—Junius West, Colon ....KO 3
Aug. 1—Arthur Persley, New Orleans ...L 12
Oct. 31—Jimmy Hackney, New Orleans . W 10
Nov. 8—Ray Riojas, Houston ....KO 7
Dec. 13—Ray Portilla, Houston ....KO 5
1956
Feb. 6—Arthur Persley, New Orleans ..KO 9
May 2—Wallace (Bud) Smith, Houston . W 10
June 5—Eddie Brant, Beaumont ......KO 3
Aug. 24—Wallace (Bud) Smith, N. Orl.... W 15
(Won World Lightweight Title)
1957
Feb. 13—Wallace (Bud) Smith,
Miami Beach ....KO 11
(World Lightweight Title)
Mar. 12—Armand Savoie, Houston ...... W 10
June 19—Orlando Zulueta, Denver .....KO 15
(World Lightweight Title)
July 30—Gilberto Holguin, San Antonio . W 10
Aug. 21—Joe Lopes, Chicago .... D 10
Nov. 12—Kid Centella, Houston .... W 10
Dec. 4—Joe Lopes, Chicago ....KO 11
(World Lightweight Title)
1958
Jan. 24—Ernie Williams, Washington ...KO 5
Feb. 26—Orlando Echevarria, Havana ..KO 1
Apr. 7—Joe Cook, New Orleans ......Exh. 3
May 7—Ralph Dupas, Houston ......KO 8
(World Lightweight Title)
July 23—Kenny Lane, Houston .... W 15
(World Lightweight Title)
Nov. 5—Johnny Busso, Miami Beach ....L 10
1959
Feb. 11—Johnny Busso, Houston .... W 15
(Title Bout)
June 3—Paolo Rosi, Washington ......KO 8
(Title Bout)
Aug. 27—Santiago Ramirez,
Baton Rouge ....KO 8

673

Sept. 9—Gale Kerwin, Columbus ..... KO 4
Sept. 26—Joey Parks, Albuquerque ..... D 10
Dec. 2—Dave Charnley, Houston .....KO 5
(Title Bout)
Dec. 14—Joey Parks, New Orleans ...... W 10

1960
Mar. 21—Ray Portilla, San Antonio . KO by 6
(non-title)
Aug. 25—Harlow Irwin, Minneapolis ...KO 5
(non-title)
Oct. 4—Battling Torres, Houston .....KO 4
Oct. 28—Cisco Andrade, Los Angeles ... W 15
(World Lightweight Title)
Dec. 7—Giordano Campari, Rome ......L 10
(non-title)

1961
Mar. 7—Joey Parks, Houston .... W 10
(non-title)
Apr. 18—Dave Charnley, London ......'. W 15
(World Lightweight Title)
Oct. 28—Bert Somodio, Quezon City ... W 15
(World Lightweight Title)

1962
Apr. 21—Carlos Ortiz, Las Vegas ....L 15
(Lost World Lightweight Title)
Aug. 24—Louis Molina, San Jose ....L 10

1963
Jan. 22—Tony Noriega, Houston .....KO 6
Feb. 25—Dave Charnley,
Manchester .... KO by 6
Apr. 20—Manuel Alvarez, Monterrey ...KO 8
May 21—Joe Lopes, Sacramento ......KO 8
June 22—Alfredo Urbina, Monterrey .....L 10
Aug. 10—Nicolino Loche, Buenos Aires ...L 10
Sept. 14—Pedro Galasso, Rio de Janeiro .KO 5
Nov. 14—Carlos Hernandez,
Maracaibo .... KO by 3

1964
Apr. 2—Manuel Gonzales, Odessa ....L 10
Apr. 28—Paul Armstead, Sacramento ...L 10
May 5—Tony Perez, San Jose .... W 10
May 25—Paul Armstead, San Francisco ..L 10
June 21—Esteban Santamaria, Colon .... W 10
Aug. 25—Richie Mederano, Austin ...L Dis. 10
Sept. 14—Chino Diaz, Omaha ....KO 8
Oct. 3—Percy Hayles, Kingston.........L 10
Nov. 21—Levi Madi, Johannesburg ...... W 10
Dec. 19—Joas Maote, Johannesburg ....KO 6

1965
Feb. 9—Levy Madi,
Cape Town, S. Africa .... W 10
Feb. 27—Joe Ngidi, Asheshov,
Johannesburg, S. Africa ....L 10
Mar. 9—Vic Andretti, London, Eng. KO by 5
May 18—Joey Olguin, Sacramento ......L 10
June 29—Blackie Zamora, Corpus Chirsti W 10
Aug. 27—Antonio Mochila,
Herrera, Cali, Colombia ....L 10
Oct. 2—Mario Rossito, Barranquilla ....L 10
Nov. 13—Frankie Narvaez, San Juan .....L 10

1966
Mar. 11—Bruno Arcari, Turin ....L 10
Apr. 6—Enoch Nhlapo, Johannesburg .. W 10
Apr. 15—Jarmo Bergloef, Helsinki ...... D 10
May 14—Josiak Nakedi, Bloemfontein .KO 9
June 25—Joe N'Gidi, Durban ....KO 10
July 30—Joe N'Gidi, Johannesburg .....L 10
Aug. 30—Rodwell Lekay, Marques ...... W 10

1967
June 16—Blackie Zamora, Baton Rouge KO 8
June 26—Joe Barrientes, New Orleans ... W 10
Aug. 1—Percy Pugh, New Orleans ....L 10
Sept. 11—Benito Juarez, New Orleans .... W 10
Dec. 13—Nathaniel Jackson, Pensacola .KO 5

1968
Apr. 23—Vic Graffio, Beaumont ....KO 8
June 9—Erubey Carmona,
Mexico City .... KO by 4
Sept. 11—Ricardo Medrano, Beaumont ...L 10
Nov. 6—Jose Garcia, Beaumont ....KO by 9

1969
Aug. 12—Steve Freeman, Houston ...... D 10

1970
Apr. 24—Ramon Flores, Tucson .... W 10

TB	KO	WD	WF	D	LD	LF	KOBY	ND	NC
160	48	56	0	12	32	1	9	0	2

674

CARLOS ORTIZ
Born, September 9, 1936, Ponce, Puerto Rico.
Weight, 135 lbs. Height, 5 ft. 7½ in.

1955
Feb. 14—Harry Bell, New York .... KO 1
Feb. 28—Morris Hodnett, New York .... KO 1
May 13—Danny Roberts, New York .... KO 3
May 30—Juan Pacheco, New York .... KO 2
June 24—Jimmy DeMura, Syracuse .... W 6
Aug. 10—Tony DeCola, New York .... W 6
Aug. 22—Armand Bush, New York .... W 6
Sept. 19—Hector Rodriguez, New York ..... KO 2
Oct. 3—Leroy Graham, New York .... KO 2
Oct. 29—Al Duarte, Boston .... KO 4
Nov. 12—Lem Miller, Boston .... W 8
Dec. 10—Charley Titone, Paterson .... KO 2

1956
Jan. 9—Ray Portilla, New York .... W 8
Feb. 17—Ray Portilla, New York .... W 8
May 25—Johnny Gorman, New York ...... W 6
July 30—Tommy Salem, New York .... W 10
Oct. 27—Mickey Northrup, Hollywood ...... W 10
Dec. 15—Phil Kim, Hollywood .... KO 9
Dec. 31—Gale Kerwin, New York .... W 10

1957
Jan. 23—Bobby Rogers, Chicago .... W 10
Mar. 2—Lou Filippo, Hollywood .... NC 9
Apr. 9—Lou Filippo, Hollywood .... KO 7
May 7—Ike Vaughn, Miami Beach .... W 10
May 29—Felix Chiocca, Chicago .... W 10
Sept. 23—Harry Bell, New York .... W 10

1958
Feb. 28—Tommy Tibbs, New York .... W 10
May 9—Joe Lopes, Hollywood .... W 10
June 27—Johnny Busso, New York .... W 10
Sept. 19—Johnny Busso, New York .... L 10
Oct. 28—Dave Charnley, London .... W 10
Dec. 31—Kenny Lane, Miami Beach .... L 10

1959
Apr. 13—Len Matthews, Philadelphia ...... KO 6
June 12—Kenny Lane, New York .... KO 2
(Won Vacant World Junior Welterweight Title)

1960
Feb. 4—Battling Torres, Los Angeles ..... KO 10
(Retained World Junior Welterweight Title)
June 15—Duilio Loi, San Francisco .... W 15
(Retained World Junior Welterweight Title)
Sept. 1—Duilio Loi, Milan .... L 15
(Lost World Junior Welterweight Title)

1961
Feb. 2—Cisco Andrade, Los Angeles .... W 10
May 10—Duilio Loi, Milan .... L 15
(For World Junior Welterweight Title)
Sept. 2—Doug Vaillant, Miami Beach ...... W 10
Nov. 18—Paolo Rosi, New York .... W 10

1962
Apr. 21—Joe Brown, Las Vegas .... W 15
(Won World Lightweight Title)
Aug. 1—Arthur Persley, Manila .... W 10
Nov. 7—Kazuo Takayama, Tokyo .... W 10
Dec. 3—Teruo Kosaka, Tokyo .... KO 5
(Retained World Lightweight Title)

1963
Apr. 7—Doug Vaillant, San Juan .... KO 13
(Retained World Lightweight Title)
Sept. 18—Pete Acera, Honolulu .... KO 7
Oct. 22—Maurice Cullen, London .... W 10

1964
Feb. 15—Flash Elorde, Manila .... KO 14
(Retained World Lightweight Title)
Apr. 11—Kenny Lane, San Juan .... W 15
(Retained World Lightweight Title)
Dec. 14—Dick Divola, Boston .... KO 1

1965
Apr. 10—Ismael Laguna, Panama City ...... L 15
(Lost World Lightweight Title)
Nov. 13—Ismael Laguna, San Juan .... W 15
(Regained World Lightweight Title)

1966
Apr. 7—Nicolino Loche, Buenos Aires ...... D 10

June 20—Johnny Bizzarro, Pittsburgh ...... KO 12
    (Retained World Lightweight Title)
Oct. 22—Sugar Ramos, Mexico City .... KO 5
    (Retained World Lightweight Title)
Nov. 28—Flash Elorde, New York .... KO 14
    (Retained World Lightweight Title)

1967

July 1—Sugar Ramos, San Juan .... KO 4
    (Retained World Lightweight Title)
Aug. 16—Ismael Laguna, New York .... W 15
    (Retained World Lightweight Title)

1968

June 29—Carlos Teo Cruz, Santo Domingo ... L 15
    (Lost World Lightweight Title)

1969

Nov. 21—Edmundo Leite, New York .... W 10

1970

(Inactive)

1971

Dec. 1—Jimmy Ligon, Las Vegas .... KO 3

1972

Jan. 8—Bill Whittenburg, Miami .... KO 7
Jan. 20—Terry Rondeau, Portland, Me. .... KO 4
Jan. 31—Ivelaw Eastman, Waltham .... KO 2
Feb. 19—Leo DiFiore, San Juan .... KO 2
Mar. 20—Junior Varney, Ponce .... KO 2
May 1—Greg Potter, Los Angeles .... W 10
June 3—Gerardo Ferrat, Chicago .... KO 3
Aug. 1—Johnny Copeland, Oklahoma City KO 3
Sept. 20—Ken Buchanan, New York .... KO by 6

TB	KO	WD	WF	D	LD	LF	KO BY	ND	NC
70	30	31	0	1	6	0	1	0	1

KENNY LANE

Born, April 9, 1932, Big Rapids, Michigan. Weight, 135-140 lbs. Height, 5 ft. 7 in. Southpaw. Managed by Jack Kearns and Pete Petroskey.

1953

Apr. 9—Clinton McDade, Grand Rapids .... W 4
Apr. 16—Jimmy DeMura, Detroit .... W 4
Apr. 30—Jimmy DeMura, Detroit .... W 4
May 11—John Walls, Chicago .... W 4
May 23—Milton Scott, Chicago .... W 4
June 15—Benny Uhl, Chicago .... W 5
June 18—Johnny Valentine, Detroit .... W 4
July 16—Frank O'Neal, Detroit .... KO 3
July 23—Ron McGilvery, Detroit .... W 4
Aug. 6—Dick Holling, Detroit .... KO 2
Aug. 20—Don Grinton, Detroit .... KO 4
Sept. 10—Eddie Crawford, Detroit .... W 6
Sept. 14—Ralph Cervantes, Saginaw .... W 6
Sept. 29—Ken Hohner, Grand Rapids .... W 8
Oct. 20—Ron Stribling, Lansing .... KO by 2
Dec. 1—Ron Stribling, Grand Rapids ...... W 8

1954

Jan. 2—Mike Turcotte, New Orleans ...... W 6
Jan. 14—Jesse Underwood, Saginaw .... W 10
Feb. 1—John Barnes, Detroit .... KO by 1
Mar. 22—John Barnes, Detroit .... L 8
May 27—Sammy Rodgers, Muskegon .... W 10
June 22—Elmer Lakatos, Detroit .... W 10
Aug. 22—John Barnes, Muskegon .... W 10
Oct. 4—Georgie Collins, New York .... W 10
Nov. 8—Orlando Zulueta, New York ...... W 10
Dec. 13—Danny Jo Perez, New York .... W 10

1955

Feb. 14—Jackie Blair, New York .... W 10
Mar. 14—Ralph Dupas, New Orleans ...... L 10
Mar. 29—Armand Savole, Grand Rapids ..... W 10
May 31—Richie Howard, Halifax .... W 10
June 7—Eli Leggett, Detroit .... W 10
June 21—Larry Boardman, Miami Beach .... W 10
June 28—Richie Howard, Halifax .... W 10
July 12—Jimmy Ford, Miami Beach .... W 10
July 28—Elmer Lakatos, Milwaukee .... KO 8
Aug. 8—Noel Humphreys, Mt. Pleasant ... W 10
Aug. 16—Hoacine Khalfi, Miami Beach ..... W 10
Oct. 3—Paddy DeMarco, New York ...... L 10
Nov. 7—Kid Centella, New Orleans .... W 10

Dec. 6—Don Mason, Milwaukee .... W 10

1956

Feb. 25—Isaac Vaughn, Lansing .... W 10
Mar. 25—Enrique Esqueda, Mexico .... W 10
May 10—Danny Davis, St. Paul .... W 10
July 9—Ralph Dupas, New Orleans .... W 10
Aug. 2—Glen Flanagan, Minneapolis ...... W 10
Aug. 30—Ralph Capone, Muskegon .... KO 5
Sept. 19—Ludwig Lightburn, Miami .... W 10
Nov. 14—Frankie Ryff, Miami .... W 10

1957

Jan. 30—Frankie Ryff, Norfolk .... KO 6
Apr. 6—Danny Davis, Muskegon .... KO 4
May 22—Henry Brown, Detroit .... KO 6
Aug. 3—Teddy Davis, Muskegon .... W 10
Aug. 20—Johnny Gonsalves, Oakland .... W 10
Oct. 30—Orlando Zulueta, Chicago .... W 10
Dec. 9—Luke Easter, San Francisco ...... KO 8

1958

Jan. 9—Johnny Gonsalves, Oakland .... W 10
May 26—Dave Dupas, Dallas .... KO 6
July 23—Joe Brown, Houston .... L 15
    (For World Lightweight Title)
Sept. 6—Orlando Zulueta, Muskegon .... W 10
Nov. 7—Lahouari Godih, Syracuse .... W 10
Dec. 31—Carlos Ortiz, Miami Beach .... W 10

1959

Apr. 17—Johnny Busso, Hollywood .... KO 6
June 12—Carlos Ortiz, New York .... KO by 2
    (For Vacant World Junior Welterweight Title)
Oct. 28—Virgil Akins, Washington .... W 10
Dec. 29—Ray Lancaster, St. Paul .... KO 3

1960

Jan. 13—Ralph Dupas, Mobile .... L 10
Apr. 25—Jerry Black, Philadelphia .... W 10
Aug. 16—Doug Vaillant, Miami Beach ...... W 10
Sept. 27—Sid Adams, Philadelphia .... KO 1
Oct. 8—Len Matthews, Los Angeles ... KO by 3
Dec. 6—Lahouari Godih, Philadelphia ..... W 10

1961

Jan. 23—Jose Stable, New York .... L 10
Feb. 20—Carlos Hernandez, Caracas .... D 10
May 1—Rip Randell, Dallas .... W 10
May 16—Manuel Gonzales, Odessa .... W 10
June 8—Curtis Cokes, Dallas .... D 10
June 16—Ray Portilla, San Antonio .... KO 6
June 30—Wilbert Robertson, Muskegon ..... W 6
Aug. 14—T. J. Jones, Chicago .... W 10
Sept. 22—Virgil Akins, Annapolis .... W 10
Oct. 16—Aissa Hashas, Paris .... W 10

1962

Jan. 23—Rip Randall, Houston .... L 10
Apr. 14—Louis Molina, San Jose .... W 10
June 11—Tommy Tibbs, Boston .... W 10
July 14—Carlos Hernandez, New York ..... W 10
Sept. 15—Len Matthews, Philadelphia ...... KO 9

1963

Mar. 2—Vicente Derado, New York .... W 10
Aug. 19—Paul Armstead, Saginaw .... W 15
    (Won Vacant Michigan World Lightweight Title)

1964

Feb. 19—Johnny Bizzarro, Erie .... W 10
Apr. 11—Carlos Ortiz, San Juan .... L 15
    (For World Lightweight Title)
May 9—Stoffel Steyn, Johannesburg ...... KO 9
June 2—Dave Charnley, London .... L 10
Oct. 1—Carlos Hernandez, Maracaibo KO by 2

1965

Oct. 25—Eddie Perkins, New Orleans ...... L 10

TB	KO	WD	WF	D	LD	LF	KO BY	ND	NC
94	16	61	0	2	10	0	5	0	0

ISMAEL LAGUNA

Born, June 28, 1943, Colon, Panama. Weight, 135 lbs. Height, 5 ft. 9 in. Managed by Hector (Tato) Valdes.

1961

Jan. 8—Al Morgan, Colon .... KO 2
Jan. 22—Eduardo Frutos, Colon .... W 4
Mar. 5—Javier Valle, Panama City .... W 4

Mar. 26—Carlos Real, Panama City .... W 4
Apr. 16—Jose Pacheco, Panama City ...... KO 3
Apr. 30—Ernest Campbell, Panama City .... W 6
May 21—Battling Escudero, Colon .... KO 2
June 4—Killer Solomon, Colon .... KO 7
June 25—Claudio Martinez, Colon .... KO 4
Aug. 27—Enrique Hitchman, Panama City .. W 10
Oct. 15—Euro Partides, Panama City ...... KO 4
Dec. 1—Hector Hicks, Colon .... KO 5

1962
Jan. 14—Eloy Sanchez, Colon .... KO 3
Mar. 2—Castor Castillo, Maracaibo .... W 10
Apr. 15—Nelson Estrada, Panama City .... KO 7
June 3—Jorge Uzcategui, Colon .... KO 2
June 10—Agustin Carmona, Panama City .. KO 6
June 24—Carlos Celis, Panama City ...... KO 3
July 29—Jorge Salazar, Panama City ...... KO 6
Sept. 16—Pedro Ortiz, Panama City .... KO 7
(Won Panamanian Featherweight Title)
Oct. 28—Beresford Francis, Colon .... KO 5
Nov. 18—Enrique Hitchman, Colon .... KO 2
Dec. 16—Tony Herrera, Panama City ...... KO 2

1963
Jan. 20—Bobby Gray, Colon .... KO 9
Feb. 22—Juan Ramirez, Panama City ...... W 10
Mar. 17—Auburn Copeland, Panama City ... W 10
May 21—Fili Nava, Panama City .... KO 3
June 8—Antonio Herrera, Bogota .... L 10
July 21—Don Johnson, Panama City ...... KO 3
Aug. 24—Lalo Guerrero, Panama City ...... W 10
Sept. 15—Antonio Herrera, Panama City ... KO 7
Nov. 18—Rafiu King, Paris, France .... W 10

1964
Jan. 26—Pedro Miranda, Colon .... KO 4
Feb. 21—Orispo Dos Santos, Sao Paulo .... KO 7
Mar. 9—Angel Robinson Garcia, Paris ..... W 10
June 1—Vicente Saldivar, Tijuana .... L 10
July 6—Kid Anahuac, Los Angeles ...... KO 8
Aug. 2—Vicente Derado, Panama City ...... W 10
Oct. 25—Percy Hayles, Panama City ...... KO 7
Dec. 19—Sebastiano Mascimento, Panama City .... W 10

1965
Apr. 10—Carlos Ortiz, Panama City .... W 15
(Won World Lightweight Title)
June 20—Raul Soriano, Panama City ...... KO 8
July 17—Nicolino Loche, Buenos Aires ...... D 10
Nov. 13—Carlos Ortiz, San Juan .... L 15
(Lost World Lightweight Title)

1966
Feb. 19—Carlos Hernandez, Panama City .. KO 8
Mar. 19—Flash Elorde, Manila .... L 10
July 28—Al Grant, Los Angeles .... W 10
Oct. 2—Percy Hayles, Kingston .... KO 6
Dec. 3—Daniel Guanin, Panama City ..... KO 8

1967
Mar. 10—Frankie Narvaez, New York .... W 10
Apr. 2—Vicente Rivas, Panama City ...... KO 5
June 3—Alfredo Urbina, Panama City ...... W 10
Aug. 16—Carlos Ortiz, New York .... L 15
(For World Lightweight Title)
Oct. 28—Paul Armstead, Panama City ...... W 10

1968
Feb. 26—Ray Adigun, Paris, France .... W 10
Apr. 15—Bud Anderson, Philadelphia ...... KO 10
Apr. 29—Frankie Narvaez, San Juan ...... KO 10
July 17—Victor Melendez, New York ...... W 10
Aug. 20—Lloyd Marshall, New York .... W 9
Oct. 7—Gabe LaMarca, Portland, Me. ...... KO 7
Oct. 22—Grady Ponder, Miami Beach .... W 10
Nov. 15—Ramon Blanco, New York .... W 10

1969
Mar. 1—Curley Aguirre, Panama City .... KO 4
Mar. 31—Maurice Tavant, Lyons .... W 10
May 24—Eugenio Espinoza, Quito .... L 10
July 5—Eugenio Espinoza, Panama City ... W 10
July 14—Genaro Soto, New York .... W 10

1970
Mar. 3—Mando Ramos, Los Angeles ...... KO 9
(Regained World Lightweight Title)

June 7—Ishimatsu Suzuki, Panama City .. KO 13
(Retained World Lightweight Title)
Sept. 26—Ken Buchanan, San Juan, P.R. ..... L 15
(Lost World Lightweight Title)

1971
Mar. 6—Lloyd Marshall, Panama City ..... W 10
Apr. 3—Chango Carmona, Panama City ... W 10
June 22—Eddie Linder, Miami Beach .... L 10
Sept. 13—Ken Buchanan, New York .... L 15
(For World Lightweight Title)

1972
Apr. 15—Announced retirement.

TB	KO	WD	WF	D	LD	LF	KO BY	ND	NC
74	36	28	0	1	9	0	0	0	0

CARLOS TEO CRUZ
(Carlos Teofilo Rosario Cruz)

Born, November 4, 1937, Santiago de los Caballeros, Dominican Republic. Weight, 135 lbs. Managed by Pete Martinez.

1959
Oct. 23—Juan Jose Jiminez, Santo Domingo L 8
Dec. 3—Rafael Acevedo, Santo Domingo ... W 10

1960
Mar. 26—Jesus Serrano, Santo Domingo ..... W 6
May 6—Daniel Berrios, San Juan .... L 10
May 29—Eutaqui Gonzalez, San Juan ...... KO 5
June 11—Bob Ashford, San Juan .... KO 3
July 5—Marcos Morales, San Juan .... L 10
Sept. 2—Lionel Rivera, San Juan .... W 10
Sept. 15—Daniel Berrios, San Juan .... L 10
Nov. 25—Gerardo Clemente, San Juan ..... KO 10

1961
Feb. 24—Daniel Berrios, San Juan ..... L disq. 2
May 26—Vernon Lynch, San Juan .... L 10
Aug. 20—Daniel Berrios, San Juan .... L 4
Aug. 26—Gerardo Clemente, San Juan ...... W 8
Oct. 17—Lionel Rivera, San Juan .... KO 4

1962
Jan. 15—Jose Aneiro, San Juan .... KO 8
Feb. 17—Rafael Acevedo, Santo Domingo ... W 12
June 1—Alejandro Gonzalez, San Juan ..... W 6
Sept. 14—Sammy Burgess, San Juan .... W 10
Nov. 24—Freddy Jackson, Totowa .... D 6
Dec. 18—Candy Padilla, New York .... W 6

1963
Jan. 12—Calvin Woodland, New York ...... W 6
Feb. 5—Roland Kellem, New York .... W 8
Mar. 2—George Foster, New York .... W 6
July 6—Johnny Bean, San Juan .... W 10
Nov. 1—Vicente Derado, New York .... L 10

1964
Feb. 14—Graham Dickers, Brisbane .... L 12
Mar. 2—Guizani Rezgui, Sydney .... KO 11
Mar. 6—Gilberto Biondi, Melbourne .... W 12
June 1—Carlos Hernandez, Caracas .... KO by 2
June 14—Tony Publico, Manila .... L 10
Sept. 20—Julio Ruiz, Balboa .... L 10
Dec. 12—Marcos Morales, Santo Domingo .. KO 2

1965
Feb. 3—Cresencio Fernandez, St. Croix ... L 3
Apr. 3—Alejandro Parra, Santo Domingo KO 4
June 18—Daniel Berrios, Caguas, P.R. ...... KO 1
July 6—Frankie Taylor, London .... W 10
Aug. 14—Chico Veliz, Mayaguez, P.R. .... W 10
Sept. 4—Vicente Derado, San Juan .... W 10

1966
Feb. 12—Paul Armstead, San Juan .... W 10
Apr. 2—Jaime Valladares, Quito .... D 10
May 7—Bunny Grant, San Juan .... W 10
Aug. 13—Vicente Derado, San Juan .... W 10
Oct. 1—Fernand Simard, San Juan .... KO 5
Dec. 12—Frankie Narvaez, San Juan .... L 10

1967
May 6—Frankie Narvaez, San Juan .... W 10
June 23—Grady Ponder, San Juan .... W 10
Dec. 11—Kennedy Clark, San Juan .... W 10

1968
Mar. 3—Johnny Bean, Santo Domingo .... KO 2

Apr.	15—Julio Viera, San Juan	W	10
June	29—Carlos Ortiz, Santo Domingo	W	15
	(Won World Lightweight Title)		
Sept.	28—Mando Ramos, Los Angeles	W	15
	(Retained World Lightweight Title)		
	1969		
Feb.	18—Mando Ramos, Los Angeles	KO by	11
	(Lost World Lightweight Title)		
Aug.	9—Grady Ponder, San Juan	W	10
Sept.	20—Len Kesey, San Juan	KO	4
Oct.	20—Victor Melendez, New York	W	10
	1970		
Jan.	17—Benito Juarez, San Juan	W	10

TB	KO	WD	WF	D	LD	LF	KO BY	ND	NC
57	13	28	2	11	1	2	0	0	

Died, February 15, 1970, with his wife and two children in an airplane crash off the coast of the Dominican Republic.

ARMANDO (MANDO) RAMOS

Born, November 15, 1948, Long Beach, California. Weight, 135 lbs. Managed by Jackie McCoy and Lee Prlia.

	1965		
Nov.	17—Berlin Roberts, Los Angeles	W	4
Dec.	2—Chuey Loera, Los Angeles	KO	2
	1966		
Jan.	27—Berlin Roberts, Los Angeles	KO	1
Mar.	3—Fidel Cruz, Los Angeles	KO	3
Mar.	17—Jose Barrera, Los Angeles	KO	2
May	12—Bosco Basillo, Los Angeles	W	6
June	23—Jerry Stevens, Los Angeles	KO	1
July	7—Joey Aguilar, Los Angeles	KO	8
July	22—Ray Coleman, Los Angeles	KO	6
Aug.	11—Manny Linson, Los Angeles	KO	2
Sept.	8—Baby Salazar, Los Angeles	W	10
Oct.	13—Allen Syres, Los Angeles	KO	5
Nov.	17—Al Franklin, Los Angeles	W	10
Nov.	28—Al Franklin, Oakland	KO	4
	1967		
Jan.	17—Ray Echevarria, Los Angeles	W	10
Mar.	30—Pete Gonzalez, Los Angeles	W	10
June	22—Len Kesey, Los Angeles	KO	5
July	6—Suh-Il Kang, Los Angeles	L	10
Aug.	15—Alex Luna, Sacramento	KO	2
Sept.	14—Eliseo Estrada, Los Angeles	KO	5
Oct.	5—Frankie Crawford, Los Angeles	L	10
	1968		
Feb.	1—Frankie Crawford, Los Angeles	W	10
May	2—Phil Garcia, Los Angeles	KO	9
June	20—Hiroshi Kobayashi, Los Angeles	W	10
Sept.	28—Carlos Teo Cruz, Los Angeles	L	15
	(For World Lightweight Title)		
Oct.	29—Billy Coleman, San Antonio	KO	3
Dec.	12—Beau Jaynes, Los Angeles	KO	2
	1969		
Feb.	18—Carlos Teo Cruz, Los Angeles	KO	11
	(Won World Lightweight Title)		
May	21—Jerry Graci, Honolulu	KO	7
Oct.	4—Yoshiaki Numata, Los Angeles	KO	6
	(Retained World Lightweight Title)		
	1970		
Jan.	13—Leonardo Aquero, San Antonio	W	10
Mar.	3—Ismael Laguna, Los Angeles	KO by	9
	(Lost World Lightweight Title)		
Aug.	7—Sugar Ramos, Los Angeles	W	10
Dec.	10—Raul Rojas, Los Angeles	KO	6
	1971		
Sept.	30—Ruben Navarro, Los Angeles	W	10
Nov.	5—Pedro Carrasco, Madrid	L disq.	11
	(For Vacant WBC Lightweight Title)		
	1972		
Feb.	19—Pedro Carrasco, Los Angeles	W	15
	(Won WBC Lightweight Title)		
June	28—Pedro Carrasco, Madrid	W	15
	(Retained WBC Lightweight Title)		
Sept.	15—Chango Carmona, Los Angeles	KO by	8
	(Lost WBC Lightweight Title)		

	1973		
Aug.	9—Arturo Pineda, Los Angeles	KO by	5
	1974		
May	3—Jaroslav Travnik, Vienna	D	8
May	10—Whan-Ki Min, Lubeck	KO	2
May	16—Arpad Majai, Hamburg	KO	4
June	3—Wolfgang Gans, Lubeck	KO by	2
July	12—Wolfgang Gans, Palma	KO by	6
	1975		
July	30—Tony Martinez, Las Vegas	L	10
Sept.	2—Al Franklin, Oklahoma City	W	10
Oct.	15—Antonio Leyva, Las Vegas	KO	7
Oct.	29—Wayne Beale, Las Vegas	KO by	2

TB	KO	WD	WF	D	LD	LF	KO BY	ND	NC
49	23	14	0	1	4	1	6	0	0

KEN BUCHANAN

Born, June 28, 1945, Edinburgh, Scotland. Weight, 135 lbs. Height, 5 ft. 7½ in.

	1965		
Sept.	20—Brian Tonks, London	KO	2
Oct.	18—Vic Woodhall, Manchester	KO	2
Nov.	1—Billy Williams, London	KO	2
Nov.	22—Joe Okezie, London	KO	3
Dec.	13—Junior Cassidy, London	W	8
	1966		
Jan.	24—Tommy Tiger, London	W	8
Mar.	7—Manley Brown, London	KO	4
Apr.	4—Tommy Tiger, London	W	8
Apr.	19—Chris Elliott, London	W	8
May	11—Junior Cassidy, Manchester	W	8
July	12—Brian Smyth, Aberavon	KO	1
Aug.	6—Ivan Whiter, London	W	8
Sept.	6—Mick Laud, London	W	8
Oct.	17—Antonio Paiva, London	W	10
Nov.	29—Al Keen, Leeds	W	8
Dec.	19—Phil Lundgren, London	W	10
	1967		
Jan.	23—John McMillan, Glasgow	W	10
	(Won Vacant Scottish Lightweight Title)		
Feb.	14—Tommy Garrison, London	W	10
May	11—Franco Brondi, Paisley	KO	3
June	28—Winston Laud, London	W	8
July	26—Rene Roque, Aberavon	W	10
Sept.	14—Al Rocca, London	KO	7
Oct.	30—Spike McCormack, London	W	12
	1968		
Feb.	19—Maurice Cullen, London	KO	11
	(Won British Lightweight Title)		
Apr.	22—Leonard Tavarez, London	W	8
June	10—Ivan Whiter, London	W	8
Oct.	23—Angel Robinson Garcia, London	W	10
Dec.	11—Ameur Lamine, Hamilton	KO	3
	1969		
Jan.	2—Frankie Narvaez, London	W	10
Feb.	17—Mike Cruz, London	KO	4
Mar.	1—Jose Luis Torcida, Solihull	W	8
July	14—Jerry Graci, Nottingham	KO	1
Nov.	11—Vincenzo Pitardi, London	KO	2
	1970		
Jan.	29—Miguel Velasquez, Madrid	L	15
	(For Vacant European Lightweight Title)		
Feb.	23—Leonard Tavarez, London	W	10
Apr.	6—Chris Fernandez, Nottingham	W	10
May	12—Brian Hudson, London	KO	5
	(Retained British Lightweight Title)		
Sept.	26—Ismael Laguna, San Juan	W	15
	(Won World Lightweight Title)		
Dec.	7—Donato Paduano, New York	W	10
	1971		
Feb.	12—Ruben Navarro, Los Angeles	W	15
	(Retained World Lightweight Title)		
May	11—Carlos Hernandez, London	KO	8
Sept.	13—Ismael Laguna, New York	W	15
	(Retained World Lightweight Title)		
	1972		
Mar.	28—Al Ford, London	W	10
Apr.	29—Andries Steyn, Johannesburg	KO	3

June	26—Roberto Duran, New York ..... KO by	13	

(Lost World Lightweight Title)

Sept.	20—Carlos Ortiz, New York .... KO	6
Dec.	4—Chang-Kil Lee, New York .... KO	2

1973

Jan.	29—Jim Watt, Glasgow .... W	15

(Regained British Lightweight Title)

Mar.	28—Hector Matta, London .... W	10
May	31—Frankie Otero, Miami Beach ...... W	10
Sept.	1—Chu Chu Malave, New York ..... KO	7
Oct.	11—Frankie Otero, Toronto .... KO	6
Dec.	6—Miguel Araujo, Copenhagen ...... KO	1

1974

Feb.	7—Jose Peterson, Copenhagen .... W	10
Apr.	4—Joe Tetteh, Copenhagen .... KO	3
May	1—Antonio Puddu, Cagliari .... KO	6

(Won European Lightweight Title)

Sept.	—Relinquished British lighweight title.	
Nov.	21—Winston Noel, Copenhagen .... KO	2
Dec.	16—Leonard Tavarez, Paris .... KO	14

(Retained European Lightweight Title)

1975

Feb.	27—Ishimatsu Suzuki, Tokyo L	15

(For WBC Lightweight Title)

July	25—Giancarlo Usai, Cagliari .... KO	12

(Retained European Lightweight Title)

1976-1978

(Inactive)

1979

June	28—Benny Benitez, Randers .... W	8
Sept.	6—Eloi de Souza, Randers .... W	8
Dec.	6—Charlie Nash, Copenhagen L	12

(For European Lightweight Title)

1980

May	15—Najib Daho, London .... KO	7
Oct.	20—Des Gwilliam, Birmingham .... W	8

TB	KO	WD	WF	D	LD	LF	KO BY	ND	NC
65	27	34	0	0	3	0	1	0	0

EDUARDO (PEDRO) CARRASCO

Born, July 11, 1943, Huelva, Spain. Weight, 135 lbs. Height, 5 ft. 8½ in. Managed by Umberto Branchini.

1962

Oct.	24—Carlo Leggenda, Imola .... KO	2
Nov.	27—Domenico Pillon, Turin .... KO	4

1963

Jan.	9—Franco Rosini, Milan .... W	6
Jan.	30—Tristano Tartarini, Milan .... W	6
Feb.	22—Emilio Riccetti, Milan .... W	6
Mar.	2—Pietro Ziino, Milan .... W	4
Mar.	29—Luciano Lambertini, Milan .... W	4

(Won European Lightweight Prospects Tournament)

May	10—Franco Rosini, Turin .... D	6
May	27—Franco Rosini, Modena .... W	6
Aug.	2—Juan Carbajal, Barcelona .... W	6
Aug.	24—Juan Pinto, Barcelona .... W	6

1964

Feb.	7—Giuseppe Amante, Milan .... W	8
Mar.	1—Aldo Pravisani, Rome L	8
Apr.	22—Giuliano Scatolini, Milan .... KO	4
May	16—Teresito Colombo, Gallarate .... W	6
June	28—Serafino Lucherini, St. Vincent .... W	8
July	6—Fortunato Munzone, St. Angelo Lodigiano .... KO	6
July	18—Giancarlo Stelluti, Falconara .... KO	5
Aug.	14—Tristano Tartarini, Falconara ...... W	8
Sept.	19—Cosimo Lacirignola, Milan .... W	8
Oct.	16—Aldo Pravisani, Turin .... W	8
Nov.	26—Pedro Gomez Acebo, Barcelona .... W	8
Dec.	10—Mohamed Laroussi, Basel ...... KO	3
Dec.	23—Miguel Kimbo, Barcelona .... W	8

1965

Feb.	4—Juan Pinto, Barcelona .... W	8
Feb.	17—Vincenzo Pitardi, Turin .... W	8
June	28—Lat Shonibare, Naples .... KO	4
July	9—Cosimo Lacirignola, Bergamo .... KO	4
Aug.	28—Serfafino Lucherini, Gubbio ...... KO	7
Sept.	18—Mario Oberti, Varese .... KO	7
Oct.	30—Pedro Gomez Acebo, Como .... W	8

Dec.	13—Rene Roque, Milan .... W	8

1966

Jan.	20—Roger Younsy, Barcelona .... KO	1
Feb.	3—Serafino Lucherini, Barcelona ..... W	8
Feb.	17—Georges Payen, Barcelona .... KO	3
Mar.	3—Pierre Tirlo, Barcelona .... KO	8
Mar.	12—Ameur Lamine, Barcelona .... W	8
Mar.	31—Mario Oberti, Barcelona .... W	8
May	13—Emilio Riccetti, Madrid .... W	10
May	26—Quintino Soarez, Barcelona ...... KO	6
June	2—Victor Alves, Madrid .... KO	3
June	10—Dris Ben Amar, Madrid .... KO	3
June	17—Karl Furcht, Barcelona .... KO	3
June	28—Waldir Derceira, Valencia .... KO	5
July	8—Ricardo Navarro, Madrid .... KO	3
July	17—Manuel Prieto, Valencia .... W	10
Aug.	5—Pedro Gomez Acebo, Madrid ...... KO	3
Aug.	13—Joao Martin, Valencia .... KO	5
Sept.	2—Tony Falcon, Madrid .... KO	2
Sept.	9—Boaulem Belouard, Madrid .... KO	3
Sept.	22—Daniel Deneux, Barcelona .... KO	6
Oct.	7—Roy Ate, Madrid .... KO	3

1967

Apr.	8—Yanclo II, Salamanca .... KO	5
Apr.	29—Abdel Bachir, Seville .... KO	3
May	13—Angel Neches, Salamanca .... W	8
June	2—Jesse Green, Madrid .... KO	3
June	30—Borge Krogh, Madrid .... KO	8

(Won European Lightweight Title)

Dec.	1—Aldo Pravisani, Madrid .... W	10
Dec.	16—Omar Oliva, Bilbao .... KO	4
Dec.	22—Franco Brondi, Madrid ., ... KO	4

1968

Feb.	3—Paul Rourre, Las Palmas .... KO	4
Mar.	9—Edoardo Batista, Tenerife .... KO	4
Mar.	19—Giampiero Salami, Valencia ...... KO	4
Apr.	7—Enrique Levy, Huelva .... KO	4
May	10—Kid Tano, Madrid .... KO	8

(Retained European Lightweight Title)

July	20—Jose Luis Penteado, Vigo .... KO	3
July	31—Serafino Lucherini, Valencia ...... W	10
Aug.	10—Valerio Nunez, Valladolid .... KO	3
Sept.	13—Bruno Melissano, Barcelona ..... KO	3

(Retained European Lightweight Title)

Oct.	19—Olli Maeki, Valencia .... W	15

(Retained European Lightweight Title)

Nov.	16—Kid Rainbow, Vigo .... KO	3
Dec.	6—Al Rocca, Barcelona .... KO	3

1969

Jan.	2—Jose Luis Penteado, Copenhagen .... W disq.	4
Mar.	6—Tore Magnussen, Barcelona ...... KO	3

(Retained European Lightweight Title)

Mar.	29—Ould Makloufi, Malaga .... KO	6
Apr.	30—Klaus Jacobi, Barcelona .... KO	2
June	13—Miguel Velasquez, Madrid .... W	15

(Retained European Lightweight Title)

July	24—Paul Rourre, Villafranca .... KO	6
Aug.	6—Massimo Consolati, Bilbao .... KO	5
Sept.	11—Angel Robinson Garcia, Bilbao ... W	10
Sept.	27—Paul Rourre, Valencia .... KO	9
Oct.	—Relinquished European lightweight title.	
Oct.	24—Victor Baerga, Vigo .... KO	4
Nov.	6—Bill Whittenburg, Madrid .... KO	5
Nov.	22—Giampiero Salami, Rome .... KO	6
Dec.	20—Vic Andretti, Madrid .... KO	10
Dec.	30—Dino Del Cid, Barcelona ...... W disq.	2

1970

Jan.	15—Massimo Consolati, Las Palmas .. KO	3
Jan.	29—Giacomo Gulino, Madrid .... KO	6
Feb.	19—Dave Wyatt, Barcelona .... KO	3
Mar.	5—Luis Vallejo, Bilbao .... KO	2
Mar.	18—Lakdar El Harizi, Valencia ...... KO	6
May	23—Jaime Marquez, Madrid .... KO	5
June	13—Carlos Almeida, Almeria .... KO	2
June	26—Jean Pierre Le Jaouen, Madrid ... KO	2
Aug.	22—Olli Maeki, Valencia .... W	10
Sept.	3—Matthew Thomas, Madrid .... KO	2
Nov.	21—Joe Tetteh, Barcelona .... D	10
Dec.	26—Joe Tetteh, Madrid .... W	10

1971

Date	Opponent	Result
Feb. 19	Pietro Vargellini, Madrid	KO 5
Apr. 17	Giacomo Gulino, Milan	KO 9
May 21	Rene Roque, Madrid	W 15
	(Won European Junior Welterweight Title)	
June 18	David Pesenti, Barcelona	W disq. 10
July 8	Klaus Jacobi, Zaragoza	KO 3
July 30	Bruno Meggiolaro, Madrid	W 10
Sept. 10	Jerry Wells, Bilbao	KO 5
Nov. 5	Mando Ramos, Madrid	W disq. 11
	(Won Vacant WBC Lightweight Title)	

1972

Date	Opponent	Result
Feb. 18	Mando Ramos, Los Angeles	L 15
	(Lost WBC Lightweight Title)	
June 28	Mando Ramos, Madrid	L 15
	(For WBC Lightweight Title)	
Sept. 22	Enrico Barlatti, Barcelona	KO 4
Dec. 1	Beau Jaynes, Madrid	KO 6

TB	KO	WD	WF	D	LD	LF	KO BY	ND	NC
110	66	35	4	2	3	0	0	0	0

ROBERTO DURAN
(Record Under Welterweight Champions)

ERUBEY (CHANGO) CARMONA
(Eudibiel Guillen Chapin)
Born, September 29, 1944, Mexico City, Mexico.

1964

Date	Opponent	Result
Jan. 18	Tony Lopez, Monterrey	W 6
Apr. 22	Joel Osorio, Mexico City	KO 2
Aug. 1	Arturo Salas, Mexico City	W 6
Aug. 15	Kid Chocolate, Acapulco	KO 6
Sept. 19	Jesus Gonzalez, Mexico City	KO 2
Oct. 7	Jorge Jimenez, Mexico City	L 8
Oct. 24	Gustavo Garcia, Oaxaca	KO 8
Nov. 11	Joaquin Velazquez, Mexico City	KO 6

1965

Date	Opponent	Result
Feb. 3	Gustavo Garcia, Mexico City	KO 5
Apr. 17	Lupe Ramirez, Mexico City	W 8
May 4	Rogelio Reyes, Juarez	D 10
July 24	Jorge Jimenez, Mexico City	KO 8
Aug. 28	Manuel Andrade, Mexico City	KO 5
Oct. 23	Arturo Morales, Mexico City	L 10

1966

Date	Opponent	Result
Jan. 26	Arturo Morales, Mexico City	L 10
Mar. 19	Marcos Gomez, Guadalajara	KO 5
June 15	Nicolas Sanchez, Mexico City	KO 6
July 6	Battling Kid, Leon	KO 5
Aug. 10	Lupe Ramirez, Mexico City	W 10
Oct. 17	Juan Ortiz, Mexico City	KO 5
Nov. 5	Charro Gomez, Mexico City	KO 3

1967

Date	Opponent	Result
Feb. 11	Lalo Moreno, Mexico City	KO 4
Mar. 11	Bernabe Vazquez, Mexico City	W 10
May 6	Alfredo Urbina, Mexico City	L 10
July 1	Chucho Garcia, Mexico City	W 10
Sept. 4	Arturo Lomeli, Tijuana	W 12
	(Won Mexican Lightweight Title)	
Oct. 21	Alfredo Urbina, Mexico City	L 12
	(Lost Mexican Lightweight Title)	

1968

Date	Opponent	Result
Feb. 24	Javier Ayala, Mexico City	KO 3
June 9	Joe Brown, Mexico City	KO 4
Aug. 10	Renaldo Victoria, Mexico City	KO 3
Sept. 21	Norio Endo, Mexico City	KO 2
Nov. 13	Percy Hayles, San Antonio	KO 4
Dec. 21	Hugo Rambaldi, Mexico City	KO by 1

1969

Date	Opponent	Result
Mar. 2	Frankie Narvaez, San Antonio	L 10
Mar. 7	Juan Escobar, Acapulco	KO 5
May 19	Ramon Blanco, San Diego	KO 8
June 20	Genato Soto, San Antonio	D 10
July 26	Alfonso Frazer, Mexico City	KO 3
Sept. 9	Doug Agin, San Antonio	KO 2
Sept. 30	Sugar Ramos, Tijuana	KO by 7

1070

Date	Opponent	Result
Mar. 22	Jose Luis Herrera, Monterrey	KO 5

Date	Opponent	Result
Apr. 11	Orlando Ribeiro, Mexico City	KO 4
July 13	Ray Adigun, Tijuana	KO 4
Aug. 22	Fermin Soto, Mexico City	KO 9
Oct. 10	Jaguar Kakizawa, Mexico City	KO 10
Nov. 17	Arturo Lomeli, Tijuana	KO 8

1971

Date	Opponent	Result
Jan. 10	Gerardo Ferrat, Mexico City	KO 3
Feb. 13	Fermin Soto, Mexico City	W 12
Apr. 3	Ismael Laguna, Panama City	L 10
June 19	Antonio Amaya, Monterrey	KO 7
Aug. 6	Ismael Rivera, Acapulco	KO 4
Aug. 31	Raimundo Diaz, Juarez	KO by 5

1972

Date	Opponent	Result
Feb. 12	Lalo Moreno, Mexico City	KO 7
Apr. 4	Raimundo Diaz, Tijuana	KO 8
May 18	Masataka Takayama, Los Angeles	KO 3
July 6	Jimmy Robertson, Los Angeles	KO 8
Sept. 15	Mando Ramos, Los Angeles	KO 8
	(Won WBC Lightweight Title)	
Nov. 10	Rodolfo Gonzalez, Los Angeles	KO by 13
	(Lost WBC Lightweight Title)	

1973

Date	Opponent	Result
Mar. 17	Jimmy Heair, Los Angeles	L 10
July 31	Shinichi Kadota, Honolulu	KO by 7

1974-1978
(Inactive)

1979

Date	Opponent	Result
Dec. 20	Francisco Candela, Acapulco	KO 2

TB	KO	WD	WF	D	LD	LF	KO BY	ND	NC
61	38	8	0	2	8	0	5	0	0

RODRIGO GONZALEZ
Born, 1945, Mexico. Weight, 117-135 lbs.

1960

Date	Opponent	Result
Dec. 16	Javier Garcia, Jiquilpan	KO 2

1961

Date	Opponent	Result
Jan. 15	Juan Arias, Leon, Guanajuato	KO 1
	Jose Munoz, Atemaja	KO 1
	Javier Garcia, Jiquilpan	KO 1
	Roberto Nuno, Atemaja	KO 2
	Tony G. Perez, Atemaja	KO 2
	Jose Luis Castillo, Guadalajara	KO 3
	Roberto Nuno, Guadalajara	KO 3
	Jose Vargas, Atontonilco	KO 1
	Serafino Sanchez, Jiquilpan	KO 4
	Kid Irapuato, Jiquilpan	KO 8
	Gregorio Lopez, Guadalajara	KO 2
	Vaquero Montoya, Guadalajara	KO 4
	Guadalupe Barrajas, Guadalajara	KO 3
	Salvador Banvelos, Guadalajara	KO 3
	Alfredo Sanchez, Guadalajara	W 10
	Antonio Luna, Guadalajara	KO 7
	Ruben Ramirez, Guadalajara	KO 4
	Diablito Campos, Mazatlan	KO 5
	Paco Gomez, Mazatlan	W 10
	Ramon Cabiedes, Atotonilco	W 10
	Jose Luis Castillo, Guadalajara	W 10
	Evaristo Perez, Guadalajara	KO 8
	Generalito Nunez. Autlan de la Grana	KO 4
	Jose Luis Castillo, Guadalajara	L 8

1962

Date	Opponent	Result
May 12	Babe Lopez, Guadalajara	W 8
June 23	Evaristo Perez, Guadalajara	KO 3
Sept. 1	Babe Lopez, Guadalajara	KO 2

1963

Date	Opponent	Result
Feb. 15	Lecho Guerrero, Los Angeles	L 10

1964
(Inactive)

1965

Date	Opponent	Result
Nov. 16	Bobby Valdez, Los Angeles	L 10
Dec. 20	Bobby Valdez, Los Angeles	D 10

1966

Date	Opponent	Result
May 20	Bobby Valdez, San Bernardino	KO by 9
July 7	Ray Coleman, Las Vegas	W 6
Aug. 11	Raul Carreon, Las Vegas	W 8
Sept. 1	Ray Coleman, Las Vegas	KO 4
Oct. 13	Alton Colter, Las Vegas	L 10
Nov. 10	Daniel Valdez, Los Angeles	W 10

1967

Feb.	9—Marcelo Cid, Los Angeles	KO	4
May	10—Ram Sarmiento, Long Beach	KO	1
July	19—Claude Adams, Long Beach	KO	8

1968

Oct.	3—Ray Adigun, Los Angeles	KO	10
Dec.	19—Rene Macias, Los Angeles	KO	9

1969

Apr.	17—Pete Gonzales, Los Angeles	KO	4
May	15—Juan Collado, Los Angeles	KO	9
July	3—Julio Viera, Los Angeles	KO	2
Aug.	28—Steve Freeman, Los Angeles	KO	5
Nov.	11—Javier Jimenez, San Antonio	KO	6

1970

May	7—Fermin Soto, Los Angeles	KO	7
Dec.	17—Antonio Cervantes, Los Angeles KO by		8

1971

Apr.	26—Ernesto Villaflor, Honolulu	KO	2
May	26—Beto Gonzalez, Sacramento	W	10
Oct.	2—Juan Collado, Northridge	W	10
Dec.	11—Nick Aghai, Long Beach	W	10

1972

Feb.	24—Manny Leal, Los Angeles	KO	7
Mar.	16—Chun-Kyo Shin, Los Angeles	KO	7
Apr.	27—Jimmy Robertson, Los Angeles	W	10
July	31—Ruben Navarro, Anaheim	W	10
Nov.	10—Chango Carmona, Los Angeles ...	KO	13
	(Won WBC Lightweight Title)		
Dec.	16—Jose Acosta, Monterrey	KO	1

1973

Mar.	17—Ruben Navarro, Los Angeles	KO	9
	(Retained WBC Lightweight Title)		
Aug.	31—Don Sennett, Los Angeles	KO	3
Oct.	27—Antonio Puddu, Los Angeles	KO	10
	(Retained WBC Lightweight Title)		

1974

Apr.	11—Ishimatsu Suzuki, Toky	KO by	8
	(Lost WBC Lightweight Title)		
Aug.	26—Clemente Mucino, Tijuana ...	W disq.	2
Nov.	28—Ishimatsu Suzuki, Osaka	KO by	13
	(For WBC Lightweight Title)		
Dec.	16—Javier Garcia, Jiquilpan	KO	2

TB	KO	WD	WF	D	LD	LF	KO BY	ND	NC
66	43	13	1	1	4	0	4	0	0

YUJI (ISHIMATSU) SUZUKI

Born, June 5, 1949, Tochigi Prefecture, Japan.
Weight, 135 lbs. Height, 5 ft. 8 in.

1966

Dec.	11—Masao Fujiwara, Tokyo	KO	1

1967

Jan.	9—Yoichi Ichikawa, Tokyo	KO	1
Feb.	12—Akio Fujita, Tokyo	W	4
Mar.	5—Toru Kimura, Tokyo	KO	3
May	17—Hajime Kagawa, Tokyo	L	4
June	12—Hajime Kagawa, Tokyo	D	4
Aug.	9—Keji Murabayashi, Tokyo	KO by	1
Oct.	2—Kazuo Yashiro, Tokyo	L	4
Nov.	8—Tadao Nakemura, Tokyo	KO	1
Dec.	5—Tetsuji Okamoto, Tokyo	W	4

1968

Jan.	17—Haruo Kikumoto, Tokyo	KO	3
Jan.	31—Toshio Araguchi, Tokyo	W	4
Apr.	2—Noboru Nakamoto, Tokyo	KO	2
June	15—Koichi Otomaru, Tokyo	L	4
July	15—Hitoshi Komase, Tokyo	D	4
Oct.	13—Tsunehisa Ninomiya, Tokyo	KO	2
Nov.	17—Makoto Yumi, Tokyo	KO	1

1969

Feb.	13—Tsuyoshi Yamamoto, Tokyo	KO	2
Mar.	3—Haruo Kikumoto, Tokyo	D	8
May	6—Hitoshi Komase, Tokyo	D	8
July	23—Isao Shuya, Tokyo	L	8
Sept.	10—Haruo Kikumoto, Tokyo	W	10
Oct.	9—Kenichiro Date, Tokyo	W	10
Dec.	10—Isao Ichihara, Tokyo	KO	6

1970

Jan.	25—Jaguar Kaizawa, Tokyo	L	10

June	7—Ismael Laguna, Panama City	KO by	13
	(For World Lightweight Title)		
Oct.	10—Lionel Rose, Melbourne	L	10
Oct.	30—Rene Barrientos, Honolulu	L	10

1971

Mar.	3—Masataka Takayama, Tokyo	D	10
	(For Japanese Lightweight Title)		
Apr.	7—Hitoshi Komase, Tokyo	W	10
Aug.	13—Shinichi Kadota, Tokyo	KO by	8
Jan.	16—Shinichi Kadota, Tokyo	W	12
	(Won Oriental Lightweight Title)		
Apr.	6—Hiroyuki Murakami, Tokyo	W	10
May	19—Rudy Gonzales, Tokyo	W	12
	(Retained Oriental Lightweight Title)		
Dec.	18—Kenji Iwata, Tokyo	KO	1

1973

Apr.	23—Fred Pastor, Tokyo	W	12
	(Retained Oriental Lightweight Title)		
July	30—Hiroshi Tonooka, Tokyo	KO	3
Sept.	8—Roberto Duran, Panama City ..	KO by	10

1974

Feb.	28—Jinny Cruz, Tokyo	KO	4
Apr.	11—Rodolfo Gonzalez, Tokyo	KO	8
	(Won WBC Lightweight Title)		
Sept.	12—Tury Pineda, Nagaya	D	15
	(Retained WBC Lightweight Title)		
Nov.	28—Rodolfo Gonzalez, Osaka	KO	13
	(Retained WBC Lightweight Title)		

1975

Feb.	27—Ken Buchanan, Tokyo	W	15
	(Retained WBC Lightweight Title)		
June	5—Tury Pineda, Osaka	W	15
	(Retained WBC Lightweight Title)		
Dec.	4—Alvaro Rojas, Tokyo	KO	14
	(Retained WBC Lightweight Title)		

1976

May	8—Esteban De Jesus, Puerto Rico	L	15
	(Retained WBC Lightweight Title)		

1977

Apr.	2—Saensak Muangsurin, Tokyo ..	KO by	6
	(For WBC Junior Welterweight Title)		

1978

June	20—Yohi Arai, Tokyo	L	10

TB	KO	WD	WF	D	LD	LF	KO BY	ND	NC
48	16	12	0	6	9	0	5	0	0

ESTEBAN DE JESUS

Born, August 2, 1951, Carolina, Puerto Rico.
Weight, 135-140 lbs. Height, 5 ft. 5½ in.

1969

Feb.	10—El Tarita, San Juan	KO	2
July	21—Braulio Rodriguez, San Juan	KO	4
Aug.	2—Francisco Maldonado, San Juan ..	KO	3
Aug.	23—Johnny Sandoval, San Juan	W	6
Sept.	27—Ramon Montes, San Juan	KO	3
Oct.	18—Kid Sheffield, San Juan	KO	2
Nov.	22—Ivelaw Eastman, San Juan	KO	5

1970

Jan.	24—Martin Cuello, San Juan	KO	2
Feb.	14—Chino Guerrero, San Juan	KO	3
Feb.	28—Braulio Rodriguez, San Juan	KO	8
Mar.	28—Bobby Parnell, San Juan	KO	1
Apr.	6—Ike Estrada, San Juan	KO	5
Apr.	30—Chino Jimenez, Ponce	W	10
May	12—Coverly Daniels, San Juan	KO	6
July	9—Tommy Shaffer, San Juan	KO	8
Sept.	30—Johnny Sandoval, San Juan	KO	10
Oct.	19—Jose Llano, San Juan	KO	7

1971

Apr.	12—Johnny Harp, San Juan	W	10
May	5—Gustavo Briceno, San Juan	W	10
July	24—Josue Marquez, San Juan	W	12
Aug.	7—Victor Ortiz, San Juan	KO	4
Sept.	4—Josue Marquez, San Juan	W	12
Oct.	6—Lionel Hernandez, Caracas	W	10
Oct.	20—Frank LeRoy, Caracas	KO	7
Oct.	30—Milton Mendez, Caracas	KO	5
Dec.	10—Antonio Gomez, Caracas	L	10

1972

Feb.	14—Percy Hayles, San Juan	W	10
Apr.	10—George Foster, New York	KO	8
May	1—Josue Marquez, New York	KO	12
July	8—Angel Robinson, San Juan	W	10
July	28—Chuck Wilburn, New York	W	10
Sept.	18—Raymundo Dias, San Juan	W	10
Oct.	30—Doc McClendon, San Juan	W	10
Nov.	17—Roberto Duran, New York	W	10

1973

Feb.	16—Ray Lampkin, San Juan	W	12
	(Won Vacant NABF Lightweight Title)		
Apr.	16—Johnny Gant, San Juan	W	10
May	21—Raul Montoya, San Juan	W	10
July	14—Ray Lampkin, New York	W	12
	(Retained NABF Lightweight Title)		
Sept.	8—Radames Checo, Panama City	KO	1
Oct.	29—Mike Mavon, San Juan	W	10
Nov.	22—Al Foster, San Juan	KO	1

1974

Jan.	7—Alfonso Frazer, San Juan	KO	10
Mar.	16—Roberto Duran, Panama City ..	KO by	11
	(For World Lightweight Title)		
June	10—Gerardo Ferratt, San Juan	KO	5
Sept.	2—Javier Ayala, San Juan	W	10

1975

Mar.	15—Jesse Lara, Caracas	KO	3
May	17—Antonio Cervantes, Panama City ...	L	15
	(For World Junior Welterweight Title)		
Oct.	11—Rudy Barros, Ponce	KO	5

1976

Mar.	6—Valentin Ramos, San Juan	KO	2
May	8—Ishimatsu Suzuki, San Juan	W	15
	(Won WBC Lightweight Title)		
Sept.	10—Hector Medina, San Juan	KO	7
	(Retained WBC Lightweight Title)		

1977

Feb.	12—Buzzsaw Yamabe, San Juan	KO	6
	(Retained WBC Lightweight Title)		
June	24—Vicente Saldivar, San Juan	KO	11
	(Retained WBC Lightweight Title)		
Sept.	10—James Brackett, San Juan	W	10

1978

Jan.	21—Roberto Duran, Las Vegas	KO by	12
	(For World Lightweight Title)		
June	3—Joe Baez, San Juan	KO	3
July	8—Chuchu Hernandez, San Juan	KO	2
Oct.	27—Edwin Viruet, New York	W	10

1979

Oct.	4—Jimmy Blevins, New York	W	10
Nov.	9—Ruby Ortiz, New York	W	10

1980

May	10—Jose Vallejo, San Juan	KO	7
July	7—Saoul Mamby, Bloomington ...	KO by	13
	(For WBC Junior Welterweight Title)		

TB	KO	WD	WF	D	LD	LF	KO BY	ND	NC
62	32	25	0	0	2	0	3	0	0

JIM WATT

Born, July 18, 1948, Glasgow, Scotland. Weight, 135 lbs. Southpaw. Managed by Terry Lawless.

1968

Oct.	30—Santos Martin, Hamilton	KO	4
Dec.	11—Alex Gibson, Hamilton	KO	2

1969

Apr.	10—Victor Paul, Glasgow	W	8
Sept.	15—Winston Thomas, London	KO	6
Nov.	24—Tommy Tiger, London	W	8

1970

Feb.	16—Victor Paul, London	KO by	6
June	1—Victor Paul, London	KO	5
June	15—Bryn Lewis, Nottingham	KO	6
Oct.	20—Sammy Lockhart, Belfast	KO	2
Dec.	1—Ron Clifford, Leeds	KO	4

1971

Jan.	11—David Pesenti, Nottingham	W	8
Mar.	22—Henri Nesi, London	KO	6
Sept.	21—Willie Reilly, London	KO	7
Nov.	1—Leonard Tavarez, London	KO	9

1972

Feb.	1—Willie Reilly, Nottingham	KO	10
	(Won British Lightweight Title)		
May	3—Tony Riley, Solihull	KO	12
	(Retained British Lightweight Title)		
Dec.	11—Novel McIvor, London	KO	3

1973

Jan.	29—Ken Buchanan, Glasgow	L	15
	(Lost British Lightweight Title)		
May	9—Johnny Cheshire, Solihull	W	8
June	7—Noel NcIvor, Glasgow	KO	4
Oct.	5—Angus McMillan, Glasgow	W	8

1974

Feb.	16—Andries Steyn, Johannesburg	KO	7
Mar.	2—Kokkie Olivier, Johannesburg	W	10
June	19—Billy Waith, Caerphilly	W	12
Oct.	26—Anthony Morodi, Johannesburg	L	10

1975

Jan.	27—Johnny Cheshire, Glasgow	KO	7
	(Regained Vacant British Lightweight Title)		
Mar.	19—Billy Waith, London	W	10
May	3—Jonathan Dale, Lagos	L	15
Oct.	31—Andre Holyk, Lyons	L	12

1976

Mar.	2—George Turpin, London	KO	4
Mar.	30—Jimmie Revie, Hammersmith	KO	7
May	10—Hector Diaz, London	KO	4
June	22—Johnny Claydon, London	KO by	3
Oct.	12—Franco Diana, London	KO	6

1977

Feb.	21—Johnny Claydon, London	KO	10
	(Retained British Lightweight Title)		
Aug.	5—Andre Holyk, Glasgow	KO	1
	(Won Vacant European Lightweight Title)		
Nov.	16—Jeronimo Lucas, Solihull	KO	10
	(Retained European Lightweight Title)		

1978

Feb.	17—Perico Ferndandez, Madrid	W	15
	(Retained European Lightweight Title)		
June	12—Billy Vivian, London	W	8
Oct.	18—Antonio Guinaldo, Glasgow	KO	5
	(Retained European Lightweight Title)		

1979

Apr.	17—Alfredo Pitalua, Glasgow	KO	12
	(Won Vacant WBC Lightweight Title)		
Nov.	3—Robert Vasquez, Glasgow	KO	9
	(Retained WBC Lightweight Title)		

1980

Mar.	14—Charlie Nash, Glasgow	KO	4
	(Retained WBC Lightweight Title)		
June	7—Howard Davis, Glasgow	W	15
	(Retained WBC Lightweight Title)		
Nov.	1—Sean O'Grady, Glasgow	KO	12
	(Retained WBC Lightweight Title)		

TB	KO	WD	WF	D	LD	LF	KO BY	ND	NC
45	28	11	0	0	4	0	2	0	0

ERNESTO ESPANA

Born, 1954, Venezuela. Weight, 135 lbs. Height, 5 ft. 11 in. Managed by Pepi Cordero.

1975

Mar.	17—Hernan Rodriguez, Caracas	KO	1
July	14—Jose Figuerero, Caracas	W	1
Aug.	8—Freddy Briceno, Caracas	KO	3
Aug.	25—Luis Beltran Rodriguez, Caracas ...	L	6
Oct.	4—Luis Romero, Caracas	KO	2
Nov.	17—Ruben Arias, Santo Domingo	KO	1

1976

Feb.	18—Cesar Chavez, Maturin	KO	2
Feb.	28—Danton Morillo, Caracas	KO	2
Mar.	6—Luis Beltran Rodriguez, Caracas ...	W	10
June	13—Juan Sarmiento, Caracas	KO	3
July	11—Julio Pena, Caracas	KO	1
Aug.	22—Clemente Mucino, Caracas	KO	1
Aug.	29—Rolando Martinez, Caracas	KO	1
Oct.	16—Andrew Fernandez, Caracas	KO	1
Nov.	14—Ricardo Arrendondo, Caracas	W	10

1977

Jan.	30—Isaac Marin, Caracas	KO	5

May 15—Milton Mendez, Caracas .... KO 1
July 3—Salvador Torres, Caracas .... KO 1
Aug. 27—Angel Rosas, San Juan .... KO 5
1978
Apr. 22—Geraldo Aceves, San Juan .... KO 2
July 8—Teo Ozuna, San Juan .... KO 1
Sept. 9—Bienvenido Quinto, San Juan .... KO 1
Oct. 28—Johnny Barr, San Juan .... KO 1
1979
Feb. 19—Fernando Jiminez, San Juan ..... KO 6
Mar. 25—Ed Bracetty, San Juan .... KO 1
June 16—Claude Noel, San Juan .... KO 13
(Won Vacant WBA Lightweight Title)
Aug. 4—Johnny Lira, Chicago .... KO 10
(Retained WBA Lightweight Title)
1980
Mar. 2—Hilmer Kenty, Detroit .... KO by 9
(Lost WBA Lightweight Title)
Sept. 20—Hilmer Kenty, San Juan ...... KO by 4
(For WBA Lightweight Title)

TB	KO	WD	WF	D	LD	LF	KO BY	ND	NC
29	23	3	0	0	1	0	2	0	0

HILMER KENTY

(James Hilmer Kenty)
Born, July 30, 1955, Austin, Texas. Weight, 135
lbs. Height, 5 ft 11 in. Managed by Emanuel Steward.

1977
Oct. 13—Steve Homan, Columbus .... W 6
Nov. 26—Ray Carrington, Columbus .... W 6
Dec. 16—Earl Stringer, Detroit .... KO 3
1978
Apr. 17—Mike Gray, Columbus .... KO 2
July 27—Ron Pettigrew, Canton .... W 6
Oct. 26—Jessie Rogers, Detroit .... KO 1
Dec. 9—Eddie Murray, Detroit .... KO 3
1979
Jan. 11—Jose Pena, Detroit .... KO 3
Jan. 25—Jose Gonzales, Detroit .... KO 7
Mar. 3—Alberto Herrera, Detroit .... KO 4
May 8—Danny Benitez, Detroit .... KO 4
June 28—Arturo Leon, Detroit .... W 10
Aug. 2—Ralph Racine, Detroit .... W 10
Aug. 23—Bobby Flores, Detroit .... KO 1
Oct. 18—Sebastian Mosquiera, Detroit ..... KO 4
Nov. 30—Scotty Foreman, New Orleans .... KO 3
1980
Mar. 2—Ernesto Espana, Detroit .... KO 9
(Won WBA Lightweight Title)
Aug. 2—Young-Ho Oh, Detroit .... KO 9
(Retained WBA Lightweight Title)
Sept. 20—Ernesto Espana, San Juan .... KO 4
(Retained WBA Lightweight Title)
Nov. 8—Vilomar Fernandez, Detroit .... W 15
(Retained WBA Lightweight Title)

TB	KO	WD	WF	D	LD	LF	KO BY	ND	NC
20	14	6	0	0	0	0	0	0	0

JUNIOR LIGHTWEIGHTS

ARTIE O'LEARY	*1917-1919*	**HIROSHI KOBAYASHI**	1967-1971
JOHNNY DUNDEE	1921-1923	*RENE BARRIENTOS (WBC)*	*1969-1970*
JACK BERNSTEIN	1923	*YOSHIAKI NUMATA (WBC)*	*1970-1971*
JOHNNY DUNDEE	1923-1924	**ALFREDO MARCANO**	1971-1972
STEVE (KID) SULLIVAN	1924-1925	*RICARDO ARRENDONDO (WBC)*	*1971-1974*
MIKE BALLERINO	1925	**BEN VILLAFLOR**	1972-1973
TOD MORGAN	1925-1929	**KUNIAKI SHIBATA**	1973
BENNY BASS	1929-1931	**BEN VILLAFLOR**	1973-1976
KID CHOCOLATE	1931-1933	*KUNIAKI SHIBATA (WBC)*	*1974-1975*
FRANKIE KLICK	1933-1934	*ALFREDO ESCALERA (WBC)*	*1975-1978*
SANDY SADDLER	1949-1950	**SAMUEL SERRANO**	1976-1980
HAROLD GOMES	1959-1960	*ALEXIS ARGUELLO (WBC)*	*1978-1980*
GABRIEL (FLASH) ELORDE	1960-1967	**YASUTSUNE UEHARA**	1980-
YOSHIAKI NUMATA	1967	*RAFAEL (BAZOOKA) LIMON (WBC)*	*1980-*

Claimants not generally recognized are in *italics*.

684

WORLD JUNIOR LIGHTWEIGHT CHAMPIONSHIP BOUTS

Date	Winner	Weight	Loser	Weight		Time KO	Site	Referee
11/18/21	**Johnny DUNDEE**	128¼	**George K.O. CHANEY**	130	WF 5	1:07	Madison Square Garden, New York	Kid McPartland
7/6/22	**Johnny DUNDEE**	129	**Jack SHARKEY**	127	unan 15		Ebbets Field, Brooklyn, N.Y.	Kid McPartland
8/28/22	**Johnny DUNDEE**	124¾	**Pepper MARTIN**	130	unan 15		Velodrome, New York City, N.Y.	Patsy Haley
2/2/23	**Johnny DUNDEE**	129¾	**Elino FLORES**	129½	unan 15		Madison Square Garden, New York	Patsy Haley
5/30/23	**Jack BERNSTEIN**	128	**Johnny DUNDEE**	128½	unan 15		Velodrome, New York City, N.Y.	Patsy Haley
6/25/23	**Jack BERNSTEIN**	129	**Freddy JACKS**	130	KO 5		Shetzline Park, Philadelphia, Pa.	Pop O'Brien
12/17/23	**Johnny DUNDEE**	127½	**Jack BERNSTEIN**	129	15		Madison Square Garden, New York	Jock O'Sullivan
6/20/24	**Kid SULLIVAN**	129½	**Johnny DUNDEE**	129	10		Henderson's Bowl, Brooklyn, N.Y.	Jock O'Sullivan
8/18/24	**Kid SULLIVAN**	129	**Pepper MARTIN**	130	unan 15		Queensboro Stadium, New York	Tommy Sheridan
10/15/24	**Kid SULLIVAN**	129½	**Mike BALLERINO**	129	KO 5	0:38	Madison Square Garden, New York	Tommy Sheridan
4/1/25	**Mike BALLERINO**	129½	**Kid SULLIVAN**	129½	unan 10		Armory A.A., Philadelphia, Pa.	Pop O'Brien
7/6/25	**Mike BALLERINO**	129¾	**Pepper MARTIN**	239¾	unan 15		Queensboro Stadium, New York	Johnny McAvoy
12/2/25	**Tod MORGAN**	128	**Mike BALLERINO**	129¾	TKO 10		Olympic Auditorium, Los Angeles	
6/3/26	**Tod MORGAN**	127½	**Kid SULLIVAN**	128½	TKO 6	2:05	Ebbets Field, Brooklyn, New York	Jim Crowley
9/30/26	**Tod MORGAN**	128½	**Joe GLICK**	129½	unan 15		Madison Square Garden, New York	Patsy Haley
10/19/26	**Tod MORGAN**	128½	**Johnny DUNDEE**	126¼	unan 10		Recreation Park, San Francisco	Harry Ertle
11/19/26	**Tod MORGAN**	127½	**Carl DUANE**	129	unan 15		Madison Square Garden, New York	Lou Magnolia
5/28/27	**Tod MORGAN**	129¾	**Vic FOLEY**	125½	ref 12		Arena, Vancouver, B.C.	Joe Waterman
2/16/27	**Tod MORGAN**	128¾	**Joe GLICK**	129½	WF 14	2:09	Madison Square Garden, New York	Eddie Forbes
5/24/28	**Tod MORGAN**	129¾	**Eddie MARTIN**	130	15		Madison Square Garden, New York	Lou Magnolia
7/18/28	**Tod MORGAN**	128	**Eddie MARTIN**	128	unan 15		Ebbets Field, Brooklyn, New York	Eddie Forbes
12/3/28	**Tod MORGAN**	130	**Santiago ZORILLA**	127¼	draw 10		State Armory, San Francisco	Toby Irwin
1/1/29	**Tod MORGAN**	128½	**Joey SANGOR**	128	ND 10		Milwaukee Auditorium, Wisconsin	Walter Houlehen
4/5/29	**Tod MORGAN**	128	**Santiago ZORILLA**	129	10		Olympic Auditorium, Los Angeles	Lt. Jack Kennedy
5/20/29	**Tod MORGAN**	129	**Baby Sal SORIO**	128¾	10		Wrigley Field, Los Angeles	Benny Whitman
12/20/29	**Benny BASS**	127	**Tod MORGAN**	128	KO 2	0:51	Madison Square Garden, New York	Jim Crowley
3/28/30	**Benny BASS**	128	**Eddie SHEA**	126½	ND 10		Arena, St. Louis, Missouri	Harry Ertle
1/5/31	**Benny BASS**	127½	**Lew MASSEY**	128	unan 10		Philadelphia Arena, Pa.	Leo Houck
7/15/31	**Kid CHOCOLATE**	125½	**Benny BASS**	128½	TKO 7	2:58	Baker Bowl, Philadelphia, Pa.	Leo Houck
4/10/32	**Kid CHOCOLATE**	128½	**Davey ABAD**	129¾	15		Polar Stadium, Havana, Cuba	
8/4/32	**Kid CHOCOLATE**	127½	**Eddie SHEA**	128	unan 10		Chicago Stadium, Illinois	Phil Collins
10/13/32	**Kid CHOCOLATE**	125¾	**Lew FELDMAN**	125½	TKO 12	2:45	Madison Square Garden, New York	Patsy Haley
12/9/32	**Kid CHOCOLATE**	125½	**Fidel LA BARBA**	124	maj 15		Madison Square Garden, New York	Willie Lewis
5/1/33	**Kid CHOCOLATE**	124	**Johnny FARR**	130	unan 10		Arena, Philadelphia, Pa.	Joe McGuigan
5/19/33	**Kid CHOCOLATE**	123½	**Seaman Tom WATSON**	125½	unan 15		Madison Square Garden, New York	Pete Hartley
12/4/33	**Kid CHOCOLATE**	130	**Frankie WALLACE**	130	unan 10		Public Hall, Cleveland, Ohio	Tommy Mulgrew
12/25/33	**Frankie KLICK**	127¾	**Kid CHOCOLATE**	130	TKO 7	2:58	Arena, Philadelphia, Pa.	Spud Murphy
12/6/49	**Sandy SADDLER**	127½	**Orlando ZULUETA**	129½	split 10		Arena, Cleveland Ohio	Vito Mazzeo
4/18/50	**Sandy SADDLER**	130	**Lauro SALAS**	130	TKO 9	2:51	Arena, Cleveland Ohio	Jackie Davis
7/20/59	**Harold GOMES**	127½	**Paul JORGENSEN**	129½	unan 15		Pierce Field, Providence	Sharkey Buonanno
3/16/60	**Flash ELORDE**	130	**Harold GOMES**	128½	KO 7	1:50	Araneta Coliseum, Quezon	Barney Ross
8/17/60	**Flash ELORDE**	130	**Harold GOMES**	130	KO 1	1:20	Cow Palace, San Francisco	Matt Zidich
3/19/61	**Flash ELORDE**	130	**Joey LOPES**	130	unan 15		Rizal Coliseum, Manila	Felipe Hernandez
12/16/61	**Flash ELORDE**	130	**Sergio CAPRARI**	129½	TKO 1	2:22	Rizal Coliseum, Manila	Felipe Hernandez
6/23/62	**Flash ELORDE**	130	**Auburn COPELAND**	129½	maj 15		Rizal Coliseum, Manila	Felipe Hernandez
2/16/63	**Flash ELORDE**	130	**Johnny BIZZARO**	129½	unan 15		Rizal Coliseum, Manila	Irineo Gallego
11/16/63	**Flash ELORDE**	130	**Love ALLOTEY**	128	W dis 11	0:36	Areneta Coliseum, Quezon	Jamie Valencia
7/27/64	**Flash ELORDE**	130	**Teruo KOSAKA**	129½	TKO 12	1:45	Kuramae Arena, Tokyo	Pempe Padilla
6/5/65	**Flash ELORDE**	130	**Teruo KOSAKA**	127½	KO 15	2:14	Araneta Coliseum, Quezon	Totoy Reyes
12/4/65	**Flash ELORDE**	130	**Kang-Il SUH**	129¾	unan 15		Araneta Coliseum, Quezon	Alex Villacampa
10/22/66	**Flash ELORDE**	130	**Vicente DERADO**	128	maj 15		Araneta Coliseum, Quezon	Toti Cayetano
6/15/67	**Yoshiaki NUMATA**	129½	**Flash ELORDE**	130	maj 15		Kuramae Arena, Tokyo	Alex Villacampa
12/14/67	**Hiroshi KOBAYASHI**	129	**Yoshiaki NUMATA**	129½	KO 12	1:56	Kuramae Arena, Tokyo	Ko Toyama
3/30/68	**Hiroshi KOBAYASHI**	129	**Rene BARRIENTOS**	130	draw 15		Martial Arts Hall, Tokyo	Ko Toyama
10/6/68	**Hiroshi KOBAYSHI**	129	**Jaime VALLADARES**	129½	unan 15		Martial Arts Hall, Tokyo	Nick Pope
2/15/69	**Rene BARRIENTOS**	129½	**Ruben NAVARRO**	129½	unan 15		Araneta Coliseum, Quezon	
4/6/69	**Hiroshi KOBAYASHI**	128¾	**Antonio AMAYA**	127½	split 15		Kuramae Arena, Tokyo	Ko Toyama
11/9/69	**Hiroshi KOBAYASHI**	128¼	**Carlos CANETE**	129	unan 15		Nihon University Auditorium, Tokyo	Nick Pope
‡ 4/5/70	**Yoshiaki NUMATA**	130	**Rene BARRIENTOS**	129	split 15		Municipal Gymnasium, Tokyo	Dick Young
8/23/70	**Hiroshi KOBAYASHI**	128¾	**Antonio AMAYA**	129½	unan 15		Korakuen Hall, Tokyo	Nick Pope
‡ 9/27/70	**Yoshiaki NUMATA**	130	**Raul ROJAS**	130	KO 5	2:47	Nihon University Auditorium, Tokyo	Hiroyuki Tezaki
‡ 1/3/71	**Yoshiaki NUMATA**	130	**Rene BARRIENTOS**	130	split 15		Sumpu Kaikan, Shizuaka, Japan	John Crowder
3/3/71	**Hiroshi KOBAYASHI**	129¼	**Ricardo ARRENDONDO**	128½	unan 15		Nihon University Auditorium, Tokyo	Yusaku Yoshida
‡ 5/30/71	**Yoshiaki NUMATA**	129¾	**Lionel ROSE**	130	unan 15		Hiroshima Prefectural Gym	Hiroyuki Tezaki
7/29/71	**Alfredo MARCANO**	128¾	**Hiroshi KOBAYASHI**	129¼	KO 10	1:25	Prefectural Gymnasium, Aomori, Japan	Yusaku Yoshida
‡10/10/71	**Ricard ARRENDONDO**	130	**Yoshiaki NUMATA**	130	KO 10	2:17	Miyagi Center, Sendai	Hiroyuki Tezaki
11/7/71	**Alfredo MARCANO**	128¼	**Kenji IWATA**	129¾	TKO 4	1:50	Nuevo Circo Ring, Caracas	Luis Sulbaran
‡ 1/29/72	**Ricardo ARRENDONDO**	129	**Jose Issac MARIN**	128½	unan 15		San Jose, Costa Rica	Jay Edson
4/22/72	**Ricardo ARRENDONDO**	129	**William MARTINEZ**	129	KO 5	2:35	Mexico City, Mexico	
4/25/72	**Ben VILLAFLOR**	128¾	**Alfredo MARCANO**	128	unan 15		Blaisdell Cntr, Honolulu	James Scaramozi
9/5/72	**Ben VILLAFLOR**	128¾	**Victor ECHEGARAY**	130	draw 15		Blaisdell Cntr, Honolulu	Wilbert Minn
‡ 9/15/72	**Ricardo ARRENDONDO**	129¾	**Susumu OKABE**	129¾	KO 12	1:39	Nihon University Auditorium, Tokyo	John Crowder
‡ 3/6/73	**Ricardo ARRENDONDO**	129¼	**Apollo YOSHIO**	129¼	unan 15		Kyuden Gym, Fukuoka City	Jim Rondeau
3/12/73	**Kuniaki SHIBATA**	130	**Ben VILLAFLOR**	130	unan 15		Blaisdell Cntr, Honolulu	Walter Cho
6/19/73	**Kuniaki SHIBATA**	129½	**Victor ECHEGARAY**	128½	unan 15		Nihon University Auditorium, Tokyo	Yusaku Yoshida
‡ 9/1/73	**Ricardo ARRENDONDO**	129¼	**Morito KASHIWABA**	129¾	KO 6	1:26	Martial Arts Hall, Tokyo	Jim Rondeau
10/18/73	**Ben VILLAFLOR**	129½	**Kuniaki SHIBATA**	130	KO 1	1:56	Blaisdell Center, Honolulu	
‡ 2/28/74	**Kuniaki SHIBATA**	129½	**Ricardo ARRENDONDO**	29½	unan 15		Nihon University Auditorium, Tokyo	Ray Solis
3/14/74	**Ben VILLAFLOR**	127¾	**Apollo YOSHIO**	130	draw 15		City Gymnasium, Toyama, Japan	Shoichi Kato
‡ 6/27/74	**Kuniaki SHIBATA**	129¾	**Antonio AMAYA**	128¾	maj 15		Nihon University Auditorium, Tokyo	Yusaku Yoshida
‡ 8/3/74	**Kuniaki SHIBATA**	130	**[illegible] BOLANOS**	[illegible]	TKO 15	2:29	Nihon University Auditorium, Tokyo	Anselmo Perez

Date	Champion		Challenger		Result		Venue	Referee
8/24/74	Ben VILLAFLOR	129¾	Yasutsune UEHARA	129½	KO 2	1:17	Blaisdell Center, Honolulu	Walter Cho
3/13/75	Ben VILLAFLOR	129¾	Hyun-Chi KIM	128½	split 15		Araneta Coliseum, Quezon	Herbert Minn
‡ 3/27/75	Kuniaki SHIBATA	129½	Ould MAKLOUFI	129	unan 15		Kyuden Gym, Fukuoka City	Yusaku Yoshida
‡ 7/5/75	Alfredo ESCALERA	128¾	Kuniaki SHIBATA	129¾	KO 2	2:56	Kasamatsu Gymnasium, Mito	Ken Morita
‡ 9/20/75	Alfredo ESCALERA	129	Lionel HERNANDEZ	130	draw 15		Nuevo Circo Ring, Caracas	Ray Solis
‡12/12/75	Alfredo ESCALERA	128	Sven-Erik PAULSEN	129	TKO 9		Oslo, Norway	Harry Gibbs
1/12/76	Ben VILLAFLOR	128	Morito KASHIWABA	130	TKO 13	1:29	Korakuen Hall, Tokyo	Carlos Padilla
‡ 2/20/76	Alfredo ESCALERA	130	Jose FERNANDEZ	130	TKO 13	2:13	Roberto Clemente Stadium	Waldemar Schmidt
‡ 4/1/76	Alfredo ESCALERA	128½	Buzzsaw YAMABE	130	TKO 6	2:39	Kashiwara Gym, Nara	Ismael Quinones Falu
4/13/76	Ben VILLAFLOR	129	Samuel SERRANO	130	draw 15		Blaisdell Center, Honolulu	Wilbert Minn
‡ 7/1/76	Alfredo ESCALERA	130	Buzzsaw YAMABE	130	unan 15		Kashiwara Gymnasium, Nara	Rudy Ortega
‡ 9/18/76	Alfredo ESCALERA	130	Ray LUNNY III	130	TKO 13		Roberto Clemente Stadium	Waldemar Schmidt
10/16/76	Samuel SERRANO	130	Ben VILLAFLOR	129½	unan 15		Hiram Bithorn Stadium	Stan Christodoulou
‡11/30/76	Alfredo ESCALERA	130	Tyrone EVERETT	130	split 15		Spectrum, Philadelphia	Ray Solis
1/15/77	Samuel SERRANO	129½	Alberto HERRERA	128½	TKO 11	2:17	Guayaquil, Ecuador	Martin Denkin
‡ 3/17/77	Alfredo ESCALERA	130	Ronnie McGARVEY	127	TKO 6	2:03	Roberto Clemente Stadium	Abraham Echavarria
‡ 5/16/77	Alfredo ESCALERA	128½	Carlos BECERRIL	127¾	KO 8	0:38	Capital Centre, Landover	Larry Barnett
6/26/77	Samuel SERRANO	129	Lionel HERNANDEZ	128	unan 15		Puerto la Cruz, Venezuela	Larry Rozadilla
8/27/77	Samuel SERRANO	129	Apollo YOSHIO	129¾	unan 15		Roberto Clemente Stadium	Waldemar Schmidt
‡ 9/10/77	Samuel SERRANO	127	Sigfredo RODRIGUEZ	125	unan 15		Roberto Clemente Stadium	Arthur Mercante
11/19/77	Samuel SERRANO	130	Tae-Ho KIM	130	TKO 10	1:50	Roberto Clemente Stadium	Larry Rozadilla
‡ 1/28/78	Alexis ARGUELLO	129½	Alfredo ESCALERA	130	TKO 13	2:24	Loubriel Stadium, Bayamon	Arthur Mercante
2/18/78	Samuel SERRANO	129½	Mario MARTINEZ	130	unan 15		Roberto Clemente Stadium	Roberto Ramirez
‡ 4/29/78	Alexis ARGUELLO	129½	Rey TAM	129¾	TKO 5	1:54	Forum, Inglewood, Calif.	Rudy Jordan
‡ 6/3/78	Alexis ARGUELLO	129	Diego ALCALA	130	KO 1	1:55	Forum, Inglewood, Calif.	Roberto Ramirez
7/8/78	Samuel SERRANO	130	Oh-Young HO	129¼	unan 15		Roberto Clemente Stadium	Luis Sulbaran
‡11/10/78	Alexis ARGUELLO	130	Arturo LEON	128¼	unan 15		Caesars Palace, Las Vegas	David Pearl
11/29/78	Samuel SERRANO	129	Takao MARUKI	129¼	unan 15		Aichi Gymnasium, Nagoya	Larry Rozadilla
‡ 2/4/79	Alexis ARGUELLO	129	Alfredo ESCALERA	129¾	KO 13	1:24	Rimini, Italy	Angelo Poletti
2/18/79	Samuel SERRANO	129½	Julio VALDEZ	130	unan 15		Hiram Bithorn Stadium, San Juan	Larry Rozadilla
4/14/79	Samuel SERRANO	128¾	Nkosana MGXAJI	127¾	TKO 8	1:34	Good Hope Centre, Cape Town	Larry Rozadilla
‡ 7/8/79	Alexis ARGUELLO	130	Rafael LIMON	129	TKO 11	1:40	Felt Forum, New York, N.Y	Tony Perez
‡11/16/79	Alexis ARGUELLO	129¾	Bobby CHACON	129½	TKO 8	*	Forum, Inglewood, Calif.	John Thomas
‡ 1/12/80	Alexis ARGUELLO	130	Ruben CASTILLO	129½	TKO 11	2:03	Community Center, Tucson, Arizona	Octavio Meyran
4/3/80	Samuel SERRANO	129½	Battle Hawk KAZAMA	129¾	TKO 13	0:45	Central Gymnasium, Nara, Japan	Stan Christodoulou
‡ 4/27/80	Alexis ARGUELLO	130	Rolando NAVARETTE	130	TKO 5	*	Hiram Bithorn Stadium, San Juan	Roberto Ramirez
8/02/80	Yasutsune UEHARA	129¼	Samuel SERRANO	130	KO 6	2:59	Joe Louis Arena, Detroit, Mich.	Luis Sulbaran
11/20/80	Yasutsune UEHARA	129¼	Leonel HERNANDEZ	129¼	split 15		Kuramae Arena, Tokyo, Japan	Chun-Kook Kim
‡12/11/80	Rafael LIMON	129¼	Ildefonso BETHELMY	129¼	TKO 15	1:21	Olympic Auditorium, Los Angeles	Larry Rozadilla

* Loser failed to answer bell for round indicated   †WBA world junior lightweight title bout   ‡WBC world super featherweight title bout

JUNIOR LIGHTWEIGHT DIVISION

ARTIE O'LEARY
(Arthur Lieberman)
(Record Not Available))

JOHNNY DUNDEE
(Record Under Featherweight Champions)

JACK BERNSTEIN
(John Dodick)
(Junior Lightweight Champion)
Born, November 5, 1899, New York City.
Nationality, Jewish-American. Weight, 130 lbs.
Height, 5 ft. 4½ in. Managed by "Doc" Hirsch.

1914
No decisions: Young West, 4; Young Philips, 4; Benny Leonard, 6; Young Fulton, 6; Willie Beecher, 6.

1915
No decisions: Young West, 4; Young Phillips, 4; Willie Astey, 6; Titchie Ryan, 8.

1917
Knockout: John Sillo, 4. Won: Young Hockey, 6.

1918
Knockout: L. McCarthy, 3. Won: Red Margolis, 5. Lost: Mick Sunday, 4.

1919
Won: Red Margolis, 4; Kid Parr, 8; Joe Neil, 6; Joe Neil, 8; Nick Gundy, 20. Lost: Nick Gundy, 10.

1920
Knockouts: J. Moore, 2; Kid Speero, 3; Kid Marcel, 4; Soldier Shaw, 1; Joe Lyons, 5. Won: Sol Friedman, 10; Sol Friedman, 8; Young Schrabe, 6.

1921
Knockouts: Willie Mack, 4; Red Wilke, 2. Won: Eddie Gorman, 10; Young Britton, 10; Young Britton, 12. Lost: Red Monroe, 12; Billy Fitzsimmons, 12; Benny Valgar, 12.

1922
Feb.	23—Jimmy Cooney, Yonkers	W 12
Mar.	7—Johnny Darcy, N. Y. C.	W 12
.Apr.	6—Young Eddy, Yonkers	KO 9
Apr.	22—Bert Spencer, N. Y. C.	W 12
May	14—Archie Walker, Brooklyn	L 12
June	21—Jimmy Carroll, N.Y.C.	KO 10
June	28—Archie Walker, Yonkers	W 12
July	8—Solly Seeman, N. Y. C.	W 12
July	20—Fred Jacks, N. Y. C.	W 12
Sept.	7—Tony Caponi, Yonkers	KO 9
Sept.	16—Johnny Conney, N. Y. C.	KO 6
Oct.	14—Pal Moran, N. Y. C.	W 12
Oct.	20—Joe Mandell, Yonkers, N. Y.	KO 5
Nov.	16—Elino Flores, N. Y. C.	D 12
Nov.	28—Babe Herman, N. Y. C.	W 12
Dec.	11—Kid Wagner, N. Y. C.	W 10

1923
Jan.	5—Pepper Martin, N. Y. C.	W 12
Feb.	13—Gene Delmont, N. Y. C.	W 12
Feb.	22—Earl Baird, N. Y. C.	W 12
Mar.	17—Eddie Brady, N. Y. C.	W 12
Mar.	27—Sammy Greene, N. Y. C.	W 4
Apr.	6—Tommy Noble, N. Y. C.	W 12
May	8—Elino Flores, N. Y. C.	W 15
May	30—Johnny Dundee, N. Y. C.	W 15
	(Won Junior Lightweight title)	
June	25—Freddie Jacks, Philadelphia	KO 5
July	31—H. Kid Brown, Philadelphia	ND 8
Aug.	9—Jimmy Goodrich, N. Y. C.	D 10
Oct.	12—Rocky Kansas, N. Y. C.	W 15
Nov.	3—Billy Defoe, N. Y. C.	W 10
Nov.	27—Harry Kabakoff, St. Louis	ND 10
Dec.	17—Johnny Dundee, N. Y. C.	L 15
	(Lost Junior Lightweight title)	

1924
Jan.	11—Sammy Mandell, N. Y. C.	D 15
Feb.	18—Rocky Kansas, Buffalo	D 10
Mar.	24—Teddy Myers, Buffalo	W 10
Apr.	12—Jack Hausner, New York	W 12
May	5—Sammy Mandell, Louisville	ND 12
June	4—Sid Barbarian, New York	L 12
June	23—Cuddy DeMarco, New Haven	L 12
July	23—Jack Zivic, Brooklyn	W 12
Aug.	14—Luis Vincentini, Brooklyn	W 12
Sept.	15—Johnny Dundee, N. Y. C.	W 15
Nov.	7—Sammy Mandell, New York	L 12
Nov.	26—Rocky Kansas, Buffalo	L 12
Dec.	16—Tony Russo, Buffalo	W 6

1925
Jan.	9—Tommy O'Brien, N. Y. C.	W 10
Apr.	22—Tony Palmer, N. Y. C.	W 10
May	7—Earl Baird, Yonkers	W 6
May	18—Harry Cook, Albany, N. Y.	D 6
Aug.	31—Sid Terris, N. Y. C.	L 12
Oct.	12—Sid Terris, N. Y. C.	L 10

1926
Feb.	15—Ray Romney, Buffalo, N. Y.	D 10
Mar.	6—Bobby Burns, N. Y. C.	KO 4
Apr.	12—Tony Vaccarelli, N. Y. C.	W 10
May	3—Johnny Rocco, N. Y. C.	KO 8
June	17—Stanislaus Loayza, N. Y. C.	L 10
Oct.	11—Cuddy De Marco, Pittsburgh	W 10
Dec.	12—Ray Miller, New York	W 12

1927
Feb.	21—Jimmy Goodrich, N. Y. C.	W 10
Mar.	1—Lee Murray, N. Y. C.	W 10
Apr.	1—Jimmy Goodrich, Buffalo	W 10
Apr.	25—Bobby Tracey, N. Y. C.	W 10
May	13—Bruce Flowers, N. Y. C.	L 10
Aug.	2—Bruce Flowers, N. Y. C.	L 10
Aug.	15—Freddie Mueller, N. Y. C.	L 10
Nov.	14—Joe Glick, N. Y. C.	L 10

1928
July	3—Armand Schackels, New York	L 10
Dec.	1—Bruce Flowers, New York	KO by 6

1929
Feb.	21—Al Tripoli, Yonkers, New York	W 6
	—Harry Carlton, New York	L 10
	—Frankie LaFay	D 10

1931
Nov.	10—Johnny Gaito, Yonkers	L 6

TB	KO	WD	WF	D	LD	LF	KOBY	ND	NC
107	17	48	0	7	22	0	1	12	0

Died, Yonkers, N. Y., December 26, 1945.

STEVE (KID) SULLIVAN
(Stephen J. Tricamo)
(Junior Lightweight, Champion)
Born, May 21, 1897, Brooklyn, N. Y.
Nationality, Italian-American. Weight, 130 lbs.
Height, 5 ft. 5 in.

1911
Knockout: Young Kenny, 3. No decisions: Andy Griffin, 4; Tommy Hynes, 4; Dick Lewis, 6; Young Cirina, 4; Jerry Clifford, 4.

1912
June 14—Charley Goldman, N. Y. C. ...ND 6
No decision: Young (Charlie) Marlow, 10.

1913
Knockouts: Willie Smith, 4; Young Alberts, 2. No decisions: Young (Charlie) Marlow, 10; Bobby Gair, 10; Young Neiman, 10; Young Jersey, 10; Mike Clancy, 10; Walter Nelson, 10; Young Mundy, 10; "Dutch" Brandt, 10; Battling Lahn, 10; Young Rector, 10. Exhibition: Battling Levinsky, 3.

1914
Knockouts: Eddie Brooks, 1; Eddie Lennon, 3. Won: Bobby Burns, 8. Draw: Young Rector, 10; Young Limbo, 10; "Dutch" Brandt, 10; Willie Doyle, 10. No decisions: Eddie Moran, 10; Battling Lahn, 10; Eddie Moran, 10; Nick Nelson, 10; Johnny Solsberg, 10; Young O'Leary, 10; Jim Kendrick, 10; Young Marino, 10; Jimmy Murray, 10; Joe Mooney, 10; Mickey Donnelly, 10; Kid Murphy, 10; Kid Taylor, 10; Frankie Mason, 10. Lost: Monk Fowler, 8. Exhibitions: Young Zulu Kid, 3; Harry Thomas, 3.

1915
Feb.	23—Eddie Campi, Brooklyn	ND 10
Mar.	26—Red Dolan, New Orleans	D 20
Apr.	19—Red Dolan, New Orleans	L 20
June	24—Eddie Wallace, Brooklyn	ND 10

Draw: Johnny Solsberg, 8. No decisions: Walter Nelson, 10; Young Limbo 10; K.O. Joe Daly, 10. Exhibition: John Murray, 3.

1916
Jan.	23—Frankie Callahan, Brooklyn	ND 10
Jan.	26—Kid Wilson, New Orleans	KO by 5
Feb.	14—Eddie Campi, Brooklyn	ND 10
Apr.	1—Young Martin, Brooklyn	KO 1

Won: K. O. Joe Daly, 2; Johnny Donovan, 8; Gus Lewis, 6. No decisions: Willie Jones, 10; Harry Glenn, 10; Walter Nelson, 10; Young Cardell, 10; Walter Nelson, 10; Marty Allen, 10. Draw: K.O. Eggers, 10.

Won: Young Steele, 10. No decisions: Battling Lahan, 10; Young Al Kale, 10.
1918
Knockout: Vincent Pepper Martin, 4. No decision: Joe Garry, 10.
(Joined U. S. Navy during World War I, 1918. Discharged in 1919.)
1920

Dec. 11—Willie Kohler, Woodhaven . KO by 4
1921
Mar. 12—Young Limbo, Woodhaven .... W 10
Apr. 9—Terry Davis, Jamaica, N. Y. .... W 10
Apr. 23—Willie Daney, Woodhaven ..... W 10
Apr. 26—Irish Kid Williams, Brooklyn ... W 15
May 14—Silent Regan, Woodhaven ......L 12
Aug. 15—Stockings Conroy, Freeport ....KO 7
Aug. 29—Eddie Gorman, Freeport .....KO 4
Sept. 26—Dutch Brandt, Freeport ......W 12
Oct. 31—Bobby Michaels, Freeport ....WF 3
Dec. 19—Irish Patsy Philbin, Freeport..........................D 10
Knockouts: Pete McDonald, 2. Won: Lew McFarland, 7.
1922
Jan. 19—Pepper Martin, Brooklyn ......L 12
Feb. 6—Harvey Bright, Brooklyn ...... D 12
Feb. 26—Sammy Sieger, Brooklyn ..... W 12
Apr. 17—Harvey Bright, Brooklyn ..... W 12
Apr. 28—Joe King Leopold, Brooklyn ..WF 9
May 19—Joe King Leopold, New York ...L 4
June 1—Battling Reddy, New Yrok .... W 12
July 9—Eddie Brady, Coney Island .....L 12
Aug. 1—Pepper Martin, Brooklyn ......L 12
Sept. 11—Sammy Sieger, New York ...KO 3
Sept. 26—Pepper Martin, Brooklyn ......L 12
Nov. 24—Louis Kid Kaplan, New York ...L 12
1923
Jan. 22—Sammy Sieger, Brooklyn ......L 12
Mar. 8—Dutch Brandt, Brooklyn ...... W 12
Aug. 7—Pepper Martin, N. Y. C. ....LF 8
Dec. 17—Babe Herman, N. Y. C. ....KO 8
—Jimmy Mars, Brooklyn ....L 12
1924
May 30—Mike Ballerino, Brooklyn ......L 12
June 20—Johnny Dundee, Brooklyn .... W 10
(Won junior lightweight title)
Aug. 18—Pepper Martin, L. I. City ..... W 15
Oct. 15—Mike Ballerino, N. Y. C. ......KO 5
(Retained junior lightweight title)
Dec. 15—Mike Ballerino, Milwaukee ...ND 10
1925
Mar. 23—Willie Ames, Canton, O. ......ND 12
Apr. 1—Mike Ballerino, Philadelphia ....L 1(
(Lost junior lightweight title)
May 22—Louis Kid Kaplan, Wat'b'y . KO by 5
1926
Feb. 1—Georgie Balduc, N. Y. C........ W 1(
Feb. 13—Frankie Brown, N. Y. C........ D
June 3—Tod Morgan Brooklyn ....KO by

TB	KO	WD	WF	D	LD	LF	KOBY	ND	NC
111	13	18	·2	10	13	1	4	50	0

1923
Jan. 5—Frankie Jerome, New York .... D 12
Jan. 19—Carl Tremaine, New York . KO by 3
Dec. 28—Mickey Brown, New York ..... W 10
Won: Joe Nelson, 10; B. Fitzsimmons, 10.
No Decision: Bobby Wolgast, 8; Cuddy De Marco, 10; Cuddy De Marco, 8; Joe O'Donnell, 8.
Lost: Harvey Bright, 12.
1924
Apr. 10—Joe Souza, N. Y. C. ....W 10
Apr. 22—Joe Celmars, Bayonne, N. J. ..ND 10
May 30—Kid Sullivan, N.Y.C. .... W 10
June 24—Vincent Pepper Martin, N.Y.C. ....W 12
July 15—Johnny Leonard, N.Y.C. ...... W 10
Aug. 5—Johnny Leonard, N.Y.C. ...... W 12
Sept. 9—Tony Vaccarelli, N.Y.C. .... W 10
Oct. 15—Kid Sullivan, N.Y.C. ......KO by 5
Dec. 15—Kid Sullivan, Milwaukee ....ND 10
1925
Jan. 1—Frankie Monroe, Milwaukee ..ND 10
Feb. 5—Vincent Martin, Brooklyn ....KO 11
Apr. 1—Kid Sullivan, Phila. .... W 12
(Won Junior Lightweight title)
May 15—Mickey Brown, Bayonne .....ND 10
May 30—Frankie Callahan, Colum., O. .ND 10
June 12—Frankie Schaffer, Aurora, Ill. .ND 10
June 16—Billy Henry, Kansas City .....ND 10
June 23—Babe Ruth, Philadelphia, Pa. ... D 10
July 6—Pepper Martin, Brooklyn .... W 15
Aug. 14—Billy Henry, Bayonne, N. J. ...ND 10
Oct. 21—Ace Hudkins, Los Angeles .....L 10
Dec. 2—Tod Morgan, Los Angeles ..KO by 10
(Lost Junior Lightweight title)
1928
June 6—Johnny Leonard, N. Y. C. ......L 10
June 25—Petey Mack, Bayonne, N. J. ..ND 10
July 9—Augie Pisano, Lg. Beach, N. Y. ..L 6
July 21—Johnny Leonard, Bayonne ....ND 10
Aug. 30—George Day, New Haven, Conn. .L 10
Sept. 15—Johnny Kochansky, Bayonne .ND 10
Sept. 30—Eddie Lord, N. Haven, Conn. .. W 10
Nov. 8—Tommy Herman, Philadelphia .L 10
Nov. 13—Joe Glick, Brooklyn, N. Y....... D 10
Nov. 29—Georgie Balduc, N.Y.C. .... W 10
Dec. 20—Joe Glick, N.Y.C. .... D 10
1927
Jan. 24—Al Foreman, Philadelphia ..... W 10
Feb. 2—Maxie Holub, Akron, Ohio ....L 10
Mar. 5—Martie Silvers, Brooklyn .... D 6
Mar. 19—Nat Kawler, Schenectady ......L 10
Apr. 19—Jack Duffy, Arkon, Ohio ......ND 10
Apr. 26—King Tut, St. Paul, Minn. ......L 10
Oct. 17—Benny Bass, Philadelphia ......L 10
Nov. 11—Joey Medill, Chicago, Ill. ....L 10
Nov. 21—Mike Dundee, Dayton, O. . KO by 10
1928
Jan. 20—Tommy Grogan, Omaha ... KO by 4
1929
—Murray Fuchs .... W 10

TB	KO	WD	WF	D	LD	LF	KOBY	ND	NC
96	8	32	0	14	19	0	5	18	0

Died April 4, 1965 in Tampa, Florida.

MIKE BALLERINO
(Junior Lightweight Champion)
Born, 1901, Bayonne, N. J. Nationality, Italian American. Weight, 126 lbs. Height, 5 ft. 4 in. Managed by Frank Churchill.
1920
Knockouts: Kid Ponso, 3; Young Gilbert, 3. Won: Kid Aguilar, 4; Kid Saunders, 4; Kid Ponso, 4; Kid Taylor, 4; Leoncio Bernabe, 6; Eddie More, 10. Draw: Ireno Flores, 4. Lost: Syd Keenan, 8; Pancho Villa, 6; Pancho Villa, 6. No decision: Pancho Villa, 6; Pancho Villa, 6.

1921
Knockouts: Kid Garcia, 11; Kid Tango, 3; Young Givinni, 1. Won: Tip O'Neill, 8. Draw: Pancho Villa, 15; Cowboy Reyes, 10; Pancho Villa, 15; Peter Sarmiento, 8. Lost: Pancho Villa, 15; Pancho Villa, 10; Pancho Villa, 20; Pancho Villa, 20.

1922
Knockouts: Joe Loth, 3; Tom Shea, 3. Won: Eddie More, 6; Mike Mitchell, 6; Jimmy Cole, 4; Kid La Rose, 4; Frankie Pantley, 6; Mike De Pinto, 6; Mike De Pinto, 6; Sam Gordon, 4; Sam Gordon, 4; Ernie Dailey, 6. Draw: Frankie Britt, 6; Vic Foley, 4; Vic Foley, 10; Bud Ridley, 10. Lost: Sam Gordon, 4.

TOD MORGAN
(Bert Pilkington)
Born, December 25, 1902. Sequim, Washington. Ancestry, English-Scotch. Weight, 130 lbs. Height, 5 ft. 7½ in. Managed by Frank Churchill.
1920
Won: George Green, 4; George Green, 4; Young Mike Gibbons, 4; Young Mike Gibbons, 4.
1921
Knockouts: Lou Hogan, 2; Bud Miller, 2. Won: Joe Bell, 4; Sammy Girsch, 4; Frankie Novey, 4; Alex McDonald, 4; Alex McDonald, 4; Trench King, 4; Young Carpenter, 4; Young Carpenter, 4; Willie Shyrock, 4; Willie Shyrock, 4; Jimmy Hackley, 4; Willie Shyrock, 4. Draw: Alex McDonald, 4; Frankie Nell, 4; Trench King, 4; Trench King, 4; Ad Remy, 4; Willie Shyrock, 4; Alex McDonald, 4.
1922
Won: Young Russ Pierce, 4; Johnny MacManus, 4; Calif. Joe Lynch, 4; Georgie Sollis, 4; Dynamite Murphy, 4; Al Roubideux, 4; Trench King, 4; Dynamite Murphy, 4; Johnny MacManus, 4; Spec. Ramies, 4; Vic Moran, 4; Jimmy Mendo, 4. Draw: Georgie Thompson, 4; Georgie Thompson, 4; Joe Lynch, 4; Young

Farrell, 4; Jimmie Mendo, 4. Lost: Calif. Joe
Lynch, 4; Eddie Macy, 4; George Thompson, 4.
Knockouts: Sailor Victrolia, 2.

1923

Won: Joe Lynch, 4; Dandy Dillon, 4;
Jimmy Rackley, 4; Joe Coffeyn, 4; Frankie
McCann, 4; Willie O'Brien, 4; Frankie McCann, 4;
Bud Ridley, 6; Bud Ridley, 6; Dandy Dillon, 4;
George Sollis, 6. Draw: Dandy Dillon, 6.

1924

Knockouts: Frankie Britt, 3; Dandy
Edwards, 5. Won: Dandy Munce, 6; John Bedent,
4; Stewart McLean, 4; Georgie Spencer, 4; Al
Walker, 4; Joe Gorman, 6; Georgie Spencer, 6;
Ad Mackie, 6; Doc Snell, 6. Draw: Frankie Britt,
6; Joe Gorman, 6; Doc Snell, 6.

1925

Mar.	13—Gene Delmont, Hollywood	W 10
Apr.	22—Stewart McLean, Oakland	D 10
June	10—Joe Gorman, Oakland	W 10
June	19—Stewart McLean, Hollywood	W 10
Sept.	9—Harry Wallach, Los Angeles	W 10
Dec.	2—Mike Ballerino, Los Angeles	KO 10

(Won World Junior Lightweight Title)

1926

Jan.	7—Sammy Campagno, Portland	KO 7
Jan.	13—Stewart McLean, Oakland	W 10
Feb.	22—Jimmy Goodrich, Milwaukee	ND 10
Feb.	26—Don Davis, East Chicago	ND 10
Mar.	17—Charlie O'Connell, Cleveland	D 12
Mar.	29—Eddie Brady, Youngstown	W 12
June	3—Steve (Kid) Sullivan, Brooklyn	KO 6

(Retained World Junior Lightweight Title)

June	24—Babe Herman, Revere Beach	L 10
July	6—Ted Blatt, Cleveland	W 10
July	9—John Kochansky, Jersey City	ND 10
Aug.	4—Tommy O'Brien, Los Angeles	L 10
Sept.	30—Joe Glick, New York	W 15

(Retained World Junior Lightweight Title)

Oct.	19—Johnny Dundee, San Francisco	W 10

(Retained World Junior Lightweight Title)

Nov.	19—Carl Duane, New York	W 15

(Retained World Junior Lightweight Title)

1927

Jan.	7—Phil McGraw, New York	L 10
May	28—Vic Foley, Vancouver	W 12

(Retained World Junior Lightweight Title)

June	29—Doc Snell, Seattle	L 6
Sept.	20—Stanislaus Loayza, Chicago	LF 9
Dec.	2—Honeyboy Finnegan, Boston	L 10
Dec.	16—Joe Glick, New York	WF 14

(Retained World Junior Lightweight Title)

1928

Feb.	24—Ritchie King, Vancouver	W 10
Apr.	3—Jimmy Duffy, Toledo	ND 10
May	24—Eddie Martin, New York	W 15

(Retained World Junior Lightweight Title)

July	18—Eddie Martin, Brooklyn	W 15

(Retained World Junior Lightweight Title)

Sept.	3—Leslie (Wildcat) Carter, Vancouver	D 10
Oct.	2—King Tut, Minneapolis	ND 10
Dec.	3—Santiago Zorilla, San Francisco	D 10

(Retained World Junior Lightweight Title)

1929

Jan.	1—Joey Sangor, Milwaukee	ND 10

(Retained World Junior Lightweight Title)

Jan.	8—Eddie Mack, Denver	L 10
Apr.	5—Santiago Zorilla, Los Angeles	W 10

(Retained World Junior Lightweight Title)

Apr.	24—Eddie Mack, Denver	D 10
May	20—Baby Sal Sorio, Los Angeles	W 10

(Retained World Junior Lightweight Title)

July	9—Goldie Hess, Los Angeles	L 10
Nov.	1—Billy Townsend, Vancouver	D 10
Nov.	26—Eddie Mack, Los Angeles	L 10
Dec.	20—Benny Bass, New York	KO by 2

(Lost World Junior Lightweight Title)

1930

June	6—Santiago Zorilla, Vancouver	D 15¹
July	23—Don Fraser, Spokane	W 6
July	25—Joey Coffman, Tacoma	W 6
Aug.	14—Leslie (Wildcat) Carter, Seattle	W 6

Aug.	29—Eddie Mack, Seattle	W 6
Sept.	23—Santiago Zorilla, Seattle	W 8
Oct.	31—Hector McDonald, Los Angeles	W 10

1931

Feb.	17—Billy Townsend, Los Angeles	L 10
Mar.	24—Goldie Hess, Los Angeles	W 10
Apr.	10—Ramon Ortega, San Francisco	KO 2
May	12—Cecil Payne, Los Angeles	L 10
July	1—Goldie Hess, Seattle	W 8
Aug.	11—Bobby Pacho, Los Angeles	L 10
Aug.	18—Frankie Stetson, Oakland	W 10
Sept.	3—Cecil Payne, Sacramento	W 10
Sept.	23—Eddie Thomas, Portland	W 10
Sept.	30—Sammy Santos, Seattle	W 6
Oct.	13—Sammy Santos, Seattle	W 8
Nov.	10—Bobby Pacho, Los Angeles	KO by 7

1932

Jan.	1—Eddie Volk, Portland	W 6
Jan.	21—Don Fraser, Tacoma	L 6
May	6—Mushy Callahan, Hollywood	L 10
June	23—Don Fraser, Spokane	L 6
July	8—Sammy Mandell, Hollywood	W 10
Aug.	19—Baby Sal Sorio, Hollywood	WF 2
Sept.	9—Kenneth LaSalle, Hollywood	L 10
Dec.	6—Harry Woods, Seattle	D 6

1933

Sept.	4—Bobby Blay, Sydney	W 15
Sept.	25—Nel Tarleton, Sydney	D 15
Oct.	9—Jack Carroll, Sydney	L 15
Oct.	30—Jimmy Kelso, Sydney	L 15
Nov.	11—Jimmy Kelso, Melbourne	W 15
Nov.	20—Jimmy Kelso, Sydney	D 15

1934

Apr.	30—Joe Ghnouly, Sydney	L 15
July	2—Jimmy Kelso, Sydney	KO 8
July	16—Tom Johns, Sydney	KO 1
July	30—Herb Bishop, Sydney	W 15
Aug.	8—Reg Hickey, Brisbane	D 15
Aug.	27—Jack Carroll, Sydney	L 15
Oct.	15—Herb Bishop, Sydney	NC 5
Nov.	5—Herb Bishop, Sydney	L 10
Nov.	12—Jack Portney, Sydney	D 15
Dec.	3—Jack Portney, Sydney	L 15
Dec.	10—Reg Hickey, Sydney	KO 8

1935

Feb.	4—Willard Brown, Sydney	L 15
	—Kid Moro, Honolulu	W

1936

Feb.	3—Saverio Turiello, Sydney	L 15

1937

Mar.	20—Mick Leonard, Broken Hill	KO 2
Apr.	23—Sid Clarke, Wollongong	KO 5
May	19—Herb Bishop, Sydney	W 15
June	9—Bert Osborne, Leichhardt	W 15
June	30—Clever Henry, Leichhardt	W 15
Sept.	21—Jimmy Dundee, Leichhardt	KO 4
Oct.	5—Herb Bishop, Leichhardt	W 12

1938

Mar.	5—Manuel Cuzzolino, Newcastle	KO 4
Mar.	12—Jimmy Dundee, Newcastle	KO 6
Apr.	29—Jimmy Dundee, Lithgow	KO 6
May	11—Ron McLaughlin, Leichhardt	KO 10
June	7—Herb Bishop, Kalgoorlie	W 12
July	22—Mick Leonard, Perth	KO 8
Sept.	9—Herb Bishop, Kalgoorlie	L 12
Dec.	9—Bob King, Perth	KO 6
Dec.	26—Herb Bishop, Perth	W 15

1939

Feb.	24—Graham Evans, Perth	KO 9
May	12—Johnny Hutchinson, Brisbane	L 12
June	30—Paddy Boxall, Perth	L 15
Oct.	6—Danny LaVerne, Perth	L 12
Nov.	10—Danny LaVerne, Perth	W 12
Dec.	26—Paddy Boxall, Perth	KO by 5

1940

Jan.	26—Claude Varner, Perth	W 12
Feb.	15—Claude Varner, Perth	KO 8
Feb.	23—Herb Bishop, Perth	W 12
Mar.	26—Fighting Carlos, Sydney	KO 12
Apr.	13—Clever Henry, Melbourne	L 12

Apr.	24—Johnny Hutchinson, Melbourne .... W	12
Oct.	29—Tiger Parkes, Kalgoorlie .... KO	4
Nov.	25—Len Fay, Adelaide .... W	12
Dec.	14—Tiger Parkes, Broken Hill .... WF	3
Dec.	26—Joe Hall, North Sydney .... KO	11

1941

Jan.	18—Ron McLaughlin, Newcastle .... D	12
Feb.	1—Alan Westbury, Newcastle .... W	12
Feb.	8—Alan Westbury, Newcastle L	12
Mar.	15—Ron McLaughlin, Melbourne ..... W	12
June	5—Vic Patrick, Sydney .... WF	5
July	3—Vic Patrick, Sydney L	15
Sept.	11—Vic Patrick, Sydney L	15

1942

Mar.	9—Vic Patrick, Sydney .... KO by	11
July	18—Lew Edwards, Melbourne .... W	12

TB	KO	WD	WF	D	LD	LF	KO BY	ND	NC
203	27	98	4	30	32	1	4	6	1

Died, August 3, 1953, Seattle, Washington.

BENNY BASS
(Record Under Featherweight Champions)

KID CHOCOLATE
(Record Under Featherweight Champions)

FRANKIE KLICK

Born, May 5, 1909, San Francisco, California.
Ancestry, Polish-French. Weight, 120-140 lbs. Height, 5
ft. 6 in. Managed by Joe Doran in California, 1924-1932;
by Ray Carlin in New York.

1924

Oct.	29—Young Manila, San Francisco ...... W	4
Nov.	12—Tony Baroni, San Francisco .... W	4
Nov.	26—Dick Cruz, San Francisco .... W	4
Dec.	10—Frankie Wilson, San Francisco .... W	4

1925

Jan.	8—Jimmy Barry, San Francisco ...... W	4
Jan.	14—Phil Doro, San Francisco .... KO	3
Feb.	20—Jack Flynn, San Francisco .... W	4
Mar.	4—Kid Magsambol, San Francisco .:.. W	4
Dec.	2—Jimmy Briggs, San Francisco ...... W	4
Dec.	9—Fred Bindon, San Francisco ...... W	4
Dec.	30—Pal Bayardo, San Francisco .... KO	1

1926

Jan.	13—Jimmy Dwyer, San Francisco ...... W	6
Feb.	5—Fred Bindon, San Francisco ...... W	4
Feb.	12—Johnny Lawson, San Francisco ... KO	3
Feb.	19—Johnny Fiske, San Francisco ..... KO	4
Mar.	23—Jimmy Briggs, San Rafael .... KO	8
Apr.	30—Sydney White, San Francisco ..... W	6
May	12—Sydney White, San Francisco ..... D	10
Nov.	12—Sydney White, San Francisco ..... W	6
Nov.	26—Davie Flash, San Francisco ...... KO	4
Dec.	17—Lou Richards, San Francisco ..... KO	5
Dec.	21—Joe French, San Francisco .... W	6

1927

Jan.	7—Leonardo Garcia, San Francisco ... W	6
Jan.	28—California Joe Lynch, San Francisco W	6
Apr.	1—Ollie Bartlett, San Francisco ...... W	6
Apr.	22—Billy Evans, San Francisco .... KO	9
May	25—Joe Pimenthal, San Francisco ..... W	10
June	1—Dynamite Murphy, Oakland ... KO by	4
July	4—Georgie Lee, Reno, Nev. .... W	6
Aug.	26—Santiago Zorilla, San Francisco .... D	10
Sept.	23—Tommy O'Brien, San Francisco ... KO	7

1928

Jan.	17—Vic Foley, Seattle, Wash. ....: L	6
Feb.	3—Charley Miller, San Francisco .... KO	3
Feb.	10—Midget Mike O'Dowd, San Fran. KO by	3
Mar.	23—California Joe Lynch, San Francisco W	4
Apr.	19—California Joe Lynch, Stockton ..... D	10
June	4—Ignacio Fernandez, San Francisco .. W	10
June	20—Bobby Herman, San Francisco .... KO	6
Aug.	1—Charley Miller, San Francisco .... KO	4
Sept.	6 Sydney White, El Cerrito W	10

Oct.	2—Willie Gordon, Portland, Oregon ... W	10
Oct.	17—California Joe Lynch, San Francisco D	10
Dec.	14—Bobby Herman, San Francisco ..... W	6

1929

Jan.	30—Battling Bullahan, San Francisco .. W	10
Mar.	14—Bert Foster, Sacramento .... W	10
Mar.	27—Charley Miller, Reno, Nev. .... D	10
Apr.	24—Charley Miller, San Francisco .... KO	8
May	24—Bert Foster, San Francisco .... KO	3
June	14—Red Humphries, San Francisco .... W	10
July	5—Tommy Fielding, San Francisco .... W	10
Nov.	22—Huerta Evans, San Francisco ..... W	10
Nov.	29—Ignacio Fernandez, Los Angeles.... W	10

1930

Jan.	3—Maurice Holtzer, Hollywood L	10
Mar.	6—Ward Sparks, San Francisco ...... W	10
June	13—Eddie Graham, San Francisco .... KO	6
Sept.	3—Jackie Spencer, Reno, Nev. .... NC	10
Nov.	4—Bobby Gray, San Jose .... KO	7
Nov.	18—Joe Noto, San Jose .... KO	8
Nov.	23—Harry Wallace, Eureka .... KO	1
Dec.	14—Joe Noto, Eureka .... W	6
Dec.	19—Santiago Zorilla, San Francisco .... D	4

1931

Jan.	16—Santiago Zorilla, San Francisco .... D	10
Jan.	24—Ramon Montoya, Hollywood .... W	6
Feb.	20—Ramon Montoya, Los Angeles ..... W	10
Mar.	13—Bobby Pacho, Hollywood .... W	10
May	14—Pierre Pothier, Klamath Falls ..... W	10
June	—Johnny Christmas, Santa Rosa ... KO	8
July	14—Benny Gallup, Santa Rosa .... W	10
Aug.	20—Joe Noto, San Rafael .... W	10
Sept.	3—Joe Noto, Vallejo .... W	10
Sept.	11—Varias Milling, Hollywood .... W	10
Nov.	25—Buddy Ryan, San Francisco .... W	10

1932

Feb.	4—Hymie Miller, Sacramento .... WF	7
May	18—Young Peter Jackson, San Francisco L	10
July	18—Tony Falco, New York .... D	8
Oct.	7—Bobby Pacho, New York .... D	8

1933

Jan.	10—Paolo Villa, New York .... W	10
Jan.	13—Lou Jallos, New York .... W	5
Feb.	3—Tony Melore, New York .... KO	6
Mar.	2—Tony Scarpati, Brooklyn .... W	6
Mar.	25—Patsy Rubinetti, Brooklyn .... W	6
Apr.	8—Pete Gullotta, Brooklyn L	6
May	19—Tony Scarpati, New York .... KO	3
May	27—Johnny Bonito, Brooklyn .... W	6
June	1—Ernie Tedesco, Brooklyn .... KO	5
June	5—Pedro Nieves, Jersey City .... KO	4
Aug.	12—Joey Kaufman, Brooklyn .... W	6
Aug.	29—Al Cuillo, Brooklyn .... D	6
Sept.	8—Eddie Cool, Baltimore .... W	10
Sept.	18—Tony Falco, Baltimore .... W	10
Oct.	28—Tony Canzoneri, Brooklyn L	10
Nov.	13—Jimmy Leto, Holyoke L	10
Nov.	27—Eddie Cool, Philadelphia L	10
Dec.	25—Kid Chocolate, Philadelphia ...... KO	7
	(Won World Junior Lightweight Title)	

1934

Jan.	22—Frankie Wallace, Cleveland L	10
Mar.	5—Barney Ross, San Francisco .... D	10
	(For World Junior Welterweight Title)	
June	28—Tony Canzoneri, Brooklyn ..... KO by	9
July	31—Cleto Locatelli, Philadelphia L	10
Nov.	2—Harry Dublinsky, New York .... W	10

1935

Jan.	28—Barney Ross, Miami L	10
	(For World Junior Welterweight Title)	
June	10—Tony Canzoneri, Washington L	12
Aug.	19—Tony Canzoneri, San Francisco L	10
Nov.	22—Al Roth, New York .... W	10

1936

Jan.	3—Lou Ambers, New York L	10
Apr.	30—Indian Hurtado, New York .... W	10
June	8—Pedro Montanez, New York L	10
July	20—Jimmy Vaughn, Louisville L	10
Aug.	3—Howard Scott, Washington L	10
Aug.	24—Eddie Zivic, Pittsburgh L	10

| Sept. | 1—Jimmy Garrison, Kansas City ...... | L | 10 |
| Nov. | 13—Enrico Venturi, New York .... | L | 10 |

1937

| May | 4—Henry Armstrong, Los Angeles | KO by | 4 |
| Sept. | 27—Billy Beauhold, New York .... | L | 10 |

1938

| Jan. | 17—Felix Garcia, New York .... | W | 8 |
| Mar. | 17—Johnny Bellus, New Haven .... | L | 10 |

1939

| Jan. | 13—Clever Henry, Honolulu .... | L | 10 |

1940-1942
(Inactive)

1943

| Feb. | 19—Al Citrino, San Francisco .... | D | 8 |
| Apr. | 16—Al Citrino, San Francisco .... | L | 8 |

TB	KO	WD	WF	D	LD	LF	KO BY	ND	NC
118	24	54	1	12	22	0	4	0	1

SANDY SADDLER
(Record Under Featherweight Champions)

HAROLD GOMES
(Harold James Gomes)
Born, August 22, 1933, Providence, R.I. Weight, 126-130 lbs. Height, 5 ft. 5 in. Ancestry, Portuguese-Greek. Managed by Sammy Richman and Frank Travis.

1951

Sept.	17—Kobilly Pierre, Providence	KO	2
Oct.	15—Paul Hallie, Providence	KO	2
Nov.	5—Manuel Baptista, Providence	KO	2
Nov.	26—Al Duarte, Providence	W	4
Dec.	10—Billy Cruz, Providence	KO	3

1952

Feb.	4—Al Duarte, Providence	KO	2
Mar.	3—Don Nelson, Providence	W	4
Mar.	10—Don Nelson, Providence	W	4
Mar.	31—Manuel Baptista, Providence	W	6
Apr.	21—Tommy Tibbs, Providence	W	6
May	7—George Araujo, Providence	Exh.	3
May	12—Tommy Tibbs, Providence	W	6
Dec.	1—Manuel Baptista, Providence	W	6
Dec.	29—Mickey Devano, Providence	KO	2

1953

Feb.	2—Tommy Tibbs, Providence	W	8
Apr.	6—Bob Davis, Providence	KO	3
May	6—Filberto Osario, Fall River	W	10
June	12—Art Mullin, New York	W	4
Sept.	10—George Allen, Boston	KO	2
Sept.	28—Art Mullin, Providence	W	6
Nov.	5—Bobby Chabot, Fall River	KO	5
Dec.	10—Stony Gaudette, Fall River	KO	1

1954

Jan.	28—Tommy Tibbs, Fall River	L	10
Mar.	1—Young Saint, Boston	KO	3
Mar.	15—Johnny O'Brien, Boston	W	12
	(Won New England Featherweight Title)		
Apr.	10—Black Pico, Boston	KO	10
May	11—Bill Bossio, Boston	W	10
June	12—Tommy Tibbs, Boston	KO by	10
July	12—Joe Wilkinson, Boston	W	10
Oct.	5—Tommy Tibbs, Boston	KO by	9

1955

Mar.	28—Art Mullin, Brockton	W	8
Oct.	24—Jimmy Ithia, Providence	KO	7
Nov.	7—Sergio Penalver, Providence	KO	2
Nov.	28—Carlo Fusco, Providence	W	10

1956

Jan.	9—Joe Wilkinson, Providence	KO	5
Feb.	6—Pat Marcune, Providence	KO	9
Mar.	12—Johnny O'Brien, Providence	W	12
Apr.	16—Dom Sacco, Providence	KO	4
Oct.	29—Charley McGarrity, Providence ..	KO	10
Nov.	12—Segundo Perez, New Britain	KO	3

1957

Apr.	24—Bobby Rogers, Providence	KO	9
July	12—Lulu Perez, Cleveland	KO	6
Aug.	28—Isidro Martinez, Boston	L	10

1958

Jan.	20—Harold Smith, New York	KO	7
Mar.	7—Ike Chestnut, New York	W	10
Oct.	14—Johnny Bean, Holyoke	W	10
Oct.	28—Louis Carmona, Holyoke	W	10

1959

Mar.	27—Paul Jorgensen, Miami Beach	W	10
June	29—Jimmy Kelly, Providence	KO	3
July	20—Paul Jorgensen, Providence	W	15
	(Won Vacant World Junior Lightweight Title)		
Oct.	2—Jay Fullmer, Providence	W	10

1960

Mar.	16—Flash Elorde, Manila	KO by	7
	(Lost World Junior Lightweight Title)		
Aug.	17—Flash Elorde, San Francisco ...	KO by	1
	(For World Junior Lightweight Title)		

1961
(Inactive)

1962

Feb.	27—Paul Alba, Houston	KO	2
May	25—Lalo Guerrero, Los Angeles	W	10
July	10—Johnny Bean, New Bedford	W	10
Sept.	19—Daniel Berrios, Miami Beach	W	10
Oct.	18—Johnny Bizzarro, Erie	L	10

1963

Apr.	19—Valerio Nunez, Milan	KO by	5
Oct.	8—Frankie Taylor, London	KO by	9
Oct.	29—Dave Coventry, London	KO by	1

TB	KO	WD	WF	D	LD	LF	KO BY	ND	NC
60	24	26	0	0	3	0	7	0	0

GABRIEL (FLASH) ELORDE
Born, March 22, 1935, Bogo, Cebu, Philippines. Weight, 118-135 lbs. Height, 5 ft. 6 in. Southpaw. Managed by Lope Sarreal.

1951

June	16—Kid Gonzaga, Cebu City ....•.	KO	4
June	23—Young Basilian, Cebu City	KO	3
June	30—Mike Sanchez, Cebu City	W	5
July	14—Kid Santos, Cebu City	KO	5
July	28—Star Mercado, Cebu City	KO	1
Aug.	11—Fighting Echaves, Cebu City	KO	1
Sept.	8—Little Patilla, Cebu City	KO	6
Sept.	15—Star Flores, Cebu City	W	10
Oct.	31—Kid Independence, Cebu City ..	KO by	10
Dec.	1—Lucky Strike, Cebu City	KO	5

1952

Jan.	30—Tenejeros Boy, Davao City	W	8
Feb.	24—Little Dundee, Davao City	L	8
Mar.	16—Tommy Romulo, Davao City	D	10
May	3—Benny Escobar, Caloocan	W	8
May	10—Paulito Escarlan, Caloocan	W	8
May	31—Tanny Campo, Caloocan	W	10
July	26—Tanny Campo, Manila	W	12
	(Won Filipino Bantamweight Title)		
Aug.	12—Little Dundee, Davao City	KO	4
	(Retained Filipino Bantamweight Title)		
Oct.	18—Horishi Hiroguchi, Tokyo	W	12
	(Won Oriental Bantamweight Title)		
Nov.	18—Akiyoshi Akanuma, Tokyo	D	12
	(Retained Oriental Bantamweight Title)		

1953

Feb.	18—Willie Brown, Manila	KO	4
Mar.	15—Al Cruz, Manila	W	10
May	20—Larry Bataan, Manila	L	12
	(For Oriental Featherweight Title)		
July	6—Akiyoshi Akanuma, Tokyo	W	12
	(Retained Oriental Bantamweight Title)		
Oct.	8—Noboru Tanaka, Tokyo	W	10
Nov.	25—Masashi Akiyama, Tokyo	L	10

1954

Jan.	21—Kiyoaki Nakanishi, Tokyo	W	10
Apr.	21—Hiroshi Okawa, Tokyo	W	10
June	—Relinquished Oriental bantamweight title.		
June	29—Shigeji Kaneko, Tokyo	L	12
	(For Oriental Featherweight Title)		
Aug.	5—Roy Higa, Tokyo	W	10
Aug.	18—Tommy Romulo, Manila	W	12
	(Won Filipino Lightweight Title)		

Nov.	20—Katsumi Kosaka, Manila .... KO 8

1955

Jan. 12—Masashi Akiyama, Tokyo .... L 10
Apr. 15—Severo Fuentes, Manila .... W 10
June 15—Leo Alonzo, Manila .... L 12
(Lost Filipino Lightweight Title)
July 20—Sandy Saddler, Manila .... W 10
Oct. 3—Shigeji Kaneko, Tokyo .... L 10

1956

Jan. 18—Sandy Saddler, San Francisco KO by 13
(For World Featherweight Title)
Apr. 23—Cleo Lane, San Francisco .... KO 1
May 8—Chico Rosa, Stockton, Calif. .... W 10
June 11—Gil Velarde, San Francisco ...... KO 7
June 26—Cecil Schoonmaker, Stockton ..... KO 9
July 24—Dave Gallardo, San Jose .... W 10
Aug. 22—Miguel Berrios, San Francisco ..... L 10
Oct. 16—Luke Sandovan, San Jose .... KO 2
Nov. 9—Miguel Berrios, New York .... L 10

1957

Feb. 5—Hidemi Wade, Osaka .... KO 5
Mar. 16—Tommy Romulo, Manila .... W 12
(Regained Filipino Lightweight Title)
Apr. 27—Hideto Kobayashi, Nagoya .... W 12
(Won Vacant Oriental Lightweight Title)
June 23—Omsap Laempapha, Bangkok ...... L 12
(Lost Oriental Lightweight Title)
Aug. 4—Salika Yontrakit, Bangkok .... KO 3
Sept. 24—Shigeji Kaneko, Tokyo .... L 10
Oct. 23—Leo Alonzo, Manila .... W 12
(Regained Filipino Lightweight Title)

1958

Mar. 2—Hiroshi Okawa, Tokyo .... W 12
(Regained Oriental Lightweight Title)
May 3—Javellana Kid, Manila .... W 12
(Retained Oriental Lightweight Title)
May 17—Paulito Escarlan, Manila .... Exh. 6
June 10—Ike Chestnut, Honolulu .... W 10
Sept. 2—Hisao Kobayashi, Tokyo .... W 12
(Retained Oriental Lightweight Title)
Nov. 15—Keiichi Ishikawa, Manila .... KO 6
(Retained Oriental Lightweight Title)
Dec. 27—Seichiro Nakaniski, Manila ...... KO 4

1959

Feb. 6—Takeo Sugimori, Tokyo .... W 12
(Retained Oriental Lightweight Title)
Feb. 23—Paolo Rosi, San Francisco .... L 10
Mar. 31—Teddy Davis, Stockton .... W 10
May 25—Sonny Leon, Caracas .... W 10
June 15—Vicente Rivas, Caracas .... L 10
July 29—Solomon Boysaw, Cleveland .... L 10
Oct. 7—Hisao Kobayashi, Tokyo .... W 12
(Retained Oriental Lightweight Title)
Dec. 15—Nursery Kid, Manila .... W 10

1960

Mar. 16—Harold Gomes, Quezon City ...... KO 7
(Won World Junior Lightweight Title)
July 9—Hachiro Ito, Manila .... KO 5
Aug. 17—Harold Gomes, San Francisco .... KO 1
(Retained World Junior Lightweight Title)
Oct. 17—Sakuji Shinozawa, Manila .... W 12
(Retained Oriental Lightweight Title)
Dec. 16—Vicente Rivas, Manila .... W 10

1961

Mar. 19—Joey Lopes, Manila .... W 15
(Retained World Junior Lightweight Title)
May 31—Giordano Campari, Manila .... W 10
Dec. 16—Sergio Caprari, Manila .... KO 1
(Retained World Junior Lightweight Title)

1962

Mar. 10—Somkiat Katmuangyon, Manila .. KO 2
(Retained Oriental Lightweight Title)
Apr. 30—Teruo Kosaka, Tokyo .... L 12
(Lost Oriental Lightweight Title)
June 23—Auburn Copeland, Manila .... W 15
(Retained World Junior Lightweight Title)
Aug. 4—Teruo Kosaka, Cebu City .... W 12
(Regained Oriental Lightweight Title)
Nov. 17—Isarasak Puntainorasing, Manila KO 3
Dec. 21—Solomon Boysaw, Manila .... W 10

1963

Feb. 16—Johnny Bizzarro, Manila .... W 15
(Retained World Junior Lightweight Title)
June 1—Tsunstomi Miyamoto, Manila .... KO 9
(Retained Oriental Lightweight Title)
Aug. 3—Love Allotey, Manila .... W 10
Nov. 16—Love Allotey, Quezon City .... W disq. 11
(Retained World Junior Lightweight Title)

1964

Feb. 15—Carlos Ortiz, Manila .... KO by 14
(For World Lightweight Title)
May 8—Tawashi Maisumoto, Manila .... W 12
(Retained Oriental Lightweight Title)
July 27—Teruo Kosaka, Tokyo .... KO 12
(Retained World Junior Lightweight Title)
Nov. 21—Kang-Il Suh, Manila .... W 12
(Retained Oriental Lightweight Title)

1965

Feb. 27—Rene Barrientos, Manila .... W 12
June 5—Teruo Kosaka, Quezon City ...... KO 15
(Retained World Junior Lightweight Title)
Aug. 5—Frankie Narvaez, New York .... W 10
Dec. 4—Kang-Il Suh, Quezon City .... W 15
(Retained World Junior Lightweight Title)

1966

Mar. 19—Ismael Laguna, Tokyo .... W 10
June 9—Yoshiaki Numata, Tokyo .... L 12
(Lost Oriental Lightweight Title)
Aug. 7—Percy Hayles, Quezon City .... W 10
Oct. 22—Vicente Derado, Quezon City ...... W 15
(Retained World Junior Lightweight Title)
Nov. 14—Carlos Ortiz, New York .... KO by 14
(For World Lightweight Title)

1967

Feb. 2—Kang-Il Suh, Manila .... W 10
Apr. 25—Fujio Mikami, Honolulu .... W 10
June 15—Yoshiaki Numata, Tokyo .... L 15
(Lost World Junior Lightweight Title)
Oct. 28—Akihisa Someya, Manila .... L 10

1968

(Inactive)

1969

Feb. 15—Eugenio Espinosa, Quito, Ecuador .. L 10
Apr. 26—Jaguar Kakizama, Quezon City ... L 10

1970

June 27—Kenji Iwata, Manila .... W 10
Aug. 28—Chico Andrade, Manila .... KO 5
Oct. 31—Tatsunao Mitsuyama, Quezon City W 10

1971

Feb. 14—Isao Ichihara, Quezon City .... KO 6
May 20—Hiroyuki Murakami, Tokyo .... L 10

TB	KO	WD	WF	D	LD	LF	KO BY	ND	NC
109	29	52	1	2	21	0	4	0	0

YOSHIAKI NUMATA

Born, April 19, 1945, Tomikawa-cho, Sara-Gun, Hokkaido, Japan. Weight, 126-135 lbs. Height, 5 ft. 7½ in. Managed by Iwao Kodaka.

1962

July 26—Toshio Aida, Tokyo .... KO 3
Aug. 22—Kaoru Narita, Tokyo .... W 4
Oct. 18—Kazuji Toji, Tokyo .... KO 1
Nov. 8—Nabuyoshi Nagasaki, Tokyo ...... W 2
Nov. 24—Tadao Abe, Tokyo .... W 4

1963

Jan. 4—Hiroshi Kaneko, Tokyo .... KO 1
Feb. 5—Susumu Akimoto, Tokyo .... W 4
Mar. 7—Yasushi Matsuzoe, Tokyo .... W 4
Apr. 11—Tatsuo Hokkai, Tokyo .... W 4
May 9—Kuniaki Masuda, Tokyo .... KO 2
May 30—Katsuhiro Sugawara, Tokyo ...... KO 6
July 11—Noriyoshi Toyoshima, Tokyo ...... W 4
Sept. 12—Kenzo Shimakura, Tokyo .... KO 3
Nov. 7—Katsuzo Nakamura, Tokyo .... W 10
Dec. 19—Yasuyuki Orito, Tokyo .... W 10

1964

Mar. 10—Pedro Adigue, Tokyo .... W 10

Apr. 23—Byang Chun, Tokyo .... W 10
May 28—Lennie Campos, Tokyo .... W 10,
July 30—Larry Fernando, Sapporo .... W 10
Sept. 3—Katsuo Yabe, Tokyo .... KO 4
Nov. 5—Atom Harai, Tokyo .... KO 4,
Dec. 3—Takeo Sugimori, Tokyo .... W 10
1965
Jan. 28—Young-Pal Lee, Tokyo .... W 10
Apr. 1—Larry Flaviano, Sapporo .... W 12
  (Won Oriental Junior Lightweight Title)
May 20—Hidemori Tsujimoto, Tokyo .... W 10
July 29—Yuji Amashima, Tokyo .... KO by 4
Nov. 11—Antonio Paiva, Tokyo .... W 10
Dec. 23—Love Allotey, Tokyo .... KO by 4
1966
Feb. 10—Kang-Il Suh, Tokyo .... L 10
Mar. 24—Chong-Tae Lim, Oita .... KO 2
  (Retained Oriental Junior Lightweight Title)
June 9—Flash Elorde, Tokyo .... W 12
  (Won Oriental Lightweight Title)
July 4—Relinquished Oriental lightweight title.
Aug. 11—Kid Rosario, Tokyo .... L 10
Oct. 10—Kid Rosario, Tokyo .... W 12
  (Retained Oriental Junior Lightweight Title)
1967
Jan. 12—Ju-Yi Kwang, Tokyo .... W 10
Mar. 23—Chokchai Krischai, Oita .... W 10
June 15—Flash Elorde, Tokyo .... W 15
  (Won World Junior Lightweight Title)
Oct. 5—Yi-Sae Chung, Sapporo .... W 10
Dec. 14—Hiroshi Kobayashi, Tokyo ..... KO by 12
  (Lost World Junior Lightweight Title)
1968
Mar. 21—Hajime Iwata, Tokyo .... W 10
June 13—Kang-Il Suh, Tokyo .... KO 7
  (Retained Oriental Junior Lightweight Title)
Sept. 12—Rosalava Kid, Tokyo .... W 10
Dec. 5—Ruben Navarro, Tokyo .... D 10
1969
Apr. 2—Relinquished Oriental junior lightweight title.
Apr. 24—Jun Koiwa, Tokyo .... D 10
July 17—Ricardo Bermisa, Tokyo .... W 10
Oct. 4—Mando Ramos, Los Angeles ... KO by 6
  (For World Lightweight Title)
Nov. 27—Jun Koiwa, Kumamoto City ...... KO 2
1970
Jan. 1—Sumio Nobata, Tokyo .... D 10
Apr. 5—Rene Barrientos, Tokyo .... W 15
  (Won WBC Junior Lightweight Title)
June 13—Jung-Bok Lee, Tomakomai .... W 10
Aug. 16—Raymond Rivera, Tokyo .... W 10
Sept. 27—Raul Rojas, Tokyo .... KO 5
  (Retained WBC Junior Lightweight Title)
1971
Jan. 3—Rene Barrientos, Shizuoka .... W 15
  (Retained WBC Junior Lightweight Title)
May 30—Lionel Rose, Hiroshima ......'.... W 15
  (Retained WBC Junior Lightweight Title)
Oct. 10—Ricardo Arrendondo, Sendai ... KO by 10
  (Lost WBC Junior Lightweight Title)
1972
Mar. 2—Kenji Iwata, Tokyo .... KO by 3

TB	KO	WD	WF	D	LD	LF	KO BY	ND	NC
55	14	30	0	3	2	0	6	0	0

HIROSHI KOBAYASHI
Born, August 23, 1944, Isesaki, Gumma, Japan. Weight, 125-130 lbs. Height, 5 ft. 6½ in. Managed by Shinichi Nakamura.
1962
July 2—Hisatsugu Kyoya, Tokyo .... W 4
July 13—Michio Ishii, Tokyo .... KO 2
July 30—Yuji Takase, Tokyo .... W 4
Aug. 20—Saburo Yanagi, Tokyo .... W 4
Sept. 11—Kiyokazu Komura, Tokyo .... W 4
Sept. 25—Kazuyoshi Ohashi, Tokyo .... W 4
Oct. 16—Masayoshi Otake, Tokyo .... W 4

Nov. 7—Kazuo Hayaseko, Tokyo .... W 4
Nov. 29—Saburo Yanagi, Tokyo .... W 4
Dec. 15—Hisao Omori, Tokyo .... W 4
Dec. 31—Noriyoshi Toyoshima, Tokyo ...... W 6
1963
Jan. 28—Tsutomu Yoshida, Tokyo .... W 6
Feb. 19—Isamu Kato, Tokyo .... W 6
Mar. 18—Hideo Fukuchi, Tokyo .... W 6
Apr. 4—Kazuhiro Furuya, Tokyo .... W 6
May 2—Teruo Hino, Tokyo .... W 8
May 13—Yuji Masuko, Tokyo .... KO 2
June 24—Tommy Barahaja, Tokyo .... W 10
Aug. 19—Manzo Kikuchi, Tokyo .... L 10
Nov. 2—Johnny Jamito, Manila .... KO by 6
1964
Jan. 25—Kang-Il Suh, Tokyo .... L 10
Feb. 20—Lalo Guerrero, Tokyo .... L 10
Apr. 6—Porte Villa, Tokyo .... W 10
Apr. 25—Mitsunori Seki, Tokyo .... W 10
July 9—Dong-Chun Lee, Tokyo .... W 10
Sept. 28—Yugi Masuko, Tokyo .... W 10
  (Won Japanese Featherweight Title)
Nov. 9—Atsushi Gunzi, Tokyo .... W 10
Dec. 12—Hyon Kim, Maebashi .... W 10
1965
Jan. 18—Yugi Masuko, Tokyo .... W 10
  (Retained Japanese Featherweight Title)
Mar. 1—Soo-Bok Kwan, Tokyo .... KO 7
May 9—Shigeo Shioyama, Tokyo .... W 10
  (Retained Japanese Featherweight Title)
June 27—Chong-Tai Lim, Tokyo .... W 10
July 18—Kunio Sakata, Tokyo .... W 10
Aug. 30—Atsushi Gunzi, Tokyo .... W 10
Sept. 23—Hyon Kim, Tokyo .... W 10
Oct. 29—Sugar Carreon, Tokyo .... W 10
Dec. 9—Orlando Medina, Tokyo .... W 10
1966
Jan. 27—Katsutoshi Aoki, Tokyo .... W 10
Feb. 28—Shigeo Shioyama, Fukuoka City ... W 10
  (Retained Japanese Featherweight Title)
Mar. 31—Hiroshi Mori, Tokyo .... W 10
May 14—Jaime Valladares, Quito .... D 10
May 30—Freddy Rengifo, Caracas .... L 10
June 25—Pedro Gomez, Caracas .... KO by 7
July 3—Fino Rasales, Culiacan .... KO 9
July 10—Aurelio Cazares, Sinaloa .... D 10
Aug. 18—Bobby Valdez, Los Angeles .... KO 7
Oct. 10—Nobuo Chiba, Tokyo .... W 10
Nov. 10—Sumio Nobata, Nagoya .... W 10
  (Retained Japanese Featherweight Title)
Nov. 28—Del Rosario Kid, Tokyo .... W 10
1967
Jan. 17—Chun-Kyo Shin, Tokyo .... W 10
Feb. 2—Kang-Il Suh, Tokyo .... W 10
Feb. 27—Vicente Derado, Tokyo .... W 10
May 8—Takao Mihashi, Tokyo .... W 10
  (Retained Japanese Featherweight Title)
June 26—Dony Tesorio, Fukushima .... W 10
Sept. 4—Soo-Yun Chang, Tokyo .... KO 7
Oct. 16—Ki-Chin Song, Tokyo .... KO 8
Dec. 14—Yoshiaki Numata, Tokyo .... KO 12
  (Won World Junior Lightweight Title)
1968
Mar. 30—Rene Barrientos, Tokyo .... D 15
  (Retained World Junior Lightweight Title)
June 20—Mando Ramos, Los Angeles .... L 10
July 21—Ulysses Botero, Tokyo .... KO 10
Aug. 26—Ruben Navarro, Tokyo .... L 10
Oct. 6—Jaime Valladares, Tokyo .... W 15
  (Retained World Junior Lightweight Title)
1969
Jan. 27—Toro George, Tokyo .... W 10
Apr. 6—Antonio Amaya, Tokyo .... W 15
  (Retained World Junior Lightweight Title)
July 7—Victor Ramos, Tokyo .... KO 2
Nov. 9—Carlos Canete, Tokyo .... W 15
  (Retained World Junior Lightweight Title)
1970
Feb. 15—Hiroshi Shoji, Tokushima .... D 10
June 21—Ray Adigun, Tokyo .... W 10

Aug.	23—Antonio Amaya, Tokyo .... W 15

(Retained World Junior Lightweight Title)

Dec. 3—Shozo Saijyo, Tokyo .... W 10

1971

Mar. 3—Ricardo Arrendondo, Tokyo .... W 15
(Retained World Junior Lightweight Title)

July 29—Alfredo Marcano, Aomori ..... KO by 10
(Lost World Junior Lightweight Title)

TB	KO	WD	WF	D	LD	LF	KO BY	ND	NC
72	10	49	0	4	6	0	3	0	0

IRENEO (RENE) BARRIENTOS
Born. February. 1942. Balite. Aklan. Philippines.
Weight. 130-135 lbs. Southpaw.

1962

Oct. 2—Charlie Kid. Tupi. Cotabato ...... KO 2

1963

(Record Not Available)

1964

Jan. 25—Arthur Fuego. Cagayan de Oro ... KO 3

Mar. 28—Sampandh Laemfapha.
Cagayan de Oro .... L 10

May 3—Rudy Perucho. Davao City .... KO 8

June 27—Koshiro Shimoji. Davao City ...... W 10

Aug. 25—Arthur Fuego. Cagayan de Oro ... KO 3

Sept. 19—Young Terror. Cagayan de Oro .... W 12
(Won Filipino Junior Lightweight Title)

Oct. 31—Joe Flash Juezan. Cebu .... W 10

1965

Jan. 16—Francisco Balug. Cebu .... W 10

Feb. 27—Flash Elorde. Manila .... L 12
(For Oriental Lightweight Title)

May 15—Carl Penalosa. Cebu .... KO 4

June 19—Carl Penalosa. Cebu .... W 10

Aug. 2—Larry Flaviano. Manila .... KO 7

Oct. 2—Noriyoshi Toyoshima. Luzon City .. W 10

Nov. 20—Love Allotey. Manila .... W 10

1966

Jan. 1—Ric Penalos. Manila .... W 3

Jan. 1—Baby Paramount. Manila .... W 3

Jan. 1—Ely Yares. Manila .... W 3

Feb. 19—Young Terror. Quezon City .... KO 3

Aug. 26—Raymond Rivera. Cagayan de Oro W 12
(Retained Filipino Junior Lightweight Title)

Oct. 1—Kang-Il Suh. Manila .... W 10

1967

Jan. 21—Pedro Adigue. Manila .... L 12
(For Oriental Lightweight Title)

Feb. 17—Pedro Adigue. Manila .... D 10

Apr. 29—Raymond Rivera. Davao City ...... W 12
(Retained Filipino Junior Lightweight Title)

June 19—Francisco Bolivar. Caracas .... W 10

July 22—Antonio Amaya. Panama City ..... L 10

Oct. 23—Koji Okana. Chiba City .... W 10

Nov. 13—Sumio Nobata. Tokyo .... KO 6

1968

Jan. 14—Herbert Kang. Manila .... W 10

Mar. 30—Hiroshi Kobayashi. Tokyo .... D 15
(For World Junior Lightweight Title)

June 22—Antonio Amaya. Manila .... KO 10

1969

Feb. 15—Ruben Navarro. Manila .... W 15
(Won Vacant WBC Junior Lightweight Title)

Apr. 16—Len Kesey. Honolulu .... KO 9

July 29—Adolph Pruitt. Honolulu ...... KO by 8

Dec. 20—Eugenio Espinosa. Manila .... W 10

1970

Apr. 5—Yoshiaki Numata. Tokyo .... L 15
(Lost WBC Junior Lightweight Title)

June 6—Shinichi Kodota. Manila .... W 10

Aug. 14—Saleman Ithianuchit. Manila ..... KO 8
(Won Oriental Junior Lightweight Title)

Sept. 30—Roger Zami. Honolulu .... KO 8

Oct. 30—Ishimatsu Suzuki. Honolulu .... W 10

1971

Jan. 3—Yoshiaki Numata. Shizuoka .... L 15
(For WBC Junior Lightweight Title)

June 4—Tatenao Mitsuyama. Manila ..... KO 4

1972

June 7—Armando Zerqua, Honolulu ...... KO 9

July 25—Javier Ayala, Honolulu .... W 10

TB	KO	WD	WF	D	LD	LF	KO BY	ND	NC
44	13	22	0	2	6	0	1	0	0

ALFREDO MARCANO
Born. January 17. 1947. Sucre. Venezuela.

1966

Mar. 4—Pedro Chirinos. Caracas .... W 4

Apr. 2—Jose Ramon Arias, Caracas ...... KO 1

Apr. 29—Abraham Veliz. Caracas .... D 4

May 9—Abraham Veliz. Caracas .... D 4

May 30—Pedro Chirinos, Caracas .... W 6

July 23—Carlos Rojas. Caracas .... W 6

Aug. 19—Francisco Escalona. Caracas ...... L 6

Oct. 3—Pedro Escalona. Caracas .... W 6

Nov. 11—Martin Rivas. Caracas .... W 8

1967

Jan. 14—Aristidas Garcia. Cumana .... KO 2

Mar. 17—Nestor Rojas. Maracay .... L 8

May 12—Victor Palencia. Caracas .... KO 1

June 19—Nestor Rojas. Caracas .... D 8

July 18—Juan Conception. Maracay ...... KO 1

Sept. 9—Claudio Lopez. Cumana .... KO 2

Nov. 18—Emiliano Marron. Cumana ...... W 8

Nov. 30—Jose Ramon Arias. Caracas ..... KO 2

Dec. 11—Frank Leroy. Caracas .... KO 5

1968

Jan. 22—Arnaldo Lujan. Caracas .... KO 1

Apr. 5—Nestor Rojas. Caracas .... KO 3

June 7—Benny McCall. Caracas .... KO 3

July 19—Raymundo Vera. Caracas .... KO 2

Aug. 2—Jaime Perez. Caracas .... KO 7

Aug. 16—Francisco Bolivar. Caracas ...... KO 7

Sept. 14—Bernardo Caraballo. Caracas ... KO 7

Oct. 4—Enrique Higgins. Caracas .... KO 6

Oct. 28—Antonio Herrera. Caracas .... W 10

Nov. 25—Calvin Woodland. Caracas ...... KO 1

1969

Jan. 20—Miguel Botta. Caracas .... KO 10

Feb. 14—Miguel Herrera. Caracas .... KO 10

Mar. 7—Fernando Sotelo. Caracas ...... KO by 5

May 3—Rocky Orengo. Caracas .... W 10

June 13—Richard Sue. Caracas .... W 10

July 21—Ken Nagamine. Caracas .... KO 1

Aug. 15—Cruz Marcano. Caracas .... D 10

Sept. 29—Joel Gomez. Caracas .... W 10

Dec. 8—Ricardo Arredondo. Tijuana ..... L 10

1970

Jan. 1—Ricardo Arredondo. Mexicali ... W 10

Feb. 23—Raul Cruz. Tijuana .... KO by 7

June 25—Ray Vega. Los Angeles .... L 10

Sept. 17—Ray Vega. Los Angeles .... W 10

Oct. 31—Ernesto Marcel. Panama City ... L 10

1971

Mar. —Nobuo Chiba. Caracas .... KO 6

Apr. —Memo Morales. Caracas .... KO 3

May 4—Ernesto Marcel. Caracas .... L 10

July 29—Hiroshi Kobayashi. Aomori ..... KO 10

July 29—Hiroshi Kobayashi. Aomori ..... KO 10
(Won World Junior Lightweight Title)

Nov. 7—Kenji Iwata. Caracas .... KO 4
(Retained World Junior Lightweight Title)

1972

Apr. 25—Ben Villaflor. Honolulu .... L 15
(Lost World Junior Lightweight Title)

June 3—Flash Gallego. Caracas .... KO 4

Dec. 12—Raul Martinez Mora. Monterrey .. KO 3

1973

Jan. 31—Sumio Nabata. Caracas .... W 10

Aug. 4—Jose Salas. Maracaibo .... KO 3

Sept. 1—Herman Torres. Bogota .... NC 5

Sept. 3—Enrique Garcia. Caracas .... L 10

Sept. 29—Hernan Torres. Caracas .... KO 5

Nov. 17—Lupe Mendez. Caracas .... KO 1

1974

Feb. 9—Vicente Blanco. Caracas .... D 10

Mar.	15—Octavio Gomez, Maracaibo	W	10
Sept.	7—Bobby Chacon, Los Angeles ... KO by		9
	(For Vacant WBC Featherweight Title)		
Dec.	12—Ben Ortiz, Caracas	KO by	7
1975			
Mar.	22—Art Hafey, Caracas	KO by	4

TB	KO	WD	WF	D	LD	LF	KO BY	ND	NC
62	29	14	0	5	8	0	5	0	1

RICARDO ARRENDONDO
Born, 1951, Apatzingan, Michoacan, Mexico.

1966
Aug.	10—Manuel Justo, Mexico City	W	6
Sept.	—Ray Garcia, Tuxtla Gutierrez	KO	9
Oct.	3—Raul Anaya, Tuxtla Gutierrez	KO	3
Nov.	—Pichon Contreras, Mexico City W disq.		6

1967
Feb.	—Paul Mora, Mexico City	W	8
Mar.	—Pedro Torres, Mexico City	W	8
Apr.	22—Kid Clay, Mexico City	W	10
June	—Tino Anguiano, Apatzingan	KO	7
July	—Raul Anaya, Tuxtla Gutierrez	KO	2
Aug.	4—Clemente Sanchez, Nuevo Laredo ... L		10
Aug.	—Manuel Flores, Nuevo Laredo	KO	5
Sept.	—Sugar Pino, Guamuchil	KO	4
Oct.	—Jose Garcia, Tuxtla Gutierrez	KO	4
Nov.	22—Emilio Olvera, Mexico City	KO	4

1968
Jan.	6—Raul Cruz, Mexico City	L disq.	10
Feb.	18—Gustavo Sosa, Puebla	KO	5
Mar.	18—Luis Barrios, Managua	KO	6
Mar.	28—Kid Clay, Managua	KO	5
Apr.	20—Chuy Rocha, Monterrey	KO	5
May	18—Chucho Hernandez, Mexico City ..	KO	8
June	22—Alfredo Meneses, Mexico City	W	10
July	13—Chiquis Rosales, Mexico City	KO	8
July	27—Enrique Garcia, Mexico City	W	10
Sept.	7—Jose Luis Lopez, Mexico City	L	10
Oct.	10—Roberto San Martin, Obregon	KO	2
Nov.	7—Billy Brown, Los Angeles	KO	5
Nov.	30—Memo Tellez, Mexico City	W	10

1969
Jan.	19—Felipe Gonzalez, Mexicali	W	10
Feb.	21—Johnny Sandoval, Mexicali	KO	7
Mar.	10—Juan Baez, Tijuana	KO	4
Mar.	23—Esteban Favela, Mexicali	KO	3
Apr.	22—Flash Besande, Honolulu	W	10
May	26—Roberto Andrade, Tijuana	KO	6
June	14—Jalapa Montes, Apatzingan	KO	3
Aug.	16—Jorge Villanueva, Mexico City	KO	10
Sept.	13—Felipe Torres, Mexico City	W	10
Oct.	14—Curly Dequino, Honolulu	W	10
Nov.	20—Jet Parker, Obregon	W	10
Dec.	8—Alfredo Marcano, Tijuana	KO	10

1970
Jan.	1—Alfredo Marcano, Mexicali	L	10
Mar.	7—Roberto Santana, Mexico City	KO	2
Apr.	16—Ruben Ruiz, Torreon	KO	3
May	9—Joel Gomez, Mexico City	KO	4
July	18—Victor Echegaray, Mexico City	KO	1
Sept.	19—Enrique Garcia, Mexico City	KO	10
Oct.	24—Miguel Riasco, Mexico City	KO	6
Nov.	17—Sammy Goss, Philadelphia	KO	5
Dec.	2—Huracan Sanchez, Oaxaca	KO	1
Dec.	12—David Duran, Apatzingan	KO	4

1971
Jan.	18—Augie Pantellas, Philadelphia	KO	10
Mar.	3—Hiroshi Kobayashi, Tokyo	L	15
	(For World Junior Lightweight Title)		
May	9—Sigfrido Rodriguez, Aguascalientes	D	10
May	27—Pedro Valverde, Chihuahua	KO	4
June	20—Samuel Reyes, Jiquilpan de Juarez	KO	3
June	26—Gato Fajardo, Los Reyes	KO	4
July	9—Lenny Brown, Obregon	KO	2
Aug.	19—David Duran, Chihuahua	KO	4
Aug.	29—Enrique Pinto, Morelia	KO	2
Oct.	10—Yoshiaki Numata, Sendai, Japan	KO	10
	(Won WBC Junior Lightweight Title)		

1972
Jan.	29—Jose Issac Marin, San Jose, C.R.	W	15
	(Retained WBC Junior Lightweight Title)		
Apr.	22—William Martinez, Mexico City ...	KO	5
	(Retained WBC Junior Lightweight Title)		
Aug.	5—Jesus Alonso, Mexico City	KO	7
Sept.	15—Susumu Okabe, Tokyo	KO	12
	(Retained WBC Junior Lightweight Title)		

1973
Mar.	6—Apollo Yoshio, Fukuoka City	W	15
	(Retained WBC Junior Lightweight Title)		
May	28—Andres Steyn, Johannesburg	L	10
July	21—Jesus Alonso, Monterrey	L	10
Sept.	1—Morito Kashiwaba, Tokyo	KO	6
	(Retained WBC Junior Lightweight Title)		
Nov.	29—Yasutsune Uehara, Naha, Okinawa	L	10

1974
Feb.	28—Kuniaki Shibata, Tokyo	L	15
	(Lost WBC Junior Lightweight Title)		
Aug.	3—Alfredo Escalera, San Juan ... L disq.		8

1975
Feb.	15—Johnny Martinez, Morelia	KO	7
May	9—Miguel Aceves, Puebla	KO	2
May	30—Jose Luis Soberanes, Culiacan	W	10
July	19—Gil Becerra, La Paz	KO	6
Nov.	28—Ramiro Bolanos, Guataquil	L	10

1976
Jan.	25—Eleuterio Hernandez, Taqachula ..	KO	5
Feb.	23—Jean Baptiste Piedvache, Paris	L	10
Apr.	23—Jorge Martinez, Reynosa	KO	7
May	8—Ould Makhloufi, Algiers	L	10
June	26—Beto Gutierrez, Los Mochis	L	10
Aug.	22—Juan Rodriguez, Tuxpan	KO	3
Oct.	1—Leonardo Bermudez, Apatzingan ...	L	10
Nov.	14—Ernesto Espana, Caracas	L	10

1977
Mar.	24—Ramiro Bolanos, Los Angeles	L	10
June	10—Rogelio Castaneda, San Diego	L	10
Sept.	16—Miguel Montilla, Santo Domingo ...	L	10
Nov.	25—Carlos Gil, Santo Domingo	KO by	10

1978
| May | 26—Hans Henrik Palm, Copenhagen | KO by | 5 |

1979
| Feb. | 26—Robert Perez, Houston | KO | 4 |
| Mar. | 17—Sang-Hyun Kim, Seoul | KO by | 10 |

TB	KO	WD	WF	D	LD	LF	KO BY	ND	NC
90	50	16	1	1	17	2	3	0	0

BEN VILLAFLOR
Born, November 10, 1952, Negros, Philippines.
Weight, 130 lbs. Southpaw.

1968
| Feb. | —Rod Sario, Manila | W | 4 |
| May | —George Arindidon, Manila | D | 4 |

1969
July	7—Willy Cangas, Quezon City	W	10
Aug.	—Marcial Macatangay, Manila	KO	7
Oct.	4—Fil Del Mundo, Manila	W	10
Dec.	20—Arturo Eracho, Manila	W	10

1970
Feb.	28—Tony Jumao-as, Manila	TD	
Mar.	7—Pedro Martinez, Manila	L	10
May	—Alfredo Avila, Manila	L	10
June	6—Ernie Cruz, Quezon City	W	10
July	12—Willie Asuncion, Manila	W	10
July	25—Tony Jumao-as, Quezon City	W	10
Sept.	19—Don Johnson, Manila	KO	4
Nov.	14—Baby Lorona, Quezon City	W	10

1971
Apr.	13—Rafael Lopez, Honolulu	KO	1
Apr.	26—Memo Morales, Honolulu	KO	6
May	19—Jose Luis Martinez, Honolulu	KO	5
June	8—Delfino Camacho, Honolulu	KO	2
June	22—Jesus Mariscal, Honolulu	KO	4
July	6—Memin Hernandez, Honolulu	KO	1
Aug.	10—Manuel Mendoza, Honolulu	W	10

Sept.	14—Tad Okamoto, Honolulu	KO	1
Oct.	5—Ricardo Garcia, Honolulu	W	10
Nov.	16—Raul Cruz, Honolulu	KO	10
Dec.	14—Ray Vega, Inglewood	KO	7

1972

Jan.	26—Frankie Crawford, Honolulu	KO	1
Mar.	7—Jose Luis Lopez, Honolulu	KO	2
Apr.	25—Alfredo Marcano, Honolulu	W	15

(Won World Junior Lightweight Title)

July	5—Carlos Fernandez, Honolulu	KO	3
Sept.	5—Victor Echegaray, Honolulu	D	15

(Retained World Junior Lightweight Title)

Nov.	15—Jimmy Robertson, Honolulu	W	10

1973

Jan.	31—Juan Collado, Honolulu	W	10
Mar.	12—Kuniaki Shibata, Honolulu	L	15

(Lost World Junior Lightweight Title)

July	18—Kenji Iwata, Honolulu	KO	1
Aug.	21—Akhiro Kawaski, Honolulu	KO	3
Oct.	17—Kuniaki Shibata, Honolulu	KO	1

(Regained World Junior Lightweight Title)

1974

Mar.	14—Apollo Yoshio, Tokyo	D	15

(Retained World Junior Lightweight Title)

July	19—Takao Maruki, Manila	KO	7
Aug.	24—Yasutsune Uehara, Honolulu	KO	2

(Retained World Junior Lightweight Title)

1975

Mar.	10—Hyun-Chi Kim, Quezon City	W	15

(Retained World Junior Lightweight Title)

1976

Jan.	12—Morito Kashiwaba, Tokyo	KO	13

(Retained World Junior Lightweight Title)

Apr.	13—Samuel Serrano, Honolulu	D	15

(Retained World Junior Lightweight Title)

Aug.	31—Rogelio Castaneda, Honolulu	W	10
Oct.	16—Samuel Serrano, San Juan	L	15

(Lost World Junior Lightweight Title)

TB	KO	WD	WF	D	LD	LF	KO BY	ND	NC
44	20	15	0	5	4	0	0	0	0

KUNIAKI SHIBATA
(Record Under Featherweight Champions)

ALFREDO ESCALERA
Born, November 21, 1952, Carolina, Puerto Rico.

1970

Sept.	24—Bob Paysant, Portland, Me.	KO	3
Dec.	1—Rod Walsh, Scranton	W	4

1971

Jan.	26—Don McClendon, New York	L	6
Mar.	20—Willie Lugo, New York	W	6
Mar.	24—Jimmy Jaynes, Boston	W	6
July	26—Henry Ocasio, New York	W	6
Sept.	2—Eddie James, Baltimore	W	6
Sept.	7—Reynald Cantin, Sorel	W	10
Sept.	23—Edwin Viruet, Paterson	L	8
Oct.	25—Henry Ocasio, New York	W	6

1972

Feb.	15—Diego Alcala, New York	L	10
June	13—Alejandro Falcon, San Juan	KO	7
July	14—Carlos Penso, Ponce	KO	1
Sept.	18—Miguel Morales, San Juan	W	10

1973

Mar.	17—Miguel Montilla, Carolina	L	10
Mar.	31—Rocky Orengo, Carolina	W	10
Apr.	28—Gino Febus, Carolina	L	10
July	14—Miguel Montilla, Caguas	KO	8
July	21—Leo Randolph, San Juan	KO	2
Aug.	21—Frankie Otero, San Juan	KO	5
Sept.	15—Jose Luis Lopez, San Juan	KO	6
Nov.	12—Antonio Amaya, San Juan	W	10
Nov.	30—Mike Mayan, San Juan	KO	4
Dec.	17—Johnny Copeland, San Juan	KO	5
Feb.	1—Stanley Vanushook, San Juan	KO	2
Mar.	3—Sigfredo Rodriguez, San Juan	KO	1

Apr.	1—Jorge Ramos, San Juan	KO	3
May	30—Carlos Mendoza, San Juan	KO	8
Aug.	3—Ricardo Arredondo, San Juan	W disq.	8
Sept.	9—Oscar Pitton, San Juan	KO	5
Oct.	18—Eleuterio Hernandez, Pueblo	KO	8
Oct.	30—Memo Cruz, Oaxaca	L	10
Nov.	15—Rodriguez Valdez, Pueblo	KO	1
Dec.	14—Mario Roman, Mexico City	KO by	2

1975

Feb.	24—Mario Roman, San Juan	KO	3
Mar.	31—Francisco Villegas, San Juan	D	10
July	5—Kuniaki Shibata, Tokyo	KO	5

(Won WBC Junior Lightweight Title)

Sept.	20—Lionel Hernandez, Caracas	D	15

(Retained WBC Junior Lightweight Title)

Nov.	17—Gaetan Hart, San Juan	KO	6
Dec.	12—Sven-Erik Paulsen, Oslo	KO	9

(Retained WBC Junior Lightweight Title)

1976

Feb.	20—Jose Fernandez, San Juan	KO	13

(Retained WBC Junior Lightweight Title)

Apr.	1—Buzzsaw Yamabe, Nara	KO	6

(Retained WBC Junior Lightweight Title)

July	1—Buzzsaw Yamabe, Nara	W	15

(Retained WBC Junior Lightweight Title)

Sept.	18—Ray Lunny, San Juan	KO	12

(Retained WBC Junior Lightweight Title)

Nov.	30—Tyrone Everett, Philadelphia	W	15

(Retained WBC Junior Lightweight Title)

1977

Mar.	17—Ronnie McGarvey, San Juan	KO	6

(Retained WBC Junior Lightweight Title)

May	16—Carlos Becerril, Landover	KO	8

(Retained WBC Junior Lightweight Title)

Sept.	10—Sigfredo Rodriguez, San Juan	W	15

(Retained WBC Junior Lightweight Title)

1978

Jan.	28—Alexis Arguello, San Juan	KO by	13

(Lost WBC Junior Lightweight Title)

June	3—Rogelio Castaneda, San Juan	W	10
July	26—Larry Stanton, New York	KO	3
Oct.	27—Julio Valdez, New York	L	10

1979

Feb.	4—Alexis Arguello, Rimini	KO by	13

(For WBC Junior Lightweight Title)

Oct.	13—Antonio Cruz, San Juan	D	10

TB	KO	WD	WF	D	LD	LF	KO BY	ND	NC
54	26	14	1	3	7	0	3	0	0

SAMUEL SERRANO
Born, November 7, 1952, Toa Alta, Puerto Rico.
Weight, 126-130 lbs. Height, 5 ft. 8½ in.

1969

Nov.	1—Ramon Laureano, San Juan	KO	4
Nov.	13—Radames Pizarro, San Juan	W	4

1970

Jan.	17—Sammy Correa, San Juan	KO	3
Feb.	14—Modesto Escalera, San Juan	W	6
Mar.	14—Ramon Montes, San Juan	W	6
Mar.	30—Francisco Villegas, San Juan	W	12

(Won Puerto Rican Featherweight Title)

Apr.	11—Roberto Guerrero, San Juan	W	6
Apr.	15—Francisco Villegas, San Juan	L	12

(Lost Puerto Rican Featherweight Title)

Nov.	1—Modesto Concepcion, San Juan	W	8

1971

Jan.	27—Wilson Yambo, Ponce	W	8
July	3—Braulio Rodriguez, San Juan	W	10
Dec.	4—Angel Rivera, San Juan	W	10

1972

Apr.	8—Francisco Villegas, San Juan	L	12

(For Puerto Rican Featherweight Title)

1973

Feb.	16—Nestor Rojas, San Juan	W	10
Apr.	14—Terry Rondeau, Carolina	KO	2
June	9—Freddie Major, San Juan	KO	2
July	21—Jose Marin, San Juan	W	10
Dec.	8—Ernesto Marcel, Panama City	L	10

1974

Apr.	15—Lorenzo Trujillo, San Juan	W	10
July	15—Gustavo Briceno, San Juan	KO	10
July	24—Cocoa Sanchez, San Juan	W	10
Nov.	15—Memo Cruz, San Juan	W	10

1975

Apr.	13—Jose Pena, San Juan	W	10
June	28—Victor Echegaray, San Juan	W	10
Sept.	1—Ahmet Tosci, San Juan	KO	2
Oct.	11—Diego Alcala, Ponce	W	10
Dec.	13—Manuel Rodriguez, San Juan	KO	3

1976

Apr.	13—Ben Villaflor, Honolulu	D	15
	(For World Junior Lightweight Title)		
May	8—Mar Bassa, San Juan	KO	9
Sept.	10—Adrian Villanueva, San Juan	KO	3
Oct.	16—Ben Villaflor, San Juan	W	15
	(Won World Junior Lightweight Title)		

1977

Jan.	15—Alberto Herrera, Guayaquil	KO	11
	(Retained World Junior Lightweight Title)		
June	26—Leonel Hernandez, Puerto La Cruz	W	15
	(Retained World Junior Lightweight Title)		
Aug.	27—Apollo Yoshio, San Juan	W	15
	(Retained World Junior Lightweight Title)		
Nov.	19—Tae-Ho Kim, San Juan	KO	10
	(Retained World Junior Lightweight Title)		

1978

Feb.	18—Mario Martinez, San Juan	W	15
	(Retained World Junior Lightweight Title)		
July	8—Young-Ho Oh, San Juan	KO	9
	(Retained World Junior Lightweight Title)		
Nov.	29—Takao Maruki, Nagoya	W	15
	(Retained World Junior Lightweight Title)		

1979

Feb.	18—Julio Valdez, San Juan	W	15
	(Retained World Junior Lightweight Title)		
Apr.	14—Nkosana Mgxaji, Capetown	KO	8
	(Retained World Junior Lightweight Title)		

1980

Apr.	3—Kiyoshi Kazama, Nara, Japan	KO	13
	(Retained World Junior Lightweight Title)		
Aug.	2—Yasutsune Uehara, Detroit	KO by	6
	(Lost World Junior Lightweight Title)		
Sept.	20—Jesus Delgado, San Juan	KO	2

TB	KO	WD	WF	D	LD	LF	KO BY	ND	NC
43	15	23	0	1	3	0	1	0	0

ALEXIS ARGUELLO
(Record Under Featherweight Champions)

YASUTSUNE UEHARA
Born, October 12, 1949, Naha, Okinawa, Japan. Weight, 130 lbs. Height, 5 ft. 6½ in. Managed by Masaki Kanehira.

1972

Nov.	14—Sam Furachiseli, Honolulu	KO	4
Nov.	21—Mar Yuzon, Honolulu	L	6
Dec.	12—Shichiro Saito, Honolulu	W	6

1973

Feb.	13—Rudy Tolongari, Honolulu	KO	1
Mar.	12—Danny Campos, Honolulu	KO	6
June	14—Noriaki Yoshimura, Tokyo	KO	5
Aug.	4—Rocky Sawa, Naha, Okinawa	KO	6
Oct.	28—Tokichi Uehara, Tokyo	KO	3
Nov.	29—Ricardo Arrendondo, Naha, Okinawa	W	10

1974

Mar.	26—Kae-Shik Yua, Nagoya	KO	6
May	28—Hasaharu Tsuchiya, Tokyo	KO	1
Aug.	24—Ben Villaflor, Honolulu	KO by	2
	(For World Junior Lightweight Title)		
Nov.	30—Freddy Mason, Akita City	W	10

1975

July	21—Susumu Okabe, Tokyo	KO	1
	(Won Japanese Junior Lightweight Title)		

Oct.	19—Masa Ito, Naha, Okinawa	KO	5
	(Retained Japanese Junior Lightweight Title)		
Dec.	9—Susumu Okabe, Tokyo	KO	8
	(Retained Japanese Junior Lightweight Title)		

1976

Apr.	23—Masa Ito, Tokuyama	L	10
	(Lost Japanese Junior Lightweight Title)		
July	29—Masa Ito, Tokyo	W	10
	(Regained Japanese Junior Lightweight Title)		
Dec.	7—Joe Lim, Manila	L	10

1977

May	29—Shoji Okano, Naha, Okinawa	KO	2
	(Retained Japanese Junior Lightweight Title)		
Sept.	9—Suketoshi Maruyama, Nagoya	KO	6
Dec.	4—Tadashi Akiyama, Tokyo	KO	7
	(Retained Japanese Junior Lightweight Title)		

1978

Apr.	28—Ryu Fukida, Tokyo	KO	7
	(Retained Japanese Junior Lightweight Title)		
Aug.	9—Tatsuya Moriyasu, Omiya	KO	2
Nov.	25—Hideyoshi Horinaga, Tokyo	KO	2
	(Retained Japanese Junior Lightweight Title)		

1979

Feb.	27—Yosuhide Takahashi, Tokyo ...	KO	6
July	12—Yoshitaka Ikehara, Tokyo	W	10
	(Retained Japanese Junior Lightweight Title)		
Nov.	10—Kojiro Sasaki, Naha, Okinawa ...	KO	10
	(Retained Japanese Junior Lightweight Title)		

1980

Mar.	13—Junichi (Blazer) Okubo, Tokyo ...	KO	5
	(Retained Japanese Junior Lightweight Title)		
Aug.	2—Samuel Serrano, Detroit	KO	6
	(Won World Junior Lightweight Title)		
Nov.	20—Leonel Hernandez, Tokyo	W	15
	(Retained World Junior Lightweight Title)		

TB	KO	WD	WF	D	LD	LF	KO BY	ND	NC
31	21	6	0	0	3	0	1	0	0

RAFAEL (BAZOOKA) LIMON
Born, January 13, 1954, Mexico City, Mexico. Weight, 130 lbs. Southpaw.

1972

Dec.	5—Jose Garcia, Mexico City	KO	1

1973

Feb.	3—Raul Juarez, Mexico City	KO	5
Feb.	24—Joel Carmona, Mexico City	KO	1
Mar.	21—Magdaleno Andrette, Mexico City	KO	4
June	20—Carlos Mimila, Mexico City ...	KO by	2
Sept.	1—Ventura Perez, Mexico City	KO	1
Sept.	20—Juan Ordanez, Mexico City	KO by	4
Oct.	31—Canelo Salinas, Mexico City	L	8

1974

Jan.	19—Armando Estavez, Mexico City ...	KO	3
Mar.	9—Chamaco Casanova, Mexico City	KO	7
Apr.	7—Antonio Nava, Mexico City	KO by	3
June	1—Canelo Salinas, Mexico City	KO	3
July	20—Gaby Morgan, Mexico City	L	10
Sept.	14—Jose Pesos, Mexico City	KO	1
Sept.	29—Alejandro Perez, Mexico City	KO	4
Oct.	28—Salvador Medina, Mexico City	KO	3
Dec.	4—Memo Ramirez, Mexico City	KO	3
Dec.	17—Edel Burunda, Juarez	KO	3

1975

Feb.	8—Chuy Rodriguez, Mexico City	KO	4
Mar.	15—Tomas Frias, Mexico City	W	10
May	4—Memo Rodriguez, Tuxtla Gutierrez	L	10
June	11—Victor Ramirez, Mexico City	W	10
July	12—Jose Luis Meza, Mexico City	W	10
Sept.	13—Victor Ramirez, Mexico City	L	10
Nov.	15—Juan Pablo Oropeza, Mexico City ..	W	10
Dec.	7—Bobby Chacon, Mexicali	W	10

1976

Feb.	1—Yambito Blanco, Mexicali	W	10
June	7—Saul Montana, Tijuana	W	10
July	10—Ray Thomas, Juarez	KO	1
Aug.	6—Ruben Coria, Inglewood	KO	4
Aug.	28—Lionel Rose, Inglewood	KO	3
Oct.	2—Teruyoshi Nohi, Los Angeles	KO	2

Nov. 13—Chuy Rodriguez, Culiacan .... KO 5

1977

Mar. 13—Leonardo Bermudez, Culiacan ..... D 10
May 31—Augustin Estrada, San Antonio .... W 10
Aug. 6—Mar Basa, Los Angeles .... KO 3
Sept. 2—Antonio Llamas, Coatzacoalcos ... KO 3
Sept. 15—Hector Munoz, Reynosa .... KO 3
Oct. 8—Ray Saldivar, Los Angeles ...... KO 3
Oct. 22—Aurelio Muniz, Obregon Mante L disq. 6
Oct. 29—Ben Ortiz, Los Angeles .... W 10

1978

Mar. 4—Ernest Bing, Los Angeles .... KO 10
(Won Vacant NABF Junior Lightweight Title)
Apr. 15—Jose Marin, Los Angeles .... KO 1
June 10—Rocky Ramon, Oklahoma City ..... W 10
Aug. 6—Juan Villa, Stockton .... KO 7
Aug. 26—Jaime Nava, Fresno .... KO 10
Dec. 4—Abe Perez, Tijuana .... KO 6

Dec. 19—Robert Vasquez, Houston .... KO 5

1979

Feb. 26—Miguel Estrada, Houston .... KO 5
Apr. 9—Bobby Chacon, Inglewood .... TD 7
(Retained NABF Junior Lightweight Title)
July 8—Alexis Arguello, New York .... KO by 11
(For WBC Junior Lightweight Title)
Nov. 27—Faustino Pena, Houston .... W 10

1980

Mar. 21—Bobby Chacon, Los Angeles .... L 10
Apr. 25—Frank Ahumada, Los Angeles ..... W 10
July 24—Frankie Baltazar, Los Angeles ... KO 4
(Retained NABF Junior Lightweight Title)
Dec. 11—Ildefonso Bethelmy, Los Angeles .. KO 15
(Won Vacant WBC Junior Lightweight Title)

TB	KO	WD	WF	D	LD	LF	KO BY	ND	NC
56	32	12	0	2	5	1	4	0	0

FEATHERWEIGHTS

TORPEDO BILLY MURPHY	1890	*JACKIE WILSON (NBA)*	*1941-1943*
YOUNG GRIFFO	1890-1891	**WILLIE PEP**	1942-1948
GEORGE DIXON	1891-1897	*JACKIE CALLURA (NBA)*	*1943*
SOLLY SMITH	1897-1898	*PHIL TERRANOVA (NBA)*	*1943-1944*
BEN JORDAN (GREAT BRITAIN)	*1898-1899*	*SAL BARTOLO (NBA)*	*1944-1946*
EDDIE SANTRY (GREAT BRITAIN)	*1899-1900*	**SANDY SADDLER**	1948-1949
DAVE SULLIVAN	1898	**WILLIE PEP**	1949-1950
GEORGE DIXON	1898-1900	**SANDY SADDLER**	1950-1957
TERRY MC GOVERN	1900-1901	**HOGAN (KID) BASSEY**	1957-1959
YOUNG CORBETT II	1901-1902	**DAVEY MOORE**	1959-1963
ABE ATTELL	1901-1912	**ULTIMINIO (SUGAR) RAMOS**	1963-1964
JOHNNY KILBANE	1912-1923	**VICENTE SALDIVAR**	1964-1967
EUGENE CRIQUI	1923	*HOWARD WINSTONE*	
JOHNNY DUNDEE	1923-1924	*(GREAT BRITAIN)*	*1968*
LOUIS (KID) KAPLAN	1925-1927	*RAUL ROJAS (WBA)*	*1968*
BENNY BASS	1927-1928	*JOSE LEGRA (WBC)*	*1968-1969*
TONY CANZONERI	1928	*SHOZO SAIJYO (WBA)*	*1968-1971*
ANDRE ROUTIS	1928-1929	**JOHNNY FAMECHON (WBC)**	1969-1970
BATTLING BATTALINO	1929-1932	**VICENTE SALDIVAR (WBC)**	1970
TOMMY PAUL (NBA)	*1932-1933*	**KUNIAKI SHIBATA (WBC)**	1970-1972
KID CHOCOLATE (NEW YORK)	*1932-1933*	*ANTONIO GOMEZ (WBA)*	*1971-1972*
FREDDIE MILLER (NBA)	*1933-1936*	**CLEMENTE SANCHEZ (WBC)**	1972
ALBERTO (BABY)		*ERNESTO MARCEL (WBA)*	*1972-1974*
ARIZMENDI (CALIF.-MEXICAN)	*1935-1936*	**JOSE LEGRA (WBC)**	1972-1973
MIKE BELLOISE (NEW YORK)	*1936-1937*	**EDER JOFRE (WBC)**	1973-1974
PETEY SARRON (NBA)	*1936-1937*	*RUBEN OLIVARES (WBA)*	*1974*
HENRY ARMSTRONG	1937-1938	*BOBBY CHACON (WBC)*	*1974-1975*
JOEY ARCHIBALD (NEW YORK)	*1938-1939*	**ALEXIS ARGUELLO (WBA)**	1974-1976
LEO RODAK (NBA)	*1938-1939*	*RUBEN OLIVARES (WBC)*	*1975*
JOEY ARCHIBALD	1939-1940	*DAVID (POISON) KOTEY (WBC)*	*1975-1976*
PETEY SCALZO (NBA)	*1940-1941*	**DANNY LOPEZ (WBC)**	1976-1980
HARRY JEFFRA	1940-1941	*RAFAEL ORTEGA (WBA)*	*1977*
JOEY ARCHIBALD	1941	*CECILIO LASTRA (WBA)*	*1977-1978*
RICHIE LEMOS (NBA)	*1941*	*EUSEBIO PEDROZA (WBA)*	*1978-*
CHALKY WRIGHT	1941-1942	**SALVADOR SANCHEZ (WBC)**	1980-

Claimants not generally recognized are in *italics*.

HISTORY OF THE FEATHERWEIGHT CLASS

John Keating claimed the featherweight championship of America in the early 1860's, but he declined to meet Nobby Clark of England in a fight for world honors. Jimmy Elliott, later American Heavyweight Champion, was substituted, but lost to Clark.

May 28, 1860, Nobby Clark beat Jimmy Elliott, 34 rounds, 1 hour and 2 minutes at Palisades, New Jersey. Nobby Clark was never beaten in America, and he returned to England and retired from the game.

Dick Hollywood and John Keating then claimed the title, but Hollywood gave Keating several terrific beatings in championship fights in the early 1860's. Hollywood then retired, and the title was claimed by Tommy Kelly (the original Tommy Kelly, not the one who boxed George Dixon in 1888).

Oct. 7, 1868, George Seddons beat Tommy Kelly, 96 rounds, lasting 1 hour and 39 minutes, at Portmouth, N. H., for the championship.

George Seddons outgrew the class, and eventually boxed Arthur Chambers for the lightweight championship. After being beaten, Seddons retired. In the early 1870's the championship was claimed by Tommy Kelly, and later by John Keating and Long Tom Ryan.

In the early 1880's the featherweight championship was claimed by Jack Keenan, until 1885, when he was beaten by Young Mitchell (John Herget). Mitchell outgrew the class, and Harry Gilmore of Canada, claimed the title in 1887, but he, too, outgrew the class after a time. Then came the era in which Ike Weir, Dal Hawkins, Cal McCarthy and George Dixon contended for the title.

On June 3, 1889, Dal Hawkins and Fred Bogan engaged in what was advertised as a featherweight title bout and at the end of the 75th round the bout was halted due to darkness and called a draw. It took place in San Francisco. The next day the bout was resumed and Hawkins was stopped by Bogan in the 15th round.

Bogan returned to Australia and Hawkins claimed the title, but both had by then outgrown the class which then had a limit of 118 pounds.

March 31, 1889—Ike Weir and Frank Murphy fought to a draw, at Kouts, Ind., 80 rounds. (Designated as world title bout.)

On July 30, Billy Murphy and Frank Murphy fought a draw of 27 rounds and then Frank returned to England, refusing to fight Weir again for the right to meet Billy Murphy. Hence the Police Gazette arranged for a championship match between Australian Billy and Weir which the latter lost.

January 13, 1890—Billy Murphy, New Zealand, knocked out Ike Weir, Ireland, at San Francisco, in 14 rounds.

The American contention was that neither Weir nor Murphy had a right to a world title claim but only to the British Empire title.

In America, George Dixon, of Boston, and Cal McCarthy, of Troy, N. Y., each of whom had graduated from the bantamweight class which at the time was recognized at 110 pounds, were the leading contenders. When Dixon stopped McCarthy at Troy in 22 rounds the ringside weight was 115 pounds and he gained recognition as the American titleholder.

April 25, 1891—Ike Weir and Johnny Griffin fought at Nantucket, Mass. The bout was stopped by police in round 4.

(Griffin had claimed title during Billy Murphy's absence in Australia.)

Dixon, on July 28, 1891, knocked out Abe Willis, featherweight champion of England, in five rounds, and thus became the world champion of the class.

Sept. 6, 1892—George Dixon knocked out Jack Skelly at New Orleans, in 8 rounds, for the world featherweight championship.

Tom O'Rourke, Dixon's manager, then gradually raised the weight limit and stipulated 120 pounds for a title match between Dixon and Solly Smith at San Francisco, October 4, 1897, Smith getting the referee's decision at the end of 20 rounds.

Smith then made a match with Dave Sullivan which was fought at Coney Island, N. Y., September 26, 1898, Smith breaking his arm and being compelled to quit in the fifth round.

Dixon challenged Sullivan and they met in the Lenox A. C., New York, November 11, 1898, and Dixon regained his title by stopping Sullivan in the tenth round, Sullivan's seconds entering the ring to prevent a knockout.

Dixon retained the title until January 9, 1900, when he was knocked out by Terry McGovern at the Broadway A. C., New York, in the eighth round. The weight was 118 pounds.

Nov. 28, 1901—Young Corbett knocked out Terry McGovern at Hartford, Conn., in 2 rounds.

(The weight was 126 pounds, nevertheless, the bout was billed as being for the featherweight championship. Corbett could never make the feather limit, and did not attempt to do so. When he and McGovern both competed in the lightweight class, Abe Attell claimed the featherweight championship.)

Attell gained the vacant title in matches with George Dixon, having drawn with him, 20 rounds, on Oct. 20, 1901, at Cripple Creek, Colo., and decisioning him, 15 rounds, Oct. 28, 1901, at St. rounds, Oct. 28, 1901, at St. Louis.

April 30, 1908—Abe Attell knocked out Brooklyn Tommy Sullivan at San Francisco, in 4 rounds in a non-title bout.

February 22, 1912—Johnny Kilbane outpointed Abe Attell at Vernon, Cal., in 20 rounds.

June 2, 1923—Eugene Criqui knocked out Johnny Kilbane at Polo Grounds, New York City, 6 rounds.

July 26, 1923—Johnny Dundee outpointed Eugene Criqui at Polo Grounds, New York City, in 15 rounds.

(In 1925, when Dundee outgrew featherweight class, an elimination tourney to determine his successor was won by Louis (Kid) Kaplan.)

Jan. 2, 1925—Louis (Kid) Kaplan knocked out Danny Kramer, in Madison Square Garden, New York City, in 9 rounds.

(By 1927 Kaplan outgrew the class. An elimination tourney made Benny Bass the leading contender.)

Sept. 12, 1927—Benny Bass outpointed Red Chapman at Philadelphia, Pa., in 10 rounds, Chapman being the N. B. A. champion.

Feb. 10, 1928—Tony Canzoneri outpointed Benny Bass in Madison Square Garden. New York City, in 15 rounds, to clinch world title.

Sept. 28, 1928—Andre Routis outpointed Tony Canzoneri at N. Y. C., in 15 rounds.

Sept. 23, 1929—Battling Battalino outpointed Andre Routis at Hartford, Conn., in 15 rounds.

(By 1932 Battalino outgrew the class. An N.B.A. elimination tournament was won by Tommy Paul of Buffalo.)

May 26, 1932—Tommy Paul outpointed Johnny Pena at Detroit, Mich., in 15 rounds. for N.B.A. title.

Oct. 13, 1932—Kid Chocolate knocked out Lew Feldman at New York, N.Y. in 12 rounds. This bout was recognized by the New York Commission as for the featherweight championship because Paul had previously lost to Feldman. The N.B.A. had not sanctioned the Feldman-Paul fight as for the crown. Chocolate later relinquished his claim to the title.

Jan. 13, 1933—Freddie Miller outpointed Tommy Paul at Chicago, Ill., in 10 rounds in an N.B.A. championship fight which New York refused to recognize.

Miller proceeded to clean up the cream of the world's contenders. He traveled all over Europe and beat all rivals, losing only two fights out of 34 and engaged in two draws. He lost only to one outstanding champion in Europe, Maurice Holtzer of France, in an overweight bout.

May 11, 1936—Miller lost to Petey Sarron, Washington, D. C., in 15 rounds.

October 29, 1937—Henry Armstrong knocked out Sarron, Madison Square Garden, in 6 rounds, to win world title.

1938—Henry Armstrong resigned as featherweight champion.

The New York State Commission, recognizing Mike Belloise of New York and Joey Archibald of Pawtucket, R. I., as the outstanding contenders, arranged a match for the St. Nicholas A. C. of New York and Archibald won the fight and recognition.

Oct. 17, 1938—Joey Archibald won decision from Mike Belloise, 15 rounds.

May 20, 1940—Joey Archibald lost to Harry Jeffra, 15 rounds, Baltimore, Md.

May 12, 1941—Joey Archibald beat Harry Jeffra, 15 rounds, Washington, D. C.

Sept. 11, 1941—Chalky Wright knocked out Joey Archibald, Washington, D.C., 11 rounds.

Petey Scalzo, on Dec. 5, 1938, knocked out Archibald in 2 rounds in an overweight match, and thereafter, tried desperately to meet Archibald in a title bout but was unsuccessful. When he refused to meet Scalzo, the N.B.A. declared Scalzo the champion and vacated Archibald's title on May 1, 1940. When Archibald fought Jeffra in Baltimore, only New York and Maryland recognized it as for the crown. But there could be no doubt that Archibald was champion and Jeffra, when he won, became successor to the crown.

As a result of this dispute, the N.B.A. had Scalzo as its champion and when Scalzo was knocked out by Richie Lemos at Los Angeles, in 5 rounds, July 1, 1941, Lemos received N.B.A. recognition. On Nov. 18, Lemos lost the N.B.A. title to Jackie Wilson. However, in 1941 Chalky Wright was the world champion.

Nov. 20, 1942—Willie Pep defeated Chalky Wright, Madison Square Garden, 15 rounds, decision. On January 18, 1943, Wilson lost the N.B.A. crown to Jackie Callura of Canada. The N.B.A. crown passed from Callura to Phil Terranova, by a knockout in 8 rounds on August 16, 1943, and Terranova lost it to Sal Bartolo on March 10, 1944 in 15 rounds at Boston.

Willie Pep, who was recognized as the international champion, joined the Navy on June 16, 1943, and was honorably discharged on February 15, 1944. He defended his title against Chalky Wright in the Garden on September 29, 1944 and won in 15 rounds. He then joined the Army. Thereafter Pep successfully defended the crown against Sal Bartolo (twice), Chalky Wright and Phil Terranova.

Oct. 29, 1948—Sandy Saddler scored a four-round knockout over Willie Pep at Madison Square Garden, New York, to win the world title.

Feb. 11, 1949—Willie Pep regained the title by winning a 15 round decision over Sandy Saddler at Madison Square Garden, New York.

September 8, 1950—Sandy Saddler regained the title by halting Willie Pep at Yankee Stadium, New York, N. Y., Pep being unable to answer the bell for the eighth round due to injury.

Saddler was inducted into the Army in 1952 and the N.B.A. recognized Percy Bassett as "Interim Champion."

Following an auto accident in which he was injured in 1956, Saddler relinquished the title in 1957.

After an elimination tournament, with Hogan (Kid) Bassey and Cherif Hamia as finalists, Bassey won the vacant title by stopping Hamia, 10 rounds, on June 24, 1957, at Paris, France.

March 18, 1959—Davey Moore won the title by knocking out Hogan (Kid) Bassey at the end of the 13th round, at Los Angeles, Calif.

March 21, 1963—Sugar Ramos won the title by stopping Davey Moore in the 11th round at Los Angeles, Calif.

September 26, 1964—Vicente Saldivar won the title by stopping Sugar Ramos in the 12th round at Mexico City, Mexico.

Feb. 12, 1966—Vicente Saldivar, Mexico City, knocked out Floyd Robertson, Ghana, in 2:29 of the second round in Mexico City. Saldivar, 125¾; Robertson, 124¼.

Aug. 7, 1966—Vicente Saldivar, Mexico City, defeated Mitsunori Seki, Japan, in Mexico City in 15 rounds by a decision. Saldivar, 124½; Seki, 124.

Jan. 29, 1967—Vicente Saldivar, Mexico City, 125, retained his crown by knocking out Mitsunori Seki, Japan, 126, in Mexico City, in the seventh round. Referee—Ramon Beruman.

June 15, 1967—Vicente Saldivar, Mexico City, 126, retained his title, defeating Howard Winstone, Wales, 125¼ by a decision in 15 rounds, in Cardiff, Wales. Referee—Wally Thom.

Oct. 14, 1967—Vicente Saldivar, Mexico City, 125, retained his crown, stopping Howard Winstone, Wales, 125¼, in 12 rounds in the Aztec Arena of Mexico City. Winstone's second tossed in the towel. Saldivar announced his retirement following his victory.

Jan. 23, 1969—Johnny Famechon, 125, Australia, decisioned Jose Legra, 124, Spain over 15 rounds to win the vacant world title. The bout was awarded to Famechon by referee George Smith by the score of 74½ to 73½. Bout held in London, England.

May 9, 1970—Vicente Saldivar of Mexico regained the world featherweight championship, defeating Johnny Fam-echon of Australia, winning the decision at the end of 15 rounds. Famechon announced his retirement after the loss.

Famechon scaled 124½ and Saldivar 126.

Dec. 11, 1970—Kuniaki Shibata, 126, Japan, halted Vicente Saldivar, 125, Mexico. in the 13th round to win world title. Bout was held in Tijuana, Mexico.

May 19, 1972—Clemente Sanchez, Mexico knocked out Kuniaki Shibata, Japan, at 2:26 of the third round to win the title. Weights, Shibata and Sanchez 126. Bout held in Tokyo, Japan.

Dec. 16, 1972—Clemente Sanchez vacated his title. He no longer could make the weight. W.B.A. recognition given to Ernesto Marcel, Panama: W.B.C. awarded Spain's Jose Legra its crown.

May 31, 1975—Alexis Arguello, Nicaragua won the vacant world title via a TKO at 2:00 of the second round over Panama's Rigoberto Riasco. Arguello also holds a win over the W.B.C. champion Ruben Olivares. Arguello and Riasco weight 126. Referee Ferly Carpentier. Contest was held in Managua, Nicaragua.

June 20, 1977—Alexis Arguello, Nicaragua, give up his title and retired as undefeated champion to move up to the lightweight division. He no longer could make the featherweight limit. See W.B.A. and W.B.C. for their champions. The Ring has the title vacant.

November 5, 1976—Danny Lopez, 124, Los Angeles, Cal., outpointed David (Poison) Kotey, 126, Ghana, over 15 rounds to win the WBC title. Site: Accra, Ghana.

April 15, 1978—Eusebio Pedroza, 126, Panama, TKO'd Cecilio Lastra, 126, Spain, in the 13th round to win the WBA title. Bout held in Panama City. Referee: Larry Rozadilla.

February 2, 1980—Salvador Sanchez, 125¼, Mexico, TKO'd Danny Lopez, 125¾, Los Angeles, Calif., at 0:51 of round 13 in Phoenix, Arizona, to win the WBC title. Waldemar Schmidt, referee.

FEATHERWEIGHT DIVISION

"TORPEDO" BILLY MURPHY
(Thomas W. Murphy)
Born, 1863, Auckland, N. Z. Height, 5 ft. 6½ in. Reach, 69½ in.

1887-1888
Won: Jack O'Meagher, 45 m; Frank Burns, KO 6; M. O'Brien, W4; J. Guller, KO 12; W. Burt, W 3; Charles Carter, W 3; J. Gardner, W 3; Walter Evans, W 3; Fuller, (twice) W 13; Sam Stewart, W 17; B. Johnson, W 3; F. King, W 3; bested by Young Mitchell, 5; Charlie Taylor, W 12; F. Bruce, W 7; C. Allen, W 7; Harry Laing, D 3; J. Fadders, KO 2; Bill Mitchell, W 4; Ike Fake, 3; Brooks, KO 1 and Parker, KO 3, in same night; J. Ford, W 11; Saxon, W 4; Jack Hall, D 8; Jerry Marshall, W 1; Basket, W 3; Smith, W 8, Eugene Donovan, L 11; Young Griffo, D 4.

1888
Nov. 20—Ben Seth, of Eng., Melbourne .... Ko by 6

1889
June 7—Arrived in San Fran. on Zelandia.
July 12—Johnny Griffin (117-120), Cal. A.C. ....KO 3
July 30—Frank Murphy, Eng. (119), Cal. A. C. $1,250 each .... D 27

1890
Jan. 13—Ike Weir, (118-124), $2,250, Calif. A. C., San Francisco ....KO 14
For R. K. Fox, belt and featherweight championship of the world.
Mar. 14—Tommy Warren, (116-118), $1,800, Occidental club, San Fran. .... W 4
Apr. 21—Bested Tommy White, Chicaco 4
May 29—Eddie Greaney, Cal. A. C. ...... W 4
June 28—Returned to Auckland, N. Z.
Sept. 3—*Young Griffo, $1,500, Sydney .L 15
Murphy took off gloves.

*For featherweight championship of Australia.
—Nipper Peakes, Melbourne ..... D 19
Nov. 10—Dummy Mace, (117-143), Melb. W 8
Dec. 17—Pat Carroll, (117-146) .... W 4

1891
Jan. 19—Jim Burge, $750, Broken Hill ....KO by 30
May 4—Artie Tully, Melbourne ....L 8
July 22—Young Griffo, Sydney, $750 ...L 22
Oct. 2—Spider Kelly, Guttenberg, N. J. ....KO by 3
Oct. 19—Bill Jennings, Sydney, £25 ....KO 2
Nov. 23—Jim Burge, Sydney ....NC 29
Dec. 20—Spider Kelly, Hoboken, N. J. ....KO by 2
Dec. 26—Chris Cunningham, Newcastle KO 2

1892
Jan. 23—Young Griffo failed to meet him, Melbourne
Feb. 16—Jim Barron, (136), Sydney KO by 3
May 31—Johnny Murphy, Boston .....D 40
$1,250, Pacific club, S. F. Johnny Murphy gave Billy Half of purse.
July 25—Spider Kelly, New York City ...L 6
—Jack Downey ....D 4
Dec. 28—Tommy White ....D NC 32
Pacific A. C., San Fran. White received $200, Murphy nothing.

1893
Feb. 6—Johnny Griffin, (122) $3,500-$500, C. I. A. C. ....KO by 7
Apr. 29—Bested by Jerry Barnett, N. Y. .. 4
May 30—Johnny Van Heest, Phil. ....ND 4
July 17—Ed Listman, Newark, N. J. ...... W 3
Sept. 13—Jack Collins, Brooklyn ....KO 2
Sept. 22—Jack Grace, Brooklyn, police .. W 2
Nov. 2—Ike Weir, (120), $650-$100, Boston.......................KO by 6
Dec. 15—George Dixon, Paterson, N. J. (row) ....L 3
Dec. 23—Jack Woods, Boston ....KO 2

1894
Feb. 19—Johnny Breslin, Boston ......KO 4
May 7—Young Griffo, Boston, Gate. Referee, Capt. Bill Daly ....L 20
Nov. 8—Jack McCabe, Cincinnati ....KO 2
Nov. 12—Anthony Lefevre, Cincinnati .. W 2
Nov. 19—Jerry Barnett, $250, Atl. A. C., New York .... D 10
Dec. 8—Bested Kentucky Rosebud, Phila. ... 4

1895
Jan. 3—Frank Machiewski, Phila. police 4
Feb. 6—"Kid" McGraw, Cincinnati ...KO 4

Feb. 26—"Kid" Hogan, Cincinnati ....L 10
May 6—Jack Dougherty, Cincinnati .... D 10
May 30—Jack Dougherty, Cincinnati .... D 6
July 11—Tommy White, Columbus, O. .. D 20
Aug. 6—Harry Sheldon, Louisville .... W 5
Aug. 22—Harry Sheldon, Louisville ...KO 3
Nov. 13—Jack Doherty, Lexington, Ky. . W 10
Dec. 23—Sol Smith, New Orleans ....L 14

1896
Jan. 21—Mike Crotty, KO 1; Harry Dally, W 4; Joe Slink, W 4; Cincinnati, Ohio ....Exh. 1
Feb. 11—Jimmy Devers, Jackson, Miss. ... W 10
Mar. 17—Paddy Smith, Cincinnati ... W 10
Apr. 29—James Connors, Jackson, Mich.KO 4
Oct. 8—Johnny Lavack, Lexington, Ky. D 20

1897
Jan. 22—George Dixon, Broadway A. C., New York ....KO by 6
Jan. 30—Jack Delaney, Polo A. C., N. Y...L 5
Feb. 6—Dave Wall, Polo A. C., N. Y. .... D 10
Feb. 8—Danny McMahon, Philadelphia ..L 6

1899
Jan. 16—Casper Leon, Cincinnati ....L 10
Apr. 29—Harry Forbes, Chicago ....L 4

1904
Returned to Sydney.
Knocked out by: Tim Hegarty, 3. Lost: Peter Toohey, 2.

1906
Knockout: Tom Toohey, 1, New Plymouth, and fought draw with Jim Ross Auckland, 4.

TB	KO	WD	WF	D	LD	LF	KOBY	ND	NC
90	17	32	0	14	15	0	9	1	2

Died July 26, 1939, Auckland, N. Z.

YOUNG GRIFFO
(Albert Griffiths)
N.S.W. Nationality, Australian. Height 5 ft. 4 in.
Born, March 31, 1871, Miller's Point, Sydney.
(Claimant World Featherweight Title)

Prior to 1889
Won: Bob O'Neil, 15; Francis (bare knuckles), 7; Sam Matthews, 140 lb. competition; Chappie, Adelaide, 3; Smith, Adelaide, 4; Young O'Brien (twice) 3; Kiama Pet, 2; Sandy Ross, 4; Lewis, 3; Lane, 2; Sullivan, 4; Holden, 12; Draw: Young Pluto, 8, 6, 23 and 13; McShane, 8; Michie, 8; Lawrence, 8; Billy Murphy, 4; Ambrose Taylor, 8.

1889
June 15—Unknown, Sydney, Aust......KO 2
July 27—Abe Willis, Sydney, Aust...... D 20
Aug. 7—Doss Patterson, Sydney, Aust. .. W 4
Nov. 19—Jem Dempsey, Sydney, Aust. .. W 12
Dec. 12—Young Pluto, Melbourne, Aust. D 70
Dec. 31—Nipper Peakes, Melbourne ..... W 8

1830
Jan. 11—Abe Willis, Sydney .... W 3
Feb. —George McKenzie, Sydney ... W 15
June —Young Patterson, Sydney ... W 2
June 12—McLeod, Sydney ....KO 2
Sept. 13—Billy Murphy, Sydney ....W 15
Nov. 14—Paddy Moran, Sydney ......KO 13

1891
Mar. 12—George Powell, Sydney ......WF 20
July 22—Billy Murphy, Sydney .... W 22
Dec. 15—Billy Williams, Melbourne ..... W 8

1892
Jan. 23—Failed to meet Billy Murphy, $750; Melbourne.
Mar. 22—Mick McCarthy, $500 .... W 4
May 17—Mick Ryan, Sydney .... W 8
July 25—Jem Bavion, Sydney ....D 22
Nov. 8—Martin Denny, Sydney .... D 25
Dec. 24—Jerry Marshall, Sydney ...... W 12

1893
Feb. 28—Jerry Marshall, Sydney ...WF 4
Nov. 13—Young Scotty, Chicago ...... W 6
Dec. 18—Tommy White, Chicago ...... D 8
Dec. 28—Al Jansen, Chicago .... W 6

1894
Jan. 3—Solly Smith, Chicago ....D 6
Jan. 23—Johnny Van Heest, Chicago .... D 8

Feb. 10—George Lavigne, New York .... D 8
Mar. 7—Ed McCabe, Chicago .... W 8
Mar. 17—Ike Weir, Chicago .... W 3
Apr. 23—Johnny Griffin, Boston .... D 8
May 7—Billy Murphy, Boston ...... W 20
May 29—George Dixon, Boston .... D 20
June 29—Walter Campbell, Philadelphia . D 4
Aug. 4—Walter Campbell, Seaside A.C. ND 10
Aug. 27—Jack McAuliffe, New York ....L 10
Sept. 17—Eddie Loeber, Philadelphia ..ND 4
Nov. 24—"Bull" McCarthy, Phila......ND 4
Nov. 29—Kentucky Rosebud, Phila.....ND 4
Dec. 8—Jack Hanley, Philadelphia ....ND 6

1895
Jan. 19—George Dixon, Coney Island ... D 25
Feb. 23—Jerome Quigley, Philadelphia .. D 4
Mar. 4—Horace Leeds, Coney Island ... W 12
Mar. 8—Jimmy Dime, Boston .... D 8
Mar. 16—"Bull" McCarthy, Phila....... D 4
Mar. 20—Jack Hanley, Philadelphia ....ND 6
Mar. 23—Jerome Quigley, Philadelphia .ND 4
Mar. 26—Joe Harmon, New York ...... W 6
Mar. 30—Eddy Curry, New York A. C.... W 6
Apr. 11—George Reynolds, Albany .... W 6
May 4—Charley Barnett, New York ... W 6
Oct. 12—"Kid" Lavigne, Maspeth...... D 20
Oct. 28—George Dixon, New York ..... D 10
Nov. 7—Jack Randall, Philadelphia ....ND 4
Nov. 13—Jack Hanley, Philadelphia ...ND 4
Nov. 18—Joe Gans, Baltimore .... D 10

1896
Feb. 3—Frank McConnell, San Fran. ....L 15
Apr. 13—Charley McKeever, Maspeth, L. I. ....L 20
Apr. 23—Bill McCarthy, Sacramento ...KO 20
(McCarthy died following day of injuries suffered in bout.)
May 25—Jack Everhardt, Brooklyn ..... D 6
June 1—Sam Tonkins, Brooklyn .... W 10
June 8—Billy Ernst, Brooklyn .... D 12
July 10—Jack Everhardt, Buffalo .... D 20

1897
June 21—Phila. Tommy Ryan, Brooklyn ..L 3
(Griffo Quit)
July 12—Owen Ziegler, Phiadelphia ....ND 6
Sept. 10—Charley McKeever, Athens, Pa. .... D 15
Sept. 21—Joe Gans, Philadelphia .... D 15
Sept. 27—"Wilmington" Jack Daly, Philadelphia ....ND 6
Oct. 12—Adam Ryan, Chicago ....L 3
Oct. 23—Frank Gerrard, Chicago .... D 6
Nov. 18—Tom Tracey, St. Louis ....L 1
(Early in day Griffo had been injured in street car collision, but insisted on going through with bout; intense pain made him retire after one round.)

1898
Jan. 6—Jack Lewis, Chicago .... W 6
June 4—Jack Lewis, Chicago .... W 6
June 20—Jack Lewis, Chicago .... D 6

1900
Feb. 6—Jack Lewis, Philadelphia ...... W 6
May 9—Jack Lewis, Philadelphia ...... D 6
July 10—Joe Gans, New York ...... KO by 8
Aug. 4—Jim Popp, Chicago .... W 6

1901
Dec. 4—Jim Popp, New York .... W 6
Dec. 11—Kid Ashe, Cincinnati .... W 10

1902
Sept. 30—Joe Tipman, Baltimore .... KO by 5
Oct. 22—Joe Bernstein, Baltimore ...... D 6

1903
Jan. 1—Jack Bain, Baltimore ....KO 8
Dec. 26—George Memsic, Chicago ...... D 6

1904
Feb. 10—Tommy White, Chicago ...KO by 1

1911
Returned to ring after absence of 7 years.
May 10—Mike Leonard, New York .....ND 6
May 25—Honey Mellody, Phila. ....ND 6

TB	KO	WD	WF	D	LD	LF	KOBY	ND	NC
107	5	42	2	37	6	0	3	12	0

Died Dec. 7, 1927. Buried in Woodlawn cemetery, N. Y. C.
Elected to Boxing Hall of Fame 1954.

GEORGE DIXON
(Little Chocolate)
Born, July 29, 1870, Halifax, N. S. Weight, 120 pounds. Height, 5 ft. 3½ in. Nationality, Canadian, managed by Tom O'Rourke.

1886
Nov. 1—Young Johnson, Halifax ......KO 3
1887
Sept. 21—Elias Hamilton, $30, Boston ... W 8
—Young Mack, Boston .... W 3
1888
Jan. 2—Jack Lyman, Boston .... W 5
Jan. 20—Charley Parton of Eng., $75, Boston .... W 6
Feb. 17—Barney Finnegan, $50, Athenian Club, Boston .... W 6
Mar. 10—Ned Morris, $75, Athenian, Boston .... W 3
Mar. 21—Paddy Kelly, Boston .... D 15
Apr. 27—Tommy Doherty, Boston ...... D 8
May 10—Tommy Kelly "Harlem Spider") Athenian (claimed bantamweight title) Club, Boston .... D 9
June 13—Jimmy Brackett, Boston ...... W 5
June 21—"Hank Brennan," Pelican, Boston .... D 14
Dec. 14—"Hank Brennan," $100, Athenian Boston .... D 9
Dec. 28—"Hank Brennan," $100, Athenian, Boston .... D 15
1889
Jan. 27—Paddy Kelly, Pelican Club, Boston .... W 10
—Frank Maguire, Putnam, Conn.. D 10
May —Billy James, Haverhill, Mass. .... W 3
June 3—Geo. Wright of Can. (foul), Parnell, Dixon had best, Boston ...... LF 1
Oct. 14—"Hank Brennan," $350, Parnel Club, Boston .... D 26
Dec. 11—Mike Sullivan, p, New Bedford . W 6
Dec. 27—Eugene Hornbacher of New York, $500 purse, $250 a side, skin gloves, New York City ....KO 2
1890
Jan. 7—Joe Murphy, Gladstone, Prov.... W 4
Feb. 7—Cal McCarthy of New York, $1,000 p., 2 oz., Ref. Al. Smith, Boston ... D 70
Mar. 1—Paddy Kearney, Paterson, N. J.. W 4
Mar. 3—Joe Farrell, New Jersey ...... W 2
Mar. 5—Jack Carey, Hoboken, N. J. ...KO 3
Mar. 31—Matt McCarthy, Philadelphia .. W 3
May 3—With Tom O'Rourke, sailed for Eng.
May —Billy Willis (in private) ......Exh. 3
June 27—Nunc Wallace (113-112), $2,000-500, champion of England and America, 4 oz., Pelican Club. Dixon's seconds, Tom O'Rourke, Tom McGeough. Referee, G. H. Vize, London ......KO 18
(Won World Bantamweight title)
—Toured England with Nunc Wallace.
Oct. 23—Johnny Murphy (114), $1,500-200, $1,200 a side, 2 oz., Gladstone Athletic Club. Referee, Dan H. (Bantam Weight Title Bout) Coakley, Providence, R. I.W 40
(Gave Up Bantam Title)
Nov. 1—J. Allan, Baltimore ..... W 2
Nov. 7—"Virginia Rosebud," Baltimore W 3
Nov. 11—Lee Andrews (col.), Wash. ....KO 4
Nov. 13—W. Dyson (col.), Washington ..KO 2
Dec. 3—Nick Collins, New York .... W 4
1891
Mar. 31—Cal McCarthy (115), $3,800-200, $2,000 a side, 2 oz. For Featherweight championship, Referee Jere Dunn, Troy, N. Y. .... W 22
Apr. 20—Martin Flaherty, Chicago ..... W 6
May 19—Bobby Burns, Providence ..... D 4
July 28—Abe Willis of Australia (115), $4,250-750, California Athletic Club. For world's Featherweight championship. Ref. H. Cook, San Fr. ....KO 5
Sept. 28—Marcellus Baker, Montreal ..... W 3
Oct. 1—Dan Coakley, Montreal .... W 4
Oct. 2—Jack Fitzpatrick, Montreal ..... D 4
Nov. 3—Hornbacher, New York .... W 4
Nov. 5—Nick Collins, New York ...... W 4
Nov. 6—Frank Wall, New York ...... W 2
Nov. 12—Billy Ross Stayed allotted rounds, but Dixon outclassed Ross ..... W 4
Died, Sept. 24, 1908, Charlestown, Mass.
Dec. 17—Lee Damro, Washington .... W 4
1892
Jan. —Tom Warren, Philadelphia ....KO 3

Jan.	11—E. McClusky, Philadelphia . . . . . W	4
Jan.	16—Young, Philadelphia . . . . W	4
Feb.	4—Watson of Paterson, Paterson .KO	1
May	6—Billy Russell of N. Haven, N. Y. W	2
June	27—Fred Johnson (117), $4,500-500, Coney Island Ath. Club. For world's Featherweight championship, Coney Island . . . . KO	14
Aug.	—Offered to box Jimmy Carroll 6r., and a side bet that Carroll couldn't stop him.	
Sept.	6—Jack Skelly, $17,500, Olympic Club New Orleans . . . . KO (Featherweight Title)	8
Oct.	29—"Kentucky Rosebud," Phila. . . D	4
Nov.	11—"Kentucky Rosebud," Phila. . . D	4
1893		
Jan.	25—Eddie Eckhardt, Brooklyn . . . . . W	4
Mar.	—Presented with feather-weight championship belt at N. Y.	
Mar.	20—George Siddons, $1,500-500, Coney Island Ath. Club, C. Island . . . . D	12
Mar.	22—Eddie Boerum, New York . . . .KO	4
Apr.	28—Bill Young (ended in row), Washington . . . . ,	4
Apr.	16—Mike Gillespie, Cincinnati . . . . . W	4
June	17—Jerry Barnet (Dixon had best), New York . . . . D	4
June	30—"Kentucky Rosebud," Phila. . . W	4
Aug.	—*Eddie Pierce, $6,500 Coney Island Ath. Club, Coney Island . . . . .KO	3
Aug.	22—Billy Plimmer of England, Ref., Steve O'Donnell of Australia, New York L	4
Sept.	25—*Solly Smith, percentage, Coney Island Ath. Club. Smith was guaranteed $8,000 if he won & $1,000 if he lost by O'Rourke, Coney Island . . . . KO	7
Nov.	16—Jack Downey, New York . . . . . .KO	2
Nov.	21—P.J. Hennessy, Lawr'ce, Mass. .KO	2
Dec.	15—Billy Murphy of Australia (row), Paterson, N. J. . . . . W *Title bouts.	3
1894		
Jan.	4—Robert Heeny, Huntingt'n, Pa. KO	2
Jan.	16—Paddy Lemmons, Cleveland . .KO	1
Mar.	4—Ed. Doyle of England, Doyle jumped ring in first round, New York . . . . W	1
Mar.	22—"Kentucky Rosebud," In three-round sparring exhibition for "Bread Fund" in Philadelphia.	
June	13—"Kentucky Rosebud," flunked out of contest to be held at Boston.	
June	29—*Young Griffo, gate, Boston . . . D	10
Oct.	25—Joe Flynn, Wilmington, Del. . . . W *Title bouts.	4
1895		
Jan.	19—Young Griffo (126-135), gate, Seaside A. C., Coney Island . . . . D	25
Jan.	28—Walter Sanford, Dayton . . . . . .KO	2
Mar.	6—John Conroy, New York . . . . . .KO	2
Mar.	7—Sam Bolen, N. Y. A. C., N. Y. . . . W	6
May	8—Failed to stop C. Slusher, Louisv. . . .	4
May	—Charlestown and Frede, St. Louis . . . . KO each	2
July	31—Tommy Connelly, gate, Boston KO	4
Aug.	19—Boxed Mike, Leonard, N. Y. . .ND	2
Aug.	27—*Johnny Griffin, gate, Boston . W	25
Oct.	28—Young Griffo, Manhattan A. C., N. Y. . . . . D	10
Dec.	5—Frank Erne, New York . . . . D *Title bouts.	10
1896		
Jan.	30—Pedlar Palmer, New York . . . . . . D	6
Mar.	17—Jerry Marshall, Boston . . . . . . .KO	7
June	16—Martin Flaherty, Boston . . . . D	20
Sept.	25—Tommy White, New York . . . . . D	20
Nov.	27—Frank Erne, New York L	20
1897		
Jan.	22—Billy Murphy, New York . . . . .KO	6
Feb.	15—Jack Downey, New York . . . . . . D	20
Apr.	7—Frank Erne, New York . . . . W	25
Apr.	26—Johnny Griffin, New York . . . . . W	20
June	6—Ed Santry . . . . W	20
June	21—Walt. Edgerton, Philadelphia . .ND	6
July	23—Dal Hawkins, San Francisco . . D	20
Oct.	4—Solly Smith, San Francisco . . . . .L (Lost featherweight title)	20
1898		
Mar.	31—Tommy White, Syracuse . . . . . . D	20
June	6—Eddie Santry, New York . . . . . . W	20
July	1—Ben Jordan, New York L	25
Aug.	29—Jimmy Dunn, Fall River . . . . .ND	6

Sept.	5—Joe Bernstein, Philadelphia . . .ND	6
Nov.	11—Dave Sullivan, New York . . .WDis. (Rewon Featherweight title)	10
Nov.	29—*Oscar Gardner, New York . . . . W *Title bouts.	25
1899		
Jan.	17—*Young Pluto, New York . . . . .KO	10
May	15—*Kid Broad, Buffalo . . . . W	20
June	2—*Joe Bernstein, New York . . . . . W	25
July	3—Sam Bolen, Louisville . . . . . . .KO	3
July	1—*Tommy White, Denver . . . . . . W	20
July	14—Eddie Santry, Chicago . . . . W	6
Aug.	11—*Eddie Santry, New York . . . . D	20
Oct.	13—Tim Callahan, Philadelphia . . .ND	6
Nov.	2—*Will Curley, New York . . . . . . W	25
Nov.	21—*Eddie Lenny, New York . . . . . W *Title bouts.	25
1900		
Jan.	9—Terry McGovern, N. Y. C. .KO by (Lost Featherweight Title)	8
Feb.	21—Terry McGovern, New York .Exb.	3
June	4—Tim Callahan, Philadelphia . . .ND	6
June	12—Benny Yanger, Chicago . . . . D	6
June	23—Terry McGovern, Chicago L	6
July	31—Tommy Sullivan, Coney Island . .L	6
1901		
Feb.	8—Harry Lons, Baltimore . . . . D	20
Aug.	16—Young Corbett, Denver L	10
Aug.	24—Abe Attell, Denver . . . . D	10
Sept.	26—Benny Yanger, St. Louis L	15
Oct.	20—Abe Atell, Cripple Creek . . . . . . D (For Vacant Featherweight Title)	20
Oct.	28—*Abe Attell, St. Louis . . . . .L (For Vacant Featherweight Title)	15
Dec.	19—Austin Rice, New London L	20
1902		
Jan.	17—Joe Tipman, Baltimore . . . . D	20
Jan.	24—Eddie Lenny, Baltimore L	9
Feb.	13—Chic Tucker, New Britain . . . . . W	20
May	16—Billy Ryan, Ottawa . . . . D	15
May	27—Dan Dougherty, Philadelphia .ND	6
June	—Eddie Lenny, Chester . . . . D	6
June	10—Biz Mackey, Findlay, O. . . . KO by	5
June	30—Tim Callahan, Philadelphia . . .ND	6
Sept.	8—Pedlar Palmer, Glasgow L	15
Sept.	29—Will Curley, England . . . . D	15
1903		
Feb.	9—Harry Ware, England . . . . D	20
Mar.	7—Fred Delaney, England L	6
Apr.	6—Jack Pearson, England . . . . W	8
Apr.	25—Spike Robson, England L	15
May	2—Ben Jordan, England L	3
June	27—Pedlar Palmer, Wonderland L	6
Aug.	1—Digger Stanley, London . . . . . . W	6
Oct.	—Billy Barrett, England . . . . D	20
Oct.	12—Digger Stanley, London L	4
Nov.	9—Pedlar Palmer, Newcastle . . . . . W	20
Dec.	7—Cockney Cohen, England . . . . . . W	15
Dec.	20—Dal Morgan, London . . . . D	15
1904		
Jan.	16—Cockney Cohen, Newcastle . . . . W	20
Feb.	—Jem Driscoll, Bristol L	6
Feb.	23—Harry Mansfield, England . . . . . D	20
Mar.	7—Cockney Cohen, England L	15
Mar.	19—Spike Robson, Newcastle . . . .KO	11
Apr.	7—Billy Barrett, London . . . . . . .KO	12
Oct.	17—Owen Moran, London L	6
1905		
Sept.	20—Tommy Murphy, Phila. . . .KO by	2
Dec.	28—Frankie Howe, New York . . . .ND	3
1906		
Jan.	4—Harry Shea, N. Y. C. . . . . .KO	3
Dec.	10—Monk Newsboy, Providence L	15

TB	KO	WD	WF	D	LD	LF	KOBY	ND	NC
149	30	47	1	37	21	1	3	9	0

Died in N. Y. C., January 6, 1909.
Elected to Boxing Hall of Fame 1956.

SOLLY SMITH

Born, 1871, Los Angeles, Cal. Weight, 122 lbs. Height, 5 ft. 4 in.
Early bouts:

	—Young Manning, Los Angeles . . W	6
	—Billy Smith, Los Angeles . . . . . . W	7
	—Kid Hogan, Los Angeles . . . . D	30
	—Joe Soto, Los Angeles . . . . D	6

—Young Moore, Los Angeles .... W   5
—Pete Cummings, Los Angeles ... W   1
—Billy Jones, Los Angeles .... W 13
—Young Abbott, Los Angeles ... W   4

1891

Dec.   3—Dan Mahoney, Los Angeles ...KO 15

1892

May   24—Dal Hawkins, San Francisco ..KO 13
July   8—Dan Dailey, San Francisco ....KO   3
Sept. 29—George Siddons, San Francisco . D 56
Dec. 29—Johnny Van Heest, San. Fran..KO 14

1893

Apr.   15—Frankie McHugh, Chicago ....ND   6
July   10—Johnny Griffin, Roby, Ind. ...KO   6
Sept. 25—George Dixon, Coney Isl. .. KO by 7
Nov. 13—Murphy of Los Ang., Chicago .KO 2

1894

Jan.   3—Young Griffo, Chicago .... D   6
Mar.   7—George Lavigne, Saginaw ...... D   8
Oct.   2—Frank Erne, Buffalo .... D 10
Oct.   26—Johnny Van Heest, Buffalo .... D 15
Nov. 27—Oscar Gardner, Buffalo .... LF   5

1895

Mar.   4—Tom Denny, Coney Island ..... D 10
May 15—Geprge Siddons, New York ...ND   8
Dec. 23—Torpedo Bily Murphy,
New Orleans .... W 14

1896

Feb.   23—Johnny Lavack, Boston .... D 15
Mar. 21—Jerry Barnett, New York ...... W   3
June   1—Dolly Lyons, Brooklyn .... D 10
June 22—Frank Paterson, Brooklyn ..... W 10
June 30—Johnny Lavack, Cleveland ..... D 10
Nov.   9—Willie Smith, London .... W   8

1897

Jan.   12—Tommy White, New York ..... D 25
Mar. 13—Oscar Gardner, New York ..... W 20
Aug. 20—Johnny Griffin, San Fran. ..... W   7
Oct.   4—George Dixon, San Fran. ...... W 20
(Smith won Featherweight Title.)

1898

Apr.   18—Eddie Santry, Chicago .... D   6
July   7—Billy O'Donnell, Buffalo ....WF 7
Aug.   1—Tommy White, Coney Island .. D 25
Sept. 26—Dave Sullivan, Coney Island L   5
Smith suffered broken arm and had to
retire, Sullivan winning the championship.
(Lost Featherweight Title.)
Oct.   12—Aurelio Herrera, Bakersfield,
Cal. .... D 10

1899

Feb.   7—Oscar Gardner, New York L   6
May 10—Frank Patterson, Brooklyn .... D 20
July   10—Frank Patterson, Coney Island . D 25
Aug. 18—Joe Bernstein, New York .. KO by 13
Oct.   2—Jack McClelland, Pittsburgh .. LF   6

TB	KO	WD	WF	D	LD	LF	KOBY	ND	NC
45	6	13	1	17	3	2	1	2	0

Died, 1929.

BEN JORDAN

Born, April 1, 1873, Bermondsey, London,
England. Weight, 122 lbs. Height, 5 ft. 5½ in.

1892-1894

—Alf Buckingham .... KO   1
—George Murray .... KO   2
—Bert Smith .... KO   3
—W.C. Wood `...................... KO   3
—Dave Wallace .... KO by 9
—Tiny Bishop .... KO   4
—Snowball .... KO   1
—Harry Munroe .... KO   1
—Alf Johnson .... KO   6
—Jack Welland .... KO   2
—Tom Cooper .... KO   4
—Bill Connolly .... KO   3
—Snipe Reynolds .... KO   2
—Darkey Wallace .... W   6
—Curley Perrin .... W   4
—Charlie Meacock .... W 10
—Bill Connolly .... W   6
—Bill Connolly .... W   6

1894

Oct.   29—Dave Wallace, London .... W   6

1895

Oct.   28—Jim Gough, London .... KO   3

1896

Feb.   13—Charlie Meacock, London .... KO 10
June   2—Joe Portley, London .... KO 19

1897

Feb.   22—Fred Johnson, London .... KO 13
(Won British Featherweight Title)
Nov. 29—Tommy White, London .... KO 19
(Retained British Featherweight Title)

1898

Apr.   4—Eddie Curry, London .... KO 17
(Retained British Featherweight Title)
July   1—George Dixon, New York .... W 25
(Won British World Featherweight Title)
July   8—Eldred McCloskey, Philadelphia .. ND   6

1899

May   29—Harry Greenfield, London .... KO   9
(Retained British World Featherweight Title)
Oct.   10—Eddie Santry, New York ...... KO by 16
(Lost British World Featherweight Title)

1900

Apr.   23—Bill Fielder, London .... D   6
May   28—Tommy Hagan, London .... KO   4

1901

(Inactive)

1902

June   23—Kid McFadden, London .... KO 15
Oct.   20—Jack Roberts, London .... KO   5
(Regained British Featherweight Title)

1903

May   2—George Dixon, London .... W   6
May   11—George Justice, London .... W   6

1904

Dec.   12—Pedlar Palmer, London .... W 15
(Retained British Featherweight Title)
Dec.   29—Frankie Howe, New York .... Exh. 3

1905

Jan.   4—Harry Shea, New York .... Exh. 3

TB	KO	WD	WF	D	LD	LF	KO BY	ND	NC
36	22	10	0	1	0	0	2	1	0

Died, January 18, 1945, London, England

EDDIE SANTRY

(Edward M. Santry)
Born, December 11, 1876, Aurora, Illinois.
Weight, 126 lbs. Height, 5 ft. 8 in.

1895

Mar.   22—Young Casey, Chicago .... KO   3
July   8—Spider Kelly, Chicago .... KO   1
Dec.   10—Kid Reynolds, Chicago .... KO   2
Dec.   29—Eddie Curry, Springfield, Ill. ..... KO   4

1896

Jan.   12—Jim Gilchrist, Chicago .... KO   6
Mar.   30—Kid Ryan, Chicago .... D   8
Apr.   29—Jack Smith, Chicago .... KO   1
July   10—Frank Mullaney, Chicago .... W 10
Aug.   1—Tommy Irwin, Kenosha, Wisc. .... KO   4
Aug.   8—Tommy White, Lemont, Ill. ..... KO by 7
Aug.   18—Charley Marsh, Chicago .... KO   2
Sept. 20—Jack Martin, Chicago .... KO   5
Nov. 10—Danny Carroll, Chicago .... KO   9
Dec.   29—Young Dempsey, Chicago .... KO   5

1897

May   19—Billy Slater, Muscatine, Iowa .... KO   4
June   1—Hays Moose, Muscatine, Iowa .... KO   8
Aug.   1—Billy Lambert, Davenport .... W 20
Oct.   15—Pete Johnson, Chicago .... KO   3
Dec.   27—Henry Lyons, Chicago .... D   6

1898

Jan.   22—Tommy Dixon, Toronto .... W 20
Jan.   28—Pete Boyle, Chicago .... W   6
Apr.   18—Solly Smith, Chicago .... D   6

Apr. 26—Aus. Billy Murphy, St. Louis ..... KO 3
June 6—George Dixon, New York .... L 20
    (Advertised For World Featherweight Title)
July 22—Joe Bernstein, New York .... L 20
1899
Feb. 2—Jack Bain, Springfield, Ill. .... KO 5
Mar. 2—Joe Cain, Chicago .... W 6
Mar. 16—Louden Campbell, Springfield, Ill. W 6
July 14—George Dixon, Chicago .... L 6
Aug. 11—George Dixon, New York .... D 20
    (For World Featherweight Title)
Oct. 10—Ben Jordan, New York .... KO 16
    (Won British World Featherweight Title)
Dec. 11—Jack O'Malley, Chicago .... KO 1
1900
Feb. 1—Terry McGovern, Chicago ..... KO by 5
    (For World Featherweight Title)
May 3—Oscar Gardner, Louisville ..... KO by 5
July 8—Oscar Gardner, Kansas City .... W 20
Dec. 29—Jack McClelland, Pittsburgh .. KO by 5
1901
Apr. 12—Young Corbett II, Denver ..... KO by 2
July 10—Joe Hedmark, Chicago .... W 6
Aug. 14—Adam Ryan, Chicago .... D 6
Sept. 18—Ole Olson, Omaha .... KO 2
Nov. 29—Battling Nelson, Chicago .... W 6
1902
Jan. 10—Jack Bain, Peoria .... W 10
Feb. 1—Kid Goulette, Chicago .... KO 1
Feb. 22—Dick Fitzpatrick, Chicago .... KO 2
July 3—Young Munzie, Hammond, Ind. ... KO 5
Aug. 10—Adam Ryan, Indianapolis .... D 10
Nov. 21—Charley Neary, Milwaukee .... D 6
1903
Mar. 23—Tommy Sullivan, Chicago .... WF 3
Apr. 15—Kid Able, Chicago .... D 6
July 5—Tommy Mowatt, Indianapolis ...... W 10
Aug. 1—Ole Olson, Indianapolis .... D 10
Aug. 17—Hugh McPadden, Indianapolis ..... D 10
Sept. 11—Jack McClelland, Chicago .... D 6
Sept. 25—Mickey Riley, Milwaukee .... D 6
Oct. 23—Jack Doherty, Milwaukee .... W 6
Oct. 29—Aurelio Herrera, Anaconda ... KO by 13
Nov. 28—Billy Ryan, Toronto .... KO by 16
1904
Jan. —Kid Sayers, Milwaukee .... D 6
Feb. 25—Kid Farmer, Chicago .... KO by 5
Nov. 29—Jack Cardell, San Francisco .... L 10
Dec. —Maurice Sayers, Milwaukee ...... WF 2
Dec. 11—Kid Black, Chicago .... D 6
Dec. 29—Eddie Toy, Chicago .... D 6
1905
Apr. 10—Jack Parry, Boston .... KO 11
May 14—Jack Hennessy, Chelsea, Mass. ... KO 7
Sept. 8—Jack Ryan, Kalamazoo, Mich. .... KO 7
Sept. 30—Elmer Grosbeck, Fond du Lac .... KO 2
Oct. 14—Eddie Kenny, Chicago .... W 6
Oct. 20—Johnny Stone, Milwaukee .... KO 2
Nov. 17—Jack Dougherty, Milwaukee ... KO by 4
1906
(Inactive)
1907
Nov. 13—Joe Parrente, Ashland, Wisc. ...... W 10
Dec. 10—Tommy Lynch, Duluth, Minn. .... KO 4
1908
Apr. 14—Jack O'Keefe, Hibbing, Minn. ..... W 6
May 28—Red Robinson, Hot Springs .... KO 3
Oct. 27—Tommy Hudson, Detroit, Mich. ... KO 11

1909
Mar. 22—Eli Hamblin, Menominee, Mich. .. KO 3
Sept. 10—Packey McFarland, Wheaton .... Exh. 4
Nov. 10—Jim McVicker, Buffalo .... KO 5
1910
(Inactive)
1911
May 12—Jack Ryan, South Bend .... KO 4

TB	KO	WD	WF	D	LD	LF	KO BY	ND	NC
78	33	15	2	15	4	0	9	0	0

708

DAVE SULLIVAN
Born, May 19, 1877, Cork, Ireland.
Weight, 126-130 lbs. Height, 5 ft. 4½ in.
1894
Won: Frank Coffee, 3. Knockout: Frank
Stone, 6. No decision: Micky Callahan, 3.
1895
Won: Dave Parkman, 3; Phil Smith, 2.
Knockout: Barty McGriel, 2.
1896
Won: Austin Kavaney, 4; Allie Alberts, 11.
Knockouts: Joe Elms, 9; Bob Cunningham, 8;
Young Dixon, 4; Tom Tully, 2. Draw: Allie
Alberts, 6; Austin Rice, 10; Billy Smith, 6; Jack
Ward, 20; Austin Rice, 12; Caspter Leon, 20.
1897
Won: Jimmy Rose, 17; Maxey Haugh, 5.
Knockouts: Patsy Haley, 13; Patsy Haley, 22.
Draw: Tom McCune, 4. Lost: Pedlar Palmer, 20.
1898
Mar. 4—Patsy Broderick, Yonkers ..... W 9
May 16—Sammy Kelly, New York ...... W 20
Sept. 26—Solly Smith, Coney Island .... W 5
    Smith suffered broken arm and retired,
Sullivan winning the championship.
    (Won World Featherweight Title)
Nov. 11—George Dixon, New York..... LF 10
    Sullivan's second entered the ring, the
referee disqualified him and Dixon regained his
title.
    (Lost World Featherweight Title)
1899
Jan. 9—Oscar Gardner, New York . KO by 17
Feb. 11—Marty McCue, Brooklyn .... D 25
Mar. 27—Joe Bernstein, Brooklyn .... D 20
Apr. 19—Jack O'Brien, Hartford .... D 20
Sept. 30—Joe Bernstein, New York ...... D 25
Nov. 10—Joe Bernstein, New York ...... D 25
Nov. 28—Kid Broad, New York ....L 25
1900
Jan. 30—Jack Hamilton, Troy .... W 25
Mar. 10—Kid Broad, New York .... W 25
Mar. 30—Tim Callahan, Philadelphia .....L 3
Apr. 2—Eddie Gardner, Brooklyn ...... W 19
May 3—Billy Whistler, Baltimore ...... D 17
July 3—Kid Broad, Coney Island ..... LF 16
July 23—Luke Burke, Buffalo ....KO 4
Oct. 8—Oscar Gardner, Louisville ..... W 14
Nov. 30—Ole Oleson, Chicago .... LF 4
Dec. 10—Tim Callahan, Louisville ......WF 18
1901
Jan. 14—Kid Broad, Louisville .... D 25
Apr. 30—Jack McClelland, Louisville ...KO 20
Sept. 30—Kid Broad, Louisville ....L 25
Oct. 14—Kid Broad, Fort Lee .... D 20
1902
Feb. 22—Terry McGovern, Louisville ....L 15
Apr. 17—Austin Rice, Waterbury .... D 20
Nov. 7—Jimmy Briggs, Boston ....WF 7
1903
June 26—Crockey Boyle, Philadelphia ..ND 6
Dec. 25—Austin Rice, Portland, Me...... W 15
1904
Jan. 12—Jimmy Briggs, Boston .... W 15
Feb. 29—Young Corbett,
    San Francisco, ...KO by 11
Mar. 18—Chas. Neary, Milwaukee ....L 6
1905
Mar. 13—Kid Herman, Hot Springs ....L 9

TB	KO	WD	WF	D	LD	LF	KO BY	ND	NC
58	10	16	2	16	7	3	2	2	0

TERRY McGOVERN
(John Terrence McGovern)
(Terrible Terry)
Born, March 9, 1880, Johnstown, Pa.
Nationality, Irish-American. Weight, 128 lbs.
Height, 5 ft. 4 in. Managed by Jimmy Dunn, Sam
Harris and Joe Humphreys.
1897
Apr. 24—Frank Barnes, Brooklyn .... W 10
May 3—Eddie Avery, N. Y. C. .... W 4
May 22—Kid Dougherty, Brooklyn ..... W 10
June 7—Tom McDermott, Brooklyn ... W 10
June —Tommy Sullivan, Brooklyn .... D 10
Aug. 16—Eddie Goodbody, Brooklyn ... W 10
Aug. 23—Billy Barrett, Brooklyn .... W 10
Sept. 18—Jack Leon, Brooklyn.........KO 7
Oct. 2—Jack Reagan, Brooklyn .... W 6

Oct.   9—Jack Doyle, Brooklyn .... W   7
Oct.   23—Eddie Goodbody, Brooklyn ... D   4
Nov.   13—Harry Peterson, N. Y. C....... W   6
Dec.   7—Charley Roden, N. Y. C....... W   6
Dec.   31—Jack Kelly, Brooklyn ....KO   2
1898
Feb.   25—Billy Maynard, Yonkers .... W   8
Mar.   12—Pinkey Evans, Yonkers .... W   8
Apr.   15—Fred Mayo, Waterbury ....KO   6
May   5—George Munroe, Yonkers ...... D   20
June   11—George Munroe, Coney Island .KO 24
July   23—Tim Callahan, Brooklyn ...... LF   11
Aug.   4—George Munroe, Brooklyn ....WF   7
Aug.   20—Tim Callahan, Brooklyn ...... D   20
Sept. 15—Eugene Garcia, Brooklyn .....KO   5
Oct.   1—Harry Forbes, Brooklyn .....KO   15
Nov.   19—Tim Callahan, Brooklyn .....KO   10
Nov.   26—Paddy Donovan, Philadelphia .KO   3
Dec.   17—Jimmy Rose, Brooklyn ....KO   6
Dec.   31—Austin Rice, Brooklyn .... W   14
1899
Jan.   30—Casper Leon, Brooklyn ....KO   12
Feb.   18—Fred Snyder, Phila........... W   6
Mar.   12—Patsy Haley, N. Y. C........KO   18
Apr.   28—Joe Bernstein, N. Y. C....... W   25
May   26—Sammy Kelly, N. Y. C........KO   5
June   8—Billy Barrett, N. Y. C. ....KO   10
July   1—Johnny Richie, Tuckahoe ..... W   3
Sept. 12—Pedlar Palmer, Tuckahoe .....KO   1
Won Vacant World Bantamweight Title)
(Scheduled for September 11 but it rained)
Sept. 29—Fred Snyder, Phila. .... W   2
Oct.   9—Billy Rotchford, Chicago .....KO   1
Nov.   18—Patsy Haley, Chicago ....KO   1
Nov.   18—Bill Smith, Chicago ....KO   3
Nov.   30—Eddie Sprague, Hartford .....KO   2
Dec.   12—Jas. J. Corbett, Jr., Chicago ...KO   2
Dec.   18—Charlie Mason, Cincinnati ....KO   2
Dec.   18—Freckles O'Brien, Cincinnati ..KO   1
Dec.   22—Harry Forbes, N. Y. C. ....KO   2
(Vacated Bantamweight Title).
1900
Jan.   9—George Dixon, N. Y. C. ....KO   8
(Won World Featherweight Title)
Jan.   29—Jack Ward, Baltimore ....KO   1
Feb.   1—*Eddie Santry, Chicago ....KO   5
Feb.   21—George Dixon, N. Y. C.......Exh.
Mar.   9—*Oscar Gardner, N. Y. C. .....KO   3
Mar.   15—Eddie Lenny, Phila. .... W   2
Apr.   17—Tommy White, Chicago ......ND   6
Apr.   20—Tommy Warren, N. Y. C. ...... W   1
May   21—El. McCloskey, Phila. ....ND   1
June   12—*Tommy White, Coney Island KO   6
June   23—George Dixon, Chicago .... W   3
July   16—Frank Erne, N. Y. C. ....KO   6
Nov.   2—*Joe Bernstein, Louisville ....KO   7
Nov.   13—Kid Broad, Chicago .... W   6
Dec.   8—Tommy White, Milwaukee ..Exh.   4
Dec.   13—Joe Gans, Chicago ....KO   2
*Title bouts.
1901
Apr.   30—*Oscar Gardner, San Fran.....KO   4
May   29—*Auerio Herrera, San Fran. ...KO   5
Sept. 28—Joe Tipman, Baltimore .....Exh.   2
Nov.   10—Kid Abel, Chicago ....Exh.   4
Nov.   28—*Young Corbett, Hartford . KO by   2
(Lost World Featherweight Title)
*Title bouts.
1902
Feb.   22—Dave Sullivan, Louisville ...... W   15
1903
Feb.   6—Joe Bernstein, Phila...........ND   6
Feb.   25—Billy Maynard, Phila..........KO   4
Mar.   31—Young Corbett, San Fran. . KO by   11
Sept. 26—Lew Ryall, Phila. ....ND   6
Oct.   3—Billy Willis, Phila. ....ND   6
Oct.   20—Jimmy Briggs, Boston .... W   15
1904
Apr.   10—George Barton, St. Paul L   4
Oct.   10—Eddie Hanlon, Phila. .... W   4
1905
Oct.   18—Tommy Murphy, Phila. ......KO   1
1906
Mar.   14—Battling Nelson, Phila. ....ND   6
May   28—Jimmy Britt, N. Y. C. ....ND   10
Oct.   17—Young Corbett, Phila........ND   6
1908
May   16—Young Loughrey, Phila. ......ND   6
May   27—Spike Robson, N. Y. C. ......ND   6

TB	KO	WD	WF	D	LD	LF	KO BY	ND	NC
77	34	24	1	4	1	1	?	10	0

Died Feb. 26, 1918, Brooklyn, N. Y.
Elected to Boxing Hall of Fame 1955.

YOUNG CORBETT
(Young Corbett II)
(William H. Rothwell)

Born, October 4, 1880, Denver, Colorado.
Nationality, American. Weight, 133 pounds.
Height, 5 ft. 2½ in.
1897
Won: Bert Crater, 3. Knockouts: Kid
Harris, 4; Julius Segil, 4.
1898
July   24—Fred O'Neil, Omaha ....KO   4
Nov.   14—Reddy Coogan, Aspen .... D   20
Dec.   12—Dago Mike, Aspen ....KO   2
1899
Feb.   27—Abe Spitz, Denver .... D   20
Apr.   7—Tom Glen, Leadville ....KO   5
May   2—Billy Irwin, Aspen ....KO   4
June   10—Abe Spitz, Aspen ....KO   4
June   23—Jack Dempsey, Aspen .... D   20
July   24—Billy Rotchford, Denver L   20
Aug.   19—Paddy Hughes, Hastings .....KO   1
Sept.   1—Jack Flint, Omaha .... W   4
Sept.   3—Billy Harris, Omaha ....KO   2
Oct.   4—Al Rivers, Des Moines ....KO   4
Oct.   6—Billy Brown, Des Moines ...... W   4
Nov.   27—Kid Bennett, Cripple Creek ...KO   3
1900
Jan.   10—Spike Wallace, Denver ....KO   1
Jan.   22—Jack Munson, Denver ....KO   2
Feb.   11—Kid Kelly, Denver ....KO   2
Feb.   29—Jack Dempsey, Pueblo .... KO by   2
Mar.   14—Jack Dempsey, Pueblo ....KO   3
Apr.   13—Benny Yanger, Denver .... KO by   8
Apr.   24—Jimmy Coogan, Denver .... W   6
May   30—Frank Newhouse, Aspen .....KO   17
July   5—Ray Streetor, Cripple Creek ..KO   2
July   28—Kid Lee, Cripple Creek ....KO   4
Aug.   27—Larry Lacy, Denver ....KO   1
Sept.   5—Jimmy Riley, Denver .... D   10
Sept. 15—Jack Kane, Cripple Creek .... D   20
Sept. 28—Jimmy Riley, Denver ....KO   3
Oct.   6—Jimmy Coogan, Pueblo ...... W   20
Nov.   27—Benny Yanger, Denver .... D   10
Dec.   15—Reddy Coogan, Cripple Creek .. W   3
1901
Jan.   18—Joe Bernstein, Denver .... W   7
Mar.   22—Kid Broad, Denver .... KO by   4
Apr.   12—Eddie Santry, Denver ....KO   2
June   26—Oscar Gardner, Denver ....KO   6
July   26—Kid Broad, Denver .... W   10
Aug.   16—George Dixon, Denver .... W   10
Nov.   28—Terry McGovern, Hartford ...KO   2
(Won Featherweight Title)
1902
May   23—Kid Broad, Denver .... W   10
Oct.   7—Eddie Lenny, Philadelphia .....ND   6
Oct.   16—Joe Bernstein, Baltimore ..... W   7
Oct.   27—Young Erne, Philadelphia ....ND   6
Nov.   17—Crockey Boyle, Philadelphia ..ND   6
(Vacated Featherweight Title)
1903
Jan.   14—Austin Rice, Hot Springs ...... W   18
Feb.   2—Billy Maynard, Philadelphia ..ND   6
Feb.   26—Eddie Hanlon, San Fran. ...... D   20
Mar.   31—Terry McGovern, San Fran. ...KO   11
Apr.   23—George Memsic, Portland .....D   4
May   2—Tommy Jacobs, Ogden .... D   3
May   19—Jack Keefe, St. Louis ....KO   3
June   25—Hughey Murphy, Boston ....KO   6
June   29—Jimmy Briggs, Boston .... W   10
July   6—Sammy Smith, Philadelphia ..ND   6
July   22—Jimmy Briggs, Boston .... W   10
July   24—Billy Maynard, Philadelphia ..KO   1
July   29—Jack O'Neill, Philadelphia ....KO   5
Oct.   10—Kid Stein, Philadelphia ....ND   6
Oct.   21—Tim Callahan, Philadelphia ...ND   6
Oct.   28—Hugh Murphy, Boston ....KO   11
Dec.   29—Eddie Hanlon, San Fran. ....KO   16
1904
Feb.   29—Dave Sullivan, San Fran. .....KO   11
Mar.   25—Jimmy Britt, San Fran. L   20
Apr.   2—Tommy Mowatt, Chicago .... W   6
Nov.   26—Frank George, San Fran. .....KO   3
Nov.   29—Battling Nelson, San Fran. . KO by   10
1905
Feb.   28—Battling Nelson, San Fran. . KO by   9
Mar.   31—Kid Sullivan, Baltimore ....D   10
Apr.   3—Young Erne, Philadelphia ....ND   6
June   2—Eddie Hanlon, San Fran. L   20
June   13—Maurice Thompson, Butte ....KO   10
Oct.   25—Young Erne, Philadelphia ....ND   6
Oct.   27—Joe Tipman, Baltimore .... W   8
Oct.   31—Kid Goodman, Chelsea ....D   15

Nov. 5—Unk Russell, Philadelphia ....ND 6
Nov. 18—Charlie Sieger, N. Y. C. ....W 3
Dec. 1—Charlie Sieger, N. Y. C. ....ND 4
1906
Jan. 12—Aurelio Herrera, Los Ang. .KO by 5
Apr. 30—Dick Hyland, Oregon .....KO by 5
May 29—Eddie Johnson, N. Y. C. ......ND 6
Oct. 17—Terry McGovern, Phila. ......ND 6
1907
Jan. 9—Tommy Murphy, Phila. ......ND 6
Apr. 27—Young Erne, Philadelphia ...ND 6
May 3—Kid Sullivan, Baltimore ...KO by 11
Dec. 12—Phil Brock, New Orleans .... D 10
1908
Mar. 4—Mickey Gannon, Philadelphia .ND 6
1909
Jan. 24—Harry Ferns, New Orleans ....KO 11
Feb. 9—Mull Bowser, Pittsburgh ......ND 6
Feb. 15—Bob Wilson, Schenectady .....ND 10
Mar. 2—Johnny Marto, N. Y. C.......ND 10
Mar. 9—Cy Smith, Schenectady ......ND 10
Mar. 25—Bert Keyes, N. Y. C...........ND 10
Apr. 23—Bert Keyes, N. Y. C...........ND 10
May 11—Harry Scroggs, Baltimore ....W 15
May 17—Dick Nelson, Schenectady ....ND 10
June 4—Sammy Smith, N. Y. C.........ND 10
June 8—Mike Deming, Philadelphia ...ND 6
July 17—Johnny Frayne, Colma,
      Cal. ....KO by 8
Aug. 21—Muggsy Shoels, Cheyenne,
      Wyo. ....KO 15
Oct. 5—Dave Deshler, Boston ....L 5
1910
Oct. 20—Willie Beecher, N. Y. C.....KO by 4

TB KO WD WF D LD LF KOBY ND NC
104 34 19 0 12 6 0   8   25 0
Died April 10, 1927 in Denver.
Elected to Hall of Fame in 1965.

ABE ATTELL
Born, February 22, 1884, San Francisco,
Cal. Nationality, Jewish-American. Weight, 122
lbs. Height, 5 ft. 4 in. Managed by Al Lippe Jack
McKenna, Tim McGrath, Zeke Abrams, Ike
Bloom, Lob Kohn, Billy Nolan, George Weedon,
Jack Kearns, Dan Morgan and John Reisler.
1900
Aug. 19—Kid Lennett, San Francisco ...KO 2
Aug. 29—Kid Dodson, San Francisco ...KO 2
Aug. 31—Joe O'Leary, San Francisco ...KO 4
Sept. 18—Benny Dwyer, San Francisco ...KO 3
Oct. 4—Joe Hill, San Francisco ....KO 5
Oct. 10—Eddie Hanlon, San Francisco ..W 5
Oct. 19—Dick Cullen, San Francisco ...KO 1
Oct. 25—Lew White, San Francisco ....KO 1
Nov. 2—Jim Barry, San Francisco .....KO 1
      (Not the Chicago Jimmy Barry)
Nov. 8—Frank Dell, San Francisco ....KO 3
Nov. 18—Kid O'Neill, San Francisco ....KO 1
Nov. 24—George Brown, San Francisco .KO 2
Dec. 4—Kid Jones, San Francisco .....KO 1
Dec. 8—Peter Carroll, San Francisco ..KO 2
Dec. 15—Kid Dulley, San Francisco ....KO 1
Dec. 20—Kid Powers, San Francisco ...KO 2
1901
Jan. 6—Jockey Bozeman, San Fran. ...W 10
Jan. 26—Mike Smith, San Francisco ...KO 2
Feb. 15—Kid Buck, Denver...........W 5
Feb. 22—Kid Buck, Denver...........W 5
Mar. 1—Kid Delaney, Denver........KO 4
Mar. 24—Kid Pieser, Denver ....KO 2
Apr. 12—Scotty Williams, Denver .....KO 2
Apr. 26—Young Cassidy, Denver......KO 2
June 26—Jockey Bozeman, Denver.....KO 3
July 4—Kid Buck, Denver...........W 5
Aug. 12—Kid Decker, Denver ....D 10
Aug. 24—George Dixon, Denver ....D 10
Aug. 26—Kid Lewis, Denver ....KO 3
Aug. 29—Scotty Williams, Denver .....KO 1
Sept. 3—Colorado Jack Dempsey, II,
      Pueblo ....W 20
Oct. 20—George Dixon, Cripple Creek .. D 20
      (For Vacant Featherweight Title)
Oct. 28—George Dixon, St. Louis ,......W 15
      (Won Vacant Featherweight Title)
Nov. 4—Harry Forbes, St. Louis ....L 15

1902
Mar. 20—Kid Broad, St. Louis .... D 15
Apr. 10—Kid Broad, St. Louis .... W 20
Apr. 24—Benny Yanger, St. Louis ...KO by 19
Aug. 25—Kid Abel, Chicago ....W 6
Sept. 11—Kid Abel, St. Louis .... W 20
Oct. 15—Aurelio Herrera, Oakland......W 15
Nov. 10—Harry Forbes, Chicago .... D 6
Dec. 8—Buddy Ryan, Chicago.........W 6
1903
Jan. 29—Eddie Hanlon, San Francisco .. D 10
Mar. 12—Eddie Toy, San Francisco .....W 20
Sept. 3—Johnny Reagan, St. Louis .....W 20
1904
Jan. 4—Harry Forbes, Indianapolis ....D 10
Feb. 1—Harry Forbes, St. Louis ......KO 5
      (Featherweight Title)
Feb. 18—Kid Herman, Chicago ....W 6
Feb. 27—Young Erne, Philadelphia ...ND 6
Mar. 9—Patsy Haley, Hot Springs ....KO 5
Mar. 23—Maurice Rausch, Hot Springs .KO 6
Mar. 28—Aurelio Herrera, Chicago ......W 6
May 14—Young Erne, Philadelphia ....ND 6
June 2—Jack McClelland, St. Louis.....L 15
June 23—Johnnie Regan, St. Louis .....W 20
Oct. 13—Tommy Sullivan, St. Louis KO by 5
      (Sullivan Claimed Title)
Nov. 19—Young Erne, St. Louis ......W 20
Dec. 8—Tommy Feltz, St. Louis ....W 15
1905
Jan. 28—Tommy Murphy, Philadelphia ND 6
Feb. 3—Tommy Feltz, Baltimore ......ND 6
Feb. 22—Kid Goodman, Boston ....D 15
      (Featherweight Title Bout)
Feb. 24—Eddie Hanlon, Philadelphia ...ND 6
May 1—Jimmy Dunn, Sharon, Pa. .....D 15
May 10—Harry Forbes, Detroit ....W 10
May 22—Battling Nelson, Philadelphia .ND 6
      —Tommy Sullivan, Alton, Ill. ...ND 6
Oct. 4—Young Erne, Philadelphia ....ND 6
Nov. 1—Chick Tucker, N. Y. C. .....Exh. 3
Nov. 8—Tommy Mowatt, Philadelphia ND 6
Nov. 16—Tommy Mowatt, Baltimore .... W 15
Nov. 23—Kid Sullivan, Baltimore ....D 15
Dec. 20—Eddie Daly, N. Y. C. ....ND 3
1906
Jan. 16—Chester Goodwin, Chelsea .....D 15
Jan. 22—Billy Maynard, Portland, Me. .. W 10
Feb. 22—Jimmy Walsh, Chelsea ....W 15
Mar. 7—*Tony Bender, N. Y. C. ......ND 3
Mar. 7—*Billy Elmer, New York ......ND 3
      Both bouts same night
Mar. 13—Artie Edmunds, N. Y. C.......ND 3
Mar. 15—Tony Moran, Baltimore ......WF 3
Mar. 19—Phil Logan, Philadelphia......ND 6
May 11—Kid Herman, Los Angeles ... D 20
July 4—Frankie Neil, Los Angeles .....W 20
      (World Featherweight Title)
Aug. 15—Frank Carsey, Grand Rapids ... W 15
Sept. 3—Frank Carsey, Davenport .....W 3
Oct. 30—*Harry Baker, Los Angeles ....W 20
Nov. 16—Billy DeCoursey, San Diego ....W 15
Dec. 7—*Jimmy Walsh, Los Angeles ..KO 8
      *Title bout.
1907
Jan. 18—*Harry Baker, Los Angeles ...KO 8
Apr. 3—Spike Robson, Philadelphia ...ND 6
Apr. 17—Tom O'Toole, Philadelphia ...ND 6
May 24—*Kid Solomon, Los Angeles ....W 20
Sept. 12—Jimmy Walsh, Indianapolis ....W 10
Sept. 21—Bklyn. Tom Sullivan, Alton, Ill. D 6
Oct. 29—*Freddie Weeks, Los Angeles .KO 4
      *Title bout.
1908
Jan. 1—*Owen Moran, San Francisco .. D 25
Jan. 31—Frankie Neil, San Francisco ...KO 13
Feb. 28—Eddie Kelly, San Francisco ...KO 7
Mar. 31—Battling Nelson, San Francisco . D 15
Apr. 20—Eddie Kelly, Seattle..........W 8
Apr. 30—Tommy Sullivan, San Fran. ...KO 4
June 20—Matty Baldwin, N. Y. C.......ND 10
July 29—Eddie Marino, Idaho ....W 10
Sept. 7—*Owen Moran, San Fran. .....D 23
Nov. 25—Freddie Welsh, Vernon, Cal. ....L 15
Dec. 11—Ad Wolgast, Los Angeles ....ND 10
Dec. 29—Biz Mackey, New Orleans ....KO 8
      *Title bout.
1909
Jan. 14—Freddie Weeks, Goldfield .....KO 10
Feb. 4—Eddie Kelly, New Orleans .....W 7
Feb. 19—Jim Driscoll, N. Y. C. ......ND 10
Mar. 1—Young Pierce, Phila. ....ND 10
Mar. 10—Young Pierce, Phila. ....KO 6
Mar. 18—Patsy Kline, N. Y. C. ....ND 10

Mar.	23—Frankie Neil, Brooklyn	ND	10
Mar.	26—*Frankie White, Dayton	KO	8
Apr.	26—Biz Mackey, Columbus	W	8
Aug.	18—Harry Stone, Saratoga	ND	10
Sept.	6—Eddie Kelly, Pittsburgh	ND	6
Sept.	14—Tommy O'Toole, Boston	W	12
Oct.	5—Charley Miller, Phila.	ND	6
Oct.	8—Patsy Kline, Phila.	ND	6
Nov.	22—Johnny Moran, Memphis	W	8
Dec.	6—Charles White, Memphis	W	8

*Title bout.

1910
Jan.	1—Eddie Kelly, Savannah, Ga.	W	5
Feb.	24—Frankie Neil, N. Y. C.	ND	10
Feb.	28—*Harry Forbes, N. Y. C.	KO	7
Mar.	18—Johnny Marto, N. Y. C.	ND	10
Apr.	1—Owen Moran, N. Y. C.	ND	10
Apr.	28—Tommy Murphy, N. Y. C.	ND	10
May	10—Tommy Murphy, N. Y. C.	ND	10
June	24—Owen Moran, Los Angeles	ND	10
Aug.	22—Eddie Marino, Calgary, Can.	KO	3
Sept.	5—Billy Lauder, Calgary, Can.	KO	17
Sept.	16—Charley White, Milwaukee	ND	10
Oct.	5—Frankie White, Milwaukee	ND	10
Oct.	10—Jack White, Winnipeg, Can.	ND	15
Oct.	24—Johnny Kilbane, Kansas City	W	10
Oct.	27—Biz Mackey, N. Y. C.	KO	6
Oct.	28—Eddie Kelly, Amterdam, N. Y.	KO	4
Nov.	9—Owen Moran, Phila.	ND	6
Nov.	13—Frankie Conley, New Orleans	D	15
Nov.	30—Pal Moore, N. Y. C.	ND	10

*Title bout.

1911
Jan.	9—Joe Coster, Brooklyn	ND	10
Jan.	13—Patsy Kline, N. Y. C.	ND	10
Jan.	23—Billy Allen, Syracuse	ND	10
Jan.	31—*Tommy Kilbane, Cleve.	KO by	4
Mar.	31—Frankie Burns, N. Y. C.	ND	10
Sept.	20—Matt Wells, N. Y. C.	ND	10
Nov.	3—Herman Smith, Buffalo	ND	10
Nov.	15—Young Cohen, N. Y. C.	ND	10
Nov.	20—Willie Jones, N. Y. C.	ND	10
Nov.	23—Leo Johnson, N. Y. C.	KO	5
Dec.	1—Patsy Kline, N. Y. C.	ND	10
Dec.	2—Willie Jones, Brooklyn	ND	10

*Attell quit, claiming he broke shoulder.

1912
Jan.	18—K. O. Brown, N. Y. C.	ND	10
Feb.	22—Johnny Kilbane, Vernon, Cal.	L	20
	(Lost World Featherweight Title)		
Mar.	9—Tommy Murphy, San Francisco, Cal.	L	20
Apr.	23—Jimmy Carroll, Sacramento	KO	7
July	4—Eddie Marino, Tacoma, Wash.	W	10
Aug.	3—Tommy Murphy, Daly City, Cal.	D	20
Sept.	13—Harry Thomas, N. Y. C.	ND	10
Oct.	24—Johnny Walsh, Boston	D	12
Nov.	27—*Oliver Kirk, St. Louis	L	6

*Attell quit, stating he was all in.

1913
Mar.	19—Ollie Kirk, N. Y. C.	KO	3
Apr.	3—Jimmy Walsh, N. Y. C.	ND	10
Apr.	15—*Benny Kaufman, Atlanta	KO	7
Apr.	28—Geo. Chaney, Baltimore	W	15
July	24—Willie Bleecher, N. Y. C.	ND	10
Sept.	1—Bert Wetherhead, Winnipeg	KO	3
Sept.	6—Kid Callahan, Gloversville	KO	5
Sept.	17—Sid Knott, Winnipeg	W	6

*Bout ordered stopped and declared "No fight".

1917
Jan.	8—Phil Virgets, New Orleans	KO by	4

TB	KO	WD	WF	D	LD	LF	KOBY	ND	NC
169	48	43	1	17	7	0	3	50	0

Elected to Boxing Hall of Fame 1955.
Died Feb 7, 1970, New Platz, N.Y.

JOHNNY KILBANE
(John Patrick Kilbane)
Born, April 18, 1889, Cleveland, O.
Nationality, Irish-American. Weight, 122-126 lbs. Height, 5 ft. 5 in. Managed by Jimmy Dunn.

1907
Knockout: Kid Campbell, 6. Won: Mangan, 3; Tommy Burns, 3.

1908
Knockout: Herman Zahinger, 9. Won: Paul Koehler, 6; Young Saylor, 10; Tommy Kilbane, 25; Clyde Le Master, 6, Draw: Tommy Kilbane, 3; Tommy Kilbane, 10. No Decision: Tommy Lynch, 10; Paul Koehler, 6; Battling Terry, 10; Young Joe Grimm, 10.

1909
Knockouts: Mike Bartley, 5; Jeff Gaffney, 5. Won: Johnny Whittaker, 12; Clyde Le Master, 8; Matty Heffron, 8. Won (foul): Biz Mackey, 6. Draw: Jack White, 10; Jack White, 12. No Decision: Happy Davis, 6; Cleyce Yeagre, 10.

1910
Jan.	1—Tommy Kilbane, Canton, O.	W	15
Jan.	12—Tom Dougherty, Wind., Can.	ND	8
Feb.	2—Jack White, Windsor, Can.	ND	8
Mar.	3—Kid Tyler, Cleveland, O.	KO	3
Mar.	30—Biz Mackay, Lorain, O.	NC Police	6
Apr.	30—Bobby Tickle, Boston, Mass.	W	10
Apr.	19—Al Delmont, Boston, Mass.	W	10
July	4—Patsy Brannigan, Akron, O.	ND	12
Sept.	29—Benny Kaufman, Pitts.	ND	6
Oct.	22—Sam Langford, Kansas City	Exh.	3
Oct.	24—Abe Attell, Kansas City, Mo.	L	10
Nov.	25—Benny Kaufman, Akron, O.	ND	12

1911
Jan.	2—Patsy Brannigan, Canton, O.	ND	12
Jan.	7—Tommy O'Toole, Philadelphia	ND	6
Jan.	12—Gussie Wilson, Cleveland, O.	W	10
Feb.	4—Jack White, Columbus. O.	W	12
Feb.	27—Tommy Bresnahan, Yngstwn.	ND	10
Mar.	8—Johnny Albanese, Cleveland	W	10
Mar.	16—Young Ghetto, Cleveland, O.	W	10
Mar.	24—Monte Attell, Cleveland, O.	D	10
May	6—Joe Rivers, Vernon, Cal.	L	20
May	30—Jimmy Walsh, Canton, O.	ND	12
July	15—Patsy Kline, Vernon, Cal.	W	20
Sept.	4—Joe Rivers, Vernon, Cal.	KO	16
Sept.	30—Frankie Conley, Vernon, Cal.	W	20
Nov.	29—Patsy Brannigan, Yngstwn.	ND	10
Dec.	23—Charley White, Cleveland, O.	ND	12

1912
Feb.	22—Abe Attell, Vernon, Cal.	W	20
	(Won Featherweight Title)		
May	14—Frankie Burns, N. Y. C.	ND	10
May	21—Jimmie Walsh, Boston, Mass.	D	12
	(Title Bout)		
June	6—Tommy O'Toole, Philadelphia	ND	6
Sept.	14—Johnny Dundee, N. Y. C.	ND	10
July	4—Tommy Dixon, Cleveland, O.	ND	12
Sept.	11—Jack Moore, Tiffin, O.	W	10
Sept.	19—Eddie O'Keefe, N. Y. C.	ND	10
Oct.	1—Eddie O'Keefe, Cleveland, O.	W	12
Oct.	24—Johnny Albanese, Columbus	ND	10
Oct.	29—Tommy McGinty, Johnstown	KO	4
Dec.	3—Monte Attell, Cleve., O.	W	9
	(Stopped by police to save Attell from knockout.)		
*Dec.	12—Tommy Dixon, St. Louis, Mo.	ND	8

*Dixon was nearly out in eighth.

1913
Jan.	1—Oliver Kirk, St. Louis	KO	2
Feb.	4—Young Driscoll, Brooklyn	ND	10
Feb.	19—Geo. Kirkwood, N. Y. C.	KO	6
Apr.	7—†Johnny Dundee, Vernon	D	20
June	10—Jimmy Fox, Oakland, Cal.	KO	6
Sept.	16—Jimmy Walsh, Boston	W	12
Sept.	25—Joe Goldberg, Rochester	ND	10
Oct.	8—Kid Julian, N. Y. C.	ND	10
Oct.	30—Knockout Mars, Cincinnati	KO	7
Nov.	10—Eddie O'Keefe, Philadelphia	KO	1
	+Charles Eyton, referee; for title.		
Jan.	5—Eddie Moy, Philadelphia	KO	5
Feb.	2—Eddie Moy, Philadelphia	ND	6
Feb.	7—Kid Thomas, Philadelphia	ND	6
Feb.	11—Tommy Bresnahan, Syracuse	ND	10
Apr.	6—Gene Delmont, Memphis	W	8
Apr.	13—Frankie Dailey, Philadelphia	ND	6
Apr.	17—Kid Julian, Syracuse	ND	10
Apr.	22—Bobby Reynolds, Windsor	ND	8
May	29—Benny Chavez, Denver	KO	2
July	2—Knockout Mars, Cincinnati	ND	10
Dec.	1—Joe Mandot, Cleveland	ND	12
Dec.	14—Willie Houck, Philadelphia	ND	6

1915
Jan.	1—Patsy Brannigan, Pittsburgh	ND	6
Jan.	8—Frankie Dailey, Toledo, O.	ND	10
Jan.	23—Eddie Morgan, Philadelphia	ND	6
Feb.	1—Rocky Kansas, Buffalo	ND	10
Feb.	13—Eddie Morgan, Philadelphia	ND	6
Mar.	1—Kid Williams, Philadelphia	ND	6
Mar.	30—Eddie Wallace, Brooklyn	ND	10
Apr.	29—Benny Leonard, N. Y. C.	ND	10
May	11—Mel Coogan, Brooklyn	ND	10

Sept.   6—Alvie Miller, Cedar Point .....ND 12
Sept. 21—Richie Mitchell, Milwaukee ...ND 10
Oct.   11—Cal Delaney, Akron ....ND 12
Nov.   15—Bobby Reynolds, Philadelphia ND 6
Nov.   22—Packey Hommey, Toledo .....ND 10
Dec.   2—Patsy Brannigan, Scranton ....ND 10
1916
Jan.   1—Richie Mitchell, Cincinnati ...ND 10
Jan.   6—Patsy Cline, Philadelphia .....KO 2
Jan.   15—Frankie Conifrey, Phila. .....ND 6
Jan.   31—Packey Hommey, Phila. ......ND 6
Feb.   16—Johnny Creeley, Hot Springs ..ND 10
Mar.   4—Johnny Ray, Pittsburgh ......ND 6
Mar.   24—Harry Donahue, N. Y. C. .....ND 10
May   8—Willie Jackson, Philadelphia ...W 5
May   24—Eddie Wallace, Montreal .....ND 10
June   13—Johnny O'Leary, Buffalo .....ND 10
Sept.   4—*George Chaney, Cedar Point .KO 3
        *For Featherweight title.
1917
Jan.   18—Young Drummie, Waterbury ..KO 10
Feb.   3—Johnny Ray, Philadelphia .....ND 6
Feb.   27—Rocky Kansas, Buffalo ....ND 10
Mar.   12—Tim Droney, York, Pa. ....ND 6
Mar.   19—Eddie Shannon, Philadelphia .ND 6
Mar.   26—Eddie Wallace, Bridgeport .....D 12
Apr.   19—Matt Brock, Cleveland ......ND 10
May   1—Freddie Welsh, N. Y. C........ND 10
May   24—Frankie Fleming, Montreal ...ND 10
July   25—Benny Leonard, Phila. .... KO by 3
1918
Boxing instructor Camp Sherman.
1919
Mar.   10—Frank Brown, Philadelphia ...ND 6
Apr.   1—Johnny Mealey, Philadelphia .KO 2
Apr.   6—Artie O'Leary, Philadelphia ...ND 6
Apr.   12—Jack Lawlor, Charleston .....ND 10
       —Andy Chaney, Jersey City ....ND 8
May   14—Ralph Brady, Cleveland .....ND 10
July   28—Joey Fox, Philadelphia ....ND 6
Sept. 16—Frankie Burns, Jersey City ....KO 6
Sept. 20—Eddy Morgan, Philadelphia ...ND 6
1920
Jan.   1—Al Shubert, Philadelphia .....ND 6
Jan.   24—Johnny Murray, Philadelphia .ND 6
Feb.   25—Benny Valgar, Newark ......ND 8
May   24—Harry Brown, Philadelphia ...ND 6
Apr.   21—*Alvie Miller, Lorain, Ohio ...KO 7
June   2—Young Andy Chaney, Phila. ...ND 8
July   28—Artie Root, Cleveland, O......ND 10
       *Title bout.
1921
May   25—Freddie Jacks, Cleveland .....ND 10
Sept. 17—*Danny Frush, Cleveland .....KO 7
       *Title bout.
1923
Mar.   12—Johnny Downes, Chicago ....Exh. 3
June   2—*Eugene Criqui, N. Y. C. ..KO by 6
       *Lost world featherweight title.
After the Criqui battle Kilbane announced
his retirement from the ring. He then became a
referee in Ohio and also taught boxing.

TB	KO	WD	WF	D	LD	LF	KOBY	ND	NC
140	21	25	1	8	2	0	2	80	1

Died, May 31, 1957, Cleveland, Ohio.
Elected to Boxing Hall of Fame 1960.

EUGENE CRIQUI
Born, Aug. 15, 1893, near Paris. Weight,
122 lbs. Height, 5 ft. 4½ in.
1910
Won: Gouguillon, Paris, 4; Gouzene, Paris,
4; Lambert, Paris, 4; Teissedre, Paris, 6;
Durocher, Paris, 6. Draw: Francisque, Paris, 8;
Prie, Paris, 8. Lost: Vinez, Paris, 8.
1911
Won: Monceau, Paris, 6; Voirin, Paris, 4;
Teissedre, Paris, 6; Dastillon, Paris, 4; Lepreux,
Paris, 8. Knockouts: Relinger, Paris, 2; Jim
Barett, Paris, 2; Buster Brown, Paris, 1.
1912
Knockouts: Chicken Paris, 9; Lepreux,
Paris, 13; Francis Charles, Paris, 17. Won:
Durocher, Paris, 10; Voirin, Paris, 10; Gatehouse,
Paris, 8; Prie, Paris, 10; Gatehouse, Paris, 8;
Demey, Paris, 10; Tom Smith, Birmingham, 15.
Draw: Gatehouse, Paris, 10; Alf. Mansfield, Paris,

10; Lepreux, Paris, 10. Lost: Dastillon, Paris, 15.
1913
Jan.   10—Alf. Mansfield, Paris .... D 10
Jan.   18—Teissedre, Paris .... W 7
Feb.   15—Rousseau, Bordeaux .... W 10
Feb.   21—Bouzonnie, Paris .... W 10
Mar.   17—Prie, Paris .... W 10
Apr.   21—Sid Smith, Paris .... L 20
May   23—Demey, Paris ....KO 10
June   6—A. Grassi, Paris .... D 12
Aug.   1—Fred Anderson, Paris .... W 10
Oct.   4—Johnny Daly, Paris .... W 10
Nov.   29—Lepreux, Paris ....L 10
1914
Feb.   12—Percy Jones, Liverpool .... W 15
Mar.   7—Bertin, Paris .... W 10
Mar.   13—Pat MacAllister, Paris ....KO 10
Mar.   26—Percy Jones, Liverpool ....L 20
Apr.   10—Bertin, Paris .... W 10
May   1—Lepreux, Paris .... W 20
May   10—Jim Harry, Bordeaux ....KO 8
May   16—Abe Mantell, Paris .... W 20
June   4—G. Lefevre, Nantes ....KO 7
June   19—Durocher, Paris .... W 15
July   11—Charles Ledoux, Paris ....L 12
       1915-1916—Served in French army during
World War and did no fighting in ring during
those years.
1917
Feb.   26—George Gravat, Paris .... K 4
Oct.   3—Durocher, Paris .... W 6
Oct.   17—Prie, Paris .... W 6
Oct.   21—Mariex, Bordeaux ....KO 9
Dec.   8—Alfred Francis, Paris .... W 6
Dec.   26—Prie, Paris .... W 6
1918
Jan.   16—Maessent, Paris ....KO 6
Jan.   23—Rousseau, Bordeaux .... W 12
Jan.   30—Lepreux, Paris .... W 6
Apr.   3—Grassi, Paris ....KO 3
Apr.   20—Rousseau, Toulouse ....KO 7
Apr.   24—Durocher, Paris ....KO 3
Apr.   26—Grassi, Toulouse .... W 7
Apr.   29—Durocher, Perpignay .... W 6
May   26—Pain, Paris .... W 5
June   1—Marty, Paris.................W 9
July   3—Maestrnni, Paris .... W 12
July   10—Eugene Clifford, Paris ....KO 2
July   17—Arthur Wyns, Paris ....KO 10
Aug.   4—Jimmy O'Day, Paris ....KO 2
Aug.   14—Bertel, Marseilles .... W 10
Oct.   2—Grassi, Paris ....KO 2
1919
Jan.   1—Osmin Lurie, Bordeaux .... W 4
Jan.   3—Jimmy Doyle, Trompeloup.....KO 6
Feb.   6—Kid Sullivan, Paris ....KO 1
Apr.   10—Tom Noble, Holbo.n Stad. .....L 10
May   25—Poutet, Marseilles .... W 6
June   1—Grassi, Moroc .... W 8
June   27—Tom Noble, Paris .... D 20
July   18—Digger Evans, Paris ....KO 7
Sept. 18—Walter Ross, Holborn Stad ....KO 15
Oct.   29—Sam Keller, Paris .... W 5
Dec.   26—Pal Moore, London .... KO by 14
1920
Apr.   17—Joe Mendell, Paris ....KO 12
June   26—B. Baker, Paris ....KO 1
Oct.   23—Vince Blackburn, Sydney ....KO 9
Nov.   20—Jack Green, Sydney ....KO 4
Dec.   18—Bert Spargo, Sydney ....KO 16
1921
Jan.   8—J. Sullivan, Sydney ....KO 13
Feb.   5—Sid Godfrey, Sydney ....KO 10
Feb.   19—Silvino Jamito, Sydney .... W 20
Mar.   19—Dencio Cabanella, Sydney ...KO 14
Sept. 27—Aug. Grassi, Paris ....KO 1
Oct.   25—Alp Spaniers, Paris ....KO 2
Dec.   6—Geo. Gaillard, Paris .... W 6
1922
Feb.   4—*Charles Ledoux, Paris ....KO 1
Apr.   11—Ben Callicott, Paris .... KO 3
May   29—Joe Fox, Holland Park ......KO 12
June   16—Youyou, Barcelona ....KO 2
June   24—Tom Anderson, Marseilles ....KO 2
July   7—Arthur Wyns, Paris ....KO 12
Sept.   9—Arthur Wyns, Paris .... W 6
Nov.   4—Walter Rossi, Paris ....KO 1
Nov.   17—Ben Collicott, Liege ....KO 2
Dec.   2—Billy Matthews, Paris .... W 17
       *Won bantamweight title of France.
1923
June   2—Johnny Kilbane, New York ...KO 6
       (Won World Featherweight Title)

July 26—Johnny Dundee, New York .....L 15
(Lost World Featherweight Title)
Oct. 6—M. Hebrans, Paris .... W 15
1924
June 1—Danny Frush, Paris ....KO by 8
1926
Oct. 6—Carlos Uzabeaga, Buenos Aires ..L 10
1927
Apr. 2—Al Brown, Paris ....L 10
Dec. 20—Gustave Humery, Paris ....L 6
1928
Mar. 19—Benny Carter. Paris .... W 10

TB	KO	WD	WF	D	LD	LF	KOBY	ND	NC
115	40	54	0	8	11	0	2	0	0

JOHNNY DUNDEE
(Joseph Corrara)
(Scotch Wop)
Born November 22, 1893, Shaikai, Italy.
Weight, 124 lbs. Height 5 ft. 4½ in. Managed by
Scotty Monteith and Jimmy Johnston.
1910
Won all at New York City: Harry Smith, 4;
Johnnie Lore, 4; Young Ferris, 4; Charley Burns,
4; Jack Rose, 4; Young Smith, 4; Eddie Moran, 4;
Eddie Sherman, 4; Pete Powers, 4; Mike Malia, 4;
Johnny Warren, 4; Eddie Moran, 6; Willie Smith,
6; Leo Johnson, 4.
1911
Feb. 3—Battling KO Eggers, N. Y......ND 4
May 15—Young Shugrue,
Perth Amboy ....ND 6
June 10—Mike Mada, Port Jervis .... W 10
July 29—Young Shugrue, New York ...ND 10
Won all Fights at New York City: Marty
Brown, 4; Marty Allen, 6; John McLean, 6;
Young Ferris, 6; Mike Mada, 6; Frankie Fleming,
6; Johnny Martin, 6; Frankie Shean, 6; Kid
Goodman, 6; Young Egan, 4; Babe Cullen, 6;
Young McGovern, 6; Young Packey Hommey, 6;
Eddie Sherman, 6. Knockouts: Young Brown, 5;
Frank Woods, 3; Mike Derval, 3; Tommy Page, 3;
Joe Shears, 4; Frank Smith, 1; Eddie Jones, 1. No
decisions in New York City: Frankie Fleming,
10; Kid Black, 10; Kid Ghetto, 10; Ty Cobb, 10;
Tommy Houck, 10; Charles Young Shugrue, 10;
Young Brown, 10; Young O'Leary, 10; Kid Black
10; Eddie Sherman, 6; Young Cohen, 10; Fights
in Brooklyn, N. Y., Knockout: Young Ketchell,
1. No decisions: Charley Barry, 10; Young
McGovern, 10; Charley Barry, 10; Mike Made,
10. Won in New Jersey: Jinks Smith, 3; Young
Shugrue, 6. No decisions at Philadelphia: Harry
Tracey, 6; Kid Thomas, 6; Bobby Reynolds, 6;
Tommy O'Toole, 6.
1912
Feb. 8—Ty Cobb, N. Y. C. .... ND 10
Feb. 23—Irish Paddy, N. Y. C. .... ND 10
Feb. 29—Eddie O'Keefe, N. Y. C. .... ND 10
Mar. 4—Eddie O'Keefe, N. Y. C. .... ND 10
Mar. 8—Tommy Houck, Philadelphia ..... ND 6
Mar. 16—Young Brown, Brooklyn, N.Y. ... ND 10
Mar. 20—Kid Julian, Syracuse, N. Y. ...... ND 10
Mar. 27—Young Wagner, N. Y. C. .... ND 10
Apr. 5—Tommy Houck, Philadelphia ..... ND 6
Apr. 10—Tommy Houck, N. Y. C. .... ND 10
Apr. 30—Charlie White, Syracuse, N. Y. ... ND 10
May 21—Packey Hommey, N. Y. C. .... ND 10
June 18—Young Wagner, N. Y. C. .... ND 10
July 1—Young Shugrue, N. Y. C. .... ND 10
July 4—Ty Cobb, N. Y. C. .... KO 10
Aug. 13—Matt Brock, Cleveland .... D 10
Sept. 14—Johnny Kilbane, N. Y. C. .... ND 10
Sept. 25—Geo. Kirkwood, N. Y. C. .... ND 10
Sept. 30—Harry Thomas, N. Y. C. .... ND 10
Oct. 11—Pal Moore, N. Y. C. .... ND 10
Oct. 21—Matt Brock, New Orleans .... W 10
Nov. 19—Frankie Conley, Vernon Cal. ..... KO 19
Dec. 19—Eddie Morgan, N. Y. C. .... ND 10
1913
Jan. 11—Willie Jones, N. Y. C. ....ND 10
Jan. 22—Willie Jones, Brooklyn, N.Y. ..ND 10
Jan. 23—Tommy Shea, Waterbury, Conn. W 12
Jan. 27—Special Delivery Hirsch,
N. Y. C........................ND 10

Apr. 29—*Johnny Kilbane, Vernon, Cal. D 20
(For World Featherweight Title)
June 17—Jack White, Vernon, Cal. ...... W 20
July 4—Tommy Dixon, Albur'que, N.M.W 10
Aug. 12—Jack White, Vernon, Cal. .....KO 9
Oct. 14—Joe Azevedo, Vernon, Cal..... W 20
Nov. 27—Charlie White, New Orleans ...ND 10
Dec. 15—Johnny Griffith, Canton, O. ...ND 12
*Charles Eyton, referee.
1914
Jan. 1—Freddy Welsh, New Orleans ...ND 10
Jan. 23—Young Shugrue, N. Y. C. .....ND 10
Jan. 27—Sapper O'Neil, N. Y. C........ND 10
Feb. 6—Johnny Lore, N. Y. C.........ND 10
Feb. 10—J. Shugrue, Waterbury, Conn. .ND 12
Feb. 24—Rocky Kansas, Buffalo ....ND 10
Feb. 26—Pal Moore, N. Y. C. ....ND 10
Feb. 28—Eddie Moy, Philadelphia .....ND 6
Mar. 28—Eddie Moy, Philadelphia .....ND 6
Apr. 15—Matty Baldwin, Boston .... D 12
May 13—Patsy Drouillard, Windsor ....ND 8
May 16—Willie Jones, N. Y. C..........ND 10
Sept. 28—Willie Beecher, Vernon, Cal. ... D 20
Oct. 20—Joe Azevedo, Oakland, Cal..... W 15
Oct. 23—Willie Ritchie, San Francisco ..ND 4
Dec. 8—Mexican Joe Rivers,
Los Angeles .... W 20
1915
Jan. 15—Jimmy Duffy, Milwaukee ....ND 10
Feb. 14—Joe Mandot, New Orleans .....D 20
Mar. 2—Benny Leonard, N. Y. C. ......ND 10
Mar. 16—Frankie Callahan, Brooklyn ..ND 10
Mar. 22—Joe Azevedo, Memphis ....W 8
Mar. 30—Frankie Callahan, Brooklyn ..ND 10
May 8—Rocky Kansas, Buffalo ....ND 10
May 10—Frankie Callahan, Cincinnati ..ND 10
May 31—Young Drummie, Brooklyn ...KO 2
June 18—Leach Cross, Brooklyn ....ND 10
July 23—Joe Rivers, Brooklyn ....ND 10
Aug. 30—Richie Mitchell, Milwaukee ..ND 10
Sept. 23—Joe Mandot, Brooklyn ....ND 10
Oct. 26—Willie Ritchie, N. Y. C. ......ND 10
Nov. 8—Joe Rivers, Milwaukee ....ND 10
Nov. 22—Phil Bloom, Brooklyn ....ND 10
Dec. 2—Phil Bloom, N. Y. C. ....ND 10
Dec. 10—Matt Wells, New Haven .... W 6
1916
Jan. 1—Joe Azevedo, Philadelphia ....ND 6
Jan. 10—Jimmy Murphy, Philadelphia .ND 6
Jan. 22—Stanley Yoakum, Denver ......W 20
Feb. 7—Jimmy Murphy, Philadelphia .ND 6
Feb. 21—Joe Mandot, New Orleans .....L 20
Mar. 8—Benny Leonard, N. Y. C. ......ND 10
Apr. 11—Phil Bloom, Brooklyn ....ND 10
May 16—Matt Wells, Boston ....W 12
May 17—Johnny O'Leary, Buffalo ....ND 10
May 22—Buck Fleming, Philadelphia ..ND 6
May 30—Eddie Wallace, Providence ..... W 12
June 12—Benny Leonard, N. Y. C. ......ND 10
July 4—Ever Hammer, E. Chicago ....ND 10
Aug. 15—Johnny O'Leary, Boston .....KO 9
Aug. 30—Joe Welling, N. Y. C. ....ND 10
Sept. 11—Ever Hammer, Kansas City ....W 15
Nov. 15—Benny Leonard, Philadelphia .ND 6
Nov. 30—Eddie Wallace, Brooklyn .....ND 10
1917
Jan. 15—Willie Jackson, Phila. .....KO by 1
Jan. 29—Jimmy Hanlon, New Orleans ..W 20
Feb. 20—Frankie Callahan, Brooklyn ..ND 10
Mar. 5—Terry McGovern, Philadelphia ND 10
Mar. 6—Jimmy Duffy, N. Y. C. ....ND 10
Mar. 26—Lew Tendler, Philadelphia ....ND 10
Apr. 10—Jimmy Powers, N. Y. C. ......KO 9
Apr. 16—Johnny Mealey, Philadelphia .ND 6
Apr. 24—Tommy Touhey, Brooklyn ..ND 6
May 1—Chick Simier, Boston ....W 12
May 15—Chick Simier, Boston ....W 12
May 29—Rocky Kansas, Boston ....W 12
June 7—Joe Welling, N. Y. C. ....ND 12
June 12—Frankie Callahan, Brooklyn ..ND 10
June 29—Willie Jackson, N. Y. C. ......ND 10
July 12—George Chaney, Philadelphia .ND 6
July 20—Joe Welling, N. Y. C. ....ND 10
July 24—Tommy Touhey, N. Y. C. .....ND 10
Aug. 22—Johnny Mealey, Philadelphia .ND 6
Sept. 12—Young Russo, N. Y. C. ....ND 6
Sept. 18—Pete Hartley, Boston ....W 12
Sept. 20—Joe Mooney, N. Y. C. ....ND 10
Oct. 1—Lew Tendler, Philadelphia ....ND 6
Oct. 9—Irish Patsy Cline, N. Y. C. ....ND 10
Oct. 30—Jimmy Duffy, N. Y. C. ....ND 10
Nov. 6—Phila. Pal Moore, N. Y. C......ND 10
Nov. 19—K. O. Chaney, Philadelphia ...ND 6
Nov. 29—Eddie Shannon, Lawrence ....KO 7

Dec.	8—Johnny Ray, Philadelphia ....ND	6

1918

Jan.	14—Pal Moran, New Orleans .... W	20
Feb.	11—Patsy Cline, New Orleans ...... D	20
Mar.	9—George Chaney, Philadelphia .ND	6
Mar.	12—Harry Carlson, Boston .... W	12
Mar.	25—Willie Jackson, New Haven ... D	12
May	24—Eddy Wallace, New York .....ND	6
May	27—Eddy Morgan, Philadelphia ..ND	6
June	3—Billy De Foe, New Haven ...... W	12
June	18—Franky Britt, Boston .... D	12
June	24—Micky Donley, Jersey City ....ND	8
July	6—Matt Brock, Cleveland ....Exh.	4
Aug.	6—Franky Britt, Boston .... D	12
Aug.	15—Eddy Wallace, Brooklyn .....Exh.	4
Aug.	19—Tommy Touhey, Jersey City ..ND	8
Sept.	10—Rocky Kansas, Boston .... D	12
Sept.	24—Frankie Britt, Boston .... W	12
Oct.	29—Frankie Callahan, Boston ...... W	12
Nov.	6—Gussy Lewis, Philadelphia ....ND	6
Nov.	16—Joe Welling, New York ......ND	6
Nov.	22—Pete Hartley, New Haven .....ND	4
Nov.	28—Joe Phillips, Philadelphia .....ND	6
Dec.	3—Joe Welling, Boston L	12
Dec.	7—Johnny Mealey, Philadelphia .ND	7

1919

Jan.	20—Benny Leonard, Newark, N. J. ND	8
Feb.	24—Johnny Ray, Pittsburgh .....ND	10
Mar.	2—Johnny Mealey. Philadelphia .ND	6
May	9—Ritchie Mitchell, Milwaukee ..ND	10
May	15—Billy Whelan, St. Paul ....ND	10
May	30—Frankie Britt, Portland, Me. ..ND	12
June	4—Joe Tiplitz, Philadelphia ......ND	6
June	16—Benny Leonard, Philadelphia .ND	6
July	1—Ralph Brady, Syracuse, N. Y. .ND	10
July	15—Benny Valgar, Boston .... W	12
July	21—Joe Tiplitz, Boston .... W	12
Aug.	4—Mel Coogan, Jersey City .....ND	8
Aug.	11—Joe Welling, Philadelphia ....ND	6
Sept.	1—Willie Jackson, Jersey City ...ND	8
Sept.	11—Frankie Britt, Prov., R. I. .... W	12
Sept.	17—Benny Leonard, Newark .....ND	8
Sept.	24—Charley Parker, Boston .... W	12
Sept.	27—Eddy Moy, Philadelphia .....ND	6
Oct.	13—Young Kloby, Lawrence ..... W	12
Oct.	31—Willie Jackson, Milwaukee ...ND	10
Nov.	4—Tommy Touhey, Newark .....KO	5
Nov.	10—Mel Coogan, Jersey City ......ND	8
Nov.	13—Johnny Buckley, Boston ...... W	6
Nov.	26—Charley White, Milwaukee ....ND	10
Dec.	26—Pal Moran, Philadelphia .....ND	6

1920

Jan.	9—Benny Leonard, Jersey City ..ND	8
Feb.	26—Jack Lawler, Atlanta .... D	10
Mar.	8—Willie Jackson, Jersey City ....ND	8
Apr.	23—Joe Welling, Columbus, O. ... W	12
May	14—Willie Jackson, Newark ....ND	10
May	19—Mel Coogan, Detroit ....ND	10
May	29—Jack Lawler, Lawrence, Mass... W	12
June	7—Billy Defoe, Philadelphia .....ND	8
June	13—Willie Jackson, Boston .... D	12
June	15—George Erne, Trenton ....ND	12
July	13—Johnny Downes, Boston ....W	12
July	26—Eddie Fitzsimmons, Newark ...ND	10
Sept.	17—Joe Welling, N. Y. C. L	15
Nov.	29—Willie Jackson, N. Y. C........ D	15
Dec.	20—Pal Moran, New Orleans .... D	15

1921

Feb.	25—Willie Jackson, N. Y. C.........L	15
Apr.	11—Johnny Ray, Pittsburgh, Pa. ..ND	10
Apr.	26—Rocky Kansas, Milwaukee ....ND	10
May	21—Blockie Richard, Dayton, Ohio W	10
May	21—Johnny Ray, Pittsburgh, Pa. ..ND	10
May	27—Sailor Friedman ....ND	10
June	10—George Chaney, Boston, Mass. . W	10
June	15—Jimmy Hanlon, N. Y. C. ...... W	10
July	18—George Chaney, Philadelphia .ND	8
July	29—Bert Spencer, N. Y. C. ......KO	9
Aug.	10—Charlie White, N. Y. C........ D	12
Aug.	24—Joe Tiplitz, Philadelphia ......ND	8
Sept.	3—Eddie Wallace, Albany, N. Y. .. W	12
Sept.	19—Joe Tiplitz, Boston, Mass. .... W	10
Nov.	18—George Chaney, N. Y. C.......WF	5
	(Won Jr. Lightweight Title.)	
Nov.	28—Eddie Wallace, Brooklyn ...... W	12
Dec.	12—Harry Kid Brown, Phila.......ND	8
Dec.	19—Jimmie Hanlon, Philadelphia .ND	8
Dec.	30—Willie Jackson, N. Y. C........ D	15

1922

Jan.	10—Whitey Fitzgerald, Phila. .....ND	8
Jan.	16—Charlie White, Boston L	10
Jan.	25—Frankie Rice, Baltimore .... W	12
Feb.	3—Joe Benjamin, N. Y. C. .... W	10
Feb.	17—Johnny Darcey, Providence .... W	10

Feb.	24—*Jimmy Hanlon, Scranton, Pa. ND	6
Mar.	17—Charlie White, N. Y. C. .... W	15
Apr.	14—Jimmie Goodrich, Toronto .... W	10
Apr.	19—Johnny Shugrue, Worcester.....L	10
May	5—Lew Tendler, N. Y. C..........L	15
June	27—Charlie White, Rock Island ...ND	10
July	8—Jack Sharkey, New York ...... W	15
	(Title bout)	
July	12—Shamus O'Brien, N. Y. C....... W	4
July	28—Kid Koster, Houston ....ND	12
Aug.	15—Danny Frush, Brooklyn .....KO	9
Aug.	28—Pepper Martin, N. Y. C........ W	15
Nov.	27—Phil Delmont, N. Y. C. .... W	12
Dec.	2—Alex Hart, Philadelphia .....ND	8
Dec.	29—Tommy O'Brien, Milwaukee ..ND	10
	*Stopped by referee.	

1923

Jan.	19—Pepper Martin, Boston .... W	10
Feb.	2—Elino Flores, N. Y. C. .... W	15
	(Title bout)	
Feb.	6—Tony Julian, Boston L	10
Feb.	20—Basil Galiano, New Orleans .... D	15
Apr.	23—Gene Delmont, Toronto .... W	12
May	18—Jimy Brady, Detroit ....ND	10
May	30—Jack Bernstein, N. Y. C........L	15
	(Lost Junior Lightweight Title)	
June	12—Ritchie Mitchell, Milwaukee ..ND	10
July	26—Eugene Criqui, N. Y. C. ...... W	15
	(Won world's featherweight title)	
Aug.	27—Eddie Wagner, Philadelphia ...ND	8
Nov.	30—Al Shubert, New Bedford.,.....L	10
Dec.	4—Sid Barbarian, Detroit ....ND	10
Dec.	17—Jack Bernstein, N. Y. C....... W	15
	(Re-won Junior Lightweight Title)	

1924

Feb.	1—Pal Moran, N. Y. C. .... W	15
Apr.	21—Rocky Kansas, Buffalo L	10
Apr.	28—Willie Ames, Canton, O. .....ND	12
June	2—Luis Vincenti, N. Y. C. .... W	12
June	9—Sammy Mandell, E. Chicago,	
	Ind.........................ND	10
June	20—Kid Sullivan, Brooklyn L	10
	(Lost Junior Lightweight Title)	
Sept.	15—Jack Bernstein, N. Y. C........L	15
Oct.	22—Charlie O'Connell, Cleveland ...L	12
	Dundee resigned featherweight title on	
August 10, 1924.		

1925

Mar.	23—Red Chapman, Boston L	10
Apr.	28—Honey Boy Finnegan, Washing-	
	ton, D. C. L	10
May	5—Sid Terris, N. Y. C.............L	12
June	12—Sid Terris, Brooklyn, N. Y. L	15
July	20—Allentown J. Leonard, B'klyn . W	10

1926

Jan.	29—Joe Glick, N. Y. C. L	10
Mar.	3—Hilario Martinez, Havana L	10
Aug.	20—Fred Bretonnel, N. Y. C. ..... W	10
Oct.	19—Tod Morgan, San Francisco L	10

1927

Oct.	24—Tony Canzoneri, N. Y. C.......L	15

1928

Nov.	12—Gaston Charles, N. Y. C. ..... W	10
Nov.	23—Billy Kowalik, Buffalo .... D	6
Dec.	3—Jackie Pilkington, New Haven ...L	10

1929

Jan.	4—Charley Rosenberg, N. Y. C. ...L	10
Jan.	22—Frankie Garcia, Wilkes-Barre L	10
Feb.	4—Tony Ascencio, Philadelphia ... W	10
Feb.	12—Lou Moscowitz, N. Y. C. ...... W	10
Mar.	23—San Sanchez, N. Y. C. ....KO	3
Apr.	8—Joey Manuel, Rochester, N. Y. ..L	10
Apr.	22—Eddie Kid Wolfe, New Orleans .L	10
July	8—Eddie Cannonball Martin, N. Y. W	10
Sept.	25—Al Foreman, Montreal ......KO by	10
Oct.	8—Al Rube Goldberg, N. Y. C. .... W	10
Nov.	14—Georgie Goldberg, N.Y.C..........L	10

1932

Dec.	5—Mickey Greb, Orange, N. J. .... W	6
	—Al Dunbar, Brooklyn L	10

TB	KO	WD	WF	D	LD	LF	KO BY	ND	NC
322	19	93	1	18	29	0	2	160	0

Died April 22, 1965, in East Orange, N.J.
Elected to Boxing Hall of Fame 1957.

LOUIS (KID) KAPLAN

Born, 1902, in Russia. Nationality, Jewish.
Weight, 135 lbs. Height, 5 ft. 4 in. Managed by

Joe Beaseley, Dinny McMahon and Billy Gibson.

1921

Won: Romeo Roach, 10; Sammy Waltz, 12; Willie Murphy, 12; Kid Lewis, 12; Red McDonald, 12; Freddy Jacks, 12; Billy DeFoe, 5; Irish Jimmy Dwyer, 12; Al Shubert, 12; Dutch Brandt, 12; Johnny Fisse, 12; Dick Russell, 10; Al Wagner, 10; Hughey Hutchinson, 12; Earl Baird, 12; Eddie Kid Wagner 12; Eddie Kid Wagner, 12; Johnny Shugrue, 12.

1922

Feb.	13—Dick Russell, Lynn ....KO	3
Feb.	15—Hughie Hutchinson, Meriden .. D	12
Mar.	2—Mickey Travers, New Haven .... D	12
Mar.	13—Al Wagner, New York .... W	8
Mar.	20—Artie Rose, Meriden ....KO	3
Apr.	10—Dick Russell, Lynn .... W	10
Apr.	18—Johnny Williams, Portland ...ND	12
May	13—Johnny Lisse, Meriden .... W	12
May	29—Earl Baird, Bridgeport .... W	12
June	9—Eddie Kid Wagner, Meriden L	12
June	29—Earl Baird, Bridgeport ....KO	8
Aug.	10—Eddie Kid Wagner, Meriden .... W	12
Sept.	14—Johnny Shugrue, Meriden ..... W	12
Oct.	20—Andy Chaney, New Haven ..... W	12
Nov.	14—Gene Delmont, Bridgeport .... W	12
Nov.	24—Kid Sullivan, New York .... W	12
Dec.	18—Babe Herman, Meriden L	12

1923

Jan.	15—Mickey Travers, Meriden, Conn. W	12
Mar.	8—Babe Herman, Meriden, Conn. . D	12
Mar.	14—Al Shubert, Meriden, Conn......L	12
Apr.	16—Harvey Bright, Meriden, Conn. . W	12
May	17—Danny Frush, N. Y. C.........KO	6
June	2—Babe Herman, N. Y. C. .... D	12
July	3—Babe Herman, New Haven ..... D	12
Aug.	9—Tommy Noble, N. Y. C. .... W	10
Sept.	28—Jimmy Goodrich, N. Y. C. ..... W	10
Dec.	13—Johnny Leonard, Allentown, Pa.W	12

1924

Jan.	7—Cuddy de Marco, Pittsburgh, Pa. D	10
Feb.	1—Eddie Brady, N. Y. C. .... W	12
Feb.	21—Billy de Foe, Waterbury, Conn. W	12
Mar.	20—Bobby Garcia, Waterbury, Conn.D	12
Apr.	24—Cuddy de Marco, Waterbury ... D	12
June	9—Bobby Garcia, New Haven ..... W	12
Aug.	21—Pal Moran, New Haven, Conn... W	9
Sept.	15—Lew Paluso, Waterbury, Conn. . W	12
Oct.	10—Angel Diaz, N. Y. C. ....KO	3
Nov.	21—Bobby Garcia, N. Y. C. .... W	10
Dec.	12—Joe Lombardo, N. Y. C. ......KO	4

1925

Jan.	2—Danny Kramer, N. Y. C. ......KO	9

(Won vacant featherweight title)

Feb.	9—Bud Ridley, Vernon, Calif. ...ND	12
Mar.	11—Johnny Farr, Oakland, Calif. ..ND	12
Mar.	28—Ernie Goozeman, San Diego ..ND	12
May	22—Kid Sullivan, Waterbury ......KO	5
June	26—Frankie Schaefer, Aurora, Ill. .ND	10
Aug.	5—Billy Kennedy, Bayonne, N. J. ND	12
Aug.	27—Babe Herman, Waterbury ...... D	15

(Title Bout)

Dec.	13—Babe Herman, N. Y. C. ...... W	15

(Title Bout)

1926

Jan.	25—Billy Murphy, Boston .... W	10
Mar.	1—Billy Petrolle, Hartford, Conn. . W	12
Mar.	9—Eddie Kid Wagner, Phila. ...... D	10
Mar.	26—Tommy Herman, Baltimore .... W	10
Apr.	12—Mickey Chapin, Scranton, Pa. ... W	10
Apr.	21—Leo Kid Roy, Montreal ....KO	7
June	4—Billy White, Jersey City ......ND	10
June	28—Bobby Garcia, Hartford, Conn. W	10
Aug.	3—Tommy Cello, N. Y. C. .... W	10
Nov.	5—Tommy Cello, Holyoke Mass. ... W	10
Dec.	2—Billy Wallace, Cleveland ...KO by	5

1927

Jan.	10—Paris Cangey, Rochester, N. Y. KO	4
Jan.	17—Lou Paluso, Cleveland, O. ..... W	10
Mar.	18—Frankie Fink, N. Y. C......... W	8
Mar.	28—Jackie Brady, Rochester, N. Y. . W	10

(Kaplan outgrew class and gave up title)

Apr.	4—John Ceccoli, Phila., Pa. .... W	10
May	2—Tony Baccarelli, New Haven ... W	7
May	9—Al Forman, Phila., Pa. .... W	10
June	15—Jackie Fields, N. Y. C. .... W	10
June	29—Bruce Flowers, N. Y. C. ...... W	10
Sept.	8—Clicky Clark, New Haven ......KO	5
Oct.	11—Tommy Cello, N. Y. C. .... W	10
Oct.	18—Jim. McLarnin, Chicago ...KO by	8
Nov.	1—Mike Dundee, New Haven ..... W	12

1928

Feb.	20—Bobby Mays, New Haven ...... W	10
Feb.	27—Joe Trabone, Rochester, N. Y. . W	10

May	8—Geo. Day, New Haven, Conn. .. W	10
May	31—M. Quintero, New Haven L	10
July	3—M. Quintero, New Haven L	10
Sept.	21—Bert Lamb. Detroit, Mich. ....KO	7
Oct.	16—Bruce Flowers, New Haven .... W	10
Nov.	3—Bobby Mays, New Haven ..... W	10

1929

Jan.	1—Ritchie King, Phila. Pa. .... W	10
Jan.	11—Johnny Jadick, Boston, Mass. .KO	7
Jan.	14—Phil McGraw, Waterbury, Ct. .. W	10
Feb.	18—Jimmy Goodrich, Buffalo ..... W	10
Feb.	26—Freddie Mueller, New Haven .. LF	8
Apr.	2—Joe Glick, New Haven, Conn. .. W	10
Apr.	11—Joey Medill, Detroit, Mich. .... W	10
May	10—Billy Wallace, N. Y. City ...... W	10
Aug.	21—Joe Trabon, Waterbury, Conn. . W	10
Sept.	9—Henri Dewancker, Baltimore ..KO	7
Sept.	16—Emery Cabana, New Haven L	10
Oct.	30—Eddie Kid Wolfe, Chicago, Ill. .KO	7
Nov.	10—Emery Cabana, New Haven .... W	10
Dec.	13—Andy Callahan, N. Y. City ..... W	10

1930

Feb.	24—Jack Portney, Baltimore, Mo. ...L	10
Mar.	18—Johnny Farr, New Haven ...... W	10
June	2—Joey Medill, Hartford .... W	10
June	19—Tommy Crowley, Waterbury .. W	10
June	30—Maurice Holtzer, W. Springfield W	10
Aug.	5—Jimmy O'Brien, Bridgeport ...KO	9
Sept.	24—Bat Battalino, Hartford ...... W	10
Oct.	17—Justo Suarez, N. Y. C. L	10

1931

Feb.	4—Jack Portney, New Haven ..... W	10
Mar.	4—Tommy Crowley, Rochester .KO	7
Mar.	16—Buster Brown, Baltimore ...... W	10
Apr.	7—Billy Lynch, Hartford .... W	10
Apr.	20—Ralph Lenny, Hartford .... W	10
July	23—Tommy Jarrett, North Adams . W	10
Aug.	24—Sammy Mandell, Hartford .... W	10
Sept.	8—Jackie Pilkington, Hartford .... W	10

(For New England Lightweight Champion-ship)

Nov.	4—Harry Dublinsky, Chicago ..... W	10
Nov.	20—Eddie Ran, N. Y. C. ....KO by	1

1932

July	19—Emil Rossi, N. Y. C. .... W	8
Aug.	4—Frankie Petrolle, N. Y. C. ...... W	8

1933

Feb.	20—Cocoa Kid, New Haven L	10

TB	KO	WD	WF	D	LD	LF	KOBY	ND NC
132	17	85	0	10	9	1	3	7 0

BENNY BASS

Born, December 4, 1904. Kiev. Russia. Nationality, Jewish. Weight, 130 pounds. Height, 5 ft. 3½ in. Managed by Phil Glassman. Bass started boxing as amateur in 1919.

1923

Knockouts: Young Kansas, 3; Eddie O'Keefe, 3. Won: Joe Nelson, 10. No decision: Battling Mack, 8; Al Gordon, 6; Mike Moran, 8; Chick Kansas, 8; Johnny Dixon, 10; Pete Sarmiento, 8; Tommy Murray, 8. Lost: Bobby Garcia, 6.

1924

Jan.	18—Martin Judge, Philadelphia ...KO	4
Jan.	28—K. O. Leonard, Philadelphia ..KO	2
Feb.	11—Jack Lester, Philadelphia .....KO	3
Feb.	18—Joe Nelson, Philadelphia ..... W	8
Mar.	14—Young Buck Fleming, Phila. ... W	10
Apr.	4—Joe Klein, Milwaukee ....KO	2
Apr.	7—Mickey Diamond, Phila. ....KO	1
Apr.	15—Georgie Wolgast, Boston .....KO	1
Apr.	25—Sammy Craden, Milwaukee ..KO	3
Apr.	29—Johnny Brown, Philadelphia ...KO	3
June	23—Teddy Joyce, Aurora, Ill. ......KO	2
July	21—Spencer Gardner, Phila. ...... W	10
Aug.	20—Spencer Gardner, Newport ...KO	6
Sept.	4—Chick Suggs, Newport, R. I....ND	10
Sept.	8—Al Markie, Philadelphia ....KO	3
Oct.	1—Frankie Mandot, Phila. ....KO	1
Oct.	20—Pete Sarmiento, Milwaukee ...ND	10
Nov.	24—Tommy Noble, Philadelphia ... W	3
Nov.	25—Andy Martin, Providence L	10
Dec.	25—Earl Baird, Philadelphia ......KO	2

1925

Jan.	14—Willie Harvey, Philadelphia ...KO	9

Feb. 2—Joe Schwartz, Philadelphia ...KO 6
Mar. 9—Joe Schwartz, Philadelphia .... W 10
Apr. 20—Johnny Sheppard, Phila. ...... W 10
June 30—Steve Smith, Cleveland .... W 10
Aug. 11—Johnny Farr, Cleveland ......ND 10
Aug. 14—Battling Mack, Phila. ....KO 3
Sept. 24—Eddie Anderson, Phila........ W 10
Oct. 12—Eddie Anderson, Phila........ W 12
Nov. 2—Lew Mayrs, Phila.............KO 2
Nov. 16—Jose Lombardo, Phila. .... W 10

1926

Jan. 1—Joe Nelson, Camden ....KO 6
Jan. 11—Leo "Kid" Roy, Phila. .... W 10
Jan. 18—Al Corbett, Cleveland ....KO 1
Feb. 17—Eddie Anderson, Phila........ D 10
Mar. 1—Pete Sarmiento, Cleveland .... LF 6
Mar. 10—Wilbur Cohen, Phila. ....KO 7
Apr. 19—Ralph Ripman, Lancaster .....KO 3
June 8—Andy Martin, Providence ......L 10
June 24—Billy Kennedy, N. Y. C. ......KO 7
July 2—Geo. Ambiard, Atlantic City ..ND 8
July 12—Honeyboy Finnegan, Phila. .... D 10
July 29—Johnny Farr, N. Y. C. .... W 10
Sept. 2—Babe Herman, Phila. .... W 10
Sept. 20—Johnny Mosely, W. Manayuh. .KO 9
Oct. 1—Babe Herman, Phila. .... W 10
Oct. 18—Frankie Garcia, N. Y. C....... W 10
Nov. 23—Babe Herman, Cleveland .....ND 12
Dec. 8—Benny Cross, Newark ....ND 10
Dec. 10—Johnny Sheppard, Boston ..... W 10

1927

Jan. 4—Red Chapman, New York ....WF 1
Mar. 21—Joe Glick, Phila. .... W 10
Apr. 24—Joe Glick, Phila. ....NC 3
June 16—Dom. Petrone, New York ...... W 10
June 27—Joe Glick, Phila. .... W 10
July 14—Mickey Doyle, Wilkes-Barre ..KO 5
May 2—Chick Suggs, Phila. .... W 10
Aug. 3—Tom. Crawley, Phila..........KO 2
Aug. 11—Johnny Farr, Cleveland ...... W 10
Aug. 16—Joe Williams, Philadelphia ...KO 8
Sept. 19—Red Chapman, Phila. .... W 10
(Won Vacant World Featherweight Title)
Oct. 17—Mike Ballerino, Phila. .... W 10
Dec. 9—Johnny Farr, Philadelphia ..... W 10
Dec. 13—Johnny Sheppard,
Wilkes-Barre .... W 10

1928

Jan. 3—Pete Nebo, Phila. .... W 10
Jan. 20—Wilbur Cohen, Phila. .... W 8
Jan. 30—Wilbur Cohen, Atlantic City .. W 10
Feb. 10—Tony Canzoneri, New York .....L 15
(Lost Featherweight Title)
June 18—Pete Nebo, Phila. ....L 10
Sept. 10—Harry Blitman, Phila. ....KO 6
Oct. 29—Phil McGraw, Phila. .... LF 4
Nov. 16—Dom. Petrone, Wilkes-Barre ..KO 1
Dec. 10—Gaston Charles, Philadelphia ... W 10

1929

Jan. 14—Davey Abad, Phila. .... W 10
Jan. 18—Joe Rivers, St. Louis ....KO 2
Jan. 28—Red Chapman, Phila...........KO 1
Feb. 6—Henry Lenard, St. Louis ..... LF 2
Feb. 11—Harry Forbes, Chicago .... W 10
Feb. 18—Steve Smith, Phila............ W 10
Feb. 28—Davey Abad, St. Louis ....ND 10
Mar. 19—Davey Abad, St. Louis ....ND 10
Mar. 25—Harry Forbes, Phila. .... W 10
Apr. 27—Johnny Farr, Phila. .... W 10
May 26—Petey Mack, New York .... W 10
May 28—Steve Smith, Pittsburgh .... W 10
July 18—Augie Pisano, Newark .... W 10
July 20—Calvin Reed, Atlantic City ..... W 8
July 31—Benny Kid Carter, Brooklyn ...KO 7
Aug. 23—C. Goodman, Long Branch ....KO 2
Sept. 18—Arm. Santiago, Phila. ....WF 2
Sept. 27—Johnny Datto, Chicago .... LF 4
Oct. 11—Armando Santiago, Phila. ....KO 2
Nov. 5—Jimmy Mendo, St. Louis .....KO 1
Nov. 11—Eddie Reed, Phila. .... W 10
Dec. 2—Jose Martinez, Phila..........KO 4
Dec. 19—Tod Morgan, N. Y. C. ....KO 2
(Won Jr. Lightweight title)

1930

Feb. 3—Davey Abad, St. Louis ....KO 4
Feb. 7—Sammy Fuller, Boston .... LF 5
Mar. 4—Eddie Anderson, Milwaukee ... D 10
Mar. 28—Eddie Shea, St. Louis ....ND 10
June 10—Eddie Anderson, Milwaukee ..KO 3
June 23—Joey Goodman, Pittsburgh ....W 10
July 21—Tony Canzoneri, Phila. ....L 10
Sept. 3—Eddie Anderson, Des Moines ..ND 10
Sept. 10—Tommy Cello, Peoria .... LF 2
Sept. 15—Eddie Anderson, Peoria ......ND 10

Oct. 6—Mike Dundee, Davenport .....ND 10
Nov. 24—Lew Massey, Phila.............ND 10
Dec. 2—Al Bryant, Allentown .... W 10
Dec. 8—Johnny Jadick, Phila. .... W 10

1931

Jan. 5—Lew Massey, Phila.............. W 10
Feb. 16—Bud Taylor, Phila. ....KO 2
Mar. 30—Young Firpo, Phila. ....L 10
Apr. 13—Young Firpo, Phila. .... W 10
May 4—Eddie Mack, Phila. ....KO 3
June 26—Georgie Day, Atlantic City ....KO 2
July 15—Kid Chocolate, Phila. ..... KO by 7
(Lost Junior Lightwegiht Title)
Sept. 10—Midget Fox, Phila..............KO 3
Nov. 30—Jackie Pilkington, Phila. ...... LF 5
Dec. 14—Tony Herrera, Phila. ....L 10
Dec. 18—Sidney Lampe, Wilmington ...KO 3
Dec. 25—Prince Sanders, Phila. ....KO 7

1932

Mar. 9—Wesley Ramey, St. Louis .....ND 10
Mar. 14—Frankie Bojarski, Pittsburgh .. LF 3
Apr. 14—Mickey Doyle, Wilmington ...KO 2
Apr. 15—Young Zazzerino, Jersey City .KO 5
May 25—Harry Dublinsky, Phila. .... W 10
June 7—Harry Carlton, Jersey City .... D 10
July 25—Ernie Ratner, Port Richmond .. W 10
Aug. 26—Yg. Patsy Wallace, Atl. City .... W 10
Sept. 12—Tony Falco, Phila. .... W 10
Dec. 5—Eddie Reilly, New York ......KO 1
Dec. 12—Dom. Petrone, New York .....KO 3

1933

Jan. 27—Sid Lampe, N. Y. C. ....KO 2
Feb. 22—Phil Zwick, Phila. .... W 10
Mar. 8—Joe Ghnouly, St. Louis .... W 10
Apr. 4—Johnny Farr, Phila. .... W 8
May 22—Buster Brown, Baltimore ...... W 10
Aug. 21—Jack Portney, Atlantic City ..KO 2
Aug. 30—Stumpy Jacobs, VirginiaBeach . W 8
Sept. 6—Davey Abad, Houston .... LF 2
Oct. 2—Stumpy Jacobs, Atlantic City .. W 8
Dec. 27—Eddie Cool, Phila. .... W 10

1934

Mar. 12—Cleto Locatelli, Phila. .... D 10
Apr. 9—Jimmy Leto, Phila. ....KO 3
Apr. 30—Cleto Locatelli, Phila...........L 10
July 31 Johnny Jadick, Phila. .... W 10
Aug. 27—Petey Sarron, Washington .... LF 6
Aug. 31—Eddie Shea, Atlantic City .....KO 2
Sept. 24—Petey Sarron, Phila............L 10
Dec. 3—Frankie Wallace, Phila. .... W 10
Dec. 25—Baby Chocolate, Atlantic City KO 2
Dec. 25—Irish Jimmy Brady, Newark .... W 10

1935

Feb. 18—Eddie Cool, Philadelphia ....L 10
Mar. 22—Mike Marshall, Philadelphia ... W 10
Apr. 12—Mike Marshall, Philadelphia .... W 10
Apr. 29—Tony Falco, Philadelphia ...... W 10
May 27—Mose Butch, Pittsburgh .... W 10
July 23—Frankie Wallace, Lancaster .... W 8
July 26—Johnny Craven, Philadelphia ... W 10
July 29—Jimmy Leto, Hartford ....L 10
Aug. 21—Johnny Craven, Philadelphia ...L 10
Aug. 27—Mike Marshall, Leiperville ..... W 10
Oct. 11—George Gibbs, Philadelphia .... W 10
Nov. 11—Jack Portney, Baltimore ....L 10
Dec. 6—Charley Burns, Philadelphia ... W 10
Dec. 25—Johnny Craven, Philadelphia ..KO 2

1936

Dec. 4—Davey Fine, Philadelphia ..... W 10
Dec. 18—Joey Zodda, Philadelphia .....KO 1

1937

Jan. 14—Joey Allen, Philadelphia ....W 10
Jan. 22—Red Cochrane, Philadelphia ... W 10
Feb. 5—Gene Gallotto, Philadelphia ... W 10
Mar. 12—Andy Bundy, Philadelphia .... W 10
Mar. 18—Charley Gomer, Philadelphia ... W 10
Apr. 8—Johnny Cabello, Philadelphia .KO 2
Apr. 16—Gene Gallotta, Philadelphia ... W 10
June 15—Tommy Cross, Philadelphia ... W 10
July 27—Henry Armstrong, Phila. ..KO by 4

1939

Aug. 10—Young Chappie, Philadelphia .KO 2
Oct. 13—Norman Rahn, Philadelphia ...W 10

1940

Jan. 22—Tony Sarullo, Philadelphia ....W 8
Feb. 2—Norman Rahn, Philadelphia ...KO 1
Mar. 4—Jimmy Tygh, Philadelphia .....D 10
Apr. 8—Jimmy Tugh, Philadelphia .....L 10
May 7—Tommy Spiegel, Philadelphia ...L 10

TB	KO	WD	WF	D	LD	LF	KOBY	ND	NC
197	59	79	2	6	16	10	2	22	1

TONY CANZONERI
(Record under Lightweight Champions)

ANDRE ROUTIS
Born, July 16, 1900, Bordeaux, France.
Nationality, French. Weight, 118-130 lbs.
Height, 5 ft., 4 in. Managed by Joe Jacobs.
1918
Won amateur championship.
1919
Feb.	2—Vves Gram, Bordeaux	W	4
Apr.	6—Geo. Gloria	WF	6
Apr.	7—Robert Diamant	D	8
Apr.	17—Emile Julliard, Paris	L	10
Aug.	10—Lebois, Bordeaux	W	8
Aug.	13—Dorlet	W	6
Dec.	22—Emile Julliard	D	12

1920
Feb.	2—Albert Bouzonnie, Bordeaux	D	10
Mar.	2—Luciani	WF	7
Apr.	10—Marignan	W	4
July	10—Geo. Gloria	KO	3
Nov.	27—Barklett	W	4
Dec.	18—Corbiaux	W	10

1921
Feb.	—All Ben Said, Casablanca	WF	3
May	4—Andre Glaise	KO	7
June	3—Eugene Husson	WF	6
June	17—Bulger Lake, Paris	W	3
July	2—Reby, Bordeaux	W	3
Aug.	7—Piacentini, Casablanca	W	10
Dec.	2—Young Blaise	WF	3

1922
Jan.	2—Robert Dastillon, Casablanca	KO	3
Feb.	7—Julien Couleaud	LF	8
Apr.	2—Blaise Paine	WF	8
Apr.	21—Robert Dastillon	WF	5
May	5—Julien Couleaud	W	4
June	18—Charles Ledoux, Casablanca	L	15
Sept.	7—Edouard Prie, Paris	W	4
Oct.	7—Michel Montreuil	KO by	2
Nov.	4—Charles Miet	W	6
Nov.	13—Johnny Chislett, Londres	KO	9
Dec.	2—Andre Dupont, Paris	KO	3

1923
Feb.	3—Emile Juliard, Casblanca	KO	3
Mar.	24—Emile Julien, Paris	W	12
May	6—Charles Ledoux, Paris	L	15
June	23—Pierre Calloir	D	15
Sept.	2—Denain, Marseilles	L	10
Sept.	25—Pierre Calloir, Paris	WF	15
Nov.	21—Pierre Calloir, Lyon	W	12

1924
Jan.	22—Charles Ledoux, Paris	W	20

(Bantamweight Championship of France)
Feb.	29—Harry Lake, Plymouth	W	15
Apr.	29—Edouard Mascart, Paris	WF	4
Aug.	13—Henry Hebrans, Deauvile	W	15
Oct.	7—Edouard Mascart, Paris	D	15

1925
Apr.	19—Antoin Ascensio, Oran	KO	6
Apr.	30—Johnny Brown, London	LF	5
June	25—Frantz Van Dyk, London	KO	14
Sept.	12—Pierre Calloir, Casablanca	KO	4
Oct.	27—Kid Francis, Paris	L	15

(Bantamweight Championship of France)
Nov.	19—Harry Corbett, London	L	15

1926
Mar.	2—Gaston Cassini, Paris	W	12
Mar.	18—Kid Berg, London	L	15
May	18—Paul Gay, Paris	W	12
June	21—Kid Berg, London	LF	3
Aug.	20—Eddie Anderson, N. Y.	W	10
Sept.	27—Eddie Anderson, N. Y.	WF	4
Oct.	25—Johnny Leonard, N. Y.	W	10
Nov.	22—Tony Canzoneri, N.Y.	L	12
Dec.	18—Frankie Fink, N. Y.	W	10
Dec.	27—Eddie Anderson, N. Y.	W	10

1927
Jan.	24—Peter Mack, N. Y.	W	10
Mar.	17—Harry Lenard, Chicago	L	10
Apr.	1—Joe Salas, N. Y. C.	LF	2
Apr.	25—Carl Tremaine, N. Y. C.	W	12
May	0—Tommy Crawley, Phila.	W	10
June	7—Joe Glick, N. Y.	W	10
June	27—Emory Cabana, Phila.	D	10
Aug.	2—Joe Malone, N. Y. C.	W	10
Aug.	17—Joe Glick, N. Y.	W	10
Dec.	10—Al Brown, Paris	W	10

1928
Jan.	6—Jackie Kid Berg, London	LF	3
Jan.	14—Johnny Cuthbert, Paris	D	12
Mar.	23—Sammy Dorfman, N. Y. C.	WF	5
Apr.	26—Ignacio Fernandez, Cleveland	W	12
May	4—Sammy Dorfman, N. Y. C.	W	10
July	3—Carl Duane, N.Y.C.	W	10
July	25—Vic Burrone, N. Y. C.	W	10
Sept.	28—Tony Canzoneri, N. Y. C.	W	15

(Won Featherweight Championship of World)
Nov.	17—Dick Finnegan, Boston	L	10

1929
May	10—Tony Canzoneri, Chicago	L	10
May	27—Buster Brown, Baltimore	KO	3

(Title Bout)
July	6—Jackie Cohen, Montreal	L. Dis.	6
July	8—Jack Zeramby, Boston	L	10
July	24—Al Singer, N. Y. C.	KO by	2
Aug.	26—Johnny Dato, Cleveland	L	10
Sept.	23—Battling Battalino, Hartford	L	15

(Lost Featherweight Championship of World)
Nov.	5—Davey Abad, St. Louis	L	10

TB	KO	WD	WF	D	LD	LF	KOBY	ND	NC
86	10	33	11	7	17	6	2	0	0

Died July 27, 1969, Paris, France.

BATTLING BATTALINO
(Christopher Battalino)
Born, February 18, 1908, Hartford, Conn.
Nationality, Italian-American. Weight, 126 lbs.
1927
Knockouts: Archie Rosenberg, 2; Mickey Rossi, 1; Young Wagner, 4; Frisco Bautisti, 4. Won: Scotty Horsburg, 3; Tony De Palmo, 6; Joe Curry, 6; "Black Bottom" Jim Bones, 6. Draw: Joe Curry, 6; Philly Griffin, 6.
1928
Knockouts: Jimmy Scully, 5; Jimmy Garcia, 1. Won: Johnny Ciccone, 6; Milton Cohen, 6; Jules Sombathy, 10; Milton Cohen, 10. Lost: Johnny Ciccone, 6.
1929
Jan.	4—Ralph Nischo, Hartford, Conn.	KO	1
Feb.	7—Joe Curry, Hartford, Conn.	KO	2
Feb.	21—Tony Leto, Hartford, Conn.	KO	7
June	6—Eddie Lord, Hartford, Conn.	W	10
July	26—Al Brown, Hartford, Conn.	W	10
Sept.	23—Andre Routis, Hartford, Conn.	W	15

(Won World's Featherweight Championship)
1930
Jan.	9—Phil Verde, New Haven	KO	3
Jan.	20—Lew Massey, Philadelphia	L	10
Mar.	20—Bud Taylor, Detroit	L	10
Apr.	14—Benny Nabors, Waterbury	KO	4
Apr.	25—Bushy Graham, Hartford, Conn.	W	10
May	5—Lew Massey, Philadelphia	W	10
May	25—Vic Burrone, Philadelphia	W	10
June	1—Cecil Payne, Cincinnati	L	10
July	15—Ignacio Fernandez, E. Hartford		
	....	KO	7
July	24—Cecil Payne, Cincinnati	L	10
Aug.	18—Bud Taylor, Hartford	W	10
Sept.	3—Roger Bernard, Detroit	L	10
Sept.	24—Young Kaplan, Hartford	L	10
Oct.	20—Young Zazzarino, Jersey City	LF	3
Dec.	12—Kid Chocolate, N. Y. C.	W	15

(Championship bout)
1931
Jan.	23—Eddie Shea, Chicago, Ill.	L	10
Mar.	6—Young Zazzarino, Hartford	W	10
Mar.	20—Andy Callahan, Boston, Mass.	L	10
Apr.	20—Andy Martin, Hartford, Conn.	W	10
May	22—Fidel La Barba, New York	W	15

(Title)
June	15—Johnny Datto, Hartford, Ct.	KO	5
July	1—Irish Bobby Brady, Jersey City	W	10

(Title)
July	23—Freddie Miller, Cincinnati, O.	W	10

(Title)
Sept.	15—Eddie Shea, Hartford, Conn.	W	10
Sept.	24—Bushey Graham, Hartford, Ct.	L	10
Oct.	12—Roger Bernard, Philadelphia	L	10
Nov.	4—Earl Mastro, Chicago, Ill.	W	10

(Title)
Nov.	19—Bushy Graham, Chicago, Ill.	KO	1
Dec.	11—Al Singer, New York	KO	2

717

1932

Jan. 27—Freddie Miller, Cincinnati .... NC 3
(Battalino was deprived of his title)
Feb. 24—Billy Shaw, St. Louis .... KO 2
Mar. 2—Battalino relinquished all claim to the featherweight title.
Mar. 11—Eddie Ran, N. Y. .... W 10
Mar. 24—Billy Petrolle, N. Y. C. ...... KO by 12
May 20—Billy Petrolle, Chicago .... L 10
June 28—Frankie Petrolle, N. Y. C. .... L 10
July 19—Frankie Petrolle, N. Y. C. .... L 10
July 28—Willie Hines, N. Y. C. .... KO 3
Aug. 11—Billy Townsend, N. Y. C. ...... W 10
Sept. 5—Eddie Holmes, Providence ...... L 10
Oct. 21—Barney Ross, Chicago .... L 10

1933

July 28—Ben Whitler, Poughkeepsie ... KO 2
Aug. 9—Phil Rafferty, N. Y. C. .... L 8

1934

Apr. 12—Antonio Cerdan, Rio de Janeiro .... KO 4
July 24—Jackie Davis, Hartford .... W 10
Sept. 11—Lew Feldman, New Haven ...... L 10
Oct. 1—Lew Feldman, Hartford .... W 10
Oct. 16—Cocoa Kid, Hartford .... KO 7
Nov. 26—Jimmy Leto, Hartford .... L 10

1936

Jan. 30—Pete Nebo, Hartford .... KO 2
Feb. 5—Brescia Garcia, N. Y. C. .... W 8
Feb. 25—Joey Greb, N. Y. C. .... W 6
Apr. 8—Al Roth, N. Y. C. .... L 10
June 15—Howard Scott, Wash., D. C. ..... L 10
July 6—Howard Scott, Hartford .... L 10

1939

July 11—Sal Canata, Hartford .... KO 1
July 25—Oscar Suggs, Hartford .... W 6
Aug. 8—Felix Garcia, Hartford .... KO 2
Sept. 5—Johnny Castonguay, Hartford KO 4
Sept. 12—Frankie Young, Hartford ...... W 6
Sept. 26—Frankie Young, Hartford ...... W 8
Oct. 30—Jerry Maloni, Holyoke .... W 10
Nov. 16—George Pepe, New Haven ...... D 8
Dec. 4—George Martin, Holyoke .... L 10

1940

Jan. 30—Dick Turcotte, Hartford .... L 10

TB	KO	WD	WF	D	LD	LF	KOBY	ND	NC
87	24	33	0	3	24	1	1	0	1

TOMMY PAUL

(Thomas Paul)

Born, 1907, Buffalo, N. Y. Weight, 126 lbs. Height, 5 ft. 4 in. Managed by Jack Singer. Boxed as an amateur, winning many contests in Buffalo as a bantam.

1927

Knockouts: Freddie Griffiths, 4; Joey Weber, 2; Young Nancy, 5; Allen Holmes, 1. Won: Andy Tomaskey, 6. Draw: Frankie La Barba, 6; Frankie Garcia, 6.

1928

Won: Young Irish, 4; Charley Pinto, 6. Mike Marcells, W 6; Johnny Dunn, W 10; Freddie Griffiths, KO 4; Joe Weber, KO 2; Patsy Russo, KO 1; Bobby Hamilton, KO 4; Allen Homes, KO 1; Lou Atta, KO 2; Young Nancy, KO 5; Eddie Hardy, KO 2; Johnny McCoy, W 6; Jimmy Valpone, W 6; Hal Stevenson, W 6; Johnny McCoy, W 6; Wee Wee Woods, W 6; Mike Marcelles, W 6; Harry Fierro, W 6; Andy Tomasky, W 6; Frankie Garcia, D 6; Joey Ross, D 6; Frankie Garcia, D 6; Johnny Dunn, D 6; Pancho Dencio, KO 1; Tommy Ryan, W 6; Phil O'Dowd, KO 1; Ansell Bell, KO 1; Frisco Grande, LF 3; Frankie Genaro, W 6.

1929

Jan. 1—Frisco Grande, Buffalo .... LF 1
Jan. 18—Frankie Genaro, Buffalo ...... W 6
Jan. 29—Frankie Genaro, Buffalo ...... W 6
Feb. 1—Frisco Grande, Buffalo .... W 6
Feb. 22—Charley Pinto, Buffalo .... KO 1
Apr. 12—Emil Paluso, Buffalo .... W 6
Apr. 20—Charles Pinto, Buffalo .... W 6
June 7—Fidel La Barba, Buffalo .... L 6
July 12—Emil Paluso, Buffalo .... W 6
Oct. 11—Joe Scalfaro, Buffalo .... W 6
Nov. 8—Johnny Datto, Buffalo .... D 10

1930

Jan. 10—Johnny Datto, Buffalo, N. Y. ... W 6
Jan. 13—Jackie Williams, Rochester ... KO 2
Jan. 20—Eddie O'Dowd, Buffalo, N. Y. KO 1
Jan. 24—Archie Bell, Detroit, Mich. ..... W 10
Feb. 7—Jackie Britton, Detroit, Mich. .. W 6
Mar. 14—Panama Al Brown, Buffalo .... D 6
Apr. 4—Fidel La Barba, Buffalo .... L 10
May 9—Johnny Datto, Providence .... WF 3
July 7—Fidel La Barba, Buffalo, N. Y. ... L 10
Aug. 23—Steve Smith, Buffalo, N. Y. .... W 10
Nov. 7—Phil Verdi, Buffalo, N. Y. ...... KO 2
Nov. 14—Bushy Graham, Buffalo, N. Y. . W 10
Nov. 28—Jackie Britton, Buffalo, N. Y. .. W 10
Dec. 19—Midget Mike O'Dowd, Erie, Pa. . W 10

1931

Mar. 5—Freddy Miller, Cincinnati .... L 10
Mar. 23—Maurice Holtzer, Philadelphia .. W 10
Apr. 6—Phil Zwick, Philadelphia .... W 10
Apr. 13—Freddie Miller, Cincinnati ...... L 10
June 12—Mickey Cohen, Cleveland ..... KO 1
Aug. 31—Freddie Miller, Buffalo .... W 10
Oct. 23—Johnny Farr, Buffalo .... W 10

1932

Feb. 5—Pete Degrasse, Detroit .... W 10
Feb. 12—Joe Thomas, Pittsburgh .... W 10
Feb. 19—Jackie Rodgers, Buffalo .... W 10
Mar. 21—Tony Sciolino, Buffalo .... L 10
Apr. 8—Bushy Graham, Detroit .... W 10
Apr. 29—Frankie Wallace, Detroit ...... W 10
May 26—Johnny Pena, Detroit, Mich. ... W 15
(Won Vacant N.B.A. Featherweight Title)
June 14—Fidel La Barba, Los Angeles .... L 10
June 23—Varias Milling, Sacramento .... W 10
Aug. 25—Lew Feldman, N. Y. C. .... L 10
Sept. 16—Baby Arizmendi, Mexico City ... L 10
Oct. 14—Danny Dempsey, Scranton ... KO 7
Nov. 2—Tony Sciolino, Buffalo, N. Y. .. W 12
Nov. 28—Young Geno, Chicago, Ill. .... KO 3
Dec. 29—Fidel La Barba, Chicago .... W 10

1933

Jan. 2—Pete Young, Buffalo .... W 4
Jan. 13—Freddy Miller, Chicago .... L 10
(Lost N.B.A. Featherweight Title)
Feb. 2—Willie Cubic, Wilkes-Barre .... KO 7
Mar. 13—Jimmy Thomas, Pittsburgh .... W 10
Mar. 27—Mose Butch, Pittsburgh ...... KO 9
Apr. 3—Jackie Wilson, Pittsburgh .... L 10
Apr. 24—Petey Sarron, Alexandria, Va. .. D 8
June 5—Jackie Wilson, Pittsburgh .. KO by 8
July 5—Jackie Sharkey, Chicago .... W 10
Sept. 15—Little Dempsey, San Fran. .... KO 7
Oct. 3—Joey Ponce, Seattle .... W 10
Nov. 10—Georgie Hansford, Hollywood . W 10
Nov. 24—Abie Israel, Hollywood .... KO 8
Dec. 8—Geo. Hansford, Hollywood ..... L 10

1934

Jan. 5—Little Dempsey, Hollywood .. KO 4
Feb. 16—George Hansford, Hollywood ... L 10
Apr. 27—Joey Ponce, Hollywood ...... LF 7
May 22—Kid Chocolate, Los Angeles .... D 10
June 19—Freddy Miller, Los Ang. ...... WF 2
Aug. 3—Freddy Miller, Hollywood ...... L 10
Aug. 24—George Hansford, Hollywd. KO by 4
Sept. 24—Joey Brown, Syracuse .... W 6
Oct. 1—Frankie Covelli, Washington .... L 10
Oct. 15—Leo Rodak, Chicago .... L 10
Dec. 3—Everett Rightmire, Chicago ..... L 10
Dec. 11—Bus Breese, Kansas City .... L 10
Dec. 28—Tony Morgano, Hollywood ..... L 10

1935

Jan. 23—Isidro Pinto de Sa, Oakland ... KO 9
Mar. 22—Holman Williams, Detroit ...... L 10

TB	KO	WD	WF	D	LD	LF	KOBY	ND	NC
114	28	48	2	10	20	3	2	1	0

KID CHOCOLATE

(Eligio Sardinias)
(Cuban Bon Bon)

Born, Jan. 6, 1910, Cerro, Cuba. Nationality, Cuban Negro. Weight, 126 lbs. Height, 5 ft. 6 in. Managed by Louis Guitieriez.

Amateur Record: 100 bouts; K. O. 86; won 14 (in Cuba).

Professional Record: 21 bouts; K. O. 21 (in Cuba).

1928

Aug.	1—Eddie Enos, New York City	...KO	3
Aug.	6—Nick Mercer, New York City	..KO	3
Aug.	13—Mike Castle, New York City	..KO	3
Aug.	18—Johnny Green, N. Y. C.	.......KO	4
Aug.	23—Nick de Salvo, N. Y. C.	.... W	10
Aug.	28—Sammy Tisch, N. Y. C.	.... W	10
Oct.	1—Johnny Erickson, N. Y. C.	..... W	10
Oct.	7—Eddie O'Dowd, N. Y. C.	.... W	10
Oct.	29—Joey Ross, N. Y. C.	..........KO	1
Nov.	7—Frisco Grande, N. Y. C.	.......KO	4
Nov.	19—Pinky Silverberg, N. Y. C.	...... W	10
Nov.	22—Jack Schweitzer, N. Y. C.	.....KO	6
Nov.	25—Pinky May, N. Y. C.	.........KO	6
Nov.	30—Joe Scalfaro, N. Y. C.	.... D	10
Dec.	7—Johnny Holstein, Buffalo, N. Y.	W	10
Dec.	17—Emil Paluso, N. Y. C.	.......KO	8
Dec.	23—Pancho Denico, N. Y. C.	......KO	2

1929

Feb.	29—Chick Suggs, Havana	.... W	10
Mar.	9—Phil O'Dowd, N. Y. C.	........KO	1
Mar.	18—Al Rackow, Buffalo	..........KO	4
Mar.	22—Johnny Vacca, Boston	.......KO	9
Apr.	12—Bushy Graham, N. Y. C.	..... W	15
Apr.	19—Vic Burrone, N. Y. C.	.... W	10
Apr.	28—Tommy Ryan, N. Y. C.	.......KO	1
May	8—Steve Smith, Wilkes-Barre	..... W	10
May	22—Fidel La Barba, N. Y. C.	..... W	10
June	5—Vidal Gregorio, Philadelphia	... W	10
June	18—Terry Roth, N. Y. C.	.........KO	3
June	24—Jackie Johnston, Toronto	...KO	1
July	10—Ignacio Fernandez, N. Y. C.	..... W	10
July	30—Steve Smith, Chicago	.... W	10
Aug.	7—Tommy Lorenzo, N. Y. C.	....KO	6
Aug.	29—Al Singer, N. Y. C.	.... W	12
Nov.	9—Johnny Erickson, N. Y. C.	..... W	10
Nov.	19—Jose Martinez, N. Y. C.	.... W	10
Nov.	29—Eddie O'Dowd, N. Y. C.	......KO	2
Dec.	10—Herman Silverberg, N. Y. C.	..KO	1
Dec.	18—Dominick Petrone	.... W	10
Dec.	21—Johnny Lawson	..............KO	2

1930

Feb.	23—Vic Burrone, Havana, Cuba	.... W	10
Mar.	5—Benny Hall, Tampa, Fla.	.... W	10
Mar.	21—Al Ridgeway, N. Y. C.	........KO	2
Apr.	28—Johnny Erickson, Toronto, Can.	W	10
July	2—Dominick Petrone, N. Y. C.	....KO	6
July	15—Luigi Quadrini, N. Y. C.	...... W	10
Aug.	7—Jack Kid Berg, N. Y. C.	L	10
Oct.	16—Benny Nabors, N. Y. C.	.......KO	1
Oct.	27—Mickey Doyle, Newark	.......KO	1
Nov.	3—Fidel Barba, N.Y.C.	 L	10
Dec.	12—Battling Battalino, N. Y. C.	L	15
	(For World Featherweight Title)		

1931

May	29—Georgie Goldberg, N.Y.C.	....KO	7
June	12—Steve Smith, New Haven	...... W	10
June	17—Max Lerner, White Plains	...... W	10
June	29—Harry Sankey, Poughkeepsie	... W	10
July	15—Benny Bass, Philadelphia	.....KO	7
	(Won Junior Lightweight Title)		
Oct.	1—Joe Scalfaro, N. Y. C.	........KO	1
Oct.	12—Steve Smith, Trenton	.... W	10
Oct.	21—Al Rube Goldberg, Jersey C'y.	KO	3
Oct.	26—Buck Oliva, Hartford	.........KO	2
Nov.	2—Lew Feldman, N. Y. C.	.... W	10
Nov.	20—Tony Canzoneri, N. Y. C.	L	15
	(For World Lightweight Title)		
Nov.	30—Maxie Lerner, N. Y. C.	.......KO	1

1932

Mar.	6—Dominick Petrone, Havana	.... W	10
Apr.	10—Davey Abad, Havana	.... W	15
May	16—Mike Sarko, N. Y. C.	.... W	10
May	26—Steve Smith, Garfield, N. J.	.... W	10
June	1—Lew Feldman, N. Y. C.	.... W	15
June	6—Mike Sarko, Albany	.... W	10
June	16—Roger Bernard, Philadelphia	... W	10
June	22—Johnny Farr, Pittsburgh	.... W	10
July	18—Jack Kid Berg, N. Y. C.	L	15
Aug.	4—Eddie Shea, Chicago	.... W	10
Aug.	11—Johnny Farr, Cincinnati	.... W	10
Sept.	1—Frankie Marchese, N. Y. C.	...KO	4
Sept.	6—Steve Smith, Boston	.... W	10
Sept.	15—Frankie Farriello, Freeport	.... W	6
Oct.	4—Johnny Farr, Detroit	.... W	10
Oct.	5—Lew Feldman, N. Y. C.	.... W	12
	(Won New York State Featherweight Title)		
Nov.	14—Pete Nebo, N. Y. C.	.... W	10
Nov.	21—Eddie Reilly, N. Y. C.	.... W	10
Nov.	29—Johnny Alba, N. Y. C.	.... W	10
Dec.	9—Fidel La Barba, N. Y. C.	...... W	15
	(New York State Featherweight Title)		

1933

May	1—Johnny Farr, Philadelphia	..... W	10
May	19—Seaman Watson, N. Y. C.	...... W	15
	(New York recognition, Featherweight Title)		
July	15—Nick Bensa, Madrid, Spain	..... W	10
Aug.	2—Franz Machtens, Barcelona, Sp.	W	10
Sept.	29—Nick Bensa, Paris, France	.....KO	10
Nov.	1—Joe Ghnouly, Montreal, Can.	... W	10
Nov.	24—Tony Canzoneri, N. Y. C.	...KO by	2
Dec.	4—Frankie Wallace, Cleveland	.... W	10
Dec.	26—Frankie Klick, Phila.	.......KO by	7
	(Lost Jr. Lightweight Title)		
	(Chocolate outgrew featherweight division)		

1934

Feb.	12—Lou Avery, Ft. Worth	.... W	10
Apr.	16—Frankie Wallace, San Fran.	.... W	10
Apr.	24—Bobby Gray, San Jose, Cal.	.... D	10
May	11—Pete Nebo, San Francisco	...... W	10
May	22—Tommy Paul, Los Angeles	...... D	10
May	29—Emil Paluso, Bakersfield, Cal.	.KO	7
June	28—Frankie Marchese, N. Y. C.	.... W	10
July	6—Johnny Erickson, Long Branch	W	10
July	11—Petey Hayes, N. Y. C.	L	10
July	31—Buster Brown, N. Y. C.	.... W	8
Aug.	1—Andre Sarilla, Washington	....KO	7
Oct.	5—Jerry Mazza, N. Y. C.	.... W	10

1935

Mar.	18—Simon Chavez, Caracas	L	10
July	4—Pete Nebo	.... W	10
Sept.	3—Kid Jackson	..................KO	7

1936

Jan.	12—Pelon Guerra, Havana	.......KO	2
Feb.	1—Andy Martin, Havana	.... W	10
May	30—Lew Feldman, Havana	.... W	10
June	20—Johnny Erickson, Havana	...... W	10
Aug.	14—Joey Brown, Havana	.... W	10
Sept.	26—Jose Santos, Havana	.... W	10
Dec.	7—Phil Baker, N. Y. C.	L	8
Dec.	19—Johnny Erickson, N. Y. C.	..... W	8
Dec.	26—Al Gillette, N. Y. C.	.... W	8

1937

Jan.	7—Joe La Fauci, N. Y. C.	.... W	8
Jan.	13—Johnny Erickson, New Haven	.KO	5
Jan.	19—Tony Pagano, Brooklyn	......KO	4
Jan.	28—Johnny Marabella, N. Y. C.	... W	8
Feb.	27—Jimmy Lancaster, Brooklyn	... W	6
Mar.	7—Bernie Friedkin, Brooklyn	..... D	8
Mar.	18—Joey Woods, N. Y. C.	........KO	1
Mar.	27—Allie Todisco, N. Y. C.	.... W	8
Apr.	9—Frankie Anselm, New Orleans	.. W	10
May	25—Henry Hook, Brooklyn	.... W	10
June	2—Al Reid, N. Y. C.	.... W	10
June	15—Young Chappie, Brooklyn	..... W	8
June	18—Al Gillette, Long Branch	....KO	4
July	2—Joe Marciente, Long Beach	... W	8
July	7—Charley Gomer, N. Y. C.	.... W	8
July	20—Young Chappie, Brooklyn	..... W	8
July	27—Orville Drouillard, Jersey City	....D	8
Aug.	2—Charley Gomer, Baltimore	... W	10
Aug.	13—Joe Marcienti, Brooklyn	.... W	8
Aug.	16—Jimmy Trameria, Hempst'd	.KO	1
Aug.	19—Johnny De Foe, N. Y. C.	...... W	10
Sept.	5—Phil Baker, Havana	.... W	10
Nov.	10—Young Chappie, Havana	...... W	10
Dec.	23—Johnny Marabella, Havana	....KO	4

1938

Mar.	20—Filio Echeverria, Havana	...... W	10
Dec.	18—Nicky Jerome, Havana	.... D	10

TB	KO	WD	WF	D	LD	LF	KOBY	ND	NC
161	64	81	0	6	8	0	2	0	0

Elected to Boxing Hall of Fame 1959.

FREDDIE MILLER

Born, April 3, 1911, Cincinnati, Ohio. Nationality, German-American. Weight, 126 lbs. Height, 5 ft. 5 in. Managed by Pete Reilly.

1927

Knockouts: Billy Barnes, 2; Chester Drown, 4; Chester Drown, 1; Mike Prunty, 3; King Cole, 3; Kid Casey, 1; Bulldog Fisher, 1; Johnny Santer, 3. Won: Chester Drown, 4; Kid Hickman, 4; Kid Mexe, 4; Red Schroeder, 6; Kid Ritchie, 6; Kid Oder, 6; Al Proctor, 4; Boston Ponzi, 4; Kid Ritchie, 4; Charley Court, 8; Al Proctor, 4; Jimmy Brown, 8; Howard Jones, 6; Red Wise, 6; Buddy Bezenah, 6; Al Proctor, 6; Solder Lewis, 2; Jimmy Harris, 10. Lost: Jimmy Harris, 10.

1928

Knockouts: Lightning Wells, 2; Eddie Jackson, 5; Young Fisher, 2; King Cole, 8; Kid Hickman, 3; Roy Kirkpatrick, 5; King Cole, 4; Jess McMurtry, 2. Won: Kid Ritchie, 6; Red Wise, 8; Buddy Bezenah, 6; Ray Van Hok, 6; King Cole, 8; Lou Lovelace, 6; Jimmy Sanzone, 10; Chet Smallwood, 6; Red Wise, 6; Howard Jones, 6; Louis De Arco, 6; Eddie Klusman, 4; Jimmy Harris, 10; Buddy Bezenah, 6; Jimmy Harris, 8; Windy Myers, 6; Eddie Klusman, 10; Jimmy Harris, 6; Al Dundee, 10; Jimmy Harris, 10; Phil O'Dowd, 10; Andy Stahura, 10; Eddie Morgan, 8; Babe Paleco, 10; Cecil Payne, 6; Stanley Williams, 6.

1929

Jan.	1—Cecil Payne, Cincinnati	W 10
Jan.	23—Johnny Brown, Cincinnati	W 10
Feb.	6—Joe Paglino, Cincinnati	W 10
Mar.	7—Harry McCarthy, Cincinnati	KO 7
Mar.	27—Johnny Brown, Cincinnati	W 10
Apr.	17—Babe Ruth, Cincinnati	W 10
May	6—Babe Keller, Cincinnati	W 10
June	11—Eddie O'Dowd, Cincinnati	W 10
July	2—Babe Keller, Cincinnati	W 10
Aug.	6—Harry Forbes, Cincinnati	W 10
Aug.	27—Midget Mike O'Dowd, Cincin.	W 10
Sept.	9—Midget Mike O'Dowd, Cincin.	W 10
Oct.	9—Al Crisp, Cincinnati	W 10
Nov.	6—Steve Smith, Cincinnati	W 10
Dec.	11—Steve Smith, Cincinnati	W 10

1930

Jan.	1—Willie Michel, Cincinnati	KO 4
Jan.	29—Bushy Graham, Cincinnati	D 10
July	31—Henry Falegano, Cincinnati	W 10
Aug.	21—Joe Marcienti, Cincinnati	W 10
Sept.	4—Babe Ruth, Columbus, O.	W 10
Sept.	16—Cecil Payne, Cincinnati	W 10
Oct.	2—Johnny Farr, Cincinnati	W 10
Oct.	27—Babe Ruth, Wheeling, W. Va.	ND 10
Nov.	13—Johnny Farr, Cincinnati	L 10
Dec.	8—Babe Ruth, Louisville	KO 2

1931

Jan.	1—Roger Bernard, Cincinnati	W 10
Jan.	26—Phil Zwick, Wheeling, W. Va.	KO 3
Mar.	5—Tommy Paul, Cincinnati	W 10
June	1—Billy Shaw, Portsmouth, O.	W 10
June	11—Eddie Shea, Cincinnati	W 10
July	23—Battling Battalino, Cincinnati	L 10
	(For World Featherweight Title)	
Aug.	24—Emil Paluso, Cincinnati	W 10
Aug.	31—Tommy Paul, Buffalo	L 10
Nov.	30—Billy Shaw, Sidney, O.	W 10
Dec.	11—Lew Feldman, N. Y. C.	W 8
Dec.	21—Ray Meyers, N. Y. C.	W 8

1932

Jan.	13—Johnny Datto, Cincinnati	W 10
Jan.	27—Battling Battalino, Cincinnati	NC 3
	Battalino was deprived of featherweight title	
Feb.	9—Joe Ghnouly, St. Louis	W 10
Feb.	29—Miki Gelb, Detroit	W 10
Feb.	24—Johnny Datto, St. Louis	W 10
Mar.	8—Frankie Wallace, Detroit	L 10
Mar.	22—Johnny Kaiser, St. Louis	W 10
May	2—Ray Meyers, N. Y. C.	W 10
May	13—Johnny Dunn, Detroit	W 8
June	22—Frankie Wallace, Cincinnati	W 10
June	29—Nat Suess, N. Y. C.	KO 5
Aug.	4—Hymie Wiseman, Chicago	W 8
Aug.	31—Frankie Wallace, Cincinnati	D 10

1933

Jan.	13—Tommy Paul, Chicago	W 10
	(Won N. B. A. Featherweight Title)	
Feb.	3—Leo Ranerie, Chicago	W 4
Feb.	24—*Baby Arizmendi, Los Angeles	W 10
Mar.	21—*Speedy Dado, Los Angeles	W 10
Apr.	4—Cecil Payne, Los Angeles	W 10
Apr.	11—Andy Bundy, Portland, Ore.	W 10
Apr.	18—Abie Israel, Seattle	ND 6
Apr.	26—Johnny Gonzales, Wilm., Cal.	KO 4
May	9—Little Dempsey, Sacra., Cal.	W 10
May	12—Eddie Trujillo, Hollywood	W 10
May	24—Joe Guerrero, Los Angeles	W 6
June	12—Baby Arizmendi, San. Fran.	L 10
July	11—Abie Israel, Seattle	KO 4
Sept.	1—Lew Feldman, Cincinnati	W 10
Sept.	26—Frankie Wallace, Cleveland	L 10
Oct.	23—Jackie Sharkey, Milw., Wis.	W 10
Nov.	1—Petey Sarron, Alexandria, Va.	W 10
Nov.	14—Lew Feldman, Brooklyn	W 10
Dec.	6—Paul Dazzo, Chicago	W 10
Dec.	20—Sammy Levine, Chicago	W 10
	*Title bout.	

1934

Jan.	1—*Jackie Sharkey, Cincinnati	W 10
Jan.	15—Roger Bernard, Flint, Mich.	W 10
Jan.	31—Frankie Covelli, N. Y. C.	W 10
Feb.	7—Petey Sarron, Cincinnati	W 10
Mar.	19—Mose Butch, Pittsburgh	W 10
Apr.	3—Moon Mullins, Vincennes, Ind.	W 10
Apr.	13—Jackie Sharkey, Minn.	ND 10
May	4—Paul Dazzo, Louisville	KO 5
May	29—Baby Casanova, Los Angeles	W 10
June	8—Chalky Wright, El Centro	W 10
June	19—Tommy Paul, Los Angeles	LF 2
June	29—Georgie Hansford, Hollywood	W 10
July	13—Gene Espinosa, Watsen., Cal.	KO 8
July	20—Clever Sison, Pismo Bea., Cal.	W 10
Aug.	3—Tommy Paul, Hollywood	W 10
Aug.	10—Little Dempsey, Salinas, Cal.	W 10
Sept.	21—Nel Tarleton, Liverpool, Eng.	W 15
	(Miller gained international recognition as world champion)	
Sept.	24—Billy Hazelgrove, Manchester, Eng.	KO 5
Oct.	1—Dave Crowley, London	W 10
Oct.	8—Benny Sharkey, New Castle, E.	KO 2
Oct.	15—W. Gannon, Manchester, Eng.	LF 6
Oct.	18—Jimmy Walsh, Liverpool, Eng.	W 12
Oct.	20—Cuthbert Taylor, Wales, Eng.	ND 6
Oct.	25—Gilbert Johnston, Glasgow	WF 10
Nov.	22—Johnny Cuthbert, Liverpool	KO 2
Dec.	1—Jose Girones, Barcelona	WF 5
Dec.	6—Cuthbert Taylor, Liverpool	W 12
Dec.	24—Al Brown, Paris	W 10
	Title bout.	

1935

Jan.	5—Francois Augire, Paris	KO 7
Jan.	6—Joe Connolly, London	W 10
Jan.	14—Tony Rogers, Bingham, Eng.	W 12
Jan.	20—Benny Caplan, London	D 10
Jan.	26—Francois Machtens, Brussels	W 10
Feb.	11—Maurice Holtzer, Paris	L 10
Feb.	17—*Jose Girones, Barcelona	KO 1
Feb.	24—Benny Caplan, London	W 10
Feb.	26—Douglas Kestrell, Belfast	W 8
Feb.	28—Johnny Peters, Liverpool	KO 4
Mar.	2—Stan Jehu, London	W 10
Mar.	11—Johnny Edwards, Paris	W 10
Mar.	14—Xavier Torres, Barcelona	KO 6
Mar.	23—Harry Brooks, London	KO 6
Mar.	27—Luigi Quadrini, Barcelona	W 10
Apr.	3—Jose Mico, Madrid	KO 3
Apr.	11—Jimmy Stewart, Liverpool	W 10
Apr.	21—Johnny Cruz, Palma, Majorca	KO 7
May	3—Jimmy Walsh, Liverpool	W 10
June	12—*Nel Tarleton, London	W 15
June	27—Seaman Watson, Liverpool	W 10
July	12—Stanley Jehu, Duluth	KO 4
July	25—Seaman Watson, Liverpool	KO 2
Aug.	21—Roger Bernard, Cincinnati	W 10
Aug.	28—Al Hamilton, Cincinnati	W 10
Sept.	9—Eddie Zivic, Pittsburgh	W 10
Sept.	16—Cecil Payne, Louisville	W 10
Sept.	20—Willy Davies, Dayton	W 10
Oct.	11—Paul Lee, Indianapolis	W 10
Oct.	22—*Vernon Cormier, Boston	W 15
Nov.	6—Vernon Cormier, Cincinnati	W 10
Nov.	13—Roger Bernard, Toronto	W 10
Nov.	18—Normant Quarles, Pittsburgh	L 10
Nov.	29—Jimmy Christy, Chicago	W 10
Dec.	11—Claude Varner, Cincinnati	W 10
	*Title bout.	

1936

Jan.	1—Baby Casanova, Mexico City	L 10
Jan.	15—Johnny Pena, Oakland	L 10
Jan.	28—Cecil Payne, Seattle	W 10
Feb.	11—Bobby Gray, San Jose	KO 1
Feb.	18—*Johnny Pena, Seattle	W 12
Mar.	2—*Petey Sarron, Coral Gables	L 15
Mar.	14—Filio Echeverria, Havana	W 10
Mar.	20—Andy Martin, Birmingham	W 10
May	11—Petey Sarron, Wash., D. C.	L 15
	(Lost featherweight title)	
May	27—Jimmy Vaughn, Cincinnati	L 10
June	24—Everette Rightmire, Kan. City	W 10
July	13—Jimmy Buckler, Louisville	W 10
Oct.	3—Willy Smith, South Africa	KO 6
Oct.	24—Maurice Holtzer, South Africa	W 15
Nov.	14—Willy Smith, South Africa	KO 7
Nov.	28—Phil Zwick, Johannesburg	KO 4
	*Title bout.	

1937

Jan.	6—Frankie Covelli, Cincinnati	W 10
Jan.	11—Jimmy Vaughn, Louisville	W 10
Jan.	18—Davey Fine, Louisville	KO 5

720

Feb.	1—Joe Teemes, Wash., D. C.	W 10
Feb.	9—Jackie Wilson, Pittsburgh	L 10
Feb.	22—Normant Quarles, Cincinnati	L 10
Apr.	6—Lew Feldman, N. Y. C.	D 8
Apr.	12—Dominic Mancini, Louisville	W 10
Apr.	26—Jackie Wilson, Cincinnati	L 10
May	17—Maxie Fisher, Woodhaven, L. I.	W 8
June	7—Red Cochrane, Woodhaven, L.I.	W 8
July	31—Petey Sarron, Johannesburg	W 10
Sept.	4—Petey Sarron, Johannesburg	L 12
	(For Featherweight title)	
Nov.	27—Aldo Spaldi, Johannasburg	W 12

1938

Jan.	27—Billy Charlton, Liverpool	W 12
Feb.	21—Len Wickwar, Leicester	W 12
Mar.	17—Paul Dognizux, Paris	D 10
Mar.	28—Tommy Hyams, Bristol	KO 9
Apr.	28—Johnny Cusick, Liverpool	KO 7
May	12—Len Beynon, Swansea	W 12
June	13—Billy Charlton, Newcastle	W 12
June	27—Ronnie James, Swansea	WF 8
July	—Frank McCudden, Edinburgh	W 12
July	21—Jack Carrick, Liverpool	W 10
Sept.	1—Johnny King, Liverpool	W 10
Oct.	24—Leo Rodak, Wash., D. C.	L 15
Dec.	5—Sammy Angott, Louisville	L 10

1939

Jan.	3—Jackie Callura, Rochester, N. Y.	L 10
Feb.	6—Wishy Jones, Louisville	W 10
Apr.	9—Simon Chavez, Caracas, Venez.	W 10
Apr.	23—Enrique Chaffardet, Caracas	W 10
May	7—Baby Oriental, Caracas	KO 2
May	21—Simon Chavez, Caracas	L 10
Dec.	1—Georgie Hansford, Hollywood	L 10

1940

Apr.	1—Herschel Joiner, Cincinnati	KO by 8

TB	KO	WD	WF	D	LD	LF	KOBY	ND	NC
244	45	160	3	5	23	2	1	4	1

Died in Cincinnati, O. on May 8, 1962.

ALBERTO (BABY) ARIZMENDI

Born, March 17, 1914, Torreon, Coahuila, Mexico.
Weight, 110-140 lbs. Height, 5 ft. 5 in. Managed by Cal Working.

Early record incomplete.

1927

Oct.	11—Kid Laredo, San Antonio	D 10

1928

	—Cave Man Ferrici, San Antonio	W 10
Mar.	28—Newsboy Reyes, San Antonio	W 6
Apr.	10—Kid Adams, San Antonio	D 6
May	22—Kid Adams, San Antonio	W 8
July	2—Kid Adams, San Antonio	W 8
July	9—Al Bosque, San Antonio	W 4
July	30—Skeets Baker, Galveston	W 6

1929-1931

	—Babe Colima	L 10
	—Babe Colima	D 10
	—Kid Pancho, Mexico City	W 10
	(Won Mexican Bantamweight Title)	
	—Chato Laredo	L 10
	—Claude Varner	D 10

1932

Jan.	1—Fidel LaBarba, Mexico City	W 10
Feb.	9—Speedy Dado, Los Angeles	W 10
Mar.	1—Claude Varner, Los Angeles	W 10
Mar.	18—Speedy Dado, Stockton	L 10
Apr.	19—Young Tommy, Los Angeles	W 10
May	3—Lew Farber, Los Angeles	W 10
June	7—Newsboy Brown, Los Angeles	W 10
June	28—Newsboy Brown, Los Angeles	L 10
Sept.	16—Tommy Paul, Mexico City	W 10
Oct.	18—Newsboy Brown, Los Angeles	W 10
Nov.	22—Varias Milling, Los Angeles	D 10
Dec.	2—Archie Bell, Hollywood	W 10
Dec.	16—Rodolfo Taglia, Phoenix	KO 3

1933

Jan.	6 Archie Bell, San Francisco	W 10
Jan.	24—Speedy Dado, Los Angeles	W 10
Feb.	28—Freddie Miller, Los Angeles	L 10
	(For NBA Featherweight Title)	
Mar.	15—Young Tommy, San Francisco	L 10
Mar.	28—Pedro Masquerria, Los Angeles	W 10
Apr.	30—Al Greenfield, Tijuana	KO 4
May	14—Mickey Cohen, Tijuana	KO 3
June	12—Freddie Miller, San Francisco	W 10
July	3—Clever Sisson, Sacramento	L 10
July	21—Baby Palmore, Hollywood	W 10
Sept.	8—Cris Pineda, Hollywood	W 10
Nov.	7—Eddie Shea, Los Angeles	W 10
Nov.	28—Eddie Shea, Los Angeles	W 10

1934

Jan.	23—Mark Diaz, Los Angeles	W 10
Feb.	9—Mark Diaz, Pismo Beach	KO 9
Feb.	23—Al Greenfield, El Paso	KO 3
Mar.	13—Tony Canzoneri, Los Angeles	L 10
May	11—Al Roth, New York	W 10
Aug.	30—Mike Belloise, New York	W 15
	(Won New York State Featherweight Title)	
Nov.	3—Henry Armstrong, Mexico City	W 10

1935

Jan.	2—Henry Armstrong, Mexico City	W 12
	(Won Calif.-Mexican World Featherweight Title)	
Feb.	2—Chalky Wright, Mexico City	KO 4
Mar.	31—Frankie Wallace, Mexico City	KO 6
June	9—Baby Casanova, Mexico City	L 12
July	5—Fillo Echevarria, Havana	L 10
Sept.	9—Mickey Genaro, Quincy, Ill.	W 10
Oct.	4—Jimmy Christy, Chicago	W 10
Nov.	8—Davey Day, Chicago	W 10
Dec.	16—Jack Sharkey, Cleveland	KO 6

1936

Feb.	7—Lou Ambers, New York	L 10
Mar.	16—Phil Baker, New York	D 10
Apr.	1—Tiger Walker, Cincinnati	W 10
May	5—Pablo Dano, Los Angeles	W 10
May	29—Frankie Covelli, Hollywood	TD 9
June	16—Wally Hally, Los Angeles	W 10
Aug.	4—Henry Armstrong, Los Angeles	L 10
	(Lost Calif.-Mexican World Featherweight Title)	
Sept.	18—Frankie Covelli, Hollywood	D 10
Nov.	10—Frankie Wallace, Los Angeles	D 10

1937

Mar.	12—Jimmy Vaughn, Hollywood	L 10
Mar.	23—Wally Hally, Los Angeles	L 10
Aug.	31—Richie Fontaine, Los Angeles	W 10
Oct.	5—Chalky Wright, Los Angeles	W 10
Nov.	16—Baby Breese, Los Angeles	W 10

1938

Mar.	15—Henry Armstrong, Los Angeles	L 10
May	17—Wally Hally, Los Angeles	W 10
June	7—Lou Ambers, Los Angeles	D 10
July	26—Jimmy Vaughn, Los Angeles	W 10
Sept.	9—Wally Hally, San Diego	W 10
Sept.	23—Umio Gen, San Diego	W 10
Oct.	10—Wally Hally, New Orleans	W 10

1939

Jan.	10—Henry Armstrong, Los Angeles	L 10
	(For World Welterweight Title)	
Feb.	24—Lou Ambers, New York	KO by 11
May	16—Eddie Marcus, Los Angeles	D 8
Aug.	22—Jackie Carter, Los Angeles	KO 1
Sept.	12—Joey Silva, Los Angeles	W 10
Nov.	3—Sammy Angott, Chicago	L 10

1940

Apr.	2—George Latka, Los Angeles	L 10
June	11—Guy Serean, Los Angeles	W 10
June	25—Sammy Angott, Los Angeles	D 10
Aug.	2—Sailor Dub Bowen, Hollywood	KO 4
Sept.	4—Chief Evening Thunder, Wilmington	L 10
Sept.	24—Jackie Callura, Oakland	D 10
Nov.	8—Richie Polite, Hollywood	KO 2
Dec.	6—George Latka, Hollywood	W 10

1941

Jan.	24—Toby Vigil, Hollywood	W 10
Mar.	7—Red Green, Hollywood	W 10
May	19—Jackie Wilson, Los Angeles	KO by 8
Aug.	22—Johnny Hutchinson, Hollywood	W 10
Nov.	21 Baby Breese, Hollywood	W 10

1942

Feb.	27—Jimmy Garrison, Hollywood	L 10
Apr.	10—Jimmy Garrison, Hollywood	L 10
May	27—Earl Turner, Oakland	KO by 6
Aug.	21—Roman Alvarez, Hollywood	L 10

TB	KO	WD	WF	D	LD	LF	KO BY	ND	NC
99	11	49	0	13	23	0	3	0	0

Died, December 31, 1963, Los Angeles, Calif.

MIKE BELLOISE

Born, February 18, 1911, Bronx, New York.
Ancestry, Italian, Weight, 126 lbs. Height, 5 ft. 5 in.
Managed by George Hughs, Eddie Walker.

1932

	—Jimmy Hughes	KO 3
	—Sergio Dadany	KO 2
	—Eddie Voccio	W 4
	—Danny London	W 4
	—Sammy Tisch	W 5
	—Sammy Tisch	W 5
	—Danny London	W 5
	—Harry Oberman	W 6
	—Abe Levine	W 5
	—Willie Dorenzo	W 6
	—Milton Sloves	W 6
	—Irish Joe Dougherty	W 6

1933

Jan.	2—Petey Hayes, New York	W 8
Feb.	21—Benny Brostoff, New York	W 5
Mar.	31—Allan Headley, New York	D 4
May	8—Lew Farber, New York	D 6
May	19—Joe Regis, New York	W 4
July	5—Mickey Brown, New York	W 6
July	24—Al Gillette, New York	W 6
Aug.	17—Lew Farber, New York	D 6
Sept.	11—Vincent Renta, New York	W 6
Nov.	24—Pete De Grasse, New York	W 6

1934

Jan.	8—Mickey Barron, New York	W 6
Jan.	12—Lew Feldman, New York	L 6
Jan.	24—Al Roth, New York	W 6
Feb.	9—Benny Britt, New York	W 6
Feb.	13—Pete De Grasse, New York	W 10
Mar.	10—Pete De Grasse, New York	W 8
Apr.	2—Petey Hayes, New York	D 10
May	11—Petey Hayes, New York	W 10
June	28—Lew Feldman, New York	W 10
Aug.	30—Baby Arizmendi, New York	L 15
	(For New York State Featherweight Title)	
Oct.	29—Joe Marciente, Syracuse	KO 8
Nov.	19—Roger Bernard, New York	W 10

1935

Jan.	14—Jose Santos, New York	L
Feb.	6—Abe Wasserman, New York	W 8
Feb.	15—Paul Lee, Chicago	W 6
Mar.	15—Orville Drouillard, Chicago	KO 5
Apr.	1—Johnny Defoe, New York	W 8
Apr.	12—Varias Milling, Chicago	W 8
May	10—Jimmy Christy, Chicago	L 10
July	1—Dick Welsh, New York	W 8
July	11—Calif. Joe Rivers, Washington	KO by 8
Oct.	2—Jose Santos, New York	W 8
Nov.	6—Lou Camps, New York	KO 2
Nov.	15—Calif. Joe Rivers, New York	W 8

1936

Jan.	8—Claude Varner, New York	KO 14
Feb.	26—Norment Quarles, New York	W 10
Apr.	3—Everette Rightmire, Chicago	KO 14
	—New York State Athletic Commission proclaimed Belloise world featherweight champion.	
May	26—Dave Crowley, Long Island City	D 10
Aug.	11—Joe Doherty, Long Island City	KO 9
Sept.	3—Dave Crowley, New York	KO 9
	(Retained New York World Featherweight Title)	
Sept.	29—Al Spina, Portland, Ore.	W 10
Oct.	27—Henry Armstrong, Los Angeles	L 10
Nov.	9—Frankie Castillo, Los Angeles	KO 1
Nov.	20—Sonny Valdez, Hollywood	KO 5

1937

Jan.	21—Johnny Cabello, New York	W 10
Feb.	22—Jackie Wilson, Pittsburgh	L 10
Mar.	12—Henry Armstrong, New York	KO by 4
Apr.	20—Maxie Fisher, Brooklyn	W 10
Apr.	27—Freddy Foran, Jersey City	KO 3
May	10—Johnny Cabello, New York	KO 6
May	25—Jimmy McLeod, Brooklyn	W 8
June	8—Charley Gomez, Long Island	W 8
June	24—Jimmy McLeod, New York	KO 7
Aug.	10—New York State Athletic Commission withdrew recognition as world featherweight champion from Belloise.	

1938

Feb.	14—Frankie Terranova, New York	W 8
Mar.	1—Al Reid, New York	D 8
Mar.	14—Julio Gonzales, New York	W 8
Apr.	5—Al Reid, New York	D 8
Apr.	18—Young Chappie, New York	W 8
Apr.	26—Pete Scalzo, New York	W 8
May	16—Paul Lee, New York	W 8
June	6—Johnny Alba, New York	KO 2
June	20—Al Reid, New York	W 8
July	11—Joey Archibald, Washington, D.C.	L 10
Aug.	9—Paul Lee, New York	W 8
Sept.	19—Joey Wach, New York	KO 3
Oct.	17—Joey Archibald, New York	L 15
	(For Vacant New York World Featherweight Title)	
Dec.	2—Emilio Magana, Hollywood	KO 8

1939

Jan.	20—Georgie Hansford, Hollywood	W 10
Jan.	20—Al Citrino, Oakland	D 10
Feb.	17—Nick Peters, Hollywood	KO by 4
Apr.	21—Angus Smith, San Diego	KO 7
May	2—George Hansford, Los Angeles	W 10
May	26—Tony Chavez, Hollywood	KO by 7
Aug.	17—Paul Lee, Baltimore	W 10
Aug.	28—Lew Feldman, Baltimore	L 10
Sept.	19—Al Reid, New York	W 8
Oct.	31—Jimmy Vaughn, New York	W 8
Nov.	21—Lew Jenkins, New York	KO by 7

1940

Jan.	16—Bernie Friedkin, Brooklyn	D 8
Jan.	30—Bernie Friedkin, Brooklyn	D 8
Mar.	25—Young Rightmire, Providence	W 10
Apr.	22—Abe Denner, Providence	D 10
May	11—Texas Lee Harper, Brooklyn	W 8
June	3—Petey Scalzo, New York	L 8
Sept.	16—Spider Armstrong, Baltimore	W 10

1941

Feb.	17—Everette Rightmire, Baltimore	W 10
Mar.	18—Bobby Ruffin, New York	L 8
Apr.	28—Frankie Donato, Philadelphia	KO by 8
June	16—Frankie Donato, Philadelphia	W 8
July	14—Al Reid, New York	W 8
July	30—Bobby Ruffin, New York	L 8

1942

Mar.	3—Chester Rico, New York	KO by 7
Oct.	6—Johnny Forte, Philadelphia	W 8
Nov.	9—Ruby Garcia, Providence	W 10
Nov.	27—Tommy Ciarlo, Waterbury	W 8
Dec.	7—Ruby Garcia, Providence	W 10

1943

Jan.	25—Johnny Hutchinson, Phila.	KO by 2
Apr.	2—Charley Williams, Philadelphia	W 8
Apr.	6—Angelo Callura, Brooklyn	L 8
June	22—Gus Levine, Brooklyn	KO 5

1944

Jan.	17—Frankie Bove, Newark	W 8
Mar.	13—Al Brown, Balboa, Panama	L 10
May	17—Freddie Russo, Elizabeth	L 8
Aug.	7—Billy Hale, Ocean Park, Calif.	D 10
Sept.	4—Joey Dolan, Spokane, Wash.	W 10
Oct.	9—Vic Flores, Venice, Calif.	W 10
Nov.	4—Henry Armstrong, Portland	KO by 4
Nov.	29—Ray Salas, Oakland, Calif.	KO by 8

1945

Jan.	31—Juan Zurita, Houston	KO by 4
Dec.	3—Arturo Barron, Ocean Park	TD 1
Dec.	17—Lou Bernal, Ocean Park	KO by 5

1946

June 14—Kui Kong Young, Honolulu ... KO by 1

1947

June 25—Charley Noel, New York .... W 8
Aug. 26—Tommy Stenhouse, Elmira ..... KO by 5

TB	KO	WD	WF	D	LD	LF	KO BY	ND	NC
126	19	65	0	13	15	0	14	0	0

Died, June 2, 1969, Bronx, New York.

PETEY SARRON

Born, 1908, Birmingham, Ala. Nationality, Syrian-American. Weight, 126 lbs. Managed by Jimmy Erwin.

1925

—Red Burke, Birmingham .... W 8
—Leroy Jordan, Birmingham .... KO 2
—Bud Harris, Birmingham .... KO 4
—Kid Dugan, Memphis .... KO 3
—Pal Moore, Birmingham .... W 10
—Johnny Brown, Miami .... KO 2

1926

—Pal Moore, Memphis .... W 10
—Jimmy McDermott, Miami .... KO 1
—Mickey Gill, Miami .... ND 10
—Mickey Gill, Miami .... ND 10

1927

—Mutt Griffin, Miami .... ND 10
—Happy Atherton, Palm Beach ..... ND 10
—Genero Pino, Miami .... ND 10
—Genero Pino, Miami .... ND 10
—Leroy Jordan, Memphis .... KO 3
—Dudley Statler, New Orleans ..... KO 6
—Bobby Binkley, Memphis .... W 10
—Johnny Moore, Miami .... ND 10
—Harry Allan, Miami .... ND 10
—Benny Regan, Memphis .... W 10

1928

—Steve Stettson, Birmingham .... D 10
—Steve Stettson, Birmingham ...... KO 2
—Benny Regan, Birmingham .... W 10
—Mike Sansone, Greenwood, Miss. ... W 10
—Mike Sansone, Greenwood, Miss. ... W 10
—Quina Lee,Birmingham .... KO 4
—Pinkey May, Savannah .... D 10
—Pinkey May, Birmingham .... W 10
—Pinkey May .... L 10
—Babe Ruth, Greenwood, Miss. ...... W 10
—Johnny Erickson, Chicago .... W 10
—Pal Moore, Memphis .... W 10

1929

—Kid Pancho, Oklahoma City .... W 10
—Kid Pancho, Oklahoma City ...... W 10
—Mickey Gill, Memphis .... KO 3
—Johnny Frank, Memphis .... W 10
—Tommy (Kid) Williams, Pompano
Beach .... ND 10
—Tony Leto, Miami .... ND 10
May 4—Charlie Glasson, Melbourne ... KO 4
June 8—Pinky Silverberg, Melbourne ... W 15
June 22—Johnny Leckie, Sydney ....L 15
July 13—Andy Devine (Young Siki),
Melbourne .... W 15
July 27—Johnny Leckie, Sydney ......KO 13
Sept. 1—Dick Corbett, Brisbane .... D 15
Sept. 7—Billy Grime, Sydney ....L 15
Oct. 11—Billy Grime, Sydney ....KO 9
Nov. 8—Billy Grime, Brisbane .... W 15
Dec. 2—Jack Jones, Wellington ......KO 10
Dec. 17—Billy Grime, Wellington ......KO 14
Dec. 26—Billy Grime, Auckland ......KO 13

1930

Jan. 1—Johnny Leckie, Napier ....KO 14
Feb. 3—Johnny Leckie, Wellington ....L 15
Mar. 15—Tommy Donovan
New Plymouth .... LF 7
Mar. 29—Tommy Donovan, Wellington ...L 15
July 1—Tommy Donovan, Dunedin ....L 15
July —Sammy Shack, Dunedin ......'.. W 15
Aug. 2—Johnny Leckie, Palmerston ... W 15

1931

Knockouts: Tony Leto, 4; Midget Mike
O'Dowd, 3; Charley Von Reeden, 1. Won: Joe

Lucas, 10; Emil Paluso, 10; Mickey Genaro, 10;
Benny Schwartz, 10; Gilbert Castillo, 10; Eddie
Burl, 10; Chicho Cisneros, 10; Mickey Genaro,
10; Gilbert Castillo, 10. Lost: Fidel La Barba, 10.
Draw: Chicho Cisneros, 10.

1932

Apr. 27—Mickey Genaro ....W 10
Nov. 10—Mike O'Dowd ....KO 3
Nov. 17—Charlie Von Reedon .... W 10
Nov. 26—Gilbert Castillo .... W 10

1933

Jan. 25—Charlie Von Reedon,
Jacksonville....................... D 10
Mar. 7—Benny Schwartz, Alexandria ..KO 7
Mar. 28—Miki Gelb, Alexandria, Va. .... W 8
Apr. 25—Tommy Paul, Alexandria, Va... D 8
May 12—Johnny Datto, Detroit, Mich. .KO 1
June 1—Johnny Datto, Birmingham .... W 10
Nov. 1—Freddie Miller, Alexandria .....L 10
Nov. 28—Varias Milling, Alexandria ..... L 10
Jan. 23—Frank Kid Covelli,
Washington D. C. ....L 10
Feb. 7—Freddie Miller, Cincinnati, O. ...L 10
Feb. 19—Buckey Burton, Miami, Fla. ...L 10
Mar. 12—Buckey Burton, Miami, Fla. ... W 10
Mar. 27—Ray Schneider, Jacksonville ... W 10
May 11—Lew Feldman, N. Y. C. ....L 8
June 29—Al Foreman, Washington, D. C. . W 10
Aug. 27—Benny Bass, Washington ......WF 6
Sept. 24—Benny Bass, Philadelphia ...... W 10
Oct. 15—Frankie Wallace, Philadelphia .. W 10
Dec. 2—Eddie Burl, Washington, D. C. ... W 10

1935

Jan. 28—Joe Rivers, Washington, D. C. .. W 10
Feb. 15—Frankie Kid Covelli, Miami .... W 10
Feb. 18—Patsy Severo, Miami .... W 10
Feb. 25—Baby Manuel, Miami .... W 10
Mar. 25—Joe Rivers, Washington, D. C. .. W 10
—Young Chocolate, Jamaica, W.I. W 10
Aug. 12—Joe Teemes, Washington, D. C. .. W 10
Sept. 30—Joe Rivers, Washington, D.C. .. W 10
Nov. 6—Andy Martin, Birmingham ....ND 10
Dec. 5—Carl Guggino, Miami .... D 10

1936

Jan. 6—Jimmy McNamara, Miami ..... W 10
Jan. 13—Red Guggino, Miami .... W 10
Mar. 2—Freddie Miller, Coral Gables....... L 15
(For Featherweight Title)
May 11—Freddie Miller, Wash., D. C. .... W 15
(Won Featherweight Title)
June 15—Nick Camarata, New Orleans ..... W 10
June 23—Lloyd Pine, Akron .... W 10
July 7—Bobby Dean, Wash., D. C. .... KO 5
July 22—Baby Manuel, Dallas .... W 15
(Title bout)
July 31—Davey Abad, Hollywood ...... W 10
Aug. 26—Jackie Carter, Youngstown .... W 10
Sept. 14—Nick Camarata, Richmond .... D 10

1937

Jan. 5—Laurie Stevens, Johannesburg .KO 12
Feb. 20—Andy Martin, Johannesburg ..KO 4
Apr. 15—Harry Mizler, London .... L Disq. 1
May 7—Dave Crowley, London ....LF 9
June 20—Harry Mizler, Johannesburg ..KO 1
July 31—Freddie Miller, Johannesburg ...L 10
Sept. 4—Freddie Miller, Johannesburg .. W 12
(Title bout)
Sept. 10—Teddy Braun, Capetown ...... W 10
Oct. 29—Henry Armstrong, N. Y. C. KO by 6
(Lost featherweight title)
Dec. 10—Carl Red Guggino, N. Y. C. .... W 10
Dec. 20—Ray Ingram, Richmond, Va. ... W 10

1938

Feb. 15—Bobby Britton, Miami .... W 10
Mar. 15—Joey Teemes, Miss. .... W 10
Apr. 11—Joey Green, Mobile, Ala. .... W 10
May 20—Lou Gevinson, Wash., D.C. .... W 10
Oct. 3—Yucatan Kid, Washington, D. C. W 15
Dec. 5—Mike Gamiere, Cleveland ...... W 10
Dec. 16—Yucatan Kid, Miami .... W 10

1939

Mar. 20—Wishy Jones, Birmingham, Ala. W 10
June 15—Herman Palomo, Richmond, Va.W 10
July 17—Sammy Angott, Pittsburgh .....L 10

1941

(In U. S. Army.)

TB	KO	WD	WF	D	LD	LF	KO BY	ND	NC
136	27	70	1	8	15	3	1	11	0

723

HENRY ARMSTRONG
(Record under Welterweight Champions)

LEO RODAK
(N.B.A. Featherweight Champion)
Born, June 5, 1913, Chicago, Ill. Nationally, Ukrainian-American. Weight, 135 lbs. Height, 5 ft. 5 in. Managed by Nate Lewis. Amateur Record: Had 103 fights—lost 4.
1933
Knockouts: Pete Magee, 4; John Gater, 3. Won: Pete Magee, John Gater, Al DeRose, Al Schiarto (three times), Joe Bozak (twice), Johnny Fitzpatrick, Frankie Minerva (twice), Art Mitchell (twice).
1934
Jan.	15—Jackie Sharkey, Chicago	W	8
Feb.	16—Moon Mullins, Chicago	W	8
Mar.	12—Paul Dazzo, Chicago	W	10
Apr.	23—Eddie Shea, Chicago	W	10
May	11—Sammy Levine, Chicago	W	8
June	18—Dave Barry, Chicago	W	10
Sept.	20—Everett Rightmire, Chicago	W	10
Oct.	15—Tommy Paul, Chicago	W	10
Nov.	12—Pete De Grasse, Chicago	W	10

1935
Jan.	11—Georgie Hansford, Hollywood	W	10
Jan.	31—Tony Canzoneri, Chicago	L	10
June	13—Wesley Ramey, Chicago	L	10
Aug.	30—Gege Gravante	W	10
Nov.	22—Lou Lombardi, N. Y. C.	W	10

1936
Jan.	6—Indian Hurtado, N. Y. C.	L	10
Jan.	15—Allie Todesco, N. Y. C.	KO	4
Feb.	7—Bushy Graham, N. Y. C.	D	10
Feb.	21—Aldo Spoldi, N. Y. C.	W	1
June	9—Johnny Morro, Long Island	L	10
Sept.	11—Frankie Wolfram, Chicago	KO	2
Sept.	24—Armanda Sicilia, Chicago	W	10
Nov.	13—Frankie Covelli, Hollywood	W	10

1937
Jan.	20—Armanda Sicilia, Chicago	W	10
Jan.	27—Merle Thompson, Chicago	W	10
Feb.	9—Wishy Jones, Houston, Tex.	W	10
Mar.	5—Kid Irish, St. Louis, Mo.	W	10
Apr.	2—Lenny Cohn, Chicago	W	10
May	14—Jackie Callura, Chicago	W	10
July	16—Young Semyton, St. Louis, Mo.	W	10
Aug.	13—Lloyd Pine, Chicago	W	10
Aug.	9—Jackie Wilson, St. Louis, Mo.	D	10
Sept.	17—Jackie Wilson, St. Louis, Mo.	W	15
Nov.	22—Varias Milling, Chicago	W	10

1938
Jan.	10—Jackie Wilson, Chicago	D	10
Feb.	11—Al Manriquez, Memphis, Tenn.	W	10
June	17—Jackie Wilson, Baltimore, Md.	W	15
July	8—Wesley Ramsey, Dallas, Tex.	L	10
July	25—Sammy Angott, Pittsburgh, Pa.	W	10
Aug.	15—Sammy Angott, Pittsburgh	KO by	1
Sept.	27—Sammy Angott, Pittsburgh	L	10
Oct.	10—Ritchie Fontaine, New Orleans	W	10
Oct.	24—Freddie Miller, Washington	W	15
Dec.	29—Leone Efrati, Chicago	W	10
(Won the NBA Featherweight Championship)

1939
Jan.	14—Billy Miller, Pittsburgh	KO	6
Mar.	6—Al Reid, N. Y. C.	W	8
Mar.	16—Everett Rightmire, St. Louis	L	10
Apr.	18—Joey Archibald, Providence	L	15
(Archibald won the undisputed featherweight championship of the world. Rodak had been recognized by NBA and Archibald by the New York State and associate commissions.)
May	15—Al Mancini, Providence	W	10
May	29—Jimmy Perrin, New Orleans	W	10
July	6—Dave Castilloux, Toronto	W	10
Aug.	28—Nick Camarata, New Orleans	L	10
Sept.	11—Jimmy Tygh, New Orleans	W	10
Oct.	9—Nick Camarata, New Orleans	W	10
Dec.	6—Dave Castilloux, New Orleans	W	10

1940
Jan.	2—Dave Castilloux, Toronto	L	10
Mar.	11—Yucantan Kid, New Orleans	L	10
Mar.	29—George Salamone, Boston	W	10
Apr.	8—Young Rightmire, Providence	W	10
May	1—Yucantan Kid, Miami, Fla.	W	10
June	3—Jackie Wilson, Chicago	W	10
June	13—Jimmy Tygh, Philadelphia	L	10
July	17—Johnny Bellus, N. Y. C.	W	6
Aug.	20—Julie Kogon, West Haven	D	10
Aug.	27—Ervin Berlier, New Orleans	L	10

Nov.	18—Red Guggino, Miami Beach	L	10
Nov.	22—Julie Kogan, N. Y. C.	W	8
Dec.	3—Maxie Shapiro, Brooklyn	W	8

1941
Jan.	6—Herschel Joiner, Cincinnati	W	10
Jan.	13—Everett Rightmire, Providence	L	10
Feb.	7—Lenny Mancini, N. Y. C.	W	8
Mar.	10—Herschel Joiner, Cincinnati	W	12
Apr.	9—Slugger White, Baltimore	W	10
Apr.	21—Jackie Wilson, Cincinnati	W	10
June	19—Armanda Sicilia, Indianapolis	W	10
July	9—Nick Castiglione, Chicago	L	10
Aug.	14—Chalku Wright, Wash., D. C.	L	10
Oct.	14—Chalky Wright, Wash., D. C.	L	10
Oct.	27—Jackie Wilson, Toledo	W	10
Nov.	17—Guy Serean, New Orleans	W	10
Dec.	1—Joey Peralta, New Orleans	W	10
Dec.	18—Tommy Hogan, Youngstown	W	10

1942
Feb.	13—Matt Dougherty, Chicago	W	10
Apr.	20—Jimmy Hatcher, New Orleans	D	10
June	3—Tippy Larkin, Newark	L	10
June	23—Charley Varre, Cincinnati	W	10
July	9—Aldo Spoldi, West Haven	D	10
July	21—Chester Rico, N. Y. C.	D	10
July	27—Slugger White, Baltimore	W	10
Aug.	24—Slugger White, Baltimore	L	12
Sept.	4—Henry Armstrong, San Fr.	KO by	8
Dec.	14—Willie Joyce, Detroit,	KO by	4
In U. S. Marines.

1943
July	24—Sammy Brown, San Diego	KO	3
Aug.	6—Mario Ramon, San Diego	W	10

1944
Jan.	10—Terry Gibson, Santa Barbara	D	10
Mar.	3—Willie Joyce, Hollywood	W	10

1945
Jan.	12—Eddie Hudson, San Diego	D	10

1946
Feb.	15—Bob Montgomery, Chicago	L	10
Mar.	29—Bobby McIntyre, Memphis	W	10
May	6—Bobby McIntyre, Youngstown	W	10
June	10—Wesley Mouzon, Baltimore	KO by	6
Oct.	28—Chester Rico, New Orleans	L	10
Nov.	2—John Thomas, Los Angeles	KO by	5

TB	KO	WD	WF	D	LD	LF	KOBY	ND	NC
117	6	74	0	10	22	0	5	0	0

JOEY ARCHIBALD
Born, Dec. 6, 1915, Providence, R.I. Nationality, Irish-American. Weight, 126 lbs. Height, 5 ft. 4 in. Managed by Al Weill.
1932
	—Ernst Kid Herbert	KO	4
	—Jimmy Martin	KO	1
	—Frankie Smith	KO	3
	—Herb Bradley	L	6
	—Frankie Walsh	W	10

1933
	—Bobby Williams	KO	1
	—Herb Bradley	KO	3
	—Dark Cloud Bradley	L	8
	—Kid Francis	KO	2
	—Buster Madeau	KO	4
Apr.	5—Frankie Genaro, Fall River	L	10
	—Frankie Walsh	W	8
	—Johnny Bangs	D	10
	—Jimmy Loranzo	KO	5
	—Dark Cloud Bradley	KO	7
	—Johnny Bangs	W	10

1934
	—Fred Lattenzier	KO	5
	—Damasco Seda	KO	6
May	21—Sixto Escobar, Holyoke, Mass.	L	10
	—Fillipo Yarbo	L	8
	—Skippy Allen	KO	5
	—Jimmy Doyle	KO	2
	—Dick Welsh	D	8
Sept.	20—Frankie Martin, Montreal	L	10
	—Frank McKenna	W	8
	—Frank McKenna	W	8
	—Baby Cormier	KO	5

1935
Apr.	24—Jose Santos, Providence	D	8
May	4—Petey Dixon, Providence	KO	4
May	6—Joe Brown, Providence	KO	2
May	28—Sixto Escobar, N. Y. C.	KO by	8
June	14—Jimmy Martin, N. Y. C.	W	8
July	5—Johnny Bangs, N. Y. C.	W	6
Sept.	10—Jose Santos, Poughkeepsie	W	8

Oct.	12—Johnny Marro, N. Y. C. L	8
Nov.	15—Indian Quintana, N. Y. C. . . . . . W	8
Dec.	1—Johnny Bangs, N. Y. C. . . . . . . .KO	6

1936
Mar.	10—Johnny Mirabella, N. Y. C. . . . . . W	6
Mar.	24—Phil Seriani, N. Y. C. . . . . W	6
Apr.	21—Lou Camps, N. Y. C. L	8
Apr.	27—Jose Santos, N. Y. C. . . . . .KO	2
May	10—Biff Lemieaux, N. Y. C. . . . . . . W	10
June	1—Katzumi Morioka, N. Y. C. . . . . . W	8
June	18—Johnny Cabello, Middlet'n KO by	2
July	28—Nat Litfin, N. Y. C. L	10
Oct.	26—Joey Wach, N. Y. C. . . . . W	6
	—Biff Lemieaux . . . . W	12

1937
Jan.	8—Syracuse Unknown, Syracuse .KO	2
Jan.	28—Biff Lemieaux, N. Y. C. . . . . . . W	12
Feb.	10—Cyril Josephs, N. Y. C. . . . . W	6
Apr.	5—Aurel Toma, N. Y. C. L	8
Apr.	19—Tony Dupre, N. Y. C. . . . . LF	6
May	3—Buddy Grimes, N. Y. C. . . . . . . W	8
May	10—Laurence Gunn, N. Y. C. . . . . . .KO	6
June	2—Ray Ingram, N. Y. C. . . . . .KO	5
June	11—Nickey Jerome, N. Y. C. . . . . . .KO	10
June	23—Harry Gentile, N. Y. C. . . . . . .KO	6
July	2—Lou Gevinson, N. Y. C. . . . . . . .KO	8
Oct.	1—Joey Marciente, N. Y. C. . . . . . .KO	4
Dec.	10—Biff Lemieaux, N. Y. C. . . . . . . W	10

1938
Mar.	John Maribella, Wash., D. C.KO	9
Mar.	14—Sammy Crosetti, Providence . . . W	10
Mar.	28—John Schibello, Wash., D. C. . . .KO	2
July	11—Mike Belloise, Washington . . . . W	10
Sept.	12—Tony Dupre, Washington . . . . . W	10
Oct.	17—Mike Belloise, N. Y. C. . . . . W	15
	(Won Vacant N. Y. Featherweight Title)	
Nov.	21—Paul Lee, Washington . . . . W	10
Dec.	5—Pete Scalzo, N. Y. C. . . . . . . KO by	2

1939
Jan.	16—Jerry Mazza, Wash. . . . . .KO	2
Feb.	6—Al Mancini, Providence . . . . W	10
Feb.	27—Jimmy Gilligan, Buffalo L	10
Apr.	18—Leo Rodak, Providence . . . . W	15
	(Won vacant world featherweight title)	
	(Archibald had been recognized by New	
	York and Rodak by the N.B.A.)	
June	5—Joey Silva, Wash. . . . . W	10
July	9—Simon Chavez, Caracas, Ven. . . .L	10
Sept.	28—Harry Jeffra, Wash. . . . . W	15
	(World featherweight title bout)	

1940
Feb.	26—Jimmy Perrin, New Orleans L	10
May	20—Harry Jeffra, Baltimore L	15
	(Lost world featherweight title)	
Aug.	2—Joe Marinelli, Dayton, Ohio . . .L	10
Aug.	20—Poison Ivy, Hartford L	10
Oct.	1—Bill Speary, Wilkes-Barre L	10
Nov.	11—Tommy Forte, Philadelphia . . .L	10
Dec.	18—Billy Banks, Washington . . . . . . W	10

1941
Feb.	3—Larry Bolvin, Providence . . KO by	4
Mar.	10—Larry Bolvin, Providence . . . . . . W	10
May	12—Harry Jeffra, Washington . . . . . W	15
	(Re-won world featherweight title)	
June	9—Poison Ivy, Providence L	10
July	17—Lou Transparenti, Baltimore L	10
Aug.	26—Richie Lemos, L. A., Calif. L	10
Sept.	11—Chalky Wright, Wash. . . . . .KO by	11
	(Lost world featherweight title)	
Oct.	14—Billy Banks, Washington . . . . . . W	10
Nov.	10—Harry Jeffra, Providence L	10

1942
Feb.	9—Lulu Costantino, N. Y. C. L	8
Mar.	24—Frankie Rubino, Brooklyn . . . . . D	8
Apr.	14—Aaron Seltzer, N. Y. C. . . . . D	8
May	25—Mike Raffa, Pittsburgh . . . . KO by	5
June	23—Willie Pep, Hartford L	8
July	7—Johnny Forte, Philadelphia L	8
July	21—Benny Goldberg, Toledo L	10
Sept.	5—National Kid, Havana . . . . . KO by	2
Oct.	16—Willie Pep, Providence L	10
Nov.	2—Lou Transparenti, Baltimore L	10

1943
Jan.	7—Joey Pirrone, Cleveland L	8
Mar.	26—Sal Bartolo, Boston L	10
Apr.	9—Kid Alexander, Wash., D. C. L	10
May	10—Tony Costa, Providence, R. I. . . .L	10
Aug.	11—Doll Rafferty, Milwaukee . KO by	3
	In U. S. Navy.	

TB	KO	WD	WF	D	LD	LF	KOBY	ND	NC
106	28	32	0	5	32	1	8	0	0

PETEY SCALZO
Born, August 1, 1917, New York City,
Nationality, Italian-American. Weight, 130 lbs.
Height, 5 ft. 6 in. Managed by Pete Reilly.

1936
June	29—Demasco Seda, N. Y. C. . . . . . .KO	1
July	7—Dom Pasculli, N. Y. C. . . . . . . .KO	1
July	9—Andy Crispano, Brooklyn . . . .KO	1
July	21—Tommy Vello, Woodhaven,	
	L. I. . . . . .KO	1
July	28—Benny Johnson, Astoria, L. I. .KO	3
Sept.	10—Louis Pisano, Brooklyn . . . . . .KO	1
Sept.	21—Sammy Santillo, N. Y. C. . . . . . W	4
Sept.	29—Davey Crawford, N. Y. C. . . . . . W	4
Oct.	5—Abe Shone, N. Y. C. . . . . W	4
Oct.	12—Davey Crawford, N. Y. C. . . . . .KO	2
Oct.	17—Ramon Pabon, N. Y. C. . . . . . .KO	1
Oct.	22—Abe Shone, Brooklyn . . . . .KO	2
Oct.	26—Johnny Compo, N. Y. C. . . . . . . W	6
Nov.	2—Connie Holmes, N. Y. C. . . . . . .KO	4
Nov.	24—Georgie Holmes, N. Y. C. . . . . .KO	1
Dec.	9—Jimmy Lancaster, N. Y. C. . . . . W	6
Dec.	29—Al Reid, N. Y. C. . . . . D	8

1937
Jan.	11—Willie Felice, N. Y. C. . . . . W	6
Jan.	25—Jimmy English, N. Y. C. . . . . . . W	6
Mar.	3—Johnny Schibelli, N. Y. C. . . . . . W	6
Mar.	16—Willis Johnson, N. Y. C. . . . . . . W	6
Apr.	1—Bobby "Kid" Wilson, N. Y. C. .KO	2
Apr.	6—Al Gillette, N. Y. C. . . . . W	6
May	4—Joey Wach, N. Y. C. . . . . W	8
May	12—Johnny Compo, N. Y. C. . . . . . . W	6
May	17—Skippy Allen, Brooklyn . . . . . .KO	2
June	7—Harry Gentile, Brooklyn . . . . .KO	2
June	15—Al Reid, N. Y. C. . . . . .KO	2
July	1—Henry Hook, Brooklyn . . . . . .KO	3
July	19—Sam Russo, Brooklyn . . . . .KO	1
July	22—Johnny Pena, Brooklyn . . . . D	8
Aug.	23—San Sanchez, Philadelphia . . . .KO	1
Sept.	26—Harry Gentile, Brooklyn . . . . .KO	2
Oct.	2—Al Gillette, Brooklyn . . . . .KO	1
Oct.	22—"Red" Hutchins, N. Y. C. . . . . .KO	6
Nov.	19—Al Reid, N. Y. C. . . . . W	8
Dec.	28—Cristobal Jaramillo, N. Y. C. . . . W	8

1938
Jan.	14—Al Gillette, Washington . . . . . .KO	2
Mar.	4—Cristobal Jaramillo, N. Y. C. . . . W	6
Mar.	15—Nat Litfin, N. Y. C. . . . . W	8
Apr.	26—Mike Belloise, N. Y. C. L	8
May	20—Georgie Carlo, Washington . . .KO	5
May	25—Georgie Karkella, Astoria, L. I. . W	8
June	23—Alex Burns, Brooklyn . . . . W	8
June	29—Al Ragone, Astoria, L.I. . . . . W	8
July	19—Tony Dupre, Washington L	8
Aug.	18—Vernon Cormier, Brooklyn . . . . W	8
Sept.	16—Jimmy Lancaster, Brooklyn . . . W	8
Oct.	3—Davey Crawford, Brooklyn . . .KO	3
Oct.	27—Frankie Walsh, Brooklyn . . . . .KO	2
Nov.	7—Jose Santos, N. Y. C. . . . . .KO	5
Dec.	5—Joey Archibald, N. Y. C. . . . . . .KO	5
Dec.	26—Paul Lee, N. Y. C. . . . . W	8

1939
Jan.	23—Minnie Demore, Pittsburgh . . .KO	6
Jan.	31—Jimmy Buckler, Pittsburgh . . .KO	2
Feb.	17—Sal Bartolo, Boston . . . . W	10
Mar.	17—Baby Louis, N. Y. C. . . . . .KO	2
May	3—Vince Del Orto, N. Y. C. . . . . . . W	8
June	12—Emil Joseph, Pittsburgh . . . . . . W	10
June	26—Pedre De Grasse, Pittsburgh . . .KO	4
July	14—Benny Piazza, Mt. Frdm., N. J. KO	3
July	28—Frankie Wallace, Brooklyn . . . . W	8
Oct.	15—Simon Chavez, Caracas, Venez. . L	10
Nov.	8—Herbie Gilmore, Providence . .KO	5
Dec.	1—Allie Stolz, N. Y. C. . . . . .KO	4
Dec.	12—Hank Nakamura, N. Y. C. . . . . . W	8
Dec.	22—Simon Chavez, N. Y. C. . . . . W	10

1940
Jan.	13—Young Johnny Buff, Brklyn . . .KO	2
Jan.	22—Nat Litfin, N. Y. C. . . . . W	8
Jan.	29—Cristobal Jaramillo, N. Y. C. . . . W	8
Feb.	3—Tony Dupre, Brooklyn . . . . W	8
Feb.	17—Jimmy Vaughn, Brooklyn . . . . . W	8
Feb.	27—Primo Flores, N. Y. C. . . . . D	8
Apr.	9—Primo Flores, N. Y. C. . . . . W	8
Apr.	30—Berger Floran, N. Y. C. . . . . . . .KO	5
May	1—(N.B.A. vacated featherweight title	
	and declared Scalzo champion)	
May	15—Frankie Covelli, Washington . .KO	6
June	3—Mike Belloise, N. Y. C. . . . . W	8
June	17—Bernie Friedkin, Woodhaven. . . . . .D	8
July	10—Bob Poison Ivy, Hartford . . . . .KO	15
	(N.B.A. title bout)	
July	15—Maxie Fisher, Newark . . . . W	10

Aug. 5—Ginger Foran, N. Y. C. .... W 8
Aug. 26—Jimmy Perrin, New Orleans .... W 10
Oct. 4—Julie Kogon, N. Y. C............L 8
Nov. 1—Bernie Friedkin, N. Y. C. ...... W 8
Dec. 27—Richie Lemos, Hollywood ....KO 7
1941
Feb. 14—Guy Serean, Hollywood ... KO by 8
Mar. 31—Vern Bybee, San Francisco .... D 10
Apr. 18—Andy Scrivani, Hollywood ...KO 1
May 19—Phil Zwick, Milwaukee .... W 15
(N.B.A. Title Bout)
July 1—Richie Lemos, Los Angeles
.................................KO by 5
(Scalzo lost NBA World Featherweight Title)
Aug. 21—Jimmy Gilligan, Brooklyn ..... W 8
Sept. 9—Jimmy Gilligan, Astoria, L. I. .KO 5
Sept. 15—Mike Raffa, Pittsburgh .... W 10
Oct. 21—Curly Nichols, Brooklyn .....KO 5
Nov. 4—Nat Litfin, Brooklyn .... W 8
Dec. 19—Allie Stolz, N. Y. C. ....L 8
Dec. 30—Mickey Farber, Brooklyn ..... W 8
1942
Jan. 9—Toby Vigil, Hollywood ....ND 6
Mar. 3—Nat Litfin, Brooklyn .... W 8
Mar. 30—George Latka, Hollywood .....L 10
Apr. 7—Jimmy Hatcher, New Orleans ...L 8
May 1—Toby Vigil, Hollywood ......KO 9
May 25—Jimmy Hatcher, New Orleans ...L 10
June 12—John Thomas, Hollywood .....L 10
Sept. 21—Ellis Phillips, Philadelphia .....L 10
Oct. 5—Jimmy Collins, Baltimore .....L 10
Nov. 9—Ellis Phillips, Philadelphia .....L 10
In U. S. Army.
1943
Sept. 17—Alex Doyle, Brooklyn ....KO 7
Sept. 21—Eddie Dowl, Brooklyn .... W 8
Oct. 25—Bob Montgomery, Phila. .. KO by 6

TB	KO	WD	WF	D	LD	LF	KOBY	ND	NC
111	46	44	0	5	12	0	3	1	0

HARRY JEFFRA

(Ignacius Pasquali Guiffi)
Born, November 30, 1914, Baltimore, Md.
Nationality, Italian-American. Featherweight.
Managed by Max Waxman.
1933
Sept. 21—Angelo Brocato, Baltimore .... W 4
Sept. 22—Earl Wise, Baltimore .... W 4
Oct. 6—Bob Sponsler, Baltimore ...... W 4
Oct. 18—Earl Wise, Baltimore .... W 4
Nov. 9—Chester Fowbie, Baltimore .... W 4
Nov. 16—Al Beatty, Baltimore .... W 4
Dec. 21—Bob Sponsler, Baltimore ......KO 1
Dec. 27—Russ Driscoll, Baltimore ....KO 1
1934
Jan. 4—Harry Groves, Baltimore ......KO 4
Jan. 8—Lew Votta, Baltimore .... W 4
Jan. 29—Elmer Lytell, Baltimore ......KO 1
Feb. 16—Pete Galiano, Baltimore ...... W 6
Apr. 9—Leroy Dougan, Baltimore ..... W 6
July 27—Lou Young, Baltimore ....KO 2
Aug. 10—Joey Selmars, Baltimore .....KO 2
Sept. 10—Chester Fowble, Baltimore ...KO 5
1935
—Tommy Horn, Baltimore ..... W 4
Jan. 28—Tommy Horn, Baltimore ....KO 3
Feb. 11—Mike Tardugno, Wash., D. C. ... D 6
Mar. 18—Nick Montana, Baltimore ....KO 3
Apr. 8—Lloyd Pine, Washington ...... W 6
May 20—Milt Jacobs, Baltimore ....KO 1
June 7—Chester Fowbie, Baltimore ...KO 2
June 21—Eddie Burl, Baltimore .... W 8
July 11—Mickey Duca, Baltimore ...... W 8
Aug. 2—Billy Landers, Baltimore ...... W 8
Oct. 21—Danny London, Balt. ..... KO by 5
Nov. 25—Tin Can Romanelli, Balt. ...... W 10
Dec. 30—Victor Valle, Baltimore ....L 10
1936
Jan. 27—Joey Allen, Baltimore ....L 10
Mar. 30—Norman Rahn, Baltimore ...... W 8
Apr. 27—Dewey Cannon, Baltimore ....KO 3
May 4—Joe Temes, Washington ...... W 6
June 1—Joe Temes, Baltimore .... W 8
June 29—Santos Hugo, Washington ..... W 6
Sept. 7—Sammy Tucker, Baltimore ....KO 4
Sept. 21—Reds Transparenti, Balt.......KO 7
Oct. 5—Sixto Escobar, Baltimore ...... W 10
Nov. 23—Skippy Allen, Baltimore ......KO 6
Dec. 9—Sixto Escobar, N. Y. C......... W 10

1937
Jan. 18—Jackie Corcoran, Baltimore ...KO 2
Feb. 22—Lawrence Gunn, Baltimore .... W 10
Mar. 29—Al Gillette, Baltimore ....KO 1
May 10—Jimmy Martin, Baltimore .....KO 7
May 14—George Holmes, Baltimore ....KO 2
July 19—Ruby Bradley, Philadelphia ...KO 4
Sept. 23—Sixto Escobar, N. Y. C......... W 15
(Won World Bantamweight championship)
Nov. 1—Biff Bang Lemieux, Dayton .... W 10
Nov. 16—Jackie Carter, St. Louis ....KO 4
Nov. 26—Indian Quintana, Baltimore ... W 10
Dec. 20—Armanda Sicilia, Washington .. W 8
1938
Jan. 1—Pancho Villa, Mexico City ......L 10
Feb. 20—Sixto Escobar, San Juan. P. R. ..L 15
(Lost Bantamweight championship)
Sept. 17—Nicky Jerome, Brooklyn .....KO 6
Dec. 19—Johnny Mirabella, Baltimore ..KO 1
1939
Jan. 9—Danny London, Baltimore .....NC 4
Jan. 16—Danny London, Baltimore ..... W 6
Feb. 22—Lou Transparenti, Baltimore ..KO 6
May 1—Marcus Pitts, Baltimore .... W 10
June 12—Al Mancini, Baltimore .... W 10
July 11—Johnny Marcelline, Phila...... W 10
Aug. 11—Joey Marciente, Baltimore ... W 10
Sept. 11—Baby Yack, Washington .... W 8
Sept. 28—Joey Archibald, Washington ...L 15
(For Featherweight championship)
Nov. 20—Andre Sarilla, Baltimore ...... W 10
Dec. 11—Johnny Buff, Washington ..... W 8
1940
Apr. 17—Hitoshi Tanaka, Hagerstown ... W 8
May 20—Joey Archibald, Baltimore .... W 15
(Won World Featherweight title)
July 29—Spider Armstrong, Baltimore .. W 15
(Title bout)
Aug. 20—Jackie Wilson, Youngstown .... W 10
Nov. 19—Bill Speary, Wilkes-Barre .....L 10
Dec. 2—Sixto Escobar, Baltimore ...... W 10
1941
Jan. 6—Bill Speary, Baltimore .... W 12
Apr. 21—Tony Iacovacci, Baltimore ..... W 10
Apr. 29—Al Brown, Wilkes Barre ....KO 7
May 12—Joey Archibald, Washington ...L 15
(Lost featherweight title)
June 24—Bobby Ivy, Hartford ....L 10
July 29—Patsy Giovanelli, L. I. C..........L 8
Aug. 12—Mike Raffa, Pittsburgh .... D 10
Sept. 8—Tommy Forte, Phila............. W 10
Sept. 15—Lou Transparenti, Baltimore ... W 12
(Title bout—Maryland State)
Nov. 10—Joey Archibald, Providence ... W 10
1942
Feb. 2—Bill Speary, Toronto .... W 10
Feb. 27—Joey Iannotti, N. Y. C......... W 8
Mar. 9—Jose Rozo, New York City ..... W 8
Mar. 16—Billy Banks, Baltimore .... W 10
Mar. 30—Sonny Brents, Baltimore ......KO 2
Apr. 13—Lulu Costantino, N. Y. C.......L 8
Apr. 28—Frankie Rubino, Brooklyn .... W 8
June 19—Chalky Wright, Baltimore . KO by 10
(For world featherweight championship)
1943
July 31—Frankie Rubino, Brooklyn .... D 8
Aug. 24—Billy Banks, Wash. .... W 8
Sept. 28—Dave Crawford, L. I. C......... W 8
Oct. 4—Johnny Cockfield, Wash., D. C. W 10
Nov. 8—Phil Terranova, Baltimore .... W 10
Nov. 22—Paulie Jackson, Philadelphia ... W 8
1944
Jan. 24—Frankie Rubino, Baltimore .... W 10
Feb. 7—Jimmy Collins, Baltimore ..... W 10
Mar. 13—Frankie Rubino, Baltimore ... W 10
Mar. 27—Lou Salica, Baltimore .... W 10
May 31—Cleo Shans, Baltimore ....L 10
Aug. 15—Domingo Diaz, Montreal ....KO 6
Aug. 28—Charley Noel, Montreal .... W 8
Nov. 3—Charley Noel, Providence .... W 10
Nov. 20—Phil Terranova, N. Y. C. .... D 10
1945
Jan. 8—Jackie Wilson, Baltimore ....L 10
Feb. 6—Jackie Graves, Minneapolis ....L 10
Mar. 21—Leroy Jackson, Cleveland .... W 8
Apr. 4—Leroy Jackson, Cleveland ..... W 8
June 1—Sammy Garcia, Boston .... W 10
Sept. 11—Mickey Quack, Pittsburgh .... D 10
Oct. 29—Freddie Russo, Baltimore .... W 10
Nov. 27—Enrique Bolanos, Los Angeles...L 10
1946
Jan. 28—Mickey Quack, Pittsburgh .... W 10
Mar. 3—Oscar Calles, Caracas ....L 10
June 25—Nick Stato, Hartford .... D 8

1947

Jan. 20—Leslie Harris, Baltimore ....D 10
Feb. 3—Leslie Harris, Baltimore .... W 10

1950

Oct. 23—Lenny Alvarez, New Orleans ....L 8
Dec. 13—Packy McFarland, Wichita .....L 10

TB	KO	WD	WF	D	LD	LF	KOBY	ND	NC
120	27	65	0	7	18	0	2	0	1

RICHIE LEMOS

Born, February 6, 1920, Los Angeles, Calif. Nationality, American-Mexican. Weight, 126 lbs. Height, 5 ft. 5 in. Managed by Baron von Stumme.

1937

July 2—Tony Navarro, Hollywood ..... W 4
Aug. 3—Frankie Rodriguez,
    Olympic, L. A. ....KO 3
Aug. 6—Rudy Ione, Hollywood.......KO 3
Sept. 3—Donnie Maes, Hollywood.......L 4
Sept. 24—Delano Ontiveras, Hollywood.. W 4
Oct. 29—Olin Loy, Hollywood ....L 4
Nov. 10—Santos Hugo, Hollywood ..... W 4
Dec. 10—Little Caesar, Hollywood ....KO 1

1938

Apr. 1—Lupe Cardoza, Hollywood ....KO 1
Apr. 8—Jose Estrada, Hollywood ...... W 4
May 20—Serio Mendoza, Hollywood .... W 4
May 27—Shorty Ramirez, Gilm., L. A. .KO 1
June 17—Pancho Leyvas, Gilmore, L. A. KO 1
July 15—Pablo Dano, Gilmore, L. A. ... W 10
Aug. 30—Manuel Ortiz, Hollywood ...... L 6
Oct. 21—Manuel Ortiz, Hollywood .....L 10

1939

Jan. 13—Pancho Leyvas, Hollywood ...KO 6
Feb. 17—Olin Loy, Hollywood .... W 6
Mar. 17—Emilio Magana, Hollywood ...KO 1
Apr. 6—Lou Salica, Hollywood ....L 10
May 12—Frankie Kainrath, Hollywood .. W 6
June 9—Emilio Magana, Hollywood .... W 6
June 18—Eddie Marcus, Olympic, L. A. .. W 10
Aug. 1—Henry Hook, Olympic, L. A. ..KO 9
Sept. 3—Eddie Marcus, Olympic, L.A......D 3
Oct. 27—Tomboy Romero, Hollywood KO 5
Nov. 28—Richard Polite, Olympic, L. A. KO 6
Dec. 29—Eddie Marcus, Hollywood .....L 10

1940

Feb. 6—Richard Polite, Olympic, L. A. KO 3
Mar. 15—Vern Bybee, Hollywood ....L 10
May 20—Christobal Jaramillo, S. Fran. .. W 10
June 4—Memo Llanes, Olympic .... D 10
July 19—Guy Serean, Hollywood .....KO 10
Aug. 16—Charley Miegel, Hollywood ...KO 5
Oct. 11—Guy Serean, Hollywood ....L 10
Oct. 24—Serio Mendoza, Wilmington ..KO 6
Nov. 8—Jesse James Jackson, S. Diego,
    Calif....................KO 2
Nov. 22—Cleo Shans, San Diego, Cal. .... W 6
Nov. 29—Andy Vasquez, Hollywood ...KO 5
Dec. 27—Pete Scalzo, Hollywood ...KO by 7

1941

Feb. 24—Jimmy Lidell, Ocean Park ...KO 4
Feb. 28—Zeke Castro, San Diego, Cal. ..KO 1
Mar. 11—Guy Serean, Olympic, L. A. ... W 10
Apr. 1—Lew Feldman, Olympic, L. A. .. W 10
Apr. 29—Georgie Hansford, Olympic .... W 10
May 23—Cleo Shans, San Diego ....L 10
July 1—Pete Scalzo, Olympic, L. A. ..KO 5
    (Won N.B.A. Featherweight Title)
July 22—Cleo Shans, Olympic, L. A. .... W 10
Aug. 26—Joey Archibald, Olympic ...... W 10
Sept. 15—Black Joe, Fresno, Calif....... W 10
Oct. 21—Jimmy Florita, Olympic, L. A. KO 7
Nov. 4—Soldier Eddie Stanley, L. A. ..KO 8
Nov. 18—Jackie Wilson, Los Angeles ....L 12
    (Lost N. B. A. Featherweight Title.)
Dec. 16—Jackie Wilson, Los Angeles .....L 12
    (Featherweight Title Bout.)

1942

Feb. 3—Chalky Wright, L. A. ......KO by 6
Mar. 3—Ray Lunny, Los Angeles ....KO 6
Apr. 28—Ray Lunny, San Francisco .....L 10
May 26—George Latka, Los Angeles .....L 10
June 8—Vern Bybee, San Francisco ....L 10
June 26—Bobby Ivy, Hollywood ......KO 8
July 24—Juan Zurita, Hollywood ....L 10
Aug. 10—Vince Dell'Orto, New Orleans ...L 10
Sept. 2—Leroy Tonzi, Colorado Sprgs. .KO 4
Sept. 7—Johnny Farrell, Denver ....KO 2
Sept. 20—Bobby Ruffin, New Orleans ...D 10
Oct. 5—Cleo Shans, Providence.......W 10
Oct. 13—Carmine Fatta, N. Y. C. ....L 8
Nov. 6—Carmine Fatta, N. Y. C. .... W 8

Nov. 10—George Zengaras, Hartford ....W 10
Nov. 16—Cleo Shans, Holyoke ....L 10
Nov. 30—Kelly Jessup, Holyoke .... W 10
Dec. 7—Henry Vasquez, Holyoke ....L 10

1943

Jan. 29—Vince Dell'Orto, Hollywood ... W 10
Feb. 8—Bobby Ruffin, N. Orleans .KO by 9
May 7—Cleo Shans, Hollywood ...... W 10
July 9—Justo Jiminez, Hollywood .....L 10
Aug. 27—Tyree White, Hollywood ... W 10

TB	KO	WD	WF	D	LD	LF	KOBY	ND	NC
77	26	25	0	3	20	0	3	0	0

ALBERT (CHALKY) WRIGHT

Born, February 10, 1912, Durango, Mexico. Weight, 126 lbs. Height, 5 ft. 7½ in. Managed by Eddie Walker.

1928

Feb. 23—Nilo Balles, San Bernardino .... W 4
Apr. 12—Nilo Balles, San Bernardino ...... KO 3
May 3—Val Martin, San Bernardino .... W 4
May 31—Vic Acosta, San Bernardino ...... KO 2
July 12—Young Valentino, San Bernardino .. D 4
July 26—Ray Davis, San Bernardino .... L 4
Aug. 23—Joe Hernandez, San Bernardino .... L 4
Sept. 13—Joe Hernandez, San Bernardino ... D 4
Nov. 22—Ray Davis, San Bernardino .... W 4
Dec. 13—Louie Contreras, San Bernardino ... D 6
Dec. 20—Ray Davis, San Bernardino ...... W 6

1929

Jan. 17—Patsy Callope, San Bernardino ... KO 2
Feb. 7—Joey Valarde, San Bernardino ..... L 6
Mar. 28—Paul Hardy, San Bernardino ..... KO 3
Apr. 9—Harry Wallinder, Los Angeles ...... D 4
Apr. 18—Johnny Mason, San Bernardino .... W 6
May 2—Ray Billobas, San Bernardino ...... D 6
July 5—Frisco Linda, El Centro .... L 4
Sept. 12—Pal Shoaf, San Bernardino ...... W 4
Oct. 7—Kid Avelino, Los Angeles .... W 4
Oct. 10—Harry Purdue, San Bernardino .... W 4
Oct. 24—Harry Barrere, San Bernardino ... W 6
Nov. 11—Ray Cervantes, Los Angeles .... W 4

1930

May 8—Clayton Gouyd, Pasadena ...... W 6
June 12—Jimmy Mack, Pasadena .... W 4
June 17—Frisco Linda, San Bernardino ..... W 6
June 26—Ray Navarro, Pasadena .... KO 5
July 5—Frisco Landa, El Centro .... L 4
July 21—Sammy Seaman, Los Angeles ...... D 6
Aug. 12—Sid Torres, Los Angeles .... W 6
Sept. 16—Manuel Trevino, Los Angeles ..... KO
Oct. 7—Kid Avelino, Los Angeles .... W 6
Oct. 21—Marin Cane, Los Angeles ...... KO 4
Oct. 24—Mose Bailey, San Diego .... D 4
Nov. 7—Johnny Lee, San Diego .... KO 3
Nov. 10—Ray Cervantes. Los Angeles ...... W 4
Nov. 14—Jerry Duffy, San Diego .... W 6
Nov. 18—Ray Cervantes, Los Angeles ...... W 6
Dec. 12—Ramon Montoya, San Diego .... L 10

1931

Jan. 13—Huerta Evans, Los Angeles .... L 6
Feb. 13—Ray Butler, San Diego .... W 10
Mar. 10—Ernie Chacon, Los Angeles ...... W 4
Mar. 31—Mike Cordova, Los Angeles ...... W 4
May 1—Claude Roberts, San Diego ...... W 6
Aug. 6—Marty Zuniga, Sacramento .... D 6
Aug. 11—Baby Jack Dempsey, Los Angeles KO 2
Sept. 15—Mike Cordova, Los Angeles ...... W 6
Nov. 24—Clem Avila, Los Angeles .... W 6

1932

Jan. 12—Tony Tassi, Los Angeles .... KO 4
Feb. 8—Ramon Montoya, San Diego .... W 6
Feb. 16—Marty Zuniga, San Diego .... D 6
Apr. 29—Al Greenfield, San Diego ...... W 6
May 3—Willie Davies, Los Angeles .... W 4
May 18—Jose Pimenthal, San Francisco ... KO 2
June 7—Huerta Evans, Los Angeles ...... KO 5
July 12—Al Greenfield, Los Angeles ...... W 4
Aug. 26—Johnny Minolla, San Diego .... W 6
Sept. 2—Mose Bailey, San Diego .... D 6

727

Oct.	11—Jess Macy, Los Angeles	KO	1
Oct.	19—Kid Ponce, Long Beach	KO	2
Nov.	15—Baby Jack Dempsey, Los Angeles	KO	1
Nov.	22—Al Greenfield, Los Angeles	W	4

1933

	—Newsboy Brown	L	10
	—Allen Foston, Portland, Ore.	D	8
Apr.	11—Mickey Cohen, Los Angeles	KO	3
May	3—Whitey Neil, Portland, Ore.	W	6
Aug.	22—Whitey Neil, Portland, Ore.	W	6
Sept.	1—Huerta Evans, San Francisco	KO	4
Sept.	5—Willie Jabura, Los Angeles	KO	3
Oct.	17—Eddie Shea, Los Angeles	KO by	1
	(For California Junior Lightweight Title)		

1934

Apr.	17—Jimmy Alvarado, Los Angeles	KO	2
May	25—Frankie Venegas, El Centro	KO	5
June	8—Freddie Miller, El Centro	L	10
Oct.	8—Mose Butch, Pittsburgh	L	10

1935

Feb.	2—Baby Arizmendi, Mexico City	KO by	4
May	10—Pablo Dano, Watsonville	KO by	2

1936

	—Buzz Brown, Butte	W	10
	—Claude Varner, Vancouver	W	
May	21—Eddie Spina, Tacoma	W	10
Aug.	20—Cecil Payne, Tacoma	D	10

1937

May	18—Sonny Valdez, Los Angeles	W	6
June	14—Bobby Gray	KO	5
July	21—Norbert Meehan, Oakland	KO	5
Aug.	7—Freddie Steele, Seattle	Exh.	
Aug.	17—Georgie Hansford, Los Angeles	D	10
Sept.	7—Georgie Hansford, Los Angeles	W	10
Oct.	5—Baby Arizmendi, Los Angeles	L	10
Oct.	19—Babe Santella, Los Angeles	KO	1
Nov.	30—Buss Breese, Los Angeles	W	10

1938

Feb.	1—Henry Armstrong, Los Angeles	KO by	3
Aug.	17—Al Reid, New York	KO	4
Nov.	7—Cristobal Jaramillo, New York	W	8
Nov.	25—Vince Dell' Orto, New York	W	6
Dec.	5—Pete De Grasse, New York	KO	5
Dec.	26—Joey Ferrando, New York	L	8

1939

Jan.	3—Tommy Speigel, Brooklyn	W	10
Jan.	14—Johnny Rohrig, Brooklyn	W	8
Jan.	31—Lew Feldman, Brooklyn	L	8
Feb.	14—Johnny Bellus, New York	L	8
Mar.	10—Joe DeJesus, New York	KO	2
Mar.	21—Red Guggino, Brooklyn	W	8
Apr.	27—Dan McAllister, Liverpool	KO	5
May	25—George Daly, London	W	8
June	8—Kid Tanner, Liverpool	KO	7
Aug.	8—Teddy Baldwin, Garfield, N.J.	W	8
Aug.	21—Billy Bullock, Baltimore	KO	5
Sept.	18—Lew Feldman, Baltimore	L	10
Dec.	1—Young Rightmire, New York	W	6

1940

Jan.	16—Sammy Julian, Brooklyn	W	8
Jan.	29—Paul Junior, Portland, Me.	L	10
Feb.	19—Frankie Gilmore, Baltimore	W	10
Feb.	22—Mike Martinez, Baltimore	KO	3
Mar.	11—Charley Gomer, Baltimore	KO	4
Apr.	1—Tommy Speigel, Baltimore	W	10
Apr.	29—Cocoa Kid, Baltimore	L	10
June	24—Saverio Turiello, Baltimore	W	10
July	15—Joey Silva, Baltimore	KO	7
Aug.	12—Paul Junior, Philadelphia	KO	5
Sept.	9—Joey Ferrando, Baltimore	KO	4
Oct.	7—Teddy Baldwin, Philadelphia	KO	4
Dec.	9—Jimmy Leto, Baltimore	L	10

1941

Jan.	6—Johnny Williams, New York	KO	5
Jan.	14—Norment Quarles, Jersey City	W	8
Feb.	4—Norman Rahn, Jersey City	KO	2
Feb.	19—Frank Terranova, Allentown	KO	6
Feb.	24—Maurice Arnault, Baltimore	KO	2
Mar.	6—Texas Lee Harper, Washington	KO	3
Mar.	17—Charles Schnaupoff, Wilkes-Barre	KO	5

May	1—Charley Varre, New York	W	8
May	22—Sal Bartolo, New York	W	8
May	29—Norment Quarles, Atlantic City	W	8
June	3—Guillermo Puentes, Long Island City	W	8
June	17—Lloyd Pine, Wilkes-Barre	KO	2
June	24—Bobby McIntire, Long Island City	KO	5
July	17—Jackie Wilson, Baltimore	W	10
Aug.	5—Paco Villa, Long Island City	KO	6
Sept.	11—Joey Archibald, Washington	KO	11
	(Won World Featherweight Title)		
Oct.	2—Jose Peralta, Wilkes-Barre	L	10
Oct.	14—Leo Rodak, Washington	W	10
Oct.	31—Ray Lunny, San Francisco	W	10
Nov.	28—Jess Morales, San Diego	KO	6

1942

Jan.	13—Bobby Ruffin, New York	L	10
Feb.	3—Richie Lemos, Los Angeles	KO	6
Feb.	19—Ritchie Fontaine, Oakland	W	10
Mar.	24—Jorge Morelia, Los Angeles	KO	6
Apr.	6—Vern Bybee, San Francisco	L	10
May	7—Lulu Costantino, New York	W	8
June	19—Harry Jeffra, Baltimore	KO	10
	(Retained World Featherweight Title)		
July	13—Lou Transparenti, Baltimore	KO	4
Aug.	6—Allie Stolz, New York	L	10
Aug.	15—Curley St. Angelo, Springfield	KO	2
Aug.	27—Joey Marinelli, Detroit	KO	2
Sept.	25—Lulu Costantino, New York	W	15
	(Retained World Featherweight Title)		
Oct.	13—No No Cuebas, Hartford	KO	4
Oct.	20—Henry Vasquez, New Haven	KO	8
Nov.	20—Willie Pep, New York	L	15
	(Lost World Featherweight Title)		

1943

Jan.	15—Joe Peralta, New York	W	10
Feb.	15—Morris Parker, Newark	KO	4
Feb.	23—Joe Peralta, St. Louis	W	10
Mar.	10—Joey Pirrone, Cleveland	KO	3
May	17—Frankie Carto, Baltimore	KO	8
May	25—Billy Pinti, Brooklyn	KO	4
June	4—Phil Terranova, New York	KO	5
July	3—Kid National, Havana	KO	8
July	21—Lulu Costantino, Cleveland	L	10
Aug.	9—Angel Avila, Washington	KO	7
Oct.	26—Patsy Spataro, Brooklyn	KO	2
Nov.	8—Billy Banks, Philadelphia	KO	5
Nov.	19—Al Reasoner, New Orleans	KO	2

1944

Jan.	25—Al Brown, Panama City	KO	5
Feb.	10—Al Carlos, Panama City	KO	6
Mar.	5—Young Finnegan, Panama City	D	10
May	1—Clyde English, Scranton	KO	7
May	22—Sammy Daniels, Baltimore	KO	8
June	5—Vince Dell' Orto, Washington	KO	3
July	10—Ruby Garcia, Houston	KO	8
July	17—Johnny Cockfield, Norfolk	KO	5
Sept.	29—Willie Pep, New York	L	15
	(For World Featherweight Title)		
Dec.	5—Willie Pep, Cleveland	L	10

1945

Feb.	5—Willie Joyce, Philadelphia	L	10
Apr.	9—Jackie Wilson, Batimore	NC	7
Apr.	17—Willie Joyce, Los Angeles	W	10
July	31—Henry Jordan, Brooklyn	KO	6
Aug.	28—Enrique Bolanos, Los Angeles	W	10
Sept.	21—Humberto Zavala, New York	W	10
Oct.	5—Bobby Ruffin, Detroit	W	10
Nov.	2—Leroy Willis, Detroit	W	10
Dec.	14—Johnny Bratton, New Orleans	W	10

1946

Jan.	25—Pedro Firpo, New York	W	10
Feb.	19—Enrique Bolanos, Los Angeles	L	10
Mar.	5—George Hansford, Milwaukee	KO	4
Mar.	27—Frankie Moore, Oakland	KO by	1
Apr.	17—Frankie Moore, Oakland	L	10
Aug.	27—Johnny Dell, New York	L	10
Oct.	15—Enrique Bolanos, Los Angeles	L	10
Nov.	27—Willie Pep, Milwaukee	KO by	3

1947

May	19—Frankie Saucedo, Juarez	D	10
June	24—Larry Cisneros, Albuquerque	L	10

1948

Mar.   9—Ernie Hunick, Salt Lake City   KO by 3

TB	KO	WD	WF	D	LD	LF	KO BY	ND	NC
198	73	70	0	15	32	0	7	0	1

Died, August 12, 1957, Los Angeles, California.
Elected to Boxing Hall of Fame, 1977.

JACKIE WILSON
(Jack Benjamin Wilson)
Pittsburgh Featherweight
Born, 1909, Arkansas. Height, 5 ft. 5 in.
Managed by Bill Daly, Jack Laken, Pete Reilly and Harry Burnkrant.
Started professional boxing career in 1930.

1931
    —Pat Flaherty ....L 10
Sept. 24—John Datto, Pittsburgh .... KO by 3

1932
Feb. 26—Willie Davies ....W 10
June 28—Ross Fields, Pittsburgh .... KO by 10
July 6—Steve Senick, Pittsburgh ....W 10

1933
Jan. 14—Ross Fields, Pittsburgh ....W 10
    —Johnny Mitchell, Pittsburgh ... W 10
Feb. 3—Midget Wolgast, Pittsburgh .... D 10
Apr. 1—Johnny Pena, Chicago ....W 10
Apr. 3—Tommy Paul, Pittsburgh ....W 10
May 8—Eddie Shea, Pittsburgh ....W 10
June 5—Tommy Paul, Pittsburgh ....KO 8
    —Benny Britt, Pittsburgh ......W 10
    —Ernie Ratner, Pittsburgh ......W 10
    —Johnny Fitzpatrick, Pittsburgh W 8
    —Dario Moreno, Pittsburgh ....KO 6
    —Young Rightmire, Pittsburgh .ND 8

1934
Jan. 8—Johnny Mitchell, Chicago ...KO 6
July 19—Mose Butch, Pittsburgh ......W 10
Dec. 16—Jose Conde, Mexico City ......L 10
Dec. 23—Mose Butch, Pittsburgh ......W 10
Dec. 29—Bud Dempsey ....W 10

1935
Oct. 10—Billy Gannon, Liverpool......W 10
    —Johnny McGregory, Glasgow .KO 10
Nov. 7—Cuthbert Taylor, Liverpool....W 10
Dec. 12—Gilbert Johnson, Liverpool...KO 5

1936
Jan. 12—Ronnie James, London........L 10
    —Jack Linahan, Cork ....W 10
    —Stan Jehu, Manchester ....W 10
    —Douglas Kestrell, Manchester .. W 10
    —George Gee, Plymouth ....KO 7
    —Tommy Rogers, Wolverhampton ......KO 4
    —Spike Robinson, Belfast ....W 12
Scored two knockouts in last two appearances in Belfast.
Oct. 12—Bobby Dean, Pittsburgh .....KO 2
Dec. 3—Lee Sheppard, Pittsburgh ......W 10

1937
Feb. 9—Freddie Miller, Pittsburgh ....W 10
Feb. 22—Mike Belloise, Pittsburgh .....W 10
Mar. 22—Charley Burns, Lancaster .....W 8
Apr. 12—Armanda Sicilia, Springfield ...D 7
Apr. 26—Freddie Miller, Cincinnati .....W 10
May 10—Joey Brown, Lancaster ....KO 4
June 15—Pete De Grasse, Los Angeles .. W 10
July 6—Speedy Dado, Stockton, Cal. .. W 10
July 16—Kenny Reed, San Diego ....L 3
July 26—Ritchie Fontaine, Los Angeles .L 10
Aug. 6—Al Manriquez, Sioux City ......W 10
Aug. 19—Leo Rodak, St. Louis ....D 10
Sept. 17—Leo Rodak, St. Louis ....D 15
Oct. 12—Young Rightmire, St. Louis.....L 10

1938
Jan. 10—Leo Rodak, Chicago ....D 10
Jan. 21—Varias Milling, Chicago ....W 10
Mar. 22—Sammy Angott, Milwaukee ....L 10
May 9—Norment Quarles, Baltimore ...W 10
June 17—Leo Rodak, Baltimore ....L 15
Nov. 4—Jiggs McKnight, Clarksburg, W. Va..............................KO 8

1939
Feb. 8—Mickey Miller, Sydney ....KO 4
Mar. 1—Joe Hall, Melbourne ....W 10
Mar. 15—Claude Varner, Melbourne ....W 12
Mar. 24—Joe Velasco, Brisbane ....W 12
    —Sammy Garcia, Brisbane ......W 12
Mar. 31—Henry Moreno, Brisbane ......W 12
Apr. 26—Joe Hall, Melbourne ....WF 10
Apr. 11—Joe Velasco, Sydney ....WF 8

May 31—Mickey Miller, Melbourne .....W 12
June 28—Henry Moreno, Melbourne ....W 12
Nov. 8—Armanda Sicilia, Pittsburgh ...W 10
Nov. 20—Emil Joseph, Pittsburgh ....W 10

1940
Feb. 12—Frankie Covelli, Chicago ......W 10
Mar. 31—Harris Blake, New Orleans ....L 10
Apr. 25—Bobby Green, Lancaster.......W 10
June 3—Leo Rodak, Chicago ....L 10
Aug. 20—Harry Jeffra, Youngstown .....L 10
Dec. 12—Frank Terranova, Baltimore ...W 8

1941
Jan. 23—Maxie Shapiro, Baltimore .....W 10
Feb. 11—Joe Marinelli, Youngstown ....W 10
Mar. 31—Matt Perfecti, Baltimore.......W 10
Apr. 21—Leo Rodak, Cincinnati ....L 10
May 19—Baby Arizmendi, Los Ang.....KO 8
July 17—Chalky Wright, Baltimore ......L 10
Oct. 27—Leo Rodak, Toledo ....L 10
Nov. 18—Richie Lemos, Los Angeles ....W 12
(Won N.B.A. Featherweight Championship)
Dec. 16—Richie Lemos, Los Angeles, Cal. (title bout)...................W 12

1942
Feb. 20—Abe Denner, Boston ....L 10
Feb. 24—Ceferino Garcia, Los Angeles ..W 10
Mar. 2—Terry Young, N. Y. C..........L 8

1943
Jan. 18—Jackie Callura, Providence ......L 15
(Lost N. B. A. Featherweight Title)
Mar. 18—Jackie Callura, Boston ....L 15
(For N.B.A. Featherweight Title)
Apr. 26—Willie Pep, Pittsburgh ....L 12
May 17—Danny Petro, Washington ....KO 10
June 7—Jimmy Phillips, Washington ... W 10
June 28—Lew Hanbury, Washington ...KO 7
July 26—Tony Costa, Providence ....W 10
Aug. 30—Lulu Costantino, Washington .. W 10
Oct. 4—Larry Bolvin, Providence ....L 10
Oct. 22—Freddie Pope, Cleveland ......L 10
Dec. 6—Tony Costa, Providence ......LF 6

1944
Sept. 19—Cleo Shans, Washington, D. C. . W 10
Oct. 17—Pedro Hernandez, Washington ..L 10

1945
Jan. 8—Harry Jeffra, Baltimore ....W 10
Jan. 22—Pedro Hernandez, Washington . W 10
Mar. 12—Cleo Shans, Baltimore ....W 10
Apr. 9—Chalky Wright, Baltimore ......NC 7
June 25—Freddie Russo, Baltimore .....L 10

1946
Mar. 11—Willie Joyce, Wash. ....KO by 5
Mar. 26—Willie Pep, Kansas City ....L 10
May 3—Jackie Graves, Minn. ....L 8
June 18—Enrique Bolanos, Los Ang. KO by 7
Sept. 11—Star Misamis, Oakland ....L 10
Sept. 25—Star Misamis, Oakland ....L 10
Oct. 22—Luis Castillo, San Jose ....W 10
Nov. 18—Luis Castillo, San Jose ....L 10
Dec. 17—Mario Trigo, San Jose ....L 10

1947
Jan. 8—Speedy Cabanella, Sacremento ..L 10
Jan. 20—Buddy Jacklich, San Fran......L 10
Apr. 7—Freddie Steele, Vancouver....KO 7
Apr. 25—Manny Ortega, El Paso ...KO by 10
May 12—Jackie Turner, Vancouver .....L 10
May 30—Jackie Turner, Vancouver ......L 10
Sept. 1—Joey Dolan, Spokane ....L 10
Sept. 22—Simon Vegara, Ocean Park . KO by 9

TB	KO	WD	WF	D	LD	LF	KOBY	ND	NC
122	17	55	2	5	34	1	6	1	1

WILLIE PEP
(Guglielmo Papaleo)
(Will o' the Wisp)

Born, Sept. 19, 1922, Middletown, Conn.
Nationality, Italian-American. Featherweight.
Height, 5 ft. 5½ in. Managed by Lou Viscusi.
Started amateur in 1937.

1938
Won the Connecticut State Amateur Flyweight Championship.

1939
Won the Connecticut State Amateur Bantamweight Championship.

1940
July 3—James McGovern, Hartford ....W 4
July 25—Joey Marcus, Hartford, Conn. ..W 4
Aug. 8—Joey Wasnick, New Haven ....KO 3

Aug.	29—Tommy Burns, Hartford, Ct. . . KO	1
Sept.	5—Joey Marcus, New Britain . . . . . W	6
Sept.	18—Jack Moore, Hartford . . . . W	6
Oct.	3—Jimmy Riche, Waterbury . . . . . KO	3
Nov.	22—Carlo Duponde, New Britain . . KO	6
Nov.	29—Frank Topazio, New Britain . . KO	5
Dec.	6—Jim Mutane, New Britain . . . . . KO	2

1941

Jan.	28—Augie Almeda, New Haven . . . . KO	6
Feb.	3—Joe Echevarria, Holyoke, Mass. W	6
Feb.	10—Don Lyons, Holyoke, Mass. . . . KO	2
Feb.	17—Ruby Garcia, Holyoke, Mass. . . W	6
Mar.	3—Ruby Garcia, Holyoke, Mass. . . W	6
Mar.	25—Marty Shapiro, Hartford, Conn. W	6
Mar.	31—Joey Gatto, Holyoke, Mass. . . . KO	2
Apr.	14—Henry Vasquez, Holyoke . . . . . . W	6
Apr.	22—Mexican Joey Silva, Hartford . . W	6
May	6—Lou Puglose, Hartford . . . . KO	2
May	12—Johnny Cockfield, Holyoke . . . . W	6
June	24—Eddie De Angelis, Hartford . . . KO	3
July	16—Jimmy Gilligan, Hartford . . . . . W	8
Aug.	1—Harry Hitlian, Manchester . . . . . W	6
Aug.	5—Paul Frechette, Hartford . . . . KO	3
Aug.	12—Eddie Flores, Thompsonville . KO	1
Sept.	26—Jackie Harris, New Haven . . . . . KO	1
Oct.	10—Carlos Manzana, New Haven . . . W	8
Oct.	22—Connie Savoie, Hartford . . . . . KO	2
Nov.	7—Billie Spencer, Los Angeles . . . W	4
Nov.	24—Dave Crawford, Holyoke . . . . . . W	8
Dec.	12—Ruby Garcia, N. Y. C. . . . . W	4

1942

Jan.	8—Joey Rivers, Fall River . . . . KO	4
Jan.	16—Sammy Parrota, N. Y. C. . . . . . . W	4
Jan.	27—Abie Kaugman, Hartford . . . . . . W	8
Feb.	10—Angelo Callura, Hartford . . . . . W	8
Feb.	24—Willie Roach, Hartford . . . . W	8
Mar.	18—Johnny Compo, New Haven . . W	8
Apr.	14—Spider Armstrong, Hartford . . KO	4
May	4—Curley Nichols, New Haven . . . . W	8
May	12—Aaron Seltzer, Hartford . . . . . . W	8
May	26—Joey Iannotti, Hartford . . . . . . W	8
June	23—Joey Archibald, Hartford . . . . . W	10
July	21—Abe Denner, Hartford . . . . W	12
Aug.	1—Joey Silva, Waterbury . . . . KO	7
Aug.	10—Pedro Hernandez, Hartford . . . . W	10
Aug.	20—Nat Litfin, West Haven . . . . W	10
Sept.	1—Bobby Ivy, Hartford . . . . KO	10
Sept.	10—Frank Franconeri, N. Y. C. . . . KO	1
Sept.	22—Vince Dell'Orto, Hartford . . . . W	10
Oct.	16—Joey Archibald, Providence . . . . W	10
Oct.	5—Bobby McIntire, Holyoke . . . . . W	10
Oct.	27—George Zengaras, Hartford . . . . W	10
Nov.	20—Chalky Wright, New York City . W	15

(Won world featherweight championship)

Dec.	14—Joe Aponte Torres, Wash., D. C. . . . . KO	7
Dec.	21—Joey Silva, Jacksonville . . . . . . KO	9

1943

Jan.	4—Vince Dell'Orto, New Orleans . . W	10
Jan.	19—Bill Speary, Hartford . . . . W	10
Jan.	29—Allie Stolz, N. Y. C. . . . . W	10
Feb.	11—Davey Crawford, Boston . . . . . . W	10
Feb.	15—Bill Speary, Baltimore . . . . W	10
Mar.	2—Lou Transparenti, Hartford . . . KO	6
Mar.	19—Sammy Angott, N. Y. C. L	10
Mar.	29—Bobby McIntire, Detroit . . . . . . W	10
Apr.	9—Sal Bartolo, Boston . . . . W	10
Apr.	19—Angel Aviles, Tampa . . . . W	10
Apr.	26—Jackie Wilson, Pittsburgh . . . . . W	12
June	8—Sal Bartolo, Boston . . . . W	15

(Title fight)

In U. S. Navy after having served in Army.
Honorably discharged—Jan., 1944.

1944

Apr.	4—Leo Francis, Hartford . . . . W	10
Apr.	20—Harold Snooks Lacey, New Haven . . . . W	10
May	1—Jackie Leamus, Philadelphia . . W	10
May	19—Frankie Rubino, Chicago . . . . . . W	10
May	23—Joey Bagnato, Buffalo . . . . KO	2
June	6—Julie Kogon, Hartford . . . . W	10
July	7—Willie Joyce, Chicago . . . . W	10
July	17—Manuel Ortiz, Boston . . . . W	10
Aug.	4—Lulu Constantino, Waterbury . . W	10
Aug.	29—Joey Peralta, Springfield . . . . . . W	10
Sept.	19—Charley Cabey Lewis, Hartford . . . . KO	8
Sept.	29—Chalky Wright, New York City . W	15

(Title bout)

Oct.	25—Jackie Leamus, Montreal . . . . . . W	10
Nov.	14—Charley Cabey Lewis, Hartford W	10
Nov.	27—Pedro Hernandez, Washington . W	10
Dec.	5—Chalky Wright, Cleveland . . . . . . W	10

1945

Jan.	23—Ralph Walton, Hartford . . . . W	10
Feb.	5—Willie Roache, New Haven . . . . . W	10
Feb.	19—Phil Terranova, New York . . . . . W	15

(Title Bout)

Mar.	14—Inducted into U. S. Army.	
Oct.	30—Paulie Jackson, Hartford . . . . . . W	8
Nov.	5—Mike Martyk, Buffalo . . . . KO	5
Nov.	26—Eddie Giosa, Boston . . . . W	10
Dec.	5—Harold Gibson, Lewiston . . . . . . W	10
Dec.	13—Jimmy McAllister, Baltimore . . D	10

1946

Jan.	15—Johnny Virgo, Buffalo . . . . KO	2
Feb.	13—Jimmy Joyce, Buffalo . . . . W	10
Mar.	1—Jimmy McAllister, N. Y. City . KO	2
Mar.	26—Jackie Wilson, Kansas City . . . . W	10
Apr.	8—Georgie Knox, Providence . . . . KO	3
May	6—Ernie Petrone, New Haven . . . . W	10
May	13—Joey Angelo, Providence . . . . . . W	10
May	22—Aponte Torres, St. Louis . . . . . . W	10
May	27—Jimmy Joyce, Minneapolis . . . . W	8
June	7—Sal Bartolo, N. Y. City . . . . KO	12

(Title bout)

July	10—Harold Gibson, Buffalo . . . . . . KO	7
July	25—Jackie Graves, Minneapolis . . KO	8
Aug.	26—Doll Rafferty, Milwaukee . . . . KO	6
Sept.	4—Walter Kolby, Buffalo . . . . KO	5
Sept.	17—Lefty LaChance, Hartford . . . . KO	3
Nov.	1—Paulie Jackson, Minneapolis . . . W	10
Nov.	15—Tomas Beato, Waterubury . . . . KO	2
Nov.	27—Chalky Wright, Milwaukee . . . . KO	3

1947

Jan.	8—Severely injured in airplane crash.	
June	17—Victor Flores, Hartford . . . . W	10
July	1—Joey Fortuna, Albany . . . . KO	5
July	8—Leo LeBrun, Norwalk . . . . W	10
July	11—Jean Barriere, No. Adams . . . . . KO	4
July	15—Paulie Jackson, New Bedford . . W	10
July	23—Humberto Sierra, Hartford . . . . W	10
Aug.	22—Jock Leslie, Flint . . . . KO	12

(Title)

Oct.	21—Jean Barriere, Portland, Me. . . KO	1
Oct.	27—Archie Wilmer, Phila. . . . . W	10
Dec.	22—Alvara Estrada, Lewiston . . . . . . W	10
Dec.	30—Lefty La Chance, Manchester . KO	8

1948

Jan.	6—Pedro Biesca, Hartford . . . . W	10
Jan.	12—Jimmy McAllister, St. Louis . . . W	10
Jan.	19—Joey Angelo, Boston . . . . W	10
Feb.	24—Humberto Sierra, Miami . . . . . . KO	10

(World Featherweight Title Bout)

May	7—Leroy Willis, Detroit . . . . W	10
May	19—Charley (Cabey) Lewis, Milw. . . W	10
June	17—Miguel Acevedo, Minneapolis . . W	10
June	25—Luther Burgess, Flint . . . . W	10
July	28—Young Junior, Utica . . . . KO	1
Aug.	3—Ted Davis, Hartford . . . . W	10
Aug.	17—Ted Davis, Hartford . . . . W	10
Sept.	2—Johnny Dell, Waterbury . . . . . . KO	8
Sept.	10—Paddy DeMarco, N. Y. C. . . . . . . W	10
Oct.	12—Chuck Burton, Jersey City . . . . W	8
Oct.	19—John LaRusso, Hartford . . . . W	10
Oct.	29—Sandy Saddler, New York . KO by	4

(Lost World Featherweight Title)

Dec.	20—Hermie Freeman, Boston . . . . . . W	10

1949

Jan.	17—Teddy Davis, St. Louis . . . . W	10
Feb.	11—Sandy Saddler, N. Y. C. . . . . W	15

(Re-won World Featherweight title)

Apr.	27—Elis Ask, Detroit . . . . Exh.	4
May	25—Mel Hammond, St. Paul . . . . . Exh.	4
June	6—Luis Ramos, New Haven . . . . . . W	10
June	14—Al Pennino, Pittsfield . . . . W	10
June	20—John LaRusso, Springfield . . . . . W	10
July	12—Jean Mougin, Syracuse . . . . W	10
Sept.	2—Miguel Acevedo, Chicago . . . . Exh.	4
Sept.	20—Eddie Compo, Waterbury . . . KO	7

(Title bout)

Dec.	12—Harold Dade, St. Louis . . . . W	10

1950

Jan.	16—Charley Riley, St. Louis . . . . . . KO	5

(Title bout)

Feb.	6—Roy Andrews, Boston . . . . W	10
Feb.	22—Jimmy Warren, Miami . . . . W	10
Mar.	17—Ray Famechon, New York . . . . W	15

(Title bout)

May	15—Art Llanos, Hartford . . . . KO	2
June	1—Terry Young, Milwaukee . . . . . . W	10
June	26—Bobby Timpson, Hartford . . . . . W	10
July	25—Bobby Bell, Washington . . . . W	10
Aug.	2—Proctor Heinold, Scranton . . . . W	10
Sept.	8—Sandy Saddler, New York . KO by	8

(Lost Featherweight title)

1951

Jan.	30—Tommy Baker, Hartford .....KO	4
Feb.	26—Billy Hogan, Sarasota ....KO	2
Mar.	5—Carlos Chavez, New Orleans ... W	10
Mar.	26—Pat Iacobucci, Miami ....W	10
Apr.	17—Baby Ortiz, St. Louis ....KO	5
Apr.	27—Eddie Chavez, San Francisco .. W	10
June	4—Jesus Compos, Baltimore ...... W	10
Sept.	4—Corky Gonzales, New Orleans .. W	10
Sept.	26—Sandy Saddler, New York . KO by	9

(For Featherweight title)

1952

Apr.	29—Santiago Gonzales, Tampa..... W	10
May	5—Kenny Leach, Columbus, Ga. .. W	10
May	10—Buddy Baggett, Aiken, S. C. ..KO	5
May	21—Claude Hammond, Miami Beach .... W	10
June	30—Tommy Collins, Boston ... KO by	6
Sept.	3—Billy Lima, Pensacola .... W	10
Sept.	11—Bobby Woods, Vancouver ..... W	10
Oct.	1—Armand Savoie, Chicago ...... W	10
Oct.	20—Billy Lima, Jacksonville ..... W	10
Nov.	5—Manny Castro, Miami Beach ..KO	5
Nov.	19—Fabala Chavez, St. Louis ..... W	10
Dec.	5—Jorge Sanchez, W. Palm Beach . W	10

1953

Jan.	19—Billy Lauderdale, Nassau ...... W	10
Jan.	27—Davey Mitchell, Miami Beach .. W	10
Feb.	10—Jose Alvarez, San Antonio ..... W	10
Mar.	31—Joey Gambino, Tampa .... W	10
Apr.	7—Noel Paquette, Miami Beach ... W	10
May	13—Jackie Blair, Dallas .... W	10
June	5—Pat Marcune, New York ......KO	10
Nov.	21—Sonny Luciano, Charlotte ..... W	10
Dec.	4—Davey Allen, West Palm Beach . W	10
Dec.	8—Billy Lima, Houston ....KO	2
Dec.	15—Tony Longo, Miami Beach..... W	10

1954

Jan.	19—David Seabrooke, Jacksonville . W	10
Feb.	26—Lulu Perez, New York ..... KO by	2
July	24—Mike Turcotte, Mobile .... W	10
Aug.	18—Til LeBlanc, Moncton, N. B. ... W	10
Nov.	1—Mario Colon, Daytona Beach .. W	10

1955

Mar.	11—Myrel Olmstead, Bennington, Vt. .... W	10
Mar.	22—Charley Titone, Holyoke ...... W	10
Mar.	30—Gil Cadilli, Parks Airforce Base, Calif. L	10
May	18—Gil Cadilli, Detroit .... W	10
June	1—Joey Cam, Boston ....KO	4
June	14—Mickey Mars, Miami Beach ...KO	7
July	12—Hector Rodriquez, Bridgeport . W	10
Sept.	13—Jimmy Ithia, Hartford ....KO	6
Sept.	27—Henry (Pappy) Gault, Holyoke . W	10
Oct.	10—Charley Titone, Brockton ..... W	10
Nov.	29—Henry (Pappy) Gault, Tampa .. W	10
Dec.	12—Leo Carter, Houston ....KO	4
Dec.	28—Andy Arel, Miami Beach ...... W	10

1956

Mar.	13—Kid Campeche, Tampa .... W	10
Mar.	27—Buddy Baggett, Beaumont ..... W	10
Apr.	17—Jackie Blair, Hartford .... W	10
May	22—Manuel Armenteros, San Ant. ..KO	7
June	19—Russ Tague, Miami Beach ...... W	10
July	4—Hector Bacquettes, Lawton, Okla. ....KO	4

1957

Apr.	23—Cesar Morales, Ft. Lauderdale .. W	10
May	10—Manny Castro, Florence, S. C... W	10
July	16—Manny Castro, El Paso .... W	10
July	23—Russ Tague, Houston .... W	10
Dec.	17—Jimmy Connors, Boston .... W	10

1958

Jan.	14—Tommy Tibbs, Boston L	10
Mar.	31—Prince Johnson, Holyoke ...... W	10
Apr.	8—George Stephany, Bristol ..... W	10
Apr.	14—Cleo Ortiz, Providence .... W	10
Apr.	29—Jimmy Kelly, Boston .... W	10
May	20—Bobby Singleton, Boston ..... W	10
June	23—Pat McCoy, New Bedford..... W	10
July	1—Bobby Soares, Athol .... W	10
July	17—Bobby Bell, Norwood .... W	10
Aug.	4—Luis Carmona, Presque Isle .... W	10
Aug.	9—Jesse Rodrigues, Painesville .... W	10
Aug.	26—Al Duarte, No. Adams .... W	10
Sept.	30—Hogan (Kid) Bassey, Boston .... KO by	9

1959

Jan.	26—Sonny Leon, Caracas..........L	10

Announced retirement, January 27, 1959.
Decided on a comeback, January 12, 1965.

1965

Jan.	28—Jerry Powers, Miami ....Exh.	4
Mar.	12—Hal McKeever, Miami .... W	8
Apr.	26—Jackie Lennon, Philadelphia ... W	6
May	21—Johnny Gilmore, Norwalk ..... W	6
May	28—Irish Bob Shaugnessy ....Exh.	4
July	26—Benny Randell, Quebec—..... W	10
Sept.	28—Johnny Gilmore, Philadelphia . W	6
Oct.	1—Willie Little, Johnston ....KO	3
Oct.	4—Tommy Haden, Providence ...KO	3
Oct.	14—Sergio Musquiz, Phoenix .....KO	5
Oct.	25—Ray Coleman, Tucson ....KO	5

1966

Mar.	16—Calvin Woodland, Richmond ...L	6

TB	KO	WD	WF	D	LD	LF	KOBY	ND	NC
241	65	164	0	1	5	0	6	0	0

Elected to Boxing Hall of Fame 1963.

JACKIE CALLURA

Born, September 24, 1917, Hamilton, Ontario, Can. Featherweight. Height, 5 ft. 6½ in.

1936

Won: Red Casson, 6; Gib Black, 6; Frankie Jarr, 6; Len Rittenhouse, 10; Len Hendrickson, 10. Lost: Len Hendrickson, 10; Billy Marquart, 6.

1937

Won: Lloyd Pine, 10; Pat Robinson, 8; Ray Cook, 10; Davey Paul, 10; Dave Lyons, 8; Lloyd Pine, 10; Barney Ruffner, 10. Lost: Lloyd Pine, 10; Leo Rodak, 10; Kayo Morgan, 10. Knockouts: Al Manriquez, 2; Jimmy Gilligan, 2.

1938

Jan.	14—Varias Milling, Chicago, Ill. L	10
Feb.	8—KO Morgan, Muskegon L	10
Mar.	7—Frankie Martin, Toronto, Can. . W	10
May	9—Dave Castilloux, Montreal, Can. .L	10
July	7—Harry Gerson, Montreal ...... W	8
Aug.	1—Frankie Jarr, Toronto .... W	8
Aug.	16—Henry Hook, Toronto .... W	10
Sept.	19—Joe Tambe, Buffalo .... W	6
Nov.	14—Jimmy Gilligan, Buffalo, N. Y. . W	6

1939

Jan.	3—Freddie Miller, Rochester ..... W	10
Mar.	28—Mickey Gamiere, Rochester ... D	10
June	15—Mel Glionna, Toronto .... W	10
	—Leon Efrati, Milwaukee ...... W	10
Sept.	18—Henry Huerta, Milwaukee .... W	10
Dec.	26—Henry Smith, Buffalo .... W	6
	—Spider Armstrong ....KO	2
	—Charley Roberts .... W	8
	—Lee Sheppard .... W	10
	—Eddie Scott .... W	8
	—Mike Martyk ....WF	9
	—Lefty Gwynne .... W	6
	—Eddie Carson .... W	8
	—Joe Marinelli L	10

1940

Jan.	1—Lee Sheppard, Buffalo .... W	8
Jan.	8—Harris Blake, Buffalo L	6
Jan.	15—Charley Roberts, Buffalo ..... W	6
Jan.	22—Joe Marinelli, Dayton, O. L	10
Feb.	15—Lee Sheppard, Rochester, N. Y. W	8
Mar.	4—Maxie Shapiro, N. Y. C. L	8
Apr.	4—Lou Salica, Rochester .... D	10
May	29—Aurel Toma, Oakland, Cal. L	10
July	1—Ritchie Shinn, San Francisco .. D	4
Aug.	21—Chick Delaney, Oakland, Cal. .. D	10
Sept.	11—Chick Delaney, Oakland ......KO	2
Sept.	24—Baby Arizmendi, Oakland .... D	10
Oct.	11—Gene Espinoza, San Francisco . W	10
Nov.	11—Georgie Pace, Toronto .... D	10
Dec.	9—Jimmy Fox, Toronto ....KO	3

1941

Feb.	24—Kid Hatcher, Miami Beach L	10
Mar.	10—Jimmy Perrin, New Orleans ... D	10
Apr.	7—Jimmy Perrin, New Orleans ...KO	4
May	6—Guy Serean, New Orleans...... W	10
Sept.	8—Guy Serean, New Orleans ..... W	10
Oct.	6—Nick Camarata, New Orleans .. W	10
Oct.	26—Frankie Garcia, Louisville ....KO	2

1942

Jan.	26—Larry Bolvin, Providence	W 10
Feb.	27—Larry Bolvin, Providence	KO 4
Mar.	23—Ted Christie, Providence	KO 3
Apr.	13—Bill Speary, New Orleans	W 10
May	4—Bobby Ivy, Providence	L 10
May	28—Sammy Garcia, Hamilton	KO 5
June	29—Vince Dell'Orto, New Orleans	L 10
July	27—Bobby Ivy, Providence	L 10
Aug.	31—Davey Crawford, Providence	W 10
Sept.	21—Davey Crawford, Providence	D 10
Sept.	28—Vince Dell'Orto, New Orleans	W 10
Nov.	23—Curley St. Angelo, Providence	KO 2
Dec.	11—Cleo Shans, Boston	L 10

1943

Jan.	18—Jackie Wilson, Providence	W 15
	(Won NBA Featherweight Title)	
Mar.	18—Jackie Wilson, Boston	W 15
	(Retained Title)	
Apr.	26—Tony Costa, Providence	L 10
May	20—Lew Hanbury, Wash., D. C.	L 10
June	30—Phil Terranova, Hartford	KO by 3
July	31—Frankie Ryan, Mobile, Ala.	KO 10
Aug.	16—Phil Terranova, N. Orleans	KO by 8
	(Lost NBA Featherweight Title)	
Oct.	1—Mike Martyk, Hamilton, Ont.	W 10
Oct.	20—Juan Villalba, New Orleans	W 10
Dec.	27—Phil Terranova, N. Orleans	KO by 6
	(For N.B.A. Featherweight Title)	

1944

Jan.	31—Chas. Cabey Lewis, Providence	L 10
June	6—Pat Demers, New Bedford	L 10

1945

Mar.	20—Paul Reguejo, Los Angeles	D 6
Apr.	24—Paul Reguejo, San Jose	L 10

1946

May	13—Jackie Harris, Boston	KO 8
June	4—Tommy Greb, Salem	L 10
June	25—Jimmy Corti, Trenton	L 8
July	2—Florient Desmarais, Man.	L 10
Oct.	16—Chico Morales, Memphis	L 10
Nov.	7—Bobby Jackson, El Paso	D 10
Nov.	29—Jackie Graves, Minneapolis	
		KO by 7
Dec.	4—Manny Ortega, El Paso	KO by 2

1947

June	4—Humberto Sierra, Miami	KO by 7

TB	KO	WD	WF	D	LD	LF	KOBY	ND	NC
100	13	43	1	10	27	0	6	0	0

PHIL TERRANOVA

Born, Sept. 4, 1919, New York City, Nationality, Italian-American. Featherweight. Managed by Bobby Gleason.

1941

July	14—Marty Kopp, N. Y. City	KO 1
July	21—Joey Agro, N. Y. C.	D 4
Aug.	4—Jimmy Kemp, New York	L 4
Sept.	2—Tommy Marino, New York	D 4
Sept.	9—Tommy Marino, New York	D 4
Sept.	23—Jimm Pereciego, White Plains	W 4

1942

Jan.	20—Harry Diduck, N. Y. C.	W 6
Feb.	17—Billy Sanders, N. Y. C.	W 6
Mar.	3—Charley Aldrich, N. Y. C.	KO 3
Mar.	24—Sonny Brents, N. Y. C.	W 6
Apr.	7—Joe Aponte Torres, N. Y. C.	D 6
Apr.	21—Joe Aponte Torres, N. Y. C.	D 8
May	26—Johnny Marcelline, N. Y. C.	D 8
June	20—Bobby Henderson, Brooklyn	W 6
June	30—Chico Morales, N. Y. C.	W 8
July	21—Johnny Dell, N. Y. C.	L 8
Aug.	11—Johnny Dell, N. Y. C.	L 8
Sept.	10—Gus Levine, N. Y. C.	W 6
Oct.	10—Frankie Rubino, Brooklyn	D 8
Oct.	27—Billy Pinti, White Plains	L 8
Nov.	13—Frank Franconeri, N. Y. C.	W 6
Dec.	8—Aaron Seltzer, White Plains	W 8

1943

Jan.	5—Johnny Dell, Brooklyn	KO 6
Jan.	23—Curley St. Angelo, Brooklyn	KO 5
Mar.	5—Al Guido, N. Y. C.	W 8
Mar.	23—Lulu Costantino, Brooklyn	W 8
Apr.	20—Angelo Callura, Hartford	W 10
May	4—Billy Pinti, Hartford	W 10
May	25—Chico Morales, Hartford	W 10
June	4—Chalky Wright, N. Y. C.	KO by 5
June	30—Jackie Callura, Hartford	KO 3

July	13—Angelo Aviles, Hartford	D 10
Aug.	16—Jackie Callura, N. Orleans	KO 8
	(For N.B.A. Featherweight Title)	
Sept.	13—Juan Villaba, N. Orleans	W 10
Sept.	21—Lefty La Chance, Hartford	L 10
Oct.	6—Sammy Garcia, New Britain	KO 5
Oct.	18—Tony Costa, Providence	L 10
Nov.	8—Harry Jeffra, Baltimore	L 10
Dec.	27—Jackie Callura, N. Orleans	KO 6
✦	(Title)	

1944

Jan.	18—Richie Myashiro, Hartford	KO 4
Feb.	1—Pat Foley, Worcester	KO 9
Feb.	14—Snooks Lacey, New Haven	W 10
Feb.	28—Milton Bell, Louisville	KO 5
Mar.	10—Sal Bartolo, Boston	L 15
	(Lost N.B.A. Featherweight title)	
May	5—Sal Bartolo, Boston	L 15
	(For N.B.A. Featherweight Title)	
July	11—Snooks Lacey, New Bedford	W 10
July	21—Snooks Lacey, Worcester	W 10
July	27—Charley Noel, Brooklyn	W 8
Aug.	14—Vince Dell'Orto, Providence	L 10
Sept.	21—Frankie Rubino, Brooklyn	KO 4
Oct.	16—Vince Dell' Orto, Providence	W 10
Oct.	27—Georgie Knox, Worcester	KO 3
Nov.	20—Harry Jeffra, N. Y. City	D 10
Dec.	7—Charley Noel, Worcester	W 10
Dec.	19—Leo Francis, Brooklyn	KO 2

1945

Jan.	12—Charley Cabey Lewis, N. Y.	W 10
Feb.	19—Willie Pep, New York	L 15
	(For World Featherweight Championship)	
Mar.	23—Leroy Willis, Detroit	W 10
Apr.	13—Maxie Shapiro, Detroit	W 10
May	11—Vince Del Orto, Boston	W 10
June	25—Bernard Docusen, New Orleans	L 8
Aug.	16—Augie Lapara, Fort Hamilton	KO 1
Aug.	27—Jean Barriere, New York	KO 4
Sept.	24—Leon Spencer, Detroit	KO 8
Nov.	19—Oscar Lewis, Stamford	KO 5
Nov.	23—Bill Eddy, Detroit	W 10
Dec.	11—Ellis Phillips, Boston	W 10
Dec.	22—Miguel Acevedo, Havana	D 10

1946

Jan.	25—Steve Curley, New Orleans	KO 3
Feb.	8—Frankie Carto, New Orleans	W 10
Feb.	22—Charley Riley, St. Louis	KO 6
Mar.	8—Jimmy Joyce, St. Louis	W 10
Apr.	2—Aponte Torres, St. Louis	W 10
Apr.	20—Leroy Jackson, Cleveland	KO 6
May	13—Freddy Russo, St. Louis	W 10
June	3—Jimmy McAllister, St. Louis	KO 4
July	23—Sandy Saddler, Detroit	W 10
Sept.	23—Willie Roache, St. Louis	W 10
Oct.	30—Willie Roache, St. Louis	W 10
Nov.	25—Oscar Calles, Caracas	KO 10

1947

Jan.	27—Jimmy Allen, New Britain	KO 5
Feb.	7—Maxie Shapiro, N. Y. C.	L 10
Mar.	5—Humberto Zavala, St. Louis	W 10
Mar.	19—Paulie Jackson, St. Louis	KO 8
Apr.	30—Charley Riley, St. Louis	KO by 7
July	2—Bernie Bernard, N. Y. C.	W 8
July	22—Clem Custer, Toledo	W 10
July	28—Jose Gonzales, New Orleans	L 10
Aug.	25—Tommy McGovern, Brooklyn	W 10
Sept.	3—Charley Riley, St. Louis	KO by 1
Dec.	11—Buddy Hayes, Worcester	KO 6

1948

Jan.	5—Arthur King, Toronto	L 8
Mar.	15—Spider Armstrong, Boston	L 8
Apr.	19—Eddie Compo, New Haven	L 8
May	24—Cliff Griffin, Lewiston	KO 3

1949

May	25—Percy Paris, Worcester	KO 6
June	8—Dom Saia, Worcester	KO 3
June	20—Johnny De Fazio, Newark	D 8
July	15—Guillermo Gimenez, N. Y. C.	L 8

TB	KO	WD	WF	D	LD	LF	KOBY	ND	NC
99	29	38	0	11	18	0	3	0	0

SAL BARTOLO

Born November 5, 1917, Boston, Mass. Nationality, Italian-American. Weight, 126 lbs. Managed by Lew Burston.

1937

Apr.	3—Art Nadeau, Boston	KO 3
May	7—Sammy Caro, Boston	KO 5

June   8—Emil Dumont, Boston........KO 3
July   9—Norman Cournier, Boston.....W 6
Sept. 20—Red Hutchins, Holyoke.......L 6
Oct.   22—Eddie Hass, Boston...........L 6
Nov.   14—Tony Saunders, Boston.......W 6
Dec.   6—John Sorenson, Boston....... D 6
1938
Jan.   8—Sammy Garcia, Worcester.....W 6
Feb.   18—Tony Costa, Boston..........W 6
Mar.   4—Eddie Hass, Boston..........W 8
Apr.   1—Tony Dupre, Boston..........L 10
May   2—Frankie Merrill, Boston.....KO 3
June   3—Tony Dupre, Boston.......... D 10
July   15—Biff Lemieux, New Bedford...W 10
Aug.   14—Tony Costa, Worcester........L 8
Sept.   3—Sammy Garcia, Boston........W 6
Oct.   17—Tony Costa, Worcester.......W 8
Nov.   11—Tony Costa, Worcester.......W 10
1939
Feb.   3—Dave Barry, Worcester.......W 10
Feb.   17—Pete Scalzo, Boston..........L 10
Mar.   10—Tony Dupre, Worcester.......W 12
Apr.   14—Poison Ivy, Worcester.......W 10
Apr.   21—Johnny Compo, New Britain...W 10
May   2—Eddie Reed, Boston..........W 10
June   24—Poison Ivy, Hartford.........L 10
Aug.   8—Dusty Brown, Boston.........W 8
Sept. 25—Ginger Foran, New Bedford...W 10
Oct.   3—Al Reid, New York City.......L 8
Nov.   11—Dusty Brown, New Bedford...W 8
Dec.   28—Abe Denner, Boston..........W 10
1940
Jan.   18—Poison Ivy, Boston...........W 10
Feb.   1—*Abe Denner, Boston.....KO by 8
June   18—Paco Villa, N.Y.C...........W 8
July   17—Everett Rightmire, N.Y.C....D 6
July   31—Everett Rightmire, N.Y.C...KO 8
Aug.   20—Bobby Ruffin, N.Y.C........D 8
Aug.   29—Monty Pignatore, N.Y.C.....W 8
Oct.   12—Maxie Shapiro, N.Y.C.......D 8
Nov.   11—Maxie Shapiro, N.Y.C.......W 10
Nov.   25—Joey Fontana, N.Y.C.........L 8
*Bout stopped—broke ear drum.
1941
Feb.   5—Vince Dell Orto, N.Y.C......W 8
Feb.   13—George Salamone, Boston.....W 10
Apr.   7—Johnny Cockfield, Baltimore.KO 4
Apr.   21—Davey Crawford, Baltimore...W 10
May   22—Chalky Wright, N.Y.C........L 8
July   9—Spider Armstrong, B'klyn....W 8
Sept. 11—Davey Crawford, Ft. Hamilton.W 8
Oct.   20—Pedro Hernandez, Baltimore....L 10
1942
Jan.   16—Maxie Shapiro, N.Y.C........L 8
Feb.   3—Maxie Shapiro, N.Y.C........L 8
Feb.   20—Maxie Shapiro, N.Y.C........L 8
June   9—Frankie Rubino, N.Y.C......W 8
June   26—Jerry Zullo, Boston.........KO 9
July   29—Jimmy Gilligan, N.Y.C......W 8
Aug.   4—Johnny Marcelline, N.Y.C....W 8
Aug.   10—Larry Bolvin, Holyoke.......W 10
Sept. 10—Billy Pinto, Ft. Hamilton....W 8
Sept. 21—Willie Roache, N.Y.C.......KO 6
Nov.   23—Davey Crawford, Holyoke....W 10
Nov.   30—Larry Bolvin, Providence....W 10
Dec.   14—Davey Crawford, Providence...W 10

1943
Jan.   22—Carmine Fatta, Boston......KO 2
Feb.   26—Pedro Hernandez, N.Y.C.....W 10
Mar.   26—Joey Archibald, Boston......W 10
Apr.   9—Willie Pep, Boston..........L 10
June   8—Willie Pep, Boston..........L 15
(For world featherweight title)
July   20—Lefty La Chance, Hartford...KO 8
July   27—Jose Rozo, Brooklyn.........KO 1
Aug.   3—Henry Vasquez, Springfield...W 10
Aug.   10—Bobby McIntire, Brooklyn....W 10
Sept. 10—Aaron Seltzer, N.Y.C........W 10
Oct.   13—Billy Bates, Hartford.......KO 3
Nov.   1—Jimmy O'Tash, New Britain..KO 6
U.S. Maritime Service.

1944
Jan.   31—Willie Roache, N.Y.C.......W 8
Feb.   14—Frankie Rubino, N.Y.C......W 10
Mar.   10—Phil Terranova, Boston......W 15
(Won N.B.A. Featherweight Title)
Apr.   13—Johnny Cockfield, Harrisburg..W 10
May   5—Phil Terranova, Boston......W 15
(Title bout)
July   21—Mike Martyk, Buffalo.......W 10
Oct.   31—Mario Colon, Albany........W 8
Dec.   15—Willie Roache, Boston.......W 15
(Title bout)

1945
Apr.   13—Gus Mell, Boston...........L 10
May   4—Gus Mell, Boston...........W 10
July   10—Al Pennino, Brooklyn.......W 8
July   27—Freddie Russo, N.Y.C.......W 10
Sept. 28—Maxie Shapiro, Boston......W 10
Oct.   26—Pedro Firpo, Boston........W 10
Nov.   19—Jock Leslie, New Orleans....W 10
1946
Jan.   17—Vince Dell'Orto, Rochester....W 10
Feb.   8—Paulie Jackson, Detroit......W 10
Apr.   5—Dennis Pat Brady, Boston....W 10
Apr.   15—Art Cooper, St. Louis.......KO 4
May   3—Spider Armstrong, Boston...KO 6
(Title bout)
June   7—Willie Pep, N.Y.C.........KO by 12
(For World Featherweight Title)
1949
Jan.   17—Bobby English, Boston.......KO 10
Jan.   25—Paulie Jackson, Salem........W 10

TB	KO	WD	WF	D	LD	LF	KOBY	ND	NC
97	16	58	0	5	16	0	2	0	0

SANDY SADDLER
Born, June 25, 1926, Boston, Mass.
Height, 5 ft. 7½ in. Managed by Charley Johnston.
1944
Mar.   7—Earl Roys, Hartford.........W 8
Mar.   21—Jock Leslie, Hartford.....KO by 3
Mar.   27—Al King, Holyoke..........KO 2
Apr.   17—Joe Landry, Holyoke.......KO 1
May   8—Joe Aponte Torres, Trenton...W 6
May   15—Joe Aponte Torres, Holyoke...W 6
May   23—Domingo Diaz, Jersey City...W 6
June   13—Joe Aponte Torres,
Union City....................W 8
June   15—Lou Alter, Fort Hamilton....L 6
June   23—Lou Alter, New York City....D 4
July   11—Clyde English, Dexter.......W 6
July   18—Benny Saladino, Brooklyn....KO 3
July   25—Al Pennino, Brooklyn.......W 6
Aug.   8—Georgie Knox, Brooklyn.....KO 3
Aug.   18—Clifford Smith, New York City.W 6
Nov.   11—Manuel Torres, Brooklyn....W 6
Nov.   13—Ken Tempkins, Newark......KO 1
Nov.   24—Manuel Torres, N.Y. City...KO 5
Nov.   28—Percy Lewis, Jersey City....KO 1
Dec.   12—Young Tony, Jersey City....KO 2
Dec.   16—Earl Mintz, Brooklyn.......KO 2
Dec.   26—Midget Mayo, Newark.......KO 3
1945
Jan.   13—Tony Oshiro, Brooklyn......W 6
Jan.   15—Lucky Johnson, Newark.....KO 1
Jan.   22—Joey Puig, New York.......KO 1
Jan.   26—Benny May, New Brunswick...W 6
Feb.   19—Joey Gatto, New York.......KO 1
Mar.   10—Harold Gibson, Brooklyn....W 6
Mar.   19—Joe Montiero, New York....KO 4
Mar.   22—Georgie Knox, Camden......KO 4
Apr.   2—Jimmy Allen, Newark.......KO 1
Apr.   19—Willie Anderson, Detroit....KO 1
Apr.   30—Chillendrina Valencia, Detroit KO 9
June   18—Caswell Harris, Baltimore...KO 3
June   25—Bobby Washington, Allentown KO 2
June   29—Leo Methot, New York......KO 1
July   23—Herbert Jones, Baltimore....KO 3
July   24—Joe Monteiro, Brooklyn.....KO 5
July   30—Lou Rivers, New York.......KO 4
Aug.   16—Louis Langley, Brooklyn....KO 1
Aug.   20—Bobby English, Providence...KO 3
Aug.   27—Earl Mintz, Providence.....KO 1
Sept. 21—Ritchie Myashiro, New York..W 6
Dec.   3—Benny Daniels, Holyoke.....W 6
Dec.   14—Joe Monterio, Boston.......W 8
Dec.   21—Filberto Osorio, New York....W 6
1946
Jan.   17—Sam Zelman, Orange........KO 1
Feb.   18—Bobby McQuillan, Detroit....L 10
Apr.   8—Ralph LaSalle, N.Y.C.......KO 1
Apr.   11—Johnny Wolgast, Atlantic City W 8
Apr.   25—Pedro Firpo, Atlantic City...W 8
June   13—Cedric Flournov, Detroit....KO 4
July   10—George Cooper, Brooklyn....KO 7
July   23—Phil Terranova, Detroit......L 10
Aug.   5—Dom Amoroso, Providence...KO 2
Aug.   22—Pedro Firpo, Brooklyn......W 10
Oct.   10—Jose Rodriguez, Atlantic City .KO 3

733

Nov. 12—Art Price, Detroit .... W 10
Dec. 9—Clyde English, Holyoke ..... KO 3
Dec. 26—Lou Marquez, Jamaica ..... KO 2
Dec. 30—Leonard Caesar, Newark ..... KO 2

1947
Jan. 20—Dusty Brown, Holyoke ..... KO 4
Jan. 27—Humberto Zavala, N. Y. C. ..... KO 7
Feb. 7—Larry Thomas, Asbury Park ..KO 2
Mar. 8—Leonardo Lopez, Mex. City ...KO 2
Mar. 29—Carlos Malacara, Mexico City .. W 10
Apr. 14—Charley Cabey Lewis, N. Y. C. .. W 10
May 2—Joe Brown, New Orleans .....KO 3
May 9—Melvin Bartholomew, New Orl. W 10
June 3—Jimmy Carter, Washington .... D 10
July 26—Oscar Calles, Caracas .... KO 5
Aug. 14—Leslie Harris, Atlantic City ...KO 5
Aug. 29—Miguel Acevedo, N. Y. C. ..... KO 8
Sept. 17—Angelo Ambrosano, Jamaica..KO 2
Oct. 3—Humberto Sierra, Minneapolis ..L 10
Oct. 13—Al Penninno, N. Y. C. ....KO 4
Oct. 26—Lino Garcia, Caracas ....KO 5
Nov. 9—El Barquerito, Caracas ....KO 5
Dec. 5—Lino Garcia, Havana ....KO 3
Dec. 13—Orlando Zuluta, Havana ...... W 10

1948
Feb. 2—Charlie Noel, Holyoke .... W 10
Feb. 9—Joey Angelo, New York .... W 10
Mar. 5—Archie Wilmer, New York .... W 8
Mar. 8—Thompson Harmon, Holyoke .KO 8
Mar. 23—Bobby Thompson, Hartford ... W 10
Apr. 10—Luis Monagas, Caracas ......KO 3
Apr. 17—Jose Diaz, Caracas ....KO 8
Apr. 26—Young Tanner, Aruba, D.W.I..KO 5
May 24—Harry La Sane, Holyoke ...... W 10
June 29—Chico Rosa, Honolulu ....L 10
Aug. 16—Kid Zefine, Panama ....KO 2
Aug. 23—Aguila Allen, Panama ....KO 2
Oct. 11—Willie Roache, New Haven ....KO 3
Oct. 29—Willie Pep, New York ....KO 4
(Won World Featherweight Title)
Nov. 19—Tomas Beato, Bridgeport .....KO 2
Nov. 29—Dennis Pat Brady, Boston ..... W 10
Dec. 7—Eddie Giosa, Cleveland ......KO 2
Dec. 17—Terry Young, New York .....KO 10

1949
Jan. 17—Young Finnegan, Panama ....KO 5
Feb. 11—Willie Pep, N. Y. C. ....L 15
(Lost World Featherweight title)
Mar. 21—Felix Ramirez, Newark .... W 10
Apr. 18—Ermano Bonetti, Philadelphia.KO 2
June 2—Jim Keery, London ....KO 4
June 23—Luis Ramos, N. Y. C. ....KO 5
July 15—Gordon House, N. Y. C. ....KO 5
Aug. 2—Chuck Burton, Pittsfield .....KO 5
Aug. 8—Johnny Rowe, Brooklyn .....KO 8
Aug. 24—Alfredo Escobar, Los Angeles .KO 9
Sept. 2—Harold Dade, Chicago .... W 10
Sept. 20—Proctor Heinold, Schenectady KO 2
Oct. 28—Paddy DeMarco, New York ...KO 9
Nov. 7—Leroy Willis, Toledo .... W 10
Dec. 6—Orlando Zulueta, Cleveland .... W 10

1950
Jan. 16—Paulie Jackson, Caracas ......KO 1
Jan. 22—Pedro Firpo, Caracas ....KO 1
Feb. 6—Chuck Burton, Holyoke ......KO 1
Feb. 20—Luis Ramos, Toronto ....KO 3
Apr. 10—Reuben Davis, Newark ......KO 8
Apr. 18—Lauro Salas, Cleveland ....KO 9
Apr. 29—Jesse Underwood, Waterbury .. W 10
May 25—Miguel Acevedo, Minneapolis .KO 6
June 19—Johnny Forte, Toronto ......KO 3
June 30—Leroy Willis, Long Beach .....KO 2
Sept. 8—Willie Pep, New York ....KO 8
(Re-won Featherweight Title)
Oct. 12—Harry LaSane, St. Louis .... W 10
Nov. 1—Charley Riley, St. Louis ...... W 10
Dec. 6—Del Flanagan, Detroit ....L 10

1951
Jan. 23—Jesse Underwood, Buffalo ..... W 10
Feb. 28—Diego Sosa, Havana ....KO 2
Mar. 27—Lauro Salas, Los Angeles ....KO 6
Apr. 3—Freddie Herman, Los Angeles .KO 5
May 5—Harry La Sane, Hershey, Pa........W 10
June 2—Alfredo Prada, Buenos Aires ..KO 4
June 16—Oscar Flores, Buenos Aires ...KO 1
June 22—Mario Salinas, Santiago ....KO 5
June 30—Angel Olivieri, Buenos Aires ..KO 5
Aug. 20—Hermie Freeman, Phila. ......KO 5
Aug. 27—Paddy DeMarco, Milwaukee ...L 10
Sept. 26—Willie Pep, New York ....KO 9
(Title bout)
Dec. 7—Paddy DeMarco, New York .....L 10

1952
Jan. 14—George Araujo, Boston ....L 10
Mar. 3—Armand Savoie, Montreal ..L Dis. 4
Mar. 17—Tommy Collins, Boston ......KO 5
In U. S. Army.

1954
Jan. 15—Bill Bossio, New York ...... KO 9
Mar. 4—Charlie Slaughter, Akron .....KO 4
Apr. 1—Augie Salazar, Boston ....KO 7
May 17—Hoacine Khalfi, New York ......L 10
July 5—Libby Manzo, New York .....KO 10
Aug. 30—Jackie Blair, Caracas ....KO 1
Sept. 27—Baby Ortiz, Caracas ....KO 3
Oct. 25—Ray Famechon, Paris ....KO 6
Dec. 10—Bobby Woods, Spokane .... W 10

1955
Jan. 17—Lulu Perez, Boston ....KO 4
Feb. 25—Teddy Davis, New York .... W 15
(World Featherweight Title)
Apr. 5—Kenny Davis, Butte ....KO 5
May 24—Joe Lopes, Sacramemnto ......L 10
July 8—Shigeru Kaneko, Tokyo ......KO 6
July 20—Flash Elorde, Manila ....L 10
Dec. 12—Dave Gallardo, San Francisco .KO 7

1956
Jan. 18—Flash Elorde, San Francisco ..KO 13
(Title Bout)
Feb. 13—Georgie Monroe, Providence ..KO 3
Apr. 14—Larry Boardman, Boston ....L 10
1957
Jan. —Relinquished world featherweight title and announced retirement from ring because of eye injury suffered in automobile crash.

TB	KO	WD	WF	D	LD	LF	KOBY	ND	NC
162	103	41	0	2	14	1	1	0	0

Elected to Hall of Fame 1971

HOGAN (KID) BASSEY
(Okon Bassey Asuquo)
Born, Calabar, Nigeria, June 3, 1932.
1949
—Dick Turpin, Lagos .... W 12
—Dick Turpin, Lagos .... LF 5
1950
Nov. 10—Joe Bennetts, Lagos ....KO 10
(Nigerian bantam title)
1951
May 4—Kid Chukudi, Lagos ....KO 3
May 16—Jack Salami, Lagos .... W 8
May 30—Adjetey Sowah, Lagos .... W 10
Aug. 29—Steve Jeffra, Lagos .... W 12
(Nigerian bantam title)
Sept. 28—Young Spider Neequauo, Lagos W 12
(West African bantam title)
1952
Jan. 31—Ray Hillyard, Liverpool ......KO 4
Feb. 19—Peter Fay, Hanley .... W 8
Mar. 5—Tommy Higgins, Blackpool .... W 8
Mar. 24—Len Shaw, Preston .... W 8
Apr. 1—Glyn Evans, Hanley .... D 8
Apr. 17—Bobby Boland, Liverpool .....KO 5
Apr. 26—Johnny Kelly, Belfast ....L 8
May 15—Frank Williams, Liverpool ......L 8
June 23—Ivor Davies, W. Hartlepool ...KO 2
July 28—Johnny Barclay,
W. Hartlepool ....KO 6
Aug. 7—Jimmy Cardew, Liverpool .... W 8
Aug. 28—Tommy Higgins, Liverpool .... W 8
Sept. 11—Stan Skinkiss, Liverpool ......KO 7
Sept. 22—Eddie McCormick, Manchester . W 8
Oct. 9—Eddie Carson, Liverpool .... W 10
Oct. 27—Tommy Proffitt, Manchester .. W 8
Nov. 14—Tommy Proffitt, Manchester .KO 7
Dec. 8—Pierre Cossemyns, Leeds ....L 10
Dec. 15—Bobby Boland, Manchester ...KO 5

1953
Jan. 8—Jackie Briers, Liverpool .... W 10
Jan. 30—Johnny Haywood, Blackpool . LF 3
Feb. 27—Luis Romero, Manchester .....KO 8
Mar. 24—Emile Chemema, London . KO by 5
July 9—Denny Dawson, Liverpool ....KO 4
Aug. 27—Tommy Higgins, Liverpool .... W 8
Sept. 7—Juan Alvarez, Newcastle ....L 10
Oct. 6—Sammy McCarthy, London .... W 10
Dec. 8—Billy Kelly, London ....L 8

1954

Date	Opponent	Result
Mar. 4	Johnny Butterworth, Liverpool	W 10
Apr. 29	Jean Sneyers, Liverpool	W 10
June 3	Enrico Macale, Liverpool	W 8
July 2	Jacques Legendre, Manchester	W 10
Aug. 12	Joe Woussem, Liverpool	L 8
Sept. 3	Luis Romero, Manchester	W 10
Oct. 27	Harry Ramsden, Blackpool	W 8
Nov. 30	Aime Devisch, Leeds	W 10

1955

Date	Opponent	Result
Jan. 31	Percy Lewis, Nottingham	W 8
Mar. 22	Marcel Ranvial, London	KO 5
June 3	Andre Pierson, Manchester	W 10
Aug. 25	Juan Alvarez, Liverpool	W 10
Oct. 8	Joe Quinn, Belfast	KO 1
Nov. 19	Billy Kelly, Belfast	KO 8

(British Empire featherweight title)

1956

Date	Opponent	Result
Feb. 7	Jean Sneyers, London	KO 4
Mar. 22	Louis Cabo, Liverpool	KO 4
May 3	Aldo Pravisani, Liverpool	W 8
Sept. 6	Alby Tissong, Liverpool	W 8
Oct. 21	Jean Sneyers, Liege	KO by 4
Nov. 26	Dos Santos, Leicester	W 10

1957

Date	Opponent	Result
Apr. 1	Percy Lewis, Nottingham	W 15

(British Empire Featherweight Title)

Date	Opponent	Result
Apr. 26	Miguel Berrios, Washington	W 12
June 24	Cherif Hamia, Paris	KO 10

(Won Vacant World Featherweight Title)

Date	Opponent	Result
Oct. 7	Victor Pepeder, Nottingham	W 10
Oct. 31	Relinquished British Empire Feather	

Title.

1958

Date	Opponent	Result
Jan. 23	Pierre Cossemyns, Liverpool	W 10
Apr. 1	Ricardo Moreno, Los Angeles	KO 3

(World Featherweight Title)

Date	Opponent	Result
June 24	Jules Touan, London	KO 7
Sept. 20	Willie Pep, Boston	KO 9
Oct. 31	Carmelo Costa, New York	W 10
Dec. 13	Ernesto Parra, Hollywood	W 10

1959

Date	Opponent	Result
Mar. 18	Davey Moore, Los Angeles	KO by 13

(Lost World Featherweight Title)

Date	Opponent	Result
Aug. 19	Davey Moore, Los Angeles	KO by 11

(For World Featherweight Title)

Appointed director of Physical Education in Nigeria by the Nigerian Government, 1963.

TB	KO	WD	WF	D	LD	LF	KOBY	ND	NC
68	20	35	0	1	6	2	4	0	0

DAVEY MOORE

Springfield, Ohio, Featherweight
Born, November 1, 1933, Lexington, Ky.
Height, 5 ft. 2½ in.
1952 National A. A. U. 118 lbs. Champion.
(Represented U. S. in 1952 Olympic Games in Helsinki; eliminated in third round of bantamweight series by Ho King of Korea.)

1953

Date	Opponent	Result
May 11	Willie Reece, Portsmouth	W 6
May 25	Ralph Capone, Chicago	W 4
June 1	Terry Book, Chicago	W 5
June 15	Dick Armstrong, Portsmouth	KO 4
July 10	Eddie Gonzales, Ft. Williams	KO 1
Aug. 29	Ed Hughes, Chicago	KO 4
Oct. 3	Russ Tague, Chicago	L 6
Nov. 20	Eddie Cooper, Dayton	KO 3

1954

Date	Opponent	Result
Jan. 5	Eddie Crawford, Columbus	KO 2
Feb. 4	Jackie Blair, Akron	L 10
Mar. 13	Bob Keeling, Cincinnati	KO 3
Apr. 1	Leo Carter, Cincinnati	KO 2
Apr. 8	Jack Ingram, Springfield	KO 1
Apr. 20	Charley Riley, St. Louis	W 10
May 18	Herky Kaminsky, Springfield	D 10
June 29	Herky Kaminsky, Springfield	W 10
Oct. 25	Dick Armstrong, Dayton	KO 6
Dec. 7	Eddie Burgin, Cincinnati	KO 9

1955

Date	Opponent	Result
Jan. 16	John Barnes, Detroit	W 6
Mar. 1	Isidro Martinez, Colon	L 10
July 16	Santiago Martinez, Havana	L 10
May 15	Pedro Tesis, Colon	W 10
Sept. 19	Ray Riojas, El Paso	W 10
Oct. 17	Nat Jackson, New Orleans	KO 2
Dec. 16	Jimmy Hackney, New York	W. Dis. 6

1956

Date	Opponent	Result
June 5	Charlie Slaughter, Montreal	KO 4
Oct. 10	Jimmy DeMura, Chicago	W 6
Nov. 7	Bobby Rogers, Chicago	L 8

1957

Date	Opponent	Result
Apr. 10	Gil Cadilli, Miami	W 10
June 13	Buddy McDonald, Spokane	W 10
July 5	Isidro Martinez, Washington	W 10
Aug. 14	Victor Manuel Quijano, Syr.	W 10
Nov. 8	Jose Cotero, Washington	W 10

1958

Date	Opponent	Result
Jan. 9	Victor Manuel Quijano, Los Angeles	KO 9
Feb. 20	Fili Nava, Los Angeles	W 10
Mar. 6	Vince Delgado, Los Angeles	KO 3
May 25	Roberto Garcia, Mex. City	W 10
June 19	Lauro Salas, Los Angeles	W 10
July 28	Kid Anahuac, Tijuana	W 10
Sept. 25	Kid Anahuac, Los Angeles	W 10
Dec. 11	Ricardo Moreno, Los Angeles	KO 1

1959

Date	Opponent	Result
Mar. 18	Hogan (Kid) Bassey, Los Ang.	KO 13

(Won World Featherweight Title)

Date	Opponent	Result
Aug. 19	Hogan (Kid) Bassey, Los Ang.	KO 11

(Title Bout)

Date	Opponent	Result
Oct. 20	Bobby Neill, London	KO 1
Dec. 14	Hilario Morales, San Francisco	W 10

1960

Date	Opponent	Result
Feb. 22	Sergio Caprari, Caracas	KO 8

(non-title)

Date	Opponent	Result
Mar. 14	Carlos Hernandez, Caracas	KO by 7

(non-title)

Date	Opponent	Result
July 20	Frank Valdez, Albuquerque	KO 7

(non-title)

Date	Opponent	Result
Aug. 1	Kid Irapuato, Tijuana	W 10
Aug. 29	Kazuo Takayama, Tokyo	W 15

(Retained Title)

Date	Opponent	Result
Nov. 27	Dave Camacho, Nogales	KO 8
Dec. 3	Rudy Carona, Obregon	KO 7

(non-title)

1961

Date	Opponent	Result
Jan. 9	Gracieux Lamperti, Paris	W 10

(non-title)

Date	Opponent	Result
Jan. 27	Fred Galiana, Madrid	KO 4

(non-title)

Date	Opponent	Result
Feb. 10	Ray Nobile, Rome	W 10

(non-title)

Date	Opponent	Result
Apr. 8	Danny Valdez, Los Angeles	KO 1

(Retained title)

Date	Opponent	Result
July 6	Gil Cadilli, Las Vegas	W 10

(non-title)

Date	Opponent	Result
July 16	Pelon Cervantes, Mexicali	W 10

(non-title)

Date	Opponent	Result
Sept. 20	Kid Irapuato, Juarez	KO 7

(Non-Title)

Date	Opponent	Result
Oct. 12	Pelon Cervantes, Los Angeles	KO 5

(Non-Title)

Date	Opponent	Result
Nov. 13	Kazuo Takayama, Tokyo	W 15

(Retained Title)

1962

Date	Opponent	Result
Mar. 9	Cisco Andrade, Los Angeles	KO 7

(non-title)

Date	Opponent	Result
July 9	Mario Diaz, Los Angeles	KO 2

(non-title)

Date	Opponent	Result
Aug. 17	Olli Makim Helsinki	KO 2

(Retained Featherweight Title)

Date	Opponent	Result
Dec. 11	Fili Nava, San Antonio	W 10

(non-title)

1963

Date	Opponent	Result
Feb. 18	Gil Cadilli, San Jose	KO 5
Mar. 21	Sugar Ramos, Los Angeles	KO by 10

(Lost World Featherweight Championship)

Mar. 23—Moore died in Los Angeles, Calif. of brain injuries received in the Ramos fight.

TB	KO	WD	WF	D	LD	LF	KOBY	ND	NC
67	30	28	1	1	5	0	2	0	0

ULTIMINIO (SUGAR) RAMOS

(Ultimo Ramos Zaqueira)
Cuban Featherweight
Born, December 2, 1941, Matanzas, Cuba

1957

Date	Opponent	Result
Oct. 5	Rene Arce, Havana	KO 2
Nov. 30	Inocencio Cartas, Havana	KO 3

1958

Date	Opponent	Result
Jan. 11	Juan Machado, Havana	KO 2
Feb. 7	Carlos Suarez, Ranchuelo	KO 2
Apr. 12	Felix Pomares, Havana	KO 2

May   24—Humberto DelaRosa, Havana .KO 4
July   5—Hector Medina, Havana ......KO 3
July 19—Manuel Perdomo, Havana ..... W 6
Aug.   9—Wilfredo Gonzalez,
        Cienfuegos......................KO 2
Sept. 20—Al Castillo, Havana ....KO 5
Oct. 11—Augusto Narvalle, Havana . W Dis. 6
Nov.   8—Jose Blanco, Havana ....KO 8
Dec. 13—Tono Coria, Havana..........KO 4
1959
Feb. 14—Orlando Castillo, Havana ....KO 10
Mar. 28—Wally Livingston, Havana ....KO 10
May   9—Angel Guerrero, Havana .....KO 4
June 29—Sonny Leon, Caracas........ W 10
Aug.   1—Johnny Bean, Havana ....KO 3
Oct. 31—Ike Chestnut, Caracas .... D 10
Nov. 20—Francisco Barraez, Matanzas ... W 10
1960
Feb. 27—Orlando Castillo, Havana ...... W 12
        (Won Cuban Featherweight Title)
Apr.   1—Tony Padron, Caracas ....KO 8
May   28—Vernon Lynch, Havana ......KO 7
Aug. 17—Tony Padron, Havana ....KO 8
Aug. 29—Jesus Santamaria, Colon .....KO 9
Dec. 30—Chato Gomez, Havana ....KO 9
1961
Jan. 23—Jesus Santamaria,
        Panama City ....KO 6
Feb.   8—Edwin Sykes, Panama City ...KO 4
Apr. 22—Juan Ramirez, Mexico City ...TD 6
May   8—Felix Cervantes, Tijuana .....KO 3
May   27—Bobby Cervantes,
        Guadalajara....................KO 4
June 17—Alfredo Urbina, Mexico City......W 12
Sept. 2—Alfredo Urbina, Mexico City ... D 10
Sept. 30—Kid Anahuac, Guadalajara ..... W 10
Dec. 13—Rafael Camacho, Puebla ... L. Dis. 4
1962
Jan. 12—Eddie Garcia, Los Angeles ....KO 9
Mar. 26—Rafiu King, Paris .... W 10
May   11—Danny Valdez, Los Angeles ...KO 7
July 15—Baby Vasquez, Mexico City ... W 10
Sept. 3—Baby Vasquez, Tijuana ......KO 10
Oct. 20—Eloy Sanchez, Mexico City ...KO 3
Dec. 30—Jose Luis Cruz, Mexico City ..KO 2
1963
Mar. 21—Davey Moore, Los Angeles ....KO 10
        (Won World Featherweight Championship)
July 13—Rafiu King, Mexico City ...... W 15
        (Retained World Featherweight
        Championship)
Oct. 22—Sammy McSpadden, London .KO 2
Nov.   9—Kid Anahuac, Los Mochis ....KO 8
1964
Jan. 10—Vicente Derado, Los Angeles .. W 10
Feb. 28—Mitsunori Seki, Tokyo ....KO 6
        (Retained World Featherweight Title)
May   9—Floyd Robertson, Accra....... W 15
        (Retained World Featherweight Title)
Sept. 26—Vicente Saldivar,
        Mexico City ....KO by 12
        (Lost World Featherweight Title)
1965
Apr. 18—Chiquis Rosales, Acapulco ..... W 10
Aug. 24—Raul Soriano, Tijuana ......KO 6
Dec. 11—Raul Soriano, Mexico City ....KO 2
1966
Feb. 12—Antonio Herrera, Mexico City . W 10
Oct. 22—Carlos Ortiz, Mexico City .. KO by 5
        (World Lightweight Title)
1967
July   1—Carlos Ortiz, San Juan ..... KO by 4
        (World Lightweight Title)
1968
        (Inactive)
1969
June 29—Rudy Gonzalez, Mexico City .KO 2
        (Started comeback as a lightweight)
Sept. 30—Chango Carmona, Tijuana ....KO 7
Dec. 14—German Gastelbondo,
        Vera Cruz......................KO 1
1970
Mar. 26—Raul Rojas, Los Angeles .... W 10
Aug.   7—Mando Ramos, Los Angeles.......L 10
1971
Jan.   5—Antonio Amaya, Monterrey ....L 10
Oct. 15—Jimmv Robertson, Los Angeles D 10
1972
Mar. 24—Lyle Randolph, Chicago ......KO 7
Apr. 25—Cesar Sinda, Los Angeles .. KO by 10

VICENTE SALDIVAR

(Vincente Samuel Saldivar Garcia)
Born, May 3, 1943, Mexico City, Mexico. Weight,
126 lbs. Height, 5 ft. 3 in. Southpaw. Managed by Adolfo
Perez.

1961
Feb. 18—Baby Palacios, Oaxaca .... KO 1
Mar. 22—Frijol Gonzalez, Oaxaca .... KO 4
Apr. 16—Cachorro Meza, Oaxaca .... KO 3
May   20—Babe Lopez, Leon .... KO 3
Oct. 14—Jose Luis Mora, Huachinango ... W 10
Dec.   3—Juan Rodriguez, Leon .... KO 6
1962
Jan.   6—Ernesto Beltran, Acapulco .... KO 6
Feb.   8—Rosendo Martinez, Huachinango .. KO 5
Mar. 18—Juan Zavala, Tuxtla Gutierrez ... KO 10
Apr.   4—Jorge Salazar, Matamoros .... KO 4
May   2—Genaro Gonzalez, Mexico City W disq. 8
June 27—Indio Fernandez, Mexico City .... KO 6
Aug. 22—Alberto Soto, Mexico City .... KO 2
Oct. 11—Chamco Hernandez, Los Mochis .. KO 1
Nov. 17—Toluco II, Monterrey .... W 10
Dec. 29—Baby Luis, Mexico City .... L disq. 7
1963
Mar. 16—Luis Hernandez, Los Mochis ...... KO 2
Apr. 19—Dwight Hawkins, Monterrey ..... KO 5
June 12—Baby Luis, Mexico City .... KO 8
July 13—Eloy Sanchez, Mexico City .... KO 1
Sept. 21—Beresford Francis, Mexico City ... KO 2
Dec. 16—Felix Gutierrez, Cuernavaca ..... KO 3
1964
Feb.   8—Juan Ramirez, Mexico City ...... KO 2
        (Won Mexican Featherweight Title)
Apr.   4—Eduardo Guerrero, Mexico City .... W 12
        (Retained Mexican Featherweight Title)
June   1—Ismael Laguna, Tijuana .... W 10
Sept. 26—Sugar Ramos, Mexico City .... KO 12
        (Won World Featherweight Title)
Dec.   6—Delfino Rosales, Leon .... KO 11
        (Retained World Featherweight Title)
1965
May   7—Raul Rojas, Los Angeles .... KO 15
        (Retained World Featherweight Title)
Sept. 7—Howard Winstone, London .... W 15
        (Retained World Featherweight Title)
1966
Feb. 12—Floyd Robertson, Mexico City ... KO 2
        (Retained World Featherweight Title)
Aug.   7—Mitsunori Seki, Mexico City ...... W' 15
        (Retained World Featherweight Title)
1967
Jan. 29—Mitsunori Seki, Mexico City ...... KO 7
        (Retained World Featherweight Title)
June 15—Howard Winstone, Cardiff .... W 15
        (Retained World Featherweight Title)
Oct. 14—Howard Winstone, Mexico City ... KO 12
        (Retained World Featherweight Title)
Oct. 14—Announced retirement.
1968
        (Inactive)
1969
July 18—Jose Legra, Los Angeles .... W 10
1970
May   9—Johnny Famechon, Rome .... W 15
        (Regained World Featherweight Title)
Dec. 11—Kuniaki Shibata, Tijuana ..... KO by 13
        (Lost World Featherweight Title)
1971
July 15—Frankie Crawford, Los Angeles .... W 10
1972
        (Inactive)
1973
Oct. 20—Eder Jofre, Salvador .... KO by 4
        (For World Featherweight Title)

	TB	KO	WD	WF	D	LD	LF	KO BY	ND	NC
	65	39	14	1	4	2	1	4	0	0
	39	25	10	1	0	0	1	2	0	0

HOWARD WINSTONE

Born, April 15, 1939, Merthyr Tydfil, Glamorganshire, Wales. Weight, 126 lbs.
1958 British ABA bantamweight champion. 1958 British Empire Games bantamweight champion.

1959
Feb.	24—Billy Graydon, London	W	6
Mar.	14—Peter Sexton, Newport	W	6
Apr.	15—Tommy Williams, Cardiff	W	6
May	27—Jackie Bowers, Cardiff	W	6
June	24—Jake O'Neal, Porthcawl	W	6
July	14—Ollie Wylie, Aberdare	W	6
Aug.	8—Hugh O'Neill, Ebbw Vale	W	6
Sept.	1—Billy Calvert, Aberdare	KO	7
Sept.	14—Joe Taylor, Ebbw Vale	KO	4
Dec.	14—Billy Calvert, London	W	8

1960
Jan.	14—George O'Neill, Cardiff	KO	7
Jan.	25—Robbie Wilson, London	W	8
Feb.	4—Colin Salcombe, Birmingham	KO	6
Feb.	24—Terry Rees, Cardiff	KO	8
Mar.	31—Gordon Blakey, Cardiff	KO	8
May	9—George Carroll, Swansea	KO	4
May	19—Con Mount Bassie, Birmingham	W	10
June	23—Noel Hazard, Birmingham	KO	3
July	27—Phil Jones, Porthcawl	W	10
Aug.	15—Sergio Milan, Aberdare	KO	6
Sept.	22—Jean Renard, Cardiff	KO	8
Oct.	25—Jean Renard, London	W	8
Nov.	28—Roy Jacobs, Carmarthen	W	10

1961
Jan.	19—Floyd Robertson, Cardiff	W	10
May	2—Terry Spinks, London	KO	10
	(Won British Featherweight Title)		
Aug.	24—Aryee Jackson, Liverpool	W	10
Sept.	4—Gene Fosmire, Cardiff	W	10
Nov.	20—Olli Maki, Nottingham	W	8

1962
Jan.	9—Oripies Dos Santos, London	W	8
Apr.	10—Derry Treanor, London	KO	14
	(Retained British Featherweight Title)		
May	30—Harry Carroll, Cardiff	KO	6
	(Retained British Featherweight Title)		
Aug.	2—Dennis Adjei, Cardiff	W	8
Aug.	18—George Bowes, Newtown	W	10
Sept.	11—Bill Davis, London	KO	7
Nov.	5—Leroy Jeffery, Leeds	KO by	2
Dec.	10—Freddie Dobson, Manchester	KO	3
Dec.	27—Teddy Rand, London	KO	3

1963
Jan.	31—Johnny Morrissey, Glasgow	KO	11
	(Retained British Featherweight Title)		
Apr.	29—Gracieux Lamperti, Cardiff	KO	8
May	13—Juan Cardenas, London	W	8
July	19—Alberto Serti, Cardiff	KO	14
	(Won European Featherweight Title)		
Aug.	20—Billy Calvert, Porthcawl	W	15
	(Retained British and European Featherweight Titles)		
Sept.	20—Miguel Kimbo Calderin, Corwen	W	10
Dec.	9—John O'Brien, London	W	15
	(Retained British and European Featherweight Titles)		

1964
Jan.	28—Don Johnson, London	L	10
Mar.	24—Joe Rafiu King, London	W	10
May	12—Lino Mastellaro, London	KO	8
	(Retained European Featherweight Title)		
June	22—Phil Lundgren, London	KO	7
Sept.	21—Jose Bisbal, Manchester	W	10
Dec.	1—Baby Luis, London	W	10
Dec.	14—Boualem Belouard, Nottingham	W	10

1965
Jan.	22—Yves Desmarets, Rome	W	15
	(Retained European Featherweight Title)		
Mar.	29—Don Johnson, Carmarthen	W	10
June	1—Lalo Guerrero, Mexico City	KO	5
June	00—Jose Legra, Blackpool	W	10
Sept.	7—Vicente Saldivar, London	L	15
	(For World Featherweight Title)		
Dec.	14—Brian Cartwright, London	KO	9

1966
Mar.	7—Andrea Silanos, Sassari	KO	15
	(Retained European Featherweight Title)		
Sept.	6—Jean de Deers, London	KO	3
	(Retained European Featherweight Title)		
Oct.	10—Don Johnson, Manchester	W disq.	4
Dec.	7—Lenny Williams, Aberavon	KO	8
	(Retained British and European Featherweight Titles)		

1967
Jan.	17—Richard Sue, London	W	10
June	15—Vicente Saldivar, Cardiff	L	15
	(For World Featherweight Title)		
Oct.	14—Vicente Saldivar, Mexico City	KO by	12
	(For World Featherweight Title)		

1968
Jan.	23—Mitsunori Seki, London	KO	9
	(Won Vacant British World Featherweight Title)		
Apr.	9—Jimmy Anderson, London	W	10
July	24—Jose Legra, Porthcawl	KO by	5
	(Lost British World Featherweight Title)		
	(For Vacant WBC Featherweight Title)		

1969
Mar.	—Relinquished British featherweight title.	
	—Announced retirement.	

TB	KO	WD	WF	D	LD	LF	KO BY	ND	NC
67	27	33	1	0	3	0	3	0	0

RAUL ROJAS

Born, November 5, 1941, San Pedro, California. Weight, 126-130 lbs. Height, 5 ft. 4 in. Managed by Jackie McCoy and Lou Prlia.

1963
Jan.	15—Ray Coleman, San Diego	KO	1
Jan.	22—Frankie Corpus, San Diego	W	4
Mar.	8—Freddie Burris, Los Angeles	KO	6
Apr.	19—Julio Zuniga, Los Angeles	TD	3
May	3—Frankie Souza, Los Angeles	W	6
June	6—Apolonio Reyes, Los Angeles	KO	2
Aug.	16—Tom O'Connor, Los Angeles	KO	3
Sept.	5—Louis Arreola, Los Angeles	KO	5
Sept.	26—Charley Robinson, Los Angeles	KO	2
Oct.	10—Lalo Larranaga, Los Angeles	KO	7
Oct.	24—Ronnie Taylor, Los Angeles	KO	4
Oct.	31—Joe Jacobs, Los Angeles	KO	1
Nov.	21—Sergio Gomez, Los Angeles	W	10
Dec.	12—Julio Zuniga, Los Angeles	KO	5

1964
Jan.	10—Al Medrano, Los Angeles	KO	7
Feb.	18—Ray Coleman, No. Hollywood	KO	5
Mar.	19—Pepino Morales, Los Angeles	KO	1
Apr.	10—Joey Olguin, Los Angeles	KO	6
May	29—Eloy Sanchez, Los Angeles	W	10
June	18—Danny Kid, Los Angeles	W	10
Sept.	11—Eloy Sanchez, Los Angeles	W	10
Oct.	13—Fidel Cruz, San Jose	KO	2
Nov.	12—Porfirio Zamora, Los Angeles	KO	6
Dec.	4—Chu Chu Garcia, Los Angeles	W	10

1965
May	7—Vicente Saldivar, Los Angeles	KO by	15
	(For World Featherweight Title)		

1966
Jan.	28—Alton Colter, Los Angeles	W	10
Mar.	18—Ricardo Moreno, Los Angeles	KO	3
June	3—Ricardo Moreno, Los Angeles	KO	2
July	26—Arturo Vingochea, Sacramento	KO	6
Aug.	24—Pete Gonzalez, San Jose	W	10

1967
Feb.	9—Jerry Stevens, Las Vegas	KO	2
Feb.	27—Ray Coleman, Oakland	KO	7
May	25—Vicente Derado, Los Angeles	KO	15
	(Won California Junior Lightweight Title)		
Sept.	14—Suh-Il Kang, Los Angeles	W	15
	(Retained California Junior Lightweight Title)		
Dec.	14—Antonio Herrera, Los Angeles	W	15
	(Retained California Featherweight Title)		

1968
Mar.	28—Enrique Higgins, Los Angeles	W	15
	(Won Vacant WBA Featherweight Title)		
June	6—Shozo Saijyo, Los Angeles	L	10
Aug.	17—Eliseo Estrada, Ventura	W	10

737

Sept. 28—Shozo Saijyo, Los Angeles .... L 15
    (Lost WBA Featherweight Title)

1969

Apr. 1—Roberto Arias, Sacramento ...... KO 10
Nov. 11—Rogelio Tulunghai, San Antonio .. KO 7

1970

Jan. 20—Enrique Jana, Sacramento .... D 10
Mar. 3—Leonardo Aguero, Los Angeles ..... W 10
Mar. 26—Sugar Ramos, Los Angeles .... L 10
July 9—Ruben Navarro, Los Angeles .... L 10
Dec. 10—Mando Ramos, Los Angeles ... KO by 6

TB	KO	WD	WF	D	LD	LF	KO BY	ND	NC
46	24	14	0	2	4	0	2	0	0

JOSE LEGRA

European Featherweight Champion, former WBC world featherweight champion. Born in Cuba April 19, 1943. Early record in Cuba, Mexico and Florida:
Knockouts—Indio Iguamo, 2; Eugenio Jiminez, 3; Huracan Diez, 3; Baby Recio, 3. Won decisions—Tomas Perez, Jose Martinez, Julian Perez (twice), Indio del Sur, Raul Nunez, Luis Odio, Lopido Galvez (twice), Oribazo, Esteban Castillo, Raimondo Pelegrini, Vicente Nunez, Pedro Soto, Andres Perez, Pedro Pinera, Miguel Oliva (twice), Jimmy Escudero, Juan Fernandez, Enrique Yamuri.
Drew—Ramon Ferrer, Juan Fernandez.
Lost decisions—Vicente Nunez, Augustin Carmona, Baby Luis (twice).
Knocked out by—Angel Ray.
Record in Europe:

1963

Undated bouts:
Knockout—Laichi, 5. Won decisions—Jose Luis Martinez, 8 (twice), Jose Luis Biescas, 8; Tony Alonso, 8.

1963

Nov. 2—Baldomero Arroyo, Madrid ....W 8
Dec. 4—Luis Aisa, Barcelona ....W 8
Dec. 12—Juan Aguiliera, Barcelona ....W 8

1964

Jan. 11—Jose Luis Martinez, Madrid ....W 8
Feb. 5—Jose Luis Martinez, Barcelona ....W 8
Feb. 15—Tony Alonso, Madrid....................W 8
Feb. 26—Luis Biescas, Bilbao.................W 8
Mar. 14—Jose Luis Martinez, Bilbao ....W 8
Mar. 31—Kid Tano, Teneriffe....................D 8
May 7—Kimbo Calderin, Madrid ....W 8
May 23—Kid Tano, Las Palmas ....W 10
July 2—Angel Rodriguez, Valencia............KO 1
July 18—Rafael Gayo, LaCorunna ....W 8
Aug. 8—Kimbo Calderin, Valencia ....W 10
Aug. 23—Kid Tano, Las Palmas ....W 8
Sept. 5—Luis Ansa, Madrid ....W 8
Sept. 18—Vincenzo Putardi, Madrid ....W 8
Oct. 10—Antoine Lucausi, Madrid ....W 8
Oct. 31—Luis Ansa, Madrid ....W 8
Nov. 14—Sanchez Merayo, Madrid ....KO 2
Nov. 26—Renato Galli, Barcelona ....W 8
Dec. 4—Tony Alonso, Madrid...................W 8

1965

Jan. 22—Juan Pinto, Madrid ....W 8
Jan. 30—Angel Neches, Bilbao ....D 8
Feb. 26—Mario Sitri, Madrid ....W 10
Mar. 6—D. Cabrera, Tenerife ....KO 6
Mar. 13—Kimbo Calderin, Tenerife ....W 10
Apr. 2—Antonio Paiva, Madrid ....W 8
June 2—Dos Santos, Madrid ....W 10
June 23—Howard Winstone, Blackpool..........L 10
Aug. 17—Lope DePablo, Madrid ....W 8
Sept. 5—Tano Tartarini, LaCoruna ....KO 1
Sept. 19—Juan Leon, San Sebastian ....KO 5
Sept. 25—Luis Segura, Valladolid ....W 8
Oct. 19—Barretto, San Sebastian ....KO 4
Oct. 30—Jose Bisbal, San Sebastian ....W 10
Nov. 12—Ramon Casal, Madrid ....W 8
Nov. 26—Manuel Calvo, Madrid ....W 10
Dec. 18—Manuel Calvo, Salamonica .....:.....W 8

1966

Jan. 6—Juan Rodriguez, Almeria ....W 8
Feb. 13—Cristobal Gomez, Almeria ....W 8
Mar. 3—Antonio Paiva, Barcelona ....KO 7
Mar. 17—Ove Turpin, Barcelona................KO 2
Apr. 3—Jesus Zarco, Santander ....W 10
Apr. 15—Omar Oliva, Madrid ....W 8

Apr. 30—Cristobal Kirby, Malaga................W 8
May 7—Ben Amar, San Sebastian ....W 8
May 21—Angel Chinea, Santander...............W 8
June 4—Jose Torcida, Santander...............W 10
July 9—Jose Ribeiro, Oviedo..................KO 7
July 29—Celmiro Rios, Barcelona ....KO 3
Aug. 21—Tommy Thompson, San Sebastian.......KO 1
Sept. 2—Julio Chico, Madrid ....KO 7
Sept. 9—Vicenzo Pitardi, Madrid ....KO 5
Oct. 1—Raul Tejera, Gijon ....KO 2
Oct. 15—Segu Valli, Sargossa ....KO 2
Oct. 16—Cristobal Gomez, Sargossa............KO 2
Oct. 26—Roberto Marthon, Bilbao ....KO 2
Oct. 29—Segu Valli, Sargossa ....KO 2
Nov. 12—Chico Carvajal, Gijon ....W 8
Nov. 24—Omar Oliva, Barcelona ....KO 9
Nov. 30—Became Spanish citizen.
Dec. 2—Jean DeKeers, Madrid ....KO 1
Dec. 23—Love Allotey, Madrid ....W 12

1967

Jan. 8—La Russ, Las Palmas..................KO 3
Jan. 16—Roger Younsi, Tenerife ....W 10
Jan. 22—Julio Gonzalez, Tenerife ....W 10
Feb. 12—Salvatore Gennatiempo, Madrid.......KO 6
Mar. 10—Rafiu King, Madrid ....W 10
Mar. 18—Ameur Lamine, Tenerife ....KO 1
Apr. 28—Ben Said Souita, Tenerife ....KO 1
June 3—Maurice Tavant, Madrid ....W 10
June 10—Paul Rourre, San Sebastian ....W 10
June 24—Jose Torcida, Leon ....W 10
June 30—Don Johnson, Madrid ....W 10
Sept. 2—Fernando Tavares, Tenerife ....KO 7
Sept. 30—Paul Rourre, Santa Cruz..............W 10
Nov. 9—Benito Gallardo, Barcelona ....KO 3
Dec. 22—Yves Desmerets, Madrid ....KO 3
    (Vacant European Featherweight Title)

1968

Feb. 2—Ernesto Miranda, Bilbao ....W 10
Mar. 14—Ernesto Miranda, Barcelona ....KO 4
Apr. 25—Joe Tetteh, Barcelona ....W 10
May 10—Klaus Jacoby, Madrid ....KO 6
June 10—Fernando Tavares, Logrno ....KO 2
July 24—Howard Winstone, Porthcawl........KO 5
Oct. 6—Bob Allotey, Bilbao ....W 10
Oct. 28—Felix Brami, Paris ....KO 1

1969

Jan. 21—Johnny Famechon, London ....L 15
    (Lost WBC world featherweight title)
May 30—Vicente Pina, Madrid ....KO 4
June 13—Domenico Scalco, Madrid ....KO 1
July 19—Vicente Saldivar, Los Angeles ....L 10
Oct. 5—Reyes Miller, Madrid ....KO 2
Dec. 11—Miguel Herrera, Barcelona ....KO 2

1970

Feb. 5—Evan Armstrong, Barcelona ....W 10
Mar. 5—Jimmy Bell, Barcelona ....W 10
Apr. 11—Rolf Kersten, Tenerife ....KO 1
May 26—Dom Chilorio, Madrid ....KO 7
June 26—Tommaso Galli, Madrid ....W 15
    (won European featherweight title)
Oct. 25—Ugo Poli, Madrid ....W 10
Nov. 14—Bruno Melissano, Madrid ....W 10
Dec. 12—Abel Almarez, Santa Cruz ....KO 4
Dec. 26—Renato Galli, Alicante ....W 10

1971

Jan. 25—Jimmy Revie, London ....W 15
    (European featherweight title)
Apr. 15—Maurice Cordier, Barcelona ....KO 3
May 8—David Pesenti, Bilbao ....KO 8
May 21—Ben Tahar Hassan, Madrid ....KO 4
    (Non title)
Aug. 14—Giovanni Girgenti, Alicante ....KO 9
    (European feather title)
Aug. 26—Marius Cordier, Alicante ....KO 5

1972

Jan. 15—Ben Salah, Alicante ....KO 1
Feb. 15—Evan Armstrong, London ....W 15
    (European featherweight title)
May 17—Tommy Glencross, Birmingham ......KO 10
June 22—Jonathan Dele, Barcelona ....L 10
Oct. 6—Daniel Vermandere, Madrid ....W 15
    (European featherweight title)
Dec. 16—Clemente Sanchez, Monterrey ....KO 10
    (Awarded WBC Title)

1973

May 4—Eder Jofre, Brasioia .... L 15
Aug. 1—Jimmy Bell, Palma .... W 10
Nov. 24—Alexis Arguello, Managua ..... KO by 1

1975

Nov. 10—Daniel Valdez, Los Angeles .... W 10

TB	KO	WD	WF	D	LD	LF	KO BY	ND	NC
153	50	87	0	4	9	0	3	0	0

SHOZO SAIJYO

Born, January 28, 1947, Kita-adachi-Gun, Saitama, Japan. Weight, 126 lbs. Height, 5 ft. $7\frac{1}{2}$ in.

1964

Aug. 13—Masaru Nakatsuka, Tokyo .... W 4
Sept. 28—Masao Totsuka, Tokyo .... W 4
Oct. 26—Saburo Nakatsu, Tokyo .... W 4
Nov. 17—Masahiko Takamatsu, Tokyo .... D 4
Dec. 4—Koji Ikeda, Tokyo .... D 4
Dec. 28—Mineharu Okimoto, Tokyo .... L 6

1965

Apr. 4—Fighting Harada, Tokyo .... Exh. 2
May 27—Kohei Ogasawara, Tokyo .... W 6
July 4—Hatsuo Kanai, Tokyo .... W 6
July 25—Masamitsu Takamatsu, Tokyo ..... W 6
Oct. 3—Sueyoshi Seki, Tokyo .... W 6
Dec. 26—Mikio Sakai, Tokyo .... W 6

1966

June 27—Haruhiko Kakagome, Tokyo .... W 6
Sept. 19—Kyuzo Hashimoto, Tokyo .... L 8
Oct. 31—Toshimasa Hasegawa, Tokyo .... L 8

1967

Jan. 23—Tadahiko Tsushima, Tokyo .... W 8
Feb. 27—Yoshihiro Kawakami, Tokyo ...... W 10
Mar. 20—Takeo Bando, Tokyo .... KO 4
Sept. 11—Toyoharu Mizuta, Tokyo .... KO 3

1968

Jan. 7—Ignacio Pina, Sinaloa .... L 10
Jan. 25—Tony Alvarado, Los Angeles ...... KO 4
Feb. 15—Jose Luis Pimental, Los Angeles ... L 10
Mar. 21—Jose Luis Pimental, Los Angeles ... W 10
June 6—Raul Rojas, Los Angeles .... W 10
Sept. 28—Raul Rojas, Los Angeles .... W 15
(Won WBA Featherweight Title)
Nov. 18—Flash Besande, Tokyo .... KO 8

1969

Feb. 9—Pedro Gomez, Tokyo .... W 15
(Retained WBA Featherweight Title)
Apr. 14—Pedro Rodriguez, Osaka .... W 10
June 16—Marcelo Kid, Tokyo .... KO 1
Sept. 7—Jose Luis Pimental, Sapporo ..... KO 2
(Retained WBA Featherweight Title)
Nov. 4—Felipe Torres, Honolulu .... W 10

1970

Feb. 8—Godfrey Stevens, Tokyo .... W 15
(Retained WBA Featherweight Title)
Apr. 19—Lion San, Tokyo .... KO 3
July 5—Frankie Crawford, Sendai .... W 15
(Retained WBA Featherweight Title)
Oct. 21—Isami Nutta, Utsunomiya .... KO 4
Dec. 3—Hiroshi Kobayashi, Tokyo .... L 10

1971

Feb. 28—Frankie Crawford, Utsunomiya .... W 15
(Retained WBA Featherweight Title)
July 1—Ray Vega, Sapporo .... W 10
Sept. 2—Antonio Gomez, Tokyo .... KO by 5
(Lost WBA Featherweight Title)

TB	KO	WD	WF	D	LD	LF	KO BY	ND	NC
38	8	21	0	2	6	0	1	0	0

JOHNNY FAMECHON

Australian Featherweight Champion

Born, France, March 28, 1945 (Son of Andre of noted French boxing clan). Began career in Australia in 1961.

1961

June 7—Sammy Lang, Melbourne .... D 3
Aug. 4—Salvatore Casabene, Melbourne ....KO 2
Sept. 15—Peter Barnes, Melbourne .....KO 4

1962

Apr. 6—Brian Levier, Melbourne .... D 4
June 1—Gordon Crooks, Melbourne ...KO 2
June 22—Roy Spackman, Melbourne .....L 6
Oct. 5—Nick Wells, Melbourne ....KO 3
Nov. 16—Roy Spackman, Melbourne .... W 6

1963

Mar. 8—Ken Edwards, Melbourne .....KO 6
Apr. 27—Bobby Daldy, Melbourne ...... W 6
July 19—Kevin Bell, Melbourne .... W 8
Aug. 23—Bobby Daldy, Melbourne ...... W 8
Sept. 6—Roy Spackman, Melbourne .... W 8
Oct. 4—Jimmy Smith, Melbourne ..... W 10
Oct. 25—Osei Renner, Melbourne .... W 10
Nov. 29—Jackie Gulino, Melbourne ..... W 12

1964

Feb. 21—Johnny Evans, Melbourne ....KO 7
Mar. 20—Jackie Gulino, Melbourne ..... W 12
May 22—Les Dunn, Melbourne ....KO 10
Aug. 9—Arthur Clarke, Melbourne ....KO 9
Aug. 28—Max Murphy, Melbourne ...... W 12
Sept. 18—Ollie Taylor, Melbourne .... W 15
(Australian featherweight title)
Nov. 6—Pat Gonzales, Melbourne ...... W 12

1965

Feb. 8—Billy Males, Sydney ....KO 6
Mar. 19—Domenico Chiliorio, Melb'ne .. W 15
(Australian featherweight title)
Apr. 1—Dion Murphy, Christchurch ....L 10
June 4—Domenico Chilorio, Melbourne D 12
June 11—Singtong Por Tor, Melbourne .. W 12
July 19—Max Murphy, Sydney ....L 12
Sept. 24—Max Murphy, Melbourne .....KO 7
(Australian featherweight title)
Oct. 15—Harold Hopkins, Melbourne ..KO 4
Oct. 29—Gilberto Biondi, Melbourne ....L 12

1966

Feb. 11—Mario Sitri, Melbourne .... W 12
Feb. 25—Carmelo Coscia, Melbourne .... W 12
Mar. 11—Noel Kunde, Brisbane ....KO 8
Apr. 1—Domenico Chiloiro, Melbourne W 15
(Australian Featherweight Title)
May 4—Noel Kunde, Brisbane ....KO 4
June 10—Domenico Chiloiro, Melbourne D 12
Oct. 7—Dos Santos, Melbourne .... W 10
Dec. 9—Giovanni Girgenti, Melbourne . D 10

1967

Jan. 20—Giovanni Girgenti, Melbourne . W 10
Mar. 4—Andrea Silanos, Melbourne ...KO 2
Apr. 14—Roberto Wong, Melbourne .... W 10
May 26—Lothar Abend, Melbourne ..... W 10
July 7—James Skelton, Melbourne ..... W 10
July 21—Gilberto Biondi, Melbourne ... W 10
Sept. 22—Don Johnson, Melbourne ...... W 10
Oct. 20—Michel Houdeau, Melbourne ..KO 6
Nov. 24—Johnny O'Brien, Melbourne ..KO 11
(Won British Empire Featherweight Title)

1968

Feb. 20—Isao Ichihara, Melbourne ...... W 10
Mar. 11—Rene Roque, Paris .... D 10
Apr. 5—Antonio Herrara, Melbourne ... W 10
May 20—Bobby Valdez, Sydney .....W dis. 13
July 2—Freddy Rengife, Sydney .....KO 10
July 26—Vincenzo Pitardi, Melbourne .. W 10
Sept. 13—Billy McGrandle, Melbourne ..KO 12
(British Empire Featherweight Title)
Oct. 18—Nevo Carbi, Melbourne .... W 10

1969

Jan. 21—Jose Legra, London .... W 15
(World featherweight title)
Mar. 21—Jose Jiminez, Melbourne ...... W 10
Apr. 21—Giovanni Girgenti, London .... W 10
Relinquished British Empire title to campaign as world champion.
May 20—Jimmy Anderson, London ..... W 10
July 28—Fighting Harada, Sydney ...... W 15
(World featherweight title)
Nov. 11—Miguel Herrera, London .... W 10
Dec. 9—Pete Gonzales, London ....KO 3

1970

Jan. 6—Fighting Harada, Tokyo ......KO 14
(Retained World Featherweight Title)
Apr. 11—Arnold Taylor, Johannesburg .. W 10
May 9—Vicente Saldivar, Rome ....L 15
(Lost World Featherweight Title)

TB	KO	WD	WF	D	LD	LF	KO BY	ND	NC
67	20	35	1	6	5	0	0	0	0

KUNIAKI SHIBATA
Born, March 29, 1947, Hitachi, Ibaraki, Japan.
Weight, 126-130 lbs. Height, 5 ft. 4 in.
1965
Mar.	6—Seiichi Iizuka, Tokyo	KO	1
Apr.	5—Hitoshi Yoshino, Tokyo	KO	1
July	28—Norio Sugimoto, Tokyo	KO	1
Sept.	2—Masaru Miyazaki, Tokyo	W	4
Sept.	27—Yoshinobu Yokoyama, Tokyo	KO	1
Nov.	11—Toshihiko Noziri, Tokyo	W	4
Dec.	20—Takao Suzuki, Tokyo	KO	1

1966
Jan.	31—Masachika Tokutome, Osaka	KO	5
Oct.	23—Atsushi Gunji, Tokyo	KO	6
Dec.	11—Kenji Fuse, Tokyo	KO	2

1967
Jan.	15—Alberto Reyes, Tokyo	W	10
Feb.	12—Hiroshi Miyata, Tokyo	KO	4
Mar.	5—Hyun Kim, Tokyo	W	10
June	7—Katsutoshi Aoki,Tokyo	KO	1
Aug.	9—Roberto Andrade, Tokyo	KO	5
Sept.	20—Roy Amalong, Tokyo	W	10
Nov.	15—Soon-In Chang, Seoul	KO	9
Dec.	5—Chang-Bok Lee, Hitachi	KO by	2
Dec.	27—Soo-Bok Kwon, Tokyo	KO	2

1968
Jan.	31—Tiny Palacio, Tokyo	KO	5
Mar.	1—Ramiro Nides, Guam	W	10
Mar.	27—Dwight Hawkins, Tokyo	KO by	7
July	2—Beto Maldonado, Tokyo	W	10
Aug.	14—Meriken Mori, Tokyo	TD	3
Oct.	23—Orlando Medina, Tokyo	W	10

1969
Jan.	15—Herbert Kang, Tokyo	KO by	6
	(For Oriental Featherweight Title)		
Mar.	24—Koji Ikeda, Tokyo	W	10
Apr.	28—Kid Barrios, Tokyo	KO	1
June	11—Yoshio Ando, Tokyo	KO	8
Sept.	10—Fernando Sotelo, Tokyo	KO	9
Oct.	22—Flash Besande, Osaka	KO	3

1970
Feb.	4—Felipe Torres, Tokyo	W	10
Apr.	15—Yasuo Sakurai, Tokyo	KO	10
	(Won Vacant Japanese Featherweight Title)		
July	8—Jose Acosta, Tokyo	D	10
Sept.	9—Hyun Kim, Tokyo	W	10
Dec.	11—Vicente Saldivar, Tijuana	KO	13
	(Won World Featherweight Title)		

1971
Mar.	7—Vicente Garcia, Hitachi	W	10
June	3—Raul Cruz, Tokyo	KO	1
Aug.	1—Hyun Kim, Nagoya	W	10
Nov.	10—Ernesto Marcel, Matsuyama	D	15
	(Retained World Featherweight Title)		

1972
May	19—Clemente Sanchez, Tokyo	KO by	3
	(Lost World Featherweight Title)		
July	11—Bert Nabalatan, Honolulu	W	10
Oct.	7—Andres Steyn, Johannesburg	L	10

1973
Feb.	2—Kimio Shindo, Sendai	KO	7
Mar.	12—Ben Villaflor, Honolulu	W	15
	(Won World Junior Lightweight Title)		
June	19—Victor Echegaray, Honolulu	D	15
	(Retained World Junior Lightweight Title)		
Sept.	3—Chung-Nam Choul, Hitachi	KO	2
Oct.	18—Ben Villaflor, Honolulu	KO by	1
	(Lost World Junior Lightweight Title)		

1974
Feb.	28—Ricardo Arrendondo, Tokyo	W	15
	(Won WBC Junior Lightweight Title)		
June	27—Antonio Amaya, Tokyo	W	15
	(Retained WBC Junior Lightweight Title)		
Aug.	3—Ramiro Bolanos, Tokyo	KO	15
	(Retained WBC Junior Lightweight Title)		

1975
Mar.	27—Ould Makloufi, Fukuoka City	W	15
	(Retained WBC Junior Lightweight Title)		
July	5—Alfredo Escalera, Mito	KO by	2
	(Lost WBC Junior Lightweight Title)		

1976
Mar.	22—Tamio Nagishi, Akita	W	10
Oct.	12—Susumu Okabe, Tokyo	W	10

1977
Nov.	29—Al Espinosa, Tokyo	W	10

TB	KO	WD	WF	D	LD	LF	KO BY	ND	NC
56	24	21	0	4	1	0	6	0	0

ANTONIO GOMEZ
Born, September 30, 1945, Cumana, Venezuela.
Weight, 126 lbs.

1967
Feb.	28—Eduardo Blanco, Caracas	KO	3
Mar.	20—Julio Cordoba, Caracas	W	4
Apr.	7—Modesto Santos, Caracas	W	4
May	12—Irene Maestre, Caracas	W	6
May	26—Edmundo Martinez, Caracas	W	6
June	19—Eduardo Blanco, Caracas	W	6
Aug.	14—Julio Cordoba, Caracas	KO	2
Sept.	1—Domingo Bastidas, Caracas	KO by	3
Dec.	11—Edmundo Martinez, Maracaibo	KO	4
Dec.	18—Eduardo Blanco, Caracas	W	6

1968
Jan.	22—Elias Alfonso, Caracas	W	4
Feb.	6—Domingo Bastidas, Caracas	W	8
Apr.	1—Julio Cordoba, Caracas	KO	4
Apr.	7—Gustavo Briceno, Caracas	W	6
June	7—Jaime Amaya, Caracas	KO	1
June	28—Jose Molina, Caracas	W	8
July	12—Raul Lizardo, Caracas	W	8
Aug.	11—Raul Lizardo, Maracaibo	KO	4
Oct.	5—Jose Molina, Caracas	W	8
Oct.	21—Isibro Rondon, Caracas	KO	6

1969
Jan.	20—Manuel Arnal, Caracas	W	10
Mar.	7—Mario Manrique, Caracas	W	10
May	30—Gustavo Briceno, Caracas	KO	9
June	13—Frank Leroy, Caracas	KO	9
July	11—Rocky Orengo, Caracas	W	10
Aug.	22—Dwight Hawkins, Los Angeles	KO	9
Sept.	13—Bobby Vasquez, Vera Cruz	L	10
Sept.	29—Francisco Bolivar, Caracas	W	10
Nov.	10—Antonio Cervantes, Caracas	W	10

1970
Feb.	14—Gil Noriega, Los Angeles	KO	8
Apr.	21—Memo Morales, Tijuana	KO	4
Apr.	27—Juan Collado, Caracas	W	10
June	4—Centavito Hernandez, Los Angeles	W	10
Sept.	5—Fernando Sotelo, Los Angeles	KO	9
Oct.	6—Julio Segura, Tijuana	KO	5

1971
Jan.	10—Raul Vega, Caracas	KO	7
May	28—Vicente Garcia, Caracas	KO	1
Sept.	2—Shozo Saijyo, Tokyo	KO	5
	(Won WBA Featherweight Title)		
Nov.	6—Jose Smecca, Caracas	KO	7
Nov.	20—Raul Martinez, Monterrey	L	10
Dec.	10—Esteban DeJesus, Caracas	W	10

1972
Feb.	6—Raul Martinez, Maracay	KO	7
	(Retained WBA Featherweight Title)		
June	—Enrique Garcia, Maracay	W	10
Aug.	19—Ernesto Marcel, Maracay	L	15
	(Lost WBA Featherweight Title)		

1973
June	16—Hyun Kim, Maracay	D	10
July	14—Ernesto Marcel, Panama City	KO by	12
	(For WBA Featherweight Title)		

TB	KO	WD	WF	D	LD	LF	KO BY	ND	NC
46	19	21	0	1	3	0	2	0	0

CLEMENTE SANCHEZ
Born Monterrey Mexico
1962 Champion Golden Gloves Featherweight
Born July 9, 1947, Monterrey, Mexico
1963
Mar.	23—Tony Herrera, Monterrey ...... W	6
May	17—Panchito Flores, Monterrey .... W	4
May	30—Frank Ky Gutierrez, Saltillo L	10
June	16—Ramon Garza, Salinas .... W	8
June	30—Chuy Rodriguez, Saltillo Coah . D	10
July	25—Ubaldo Cruz, Monterrey ...... W	6
1964
July	4—Ardillagarcia, Matamoros TampsW	10
1965
Apr.	10—Rocky Garcia, Monterrey ..... W	10
July	31—Santos Sandoval, Monterrey L	12
Oct.	16—Luis Briones, Monterrey .... W	10
Dec.	4—Gallito Camacho, Monterrey ... W	10
1966
Feb.	5—Lupe Mendez, Monterrey ...... W	10
Feb.	26—Chilango Gomez, Guadalajara JalW	10
Mar.	19—Chocolate Zambrano, Laredo .. W	10
June	25—Lobito Montoya, Monterrey L	10
1967
Mar.	4—Rocky Garcia, Monterrey ..... D	10
Apr.	22—Chuy Rocha, Monterrey L	10
Aug.	4—Ricardo Arredondo, Nuevo Laredo .... W	10
1968
Feb.	17—Manuel Flores, Monterrey ....KO	5
Mar.	8—Rogelio Lara, Matamoros Tamps L	10
Apr.	5—Rogelio Lara, Matamoros Tamps L	10
May	3—Juan Kid Sanchez, San Nicolas KO	3
June	22—Ramon Reyes, Monterrey ....KO	1
Sept.	21—Federico Palomares, Monterrey ....KO	2
Oct.	19—Manuel Barajas, Monterrey ..KO	5
Nov.	9—Cubano Gonzalez, Monterrey .KO	4
Dec.	28—Santos Sandoval, Monterrey ..KO	5
1969
Jan.	12—Chuy Rodriguez, Rosita Coah .KO	1
Jan.	26—Chicharito Martinez, Rosita Coah ....KO	4
Feb.	15—Chocolate Zambrano, Monterrey ....KO	4
Mar.	8—German Bastidas, Monterrey ..KO	6
May	1—Raul Vega, Monterrey ....KO	3
June	28—Ray Vega, Monterrey ....KO	6
Sept.	14—Miguel Riasgo, Monterrey L	10
Nov.	15—Hipolito Hernandez, Monterrey ....KO	1
1970
Jan.	17—Rogelio Fernandez, MonterreyKO	7
Feb.	28—Jose Valenzuela, Monterrey ..KO	4
Apr.	17—Pedro Cruz, Monclova Coah ..KO	3
June	28—Raul Cruz, Monterrey ....KO	5
Nov.	22—Fernando Sotelo, Monterrey ..KO	7
Dec.	25—Love Allotey, Monterrey ...... D	10
1971
Mar.	8—Jesse Lara, Piedras Negras CoahKO	4
June	16—Johnny Bean, Monterrey .....KO	2
Aug.	3—Armando Muliz, Monclova Coah ....KO	5
Sept.	25—Jose Jimenez, Monterrey .....KO	3
Oct.	31—Mouico Martinez, Saltillo .....KO	5
Nov.	20—Tahar Ben Hasson, Monterrey .KO	8
Dec.	21—Joao Ulloa, Valles ....KO	2
1972
May	19—Kuniaki Shibata, Tokyo ......KO	3
	(Won World Featherweight Title)	
Aug.	12—Enrique Garcia, Monterrey L	10
Dec.	16—Vacated his Title	
Dec.	16—Jose Legra, Monterrey ....KO by	10
1973
Inactive
1974
June	10—Memin Vega, Matamoros ....KO	4
Aug.	31—Jose Marin, Monterrey ......KO	5
Aug.	11—Jose Luis Meza, La Paz .....W dis.	5
July	8—Victor Ortiz, San Juan L	10
1975
Apr.	—Juventino Castillo, Rio Bravo ....KO	3
May	2—Hector 'Tuloco' Munoz, Reynosa ......W	10
July	13—Ramiro Bolanos, Monterrey ....W	10
Aug.	—Alvaro Rojas, Monterrey L	10

TB	KO	WD	WF	D	LD	LF	KOBY	ND	NC
58	30	14	1	3	9	0	1	0	0

Died Dec. 25, 1978 in Monterey, Mexico. Shot to death in a traffic dispute.

ERNESTO MARCEL
Born, May 23, 1948, Colon, Panama. Weight, 126 lbs.
1966
Apr.	12—Valentin Worrell, Panama City ... KO	1
May	22—Guillermo Porter, Panama City .... W	4
July	14—Carlos Harris, Colon .... D	4
Aug.	28—Leroy Carquill, Colon .... W	4
Sept.	25—Luis Rodriguez, Colon .... W	4
Dec.	4—Herbert Luck, Panama City ...... KO	5
1967
Feb.	26—Lazaro Fruto, Panama City ...... KO	2
Apr.	1—Santos Pena, Panama City .... KO	3
May	20—Agustin Cedeno, Colon .... W	8
July	2—Miguel Riasco, Colon L	8
Sept.	13—Mario Molo, Colon .... W	6
1968
Mar.	17—Encarnacion Guerrero, Colon ...... W	6
Apr.	22—Agustin Cedeno, Panama City L	8
Oct.	17—Frank Leroy, Caracas .... W	8
Nov.	16—Zenen Rios, Colon .... KO	9
Dec.	21—Agustin Cedeno, Colon .... KO	9
1969
Jan.	19—Camy Beto, Colon .... W	10
Feb.	13—Juvencio Guerrero, Colon .... KO	5
Mar.	22—Eliodoro Pitalua, Colon .... KO	6
Apr.	26—Eugenio Hurtado, Colon .... KO	6
May	11—Eugenio Hurtado, Panama City .... W	10
June	17—Jose Gonzalez, Colon .... KO	7
July	19—Julio Davis, Colon .... KO	3
Aug.	17—Bernardo Caraballo, Colon .... KO	2
Oct.	4—Freddie Rengifo, Colon .... KO	2
Dec.	13—Miguel Riasco, Colon .... KO	8
1970
Mar.	7—Aurelio Muniz, Monterrey .... W	10
Mar.	20—Chano Herrera, Acapulco .... KO	2
May	16—Roberto Duran, Panama City .. KO by	10
Aug.	—Miguel Riasco, Panama City .... W	12
Oct.	31—Alfredo Marcano, Panama City .... W	10
Nov.	21—Wilson Yambo, Panama City ..... KO	3
1971
Jan.	23—Angel Macias, Panama City ...... KO	6
May	4—Alfredo Marcano, Caracas .... W	10
Sept.	12—Jose Arranz, Panama City .... KO	5
Oct.	2—Mani Roque, Colon .... KO	3
Nov.	10—Kuniaki Shibata, Matsuyama ...... D	15
	(For World Featherweight Title)	
1972
Feb.	5—Jose Smecca, Panama City .... KO	1
June	10—Jose Luis Lopez, Panama City .... KO	2
Aug.	19—Antonio Gomez, Maracay .... W	15
	(Won WBA Featherweight Title)	
Dec.	3—Enrique Garcia, Panama City ..... KO	6
	(Retained WBA Featherweight Title)	
1973
Mar.	17—Leonel Hernandez, Maracay L	10
May	19—Ramiro Bolanos, Panama City ..... W	10
July	14—Antonio Gomez, Panama City .... KO	12
	(Retained WBA Featherweight Title)	
Sept.	8—Spider Nemoto, Panama City ..... KO	9
	(Retained WBA Featherweight Title)	
Dec.	8—Samuel Serrano, Panama City .... W	10
1974
Feb.	16—Alexis Arguello, Panama City ..... W	15
	(Retained WBA Featherweight Title)	

TB	KO	WD	WF	D	LD	LF	KO BY	ND	NC
47	24	17	0	2	3	0	1	0	0

EDER JOFRE
Brazilian Bantamweight
Born, March 26, 1936, Sao Paulo, Brazil.
1957
Mar.	26—Raul Lopez, San Pablo ....KO	5
Apr.	23—Raul Lopez, San Pablo ....KO	3
May	5—Osvaldo Perez, San Pablo ...KO	10
June	7—Osvaldo Perez, San Pablo .....KO	2
June	14—J. C. Gonzalez, San Pablo .....KO	5
July	5—Raul Jamie, San Pablo .... W	10
July	19—Raul Jamie, San Pablo .... W	10

Aug. 16—Ernesto Miranda, San Pablo .... D 10
Sept. 6—Ernesto Miranda, San Pablo .... D 10
Oct. 30—Luis Jiminez, San Pablo ......KO 8
Dec. 13—Adolfo Pendas, San Pablo ..... W 10
Dec. 22—Carlos Garbisans,
Rio De Janeiro .... W 10
1958
Jan. 24—Avelino Romero, Sao Paulo ...KO 2
Mar. 7—Carlos Gavisans, Sao Paulo ....KO 6
Apr. 13—German Escudero, Sao Paulo .KO 2
Apr. 27—German Escudero,
Rio deJaneiro .... KO 2
May 14—Ruben Caceres, Montevideo ... D 10
July 10—J. C. Acebal, Sao Paulo ....KO 2
Aug. 9—Roberto Olmedo, Sao Paulo ..KO 5
Sept. 12—Jose Casas, Sao Paulo .... W 10
Oct. 10—Jose Casas, Sao Paulo ....KO 5
Nov. 14—Jose Smecca, Sao Paulo .....KO 7
Dec. 12—Roberto Castro, Sao Paulo ...KO 2
1959
Mar. 23—Aniceto Pereyra, Sao Paulo .... W 10
Apr. 20—Sal Suarez, Sao Paulo ....KO 4
June 4—Leo Espinosa, Sao Paulo ...... W 10
June 19—Angel Bustos, Sao Paulo ......KO 4
July 6—Angel Bustos, Rio De Janeiro .KO 1
July 31—Ruben Caceres, Sao Paulo .....KO 7
Oct. 9—Angel Bustos, Sao Paulo .....KO 4
Oct. 30—Gianni Zuddas, Sao Paulo .... W 10
Dec. 12—Danny Kid, Sao Paulo .... W 10
1960
Feb. 19—Ernesto Miranda, Sao Paulo .... W 15
(Won South American Bantamweight Title)
June 10—Ernesto Miranda, Sao Paulo ...KO 3
(Retained South American Title)
July 15—Claudio Barrientos,
Sao Paulo ....KO 8
Aug. 18—Joe Medel, Los Angeles ....KO 10
Sept. 30—Ricardo Moreno, Sao Paulo ...KO 6
Nov. 18—Eloy Sanchez, Los Angeles ...KO 6
(Won N.B.A. Bantamweight Title)
Dec. 16—Billy Peacock, Sao Paulo .....KO 2
1961
Mar. 25—Piero Rollo, Rio De Janeiro ...KO 10
(Won Vacant World Bantamweight Title)
Apr. 18—Sugar Ray, Buenos Aires ....KO 2
July 26—Sadao Yaoita, Sao Paulo .....KO 10
Aug. 19—Ramon Arias, Caracas ....KO 7
(Retained Title)
Dec. 7—Fernando Soto, Sao Paulo ...KO 8
1962
Jan. 18—Johnny Caldwell, Sao Paulo ..KO 10
(Retained Title)
May 4—Herman Marques, San Fran. ..KO 10
(Retained Title)
Sept. 11—Joe Medel, Sao Paulo ....KO 6
(Retained Bantamweight title)
1963
Apr. 4—Katsutoshi Aoki, Tokyo .....KO 3
(Retained Title)
May 18—Johnny Jamito, Manila ......KO 12
(Retained Title)
1964
Nov. 27—Bernardo Caraballo, Bogota ..KO 7
(Retained World Title)
1965
May 17—Fighting Harada, Nagoya, Japan .L 15
(Lost World Bantamweight Title)
Nov. 5—Manny Elias, Sao Paulo .... D 10
1966
June 1—Fighting Harada, Tokyo ....L 15
(For World Bantamweight Title)
1967-1968
(Retired following the Harada bout)
1969
Aug. 27—Rudy Corona, Sao Paulo .....KO 6
(Started comeback as a featherweight)
1970
Jan. 30—Nevio Carbi, Sao Paulo .... W 10
May 29—Manny Elias, Sao Paulo .... W 10
Sept. 25—Roberto Wong, Sao Paulo ...KO 3
Dec. 5—Giovanni Girgenti, Sao Paulo .. W 10
1971
Mar. 26—Jerry Stokes, Sao Paulo .....·KO 2
June 10—Domenico Chiloiro, Sao Paulo . W 10
Sept. 10—Tony Jamao, Sao Paulo .... W 10
Nov. 16—Robert Porcel, Sao Paulo ....KO 2
1972
Mar. 24—Guillermo Morales, Sao Paulo .KO 6
Apr. 28—Felix Figueroa, Sao Paulo ..... W 10
June 30—Jose Bisbal, Saos Paulo ....KO 2
Aug. 18—Shig Fukuyama, Sao Paulo ...KO 9
Sept. 29—Ejiemei Belhadf, Sao Paulo ...KO 3

1973
May 5—Jose Legra, Brasilia .... W 15
(W.B.C. Featherwieght Title)
July 21—Godfrey Stevens, Sao Paulo ...KO 4
Aug. 26—Frankie Crawford, Bauru ...... W 10
Oct. 20—Vicente Saldivar, Salvador ....KO 4
(W.B.C. Featherweight Title)
1975
Jan. 3—Filiberto Herrera, Jundial ....W 10
1976
Feb. 24—Enzo Farinelli, Porto Alegre ....KO 4
May 1—Michel Lefebvre, Brasilia ....KO 3
May 29—Pasqualino Morbidelli, Sao Paulo ...KO 4
July 2—Gitanio Jiminez, Sao Paulo ....W 10
Aug. 13—Juan Lopez, Sao Paulo ....W 10
Oct. 8—Octavio Gomez, Sao Paulo ....W 10

TB	KO	WD	WF	D	LD	LF	KOBY	ND	NC
75	48	21	0	4	2	0	0	0	0

RUBEN OLIVARES
Born, January 14, 1947, Mexico City, Mexico.
Weight, 118-126 lbs. Height, 5 ft. 5½ in.
1964
Feb. 29—Freddy Garcia, Cuernavaca ...... KO 1
Apr. 13—Jose Sotelo, Cuernavaca .... KO 1
May 18—Jeronimo Cisneros, Mexico City .. KO 3
1965
Feb. 13—Torrito Silva, Torreon .... KO 6
Apr. 1—Tony Gallegos, Gomez Palacio .... KO 4
Aug. 14—Nemesio Zenil, Mexico City ...... KO 2
Sept. 8—Jorge Ruiz, Torreon .... KO 9
Oct. 20—Mateo Jaimes, Mexico City ...... KO 5
Nov. 24—Pablo Martinez, Mexico City ..... KO 2
1966
Jan. 17—Reynaldo de la Garza, Mexico City KO 3
Feb. 16—Eduardo Alvarado, Mexico City ... KO 2
Mar. 12—Gallito Camacho, Mexico City ... KO 1
Apr. 4—Juan Molina, Mexico City .... KO 2
June 2—Emeterio Campos, Tampico ...... KO 4
June 16—Alfonso Cazares, Mexico City .... KO 2
July 10—Gerardo Lujano, Tampico .... KO 5
Aug. 7—Oscar Rivas, Mexico City .... KO 3
Sept. 1—Ramiro Garcia, Mexico City ...... KO 9
Sept. 30—Monito Aguilar, Mexico City ..... KO 3
Oct. 18—Rafael Garcia, Mexico City ...... KO 5
Dec. 17—Daniel Gutierrez, Mexico City ... KO 10
1967
Feb. 5—Antonio Leal, Mexico City ...... KO 1
Mar. 8—Felipe Gonzalez, Mexicali .... W 10
June 7—Julio Guerrero, Mexico City ..... KO 4
July 1—Angel Hernandez, Leon .... KO 5
July 29—German Bastidas, Mexico City ..... D 10
Sept. 6—Grillo Aguilar, Poza Rica .... KO 5
Sept. 20—Gustavo Sosa, Puebla .... KO 3
Oct. 14—Ushiwakamaru Harada, Mexico
City .... KO 2
Nov. 3—Chamaco Castillo, Vera Cruz ..... KO 4
Nov. 19—Felipe Gonzalez, La Paz .... KO 4
1968
Jan. 28—German Bastidas, Mexico City ... KO 4
Mar. 3—Pornchai Poppraigam, La Paz .... KO 9
Mar. 30—Salvatore Burruni, Mexico City ... KO 3
Apr. 27—Manuel Arnal, Mexico City ... W disq. 6
May 20—Kid Gavilan, Puebla .... KO 4
June 8—Octavio Gomez, Mexico City ...... KO 5
June 25—Enrique Yepes, Jalapa .... KO 5
July 11—Garry Garber, Torreon .... KO 6
Aug. 10—Tiny Palacio, Mexico City .... KO 6
Aug. 24—Bernabe Fernandez, Inglewood ... KO 3
Sept. 15—Antoine Porcel, Mexico City ...... KO 5
Oct. 11—Wally Brooks, Mexico City .... KO 1
Nov. 23—Joe Medel, Monterrey .... KO 8
1969
Jan. 26—Kazuyoshi Kanazawa, Mexico City KO 2
Feb. 23—Jose Bisbal, Mexico City .... KO 3
Mar. 9—Carlos Zayas, Tuxtla Gutierrez ... KO 7
Mar. 17—Ernie de la Cruz, Inglewood ...... KO 9

742

May	6—Frank Adame, Nogales .... KO	3
May	23—Takao Sakurai, Inglewood .... KO	6
June	29—Nene Jun, Mexico City .... KO	1
Aug.	22—Lionel Rose, Inglewood .... KO	5

(Won World Bantamweight Title)

| Oct. | 27—Shigeyoshi Oki, Juarez .... KO | 3 |
| Dec. | 12—Alan Rudkin, Inglewood .... KO | 2 |

(Retained World Bantamweight Title)

1970

Feb.	22—Angel Hernandez, Acambaro ..... KO	3
Mar.	18—Romy Guelas, San Antonio .... KO	5
Apr.	18—Chucho Castillo, Inglewood .... W	15

(Retained World Bantamweight Title)

July	22—Shuji Chiyoda, Chicago .... W	10
Aug.	14—Jose Arranz, Inglewood .... KO	3
Sept.	11—Guillermo Rodriguez, Acapulco ... KO	5
Oct.	16—Chucho Castillo, Inglewood .... KO by	14

(Lost World Bantamweight Title)

1971

| Mar. | 4—Chung Park, Guadalajara .... KO | 6 |
| Apr. | 3—Chucho Castillo, Inglewood .... W | 15 |

(Regained World Bantamweight Title)

May	19—Yoji Mineyama, Tijuana .... KO	3
June	7—Yambito Blanco, Managua .... KO	5
July	11—Efren Torres, Guadalajara .... KO	4
Aug.	23—Valentin Galeano, Inglewood ..... KO	9
Oct.	25—Kazuyoshi Kanazawa, Nagoya ... KO	14

(Retained World Bantamweight Title)

| Dec. | 14—Jesus Pimentel, Inglewood .... KO | 11 |

(Retained World Bantamweight Title)

1972

| Mar. | 19—Rafael Herrera, Mexico City ... KO by | 8 |

(Lost World Bantamweight Title)

| Aug. | 19—Godfrey Stevens, Monterrey .... W | 10 |
| Nov. | 14—Rafael Herrera, Inglewood .... L | 10 |

1973

| Apr. | 28—Walter Seeley, Ingelwood .... KO | 2 |
| June | 23—Bobby Chacon, Inglewood .... KO | 9 |

(Won Vacant NABF Featherweight Title)

| Sept. | 4—Art Hafey, Monterrey .... KO by | 5 |
| Dec. | 2—Frank Durango, Matamoros .... W | 10 |

1974

| Mar. | 4—Art Hafey, Inglewood .... W | 12 |

(Retained NABF Featherweight Title)

| May | 14—Ad Zapanta, Juarez .... KO | 2 |
| July | 9—Zensuke Utagawa, Inglewood ..... KO | 7 |

(Won Vacant WBA Featherweight Title)

Sept.	1—Enrique Garcia, Monterrey .... KO	5
Oct.	6—Carlos Mendoza, Juarez .... KO	6
Nov.	23—Alexis Arguello, Inglewood .... KO by	13

(Lost WBA Featherweight Title)

1975

| Apr. | 7—Benjamin Ortiz, Tijuana .... KO | 6 |
| June | 20—Bobby Chacon, Inglewood .... KO | 2 |

(Won WBC Featherweight Title)

| Sept. | 20—David Kotey, Inglewood .... L | 15 |

(Lost WBC Featherweight Title)

| Dec. | 4—Danny Lopez, Inglewood ...... KO by | 7 |

1976

June	2—Pajet Lupikanete, Los Angeles ... KO	1
July	30—Fernando Cabanela, Los Angeles .. W	10
Nov.	19—Jose Cervantes, Los Angeles ... KO by	6

1977

| Aug. | 20—Bobby Chacon, Inglewood .... L | 10 |
| Dec. | 6—Ricky Gutierrez, San Antonio ...... W | 10 |

1978

Apr.	28—Jose Luis Ramirez, Obregon ...... KO	2
Oct.	18—Shig Furuyama, Houston .... KO	2
Nov.	20—Isaac Vega, Houston .... KO	3

1979

Apr.	22—Guillermo Morales, Tuxtla Gutierrez D	10
June	30—Adrian Zapanta, Albuquerque .... KO	2
July	21—Eusebio Pedroza, Houston .... KO by	12

(For WBA Featherweight Title)

1980

Mar.	7—Carlos Serrano, Chicago .... KO	5
Apr.	25—Sergio Reyes, Nuevo Laredo ...... KO	7
Aug.	24—Rafael Gandarilla, McAllen ... KO by	9

TB	KO	WD	WF	D	LD	LF	KO BY	ND	NC
100	77	9	1	2	3	0	8	0	0

BOBBY CHACON

Born, November 28, 1951, Los Angeles, Calif.
Weight, 126-130 lbs. Height, 5 ft. 5 in.

1972

Apr.	17—Jose Rosa, Los Angeles .... KO	5
Apr.	19—Limon Salas, Los Angeles .... KO	1
May	8—Ruben Coria, Los Angeles .... KO	2
May	15—Moses Felix, Los Angeles .... KO	1
May	23—Luis Robles, Los Angeles .... KO	1
June	5—Ray Llamas, Los Angeles .... KO	1
June	19—Alfredo de la Rosa, Los Angeles .... W	5
June	30—Jesus Robles, Los Angeles .... KO	2
July	17—Alberto Perez, Los Angeles .... KO	5
July	31—Alfredo de la Rosa, Anaheim ..... KO	4
Aug.	11—Modesto Dayaganon, Maui .... KO	2
Aug.	21—Juan Montoya, Los Angeles ..... KO	8
Sept.	11—Valente Viera, Anaheim .... KO	5
Oct.	16—Albert Reyes, Woodland Hills .... KO	9
Nov.	9—Ray Echavarria, Los Angeles ..... KO	1

1973

Feb.	15—Arturo Pineda, Los Angeles ..... KO	5
Feb.	28—Jose Del Campo, Los Angeles ..... KO	4
Mar.	30—Frankie Crawford, Anaheim .... W	10
Apr.	28—Chucho Castillo, Los Angeles ..... KO	9
June	23—Ruben Olivares, Inglewood .... KO by	9

(For Vacant NABF Featherweight Title)

| Sept. | 28—Jorge Ramos, San Diego .... KO | 10 |
| Oct. | 13—Jose Del Campo, Los Angeles ..... KO | 9 |

1974

Feb.	1—Jorge Ramos, San Diego .... KO	5
Mar.	4—Genzo Kurozawa, Los Angeles .... KO	5
May	24—Danny Lopez, Los Angeles .... KO	9
Sept.	7—Alfredo Marcano, Los Angeles .... KO	9

(Won WBC Featherweight Title)

1975

| Mar. | 1—Jesus Estrada, Los Angeles ...... KO | 2 |

(Retained WBC Featherweight Title)

| June | 20—Ruben Olivares, Inglewood .... KO by | 2 |

(Lost WBC Featherweight Title)

| Nov. | 18—Fel Clemente, Honolulu .... KO | 5 |
| Dec. | 7—Rafael (Bazooka) Limon, Mexicali .. L | 10 |

1976

Jan.	27—Gene Prado, Fresno .... KO	5
Feb.	17—Modesto Concepcion, San Jose .... KO	10
Feb.	25—David Sotelo, Los Ang eles .... W	10
Nov.	10—Bonnie Necessario, Stockton ...... KO	2
Dec.	16—Miguel Meza, Los Angeles .... KO	3

1977

Jan.	13—Julio Lael, Los Angeles .... KO	7
May	19—Roman Contreras, Los Angeles ... KO	8
June	9—Miguel Estrada, Los Angeles ..... KO	2
July	15—Alejandro Lopez, San Diego ...... KO	7
Aug.	20—Ruben Olivares, Ingelwood .... W	10
Nov.	15—Arturo Leon, Anaheim L	10

1978

| May | 12—Ignacio Campos, San Diego ...... KO | 7 |
| Dec. | 6—Gerald Hayes, Stockton .... W | 10 |

1979

| Feb. | 26—Shig Fukuyama, Los Angeles ..... KO | 5 |
| Apr. | 9—Rafael (Bazooka) Limon, Los Angeles .... TD | 7 |

(For NABF Junior Lightweight Title)

June	18—Jose Torres, Los Angeles .... W	10
Sept.	27—Augie Pantellas, Philadelphia .... KO	7
Nov.	16—Alexis Arguello, Inglewood .... KO by	7

(For WBC Junior Lightweight Title)

1980

| Mar. | 21—Rafael (Bazooka) Limon, Inglewood W | 10 |

TB	KO	WD	WF	D	LD	LF	KO BY	ND	NC
49	36	7	0	1	2	0	3	0	0

ALEXIS ARGUELLO

Born, April 19, 1952, Managua, Nicaragua.
Weight, 126-135 lbs. Height, 5 ft. 10 in.

1968

| Nov. | 18—Israel Medina, Managua .... KO | 1 |
| Dec. | 14—Alacran Espinosa, Managua .... W | 4 |

1969

Jan.	23—Burrito Martinez, Managua ...... KO	3
Apr.	26—Alacran Espinosa, Managua L	6

1970

July	29—Carlos Huete, Managua .... W	8
Aug.	12—Ricardo Donoso, Managua .... KO	2
Sept.	7—Marcelino Beckles, Managua ..... KO	8
Oct.	17—Mario Bojorge, Managua .... KO	3
Nov.	14—Jose Urbina, Managua .... KO	1
Dec.	5—Julio Morales, Managua .... KO	3
Dec.	19—Armando Figueroa, Managua .... KO	1

1971

Feb.	12—Tony Quiroz, Managua .... KO	6
Mar.	13—Raton Hernandez, Managua ...... W	10
Apr.	17—Raton Hernandez, Managua ...... W	10
May	1—Halcon Buitrago, Managua ...... KO	7
June	5—Kid Chapula, Managua .... KO	1
June	26—Marcial Loyola, Managua .... KO	2
July	17—Hurricane Clay, Managua .... KO	5
Aug.	14—Catalino Alvarado, Managua .... KO	1
Sept.	4—Rey Mendoza, Managua .... KO	4
Oct.	2—Hurricane Clay, Managua .... W	10
Nov.	18—Vicente Worrel, Managua .... KO	2

1972

Feb.	8—Guillermo Barrera, Managua ..... KO	1
Apr.	11—Tanquecito Gonzalez, Managua ... KO	2
June	22—Jorge Reyes, Managua .... KO by	6
Aug.	16—Fernando Fernandez, Managua ... KO	1
Sept.	23—Jorge Benitez, Managua .... KO	1
Nov.	17—Memo Ortiz, Managua .... KO	2
Dec.	12—Rafael Gonzalez, Managua .... KO	7

1973

Mar.	30—Fernando Fernandez, Managua ... KO	2
Apr.	22—Magallo Lozada, Managua .... W	10
May	26—Kid Pascualito, Managua .... KO	3
June	30—Octavio Gomez, Managua .... KO	2
Aug.	25—Nacho Lomeli, Masaya .... KO	1
Oct.	17—Sigfredo Rodriguez, Managua .... KO	9
Nov.	27—Jose Legra, Masaya .... KO	1

1974

Jan.	8—Raul Martinez, Managua .... KO	1
Feb.	16—Ernesto Marcel, Panama City L	15
	(For WBA Featherweight Title)	
Apr.	27—Enrique Garcia, Masaya .... KO	3
May	20—Art Hafey, Masaya .... KO	5
Aug.	29—Oscar Aparicio, Masaya .... W	12
	(Won Central American Featherweight Title)	
Sept.	21—Otoniel Martinez, Masaya .... KO	1
Nov.	23—Ruben Olivares, Inglewood .... KO	13
	(Won WBA Featherweight Title)	

1975

Feb.	8—Oscar Aparicio, San Salvador ...... W	10
Mar.	15—Lionel Hernandez, Caracas .... KO	8
	(Retained WBA Featherweight Title)	
May	31—Rigoberto Riasco, Granada .... KO	2
	(Won Vacant World Featherweight Title)	
July	18—Rosalio Muro, San Francisco ..... KO	2
Oct.	12—Royal Kobayashi, Tokyo .... KO	5
	(Retained World Featherweight Title)	
Dec.	20—Saul Montano, Managua .... KO	3

1976

Feb.	1—Jose Torres, Mexicali .... W	10
Apr.	10—Modesto Concepcion, Managua ... KO	2
June	19—Salvador Torres, Ingelwood .... KO	3
	(Retained World Featherweight Title)	

1977

Feb.	19—Godfrey Stevens, Managua .... KO	2
May	14—Alberto Herrera, Managua .... KO	1
June	20—Relinquished world featherweight title.	
June	22—Ezequiel Sanchez, New York ..... KO	4
Aug.	3—Jose Fernandez, New York ...... KO	1
Aug.	27—Ben Ortiz, San Juan .... W	10
Sept.	29—Jerome Artis, New York .... KO	2
Dec.	18—Enrique Solis, Managua .... KO	5

1978

Jan.	28—Alfredo Escalera, Bayamon .... KO	13
	(Won WBC Junior Lightweight Title)	
Mar.	25—Mario Mendez, Las Vegas .... KO	3
Apr.	29—Rey Tam, Inglewood .... KO	5
	(Retained WBC Junior Lightweight Title)	

June	3—Diego Alcala, San Juan .... KO	1
	(Retained WBC Junior Lightweight Title)	
July	26—Vilomar Fernandez, New York L	10
Nov.	10—Arturo Leon, Las Vegas .... W	15
	(Retained WBC Junior Lightweight Title)	

1979

Feb.	4—Alfredo Escalera, Rimini .... KO	13
	(Retained WBC Junior Lightweight Title)	
July	8—Rafael (Bazooka) Limon, New York KO	11
	(Retained WBC Junior Lightweight Title)	
Nov.	16—Bobby Chacon, Inglewood .... KO	7
	(Retained WBC Junior Lightweight Title)	

1980

Jan.	20—Ruben Castillo, Tucson .... KO	11
	(Retained WBC Junior Lightweight Title)	
Mar.	31—Gerald Hayes, Las Vegas .... W	10
Apr.	27—Rolando Navarette, San Juan .... KO	5
	(Retained WBC Junior Lightweight Title)	
Aug.	9—Cornelius Boza-Edwards, Atlantic City .... KO	8
	—Relinquished WBC junior lightweight title.	
Nov.	14—Jose Ramirez, Miami .... W	10

TB	KO	WD	WF	D	LD	LF	KO BY	ND	NC
73	56	13	0	0	3	0	1	0	0

DAVID (POISON) KOTEY

Born, December 7, 1950, Accra, Ghana. Weight, 126-130 lbs. Height, 5 ft. 8 in.

1966

Feb.	5—Young Famous Lartey, Accra ...... W	6
Sept.	3—Abu Morgan, Accra .... KO	4
Dec.	10—Bob Cofie, Accra .... KO	6

1967

Feb.	5—Emmanuel Dudzro, Togo .... W	8
Mar.	2—Shido Armah, Accra .... KO	3
June	5—Peter Aywith, Togo .... W	10

1968

Mar.	1—Kid Killer, Precipe .... KO	8
May	4—Abu Morgan, Tomale .... W	8
Aug.	31—Teddy Walker, Accra .... W	8

1969

Mar.	1—Teddy Walker, Brigade Gas Factory W	8
June	14—Teddy Walker, Black Star .... KO	4
Aug.	30—Asebi Bookye, Precipe .... KO	10
Dec.	2—Cassimo Alhasson, Takoradi ..... KO	3

1970

Mar.	7—Buddy Guy, Accra .... W	8
Aug.	29—Buddy Guy, Accra .... W	8
Sept.	3—Joe Banks, Tamale .... KO	3
Oct.	30—Joe Issaka, Koforidua .... KO	2
Nov.	28—Bob Seifu, Accra .... KO	3

1971

June	5—Freddie Mensah, Accra .... D	8
Dec.	3—Cassimo Alhassan, Accra .... KO	3

1972

May	29—Andy Broome, Melbourne L	10
June	22—Alan Pressnell, Melbourne .... W	10
June	29—Ted Bonner, Sydney .... W	10
July	13—Rex Downward, Sydney L	10
July	27—Tony Cunningham, Sydney .... W	10
Aug.	23—Ray Ross, Melbourne .... KO	3
Oct.	18—Sakae Makamura, Melbourne ..... W	10

1973

Oct.	6—Bingo Crooks, Accra .... KO	6
Dec.	14—Peter Koloko, Kumasi .... KO	2

1974

Feb.	2—Tahar Ben Hassen, Tunis .... KO	1
	(Won African Featherweight Title)	
Nov.	9—Osmanu Toure, Accra .... KO	5
Dec.	7—Evan Armstrong, Accra .... KO	10
	(Won Commonwealth Featherweight Title)	

1975

Sept.	20—Ruben Olivares, Inglewood .... W	15
	(Won WBC Featherweight Title)	
Dec.	21—David Sotelo, Accra .... W	10

1976

Mar.	6—Flipper Uehara, Accra .... KO	12
	(Retained WBC Featherweight Title)	

July   16—Shig Fukuyama, Tokyo .... KO   3
(Retained WBC Featherweight Title)
Nov.   13—Danny Lopez, Accra L   15
(Lost WBC Featherweight Title)
1977
Apr.   30—Billy Wade, Accra .... KO   5
July   30—Laurent Bazie, Accra .... W   15
(Regained African Featherweight Title)
Oct.   30—Jose Resto, Accra .... W   10
Dec.   4—Victor Diaz, Accra .... KO   3
1978
Feb.   15—Danny Lopez, Las Vegas .... KO by   6
(For WBC Featherweight Title)
Sept.   29—Eddie Ndukwu, Lagos L   15
(For Commonwealth Featherweight Title)
1979
Feb.   3—Tapsoba Tiga, Accra .... KO   8

TB	KO	WD	WF	D	LD	LF	KO BY	ND	NC
44	23	15	0	1	4	0	1	0	0

DANNY (LITTLE RED) LOPEZ

Born, July 6, 1952, Fort Duchesne, Utah. Weight, 126 lbs. Height, 5 ft. 8 in. Managed by Howie Steindler, Bennie Georgino.

1971
May   27—Steve Flajole, Los Angeles .... KO   1
June   17—Fili Castro, Los Angeles .... KO   1
July   9—Mauro Olivares, Los Angeles ..... KO   1
July   29—Jose Luis Estrada, Los Angeles ... KO   2
Aug.   12—Modesto Ortiz, Los Angeles ...... KO   4
Sept.   16—Rafael Lopez, Los Angeles .... KO   5
Oct.   14—Frank Granados, Los Angeles .... KO   2
Nov.   18—Marcarito Rios, Los Angeles ..... KO   1

1972
Jan.   20—Jose Orantes, Los Angeles .... KO   2
Feb.   18—Rafael Lopez, Los Angeles .... KO   2
Mar.   10—Arturo Pineda, Los Angeles ..... KO   4
May   11—Jose Luis Valdovinos, Los Angeles KO   4
July   20—Benny Rodriguez, Los Angeles .... KO   1
July   28—Yoshinabu Goto, Los Angeles ..... KO   8
Oct.   19—Jorge Reyes, Los Angeles .... KO   7

1973
Feb.   9—Jorge Carrasco, Los Angeles ...... KO   1
Mar.   17—Kenji Endo, Los Angeles .... KO   2
May   10—Cesar Ordunez, Los Angeles ..... KO   6
June   21—Juan Ordonez, Los Angeles .... KO   4
July   31—Ushiwakamaru Harada, Honolulu KO   3
Sept.   27—Goya Vargas, Los Angeles .... KO   1

1974
Jan.   17—Genzo Kurosawa, Los Angeles ..... W   10
Feb.   4—Memo Rodriguez, Mexicali .... KO   10
May   24—Bobby Chacon, Los Angeles ... KO by   9
Aug.   8—Masanao Toyoshima, Los Angeles KO   3
Sept.   9—Shig Fukuyama, Los Angeles ... KO by   9

1975
Jan.   18—Octavio Gomez, Anaheim L   10
Apr.   24—Chucho Castillo, Los Angeles ..... KO   2
July   26—Raul Cruz, Los Angeles .... KO   6
Sept.   13—Antonio Nava, Los Angeles ...... KO   6
Dec.   4—Ruben Olivares, Inglewood .... KO   7

1976
Feb.   25—Sean O'Grady, Inglewood .... KO   4
Apr.   28—Octavio Gomez, Inglewood .... KO   3
Aug.   6—Art Hafey, Inglewood .... KO   7
Nov.   5—David (Poison) Kotey, Accra ...... W   15
(Won WBC Featherweight Title)

1977
July   29—Jose Olivares, San Diego .... KO   2
Aug.   28—Jorge Altamirano, Stateline ...... KO   6
Sept.   13—Jose Torres, Los Angeles .... KO   7
(Retained WBC Featherweight Title)

1978
Feb.   15—David (Poison) Kotey, Las Vegas   KO   6
(Retained WBC Featherweight Title)
Apr.   22—Jose DePaula, Los Angeles .... KO   6
(Retained WBC Featherweight Title)
Sept.   15—Juan Malvarez, New Orleans ..... KO   2
(Retained WBC Featherweight Title)
Oct.   21—Fel Clemente, Pesaro .... W disq.   4
(Retained WBC Featherweight Title)

1979
Mar.   10—Roberto Castanon, Salt Lake City KO   2
(Won Vacant World Featherweight Title)
June   17—Mike Ayala, San Antonio .... KO   15
(Retained World Featherweight Title)
Sept.   25—Jose Caba, Los Angeles .... KO   3
(Retained World Featherweight Title)

1980
Feb.   2—Salvador Sanchez, Phoenix .... KO by   13
(Lost World Featherweight Title)
June   21—Salvador Sanchez, Las Vegas .. KO by   14
(For World Featherweight Title)

TB	KO	WD	WF	D	LD	LF	KO BY	ND	NC
47	39	2	1	0	1	0	4	0	0

RAFAEL ORTEGA

Born, September 25, 1950, Panama. Weight, 126 lbs. Height, 5 ft. 4½ in.

1970
Jan.   30—Roberto Jaier, Colon .... W   4
Oct.   31—Jose Jimenez, Panama City .... D   4
1971
Mar.   21—Ismael Escobar, Panama City ...... D   4
June   27—Jose Jimenez, Panama City .... W   4
Sept.   25—Mario De Leon, Panama City ...... D   10
Dec.   18—Victor Hoyth, Panama City ...... KO   8
1972
Feb.   16—Fernando Jimenez, New York ..... W   8
Feb.   29—Heriberto Cintron, White Plains ... W   8
Mar.   22—Carlos Zayas, New York .... KO   2
June   17—Ismael Escobar, Panama City ...... W   10
Sept.   2—Norberto Reyes, Panama City .... W   7
Sept.   16—Ray Mendoza, San Salvador .... W   10
1973
May   12—Jesus Santis, Panama City ...... KO   6
June   16—Benjamin Ramirez, Panama City .. W   10
Sept.   1—Orlando Natera, Panama City ..... W   10
Dec.   15—Rigoberto Riasco, Panama City L   12
(For Panamanian Flyweight Title)
1974
June   29—Jose Torres, Guadalajara .... KO   2
Sept.   14—Chucho Castillo, Mexico City L   10
1975
Feb.   16—Rodolfo Francis, Panama City ..... W   10
Aug.   23—Gideon Borias, Johannesburg ...... W   10
Nov.   15—Niliberto Herrera, Caracas .... D   10
1976
Jan.   17—Reynaldo Hidalgo, Panama City .. KO   8
June   26—Armando Perez, Panama City ..... W   10
1977
Jan.   15—Francisco Coronado, Panama City   W   15
(Won Vacant WBA Featherweight Title)
May   29—Flipper Uehara, Naha, Okinawa ... W   15
(Retained WBA Featherweight Title)
Dec.   17—Cecilio Lastra, Torrelavega L   15
(Lost WBA Featherweight Title)

TB	KO	WD	WF	D	LD	LF	KO BY	ND	NC
26	6	13	0	4	3	0	0	0	0

CECILIO LASTRA

Born, August 12, 1951, Monte, Santander, Spain.
Weight, 126 lbs. Height, 5 ft. 5 in.

1975
Dec. 20—Juan Barros, Santander .... W 6

1976
Jan. 17—Jimmy Cruz, Santander .... KO 1
Jan. 24—Mohatar II, Santander .... KO 1
Feb. 14—Antonio Munoz Jurado, Santander KO 1
Mar. 4—Jose Francisco Artigao II, Bilbao KO 2
Mar. 20—Mariano Gasco, Santander .... KO 1
Apr. 2—Miguel Quintana, Bilbao .... KO 1
Apr. 24—Cayetano Alcala, Santander ..... KO 1
May 6—Juan Francisco Aparicio, Bilbao .. KO 2
May 29—Guy Caudron, Santander .... W 8
June 25—Tommy Wright, Santander ...... KO 4
July 31—Tommy Glencross, Santander ..... KO 2
Sept. 3—Jose Carlos Hernandez, Madrid .... L 8
Sept. 18—Ramon Garcia Marichal, Santander KO 6
Oct. 9—Adolfo Osses, Santander .... KO 2
Oct. 23—Frank Realinho, Santander ...... KO 3
Nov. 6—Jean Pierre Hainault, Santander .. W 8
Nov. 20—Roland Cazeaux, Santander .... W 8
Dec. 11—Ramiro Suarez, Santander ...... KO 1
Dec. 18—Renzo Battistelli, Santander ...... KO 1

1977
Feb. 5—Mario Oliveira, Santander .... KO 7
Mar. 12—Isidoro Cabeza, Santander .... W 12
(Won Spanish Featherweight Title)
Apr. 16—Joseph Tabla, Santander .... KO 3
Apr. 30—Rodolfo Sanchez, Santander ...... W 8
June 16—Hugo Carrizo, Santander .... W 8
Aug. 20—Roberto Castanon, Santander .. KO by 11
(Lost Spanish Featherweight Title)
Sept. 24—Antonio Medina Rodriguez,
Santander .... W 8
Dec. 17—Rafael Ortega, Torrelavega .... W 15
(Won WBA Featherweight Title)

1978
Apr. 15—Eusebio Pedroza, Panama City KO by 13
(Lost WBA Featherweight Title)
May 31—Helenio Ferreira, Barcelona ...... KO 1
June 10—Guy Caudron, Santander .... W 8
Oct. 28—Hector Molina, Santander .... KO 4
Dec. 2—Rodolfo Sanchez, Bilbao .... L 8

1979
Feb. 17—Nani Rodriguez, Santander .... KO 5
(Regained Spanish Featherweight Title)
Mar. 3—Maurice Apeang, Papeete ..... KO by 4
Apr. 7—Salid Mimun Amar, Santander .... W 8
Apr. 28—Isidoro Cabezas, Santander .... W 8
May 26—Alain Le Fol, Santander .... W 8
June 2—Michel Lefebvre, Santander ...... KO 2
July 27—Marvin Edwards, Santander ...... KO 3
Aug. 31—Samuel Meck, Madrid .... D 8
Sept. 29—Roberto Castanon, Santander .... L 12
(For European Featherweight Title)

1980
Apr. 12—Laurent Grimbert, Santander .... KO 2
May 23—Jose Luis Vicho, Mallorca .... KO 1
July 11—Isidoro Cabeza, Mallorca ...... KO by 5
Sept. 6—Francisco Moya, Santander .... W 8
Sept. 27—Esteban Eguia, Santander .... D 10
(Retained Spanish Featherweight Title)
Nov. 29—Roberto Castanon, Leon .... KO by 4
(For European Featherweight Title)

TB	KO	WD	WF	D	LD	LF	KO BY	ND	NC
48	24	14	0	2	3	0	5	0	0

EUSEBIO PEDROZA

Born, March 2, 1953, Panama City, Panama.
Weight, 126 lbs. Height, 5 ft. 9 in. Managed by Santiago del Rio.

1973
Dec. 1—Julio Garcia, Panama City .... KO 4
Dec. 22—Jose Santana, Panama City .... W 4

1974
Feb. 8—Jorge Bernal, Panama City .... W 6
Mar. 1—Chacon Plata, Panama City ...... W 8
Mar. 30—Jacinto Fuentes, Panama City .... KO 1
May 4—Ricardo Vega, Panama City ..... KO 2
June 14—Ernesto Davis, Panama City .... KO 1
July 20—Vicente Worrell, Panama City .... KO 1
Sept. 14—Senen Rios, Panama City .... KO 6

1975
Jan. 18—Alfonso Perez, Panama City ... KO by 3
Feb. 22—Ernesto Mathias, Panama City ... TW 8
Mar. 21—Benicio Sosa, Panama City ...... W 10
Apr. 26—Marcos Britton, Panama City .... KO 4
July 19—Guillermo Almongod, Panama City KO 7
Nov. 5—Orlando Amoros, Panama City ... KO 9

1976
Apr. 3—Alfonso Zamora, Mexicali ..... KO by 2
(For World Bantamweight Title)
July 11—Oscar Arnal, Caracas .... KO by 6

1977
Apr. 2—Jose Santana, Panama City .... W 10
May 14—Reynaldo Hidalgo, Panama City .. KO 9
Nov. 26—Rodolfo Francis, Panama City .... KO 7

1978
Apr. 15—Cecilio Lastra, Panama City ..... KO 13
(Won WBA Featherweight Title)
July 2—Ernesto Herrera, Panama City ... KO 12
(Retained WBA Featherweight Title)
Nov. 27—Enrique Solis, San Juan .... W 15
(Retained WBA Featherweight Title)

1979
Jan. 9—Royal Kobayashi, Tokyo .... KO 13
(Retained WBA Featherweight Title)
Apr. 8—Hector Carrasquilla, Panama City KO 11
(Retained WBA Featherweight Title)
July 21—Ruben Olivares, Houston .... KO 12
(Retained WBA Featherweight Title)
Nov. 17—Johnny Aba, Port Moresby .... KO 11
(Retained WBA Featherweight Title)

1980
Jan. 22—Spider Nemoto, Tokyo .... W 15
(Retained WBA Featherweight Title)
Mar. 29—Juan Malvares, Panama City ..... KO 9
(Retained WBA Featherweight Title)
July 20—Sa-Wang Kim, Seoul, Korea ...... KO 8
(Retained WBA Featherweight Title)
Oct. 4—Rocky Lockridge, McAfee, N.J. .... W 15
(Retained WBA Featherweight Title)

TB	KO	WD	WF	D	LD	LF	KO BY	ND	NC
31	19	9	0	0	0	0	3	0	0

SALVADOR SANCHEZ

Born, February 3, 1958, Santiago Tianquistenco, Mexico. Weight, 126 lbs. Height, 5 ft. 7 in.

1975
May 4—Al Gardeno, Veracruz .... KO 3
May 25—Miguel Ortiz, Misantla .... KO 3
Aug. 10—Victor Martinez, Misantla .... KO 2
Oct. 19—Cesar Lopez, Misantla .... KO 4
Nov. 25—Candido Sandoval, Mexico City ... KO 8
Dec. 11—Fidel Trejo, Mexico City .... W 8

1976
Jan. 24—Juan Granados, Mexico City ..... KO 3
Feb. 25—Javier Solis, Mexico City .... KO 7
Mar. 31—Serafin Pacheco, Mexico City .... KO 4
Apr. 24—Jose Chavez, Mexico City .... KO 7
May 26—Fidel Trejo, Mexico City .... KO 6
July 5—Pedro Sandoval, Mexico City ..... KO 9
Aug. 11—Joel Valdez, Mexico City .... KO 9
Oct. 31—Saul Montana, Nuevo Laredo ..... KO 9
Dec. 25—Antonio Leon, Mexico City .... KO 10

1977
Feb. 5—Raul Lopez, Mexicali .... KO 10
Mar. 12—Daniel Felizardo, Mexico City .... KO 5
May 21—Rosalio Badillo, Mexico City ..... KO 5
Sept. 9—Antonio Becerra, Mazatlan .... L 12
(For Vacant Mexican Bantamweight Title)
Nov. 11—Jose Luis Soto, Los Mochis .... W 10
Dec. 3—Eliseo Cosme, Mexico City .... W 10

1978

Apr.	15—Juan Escobar, Los Angeles	D	10
July	1—Jose Sanchez, Mexico City	W	10
Aug.	13—Hector Cortez, Mazatlan	KO	7
Sept.	26—Francisco Ponce, Houston	KO	2
Nov.	21—Edwin Alarcon, San Antonio	KO	9
Dec.	16—Jose Santana, Mexico City	KO	2

1979

Feb.	3—Carlos Mimila, Mexico City	KO	3
Mar.	13—James Martinez, San Antonio	W	10
May	19—Salvador Torres, Mexico City	KO	7
June	17—Fel Clemente, San Antonio	W	12
July	22—Rosalio Muro, San Luis Potosi	KO	3
Aug.	7—Felix Trinidad, Houston	KO	5
Sept.	25—Richard Rozelle, Los Angeles	KO	3
Dec.	15—Rafael Gandarilla, Guadalajara ...	KO	5

1980

Feb.	2—Danny Lopez, Phoenix	KO	13
	(Won World Featherweight Title)		
Apr.	12—Ruben Castillo, Tucson	W	15
	(Retained World Featherweight Title)		
June	21—Danny Lopez, Las Vegas	KO	14
	(Retained World Featherweight Title)		
Sept.	13—Patrick Ford, San Antonio	W	15
Dec.	13—Juan LaPorte, El Paso	W	15
	(Retained World Featherweight Title)		

TB	KO	WD	WF	D	LD	LF	KO BY	ND	NC
40	29	9	0	1	1	0	0	0	0

747

JUNIOR FEATHERWEIGHTS

JACK (KID) WOLFE	*1922-1923*	**WILFREDO GOMEZ (WBC)**	1977-
CARL DUANE	*1923-1924*	*SOO-HWAN HONG (WBA)*	*1977-1978*
RIGOBERTO RIASCO (WBC)	*1976*	*RICARDO CARDONA (WBA)*	*1978-1980*
ROYAL KOBAYASHI (WBC)	*1976*	*LEO RANDOLPH (WBA)*	*1980*
DONG-KYUN YUM (WBC)	*1976-1977*	*SERGIO PALMA (WBA)*	*1980-*

Claimants not generally recognized are in *italics.*

Date	Winner	Wt	Loser	Wt	Result	Venue	Referee
9/21/22	Jack (Kid) WOLFE	122	Joe LYNCH	118	15	Madison Square Garden, New York	Patsy Haley
8/29/23	Carl DUANE	122¾	Jack (Kid) WOLFE	123½	unan 12	Queensboro A.C., Long Island City	
‡ 4/3/76	Rigoberto RIASCO	121¾	Waruinge NAKAYAMA	121¼	TKO 9	Panama City, Panama	
‡ 6/12/76	Rigoberto RIASCO		Livio NOLASCO		KO 10	Panama City, Panama	
‡ 8/1/76	Rigoberto RIASCO	120¾	Dong-Kyun YUM	121½	split 15	Pusan, Korea	Larry Rozadilla
‡10/10/76	Royal KOBAYASHI	122	Rigoberto RIASCO	122	TKO 8 0:48	Kuramae Arena, Tokyo, Japan	Jay Edson
‡11/24/76	Dong-Kyun YUM	121¼	Royal KOBAYASHI	122	maj 15	Changchung Gymnasium, Seoul	Yusaku Yoshida
‡ 2/13/77	Dong-Kyun YUM	121¼	Jose CERVANTES	120	unan 15	Changchung Gymnasium, Seoul	Jay Edson
‡ 5/21/77	Wilfredo GOMEZ	120	Dong-Kyun YUM	121	KO 12 2:40	Roberto Clemente Coliseum	Dick Young
‡ 7/11/77	Wilfredo GOMEZ	120	Raul TIRADO	120	KO 5 0:42	Roberto Clemente Coliseum	Chuck Hassett
‡11/26/77	Soo-Hwan HONG	121¾	Hector CARRASQUILLA	121	KO 3 1:04	Panama City, Panama	Jay Edson
‡ 1/19/78	Wilfredo GOMEZ	121½	Royal KOBAYASHI	121¾	KO 3 1:25	Kitakyushu Municipal Gymnasium	Harry Gibbs
‡ 2/1/78	Soo-Hwan HONG	121¾	Yu KASAHARA	121½	unan 15	Kuramae Arena, Tokyo, Japan	Martin Denkin
‡ 4/8/78	Wilfredo GOMEZ	122	Juan Antonio LOPEZ	122	TKO 7 2:51	Loubriel Stadium, Bayamon	Zack Clayton
‡ 5/6/78	Ricardo CARDONA	120	Soo-Hwan HONG	121	TKO 12 1:23	Changchung Gymnasium, Seoul	Tony Perez
‡ 6/2/78	Wilfredo GOMEZ	121½	Sakad PORNTAVEE	122	TKO 3 2:32	Main Stadium, Korat, Thailand	Ray Solis
‡ 9/2/78	Ricardo CARDONA	121½	Ruben VALDEZ	122	unan 15	Cartagena, Colombia	Isidoro Rodriguez
‡ 9/9/78	Wilfredo GOMEZ	122	Leonardo CRUZ	121¼	TKO 13 0:21	Hiram Bithorn Stadium, San Juan	Anselmo Escobedo
‡10/28/78	Wilfredo GOMEZ	122	Carlos ZARATE	122	TKO 5 0:44	Roberto Clemente Stadium	Harry Gibbs
‡11/12/78	Ricardo CARDONA	121¼	Soon-Hyun CHUNG	122	split 15	Changchung Gymnasium, Seoul	Luis Sulbaran
3/9/79	Wilfredo GOMEZ	122	Nestor JIMENEZ	121¾	TKO 5 2:51	Madison Square Garden, New York	Tony Perez
6/16/79	Wilfredo GOMEZ	122	Jesus HERNANDEZ	122	TKO 5 2:15	Roberto Clemente Coliseum	Henry Elespuro
‡ 6/23/79	Ricardo CARDONA	120½	Soon-Hyun CHUNG	121¾	unan 15	Changchung Gymnasium, Seoul	Stan Christodoulou
‡ 9/6/79	Ricardo CARDONA	121½	Yukio SEGAWA	121¾	unan 15	City Gymnasium, Hachinohe, Japan	Larry Rozadilla
9/28/79	Wilfredo GOMEZ	122	Carlos MENDOZA	120½	TKO 10 2:29	Caesars Palace, Las Vegas, Nevada	Richard Green
10/26/79	Wilfredo GOMEZ	122	Nicky PEREZ	120	TKO 5 3:00	Madison Square Garden, New York	Arthur Mercante
‡12/15/79	Ricardo CARDONA	122	Sergio PALMA	122	unan 15	Barranquilla, Colombia	Waldemar Schmidt
2/3/80	Wilfredo GOMEZ	122	Ruben VALDEZ	121¾	TKO 7	Caesars Palace, Las Vegas, Nevada	Ferd Hernandez
† 5/04/80	Leo RANDOLPH	121½	Ricardo CARDONA	121¾	TKO 15 1:31	Center Arena, Seattle, Wash.	Larry Rozadilla
† 8/09/80	Sergio PALMA	121½	Leo RANDOLPH	122	TKO 5 1:12	Coliseum, Spokane, Washington	Stan Christodoulou
8/22/80	Wilfredo GOMEZ	121¾	Derrik HOLMES	120¼	TKO 5 2:29	Caesars Palace, Las Vegas, Nev.	Joey Curtis
†11/08/80	Sergio PALMA	121¾	Ulises MORALES	119¾	TKO 9 1:20	Luna Park Stadium, Buenos Aires	Luis Sulbaran
¡12/13/80	Wilfredo GOMEZ	122	Jose CERVANTES	120½	KO 3 1:50	Jai Alai Fronton, Miami, Florida	Ismael Quinones Falu

Carl Duane and Jack (Kid) Wolfe were over the weight limit on August 29, 1923.   †WBA world junior featherweight title bout
* Loser failed to answer bell for round indicated   ‡WBC world super bantamweight title bout

JUNIOR FEATHERWEIGHT DIVISION

JACK (KID) WOLFE
(Jackson Kenneth Wolfe)
Born, June 11, 1895, Cleveland, Ohio. Weight 120
lbs. Height, 5 ft. 2 in.

1911
—Kid Schwertle	KO	3
—Julius Hess	W	10
—Tommy Lynn	W	10
—Tommy Lynn	W	10
—Johnny Griffith	WF	6
—Cal Delaney	D	6
—Cal Delaney	D	10
—Cal Delaney	D	10
—Kid Coffey	ND	10
—Jimmy Hector	ND	10

1912
—George St. Pierre	KO	6
—Rip Starke	KO	8
—Julius Hess	KO	3
—Kid Tepper	KO	3
—Frankie Mason	ND	10
—Rip Stark	ND	10
—Porter Root	ND	10

1913
—K. O. Eggers	KO	4
—Alvie Miller	ND	10
—Alvie Miller	ND	10
—Jimmy Murphy	ND	10
—Jerry Murphy	ND	6

1914
—Indian Kid	ND	10

1915
—Joe Kudria	KO	3
—Finney Boyle	KO	2
—K. O. Eggers	KO	5
—Al Shubert	D	12
—Al Shubert	L	12
—Eddie O'Keefe	ND	10
—Johnny Collins	ND	10
—Kid Herman	ND	10
—Battling Lahn	ND	10

1916
—Frankie Brown	W	10
—Battling Lahn	W	10
—Mickey Byrne	ND	10
—Luke Ginley	ND	10
—Young Sylvester	ND	10
—Young Mendo	ND	6
—Young Mendo	ND	10
—Battling Lahn	ND	10
—Luke Ginley	ND	10

1917
—Pal Moore	KO	4
—Johnny Allen	KO	8
—Al Shubert	W	15
—Dick Loadman	W	15
—Terry Martin	W	15
—Sammy Sandow	W	15
—Mickey Byrne	WF	3
—Pal Moore	L	8
—Chick Hayes	ND	10
—Dick Loadman	ND	10
—Eddie Wimler	ND	6
—Willie Devore	ND	10
—Willie Devore	ND	10
—Johnny Ertle	ND	10
—Benny Coster	ND	10

1918
—Danny Frush	W	15
—Andy Chaney	D	15
—Dick Loadman	ND	10
—Joe Lynch	ND	10
—Artie Root	ND	10
—Johnny Ertle	ND	10

1919
—Billy Hill	KO	5
—Jackie Saunders	KO	11
—Patsy Johnson	W	15

—K. O. Circus	ND	10
—Eddie Lavery	ND	10
—Pete Herman	ND	10
—Jack Sharkey	ND	10
—Earl Puryear	ND	10
—Joe Lynch	ND	10
—Joe Burman	ND	10

1920
—Harry Bramer	W	8
—Harry Bramer	W	8
—Harry Coulon	W	10
—Kid Dayton	WF	5
—Joe Burman	ND	10
—Joe Burman	ND	10
—Joe Lynch	ND	10
—Mike Dundee	ND	10

1921
—Johnny O'Leary	KO	2
—Paddy Owens	KO	11
—Kid Williams	W	12
—Frankie Dailey	W	10
—Carl Tremaine	D	12
—Terry Martin	L	12
—Bernie Hahn	ND	10
—Charlie Beecher	ND	10
—Joe Dailey	ND	10
—Terry McHugh	ND	8
—Harry Coulon	ND	10
—Eddie Pinchot	ND	8
—Babe Asher	ND	10
—Joe Lynch	ND	6
—Willie Doyle	ND	10
—Willie Doyle	ND	10
—Gussie Lewis	ND	10
—Danny Kramer	KO by	5

1922
Mar.	22—Alvie Miller, Lorain, Ohio	ND	10
Apr.	15—Terry Smith, Sandusky, Ohio	KO	2
May	5—Bernie Hahn, Chillicothe, Ohio	ND	10
June	13—Johnny (Pee Wee) Kaiser, Cincinnati	ND	10
July	3—Johnny (Pee Wee) Kaiser, St. Louis	ND	10
July	10—Frankie Jerome, New York	L	12
Aug.	8—Pal Moore, New York	D	12
Aug.	15—Frankie Jerome, New York	W	12
Sept.	22—Joe Lynch, New York	W	15

(Won Vacant World Junior Featherweight Title)

Oct.	6—Midget Smith, Canton, Ohio	ND	12
Oct.	30—Sammy Mandell, Kenosha, Wisc.	ND	10
Dec.	8—Mickey Dillon, Erie, Penn.	ND	12
	—Sammy Harris	D	12
Dec.	26—Benny Gould, Toronto	L	10

1923
Jan.	22—Benny Schwartz, Baltimore	W	12
Feb.	1—Eddie O'Dowd, Columbus	W	12
Feb.	5—Terry Martin, Jersey City	ND	12
Feb.	20—Pancho Villa, Philadelphia	KO by	3
June	13—Sammy Mandell, Cincinnati	ND	12
July	31—Pete Zivic, Columbus	W	6
Aug.	29—Carl Duane, Long Island City	L	12

(Lost World Junior Featherweight Title)

	—Frankie Jerome	D	12

1924
Jan.	14—Young Montreal, Columbus	W	12
Jan.	21—Benny Schwartz, Baltimore	WF	3
Mar.	12—Leo Roy, Montreal	L	10
Apr.	8—Bobby Burke, Reading, Penn.	ND	10
July	28—Carl Tremaine, Cleveland	KO by	6
Oct.	7—Vincent Salvadore, Reading	W	8
Oct.	22—Emil Paluso, Reading	D	10
Nov.	18—Newsboy Brown, Reading	D	10

TB	KO	WD	WF	D	LD	LF	KO BY	ND	NC
128	16	23	4	11	7	0	3	64	0

750

CARL DUANE
(Carl Duane Yacconetti)
Born, June 25, 1902, New York City, New York.
Weight, 122 lbs. Height, 5 ft. ½ in. Managed by Mike Valentine.

1920
—Al Kane	KO	4
—Andy Davis	KO	4

1921
—Silent Lamont	W	6
—Joe Frisco	W	6
—Young Zaccone	W	6
—Peter Husie	ND	10
—Tommy Lynch	LF	2

1922
—Johnny Noble	KO	1
—Moe Ginsburg	KO	2
—Scotty Williams	KO	1
—Nil Alexander	KO	2
—Johnny Noble	W	6
—George Daly	L	6

1923
Jan.	3—George Daly, New York	W	6
Jan.	17—Urban Grass, New York	KO	2
Mar.	9—Jackie Cope, New York	KO	1
Apr.	16—Charley Hayes, New York	W	6
Apr.	30—Lew Hurley, New York	W	6
May	21—Harry London, New York	W	6
June	9—Charlie Rosenberg, New York	D	6
June	23—Danny Edwards, New York	W	12
July	4—Billy Ryckoff, New York	KO	2
July	18—Charles Rosenberg, New York	W	12
Aug.	11—Carty Collins, New York	KO	2
Aug.	29—Jack (Kid) Wolfe, New York	W	12
	(Won World Junior Featherweight Title)		
Sept.	12—Young Montreal, New York	W	12
Sept.	21—Frankie Jerome, New York	D	6
Oct.	22—Mickey Brown, New York	W	12
Nov.	5—Frankie Conway, New York	W	12
Nov.	23—Frankie Jerome, New York	W	15

1924
Feb.	2—Andy Tucker, New York	KO	7
Feb.	15—Vincent (Pepper) Martin, New York	W	12
Mar.	22—Johnny Leonard, New York	D	12
Apr.	24—Packey O'Gatty, New York	KO	1
May	2—Johnny Leonard, New York	KO by	6

1925
Mar.	26—Lew Avery, Yonkers, New York	KO	2
Apr.	27—Izzy Cooper, New York	W	6
Mar.	11—Izzy Cooper, New York	W	10
June	1—Edouard Mascart, Brooklyn	L	10
Aug.	3—Bud Dempsey, New York	KO	5
Aug.	17—Johnny Leonard, Brooklyn	D	12
Nov.	16—Lew Kemp, New York	W	10

1926
Feb.	8—Joey Kaufman, New York	W	10
Mar.	1—Joe Malone, New York	W	10
Apr.	12—Georgie Bolduc, New York	W	10
May	25—Joe Glick, Brooklyn	WF	6
Nov.	19—Tod Morgan, New York	L	15
	(For World Junior Lightweight Title)		

1927
Feb.	4—Johnny Filucci, New York	L	10
June	7—Sammy Dorfman, New York	L	10
Aug.	19—Joe Bush, Allentown	W	10
Sept.	12—Joey Kauffman, Jersey City	ND	10
Sept.	23—Sammy Dorfman, New York	L	6
Dec.	19—Jackie Snyder, New York	W	10

1928
Jan.	23—Petey Mack, Jersey City	ND	10
Mar.	15—Pete Couvaris, Yonkers	W	6
Mar.	21—Pete Couvaris, New York	W	6
Mar.	31—Dominick Petrone, New York	L	10
Apr.	28—Lou Moscowitz, New York	W	10
Apr.	29—Joe Glick, New York	D	10
July	3—Andre Routis, New York	L	10
Oct.	11—Eddie Guida, New York	L	10

1929
Feb.	5—Angelo Gentile, New York	L	10
Apr.	15—Angelo Gentile, New York	W	10

TB	KO	WD	WF	D	LD	LF	KO BY	ND	NC
63	14	28	1	5	10	1	1	3	0

RIGOBERTO RIASCO
Born, Panama. Weight, 122-126 lbs.

1966
May	10—Jose Brown, Panama City	L	4
June	12—Marcos Herrera, Panama City	KO	1
Aug.	8—Agustin Lara, Panama City	W	4
Aug.	15—Kid Lalo, Colon	KO	5
Sept.	27—Offin Iborguez, Panama City	W	6
Oct.	10—Martin Ortega, Panama City	L	6

1967
Apr.	9—Franklin Espinosa, Panama City	W	6
Apr.	29—Eladio Espinosa, Panama City	KO	6
May	20—Franklin Espinosa, Panama City	W	8
June	3—Eladio Espinosa, Panama City	W	8
Aug.	25—Martin Ortega, Panama City	L	8
Oct.	28—Enrique Warren, Panama City	L	8

1968
Aug.	25—Carlos Mendoza, Panama City	D	4
Nov.	30—Santos Pena, Panama City	W	4
Dec.	15—Manuel Jimenez, Panama City	KO	1

1969
Feb.	4—Manuel Jimenez, Panama City	D	4
Mar.	1—Manuel Jiminez, Panama City	W	4
Aug.	6—Catalino Alvarado, Panama City	W	6
Oct.	6—Enrique Warren, Panama City	D	6
Dec.	13—Carlos Mendoza, Panama City	KO	6

1970
June	25—Humberto Arbaleda, Panama City	KO	3
Oct.	10—Jorge Reyes, Mexico City	L	10
Nov.	24—Francico Amano, Tijuana	KO	7

1971
Jan.	30—Jose Luis Meza, Mexico City	L	10

1972
Apr.	29—Enrique Alonso, Colon	L	10
Aug.	18—Alberto Herrera, Quito	KO	4
Oct.	28—Enrique Alonso, Panama City	KO	4
Nov.	19—Herman Espinosa, Panama City	W	10

1973
May	3—Jose Angel Herrera, Los Angeles	W	10
July	14—Lionel Hernandez, Panama City	W	10
Aug.	4—Santos Luis Rivera, San Juan	KO by	1
Sept.	14—Yambito Blanco, Panama City	KO	6
Dec.	15—Rafael Ortega, Panama	W	12

1974
May	11—Jesus Estrada, Monterrey	KO	6
June	24—Sanjo Takemori, Tokyo	D	10
Oct.	21—Flipper Uehara, Tokyo	L	10

1975
Jan.	26—Renan Marota, Panama City	W	10
Mar.	9—Raul Silva, Panama City	KO	10
May	31—Alexis Arguello, Managua	KO by	2
	(For Vacant World Featherweight Title)		
Aug.	23—Luis Avila, Panama City	W	12
Nov.	15—Santos Luis Rivera, Panama City	KO	7

1976
Apr.	3—Waruinge Nakayama, Panama	KO	9
	(Won Vacant WBC Super Bantamweight Title)		
June	12—Livio Nolasco, Panama City	KO	10
	(Retained WBC Super Bantamweight Title)		
Aug.	1—Dong-Kyun Yum, Pusan	W	15
	(Retained WBC Super Bantamweight Title)		
Oct.	10—Royal Kobayashi, Tokyo	KO by	8
	(Lost WBC Super Bantamweight Title)		

TB	KO	WD	WF	D	LD	LF	KO BY	ND	NC
45	15	16	0	4	7	0	3	0	0

KAZUO (ROYAL) KOBAYASHI
Born, October 10, 1949, Fukuoka Prefecture, Japan. Weight, 122-126 lbs. Height, 5 ft. 4½ in.

1973
Feb.	25—Baron Kumazawa, Tokyo	W	8
Apr.	27—Hiromichi Sato, Nagoya	KO	2
June	15—Hiroshi Miura, Tokyo	KO	2
July	21—Victor Dunu, Kumamoto	KO	7

Sept. 7—Katsutoshi Inuzuka, Tokyo .... KO 5
Oct. 19—Chung Nam Choul, Tokyo .... W 10
Nov. 23—Nobuyoshi Sekino, Tokyo .... KO 2
1974
Feb. 1—Hiroshi Nunose, Tokyo .... KO 4
Mar. 17—Sung Jong Hong, Tokyo .... KO 3
May 19—Jose Medel, Tokyo .... KO 6
Aug. 4—Freddie Mason, Tokyo .... KO 7
Sept. 16—Bert Nabalatan, Tokyo .... W 10
Dec. 30—Sanjyo Takemori, Tokyo .... KO 2
1975
Feb. 17—Masanao Toyoshima, Tokyo ...... KO 6
Apr. 4—June Gallego, Sendai City .... KO 9
May 2—Zensuke Utagawa, Tokyo .... KO 2
June 16—Yuh Hwa Wyong, Tokyo .... KO 4
Oct. 12—Alexis Arguello, Tokyo .... KO by 5
(For WBA Featherweight Title)
Dec. 21—Ushiwakamaru Harada, Tokyo .... W 10
1976
Feb. 15—Emirio Sarusero, Panama .... L 10
July 10—Jager Sekino, Tokyo .... KO 5
Oct. 10—Rigoberto Riasco, Tokyo .... KO 8
(Won WBC Super Bantamweight Title)
Nov. 24—Dong-Kyun Yum, Seoul .... L 15
(Lost WBC Super Bantamweight Title)
1977
Feb. 8—Junichi Ohkubo, Osaka .... KO 7
May 23—Shigeru Sasaki, Tokyo .... KO 1
Nov. 3—Toshi Nakai, Tokyo .... KO 1
1978
Jan. 19—Wilfredo Gomez, Kitakyushu .. KO by 3
(For WBC Super Bantamweight Title)
Apr. 27—Bok-Soo Hwang, Tokyo .... KO 10
(Won OPBF Featherweight Title)
Aug. 6—Spider Nemoto, Tokyo .... W 12
(Retained OPBF Featherweight Title)
1979
Jan. 9—Eusebio Pedroza, Tokyo .... KO by 13
(For WBA Featherweight Title)
Apr. 27—Bok-Soo Hwang, Kuamoto .... W 12
(Retained OPBF Featherweight Title)
July 26—Hikaru Tomonari, Tokyo .... L 10
Oct. 28—Suk Tae Yun, Aomori Ken .... W 12
(Retained OPBF Featherweight Title)
Dec. 20—Kashi Keno, Tokyo .... KO 6
1980
Feb. 24—Masa Ito, Yamaguchi .... KO 7
June 9—Tenyu Maruki, Nagoya .... KO 6
(Retained OPBF Featherweight Title)
Aug. 19—Tae-Hwan Lee, Tokyo .... W 12
(Retained OPBF Featherweight Title)

TB	KO	WD	WF	D	LD	LF	KO BY	ND	NC
37	23	8	0	0	3	0	3	0	0

DONG-KYUN YUM
(Early Record Not Available)
1970
—Chong-Ho Lee .... W 10
—Sung-Jong Hong .... W 10
1971
Aug. 19—Duk-Lee Byung, Seoul .... KO 8
Oct. 20—Sung-Jong Hong, Daeku City ...... W 10
(Won Korean Junior Featherweight Title)
Dec. 10—Chung Park, Daeku City .... W 10
1972
Jan. 8—Speedy Daeoka, Seoul .... KO 7
Feb. 27—Soo-Man Hyun, Pusan .... W 10
(Retained Korean Junior Featherweight Title)
Mar. 10—Dong-Il Park, Seoul .... KO 6
(Retained Korean Junior Featherweight Title)
Apr. 2—Sung-Jong Hong, Pusan .... D 10
(Retained Korean Junior Featherweight Title)
Apr. 21—Genzo Kurosawa, Seoul .... W 10
Aug. 6—Soo-Man Hyun, Seoul .... W 10
Sept. 24—Dong-Il Park, Pusan .... KO 3
(Retained Korean Junior Featherweight Title)
Oct. 22—Hiroshi Ishibashi, Seoul .... KO 6
Nov. 19—Sung-Jong Hong, Daeku City ...... W 10
(Retained Korean Junior Featherweight Title)

1973
Feb. 15—Sung-Kyun Kim, Seoul .... KO 4
(Retained Korean Junior Featherweight Title)
Apr. 15—Hariken Choi, Seoul .... KO 7
(Retained Korean Junior Featherweight Title)
May 27—Min-Choul Choi, Pusan .... W 10
(Retained Korean Junior Featherweight Title)
July 15—Koji Ishibashi, Seoul .... W 10
Aug. 18—Sung-Kyun Kim, Pusan .... KO 6
(Retained Korean Junior Featherweight Title)
Oct. 13—Yung-Choul Choi, Gwang-Joo ..... W 10
(Retained Korean Junior Featherweight Title)
Oct. 27—Chong-Tae Yuh, Daejon .... W 10
(Retained Korean Junior Featherweight Title)
Dec. 8—Shoji Sakugawa, Seoul .... KO 6
1974
Feb. 3—Chin-Kyun Kim, Daeku City ...... W 10
Mar. 17—Kyu-Chul Chang, Pusan .... W 12
(Won Oriental Junior Featherweight Title)
May 26—Polrub Luknaka, Pusan .... W 12
(Retained Oriental Junior Featherweight Title)
July 16—Tomoharu Eda, Daejon .... W 12
(Retained Oriental Junior Featherweight Title)
1975
June 5—Seiichi Watanuki, Osaka .... KO 10
(Retained Oriental Junior Featherweight Title)
Aug. 2—Hiroshi Ishibashi, Tokyo .... KO 9
Nov. 7—Futaro Tanaka, Osaka .... W 12
(Retained Oriental Junior Featherweight Title)
1976
Apr. 8—Kenji Kato, Seoul .... KO 4
June 12—Shigeru Sasaki, Seoul .... KO 9
Aug. 1—Rigoberto Riasco, Pusan .... L 15
(For WBC Super Bantamweight Title)
Nov. 24—Royal Kobayashi, Seoul .... W 15
(Won WBC Super Bantamweight Title)
Dec. 26—Tiger Osano, Pusan .... KO 6
1977
Feb. 13—Jose Cervantes, Seoul .... W 15
(Retained WBC Super Bantamweight Title)
Apr. 15—Shujo Yoshida, Seoul .... W 10
May 21—Wilfredo Gomez, San Juan .... KO by 12
(Lost WBC Super Bantamweight Title)
June 27—Soo-Hwan Hong, Seoul .... L 10
(For Korean Junior Featherweight Title)
July 19—Shuzo Yoshida, Yokohama .... KO by 2
1978
Feb. 25—Edwin Alarcon, Seoul .... W 10
May 8—Orlando Javierto, Changchung .... W 10
July 12—Fernando Cabanela, Seoul .... W 10
1979
(Inactive)
1980
Dec. 19—Soo-Hwan Hong, Seoul .... D 10

TB	KO	WD	WF	D	LD	LF	KO BY	ND	NC
43	14	23	0	2	2	0	2	0	0

WILFREDO GOMEZ
Born, October 29, 1956, Las Monjas, Puerto Rico.
Weight, 122-126 lbs. Height, 5 ft. 5 in.
1974
Nov. 16—Jacinto Fuentes, Panama City ..... D 6
Dec. 21—Mario Hernandez, San Jose ...... KO 1
1975
Feb. 16—Jorge Bernal, Panama City ...... KO 1
Mar. 2—Antonio DaSilva, Panama City ... KO 2
May 3—Jose Jimenez, Panama City ...... KO 1
June 21—Jacinto Fuentes, Panama City .... KO 2
Aug. 2—Clotilde Garcia, Managua .... KO 2
Sept. 19—Joe Guevara, San Juan .... KO 6
Dec. 20—Andres Hernandez, San Juan ..... KO 8
1976
Feb. 20—Cornell Hall, San Juan .... KO 3
Apr. 5—Rick Quijano, San Juan .... KO 1
May 8—Sak Lempthong, San Juan .... KO 3
July 19—Albert Davila, San Juan .... KO 9
Aug. 16—Tony Rocha, San Juan .... KO 2
Oct. 11—Jose Murillo, San Juan .... KO 4

1977

Feb.	12—John Meza, San Juan .... KO	2
May	21—Dong-Kyun Yum, San Juan ...... KO	12
	(Won WBC Super Bantamweight Title)	
July	11—Raul Tirado, San Juan .... KO	5
	(Retained WBC Super Bantamweight Title)	

1978

Jan.	19—Royal Kobayashi, Kitakyushu .... KO	3
	(Retained WBC Super Bantamweight Title)	
Apr.	8—Juan A. Lopez, San Juan .... KO	7
	(Retained WBC Super Bantamweight Title)	
June	2—Sakad Porntavee, Korat .... KO	3
	(Retained WBC Super Bantamweight Title)	
Sept.	9—Leo Cruz, San Juan .... KO	13
	(Retained WBC Super Bantamweight Title)	
Oct.	28—Carlos Zarate, San Juan .... KO	5
	(Retained WBC Super Bantamweight Title)	

1979

Mar.	9—Nestor (Baba) Jimenez, New York KO	5
	(Won Vacant World Junior Featherweight Title)	
May	21—Nelson Cruz Tamariz, New York KO	2
June	16—Julio Hernandez, San Juan .... KO	5
	(Retained World Junior Featherweight Title)	
Sept.	28—Carlos Mendoza, Las Vegas ...... KO	10
	(Retained World Junior Featherweight Title)	
Oct.	26—Nicky Perez, New York .... KO	5
	(Retained World Junior Featherweight Title)	

1980

Feb.	3—Ruben Valdez, Las Vegas .... KO	6
	(Retained World Junior Featherweight Title)	
Apr.	27—Eddie Ndukwu, San Juan .... KO	4
Aug.	22—Derrik Holmes, Las Vegas ...... KO	5
	(Retained World Junior Featherweight Title)	
Dec.	13—Jose Cervantes, Miami .... KO	3
	(Retained World Junior Featherweight Title)	

TB	KO	WD	WF	D	LD	LF	KO BY	ND	NC
32	31	0	0	1	0	0	0	0	0

SOO-HWAN HONG
(Record Under Bantamweight Champions)

RICARDO CARDONA
Born, November 9, 1952, Palenque de San Basilio, Bolivar, Colombia. Weight, 122 lbs. Height, 5 ft. 8 in.

1973

Sept.	15—Osvaldo Rojas, Valencia .... W	4
Nov.	17—Manuel Olivares, Caracas .... KO	4

1974

Feb.	9—Juan J. Rojas, Caracas .... W	6
Mar.	26—Osvaldo Rojas, Caracas .... W	6
May	19—Leslie Moreno, Barquisimeto L	10
Nov.	28—Miguel Espinosa, Bogota .... W	10

1975

Feb.	15—Chita Tovar, Caracas .... KO	7
Mar.	1—Silvio Diaz, Caracas .... D	
Apr.	13—Guillermo Gomez, Caracas .... KO	5
July	14—Idelfonso Bethelmy, Caracas ..... KO	8
Oct.	11—Jose Quijano, Caracas L	
Dec.	14—Abraham Meza, Caracas .... KO	8

1976

Jan.	31—Oscar Arnal, Caracas L	10
Apr.	11—Pedro Vasquez, Caracas .... W	10
July	25—Jesus Medina, Valencia .... KO	4
Nov.	7—Rafael Montes, Cartagena .... KO	7
	(Won Colombian Junior Featherweight Title)	

1977

Feb.	18—Nestor (Baba) Jimenez, Cartagena .. L	10
Mar.	19—Guillermo Gomez, Barranquila ... KO	5
June	3—Francisco Hernandez, Caracas .... KO	8
Nov.	5—Jesus Caicedo, Maracay .... W	10

1978

May	7—Soo-Hwan Hong, Seoul .... KO	12
	(Won WBA Junior Featherweight Title)	
Sept.	9—Ruben Valdes, Cartagena .... W	15
	(Retained WBA Junior Featherweight Title)	
Nov.	12—Soon-Hyun Chung, Seoul .... W	15
	(Retained WBA Junior Featherweight Title)	

1979

June	23—Soon-Hyun Chung, Seoul .... W	15
	(Retained WBA Junior Featherweight Title)	
Sept.	6—Yukio Segawa, Hachinohe .... W	15
	(Retained WBA Junior Featherweight Title)	
Dec.	15—Sergio Palma, Barranquilla .... W	15
	(Retained WBA Junior Featherweight Title)	

1980

May	4—Leo Randolph, Seattle .... KO by	15
	(Lost WBA Junior Featherweight Title)	
Nov.	14—Ralph Barrios, Miami .... KO	1

TB	KO	WD	WF	D	LD	LF	KO BY	ND	NC
28	11	11	0	1	4	0	1	0	0

LEO RANDOLPH
Born, February 27, 1958, Tacoma, Washington. Weight, 118-122 lbs. Height, 5 ft. 5 in.
1976 Olympic Flyweight Gold Medalist

1978

June	20—Alfonso Delgadillo, Seattle .... KO	2
July	12—Tony Reed, Kansas City .... W	8
Aug.	17—Marcial Santiago, Totowa .... W	6
Oct.	5—Eddie Logan, Seattle .... W	8
Oct.	31—Carlos Zayas, St. Louis .... KO	1
Nov.	14—Fernando Martinez, Totowa .... W	8
Nov.	30—Ralph Roman, Cohoes .... KO	2
Dec.	15—Tony Hernandez, White Plains ... KO	4

1979

Apr.	20—David Capo, New York L	8
May	14—Alfonso Cirillo, Philadelphia ..... KO	5
May	25—Daryl Jones, Santa Monica .... W	10
Sept.	22—Jose Bautista, Los Angeles .... W	10
Oct.	27—Oscar Muniz, Los Angeles .... W	10
Nov.	27—Tony Cisneros, Los Angeles ...... KO	1

1980

Jan.	12—Joe Zaldivar, Incline Village ..... KO	2
Jan.	26—Baby Kid Chocolate, Los Angeles .. W	10
Mar.	28—Tony Rocha, Tacoma, Washington KO	2
May	4—Ricardo Cardona, Seattle, Wash... KO	15
	(Won WBA Junior Featherweight Title)	
Aug.	9—Sergio Palma, Spokane, Wash. KO by	5
	(Lost WBA Junior Featherweight Title)	

TB	KO	WD	WF	D	LD	LF	KO BY	ND	NC
19	9	8	0	0	1	0	1	0	0

SERGIO PALMA
(Sergio Victor Palma)
Born, January 1, 1956, La Tigra, Chaco, Argentina.

1976

Jan.	15—Ricardo Gomez, Pergamino .... W	6
Feb.	25—Manuel Munoz, Mar del Plata .... KO	4
Apr.	7—Jose Izquierdo, Buenos Aires ...... W	6
May	8—Emilio Haedo, Buenos Aires ...... W	6
June	11—Hector R. Barreto, Villaguay ..... W	6
July	17—Ricardo Gomez, Buenos Aires ...... W	8
Aug.	6—Romualdo Agramonte, T. Lauquen KO	7
Sept.	29—Jose Vicario, Buenos Aires .... W	10
Dec.	4—Jose Casas, Villa Carlos Paz .... D	10

1977

Jan.	19—Gilberto Lopez, Villa Carlos Paz .... D	10
Mar.	9—Felix Gonzalez, Villa Carlos Paz L	10
Mar.	23—Juan Aravena, Bariloche .... W	10
Apr.	22—Ricardo Gomez, Reconquista ...... W	10
July	13—Hugo Emer, Villa Carlos Paz ...... D	10
Sept.	12—Jose Casas, Buenos Aires .... KO	9
Oct.	15—Arnoldo Aguero, Buenos Aires .... W	12
	(Won Argentine Junior Featherweight Title)	
Dec.	10—Carlos Cordoba, Rio Tercero .... D	10
Dec.	23—Manuel Almada, C. Pringles .. L disq.	4

1978

Feb.	3—Arnoldo Aguero, Mar del Plata ... TW	7
	(Retained Argentine Junior Featherweight Title)	
Apr.	8—Benicio Sosa, Sierras Bayas ...... KO	6
Apr.	22—David Gonzalez, Maximo Pax ...... W	10
May	13—Hugo Melgarejo, Bariloche .... W	12
	(Won South American Junior Featherweight Title)	

June 16—Diego Vega Ramirez, Villa Carlos
    Paz .... W 10
July   7—Pablo Lencina, Curuzu Cuatia .... KO 2
July 21—Juan C. Acosta, Villa Angela ..... KO 3
Aug. 12—Ruben Granado, Buenos Aires .... KO 10
    (Retained Argentine Junior Featherweight Title)
Sept. 30—Arnoldo Aguero, Buenos Aires ..... W 12
    (Retained Argentine Junior Featherweight Title)
Oct. 28—Raul Perez, Mar del Plata .... W 10
Nov. 10—Carlos Betbeder, Costa Rivadavia .. W 10
Dec. 15—Gilberto Lopez, Curuzu Cuatia ..... W 10

1979

Jan. 27—Diego Ramirez, V. Huidobro .. W disq. 3
Mar. 16—Ruben Butiler, Bariloche .... KO 10
    (Retained Argentine Junior Featherweight Title)
Apr.   6—Hector Lopez, Tucuman .... KO 5
May   4—Gilberto Lopez, Caleta Oliva .... W 10
May 18—Gilberto Lopez, Barranqueras ...... W 10
June 15—Raul Perez, Cordoba .... W 10
July 13—Roberto Haidar, General Pico .... KO 3

Aug. 10—Francisco Acosta, San Pena ...... KO 7
    (Retained Argentine Junior Featherweight Title)
Sept. 28—Gilberto Lopez, Villa Regina .... W 10
Oct. 20—Nestor Jimenez, Buenos Aires ..... W 10
Nov.   9—Miguel Lovera, Villa Angela ..... KO 3
    (Retained South American Junior Featherweight Title)
Dec. 15—Ricardo Cardona, Barranquilla ..... L 15
    (For WBA Junior Featherweight Title)

1980

May 17—Carlos Totaro, Mar del Plata ...... W 10
June 7—Juan Brizuela, Pergamino .... W 10
Aug.   9—Leo Randolph, Spokane, Wash..... KO 5
    (Won WBA Junior Featherweight Title)
Nov.   8—Ulises Morales, Buenos Aires ..... KO 9
    (Retained WBA Junior Featherweight Title)
Dec. 20—Hugo Fica, Resistencia .... KO 3

TB	KO	WD	WF	D	LD	LF	KO BY	ND	NC
47	15	24	1	4	1	2	0	0	0

BANTAMWEIGHTS

TOMMY (SPIDER) KELLY	1887	BALTAZAR SANGCHILLI	1935-1936
HUGHEY BOYLE	1887-1888	*LOU SALICA (NBA)*	*1935*
TOMMY (SPIDER) KELLY	1889	*SIXTO ESCOBAR (NBA)*	*1935-1936*
CHAPPIE MORAN	1889-1890	TONY MARINO	1936
TOMMY (SPIDER) KELLY	*1890-1892*	SIXTO ESCOBAR	1936-1937
GEORGE DIXON	1890-1891	HARRY JEFFRA	1937-1938
BILLY PLIMMER (GREAT BRITAIN)	*1892-1895*	SIXTO ESCOBAR	1938-1939
JIMMY BARRY	1894-1899	GEORGIE PACE (NBA)	1940
THOMAS (PEDLAR) PALMER	*1895-1899*	LOU SALICA	1940-1942
TERRY MC GOVERN	1899-1900	MANUEL ORTIZ	1942-1947
HARRY HARRIS	1901-1902	HAROLD DADE	1947
HARRY FORBES	1902-1903	MANUEL ORTIZ	1947-1950
FRANKIE NEIL	1903-1904	VIC TOWEEL	1950-1952
JOE BOWKER	1904-1905	JIMMY CARRUTHERS	1952-1954
JIMMY WALSH	1905-1907	ROBERT COHEN	1954-1956
KID MURPHY (CLAIMANT)	*1907-1908*	*RAUL (RATON) MACIAS (NBA)*	*1955-1957*
FRANKIE CONLEY (CALIFORNIA)	1910-1911	MARIO D'AGATA	1956-1957
JOHNNY COULON	1910-1914	ALPHONSE HALIMI	1957-1959
GEORGE (DIGGER) STANLEY (GREAT BRITAIN)	*1910-1912*	JOE BECERRA	1959-1960
CHARLES LEDOUX (GREAT BRITAIN)	*1912-1913*	EDER JOFRE	1961-1965
		MASAHIKO (FIGHTING) HARADA	1965-1968
KID WILLIAMS	1914-	LIONEL ROSE	1968-1969
JOHNNY (KEWPIE) ERTLE	*1915*	RUBEN OLIVARES	1969-1970
PETE HERMAN	1917-1920	JESUS (CHUCHO) CASTILLO	1970-1971
JOE LYNCH	1920-1921	RUBEN OLIVARES	1971-1972
PETE HERMAN	1921	RAFAEL HERRERA	1972
JOHNNY BUFF	1921-1922	ENRIQUE PINDER	1972-1973
JOE LYNCH	1922-1924	ROMEO ANAYA	1973
ABE GOLDSTEIN	1924	*RAFAEL HERRERA (WBC)*	*1973-1974*
EDDIE (CANNONBALL) MARTIN	1924-1925	ARNOLD TAYLOR	1973-1974
CHARLIE (PHIL) ROSENBERG	1925-1927	SOO-HWAN HONG	1974-1975
TEDDY BALDOCK (GREAT BRITAIN)	*1927*	*RODOLFO MARTINEZ (WBC)*	*1974-1976*
CHARLES (BUD) TAYLOR (NBA)	1927-1928	ALFONSO ZAMORA	1975-1977
WILLIE SMITH (GREAT BRITAIN)	*1927-1928*	*CARLOS ZARATE (WBC)*	*1976-1979*
BUSHY GRAHAM (NEW YORK)	*1928-1929*	JORGE LUJAN	1977-1980
(PANAMA) AL BROWN	1929-1935	*LUPE PINTOR (WBC)*	*1979*
SIXTO ESCOBAR (NBA)	*1934-1935*	JULIAN SOLIS	1980
		JEFF CHANDLER	1980-

Claimants not generally recognized are in *italics*.

HISTORY OF THE BANTAMWEIGHT CLASS

No authentic, continuous records of the bantamweight division during London Prize Ring days were ever kept, but it is known that Charley Lynch was American champion in 1856 when he went to England, where he won and lost several battles. He claimed the world bantam title when he defeated Simon Finighty in 43 rounds. Lynch returned home and retired soon afterwards. He was born in New York, weighed 112 pounds and was five feet, four inches in height. The title then lapsed, until claimed in 1887 by Tommy Kelly, the "Harlem Spider." Championship bouts were staged as follows:

During the period from 1870 to 1890 there was much confusion with a number of claims made to the American and World titles. Those whose claims received the most credit were George Siddons in 1870, Tommy Kelly of Boston in 1870, Dick Hollywood in 1871, Tommy (Spider) Kelly of New York in 1887, Hughey Boyle in 1888, Chappie Moran of England in 1889, Cal McCarthy in 1889, Spider Kelly again in 1889, Tim Murphy in 1890, Fred Bogan of Australia in 1890 and then George Dixon in 1890.

May 10, 1888. Tommy Kelly drew with George Dixon at Boston, in 9 rounds. (The weight was 105 pounds, and Dixon's manager, Tom O'Rourke, claimed the bantam crown for the colored lad at that mark, which was afterwards advanced to 112 then to 115 pounds, and finally to the present scaling of 118 pounds.)

June 27, 1890. George Dixon stopped Nunc Wallace at London, England, in 18 rounds. (This was for the world's bantam championship, Wallace scaling 113 against Dixon's 112 pounds.)

Oct. 23, 1890. George Dixon outpointed Johnny Murphy at Providence, R. I., in 40 rounds.

March 31, 1891. George Dixon stopped Cal McCarthy at Troy, N. Y., in 22 rounds.

July 28, 1891. George Dixon knocked out Abe Willis at San Francisco, in 5 rounds. (In the following year Dixon outgrew the bantam grade and entered the featherweight division.)

Sept. 15, 1894. Jimmy Barry knocked out Casper Leon at Lamont, Ill., in 28 rounds. (With this victory, Jimmy Barry claimed the bantam championship, vacant since Dixon relinquished the title in 1892.)

Dec. 6, 1897. Jimmy Barry knocked out Walter Croot at London, England, in 20 rounds. (This bout gave Barry the world's title. Croot died after the knockout, but Barry was exonerated by a coroner's jury.)

Sept. 12, 1899. Terry McGovern knocked out Pedlar Palmer at Tuckahoe, N. Y., in 1 round. (This victory over England's champion gave McGovern the world title, Jimmy Barry having retired undefeated. In 1900 McGovern vacated the bantam title, and joined the featherweight ranks.

March 18, 1901—Harry Harris outpointed Pedlar Palmer at London, England, in 15 rounds. (This was an international match, with the world bantam title at stake, McGovern having entered the featherweight division. Harris also became a featherweight in the year following.)

Jan. 23, 1902. Harry Forbes knocked out Danny Dougherty at St. Louis, in 4 rounds. (Forbes had beaten most of the crack bantams, and his claim to the American title was universally recognized. But in 1903, he beat Andy Tokell in 10 rounds in Detroit, thus winning the world crown, Tokell being the British champion.)

Aug. 13, 1903. Frankie Neil knocked out Harry Forbes at San Francisco, Cal., 2 rounds.

Oct. 17, 1904. Joe Bowker outpointed Frankie Neil at London, England, in 20 rounds. (Bowker, British champion, won the world title, but outgrew the bantam class the same year. Both Digger Stanley of England and Jimmy Walsh of Boston, claimed the title. One was recognized in the U.S. the other in England.)

Oct. 20, 1905. Jimmy Walsh outpointed Digger Stanley at Chelsea, Mass., in 15 rounds. (Walsh claimed the bantamweight title after beating Stanley, England's champion. By 1907 Walsh had outgrown the class.)

In 1908 Kid Murphy claimed the U. S. championship. It was not until 1910, when Johnny Coulon beat Jim Hendrick, British champion in 10 rounds and stopped him in 19 rounds on March 6, 1910, that the international title was at stake and Coulon was accepted as the titleholder since he had whipped Kid Murphy three times previously in U. S. title bouts.

June 9, 1914, Kid Williams knocked out Johnny Coulon at Vernon, Cal., in 3 rounds.

Sept. 10, 1915. Johnny Ertle won from Kid Williams on a foul at St. Paul, Minn., in 5 rounds. (Ertle claimed title, but as decision was a disputed one, his claim was not generally recognized.)

Jan. 9, 1917, Pete Herman outpointed Kid Williams at New Orleans, in 20 rounds. (Herman was recognized by entire press as bantamweight titleholder, and Ertle's claim disallowed.)

Dec. 22, 1920, Joe Lynch outpointed Pete Herman, in Madison Square Garden, in 15 rounds.

July 25, 1921. Pete Herman outpointed Joe Lynch at Ebbets Field, Brooklyn, N.Y., in 15 rounds.

Sept. 23, 1921. Johnny Buff outpointed Pete Herman in Madison Square

Garden, in 15 rounds.

July 10, 1922. Joe Lynch knocked out Johnny Buff in New York Velodrome, New York City, in 14 rounds.

March 21, 1924. Abe Goldstein outpointed Joe Lynch in Madison Square Garden, in 15 rounds.

Dec. 19, 1924. Eddie (Cannonball) Martin outpointed Abe Goldstein in Madison Square Garden, in 15 rounds.

March 20, 1925. Charlie (Phil) Rosenberg outpointed Eddie (Cannonball) Martin in Madison Square Garden, in 15 rounds. (Rosenberg was deprived of his title by boxing commission when he was unable to make weight for a scheduled championship bout with Bushy Graham.)

On June 24, 1927, in Chicago, Bud Taylor beat Tony Canzoneri to win N.B.A. recognition. Taylor vacated the N.B.A. title on August 21, 1928.

On May 23, 1928, Bushy Graham outpointed Corp. Izzy Schwartz in fifteen rounds for the N. Y. recognition as world champion. Graham outgrew the class without ever defending the title, and with Taylor having given up his claim, an Al Brown-Vidal Gregorio bout was for worldwide recognition.

June 18, 1929. Al Brown outpointed Vidal Gregario at New York City, in 15 rounds. (This was the outcome of an elimination tourney ordered by the New York State Commission, to determine a successor to Rosenberg, and Al Brown thereby became champion.)

June 1, 1935. Baltazar Sangchili outpointed Al Brown at Valencia, Spain, in 15 rounds.

June 29, 1936. Tony Marino knocked out Baltazar Sangchili at Queensboro Club, New York City, in 14 rounds.

August 31, 1936. Sixto Escobar knocked out Tony Marino at Dykeman Oval, New York City, in 13 rounds.

Sept. 23, 1937. Harry Jeffra outpointed Sixto Escobar at Polo Grounds, New York City, in 15 rounds.

February 20, 1938. Sixto Escobar outpointed Harry Jeffra in Puerto Rico in 15 rounds.

Sixto Escobar retired in 1940. Georgie Pace and Lou Salica were the outstanding contenders. Pace was the N. B. A. champion and Salica had the support of N. Y. and California. They fought and Salica won. By conquering Tommy Forte, he gained international recognition.

Aug. 7, 1942. Lou Salica was outpointed in 12 rounds by Manuel Ortiz, Hollywood, in title bout, Ortiz gaining the title.

In 1943, Ortiz successfully defended his title eight times.

In 1944, Ortiz successfully defended his world crown four times.

In 1945, Ortiz went into the Army and after his discharge, he defended his title successfully three times, all in 1946. His victims were Luis Castillo, whom he

knocked out in the 13th round; Kenny Lindsay, whom he stopped in five and Jackie Jurich, whom he halted in 11 rounds.

On January 6, 1947, Ortiz lost his title to Harold Dade via the decision route in 15 rounds at San Francisco.

Ortiz regained the title on March 11, 1947, by winning a 15 round decision from Dade at Los Angeles.

May 31, 1950—Vic Toweel won the title by defeating Manuel Ortiz in 15 rounds at Johannesburg, So. Africa.

Nov. 15, 1952—Jimmy Carruthers won the title by knocking out Vic Toweel in one round at Johannesburg, So. Africa.

Jimmy Carruthers retired as undefeated champion on May 16, 1954, shortly after successfully defending his crown against Chamrern Songkitrat at Bangkok, Thailand.

Sept. 19, 1954—Robert Cohen defeated Chamrern Songkitrat, 15 rounds, for the vacant bantamweight championship, at Bangkok, Thailand.

June 29, 1956—Mario D'Agata won title by halting Robert Cohen in sixth round at Rome, Italy.

April 1, 1957—Alphonse Halimi won the title by decisioning Mario D'Agata, 15 rounds, at Paris, France.

July 8, 1959—Joe Becerra won the title by knocking out Alphonse Halimi in 3 rounds at Los Angeles, Calif.

Becerra announced his retirement on August 30, 1960 after being stopped in the eighth round of a non-title bout by Eloy Sanchez in Juarez, Mexico.

The National Boxing Association and the European Boxing Union arranged eliminations to decide Becerra's successor. On October 15, 1960, Alphonse Halimi of France gained the decision, in London, over Freddie Gilroy of Ireland, to win the European title. In Los Angeles on November 18, 1960, Eder Jofre of Brazil knocked out Eloy Sanchez of Mexico in the sixth round to win the American title.

Though the winners were to clash for the world championship, Halimi refused to accept Jofre and because of his refusal to fight the Brazilian, a match was arranged with Piero Rollo, champion of Italy, sanctioned by the Italian Federation, as a title bout. Rollo was stopped in the tenth round at Rio de Janeiro, March 25, 1961, and Jofre was acknowledged world title holder by the N.B.A., New York State, the South American Federation and Ring Magazine.

On May 30, 1961, Halimi was outpointed by Johnny Caldwell of Ireland who was given recognition by the European Boxing Union.

January 18, 1962—Eder Jofre gained international recognition by knocking out Johnny Caldwell in the tenth round at Sao Paulo, Brazil.

May 17, 1965—Fighting Harada defeated Eder Jofre by a decision in 15

rounds in Tokyo, to win the bantam title.

February 26, 1968—Lionel Rose, Australia, 117¾, beat Fighting Harada, Japan, 118, to win the world bantamweight crown by a unanimous decision in 15 rounds. The fight was held in Tokyo. Referee Ko Toyama scored it 72—71, Judge Hiroyuki Tezaki, 72—69 and Judge Ken Morita, 72—70, all for Rose. The attendance was 7,000.

Aug. 22, 1969—Ruben Olivares, 118, Mexico kayoed Lionel Rose, 118, Australia at 2:24 of the fifth round to win the world title in Los Angeles, Calif. The referee was Larry Rozadilla. Att.—17,000.

October 16, 1970—Chucho Castillo, Mexico, stopped Ruben Olivares, Mexico in the 14th round to win the title. Bout held in Los Angeles, Calif. Weights: Olivares—118, Castillo—118. Referee Dick Young stopped the bout at 2:27 of the 14th round on the recommendation of the ring physician.

April 2, 1971—Mexico's Ruben Olivares regained the crown with a 15-round decision over Chucho Castillo at Los Angeles, Calif. Both fighters weight 117.

March 19, 1972—Rafael Herrera, Mexico won the title, stopping Ruben Olivares at 1:28 of the 8th round. Weights, both 118. Contest held at Mexico City.

July 30, 1972—Enrique Pinder, Panama, decisioned Rafael Herrera, Mexico to win the world title in 15 rds. Pinder 118, Herrera 117½. Bout held in Panama City, Panama.

January 20, 1973—Romeo Anaya, Mexico kayoed Enrique Pinder, Panama in the third round. Bout held in Panama City, Panama. Anaya and Pinder both weighed 118.

November 3, 1973—Arnold Taylor, South Africa halted Romeo Anaya, Mexico, in the 13th round. Contest held in Johannesburg, South Africa. Taylor 114, Anaya 117 ¾.

July 3, 1974—Soo Hwang Hong, Korea outpointed Arnold Taylor, South Africa, in 15 rounds to win the bantamweight crown. Contest was held in Durban, South Africa. Taylor—117, Hong—118.

March 15, 1975—Alfonso Zamora became the youngest bantamweight to win the title with his kayo over Soo Hwan Hong at 2:34 of 4th round. Contest held at Los Angeles, Calif. Zamora and Hong 118. Referee George Latka.

November 19, 1977—Jorge Lujan, Panama, 117, won the title from Alfonso Zamora, Mexico, 118, via kayoed the 10th round. The bout held in Los Angeles, Calif. Referee John Thomas.

June 2, 1979—Guadalupe (Lupe) Pintor, 118, Mexico, won a split decision over Carlos Zarate, 117½, Mexico, to win the WBC title. Site: Las Vegas, Nev. Referee: Mills Lane.

August 29, 1980—Julian Solis, 117¾, Puerto Rico, won a split decision over Jorge Lujan, 118, Panama, for the world crown in Miami Beach, Florida. Jimmy Rondeau, referee.

November 14, 1980—Jeff Chandler, 118, Philadelphia, Pa., TKO'd Julian Solis, 117½, Puerto Rico, at 1:05 of the 14th round in Miami, Florida, to win the world title. Carlos Berrocal, referee.

BANTAMWEIGHT DIVISION

TOMMY "SPIDER" KELLY
("The Harlem Spider")
Born, New York City, September 6, 1867.
Height, 5 ft. 4 in. Weight, 105 lbs. Nationality,
Irish-American. Managers, P. Black, Billy
Murray. In 1887 Kelly laid claim to the World
Bantamweight title.

1887
—Dick Roche, Westchester	W	2
—Paddy Carr, Westchester	W	13
—Frank Donovan, Glouster, N. J.	W	10
—Tommy Russell, Glouster, N. J.	W	10
Dec. 24—Hughey Boyle (Oliver's Cottage) Harlem, N. Y.	KO by	8

(Lost world Bantamweight title—105 lbs. ringside.)

1888
—Eugene Hornbacher, New York	W	15
—Harry Walton, Troy	W	17
May 10—George Dixon (Anthenian Club) Boston	D	9

(Hughey Boyle, the world bantamweight champion, decided to retire as the undisputed, undefeated champion and went back to his old trade, painting. Both Dixon and Kelly claimed the vacant bantamweight title. Kelly on tour of the country defeated Sammy Watson at Paterson, Joe Byrnes at Hoboken, Joe Glossy at New York, Freddie Jamison at Pottsville, Johnny Van Heest in Philadelphia, which broke up in a row, Tommy (Young) Milton at Wilmington, Del, and Tommy James at Troy.)

Dec. 24—Cal McCarthy (Oliver's Cottage) Harlem, N. Y.	D	8

(For Bantamweight championship of America—105 lbs. ringside.)

1889
Jan. 29—Billy Murray (100 miles from N. Y.)	W	10
Mar. 17—Cal McCarthy, Jersey City	D	6
—Chappie Moran, Hoboken, N.J.	W	4

(Moran was British Bantam Champion, and the fight was recognized as for the world bantam title.)

June 5—Chappie Moran (Smithsonian Hall), Greenpoint, Bkln.	L	10

(Lost world bantamweight title—105 lbs. ringside.)

1890
Jan. 31—Chappie Moran, New York	KO	10

(Re-won World Bantam Title)

Mar. 5—Benny Murphy, New York	KO	3

(Skin-tight gloves, Bantam Title bout)

May 6—Hughey Boyle, Quinnsport	Exh.	3
June 26—Benny Murphy, Centerport, L. I.	KO	3
July 3—Pete Carroll, Weehawken	KO	2
Aug. 16—Benny Murphy, Hoboken	W	6
Aug. 25—Benny Murphy (Palace Rink) Brooklyn	Exh.	6

(Testimonial Benefit for Nonpariel Jack Dempsey.)

Sept. 4—Tommy Russell, Hoboken	KO	11
Oct. 12—Billy Murphy, Guttenberg	KO	3
Dec. 10—Billy Murphy, Guttenberg	KO	3
Dec. 20—Billy Murphy, Hoboken	KO	1

1891
Frank Donovan, Hoboken	W	10
—Mike Scanlon, Lynn	W	4
June 6—Patsy Daly, Guttenberg	KO	3

1892
Feb. 15—Ike "Spider" Weir, N. Y.	Exh.	3
May 9—Billy Plimmer, Coney Island	L	10

(Lost world bantam title. Referee Al Smith. They fought at 110 pounds at 2 p.m. This was the beginning of weight raising limit from 105 pounds to 110 pounds.)

July 25—Billy Murphy, New York	W	6
July 15—Eddie Avery, New York	Exh.	6
Sept. 24—Tim Murphy, New York	KO by	4

(For American Bantam championship)

1893
Feb. 10—Maxie Haugh, Buffalo	KO by	1

(6 min. 3/5 sec., a record K.O. at that time.)

1894
Feb. 17—Tim Murphy, New York	L	4
Aug. 6—Kid Gleason, New York	L	8

1895
Jan. 20—Harry Fisher, New York	L	4
July 4—Jimmy Haughie, Jersey City	KO	3

1896
July 20—Jack Burns, Philadelphia	KO	2
—Casper Leon, New York	KO by	5
Nov. 15—(Sunday)—Hugh McDonnough, Union Hill, N. J.	ND	7

(Referee left the ring without giving a decision.)

1900
May —Kid Able, Chicago	D	6

1909
Dec. 21—Casper Leon (New Polo A.A.) New York	Exh.	2

(Testimonial Benefit for Casper Leon)

TB	KO	WD	WF	D	LD	LF	KOBY	ND	NC
44	11	19	0	4	5	0	4	1	0

HUGHEY BOYLE
(Record Not Available)

CHAPPIE MORAN
British Bantamweight Champion
Born Manchester, England 1869.
Won U. S. Amateur Bantamweight championship in 1886.
Fights in England 1887-88
—Tom Fisher, London	W	
—1 Hour 33 minutes		
—Patsy Sheehan, London	L	
—Tom Varley, London	W	9
—Fred Brown, London	W	4

1889
May 21—Frank Donovan, Staten Island	KO	14
June —Tommy (Spider) Kelly, Hoboken	L	4

(For Vacant World Bantamweight Title)

June 5—Tommy (Spider) Kelly, Greenpoint, Brooklyn	W	10

(Won World Bantamweight Title)

July 29—Peter Sherry, Jersey City	W	4

1890
Jan. 31—Tommy (Spider) Kelly, New York	KO by	10

(Lost World Bantamweight Title)

TB	KO	WD	WF	D	LD	LF	KOBY	ND	NC
9	1	5	0	0	2	0	1	0	0

GEORGE DIXON
(Record under Featherweight Champions)

BILLY PLIMMER
Born, February 6, 1869, Birmingham, Lancashire, England. Weight, 105-115 lbs. Height, 5 ft. 3½ in.

1888
—Jack Shannon	W	6
—Charley Sallade	W	4
—Chappie Moran	KO	3
—Chappie Moran	W	8
—Jack Brown	W	4
—Sol Phillips	W	8
—Bill Moore	W	8

1889
Feb. 18—Jack Sweeney, London	W	3
Feb. 18—Tim Buckley, London	W	4
Feb. 18—Patsy Sheehan, London	L	4

(Hinde's 104-Pound Competition)

June 2—Joe Farrell, London	W	6
Aug. 13—Billy Willis, London	W	12

1890
Aug. 11—Arthur Westley, London	KO	13

1891
Feb. 13—Charles Mansford, London	W	10
Apr. 2—Jem Stevens, London	KO	15

(Won Vacant British Bantamweight Title)

Oct. 27—Jim Watson, Paterson	W	4
Nov. 13—Jack Lynch, Philadelphia	W	4

Dec. 19—Jimmy Dwyer, Philadelphia ...... ND 4
Dec. 30—Matt McCarthy, Philadelphia ...... W 2
1892
Jan. 12—Kid Hogan, Brooklyn .... D 8
May 9—Tommy Kelly, Coney Island .... W 10
(Won British World Bantamweight Title)
June 14—Willie Tucker, Newark, N.J. ..... KO 3
Aug. 8—Jerry Barnett, Coney Island ...... D 8
Dec. 28—Joe McGrath, Coney Island .... KO 8
1893
Jan. 18—Jack Harding, Philadelphia ...... KO 2
Jan. 21—Dan Cleland, Philadelphia .... KO ·2
Apr. 29—Joe Murphy, Philadelphia .... KO 1
June 3—Barney Reily, Philadelphia .... ND 4
Aug. 22—George Dixon, New York .... KO 4
Nov. 28—Joe Tracy, New York .... KO 2
Dec. 18—Pete Mace, New York .... KO 2
Dec. 18—Fred Thompson, New York .... KO 2
1894
Feb. 6—Van Hoest, Chicago .... W 3
Sept. 24—Johnny Murphy, New Orleans ..... D 25
Nov. 26—Charley Kelly, Coney Island ..... KO 3
Dec. 1—Billy Whistler, Philadelphia .... D 4
1895
Jan. 2—Allan Johnson, Cincinnati .... KO 3
Jan. 12—Barney Reilly, Philadelphia ...... ND 4
Feb. 23—Elwood McClockey, Philadelphia ... W 4
May 28—George Corfiel, London .... KO 7
(Retained British Bantamweight Title)
(Retained British World Bantamweight Title)
Nov. 25—Pedlar Palmer, London .... LF 14
(Lost British World Bantamweight Title)
(Lost British Bantamweight Title)
1896
Sept. 7—George Corfield, Sheffield .... W 20
1897
Mar. 9—Sam Kelly, Birmingham ...... KO by 20
1898
Dec. 12—Pedlar Palmer, London .... KO by 17
1899
Apr. 3—Harry Ware, Birmingham ..... KO by 19
1900
Sept. 21—George Corfield, Stalybridge .... D 20

TB	KO	WD	WF	D	LD	LF	KO BY	ND	NC
46	15	18	0	5	1	1	3	3	0

JIMMY BARRY

Born, March 7, 1870, Chicago, Ill.
Nationality, Irish-American. Weight, 105 to 115 lbs. Height, 5 ft. 2 in.
1891
Knockouts: Fred Larson, 1; Dick Ward, 3; Tom Cassidy, 2; Young Cransden, 3; Joe O'Leary, 3; Jockey Sloane, 3; Joe Gates, 2; Jack Ghetlain, 1; Jack Kelly, 1; Young Lyons, 1; Al Newman, 1; Won: Jack Miller, 4; Tom Cassidy, 6; Barney McCall, 4; Spud Murphy, 4.
1892
Feb. 1—Billy Wellington, Chicago ..... W 6
Feb. 10—Shorty Cleveland, Chicago ....KO 4
Feb. 20—Dan Rowan, Chicago ....KO 4
Mar. 2—Billy Joyce, Chicago ....KO 3
Mar. 12—Paddy Snow, Chicago ....KO 2
Apr. 3—Jack Smith, Chicago .... W 5
May 10—Kid Corbett, Chicago .... W 4
June 8—Romeo Durand, Chicago ..... W 4
July 4—Dick Reedy, Chicago ....KO 4
Aug. 8—Young Moron, Chicago ......KO 2
Sept. 3—Frank Murphy, Springfld., Ill..KO 7
Oct. 11—Joe Gates, Chicago............ W 6
1893
Jan. 8—Max Eaufeldt, Chicago ......KO 1
Jan. 20—Dave Ross, Chicago ....KO 2
Feb. 12—Billy Murphy, Chicago ....KO 1
Mar. 20—Jockey Stanton, Chicago ....KO 2
Apr. 5—Lou Simmons, Chicago ...... W 6
July 10—Jimmy Shea, Roby, Ind....KO 4
Aug. 7—Con Sheenan, Chicago ...... W 5
Sept. 6—Tom Cassidy, Chicago ......KO 6
Nov. 13—Jack Fitzgerald, Chicago ... W 4
Dec. 5—Jack Levy, Roby, Ind........KO 17
(Won World 100-lb. Championship, Private Fight, Skin-tight Gloves, $500 Aside)

1894
Jan. 22—Joe Cranston, Chicago ....KO 3
Feb. 6—Joe McGrath, Chicago........KO 3
Feb. 28—Bob Costello, Chicago.......KO 2
June 2—Jimmy Gorman, New Orleans .. W 11
July 3—Harry Brooks, Bradford Falls .. W 4
Sept. 15—Casper Leon, Lamont, Ill, ...KO 28
(Claimed Bantamweight Title)
Nov. 14—George Church, Chicago ...... W 8
1895
Mar. 21—Joe Bertrand, Chicago ....KO 5
Mar. 30—Casper Leon, Chicago .... D 14
(Police interferred)
(title bout)
July 25—Dave Ross, Boston, Mass. .....KO 2
Sept. 30—Jack Lynch, Philadelphia .....ND 4
Oct. 21—Jack Madden, Maspeth, L. I. ..KO 4
1896
Jan. 12—Young Lyons, Chicago ....KO 1
Feb. 18—Young Spitz, Chicago ....KO 8
Mar. 15—Jim McGuire, Chicago........KO 2
Apr. 20—Joe O'Donnell, Chicago ......KO 3
July 24—Casper Leon, Elmira ....ND 6
Aug. 11—Steve Flanagan, Philadelphia ... W 6
1897
Jan. 10—Harry Dally, Chicago........KO 2
Jan. 18—Jack Berger, Chicago ....KO 1
Jan. 30—Sammy Kelly, New York ...... D 20
Mar. 1—Jack Ward, New York ...... W 20
Apr. 27—Jimmy Anthony, San Fran..... W 20
Dec. 6—Walter Croot, London, Eng. ..KO 20
(Won World Bantamweight Title)
(Croot died of brain injury. Barry exonerated.)
1898
Mar. 17—Johnny Connors, Chicago ..... W 6
Mar. 26—Johnny Ritchie, Chicago ...... W 6
Apr. 18—Billy Rotchford, Chicago ...... D 6
May 30—Casper Leon, New York .... D 20
(title bout)
June 3—Steve Flanagan, Philadelphia ... D 6
Oct. 31—Frank Bartley, Chicago .... D 4
Nov. 21—Casper Leon, Chicago ...... D 6
Dec. 29—Casper Leon, Davenport, Iowa . D 20
(title bout)
1899
Sept. 1—Harry Harris, Chicago .... D 6
Barry retired, undefeated.

TB	KO	WD	WF	D	LD	LF	KO BY	ND	NC
70	39	20	0	9	0	0	0	2	0

Died April 5, 1943, Chicago, Ill.

THOMAS (PEDLAR) PALMER

Born, November 19, 1876, Canning Town.
Weight, 115 lbs. Height, 5 ft. 3 in.
1891
—W.C. Bond .... W 11
1892
(Number of rounds not recorded).
Defeated San Swamburg, Arthur Wigg, Ernie, Stanton, Tom Shane, Ginger Wright, Will Morse, Ted Saunders, Dick Edwards, George Wood, Ted Willis.
1893
May 1—Walter Croot, London ....KO 17
May 29—Mike Small, London .... W 6
July 17—Albert Gould, London .... W 6
Sept. 7—Ted Wood, London .... W 6
1894
June 25—Bill Mortimer, London .... W 5
Oct. 15—Ernie Stanton, London .... W 20
1895
Nov. 25—Billy Plimmer, London .... W 14
(Won British Bantamweight Title)
1896
Jan. 30—George Dixon, New York ...... D 6
Oct. 12—Johnny Murphy, London ...... W 20
1897
Jan. 25—Ernie Stanton, London .... W 14
Oct. 18—Dave Sullivan, London .... W 20
1898
Dec. 12—Billy Plimmer, London .... W 17
1899
Apr. 17—Billy Rotchford, London .....WF 3
Sept. 12—Terry McGovern, Tuckahoe KO by 1
(For World's Bantamweight Title)
Scheduled for Sept. 11 but it rained.
1900
May 28—Harry Ware, London .... W 15

Nov. 12—Harry Ware, London ....L 20
1901
Mar. 18—*Harry Harris, London ....L 15
*For world's bantamweight title.
1902
Jan. 27—Jim Williams, London ....L 15
June 16—Digger Stanley, London ....W 10
Sept. 8—George Dixon, Glasgow ....W 15
Dec. 15—Will Curley, Newcastle ....KO by 8
1903
Feb. 16—Harry Ware, London .... W 12
Apr. 2—Fred Delaney, Barking .... W 6
May 11—Digger Stanley, London .... W 12
June 27—George Dixon, London .... W 8
Sept. 14—Spike Robson, Newcastle...... W 20
Nov. 9—George Dixon, Newcastle.......L 20
1904
Mar. 14—H. Alexander, Hull .... KO by 4
May 26—Dan Hyman, Johannesburg KO by 9
July 11—Watty Austin, Cape Town ..... D 20
Aug. 8—Watty Austin, Cape Town ..... W 20
Oct. 17—Young Joseph, London .... W 15
Dec. 12—Ben Jordan, London ....L 15
(For British Featherweight Title)
1905
Mar. 20—Joe Bowker, London..........L 12
(Lost British Bantamweight Title)
May 29—George Moore, London .... D 15
June 17—George Moore, London ...... W 6
Aug. 5—Bob White, W. Hartlepool ....KO 6
Sept. 25—Cockney Cohen, London ..... W 15
Nov. 13—Cockney Cohen, London ......L 6
1906
Feb. 28—Charlie Lampey, London ......L 15
Mar. 26—Cockney Cohen, London ...... D 15
Apr. 28—Driver Himpfen, London ...... W 6
May 28—Cockney Cohen, Plymouth .... W 4
1911
Dec. 7—Darkey Haley, London .... KO by 10
1912
Jan. 6—Darkey Haley, London .... W 6
Jan. 24—Alec Lambert, London .... W 6
Mar. 2—George Moore, London ......WF 5
Mar. 25—Pte. Walton, London .... W 7
July 27—Sam Russell, London ......WF 3
Aug. 2—Jim Lloyd, Liverpool .... W 4
Nov. 9—George Dixon, Newcastle ...... W 7
Nov. 19—Digger Stanley, London ....L 4
1919
Mar. 10—Jim Driscoll, London ....L 4

TB	KO	WD	WF	D	LD	LF	KOBY	ND	NC
64	2	40	3	4	10	0	5	0	0

TERRY McGOVERN
(Record under Featherweight Champions)

HARRY HARRIS
(Human Scissors)
Born, November 18, 1880, Chicago, Ill.
Weight 115 lbs. Height, 5 ft. 7½ in.
1896
Apr. 5—Dennis Mahoney, Chicago ..... W 5
June 12—Young Sweeney, Chicago......W 4
Sept. 2—Archie Bernard, Chicago .....KO 2
1897
Oct. 4—Dave Rosenberg, Chicago ...... W 3
Oct. 16—Lee LaBlanche, Chicago ...... W 4
Nov. 3—Chick Brooker, Chicago ...... W 3
Nov. 18—Lee LaBlanche, St. Louis ..... W 4
Dec. 14—John Whitecraft, Flint, Mich. .KO 3
Dec. 27—Morris Rauch, Chicago .... D 6
1898
Mar. 7—Link Pope, Chicago .... W 6
Mar. 19—Harry Sincere, Chicago .... W 6
Apr. 2—Morris Rauch, Chicago .... W 6
Apr. 16—Dan Lucas, Chicago .... W 6
Sept. 9—Geo. Ross, New York .... W 10
Sept. 24—"Tut" Reilly, New York......KO 9
Oct. 14—Billy Trueman, New York ....KO 6
Nov. 12—Pinky Evans, Brooklyn .... W 10
Nov. 22—Charley Roden, N. Y. ....KO 9
1899
Jan. 24—Kid Purdy, Chicago .... W 6
Jan. 28—George Pardy, Chicago .... W 6
Feb. 7—Steve Flanagan, Chicago ....L 6
Feb. 24—Dick Sleif, Chicago ....KO 1

Mar. 17—Larry Lacey, Chicago .... W 6
May 19—Aus. Billy Murphy, Chicago ...KO 4
July 7—Sig. Hart, Davenport .... W 15
Aug. 4—Sig. Hart, Clinton ....KO 6
Aug. 10—Joe Huguelett, Davenport ..... K 3
Sept. 1—Jimmy Barry, Chicago .... D 6
Sept. 22—Steve Flanagan, Chicago ...... D 6
Oct. 14—Steve Flanagan, Chicago ...... D 6
Nov. 14—Billy Casey, Chicago ....KO 5
1900
Jan. 20—Kid Abel, Chicago ....KO 3
Jan. 27—Kid Carter, Chicago ....KO 2
May 25—Morris Rauch, Chicago .... D 6
May 29—Buddy Ryan, Chicago .... W 6
July 7—Tony Moran, New York ...... W 10
Sept. 21—Paddy Donovan, Philadelphia .ND 6
Oct. 2—Jack Ryan, Chicago .... W 6
Oct. 16—Casper Leon, Chicago .... W 6
Oct. 26—Johnny Reagan, Chicago ...... W 6
Oct. 30—Kid McFadden, Chicago ...... W 6
Nov. 27—Clarence Forbes, Chicago ......L 6
Feb. 28—Kid Abel, Chicago .... D 6
1901
Mar. 18—Pedlar Palmer, London .... W 15
(For Vacant World's Bantamweight Title)
Gave up crown to fight as featherweight.
Apr. 15—Harry Ware, London .... W 15
—Al Kirk, Chicago ....KO 3
1902
Feb. 27—Austin Rice, Chicago .... D 6
Mar. 26—Dan Doughtery, Phila. ....ND 6
—Kid Abel ....KO 3
—Jack Chambers ....KO 6
1906
Mar. 31—Jack Goodman, New York ....ND 3
1907
Feb. 14—Jack Goodman, New York ....ND 6
Mar. 11—Jack Goodman, New York ....ND 6
June 3—Harlem Tommy Murphy,
New York ....WF 8

TB	KO	WD	WF	D	LD	LF	KOBY	ND	NC
54	15	24	1	7	2	0	0	5	0

Died, June 5, 1959, New York, N. Y.

HARRY FORBES
Born, May 13, 1879, Rockford, Ill.
Nationality, Irish-American. Weight, 118
pounds. Height, 5 ft. 4 in.
1897
Jan. 16—Joe Sturch, Chicago ....L 4
Apr. 10—Morris Rauch, Chicago .... W 6
May 1—Fred Wolf, Chicago .... W 4
July 10—Mike Bartley, Chicago ....KO 2
Aug. 28—Ned Hanlon, Chicago ....KO 1
Sept. —Fred Woods, Chicago .... D 5
Oct. 23—Joe Sturch, Chicago .... W 4
Nov. 30—Morris Rauch, Chicago .... W 6
Nov. —Eddie Carroll, Chicago .... W 6
Dec. 12—John Gallagher, Chicago .....KO 5
Dec. 21—Billy Boyd, Chicago .... W 4
Dec. 30—Barney McCall, Chicago .... W 6
1898
Jan. 15—Tom Cooney, Chicago .... W 2
Jan. 20—Barney McCall, Chicago .... D 5
Feb. —Johnny Richie, Chicago ....L 6
Feb. 21—Joe Bertrand, Chicago .... D 6
July 13—Barney McCall, Chicago .....KO 6
July 18—Larry Lacey, Chicago ....KO 4
Aug. 6—Maxey Haugh, Brooklyn ....KO 7
Aug. 13—Billy Barrett, Brooklyn .... W 10
Sept. 2—Patsy Donovan, New York .... W 4
Sept. 10—Jack Ward, Brooklyn ....WF 6
Oct. 1—Terry M'Govern, Brooklyn KO by 15
Oct. 8—John Whittaker, Chicago ...... D 6
Oct. 22—Casper Leon, Chicago .... D 6
Nov. 5—Jimmy Rose, Brooklyn ......WF 14
Nov. 11—Syd. Huntington, Milwaukee .ND 4
Nov. 16—George Hall, Chicago .... W 6
Dec. 10—Willie Purdy, Chicago .... W 6
Dec. 15—John Whittaker, Milwaukee ... W 6
Dec. 19—Tim Callahan, Chicago .... D 6
Dec. 24—Eddie Sprague, Chicago ...... W 6
1899
Jan. 30—Billy Smith of Phil., Chicago ... W 6
Feb. 3—Billy Boyd, Chicago .... W 6
Mar. 11—Billy Smith, Chicago .... W 6
Mar. 25—Eddie Sprague, Chicago ...... W 6
Mar. 31—Eddie Lenny, Toronto .... W 20
Apr. 19—Kid Ryan, Springfield, Ill. ..... W 6
Apr. 29—"Aus" Billy Murphy, Chicago .. W 4

May   6—Billy Smith, Chicago .... D   6
May   29—Billy Smith, St. Louis .... W 13
July   4—Ed. Sprague, Bloomington, Ill. KO 12
July   28—Billy Rochford, Chicago ...... WF   1
Aug.   25—Billy Rochford, Chicago .... W   6
Sept. 11—Billy Lenny, Coney Island .... D 25
Sept. 19—Ed. Sprague, Peoria, Ill. ...... W 12
Dec.   1—Oscar Gardner, Chicago .... D   6
Dec.   10—Tim Callahan, Chicago .... D   6
Dec.   18—Dan McMahon, Michigan City .ND   6
Dec.   22—Terry McGovern, N. Y. .... KO by 2
                (For Bantamweight Title)
1900
Jan.   6—Young Simister, Brooklyn ..... D 20
Jan.   20—Walter Bloom, Chicago .... W   6
Jan.   26—Morris Rauch, Chicago .... D   6
Mar.   17—Benny Yanger, Chicago ... KO by   5
Apr.   22—Jim Ryan, Kensington .... KO   3
May   15—Fred O'Neil, Chicago .... W   1
June   1—Oscar Gardner, Chicago ... KO by   1
June   2—Young Herzog, Chicago ...... KO   3
June   15—Young Gustavson, Chicago ...KO   3
July   4—Walter Bloom, Bloomington ... W 20
July   26—Jack Ryan, Aurora .... D   6
Sept.   6—Casper Leon, St. Joseph .... D 20
                (For Vacant Bantamweight Title)
Nov.   12—Casper Leon, Chicago .... W   6
1901
Apr.   2—Casper Leon, Memphis .... W 15
                (Won Vacant Bantamweight Title)
June   30—Jack O'Keefe, Rockford .... D 15
Nov.   4—Abe Attell, St. Louis .... W 15
Nov.   11—Dan Dougherty, St. Louis ....KO   2
Dec.   19—Billy Rotchford, Chicago .....KO   1
1902
Jan.   23—*Dan Dougherty, St. Louis ...KO   4
Feb.   27—*Tommy Feltz, St. Louis ...... W 15
Mar.   13—Kid Goodman, Chicago .... W   6
May   1—Johnny Reagan, St. Louis .... D 20
June   13—Young Devaney, Denver .... W 10
July   28—Mike Memsic, Chicago .... W   6
Aug.   11—Tommy Feltz, Chicago .... W   6
Sept.   4—Biz Mackey, South Bend ...... W   2
Nov.   3—Geo. Halliday, Chicago .... W   1
Nov.   3—Billy Finucane, Chicago ...... W   6
Nov.   10—Abe Attell, Chicago .... D   6
Nov.   28—Morris Rauch, Chicago .... W   6
Dec.   23—*Frank Neil, Oakland .... W   7
                *Title Bout.
1903
Feb.   27—*Andy Tokell, Detroit .... W 10
Mar.   24—Johnny Kelly, Kansas City ....KO   9
Apr.   13—Jimmy Devine, Philadelphia ..KO   4
Apr.   16—Biz Mackey, Findlay .... W   6
Apr.   20—Tommy Love, Philadelphia ...ND   6
May   26—Morris Rauch, Kansas City ... W 15
June   22—Danny Dougherty, Phila. .....ND   6
Aug.   13—Frankie Neil, San Fran..... KO by   2
                (Lost Bantamweight Title)
Sept. 10—Kid McFadden, Boston ......KO 10
Sept. 18—Tommy Love, Philadelphia ...ND   6
Oct.   14—Tommy Feltz, Detroit .... D 10
                *Title Bout.
1904
Jan.   4—Abe Attell, Indianapolis .... D 10
Feb.   1—Abe Attell, St. Louis ...... KO by   5
                (For World Featherweight Title)
Feb.   13—Johnnie Kelly, Chicago ....KO   3
June   17—Frankie Neil, Chicago ..... KO by   3
                (For World Bantamweight Title)
Sept.   9—Mike Margovey, Denver ......KO   3
Nov.   25—Joe Cherry, Saginaw ....KO 13
Dec.   2—Paddy Nee, Kalamazoo .... D 10
1905
Jan.   27—Joe Cherry, Saginaw ....KO   1
Feb.   21—Paddy Nee, Indianapolis .... W 10
May   10—Abe Attell, Detroit ....L 10
June   15—Biz Mackey, Findlay ....L 10
Sept.   5—Bruce Shearer, Bloomington ..KO   5
Oct.   31—Young Garfield, Peoria ....KO   6
1906
Mar.   5—Tommy O'Toole, Phila. ....ND   6
Mar.   26—Morris Rauch, Springfield, Ill. .. D   6
Sept.   4—Bruce Shearer, Chenoa, Ill. ...KO   4
1907
May   28—Tom Ryan, Menominee, Mich. . W   6
1910
Feb.   8—George Ramsey, Troy, N. Y. ..KO   2
Feb.   14—Jos. Coster, New York ....KO   6
Feb.   28—Abe Attell, Troy, N. Y. ..... KO by   7
Sept. 11   Joe Hennesy, Chicago ,,,,,,,,KO   3
Nov.   8—Kid Hogan, Pittsburgh .... W   6
Dec.   21—Earl Denning, Windsor, Ont. .. W   8

1911
Jan.   25—Mike Bartley, Fort Wayne ....KO   4
Mar.   28—Johnny Coulon, Kenosha, Wis. ND 10
Apr.   18—Young Britt, South Bend, Ind. KO   1
May   8—Young Fitzgerald, Gary, Ind. .KO   3
June   15—Joe Homeland, Janesville, Wis.
        ....ND   8
July   4—Young Togo, McAlester, Okla. . D 15
July   27—Joe Homeland, Aurora, Ill. ....KO   5
Sept.   4—Earl Denning, Aurora, Ill......ND   6
Oct.   10—Sammy Kellar, Cleveland, O.... D 10
Nov.   14—Charley Goldman, New York .ND 10
Nov.   17—Young Ketchel, New York ....ND 10
Nov.   30—Eddie O'Keefe, New Orleans ..ND 10
1912
Jan.   22—Johnny Coulon, Kenosha, Wis.
        ....KO by   3
July   22—Oscar Williams, Paducah, Ky.
        ....KO by   2
1913
Sept. 22—Paddy Meehan, Glen Cove . KO by   2

TB KO WD WF D LD LF   KOBY   ND NC
130 30 47   3 23   4   0   11   12 0
        Died Dec. 19, 1946, Chicago, Ill.

FRANKIE NEIL
                (Francis James Neil)
        Born, July 25, 1883, San Francisco.
Nationality, Irish-American. Weight, 115-118
lbs. Height, 5 ft. 5½ in.
1900
Nov.   8—Chas. Anderson, San Fran.....KO   1
Nov.   19—John Scott, San Francisco ...KO   1
Dec.   20—George Gibbs, San Francisco .KO   1
Dec.   23—Ivy Powell, San Francisco ....KO   2
Dec.   27—Eddie Hanlon, San Francisco ...L   4
1901
Jan.   12—Kid Goldie, San Francisco ....KO   1
Jan.   17—Kid Goldie, San Francisco ....KO   1
Jan.   26—Kid Malone, San Francisco ...KO   1
Feb.   2—Jack Kane, San Francisco ...... D   4
Feb.   15—George Dougherty, San Fran. .KO   3
Mar.   3—John Margarini, San Fran.....KO   1
Mar.   15—Jack Kane, San Francisco .....KO   1
Mar.   21—Geo. White, San Francisco .... D   4
Apr.   19—Dave Gilmore, San Fran. .....KO   1
Apr.   26—Henry Baker, San Francisco ..KO   1
June   6—H. McLaughton, San Fran.....KO   2
June   20—Tommy Dixon, San Fran. .....KO   1
July   31—Eddie Hanlon, San Francisco ...L   4
1902
Mar.   12—Robbie Johnson, San Fran.....KO   2
Apr.   11—Eddie Hanlon, Oakland, Cal. ... D 15
Dec.   23—Harry Forbes, Oakland, Cal. L   7
                (Bantamweight Title Bout)
1903
Jan.   15—Clarence Forbes, San Fran. ...KO   6
Aug.   13—Harry Forbes, San Francisco ..KO   2
                (Won Bantamweight Title)
Sept.   4—*Billy DeCoursey, Los Ang. ..KO 15
Oct.   16—*Johnny Reagan, Los Angeles . D 20
                *Title Bout.
1904
May   27—Tommy Moore, Chicago .....KO   1
June   17—*Harry Forbes, Chicago ......KO   3
July   27—Hugh McGovern, Phila. ....ND   6
Aug.   31—Tom Murphy, Philadelphia ...ND   6
Oct.   17—Joe Bowker, London ....L 20
                (Lost Bantamweight Title)
                *Title Bout.
1905
Jan.   31—Dick Hyland, San Francisco ..KO 15
July   28—Harry Tenny, Colma, Cal. ..... W 25
1906
Feb.   28—Harry Tenny, San Francisco ..KO 14
                (Tenny died of injuries suffered in bout)
July   4—Abe Attell, Los Angeles ....L 20
                (For World Featherweight Title)
Aug.   7—Harry Baker, Los Angeles.......L 20
1907
Nov.   22—Owen Moran, San Fran. ...KO by 16
1908
Jan.   31—Abe Attell, San Francisco . KO by 13
May   6—Ad Wolgast, Milwaukee ....L 10
Aug.   13—Fred O'Brien, N. Y. C.........ND   6
Sept.   5—Jack Langdon, Philadelphia ...KO   6
Sept. 10—Tommy O'Toole, Philadelphia ND   6
Oct.   2—Frankie Moore, Philadelphia ..ND   6

Oct. 3—Joe Wagner, Pittsburgh, Pa. ...ND 6
Oct. 19—Joe Wagner, N. Y. C. ....ND 6
Dec. 15—Owen Moran, Boston ....L 12
1909
Feb. 18—Boyo Driscoll, N. Y. C. ....ND 10
Mar. 1—Kid Beebe, Schenectady, N. Y. ND 10
Mar. 23—Abe Attell, Brooklyn ....ND 10
Apr. 26—Owen Moran, New Haven .....ND 12
May 4—Young Britt, Baltimore ....WF 11
May 14—Bert O'Donnell, Wilkes-Barre .ND 6
June 19—Monte Attell, Colma, Cal. ...KO by 18
Sept. 10—Patsy McKenna, Vancouver,
B. C. ....KO 1
Sept. 30—Billy Lauder, Vancouver, B. C. ..L 15
1910
Feb. 24—Abe Attell, New York ....ND 10
Feb. 26—Willie Jones, Baltimore ....KO by 13

TB	KO	WD	WF	D	LD	LF	KOBY	ND	NC
56	24	1	1	4	9	0	4	13	0

Died, March 6, 1970, Richmond, Calif.

JOE BOWKER
(Tommy Mahon)

Born, July 20, 1883, Salford, England.
Nationality, English. Weight, 122 lbs. Height, 5 ft. 3½ in.
1900
Won: Owens, 10; Daly 10; Perkins, 6;
Doyle, 10; Turner, 10. Knockouts: Thompson, 5; Albert Wheeler, 4.
1901
Jan. 14—Won 115 pound novices' competition at N. S. club (64 entires).
Jan. 21—Jack Guyon, London ....W 6
Dec. 14—Jack Guyon, London ....W 6
1902
Feb. 2—A. Wheeler, London ....W 5
Mar. 10—Harry Paul, London...........W 10
Apr. 21—Bill Lampshire, London ......W 10
May 10—Jack Guyon, London ....W 6
June 2—Bill Fielder, London ....W 6
June 27—Harry Ware, London ....W 15
(For British Bantam Title)
Aug. 12—Charlie Hickman, London ....KO 3
1903
May 25—A. Tokell, London ....W 20
(Won British Bantamweight Title)
Oct. 5—Bill King, London ....W 15
(For British Bantam Title)
Nov. 9—Alf Fellows, London ....W 20
1904
May 20—Owen Moran, London........W 20
Oct. 17—Frank Neil, London ....W 20
(Won World Bantamweight title)
1905
Mar. 12—Pedlar Palmer, London .....W 12
Mar. 20—Pedlar Palmer, London ......KO 12
(Won British Featherweight title)
(Bowker outgrew bantam division and
gave up title)
May 29—Pinky Evans, London ......W 20
Oct. 23—Bill Robson, London ....W 20
(For British Bantam Title)
Nov. 27—Wally Pickard, London ....W 6
1906
Apr. 21—Owen Moran, London............ND 4
May 28—Jim Driscoll, London ....L 15
(Lost British Featherweight Title)
June 12—Cockney Cohen, London .....W 10
Sept. 10—Bill Fielder, London ....D 6
1907
Feb. 2—Harry Smith, Canning Town ..KO 5
Mar. 5—Owen Moran, Cardiff, Eng. ...ND 4
June 3—Jim Driscoll, London ....KO by 17
(For British Bantam Title)
1908
Apr. 27—Charley Griffin, London ....L 8
1909
Mar. 16—Al Delmont, Boston ....L 12
Mar. 20—Tommy O'Toole, Phila. ...KO by 2
Apr. 7—Jean Audouy, London ....KO 8
Oct. 17—Digger Stanley, London ...KO by 8
1910
Jan. 17—Jean Audouy, London ....W 8
May 16—Alec Lambert, London ......W 8
Oct. 17—Digger Stanley, London ...KO by 8
1911
Mar. 27—Con Houghton, London ....W 7
May 29—Paul Til, London ....W 14

Dec. 18—George Allen, Wandsworth ....W 2
1912
Jan. 29—Charles Ledoux, London ....L 10
1913
Feb. 3—Young Cohen, London ....W 15
Nov. 24—Francis Charles, London ....W 10
1914
Feb. 16—Biz Mackey, London ....KO 5
May 11—Robert Dastillon, London .....W 15
1916
July 17—Harold Walker, Manchester ..W 6
1919
Oct. 9—Charlie Ward, London ....KO 15

TB	KO	WD	WF	D	LD	LF	KOBY	ND	NC
51	8	32	0	1	4	0	4	2	0

Died October 30, 1955, London England.

JIMMY WALSH
Born, 1886, Newton, Mass. Nationality, Irish-American. Weight, 115 lbs. Height, 5 ft. 2 in.
1901
Oct. 23—Young Schlindler, Boston ....W 3
Oct. 26—Johnny Powers, Boston ....W 3
Oct. 26—Tom Cunningham, Boston ....W 3
Nov. 27—B. Nadeau, Boston ....W 3
Nov. 27—Johnny Lynch, Boston ....W 3
Nov. 30—Albert Delmont, Boston ......W 3
1902
Jan. 11—Johnny Powers, Boston ......W 3
Jan. 31—Denny Ryan, Boston ....W 4
Mar. 8—C. Hoffman, Boston ....W 3
Apr. 19—Albert Delmont, Boston ......W 6
May 20—Albert Delmont, Cambridge ..W 6
May 24—Young Sullivan, Boston ......W 6
May 30—Kid York, Cambridge ....W 6
June 25—Albert Delmont, Boston ......D 7
Aug. 1—Jimmy Malloy, Providence ...D 6
Oct. 7—Albert Delmont, Boston ......D 6
Oct. 13—Johnny Lynch, Cambridge ...D 6
Nov. 3—W. Schumacker, Boston ....ND 3
Dec. 25—Denny Ryan, Boston ....KO 2
Dec. 30—Patsy McKenna, Boston ......W 6
1903
Jan. 23—Kid Terrill, Boston ....W 6
Jan. 25—Young Brooks, Boston ......W 6
Feb. 20—Johnny Sheehan, Boston .....W 8
Mar. 17—Johnny Powers, Boston ......W 10
Mar. 26—W. Schumacker, Boston .....W 10
Apr. 17—Johnny Powers, Boston ......W 10
Apr. 24—Terry Edwards, Boston ......W 10
May 6—Terry Edwards, Boston ......W 10
June 7—Harry Ogden, England ......W 6
June 18—Oscar Hines, England ......W 6
Sept. 11—Albert Delmont, Boston ......W 12
Oct. 2—Eddie Carr, Boston ....KO 10
Nov. 9—Young Hines, Boston ....KO 2
Nov. 14—Young Wagner, Salem ....W 2
Nov. 21—Harry Brown, Salem ....KO 9
Dec. 30—Patsy McKenna, Salem .....W 6
1904
Jan. 9—Kid Paul, Boston ....KO 6
Feb. 9—Jim Connolly, Boston ....KO 1
Feb. 23—Tom Quigley, Boston ....KO 13
Mar. 2—Jack Desmond, Dracut, Mass. .. D 12
Apr. 18—Digger Stanley, London .....L 15
June 2—Digger Stanley, London .....D 15
Sept. 27—D'y Dougherty, Philadelphia ..ND 6
Oct. 8—Bob Kendrick, Philadelphia ...ND 6
Dec. 26—Harry Brodigan, Salem...........KO 6
1905
Mar. 7—Tommy Feltz, Chelsea ......WF 11
Mar. 20—Monte Attell, Philadelphia ....ND 6
Mar. 25—Joe Wagner, Philadelphia ....KO 2
Mar. 29—Monte Attell, Philadelphia ....KO 6
Apr. 1—Phil Logan, Philadelphia ......ND 6
May 1—Phil Logan, Philadelphia ......ND 6
May 23—Willie Gibbs, Chelsea ....W 15
Sept. 4—Tommy O'Toole, Philadelphia ND 6
Oct. 20—Digger Stanley, Chelsea ....W 15
(Won vacant world bantamweight title)
1906
Jan. 29—Tommy O'Toole, Phila. ......ND 6
Feb. 2—Johnny Reagan, Chelsea......KO 5
Feb. 19—Jack Langdon, Phila. ....ND 6
Feb. 22—Abe Attell, Chelsea ....L 15
Apr. 7—Willie Moody, Phila. ....ND 6

764

Dec. 7—Abe Attell, Los Angeles ...KO by 8
(For World Featherweight Title)
Gave up Bantam Title.
1907
Mar. 8—Eddie Menney, Los Angeles.... W 10
June 18—Freddie Weeks, Denver ....L 10
Sept. 2—Young Erlenb'n, Chelsea .....ND 10
Sept. 12—Abe Attell, Indianapolis ....L 10
Oct. 2—Babe Cullen, Chelsea ....ND 10
1908
Mar. 31—Al Delmont, Boston ....D 10
Apr. 6—Young Pierce, Phila. ....ND 6
May 19—Eddie Menney, Los Angeles...ND 10
June 26—Jimmy Carroll, San Fran. .....KO 11
Sept. 9—Joe Wagner, N. Y. C. ....ND 6
Oct. 9—Young Britt, Baltimore .... W 15
Dec. 21—Monte Attell, San Fran. .... D 15
1909
Jan. 29—Johnny Reagan, San Fran. ......L 12
Mar. 27—Young Pierce, London ....ND 15
May 24—Digger Stanley, London ...... D 15
July 13—Ed Whittaker, Pittsburg ......ND 6
Nov. 9—Tommy O'Toole, Boston ...... D 12
Dec. 13—Billy Allen, Syracuse ....ND 10
Dec. 23—Alfie Lynch, Quebec, Can.....ND 10
1910
Jan. 28—Patsy Brannigan, Pittsburgh.... ND 6
Feb. 2—French Kid, Rutland ....ND 10
Feb. 10—Joe Coster, Boston............ W 6
Mar. 15—Al Delmont, Boston .... D 8
Mar. 28—Billy Allen, Woonsocket.....D 10
Apr. 4—Young Britt, Schenectady ....ND 10
Apr. 8—Eddie Greenwald, Milwaukee .ND 10
Apr. 21—Pal Moore, New York ....ND 10
May 15—Al Delmont .... D 8
May 31—Pal Moore, Boston .... W 12
Sept. 20—Young Britt, Boston .... W 10
Nov. 15—Sammy Keller, New York ....ND 10
Nov. 23—Monte Attell, Kansas City .....L 10
Dec. 10—Joe Coster, Brooklyn ....ND 10
1911
Jan. 28—Bert O'Donnell, Wilkes-Barre .ND 8
May 16—Al Delmont, Boston .... D 12
May 30—Johnny Kilbane, Canton, O. ..ND 12
June 15—Fred Landowne, Toronto, Can. W 7
Nov. 18—Eddie Stanton, Portland ......ND 10
Dec. 11—Jim Kendrick, Boston .... W 8
1912
Jan. 3—Alfie Lynch, Boston .... W 8
Feb. 1—Young Cohen, New York .....ND 10
Mar. 18—Eddie Sherman, Boston ...... W 6
Apr. 10—Joe Coster, New York ....ND 8
May 21—Johnny Kilbane, Boston....... D 12
(For World Featherweight Title)
Aug. 14—Patsy Brannigan, Boston .... D 10
Oct. 24—Abe Attell, Boston............. D 12
Nov. 13—Tommy Dixon, Windsor, Can. ND 8
Dec. 16—Young Sheppard, Albany .....ND 10
1913
Apr. 3—Abe Attell, New York ....ND 10
Apr. 7—Bobby Pittsly, Syracuse ......ND 10
Apr. 28—Kid Julian, Syracuse ....ND 10
June 28—Ad Zottee, Salt Lake City .....D 10
Sept. 2—Jim Kendrick, New York .....ND 10
Sept. 16—Johnny Kilbane, Boston.......L 12
Oct. 4—Eddie Wallace, Brooklyn .....ND 10
Oct. 27—Joe Goldberg, Syracuse ......ND 10
Nov. 5—Young Goldie, Pittsburgh ....ND 6
1914
Jan. 1—Young McAuliffe, Bridgeport .. W 10
1915
Feb. 25—Johnny Ertle, Milwaukee .....ND 8

TB	KO	WD	WF	D	LD	LF	KOBY	ND	NC
119	12	39	1	18	7	0	1	41	0

KID MURPHY
(Peter Frascella)
(Claimant to Bantamweight Title)
Born, May 2, 1886, Boston, Mass. Height,
5 ft 1½ ins. Nationality, Italian-American.
1903
Knockouts: Young James, 1; Ray George, 2; Joe Smith, 1; Kid Lewis, 1; Kid Chappel, 2. Won: Pat McKenna, 6; Kid Lewis, 4; Kid Lewis, 6. Drew Teddy Edwards, 6. Lost: Willie Schumaker, 15. Lost Foul. Pat McKenna, 7,
1904
Knockouts: Young Brunzy, 3; Kid O'Brien, 3; Johnny Lessner, 2; Jack Dorsey, 1;

Todo Leonard, 1; Cy Williams, 2; Kid Allen, 2; Harry Bresen, 2; Eddie Power, 1; George Kitson, 2; Jimmy Moran, 2. Won: Benny Franklin, 15; Kid Hickey, 3; Jimmy Moran, 3; Kid Hickey, 3; Terry Young, 3; Terry Young, 3; Jimmy Farren, 15. Draw: Joe Wagner, 10; Benny Franklin, 25; Jimmy Farren, 15; Jimmy Farren, 15. No Decision: Willie Gibbs, 6; Kid McLuckin, 6; Willie Gibbs, 6; Kid Stinger, 6; Griff Jones, 6.
1905
Mar. 7—Jimmy Farren, Baltimore .....KO 2
Mar. 7—Kid Egan, Baltimore .... D 10
Mar. 16—Frankie McHugh, New Orl. ...KO 2
Mar. —Kid Hickey, New York ....KO 2
Apr. 4—Kid Egan, Baltimore ....KO 4
Apr. —Charley Flanagan, N. Y. C...KO 2
Apr. 27—Tommy Lowe, Baltimore .. KO by 1
May 9—Peter Burke, Baltimore .... W 10
Oct. 21—Harry Decker, Philadelphia ...ND 6
Nov. 30—Tommy O'Toole, PHila. ......ND 6
Dec. 19—Al Delmont, Providence ......L 12
Dec. 20—Al Fellows, New York .... W 3
1906
Apr. 6—Willie Schumaker, New York .. D 4
May 3—Willie Schumaker, New York .KO 4
May 4—Owney Flynn, New York .....ND 4
May 26—Tom Langdon, Philadelphia ..ND 6
May 31—Emergency Kelly, New York..ND 4
Dec. 6—Young Britt, Baltimore ....KO 4
Dec. 24—Sammy Smith, Albany ....KO 11
Dec. 31—Jimmy Farren, Annapolis ....KO 2
1907
Jan. 1—Young McCue, Baltimore ...... D 15
Feb. 15—Young Fitzgerald, Milwaukee .. D 10
Mar. 1—Johnny Coulon, Milwaukee .... W 10
(Murphy claimed Bantamweight Title)
Mar. 15—Eddie Greenwald, Milwaukee .. W 10
July 3—Young Britt, Baltimore .... D 15
1908
Jan. 8—Johnny Coulon, Peoria ....L 10
(For American Title)
Jan. 29—Johnny Coulon, Peoria ....L 10
Mar. 18—Sally Weinrid, Baltimore .. KO by 8
Dec. 2—Joe Coster, Albany ....ND 10
1909
Feb. 11—Johnny Coulon, N. Y. C. .. KO by 5
1913
Nov. 11—Johnny Keyes, New York .....ND 10
Dec. 25—Pinkey Burns, New York .....ND 10
Died, October 30, 1963 in Trenton, N. J.

TB	KO	WD	WF	D	LD	LF	KOBY	ND	NC
70	24	14	0	10	4	1	3	14	0

FRANKIE CONLEY
(Francesco Conte)
(Claimant World Bantam Title)
Born, Platania, Italy, October 4, 1890.
Height, 5 feet, 5½ inches. Weight, 116-122
pounds.
1906
Aug. 11—Kid Hertz, Kenosha, Wis. ......W 6
Aug. 16—Irish Landers, Waukegan ...... D 6
Aug. 23—Irish Landers, Waukegan, Ill... W 6
Sept. 4—Kid Finnegan, Belvidere, Ill. ...KO 5
Oct. 4—Gene McGovern, Racine, Wis. .. W 8
Oct. 12—Patsy Broderick, Kenosha, Wis. W 8
Oct. 25—Sport Christensen, Waukegan .KO 4
Nov. 8—Kid Jackson, Racine, Wis. ..... W 6
1907
Jan. 4—Johnnie Primrose, Elgin, Ill. ..KO 4
Jan. 18—Gene McGovern, Racine, Wis... W 8
Jan. 29—Sport Christensen, Waukegan .. W 4
Feb. 18—Kid Stage, Belvidere, Ill. ....KO 4
Feb. 27—Jack Millward, Fond du Lac ..KO 5
Mar. 8—Chuck Larson, Kenosha, Wis. .. W 8
Mar. 20—Kid Taylor, Fond du Lac ...... W 8
Apr. 6—Kid Clipper, St. Joseph, Mo. ... W 15
Apr. 23—Jack Nolan, Racine, Wis. ..... W 8
Sept. 10—Ad Wolgast, Milwaukee ....L 8
Sept. 28—Jeff O'Connell, Racine, Wis. ... D 8
Oct. 15—Ad Wolgast, Milwaukee ...... D 8
1908
Jan. 9—Gene McGovern, Kenosha, Wis. W 8
Jan. 11—Charley White, Windsor, Ont. ..ND 8
Jan. 28—Willie Gardner, Rockford ......KO 3
Feb. 21—Johnny Gorman, Aurora ......KO 5
Mar. 17—Harry Nelson, Aurora ....KO 8
Mar. 20—Gene McGovern, Racine ...... D 6
Apr. 6—Jeff O'Connell, Waukegan ..... W 10
Apr. 26—Johnny Illig, Elgin .... W 8
May 29—Ad Wolgast, Racine, Wis. ..... D 8

1909

Feb. 9—Howard Smith, New York ....DN 6
Feb. 15—Kid Bosse, New York ....ND 6
Mar. 6—Joe Hyland, New York ......ND 6
Mar. 26—Kid Maloney, New York.....ND 6
May 5—Charlie White, Windsor, Ont. ...ND 8
June 21—Blink McCloskey, St. Joseph, Mo. ....W 15
June 27—Peter Savoy, St. Joseph, Mo. ... W 15
July 9—Peter Savoy, St. Joseph, Mo. ...KO 8
Aug. 10—Frankie White, St. Joseph, Mo. . W 15
Sept. 4—Harry Forbes, Kenosha, Wis. .Exh. 3
Sept. 25—Harry Forbes, Kenosha, Wis. .Exh. 6
Oct. 26—Jockey Bennett, Oakland, Cal. . W 6
Dec. 21—Kid Cleveland, Los Angeles ...ND 10

1910

Feb. 3—Danny Webster, Portland, Ore. ND 10
Feb. 22—Monte Attell, Los Angeles ....KO 42
(advertised for vacant world bantamweight title)
Apr. 28—Danny Webster, Los Angeles ..ND 10
June 7—Owen Moran, Los Angeles ....ND 10
Sept. 2—Charley White, Milwaukee ...ND 10
Oct. 8—Johnny Lynch, New Orleans ..KO 2
Oct. 22—Joe Mandot, New Orleans .....W 10
Nov. 13—Abe Attell, New Orleans...... D 15

1911

Jan. 13—Freddie Andrews, MilwaukeeStpd. 8
Jan. 18—Tommy Dixon, Kansas City ... D 10
Feb. 26—Johnny Coulon, New Orleans ...L 20
(For world bantamweight title)
May 28—Joe Coster, New Orleans........L 20
Aug. 26—Patsy Kline, Vernon, Cal.....KO 14
Sept. 30—Johnny Kilbane, Vernon, Cal...L 20
Nov. 18—Joe Rivers, Vernon, Cal....... D 20

1912

Jan. 1—Joe Rivers, Vernon, Cal. ... KO by 11
Feb. 3—Johnny Coulon, Vernon, Cal. ...L 20
(For world bantamweight title)
May 10—Jack White, Vernon, Cal. .. KO by 12
Aug. 17—Harry Thomas, Vernon.........L 20
Nov. 19—Johnny Dundee, Vernon . KO by 19

1913

Jan. 28—Kid Payo, El Paso .... W 6
Feb. 24—Ernest Lucien, New Orleans ....Pol. Stpd 7
Mar. 5—Eddie O'Keefe, New Orleans ..ND 10
Aug. 15—Young Togo, Ft. Smith, Ark. ... W 10
Sept. 1—Ollie Kirk, Ft. Smith, Ark...... W 10
Sept. 25—Eddie Menny, St. Joseph, Mo..KO 13
Oct. 7—Benny Chavez, Denver ....L 10
Nov. 7—Cal Delaney, Racine, Wis.....ND 10
Nov. 26—Young Goldie, Pittsburgh ....ND 10
Dec. 8—K.O. Mars, Cincinnati ....ND 10
Dec. 20—Cal Delaney, Racine ....ND 10
Dec. 27—Young Goldie, Pittsburgh ....ND 10

1914

Jan. 21—George Stewart, Wheeling, W. Va............................... D 10
Feb. 23—Benny Kaufman, Columbus ..ND 12

1915

Feb. 26—Tex Vernon, Marinette, Ind. ..KO 7
Mar. 8—Chick Hayes, Newcastle, Ind. .ND 10
Apr. 27—Johnny Ritchie, Kenosha.....D 10
May 31—Frankie Mason, Lima ....KO 3
Aug. 26—K. O. Eggers, Quebec.......ND 10
Sept. 22—Young O'Leary, Quebec......ND 10

1919

—Jimmy Hanlon ....KO by 2

TB	KO	WD	WF	D	LD	LF	KOBY	ND	NC
81	15	22	0	10	7	0	4	21	2

Died, Kenosha, Wis., August 21, 1952.

JOHNNY COULON

Born, Feb. 12, 1889, Toronto, Can. Nationality, Irish and French. Weight 118 pounds. Height, 5 feet. Managed by "Pop" Coulon.

1905

Jan. 18—Young Bennie, Chicago ......KO 6
Jan. 24—Kid Burns, Chicago ....W 6
Feb. 15—Frankie Nee, Chicago ....W 6
Mar. 2—Kid Irwin, Chicago..........KO 2
Mar. 14—George Fox, Chicago.........KO 4
Apr. 12—Kid Carpenter, N. Y. C........KO 3
May 18—Young Kelley, College Point ..KO 3
Nov. 13—Dannie Goodman, Chicago ....W 3
Nov. 17—Jack Ryan, Chicago ....KO 3

Nov. 24—Jimmie Dunn, Chicago ....KO 1
Dec. 8—Bob Prosser, Chicago ....KO 2
Dec. 9—Frang Moran, Chicago......... W 3

1906

Jan. 13—Eddie Grenwald, Chicago...... W 3
Jan. 21—Jack Francis, Chicago .... W 3
Feb. 3—Eddie Barndt, Milwaukee ...... W 3
Mar. 2—Kid Bardt, Chicago ....W 2
Mar. 20—Johnny Eagen, Chicago ....W 2
Aug. 6—Fred Gaylor, Box Lake, Ill. ...KO 2
Sept. 3—Danny Goodman, Davenport ..W 8
Oct. 11—Ralph Grant, Davenport......KO 4
Oct. 14—Fred Gaylor, Fox Lake, Ill. ...KO 1
Oct. 24—Kid Bruno, Fox Lake, Ill......KO 3
Nov. 15—Charlie Kriegel, Davenport ....W 8
Dec. 9—Frank Moran, Chicago.........W 3

1907

Feb. 12—Young Fitzgerald, Milwaukee .. W 10
Mar. 12—Young Fitzgerald, Milwaukee .. W 8
Mar. 15—Kid Murphy, Milwaukee.......L 10
Nov. 1—Young Fitzgerald, Milwaukee .. W 10

1908

Jan. 8—Kid Murphy, Peoria .... W 10
(Won American Bantamweight Title)
Jan. 29—*Kid Murphy, Peoria.......... W 10
Feb. 20—*Cooney Kelly, Peoria.........KO 9
Mar. 14—Yng. T. McGovern, L. A. ...... W 10
Apr. 29—Tommy Scully, Waukegan ..... W 5
Aug. 6—Young Joe Gans, Waukegan .... W 5
Sept. 24—Terry Edwards, Milwaukee ....KO 4
Oct. 5—Yankee Schwartz, Phila.......ND 6
Oct. 13—Eddie Doyle, Phila...........ND 3
Oct. 13—Young McGovern, Phila.......ND 4
Nov. 4—Young O'Leary, N. Y. C. .....ND 6
*American title bout

1909

Jan. 1—Mike Orrison, Kansas City .... W 6
Feb. 11—*Kid Murphy, N.Y.C................W 5
Feb. 18—Johnny Daly, N. Y. C. ....ND 6
Mar. 1—Joe Coster, Brooklyn ....ND 10
Mar. 4—Eddie Doyle, N. Y. C. ....ND 10
May 20—Jack Phenecie, Johnstown ....ND 6
May 28—Tebby Watson, Dayton ....KO 10
Oct. 22—Young Ziringer, Pittsburgh ...ND 6
Nov. 23—Patsy Brannigan, Pittsburgh ..ND 6
—Kid Graves ....D 6
*American title bout.

1910

Jan. 15—George Kitson, New Orleans ... W 10
Jan. 30—*Earl Denning, New Orleans ..KO 9
Feb. 19—*Jim Kendrick, New Orleans .... W 10
Mar. 6—Jim Kendrick, New Orleans ...KO 19
(Won Vacant World Bantamweight Title)
Apr. 11—Young O'Leary, N. Y. C. .....ND 10
Apr. 25—Frankie Burns, Brooklyn .....ND 10
May 12—Phil McGovern, N. Y. C. .....ND 10
June 8—Frankie Burns, N. Y. C. ....ND 10
Dec. 5—Charley Harvey, New Orleans .. W 10
Dec. 19—*Earl Denning, Memphis .... W 5

1911

Jan. 19—Terry Moran, Memphis ....KO 2
Feb. 26—*Frankie Conley, New Orleans . W 20
Mar. 22—George Kitson, Akron ....KO 5
Mar. 28—Harry Forbes, Kenosha.......ND 10
Apr. 20—Phil McGovern, Kenosha .....W 10
Apr. 25—Eddie O'Keefe, Kansas City ....D 10
May 25—Johnny Daly, Fort Wayne ....ND 10
*Title bout.

1912

—Young Terry McGovern ......NC 6
Jan. 11—George Kitson, South Bend ...KO 3
Jan. 22—Harry Forbes, Kenosha, Wis. ..KO 3
Feb. 3—*Frankie Conley, Vernon, Cal. . W 20
Feb. 18—*Frankie Burns, New Orleans .. W 20
May 8—Young Solsberg, Brooklyn ....ND 10
June 11—Frankie Hayes, New Haven ...KO 4
July 2—Young Wagner, N.Y.C..............ND 10
Oct. 18—*Kid Williams, N. Y. C. ....ND 10
Nov. 20—Charley Goldman, Brooklyn ..ND 10
*Title bout.

1913

Apr. 30—Tommy Hudson, Winds'r. Can.KO 5
May 12—Frankie Bradley, Phila.......ND 6
June 23—Frankie Burns, Kenosha, Wis. .ND 10
Nov. 20—Charley Goldman, Brooklyn ..ND 10

1914

Jan. 21—Young Sinnet, Racine, Wis. ....ND 10
June 9—*Kid Williams, Vernon ....KO by 3
(Lost Bantamweight Title.)

1916

Apr. 25—Johnny Ritchie, Kenoska, Wis. ND 10
July 4—Billy Mascott, Portland, Ore...ND 6
July 21—Billy Mascott, Portland, Ore...ND 6
July 28—Eddie Campi, San Francisco.......D 4

Aug. 4—Georgie Thompson, San Diego ND 4
Aug. 11—Kid Julian, San Diego, Cal. ..... W 4
Sept. 8—Georgie Thompson, San Diego ND 4

1917
Jan. 1—Joe Wagner, N.Y.C. ....ND 10
Feb. 5—Jack Sharkey, N.Y.C. ....ND 10
Feb. 26—Steve Flessner, Baltimore ...... D 15
Mar. 30—Franky Mason, Fort Wayne ...ND 10
Apr. 9—Bobby Hughes, New Orleans ... W 10
May 14—Pete Herman, Racine, Wis. ......L 3

1918-1919
(Inactive. In U. S. Army as an instructor.)
1920
Feb. 3—Emile Juliard, Paris ....KO 2
Mar. 16—Charles Ledoux, Paris ..... KO by 6
Retired and opened a gymnasium and fight club for amateurs in Chicago. Also refereed bouts and did a specialty act in vaudeville.

TB	KO	WD	WF	D	LD	LF	KOBY	ND	NC
97	24	32	0	1	2	0	2	32	1

Elected to Hall of Fame in 1965.
Died, Oct. 29, 1973, Chicago, Ill.

GEORGE (DIGGER) STANLEY
Born, February 28, 1883, Norwich, Norfolk, England. Weight, 116 lbs. Height, 5 ft. 6½ in.

1901
June 17—Owen Moran, Birmingham .... W 20
1902
Jan. 23—F. Morcombe, London .... D 12
Mar. 22—Tibby Watson, London .... W 6
Mar. 29—Jim Kenrick, London .... W 6
Apr. 14—Tibby Watson, London .... W 10
May 3—Jack Christian, London .... W 6
May 5—Tibby Watson, Hammersmith ...... W 6
May 10—Dick Golding, London .... W 10
May 24—J. Fitzpatrick, London .... W 8
June 16—Pedlar Palmer, London .... L 10
Aug. 30—Cockney Cohen, London .... W 6
Nov. 10—Jack Guyon, London .... W 10
1903
Mar. 2—Jack Walker, London .... W 12
Mar. 14—Jim Kenrick, London .... W 6
Mar. 28—Jack Guyon, London .... W 10
May 11—Pedlar Palmer, London .... L 12
July 11—Jim Williams, London .... W 6
Aug. 1—George Dixon, London .... L 6
Oct. 12—George Dixon, London .... W 6
Nov. 9—Owen Moran, London .... W 15
Dec. 14—Jack Walker, London .... W 15
1904
Apr. 18—Jimmy Walsh, London .... W 15
June 6—Jimmy Walsh, London .... D 15
July 11—H. McDermott, Newcastle .... KO 6
Oct. 17—H. McDermott, Newcastle .... KO 19
Nov. 19—Sid Wilmott, Newcastle .... KO 4
1905
Jan. 23—Owen Moran, London .... L 20
Feb. 27—Lew Branson, London .... KO 4
Mar. 25—Alf Smith, Hounslow .... KO 4
Apr. 17—Louis d'Or, London .... W 10
June 24—Darkey Haley, London .... W 6
July 1—George Moore, London .... L 6
Oct. 20—Jimmy Walsh, Chelsea .... L 15
Dec. 18—Darkey Haley, London .... D 6
1906
Jan. 20—Ike Bradley, Newcastle .... W 20
Feb. 10—Billy Hughes, Newcastle .... KO 16
May 21—Harry Slough, Newcastle .... KO 18
Dec. 13—Ike Bradley, Liverpool .... W 20
1907
June 6—Al Delmont, Liverpool .... KO by 17
Sept. 12—Bob Kendrick, Liverpool .... KO by 9
Nov. 30—Wally Morgan, London .... W 6
1908
Feb. 22—Wally Morgan, London .... W 6
Mar. 7—Driver Himpfen, London .... W 6
Mar. 20—Ike Bradley, London .... W 15
Apr. 4—Young Sullivan, London .... W 6
Oct. 19—Sam Keller, London .... W 20

Nov. 19—Wally Morgan, London .... D 6
1909
Mar. 22—Bill Jordan, London .... W 10
May 24—Jimmy Walsh, London .... D 15
June 14—Alf Mitchell, London .... W 6
Nov. 5—Oswald Stapleton, London .... KO 5
Dec. 26—Dick Golding, London .... KO 3
1910
Feb. 14—G. Young Pierce, London .... D 20
Oct. 17—Joe Bowker, London .... KO 8
(Won British World Bantamweight Title)
Dec. 5—Johnny Condon, London .... W 20
(Retained British World Bantamweight Title)
1911
Jan. 27—Frankie Burns, New York .... ND 10
Feb. 8—Tommy O'Toole, Philadelphia .... ND 6
Sept. 14—Ike Bradley, London .... W 20
(Retained British World Bantamweight Title)
1912
Feb. 23—Jean Poesy, London .... L 15
Apr. 22—Charles Ledoux, London .... W 20
(Retained British World Bantamweight Title)
June 23—Charles Ledoux, Dieppe, France KO by 7
(Lost British World Bantamweight Title)
Aug. 30—Oswald Stapleton, Chelmsford .... KO 9
Oct. 21—Alec Rafferty, London .... W 20
1913
June 2—Bill Benyon, London .... L 20
(For British Bantamweight Title)
Oct. 23—Bill Benyon, London .... W 20
(Won British Bantamweight Title)
1914
Apr. 20—Curley Walker, London .... LF 13
(Lost British Bantamweight Title)
1915
Mar. 29—Jimmy Barry, London .... D 15
Sept. 16—Joe Fox, Liverpool .... W 15
Nov. 11—Tommy Harrison, Liverpool .... LF 4
Dec. 17—Joe Symonds, Plymouth .... LF 11
1916
Mar. 13—Young Brooks, Hoxton .... L 15
Sept. 18—Sid Whatley, London .... KO 3
Oct. 9—Joe Fox, Bradford .... LF 10
Oct. 23—Tommy Noble, London .... W 20
1917
(Inactive)
1918
Jan. 28—Walter Ross, Hoxton .... L 15
Feb. 18—Tommy Noble, London .... L 20
Feb. 25—Bill Beynon, Cardiff .... KO 5
Mar. 23—Johnny Hughes, London .... W 20
Apr. 22—Walter Ross, Hoxton .... LF 6
June 22—George Kilts, Newcastle .... LF 9
July 13—George Kilts, Newcastle .... LF 6

TB	KO	WD	WF	D	LD	LF	KO BY	ND	NC
81	13	38	0	7	11	7	3	2	0

CHARLES LEDOUX
Born, October 27, 1892, Nievre, France. Weight, 116 lbs. Height, 5 ft. ½ in.

1909
   —Charles Meyer, Paris .... KO 1
   —Vauthier, Paris .... KO 4
   —Costet, Paris .... KO 2
   —Frigol, Paris .... KO 1
   —Thibault, Paris .... KO 1
   —Vimard, Paris .... KO 1
   —Robert, Paris .... KO 1
   —M. Meyer, Paris .... KO 1
   —Dages, Paris .... KO 1
   —Guiraud, Paris .... KO 1
   —Rigot, Paris .... KO 7
Oct. 16—Buster Brown, Paris .... KO 1
Nov. 22—Lepine, Paris .... KO 2
Nov. 24—Georges Carpentier, Paris .... L 15
Nov. 27—Sejourne, Paris .... KO 1
   —Marcel Mouginot, Paris .... KO 2
Dec. 7—Achalme, Paris .... KO 1

Dec. 12—Marcel Mouginot, Paris .... D 6
Dec. 18—Charles Olive, Paris .... KO 4
Dec. 22—Georges Gaillard, Paris .... W 6
1910
Jan. 8—Bill Ladbury, Paris .... KO by 4
　　　—Charles Meyer, Paris .... KO 2
Apr. 16— Lucien Dorgueille, Paris .... W 8
Apr. 23—Jack Guyon, Paris .... KO 3
May 1—Lucien Dorgueille, Paris .... D 8
June 4—Buck Shine, Paris .... W 10
July 1—Paul Til, Paris .... L 10
July 19—Bill Kard, Paris .... W 6
Sept. 14—Harry Ray, Paris .... KO 5
Oct. 29—Auguste Grassi, Paris .... W 6
Nov. 3—Auguste Grassi, Nancy .... KO 5
Nov. 12—Alf Shipp, Paris .... KO 3
Nov. 26—Johnny Hughes, Paris .... WF 2
1911
Jan. 6—Johnny Hughes, Paris .... L 10
Jan. 21—Tom Paul, Paris .... KO 2
Feb. 4—Buck Shine, Paris .... W 10
Feb. 24—Jim Butler, Paris .... KO 4
Mar. 18—Jack Morris, Paris .... KO 2
Apr. 8—Lucien Dorgueille, Paris .... KO 4
Apr. 15—Christian, St. Denis .... W 10
May 8—Charles Legrand, Paris .... W 15
June 22—Bill Kard, Paris .... KO 2
Oct. 14—Arthur Exhall, Paris .... KO 1
Oct. 28—Stoker Hoskyne, Paris .... KO 3
Nov. 8—Bill Ladbury, Paris .... KO 4
Nov. 22—Kid Logan, Paris .... KO 2
Nov. 30—Louis Carbonell, Paris .... KO 3
Dec. 23—George Burns, Lille .... KO 2
1912
Jan. 29—Joe Bowker, London .... KO 10
Mar. 1—Eddie Stanton, Paris .... KO 3
Mar. 20—Georges Gaillard, Paris .... L 10
Apr. 22—Digger Stanley, London .... L 20
　　(For European Bantamweight Title)
May 4—Young Greenstock, Paris .... KO 8
June 1—Georges Gaillard, Paris .... KO 11
　　(Won French Bantamweight Title)
June 23—Digger Stanley, Dieppe .... KO 7
　　(Won European Bantamweight Title)
　　(Won British World Bantamweight Title)
Aug. 22—Jim Heldey, Boulogne .... KO 1
　　　—Jim Maher, Lyons .... KO 1
Sept. 9—George Burns, Aix les Bains ..... KO 1
Oct. 12—Sam Minto, Paris .... KO 9
Oct. 16—Georges Gaillard, Paris .... WF 7
Nov. 20—Battling Reddy, New York ...... ND 10
Nov. 28—Frankie Conway, Philadelphia ... ND 6
Dec. 11—Kid Williams, Philadelphia ...... ND 6
1913
May 1—Albert Wyns, Paris .... KO 6
May 21—Robert Dastillon, Paris .... KO 6
June 10—Phil McGovern, Boston .... D 12
June 24—Eddie Campi, Vernon, Calif. .... L 20
July 15—Kid Williams, Vernon .... KO by 15
　　(Lost British World Bantamweight Title)
Oct. 25—Sid Smith, Paris .... KO 20
Dec. 12—Marcel Lepreux, Paris .... KO 11
Dec. 27—Bill Beynon, Cardiff .... KO 8
1914
Feb. 7—Bill Beynon, Cardiff .... KO 8
May 2—Johnny Hughes, Cardiff .... KO 7
June 6—M. Durocher, Paris .... KO 3
June 14—Lucien Armanet, Baziers .... KO 5
June 29—Curley Walker, London ..... KO 5
July 10—Eugene Criqui, Paris .... KO 12
　　(Won French Flyweight Title)
1915-1917
(Inactive)
1918
Oct. 4—Spike Webb, Verdun .... D 6
1919
July 16—M. Durocher, Paris .... KO 7
July 31—Tommy Noble, Paris .... KO 10
Aug. 18—Cuendet, Deauville .... KO 3
Sept. 12—Gredeville, Nevers .... KO 4
Oct. 1—Joe Bambridge, Paris .... KO 3

768

Oct. 20—Jem Driscoll, London .... KO 16
　　(Retained European Bantamweight Title)
Nov. 9—Gaston Cassini, Marseille .... KO 5
Dec. 13—Walter Ross, Paris .... KO 12
1920
Jan. 18—George Langham, Monte Carlo ... KO 4
Feb. 2—Christian, Bordeaux .... KO 6
Mar. 16—Johnny Coulon, Paris .... KO 6
Apr. 17—Percy Barnes, Lyons .... KO 4
May 31—Jim Higgins, London .... KO 11
June 23—Joe Burman, Philadelphia ...... ND 8
July 5—Young Lewis, Montreal .... KO 5
Aug. 2—Joe Lynch, Jersey City .... ND 12
Aug. 4—Johnny Frissee, Montreal ...... KO 5
Sept. 20—Joe Burman, Philadelphia ...... ND 8
Oct. 15—Jack Sharkey, New York .... L 15
Nov. 18—Micky Belmont, Montreal ...... ND 10
Nov. 26—Joe Burman, Providence .... D 10
Dec. 16—Kid Williams, Baltimore .... L 12
1921
Mar. 24—Bill Beynon, Paris .... KO 4
Apr. 12—Robert Dastillon, Paris .... KO 1
May 18—Christian, Barcelona .... KO 4
June 11—Percy Barnes, Bordeaux .... KO 5
June 24—Danny Kramer, Philadelphia ..... ND 8
July 13—Joe Burman, New York .... L 12
Aug. 10—Johnny Buff, New York .... L 10
Aug. 24—Danny Kramer, Philadelphia ..... ND 8
Sept. 5—Pete Herman, New Orleans ..... L 10
Oct. 24—Tommy Harrison, Hanley .... L 20
　　(Lost European Bantamweight Title)
1922
Feb. 4—Eugene Criqui, Paris .... KO by 1
　　(For French Featherweight Title)
Apr. 24—Tommy Harrison, Liverpool .... W 20
　　(Regained European Bantamweight Title)
June 18—Andre Routis, Casablanca .... W 15
　　(Retained European Bantamweight Title)
Sept. 24—Ben Thomas, Paris .... W disq. 8
Oct. 9—Tommy Harrison, Hanley .... KO 18
　　(Retained European Bantamweight Title)
Nov. 10—George French, Paris .... KO 3
1923
Feb. 27—Michel Montreuil, Paris .... KO 11
　　(Retained European Bantamweight Title)
Mar. 10—M. Calloir, Lyons .... W 10
May 6—Andre Routis, Paris .... W 15
　　(Retained European Bantamweight Title)
July 31—Harry (Bugler) Lake, London .... L 20
　　(Lost European Bantamweight Title)
1924
Jan. 22—Andre Routis, Paris .... L 20
　　(For French Featherweight Title)
Feb. 19—Edouard Mascart, Paris .... W 20
　　(Won European Featherweight Title)
May 8—Henry Hebrans, Brussels .... L 15
　　(Lost European Featherweight Title)
June 6—Ernie Goozeman, Chicago .... ND 10
June 20—John Curtin, Jersey City .... ND 10
July 16—Abe Goldstein, New York .... L 15
　　(For World Bantamweight Title)
Oct. 12—Julien Couleand, Monteau .... KO 3
Nov. 18—Edouard Mascart, Paris .... L 20
　　(For French Featherweight Title)
1925
Feb. 11—Gredeville, Dijon .... KO 3
Apr. 2—Paul Marignan, Tours .... KO 3
June 9—Kid Francis, Paris .... L 12
1926
Feb. 6—Young Cyclone, Barcelona .... L 12
Apr. 8—M. Durocher, Strasbourg .... KO 2

TB	KO	WD	WF	D	LD	LF	KO BY	ND	NC
133	79	14	3	4	19	0	3	11	0

KID WILLIAMS
(Johnny Gutenko)
Born, Dec. 5, 1893, Copenhagen,
Denmark. Weight, 117 lbs. Height, 5 ft. 1 in.
1910
July 18—Shep Farren, Baltimore ......KO 5

July	25—Kid McFarland, Baltimore	....KO	1
Aug.	1—Ike Miller, Baltimore	...........KO	2
Aug.	15—Shep Farren, Baltimore	.....KO	6
Sept.	12—Tommy Buck, Baltimore	.....W	6
Sept.	19—Buddy Jones, Baltimore	.....KO	2
Sept.	22—Joe Britton, Baltimore	......KO	1
Sept.	24—Sam Miller, Baltimore	......KO	1
Oct.	2—Babe Stinger, Philadelphia	....KO	5
Oct.	9—Tommy Buck, Baltimore	..... D	15
Nov.	2—Frank Bradley, Baltimore	.....KO	5
Nov.	9—Tommy Buck, Baltimore	..... W	10

1911

Jan.	2—Young McGovern, Baltimore	.KO	3
Jan.	9—Young McCue, Baltimore	....KO	2
Jan.	16—Lee Morton, Baltimore	......KO	5
Jan.	24—Lee Walton, Baltimore	......KO	5
Mar.	14—Charley Harvey, Baltimore	..... D	13
Mar.	20—Jimmy Cross, Baltimore	......KO	5
May	26—Kid Murphy, Baltimore	...... W	12
July	10—George Chaney, Baltimore	L	20
July	27—Yg. Packy McFarland, N.Y.C. KO		5
July	28—Babe Davis, N.Y.C.	..........KO	5
July	31—Young Solly, Perth Amboy	..KO	1
Aug.	1—Willie Carroll, N.Y.C.	.........KO	4
Aug.	2—Frankie Callahan, Rockaway	.ND	6
Aug.	6—Young Solberg, Brooklyn	....ND	10
Aug.	15—Willie Faust, N.Y.C.	.........KO	4
Aug.	19—K.O. Sweeney, N.Y.C.	......ND	10
Aug.	22—Willie Carroll, N.Y.C.	.......KO	2
Oct.	13—Barry Hill, Baltimore	.........KO	13
Nov.	11—Harry Smith, Baltimore	......KO	6
Nov.	24—Eddie McCloskey, Baltimore	..KO	5
Dec.	23—Barry Hill, N.Y.C.	............ND	10

1912

Jan.	6—Banty Lewis, N.Y.C.	........ND	10
Jan.	15—Charley Harvey, Brooklyn	....ND	10
Jan.	17—Yg. Mick McDongh, Brooklyn	ND	10
Jan.	19—Bennie Riley, Baltimore	......ND	12
Jan.	20—Young Solsberg, Brooklyn	....ND	10
Feb.	10—Young Stanley, N.Y.C.	......ND	10
Mar.	6—Kokomo Kid, Baltimore	......KO	4
Apr.	9—Johnny Daly, Baltimore	..... W	15
Apr.	23—Battling Reddy, N.Y.C.	.....ND	10
May	2—Young Ketchell, Baltimore	..KO	2
May	31—Charley Goldman, Baltimore	. W	15
July	20—Artie Edwards, N.Y.C.	...... W	8
July	29—Young Solsberg, N.Y.C.	..... W	7
Aug.	9—Young Marino, Baltimore	...KO	5
Aug.	17—Battling Reddy, N.Y.C.	......ND	10
Aug.	26—Kid Kelly, N.Y.C.	...........W	9
Sept.	14—Mickey Brown, N.Y.C.	......KO	8
Sept.	16—Billy Fitzsimmons, N.Y.C.	..KO	8
Sept.	24—Young Diggins, Philadelphia	.ND	6
Oct.	18—Johnny Coulon, N.Y.C.	......KO	10
Nov.	1—Johnny Hughes, Philadelphia	.ND	6
Nov.	6—Billy Fitzsimmons, N.Y.C.	..ND	10
Nov.	22—Harry Smith, Philadelphia	....ND	6
Dec.	11—Charley Ledoux, Philadelphia	.ND	6

1913

Jan.	4—Frankie Conway, Philadelphia	ND	6
Feb.	12—Eddie Campi, Vernon	.... W	20
Mar.	28—Frankie Conway, Philadelphia	ND	6
Apr.	14—Frankie Bradley, Philadelphia	ND	6
Apr.	26—Louisiana, Philadelphia	......ND	6
May	14—Young Diggins, Baltimore	....KO	4
June	11—Jim Kendrick, Baltimore	...... W	6
July	15—Charley Ledoux, Vernon	.....KO	15
Oct.	3—Mickey Dunn, Baltimore	.....KO	2
Oct.	6—Willie Mack, Philadelphia	....ND	6
Oct.	25—Patsy Brannigan, Phila.	......ND	6
Nov.	24—Battling Reddy, Philadelphia	..ND	6
Nov.	27—Kid Lodiman, Milwaukee	.....ND	6

1914

Jan.	6—Chick Hayes, Baltimore	.... W	7
Jan.	31—Eddie Campi, Vernon	............KO	12
Mar.	23—Fred Diggins, Philadelphia	......ND	6
Apr.	6—Louisiana, Philadelphia	.......ND	6
June	9—Johnny Coulon, Vernon	........KO	3

(Won Bantamweight Title)

June	30—Pete Kid Herman, New Orl.	...ND	10
Sept.	14—Louisiana, Philadelphia	......ND	6
Sept.	28—Pete Kid Herman, Phila.	....KO	4
Oct.	27—Dutch Brandt, Brooklyn	....ND	10
Nov.	30—Young Diggins, Philadelphia	..ND	6
Dec.	19—K.O. O'Donnell, Philadelphia	.. W	3
Dec.	25—Johnny Daly, N.Y.C.	........ND	10

1915

Jan.	31—Eddie Campi, Baltimore	......KO	15
Feb.	2—Eddie Wallace, Philadelphia	...ND	10
Feb.	15—Jimmy Murray, N.Y.C.	......ND	10
Mar.	17—Johnny Kilbane, Philadelphia	.ND	6
Mar.	23—Young Diggins, Baltimore	....ND	10
Apr.	5—Louisiana, Philadelphia	......ND	6

June	4—Jimmy Murray, Philadelphia	... W	6
July	24—Jimmy Taylor, Baltimore	...... W	15
Sept.	10—Johnny Ertle, St. Paul	.... LF	5

(Ertel Claimed Title)

Oct.	5—Dutch Brandt, Baltimore	..... W	10
Oct.	28—Young Pal Moore, Memphis	...ND	8
Dec.	6—*Frankie Burns, New Orleans	.. D	20

*Title bout.

1916

Feb.	7—*Pete Kid Herman, New Orl.	... D	20
Apr.	11—Battling Lahn, N.Y.C.	.......ND	10
May	15—Billy Bevan, Wilkes-Barre, Pa.	.ND	10
May	30—Benny McCoy, Baltimore	.....KO	7
July	12—Alf Mansfield, Baltimore	.....KO	5
Aug.	28—Young Mendo, Buffalo	.......KO	5
Sept.	4—Franky Brown, Baltimore	...ND	10
Sept.	11—Joe O'Donnell, Philadelphia	..ND	6
Sept.	15—Dick Loadman, Buffalo	......ND	10
Oct.	3—Benny Kaufman, Philadelphia	ND	6
Oct.	16—Al Shubert, Philadelphia	.....ND	6
Oct.	26—Al Shubert, Baltimore	.......ND	10
Dec.	7—Billy Fitzsimmons, Baltimore	.ND	10

*Title bout.

1917

Jan.	9—*Pete Kid Herman, New Orleans L		20
Jan.	30—Benny McNeill, Kansas City	... W	15
Feb.	19—Eddie O'Keefe, Philadelphia	..ND	6
Mar.	8—Benny Kaufman, Baltimore	...KO	10
Mar.	13—Joe Lynch, N.Y.C.	...........ND	10
Mar.	27—Jimmy Murray, N.Y.C.	......ND	10
Apr.	2—Benny McNeill, Philadelphia	..ND	6
Apr.	23—Jimmy Taylor, York, Pa.	....ND	10
May	14—Barney Hahn, Philadelphia	....ND	6
May	24—Benny McNeill, Baltimore	..... W	15
June	13—Pete Kid Herman, Phila.	......ND	6
July	27—Jack Sharkey, Baltimore, Md.	.. W	6
Sept.	24—Gussie Lewis, Philadelphia	....ND	6
Oct.	1—Dick Loadman, Baltimore	.....W	12
Oct.	16—Benny McNeill, St. Louis	....ND	10
Dec.	17—Johnny Ertle, Baltimore	...... D	12

*Lost bantamweight title; Billy Rocap, referee.

1919

Jan.	29—Joe Lynch, Philadelphia	... KO by	4
Feb.	25—Joe (King) Leopold, Denver	... W	10
Apr.	1—Jack Sharkey, Baltimore	..... W	12
May	20—Joe Tuber, Philadelphia	......ND	6
June	1—Young Chaney, Baltimore	..... W	12

1920

May	24—Patsy Johnson, Philadelphia	..ND	8
June	28—Dutch Brandt, Baltimore, Md..	KO	3
Aug.	13—Johnny Ertle, Baltimore, Md.	... W	12
Oct.	28—Sammy Sandow, Baltimore	.... W	12
Nov.	13—Earl Puryear, Phila.	...........ND	8
Dec.	16—Charley Ledoux, Baltimore	.... W	12

1921

Jan.	24—Carl Tremaine, Phila.	........ND	8
Feb.	21—Abe Goldstein, Phila.	.......ND	8
Mar.	2—Tom. Ryan, McKeesport, Pa.	.ND	10
Mar.	15—Marty Collins, Phila.	.........ND	8
Mar.	18—Joe O'Donnell, Phila.	........ND	8
Apr.	18—Earl Puryear, Baltimore	.......ND	12
Apr.	25—Joe Burman, Phila.	..........ND	8
May	11—Packy O'Gatty, N.Y.C.	.......KO	9
May	18—Jack Wolfe, Cleveland	........ND	12
May	20—Patsy Scanlon, Pittsburgh	...ND	10
June	11—Frankie Edwards, Brooklyn	... W	9
June	29—Louisiana, Phila.	..............ND	8
Oct.	4—Andy Chaney, Boston	L	10
Oct.	12—Mickey Brown, Brooklyn	..... W	12
Oct.	19—Jimmy Mendo, Reading, Pa.	..ND	8

1922

Feb.	15—Terry Martin, Mariesville, R.I.	. D	12
July	8—Joe Mandell, Brooklyn	.......WF	6
Aug.	14—Essie Ray, Shreveport	.... W	10
Sept.	4—Joe Dundee, Baltimore	......WF	10
Sept.	18—Roy Moore, Baltimore	........KO	7
Nov.	20—Pascal Colletti, New Orleans	L	10
Nov.	24—Eddie O'Dowd, Providence	....WF	9
Dec.	22—Battling Leonard, New York	..WF	1

1923

Jan.	15—Young Montreal, Baltimore	.... W	12
Mar.	12—Sammy Sandow, Baltimore	.... W	12
Apr.	5—Bobby Garcia, Baltimore	..... LF	9
Apr.	17—Battling Mack, Phila.	..........ND	8
Apr.	25—Bob Garcia, Baltimore	L	12
July	13—Bud Dempsey, New York	..... W	12
July	31—Pancho Villa, Phila.	..........ND	8
Sept.	26—Frankie Daly, Baltimore	...... W	12
Oct.	24—Charlie Holman, Baltimore	.... LF	8
Dec.	22—Danny Lee, New York	.........KO	1
Dec.	29—Joey Schwartz, Baltimore	.... W	12

1924

Jan.	1—Midget Smith, New York	...... W	12
Jan.	14—Charlie Goodman, New York	.. W	10

Feb.   6—Young Montreal, Providence . . . W   12
Feb. 27—Abe Friedman, Provide., R. I. . LF   8
Apr.   5—Al Markie, Phila. . . . . W   10
1925
Jan. 21—Jack West, Atlantic City . . . . . . ND   8
Feb.   9—Al Monahan, Atlantic City . . . . ND   8
Apr. 20—Lew Mayrs, Baltimore . . . . D   12
Apr. 22—Terry McHugh, Pottsville, Pa. . . . W   3
June 26—Frankie Genaro, Baltimore L   12
Aug. 21—Midget Smith, Baltimore . . . . . . W   12
Aug. 28—Red Leonard, Portsmouth . . . . . . W   10
Sept. 28—Midget Smith, Baltimore . . . . . WF   7
Oct.   5—Jack West, Portsmouth . . . . W   10
Dec. 28—Jack West, Washington . . . . W   10
1926
Jan.   4—Nate Corp. Baltimore . . . . L Disq.   11
Mar.   5—Al Monohan, Philadelphia . . . . . W   10
Mar.   —Billy Pinkus, Baltimore . . . . KO   3
1927
Feb. 25—Jack Skinner, Baltimore . . . . . . KO   3
July 15—Jimmy Hogan, Baltimore . . . . . . W   3
1928
July 19—Eddie Buell, Baltimore . . . KO by   4
Aug.   —Joe O'Donnell, Philadelphia . . . W   8
Aug. 27—Tony Ross, Baltimore . . . . D   12
Sept. 7—Jack Daily, Baltimore . . . . W   8
Sept. 28—Lou Guggliemini, Baltimore . . . W   8
Oct. 26—Joe Caniano, Centreville, Md. . . W   8
Nov. 29—Eddie Bowling, Baltimore . . . . . W   8
Dec.   7—Joe Caniano, Centreville . . . . . . W   8
Dec. 14—Willie Parrish, Baltimore . . . . . . KO   5
Dec. 27—Lou Guggliemini, Baltimore . . . W   8
1929
Jan. 14—Bobby Garcia, Baltimore . . . . . . W   10
Feb. 11—Sid Lampe, Baltimore . . . . WF   7
Mar.   6—Sid Lampe, Baltimore L   10
Apr.   9—Joe Belmont, Hagerstown L   8
July 12—Frankie Garcia, Greensboro,
          Md. . . . . W   8
Sept. 3—Bobby Burns, Baltimore . . . KO by   2
Tried an unsuccessful comeback in 1935.

TB	KO	WD	WF	D	LD	LF	KOBY	ND	NC
204	48	53	6	8	8	5	3	73	0

Died, Oct. 18, 1963 in Baltimore, Md.
Elected to Boxing Hall of Fame 1970.

JOHNNY (Kewpie) ERTLE
(Claimant World Bantamweight Title)
Born, March 21, 1896, Dunafaldyar,
Austria. Weight, 112-16 lbs. Height, 4 ft. 11 in.
Managed by Mike McNulty.
1913
Oct. 31—La Sotte, St. Paul, Minn. . . . . . . KO   3
Nov. 25—La Sotte, St. Paul, Minn. . . . . . . KO   4
1914
Jan. 11—Dan Cushway, Superior, Wis. . ND   6
Feb. 22—Jim Azine, Minneapolis, Minn. . . W   8
Mar.   4—Kid Watson, Superior, Wis. . . . KO   2
May   19—Johnny Cashell, Minneapolis . . . W   8
June 14—Kid Blinkey, Superior, Wis. . . . KO   2
June 20—Johnny Cashill, Minneapolis . . . D   10
Aug. 31—Johnny Cashill, Superior, Wis. ND   8
Sept. 2—Jim Azine, Hudson, Wis. . . . . . . ND   4
Sept. 7—Jim Azine, Superior, Wis. . . . . . ND   8
Oct. 15—Jim Azine, Minneapolis, Minn. ND   9
Nov.   9—Kayo Krause, Milwaukee . . . . . ND   6
Nov. 26—Young Virigo, La Salle, Ill. . . . . KO   5
Nov. 30—Frankie Izzo, Milwaukee, Wis. ND   10
Dec. 11—Artie Armstrong, Milwaukee . . ND   10
Dec. 15—Johnny Cashill, Minneapolis . . ND   10
1915
Jan. 21—Young Herzog, Milwaukee . . . . KO   1
Jan. 29—Young Krause, Milwaukee . . . . . W   6
Feb.   5—Chick Hayes, Milwaukee . . . . . . ND   10
Feb. 15—Ruby Hirsch, Kenosha, Wis. . . ND   10
Feb. 19—Johnny Ritchie, Milwaukee . . . ND   10
Feb. 25—Jimmy Walsh, Milwaukee . . . . . ND   8
Feb. 26—Frankie Izzo, Milwaukee . . . . WF   7
Apr.   6—Pal Moore, Memphis, Tenn. L   8
Apr. 26—Young Solsberg, Milwaukee . . ND   10
May   3—Eddie Coulon, Milwaukee . . . ND   10
Aug. 20—Eddie Coulon, St. Paul . . . . . . ND   10
Sept. 10—Kid Williams, St. Paul . . . . WF   5
          (Ertle claimed title)
Oct. 12—Jimmy Pappas, St. Louis . . . . . ND   8
Nov.   8—Abe Friedman, B'klyn, N.Y. . . ND   10
Nov. 15—Young Solsberg, B'klyn, N. Y. ND   10
Dec.   4—Young O'Leary, B'klyn, N.Y. . . KO   3

Dec.   6—Young Diggins, Phila., Pa. . . . KO   1
Dec. 25—Joe O'Donnell, Phila., Pa. . . . . . ND   6
1916
Jan. 21—Jack Sayles, N. Y. C. . . . . ND   10
Feb.   9—Teddy Martin, N. Y. C. . . . . ND   10
Feb. 14—Joe Tuber, Phila., Pa. . . . . ND   6
Feb. 22—Al Shubert, New Bedford . . . . . D   12
Mar. 13—Yg. Zulu Kid, B'klyn, N. Y. . . . ND   10
Mar. 16—Alf Mansfield, Reading, Pa. . . ND   6
Mar. 20—Young McGovern, Phila., Pa . . ND   6
May   9—Bobby Burns, St. Paul . . . . KO   4
June 17—Johnny Ritchie, St. Louis . . . . . W   12
Sept. 4—Benny Kaufman, Phila., Pa. . . . ND   6
Oct. 10—Joe Lynch, N.Y.C. . . . . ND   10
Nov. 10—Mickey Byrne, Cleveland, O. . . KO   9
Nov. 21—Dick Loadman, Baltimore . . . . ND   10
1917
Feb. 16—Pekin Kid Herman, Milw'kee . . ND   10
May   14—Tony Baron, Pittsburgh, Pa. . . ND   6
June 13—Jack Douglas, Dubuque . . . . . . KO   8
July   3—Sammy Sandow, Cincinnati . . ND   15
July 31—Roy Moore, St. Paul . . . . ND   10
Sept. 11—Roy Moore, St. Paul . . . . ND   10
Sept. 28—Tony Barrone, Waterloo . . . . . ND   10
Oct. 29—Geo. Thompson, Racine . . . . . . ND   10
Nov. 21—Joe Burman, Milwaukee . . . . . ND   10
Dec.   7—Jack Wolfe, Cleveland . . . . ND   10
Dec. 17—Kid Williams, Baltimore . . . . . . D   12
1918
Jan. 25—Jack Wolf, Cleveland . . . . ND   10
Feb.   4—Arthur Simons, New Orleans . . ND   10
Apr. 10—Pal Moore, Baltimore L   15
May   10—Dick Loadman, Milw'kee . . KO by   3
Sept. 14—Benny Vogel, Omaha . . . . KO   8
Nov.   9—Franky Burns, Weeh'ken . . KO by   7
1919
May   23—Pete Herman, Minneapolis . KO by   5
Apr. 24—Frankie Mason, South Bend . . ND   10
June 20—Frankie Mason, Grand Rapids . . . L   10
1920
Aug. 13—Kid Williams, Baltimore L   12
1921
Sept. 29—Johnny Ritchie, Des Moines . . KO   3
Oct. 18—Babe Asher, Winnipeg L   12
1922
Jan. 20—Benny Vogel, Milwaukee . . . . . ND   10
Mar. 17—Joey Schwartz, Detroit . . . . ND   10
Aug. 23—Jimmy Valentine, Eveleth . . . . ND   10
Nov.   3—Bobby Eber, Hamilton L   10
1923
Jan. 26—Saph McKenna, St. Paul . . . . . . ND   10
Mar. 16—Carl Tremaine, Windsor, Ont. . . . L   10
Apr.   5—Johnny Andrews, Toledo . . . . . ND   10
May   7—Carl Tremaine, Columbus L   12

TB	KO	WD	WF	D	LD	LF	KOBY	ND	NC
79	14	4	2	3	8	0	3	45	0

PETE HERMAN
(Peter Gulotta)
Born, Feb. 12, 1896, New Orleans, La.
Nationality, Italian-American. Weight 116-118
lbs. Height, 5 ft. 2 in. Managed by Jerome
Gargano, Doc Cutch, Sammy Goldman and Red
Walsh.
1912
Record of several early bouts (all in New
Orleans) unavailable.
Draw: Eddie Coulon, 10. Lost: Eddie
Coulon, 10.
1913
July   3—Young Rosner, New Orleans . . ND   10
Oct.   6—Ruby Hirsch, New Orleans . . . . ND   10
Nov.   3—Joe Wagner, New Orleans . . . . ND   10
Knockouts: Kid Acktins, 3; Bobby
Dibbons, 6. Won: Kid Gormley, 15; Bill Stevens,
10; Buddy Garic, 10; Stanley Everett, 10; Kid
Koster, 8; Phil Virgets, 10; Kid Gormley, 15; Abe
Kabakoff, 8; Jimmy Walsh, 8; Johnny Fisse, 8
(twice) and 15; Eddy Coulon, 8; Nate Jackson, 8;
Nate Jackson, 8; Kid Greaves, 10. Draw: Eddie
Coulon, 8 (twice); Kid Gormley, 15; Nate
Jackson, 15. Lost: Johnny Fisse, 8 and 10. No
Decision: Johnny Fisse, 8 and 10.
1914
Won: Johnny Fiss, 10; Franky Sinnett, 10;
Arthur Simons, 10.
Feb.   2—Young Allen, New Orleans . . . . KO   10
Feb. 18—Marty Kid Taylor, New Orl. . . . . . W   10

770

Mar.	9—K.O. Eggers, New Orleans ....ND	10
June	30—Kid Williams, New Orleans....ND	10
Sept.	13—Eddie Campi, New Orleans .... W	20
Nov.	15--Frankie Burns, N. Orleans . KO by	13
Nov.	24—Young Zulu Kid, New Orleans . W	15
	—Jimmy Pappas, New Orleans ... W	10
	—Johnny Fisse, New Orleans ... W	10
	—Johnny Fisse, New Orleans .... W	15

1915

Jan.	12—K. O. Eggers, Atlanta .... W	10
Feb.	6—Kid Taylor, New Orleans ...... W	10
Mar.	1—Johnny Solsberg, Memphis ....W	8
May	1—Young Zulu Kid, New Orleans . D	10
May	18—Al Shubert, New Orleans ...... W	15
June	18—Harry Bramer, Denver ....KO	4
July	2—Louisiana, New Orleans .... W	20
July	21—Jack Doyle, New Orleans ..... W	15
Sept.	6—Nate Jackson, Denver .... LF	3
Sept.	13—Nate Jackson, Denver .... W	15
Oct.	7—Young Sandow, New Orleans .. W	15
Nov.	6—Young Zulu Kid, New Orleans . W	15
Nov.	15—Young Pal Moore, Memphis L	3
Dec.	13—Eddy Coulon, New Orleans ...KO	4

1916

Feb.	7—Kid Williams, New Orleans..... D	20
	(For Bantamweight Title)	
Feb.	28—Lew Tendler, Philadelphia ....ND	6
Mar.	23—Frankie Brown, Baltimore ..... D	15
June	12—Frankie Brown, New Orleans .. W	15
July	10—George Brown, Memphis ....KO	5
July	31—Roy Moore, New Orleans ..... W	15
Sept.	4—Jimmy Pappas, Atlanta .... W	10
Sept.	30—Bernie Hahn, Philadelphia ....ND	6
Nov.	6—Johnny Eggers, New Orleans .. W	20
Dec.	10—Leo Schaeffer, Memphis .... W	8

1917

Jan.	9—Kid Williams, New Orleans..... W	20
	(Won bantamweight title; Bill Rocap, referee)	
Feb.	12—Sammy Sandow, Cincinnati ...ND	10
Feb.	20—Harry Kabakoff, St. Louis, Mo. W	12
Mar.	6—Jabez White, Albany, N. Y. ....ND	10
Mar.	14—Dutch Brandt, Brooklyn ....ND	10
Apr.	27—Pekin Kid Herman, Peoria, Ill. ....ND	10
May	4—Harry Coulon, Buffalo ......ND	10
May	14—Johnny Coulon, Racine, Wis. .. W	3
May	21—Gussie Lewis, Philadelphia ....ND	6
June	1—Joe Lynch, N. Y. C. ....ND	10
June	13—Kid Williams, Philadelphia ....ND	6
Aug.	21—Jack Douglas, New Orleans ...ND	10
Sept.	3—Nate Jackson, Tulsa, Okla. ....ND	10
Sept.	10—Earl Puryear, Tulsa, Okla. ....ND	10
Sept.	17—K. O. Eggers, Philadelphia ....ND	6
Nov.	5—*Frankie Burns, New Orleans .. W	20
Dec.	10—Joe Tuber, Philadelphia ......ND	6
Dec.	14—Frankie Mason, Ft. Wayne, Ind. ....KO	3
Dec.	19—Gussie Lewis, Philadelphia ....ND	6
	*Title contest.	

1918

Apr.	12—Yg. Zulu Kid, Peoria ....ND	10
May	4—Jack Sharkey, Philadelphia ...ND	6
May	8—Young Chaney, Baltimore ....ND	10
July	3—Franky Burns, Jersey City ....ND	8
Sept.	2—Jack Sharkey, Philadelphia ....ND	6
Sept.	6—Zulu Kid, Jersey City ....ND	8

1919

Feb.	10—Patsy Scanlon, Pittsburgh ....ND	10
Mar.	4—Jack (Kid) Wolfe, Cleveland ...ND	10
Mar.	10—Al Shubert, New Bedford .....ND	10
Mar.	24—Pal Moore, Memphis, Tenn. ...ND	8
Apr.	8—Al Shubert, Baltimore ....ND	10
Apr.	16—Al Shubert, Baltimore ....ND	10
Apr.	21—Patsy Johnson, Trenton, N. J. .ND	8
Apr.	25—Kid Regan, St. Louis, Mo. ...ND	8
May	8—Patsy Wallace, Philadelphia ...ND	6
May	18—Johnny Solsberg, Syracuse ...ND	10
May	23—Johnny Ertle, Minneapolis ....KO	5
May	29—Kid Regan, St. Louis ....ND	8
June	10—Terry McHugh, Allentown, Pa. ....ND	6
July	4—Dick Griffin, Fort Worth .....ND	10
Aug.	6—Bernie Hahn, Atlanta, Ga. ....ND	10
Aug.	15—Jack Sharkey, Milwaukee ....ND	10
Sept.	1—Joe Lynch, Waterbury, Conn. .ND	10
Sept.	15—Jack Sharkey, Detroit ....ND	10
Sept.	30—Sammy Sandow, Newport, Ky. ....ND	10
Oct.	13—Harold Forese, Newark, N.J....ND	8
Nov.	12—Joe Lynch, Philadelphia .....ND	6
Nov.	24—Johnny Buff, Trenton, N. J. ..ND	8
Nov.	27—Mickey Russell, Jersey City ...ND	8

Dec.	1—Patsy Johnson, Philadelphia ..ND	6
Dec.	4—Kid Regan, St. Louis ....KO	3

1920

Jan.	7—Johnny Ritchie, New Orleans .KO	8
Feb.	10—Johnny Solsberg, St. Louis ...ND	8
Mar.	1—Earl Puryear, Trenton ....ND	8
Mar.	19—Young Angelo, Paterson ......KO	8
Mar.	25—Patsy Johnson, Jersey City ...ND	8
Mar.	31—Joe O'Donnell, Camden ......ND	8
Apr.	19—Paul Demers, Bedford, Mass.... W	10
May	10—Jabez White, Philadelphia ....ND	8
May	19—Roy Moore, Philadelphia .....ND	6
Aug.	19—Roy Moore, Colorado Springs.. W	10
Sept.	6—Joe Burman, St. Louis ....ND	8
Sept.	11—Jack Sharkey, E. Chicago, Ind. ....ND	10
Sept.	21—Jimmy Kelly, Beardstown, Ill. ....ND	10
Dec.	22—Joe Lynch, N. Y. C. L	15
	(Lost Bantamweight Title)	

1921

Jan.	13—Jimmy Wilde, London ....KO	17
Mar.	24—George Adams, N. Y. C. ......KO	1
Mar.	30—Willie Spencer, N. Y. C.......KO	12
Apr.	4—Johnny Solsberg, Freept., L. I. KO	7
Apr.	7—Barney Snyder, Worcester ....KO	5
Apr.	15—Young Montreal, Boston L	10
Apr.	29—Frankie Dailey, N. Y. C. ...... W	15
May	27—Young Montreal, Boston L	10
July	11—Jimmie Higgins, London .....KO	11
July	25—*Joe Lynch, Brooklyn .... W	15
Sept.	5—Charlie Ledoux, New Orleans .. W	10
Sept.	23—†Johnny Buff, N. Y. C. L	15
Dec.	9—Packy O'Gatty, N. Y. C. ....KO	1
Dec.	13—Abe Friedman, Boston ...... W	10
Dec.	22—Midget Smith, N. Y. C. L	15
	*Herman regained title.	
	†Herman lost title to Buff.	

1922

Feb.	20—Babe Asher, New Orleans .....KO	7
Apr.	24—Roy Moore, Boston .... W	10

Herman became blind and retired from game. Became cafe owner in New Orleans; later appointed life member of Louisiana State Athletic Commission.

TB	KO	WD	WF	D	LD	LF	KOBY	ND	NC
149	19	50	0	8	9	1	1	61	0

Elected to Boxing Hall of Fame 1960.
Died, New Orleans, April 13, 1973.

JOE LYNCH

Born, November 30, 1898. Nationality, Irish-American. Weight, 118 lbs. Height, 5 ft. 8 in. Managed by Eddie Mead.

After brief amateur career, turned professional in 1915; early record unavailable.

1916

	—Terry Martin, N. Y. C. ......ND	10
Oct.	10—Johnny Ertle, N. Y. C. ....ND	10
Nov.	24—Johnny Solsberg, N. Y. C. ....ND	10
Oct.	26—Jack Sharkey, N. Y. C. ....ND	10

1917

Feb.	1—One Punch Hogan, New Orl'ns . W	15
Feb.	23—Young Marino, New York ....KO	3
Feb.	27—Jack Sharkey, New York .....ND	10
Mar.	13—Kid Williams, New York .....ND	10
Apr.	7—Dutch Brandt, Brooklyn ......ND	10
May	15—Frankie Burns, New York ....ND	10
June	1—Pete Herman, New York ......ND	10
June	16—Willie Astey, New York ......ND	10
June	26—Frankie Daley, New York .....ND	10
Sept.	23—Jack Sharkey, Albany, N. Y. ...ND	10
Oct.	11—Joe Leonard, Brooklyn ....ND	10
Oct.	27—Pal Moore, New York ....ND	10
Nov.	26—Eddie O'Keefe, Philadelphia ..KO	4
Nov.	29—Terry Martin, Providence, R.I. . W	12
Dec.	8—Willie Astey, Providence ......KO	3
Dec.	21—Pal Moore, (Memph.), Providence, R. I. ...... W	12

1918

Jan.	1—Andy Burns, Philadelphia ....KO	3
Jan.	11—Pal Moore, Providence, R. I. L	12
Jan.	29—Kid Williams, Philadelphia ....KO	4
Feb.	18—Benny Valgar, Philadelphia ...ND	6
Mar.	2—Joe Tuber, Philadelphia ......ND	6
Mar.	4—Eddie Wimler, Pittsburgh .....ND	6
Apr.	2—George Kirkwood, Carbondale, Pa. ....KO	3
Apr.	4—Dick Loadman, Providence .... W	12

Apr. 6—Frankie Burns, Philadelphia ..ND 6
Apr. 16—Jack (Kid) Wolfe, Cleveland ..ND 10
May 15—Benny McNeill, No. Adams ...KO 5
May 30—Willie Devore, Cleveland ......ND 10
June 20—Young Farina, New York .....ND 4
July 16—Dick Loadman, New York ....ND 4
Dec. 11—Jimmy Wilde, London ....L 3
1919
Feb. —Tommy Noble, London, Eng. ... W 20
Mar. 31—Jimmy Wilde, London, Eng. .....L 15
June 3—Joe O'Donnell, Philadelphia ..ND 6
June 14—Mickey Delmont, Bayonne,
            N. J.............................ND 8
July 4—Charley Beecher, Jersey City ..ND 8
July 8—Bobby Joseph, Boston ....KO 12
Aug. 4—Jabez White, Boston .... D 12
Sept. 1—Pete Herman, Waterbury,
            Conn. ....ND 10
Sept. 16—Patsy Johnson, Jersey City ...ND 8
Sept. 19—Frankie Mason, Baltimore ..... D 12
Sept. 29—Joe Burman, Philadelphia ....ND 6
Oct. 11—Dick Griffith, Detroit ....KO 2
Oct. 25—Joe Burman, Philadelphia ....ND 6
Nov. 5—Jack Kid Wolfe, Detroit .....ND 10
Nov. 12—Pete Herman, Philadelphia ....ND 6
Nov. 24—Jack Kid Wolfe, Philadelphia ..ND 6
Dec. 22—Joey Fox, Newark ....ND 8
1920
Feb. 5—Eddie Segal, Jersey City ......KO 3
Feb. 9—Louisiana, Philadelphia ....ND 6
Feb. 18—Jack Wolfe, Cleveland ....ND 10
Feb. 22—Hugh Hutchinson, Phila. .....ND 6
Mar. 4—Eddie Segal, Boston..........KO 3
Mar. 6—Joe O'Donnell, Philadelphia ..ND 6
Mar. 8—Samy Waltz, Hartford, Conn. .ND 10
May 7—Billy Fitzsimmons, Marlboro,
            Mass.............................W 12
May 24—Pal Moore, Jersey City ....ND 12
June 7—Joe O'Donnell, Philadelphia ..ND 8
Aug. 2—Charley Ledoux, Jersey City ..ND 12
Sept. 28—Jack Sharkey, New York ...... D 15
Oct. 15—Jabez White, New York ...... D 15
Oct. 26—Pal Moore, St. Louis ....ND 8
Nov. 5—Abe Goldstein, New York ....KO 11
Dec. 2—Jack Sharkey, New York .....KO 15
Dec. 22—Pete Herman, New York ..... W 15
         (Won World Bantamweight Title)
         —Johnny Ritchie..............KO 4
         —Harry Bremer ....KO 3
         —Kid Reagan ....KO 5
1921
Feb. 9—Jabez White, St. Louis .... D 8
Feb. 22—Jabez White, Philadelphia ....ND 10
Feb. 28—Young Montreal, Detroit .....ND 10
Mar. 10—Joe Burman, Cleveland ......ND 10
Mar. 28—Young Pinchott, Pittsburgh ...ND 10
Apr. 8—Young Montreal, Cleveland ...ND 10
         —Midget Smith .... D 10
May 6—Pal Moore, Lousiville, Ky. ....ND 12
June 21—Sammy Sandow, New York ...KO 1
June 28—Joe Burman, E. Chicago, Ind. .ND 10
July 25—Pete Herman, Brooklyn ....L 15
         (Lost World Bantamweight title)
Oct. 26—Phil O'Dowd, New York........L 12
Dec. 9—Maxie Williamson, New York .KO 8
         —Dick Griffin................Exh. 4
1922
Jan. 2—Al Walker, New York ....KO 1
Jan. 9—Patsy Wallace, Philadelphia ...ND 8
Jan. 13—Patsy Johnson, Syracuse .....KO 6
Mar. 14—Terry Martin, Providence ...... W 12
Apr. 8—Terry Martin, N. Y. ....W 12
Apr. 11—Terry Martin, Boston ....L 10
Apr. 20—Jimmy Mendo, Philadelphia ..ND 8
June 1—Midget Smith, New York ...... W 12
July 10—*Johnny Buff, New York .....KO 14
Aug. 21—Frankie Murray, Shreveport,
            La...............................KO 6
Aug. 24—Ben Levy, Ft. Worth ....KO 4
Aug. 30—Eddie Macey, San Francisco ... D 4
Sept. 4—Pal Moore, Michigan City .....ND 10
Sept. 21—Jack Wolfe, New York ....L 15
Nov. 24—Bennie Schwartz, Springfield,
            Ohio.............................KO 5
Dec. 2—Frankie Daley, Indianapolis ..ND 10
Dec. 7—Joey Sangor, Milwaukee ......ND 10
Dec. 22—Midget Smith, New York ..... W 15
         (Title Bout)
         *Regained bantamweight title.
1923
Feb. 27—Pete Husic, Harrisburg, Pa.....ND 8
Mar. 5—Jimmy Mendo, Philadelphia ..ND 8
Mar. 19—Joe Burman, Chicago ....ND 10
Apr. 4—Midget Smith, Chicago ....ND 10

Apr. 10—Joe O'Donnell, Portland, Me. .ND 12
May 29—Young Montreal, Providence ... D 10
July 9—Bobby Wolgast, Philadelphia ..ND 8
July 13—Patsy Johnson, Erie, Pa. ......KO 6
Aug. 2—Battling Reddy, W. New York .ND 12
Aug. 31—Harold Smith, Aurora, Ill. ....ND 10
Sept. 7—Eddie Segal, Philadelphia .....KO 3
Nov. 23—Frankie Murray, Peoria, Ill. ...KO 5
Nov. 28—Pal Moore, St. Louis .... D 10
Dec. 3—Eddie Coulon, Newark, N. J. ...ND 10
1924
Jan. 1—Jimmie Murphy, Akron, O. ...KO 3
Jan. 4—Earl McArthur, Omaha, Neb. .. W 10
Jan. 18—Eddie McKenna, New Orleans ...L 10
Jan. 23—Parky Owens, El Dorado, Ark. KO 2
Mar. 21—†Abe Goldstein, New York .....L 15
July 11—Johnny Sheppard, Boston ......L 10
Sept. 8—Pete Sarmiento, Phila............L 10
         (†Lost world bantamweight title)
         —Al Crisp .... D 4
         —Georgie Rivers .... W 4
         —Joe Bell..................... D 4
1925
Apr. 6—Lou Brenner, Lancaster ....L 8
May 5—Larry Goldberg, Albany .... D 10
May 18—Willie Cunningham, Buffalo ....L 6
July 2—Jack Sharkey, N. Y. .... D 4
1926
Feb. 24—Pal Moore, Ft. Lauderdale ..... D 10
Mar. 4—Pal Moore, Miami .... D 10

TB	KO	WD	WF	D	LD	LF	KOBY	ND	NC
133	29	13	0	15	13	0	0	63	0

Appointed Postmaster at New City, Y. Y.
Found dead from drowning at Sheepshead
Bay, Brooklyn, N. Y., August 1, 1965.

JOHNNY BUFF
(John Lesky)
Born, June 12, 1888, Perth Amboy, N. J.
Weight, 112-118 lbs. Height, 5 ft. 3 in.
Nationality, Polish-American. Managed by Lew
Diamond.
    Was in U. S. Navy and fought as an
amateur.
1918
    Started as professional. Won: Johnny
Rosner, 8. No decision: Patsy Wallace, 8; Mickey
Russell, 8.
1919
    Knockouts: Johnny Burns, 7; Dick
Gotwalt, 4; Kid Troubles, 4; Al Cook, 6; Tommy
Gorman, 2. No decisions: Rockey Walker, 4;
Mickey Brown, 8; Jimmy Sullivan, 8; Mickey
Delmont, 6; Al Cook, 8; Mickey Russell, 8; Patsy
Johnson, 8; Mickey Russell, 8; Joe Ryder, 8;
Mickey Russell, 8; Johnny Rosner, 8; Jack Eile,
8; Battling Murray, 8; Patsy Wallace, 8; Mickey
Dunn, 8; Harvey Crosby, 8; Willie Spencer, 8;
Mickey Russell, 8; Patsy Wallace, 6; Lew Angelo,
8; Max Williamson, 8; Mickey Russell, 6; Pete
Herman, 8; Bobby Doyle, 6; Johnny Ritchie, 6;
Jack Eile, 8.
1920
    Knockouts: Victor Ritchie, 5; Dummy
Lamont, 2; Willie Burns, 6; Mike Ertle, 7; Kid
Wolfe, 2. Won: Midget Smith, 10. No decision:
Jack Sharkey, 8; Earl Puryear, 8; Willie Spencer,
8; Pal Moore, 8; Willie Spencer, 8; Abe Goldstein,
12; Billy Bevan, 10; Frankie Mason, 6; Tommy
Murray, 8. Knocked out by: Mickey Delmont, 3.
1921
Jan. 10—Battling Murray, Trenton.....ND 12
Jan. 21—Georgie Lee, New Orleans ..... W 15
Feb. 11—*Frankie Mason, New Orleans . W 15
Mar. 2—Frankie Daly, New York ...... W 10
Mar. 30—Abe Goldstein, N. Y. C. ......KO 2
         (American Flyweight Title Bout)
Apr. 16—Young Zulu Kid, Brooklyn ... W 15
May 2—Eddie O'Dowd, New York .... W 15
June 29—Frankie Daly, Coney Island .... W 12
July 10—Harry Mansell, Jersey City ....KO 3
Aug. 1—Jabez White, Jersey City ...... W 12
Aug. 11—Charley Ledoux, N. Y. C. ...... W 10
Sept. 5—Indian Russell, Jersey City ....KO 5
Sept. 23—†Pete Herman, N. Y. C. .... W 15
Nov. 10—Jack Sharkey, N. Y. C. .... W 15
         (World Bantamweight Title Bout)
Dec. 15—Pal Moore, Milwaukee, Wis. ...ND 10
         *Won American flyweight title.
         †Won world bantamweight title.

1922

July	10—*Joe Lynch, N. Y. C. ......KO by	14
Sept.	14—†Pancho Villa, Brooklyn ..KO by	11

*For bantamweight title.
†For flyweight title.

1923

Jan.	31—California J. Lynch, Oakl., Cal. ..L	4
Feb.	6—Teddy Silva, Fresno, Cal. ......D	4
Mar.	26—*Jean Larue, Detroit ....NC	8
Apr.	11—Geo. Murray, Fall River, Mass. ..L	10
May	24—Patsy Wallace, Phila., Pa. .....ND	8
June	11—Patsy Wallace, Jersey City ....ND	12
July	17—Henry Catena, N. Y. C. ....KO by	10

*Stopped by referee.

1924

Jan.	22—Willie Woods, Jersey City .....ND	10
Feb.	11—Frankie Ash, Jersey City, N. J. ND	10
Mar.	3—Emil Paluso, Trenton, N.J. ....ND	10
Mar.	17—Benny Schwartz, Balt., Md. .... W	12
Mar.	27—Harry Forbes, Columbus, O. ..ND	10
Mar.	31—Johnny Lear, Hamilton, Ont. ...L	10
Apr.	5—Young Dencio, Boston, Mass. ... W	10
May	10—Frankie Demari, New Orl., La. .. W	15
June	11—Tony Carney, Providence, R. I. ..L	12
June	23—Kid Carlin, New Orleans ... KO by	9

1925

Feb.	23—Frankie Novey, San Francisco . D	4
Mar.	5—Eddie Kelly .... D	6
Mar.	12—Mickey Gill, San Jose L	6
June	13—Benny Hall, Brooklyn, N. Y. L	6
July	24—Izzy Cooper, Brooklyn, N. Y. ... D	10
Sept.	25—Johnny Breslin, Bayonne . .KO by	5
Oct.	30—Jackie Johnston, Toronto, Can. .L	10
Nov.	26—Benny Schwartz, Phila., Pa. L	10

1926

Apr.	12—Joe Lynch, New York City L	10
May	15—Johnny Hamm, Pittsburgh . KO by	2

Reenlisted in U. S. Navy.

TB	KO	WD	WF	D	LD	LF	KOBY	ND	NC
94	13	15	0	4	9	0	7	45	1

Died January 14, 1955, East Orange, N. J.

ABE GOLDSTEIN

Born, 1900, New York. Nationality, Jewish-American. Weight, 118 lbs. Height, 5 ft. 5 in. Managed by Willie Lewis.

1916

June	30—Georgie Lewis, New York ....KO	8
Aug.	26—Smiling Willie, New York .....KO	2
Nov.	13—Murray Perkie, New York ....ND	10

1917

May	26—Tommy Geary, New York ....ND	6
June	18—Patsy Finnegan, New York KO by	7
Aug.	31—Terry Miller, New York ......ND	10
Oct.	6—Young Greenfield, Brooklyn ..ND	10

1919-1920

Knockouts: Kid Barren, 6; Al Ziemer, 6; Joe Leon, 2; Harry Martin, 1; Joe Dundee, 2; Frankie Sullivan, 2; Marshall Watier, 6; Pinkey Brown, 4; Mike Dundee, 1; Joe Ryder, 7; Bobby Hanson, 7; Tommy Murray, 4; Willie Burns, 7; Bobby Hughes, 12; Paddy Owens, 2.

Won: Eddie Fletcher, 10; Tommy Geary, 10; Young Rago, 10; Terry Miller, 9; Patsy Finnegan, 10; Jack Eile, 6; Kid Rash, 10; Billy Fitzsimmons, 10; Paddy Owens, 12; Jack Perry, 6; Batt. Mack, 10; Frankie Daly, 10; George Thompson, 12; Artie Simons, 12; Joe Leonard, 10; Terry Miller, 12; Harvey Crosby, 6; Red Monroe, 10; Wille Spencer, 6; Patsy Johnson, 12; George Thompson, 12; Frankie Daly, 10; Battling Mack, 8; Paddy Owens, 12; Barney Snyder, 12; Eddie Fletcher, 12.

	—Patsy Wallace, Philadelphia ...ND	6
	—Johnny Buff, Jersey City .....ND	12

1921

Jan.	31—Hank McGovern, Phila........ND	8
Feb.	11—Patsy Wallace, New York .....KO	7
Feb.	15—Frankie Daly, New York ...... W	10
Feb.	21—Kid Williams, Philadelphia ....ND	8
Mar.	31—Johnny Buff, New York .... KO by	2
	—Eddie Anderson, Brooklyn .... D	12
Apr.	29—Georgie Thompson, Brooklyn . W	12
June	10—Bobby Hughes, Rockwy. Bch. KO	12
June	10—Billy Marlowe ....KO	3
July	3—Earl Puryear, Rockaway ..... W	12
	—Young Montreal, Hartford ....ND	12
	—Frankie Jerome, N. Y. C. ...... D	12
Oct.	14—Eddie O'Dowd, New York ..... D	8

Nov.	28—Harry London, N.Y.C. ....W	12
Nov.	5—Joe Lynch, New York City KO by	11
Nov.	15—Battling Mack, Philadelphia ...ND	8
Dec.	9—Frankie Daly, N. Y. C......... W	10

1922

Jan.	6—Andy Davis, New York ....KO	6
Jan.	17—Frankie Fay, New York ......KO	7
Jan.	28—Frankie Curry .... D	12
Mar.	13—Georgie Marks, New York ..... W	8
Mar.	27—Patsy Wallace, Philadelphia ...ND	8
Apr.	7—Johnny Sheppard, Boston ..... W	10
May	19—Frankie Genaro, New York ... W	4
June	6—Pancho Villa, Jersey City .....ND	12
July	14—Johnny Gray, New York ....W	12
July	25—Danny Edwards, Jersey City ..ND	12
	—Terry Martin, Brooklyn .... D	12
Nov.	16—Pancho Villa, New York L	15
	—Johnny Green, Brooklyn .....KO	7

1923

Jan.	15—Frankie Daly, Troy, N. Y. ..... W	12
Jan.	29—Mike Moran, Pittsburgh ......ND	10
Mar.	1—Tommy Ryan, McKeesport ...ND	10
Mar.	29—Pete Zivic, McKeesport ....ND	10
Apr.	23—Frankie Coster, N. Y. C.......KO	5
May	11—Art Wanderer, Syracuse .... W	10
May	29—Willie Darcey, N. Y. C........KO	3
June	4—Tommy Ryan, Pittsburgh ....ND	10
June	22—Frankie Daly, N. Y. C......... W	12
July	16—Kid Rash, Atlantic City ......ND	8
July	27—Wilbur Cohen, Rockaway .....W	12
Aug.	14—Danny Edwards, N. Y. C.......KO	14
Sept.	4—Frankie Conway, N. Y. C....... W	10
Oct.	1—Tommy Lynch, N. Y. C........ W	10
Oct.	5—Chick Suggs, Fall River .... W	10
Oct.	15—Johnny Naselle, N. Y. C.......KO	2
Oct.	19—Joe Burman, N. Y. C.......... W	12

For recognition as N. Y. bantam champ.

1924

Jan.	8—Wilbur Cohen, N. Y. C........ W	10
Feb.	19—Danny Edwards, N. Y. C. ...... W	10
Mar.	21—*Joe Lynch, N. Y. C........... W	15
Apr.	7—Tommy Murray, Toledo, O. ..ND	10
May	5—Clarence Rosen, Detroit, Mich.ND	10
May	30—Johnny Sheppard, Boston, Mass. L	10
June	20—Tommy Murray, Portland, Me. ND	10
July	16—Charley Ledoux, N. Y. C. ...... W	15
	(Title Bout)	
Sept.	8—Tommy Ryan, L. I. City .... W	15
	(Title Bout)	
Nov.	14—Eddie Shea, East Chicago, Ill. .ND	10
Dec.	19—†Eddie Cannonball Martin, N. Y. C. L	15

*Won bantamweight championship.
†Lost championship.

1925

Mar.	19—Tommy Milton, Brooklyn .... W	12
Apr.	1—Al Felder, New York ....KO	1
Apr.	14—Joie Russell, New York ....KO	3
May	6—Buck Josephs, Newark, N. J. ..ND	12
May	26—Bud Taylor, New York L	10
July	23—Bushy Graham, New York L	8
Oct.	8—Dixie La Hood, Butte, Mont.....L	12
Oct.	13—Teddy Silva, Vernon, Cal. .... W	10
Oct.	22—Chuck Hellman, San Francisco . W	10
Nov.	10—Yg. Nationalista, Portland, Ore. .L	10

1926

Jan.	11—Dominick Petrone, New York ...L	12
Feb.	2—Chick Suggs, New York L	10
Apr.	8—Bud Taylor, Terre Haute .....ND	10
Apr.	8—Al Brown, New York L	12
Dec.	5—San Sanchez, Perth Amboy ...ND	10
Dec.	14—Johnny Dunn, Wilkes-Barre .. W	10

1927

Feb.	14—Charley Pinto, Buffalo .... W	10
Feb.	28—Pete Sarmiento, Boston ....ND	12
Mar.	26—Pete Sarmiento, Chicago ..... W	8
May	3—Bud Taylor, Chicago L	10
May	27—Willie Spencer, Holyoke ......KO	2
June	24—Ignacio Fernandez, Chi. ...KO by	7

1942

In U. S. Army.

TB	KO	WD	WF	D	LD	LF	KO BY	ND	NC
130	30	55	0	5	10	0	4	26	0

EDDIE CANNONBALL MARTIN
(Edward Vittorio Martino)
Born, March 3, 1903, Brooklyn, N. Y. Nationality, Italian-American. Weight, 118 lbs. Height, 5 ft. 4 in.

1922

Knockouts: Sammy Jackson, 2; Jack North, 3; Joe Layden, 1; Young Schaen, 4; Kewpie Collins, 2; Freddie Seid, 1; Joe Wright, 3; Billy Bell, 4. Won: Paul Raymon, 4; Young Tell, 4; Charley Furey, 4; Young Skelly, 4; Willie Mack, 4; Pete Mack, 4; Willie Mack, 4; Jackie Stone, 6; Willie O'Connell, 6; Scotty Malcomb, 6; August Pisano, 6. Lost: Artie Downs, 4; Howard Mayberry, 4.

1923

Jan.	13—Jerry Sullivan, Brooklyn	....KO	4
Jan.	27—Johnny Vinney, Brooklyn	....W	4
Feb.	3—Willie Clarkson, Brooklyn	....KO	1
Feb.	10—Paulie Porter, Brooklyn	......KO	3
Feb.	24—Jackie Marlowe, Brooklyn	....KO	2
Mar.	29—Wally Land, Brooklyn	........KO	1
Apr.	2—Jimmy Barton, Brooklyn	......W	6
Apr.	7—Mickey Romano, Brooklyn	.... W	6
Apr.	21—Jackie Murray, Brooklyn	...... W	6
May	3—Sonny Smith, New York	...... W	6
May	24—Joe Ryder, Brooklyn	.... D	4
July	18—Joe Ryder, New York	.... W	6
July	28—Joey Zellars, Brooklyn	......KO	2
Aug.	6—Jackie Gordon, Brooklyn	.....KO	6
Aug.	18—Frankie Coster, Brooklyn	..... W	6
Sept.	17—Johnny Vestri, Brooklyn	...... W	6
Oct.	13—Tommy Lynch, Brooklyn	..... W	6
Oct.	22—Billy Ryckoff, Brooklyn	....KO	5
Nov.	1—Johnny Vestri, Brooklyn	...... W	6
Nov.	12—Harry London, Brooklyn	....KO	1
Nov.	29—Charley Rosenberg, New York	. W	6
Dec.	6—Tommy Galston, Brooklyn	.... W	6
Dec.	11—Wilbur Cohen, Brooklyn	..... W	6
Dec.	17—Sonny Smith, New York	...... W	6

1924

Jan.	17—Sonny Smith, Brooklyn	.... W	6
Jan.	28—Charley Rosenberg, Brooklyn	.. W	6
Feb.	4—Midget Smith, N. Y. C.	...... W	6
Feb.	18—Buck Josephs, Brooklyn	...... W	6
Apr.	14—Joe Souza, Brooklyn	.... W	10
Apr.	22—Al Pettingel, N. Y. C.	.........KO	4
Apr.	29—Charley Phil Rosenberg, N. Y. C.	D	10
May	23—Jackie Snyder, Brooklyn	...... W	10
June	20—Sammy Nable, Brooklyn	.....KO	5
June	24—Charley Goodman, Brooklyn	.. W	12
July	11—Harry Batt. Leonard, Rockaway Beach	.... W	12
Sept.	13—Charley Kid Kohler, Brooklyn KO		4
Sept.	25—Harry Batt. Leonard, B'klyn	..KO	8
Oct.	5—Bobby Wolgast, Boston	....KO	8
Nov.	6—Johnny Curtin, Brooklyn	...... W	12
Dec.	19—*Abe Goldstein, N. Y. C.	...... W	15

*Won bantamweight title.

1925

Jan.	6—Augie Pisano, N. Y. C.	........NC	4
Jan.	12—Tommy Murphy, Phila.	.... W	10
Feb.	16—Willie Spencer, N. Y. C.	.......ND	12
Feb.	24—Carl Tremaine, Cleveland, O.	..ND	12
Mar.	6—Pete Sarmiento, Milwaukee	...ND	10
Mar.	20—Charlie Phil Rosenberg, N.Y.C.	.L	15

(Lost the Bantamweight championship of the World)

July	13—Johnny Curtin, Brooklyn	.....KO	7
Sept.	14—Lew Perfetti	 L	10

1927

Mar.	26—Joe Souza, Brooklyn	.........KO	1
Apr.	9—Johnny Curtin, Brooklyn	.... W	6
May	7—Al Rube Goldberg, Brooklyn	.. W	6
May	14—Spencer Gardner, Brooklyn	.... W	6
Oct.	6—Pancho Dencio, Brooklyn	.... W	6
Oct.	31—Eddie Anderson, Brooklyn	.... W	10

1928

Jan.	23—Dominick Petrone, N. Y. C.	..... W	10
Feb.	27—Jack Petibone, N. Y. C.	......KO	3
Mar.	5—Johnny Huber, N. Y. C.	......KO	2
Mar.	16—Davey Abad, N. Y. C.	.... W	10
May	24—Tod Morgan, N. Y. C.	L	15
July	18—Tod Morgan, Brooklyn	L	15

(For Junior lightweight title)

1929

July	8—Johnny Dundee, New York	L	10
Sept.	5—Young Zazzarino, Bayonne KO by		7

1930

	—Jack Giralda, New York	......KO	2
	—Marty Goldman, N. Y. C.	..KO by	7

1931

Mar.	23—Jackie Cohen, New York	...... W	10
May	1—Joey Kaufman, New York	..... D	6
Aug.	28—Al Singer, New York	......KO by	6

774

1932

July	11—Harry Baron, Brooklyn	.... W	6
	—Al Dunbar, Brooklyn	L	10

TB	KO	WD	WF	D	LD	LF	KOBY	ND	NC
90	27	45	0	3	8	0	3	3	1

CHARLEY PHIL ROSENBERG
(Charles Green)

Born, August 15, 1902, New York City. Nationality, Jewish-American. Weight, 118 lbs. Height, 5 ft. 4 in. Managed by Harry Segal.

1921

Lost: Charles Bengo, 4; Al Diamond, 8; Bobby Bolin, 6; Bobby Bolin, 12. Draw: Harry Martin, 4.

1922

Won: Mickey Nelson, 10; Sammy Butts, 12; Willie Darcy, 10; Henny Catena, 12.

May	23—Frankie Genaro, New York	L	12
Oct.	21—Frankie Genaro, New York	L	12
Dec.	22—Curley Wilshur, New York	L	6
Dec.	30—Johnny Inhouse, New York	.... W	6

1923

Knockout: Billy Pimpus, 4. Won: Mike Moran, 12; Joe Souza, 12; Wilbur Cohen, 10; Buck Josephs, 10.

Jan.	5—Johnny Rose, New York	L	6
Jan.	15—Willie Darcey, New York	L	12
Feb.	16—Sammy Cohen, New York	.... D	6
Feb.	26—Willie Darcey, New York	L	12
Apr.	9—Mannie Wexler, New York	.... W	12
June	9—Carl Duane, New York	.... D	6
July	18—Carl Duane, New York	L	12
Sept.	22—Harry London, New York	..... W	12
Oct.	19—Bud Taylor, New York	L	12
Oct.	30—Danny Edwards New York	.... W	12
Nov.	29—Eddie Martin, New York	L	6

1924

Jan.	29—Eddie Martin, Brooklyn	L	10
Mar.	18—Gaylor Kid Lewis, New York	.. W	10
Apr.	29—Eddie Martin, New York	.... D	10
June	3—Sonny Smith, Brooklyn	.... W	10
Aug.	15—Joe Souza, Rockaway Beach	... W	12
Aug.	25—Mike Moran, New York	..... W	12
Sept.	27—Gaylor Kid Lewis, New York	.KO	9
Oct.	10—Irish Johnny Curtin, New York	W	10
Oct.	20—Joe Souza, New York	........KO	8
Nov.	15—Wilbur Cohen, New York	...... W	10

1925

Jan.	2—Buck Josephs, N. Y. C.	...... W	10
Mar.	5—Nat Pincus, N. Y. C.	.........KO	11
Mar.	20—Eddie Martin, N.Y.C.	...... W	15

(Won world bantamweight title.)

Apr.	27—Clarence Rosen, Toledo	..... W	12
May	11—Harry Gordon, Covington	....ND	10
May	16—Harry Gordon, N. Y. C.	...... W	10
May	22—Harold Smith, E. Chicago	.....ND	10
May	29—Herbie Schaeffer, Aurora, Ill.	.ND	10
June	1—R. Pettingill, Covington	......KO	2
July	8—Pete Sariento, Cleveland	......ND	10
July	23—*Eddie Shea, N. Y. C.	......KO	4
Dec.	2—"Calif." Joe Lynch, Oakland	L	10
Dec.	30—Doc Snell, Los Angeles	.... LF	6

*Title bout.

1926

Mar.	2—*George Butch, St. Louis	...... W	10
May	1—George Butch, Youngstown	... W	10
May	21—Bobby Ebber, Cleveland	.....KO	10
May	27—Willie Ames, Toronto	........ND	5
July	30—Midget Smith, Cleveland	.....WF	5
Aug.	13—Joey Sangor, Chicago	.... D	10
Aug.	25—Pete Sarmiento, Chicago	.... D	10
Nov.	29—George Mack, Jersey City	........ND	10
Dec.	20—Petie Mack, Jersey City	.......ND	10

*Title bout.

1927

Jan.	3—Benny Schwartz, Baltimore	.... W	12
Feb.	4—Bushy Graham, N. Y. C.	.... W	15

(Rosenberg unable to make weight; title declared vacant and both Rosenberg and Graham suspended for one year due to secret agreement.)

1928

Mar.	10—Harry Scott, N. Y. C.	.... W	6

1929

Jan.	4—Johnny Dundee, N. Y. C.	...... W	10

1942

In U. S. Army.

TB	KO	WD	WF	D	LD	LF	KOBY	ND	NC
65	7	28	1	6	15	1	0	7	0

TEDDY BALDOCK
Born, May 20, 1908, Poplar, London, England.
Weight, 118 lbs.
1921
Mar.	14—Young Makepeace, London	W	6
Dec.	15—Young Makepeace, London	W	6

1922
Feb.	16—Johnny O'Brien, London	W	6
June	29—Johnny O'Brien, London	W	8

1923
Jan.	8—Johnny O'Brien, London	KO	3
Feb.	13—Young Stoneham, London	KO	4
Mar.	24—Arthur Webb, Edinburgh	W	10
Apr.	24—Arthur Webb, London	W	10
Sept.	—Young Faithful, Addlestone	KO	2
Oct.	14—Young Riley, London	W	10
Nov.	8—Kid Roberts, London	KO	3
Dec.	13—Percy Faithfull, London	W	10
Dec.	17—Joe Goddard, London	KO	3

1924
Jan.	10—Arthur Cowley, London	KO	2
Jan.	24—Young Bowler, London	KO	1
Feb.	17—Young Bill Lewis, London	W	10
Mar.	24—George (Kid) Socks, London	D	10
July	17—Young Bill Lewis, London	W	15
July	20—Dod Oldfield, Leeds	W	10
Aug.	7—Dod Oldfield, London	W	15
Sept.	8—Kid Hughes, London	KO	7
Sept.	25—Vic Wakefield, London	KO	10
Nov.	6—Harry Hill, London	W	15

1925
Jan.	15—Fred Hinton, London	KO	8
Feb.	1—Willie Evans, London	KO	5
Mar.	25—Fred Hinton, London	KO	5
Apr.	6—Willie Evans, London	KO	12
May	21—Ernie Jarvis, London	W	15
June	7—Johnny Haydn, London	KO	7
June	24—Johnny Murton, Brighton	KO	2
July	9—Frankie Kestrell, London	KO	3
July	30—Frank Ash, London	W	15
Sept.	3—Tiny Smith, London	W	15
Oct.	1—Jim Haddon, London	KO	5
Oct.	25—Billy Shaw, London	KO	1
Nov.	23—Ernie Veitch, London	KO	7
Dec.	17—Antoine Merlo, London	W	15

1926
Feb.	11—Frank Ash, London	W	15
Mar.	18—Alf Barber, London	KO	5
Apr.	29—Francois Morrachini, London	W	15
June	10—Tiny Smith, London	KO	6
July	15—George (Kid) Nicholson, London	LF	9
Aug.	27—Mickey Gill, New York	W	6
Sept.	22—Tommy Atova, New York	W	6
Sept.	30—Arthur de Champlaine, New York	KO	1
Oct.	6—Johnny Eriksen, New York	W	8
Oct.	19—San. Sanchez, New York	W	6
Oct.	25—Jackie Cohen, New York	D	6
Nov.	4—Billy Marlow, New York	WF	1
Nov.	12—Tommy Lorenzo, New York	W	6
Nov.	17—Billy Reynolds, New York	W	6
Nov.	22—Ralph Nischio, New York	W	6
Dec.	—Pierre Calloir, New York	W	6
Dec.	13—Joe Clifford, New York	KO	2

1927
Feb.	16—Young Johnny Brown, London	KO	3
Mar.	30—Felix Friedemann, London	KO	2
May	5—Archie Bell, London	W	15

(Won Vacant British World Bantamweight Title)
June	30—Johnny Cuthbert, London	D	6
July	21—Len Oldfield, London	KO	2
Oct.	6—Willie Smith, London	L	15

(Lost British World Bantamweight Title)
Dec.	5—Len Fowler, London	KO	8

1928
Feb.	13—Phil Lolosky, London	W	15
July	15—Pierre Calloir, London	KO	4
Aug.	12—Bugler Harry Lake, Blackpool	KO	5
Aug.	29—Johnny Brown, London	KO	2

(Won British Bantamweight Title)
Oct.	8—Mick Hill, London	KO	14
Oct.	25—Phil Lolosky, London	KO	3

1929
Mar.	21—Van Paemel, London	KO	9
May	16—Alf (Kid) Pattenden, London	W	15

(Retained British Bantamweight Title)
Aug.	5—Gideon Potteau, Blackpool	KO	11

1930
Jan.	22—Emile (Spider) Pladner, London	WF	6
Mar.	6—Charlie Rowbotham, London	KO	11
Apr.	3—Lew Pinkus, London	W	15
July	5—Jimmy Docherty, Norwich	KO	6
Sept.	1—Benny Sharkey, Newcastle	L	15
Dec.	7—Alf (Kid) Pattenden, London	W	15

1931
Mar.	26—Gideon Potteau, London	KO	2
Apr.	30—Terence Morgan, London	W	15
May	21—Panama Al Brown, London	KO by	12
Sept.	7—Dick Corbett, London	L	12

TB	KO	WD	WF	D	LD	LF	KO BY	ND	NC
80	37	33	2	3	3	1	1	0	0

Died, March 15, 1971, Romford, England.

CHARLES B. (BUD) TAYLOR
Born, July 22, 1903, Terre Haute, Ind.
Nationality, American. Height, 5 ft. 6 in.
Managed by Eddie Long.
1920
Knockouts: Walter Gorring, 3; Kid Shepard, 3; Dutch Davison, 3; Jack Edwards, 2; Dave Templeton, 2; Jimmie Burns, 8; Bruce Mickles, 4 and 3; Young Dempsey, 3. No decisions: Dave Templeton, 4; Artie Armstrong, 8 and 10; Whittie Morrett, 6.
1921
Knockouts: Patsy Brennan, 1; Solly Epstein, 9. Won: Herbie Schaefer, 8. Draw: Herb Schaffer, 10. No decisions: Battling Chink 12; Whittie Morrett, 10; Frankie Mason, 10; Phil O'Dowd, 10; Eddie O'Dowd, 10; Battling Chink, 10; Chick Allman, 10; Harold Smith, 8; Stanley Everett, 10; Harold Smith, 10.
1922
Jan.	5—Solly Epstein, Terre Haute	KO	1
Jan.	13—George Corbett, Chicago	KO	3
Jan.	24—Ollie O'Neill, Chicago	ND	8
Feb.	1—Harold Smith, La Salle, Ill.	ND	10
Feb.	10—Jimmy Kelly, Chicago	KO by	6
Mar.	10—Herb Schaeffer, Chicago	ND	10
Mar.	12—Jimmy Kelly, Kenosha, Wis.	ND	10
Apr.	21—Franke Henke, Chicago	KO	7
May	17—Kid Buck, Logansport, Ind.	ND	10
June	15—Herb Schaeffer, Indianapolis	ND	10
June	23—Pal Moore, Aurora, Ill.	ND	10
July	4—Babe Asher, Terre Haute	ND	10
Sept.	4—Jimmy Kelly, Terre Haute	ND	10
Sept.	21—Harold Smith, E. Chicago	ND	10
Oct.	13—Stanley Everett, Chicago	KO	5
Nov.	1—Battling Chink, Terre Haute	ND	10
Nov.	27—Billy O'Brien, Peoria, Ill.	ND	10
Dec.	2—Eddie Santry, Terre Haute	KO	5

1923
Jan.	1—Benny Vogel, Indianapolis	KO	1
Jan.	8—Jimmy Kelly, Racine, Wis.	ND	10
Jan.	15—Pal Moore, Chicago	ND	10
Feb.	13—Pal Moore, Indianapolis	ND	10
Apr.	4—Frankie Genaro, Chicago	ND	10
July	5—John Sheppard, Indianapolis	ND	10
July	20—Harry Gordon, Aurora, Ill.	ND	10
July	31—Tommy Murray, Terre Haute	ND	10
Aug.	24—Hilly Levine, Aurorra, Ill.	ND	10
Sept.	3—Harry Gordon, Terre Haute	ND	10
Sept.	8—Pancho Villa, Chicago	ND	10
Oct.	19—Charley Rosenberg, N. Y. C.	W	12
Dec.	5—Ray Moore, Terre, Haute	ND	10

1924
Jan.	1—Sammy Nable, N. Y. C.	W	12
Jan.	9—Johnny Brown, Indianapolis	KO	3
Jan.	11—*Frankie Jerome, N. Y. C.	KO	12
Jan.	28—Herbie Schaefer, E. Chic., Ind.	ND	10
Feb.	7—Eddie O'Dowd, Columbus, O.	L	10
Feb.	18—Sammy Nable, Indianapolis	ND	10
Mar.	6—Pancho Villa, Milwaukee	ND	10
Apr.	7—Al Pettingill, Indianapolis	KO	2
Apr.	15—Rosey Stoy, Youngstown	ND	12
May	26—Connie Curry, Aurora	ND	10
May	30—Tommy Ryan, Indianapolis		
June	10—Pancho Villa, New York	L	12
June	23—Eddie Coulon, Indianapolis	KO	1

June	27—Al Ziemer, Cleveland ....ND	10
Aug.	1—Tommy Ryan, Philadelphia .... W	10
Aug.	11—Pete Sarmiento, Chicago .....ND	10
Aug.	28—Carl Tremaine, Cleveland .....ND	10
Sept.	23—Georgie Rivers, Vernon .... W	4
Oct.	7—George Rivers, Vernon .... W	4
	*Jerome died after bout.	

1925

Jan.	1—Al Ziemer, Indianapolis ......ND	10
Apr.	20—Midget Smith, E. Chic., Ind. ..ND	10
May	18—Mike Moran, Terre Haute .....ND	10
May	26—Abe Goldstein, N. Y. C. .... W	10
June	2—Jimmy McLarnin, Vernon, Cal. W	10
June	16—Ernie Goozeman, Vernon, Cal. KO	7
June	24—Dynamite Murphy, Oakland ... W	10
July	31—Bushy Graham, Aurora, Ill. ...ND	10
Aug.	4—Bobby Wolgast, Terre Haute ..ND	10
Aug.	24—*Bushy Graham, N. Y. C. L	12
Oct.	27—Doc Snell, Vernon, Cal. ...... W	10
Nov.	18—Pete Sarmiento, Los Angeles ... W	10
Dec.	8—Jimmy McLarnin, Vernon, Cal. LF	2
	*Taylor broke left hand in 3rd round.	

1926

Jan.	12—Jimmy McLarnin, Vernon, Cal. W	10
Feb.	3—Joey Sangor, Los Angeles ...... W	10
Mar.	9—Johnny Brown, Los Angeles ... W	10
Mar.	26—Doc Snell, Cleveland .... W	12
Apr.	8—Abe Goldstein, Terre Haute ...ND	10
Apr.	19—Clever Sencio, Milwauke .....ND	10
	Died after above bout.	
May	14—Tommy Ryan, Louisville ...... W	12
June	18—Cal Joe Lynch, San Francisco .. W	10
June	25—Chuck Hellman, Portland, Ore.. D	10
June	29—Young Nationalista, Seattle .... W	6
July	24—Tommy Ryan, Chicago ....WF	3
Aug.	19—Dixie La Hood, Los Angeles ..KO	8
Oct.	22—Vic Burrone, St. Paul ....ND	10
Nov.	6—Young Montreal, Vernon, Cal. . W	2
Nov.	29—Joey Sangor, Milwaukee ....ND	10

1927

Jan.	20—Jack Phillips, N. Y. C. ....KO	2
Feb.	15—Midget Smith, Indianapolis ...ND	10
Feb.	24—Eddie Shea, Chicago, Ill. ....W	10
Mar.	15—Pete Sarmiento, Terre Haute .. W	10
Mar.	26—Tony Canzoneri, Chicago ...... D	10
	(For Vacant N.B.A. Bantamweight Title)	
Apr.	18—Young Nationalista, Los Ang. ..KO	5
May	3—Abe Goldstein, Chicago ...... W	10
June	1—Chick Suggs, Los Angeles ....KO	5
June	11—Johnny Hughes, St. Paul .....KO	2
June	24—Tony Canzoneri, Chicago ...... W	10
	(Won Vacant N.B.A. Bantamweight Title)	
Sept.	1—Midget Don Smith,	
	Culver City, Cal. ....KO	1
Sept.	20—Joey Sangor, Los Angeles L	10
Nov.	8—Johnny Farr, Los Angeles ..... W	10
Dec.	30—Tony Canzoneri, N. Y. C. L	10

1928

Jan.	10—Babe Ruth, Chicago .... W	10
Jan.	24—Phil Zwick, Milwaukee ......KO	2
Feb.	9—Joey Sangor, Chicago ......KO by	7
Mar.	6—Ignacio Fernandez, Los Ang.... W	10
Mar.	23—Vic Foley, Vancouver, B. C. L	10
Apr.	3—Santiago Zorilla, Los Angeles .. W	10
May	21—Joe Lucas, Chicago .... W	10
June	29—Santiago Zorilla, San Fran. .... W	10
July	10—Johnny Vacca, Los Angeles .... W	10
July	27—Santiago Zorilla, San Fran. L	10
Aug.	21—Taylor vacated N. B. A. Bantam-	
	weight Title.	

1929

Jan.	29—Billy Shaw, Indianapolis .....ND	10
Jan.	31—Bobby Dempsey, Davenport ..KO	4
Feb.	8—Al Singer, N. Y. C. ....LF	4
Mar.	15—Al Singer, N. Y. C. L	10
Apr.	2—Henry Falegano, Milwaukee.... ND	8
Apr.	10—Young Montreal, Providence ...L	10
Apr.	16—Tommy Murray, Indianapolis .KO	1
June	11—Goldie Hess, Los Angeles ...... D	10
July	22—Andy Martin, Boston L	10
Oct.	8—Earl Mastro, Chicago .... D	10
Nov.	15—Santiago Zoorilla, Chicago ..... W	10
Dec.	27—Earl Mastro, Chicago .....KO by	9

1930

Mar.	20—Bat Battalino, Detroit .... W	10
Apr.	11—Paul Wangley, Minneapolis ...KO	5
Apr.	21—Fidel La Barba, Chicago L	10
June	3—Jackie Johnson, Chicago ......KO	2
June	12—Johnny Kaiser, Springfield ...KO	2
July	1—Earl Mastro, Detroit L	10
July	29—Mickey Genaro, Indianapolis .. W	10
Aug.	18—Bat Battalino, Hartford, Conn. ..L	10
Oct.	14—Eddie Edelman, Spokane ...... W	8
Oct.	21—Santiago Zorilla, Seattle .... D	8

Nov.	10—Maurice Holtzer, Los Angeles ...L	10
Nov.	28—Fidel La Barba, N. Y. C. L	10
Dec.	12—Maurice Holtzer, New York ...L	10

1931

Jan.	13—Joe Lucas, Indianapolis .... W	10
Jan.	30—Sam Hackett, Buffalo ....KO	3
Feb.	16—Benny Bass, Phila. ....KO by	2
Mar.	16—Lew Massey, Phila........ L Disq.	8

(Retired to become a manager and promoter of boxing.)

TB	KO	WD	WF	D	LD	LF	KOBY	ND	NC
157	35	34	1	6	16	3	4	58	0

Died in Los Angeles, Calif. on March 8, 1962.

WILLIE SMITH

Born, 1906, Johannesburg, South Africa. Weight, 118-126 lbs.

1924 Olympic Bantamweight Gold Medalist

1925

June	20—Scotty Fraser, Johannesburg .... D	8
Aug.	1—Clarence Walker, Johannesburg ... W	10
Sept.	26—Scotty Fraser, Johannesburg ..... KO	13
Oct.	10—Sam Lee, Johannesburg .... KO	5
Dec.	12—Young Johnny Brown, Johannesburg W	20

1926

Feb.	13—Taffy Jones, Johannesburg ...... KO	12
Apr.	10—Jim McKenzie, Johannesburg ...... W	20
May	15—Jim McKenzie, Johannesburg ...... W	20
July	17—George (Kid) Socks, Johannesburg W	20
Dec.	18—Arthur Webb, Johannesburg .... W	15

1927

Jan.	29—Johnny Brown, Johannesburg ..... W	15
Feb.	5—Reinnen Kokke, Johannesburg ... KO	4
Mar.	5—Ralph Minshull, Johannesburg .... W	10
June	4—Ernie Jarvis, Johannesburg ..... W	15
Oct.	6—Teddy Baldock, London .... W	15
	(Won British World Bantamweight Title)	
Nov.	7—Dominick Petrone, Cleveland L	10

1928

May	5—Young Johnny Brown, Johannesburg W	15
May	31—Pierre Pothier, Johannesburg ..... D	15
Aug.	4—Sammy Ticken, Johannesburg .... WF	9
Oct.	6—Mickey Doyle, Johannesburg ...... W	15

1929

Jan.	12—Archie Cowan, Sydney .... KO	8
Feb.	9—Fidel LaBarba, Sydney L	15
Mar.	3—Fidel LaBarba, Sydney .... KO by	12
Apr.	—Jack Roberts, Sydney .... KO by	5
Nov.	13—Mickey Doyle, Johannesburg ...... W	15
Nov.	30—Dolf du Plessis, Durban .... W	15
	(Won South African Featherweight Title)	

1930

Mar.	5—George (Kid) Nicholson, Cape Town W	15
May	22—Dick Corbett, London L	15
	(For Vacant British Empire Bantamweight Title)	
Dec.	1—Johnny Bosman, Cape Town .... W	15

1931

Mar.	21—George (Panther) Purchase,	
	Johannesburg .... W	15
Apr.	18—Sammy Shack, Johannesburg ...... W	15
June	6—Dick Corbett, Johannesburg L	15
June	27—Dick Corbett, Cape Town .... W	15
July	15—Ginger Jones, N'Kana .... W	15
Aug.	29—Kid Como, Durban .... KO by	8
Sept.	5—Kid Como, Bulawayo .... W	15
Sept.	19—Kid Como, N'Kana .... W	15
Oct.	3—Benny Sharkey, Johannesburg ..... W	12

1932

Mar.	14—Phineas John, Johannesburg L	12
June	4—Kid Como, Johannesburg .... W	12
July	30—Len McLoughlin, Durban L	12
	(Lost South African Featherweight Title)	
Oct.	1—Len McLoughlin, Bloemfontein L	12

1933

Dec.	26—Ivan Swanepoel, Johannesburg .... W	6

1934

Jan.	13—Dave Burgher, Johannesburg ..... W	6
Feb.	3—Gerry Stone, Johannesburg ...... W	6

Feb. 17—Len McLoughlin, Johannesburg .... D 8
Apr. 7—Guiliano Secchi, Johannesburg .... W 8
May 5—Len McLoughlin, Johannesburg .... W 12
      (Regained South African Featherweight Title)
July 28—Guiliano Secchi, Pietermaritzburg W 10
1935
Oct. 12—Babe Smith, Johannesburg .... W 12
1936
Feb. 29—Ernst Wohner, Johannesburg ..... W 12
Aug. 29—Maurice Holtzer, Johannesburg .... W 12
Oct. 10—Freddie Miller, Johannesburg KO by 6
Nov. 21—Freddie Miller, Johannesburg KO by 6
Dec. 26—Johnny McGrory, Johannesburg .... L 12
      (For British Empire Featherweight Title)

TB	KO	WD	WF	D	LD	LF	KO BY	ND	NC
55	5	33	1	3	8	0	5	0	0

BUSHY GRAHAM
(Angelo Geraci)
Born, June 18, 1903, Italy. Nationality, Italian-American. Weight, 126 lbs. Height, 5 ft. 5 in. Managed by Joe Metro.
1922
Knockouts: Pete Harmon, 6; Pete Harmon, 8; Jone Connors, 3; Henry Samuels, 2. Won: Spike Sullivan, 6; Kid Crouzier, 6; Spider Ryan, 6; Spider Ryan, 4; Spider Ryan, 4; Spider Ryan, 6; Spider Ryan, 6; Spider Ryan, 6; Frank Mozdy, 6. Draw: Spike Sullivan, 10; Kid Crouzier, 6; Frank Mozdy, 8. Knocked Out by: Spike Sullivan, 1.
1923
Knockouts: Biff Bang Burns, 3; Bobby Hamilton, 1; Joe Maggio, 2; Murray Bresson, 1; Johnny Jones, 2; Andy Jackson, 1; Young Murphy, 6; Patsy Vic Adams, 6; Patsy Vic Adams, 6; Don Causon, 6; Kid Julian, 3. Won: Kid Vig, 6; Phil Verdi, 6; Barney Buttler, 8; Harry Burns, 6; Red Mahoney, 8; Donny Mack, 10; Frank Mozdy, 10; Dave Astor, 10; Cyclone Lambert, 4.
1924
Knockouts: Pete Zivic, 9; Sammy Nable, 4. Won: Frankie Ash, 6; Irish Johnny Curtin, 6; Phil Verdi, 6; Terry Miller, 10; Harold Farese, 12; Jackie Snyder (foul) 8. No decision: Frankie Genaro, 10. Lost: Irish Johnny Curtin, 6; Frankie Genaro, 12.
1925
Jan. 1—Tommy Ryan, Syracuse ...... W 8
Jan. 9—Nat Pincus, N. Y. .... KO 8
Mar. 7—Phil Verdi, Rochester .... W 10
Mar. 9—Spark Plug Russell, Newark ... ND 12
Mar. 20—Harold Smith, N. Y. .... W 10
Apr. 13—Eddie Anderson, Milwaukee ..ND 10
June 11—Larry Goldberg, Albany .... W 12
June 19—Joe Ryder, E. Chicago .... ND 10
June 17—Eddie O'Dowd, Cleveland ..... W 10
June 23—Abe Goldstein, N. Y. C. .... W 8
June 24—Pete Zivic, Utica .... W 10
July 31—Bud Taylor, Aurora .... ND 10
Aug. 24—Bud Taylor, N. Y. C. .... W 12
Sept. 19—Frankie Fasano, Syracuse ....KO 3
Oct. 14—Joe Ryder, N. Y. C. .... W 10
Nov. 25—Willie Spencer, Albany .... KO 5
1926
Jan. 22—Joe Lynch, New York .... W 10
Mar. 1—Tommy Ryan, Buffalo .... W 10
Mar. 26—Johnny Rosen, Syracuse .....KO 1
Mar. 29—Cal. Joe Lynch, Toronto .... D 10
May 17—Frankie Genaro, New York ... W 10
May 25—Mickie Garcia, New York ...... W 10
June 8—Eddie O'Dowd, Syracuse ......W 6
Aug. 5—Dominick Petrone, N. Y. C. ...KO 8
Aug. 16—Davey Abad, Utica, N. Y. ...... W 10
Aug. 24—Tommy Ryan, Utica, N. Y. .... W 10
Sept. 2—Chick Suggs, New York ...... W 10
Sept. 7—Young Montreal, Providence... W 12
Sept. 21—Young Montreal, Providence ...L 12
Nov. 6—Giovanni Salerino, Syracuse ... W 10
Dec. 17—Tony Cansoneri, N. Y. C. ......L 10
1927
Feb. 4—Charley Rosenberg, New York ..L 15
      (Graham and Rosenberg suspended for one
      year due to a secret agreement.)
1928
Mar. 22—Joe Ryder, Toledo, O. ....ND 12
May 12—Pete Zivic, New York ....KO 4

May 23—Corp. Izzy Schwartz, N. Y. C. ...W 15
      (Won Vacant N. Y. Commission Bantam-
      weight Title)
July 24—Billy Kowalik, Buffalo .... W 6
Aug. 14—Charlie Pinto, Los Angeles ..... W 10
Aug. 21—Calif. Joe Lynch, Los Angeles .KO 7
Sept. 11—Fidel La Barba, Los Angeles ...L 10
Oct. 5—Young Montreal, Syracuse ..... W 10
1929
Feb. 13—Babe Keller, Cincinnati ....KO 2
Mar. 18—Eddie O'Dowd, Cincinnati, O. .. W 10
Apr. 12—Kid Chocolate, New York ....L 15
      (Outgrew class and gave up claim to title)
May 15—Young Montreal, Providence ... W 10
June 11—Archie Bell, Wilkes-Barre ...... W 10
Aug. 19—Eddie O'Dowd, Columbus, O. .. W 10
Aug. 26—Vidal Gregorio, Philadelphia ... W 10
Sept. 20—Andy Martin, Boston ....L 10
Nov. 1—Cecil Payne, Louisville, Ky. .... W 10
Nov. 28—Pete Zivic, New York ....KO 4
Dec. 4—Young Montreal, Providence ... W 10
Dec. 21—Tommy Ryan, Troy, N. Y. .....KO 4
1930
Jan. 29—Freddie Miller, Cincinnati ..... D 10
Feb. 6—Al Rackon, Hartford, Conn. ...KO 3
Apr. 9—Billy Shaw, Cincinnati ....KO 1
Apr. 25—Bat Battalino, Hartford, Conn. ..L 10
May 28—Fidel La Barba, New York ......L 10
Aug. 20—Johnny Vacca, Utica .... W 10
Nov. 14—Tommy Paul, Buffalo, N. Y. ....L 10
1931
Jan. 2—Davey Abad, St. Louis .... W 8
Mar. 16—Jimmy Katz, Rochester, N. Y. KO 6
Apr. 6—Johnny Farr, Columbus, O. ...KO 8
Apr. 22—Johnny Datto, Cleveland ...... W 6
May 11—Hymie Wiseman, Des Moines ... W 8
July 17—Emil Paluso, Utica ....KO 8
Sept. 24—Battling Battalino, Hartford ... W 10
Nov. 19—Battling Battalino, Chicago KO by 1
1932
Apr. 8—Tommy Paul, Detroit ....L 10
1935
Nov. 12—Steve Smith, Buffalo .... W 10
1936
Feb. 7—Leo Rodak, N. Y. C. .... D 10
Feb. 28—Pete Nebo, Utica ....KO 2
Apr. 17—Tony Herrera, N. Y. C. ....KO 2
June 1—Orville Drouillard, N. Y. C. ...KO 7
June 15—Johnny Jadick, N. Y. C. ...... W 8
Aug. 7—Joe Zodda, Utica ....KO 2
Aug. 19—Tommy Howell, Utica ....KO 2
Sept. 9—Johnny Alba, Utica .... W 8
Oct. 15—Honeyboy Hughes, Utica ...... W 8
Nov. 6—Eddie Zivic, Utica .... W 8
Nov. 27—Enrico Venturi, N. Y. C. ....L 8

TB	KO	WD	WF	D	LD	LF	KO BY	ND	NC
128	37	63	1	6	12	1	2	6	0

PANAMA AL BROWN
(Alphonse Theo Brown)
Born, July 5, 1902, Panama Nationality, Panamanian. Weight, 118-112 lbs. Height, 5 ft. 11 in. Managed by Dave Lumiansky.
(Started boxing in 1919)
1922
      —Jose Moreno, Panama .... W 6
      —Young Jeff Clarke, Panama ...KO 4
Dec. 6—Sailor Patchett, Panama ...... W 15
      (Won Isthmus Flyweight Title)
1923
Aug. 22—Johnny Breslin, New York ..... D 4
Sept.   —Tommy Milton, New York ...KO 1
Oct. 13—Billy Hines, New York ......KO 3
Nov.   —Bobby Risden, New York .... D 6
Dec. 12—Willie Darcy, New York ...... W 12
1924
Apr. 12—Willie Farley, N.Y.C. ....KO 1
May 3—Bobby Burns, N. Y. C. ....KO 7
May 24—Joe Colletti, N. Y. C. .... W 12
June 7—Willie La Morte, N. Y. C. .....KO 2
June 28—Al Kaufman, N. Y. C. ....KO 1
Aug.   —George McNally, New York ....KO 4
Aug. 30—Sparkplug Russell, N. Y. C. ... W 10
Sept. 13—Willie Salter, New York ......KO 1
Sept. 27—Billy Marlowe, N. Y. C. ...... W 12
Oct. 25—Frankie Ash, N. Y. C. ....KO 1
Nov. 11—Tommy Milton, N.Y.C..............W 15
      —Tommy Murphy ....KO 4

1925

Jan.	3—Jimmy Russo, N. Y. C. L	10
Feb.	19—Davey Abad .... W	6
June	3—Jimmy Russo, N. Y. C. .... W	10
Aug.	22—Eddie Flank, N. Y. C. .... W	10
	—Johnny Forbes, Albany .... W	12
Oct.	5—Bobby Green, N. Y. C. ...... W	10
Oct.	16—Johnny Breslin, N. Y. C. ...... W	10
Dec.	11—Tommy Hughes, N. Y. C. ..... W	10
	—Dominick Petrone, N. Y. C. .... W	6
	—Joey Ross .... ND	10

1926

Jan.	26—Domingo Compas, Vernon, Cal. .... D	10
Feb.	6—Dominick Petrone, N. Y. C. L	10
Feb.	9—Jackie Sherman, Vernon, Cal. L	10
Apr.	23—Abe Goldstein, N. Y. C. L	10
May	21—Teddy Silva, N. Y. C. .... KO	3
June	6—Jack Pettibone, N. Y. C. .... KO	4
July	7—Pete Zivic, N. Y. C. .... W	10
July	31—Awk Derrich, Huron, S. D. .... KO	3
Aug.	6—Harry Forbes, Albany, N. Y. .... W	12
Sept.	2—Joe Ryder, N. Y. C. .... W	4
	—Davey Adelman, Atlantic City ..... W	10
	—Willie LaMorte .... ND	10
Nov.	—Antonio Merlo, Paris .... KO	3

1927

Jan.	25—Edouard Mascart, Paris .... KO	5
Mar.	8—Kid Socks, Paris .... KO	5
Apr.	2—Eugene Eriqui, Paris .... W	10
May	10—Young Cyclone, Paris .... W	10
Oct.	18—Albert Ryall, Paris .... KO	2
Nov.	22—Henri Scillie, Paris L	12
Dec.	10—Andre Routis, Paris L	10
	—Yg. Henri Scillie, Paris .... D	10

1928

Mar.	23—Benny Schwartz, N. Y. C. .... W	10
Mar.	29—Billy Shaw, N. Y. C. .... KO	1
May	2—Eddie O'Dowd, N. Y. C. .... W	10
June	21—Billy Shaw, N. Y. C. .... KO	1
Sept.	13—Kid Francis, N. Y. C. .... W	12
Nov.	17—Johnny Cuthbert, Paris .... D	15
Dec.	28—Harry Corbett, Paris .... W	12

1929

Jan.	29—Tiger Humery, Paris, France ..KO	1
Mar.	6—Francis Biron, Paris, France ..KO	3
Mar.	24—Don Bernasconi, Madrid, Spain	W	10
Apr.	9—Joe Cadman, Paris, France ....KO	4
May	26—Vernon Cormier, Portld., Me. .KO	3
June	18—Vidal Gregorio, N. Y. C. .... W	15
	(Won Vacant World Bantamweight Title)	
July	3—Vic Burrone, Newark, N. J. .... W	10
July	16—Vernon Cormier, Portld., Me. .KO	4
July	26—Battling Battalino, Hartford ...L	10
Aug.	28—*Knud Larsen, Copenhagen ... W	10
	*Title bout.	

1930

Jan.	25—Pinkey Silverberg, Havana ..... W	10
Feb.	8—Johnny Erickson, N. Y. C. ....WF	4
Feb.	18—Johnny Canzoneri, Allentown . W	10
Mar.	14—Tommy Paul, Buffalo, N. Y. ... D	6
Apr.	15—K. O. Morgan, Boston ....KO	7
Apr.	21—Al Gillette, New Bedford ....KO	9
May	10—Calvin Reed, New Bedford ....KO	4
June	4—Frankie Wilson, N. Y. C. .....KO	1
June	5—Milton Cohen, Waterbury ....KO	1
June	17—Johnny McCoy, West Spgfield KO	6
June	18—Benny Brostoff, Bayonne ....KO	2
June	23—K. O. Wallace, N. Y. C. ......KO	3
June	25—Mickey Doyle, Scranton .... W	10
July	14—Luigi Quadrini, N. Y. C. .... W	10
July	23—Domenico Bernasconi, N. Y. C. W	10
Aug.	29—Johnny Vacca, Bridgeport ....KO	3
Oct.	4—Eugene Huat, Paris, France ... W	15
	(Title bout)	
Oct.	22—Jose Girones, Barcelona, Spain . D	10
Nov.	8—Nick Bensa, Paris .... W	10

1931

Feb.	11—*Nick Bensa, Paris .... W	10
Mar.	10—Willie Farrell, Manchester .... KO	3
Mar.	31—Parker, Newcastle .... KO	
Apr.	13—Jack Garland, London .... W	15
Apr.	15—Roger Simende, Paris, France .KO	3
Apr.	30—Julien Verbist, Paris, France ..KO	8
May	21—Teddy Baldock, London ....KO	12
June	15—Johnny Cuthbert, London .... LF	8
Aug.	15—*Pete Sanstol, Montreal .... W	15
Oct.	27—*Eugene Huat, Montreal ...... W	15

778

Nov.	18—Art Chapdelaine, Quebec .....KO	7
Dec.	15—Newsboy Brown, Los Angeles ...L	10
	*Title.	

1932

Jan.	4—Speedy Dado, Los Angeles......L	10
Mar.	15—Golfball Bernard, New Bedfd... W	10
May	18—DiCea, Paris, France .... W	10
May	28—Luigi Quadrini, Cardiff ....KO	6
May	31—Rene Machtens, Paris .... W	10
June	13—Nel Tarleton, Liverpool, Eng. .. D	15
June	18—Eugene Huat, Paris........... W	10
June	25—Vittorio Tamagnini, Milan L	10
July	10—*Kid Francis, Marseilles .... W	15
	(One judge and referee favored Brown; one	
	for Francis. Riot started).	
July	11—The international Boxing Union	
	awarded the fight to Brown.	
Aug.	17—Roland Lecuyer, Montreal ....KO	6
Sept.	19—*Emile Pladner, Toronto .....KO	1
Sept.	26—Mose Butch, Pittsburgh .... W	10
Oct.	20—Young Machtens, Antwerp .... W	10
Oct.	23—Petit Biquet, Brussels .... W	10
Nov.	14—Emile Pladner, Paris ....KO	2
Dec.	1—Dick Burke, Sheffield .... W	12
Dec.	3—Young Henri Scillie, Brussels... D	10
Dec.	8—Franz Matchens, Paris .... W	10
	*Title bout.	

1933

Feb.	9—Henri Pontrain, Paris .... W	10
Mar.	4—Johnny Peters, London .... W	15
Mar.	18—*Dom Bernasconi, Milan ...... W	12
May	—Tommy Hymans, England ....KO	9
June	—Art Boddington, London .....KO	4
June	12—Dave Crowley, London .... W	10
July	3—*Johnny King, London .... W	15
Dec.	19—Luigi Quadrini, Oran .... W	10
	*Title bout.	

1934

Feb.	19—*Young Perez, Paris .... W	15
Apr.	16—Kid Francis, Paris .... W	10
May	17—Gustave Humery, Paris .... LF	6
June	30—Johnny Edwards, Zurich L	10
Nov.	1—Young Perez, Tunis .... KO	10
Dec.	24—Freddie Miller, Paris L	10
	*Title bout.	

1935

Mar.	18—Baltazar Sangchilli, Valencia ... D	10
Apr.	12—Luigi Quadrini, Madrid .... W	10
June	1—Baltazar Sangchilli, Valencia L	15
	(Lost world bantamweight championship)	
Sept.	10—Pete Sanstol, Oslo, Norway L	10

1937

Sept.	9—Andre Regis, Paris ....KO	1
Sept.	23—Maurice Huguenin, Paris ......KO	3
	—Augier, Geneva ....KO	2
Nov.	26—Poppy Decico, Paris .... W	10
Dec.	22—Young Perez, Paris ....KO	5

1938

Mar.	4—Baltazar Sangchilli, Paris ...... W	15
Apr.	13—Valentine Anglemann, Paris ..KO	8

1939

Apr.	22—Christobal Jaramillo, N. Y. C. .KO	4
May	6—Mariano Arilla, N. Y. C. ......KO	3
Apr.	29—Harry Jefra, New York ....KO by	7

1941

July	14—Leocadio Torres, Panama .... KO	8
July	26—Battling Nelson, Panama .... KO	4
Sept.	7—Kid Fortune, Panama .... KO	2
Oct.	26—Eduardo Carrasco, Panama L	10

1942

Mar.	8—Eduardo Carrasco, Panama L	10
Aug.	30—Leocadio Torres, Panama .... D	15
	(Panama Featherweight Title Fight)	
Dec.	4—Kid Fortune, Panama .... W	10

TB	KO	WD	WF	D	LD	LF	KO BY	ND	NC
152	57	62	1	11	16	2	1	2	0

Died April 11, 1951, New York N. Y.
Buried Amador Guerrero Cemetery, Panama
City.

SIXTO ESCOBAR

Born, Barcelona, Puerto Rico, March 23,
1913. Weight, 118 lbs. Height, 5 ft. 4 in. Managed
by Lew Brix.

1931

Knockouts: Ramon Rodriquez, 6; Luis

Perez, 2. Won: Luis Perez, 6; Luis Perez, 6; Rafael Morales, 10. Lost: Rafael Morales, 8. All fights in San Juan, P.R.

1932
Knockouts: Pica Rica, 5; Rafael Morales, 2; Firpo Suhano, 5. Won: Simon Chaves, 10; Firpo Suhano, 5; Phil Tobias, 10. Lost: Simon Chaves, 10. Pica Rica fight in San Juan—all others Venezuela.

1933
Knockouts: Jose Lago, 10; K. O. Tiger, 2. Won: K. O. Tiger, 8; Baby Face Mendoza, 10; Pedro Riuz, 10; Sindolfo Diaz, 10; Vincinte Abadia, 10. Lost: Pancho Villa, 10. Draw: Henry Chaft, 10; Felipe Andrade, 10 (San Juan). All others in Venezuela.

1934
Jan.	6—Billy Nelson, Porto Rico	KO	10
Feb.	9—Ray Lullolo, Porto Rico	W	10
Mar.	12—Kid Truyol, Porto Rico	KO	8
May	7—Bobby Leitham, Holyoke	KO	7
May	21—Joey Archibald, Holyoke	W	10
June	5—Boby Leitham, Montreal	KO	5
June	26—Baby Casanova, Montreal	KO	9
(Won N. B. A. Bantamweight Title)
Aug.	8—Eugene Huat, Montreal	W	15
(N.B.A. Title Bout)

1935
Mar.	30—Juan Zurita, Mexico City	L	10
May	28—Joey Archibald, N. Y. C.	KO	6
June	21—Johnny Bang, N. Y. C.	KO	5
Aug.	7—Pete Sanstol	W	12
Aug.	26—Lou Salica, N. Y. C.	L	15
(Lost N.B.A. Bantamweight title)
Nov.	15—Lou Salica, N. Y. C.	W	15
(Re-won N.B.A. Bantamweight title)

1936
Feb.	5—Al Gillette, Cuba	KO	5
July	15—Indian Quintana, L. I.	KO	10
Aug.	31—Tony Marino, N. Y. C.	KO	13
(Won World Bantamweight Title)
Oct.	5—Harry Jeffra, Baltimore	L	10
Oct.	13—*Indian Quintana, N. Y. C.	KO	1
Dec.	9—Harry Jeffra, N. Y. C.	L	10
*Title Bout.

1937
| Feb. | 21—Lou Salica, Puerto Rico | W | 15 |
| (Bantam Title) |
May	12—Nicky Jerome, N. Y. C.	KO	2
June	21—Pat Robertson, Chicago	KO	8
July	21—George Holmes, N. Y. C.	KO	3
Sept.	1—Eddie Reid, Hartford	KO	8
Sept.	23—Harry Jeffra, N. Y. C.	L	15
(Lost Bantamweight Title)
Nov.	13—Johnny De Foe, Brooklyn	D	8

1938
| Feb. | 20—Harry Jeffra, San Juan | W | 15 |
| (Re-won World Bantamweight Title) |
Apr.	19—Kayo Morgan, Detroit	L	10
May	4—Nat Litfin, N. Y. C.	L	10
Sept.	5—Lew Transparenti, Baltimore	W	10
Nov.	1—Henry Hook, Toronto	L	10
Dec.	19—Al Mancini, Washington, D. C.	L	10

1939
| Apr. | 2—Kayo Morgan, San Juan | W | 15 |
| (For Title) |
July	7—Johnny Buff, Mt. Frdm., N. J.	W	8
July	25—Frankie Bove, Garfield, N. J.	L	8
Aug.	14—Jimmy Perrin, New Orleans	L	10
Oct.	4—Tony Olivera, Oakland, Cal.	L	10
(Vacated title because of weight)
Dec.	11—Frankie Covelli, Pittsburgh	L	10

1940
| Apr. | 7—Simon Chavez, Caracas, Venez. | D | 10 |
| Dec. | 2—Harry Jeffra, Baltimore | L | 10 |

1941
In U. S. Army.

TB	KO	WD	WF	D	LD	LF	KOBY	ND	NC
64	21	21	0	4	18	0	0	0	0

Elected to Boxing Hall of Fame, 1975.
Died, November 17, 1979, Puerto Rico.

BALTAZAR SANGCHILLI
(Baltasar Belenguer Hevoas)
Born, October 15, 1911, Valencia, Spain. Nationality, Spanish. Weight, 118 lbs. Height, 5 ft. 3 in. Managed by Bertys Remy.

1929
Apr.	29—Casanova, Valencia	KO	2
June	8—Saenz, Valencia	LF	2
Aug.	4—Samber, Valencia	W	4

Sept.	21—Viana, Valencia	W	4
Oct.	5—Viana, Valencia	D	4
Nov.	17—Antonio Bernaben, Valencia	KO	6
Nov.	24—Las Heras, Valencia	L	6

1930
Jan.	2—Saulo, Valencia	W	6
Mar.	2—Viana, Valencia	WF	4
June	7—Barber, Alicante	W	4
June	3—Vicenie Santacruz, Alicante	W	6
July	5—Battista, Alicante	KO	5
July	12—Jaime Garcia, Alicante	KO	1
July	17—Pascual Latorre, Alicante	W	6
Aug.	1—Liberato, Malaga	W	10
Aug.	20—Parejo, Grenade	KO	1
Sept.	17—Lagaves, Malaga	KO	3
Sept.	30—Kid Brand, Malaga	KO	2
Nov.	2—Ignacio Gomez, Malaga	KO	3
Nov.	23—Sam'ber, Malaga	W	8

1931
Jan.	10—Koliche, Seville	KO	1
Jan.	17—Alejandro Soler, Seville	KO	4
Mar.	20—Vercher, Seville	KO	2
Mar.	28—Francisco Bella, Seville	W	10
July	26—Morales, Volmau	W	8
July	31—Abraham, Casablanca	KO	6
Aug.	20—Lorente, Gibraltar	KO	8
Aug.	29—Jose Hugo, Melilla	W	10
Sept.	16—Liberato, Lisbon	W	8

1932
Feb.	12—Fortunato Ortega, Barcelona	L	8
July	4—Miguel Safont, Barcelona	W	8
Aug.	20—Miguel Safont, Barcelona	W	10
Sept.	3—Albert Biesmans, Barcelona	W	10
Nov.	3—Manuel Gonzales, Barcelona	W	10
Dec.	20—Lorenzo Vitria, Barcelona	L	10

1933
Jan.	17—Jean Cuart, Barcelona	KO	5
Feb.	7—Emilio Iglesias, Barcelona	W	10
Mar.	18—Young Perez, Valencia	W	10
Apr.	22—Carlos Flix, Valencia	W	12
(Bantamweight Championship of Spain)
June	11—Ottavio Gori, Valencia	W	10
July	15—Nic Petit-Biquet, Valencia	D	15
(Declared void by I.B.U.)
Aug.	2—Ottavio Gori, Malaga	KO	5
Sept.	10—Ottavio Gori, Valencia	KO	10
Oct.	17—Alfredo Magnolfi, Madrid	W	10
Oct.	25—Vigili, Castellon	KO	2

1934
Jan.	11—Simons, Alicante	KO	1
Jan.	19—Victor Ferrand, Madrid	W	10
Feb.	6—Carlos Flix, Madrid	D	12
(Spanish Bantamweight Championship)
Feb.	23—Henri Barras, Madrid	WF	4
Mar.	18—Giovanni Sili, Valencia	KO	2
Apr.	14—Victor Ferrand, Valencia	KO	4
June	17—Young Perez, Oran	W	10
Aug.	18—Nic. Petit-Biquet, Algeria	L	10
Nov.	28—Joseph Decico, Paris	D	10

1935
Jan.	4—Young Borel, Paris	W	10
Jan.	16—Kid David, Brussels	W	15
Mar.	18—Al Brown, Valencia	D	10
June	1—Al Brown, Valencia	W	15
(Won World Bantamweight Championship)
June	28—Rene Gabes, Valencia	KO	3
July	16—Vincent Riambau, Melilla	W	10
Aug.	3—Young Borel, Oran	W	10
Aug.	31—Nic. Petit-Biquet, Algeria	KO	10
Sept.	14—Young Perez, Casablanca	W	10
Oct.	18—Alfredo Magnolfi, Madrid	W	10

1936
Mar.	20—George Butcher, Spain	KO	4
Mar.	31—Ronnie Jones, London	W	10
Apr.	10—Benny Sharkey, England	L	10
May	11—Jimmy Martin, Brooklyn	KO	8
May	29—Lew Farber, N. Y. C.	W	10
June	29—Tony Marino, N. Y. C.	KO by	14
(Lost World Bantamweight Title)
Sept.	28—Frankie Martin, Canada	L	10
Oct.	15—Tony Marino, Pittsburgh	W	10

1938
Jan.	1—Juan Zurita, Mexico City	L	10
Mar.	4—Al Brown, Paris	L	10
Dec.	9—Ernst Weiss, Berlin	L	10

1939
| Mar. | 13—Jim Brady, Manchester | L | 12 |
| Apr. | 3—Peter Kane, London | L | 10 |

TB	KO	WD	WF	D	LD	LF	KOBY	ND	NC
77	24	33	2	9	11	1	1	0	0

779

LOU SALICA

Born, July 26, 1913, New York City.
Natinality, Italian-American. Weight, 118
pounds. Managed by Hymie Caplin.

1931
Won the Metropolitan A. A. U. Flyweight
Championship.

1932
Won the Metropolitan A. A. U. Flyweight
Championship.
Won the Golden Gloves Flyweight
Championship.
Won the Inter-City Golden Gloves
Flyweight Championship.
Defeated Steve Enekes, Olympic Champion.
Won the Italian-American Flyweight
Championship.

1933
Jan.   5—Lew Franklin, N. Y. C. .... W   4
Apr. 14—Ernest Torres, N. Y. C. .... W   5
May 27—Johnny Ladao, N. Y. C. .... W   6
Aug.   1—Skippy Allen, N. Y. C. .... W   6
Aug. 26—Sammy Goldman, N. Y. C. ..... W   6
Sept. 19—Antol Koscis, N. Y. C. .... W   6
Nov.   2—Antol Koscis, N. Y. C. .... D   6
Dec. 19—Tony Passano, N. Y. C. .... W   6
Dec. 27—Pete De Grasse, N. Y. C. ...... W   6
       —Damasco Seda .... KO   2
       —Frankie Puccio .... W   4
       —Frankie Puccio .... W   5
       —Jimmy Martin .... W   6
       —Jimmy Martin .... W   6
       —Ralph Giffone .... W   6

1934
Feb.   2—Julie Katz, N. Y. C. .... W   6
Feb. 14—Midget Wolgast, N. Y. C. L   8
Apr.   2—Harry Bauman, N. Y. C. .... W   6
May   1—Midget Wolgast, N. Y. C. ...... D   8
May 11—Julie Katz, N. Y. C. .... W   8
Aug. 10—Joe Tei Ken, Hollywood .... W 10
Sept. 7—Young Tommy, Hollywood ... W 10
Oct.   5—B'y Face Mathes'n, Hollywood KO   6
Oct. 17—Speedy Dado, Hollywood ...... L 10
Dec. 20—Baby Quintana, Montreal ...... W 10

1935
Jan. 28—Johnny Erickson, N. Y. C. ..... W   8
Mar.   1—Dick Welsh, N. Y. C. .... W   6
May   3—Midget Wolgast, Hollywood ... W 10
June 11—Pablo Dano, Los Angeles ...... W 10
July 30—Jerry Mazza, N. Y. C. .... D   8
Aug. 26—Sixto Escobar, N. Y. C. .... W 15
(Won N.B.A. Bantamweight Title)
Nov. 15—Sixto Escobar, N. Y. C. .... L 15
(Lost N.B.A. Bantamweight Title)

1936
Feb. 28—Henry Hook, Hollywood ...... D 10
Mar. 11—Tuffy Pierpont, Oakland ...... KO   6
Mar. 20—Small Montana, San Francisco . W 10
Apr.   3—Henry Hook, Hollywood ...... W 10
June   2—Tony Marino, Long Island ..... L 10
June 23—Yg. Jack Sharkey, Brooklyn ... D   8
Sept. 8—Sammy Garcia, Brooklyn ...... W   8
Sept. 19—Nicky Jerome, Brooklyn L   8
Oct. 10—Nicky Jerome, Brooklyn L   8
Dec.   4—Joe Mendiola, Hollywood ..... W 10

1937
Jan.   1—Mauricio Seria, Stockton ...... W 10
Jan. 15—Bobby Leyvas, Hollywood ..... D 10
Feb. 21—Sixto Escobar, San Juan .... L 15
(For World Bantamweight title)
Apr. 16—Bobby Leyvas, Hollywood ... KO 10
May 11—Pete DeGrasse, Los Angeles .... W 10
June 18—Pancho Leyvas, Hollywood .... D 10
Oct. 12—Jackie Corcoran, Elizabeth .... W 10
Nov.   2—Joey Wach, Brooklyn .... KO   4
Nov. 16—Sammy Garcia, Brooklyn...... W 10

1938
Feb.   5—Ernest Weiss, Brooklyn .... W   8
Mar. 26—Jimmy Urso, Brooklyn .... W   8
May 15—Fillo Echeverria, Havana .... KO   9
July 22—Emilio Magana, Hollywood ... KO   9
Aug. 12—Pablo Dano, Hollywood ...... W 10
Aug. 26—Jim Roche, San Francisco .... KO   8
Nov. 17—Katsumi Morioka, Brooklyn ... W 10

1939
Mar.   1—Little Dado, Oakland .... D 10
Apr.   6—Richard Lemos, Hollywood ... W 10
May 19—Little Pancho, Hollywood .... W 10
June 16—Little Dado, Hollywood .... L 10
Aug. 18—Jackie Jurich, Hollywood .... KO   9
Sept. 15—Manuel Ortiz, Hollywood ..... W 10

Oct. 20—Little Dado, Hollywood .... D 10
Nov. 17—Tony Olivera, Hollywood ..... W 10
Dec. 14—Tony Olivera, Hollywood .....L 10

1940
Mar.   4—Georgie Pace, Toronto .... D 15
(For Vacant N.B.A. Bantamweight title)
Apr.   4—Jackie Callura, Rochester ...... D 10
Sept. 24—Georgie Pace, N. Y. C. .... W 15
(Won Vacant Bantamweight title, New York
State)
Oct. 21—Tommy Forte, Philadelphia ....L 10
Dec.   2—Small Montana, Toronto ..... KO   3

1941
Jan. 13—Tommy Forte, Philadelphia ... W 15
(Won World Bantamweight title)
Mar.   6—Lou Transparenti, Cleveland ....L 10
Apr. 25—*Lou Transparenti, Baltimore . W 15
June 16—*Tommy Forte, Philadelphia .. W 15
Aug.   8—Henry Hook, Coney Island .... W 10
Oct.   6—Rush Dalma, Honolulu ....L 10
Nov.   3—Kui Kong Young, Honolulu ....L 10
*Title bout.

1942
Jan. 20—Aaron Seltzer, N. Y. C. .... W 10
Apr. 17—Carlos Chavez, Hollywood ......L 10
June   3—Kenny Lindsay, Vancouver .... W 10
July 10—Nat Corum, San Jose .... W 10
Aug.   7—Manuel Ortiz, Hollywood .....L 12
(Lost world bantamweight championship)

1943
Mar. 10—Manuel Ortiz, Oakland ..... KO by 11
(For Bantamweight title)

1944
Jan. 27—Don McLean, Scranton .... W 10
Feb.   3—Larry Torpey, Philadelphia ... KO   7
Feb. 25—Maxie Tanaka, Scranton ...... KO   9
Feb. 28—Mario Colon, Holyoke .... KO 10
Mar. 27—Harry Jeffra, Baltimore ....L 10

TB	KO	WD	WF	D	LD	LF	KOBY	ND	NC
90	13	49	0	11	16	0	1	0	0

TONY MARINO

Born, 1912, Pittsburgh, Pa. Weight, 118
lbs. Height, 5 ft. 3 in. Managed by Bill Newman.

1931
Won: Young Ketchel, 6.

1932
Knockouts: Eller McNeil, 2; George Shea,
4. Won: George Litch, 6; Young Ketchel, 6;
George Tomasky, 6; Johnny Edwards, 10.

1933
Knockout: Mickey Farr, 3. Won: Frisco
Grande, 10; Marty Gold, 10; Franklin Young, 10;
Joey Ross, 8; Young Ketchell, 8. Lost: Willie
Davies, 10; Wolgast, 10.

1934
Knockout: Bobby Olivas, 4. Won: Ray
Mayo, 8. Lost: Small Montana, 10; Small
Montana, 10; Pablo Dano, 10. Draw: Joey
Dodge, 10.

1935
Apr. 12—Joey Dodge, Sacramento ...... W 10
Apr. 26—Pablo Dano, Sacramento ......L 10
July 12—Young Tommy, Hollywood ....L 10
Aug.   5—General Padilla, San Francisco . W   8
Oct.   2—Midget Wolgast, Oakland ......L 10
Oct. 22—"Speedy" Dado, Sacramento .. D 10

1936
Mar. 14—Richard Li Brandi, Brooklyn .. W   6
Mar. 28—Skippy Allen, Brooklyn ...... KO   6
Apr. 11—Willie Felice, Brooklyn .... KO by   3
May   2—Willie Felice, Brooklyn .... W   6
May 16—Santos Hugo, Brooklyn ...... KO   4
June   2—Lou Salica, L. I., N.Y. .... W 10
June 29—Baltazar Sangchilli, N. Y. C. .. KO 14
(Won Bantamweight Title)
Aug. 31—Sixto Escobar, N. Y. C. ...... KO by 13
(Lost Bantamweight Title)
Oct. 15—Baltazar Sangchilli, Brooklyn ..L 10
Oct. 31—Nickey Jerome, Brooklyn ..... W   8
Nov. 21—Jimmy Martin, Brooklyn ..... W   8
Dec.   3—Cristobal Jaramillo, N. Y. C. ... W   8
Dec. 19—Nickey Jerome, Brooklyn ..... W   8

1937
Jan. 30—Indian Quintana, Brooklyn L   8

TB	KO	WD	WF	D	LD	LF	KOBY	ND	NC
41	7	20	0	2	10	0	2	0	0

Marino suffered cerebral hemorrhage; died
Feb. 1, 1937, New York.

HARRY JEFFRA
(Record under Featherweight Champions)

GEORGIE PACE
Born, February 2, 1916. Cleveland, Ohio. Nationality, American-Negro. Weight, 118 lbs. Height, 5 ft. 5 in. Managed by Jimmy White, Tom Stanley and Bobby Michaels.
1936
Knockout: Nat Litfin, 1. Won: Mel Glionna, 6; Al McKenzie, 6; Leo Abrams, 6; Al Harris, 6. No decision: K. O. Morgan, 10.
1937
Jan.	6—Jimmy Young, Toronto	KO 2
Feb.	3—Leo Ritnour, Cleveland	W 8
Mar.	12—Franklin Young, Youngstown	W 10
May	7—Willie Felice, Detroit	KO 1
June	1—Angelo Calura, Toronto	W 8
July	5—Joey Lombardo, Toledo	KO 2
Aug.	11—Frankie Martin, Toronto	KO 6
Sept.	8—Johnny Edwards, Toronto	KO 1
Nov.	23—Spider Armstrong, Toronto	KO by 6
1938
Feb.	14—Katsumi Morioka, Toronto	W 10
Feb.	21—Johnny Gaudes, Toronto	W 10
Mar.	28—Katsumi Morioka, Toronto	W 10
Apr.	18—Henry Hook, Toronto	W 10
May	23—Indian Quintana, Toronto	W 10
Sept.	23—Baby Yack, Toronto	W 10
Oct.	24—Jimmy Thomas, Cleveland	KO 2
Nov.	21—Henry Hook, Toronto	W 10
Dec.	14—Jackie Landers, Lorain, O.	KO 2
1939
Mar.	1—Henry Hook, Cleveland	W 10
Nov.	13—Bobby Doherty, Columbus	KO 2
Nov.	24—Jimmy Webster, Cleveland	KO 8
1940
Jan.	1—Johnny Gaudes, Milwaukee	W 10
Mar.	4—Lou Salica, Toronto	D 15
	(NBA Bantamweight Title)	
May	1—Pablo Dano, N. Y. C.	W 10
Jan.	27—Lawrence Gunn, Balti., Md.	KO 1
Sept.	24—Lou Salica, N. Y. C.	L 15
	(N.Y. Commission Bantamweight Title)	
Oct.	14—Joey Puig, Stamford	KO 6
Nov.	11—Jackie Callura, Toronto	D 10
Dec.	4—Rush Dalma, Oakland, Cal.	L 10
1941
Feb.	18—Spider Armstrong, Toronto	KO 6
Mar.	21—Tony Dupre	KO 2
Apr.	22—Matty Perfetti, Toronto	KO 7
July	10—Jimmy Hatcher, Wtrby, Conn.	L 8
Aug.	22—Danny London, Brooklyn	W 8
Nov.	10—Bill Speary, Toronto	L 10
1942
In U. S. Army.
1943
Aug.	1—Al Reasoner, New Orleans	L 10

TB	KO	WD	WF	D	LD	LF	KOBY	ND	NC
42	15	18	0	2	5	0	1	1	0

MANUEL ORTIZ
Born, July 2, 1916, Corona, California. Ancestry, Mexican. Weight, 112-120 lbs. Height, 5 ft. 4 in. Managed by Noel Johnson, Tommy Farmer and Johnny Rogers.
1938
Feb.	25—Benny Goldberg, Hollywood	L 4
Mar.	25—Frenchy Savidan, Hollywood	W 4
Apr.	14—Serio Mendoza, Hollywood	W 4
May	3—General Padilla, Los Angeles	KO 4
May	17—Santos Hugo, Los Angeles	KO 4
June	3—Sammy LaPorte, Hollywood	W 4
June	24—Frenchy Savidan, Hollywood	W 4
July	5—Pablo Dano, Los Angeles	L 6
Aug.	5—Benny Goldberg, Hollywood	L 4
	—Tony Navarro	KO 3
Sept.	30—Richie Lemos, Hollywood	W 6
Oct.	21—Richie Lemos, Hollywood	W 10
Nov.	8—Kui Kong Young, Los Angeles	L 10
Dec.	6—Bernie Reyes, Los Angeles	W 10
1939
Jan.	2—Small Montana, Stockton	L 10
	—Donnie Maes	L 10
	—Kent Martinez	KO 3

Mar.	14—Jackie Jurich, San Jose	KO 7
Apr.	11—Tommy Cobb, San Jose	W 10
	—Sammy LaPorte, El Centro	KO 7
June	9—Jackie Jurich, Hollywood	L 10
	—Pancho Leyvas, Yuma	L 10
Sept.	15—Lou Salica, Hollywood	L 10
Oct.	26—Horace Mann, San Jose	W 10
Dec.	—Young Canada Lee, San Jose	KO 5
Dec.	14—Elwood Romero, Sacramento	W 10
1940
Jan.	30—Little Dado, Stockton	D 10
Mar.	22—Andy Vasquez, Hollywood	KO 5
Apr.	5—Jackie Jurich, Hollywood	KO 9
Apr.	20—Panchito Villa, Mexico City	W 10
May	18—Panchito Villa, Mexico City	L 10
July	30—Jackie Jurich, San Jose	W 12
Oct.	9—Panchito Villa, Monterrey	KO 7
Nov.	22—Cleo Shans, San Diego	W 6
1941
Jan.	10—Rush Dalma, Hollywood	KO 3
Feb.	—Joe Robleto, Calexico	KO 6
Mar.	14—Lupe Cardoza, Sacramento	KO 9
Apr.	4—Carlos Chavez, Hollywood	D 10
May	1—Jesus Llanes	W 8
May	9—Carlos Chavez, Hollywood	W 10
June	6—Lou Transparenti, Hollywood	KO 7
Aug.	8—Tony Olivera, Hollywood	L 10
Nov.	7—Donny Maes, Hollywood	W 10
Nov.	21—Johnny Grady, Hollywood	W 10
1942
Jan.	2—Tony Olivera, Hollywood	W 10
Mar.	6—Little Pancho, Hollywood	KO 7
May	8—Kenny Lindsay, Hollywood	KO 6
May	30—Leonard Lopez, Tijuana	KO
July	3—Elwood Romero, Hollywood	KO 6
Aug.	7—Lou Salica, Hollywood	W 12
	(Won World Bantamweight Title)	
Sept.	25—Bobby Carroll, San Diego	KO 5
Oct.	9—Nat Corum, Portland, Ore.	W 10
Oct.	30—Nat Corum, Hollywood	KO 6
1943
Jan.	1—Kenny Lindsay, Portland, Ore.	W 10
	(Retained World Bantamweight Title)	
Jan.	27—Georgie Frietas, Oakland	KO 10
	(Retained World Bantamweight Title)	
Mar.	10—Lou Salica, Oakland	KO 11
	(Retained World Bantamweight Title)	
Apr.	2—Pedro Ramirez, Hollywood	KO 6
Apr.	16—Joe Robleto, San Diego	W 10
Apr.	28—Lupe Cardoza, Fort Worth	KO 6
	(Retained World Bantamweight Title)	
May	26—Joe Robleto, Long Beach	W 15
	(Retained World Bantamweight Title)	
June	25—Tony Olivera, Hollywood	KO 7
July	12—Joe Robleto, Seattle	KO 7
	(Retained World Bantamweight Title)	
Aug.	13—Leonard Lopez, Hollywood	W 10
Sept.	4—Fillo Gonzales, Hollywood	W 10
Oct.	1—Leonardo Lopez, Hollywood	KO 4
	(Retained World Bantamweight Title)	
Nov.	23—Benny Goldberg, Los Angeles	W 15
	(Retained World Bantamweight Title)	
1944
Mar.	14—Ernesto Aguilar, Los Angeles	W 15
	(Retained World Bantamweight Title)	
Apr.	4—Tony Olivera, Los Angeles	W 15
	(Retained World Bantamweight Title)	
May	19—Pee Wee Lewis, Hollywood	KO 9
June	9—Larry Bolvin, Boston	W 10
July	17—Willie Pep, Boston	L 10
Aug.	29—Enrique Bolanos, Los Angeles	KO 6
Sept.	12—Luis Castillo, Los Angeles	KO 4
	(Retained World Bantamweight Title)	
Sept.	30—Carlos Chavez, Hollywood	W 10
Nov.	14—Luis Castillo, Los Angeles	KO 9
	(Retained World Bantamweight Title)	
Nov.	22—Lorenzo Safora, Oakland	W 10
1945
Jan.	19—Baby Gonzales, Hollywood	W 10
Jan.	26—Bert White, San Diego	KO 7

781

Nov.	2—Little Giant, San Diego	W 10
Nov.	12—Jose Andreas, Dallas	W 10
Nov.	20—Proctor Heinhold, San Antonio	W 10

1946

Feb.	15—Eli Galindo, Hollywood	KO 4
Feb.	25—Luis Castillo, San Francisco	KO 13
	(Retained World Bantamweight Title)	
Mar.	19—Carlos Chavez, Los Angeles	D 15
Apr.	22—Horace Greeley Leftwich, San Fran.	W 10
May	26—Kenny Lindsay, Hollywood	KO 5
	(Retained World Bantamweight Title)	
June	10—Jackie Jurich, San Francisco	KO 11
	(Retained World Bantamweight Title)	
July	12—Kui Kong Young, Honolulu	KO 7
Oct.	22—Carlos Chavez, Los Angeles	L 12

1947

Jan.	6—Harold Dade, San Francisco	L 15
	(Lost World Bantamweight Title)	
Mar.	11—Harold Dade, Los Angeles	W 15
	(Regained World Bantamweight Title)	
May	30—Kui Kong Young, Honolulu	W 15
	(Retained World Bantamweight Title)	
Oct.	15—Manny Ortega, El Paso	KO by 8
Dec.	20—Tirso Del Rosario, Manila	W 15
	(Retained World Bantamweight Title)	

1948

Apr.	27—Joey Dolan, Portland, Ore.	KO 6
May	25—Henry Davis, Honolulu	W 10
July	4—Memo Valero, Mexicali	KO 8
	(Retained World Bantamweight Title)	
Sept.	28—Lauro Salas, Los Angeles	L 10
Oct.	29—Buddy Jacklich, Hollywood	KO 8
Dec.	14—Maxie Docusen, Los Angeles	L 10

1949

Jan.	1—Jose Cardenas, Mexicali	W 10
Mar.	1—Dado Marino, Honolulu	W 15
	(Retained World Bantamweight Title)	
Mar.	29—Henry Davis, Honolulu	L 10
Apr.	26—Lauro Salas, Los Angeles	KO 10
May	15—Baby Mickey, Guaymas, Sonora	KO 5
May	20—Pinky Peralta, Mexico City	KO 5
June	25—Baby Coaury, Veracruz	L 10
June	29—Beto Carvajal, Merida, Yucatan	W 10
July	16—Memo Valero, Mexico City	KO 7
July	23—Tony Vasquez, Tampico	KO 4
Aug.	29—Jimmy Cooper, Washington, D.C.	L 10
Sept.	2—Chuck Wilkerson, Chicago	Exh.
Oct.	3—Ronnie Clayton, Manchester	L 10
Oct.	26—Jackie Paterson, Glasgow	W 10
Nov.	14—Theo Medina, Paris	W 10

1950

Mar.	7—Harold Dade, Los Angeles	W 10
May	31—Vic Toweel, Johannesburg	L 15
	(Lost World Bantamweight Title)	
Nov.	10—Jackie McCoy, Hollywood	W 10
Dec.	5—Eddie Chavez, San Jose	L 10

1951

Jan.	26—Lauro Salas, Hollywood	L 10
Mar.	3—Bonnie Espinosa, Manila	KO 8
June	2—Tirso del Rosario, Manila	L 10
July	17—Jackie Graves, Los Angeles	L 10
Sept.	3—Eddie Chavez, Santa Clara	L 10

1952

(Inactive)

1953

Mar.	6—Manuel Hernandez, Mexicali	KO 6

1954

(Inactive)

1955

June	10—Manuel Hernandez, Ensenada	KO
July	22—Memo Valero, Mexicali	KO 3
Aug.	16—Papelero Sanchez, Mexicali	KO 3
Dec.	10—Enrique Esqueda, Mexico City	L 10

TB	KO	WD	WF	D	LD	LF	KO BY	ND	NC
128	49	48	0	3	27	0	1	0	0

Died, May 31, 1970, San Diego, California.

HAROLD DADE

Born Oct. 9, 1924, Chicago, Ill. Height 5 ft. 5 in. Bantamweight. Managed by Gus Wilson. Fought as amateur, 1940-1941.

1942

Dec.	18—Ceferino Robleto, Hollywood	. W 4

1943

Jan.	4—Joe Robleto, Ocean Pk., Cal.	D 6
Jan.	8—Orville Young, Hollywood	KO 4
Jan.	18—Ceferino Robleto, Ocean Pk., Cal.	D 8
Feb.	19—Chester Ellis, San Diego	W 10
Mar.	22—Victor Flores, Ocean Pk., Cal.	W 8
Apr.	22—Victor Flores, San Diego	W 10
May	11—Dave Hernandez, Los Angeles	W 10
May	14—Joey Dolan, Portland, Ore.	W 10
	—Ceferino Robleto, Los Angeles	W 4
	—Pedro Ramirez, Hollywood	L 6
	—Joe Robleto, Hollywood	W 10

1944

U. S. Marines

	—Al Gregorio, Overseas	KO 2
	—Mc. Don, Overseas	KO 1

1946

Apr.	9—Ruperto Garcia, San Jose	KO 3
Apr.	16—Billy Clark, Fresno	KO 2
Apr.	26—Jess Salazar, Hollywood	KO 3
Apr.	30—Joe Borjon, Fresno	W 8
May	7—Billy Gibson, Fresno	W 8
Sept.	9—Juan Leanos, Ocean Park	W 10
Dec.	13—Joey Dolan, Portland	W 10
	—Chivo Carvajal, San Diego	KO 7

1947

Jan.	6—Manuel Ortiz, San Francisco	W 15
	(Won Bantamweight Title)	
Feb.	12—Speedy Cabanella, Oakland	W 10
Mar.	11—Manuel Ortiz, Los Angeles	L 15
	(Lost Bantamweight Title)	
Apr.	2—Tony Olivera, Oakland	W 10
May	6—Carlos Chavez, Los Angeles	D 12
May	27—Jackie McCoy, San Jose	W 10
July	22—Carlos Chavez, Los Angeles	L 12
Aug.	26—Simon Vegara, Los Angeles	L 10
Oct.	18—Speedy Cabanella, Manila	W 10
Nov.	19—Star Navan, Manila	W 10
Dec.	23—Manny Ortega, Los Angeles	W 10

1948

Jan.	6—Bobby Jackson, Los Angeles	KO 7
Mar.	3—Lauro Salas, Sacramento	W 10
Mar.	16—Jackie McCoy, San Jose	W 10
Apr.	3—Luis Galvani, Havana	L Dis. 8
Apr.	14—Carlos Chavez, Los Angeles	L 10
June	3—Jackie Graves, Minneapolis	L 10
June	21—Charley Riley, Chicago	W 10
July	12—Charley Riley, St. Louis	D 10
Aug.	28—Luis Galvani, Havana	L 10
Sept.	28—Henry Davis, Honolulu	L 10
Oct.	29—Charley Riley, Chicago	W 8
Dec.	7—Lauro Salas, Los Angeles	W 12

1949

Jan.	18—Joey Clemo, Seattle	W 10
Feb.	16—Joe Velez, Spokane	W 10
Mar.	1—Aaron Joshua, Portland	KO 5
Apr.	14—Joey Ortega, Tacoma	W 10
May	31—Jesus Fonseca, Los Angeles	W 10
July	21—Corky Gonzales, Denver	L 10
Sept.	2—Sandy Saddler, Chicago	L 10
Sept.	30—Frank Flannery, Melbourne	W 12
Oct.	17—Elley Bennett, Sydney	W 12
Nov.	22—Corky Gonzales, St. Paul	L 10
Dec.	12—Willie Pep, St. Louis	L 10

1950

Jan.	2—Keith Nuttall, Salt Lake City	L 10
Jan.	18—Baby Leroy, Sacramento	D 10
Jan.	31—Keith Nuttall, Salt Lake City	L 10
Feb.	14—Chico Rosa, San Jose	D 10
Mar.	7—Manuel Ortiz, Los Angeles	L 10
Apr.	4—Eddie Chavez, San Jose	KO by 5
Apr.	24—Eddie Chavez, San Francisco	L 10
July	14—Rudy Garcia, Hollywood	KO by 11
Sept.	—Kid Chocolate, Panama	W 10
Oct.	4—Rocky McKay, Panama	L 10
Dec.	3—Rocky McKay, Balboa	L 10

1951

Jan.	30—Percy Bassett, Phila.	KO by 8
Mar.	6—Felix Ramirez, San Jose	L 10
Apr.	22—Memo Valero, Mex. City	L Dis.
June	1—Fabala Chavez, Hollywood	L 10
June	28—Diego Sosa, Havana	L 10

1952

Feb.	28—Bobby Woods, Spokane	W 10
June	22—Lauro Salas, Monterrey	KO by 3
Nov.	27—Bobby Woods, Vancouver	L 10

Apr. 9—Ernie Kemick, Calgary ....L 10
1955
Mar. 29—Paul Jorgensen, Houston—Ko by 4

TB	KO	WD	WF	D	LD	LF	KOBY	ND	NC
77	9	32	0	6	23	2	5	0	0

Died in Los Angeles, Calif. on July 17, 1962.

VIC TOWEEL

Born, January 12, 1929; Benoni, South Africa. As an amateur, engaged in 190 bouts, losing only two decisions. Won 160 by knockouts.

1949
Jan. 21—Johannes Landman, Johannesburg ....KO 2
Feb. 26—Herbie Andre, Johannesburg..KO 2
Mar. 19—Kalla Persson, Germiston .....KO 1
Mar. 26—Jimmy Webster, Johannesburg ....WF 3
(South African bantam title)
May 12—Jackie Johnson, Jo'burg ......KO 1
June 8—Johnny Holt, Durban ....W 10
June 27—Jackie Johnston, Springs .....KO 4
June 30—Plassie Fouri, Germiston .....KO 1
Aug. 6—Tony Lombard, Johannesburg . W 12
(South African feather title)
Sept. 30—Tony Lombard, Johannesburg . W 12
(South African feather title)
Nov. 12—Stan Rowan, Johannesburg .... W 15
(British Empire bantam title)
Dec. 17—Jackie Paterson, Johannesburg . W 10
1950
Apr. 8—Fernando Gagnon, Jo'burg .... W 15
(British Empire bantam title)
May 31—Manuel Ortiz, Johannesburg ... W 15
(World bantamweight title)
Oct. 21—Alvaro Nuvoloni, Jo'burg...... W 10
Nov. 13—Bunty Doran, Durban ....KO 9
Dec. 2—Danny O'Sullivan, Jo'burg....KO 10
(World title)
1951
June 16—Fanie van Graan, Johan'burg ..KO 2
(South African featherweight title)
June 30—Jim Kenny, Johannesburg ....KO 7
Sept. 1—Bobby Boland, Johannesburg . KO 1
Nov. 2—Georges Mousse, Pt. Elizabeth . W 10
Nov. 17—Luis Romero, Johannesburg ... W 15
(World Title)
1952
Jan. 26—Peter Keenan, Johannesburg ... W 15
(World bantamweight title)
Mar. 24—Tony Lombard, Cape Town ..KO 8
(South African featherweight title)
May 31—Thoe Medina, Johannesburg ..KO 7
July 19—Georges Mousse, Salisbury ..... D 10
Aug. 19—Georges Mousse, Johannesburg W 10
Nov. 15—Jimmy Carruthers, Johannesburg ....KO by 1
(Lost World Bantamweight Title)
1953
Mar. 21—Jimmy Carruthers, Johannesburg ....KO by 10
(For World Bantamweight Title)
Dec. 11—Ronnie Clayton, Johannesburg W 10
1954
July 26—Carmelo Costa, Brooklyn.......L 10
Nov. 6—Harry Walker, Johannesburg ..KO 8

TB	KO	WD	WF	D	LD	LF	KOBY	ND	NC
32	14	13	1	1	1	0	2	0	0

JIMMY CARRUTHERS

Born, Paddington, N.S.W., Australia, July 5, 1929. Managed by Dr. John McGirr and Bill McConnell.

Was a member of Australian Olympic team in 1948.

1950
Aug. 15—Ted Fitzgerald, Leichhardt ...KO 3
Oct. 13—Ron Wilson, Melbourne .....KO 5
Oct. 19—Fred Kay, Leichhardt ,,,,,,,KO 12
Nov. 20—Keith Francis, Sydney ....KO 10
Dec. 12—Jimmy McFadden, Sydney ...KO 6

1951
Jan. 22—Bluey Wilkins, Sydney .... W 12
Mar. 5—Bob Scrivano, Sydney ....KO 1
Apr. 2—Billy Herbert, Sydney ....KO 10
May 14—Elley Bennett, Sydney .... W 15
(Australian bantam title)
Aug. 27—Enrique Morales, Sydney .....KO 7
Nov. 26—Luis Castillo, Sydney ....W 12
1952
Mar. 13—Taffy Hancock, Leichardt ....KO 7
Apr. 7—Ray Coleman, Sydney .... W 12
May 12—Johnny O'Brien, Sydney ......W 12
Nov. 15—Vic Toweel, Johannesburg ....KO 1
(World bantam title)
1953
Mar. 21—Vic Toweel, Johannesburg ....KO 10
(Title Bout)
Nov. 13—Henry (Pappy) Gault, Sydney .. W 15
(Title Bout)
1954
Mar. 29—Bobby Sinn, Sydney ....W 12
May 2—Chamrern Songkitrat, Bangkok...................... W 12
(World Bantamweight Title Bout)
Carruthers announced his retirement from boxing on May 16 and opened a pub. Also refereed.
1961
(Returned to the ring after an absence of 7 years.)
Sept. 11—Aldo Pravisani, Sydney ....L 12
Nov. 20—Wally Taylor, Sydney ....L 12
Dec. 15—Don Johnson, Melbourne .. KO by 5
1962
Mar. 10—Louis Magnifico, Adelaide ....KO 2
Mar. 29—Johnny Jarrett, Woodville ....KO 2
June 18—Jimmy Cassidy, Wellington ....LF 7

TB	KO	WD	WF	D	LD	LF	KOBY	ND	NC
25	13	8	0	0	2	1	1	0	0

ROBERT COHEN

Born, Bone, Algeria, Nov. 15, 1930. Height, 5 feet, 3½ ins. Managed by Gaston Charles Raymond.

1951
Sept. 12—Gauche, Paris ....KO 2
Sept. 20—Francis Pondocchi, Paris ...... W 6
Sept. 26—E. Cordillot, Paris............. W 6
Oct. 11—Henri Pageot, Paris ....KO 5
Oct. 17—Georges Drouart, Paris ....KO 5
Nov. 4—Yansonne, Metz ....KO 6
Dec. 2—R. Meunier, Paris ....L 8
Dec. 16—R. Martin, Paris ....KO 6
Dec. 29—L. Gougelin, Paris .... W 8
1952
Jan. 5—Edmond Moletto, Paris .... W 8
Jan. 19—Georges Lafage, Paris .... W 6
Feb. 3—Jean Binet, Paris ....W 10
Feb. 25—R. Lefeuvre, Paris .... W 8
Mar. 17—F. Vanderdonck, Paris ....KO 4
Apr. 6—Robert Garcia, Oran .... W 10
May 15—Robert Meunier, Paris ....KO 8
May 29—Andre Jasse, Paris ....KO 9
June 30—Tino Cardinale, Paris .... W 8
Sept. 18—Roland Gibert, Paris ....KO 1
Oct. 2—Dante Bini, Paris .... W 10
Oct. 20—Thoe Medina, Paris .... W 10
Nov. 17—Andre Valignat, Paris .... W 10
Dec. 19—Marcel Mathieu, Paris ....KO 7
1953
Jan. 19—Maurice Sandeyron, Paris .....KO 9
Feb. 23—Jean Sneyers, Paris ....W 10
Mar. 19—Gaetano Annalaro, Paris ...... W 10
Mar. 28—Jean Sneyers, Brussels .... D 10
Apr. 15—Pappy Gault, Paris .... W 10
May 30—Gaetano Annaloro, Marseilles .. W 10
Sept. 25—Teddy Peckham, Manchester .KO 6
Oct. 17—Dante Bini, Casablanca .... W 10
Nov. 6—Maurice Sandeyron, Paris ..... W 15
(French bantam title)
Dec. 14—Jake Tuli, Manchester .... W 10
1954
Feb. 27—John Kelly, Belfast ....KO 3
(European bantam title)
Mar. 7—Relinquished French bantam title.
Apr. 7—Eddie Carson, Glasgow .... W 10
Apr. 30—Mannie Francis, Manchester ... W 10
May 15—Mario D'Agata, Tunis .... W 10

Sept. 19—Chamrern Songkitrat, Bangkok W 15
   (vacant world bantam title)
Dec. 20—Roy Ankrah, Paris .... KO 4
1955
Sept. 3—Willie Toweel, Johannesburg ... D 15
   (World bantam title)
Dec. 10—Cherif Hamia, Paris .... KO by 10
1956
June 29—Mario D'Agata, Rome .... KO by 5
   (World bantamweight title)
1959
July 13—Peter Lock, Ndola,
   N. Rhodesia .... L 10

TB	KO	WD	WF	D	LD	LF	KOBY	ND	NC
43	14	22	0	3	2	0	2	0	0

RAUL (RATON) MACIAS
Born, July 28, 1934, Mexico City, Mexico.
Height, 5 feet, 3½ ins. Managed by Luis Andrade
and George Parnassus.
   Lost to G. Garbuzov (U.S.S.R.) in second
series, in bantamweight division at 1952
Olympics.
1953
Apr. 15—Manuel Armenteros, Mexico
   City .... W 10
May 13—Trini Ruiz, Mexico City .... W 10
Aug. 1—Zurdo Galvan, Mexico City .... W 12
Sept. 12—Genaro Serafin, Mexico City ... W 10
Oct. 17—Beto Couary, Mexico City ..... W 12
   (Mexican Bantamweight Title)
Nov. 21—Alberto Reyes, Mexico City ..KO 3
1954
Jan. 16—Alberto Reyes, Mexico City ... W 10
Mar. 13—Billy Peacock, Mexico City ...KO 7
Apr. 10—Fili Nava, Mexico City .... W 12
   (Mexican Bantamweight Title)
May 22—Fili Nava, Mexico City .... W 10
Sept. 26—Nate Brooks, Mexico City ..... W 12
   (North American Bantamweight Title)
1955
Mar. 9—Chamrern Songkitrat, San
   Francisco .... KO 11
   (Won N.B.A. Bantamweight Title)
Apr. 10—Memo Sanchez, Mexicali ..... KO 6
May 12—Baby Moe Mario, San Antonio KO 5
June 15—Billy Peacock, Los Ang. ... KO by 3
Oct. 17—Cecil Schoonmaker, Corpus
   Christi .... W 10
Nov. 21—Pedro Soto, Orizaba .... KO 6
Dec. 11—Babe Ruiz, Acapulco .... KO 6
1956
Jan. 15—Lucio Torres, Vera Cruz ...... KO 6
Jan. 29—Joe Chamaco, Irapauto ...... KO 4
Mar. 25—Leo Espinosa, Mexico City ...KO 10
   (N. B. A. Bantamweight Title)
Apr. 21—Mike Hernandez, Merida ..... KO 6
May 26—Bombom Kiriz, Monterrey ...KO 3
June 30—Tanny Campo, Mexico City .... W 10
Sept. 5—Larry Bataan, Hollywood ...KO 6
Oct. 27—Chango Ceballos, Hermosillo .KO 4
Nov. 3—Ramon Young, Obregon ..... KO 2
Nov. 13—Johnny (Ace) Hand, El Paso .. KO 1
Nov. 21—Gaetano Annaloro, San
   Antonio .... W 10
1957
Feb. 10—Juan Cardenas, Mexico City ..KO 6
June 15—Dommy Urusa, San Francisco .KO 11
   (N. B. A. Bantamweight Title)
Sept. 7—Panchito Gonzalez, Juarez ....KO 5
Nov. 6—Alphonse Halimi, Los Angeles ..L 15
   (World Bantamweight Title)
1958
Nov. 10—Kid Irapuato, Tijuana .... W 10
1959
Jan. 25—Luis Trejo, Leon .... KO 8
Feb. 8—Carmen Iacobucci, Mexicali ..KO 2
Feb. 28—Ernesto Parra, Mexico City .... W 10
1962
Oct. 13—Chocolate Zambrano,
   Guadalajara .... KO 5
   (Special bout on Benefit show)

TB	KO	WD	WF	D	LD	LF	KOBY	ND	NC
38	22	14	0	0	1	0	1	0	0

MARIO D'AGATA
Born, Arezzo, Italy, May 29, 1926.

784

Managed by Libero Cecchi.
   In five years of amateur competition,
engaged in 110 bouts.
1950
Oct. 14—Salardi, Siena .... W 6
Oct. 28—Marabitti, Arezzo .... W 6
Nov. 4—Marabitti, Rome .... W 8
Dec. 16—Garutti, Montevarchi .... KO 4
1951
Jan. 12—Cesarini, S. Giovanni .... KO 5
Jan. 31—Giovanni Capobianchi, Firenze W 8
Feb. 28—Arturo Peratici, Arezzo .... W 8
May 2—Benito Fattori, Arezzo .... W 8
May 31—Benvenuto Cardinale, Firenze .. W 8
June 22—Arturo Paoletti, Arezzo ..... WF 7
Aug. 2—Kid Arcelli, Firenze .... L 10
Oct. 2—D'Augusta, Catania .... D 8
Nov. 30—Luigi Fasulo, Grosseto ....KO 3
Dec. 28—Kid Arcelli, Siena .... L 10
1952
Feb. 20—Giuliano Catini, Firenze ...... KO 2
May 17—Denti, Firenze .... LF 5
June 11—Enzo Ganadu, Milan .... KO 3
Nov. 8—Stiaccini, Milan .... W 6
Nov. 26—Gaetano Annaloro, Milan ....WF 7
Dec. 26—D'Augusta, Milan .... W 10
1953
Jan. 15—Jacques Louni, Aprezzo .... W 10
Mar. 31—Edmond Moletto, Arezzo ..... W 10
July 5—Arthur Emboule, Arezzo ..... W 8
Sept. 26—Gianni Zuddas, Arezzo ....WF 9
   (Italian bantamweight title)
Oct. 30—Pierre Gress-Gyde, Geneva ....KO 6
Nov. 15—Andre Valignat, Paris .... D 10
1954
Jan. 23—Luigi Fasulo, Naples .... KO 4
   (Italian bantam title)
Apr. 10—Gianni Zuddas, Milan .... W 12
   (Italian bantam title)
Apr. 30—Kid Andre, Milan .... KO 10
May 15—Robert Cohen, Tunis .... L 10
June 12—Emile Chemama, Tunis .... W 10
July 31—Andre Valignat, Arezzo .... W 10
Oct. 1—Alex Bollaert, Milan .... KO 5
Nov. 19—Bobby Sinn, Melbourne ..... W 12
Dec. 10—Billy Peacock, Melbourne ..... W 12
Dec. —Italian title forfeited because of failure
   to defend.
1955
May 25—Arthur Emboule, Turin ....KO 8
June 11—Ullah Fakjh, Leghorn .... KO 4
June 28—Robert Meunier, Rome .... W 10
July 21—Henri Schmid, Prato .... W 10
July 30—Juan Crespi, Bari .... KO 5
Aug. 9—Mahmoud Farid, Naples ..... KO 4
Aug. 18—Jose Martinez, Messina ...... KO 8
Sept. 15—Pedro Paris, Bologna .... KO 3
Oct. 15—Jean Kidy, Milan .... KO 5
Oct. 29—Andre Valignat, Milan .... WF 5
   (Vacant European bantam title)
1956
Jan. 21—Little Cezar, Manila .... W 10
Mar. 21—Jesus Rubio, Ravenna .... W 10
May 18—Jesus Rubio, Milan .... W 10
June 29—Robert Cohen, Rome .... KO 6
   (Won World Bantamweight Title)
Oct. 27—Juan Cardenas, Milan .... W 10
Dec. 8—Robert Tartari, Geneva .... D 10
1957
Apr. 1—Alphonse Halimi, Paris .... L 15
   (Lost World Bantamweight Title)
June 29—Roland Roy, Genoa .... KO 7
Oct. 27—Federico Scarponi, Cagliari ...KO 8
   (For Vacant European Bantamweight Title)
Dec. 10—Jean Renard, Bergamo .... KO 7
Dec. 26—Roger Cappato, Milan .... W 10
1958
Feb. 13—Michel Lamora, Naples ....KO 4
Sept. 13—Ben Ali, Cagliari .... W 10
Oct. 12—Piero Rollo, Cagliari .... L 15
   (European Bantamweight Title)
1959
Feb. 5—Joe Becerra, Los Angeles.....KO by 11
Sept. 15—Freddie Gilroy, London .... L 10
1960
June 9—Jackie Brown, Glasgow .... L 10
1961
Oct. 24—Mohamed ben Leyesi, Rome ..KO 6
Nov. 24—Francois Carreno, Rome ...... W 8
1962
Jan. 19—Ugo Milan, Rome .... KO 6
Mar. 27—Andre Gasperini, Milan .... W 8
July 19—Federico Scarponi, Rome ..... L 12
   (For Vacant European Bantamweight Title)

Aug.   1—announced retirement.

TB	KO	WD	WF	D	LD	LF	KOBY	ND	NC
67	23	27	4	3	8	1		1	0	0

ALPHONSE HALIMI
French-Algerian Bantamweight
Born, Constantine, February 18, 1932.
As an amateur engaged in 189 bouts. Held French bantam title in 1953, 1954 and 1955; also won All-Mediterranean championship in 1955.

1955
Sept. 26—Georges Lafage, Paris .... KO 1
Oct.   24—Felix Vanderdonckt, Tunis ... KO 1
Nov.   5—Charles Vandeville, Paris .... KO 1
Nov.   17—Jose Luis Martinez, Paris .... KO 1
Nov.   26—Rino Stiaccini, Milan .... KO 2
Dec.   10—Stan Sobolak, Paris .... KO 1
Dec.   19—Jose Crespo, Tunis .... KO 6
Dec.   26—Letterio Petilli, Milan .... W 10
1956
Jan.   26—Antonio Diaz, Paris .... KO 6
Feb.   26—Pierre Gress-Gyde, Paris ...... KO 2
Mar.   16—Billy Peacock, Paris .... W 10
June   2—Kim Navarro, Tunis .... KO 2
Oct.   8—Robert Meunier, Paris .... W 10
Oct.   22—Tanny Campo, Paris .... W 10
Dec.   13—Andre Younsi, Paris .... WF 9
Dec.   27—Andre Jasse, Paris .... KO 6
1957
Jan.   21—Alfred Schweer, Paris .... W 10
Feb.   14—Alex Bollaert, Paris .... W 10
Apr.   1—Mario D'Agata, Paris .... W 15
          (Won World Bantamweight Title)
June   4—Jimmy Carson, London .... KO by 9
Sept. 16—Chic Brogan, Paris .... KO 2
Nov.   6—Raton Macias, Los Angeles .... W 15
          (World Bantamweight Title)
Dec.   8—Tanny Campo, Marseilles ..... W 10
1958
Oct.   13—Dante Bini, Paris .... KO 5
Nov.   17—Peter Keenan, Paris .... W 10
1959
Feb.   9—Pierre Cossemyns, Paris ...... KO 3
Mar.   12—Jose Luis Martinez, Rome ..... W 10
May   11—Al Asuncion, Paris .... KO 5
July   8—Joe Becerra, Los Angeles .. KO by 8
          (Lost World Bantamweight Title)
1960
Feb.   4—Joe Becerra, Los Angeles .. KO by 9
          (For World Bantamweight Title)
Apr.   11—Louis Poncy, Paris .... W 10
July   2—Juan Cardenas, Algiers ...... KO 3
Sept. 10—Jimmy Carson, Algiers .... KO 9
Oct.   14—Robert Meunier, Paris .... W 10
Oct.   25—Freddie Gilroy, London .... W 15
          (Won European version of world Bantamweight Title)
1961
Feb.   4—Jean Renard, Burssels .... W 10
Mar.   5—Jean Renard, Tunis .... KO 4
Apr.   29—Michel Lamora, Oran .... KO 5
May   30—Johnny Caldwell, London ..... L 15
          (Lost European version of world title)
Oct.   31—Johnny Caldwell, London ..... L 15
          (European Version title bout)
Dec.   2—Joe Buck, Tunis .... KO 7
1962
May   12—Jean dos Santos, Tunis .... W 10
June   26—Piero Rollo, Tel Aviv .... W 15
          (Re-won European Bantamweight Title)
Oct.   20—Piero Rollo, Cagliari .... L 15
          (Lost European Bantamweight Title)
Dec.   8—Jose Luis Martinez, Paris ..... W 10
1963
Jan.   5—Rafael Fernandez, Tours ..... W 10
Feb.   1—Michel Lemora, Geneva ...... D 10
1964
Jan.   31—Klaus Jaegar, Paris .... KO 1
Feb.   24—Ramon Casal, Paris .... L 10
Nov.   27—Victor Cano, Bogota .... L 10

TB	KO	WD	WF	D	LD	LF	KOBY	ND	NC
50	21	19	1	1	5	0		3	0	0

JOE BECERRA
(Jose Becerra Covarrubias)
Born, April 15, 1936. Guadalajara, Jalisco,

Mexico. Height, 5 ft. 5 inches.
1953
Aug.   30—Ray Gomez, Guadalajara .... KO 4
Sept. 6—M. Estrada, Atemajac .... KO 5
Oct.   3—R. Gonzalez, Guadalajara ..... W 4
Oct.   24—Raul Salazar, Atemajac .... W 6
1954
Mar.   13—J. Plascencia, Guadalajara ..... W 4
Apr.   24—Marcelino Garcia, Guadalajara . W 4
May   2—R. Espinosa, Guadalajara ..... W 6
May   15—Kid Pompeyo, Guadalajara ... KO 4
May   23—Al Escalante, Guadalajara ..... W 6
June   5—Joe Mariscal, Guadalajara .... KO 4
June   12—Raul Perez, Guadalajara ...... KO 2
July   3—Kid Popeye, Guadalajara ..... KO 4
July   19—Al Escalante, Guadalajara ..... W 6
Aug.   2—Kid Pichilingo, Guadalajara .. KO 6
Aug.   23—Jose Luis Navarro,
          Guadalajara .... W 6
Sept. 6—Mario Leon, Guadalajara ..... KO 2
Sept. 12—J. Plascencia, Guadalajara ..... W 6
Sept. 20—Tomas Cervantes,
          Guadalajara .... KO 3
Oct.   3—L. Ibarra, Guadalajara .... L 6
Oct.   18—Jose Luis Navarro,
          Guadalajara .... W 6
Dec.   4—Kid Senorito, Guadalajara .... KO 4
1955
Feb.   12—M. Gonzalez, Guadalajara .... W 8
Mar.   5—Chucho Guerrero,
          Guadalajara .... KO 4
May   28—Joe Chamaco, Guadalajara .... KO 5
June   11—Danny Bedolla, Morelia ...... D 10
June   25—Chava Santiago, Guadalajara .. KO 6
July   2—Fili Presa, Leon .... KO 4
July   16—Firpito Gaytan, Guadalajara ... W 10
Oct.   4—Pepe Villa, Pala .... KO 7
Oct.   8—Antonio Guevara, Leon ...... KO 10
Oct.   15—R. Garcia, Guadalajara .... W 10
1956
Feb.   11—Antonio Guevara, Leon ...... KO 10
Feb.   18—C. Martinez, Guadalajara .... L 10
Mar.   22—German Ohm, Gomez Pacaco KO 6
May   11—Jorge Valverde,
          Gomez Palacio .... KO 7
May   31—Rogelio Sancedo,
          Gomez Palacio .... W 10
June   21—Mario Ruiz, Gomez Palacio .... W 10
Aug.   9—Jorge Gabino, Gomez Palacio .KO 5
Sept. 6—Memo Sanchez, Gomez Palacio W 10
Oct.   18—German Ohm, Gomez Palacio ...L 10
Nov.   7—Chuy Guerrereo, Torreon ..... W 10
1957
Jan.   1—Jorge Herrera, Torreon .... KO 7
Jan.   12—Manuel Armenteros,
          Monterrey .... W 10
Feb.   9—Joe Medel, Monterrey .... W 10
Mar.   2—Joe Medel, Mexico City .... W 10
Apr.   2—Juan Perez, Juarez .... KO 4
Apr.   27—Chuy Rodriguez, Mexico City .. W 10
May   25—Jose Luis Mora, Mexico City ... W 10
June   15—Johnny Ortega, San Francisco KO 4
July   1—Kid Irapuato, Tijuano .... KO 8
Aug.   17—Raul Leanos, Monterrey .... D 10
Oct.   12—Ramon Calatayud, Mexico City W 10
Nov.   6—Dwight Hawkins, Los Ang. KO by 4
1958
Jan.   25—Jorge Herrera .... KO 4
Feb.   8—Joe Medel, Mexico City ...... W 10
Mar.   8—Dwight Hawkins, Guadalajara .KO 9
Mar.   31—Hector Agundez, Tapachula ... W 10
Apr.   12—Miguel Lazu, Mexico City .... KO 7
May   25—Charlie De Bow, Mexico City .KO 2
June   28—Gaetano Annaloro,
          Guadalajara .... KO 10
July   21—Joey Agustin, Tijuana .... KO 5
Aug.   14—Willie Parker, Los Angeles ..... KO 2
Sept. 5—Little Cezar, Los Angeles ..... KO 4
Oct.   25—Jose Luis Mara, Guadalajara .. KO 3
Nov.   30—Ross Padilla, Mexicali .... KO 1
1959
Feb.   5—Mario D'Agata, Los Angeles .. KO 10
Mar.   19—Chuy Rodriguez, Guadalajara .KO 5
Apr.   20—Billy Peacock, Tijuana .... KO 1
July   8—Alphonse Halimi, Los Angeles KO 8
          (Won World Bantamweight Title)
Oct.   24—Walt Ingram, Guadalajara ..... KO 9
          Ingram died two days after bout.
Dec.   12—Frankie Duran, Nogales .... W 10
1960
Feb.   4—Alphonse Halimi, Los Angeles KO 9
          (Retained Bantamweight Title)
Mar.   15—Ward Yee, San Antonio ...... W 10

785

Apr. 10—Pimi Barajas, Terreon ....KO 7
May   23—Kenji Yonekura, Tokyo ....W 15
　　　　(Retained Bantamweight Title)
Aug. 12—Chuy Rodriguez, Tampico ....KO 4
Aug. 30—Eloy Sanchez, Juarez .....KO by 8
　　　　(Announced retirement)
1962
Oct. 13—Alberto Martinez,
　　　　Guadalajara ....W 6
　　　　(Special bout on benefit show)

TB	KO	WD	WF	D	LD	LF	KOBY	ND	NC
78	42	29	0	2	3	0	2	0	0

EDER JOFRE
(Record Under Featherweight Champions)

MASAHIKO (FIGHTING) HARADA
Born, April 5, 1943, Setagaya Ward, Tokyo, Japan. Weight, 112-126 lbs. Height, 5 ft. 4 in. Managed by Takeshi Sasazaki.

1960
Feb. 21—Isami Masui, Tokyo ....KO 4
Mar. 2—Mitsuo Motohashi, Tokyo ....W 4
Mar. 27—Goro Iwamoto, Tokyo ....KO 3
Apr. 4—Yuichi Noguchi, Tokyo ....W 4
Apr. 13—Ken Morita, Tokyo ....W 4
June 10—Masatake Ogura, Tokyo ....KO 3
June 26—Ken Morita, Tokyo ....KO 1
July 18—Masaru Kodangi, Tokyo ....KO 3
Sept. 1—Yukio Suzuki, Tokyo ....W 4
Oct. 28—Sadayoshi Yoshida, Tokyo ....KO 4
Nov. 7—Hachiro Arai, Tokyo ....W 4
Dec. 11—Yoshinori Hikita, Tokyo ....KO 3
Dec. 24—Hiroyuki Ebihara, Tokyo ....W 6
1961
Jan. 5—Takeshi Nakamura, Tokyo ....W 6
Jan. 28—Riichi Tanaka, Tokyo ....W 6
Mar. 5—Yasuo Fujita, Tokyo ....W 6
Apr. 3—Sadao Yaoita, Tokyo ....Exh. 4
May   1—Ray Perez, Tokyo ....W 10
June 19—Shigeru Ito, Tokyo ....W 10
July 31—Akio Maki, Tokyo ....KO 8
Sept. 9—Sombang Banbung, Tokyo ....KO 5
Oct. 9—Akio Maki, Osaka ....W 10
Dec. 10—Ryoji Shiratori, Nagoya ....KO 6
1962
Jan. 12—Kozo Nagata, Tokyo ....W 10
Mar. 18—Tadao Kawamura, Tokyo ....W 10
May   4—Baby Espinosa, Tokyo ....W 10
June 15—Edmundo Esparza, Tokyo ....L 10
July 23—Little Rufe, Tokyo ....W 10
Aug. 23—Leo Espinosa, Tokyo ....Exh. 6
Oct. 10—Pone Kingpetch, Tokyo ....KO 11
　　　　(Won World Flyweight Title)
Nov. 18—Kenichi Iida, Tokyo ....Exh. 3
1963
Jan. 12—Pone Kingpetch, Bangkok ....L 15
　　　　(Lost World Flyweight Title)
Mar. 21—Tetsuro Kawai, Tokyo ....W 10
May   5—Jose Cejuda, Okinawa ....KO 1
June 19—Thira Loedjalengabo, Nagoya .....KO 6
Aug. 7—Dommy Balajada, Tokyo ....W 10
Sept. 26—Joe Medel, Tokyo ....KO by 6
Nov. 25—Emile de Leon, Tokyo ....W 10
Aug. 25—Goro Tsutsumi, Tokyo ....Exh. 4
Sept. 26—Joe Medel, Tokyo ....KO by 6
Nov. 4—Taizo Kakizawa, Tokyo ....Exh. 3
Nov. 25—Emile de Leon, Tokyo ....W 10
1964
Jan. 2—Avelino Estrada, Tokyo ....KO 5
Feb. 14—Somsak Laemphafa, Osaka ....KO 2
July 6—Ray Asis, Los Angeles ....W 10
Sept. 17—Oscar Reyes, Tokyo ....W 10
Oct. 29—Katsutoshi Aoki, Tokyo ....KO 3
1965
Jan. 4—Dommy Froilan, Tokyo ....KO 6

Mar. 4—Toru Nakamura, Tokyo ..... Exh. KO 2
Apr. 4—Katsuro Takahashi, Tokyo ...... Exh. 2
Apr. 4—Shozo Saijyo, Tokyo .... Exh. 2
May   17—Eder Jofre, Nagoya .... W 15
　　　　(Won World Bantamweight Title)
July 11—Kazutoshi Nakayama, Tokyo .... Exh. 4
July 28—Katsuo Saito, Tokyo .... W 12
Nov. 30—Alan Mudkin, Tokyo .... W 15
　　　　(Retained World Bantamweight Title)
1966
Feb. 15—Soo-Kang Soo, Nagoya .... W 12
Mar. 11—Kazuo Fujiwara, Tokyo .... Exh. 4
Apr. 10—Nobuo Chiba, Tokyo .... Exh. 4
June 1—Eder Jofre, Tokyo .... W 15
　　　　(Retained World Bantamweight Title)
Aug. 1—Dio Espinosa, Sapporo .... W 10
Oct. 25—Antonio Herrera, Osaka .... W 12
1967
Jan. 3—Joe Medel, Nagoya .... W 15
　　　　(Retained World Bantamweight Title)
Apr. 4—Tiny Palacio, Fukuoka City ...... W 12
July 4—Bernardo Caraballo, Tokyo .... W 15
　　　　(Retained World Bantamweight Title)
Sept. 25—Hajime Taroura, Osaka .... KO 2
Nov. 28—Soo-Bok Kwon, Okayama City .... KO 8
1968
Feb. 26—Lionel Rose, Tokyo .... L 15
　　　　(Lost World Bantamweight Title)
June 5—Dwight Hawkins, Tokyo .... W 10
Sept. 4—Nobuo Chiba, Sano .... KO 7
Dec. 4—Roy Amolong, Tokyo .... KO 2
1969
Apr. 2—Alton Colter, Tokyo .... L 10
June 5—Vil Tumulak, Nagoya .... W 10
July 28—Johnny Famechon, Sydney .... L 15
　　　　(For World Featherweight Title)
Oct. 1—Pat Gonzales, Fukui City .... KO 8
1970
Jan. 6—Johnny Famechon, Tokyo ..... KO by 14
　　　　(For World Featherweight Title)

TB	KO	WD	WF	D	LD	LF	KO BY	ND	NC
62	22	33	0	0	5	0	2	0	0

LIONEL ROSE
Born, June 21, 1948, Drouin, Australia. Weight, 118-130 lbs.

1964
Sept. 9—Mario Magriss, Waragul .... W 8
Oct. 9—Mario Magriss, Melbourne .... W 8
Nov. 6—Joe Oliveri, Melbourne .... KO 2
1965
Apr. 2—Jackie Bruce, Melbourne .... KO 1
June 25—Singtong Por Tor, Melbourne ...... W 12
July 23—Singtong Por Tor, Melbourne ...... L 6
July 27—Teddy Rainbow, Kogarah .... W 12
Aug. 20—Bobby Wells, Melbourne .... KO 8
Oct. 1—Billy Brown, Melbourne .... KO 10
Oct. 14—Laurie Ny, Christchurch .... W 10
Nov. 5—Billy Brown, Melbourne .... W 12
Dec. 2—Arthur Clark, Sydney .... W 8
1966
Feb. 18—Ray Perez, Melbourne .... W 12
Apr. 4—Ray Perez, Sydney .... L 10
May   13—Jerry Stokes, Melbourne .... W 12
June 17—Flash Dum Dum, Melbourne ..... W 12
July 8—Ray Perez, Melbourne .... W 12
Aug. 26—Noel Kunde, Melbourne .... W 12
Oct. 14—Jackie Burke, Melbourne .... KO 4
Oct. 28—Noel Kunde, Melbourne .... W 15
　　　　(Won Australian Bantamweight Title)
Nov. 18—Felipe Gonzalez, Melbourne ...... W 10
1967
Mar. 17—Nevio Carbi, Melbourne .... W 10
May   11—Akihide Tamoake, Melbourne .... KO 6
June 8—Rudy Corona, Melbourne .... W 10
July 28—Tiny Palacio, Melbourne .... W 10
Sept. 1—Ronnie Jones, Melbourne .... W 10
Oct. 13—Kamara Diop, Melbourne .... KO 3

Nov. 20—Garry Garber, Sydney .... W 10
Dec. 11—Rocky Gattellari, Sydney .... KO 13
      (Retained Australian Bantamweight Title)

1968

Feb. 26—Fighting Harada, Tokyo .... W 15
      (Won World Bantamweight Title)
Apr. 26—Tommasco Galli, Melbourne .... W 10
July   2—Takao Sakurai, Tokyo .... W 15
      (Retained World Bantamweight Title)
Aug. 28—Joe Medel, Inglewood .... W 10
Dec.   6—Chucho Castillo, Inglewood .... W 15
      (Retained World Bantamweight Title)

1969

Mar.   8—Alan Rudkin, Kooyong .... W 15
      (Retained World Bantamweight Title)
June 10—Ernie Cruz, Honolulu .... W 10
Aug. 22—Ruben Olivares, Inglewood .... KO by 5
      (Lost World Bantamweight Title)
Nov.   1—Vicente Garcia, Melbourne .... KO 5
Dec.   7—Fernando Sotelo, Sydney ..... KO by 7

1970

Mar.   7—Don Johnson, Melbourne .... W 10
May 16—Raul Cruz, Inglewood .... KO by 4
July 14—Fred Wicks, Sydney .... W 10
Aug.   4—Richard Borias, Melbourne .... KO 3
Oct. 10—Ishimatsu Suzuki, Melbourne ..... W 10

1971

Feb. 12—Jeff White, Brisbane .... L 15
      (For Australian Lightweight Title)
May   4—Tanny Cuaresma, Nunawingding KO 1
May 30—Yoshiaki Numata, Hiroshima ...... L 15
      (For WBC Junior Lightweight Title)

1972-1974
(Inactive)

1975

July   1—Shoji Uchida, Kuala Lumpur ...... W 10
Aug. 29—Blakeney Matthews, Melbourne .... L 10
Oct.   8—Billy Moeller, Marrickville .... L 10
Nov. 13—Giuseppe Agate, Melbourne ...... KO 3

1976

Aug. 30—Rafael Limon, Inglewood ...... KO by 3
Dec. 18—Maurice Apeang, Noumea ..... KO by 2

TB	KO	WD	WF	D	LD	LF	KO BY	ND	NC
53	12	30	0	0	6	0	5	0	0

RUBEN OLIVARES
(Record Under Featherweight Champions)

JESUS (CHUCHO) CASTILLO
Born, June 17, 1944, Mexico. Weight, 118 lbs.

1962

Apr. 26—Carlos Navarrete .... L 6
Aug. 10—Arnulfo Daza, Oaxaca .... W 8
Oct. 20—Zurdo Suarez, Oaxaca .... W 10

1963

Mar.   2—Pichon Contreras, Oaxaca .... KO 10
June 12—Eduardo Torres, Mexico City ...... W 6
Sept.   2—Samuel Castillo, Oaxaca .... KO 9
Sept. 15—Catarino Lopez, Mexico City .... W 6
Oct. 20—Felipe Silva .... W
Nov. 21—Juan C. Villanueva .... W 8

1964

       —Chucho Cardenas, Acapulco ...... WF 3
Mar. 18—Samuel Castillo, Mexico City ...... W 8
May 23—Jose Gonzalez, Mexico City .... KO 8
June 13—Jorobado Olvera, Mexico City ...... W 10
July   8—Genaro Gaytan, Mexico City ...... W 10
Sept. 30—Adalberto Martinez, Mexico City KO 8
Oct. 17—Zorrito Castanon, Oaxaca .... KO by 10
Nov. 11—Jose Gonzalez, Mexico City .... KO by 7

1965

Mar.   4—Goyo Sanchez, Mexico City .... KO 1
Mar. 24—Daniel Valdez, Mexico City .... W 10
June   8—Chucho Hernandez, Mexico City .. KO 6
June 16—Mundo Esparza .... KO 2
Sept. 26—Memo Tellez, Mexico City ..... KO by 0
Nov. 20—Lenny Brice, Guadalajara .... W 10

1966

Mar. 20—Miguel Castro, Mexico City ... KO by 5
May   8—Felipe Gonzalez, Culiacan ..... KO by 4
May 22—Chucho Hernandez .... KO 7
July 27—Edmundo Esparza, Juarez .... KO 3
Aug. 28—Jerry Stokes, Mexico City .... KO 2
Nov. 13—Valdemiro Pino, Juarez .... KO 3
Dec. 26—Miguel Castro, Mexico City .... W 10

1967

Apr. 29—Joe Medel, Mexico City .... W 12
        (Won Mexican Bantamweight Title)
Aug. 14—Pornchai Poppaingam, Tijuana ... KO 5
Oct. 14—Bernardo Caraballo, Mexico City KO 8
Nov. 26—Miguel Castro, Juarez .... KO 6
      (Retained Mexican Bantamweight Title)

1968

Mar.   6—Joe Valdez, Leon .... W 10
Mar. 31—Yoshio Nakane, Juarez .... W 10
May 14—Memo Tellez, Juarez .... WF 10
      (Retained Mexican Bantamweight Title)
June 14—Jesus Pimentel, Inglewood .... W 12
Aug. 28—Evan Armstrong, Inglewood ...... KO 2
Dec.   6—Lionel Rose, Inglewood .... L 15
      (For World Bantamweight Title)

1969

Feb. 15—Rafael Herrera, Monterrey .... KO 3
      (Retained Mexican Bantamweight Title)
Apr. 16—Ushiwakamaru Harado, Tokyo ..... D 10
June 10—Kenishi Watanuki, Juarez .... KO 4
June 29—Ernie de la Cruz, Mexico City .... KO 5
July 26—Albert Jangalay, Mexico City ..... KO 5
Sept. 30—Joe Medel, Juarez .... D 12
      (Retained Mexican Bantamweight Title)
Oct. 18—Raul Cruz, Inglewood .... L 12
Dec. 12—Raul Cruz, Inglewood .... W 10

1970

Apr. 19—Ruben Olivares, Inglewood .... L 15
      (For World Bantamweight Title)
Aug. 14—Rogelio Lara, Inglewood .... W 12
Oct. 16—Ruben Olivares, Inglewood .... KO 14
      (Won World Bantamweight Title)

1971

Feb. 28—Felipe Ursua, Monterrey .... KO 6
Apr.   3—Ruben Olivares, Inglewood .... L 15
      (Lost World Bantamweight Title)
Aug.   4—Earl Large, Juarez .... W 10
Aug. 23—Rafael Herrera, Inglewood .... L 12
      (For NABF Bantamweight Title)

1972

       —Jose Lopez, Juarez .... KO 1
June   6—Earl Large, Juarez .... W 10
Nov. 14—Enrique Pinder, Inglewood .... L 10

1973

Mar.   2—Jose Luis Soto, Culiacan .... L 10
Apr. 28—Bobby Chacon, Inglewood ..... KO by 10

1974

May 14—Victor Rodrigo, Juarez .... W 10
June 22—Yambito Blanco, Managua .... L 10
Sept. 14—Rafael Ortega, Mexico City .... W 10

1975

Apr. 24—Danny Lopez, Los Angeles ... KO by 2
Dec. 12—Ernesto Herrera, Laredo .... L 10

TB	KO	WD	WF	D	LD	LF	KO BY	ND	NC
65	22	22	2	2	10	0	7	0	0

RAFAEL HERRERA
Born, January 7, 1945. Mexico. Weight, 118 lbs.

1963

Mar. 20—Memo Gonzalez, Mexico City ...... W 4
Apr. 17—Raul Martinez, Mexico City .... W 4
May 25—Wenceslao Angeles, Mexico City ... W 4
July 13—David Monroy, Mexico City .... W 6
Sept. 21—Alfonso Cazarez, Mexico City ...... L 6

1964

Jan.   —Peleas Granadas, Mexico City .... W 4
Feb.   7—Frijol Madrid, Poza Rica ...... KO by 5
        Memo Gonzalez, Mexico City ...... W 6
       —Raul Martinez, Mexico City .... W 6

—Wenceslao Angeles, Mexico City .. KO 6
—David Montroy, Mexico City .... W 6
Aug. 26—Frijol Madrid, Mexico City .... KO 2
Sept. 20—Miguel Zamudio, Mexico City .... KO 8
Oct. 10—Alfonso Izquierdo, Mexico City ..... W 6
Nov. 21—Andres Molina, Mexico City ...... KO 7
1965
Jan. 28—Cid Cardenas, Mexico City .... W 8
Apr. 4—Rogelio Rea, Mexico City .... KO 5
May 2—Gerardo Luna, Mexico City .... L 10
—Andres Molina, Mexico City ..... KO 8
Oct. 10—Alfredo Meneses, Mexico City .... W 10
Nov. 8—Coruco Contreras, Tuxtla Gutierrez KO 6
1966
—Coruco Contreras, Mexico City .... KO 10
July 9—Gerardo Luna, Mexico City .... W 10
July 14—Memo Vega, Mexico City .... W 10
Nov. 16—Alfredo Meneses, Mexico City .... W 10
1967
Jan. 21—Gerardo Luna, Mexico City .... D 10
Mar. 2—Changa Magallanes, Los Angeles .. W 4
May 16—Raton Perez, San Jose .... W 10
June 8—Pedro Rodriguez, Los Angeles ..... W 10
June 12—Alex Rivera, Stockton .... W 10
July 6—Cheparro Bargas, Mexico City .... KO 10
Aug. 12—Shorty Vargas, San Bernardino ... KO 3
Sept. 14—Rollie Penaroya, Los Angeles ...... L 10
Sept. 19—Lupe Gonzalez, San Jose .... TD 8
Oct. 17—Ricardo Solis, San Jose .... KO 5
Dec. 9—Al Rivera, San Jose .... W 10
1968
Mar. 30—Raul Vega, Mexico City .... W 10
May 16—Wayman Gray, Los Angeles .... L 6
June 29—Santos Sandoval, Mexico City ... KO 2
Aug. 3—Ronnie Jones, Mexico City ...... KO 3
Sept. 28—Memo Tellez, Mexico City .... KO 9
Nov. 21—Lenny Brice, Los Angeles .... W 10
Dec. 20—Jerry Stokes, Los Angeles .... W 10
1969
Feb. 15—Chucho Castillo, Monterrey ... KO by 3
Mar. 5—Ken Nagamine, Los Angeles .... W 10
Apr. 10—Billy McGrandle, Edmonton .... D 10
July 26—Raul Cruz, Mexico City .... L 10
Sept. 25—Lenny Price, Los Angeles .... KO 3
1970
Jan. 20—Yoshiaki Suda, Tijuana .... KO 3
Mar. 17—Chuy Chavez, Tijuana .... KO 2
Apr. 18—Jose Lopez, Los Angeles .... W 10
Sept. 5—Famoso Gomez, Inglewood .... W 10
1971
Jan. 20—Rodolfo Martinez, Inglewood .... W 12
(Won Vacant NABF Bantamweight Title)
Apr. 2—Cesar Deciga, Inglewood .... KO 10
July 12—Modesto Dayaganon, Tijuana ..... KO 2
Aug. 23—Chucho Castillo, Inglewood .... W 12
(Retained NABF Bantamweight Title)
1972
Mar. 19—Ruben Olivares, Mexico City ..... KO 8
(Won World Bantamweight Title)
July 30—Enrique Pinder, Panama City ...... L 15
(Lost World Bantamweight Title)
Nov. 14—Ruben Olivares, Inglewood .... W 10
1973
Apr. 15—Rodolfo Martinez, Monterrey ..... KO 12
(Won Vacant WBC Bantamweight Title)
Oct. 13—Venice Borkorsor, Inglewood ...... W 15
(Retained WBC Bantamweight Title)
1974
May 25—Romeo Anaya, Mexico City ...... KO 6
(Retained WBC Bantamweight Title)
Dec. 7—Rodolfo Martinez, Merida ..... KO by 4
(Lost WBC Bantamweight Title)
1975
July 5—Famoso Gomez, Los Angeles .... L 10
Nov. 10—Jose Luis Soto, Los Mochis .... L 10
1976
May 23—Jose Cervantes, Maracaibo .... D 12

TB	KO	WD	WF	D	LD	LF	KO BY	ND	NC
66	22	29	0	4	8	0	3	0	0

788

ENRIQUE PINDER
Born, August 7, 1947, Panama. Weight, 118 lbs.
1966
Aug. 20—Jorge Jacobos, Panama City ...... KO 1
Aug. 27—Euclides Escobar, Panama City ... KO 1
Sept. 25—Carlos Melendez, Colon .... KO 1
Dec. 4—Jim Thousend, Panama City ..... KO 4
1967
Jan. 17—Herbert Looke, Panama City ...... W 6
Mar. 7—Herbert Looke, Panama City ...... W 6
Apr. 20—Carlos Real, Panama City .... W 6
Aug. 5—Arnold Prescott, Colon .... D 8
Oct. 28—Carlos Real, Panama City .... W 8
1968
Feb. 10—Arnold Prescott, Colon .... KO 2
Feb. 17—Felix Archer, Panama City .... W 8
Apr. 26—Carlos Cruz, Panama City .... W 10
Sept. 6—Carlos Zayas, New York .... W 8
Nov. 17—Eugenio Hurtado, Panama City .. KO 8
1969
Feb. 28—Carlos Mendoza, Colon .... W 8
Apr. 20—Orlando Amores, Panama City KO by 9
June 15—Jose Luis Meza, Panama City .... KO 3
Aug. 23—Carlos Real, Colon .... KO 1
Oct. 4—Fernando Cuevas, Colon .... KO 9
Dec. 20—Eugenio Hurtado, Colon .... KO 8
1970
Jan. 30—Agustin Cedeno, Colon .... KO 3
Feb. 20—Antonio Munoz, Acapulco .... KO 2
Mar. 7—Victor Rocha, Monterrey .... KO 3
Mar. 20—Memo Rodriguez, Acapulco .... D 10
May 31—Camilo Valdespino, Panama City .. W 12
July 19—Hilario Diaz, Panama City .... W 10
Aug. 15—Baba Jimenez, Panama City ...... W 10
Oct. 31—Luis Osses, Panama City .... KO 1
Dec. 5—Pablo Vega, Panama City .... W 10
1971
Mar. 4—Salvador Lozano, San Jose .... KO by 4
Apr. 24—Adolfo Osses, Panama City .... W 12
June 27—Angel Sanchez, Panama City ...... W 10
Oct. 3—David Vasquez, New York .... W 12
Nov. 13—David Vasquez, New York .... W 12
Dec. 18—Justo Valdez, Panama City .... W 10
1972
Jan. 29—Senon Rios, Panama City .... W 12
Mar. 10—Heleno Ferreyro, Panama City .... W 10
Apr. 22—Memo Espinosa, Panama City ..... W 10
July 30—Rafael Herrera, Panama City ..... W 15
(Won World Bantamweight Title)
Nov. 14—Chucho Castillo, Inglewood .... W 10
1973
Jan. 20—Romeo Anaya, Panama City ... KO by 3
(Lost World Bantamweight Title)
Aug. 18—Romeo Anaya, Inglewood ...... KO by 3
(For World Bantamweight Title)
Nov. 22—Francisco Villegas, San Juan .... L 10
Dec. 10—Announced retirement.

TB	KO	WD	WF	D	LD	LF	KO BY	ND	NC
43	14	22	0	2	1	0	4	0	0

ROMEO ANAYA
Born, April 5, 1946, Mexico. Weight, 118 lbs.
1967
July 25—Costenito Pena, Tuxtla Gutierrez KO 6
Aug. 23—Alejandro Baena, Tuxtla Gutierrez L 10
Oct. 23—Firpito Flores, Tuxtla Gutierrez .. KO 5
1968
Aug. 14—Enrique Hernandez, Mexico City KO 4
Sept. 18—Benito Hernandez, Mexico City ... KO 2
Oct. 30—Tomas Frias, Mexico City .... D 6
Nov. 30—Jeronimo Cisneros, Mexico City ... W 6
Dec. 11—Miguel Zacarias, Tapachula .... W 10
Dec. 25—Dragon Galeana, Acapulco .... KO 1
1969
Jan. 18—Alex Bahena, Tapachula .... KO 5
Feb. 26—Jorge Reyes, Mexico City .... KO 2
Mar. 29—Farolito Coutino, Tapachula ...... KO 1
May 21—Armando Ramirez, Mexico City ... KO 2

June	18—Guillermo Barrera, Mexico City .. KO	2
July	14—Dumbo Perez, Tuxtla Gutierrez ... KO	3
Oct.	11—Jose Garcia, Mexico City ... KO	2
Dec.	7—Memo Espinosa, Tuxtla Gutierrez KO	1

1970

Jan.	7—Pajarito Solis, Mexico City ...... KO	2
Jan.	24—Raul Bolanos, Mexico City ...... KO	2
Feb.	21—Felipe Ursua, Mexico City ...... KO	2
Feb.	28—Arlindo Borges, Mexico City ...... KO	6
Mar.	19—Armando Villa, Gomez Palacio ... KO	1
June	27—Famoso Gomez, Mexico City ... KO by	9
Aug.	18—Victor Rios, Huatabampo .... KO	5
Sept.	8—Alejandro Lopez, Tijuana .... KO	7
Sept.	23—Hiroshi Ishibashi, Ciudad Obregon KO	1
Oct.	13—Cesar Deciga, Tijuana .... KO by	3

1971

Mar.	26—Francisco (Sugar) Pino, Acapulco KO	4
Apr.	9—Memo Espinosa, Acapulco .... KO	10
May	15—Mario Manrique, Mexico City .... KO	2
June	19—Chuy Rocha, Monterrey .... KO by	1
Sept.	4—Carlos Mendoza, Mexico City ..... KO	7
Oct.	31—Alfredo Meneses, Tuxtla Gutierrez KO	3
	(Won Mexican Bantamweight Title)	

1972

Jan.	2—Baba Jimenez, Tuxtla Gutierrez ... W	10
Feb.	13—Kazuyoshi Kanazawa, Tuxtla .... KO	5
Apr.	22—Franco Zurlo, Los Angeles ...... W	10
June	18—Julio Guerrero, Tuxtla Gutierrez ... W	10
Oct.	28—Salvador M. Carrillo, Guadalajara KO	6
	(Retained Mexican Bantamweight Title)	

1973

Jan.	20—Enrique Pinder, Panama City .... KO	3
	(Won World Bantamweight Title)	
Feb.	10—Jorge Torres, Guadalajara .... W	10
Apr.	28—Rogelio Lara, Los Angeles .... W	15
	(Retained World Bantamweight Title)	
July	10—Kyu-Chul Chang, Tijuana .... KO	8
Aug.	18—Enrique Pinder, Los Angeles ..... KO	3
	(Retained World Bantamweight Title)	
Nov.	3—Arnold Taylor, Johannesburg .. KO by	14
	(Lost World Bantamweight Title)	

1974

May	25—Rafael Herrera, Mexico City ... KO by	6
	(For WBC Bantamweight Title)	
Sept.	29—Marcos Britton, Tuxtla Gutierrez KO	2

1975

June	27—Arnold Taylor, Johannesburg .. KO by	8
Sept.	27—Miguel Angel Rivera, Chicago .... KO	6

1976

Mar.	12—Juan Antonio Lopez, Culiacan L	10
Apr.	2—Jose Rosa, Los Angeles L	10
Oct.	31—Ramon Guillen, Nuevo Laredo .... KO	8
Dec.	17—Mario Castro, Piedras Negras KO by	6

1977

Mar.	25—Mike Ayala, San Antonio ..... KO by	6
	(For Vacant NABF Junior Featherweight Title)	
Oct.	13—Chilango Pacheco, Nuevo Laredo ... L	10
Dec.	9—Jose A. Cazares, Juarez .... KO by	3

1978

Jan.	22—Roberto Castillo, Guanajuato ..... KO	3
Mar.	2—Fel Clemente, Stockton L	10
Apr.	4—Samuel Castillo, Vera Cruz ...... KO	3
Apr.	15—Sean O'Grady, Los Angeles ... KO by	3
Oct.	17—Bobby Flores, Houston .... KO	4
Dec.	2—Rodolfo Chavez, Culiacan L	10
Dec.	23—Torito Melendez, Matamoros .. KO by	1

1979

May	20—Ruben Valdez, Cartagena ..... KO by	7
Oct.	19—Carmelo Montes, Acapulco .... KO	2
Dec.	20—Raul Silva, San Jose .... KO by	4

1980

Feb.	22—Benny Arguelles, Coatzacoalcos KO by	4

TB	KO	WD	WF	D	LD	LF	KO BY	ND	NC
66	37	8	0	1	6	0	14	0	0

ARNOLD TAYLOR
Born, July 15, 1943, South Africa. Weight.
114-126 lbs.

1967

May	20—Ray Buttle, Potgietersrus .... D	6
June	30—Ray Buttle, Johannesburg .... KO	9
	(Won Transvaal State Bantamweight Title)	
Dec.	11—Ray Buttle, Johannesburg .... W	8

1968

Feb.	19—Andres Steyn, Johannesburg ...... W	12
Apr.	29—Bobby Davies, Johannesburg ...... W	10
June	3—Gerry McBride, Johannesburg ..... W	10
July	1—Dennis Adams, Johannesburg KO by	1
Aug.	13—Herbie Clark, Johannesburg ..... KO	9
Aug.	26—Robert Trott, Johannesburg ...... W	8
Oct.	7—Robert Trott, Johannesburg ...... KO	3
Oct.	30—Anthony Morodi, Maseru .... W	6
Nov.	2—Colin Lake, Johannesburg .... W disq.	3

1969

Feb.	15—Henri Nesi, Johannesburg .... W	10
Apr.	11—Herbie Clarke, Durban ..... W disq.	6
May	12—Herbie Clarke, Durban .... W	12
	(Won South African Lightweight Title)	
May	24—Dennis Adams, Johannesburg .... KO	8
	(Won South African Featherweight Title)	
July	4—Andres Steyn, Durban .... KO by	8
Aug.	30—Johnny O'Brien, Johannesburg ... L	10
Nov.	15—Mike Buttle, Johannesburg ...... KO	5
Nov.	29—Ernie Baronet, Durban .... W	10
Dec.	6—Mike Buttle, Johannesburg ...... KO	6
	(Won South African Bantamweight Title)	

1970

Apr.	11—Johnny Famechon, Johannesburg ... L	10
Aug.	15—Ray Buttle, Johannesburg .... KO	9
Sept.	21—Chris Nel, Durban .... KO	7
Dec.	28—Chris Nel, Durban .... KO	10

1971

May	3—Willie Cordova, Melbourne .... W	10
May	17—Willie Cordova, Melbourne .... W	10
June	14—Toro George, Melbourne .... W	10
Aug.	2—Memo Espinosa, Melbourne .... W	10
Aug.	30—Alberto Jangalay, Melbourne ...... W	10
Oct.	30—Luis Aisa, Johannesburg .... W	10
Nov.	27—Chris Nel, Salisbury .... KO	7

1972

Jan.	29—Ugo Poli, Johannesburg .... KO	4
Mar.	27—Hansie Van Rooyen, Johannesburg W	12
	(Retained South African Featherweight Title)	
May	13—Hansie Van Rooyen, Johannesburg KO	6
	(Retained South African Featherweight Title)	
Oct.	28—Evan Armstrong, Johannesburg .. KO	4

1973

Apr.	28—Jimmy Bell, Johannesburg .... W	10
June	16—Billy Waith, Johannesburg .... W	10
Nov.	3—Romeo Anaya, Johannesburg ..... KO	14
	(Won World Bantamweight Title)	

1974

Feb.	16—Gey Caudron, Johannesburg .... W	10
Mar.	18—Paul Ferreri, Cape Town .... W	10
June	1—Lorenzo Trujillo, Port Elizabeth L	10
July	3—Soo-Hwan Hong, Durban L	15
	(Lost World Bantamweight Title)	

1975

Feb.	22—John Mitchell, Johannesburg ..... KO	4
May	5—Lothar Abend, Johannesburg ..... KO	3
June	27—Romeo Anaya, Johannesburg ..... KO	8

1976

May	8—Dave Neeham, Johannesburg ..... W	10
Oct.	23—Eric Paulsen, Oslo L	10
Nov.	24—Vernon Sollas, London .... KO by	8

TB	KO	WD	WF	D	LD	LF	KO BY	ND	NC
49	17	21	2	1	5	0	3	0	0

SOO-HWAN HONG
Born, May 26, 1950, Seoul, Korea. Weight.
118-122 lbs. Height, 5 ft. 7 in.

1969

May	10—Sang-Il Kim, Seoul .... D	4
June	3—Chang-Soo Choi, Seoul .... W	4
June	21—Young-Suh Park, Seoul .... W	4
Aug.	12—Ju-Hong Taek, Seoul .... W	1

Sept. 7—Young-Tae Kim, Seoul .... KO 1
Oct. 6—Rak-Ki Beak, Seoul .... W 4
1970
Mar. 3—Hae-Suh Shim, Seoul .... W 6
Apr. 19—Choul-Ho Shin, Taegu .... D 10
June 9—Ushiwakamaru Harada, Oita ...... L 10
Aug. 8—Shintaro Oshima, Yokohama ..... KO 1
Oct. 17—Hae-Suh Shim, Seoul .... W 8
Dec. 1—Kyu-Choul Chang, Seoul .... W 10
1971
Sept. 14—Jung-Ho Moon, Seoul .... KO 5
(Won Korean Bantamweight Title)
Nov. 7—Saturnino Ortega, Seoul .... W 10
Dec. 12—Colley Saloma, Guam .... L 10
1972
Jan. 15—Yung-Suh Park, Seoul .... KO 4
(Retained Korean Bantamweight Title)
Mar. 12—Jae-Bae Kil, Seoul .... W 10
(Retained Korean Bantamweight Title)
Apr. 2—Jung-Ho Moon, Pusan .... W 10
(Retained Korean Bantamweight Title)
June 4—Al Diaz, Seoul .... W 12
(Won Vacant Oriental Bantamweight Title)
June 8—Ace Endo, Seoul .... KO 1
Oct. 1—Shigeyoshi Ohki, Seoul .... W 12
(Retained Oriental Bantamweight Title)
Nov. 26—Ushiwakamaru Harada, Seoul ..... W 10
1973
Feb. 9—Thanomjit Sukhothai, Bangkok ... KO 8
(Retained Oriental Bantamweight Title)
Aug. 19—Susumu Inoue, Seoul .... KO 3
Oct. 7—Berkrerk Chartvanchai, Seoul ..... W 10
Nov. 24—Eddie Saloma, Taegu .... W 12
1974
Feb. 3—Seiichi Watanuki, Taegu .... W 12
(Retained Oriental Bantamweight Title)
Apr. 20—Go Mifune, Pusan .... W 12
(Retained Oriental Bantamweight Title)
July 3—Arnold Taylor, Durban .... W 15
(Won World Bantamweight Title)
Oct. 8—Genzo Kurosawa, Seoul .... W 10
Dec. 28—Fernando Cabanela, Seoul .... W 15
(Retained World Bantamweight Title)
1975
Mar. 14—Alfonso Zamora, Inglewood .... KO by 4
(Lost World Bantamweight Title)
May 21—Johnny Meza, Seoul .... KO 2
Aug. 30—Orlando Amores, Seoul .... W 10
Nov. 27—Vitaya Plernchit, Seoul .... KO 4
1976
Feb. 21—Eddie Alarcon, Seoul .... KO 4
Feb. 29—Shinobu Fuchita, Pusan .... KO 2
Apr. 6—Sutan Rambing, Seoul .... KO 6
May 30—Venice Borkorsor, Seoul .... W 12
(Regained Oriental Bantamweight Title)
Aug. 21—Ric Quijano, Seoul .... D 10
Oct. 16—Alfonso Zamora, Inchon .... KO by 12
(For World Bantamweight Title)
1977
Mar. 15—Conrado Vasquez, Honolulu .... W 10
June 27—Dong-Kyun Yum, Seoul .... W 10
Oct. 10—Futaro Tanaka, Seoul .... W 12
(WBA Junior Featherweight Elimination Tournament)
Nov. 26—Hector Carrasquilla, Panama City KO 3
(Won Vacant WBA Junior Featherweight Title)
1978
Feb. 1—Yutaka Kasahara, Tokyo .... W 15
(Retained WBA Junior Featherweight Title)
May 7—Ricardo Cardona, Seoul ...... KO by 12
(Lost WBA Junior Featherweight Title)
1979
(Inactive)
1980
Dec. 19—Dong-Kyun Yum, Seoul .... D 10

TB	KO	WD	WF	D	LD	LF	KO BY	ND	NC
48	13	26	0	4	2	0	3	0	0

790

RODOLFO MARTINEZ
Born, August 24, 1946, Tepito, Mexico. Weight,
118 lbs. Height, 5 ft. 6 in.
1965
Aug. 14—Roman Mejia, Mexico City .... KO 3
Sept. 11—Isidro Encisco, Mexico City ...... KO 2
Oct. 30—Mario Campero, Mexico City ..... KO 2
Dec. 18—Adan Garcia, Mexico City .... KO 2
1966
Jan. 8—Tomas Gonzalez, Mexico City ..... KO 4
Feb. 26—Armando Navarro, Mexico City ... KO 2
Apr. 11—Raul Perez, Mexico City .... KO 2
July 2—Mateo Jaimes, Mexico City .... KO 2
Aug. 20—Anacieto Resendiz, Mexico City ... KO 2
Sept. 17—Eduardo Alvarado, Mexico City ... KO 4
Oct. 8—Eduardo Ramirez, Mexico City ... KO 3
Nov. 26—Manuel Sanchez, Mexico City .... KO 2
1967
Feb. 18—Chema Espinosa, Mexico City .... KO 2
July 5—Ramiro Garcia, Mexico City ..... KO 4
Aug. 16—Jose (Carbonero) Vargas, Mexico
City .... KO 4
Oct. 7—Carlos (Zorrito) Garrido, Mexico
City .... KO 8
Nov. 25—Luciano Reyes Escandon, Mexico
City .... KO 6
1968
Apr. 6—Hilario Diaz, Mexico City .... KO 5
June 15—Raul Cruz, Mexico City .... KO 5
Aug. 31—Camy Beto, Mexico City .... KO 2
Nov. 24—Heleno Ferreyra, Monterrey .... D 10
1969
Jan. 26—Yoshio Nakane, Mexico City ...... W 10
Oct. 5—Yoshiaki Suda, Los Angeles ...... KO 6
Nov. 28—Shitaro Oshima, Guadalajara ..... KO 1
1970
Feb. 16—Roger Moreno, Tijuana .... KO 2
Apr. 9—Kazuyoshi Kanazawa, Los Angeles KO 5
July 2—Lenny Brice, Los Angeles .... KO 10
Sept. 5—Shintaro Uchiyama, Inglewood .... W 10
Oct. 16—Rogelio Lara, Inglewood .... W 12
1971
Jan. 20—Rafael Herrera, Inglewood .... L 12
(For Vacant NABF Bantamweight Title)
June 12—Jose Luis Meza, Mexico City ..... KO 2
Oct. 30—Pedro Cordero, Mexico City ...... KO 2
Nov. 27—Manuel Mendoza, Mexico City .... KO 6
1972
Jan. 31—Ramon Bravo, Caracas .... KO 5
Apr. 22—Kenji Ando, Mexico City .... KO 4
June 30—Famoso Gomez, Inglewood .... KO 6
Nov. 14—Yoshio Kajimoto, Inglewood .... W 10
1973
Apr. 14—Rafael Herrera, Monterrey .... KO by 12
(For Vacant WBC Bantamweight Title)
Aug. 18—Guy Caudron, Inglewood .... W 10
Dec. 5—Jorge Miranda, Panama City ...... W 10
1974
Feb. 18—Francisco Villegas, San Juan .... L 10
May 25—Saul Montano, Mexico City ...... KO 10
Dec. 7—Rafael Herrera, Merida .... KO 4
(Won WBC Bantamweight Title)
1975
May 31—Nestor Jiminez, Bogota .... KO 7
(Retained WBC Bantamweight Title)
Oct. 8—Hisami Numata, Sendai .... W 15
(Retained WBC Bantamweight Title)
1976
Jan. 30—Venice Borkorsor, Bangkok .... W 15
(Retained WBC Bantamweight Title)
May 8—Carlos Zarate, Inglewood ...... KO by 9
(Lost WBC Bantamweight Title)
Sept. 18—Roberto Rubaldino, Reynosa ... KO by 4
(For Mexican Bantamweight Title)
1977
May 17—Mike Ayala, San Antonio .... KO 7
Aug. 9—Gilberto Illueca, San Antonio ...... W 10
Nov. 17—Albert Davila, Los Angeles .... KO by 7
1978
(Inactive)

1979
July   —Manuel Lara, Ciudad Constitucion .. L 10

TB	KO	WD	WF	D	LD	LF	KO BY	ND	NC
52	35	9	0	1	3	0	4	0	0

ALFONSO ZAMORA
Born, February 9, 1954, Mexico City, Mexico.
Weight, 118 lbs. Height, 5 ft. 2 in.

1972 Olympic Bantamweight Silver Medalist
1973
Apr.   16—Heraclio Amaya, San Luis Potosi   KO   2
June   2—Antonio Enriquez, La Paz .... KO   3
June   25—Juan Perez, La Paz .... KO   2
July   8—Sixto Esqueda, La Paz .... KO   1
Aug.   21—Pajarito Plascencia, Tijuana ..... KO   1
Sept. 16—Cruz Vega, Monterrey .... KO   3
Oct.   10—Tortillo Armenta, Monterrey ..... KO   2
Oct.   30—Julio Romero, Tijuana .... KO   2
Dec.   11—Salvador Lozano, Tijuana .... KO   9
1974
Jan.   23—Pedro Lara, Zihuatanejo .... KO   2
Feb.   24—Fili Castro, Mexicali .... KO   3
Mar.   31—Tetsuro Kawakami, Mexicali .... KO   3
Apr.   17—Pedro Ibanez, Matamoros .... KO   2
May   7—Cesar Ordonez, Tijuana .... KO   3
May   25—Raul Tirado, Mexico City .... KO   2
July   9—Shintaro Uchiyama, Inglewood ... KO   6
Aug.   31—Ad Zapanta, Monterrey .... KO   1
Oct.   5—Francisco Villegas, Juarez .... KO   2
Nov.   23—Jose Rosa, Inglewood .... KO   3
1975
Feb.   4—Tanny Amancio, Ciudad Victoria   KO   4
Mar.   14—Soo-Hwan Hong, Inglewood ..... KO   4
        (Won World Bantamweight Title)
June   2—Jorge Torres, Tijuana .... KO   10
Aug.   30—Thanomjit Sukhothai, Anaheim .. KO   4
        (Retained World Bantamweight Title)
Dec.   6—Socrates Batoto, Mexico City .... KO   2
        (Retained World Bantamweight Title)
1976
Apr.   3—Eusebio Pedroza, Mexicali .... KO   2
        (Retained World Bantamweight Title)
July   10—Gilberto Illueca, Juarez .... KO   3
        (Retained World Bantamweight Title)
Sept. 5—Candido Sandoval, Durango ...... KO   3
Oct.   16—Soo-Hwan Hong, Inchon .... KO   12
        (Retained World Bantamweight Title)
1977
Feb.   12—Alejandro Orejel, Tijuana .... KO   2
Apr.   23—Carlos Zarate, Inglewood ..... KO by   4
Nov.   19—Jorge Lujan, Los Angeles ... KO by   10
        (Lost World Bantamweight Title)
1978
June   23—Hector Medina, Obregon .... KO   6
Oct.   26—Alberto Sandoval, Inglewood ..... KO   9
1979
Jan.   18—Luis Rosario, New York .... W   10
July   22—Juan Alvarez, San Luis Potosi L disq.   5
Nov.   16—Eddie Logan, Inglewood .... KO by   9
1980
July   17—Melvin Johnson, Los Angeles ..... KO   3
Sept. 19—Giglio Estrada, Los Angeles ... KO by   3

TB	KO	WD	WF	D	LD	LF	KO BY	ND	NC
38	32	1	0	0	0	1	4	0	0

CARLOS ZARATE
Born, May 23, 1951, Tepito, Mexico. Weight, 118 lbs. Height, 5 ft. 8 in.
1970
Feb.   3—Luis Castaneda, Guernavaca ..... KO   3
Mar.   23—Jose Luis Davon, Guernavaca .... KO   2
       —Costenito Sotelo, Villahermosa ... KO   0
       —Nuno Temix, Villahermosa .... KO   2
Dec.   18—Alfredo Perez, Acapulco .... KO   2

1971
Feb.   15—Antonio Lucas, Guernavaca ...... KO   3
Mar.   20—Fermin Ramos, Toluca .... KO   2
May   5—Ramon Pinedo, Guernavaca ..... KO   2
Aug.   7—Julio Martinez, Morelia .... KO   2
Nov.   26—Victor Nava, Acapulco .... KO   2

1972
Jan.   29—Emiliano Mayoral, Acapulco ..... KO   3
Feb.   7—Jose Luis Gonzalez, Tampico ..... KO   2
Mar.   19—Jose Luis Morales, Mexico City ... KO   2
June   8—Jesus Escobedo, Monterrey .... KO   2
Aug.   9—Chato Patino, Madero .... KO   2
Oct.   31—Armando Carrasco, Villahermosa   KO   3
Dec.   4—Chilango Perez, La Paz .... KO   2

1973
Feb.   6—Chilango Perez, La Paz .... KO   2
June   2—Juan Ramon Perez, La Paz .... KO   2
July   12—Sugar Pino, Guernavaca .... KO   2
Aug.   21—Al Torres, Tijuana .... KO   5
Oct.   2—Caguano Castaneda, Tijuana ..... KO   9
Dec.   11—Sixto Perez, Tijuana .... KO   2

1974
Jan.   30—Victor Ramirez, Mexico City .... W   10
Feb.   22—Carlos Armenta, Matamoros ..... KO   1
Apr.   9—Alfonso Ibarra, Tijuana .... KO   2
May   3—Chomaco Limon, Monterrey ...... KO   3
May   25—Juan Ordonez, Mexico City .... KO   3
Aug.   3—Magallo Lozada, Mexico City ..... KO   5
Oct.   26—Francisco Cruz, Mexicali .... KO   2
Nov.   23—James Martinez, Los Angeles ..... KO   7

1975
Feb.   4—Alberto Cabanig, Ciudad Victoria   KO   5
Mar.   14—Joe Guevara, Inglewood .... KO   3
June   20—Orlando Amoros, Inglewood ...... KO   3
Aug.   16—Jose Sanchez, Mexico City .... KO   3
Sept. 20—Benicio Sosa, Inglewood .... KO   4
Oct.   11—Jorge Torres, Guadalajara .... KO   9
Dec.   7—Nestor (Baba) Jimenez, Mexicali .. KO   2

1976
Mar.   29—Cesar Desiga, Monterrey .... KO   4
May   8—Rodolfo Martinez, Inglewood ..... KO   9
        (Won WBC Bantamweight Title)
June   26—Felix Illanos, Mexicali .... KO   2
Aug.   2—Antonio Paredes, Chihuahua ..... KO   2
Aug.   28—Paul Ferreri, Inglewood .... KO   12
        (Retained WBC Bantamweight Title)
Nov.   13—Waruinge Nakayama, Culiacan .. KO   4
        (Retained WBC Bantamweight Title)

1977
Feb.   5—Fernando Cabanela, Mexico City   KO   3
        (Retained WBC Bantamweight Title)
Apr.   23—Alfonso Zamora, Inglewood .... KO   4
Oct.   29—Danilo Batista, Los Angeles ...... KO   6
        (Retained WBC Bantamweight Title)
Dec.   2—Juan Francisco Rodriguez, Madrid   KO   5
        (Retained WBC Bantamweight Title)

1978
Feb.   25—Albert Davila, Inglewood .... KO   8
        (Retained WBC Bantamweight Title)
Apr.   22—Andres Hernandez, San Juan ..... KO   13
        (Retained WBC Bantamweight Title)
June   9—Emilio Hernandez, Las Vegas .... KO   4
        (Retained WBC Bantamweight Title)
Sept. 30—Rudy Gonzalez, Matamoros .... KO   4
Oct.   28—Wilfredo Gomez, San Juan .... KO by   5
        (For WBC Super Bantamweight Title)

1979
Mar.   10—Mensah Kpalongo, Inglewood ..... KO   3
        (Retained WBC Bantamweight Title)
May   1—Celso Chairez, Houston .... KO   5
June   3—Lupe Pintor, Las Vegas L   15
        (Lost WBC Bantamweight Title)

TB	KO	WD	WF	D	LD	LF	KO BY	ND	NC
56	53	1	0	0	1	0	1	0	0

JORGE LUJAN
Born, March 18, 1955, Colon, Panama.
1973
June	16—Alcibiades Smith, Panama City ... KO	1
Sept.	1—Guillermo Shakespere, Panama City .... KO	1
Oct.	6—Carlos Rios, Panama City .... W	6
Nov.	16—Felipe Perez, Panama City .... W	6

1974
Jan.	19—Alex Santana Guido, Panama City KO	2
July	20—Socrates Batoto, Panama City .... KO	4
Sept.	14—Aurellio Castillo, Panama City .... W	10

1975
Feb.	15—John Cajina, Panama City .... W	10
May	3—Eliseo Padilla, Panama City ...... KO	2
June	21—Reyes Arnal, Panama City .... KO	5
Aug.	26—Catalino Flores, Panama City .... KO	4

1976
Jan.	17—Enrique Torres, Panama City .... KO	7
May	15—Pablo Jiminez, Panama City ...... W	10
July	17—Antonio Sanchez, Panama City .... W	10

1977
Jan.	29—Juanito Herrera, Panama City ..... W	10
May	14—Gilbert Illueca, Panama City L	10
July	30—Jaime Ricardo, Cartagena .... KO	7
Sept.	3—Jose Cervantes, Bogota L	10
Nov.	19—Alfonso Zamora, Los Angeles ..... KO	10
	(Won World Bantamweight Title)	

1978
Mar.	18—Roberto Rubaldino, San Antonio .. KO	11
	(Retained World Bantamweight Title)	
Sept.	15—Albert Davila, New Orleans .... W	15
	(Retained World Bantamweight Title)	

1979
Apr.	8—Cleo Garcia, Las Vegas .... KO	15
	(Retained World Bantamweight Title)	
Oct.	6—Roberto Rubaldino, McAllen ...... KO	15
	(Retained World Bantamweight Title)	

1980
Apr.	2—Shuichi Isogami, Tokyo .... KO	9
	(Retained World Bantamweight Title)	
Aug.	29—Julian Solis, Miami Beach L	15
	(Lost World Bantamweight Title)	

TB	KO	WD	WF	D	LD	LF	KO BY	ND	NC
25	14	8	0	0	3	0	0	0	0

LUPE PINTOR
(Jose Guadalupe Pintor)
Born, April 13, 1955, Cuajimalpa, Mexico.
Weight, 118 lbs. Height, 5 ft. 4½ in.
1974
Mar.	2—Manuel Vasquez, Tijuana .... KO	2
May	7—Francisco Nunez, Tijuana .... W	10
July	24—Manuel Castaneda, Tijuana ...... KO	4
Sept.	10—Salvador Martinez, Mexico city .... W	10
Oct.	16—Margarito Lozano, Mexico City L disq.	4
Dec.	2—Juan Diaz, Mexico City .... KO	2

1975
Feb.	19—Martin Valencia, Mexico City .... KO	6
Mar.	10—Andres Reyes, Durango .... W	10
Apr.	16—Rocky Mijares, Torreon .... KO	7
July	25—Roberto Alvarez, Guadalajara .... KO	1
Sept.	20—Willie Jensen, Inglewood .... KO	7
Oct.	11—Alvaro Lopez, Guadalajara .... KO	2
Dec.	4—Catalino Flores, Inglewood .... KO	2

1976
Feb.	25—Albert Davila, Inglewood L	10
Mar.	27—Jose Luis Cruz, Tijuana .... KO	9
June	2—Gallito Castro, Tijuana .... KO	1
June	26—Manuel Killer, Mexicali .... KO	2
July	31—Samuel Machorro, Mexico City .... W	10
Oct.	2—Jose Rosa, Los Angeles .... KO	6
Nov.	13—Nacho Beltran, Culiacan .... KO	3

1977
Jan.	1—Jose Luis Cazares, Torreon .... KO	1
Jan.	29—Maestrito San Martin, Reynosa ... KO	7
Feb.	26—Evaristo Perez, Mexico City ...... KO	1
Mar.	11—Orlando Amores, Culiacan .... KO	1
Apr.	12—Gabe Cantera, San Antonio ...... KO	7

May	21—Enrique Brown, Madero .... KO	1
June	17—Eduardo Limon, Reynosa .... KO	1
July	2—Ramon Guillen, Mexico City ..... KO	1
Aug.	20—Andres Torres, Inglewood .... KO	4
Oct.	8—Tony Rocha, Los Angeles .... KO	4
Nov.	8—Baby Kid Chocolate, San Antonio KO	2
Dec.	15—Joaquin Martinez, Matamoros .... KO	2

1978
Jan.	30—David Vasquez, San Antonio ..... KO	2
Feb.	25—Gerald Hayes, Inglewood .... W	10
Mar.	31—Antonio Becerra, Mazatlan .... W	10
Apr.	22—Leo Cruz, San Juan L	10
June	30—Jose Luis Soto, Sinaloa L	10
July	22—Richard Rozelle, Houston .... KO	4
Sept.	26—Roger Bucheli, Houston .... KO	2
Nov.	11—Agustin Vega, Matamoros .... KO	3

1979
Mar.	10—Livio Nolasco, Los Angeles .... KO	6
May	1—Rodrigo Gonzalez, Houston .... KO	3
June	3—Carlos Zarate, Las Vegas .... W	15
	(Won WBC Bantamweight Title)	
Oct.	5—Auscencio Melendez, Reynosa .... KO	1
Oct.	29—Jose Luis Soto, Ciudad Obregon ... W	10
Dec.	29—Manuel Vasquez, Hermosillo .. KO by	6

1980
Feb.	9—Alberto Sandoval, Los Angeles ... KO	12
	(Retained WBC Bantamweight Title)	
June	11—Eijiro Murata, Tokyo .... D	15
	(Retained WBC Bantamweight Title)	
Sept.	19—Johnny Owen, Los Angeles .... KO	12
	(Retained WBC Bantamweight Title)	
Dec.	19—Albert Davila, Las Vegas .... W	15
	(Retained WBC Bantamweight Title)	

TB	KO	WD	WF	D	LD	LF	KO BY	ND	NC
50	35	9	0	1	3	1	1	0	0

JULIAN SOLIS
Born, January 7, 1957, Rio Piedras, Puerto Rico.
Weight, 118 lbs. Height, 5 ft. 5 in.
1975
Nov.	11—Ray Negron, San Juan .... W	4
Dec.	20—Ruben Maldonado, San Juan ...... W	4

1976
Apr.	5—Luis Cruz, San Juan .... W	4
June	5—Jorge Cruz, San Juan .... KO	4

1977
Oct.	8—Luis Rosario, Carolina .... W	10
Dec.	3—Sergio Villeta, San Juan .... KO	6

1978
Feb.	12—Livio Nolasco, Carolina .... W	10
Mar.	15—Leopoldo Frias, Santo Domingo ... W	10
June	10—Jose Jiminez, Carolina .... KO	2
Aug.	26—Jaime Ricardo, Carolina .... KO	8
Oct.	16—Julio Soto Solano, Santo Domingo .. W	12
	(Won Central American & Caribbean Bantamweight Title)	
Nov.	27—Gilberto Illueca, San Juan .... W	10

1979
Mar.	25—Guillermo Almongot, San Juan .... W	10
June	2—Julio Saba, Buenos Aires .... KO	8
Sept.	25—Bobby Flores, Miami Beach ...... KO	1
Dec.	18—Juan Ramirez, Rio Piedras .... KO	2

1980
Feb.	1—Edgar Roman, Caracas .... KO	11
	(Retained Central American & Caribbean Bantamweight Title)	
May	31—Welile Nkosinkulu, East London ... W	10
Aug.	29—Jorge Lujan, Miami Beach .... W	15
	(Won World Bantamweight Title)	
Nov.	14—Jeff Chandler, Miami .... KO by	14
	(Lost World Bantamweight Title)	

TB	KO	WD	WF	D	LD	LF	KO BY	ND	NC
20	8	11	0	0	0	0	1	0	0

JEFF CHANDLER

Born, September 3, 1956, Philadelphia, Pa. Weight, 118 lbs. Height, 5 ft. 7 in. Managed by K. O. Becky O'Neill.

1976

Feb.	25—Mike Dowling, Scranton	D	4
Apr.	13—Chico Vivas, Philadelphia	W	4
June	8—Mike Frazier, Philadelphia	W	4
Aug.	6—John Glover, Atlantic City	W	4
Oct.	14—Larry Huffin, Wilmington	KO	3
Nov.	30—Pee Wee Stokes, Philadelphia	W	4

1977

Feb.	21—Fernando Sanchez, Philadelphia ...	W	6
June	15—John Glover, Philadelphia	W	6
Oct.	25—Tony Reed, Philadelphia	W	8

1978

Mar.	14—Tony Hernandez, Philadelphia	KO	2
May	24—Jose Luis Garcia, Philadelphia ...	KO	5
June	19—Roque Moreno, Philadelphia	KO	5
Aug.	24—Sergio Reyes, Philadelphia	W	8

Oct.	24—Andres Torres, Philadelphia	W	10
Dec.	5—Rafael Gandarillo, Philadelphia ..	KO	9

1979

Apr.	3—Davey Vasquez, Philadelphia	W	10
May	14—Justo Garcia, Philadelphia	W	10
July	31—Alberto Cruz, Atlantic City	WF	3
Sept.	26—Baby Kid Chocolate, Upper Darby	KO	9
	(Won Vacant USBA Bantamweight Title)		
Dec.	4—Francisco Alvarado, Upper Darby	KO	7

1980

Feb.	1—Javier Flores, Philadelphia	KO	10
	(Won Vacant NABF Bantamweight Title)		
Mar.	29—Andres Hernandez, Atlantic City ..	W	12
	(Retained USBA and NABF Bantamweight Titles)		
July	12—Gilberto Villacana, Atlantic City	KO	4
July	31—Gustavo Martinez, Atlantic City ..	KO	8
Nov.	14—Julian Solis, Miami, Florida	KO	14
	(Won World Bantamweight Title)		

TB	KO	WD	WF	D	LD	LF	KO BY	ND	NC
25	12	12	0	1	0	0	0	0	0

FLYWEIGHTS

SID SMITH (GREAT BRITAIN)	*1913*	PONE KINGPETCH	1960-1962
BILL LADBURY (GREAT BRITAIN)	*1913-1914*	MASAHIKO (FIGHTING) HARADA	1962-1963
PERCY JONES (GREAT BRITAIN)	*1914*	PONE KINGPETCH	1963
JOE SYMONDS (GREAT BRITAIN)	*1914-1916*	HIROYUKI EBIHARA	1963-1964
JIMMY WILDE	1916-1923	PONE KINGPETCH	1964-1965
PANCHO VILLA	1923-1925	SALVATORE BURRINI	1965-1966
FIDEL LA BARBA	1925-1927	*HORACIO ACCAVALLO (WBA)*	*1966-1968*
ALBERT (FRENCHY)		WALTER MC GOWAN	1966
BELANGER (NBA, IBU)	1927-1928	CHARTCHAI CHIONOI	1966-1969
CORPORAL IZZY		ALACRAN (EFREN) TORRES	1969-1970
SCHWARTZ (NEW YORK)	1927-1929	*HIROYUKI EBIHARA (WBA)*	*1969*
JOHNNY MC COY (CALIF.)	*1927-1928*	*BERNABE VILLACAMPO (WBA)*	*1969-1970*
NEWSBOY BROWN (CALIF.)	*1928*	CHARTCHAI CHIONOI	1970
FRANKIE GENARO (NBA, IBU)	1928-1929	*BERKERK CHARTVANCHAI (WBA)*	*1970*
JOHNNY HILL (GREAT BRITAIN)	*1928-1929*	*MASAO OHBA (WBA)*	*1970-1973*
EMILE (SPIDER) PLADNER		ERBITO SALAVARRIA	1970-1973
(NBA, IBU)	1929	*BETULIO GONZALEZ (WBC)*	*1972*
FRANKIE GENARO (NBA, IBU)	1929-1931	*VENICE BORKORSOR (WBC)*	*1972-1973*
WILLIE LA MORTE (CLAIMANT)	*1929-1930*	VENICE BORKORSOR	1973
MIDGET WOLGAST (NEW YORK)	*1930-1935*	*CHARTCHAI CHIONOI (WBA)*	*1973-1974*
VICTOR (YOUNG) PEREZ		*BETULIO GONZALEZ (WBC)*	*1973-1974*
(NBA, IBU)	1931-1932	*SHOJI OGUMA (WBC)*	*1974-1975*
JACKIE BROWN	1932-1935	*SUSUMU HANAGATA (WBA)*	*1974-1975*
BENNY LYNCH	1935	MIGUEL CANTO (WBC)	1975-1979
SMALL MONTANA (CLAIMANT)	*1935-1937*	*ERBITO SALAVARRIA (WBA)*	*1975-1976*
VALENTIN ANGELMANN (IBU)	*1937*	*ALFONSO LOPEZ (WBA)*	*1976*
BENNY LYNCH	1937-1938	*GUSTAVO (GUTY) ESPADAS (WBA)*	*1976-1978*
PETER KANE	1938-1943	*BETULIO GONZALEZ (WBA)*	*1978-1979*
JACKIE PATERSON	1943-1948	CHAN-HEE PARK (WBC)	1979-1980
RINTY MONAGHAN	1948-1950	*LUIS IBARRA (WBA)*	*1979-1980*
TERRY ALLEN	1950	*TAE-SHIK KIM (WBA)*	*1980*
SALVADOR (DADO) MARINO	1950-1952	SHOJI OGUMA (WBC)	1980-
YOSHIO SHIRAI	1953-1954	*PETER MATHEBULA (WBA)*	*1980-*
PASCUAL PEREZ	1954-1960		

Claimants not generally recognized are in *italics*.

HISTORY OF THE FLYWEIGHT CLASS

The flyweight class was created in England during 1910, when it was given official recognition, with the scaling mark set at 108 pounds. Prior to this the smallest of the small battlers had to do the best they could against the 118 pounders of the bantam division. America followed suit the same year by recognizing the flyweight grade. The first championship fight at the weight brought together Jimmy Wilde of England, and Young Zulu Kid, of the U. S. A. Battles staged were as follows:

Dec. 18, 1916—Jimmy Wilde knocked out Young Zulu Kid, at London, England, in 11 rounds.

Feb. 11, 1921—Johnny Buff outpointed Frankie Mason at New Orleans, in 15 rounds.

(This was for American flyweight title.)

Sept. 14, 1922—Pancho Villa knocked out Johnny Buff, at Ebbets Field, Brooklyn, in 11 rounds.

March 1, 1923—Frankie Genaro outpointed Pancho Villa at Madison Square Garden, New York City, in 15 rounds.

June 18, 1923—Pancho Villa knocked out Jimmy Wilde at Polo Grounds, New York City, in 7 rounds.

(Villa was recognized as world's flyweight champion, although he had lost a decision to Frankie Genaro. Villa died in July, 1925, and Genaro claimed the title.)

August 22, 1925—Fidel La Barba outpointed Frankie Genaro at Los Angeles, Cal., in 10 rounds.

(La Barba was recognized as world flyweight champion, but temporarily retired from the ring in 1927.)

Dec. 16, 1927—Corporal Izzy Schwartz outpointed Newsboy Brown at New York City, in 15 rounds.

(Schwartz was recognized as flyweight champion by the New York State Commission, but conditions in the class became completely confused, and did not become stabilized until the commission staged an elimination tourney at the beginning of November, 1929.)

Feb. 6, 1928—Genaro gained N. B. A. recognition by outpointing Frenchy Belanger, 10 rounds, at Toronto, Canada.

Mar. 2, 1929—Emile (Spider) Pladner kayoed Genaro in one round at Paris, France, in a bout advertised as for the world title.

Mar. 20, 1929—With Pladner having defeated Izzy Schwartz, recognized by the New York Commission; Genaro, recognized by the N. B. A.; and Johnny Hill, the European champion, the International Boxing Union officially recognized Emile as the world champion.

Apr. 18, 1929—Frankie Genaro won from Pladner on a foul, 5 rounds, in Paris, France, in a bout advertised as for the world title.

March 21, 1930—Midget Wolgast outpointed Black Bill at New York City, in 15 rounds.

(This was the finals of the elimination tourney ordered by the New York State Commission, which thus recognized Wolgast as champion of the flyweights.)

Dec. 26, 1930—Frankie Genaro and Midget Wolgast fought a draw at New York City, in 15 rounds.

(Genaro was the National Boxing Association champion. Both claimed the title.)

Oct. 26, 1931—Young Perez knocked out Frankie Genaro at Paris, France, in 2 rounds.

(The bout was staged at the title limit, and Perez was recognized by the I. B. U. of Europe as world title holder.)

Oct. 31, 1932—Jackie Brown knocked out Young Perez at Manchester, England, in 13 rounds, and Brown was recognized throughout Europe as title holder.

Sept. 16, 1935—Small Montana, Philippines, outpointed Midget Wolgast at Oakland, Cal., in 10 rounds.

(This bout was advertised as being for world flyweight championship, and Montana claimed the title. This, however, was erroneous, as only the American title was at stake.)

Sept. 8, 1935—Benny Lynch knocked out Jackie Brown at Manchester, England, in 2 rounds and was generally accepted as world title holder.

Jan. 19, 1937—Benny Lynch outpointed Small Montana at London, England, in 15 rounds to gain international recognition.

June 29, 1938—Lynch retired from the class after his fight with Jackie Jurich, in Paisley, Scotland, because he was far overweight and was ruled out by the British Board of Boxing Control.

September 22, 1938—Jackie Jurich U.S., went to England to fight Peter Kane for what the British recognized as a world title bout, though Jurich was not the U.S. champion at the time. He was defeated by Kane in 15 rounds.

In America, the dispute between Jurich and Montana as to the U.S. championship, was decided on March 3, 1939, when Montana was knocked out in the 7th round at Hollywood. Then on October 4, Jurich again beat Montana, this time in 10 rounds at Oakland, and Jurich became the undisputed U.S. title holder of the flyweight division.

On September 22, 1939, when Jurich drew with Little Dado, who had beaten Montana at the flyweight limit on November 30, 1938. Jurich claimed the title as Dado no longer could make the weight.

Dado, following his victory over Montana, was matched to fight Enrico Urbinati of Italy for the vacant world title.

but the outbreak of World War II cancelled out this match and the N.B.A. gave him its backing as champion although Montana still claimed the title.

Kane's record was so far superior to that of Jurich or Montana, that he was generally recognized as world champion, especially because only three months before Lynch's retirement, Peter had fought Lynch a draw in 12 rounds, as the weight.

When World War II started, Kane was forced into temporary retirement after he had given up the flyweight title to enter the bantam class. Thus, in 1942, the title of world flyweight champion was vacant.

On June 19, 1943, Jackie Paterson knocked out Peter Kane in one round in Scotland to gain international recognition as world champion.

On July 10, 1946 Paterson successfully defended his title when he defeated Joe Curran in 15 rounds.

On Oct. 20, 1947, Rinty Monaghan defeated Dado Marino in London in 15 rounds to win N.B.A. recognition as title holder after Paterson had failed to go through with contest he had arranged with Marino for the title. Paterson however, was still recognized as world champion by the British Board.

On March 23, 1948, Monaghan stopped Paterson at Belfast in 7 rounds to win the crown.

With Rinty Monaghan retired, on April 25, 1950, Terry Allen won the vacant crown by defeating Honore Pratesi over 15 rounds at Harringay Arena, London, England.

August 1, 1950—Dado Marino won the title, outpointing Terry Allen over 15 rounds at Honolulu, Hawaii.

May 19, 1952—Yoshio Shirai won a 15-round decision over Dado Marino to gain the title, Korakuen Stadium, Tokyo, Japan.

Nov. 26, 1954—Pascual Perez defeated Yoshio Shirai, Korakuen Stadium, Tokyo, Japan, 15 rounds. Major John Sullivan, referee.

April 16, 1960—Pone Kingpetch won the title by a split 15-round decision over Pascual Perez at Bangkok, Thailand.

Oct. 10, 1962—Fighting Harada won the title by knocking out Pone Kingpetch in 2:59 of the 11-round at Tokyo, Japan.

January 12, 1963—Pone Kingpetch became the first to regain the flyweight title when he dicisioned Fighting Harada over 15 rounds at Bangkok, Thailand.

September 18, 1963—Hiroyuki Ebihara won the title when he knocked out Pone Kingpetch in 2:07 of the first round at Tokyo, Japan.

January 23, 1964—Pone Kingpetch regained the title when he decisioned Hiroyuki Ebihara over 15 rounds at Bangkok, Thailand.

April 23, 1965—Salvatore Burruni won a unanimous decision over Pone Kingpetch in a bout of 15 rounds in Rome, winning the flyweight title.

June 14, 1966—Walter McGowan, Scotland, defeated Salvatore Burruni, Italy, at Tokyo in 15 rounds by a unanimous decision. McGowan, 111¾; Burruni, 110.

Dec. 30, 1966—Walter McGowan, Scotland, was stopped by Chartchai Chionoi of Thailand in nine rounds at Bangkok. McGowan, 110; Chionoi, 111.

Feb. 23, 1969—Efren Torres, 111, Mexico, stopped Chartchai Chionoi, 110, Thailand, in the eighth round to win the world title. The bout was held in Mexico City, Mexico. The referee was Arthur Mercante.

March 20, 1970—Chartchai Chionoi, Thailand, regained his title by outpointing Efren Torres, Mexico in 15 rounds at Bangkok, Thailand. Weights: Chionoi—112, Torres—112.

Dec. 7, 1970—Erbito Salvarria, 111¼, Philippines kayoed Chartchai Chionoi, 111¼, Thailand, in second round. Bout held in Bangkok, Thailand.

February 9, 1973—Venice Borkorsor, Thailand won a 15-round decision over Erbito Salvarria, Philippines. Contest held in Bangkok, Thailand. Borkorsor 111 and Salvarria 110.

July 10, 1973—Venice Borkorsor, Thailand gave up his world flyweight crown. He moved up to the bantamweight division.

January 8, 1975—Miguel Canto, Mexico, won the vacant title via 15 round majority decision over Japan's Shoji Oguma (W.B.C. Champion) at the time of the contest, they were ranked 1 & 2. Contest was held in Sendai, Japan. Weights, both 111. Referee Jay Edson.

March 18, 1979—Chan-Hee Park, 112, Korea, won a unanimous decision over Miguel Canto, 111, Mexico, to take the WBC title in Pusan, Korea. The referee was Rudy Ortega.

November 17, 1979—Luis Ibarra, 110½, Panama, won a unanimous decision over Betulio Gonzales, 110, Venezuela to take WBA title. Site: Maracay, Venezuela. Referee: Ernesto Magana.

February 16, 1980—Tae-Shik Kim, 111¾, Korea, knocked out Luis Ibarra, 110¾, Panama, in 1:50 of the second round in Seoul, Korea, for the WBA title. Servio Tulio Lay, referee.

May 18, 1980—Shoji Oguma, 111¾, Japan, won the world title by kayoing Chan-Hee Park, also 111¾, Korea, in 0:53 of the ninth round in Seoul, Korea. Harold Nadaya, referee.

December 13, 1980—Peter Mathebula, 112, South Africa, won the WBA title with a split decision over Tae-Shik Kim, 111, Korea, in Los Angeles, Calif. Terry Smith, referee.

FLYWEIGHT DIVISION

SID SMITH
Born, February 2, 1889, Bermondsey, London, England. Weight, 112 lbs.

1907
—Jack Brooks, London	W	6
Mar. 30—Drummer LeHay, London	W	6
Apr. 13—Drummer LeHay, London	W	6
May 25—Curley Osborne, London	W	6
Nov. 16—Curley Osborne, London	W	6
Nov. 30—Curley Osborne, London	W	6
Dec. 14—Charlie Dew, London	W	6

1908
Jan. 4—Arthur Jones, London	KO	3
Jan. 13—Charlie Dew, London	L	10
Jan. 18—Frank Morecombe, London	W	6
Jan. 25—Jim Glover, London	W	6
Feb. 1—Frank Morecombe, London	W	6
Feb. 15—Drummer LeHay, London	W	6
Mar. 9—Young Healey, London	KO	2
—Jim Forrester	KO by	5
Apr. 27—Albert Cocksedge, London	D	6
May 25—Charlie Dew, London	L	10
July 4—Jack Fox, London	W	6
—Harry Lyons	W	6
—Bill Shard	W	6
—Curley Osborne, London	W	6
Oct. 30—Frank Morecombe, London	W	10
Nov. 30—Jack Morris, London	W	6
Dec. 21—George Hearne, London	W	6

1909
Jan. 9—Albert Cocksedge, London	L	6
Feb. 8—Albert Cocksedge, London	W	15
Mar. 15—Jack Wise, London	W	6
Mar. 23—Albert Cocksedge, Leicester	W	10
—Ernie Godwin	W	6
—Frank Exall	D	6
—Albert Cocksedge	D	6
June 5—Bill Kyne, London	L	6
Sept. 20—Frank Exall, London	KO	2
Oct. 4—Albert Dabbs, London	W	6
Nov. 8—Ted Timmins, Birmingham	W	6
Dec. 19—Bill Kyne, London	W	6

1910
Jan. 10—Jimmy Butler, Birkenhead	W	20
Jan. 27—Joe Shear, London	W	10
Feb. 17—Paddy Carroll, Liverpool	W	20
Feb. 23—Albert Cocksedge, Leicester	D	20
Mar. 20—Bill Kyne, London	W	6
June 6—Patsy Carroll, London	W	6
—Curley Osborne	W	6
—Bob Finch	W	6
—Bill Kyne	W	6
Oct. 12—Curley Osborne, London	W	6
Nov. 10—Paddy Carroll, Liverpool	L	20
Nov. 12—Bert Moughton, London	W	10
Nov. 16—George Hearn, London	W	6
Dec. 5—Alex Lafferty, Glasgow	W	20
Dec. 26—Bob Finch, London	KO	2

1911
Jan. 11—Stoker Hoskyne, London	W	6
Jan. 30—George Peters, London	W	15
Feb. 1—Kid Hogan, Leicester	KO	7
Mar. 8—Kid Logan, London	W	6
Mar. 20—Kid Logan, London	W	10
Aug. 4—Kid Hogan, Portsmouth	KO	8
Sept. 25—Stoker Hoskyne, London	W	20
Oct. 2—Georges Galliard, London	W	10
Oct. 19—Louis Ruddick, Liverpool	W	20
Dec. 4—Joe Wilson, London	W	20
(Won British Flyweight Title)		

1912
Feb. 24—Louisiana, Philadelphia	ND	6
Sept. 19—Curley Walker, London	W	20
Dec. 20—Albert Bouzonnie, London	W	10

1913
Feb. 12—Albert Bouzonnie, Paris	W	10
Feb. 14—Charlie Ward, London	W	6
Feb. 24—Sam Kellar, London	W	20
Mar. 15—Kid Hogan, Brighton	W	6
Mar. 28—Charlie Ward, London	W	10
Apr. —Relinquished British flyweight title.		
Apr. 11—Eugene Criqui, Paris	W	20
(Won European Flyweight Title)		
(Won World Flyweight Title)		
May 16—Joe Symonds, Plymouth	W	15
June 2—Bill Ladbury, London	KO by	11
(For British Flyweight Title)		
(Lost European Flyweight Title)		
(Lost World Flyweight Title)		
Oct. 9—Ike Bradley, Liverpool	W	10
Oct. 24—Charles Ledoux, Paris	KO by	6
Nov. 3—Alf Wye, London	L	15
—Danny Elliott	W	6
—Danny Elliott	W	8

1914
Feb. 16—Alf Wye, London	W	20
Mar. 23—Alf Wye, London	L	20
—Billy Rowlands	W	15
Dec. 3—Jimmy Wilde, Liverpool	KO by	9
Dec. 19—Johnny Marshall, Glasgow	WF	4

1915
Feb. 15—Joe Symonds, London	KO by	5
Mar. 17—Young Riley, Plymouth	W	6
Mar. 20—Johnny Best, London	D	20
Dec. 20—Jimmy Wilde, London	KO by	8

1916
Feb. 17—Sid Shields, London	W	15
Mar. 27—Jimmy Wilde, London	KO by	3
May 20—Dido Gains, London	W	15
June 1—Ivor Day, Liverpool	W	15
June 22—Young Josephs, Liverpool	W	15

1917
Jan. 8—Sid Whatley, London	KO	16
Jan. 29—George Clarke, London	L	20
Feb. 12—Billy Affleck, London	KO	13
Apr. 23—Tommy Noble, London	KO by	5
Oct. 15—Joe Conn, London	KO by	4

1918
Apr. 22—Sid Whatley, London	W	10
Oct. 12—Jerry Lyons, Redhill	KO	9

1919
Dec. 26—Johnny Marshall, London	KO	11

TB	KO	WD	WF	D	LD	LF	KO BY	ND	NC
99	10	65	1	5	8	0	9	1	0

Died, April 28, 1948, Hendon, London, England.

BILL LADBURY
Born, October 14, 1891, New Cross, London, England. Weight, 112 lbs.

1908
—Bob Campion	W	6
Nov. 30—Jack Fox, London	D	6

1909
Jan. 18—Jack Fox, London	W	15
Mar. 8—Young Langhorn, London	W	10
Mar. 29—Albert Bass, London	KO	4
Nov. 29—Johnny Condon, London	L	15

1910
Jan. 1—Charles Ledoux, Paris	KO	4
Feb. 28—Sam Kellar, London	L	20

1911
Jan. 30—Stoker Hoskyne, London	W	10
Feb. 18—Jack Arundel, London	W	10
July 15—Sweeper Madge, London	W	10
Oct. 17—Albert Cocksedge, Leicester	KO	7
Nov. 4—Georges Galliard, Paris	D	10
Nov. 8—Charles Ledoux, Paris	KO by	4
Nov. 16—Johnny Hughes, London	KO by	3

1912
Jan. 16—Nat Brooks, London	KO	6
Jan. 27—Stoker Hoskyne, London	W	10
Feb. 10—Joe Wilson, London	D	12
Mar. 9—Joe Fox, London	W	15

798

Apr.	20—Frank Warner, London	W	10
Apr.	27—Joe Fox, London	W	10
June	1—Joe Wilson, London	L	10
June	15—Joe Fox, London	KO by	5
June	29—Bill Kyne, London	W	10
July	20—Nat Brooks, London	L	12
Oct.	7—Joe Wilson, London	KO	12
Nov.	11—Sam Kellar, London	W	20
Nov.	21—Tommy Harrison, Liverpool	W	10
Dec.	9—Jack Arundel, London	KO	6

1913

Jan.	6—Young Dando, London	KO	14
Feb.	3—Joe Wilson, London	KO	17
Mar.	10—Louis Ruddick, London	W	20
Apr.	7—George Peters, London	W	10
June	2—Sid Smith, London	KO	11

(Won British and European Flyweight Titles)
(Won World Flyweight Title)

Nov.	24—Tommy Harrison, London	W	20
Dec.	15—Jimmy Berry, London	KO by	10

1914

Jan.	26—Percy Jones, London	L	20

(Lost British and European Flyweight Titles)
(Lost World Flyweight Title)

Mar.	2—Joe Symonds, London	D	20
Mar.	30—Tommy Harrison, London	W	15
Apr.	27—Tancy Lee, London	KO by	8
Dec.	10—Johnny Hughes, London	W	20

1915

Mar.	28—Joe Symonds, London	KO by	1
June	11—Joe Symonds, Plymouth	KO by	2
Oct.	11—Percy Jones, London	KO by	5

1916

Jan.	10—Harry Curley, London	W	15
Feb.	21—Peter Cain, London	D	15
July	17—Nat Brooks, London	KO by	6
Oct.	9—Tommy Noble, London	KO by	13
Nov.	9—Harry Curley, London	KO	11
Nov.	27—Alf Mansfield, London	W	15

TB	KO	WD	WF	D	LD	LF	KO BY	ND	NC
50	10	20	0	5	5	0	10	0	0

Killed in action, July, 1917, France.

PERCY JONES

Born, December 26, 1892, Porthcawl, Glamorganshire, Wales. Weight, 112 lbs.

1912

	—Dai Davies	KO	9
	—Con Rowlands	KO	5
	—Lew Williams	W	6
	—Gordon Francis	KO	3
Sept.	20—Shon Price, Pentre	W	10
Oct.	5—Charlie Yeomans, Pentre	D	10
Nov.	16—Will Gould, Tonypandy	KO	5
Nov.	23—Harry Stuckey, Tonypandy	W	6
Nov.	30—Sam Morgan, Tonypandy	W	6
Dec.	7—Jim England, Tonypandy	KO	7
Dec.	14—Dai Matthews, Cardiff	KO	6
	—Curley Pullman	W	10

1913

Jan.	11—George Williams, Tonypandy	KO	11
Jan.	25—Young Rule, Tonypandy	KO	9
Feb.	1—Young Kendal, Tonypandy	KO	4
Feb.	8—Will Jones, Tonypandy	KO	2
Mar.	19—Joe Symonds, Tonypandy	WF	4
Mar.	29—Stoker Hoskyne, Tonypandy	KO	3
Apr.	5—Tom Lewis, Tonypandy	W	12
Apr.	28—Gus Govarts, London	W	6
May	8—Tommy Harrison, Liverpool	KO	11
June	2—Joe Symonds, London	W	10
June	5—Dido Gains, Liverpool	KO	6
June	7—Alf Mansfield, Tonypandy	KO	5
June	23—Bill Kyne, London	W	10
July	5—Alf Mansfield, Tonypandy	KO	8
July	10—Tom Cherry, Liverpool	KO	6
July	22—Bill Kyne, Tonypandy	W	10
Sept.	18—Joe Symonds, Hanley	KO	8
Sept.	20—Dolly Benyon, Tonypandy	W	15

Oct.	11—Tom Cherry, Tonypandy	W	15
Oct.	18—Joe Wilson, Tonypandy	KO	13
Nov.	8—Joe Wilson, Tonypandy	KO	12
Nov.	24—Sam Kellar, London	W	15
Nov.	27—Alf Mansfield, Liverpool	KO	8
Dec.	6—Driver Knox, Tonypandy	KO	1

1914

Jan.	8—Million, Liverpool	KO	2
Jan.	26—Bill Ladbury, London	W	20

(Won British and European Flyweight Titles)
(Won World Flyweight Title)

Feb.	12—Eugene Criqui, Liverpool	L	15
Mar.	26—Eugene Criqui, Liverpool	W	20

(Retained European Flyweight Title)
(Retained World Flyweight Title)

May	15—Joe Symonds, Plymouth	KO by	18

(Lost British and European Flyweight Titles)
(Lost World Flyweight Title)

June	2—George Reeves, Tonypandy	KO	7
June	3—Young Kendall, Tonyrefail	KO	4
June	8—Billy Jones, Mountain Ash	KO	3
Oct.	19—Tancy Lee, London	KO by	14

1915

Oct.	1—Young Swift, Plymouth	D	15
Oct.	11—Bill Ladbury, London	KO	5

TB	KO	WD	WF	D	LD	LF	KO BY	ND	NC
47	25	16	1	2	1	0	2	0	0

Died (of war wounds), December 25, 1922.

JOE SYMONDS

Born, December 28, 1894, Plymouth, Devonshire, England. Weight, 112 lbs.

1911

Jan.	6—Young Bob, Plymouth	W	4
Jan.	20—Young Coombs, Plymouth	KO	4
Jan.	27—Young Stanley, Plymouth	W	4
Mar.	10—Young Slocombe, Plymouth	W	4
Mar.	17—Stanley Hood, Plymouth	W	4
May	5—Young Riley, Plymouth	W	4
May	19—Young Coombs, Plymouth	KO	5
July	7—Young Otto, Plymouth	W	6
July	21—Young Riley, Plymouth	D	6
Sept.	15—George French, Plymouth	W	8
Nov.	10—Young Jago, Plymouth	L	6

1912

Jan.	27—Young Duffin, Portsmouth	W	6
Mar.	22—Young Riley, Plymouth	D	6
Apr.	19—Young Harrison, Plymouth	KO	1
May	3—Young Snowball, Plymouth	W	6
May	10—Young Britt, Plymouth	KO	1
May	17—Dido Gains, Plymouth	L	15
	—Young Swift, Plymouth	KO	4
Oct.	16—Young Jago, Paignton	W	8
Oct.	25—George French, Plymouth	KO	3
Nov.	8—Dido Gains, Plymouth	W	15
Nov.	10—Young Jago, Devonport	W	10
Nov.	29—Arthur Ireland, Plymouth	D	15
Dec.	13—Josephs' Nipper, Plymouth	KO	9

1913

Jan.	3—Alf Mansfield, Plymouth	W	15
Jan.	24—Joe Ross, Plymouth	W	15
Mar.	3—Alf Mansfield, London	W	15
Mar.	7—Bill Kyne, Plymouth	W	15
Mar.	19—Percy Jones, Tonypandy	LF	4
Mar.	24—Tommy Hughes, Blackburn	W	15
Apr.	21—Jim Hales, London	W	6
Apr.	28—Tom Cherry, Southampton	W	10
May	2—Harry Brooks, Plymouth	KO	12
May	16—Sid Smith, Plymouth	L	15
June	2—Percy Jones, London	L	10
June	11—Bob Finch, Plymouth	W	15
Aug.	1—Joe Wilson, Plymouth	KO	9
Sept.	18—Percy Jones, Hanley	KO by	8
Oct.	24—Fred Anderson, Plymouth	KO	2
Nov.	14—Jim Hales, Plymouth	KO	4
Dec.	11—Charlie Ward, Exeter	W	15

1914

Jan.	9—Sam Kellar, Plymouth	W	15
Feb.	6—Sid Peploe, Plymouth	KO	6
Mar.	2—Bill Ladbury, London	D	20
Apr.	3—Abe Mantell, Plymouth	W	15
Apr.	8—Bert Moughton	KO	7
May	15—Percy Jones, Plymouth	KO	18

(Won British and European Flyweight Titles)
(Won World Flyweight Title)

June	12—Tommy Harrison, Plymouth	W	15
June	30—Albert Bouzonnie, Plymouth	WF	7
July	17—Johnny Baker, Plymouth	W	15
Nov.	16—Jimmy Wilde, London	L	15
Dec.	11—Bob Finch, Plymouth	KO	5

1915

Jan.	8—Ike Bradley, Plymouth	W	15
Jan.	29—Sid Shields, Plymouth	KO	14
Feb.	15—Sid Smith, London	KO	5
Mar.	11—Tommy Harrison, Liverpool	D	15
Mar.	22—Bill Ladbury, London	KO	1
May	14—Jim King, Plymouth	KO	3
June	11—Bill Ladbury, Plymouth	KO	2
July	2—Johnny Best, Plymouth	W	15
July	23—Johnny Hughes, Plymouth	W	20
Aug.	13—Dido Gains, Plymouth	W	20
Sept.	10—Johnny Best, Plymouth	KO	11
Oct.	18—Tancy Lee, London	KO	16

(Retained British and European Flyweight Titles)
(Retained World Flyweight Title)

Nov.	12—Johnny Gratton, Plymouth	KO	3
Nov.	25—Johnny Hughes, Liverpool	W	15
Dec.	9—Sam Kellar, London	LF	6
Dec.	17—George (Digger) Stanley, Plymouth	WF	11

1916

Feb.	7—Young Dando, Newcastle	KO	1
Feb.	14—Jimmy Wilde, London	KO by	12

(Lost British and European Flyweight Titles)
(Lost World Flyweight Title)

Mar.	24—Ivor Day, Plymouth	LF	4
Apr.	14—Tommy Noble, Plymouth	KO	6
May	5—Tancy Lee, Plymouth	KO by	17
June	16—Ivor Day, Plymouth	KO	9
July	8—Tommy Noble, London	W	20
Aug.	11—Sid Shields, Plymouth	KO	4
Sept.	1—Eugene Husson, Plymouth	KO	4
Sept.	30—Louis Ruddick, Swansea	D	20
Oct.	27—Johnny Hughes, Plymouth	WF	7
Nov.	17—Bill Beynon, Plymouth	W	15
Dec.	26—Louis Ruddick, Plymouth	W	15

1917

Feb.	23—Bill Beynon, Plymouth	KO	16
Mar.	16—Joe Dasher, Plymouth	KO	6
Apr.	9—Ted Bull, Plymouth	KO	5
June	8—Sid Whatley, Plymouth	KO	1
June	25—Joe Fox, London	KO by	18

(For British Bantamweight Title)

Aug.	6—Louis Ruddick, London	WF	15
Sept.	1—Jack Marks, Cleethorpe	KO	10
Oct.	20—Jim Calbert, Grimsby	KO	1
Oct.	29—Frankie Neil, London	KO	3
Nov.	3—Bill Beynon, Llwynpia	D	15
Dec.	26—George Langham, Plymouth	KO	1

1918

Apr.	1—Chris Langdon, Plymouth	KO	9
Apr.	8—Tommy Noble, London	W	15
Aug.	2—George Clarke, Plymouth	W	15
Oct.	4—Charlie Stone, Plymouth	KO	3
Nov.	25—Tommy Noble, London	L	20

(For British Bantamweight Title)

Dec.	26—Fred Jacks, Plymouth	W	15

1919

Jan.	10—Terry Martin, Plymouth	WF	14
Jan.	20—Seaman Arthur Hayes, London	KO by	9
Apr.	4—Mike Blake, Plymouth	D	15
Nov.	7—George Clarke, Plymouth	W	15
Nov.	15—Billy Eynon, Mountain Ash	D	15
Dec.	12—Chris Langdon, Plymouth	W	15
Dec.	26—Walter Ross, Plymouth	ND	10

1920

Jan.	1—George Clarke, London	LF	13

Apr.	17—Silvino Jamito, Sydney	KO	8
May	22—Digger Evans, Sydney	KO	8
June	12—Jack Green, Sydney	D	20
June	26—Jack Green, Sydney	W	20
July	17—Sid Godfrey, Sydney	LF	9
Aug.	7—Jerry Sullivan, Sydney	D	20
Aug.	28—Jerry Sullivan, Sydney	KO	9
Sept.	25—Joe Alvarez, Sydney	KO	7
Oct.	16—Jack Green, Sydney	L	20
Dec.	4—Arthur Wyns, Sydney	LF	7

1921

Mar.	5—Vince Blackburn, Sydney	KO	7
Mar.	26—Bert Spargo, Melbourne	KO by	9
May	21—Bert Spargo, Sydney	KO by	7
Oct.	21—Walter Ross, Plymouth	W	15
Nov.	28—Billy Eynon, London	L	20
Dec.	27—Ben Callicott, Plymouth	KO by	2

1922

June	30—Benny Thomas, Plymouth	W	15
July	28—Kid Davis, Plymouth	W	15
Sept.	1—Albert Colcombe, Plymouth	KO	6
Oct.	20—Billy Morgan, Plymouth	KO	7
Nov.	—Tommy Gerrard, U.S.A.	W	12

1923

May	11—Jim Higgins, Plymouth	WF	2
June	1—Billy Palmer, Plymouth	KO by	12
June	22—Billy Palmer, Plymouth	KO by	2

1924

May	16—Franco Vitale, Plymouth	WF	2
Oct.	31—Bugler Harry Lake, Plymouth	KO by	7

TB	KO	WD	WF	D	LD	LF	KO BY	ND	NC
133	45	44	7	11	8	6	11	1	0

Died, March 4, 1953, Plymouth, England.

JIMMY WILDE
(Mighty Atom)

Born, May 15, 1892, Pontypridd, Wales.
Weight, 108 lbs. Height 5 ft. 2½ ins. Managed by Teddy Lewis.

1911

Knockouts: Lewis Williams, 3; Sid Jenkins, 11; Young Avent, 4; Ted Powell, 3; Joe Rogers, 5; Kid Pearson, 2; Joe Gans, 7; Lewis Williams, 5; Mike Flynn, 8; Young Powell, 3; Ted Roberts, 3; Ted Roberts, 4; Dai Robers, 3; Young Langford, 2; Eddie Thomas, 2; Steve Thomas, 3; Billy Papke, 3; Archie Grant, 2; Young Towell, 4; Young Towell, 3; Young Rice, 4; Walter Hall, 3; Harry Stuckey, 7. Won: Dai Thomas, 3; Dick Jenkins; Fred Chappell, 6; Jim Easton, 10; Young Baker, 6. Draw: George Luke, 6.

1912

Jan.	20—Matt Wells, Nipper, London	KO	1
Feb.	18—George Luke, Pontypridd	D	6
Mar.	20—D. Thomas, Pontypridd	W	3
July	20—Jim Morris, Cardiff	KO	5
Aug.	17—Jim Stuckey, Tonypandy	KO	8
Nov.	9—Phil Davis, Merthyr	KO	2
Nov.	16—Young Ransford, Tonypandy	KO	2
Nov.	30—Alf Williams, Tonypandy	W	12
Dec.	14—Stoker Staines, Tonypandy	KO	1
Dec.	21—Billy Yates, Cardiff	KO	4
Dec.	31—Billy Padden, Glasgow	KO	19

1913

Jan.	18—Tom Hughes, Tonypandy	KO	7
Feb.	1—Dick Jenkins, Tonypandy	ND	10
Feb.	15—Kid Fitzpatrick, Tonypandy	KO	2
Feb.	—Harry Stuckey, Tonypandy	ND	6
Feb.	—Ben Hardwick, Tylorstown	ND	4
Mar.	8—Dai Matthews, Tonypandy	KO	4
Mar.	—Harry Taylor, Swansea	KO	3
Apr.	12—Will Rees, Tonypandy	KO	3
Apr.	19—Billy Yates, Tonypandy	KO	3
Apr.	27—Dai Davies, Tonypandy	W	12
May	6—Kid Levine, Tonypandy	KO	8
May	19—Harry Brooks, Manchester	KO	8
May	30—Harry Curley, Hanley	KO	12
June	14—Billy Padden, Tonypandy	W	15
June	21—Gwilym Thomas, Tonypandy	KO	3
July	1—Dick Lewis, Tonypandy	KO	3
July	12—Tommy Lewis, Tonypandy	W	12
July	19—Young Dando, Tonypandy	W	15
Aug.	4—Darky Sanders, Cardiff	W	10

Aug. 28—Young Dyer, Liverpool......KO 3
Sept. 6—Dick Jenkins, Ferndale........W 10
Sept. 8—Dido Gains, Cardiff..........W 15
Sept. 18—Kid Levine, Hanley.........KO 7
Sept. 22—Young Dando, Cardiff.......W 10
Nov. 1—Darky Sanders, Tonypandy...KO 11
Nov. 13—Young Baker, Liverpool......KO 10
Nov. 21—Young Dyer, Manchester......W 10
Nov. 22—Dido Gains, Swansea..........W 15
Dec. 6—Young Dando, Merthyr.....WF 10
Dec. 13—Billy Charles, Tonypandy....KO 6

1914

Jan. 3—Kid Nutter, Tonypandy.......W 15
Jan. 8—Young Reynon, Liverpool.....W 15
Jan. 29—Billy Padden, Liverpool......W 3
Feb. 2—Kid Nutter, Birkenhead.....W 15
Feb. 9—Tom Thomas, Manchester....KO 7
Feb. 16—Paddy Carroll, Liverpool.....KO 2
Feb. 16—Geo. Jaggers, Sheffield.......W 5
Mar. 26—Bill Kyne, Liverpool.........W 4
Mar. 30—Eugene Husson, N.S.C.......KO 6
Apr. 13—Jack Madden, Ashton-u-L....KO 4
Apr. 16—Bouzonnie, Liverpool.......KO 6
Apr. 27—Alf. Mansfield, Leeds........W 20
May 11—Gloria, N.S.C. ....KO 9
June 22—Charlie Banyard, Aberdare....W 9
July 18—Charley Jordan, Tonypandy..KO 10
July 23—Artie Edwards, Liverpool......W 15
Aug. 19—Young Baker, Leicester.......W 15
Sept. 28—Alf Mansfield, London.......KO 10
Nov. 16—Joe Symonds, London........W 15
Dec. 3—Sid Smith, Liverpool.........KO 9

1915

Jan. 25—Tancy Lee, London......KO by 17
Mar. 25—Sid Shields, Liverpool........KO 2
July 24—Dvr. Benthew, Sheffield.......W 5
Aug. 14—George Clark, Sheffield.......W 8
Sept. 25—Walter Buchan, Liverpool....KO 5
Oct. 20—Peter Cullen, Dublin..........W 9
Nov. 27—Tommy Hughes, Barrow......W 8
Dec. 9—Johnny Best, Liverpool.......W 14
Dec. 13—Danny Elliott, Bradford......KO 2
Dec. 20—Sid Smith, Liverpool..........W 8

1916

Jan. 8—Billy Rowlands, Swansea.....W 7
Jan. 24—Tom Noble, New Cross.......W 11
Jan. 27—Jimmy Morton, Liverpool....KO 2
Feb. 14—Young Symonds, London.....KO 12
Mar. 9—Sam Keller, W. L. Stadium....W 8
Mar. 27—Sid Smith, Hoxton..........KO 3
Apr. 27—Johnny Rosner, London....KO 11
Apr. 29—Benny Thomas, London......W 8
May 13—Darkey Saunders, New Cross...W 5
May 13—Joe Magnus, New Cross......W 5
May 29—Tommy Harrison, London....W 8
June 26—Tancy Lee, London..........KO 11
July 31—Johnny Hughes, London....KO 10
—Tommy Noble, New Cross.....W 15
Dec. 18—Young Zulu Kid, London....KO 11
(Won Vacant World Flyweight Title)

1917

Mar. 13—George Clark, London........W 4
Mar. 22—Frankie Russell, London....KO 3
Aug. 11—Sid Smith, London..........Exh. 4
Sept. 17—Sid Smith, London.........Exh. 4

1918

Mar. 28—L-Cpl. Jacobs, Aldersoht.....KO 4
Apr. 29—Pte. Dick Heasman, London..KO 2
May 9—Pedlar Palmer, London......Exh. 4
Aug. 31—Joe Conn, London..........KO 12
Dec. 11—Joe Lynch, London...........W 3
Dec. 11—Digger Evans, London........W 3
Dec. 12—Pal Moore, London.........L 3
(Final of bantamweight class in Inter-Allied King's Trophy Competition.)

1919

Mar. 31—Joe Lynch, N. S. C. ....W 15
Apr. 21—Jimmy Buck, Liverpool......KO 5
May 17—Alf Mansfield, Hol. Stad. .....KO 13
July 17—Pal Moore, Olympia...................W 20
Dec. 6—Jack Sharkey, Milwaukee.....ND 10

1920

Jan. 8—Babe Asher, St. Louis........ND 8
Jan. 29—Mike Ertle, Milwaukee.......KO 3
Feb. 19—Mickey Russell, Jersey City...KO 7
Mar. 3—Patsy Wallace, Philadelphia...ND 6
Mar. 12—Frankie Mason, Toledo, O. ...ND 12
Apr. 12—Zulu Kid, Windsor, Ont. ......ND 10
Apr. 21—Battling Murray, Camden, N.J..KO 8
May 1—Bobby Dyson, Lawrence.....KO 1
May 12—Battling Murray, Philadelphia.KO 2
May 24—Patsy Wallace, Toronto, Ont. ..W 10

1921
Jan. 13—Pete Herman, London.....KO by 17
1923
Mar. 29—Pedlar Palmer, London......Exh. 3
June 18—Pancho Villa, N.Y..............KO by 7
(Lost world flyweight title)

TB	KO	WD	WF	D	LD	LF	KOBY	ND	NC
140	77	48	1	2	1	0	3	8	0

Elected to Boxing Hall of Fame 1959.
Died, Mar. 10, 1969, Cardiff, Wales.

PANCHO VILLA
(Francisco Guilledo)
Born, August 1, 1901, at Iloilo, Philippine Islands. Nationality, Filipino. Weight, 110 lbs. Height, 5 ft. 1 in. Managed by Frank Churchill.

1919
Started as professional
Won: Kid Castro, 4; Terrible Pondong, 4; Kid Cortez, 4; Peter Alberto, 4; Young Edwards, 4; Young Duarte, 4; Kid Elino, 4; Jose de la Cruz, 4; Pedro Olengapo, 4. Knockouts: Kid Moro, 2; Alberto Castro, 3; Cesareo Siguion, 2; Jaime Desiderio, 2. Lost: Frisco Concepcion, 4.
1920
Won: Kid Castro, 6; Jose de la Cruz, 6; Mike Ballerino 6 (twice); Stiff Irineo, 6; Juan Candelaria, 6; Kid Cortez, 6. Knockouts: Pedro Capitan, 4; Salvador Santo Tomas, 2. No decision: Big Cortez, 6; Mike Ballerino, 6 (twice).
1921
Jan. 10—Mike Ballerino, Manila, P. I.....D 15
Jan. 23—Juan Candelaria, Manila, P. I..KO 4
Feb. 7—Kid Moro, Manila, P.I.........KO 3
Feb. 21—Terrible Pondong, Manila, P.I...W 8
(Won Orient Flyweight Title)
Mar. 5—Mike Ballerino, Manila, P. I.....W 10
Mar. 26—Young Santos, Manila, P. I. ...KO 7
Apr. 10—Kid Garcia, Manila, P. I........W 8
Apr. 24—Stiff Irineo, Manila, P. I.......KO 2
May 8—Mike Ballerino, Manila, P. I.....W 15
May 22—Knock-out Lewis, Manila, P.I..KO 4
June 6—Pedro Alberto, Manila, P. I....W 8
June 20—Leoncio Bernabe, Manila, P. I..D 6
July 11—Young Modejar, Manila, P. I...W 6
July 25—Mike Ballerino, Manila, P. I....D 15
Aug. 9—Eddie Moore, Manila, P. I.....LF 10
Aug. 23—Mike Ballerino, Manila, P. I.....W 20
Sept. 7—Syd Keenan, Manila, P. I......W 8
Sept. 21—Leoncio Bernabe, Manila, P. I..W 8
Oct. 5—Mike Ballerino, Manila, P. I....W 20
Oct. 19—Kid Aguila, Manila, P. I.......W 8
Nov. 3—Cowboy Reyes, Manila, P. I...W 15
Nov. 10—Kid Aguila, Manila, P. I.......W 8
Nov. 17—Kid Garcia, Manila, P. I.......W 8
Dec. 8—George Mendies, Manila, P. I..KO 3
(Won Orient Bantamweight Title)
Dec. 15—Jimmy Taylor, Manila, P. I....W 8
Dec. 29—Battling Ongay, Manila, P. I..KO 1
1922
Jan. 12—Kid Abayan, Manila, P. I.......W 8
Feb. 12—George Washington Lee, Manila W 15
Mar. 19—Max Mason, Iloilo, P. I.......KO 4
Apr. 1—Peter Sarmiento, Manila, P. I...W 15
June 7—Abe Attel Goldstein, Jersey City......................ND 12
July 6—Frankie Genaro, Jersey City....ND 12
July 19—Frankie Murray, Long Island...W 6
July 29—Terry Miller, Jersey City......ND 12
Aug. 2—Johnny Hepburn, New York...W 6
Aug. 15—Sammy Cohen, New York....W 8
Aug. 22—Frankie Genaro, New York.....L 10
Sept. 14—Johnny Buff, New York..........KO 11
(Won American Flyweight title)
Sept. 21—Terry Smacka, Newark.......ND 4
Nov. 17—Abe Goldstein, New York....W 15
Nov. 27—Young Montreal, Boston.....W 10
Dec. 29—Terry Martin, New York......W 15
1923
Jan. 1—Battling Murray, Philadelphia.ND 8
Feb. 13—Frankie Mason, Boston.......KO 5
Feb. 20—Kid Wolfe, Philadelphia.......KO 3
Mar. 1—Frankie Genaro, New York.....L 15
(Lost American flyweight championship)
Mar. 19—Young Montreal, Phila........ND 8
Apr. 23—Clarence Rosen, Detroit......ND 10

May 11—Battling Murray, Chicago .....ND 10
May 24—Bobby Wolgast, Philadelphia..ND 8
June 18—Jimmy Wilde, New York .....KO 7
(Won flyweight championship of world.)
July 20—Abe Friedman, Boston .... W 10
July 31—Kid Williams, Philadelphia ....ND 8
Aug. 22—Jackie Feldman, New York ...KO 3
Sept. 8—Bud Taylor, Chicago ....ND 10
Sept. 24—Tony Thomas, Boston .... W 10
Oct. 13—Benny Schwartz, Baltimore .... W 15
(World Flyweight Title)
Oct. 22—Jabez White, Philadelphia ....ND 8
Nov. 19—Joie Shcwartz, Detroit ....ND 10
Dec.   5—Young Mack, Toronto, Can. ..KO 4
Dec. 10—Patsy Wallace, Philadelphia ...ND 8

1924
Jan.   1—Tony Norman, Pittsburgh ....ND 10
Jan. 21—Mike Moran, Pittsburgh ......ND 10
Feb.   8—Georgie Marks, New York ....W 15
Mar.   6—Bud Taylor, Milwaukee .....ND 10
Mar. 21—Georgie Lee, Sacramento ..... D   4
Apr. 23—Eddie McKenna, Cleveland ...ND 10
May 30—Frankie Ash, Brooklyn .... W 15
(Title Bout)
June 10—Bud Taylor, N. Y. C. .... W 12
July   2—Henry Catena, West New York
N. J..............................KO 5
July 21—Willie Woods, Boston .... W 10
July 28—Frankie Murray, Atl. City ....ND 10
Aug. 18—Amos Carlin, New Orleans ....ND 10
—Willie Darcy, Waterbury ....W 12

1925
Mar.   9—Francisco Pilapel, Manila, P.I. .KO 1
May   1—Jose Sencio, Manila, P. I. ...... W 15
July   4—Jimmy McLarnin, Oakland, Cal. .L 10

TB	KO	WD	WF	D	LD	LF	KOBY	ND	NC
103	22	49	0	4	4	1	0	23	0

Died July 14, 1925 from blood poisoning caused by an infected tooth following fight with McLarnin.
Elected to Boxing Hall of Fame 1961.

FIDEL LA BARBA
Born, September 29, 1905, New York City, Nationality, Italian-American. Weight, 112 lbs. Height, 5 ft. 3 in. Reach, 66 inches. Managed by George Blake.

1924
May 21—Ray Fee, Boston.............KO 2
(National Amateur Flyweight Champion)
July 15—McKenzie, Paris .... W 3
July 24—Won Amateur Flyweight Championship of World at 1924 Olympic Games in Paris.
(Professional Career)
Sept. 14—Pat Pringle, Los Angeles ......KO 1
Oct. 14—Frankie Grandetta, Vernon, Cal.W 4
Oct. 28—Jimmy McLarnin, Vernon, Cal. .L 4
Nov. 11—Jimmy McLarnin, Vernon, Cal. D 4
Dec.   4—Pedro Villa, San Pedro, Cal. .... W 4

1925
Jan. 13—Jimmy McLarnin, Vernon, Cal. .L 10
Feb. 20—Young Nationalista, Hollywood W 10
Mar. 20—George Rivers, Hollywood .....W 10
Apr. 17—Newsboy Brown, Hollywood .. D 10
May 29—Teddy Silva, Hollywood ....W 10
July 17—Georgie Rivers, Hollywood .... W 10
Aug. 22—Frankie Genaro, Los Angeles .. W 10
(Won American Flyweight Title)
Nov. 20—Ray Fee, Hollywood, Cal. ....KO 1
Dec. 23—Lew Perfetti, N. Y. C. .... W 6

1926
Jan. 20—Clever Sencio, Los Angeles ....W 10
Mar. 12—Vic King, Hollywood ....KO 4
Mar. 31—Clever Sencio, Los Angeles .... W 10
May   4—Emil Paluso, Los Angeles ...... W 10
July   7—Georgie Rivers, Los Angeles ... W 10
Aug. 13—Emil Paluso, Chicago .... W 10
Aug. 25—Happy Atherton, Chicago ..... W 10
Sept. 2—Paul Milnar, Peoria............ W 8
Oct.   5—Newsboy Brown, Vernon, Cal. . D 10
Oct. 26—Yg. Nationalista, Los Angeles . D 10
Nov. 19—Calif. Joe Lynch, San Francisco W 4
Dec.   7—Delos Williams, Fresno, Cal. ... W 10

1927
Jan. 21—Elky Clark, New York .... W 12
(Won vacant world's flyweight title)
Feb.   3—Harry Kid Brown, Hollywood .. W 10
Feb. 14—Johnny Vacca, Boston ....L 10

Mar. 22—Johnny Vacca, Boston ....L 10
Apr. 24—Young Montreal, Providence ... W 10
Apr. 29—Mickie Billy Shaw, Detroit ....ND 10
May 11—Babe Keller, Kalamazoo, Mich. . W 10
June 11—Paul Milnar, St. Paul. Minn. ...ND 4
June 21—Mike Brody, St. Louis, Mo. .... W 10
June 27—Clarence Rosen, Detroit .... D 10
July 12—Pal Moore, Chicago .... W 10
Aug. 23—†Johnny Vacca, Los Angeles... W 10
†La Barba announced retirement to enter Stanford University.

1928
July 17—†Huerta Evans, Los Angeles ... W 10
Aug.   7—Earl Mastro, Los Angeles ...... W 10
Sept. 11—Bushy Graham, Los Anglees ... W 10
Sept. 25—Yg. Nationalista, Los Angeles .. W 10
Nov. 23—Ray Ravini, San Francisco ....KO 8
†Resumed his boxing career.

1929
Jan. 26—Billy McAllister, Sydney .....KO 9
Feb.   8—Willie Smith, Sydney, Aus. .... W 15
Mar.   2—Billy Grimes, Melbourne, Aus. . W 15
Mar. 16—Willie Smith, Sydney, Aus. ...KO 12
May 22—Kid Chocolate, New York ......L 10
June   7—Tommy Paul, Buffalo .... W 6
June 25—Earl Mastro, Los Angeles ......L 10
Aug. 30—Jackie Mandell, Hollywood ...KO 8
Oct. 12—Kid Francis, Paris ....L 12

1930
Jan. 14—Ignacio Fernandez, L. A. ...... W 10
Jan. 28—Johnny Torres, Los Angeles ... W 10
Feb. 14—Charley Sullivan, Hollywood .KO 5
Mar.   4—Santiago Zorilla, Los Angeles .. W 10
Apr.   4—Tommy Paul, Buffalo .... W 10
Apr. 21—Bud Taylor, Chicago .... W 10
May 28—Bushy Graham, New York ..... W 10
July   7—Tommy Paul, Buffalo .... W 10
Aug.   7—Earl Mastro, Chicago .... D 10
Nov.   3—Kid Chocolate, New York ..... W 10
Nov. 28—Bud Taylor, New York .... W 10
Dec.   9—Eddie Shea, Cleveland ....L 10

1931
Feb.   3—Claude Varner, Los Angeles .... D 10
Mar. 27—Kid Francis, New York .... W 10
May 22—Bat Battalino, New York ....L 15
(For Featherweight Title)
June 26—Claude Varner, Hollywood .....L 10
July 24—Ray Montoya, P. Beach, Cal. ... W 10
Aug.   6—Santiago Zorilla, Sacramento .. W 10
Aug. 21—Pinto De Sa., San Fran. .... W 10
Sept. 16—Johnny Previs, Wilmgton., Cal. . W 10
Oct.   9—Joe Guerrero, Sacramento ..... W 10
Nov. 10—Leslie Carter, Seattle .... W 6
Nov. 27—Santiago Zorilla, Hollywood ..KO 6
Dec. 11—Wildcat Carter, Oakland, Cal. .KO 1
Dec. 15—Benny Pelz, Portland, Ore. .... W 6
Dec. 17—Davie Jones, Tacoma, Wash. ... W 6

1932
Jan.   1—Baby Arizmendi, Mexico City ...L 10
Jan. 24—Newsboy Brown, Hollywood .. D 10
Feb. 11—Wildcat Carter, Hollywood ....KO 1
Mar. 11—Varias Miling, Hollywood ....W 10
Apr.   8—Max Tarley, Stockton, Cal. ... W 10
Apr. 22—Petey Sarron, Detroit .... W 10
Apr. 29—Johnny Pena, Detroit ....L 10
June   2—Varias Milling, Sacramento ... W 10
June 14—Tommy Paul, Los Angeles ..... W 10
June 28—Bobby Gray, San Jose ....KO 8
July 29—Varias Milling, Hollywood .... W 10
Aug. 12—Al Citrino, San Francisco .....KO 6
Sept. 2—Vicente Venturillo, Honolulu .KO 10
Oct. 16—Little Dempsey, Honolulu ..... W 10
Nov. 10—Conrad Senico, Honolulu .....KO 6
Dec.   9—Kid Chocolate, New York ......L 15
(For N. Y. State Featherweight title)
Dec. 29—Tommy Paul, Chicago..........L 10

1933
Jan. 27—Seaman Watson, New York .....L 12
Feb. 13—Mose Butch, Pittsburgh .... W 10

1942
In U. S. Army.

TB	KO	WD	WF	D	LD	LF	KOBY	ND	NC
97	15	57	0	8	15	0	0	2	0

Elected to Hall of Fame in 1972

802

ALBERT FRENCHIE BELANGER
(N.B.A. Flyweight Champion in 1927)
Born, May 17, 1906, Toronto, Canada.
Height, 5 ft. 4 in. Started boxing as an ameteur in
1925.
Fights before 1927:
Knockouts: Lou Passavanti, 2; Joe
McKeon, 1; Hank Jarvis, 3; Jack Silver, 3; Abe
Heilman, 1; Jack Martin, 2; Bobby Leithman, 2;
Bobby Clary, 3; Billy Barncott, 2; Kid Vick
Belanger, 1. Won: Allen Holmes, 4; Billy
Barncott, 4; Ken Ralfman, 4; Dick Ray, 4;
Charlie Pinto, 4; Charlie Stevenson, 4; Ty
Coleman, 6; Allen Holmes, 6; Hugh Mason, 8;
Whitey Moret, 8; Willie Woods, 10; Harry
Goldstein, 10; Spider Tyan, 10. Draw: Willie
Davies, 10; Charlie Pinto, 10; Teddy Beardwood,
10; Harry Goldstein, 10; Ty Coleman, 10; Hal
Stevenson, 10; Joe McKeon, 10. Lost: Manny
Wexler, 10; Alex Burley, 10; Ty Coleman; Hal
Stevenson.
1927
	—Newsboy Brown, Toronto	W	10
Sept.	22—Ray Shauers, Toronto	KO	5
Nov.	28—Frankie Genaro, Toronto	W	10

(Won Vacant N.B.A. Flyweight Championship)
| Dec. | —Ernie Jarvis, Toronto | W | 10 |

(N.B.A. title)
1928
| Jan. | 16—Frisco Grande, Buffalo | LF | 5 |
| Feb. | 6—Frankie Genaro, Toronto | L | 10 |

(Lost NBA Championship)
Feb.	17—Joey Ross, Detroit	L	8
May	11—Frisco Grande, Toronto	W	10
June	5—Steve Rocco, Toronto	L	10

(Lost Canadian Flyweight Title)
June	25—Johnny McCoy, Toronto	L	10
Oct.	3—Marty Gold, Toronto	W	10
Oct.	15—Frankie Genaro, Toronto	L	10
Dec.	3—Willie Davies, Toronto	W	12

1929
| Jan. | 2—Steve Rocco, Toronto | W | 10 |

(Canadian Championship)
Feb.	8—Izzy Schwartz, Toronto	L	10
Mar.	8—Harry Hill, Montreal	L	10
Mar.	12—Izzy Schwartz, Toronto	L	12

(For American Flyweight Title)
| May | 13—Johnny Hill, Toronto | KO | 6 |
| Oct. | 18—Eugene Huat, Toronto | KO by | 6 |

1930
Feb.	24—Kid Lencho, Toronto	KO	2
Apr.	15—Quina Lee, Winnepeg, Can.	W	10
May	12—Franklin Young, Toronto	W	10
June	10—Frankie Genaro, Toronto	L	10
Sept.	28—Malcolm Mattherson, Toronto	W	10
Oct.	15—Frisco Grande, Stratford, Connecticut	W	8
Oct.	27—Marty Gold, Toronto	L	8
Dec.	2—Frisco Batista, Toronto	L	6

1932
| | —Frankie Wolfram, Toronto | KO by | 7 |

TB	KO	WD	WF	D	LD	LF	KOBY	ND	NC
62	13	24	0	7	15	1	2	0	0

CORPORAL IZZY SCHWARTZ
Born, October 23, 1902, New York.
Nationality, Jewish-American. Height, 5 ft. 1 in.
Managed by Phil Bernstein.
1922
Knockout: Billy Stone, 4; No decision:
Billy Stone, 10; Sammy Lasco, 10; Joe Lucas, 10;
Sammy Lasco, 10; Billy Steepie, 10; Joe Loucas,
10; Billy Steepie, 10.
1923
Knockouts: Joe Dundee, 3; Joe Dillon, 4.
Won: Vincent Salvatore, 10; Willie Farley, 6; Kid
Corona, 12; Indian Russell, 12; Al Felder, 10;
Bobby Green, 5; Willie La Morte, 4; Babe Willard,
10; Billy Bell, 6; Mickey Nelson, 10; Terry Miller,
10; Willie Darcey, 10; Bobby Ruttenberg, 12. No
decisions: Al Felder, 10; Joe Jackson, 10. Draw:
Sammy Bienfeld, 6; Bobby Ruttenberg, 10;
Bobby Green, 10. Lost: Henry Catena, 15; Al
Felder, 10; Bobby Green, 10; Sammy Bienfeld,
10; Henry Catena, 10.

1924
Won: Mickey Morris, 10; Al Felder, 6;
Johnny Breslin, 6; Johnny Hamm, 10; Henry
Catena, 10; Frankie Ash, 10. No decisions:
Bobby Walker, 10; Joe Jackson, 10; Willie
Woods, 12; Willie Woods, 12. Draw: Terry Miller,
10; Henry Catena, 10; Frankie Ash, 10; Young
Denico, 12. Lost: Ty Coleman, 10; Tommy
Milton, 10; Tommy Milton, 10; Eddie Flank, 10;
Kid Durand, KO by 7.

1925
Knockout: Lew Perfetti, 2. Won: Jimmy
Russo, 10; Frankie Murray, 10; Black Bill, 10;
Ernie Jarvis, 10. No decisions: Joey Ross, 10;
Charlie Ray, 12; Mickey Lewis, 10; Mickey
Lewis, 10; Draw: Ernie Jarvis, 10; Lew Perfetti,
10. Lost: Willie Davies, 10; Black Bill, 10; Black
Bill, 10; Newsboy Brown, 10; Willie Davies, 10;
Johnny Breslin, 10; Black Bill, 10; Clever Sencio,
10

1926
Won: Young Dencio, 10; Willie Woods, 10;
Delos Kid Williams, 10; Ernie Hood, 10; Chuck
Hellman, 10; Joey Ross, 10; Mannie Wexler, 10;
Willie Woods, 10; Johnny McCoy, 12. Draw:
Dixie La Hood, 12. Lost: Alec Burley, 10;
George Rivers, 10.

1927
Jan.	11—Willie Gordon, Portland, Ore.	W	10
Jan.	21—Tommy Aboda, N.Y.C.	KO	2
Feb.	19—Blas Rodriguez, N.Y.C.	W	10
Mar.	5—Joey Ross, N.Y.C.	W	10
Mar.	17—Kid Anselm, Harrisburg, Pa.	W	8
Mar.	25—Pinkey May, Savannah, Ga.	D	10
June	6—Chuck Hellman, N.Y.C.	L	10
Aug.	26—Willie Davies, Hollywood	L	10
Sept.	12—Billy Kelly, Hollywood	W	10
Oct.	4—Blas Rodriguez, Hollywood	W	10
Nov.	9—Willie Davies, Hollywood	W	10
Nov.	22—Benny Hall, Hollywood	W	4
Dec.	16—Newsboy Brown, N.Y.C.	W	15

(Won American Flyweight Title)
1928
Jan.	26—Harry Goldstein, Boston	W	10
Feb.	17—Billy Shaw, Detroit	W	10
Feb.	23—Benny Hall, Brooklyn	W	4
Apr.	9—*Routier Parra, N.Y.C.	W	15
May	9—Happy Atherton, Ft. Wayne	ND	10
May	23—Bushy Graham, Brooklyn	L	15

(For Vacant World Bantamweight Title)
July	20—*Frisco Grande, N.Y.C.	WF	4
Aug.	3—Little Jeff, N.Y.C.	KO	4
Aug.	31—Frisco Grande, Long Branch	KO	8
Oct.	4—Willie La Morte, Jersey City	W	12
Dec.	1—Emile Pladner, Paris	L	12
	—Black Bill, N.Y.C.	W	10

1929
Feb.	8—Frenchy Belanger, Toronto	W	10
Mar.	12—*Frenchy Belanger, Toronto	W	12
Apr.	12—Boy Wally, San Francisco	W	10
Apr.	19—Pablo Dano, San Francisco	D	10
Aug.	20—Willie La Morte, Newark	L	15
Sept.	16—Willie Davies, Pittsburgh	L	10
Oct.	3—Willie La Morte, Newark	L	10
Nov.	4—Eugene Huat, N.Y.C.	L	10

(Gave up flyweight title)
*Flyweight Title bout.

1931
| | —Unknown | W | 6 |

TB	KO	WD	WF	D	LD	LF	KOBY	ND	NC
117	7	51	1	12	27	0	1	18	0

JOHNNY MC COY
(Record Not Available)

NEWSBOY BROWN
(Record Not Available)

FRANKIE GENARO
(Frank Di Gennara)

Born, August 26, 1901, New York. Nationality, Italian-American. Weight, 112 lbs. Height, 5 ft 2½ in. Managed by Harry Garsh, Phil Bernstein, Joe Jacobs and Billy McCarney. Boxed as an amateur in 1919-1920, winning state and national amateur tourneys. Won Olympic Championship at Antwerp, 1920.

1920
Won: Billy Murphy, 6. Knockout: Joe Colletti, 2.

1921
Won: Jimmy Patterson, 10; Johnny Rosner, 12; Joe Dillon, 15; Bobby Doyle, 15; Joe Colletti, 10 and 12; Joe Leon, 12; Andy Davis, 10; Johnny Rosner, 10. Draw: Joe Colletti, 12. No decision: Kid Wolfe, 6.

1922
Feb. —Leo Reynolds, New York ..... W 12
Mar. 13—Jack Sayles, New York ....W 12
Apr. —Sammy Cohen, New York ..... W 12
Apr. 18—Mannie Wexler, New York ..... W 12
May 19—Abe Goldstein, New York ......L 4
May 23—Charley Phil Rosenberg, New York .... W 12
June 9—Eddie Lynch, Jersey City.............ND 12
July 6—Pancho Villa, Jersey City ......ND 12
July 21—Battling Murray, Jersey City ....ND 12
Aug. 22—Pancho Villa, Brooklyn .... W 10
Sept. —Harry Battling Leonard, New York ....L 12
Oct. 5—Indian Russell, New York ....KO 14
Oct. 21—Charley Phil Rosenberg, New York .... W 12
Dec. 15—Terry Martin, Boston .... W 10

1923
Feb. 12—Tommy Shay, Harrisburg, Pa. ..KO 4
Mar. 1—Pancho Villa, New York .... W 15
(Won American Flyweight title)
Mar. 6—Bobbie Williams, Harrisburg ..KO 3
Apr. 4—Bud Taylor, Chicago ....ND 10
Apr. 17—Bobby Wolgast, Philadelphia ..ND 8
Apr. 23—Pal Moore, Chicago ....WF 6
July 7—Tony Norman, Pittsburgh ...ND 10
July 19—Bobby Gershane, New York ..KO 3
July 27—Frankie Daly, New Haven ... W 12
July 31—Buddy Wallace, Columbus, O. ..KO 4
Aug. 28—Bobby Wolgast, Boston .... W 10
Sept. 27—Vincent Salvadore .... W 12
Nov. 30—Carl Treamine, New York ..... W 12
Dec. 18—Joe Clifford, Detroit ....ND 10

1924
Jan. 22—Johnny Shepard, Boston ...... W 10
May 22—Howard Mayberry, Toronto ... D 10
June 12—Joe Clifford, Berwin, Md. ..... W 10
July 7—Bushy Graham, Rochester, N.Y. D 10
Aug. 6—Irish Johnny Curtin, New York W 12
Aug. 22—Hilly Levine, Rockaway Beach . W 12
Sept. 23—Bushy Graham, New York ..... W 12
Oct. 6—Eddie O'Dowd, New Orleans ... W 15

1925
Feb. 16—Kid Wolfe, Philadelphia .... W 10
Mar. 4—Eddie O'Dowd, Youngstown .. W 10
Mar. 20—Joe Lucas, Detroit .... W 10
Apr. 13—Al Dundee, Mansfield, O. ..... W 12
May 28—Harold Smith, New York ..... W 10
June 16—Georgie Marks, N.Y.C. ...... W 10
June 26—Kid Williams, Baltimore .... W 12
July 31—Hilly Levine, New York ....WF 11
Aug. 7—Georgie Marks, Red Bk., N.J. .ND 10
Aug. 22—Fidel LaBarba, Los Angeles .....L 10
(Lost American Flyweight Title)
Oct. 14—Newsboy Brown, Los Angeles...L 10
Nov. 16—Vic St. Onge, Buffalo ....KO 4

1926
Apr. 5—Hilly Levine, Bayonne, N.J. ..ND 10
Apr. 16—Willie Darcy, Bayonne, N.J. ..ND 10
May 17—Bushy Graham, New York .....L 10
June 11—Scotty McKeon, New York .... W 10
July 8—Scotty McKeon, Albany .....KO 10
July 22—Willie Darcy, Albany, N.Y. .... D 12
Oct. 7—Mickey Lewis, New York .....ND 10

1927
Jan. 21—Newsboy Brown, New York ...L 10
Feb. 16—Joe Scalfaro, New York .... W 10
Feb. 23—Tommy Hughes, Cleveland .... W 8
Mar. 11—Dark Cloud, Providence, R.I. .. W 12
Mar. 21—Willie La Morte, Chicago ..... D 10
Apr. 9—Dark Cloud, New York .... W 10
July 22—Joey Ross, Springfield, Mass. ... W 10
Aug. 23—Pal Graham, Utica, N.Y. .....KO 2
Aug. 30—Willie La Morte, Chicago ...... D 10

Sept. 2—Tommy Hughes, Akron, O. .... W 10
Sept. 12—Eddie Flank, New York .... W 10
Sept. 16—Joe Eulo, Harrison, N.J.......ND 10
Oct. 7—Marty Gold, Raleigh, N.C. ..... W 10
Oct. 28—Billy Kelly, Scranton...........L 10
Nov. 28—Frenchy Belanger, Toronto .....L 10
(For Vacant N.B.A. Flyweight title)
Dec. 20—Willie La Morte, Newark ......ND 10

1928
Feb. 6—Frenchy Belanger, Toronto .... W 10
(Won N.B.A. World's Flyweight title)
Mar. 6—Duke Menard, Portlano ......ND 10
Mar. 9—Frisco Grande, Buffalo .... W 10
Mar. 30—Jackie Johnston, Toronto ......L 10
Apr. 9—Johnny Vacca, Boston .... W 10
June 18—Lew Goldberg, Spfield., Mass..KO 3
July 23—Steve Rocco, Toronto .... D 10
Aug. 21—Ernie Peters, Chicago .... W 10
Oct. 15—Frenchy Belanger, Toronto .... W 10
Nov. 27—Art Giroux, Portland, Me. .....L 12
Dec. 14—Steve Rocco, Detroit ....WF 2

1929
Jan. 9—Al Goldberg, Portland, Me. ...KO 5
Jan. 18—Tommy Paul, Buffalo ....L 6
Jan. 23—Eddie Franks, Springfield ....KO 7
Jan. 29—Tommy Paul, Buffalo ....L 6
Mar. 2—Spider Pladner, Paris ......KO by 1
(Lost N.B.A. Flyweight title)
Apr. 18—Spider Pladner, Paris ....WF 5
(Re-won N.B.A. Flyweight title)
Aug. 5—Willie Davies, Pittsburgh ....L 10
Sept. 9—Jack Sharkey, Minneapolis ... W 10
Oct. 17—Ernie Jarvis, London, Eng...... W 15

1930
Jan. 18—Yvon Trevidic, Paris ....KO 12
Feb. 6—Harry Stein, Berlin ....LF 8
Feb. 23—Orlando Magliozzi, Milan, Itlay WF 10
Apr. 8—Gleizes of France, Naples, Italy ....KO 3
May 16—Frisco Grande, Camden ......KO 4
June 10—*Frenchy Belanger, Toronto ...W 10
June 24—Little Jeff, Hartford ....KO 2
July 28—Davey Adleman, Brooklyn .... W 10
Aug. 6—Willie La Morte, Newark .... W 10
Sept. 4—Rube Bradley, N.Y.C. ....L 10
Sept. —Tony de La Cruz ....KO 3
Dec. 26—*Midget Wolgast, New York ... D 15
*For N.E.A. title.

1931
Mar. 25—*Victor Ferrand, Madrid, Spain D 15
July 16—Routier Parra, North Adams ..KO 4
July 30—*Jackie Harmon, Waterbury ..KO 6
Oct. 3—*Valentin Angelman, Paris.........W 12
Oct. 27—Young Perez, Paris ....KO by 2
(Lost flyweight title)
Nov. 16—Arilla, Paris ....LF 7
*Title bout.

1932
Mar. 29—Young Tommy, Los Ang...KO by 3

1933
Jan. 25—Joe Fino, Alexandria .... W 8
Apr. 5—Joe Archibald, Fall River ...... W 10
June 9—Tommy Lemieux, Biddefd, Ore. W 6
Oct. 5—Ernie Mauer, Ypsilanti ....L 10
Nov. 7—Frankie Jarr, Fort Wayne .....L 10

1934
Feb. 13—Speedy Dado, San Jose ....KO by 3

TB	KO	WD	WF	D	LD	LF	KOBY	ND	NC
129	19	59	5	9	16	2	4	15	0

Died, December 27, 1966, New York City, N.Y.
Elected to Boxing Hall of Fame, 1973.

JOHNNY HILL
Born, December 14, 1905, Strathmigloe, Fife, Scotland. Weight, 112 lbs.

1926 British ABA Flyweight Champion
1926
Sept. 30—Bill Huntly, London .... KO 5
Oct. 17—Mark Lesnick, London .... NC 15
Nov. 2—Arthur Cunningham, London ..... KO 15
Nov. 7—Billy James, London .... D 15
Nov. 15—Frank Maurier, London .... W 12
Nov. 25—Tiny Smith, London .... D 12
Nov. 29—Young Jackie Brown, London .... KO 12
Dec. 18—Henri Poutrain, Brighton .... W 12

1927

Jan.	19—Tiny Smith, London	W	15
Jan.	31—Young Denain, London	KO	6
Feb.	16—Phil Lolosky, London	KO	15
Mar.	30—Petit Biquet, London	WF	11
Apr.	11—Jim Hanna, Edinburgh	KO	11
May	23—Alf Barber, London	KO	14
	(Won Vacant British Flyweight Title)		
July	3—Phil Lolosky, London	D	15
Oct.	13—Francois Morrachini, London	KO	9
Oct.	31—Petit Biquet, London	W	15
Dec.	19—Emile (Spider) Pladner, London	W	15

1928

Mar.	19—Emile (Spider) Pladner, London	W	15
	(Won European Flyweight Title)		
Aug.	29—Newsboy Brown, London	W	15
	(Won Calif.-British World Flyweight Title)		

1929

Feb.	7—Emile (Spider) Pladner, Paris	KO by	6
Mar.	21—Ernie Jarvis, London	W	15
	(Retained British and European Flyweight Titles)		
	(Retained Calif.-British World Flyweight Title)		
June	29—Ernie Jarvis, Glasgow	WF	10
	(Retained British and European Flyweight Titles)		
	(Retained Calif.-British World Flyweight Title)		

TB	KO	WD	WF	D	LD	LF	KO	BY	ND	NC
23	8	8	2	3	0	0	1		0	1

Died, September 27, 1929, Edinburgh, Scotland.

EMILE (SPIDER) PLADNER
Born, September 2, 1906, Clermont-Ferrand, France.

1926

Jan.	29—Boriello, Casablanca	W	10
Mar.	19—Privat	W	10
Mar.	31—Provenzano, Meknes	KO	7
Apr.	7—Sempere, Casablanca	KO	7
May	16—Di Pascal, Fez	W	10
July	11—Morrachini, Casablanca	W	10
Sept.	15—George Kent, Paris	W	10
Sept.	22—Chartier, Le Havre	KO	7
Nov.	3—Treve, Paris	W	10
Nov.	16—Minow	KO	6
Nov.	20—Maurice Josie, Clermont	KO	3
Dec.	14—Tiny Smith, Paris	W	10

1927

Jan.	5—Billy Clark, Paris	KO	4
Jan.	27—Kid Socks, London	D	15
Feb.	11—Franc Morrachini, Paris	W	15
Feb.	22—Michel Montreuil	W	15
Mar.	20—Jean Soler, Marseille	KO	3
Mar.	29—Alf Barber, Paris	W	12
Apr.	6—Buck Jones, Lyon	KO	4
May	10—Kid Rich, Paris	KO	6
June	6—Nic Petit-Biquet	W	12
June	18—Marcel Josie, Limoges	KO	10
July	2—Kid Perez, Clerm-Fer	KO	5
July	23—Jean Gregoire, Vichy	W	10
Aug.	7—Franc Morrachini, Marseille	W	10
Sept.	14—Frankie Ash, Paris	W	10
Sept.	24—Nic Petit-Biquet, Liege	D	12
Nov.	16—Franc Morrachini, Paris	W	12
Dec.	19—Johnny Hill, London	L	15

1928

Jan.	4—Frankie Ash, Paris	W	12
Feb.	15—Francis Biron, Paris	W	10
Mar.	19—Johnny Hill, London	L	15
	(For European Flyweight Title)		
Apr.	11—Giovanni Sili, Paris	W	5
Apr.	21—Luigi Cecchi, Florence	KO	9
Apr.	30—Johnny Croxon, Paris	KO	4
May	14—Marcel Josie, Paris	KO	12
June	4—Billy James, London	W	12
June	27—Billy James, Paris	W	10
July	14—Francis Biron, Algiers	W	10
Sept.	2—Dod Oldfield, Marseille	W	10
Oct.	8—Robert Tassin, Paris	W	10
Dec.	1—Izzy Schwartz, Paris	W	12
Dec.	22—Ernie Jarvis, Paris	W	12

1929

Feb.	7—Johnny Hill, Paris	KO	6
Mar.	2—Frankie Genaro, Paris	KO	1
	(World's Flyweight Title)		
Mar.	20—The International Boxing Union Recognized Pladner as the World Flyweight Champion.		
Apr.	18—Frankie Genaro, Paris	LF	5
	(World's Flyweight Title)		
May	15—Kid Francis, Paris	D	12
May	26—Jimmy Taylor, Marseille	KO	6
June	20—Eugene Huat, Paris	KO by	15
	(French & European Flyweight Titles)		
Oct.	29—Kid Socks, Paris	W	12
Dec.	17—Carlos Flix, Paris	W	12

1930

Jan.	22—Teddy Baldock, London	L Dis.	6
Feb.	5—Arthur Boddington, Paris	W	12
Feb.	18—Dick Corbett, London	L	12
Mar.	22—Andre Regis, Paris	W	10
Apr.	5—Joseph Denain, Beausoleil	W	10
May	10—Eugene Huat, Paris	L	12
June	14—Ted Higgins, Paris	W	10
June	28—Gh. Stamate, Bucharest	KO	10
July	6—Arly Hollinsgsworth, Paris	L	10
July	20—Francis Biron, Bordeaux	W	10
Oct.	18—Nic Petit-Biquet, Paris	W	10
Dec.	17—Alf Magnolfi, Paris	W	10

1931

Jan.	22—Cuthbert Taylor, Paris	W	12
Mar.	5—Eguene Huat, Paris	D	12
Mar.	18—Antoine Ascencio, Casablanca	KO	6
Mar.	25—Manuel Gonzalez, Barcelona	W	10
Apr.	16—J. Pannecouke, Paris	KO	5
Apr.	22—Benny Sharkey, London	L	8
May	9—Tom Cowley, Sheffield	W	12
May	28—Francis Biron, Paris	W	12
	(French Bantamweight Title)		
July	10—Orlando Magliozzi, Paris	KO	5
Sept.	3—Francis Biron, Paris	W	12
Oct.	15—Willie Metzner, Paris	KO	1
Nov.	9—Johnny Peters, London	D	8
Nov.	21—Guiseppe Sili, Zurich	W	10
Nov.	30—Alfredo Magnolfi, Paris	W	10
Dec.	5—Albert Biesmans, Amiens	W	10
Dec.	21—Young Perez, Paris	W	10

1932

Feb.	26—Anton Kocsis, New York	W	10
Mar.	8—Jim Thomas, Pittsburgh	KO	3
Apr.	18—George Ostrow, Boston	W	10
May	14—Bobby Leitham, Montreal	W	10
June	13—Willie Davies, Toronto	W	10
June	29—Bobby Leitham, Montreal	W	12
July	20—Pete Sanstol, Montreal	D	10
Aug.	17—Newsboy Brown, Montreal	W	12
Sept.	19—Al Brown, Toronto	KO by	1
Nov.	9—Francois Machtens, Paris	W	10
Nov.	14—Al Brown, Paris	KO by	2

1933

Jan.	24—Young Perez, Tunis	L	10
Mar.	6—Werner Riethdorf, Paris	W	10
	Fought several exhibition bouts in Japan.		

1934

Apr.	16—Ali Ben Said, Paris	W	7
Apr.	28—Joseph Decico, Paris	W	10
May	25—Teodoro Murrali, Paris	KO	10
June	2—Maurice Dubois, Zurich	W	10
July	11—Young Perez, Paris	L	10
July	29—Eugene Lorenzoni, Rouen	W	10
Aug.	6—Kid Francis, Marseille	L	10
Sept.	3—Kid Francis, Paris	D	12
Sept.	17—Werner Riethdorf, Berlin	KO	9
Oct.	5—Joseph Decico, Paris	W	12
	(French Bantamweight Title)		
Nov.	2—Padrone Finnegan, Paris	KO	10
Nov.	23—Frank Harsen, Paris	D	12
Dec.	5—Maur. Waroqueaux, Bordeaux	KO	4
Dec.	22—Albert Biesmans, Brest	KO	10

1935

Jan.	28—Eugene Huat, Paris	KO	7
Feb.	7—Henri Barras, Strasbourg	W	10
Feb.	20—Paul Dogniaux, Paris	KO	6
Mar.	3—Henri Sanchez, Toulouse	W	10

805

Mar. 10—Raymond Gilbert, Roubaix ...KO 6
Mar. 14—Young Borel, Bordeaux .... W 10
Mar. 30—Rene Chalange, Rouen ....KO 6
Apr. 8—Joseph Decico, Paris ....L 10
Apr. 30—Eug. Lorenzoni, St. Etienne ..KO 10
July 5—Young Perez, Casablanca ...... D 10
July 19—Emile Martinez, Casablanca ... W 10
Oct. 5—Maurice Dubois, Geneva ....L 15
Oct. 12—Orlando Magliozzi, Laval .....KO 8
Nov. 7—Carlo Cavagnoli, Bordeaux .... W 10
Nov. 15—Young Borel, Paris .... W 10
Dec. 3—Salvador Lozano, Barcelona ... D 10

TB KO WD WF D LD LF KOBY ND NC
122 34 61 1 10 11 2   3   0 0

Died, March 15, 1980, Auch, France.

WILLIE LA MORTE

Born, June 16, 1904, New York City, N.Y. Weight, 112 lbs. Height, 5 ft. 3 in. Managed by Dan Morgan, Tom Stanley, Lawrence Lupo, Phil Bernstein.

1923
Aug. 9—Corp. Izzy Schwartz, New York ..... L 4
1924
  —Joe Jackson .... KO 2
  —Tony Mack .... KO 3
  —Young Anthony .... KO 8
  —Tiny Tinkle .... KO 3
  —Dodo Jackson .... KO 2
  —Joe Jackson .... W 10
  —Jimmy Clarke .... W 8
1925
  —Johnny Brennan .... KO 2
  —Kid Durand .... KO 5
  —Willie Woods .... W 10
  —Henry Catena .... W 10
  —Jackie Feldman .... W 8
  —Jimmy Russo .... W 8
  —Sam Sanchez .... D 10
  —Tommy Hughes .... W 6
  —Al Brown .... ND 8
  —Joey Ross .... ND 8
1926
Jan. 9—Davey Abad, Brooklyn .... L 10
  —Archie Bell .... KO 3
  —Frankie Mason .... KO 2
  —Pinky Silverberg .... KO 2
  —Wilbur Cohen .... W 10
  —Wilbur Cohen .... W 12
  —Irish Mickey Gill .... W 10
  —Pee Wee Ross .... W 8
  —Benny Pascal .... W 8
  —Mickey Lewis .... W 8
  —Jimmy Bones .... W 10
  —Emil Paluso .... ND 8
  —Emil Paluso .... ND 8
  —Dave Adelman .... ND 10
  —Wilbur Cohen .... D 12
  —Harry Goldstein .... D 6
  —Willie Davies .... D 6
  —Al Brown .... KO by 2
  —Wilbur Cohen .... L 12
  —Willie Davies .... D 6
1927
  —Happy Atherton .... W 8
  —Happy Atherton .... W 8
  —Marty Gold .... W 8
  —Benny Tressito .... W 10
Mar. 21—Frankie Genaro, Chicago .... D 10
Aug. 30—Frankie Genaro, Chicago .... D 10
  —Willie Davies .... L 10
Dec. 20—Frankie Genaro, Newark .... ND 10
1928
  —Routier Parra .... KO 3
  —Ivan Hawes .... KO 6
Oct. 4—Corp. Izzy Schwartz, Jersey City .... L 12

1929
  —Willie Cubic, Toronto .... W 10
  —Harry Bill, Toronto .... W 6
  —Pablo Dano, San Francisco .... L 10
Aug. 22—Corp. Izzy Schwartz, Newark ..... W 15
  (Claimed World Flyweight Title)
  —Frisco Grande, Paterson .... KO 7
Oct. 3—Corp. Izzy Schwartz, Newark ..... W 15
  (Retained Claim to World Flyweight Title)
1930
May 16—Midget Wolgast, New York .... KO by 6
  (For New York World Flyweight Title)

TB KO WD WF D LD LF KOBY ND NC
56 13 23 0 6 6 0   2   6 0

MIDGET WOLGAST
(Joseph Robert Loscalzo)
Born, July 18, 1910, Philadelphia, Pa. Nationality, Italian-American. Weight 112 lbs. Height, 5 ft. 3½ in. Managed by Johnny Keyes, Al Lippe and Eddie Walker.

1927
Nov. 3—Willie Davies, N. Y. C. .... W 10
1928
Jan. 15—Billy Kelly, Scranton...........L 10
Feb. 20—Willie Davies, Pittsburgh .... W 10
May 28—Willie Davies, Philadelphia ..... W 10
July 30—Phil Tobias, Atlantic City ...... W 10
Aug. 22—Phil Tobias, Jersey City, N. J. .. W 8
Nov. 29—Phil Tobias, N. Y. C. ....L 10
1929
Feb. 11—Phil Tobias, New York .... D 10
Feb. 18—Ruby Bradley, Toronto .... W 10
Feb. 28—Routier Parra, Philadelphia ... W 8
Apr. 22—Phil Tobias, Toronto .... W 10
July 26—Tommy Milton, New York ...KO 3
Aug. 1—Frankie Anselm, Philadelphia .. W 8
Aug. 9—Tommy Abobo, New York .... W 10
Nov. 4—Johnny McCoy, New York .... W 10
Nov. 20—Jose Albano, Harrisburg .... W 10
Dec. 3—Tommy Abobo, Harrisburg .... W 10
Dec. 13—Kid Singh, New York .... W 10
1930
Feb. 10—Frisco Grande, New York .... W 10
Mar. 11—Pinkey Silverberg, New York .. W 10
Mar. 21—Black Bill, New York .... W 15
  (New York State recognition as World Flyweight Champion)
May 8—Pinkey Silverberg, Phiadel. ....W 8
May 16—Willie LaMorte, New York ....KO 6
  (N. Y. Title bout)
June 16—Frankie Bauman, Jersey City .. W 10
July 7—Routier Parra, Jersey City ..... W 10
July 17—Ernie Peters, New York .... W 8
July 29—Speedy Dado, Los Angeles....KO 5
Aug. 8—Canto Robleto, Hollywood .... W 10
Aug. 19—Newsboy Brown, Los Angeles...L 10
Nov.   —Frankie Bauman .... W 10
Dec. 1—Al Tedesco, Jersey City .... W 10
Dec. 19—Willie Davies, Toronto .... W 10
Dec. 26—Frankie Genaro, New York .... D 15
  (For Vacant World Flyweight Title)
1931
Feb. 13—Al Beauregard, Bridgeport ....KO 3
Feb. 23—Ruby Bradley, Holyoke .... W 10
Mar. 3—Willie Davies, Pittsburgh .... W 10
Mar. 9—Pinkey Silverberg, Bridgeport .. W 10
Apr. 13—Archie Bell, Pittsburgh .... W 10
May 4—Lew Farber, Holyoke .... W 10
June 1—Lew Farber, Holyoke .... W 10
June   —Jackie Harmon, Holyoke .....KO 6
June 19—Lew Franklin, Atlantic City ..ND 10
July 13—Ruby Bradley, Brooklyn ...... W 15
  (N. Y. Title bout)
July 23—Joie Eulo, Paterson, N. J. ..... W 10
Aug. 4—Johnny Brennan, Jersey City .. W 10
Aug. 17—Dick Welsh, Norfolk, Va. ...... W 10
Aug. 20—Cris Pineda, N. Adams, Mass. ....L 10
Sept. 8—Happy Atherton, Indianapolis .. W 10
Sept. 17—Frisco Grande, Terre Haute .... W 10

Sept. 21—Joe Dragon, Muncie, Ind. ...... W 10
Sept. 22—Johnnie Edwards, Indianapolis . W 10
Oct.   7—Speedy Dado, Oakland .... W 10
Oct. 14—Johnny Russell, Oakland, Cal. KO   3
Oct. 22—Chato Laredo, Sacramento .... W 10
Dec.   2—Speedy Dado, Oakland, Cal. ... W 10
Dec.   7—Speedy Dado, Oakland, Cal. ... W 10
Dec. 12—Canto Robleto, San Francisco KO   5
Dec. 18—Chato Laredo, San Francisco .. W 10

1932
Jan. 12—Sailor Billy Landers,
          Alexandria, Va. .... W   8
Feb. 12—Tommy Hughes, Hollywood ... W 10
Mar. 18—Little Pancho, Honolulu .... W 1C
Apr. 15—Little Pancho, Honolulu .... D 10
June   6—Tony Marino, Pittsburgh ...... W 10
June 14—Marty Gold, Passaic .... W 10
Aug.   3—Young Tommy, Oakland ...... W 10
Sept. 21—Speedy Dado, Oakland .... D 10
Sept. 30—Pedro Villanueva, Hollywood .. W 10
Oct. 14—Lou Snyder, San Diego .... D 10
Oct. 26—Young Tommy, Oakland .... L 10

1933
Feb.   3—Jackie Wilson, Pittsburgh ...... D 10
Feb.   9—Billy Passamento, Phila. ......KO   7
Feb. 14—Nick Montano, Plainfield, N. J.. W   6
May   12—Eddie Burl, Baltimore .... W 10
May   20—Ernie Maurer, Detroit .... D 10
June   9—Brit Gorman, Detroit ..... KO by   6
June 28—Skippy Allen, N. Y. C. .... W   8
June 29—Marty Gold, N. Adams, Mass. .. W 10
July 13—Lew Farber, Brooklyn .... L 10
Aug. 15—Pete Sanstol, Brooklyn .... W 10
Aug. 30—Freddie Latanzio, Mt. Vernon . W   6
Sept. 27—Bobby Leitham, Montreal ..... L 10
Oct. 30—Jackie Brown, London, Eng.... W 12
Nov. 13—Valentin Angelmann, Paris, Fr.. D 10

1934
Jan. 15—Jimmy Perrin, New Orleans .... W   8
Jan. 18—Dewey Cannon, Mobile .... W   8
Feb. 13—Lou Salica, New York .... W   8
May   1—Lou Salica, New York .... D   8
June 13—Sammy Seaman, Alexandria ... W 10
Aug. 27—Henry Hook, New Orleans .... W 10
Sept. 4—Henry Moreno, New Orleans ..L 10
Sept. 11—Kid Laredo, Houston .... W 10
Sept. 17—Henry Moreno, New Orleans ..L 10
Oct.   1—Babe Triscaro, Cleveland ..... W 10
Nov.   9—Pablo Dano, Holly.vood .... L 10
Nov. 27—Pablo Dano, Los Angeles ..... D 10
Dec. 12—Johnny Pena, Oakland .... D 10
Dec. 21—Henry Armstrong, San Fran.... L 10

1935
Jan. 11—Johnny Pena, San Francisco .. D 10
Jan. 25—Young Tommy, Hollywood ... W 10
Feb. 21—Juan Zurita, Los Angeles ..... W 10
Apr. 11—Baby Casanova, Mex. City .....L 10
Apr. 25—Bobby Fernandez, Juarez ..... W 10
May   3—Lou Salica, Hollywood .... L 10
May   25—Juan Zurita, Hollywood ...... W 10
June 28—Juan Zurita, Hollywood ...... W 10
July   3—Small Montana, Sacramento ...L 10
July 26—Baby Casanova, Hollywood ... W 10
Aug.   9—Frankie Covelli, Hollywood ... W 10
Aug. 23—Young Gildo, Watsonville .... W 10
Sept. 3—Little Dempsey, Los Angeles ..KO   9
Sept. 16—Small Montana, Oakland ......L 10
         (Lost American Flyweight Title)
Oct.   2—Tony Marino, Oakland .... W 10
Oct. 25—Pancho Leyvas, Hollywood .... W 10
Nov.   5—Small Montana, Los Angeles .. W 10
Nov. 27—Henry Armstrong, Oakland ....L 10

1936
Jan. 28—Ritchie Fontaine, Portland KO by   7
Feb. 21—Varias Milling, San Luis Obispo W 10
Mar. 11—Jimmy Thomas, Sacramento ... W 10
Mar. 28—Juan Zurita, Mex. City .... KO by   5
May   7—Mark Diaz, Pasadena .... W 10
June   5—Varias Milling, Hollywood ..... W 10
July 24—Juan Zurita, Hollywood ...... L 10
Aug. 18—Abie Israel, Los Angeles ...... W   8
Aug. 28—Bobby Gray, Pasadena ......KO   7
Sept. 11—Davey Abad, S. Luis Obispo ... D 10
Sept. 28—Perfecto Lopez, L. A. L   8
Oct. 19—Perfecto Lopez, L. A. .... L 10
Nov. 17—Young Rightmire, St. Louis ....L 10
Dec.   3—Davey Abad, St. Louis .... L 10
Dec. 15—Norment Quarles, Norfolk ..... D 10

1937
Feb.   4—Johnny Hutchinson, Phila. .... W 10
Feb. 25—Tommy Cross, Phila. .... W 10
May   10 Tommy Cross, Phila. .... L 10
June 16—Dick Welsh, Richmond .... D 10

June 25—Lew Feldman, Long Beach .....L 10
July   6—Maxie Berger, Brooklyn L   8
Oct. 16—George Daly, Phila. .... W 10
Nov.   4—Tommy Cross, Phila. ....L 10

1938
Jan.   6—Norment Quarles, Phila. .... W   9
Feb.   3—Lew Massey, Philadelphia ......L 10
Mar.   4—Eddie Dolan, Phila. ....L 10
June 16—Johnny Craven, Norristown
          ....KO by   1

1939
Jan. 19—Teddy Baldwin, Phila. L   8
Mar.   4—Walter Padlo, Phila. .... KO by   3
July 19—Billy Mims, Phila. .... KO by   5
Sept. 7—Tony Maglione, Bristol ......KO   1

1940
Mar. 14—Bill Morris, Lancaster L   6

TB	KO	WD	WF	D	LD	LF	KOBY	ND	NC
147	11	85	0	15	29	0	6	1	0

Died, October 19, 1955, Philadelphia, Pa

VICTOR (YOUNG) PEREZ
Born, Tunis, October 18, 1911.

1928
Feb.   4—Zerbib, Tunis .... D   6
Feb. 15—Zerbib, Tunis .... W   6
Mar.   1—Zerbib, Sousse .... W   6
Mar. 15—Gondore, Tunis ....KO   2
Apr.   2—Bob Zerbi, Tunis ....KO   1
Apr. 18—Kid Roger, South Ahrhas...........D   6
         —Kid Roger, Bone ....KO   3
         —Taieb, Bizerte ....KO   3
         —Maurice Petit, Tunis ....KO   3
         —Clunchi, Souk l'Arba .... W   6
         —Mola, Sfax .... W   6
         —Brami, Sfax ....KO   2
         —Fredo, Souk l'Arba .... W   6
         —Glenchi, Souk l'arba .... KO   3
         —Bob Omar, Tunis .... D   6
         —Kid Santi, Tunis .... W   6
Dec. 22—Beauvais, Paris .... D   8
Dec. 29—Dherbomez, Paris............. W   8

1929
Jan.   5—Laurenzoin, Paris............. W   8
Jan. 12—Mousseron, Paris ....KO   5
Jan. 19—Carbonnel, Paris .... W   8
Jan. 26—Couturier, Paris .... W   8
Mar. 14—Heddebaut, Paris .... W   8
Apr.   9—Verdier, Paris................ W   8
Apr. 17—Verdier, Paris................ W   8
May   18—Escargeuil, Paris .... W   8
Aug. 11—Leo Hermal, Paris.............L 10
Sept. 1—Heddebaut, Paris .... W   8
Sept. 8—Gerdal, Paris .... W 10
Oct.   1—Barras, Paris .... D 10
Nov.   3—Verdier, Paris................ D 10
Dec. 22—Chalange, Paris .... W 10
Dec. 31—Bob Omar, Oran .... D 10

1930
Jan. 16—Beauvais, Paris .... W 10
Feb.   8—Kid Oliva, Limoges ....KO by   4
         (French flyweight title)
Feb. 18—Nour, Paris ....KO   7
Mar. 11—Gabes, Paris .... W 10
July   2—Praxille Gyde, Tunis .... W 10
Aug. 17—Larrani, Tunis .... W 10
Nov.   3—Johnny King, Manchester ... D 15
Nov. 10—Potier, Paris................. W 10
Nov. 25—Henri Barras, Paris .... W 10
Dec.   6—Etienne Mura, Paris .... D 10

1931
Jan.   3—Bob Omar, Oran .... D 10
Jan.   7—Joe Mendiola, Paris ...... KO by   1
Jan. 17—Rene Bastiaens, Paris.........KO   6
Feb. 11—Joe Mendiola, Paris .... W 10
Mar. 10—Willie Metzner, Paris .... W 10
Mar. 21—Etienne Mura, Paris .... W 10
Apr.   1—Emile Degand, Rouen .... W 10
Apr.   8—Carlos Flix, Paris .... W 10
Apr. 22—Jack Himpfen, Paris ....KO   2
Apr. 30—Tommy Brown, Paris ....KO   6
May   26—Victor Ferrand, Tunis .... W 10
June 11—Valentin Angelmann, Paris .... W 15
         (French flyweight title)
Aug. 25—Jean Cuart, Paris............. W 10
Sept. 10—Willie Metzner, Paris .... W 12

807

Oct.   26—Frankie Genaro, Paris ....KO   2
       (IBU, World flyweight title)
Nov.   3—Johnny King, Manchester .... D 15
Nov.   21—Rene Chalange, Casablanca .... W 10
Dec.   21—Emile Pladner, Paris............L 10
1932
Jan.   6—Giovanni Savo, Paris .... W 10
Jan.   28—Len Beynon, London .... W 10
Feb.   27—Paul Schafer, Zurich .... W 10
Mar.   18—Guiseppe Parigi, Tunis ....KO   8
Apr.   10—Willie Metzner, Algiers .... W 10
May   14—Mariano Arilla, Algiers .... W 10
June   5—Manuel Gonzalez, Oran..............W 10
June   26—Nicholas Petit-Biquet, Algiers .. W 10
July   3—Mariano Arilla, Oran .... D 10
Sept. 2—Mariano Arilla, Paris .... W 10
Sept. 12—Mickey McGuire, N'castle ...KO by 2
Oct.   3—Percy Dexter, Vienna ....KO   9
Oct.   12—Sandy McEwan, Paris . ...KO   6
Oct.   31—Jackie Brown, Manchester . KO by 13
       (Lost IBU, World Flyweight Title)
Nov.   19—Jack Cowley, Paris ....KO   6
Dec.   14—Carlo Cavagnoli, Paris .... W 10
Dec.   22—Orlando Magliozzi, Toulouse .KO   1
1933
Jan.   24—Emile Pladner, Tunis .... W 10
Feb.   14—Albert Biesmans, Troyes ...... W 10
Feb.   23—Kid Socks, Paris .... W 10
Mar.   18—Baltasar Sangchili, Valencia ....L 10
Mar.   23—Vittorio Tamagnini, Paris ......L 10
Apr.   4—Nicolas Petit-Biquet, Tunis .... D 10
June   9—Charley Sauvage,
           Castantinople .... W 10
July   3—Jackie Brown, London ....L 10
Oct.   16—Kid Francis, Paris .... W 10
Oct.   31—Young Borel, Lyons .... D 10
Nov.   10—Young Borel, Paris .... W 10
Nov.   28—Vittorio Tamagnini, Tunis ...... W 10
Dec.   3—Nicolas Petit-Biquet, Lille .....L 12
Dec.   7—Teodore Murrall, St. Etienne .. KO   4
1934
Jan.   19—Eugene Huat, Paris .... W 12
Feb.   19—Al Brown, Paris................L 15
       (For World Bantamweight Title)
Mar.   21—Leone Blasi, Paris .... W 10
Apr.   10—Leone Blasi, Lyons ....WF   3
June   7—Marius Monti, Nice ....KO   5
June   10—Albert Biesmans, Marseilles .... W 10
June   17—Baltazar Sangchili, Oran ....L 10
July   11—Emile Pladner, Paris.......... W 10
Aug.   16—Victor Ferrand, Cannes ......KO   3
Aug.   21—Charles Fougere, Bagnoles .... W   6
Sept. 1—Pete Sanstol, Oslo ....L 10
Nov.   1—Al Brown, Tunis ....KO by 10
Dec.   1—Ottavio Gori, Paris .... W 10
Dec.   11—Lorenzo Boira, Paris ....KO   6
Dec.   24—Joseph Decico, Paris ....L 10
1935
Jan.   5—Carlo Cavagnoli, Paris .... W 10
Feb.   16—Gustavo Ansini, Paris ....L 10
Mar.   13—Mariano, Nancy ....KO   3
Apr.   2—Paul Dogniaux, Paris...........L 10
July   5—Emile Pladner, Casablanca ..... D 10
Aug.   5—Spud Arenas, Casablanca ..... W 10
Sept. 15—Baltazar Sangchili, Casablanca ..L 10
Oct.   9—Salvadore Lozano, Barcelona ..L 10
Nov.   26—Orlando Magliozzi, Paris .... W 10
Dec.   14—Eugene Huat, Paris..............L 10
Dec.   31—Aurel Toma, Paris ....L 10
1936
Feb.   3—Giovanni Sili, Orleans ....KO   5
Feb.   8—Robert Raquet, Amiens .... W 10
Mar.   2—Henri Soya, Le Mans ....KO   4
Mar.   5—Maurice Filhol, Strasbourg .... W 10
Apr.   14—Eugene Huat, Tunis .... W 10
May   2—Giovanni Mazella, Tunis ...... W 12
July   1—Pedrito Ruiz, Paris .... D 10
Aug.   12—Ernst Weiss, Vienna ....L 10
Oct.   11—Pedrito Ruiz, Antwerp .... W 10
Dec.   3—Maurice Huguenin, Lyons .....L 10
1937
Oct.   4—Aurel Toma, Bucharest .... KO by 5
Dec.   22—Al Brown, Paris............ KO by 5
1938
Nov.   11—Ernest Weiss, Berlin ....L 10

TB	KO	WD	WF	D	LD	LF	KOBY	ND	NC
131	26	62	1	16	19	0	7	0	0

Believed to have died in German prison
camp, 1942.

JACKIE BROWN
Born, Ancoats, Manchester, England,
Weight, 120 lbs. Height, 5 ft. 5 in. Managed by
Harry Fleming.
1926
Mar.   23—Dick Manning, Manchester .... W   6
1927
Mar.   4—Tommy Brown, Salford ....L 10
Mar.   15—Fred Webb, Manchester L   3
Mar.   22—Francois Biron, Paris, France ...L 10
May   15—Ernie Hendricks, Salford ...... D 10
July   7—Young Fagill, Liverpool ......WF   1
Sept. 27—Joe Fleming, Manchester ...... W   6
Oct.   7—Harry Yates, Manchester ...... W 10
Nov.   1—Fred Webb, Manchester ...... W 10
Nov.   19—Jack Cantwell, Mountain Ash. . W 10
Dec.   11—Glover's Nipper, Salford ....L 15
Dec.   29—Jim Crawford, Liverpool ......KO   5
1928
Feb.   14—Young Fitz, Manchester ...... W   6
Mar.   16—Ernie Barker, Blackpool ...... W 10
Apr.   2—Jim Crawford, Salford .... W 10
Apr.   21—Fred Morgan .... W 15
May   1—Martin Gallagher, Leigh ...... W 12
May   20—Fred Webb, Salford .... W 10
June   14—Glover's Nipper, Liverpool .... D 10
July   3—Siki Coulton, Ashton-u-Lyne ....W
July   5—Ernie Barker, Manchester .... W   6
July   —Jean Locatelli, Morecambe .... W 10
Aug.   2—Jim Crawford, Liverpool ...... W 10
Sept. 21—Harry Inkles, Ashton-u.-Lyne .. W 10
Oct.   13—Fred Morgan, Ogmore Vale ... D 15
Oct.   20—Dickie Inkles, Ashton-u.-Lyne ..L 15
Nov.   3—Jerry O'Neill, Pontypridd ...... W 15
Nov.   24—Phineas John, Pontypridd..........L 15
Dec.   4—Tommy Brown, Manchester ... W 15
Dec.   9—Dickie Inkles, Leeds .... W 15
Dec.   15—Kid Hughes, Bridgend .... W 15
Dec.   29—Cuthbert Taylor, Merthyr ..... D 15
1929
Jan.   6—Boy Edge, Leeds ....KO   3
Feb.   12—George Greaves, Manchester ... W 20
       (Northern Flyweight Championship)
Mar.   5—Walter Lemon, Manchester ....KO 13
Mar.   19—Tony Roberti, Manchester ....KO   4
Apr.   22—Phineas John, London .... W 12
June   18—Jim Campbell, Manchester ....KO   9
Oct.   13—Bert Kirby, West Bromwich ..KO   3
       (British Flyweight Championship)
Nov.   13—Phineas John, Holborn .... W 15
Dec.   20—Harry Hill, West Bromwich ..KO 11
1930
Mar.   3—Bert Kirby .... KO by 3
       (British Flyweight Title and Lonsdale Belt)
Apr.   14—Emile Degand, Manchester .... W 15
May   18—Percy Dexter, W. Bromwich ...KO   7
June   23—Rene Chalange, Manchester ... W 15
July   20—Billy James, W. Bromwich .....L 15
Sept. 22—Kid Hughes, Manchester......KO 11
1931
Feb.   2—Bert Kirby, Manchester .... W 15
       (British Flyweight Title and Lonsdale Belt)
May   4—Lucien Popescu, Manchester ... W 15
June   15—Emile Degand, Olymp., London W 15
       (European flyweight championship)
July   6—Vincenzo Savo, Manchester ... W 15
       (European flyweight championship)
July   20—Colignon, Sheffield .... W 15
Aug.   24—Jim Maharg, Manchester ......WF   8
Oct.   12—Ottavio Gori, Manchester .....KO   8
Nov.   8—Benny Thackeray, Royton .... W 15
Nov.   13—George Aziz, Blackpool .... W 12
Dec.   2—Percy Dexter, Morecambe ...KO   9
1932
Feb.   1—Jean Cuart, Manchester ......KO 11
Feb.   15—Benny Thackeray, Leeds ...... W 15
Feb.   22—Mickey McGuire, Newcastle ....L 15
Mar.   7—Emile Degand, Manchester ... W 15
Apr.   18—Len Beynon, Manchester ..... W 15
June   9—George Marsden, D'glas I.O.M. KO   6
Aug.   1—Bob Fielding, Blackpool ....KO   8
Aug.   13—Tucker Winch, Sheffield ......LF   4
Sept. 19—Jim Maharg, Manchester ......WF   8
       (British flyweight title and Lonsdale belt)
Oct.   31—Young Perez, Manchester ....KO 13
       (Won World's Flyweight Championship)
1933
b.   16—Ettienne Mura, Paris, France ....L 12
May   1—Dave Crowley, Manchester ...LF   9
May   7—Billy Bryon, Ring, London ...KO 14

June 12—Valentin Angelmann, London . W 15
(World's Flyweight Championship)
July 3—Young Perez, Manchester ...... W 12
July 24—Mickey M'Guire, Manchester . LF 7
Sept. 11—Valentin Angelmann, M'nchst'r. W 15
(World's Flyweight Championship)
Sept. 27—Jimmy Knowles, Edinburgh ... W 12
Oct. 30—Midget Wolgast, Albert Hall ....L 12
Dec. 11—Ginger Foran, Manchester ..... W 15
(World's Empire and British Flyweight Titles)

1934
Apr. 16—Aurel Toma, Manchester ...... W 12
June 18—Valentin Angelmann, Mnchstr.. D 15
(World's Flyweight Championship)

1935
Feb. 11—Orlando Magliozzi, Mnchstr. ...KO 4
Feb. 22—Henri Barrass, Blackpool ...... W 12
Mar. 4—Benny Lynch, Glasgow .... D 12
Mar. 11—Kid Francis, Manchester .... D 12
Mar. 25—Maurice Filhol, Birmingham ... W 12
May 30—George Marsden, Liverpool ...KO 6
June 24—Ernst Weiss, Manchester ...... W 10
July 19—Jackie Quinn, Manchester ....KO 2
July 29—Syd Rose, Manchester ....KO 3
Aug. 15—Eric Jones, Sheffield ....KO 3
Sept. 8—Benny Lynch, Manchester .KO 2
(Lost World, European and British Flyweight Titles)
Oct. 14—Bert Kirby, Sparkbrook ......KO 12
Nov. 4—Tommy Pardoe, Sparkbrook ..KO 4
Nov. 22—Johnny King, Manchester . KO by 6
Dec. 22—Ellis Ashurst, Leeds ....KO 2

1936
Feb. 7—Nic Petit-Biquet, Manchester .KO 6
Feb. —Jackie Ryan, Liverpool ....KO 4
Mar. 6—Fred Morris, Manchester .....KO 8
—Tucker Winch ....KO 8
—Ted Green ....KO 1
May 18—Johnny Cusick, Manchester ....L 15
July 13—Johnny Cusick, Manchester ... W 15
Oct. 5—Len Hampston, Manchester ... W 15
Nov. —Jim McNally, Manchester .....KO 15
—Rafael Valdez .... W 10
Nov. —Len Beynon, Manchester ..... W 15

1937
Mar. 8—Bobby Hinds, Batley .... W 12
Mar. 15—Van Meensal, Rotherham ....KO 10
Mar. 21—Juanita Hernandez, Mnchstr. .KO 8
May 31—Johnny King, Manchester . KO by 13
Oct. 11—Pat Palmer, London ....KO 6
Nov. 24—Len Hampston, Bradford ..... LF 13

1938
Jan. 10—Battling Jim Hayes, Leeds .....L 12
Feb. 15—Joe Skelly, Douglas .... W 10
Mar. 3—Pat Palmer, London .... W 8
Mar. 14—Fred Tennant, Darlington ..... W 10
Apr. 7—Jim Brady, London ....L 8
Apr. 17—Joe Skelly, Burnsley ....KO 10
June 29—Joe Connolly, Paisley ....L 8
July 25—Battling Jim Hayes, Mnchstr. .. W 10
Oct. 5—Dave Kellar, London ....KO 3
Oct. 31—Pierce Ellis, Manchester ...... W 10
Nov. 28—Ginger Murphy, Manchester ..KO 4

1939
Mar. 5—Battling Jim Hayes, Leeds ..... W 15
Apr. 24—Tommy Smith, Manchester ....L 10
May 8—Teddy O'Neil, Manchester .... W 10
July 20—Kid Tanner, Liverpool ....L 10
July 24—Benny Jones, Manchester ..... W 10

TB	KO	WD	WF	D	LD	LF	KOBY	ND	NC
129	36	58	3	7	17	4	4	0	0

Died, Mar. 15, 1971 Manchester, England.

BENNY LYNCH
Born, April 2, 1913, Clydesdale, Scotland.
Weight 112 lbs. Height, 5 ft. 5 in.
Additional early records missing for 1931 and 1932. First Scottish Champion. Had 37 amateur bouts and lost only 2.

1931
June 11—Young M'Coll, Glasgow ,,,,,.KO 3
Aug. 14—Young Donnelly, Glasgow ..... D 0
Oct. 1—Paddy Docherty, Glasgow ......L 8

1932
Feb. 27—Jimmy Barr, Glasgow .... W 6
Mar. 11—Scotty Deans, Glasgow .... W 6
Apr. 16—Young Griffo, Glasgow .... W 6
June 11—Joe Aitken, Glasgow .... W 10
July 28—Jim Jeffries, Blantyre .... W 6
Aug. 18—Tony Fleming, Glasgow .... D 6
Nov. 3—Tommy Higgins, Bridgeton ....W 10
Nov. 9—Ginger M'Leod, Edinburgh ...KO 5
Nov. 17—Paddy Docherty, Glasgow ..... D 10
Dec. 1—Paddy Docherty, Glasgow .... W 10
Dec. 8—Jim Naughton, Glasgow ...... W 6
Dec. 21—Fred Tennant, Glasgow .... D 10

1933
Jan. 11—Dan Conlin, Glasgow .... W 10
Feb. 15—Joe Aitken, Glasgow .... D 10
Mar. 29—Paddy Docherty, Glasgow ..... D 10
Apr. 19—Walter Lemon, Glasgow ...... W 10
May 3—Fred Tennant, Glasgow ...... W 10
May 10—Alec Farris, Glasgow .... W 8
May 24—Jim Maharg, Glasgow .... W 12
June 14—Billy Warnock, Glasgow ......KO 11
June 28—Kid Hughes, Glasgow ....KO 9
Oct. 12—Willie Vagan, Edinburgh ......KO 2
Oct. 24—Boy McIntosh, Blantyre ......KO 4
(stopped by referee)
Oct. 29—Bert Kirby, West B'wich .... W 12
Nov. 9—Bob Fielding, Liverpool .... D 10

1934
Feb. 1—Jim Brady, Edinburgh .... W 12
Feb. 8—Fred Webb, Glasgow ....KO 3
Mar. 21—Carlo Cavagnoli, Glasgow ..... W 12
Apr. 17—George Lowe, Glasgow ......KO 2
May 16—Jim Campbell, Glasgow .... W 15
(Scottish flyweight championship)
May 27—Evan Evans, Glasgow ....KO 3
May 29—Peter Miller, Glasgow ....KO 8
June 27—Jim Campbell, Glasgow .... W 15
(Scottish flyweight championship)
Aug. 8—Maurice Huguenin, Glasgow ... W 12
Aug. 30—Jim Brady, Glasgow .... W 12
Sept. 26—Valentin Angelmann, Glasgow . W 12
Oct. 25—Billy Johnstone, Glasgow .....KO 5
Nov. 7—Pedrito Ruiz, Glasgow .... W 12
Nov. 12—Peter Miller, Newcastle ......KO 8
Nov. 29—Johnny Griffiths, Edinburgh ..KO 1
Dec. 5—Tut Whalley, Dundee ....WF 8
Dec. 13—Sandy M'Ewan, Edinburgh .... W 12

1935
Jan. 7—Bobby Magee, Glasgow .... W 12
Mar. 4—Jackie Brown, Glasgow .... D 12
Apr. 15—Tommy Pardoe, Brimingham .KO 14
May —Charlie Hazelgrove, Glasgow ..KO 1
Sept. 8—Jackie Brown, Manchester ....KO 2
(British, European and world's flyweight titles)
Dec. 3—Gaston Maton, Glasgow ...... W 12
Dec. 12—Harry Orton, Leith .... W 10
Dec. 19—Phil Milligan, Glasgow .... W 12

1936
Mar. 2—Jim Warnock, Belfast ....L 12
May 25—Mickey Maguire, New Castle ..KO 4
May 28—Pat Warburton, London ......KO 3
June 16—Syd Parker, Glasgow ....KO 9
Sept. 16—Pat Palmer, Glasgow ....KO 8
(British, European and world title bout)
Nov. 16—Phil Milligan, Manchester .....KO 7
Dec. 10—Eric Jones, London ....KO 2

1937
Jan. 19—Small Montana, London .... W 15
(World flyweight title bout)
Feb. 10—Fortunato Ortega, Glasgow .... W 12
Mar. 1—Len Hampston, Manchester ... LF 5
Mar. 2—Jim Hampston, Leeds ....KO 10
June 2—Jim Warnock, Glasgow ....L 10
Aug. 20—Roy Underwood, Glasgow ....KO 6
Oct. 13—Peter Kane, Glasgow ....KO 13
(World flyweight title bout)
Dec. 13—Georges Bataille, Leicester ....KO 8

1938
Feb. 9—Maurice Filhol, Glasgow ......KO 5
Mar. 24—Peter Kane, Liverpool .... D 15
(World Flyweight Title)
June 29—Jackie Jurich, Paisley, Scot....KO 12
Lynch failed to make the weight and announced his retirement as champion.
Sept. 28—Kayo Morgan, Glasgow ....L 12
Oct. 3—Aurel Toma, London .....KO by 3

TB	KO	WD	WF	D	LD	LF	KOBY	ND	NC
73	28	29	1	9	1	1	1	0	0

Died Aug. 6, 1946 in Glasgow, Scotland.

SMALL MONTANA
(Benjamin Gan)
Born, Feb. 24, 1913, Negros, Philippine
Islands. Nationality, Filipino. Weight, 112 lbs.
Height, 5 ft. 4 in. Managed by Paddy Ryan.
1931
Won: Little Ligaspe, 4 (twice); Jack Silver,
4; Rush Jolly, 4; Little Damaguillas, 4 (twice);
Doc Olaso, 4 (twice); Yg. Bono, 4; Young
Johnson, 6. Knockout: Fighting Sorsegon, 3.
1932
Won: Young Silva, 6; Kid Bakong, 10;
Rush Jolly, 10; Kid Augustine, 6; Kid Filipe, 6;
Kid Paline, 6; Kid Leonard, 6; Young Alvares, 4;
Young Vicente, 8.
1933
Won: Young Alexander, 4; Al Garcia, 4;
Camel Joe, 4; Rush Ribo, 6; Gene Torres, 6;
Dommy Reyes, 10; Young Silva, 10; Young
Radiola, 8; Kid Oriolo, 6; Kid Oriolo, 8; Fighting
Quenubatan, 6; Kid Oriolo, 6; Lost—David
Dencio, 4; Dommy Reyes, 8. Draw: Young
Domingo, 10; Kid Kelly, 10.
1934
Knockouts: Young Dencio, 4; Tuffy
Pierpont, 3; Al Robinson, 2; Young Sport, 4;
Felix Ignacio, 4; Won: Kid Kuratsu, 8 (twice);
Young Sport, 8; Joe Duclan, 8; Henry Kudo, 8;
Frank Baron, 6; Joe Tei Ken, 10; Billy McLeod,
10; Chato Laredo, 10; Augie Curtis, 10; Tony
Marino, 10 (twice). Draw: Billy McLeod, 10
(twice); Chato Laredo, 10. Lost: Tuffy Pierpont,
4; Joe Tei Ken, 10.
1935
Mar.	8—Joe Tei Ken, Sacramento	W 10
May	2—Anton Kocsis, Sacramento	W 10
May	24—Joe Tei Ken, San Francisco	W 10
July	3—Midget Wolgast, Sacramento	W 10
Aug.	5—Anton Kocsis, San Francisco	W 10
Aug.	12—Bobby Olivas, Oakland	KO 3
Aug.	31—Speedy Dado, Stockton, Cal.	W 10
Sept.	16—Midget Wolgast, Oakland	W 10
	(Won American Flyweight Title)	
Oct.	1—Bobby Olivas, Los Angeles	W 10
Oct.	21—Tuffy Pierpont, Oakland	W 10
Nov.	5—Midget Wolgast, Los Angeles	L 10
Dec.	16—Tuffy Pierpont, Oakland	W 10
1936
Feb.	12—Pancho Leyvas, Oakland	L 10
Mar.	20—Lou Salica, San Francisco	L 10
June	27—Abe Konehali, Hawaii	W 10
July	11—Augie Curtis, Hawaii	W 10
July	25—Jimmy Uchida, Hawaii	W 10
Aug.	8—Augie Curtis, Hawaii	D 8
Oct.	10—Mauricio Seria, Stockton	W 10
Oct.	28—Peppy Sanchez, Oakland	W 10
Nov.	20—Star Frisco, Pismo Beach	L 10
1937
Jan.	19—Benny Lynch, London	L 15
	(For World Flyweight Title)	
Feb.	8—Tiny Bostock, Manchester	L 12
Mar.	4—Pat Palmer, London	W 10
Apr.	27—Pat Palmer, London	W 10
Aug.	27—Little Dado, Honolulu	D 10
Oct.	26—Jackie Jurich, San Jose	D 10
Dec.	14—Jackie Jurich, San Jose	L 10
1938
May	9—Frankie Jarr, Toronto	W 10
May	30—Baby Yack, Toronto	W 10
June	13—Pancho Villa II, Toronto	W 10
Aug.	3—Katzumi Morioka, L. I. C.	W 15
Aug.	17—Tommy Forte, New York	W 8
Oct.	3—Aurelin Lamothe, Washington	KO 8
Oct.	17—Pete Powell, Richmond	D 10
Nov.	30—Little Dado, Oakland	L 10
	(Lost American and N.B.A. Title)	
1939
Mar.	3—Jackie Jurich, Hollywd	KO by 7
July	21—Al Robinsin, Watsonville	W 10
Aug.	25—Al Robinson, Reno	KO 10
Oct.	4—Jackie Jurich, Oakland	L 10
	—Manuel Ortiz	W 10
1940
Jan.	10—Little Pancho, Oakland	L 10
Oct.	19—Young Canada Lee, Pittsburgh	W 6
Dec.	2—Lou Salica, Toronto	KO by 3
Dec.	10—Freddy Pope, Columbus	L 10
1941
Jan.	30—Lou Transparenti, Baltimore	L 10
Feb.	13—Tommy Forte, Philadelphia	L 10
Apr.	5—Luis Castillo, Havana	L 12
Apr.	19—Bobby Peyvas, Havana	KO 2
May	3—Luis Castillo, Havana	L 12

May	10—Lorenzo Safora, Havana	D 10
Aug.	17—Chico Morales, Jacksonville	W 8
Oct.	12—Luis Castillo, Mexico City	KO by 2
1942
In U. S. Army.

TB	KO	WD	WF	D	LD	LF	KOBY	ND	NC
111	10	70	0	9	19	0	3	0	0

VALENTIN ANGELMANN
Born, March 7, 1910, Colmar, France. Weight, 112
lbs. Height, 5 ft. 1 in.
1927
Jan.	6—Eugene Catrain, Lyons	D 8
1928
Mar.	13—Leroux, Lyons	KO by 4
Dec.	5—Clement, Lyons	KO 2
1929
Jan.	2—Settemana, Lyons	WF 1
Feb.	6—Serra, Lyons	W 8
Mar.	5—Joseph Tournel, Roanne	W 8
	—Garde, Lyons	W 8
	—Young Philippe, Lyons	W 8
	—Garde, Lyons	KO 4
	—Leroy, Lyons	KO 1
	—Harica, Lyons	KO 3
	—Eugene Catrain, Lyons	W 8
	—Foullon, Lyons	W 8
	—Kid Roger, Essonne	W 10
1930
Jan.	8—Leroy, Paris	KO 2
Feb.	2—Bob Rousseau, Limoges	W 10
Feb.	23—Etienne Lapouble, Limoges	KO 7
Mar.	4—Jack Poillion, Paris	W 10
Apr.	3—Etienne Lapouble, Paris	W 10
Apr.	12—Young Philippe	W 10
Apr.	23—Etienne Mura, Paris	W 10
June	4—Jean Cuart, Limoges	W 8
June	21—Marcel Naegelen, Limoges	KO 4
Oct.	18—Lucian Popescu, Bucharest	L 10
Nov.	10—Tommy Brown, Manchester	L 10
Dec.	23—Joe Mendiola, Paris	D 10
1931
Jan.	4—Rene Gabes, Paris	W 10
Feb.	3—Rene Challange	W 12
	(Won French Bantamweight Title)	
Feb.	24—Desire Collignon, Paris	W 10
Mar.	30—Willie Metzner, Paris	W 10
Apr.	23—Willie Metzner, Lyons	W 10
May	5—Maurice Justice, Cherbourg	W 12
	(Won French Flyweight Title)	
May	14—Ben Omar, Algiers	L 10
June	4—Victor (Young) Perez, Paris	L 15
	(Lost French Flyweight Title)	
Sept.	12—Jean Cuart, Paris	W 10
Oct.	3—Frankie Genaro, Paris	L 15
	(For NBA World Flyweight Title)	
Nov.	5—Mariano Arilla, Paris	L 10
Nov.	7—Joseph Jacobs, Zurich	KO 5
Dec.	17—Bert Kirby, Paris	KO 5
1932
Jan.	13—Joseph Jacobs, Paris	KO 2
Feb.	3—Mariano Arilla, Paris	W 10
Feb.	12—Carlo Cavagnoli, Geneva	W 10
Mar.	16—Mickey Maguire, Paris	W 8
Apr.	13—Tucker Winch, Paris	KO 7
May	25—Praxille, Gyde, Paris	W 10
June	25—Young Philippe, Nancy	KO 4
June	29—Maurice Huguenin, Paris	W 15
	(Regained French Flyweight Title)	
Sept.	16—Helmut Hinz, Paris	W 10
Nov.	2—Percy Dexter, Paris	KO 9
Nov.	18—Carlo Cavagnoli, Paris	W 10
Nov.	30—Joe Mendiola, Paris	W 10
Dec.	28—Rene Challange, Paris	W 10
1933
Jan.	6—Giannarelli, Strasbourg	KO 4

Feb.	9—Kid Martino, Geneva	W	10
Mar.	8—Kid Martin, Paris	W	10
Apr.	6—Giovanni Savo, Paris	W	10
Apr.	19—Kid Oliva, Paris	W	12
	(Retained French Flyweight Title)		
May	12—Emil Degand, Geneva	W	10
June	12—Jackie Brown, London	L	15
	(For NBA-IBU World Flyweight Title)		
Aug.	6—Marcel Aubry, Deauville	KO	6
Sept.	11—Jackie Brown, Manchester	L	15
	(For NBA-IBU World Flyweight Title)		
Oct.	30—Herbie Hill, London	KO	5
Nov.	13—Midget Wolgast, Paris	D	10
Nov.	28—Maurice Huguenin, Paris	D	12
Dec.	18—Mickey Maguire, Newcastle	LF	8

1934

Feb.	16—Jerry O'Neill, Paris	W	10
Mar.	5—Mickey Maguire, Newcastle	W	12
Mar.	19—Marcel Aubry, Le Havre	W	10
Apr.	4—Georges Bataille, Paris	KO	9
Apr.	16—Mickey Maguire, Manchester	KO	10
Apr.	21—Eloi Eddebaut, Brest	KO	3
June	18—Jackie Brown, Manchester	D	15
	(For NBA-IBU World Flyweight Title)		
Sept.	26—Benny Lunch, Glasgow	L	12
Oct.	17—Pedrito Ruiz, Paris	W	10
Nov.	7—Maurice Huguenin, Paris	L	15
	(Lost French Flyweight Title)		
Nov.	20—Pedrito Ruiz, Paris	W	10
Dec.	12—Joe Mendiola, Paris	D	10
Dec.	29—Maurice Dupuis, Paris	W	10

1935

Jan.	29—Maurice Filhol, Paris	W	10
Feb.	23—Jean Cuart, Rouen	KO	5
Mar.	21—Marcel Aubry, Nice	KO	4
Oct.	8—Willie Smith, Paris	KO	5
Oct.	31—Pedrito Ruiz, Paris	W	10

1936

Jan.	6—Kid David, Paris	KO	5
	(Won Vacant IBU World Flyweight Title)		
Feb.	14—Fortunato Ortega, Paris	D	10
Mar.	13—Leopold Courtwriendt, Paris	KO	8
Apr.	9—Aurel Toma, Lyons	L	10
May	14—Gabriel Burah, Lyons	KO	3
July	2—Pierre Louis, Paris	W	10
July	11—Enrico Urbinati, Marseilles	L	10
Sept.	1—Giovanni Sili, Paris	KO	3
Sept.	14—Joseph Quintallet, Mulhouse	KO	5
Sept.	19—Etienne Loiseau, Colmar	KO	4
Oct.	22—Etienne Ferraro, Paris	L	10
Nov.	6—Juanito Hernandez, Mulhouse	W	10
Nov.	12—Peter Kane, Liverpool	L	12
Dec.	12—Ernst Weiss, Paris	W	15
	(Won European Flyweight Title)		
	(Retained IBU World Flyweight Title)		

1937

Jan.	18—Peter Kane, Paris	L	12
May	5—Tiny Bostock, Paris	L	10
Sept.	3—Ernst Weiss, Wien	L	12
Sept.	25—Solomon Rubin, Amiens	KO	6
Oct.	20—Jim McStravick, Belfast	W	10
Dec.	7—Bob Rousseau, Rochefort	KO	4

1938

Jan.	7—Young Gonzalez, Paris	KO	9
Jan.	18—Gaston Van den Bos, Brussels	D	10
Feb.	3—Gaston Van den Bos, Paris	W	10
Feb.	23—Maurice Huguenin, Paris	W	10
Mar.	30—Jimmy Warnock, Belfast	KO	5
Apr.	13—Panama Al Brown, Paris	KO by	8
May	11—Dumitru Panaitescu, Bucharest	L	10
July	2—Bernard Leroux, Paris	L	10
Oct.	6—Baltazar Sangchilli, Paris	WF	4
	(Retained European Flyweight Title)		
Nov.	3—Poppy Decico, Paris	W	10
Dec.	3—Ernst Weiss, Hamburg	W	8

1939

Feb.	2—Robert Bourdet, Paris	L	10
Mar.	17—Ernst Weiss, Berlin	D	10
Mar.	22—Albert Legrand, Brussels	L	10
Apr.	19—Young Gonzalez, Paris	LF	5

May	15—Jackie Paterson, Glasgow	D	10
June	11—Robert Bourdet, Chantilly	KO	8
Aug.	13—Jim Campbell, Deauville	KO	7

1940

Feb.	3—Bernard Leroux, Paris	W	10
Mar.	9—Sammy Benchetrit, Paris	W	10
Nov.	2—Vincent Aucejo, Paris	D	10
Nov.	23—Rene Taysse, Paris	W	10
Dec.	7—Roger Tison, Paris	L	10
Dec.	20—Roger Cotti, Bordeaux	W	10

1941

Jan.	12—Roger Cotti, Paris	W	10
Feb.	1—Roger Tison, Paris	W	10
Feb.	15—Roger Fournier, Paris	W	10
Mar.	9—Al Legrand, Brussels	L	10
Mar.	29—Theo Medina, Paris	W	10
Apr.	28—Rene Jacquart, Paris	KO	10
May	11—Jean Le Balanger, Le Havre	W	10
June	13—Jean Le Balanger, Paris	L	10
July	13—Theo Medina, Angouleme	L	10
July	20—Roger Fournier, Poitiers	W	10
July	27—Juanito Hernandez, Dijon	W	10
Sept.	19—Vincent Aucejo, Paris	L	10
Oct.	2—Marius Tassart, Besancon	L	10
Oct.	26—Florentin Declais, Paris	D	10
Nov.	9—Theo Medina, Paris	W	10
Nov.	28—Luis Fernandez, Paris	D	10
Dec.	19—Juanito Hernandez, Paris	W	10

1942

Jan.	13—Florentin Declais, Paris	W	10
Feb.	1—Roger Tison, Paris	W	10
Feb.	13—Roger Fournier, Paris	W	12
Mar.	13—Jean Le Balanger, Paris	W	10
Mar.	23—Florentin Declais, Bordeaux	W	12
May	24—Jean Engelen, Paris	W	10
June	21—Theo Medina, Tours	L	12
July	19—Francis Ruiz, Bordeaux	W	10
Oct.	3—Poppy Decico, Lyons	L	10
Nov.	2—Roger Fournier, Bordeaux	W	10
Nov.	19—Eugene Huat, Toulouse	W	10
Dec.	20—Etienne Ferraro, Marseilles	D	10
Dec.	27—Francois Atenza, Paris	W	10

1943

Mar.	7—Robert Raquet, Paris	W	10
Apr.	11—Brahim Ben Yahi, Paris	W	10
June	9—Pierre Paul, Paris	W	10
June	20—Roger, Brussels	L	10
Aug.	8—Joe Cornelis, Liege	L	10
Sept.	22—Emil Famechon, Paris	W	10
Oct.	9—Florentin Declais, Paris	W	10
Nov.	28—Pierre Fouilloux, Paris	KO	3
Dec.	17—Luis Fernandez, Paris	L	10

1944

Feb.	6—Gabriel Fayaud, Toulouse	KO	7
Feb.	26—Camille Dormont, Paris	W	10
Mar.	19—Roger, Paris	KO	8
Apr.	22—Florentin Declais, Paris	W	10
Apr.	30—Luis Fernandez, Paris	KO by	7
Nov.	1—Etienne Ferraro, Paris	W	10
Dec.	1—Rene Megret, Paris	L	12
	(For French Bantamweight Title)		

1945

Jan.	30—Etienne Ferraro, Toulouse	L	10
Oct.	22—Robert Crochard, Montlucon	D	10

1946

Aug.	3—Camille Dormont, Limoges	D	10

TB	KO	WD	WF	D	LD	LF	KO BY	ND	NC
176	38	81	2	16	34	2	3	0	0

PETER KANE

Born, Golborne, Lancaster, England, Feb. 28, 1918.

1934

Dec.	13—Joe Jacobs, Liverpool	KO	5

Feb. 19—Kid Patterson, Liverpool .....KO 3
Mar. 19—Charlie Powell, Liverpool.....KO 2
Mar. 28—Nipper Carroll, Liverpool.....KO 3
May 2—Bobby Doyle, Liverpool......KO 6
May 30—Jacky Burns, Liverpool.......KO 1
June 27—Billy Charnock, Liverpool....KO 2
July 11—Kid Bonser, Liverpool.......KO 4
July 25—Jacky Shea, Liverpool........KO 2
Sept. 12—Charlie Reed, Liverpool.....KO 2
Oct. 10—Billy Charnock, Liverpool....KO 2
Nov. 7—Jacky Forshaw, Liverpool.....KO 1
Dec. 5—Clarry Gill, Liverpool ....KO 4

1936
Jan. 24—Joe Curran, Warrington .... W 10
Feb. 14—Tiny Bostock, Blackpool ...... W 10
Apr. 29—Willie Smith, Liverpool......KO 4
May 6—Praxille Gyde, Liverpool .....KO 3
May 21—Jim Laird, Liverpool ....KO 3
June 11—Herbie Hill, Liverpool ....KO 2
June 21—Cyclone Kelly, Manchester ...KO 4
June 30—Jim Maharg, Glasgow ....KO 3
Aug. 13—Enrico Urbinati, Liverpool ...KO 8
Aug. 27—Tommy Stewart, Belfast .....KO 10
Sept. 3—Ernst Weiss, Liverpool .... W 12
Sept. 16—Willie M'Camley, Glasgow ....W 10
Oct. 22—Pedrito Ruiz, Liverpool ......KO 7
Nov. 2—Pat Warburton, N.S.C., Lond. .KO 1
Nov. 12—Valentin Angelmann, Liverpool......................W 12
Nov. 23—Eugene Huat, N.S.C. ....KO 7
Dec. 14—Gaston Vandenbos, N.S.C. ...KO 6
Dec. 17—Al Hopp, Liverpool ....KO 2

1937
Jan. 18—Valentin Angelmann, Paris .... W 12
Feb. 18—Paul Schafer, Liverpool ......KO 1
Mar. 1—Pierre Louis, Paris ....KO 7
Mar. 18—Fortunato Ortega, Liverpool ...W 12
Apr. 3—Poppi Decico, Paris ....KO 1
Apr. 20—Phil Milligan, Liverpool .....KO 11
(For N. Area Flyweight Title)
May 27—Ernst Weiss, London ....W 10
June 17—Maurice Huguenin, Liverpool .KO 1
June 28—Petit Biquet, London ....KO 9
Aug. 26—Jim Warnock, Liverpool .....KO 4
Oct. 13—Benny Lynch, Glasgow .... KO by 13
(For World's Flyweight Title)

1938
Feb. 3—Hubert Offermanns, Liverpl...KO 10
Feb. 17—Georges Bataille, Paris........ W 10
Mar. 24—Benny Lynch, Liverpool ...... D 15
(World Flyweight Title Bout)
May 3—Georges Bataille, Liverpool ...KO 2
June 2—Bernard Leroux, Liverpool .... W 10
Sept. 22—Jackie Jurich, Liverpool .... W 15
(Claimed Vacant Flyweight Title)

1939
Jan. 31—Raoul Degryse, Leicester ...... W 10
Feb. 20—Gino Cattaneo, Liverpool ..... W 10
Apr. 3—Baltazar Sangchilli, London ... W 10
Apr. 27—Albert Legrand, London .....KO 8
May 18—El Houssaine, Paris .... W 10
Aug. 4—Pierre Lous, Monte Carlo .....KO 3

1940
Feb. 12—Jackie Rankin, London ... KO by 6
Apr. 4—Battling Jim Hayes, Liverpool .... W 10

1941
Feb. 20—Teddy O'Neil, London .... W 6
Mar. 2—Jimmy Lyden, Liverpool ......L 10
In British Army.
Nov. 16—Tommy McClinchey, Liverpl. .KO 2
Dec. 14—Jimmy Stubbs, Liverpool...... W 10

1942
Mar. 30—Willie Gray, London ....KO 5
Apr. 6—Eddie Petrin, Bristol ....KO 5
Apr. 26—Joe Curran, Liverpool .... W 10
June 1—Sammy Reynolds, Liverpool ... W 10
July 11—Sammy Reynolds, Wolver-hampton .... W 8
Aug. 3—Joe Curran, Liverpool ....KO 11
Sept. 10—Hugh Cameron, Liverpool .... W 10
Oct. 1—Frank Bonsor, Liverpool .....KO 7
Oct. 29—Paddy Ryan, Liverpool ....KO 6

1943
Jan. 14—Willie Grey, Liverpool .... W 10
Feb. 23—Willie Grey, London .... NC 5
Mar. 26—Gus Foran, Blackpool .... W 10
June 19—Jackie Paterson, Glasgow .. KO by 1
(Lost World Flyweight Title)
Oct. 10—Johnny Summers, Bristol .....KO 1

Oct. 13—Sammy Reynolds, London .... W 10
Nov. 3—Jim Brady, London .... W 10

1946
Aug. 13—Jackie Hughes, Brighton......WF 5
Sept. 4—Ron Bissell, Cardiff.........KO 2
Oct. 28—Norman Lewis, London ......KO 5
Nov. 18—Jean Jouas, Paris.............. W 10

1947
Jan. 6—Tommy Madine, Nottingham .KO 4
Feb. 10—Eddie Bunty Doran, Manch. ... W 8
Apr. 28—Joe Cornelis, Manchester ...... W 10
May 19—Theo Medina, Manchester ....KO 7
June 9—Theo Medina, Manchester ....KO 7
June 27—Albert Braedt, Brighton ......KO 3
Aug. 8—Dado Marino, Manchester ..... W 10
Sept. 26—Theo Medina, Manchester .... W 15
(Won European Bantamweight title)
Dec. 15—Joe Cornelis, Manchester ...... W 15
(European Bantamweight title)

1948
Jan. 26—Sammy Reynolds, Nottingham W 10
Feb. 20—Guido Ferracin, Manchester ...L 15
(Lost European Bantamweight Title)
Apr. 16—Bunty Doran, Manchester ....KO 8
May 26—Amleto Falcinelli, Paisley .....D 10
July 16—Gudio Ferracin, Manchest. KO by 5
Nov. 19—Stan Rowan, Manchester......L 12

TB	KO	WD	WF	D	LD	LF	KOBY	ND	NC
95	51	33	1	2	3	0	4	0	1

JACKIE PATERSON
Born, Springfield, Ayrshire, Scotland, September 5, 1920, Managed by Pat Collins.

1938
May 26—Joe Kiely, Greenock .... W 10
July 23—Rinty Monaghan, Belfast .....KO 5
Aug. 2—Pat McStravick, Glasgow .....KO 8
Aug. 17—Joe Curran, Glasgow .... LF 4
Aug. 19—Tommy Stewart, Belfast ......KO 1
Aug. 26—Joe Curran, Glasgow ......KO by 4
Sept. 27—Mickey O'Neill, Glasgow ...... W 10
Dec. 14—Billy Nash, Glasgow ....KO 8
Dec. 19—Phil Milligan, Newcastle ......KO 6

1939
Jan. 16—Tut Whalley, Newcastle .... D 10
Feb. 24—Jackie Kenny, Port Glasgow ...KO 1
Mar. 10—Gavino Matta, Leith ....KO 7
May 3—Raoul Degryse, Glasgow .... W 10
May 15—Valentin Angelmann, Glasgow .D 10
May 31—Freddy Tennant, Dundee .....KO 11
June 19—Tut Whalley, Glasgow ....KO 1
July 19—Joe Curran, Dundee .... W 10
Aug. 15—Eric Jones, Glasgow ....KO 1
Sept. 30—Paddy Ryan, Glasgow ....KO 13
Won the vacant British Flyweight Championship.
Nov. 27—Charley Brown, London ....L 10

1940
Mar. 11—Kid Tanner, Manchester .... W 15
Won the vacant Empire Flyweight Title
June 1—Walley Knightley, Chester-field ....KO 8
June 30—Young Chocolate, Edinburgh .KO 2
July 5—Kid Tanner, Liverpool ....KO 10
Nov. 13—Jimmy Stewart, Newcastle ....KO 1
Dec. —Teddy O'Neil, Glasgow ....W 6
Dec. 28—Jimmy Stewart, Glasgow .....KO 3

1941
Jan. 1—Billy Clinton, Dundee ....KO 1
Feb. 3—Paddy Ryan, Nottingham ....KO 6
Title bout—British and Empire Flyweight Championship.
Feb. 12—Jim Brady, Newcastle .... W 10
Mar. 15—Phil Milligan, Manchester ....KO 4
May 19—Billy Hazelgrove, Bristol ......KO 7
June 3—Kid Tanner, Glasgow ....KO 2
June 20—Jimmy Lyden, Manchester ....KO 9
June 27—Jimmy Stubbs, Liverpool ...... W 10
July 16—Jim Brady, Glasgow ....L 15
(For British Empire bantam title)
Sept. 19—Kid Tanner, Manchester .... W 10
Oct. 6—Billy Hazelgrove, London ....KO 9
Dec. 18—Dudley Lewis, London ....KO 1

1942
Feb. 23—Joe Hardy, London ....KO 6
Mar. 12—Kid Tanner, Glasgow ....KO 4
May 18—*Frank Bonsor, Notting-ham ....KO by 6

June	18—Billy Tansey, Glasgow ....KO 2
July	20—Eddie Petrin, London ....KO 2
July	6—Frank Bonsor, Nottingham ...KO 2
Sept.	24—Norman Lewis, Glasgow ......W 10
Nov.	26—Jim Hayes, Glasgow ....KO 1
	*Paterson quit with a broken hand.

1943

Jan.	13—Phil Milligan, London ....KO 2
Mar.	17—Al Phillips, London ....KO 3
June	19—Peter Kane, Glasgow ....KO 1
	(Won World flyweight title)
July	22—George Williams, Hamilton ...KO 2
Aug.	11—Gus Foran, London ....W 8
Sept.	27—Len Davies, Leicester ....L 10
Oct.	28—Jimmy Hayes, London ....W 3
	(Exhibition on Army Show)
Nov.	24—George Pook, London ....KO 6

1944

Apr.	24—Ben Duffy, Wolverhampton ... W 10
July	6—Ben Duffy, Hamilton ....W 10
Aug.	12—Norman Clayton, Liverpool ...KO 12
Oct.	25—Danny Webb, London .....KO by 3
Dec.	14—P. O. Ben Duffy, Glasgow .. KO by 7

1945

Jan.	29—Jackie Grimes, London ....W 8
Aug.	24—Gus Foran, Brighton ....L 8
Sept.	12—Jimmy Brady, Glasgow ....W 15
	(For British Empire bantam title)
Nov.	6—Sammy Reynolds, London ...KO 3
Nov.	19—Theo Medina, Paris ....L 10

1946

Mar.	8—Bunty Doran, Dublin ....L 10
Mar.	19—Theo Medina, London ....WF 8
	(Won European Bantamweight Title)
May	22—Jimmy Webster, Glasgow .....KO 5
June	7—Rinty Monaghan, Belfast .. KO by 6
July	10—Joe Curran, Glasgow .... W 15
	(World flyweight title)
Oct.	30-Theo Medina, Glasgow ......KO by 4
	(For European bantam title)

1947

Jan.	20—Cliff Anderson, London ....L 8
Feb.	10—Johnny King, Manchester ...KO 7
	(Won British bantamweight title)
Apr.	17—Corrado Conti, Glasgow ......W 10
May	15—Emidio Cacciatori, Glasgow ..KO 3
Sept.	8—Stan Rowan, London .....KO by 4
Oct.	20—Norman Lewis, London ......KO 5
	(British bantamweight title)
Dec.	15—Al Chavez, Manchester ....W 8

1948

Mar.	23—Rinty Monaghan, Belfast .. KO by 7
	(Lost world flyweight title)
May	5—Fernando Rosa, Glasgow .....KO 8
July	27—Jean Machtelinck, Firm....KO by 4
Aug.	23—Teddy Gardner, W. Hartlepool ..L 8
Oct.	18—Danny O'Sullivan, London ...KO 7
Nov.	29—Ronnie Draper, London ....L 8

1949

Feb.	7—Danny O'Sullivan, London .....L 8
Mar.	24—Stan Rowan, Liverpool ....L 15
	(Lost British & British Empire Bantam Titles)
Aug.	26—Mustapha Mustaphaoui, Paisley ....KO 4
Oct.	26—Manuel Ortiz, Glasgow ....L 10
Dec.	17—Vic Toweel, Johannesburg .....L 10

1950

May	10—Eddie Carson, Glasgow ....KO by 2

1951

Feb.	7—Willie Myles, Dundee ....L 8

TB	KO	WD	WF	D	LD	LF	KOBY	ND	NC
91	41	21	1	3	14	1	10	0	0

Died, November 19, 1966 after being shot.

RINTY MONAGHAN
(John Joseph Monaghan)
Born, Belfast, August 21, 1920. Managed
by Frank McAloran.

1935

Feb.	17—Vic Large, Belfast ....KO 4

1936

Jan.	13—Sam Ramsey, Belfast .....,,,W 6
Apr.	8—Young Kelly, Belfast ....W 6
May	16—Young Josephs, Belfast ....KO 3

1937

May	10—Mick Gibbons, Belfast ....W 6
June	21—Mick Gibbons, Belfast ....W 6
July	7—Sam Ramsey, Belfast ....W 6
July	13—Ted Meikle, Belfast ....KO 4
Aug.	9—Ted Meikle, Belfast ....W 8
Aug.	18—Frank Benson, Belfast ....KO 6
Sept.	17—Ted Meikle, Belfast ....W 8
Oct.	1—Paddy O'Toole, Belfast ....KO 4
Nov.	17—George Lang, Belfast ....KO 1
Dec.	2—Tommy Allen, Belfast ....KO 5

1938

Jan.	21—Alf Hughes, Belfast ....KO 9
Feb.	4—Pat Murphy, Belfast ....KO 4
Mar.	1—Spider Allen, Belfast ....KO 2
Mar.	3—Cyclone Kelly, Liverpool ......W 10
Apr.	15—Cyclone Kelly, Belfast ....W 10
May	27—Peter Peters, Belfast ....KO 1
June	18—Ivor Neil, Belfast ....KO 1
July	23—Jackie Paterson, Belfast ...KO by 9
Aug.	11—Joe Curran, Belfast ....W 10
Sept.	2—Tommy Stewart, Belfast ....L 10

1939

Feb.	27—Joe Curran, Newcastle ....KO 5
Mar.	20—Sammy Reynolds, Newcastle .. W 10
June	28—Tommy Stewart, Belfast ......W 10
July	20—Billy Ashton, Liverpool ......W 10
Nov.	8—Seaman Chetty, Newcastle ... W 10
	In War Service.

1940

Jan.	10—Paddy Ryan, Newcastle ....L 10
Apr.	28—Jimmy Gill, Newcastle ....L 10

1943

July	13—Ike Weir, Belfast ....L 10

1945

May	—Joe Meikle, Belfast ....KO 1
July	—Joe Boy Collins, Dublin ....W 10
Sept.	13—Tommy Burney, Liverpool .... W 10
Oct.	18—Joe Curran, Liverpool ....L 10
Nov.	6—Bunty Doran, Belfast ....KO 4

1946

Apr.	4—Tom Burney, Liverpool ......W 8
June	7—Jackie Paterson, Belfast ......KO 6
Sept.	11—Alec Murphy, Glasgow ....W 8
Sept.	24—Sammy Reynolds, Belfast ....WF 8

1947

Mar.	11—Terry Allen, London ....KO 1
July	—Emilie Famechon, London .....W 10
July	16—Dado Marino, Glasgow ......W 10
Oct.	20—Dado Marino, London ....W 15
	(Won N.B.A. Flyweight Title)

1948

Mar.	23—Jackie Paterson, Belfast ......KO 7
	(Won world flyweight title)
June	28—Charley Squire, Birmingham ..KO 7

1949

Feb.	7—Terry Allen, London ....L 10
Apr.	5—Maurice Sandeyron, Belfast ....W 15
	(World flyweight title)
Aug.	19—Otello Belardinelli, Belfast .....W 10
Sept.	30—Terry Allen, Belfast ....D 15
	(World flyweight title)

1950

Apr.	25—Announced retirement.

TB	KO	WD	WF	D	LD	LF	KOBY	ND	NC
51	19	22	1	1	6	1	1	0	0

TERRY ALLEN
Edward Goveir
Born, Aug. 11, 1925, Islington, England.
Managed by Johnny Sharpe. Height, 5 feet, 3 ins.

1942

Sept.	3—Jim Thomas, Islington ....W 6
Mar.	8—Douglas Claxton, Islington ...KO 4
Mar.	19—Ronnie Kingston, Hayes......KO 4
Apr.	7—George Howell, York ....KO 1
May	10—Les Johnson, Islington ....W 6
Sept.	9—Tommy Burney, Liverpool ....W 8
Sept.	30—Ronnie Bishop, Liverpool .....W 8

1943

Nov.	4—Roy Ball, Liverpool ....W 8
Nov.	9—Mickey Jones, Hayes ....W 8
Nov.	19—Jack McKenzie, Blackpool .....W 10
Dec.	31—Billy Hazlegrove, Blackpool ..KO 9

1944

Jan.	4—Jackie Evans, Liverpool	W 8
Mar.	17—Joe Josephs, Hornsby	KO 4
Apr.	6—Tommy Burmey, Liverpool	W 10
Apr.	21—Roy Ball, Blackpool	KO 5
May	2—Mickey Jones, South End	W 8
May	10—Georges Shamar, Egypt	W 4
July	8—Ahmed Marli, Egypt	KO 1
Dec.	10—Hassan Ramadin, Egypt	W 4
Dec.	23—Chehata Hafez, Egypt	KO 3

1945

Jan.	4—Christie Kyrisco, Egypt	W 6
Feb.	4—Hassan Abou Saada, Egypt	W 6
Mar.	3—Sapper Johnstone, Egypt	W 6
Mar.	8—Phil Milligan, Egypt	W 6
Apr.	28—Lt. Mustapha Ezzatt, Egypt	W 6
May	24—Lt. Mustapha Ezzatt, Egypt	W 6
July	16—Abdel Hassen, Alexandria	KO 8
Sept.	29—Lt. Mustapha Ezzatt, Alexand.	W 8
Oct.	12—Sayrd Mustapha, Alexandria	KO 2
Nov.	8—Hassan Robbou, Alexandria	KO 1
Dec.	13—Abdel F. Hassen, Alexandria	KO 3
Dec.	18—Billy Hazlegrove, Islington	W 8

1946

May	20—Alec Murphy, Harringay	KO by 6
Aug.	13—Leo Johnson, Wembley	W 8
Oct.	30—Frank Tierney, Glasgow	W 8
Dec.	4—Billy Davies, Shepherd's Bush	KO 4
Dec.	18—Billy Hazelgrove, Islington	W 8

1947

Mar.	11—Rinty Monaghan, London	Kobv 1
June	17—Pinchie Thompson, Willesden	W 8
July	7—Alf Hughes, W. Hartlepool	W 8
Aug.	25—Johnny Bollen, W. Hartlepool	KO 1
Aug.	26—Johnny Summers, Wembley	W 8
Oct.	14—Andy McCulloch, Islington	KO 5
Nov.	3—Les Johnson, Kentish Town	W 8
Nov.	12—Frank Tierney, Islington	W 8
Dec.	15—Tom Whittle, Kentish Town	KO 3

1948

Jan.	21—Jackie Bryce, Islington	W 8
Feb.	18—Jimmy Gill, Islington	KO 4
Mar.	16—Dickie O'Sullivan, Harringay	WF 2
June	25—Jackie Bryce, Coatbridge	L 12
Nov.	4—Charley Wilson, Islington	W 8
Dec.	14—Tommy Farricker, Kent Town	W 8

1949

Jan.	10—Billy Hazelgrove, Walworth	W 8
Jan.	24—Dickie O'Sullivan, Albert Hall	W 12
Feb.	7—Rinty Monaghan, Harringay	W 10
Mar.	3—Jackie Foster, Islington	W 8
May	3—Honore Pratesi, Earl's Court	L 10
June	8—Norman Tennant, Dundee	W 12
Sept.	30—Rinty Monaghan, Belfast	D 15
	(For World Flyweight Title)	

1950

Feb.	15—Peter Fay, Kentish Town	W 8
Apr.	25—Honore Pratesi, Harringay	W 15
	(Won vacant world flyweight title)	
Aug.	1—Dado Marino, Honolulu	L 15
	(Lost world flyweight title)	
Oct.	30—Jean Sneyers, Nottingham	L 12

1951

Apr.	11—Jimmy Pearce, Kentish Town	W 8
Apr.	30—Henry Carpenter, London	W 10
June	11—Vic Herman, Leicester	W 15
	(Won vacant British flyweight Title)	
Nov.	1—Dado Marino, Honolulu	L 15
	(For World Flyweight Title)	

1952

Jan.	29—Maurice Sandeyron, London	L 10
Mar.	17—Teddy Gardner, W. Hartlepool	L 15
	(Lost British flyweight title)	
Aug.	25—Jimmy Pearce, W. Hartlepool	W 12
Oct.	21—Eric Marsdne, London	KO 6
	(Won Vacant British Flyweight Title)	

1953

Apr.	28—Gaetano Annaioro, London	L 10
Oct.	27—Yoshio Shirai, Tokyo	L 15
	(For World Flyweight Title)	

1954

Feb.	16—Eric Marsden, London	WF 5
	(British Flyweight Title)	
Mar.	23—Dai Dower, London	KO by 2
Sept.	10—Nazzarino Gianelli, Milan	L 15
	(For vacant European Flyweight Title)	
Sept.	20—Announced retirement from ring.	

TB	KO	WE	WF	D	LD	LF	KOBY	ND	NC
76	18	42	2	1	10	0	3	0	0

814

SALVADOR (DADO) MARINO

Born, Honolulu, August 26, 1916.
Managed by Sam Ichinose. Filipino. Height, 5
feet, 3 in. Weight, 112.

1941

June	20—Paul Francis, Honolulu	KO 2
July	3—Hilo Francisco, Honolulu	KO 1
July	18—Al Rufino, Honolulu	KO 2
Aug.	11—Charley Higa, Honolulu	W 6
Aug.	15—Sergio Delania, Honolulu	KO 1
Aug.	22—Kid Rustia, Honolulu	KO 1
Sept.	5—Frankie Baron, Honolulu	KO 6
Oct.	6—Little Reynes, Honolulu	KO 2
Oct.	16—Jimmy Clinton, Honolulu	KO 5
Nov.	3—Toy Tomanaha, Honolulu	W 6
Nov.	14—Toy Tomanaha, Honolulu	W 6

1942

Jan.	11—Charley Higa, Honolulu	W 6
Aug.	9—Joe Sanchez, Honolulu	KO 5
Sept.	6—Willie Gonzales, Honolulu	KO 8
Sept.	27—Adolph Samuels, Honolulu	W 10

1943

Jan.	24—Quentin Hernandez, Honolulu	L 8
Feb.	7—Adolph Samuels, Honolulu	W 8
May	2—David Young, Honolulu	KO by 8
Aug.	22—Adolph Samuels, Honolulu	W 10
Nov.	21—Alfred Chavez, Honolulu	W 8
Dec.	5—Richard Silva, Honolulu	L 8

1944

Mar.	12—Quentin Hernandez, Honolulu	KO 2
Apr.	9—Alfred Chavez, Honolulu	W 10
Apr.	29—Alfred Chavez, Honolulu	W 12
	(Hawaiian Flyweight Title)	
May	13—Chico Rosa, Honolulu	W 10
June	18—Joho Shiroma, Honolulu	W 8
Nov.	19—Eddie Silva, Honolulu	KO 4
Dec.	9—Eddie Silva, Honolulu	KO 4

1945

Mar.	17—Gus Rosa, Honolulu	D 6
Apr.	8—Lou Renai, Honolulu	W 6
Apr.	28—Gus Rosa, Honolulu	W 8
Dec.	29—Gus Rosa, Honolulu	W 6

1946

Jan.	12—Jose Onacanim, Honolulu	KO 3
Mar.	9—Al Chavez, Honolulu	L 6
May	5—Al Chavez, Honolulu	W 10
July	5—Ankie Hashijo, Honolulu	W 6
Sept.	30—Val Alvarado, Honolulu	W 8
Nov.	11—Eddie Reyes, Honolulu	W 8
Dec.	9—Eddie Reyes, Honolulu	W 8

1947

Feb.	25—Gus Rosa, Honolulu	W 8
July	16—Rinty Monaghan, Glasgow, Scotland	WF 9
Aug.	8—Peter Kane, Manchester	L 10
Oct.	20—Rinty Monaghan, London	L 15
	(For N.B.A. Flyweight Title)	

1948

Apr.	6—Mike Bernal, Stockton	W 10
Apr.	13—Sonny Gomez, Sacramento	W 10
Apr.	26—Tommy Rhett, Stockton	KO 1
May	10—Kenny Lindsay, San Fran.	KO 1
May	24—Cecil Schoonmaker, San Fran.	L 10
June	1—Marino Tiwanak, Honolulu	KO 5
June	22—Jackie Turner, Honolulu	W 10
July	16—Gus Rosa, Honolulu	W 10
Sept.	21—Chico Rosa, Honolulu	W 10

1949

Mar.	1—Manuel Ortiz, Honolulu	L 15
	(For World Bantamweight Title)	
July	26—George Sanchez, Honolulu	KO 3
Aug.	4—Jackie Turner, Vancouver	W 10
Aug.	18—Stan Almond, Vancouver	W 10
Sept.	6—Lou Langley, Honolulu	W 5
Sept.	16—Tirso de Rosario, Manila	KO by 5
Dec.	22—Tirso del Rosario, Manila	L 10

1950

Aug.	1—Terry Allen, Honolulu	W 15
	(Won World Flyweight title)	
Sept.	18—Tim Ramos, Guam	KO 4
Oct.	4—Al Chavez, Guam	W 10
Oct.	31—Bobby Garza, Honolulu	KO 7

1951

Jan.	31—Tanny Campo, Manila	W 10
Apr.	30—Eddie Reyes, Honolulu	L 6
May	21—Yoshio Shirai, Tokyo	W 10
June	9—Hideo Goto, Tokyo	D 10
June	25—Hiroshi Horiguchi, Tokyo	KO 3
July	30—Hideo Goto, Tokyo	W 10
Aug.	27—Fernando Gagnon, Quebec	D 10

Nov. 1—Terry Allen, Honolulu .... W 15
      (Won World Flyweight Title)
Dec. 4—Yoshio Shirai, Honolulu ... KO by 7
               1952
May 19—Yoshio Shirai, Tokyo ....L 15
      (Lost World Flyweight Title)
Nov. 15—Yoshio Shirai, Tokyo ....L 15
      (For world flyweight title)

TB	KO	WD	WF	D	LD	LF	KOBY	ND	NC
74	21	35	1	3	11	0	3	0	0

YOSHIO SHIRAI

Born, November 23, 1923, Arakawa Ward, Tokyo,
Japan. Weight, 112 lbs. Height, 5 ft. 6 in. Managed by Dr.
Alvin R. Cahn.

               1943
Nov. 26—Junpo Umiyama, Tokyo .... KO 1
Dec.   —Saichi Kubota, Tokyo .... KO 1
Dec.   —Minoru Tanaka, Tokyo .... KO 1
Dec.   —Sadasuke Aoki, Tokyo .... W 4
Dec.   —Ito, Tokyo .... KO 1
               1944
Mar. 28—Sakae Suzuki, Tokyo .... KO 1
               1945
             (Inactive)
               1946
Aug.   —Nakamura, Tokyo .... W 6
Dec. 14—Noboru Kushida, Tokyo .... KO by 5
               1947
June 27—Kazumi Ueda, Tokyo .... W 6
        —Toshimitsu Kushihashi, Tokyo ..... W 8
July 18—Yoichiro Hanada, Tokyo .... L 8
Sept. 11—Eijiro Yajima, Tokyo .... L 8
Dec. 25—Michiyoshi Koizumi, Tokyo ...... KO 2
               1948
Feb. 15—Kazumi Ueda, Tokyo .... W 6
May   7—Sadaji Wada, Tokyo .... W 8
June 6—Eijiro Yajima, Tokyo .... D 8
July 30—Nobuyuki Ishimori, Tokyo ...... KO 2
Sept. 11—Eijiro Yajima, Tokyo .... W 8
Oct. 9—Noboru Kushida, Tokyo .... W 8
               1949
Jan. 28—Yoichiro Hanada, Tokyo .... KO 5
      (Won Japanese Flyweight Title)
Feb. 21—Mitsuo Oikawa, Tokyo .... Exh.
Mar. 21—Tomoyoshi Yanagida, Tokyo ..... KO 2
May   2—Eijiro Yajima, Tokyo .... W 10
June 25—Noboru Kushida, Tokyo .... W 10
      (Retained Japanese Flyweight Title)
Sept. 28—Kyoichi Muto, Tokyo .... KO 3
Dec. 15—Hiroshi Horiguchi .... W 10
      (Won Japanese Bantamweight Title)
               1950
Jan. 4—Keizo Yasui, Tokyo .... Exh. 3
Feb. 6—Mamoru Murata, Tokyo .... KO 2
Apr. 14—Yoshiaki Naruo, Tokyo .... W 8
May 25—Yoichiro Hanada, Tokyo .... W 10
      (Retained Japanese Bantamweight Title)
June 28—Hideo Kijima, Tokyo .... KO 2
      (Retained Japanese Flyweight Title)
July 17—Katsumi Kobayashi, Tokyo ..... Exh.
July 31—Kyoichi Muto, Tokyo .... Exh. 4
Aug. 26—Takeshi Nomura, Tokyo .... KO 5
Sept. 25—Katsumi Kobayashi, Tokyo .... KO 2
Oct. 26—Takashi Seno, Tokyo .... W 10
      (Retained Japanese Bantamweight Title)
               1951
Feb. 3—Yukio Takahashi, Tokyo ..... W disq. 7
Mar. 17—Hidemasa Nagashima, Tokyo L disq. 8
      (Lost Japanese Bantamweight Title)
May 21—Dado Marino, Tokyo .... L 10
Sept. 20—Hidemasa Nagashima, Tokyo ...... W 10
      (Regained Japanese Bantamweight Title)
Oct. 25—Takahisa Horiguchi, Tokyo ...... KO 6
      (Retained Japanese Flyweight Title)
Nov. 1—Richard Sakai, Honolulu .... KO ?
Dec. 4—Dado Marino, Honolulu .... KO 7

               1952
Feb. 7—Hiroshi Horiguchi, Tokyo .... W 10
Apr. 4—Kiyochi Muto, Tokyo .... KO 6
May 19—Dado Marino, Tokyo .... W 15
      (Won World Flyweight Title)
Aug. 23—Haruo Oba, Tokyo .... W 8
Aug. 25—Relinquished Japanese bantamweight title.
Sept. 27—Roy Higa, Tokyo .... W 10
Nov. 15—Dado Marino, Tokyo .... W 15
      (Retained World Flyweight Title)
               1953
Jan. 4—Masaru Kaneko, Tokyo .... Exh. 4
Apr. 17—Baby Moe Mario, Tokyo .... W 10
May 18—Tanny Campo, Tokyo .... W 15
      (Retained World Flyweight Title)
July 17—Vic Herman, Tokyo .... KO 10
Aug. 12—Tamio Sasaki, Tokyo .... Exh. 4
Sept. 19—Leo Espinosa, Osaka .... KO by 7
Oct. 27—Terry Allen, Tokyo .... W 15
      (Retained World Flyweight Title)
               1954
Apr. 8—Masaru Kaneko, Osaka .... KO 8
May 23—Leo Espinosa, Tokyo .... W 15
      (Retained World Flyweight Title)
July 24—Pascual Perez, Buenos Aires .... D 10
Aug. 11—Albert Barenghi, Buenos Aires .... W 10
Sept. 27—Hitoshi Misako, Tokyo .... Exh. 4
Nov. 26—Pascual Perez, Tokyo .... L 15
      (Lost World Flyweight Title)
               1955
May 10—Kunio Suzuki, Tokyo .... Exh. 3
May 30—Pascual Perez, Tokyo .... KO by 5
      (For World Flyweight Title)

TB	KO	WD	WF	D	LD	LF	KO BY	ND	NC
56	20	25	1	2	4	1	3	0	0

Elected to Boxing Hall of Fame, 1977.

PASCUAL PEREZ

Born, March 4, 1926, Tupungate, Mendoza
Argentina.
(Olympic Flyweight Champion in London)
      Games in 1948
               1952
Dec. 5—Jose Ciorino, Gerli .... KO 5
Dec. 20—Jorge Flores, San Fernando ... KO 3
               1953
Jan. 3—Ramon Stronatti, Mendoza ... KO 2
Feb. 20—Mario Ahumada, Mendoza .... KO 1
Mar. 16—Miguel Carrasco, Mendoza ... KO 5
Mar. 30—Juan Godoy, Buenos Aires .... KO 2
Nov. 11—Marcelo Quiroga,
         Buenos Aires .... KO 4
      (Argentine Flyweight Title)
Nov. 25—Eduardo Lliuzzi, Buenos Aires KO 1
Dec. 23—Hernan Rojas, Catamarca ..... KO 2
Dec. 30—Roberto Romero, Mendoza ... KO 2
               1954
Jan. 8—Nestor Rojas, Catamarca ..... KO 2
Jan. 19—Jose Domingo Luna,
         Tucuman .... KO 2
Jan. 26—Antonio Zapata, Catamarca .. KO 5
Feb. 6—Marcelo Quiroga, Buenos Aires KO 2
Feb. 12—Nestor Rojas, Tandil .... KO 3
Feb. 24—Nicolas Paez, Buenos Aires ... KO 7
Mar. 12—Pablo Sosa, Catamarca .... KO
Mar. 24—Pablo Sosa, Buenos Aires .... KO 2
Apr. 22—Juan Bishop, Buenos Aires ... W 16
May 19—Vincente Bruno, Buenos Aires ... KO
June   —Domingo Sandoval,
         Comodoro Rivadavia .... KO 4
June 12—Pablo Sosa,
         Comodoro Rivadavia .... KO
June 26—Marcelo Quiroga, Eva Peron .. KO 4
July 24—Yosho Shirai, Buenos Aires ... D 10
Nov. 26—Yosho Shirai, Tokyo .... W 15
      (Won World Flyweight Title)
               1955
*Apr. 13—Alberto Barenghi,
         Buenos Aires .... KO 3
May 30—Yoshio Shirai, Tokyo .... KO 5
      (Retained World Flyweight Title)
July 12—Albert Palomeque, Catamorca KO 4
*Oct. 22—Danny Kid, Buenos Aires ...... W 10

1956

Jan.	11—Leo Espinosa, Buenos Aires .... W	15
	(Retained World Flyweight Title)	
*Feb.	10—Antonio Gomez, Mar del Plata . W	10
Mar.	21—Antonio Gomez, Buenos	
	Aires ....KO	8
*Mar.	31—Marcelo Quiroga, Mendoza .... W	10
June	8—Ricardo Valdez, Bahia Blanca .KO	6
June	15—Pablo Sosa, Martinez ....KO	4
June	30—Oscar Suarez, Montevideo ....KO	11
	(Retained Wrold Flyweight Title)	
Aug.	3—Ricardo Valdez, Tandil ......KO	5
	(Retained World Flyweight Title)	
*Aug.	25—Hecotr Almaraz, Rosario .....KO	3
Sept.	6—Conrado Morera, Sao Paulo .... W	10
Sept.	28—Gernan Rojas, Ascunsion,	
	Paraguay ....KO	8
Dec.	12—Conrado Morera, Buenos Aires . W	10

1957

Mar.	30—Dai Dower, Buenos Aires .....KO	1
	(Retained World Flyweight Title)	
*July	12—Luis Angel Jinenez, Buenos	
	Aires .... W	10
Aug.	6—Urbieta Sosa, Sante Fe ....KO	4
*Aug.	16—Pablo Sosa, Tandil ....KO	3
Sept.	13—Conrado Moreira, La Plata V	10
Dec.	7—Young Martin, Buenos Aires ..KO	3
	(Retained World Flyweight Title)	

1958

Mar.	23—Ricardo Valdez, Buenos Aires .KO	8
Apr.	19—Ramon Arias, Caracas .... W	15
	(World Flyweight Title)	
June	15—Carlos Miranda, Aruba ......Exh.	4
Aug.	10—Tito Ragone, Ciudad Trujillo .. W	10
Nov.	22—Tito Ragone, Curacao .... W	10
Dec.	15—Dommy Ursua, Manila .... W	15
	(Retained World Flyweight Title)	

1959

Jan.	16—Sadao Yaoita, Tokyo L	10
Feb.	18—Kenji Yonekura, Tokyo .... W	10
Aug.	10—Kenji Yonekura, Tokyo .... W	15
	(Retained World Flyweight Title)	
Nov.	5—Sadao Yaoita, Osaka ....KO	13
	(Retained World Flyweight Title)	

*Scheduled as non-title bouts, but as both men weighed in under the division limit, 112, title was at stake.

1960

Apr.	16—Pone Kingpetch, Bangkok L	15
	(Lost World Flyweight Title)	
Sept.	22—Pone Kingpetch,	
	Los Angeles....................KO by	8
	(For World Flyweight Title)	

1961

Mar.	18—Hugo Villarreal, Avellaneda ...KO	4
Apr.	1—Juan Moreyra, Quilmes .... W	10
Apr.	9—Pablo Sosa, San Pedro ....KO	3
May	13—Juan C. Montevero,	
	General Roco ....KO	6
May	19—Francisco Behamondez,	
	Cipolletti ....KO	3
July	7—Hugo Villarreal, Punta Alta ...KO	3
July	29—Waldemiro Torres, Rio	
	Gallegos ....KO	8
Aug.	19—Simon Rios, Trelew ....KO	5
Sept.	5—Waldemire Torres, Bolivar ....KO	3
Oct.	13—Hector Diaz, Esquel ....KO	7
Oct.	20—Antonio Garcia, Rosario .....KO	6
Dec.	22—Rodolfo Trivis, Cordova .... W	10

1962

Jan.	27—Ruben Acosta, Nueve DeJulio KO	2
Feb.	23—Ursino Bernal, Balcarce .... W	10
Mar.	2—Rodolfo Trivia, Miramar ..... W	10
Apr.	21—Ursino Bernal, Tucuman ......KO	7
Apr.	27—Juan Carlos Moreyrz, Salta ...KO	3
May	2—Martin Luque, Del Estero .....KO	5
May	18—Cirilo Avellanda, Formosa ....KO	5
June	9—Rodolfo Trivia, Tucuman .....KO	10
June	15—Martin Luque, Jujuy ....KO	5
Dec.	7—Juan Moreira, Cordoba ......KO	9

1963

Jan.	25—Cirile Avellanda,	
	Villa Dolores .... W	10
Feb.	1—Miguel Herrera, San Luis ...... W	10
Feb.	16—Rodolfe Trviis, Montevido ..... W	10
Apr.	5—Juan C. Moreyra, Villa	
	Mercedes, San Luis .... W	10
Apr.	12—Cirilo Avellaneda,	
	Bahia Blanco ....KO	7
Apr.	30—Leo Zulueta, Manila L	10
June	16—Manuel Moreno, Panama City .. W	10
July	26—Bernardo Caraballo, Bogota L	10
Aug.	10—Adolfo Osse, Guayaquil..............W	10

Oct.	19—Efren Torres, Guadalajara ...KO by	3
Mar.	15—Eugenio Hurtado,	
	Panama City ....KO by	6
Apr.	11—Announced retirement.	

TB	KO	WD	WF	D	LD	LF	KO BY	ND	NC
91	56	27	0	1	4	0	3	0	0

Died, January 22, 1977, Argentina.
Elected to Boxing Hall of Fame, 1977.

PONE KINGPETCH

Orient Flyweight Champion
(Early record unavailable)
Born February 12, 1936, Hui Hui Province, North Thailand. Height, 5 ft. 6½ in.

1955

	—G. Noknid, Tor Sor ....KO	2
	—C. Saatonghin, Tor Sor .... W	8
	—Yutaphol Raksu, Bangkok ..... W	10
	—Suwan Nappaphol, Bangkok ...L	10
	—Okas ETB, Bangkok .... W	10

1956

	—Kunio Vithichai, Bangkok L	10
	—Kunio Vithichai, Bangkok ....KO	6
	—Posu Punthulkiet, Bangkok .... W	10
	—Minton of Cambodia, BangkokKO	4
	—Kunio Vithichai, Bangkok ..... W	10
	—Yuthaphol Raksu, Bangkok ... W	10
	—Suwan Nappaphol, Bangkok ... W	10
	—Okas ETB, Bangkok .... W	10
May	9—Kunio Vitichai, Bangkok ..KO by	9
July	18—Kunio Vitichai, Bangkok ....KO	6
Sept.	10—Posu Printhulkiet, Bangkok .... W	10
Oct.	12—C. Minton, Bangkok ....KO	4
Nov.	6—*Kunio Vitichai, Bangkok ..... W	10
	(*For Flyweight Title of Thailand)	

1957

Jan.	6—Danny Kid, Bangkok ....W	12
	(Orient flyweight title)	
July	7—Leo Espinosa, Bangkok L	12
Sept.	14—Hitoshi Misako, Bangkok ...... W	12
	(Orient flyweight title)	

1958

Jan.	11—Dommy Ursua, Bangkok .....WF	5
Mar.	14—Masaja Iwamoto, Bangkok ..... W	10
July	3—S. Somyos, Bangkok ....KO	5
Nov.	4—Daengtoi Srisothorn, Bangkok . W	8

1959

Feb.	17—Manuel Armenteros, Bangkok . W	10

1960

Jan.	31—Baby Ross, Bangkok ....KO	4
Apr.	16—Pascual Perez, Bangkok .... W	15
	(Won World Flyweight Title)	
Sept.	22—Pascual Perez, Los Angeles....KO	8
	(Retained World Flyweight Title)	

1961

Mar.	2—Jose Luis Martinez, Bangkok ... W	10
	(non-title)	
June	27—Mitsunori Seki, Tokyo .... W	15
	(retained title)	

1962

Feb.	19—Baby Demillones, Bangkok ....KO	8
	(non-title)	
May	30—Kyo Noguchi, Tokyo .... W	15
	(Retained Title)	
Oct.	10—Fighting Harada, Tokyo ...KO by	11
	(Lost World Flyweight Title)	

1963

Jan.	12—Fighting Harada, Bangkok ..... W	15
	(Rewon World Flyweight Championship)	
	(Became first to regain flyweight title)	
Sept.	18—Hiroyuki Ebihara, Tokyo ...KO by	1
	(Lost World Flyweight Championship)	

1964

Jan.	23—Hiroyuki Ebihara, Bangkok .... W	15
	(Regained World Flyweight Title)	

1965

Apr.	23—Salvatore Burruni, Rome L	15
	(Lost World Flyweight Title)	

1966

Feb.	17—Baby Lorona, Bangkok ....KO	4
Apr.	13—Kumantong Yontrakit,	
	Bangkok.........................KO	4
	(Announced retirement May 30, 1966)	

TB	KO	WD	WF	D	LD	LF	KOBY	ND	NC
40	11	20	1	0	5	0	3	0	0

MASAHIKO (FIGHTING) HARADA
(Record Under Bantamweight Champions)

HIROYUKI EBIHARA
Born, March 26, 1940, Nishitama-Gun, Tokyo,
Japan. Weight, 112 lbs. Height, 5 ft. 4 in. Southpaw.
Managed by Masaki Kanehira.
1959

Sept.	20—Kazuhiko Kurihara, Tokyo	KO	4
Oct.	1—Yasuhiko Murai, Tokyo	W	4
Oct.	16—Shoichi Saito, Tokyo	W	4

1960

June	17—Kiyoshi Fujio, Tokyo	KO	1
Aug.	29—Masayuki Matsuzawa, Tokyo	W	4
Oct.	26—Kazutoshi Ohi, Tokyo	W	4
Nov.	7—Nagao Nagahata, Tokyo	KO	1
Nov.	23—Takeshi Nakamura, Tokyo	W	4
Dec.	11—Masayuki Matsuzawa, Tokyo	KO	2
Dec.	24—Fighting Harada, Tokyo	L	6

1961

Jan.	27—Shigeo Mirasawa, Tokyo	W	6
Feb.	22—Kinichiro Toyama, Tokyo	W	6
Apr.	5—Katsutoshi Aoki, Tokyo	KO	2
May	18—Takeshi Nakamura, Tokyo	D	6
June	9—Yoshikatsu Furukawa, Tokyo	KO	3
June	27—Seinosuke Tsuchiya, Tokyo	W	6
July	28—Hajime Taroura, Tokyo	KO	3
Aug.	27—Shington P.T., Tokyo	W	10
Sept.	29—Shigeru Ito, Tokyo	KO	2
Oct.	30—Johnny Jamito, Tokyo	W	10
Dec.	15—K. Yamakawa, Tokyo	KO	1

1962

Jan.	6—Sombang Banbung, Tokyo	KO	4
Feb.	8—Marcel Juban, Tokyo	KO	6
Mar.	9—Takeshi Nakamura, Tokyo	W	10
Apr.	12—Ray Ortiz, Tokyo	KO	3
May	4—Katsuo Haga, Tokyo	W	10
July	27—Cherngchai Laemfapha, Tokyo	KO	2
Aug.	13—Little Rufe, Tokyo	KO	3
Sept.	6—Ray Perez, Tokyo	KO	8
Sept.	28—Shinsuke Taniwaki, Tokyo	KO	1
Oct.	26—Narongrit Jalengkabo, Tokyo	KO	3
Nov.	21—Changa Magallanes, Tokyo	W	10
Dec.	6—Roberto Luna, Tokyo	KO	3
Dec.	31—Chartchai Chionoi, Tokyo	W	10

1963

Feb.	1—Vic Campos, Tokyo	W	10
Mar.	27—Billy Brown, Tokyo	W	10
July	17—Young Bonnie, Tokyo	KO	1
Aug.	1—Masao Ogawa, Tokyo	KO	9
Sept.	18—Pone Kingpetch, Tokyo	KO	1
	(Won World Flyweight Title)		
Nov.	20—Henry Acida, Nagoya	KO	10

1964

Jan.	23—Pone Kingpetch, Bangkok	L	15
	(Lost World Flyweight Title)		
Mar.	19—Fabian Esquivel, Los Angeles	W	10
Apr.	30—Efren Torres, Los Angeles	W	12
July	19—Kang-Nam Kung, Osaka	KO	10
Sept.	7—Ric Magramo, Tokyo	W	10
Nov.	1—Ki-Soo Kan, Nagoya	W	10
Nov.	13—Bonnie Boromeo, Toyoda	W	10

1965

Jan.	3—Takeshi Nakamura, Tokyo	W	10
Feb.	7—Katsuo Haga, Tokyo	W	10
Mar.	13—Hideki Osaka, Tokyo	KO	3
Mar.	28—Siego Nirasawa, Tokyo	KO	7
May	7—Efren Torres, Los Angeles	KO	7
July	4—Yoshio Nakane, Tokyo	W	10
Aug.	15—Un-Mo Oh, Tokyo	KO	6
Nov.	13—Bonnie Boromeo, Toyoda	W	10

1966

Apr.	24—Dio Espinosa, Tokyo	KO	3
July	16—Horacio Accavallo, Buenos Aires	L	15
	(For WBA Flyweight Title)		

1967

Apr.	10—Speedy Hayase, Tokyo	W	10
May	22—Manuel Balaba, Tokyo	W	10

July	10—Un-Mo Oh, Tokyo	KO	5
Aug.	12—Horacio Accavallo, Buenos Aires	L	15
	(For WBA Flyweight Title)		

1968

Mar.	4—Chango Magallanes, Tokyo	KO	4
Apr.	8—Yuzo Narumi, Tokyo	W	10
May	20—Rudy Ventura, Tokuyama	W	10
July	29—Bart Limon, Tokyo	KO	7
Dec.	23—Eli Axinto, Sendai	KO	3

1969

Mar.	30—Jose Severino, Sapporo	W	15
	(Won Vacant WBA Flyweight Title)		
June	30—Juan Garcia Lopez, Okayama	KO	1
Oct.	20—Bernabe Villacampo, Tokyo	L	15
	(Lost WBA Flyweight Title)		

TB	KO	WD	WF	D	LD	LF	KO BY	ND	NC
69	34	29	0	1	5	0	0	0	0

SALVATORE BURRUNI
Born, Alghero, April 11, 1933.

1957

Apr.	3—Maurice Sevelle, Milan	KO	4
Apr.	27—Luigi Squaita, Milan	W	6
May	29—Salv. Petrangeli, Milan	W	6
June	26—Giacomo Spano, Milan	D	6
July	19—Giacomo Spano, Alghero	W	6
Oct.	10—Angelo Rampin, Alghero	W	6
Dec.	13—Elio DeWitt, Alghero	W	6

1958

Feb.	15—Aristide Pozzali, Milan	L	8
Mar.	1—Giacomo Spano, Milan	W	8
Apr.	27—Pompeo Cicognani, Milan	W	6
July	5—Salvatore Petrangeli, Algheri	KO	6
Aug.	27—Stefano Urbani, Sassari	W	8
Sept.	27—Giacomo Spano, Alghero	W	12
	(vacant Italian flyweight title)		
Oct.	12—Horacio Accavallo, Cagliari	L	8

1959

Jan.	31—Giancarlo Montanari, Milan	W	6
Feb.	28—Valentino Campagni, Milan	W	8
Apr.	18—Raton Osuna, Alghero	W	10
May	27—Salvatore Manca, Milan	W	12
	(Italian flyweight title)		
Aug.	1—Horacio Accavallo, Sessari	W	10
Aug.	29—Santos Seoane, Alghero	W	10
Sept.	26—Juanito Cid, Alghero	KO	9
Dec.	23—Giacomo Spano, Alghero	W	12
	(Italian flyweight title)		

1960

Mar.	16—Albert Younsi, Milan	L	10
May	19—Henry Schmidt, Sassari	W	10
July	10—Angelo Rampin, Alghero	W	12
	(Italian flyweight title)		
Aug.	5—Pancho Bhattachaji, Cagliari	W	8
Aug.	14—Edgar Basel, Sassari	W	10
Oct.	30—Salvatore Manca, Cagliari	W	12
	(Italian flyweight title)		

1961

Feb.	25—Albert Younsi, Alghero	W	10
Apr.	2—Kamara Diop, Alghero	W	10
June	4—Jacques Jacob, Alghero	W	10
June	29—Risto Luukkonen, Alghero	W	15
	(European flyweight title)		
	—Derek Lloyd, San Remo	KO	6
	(European flyweight title)		
Sept.	2—Ben Layesi, Cagliari	KO	9
Sept.	20—Francesco Carreno, Rome	W	10
Sept.	30—Henri Schmid, Cagliari	W	10
Oct.	21—Albert Younsi, Milan	KO	7
Oct.	27—Michel Lamora, Rome	W	8
Dec.	20—Christian Marchand, Milan	W	10

1962

Mar.	7—Henri Schmid, Milan	KO	5
Apr.	7—Jean-Claude Leroy, Genoa	W	10
Apr.	29—Bernard Jubert, Milan	W	10
June	30—Mimun ben Ali, St. Vincent	W	15
	(European flyweight title)		

July   23—Rafael Fernandez, Napels ..... W 10
Aug.   4—Ramon Casal, Genoa .... W 10
Sept.   14—Pierre Rossi, Milan .... W 15
        (European flyweight title)
Nov.   27—Manuel Alvarez, Turin ....KO 6

1963

Jan.   11—Carlos Zayas, Milan .... W 10
Jan.   26—Rafael Fernandez, Alghero .... W 10
Feb.   22—Jean-Claude Leroy,
        Alessandria .... W 10
Mar.   21—Jose Rodriguez, Jesolo ......KO 8
Apr.   5—Neves Martin, Turin ....KO 9
May   11—Jean Leroux, Alghero ....KO 5
June   8—Jose Luis Martinez,
        Alessandria .... W 10
July   5—Rene Libeer, Alessandria ...... W 15
        (European flyweight title)
Aug.   3—Baby John, Cagliari .... KO 6
Aug.   18—Jacques Jacob, St. Remo ..... KO 9
Sept.   1—Jose Luis Martinez, Alghero ..KO 7
Sept.   14—Felix Alonso, Canelli .... W 10
Oct.   8—Mick Hussey, Rome .... KO 6
Oct.   19—Luis Rodriguez, Turin .... KO 8
Nov.   15—Koli Mustapha, Sassari ...... KO 4
Dec.   13—Chilango Gomez, Rome ...... KO 4
Dec.   23—Alex O'Neill, Sassari .... KO 5

1964

Jan.   17—Francisco Carreno, Padua ..... W 10
Jan.   25—Jean-Claude Leroy, Naples ...KO 6
Feb.   21—Brian Cartwright, Rome ...... W 10
Apr.   24—Walter McGowan, Rome ...... W 15
        (European flyweight title)
June   13—Lazaro Blanquer, Sassari ...... W 10
June   26—Natalio Jiminez, Turin .... W 10
July   4—Angel Campos Chinea,
        Ceccano ....KO 3
July   19—Rafael Fernandez, Rimini ....W 10
Aug.   8—Rafael Fernandez, Rimini ..... W 10
Sept.   12—Baby John, Rome .... W 10
Sept.   29—Lazaro Blanquer, Terracina ..... W 10
Nov.   12—Francisco Berdonces, Milan .... W 10
Nov.   25—Antonio Lazaro, Bologna .....KO 7
Dec.   12—Jose Robledo, Treviso .... W 10
Dec.   26—Francisco Berdonles .... W 10

1965

Mar.   18—Jo Horny, Milan ....KO 5

Apr.   23—Pone Kingpetch, Rome .... W 15
        (Won World Flyweight Title)
May   29—Francisco Berdonces,
        Fosinone ....KO 8
June   11—Demetrio Carbajal, Rome ....KO 7
June   28—Jerry Stokes, Naples .... W 10
July   7—Michel Lamora, Rimini .... W 10
Aug.   7—Horacio Accavallo,
        Buenos Aires ....L 10
Oct.   7—Katsuyoshi Takayama, Tokyo ..L 10
Dec.   2—Rocky Gattellari, Sydney ....KO 13
        (Retained World Flyweight Title)

1966

Jan.   26—Ray Jutras, Turin............... KO 4
Feb.   8—Chartchai Chionoi, Bangkok ....L 10
June   14—Walter McGowan, London ......L 15
        (Lost World Flyweight Title)
Aug.   14—Wellington Vilela, Portoscuzo .. W 10
Sept.   25—Felix Alonso, Viterbo ....KO 5
Oct.   27—Spider McNorthy, Sassari ...... W 10
Dec.   23—Carl Taylor, Rome ....KO 5

1967

Feb.   11—Antonio Lopez, Cagliari .... W 8
Feb.   25—Pierre Vetroff, Torin ......KO by 7
Apr.   28—Wellington Vilella, Genoa .... W 10
July   28—Jose Arranz, Cagliari .... W 10
Aug.   27—Felix Alonso, Antioco ....KO 2
Nov.   28—Marc Vandomme, Sassari ...... W 10

1968

Jan.   10—Mimun ben Ali, Naples .... W 15
        (Won European Bantamweight Title)
Mar.   10—Manuel Alvarez, Padua .... W 10
Mar.   31—Ruben Olivares,
        Mexico City ....KO by 3
June   27—Billy Borwn, Sassari .... W 10
July   31—Franco Zurlo, San Benedetto
        Del Tronto .... W 15
        (European Bantamweight Title)
Oct.   5—Gerard Macrez, Oristano ...... W 10

1969

Feb.   4—Wellington Vilella, Taranto .... W 10
Apr.   9—Pierre Vetroff,
        Reggio Calabria ....KO 9
        (European bantamweight title)
Aug.   —Announced retirement from boxing.

TB	KO	WD	WF	D	LD	LF	KOBY	ND	NC
109	31	68	0	1	7	0	2	0	0

HORACIO ACCAVALLO

(W.B.A. Flyweight Champion)

Argentine Flyweight

Born, October 14, 1934.

1956

Sept.   21—Emilio Avila, Buenos Aires ...KO 5
Oct.   15—Mario Cabrera, Buenos Aires ..KO 4
Oct.   12—Pablo Sosa, Martinez ....KO 3
Nov.   16—Cecilio Serantes, V. Alsina ...KO 7
Nov.   30—Lorenzo Ordenes, V. Alsina ...KO 2
Dec.   5—Luis Jimenez, Buenos Aires .... D 8
Dec.   28—Alfredo Rios, Mataderos .....KO 4

1957

Jan.   11—Hector Coria, Lanus ....KO 6
Jan.   25—Alfredo Romero Luque, Lanus KO 7
Feb.   1—Carlos Cappozuca, Martinez ..KO 3
Feb.   22—Jose Costa, Lanus ....KO 4
Mar.   30—German Escudero,
        Buenos Aires .... D 10
Apr.   20—Abraham Esteban, Lanus ...... W 10
May   15—Marcelo Quiroga,
        Buenos Aires ....KO 6
Aug.   16—Ramon Juarez, Tucuman ...... W 10
Nov.   9—Hector Barrera, V. Alsina ...... W 10
Dec.   6—Eduardo Lliuzzi, V. Alsina ...KO 6

1958

Jan.   17—Juan C. Acebal, Val. Alsina ....W 10
Apr.   1—Vicente Bruno, Tucuman .....KO 7
May   13—Hector Coria, Tucuman ......KO 8
July   9—Avelino Romero, B. Aires .....KO 5
Aug.   27—Ricardo Valdes, B. Aires ......KO 9
Oct.   12—Salvador Burruni, Cagliari ..... W 10
Nov.   20—Giacomo Spano, Sassari .... W 10
Dec.   12—Francisco Carreno, Cagliari .... W 10

1959

Jan.   14—Angelo Rampin, Milan .... W 10
Feb.   5—Giacomo Spano, Cagliari ..... D 10
Feb.   12—Salvatore Manca, Rome .... D 10
Apr.   13—Salvatore Manca, Bergamo ..... W 10
May   1—Raton Osuna, Cagliari .... W 8
May   30—Giacomo Spano, Cagliari ...... D 10
Aug.   1—Salvatore Burruni, Sassari .....L 10

1960

Apr.   9—Antonio Gomez, Buenos Aires KO 7
July   1—Carlos Rodriguez, Buenos Aires W 12
        (Won Argentine Flyweight Title)
July   16—Giacomo Spano, Buenos Aires . D 10
Sept.   7—Julio Barrera, Buenos Aires ...KO 5
Oct.   7—Jupiter Mansilla, Buenos Aires . W 15
        (Won Vacant South American Flyweight
Title)
Oct.   22—Carlos Miranda, Buenos Aires .. W 10
Dec.   2—Chucho Hernandez,
        Buenos Aires .... W 10

1961

Apr.   8—Jose Acebal, Pargamino .... W 10
        —Carlos Rodriguez,
        Buenos Aires .... W 12
May   10—Jupiter Mansilla,
        Buenos Aires .... W 15
        (South American Flyweight Title Bout)
        —Juan Hernandez, Buenos Aires . W 10
Sept.   8—Ursino Bernal, La Emilia ...... W 10

1962

Apr.   14—Salvatore Manca,
        Buenos Aires .... W 8
May   19—Demetrio Carabajal,
        Buenos Aires .... W 10
July   21—Chucho Hernandez,
        Buenos Aires ....KO 9
Sept.   7—Carlos Rodriguez,
        Buenos Aires .... W 12
Nov.   16—Jupiter Mansilla, Montevideo .. W 10

1963
Apr.	6—Jupiter Mansilla, Buenos Aires	W	10
May	24—Fidel Folch, Rosario	KO	6
June	22—Ramon Arias, Caracas	W	10
July	13—Armando Mansilla, Mar Del Plata	W	10
Aug.	2—Fidel Folch, Tucuman	KO	4
Sept.	7—Jupiter Mansilla, Buenos Aires	W	15

(Retained South American Flyweight Title)

Sept.	28—Ursino Bernal, La Emilia	KO	8
Oct.	11—Julio Romero, Rosario	W	10
Oct.	26—Demetrio Carbajal, Buenos Aires	KO	11

(Retained Argentina Flyweight Title)
1964
Jan.	15—Abelardo Martinez, Bahia Blanca	KO	8
Feb.	7—Julio Romero, Mar Del Plata	KO	8
Mar.	27—Armando Mansilla, Salta	KO	5
May	16—Eugene Hurtado, Buenos Aires	W	10
June	12—Juan Moreira, LaPlata	W	10
Aug.	1—Juan Moreira, Bahia Blanca	W	10
	Buenos Aires	KO	6
Dec.	12—Nelson Alarcon, Buenos Aires	W	12

(Retained Argentine Flyweight Title)
1965
Apr.	9—Demetrio Carbajal, Del Plata	KO	9
May	8—Juan Moreyra, Rosario	KO	8
June	19—Ursino Bernal, Rio Cuarto	W	10
July	2—Juan Moreyra, Bahia Blanca	W	10
July	16—Ursino Bernal, Rio Cuarto	W	10
Aug.	7—Salvatore Burruni, Buenos Aires	W	10
Aug.	20—Pedro Guevara, Rio Cuarto	KO	8
Nov.	12—Juan Moreyra, Rosario	KO	6
Dec.	17—Ursino Bernal, Asuncion	KO	8
1966
Mar.	1—Katsuyoshi Takayama, Tokyo	W	15

(W.B.A. Flyweight Title)

Apr.	22—Ursino Bernal, Tres Arroyos	W	10
May	13—Pedro Guevara, Necohea	KO	9
July	16—Hiroyuki Ebihara, Buenos Aires	W	15

(W.B.A. Flyweight Title)

Oct.	6—Ursino Bernal, Rucaman	KO	7
Dec.	10—Efren Torres, Buenos Aires	W	15

(Retained WBA Flyweight Title)
1967
Feb.	20—Kiyoshi Tanabe, Tokyo	KO by	6
July	9—Heleno Ferreyire, Buenos Aires	W	10
Aug.	12—Hiroyuki Ebihara, Buenos Aires	W	15

(Retained W.B.A. Flyweight Title)
1968
Oct. 1—Retired

TB	KO	WD	WF	D	LD	LF	KOBY	ND	NC
84	33	43	0	6	1	0	1	0	0

WALTER McGOWAN
Flyweight, Scotland
British and Empire Flyweight Chamion Born Burnbank, Lanarkshire, October 13, 1942. As amateur, lost only 2 of 124 bouts; won several Scottish titles, became British A.B.A. champion in 1961, and represented Scotland in 9 international tourneys.
1961
Aug.	9—George McDade, Glasgow	KO	3
Sept.	22—Eddie Barraclough, Hamilton	W	8
Oct.	25—Jackie Brown, Paisley	L	8
Dec.	16—Brian Bissmire, Glasgow	W	8
1962
June	14—Danny Lee, Glasgow	W	8
Sept.	20—Jacques Jacob, Glasgow	KO	6
Oct.	16—Rene Libeer, London	KO	6
Nov.	14—Ray Jutras, Glasgow	KO	6
1963
Jan.	31—Bernard Jubert, Glasgow	W	8
May	2—Jackie Brown, Paisley	KO	12

(British and Empire flyweight titles)

June	27—Ray Perez, Paisley	KO	9
Sept.	12—Kid Solomon, Paisley	KO	9

(British Empire flyweight title)

Nov.	28—Ric Magramo, Paisley	W	10

1964
Mar.	4—Risto Luukkonen, Paisley	W	10
Apr.	24—Salvatore Burruni, Rome	L	15

(European flyweight title)

Sept.	3—Natalio Jiminez, Paisley	W	10
Nov.	25—Luis Rodriguez, Solihull	KO	2
1965
Jan.	20—Mick Hussey, Solihull	KO	3
Feb.	23—Felix Brami, London	W	10
Apr.	23—Benny Lee, Rome	W	10
June	1—Joe Medel, London	KO by	6
Aug.	21—Ronnie Jones, Paisley	KO by	6
Dec.	3—Tommaso Galli, Rome	D	15

(European bantamweight title)
1966
Jan.	6—Nevio Carbi, London	KO	6
Mar.	28—Ernesto Miranda, London	W	8
June	14—Salvatore Burruni, London	W	15

(Won World Flyweight Title)

Sept.	6—Alan Rudkin, London	W	15

(British Empire Bantamweight Title Match)

Nov.	16—Jose Bisbal, London	KO	6
Dec.	30—Chartchai Chionoi, Bangkok	KO by	9

(Lost World Flyweight Title)
1967
Mar.	15—Osame Myashita, London	W	10
May	10—Giancario Centa, Birmingham	W	10
July	10—Antoine Porcel, London	W	10
Sept.	19—Chartchai Chionoi, London	KO by	7

(World flyweight title)
1968
May	13—Alan Rudkin, Manchester	L	15

(British and Empire Bantamweight Titles)

Oct.	23—Gerard Macrez, Mayfair	KO	4
Nov.	26—Marc Vandomme, Belfast	KO	2
Dec.	17—Messaoud Boussaboua, Brighton	W	8
1969
Apr.	28—Michel Houdeau, Mayfair	KO	4
Aug.	13—Umberto Simbola, San Remo	W	8
Nov.	11—Antonio Chiloiro, London	W	8
	Retired.		

TB	KO	WD	WF	D	LD	LF	KOBY	ND	NC
40	14	18	0	1	3	0	4	0	0

CHARTCHAI (LAEMFAPHA) CHIONOI
Born, Bangkok, Thailand, October 10, 1942.
1957
Oct.	12—Suratin Meeprasert, Bangkok	KO	2
1958
Oct.	13—Paiboon Krasaesuk, Bangkok	KO	2
1959
Mar.	27—Somsak Krisinasuwan, Bangkok	KO	2
April	8—Surin Praromdee, Bangkok	KO	2
May	31—Sala Kampuj, Cambodia	D	
Sept.	16—Prapass Sae Tang, Bangkok	KO	2
Sept.	27—Opas Eto, Bangkok	W	6
Nov.	1—Yoo Sam-ang, Cambodia	KO	4
Dec.	29—Van Po, Cambodia	W	6
1960
Feb.	2—Villy Lertrit, Bangkok	KO	2
June	4—Supparit Benjamasit, Bangkok	KO	4
Aug.	2—Masanobu Kanbayachi, Tokyo	KO	8
Sept.	2—Masanobu Kanbayachi, Tokyo	KO	8
Sept.	29—Atsushi Fokukaiwa, Tokyo	KO	2
Oct.	19—Yoshikatsu Furukaiwa, Tokyo	W	8
Dec.	4—Masso Ogawa, Tokyo	W	10
1961
Jan.	4—Mitsunori Seki, Tokyo	L	10
Apr.	19—Katsuyoshi Amada, Tokyo	KO	6
May	15—Shutara Kida, Nagoya	KO	2
June	8—Akira Oguchi, Tokyo	L	10
July	21—Masakatsu Kuboki, Osaka	KO	7
Aug.	17—Haruo Sakamoto, Tokyo	L	10
Sept.	7—Hiroyuki Hogkawa, Tqkyo	KO	2
Sept.	28—Akira Oguchi, Bangkok	KO	5
Dec.	9—Kyo Noguchi, Bangkok	W	10
1962
Apr.	24—Mitsunori Seki, Bangkok	W	10
July	12—Ernesto Miranda, Bangkok	L	10
Sept.	22—Primo Famiro, Manila	W	12

(Orient flyweight title)

Dec. 31—Hiroyuki Ebihara, Tokyo ......L 12
      (Orient flyweight title)
                  1963
Feb. 19—Seisaku Saito, Tokyo ....KO   8
June   7—Takeshi Nakamura, Tokyo .....L 10
July   8—Takeshi Nakamura, Osaka .....L 12
      (Orient flyweight title)
July 26—Tadao Kawamura, Kita-
      Kyusyu............................ W 10
Aug. 28—Tatsumi Yamagami, Tokyo .... D 10
Dec. 10—Yuji Ashiyama, Tokyo .... W 10
                  1964
Feb.   8—Rudy Villagonga, Manila ......L 10
June 10—Little Paramount, Manila .....KO   2
July 12—Bernardo Carballo, Manila .....L 10
Sept. 10—Little Paramount, Manila ......KO   2
Sept. 12—Anantadej Sithiran, Bangkok .. W 10
                  1965
Feb.   2—Anan Sithiran, Bangkok ....W 10
Apr. 24—Rudy Villagonza, Quezon ....KO   4
May   12—Rudy Villagonza, Manila .....KO   3
June 10—Chery Montana, Manila ....KO   2
July   8—Cherry Montano, Manila .....KO   2
Aug. 22—Hajime Taroura, Tokyo ....L 10
Sept. 28—Michel Lamora, Bangkok ...... W 10
                  1966
Jan.   7—Pornchai Popraingam,
      Bangkok........................KO   1
Feb.   8—Salvatore Burruni, Bangkok .. W 10
Mar. 15—Ernesto Miranda, Bangkok .... W 10
Apr. 10—Clever Luna, Bangkok ....KO   4
May   21—Chaithong Singshueplerng,
      Bangkok........................KO   3
Aug. 16—Sakdinoi Kosum, Bangkok ....KO   1
Nov. 15—Terry Go, Bangkok ....KO   6
Dec. 30—Walter McGowan, Bangkok ...KO   9
      (Won World Flyweight Title)
                  1967
Feb.   3—Bonnie Borromeo, Pitsamboke KO   4
Feb. 28—Baby Lorona, Bangkok .... W 10
July 26—Puntip Keosuriya, Bangkok ...KO   3
      (World flyweight title)
Sept. 19—Walter McGowan, London ....KO   7
      (World flyweight title)
Dec.   8—Mimun Ben Ali, Bangkok .....KO   4
                  1968
Jan. 28—Efren Torres, Mexico City ....KO 13
      (Retained World Flyweight Title)
June   8—Raton Mojica, Managua ....L 10
Nov. 10—Bernabe Villacampo, Bangkok . W 15
      (Retained World Flyweight Title)
                  1969
Feb. 23—Efren Torres, Mexico City . KO by 8
      (World flyweight title)
June 24—Willy Del Prado, Bangkok .....L 10
Sept. 7—Rudy Alarcon, Bangkok .....KO   9
                  1970
Jan. 13—Ely Axinto, Bangkok .... KO   6
Mar. 20—Efren Torres, Bangkok .... W 15
      (World Flyweight Title)
June 20—Al Diaz, Bangkok .... W 10
Dec.   7—Erbito Salavarria, Bangkok ... KO by   2
      (World Flyweight Title)
                  1971
Apr. 19—Eiichi Asano, Bangkok .... D 10
Nov. 15—Berkrerk Chartvanchai,
      Bangkok........................... W 10
                  1972
Jan. 31—Kenji Endo, Bangkok .... W 10
Apr.   5—Edmundo Ejandra, Bangkok ...KO   9
July   5—Shiomi Tanaka, Bangkok ..... W 10
Oct. 18—Esteban Rangel, Bangkok ....KO   2
                  1973
Jan.   2—Masao Ohba, Tokyo ...... KO by 12
May   17—Fritz Chervet, Bangkok ......KO   5
      (WBA world flyweight title)
Oct. 27—Susumu Hanagata, Bangkok ... W 15
      (WBA world flyweight title)
                  1974
Jan. 29—Fernando Cabanela, Honolulu ..L 10
Apr   27—Fritz Chervet, Zurich .... W 15
      (W.B.A. Flyweight Title)
Oct. 18—Susumu Henagata, Tokyo . KO by   6
      (W.B.A. Flyweight Title)
                  1975
Aug. 16—Rodolfo Frencis, Panama City   KO by   6

TB	KO	WD	WF	D	LD	LF	KO BY	ND	NC
83	39	23	0	3	13	0	5	0	0

820

ALACRAN (EFREN) TORRES
Guadalajara, Mexico, Flyweight
(Early Record Unavailable)
Born November 29, 1943
                  1961
Oct.   7—Felix Padilla, Guadalajara ..... W 10
Sept. 16—Chabelo Mejia, Guadalajara ...KO   3
Nov. 11—Raton Mojica, Guadalajara .... W 10
                  1962
Jan. 13—Chico Jasso, Guadalajara ...... W 10
Feb.   1—Joe Valenzuela,
      Gomez-Palacio ....KO   2
Mar.   3—Luis Mendez, Guadalajara ..... W 10
May   5—Raton Mojica, Guadalajara ... W 10
June   9—Ernesto Barrera, Guadalajara .. W 10
July 29—Raton Mojica, Managua ....L 10
Oct. 13—Ernesto Garrera, Guadalajara .. W 10
Nov. 24—Carlos Gomez, Guadalajara ...KO   7
                  1963
Feb. 16—Fidel Alfaro, Mexico City ....KO   6
Mar. 21—Changa Munoz, Mexico City ..KO   4
Apr.   5—Juan Amador, Los Angeles ...KO   1
Apr. 21—Joe Valenzuela, Juarez ......KO   1
July   6—Carlos Gomez, Mexico City ...KO   6
      (Won Mexican Flyweight Title)
Aug. 17—Raul Veloz, Juarez ....KO   1
Sept. 28—Natalio Jiminez, Guadalajara .KO   2
Oct. 19—Pascual Perez, Guadalajara ...KO   3
Nov. 30—Fabian Esquivel, Mexico City .KO   1
      (Retained Mexican Flyweight Title)
      Luis Gonzalez. Mexico City ....KO   2
                  1964
Feb.   2—Changa Magallanes, Mexicali ..KO   7
Feb. 15—Jose Hernandez, Culiacan ....KO   3
Mar. 15—Leo Zulueta, Guadalajara ...... W 10
Apr. 30—Hiroyuki Ebihara, Los Angeles ..L 12
Aug. 15—Cuervo Salinas, Guadalajara ... W 12
      (Mexican Flyweight Title Bout)
Sept. 11—Luis Gonzalez, Los Angeles ...KO   7
Nov. 14—Mauro Miranda, Mex. City ....KO   2
                  1965
Jan. 29—Ismael Guiterrez, Juarez ......KO   2
Feb. 28—Changa Magallanes,
      Monterrey ....KO   2
May   7—Hiroyuki Ebihara,
      Los Angeles .... KO by   7
Oct. 16—Manuel Flores, Guadalajara ...KO   6
Dec. 11—Bob Allotey, Mexico City ..... W 10
                  1966
Mar. 12—Manuel Tarazon, Guadalajara .KO   3
Apr.   3—Jose Lopez, Mexicali ....KO   6
May   14—Fermin Gomez, Guadalajara .. D 12
July   2—Ramiro Nides, Hermosillo ...KO   5
Aug.   7—Luis Gonzalez, Mexico City ...KO   2
Dec. 10—Horacio Accavallo, Buenos
      Aires ....L 15
      (W.B.A. Flyweight Title)
                  1967
Apr. 29—Octavio Gomez, Mexico City, .KO   5
      Mexican Flyweight Title
July 10—Pornchai Poppragram, Tijuana . W 10
      Guadalajara....................... W 10
Sept. 16—Jupiter Mansilla,
      Guadalajara ....KO   3
Oct.   7—Joe Medel, Guadalajara .... W 10
                  1968
Jan. 28—Chartchai Chionoi,
      Mexico City .... KO by 13
      (World Flyweight Title)
May   28—Pedro Cordero, Vallarta ......KO   6
Sept. 15—Raton Mojica, Mexico City .... W 10
Nov.   8—Daniel Gutierrez, Reynosa ..... W 10
Nov. 19—Jose Salinas, San Antonio ....KO   1
                  1969
Feb. 23—Chartchai Chionoi,
      Mexico City ....KO   8
      (Won World Flyweight Title)
June 20—Susumo Hanagata, Los Angeles .L 10
Sept. 30—Heleno Ferreyra, Mexico City .. W 10
Nov. 28—Susumo Hanagata,
      Guadalajara .... W 15
      (Retained World Flyweight Title)
                  1970
Mar. 20—Chartchai Chionoi, Bangkok ....L 15
      (Lost World Flyweight Title)
June 28—Rocky Garcia, Monterrey ..... W 10
Oct. 31—Joel Medel, Tijuana ....KO   4
                  1971
Feb.   2—Julio Guerrero, Tijuana ....L 10
July 11—Ruben Olivares, Guadalajara KO by   4

Apr. 21—Isao Kimura, Guadalajara.....KO 2

TB	KO	WD	WF	D	LD	LF	KOBY	ND	NC
58	31	17	0	1	6	0	3	0	0

BERNABE VILLACAMPO
Filipino Flyweight
Born, June 11, 1943—, Toledo City, Philippine Island.

1963
Apr. 20—Little Rufe, Cebu.....KO 6
Aug. 10—Ric Magramo, Cebu.....L 10
Sept. 21—Primi Famiro, Luzon City.....L 10
Dec. 28—Rom Rico, Luzon City.....W 10
1964
Feb. 1—Ric Magramo, Cebu.....W 10
Apr. 4—Little Paramount, Cebu.....L 10
May 2—Young Bonnie, Cebu.....W 10
June 27—Chosie Yoshio, Debu.....KO 7
Nov. 7—Rudy Billones, Luzon City.....KO 4
Nov. 28—Little Paramount, Cebu.....W 10
1965
Mar. 6—Jet Parker, Cebu.....L 10
Apr. 24—Speedy Haynes, Cebu.....KO 6
May 15—Jet Parker, Cebu.....L 10
July 31—Primo Famiro, Cebu.....WF 8
1966
(Unavailable)
1967
Feb. 19—Manuelo Balaba, Qeuzon City.....D 10
Sept. 30—Dong Ki Cho, Cebu City.....W 10
Oct. 1—Ric Magramo, Manila.....KO by 3
Nov. 7—Katsuyoshi Takayama, Okayama.....KO 6
Dec. 4—Yoshio Nakane, Tokyo.....KO 6
1968
Feb. 10—Al Diaz, Milan.....W 10
May 15—Takeshi Nakamura, Tokyo.....D 12
(Orient Flyweight Title)
June 24—Yuzo Narumi, Tokyo.....KO 6
Nov. 10—Chartchai Chinonoi Bangkok.....L 15
(World Flyweight Title)
1969
Jan. 18—Fernando Atzori, Manila.....KO 7
May 6—Berglerk Chartwanchai, Bangkok.....L 10
Aug. 16—Yasuo Narumi, Quezon City.....KO 4
Oct. 20—Hiroyuki Ebihara, Tokyo.....W 15
(W.B.A. Flyweight Title)
Dec. 14—Masao Ohba, Tokyo.....L 10
1970
Feb. 7—Raton Mojica, Manila.....W 10
Apr. 7—Berkrerk Chartvanchai, Bangkok.....L 15
(W.B.A. Flyweight Title)
June 27—Seichi Watanuki, Manila.....KO 8
Aug. 29—Baby Lorona, Manila.....KO 6
Dec. 21—Betulio Gonzalez, Caracas.....L 12
1971
Jan. 20—Cesar Desiga, Inglewood.....L 10
Apr. 11—Kuniaki Shimada, Manila.....KO 3
May 13—Beaver Kajimoto, Tokyo.....W 10
July 27—Octavio Gomez, Tijuana.....L 10
Dec. 3—Billy Abato, Cebu City.....KO by 8
1978
Mar. 7—Shigeo Nakajima, Tokyo.....KO 4
1979
Apr. 7—Arnel Arrozal, Pampanga.....KO by 4
July 15—Netrnoi Vorasingh, Bangkok.....KO by 6
Nov. 24—Danilo Inocian, Santos City.....KO by 5

TB	KO	WD	WF	D	LD	LF	KO BY	ND	NC
42	13	9	1	2	12	0	5	0	0

BERKRERK CHARTVANCHAI
Thai Bantamweight
Born: 1946, Bangkok
Height: 5 ft. 6 in.
1966
Jan 5—Kachasuk Sakoonthai, Bangkok.....W 6
Feb. 11—Kamon Rajadej, Bangkok.....KO 2
Mar. 15—Vitijanoi Singiotpha, Bangkok.....D 8
Apr. 1—Channaring Srisothern, Bangkok.....KO 6

May 5—Chakraphet Lookakmoung, Bangkok.....W 6
May 30—Suwat Sakoonthai, Bangkok.....W 8
June 15—Chomphon Sitkasaw, Bangkok.....D 8
July 10—Kingthon Aripai, Bangkok.....W 8
Aug. 5—Anatachai Saungprachpn, Bangkok.....W 8
Sept. 3—Luckchai Singkoungsong, Bangkok.....W 8
Oct. 15—Songchai S. Pichitchai, Bangkok.....D 8
Nov. 2—Phetchart Ratana, Bangkok.....W 8
Dec. 1—Sardez Moungpratom, Bangkok.....KO 6
1967
Jan. 2—Adulsak Itti-Anuchit, Bangkok.....W 10
Feb. 15—Somreck Eto, Bangkok.....KO 5
Mar. 1—Virachon Lukamsirek, Bangkok.....W 8
Apr. 6—Kaikeow Yongrakit, Bangkok.....W 10
June 6—Suknoi Eto, Bangkok.....W 10
1968
Sept. 13—Jaime Pitalbo, Bangkok.....W 10
1969
Jan. 22—Ric Magrano, Bangkok.....W 10
Mar. 27—Vitayanoi Sinyfoda, Bangkok.....KO 4
May 6—Bernabe Villacampo, Bangkok.....W 10
July 7—Kriankai Yingsakdi, Bangkok.....W 10
Aug. 4—Willy Del Prado, Bangkok.....W 10
Oct. 13—Felipe Gonzalez, Bangkok.....W 10
1970
Jan. 26—Rudy Tumulak, Bangkok.....W 10
Apr. 14—Bernabe Villacampo, Bangkok.....W 15
(Won WBA World Flyweight Title)
July 25—Erbito Salavaria, Manila.....L 10
Oct. 22—Masao Oba, Tokyo.....KO by 13
(Lost WBA World Flyweight Title)
1971
Feb. 1—Kazuyoshi Kanazawa, Bangkok.....KO by 4
May 31—Pedro Cerio, Bangkok.....W 10
Aug. 2—Takeo Sukegawa, Bangkok.....KO 8
Sept. 20—Yoshiaki Mutsumoto, Bangkok.....W 10
Nov. 15—Chartchai Chionoi, Bangkok.....L 10
1972
June 26—Franco Cruz, Bangkok.....W 10
Aug. 7—Zensuke Utagawa, Bangkok.....L 10
1973
July 31—Thanomchit Sukothai, Bangkok.....KO by 10
Dec. 17—Fernando Cabanella, Bangkok.....KO by 5

TB	KO	WD	WF	D	LD	LF	KO BY	ND	NC
38	6	22	0	3	3	0	4	0	0

MASAO OHBA
Born, October 21, 1949, Yokogawa-cho, Sumida-ku, Tokyo, Japan. Weight, 112 lbs. Height, 5 ft. 5¾ in.
1966
Nov. 7—Kazuyoshi Watanabe, Tokyo.....KO 1
Dec. 12—Joji Kuroki, Tokyo.....KO 3
1967
Jan. 2—Ryoichi Takahashi, Tokyo.....KO 2
Feb. 20—Sumio Arai, Tokyo.....KO 3
Mar. 27—Kenji Otsuka, Tokyo.....W 4
Apr. 30—Kunio Shimada, Tokyo.....W 4
June 16—Masakazu Tani, Osaka.....L 4
July 31—Tadashi Nishikawa, Tokyo.....KO 1
Sept. 3—Yasuo Jo, Tokyo.....W 4
Sept. 22—Masao Ohara, Tokyo.....KO 2
Oct. 13—Eiichi Asano, Tokyo.....D 4
Nov. 13—Toshimi Yasuda, Tokyo.....KO 4
Dec. 14—Shunichi Minagawa, Tokyo.....W 4
1968
Jan. 8—Yoshiaki Hagiri, Tokyo.....W 6
Mar. 11—Shoji Wada, Tokyo.....W 6
May 13—Takeo Tamashiro, Tokyo.....KO 4
June 17—Shoichi Fujimaki, Tokyo.....KO 3
Aug. 5—Shoji Wada, Tokyo.....W 8
Sept. 2—Susumu Hanagata, Tokyo.....L 10
Oct. 28—Yuzo Narumi, Tokyo.....W 10
Dec. 23—Shuta Yoshino, Sendai.....W 10
1969
Mar. 3—Speedy Hayase, Tokyo.....W 10
May 5—Yoshiaki Matsumoto, Tokyo.....W 10
June 23—Sakdinoi Eto, Tokyo.....W 10
Aug. 18—Takeshi Nakamura, Tokyo.....W 10
Dec. 14—Bernabe Villacampo, Tokyo.....W 10
1970
Mar. 1—Rudy Billones, Tokyo.....W 10
June 21—Baby Carona, Tokyo.....W 10
Oct. 22—Berkrek Chartvanchai, Tokyo.....KO 13
(Won WBA Flyweight Title)

Jan. 21—Fritz Chervet, Tokyo .... KO 8
Apr. 1—Betulio Gonzalez, Tokyo .... W 15
    (Retained WBA Flyweight Title)
June 18—Rocky Garcia, San Antonio ...... KO 9
Aug. 19—Tony Moreno, Tokyo .... W 10
Oct. 23—Fernando Cabanela, Tokyo .... W 15
    (Retained WBA Flyweight Title)
1972
Mar. 3—Susumu Hanagata, Tokyo .... W 15
    (Retained WBA Flyweight Title)
June 20—Orlando Amores, Tokyo .... KO 5
    (Retained WBA Flyweight Title)
Sept. 26—Natalio Jimenez, Tokyo .... KO 5
1973
Jan. 2—Chartchai Chionoi, Tokyo .... KO 12
    (Retained WBA Flyweight Title)

TB	KO	WD	WF	D	LD	LF	KO BY	ND	NC
38	15	20	0	1	2	0	0	0	0

Died, January 24, 1973, in automobile accident, outside of Tokyo, Japan.

ERBITO SALAVARRIA

Born, January 20, 1946, Manila, Philippines. Weight, 112 lbs.
1963
Sept. 14—Pablito Seldo, Quezon City .... KO 4
Dec. 7—Fil Bartolome, Quezon City .... W 4
Dec. 17—Adolfo Cruz, Manila .... W 4
1964
Feb. 15—Mar Anacay, Manila .... W 4
Apr. 18—Urbina, Jr., Quezon City .... W 4
May 23—Speedy Castro, Quezon City ...... W 6
July 31—Jesse Fernandez, Manila .... W 6
Aug. 21—Ruben Dingal, Manila .... D 6
Oct. 28—Johnny Bulawan, Quezon City ..... L 8
Dec. 5—Joe Cagulada, Manila .... KO 3
1965
Apr. 27—Speedy Castro, Quezon City .... W 8
July 3—Baby Castro, Manila .... W 10
Aug. 20—Rudy Billiones, Manila .... W 10
Oct. 15—Manuelo Balaba, Manila .... W 10
1966
Jan. 8—Henry Acido, Manila .... W 10
Feb. 19—Primo Famiro, Manila .... W 10
Apr. 9—Al Diaz, Manila .... KO by 9
July 22—Cesar Soliman, Manila .... KO 9
Oct. 8—Tom Rico, Quezon City .... W 10
Nov. 18—Ric Magramo, Manila .... L 12
    (For Filipino Flyweight Title)
1967
May 13—Ric Magramo, Manila .... W 12
    (Won Filipino Flyweight Title)
Aug. 12—Dong-Ki Cho, Quezon City .... W 10
Oct. 14—Ric Magramo, Quezon City .... L 12
    (Lost Filipino Flyweight Title)
Dec. 20—Takeshi Nakamura, Tokyo .... L 12
    (For Oriental Flyweight Title)
1968
May 16—Speedy Hayase, Quezon City ...... W 10
Aug. 17—Ric Magramo, Quezon City .... W 12
    (Regained Filipino Flyweight Title)
Oct. 7—Speedy Hayase, Tokyo .... W 10
Nov. 4—Yoshiaki Matsumoto, Tokyo .... D 10
1969
Feb. 16—Yoshiaki Matsumoto, Manila ..... KO 4
Apr. 26—Sakdinoi Eto, Quezon City .... KO 9
May 16—Al Diaz, Quezon City .... W 12
    (Retained Filipino Flyweight Title)
Oct. 18—Takeshi Nakamura, Manila ...... KO 12
    (Won Oriental Flyweight Title)
1970
Mar. 4—Shigeru Taremizu, Tokyo .... KO 2
    (Retained Oriental Flyweight Title)
June 21—Witaya Plernjit, Manila .... W 12
    (Retained Oriental Flyweight Title)

July 25—Berkrerk Chartvanchai, Manila ... W 10
Dec. 7—Chartchai Chionoi, Bangkok ..... KO 2
    (Won World Flyweight Title)
1971
Feb. 20—Harry Hayes, Manila .... W 12
Apr. 30—Susumu Hanagata, Manila .... W 15
    (Retained World Flyweight Title)
June 4—Halimi Gutierrez, Los Angeles ..... L 10
Sept. 11—Natalio Jimenez, Manila .... W 12
Nov. 20—Betulio Gonzalez, Caracas .... D 15
    (Retained World Flyweight Title)
1972
Aug. 5—Dong-Ki Cho, Davao City .... W 12
    (Retained Oriental Flyweight Title)
1973
Feb. 9—Venice Borkorsor, Bangkok .... L 15
    (Lost World Flyweight Title)
Aug. 8—Stripped of Oriental flyweight title.
Oct. 9—Fortunato Hernandez, Honolulu .. KO 2
Nov. 7—Enrique Torres, Honolulu .... W 12
1974
June 8—Vicente Pool, Merida .... KO 6
June 29—Alfonso Lopez, Panama city .... L 10
Nov. 15—Katsumasa, Manila .... KO 5
1975
Apr. 1—Susumu Hanagata, Toyama .... W 15
    (Won WBA Flyweight Title)
May 17—Alberto Morales, Los Angeles ...... L 10
Oct. 7—Susumu Hanagata, Yokohama ..... W 15
    (Retained WBA Flyweight Title)
1976
Feb. 27—Alfonso Lopez, Manila .... KO by 15
    (Lost WBA Flyweight Title)
1977
(Inactive)
1978
Dec. 3—Netrnoi Sor Vorasingh, Bangkok KO by 4

TB	KO	WD	WF	D	LD	LF	KO BY	ND	NC
53	11	28	0	3	8	0	3	0	0

BETULIO GONZALEZ

Born, October 24, 1949, Maracaibo, Venezuela. Weight, 112 lbs. Height, 5 ft. 3¾ in.
1968
    —E. Monzat, Maracaibo .... KO 3
    —F. Ramirez, Maracaibo .... W 6
Sept. 2—J. Hernandez, Maracaibo .... W 4
Oct. 22—Hector Criollo, Maracaibo .... KO 5
Nov. 25—Evencio Bruguillos, Caracas .... W 10
1969
Feb. 3—Hilario Diaz, Caracas .... W 10
Feb. —Pollito Lara, Caracas .... W 10
Mar. 31—Mario de Leon, Maracaibo .... W 10
May 26—Tony Barboza, Maracaibo .... W 10
July 15—Nelson Alarcon, Maracaibo .... W 10
Aug. 1—Jose Brizuela, Caracas .... D 10
Sept. 8—Ramon Bravo, Caracas .... KO 5
Sept. 16—Jose Brizuela, Maracaibo .... W 10
Oct. 10—Hector Crillo, Caracas .... KO 7
Nov. 4—Ismael Escobar, Maracaibo ...... KO 4
Dec. 12—Catalino Alvarado, Caracas ...... KO 6
1970
Feb. 8—Plinio Hernandez, Caracas .... KO 3
Mar. 6—Felix Marquez, Caracas .... KO by 6
Apr. 17—Jose Jimenez, Caracas .... W 10
May 8—Ignacio Espinal, Caracas .... L 10
June 15—Felix Marquez, Caracas .... W 10
Aug. —Ignacio Espinal, Caracas .... KO 10
Sept. 25—Ubaldo Duarte, Caracas .... W 10
Oct. 8—Salvador Lozano, Costa Rico .... W 10
Nov. —Jose Garcia, Caracas .... KO 4
Nov. 30—Chamaco Lopez, Caracas .... KO 3
Dec. 21—Bernabe Villacampo, Caracas ..... W 12
1971
Jan. 31—Lucio del Rio Mosca, Caracas ..... KO 9

Apr. 1—Masao Ohba, Tokyo .... L 15
(For WBA Flyweight Title)
June 7—Tony Moreno, Caracas .... W 10
July 17—Natalio Jimenez, Maracaibo ...... W 10
Aug. 30—San Sacristan, Caracas .... W 10
Nov. 20—Erbito Salavarria, Caracas .... D 15
(For World Flyweight Title)
1972
Jan. 31—Salvatore Lozano, Caracas ...... KO 6
Mar. 15—Willie Pastana, Maracaibo ...... KO 4
June 3—Socates Batoto, Caracas .... KO 4
(Won Vacant WBC Flyweight Title)
Sept. 29—Venice Borkorsor, Bangkok ... KO by 10
(Lost WBC Flyweight Title)
1973
Jan. 31—Osamu Haba, Caracas .... KO 3
Mar. 10—Halim Gutierrez, Maracaibo ...... KO 3
July 10—Ricardo Delgado, Maracar .... W 10
Aug. 4—Miguel Canto, Caracas .... W 15
(Regained Vacant WBC Flyweight Title)
Oct. 10—Reynaldo Ramirez, Caracas ...... KO 3
Nov. 17—Alberto Morales, Caracas .... KO 11
(Retained WBC Flyweight Title)
1974
Mar. 30—Luis Cortez, Caracas .... KO 2
May 20—Shoji Oguma, Koriyama .... W 10
July 21—Franco Udella, Sabbiardoro ...... KO 10
(Retained WBC Flyweight Title)
Oct. 1—Shoji Oguma, Tokyo .... L 15
(Lost WBC Flyweight Title)
1975
Feb. 22—Mario Mendez, Caracas .... KO 8
May 26—Miguel Canto, Monterrey .... L 15
(For World Flyweight Title)
July 28—Mariano Garcia, Caracas .... KO 2
Sept. 6—Sergio Villouta, Caracas .... KO 4
Oct. 4—Reinaldo Romero, Caracas ...... KO 1
Nov. 15—Andrea Reyes, Panama City ..... KO 4
Dec. 1—Luis Torres, Caracas .... KO 3
1976
Feb. 14—Antonio Sanchez, Caracas .... W 10
Apr. 11—Henry Diaz, Caracas .... KO 8
May 15—Felix Madrigal, Maracaibo .... KO 2
June 20—Hildo Roche, Caracas .... KO 2
July 25—Peanuts Emerson, Maracaibo ..... KO 3
Aug. 21—Mario Chavez, Caracas .... KO 2
Oct. 3—Miguel Canto, Caracas .... L 15
(For World Flyweight Title)
1977
Feb. 13—Valentin Marintez, Maracaibo .... KO 7
Mar. 12—Prudencio Cardona, Maracaibo ... KO 3
Apr. 16—Samuel Machorro, Maracaibo ..... W 10
June 25—Rodolfo Rodriguez, Maracaibo ... KO 7
Sept. 30—Carlos Escalante, Maracaibo ..... KO 6
1978
Mar. 4—Raul Valdez, Caracas .... W 10
May 13—Humberto Mayorga, Maracaibo ... KO 2
July 8—Rocky Mijares, Maracaibo .... KO 8
Aug. 12—Guty Espadas, Maracay .... W 15
(Won WBA Flyweight Title)
Nov. 4—Martin Vargas, Venezuela .... KO 12
(Retained WBA Flyweight Title)
1979
Jan. 29—Shoji Oguma, Hamamatsu .... D 15
(Retained WBA Flyweight Title)
July 6—Shoji Oguma, Utsunomiya .... KO 12
(Retained WBA Flyweight Title)
Nov. 17—Luis Ibarra, Maracay .... L 15
(Lost WBA Flyweight Title)

1980
—Elias de Leon, Caracas .... W 10
Oct. 31—Arturo Gonzalez, Maracaibo ...... KO 5
Nov. 14—Pascual Polanca, Maracaibo ..... KO 5
Dec. 6—Manuel Rios, Maracaibo .... KO 5

TB	KO	WD	WF	D	LD	LF	KO BY	ND	NC
78	42	25	0	3	6	0	2	0	0

VENICE BORKORSOR
Born, 1950, Thailand. Weight, 112-120 lbs.
Southpaw. Managed by Chana Thupkeow.
1970
Mar. 4—Lugnakorn Chaiari, Rajburi ..... KO 7
Apr. 6—Vittya Pleonchit, Bangkok .... KO 3
1971
Mar. 2—Shigeru Taremitzu, Bangkok ..... KO 1
Apr. 2—Dong-Ki Cho, Bangkok .... KO 8
July 9—Johnny Agbon, Bangkok .... W 10
Sept. 14—Chong-Ho Moon, Bangkok .... KO 6
Oct. 19—Johnny Agbon, Bangkok .... KO 8
Dec. 17—Snappy Asano, Bangkok .... W 10
1972
Feb. 15—Fernando Cabanela, Bangkok ..... W 10
June 9—San Sacritan, Bangkok .... KO 7
Sept. 29—Betulio Gonzalez, Bangkok .... KO 10
(Won WBC Flyweight Title)
Dec. 15—Abdsellem Ben Sallah, Bangkok .. KO 3
1973
Feb. 9—Erbito Salavarria, Bangkok .... W 15
(Won World Flyweight title)
July 10—Julio Guerrero, Tijuana .... KO 6
—Relinquished world flyweight title.
Oct. 13—Rafael Herrera, Inglewood .... L 15
(For WBC Bantamweight Title)
1974
Feb. 23—Raul Montana, Monterrey .... L 10
Mar. 23—Joe Gumede, Mexico City .... KO 10
Nov. 29—Conrado Vasquez, Bangkok .... W 12
(Won Vacant Oriental Bantamweight Title)
1975
Feb. 11—Bok-Soo Hwan, Bangkok .... KO 9
(Retained Oriental Bantamweight Title)
Sept. 20—Seing-Keun Koh, Seoul .... W 10
1976
Jan. 30—Rodolfo Martinez, Bangkok .... L 15
(For WBC Bantamweight Title)
May 30—Soo-Hwan Hong, Seoul .... L 12
(Lost Oriental Bantamweight Title)
Oct. 12—Yung-Shik Kim, Bangkok .... W 10
1977
June 22—Bill Abrogar, Bangkok .... KO 6
1978
May 9—Paul Ferreri, Melbourne .... L 10
1979
—Duan-e-san Luklongjun, Bangkok KO 4
(Won Thai Bantamweight Title)
Oct. 21—Sang-Bong Lee, Seoul .... KO 6
Dec. 7—Neptali Alamag, Manila .... L 10
1980
Jan. 22—Dedked Kiatbungyong, Bangkok KO by 4
Aug. 11—Suriya Pratumvadee, Bangkok ... KO 6
(Retained Thai Bantamweight Title)
(Stripped of crown for failure to make weight)

TB	KO	WD	WF	D	LD	LF	KO BY	ND	NC
30	16	7	0	0	6	0	1	0	0

SHOJI OGUMA
Born, July 22, 1951, Koriyama, Fukushima,
Japan. Weight, 112 lbs. Height, 5 ft. 4 in. Southpaw.
Managed by Shichiro Kimura.
1970
Dec. 26—Kenji Yoshida, Tokyo .... KO 1
1971
Feb. 12—Kenetsuro Kikuchi, Tokyo .... W 4
Mar. 20—Masamitsu Sugawara, Tokyo ...... W 4
May 13—Toshiaki Nishio, Tokyo .... KO 1
July 30—Yoshio Tabata, Tokyo .... W 4
Aug. 19—Massakuni Kawakami, Tokyo ..... L 4
Oct. 14—Fujio Matsuoka, Tokyo .... W 4
Nov. 18—Masao Obara, Tokyo .... KO 3
Dec. 27—Masamitsu Katyama, Koriyama .. KO 2
1972
Mar. 23—Moritaka Sasaki, Tokyo .... KO 1
Apr. 14—Masakuni Kawauchi, Sendai ...... W 6
June 29—Masaichi Kobayashi, Tokyo ...... KO 1
Aug. 5—Yoichiro Hamada, Utsonomiya ... KO 8
Sept. 15—Matsushi Yoshida, Tokyo .... W 6

1973

Jan.	18—Jiro Shimizu, Tokyo	KO	4
Apr.	5—Kazuaki Koyanagi, Tokyo	KO	4
May	6—Tatsuo Shimizu, Utsonomiya	KO	4
July	2—Takeshi Mifune, Tokyo	W	10
Sept.	7—Dong-Ki Cho, Tokyo	W	10
Nov.	23—Kazumasa Shukamoto, Tokyo	W	10

1974

Mar.	24—Kenji Kato, Tokyo	W	10
May	19—Betulio Gonzalez, Koriyama City	L	10
Oct.	1—Betulio Gonzalez, Tokyo	W	15
	(Won WBC Flyweight Title)		

1975

Jan.	8—Miguel Canto, Sendai	L	15
	(For Vacant World Flyweight Title)		
Apr.	25—Peter Noble, Tokyo	KO	9
Aug.	22—Kazuo Aikawa, Tokyo	KO	5
Nov.	7—Yuji Matsunaga, Tokyo	KO	1

1976

Feb.	13—Domy Morolena, Tokyo	KO	10
Apr.	21—Alfonso Lopez, Tokyo	L	15
	(For WBA Flyweight Title)		
July	18—Dong-Rae Yim, Koriyama City	KO	4
Sept.	7—Chun-Ha Park, Tokyo	KO	3
Dec.	14—Kimio Furesawa, Tokyo	KO by	8

1977

| Feb. | 15—Sung-Jun Kim, Tokyo | W | 10 |
| Aug. | 29—Puma Koya, Tokyo | KO | 5 |

1978

Jan.	4—Miguel Canto, Koriyama	L	15
	(For WBC Flyweight Title)		
Apr.	18—Miguel Canto, Tokyo	L	15
	(For WBC Flyweight Title)		
Sept.	25—Puma Koya, Shizueka City	W	10
Nov.	23—Shinji Suga, Tokyo	KO	3

1979

Jan.	29—Betulio Gonzalez, Hamamatsu	D	15
	(For WBA Flyweight Title)		
July	6—Betulio Gonzalez, Utsonomiya	KO by	12
	(For WBA Flyweight Title)		
Dec.	17—Riki Igarashi, Tokyo	KO	8

1980

May	18—Chan-Hee Park, Seoul	KO	9
	(Won World Flyweight Title)		
July	28—Sung-Jun Kim, Tokyo	W	15
	(Retained World Flyweight Title)		
Oct.	18—Chan-Hee Park, Sendai	W	15
	(Retained World Flyweight Title)		

TB	KO	WD	WF	D	LD	LF	KO BY	ND	NC
44	20	15	0	1	6	0	2	0	0

SUSUMU HANAGATA

Born, January 21, 1946, Kanazawa Ward, Yokohama, Kanagawa, Japan. Weight, 112 lbs. Height, 5 ft. 3½ in.

1963

Nov.	1—Kohachi Haga, Yokohama	W	4
Nov.	28—Tsuyoshi Suzuki, Tokyo	L	4
Dec.	30—Tetsuo Moori, Tokyo	L	4

1964

Feb.	16—Hideo Isono, Yokohama	W	4
Apr.	14—Yoshihiro Kawakami, Tokyo	L	4
May	5—Sumiaki Moori, Tokyo	W	4
June	29—Kobayashi, Tokyo	W	4
Oct.	25—Junya Shin, Tokyo	W	4
Dec.	20—Star Yasunaka, Tokyo	D	4

1965

Jan.	26—Wasaburo Kokubo, Tokyo	D	4
Feb.	8—Hideo Isono, Yokohama	W	4
May	30—Kenzo Fukuyama, Tokyo	W	6
June	13—Shigeru Sawazaki, Tokyo	W	6
Aug.	22—Yoichi Nagumo, Tokyo	KO by	3
Sept.	9—Shigeru Taremizu, Tokyo	L	4
Dec.	5—Haruo Tashiro, Yokohama	D	4

1966

| Jan. | 10—Kenji Ashikaga, Tokyo | D | 6 |
| Feb. | 3—Nagayoshi Hara, Tokyo | L | 6 |

Mar.	11—Katsumi Takaishi, Yokohama	D	6
May	15—Goro Kawasaki, Yokohama	W	6
June	30—Kunio Ishida, Tokyo	W	6
Aug.	18—Michio Wakayama, Ito	W	6
Sept.	11—Katsuyoshi Nakajima, Tokyo	D	6
Oct.	23—Katsuyuki Kawabata, Tokyo	W	6
Nov.	14—Kenji Ashikaga, Tokyo	L	6

1967

May	18—Toshio Yamazaki, Tokyo	W	6
June	18—Yoshiaki Matsumoto, Tokyo	L	6
July	17—Yoshiaki Matsumoto, Yokohama	D	8
Sept.	18—Katsuji Ishioka, Tokyo	W	8

1968

Jan.	25—Shinzaburo Kaneko, Tokyo	KO	8
Aug.	3—Mitsuyoshi Iritsuki, Kawasaki	KO	4
Sept.	2—Masao Ohba, Tokyo	W	10
Oct.	21—Shoji Wada, Tokyo	W	10
Dec.	9—Terry Go, Tokyo	W	10

1969

Apr.	7—Speedy Hayase, Tokyo	W	10
	(Won Japanese Flyweight Title)		
June	20—Alacran (Efren) Torres, Los Angeles	W	10
Sept.	8—Roger Moreno, Tokyo	KO	4
Nov.	28—Alacran (Efren) Torres, Guadalajara	L	15
	(For World Flyweight title)		

1970

Jan.	11—Raton Mojica, Tokyo	W	10
Apr.	12—Seiichi Watanuki, Yokohama	W	10
	(Retained Japanese Flyweight Title)		
May	24—Fernando Lumacad, Tokyo	KO	7
Nov.	25—Shigeru Taremizu, Tokyo	W	10
	(Retained Japanese Flyweight Title)		

1971

Jan.	27—Tatsuro Uchida, Yokohama	W	10
Apr.	30—Erbito Salavarria, Manila	L	15
	(For World Flyweight Title)		
Sept.	23—Hideki Watanuki, Yokohama	W	10
	(Retained Japanese Flyweight Title)		

1972

Feb.	6—Takeo Sukegawa, Akita City	W	10
Mar.	3—Masao Ohba, Tokyo	L	15
	(For WBA Flyweight Title)		
May	18—Takeo Sukegawa, Tokyo	KO	2
July	3—Osamu Haba, Yokohama	KO by	8
	(Lost Japanese Flyweight Title)		
Oct.	6—Osamu Haba, Yokohama	W	10
	(Regained Japanese Flyweight Title)		

1973

June	17—Mikio Nakada, Tokyo	W	10
	(Retained Japanese Flyweight Title)		
Oct.	27—Chartchai Chionoi, Bangkok	L	15
	(For WBA Flyweight Title)		

1974

Feb.	—Relinquished Japanese flyweight title.		
Mar.	19—Rudy Billiones, Tokyo	KO	3
Sept.	5—Ernie Timbal, Toyama City	KO	4
Oct.	18—Chartchai Chionoi, Yokohama	KO	6
	(Won WBA Flyweight Title)		

1975

Apr.	1—Erbito Salavarria, Toyama City	L	10
Oct.	7—Erbito Salavarria, Yokohama	L	15
	(Lost WBA Flyweight Title)		
May	15—Miguel Canto, Merida	L	15
	(For World Flyweight Title)		

TB	KO	WD	WF	D	LD	LF	KO BY	ND	NC
58	8	27	0	7	14	0	2	0	0

MIGUEL CANTO

Born, January 30, 1949, Merida, Yucatan, Mexico. Weight, 112 lbs. Height, 5 ft. 1 in.

1969

Feb.	5—Canejo Hernandez, Merida	KO by	3
May	5—Gavilan Martinez, Merida	W	4
Aug.	13—Pedro Carrillo, Mexico City	KO by	4
Dec.	6—Vicente Pool, Chestumal	W	8

1970

Jan.	21—Rudy Granados, Merida	W	10
Feb.	4—Joe Calvario, Merida	D	10
Mar.	4—Vicente Pool, Merida	W	10
Mar.	21—Baby Albornoz, Chetumal	KO	9
Apr.	8—Alex Basilio, Merida	KO	6
Apr.	29—Ranita Torres (Jose Luis Morales), Merida	D	10

(For Yucatan Flyweight Title)

May	27—Vicente Pool, Merida	W	12
June	24—Chamaco Cetina, Merida	W	12

(Retained Yucatan Flyweight Title)

Oct.	14—Tarcisio (Famosito) Gomez, Merida	L	10
Nov.	11—Arturo Velazquez, Merida	W	10
Dec.	9—Joe Medrano, Merida	W	10

1971

Jan.	21—Pedro Martinez, Cansahcab	KO	2
Feb.	14—Francisco Montalvo, Cansahcab	KO	6
Mar.	17—Jose Luis Gomez, Merida	W	6
Apr.	4—Tigre Bracamontes, Tizimin	W	8
Apr.	29—Jose Luis Cetina, Merida	W	10
May	14—Gavilan Martinez, Tekax	W	10
June	2—Mario Garcia, Merida	KO	10
July	14—Pedro Lopez, Merida	KO	3
July	28—Domingo Ledezma, Merida	W	10
Sept.	1—Roberto Alvarez, Merida	W	10
Oct.	20—Alberto Morales, Merida	W	10
Dec.	1—Luis Carlos Urrunaga, Merida	W	10

1972

Jan.	22—Rocky Garcia, Merida	W	12

(For Mexican Flyweight Title)

Mar.	15—Jose (Carbonero) Vargas, Merida	W	10
Apr.	5—Armando Villa, Merida	KO	4
May	20—Ricardo Delgado, Merida	W	12

(Retained Mexican Flyweight Title)

July	26—Jose Luis Valencia, Merida	W	10
Sept.	27—Jose Antonio Corral, Merida	KO	3
Nov.	18—Alberto Morales, Merida	W	12

1973

Jan.	31—Ignacio Espinal, Merida	D	10
Mar.	24—Tarcisio Gomez, Merida	KO	2
May	2—Rudy Billones, Merida	W	10
May	10—Luis Garcia, Villarhermosa	KO	7
June	29—Chamaco Rodriguez, Chetumal	KO	5
Aug.	4—Betulio Gonzalez, Caracas	L	15

(For Vacant WBC Flyweight Title)

Nov.	17—Lupe Hernandez, Merida	W	12

1974

Feb.	13—Tony Moreno, Meridan	KO	5
Apr.	27—Manuel Montiel, Merida	W	10
June	10—Pablito Jiminez, Merida	W	10
Aug.	17—Alberto Morales, Mexico City	W	10
Oct.	25—Ricardo Delgado, Valladoli	W	10

1975

Jan.	8—Shoji Oguma, Sendai	W	15

(Won Vacant World Flyweight Title)

Mar.	9—Ignacio Espinal, Merida	W	10
May	26—Betulio Gonzalez, Monterrey	W	15

(Retained World Flyweight Title)

July	18—Lupe Madera, Cozumel	KO	9
Aug.	23—Jiro Takada, Merida	KO	11

(Retained World Flyweight Title)

Dec.	12—Ignacion Espinal, Merida	W	15

(Retained World Flyweight Title)

1976

Mar.	13—Francisco Marquez, Merida	W	10
May	15—Susumu Hanagata, Merida	W	15

(Retained World Flyweight Title)

Oct.	3—Betulio Gonzalez, Caracas	W	15

(Retained World Flyweight Title)

Nov.	20—Orlando Javierto, Los Angeles	W	15

(Retained World Flyweight Title)

1977

Apr.	24—Reyes Arnal, Caracas	W	15

(Retained World Flyweight Title)

June	15—Kimio Furesawa, Tokyo	W	15

(Retained World Flyweight Title)

Sept.	18—Martin Vargas, Merida	W	15

(Retained World Flyweight Title)

Nov.	30—Martin Vargas, Santiago	W	15

(Retained World Flyweight Title)

1978

Jan.	4—Shoji Oguma, Tokyo	W	15

(Retained World Flyweight Title)

Apr.	18—Shoji Oguma, Tokyo	W	15

(Retained World Flyweight Title)

Nov.	20—Tacomron Vibonchai, Houston	W	15

(Retained World Flyweight Title)

1979

Feb.	10—Antonio Avelar, Merida	W	15

(Retained World Flyweight Title)

Mar.	18—Chan-Hee Park, Pusan	L	15

(Lost World Flyweight Title)

Sept.	9—Chan-Hee Park, Seoul	D	15

(For World Flyweight Title)

1980

Aug.	16—Alfredo Hernandez, Merida	W	10
Oct.	18—Orlando Maldonado, Guadalajara	W disq.	6

TB	KO	WD	WF	D	LD	LF	KO BY	ND	NC
68	14	44	1	4	3	0	2	0	0

ALFONSO LOPEZ

Born, January 8, 1953, Taimiti, Panama.

1972

Mar.	8—C. Perez, Panama City	KO	2
Apr.	15—Ramon Montenegro, Panama City	W	4
July	30—San Blas III, Panama City	W	4

1973

Jan.	14—Antonio Shakespeare, Panama City	W	8
Mar.	31—Enrique Brown, Panama City	W	6
May	12—Maximo Figueroa, Panama City	KO	2
Oct.	6—Eduardo Parra, Panama City	KO	1

1974

Feb.	17—J. Martinez, Panama City	KO	8
May	5—L. Ramirez, Panama City	KO	5
June	29—Erbito Salavarria, Panama City	W	10
Aug.	31—Eduardo Cuardo, Panama City	KO	7
Dec.	2—Juan Villouta, Panama City	KO	1

1975

Feb.	2—Calixto Perez, Panama City	W	10
Mar.	9—Enrique Torres, Panama City	KO	6
May	17—Eliud Garces, Panama City	KO	2
July	26—Hildo Roche, Panama City	KO	2
Aug.	23—Juanito Herrera, Panama City	KO	1

1976

Feb.	27—Erbito Salavarria, Manila	KO	15

(Won WBA Flyweight Title)

Apr.	21—Shoji Oguma, Tokyo	W	15

(Retained WBA Flyweight Title)

Aug.	25—Kenji Kato, Merida, Yucatan	KO	2
Oct.	2—Guty Espadas, Los Angeles	KO by	13

(Lost WBA Flyweight Title)

1977

Jan.	15—Alex Santana Guido, Panama City	W	10
Apr.	30—Guty Espadas, Merida	KO by	13

(For WBA Flyweight Title)

Oct.	29—Amado Ursua, Panama City	KO by	7

1978

Mar.	10—Prudencio Cardona, Barranquilla	L	10
Apr.	22—Martin Vargas, Santiago	KO	1

(For South American Flyweight Title)

Oct.	28—Hilario Zapata, Panama City	W	15

(Won Vacant Latin American Junior Flyweight Title)

1979

Feb.	3—Orlando Rudas, Panama City	KO	2

(Won Panamanian Junior Flyweight Title)

Apr.	8—Yoko Gushiken, Tokyo	KO by	7

(For WBA Junior Flyweight Title)

1980

Feb.	16—Antonio Avelar, Mexico City	KO by	5
Apr.	26—Freddy Castillo, Merida	W	10
June	20—Jorge Vora, Campeche	L	10
Aug.	16—Pedro Galaviz, Merida	KO	9

Sept. 16—Charlie Magri, London .... L 10
Nov. 22—Gustavo Ballas, Buenos Aires ...... L 10
Dec. 1—Jovito Rengifo, Caracas .... W 10

TB	KO	WD	WF	D	LD	LF	KO BY	ND	NC
36	15	11	0	0	4	0	6	0	0

GUSTAVO (GUTY) ESPADAS
(Gustavo Hernan Espadas Cruz)
Born, December 20, 1954, Merida, Yucatan, Mexico. Weight, 112 lbs.
1971
Apr. 4—Chucho Loria, Tizimin, Yucatan ... W 6
June 2—Miguel Caballero, Merida, Yucatan KO 4
June 30—Miguel Camarge, Merida .... W 4
July 28—Chucho Loria, Merida .... D 4
Sept. 15—Panterita de Santa Cruz, Baca ..... D 6
Sept. 22—Freddy Castillo, Merida .... KO 4
Nov. 5—Zorrita Kid, Cozumel .... KO 3
Nov. 17—Baby Salazar, Merida .... KO 1
Dec. 15—Miguel Caballero, Merida .... KO 4
1972
Jan. 12—Chucho Loria, Merida .... W 6
Feb. 4—Kid Valente, Cozumel, Quintana Roo W 10
May 3—Kid Valente, Merida .... W 8
June 14—Juan Gomez, Merida .... KO 1
July 26—Fortino Mendez, Merida .... KO 2
Aug. 23—Daniel Acuna, Merida .... KO 4
1973
Jan. 24—Raul Tirado, Merida .... D 10
June 29—Kid Valente, Chetumal .... KO 7
Oct. 5—Chucho Loria, Progrese, Yucatan ... D 6
Nov. 17—Luis Enrique Garcia, Merida ..... KO 4
Dec. 8—Hector Mendieta, Merida .... W 12
(Won Yucatan Flyweight Title)
1974
Apr. 27—Roberto Alvarez, Merida .... KO 10
June 29—Alfonso Aguilar, Valladolid ...... KO 2
Aug. 7—Ricardo Delgado, Merida .... W 10
Oct. 5—Pablito Jimenez, Merida .... L 10
1975
Mar. 29—Alberto (Costeno) Morales, Acapulco L 10
Aug. 6—Juan Jose Guzman, Merida ...... KO 2
1976
Feb. 4—Orlando Hernandez, Merida ...... KO 1
May 8—Willie Jensen, Los Angeles .... D 10
July 21—Alfonso Gutierrez, Merida .... KO 4
Aug. 25—Ryuji Iwamoto, Merida .... KO 2
Oct. 2—Alfonso Lopez, Los Angeles ...... KO 13
(Won WBA Flyweight Title)
1977
Jan. 1—Jiro Takada, Tokyo .... KO 7
(Retained WBA Flyweight Title)
Apr. 30—Alfonso Lopez, Merida .... KO 13
(Retained WBA Flyweight Title)
Nov. 19—Alex Santana, Los Angeles ...... KO 8
(Retained WBA Flyweight Title)
1978
Jan. 2—Kimio Furesawa, Tokyo .... KO 7
(Retained WBA Flyweight Title)
Aug. 12—Betulio Gonzalez, Maracay .... L 15
(Lost WBA Flyweight Title)
1979
Feb. 10—Gato Mancilla, Merida .... KO 3
Mar. 5—Roberto Ruiz, Houston .... KO 7
Aug. 12—Jose Luis Cruz, Merida .... KO 6
Dec. 16—Chan-Hee Park, Pusan .... KO by 2
(For World Flyweight Title)
1980
Aug. 19—Franco Torregoza, Stockton .... W 10
Dec. 20—Rodolfo Martinez, Merida .... KO 10

TB	KO	WD	WF	D	LD	LF	KO BY	ND	NC
42	25	8	0	5	3	0	1	0	0

CHAN-HEE PARK
Born, March 23, 1957, Pusan, Korea. Weight, 112 lbs. Height, 5 ft. 3¼ in.
1977
July 8—Chuji Muto, Pusan .... KO 1
Sept. 10—Yukimitsu Kondo, Seoul .... KO 3
Oct. 1—Sang-Il Chung, Seoul .... W 10
Nov. 26—Daniel Pedro Solo, Pusan .... W 10
1978
Feb. 18—George Pedroso, Seoul .... W 10
Apr. 16—Puma Koya, Pusan .... KO 2
Aug. 12—Mikio Uchida, Seoul .... KO 3
Sept. 8—Torayuki Nanasha, Seoul .... KO 6
Oct. 21—Rolly Garcia Ramos, Pusan .... W 10
1979
Feb. 18—Siony Carupo, Seoul .... D 10
Mar. 18—Miguel Canto, Pusan .... W 15
(Won World Flyweight Title)
May 20—Riki Igarashi, Seoul .... W 15
(Retained World Flyweight Title)
Sept. 9—Miguel Canto, Seoul .... D 15
(Retained World Flyweight Title)
Dec. 16—Guty Espadas, Pusan .... KO 2
(Retained World Flyweight Title)
1980
Feb. 10—Arnel Arrozal, Seoul .... W 15
(Retained World Flyweight Title)
Apr. 13—Alberto Morales, Taegu .... W 15
(Retained World Flyweight Title)
May 18—Shoji Oguma, Seoul .... KO by 9
(Lost World Flyweight Title)
July 26—Pilardo Lavrador, Seoul .... TW 6
Oct. 18—Shoji Oguma, Sendai .... L 15
(For World Flyweight Title)

TB	KO	WD	WF	D	LD	LF	KO BY	ND	NC
19	6	9	0	2	1	0	1	0	0

LUIS IBARRA
Born, 1953, Panama. Weight, 112 lbs. Southpaw.
1975
July 20—Antonio Walker, Panama City ..... W 4
—Victor Barrows, Panama City ... KO 4
Oct. —Baby San Blas III, Panama City .. KO 2
1976
Jan. 31—Ulises Morales, Panama City ...... W 4
Mar. 12—Ricardo Vega, Colon, Panama ..... W 6
—Arnulfo Ayala .... KO 3
Sept. 4—Juan Pimental, Colon, Panama ... KO 1
Sept. 18—Carlos Rios, Panama City .... KO 3
Oct. 30—Enrique Torres, Panama City ..... W 12
1977
Jan. 28—Jaime Ricard, Colon, Panama ..... W 10
Apr. 1—Manuel Buitrago, Colon, Panama .. W 10
July 17—Felix Madrigal, Colon, Panama ... KO 6
Oct. 1—Rafael Pedroza, Colon, Panama ... W 10
Dec. 17—Henry Diaz, Colon, Panama .... W 10
1978
Jan. 26—Felix Madrigal, Costa Rica .... W 10
June 30—Prudencio Cardona, Barranquilla ... L 10
1979
Feb. 17—Prudencio Cardona, Colon .... W 10
May 5—Tomas Massa, Colon, Panama ..... KO 2
Aug. 4—Maximo Rodriguez, Colon .... W disq. 6
Nov. 17—Betulio Gonzalez, Maracay .... W 15
(Won WBA Flyweight Title)
1980
Feb. 16—Tae-Shik Kim, Seoul, Korea ... KO by 2
(Lost WBA Flyweight Title)
June 1—Amado Ursua, Colon, Panama ..... W 10
Nov. 1—Modesto Gaytan, Colon, Panama KO 1

TB	KO	WD	WF	D	LD	LF	KO BY	ND	NC
23	8	12	1	0	1	0	1	0	0

TAE-SHIK KIM
Born, July 4, 1957, Kanwon-Do, Korea. Weight, 112 lbs. Height, 5 ft. 3½ in.
1977
Sept.	30—Kee-Bong Koh, Seoul .... KO by	3
Nov.	6—Kap-Chul Shin, Seoul .... W	4
Dec.	16—Yung-Shik Moon, Seoul .... KO	1
Dec.	19—Chong-Keun Kim, Seoul .... W	6
Dec.	24—Sung-Kouk Lee, Seoul .... KO	3

1978
Feb.	12—Chung-Woon Moon, Seoul .... KO	3
May	13—Mikio Uchida, Seoul .... KO	2
Oct.	3—Nobuyuki Watanabe, Seoul ...... KO	1
Nov.	18—Kriankai Yingsakdi, Seoul .... KO	2

1979
Jan.	14—Tito Abella, Pusan .... KO	5
Mar.	11—Flash Jagdon, Seoul .... KO	2
Aug.	26—William Develos, Seoul .... KO	5
Nov.	18—Riki Igarishi, Seoul .... KO	4

1980
Feb.	16—Luis Ibarra, Seoul .... KO	2
	(Won WBA Flyweight Title)	
June	29—Arnel Arrozal, Seoul .... W	15
	(Retained WBA Flyweight Title)	
Dec.	13—Peter Mathebula, Los Angeles L	15
	(Lost WBA Flyweight Title)	

TB	KO	WD	WF	D	LD	LF	KO BY	ND	NC
16	11	3	0	0	1	0	1	0	0

PETER MATHEBULA
Born, July 3, 1952, South Africa. Weight, 112 lbs. Height, 5 ft 2½ in. Managed by Albert Mthembu.
1971
July	10—Sydwell Mhlongo, Thembisa .... W	4

1972
Feb.	11—Alois Vundla, Dobsonville .... W	4
June	23—Daniel Hlahane, Dobsonville L	6
Sept.	15—William Sefefe, Dobsonville L	4

1973
Mar.	31—Joe Ngidi, Durban .... W	6

1974
Feb.	22—Esau Lekepetsi, Dobsonville ...... KO	1
May	10—Paulos Tshehla, Mamelodi .... W	4
June	29—Joe Ngidi, Durban .... KO by	4

Aug.	30—David Moyo, Orlando West .... W	6
Nov.	15—Abednigo Hlape, Orlando West ... KO	2
Feb.	21—MacDonald Mpanza, Orlando West KO	1
Apr.	25—Johannes Sithebe, Dobsonville ..... W	10
June	6—William Molatudi, Kwa-Thema .... W	10
July	11—William Matlokotsi, Orlando West KO	4
Nov.	7—Johannes Sithebe, Dobsonville ..... W	10

1976
May	1—Joe Ngidi, Durban .... KO	10
June	5—Richard Modise, Jabulani .... W	6
July	17—Leslie Pikoli, Port Elizabeth .... W	8

1977
Mar.	4—Johannes Sithebe, Pretoria .... W	12
Apr.	16—Daniel Hlahane, Johannesburg .... W	6
May	9—Joe Ngidi, Durban .... KO	7
May	21—Freddy Hernandez, Johannesburg .. L	10
Oct.	3—Blessing Vezi, Durban .... KO	1
Oct.	15—Reuben Matewu, East London .... KO	1
Nov.	28—Johannes Sithebe, Durban .... W	12

1978
Apr.	29—Johannes Sithebe, Johannesburg ... W	12
	(Won Vacant South African Flyweight Title)	
Aug.	26—Phindile Gaika, East London ..... KO	5
Dec.	4—Johannes Sithebe, Durban .... W	6

1979
Feb.	3—Leslie Pikoli, Port Elizabeth ...... KO	8
	(Won Vacant South African Bantamweight Title)	
Apr.	7—Phindile Gaika, Port Elizabeth ... KO	9
	(Retained South African Bantamweight Title)	
Sept.	7—Vincent Ngcobo, Springs .... KO	5
	(Retained South African Bantamweight Title)	
Sept.	29—Monde Mpulampula, East London KO	2
Dec.	8—Welile Nkosinkulu, East London KO by	9
	(Lost South African Bantamweight title)	

1980
Mar.	28—Godfrey Nkate, Springs .... KO	4
	(Retained South African Flyweight Title)	
Sept.	20—Johannes Sithebe, Johannesburg KO	9
	(Retained South African Flyweight Title)	
Dec.	13—Tae-Shik Kim, Los Angeles .... W	15
	(Won WBA Flyweight Title)	

TB	KO	WD	WF	D	LD	LF	KO BY	ND	NC
36	15	16	0	0	3	0	2	0	0

JUNIOR FLYWEIGHTS

FRANCO UDELLA (WBC)	*1975*	*FREDDY CASTILLO (WBC)*	*1978*
JAIME RIOS (WBA)	*1975-1976*	*NETRNOI SOR VORASINGH (WBC)*	*1978*
LUIS ESTABA (WBC)	*1975-1978*	*SUNG-JUN KIM (WBC)*	*1978-1980*
JUAN JOSE GUZMAN (WBA)	*1976*	*SHIGEO NAKAJIMA (WBC)*	*1980*
YOKO GUSHIKEN (WBA)	*1976-*	*HILARIO ZAPATA (WBC)*	*1980-*

Claimants not generally recognized are in *italics*.

WORLD JUNIOR FLYWEIGHT CHAMPIONSHIP BOUTS

‡	4/4/75	**Franco UDELLA**	107	**Valentin MARTINEZ**	106½	WF 12	2:56	San Siro Stadium, Milan, Italy	Raymond Baldeyrou
†	8/23/75	**Jaime RIOS**		**Rigoberto MARCANO**		15		Panama City, Panama	
‡	9/13/75	**Luis ESTABA**	107¾	**Rafael LOVERA**	107¼	KO 4		Caracas, Venezuela	Anselmo Escobedo
‡	12/17/75	**Luis ESTABA**	107½	**Takenobu SHIMABUKURO**	108	TKO 10	1:25	Onoyama Gymnasium, Okinawa	Anselmo Escobedo
†	1/3/76	**Jaime RIOS**	107¼	**Kazunori TENRYU**	106¾	split 15		Prefectural Gymnasium, Kagoshima	Larry Rozadilla
‡	2/14/76	**Luis ESTABA**	107¾	**Leo PALACIOS**	106	unan 15		Caracas, Venezuela	Isidoro Rodriguez
‡	5/2/76	**Luis ESTABA**		**Juan ALVAREZ**		unan 15		Caracas, Venezuela	Rafael Toro Lugo
†	7/1/76	**Juan Jose GUZMAN**		**Jaime RIOS**		split 15		Santo Domingo, Dominican Rep.	Isidro Rodriguez
‡	7/17/76	**Luis ESTABA**		**Franco UDELLA**		TKO 3		Maracay, Venezuela	Jay Edson
‡	9/26/76	**Luis ESTABA**	107¼	**Rodolfo RODRIGUEZ**	106¾	TKO 11		Caracas, Venezuela	Rafael Toro Lugo
†	10/10/76	**Yoko GUSHIKEN**	107¼	**Juan Jose GUZMAN**	107	KO 7	0:32	Yamanash University Gym, Kofu	Rudy Ortega
‡	11/21/76	**Luis ESTABA**	107½	**Valentin MARTINEZ**		TKO 11		Caracas, Venezuela	Isidoro Rodriguez
†	1/30/77	**Yoko GUSHIKEN**	107	**Jaime RIOS**	106¼	split 15		Martial Arts Hall, Tokyo, Japan	Rudy Ortega
‡	5/15/77	**Luis ESTABA**	107	**Rafael PEDROZA**	107¾	unan 15		Caracas, Venezuela	Ismael Quinones Falu
†	5/22/77	**Yoko GUSHIKEN**	107¾	**Rigoberto MARCANO**	106¾	split 15		Makomanai Ice Arena, Sapporo	Martin Denkin
‡	7/17/77	**Luis ESTABA**	107¼	**Ricardo ESTUPINAN**	108	unan 15		Puerto la Cruz, Venezuela	Jay Edson
‡	8/21/77	**Luis ESTABA**	107¼	**Juan ALVAREZ**	107½	TKO 11		Puerto la Cruz, Venezuela	Ismael Quinones Falu
‡	9/18/77	**Luis ESTABA**	107½	**Orlando HERNANDEZ**	108	TKO 15		Puerto la Cruz, Venezuela	Moises Sister
†	10/9/77	**Yoko GUSHIKEN**	107	**Montsayarm MAHACHAI**	107	TKO 4	2:17	Beppu City Spa, Oita, Japan	Yusaku Yoshida
‡	10/30/77	**Luis ESTABA**	108	**Netrnoi VORASINGH**	107½	unan 15		Nuevo Circo, Caracas, Venezuela	Anselmo Escobedo
†	1/29/78	**Yoko GUSHIKEN**	106¾	**Aniceto VARGAS**	106½	TKO 14	0:27	Aichi Prefectural Gym, Nagoya	Masao Kato
‡	2/19/78	**Freddie CASTILLO**	106½	**Luis ESTABA**	107	TKO 14	2:30	Nuevo Circo, Caracas Venezuela	Jay Edson
‡	5/6/78	**Netrnoi VORASINGH**	107¼	**Freddie CASTILLO**	108	split 15		Ourdoor Army Camp, Bangkok	Rudy Jordan
†	5/7/78	**Yoko GUSHIKEN**	108	**Jaime RIOS**	107¼	TKO 13	2:59	Hiroshima Prefectural Gymnasium	Ernesto Magana
‡	7/29/78	**Netrnoi VORASINGH**	106¾	**Luis ESTABA**	107	TKO 5	1:10	Nuevo Circo, Caracas, Venezuela	Jay Edson
‡	9/30/78	**Sung-Jun KIM**	107½	**Netrnoi VORASINGH**	107¾	KO 3	2:29	Munhwa Stadium, Seoul, Korea	Pedro Flores
†	10/15/78	**Yoko GUSHIKEN**	107¾	**Sang-Il CHUNG**	107½	KO 5	0:22	Kuramae Arena, Tokyo, Japan	Ken Morita
†	1/7/79	**Yoko GUSHIKEN**	107¾	**Rigoberto MARCANO**	107	KO 7	0:36	Municipal Gym, Kawasaki, Japan	Tony Perez
‡	3/31/79	**Sung-Jun KIM**	108	**Rey MELENDEZ**	107	draw 15		Munhwa Stadium, Seoul, Korea	Jay Edson
†	4/8/79	**Yoko GUSHIKEN**	108	**Alfonso LOPEZ**	108	TKO 7	2:47	Kuramae Arena, Tokyo, Japan	Ken Morita
‡	7/28/79	**Sung-Jun KIM**	108	**Siony CARUPO**	108	split 15		Changchung Gym, Seoul, Korea	Takeshi Shimakawa
†	7/29/79	**Yoko GUSHIKEN**	107¼	**Rafael PEDROZA**	107½	unan 15		Municipal Gymnasium, Kitakyushu	Vincent Rainone
‡	10/21/79	**Sung-Jun KIM**	107½	**Rey MELENDEZ**	105½	unan 15		Munhwa Stadium, Seoul, Korea	H. Beltini
†	10/28/79	**Yoko GUSHIKEN**	108	**Tito ABELLA**	107¼	KO 7	0:53	Kuramae Arena, Tokyo, Japan	Tomoyuki Tezaki
‡	1/3/80	**Shigeo NAKAJIMA**	107¾	**Sung-Jun KIM**	107¾	unan 15		Korakuen Hall, Tokyo, Japan	Dick Young
†	1/27/80	**Yoko GUSHIKEN**	107½	**Yong-Hyun KIM**	107½	unan 15		Prefectural Gym, Osaka, Japan	Paul Field
‡	3/24/80	**Hilario ZAPATA**	108	**Shigeo NAKAJIMA**	108	unan 15		Kuramae Arena, Tokyo, Japan	Henry Elespuro
†	6/01/80	**Yoko GUSHIKEN**	107¾	**Martin VARGAS**	107¾	TKO 8	1:42	Prefectural Gymnasium, Kochi City	Larry Hazzard
‡	6/07/80	**Hilario ZAPATA**	107½	**Chi-Bok KIM**	107	unan 15		Munhwa Gymnasium, Seoul, Korea	Richard Steele
‡	8/04/80	**Hilario ZAPATA**	108	**Hector MELENDEZ**	107¾	unan 15		Circo Nuevo, Caracas, Venezuela	Rudy Jordan
‡	9/17/80	**Hilario ZAPATA**	107¼	**Shigeo NAKAJIMA**	107¾	TKO 11	2:56	Civil Center, Gifu, Japan	Rudy Jordan
†	10/12/80	**Yoko GUSHIKEN**	107½	**Pedro FLORES**	107¾	unan 15		Jissen Memorial Arena, Kanazawa	Vincent Rainone
‡	12/01/80	**Hilario ZAPATA**	108	**Reynaldo BECERRA**	107	split 15		Circo Nuevo, Caracas, Venezuela	Richard Steele

†WBA world junior flyweight title bout ‡WBC world junior flyweight title bout *Loser failed to answer bell for round indicated

JUNIOR FLYWEIGHT DIVISION

FRANCO UDELLA
Born February 25, 1947, Cagliari, Italy. Weight, 108-112 lbs. Height, 5 ft. ½ in.
1972
Dec.   4—Ray Salami, Bologne .... W 6
Dec. 29—Mohamed Ben Salah, Cagliari .... KO 2
1973
Jan.   19—Angelo D'Aleo, Milan .... W 6
Feb.   8—Antonio Galletta, Milan .... KO by 2
Apr.   4—Grazietto Soro, Cagliari .... W 6
May   2—Antonio Galletta, Cagliari .... KO 3
May 11—Francisco Herrera, Milan .... W 6
July 12—Filippo Belvedere, Milan .... KO 5
Sept. 14—Grazietto Soro, Monza .... W 6
Sept. 28—Pedro La Tore, Milan .... KO 5
Oct. 26—Dominique Cesari, Milan .... W 10
Nov. 30—Pedro Molledo, Milan .... W 10
Dec. 28—Fernando Gabino, Cagliari .... W 8
1974
Feb.   1—Altero Marini, Milan .... LF 3
Feb. 28—Altero Marini, Cagliari .... W 8
Apr.   5—Fernando Gabino, Milan .... W 8
Apr. 19—Altero Marini, Milan .... KO 1
June 7—Rino Ferrari, Milan .... KO 5
July 20—Betulio Gonzalez,
        Lignano Sabbiadoro .... KO by 10
        (For WBC Flyweight Title)
Oct. 27—Pedro Molledo, Milan .... KO 5
        (Won European Flyweight Title)
Dec.   6—Willie Pastrana, Milan .... KO 4
1975
Feb.   1—Heriberto Mascarell, Cagliari ...... W 10
Apr.   4—Valentin Martinez, Milan .... WF 12
        (Won Vacant WBC Junior Flyweight Title)
May 31—Fritz Chervet, Zurich .... NC 2
        (Retained European Flyweight Title)
        —Stripped of WBC Junior Flyweight Title
Nov. 14—Christian Martin, Milan .... KO 6
Nov. 29—Daniel Rodriguez Figueroa,
        Cagliari .... KO 1
1976
Jan. 14—Fritz Chervet, Italy .... W 15
Mar.   5—Pee Wee Emerson, Sassari .... KO 3
Mar. 26—Jerry Strickland, Cagliari .... KO 3
Apr. 30—Jacky Bihin, Cagliari .... KO 7
June 12—Franco Sperati, Santa Teresa ... KO 8
        (Retained European Flyweight Title)
July 19—Luis Estaba, Caracas .... KO by 3
        (Lost WBC Flyweight Title)
Oct. 29—Dominique Cesari, Cagliari .... W 10
Dec.   3—Pedro Molledo, Milan .... W 10
1977
Feb.   6—Fernando Bernardez, Cagliari .... KO 4
June 10—Jose Cantero, Milan .... KO 5
        (Retained European Flyweight Title)
Aug. 21—Antonio Franca, Rijeka .... W 8
Sept. 28—Antonio Franca, Fort Village ...... W 8
Oct. 26—Nessim Zebelini, Vigevano .... KO 9
        (Retained European Flyweight Title)
Dec. 24—Emilio Pireddu, Cagliari .... W 15
        (Retained European Flyweight Title)
1978
May 24—Mariano Garcia, Cagliari .... KO 6
        (Retained European Flyweight Title)
Nov. 15—Manuel Carrasco, Bellaria .... W 15
        (Retained European Flyweight Title)
1979
May   1—Charlie Magri, London .... L 12
        (Lost European Flyweight Title)

TB	KO	WD	WF	D ·	LD	LF	KO BY	ND	NC
43	18	18	1	0	1	1	3	0	1

JAIME RIOS
Born, August 14, 1953, Panama. Weight, 108 lbs.
1973
July 28—Ramon Montenegro, Panama City KO 2

Sept.   1—Orlando Quijada, Panama City .... W 4
Oct.   6—Dionisio Palma, Panama City .... KO 2
Oct. 27—Charolito Mendez, Panama City ... W 4
Dec. 15—Jose Jimenez, Panama City .... W 8
1974
Feb. 16—Luis Cortez, Panama City .... W 8
May   4—Orlando Quijada, Panama City ... W 8
June 14—Rene Herrera, Panama City ...... KO 4
June 29—Manuel Castanedas, Panama City W 10
July 20—Andres Reyes, Panama City ...... KO 7
Aug. 31—Enrique Torres, Panama City ..... L 12
Sept. 27—Carlos Osorio, Ecuador .... D 10
Nov. 16—Orlando Hernandez, Panama City W 10
1975
Feb.   1—Dagoberto Perinan, Panama City KO 6
Mar.   8—Orlando Tejedor, Panama City .. KO 3
May 17—Kazunori Tenryu, Panama City .. KO 3
July 26—Juan Disla, Panama City .... KO 5
Aug. 23—Rigoberto Marcano, Panama City .. W 15
        (Won Vacant WBA Junior Flyweight Title)
1976
Jan.   3—Kazunori Tenryu, Tokyo .... W 15
        (Retained WBA Junior Flyweight Title)
July   2—Juan Jose Guzman, Santo Domingo L 15
        (Lost WBA Junior Flyweight Title)
1977
Jan. 30—Yoko Gushiken, Tokyo .... L 15
        (For WBA Junior Flyweight Title)
Aug.   6—Calixto Perez, Panama City .... W 10
Oct. 29—Alfredo Thomas, Panama City .... KO 4
1978
Jan. 28—Humberto Mayorga, Panama City KO 9
May   7—Yoko Gushiken, Hiroshima .... KO by 13
        (For WBA Junior Flyweight Title)

TB	KO	WD	WF	D	LD	LF	KO BY	ND	NC
25	10	10	0	1	3	0	1	0	0

LUIS ALBERTO (LUMUMBA) ESTABA
Born, August 13, 1941, Puerto la Cruz, Venezuela.
1967
Feb. 28—Pedro Garcia, Caracas, Venezuela KO 1
Mar. 17—Enrique Calatayud, Maracay ...... W 4
Apr. 15—Luis Sanchez, Maracaibo .... KO 1
Sept. 29—Fernando Cuevas, Caracas .... W 6
Nov. 18—Enrique Calatadyud, Cumana ... KO 1
1968
Jan. 22—Jesus Ferrera, Caracas .... KO 2
Sept. 13—Fernando Cuevas, Caracas .... W 8
Oct. 11—Romero Diaz, Maracaibo .... KO 3
Nov. 18—Natalio Jiminez, Caracas .... L 10
Dec. 20—Natalio Jiminez, Caracas .... W 10
1969
Mar.   1—Mario Garcia, Caracas .... KO 5
June 6—Hilario Diaz, Caracas .... W 10
June 16—Natalio Jiminez, Santo Domingo ... D 10
July 21—Carlos Zayas, San Juan .... W 10
1970
Feb.   9—Ricardo Delgado, Tijuana .... KO 9
Apr. 20—Chico Ortega, Tijuana .... KO 1
June 1—Alejandro Lopez, Tijuana .... KO 6
July 30—Henry Williams, Caracas .... KO 4
Sept. 18—Raul Noria, Caracas .... KO 5
1971
May 28—Pablo Jiminez, Caracas .... W 10
July 10—Gerardo Ferrat, Valencia, Venezuela W 10
Sept. 18—Orlando Amores, Panama City ..... L 10
1972
Aug. 26—Pablito Jiminez, Santo Domingo .... L 10
1973
Apr. 13—Carlos Osorio, Caracas .... KO 8
June 8—Gonzalo Cruz, Guayaquil, Ecuador KO 5
Sept. 28—Cesar Gonzalez, Guayaquil .... KO 8
1974
July   8—Calixto Perez, Maracaibo .... D 10

1975

Jan.	31—Arturo Patino, Caracas	KO	7
Mar.	1—Javier Valdez, Caracas	KO	8
Mar.	22—Jose Luna, Caracas	KO	3
Apr.	12—Orlando Hernandez, Caracas	KO	10
July	16—Orlando Quijada, Caracas	KO	2
Aug.	2—Calixto Perez, Caracas	KO	8
Sept.	13—Rafael Lovera, Caracas	KO	4

(Won Vacant WBC Junior Flyweight Title)

Dec.	17—Takenobu Shimabukuro, Naha ...	KO	10

(Retained WBC Junior Flyweight Title)

1976

Feb.	14—Leo Palacios, Caracas	W	15

(Retained WBC Junior Flyweight Title)

May	2—Juan Alvarez, Caracas	W	15

(Retained WBC Junior Flyweight Title)

July	17—Franco Udella, Caracas	KO	3

(Retained WBC Junior Flyweight Title)

Sept.	26—Rodolfo Rodriguez, Caracas	KO	10

(Retained WBC Junior Flyweight Title)

Nov.	21—Valentin Martinez, Caracas	KO	11

(Retained WBC Junior Flyweight Title)

1977

May	15—Rafael Pedroza, Caracas	W	15

(Retained WBC Junior Flyweight Title)

July	17—Ricardo Estupian, Puerto la Cruz ..	W	15

(Retained WBC Junior Flyweight Title)

Aug.	21—Juan Alvarez, Puerto la Cruz	KO	11

(Retained WBC Junior Flyweight Title)

Sept.	18—Orlando Hernandez, Caracas	KO	15

(Retained WBC Junior Flyweight Title)

Oct.	29—Netrnoi Sor Vorasingh, Caracas ...	W	15

(Retained WBC Junior Flyweight Title)

1978

Feb.	19—Freddy Castillo, Puerto la Cruz	KO by	14

(Lost WBC Junior Flyweight Title)

May	14—Ricardo Estupian, Caracas	W	15

(Won Central American Junior Flyweight Title)

July	30—Netrnoi Sor Vorasingh, Caracas	KO by	5

(For WBC Junior Flyweight Title)

TB	KO	WD	WF	D	LD	LF	KO BY	ND	NC
48	27	14	0	2	3	0	2	0	0

JUAN JOSE GUZMAN
Born, Dominican Republic. Weight, 108 lbs.
1969

Nov.	8—Antonio Alcala, Guadalajara	D	6

1970

	—Teo Jimenez, Guadalajara	L	10
	—Chamaco Limon, Guadalajara	KO	2

1971

	—Gilberto Reyes, Guadalajara	KO	7
	—Chango Rodriguez, Guadalajara ..	KO	8
	—Hipolito Hernandez, Guadalajara ...	L	10
	—Jose (Titino) Gonzalez, Guadalajara	W	10

1972

	—Panchito Granados, Guadalajara	L	10
Aug.	9—Vicente Pool, Merida, Yucatan	L	10
	—Teo Jimenez, Guadalajara	W	12

(Won Jalisco State Flyweight Title)

Nov.	17—Juanito Alvarez, Guadalajara	W	10

1973

Feb.	16—Jorge Padron, Guadalajara	KO	2
Mar.	23—Venancio Carvente, Guadalajara ...	W	10
	—Abundio Cortes, Guadalajara	L	10
	—Margarito Lozano, Mexico City	W	10

1974

Feb.	2—Abundio Cortes, Guadalajara	W	10
Mar.	1—Jesus Cuica, Guadalajara	W	10
Apr.	9—Martin Garcia, Tijuana	W	10
May	21—Evaristo Perez, Tijuana	W	10
July	6—Juan Garcia, Santo Domingo	KO	4
July	24—Valentin Martinez, Tijuana	KO	6
Aug.	24—Roberto Minaya, Santo Domingo ..	KO	1
Sept.	7—Juan Disla, Santo Domingo	KO	3
Nov.	20—Catalino Flores, Tijuana	KO	6

1975

Feb.	8—Juan Disla, Santo Domingo	KO	2

Feb.	22—Alberto Morales, Mexico City	L	12

(For Mexican Flyweight Title)

Mar.	23—Rocky Thompson, Culiacan	KO	5
June	16—Domingo Santana, Santo Domingo	KO	3
July	4—Francisco Marquez, Guadalajara	L	10
Aug.	6—Guty Espadas, Merida, Yucatan	KO by	2
Aug.	18—Luis A. Rosario, Santo Domingo	L	10
Dec.	13—Frank Palafox, San Juan, P.R. ...	KO	3

1976

Feb.	21—Adelaido Galindo, Mexico City	L	10
Apr.	23—Hector Medina, San Bernardino	KO by	5
May	22—Arturo Delgado, Mexico City ..	KO by	6
May	31—Anacito Vargas, San Juan, P.R. ..	KO	6
July	2—Jaime Rios, Santo Domingo	W	15

(Won WBA Junior Flyweight Title)

Oct.	10—Yoko Gushiken, Kofu, Japan ..	KO by	7

(Lost WBA Junior Flyweight Title)

Nov.	12—Antonio Avelar, Guadalajara	KO	7

1977

Mar.	25—Freddie Castillo, Guadalajara	L	10
Nov.	19—Santos Nunez, San Juan, P.R.	W	10

1978

Feb.	14—Jose Ortiz, San Juan, P.R.	L	10
May	3—Lupe Madera, Merida, Yucatan	KO by	9
July	1—Hilario Zapata, Panama City	L	10
Oct.	6—Jose Luis Cruz, Guadalajara	W	10

1979

Feb.	16—Ubaldo Gonzalez, Guamuchil ..	KO by	6

(For Mexican Flyweight Title)

Mar.	17—Alberto Morales, Mexico City	L	10
Apr.	6—Jose Luis Cruz, McAllen, Texas	KO by	2

1980

Feb.	1—Jovito Rengifo, Caracas	KO by	8
Mar.	—Ignacio Espinal, Coatzacoalcos	KO by	3
Sept.	4—Candido Tellez, Los Angeles ...	KO by	1
	—Rosendo Alonso, Guadalajara ..	KO by	5

TB	KO	WD	WF	D	LD	LF	KO BY	ND	NC
52	15	12	0	1	13	0	11	0	0

YOKO GUSHIKEN
Born, June 26, 1955, Yaeyama-Gun, Okinawa, Japan. Weight 108 lbs. Height, 5 ft. 4 in. Southpaw. Managed by Masaki Kanehira.
1974

May	28—Koichi Maki, Tokyo	W	4
Sept.	10—Koichi Maki, Okinawa	W	4
Dec.	9—Tadahiro Mihara, Tokyo	KO	5

1975

Mar.	9—Yasunobu Nitta, Okinawa	KO	4
June	29—Joe Yasuo, Okinawa	W	6
Oct.	19—Shogi Warabino, Okinawa	KO	6

1976

Jan.	23—Cesar Gomez Kee, Kawasaki	KO	7
July	16—Toshihisa Takii, Tokyo	KO	3
Oct.	10—Juan Jose Guzman, Kotu	KO	7

(Won WBA Junior Flyweight Title)

1977

Jan.	30—Jaime Rios, Tokyo	W	15

(Retained WBA Junior Flyweight Title)

May	21—Rigoberto Marcano, Sapporo	W	15

(Retained WBA Junior Flyweight Title)

Oct.	9—Montsayarm Mahachai, Beppu ..,	KO	4

(Retained WBA Junior Flyweight Title)

1978

Jan.	29—Anaceto Vargas, Nagoya	KO	14

(Retained WBA Junior Flyweight Title)

May	6—Jaime Rios, Tokyo	KO	13

(Retained WBA Junior Flyweight Title)

Aug.	14—Mak-Dong Kim, Omiya	KO	6
Oct.	15—Sang-Il Chung, Tokyo	KO	5

(Retained WBA Junior Flyweight Title)

1979

Jan.	7—Rigoberto Marcano, Kawasaki	KO	7

(Retained WBA Junior Flyweight Title)

Apr.	8—Alfonso Lopez, Tokyo	KO	7

(Retained WBA Junior Flyweight Title)

July	00—Rafael Pedroza, Kitakyushu	W	15

(Retained WBA Junior Flyweight Title)

Oct. 28—Tito Abella, Tokyo .... KO   7
      (Retained WBA Junior Flyweight Title)
                    1980
Jan. 27—Yong-Hyun Kim, Osaka .... W   15
      (Retained WBA Junior Flyweight Title)
June   1—Martin Vargas, Kochi .... KO   8
      (Retained WBA Junior Flyweight title)
Oct. 12—Pedro Flores, Kanazawa .... W   15
      (Retained WBA Junior Flyweight Title)

TB	KO	WD	WF	D	LD	LF	KO BY	ND	NC
23	15	8	0	0	0	0	0	0	0

FREDDY CASTILLO
(Rodolfo Alfredo Martinez Castillo)
Born, June 15, 1955, Merida, Yucatan, Mexico.
Weight, 108 lbs. Managed by Jorge (Fito) Jimenez.
                    1971
Sept. 22— Guty Espadas, Merida .... KO by   4
Oct. 20—Ranulfo Cano, Merida .... KO   4
      —Augustin Cruz, Tenosique .... KO   1
Dec.   1—Magallito Lozada, Merida .... W   4
                    1972
Jan. 12—Romulo Cortes, Merida L   4
Jan. 28—Miguel Camargo, Chetumal ...... KO   4
May   3—Irving Cetina, Merida .... D   6
      —Gonzalo (Zurdo) Gonzalez, Progreso W   6
Aug. 23—Chucho Loria, Merida .... D   6
Sept. 20—Lupe Madera, Merida .... W   6
                    1973
Mar. 16—Chucho Loria, Progreso .... D   6
Apr. 25—Kid Copetes, Merida .... KO   4
June   6—Babe Gil, Merida .... KO   2
June 22—Chucho Loria, Merida L   8
July 28—Kid Valente, Merida .... W   8
Aug. 20—Evelio (Zurdo) Munoz, Buctzotz .... W   6
Sept. 8—Gonzalo (Zurdo) Gonzalez, Merida .. W   8
                    1974
Mar. 23—Luis Enrique Garcia, Merida L   10
July 20—Chucho Loria, Valladolid .... KO   7
Aug. 23—Joe Mendoza, Valladolid .... KO   7
Sept. 7—"Rancherito" Fernandez, Merida .. KO   3
Oct.   5—Jose Curiel, Merida .... KO   3
                    1975
Jan. 15—Juan (Monito) Diaz, Merida ... L disq.   4
May   7—Rocky Thompson, Merida .... KO   1
July   9—Fransisco Granada, Merida ...... KO   3
Aug.   6—Juan Zarate, Merida .... W disq.   2
                    1976
Feb.   4—Freddie Hernandez, Merida ... KO by   5
Sept. 23—Arturo Delgado, Cancun .... W   10
                    1977
Jan. 15—Freddy Polanco, Acapulco .... KO   1
Feb.   4—Antonio Avelar, Guadalajara ...... W   10
Mar. 25—Juan Jose Guzman, Guadalajara ... W   10
Apr. 30—Adelaido Galindo, Merida .... KO   8
July   6—Pedro Flores, Merida .... KO   8
Aug. 13—Aureliano (Pulga) Sanchez,
      Tenosique .... KO   3
Sept. 17—Wilbert Canche, Merida .... KO   3
                    1978
Feb. 19—Luis (Lumumba) Estaba, Caracas KO   14
      (Won WBC Junior Flyweight Title)
May   6—Netrnoi Sor Vorasingh, Bangkok ... L   15
      (Lost WBC Junior Flyweight Title)
July 29—Juan Alvarez, Merida .... KO   10
                    1979
Mar.   5—Jose Gallegos, Houston L   10
Nov. 10—Ramon Soria, Buenos Aires ...... KO   5
                    1980
Feb. 10—Jimmy Fernandez, Tuxtla
      Gutierrez .... KO   4
Apr. 26—Alfonso Lopez, Merida .... KO   10
Sept. 6—Samuel Machorro, Mexico City ... KO   6
Oct. 25—Amado Ursua, Mexico City .... KO by   3
Dec. 20—Alfredo Hernandez, Merida .... W   10

TB	KO	WD	WF	D	LD	LF	KO BY	ND	NC
45	21	10	1	3	6	1	3	0	0

NETRNOI SOR VORASINGH
Born, Thailand. Weight, 108-112 lbs. Height, 5 ft.
Southpaw. Managed by Sophon Phothisophon.
                    1976
Feb. 12—Pharsrithong Singphanom,
      Bangkok .... KO by   3
June 24—Den Chai Petch-u-bul, Bangkok ... W   10
Oct. 28—Suriya Pratumvadee, Bangkok .... W   10
Nov. 26—Sang-Il Chung, Chongju .... D   12
      (For Oriental Junior Flyweight Title)
                    1977
Feb. 24—Pharsrithong Fairtex, Bangkok ... KO   7
      (Won Thai Junior Flyweight Title)
July 18—Fior Escobido, Bangkok .... KO   9
Oct. 30—Luis Estaba, Caracas L   15
      (For WBC Junior Flyweight Title)
                    1978
Feb. 18—Tito Abella, Bangkok .... KO   5
May   6—Freddie Castillo, Bangkok .... W   15
      (Won WBC Junior Flyweight Title)
July 29—Luis Estaba, Caracas .... KO   5
      (Retained WBC Junior Flyweight Title)
Sept. 30—Sung-Jun Kim, Seoul .... KO by   3
      (Lost WBC Junior Flyweight Title)
Dec.   3—Erbito Salavarria, Bangkok ...... KO   4
                    1979
Feb. 10—Seung-Hoon Lee, Bangkok .... W   12
July 15—Bernabe Villacampo, Bangkok .... KO   5
Oct. 28—Julio Rodriguez, Bangkok .... W   10
                    1980
Feb. 15—Mannaseh Base, Manila .... KO   11
July   4—Brigildo Canada, Manila .... W   10
Oct.   3—Brigildo Canada, Quezon City ... D   10
Nov. 29—Dae-Chun Park, Sakol Nakhon ... KO   5

TB	KO	WD	WF	D	LD	LF	KO BY	ND	NC
19	8	6	0	2	1	0	2	0	0

SUNG-JUN KIM
Born, June 3, 1953, Seoul, Korea. Weight, 108-112
lbs. Height, 5 ft. 5¾ in.
                    1971
Dec. 28—In-Soo Yim, Seoul L   4
                    1972
Feb.   5—In-Soo Yim, Seoul .... D   4
                    1973
                 (Inactive)
                    1974
June   6—Young-Woon Lee, Pusan .... W   4
June   7—Hak-Soo Sul, Pusan L   4
Sept. 4—Shi-Ho Kim, Taegu .... KO   5
Dec. 28—Young-Woon Lee, Seoul .... W   4
                    1975
Mar. 30—Yong-Keun Lee, Taegu .... KO   2
Apr. 19—Choon-Woo Lee, Pusan .... W   8
June   7—Little Park, Seoul L   10
July 23—Han-Soo Lee, Pusan .... KO   3
Aug. 31—Myung-Ahn Moon, Pusan .... W   10
      (Won Korean Junior Flyweight Title)
Nov. 23—Ki-Hyung Lee, Seoul .... W   10
      (Retained Korean Junior Flyweight Title)
                    1976
Jan. 25—Little Park, Pusan .... W   10
      (Retained Korean Junior Flyweight Title)
June 24—Young-Hwan Kim, Seoul .... D   8
      (Stripped of Korean Junior Flyweight Title)
Sept. 1—Ki-Hyung Lee, Seoul .... KO   4
Nov. 27—Suriya Prateumvadee, Chung-Ju KO   5
                    1977
Jan. 22—Little Park, Chung-Ju .... W   10
      (Regained Korean Junior Flyweight Title)
Feb. 15—Shoji Oguma, Tokyo L   10
Mar. 27—Mak-Dong Kim, Taegu .... W   10
      (Retained Korean Junior Flyweight Title)
Apr. 19—Kazunori Tenryu, Tokyo L   10
July 15—Yong-Hyun Kim, Pusan .... D   10
Aug. —Ryuji Iwamoto, Pusan .... W   10
Nov. 14—Demetrio Alferez, Seoul .... KO   7
Dec. 28—Kyung-Joo Ha, Seoul .... KO   5

1978

Jan. 26—Sang-Il Chung, Seoul .... W 12
(Won OPBF Junior Flyweight Title)
Mar. 25—Kazunori Tenryu, Seoul .... KO 3
(Retained OPBF Junior Flyweight Title)
Apr. 29—Francisco Teregosa, Pusan .... D 10
June 15—Eddie Carazal, Seoul .... KO 10
July 9—Sang-Il Chung, Seoul .... L 12
(Lost OPBF Junior Flyweight Title)
Sept. 30—Netrnoi Sor Vorasingh, Seoul .... KO 3
(Won WBC Junior Flyweight Title)
Nov. 30—Ric Brimbad, Seoul .... W 10

1979

Feb. 24—Peter Siscon, Seoul .... KO 4
Mar. 31—Hector Rey Melendez, Seoul .... D 15
(Retained WBC Junior Flyweight Title)
June 3—Jiro Takada, Seoul .... W 10
July 28—Siony Carupo, Seoul .... W 15
(Retained WBC Junior Flyweight Title)
Oct. 21—Hector Rey Melendez, Seoul .... W 15
(Retained WBC Junior Flyweight Title)

1980

Jan. 3—Shigeo Nakajima, Tokyo .... L 15
(Lost WBC Junior Flyweight Title)
May 9—Seung-Hoon Lee, Seoul .... L 10
June 20—Hong-Soo Yang, Seoul .... TD 6
July 28—Shoji Oguma, Tokyo .... L 15
(For World Flyweight Title)
Sept. 26—Arnel Arrozal, Seoul .... W 10

TB	KO	WD	WF	D	LD	LF	KO BY	ND	NC
41	11	15	0	6	9	0	0	0	0

SHIGEO NAKAJIMA

Born, January 18, 1954, Yuki-Gun, Ibaraki, Japan. Weight, 108 lbs. Height, 5 ft. 3½ in. Managed by Kenji Yonekura.

1976

July 12—Shigeo Maezawa, Tokyo .... KO 2
Sept. 16—Chi-Bok Kim, Pusan .... D 8
Oct. 12—Toshihiro Fujii, Tokyo .... KO 5
Dec. 14—Beaver Kajimoto, Tokyo .... W 10

1977

Apr. 2—Masayuki Kobayashi, Tokyo .... W 10
June 21—Koichi Maki, Tokyo .... W 10
Aug. 23—Kazunori Tenryu, Tokyo .... KO 3
Nov. 29—Nanasha Torayuki, Tokyo .... KO 4

1978

Jan. 24—Yukimitsu Kondo, Tokyo .... KO 3

Mar. 7—Bernabe Villacampo, Tokyo ... KO by 4
June 20—Puma Koya, Tokyo .... W 10
Aug. 29—Hwan-Chin Kim, Tokyo .... L 10

1979

Mar. 27—Rocky Sekiyama, Tokyo .... KO 7
June 12—Kobomura Tomishisa, Tokyo ..... KO 3
Nov. 6—Hong-Soo Yang, Tokyo .... W 10

1980

Jan. 3—Sung-Jun Kim, Tokyo .... W 15
(Won WBC Junior Flyweight Title)
Mar. 24—Hilario Zapata, Tokyo .... L 15
• (Lost WBC Junior Flyweight Title)
Sept. 17—Hilario Zapata, Gifu .... KO by 11
(For WBC Junior Flyweight Title)

TB	KO	WD	WF	D	LD	LF	KO BY	ND	NC
18	7	6	0	1	2	0	2	0	0

HILARIO ZAPATA

Born, August 19, 1958, Panama. Weight, 108 lbs. Height, 5 ft. 6½ in.

1977

Oct. 28—Victor Lopez, Panama City .... KO 2
Nov. 26—Cesar Becerra, Panama City ..... KO 3

1978

Mar. 4—Humberto Mayorga, Panama City W 6
Apr. 15—Alfredo Thomas, Panama City .... KO 3
July 1—Juan Jose Guzman, Panama City .. W 10
Aug. 19—Yong-Hwang Kim, Seoul, Korea ... W 10
Oct. 28—Alfonso Lopez, Panama City .... L 12
(For Latin American Junior Flyweight Title)

1979

Jan. 14—Ramon Perez, San Juan .... KO 9
Apr. 7—Nestor W. Obregon, Panama City .. W 10
June 24—Freddie Castillo, Panama City ..... W 10
Oct. 6—Jose Ricardo, Panama City .... KO 6

1980

Mar. 24—Shigeo Nakajima, Tokyo, Japan ... W 15
(Won WBC Junior Flyweight Title)
June 7—Chi-Bok Kim, Seoul, Korea .... W 15
(Retained WBC Junior Flyweight Title)
Aug. 4—Hector Rey Melendez, Caracas ..... W 15
(Retained WBC Junior Flyweight Title)
Sept. 17—Shigeo Nakajima, Tokyo, Japan .. KO 11
(Retained WBC Junior Flyweight Title)
Dec. 1—Reynaldo Becerra, Caracas .... W 15
(Retained WBC Junior Flyweight Title)

TB	KO	WD	WF	D	LD	LF	KO BY	ND	NC
16	6	9	0	0	1	0	0	0	0

A LIST OF OF BOXING'S IMMORTALS ENSHRINED IN THE HALL OF FAME

Aaron, Barney (Young) — Pioneer Group
Career: 1856-1867 — Elected 1967

TB	KO	WD	WF	D	LD	LF	KO BY	ND	NC
6	4			1	1				

Ambers, Lou — Modern Group
Career: 1932-1941 — Elected 1964

TB	KO	WD	WF	D	LD	LF	KO BY	ND	NC
102	29	59		6	6		2		

Angott, Sammy — Modern Group
Career: 1935-1950 — Elected 1973

TB	KO	WD	WF	D	LD	LF	KO BY	ND	NC
125	22	72		8	22		1		

Apostoli, Fred — Modern Group
Career: 1934-1948 — Elected 1978

TB	KO	WD	WF	D	LD	LF	KO BY	ND	NC
72	31	30	30	1	6		4		

Armstrong, Henry — Modern Group
Career: 1931-1945 — Elected 1954

TB	KO	WD	WF	D	LD	LF	KO BY	ND	NC
174	97	47		8	18	1	2	1	

Attell, Abe — Old-timers
Career: 1900-1913 — Elected 1955

TB	KO	WD	WF	D	LD	LF	KO BY	ND	NC
169	48	43	1	17	7		3	50	

Baer, Max — Modern Group
Career: 1929-1942 — Elected 1968

TB	KO	WD	WF	D	LD	LF	KO BY	ND	NC
83	52	18		8	2		3		

Basilio, Carmen — Modern Group
Career: 1948-1961 — Elected 1969

TB	KO	WD	WF	D	LD	LF	KO BY	ND	NC
79	27	29		7	14		2		

Berg, Jackie Kid — Modern Group
Career: 1924-1945 — Elected 1975

TB	KO	WD	WF	D	LD	LF	KO BY	ND	NC
197	59	89	14	9	18		8		

Berlenbach, Paul — Old-timers
Career: 1923-1933 — Elected 1971

TB	KO	WD	WF	D	LD	LF	KO BY	ND	NC
50	30	7		3	4		4	1	1

Britt, Jimmy — Old-timers
Career: 1902-1909 — Elected 1976

TB	KO	WD	WF	D	LD	LF	KO BY	ND	NC
23	3	10		1	1	2	4	2	

Britton, Jack — Modern Group
Career: 1905-1930 — Elected 1960

TB	KO	WD	WF	D	LD	LF	KO BY	ND	NC
325	21	77	1	20	25	2	1	177	1

Broughton, Jack — Pioneer Group
Career: 1729-1750 — Elected 1954

Record Not Available

Burke, James (Deaf) — Pioneer Group
Career: 1828-1843 — Elected 1966

TB	KO	WD	WF	D	LD	LF	KO BY	ND	NC
20	15			1	1	1		2	

Burns, Tommy — Old-timers
Career: 1900-1920 — Elected 1960

TB	KO	WD	WF	D	LD	LF	KO BY	ND	NC
57	35	8		8	3		2	1	

Canzoneri, Tony — Modern Group
Career: 1925-1939 — Elected 1956

TB	KO	WD	WF	D	LD	LF	KO BY	ND	NC
176	44	95		10	22	1	1	3	

Carpentier, Georges — Old-timers
Career: 1908-1926 — Elected 1964

TB	KO	WD	WF	D	LD	LF	KO BY	ND	NC
109	56	28	4	6	4	2	8	1	

Cerdan, Marcel — Modern Group
Career: 1934-1949 — Elected 1962

TB	KO	WD	WF	D	LD	LF	KO BY	ND	NC
123	74	45		1	2		1		

Chambers, Arthur — Pioneer Group
Career: 1864-1879 — Elected 1972

TB	KO	WD	WF	D	LD	LF	KO BY	ND	NC
14	9	1	2				1		

Chandler, Tom — Pioneer Group
Career: 1862-1867 — Elected 1972

TB	KO	WD	WF	D	LD	LF	KO BY	ND	NC
4	2	1		1					

Chaney, George K.O. — Old-timers
Career: 1910-1925 — Elected 1974

TB	KO	WD	WF	D	LD	LF	KO BY	ND	NC
181	86	23		3	6		8	55	

Charles, Ezzard — Modern Group
Career: 1940-1959 — Elected 1970

TB	KO	WD	WF	D	LD	LF	KO BY	ND	NC
122	58	38		1	17	1	7		

Chocolate, Kid — Modern Group
Career: 1928-1938 — Elected 1959

TB	KO	WD	WF	D	LD	LF	KO BY	ND	NC
161	64	81		6	8		2		

Choynski, Joe — Old-timers
Career: 1888-1904 — Elected 1959

TB	KO	WD	WF	D	LD	LF	KO BY	ND	NC
79	55	22	3	6	4		10	8	1

Clark, Nobby — Pioneer Group
Career: 1860-1869 — Elected 1971

TB	KO	WD	WF	D	LD	LF	KO BY	ND	NC
7	4			1				2	

Collyer, Sam — Pioneer Group
Career: 1866-1892 — Elected 1964

TB	KO	WD	WF	D	LD	LF	KO BY	ND	NC
15	9			1	4		1		

Conn, Billy — Modern Group
Career: 1935-1948 — Elected 1965

TB	KO	WD	WF	D	LD	LF	KO BY	ND	NC
74	14	49		1	8		2		

Corbett, James J. — Old-timers
Career: 1886-1903 — Elected 1954

TB	KO	WD	WF	D	LD	LF	KO BY	ND	NC
19	7	4		2	1		3	2	

Corbett, Young II — Old-timers
Career: 1897-1910 — Elected 1965

TB	KO	WD	WF	D	LD	LF	KO BY	ND	NC
104	34	19		12	6		8	25	

Coulon, Johnny — Old-timers
Career: 1905-1920 — Elected 1965

TB	KO	WD	WF	D	LD	LF	KO BY	ND	NC
97	24	32		4	2		2	32	1

Cribb, Tom — Pioneer Group
Career: 1805-1820 — Elected 1954

TB	KO	WD	WF	D	LD	LF	KO BY	ND	NC
11	10					1			

Curtis, Dick — Pioneer Group
Career: 1820-1828 — Elected 1974

TB	KO	WD	WF	D	LD	LF	KO BY	ND	NC
18	2	16							

Darcy, Les — Old-timers
Career: 1910-1916 — Elected 1957

TB	KO	WD	WF	D	LD	LF	KO BY	ND	NC
50	29	16	1	2	2				

Delaney, Jack — Old-timers
Career: 1919-1932 — Elected 1973

TB	KO	WD	WF	D	LD	LF	KO BY	ND	NC
86	42	27	1	3	7		3	2	1

Dempsey, Jack — Modern Group
Career: 1919-1940 — Elected 1954

TB	KO	WD	WF	D	LD	LF	KO BY	ND	NC
80	49	10	1	7	6		1	5	1

Dempsey, (Nonpareil) Jack — Old-timers
Career: 1883-1895 — Elected 1954

TB	KO	WD	WF	D	LD	LF	KO BY	ND	NC
68	8	42		12	1		2	3	

Dillon, Jack — Old-timers
Career: 1908-1923 — Elected 1959

TB	KO	WD	WF	D	LD	LF	KO BY	ND	NC
240	60	32		14	6			127	1

Dixon, George — Old-timers
Career: 1886-1906 — Elected 1956

TB	KO	WD	WF	D	LD	LF	KO BY	ND	NC
149	30	47	1	37	21	1	3	9	

Donnelly, Dan — Pioneer Group
Career: 1815-1819 — Elected 1960

Record Not Available

Donovan, (Prof.) Mike — Pioneer Group
Career: 1866-1891 — Elected 1970

TB	KO	WD	WF	D	LD	LF	KO BY	ND	NC
33	2	22		7				2	

Driscoll, Jem — Old-timers
Career: 1909-1919 — Elected 1956

TB	KO	WD	WF	D	LD	LF	KO BY	ND	NC
70	27	25	1	6		1		1	9

Dundee, Johnny — Modern Group
Career: 1910-1932 — Elected 1957

TB	KO	WD	WF	D	LD	LF	KO BY	ND	NC
322	19	93	1	18	29		2		160

Escobar, Sixto — Modern Group
Career: 1930-1940 — Elected 1975

TB	KO	WD	WF	D	LD	LF	KO BY	ND	NC
64	21	21		4	18				

Fields, Jackie — Old-timers
Career: 1924-1933 — Elected 1977

TB	KO	WD	WF	D	LD	LF	KO BY	ND	NC
85	28	42	1	2	8		1	2	1

Figg, James — Pioneer Group
Career: 1719-1730 — Elected 1954

TB	KO	WD	WF	D	LD	LF	KO BY	ND	NC

Record Not Available

Fitzsimmons, Bob — Old-timers
Career: 1889-1914 — Elected 1954

TB	KO	WD	WF	D	LD	LF	KO BY	ND	NC
62	32	8			2	1	8	10	1

Flowers, Tiger — Old-timers
Career: 1918-1927 — Elected 1971

TB	KO	WD	WF	D	LD	LF	KO BY	ND	NC
149	49	61	5	6	3	2	8	14	1

Frazier, Joe — Modern Group
Career: 1965-1976 — Elected 1980

TB	KO	WD	WF	D	LD	LF	KO BY	ND	NC
36	27	5				1	3		

Fullmer, Gene — Modern Group
Career: 1951-1963 — Elected 1974

TB	KO	WD	WF	D	LD	LF	KO BY	ND	NC
64	24	31		3	4		2		

Gans, Joe — Old-timers
Career: 1891-1909 — Elected 1954

TB	KO	WD	WF	D	LD	LF	KO BY	ND	NC
156	55	60	5	10	3		5	18	

Garcia, Ceferino — Modern Group
Career: 1927-1945 — Elected 1977

TB	KO	WD	WF	D	LD	LF	KO BY	ND	NC
122	62	26		9	19	1	5		

Gavilan, Kid — Modern Group
Career: 1943-1958 — Elected 1966

TB	KO	WD	WF	D	LD	LF	KO BY	ND	NC
143	27	79		6	30				1

Genaro, Frankie — Old-timers
Career: 1920-1934 — Elected 1973

TB	KO	WD	WF	D	LD	LF	KO BY	ND	NC
129	19	59	5	9	16	2	4		15

Gibbons, Mike — Old-timers
Career: 1908-1920 — Elected 1958

TB	KO	WD	WF	D	LD	LF	KO BY	ND	NC
114	35	18	1	4	2				54

Gibbons, Tom — Old-timers
Career: 1911-1925 — Elected 1963

TB	KO	WD	WF	D	LD	LF	KO BY	ND	NC
106	47	10		1	2	1	1	43	1

Goss, Joe — Pioneer Group
Career: 1859-1881 — Elected 1969

TB	KO	WD	WF	D	LD	LF	KO BY	ND	NC
15	1	5		2	4		1		

Graziano, Rocky — Modern Group
Career: 1942-1952 — Elected 1971

TB	KO	WD	WF	D	LD	LF	KO BY	ND	NC
83	52	14	1	6	7		3		

Greb, Harry — Modern Group
Career: 1913-1926 — Elected 1955

TB	KO	WD	WF	D	LD	LF	KO BY	ND	NC
294	47	64	1	3	5	1	2	170	1

Griffo, Young — Old-timers
Career: 1889-1911 — Elected 1954

TB	KO	WD	WF	D	LD	LF	KO BY	ND	NC
107	5	42	2	37	6		3	12	

Gully, John — Pioneer Group
Career: 1805-1809 — Elected 1959

TB	KO	WD	WF	D	LD	LF	KO BY	ND	NC

Record Not Available

Heenan, John C. — Pioneer Group
Career: 1860-1863 — Elected 1954

TB	KO	WD	WF	D	LD	LF	KO BY	ND	NC

Record Not Available

Herman, Pete — Old-timers
Career: 1912-1922 — Elected 1959

TB	KO	WD	WF	D	LD	LF	KO BY	ND	NC
149	19	50		8	9	1	1		61

Houck, Leo — Old-timers
Career: 1902-1926 — Elected 1969

TB	KO	WD	WF	D	LD	LF	KO BY	ND	NC
212	21	136		11	9	1			34

Hyer, Jacob — Pioneer Group
Career: 1816 (Est.) — Elected 1968

TB	KO	WD	WF	D	LD	LF	KO BY	ND	NC

Record Not Available

Hyer, Tom — Pioneer Group
Career: 1841-1849 (Est.) — Elected 1954

TB	KO	WD	WF	D	LD	LF	KO BY	ND	NC

Record Not Available

Jack, Beau — Modern Group
Career: 1940-1955 — Elected 1972

TB	KO	WD	WF	D	LD	LF	KO BY	ND	NC
111	40	43		5	20		3		

Jackson, (Gentleman) John — Pioneer Group
Career: 1788-1795 (Est.) — Elected 1954

TB	KO	WD	WF	D	LD	LF	KO BY	ND	NC

Record Not Available

Jackson, Peter — Pioneer Group
Career: 1883-1899 — Elected 1957

TB	KO	WD	WF	D	LD	LF	KO BY	ND	NC
27	12	5	1	4			3	1	1

Jeannette, Joe — Old-timers
Career: 1904-1919 — Elected 1967

TB	KO	WD	WF	D	LD	LF	KO BY	ND	NC
156	58	12	3	9	8		1		65

Jeffries, James J. — Old-timers
Career: 1896-1910 — Elected 1954

TB	KO	WD	WF	D	LD	LF	KO BY	ND	NC
21	15	3		2			1		

Jenkins, Lew — Modern Group
Career: 1934-1950 — Elected 1976

TB	KO	WD	WF	D	LD	LF	KO BY	ND	NC
109	47	18		5	27		12		

Johnson, Jack — Old-timers
Career: 1897-1928 — Elected 1954

TB	KO	WD	WF	D	LD	LF	KO BY	ND	NC
113	46	29	4	12	2	1	5		14

Ketchel, Stanley — Old-timers
Career: 1903-1918 — Elected 1954

TB	KO	WD	WF	D	LD	LF	KO BY	ND	NC
61	46	3		4	2		2		4

Kid, The Dixie — Old-timers
Career: 1899-1914 — Elected 1975

TB	KO	WD	WF	D	LD	LF	KO BY	ND	NC
126	63	13	2	6	13	2	3	23	1

Kilbane, Johnny — Old-timers
Career: 1907-1923 — Elected 1960

TB	KO	WD	WF	D	LD	LF	KO BY	ND	NC
140	21	25	1	8	2		2	80	1

Kilrain, Jake — Pioneer Group
Career: 1883-1898 — Elected 1965

TB	KO	WD	WF	D	LD	LF	KO BY	ND	NC
36	3	15		12	3		3		1

King, Tom — Pioneer Group
Career: 1860-1863 — Elected 1976

TB	KO	WD	WF	D	LD	LF	KO BY	ND	NC
5	4					1			

Klaus, Frank — Old-timers
Career: 1904-1918 — Elected 1974

TB	KO	WD	WF	D	LD	LF	KO BY	ND	NC
90	27	20	4	2	2		2		33

LaBarba, Fidel — Old-timers
Career: 1924-1933 — Elected 1972

TB	KO	WD	WF	D	LD	LF	KO BY	ND	NC
97	15	57		8	15				2

Langford, Sam — Old-timers
Career: 1902-1924 — Elected 1955

TB	KO	WD	WF	D	LD	LF	KO BY	ND	NC
250	102	25	1	31	20		5	58	1

Lavigne, George (Kid) — Old-timers
Career: 1885-1910 · Elected 1959

TB	KO	WD	WF	D	LD	LF	KO BY	ND	NC
56	16	19		8	4		2		7

Leonard, Benny — Modern Group
Career: 1911-1932 · Elected 1955

TB	KO	WD	WF	D	LD	LF	KO BY	ND	NC
210	71	18		1		1	4		115

Lesnevich, Gus — Modern Group
Career: 1934-1949 · Elected 1973

TB	KO	WD	WF	D	LD	LF	KO BY	ND	NC
76	21	36		5	9		5		

Levinsky, Battling — Old-timers
Career: 1910-1929 · Elected 1966

TB	KO	WD	WF	D	LD	LF	KO BY	ND	NC
274	23	42	1	13	13	2	4		176

Lewis, Ted (Kid) — Old-timers
Career: 1909-1929 · Elected 1964

TB	KO	WD	WF	D	LD	LF	KO BY	ND	NC
254	68	86	2	9	13	7	4		65

Louis, Joe — Modern Group
Career: 1934-1951 · Elected 1954

TB	KO	WD	WF	D	LD	LF	KO BY	ND	NC
71	54	13	1		1		2		

McAuliffe, Jack — Old-timers
Career: 1884-1914 · Elected 1954

TB	KO	WD	WF	D	LD	LF	KO BY	ND	NC
53	9	32							3

McCoy, Charles (Kid) — Old-timers
Career: 1891-1916 · Elected 1957

TB	KO	WD	WF	D	LD	LF	KO BY	ND	NC
105	55	24	2	6		2	4	9	3

McFarland, Packey — Old-timers
Career: 1904-1915 · Elected 1957

TB	KO	WD	WF	D	LD	LF	KO BY	ND	NC
104	47	17		5			1		34

McGovern, Terry — Old-timers
Career: 1897-1908 · Elected 1955

TB	KO	WD	WF	D	LD	LF	KO BY	ND	NC
77	34	24	1	4	1	1	2		10

McLarnin, Jimmy — Modern Group
Career: 1923-1936 · Elected 1956

TB	KO	WD	WF	D	LD	LF	KO BY	ND	NC
77	20	42	1	3	10		1		

Mace, Jem — Pioneer Group
Career: 1855-1890 · Elected 1954

TB	KO	WD	WF	D	LD	LF	KO BY	ND	NC
19		12		2	3		1	1	

Maher, Peter — Old-timers
Career: 1888-1908 · Elected 1978

TB	KO	WD	WF	D	LD	LF	KO BY	ND	NC
77	31	13	3	5			15		10

Marciano, Rocky — Modern Group
Career: 1947-1955 · Elected 1959

TB	KO	WD	WF	D	LD	LF	KO BY	ND	NC
49	43	6							

Maxim, Joey — Modern Group
Career: 1941-1959 · Elected 1975

TB	KO	WD	WF	D	LD	LF	KO BY	ND	NC
115	21	61	4	27	1		1		

Mendoza, Daniel — Pioneer Group
Career: 1787-1820 (Est.) · Elected 1954

TB	KO	WD	WF	D	LD	LF	KO BY	ND	NC
10		7		2			1		

Mitchell, Charley — Old-timers
Career: 1878-1894 · Elected 1957

TB	KO	WD	WF	D	LD	LF	KO BY	ND	NC
27		13		11	2		1		

Molineaux, Tom — Pioneer Group
Career: 1810-1815 · Elected 1958

TB	KO	WD	WF	D	LD	LF	KO BY	ND	NC
7		3		1	3				

Moore, Archie — Modern Group
Career: 1936-1965 · Elected 1966

TB	KO	WD	WF	D	LD	LF	KO BY	ND	NC
231	143	53		8	16	2	8		1

Moran, Owen — Old-timers
Career: 1900-1916 · Elected 1965

TB	KO	WD	WF	D	LD	LF	KO BY	ND	NC
106	25	37		6	10	5	2		21

Morrissey, John — Pioneer Group
Career: 1852-1858 (Est.) · Elected 1954

Record Not Available

Nelson, Battling — Old-timers
Career: 1896-1923 · Elected 1957

TB	KO	WD	WF	D	LD	LF	KO BY	ND	NC
132	38	20	1	19	15	2	2		35

O'Brien, (Philadelphia) Jack — Old-timers
Career: 1896-1912 · Elected 1968

TB	KO	WD	WF	D	LD	LF	KO BY	ND	NC
181	36	59	6	16	3		4		57

Papke, Billy — Old-timers
Career: 1905-1919 · Elected 1972

TB	KO	WD	WF	D	LD	LF	KO BY	ND	NC
64	29	9	1	7	6	2	1		9

Patterson, Floyd — Modern Group
Career: 1952-1972 · Elected 1976

TB	KO	WD	WF	D	LD	LF	KO BY	ND	NC
64	40	15	1	3			5		

Pep, Willie — Modern Group
Career: 1940-1966 · Elected 1963

TB	KO	WD	WF	D	LD	LF	KO BY	ND	NC
241	65	164	1	5			6		

Perez, Pascual — Modern Group
Career: 1952-1963 · Elected 1977

TB	KO	WD	WF	D	LD	LF	KO BY	ND	NC
91	56	27	1	4			3		

Petrolle, Billy — Modern Group
Career: 1924-1934 · Elected 1962

TB	KO	WD	WF	D	LD	LF	KO BY	ND	NC
157	63	22	4	10	17	3		37	1

Price, Ned — Pioneer Group
Career: 1855-1859 (Est.) · Elected 1962

Record Not Available

Richmond, Bill — Pioneer Group
Career: 1804-1818 · Elected 1956

TB	KO	WD	WF	D	LD	LF	KO BY	ND	NC
12	3	8					1		

Ritchie, Willie — Old-timers
Career: 1907-1927 · Elected 1962

TB	KO	WD	WF	D	LD	LF	KO BY	ND	NC
71	8	27	1	4	8		1		22

Robinson, Ray (Sugar) — Modern Group
Career: 1940-1965 · Elected 1967

TB	KO	WD	WF	D	LD	LF	KO BY	ND	NC
201	109	65		6	18		1	1	1

Root, Jack — Old-timers
Career: 1897-1906 · Elected 1961

TB	KO	WD	WF	D	LD	LF	KO BY	ND	NC
53	24	17	3	5			3		1

Rosenbloom, Maxie — Modern Group
Career: 1923-1939 · Elected 1972

TB	KO	WD	WF	D	LD	LF	KO BY	ND	NC
289	18	187	5	23	33	2		19	2

Ross, Barney — Modern Group
Career: 1929-1938 · Elected 1956

TB	KO	WD	WF	D	LD	LF	KO BY	ND	NC
82	24	50		3	4		1		

Ryan, Paddy — Pioneer Group
Career: 1880-1886 (Est.) · Elected 1973

Record Not Available

Ryan, Tommy — Old-timers
Career: 1887-1907 · Elected 1958

TB	KO	WD	WF	D	LD	LF	KO BY	ND	NC
109	68	17	1	5	1	1	1	6	9

Sam, Young Dutch — Pioneer Group
Career: 1825-1838 (Est.) · Elected 1975

TB	KO	WD	WF	D	LD	LF	KO BY	ND	NC
11		11							

Sayers, Tom — Pioneer Group
Career: 1849-1860 (Est.) · Elected 1954

TB	KO	WD	WF	D	LD	LF	KO BY	ND	NC
16		12		3	1				

Schmeling, Max — Modern Group
Career: 1924-1948 · Elected 1970

TB	KO	WD	WF	D	LD	LF	KO BY	ND	NC
70	38	15	3	4	5		5		

Sharkey, Jack
Career: 1924-1936 — Old-timers — Elected 1980

TB	KO	WD	WF	D	LD	LF	KO BY	ND	NC
55	15	20	3	3	8	1	4	1	

Sharkey, Tom
Career: 1893-1923 — Old-timers — Elected 1959

TB	KO	WD	WF	D	LD	LF	KO BY	ND	NC
54	37	1	2	5	3	1	2	3	

Shirai, Yoshio
Career: 1943-1955 — Modern Group — Elected 1977

TB	KO	WD	WF	D	LD	LF	KO BY	ND	NC
56	20	25	1	2	4	1	3		

Smith, Jeff
Career: 1910-1927 — Old-timers — Elected 1969

TB	KO	WD	WF	D	LD	LF	KO BY	ND	NC
178	46	51	2	3	8	1	1	65	1

Spring, Tom
Career: 1814-1824 — Pioneer Group — Elected 1961

TB	KO	WD	WF	D	LD	LF	KO BY	ND	NC
12		11				1			

Sullivan, John L.
Career: 1878-1905 — Old-timers — Elected 1954

TB	KO	WD	WF	D	LD	LF	KO BY	ND	NC
46	33	8		3			1	1	

Tendler, Lew
Career: 1913-1928 — Modern Group — Elected 1961

TB	KO	WD	WF	D	LD	LF	KO BY	ND	NC
168	37	22		2	7	3	1	95	1

Thompson, William (Bendigo)
Career: 1832-1850 — Pioneer Group — Elected 1955

TB	KO	WD	WF	D	LD	LF	KO BY	ND	NC
20	15	4				1			

Tiger, Dick
Career: 1952-1970 — Modern Group — Elected 1974

TB	KO	WD	WF	D	LD	LF	KO BY	ND	NC
81	26	35	3	16		1			

Tunney, Gene
Career: 1915-1928 — Modern Group — Elected 1955

TB	KO	WD	WF	D	LD	LF	KO BY	ND	NC
77	42	14	1	1	1			17	1

Villa, Pancho
Career: 1919-1925 — Old-timers — Elected 1961

TB	KO	WD	WF	D	LD	LF	KO BY	ND	NC
103	22	49	4	4		1		23	

Walcott, Joe (Barbados)
Career: 1890-1911 — Old-timers — Elected 1955

TB	KO	WD	WF	D	LD	LF	KO BY	ND	NC
150	34	45	2	30	17	3	4	15	

Walcott, (Jersey) Joe
Career: 1930-1953 — Modern Group — Elected 1969

TB	KO	WD	WF	D	LD	LF	KO BY	ND	NC
67	30	18	1	1	11		6		

Walker, Mickey
Career: 1919-1935 — Modern Group — Elected 1955

TB	KO	WD	WF	D	LD	LF	KO BY	ND	NC
162	60	33		4	11	3	5	45	1

Ward, Jem
Career: 1822-1831 (Est.) — Pioneer Group — Elected 1963

TB	KO	WD	WF	D	LD	LF	KO BY	ND	NC

Record Not Available

Welsh, Freddie
Career: 1905-1922 — Old-timers — Elected 1960

TB	KO	WD	WF	D	LD	LF	KO BY	ND	NC
167	24	50	3	7	3		1	79	

Wilde, Jimmy
Career: 1911-1923 — Old-timers — Elected 1959

TB	KO	WD	WF	D	LD	LF	KO BY	ND	NC
140	77	48	1	2	1		3	8	

Willard, Jess
Career: 1911-1926 — Old-timers — Elected 1977

TB	KO	WD	WF	D	LD	LF	KO BY	ND	NC
35	20	3		1	2	1	3	5	

Williams, Ike
Career: 1940-1955 — Modern Group — Elected 1978

TB	KO	WD	WF	D	LD	LF	KO BY	ND	NC
153	60	64		5	18		6		

Williams, Kid
Career: 1910-1929 — Old-timers — Elected 1970

TB	KO	WD	WF	D	LD	LF	KO BY	ND	NC
204	48	53	6	8	8	5	3	73	

Wills, Harry
Career: 1910-1932 — Old-timers — Elected 1970

TB	KO	WD	WF	D	LD	LF	KO BY	ND	NC
102	45	17		2	1	3	4	27	3

Wolgast, Ad
Career: 1906-1920 — Old-timers — Elected 1958

TB	KO	WD	WF	D	LD	LF	KO BY	ND	NC
135	38	21	1	14	6	4	2	49	

Wright, Chalky
Career: 1929-1948 — Modern Group — Elected 1976

TB	KO	WD	WF	D	LD	LF	KO BY	ND	NC
198	73	70		15	32		7	1	

Zale, Tony
Career: 1934-1948 — Modern Group — Elected 1958

TB	KO	WD	WF	D	LD	LF	KO BY	ND	NC
89	46	24		2	13		4		

Zivic, Fritzie
Career: 1931-1949 — Modern Group — Elected 1972

TB	KO	WD	WF	D	LD	LF	KO BY	ND	NC
230	80	74	1	10	61		4		

Elected for Meritorious Service to Boxing

Dan Daniel, Writer (Elected 1977)

Nat Fleischer, Editor-Writer (Elected 1975)

Tex Rickard, Promoter (Elected 1980)

Sam Taub, Announcer-Writer (Elected 1978)

THE RING'S ANNUAL RATINGS 1924 TO PRESENT

RING RATINGS
1 9 2 4

Heavyweights
1. Jack Dempsey, *Champion*
2. Harry Wills
3. Tom Gibbons
4. Charley Weinert
5. Quinton Romero Rojas
6. Jack Renault
7. Luis Angel Firpo
8. George Godfrey
9. Jim Maloney
10. Erminio Spalla

Light Heavyweights
1. Gene Tunney
2. Young Stribling
3. Kid Norfolk
4. Mike McTigue, *Champion*
5. Ad Stone
6. Jeff Smith
7. Paul Berlenbach
8. Young Marullo
9. Tommy Loughran
10. Jimmy Delaney

Middleweights
1. Harry Greb, *Champion*
2. Tiger Flowers
3. Jimmy Slattery
4. Jack Delaney
5. Johnny Wilson
6. Frankie Schoell
7. Jock Malone
8. Bert Colima
9. (Allentown) Joe Gans
10. Ted Moore

Welterweights
1. Mickey Walker, *Champion*
2. Dave Shade
3. Willie Harmon
4. Lew Tendler
5. Pete Latzo
6. Morrie Schlaiffer
7. Billy Wells
8. Jimmy Jones
9. Eddie Shevlin
10. Jack Zivic

Lightweights
1. Benny Leonard, *Champion*
2. Sid Terris
3. Sammy Mandell
4. Sid Barbarian
5. Johnny Dundee
6. Louis Vicentini
7. Tommy O'Brien
8. Charley O'Connell
9. Basil Galiano
10. Archie Walker

Junior Lightweights
1. Kid Sullivan, *Champion*
2. Jack Bernstein
3. Solly Seaman
4. Lew Paluso
5. Eddie Wagner
6. Joey Silvers
7. Mike Ballerino
8. Tony Vaccarelli
9. Johnny Leonard
10. "Pepper" Martin

Featherweights
Title Vacant
1. Louis (Kid) Kaplan
2. Babe Herman
3. Mike Dundee
4. Danny Kramer
5. Jose Lombardo
6. Bobby Garcia
7. "Red" Chapman
8. Joey Sanger
9. Ray Miller
10. Bud Ridley

Bantamweights
1. Eddie (Cannonball) Martin, *Champion*
2. Abe Goldstein
3. Bud Taylor
4. Carl Tremaine
5. Amos Carlin
6. Harold Smith
7. Pete Sarmiento
8. Vic Foley
9. Bushy Graham
10. Johnny Brown

Flyweights
1. Pancho Villa, *Champion*
2. Frankie Genaro
3. Panama Al Brown
4. Jimmy Russo
5. Tommy Milton
6. Cpl. Izzy Schwartz
7. Lew Perfetti
8. Emil Paluso
9. Young Dencio
10. Kid Wolfe

R I N G   R A T I N G S
1 9 2 5

Heavyweights
1. Jack Dempsey, *Champion*
2. Harry Wills
3. Gene Tunney
4. Jack Renault
5. Bud Gorman
6. George Godfrey
7. Jack Sharkey
8. Bob Fitzsimmons
9. Paolino Uzcudun
10. Jim Maloney
11. Harry Persson
12. King Solomon
13. Johnny Risko
14. Ray Neuman
15. Jim Keeley

Light Heavyweights
1. Paul Berlenbach, *Champion*
2. Jack Delaney
3. Mike McTigue
4. Young Stribling
5. Eddie Huffman
6. Ad Stone
7. Tommy Loughran
8. Jimmy Delaney
9. Jimmy Slattery
10. Maxie Rosenbloom
11. Yale Okun
12. Young Marullo
13. "Hambone" Kelly
14. Ernie Owens
15. Murray Gitlitz

Middleweights
1. Harry Greb, *Champion*
2. Dave Shade
3. Tiger Flowers
4. Leo Lomski
5. (Allentown) Joe Gans
6. K. O. Phil Kaplan
7. Frank Moody
8. Jock Malone
9. Roland Todd
10. Bert Colima
11. Art Weigand
12. Ted Moore
13. Frank Campbell
14. Bob Sage
15. Bruno Frattini

Welterweights
1. Mickey Walker, *Champion*
2. Tommy Milligan
3. Jack Zivic
4. Joe Dundee
5. Georgie Ward
6. Willie Harmon
7. Sailor Friedman
8. (Mushy) Callahan
9. Frankie Schoell
10. Jack McVey
11. Billy Wells
12. Pete Latzo
13. Sgt. Sammy Baker
14. Lew Tendler
15. Al Mello

Lightweights
1. Sammy Mandell
2. Sid Terris
3. Rocky Kansas, *Champion*
4. Jimmy Goodrich
5. Solly Seaman
6. Luis Vicentini
7. Phil McGraw
8. Stanislaus Loayza
9. Jack Bernstein
10. Harry Felix
11. Ace Hudkins
12. Tommy O'Brien
13. Lucien Vinez
14. Tommy (Kid) Murphy
15. Alf Mancini

Junior Lightweights
1. Tod Morgan, *Champion*
2. Joe Glick
3. Mike Dundee
4. Honeyboy Finnegan
5. Johnny Drew
6. Ruby Goldstein
7. Lew Mayrs
8. George Balduc
9. Joe Celmars
10. Carl Duane
11. Babe Ruth
12. Jackie Fields
13. Tony Vaccarelli
14. Mike Ballerino
15. Joey Kaufman

Featherweights
1. Louis (Kid) Kaplan, *Champion*
2. Babe Herman
3. Jimmy McLarnin
4. Bobby Garcia
5. Benny Bass
6. Red Chapman
7. Ray Miller
8. Danny Kramer
9. Eddie Anderson
10. Kid Roy
11. Eddie Shea
12. Petey Mack
13. Lew Hurley
14. Edouard Mascart
15. Benny Geishe

Bantamweights
1. Chick Suggs
2. Bushy Graham
3. Bud Taylor
4. Charley Phil Rosenberg, *Champion*
5. Pete Sarmiento
6. Andy Martin
7. Archie Bell
8. Carl Tremaine
9. Dixie La Hood
10. Johnny Brown
11. Amos Carlin
12. Vic Burrone
13. Abe Goldstein
14. Joe Lynch
15. Sencio Moldez

Flyweights
Title Vacant
1. Fidel La Barba
2. Frankie Genaro
3. Newsboy Brown
4. Cpl. Izzy Schwartz
5. Panama Al Brown
6. Black Bill
7. Willie Davies
8. Ernie Jarvis
9. Joey Ross
10. Tommy Milton
11. Johnny Breslin
12. Willie La Morte
13. Elky Clarke
14. Emil Paluso
15. Dave Adelman

R I N G   R A T I N G S
1 9 2 6

Heavyweights
1. Gene Tunney, *Champion*
2. Jack Dempsey
3. Jack Sharkey
4. Jim Maloney
5. Paolino Uzcudun
6. Harry Wills
7. Jack Renault
8. Harry Jerrson
9. Knute Hanson
10. Johnny Risko
11. Sully Montgomery
12. Sandy Seifert
13. Jack De Mave
14. Monte Munn
15. Artie De Kuh

Light Heavyweights
1. Jack Delaney, *Champion*
2. Paul Berlenbach
3. Tommy Loughran
4. Mike McTigue
5. Young Stribling
6. Jimmy Slattery
7. Eddie Huffman
8. Yale Okun
9. Martin Burke
10. Art Wiegand
11. Jimmy Delaney
12. Pat McCarthy
13. Earl Blue
14. Young Marullo
15. Matt Adgie

Middleweights
1. Tiger Flowers
2. Mickey Walker, *Champion*
3. Maxie Rosenbloom
4. K. O. Phil Kaplan
5. George Courtney
6. Dave Shade
7. Joe Anderson
8. Leo Lomski
9. Tommy Milligan
10. Osk Till
11. Frankie Schoell
12. (Allentown) Joe Gans
13. Jock Malone
14. Joe Roche
15. Jack Willis

Welterweights
1. Pete Latzo, *Champion*
2. Joe Dundee
3. Eddie Roberts
4. Tommy Freeman
5. Georgie Ward
6. Al Mello
7. Jack McVey
8. Ace Hudkins
9. Mushy Callahan
10. Andy Divodi
11. Willie Harmon
12. Jack Hood
13. Sammy Baker
14. Jack Zivic
15. Meyer Cohen

Lightweights
1. Sammy Mandell, *Champion*
2. Sid Terris
3. Billy Wallace
4. Stanislaus Loayza
5. Phil McGraw
6. Louis (Kid) Kaplan
7. Billy Petrolle
8. Baby Joe Gans
9. Jackie Fields
10. Bruce Flowers
11. Spug Myers
12. Tommy Herman
13. Sid Barbarian
14. Young Harry Wills
15. Young Jack Thompson

Junior Lightweights
1. Tod Morgan, *Champion*
2. Jack Bernstein
3. Babe Herman
4. Carl Duane
5. Al Winkler
6. Joe Glick
7. Ray Miller
8. Johnny Drew
9. Mike Dundee
10. Jackie Snyder
11. Bobby Garcia
12. Lew Mayrs
13. Frankie Fink
14. Doc Snell
15. Young Datto

Featherweights
Title Vacant
1. Honeyboy Finnegan
2. Benny Bass
3. Chick Suggs
4. Red Chapman
5. Joey Sanger
6. Andre Routis
7. Eddie Shea
8. Johnny Farr
9. Andy Martin
10. Johnny Hill
11. Sammy Fuller
12. Sammy Dorfman
13. Eddie Anderson
14. Al Foreman
15. Lew Hurley

Bantamweights
1. Charley Phil Rosenberg, *Champion*
2. Tony Canzoneri
3. Bushy Graham
4. Bud Taylor
5. Johnny Green
6. Panama Al Brown
7. Chuck Hellman
8. Davey Abad
9. Dixie La Hood
10. Archie Bell
11. Pete Sarmiento
12. Teddy Baldock
13. Vic Burrone
14. Dominick Petrone
15. Tommy Ryan

Flyweights
Title Vacant
1. Fidel La Barba
2. Elky Clarke
3. Frankie Genaro
4. Newsboy Brown
5. Willie Davies
6. Cpl. Izzy Schwartz
7. Alex Burley
8. Ernie Jarvis
9. Black Bill
10. Joey Ross
11. Harry Goldstein
12. Dave Adelman
13. Ernie Peters
14. Blas Rodriguez
15. Routier Parra

RING RATINGS
1 9 2 7

Heavyweights
1. Gene Tunney, *Champion*
2. Jack Dempsey
3. Jack Sharkey
4. Tom Henney
5. Johnny Risko
6. Paolino Uzcudun
7. Jack Delaney
8. Vittorio Campolo
9. George Godfrey
10. Knute Hanson
11. Jack Dorval
12. Jack Renault
13. Arthur De Kuh
14. Phil Scott
15. George Cook

Light Heavyweights
1. Tommy Loughran, *Champion*
2. Leo Lomski
3. Jimmy Slattery
4. Mike McTigue
5. Yale Okun
6. Young Stribling
7. Martin Burke
8. Joe Sekyra
9. Armand Emmanuel
10. Roleux Saguero
11. Sunny Jim Williams
12. George Manley
13. Battling Levinsky
14. Jimmy Braddock
15. Otto Van Porat

Middleweights
1. Mickey Walker, *Champion*
2. Tiger Flowers
3. Dave Shade
4. George Courtney
5. Jack McVey
6. Maxie Rosenbloom
7. K. O. Phil Kaplan
8. Joe Anderson
9. Tommy Milligan
10. Pete Latzo
11. Babe McGorgary
12. Harry Ebbetts
13. Cowboy Jack Wills
14. Rene De Vos
15. Osk Till

Welterweights
1. Joe Dundee, *Champion*
2. Sgt. Sammy Baker
3. Ace Hudkins
4. Tommy Freeman
5. Hilario Martinez
6. Jack Hood
7. Clyde Hull
8. Farmer Joe Cooper
9. Alf Mancini
10. Eddie Roberts
11. Willie Harmon
12. Lew Tendler
13. Vince Dundee
14. Arturo Shekels
15. Johnny Indrasano

Lightweights
1. Sammy Mandell, *Champion*
2. Jimmy McLarnin
3. Sid Terris
4. Billy Wallace
5. Bruce Flowers
6. Lope Tenario
7. Louis (Kid) Kaplan
8. Billy Petrolle
9. Phil McGraw
10. Lew Paluso
11. Tommy Cello
12. Baby Joe Gans
13. Joey Kaufman
14. Doc Snell
15. Al Winkler

Junior Lightweights
1. Tod Morgan, *Champion*
2. Honeyboy Finnegan
3. Joe Glick
4. Mike Dundee
5. Ray Miller
5. Jack Bernstein
7. Babe Herman
8. Young Johnny Dado
9. Pedro Amador
10. Johnny Drew
11. Billy Grimes
12. Leo Kid Roy
13. Frankie Fink
14. Bobby Garcia
15. Al Winkler

Featherweights
1. Tony Canzoneri
2. Benny Bass, *Champion*
3. Joey Sangor
4. Andy Martin
5. Red Chapman
6. Harry Blitman
7. Sammy Dorfman
8. Ignatio Fernandez
9. Lew Perfetti
10. Dominick Petrone
11. Santiago Zorilla
12. Charley Phil Rosenberg
13. (Cannonball) Eddie Martin
14. Johnny Cuthbert
15. Chick Suggs

Bantamweights
Title Vacant
1. Bud Taylor
2. Kid Francis
3. Archie Bell
4. Panama Al Brown
5. Willie Smith
6. Teddy Baldock
7. Joey Rychell
8. Johnny Vacca
9. Vic Foley
10. Young Nationalista
11. Chuck Hellman
12. Midget Mike O'Dowd
13. Johnny Green
14. Benny Schwartz
15. Emil Paluso

Flyweights
Title Vacant
1. Cpl. Izzy Schwartz
2. Frenchy Belanger
3. Spedy Dado
4. Johnny Hill
5. Frankie Genaro
6. Newsboy Brown
7. Johnny McCoy
8. Billy Kelly
9. Willie Davies
10. Ernie Jarvis
11. Petit Biquet
12. Spider Pladner
13. Alex Burley
14. Blas Rodriguez
15. Black Bill

R I N G R A T I N G S
1 9 2 8

Heavyweights
Title Vacant
1. Young Stribling
2. George Godfrey
3. Paolino Uzcudun
4. Jack Sharkey
5. Knute Hanson
6. Jim Maloney
7. Johnny Risko
8. Phil Scott
9. Tom Heeney
10. Otto Von Porat

Light Heavyweights
1. Tommy Loughran, *Champion*
2. Jimmy Braddock
3. Leo Lomski
4. Jimmy Slattery
5. Jack Delaney
6. Tuffy Griffith
7. Maxie Rosenbloom
8. Cuban Bobby Brown
9. Tiger Jack Payne
10. Pete Latzo

Middleweights
1. Mickey Walker, *Champion*
2. Rene De Vos
3. George Courtney
4. Dave Shade
5. K. O. Phil Kaplan
6. Jack McVey
7. Frankie Schoell
8. Ace Hudkins
9. Harry Ebbets
10. Jack Willis

Welterweights
1. Joe Dundee, *Champion*
2. Jackie Fields
3. Young Jack Thompson
4. Al Mello
5. Gorilla Jones
6. Tommy Freeman
7. Jack Hood
8. Billy Light
9. Farmer Joe Cooper
10. Sammy Baker

Junior Welterweights
1. Mushy Callahan, *Champion*
2. Ruby Goldstein
3. Jimmy Goodrich
4. Jackie Brady
5. Sam Bruce
6. Freddy Mueller
7. Paul Pirrone
8. Harry Wallach
9. Tommy Kid Murphy
10. Freddy Fitzgerald

Lightweights
1. Sammy Mandell, *Champion*
2. Ray Miller
3. Joe Glick
4. Baby Joe Gans
5. King Tut
6. Joe Medill
7. Billy Wallace
8. Billy Petrolle
9. Jack Kid Berg
10. Manuel Quintero

Junior Lightweights
1. Tod Morgan, *Champion*
2. Honeyboy Finnegan
3. Davey Abad
4. Tony Canzoneri
5. (Cannonball) Eddie Martin
6. Al Foreman
7. Wildcat Carter
8. Mike Dundee
9. Sammy Dorfman
10. Eddie Anderson

Featherweights
1. Andre Routis, *Champion*
2. Benny Bass
3. Santiago Zorilla
4. Joey Sangor
5. Pete Nebo
6. Eddie Shea
7. Harry Blitman
8. Al Singer
9. Bud Taylor
10. Rosey Stoy

Bantamweights
Title Vacant
1. Bushy Graham
2. Fidel La Barba
3. Al Brown
4. Kid Francis
5. Kid Chocolate
6. Joe Scalfaro
7. Teddy Baldock
8. Archie Bell
9. Young Nationalista
10. Kid Pattenden

Flyweights
1. Cpl. Izzy Schwartz, *Champion*
2. Frankie Genaro
3. Johnny Hill
4. Steve Rocco
5. Newsboy Brown
6. Phil Tobias
7. Willie Davies
8. Emile (Spider) Pladner
9. Midget Wolgast
10. Ernie Peters

R I N G   R A T I N G S
1 9 2 9

Heavyweights
Title Vacant
1. Jack Sharkey
2. Max Schmeling
3. George Godfrey
4. Tuffy Griffiths
5. Phil Scott
6. Otto Von Porat
7. Young Stribling
8. Johnny Risko
9. Primo Carnera
10. Vittorio Campolo

Light Heavyweights
Title Vacant

1. Maxie Rosenbloom
2. Jimmy Slattery
3. Lou Scozza
4. Larry Johnson
5. Leo Lomski
6. George Courtney
7. Charley Belanger
8. George Manley
9. Fred Lenhart
10. Yale Okun

Middleweights
World Champion
Mickey Walker
1. Rene De Vos
2. Dave Shade
3. Harry Ebbets
4. Ace Hudkins
5. Doc Conrad
6. Len Harvey
7. Harry Smith
8. Johnny Burns
9. Haakon Hansen
10. Jack McVey

Welterweights
World Champion
Jackie Fields
1. Jimmy McLarnin
2. Young Corbett
3. Gorilla Jones
4. Tommy Greeman
5. Vince Dundee
6. Young Jack Thompson
7. Jack Hood
8. Canada Lee
9. Sammy Baker
10. My Sullivan

Junior Welterweights
World Champion
Mushy Callahan
1. Baby Joe Gans
2. Ruby Goldstein
3. Manuel Quintero
4. Freddy Fitzgerald
5. Stanislaus Loayza
6. Eddie Murdock
7. Harry Kid Brown
8. Jackie Brady
9. Joe Trippe
10. Joe Glick

Lightweights
World Champion
Sammy Mandell
1. Tony Canzoneri
2. Jack Kid Berg
3. Louis Kid Kaplan
4. Billy Wallace
5. Johnny Jadick
6. King Tut
7. Al Singer
8. Bruce Flowers
9. Andy Callahan
10. Tommy Grogan

Junior Lightweights
World Champion
Benny Bass
1. Eddie Mack
2. Sammy Fuller
3. Tod Morgan
4. Cecil Payne
5. Pete Nebo
6. Sammy Dorfman
7. Johnny Farr
8. Mickey Cohen
9. Al Ridgeway
10. Roger Bernard

Featherweights
World Champion
Battling Battalino
1. Kid Chocolate
2. Earl Mastro
3. Freddy Miller
4. Lew Massey
5. Bud Taylor
6. Johnny Datto
7. Eddie Shea
8. Fidel La Barba
9. Nel Tarleton
10. Andy Martin

Bantamweights
Title Vacant

1. Bushy Graham
2. Panama Al Brown
3. Kid Francis
4. Tommy Paul
5. Teddy Baldock
6. Pete Sanstrol
7. Vidal Gregario
8. Archie Bell
9. Emile (Spider) Pladner
10. Joe Scalfaro

Flyweights
Title Vacant

1. Black Bill
2. Midget Wolgast
3. Willie Davies
4. Frankie Genaro
5. Willie La Morte
6. Steve Rocco
7. Phil Tobias
8. Pablo Dano
9. Johnny McCoy
10. Ruby Bradley

R I N G   R A T I N G S
1 9 3 0

Heavyweights
World Champion
Max Schmeling
1. Jack Sharkey
2. Ernie Schaaf
3. Primo Carnera
4. King Levinsky
5. Mickey Walker
6. Tommy Loughran
7. Young Stribling
8. Stanley Poreda
9. Tuffy Griffiths
10. Max Baer

Light Heavyweights
World Champion
Maxie Rosenbloom
1. Billy Jones
2. Dave Maier
3. Lew Scozza
4. George Courtney
5. George Manley
6. Al Gainer
7. Bob Olin
8. Larry Johnson
9. Battling Bozo
10. Joe Knight

Middleweights
Title Vacant
1. Dave Shade
2. Marcel Thil
3. Vince Dundee
4. Young Terry
5. Ben Jeby
6. Harry Smith
7. Gorilla Jones
8. Frank Battaglia
9. Chic Devin
10. Paul Pirrone

Welterweights
World Champion
Lou Brouillard
1. Baby Joe Gans
2. Jimmy McLarnin
3. Young Corbett
4. Jackie Fields
5. King Tut
6. Billy Townsend
7. Franta Nekolny
8. Paulie Walker
9. Jimmy Belmont
10. Teddy Yarosz

Junior Welterweights
World Champion
Jack Kid Berg
1. Billy Petrolle
2. Tony Herrera
3. Manuel Quintero
4. Jack Portney
5. Andy Callahan
6. Steve Haliako
7. Pat Igo
8. Mickey Cohen
9. Eddie Kid Wolfe
10. Louis Kid Kaplan

Lightweights
World Champion
Tony Canzoneri
1. Battling Battalino
2. Kid Chocolate
3. Billy Petrolle
4. Ray Miller
5. Billy Wallace
6. Battling Gizzy
7. Sammy Dorfman
8. Wesley Ramey
9. Johnny Jadick
10. Bobby Pacho

Junior Lightweights
World Champion
Kid Chocolate
1. Benny Bass
2. Al Forman
3. Roger Bernard
4. Freddy Miller
5. Andy Martin
6. Petey Sarron
7. Joey Costa
8. Joe Ghnouly
9. Lew Feldman
10. Ernie Mandell

Featherweights
World Champion
Battling Battalino
1. Earl Mastro
2. Fidel La Barba
3. Kid Francis
4. Eddie Shea
5. Tommy Paul
6. Claude Varner
7. Nel Tarleton
8. Johnny Pena
9. Frankie Wallace
10. Varias Milling

Bantamweights
World Champion
Panama Al Brown
1. Newsboy Brown
2. Pete Sanstol
3. Eugene Huat
4. Antol Kocsis
5. Vidal Gregario
6. Emile (Spider) Pladner
7. Moss Butch
8. Archie Bell
9. Ross Fields
10. Bobby Leitham

Flyweights
Title Vacant
1. Midget Wolgast
2. Young Perez
3. Jackie Brown
4. Marianna Arilla
5. Phil Tobias
6. Speedy Dado
7. Young Pancho
8. Valentin Anglemann
9. Babe Triscaro
10. Johnny Goodrich

RING RATINGS
1 9 3 1

Heavyweights
World Champion
Max Schmeling
1. Jack Sharkey
2. Ernie Schaaf
3. Primo Carnera
4. King Levinsky
5. Mickey Walker
6. Tommy Loughran
7. Young Stribling
8. Stanley Poreda
9. Tuffy Griffiths
10. Max Baer

Light Heavyweights
World Champion
Maxie Rosenbloom
1. Billy Jones
2. Dave Maier
3. Lew Scozza
4. George Courtney
5. George Manley
6. Al Gainer
7. Bob Olin
8. Larry Johnson
9. Battling Bozo
10. Joe Knight

Middleweights
Title Vacant
1. Dave Shade
2. Marcel Thil
3. Vince Dundee
4. Young Terry
5. Ben Jeby
6. Harry Smith
7. Gorilla Jones
8. Frank Battaglia
9. Chic Devlin
10. Paul Pirrone

Welterweights
World Champion
Lou Brouillard
1. Baby Joe Gans
2. Jimmy McLarnin
3. Young Corbett
4. Jackie Fields
5. King Tut
6. Billy Townsend
7. Franta Nekolny
8. Paulie Walker
9. Jimmy Belmont
10. Teddy Yarosz

Junior Welterweights
World Champion
Jack Kid Berg
1. Billy Petrolle
2. Tony Herrera
3. Manuel Quintero
4. Jack Portney
5. Andy Callahan
6. Steve Haliako
7. Pat Igo
8. Mickey Cohen
9. Eddie Kid Wolfe
10. Louis Kid Kaplan

Lightweights
World Champion
Tony Canzoneri
1. Battling Battalino
2. Kid Chocolate
3. Billy Petrolle
4. Ray Miller
5. Billy Wallace
6. Battling Gizzy
7. Sammy Dorfman
8. Wesley Ramey
9. Johnny Jadick
10. Bobby Pacho

Junior Lightweights
World Champion
Kid Chocolate
1. Benny Bass
2. Al Forman
3. Roger Bernard
4. Freddie Miller
5. Andy Martin
6. Petey Sarron
7. Joey Costa
8. Joe Ghnouly
9. Lew Feldman
10. Ernie Mandell

Featherweights
World Champion
Battling Battalino
1. Earl Mastro
2. Fidel La Barba
3. Kid Francis
4. Eddie Shea
5. Tommy Paul
6. Claude Varner
7. Nel Tarleton
8. Johnny Pena
9. Frankie Wallace
10. Varias Milling

Bantamweights
World Champion
Panama Al Brown
1. Newsboy Brown
2. Pete Sanstol
3. Eugene Huat
4. Antol Kocsis
5. Vidal Gregario
6. Emile (Spider) Pladner
7. Moss Butch
8. Archie Bell
9. Ross Fields
10. Bobby Leitham

Flyweights
Title Vacant
1. Midget Wolgast
2. Young Perez
3. Jackie Brown
4. Marianna Arilla
5. Phil Tobias
6. Speedy Dado
7. Young Pancho
8. Valentin Anglemann
9. Babe Triscaro
10. Johnny Goodrich

RING RATINGS
1 9 3 2

Heavyweights
World Champion
Jack Sharkey
1. Max Schmeling
2. Max Baer
3. Stanley Poreda
4. Primo Carnera
5. Ernie Schaaf
6. Johnny Risko
7. King Levinsky
8. Walter Neusel
9. Larry Gains
10. Unknown Winston

Light Heavyweights
World Champion
Maxie Rosenbloom
1. Adolph Heuser
2. Joe Knight
3. Bob Godwin
4. John Henry Lewis
5. Al Gainer
6. Billy Jonew
7. Norman Conrad
8. Lew Scozza
9. Wesley Ketchell
10. Ham Jenkins

Middleweights
World Champion
Marcel Thil
1. Frank Battaglia
2. Vince Dundee
3. Dave Shade
4. Sammy Slaughter
5. Ben Jeby
6. Gorilla Jones
7. Chick Devlin
8. Marty Sampson
9. Jimmy Smith
10. Enzo Fiermonte

Welterweights
World Champion
Jackie Fields
1. Jimmy McLarnin
2. Young Corbett
3. Andy Callahan
4. Johnny Indrisano
5. Baby Joe Gans
6. Teddy Yarosz
7. Eddie Kid Wolfe
8. Lou Brouillard
9. Paulie Walker
10. Bep Van Klaveren

Lightweights
World Champion
Tony Canzoneri
1. Johnny Jadick
2. Sammy Fuller
3. Barney Ross
4. Benny Bass
5. Tracey Cox
6. Eddie Cool
7. Lew Massey
8. Wesley Ramey
9. Tony Herrera
10. Bobby Pacho

Featherweights
World Champion
Kid Chocolate
1. Fidel La Barba
2. Seaman Watson
3. Baby Arizmendi
4. Lew Feldman
5. Nel Tarleton
6. Varias Milling
7. Eddie Shea
8. Tommy Paul
9. Albert Ladou
10. Paul Dazzo

Bantamweights
World Champion
Panama Al Brown
1. Speedy Dado
2. Pete Sanstol
3. Newsboy Brown
4. Young Casanova
5. Young Tommy
6. Eugene Huat
7. Jimmy Thomas
8. Johnny King
9. Willie Davies
10. Bobby Leitham

Flyweights
Title Vacant
1. Midget Wolgast
2. Jackie Brown
3. Little Pancho
4. Mickey McGuire
5. Babe Triscaro
6. Phil Tobias
7. Valentin Anglemann
8. Praxille Gyde
9. Jose Arilla
10. Maurice Huguenin

RING RATINGS
1 9 3 3

Heavyweights
World Champion
Primo Carnera
1. Max Baer
2. Tommy Loughran
3. King Levinsky
4. Max Schmeling
5. Don McCorkindale
6. Patsy Perroni
7. Walter Neusel
8. Charley Massare
9. Steve Hamas
10. Lee Ramage

Light Heavyweights
World Champion
Maxie Rosenbloom
1. John Henry Lewis
2. Tony Shucco
3. Joe Knight
4. Bob Olin
5. Bob Godwin
6. Clyde Chastain
7. Young Firpo
8. Al Gainer
9. Lou Brouillard
10. Mickey Walker

Middleweights
World Champion
Marcel Thil
1. Vince Dundee
2. Teddy Yarosz
3. Gorilla Jones
4. Jimmy Smith
5. Young Terry
6. Ben Jeby
7. Dave Shade
8. Len Harvey
9. Kid Tunero
10. Frank Battaglia

Welterweights
World Champion
Jimmy McLarnin
1. Billy Petrolle
2. Bep Van Klaveren
3. Cerefino Garcia
4. Kid Azteca
5. Eddie Kid Wolfe
6. Jimmy Leto
7. Tony Herrera
8. Baby Joe Gans
9. Andy Callahan
10. Billy Hogan

Lightweights
World Champion
Barney Ross
1. Tony Canzoneri
2. Young Peter Jackson
3. Wesley Ramey
4. Sammy Fuller
5. Benny Bass
6. Eddie Cool
7. Frankie Klick
8. Johnny Jadick
9. Lew Ambers
10. Joe Ghnouly

Featherweights
World Champion
Kid Chocolate
1. Seaman Watson
2. Freddy Miller
3. Frankie Wallace
4. Baby Arizmendi
5. George Hansford
6. Tommy Paul
7. Petey Hayes
8. Lew Feldman
9. Jackie Wilson
10. Petey Sarron

Bantamweights
World Champion
Panama Al Brown
1. Young Casanova
2. Pete Sanstol
3. Lew Farber
4. Speedy Dado
5. Young Tommy
6. Little Pancho
7. Star Frisco
8. Joe Tei Ken
9. Bobby Leitham
10. Ernie Maurer

Flyweights
Title Vacant
1. Midget Wolgast
2. Jackie Brown
3. Valentin Anglemann
4. Ginger Foran
5. Mickey McGuire
6. Maurice Huguenin
7. Praxille Gyde
8. Tom Pardoe
9. Ellis Ashurst
10. Tommy Steele

RING RATINGS
1 9 3 4

Heavyweights
World Champion
Max Baer
1. Steve Hamas
2. Primo Carnera
3. Art Lasky
4. Max Schmeling
5. King Levinsky
6. Patsy Perroni
7. Jack Peterson
8. Natie Brown
9. Joe Louis
10. Lee Ramage

Light Heavyweights
World Champion
Bob Olin
1. Maxie Rosenbloom
2. Tony Shucco
3. Joe Knight
4. John Henry Lewis
5. Lou Brouillard
6. Ambrose Palmer
7. Al Gainer
8. Johnny Miler
9. Fred Lenhart
10. Al McCoy

Middleweights
World Champion
Marcel Thil
1. Teddy Yarosz
2. Paul Pirrone
3. Young Corbett
4. Oscar Rankins
5. Crmelo Candel
6. Jock McAvoy
7. Vince Dundee
8. Fred Henneberry
9. Freddie Steele
10. Lou Halper

Welterweights
World Champion
Jimmy McLarnin
1. Kid Azteca
2. Bep Van Klaveren
3. Harry Dublinsky
4. Cerefino Garcia
5. Eddie Kid Wolfe
6. Bobby Pacho
7. Tony Falco
8. Willard Brown
9. Werther Arcelli
10. Andy Callahan

Lightweights
World Champion
Barney Ross
1. Tony Canzoneri
2. Frankie Klick
3. Young Peter Jackson
4. Sammy Fuller
5. Tiger Humery
6. Cleto Locatelli
7. Lew Ambers
8. Eddie Cool
9. Lew Massey
10. Tracey Cox

Featherweights
World Champion
Freddie Miller
1. Baby Arizmendi
2. Mike Belloise
3. Petey Hayes
4. Nel Tarleton
5. Petey Sarron
6. Henry Armstrong
7. Merv Blandon
8. Johnny Pena
9. Jackie Wilson
10. Maurice Holtzer

Bantamweights
World Champion
Panama Al Brown
1. Sixto Escobar
2. Young Tommy
3. Pablo Dano
4. Lou Salica
5. Speedy Dado
6. Star Frisco
7. Baby Quintana
8. Little Pancho
9. Henry Moreno
10. Joe Tei Ken

Flyweights
Title Vacant
1. Midget Wolgast
2. Jackie Brown
3. Benny Lynch
4. Maurice Huguenin
5. Valentin Anglemann
6. Joe Mendiola
7. Bobby McGhee
8. Young Siki
9. Tommy Pardoe
10. Phil Milligan

R I N G   R A T I N G S
1 9 3 5

Heavyweights
World Champion
Jimmy Braddock
1. Joe Louis
2. Max Schmeling
3. Primo Carnera
3. Charley Retzlaff
5. Tommy Loughran
6. Eddie Mader
7. Hank Hankinson
8. Ray Impellitiere
9. Al Ettore
10. Ford Smith

Light Heavyweights
World Champion
John Henry Lewis
1. Maxie Rosenbloom
2. Jock McAvoy
3. Al McCoy
4. Bob Olin
5. Tony Shucco
6. Ambrose Palmer
7. Adolf Heuser
8. Joe Knight
9. Al Gainer
10. Fred Lenhart

Middleweights
World Champion
Marcel Thil
1. Freddie Steele
2. Lou Brouillard
3. Babe Risko
4. Frank Battaglia
5. Fred Henneberry
6. Paul Pirrone
7. Erich Seelig
8. Ken Overlin
9. Fred Apostoli
10. Al Quaill

Welterweights
World Champion
Barney Ross
1. Jimmy McLarnin
2. Bep Van Klaveren
3. Jack Carroll
4. Ceferino Garcia
5. Kid Azteca
6. Cleto Locatelli
7. Harry Dublinsky
8. Jack Portney
9. Eddie Kid Wolfe
10. Jimmy Leto

Lightweights
World Champion
Tony Canzoneri
1. Lou Ambers
2. Wesley Ramey
3. Frankie Klick
4. Leo Rodak
5. Pedro Montanez
6. Al Roth
7. Joey Ferrando
8. Joe Ghnouly
9. Ralph Hurtado
10. Lew Feldman

Featherweights
World Champion
Freddie Miller
1. Maurice Holtzer
2. Henry Armstrong
3. Baby Arizmendi
4. Midget Wolgast
5. Mike Belloise
6. Young Casanova
7. Petey Hayes
8. Petey Sarron
9. Vernon Cormier
10. Moon Mullins

Bantamweights
World Champion
Baltazar Sangchilli
1. Sixto Escobar
2. Lou Salica
3. Pablo Dano
4. Johnny King
5. Little Pancho
6. Frankie Castillo
7. Joey Archibald
8. Henry Hooks
9. Bobby Leyvas
10. Frankie Martin

Flyweights
Title Vacant

1. Benny Lynch
2. Small Montana
3. Jackie Brown
4. Joe Mendiola
5. Valentin Anglemann
6. Tuffy Pierpont
7. Jim Campbell
8. Syd Parker
9. Jim Warnock
10. Rafaleto Valdes

RING RATINGS
1 9 3 6

Heavyweights
World Champion
Jimmy Braddock
1. Max Schmeling
2. Joe Louis
3. Gunnary Barlund
4. Jack Trammell
5. Maxie Rosenbloom
6. Ray Impellitiere
7. Leroy Haynes
8. Sonny Walker
9. Al Ettore
10. Arturo Godoy

Light Heavyweights
World Champion
John Henry Lewis
1. Al Gainer
2. Leo Kelly
3. Jock McAvoy
4. Gus Lesnevich
5. Ray Actis
6. Lou Brouillard
7. Fred Lenhart
8. Marty Simmons
9. Allen Mathews
10. Johnny Romero

Middleweights
World Champion
Marcel Thil
1. Freddie Steele
2. Fred Apostoli
3. Teddy Yarosz
4. Solly Krieger
5. Ken Overlin
6. Babe Risko
7. Oscar Rankin
8. Harry Balsamo
9. Frank Battaglia
10. Erich Seelig

Welterweights
World Champion
Barney Ross
1. Jack Carroll
2. Jimmy McLarnin
3. Ceferino Garcia
4. Fritzie Zivic
5. Izzy Jannazzo
6. Cleto Locatelli
7. Cocoa Kid
8. Jack Portney
9. Glen Lee
10. Milt Aron

Lightweights
World Champion
Lou Ambers
1. Eddie Cool
2. Tony Canzoneri
3. Pedro Montanez
4. Enrico Venturi
5. Laurie Stevens
6. Wesley Ramey
7. Aldo Spoldi
8. Davey Day
9. Red Guggino
10. Jimmy Walsh

Featherweights
World Champion
Petey Sarron
1. Henry Armstrong
2. Mike Belloise
3. Freddie Miller
4. Dick Corbett
5. Johnny McGrory
6. Tony Chavez
7. Young Rightmire
8. Nel Tarleton
9. Sonny Valdez
10. Pete De Grasse

Bantamweights
World Champion
Sixto Escobar
1. Harry Jeffra
2. Frankie Martin
3. Lou Salica
4. Baltazar Sangchilli
5. Tony Marino
6. K. O. Morgan
7. Johnny Cusick
8. Star Frisco
9. Joe Mendiola
10. Henry Hook

Flyweights
Title Vacant

1. Benny Lynch
2. Small Montana
3. Peter Kane
4. Valentin Anglemann
5. Ernst Weiss
6. Jim Warnock
7. Tiny Bostock
8. Pat Palmer
9. Phil Milligan
10. Tut Whalley

RING RATINGS
1 9 3 7

Heavyweights
World Champion
Joe Louis
1. Max Schmeling
2. Tommy Farr
3. Nathan Mann
4. Alberto Lovell
5. Tony Galento
6. Jimmy Adamick
7. Lou Nova
8. Bob Pastor
9. Roscoe Toles
10. Andre Lenglet

Light Heavyweights
World Champion
John Henry Lewis
1. Al Gainer
2. Tiger Jack Fox
3. Jock McAvoy
4. Eddie Wenstob
5. Ray Actis
6. Ralph De John
7. Billy Conn
8. Gus Lesnevich
9. Melio Bettina
10. Fred Lenhart

Middleweights
World Champion
Freddie Steele
1. Fred Apostoli
2. Al Hostak
3. Carmelo Candel
4. George Black
5. Young Corbett
6. Ben Brown
7. Glen Lee
8. Teddy Yarosz
9. Lou Brouillard
10. Ken Overlin

Welterweights
World Champion
Barney Ross
1. Ceferino Garcia
2. Jack Carroll
3. Gustave Eder
4. Saverio Turiello
5. Izzy Jannazzo
6. Holman Williams
7. Cocoa Kid
8. Jimmy Leto
9. Fritzie Zivic
10. Ralph Zannelli

Lightweights
World Champion
Lou Ambers
1. Pedro Montanez
2. Davey Day
3. Wesley Ramey
4. Billy Beauhuld
5. Eddie Cool
6. Johnny Bellus
7. Paul Junior
8. Petey Sarron
9. Frankie Wallace
10. Eddie McGeever

Featherweights
World Champion
Henry Armstrong
1. Freddie Miller
2. Leo Rodak
3. Young Rightmire
4. Jackie Wilson
5. Tony Chavez
6. Ginger Foran
7. Benny Sharkey
8. Kid Chocolate
9. Joey Archibald
10. Johnny Cusick

Bantamweights
World Champion
Harry Jeffra
1. K. O. Morgan
2. Sixto Escobar
3. Lou Salica
4. Indian Quintana
5. Georgie Pace
6. Spider Armstrong
7. Baby Yack
8. Johnny King
9. Tobe De La Rosa
10. Aurel Toma

Flyweights
World Champion
Benny Lynch
1. Peter Kane
2. Pierre Louis
3. Tiny Bostock
4. Small Montana
5. Jackie Jurich
6. Jim Warnock
7. Valentin Anglemann
8. Joe Curran
9. Tut Whalley
10. Frank Kid Bonser

RING RATINGS
1 9 3 8

Heavyweights
World Champion
Joe Louis
1. Lou Nova
2. Max Baer
3. Bob Pastor
4. Tony Galento
5. Maxie Rosenbloom
6. Len Harvey
7. Red Burman
8. Roscoe Toles
9. Gus Dorazio
10. Tommy Farr

Light Heavyweights
World Champion
John Henry Lewis
1. Tiger Jack Fox
2. Melio Bettina
3. Ron Richards
4. Gus Lesnevich
5. Len Harvey
6. Adolph Heuser
7. Jock McAvoy
8. Al Gainer
9. Billy Conn
10. Ambrose Palmer

Middleweights
Title Vacant
1. Fred Apostoli
2. Solly Krieger
3. Ron Richards
4. Ken Overlin
5. Teddy Yarosz
6. Walter Woods
7. Ben Brown
8. Al Hostak
9. Jock McAvoy
10. Ginger Sadd

Welterweights
World Champion
Henry Armstrong
1. Ceferino Garcia
2. Fritzie Zivic
3. Charley Burley
4. Ernie Roderick
5. Steve Mamakos
6. Saverio Turiello
7. Sammy Luftspring
8. Jake Kilrain
9. Kid Frattini
10. Jimmy Leto

Lightweights
World Champion
Henry Armstrong
1. Lou Ambers
2. Pedro Montanez
3. Davey Day
4. Baby Arizmendi
5. Sammy Angott
6. Billy Beauhuld
7. Aldo Spoldi
8. Petey Sarron
9. Maxie Berger
10. Tommy Cross

Featherweights
Title Vacant
1. Leo Rodak
2. Pete Scalzo
3. Dave Castilloux
4. Joey Archibald
5. Mike Belloise
6. Chalky Wright
7. Johnny Hutchinson
8. Al Reid
9. Freddie Miller
10. Claude Varner

Bantamweights
World Champion
Sixto Escobar
1. K. O. Morgan
2. Lou Salica
3. Georgie Pace
4. Kid Tanner
5. Aurel Toma
6. Henry Hook
7. Pancho Villa
8. Johnny Gaudes
9. Teddy O'Neil
10. Spider Kelly

Flyweights
World Champion
Peter Kane
1. Little Dado
2. Small Montana
3. Kid Tanner
4. Tut Whalley
5. Jackie Jurich
6. Dennis Cahill
7. Carlo Urbinati
8. Tiny Bostock
9. Paddy Ryan
10. Tommy Farriker

RING RATINGS
1 9 3 9

Heavyweights
World Champion
Joe Louis
1. Tony Galento
2. Bob Pastor
3. Lou Nova
4. Tommy Farr
5. Max Schmeling
6. Johnny Paychek
7. Red Burman
8. Gunnar Barlund
9. Roscoe Toles
10. Lee Savold

Light Heavyweights
World Champion
Billy Conn
1. Gus Lesnevich
2. Melio Bettina
3. Len Harvey
4. Jock McAvoy
5. Dave Clark
6. Tiger Jack Fox
7. Teddy Yarosz
8. Al Gainer
9. Larry Lane
10. Lee Oma

Middleweights
Title Vacant

1. Ceferino Garcia
2. Al Hostak
3. Ken Overlin
4. Ron Richards
5. Ben Brown
6. Lloyd Marshall
7. Ossie Stewart
8. Victor Dellicurti
9. Nate Bolden
10. Tony Zale

Welterweights
World Champion
Henry Armstrong
1. Fritzie Zivic
2. Holman Williams
3. Milt Aron
4. Ernie Roderick
5. Charley Burley
6. Mike Kaplan
7. Cocoa Kid
8. Maxie Berger
9. Jimmy Leto
10. Steve Mamakos

Lightweights
World Champion
Lou Ambers
1. Davey Day
2. Sammy Angott
3. Eric Boon
4. Wesley Ramey
5. Jackie Wilson
6. Bob Montgomery
7. Pete Lello
8. George Crouch
9. Leo Rodak
10. Billy Maher

Featherweights
World Champion
Joey Archibald
1. Al Mancini
2. Simon Chavez
3. Pete Scalzo
4. Jackie Wilson
5. Harry Jeffra
6. Chalky Wright
7. Jimmy Perrin
8. Frankie Covelli
9. Richard Lemos
10. Bobby Green

Bantamweights
Title Vacant

1. K. O. Morgan
2. Georgie Pace
3. Lou Salica
4. Peter Kane
5. Tony Olivera
6. Little Pancho
7. Kui Kong Young
8. Jim Brady
9. Benny Goldberg
10. Tommy Kiene

Flyweights
Title Vacant

1. Little Dado
2. Enrico Urbinati
3. Jackie Paterson
4. Joe Curran
5. Tiny Bostock
6. Small Montana
7. Jackie Jurich
8. Raoul Degryse
9. Paddy Ryan
10. Rinty Monaghan

R I N G   R A T I N G S
1 9 4 0

Heavyweights
World Champion
Joe Louis
1. Max Baer
2. Arturo Godoy
3. Red Burman
4. Abe Simon
5. Buddy Walker
6. Buddy Baer
7. Pat Comiskey
8. Lee Savold
9. Otis Thomas
10. Lem Franklin

Light Heavyweights
World Champion
Billy Conn
1. Jimmy Webb
2. Anton Christoforidis
3. Melio Bettina
4. Gus Lesnevich
5. Teddy Yarosz
6. Turkey Thompson
7. Tommy Tucker
8. Jimmy Reeves
9. Solly Krieger
10. Lloyd Marshall

Middleweights
Title Vacant

1. Ken Overlin
2. Tony Zale
3. Billy Soose
4. Archie Moore
5. Steve Belloise
6. Jimmy Bivins
7. Al Hostak
8. Georgie Abrams
9. Tami Mauriello
10. Ernie Vigh

Welterweights
World Champion
Fritzie Zivic
1. Henry Armstrong
2. Izzy Jannazzo
3. Charley Burley
4. Jimmy Leto
5. Mike Kaplan
6. Maxie Berger
7. Holman Williams
8. Cocoa Kid
9. Tony Marteliano
10. Baby Breese

Lightweights
World Champion
Lew Jenkins
1. Sammy Angott
2. Jackie Wilson
3. Pete Lello
4. Tommy Speigal
5. Dave Castilloux
6. Bob Montgomery
7. Toby Vigil
8. Baby Arizmendi
9. Aldo Spoldi
10. Yucatan Kid

Featherweights
World Champion
Harry Jeffra
1. Bill Speary
2. Chalky Wright
3. Pete Scalzo
4. Joe Marinelli
5. Jimmy Perin
6. Larry Bolvin
7. Bobby Ivy
8. Young Rightmire
9. Vincenzo Dell Orto
10. Al Mancini

Bantamweights
Title Vacant

1. Tommy Forte
2. Tony Olivera
3. Lou Salica
4. Rush Dalma
5. Kui Kong Young
6. Jim Brady
7. Kid Tanner
8. Chick Delaney
9. Freddie Pope
10. Johnny Juliano

Flyweights
Title Vacant

1. Jackie Paterson
2. Little Pancho
3. Little Dado
4. Manuel Oritz
5. Jackie Jurich
6. Paddy Ryan
7. Tiny Bostock
8. Joe Curran
9. Jimmy Stewart
10. Small Montana

R I N G   R A T I N G S
1 9 4 1

Heavyweights

World Champion
Joe Louis
1. Billy Conn
2. Lem Franklin
3. Bob Pastor
4. Melio Bettina
5. Abe Simon
6. Turkey Thompson
7. Buddy Baer
8. Lou Nova
9. Arturo Godoy
10. Roscoe Toles

Light Heavyweights

World Champion
Gus Lesnevich
1. Booker Beckwith
2. Ken Overlin
3. Jimmy Bivins
4. Mose Brown
5. Billy Soose
6. Anton Christoforidis
7. Tommy Tucker
8. Joey Maxim
9. Erv Sarlen
10. Lloyd Marshall

Middleweights

World Champion
Tony Zale
1. Georgie Abrams
2. Ezzard Charles
3. Ernie Vigh
4. Coley Welch
5. Ceferino Garcia
6. Steve Belloise
7. Antonio Fernandez
8. Fred Apostoli
9. Ron Richards
10. Ossie Stewart

Welterweights

World Champion
Freddie Cochrane
1. Ray Robinson
2. Jackie Wilson
3. Fritzie Zivic
4. Young Kid McCoy
5. Charley Burley
6. Holman Williams
7. Cocoa Kid
8. Izzy Jannazzo
9. Ron Richards
10. Norman Rubio

Lightweights

World Champion
Sammy Angott
1. Bob Montgomery
2. Lenny Mancini
3. Dave Castilloux
4. Ray Lunny
5. Juan Zurita
6. George Latka
7. Chester Rico
8. Bobby Ruffin
9. Harry Hurst
10. Lew Jenkins

Featherweights

World Champion
Chalky Wright
1. Jackie Wilson
2. Richie Lemos
3. Pedro Hernandez
4. Harry Jeffra
5. Sal Bartolo
6. Bobby Ivy
7. Mike Raffa
8. Jimmy Hatcher
9. Charley Costantino
10. Bill Speary

Bantamweights

World Champion
Lou Salica
1. Kui Kong Young
2. Manuel Ortiz
3. Rush Dalma
4. Jim Brady
5. Horace Mann
6. Tony Olivera
7. Tommy Forte
8. Kenny Lindsay
9. Peter Kane
10. Jimmy Stubbs

Flyweights

Title Vacant

1. Jackie Paterson
2. Little Dado
3. Joe Curran
4. Luis Castillo
5. Paddy Ryan
6. Johnny Shaughnessy
7. Tiny Bostock
8. Small Montana
9. Lupe Cordoza
10. Humberto Espinosa

R I N G   R A T I N G S
1 9 4 2

Heavyweights
World Champion
Joe Louis*
1. Jimmy Bivins
2. Tami Mauriello
3. Turkey Thompson
4. Roscoe Toles
5. Harry Bobo
6. Big Boy Brown
7. Lee Savold
8. Lou Brooks
9. Tony Musto
10. Joey Maxim

Light Heavyweights
World Champion
Gus Lesnevich*
1. Jimmy Bivins
2. Anton Christoforidis
3. Ezzard Charles
4. Freddie Mills
5. Lloyd Marshall
6. Jack Coggins
7. Nate Bolden
8. Alabama Kid
9. Johnny Romero
10. Herbie Katz

Middleweights
World Champion
Tony Zale*
1. Archie Moore
2. Charley Burley
3. Holman Williams
4. Kid Tunero
5. Jose Basora
6. Jake LaMotta
7. Jack Chase
8. Eddie Booker
9. Harry Kid Matthews
10. Antonio Fernandez

Welterweights
World Champion
Freddie Cochrane*
1. Ray Robinson
2. Henry Armstrong
3. Jackie Wilson
4. Cocoa Kid
5. Earl Turner
6. Joe Legon
7. Jimmy Edgar
8. Fritzie Zivic
9. Tony Motisi
10. Sheik Rangel

Lightweights
Title Vacant
1. Beau Jack
2. Bob Montgomery
3. Allie Stolz
4. Slugger White
5. Willie Joyce
6. John Thomas
7. Juan Zurita
8. Maxie Shapiro
9. Joey Peralta
10. Chester Rico

Featherweights
World Champion
Willie Pep
1. Chalky Wright
2. Lulu Costantino
3. Sal Bartola
4. Mike Raffa
5. Benny Goldberg
6. Carlos Chavez
7. Jackie Callura
8. Mike Belloise
9. Nel Tarleton
10. Lefty LaChance

Bantamweights
World Champion
Manuel Ortiz
1. Lou Salica
2. Kui Kong Young
3. Jim Brady
4. Ham Wiloby
5. Rush Dalma
6. Mario Morales
7. Kid Zefine
8. Leonardo Lopez
9. Tony Olivera
10. Stan Mott

Flyweights
Title Vacant

1. Peter Kane
2. Jackie Paterson
3. Little Dado
4. Joe Curran
5. Sammy Reynolds
6. Norman Lewis
7. Humberto Espinosa
8. Jimmy Gill
9. Paddy Ryan
10. Larry Torpey

*Indicates title frozen for duration.

R I N G   R A T I N G S
1 9 4 3

Heavyweights
World Champion
Joe Louis*
1. Jimmy Bivins
2. Tami Mauriello
3. Lee Q. Murray
4. Curtis Shepard
5. Gus Dorazio
6. Joe Baksi
7. Joey Maxim
8. Turkey Thompson
9. Lee Savold
10. Buddy Scott

Light Heavyweights
World Champion
Gus Lesnevich*
1. Lloyd Marshall
2. Alabama Kid
3. Eddie Booker
4. Nate Bolden
5. Freddie Mills
6. Bob Jacobs
7. Bob Garner
8. Jack McNamee
9. Jack Coggins
10. Billy Grant

Middleweights
World Champion
Tony Zale*
1. Jake LaMotta
2. Holman Williams
3. Coley Welch
4. Jose Basora
5. Steve Belloise
6. Marcel Cerdan
7. Joe Carter
8. Ruben Shank
9. Georgie Kochan
10. Archie Moore

Welterweights
World Champion
Freddie Cochrane*
1. Tippy Larkin
2. Leo Rodak
3. Tommy Bell
4. Frankie Wills
5. Ralph Zannelli
6. Paul Lewis
7. Cecil Hudson
8. Izzy Jannazzo
9. Al Davis
10. Freddie Archer

Lightweights
Title Vacant
1. Beau Jack
2. Sammy Angott
3. Bob Motgomery
4. Allie Stolz
5. Willie Joyce
6. Ike Williams
7. Lulu Costantino
8. Slugger White
9. Juan Zurita
10. John Thomas

Featherweights
World Champion
Willie Pep*
1. Chalky Wright
2. Sal Bartola
3. Phil Terranova
4. Harry Jeffra
5. Larry Bolvin
6. Lefty LaChance
7. Enrique Bolanos
8. Billy Miller
9. Ham Wiloby
10. Steve Belloise

Bantamweights
World Champion
Manuel Ortiz
1. Rush Dalma
2. Tony Olivera
3. Lou Salica
4. Al Phillips
5. Kui Kong Young
6. Luis Castillo
7. Ernesto Aguilar
8. Jim Brady
9. Leonardo Lopez
10. Johnny King

Flyweights
World Champion
Jackie Paterson
1. Peter Kane
2. Sammy Reynolds
3. Little Dado
4. Mickey Jones
5. Joe Curran
6. George Parks
7. Norman Lewis
8. Johnny Shaughnessy
9. Larry Torpey
10. Humberto Espinosa

*Indicates title frozen for duration.

R I N G   R A T I N G S
1 9 4 4

Heavyweights
World Champion
Joe Louis*
1. Melio Bettina
2. Tami Mauriello
3. Curtis Sheppard
4. Joe Baksi
5. Lee Oma
6. Lee Q. Murray
7. Jack London
8. Elmer Ray
9. Al Hart
10. Buddy Scott

Light Heavyweights
World Champion
Gus Lesnevich*
1. Lloyd Marshall
2. Bruce Woodcock
3. Alabama Kid
4. Jack Johnson
5. Freddie Mills
6. Bob Garner
7. Billy Grant
8. Watson Jones
9. Fitzie Fitzpatrick
10. Walter Woods

Middleweights
World Champion
Tony Zale*
1. Holman Williams
2. Jake LaMotta
3. Charley Burley
4. Jose Basora
5. Joe Carter
6. Vince Hawkins
7. Cocoa Kid
8. Coley Welch
9. Jack Chase
10. Vic Dellicurti

Welterweights
World Champion
Freddie Cochrane*
1. Henry Armstrong
2. Ray Robinson
3. Johnny Greco
4. Jimmy McDaniels
5. Fritzie Zivic
6. Bee Bee Wright
7. Harold Green
8. Tippy Larkin
9. Sammy Angott
10. Billy Arnold

Lightweights
Title Vacant
1. Beau Jack
2. Bob Montgomery
3. Juan Zurita
4. Willie Joyce
5. Johnny Thomas
6. Bobby Ruffin
7. Ike Williams
8. Ronnie James
9. Lulu Costantino
10. Joey Peralta

Featherweights
World Champion
Willie Pep
1. Sal Bartolo
2. Phil Terranova
3. Al Phillips
4. Chalky Wright
5. Willie Roache
6. Danny Webb
7. Charley Cabey Lewis
8. Enrique Bolanos
9. Nel Tarleton
10. Harry Jeffra

Bantamweights
World Champion
Manuel Ortiz
1. Sammy Reynolds
2. Tony Olivera
3. Chico Rosa
4. Carlos Chavez
5. Luis Castillo
6. Rush Dalma
7. Kui Kong Young
8. Jorge Robles
9. Lorenzo Safora
10. Ronnie Clayton

Flyweights
World Champion
Jackie Paterson
1. Joe Curran
2. Tommy Burney
3. Norman Lewis
4. George Parkes
5. Stumpy Butwell
6. Alec Murphy
7. Dado Marino
8. Timmy Plowright
9. Johnny Summers
10. Hugh Cameron

*Indicates title frozen for duration.

R I N G   R A T I N G S
1 9 4 5

Heavyweights
World Champion
Joe Louis
1. Billy Conn
2. Tami Mauriello
3. Jimmy Bivins
4. Elmer Ray
5. Bruce Woodcock
6. Lee Oma
7. Freddie Schott
8. Arturo Godoy
9. Jersey Joe Walcott
10. Joe Baksi

Light Heavyweights
World Champion
Gus Lesnevich
1. Archie Moore
2. Phil Muscato
3. Billy Grant
4. Lloyd Marshall
5. Joe Kahut
6. Nate Bolden
7. Jack Johnson
8. Freddie Mills
9. Billy Smith
10. Fitzie Fitzpatrick

Middleweights
World Champion
Tony Zale
1. Holman Williams
2. Charley Burley
3. Jake LaMotta
4. Rocky Graziano
5. Marcel Cerdan
6. Bee Bee Washington
7. Aaron Wade
8. Wildcat George Henry
9. Jimmy Edgar
10. Bert Lytell

Welterweights
World Champion
Freddie Cochrane

1. Ray Robinson
2. Jimmy Doyle
3. Tippy Larkin
4. Freddie Archer
5. Nick Moran
6. Arthur Danabar
7. Johnny Greco
8. Sammy Angott
9. Tony Janiro
10. Chuck Hunter

Lightweights
Title Vacant
1. Allie Stolz
2. Dave Castilloux
3. Willie Joyce
4. Ike Williams
5. Bob Montgomery
6. Bobby Ruffin
7. Ronnie James
8. Freddie Dawson
9. Bobby Yaeger
10. Enrique Bolanos

Featherweights
World Champion
Willie Pep
1. Sal Bartolo
2. Chalky Wright
3. Phil Terranova
4. Carlos Chavez
5. Kid Zefine
6. Al Phillips
7. Freddie Russo
8. Jackie Graves
9. Jimmy Stubbs
10. Charley Riley

Bantamweights
World Champion
Manuel Ortiz
1. Benny Goldberg
2. Tony Olivera
3. Luis Catillo
4. Simon Vergera
5. Sammy Reynolds
6. Norman Lewis
7. Gus Foran
8. Ronnie Clayton
9. Young Giant
10. Cliff Anderson

Flyweights
World Champion
Jackie Paterson
1. Seaman Terry Allen
2. Bunty Doran
3. Joe Curran
4. Rinty Monaghan
5. Luis Galvani
6. Alec Murphy
7. Hugh Cameron
8. Tommy Burney
9. George Parkes
10. Billy Clinton

RING RATINGS
1 9 4 6

Heavyweights
World Champion
Joe Louis
1. Tami Mauriello
2. Elmer Ray
3. Jersey Joe Walcott
4. Bruce Woodcock
5. Lee Q. Murray
6. Curtis Sheppard
7. Melio Bettina
8. Joe Baksi
9. Joe Kahut
10. Joey Maxim

Light Heavyweights
World Champion
Gus Lesnevich
1. Billy Fox
2. Ezzard Charles
3. Archie Moore
4. Jack Chase
5. Billy Smith
6. Tommy Yarosz
7. Johnny Colan
8. Booker Beckwith
9. Freddie Mills
10. Fitzie Fitzpatrick

Middleweights
World Champion
Tony Zale
1. Jake LaMotta
2. Charley Burley
3. Rocky Graziano
4. Marcel Cerdan
5. Georgie Abrams
6. Steve Belloise
7. Jimmy Edgar
8. Bert Lytell
9. Sam Baroudi
10. Al Priest

Welterweights
World Champion
Ray Robinson
1. Tommy Bell
2. Tippy Larkin
3. Beau Jack
4. Tony Janiro
5. Johnny Greco
6. Tony Pellone
7. Jimmy Doyle
8. Jackie Wilson
9. Willie Joyce
10. Charley Fusari

Lightweights
Title Vacant
1. Bob Montgomery
2. Ike Williams
3. Johnny Bratton
4. John Thomas
5. Larry Cisneros
6. Enrique Bolanos
7. Chester Rico
8. Vic Patrick
9. Jesse Flores
10. Billy Graham

Featherweights
World Champion
Willie Pep
1. Phil Terranova
2. Carlos Chavez
3. Oscar Calles
4. Miguel Acevedo
5. Jackie Graves
6. Jock Leslie
7. Sandy Saddler
8. Spider Armstrong
9. Charles Cabey Lewis
10. Al Phillips

Bantamweights
World Champion
Manuel Ortiz
1. Harold Dade
2. Luis Castillo
3. Kui Kong Young
4. Dado Marino
5. Cliff Anderson
6. Tony Olivera
7. Peter Kane
8. Theo Medina
9. Stan Rowan
10. Luis Galvani

Flyweights
World Champion
Jackie Paterson
1. Rinty Monaghan
2. Jimmy Gill
3. Bunty Doran
4. Joe Curran
5. Emile Famechon
6. Raoul Degryse
7. Jackie Bryce
8. Terry Allen
9. Mickey Hill
10. Billy Davies

R I N G   R A T I N G S
1 9 4 7

Heavyweights
World Champion
Joe Louis
1. Jersey Joe Walcott
2. Elmer Ray
3. Lee Q. Murray
4. Pat Comiskey
5. Joe Baksi
6. Tommy Gomez
7. Joey Maxim
8. Turkey Thompson
9. Bruce Woodcock
10. Phil Muscato

Light Heavyweights
World Champion
Gus Lesnevich
1. Ezzard Charles
2. Archie Moore
3. Billy Fox
4. Freddie Mills
5. Tommy Yarosz
6. Dave Sands
7. Lloyd Marshall
8. Bob Foxworth
9. Billy Smith
10. Billy (Chicken) Thompson

Middleweights
World Champion
Rocky Graziano
1. Tony Zale
2. Bert Lytell
3. Marcel Cerdan
4. Steve Belloise
5. Jake LaMotta
6. Al Hostak
7. Major Jones
8. Anton Raadik
9. Jackie Darthard
10. Tony Janiro

Welterweights
World Champion
Ray Robinson
1. Gene Burton
2. Tommy Bell
3. Bernard Docusen
4. Ralph Zannelli
5. George Costner
6. Tippy Larkin
7. Kid Gavilan
8. Beau Jack
9. Aldo Minelli
10. Johnny Greco

Lightweights
World Champion
Ike Williams
1. Enrique Bolanos
2. Rudy Cruz
3. Freddie Dawson
4. Billy Thompson
5. Buddy Garcia
6. Maxie Docusen
7. Johnny Bratton
8. Jesse Flores
9. Terry Young
10. Lalo Gallardo

Featherweights
World Champion
Willie Pep
1. Humberto Sierra
2. Sandy Saddler
3. Charley Riley
4. Jose Baby Gonzales
5. Henry Davis
6. Miguel Acevedo
7. Carlos Chavez
8. Harold Dade
9. Chico Rosa
10. Jock Leslie

Bantamweights
World Champion
Manuel Ortiz
1. Peter Kane
2. Jackie Paterson
3. Luis Galvani
4. Kui Kong Young
5. Luis Castillo
6. Bunty Doran
7. Armondo Puenti Pi
8. Fernando Gagnon
9. Tsuneshi Maruo
10. Joe Cornelis

Flyweights
World Champion
Jackie Paterson
1. Rinty Monaghan
2. Dado Marino
3. Maurice Sandeyron
4. Monito Flores
5. Dickie O'Sullivan
6. Mustapha Mustaphaoui
7. Raoul Degryse
8. Emile Famechon
9. Spider Tymms
10. Taffy Hancock

RING RATINGS
1 9 4 8

Heavyweights
World Champion
Joe Louis
1. Jersey Joe Walcott
2. Ezzard Charles
3. Lee Savoid
4. Johnny Flynn
5. Joey Maxim
6. Jimmy Bivins
7. Joe Kahut
8. Rusty Payne
9. Pat Valentino
10. Freddie Beshore

Light Heavyweights
World Champion
Freddie Mills
1. Gus Lesnevich
2. Leonard Morrow
3. Archie Moore
4. Dave Sands
5. Lloyd Marshall
6. Doc Williams
7. Billy Smith
8. Artie Levine
9. Henry Hall
10. Dave Whitlock

Middleweights
World Champion
Marcel Cerdan
1. Bert Lytell
2. Steve Belloise
3. Jake LaMotta
4. Tony Zale
5. Cyrille Delannoit
6. Sylvester Perkins
7. Dick Turpin
8. Robert Villemain
9. Lee Sala
10. Rocky Graziano

Welterweights
World Champion
Ray Robinson
1. Kid Gavilan
2. Frankie Fernandez
3. Bernard Docusen
4. Johnny Greco
5. Beau Jack
6. Gene Burton
7. Johnny Cesario
8. Charley Fusari
9. Charley Williams
10. Vince Foster

Lightweights
World Champion
Ike Williams
1. Enriqu� Bolanos
2. Freddie Dawson
3. Maxie Docusen
4. Tommy Campbell
5. Arthur King
6. Jesse Flores
7. Johnny Williams
8. Paddy DeMarco
9. Carlos Chavez
10. Pierre Montane

Featherweights
World Champion
Sandy Saddler
1. Willie Pep
2. Ray Famechon
3. Jackie Graves
4. Tirso del Rosario
5. Eddie Miller
6. Johnny Molloy
7. Elis Ask
8. Eddie Compo
9. Henry Davis
10. Miguel Acevedo

Bantamweights
World Champion
Manuel Ortiz
1. Cecil Schoomaker
2. Luis Romero
3. Guido Ferracin
4. Memo Valero
5. Kui Kong Young
6. Chico Rosa
7. Jackie Paterson
8. Stan Rowan
9. Theo Medina
10. Luis Galvani

Flyweights
World Champion
Rinty Monaghan
1. Maurice Sandeyron
2. Dickie O'Sullivan
3. Dado Marino
4. Black Pico
5. Louis Skena
6. Al Chavez
7. Emile Famechon
8. Charley Squire
9. Honore Pratesi
10. Norman Tennant

R I N G   R A T I N G S
1 9 4 9

Heavyweights
Title Vacant

1. Ezzard Charles
2. Lee Oma
3. Turkey Thompson
4. Jersey Joe Walcott
5. Bruce Woodcock
6. Lee Savold
7. Jimmy Bivins
8. Pat Valentino
9. Omelio Agramonte
10. Roland LaStarza

Light Heavyweights
World Champion
Freddie Mills

1. Joey Maxim
2. Archie Moore
3. Harold Johnson
4. Leonard Morrow
5. Bert Lytell
6. (Irish) Bob Murphy
7. Dave Whitlock
8. Billy Smith
9. Nick Barone
10. Tommy Yarosz

Middleweights
World Champion
Jake LaMotta

1. Ray Robinson
2. Dave Sands
3. Robert Villemain
4. Tiberio Mitri
5. Steve Belloise
6. Art Towne
7. Laurent Dauthuille
8. Lee Sala
9. Randy Turpin
10. Tuzo Portuguez

Welterweights
World Champion
Ray Robinson

1. Kid Gavilan
2. George Costner
3. Bernard Docusen
4. Johnny Bratton
5. Lester Felton
6. Ronnie Delaney
7. Charley Fusari
8. Ross Virgo
9. Frankie Fernandez
10. Gene Burton

Lightweights
World Champion
Ike Williams

1. Maxie Docusen
2. Arthur King
3. Freddie Dawson
4. Enrique Bolanos
5. Roberto Proietti
6. Rudy Cruz
7. Sonny Boy West
8. Bud Smith
9. Solly Cantor
10. Art Aragon

Featherweights
World Champion
Willie Pep

1. Sandy Saddler
2. Ray Famechon
3. Ronnie Clayton
4. Henry Davis
5. Miguel Acevedo
6. Percy Bassett
7. Charley Riley
8. Tirso del Rosario
9. Glen Flanagan
10. Luis De Santiago

Bantamweights
World Champion
Manuel Ortiz

1. Danny O'Sullivan
2. Luis Romero
3. Elley Bennett
4. Luis Galvani
5. Theo Medina
6. Vic Toweel
7. Guido Ferracin
8. Memo Valero
9. Reuben Smith
10. Teddy Gardner

Flyweights
World Champion
Rinty Monaghan

1. Honore Pratesi
2. Terry Allen
3. Maurice Sandeyron
4. Jean Sneyers
5. Taffy Hancock
6. Norman Lewis
7. Peter Keenan
8. Norman Tennant
9. Mickey Hill
10. Black Pico

RING RATINGS
1 9 5 0

Heavyweights
World Champion
Ezzard Charles
1. Joe Louis
2. Lee Savoid
3. Joey Maxim
4. Clarence Henry
5. Bob Baker
6. Rex Layne
7. Jersey Joe Walcott
8. Jack Gardner
9. Lee Oma
10. Rocky Marciano`

Light Heavyweights
World Champion
Joey Maxim
1. Archie Moore
2. Harry (Kid) Matthews
3. (Irish) Bob Murphy
4. Bob Satterfield
5. Nick Barone
6. Jimmy Slade
7. Doc Williams
8. Dan Bucceroni
9. Connie Rux
10. Don Cockell

Middleweights
World Champion
Jake LaMotta
1. Ray Robinson
2. Laurent Dauthuille
3. Dave Sands
4. Randy Turpin
5. Jimmy Beau
6. Gene Hairston
7. Ray Barnes
8. Robert Villemain
9. Walter Cartier
10. Paddy Young

Welterweights
World Champion
Ray Robinson
1. Kid Gavilan
2. Billy Graham
3. Charley Fusari
4. Johnny Bratton
5. Eddie Thomas
6. Johnny Saxton
7. Mickey Tollis
8. Charley Cotton
9. Joe Miceli
10. Charley Salas

Lightweights
World Champion
Ike Williams
1. John L. Davis
2. Freddie Dawson
3. Tommy Campbell
4. James Carter
5. Art Aragon
6. Johnny Gonsalves
7. Eddie Chavez
8. Del Flanagan
9. Rudy Cruz
10. Arthur King

Featherweights
World Champion
Sandy Saddler
1. Willie Pep
2. Ray Famechon
3. Percy Bassett
4. Charley Riley
5. Luis de Santiago
6. Ronnie Clayton
7. Al Phillips
8. Ciro Morasen
9. Rudy Garcia
10. Lauro Salas

Bantamweights
World Champion
Vic Toweel
1. Luis Romero
2. Manuel Ortiz
3. Peter Keenan
4. Luis Galvani
5. Elley Bennett
6. Emile Chemama
7. Maurice Sandeyron
8. Tommy Proffitt
9. Hadi Tijani
10. Gianni Zuddas

Flyweights
World Champion
Dado Marino
1. Jean Sneyers
2. Terry Allen
3. Louis Skena
4. Vic Herman
5. Honore Pratesi
6. Stumpy Butwell
7. Teddy Gardner
8. Norman Tennant
9. Henry Carpenter
10. Black Pico

RING RATINGS
1 9 5 1

Heavyweights
World Champion
Jersey Joe Walcott
1. Ezzard Charles
2. Rocky Marciano
3. Clarence Henry
4. Roland LaStarza
5. Karel Sys
6. Joe Louis
7. Cesar Brion
8. Joe Baksi
9. Bob Baker
10. Johnny Williams

Light Heavyweights
World Champion
Joe Maxim
1. Harry (Kid) Matthews
2. Archie Moore
3. Harold Johnson
4. Dan Bucceroni
5. Danny Nardico
6. (Irish) Bob Murphy
7. Wesbury Bascom
8. Bob Satterfield
9. Yolande Pompey
10. Don Cockell

Middleweights
World Champion
Ray Robinson
1. Randy Turpin
2. Dave Sands
3. Laurent Dauthuille
4. Eugene Hairston
5. Rocky Castellani
6. Ernie Durando
7. Walter Cartier
8. Ronnie Delaney
9. Robert Villemain
10. Rocky Graziano

Welterweights
Title Vacant

1. Kid Gavilan
2. Charley Humez
3. Billy Graham
4. Johnny Bratton
5. Gil Turner
6. Freddie Dawson
7. Johnny Saxton
8. Charley Fusari
9. Pierre Langlois
10. Bobby Jones

Lightweights
World Champion
James Carter
1. Luther Rawlings
2. Virgil Akins
3. Joe Brown
4. Paddy DeMarco
5. Art Aragon
6. Henry Davis
7. Tommy Campbell
8. George Araujo
9. Del Flanagan
10. Eddie Chavez

Featherweights
World Champion
Sandy Saddler
1. Willie Pep
2. Ray Famechon
3. Roy Ankarah
4. Ernesto Formenti
5. Ciro Morasen
6. Percy Bassett
7. Gabriel Diaz
8. Lauro Salas
9 Ronnie Clayton
10. Glen Flanagan

Bantamweights
World Champion
Vic Toweel
1. Jimmy Carruthers
2. Peter Keenan
3. Luis Romero
4. Maurice Sandeyron
5. Jean Sneyers
6. Emile Chemama
7. Gianni Zuddas
8. Hadi Tijani
9. Alvaro Nuvoloni
10. Frank Williams

Flyweights
World Champion
Dado Marino
1. Yoshio Shirai
2. Terry Allen
3. Teddy Gardner
4. Vic Herman
5. Tanny Campo
6. Taffy Hancock
7. Johnny Gleeson
8. Jimmy Laffin
9. Louis Skena
10. Juan Diaz

R I N G   R A T I N G S
1 9 5 2

Heavyweights
World Champion
Rocky Marciano
1. Jersey Joe Walcott
2. Rex Layne
3. Ezzard Charles
4. Bob Dunlop
5. Clarence Henry
6. Johnny Williams
7. Roland LaStarza
8. Heinz Neuhaus
9. Karel Sys
10. Jimmy Bivins

Light Heavyweights
World Champion
Archie Moore
1. Joey Maxim
2. Harold Johnson
3. Harry Matthews
4. Yolande Pompey
5. Jake LaMotta
6. Danny Nardico
7. Jimmy Slade
8. Randy Turpin
9. Rocky Jones
10. Tommy Harrison

Middleweights
Title Vacant

1. Randy Turpin
2. Charley Humez
3. Carl (Bobo) Olson
4. Ernie Durando
5. Rocky Castellani
6. Lee Sala
7. Norman Hayes
8. George Angelo
9. Joe Giardello
10. Mickey Laurent

Welterweights
World Champion
Kid Gavilan
1. Johnny Bratton
2. Bobby Dykes
3. Joe Micelli
4. Gil Turner
5. Chuck Davey
6. Billy Graham
7. Johnny Saxton
8. Cliff Curvis
9. Art Aragon
10. Danny Womber

Lightweights
World Champion
James Carter
1. Lauro Salas
2. Johnny Gonsalves
3. George Araujo
4. Arthur King
5. Jorgen Johansen
6. Frank Johnson
7. Joey Brown
8. Virgil Akins
9. Georgie Dunn
10. Eddie Chavez

Featherweights
World Champion
Sandy Saddler
1. Ray Famechon
2. Tommy Collins
3. Willie Pep
4. Luis Romero
5. Glen Flanagan
6. Percy Bassett
7. Teddy (Red Top) Davis
8. Gene Smith
9. Charley Riley
10. Roy Ankarah

Bantamweights
World Champion
Jimmy Carruthers
1. Vic Toweel
2. Maurice Sandeyron
3. Jean Sneyers
4. Puppy Garcia
5. Gianni Zuddas
6. Gaetano Annaloro
7. Peter Keenan
8. Frankie Williams
9. Henry (Pappy) Gault
10. Andre Valignat

Flyweights
World Champion
Yoshio Shirai
1. Dado Marino
2. Jake Tull
3. Terry Allen
4. Joe Cairney
5. Vic Herman
6. Teddy Gardner
7. Jimmy Pearce
8. Tanny Campo
9. Louis Skena
10. Nazzareno Gianelli

RING RATINGS
1 9 5 3

Heavyweights
World Champion
Rocky Marciano
1. Nino Valdes
2. Ezzard Charles
3. Dan Bucceroni
4. Roland LaStarza
5. Earl Walls
6. Don Cockell
7. Clarence Henry
8. Tommy Harrison
9. Bob Satterfield
10. Coley Wallace

Light Heavyweights
World Champion
Archie Moore
1. Harold Johnson
2. Joey Maxim
3. Yolande Pompey
4. Danny Nardico
5. Jimmy Slade
6. Gerhard Hecht
7. Floyd Patterson
8. Alex Buxton
9. Willi Hoepner
10. Paul Andrews

Middleweights
World Champion
Carl (Bobo) Olson
1. Rocky Castellani
2. Joey Giardello
3. Randy Turpin
4. Gil Turner
5. Bobby Dykes
6. Joey Giambra
7. Willie Troy
8. Holley Mims
9. Paddy Young
10. Pierre Langlois

Welterweights
World Champion
Kid Gavilan
1. Carmen Basilio
2. Billy Graham
3. Johnny Bratton
4. Del Flanagan
5. Johnny Saxton
6. Ramon Fuentes
7. Art Aragon
8. Freddie Dawson
9. Chico Varona
10. Gilbert Lavoine

Lightweights
World Champion
James Carter
1. Wallace (Bud) Smith
2. Eddie Chavez
3. Orlando Zulueta
4. Paddy DeMarco
5. Ralph Dupas
6. Johnny Gonsalves
7. Arthur Persley
8. George Araujo
9. Joe Brown
10. Arthur King

Featherweights
World Champion
Sandy Saddler
1. Willie Pep
2. Percy Bassett
3. Teddy (Red Top) Davis
4. Baby Ortiz
5. Lulu Perez
6. Dave Gallardo
7. Roy Ankarah
8. Jean Sneyers
9. Ray Famechon
10. Bill Bossio

Bantamweights
World Champion
Jimmy Carruthers
1. Robert Cohen
2. Chamrern Songkitrat
3. Billy Peacock
4. John Kelly
5. Henry (Pappy) Gault
6. Paul (Raton) Macias
7. Pierre Cossemyns
8. Andre Valignat
9. Gaetano Annaloro
10. Maurice Sandeyron

Flyweights
World Champion
Yoshiro Shirai
1. Jake Tuli
2. Leo Espinosa
3. Tanny Campo
4. Terry Allen
5. Louis Skena
6. Vic Herman
7. Charley Bohbot
8. Nazzarino Giannelli
9. Young Martin
10. Dai Dower

RING RATINGS
1 9 5 4

Heavyweights
World Champion
Rocky Marciano
1. Nino Valdes
2. Don Cockell
3. Ezzard Charles
4. Bob Baker
5. Earl Walls
6. Heinz Neuhaus
7. Rex Layne
8. Tommy Jackson
9. Charley Norkus
10. Jimmy Slade

Light Heavyweights
World Champion
Archie Moore
1. Joey Maxim
2. Paul Andrews
3. Harold Johnson
4. Floyd Patterson
5. Billy Smith
6. Gerhard Hecht
7. Marty Marsnall
8. Yolande Pompey
9. Willi Hoepner
10. Bob Satterfield

Middleweights
World Champion
Carl (Bobo) Olson
1. Joey Giardello
2. Rocky Castellani
3. Holley Mims
4. Charley Humez
5. Pierre Langlois
6. Tiberio Mitri
7. Bobby Jones
8. Willie Troy
9. Eduardo Lausse
10. Johnny Sullivan

Welterweights
World Champion
Johnny Saxton
1. Carmen Basilio
2. Kid Gavilan
3. Vince Martinez
4. Ramon Fuentes
5. Freddy Dawson
6. Tony DeMarco
7. Maurice Harper
8. Del Flanagan
9. Hector Constance
10. Joe Miceli

Lightweights
World Champion
Jimmy Carter
1. Paddy De Marco
2. Duilio Loi
3. Ralph Dupas
4. Frankie Ryff
5. Wallace (Bud) Smith
6. Johnny Gonsalves
7. Richie Howard
8. Orlando Zulueta
9. Cisco Andrade
10. Arthur Persley

Featherweights
World Champion
Sandy Saddler
1. Teddy (Red Top) Davis
2. Percy Bassett
3. Ray Famechon
4. Ciro Morasen
5. Hogan (Kid) Bassey
6. Jean Sneyers
7. Rudy Garcia
8. Bobby Bell
9. Orlando Eschevarria
10. Billy Kelly

Bantamweights
World Champion
Robert Cohen
1. Raul (Raton) Macias
2. Mario D'Agata
3. Chamrern Songkitrat
4. Pierre Cossemyns
5. Willie Toweel
6. Andre Valignat
7. Peter Keenan
8. Bobby Sinn
9. Hilaire Pratesi
10. Nate Brooks

Flyweights
World Champion
Pascual Perez
1. Yoshio Shirai
2. Leo Espinosa
3. Dai Dower
4. Nazzareno Gianelli
5. Danny Kid
6. Tanny Campo
7. Eric Marsden
8. Jake Tuli
9. Oscar Suarez
10. Antonio Diaz II

RING RATINGS
1 9 5 5

Heavyweights
World Champion
Rocky Marciano
1. Archie Moore
2. Bob Baker
3. Tommy Jackson
4. John Holman
5. Willie Pastrano
6. Nino Valdes
7. Johnny Summerlin
8. Bob Satterfield
9. Young Jack Johnson
10. Ezzard Charles

Light Heavyweights
World Champion
Archie Moore
1. Floyd Patterson
2. Yolande Pompey
3. Gerhard Hecht
4. Willi Hoepner
5. Chuck Spieser
6. Joey Maxim
7. Harold Johnson
8. Albert Finch
9. Charles Colin
10. Dave Whitlock

Middleweights
World Champion
Ray Robinson
1. Carl (Bobo) Olson
2. Charley Humez
3. Eduardo Lausse
4. Milo Savage
5. Rocky Castellani
6. Holley Mims
7. Gene Fullmer
8. Bobby Boyd
9. Ralph Jones
10. Artie Towne

Welterweights
World Champion
Carmen Basilio
1. Tony DeMarco
2. Johnny Saxton
3. Ramon Fuentes
4. Vince Martinez
5. Isaac Logart
6. Virgil Akins
7. Del Flanagan
8. George Barnes
9. Art Aragon
10. Joe Miceli

Lightweights
World Champion
Wallace (Bud) Smith
1. Duilio Loi
2. James Carter
3. Frankie Ryff
4. Ralph Dupas
5. Ludwig Lightburn
6. Johnny Gonsalves
7. Cisco Andrade
8. Kenny Lane
9. Orlando Zulueta
10. Joe Lopes

Featherweights
World Champion
Sandy Saddler
1. Fred Galiana
2. Carmelo Costa
3. Ciro Morasen
4. Hogan (Kid) Bassey
5. Gabriel (Flash) Elorde
6. Ray Famechon
7. Martin Rodriguez
8. Victor (Sonny) Leon
9. Teddy (Red Top) Davis
10. Paul Jorgensen

Bantamweights
World Champion
Robert Cohen
1. Mario D'Agata
2. Billy Peacock
3. Raul (Raton) Macias
4. Andre Valignat
5. Emil Chemama
6. Little Cezar
7. Jose Lopez
8. Pierre Cossemyns
9. Peter Keenan
10. Fili Nava

Flyweights
World Champion
Pascual Perez
1. Young Martin
2. Leo Espinosa
3. Danny Kid
4. Dai Dower
5. Tanny Campo
6. Jake Tuli
7. Oscar Suarez
8. Memo Diez
9. Hitoshi Misako
10. Guy Schatt

RING RATINGS
1 9 5 6

Heavyweights
World Champion
Floyd Patterson
1. Tommy Jackson
2. Archie Moore
3. Harold Carter
4. Willie Pastrano
5. Eddie Machen
6. Bob Satterfield
7. Ingemar Johansson
8. Bob Baker
9. Zora Folley
10. Wayne Bethea

Light Heavyweights
World Champion
Archie Moore
1. Gerhard Hecht
2. Chuck Spieser
3. Hans Stretz
4. Tony Anthony
5. Yolande Pompey
6. Willi Besmanoff
7. Dogomar Martinez
8. Randy Turpin
9. Charles Colin
10. Willi Hoepner

Middleweights
World Champion
Ray Robinson
1. Gene Fullmer
2. Charley Humez
3. Ralph Jones
4. Ellsworth (Spider) Webb
5. Rory Calhoun
6. Joey Giardello
7. Joey Giambra
8. Neal Rivers
9. Chebo Hernandez
10. Charley Joseph

Welterweights
World Champion
Carmen Basilio
1. Johnny Saxton
2. Gaspar Ortega
3. Tony DeMarco
4. Isaac Logart
5. Virgil Akins
6. Art Aragon
7. Vince Martinez
8. Ramon Fuentes
9. George Barnes
10. Joe Miceli

Lightweights
World Champion
Joe Brown
1. Duilio Loi
2. Kenny Lane
3. Johnny Gonsalves
4. Larry Boardman
5. Wallace (Bud) Smith
6. Orlando Zulueta
7. Cisco Andrade
8. Ralph Dupas
9. Willie Toweel
10. Jimmy Carter

Featherweights
World Champion
Sandy Saddler
1. Cherif Hamia
2. Hogan (Kid) Bassey
3. Miguel Berrios
4. Carmelo Costa
5. Paul Jorgensen
6. Jean Sneyers
7. Gabriel (Flash) Elorde
8. Gil Cadilli
9. Altidoro Polidori
10. Victor (Sonny) Leon

Bantamweights
World Champion
Mario D'Agata
1. Raul (Raton) Macias
2. Leo Espinosa
3. Alphonse Halimi
4. German Ohm
5. Billy Peacock
6. Tanny Campo
7. Robert Tartari
8. Danti Bini
9. Al Asuncion
10. Jose Lopez

Flyweights
World Champion
Pascual Perez
1. Memo Diez
2. Dia Dower
3. Young Martin
4. Hitoshi Misako
5. Dommy Ursua
6. Aristide Pozzali
7. Pone Kingpetch
8. Danny Kid
9. Robert Pollazon
10. Oscar Suarez

R I N G   R A T I N G S
1 9 5 7

Heavyweights
World Champion
Floyd Patterson
1. Eddie Machen
2. Zora Folley
3. Willie Pastrano
4. Roy Harris
5. Pat McMurtry
6. Nino Valdes
7. Mike DeJohn
8. Wayne Bethea
9. Alex Miteff
10. Ingemar Johansson

Light Heavyweights
World Champion
Archie Moore
1. Harold Johnson
2. Yolande Pompey
3. Yvon Durelle
4. Tony Anthony
5. Willie Hoepner
6. Artenio Calzavara
7. Chuck Spieser
8. Clarence Hinnant
9. Gerhard Hecht
10. Erich Schoppner

Middleweights
World Champion
Carmen Basilio
1. Ray Robinson
2. Gene Fullmer
3. Ellsworth (Spider) Webb
4. Joey Giardello
5. Charley Humez
6. Rory Calhoun
7. Joey Giambra
8. Bobby Boyd
9. Charley Joseph
10. Willie Vaughn

Welterweights
Title Vacant

1. Virgil Akins
2. Isaac Logart
3. Vince Martinez
4. Charley Smith
5. Tony DeMarco
6. Gil Turner
7. Gaspar Ortega
8. Kid Gavilan
9. George Barnes
10. Garnet (Sugar) Hart

Lightweights
World Champion
Joe Brown
1. Duilio Loi
2. Kenny Lane
3. Ralph Dupas
4. Willie Toweel
5. Paolo Rosi
6. Joe Lopes
7. Baby Vasquez
8. Al Nevarez
9. Orlando Zulueta
10. Johnny Busso

Featherweights
World Champion
Hogan (Kid) Bassey
1. Cherif Hamia
2. Davey Moore
3. Gabriel (Flash) Elorde
4. Paul Jorgensen
5. Ike Chestnut
6. Ricardo Gonzalez
7. Ricardo Moreno
8. Jean Sneyers
9. Shigeji Kaneko
10. Gracieux Lamperti

Bantamweights
World Champion
Alphonse Halimi
1. Raul (Raton) Macias
2. Mario D'Agata
3. Leo Espinosa
4. Al Asuncion
5. Jose Lopez
6. Piero Rollo
7. Manuel Armenteros
8. Joe Beccera
9. Eugene LeCozannet
10. Peter Keenan

Flyweights
World Champion
Pascual Perez
1. Ramon Arias
2. Young Martin
3. Pone Kingpetch
4. Dommy Ursua
5. Aristide Pozzali
6. Ramon Calatayud
7. Masaju (Lefty) Iwamoto
8. Sadao Yaoita
9. Memo Diez
10. Dennis Adams

R I N G   R A T I N G S
1 9 5 8

Heavyweights
World Champion
Floyd Patterson
1. Ingemar Johannson
2. Nino Valdes
3. Zora Folley
4. Henry Cooper
5. Willie Pastrano
6. Archie Moore
7. Eddie Machen
8. Brian London
9. Sonny Liston
10. Mike DeJohn

Light Heavyweights
World Champion
Archie Moore
1. Tony Anthony
2. Harold Johnson
3. Yvon Durelle
4. Erich Shoppner
5. Sonny Ray
6. Mike Holt
7. Johnny Halafihi
8. Jesse Bowdry
9. Yolande Pompey
10. Jerry Luedee

Middleweights
World Champion
Ray Robinson
1. Carmen Basilio
2. Gene Fullmer
3. Ellsworth (Spider) Webb
4. Gustav Scholz
5. Joey Giardello
6. Holley Mims
7. Bobby Boyd
8. Rory Calhoun
9. Gene Armstrong
10. Ralph (Tiger) Jones

Welterweights
World Champion
Don Jordan
1. Virgil Akins
2. Garnet (Sugar) Hart
3. Isaac Logart
4. Ralph Dupas
5. Del Flanagan
6. Gaspar Ortega
7. Vince Martinez
8. Gil Turner
9. Gerald Gray
10. Emilio Marconi

Lightweights
World Champion
Joe Brown
1. Kenny Lane
2. Carlos Ortiz
3. Duilio Loi
4. Johnny Busso
5. Paolo Rosi
6. Dave Charnley
7. Willie Toweel
8. Paul Armstead
9. Johnny Gonsalves
10. Bobby Scanlon

Featherweights
World Champion
Hogan (Kid) Bassey
1. Davey Moore
2. Paul Jorgensen
3. Gabriel (Flash) Elorde
4. Gracieux Lamperti
5. Ike Chestnut
6. Ricardo Gonzalez
7. Sergio Caprari
8. Manolo Garcia
9. Victor (Sonny) Leon
10. Percy Lewis

Bantamweights
World Champion
Alphonse Halimi
1. Piero Rollo
2. Leo Espinosa
3. Mario D'Agata
4. Jose Lopez
5. Manuel Armenteros
6. Joe Becerra
7. Boots Monroe
8. Kiyoshi Miura
9. Ernesto Miranda
10. Al Asuncion

Flyweights
World Champion
Pascual Perez
1. Sadao Yaoita
2. Ramon Arias
3. Young Martin
4. Pone Kingpetch
5. Dommy Ursua
6. Mario DeLeon
7. Ramon Calatayud
8. Mimun Ben Ali
9. Carlos Miranda
10. Horacio Accavallo

R I N G   R A T I N G S
1 9 5 9

Heavyweights
World Champion
Ingemar Johansson
1. Zora Folly
2. Floyd Patterson
3. Sonny Liston
4. Henry Cooper
5. Eddie Machen
6. Billy Hunter
7. Roy Harris
8. Mike DeJohn
9. Joe Erskine
10. Alex Miteff

Light Heavyweights
World Champion
Archie Moore
1. Harold Johnson
2. Erich Schoppner
3. Mike Holt
4. Von Clay
5. Sixto Rodriguez
6. Jesse Bowdry
7. Johnny Halafihi
8. Sonny Ray
9. Chic Calderwood
10. Sante Amonti

Middleweights
World Champion
Ray Robinson
1. Gene Fullmer
2. Gustav Scholz
3. Ellsworth (Spider) Webb
4. Joey Giardello
5. Henry Hank
6. Carmen Basilio
7. Dick Tiger
8. Paul Pender
9. Joey Giambra
10. Holley Mims

Welterweights
World Champion
Don Jordan
1. Luis Rodriguez
2. Charley Scott
3. Rudell Stitch
4. Ralph Dupas
5. Denny Moyer
6. Garnet (Sugar) Hart
7. Kenny Lane
8. Federico Thompson
9. Benny (Kid) Paret
10. Florentino Fernandez

Lightweights
World Champion
Joe Brown
1. Paolo Rosi
2. Carlos Ortiz
3. Dave Charnley
4. Battling Torres
5. Willie Toweel
6. Len Matthews
7. Paul Armstead
8. Johnny Gonsalves
9. Mario Vecchiato
10. Johnny Busso

Featherweights
World Champion
Davey Moore
1. Ricardo Gonzalez
2. Harold Gomes
3. Gracieux Lamperti
4. Hogan (Kid) Bassey
5. Sergio Caprari
6. Paul Jorgensen
7. Rafiu King
8. Ike Chestnut
9. Gabriel (Flash) Elorde
10. Sugar Ramos

Bantamweights
World Champion
Joe Becerra
1. Alphonse Halimi
2. Freddie Gilroy
3. Eder Jofre
4. Piero Rollo
5. Danny Kid
6. Leo Espinosa
7. Jose Lopez
8. Kenji Yonekura
9. Ernesto Miranda
10. Herman Marques

Flyweights
World Champion
Pascual Perez
1. Sadao Yaoita
2. Pone Kingpetch
3. Ramon Arias
4. Dommy Ursua
5. Mimum Ben Ali
6. Hiram Bacallao
7. Risto Luukkonen
8. Larry Pineda
9. Joe Medel
10. Ramon Calatayud

RING RATINGS
1 9 6 0

Heavyweights
World Champion
Floyd Patterson
1. Sonny Liston
2. Ingemar Johansson
3. Eddie Machen
4. Zora Folley
5. Henry Cooper
6. Mike DeJohn
7. Robert Cleroux
8. Alex Miteff
9. Dick Richardson
10. Joe Erskine

Light Heavyweights
World Champion
Archie Moore
1. Harold Johnson
2. Chic Calderwood
3. Erich Schoppner
4. Willie Pastrano
5. Giulio Rinaldi
6. Doug Jones
7. Mike Holt
8. Carl (Bobo) Olson
9. Johnny Halafihi
10. Germinal Ballarin

Middleweights
World Champion
Paul Pender
1. Gene Fullmer
2. Gustav Scholz
3. Hank Casey
4. Joey Giardello
5. Ray Robinson
6. Henry Hank
7. Joey Giambra
8. Terry Downes
9. Don Fullmer
10. Dick Tiger

Welterweights
World Champion
Benny (Kid) Paret
1. Luis Rodriquez
2. Federico Thomspon
3. Ralph Dupas
4. Denny Moyer
5. Don Jordan
6. Emile Griffith
7. Duilio Loi
8. Florentino Fernandez
9. Jorge Fernandez
10. Gaspar Ortega

Lightweights
World Champion
Joe Brown
1. Dave Charnely
2. Carlos Ortiz
3. Len Matthews
4. Carlos Hernandez
5. Gabriel (Flash) Elorde
6. Cisco Andrade
7. Kenny Lane
8. Eddie Perkins
9. Battling Torres
10. Nursey Kid

Featherweights
World Champion
Davey Moore
1. Gracieux Lamperti
2. Sugar Ramos
3. Sergio Caprari
4. Percy Lewis
5. Ricardo Gonzalez
6. Rafiu King
7. Felix Cervantes
8. Ray Nobile
9. Terry Spinks
10. Danny Valdez

Bantamweights
Title Vacant
1. Eder Jofre
2. Alphonse Halimi
3. Piero Rollo
4. Freddie Gilroy
5. Kenju Yonekura
6. Joe Medel
7. Eloy Sanchez
8. Ignacio Pina
9. Jose Lopez
10. Leo Espinosa

Flyweights
World Champion
Pone Kingpetch
1. Mimum Ben Ali
2. Pascual Perez
3. Sadao Yaoita
4. Johnny Caldwell
5. Dommy Ursua
6. Edmundo Esparza
7. Ramon Arias
8. Mitsunroi Seki
9. Leo Zulueta
10. Risto Luukkonen

RING RATINGS
1 9 6 1

Heavyweights
World Champion
Floyd Patterson
1. Sonny Liston
2. Eddie Machen
3. Zora Folley
4. Alejandro Lavorante
5. Robert Cleroux
6. Ingemar Johansson
7. Cleveland Williams
8. Henry Cooper
9. Cassius Clay
10. George Logan

Light Heavyweights
World Champion
Archie Moore
1. Harold Johnson
2. Giulio Rinaldi
3. Doug Jones
4. Eddie Cotton
5. Erich Schoppner
6. Chic Calderwood
7. Gustav Scholz
8. Mauro Mina
9. Von Clay
10. Willie Pastrano

Middleweights
World Champion
Terry Downes
1. Gene Fullmer
2. Dick Tiger
3. Paul Pender
4. Ray Robinson
5. Henry Hank
6. Florentino Fernandez
7. Yama Bahama
8. Joey Giardello
9. Denny Moyer
10. Jesse Smith

Welterweights
World Champion
Benny (Kid) Paret
1. Emile Griffith
2. Ralph Dupas
3. Jorge Fernandez
4. Luis Rodriguez
5. Duilio Loi
6. Federico Thompson
7. Brian Curvis
8. Ted Wright
9. Luis Folledo
10. Curtis Cokes

Lightweights
World Champion
Joe Brown
1. Carlos Ortiz
2. Davey Charnley
3. Gabriel (Flash) Elorde
4. Eddie Perkins
5. Doug Vaillant
6. Kenny Lane
7. Carlos Hernandez
8. Paolo Rosi
9. Bert Somodio
10. Len Matthews

Featherweights
World Champion
Davey Moore
1. Rafiu King
2. Howard Winstone
3. Sugar Ramos
4. Kazuo Takayama
5. Sergio Caprari
6. Gracieux Lamperti
7. Danny Valdez
8. Jet Bally
9. Lalo Guerrero
10. Jose Luis Cruz

Bantamweights
Title Vacant
1. Eder Jofre
2. Joe Medel
3. Johnny Caldwell
4. Pierre Cossemyns
5. Alphonse Halimi
6. Piero Rollo
7. Leo Espinosa
8. Ismael Laguna
9. Freddie Gilroy
10. Herman Marques

Flyweights
World Champion
Pone Kingpetch
1. Ramon Arias
2. Mimum Ben Ali
3. Sadao Yaoita
4. Salvatore Burruni
5. Pascual Perez
6. Chatchai Lamphafa
7. Kyo Noguchi
8. Jean Guerard
9. Chucho Hernandez
10. Horacio Accavallo

RING RATINGS
1 9 6 2

Heavyweights
World Champion
Sonny Liston
1. Floyd Patterson
2. Cassius Clay
3. Doug Jones
4. Ingemar Johansson
5. Zora Folley
6. Cleveland Williams
7. Robert Cleroux
8. Billy Daniels
9. Archie Moore
10. Henry Cooper

Light Heavyweights
World Champion
Harold Johnson
1. Mauro Mina
2. Giulio Rinaldi
3. Eddie Cotton
4. Gustav Scholz
5. Carl (Bobo) Olson
6. Willie Pastrano
7. Erich Schoppner
8. Henry Hank
9. Chic Calderwood
10. Allen Thomas

Middleweights
World Champions
Paul Pender & Dick Tiger
1. Gene Fullmer
2. Terry Downes
3. George Benton
4. Joey Giardello
5. Luis Folledo
6. Denny Moyer
7. Laszlo Papp
8. Joey Archer
9. Joey Giambra
10. Bruno Visintin

Welterweights
World Champion
Emile Griffith
1. Luis Rodriguez
2. Brian Curvis
3. Ralph Dupas
4. Ted Wright
5. Jorge Fernandez
6. Rip Randall
7. Frederico Thompson
8. Curtis Cokes
9. Bob Fosmire
10. Issac Logart

Junior Welterweights
World Champion
Duilio Lio
1. Eddie Perkins
2. Kenny Lane
3. Louis Molina
4. Battling Tores
5. Jose Stable
6. Angel Garcia
7. Manuel Alvarez
8. Aissa Hashas
9. Ben Medina
10. Jose Napoles

Lightweights
World Champion
Carlos Ortiz
1. Bunny Grant
2. Carlos Hernandez
3. Doug Vaillant
4. Joe Brown
5. Alfredo Urbina
6. Paul Armstead
7. Arthur Persley
8. Dave Charnley
9. Teruo Kosaka
10. Sebastiao Nascimento

Junior Lightweights
World Champion
Gabriel (Flash) Elorde
1. Ray Nobile
2. Auburn Copeland
3. Love Allotey
4. Jose Luis Cruz
5. Johnny Bizzarro
6. Yukio Katsumato
7. Harold Gomes
8. Oscar Reyes
9. Vince Derardo
10. Mel Middleton

Featherweights
World Champion
Davey Moore
1. Sugar Ramos
2. Rafiu King
3. Kazuo Takayama
4. Jet Bally
5. Howard Winstone
6. Mitsunori Seki
7. Danny Valdez
8. Don Johnson
9. Alberto Serti
10. Billy Calvert

Bantamweights
World Champion
Eder Jofre
1. Ismael Laguna
2. Piero Rollo
3. Alphonse Halimi
4. Joe Medel
5. Katsutoshi Aoki
6. Pierre Cossemyns
7. Johnny Caldwell
8. Freddie Gilroy
9. Jorge Salazar
10. Edmundo Esparza

Flyweights
World Champion
Fighting Harada
1. Pone Kingpetch
2. Salvatore Burruni
3. Bernardo Carballao
4. Ramon Arias
5. Pascual Perez
6. Hiroyuki Ebihara
7. Horacio Accavallo
8. Mimun Ben Ali
9. Seisaku Saito
10. Kyo Noguchi

RING RATINGS
1 9 6 3

Heavyweights
World Champion
Sonny Liston
1. Cassius Clay
2. Doug Jones
3. Ernie Terrell
4. Cleveland Williams
4. Zora Folley
6. Eddie Machen
7. Floyd Patterson
8. Karl Mildenberger
9. George Chuvalo
10. Brian London

Light Heavyweights
World Champion
Willie Pastrano
1. Eddie Cotton
2. Harold Johnson
3. Guilio Rinaldi
4. Mauro Mina
5. Gregorio Peralta
6. Carl (Bobo) Olson
7. Henry Hank
8. Wayne Thornton
9. Terry Downes
10. Gustav Scholz

Middleweights
World Champion
Joey Giardello
1. Dick Tiger
2. Joey Archer
3. Rubin (Hurricane) Carter
4. Laszlo Papp
5. Gene Fullmer
6. Sandro Mazzinghi
7. Nino Benvenuti
8. Luis Folledo
9. Jose Torres
10. Joe Gonzalez

Welterweights
World Champion
Emile Griffith
1. Luis Rodriguez
2. Jose Stable
3. Brian Curvis
4. Ralph Dupas
5. Rip Randall
6. Federico Thompson
7. Curtis Cokes
8. Gaspar Ortega
9. Dick Turner
10. Stan Harrington

Junior Welterweights
World Champion
Eddie Perkins
1. Louis Molina
2. Angel Garcia
3. Roberto Cruz
4. Jose Napoles
5. Aissa Hashas
6. Battling Torres
7. Bobby Scanlon
8. Rodolfo (Tito) Marshall
9. Mario Rositto
10. Enoch Nhlapo

Lightweights
World Champion
Carlos Ortiz
1. Kenny Lane
2. Carlos Hernandez
3. Alfredo Urbina
4. Dave Charnley
5. Bunny Grant
6. Paul Armstead
7. Teruo Kosaka
8. Nicolino Loche
9. Doug Vaillant
10. Sandro Lopopolo

Junior Lightweights
World Champion
Gabriel (Flash) Elorde
1. Johnny Bizzarro
2. Love Allotey
3. Vincente Derado
4. Jose Luis Cruz
5. Auburn Copeland
6. Yukio Katsumato
7. Kazuo Takayama
8. Young Terror
9. Ray Adigun
10. Mel Middleton

Featherweights
World Champion
Sugar Ramos
1. Mitsunori Seki
2. Ismael Laguna
3. Howard Winstone
4. Rafiu King
5. Don Johnson
6. Danny Valdez
7. Floyd Robertson
8. Willi Quatour
9. Antonio Herrera
10. Billy Calvert

Bantamweights
World Champion
Eder Jofre
1. Joe Medel
2. Fighting Harada
3. Alphonse Halimi
4. Ronnie Jones
5. Piero Rollo
6. Jesus Pimentel
7. Manny Barrios
8. Mimun Ben Ali
9. Risto Luukkonen
10. Ray Asis

Flyweights
World Champion
Hiroyuki Ebihara
1. Salvatore Burruni
2. Bernardo Caraballo
3. Horacio Accavallo
4. Pone Kingpetch
5. Alacran Efren Torres
6. Leon Zulueta
7. Walter McGowan
8. Takeshi Nakamura
9. Pascual Perez
10. Raton Mojica

RING RATINGS
1 9 6 4

Heavyweights
World Champion
Muhammad Ali
1. Sonny Liston
2. Floyd Patterson
3. Ernie Terrell
4. Cleveland Williams
5. George Chuvalo
6. Zora Folley
7. Karl Mildenberger
8. Roger Rischer
9. Eddie Machen
10. Doug Jones

Light Heavyweights
World Champion
Willie Pastrano
1. Gregorio Peralta
2. Harold Johnson
3. Eddie Cotton
4. Mauro Mina
5. Wayne Thornton
6. Jose Torres
7. Gustav Scholz
8. Terry Downes
9. Carl (Bobo) Olson
10. Johnny Persol

Middleweights
World Champion
Joey Giardello
1. Joey Archer
2. Dick Tiger
3. Ruben Carter
4. Laszlo Papp
5. Sandro Mazzinghi
6. Nino Benvenuti
7. Hurricane Kid
8. Luis Folledo
9. Gomeo Brennan
10. Mick Leahy

Welterweights
World Champion
Emile Griffith
1. Luis Rodriguez
2. Jose Stable
3. Brian Curvis
4. Manuel Gonzales
5. William Ludick
6. Stan Hayward
7. Fortunato Manca
8. Gabriel Terronez
9. Gaspar Ortega
10. Jean Josselin

Junior Welterweights
World Champion
Eddie Perkins
1. Jose Napoles
2. Pierro Brandi
3. Sandro Popopolo
4. Tito Marshall
5. Louis Molina
6. Johnny De Peiza
7. Olli Maki
8. Valero Nunez
9. Doug Vaillant
10. Giordano Campari

Lightweights
World Champion
Carlos Ortiz
1. Dave Charnley
2. Carlos Hernandez
3. Bunny Grant
4. Angel Robinson Garcia
5. Nicolino Loche
6. Paul Armstead
7. Kenny Lane
8. Frankie Narvaez
9. Franco Brondi
10. Alfredo Urbina

Junior Lightweights
World Champion
Gabriel (Flash) Elorde
1. Johnny Bizzarro
2. Willie Quartour
3. Terou Kosaka
4. Love Allotey
5. Jose Luis Cruz
6. Ray Adigun
7. Kang Suh Il
8. Vincente Derado
9. Danny Valdez
10. Levi Midi

Featherweights
World Champion
Vicente Saldivar
1. Ismael Laguna
2. Sugar Ramos
3. Floyd Robertson
4. Mitsunori Seki
5. Don Johnson
6. Howard Winstone
7. Raul Rojas
8. Carlos Canete
9. Antonio Herrera
10. Rafiu King

Bantamweights
World Champion
Eder Jofre
1. Fighting Harada
2. Joe Medel
3. Jesus Pimental
4. Manuel Barrios
5. Bernardo Caraballo
6. Ronnie Jones
7. Risto Luukkonen
8. Felix Brami
9. Ray Asis
10. Johnny Caldwell

Flyweights
World Champion
Pone Kingpetch
1. Salvatore Burruni
2. Hiroyuki Ebihara
3. Alacran Efren Torres
4. Horacio Accavallo
5. Rocky Gattelari
6. Takeshi Nakamura
7. Raton Mojica
8. Katsuyoshi Takayama
9. Walter McGowan
10. Bob Allotey

R I N G   R A T I N G S
1 9 6 5

Heavyweights
World Champion
Muhammad Ali
1. Ernie Terrell
2. Floyd Patterson
3. George Chuvalo
4. Karl Mildenberger
5. Zora Folley
6. Amos Lincoln
7. Thad Spencer
8. Doug Jones
9. Hubert Hilton
10. Brian London

Light Heavyweights
World Champion
Jose Torres
1. Wayne Thornton
2. Mauro Mina
3. Bob Foster
4. Gregorio Peralta
5. Roger Rouse
6. Eddie Cotton
7. Carl (Bobo) Olson
8. Willie Pastrano
9. Giulio Rinaldi
10. Gert (Hotty) Van Heerden

Middleweights
World Champion
Dick Tiger
1. Nino Benvenuti
2. Joey Archer
3. Joey Giardello
4. Gomeo Brennan
5. Ruben (Hurricane) Carter
6. Luis Folledo
7. Sandro Mazzinghi
8. Don Fullmer
9. Jose Gonzalez
10. Stan Harrington

Welterweights
World Champion
Emile Griffith
1. Luis Rodriguez
2. Manuel Gonzalez
3. Willie Ludick
4. Brian Curvis
5. Curtis Cokes
6. Fortunato Manca
7. Ted Whitfield
8. Billy Collins
9. Eddie Pace
10. Tito Marshall

Junior Welterweights
World Champion
Carlos Hernandez
1. Jose Napoles
2. Adolph Pruitt
3. Eddie Perkins
4. Juan Sombrita
4. Pierro Brandi
6. Johnny Santos
7. Paul Fujii
8. Sandro Lopopolo
9. Pedro Adigue
10. Makoto Watanabe

Lightweights
World Champion
Carlos Ortiz
1. Ismael Laguna
2. Nicolino Loche
3. Paul Armstead
4. Angel Robinson Garcia
5. Frankie Narvaez
6. Bunny Grant
7. Maurice Cullen
8. Sugar Ramos
9. Ray Adigun
10. Franco Brondi

Junior Lightweights
World Champion
Gabriel (Flash) Elorde
1. Johnny Bizzarro
2. Love Allotey
3. Teruo Kosaka
4. Carlos (Teo) Cruz
5. Kid Tano
6. Vicente Derado
7. Kang Suh Il
8. Danny Valdez
9. Alfonso Frazier
10. Rene Barrientos

Featherweights
World Champion
Vincente Saldivar
1. Richard Sue
2. Carlos Canete
3. Mitsunori Seki
4. Howard Winstone
5. Ricardo Moreno
6. Floyd Robertson
7. Raul Rojas
8. Hiroshi Kobayashi
9. Rokoru Ishiyama
10. Yves Desmarets

Bantamweights
World Champion
Fighting Harada
1. Eder Jofre
2. Jesus Pimental
3. Joe Medel
4. Bernardo Caraballo
5. Alan Rudkin
6. Manny Elias
7. Tommaso Galli
8. Mimun Ben Ali
9. Manuel Barrios
10. Baby Lorona

Flyweights
World Champion
Salvatore Burruni
1. Hiroyuki Ebihara
2. Horacio Accavallo
3. Katsutoshi Takayama
4. Pone Kingpetch
5. Rocky Gattellari
6. Vitayinoi Singyodah
7. Puntip Keosuriya
8. Kiyoshi Tanabe
9. Alacran Efren Torres
10. Walter McGowan

R I N G   R A T I N G S
1 9 6 6

Heavyweights
World Champion
Muhammad Ali
1. Ernie Terrell
2. Zora Folley
3. Thad Spencer
4. Floyd Patterson
5. Karl Mildenberger
6. Joe Frazier
7. Oscar Bonavena
8. George Chuvalo
9. Johnny Persol
10. Manuel Ramos

Light Heavyweights
World Champion
Dick Tiger
1. Jose Torres
2. Roger Rouse
3. Eddie Cotton
4. Piero Del Papa
5. Andres Selpa
6. Don Fullmer
7. Bob Dunlop
8. Gregorio Peralta
9. Carl (Bobo) Olson
10. Giovanni Biancardi

Middleweights
World Champion
Emile Griffith
1. Sandro Mazzinghi
2. Dick Tiger
3. Nino Benvenuti
4. Luis Folledo
5. Ki Soo Kim
6. Ferd Hernandez
7. Jose Gonzalez
8. Joey Archer
9. Stan Harrington
10. Johnny Pritchett

Welterweights
World Champion
Curtis Cokes
1. Jean Josselin
2. Luis Rodriguez
3. Willie Ludick
4. Conny Rudhof
5. Gypsy Joe Harris
6. Ernie Lopez
7. Francois Pavilla
8. Charlie Shipes
9. Leroy Roberts
10. Ted Whitfield

Junior Welterweights
World Champion
Sandro Lopopolo
1. Paul Fujii
2. Willi Quatour
3. Daniel Guanin
4. Eugenio Espinoza
5. Juan Sombrita
6. Jose Napoles
7. Marcel Cerdan, Jr.
8. Lennox Beckles
9. Paul Armstead
10. Herbie Lee

Lightweights
World Champion
Carlos Ortiz
1. Nicolino Loche
2. Carlos (Teo) Cruz
3. Maurice Cullen
4. Borge Krogh
5. Ismael Laguna
6. Angel Robinson Garcia
7. Frankie Narvaez
8. George Foster
9. Sugar Ramos
10. Ray Adigun

Junior Lightweights
World Champion
Gabriel (Flash) Elorde
1. Jose Legra
2. Pedro Gomez
3. Johnny Famechon
4. Antonio Amaya
5. Love Allotey
6. Kang Suh Il
7. Ray Echavarria
8. Jean De Keers
9. Rene Barrientos
10. Kid Tano

Featherweights
World Champion
Vicente Saldivar
1. Carlos Canete
2. Paul Rojas
3. Mitsunori Seki
4. Howard Winstone
5. Freddy Rengifo
6. Richard Sue
7. Hiroshi Kobayashi
8. Bobby Valdez
9. Alex Benitez
10. Mario Diaz

Bantamweights
World Champion
Fighting Harada
1. Jesus Pimental
2. Mimum Ben Ali
3. Alan Rudkin
4. Bernardo Caraballo
5. Joe Medel
6. Lionel Rose
7. Katsuo Saito
8. Valdomiro Pinto
9. Yoshio Nakane
10. Kamara Diop

Flyweights
World Champion
Chartchai Chionoi
1. Walter McGowan
2. Haracio Accavallo
3. Katsutoshi Takayama
4. Salvatore Burruni
5. Kiyoshi Tanabe
6. Hiroyuki Ebihara
7. Puntip Keosuriya
8. Alacran Efren Torres
9. Rocky Gattellari
10. Rene Libeer

R I N G   R A T I N G S
1 9 6 7

Heavyweights
World Champion
Muhammad Ali
1. Joe Frazier
2. Thad Spencer
3. Jimmy Ellis
4. Manuel Ramos
5. Jerry Quarry
6. Oscar Bonavena
7. Floyd Patterson
8. Eduardo Corletti
9. Karl Mildenberger
10. Ernie Terrell

Light Heavyweights
World Champion
Dick Tiger
1. Bob Foster
2. Gregorio Peralta
3. Bob Dunlop
4. Roger Rouse
5. Piero Del Papa
6. Eddie Cotton
7. Eddie Jones
8. Roger Russell
9. Lothar Stengel
10. Jack Rodgers

Middleweights
World Champion
Emile Griffith
1. Luis Rodriguez
2. Nino Benvenuti
3. Sandro Mazzinghi
4. Don Fullmer
5. Freddie Little
6. Ferd Hernandez
7. Ki Soo Kim
8. Luis Folledo
9. Tom Bogs
10. Juan Carlos Duran

Welterweights
World Champion
Curtis Cokes
1. Ernie Lopez
2. Gypsy Joe Harris
3. Willie Ludick
4. Jose Napoles
5. Joe Shaw
6. Carmelo Bossi
7. Conny Rudhof
8. Jean Josselin
9. Charlie Shippes
10. Ramon LaCruz

Junior Welterweights
World Champion
Paul Fujii
1. Nicolino Loche
2. Eddie Perkins
3. Johann Orsolics
4. Rodrigo Valdez
5. Percy Pugh
6. Marcel Cerdan, Jr.
7. Juan Sombrita
8. Koji Okano
9. Willi Quatuor
10. Barrera Corpas

Lightweights
World Champion
Carlos Ortiz
1. Ismael Laguna
2. Carlos (Teo) Cruz
3. Borge Krogh
4. Frankie Narvaez
5. Lloyd Marshall
6. Pedro Carrasco
7. Ken Buchanan
8. Pedro Adigue
9. Ray Adigun
10. Carlos Aro

Junior Lightweights
World Champion
Yoshiaki Numata
1. Raul Rojas
2. Jose Legra
3. Hiroshi Kobayashi
4. Carlos Canete
5. Antonio Amaya
6. Armando Ramos
7. Rene Barrientos
8. Kang Suh Il
9. Renaldo Victoria
10. Alton Colter

Featherweights
Title Vacant
1. Mitsunori Seki
2. Johnny Famechon
3. Howard Winstone
4. Bobby Valdez
5. Frankie Crawford
6. Ray Echavarria
7. Tony Alvarado
8. Jose Luis Valdovinos
9. Pedro Gomez
10. Richard Sue

Bantamweights
World Champion
Fighting Harada
1. Jesus Pimentel
2. Lionel Rose
3. Bernardo Caraballo
4. Takoa Sakurai
5. Rollie Penaroya
6. Mimum Ben Ali
7. Eigo Takagi
8. Yoshio Nakane
9. Franco Zurlo
10. Angel Sanchez

Flyweights
World Champion
Chartchai Chionoi
1. Horacio Accavallo
2. Walter McGowan
3. Raton Mojica
4. Fernando Atzori
5. Alacran Efren Torres
6. Octavio Gomez
7. John McCluskey
8. Hiroyuki Ebihara
9. Bernabe Villacampo
10. Katsutoshi Takayama

RING RATINGS
1 9 6 8

Heavyweights
World Champion
Muhammad Ali
1. Joe Frazier
2. Jimmy Ellis
3. Oscar Bonavena
4. George Chuvalo
5. Sonny Liston
6. Jerry Quarry
7. Leotis Martin
8. Manuel Ramos
9. Alvin (Blue) Lewis
10. Floyd Patterson

Light Heavyweights
World Champion
Bob Foster
1. Dick Tiger
2. Gregorio Peralta
3. Mark Tessman
4. Yvan Prebeg
5. Bob Dunlop
6. Tom Bogs
7. Andy Kendall
8. Jimmy Rosette
9. Eddie Jones
10. Harold Johnson

Middleweights
World Champion
Nino Benvenuti
1. Don Fullmer
2. Luis Rodriguez
3. Stan Hayward
4. Emile Griffith
5. Sandro Mazzinghi
6. Juan Carlos Duran
7. Carlos Monzon
8. Doyle Baird
9. Denny Moyer
10. Freddie Little

Welterweights
World Champion
Curtis Cokes
1. Jose Napoles
2. Percy Pugh
3. Paul Soriano
4. Manuel Gonzalez
5. Ernie Lopez
6. Fighting Mack
7. Billy Backus
8. Johann Orsolics
9. Carmelo Bossi
10. Joe Shaw

Junior Welterweights
World Champion
Paul Fujii
1. Bruno Arcari
2. Nicolino Loche
3. Adolph Pruittt
4. Pedro Adigue
5. Joao Henrique
6. Barrera Corpus
7. Willi Quatuor
8. German Gastelbondo
9. Rodrigo Valdez
10. Marcel Cerdan, Jr.

Lightweights
World Champion
Carlos (Teo) Cruz
1. Ismael Laguna
2. Pedro Carrasco
3. Carlos Ortiz
4. Ken Buchanan
5. Mando Ramos
6. Frankie Narvaez
7. Jaguar Kakizawa
8. Carlos Hernandez
9. Chango Carmona
10. Lloyd Marshall

Junior Lightweights
World Champion
Hiroshi Kobayashi
1. Yoshiaki Numata
2. Ruben Navarro
3. Carlos Canete
4. Antonio Amaya
5. Arturo Lomeli
6. Rene Barrientos
7. Pete Gonzalez
8. Don Johnson
9. Jaime Valladares
10. Len Kesey

Featherweights
Title Vacant
1. Jose Legra
2. Johnny Famechon
3. Shozo Saijyo
4. Fighting Harada
5. Dwight Hawkins
6. Jose Jimenez
7. Howard Winstone
8. Bobby Valdez
9. Raul Rojas
10. Cruz Marcano

Bantamweights
World Champion
Lionel Rose
1. Ruben Olivares
2. Chucho Castillo
3. Kazuyoshi Kanazawa
4. Takao Sakurai
5. Alan Rudkin
6. Domi Manalang
7. Salvatore Burruni
8. Jesus Pimentel
9. Johnny Clark
10. Franco Zurlo

Flyweights
World Champion
Chartchai Chionoi
1. Alacran Efren Torres
2. Bernabe Villacampo
3. Hiroyuki Ebihara
4. Jose Severino
5. Raton Mojica
6. Yoshiaki Matsumoto
7. Fernando Atzori
8. Fermin Gomez
9. Octavio Gomez
10. Walter McGowan

RING RATINGS
1 9 6 9

Heavyweights
World Champion
Muhammad Ali
1. Joe Frazier
2. Jimmy Ellis
3. Jerry Quarry
4. Leotis Martin
5. Mac Foster
6. Sonny Liston
7. Oscar Bonavena
8. Al Jones
9. Henry Cooper
10. Gregorio Peralta

Light Heavyweights
World Champion
Bob Foster
1. Dick Tiger
2. Ray Anderson
3. Jimmy Dupree
4. Mark Tessman
5. Yvan Prebeg
6. Bob Dunlop
7. Hal Carroll
8. Larry Buck
9. Andy Kendall
10. Vicente Rondon

Middleweights
World Champion
Nino Benvenuti
1. Freddie Little
2. Denny Moyer
3. Luis Rodriguez
4. Tom Bogs
5. Emile Griffith
6. Juan Carlos Duran
7. Fraser Scott
8. Doyle Baird
9. Don Fullmer
10. Carlos Monzon

Welterweights
World Champion
Jose Napoles
1. Manuel Gonzalez
2. Ernie Lopez
3. Percy Pugh
4. Hedgemon Lewis
5. Johann Orsolics
6. Rodrigo Valdez
7. Curtis Cokes
8. Billy Backus
9. Raul Rodriguez
10. Miguel Barreto

Junior Welterweights
World Champion
Nicolino Loche
1. Bruno Arcari
2. Adolph Pruitt
3. Joao Henrique
4. Turk Kamaci
5. Larry Harding
6. Enrique Jana
7. Jimmy Robertson
8. German Castelbondo
9. Eddie Perkins
10. Rodolfo Gonzalez

Lightweights
World Champion
Mando Ramos
1. Ismael Laguna
2. Pedro Carrasco
3. Jaguar Kakizawa
4. Carlos (Teo) Cruz
5. Arturo Lomeli
6. Ken Buchanan
7. Carlos Aro
8. Carlos Hernandez
9. Sugar Ramos
10. Chango Carmona

Junior Lightweights
World Champion
Hiroshi Kobayashi
1. Ruben Navarro
2. Antonio Amayo
3. Silvero Ortiz
4. Alfredo Marcano
5. Alton Colter
5. Ray Echavarria
7. Yoshiaki Numata
8. Jose Acosta
9. Rene Barrientos
10. Jose Smecca

Featherweights
World Champion
Johnny Famechon
1. Shozo Saijyo
2. Vicente Saldivar
3. Fighting Harada
4. Cruz Marcano
5. Antonio Gomez
6. Kuniaki Shibata
7. Jimmy Revie
8. Jose Legra
9. Lionel Rose
10. Dwight Hawkins

Bantamweights
World Champion
Ruben Olivares
1. Alan Rudkin
2. Takao Sakurai
3. Raul Cruz
4. Kazuyoshi Kanazawa
5. Chucho Castillo
6. Julio Guerrero
7. Ricardo Arredondo
8. Rudy Alarcon
9. Kaisuyoshi Takayama
10. Leo Calderon

Flyweights
World Champion
Alacran Efren Torres
1. Berkrerk Chartvanchai
2. Bernabe Villacampo
3. Susumu Hanagata
4. Fermin Gomez
5. Arturo Hernandez
6. Octavio Gomez
7. Chartchai Chionoi
8. Hiroyuki Ebihara
9. Lorenzo Halimi Gutierrez
10. Betulio Gonzalez

R I N G   R A T I N G S
1 9 7 0

Heavyweights
World Champion
Joe Frazier
1. Muhammad Ali
2. George Foreman
3. Oscar Bonavena
4. Jerry Quarry
5. Mac Foster
6. Henry Cooper
7. George Chuvalo
8. Sonny Liston
9. Jose Ibar Urtain
10. Jose Luis Garcia

Light Heavyweights
World Champion
Bob Foster
1. Jimmy Dupree
2. Vicente Rondon
3. Gomeo Brennan
4. Hal Carroll
5. Dick Tiger
6. Mark Tessman
7. Andy Kendall
8. Larry Buck
9. Piero Del Papa
10. Ron Marsh

Middleweights
World Champion
Carlos Monzon
1. Nino Benvenuti
2. Emile Griffith
3. Luis Rodriguez
4. Carmelo Bossi
5. Fraser Scott
6. Juan Carlos Duran
7. Doyle Baird
8. Denny Moyer
9. Tom Bogs
10. Rafael Gutierrez

Welterweights
World Champion
Billy Backus
1. Jose Napoles
2. Percy Pugh
3. Donato Paduano
4. Hedgemon Lewis
5. Ernie Lopez
6. Dario Hidalgo
7. Robert Gallois
8. Ralph Charles
9. Roger Menetrey
10. Jean Josselin

Junior Welterweights
World Champion
Nicolino Loche
1. Bruno Arcari
2. Adolph Pruitt
3. Eddie Perkins
4. Bunny Grant
5. Ely Yares
6. Joao Henrique
7. Enrique Jana
8. Jimmy Robertson
9. Lion Furuyama
10. Anthony Morodi

Lightweights
World Champion
Ken Buchanan
1. Ismael Laguna
2. Pedro Carrasco
3. Carlos Hernandez
4. Mando Ramos
5. Al Ford
6. Sugar Ramos
7. Miguel Velazquez
8. Raul Montoya
9. Shinichi Kadota
10. Chango Carmona

Junior Lightweights
World Champion
Hiroshi Kobayashi
1. Ruben Navarro
2. Yoshiaki Numata
3. Antonio Amaya
4. Rene Barrientos
5. Sammy Goss
6. Frank Otero
7. Frankie Crawford
8. Armando Mendoza
9. Jose Acosta
10. Hiroshi Shoji

Featherweights
World Champion
Kuniaki Shibata
1. Vincente Saldivar
2. Shozo Saijyo
3. Antonio Gomez
4. Raul Cruz
5. Eder Jofre
6. Jose Legra
7. Jose Luis Pimentel
8. Jimmy Revie
9. Alfredo Marcano
10. Ricardo Arredondo

Bantamweights
World Champion
Chucho Castillo
1. Ruben Olivares
2. Rodolfo Martinez
3. Jesus Pimentel
4. Alan Rudkin
5. Franco Zurlo
6. Ramon Bravo
7. Takao Sakurai
8. Orlando Amores
9. Rafael Herrera
10. Ushiwakamaru Harada

Flyweights
World Champion
Erbito Salvarria
1. Charachai Chionoi
2. Masao Ohba
3. Alacran Efren Torres
4. Bernabe Villacampo
5. Lorenzo Gutierrez
6. Berkrerk Chartvanchai
7. Octavio Gomez
8. Fermin Gomez
9. Susumu Hanagata
10. Fernando Atzori

RING RATINGS
1 9 7 1

Heavyweights
World Champion
Joe Frazier
1. Muhammad Ali
2. Jerry Quarry
3. George Foreman
4. Oscar Bonavena
5. Mac Foster
6. Jimmy Ellis
7. Floyd Patterson
8. Jose Luis Garcia
9. Jack Bodell
10. Joe Bugner

Light Heavyweights
World Champion
Bob Foster
1. Vicente Rondon
2. Pierre Fourie
3. Andy Kendall
4. Chris Finnegan
5. Mike Quarry
6. Jimmy Dupree
7. Brian Kelly Burden
8. Conny Velensek
9. Pat O'Connor
10. Gomeo Brennan

Middleweights
World Champion
Carlos Monzon
1. Bunny Sterling
2. Emile Griffith
3. Denny Moyer
4. Jean-Claude Bouttier
5. Rodrigo Valdez
6. Bennie Briscoe
7. Rafael Gutierrez
8. Koichi Wajima
9. Miguel de Oliveire
10. Eugene Hart

Welterweights
World Champion
Jose Napoles
1. Ernie Lopez
2. Adolph Pruitt
3. Marcel Cerdan, Jr.
4. Robert Gallois
5. Hedgemon Lewis
6. Armando Muniz
7. Thurman Durden
8. Billy Backus
9. Sandro Lopopolo
10. Nate Robinson

Junior Welterweights
World Champion
Nicolino Loche
1. Bruno Arcari
2. Joao Henrique
3. Johnny Gant
4. Eddie Perkins
5. Jeff White
6. Jimmy Robertson
7. Paco Flores
8. Carlos Gimenez
9. Rodolfo Gonzalez
10. Eagle Sato

Lightweights
World Champion
Ken Buchanan
1. Pedro Carrasco
2. Ismael Laguna
3. Antonio Paddu
4. Shinichi Kadota
5. Al Ford
6. Roberto Duran
7. Alfonso Frazier
8. Raymundo Dias
9. Chango Carmona
10. Mando Ramos

Junior Lightweights
World Champion
Alfredo Marcano
1. Frankie Otero
2. Frankie Crawford
3. Ugo Poli
4. William Martinez
5. Jose Luis Lopez
6. Jose Marin
7. Rene Barrientos
8. Yoshiaki Numata
9. Sammy Goss
10. Hiroshi Kobayashi

Featherweights
World Champion
Kuniaki Shibata
1. Antonio Gomez
2. Ricardo Arredondo
3. Eder Jofre
4. Ernesto Marcel
5. Shozo Saijyo
6. Vicente Saldivar
7. Tahar Hassen
8. Ben Villaflor
9. Jose Legra
10. Clemente Sanchez

Bantamweights
World Champion
Ruben Olivares
1. Jesus Pimentel
2. Rafael Herrera
3. Rodolfo Martinez
4. Chucho Castillo
5. Augustin Senin
6. Alan Rudkin
7. Enrique Pinder
8. Octavio Gomez
9. Ramon Bravo
10. Franco Zurlo

Flyweights
World Champion
Erbito Salvarria
1. Masao Ohba
2. Betulio Gonzalez
3. Servillo de Oliveire
4. Venich Borkorsor
5. Lorenzo Gutierrez
6. Miguel Canto
7. Ricardo Delgado
8. Fernando Atzori
9. Fernando Cabanela
10. Orlando Amoros

R I N G   R A T I N G S
1 9 7 2

Heavyweights
World Champion
Joe Frazier
1. Muhammad Ali
2. George Foreman
3. Jimmy Ellis
4. Ron Lyle
5. Floyd Patterson
6. Ernie Terrell
7. Jose Roman
8. Joe Bugner
9. Ken Norton
10. Jose Luis Garcia

Light Heavyweights
World Champion
Bob Foster
1. Andy Kendall
2. Pierre Fourie
3. Eddie Owens
4. Len Hutchins
5. Rudiger Schmidtke
6. Chris Finnegan
7. Victor Galindez
8. Pat O'Connor
9. Avenamar Peralta
10. John Frankham

Middleweights
World Champion
Carlos Monzon
1. Emile Griffith
2. Tony Mundine
3. Miguel de Oliviera
4. Jean-Claude Bouttier
5. Koichi Wajima
6. George Cooper
7. Bennie Briscoe
8. Nate Collins
9. Bunny Sterling
10. Juan Carlos Duran

Welterweights
World Champion
Jose Napoles
1. Hedgemon Lewis
1. Billy Backus
3. Roger Menetrey
4. Clyde Gray
5. Ernie Lopez
6. Jack Tillman
7. Robert Gallois
8. Young Kennedy
9. Buddy Boggs
10. Ryu Sorimachi

Junior Welterweights
World Champion
Antonio Cervantes
1. Bruno Arcari
2. Victor Ortiz
3. Alfonso Frazier
4. Carlos Gimenez
5. Romano Fanali
6. Eddie Perkins
7. Joe Tetteh
8. Turk Kamaci
9. Roger Zami
10. Joao Henrique

Lightweights
World Champion
Roberto Duran
1. Esteban DeJesus
2. Rodolfo Gonzalez
3. Ken Buchanan
4. Chango Carmona
5. Ray Lampkin
6. Antonio Puddu
7. Pedro Carrasco
8. Jimmy Heair
9. Ruben Navarro
10. Mando Ramos

Junior Lightweights
World Champion
Ben Villaflor
1. Victor Echegaray
2. Sammy Goss
3. Alfredo Marcano
4. Frankie Otero
4. Walter Seeley
6. Jose Fernandez
7. Hugo Bazzaro
8. Frankie Crawford
9. Love Allotey
10. William Martinez

Featherweights
World Champion
Clemente Sanchez
1. Ricardo Arredondo
2. Ernesto Marcel
3. Bert Nabalatan
4. Eder Jofre
5. Bob Allotey
6. Enrique Garcia
7. Danny Lopez
8. Arnold Taylor
9. Ruben Olivares
10. Kuniaki Shibata

Bantamweights
World Champion
Enrique Pinder
1. Chartchai Chionoi
2. Rodolfo Martinez
3. Augustin Senin
4. Rafael Herrera
5. Johnny Clark
6. Chucho Castillo
7. Romero Anaya
8. Paddy Maguire
9. Jose Casas
10. Octavio Gomez

Flyweights
World Champion
Erbito Salvarria
1. Masao Ohba
2. Venice Borkorsor
3. Betulio Gonzalez
4. Henry Nissen
5. Fritz Chervet
6. Miguel Canto
7. Susumu Hanagata
8. Osamu Haba
9. Tony Moreno
10. Lorenzo Gutierrez

R I N G   R A T I N G S
1 9 7 3

Heavyweights
World Champion
George Foreman
1. Muhammad Ali
2. Joe Frazier
3. Ken Norton
4. Jerry Quarry
5. Ron Lyle
5. Earnie Shavers
7. Oscar Bonavena
8. Joe Bugner
9. Jimmy Ellis
10. Chuck Wepner

Light Heavyweights
World Champion
Bob Foster
1. John Conteh
2. Len Hutchins
3. Tom Bogs
4. Victor Galindez
5. Pierre Fourie
6. Macie Smith
7. Chris Finnegan
8. Bobby Cassidy
9. Richie Kates
10. Andy Kendall

Middleweights
World Champion
Carlos Monzon
1. Tony Mundine
2. Rodrigo Valdez
3. Bennie Briscoe
4. Miguel de Oliviera
5. Jean-Claude Bouttier
6. Koichi Wajima
7. Tony Licata
8. Emile Griffith
9. Charkey Ramon
10. Luis Fabre

Welterweights
World Champion
Jose Napoles
1. Angel Espada
2. Hedgemon Lewis
3. Clyde Gray
4. Roger Menetrey
5. Fausto Rodriguez
6. John Stracey
7. Eddie Perkins
8. Jack Tillman
9. Horacio Saldano
10. Elisha Obed

Junior Welterweights
World Champion
Antonio Cervantes
1. Bruno Arcari
2. Alfonso Frazer
3. Roger Zami
4. Toni Ortiz
5. Hector Thompson
6. Miguel Barreto
7. Carlos Gimenez
8. Victor Ortiz
9. Mario Guilloti
10. Johnny Gant

Lightweights
World Champion
Roberto Duran
1. Esteban DeJesus
2. Ken Buchanan
3. Jimmy Heair
4. Rodolfo Gonzalez
5. Ray Lampkin
6. Hugo Gutierrez
7. Andres Steyn
8. Ould Makloufi
9. Shinicho Kadota
10. Ray Lunny

Junior Lightweights
World Champion
Ben Villaflor
1. Kuniaki Shibata
2. Lothar Abend
3. Alfredo Escalera
4. Sammy Goss
5. Alfredo Marcano
6. Ricardo Arredondo
7. Victor Echegaray
8. Love Allotey
9. Jesus Alonso
10. Arturo Pineda

Featherweights
Title Vacant
1. Eder Jofre
2. Ernesto Marcel
3. Art Hafey
4. Danny Lopez
5. Lionel Hernandez
6. Ruben Olivares
7. Bobby Chacon
8. Jose Legra
9. Santos Luis Rivera
10. Antonio (Gitano) Jimenez

Bantamweights
World Champion
Arnold Taylor
1. Romeo Anaya
2. Rafael Herrera
3. Venice Borkorsor
4. Johnny Clark
5. Benico Sosa
6. Paul Ferreri
7. Rodolfo Martinez
8. Jose Casas
9. Benny Rodriguez
10. Francisco Villegas

Flyweights
Title Vacant
1. Betulio Gonzalez
2. Chartchai Chionoi
3. Miguel Canto
4. Henry Nissen
5. Fritz Chervet
6. Erbito Salavarria
7. Tony Moreno
8. Vicente Pool
9. Costenito Morales
10. Fernando Atzori

R I N G   R A T I N G S
1 9 7 4

Heavyweights
World Champion
Muhammad Ali
1. George Foreman
2. Joe Frazier
3. Ron Lyle
4. Oscar Bonavena
5. Joe Bugner
6. Ken Norton
7. Jerry Quarry
8. Chuck Wepner
9. Henry Clark
10. Larry Middleton

Light Heavyweights
Title Vacant

1. John Conteh
2. Victor Galindez
3. Len Hutchins
4. Jorge Ahumada
5. Karl Heinz Klein
6. Alvaro Lopez
7. Richie Kates
8. Pierre Fourie
9. Maxie Smith
10. Tom Bogs

Middleweights
World Champion
Carlos Monzon
1. Rodrigo Valdez
2. Tony Licata
3. Vito Antuofermo
4. Gratien Tonna
5. Kevin Finnegan
6. George Cooper
7. Tony Mundine
8. Bennie Briscoe
9. Emile Griffith
10. Bobby Watts

Junior Middleweights
World Champion
Oscar Alvarado
1. Elisha Obed
2. Jose Duran
3. Koichi Wajima
4. Miguel Angel Campanino
5. Miguel de Oliviera
6. Eckhard Dagge
7. Larry Paul
8. Charkey Ramon
9. Donato Paduano
10. Miguel Castellini

Welterweights
World Champion
Jose Napoles
1. Clyde Gray
2. Angel Espada
3. John Stracey
4. Fausto Rodriguez
5. Rocky Mattioli
6. Hedgemon Lewis
7. Johnny Gant
8. Armando Muniz
9. Bruno Arcari
10. Sandy Torres

Junior Welterweights
World Champion
Antonio Cervantes
1. Hector Thompson
2. Esteban DeJesus
3. Pedro Fernandez
4. Tony Petronelli
5. Monroe Brooks
6. Toni Ortiz
7. Emiliano Villa
8. Leoncio Ortiz
9. Brooks Byrd
10. Miguel Barreto

Lightweights
World Champion
Roberto Duran
1. Ray Lampkin
2. Angel Mavoral
3. Ken Buchanan
4. Hugo Gutierrez
5. Rudy Barro
6. Ishimatsu Suzuki
7. Arturo Pineda
8. Ray Lunny
9. Hugo Barraza
10. Miguel Mayan

Junior Lightweights
World Champion
Ben Villaflor
1. Kuniaki Shibata
2. Sven-Erik Paulsen
3. Tyrone Everett
4. Victor Echegaray
5. Lothar Abend
6. Samuel Serrano
7. Jean-Baptiste Piedvache
8. Alfredo Escalera
9. Apollo Yoshio
10. Pedro Aguero

Featherweights
Title Vacant

1. Bobby Chacon
2. Alexis Arguello
3. Lionel Hernandez
4. Alfredo Marcano
5. Art Hafey
6. Ruben Olivares
7. Shig Fukuyama
8. Antonio (Gitano) Jiminez
9. Eder Jofre
10. Royal Kobayashi

Bantamweights
World Champion
Soo Hwan Hong
1. Benicio Sosa
2. Rafael Herrera
3. Romeo Anaya
4. Rodolfo Martinez
5. Jose Casas
6. Arnold Taylor
7. David Vasquez
8. Alfonso Zamora
9. Paul Ferreri
10. Jose Luis Soto

Flyweights
Title Vacant

1. Miguel Canto
2. Shoji Oguma
3. Thanomjit Sukothai
4. Betulio Gonzalez
5. Susumu Hanagata
6. Vicente Pool
7. Erbito Salvarria
8. Ignacio Espinoza
9. Fritz Chervet
10. Cecil Escobido

R I N G   R A T I N G S
1 9 7 5

Heavyweights
World Champion
Muhammad Ali
1. Ken Norton
2. Jimmy Young
3. Joe Frazier
4. George Foreman
5. Ron Lyle
6. Earnie Shavers
7. Duane Bobick
8. Joe Bugner
9. Chuck Wepner
10. Randy Neumann

Light Heavyweights
Title Vacant

1. Victor Galindez
2. John Conteh
3. Len Hutchins
4. Richie Kates
5. Tom Bethea
6. Bobby Cassidy
7. Alvaro Lopez
8. Jessie Burnett
9. Domenico Adinolfi
10. Mike Colbert

Middleweights
World Champion
Carlos Monzon
1. Rodrigo Valdez
2. Gratien Tonna
3. Vito Antuofermo
4. George Cooper
5. Tony Licata
6. Willie Monroe
7. Bobby Watts
8. Emile Griffith
9. Rudy Robles
10. Bennie Briscoe

Junior Middleweights
World Champion
Jae Do Yuh
1. Elisha Obed
2. Miguel de Oliviera
3. Eckhard Dagge
4. Gene Wells
5. Mike Baker
6. Koichi Wajima
7. Sandy Torres
8. Maurice Hope
9. Miguel Campanino
0. Perry Abner

Welterweights
World Champion
John Stracey
1. Jose Napoles
2. Angel Espada
3. Armando Muniz
4. Clyde Gray
5. Johnny Gant
6. Bruno Arcari
7. Harold Weston
8. Fausto Rodriguez
9. Pete Ranzany
10. Tony Petronelli

Junior Welterweights
World Champion
Antonio Cervantes
1. Adolfo Viruet
2. Hector Thompson
3. Monroe Brooks
4. Shengsak Muangsurin
5. Lou Bizzarro
6. Esteban DeJesus
7. Leonico Ortiz
8. Cemal Kamaci
9. Nicolino Loche
10. Carlos Giminez

Lightweights
World Champion
Roberto Duran
1. Ray Lampkin
2. Angel Mayoral
3. Ishimatsu Suzuki
4. Hector Medina
5. Buzzsaw Yamabe
6. Rudy Hernandez
7. Vicente Saldivar
8. Randy Shields
9. Arturo Pineda
10. Bobby Chacon

Junior Lightweights
World Champion
Ben Villaflor
1. Tyrone Everett
2. Alfredo Escalera
3. Sven-Erik Paulsen
4. Samuel Serrano
5. Hugo Barraza
6. Ronnie McGarvey
7. Vilomar Fernandez
8. Ray Lunny
9. Apollo Yoshio
10. Kuniaki Shibata

Featherweights
World Champion
Alexis Arguello
1. Art Hafey
2. David (Poison) Kotey
3. Elio Cotina
4. Danny Lopez
5. Lionel Hernandez
6. Ruben Olivares
7. Shig Fukuyama
8. Royal Kobayashi
9. Octavio Gomez
10. Arnold Taylor

Bantamweights
World Champion
Alfonso Zamora
1. Rodolfo Martinez
2. Carlos Zarate
3. Eusebio Pedroza
4. Andres Hernandez
5. Soo Hwan Hong
6. Thanomjit Sukothai
7. Paul Ferreri
8. Paddy Maguire
9. Daniel Troulaire
10. Gilbert Illueca

Flyweights
World Champion
Miguel Canto
1. Ignacio Espinal
2. Betulio Gonzalez
3. Erbito Salvarria
4. Shoji Oguma
5. Alberto Morales
6. Jaime Rios
7. Luis Estabe
8. Franco Sperti
9. Pablo Jiminez
10. Alfonso Lopez

RING RATINGS
1976

Heavyweights
World Champion
Muhammad Ali
1. George Foreman
2. Ken Norton
3. Jimmy Young
4. Duane Bobick
5. Ron Lyle
6. Larry Holmes
7. Howard Smith
8. Johnny Boudreaux
9. Stan Ward
10. Joe Bugner

Light Heavyweights
Title Vacant

1. Victor Galindez
2. Len Hutchins
3. Richie Kates
4. John Conteh
5. Miguel Cuello
6. Jessie Burnett
7. Bobby Cassidy
8. Vonzell Johnson
9. Mike Quarry
10. Alvaro (Yaqui) Lopez

Middleweights
World Champion
Carlos Monzon
1. Mike Colbert
2. Rodrigo Valdes
3. Bennie Briscoe
4. Bobby Watts
5. David Love
6. Gratien Tonna
7. Alan Minter
8. Vito Antuofermo
9. Tony Licata
10. Leo Saenz

Junior Middleweights
World Champion
Miguel Angel Castellini
1. Eckard Dagge
2. Maurice Hope
3. Elisha Obed
4. Jose Duran
5. Rocky Mattioli
6. Monty Bethan
7. Miguel Campanino
8. Koichi Wajima
9. Bruno Arcari
10. Frank Wissenbach

Welterweights
World Champion
Carlos Palomino
1. Pete Ranzany
2. Clyde Gray
3. Pipino Cuevas
4. John Stracey
5. Armando Muniz
6. Angel Espada
7. Johnny Gant
8. Randy Shields
9. Miguel Barreto
10. Mel Dennis

Junior Welterweights
World Champion
Wilfred Benitez
1. Antonio Cervantes
2. Monroe Brooks
3. Shengsak Muangsurin
4. Hector Thompson
5. Davey (Boy) Green
6. Rudy Hernandez
7. Nicolino Loche
8. Cemal Kamaci
9. Miguel Velazquez
10. Saoul Mamby

Lightweights
World Champion
Roberto Duran
1. Esteban DeJesus
2. Vicente Saldivar
3. Edwin Viruet
4. Vilomar Fernandez
5. Perico Fernandez
6. Hector Medina
7. Jean-Baptiste Piedvache
8. Jose Marquez
9. Hugo Barraza
10. Giancarlo Usai

Junior Lightweights
World Champion
Samuel Serrano
1. Alfredo Escalera
2. Tyrone Everett
3. Ben Villaflor
4. Walter Seeley
5. Rafael (Bazooka) Limon
6. Apollo Yoshio
7. Blakeney Matthews
8. Ezequiel Sanchez
9. Reuben Castillo
10. Sigfredo Rodriguez

Featherweights
World Champion
Alexis Arguello
1. Danny Lopez
2. Jose Cervantes
3. Lionel Hernandez
4. Art Hafey
5. Eder Jofre
6. Yum Dong-Kyun
7. Pedro Jiminez
8. David (Poison) Kotey
9. Royal Kobayashi
10. Elio Cotina

Bantamweights
World Champion
Alfonso Zamora
1. Carlos Zarate
2. Wilfredo Gomez
3. Eusebio Pedroza
4. Raul Tirada
5. Paddy Maguire
6. Frank Duarte
7. Roberto Rubaldino
8. Salvatore Fabrizio
9. Daniel Trioulaire
10. Sean O'Grady

Flyweights
World Champion
Miguel Canto
1. Luis Estaba
2. Gutty Espada
3. Jorge Lujan
4. Yoko Gushiken
5. Juan Guzman
6. Alfonso Lopez
7. Betulio Gonzalez
8. Juan Alvarez
9. Willie Jansen
10. Jiro Takada

R I N G   R A T I N G S
1 9 7 7

Heavyweights
World Champion
Muhammad Ali
1. Ken Norton
2. Jimmy Young
3. Larry Holmes
4. Ron Lyle
5. Duane Bobick
6. Earnie Shavers
7. Kallie Knoetze
8. Alfredo Evangelista
9. Leon Spinks
10. Gerry Coetzee

Light Heavyweights
Title Vacant

1. Victor Galindez
2. Miguel Cuello
3. John Conteh
4. Mike Rossman
5. Richie Kates
6. Bobby Cassidy
7. Alvaro (Yaqui) Lopez
8. Vonzell Johnson
9. Mate Parlov
10. Jesse Burnett

Middleweights
World Champion
Rodrigo Valdes
1. Marvin Hagler
2. Mike Colbert
3. Ronnie Harris
4. Bennie Briscoe
5. Dave Love
6. Vito Antuofermo
7. Gratien Tonna
8. Alan Minter
9. Edgar Wallace
10. Tony Chiaverini

Junior Middleweights
World Champion
Eddie Gazo
1. Maurice Hope
2. Ayub Kalula
3. Elisha Obed
4. Rocky Mattioli
5. Miguel Angel Castellini
6. Alvin Anderson
7. Edgar Ross
8. Billy Backus
9. Frank Wissenbach
10. Ray Phillips

Welterweights
World Champion
Carlos Palomino
1. Pipino Cuevas
2. Pete Ranzany
3. Randy Shields
4. Harold Weston
5. Floyd Mayweather
6. Armando Muniz
7. Clyde Gray
8. Jose Palacios
9. Everaldo Azevedo
10. Bruce Curry

Junior Welterweights
World Champion
Wilfred Benitez
1. Shengsak Muangsurin
2. Antonio Cervantes
3. Miguel Montilla
4. Monroe Brooks
5. Laurie Austin
6. Davey (Boy) Green
7. Hector Thompson
8. Joe Kimpuani
9. Nani Marrero
10. Jimmy Corkum

Lightweights
World Champion
Roberto Duran
1. Esteban DeJesus
2. Vicente Salidvar
3. Andrew Ganigan
4. Edwin Viruet
5. Vilomar Fernandez
6. Giancarlo Usai
7. Jose Marquez
8. Antonio Guinaldo
9. Enrique Solis
10. Jim Watt

Junior Lightweights
World Champion
Samuel Serrano
1. Alfredo Escalera
2. Alexis Arguello
3. Rafael (Bazooka) Limon
4. Walter Seeley
5. Frankie Baltazar
6. Alfredo Pitalua
7. Arturo Leon
8. Bobby Chacon
9. Warren Matthews
10. Roy Hernandez

Featherweights
Title Vacant

1. Danny Lopez
2. Ruben Castillo
3. David (Poison) Kotey
4. Rafael Ortega
5. Lionel Hernandez
6. Yum-Dong Kyun
7. Mike Ayala
8. Richard Rozelle
9. Manuel Masso
10. Pedro Jiminez

Bantamweights
World Champion
Jorge Lujan
1. Carlos Zarate
2. Wilfredo Gomez
3. Alfonso Zamora
4. Sean O'Grady
5. Franco Zurlo
6. Roberto Rubaldino
7. Eusebio Pedroza
8. Alberto Davila
9. Frank Duarte
10. Lupe Pintor

Flyweights
World Champion
Miguel Canto
1. Gutty Espadas
2. Luis Estabe
3. Yoko Gushiken
4. Albert Sandoval
5. Juan Guzman
6. Alfonso Lopez
7. Betulio Gonzalez
8. Juan Alvarez
9. Patrick Mambrwe
10. Franco Udella

R I N G   R A T I N G S
1 9 7 8

Heavyweights
World Champion
Muhammad Ali
1. Larry Holmes
2. Ken Norton
3. Leon Spinks
4. Ron Lyle
5. Jimmy Young
6. Kallie Knoetze
7. Alfredo Evangelista
8. Gerry Coetzee
9. Ozzie Ocasio
10. Domingo D'Elia

Light Heavyweights
Title Vacant

1. Mike Rossman
2. Matt Franklin
3. John Conteh
4. Alvaro (Yaqui) Lopez
5. Marvin Johnson
6. Mate Parlov
7. Victor Galindez
8. James Scott
9. Vonzell Johnson
10. Bobby Cassidy

Middleweights
World Champion
Hugo Coro
1. Marvin Hagler
2. Vito Antuofermo
3. Ronnie Harris
4. Marcos Geraldo
5. Mike Colbert
6. Bennie Briscoe
7. Rudy Robles
8. Tony Chiaverini
9. Elijah Makhatini
10. Bobby Watts

Junior Middleweights
World Champion
Masashi Kudo
1. Ayub Kalule
2. Rocky Mattioli
3. Maurice Hope
4. Rocky Mosley, Jr.
5. Edgar Ross
6. Frank Wissenbach
7. Alvin Anderson
8. Loucif Hamani
9. Marijan Benes
10. Mustafa Hamsho

Welterweights
World Champion
Carlos Palomino
1. Pipino Cuevas
2. Clyde Gray
3. Ray Leonard
4. Johnny Gant
5. Harold Weston
6. Pete Ranzany
7. Randy Shields
8. David Green
9. Thomas Hearns
10. Andy Price

Junior Welterweights
World Champion
Wilfred Benitez
1. Antonio Cervantes
2. Saensak Muangsurin
3. Esteban DeJesus
4. Miguel Montilla
5. Saoul Mamby
6. Domingo Ayala
7. Adrian (Nani) Marrera
8. Joe Kimpauani
9. Adolph Viruet
10. Sean O'Grady

Lightweights
World Champion
Roberto Duran
1. Alfredo Pitalua
2. Giancarlo Usai
3. Violmar Fernandez
4. Claude Noel
5. Jim Watt
5. Johnny Lira
7. Edwin Viruet
8. Termite Watkins
9. Julio Valdez
10. Herman Montes

Junior Lightweights
World Champion
Samuel Serrano
1. Frankie Baltzar
2. Alexis Arguello
3. Rafael (Bazooka) Limon
4. Alfredo Escalera
5. Natale Vezzoli
6. Bobby Chacon
7. Arturo Leon
8. Ernesto Espana
9. Walter Seeley
10. Greg Coverson

Featherweights
Title Vacant

1. Danny Lopez
2. Wilfredo Gomez
3. Eusebio Pedroza
4. Ricardo Cardona
5. Roberto Gastanon
6. Ruben Castillo
7. Cecilio Lastra
8. Hector Carrasquilla
9. Mike Ayala
10. Juan Malvarez

Bantamweights
World Champion
Jorge Lujan
1. Lupe Pintor
2. Carlos Zarate
3. Franco Zurlo
4. Alfonso Zamora
5. Albert Sandoval
6. Frank Duarte
7. Richard Rozelle
8. Roberto Rubaldino
9. Alfredo Davila
10. Enrique Sanchez

Flyweights
World Champion
Miguel Canto
1. Yoko Gushiken
2. Betulio Gonzalez
3. Guty Espadas
4. Franco Udella
5. Kim Sung
6. Freddy Castillo
7. Netrnoi Vorasingh
8. Jose Ortiz
9. Charlie Magri
10. Shoji Oguma

RING RATINGS
1 9 7 9

Heavyweights
Title Vacant
1. Larry Holmes
2. John Tate
3. Gerrie Coetzee
4. Mike Weaver
5. Earnie Shavers
6. Leroy Jones
7. Lorenzo Zanon
8. Alfredo Evangelista
9. Gerry Cooney
10. Scott LeDoux

Light Heavyweights
World Champion
Matthew Saad Muhammad
1. Marvin Johnson
2. James Scott
3. John Conteh
4. Victor Galindez
5. Alvaro (Yaqui) Lopez
6. Eddie Gregory
7. Lotte Mwale
8. Mustapha Wassaja
9. Mike Rossman
10. Rudi Koopmans

Middleweights
World Champion
Vito Antuofermo
1. Marvin Hagler
2. Hugo Corro
3. Alan Minter
4. Ronnie Harris
5. Curtis Parker
6. Loucif Hamani
7. Mustafa Hamsho
8. Mike Colbert
9. Kevin Finnegan
10. Tony Sibson

Junior Middleweights
World Champion
Ayub Kalule
1. Maurice Hope
2. Masashi Kudo
3. Rocky Mattioli
4. Tony Chiaverini
5. Kenny Bristol
6. Nick Ortiz
7. Rocky Mosley Jr.
8. Sandy Torres
9. Marijan Benes
10. Andoni Amana

Welterweights
World Champion
Ray Leonard
1. Wilfred Benitez
2. Pipino Cuevas
3. Roberto Duran
4. Thomas Hearns
5. Jorgen Hansen
6. Pete Ranzany
7. Angel Espada
8. Davey (Boy) Green
9. Joseph Nsubuga
10. Randy Shields

Junior Welterweights
World Champion
Antonio Cervantes
1. Joe Kimpuani
2. Sang-Hyun Kim
3. Saoul Mamby
4. Miguel Montilla
5. Esteban DeJesus
6. Lennox Blackmoore
7. Teo Ozuna
8. Bruce Curry
9. Juan Jose Gimenez
10. Hugo Luero

Lightweights
Title Vacant
1. Ernesto Espana
2. Jim Watt
3. Claude Noel
4. Julio (Diablito) Valdez
5. Johnny Lira
6. Howard Davis
7. Vilomar Fermandez
8. Aaron Pryor
9. Hilmer Kenty
10. Jorge Morales

Junior Lightweights
World Champion
Samuel Serrano
1. Alexis Arguello
2. Frankie Baltazar
3. Bobby Chacon
4. Rafael (Bazooka) Limon
5. Rodolfo Sanchez
6. Victor Echegaray
7. Roberto Elizondo
8. Greg Coverson
9. Carlos Hernandez
10. Nkosana Mgxaji

Featherweights
World Champion
Danny Lopez
1. Eusebio Pedroza
2. Reuben Castillo
3. Roberto Castanon
4. Mike Ayala
5. Eddie Ndukwu
6. Juan Malvarez
7. Hector Carrasquilla
8. Salvador Sanchez
9. Nene Jun
10. Cecilio Lastra

Junior Featherweights
World Champion
Wilfredo Gomez
1. Ricardo Cardona
2. Juan (Kid) Meza
3. Nicky Perez
4. Jose Caba
5. Soo-Hyun Chung
6. Sergio Palma
7. Javier Flores
8. Leo Cruz
9. Shuchi Isogami
10. Hiroyuki Iwamote

Bantamweights
World Champion
Jorge Lujan
1. Lupe Pintor
2. Carlos Zarate
3. Alberto Davila
4. Roberto Rubaldino
5. Leo Randolph
6. Oscar Muniz
7. Eddie Logan
8. Juan F. Rodriguez
9. Ricardo Bennett
10. Jeff Chandler

Flyweights
World Champion
Chan-Hee Park
1. Yoko Gushiken
2. Luis Ibarra
3. Betulio Gonzalez
4. Sung-Jun Kim
5. Guty Espadas
6. Charlie Magri
7. Joey Olivo
8. Shoji Oguma
9. Netrnoi Vorasingh
10. Rey Melendez

RING RATINGS
1980

Heavyweights
World Champion
Larry Holmes
1. Mike Weaver
2. Gerry Cooney
3. Leon Spinks
4. Michael Dokes
5. Gerrie Coetzee
6. Marty Monroe
7. Trevor Berbick
8. Greg Page
9. Bernardo Mercado
10. Ken Norton

Light Heavyweights
World Champion
Matthew Saad Muhammad
1. Eddie Mustafa Muhammad
2. Michael Spinks
3. James Scott
4. Jerry Martin
5. Marvin Johnson
6. Carlos DeLeon
7. Yaqui Lopez
8. Lotte Mwale
9. Marvin Camel
10. Mustafa Wasajja

Middleweights
World Champion
Marvin Hagler
1. Alan Minter
2. Dwight Davison
3. Vito Antuofermo
4. Fulgencio Obelmejias
5. Curtis Parker
6. Mustafa Hamsho
7. Wilford Scypion
8. Ronnie Harris
9. Frank Fletcher
10. Tony Sibson

Junior Middleweights
World Champion
Ayub Kalule
1. Maurice Hope
2. Kenny Bristol
3. Rocky Mattioli
4. Roger Leonard
5. Rocky Mosley
6. Carlos Herrera
7. Walter Gomez
8. Bushy Bester
9. Tyrone Rackley
10. Tidashi Mihara

Welterweights
World Champion
Ray Leonard
1. Thomas Hearns
2. Wilfred Benitez
3. Pipino Cuevas
4. Roberto Duran
5. Randy Shields
6. Pete Ranzany
7. Adolfo Viruet
8. Jorgen Hansen
9. Luis Primera
10. Clint Jackson

Junior Welterweights
World Champion
Aaron Pryor
1. Saoul Mamby
2. Jo Kimpuani
3. Lennox Blackmoore
4. Sang-Hyun Kim
5. Domingo Ayala
6. Dujuan Johnson
7. Miguel Montilla
8. Willie Rodriguez
9. Bruce Curry
10. Monroe Brooks

Lightweights
Title Vacant
1. Hilmer Kenty
2. Jim Watt
3. Alexis Arguello
4. Aaron Pryor
5. Howard Davis, Jr.
6. Rodolfo Gonzalez
7. Sean O'Grady
8. Vilomar Fernandez
9. Claude Noel
10. Edwin Viruet

Junior Lightweights
World Champion
Yasutsune Uehara
1. Rafael (Bazooka) Limon
2. Samuel Serrano
3. Roberto Elizondo
4. Ildelfonso Bethelmy
5. Frankie Baltazar
6. Victor Echegaray
7. Johnny Sato
8. Greg Coverson
9. Leonel Hernandez
10. Ruben Riani

Featherweights
World Champion
Salvador Sanchez
1. Wilfredo Gomez
2. Eusebio Pedroza
3. Ruben Castillo
4. Rocky Lockridge
5. Patrick Ford
6. Roberto Castanon
7. Noel Arriesgado
8. Juan LaPorte
9. Francisco Manzo
10. Paul Ferreri

Junior Featherweights
World Champion
Wilfredo Gomez
1. Sergio Palma
2. Ricardo Cardona
3. Leo Cruz
4. Mike Ayala
5. Nicky Perez
6. Soon-Hyun Chung
7. Carmelo Negron
8. Jose Caba
9. Jose Cervantes
10. Carlos Mendoza

Bantamweights
World Champion
Jeff Chandler
1. Lupe Pintor
2. Julian Solis
3. Albert Davila
4. Jorge Lujan
5. Roberto Rubaldino
6. Oscar Muniz
7. Rafael Orono
8. Eijiro Murata
9. Jose R. Narvaez
10. Norberto Cabrera

Flyweights
World Champion
Shoji Oguma
1. Yoko Gushiken
2. Hilario Zapata
3. Peter Mathebula
4. Guty Espadas
5. Chan-Hee Park
6. Betulio Gonzalez
7. Luis Ibarra
8. Charlie Magri
9. Miguel Canto
10. Joey Olivo

A COMPENDIUM OF LITTLE KNOWN BOXING FACTS & OTHER ESOTERICA

THE RING MAGAZINE'S "FIGHT OF THE YEAR"

1945	—June 29—Graziano-Cochrane, N.Y.	1963	—Mar. 13—Clay-Jones, N.Y.
1946	—Sept. 27—Zale-Graziano, N.Y.	1964	—Feb. 25—Clay-Liston, Miami Beach
1947	—July 16—Graziano-Zale, Chicago	1965	—Feb. 1—Patterson-Chuvalo, N.Y.
1948	—Sept. 21—Cerdan-Zale, Jersey City	1966	—Aug. 15—Eddie Cotton-Jose Torres, Las Vegas
1949	—Feb. 11—Pep-Saddler, N.Y.	1967	—Nov. 17—Griffith-Benvenuti, N.Y.
1950	—Sept. 13—LaMotta-Dauthuille, Detroit	1968	—Oct. 25—Tiger-De Paula, N.Y.
1951	—July 18—Walcott-Charles, Pittsburgh	1969	—June 23—Frazier-Quarry, N.Y.
1952	—Sept. 23—Marciano-Walcott, Phila.	1970	—Nov. 7—Monzon-Benvenuti, Rome, Italy
1953	—Sept. 24—Marciano-LaStarza, N.Y.	1971	—March 8—Frazier-Ali, N.Y.
1954	—Sept. 17—Marciano-Charles, N.Y.	1972	—Sept. 26—Foster-Finnegan, London
1955	—Nov. 30—Basilio-DeMarco, Boston	1973	—Jan. 22—Frazier-Foreman, Kingston, Jamaica
1956	—Sept. 12—Basilio-Saxton, Syracuse	1974	—Oct. 30—Ali-Foreman, Kinshasa, Zaire
1957	—Sept. 23—Basilio-Robinson, N.Y.	1975	—Oct. 1—Ali-Frazier, Manila, Philippines
1958	—Mar. 25—Robinson-Basilio, Chicago	1976	—Jan. 24—Foreman-Lyle, Las Vegas
1959	—Aug. 28—Fullmer-Basilio, San Fran.	1977	—Sept. 29—Young-Foreman, San Juan, P.R.
1960	—June 20—Patterson-Johansson, N.Y.	1978	—Feb. 15—Ali-Spinks, Las Vegas
1961	—Apr. 18—Brown-Charnley, London	1979	—June 17—Lopez-Ayala, San Antonio, Tex.
1962	—Jan. 30—Giardello-Hank, Phila.	1980	—July 13—S. Muhammad-Lopez, McAfee, N.J.

THE RING MAGAZINE'S "ROUND OF THE YEAR"

1945	—Mar. 2—Joyce-Williams, N.Y., 12th round.	1963	—July 22—Liston-Patterson, Las Vegas, 1st round.
1946	—Sept. 27—Zale-Graziano, N.Y., 6th round.	1964	—Nov. 27—Torres-Olson, 1st round.
1947	—Dec. 5—Louis-Walcott, N.Y., 4th round.	1965	—Mar. 30—Torres-Pastrano, N.Y. 6th round.
1948	—June 25—Louis-Walcott, N.Y. 11th round.	1966	—Oct. 22—Ortiz-Ramos, Mexico City, 5th round.
1949	—Sept. 14—Graziano-Fusari, N.Y., 14th round.	1967	—Nov. 17—Tiger-Rouse, Las Vegas, 12th round.
1950	—Sept. 13—LaMotta-Dauthuille, Detroit, 15th.	1968	—May 24—Tiger-Foster, N.Y., 4th round.
1951	—Oct. 26—Marciano-Louis, N.Y., 8th round.	1969	—Nov. 22—Benvenuti-Rodriguez, Rome, Italy, 11th
1952	—Sept. 13—Marciano-Walcott, Phila., 13th round.	1970	—Dec. 7—Ali-Bonavena, N.Y., 15th round.
1953	—Sept. 18—Gavilan-Basilio, Syracuse, 2nd round.	1971	—March 8—Frazier-Ali, N.Y., 15th round.
1954	—Aug. 11—Moore-Johnson, N.Y., 14th round.	1972	—Nov. 21—Ali-Foster, Stateline, Nev., 5th round.
1955	—June 22—Moore-Olson, N.Y., 3rd round.	1973	—Jan. 22—Frazier-Foreman, Kingston, Jamaica, 2nd
1956	—May 18—Robinson-Olson, Los Angeles, 4th round.	1974	—Oct. 30—Ali-Foreman, Kinshasa, Zaire, 8th round.
1957	—May 1—Robinson-Fullmer, Chicago, 5th round.	1975	—Oct. 1—Ali-Frazier (3rd bout), Manila, 12th round.
1958	—Sept. 14—Johansson-Machen, Gothenburg, 1st.	1976	—Jan. 24—Foreman-Lyle, Uniondale, 4th and 5th
1959	—June 26—Johansson-Patterson, N.Y., 3rd round.	1977	—Sept. 29—Young-Foreman, San Juan, P.R., 12th.
1960	—June 20—Patterson-Johansson, N.Y., 5th round.	1978	—Feb. 15—Ali-Spinks, Las Vegas, Nev., 15th round.
1961	—Mar. 13—Patterson-Johansson, Miami Beach, 1st	1979	—Apr. 22—Franklin-Johnson, Indianapolis 8th.
1962	—Sept. 25—Liston-Patterson, Chicago, 1st round.	1980	—July 13—S. Muhammad-Lopez, McAfee 8th.

THE RING MAGAZINE "FIGHTER OF THE YEAR" AWARD

EACH YEAR a gold and silver medal is awarded by The Ring magazine to the boxer, who, during the past year, has by his conduct, and fighting qualities, earned the esteem of the sports public.

The four points which govern The Ring award for "The Fighter of the Year," are:

1. He must be foremost in his contribution to the skill and the science of boxing and he need not be a champion.

2. The recipient must combine with his high place in the ranking of fighters, a similar position as sportsman.

3. He must associate with his abilities as a fighter, good public relations and a reputation for clean and moral living.

4. The boxer receiving this award must be recognized as an example to the growing American youth.

1928	—Gene Tunney	1941	—Joe Louis	1955	—Rocky Marciano
1929	—Tommy Loughran	1942	—Ray Robinson	1956	—Floyd Patterson
1930	—Max Schmeling	1943	—Fred Apostoli	1957	—Carmen Basilio
1931	—Tommy Loughran	1944	—Beau Jack	1958	—Ingemar Johansson
1932	—Jack Sharkey	1945	—Willie Pep	1959	—Ingemar Johansson
1933	—No award	1946	—Tony Zale	1960	—Floyd Patterson
1934	—Barney Ross and	1947	—Gus Lesnevich	1961	—Joe Brown
	Tony Canzoneri	1948	—Ike Williams	1962	—Dick Tiger
1935	—Barney Ross	1949	—Ezzard Charles	1963	—Cassius Clay
1936	—Joe Louis	1950	—Ezzard Charles	1964	—Emile Griffith
1937	—Henry Armstrong	1951	—Ray Robinson	1965	—Dick Tiger
1938	—Joe Louis	1952	—Rocky Marciano	1966	—No award
1939	—Joe Louis	1953	—Carl Bobo Olson	1967	—Joe Frazier
1940	—Billy Conn	1954	—Rocky Marciano	1968	—Nino Benvenuti

1969	—Jose Napoles
1970	—Joe Frazier
1971	—Joe Frazier
1972	—Muhammad Ali and Carlos Monzon
1973	—George Foreman
1974	—Muhammad Ali
1975	—Muhammad Ali
1976	—George Foreman
1977	—Carlos Zarate
1978	—Muhammad Ali
1979	—Ray Leonard
1980	—Thomas Hearns

RECIPIENTS OF THE NAT FLEISCHER MEMORIAL AWARD
(Excellence in Boxing Journalism)

Awarded annually by the Boxing Writers' Association of New York to the person who has done the most for boxing in covering that sport during the preceding year.

1972	—Barney Nagler	1977	—Bob Waters
1973	—Dave Anderson	1978	—Jerry Izenberg
1974	—Jack Hand and Murray Rose	1979	—Ed Schuyler
1975	—Red Smith	1980	—Tom Cushman
1976	—Jesse Abramson		

RECIPIENTS OF THE JAMES J. WALKER MEMORIAL AWARD

Awarded annually since 1940 by the Boxing Writers Association of New York to an individual for long and meritorious service in boxing. Before 1947 the award was known as the Meritorious Service Award.

1940 —James J. Walker	1954 —James J. Braddock	1968 —John Condon
1941 —Gene Tunney	1955 —Harry Mendel	1969 —Murray Goodman
1942 —No award	1956 —Frank Graham	1970 —Don Dunphy
1943 —Nat Fleischer	1957 —Jack Dempsey	1971 —Teddy Brenner
1944 —John J. Phelan	1958 —Sam Taub	1972 —Dr. Edwin Campbell
1945 —James J. Johnston	1959 —Marv Jenson	1973 —Barney Nagler
1946 —Mike Jacobs	1960 —Ned Brown	1974 —Bobby Gleason
1947 —James A. Farley	1961 —Dr. Alexander Schiff	1975 —Dan Daniel
1948 —Dan Morgan	1962 —Dr. Mal Stevens	1976 —Duke Stefano
1949 —Abe J. Greene	1963 —Harry Markson	1977 —Chris Dundee
1950 —Wilbur Wood	1964 —Mickey Walker	1978 —Ray Arcel & Freddie Brown
1951 —Edward P.F. Eagan	1965 —Jack Cuddy	1979 —Marvin Kohn & Bobby Goodman
1952 —George A. Barton	1966 —Nat Fleischer	1980 —Nat Loubet
1953 —Dr. Vincent A. Nardiello	1967 —Joe Louis	

WINNERS OF THE EDWARD J. NEIL TROPHY

A MEMORIAL PLAQUE awarded by the Boxing Writers' Association of New York to the person who has done the most for boxing during the preceding year.

Edward J. Neil, the man whose memory is honored annually, was born January 17, 1900 in Methuen, Mass. He served the Associated Press, both as a sports writer and a war correspondent, with distinction and steadfast devotion to duty.

On January 3, 1938, while serving as a war correspondent with the Loyalist Army in the Spanish Civil War, Edward J. Neil died of shrapnel wounds suffered in the line of duty. The boxing writers of New York keep alive the memory of beloved "Eddie" Neil with the annual presentation of the Neil Trophy.

1938 —Jack Dempsey	1959 —Ingemar Johansson
1939 —Billy Conn	1960 —Floyd Patterson
1940 —Henry Armstrong	1961 —Gene Fullmer
1941 —Joe Louis	1962 —Dick Tiger
1942 —Sgt. Barney Ross, U.S.M.C.R.	1963 —Emile Griffith
1943 —The Boxers in All Branches of the Armed Forces of Our Country	1964 —Willie Pastrano
	1965 —Muhammad Ali
1944 —Lt. Commdr. Benny Leonard, U.S.M.S.	1966 —Dick Tiger
1945 —James J. Walker (Author of Walker Boxing Law; former Mayor of the City of New York)	1967 —Carlos Ortiz
	1968 —Bob Foster
1946 —Tony Zale	1969 —Joe Frazier
1947 —Gus Lesnevich	1970 —Ken Buchanan
1948 —Ike Williams	1971 —Joe Frazier
1949 —Ezzard Charles	1972 —Carlos Monzon
1950 —Ray Robinson	1973 —George Foreman
1951 —Joe Walcott	1974 —Muhammad Ali
1952 —Rocky Marciano	1975 —Joe Frazier & Muhammad Ali
1953 —Kid Gavilan	1976 —Olympic Team
1954 —Carl Bobo Olson	1977 —Ken Norton
1955 —Carmen Basilio	1978 —Larry Holmes
1956 —Floyd Patterson	1979 —Ray Leonard
1957 —Carmen Basilio	1980 —Thomas Hearns
1958 —Archie Moore	

AL BUCK MEMORIAL AWARD
(Manager of the Year)

1967 —Gil Clancy	1971 —Yancey Durham	1974 —Herbert Muhammad	1978 —Richie Giachett
1968 —Angelo Dundee	1972 —Paddy Flood &	1975 —Eddie Futch	1979 —Angelo Dundee
1969 —Yancey Durham	Gregorio Benitez	1976 —Bob Biron	1980 —Emanuel Steward
1970 —Dick Sadler	1973 —Gil Clancy	1977 —Bill Slayton	

MILLION DOLLAR GATES

			Attendance	Receipts	Ringside	Won By
July 2, 1921	Dempsey-Carpentier	Jersey City	80,183	$1,789,238	$ 50.00	Dempsey
Sept. 14, 1923	Dempsey-Firpo	New York	82,000	1,188,603	50.00	Dempsey
Sept. 23, 1926	Tunney-Dempsey	Philadelphia	120,757	1,895,733	27.50	Tunney
July 21, 1927	Dempsey-Sharkey	New York	75,000	1,083,530	27.50	Dempsey
Sept. 22, 1927	Tunney-Dempsey	Chicago	104,943	2,658,660	40.00	Tunney
Sept. 24, 1935	Louis-Max Baer	New York	88,150	1,000,832	25.00	Louis
June 22, 1938	Louis-Schmeling	New York	70,043	1,015,012	40.00	Louis
June 19, 1946	Louis-Conn	New York	45,266	1,925,564	100.00	Louis
Mar. 8, 1971	Frazier-Ali	New York	20,455	1,352,951	150.00	Frazier
Jan. 28, 1974	Ali-Frazier	New York	20,748	1,653,688	150.00	Ali
Oct. 1, 1975	Ali-Frazier	Manila	25,000	1,600,000	200.00	Ali
Sept. 28, 1976	Ali-Norton	New York	30,289	2,400,000	200.00	Ali
Sept. 15, 1978	Ali-Spinks	New Orleans	63,350	4,806,675	200.00	Ali

MEASUREMENTS OF HEAVYWEIGHT CHAMPIONS

	John L. Sullivan	James J. Corbett	Bob Fitz-simmons	James J. Jeffries	Marvin Hart	Tommy Burns
Height	5 ft. 10½ in.	6 ft. 1 in.	5 ft. 11¾ in.	6 ft. 2½ in.	Measurements Not Available	5 ft. 7 in.
Weight	196 lbs.	178 lbs.	167 lbs	206 lbs.		180 lbs.
Reach	74 in.	73 in.	71¾ in.	76½ in.		74½ in.
Chest, Nor.	43 in.	38 in.	41 in.	43 in.		40 in.
Chest, Exp.	48 in.	42 in.	44 in.	48½ in.		43¾ in.
Waist	36 in.	33 in.	32 in.	35 in.		33 in.
Biceps	16¼ in.	14½ in.	12 in.	16 in.		14½ in.
Neck	18 in.	17 in.	15 in.	18¼ in.		16 in.
Wrist	8 in.	6½ in.	7½ in.	7¾ in.		7¼ in.
Calf	16 in.	14½ in.	13½ in.	17 in.		16½ in.
Ankle	9 in.	8¼ in.	8¼ in.	10 in.		8¼ in.
Thigh	24 in.	21 in.	21 in.	25 in.		22 in.
Fist	14 in.	12¾ in.	12½ in.	13½ in.		12 in.
Forearm	13 in.	11½ in.	11½ in.	13½ in.		13 in.

	Jack Johnson	Jess Willard	Jack Dempsey	Gene Tunney	Max Schmeling	Jack Sharkey
Height	6 ft. 1¼ in.	6 ft. 6¼ in.	6 ft. ¾ in.	6 ft. ½ in.	6 ft. 1 in.	6 ft.
Weight	192 lbs.	230 lbs.	187 lbs.	189½ lbs.	188 lbs.	205 lbs.
Reach	74 in.	83 in.	77 in.	77 in.	76 in.	74½ in.
Chest, Nor.	37½ in.	46 in.	42 in.	42 in.	43 in.	40½ in.
Chest, Exp.	42¾ in.	49½ in.	46 in.	45 in.	47 in.	45½ in.
Waist	36 in.	35½ in.	33 in.	34½ in.	33¼ in.	34½ in.
Biceps	16 in.	17½ in.	16¼ in.	14½ in.	16 in.	14½ in.
Neck	17½ in.	17½ in.	16½ in.	17 in.	17½ in.	17 in.
Wrist	10½ in.	10 in.	9 in.	9 in.	8 in.	7¾ in.
Calf	15 in.	17½ in.	15 in.	15½ in.	16 in.	16 in.
Ankle	9½ in.	10½ in.	9 in.	9 in.	10 in.	10¼ in.
Thigh	22½ in.	26 in.	23 in.	22 in.	23½ in.	24¾ in.
Fist	14 in.	14 in.	11¼ in.	11¼ in.	12 in.	12¾ in.
Forearm	14½ in.	14 in.	14½ in.	13½ in.	12¾ in.	15¾ in.

	Primo Carnera	Max Baer	Jimmy Braddock	Joe Louis	Ezzard Charles	Joe Walcott
Height	6 ft. 5¾in.	6 ft. 2½ in.	6 ft. 2½ in.	6 ft. 1½ in.	6 ft.	6 ft.
Weight	260½ lbs.	209½ lbs.	193¾ lbs.	197¼ lbs	181¾lbs.	194 lbs.
Reach	85½ in.	81 in.	75 in.	76 in.	74 in.	74 in.
Chest, Nor.	48 in.	44 in.	41 in.	42 in.	39 in.	40 in.
Chest, Exp.	54 in.	47½ in.	44 in.	45 in.	42 in.	43 in.
Waist	38 in.	32½ in.	34½ in.	36½ in.	33 in.	35 in.
Biceps	18½ in.	14½ in.	13 in.	15 in.	15½ in.	16 in.
Neck	20 in.	17½ in.	17 in.	17 in.	16½ in.	17 in.
Wrist	9½ in.	8 in.	8 in.	8 in.	7 in.	7¾ in.
Calf	20 in.	15 in.	16 in.	14 in.	13 in.	14 in.
Ankle	11½ in.	9½ in.	10 in.	10 in.	8½ in.	9¾ in.
Thigh	30½ in.	21 in.	22¾ in.	22½ in.	20 in.	21 in.
Fist	14¾ in.	12 in.	11½ in.	11¾ in.	12 in.	12 in.
Forearm	16 in.	14 in.	12½ in.	12 in.	12 in.	13 in.

	Rocky Marciano	Ingemar Johansson	Floyd Patterson	Sonny Liston	Muhammad Ali	Joe Frazier
Height	5 ft. 10¼ in.	6 ft. ½ in.	6 ft.	6 ft. 1 in.	6 ft. 3 in.	5 ft. 11½ in.
Weight	184 lbs.	196 lbs.	182¾ lbs.	214 lbs.	210½ lbs.	205 lbs.
Reach	68 in.	72½ in.	71 in.	84 in.	82 in.	73½ in.
Chest, Nor.	39 in.	43 in.	40 in.	44 in.	43 in.	42 in.
Chest, Exp.	42 in.	45 in.	42 in.	46½ in.	45½ in.	44 in.
Waist	32 in.	34 in.	32½ in.	33 in.	34 in.	34 in.
Biceps	14 in.	16½ in.	14¼ in.	16½ in.	15½in.	15 in.
Neck	16¾ in.	17 in.	17 in.	17½ in.	17½ in.	17½ in.
Wrist	7½ in.	7 in.	6 in.	8½ in.	8 in.	7 in.
Calf	14¾ in.	16 in.	15½ in.	16 in.	17 in.	13 in.
Ankle	10 in.	10 in.	9½ in.	12 in.	10 in.	11 in.
Thigh	22 in.	24 in.	21½ in.	25½ in.	25 in.	26 in.
Fist	11½ in.	13½ in.	12¾ in.	15 in.	12½ in.	13 in.
Forearm	12 in.	15 in.	12 in.	14½ in.	15 in.	13 in.

	George Foreman	Leon Spinks	Ken Norton	Larry Holmes	John Tate	Mike Weaver
Height	6 ft. 3 in.	6 ft. 2 in.	6 ft. 3 in.	6 ft. 4 in.	6 ft. 4 in.	6 ft 1 in.
Weight	217½ lbs.	196 lbs.	215½ lbs.	209 lbs.	240 lbs.	207½ lbs.
Reach	82 in.	76 in.	80 in.	81 in.	80 in.	78½ in.
Chest, Nor.	42 in.	40½ in.	45 in.	43½ in.	42 in.	44½ in.
Chest, Exp.	44½ in.	42 in.	48 in.	45½ in.	44 in.	46½ in.
Waist	34 in.	32¼ in.	33 in.	35 in.	36 in.	32 in.
Biceps	15 in.	15½ in.	16 in.	15+ in.	16 in.	17 in.
Neck	17 in.	17 in.	18 in.	17½ in.	17½ in.	18 in.
Wrist	7½ in.	7 in.	8 in.	8 in.	7½ in.	8 in.
Calf	17 in.	15½ in.	15½ in.	16 in.	17 in.	16 in.
Ankle	9½ in.	9½ in.	10 in.	10 in.	10 in.	10½ in.
Thigh	25 in.	24 in.	25 in.	25 in.	26 in.	24 in.
Fist	12 in.	12½ in.	13 in.	13½ in.	13 in.	13½ in.
Forearm	13½ in.	12 in.	13 in.	13 in.	13 in.	13½ in.

MOST KNOCKOUTS

ARCHIE MOORE.........	1936-1963	 143
YOUNG EDDIE WILLIAMS	1929-1935	 139
YOUNG STRIBLING	1921-1933	 126
SUGAR RAY ROBINSON...	1940-1965	 109
BANTY LEWIS	1909-1922	 108
SANDY SADDLER	1944-1956	 103
SAM LANGFORD	1902-1924	 102
HENRY ARMSTRONG	1931-1945	 97
GEORGE K.O. CHANEY ...	1910-1925	 86
JOCK McAVOY	1928-1942	 86
ARCHIE SEXTON.......	1925-1935	 86
FRED GALIANA.........	1951-1965	 84
TIGER JACK FOX........	1932-1950	 81
*KID AZTECA	1932-1961	 80
FRITZIE ZIVIC.........	1931-1949	 80
CHARLES LEDOUX	1909-1926	 79
ALABAMA KID..........	1932-1950	 78
FERNANDO GAGNON.....	1942-1955	 77
RUBEN OLIVARES.......	1964-1980	 77
JIMMY WILDE..........	1911-1923	 77
GEORGE GODFREY......	1920-1937	 76

*Started boxing in 1929; early record unavailable.

MOST CONSECUTIVE KNOCKOUTS

LAMAR CLARK..........	1958-1960	 44
BILLY FOX	*1943-1946	 43
BOB ALLOTEY	1957-1963	 33
WILFREDO GOMEZ	1974-1980	 31
JOSE MANUEL IBAR	*1968-1970	 30
ALFONSO ZAMORA	*1973-1977	 29
CHARLIE PARNAM	*1940-1941	 28
JESUS PIMENTEL.......	1961-1964	 28
CARLOS ZARATE	1974-1978	 28
HENRY ARMSTRONG....	1937-1938	 27
ERNIE SHAVERS........	1970-1972	 27
GEORGE FOREMAN	1970-1974	 24
MAC FOSTER	*1966-1970	 24
CARLOS ZARATE	*1970-1973	 23
JOSE BRUNO	1951-1953	 22
RUBEN OLIVARES	*1964-1967	 22
DANNY LOPEZ	*1971-1973	 21
RICARDO MORENO.......	1964-1965	 21
RUBEN OLIVARES	1968-1970	 21
RODOLFO MARTINEZ ...	*1965-1968	 20
FAUSTO RODRIGUEZ	*1971-1973	 20
TOM SHARKEY	*1893-1896	 20

*From start of career.

MOST ONE-ROUND KNOCKOUTS

YOUNG OTTO........... 1903-1923 42

MOST CONSECUTIVE ONE-ROUND KNOCKOUTS

ONE-ROUND HOGAN......	1910	 18
YOUNG OTTO...........	1905	 16

MOST CONSECUTIVE BOUTS WITHOUT A LOSS

		Bouts	Draws or ND
HAL BAGWELL	1938-1948..	180...	5
HARRY GREB	1916-1923..	178...117	
AL McCOY	1908-1917..	*139....92	
JOHNNY DUNDEE	1910-1916..	*128....80	
LEO JOHNSON	1910-1916..	*124....69	
JACK DILLON.........	1912-1916..	107....65	
PACKEY McFARLAND ...	1905-1915...	97.....5	
FRED DYER	1908-1912..	* 94.....9	
PEDRO CARRASCO	1964-1971..	93.....1	
SUGAR RAY ROBINSON .	1943-1951..	91.....3	
BOB CUNNINGHAM	1885-1892..	* 89.....6	
JIMMY WILDE	1911-1914..	* 88.....1	
AD WOLGAST	1906-1912...	85.....9	
CARLOS MONZON	1964-1977...	82.....9	
JAIME GINE	1954-1960...	73.....6	
WILLIE PEP	1943-1948...	73.....1	

*From start of career.

UNDEFEATED THROUGHOUT CAREER

(25 or more total bouts)

		TB	KO	WD	WF	D	LD	LF	KO BY	ND	NC
YOUNG MITCHELL	1884-1893 ...41		32	3	0	6	0	0	0	0	0
JACK McAULIFFE	1884-1897 ...53		8	33	0	9	0	0	0	3	0
JIMMY BARRY	1891-1899 ...70		39	20	0	9	0	0	0	2	0
ROCKY MARCIANO	1947-1955 ...49		43	6	0	0	0	0	0	0	0
LASZLO PAPP	1957-1964 ...29		15	12	0	2	0	0	0	0	0
CRUZ MARCANO	1966-1970 ...26		12	11	0	3	0	0	0	0	0

WORLDWIDE RING DEATHS
(Amateur and Professional)

Year	Deaths	Year	Deaths	Year	Deaths
1918	1	1939	1	1960	10
1919	1	1940	4	1961	10
1920	1	1941	4	1962	14
1921	2	1942	5	1963	10
1922	3	1943	3	1964	15
1923	1	1944	2	1965	7
1924	1	1945	6	1966	9
1925	6	1946	14	1967	4
1926	4	1947	11	1968	6
1927	1	1948	14	1969	5
1928	4	1949	18	1970	7
1929	9	1950	11	1971	5
1930	10	1951	12	1972	11
1931	3	1952	17	1973	3
1932	0	1953	22	1974	5
1933	6	1954	8	1975	5
1934	2	1955	10	1976	7
1935	1	1956	11	1977	3
1936	6	1957	8	1978	9
1937	2	1958	9	1979	8
1938	3	1959	11	1980	8

EUROPEAN CHAMPIONS

Heavyweights

Gunner James Moir	Oct. 29, 1906-Apr. 19,1909
William (Iron) Hague	Apr. 19, 1909-Apr. 24, 1911
Bombardier Billy Wells	Apr. 24, 1911-June 1, 1913
Georges Carpentier	June 1, 1913-Sept. 24, 1922
*Battling Siki	Sept. 24, 1922-Jan. 11, 1923
Erminio Spalla	May 13, 1923-May 18, 1926
*Paulino Uzcudun	May 18, 1926-Dec. 5, 1928
Pierre Charles	Feb. 2, 1929-Aug. 30, 1931
Hein Mueller	Aug. 30, 1931-May 28, 1932
Pierre Charles	May 28, 1931-May 13, 1933
Paulino Uzcudun	May 13, 1933-Oct. 22, 1933
*Primo Carnera	Oct. 22, 1933-May 10, 1935
Pierre Charles	June 21, 1935-Mar. 17, 1937
Arno Koelblin	Mar. 17, 1937-Mar. 4, 1938
Heinz Lazek	Mar. 4, 1938-Mar. 17, 1939
Adolf Heuser	Mar. 17, 1939-July 2, 1939
*Max Schmeling	July 2, 1939-Mar. 18, 1941
Olle Tandberg	May 30, 1943-Nov. 14, 1943
*Karel Sys	Nov. 14, 1943-Jan., 1946
*Bruce Woodcock	July 29, 1946-Sept. , 1949
Jo Weidin	June 3, 1950-Mar. 27, 1951
Jack Gardner	Mar. 27, 1951-Sept. 23, 1951
Heinten Hoff	Sept. 23, 1951-Jan. 12, 1952
Karel Sys	Jan. 12, 1952-Mar. 9, 1952
Heinz Neuhaus	Mar. 9, 1952-June 26, 1955
Franco Cavicchi	June 26, 1955-Sept. 30, 1956
*Ingemar Johansson	Sept.30, 1956-June , 1959
Dick Richardson	Mar. 27, 1960-June 17, 1962
*Ingemar Johansson	June 17, 1962-June 25, 1963
*Henry Cooper	Feb. 24, 1964-Sept. 28, 1964
Karl Mildenberger	Oct. 17, 1964-Sept. 18, 1968
*Henry Cooper	Sept. 18, 1968-Oct. 14, 1969
Peter Weiland	Dec. 6, 1969-Apr. 3, 1970
Jose Manuel Ibar Urtain	Apr. 3, 1970-Nov. 10, 1970
Henry Cooper	Nov. 10, 1970-Mar. 16, 1971
Joe Bugner	Mar. 16, 1971-Sept. 27, 1971
Jack Bodell	Sept. 27, 1971-Dec. 17, 1971
Jose Manuel Ibar Urtain	Dec. 17, 1971-June 9, 1972
Jurgen Blin	June 9, 1972-Oct. 10, 1972
*Joe Bugner	Oct. 10, 1972-June , 1975
Richard Dunn	Apr. 6, 1975-Oct. 12, 1976
Joe Bugner	Oct. 12, 1976-Jan. , 1977
Jean Pierre Coopman	Mar. 12, 1977-May 7, 1977
Lucien Rodriguez	May 7, 1977-Sept. 9, 1977
Alfredo Evangelista	Sept. 9, 1977-Apr. 18, 1979
*Lorenzo Zanon	Apr. 18, 1979-Feb. , 1980
John L. Gardner	Apr. 22, 1980-

Light Heavyweights

Georges Carpentier	Feb. 12, 1913-Sept. 24, 1922
Battling Siki	Sept 24, 1922-June 16, 1923
Emile Morelle	June 16, 1923-Dec. 1, 1923
Raymond Bonnel	Dec. 1, 1923-Apr. 27, 1924
Louis Clement	Apr. 27, 1924-Jan. 5, 1926
Herman Van T'Hoff	Jan. 5, 1926-July 25, 1926
Fernand Delarge	July 25, 1926-June 19, 1927
*Max Schmeling	June 19, 1927-Dec. , 1928
*Michele Bonaglia	Feb. 10, 1929-Apr. 22, 1930
*Ernst Pistulla	Mar. 18, 1931-Mar. 24, 1932
*Adolf Heuser	June 25, 1932-Dec. 28, 1932
*John Andersson	Apr. 1, 1933-Oct. 18, 1933
Martinez de Alfara	Feb. 7, 1934-Mar. 26, 1934
Marcel Thil	Mar. 26, 1934-May 22, 1935
Merlo Preciso	Aug. 9, 1935-Sept. 17, 1935
Heinz Lazek	Sept. 17, 1935-Sept. 1, 1936
Gustave Roth	Sept. 1, 1936-Mar. 25, 1938
*Adolf Heuser	Mar. 25, 1938-Mar. , 1939
*Luigi Musina	Apr. 5, 1942-Sept. 5, 1943
Freddie Mills	Sept. 8, 1947-Feb. 16, 1950
Albert Yvel	July 9, 1950-Mar. 27, 1951
*Don Cockell	Mar. 27, 1951-Apr. , 1952
*Conny Rux	July 26, 1952-Oct. 16, 1952
Jacques Hairabedian	July 12, 1953-Apr. 9, 1954
Gerhard Hecht	Apr. 9, 1954-Mar. 11, 1955
Willi Hoepner	Mar. 11, 1955-June 12, 1955
Gerhard Hecht	June 12, 1955-July 12, 1957
Artemio Calzavara	July 12, 1957-May 30, 1958
Willi Hoepner	May 30, 1958-Dec. 12, 1958
"Erich Schoppner	Dec. 12, 1958-May 26, 1962

916

Giulio Rinaldi	Sept. 28, 1962-Apr. 4, 1964
*Gustav Scholz	Apr. 4, 1964-Jan. , 1965
Giulio Rinaldi	July 8, 1965-Mar. 11, 1966
Piero Del Papa	Mar. 11, 1966-Dec. 2, 1967
Lothar Stengel	Dec. 2, 1967-Sept. 12, 1968
Tom Bogs	Sept. 12, 1968-Apr. 12, 1969
Yvan Prebeg	June 28, 1969-Feb. 6, 1970
Piero Del Papa	Feb. 6, 1970-Jan. 22, 1971
Conny Velensek	Jan. 22, 1971-Feb. 1, 1972
Chris Finnegan	Feb. 1, 1972-Nov. 14, 1972
Ruediger Schmidtke	Nov. 14, 1972-Mar. 13, 1973
*John Conteh	Mar. 13, 1973-Oct. 1, 1974
Domeniço Adinolfi	Dec. 4, 1974-July 10, 1976
*Mate Parlov	July 10, 1976-July , 1977
Aldo Traversaro	Nov. 26, 1977-Mar. 8, 1979
Rudi Koopmans	Mar. 8, 1979-

Middleweights

*Georges Carpentier	Feb. 29, 1912-Aug. , 1914
Ercole (Billy) Balzac	Dec. 7, 1920-Feb. 21, 1921
Gus Platts	Feb. 21, 1921-May 31, 1921
Johnny Basham	May 31, 1921-Oct. 14, 1921
Ted (Kid) Lewis	Oct. 14, 1921-Feb. 15, 1923
Roland Todd	Feb. 15, 1923-Nov. 30, 1924
Bruno Frattini	Nov. 30, 1924-June 8, 1925
*Tommy Milligan	June 8, 1925-Dec. , 1925
*Rene Duvos	Jan. 31, 1926-Sept. , 1927
Mario Bosisio	Apr. 1, 1928-June 24, 1928
Leone Jacovacci	June 24, 1928-Mar. 27, 1929
Marcel Thil	Mar. 27, 1929-Nov. 23, 1930
Mario Bosisio	Nov. 23, 1930-June 19, 1931
Leopold Steinbach	June 19, 1931-Aug. 30, 1931
*Hein Domgoergen	Aug. 30, 1931-Nov. 21, 1931
*Ignacio Ara	May 9, 1932-Jan. 2, 1933
Gustave Roth	Mar. 17, 1934-May 3, 1934
*Marcel Thil	May 3, 1934-Feb. 17, 1938
Edouard Tenet	Apr. 7, 1938-July 17, 1938
Bep Van Klaveren	July 17, 1938-Nov. 14, 1938
Anton Christoforidis	Nov. 14, 1938-Jan. 10, 1939
*Edouard Tenet	Jan. 10, 1939-June 21, 1939
*Josef Besselmann	May 23, 1942-Aug. 10, 1943
Marcel Cerdan	Feb. 2, 1947-May 23, 1948
Cyrille Delannoit	May 23, 1948-July 10, 1948
*Marcel Cerdan	July 10, 1948-Oct. 4, 1948
Cyrille Delannoit	Nov. 6, 1948-May 7, 1949
*Tiberio Mitri	May 7, 1949-May 28, 1950
Randolph Turpin	Feb. 27, 1951-May 2, 1954
Tiberio Mitri	May 2, 1954-Nov. 13, 1954
Charles Humez	Nov. 13, 1954-Oct. 4, 1958
*Gustav Scholz	Oct. 4, 1958-Apr. 24, 1961
John McCormack	Oct. 17, 1961-Feb. 8, 1962
Chris Christensen	Feb. 8, 1962-May 16, 1962
*Laszlo Papp	May 16, 1962-Nov. , 1964
*Nino Benvenuti	Oct. 15, 1965-Apr. 18, 1967
Juan Carlos Duran	Nov. 17, 1967-Sept. 11, 1969
Tom Bogs	Sept. 11, 1969-Dec. 4, 1970
Juan Carlos Duran	Dec. 4, 1970-June 9, 1971
*Jean-Claude Bouttier	June 9, 1971-Sept. , 1972
*Tom Bogs	Jan. 18, 1973-Sept. , 1973
Elio Calcabrini	Nov. 7, 1973-Mar. 2, 1974
Jean-Claude Bouttier	Mar. 2, 1974-May 27, 1974
Kevin Finnegan	May 27, 1974-May 7, 1975
*Gratien Tonna	May 7, 1975-Oct. , 1975
Bunny Sterling	Feb. 20, 1976-June 4, 1976
Angelo Jacopucci	June 4, 1976-Oct. 1, 1976
Germano Valsecchi	Oct. 1, 1976-Feb. 4, 1977
Alan Minter	Feb. 4, 1977-Sept. 21, 1977
*Gratien Tonna	Sept. 21, 1977 Apr , 1978
*Alan Minter	July 19, 1978-Jan. , 1980
Kevin Finnegan	Feb. 7, 1980-Sept. 10, 1980

Matteo Salvemini	Sept. 10, 1980-Dec. 8, 1980
Tony Sibson	Dec. 8, 1980-

Junior Middleweight

Bruno Visintin	May 22, 1964-Jan. 1, 1966
Bo Hoberg	Jan. 1, 1966-Feb. 11, 1966
Yoland Leveque	Feb. 11, 1966-June 17, 1966
*Sandro Mazzinghi	June 17, 1966-May 25, 1968
Remo Golfarini	Nov. 29, 1968-July 16, 1969
Gerhard Piaskowy	July 16, 1969-Sept. 11, 1970
Jose Hernandez	Sept. 11, 1970-July 5, 1972
Juan Carlos Duran	July 5, 1972-July 4, 1973
Jacques Kechichian	July 4, 1973-June 7, 1974
Jose Duran	June 7, 1974-June 24, 1975
Eckhard Dagge	June 24, 1975-Jan. 16, 1976
Vito Antuofermo	Jan. 16, 1976-Oct. 1, 1976
*Maurice Hope	Oct. 1, 1976-Nov. 17, 1978
Gilbert Cohen	Nov. 21, 1978-Mar. 17, 1979
Marijan Benes	Mar. 17, 1979-

Welterweights

Young Joseph	Dec. 19, 1910-Oct. 23, 1911
*Georges Carpentier	Oct. 23, 1911-Feb. , 1912
*Albert Badoud	Apr. 20, 1915-Aug. , 1919
Johnny Basham	Sept. 2, 1919-June 9, 1920
*Ted (Kid) Lewis	June 9, 1920-Dec. , 1920
Piet Hobin	June 25, 1921-Sept. 27, 1925
*Mario Bosisio	Sept. 27, 1925-Apr. , 1928
Leo Darton	Apr. 22, 1928-Nov. 26, 1928
Alf Genon	Nov. 26, 1928-Oct. 9, 1929
Gustave Roth	Oct. 9, 1929-Oct. 26, 1932
Adrien Anneet	Oct. 26, 1932-May 22, 1933
*Jack Hood	May 22, 1933-Nov. , 1933
Gustav Eder	June 8, 1934-June , 1936
Felix Wouters	July 23, 1936-Dec. 26, 1938
Saverio Turiello	Dec. 26, 1938-June 3, 1939
*Marcel Cerdan	June 3, 1939-Dec. , 1942
Ernie Roderick	June 4, 1946-Feb. 1, 1947
*Robert Villemain	Feb. 1, 1947-Mar. , 1948
Livio Minelli	Mar. 4, 1949 14, 1950
Michele Palermo	July 14, 1950-Feb. 19, 1951
Eddie Thomas	Feb. 19, 1951-June 13, 1951
Charles Humez	June 13, 1951-Feb. , 1952
Gilbert Lavoine	Mar. 22, 1953-Aug. 26, 1954
Wally Thom	Aug. 26, 1954-June 23, 1955
Idrissa Dione	June 23, 1955-Feb. 12, 1956
Emilio Marconi	Feb. 12, 1956-Jan. 28, 1958
Peter Waterman	Jan. 28, 1958-June , 1958
Emilio Marconi	Dec. 26, 1958-Apr. 19, 1959
*Duilio Loi	Apr. 19, 1959-Jan. 23, 1963
*Fortunato Manca	Oct. 9, 1964-Oct. , 1965
Jean Josselin	Apr. 25, 1966-May 17, 1967
Carmelo Bossi	May 17, 1967-Aug. 14, 1968
Edwin (Fighting) Mack	Aug. 14, 1968-Jan. 13, 1969
Silvano Bertini	Jan. 13, 1969-May 5, 1969
Jean Josselin	May 5, 1969-Sept. 25, 1969
Johann Orsolics	Sept. 25, 1969-Nov. 20, 1970
Ralph Charles	Nov. 20, 1970-June 4, 1971
Roger Menetrey	June 4, 1971-May 27, 1974
*John H. Stracey	May 27, 1974-Dec. 6, 1975
Marco Scano	Apr. 9, 1976-June 2, 1977
Jorgen Hansen	June 2, 1977-Aug. 6, 1977
Jorg Eipel	Aug. 6, 1977-Dec. 17, 1977
Alain Marion	Dec. 17, 1977-Apr. 27, 1978
Jorgen Hansen	Apr. 27, 1978-Aug. 18, 1978
Joseph Pachler	Aug. 18, 1978-Dec. 2, 1978
Henry Rhiney	Dec. 2, 1978-Jan. 23, 1979
Dave (Boy) Green	Jan. 23, 1979-Feb. 15, 1979
Jorgen Hansen	Feb. 15, 1979-

Junior Welterweights

*Olli Maki	Feb. 14, 1964-Jan. 27, 1965
Juan Sombrita Albornoz	July 17, 1965-Dec. 26, 1965
*Willi Quatuor	Dec. 26, 1965-Nov. 10, 1966
Conny Rudhoff	Feb. 1, 1967-June 6, 1967
Johann Orsolics	June 6, 1967-May 7, 1968
*Bruno Arcari	May 7, 1968-Feb. 13, 1970
Rene Roque	Mar. 21, 1970-May 21, 1971
*Pedro Carrasco	May 21, 1971-Jan. , 1972
Roger Zami	Feb. 28, 1972-Oct. 1, 1972
Cemal Kamaci	Oct. 1, 1972-June 15, 1973
Tony Ortiz	June 15, 1973-July 26, 1974
*Perico Fernandez	July 26, 1974-Sept. 21, 1974
Jose Ramon Gomez Fouz	Mar. 8, 1975-Oct. 31, 1975
*Cemal Kamaci	Oct. 31, 1975-Nov. , 1976
*Dave (Boy) Green	Dec. 7, 1976-July , 1977
Primo Bandini	Aug. 10, 1977-Dec. 5, 1977
Jean Baptiste Piedvache	Dec. 5, 1977-June 5, 1978
Colin Powers	June 5, 1978-Sept. 9, 1978
Fernando Sanchez	Sept. 9, 1978-Mar. 3, 1979
Jose Luis Heredia	Mar. 3, 1979-May 19, 1979
*Jo Kimpuani	May 19, 1979-July , 1980
Giuseppe Martinese	Aug. 27, 1980-Dec. 15, 1980
Antonio Guinaldo	Dec. 15, 1980-

Lightweights

Freddie Welsh	Aug. 23, 1909-Feb. 27, 1911
Matt Wells	Feb. 27, 1911-Nov. 11, 1912
*Freddie Welsh	Nov. 11, 1912-July , 1914
Bob Marriot	Apr. 10, 1919-May 17, 1920
Georges Papin	May 17, 1920-May 9, 1921
Ernie Rice	May 9, 1921-Sept. 18, 1922
Seaman Hall	Sept. 18, 1922-Mar. 17, 1923
*Harry Mason	Mar. 17, 1923-Dec. , 1923
Fred Bretonnel	Feb. 27, 1924-Oct. 7, 1924
Lucien Vinez	Oct. 7, 1924-Aug. 3, 1927
*Luis Rayo	Aug. 3, 1927-May , 1928
Aime Raphael	Dec. 22, 1928-Apr. 14, 1929
Francois Sybille	Apr. 14, 1929-Jan. 16, 1930
Alf Howard	Jan. 16, 1930-June 10, 1930
Francois Sybille	June 10, 1930-July 19, 1931
Bep Van Klaveren	July 19, 1931-Aug. 18, 1932
Anacleto Locatelli	Aug. 18, 1932-Dec. 7, 1932
Francois Sybille	Dec. 7, 1932-Oct. 22, 1933
*Anacleto Locatelli	Oct. 22, 1933-Dec. , 1933
Francois Sybille	Feb. 10, 1934-Mar. 17, 1934
*Carlo Orlandi	Mar. 17, 1934-Mar. , 1935
*Enrico Venturi	Oct. 12, 1935-Apr. , 1936
Vittorio Tamagnini	Oct. 10, 1936-Apr. 22, 1937
Maurice Arnoult	Apr. 22, 1937-May 27, 1937
*Gustave Humery	May 27, 1937-May , 1938
Aldo Spoldi	Sept. 2, 1938-Sept. , 1939
Karl Blaho	Oct. 26, 1940-May 31, 1941
Bruno Bisterzo	May 31, 1941-Nov. 26, 1941
Ascenzo Botta	Nov. 26, 1941-Dec. 31, 1941
Bruno Bisterzo	Dec. 31, 1941-May 14, 1942
Ascenzo Botta	May 14, 1942-Sept. 20, 1942
Roberto Proietti	Sept. 20, 1942-May 8, 1943
Bruno Bisterzo	May 8, 1943-May 26, 1946
*Roberto Proietti	May 26, 1946-June , 1946
Emile Di Cristo	Dec. 4, 1946-Mar. 29, 1947
Kid Dussart	Mar. 29, 1947-May 21, 1947
Roberto Proietti	May 21, 1947-Feb. 12, 1948
Billy Thompson	Feb. 12, 1948-July 5, 1949
Kid Dussart	July 5, 1949-Dec. 18, 1949
*Roberto Proietti	Dec. 18, 1949-Oct. , 1950
Pierre Montane	Feb. 23, 1951-Aug. 17, 1951

Elis Ask	Aug. 17, 1951-Jan. 4, 1952
Jorgen Johansen	Jan. 4, 1952-Feb. 6, 1954
*Duilio Loi	Feb. 6, 1954-Sept. , 1959
Mario Vecchiatto	Oct. 24, 1959-Mar. 29, 1960
*Dave Charnley	Mar. 29, 1960-Apr. , 1963
*Conny Rudhoff	Sept. 29, 1963-Jan. , 1964
*Willi Quatuor	May 8, 1964-Jan. , 1965
Franco Brondi	Mar. 13, 1965-Oct. 9, 1965
Maurice Tavant	Oct. 9, 1965-Nov. 3, 1966
Borge Krogh	Nov. 3, 1966-June 30, 1967
*Pedro Carrasco	June 30, 1967-Oct. , 1969
Miguel Velasquez	Jan. 29, 1970-July 31, 1971
Antonio Puddu	July 31, 1971-May 1, 1974
*Ken Buchanan	May 1, 1974-July , 1975
Fernand Roelands	Feb. 6, 1976-July 9, 1976
*Perico Fernandez	July 9, 1976-June , 1977
*Jim Watt	Aug. 5, 1977-Apr. 17, 1979
*Charlie Nash	June 27, 1979-Mar. , 1980
Francisco Leon	June 1, 1980-Dec. 14, 1980
Charlie Nash	Dec. 14, 1980-

Junior Lightweights

Tommaso Galli	Jan. 13, 1971-Aug. 16, 1972
Antonio Chiloiro	Aug. 16, 1972-Oct. 13, 1972
Lothar Abend	Oct. 13, 1972-May 7, 1974
*Svein-Erik Paulsen	May 7, 1974-Jan. , 1976
Roland Cazeaux	Feb. 27, 1976-Sept. 24, 1976
Natale Vezzoli	Sept. 24, 1976-Mar. 10, 1979
Carlos Hernandez	Mar. 10, 1979-June 2, 1979
Rodolfo Sanchez	June 2, 1979-Dec. 21, 1979
Carlos Hernandez	Dec. 21, 1979-

Featherweights

*Jem Driscoll	June 3, 1912-July , 1913
*Ted (Kid) Lewis	Oct. 6, 1913-May , 1914
*Louis DePonthieu	Dec. 24, 1919-Feb. , 1920
Arthur Wyns	May 31, 1920-July 7, 1922
Eugene Criqui	July 7, 1922-Dec. 20, 1923
Edouard Mascart	Dec. 20, 1923-Feb. 19, 1924
Charles Ledoux	Feb. 10, 1924-May 8, 1924
Henry Hebrans	May 8, 1924-Oct. 30, 1925
Antonio Ruiz	Oct. 30, 1925-Jan. 7, 1928
Luigi Quadrini	Jan. 7, 1928-Jan. 11, 1929
Knud Larsen	Jan. 11, 1929-Dec. 1, 1929
*Jose Girones	Dec. 1, 1929-Mar. 29, 1934
*Maurice Holtzer	Mar. 26, 1935-July 11, 1938
Phil Dolhem	Sept. 6, 1938-June 3, 1939
Lucien Popescu	June 3, 1939-May 31, 1941
Ernst Weiss	May 31, 1941-June 30, 1941
Gino Bondavalli	June 30, 1941-Nov. 11, 1945
*Ermanno Bonetti	Nov. 11, 1945-May , 1946
Al Phillips	May 27, 1947-Sept. 11, 1947
Ronnie Clayton	Sept. 11, 1947-Mar. 22, 1948
Ray Famechon	Mar. 22, 1948-Oct. 17, 1953
Jean Sneyers	Oct. 17, 1953-Sept. 20, 1954
Ray Famechon	Sept. 20, 1954-Nov. 3, 1955
*Fred Galiana	Nov. 3, 1955-Oct. 1, 1956
*Cherif Hamia	Jan. 21, 1957-May 17, 1958
Sergio Caprari	Aug. 18, 1958-Sept. 15, 1959
Gracieux Lamperti	Sept. 15, 1959-Aug. 19, 1962
Alberto Serti	Aug. 19, 1962-July 9, 1963
*Howard Winstone	July 9, 1963-Oct. 25, 1967
*Jose Legra	Dec. 22, 1967-Sept. 21, 1968
Manuel Calvo	Dec. 17, 1968-Aug. 20, 1969
Tommaso Galli	Aug. 20, 1969-June 26, 1970
*Jose Legra	June 26, 1970-Dec. 16, 1972
Gitano Jimenez	May 12, 1973-Feb. 12, 1975
Elio Cotena	Feb. 12, 1975-Dec. 3, 1976
Pedro (Nino)Jimenez	Dec. 3, 1976-Sept. 16, 1977

Manuel Masso	Sept. 16, 1977-Dec. 16, 1977	Bob Allotey	Oct. 4, 1974-Feb. 9, 1975
Roberto Castanon	Dec. 16, 1977-	Daniel Trioulaire	Feb. 9, 1975-Aug. 14, 1976
		Salvatore Fabrizio	Aug. 14, 1976-Feb. 23, 1977
		Franco Zurlo	Feb. 23, 1977-Sept. 16, 1978

Bantamweights

		Juan Francisco	
Joe Bowker	Mar. 7, 1910-Oct. 17, 1910	Rodriguez	Sept. 16, 1978-Feb. 28, 1980
George (Digger) Stanley	Oct. 17, 1910-June 23, 1912	*Johnny Owen	Feb. 28, 1980-Nov. 3, 1980
Charles Ledoux	June 23, 1912-Oct. 24, 1921	Valerio Nati	Dec. 3, 1980-
Tommy Harrison	Oct. 24, 1921-Apr. 24, 1922		
Charles Ledoux	Apr. 24, 1922-July 30, 1923		
Harry (Bugler) Lake	July 30, 1923-Nov. 26, 1923		Flyweights
*Johnny Brown	Nov. 26, 1923-Oct. , 1924		
*Henri Scillie	May 11, 1925-Dec. , 1927	Sid Smith	Apr. 11, 1913-June 2, 1913
Domenico Bernasconi	Dec. 11, 1927-Sept. 26, 1929	Bill Ladbury	June 2, 1913-Jan. 26, 1914
Carlos Flix	Sept. 26, 1929-Sept. 19, 1931	Percy Jones	Jan. 26, 1914-Oct. 19, 1914
Lucien Popescu	Sept. 19, 1931-Mar. 19, 1932	Tancy Lee	Oct. 19, 1914-June 26, 1916
*Domenico Bernasconi	Mar. 19, 1932-Sept. , 1932	*Jimmy Wilde	June 26, 1916-Apr. , 1917
Nicolas Petit-Biquet	Dec. 7, 1932-May 11, 1935	Michel Montreuil	Sept. 29, 1923-Jan. 31, 1925
Maurice Dubois	May 11, 1935-Feb. 19, 1936	*Elky Clark	Jan. 31, 1925-Mar. , 1927
Joseph Decico	Feb. 19, 1936-July 26, 1936	*Victor Ferrand	Apr. 11, 1927-Feb. 14, 1928
Aurel Toma	July 26, 1936-Aug. 11, 1939	Emile (Spider) Pladner	Feb. 14, 1928-Mar. 19, 1928
Ernst Weiss	Aug. 11, 1939-Nov. 25, 1939	Johnny Hill	Mar. 19, 1928-Feb. 7, 1929
Gino Cattaneo	Nov. 25, 1939-Sept. 28, 1941	Emile (Spider) Pladner	Feb. 7, 1929-June 20, 1929
*Gino Bondavalli	Sept. 28, 1941-Sept. 5, 1943	*Eugene Huat	June 20, 1929-Dec. 2, 1929
Jackie Paterson	Mar. 19, 1946-Oct. 30, 1946	Emile Degand	Dec. 2, 1929-Mar. 5, 1930
Theo Medina	Oct. 30, 1946-Sept. 19, 1947	*Kid Oliva	Mar. 5, 1930-June 7, 1930
Peter Kane	Sept. 19, 1947-Feb. 20, 1948	Lucien Popescu	June 7, 1930-May 4, 1931
Guido Ferracin	Feb. 20, 1948-Aug. 10, 1949	*Jackie Brown	May 4, 1931-Oct. , 1932
Luis Romero	Aug. 10, 1949-Sept. 5, 1951	Praxile Gyde	Nov. 1, 1932-June 23, 1935
Peter Keenan	Sept. 5, 1951-May 21, 1952	*Kid David	June 23, 1935-Dec. 1, 1935
*Jean Sneyers	May 21, 1952-Nov. 1, 1952	Ernst Weiss	Oct. 5, 1936-Dec. 12, 1936
Peter Keenan	June 16, 1953-Oct. 3, 1953	*Valentin Angelmann	Dec. 12, 1936-Sept. 1, 1938
John Kelly	Oct. 3, 1953-Feb. 27, 1954	*Enrico Urbinati	Dec. 5, 1938-Feb. 15, 1943
*Robert Cohen	Feb. 27, 1954-Dec. 30, 1954	Raoul Degryse	Oct. 9, 1946-May 21, 1947
Mario D'Agata	Oct. 29, 1955-Oct. 12, 1958	Maurice Sandeyron	May 21, 1947-Apr. 5, 1949
Piero Rollo	Oct. 12, 1958-Nov. 3, 1959	*Rinty Monaghan	Apr. 5, 1949-Mar. 30, 1950
*Freddie Gilroy	Nov. 3, 1959-Oct. 25, 1960	Terry Allen	Apr. 25, 1950-Oct. 30, 1950
Pierre Cossemyns	May 27, 1961-Apr. 13, 1962	*Jean Sneyers	Oct. 30, 1950-Feb. 26, 1951
Piero Rollo	Apr. 13, 1962-June 26, 1962	*Teddy Gardner	Feb. 18, 1952-Sept. 12, 1952
Alphonse Halimi	June 26, 1962-Oct. 28, 1962	*Louis Skena	June 13, 1953-Apr. 28, 1954
Piero Rollo	Oct. 28, 1962-July 19, 1963	Nazzareno Giannelli	Sept. 10, 1954-Mar. 8, 1955
Mimoun Ben Ali	July 19, 1963-Dec. 9, 1963	Dia Dower	Mar. 8, 1955-Oct. 3, 1955
*Risto Luukkonen	Dec. 9, 1963-Sept. , 1964	Young Martin	Oct. 3, 1955-Sept. 3, 1959
Mimoun Ben Ali	Feb. 4, 1965-Aug. 19, 1965	Risto Luukkonen	Sept. 3, 1959-June 29, 1961
Tommaso Galli	Aug. 19, 1965-June 17, 1966	*Salvatore Burruni	June 29, 1961-May , 1964
Mimoun Ben Ali	June 17, 1966-Jan. 10, 1968	*Rene Libeer	June 13, 1965-Oct. 12, 1966
*Salvatore Burruni	Jan. 10, 1968-July 24, 1969	Fernando Atzori	Jan. 25, 1967-Mar. 3, 1972
Franco Zurlo	Dec. 17, 1969-Feb. 16, 1971	*Fritz Chervet	Mar. 3, 1972-June , 1973
Alan Rudkin	Feb. 16, 1971-Aug. 10, 1971	Fernando Atzori	June 28, 1973-Dec. 26, 1973
*Agustin Senin	Aug. 10, 1971-Jan. , 1973	*Fritz Chervet	Dec. 26, 1973-July 10, 1974
*Johnny Clark	Apr. 17, 1973-Aug. , 1974	Franco Udella	Oct. 25, 1974-May 1, 1979
		Charlie Magri	May 1, 1979-

ORIENTAL CHAMPIONS

The Oriental Boxing Federation (OBF) was established on October 27, 1954, when boxing commissioners from three Oriental countries met in Tokyo, Japan. The commissioners were Soeni Tanabe of Japan, Alfredo Guidote of the Philippines, and Phorn Panitchpakdi of Thailand.

The OBF changed its name to the Oriental & Pacific Boxing Federation (OPBF) at its 21st convention, held in the Philippines in November, 1977. This was because Australia joined the Federation.

The OPBF consists, at present, of Japan, Korea, Philippines, Thailand, Australia, Indonesia, Taiwan, Guam, Hong Kong, and Papua New Guinea.

MIDDLEWEIGHTS

Hachiro Tatsumi	Mar. 22, 1954-Apr. 20, 1955
*Somdej Yontrakit	Apr. 20, 1955-Apr. 30, 1955
Hachiro Tatsumi	Dec. 7, 1955-Jan. 8, 1956
Teruo Ohnuki	Jan. 8, 1956-Apr. 9, 1956

Hachiro Tatsumi	Apr. 9, 1956-June 1, 1957
Dowthong	
Singahapaplop	June 1, 1957-Nov. 16, 1959
Fumio Kaizu	Nov. 16, 1959-July 13, 1961
Samart Sorndaeng	July 13, 1961-Oct. 17, 1961
.Fumio Kaizu	Oct. 17, 1961-Jan. 20, 1964
Masao Gondo	Jan. 24, 1964-Aug. 3, 1964
Fumio Kaizu	Aug. 3, 1964-Jan. 10, 1965
Ki-Soo Kim	Jan. 10, 1965-Nov. 20, 1968
Hisao Minami	Nov. 20, 1968-Mar. 1, 1969
*Ki-Soo Kim	Mar. 1, 1969-Aug. 5, 1969
Sung-Kap Choi	Sept.27, 1969-Jan. 10, 1970
Keun-Taek Lee	Jan. 10, 1970-Jan. 6, 1971
Cassius Naito	Jan. 6, 1971-July 24, 1971
*Jae-Do Yuh	July 24, 1971-July , 1979
Chong-Pal Park	Aug. 22, 1979-

JUNIOR MIDDLEWEIGHTS

Se-Chul Kang	Nov. 20, 1960-Nov. 13, 1961
Keowang Yontrakit	Nov. 13, 1961-Nov 17, 1963
*Shigemasa Kawakami	Nov. 17, 1963-Nov. 8, 1965
Ansano Lee	Mar. 13, 1966-May 10, 1969
*Muneo Mizoguchi	May 10, 1969-Oct. 20, 1969
Hideo Kanazawa	Nov. 13, 1969-Feb. 23, 1975
Jae-Keun Yim	Feb. 23, 1975-Nov. 20, 1976
Tsutomu Hagusa	Nov. 20, 1976-Nov. 12, 1977
*Ho Joo	Nov. 12, 1977-Sept. 1, 1978
Jae-Keun Yim	Sept. 2, 1978-Apr. 26, 1979
Tadashi Mihara	Apr. 26, 1979-

WELTERWEIGHTS

Somdej Yontrakit	Jan. 4, 1953-Nov. 20, 1957
Kenji Fukuchi	Nov. 20, 1957-Dec. 16, 1961
Filipino Ravalo	Dec. 16, 1961-July 2, 1962
*Kenji Fukuchi	July 2, 1962-Feb. 26, 1963
Yoshinori Takahashi	Aug. 26, 1963-May 8, 1964
Eliseo Aranda	May 8, 1964-Jan. 7, 1965
Apidej Sithiran	Jan. 7, 1965-Jan. 8, 1966
*Misashi Nakano	Jan. 8, 1966-Apr. 28, 1969
Hisao Minami	May 21, 1969-Apr. 1, 1970
Byong-Mo Yim	Apr. 1, 1970-Oct. 28, 1970
Ryu Sorimachi	Oct. 28, 1970-Mar. 6, 1979
Man-Duk Lee	Mar. 6, 1979-Nov. 16, 1979
Dan de Guzman	Nov. 16, 1979-Feb. 29, 1980
Chung-Jae Hwang	Feb. 29, 1980-

JUNIOR WELTERWEIGHTS

Bert Somodio	May 7, 1960-June 22, 1964
Makoto Watanabe	June 22, 1964-June 20, 1966
Rocky Alarde	June 20, 1966-Sept. 29, 1966
*Paul Fujii	Sept. 29, 1966-Feb. 29, 1968
Larry Flaviano	June 18, 1968-Jan. 22, 1969
Shigeru Ogiwara	Jan. 22, 1969-Apr. 12, 1969
Chun-Kyo Shin	Apr. 12, 1969-Sept. 2, 1970
Lion Furuyama	Sept. 2, 1970-May 29, 1971
*Chang-Kil Lee	May 29, 1971-Jan. 16, 1973
Pedro Adigue	July 25, 1973-Sept. 27, 1973
Chang-Kil Lee	Sept. 27, 1973-July 28, 1975
Wongso Suseno	July 28, 1975-Sept. 29, 1977
Moises Cantoja	Sept. 29, 1977-Sept. 23, 1978
Sang-Hyun Kim	Sept. 23, 1978-July , 1979
Sang-Mo Koo	Aug. 3, 1979-Aug. 15, 1980
Thomas Americo	Aug. 15, 1980-

LIGHTWEIGHTS

*Chamrern Songkitrat	Mar. 1, 1953-Feb. , 1954
Masaji Akiyama	Mar. 30, 1954-Sept. 20, 1954
Bony Espinosa	Sept. 20, 1954-Apr. 10, 1955
Omsap Nalphai	Apr. 10, 1955-July 15, 1955
Masaji Akiyama	July 15, 1955-Aug. 25, 1955

Jiro Sawada	Aug. 25, 1955-Dec. 3, 1955
*Leo Alonzo	Dec. 3, 1955-Mar. 10, 1957
Flash Elorde	Apr. 27, 1957-June 23, 1957
Omsap Laempapha	June 23, 1957-Nov. 20, 1957
Hiroshi Okawa	Nov. 20, 1957-Mar. 2, 1958
Flash Elorde	Mar. 2, 1958-Apr. 30, 1962
Teruo Kosaka	Apr. 30, 1962-Aug. 4, 1962
Flash Elorde	Aug. 4, 1962-June 9, 1966
*Yoshiaki Numata	June 9, 1966-July 4, 1966
*Pedro Adigue	Dec. 17, 1966-Jan. 6, 1969
Jaguar Kakizawa	Feb. 24, 1966-Mar. 15, 1970
Yung-Chul Cho	Mar. 15, 1970-Oct. 17, 1970
Shinichi Kadota	Oct. 17, 1970-Jan. 16, 1972
*Ishimatsu Suzki	Jan. 16, 1972-Apr. 17, 1974
*Fred Pastor	July 19, 1974-Feb. 21, 1975
Morito Kashiwaba	Feb. 21, 1975-Mar. 15, 1976
Young-Ho Oh	Apr. 25, 1976-

JUNIOR LIGHTWEIGHTS

Hiroshi Okawa	June 30, 1960-May 4, 1961
Kirisak Babos	May 4, 1961-Nov. 30, 1961
Yukio Katsumata	Nov. 30, 1961-May 27, 1962
Oscar Reyes	May 27, 1962-Sept. 3, 1962
Yukio Katsumata	Sept. 3, 1962-May 17, 1964
Larry Flaviano	May 17, 1964-Apr. 1, 1965
*Yoshiaki Numata	Apr. 1, 1965-Apr. 2, 1969
Saleman Itti-anuchit	May 17, 1969-Aug. 14, 1970
*Rene Barrientos	Aug. 14, 1970-Jan. 31, 1972
*Susumu Okabe	Mar. 23, 1972-Aug. 4, 1972
*Hyun-Chi Kim	Sept. 3, 1972-Oct. 31, 1974
Apollo Yoshio	Apr. 7, 1975-Nov. 20, 1977
Rey Tam	Nov. 20, 1977-Nov. 19, 1978
Moon-Suk Choi	Nov. 19, 1978-Nov. 6, 1979
Ryu Fukida	Nov. 6, 1979-

FEATHERWEIGHTS

Larry Bataan	Nov. 11, 1952-Dec. 6, 1953
Shigeji Kaneko	Dec. 6, 1953-Nov. 21, 1957
Hisao Kobayashi	Nov. 21, 1957-Feb. 1, 1961
Army Wonderboy Ramos	Feb. 1, 1961-Dec. 12, 1961
Veeranid Charemuang	Dec. 12, 1961-Sept. 12, 1962
*Mitsunori Seki	Sept. 12, 1962-Mar. 29, 1968
Katsuo Saito	June 12, 1968-Sept. 11, 1968
Herbert Kang	Sept. 11, 1968-Mar. 11, 1970
Nobuo Chiba	Mar. 11, 1970-Apr. 24, 1971
Hyun Kim	Apr. 24, 1971-Jan. 16, 1973
Zensuke Utagawa	Jan. 16, 1973-Mar. 23, 1975
Fel Clemente	Mar. 23, 1975-May 16, 1976
Bok-Soo Hwang	May 16, 1976-Apr. 27, 1978
Royal Kobayashi	Apr. 27, 1978-

JUNIOR FEATHERWEIGHTS

Haruo Sakamoto	Aug. 25, 1960-Dec. 19, 1963
Akio Maki	Dec. 19, 1963-May 6, 1964
Prinoi Tro	May 6, 1964-Oct. 1, 1964
Rokuro Ishiyama	Oct. 1, 1964-Jan. 13, 1966
Chun-Won Kang	Jan. 13, 1966-Apr. 20, 1967
Kiyohide Yutsudo	Apr. 20, 1967-Sept. 26, 1968
Sulfredo Basco	Sept. 26, 1968-Mar. 20, 1969
Koichi Okada	Mar. 20, 1969-Nov. 20, 1971
Kyu-Chul Chang	Nov. 20, 1971-Mar. 17, 1974
*Dong-Kyun Yum	Mar. 17, 1974-Dec. , 1976
Ric Quijano	Jan. 28, 1977-Apr. 2, 1978
Soon-Hyun Chung	Apr. 2, 1978-Nov. 21, 1980
Willie Lucas	Nov. 21, 1980-

BANTAMWEIGHTS

*Flash Elorde	Oct. 18, 1952-June , 1954
*Leo Espinosa	July 8, 1954-Dec. 1, 1955
Keiichi Komoro	Dec. 3, 1955-Mar. 3, 1956

Leo Espinosa	Mar. 3, 1956-Oct. 8, 1958
Kiyoshi Miura	Oct. 8, 1958-Nov. 15, 1958
Leo Espinosa	Nov. 15, 1958-Jan. 6, 1960
Kenji Yonekura	Jan. 6, 1960-Oct. 29, 1962
Katsutoshi Aoki	Oct. 29, 1962-Sept. 5, 1963
Curley Aguire	Sept. 5, 1963-Mar. 25, 1964
Katsutoshi Aoki	Mar. 25, 1964-Apr. 28, 1966
Won-Suk Lee	Apr. 28, 1966-Oct. 23, 1969
*Takao Sakurai	Oct. 23, 1969-June 4, 1971
*Kazuyoshi Kanazawa	July 2, 1971-Feb. 29, 1972
*Soo-Hwan Hong	June 4, 1972-Oct. 1, 1974
Venice Borkorsor	Nov. 29, 1974-May 30, 1976
*Soo-Hwan Hong	May 30, 1976-Mar. , 1977
Yung-Shik Kim	June 17, 1977-Dec. 14, 1978
Eijiro Murata	Dec. 14, 1978-

JUNIOR BANTAMWEIGHTS

| Yung-Shik Kim | Mar. 30, 1980-Oct. 15, 1980 |
| William Develos | Oct. 15, 1980- |

FLYWEIGHTS

| Tanny Campo | Mar. 20, 1954-Mar. 9, 1955 |

Hitoshi Misako	Mar. 9, 1955-June 24, 1955
Danny Kid	June 24, 1955-Mar. 29, 1956
*Hitoshi Misako	Mar. 29, 1956-Nov. 10, 1956
*Pone Kingpetch	Jan. 6, 1957-May 13, 1958
*Sadao Yaoita	Sept. 11, 1958-June 27, 1962
Chartchai Chionoi	Sept. 22, 1962-July 7, 1963
Takeshi Nakamura	July 7, 1963-Oct. 18, 1969
*Erbito Salavarria	Oct. 18, 1969-Aug. 8, 1973
Socrates Batoto	Nov. 18, 1973-Sept. 30, 1974
Jiro Takada	Mar. 17, 1975-Dec. 8, 1977
Hong-Soo Yang	Dec. 8, 1977-July 25, 1978
Riki Igarashi	July 25, 1978-Aug. 4, 1979
Hong-Soo Yang	Aug. 4, 1979-

JUNIOR FLYWEIGHTS

Monsayarm	
H. Mahachai	May 30, 1975-June 5, 1976
Sang-Il Chung	June 5, 1976-Jan. 26, 1978
Sung-Jun Kim	Jan. 26, 1978-July 9, 1978
Sang-Il Chung	July 9, 1978-Nov. 27, 1979
Yong-Hyun Kim	Nov. 27, 1979-

JAPANESE CHAMPIONS

Middleweights

Shokichi Arai	Aug. 31, 1947-Mar. 28, 1948
Tsuneo Horiguchi	Mar. 28, 1948-May 22, 1948
Haruki Fumimoto	May 22, 1948-Jan. 2, 1950
Shokichi Arai	Jan. 2, 1950-Jan. 9, 1951
*Hachiro Tatsumi	Jan. 9, 1951-June 23, 1953
Mamoru Yokoyama	July 1, 1953-Jan. 18, 1954
Hachiro Tatsumi	Jan. 18, 1954-Jan. 8, 1956
Teruo Onuki	Jan. 8, 1956-Apr. 9, 1961
Hachiro Tatsumi	Apr. 9, 1961-June 3, 1962
Takao Maemizo	June 3, 1962-Dec. 2, 1962
Noboru Saito	Dec. 2, 1962-Feb. 17, 1963
Takao Maemizo	Feb. 17, 1963-Aug. 12, 1963
Mario Kaneda	Aug. 12, 1963-May 10, 1965
Fumio Kaizu	May 10, 1965-May 3, 1967
Yoshiaki Akasaka	May 3, 1967-July 19, 1967
*Fumio Kaizu	July 19, 1967-Aug. 29, 1967
Yoshiaki Akasaka	Nov. 8, 1967-May 6, 1968
Hajime Fuji	May 6, 1968-Sept. 19, 1968
Yoshiaki Eto	Sept. 19, 1968-Dec. 25, 1968
Benkei Fujikura	Dec. 25, 1968-Apr. 23, 1969
*Yoshiaki Eto	Apr. 23, 1969-Feb. 4, 1970
*Cassius Naito	Feb. 25, 1970-Feb. 1, 1971
Turtle Okabe	Feb. 24, 1971-Apr. 19, 1971
*George Carter	Apr. 19, 1971-Dec. 1, 1972
Cassius Naito	Dec. 8, 1972-Feb. 26, 1973
*Stevens Smith	Feb. 26, 1973-Sept. , 1974
*Masashi Kudo	Mar. 2, 1975-Dec. , 1978
Katsuo Esashi	Mar. 6, 1979-Oct. 13, 1979
Dynamite Matsuo	Oct. 13, 1979-Jan. 9, 1980
James Callaghan	Jan. 9, 1980-

Junior Middleweights

Muneo Mizoguchi	July 21, 1966-Oct. 10, 1968
Noriyasu Yoshimura	Oct. 10, 1968-Sept. 4, 1969
Koichi Wajima	Sept. 4, 1969-Feb. 2, 1970
George Carter	Feb. 2, 1970-Apr. 9, 1970
*Koichi Wajima	Apr. 9, 1970-Jan. 20, 1972
Turtle Okabe	Dec. 18, 1972-Apr. 4, 1973
Raizo Kajima	Apr. 4, 1973-Sept. 26, 1973
Hitoshi Nakagawa	Sept. 26, 1973-May 10, 1974
Kenji Shibata	May 10, 1974-Oct. 8, 1975

Hiroshi Hikichi	Oct. 8, 1975-July 27, 1976
Kenji Shibata	July 27, 1976-July 11, 1979
Michihiro Horihata	July 11, 1979-

Welterweights

Ichiro Kawada	Sept. 1, 1947-Apr. 29, 1949
Hachiro Tatsumi	Apr. 29, 1949-May 9, 1951
Isao Shiina	May 9, 1951-Feb. 19, 1952
Takeo Ugo	Feb. 19, 1952-June 21, 1952
*Hachiro Tatsumi	June 21, 1952-June 26, 1953
Teruo Onuki	July 3, 1953-Feb. 9, 1954
Takeo Ugo	Feb. 9, 1954-July 19, 1954
Teruo Onuki	July 19, 1954-Jan. 6, 1955
Teruo Matsuyama	Jan. 6, 1955-Feb. 28, 1956
Kenji Fukuchi	Feb. 28, 1956-Oct. 3, 1956
Teruo Matsuyama	Oct. 3, 1956-Aug. 22, 1957
Kenji Fukuchi	Aug. 22, 1957-June 10, 1958
Jiro Sawada	June 10, 1958-Apr. 21, 1959
Hiroshi Shinada	Apr. 21, 1959-Aug. 20, 1959
Jiro Sawada	Aug. 20, 1959-July 28, 1961
Makoto Watanabe	July 28, 1961-May 7, 1962
Hachiro Ito	May 7, 1962-Sept. 10, 1962
Makoto Watanabe	Sept. 10, 1962-Oct. 19, 1964
Osamu Watanabe	Oct. 19, 1964-Jan. 14, 1965
Sakuji Shinozawa	Feb. 8, 1965-June 14, 1965
Mokoto Watanabe	June 14, 1965-Oct. 3, 1966
Hisao Minami	Oct. 3, 1966-Mar. 27, 1967
Kazuyoshi Kubokura	Mar. 27, 1967-Jan. 6, 1969
*Ryu Sorimachi	Jan. 6, 1969-Dec. 22, 1970
Takatsune Shimizu	Mar. 31, 1971-Oct. 30, 1972
Shoji Tsujimoto	Oct. 30, 1972-Apr. 28, 1978
Akio Kameda	Apr. 28, 1978-

Junior Welterweights

*Koji Okano	Aug. 16, 1964-Apr. 25, 1965
*Paul Fujii	June 17, 1965-July 25, 1967
*Shigeru Ogiwara	Aug. 3, 1967-Mar. 5, 1969
*Lion Furuyama	Apr. 9, 1969-Dec. 17, 1970
Eagle Sato	Jan. 15, 1971-Feb. 13, 1972
Hiroshi Shoji	Feb. 13, 1972-Oct. 30, 1972
Lion Furuyama	Oct. 30, 1972-Oct. 27, 1977
Noboru Hatakeyama	Oct. 27, 1977-Sept. 24, 1979

Eiichi Fukumoto	Sept. 24, 1979-May 19, 1980
Minori Sugiya	May 19, 1980-Sept. 23, 1980
Eiichi Fukumoto	Sept. 23, 1980-Dec. 25, 1980
Noboru Hatakeyama	Dec. 25, 1980-

Lightweights

Takeshi Sasazaki	Aug. 31, 1947-Aug. 8, 1948
Tetsuo Naito	Aug. 8, 1948-Apr. 17, 1949
Isao Shiina	Apr. 17, 1949-Apr. 8, 1950
Masashi Akiyama	Apr. 8, 1950-July 26, 1955
Toshiharu Ogoshi	Aug. 17, 1955-Feb. 28, 1956
Keijiro Kazama	Feb. 28, 1956-Apr. 19, 1956
Toshiharu Ogoshi	Apr. 19, 1956-Nov. 30, 1956
Katsumi Kosaka	Nov. 30, 1956-Jan. 4, 1957
Hideo Kobayashi	Jan. 4, 1957-Aug. 4, 1957
*Hiroshi Okawa	Aug. 4, 1957-Aug. 13, 1957
Keiichi Ishikawa	Oct. 26, 1957-Dec. 14, 1960
*Teruo Kosaka	Dec. 14, 1960-Sept. 15, 1963
*Noriyoshi Toyoshima	Nov. 1, 1965-June 15, 1966
Fujio Mikami	Aug. 29, 1966-Dec. 22, 1966
Akihisa Someya	Dec. 22, 1966-Aug. 28, 1969
Hidemori Tsujimoto	Aug. 28, 1969-Jan. 21, 1970
Masataka Takayama	Jan. 21, 1970-July 2, 1973
Buzzsaw Yamabe	July 2, 1973-Feb. 18, 1974
*Masataka Takayama	Feb. 18, 1974-May 8, 1975
*Big Yamaryu	July 27, 1975-Oct. 30, 1975
Yasuji Yajima	Nov. 17, 1975-June 24, 1976
Tamio Negishi	June 24, 1976-Jan. 28, 1977
Masa Ito	Jan. 28, 1977-Apr. 27, 1977
Tamio Negishi	Apr. 27, 1977-July 25, 1977
*Masahiro Yokai	July 25, 1977-May 21, 1979
Battle Hawk Kazama	July 6, 1979-

Junior Lightweights

Yasunobu Takada	Aug. 20, 1964-Dec. 10, 1964
Mamoru Hayashi	Dec. 10, 1964-Aug. 2, 1965
Hiroshi Mori	Aug. 2, 1965-Dec. 13, 1965
Mamoru Hayashi	Dec. 13, 1965-Sept. 18, 1966
Yuji Amashima	Sept. 18, 1966-Jan. 15, 1967
Hiroshi Shoji	Jan. 15, 1967-June 29, 1968
Kiyoshi Ogawa	June 29, 1968-Oct. 9, 1968
Hiroshi Shoji	Oct. 9, 1968-Oct. 21, 1970
Kenji Iwata	Oct. 21, 1970-July 9, 1972
*Sumio Nobata	July 9, 1972-May 16, 1973
*Morito Kashiwaba	May 27, 1973- , 1973
Susumu Okabe	Jan. 20, 1974-July 21, 1975
Yasutsune Uehara	July 21, 1975-Apr. 23, 1976
Masa Ito	Apr. 23, 1976-July 29, 1976
Yasutsune Uehara	July 29, 1976-

Featherweights

Baby Gostero	Aug. 29, 1947-May 1, 1950
Hideo Goto	May 1, 1950-Sept. 16, 1950
Baby Gostero	Sept. 16, 1950-Feb. 3, 1951
Hideo Goto	Feb. 3, 1951-Sept. 23, 1952
Akiyoshi Akanuma	Sept. 23, 1952-Apr. 15, 1953
Noboru Tanaka	Apr. 15, 1953-Mar. 13, 1954
Hiroshi Okawa	Mar. 13, 1954-Aug. 30, 1956
Kiyoaki Nakanishi	Aug. 30, 1956-Apr. 19, 1957
Hiroshi Okawa	Apr. 19, 1957-June 17, 1958
*Kazuo Takayama	June 17, 1958-July 4, 1963
Manzo Kikuchi	Aug. 19, 1963-Jan. 6, 1964
Yuji Masuko	Jan. 6, 1964-Sept. 28, 1964
*Hiroshi Kobayashi	Sept. 28, 1964-Jan. , 1968
*Nobuo Chiba	Mar. 25, 1968-Mar. 12, 1970
*Kuniaki Shibata	Apr. 15, 1970-Feb. 1, 1971
Masanao San	Mar. 10, 1971-Jan. 27, 1972
Kimio Shindo	Jan. 27, 1972-May 4, 1972

Thad Okamoto	May 4, 1972-Sept. 9, 1972
Masanao San	Sept. 9, 1972-Jan. 4, 1974
Ushiwakamaru Harada	Jan. 4, 1974-Mar. 9, 1975
Flipper Uehara	Mar. 9, 1975-Oct. 10, 1976
Shuzo Yoshida	Oct. 10, 1976-Dec. 11, 1976
*Flipper Uehara	Dec. 11, 1976- , 1977
Spider Nemoto	Sept. 18, 1977-

Junior Featherweights

Hajime Taroura	Aug. 15, 1964-Feb. 12, 1969
Kuwashi Shimizu	Feb. 12, 1969-Apr. 30, 1969
Kenjiro Nakajima	Apr. 30, 1969-July 23, 1969
Kuwashi Shimizu	July 23, 1969-Nov. 15, 1970
Takeo (Attack) Harada	Nov. 15, 1970-Feb. 17, 1971
Sarutobi Koyama	Feb. 17, 1971- , 1973
Snappy Asano	June 8, 1973-Mar. 20, 1974
Masaji Okano	Mar. 20, 1974-July 4, 1974
Seiichi Eto	July 4, 1974-Apr. 7, 1975
Waruinge Nakayama	Apr. 7, 1975-Jan. 30, 1977
Yu Kasahara	Jan 30, 1977-Sept. 4, 1979
Hiroyuki Iwamoto	Sept. 4, 1979-July 6, 1980
Bunji Ando	July 6, 1980-Oct. 5, 1980
Hiroyuki Iwamoto	Oct. 5, 1980-

Bantamweights

Hiroshi Horiguchi	Aug. 29, 1947-Jan. 16, 1948
Yoichiro Hanada	Jan. 16, 1948-Apr. 11, 1948
Hiroshi Horiguchi	Apr. 11, 1948-Dec. 15, 1949
Yoshio Shirai	Dec. 15, 1949-Mar. 17, 1951
Hidemasa Nagashima	Mar. 17, 1951-Sept. 20, 1951
*Yoshio Shirai	Sept. 20, 1951-Aug. 25, 1952
Hiroshi Horiguchi	Sept. 23, 1952-July 27, 1954
Keiichi Komoro	July 27, 1954-Apr. 19, 1955
Showa Otsuka	Apr. 19, 1955-June 28, 1955
Keiichi Komoro	June 28, 1955-July 8, 1956
Danny Kid	July 8, 1956-Aug. 20, 1956
Saburo Otaki	Aug. 20, 1956-Aug. 25, 1957
Hiroji Ishibashi	Aug. 25, 1957-Feb. 1, 1961
Tetsuya Yamaguchi	Feb. 1, 1961-Dec. 14, 1961
*Kozo Nagata	Dec. 14, 1961-July 5, 1963
Katsuo Haga	July 7, 1963-Mar. 19, 1964
Tatsuya Takami	Mar. 19, 1964-July 10, 1964
Katsuo Haga	July 10, 1964-June 10, 1965
Tetsuya Yamagami	June 10, 1965-Apr. 7, 1966
Katsuo Saito	Apr. 7, 1966-Mar. 16, 1967
Ushiwakamaru Harada	Mar. 16, 1967-Sept. 14, 1967
Eigo Takagi	Sept. 14, 1967-Oct. 24, 1968
Ushiwakamaru Harada	Oct. 24, 1968-Nov. 26, 1969
Shintaro Uchiyama	Nov. 26, 1969-Dec. 9, 1970
Shigeyoshi Oki	Dec. 9, 1970-Feb. 10, 1971
Shintaro Uchiyama	Feb. 10, 1971-Nov. 11, 1972
Genzo Kurosawa	Nov. 11, 1972-Feb. 26, 1973
*Shintaro Uchiyama	Feb. 26, 1973-Sept. , 1974
Hisami (Go) Numata	Dec. 1, 1974-Jan. 29, 1977
Tsuyoshi Okabe	Jan. 29, 1977-May 16, 1977
Hisami (Go) Numata	May 16, 1977-Aug. 25, 1978
Jo Araki	Aug. 25, 1978-Nov. 25, 1978
Kosei Anan	Nov. 25, 1978-July 16, 1979
Hurricane Teru	July 16, 1979-Jan. 28, 1980
Hitoshi Ishigaki	Jan. 28, 1980-May 3, 1980
Hurricane Teru	May 3, 1980-

Junior Bantamweights

| Jackal Maruyama | Dec. 2, 1980- |

Flyweights		Yoshiaki Matsumoto	Feb. 26, 1968-June 3, 1968

Flyweights	
Yoichiro Handa	Sept. 1, 1947-Jan. 28, 1949
*Yoshio Shirai	Jan. 28, 1949-Aug. 5, 1952
Speedy Akira	Oct. 25, 1952-Jan. 6, 1955
*Hitoshi Misako	Jan. 6, 1955-Mar. 12, 1955
Speedy Akira	Apr. 13, 1955-Oct. 15, 1955
Mitsutada Okami	Oct. 15, 1955-Jan. 9, 1956
Speedy Akira	Jan. 9, 1956-Apr. 19, 1956
Masaji Iwamoto	Apr. 19, 1956-Jan. 7, 1958
*Sadao Yaoita	Jan. 7, 1958-Dec. 29, 1958
*Kenji Yonekura	Jan. 4, 1959-Sept. 10, 1959
Atsuto Fukumoto	Sept. 29, 1959-Apr. 28, 1961
Kyo Noguchi	Apr. 28, 1961-Dec. 28, 1962
Seisaku Saito	Dec. 28, 1962-Apr. 2, 1964
Kenichi Iida	Apr. 2, 1964-Nov. 19, 1964
Akashi Namekawa	Nov. 19, 1964-Oct. 25, 1965
*Kiyoshi Tanabe	Oct. 25, 1965-May 27, 1967
Speedy Hayase	Aug. 28, 1967-Feb. 26, 1968

Yoshiaki Matsumoto	Feb. 26, 1968-June 3, 1968
Speedy Hayase	June 3, 1968-Apr. 7, 1969
Susumu Hanagata	Apr. 7, 1969-July 3, 1972
Osamu Haba	July 3, 1972-Oct. 6, 1972
*Susumu Hanagata	Oct. 6, 1972-Feb. , 1974
*Jiro Takada	Apr. 13, 1974-Mar. , 1975
Kenji Kato	Oct. 25, 1975-Feb. 13, 1976
Riki Igarashi	Feb. 13, 1976-June 27, 1977
Kenji Kato	June 27, 1977-Mar. 27, 1978
Koichi Maki	Mar. 27, 1978-Jan. 10, 1980
Kazumasa Tamaki	Jan. 10, 1980-

Junior Flyweights

Kazunori Tenryu	Mar. 2, 1980-Feb. 28, 1980
Tadashi Tomori	Feb. 28, 1980-Aug. 29, 1980
*Shuichi Hozumi	Aug. 29, 1980-Oct. , 1980
Masaharu Inami	Nov. 27, 1980-

1980 AMATEUR CHAMPIONS

OLYMPIC CHAMPIONS

106 — Shamil Sabirov, *U.S.S.R.*
112 — Peter Lessov, *Bulgaria*
119 — Juan Hernandez, *Cuba*
125 — Rudi Fink, *East Germany*
132 — Angel Herrera, *Cuba*
139 — Patrizio Oliva, *Italy*

147 — Andres Aldama, *Cuba*
156 — Armando Martinez, *Cuba*
165 — Jose Gomez, *Cuba*
178 — Slobodan Kacar, *Yugoslavia*
HVT — Teofilo Stevenson, *Cuba*

U.S. OLYMPIC TRIALS WINNERS

106 — Robert Shannon, *Edmonds, Wash.*
112 — Richard Sandoval, *Pomona, Calif.*
119 — Jackie Beard, *Jackson, Tenn.*
125 — Bernard Taylor, *Charlotte, N.C.*
132 — Joe Manley, *Detroit, Mich.*
139 — Johnny Bumphus, *Nashville, Tenn.*

147 — Don Curry, *Ft. Worth, Texas*
156 — James Shuler, *Philadelphia, Pa.*
165 — Charles Carter, *Santa Monica, Calif.*
178 — Lee Roy Murphy, *Chicago, Ill.*
HVT — James Broad, *Army (Wildwood, N.J.)*

NATIONAL AMATEUR ATHLETIC UNION CHAMPIONS

106 — Robert Shannon, *Edmonds, Wash.*
112 — Richard Sandoval, *Pomona, Calif.*
119 — Jackie Beard, *Jackson, Tenn.*
125 — Clifford Gray, *Boynton Beach, Fla.*
132 — Melvin Paul, *New Orleans, La.*
139 — Johnny Bumphus, *Nashville, Tenn.*

147 — Gene Hatcher, *Ft. Worth, Texas*
156 — Donald Bowers, *Jackson, Tenn.*
165 — Martin Pierce, *Flint, Mich.*
178 — Jeffrey Lampkin, *Youngstown, Ohio*
HVT — Marvis Frazier, *Philadelphia, Pa.*

NATIONAL GOLDEN GLOVES CHAMPIONS

106 — Steven McCrory, *Detroit, Mich.*
112 — Jerome Coffee, *Knoxville, Tenn.*
119 — Myron Taylor, *Philadelphia, Pa.*
125 — Bernard Taylor, *Charlotte, N.C.*
132 — Melvin Paul, *New Orleans, La.*
139 — Terry Silver, *Louisville, Ky.*

147 — Don Curry, *Ft. Worth, Texas*
156 — James Shuler, *Philadelphia, Pa.*
165 — Lamong Kirkland, *Omaha, Neb.*
178 — Steve Eden, *Des Moines, Iowa*
HVT — Michael Arms, *Milwaukee, Wisc.*

NEW YORK GOLDEN GLOVES CHAMPIONS

Open
106 — Miguel Rosario, *25th Precinct, N.Y.P.D.*
112 — Kenneth Mitchell, *Fort Apache Boxing Club*
119 — Hector Camacho, *LaSombra Sporting Club*
125 — Roberto Vinas, *Solar Sporting Club*
132 — Jesus Serrano, *Bronxchester Boxing Club*

139 — Bryant Ware, *Spartan Athletic Club*
147 — Pedro Villella, *Physical Sporting Club*
156 — Alex Ramos, *Bronxchester Boxing Club*
165 — Michael Martinez, *Lunar Boxing Club*
178 — Porfirio Llanes, *Lunar Boxing Club*
HVT — Mitchell Green, *unattached*

Sub-Novice
106 — John Picart, *Solar Sporting Club*
112 — Wellington Rocafuerte, *Yonkers PAL*
119 — Alberto Maidonado, *Bronxchester Boxing Club*
125 — Pedro Hernandez, *N.Y.C. Recreation Dept.*
132 — Angel Diaz, *PAL*

139 — Mark Breland, *Spartan Athletic Club*
147 — Michael DeLaRue, *South Queens Boys Club*
156 — Rodney Brown, *unattached*
165 — Michael Trapani, *Cage Teen Center*
178 — Juan Hernandez, *unattached*
HVT — Carl Williams, *N.Y.C. Recreation Dept.*

THE
RING'S
DIRECTORY
OF MANAGERS,
PROMOTERS,
AND
COMMISSIONS

WILLIE O. ABUAN, Don Cornelio Subdivision, Dau, Mabalacat, Pampanga, Philippines; Tel.: 6937, 4923 (Promoter)

ACE BOXING CLUB, Del Porter, 1222 So. 16th, Milwaukee, Wisconsin 53204

ACTION SPORTS, 285 Milwaukee Street, Denver, Colorado 80206 (Promoter)

STEVE ACUNTO, 86 Fletcher Drive, Mount Vernon, New York 10550; Tel.: 914-MO 4-4571

MAX AGUIRRE, Luna Park y Coliseo Nacional, Coronel Naquero, 100 Plaza 2 De Mayo, Lima, Peru; Tel.: 33-579 Peru (Promoter)

JUAN C. ALBARDO, Box 1215-4004 A. B. Square, Port O'Connor, Texas 77982 (Manager)

HOWARD ALBERT, c/o Sasson Jeans, 498 Seventh Avenue, New York, New York 10018; Tel.: (Office) 212-736-0111, (Home) 516-938-4828

ROYAL ALBERT HALL BOXING PROMOTIONS LONDON, Mike Barret, 118 Wardour Street, London W1, England; Tel.: GERard 5956/7; Cables: Boxefight, London W1 (Promoter)

ALBUQUERQUE BOXING AND WRESTLING BOARD, 2823 Madison, N.E., Albuquerque, New Mexico 87110

SAL ALGIERI, 17 Summer Street, Lodi, New Jersey 07644

RON AIL, c/o Northwest Sports, 9727 No. Union Avenue, Portland, Oregon 97217; Tel.: 503-289-2322; 289-9882

MANUEL ALFARO, 3633 N.W. 9th Street, Room 22, Miami, Florida 33125; Tel.: 305-642-0917

ALL SOUTH BOXING CLUB, P. O. Box 1412, Lake Charles, Louisiana 70601; Tel.: 318-433-8344

AUGUSTUS C. (AL) ALLEN, 3016 W. 144th Street, Blue Island, Illinois 60406

EDDIE ALLEN, 24 Barry Place, Colonia, New Jersey 07067; Tel.: 201-388-5230, 201-795-2200 (Manager)

HERB ALLEN, Box 191, Tampa, Florida 33601; Tel.: 813-272-7655, 813-733-4087

STAN ALLEN, 21st Floor, L & C Tower, Nashville, Tennessee 37219; Tel.: 615-244-0847; 615-385-3954 (Manager)

JUAN BUSTANMENT ALVAREZ, 3256 "J" Street, San Diego, California 92113 (Manager)

PETER ALVAREZ, 190 Ellsworth Street, San Francisco, California; Tel.: (Gym) 775-7020, (Home) 824-8286; JO-7-1532 (Manager-Promoter)

GUSTAVE AMADUZZI, via Parisio 124-40137, Bologna, Italy (Manager)

JIMMIE AMANN, Editor, Weekly Boxing Letter, 6716 Palmetto Street, Cincinnati, Ohio 45227

AMATEUR ATHLETIC UNION OF THE UNITED STATES, INC., 3400 W. 86th, Indianapolis, Indiana; Tel.: 317-297-2900

AMERICAN ASSOCIATION FOR THE IMPROVEMENT OF BOXING, INC., 85 Fletcher Avenue, Mount Vernon, New York 10550

AMERICAN BOXING ASSOCIATION, Edward R. Howarth, Chairman, 6424 Keystone Street, Suite B1, Philadelphia, Pennsylvania 19135; Tel.: (Office) 215-457-5200, (Home) 215-338-7317

AMERICAN BOXING CLUB, Angelo Curly, 110 So. 800 Street, #403, Salt Lake City, Utah 84102; Tel.: (Office) 801-531-7270

AMERICAN BROADCASTING COMPANY (ABC), 1330 Avenue of the Americas, New York City, New York; Tel.: 212-541-7777; c/o Alex Wallau

MICHAEL ANCONA, 3686 E. Livingston, Columbus, Ohio 43227; Tel.: 614-236-8881

TIM ANDERSON, 2027 E. Franklin, Minneapolis, Minnesota

MIKE ANDRADE, United Productions, 421 Myrtle Avenue, El Paso, Texas 79901

ANGLO-AMERICAN SPORTING CLUB, Anglo-American Sporting Club (1964) Ltd., Chairman: Ivor Barnard, Esq. Headquarters: Grand Ballroom, London Hilton Hotel, Park Lane, London W1, England; Tel.: Hyde Park 8000. Executive Offices: 38 Upper Grosvenor Street, London W1; Tel.: MAYfair 2707. American Headquarters: Carillon Hotel, Miami Beach, Florida. Administrative Offices: 118 Wardour Street; Tel.: GERard 0922

DON ANTHONY, 5720 Michael Cole Drive, Fayetteville, Arkansas 72701; Tel.: 501-521-8173

JOHN APPEL, JR., Ten Rounds, Inc., 120 E. Vermont Stret, Indianapolis, Indiana 46204; Tel.: 317-251-0790

ARANETA COLISEUM, Quezon City, Philippines; J. Armado Araneta (Promoter), Jorge L. Araneta (Matchmaker)

RAY ARCEL, Casting Materials Company, New King Street, White Plains, New York 10604

ARENA BOXING CLUB, 5700 Oakland Avenue, St. Louis, Missouri 63110; Tel.: Mission 4-0900

ARENA GYMNASIUM, INC., Michael Chimarys, Jr., Vice President, General Offices, 3597 Emerson Street, Jacksonville, Florida 32207; Tel.: 1-904-398-9999

ARDORE LTD., 900 Harry S. Truman Parkway, Bay City, Michigan 48706

ERIC ARMIT, 25 Sidmouth Road, Welling, Kent, England (Manager)

NELSON AQUILES ARRIETA, Apartado Aereo No. 22-02, Cartagena, Columbia; Tel.: 13-888 (Manager-Promoter)

A & S PRO BOXING STABLES, 819 W. Travis, San Antonio, Texas; Tel.: 512-223-0230

JOHNNY L. ASA, 2457 Leon Guinto Street, Malate, Manila, Philippines (Promoter)

ELIS ASK, Loutsikatu, 3B, Helsinki 16, Finland (Manager)

WALLY ATKINSON, 31 Hull Road, Woodmansey, E. Yorks, England (0482-884000)

TED ATSALES, 8721 Oasis Avenue, Westminster, California; Tel.: 893-89109 (Manager)

AUCKLAND BOXING ASSOCIATION, J. T. Jacka, Secretary, P. O. Box 5453, Auckland, New Zealand

JACK AVOTH, 13 Jackdrow Square, Ely, Cardif, Wales; Tel.: 0222 591746

TONY AYALA, 602 Royston, San Antonio, Texas 78225; Tel.: 512-923-4906; 223-0230

AZTECA PROMOTIONS DE SAN ANTONIO, John S. Toscano, 610 Main Plaza Building, San Antonio, Texas 78205; Tel.: 512-226-5252 (Promoter)

EDDIE BABST, Boxtron Enterprises, 812 Race Street, Cincinnati, Ohio 45202; Tel.: 516-241-9112, 241-8273, 661-9018

BACHMAN BOXING ENTERPRISES, Al Bachman, 228 E. 45th Street, New York, New York 10017; Tel.: 212-986-1195/6/7, (Nights) 914 CE-8-8891

VINCE BAGNATO, All Canada Sports Promotions, 1526 DuPont Street, Toronto, Ontario, Canada M6P 3S3; Tel.: 416-766-2321, 749-1367

AL BALBACH, 5 Daniel Drive, Middletown, New Jersey 07748; Tel.: 201-671-1751

MARINO BALDAZZI, Via Carlo Lussi, II, So. Lazzaro Di Savena, Bologna, Italy (Manager)

BRENT BALDWIN, Shear Brothers Barbers, 130½ 25th Street, Ogden, Utah 84401; Tel.: 801-394-0721

RALPH (RED) BANKS, 110 W. Paterson, Columbus, Ohio 43202; Tel.: 614-299-4808

PAT BARLOW, 4961 Oakwood Trail, Indianapolis, Indiana 46268; Tel.: 317-293-4894

MITT BARNES, 3310 Salena Avenue, St. Louis, Missouri 63118; Tel.: 314-771-0818

ESTEBAN BARRAZA, MACID TESORERO DE AGUABOL, Cartagena, Columbia (Manager)

JACK BARRET, 671 Bronx River Road, Yonkers, New York 10704; Tel.: 914-237-2339, (N.Y.) BR 9-9191 (Manager)

MIKE BARRETT PROMOTIONS, 60-66 Wardour Street, London W1, England

FREDDIE BARRUE, Nu-Life Boxing Ent. Inc., 536 Washington Avenue, Miami Beach, Florida 33139

MATT BAULIE 14 BOXING ENTERPRISES, 295 Weis Avenue, Fond du Lac, Wisconsin 54935; Tel.: 414-921-4129

OTILIO BAUTISTA, 1646 E. 8th, Stockton, California 95206; Tel.: 209-463-4619

ARNOLD E. BAYER, 77 Lafayette Street, Hartford, Connecticut 06106; Tel.: 203-522-0221

BCR BOXING CLUB DU RHONE, 6 Rue Sully-Prudhomme — 69 Villeurbane, France

GEORGE C. BECKLES, International Matchmaker, Harp Place 1-7, Building 2, Apartment 3-3, Port of Spain, Trinidad, West Indies

JAY BEDECARRE, Concord Leisure Promotions, 2974 Salvio Street, Concord, California 94519; Tel.: 415-671-3270

SHARKEY BEGOVICH, Sharkey's Nugget, 1440 Highway 395, Gardnerville, Nevada 89410; Tel.: 702-782-3133

BEL-BOX EMPREENDIMENTOS LTDA., Rua Canuto do Val. 59, Sao Paulo, Brazil; Tel.: 220-7760

GILBERT BENAIM, Palais Des Sports, Boulevard Des Versailes, Paris, France (Promoter)

HUGH BENBOW, Route 3, Yoakum, Texas 77995; Tel.: 713-293-3790

GREGORIO BENITEZ, Calle 6 #248, Saint Just, Puerto Rico 00750

BEN BENTLEY, 6140 No. Francisco, Chicago, Illinois 60659

FRED BERNS, 561 W. 72nd Street, Indianapolis, Indiana 46260

WARREN (PEE WEE) BERWICK, c/o Sherbrooke Daily Record, Sherbrooke, Quebec, Canada; Tel.: Lorraine 2-8550

ARMANDO C. BESA, 172 Dasmarinas Street, Binondo, Manila, Philippines

M. B. BESA, Besa Boxing Arena, Plaza Lawton, Manila, Philippines, Armando C. Besa (Matchmaker)

AHMED BEY, Ahmed Bey Boxing Promotions, 1570 No. Sanborn, Hollywood, California 90027; Tel.: 213-666-5525; 666-0200

JERRY BILDERRIAN AND HARRY SHAPIRO, 2919 Sussex Lane, Los Angeles, California 90023 (Managers)

MIKE BIVENS, T.B.S. Productions, P. O. Box 318, Route 2, Lincolnton, North Carolina 28092; Tel.: 704-735-1117

LEE BLACK, 2660 8th Avenue, New York City, New York 10030; Tel.: 212-283-3842

BLACKHAWK SPORTS PROMOTION, 538 Trade School Drive, Bo. Obrero, Davao City, Philippines; Tel.: PLDT 7-24-85, DCTS (II) 30-12; Gym and Stable: 233 Inigo-Porras Street, Bo. Obrero, Davao City, or 628 Governor Generoso Street, Bo. Obrero, Davao City, Philippines; Engr. Andres G. Ong (Promoter)

THE BLACKWOOD BOYS CLUB, Butch Cristelli, 1130 So. Black Horse Pike, Blackwood, New Jersey 08012; Tel.: 609-227-9734

GEORGE D. BLAIR, 370 Burbank Avenue, St. Paul, Minnesota 55119

HENRY BLOWIN AND JERRY MOORE, 130 W. 52nd Street, Los Angeles, California; Tel.: 292-5040

ARNOLD BLUEFORD, 387 12th Street, Oakland, California

SAM BOARDMAN, 1011 Colorado Boulevard, Denver, Colorado 80206; Tel.: 333-4043

BOY BOLANG, B.B. Boxing Promotion, Speed Building, Jakarta, Indonesia; Tel.: 372909 ext. 50

LESLIE J. BONANO, 2800 Gravier Street, New Orleans, Louisiana 70119; Tel.: 504-821-2611; 835-2054

BONANZA BOXING CLUB, 411 Santa Clare, Apartment 4, Oakland, California

BORDER CITIES A. C., Fred Stevens, 1100 Wellington Street, Apartment 20, Sarnia, Ontario, Canada

JOHNNY BOS, 841 Bayridge Avenue, Brooklyn, New York 11220; Tel.: 212-279-9321 (Matchmaker)

TOMAS BOSA, 87-12 166th Street, Jamaica, New York 11432

GEORGE BOULANGER, 18 Guild Road, Framingham, Massachusetts

BOXING CHAMPIONS INC., 228-11 Linden Boulevard, Cambria Heights, New York 11411; Tel.: 212-527-1399

BOXING CLUB OF AMERICA, INC., 3086 Fairmount Avenue, San Diego, California 92105; Tel.: 714-284-9489; Dr. Michael Dean, Ph.D., Owner and President; William (Murf) Murphy, Managing Director

BOXING ENTERPRISES, Matt L. Baulie, 295 Weis Avenue, Fond du Lac, Wisconsin 54935; (Manager-Booker-Promoter)

BOXING GYM, of Las Vegas, 11 W. Charleston Boulevard, Las Vegas, Nevada 89102; Tel.: 385-9990

BOXRING INTERNATIONAL, I. Zeller, 1 Berlin 38, Cimbernstr. 22 Germany; Tel.: 030/803 30 68

ELMER BOYCE, Missoula Sports Association, 2821 St. Thomas Drive, Missoula, Montana 59801; Tel.: 400 540 5549 (Promoter)

JACK BRACKE, 12209 N.E. Second Street, Vancouver, Washington 98664; Tel.: 206-892-8498 (Manager)

PETE BRACKENIERS, 56 Rue Van Wezenbeke Street, Antwerp, Belgium (Promoter)

JOE BRADLEY, Redwood International Fighters, P. O. Box 118, Santana Rosa, California 95402; Tel.: 707-546-6516

JAK BRAMI, El San Juan Hotal, P. O. Box 3189, San Juan, Puerto Rico 00904; Tel.: 809-791-1100

UMBERTO BRANCHINI, Via Privata Asti 2, 20149 Milano, Italy; Tel.: 2-349-8313, 799-201 (International Boxing Manager)

MEYER (REX) BRAUN, President, Texas Boxing Enterprises, Inc., 612 Louisiana Street, Houston, Texas 77002

AL BRAVERMAN, 3081 Villa Avenue, New York, New York 10468; Tel.: (Office) 212-655-6650, (Home) 212-933-6254

BILL BRENNAN, 850 E. Broad Street, Richmond, Virginia 23219

TEDDY BRENNER, Top Rank, Inc., 450 Park Avenue, New York City, New York 10022; Tel.: 212-371-3232

JEAN BRETONNEL, 16 Rue Amiral Courbet, 94th Street, Mande, France; Tel.: 328-12-30 (Manager, Matchmaker)

FRANK BRICKER, 270 Grand Street, Brantford, Ontario, Canada N3R 4C8; Tel.: 519-752-7750; 752-7081

BRISBANE STADIUM, Bert Potts, Brisbane, Australia; Tel.: 4154 (Manager)

BRITISH BOXING BOARD OF CONTROL, Ramillies Buildings, Hill's Place, London W1, England

ALVA BROWN, Maritime Sports Enterprises, P. O. Box 23, Sydney, N.S. Canada B1P 6G9

ANDY (POP) BROWN, 2975 Northwestern, Detroit, Michigan 48206 (Booking Agent)

E. L. (BUD) BRUNER, 2023 Eastern Parkway, Louisville, Kentucky 40204; Tel.: 502-459-4254 (Manager)

TOM BRUNETTE, 378 Front Avenue, St. Paul, Minnesota; Tel.: 612-488-1650

OSCAR BRYAN, 953 Winthorpe Drive, Virginia Beach, Virginia 23452; Tel.: 703-625-0378; 464-3993

BUCKLEY, Nelson Memorial Boxing Club, 51 Russ Street, Hartford, Connecticut 06106

JUAN BUSTAMANTE, 3256 J Street, San Diego, California 92102; Tel.: 233-0850 (Manager)

RUA CAIOWAA, 1194 Apto. 261 Cep-05018, Sao Paulo, Brazil

VINCE CALA, Boxing Enterprises, Inc., 4601 Crosswood Avenue, Baltimore, Maryland 21214; Tel.: 301-337-8766; 426-0493

CAESARS PALACE, Bob Halloran, 3570 Las Vegas Boulevard So., Las Vegas, Nevada 89109; Tel.: 702-731-7110

M. CALVILLO, 5 Sara Cosa, 646 So. Blasa, Monterey, N.L. Mexico

CAMBRA, National Olympic Stadium, Panama City, Panama (Promoter)

STEVE CANTON, Canton and Lequire Enterprises, 282 Halidonhill Road, Cincinnati, Ohio 45238; Tel.: 513-922-7883

CAPE TOWN SPORTING CLUB, 706 Alexandra House, 75 Strand Street, Cape Town, South Africa

BILL CAPLAN, 253 Campana Avenue, Daly City, California; Tel.: ST 4-6907 (Manager)

MIKE CAPRIANO, 2205 Ryer Avenue, Bronx, New York 10457; Tel.: Fordham 4-0028 (Manager)

TONY CARIONE, 378 Forest Park Circle, Longwood, Florida 32750; Tel.: 305-831-1539

JOE CARROLL, 12 Montifern, Revere, Massachusetts; Tel.: ST 4-6907 (Manager)

BOB CARSON, 5236 E. 28th Street, Kansas City, Missouri 64128

CARSON BOXING CLUB, P.O. Box 290, Carson City, Nevada 89701; Tel.: 702-882-5698

CARMEN CASTELLANO, P.O. Box 202, E. Northport, New York 11731; Tel.: 516-368-0985

RAFITO CEDEINO, Avenida 25 #5JB-146 Quinta "Betty"; Tel.: F9-882; Prolongacion Gramo de Oro, Maracaibo, Venezuela; Hotel Mara, Tel.: 811051, Caracas, Venezuela

AL CERTO, K. O. Productions, 1259 Paterson Plank Road, Secaucus, New Jersey; Tel.: 201-867-4934

GARY CHAMPION, Queen City Boxing Club, 909 Queen Street E., Toronto, Ontario, Canada M4M 1J4

RICKIE CHAN, 0 Surrey Road, Singapore, Malaya

DON CHARGIN, The Olympic Auditorium, 1801 So. Grand Avenue, Los Angeles, California 90015; Tel.: 213-749-5171

CHARLAND AND FRIEND BOXING PROMOTIONS, Chalard Vongcheep, Alongside Lumpinee Boxing Stadium, Bangkok, Thailand; Tel.: Bankok 58765 (Manager-Promoter)

GEORGE CHEMERES, 604 N.E. 165th, Seattle, Washington 98155; Tel.: 206-365-6987 (Manager)

LUCIEN CHEN, 41A Half Way Tree Road, Kingston 5, Jamaica; Tel.: 65521, 65522; Cable Address: Luchen, Jamaica

JACQUES CHEVRIER, 4371 Chapleau, Montreal 34, Quebec, Canada; Tel.: LA 6-3116

FRANK CHILONE, Stage West, 165 Dexter Avenue, West Hartford, Connecticut 06110; Tel.: 203-246-2602

SAM CHIMENO, 1005 Orleans Street, Beaumont, Texas; Tel.: TE 5-7373

RICHARD CHRISTMAN, 3618 Barberry Avenue, Cincinnati, Ohio 45207; Tel.: 871-2956 (Manager)

KANG SAE CHULL BOXING CLUB, 56, 5-Ka Namdaemoon-Ro, Chung-Ku, Seoul, Korea

CHURCH STREET GYM AND PROMOTIONS, 444 W. Church Street, Orlando, Florida; Tel.: 305-422-0190; (Home) 305-644-0888

CHA CHA CIARCIA, Cha Cha Sporting Productions, 113 Mulberry Street, New York City, New York 10013; Tel.: 212-966-2677

CITY TATERSALL'S CLUB, 198 Pitt Street, Sydney, Australia

GIL CLANCY, Madison Square Garden, Boxing Department, 4 Penn Plaza, New York City, New York 10001; Tel.: 212-563-8164 (Matchmaker)

ERNIE CLARK, 20478 Basil, Detroit, Michigan

JACKIE CLARK, 513 W. State, Rockford, Illinois; Tel.: (Gym) 962-3170, (Home) 965-4938

RUSS CLARK, 1759 No. Orchid Avenue, Hollywood, California 90028

H. A. CLARKE, 1A Jeringham Avenue, Port of Spain, Trinidad, West Indies; Tel.: 4-3513

CLASSIC PROMOTIONS, 5107 Conti Street, New Orleans, Louisiana 70124; Tel.: 504-488-4379; Al Karcher (Promoter), Heard Ragas (Matchmaker)

CLEVELAND BOXING CLUB, INC., 3600 Ridge T Road, Cleveland, Ohio 44102; Tel.: 216-631-7100

CHRIS CLINE, 2000 County Road, District Heights, Maryland 20028; Tel.: (Office) 301-420-5393, (Home) 301-735-4510

PAUL CLINITE, 611 Rubin #51, El Paso, Texas 79912; Tel.: 915-581-5883

MRS. BONNIE COCCARO, MR. JOE GRAMBY, 802 No. 10th Street, Millville, New Jersey

MILLARD COLLINS, 1611 Redwood Drive, Tallahasse, Florida 32301; Tel.: 904-877-4554

JIM COLOTTO, 171 Chestnut Street, Englewood Cliffs, New Jersey; Tel.: 201-LO 8-8795 (Manager)

COLUMBIA BROADCASTING SYSTEM (CBS), 51 W. 52nd Street, New York City, New York; Tel.: 212-975-4321; c/o Mort Sharnik

COMMACK ARENA PRODUCTIONS, INC., 88 Veterans Highway, Commack, L.I., New York 11725; Tel.: 516-543-7100

COMMUNIPLEX SERVICES, Executive Building, Suite 404, 35 E. Seventh Street, Cincinnati, Ohio 45202; Tel.: 513-621-2812

JOHN F. X. CONDON, Madison Square Garden, Boxing Department, 4 Penn Plaza, New York City, New York 10001; Tel.: 212-563-8164

CONNECTICUT DEPARTMENT OF CONSUMER PROTECTION, State Office Building, Room 105, 165 Capitol Avenue, Hartford, Connecticut 06115

CONNECTICUT SPORTING CLUB, 105 Haynes Road, West Hartford, Connecticut; Tel.: (Day or Night) 247-6656

CONNOLLY BOXING CLUB, William (Billy) Connolly, 44 Waldo Street, Randolph, Massachusetts 02368; Tel.: 617-963-1284 (Manager)

JIMMY CONNOLLY, Main Event Boxing Club, 46 Beacon Street, Hyde Park, Massachusetts 02136; Tel.: 617-523-9193; 268-9043

COPPERBELT BOXING PROMOTIONS, P.O. Box 523, Kitwe, Northern Rhodesia

JULIO CORAJAL, SR., Edificio Mainero, Apartment 7, Calle Larga, Cartagena, Colombia (Manager)

JOSE (PEPITO) CORDERO, Salinas Promotions, Avenue

F.D. Roosevelt, 233 Int., Hato Rey, Puerto Rico 00919; Tel.: 809-766-4944; 763-4919

EUGENE CORREIA, 8-10 Vlissengen Road, Newton, Georgetown, Guyana; Tel.: (Office) 65735 (Manager)

MICHAEL CORREIA, Regent & Wellington Streets, Georgetown, Guyana; Tel.: (Office) 02-61960, (Home) 02-61136 (Manager)

RAMIRO MACHADO CORZO, Apartado De Correos 2863, Venezuela; Tel.: 42-39-03 (Manager)

JACK COWEN, Million Dollar Boxing Club, 4800 Lake Park Avenue, Chicago, Illinois 60615; Tel.: 312-268-5104

ALBERT COX, 2 Hoel Isas, Tonrefail, Glamorgan, S. Wales; Tel.: 0443-77630

HAROLD D. COX, 27 Chester Avenue, Bakersfield, California 93301

CLEM CROWLEY, 45 Norton Road, Quincy, Massachusetts 02169; Tel.: 617-773-3539 (Manager)

ENRIQUE SIERRS CRUZ, P.O. Box 4634, Of. Quisquis 113, Guayquil Ecuador; Tel.: 13701 (Promoter)

JACK CRUZ, 3913 James Court, Stockton, California 95204; Tel.: 209-462-5525

LINNY CRUZ, JR., Boxing Stable, 7607 Guijo Street, San Antonio Village, Makati, Metro Manila, Philippines; Tel.: 86-18-10; Linny Cruz, Jr. (Manager), Jimmy M. Narvaez (Trainer-Second)

JESUS CUATA, Manger de Box, Playa Cortez Num, 435, Colonia Marte; Tel.: 39-58-63, Y-13-1859, Mexico 13, D.F.

EDWARD J. CUDNEY, SR., 48 Lester Street, Buffalo, New York 14210

JAMES (DUKE) CUMMINGS, 6633 Langdon Avenue, Van Nuys, California 91406; Tel.: 213-781-4429; Cable: Van Duke (Manager)

GEORGE CURCIO, 3803 Summer Wind Drive, Winter Park, Florida 32792; Tel.: 305-671-5482

KALED CURI, Rua 25 De Marco 641-503, Sao Paulo, Brazil 228-9905 (Promoter)

ANGELO CURLEY, 110 So. 800 East, #403, Salt Lake City, Utah 84102; Tel.: (Office) 801-535-7854, (Home) 801-531-7270

ARTIE CURLEY, 901 Granite Springs Road, Yorktown Heights, New York 10598; Tel.: 914-962-7930

MIKE CUSIMANO, 531 Emerald Street, New Orleans, Louisiana 70124; Tel.: 282-9757, 525-8671 (Manager)

PHILIP (TEX) DALEY, All South Boxing Club, P. O. Box 1412, Lake Charles, Louisiana 70601; Tel.: 318-433-8344

BILL DALY, 316 De Diego Street, Santurce, Puerto Rico; Tel.: (Office) 725-4152, (Home) 724-2262 (Manager)

JOE DASZKIEWICZ, 3918 Xerxes Avenue, No., Minneapolis, Minnesota 55412

CHUCK DAVEY, Champion Productions, 14415 Prevost, Detroit, Michigan 48227; Tel.: 313-272-7333

MICKEY DAVIES, Five-Star Promotions, 328 So. Atlantic Boulevard, Monterey Park, California 91754; Tel.: 213-576-8762

CARLOS DAVILA, Southern Boxing Association, C-52 Villa Del Carmen, Ponce, Puerto Rico 00731; Tel.: 809-842-0983

TOM DAVILA, Torito Enter, P. O. Box 5552, San Antonio, Texas 78201; Tel.: 512-349-1333; 223-0230

DR. MICHAEL DEAN BOXING CLUB OF AMERICA, 3086 Fairmount Avenue, San Diego, California 92105; Tel.: (Afternoons) 714-222-8120

ROY DEAN, 4133 Hartz Drive, Memphis, Tennessee 38116

BENNY DEATON, 3168 W. 14th Avenue, Denver, Colorado 80204 (Boxer's Representative)

JIM DECARO, Downtown Boxing Club, 1510½ First Avenue, Seattle, Washington; Tel.: MA 2-0490

ANTHONY J. DECICCO, 5128 Coronada Parkway, Fort Myers, Florida 33904; Tel.: 813-549-6456

JOHN DE JOHN, 308 Chester Road, Syracuse, New York 13219; Tel.: HU 8-6686 (Manager)

DIOGENES DE LA FUENTE, Estadio Caupolican, Santiago de Chile

GUS DEMMY PROMOTIONS LTD., 3rd Floor, 58 Swan Street, Manchester 4, England; Tel.: BLAckfriars 9248

YOUNG DEMOE, 17 Pine Street, Steelton, Pennsylvania 17113

WILLIE JOE DE MYERS, 20145 Tracey, Detroit, Michigan 48235; Tel.: 313-342-4388

VERN DE PAUL, 117-16 Courtney Avenue, Auburndale, New York 11358

JIMMY DE PIANO, 306 Westminster Boulevard, Turnersville, New Jersey; Tel.: 609-227-8591, (Gym) 365-9311

DEPORTIVES MAZAVA, INC., P.O. Box 719, Hato Rey, San Juan, Puerto Rico

AL DE ROSE, 2140 No. Clark Street, Chicago, Illinois 60614; Tel.: 312-248-1950

BILL DICKSON, 1347 Dresslerville Road, Gardnerville, Nevada 89410; Tel.: 702-782-5358, 702-782-3133

ERNEST DICKSON, 382 12th Street, Oakland, California

DR. CHARLES E. DIETZ, 707 Highcrest Drive, Dallas, Texas 75232 (Manager)

PAT DI FURIA, Bank of America Building, 790 W. Shaw Avenue, Suite 310, Fresno, California 93704; Tel.: (Office) 209-222-5426, (Home) 209-268-1268

JOSEPH DILEO, 50-11 Broadway, Woodside, L.I., New York (Manager)

J. J. DIZON ENTERPRISES, Clark Airbase, Office Contractor, Compound: C.A.B.; Tel.: 2-22-88; Office: 245 Balibago, Angeles City, Philippines (Promoter)

ATTY. LUCIO DIZON, Buyagan, La Trinidad, Benguet, Philippines (Promoter)

FRANK DOBALES, 240 E. Gibson Street, Stockton, California; Tel.: 463-3651 (Manager)

C. DOMINY, 6727 No. 44th Avenue, Glendale, Arizona 85301; Contact: Terry Downes, Milestone, Miles Pit Hill, London N.W. 7, England; Tel.: 959-1378

WILLIAM J. DONOHO, 31 Cleveland Avenue, Nashville, Tennessee 37210; Tel.: 615-255-3450

ARTHUR DORE, 900 Harry S. Truman Parkway, Bay City, Michigan 48706; Tel.: 517-684-1799

DORIO SPORTING ENTERPRISES, CORP., Paddy Read, Room 301, 144 Westminster Street, Providence, Rhode Island 02903; Tel.: RI 8-4009, RI 8-5171 (Matchmaker)

BILLY DOUGLAS, 1692 East Maynard, Columbus, Ohio 43219; Tel.: 614-267-1546

TONY DOWLING, 105 So. Grosvenor Avenue, Burnaby, B.C., Canada V5B 3N7; Tel.: 694-926-9675

DON DOWNEY, 6399 Creighton Street, Halifax, N.S. Canada B3K 3S1; Tel.: 902-423-2586

GEORGE DROUIN, 785 St. Valliet Est., Quebec 2 P.Q., Canada; Tel.: (Office) 524-9936, (Home) 525-2812

JOHNNY DUBLIS, 140 Whiting, El Segundo, California 90245; Tel.: 213-322-3634

JAMES DUDLEY, 1344 "W" Street N.W., Washington, D.C. 20009

MICKEY DUFF, 60-66 Wardour Street, London W1, England; Tel.: (Office) 01-734 1041, 01-437 7579, 01-437 5956; (Home) 01-458 3479

FRANCIS (PAT) DUFFY, 1304 Manor Road, Yeadon, Pennsylvania 19051

ANGELO DUNDEE, 1700 Washington Avenue, Miami Beach, Florida 33139; Tel.: 305-673-4448; Cable Address: Dunbox

CHRIS DUNDEE ENTERPRISES, INC., 1901 Convention Center Drive, Miami Beach, Florida 33139; Tel.: (Office) 305-532-4571, (Gym) 305-531-9504, (Home) 305-531-3102 (Promoter)

MICHAEL DUNDEE, 1901 Convention Center Drive, Miami Beach, Florida 33139; Tel.: (Office) 305-532-4571; (Home) 305-931-3874; 305-531-3102

SUZANNE DUNDEE, Chris Dundee Enterprises, Inc., 1901 Convention Center Drive, Miami Beach, Florida 33139; Tel.: 305-532-4571; 534-1720

JOHN DUNN, L194 Franklin Avenue, Chelsea, Massachusetts; Tel.: 617-889-1348; 523-9193

DAN DUVA, Main Events, 349 Union Boulevard, Totowa Boro, New Jersey 07512; Tel.: 201-942-0770; 942-5697

LOU DUVA, 1078 Route 46, Clifton, New Jersey 07013; Tel.: (Office) 201-473-0343; (Home) 201-684-6498

CHRIS DUVALL, 1000 Center Building, Louisville, Kentucky 40202; Tel.: 582-2581

VIC EADS, 1335 No. Kilpatrick, Portland, Oregon 97217; Tel.: 503-285-3035 (Manager)

EASTERN PROMOTIONS, 72 Mitchell Street, New Glasgow, N.S., Canada; Tel.: 2-4030

EASY BAY BOXING CLUB, Henry Winsoth, 1225 16th Street, Oakland, California

EILEEN EATON, Olympic Auditorium, 1801 So. Grand Avenue, Los Angeles, California 90015; Charsin Tel.: RI 9-5171

BILL EBEL, Main Event Boxing Club, 46 Beacon Street, Hyde Park, Boston, Massachusetts 02136; Tel.: 617-523-9193; 364-0008

AL EDDY, 500 Woburn Street, No. Wilmington, Massachusetts; Tel.: Oliver 8-4607 (Manager)

EDMONTON BOXING AND WRESTLING COMMISSION, 13528 116 B Avenue, Edmonton, Alberta, Canada

JAY EDSON, 1085 Forest Lakes Drive, Apartment 305, Naples, Florida 33940; Tel.: 813-262-2110 (Referee)

BILLY EDWARDS, 1002 Park Avenue, Albuquerque, New Mexico; Tel.: 505-843-9366

JOHN EDWARDS, 4219 St. Louis Avenue, St. Louis, Missouri

STEVEN EISNER, c/o Phoenix Sports, Inc., Scottsdale, Arizona 85252; Tel.: 602-945-0122

DON ELBAUM, Premiere Studios, 2 W. 45th Street, New York, New York 10036; Tel.: 212-730-0757

CARLOS ELETA, P.O. Box 157, Arena Colon, Panama City, Panama

ALBERTO ELJURE, Calle 69 #447-H, Merida, Yucatan

WALTER ENGLERT, Xantener Strasse 7, Berlin W15, Germany; Tel.: 91-1831

BUDDY EY, 1209 Elsing Road, Baltimore, Maryland 21221

EMPRESA DEPROTIVA NACIONAL ULISES FRIAS, 25 Jose Trujillo Valdez, Cuidad Trujillo, Dominican Republic; Tel.: 2-2420, 2-6666 (Promoter)

EMPRESA MEXICANA DE BOX, S.A., Eladio Flores Lutteroth, Dr. Lavista, #181-A, Desp. 2, Mexico 7, D.F.; Tel.: 13-11-07; Cable Address: EMEBOX MEXICO, D.F. (Promoter)

EMPRESS NACIONAL DE BOXEO, Director-Milano Porto A. Cartagena, Colombia, South America; Tel.: 12571, 13659 (Promoter)

ESCOT BOXING ENTERPRISES, Emanuel Steward, President, 8925 Birwood, Detroit, Michigan 48204; Tel.: 313-491-8185, (Gym, 4-8 p.m.) 894-8674

TONY O. ESGUERRA STABLE, Cable Address: T.O.E., Angeles City, Philippines; Efren E. Nazal (Matchmaker), Chris Pineda (Trainer)

ESPECTACULOS PUBLICOS DE LA BJA, CALIFORNIA, Club el Mexicano, Calle 4A #251, Mexicali, Mexico; Tel.: 2979

ESPN, Bristol, Connecticut 06010; Tel.: 203-584-8477; Chet Simmons, President

EUZKALDUNAK, INC., c/o Al Berro, 821 Main Street, Boise, Idaho

BERNIE EWENSON, 20th Century Boxing Club, 411001 4th Street, Laval West, Quebec, Canada

MALCOLM FABER, 9129 Airline Highway, New Orleans, Louisiana 70118; Tel.: 504-482-6638, 504-821-5711

RICHIE FALCIGNO, Momentum Enterprises, Inc., 340 W. 57th Street, New York City, New York 10019; Tel.: 212-265-4621

LOUIS FALCIGNO, c/o Momentum Enterprises, 45 E. 51st Street, New York, New York 10022; Tel.: 212-759-8760, 914-948-5133

MARK FANNON, 525 So. Dexter Avenue, DeLand, Florida 32720; Tel.: 904-734-6420 (Booking)

MARTY FELDMAN, 7340 W. Chester Pike, Upper Darby, Pennsylvania 19082; Tel.: 215-352-2300

WILLIE FELICE, 5300 65th Place, Maspeth, Queens, L.I., New York; Tel.: (Home) 898-8998

AL FENN, 11821 No. 35th Street, Phoenix, Arizona 85028; Tel.: 996-9407

AL FERNANDEZ, 193 Richards, Brooklyn, New York 11231 (Manager)

GENE FERRUS, Round Ten Boxing Promotions, P. O. Box 263, Latham, New York 12110; 518-783-5433

JOSEPH P. FERRY, 1759 No. Orchid Avenue, Hollywood, California 90028

BILL FIELD, 1405 Gardenia Avenue, Long Beach, California 90813; Tel.: 213-591-8302

JOSE (PEPE) FIGUEROA, Philippine Boxing Council, Inc., 3573 Sandico Street, Makati, Metro Manila, Philippines (Promoter)

JACQUES DESCHAMPS FILS (HAITI), Boxe Internationale, 63 163rd Street, N.W., No. Miami Beach, Florida 33169

SHELLY FINKEL, Cross Country Concerts Corp., 527 Madison Avenue, Suite 1622, New York City, New York 10021; Tel.: 212-758-6211

FINNISH PROFESSIONAL BOXING UNION, Certi Augustin, Secretary-General, Porvoonkatu 11 C, 81 Helsinki 51, Finland

JOHN L. FISHER, 2140 No. Capitol Avenue, Indianapolis, Indiana 46202; Tel.: 317-925-1461

JERRY FITCH, 11851 Lake Avenue, #17, Cleveland, Ohio 44107; Tel.: 216-228-6452

FIVE STAR PROMOTIONS, 328 S. Atlantic Boulevard, Monterey Park, California 91754; Tel.: 213-576-8762

WILLIAM J. FLASSER, 11 First Federal Building, Scranton, Pennsylvania 18503; Tel.: 961-2032

MOE FLEISCHER, c/o Allen Hotel, 2001 Washington Avenue, Miami Beach, Florida 33139

RANDY FLOOD, 1480 York Avenue, New York, New York 10021; Tel.: 212-RE 4-3176

JOHNNY FLORES, c/o Flores Gym, 13717 Jouett Street, Pacoima, California 91331; Tel.: 213-899-3720

PEDRO APONTE FLORES, Box 594, Caguas, Puerto Rico; Tel.: 744 2573; 763-5832 (Fijude Promotions)

JOHN A. FLORIO, c/o Lehigh Athletic Club, P.O. Box 262, Allentown, Pennsylvania 18105; Tel.: 215-395-2680; 215-395-5404

J. A. FLYNN & SONS PROMOTIONS, P.O. Box 901, Southern Pines, North Carolina 28387; Tel.: 919-692-8527, 919-692-6021

BENNIE FORD, Superior Boxing Club, 453 O'Farrell Street, San Francisco, California 94102; Tel.: 415-771-1525; 775-4772

RED FORTNER, 5178 Chantilly Drive, Memphis, Tennessee 38127; Tel.: 901-353-4866

FORUM, THE, Montreal, Canada; Tel.: Willbank 3788

ERNIE FOSSEY, 66 Aubert Park, Highbury, London N5, England; Tel.: 01-226-6267

JAMES J. FRAIN, Sports Enterprises, Orange, New Jersey; Tel.: 201-675-8405

GERRY FRASER, Red Carpet Promotions, 64 Covington Way, Halifax, N.S. Canada B3M 3K2; Tel.: 902-443-5739

DON FRASER, The Forum, P.O. Box 10, Inglewood, California 90306; Tel.: 213-674-6000

JOE FRAZIER, Cloverlay Gym, 2917 No. Broad Street, Philadelphia, Pennsylvania 19132; Tel.: 215-225-9852; 221-5303

AUDREY FREW, 206-1140 Pendrell, Vancouver, B.C. Canada V6E 1L3; Tel.: 604-689-9894

ULISES FRIAS, Maximo Gomez, III, Santo Domingo, Dominican Republic (Promoter)

GENE FRITZ, Gene Fritz Promotions, 304 Valley Road, Olathe, Kansas 66061; Tel.: 913-782-4655

ERNIE FUENTES, 4650 39th Street, San Diego, California 92116; Tel.: 714-283-8976

FUJI PROMOTIONS, Fuji Okamoto, President, 6-3 chome, Naka-Machi, Nachidashi, Tokyo, Japan

ALFONSO FULLER, 1770 City National Bank Boulevard, Detroit, Michigan 48226; Tel.: 313-963-1885; 835-7232

EDDIE FUTCH, 14308 Homeward Street, La Puente, California 91744; Tel.: 330-6020 (Manager)

G. A. FIGHTS, Boxing Promotion & Matchmaking, Bill Glassmann, III, 1518 27th Street, Ogden, Utah 84401; Tel.: (Office) 801-394-7711, (Home) 801-399-3635

MURRAY H. GABY, 7600 Red Road, South Miami, Florida 33143; Tel.: 305-667-0959; 442-8193

JOHN GAGLIARDI, Celebrity Boxing Club, 102 Wellesley Street, Medford, Massachusetts 02155; Tel.: 617-935-8090

JIMMY GAGNON, 498 Lisbon Street, Lewiston, Maine 04240; Tel.: 207-782-1613

JANEZ GALE, 61260 Ljubljana Polje 352, Yugoslavia (Manager-Promoter)

PROFESSOR STANISLAV GALE, 61240 Kamnik, Kovinarska 10A (Slavenin) Yugoslavia; Tel.: 831 211

ROBERT GALLAGHER, 19 Dow Road, West Roxbury, Massachusetts; Tel.: FA 5-38210; also Connolly's Gym, Tel.: 269-9691 (Manager)

ERNESTO GALLARDO, Nino Perdido #153, Mexico 7, D.F.; Tel.: 905-578-4527 (Manager)

AL (SCOOP) GALLELLO, 94 Crescent Avenue, New Rochelle, New York; Tel.: BE 5-0955

RALPH GAMBINA, International Boxing and Sports Enterprises, 10727 Bluffside Drive, Studio City, California 91604; Tel.: (Office) 213-877-8470; (Gym) 926-7484

GREGO GARCIA, 13 Zambales Street, Quezon City, Philippines

RALPH GARCIA PROMOTIONS, 310 Bridge Boulevard S.W., Albuquerque, New Mexico; Tel.: CHapel 7-0028

GARDEN BOXING CLUB, 513 Emerald Street, New Orleans, Louisiana; Tel.: 282-9751; 525-8671

GARDEN CITY BOXING CLUB, 35 Louisa Street, St. Catherines, Ontario, Canada

TONY GARDNER, Pro Boxing Inc., 1114 Uvalde, Houston, Texas 77015; Tel.: 713-461-4418; 226-9170

JACK GARTLEY, 6600 E. Lincoln Drive, Paradise Valley, Arizona 85253; Tel.: 602-998-2282

ED GARZA, 757 Savage Lane, Corpus Christi, Texas 78408; Tel.: 512-883-8308

BOB GASKILL, Lazy Lane, Fort Myers, Florida 33905; Tel.: 813-694-7414

PAPPY GAULT, Logan, Virginia; Tel.: 301-336-1187

ALLAN GAVIN, 238 Autumn Avenue, Brooklyn, New York 11208

FRANK N. GELB, 1015 Chestnut Street, Philadelphia, Pennsylvania 19107; Tel.: 215-925-1758

JOSEPH GENNARO, JR., Box 46, Hillsville, Pennsylvania 16132

PINKIE GEORGE, 212 Securities Building, Des Moines, Iowa

DON GEORGINO, Five-Star Promotions, 328 So. Atlantic Boulevard, Monterey Park, California 91754; Tel.: 213-576-8762

NICKIE GERARD, P.O. Box 125, Woodside, New York 11377; Tel.: 212-478-3819 (Manager)

RICHIE GIACHETTI, 4215 W. 63rd Street, Cleveland, Ohio 44109; Tel.: 216-252-6855; 216-661-0928

VINCE GIANTOMASI, One Thompson Road, RD 1, Boonton, New Jersey 07005

RALPH GILBREATH, 3039 Ocana Avenue, Long Beach, California

MITCH GILMORE, The Steak Loft, 9974 Jasper Avenue, Edmonton, Alberta, Canada; Tel.: 422-4567 (Manager)

BILL GLASMANN, G. A. Fights, 4050 Taylor, Ogden, Utah 84403; Tel.: 801-394-7711

SAM GLASS, Tiffany Promotions, One Old Country Road, Carle Place, New York 11514; Tel.: 516-742-1666

GLEASON GYM, see New Garden Gym

JIMMY GLENN GYM, 42nd 6th Broadway, New York City, New York; Tel.: 212-221-9510

DR. MARVIN GOLDBERG, 3257 Shore Road, Oceanside, L.I., New York; Tel.: 516-RO 6-0378

SI GOLDBERG PROMOTIONS, 3362 Forest Grove, Toledo, Ohio 43623

GOLDEN CITY SPORTING CLUB, 4th Floor, Equity Building, Corner of Fox & Harrison Streets, Johannesburg, South Africa; Tel.: Johannesburg 33-1845

LOUIS GOLDSCHMIDT, President, BDV., 1 Berlin, 30, Potsdamer Strasse, 100-172, Berlin, Germany

MARTY GOLDSTEIN, 2761 S.W. 3rd Street, Fort Lauderdale, Florida

ROCKY GOLIO, 805 N.W. 3rd Street, Fort Lauderdale, Florida 33309; Tel.: 305-491-9848; 467-1275

STEPHEN M. GOLUB, 3701 Bergen Turnpike, North Bergen, New Jersey 07047; Tel.: 201-868-5329

OCTAVIO FAMOSO GOMEZ, Guillermo Pristo 7, Section Boxeo, Mexico, D.F. (Manager)

CORKY GONZALES, 1567 Downing Street, Denver, Colorado 80218; Tel.: 303-832-1145

JESS CONZALES, Colorado Recreation Boxing Coaches Association, 1567 Downing Street, Denver, Colorado 80218; Tel.: 303-832-1145

JOSE GONZALES, Latin World Night Club, 7035 Harrisburg Boulevard, Houston, Texas 77011; Tel.: 713-926-0117; 926-2193

OSCAR GONZALES, 15 Augustine La, Gonzales Place, Port of Spain, Trinidad, West Indies; Tel.: 62-44409 (Manager-Promoter-Matchmaker)

ICO GONZALEZ, 4218 Green Grove Drive, Corpus Christi, Texas 78415; Tel.: 852-1289 (Manager-Trainer)

CHARLIE GOODEN, 6655 Decelles Avenue, Montreal, Quebec, Canada

BOB GOODMAN, 232 Madison Avenue, New York, New York 10016; Tel.: (Office) 212-686-4231; (Home) 201-349-4553

FRANKIE GOODMAN, c/o Goodman's Kid Glove Boxing School and Gym, 6410 Van Nuys Boulevard, Van Nuys, California

T. DAVID GOODWIN COMPANIES, 48 So. Prescott, Suite 2, Memphis, Tennessee 38111; Tel.: 327-5636

ANTOLIN SANCHEZ-GOVIN (CHINO), 779 Riverside Drive, Apartment A-62, New York, New York 10032; Tel.: (Office) 212-947-3744; (Home) 212-927-2850

JOSEPH GRAMBY, 854 Corinthian Avenue, Philadelphia, Pennsylvania 19130; Tel.: (Office) 215-PO 5-4091; (Home) 215-PO 5-4949

TOM GRAVELY, Grizzly Promotions, 4701 Melvin Avenue, Anchorage, Alaska 99503; Tel.: 907-276-6193

W. R. GRAY, P.O. Box 784, Hemet, California 92343; Tel.: (Office) 714-658-5161; (Home) 714-658-5237

ANTHONY GRAZIANO, 1409 No. Peterboro Street, Canastota, New York; Tel.: 314-697-7936

MEL GREB, 3235 E. Robin Circle, Las Vegas, Nevada 89121; Tel.: 702-451-5129

MRS. LEROY GREEN, 1314 No. 4th Street, Kansas City, Kansas 66101

BEN GREENE, P.O. Box 727, New York, New York 10018

BABE GRIFFIN, 19950 Hale Avenue, Morgan Hill, California 95037; Tel.: 408-779-5089

EDDIE GRIFFIN, 60 Ocean Street, So. Portland, Maine 04106; Tel.: (Office) 207-799-7065; (Home) 207-799-1671

JOHNNY GRIFFIN, 26 Christow Street, Leicester LE1 2GN, England; Tel.: 29287

SONNY GRIFFIN, 118 So. Stevenson Avenue, Louisville, Kentucky 40206

ALEX GRIFFITHS, G. R. G. Promotions, Upper Lichfield Street, Willenhall, Staffs, England; Tel.: Willenhall 65377, Wolverhampton 52770

WINKY GROOM, Fort Worth Boxing Club, 115 Sandy Lane, Suite B-1, Fort Worth, Texas 76112; Tel.: 817-429-0343

HANK GROOMS, Professional Management Enterprises, Inc., P. O. Box 229, Kalamazoo, Michigan 49005; Tel.: 616-345-0806

GERRY GRUNDMAN, Montreal Forum, 2313 Ouest, Rue Ste-Catherine West, Montreal, Ont. Canada H3H 1N2; Tel.: 514-932-6181

GUAM BOXING COMMISSION, 7726 940 P.O. Box 786, Agana, Guam

RUBEN GUERRA, 7914 Canal Street, Houston, Texas 77012; Tel.: 713-926-8739

ALBERTO GUERRERO, D. Caliccuchima 1201, P.O. Box 464, Guayquil, Ecuador, South America; Tel.: 15833 (Promoter)

PAUL GUEZ, Sasson Jeans, Inc., 498 Seventh Avenue, New York, New York 10018; Tel.: 212-736-0111 (Promoter)

HAROLD E. GUNN, 411 No. Avalon Boulevard, Wilmington, Georgia 90744; Tel.: 213-830-9306 (3 p.m. to 7 p.m.)

RICHARD J. GUNN, 315 Peavey Building, Minneapolis, Minnesota 55402

MILT GUPTILL, The Portland Plaza, 1500 S.W. 5th Avenue, Portland, Oregon 97201; Tel.: 503-224-5553

HARLAN HAAS, 11211 So. Post Oak, #62, Houston, Texas 77035; Tel.: (A/C Office) 713-723-1050, (Home) 713-729-6295

A. HACK, Johannesburg S.C., P.O. Box 6483, Johannesburg, South Africa

MIKE HAFNER, 522 Van Buren Avenue, St. Paul, Minnesota 55103; Tel.: 612-488-2017

JOE WAVE HAM, 340 Aspen Street, Warminster, Pennsylvania 18974; Tel.: 215-441-0391

THE HAMILTON BOXING ASSOCIATION, P.O. Box 66, Hamilton, Ohio 45011

JOE HAND, Joe Hand Promotions, Inc., 509 Denis Drive, Philadelphia, Pennsylvania 19116; Tel.: 215-677-6438

MIKE HANEY, 420 So. 16th, Blytheville, Arkansas 72315; Tel.: 501-763-9963, 763-7733

GEORGE HANKINS, Fort Apache Boxing Club, 1111 Fox Street, Bronx, New York 10459; Tel.: 212-328-2723

JOE P. HANKE, 411 Palermo Avenue, Coral Gables, Florida 33134; Tel.: 305-448-7074

DEL HANLON, Capital City Gym, 402 Exchange Place, Minneapolis, Minnesota (Manager)

TOM HARGIS, 840 So. Millwood, Wichita, Kansas 67213

PAUL HARIMAN, 42 Main Street, Dover, New Hampshire 03820; Tel.: 603-742-9807

TOM HARMON, Mid South Pro Boxing, Inc., 5178 Chantilly Drive, Memphis, Tennessee 38127; Tel.: 901-353-4866

BILLY HARRIS, 221 McKinley Avenue, Syracuse, New York 13205

ROY HARRIS, 611 W. Davis, Conroe, Texas 77301; Tel.: 713-756-1188, 264-1235

FRANK J. HARTLEY, 5821 Main Street, Millbrook, Alabama 36054; Tel.: 205-285-3937

TONY HARTMANN, Hyatt Lake Tahoe Hotel, P. O. Box 3239, Incline Village, Nevada 89450; Tel.: 702-831-1111

REG HASWELL, 51 Twindbro House, Wanderers Street, Johannesburg, South Africa (Matchmaker-Promoter)

TOMMY HATCHER, 16A Padgett Court, Pensacola, Florida

PHIL HAUSER, 4338 E. 9th Avenue, Anchorage, Alaska 99504

MIKE HAYES, Denver Boxing Club, 285 Milwaukee Street, Denver, Colorado 80206; Tel.: 303-321-1606

BURTON D. HAYS, 5606½ 4th Avenue, Vienna, West Virginia 26105; Tel.: 304-295-9115

NICK HAYWOOD, 2811 Tracy Street, Kansas City, Missouri; Tel.: WE 0153

GARY G. HEGYI, 8012 Leonard Street, Philadelphia, Pennsylvania 19152; Tel.: 215-333-2859, 335-3107 (Manager and Booking Agent)

JOHN HEIDEL, 9027 North Avenue, St. Louis, Missouri 63114; Tel.: 314-427-1565

ROBERT HEINE, Promotion and Hibbing Municipal AC., St. Paul, Minnesota (Promoter)

RAY HELING, Boxing Enterprises, 2101 E. Hillcrest Avenue, Milwaukee, Wisconsin 53207; Tel.: 1-414-744-6815

RON HEMPEL, Broken Hill, New South Wales, Australia

BOBBY HENDERSON, 3538 Blair Circle, Salt Lake City, Utah 94115; Tel.: 801-484-2665

MARTIN HENRICH, Texas Boxing Enterprises, 707 Texas Avenue, Houston, Texas; Tel.: (Office) CA 7-1816, (Home) 713-MO 7-6316

JOE HERMAN AND BILLY NEWMAN, 312 Leavenworth Street, San Francisco, California; Tel.: Prospect 7020

ARTURO (CUYO) HERNANDEZ, Estrella 91 Col. Guerrero, Mexico 3, D.F.; Tel.: 12-23-75

LEODEGARIO HERNANDEZ, Organizaccion de Box, Combred de Maltrata No. 375 and 43-26-62, Mexico 12, D.F.; Tel.: 36-14-45 at 447

PEPE HERNANDEZ, Calle Oriente 50, No. 5111, Col. LaJoyita, Mexico 14, D.F.; Tel.: 13-18-59, 26-67-53

RALPH HERNANDEZ, 316 De Diego, Santurce, Puerto Rico

ANDRES HERRERA, Dr. Acr 46, Mexico City, Mexico

PETER G. HICKEY, 26 Bapaume Road, Mosman N.S.W. 2088, Australia (Manager)

SANGWIAN HIRANYALEKHA, President, Thailand Pro Boxing Association, Bangkok, Thailand

KEN HISSNER, 4057 Hillside Road, Lafayette Hills, Pennsylvania 19444

ABE HOCHHEISER, 10747 Debra Avenue, Granada Hills, California 91344; Tel.: 363-9638

AKIHIKI HONDA, President, Teikea Promotions, 45 Sakao-cho, Kita-ku, Tokyo, Japan

RAY E. HOLLAND, 164-1 Third Avenue, Albany, New York 12202; Tel.: (Home) 1-518-465-7881 (Manager)

HOME BOX OFFICE (HBO), 1271 Avenue of the Americas, New York city, New York 10020; Tel.: 212-484-1000; Seth Abraham, V.P., Sports

MAX HORD, 1505 Broome Street, Fernandina Beach, Florida 32034

HOUSTON BOXING ASSOCIATION, 902 Texas Avenue, Houston 2, Texas; Tel.: CA 8-7738

GERALD (JERRY) HOUSTON, 154 Apponegansett Street, New Bedford, Massachusetts 02744; Tel.: 617-997-0116

EDWARD HOWARTH, H. Boxing Corporation, 6735 No. Jackson Street, Philadelphia, Pennsylvania 19135; Tel.: (Office) 015 CI 7-5200 (Home) 215-DE 8-7317

931

JIM HOWELL, 40 Maple Drive, Florissant, Missouri 63031; Tel.: 314-837-5970

EDWARD HRICA, 110 W. 39th Street, Baltimore, Maryland 21210

ROBERT HUDSON, 4342 No. Hartford Avenue, Tulsa, Oklahoma 74106; Tel.: 918-425-7961

RICHARD HUSSAR, 751 Benton Road, Salem, Ohio 44460; Tel.: 216-337-6171

REGGIE ICHINOSE, 3-5 Joji Machi, Chiyodaku, Tokyo, Japan

SAM M. ICHINOSE, 1348 Highview Place, Honolulu, Hawaii; Tel.: 67188, 79314

IDAHO ATHLETIC CLUB, P.O. Box 1393, Boise, Idaho 83701

IGNIS COMPANY (Varese and Milan), Milan, Italy

JOHN INGRAO, 12804 Ross Avenue, Chino, California; Tel.: National 8-6277

INTERNATIONAL BOXING AGENCY, Tony Cardione, 1841 Broadway, Suite 1011, New York, New York 10023; Tel.: 212-757-0750

INTERNATIONAL MANAGEMENT, INC., Suite II, First Federal Building, Scranton, Pennsylvania 18503

INTERNATIONAL PROMOTIONS, Yoshimi Takimoto, President, Japan Boxing Association, 1-3 Koraky, Bunkyo-ku, Tokyo, Japan

INTERNATIONAL PROMOTIONS LTD., Kenny Shimbo, #73, Wakamatsu-cho, Shinjuku-ku, Tokyo, Japan

JACK W. IRWIN, Corpus Christi Club, 714 Kinney, Corpus Christie, Texas; Tel.: TU 4-5414

IKE ISAACS, 318 North Texas, Odessa, Texas 79760; Tel.: 915-366-0802

C. A. JACKSON, Texas Automotive, 3006 Gulfway Drive, Port Arthur, Texas 77640; Tel.: 713-985-6645

JACKSONVILLE BOXING ENTERPRISE, INC., Room 28, Jacksonville Coliseum, 1145 E. Adams Street, Jacksonville, Florida 32202; Tel.: 356-6072, 354-2041 ext. 28

BENNY JACOBS, 12 Albany Court, Penarth, Glam, Cardiff, England; Tel.: 709063 (Manager)

MRS. DORIS JACOBS, 7068 Cromwell Way, Sacramento, California 95822

JIM JACOBS AND BILL CAYTON, 9 E. 40th Street, New York, New York 10016

JAPAN BOXING COMMISSION, No. 2-9 1 Chomemisaki-cho, Chiyoda-ku, Tokyo, Japan; Tel.: 292-7573-7467

JAPAN BOXING ENTERPRISES, INC., Takafusa Kawari, Wada Building, I-II, Kirakawa-cho, Chiyoda-ku, Tokyo, Japan; Tel.: 261-8775-8056 (Promoter)

FELIXBERTO JARDENIL, Barrio Canlalay, Laguna, Philippines (Promoter)

CONRAD (ACE) JARESKY, Main Event Boxing Club, 46 Beacon Street, Hyde Park, Massachusetts 02136; Tel.: 617-364-0008, 523-9193

BILL JEFFERSON, 809 North 7, Rapid City, South Dakota 57701; Tel.: 605-342-3532

CHUCK JENKINS, Mile High Boxing Club, 6840 Warren Drive, Denver, Colorado 80221; Tel.: 303-429-0835 (Promoter)

MARV JENSEN ENTERPRISES, 8416 So. 1700 West, West Jordan, Utah 84084; Tel.: AM 5-5022 (Manager)

J & J PROMOTIONS, P.O. Box 2929, Vancouver 3, B.C., Canada; Tel.: 604-687-4633; George S. Hobson (Promoter), Jimmy Johnston (Matchmaker)

J & J SPORTS PRODUCTIONS, Garden City Boxing Club, 1457 W. San Carlos, San Jose, California 95126; Tel.: 408-294-7072

CLARENCE JOHNSON, 1221 E. Jersey Street, Alliance, Ohio 44601; Tel.: 216-821-7308

JAMES J. JOHNSON, Drew Road, Deerfield, New Hampshire 03037; Tel.: 603-432-2242

JIMMY JOHNSON, J & J Promotions, P.O. Box 2929, Vancouver 3, B.C., Canada; Tel.: 604-687-4633 (Matchmaker)

JOHN JOHNSON, 144 Huber Village Boulevard, Westerville, Ohio 44601

TOM JOHNSON, Denver Sporting Club, 285 Milwaukee, Denver, Colorado 80206

JIM JOHNSTON, Box 2929, Vancouver V6B 3X4, B.C., Canada

MICHAEL R. JONES, 228-11 Linden Boulevard, Cambria Heights, New York 11411; Tel.: 212-527-1101, 516-485-0340

BOB JONES, Impact Promotions, Martin Luther King Arena, 4530 Market Street, Philadelphia, Pennsylvania 19139; Tel.: 215-662-5100

THE ROBERT JONES GROUP OF INVESTMENT COMPANIES, Commercial Property Developers and Investors throughout Australia and New Zealand; Head Office: Brandon House, Dudley Street, Lower Hutt; Tel.: 666-073; Correspondence: G.P.O. Box 3200, Wellington

THOMAS JONES, 20 W. 2nd Avenue, Pine Hill, New Jersey; Tel.: 627-7916

PETE JOVANOVICH, West Valley, Anaconda, Montana 59711; Tel.: 406-563-7787

AL JOYNER, 112-28 198th Street, Hollis, L.I., New York; Tel.: 516-465-4525 (Manager)

HARRY KABAKOFF, Pimentel Boxing Promotions, 1832 So. Hope Street, Los Angeles, California 90021; Tel.: 213-747-2991

BILL KAEHN, 2348 Wellswood Curve, Bloomington, Minnesota 55431; Tel.: 612-888-3654

MASAKA KANEHIBA, President Kyoei Productions, 4-29 Sendagaya, Shibuya-ku, Tokyo, Japan

G. E. KANTER, 232 Madison Avenue, Room 804, New York, New York 10016; Tel.: (Office) 212-686-8793, (Home) 212-628-3197

ARTHUR KARP, 16 Sparwell Lane, Brunswick, Maine 04011; Tel.: 207-725-7105

RON KATZ-V.P., MOMENTUM ENTERPRISES, INC., 340 W. 57th Street, New York, New York 10019; Tel.: 212-265-4261

TAD T. KAWAMURA, 1330 Kanewai, Honolulu, Hawaii 96816; Tel.: 808-737-6471

PETER KEENAN PROMOTIONS, LTD., 97 Maxwell Drive, Glasgow 1, Scotland

JAMES KEOUGH, Fort Lauderdale, Florida; Tel.: 305-563-8331, 764-3402 (Promoter); Rocky Golio (Matchmaker)

DON KERR, 5871 Chain Rock Drive, Halifax, N.S. Canada B3H 1A3; Tel.: 902-429-1420, 429-8644

PAAVO KETONEN, 614 E. Palo Verde Drive, Phoenix, Arizona 85012; Tel.: 602-266-5543, 602-274-2113

H. KEYSER, P.O. Box 2126, Amwrikaweg No. 153, (Vesansana), Willinstad, Curacao, N. Antilles

KIMUTTA BOXING GYM, Schichiro Kimura, President, 1-8 Minami, Koenji, Sugianami-ku, Tokyo, Japan

BILL KING, State Fair Grounds Office, Louisville, Kentucky

DON KING PRODUCTIONS INC., 32 E. 69th Street, New York, New York 10021; Tel.: 212-794-2900

JOE KING, 1930 Saturn Street, Bossier City, Louisiana 71112

MICHAEL KLAHR, Route 2, 738-F, Golden, Colorado 80401

BILL KLEEMAN, 15 E. Ohio Street, Chicago, Illinois 60611

LARRY KLENDA, 1400 Vickers, Wichita, Kansas 67202; Tel.: 316-267-0331

IWAO KODAKA, President, Kyokuto Promotions, 54 Hitotsugi-cho Akasaka, Minato-ku, Japan

JOE Y. KOIZUMI, P.O. Box 5, Musashino, Tokyo 180, Japan

K. O. PRODUCTIONS INC., 1259 Paterson Plank Road, Secaucus, New Jersey 07094

KO SPORTS, INC., 252 W. 30th, New York City, New York 10001

KOREA BOXING ASSOCIATION, Roy Kim, Executive Secretary, I.P.O. Box 1490, Seoul, Korea

OSCAR KORTWICH, Canton Memorial Auditorium, Canton, Ohio

KOSHIN PROMOTIONS, Takafusa Kawarai, President, Japan Boxing Association, 1-3 Koraku, Bunkyo-ku, Tokyo, Japan

VIC KOSTICK, Seaside Gym, 335 E. Seaside Way, Long Beach, California 90802; Tel.: 213-437-9850 (Manager)

AL KOURI SPORTS, INC., 144 Wellington Street North, Sherbrooke, Quebec, Canada

NELSON KREIDMAN, 540 Ocean Parkway, Brooklyn, New York 11218

MR. KRESCH, P.O. Box 367, Colon, Republic of Panama; Tel.: 7-3319 (Manager)

SHIMIZU KUWASHI, Kuwashi Enterprises, Inc., 1421 So. Beretania, Honolulu, Hawaii 96814; Tel.: 808-491-3358

932

K. K. KYOEI PROMOTIONS, Chin Aoyama Building, No. 9-5, Minami Koyama, Minato-ku, Tokyo, Japan; Tel · 409-3988; Cable: Proboxkvo. Tokyo

LENNY LA BARRE, 1919 Martingdale Avenue S.W., Grand Rapids, Michigan 49509 (Manager)

SAM LA FATA, Aptco Athletic Club, 20911 Galdwin, Taylor, Michigan 48180; Tel.: 313-285-7300

CHARLIE LAGOR, 69 Second Avenue, Woodsocket, Rhode Island; Tel.: 766-4527 (Manager)

MIKE LA QUATRA, Sportsman Boxing Club, 7210 Normandy Drive, Cleveland, Ohio 44131; Tel.: 216-845-1649

MICKEY LA ROSA, 135 Menaham Street, Brooklyn, New York; Tel.: 212-691-9098, (Home) 453-0616

WOODROW LARROSEAUX, 254 W. 25th Street, New York 10001; Tel.: 212-691-9098 (Manager)

TED LARVE, Luprican Productions, 8 E. State Street, Trenton, New Jersey 08608; Tel.: 609-392-2747, 396-5423, 888-4050

LAS VEGAS ATHLETIC GUILD & PRESS CLUB, Charleston Boulevard at Main Street, Las Vegas, Nevada 89102

PAUL LAVIGNE, Promotions Andy Nadon, 104 Mac Laren Street, E., Buckingham, Que., Canada J8L 1K1; Tel.: 819-986-3375

TERRY LAWLESS, 13 Park Drive, Romford, England; Tel.: 534-3134 England

BILL LAWRENCE, 385 Church Street, Parramette, New South Wales, Australia

TOM LAWRENCE, Gladiator Boxing Club, 601 No. Main Street, Winston-Salem, North Carolina; Tel.: 919-724-3272, (Night) 748-8348; Tom Lawrence (Director), Hilbert Stevenson (Assistant Director)

JACK LAZAROW, Mid-South Boxing Club Association, Inc., 899 University Street, Memphis, Tennessee 38107; Tel.: 901-527-2536, 274-3186 (Promoter)

A. R. (NICK) LAZO, 1500 Pacheco Road, #52, Bakersfield, California 93307; Tel.: 805-831-1708

RICHARD LEAN STADIUM PTY., LTD., Suite 2, Southern Cross Hotel, Exhibition Street, Melbourne, Australia; Tel.: 63-5634, 52-5672; Cable: Leanstad (Promoter)

FILIBERTO LEBRON, (Manager of Alfredo Escalera), Box 594, Caguas, Puerto Rico 00625; Tel.: 744-2573

JOHN LE BRUN, P.O. Box 637, Alachua, Florida 32615; Tel.: 904-462-5555; 904-462-1798

DICK LEE, 50 S.W. 18th Terrace, Miami, Florida 33129; Tel.: 445-4311, 854-4917

EDDIE LEE, Lee's Sports Promotions, Route 1 Box 137-A1, Collinston, Louisiana 71229

LEHIGH ATHLETIC CLUB, P.O. Box 262, Allentown, Pennsylvania 18105; Tel.: 395-2680, (Night) 395-5404

LEICESTER BOXING PROMOTIONS, Mike Barret, 118 Wardour Street, London W1, England; Tel.: Gerrard 5956/7; Cables: Boxefight, London W1 (Promoter)

LEICHHARDT STADIUM, H. McHugh, Leichhardt, Australia; Tel.: LM 4323 (Manager)

AL LEMAY, Nor-Cal Boxing Promotions, P.O. Box 7417, Santa Rosa, California 95407

ERNEST LENNEY, 1530 Beach Grove, Delta, B.C., Canada V4L 1P2; Tel.: 604-943-7986

ELIAS LEON G., 28 de Enero #729, Guadalajara, Mexico; Tel.: 7-34-47 (Manager)

SUGAR RAY LEONARD, Sugar Ray Leonard, Inc., 1005 Bonifant Street, Silver Spring, Maryland 20910; Tel.: 301-587-7330

SHELLIE LEQUIRE, Canton and Lequire Enterprises, Inc., 282 Halidonhill Road, Cincinnati, Ohio 45238; Tel.: 513-874-2808

COLONEL BOONLERT LERTPRICHA, 78 Prasanmit Lane, Bangkok, Thailand; Tel.: 910005; Also Lumpini Stadium, Bangkok (Manager)

ERNEST W. LETIZIANO, Spector Promotions, 319 Clematis Street, West Palm Beach, Florida 33401; Tel.: 305-832-2000, 832-4001

GENE LETOURNEAU, 1061 Avenue, Des Drables, Quebec 6, P.Q., Canada; Tel.: 522-3665

HARRY LEVENE, 87 Wardour Street, London W1, England; Tel.: Gerrard 2304-5 (International Boxing Promoter)

REGIS LEVESQUE, Paul Suave Center, 4000 est, rue Beaubien, Montreal, Que., Canada H1X 1H6; Tel.: 514-720-0919

DAVE LEVIN PROMOTIONS, P.O. Box 8010, Johannesburg, South Africa

JEFF LEVINE, Round One Productions, 585 Stewart Avenue, Garden City, New York 11530; Tel.: 212-631-8241

MEYER LEVINE, c/o Jenny Leaf, Guest House, 15 Rabbi Tarfon Street, Pardes Hagdud, Nathaya, Israel

JACK LEVINSON, 109C Suburban Parkway, Norfolk, Virginia 23505

SY LEVINSON, 43-18 44th Street, Sunnyside, New York 11104; Tel.: 212-937-1728

DAVE LEWIN, 777 N.W. 72nd Avenue, Miami, Florida 33126; Tel.: 305-266-2368

BUTCH LEWIS, Butch Lewis Productions, 250 W. 57th Street, Suite 1508, New York City, New York 10019; Tel.: 212-582-4344

CARLOS (PANAMA) LEWIS, 1059 Belmont Avenue, Brooklyn, New York 11208; Tel.: 212-235-4106

DAVE LEWIS, 387 12th Street, Oakland, California

HEDGEMON LEWIS, c/o Richard B. Francis, 328 So. Beverly Drive, Beverly Hills, California 90212; Tel.: 213-277-7351

MACK LEWIS, 2000 E. Lanvale Street, Baltimore, Maryland 21213

RAYMOND L'HERNOULD, 59 Square Des Sports, Gonese, (La Faucconimiere) 95, France

LIFLANDER & ASSOCIATES BOXING PROMOTIONS, 61 Parsons, Suite 21, Detroit, Michigan 48201; Tel.: 313-964-3075

LI.MA, Libertine Mario, Viale Dello Staduto, 37, Italy; Tel.: 498270-495923

JOEL LIPSITT, 95-325 Kahikinui Court, Suite 223, Mililani Town, Hawaii 96789; Tel.: 808-623-0919; 449-1454

LITTLE ROCK BOXING CLUB, 3901 W. 13th Street, Little Rock, Arkansas 72205; Tel.: (Office) 663-9837, (Home) 663-0919

BARRY LOCKE, Bi-State Dev. Agency, 818 Olive Street, Suite 630, St. Louis, Missouri 63101; Tel.: (Office) 314-231-1727, (Home) 314-241-3867

GERALD F. LOCKER, JR., Southern International Boxing Association, 17135 N.W. 78th Avenue, Hialeah, Florida 33002

NORM LOCKWOOD, Lockwood's Industries, 3406 Larga Avenue, Los Angeles, California 90039

SAM LOCRICCHIO, Pine Knob Fisticuffs, 7777 Pine Knob Road, Clarkstown, Michigan 48016; Tel.: (Day and Night) 313-625-0700, (Day Only) 313-939-3340 (Promoter)

ANTHONY LOMBARDO, 1265 Central Drive, Beaumont, Texas 77706 (Promoter)

CARLOS LOMBARDO, Cleveland Boxing Club, 3600 Ridge Road, Cleveland, Ohio 44102; Tel.: 216-631-7100

NICK LONDOS, McGraw-Olympia A.C., 59 O Grand River, Detroit, Michigan

BUD LONG, T.B.S. Productions, 1210 E. Maine Street, Lincolnton, North Carolina 28092; Tel.: 704-735-6166

BEN LONIO, 5 So. Flagler Street, Homestead, Florida 33030

DOUG LORD, 11816 Cheswick, Dallas, Texas 75218; Tel.: (Office) 328-9831, (Home) 348-7136

JEAN LORING, 5 Koln, Bayenthal, Klopstockstrasse 1, Germany; Tel.: 38-1545

PIET LOURENS, P.O. Box 1408, Pretoria, South Africa

TOM LOVGREN, 5148 Hickory, Omaha, Nebraska 68106; Tel.: 402-551-4106

DON LOWRIE, 1904A Poplar, No. Little Rock, Arkansas 72114; Tel.: 501-758-8854

FRANK LUCA, 303 32nd Street N.W., Canton, Ohio 44709; Tel.: 216-492-8455

INIGO LUCCHESI, OLYMPIC BOXING CLUB, 5117 24th Avenue, S.E. Lacey, Washington 98503; Tel.: 456-1955

LUMPINI STADIUM, Lt. Col. Erb Sangritti, Vidhayu Junction Rama IV Road, Bangkok, Thailand (Promoter)

JAMES J. LUMPKINS, 2512 Waverly Way, Norfolk, Virginia 23504 (Manager)

A. F. LUPO, P.O. Box 417, Hartford, Connecticut (Manager)

SANCHEZ LUPO, Sur 75-A, No. 4349, Co. Viaducto Piedad, Mexico, D.F.; Tel.: 19-27-85 (Manager)

ELADIO FLORES LUTTEROTH, Empresa Mexicana, De Box S.A. Dr. Lavista, No. 181-A Desp 2, Mexico 7, D.F.; Tel · 588-04-78, 588-29-95 (Promoter)

SALVADOR LUTTEROTH, Dr. Lavista, 189 Mexico 7, D.F.; Tel.: 15-38

BILLY LYONS, King of the Hill Productions, P.O. Box 165, Biloxi, Mississippi 39533; Tel.: 601-432-0257

JOHN L. MC CAFFERTY, Summit Boxing Club, 596 Carpenter Street, Akron, Ohio 44310; Tel.: 216-535-1098

BARRY R. MC CALL, 4506 No. 17th Street, Philadelphia, Pennsylvania 19140

HOWARD MC CALL, Impact Promotions, Martin Luther King Arena, 4530 Market Street, Philadelphia, Pennsylvania 19139; Tel.: 215-662-5100

R. MC CALLAUM, Box 1930, Labrador City, Labrador, Newfoundland

ED MC CARTHY, Box 122, Box 901, So. Pines, North Carolina 28387; Tel.: 919-692-8527, 919-692-6021

JERRY MC CARTHY, 1084 Reedmere Road, Windsor, Ontario, Canada; Tel.: 519-945-6116

JIM MC CLENAHAN, 418 E. Baldwin Avenue, Spokane, Washington 99207; Tel.: 509-489-9046

JACK MC COY, 18713 Florwood Avenue, Torrance, California; Tel.: 323-2016

MARY MC DONALD, Club Forum, Union Street, Grace Bay, N. S., Canada

DICK MC DONNELL, 1306 E. Pike, Seattle, Washington; Tel.: 206-EA 3-2627 (Manager)

MC DONOUGH AND NEWIN, Manila, Philippines

FRANK C. MC GEE, 118 W. Grayson Street, San Antonio, Texas

ALTO MC GOWAN, 1807 Hall Street, Dallas, Texas

BOBBY MC GUIRE, 149-26 Hawthorne Boulevard, Lawndale, California 90260; Tel.: 213-679-6757

CHRIS MC INTOSH, 1619 W. 15th Street, Muncie, Indiana 47302; Tel.: 1-317-284-0355

JIM MC MANIS, 935 So. Grant, Springfield, Missouri 65806; Tel.: 865-4708

CLARENCE MC MINN, 9 Jackson, Quapaw, Oklahoma 74363; Tel.: 918-674-2558

FRED MC NALLY, McNally's Sports Attractions, 9401 S.E. 82nd Avenue, Portland, Oregon 97266; Tel.: 503-777-5516

SOLOMON MC TIER, P.O. Box 176, Eustis, Florida 32726; Tel.: 904-357-4667

CLIFF MC WHORTER, 29 Wellington Avenue, Ontario, Canada; Tel.: Netcali 9316 (Manager)

RAMIRO MACHADO, Corzo Aportado De Correos 2863, Caracas, Venezuela (Manager)

MACID TESORERO DE AGUABOL, ESTEBAN BARRAZA, Cartagena, Columbia (Manager)

GUS MacLELLAND, Maritime Sports Enterprises, P.O. Box 23, Sydney, N.S., Canada P1P 6G9

MADISON SQUARE GARDEN, Al Fenn, 118 No. 7th Avenue, Phoenix, Arizona; Tel.: 258-9014 (Promoter)

MADISON SQUARE GARDEN BOXING CLUB, Gil Clancy, 31st Street and 8th Avenue, New York, New York 10001; Tel.: 563-8165 (Matchmaker)

EDDIE MAFUZ, 1626 Madison Avenue, New York, New York 10029; Tel.: TR 6-6641

MAGNAVERDE, 250 Park Avenue, New York, New York 10017; Tel.: 212-697-1213; also, 5420 Melrose, Hollywood, California 90038

BILL MAHONEY, 329 E. Michigan, Fresno, California 83704

MAIN EVENTS, Lou and Dan Duva, 349 Union Boulevard, Totowa, New Jersey 07512; Tel.: 201-942-0770, 201-942-5697

W. M. MAJESKA, 2 Farms Village Road, Simsbury, Connecticut 06070

DON MAJESKI, 3115 Sullivan Lane, Sparks, Nevada; Tel.: 702-359-2050, 702-358-0884

MAKAMURA BOXING GYM AND PROMOTIONS, No. 8-2 Chome Minami Ebisu, Shibuya-ky, Tokyo, Japan; Tel.: 711-3710, 713-5232

J. M. MALANGSKY, 28 Arch Drive, Shrub Oak, New York 10588

JACK MALANPHY, 28 Arch Drive, Shrub Oak, New York 10588

ERELIO AREAS MANAGUA, Costa Rico (Promoter)

DENNIE MANCINI, International Agent, Worldwide Agent for Stadiums, Limited, Melbourne, Australia, 10 Laurel View, Finchley, London N12 7DT, England; Tel.: (Office) 01-434-1741, 01-437-3375, (Home) 01-445-6515 (Manager-Matchmaker)

MANUEL GARCIA BOXING STABLE, 631 Mabini Ext., Cabanatuan City, Philippines; Sammy C. Garcia (Manager), Abraham S. Manuel (Promoter)

WILLIE MANZA, 1 Richford Road, Kendall Park, New Jersey 08824 (Manager)

JARAN MANZANET, Solar Gym, 146 W. 28th Street, New York, New York 10001; Tel.: 212-243-6170 (Manager)

ANTONIO MARCILLA, 1 Havens Place, Apartment 19A, New York, New York; Tel.: 533-3586 (Manager)

MARILAG SPORTS PROMOTION, Atty. Agustin C. Garcia, Quimpo Building, Rizal Street, Davao City, Philippines; Tel.: 49-83 DCTS 7-97-41 & 7-63-63 PLDT (Promoter)

JIM MARIS, 835 So. Grant, Springfield, Massachusetts; Tel.: 865-4708 (Manager)

MARITIME SPORTS ENTERPRISES, A. M. Brown, 69 McLean Street, Halifax, N.S., Canada; Tel.: 3-4164, 2-5008, 4-3406

STUBLIN MARIUS, 27 Rue Barrier, Lyon (Rhone), France (Manager)

JOSEPH MARSARO, JR., Eastern States Coliseum, Springfield, Massachusetts

ROBERT MARSHALL, Capitol A.C., 2704 Magnolia Street, Richmond, Virginia; Tel.: MI 9-0545

J. E. MARTIN, 915 Umbilo Road, Durban, South Africa

JOE MARTIN, 207 Metropolitan Avenue, Rosindale, Massachusetts (Manager)

SYD MARTIN, 91 Gramercy Place, Teaneck, New Jersey 07666; Tel.: 212-244-9682 (Manager-Trainer)

EDDIE MARTINEZ, P.O. Box 719, Hato Rey, San Juan, Puerto Rico; Tel.: (Home) 7-6784

NARCISO L. MARTINEZ, Butuan City, Philippines (Promoter)

PETER MARTINEZ, P.O. Box 687, Carolina, Puerto Rico

RIGOBERTO MARZUEZ, The Country Club, Cancha Pepin Cestero, Carolina, Puerto Rico 00630

MASBATE PROMOTIONS, INC., Business Address: 42 Danoa Street, Masbate, Masbate, Philippines; Liaison Office: 1180 J. Bocobo Street, Ermita, Manila, Philippines; Tel.: 50-10-98

FRANK MASTERANA, 300 Tropicana East, Sp. 60, Las Vegas, Nevada 89106; Tel.: 736-2759

GLICERIO MATTEI, Office: R. Dona Veridiana, 154-Sala 2, Sao Paulo, Brazil; Tel.: 220-7760; Home: Rua Alfredo Piragibe, 363-Alto de Pinheiros, Sao Paulo-SP, Brazil (Promoter)

EDWARD C. MEARS, 200 Granger Road, Medina, Ohio 44256; Tel.: 666-1181 (Manager)

RICHARD MEEK, 2020 S. Topeka, Wichita, Kansas 67211; Tel.: 316-264-2930

BOBBY MELNICK, 1408 Fourth Avenue, Seattle, Washington; Tel.: MA 3-4725

RAYMON MENDEZ, Pan-American Promoting Syndicate, Box 2536, Cristobal, Canal Zone

EVILO ARIAS MENDOZA, Radio 590, Managua, Nicaragua (Manager)

LUIS MENDOZA, 3121 Magnolia, Corpus Christi, Texas 78408; Tel.: 512-884-1509

RAFAEL MENDOZA, Sur 75-A, No. 4320, Mexico 13, DF., Mexico; Tel.: 530-15-05, 591-06-88

FREDDIE MENNA, 167 Morris Drive, East Meadow, L.I., New York; Tel.: PE 1-4994

W. E. (DUKE) MERCER, Continental Boxing Associates, 418 Via Roma, Naples, Italy

LOUIS MESSINA, 6017 Vicksburg Street, New Orleans, Louisiana 70124 (Promoter)

METRO BOXING PROMOTIONS, Fred Bishop, 6436 Vienna Street, Halifax, N.S., Canada; Tel.: 902-454-0010

THE METROPOLE SPORTING CLUB, Brighton, Sussex, Mike Barrett, 118 Wardour Street, London W1, England; Tel.: GERard 5956/7; Cables: Boxefight, London W1 (Matchmaker)

WILLIAM MEYER, Olympiad Promotions, One Main Plaza, Suite 351, Houston, Texas 77002; Tel.: 713-222-0550

LEW MEYERS, 2325 Williamsbridge Road, Bronx, New York 10469; Tel.: (Home) OL 4-2686 (Manager)

MICHAEL J. MIANO AND A. F. LUPO, P.O. Box 417, Hartford, Connecticut (Manager)

GEORGE MIDDLETON, 441 Tachbrook Road, Leamington Spa, England; Tel.: 0926-26479

MID-SOUTH PRO BOXING ASSOCIATION INC., 1450 No. Thomas Street, Memphis, Tennessee 38107; Tel.: 353-4866

MIDWEST BOXING CLUB, Lee Sloan, 4408 Capitol Avenue, Omaha, Nebraska; Tel.: (Day) Regent 2041, (Night) Glendale 9304 (Promoter)

MICHAEL MIELE, 2153 Belmont Avenue, Bronx, New York; Tel.: FO 4-7819 (Manager)

BILL MILLER, 5231 Calle La Cima, Tucson, Arizona 85718; Tel.: 602-299-5708

DOUG MILLER, P.O. Box 885, Newcastle 2940, South Africa

TOMMY MILLER, Yorkshire's Premier Boxers' Manager and Matchmaker, 128 Clapton Mount, King Cross Road, Halifax, England; Tel.: Halifax 61147 England

JOHN S. MILLIGAN, Lupracon Productions, 16 Greenfield Productions, 16 Greenfield Drive, Allentown, New Jersey 08501; Tel.: 609-259-9262

MILLION DOLLAR BOXING CLUB, 5401 Hyde Park Boulevard, Chicago, Illinois 60615; Tel.: 312-667-4200, 312-667-7342

DANNY MILLSAP, 1859 5th Avenue, San Diego, California (Manager-Promoter)

P. MINAI, 27 Washington Street, Belleville, New Jersey 07109

MINAKI PROMOTIONS, Hisotoshi Kawano, President, 851 Ohsawa, Mikaka-shi, Tokyo, Japan

MINNEAPOLIS BOXING & WRESTLING CLUB, Dennis Stecher & Wally Karbo, 605 Hotel Dyckman, Minneapolis, Minnesota

MINOOKA, INC., 3101 Pitston Avenue, Scranton, Pennsylvania 18505; Tel.: 717-344-2544

GARY MIRES, MANAGER; JIMMY WILLIAMS, TRAINER, The Church Street Gym and Promotions, 444 W. Church Street, Orlando, Florida; Tel.: 305-422-0190

MISAKE PROMOTIONS, Hitoshi Misake, President, 10 Hamazono-cho, Fukagawa, Koto-ky, Tokyo, Japan

ALLEN MITCHELL, Ball T barin, 550 Crown Street, Quebec, P.Q., Canada (Promoter)

BILLY MITCHELL, P.O. Box 820, St. Augustine, Florida 32084; Tel.: 904-797-4804

SKIPPY MIYASHIRO, 2866 Pahoehoe Place, Honolulu, Hawaii 96817; Tel.: 808-595-6610, 735-5845

GENE MOCK, c/o Mock's Gym, 12947 Sherman Way, No. Hollywood, California; Home Address: 8112 Rhodes Avenue, No. Hollywood, California; Tel.: (Gym) 765-8185, (Home) 767-4834

CHARLES MOFFAT, Box 297, Clarks Summit, Pennsylvania 18411 (Manager)

BRENT D. MOLOVINSKY, Sports Promotions, Inc., 4235 28th Avenue, Suite 601, Marlow Heights, Maryland 20031; Tel.: 301-899-2442

BEN MONTABANA, 1351 Gibson Drive, Forestdale, Alabama 35214; Tel.: 205-798-3427

M. MONTANO, Alondra No. 909 Country Club, Rio Piedras, Puerto Rico; Tel.: 809-762-1695

FRANCISCO (PANCHO) MONTES, Empresa de Box, Av. Juarez 409, Cd. Juarez, Mexico; Tel.: 647

MONTEZUMA BOXING CLUB, Ruggles Larson, 2131 No. Prospect, Tacoma, Washington 98406; Tel.: SK 9-6452, BR 2-8047 (Promoter)

JIMMY MONTOYA, Montoya Brothers Boxing, Inc., 10730 So. Broadway, Los Angeles, California 90061; Tel.: 213-777-9690

MONTREAL FORUM BOXING OFFICE, 2313 St. Catherine Street West, Montreal, Quebec, Canada H3H 1N2; Tel.: 514-932-6131; Gerry Grundman (Promoter), Claude Mouton (Matchmaker)

AL MOORE, Box 216, Ringwood, New Jersey 07456

GENE MOORE, 170 Thomas Street, Brentwood, New York 11717; Tel.: 516-273-3685

JERRY MOORE, 740 E. 51st Street, Los Angeles, California 90011; Tel.: 234-0728

JERRY MOORE & HENRY BLOUIN, 1301 W. 52nd Street, Los Angeles, California; Tel.: 292-5040

WHITEY MOORE, 2021 Sherman, Corpus Christi, Texas; Tel.: 512-885-9252 (Manager-Trainer)

BENJAMIN MORA, 4 Surey 13 Oriente, Puebla, Mexico; Tel.: 40-48 Mexicana

DOMINIC MORALES, 98-A Forest Lane Park, Salem, New Hampshire 00079 Tel.: 893-6973

JOHNNY MORAN, P.O. Box 2994, Bayamon, Puerto Rico 00619; Tel.: 809-787-3705

JUAN MANUEL MORALES, Luna Park, Bouchard 465, Buenos Aires, Argentina; Tel.: (Stadium) 31-1990, 32-2538, (Home) 26-9889 (Promoter)

LUIS A. MORENO, 1543 W. Olympic Boulevard, Suite 229, Los Angeles, California 90015; Tel.: 213-386-9021, 383-7346 (International Boxing Agent-Matchmaker)

JAMES MORGAN, 515 Seward Square S.E., Washington, D. C. 20003

MIKE MORTON, 4010 N.E. Hancock, Portland, Oregon 97212

RODGER MORTON, 478 East Tremont Avenue, Bronx, New York 10457; Tel.: CY 9-7593 (Manager)

CLAUDE MOUTON, Montreal Forum, 2313 Quest, Rue Ste-Catherine W., Montreal, Ont., Canada H3H 1N2; Tel.: 514-932-6181

D. A. MUCEROS BOXING PROMOTIONS, IMM Building, 488 E. de los Santos Avenue, Caloocan City, Philippines; Tel.: 35-26-40

FRANK J. MUCHE, Box 1390, Arcadia, California 91006; Tel.: 213-447-8668

BAHAR MUHAMMAD, 1180 Raymond Boulevard, Newark, New Jersey 07102; Tel.: (Office) 201-623-1940, (Home) 201-623-5159 (Matchmaker)

MURAD MUHAMMAD, 1180 Raymond Boulevard, Newark, New Jersey 07102; Tel.: (Office) 201-623-1940, (Home) 201-623-5358 (Promoter)

BRUNO MULLER, Tanus Box Camp, 6232 Bad Soden, Dachbergergstrasse, 6; Tel.: 06196/3055

KEITH MURPHY, P.O. Box 161, Woolwich, Maine 04579; Tel.: 207-443-3866, 563-5575

HAROLD MURRELL, Valley Sports Inc., 505 Kearney Boulevard, Fresno, California; Tel.: AM 8-8856

ANDY NADON, 104 MacLaren East, Buckingham, Quebec, Canada J8L 1K1; Tel.: 1-819-986-3375

HORST NALBACH, Boxmanager, Lanestrabe 3, 2000 Hamburg 4, Germany

NASHOBA SPORTS ENTERPRISES, Dan Monagan and Frank Leary, 350 Water Street, Leominster, Massachusetts 01453; Tel.: 537-2925 (Managers)

NATIONAL BOXING CLUB, Aranata Coliseum, Quezon City, Philippines

NATIONAL BOXING COUNCIL (NBC), The Honorable James Tennant, President; 8, The Precinct, Packington Street, London N1 7 UP, England; Tel.: London 359-3480

NATIONAL BROADCASTING CO. (NBC), 30 Rockefeller Plaza, New York, New York 10020; Tel.: 212-664-2121; c/o Dr. Ferddie Pacheco

NATIONAL SPORTING CLUB, Cafe Royal, Regent Street, London W1, England

AL NAYER, 27 Ellen Road, Brockton, Massachusetts 02402; Tel.: (Gym) 617-323-9141; Vin Marino, 617-323-9653 and Al Nayer, 617-586-0222 (Co-Managers)

CHARLES NEFF, Lubbock Lions Club, Monterrey Center, Lubbock, Texas 79408; Tel.: 806-797-4359

BOBBY NEILL, 53 Georgia Road, Thornton Heath, Surrey, England; Tel.: (Gym) 01-607-5432, (Home) 01-764-2280

CHUCK NELSON, 3340 E. Market, Warren, Ohio 44484; Tel.: 216-394-3801

NENE PROMOTIONS-FILEMON SALAYSAY (LITTLE NENE), Happy World Stadium, Singapore, City, Malaya

N.E.S.V.I., INC., 11109 So. Hawthorne Boulevard, Lennox, California 90304

NEWCASTLE STADIUM, Harry Macka and Stan Heaney, Newcastle, Australia; Tel.: B1689 (Managers)

NEW GARDEN GYM (Formerly Gleason's), 252 W. 30th, New York City, New York; Tel.: 212-947-3744; Proprietors: Ira & William Becker

PERCY NEWLAND, 17290 24th Avenue, Surrey, B.C., Canada V4B 4Z5

NEW OAKLAND BOXING CLUB, 387 12th Street, Oakland, California

NEW ORLEANS BOXING CLUB, Lou Messina, 411 So. Genois Street, New Orleans, Louisiana 70119; Tel.: 482-7557, 488-6046, 523-2471 (Promoter)

NEW PRO SPORTS, John Forhen, Halifax, N.S., Canada; Tel.: 902-425-3017

JERRY NISS, 7955 Oakwood Avenue, Los Angeles, California 90048; Tel.: 213-938-3642

HARUO NIWA, Japan Boxing Commission, c/o Korakuen Stadium, Ltd., 3-7 Chave, Koraku, Bunkyo-ku, Tokyo, Japan

RAYMOND NOE, Vlaanderenstraat 97-101-9000 Gent, Belgium; Tel.: (Day and Night) 25.46.68, 25.61.35

NOGOCHI PROMOTIONS, Satono Noguchi, President, 127 1-chome Shimo-Meguro, Meguro-ku, Tokyo, Japan

NOGUCHI BOXING CLUB, 17-3 chome Shimo-Meguro, Meguro-ku, Tokyo, Japan

OSANU NOGUCHI, Noguchi Promotions, Ltd., 6-7 chome Nishiginza, Chyo-ky, Tokyo, Japan; Tel.: 872-8728

BOB NOLAND, 130 Bryant Street, Fort Benning, Georgia 31905; Tel.: 404-682-1721

JIM NOLAND, 2503 Jackson Keller, Suite 1101, San Antonio, Texas 78230; Tel.: 512-340-2055

NOR-CAL BOXING PROMOTIONS, J. Lawrence Bradley, P.O. Box 741, Santa Rosa, California 95407 (Promoter)

NORTH AMERICAN PRODUCTIONS, 836 Broad Ripple Avenue, Indianapolis, Indiana 46220

NORTHERN NEVADA BOXING PROMOTION, 1115 Shady Oak Drive, Carson City, Nevada 89701

NORTHERN SPORTS CENTER, LTD., P.O. Box 1730, Labrador City, Newfoundland

NORTHERN TRAVALL SPORTING CLUB, c/o Mr. Potgieter, Pretoria Weg., Brits Northern Transvaal, South Africa; Tel.: Brits 148

NORTHLAKE A.C., 715 31st Avenue So., Seattle, Washington 98144

NU-LIFE, 229 N.E. First Avenue, Miami, Florida 33101; Tel.: 379-4753 ext. 302

OSCAR AGUSTIN NUNEZ, Industria Dayma, General Cabrera No. 90 altos, Santiago, Provincia de Santiago, Republica Dominicana

THE OAKLAND BOXING CLUB, 387 12th Street, Oakland, California 94607; Tel.: (Gym) 415-832-7577, 415-832-9866, (Office) 415-832-0257, 415-836-1321, (Home) 415-658-4647

HERBERT D. ODOM, Mal-Mart Medical Group, 6333 So. Green Street, Chicago, Illinois 60621; Tel.: 312-651-8000

BOBBY O'DOWD, 1940 Lincoln Avenue, Chicago, Illinois 60614; Tel.: 312-266-2645

PAT O'GRADY SPORTS PROMOTIONS, 3920 N.W. 23rd Street, Oklahoma 73107; Tel.: (Office) 405-947-2232, (Home) 405-943-3530

MIGUEL A. RIVAS OJEDA, Apartado postal 1033, Manatua, N.N., Nicaragua

SERGIO OJEDA, 1912 Chickasaw Avenue, Los Angeles, California 90041

CHET O'KELLEY, Promoter of Amateurs, 140 N.W. Second Street, Norton, Ohio 44203; Tel.: 825-3344

JOHN OLEJACK AND JOHN DOPSOVIC, 518 Buttonwood Street, Catasauqua, Pennsylvania; Tel.: 264-9645, 264-2610

ED OLTJENBRUNS, North Group America, P.O. Box 1435, Santa Rosa, California 95402

OLYMPIAD SPORTS INTERNATIONAL, INC., Ken Guest, President, 918 Congress Avenue, Houston, Texas 77002; Tel.: 226-7556

OLYMPIC BOXING CLUB, 5711 Park Avenue, Montreal, Quebec, Canada; Tel.: (Gym) 270-4040, (Home) 676-9176, (Bur.) 725-5895, 728-9318

OLYMPIC YOUTH CENTER, Hippodrome Building, 600 Basle, Memphis, Tennessee

DICK O'NEAL, Bamboo Sports, Box 156, Agana, Guam

CECILE OPAON STABLE, 287 Leandro Ibarra Street, Tondo, Manila, Philippines (Manager)

ANGEL ORTIZ, 45-05 40th Street, Sunnyside, New York 11104; Tel.: 212-729-6087, 364-2161

DANTE ORTIZ, 525 Jackson Avenue, 4-K, Bronx, New York 10455; Tel.: (Office) 212-243-6170, (Home) 635-4181

LOUIS OUILLETTE, 1 Longfellow Avenue, Brunswick, Maine 04011; Tel.: 207-729-0223

ED OWENS, 5204 E. Randolph Court, Virginia Beach, Virginia 23462; Tel.: 804-490-1900

OZARK ATHLETIC CLUB, Promotional Group, 835 So. Grant, Springfield, Missouri; Tel.: UN 5-4708; Rex Buff (Promoter), Jim McManus (Matchmaker)

ISMAEL PACE, 465 Luna Park Boulevard, Buenos Aires Argentina (Promoter)

RENATO PACOTE TESTI ALFONSO, Rua Dos Arcos, 9 Sobrado, Rio de Janiero, G.B., Brazil; Tel.: 142-9641

TONY PADILLA, 146 North Drive, San Antonio, Texas 78201; Tel.: 512-733-1677, 223-8314

S. D. (SONNY) PALAZZO, P.O. Box 2055, Seattle, Washington 98101; Tel.: 663-5608

MOGENS PALLE, 12 Skjule T-2880 Bagsvaerd, Denmark; Tel.: Denmark 2-988200; Cable Address: World Box/Copenhagen (Promoter-Manager)

RALPH PALMISAMO, 39 W. 51st Street, Bayonne, New Jersey 07002; Tel.: (Office) 201- 333-2820, (Home) 201-339-5316

JIMMY PARKS, 451 Trudell, San Antonio, Texas; Tel.: WA 4-7121 (Manager)

FRANK PARRILLA, Calle Benito Feijoo, No. 2039, Urb.El Senorial, Rio Piedras, Puerto Rico 00928; Tel.: 809-761-8375

BARON PATE, 1401 Flagler Drive So., West Palm Beach, Florida 33401; Tel.: 305-833-6540

EDIO PAVENA, Via Roma Destra, 91 Jesolo, Venice, Italy; Tel.: 90935 (Manager)

PELTZ BOXING PROMOTIONS, 801 No. 27th Street, Philadelphia, Pennsylvania 19130; Tel.: 215-235-9933

DOUGLAS PENDARVIS, Pendarvis Boxing Enterprises, 97 Dale Street, Roxbury, Massachusetts 02119; Tel.: 617-445-4150

ETTORE PENN, 78-19 87th Road, Woodhaven, L.I., New York

PAUL PERCIFIELD, 2041 Glenwood Circle, Corsicana, Texas 75110; Tel.: 214-872-6523, 874-8291

LARRY PETERSON, 226 Sara Drive, Jacksonville, Florida 32218; Tel.: 904-751-0007

RON PETERSON, 12600 W. 62nd Street, Minneapolis, Minnesota 55343

AL PHILLIPS, 30 Sunningdale Close, Gordon Avenue, Stanmore, Middlesex HA7 3QL; Tel.: (Home) 9545535-5205 (Manager-Agent)

JOHNNY PHILLIPS, 145 Brook Street, Coogee, 2031 New South Wales, Australia; Tel.: 665-7079

PHOENIX SPORTS, P.O. Box 1606, Scottsdale, Arizona 85252

JESUS PIMENTEL, Pimentel Boxing Promotions, 1832 So. Hope Street, Los Angeles, California 90021; Tel.: 213-747-2991

PIONEER SPORTS PROMOTION, Paciencia Hitosis, 1427 Tayabas Street, Sta. Cruz, Manila, Philippines; Tel.: 26-80-92 (Promoter)

JAY P. PITTMAN, 2904 Peppercorn Court, Virginia Beach, Virginia

DON POLIAFILO, 3720 Warrensville Road, Apartment 102, Shaker Heights, Ohio 44122; Tel.: 216-361-9568

JOE PONCE, 13454 Sunburst Street, Arlita, California; Tel.: 896-7820

ALBERT PONS, Casonovay 375, Gran Price, Barcelona, Spain

JOE POODLES, 829 So. Milton Avenue, Baltimore, Maryland; Tel.: Orleans 5-5474

LUIS PORTELA, Ap. 771, San Jose, Costa Rica; Tel.: 32-41-36

PORT ELIZABETH SPORTING CLUB, c/o S. C. Dickeos, 1 Berkeley Court, Summer Strand, Port Elizabeth, South Africa

ALFREDO AND TINO PORZIO, San Martin, 780 Buenos Aires, Argentina

PRETORIA SPORTING CLUB, P.O. Box 814, Pretoria, South Africa; Tel.: Pretoria 93-33126

BILL PREZANT, Wellington Hotel, 55th Street and 7th Avenue, New York, New York (Manager)

AL PRINCIPE, Pacific Northwest Boxing Club, 738 W. Hastings Street, Vancouver 1, B.C., Canada; Tel.: 604-685-5013, (Home) 604-581-9127 (Promoter)

JOHNNY PRITCHETT, 68 Woodland Way, Winchmore Hill N21, England; Tel.: 01-886-6334

PRO-AM BOXING, Hank Grooms, 241 No. Burdick Street, Kalamazoo, Michigan 49006; Tel.: 616-345-0806 (Promoter)

PROFESSIONAL & AMATEUR BOXING, WRESTLING & WEIGHT LIFTING POOL & GAMES, 1921 Tuolumne, Fresno, California; Tel.: 209-237-3258

PROFESSIONAL MANAGEMENT ENTERPRISES, INC., P.O. Box 229, Kalamazoo, Michigan 49005; Tel.: 616-345-0806

PROMOCIONES BOXIANA, Primera Empresa De Boxeo Y Espectaculous De Colombia

PROMOCIONES INTERNACIONALES, Av. Madero No. 420 Edif. Guajardo, Mexicali, Baja California, Mexico; Despachos: 200-202-204

PUERTO ENTERTAINMENT, INC., Felix Zabala, GPO Box 4073, San Juan, Puerto Rico 00936; Tel.: 765-5479, 767-7322 (Promoter)

EARL PURYEAR AND JIM FARGART, 3118 Charles Street, Omaha, Nebraska; Tel.: W-2427

QUALITY BOXER & ENTERPRISES INC., Ernie Terrell, President, P.O. Box 12269, Chicago, Illinois 60612

QUEENS GYM, Ray Skarica and Tony Carione, 5702 Hoffman Drive, Atop the Elmwood Theatre, Elmhurst, L.I., New York; Tel.: 212-429-9308 (Managers)

JOE R. QUILLAN, 739 So. 2nd Avenue, Tucson, Arizona 85701; Tel.: 602-624-3394 (Manager)

QUIRANTE GYM, Green Dauphin Street, Mambaling, Cebu City, Philippines 6401; Tel.: 7-24-25, 9-29-70

REUBEN RABAGO, Savannah Promotions, 7526 Martin Luther King Boulevard, Houston, Texas 77033; Tel.: 713-524-9668

RAJADAMNERN STADIUM, Bangkok, Thailand; Tel.: 20600

JACK RALEIGH, St. Paul Boxing Club, 464 Hotel Capri, 9 W. 7th Street, St. Paul, Minnesota 55102; Tel.: 612-227-4433, 612-227-5970

ART RAMALHO, 52 Sidney Street, Lowell, Massachusetts 01852; Tel.: 459-3078, 453-1052

DAVE L. RAMOS, 857 E. Southlake Drive, Murray, Utah 84107; Tel.: 801-262-9299

RANCHO ARRYO BOXING CLUB, Ed. Vinson, 980 Jackson Road, Sacramento, California 95826; Tel.: 457-9548

GEORGE RANDAZZO, 147 Schubert Avenue, Glendale Heights, Illinois 60137

CARNESALE RAPHAEL BOXING CLUB, 6 Rue Sully Prudhomme, Villeurbanne, France 6G100

DENNIS RAPPAPORT, 271-33G, Grand Central Parkway, Floral Park, Queens, New York; Tel.: (Office) 212-528-4086, (Home) 212-631-7228 (Manager)

REDWOOD INTERNATIONAL FIGHTERS, J. L. Bradley, President, P.O. Box 118, Santa Rosa, California 95402; Tel.: 707-546-6516

J. W. REID, 16017 Basil Street, Fountain Valley, California 92708

HEARD REGAS, 5115 Conti Street, New Orleans, Louisiana 70124; Tel.: 504-488-4379

JACK RENNIE, 28 Marco Polo Street, Essenden, Victoria, Australia 3040; Tel.: 379-5365

RESORTS INTERNATIONAL HOTAL CASINO, No. Carolina Avenue and Boardwalk, Atlantic City, New Jersey 08404; Tel.: 609-344-6000

PETE RICCITELLI, 7 Deering Street, Portland, Maine 04101; Tel.: 207-773-1918

STEVE RICHARDS, Pilgrims Way School House, Tustin Estate, Manor Grove SE15, England; Tel.: 732-0747

JOSEPH RICHARDSON, 156 Beach Hill Drive, Manchester, New Hampshire 03103; Tel.: 603-627-1007

GERD RIETHENAUER, Frankfurt, Main No. 14, Rothchild, Alec 45, Germany

RIKI PROMOTIONS, Yoshio Yoshimura, President, 78 Owasa-cho, Shibuya-ku, Tokyo, Japan

RINGSIDE PRODUCTIONS INC., 2395 Somersworth Drive North, Columbus, Ohio 43219

RINGSIDE PROMOTIONS, LTD., P.O. Box 901, Southern Pines, North Carolina 28387; Tel.: 919-692-8527, 919-692-6021

JOE RIOS GYM, Condominio Las Lomas, Caparra Heights, Puerto Rico, Local 15; Tel.: 783-7570

RIVERINA STADIUM, A. E. French, Wagga Wagga, Australia (Promoter)

RIVERSIDE BOXING CLUB, Tommy Butler, 1975 So. Central, Phoenix, Arizona (Promoter)

BOB RITZ, Champmaker, P.O. Box 2511, Tulsa, Oklahoma 74101; Tel.: 918-583-1910

MURRAY ROARK, 1248 Margert, Greenville, Mississippi 38701; Tel.: 601-335-5150

JACK ROBERTS, 226 Caribbean Drive, Corpus Christi, Texas 78418; Tel.: 512-937-4920

J. ROBBINS, 1424 W. Cowin Street, Syracuse, New York 13207

NOAH R. ROBINSON, 10842 So. Michigan Avenue, Chicago, Illinois 60628; Tel.: 312-468-3109

REGELIO RODLOD, Asteos Promotions, Inc., 329 No. Rowan, Los Angeles, California 90063; Tel.:

213-263-9978, 263-9979

HECTOR ROCHA, 3001 Helena Street, #3, Houston, Texas 77006; Tel.: 713-526-9575

ROCKY'S BOXING SCHOOL & GYM, 805 N.W. 44th Street (Prospect Road), Fort Lauderdale, Florida 33309

DAVID RODRIGUEZ, 4585 S.W. 74th Avenue, Miami, Florida 33155; Tel.: 305-264-2166, 305-261-7383

RUBEN P. RODRIGUEZ, 531 Lively Drive, San Antonio, Texas; Tel.: DI 2-2594, CA 2-1913

MORTON ROGERS, 502 E. Tremont, Bronx, New York 10457; Tel.: CY 9-7593, CY 4-2460

PETE ROKAS, Fresno Boxing Club, 2981 E. Princeton, Fresno, California 93703; Tel.: 209-224-8159, 209-268-1268

JOE ROMANO, 2700 Ohio, Topeka, Kansas 66605; Tel.: (Office) 862-1234 ext. 4352, (Home) 232-3503

JAMES E. (JIM) ROMEL, 150 Olive Street, Weston, West Virginia 26452; Tel.: (Office) 304-269-1361, (Home) 304-269-1076

LEO ROSALES, 3828 Seward Street, Omaha, Nebraska 68111; Tel.: 402-556-9892; Gym: 1006 So. 10th Street, Omaha, Nebraska 68108 (Manager-Coach)

VICTOR R. ROSARIO, P.O. Box 751, Santo Domingo, Dominican Republic

AL ROSE, Route 1, Box 87, Valleyford, Washington 99036; Tel.: 509-488-9230

IRWIN N. ROSEE COMPANY, 515 Madison Avenue, New York, New York 10022; Tel.: 212-753-4153/4

ROSELAND SPORTS CLUB, Rosel and Ballroom, Taunton, Massachusetts; Tel.: 617-238-4355, (Night) 617-238-3074

ROSELAND SPORTS CLUB, INC., 100 Main Street, No. Easton, Massachusetts 02356; Danny La Fratta (Promoter), Vito Talarita (Matchmaker)

KEN ROSENBERG, Alessi Promotions, 2909 W. Cypress, Tampa, Florida 33609; Tel.: (Office) 813-870-3879; (Home) 813-962-1683

JIM ROWAN, 1050 Groner Drive, Knoxville, Tennessee 37915; Tel.: 615-522-1608

PAUL RUDDY, 1717 Green Ridge Street, Dunmore, Pennsylvania 18512; Tel.: 717-343-9627

HENK RUHLING, Interbox, Tjerk Hiddesstraat 2, Flat 5, Zandvoort, Holland, Postbox 141, 2040AC Zandvoort, Holland; Tel.: (Day and Night) Zandvoort 0-2507-4530; Cable Address: Interbox Zandvoort, Holland (International Matchmaker-Manager)

ROBERT J. RUIZ, Apartment 501, 1601 Park Avenue, Omaha, Nebraska 68105

STEVE J. RULJANCICH, 5807 S.E. 39th Avenue, Portland, Oregon 97202

CHUCK RUNZO, Boxing Clubs of America, P.O. Box 359, New Alexandria, Pennsylvania 15670; Tel.: 412-668-7875, 688-7123

FRANK RUSSO, Connecticut Sports Promotions, 1 Civic Center Plaza, Hartford, Connecticut 06103; Tel.: 203-566-6588

RODOLFO SABATINI'S PROMOTIONS, Via G. Battista Vico, 1 Rome, Italy; Tel.: 388007, 315363 Rome, Italy

ST. PAUL BOXING CLUB, 464 Hotel Capri, 9 W. 7th Street, St. Paul, Minnesota 55102

ROGER V. SALA ASSOCIATES, INC., 35 Colvin Avenue, Albany, New York 12206; Tel.: 518-438-6866

JULIAN SANCHEZ, Medrano y 20 de Noviembre, Guadalajara, Mexico; Tel.: 4-34-01

LUPE SANCHEZ, Sur 75-A #4349, Co. Viaducto Piedad, Mexico City, D.F., Mexico; Tel.: 1-519-8785

BILL SANFORD, 1037 Kenston. Drive, Concord, California; Tel.: (Gym) 415-775-7020, (Home) 415-685-3031

PANTALONES SANTIAGO, Coliseo Roberto Clemente, San Juan, Puerto Rico (Promoter)

EDDIE L. SAPIR, 434 So. Broad, New Orleans, Louisiana 70119; Tel.: 504-821-4840, 822-3154

MIKE SARGE, 2201 Santa Ynez Drive, Las Vegas, Nevada 89104; Tel.: 702-735-6622

JUN SARREAL AND ELORDE STABLE, 1776 Dian Street, corner of Casino Street, Makati, Metro Manila, Philippines; Tel.: 80-77-39, 80-42-85

LOPE SARREAL, JR., 1776 Dian Street, Makati, Rizal, Philippines; Tel.: 80-77-39 Cable: Lalorde, Manila

SASZAKI PROMOTIONS, Takeshi Saszaki, President, I-Sanya-cho, Megura-ku, Tokyo, Japan

(SAILOR) DON SAUER BOXING ENTERPRISES, 71 Main Street, Kingston, Massachusetts 02364; Tel.:

937

(Day) 617-746-0610 ext 35, (Night) 617-585-2039

WILLIAM (PINNY) SCHAFER, 308 Lindsey Street, Ridley Park, Pennsylvania 19107; Tel.: 545-8627, 583-8144

SCIACCA BOXING PROMOTIONS INCORPORATED, 218 Central Avenue, Brooklyn, New York 11237

FRANK SCIACCA, 793 Wyckoff Avenue, Brooklyn, New York 11227; Tel.: (Office) 212-366-9493, (Home) 212-845-4824 (Manager)

NANCY SCIACCA, Sciacca Boxing Promotions, 793 Wyckoff Avenue, Brooklyn, New York 11227; Tel.: 212-366-9493

CHARLIE SCHMIDT, 1711 So. Congress, Austin, Texas 78704; Tel.: 444-5400 (Promoter)

EDWARD SCHOFIELD AND JIM PERRIN, JR., 1329 Adams Street, New Orleans, Louisiana 70018 (Promoter)

SCHONIGER ENTERPRISES, James Wallach, c/o Murray Lincoln, 250 W. 39th Street, New York, New York; Tel.: 212-565-4818

CARL SCHULMEISTER, Kiel Strasse, Boningstedt bei, Hamburg, Germany; Tel.: 58-6000

JOE SCORCIA, 789 Bergen Street, Brooklyn, New York; Tel.: 212-622-2900 (Manager)

ROCKY SCOTT, 44 Birr Street, Rochester, New York 14613

SEASIDE GYM, 355 E. Seaside Boulevard, Long Beach, California; Tel.: 213-437-9850

DANNY SEGUNDO, 181 Magsaysay Avenue, Begulo City, Philippines (Promoter)

ERNIE SERGIO, 19 Blydenburg Road, Centereach, New York 11720

JOSEPH S. SERIAN, 1214 So. James Road, Columbus, Ohio 43227; Tel.: 614-237-4561

A. A. SERRANO BOXING STABLE, Guagua, Pampanga, Philippines; Tel.: 066-404-070; Tony A. Serrano (Promoter), A. A. Serrano, B. I. Cervantes (General Contractors)

JIM SETZER, Boxing Action Associates, Inc., 303 Cherokee Trail, Huntington, West Virginia 25705; Tel.: 523-7767, 736-5287 (Promoter-Matchmaker)

JOE SGRETTO, Super City Boxing Club, 430 So. Broad Street, New Orleans, Louisiana 70119; Tel.: 504-821-4840

LARRY SHAEFFER, Little Wing, Inc., P.O. Box 263, Tulsa, Oklahoma 74101; Tel.: 918-584-2306

RED SHANNON'S GYM, 4722 Amberwood Avenue, La Palma, California 90623; Tel.: 213-865-4639

JOHN SHAPRE, 56 Valley Drive, Kingsbury, London NW9, England; Tel.: CL 7781

CYRIL SHAW, 72 Wellington Street, Lacytown, Georgetown, Guyana; Tel.: 02-61960 (Promoter)

RUFUS SHAW, 6616 Braddock Place, Dallas, Texas 75232; Tel.: 214-331-1925

PEYTON SHER ENTERPRISES, INC., 9328 Outlook Drive, Overland Park, Kansas 66207

SHINWA PROMOTIONS, Iawo Wakamatsu, President, 4-2 Nishi-Shinbashi, Minato-ku, Tokyo, Japan

AL SILVA, 1502 E. 6th Street, Sterling, Illinois 61081; Tel.: 815-625-8071

JOE J. SILVA, 279 No. State, Salt Lake City, Utah 84103; Tel.: 801-322-4572

MARIO SILVA, Boxing Enterprises Limited, 1348 Highview Place, Honolulu, Hawaii 96816; Tel.: 808-734-5314

PHIL SILVER, c/o Forum Boxing Promotions, Elks Building, 607 So. Parkview Avenue, Los Angeles, California 90057; Tel.: 213-380-5794, 213-380-5796

DAVID M. SINGER, 12 Charlton Avenue, Spryfield, Halifax, N.S. B3R 1B1, Canada; Tel.: 902-477-6491

SINGERS GYMNASIUM, 629 Main Street, Buffalo, New York 14203; Tel.: 716-855-8677

KHEMRAJ SINGH, Triple M Promotions, Residence: D Peter's Hall, E. Bank Demerara, Guyana, South America 67679, Office: 45/47 Water Street, Georgetown, Guyana; Tel.: 60769, Cable: Guynaco (Promoter)

ROBERT H. SKEGEN, Champions' Promotions, Inc., 278 E. Main Street, Smithtown, New York 11787; Tel.: 516-360-7722

STAN SKINKISS, Longdale Club, Manchester, England; Tel.: 061-236-4186

RICHARD SKINNER, Ten Rounds, Inc., 120 E. Vermount Street, Indianapolis, Indiana 46204; Tel.: 317-371-3232

WILLIAM SLAYTON AND LINDA SIVILS; Tel.: 213-269-6803, 466-0682

GEORGE (TIGER) SMALL, 6308 Boulevard of Champions, North Lauderdale, Florida 33308; Tel.: 305-491-3521

ED SMITH, 4912 Winchester Drive, Charlotte, North Carolina 28208; Tel.: 704-399-8058

FELIX SMITH, 17 Range Crescent, Kingston 2, Jamaica; Tel.: 928-4342, (Office) 938-6231

SOCRATES BOXING CLUB, Socrates Cruz, Barrio Crespo, Cartagena, Colombia (Manager)

SOCTRON, 3215 Superior Avenue, Cleveland, Ohio 44114; Tel.: 216-621-3200

SIDNEY SOLMON, JR., 10 Vough Lane, Frontenac, Missouri; Tel.: Mission 6-3110, Mission 4-0900 (Promoter in St. Louis, Mo.)

SAM SOLOMON, 40 No. Felton Street, Philadelphia, Pennsylvania 19139; Tel.: 215-472-4221, 215-222-8760

S. O. PROMOTIONS, 1-15 Minami Nakamura, Minato-ku, Tokyo, Japan

JOE SOUZA, 6803 Whitestone, San Antonio, Texas 78227; Tel.: 512-674-3963

SPANKY'S BOXING CLUB, 114 W. Avenue C, Kennewick, Washington 99336

KENNETH (JAP) KING FOOK SPARROW, Hideaway Petit Valley, Port of Spain, Trinidad, West Indies

THE SPARTAN SPORTING ENTERPRISES, INC., 378 Union Avenue, Paterson, New Jersey 07502

SPECTRUM FIGHTS, INC., J. Russell Peltz, Director of Boxing, Broad Street and Pattison Avenue, Philadelphia, Pennsylvania 19148

FRED SPENCE, 63 Oscott Road, Birmingham B42 2TA, England

LORENZO SPGNOLI, Italian Boxing Promotion, Via Giambattista Vieo 1, Roma Italy 00196; Tel.: 3610t0t-3610694

HENRI F. SPITZER, Promotions H.F.S., Inc., 8180 Devonshire, Suite 6, Mont-Royal, Que., Canada; Tel.: 514-737-8696

AL SPOLDI, Boxing Enterprises, 6759 Yucca Street, Hollywood, California 90028

SPORTSMAN BOXING CLUB, 409 No. Tryon Street, Charlotte, North Carolina 28202

JOHN SQUAGLIA, 2378 E. Los Altos Avenue, Fresno, California 93710; Tel.: 209-299-3764

STADIUMS, LTD., R. Lean, General Manager, Hutchinson House, 76 Flinders Lane, Melbourne C1, Australia; Tel.: C7499, FL9251

STARMAKER, INC., Pat O'Grady, 3920 N.W. 23rd Street, Oklahoma City, Oklahoma 73107; Tel.: 405-947-2232, 405-943-3530

GEORGE STASSI, 246 Kelby Street, Covina, California 91723

DENNIS STECHER AND WALLY KARBO, Boxing 7 Wrestling Club, Hotel Dyckman, Minneapolis, Minnesota

STEPHENVILLE GARDENS, Box 772, Stephenville, Newfoundland; Tel.: 643-2591 (Promoter)

SILVANA STERLINI, Italian Boxing Promotion, 00196 Roma, Via G.B. Vico, 1; Tel.: -06/3610694 3610707

STERNBERG ATTRACTIONS, Rochester, Minnesota 55901

VERN STEVENSON, P.O. Box 1745, San Antonio, Texas 78296; Tel.: 512-227-5991

EMANUEL STEWARD, 19260 Bretton Drive, Detroit, Michigan 48223; Tel.: 313-531-7939

HARRY STICKEVERS, Consulate Hotel, 224 W. 49th Street, New York City, New York 10019; Tel.: 212-CI 6-5252

GREGORY STOUT, 10246 Sweet Gum, Dallas, Texas 75249; Tel.: 214-296-5331

BEN STRAZZERI, 5006 Roosevelt Boulevard, Philadelphia, Pennsylvania 19123; Tel.: 288-3375 (Manager)

TONY STRAZZERI, 5006 Roosevelt Boulevard, Philadelphia, Pennsylvania 19124; Tel.: 333-9018 (Manager)

JIM AND DEANNA STRICKLAND, Jim-Dee Sports Consultants, 7900 So. Cottage Grove, Chicago, Illinois 60619; Tel.: 312-386-5955, 723-5904

PATSY SUAREZ, 3501 E. Frierson; Tampa, Florida

JOHN SUDAC, (Home) 259 Wadsworth Avenue, Tonawanda, New York 14150; Tel.: 716-693-7080

SUMMIT BOXING CLUB, 596 Carpenter Street, Akron, Ohio 44310

BEN SUN, Ponkol Stable, 295-B-4 Jones Avenue, Cebu City, Philippines; Tel.: 71819 (Promoter)

PETE SUSENS, 401 E. Washington Street, Indianapolis, Indiana 46204; Tel.: 317-637-6464

ROBERT L. SUSSMAN, BOXING ENTERPRISES, INC., 5740 Greenspring Avenue, Baltimore, Maryland 21209

SWAN PROMOTIONS COMPANY, LTD., Tamachi Building 7-4 Chome, Alaska, Tamachi Minato-ku, Tokyo, Japan; Tel.: 481-7906, 5903, 1074; Cable: Swanpromot Tokyo

ED SWEENY, Soctron, 3215 Superior Avenue, Cleveland, Ohio 44114; Tel.: 216-621-3200

LORENZO (CHAO) SY, Cebu City, Philippines (Promoter)

SYDNEY STADIUM, H. Miller, Ruschcutters Bay, Sydney, Australia; Tel.: FM-1363 (Manager)

LEON R. TABBS, Joe Frazier's Gym, 2917 No. Broad Street, Philadelphia, Pennsylvania 19132; Tel.: (Gym) 215-225-9832, (Home) 215-222-6627 (Manager-Trainer)

VITO TALLARITA, 58 Fairview Avenue, Thompsonville, Connecticut; Tel.: 745-6972

TANABE PROMOTIONS, Kunio Tanabe, President, 109 Omoto-cho, Tokyo, Japan

TOSHIO TANAKA, Akatsuki Boxing Club, No. 884-2 Chome Kamiochiai, Shinjuki-ku, Tokyo, Japan; Tel.: 369-7960

GERALD TANIS, Box 154, Augusta, New Jersey 07822

ABRAHAM TANZMAN, 1916 N.E. 28th, Portland, Oregon 97212; Tel.: 503-284-0386, 503-284-1209

BERNIE TAYLOR, 47 Columbia Street, Wharton, New Jersey 17885; Tel.: 201-361-1738

FREDERICK E. TERHUNE, 536 Washington Avenue, Miami Beach, Florida 33139; Tel.: (Office) 305-531-1206, (Home) 305-672-2511

FREDDIE B. TERMUNE, L & M Enterprises, 229 N.E. 1 Avenue, Miami, Florida 33101; Tel.: 379-4753

ERNIE TERRELL, 4934 W. Fulton, Chicago, Illinois 60644

TEXAS DEPARTMENT OF LABOR AND STANDARDS, Box 12157, Capitol Station, Austin, Texas 78711; Tel.: 512-475-2403

THAILAND BOXING COMMISSION, P.O. Box 2-59, Bangkok, Thailand

CAROLYN K. THOMAS, Golden Circle Promotions, Inc., 272 Nye Avenue, Newark, New Jersey 07112; Tel.: 201-926-5479, 926-9707

EDDIE THOMAS, 5 King Edward Villas, The Walk, Merthyr Tydfil, So. Wales; Tel.: 0685-4586

HENRY THOMAS, 23 So. Ingram Street, Alexandria, Virginia 22304; Tel.: (Home) 703-751-6462, 202-544-9132, 202-755-5095/6 (Manager-Trainer)

JERRY THOMAS, West Virginia Sports Promotions, Inc., P.O. Box 666, Clarksburg, West Virginia 26301; Tel.: 304-623-0796, 623-0832

GERALD THOMPSON, Benton Falls Fair, Waterville, Maine 94901; Tel.: 207-453-2718

JACK THOMPSON ENTERPRISES, 5802 So. Oak Park Avenue, Chicago, Illinois 60638; Tel.: 586-5295

JOE THORNTON, King of the Hill Productions, P.O. Box 165, Biloxi, Mississippi 39533; Tel.: 601-432-0257

TIAMBOOM INTRABUTRA, Rajadamnern Stadium, No. 1 Rajadamnern Avenue, Bangkok, Thailand

PAUL TIBBS, 23-30 Goodhope Road S.E., Washington, D. C.; Tel.: 202-582-4039, 202-462-2504

TIGER'S BOXING SCHOOL, 1556 E. Commercial Boulevard, Ft. Lauderdale, Florida 33308; Tel.: 305-771-9667

JOSEPH TILLMAN, 1225 Athey Road, Mobile, Alabama 36608; Tel.: 205-342-5919

TIMES SQUARE BOXING CLUB, Jimmy Glenn, 145 W. 42nd Street, New York, New York 10036; Tel.: 212-221-8933

KIRK TINKER, P.O. Box 5599 E.S., Nassau, Bahamas; Tel.: 809-325-7939

S. TISCHLER, 1499 Pawnee Drive, Las Vegas, Nevada 89109

JOHNNY TOCCO, 408 Melody Lane, Las Vegas, Nevada 89108; Tel.: 878-6236

JOHN H. TODD, 5513 Barnhallow Road, Norfolk, Virginia 23502; Tel.: 1-804-101 7545

F. TOMASO, 2200 So. Ocean Lane, Ft. Lauderdale, Florida 33316

STEVE TOMASSI, 2968 No. Bondall Street, Philadelphia, Pennsylvania 12132

STAN TOMMASELLO PROMOTIONS, P.O. Box 1093, Maitland, Florida 32751; Tel.: 305-677-7927, (Home) 305-671-9817

TOP RANK, 450 Madison Avenue, New York, New York 10022; Tel.: 212-371-3232

JOE TORO, Eagles Boxing Club, 1416 7th Avenue, Seattle, Washington; Tel.: (call after 5 p.m.) 206-MA 3-8787, ME 3-4858 (Manager)

TORONTO A. C., Earl (Sully) Sulivan, 109 Ossington Avenue, Toronto, Canada; Tel.: LE 1-0088 (Promoter)

CHI CHI TORRES, 390 E. 162nd Street, Bronx, New York 10451; Tel.: 212-993-7764

JOSE LUIS TORRES, Avenue A, Apartment 93, Panama, Republic De Panama; Tel.: 783-1243

TORTINO ENTERPRISES, P.O. Box 5552, San Antonio, Texas

JOHN TOSCANO, 610 Main Plaza Building, San Antonio, Texas 78205; Tel.: 512-349-8907 (Promoter)

JORGE TOVAR, 2305 W. Taylor, Chicago, Illinois 60612; Tel.: 312-421-7528

MIKE TRAINER, Sugar Ray Leonard, Inc., 1005 Bonifant Street, Silver Springs, Maryland 20910; Tel.: 301-587-7330

BRUCE TRAMPLER, Ahmed Bey Boxing Promotions, 1570 No. Sanborn, Hollywood, California 90027; Tel.: 213-666-5525, 666-0200

TRANSVAAL NATIONAL SPORTING CLUB, P.O. Box 6711, Johannesburg, South Africa; Tel.: Johannesburg 33-9887

PETER TRAVIS, Point After, 7103 78th Avenue, Edmonton, Alb., Canada T6B 0B9; Tel.: 403-465-5955

TREASURE BALLEY BOXING CLUB, 604 6th Street, No. Ext. Nampa, Idaho; Tel.: 208-466-2767

TONY TRUDNICH, Las Vegas Sports Promotion, Hotel Sahara, P.O. Box 14337, Las Vegas, Nevada 89114; Tel.: (Office) 702-737-2111, (Home) 702-735-4402

EMMETT TUCKER, Midwest Promotions, P.O. Box 1534, Kansas City, Kansas 66117

FRANK TUNNEY, Maple Leaf Gardens, 466 Church Street, Toronto, Ontario, Canada

DON TURNER, 500 Central Avenue #901, Union City, New Jersey 07087; Tel.: 201-863-6994

IRVING UNGERMAN, 1526 Du Pont, Toronto 9, Ontario, Canada

UNIPROM, INC., Arenata Enterprises Building, Cabao, Quezon City, Philippines; P.O. Box 746, Manila, Philippines

TONY UNITAS, c/o Bayview Boxing Promotions, 43 Victoria Street, Toronto, Ontario, Canada; Tel.: 416-869-1925; 416-226-1471

HECTOR VACCARA, Avenue Del Liberatador, Buenos Aires, Argentina; Tel.: 4520-60-13 (International Boxing Manager)

PETE VACCARE, 189-15 50th Avenue, Flushing, New York 11365; Tel.: FL 7-8577 (Manager)

JOE J. (HORN) VACCARELLI, 604 Pike Street, Seattle, Washington; Tel.: MA 3-9941

JESUS MORALES VALARINO, San Francisco a Sociedad Edifiecio Magdalena 40 piso No. 42, Caracas, Venezuela; Tel.: (Office) 4-21-570, (Home) 2-3577

FRANK VALENTI, 83 Canal Street, Boston, Massachusetts 02114; Tel.: 617-227-9332

ALFONSO ORTEGA VALEZ, Empresa Mexicana de Box (Salvador Lutteroth Suvs.), Calle del Dr. Lavista, 181 A. Mexico City, Mexico

DANIE VAN ZYL, 46 Queens Court, Klein Street, Johannesburg, South Africa

GEORGE VASILOU, Seaside Gym, 355 E. Seaside Boulevard, Long Beach, California 90802; Tel.: 213-437-9850

JORGE VASQUEZ, 2071 Berkeley Avenue, Los Angeles, California 90026; Tel.: 384-3958

JOSE VASQUEZ, Calle Volt 48, La Mesa, Tijuana, B.C., Mexico; Tel.: 386-3391

ANGEL VAZQUEZ, Diversiones Y Espedtatulos de Mexico S.A., J. Maria Marroqui 11-3 Piso, Mexico City, Mexico

VINCENT L. VECEHIONE, 92 Alden Street, Brockton, Massachusetts 02401

ALONSO VEGA, 2017 Berkeley Avenue, Los Angeles, California 90026; Tel.: (Home) 384-3958

VENETIAN GARDENS, S.C., John Chechetto, 586 George Street, Sydney, N.S., Canada

939

VENTURA BOXING CLUB, Robert H. Krupp, P.O. Box 317, Ventura, California

PAT VERSACE, 830 Hartsdale Road, White Plains, New York 10607; Tel.: (Day) 914-592-2892, (Night) 914-949-4317

DR. TEODORO B. VESAGAS, Butuan City, Philippines (Manager)

HENRI VIAENE, Chemin de Bas Ransbeck 1, 1328 Ohain, Belgium

AL VIALARDI PRODUCTIONS, 3130 Arnow Place, Bronx, New York 10461; Tel.: 212-931-4567 (Manager-Trainer-Cutman)

MORIE VICKERS, Royal Oak, 67 Barking Road, Canning Tower, London E16, England

GENE VILLACCI, Sheraton Eastland Hotel, Portland, Maine; Tel.: 772-9325

ED VINSON, Rancho Arroyo Boxing Club, 9880 Jackson Road, Sacramento, California 95826; Tel.: 457-9548 (Manager)

DENNIS VINT, P.O. Box 699, Westerville, N.S., Canada B0K 2A0; Tel.: 902-396-3255

PETEY VIRGIN, 1570 Van Vranken Avenue, Schenectady, New York 12308; Tel.: FR 4-2926

JOE VISALLI, 12 Colonial Gardens, Brooklyn, New York; Tel.: TE 6-8043

PETE VITAL, SR., 416 No. Katherine Drive, Montebello, California 90640; Tel.: 723-2209

CHARLARD VONGCHEEP, Charland Boxing Promotions, Lumpinee Boxing Stadium, Bangkok, Thailand

BARON WALKER, 5486 Iveyridge Court, Fayetteville, North Carolina 28304; Tel.: 919-867-0065; 615-968-3106

JOHNNY WALKER, Naval School Survival Training, Naval Air Station, Pensacola, Florida 32508; Tel.: (Office) 904-452-3174; (Home) 904-455-5941

TED WALKER, Carson Boxing Club, P.O. Box 295, Carson City, Nevada 89701; Tel.: 702-882-2885, 702-782-5358

RAY WALSH, 4217 Hermitage Road, Richmond, Virginia; Tel.: 2-3227 (Manager)

JOE WAREHAM, 340 Aspen Street, Warminster, Pennsylvania 18974; Tel.: OS 2-0397 (Manager-Trainer)

AL WARNER ASSOCIATES, Worldwide Promotions, 1234 24th South, St. Petersburg, Florida 33711

BEN WASHINGTON, 17161 Pontchartram Drive, Detroit, Michigan 48203; Tel.: 313-834-4400

BILL WATKINS BOXING STABLE, 1114 Uvalde, Houston, Texas 77015

FRANK WATTS, The Silver Slipper, 3100 Las Vegas Boulevard So., Las Vegas, Nevada 89109; Tel.: 702-734-1212

RON WEATHERS, Vista Tomas, El Paso, Texas 79935

ARNOLD WEISS, 7601 Castor Avenue, Philadelphia, Pennsylvania 19152

WEST JORDAN BOXING CLUB, 8416 So. 1700 West, West Jordan, Utah 84084; Tel.: 801-255-5022

HAROLD WESTON, Madison Square Garden, Boxing Department, 4 Penn Plaza, New York City, New York 10001; Tel.: 212-563-8169

WEST RAND SPORTING CLUB, 72 8th Avenue, Roodepoort 7611

RAY WHEBBE, 3718 Stevens Avenue So., Minneapolis, Minnesota 55409; Tel.: 612-827-1144

DON WHITE, P.O. Box 5283, Spartanburg, South Carolina 29301; Tel.: 803-582-5921

JERRY WHITE, 1722 Jefferson Avenue, Miami Beach, Florida 33139; Tel.: 305-531-1981

JIMMY WHITE, 1900 Condon Avenue, Metairie, Louisiana 70003

WHITE CITY SPORTING CLUB, P.O. Box 3965, Johannesburg, South Africa; Tel.: Johannesburg 33-3551

DICK WHITEHEAD, 1913 E. Seminole, P.O. Box 3217, Glenstone Station, Springfield, Missouri; Tel.: TU 1-0772, UN 6-7853 (Manager)

FRITZ WIENE, Boxburo, Hamburg 1, Steindamm, Germany 11013; Tel.: 240791

JIM WILLIAMS, 416 Addison Avenue, Westmont, New Jersey 08108; Tel.: 609-858-0142 (Manager)

JOE WILLIAMS, Global Productions, 1818 Westlake Avenue No., Seattle, Washington 98109; Tel.: 202-582-4440

MAC WILLIAMS, 351 Chapelwood, Llandeyrn, N. Cardiff, Wales 0222-75638

NATHANIEL WILLIAMS, Nat Williams Enterprises, 2310 Minnesota Avenue S.E., Washington, D.C. 20020; Tel.: 202-582-4440

BARBARA WILLIS, Northern Nevada Boxing Promotions, 1115 Shady Oak Drive, Carson City, Nevada 89701; Tel.: 702-882-5087

ROBEY WILLIS, Northern Nevada Amateur Boxing League and Coach Stewart Boxing Club, P.O. Box 146, Stewart, Nevada 89437; Tel.: (School) 882-3411, (Home) 882-5087

JIM WINDSOR, Sherwood, 4, Broomhill Crescent, Leeds 7, England

JIMMY WINTERS, 75 Glen Cove Avenue, Glen Cove, New York; Tel.: 516-759-1340

THEO WITTENBRINK, St. Georgstrasse 8, Hamburg, Germany; Tel.: 24-67-4748

DAVID WOLF, 147 W. 79th Street, New York City, New York 10024; Tel.: 212-362-3686

BOB WOLFE, 417 Waller Street, Portsmouth, Ohio 45662; Tel.: 614-353-0684

DON WOLFGANG, 11773 Woodworth, Salem, Ohio 44460; Tel.: 216-549-2797

HAROLD E. WONNELL, 324 Jackson, Columbus, Ohio 43206; Tel.: 614-221-9381

JERRY L. WRIGHT, 5716 Devon Avenue, El Paso, Texas 79924

JOE YDIANDO, 1755 So. Bridge Street, Winnemucca, Nevada 89445; Tel.: 702-623-3174 (Promoter)

GEORGE YELTON, 3011 92nd South, Tacoma, Washington 89409; Tel.: 206-588-9019

NAT YESS, 27 Truesdale Gardens, Alsworth, Middlesex, England

JOHN YOPP, All-Star Boxing Promotions, 18290 James Couzens Highway, Detroit, Michigan 48235; Tel.: 313-863-0375

YUGOSLAV BOXING, Zuruzenje Profesionalnih, Boksarjev y Ljubljini, 61000, Ljuoijama, Nazajevai, Yugoslavia

FELIX ZABALA, G.P.O. Box 4073, San Juan, Puerto Rico 00936; Tel.: (Office) 809-723-8400; (Home) 809-764-9771, 809-764-5143

BO ZAINE, Ericsson do Brasil, Caixa Postal 5677, Sao Paulo, Brazil; Tel.: 298-3322

WILLY ZELLER, 1 Berlin 41, Forum Steglitz (Pelz-Zeller) SchloB-Str. 1-2 Germany; Tel.: 030-79130-40; 030-80330-68

IZZY ZERLING, Youth Recreation Center Inc., 1720 Church Avenue, Brooklyn, New York 11226

FRANK ZETTS, 64 E. Dewey Avenue, Youngstown, Ohio; Tel.: ST 8-83-8

NICK ZIBELLI, 143 Park Road, Brockton, Massachusetts 02401

WALDEMAR ZUMBANO, Av. Higienopolis, 240 ap. 212-B, Sao Paulo SP, Brazil

U.S. BOXING COMMISSIONS

ALABAMA: Alabama Boxing and Wrestling Commission, P.O. Box 1069, Montgomery, Alabama 36102, (205) 262-6638

ALASKA: Alaska Athletic Commission, Office of the Governor, Pouch A, Juneau, Alaska 99801, (907) 465-3500

ARIZONA: Arizona Athletic Commission, 1645 West Jefferson Street, Room 418, Phoenix, Arizona 85007, (602) 255-3095

ARKANSAS: Arkansas State Athletic Commission, P.O. Box 628, Cabot, Arkansas 72450, (501) 843-6022

CALIFORNIA: California State Athletic Commission, 107 South Broadway, Room 3030, Sacramento, California 95818, (213) 620-4590

COLORADO: Colorado State Athletic Commission, State Services Building, Room 100, 1525 Sherman Street, Denver, Colorado 80203, (303) 892-3308

CONNECTICUT: Conn. State Boxing and Wrestling Commission, Dept. of Consumer Protection, State Office Building, 165 Capitol Avenue, (203) 566-3843

DELAWARE: Delaware State Athletic Commission, 100 West Tenth Street, Room 1200, Wilmington, Delaware 19801, (302) 658-7581

DISTRICT OF COLUMBIA: D.C. Boxing and Wrestling Commission, 700 Seventh Street, S.W., Washington, D.C. 20024, (202) 554-4866

FLORIDA: (No State Commission. Each municipality has its own form of boxing regulation.) Hollywood: Hollywood Boxing Commission, 3515 South Ocean Drive, Hollywood, Florida 33022, (305) 457-8111. Miami Beach: Miami Beach Boxing Commission, 1 Lincoln Road, Miami Beach, Florida 33139, (305) 534-2139

GEORGIA: (No form of boxing regulation.)

HAWAIIAN ISLANDS: Hawaii State Boxing Commission, 1010 Richards Street, Honolulu, Oahu, Hawaiian Islands 96801, (808) 548-7461

IDAHO: Idaho State Athletic Commission, State House, Boise, Idaho 83702, (208) 384-3888

ILLINOIS: Illinois State Athletic Commission, Dept. of Registration and Education, 55 East Jackson Blvd., Suite 17, Chicago, Illinois 60604, (312) 793-8540

INDIANA: Indiana Athletic Commission, State Office Building, Room 1021, Indianapolis, Indiana 46204, (317) 633-4284

IOWA: Commissioner of Athletics, State Capitol Building, Des Moines, Iowa 50309, (515) 281-5864

KANSAS: Kansas Athletic Commission, New England Building, Room 528, 503 Kansas Avenue, Topeka, Kansas 66603, (913) 296-3596

KENTUCKY: Kentucky Athletic Commission, Kentucky Towers, Suite 306, 430 West Walnut Street, Louisville, Kentucky 40202, (502) 588-4502

LOUISIANA: Louisiana State Athletic Commission, 2501 Bell Street, New Orleans, Louisiana 70119, (504) 947-8900

MAINE: Maine Boxing Commission, State Office Building, Fourth Floor, Augusta, Maine 04333, (207) 289-3141

MARYLAND: Maryland State Athletic Commission, One South Calvert Street, Baltimore, Maryland 21202, (301) 383-4141

MASSACHUSETTS: Massachusetts State Boxing Commission, Department of Public Safety, McCormack State Office Building, 10th Floor, 1 Ashburton Place, Boston, Massachusetts 02108, (617) 727-3296

MINNESOTA: State of Minnesota Board of Boxing, Metro Square Building, Fifth Floor, St. Paul, Minnesota 55101, (612) 296-2501

MICHIGAN: Michigan Athletic Board of Control, 1200 Sixth Avenue, Executive Plaza, Detroit, Michigan 48926, (313) 256-2850

MISSISSIPPI: Mississippi Athletic Commission, War Memorial Building, Jackson, Mississippi 39201, (601) 354-6553

MISSOURI: Office of Athletics, P.O. Box 1335, Jefferson City

Missouri 65101, (314) 751-2334

MONTANA: Montana State Board of Athletics, Lalonde Building, Helena, Montana 59601, (406) 449-3737

NEBRASKA: (No State Commission. Each municipality has its own form of boxing regulation.)

NEVADA: Nevada State Athletic Commission, 2921 Industrial Road, Las Vegas, Nevada 89109, (702) 385-0434

NEW HAMPSHIRE: New Hampshire State Athletic Commission, 9 Edson Street, Nashua, New Hampshire 03060, (603) 883-5770

NEW JERSEY: New Jersey State Athletic Commission, 143 East State Street, Suite 500, Trenton, New Jersey 08608, (609) 292-0315

NEW MEXICO: (No State Commission. Each municipality has its own form of boxing regulation.) Albuquerque: Boxing and Wrestling Board, 2823 Madison, N.E., Albuquerque, New Mexico 87110, (505) 256-7876

NEW YORK: New York State Athletic Commission, 270 Broadway, Room 750, New York City, New York 10007, (212) 488-4604

NORTH CAROLINA: (No State Commisson. Each municipality has its own form of boxing regulation.)

NORTH DAKOTA: State Boxing Commissioner, State Capitol Building, Bismarck, North Dakota 58501, (701) 224-2900

OHIO: (No State Commission. State Code turns over regulation to a three-man Board of Commissioners in each of Ohio's 88 counties.)

OKLAHOMA: (No form of boxing control.)

OREGON: (No State Commission.) Portland: Municipal Boxing and Wrestling Commission, 1947 S.E. Clinton, Portland, Oregon 97202, (503) 235-5713

PENNSYLVANIA: Pennsylvania State Athletic Commission, State Office Building, Room 1103, 1400 West Spring Garden Street, Philadelphia, Pennsylvania 19130, (215) 238-6676

RHODE ISLAND: R.I. Racing and Athletics Commission, Roger Williams Building, Hayes Street, Providence, Rhode Island 02908, (401) 277-2636

SOUTH CAROLINA: (No form of boxing control.)

SOUTH DAKOTA: South Dakota State Athletic Commission, State Building, Pierre, South Dakota 57501, (605) 224-9261

TENNESSEE: Tennessee Athletic Commission, Capitol Hill Building, Room 522, 301 Seventh Avenue, Nashville, Tennessee 37219, (615) 741-2384

TEXAS: Boxing and Wrestling Division, Dept. of Labor and Standards, P.O. Box 12157, Austin, Texas 78711, (512) 475-4229

UTAH: Utah Athletic Commission, 995 West 9000 South, West Jordan, Utah 84084, (801) 255-3053

VERMONT: Vermont Boxing Control Commission, 135 Hood Street, Winooski, Vermont 05404, (802) 655-2522

VIRGINIA: Virginia Athletic Commission, 2 South Ninth Street, Richmond, Virginia 23219, (804) 786-2011

WASHINGTON: Washington State Athletic Commission, 1417 Columbia Street, South, Olympia, Washington 98504, (206) 722-1100

WEST VIRGINIA: West Virginia State Athletic Commission, State Capital Building, Charleston, West Virginia 25301, (304) 348-2001

WISCONSIN: Athletic Examining Board, Dept. of Regulation and Licensing, 201 East Washington Avenue, Madison, Wisconsin 53702, (608) 266-2852

WYOMING: (No State Commission listed.)

CANADIAN BOXING COMMISSIONS

CAPE BRETON: Cape Breton Boxing & Wrestling Commission, 14 View Street, Sydney Mines, Nova Scotia B1V 1G7

CALGARY: Calgary Boxing and Wrestling Commission, P.O. Box 2100, Calgary, Alberta T2P 0M5

EDMONTON: Edmonton Boxing and Wrestling Commission, 10630 130 Street, Edmonton, Alberta T5N 1Y2 (403) 428-5426

HALIFAX: Halifax Athletic Commission, David Johnson, Chairman, Chandler, Moore, Sutherland & Johnson, 270 Dutch Village Road, Halifax, Nova Scotia B3N 2R9

MANITOBA: Manitoba Boxing & Wrestling Commission, 912-200 Ronald Street, Winnipeg, Manitoba R3J 3J3, (204) 943-9331

MONTREAL: Montreal Athletic Commission, 7125 rue St. Hubert, Montreal, Quebec H2S 2N1, (514) 273-1577

NOVA SCOTIA: Nova Scotia Boxing Authority, P.O. Box 2175, Dartmouth East, Nova Scotia B2W 3Y2, (902) 435-1938

ONTARIO: Ontario Athletic Commission, Office of Athletic Commissioner, 555 Yonge Street, Third Floor, Toronto, Ontario M7A 2H6, (519) 963-0844

QUEBEC: Quebec Athletic Commission, 1160, DeSalaberry, Quebec, Province of Quebec, (418) 643-2839

VANCOUVER: Vancouver Athletic Commission, 4280 Venables Street, Burnaby, British Columbia V5C 2Z9

LATIN AMERICAN BOXING COMMISSIONS

ARGENTINA: Federacion Argentina de Box, Castro Barros 75, Buenos Aires, Argentina

BELIZE: Belize Boxing Board of Control, P.O. Box 223, Belize City, Belize

BRAZIL: Confederacao Brasileira de Pugilismo, Rua Pedro 1 7-GR 906, Rio de Janeiro, Brazil

COSTA RICA: Limon: Comision de Boxeo Profesional de Puerto Limon, Apartado 262, Limon, Costa Rica

COSTA RICA: San Jose: Comision de Boxeo Profesional de San Jose, Apartado 6014, San Jose, Costa Rica

COLOMBIA: Comision Nacional de Boxeo Profesional, Apartado Aereo 1458, Cartagena, Colombia

DOMINICAN REPUBLIC: Comision Nacional de Boxeo Profesional, Av. Independencia No. 6, Santo Domingo 1, Dominican Republic

ECUADOR: Federacion Deportiva Nacional del Ecuador, Palacio Municipal, Apartado 3409, Guayaquil, Ecuador

GUATEMALA: Comision de Boxeo Profesional, 3a. Calle No. 9-31, Guatemala City, Guatemala

GUYANA: Guyana Boxing Board of Control, P.O. Box 97, Georgetown, Guyana

HAITI: Haiti Professional Boxing Commission, P.O. Box 1091, Port-Au-Prince, Haiti

JAMAICA: Jamaica Boxing Board of Control, 50 Begonia Drive, Kingston 6, Jamaica, West Indies

PUERTO RICO: Puerto Rico Boxing Commission, Public Recreation and Parks Administration, Box 3207, San Juan, P.R. 00903, (809) 725-8445

TRINIDAD: Trinidad Boxing Board of Control, 99 Piccadilly Street, Port of Spain, Trinidad

VENEZUELA: Caracas: Comision de Boxeo Profesional del Distrito Federal, Estadio Nacional, El Paraiso, Caracas, Venezuela

VIRGIN ISLANDS: St. Croix: St. Croix Boxing Commission, 6 A & B Lane, Christiansted, St. Croix, V.I. 00820

EUROPEAN BOXING COMMISSIONS

AUSTRIA: Osterreichischer Berufs Box Verband, An der Hulben, Vienna 1, Austria

BELGIUM: Belgian Royal Boxing Federation, 15 Avenue Defre, Brussels, Belgium

DENMARK: Danish Professional Boxing Association, Neder Hjerkvej 2, Hjerk, 7870 Roslev, Denmark

FINLAND: Finland Boxing Commission, 34 Helsinki, A-8, Finland

FRANCE: Federation Francaise de Boxe, 62 Rue Nollet, Paris 17e, France

GERMANY: Bund Deutscher Berufsboxer, St. Georgstrasse 8, Hamburg 2, Germany

GREAT BRITAIN: British Board of Boxing Control, Ramillies Building, Hill's Place, London W1R 2BS, England

GREECE: Federation Hellenique de Boxe, 4 Rue Capsali, Athens, T.I., Greece

ITALY: Federazione Pugilistica Italiana, Foro Italico, Rome, Italy

NETHERLANDS: Nederlandes Boksbond, Emmalaan 10, Amsterdam Z, Netherlands

NORWAY: Norges Profesjonelle Boksforbund, Neuberggt, 2 opg C, Oslo, Norway

PORTUGAL: Federacao Portuguesa de Boxe, Rua do Arco C360, 90-5, Lisbon, Portugal

SPAIN: Federacion Espanola de Boxeo, Ferraz 16, Madrid 8, Spain

SWEDEN: Svenska Boxingsforbundet, Sveavagen 29, Stockholm, Sweden

SWITZERLAND: Federation Suisse de Boxe, Case Postal, Bale 2, Switzerland

TURKEY: Federation Turque de Boxe, Direction Generale de l'Education, Physique Necatibey Caddesi, Ankara, Turkey

ORIENTAL BOXING COMMISSIONS

JAPAN: Japan Boxing Commission, Office of the Commissioner, c/o Korakuen Stadium, Ltd., 3-61, 1-chome, Koraku, Bunkyo-ku, Tokyo, Japan, Cable Address: ORBOXING TOKYO

KOREA: Korea Boxing Commission, C.P.O. Box 1490, Seoul, Korea, Cable Address: ORBOX SEOUL

PHILIPPINES: Games and Amusements Board, Legaspi Towers 200, Paseo de Roxas, Makati, Manila, Philippines

THAILAND: Thailand Boxing Commission, P.O. Box 2-59, Bangkok 2, Thailand, Cable Address: ORBOX BANGKOK

World Boxing Association: Apartado 470, Panama 1, Republic of Panama, Cable Address: AEMEBE

World Boxing Council: Apartado Postal 75-254, Mexico 14, D.F., Mexico, Cable Address: CONSEMUNBO

North American Boxing Federation: 2201 West Nye Lane, Carson City, Nevada 89701, (702) 885-4817

United States Boxing Association: P.O. Box 980, Richmond, Virginia 23207, (804) 786-2011

Latin American Boxing Federation: Av. Bolivar No. 16, A "Bajos", Santo Domingo, D.N., Dominican Republic

INDEX

941

950

951

952

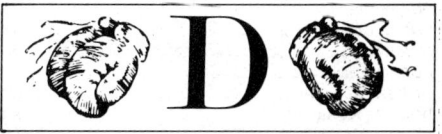

954

K

965

970

A PICTORIAL PORTFOLIO OF 1980

PRECEDING SPREAD
The Moment of 1980:
Sugar Ray Leonard
torments his tormentor, the
seemingly indestructible
Roberto Duran in the
seventh round of their
rematch in New Orleans on
November 25th, forcing
"Hands of Stone" to throw
them up in abject defeat
one round later.

THIS PAGE CLOCKWISE:
The Pin-Point Bombing of
the Year:
England's Alan Minter
takes the measure of—and
the crown—from Vito
Antuofermo, winning the
world's middleweight title
on March 16, 1980, London,
England.

FAR RIGHT:
The Surprise of the Year:
Mike Weaver stands over a
fallen Gerrie Coetzee in the
13th round of their WBA
heavyweight title bout after
decking the previously
unfloorable Coetzee with a
right hand—Botswanaland,
October 25, 1980.

BOTTOM:
The Punch of the Year:
Thomas Hearns earns his
nickname "The Hit Man,"
as he stuns Pipino Cuevas
in the second round of
their championship bout
last August 2nd, in Detroit,
Michigan, to win the WBA
version of the welterweight
crown.

FOLLOWING SPREAD:
The Blood-letting of the
Year:
"Marvelous" Marvin Hagler
finally attains the crown he
had coveted for years by
stopping Alan Minter on
cuts in the third round,
September 27, 1980, in
London, England.

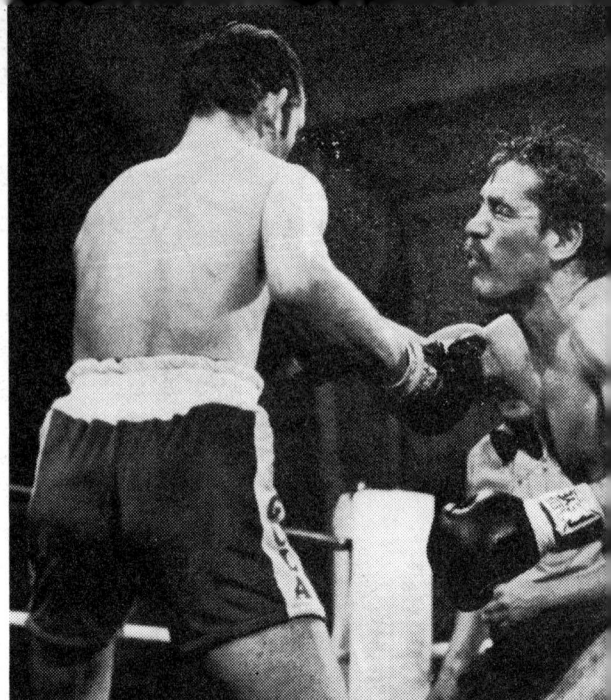

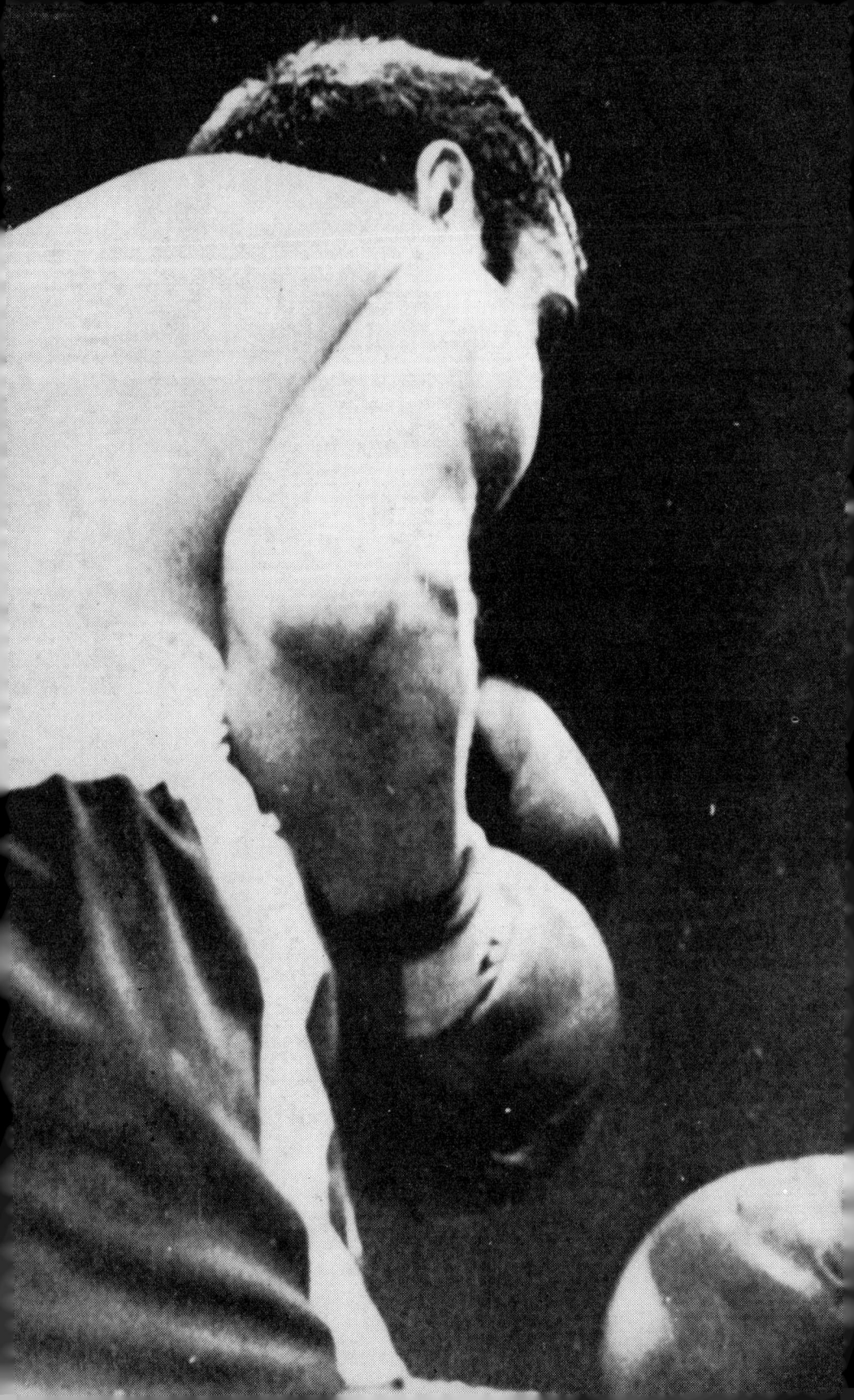

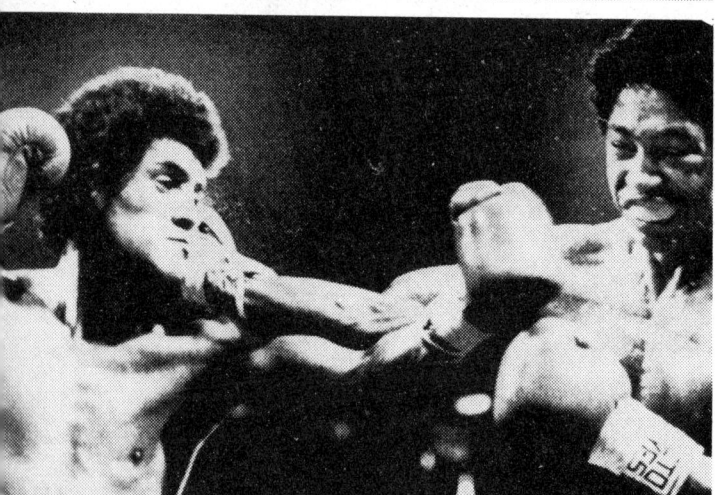

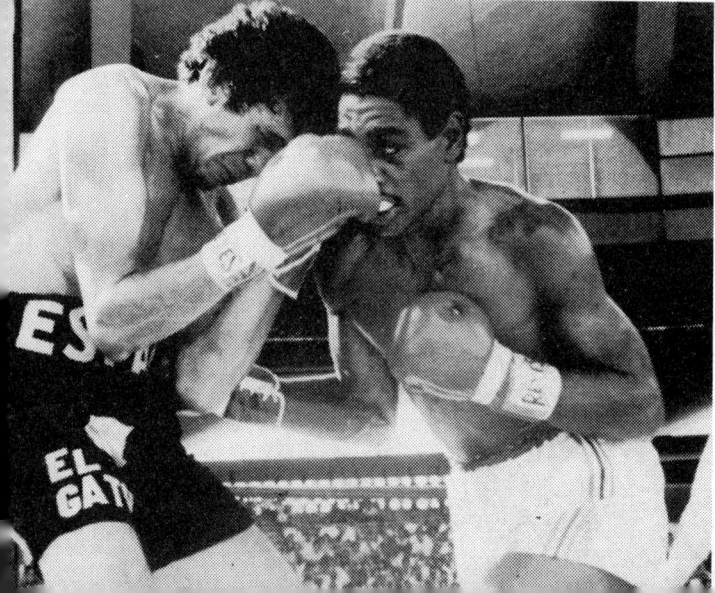

CLOCKWISE:
*The Workman-like
effort of the Year:
"The Black Dane,"
Ugandan Ayub Kalule—by
way of Denmark—knocks
down challenger Steve
Gregory on his way to a
one-sided decision in
defense of his WBA junior
Middleweight crown—Dec-
ember 6, 1980, Copenhagen
Denmark.*

RIGHT
*The Breather Of The Year:
Matthew Saad Muhammad,
whose every fighter in
defense of his WBC light
heavyweight crown is a war
takes on challenger Lotte
Mwale for a change of pace
and finishes off the
challenger at 2:25 of the
fourth round—San Diego,
California, November 28,
1980.*

BOTTOM LEFT
*The Re-Run of the Year:
Hilmer Kenty, who had
defeated Ernesto Espana
six months earlier in his
hometown of Detroit,
Michigan, to win the WBA
version of the lightweight
championship, takes his
title and act to San Juan to
repeat his victory in a
virtual replica of his first
win, September 20, 1980.*

MID-LEFT
*The Unsung
Fighter of the Year:
Salvador Sanchez, the
formerly unheralded and
unknown WBC
featherweight champion,
retains his crown via a 15-
round decision against Jua
LaPorte on December 13,
1980, to gain further
reknown as one of 1980's
best boxers. The fight took
place in El Paso, Texas.*

PRECEDING SPREAD
The Destruction of the Year: Wilfredo Gomez, WBC Junior featherweight champ, extends his record to 13 straight knockouts with a fifth-round stoppage of Derrik Holmes on August 22, 1980 in Las Vegas, Nevada.

THIS PAGE:
The Most Dramatic Changing of the Guard of the Year: Salvador Sanchez not only exchanges shots with Danny "Little Red" Lopez and survives, but wins the fight as well, knocking out Lopez and winning the WBC featherweight championship on February 2, 1980 in Phoenix, Arizona.

FOLLOWING SPREAD
The Small-But-Oh-My Victory of the Year: Little Jeff Chandler stops Julian Solis in round 14 to win the WBA bantamweight title, the first American in three decades to capture the 118-pound crown. The bout took place on November 15, 1980 in Miami, Florida.

TOP RIGHT
The Butt of the Year: Challenger Sean O'Grady, blood streaming down his face, is stopped by WBC champion Jim Watt on a cut inflicted by an impromptu meeting of the combatant's heads on November 1, 1980 in Glasgow, Scotland.

BOTTOM RIGHT
The Bust of the Year: Muhammad Ali's fourth coming ran afoul of time and Larry Holmes as the three-time former heavyweight champion showed nothing in his 11-round loss to Holmes— October 2, 1980, in Las Vegas, Nevada.

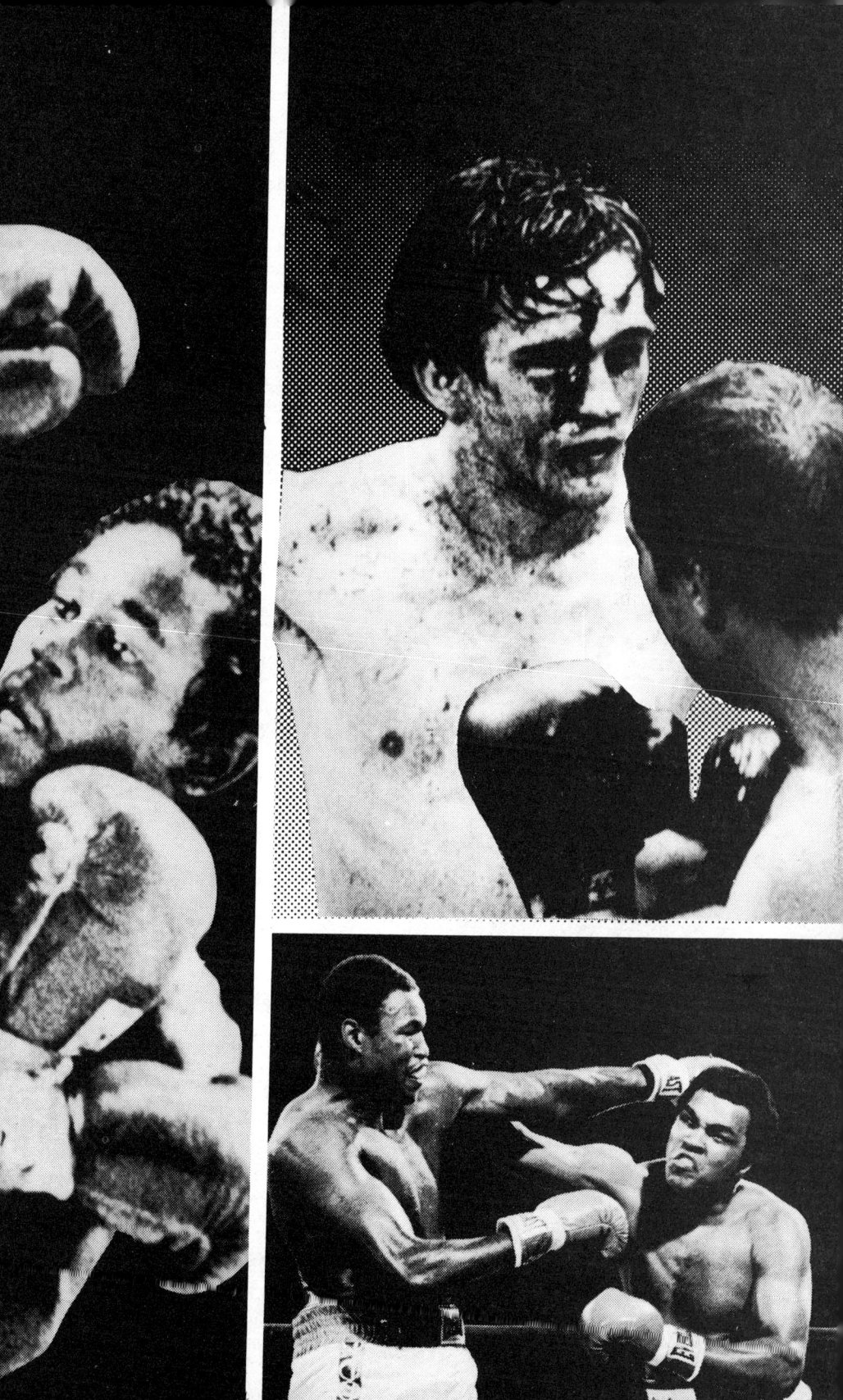